PUBLIC LIBRARY CORE COLLECTION:

NONFICTION

EIGHTEENTH EDITION

CORE COLLECTION SERIES

Formerly

STANDARD CATALOG SERIES

SHAUNA GRIFFIN, MLS, GENERAL EDITOR

CHILDREN'S CORE COLLECTION

MIDDLE AND JUNIOR HIGH CORE COLLECTION

SENIOR HIGH CORE COLLECTION

PUBLIC LIBRARY CORE COLLECTION: NONFICTION

FICTION CORE COLLECTION

YOUNG ADULT CORE COLLECTION

GRAPHIC NOVELS CORE COLLECTION

PUBLIC LIBRARY CORE COLLECTION: NONFICTION

A Selection Guide to Reference Books
and
Adult Nonfiction

EIGHTEENTH EDITION

Former title:

Public Library Catalog

EDITED BY

KENDAL SPIRES

H. W. Wilson
A Division of EBSCO Information Services
Ipswich, Massachusetts
2021

GREY HOUSE PUBLISHING

Cover: © Photo by gnagel via iStock.

ISBN 978-1-64265-646-6

Public Library Core Collection, 2021, published by Grey House Publishing, Inc., Amenia, NY, under exclusive license from EBSCO Information Services, Inc.

A catalog record for this title is available from the Library of Congress.

PRINTED IN CANADA

CONTENTS

PREFACE

PUBLIC LIBRARY CORE COLLECTION: NONFICTION is a curated list of nonfiction titles for adults that may be used to develop a collection serving general readers in public libraries of all sizes. It also includes professional materials for librarians, including titles focusing on collection development, readers' advisory, reference, and managing a public library.

This Core Collection is an abridgement of the database available from EBSCO Information Services, which has an additional two recommendation levels, Lexile measures, book reviews and articles, and expanded metadata. It is updated weekly. Contact your EBSCO or NoveList sales rep for a free trial, or visit https://www.ebscohost.com/novelist/our-products/core-collections for more information. EBSCO also invites feedback from Core Collections customers at novelist@ebsco.com

What's new in this Edition?

This edition continues to emphasize equity, diversity, and inclusion, representing and reflecting a varied community in which many voices can be heard. Significant weeding is undertaken to ensure that older, outdated books are removed in favor of more relevant recommendations.

With more than 14,000 nonfiction titles appropriate to general adult readers as well as reference books and a selection of professional materials of use to librarians and library administrators, this 18th edition contains both new titles that reflect new topics of interest or new interpretations of traditional knowledge as well as older titles – sometimes in updated versions – that remain the best in their field.

As always, a star (★) at the start of an entry indicates that a book is an *Essential* title, our highest recommendation level. These titles are the essential books in a given category or on a given subject; while there are often a number of recommended titles, this designation helps users who want only a small selection. Non-starred entries represent *Recommended* titles, which provide a fuller list of recommended books.

History

The first of several installments of the "Standard Catalog" for the general library was published in 1918. It was called STANDARD CATALOG: SOCIOLOGY SECTION. Additional installments were issued over the next fourteen years, covering Biography; Fiction; Fine Arts; History and Travel; Science and Useful Arts; Literature and Philology;, and Philosophy, Religion, and General Works. Finally, a fully integrated first edition of the STANDARD CATALOG FOR PUBLIC LIBRARIES was assembled and published in 1934. The contents were displayed in classified order, according to the Dewey Decimal Classification. The name was changed to PUBLIC LIBRARY CATALOG with the publication of the fifth edition in 1969, and then to PUBLIC LIBRARY CORE COLLECTION: NONFICTION with the thirteenth edition in 2008.

The collection subsequently evolved, along with other Core Collections, into an online resource called WilsonWeb. EBSCO Information Services acquired H.W. Wilson in 2011, and the collections became EBSCO*host* databases in 2012. In 2020, the readers' advisory experts at NoveList applied their expertise: while Core Collections continues to provide impartial collection development guidance by experts in their fields, this marriage of readers advisory and collection development expertise strengthened the application of genre and subject headings, expanded awards content, and improved search and browse capabilities in the online Core Collections databases.

Scope

PUBLIC LIBRARY CORE COLLECTION: NONFICTION is a guide to nonfiction books published in the United States or published in other countries and distributed in the United States. It excludes non-print materials; periodicals; non-English items (with the exception of dictionaries); and works of an ephemeral nature. Original paperback materials are included. Multiple subjects provide access points via the subject index.

The Core Collection is intended to serve the needs of public and undergraduate libraries and stands as a basic or "opening day" collection. The newer titles help in identifying areas in a collection that can be updated or strengthened, while the retention of useful material from the previous edition enables the librarian to make informed decisions about weeding a collection. With its classified arrangement, complete bibliographical data, and descriptive and evaluative annotations, the Core Collection provides useful information for the acquisitions librarian, the reference librarian, and the cataloger.

Although a Fiction Section was issued in 1923, followed by supplements in 1928 and 1931, fiction was omitted from the first edition of the complete Catalog in 1934. A new expanded edition of the Fiction Section was published as FICTION CATALOG in 1942. In its preface, that Catalog was referred to as a "companion volume to the Standard Catalog for Public Libraries." This complementary relationship has continued to the present: PUBLIC LIBRARY COLRE COLLECTION: NONFICTIION has always listed works of literary criticism and literary history, as well as books about literary technique.

Books are listed with an ISBN – most frequently for a hardcover edition published in the United States, or published in Canada or the United Kingdom and distributed in the U.S. Out-of-print titles are retained in the belief that good books are not obsolete simply because they happen to go out of print.

Database

This Core Collection is derived from the database available from EBSCO Information Services. Metadata for the titles in this volume is provided by the metadata librarians at NoveList, who manage and apply a controlled vocabulary that adapts as terms come in and out of style, or as events require new ones. There are additional, browsable access points, plus full-text book reviews and articles, full-color cover art, Lexile measures, and all of the *Supplemental* book recommendations and *Weeded* titles. It is updated weekly. For more information or for a free trial, contact your EBSCO or NoveList sales rep, or visit https://www.ebscohost.com/novelist/our-products/core-collections. EBSCO also invites feedback from Core Collections customers at novelist@ebsco.com.

In 2017, EBSCO renamed the PUBLIC LIBRARY CORE COLLECTION: NONFICTION database. Now called NONFICTION CORE COLLECTION, it is in line with the other database names, is less cumbersome, and signifies its applicability to general readers in libraries of all types. Although the title of this edition is different from the database from which it is derived, it contains the same content, and is not a separate set of book recommendations.

Preparation

Books included in Core Collections are selected by experienced librarians representing public library systems, school libraries, and academic libraries across the United States and Canada, as well as NoveList staff. These librarians also act as advisors on library policy, trends, and special projects. The names of participating librarians and their affiliations are listed in the Acknowledgements.

Core Collections Products

For recommendations for books for children and teens, librarians are encouraged to investigate the following databases and their associated print versions:

CHILDREN'S CORE COLLECTION
MIDDLE AND JUNIOR HIGH CORE COLLECTION
SENIOR HIGH CORE COLLECTION

For young adult fiction specifically, consult the YOUNG ADULT FICTION CORE COLLECTION, available only in print.

For adult nonfiction for the general reader, try the database NONFICTION CORE COLLECTION or the associated print volume PUBLIC LIBRARY CORE COLLECTION: NONFICTION. For fiction, please use FICTION CORE COLLECTION, either as a database or the associated print version.

For Graphic Novels for all ages, try the GRAPHIC NOVELS CORE COLLECTION in print or database form, which includes both fiction and nonfiction recommendations.

PURPOSE AND ORGANIZATION

Purpose

CORE COLLECTIONS is designed to serve a number of purposes:

As an aid in purchasing. Core Collections is designed to assist in the selection and ordering of titles. Summaries and evaluative excerpts are provided for each title along with information regarding the publisher, ISBN, page count, and publication year. In evaluating the suitability of a work, each library will want to consider the needs of the unique patron base it serves.

As an aid in verification of information. For this purpose, bibliographical information is provided in the list of works. Entries also include recommended subject headings based on NoveList's proprietary subject vocabulary. Notes may describe editions available and other content; for the most up-to-date metadata, please consult the EBSCOhost database.

As an aid in curriculum or programming support. The classified approach, subject indexing, annotations, and evaluative excerpts are helpful in identifying materials appropriate for classroom support, for book discussions, and other programming.

As an aid in collection maintenance. Information about titles available on a subject facilitates decisions to rebind, replace, or discard items. If a book has been demoted to the Supplemental or Weeded recommendation levels and therefore no longer appears in the print abridgement of the database, that demotion is not intended as a sign that the book is no longer valuable or that it should necessarily be weeded from your library's collection.

As an aid in professional development or instruction. The Core Collection is useful in courses or professional training that deal with collection development and readers' advisory; it may also be used in course that deal with literature and book selection, especially in the creation of bibliographies and reading lists.

As an aid to readers' advisory. Every title in this Core Collection is a recommended work and can be given with confidence to a user who expresses a need based on topic, genre, etc. Readers' advisory and user service are further aided by series and awards information, by the descriptive summaries and evaluative excerpts from trusted review sources, and by the subject headings in the Title and Subject Index applied by professional metadata librarians at NoveList.

Organization

This Core Collection consists of two parts: a Classified Collection, and a Title and Subject Index.

Part 1. Classified Collection

The Classified Collection is arranged with nonfiction books first, classified according to the Dewey Decimal Classification in numerical order from 000 to 999. The exception is individual biographies, which are classed at 92 and close out the collection. These will have a subject heading **B**.

An Outline of Classification, which serves as a table for contents for the Classified Collection, is reproduced following this section. It should be noted that many topics can be classified in more than one discipline. If a particular title is not found where it might be expected, the Index should be consulted to determine if it is classified elsewhere.

Within classes, works are arranged alphabetically under main entry, usually the author. Works of individual biography are arranged alphabetically under the biography's subject.

Each listing consists of a bibliographic description, suggested subject headings derived from NoveList, series information, a suggested classification number from the *Abridged Dewey Decimal Classification* and Relative Index, a brief description of the contents of the book, and where possible an evaluative excerpt from a notable source. The following is an example of a typical entry and a description of its components.

Roach, Mary

★ **Stiff:** the curious lives of human cadavers / Mary Roach. W.W. Norton & Co., 2003. 303 p.: **611**

1. Human experimentation in medicine. 2. Dead. 3. Human dissection. 4. Medical research.

ISBN 0-393-05093-9;

LC 2002-152908

A look inside the world of forensics examines the use of human cadavers in a wide range of endeavors, including research into new surgical procedures, space exploration, and a Tennessee human decay research facility.

"**Roach** writes in an insouciant style and displays her metier in tangents about bizarre incidents in pathological history. Death may have the last laugh, but, in the meantime, **Roach** finds merriment in the macabre." Booklist.

The name of the author, Mary Roach, is given in conformity with Library of Congress Authorities. The star at the start of the title indicates that this is an *Essential* title. The title of the book is *Stiff: the curious lives of human cadavers*. The book was published by W.W. Norton & Co. in 2003.

The book has 303 pages. If it were part of a series, the series name would follow the page count.

At the end of the last line of type in the body entry is 611 in boldface type. This is the classification number or category derived from the fifteenth edition of the *Abridged Dewey Decimal Classification.*

The numbered terms "1. Human experimentation in medicine. 2. Dead. 3. Human dissection. 4. Medical research." are recommended subject headings for this book.

An ISBN (International Standard Book Number) is included to facilitate ordering; however, there will often be many editions and formats of a given title; due to space constraints these ISBNs are not provided in the print edition, though many can be found in the corresponding database. The Library of Congress control number is provided when available.

These are followed by a brief summary and an evaluative excerpt from a critical reviewing source, in this case *Booklist*. Such summaries and excerpts are useful in evaluating books for selection and in determining which of several books on the same subject is best suited for the individual reader or purchasing library. Notes are also made to describe special features, such as a bibliography, if applicable. or to describe series order and companion volumes, editions available, awards, and publication history.

Part 2. Author, Title, and Subject Index

The Index is a single alphabetical list of all the books entered in the Core Collection. Each book is entered under author, title, and subject. The classification number, displayed in boldface type, is the key to the location of the main entry for the book in the Classified Collection. Biographies will have the subject indicator **B**.

The following are examples of Index entries for the book cited above:

Author	**Stiff. Roach, M.**	**611**
Subject	**HUMAN** EXPERIMENTATION IN MEDICINE Roach, M. Stiff.	**611**

ACKNOWLEDGMENTS

H.W. Wilson, NoveList, and EBSCO Information Services express special gratitude to the following librarians who both advised in editorial matters and assisted in the selection and weeding of titles for this Core Collection.

Tracy Babiasz
Acquisitions and Collections Manager
Chapel Hill Public Library
Chapel Hill, North Carolina

Jim Bobick
Head, Science and Technology Department (retired)
Carnegie Library of Pittsburgh
Pittsburgh, Pennsylvania

Mary Griffin
Librarian (retired)
Omaha Public Library
Omaha, Nebraska

Steven Jablonski
Collection Development Librarian
Skokie Public Library
Skokie, Illinois

Neal Wyatt
Columnist and Contributing Editor, Library Journal
Richmond, Virginia

The editors would also like to thank NoveList Readers' Advisory Librarians Kaitlin Conner, Ashley Lyons, and Gillian Speace and Metadata Librarians Elizabeth Coleman and Renee Young for their help in creating this collection, along with Digital Content Integration Manager Cathleen Keyser. Lastly, Collection Development Coordinator Lisa Schimmer was instrumental in the creation of this collection.

OUTLINE OF CLASSIFICATION

Reproduced below is the Second Summary of the Dewey Decimal Classification. * As Part 1 of this Core Collection is arranged according to this classification, the outline will serve as a table of contents for it. Please note, however, that the inclusion of this outline is not to be considered a substitute for consulting the Dewey Decimal Classification itself.

* Reproduced from Edition 15 of the Abridged Dewey Decimal Classification and Relative Index, published in 2012, by permission of OCLC Online Computer Library Center, Inc., owner of copyright.

PUBLIC LIBRARY CORE COLLECTION: NONFICTION

EIGHTEENTH EDITION

CLASSIFIED COLLECTION

001.1 Intellectual life

Levine, Lawrence W.

The **opening** of the American mind : canons, culture, and history / Lawrence W. Levine. Beacon Press, c1996. xxiv, 212 p. ; **001.1**

1. Education, Higher -- United States 2. United States -- Intellectual life.
ISBN 9780807031193

LC 96033866

In response to recent books attacking the contemporary university and blaming educators for a decline in American culture, the author argues that the "opening up" of American education and of a changing society are inextricably linked.

001.2 Scholarship and learning

Lima, Manuel, 1978-

The **book** of trees : visualizing branches of knowledge / Manuel Lima. Princeton Architectural Press, 2014. 192 p. **001.2**

1. Learning and scholarship -- History. 2. Knowledge theory -- History. 3. Trees -- Symbolic aspects. 4. Graphic methods -- History.
ISBN 9781616892180

LC 2013026128

"Sure to appeal to a diverse group of readers, the book beautifully combines art and science, as well as ancient and contemporary worldviews." Publishers Weekly.

001.4 Research statistical methods

Booth, Wayne C.

The **craft** of research / Wayne C. Booth, Gregory G. Colomb, Joseph M. Williams, Joseph Bizup, William T. FitzGerald. The University of Chicago Press, 2016. xvi, 316 p. : **001.4**

1. Research -- Methodology 2. Technical writing
ISBN 9780226239569

LC 2016000143

This fundamental work explains how to find and evaluate sources, anticipate and respond to reader reservations, and integrate these pieces into an argument that stands up to reader critique. --Provided by publisher.

MacLeod, Don, 1955-

How to find out anything : from extreme Google searches to scouring government documents, a guide to uncovering anything about everyone and everything / Don MacLeod. Prentice Hall Press, 2012. x, 256 p. ; **001.4**

1. Google. 2. Research -- Methodology. 3. Information resources. 4. Electronic information resources. 5. Internet searching.
ISBN 9780735204676

LC 2012010974

Includes index.

A master |cybrarian| explains how to really use the full power of Google, as well as other little-known online resources to ferret out difficult-to-find information, whether writing a term paper or trying to uncover confidential information.

Page, Scott E

The **model** thinker : what you need to know to make data work for you / Scott E. Page. Basic Books, 2018. xiii, 427 p. : **001.4**

1. Information visualization. 2. Data mining. 3. Quantitative research.
ISBN 9780465094622

LC bl2018193882

A University of Michigan social scientist demonstrates the mathematical, statistical and computational models that can organize raw data into more robust and informative designs for more accurate predictions and decision-making.

Stone, Deborah A.

Counting : how we use numbers to decide what matters / Deborah Stone. Liveright Publishing, 2020 xvi, 291 p. : **001.4**

1. Statistics 2. Counting 3. Measurement 4. Perception
ISBN 9781631495922

LC 2020014990

Most of us think of counting as a skill so basic that we see numbers as objective, indisputable facts. Not so, says scholar Deborah Stone. In this playful-yet-probing work, Stone reveals the inescapable link between quantifying and classifying, and explains how counting determines almost every facet of our lives -- from how we are evaluated at work to how our political opinions are polled to whether we get into college or even out of prison. But numbers, Stone insists, need not rule our lives.

"A delightful takedown of our unreasonable worship of numbers. . . . As Stone lays out her examples of irrational faith in numbers, readers will squirm, but not with disbelief." Kirkus

Tufte, Edward R., 1942-

The **visual** display of quantitative information / Edward R. Tufte. Graphics Press, c2001. 197 p. : **001.4**

1. Statistics -- Graphic methods.
ISBN 9780961392147

LC 2001271866

Includes index.

The classic book on statistical graphics, charts, tables. --Provided by publisher.

Whitby, Andrew, 1981-

The **sum** of the people : how the census has shaped nations, from the ancient world to the modern age / Andrew Whitby.

Basic Books, 2020. 356 p. **001.4**

1. Census 2. Demography 3. Statistics 4. Social control 5. United States Census 6. United States -- Statistical services

ISBN 9781541619340

LC bl2020007460

In April 2020, the United States will embark on what has been called "the largest peacetime mobilization in American history": the decennial population census. It is part of a tradition of counting people that goes back at least three millennia and now spans the globe. In The Sum of the People, data scientist Andrew Whitby traces the remarkable history of the census, from ancient China and the Roman Empire, through revolutionary America and Nazi-occupied Europe, to the steps of the Supreme Court. Marvels of democracy, instruments of exclusion, and, at worst, tools of tyranny and genocide, censuses have always profoundly shaped the societies we've built.

"An important, accessible, and engaging book that will find a varied audience from readers of political science, history, economics, and national security." Library Journal

001.94 Mysteries

Prothero, Donald R.

UFOs, chemtrails, and aliens : what science says / Donald R. Prothero and Timothy D. Callahan ; foreword by Michael Shermer. Indiana University Press, 2017. 448 p. **001.94**

1. Human-alien encounters. 2. Conspiracy theories 3. UFOs 4. Aliens

ISBN 9780253026927

LC 2017006388

"With their books brisk pace and energetic writing, Prothero and Callahan offer entertainment as well as wisdom for everyone who's ever wondered whats behind so many conspiracy theories and paranormal phenomena." Publishers Weekly.

001.942 Unidentified flying objects (UFOs)

Mezrich, Ben, 1969-

The **37th** Parallel : the secret truth behind America's UFO highway / Ben Mezrich. Atria Books, 2016. 288 p. **001.942**

1. Zukowski, Chuck. 2. Human/alien encounters 3. UFOs 4. UFO abductions 5. Paranormal phenomena

ISBN 9781501135521

LC 2016021639

Documents the true story of the author's investigations into paranormal UFO events in America's heartland, detailing a baffling case involving mutilated and exsanguinated livestock and how it was tied to unexplained sightings in Roswell, Area 51 and other regions associated with alien activity.

"Mezrich probably won't sway the skeptical, but fans of Art Bell and company will find all the affirmation they need." Kirkus.

Scoles, Sarah

They are already here : UFO culture and why we see saucers / Sarah Scoles. Pegasus Books, 2020. 248 p. ; **001.942**

1. UFOs -- Sightings and encounters 2. UFOs -- Social aspects 3. UFOs in popular culture 4. Belief and doubt

ISBN 9781643133058

LC bl2020005217

"More general insights into the mercurial quality of memory and belief add considerable heft to this take on an admittedly well-worn topic. Through it all, Scoles remains an open-minded skeptic, and it's this objectivity that makes her buoyant survey so delightful to read." Publishers Weekly

001.944 Monsters and related phenomena

Loxton, Daniel, 1975-

Abominable science! : origins of the Yeti, Nessie, and other famous cryptids / Daniel Loxton and Donald R. Prothero. Columbia University Press, 2013 368 p. **001.944**

1. Cryptozoology. 2. Mythical creatures 3. Pseudoscience.

ISBN 9780231153201

LC 2013008424

A look at mythic beasts and legendary creatures and the arguments both for and against their existence.

002 The book

Lansky, Aaron, 1955-

Outwitting history : the amazing adventures of a man who rescued a million Yiddish books / Aaron Lansky. Algonquin Books of Chapel Hill, 2004. 316 p. **002**

1. Lansky, Aaron, 1955- 2. National Yiddish Book Center (U.S.) -- History. 3. Book collecting. 4. Yiddish imprints. 5. Language revival. 6. Yiddish language.

ISBN 1565124294

LC 2004051587

ALA Notable Book, 2005.

In 1980 an entire body of Jewish literature--the physical remnant of Yiddish culture--was on the verge of extinction. Precious volumes that had survived Hitler and Stalin were being passed down from older generations of Jewish immigrants to their non-Yiddish-speaking children only to be discarded or destroyed. So Aaron Lansky, just twenty-three, issued a worldwide appeal for unwanted Yiddish works.

"Part memoir and part history, this is the . . . tale of how Lansky retrieved thousands of books from dumpsters and abandoned buildings across America. He also rescued books from the aftermath of the 1994 terrorist bombing of the Jewish Community Center in Buenos Aires and went to Havana to save the few remaining Yiddish books of a vestigial Jewish community there." Library Journal.

Raven, James, 1959-

The **Oxford** illustrated history of the book / edited by James Raven. Oxford University Press, 2020 480 p. : **002**

1. Books -- History. 2. Books and reading 3. Printing 4. Bookbinding 5. Essays

ISBN 9780198702986

"A profusely illustrated, handsomely produced intellectual history." Kirkus

Rosenbloom, Megan, 1981-

Dark archives : a librarian's investigation into the science and history of books bound in human skin / Megan Rosenbloom. Farrar, Straus and Giroux, 2020. 288 p. **002**

1. Rare books 2. Skin. 3. Medical ethics. 4. Anthropodermic books.

ISBN 9780374134709

LC 2020023645

Dozens of books bound with human skin live on in the world's most famous libraries and museums. Dark Archives exhumes their origins and brings to life the doctors, murderers, innocents, and indigents whose lives are sewn together in this disquieting collection. Along the way, the author tells the story of how her team of scientists, curators, and librarians test rumored anthropodermic books, untangling the myths around their creation and reckoning with the ethics of their custodianship.

"Essential for most libraries, especially where books about medical history and material culture circulate well." Library Journal

002.03 The book -- Dictionaries

Berger, Sidney E

The **dictionary** of the book : a glossary for book collectors, booksellers, librarians, and others / Sidney E. Berger. Rowman & Littlefield, 2016 xiv, 319 p. : **002.03**

1. Bibliography 2. Book collecting 3. Book industries and trade 4. Library science
ISBN 1442263393

LC 2016013533

"A former museum library director and curator of manuscripts at different institutions, Berger is highly qualified to compile this informative and important work." Booklist.

002.075 Book collecting

Willes, Margaret

Reading matters : five centuries of discovering books / Margaret Willes. Yale University Press, 2008. xvi, 295 p., 8 p. of plates : **002.075**

1. Book collecting -- History 2. Books and reading -- History 3. Bookselling 4. Book collectors -- Great Britain. 5. United States -- History 6. England -- History 7. Great Britain -- History
ISBN 9780300127294

LC 2008015557

"There's a wealth of information here, though some chapters cohere more successfully than others, and a somewhat breathless final chapter surprisingly omits Amazon and e-books as they relate to collecting." Publishers Weekly.

002.09 The book -- History

Houston, Keith, 1977-

The **book** : a cover-to-cover exploration of the most powerful object of our time. / Keith Houston. W.W. Norton & Company, [2016] xvii, 428 pages : **002.09**

1. Books -- History 2. Books and reading -- History. 3. Fiction and culture. 4. Reading.
ISBN 9780393244793

LC 2016002842

Reveals how books and the materials that make them reflect the rich history and culture of human civilization, tracing the development of writing, printing, illustrating and binding to demonstrate the transition from cuneiform tablets and papyrus scrolls to the mass-distributed books of today.

"Pulling together aspects of archaeology, history, literature, and biography, the author reveals the facts, conjecture, and educated guesses experts have made about how and when the first modern tome came to be, which is surprisingly difficult to pin down." Library Journal.

McIlwaine, Catherine

Tolkien : maker of Middle-Earth / Catherine McIlwaine. Bodleian Library, University of Oxford, 2018. 416 p. : **002.09**

1. Tolkien, J. R. R. (John Ronald Reuel), 1892-1973 Exhibitions. 2. Authors, English 3. Creation (Literary, artistic, etc.) 4. Characters and characteristics in literature 5. Writing 6. Illustrated books
ISBN 9781851244850

LC 2018411739

Catalogue published for the exhibition at the Bodleian Library, University of Oxford (2018), and at the Morgan Library & Museum, New York (2019).

This richly illustrated book explores the huge creative endeavour behind Tolkien's enduring popularity. Lavishly illustrated with over 300 images of his manuscripts, drawings, maps and letters, the book traces the creative process behind his most famous literary works -- The Hobbit, The Lord of the Rings and The Silmarillion and reproduces personal photographs and private papers (some of which have never been seen before in print).

"Richly illustrated and dense with information: Tolkien fans could have no better companion." Kirkus.

004 Computer science; computer programming, programs, data; special computer methods

Dyson, George, 1953-

Turing's cathedral : the origins of the digital universe / George Dyson. Pantheon Books, 2012. 512 p. **004**

1. Von Neumann, John, 1903-1957. 2. Turing, Alan Mathison, 1912-1954. 3. Computers -- History. 4. Turing machines. 5. Computer technology. 6. Random access memory.
ISBN 9780375422775

LC 2011030265

Includes index.

ALA Notable Book, 2013

Legendary historian and philosopher of science George Dyson vividly re-creates the scenes of focused experimentation, incredible mathematical insight, and pure creative genius that gave us computers, digital television, modern genetics, models of stellar evolution--in other words, computer code.

DK Publishing, Inc,

Help your kids with computer science : a unique visual step-by-step guide to computers, coding, and communication DK, 2018. 256 p. : **004**

1. Computer science.
ISBN 9781465473608

LC bl2018086689

Includes index.

This visual guide to modern digital life uses diagrams and colorful graphics to show children everything they need to know about how computers and the internet work, as well as help them understand how to stay safe online.

004.16 Personal computers

Mueller, Scott

Upgrading and repairing PCs / Scott M. Mueller. QUE, 2015 xiii, 1162 p. : **004.16**

1. Microcomputers -- Equipment and supplies. 2. Microcomputers

-- Maintenance and repair. 3. Microcomputers -- Upgrading.
ISBN 0789756102

LC bl2015030309

Includes index.

Provides information on how to upgrade, maintain, and troubleshoot the hardware of personal computers, discussing the differences among them as well as their various configuration options.

White, Ron, 1944-

How computers work : the evolution of technology / Ron White ; illustrated by Timothy Edward Downs. Que, 2015 xx, 361 p. : **004.16**

1. Computer input-output equipment. 2. Computers.
ISBN 078974984X

LC bl2015001329

Includes index.

Explains the structure and functions of microprocessors, hard drives, disk drives, tape drives, keyboards, CD-ROM, multimedia sound and video, serial ports, mice, modems, scanners, LANs, and printers.

004.67 Wide-area networks

Janis-Norton, Noel

Calmer, easier, happier screen time : for parents of toddlers to teens : a guide to getting back in charge of technology / Noel Janis-Norton. Yellow Kite, 2017. xiv, 257 p. ; **004.67**

1. Adjustment (Psychology) in children. 2. Computers and children. 3. Computers and civilization. 4. Information technology -- Social aspects.
ISBN 147362276X

LC bl2018052638

Includes index.

How to get back in charge of screen time.

Pariser, Eli

The **filter** bubble : what the Internet is hiding from you / Eli Pariser. Penguin Group USA, 2011. 304 p. **004.67**

1. Internet searching 2. Web search engines 3. Information technology 4. Internet filtering software
ISBN 9781594203008

LC 2011010403

Shows how Internet personalization is limiting information, revealing how sites like Google and Facebook only display results that are most likely to be selected, raising a risk that users will become biased and less informed.

"The distinction between citizen and consumer forms the core of [this book]. Are we consumers whose role in society is primarily to purchase and use products, or are we citizens who make informed decisions in an attempt to make life better for ourselves and the world? The Internet, as Eli Pariser convincingly argues in the book, is hurtling toward a consumer model, existing primarily to sell people stuff at the expense of everything else. Pariser is focused on the personalization model, as well as the filter bubble that the gives the book its name. The biggest companies on the Internet, specifically Google and Facebook, are changing the Internet to match users' specific interests, habits, and purchasing preferences, often without us even knowing we're getting personalized content. Pariser isn't simply a disgruntled anticapitalist, though he lays out the societal and cognitive reasons this particular form of personalization is threatening, using anecdotes, data, philosophy, and social as well as cognitive psychology." AV Club.

Stryker, Cole

Hacking the future : privacy, identity, and anonymity on the Web / Cole Stryker. Penguin Group USA, 2012. 255 p. **004.67**

1. Internet. 2. Internet and freedom of speech. 3. Privacy. 4. Civil rights.
ISBN 9781590209745

LC bl2012036531

A broad analysis of how issues in anonymity and privacy are influencing politics, activism, religion and art in America and the world poses strong arguments about free speech, Internet identity and online piracy while profiling some of the tools and organizations that have evolved on both sides of the debate. By the author of Epic Win for Anonymous.

"A multilayered and well-reasoned retort against all those who would seek to erase anonymity from the Web... The author explores the rich history of anonymity in politics, literature and culture, while also debunking the notion that only troublemakers fear revealing their identities to the world... One of the most well-informed examinations of the Internet available today." Kirkus.

005.1 Software development

Gribbin, John, 1946-

Schrodinger's kittens and the search for reality : solving the quantum mysteries / John Gribbin. Little, Brown & Co., 1995. ix, 261 p. : **005.1**

1. Schrodinger, Erwin, 1887-1961. 2. Heisenberg uncertainty principle 3. Quantum theory. 4. Light. 5. Reality.
ISBN 0316328383

LC 95075652

"Gribbin reviews this active and controversial field and cautiously indicates his personal preference for one of the new theoretical models. It is fascinating to see how a problem long regarded as "settled" has acquired new layers of mystery." Library Journal.

Dugger, Kayla,

Beginner's step-by-step coding course : learn computer programming the easy way / US editor: Kayla Dugger ; contributors: Clif Kussmaul, Sean McManus, Craig Steele, Dr. Claire Quigley, Dr. Tammy Pirmann, Dr. Martin Goodfellow, Jonathan Hogg, David Krowitz.. Dorling Kindersley, 2020. 359 p. : **005.1**

1. Computer programming 2. Coding theory
ISBN 9781465482211

LC bl2020002901

Includes index.

Learning to code is made easier by this full-color guide to computer programming for beginners.

"The value of this book . . . lies in the structure it provides for novice programmers to get comfortable with the language and its interface and its progression from easier to more difficult programming concepts and projects. Recommended for novice programmers who would rather work from a book than from multiple websites." Booklist

005.1092 Computer software developers

Thompson, Clive, 1968-

Coders : the making of a new tribe and the remaking of the world / Clive Thompson. Penguin Press, [2019] 448 p. **005.1092**

1. Computer programmers 2. Computer programming -- Social aspects 3. Computer programming -- Psychological aspects 4.

Interpersonal relations
ISBN 9780735220560

LC 2018051657

We live in a world constructed of code--and coders are the ones who built it for us. From acclaimed tech writer Clive Thompson comes a brilliant anthropological reckoning with the most powerful tribe in the world today, computer programmers, in a book that interrogates who they are, how they think, what qualifies as greatness in their world, and what should give us pause. They are the most quietly influential people on the planet, and Coders shines a light on their culture.

"This engaging work will appeal to readers who wish to learn more about the intersection of technology and culture, and the space in which they blur together." Library Journal.

005.13 Programming languages

Payne, Bryson

Teach your kids to code / Bryson Payne. No Starch Press, 2015. 213 p. **005.13**

1. Computer programming 2. Programming languages (Computers) 3. Python (Computer program language) 4. Computer programmers
ISBN 9781593276140

LC 2015006794

A guide to teaching basic programming skills for parents and teachers, with step-by-step explanations, visual examples, and exercises. Covers programming concepts including loops, lists, functions, and variables, and how to build games and applications.

"The full-color printing includes charming spot illustrations, code-output screenshots, and example codes in a layout and color scheme identical to the Python editor. Sophisticated concepts and serious programming make for an easy, enjoyable game for families." Kirkus.

005.7 Data in computer systems

Malone, Thomas W.

Superminds : the surprising power of people and computers thinking together / Thomas W. Malone. Little, Brown and Company, 2018. 288 p. **005.7**

1. Human/computer interaction 2. Computers and civilization 3. Swarm intelligence 4. Thought and thinking
ISBN 9780316349130

LC bl2018080009

The founding director of the MIT Center for Collective Intelligence demonstrates through examples and case studies how artificially intelligent computers can and will amplify the power of groups of people working together collectively in "superminds."

O'Neil, Cathy

★**Weapons** of math destruction : how big data increases inequality and threatens democracy / Cathy O'Neil. Crown Publishers, 2016 272 p. **005.7**

1. Big data. 2. Social indicators -- Mathematical models -- Moral and ethical aspects. 3. Democracy. 4. Mathematical models. 5. United States -- Social conditions -- 21st century.
ISBN 9780553418811

LC 2016003900

A former Wall Street quantitative analyst sounds an alarm on mathematical modeling, a pervasive new force in society that threatens to undermine democracy and widen inequality.

005.8 Data security

Mitnick, Kevin D. (Kevin David), 1963-

The **art** of invisibility : the world's most famous hacker teaches you how to be safe in the age of Big Brother and big data / Kevin Mitnick with Robert Vamosi. Little, Brown and Company, 2017 320 p. **005.8**

1. Internet -- Security measures. 2. Computer security. 3. Data protection. 4. Privacy rights.
ISBN 9780316380508

LC 2016024302

A world-famous hacker reveals unsettling truths about information vulnerability while outlining affordable online and offline strategies for maximizing privacy and computer security.

Olson, Parmy

We are Anonymous : inside the hacker world of LulzSec, Anonymous, and the global cyber insurgency / Parmy Olson. Little, Brown and Co., 2012. 512 p. **005.8**

1. Anonymous (Group) 2. Hackers. 3. Hacking. 4. Internet -- Security measures. 5. Cyberculture.
ISBN 9780316213547

LC 2012936919

Follows the stories of three key members of the hacker groups Anonymous and LulzSec, drawing on clandestine conversations with many other members, showing how their pasts led them to their roles as "hacktivists" that can bring some of the biggest nations and companies to their knees.

006.3 Artificial intelligence

Baker, Stephen, 1955 November 15-

Final jeopardy : man vs. machine and the quest to know everything / Stephen Baker. Houghton Mifflin Harcourt, 2011. 272 p. **006.3**

1. International Business Machines Corporation 2. Jeopardy (Television program) 3. Artificial intelligence 4. Technology -- Social aspects 5. Knowledge
ISBN 9780547483160

LC 2010051653

Follows the quest of a team of scientists to develop a computer so intelligent that it can beat the best of champions in the Jeopardy quiz show.

Dormehl, Luke

Thinking machines : the quest for artificial intelligence and where it's taking us next / Luke Dormehl. TarcherPerigee, 2017. 288 p. **006.309**

1. Artificial intelligence 2. Computers 3. Computers and civilization 4. Neural networks (Computer science)
ISBN 9780143130581

LC 2016044018

Technology journalist Dormehl takes you through the history of AI and how it makes up the foundations of the machines that think for us today. Furthermore, Dormehl speculates on the incredible -- and possibly terrifying -- future that's much closer than many would imagine.

"With interesting real-life characters . and stories about headline-news smart devices, Thinking Machines is an easy introduction for readers wanting insight into how technology fits into their lives." Booklist.

Kasparov, G. K. (Garri Kimovich)

Deep thinking : where machine intelligence ends and human creativity begins / Garry Kasparov, with Mig Greengard. Public Affairs, 2017. vii, 287 p. ; **006.3**

1. Kasparov, G. K. (Garri Kimovich) 2. Chess players 3. Computers 4. Artificial intelligence 5. Human/computer interaction

ISBN 9781610397865

LC 2017304768

The former world chess champion who played, and lost, against Deep Blue, a supercomputer, in 1997 discusses why he thinks humans should embrace the competition between themselves and machine intelligence and how it can open us up to exploring new challenges.

"Thoughtful reading for anyone interested in human and machine cognition and a must for chess fans." Kirkus.

Lepore, Jill, 1966-

If then : how the Simulmatics Corporation invented the future / Jill Lepore. Liveright Publishing, 2020 xii, 415 p. **006.3**

1. Simulmatics Corporation 2. Data mining 3. Algorithms 4. Big data 5. Computer simulation

ISBN 9781631496103

LC 2020008058

A revelatory account of the Cold War origins of the data-mad, algorithmic twenty-first century. The Simulmatics Corporation, founded in 1959, mined data, targeted voters, accelerated news, manipulated consumers, destabilized politics, and disordered knowledge--decades before Facebook, Google, Amazon, and Cambridge Analytica. Borrowing from psychological warfare, they used computers to predict and direct human behavior, deploying their "People Machine" from New York, Cambridge, and Saigon for clients that included John Kennedy's presidential campaign, the New York Times, Young & Rubicam, and, during the Vietnam War, the Department of Defense. Jill Lepore, distinguished Harvard historian and New Yorker staff writer, unearthed from the archives the almost unbelievable story of this long-vanished corporation, and of the women hidden behind it.

"Scholars of American history and technology will appreciate the extensive research that went into this book, while general readers will be swept up by the novelistic scope of the story." Library Journal

Mulgan, Geoff

Big mind : how collective intelligence can change our world / Geoff Mulgan. Princeton University Press, 2017. 200 p. **006.3**

1. Intelligence 2. Technology -- Social aspects. 3. Thought and thinking 4. Collaboration

ISBN 9780691170794

LC 2017954117

Gathering insights from diverse fields, including philosophy, computer science, and biology, Big Mind reveals how collective intelligence can guide corporations, governments, universities, and societies to make the most of human brains and digital technologies.

"In this brilliant, somewhat heady, but generally accessible book, Mulgan (The Locust and the Bee: Predators and Creators in Capitalism's Future, 2015, etc.), chief executive of Nesta, Britain's National Endowment for Science, Technology and the Arts, shows how the answers can be found in the emerging field of collective intelligence, which links people and machines to foster 'dramatic jumps' in group intelligence." Kirkus.

006.301 Artificial intelligence--philosophy

Bostrom, Nick, 1973-

Superintelligence : paths, dangers, strategies / Nick Bostrom, Director, Future of Humanity Institute Professor, Faculty of Philosophy & Oxford Martin School University of Oxford. Oxford University Press, 2014. xvi, 328 p. : **006.301**

1. Cognitive science. 2. Artificial intelligence -- Philosophy. 3. Technological forecasting. 4. Scientific forecasting.

ISBN 9780199678112

LC 2013955152

"Bostrom delivers a comprehensive outline of the philosophical foundations of the nature of intelligence and the difficulty not only in agreeing on a suitable definition of that concept but in living with the possibly dire consequences of that concept." Choice.

Russell, Stuart J. (Stuart Jonathan)

Human compatible : artificial intelligence and the problem of control / Stuart Russell. Viking, 2019. 352 p. **006.301**

1. Artificial intelligence 2. Automation 3. Risk management. 4. Risk analysis.

ISBN 9780525558613

LC 2019029688

A leading artificial intelligence researcher lays out a new approach to AI that will enable us to coexist successfully with increasingly intelligent machines.

Tegmark, Max

Life 3.0 : being human in the age of artificial intelligence / Max Tegmark. Alfred A. Knopf, 2017 336 p. **006.301**

1. Artificial intelligence -- Social aspects. 2. Robotics 3. Forecasting. 4. Technology -- Economic aspects.

ISBN 9781101946596

LC 2017006248

An MIT professor of physics and co-founder of the Future of Life Institute explores key questions related to a near-future world of increasing digital autonomy, exploring the likeliness of suprahuman intelligence, the role of A.I. in replacing human jobs and how legal systems might handle autonomous issues.

"Stretching the superhuman AI idea to intergalactic proportions by envisioning its colonization of the universe, Tegmark enthusiastically lays out concepts of AI, to the delight or disturbance of readers." Booklist.

006.7 Multimedia systems

Bilton, Nick

Hatching Twitter : a true story of money, power, friendship, and betrayal / Nick Bilton. Portfolio, 2013. 288 p. **006.7**

1. Dorsey, Jack, 1976- 2. Williams, Evan, 1972- 3. Stone, Biz 4. Glass, Noah 5. Twitter (Electronic resource) 6. Internet industry and trade 7. Online social networks. 8. Internet -- Social aspects 9. Instant messaging

ISBN 9781591846017

LC 2013037924

A behind-the-scenes portrait of the influential news and networking company traces its rise from a failed podcasting business to a multi-billion-dollar giant, recounting the high-stakes power struggles, betrayed friendships and global influences that shaped its evolution.

Krug, Steve
★**Don't** make me think, revisited : a common sense approach to web usability / Steve Krug. New Riders, 2014 xi, 200 p. : **006.7**

1. Web site development. 2. Web sites -- Design.
ISBN 0321965515

LC bl2014002331

Includes index.

Offers observations and solutions to fundamental Web design problems, as well as a new chapter about mobile Web design.

Maxwell, Lucas
Podcasting with youth : a quick guide for librarians and educators / Lucas Maxwell. Libraries Unlimited, 2020. 90 p. **006.7**

1. Children's libraries -- Activity programs. 2. Podcasting -- Library applications.
ISBN 9781440870354

LC 2020003262

"Learn how to set up a student-led podcast in your library, involve staff from several subject areas, market effectively, what challenges you are likely to face, and how podcasting will benefit the students and school overall".-- Provided by publisher.

Meinzer, Kristen
So you want to start a podcast : finding your voice, telling your story, and building a community that will listen / Kristen Meinzer. William Morrow, 2019 viii, 216 p. ; **006.7**

1. Podcasting 2. Podcasts
ISBN 9780062936677

LC bl2019022417

Includes index.

An award-winning commentator and producer shares her expertise, providing aspiring podcasters with advice for working smarter, not harder as they start their own audio forum.

006.8 Augmented and virtual reality

Harris, Blake J.
The **history** of the future : how a bunch of misfits, makers, and mavericks cracked the code of virtual reality / Blake J. Harris ; foreword by Ernest Cline. Dey Street Books, 2018. 320 p. **006.8**

1. Virtual reality 2. Computer software developers 3. Corporations 4. Virtual reality industry and trade
ISBN 9780062455963

LC bl2018079213

The author of Console Wars traces the development of virtual reality technology and the achievements of his Facebook-acquired startup, Oculus VR, to share engaging insights into how VR is already transforming the world.

011 Bibliographies and catalogs

O'Gorman, Jack
Reference sources for small and medium-sized libraries / Jack O'Gorman, editor. American Library Association, 2014. xxi, 289 p. ; **011**

1. Reference books -- Bibliography. 2. Small libraries -- United States -- Book lists.
ISBN 9780838912126

LC 2013049993

Includes index.

Focusing on new reference sources published since 2008 and reference titles that have retained their relevance, this new edition brings O'Gorman's complete and authoritative guide to the best reference sources for small and medium-sized academic and public libraries fully up to date. --Provided by publisher.

"An essential for the well-appointed professional shelf, O'Gorman's update of current reference materials accommodates both professionals and young readers." VOYA

Pearl, Nancy
More book lust : recommended reading for every mood, moment, and reason / Nancy Pearl. Sasquatch Books, c2005. xv, 286 p. ; **011**

1. Best books. 2. Books and reading -- United States.
ISBN 9781570614354

LC 2004066292

The Seattle librarian who created the popular program "If All of Seattle Read the Same Book" organizes readers' interests into 150 sometimes unusual categories, recommending great books in each.

Rosow, La Vergne
Accessing the classics : great reads for adults, teens, and English language learners / La Vergne Rosow. Libraries Unlimited, 2006. xi, 301 p. ; **011**

1. Best books -- United States. 2. Best books. 3. Canon (Literature) 4. English language -- Study and teaching -- Foreign speakers.
ISBN 1563088916

LC 2005030838

"This collection of annotated titles aims at providing resources for anyone who works with inexperienced or low-literacy teenagers or adults." Voice of Youth Advocates.

011.02 Bibliographies and catalogs of reference works

Whitlatch, Jo Bell,
Guide to reference : essential general reference and library science sources / Jo Bell Whitlatch and Susan E. Searing, Editors. ALA Editions, 2014. xiv, 230 p. ; **011.02**

1. Reference books -- Bibliography. 2. Reference sources -- Bibliography. 3. Reference services (Libraries).
ISBN 9780838912324

LC 2014013098

Ideal for public, school, and academic libraries looking to freshen up their reference collection, as well as for LIS students and instructors conducting research, this resource collects the cream of the crop sources of general reference and library science information. --Provided by publisher.

011.62 Works for young people

Chance, Rosemary
★**Young** adult literature in action : a librarian's guide / Rose Brock. Libraries Unlimited, 2019 xvii, 219 p. ; **011.62**

1. Teenagers -- Books and reading -- United States -- Bibliography. 2. Young adults -- Books and reading -- United States -- Bibliography. 3. Young adult literature -- Bibliography. 4. Young adult literature,

American -- Bibliography.
ISBN 9781440866937

LC 2019018612

Taking a genre approach, this overview of young adult literature shows new librarians and library science students the criteria to use for selecting quality books, including recommended titles.

Martin, William P. (William Patrick)
Wonderfully wordless : the 500 most recommended graphic novels and picture books / William Patrick Martin. Rowman & Littlefield, 2015 xvii, 315 p. : **011.62**

1. Picture books for children -- Bibliography. 2. Picture books -- Bibliography. 3. Graphic novels -- Bibliography. 4. Best books.
ISBN 9781442254770

LC 2015019482

"As this is compiled out of the choices of librarians, educators, and reviewers from around the world, no dark corner is left unexplored, illuminating a far greater array of choices than any reader might have guessed. The choices, furthermore, are ideally arranged for both browsing and targeted navigation, with more than 30 topic-focused chapters covering everything from fantasy, mystery, and comedy to curricular topics like friendship, numbers and letters, and environmental awareness." Booklist

016 Bibliographies and catalogs of works on specific subjects

Beisner, Robert L.
American foreign relations since 1600 : a guide to the literature / Robert L. Beisner, editor. ABC-CLIO, c2003. 2 v. (xviii, 2065 p.) ; **016**

1. United States -- Foreign relations Bibliography.
ISBN 9781576070802

LC 2003008684

Rev. ed. of: Guide to American foreign relations since 1700 / edited by Richard Dean Burns. 1983.

Chronicles American foreign relations literature from colonial times to the present, with updated material on post World-War II.

Clark, Craig A.
Read on...sports : reading lists for every taste / Craig Clark and Richard T. Fox. Libraries Unlimited, 2014 xv, 165 p. ; **016**

1. Sports -- Bibliography
ISBN 9781610693578

LC 2013034587

"Organized across appeal features, this comprehensive listing of stories, biographies, and fiction is the first and only guide to sports literature for adult and teen readers"-- Provided by publisher.

Frolund, Tina
Read on...history : reading lists for every taste / Tina Frolund. Libraries Unlimited, 2013. xiv, 195 p. ; **016**

1. History 2. Public libraries -- United States 3. Readers' advisory services -- United States. 4. United States -- History Bibliography. 5. Book lists.
ISBN 1610690346

LC 2013029492

Includes index.

"Make history come alive! This book helps librarians and teachers as well as readers themselves find books they will enjoy--titles that will animate and explain the past, entertain, and expand their minds".-- Provided by publisher.

Ladd, Dana L.
The **Medical** Library Association guide to finding out about diabetes : the best print and electronic resources / Dana L. Ladd and Alyssa Altshuler. Neal-Schuman, an imprint of the American Library Association, 2013. xii, 323 p. ; **016**

1. Diabetes 2. Diabetes -- Computer network resources 3. Diabetes.
ISBN 1555708900

LC 2012028333

"This basic, plainly written bibliography is a must for any collection expected to provide current resources on diabetes to health-care students, medical professionals, or patients and their families." Library Journal.

Martinez, Sara E.
Latino literature / edited by Sara E. Martinez ; foreword by Connie Van Fleet. Libraries Unlimited, c2009. xxii, 364 p. ; **016**

1. American fiction -- Hispanic American authors -- Bibliography. 2. Hispanic American fiction (Spanish) -- 20th century -- Translations into English -- Bibliography. 3. Hispanic American fiction (Spanish) -- 21st century -- Translations into English -- Bibliography. 4. American literature -- Hispanic American authors -- Bibliography.
ISBN 9781591582922

LC 2009026355

Sub-title on cover : A guide to reading interests.

Presents a list of recommended works by Hispanic American authors published between 1995 and 2008, with plot summaries, subject headings, and quotes from each work, in such genres as general fiction, mystery, romance, fantasy, and nonfiction.

"This well-written book is an essential resource for public and high-school libraries, especially if they serve Latino populations." Booklist.

McCollough, Carole J,
★The **Coretta** Scott King awards : 50th anniversary / edited by Carole J. McCollough and Adelaide Poniatowski Phelps. ALA Editions, 2019. 214 p. **016**

1. Coretta Scott King Award. 2. American literature -- African American authors -- Bibliography. 3. American literature -- African American authors -- Awards. 4. Children's literature, American -- Bibliography.
ISBN 9780838918692

LC 2019010142

"The Coretta Scott King Book Awards Committee, Ethnic and Multicultural Information Exchange Round Table."

Marking the 50th anniversary of the Coretta Scott King (CSK) Book Awards, this invaluable guide celebrates the legacy of these prestigious honors, which have enlarged the prominence of literature for children and youth about the Black experience. Provided by publisher

Niebuhr, Gary Warren
Caught up in crime : a reader's guide to crime fiction and nonfiction / Gary Warren Niebuhr. Libraries Unlimited/ABC-CLIO, c2009. xviii, 304 p. ; **016**

1. Crime writing -- Bibliography. 2. Criminal investigation -- Bibliography.
ISBN 9781591584285

LC 2009008733

Includes indexes.

"The only challenge that readers or readers advisors face when confronted with so many excellent choices is deciding where to begin reading. Whether youre after capers, serial-killer tales, white-collar crime, mobsters, dirty cops or lawyers, criminals on the lam, amateur criminals, or any other kind of crime tale, this work is recommended as a thoughtful starting point." Booklist.

Ottemiller, John H. (John Henry), 1916-1968
Ottemiller's index to plays in collections : an author and title index to plays appearing in collections published since 1900. / Denise L. Montgomery. Scarecrow Press, Inc., c2011. xlix, 781 p. ; **016**

1. Drama
ISBN 0810877201

LC 2010053010

"Returning after some 20 years, this volume (7th ed., 1988) remains the classic index to plays in collections and anthologies... Plays are indexed by title, author, and anthology title. Montgomery adds more than 2,300 new authors and 3,593 new plays, expanding the work's focus to include works from 103 countries and making works by women and LGBT authors more discoverable." Choice.

Perrault, Anna H., 1944-
Information resources in the humanities and the arts. / Elizabeth S. Aversa, Anna H. Perrault, Sonia Ramirez (CON) Wohlmuth, Cynthia (CON) Miller. Libraries Unlimited, an imprint of ABC-CLIO, LLC 2013 xvii, 461 p. ; 26 **016**

1. Arts 2. Arts -- Electronic information resources. 3. Arts -- Information services 4. Arts -- Reference books
ISBN 159884833X

LC 2012028606

Third-fifth editions, authored by Ron Blazek and Elizabeth Aversa, entitled Humanities : a selective guide to information sources; First and second editions authored by A. Robert Rogers.

"This familiar guide to information resources in the humanities and the arts, organized by subjects and emphasizing electronic resources, enables librarians, teachers, and students to quickly find the best resources for their diverse needs".-- Provided by publisher.

Riechel, Rosemarie, 1937-
Easy information sources for ESL, adult learners & new readers / Rosemarie Riechel. Neal-Schuman Publishers, c2009. ix, 285 p. ; **016**

1. Adult services in public libraries -- United States 2. High interest-low vocabulary books 3. Libraries and new literates -- United States 4. Libraries -- Special collections -- Children's literature
ISBN 9781555706500

LC 2008040028

Provides a plan for using children's literature to teach adult ESL students and new literates, and provides an annotated bibliography of suggested titles.

"This work is aimed at educators and librarians working with adults whose English is poor. Advice on ways to use children's nonfiction for adults; reference interview strategies; book selection, placement, and utilization; collection development; and readers' advisory enables this work to not only suggest sources but also offer new ways of serving this growing and diverse population." Booklist.

Stoeger, Melissa Brackney
Food lit : a reader's guide to epicurean nonfiction / Melissa Brackney Stoeger. Libraries Unlimited, 2013 xx, 350 p. **016**

1. Food -- Bibliography. 2. Recipes
ISBN 1598847066

LC 2012038052

"An essential tool for assisting leisure readers interested in topics surrounding food, this unique book contains annotations and read-alikes for hundreds of nonfiction titles about the joys of comestibles and cooking".-- Provided by publisher.

"The hundreds of annotations alone make any librarians job much, much easier, but Stoeger's inclusion of appendix materials from famous cooks and their books, food blogs, feature films and documentaries, fiction featuring food, and food-writing awards makes this an outstanding reference tool for any public library collection." Booklist.

Vnuk, Rebecca
Women's fiction : a guide to popular reading interests / Rebecca Vnuk and Nanette Donohue. Libraries Unlimited, 2013 xv, 233 p. ; **016**

1. American fiction -- 21st century -- Bibliography. 2. American fiction -- 20th century -- Bibliography. 3. Women -- Bibliography. 4. American fiction -- Women authors -- Bibliography.
ISBN 9781598849202

LC 2013023685

Offering a fresh perspective on women's fiction for a broad reading audience--fans as well as librarians--this book defines and maps the genre, and describes hundreds of relevant titles. --Provided by publisher.

016.58 Botany--bibliographies

Fraser, Susan M.
Flora illustrata : great works from the LuEsther T. Mertz Library of the New York Botanical Garden / edited by Susan M. Fraser and Vanessa Bezemer Sellers. Yale University Press, 2014. xxiii, 296 p. : **016.58**

1. LuEsther T. Mertz Library Bibliography. 2. LuEsther T. Mertz Library -- History. 3. Botanical libraries -- New York (State) -- New York. 4. Book collecting -- New York (State) -- New York. 5. Botanical illustration -- Bibliography. 6. Flowers in art -- Bibliography.
ISBN 9780300196627

LC bl2014050949

Presents the history and significance of some of the most important works held by the renowned New York City library, including handwritten manuscripts, botanical artworks, herbals, explorer's notebooks, and nineteenth-century media.

016.74 Graphic arts--bibliographies

Pawuk, Michael
Graphic novels : a guide to comic books, manga, and more / Michael Pawuk and David S. Serchay. Libraries Unlimited, 2017. xxxv, 719 p. : **016.74**

1. Comic books, strips, etc. -- Bibliography. 2. Comic books, strips, etc. -- Themes, motives.
ISBN 9781598847000

LC 2017002418

An annotated bibliographic guide to graphic novels and comics contains over three thousand titles listed by genre and sub-genre.

Weiner, Stephen, 1955-
101 outstanding graphic novels / Stephen Weiner ; introduction by Ellen Forney ; edited by Danny Fingeroth. NBM Publishing,

2015 80 p. : **016.74**

1. Graphic novels -- Bibliography. 2. Best books -- United States.
ISBN 9781561639441

LC bl2016005306

A listing of recommended graphic novels currently available in the United States includes a black-and-white illustration of the cover, a suggested age rating, and a brief review.

016.78 Music--bibliographies

Boomhower, Daniel F., 1976-

A **basic** music library : essential scores and sound recordings / compiled by the Music Library Association ; Daniel F. Boomhower, editor ; Edward Komara, Amanda Maple, and Liza Vick, associate editors. American Library Association, 2017. 359 p. ; **016.78**

1. Music 2. Music libraries -- Collection development.
ISBN 0838910394

LC 2013020223

Prepared by the Music Library Association, with thousands of records selected by experts in dozens of specialized and popular areas of music, A Basic Music Library constitutes the most authoritative music collection resource available. --Provided by publisher.

Friedwald, Will, 1961-

The **great** jazz and pop vocal albums / Will Friedwald. Pantheon Books, 2017 xxv, 402 p. : **016.78**

1. Jazz vocals 2. Popular music 3. Singers 4. Sound recordings
ISBN 0307379078

LC 2016027178

A deeply personal survey of 57 of the greatest 20th-century jazz and pop albums considers how singers and musicians shaped and organized their extraordinary collections of songs, revealing personal stories of the singers' successes and failures.

"This absolutely indispensable compendium of essential jazz and pop vocal albums is a testament to the ongoing vibrancy of jazz music and the Great American Songbook." Booklist.

016.78026 Sound recordings--music--catalogs, . . .

Woodstra, Chris

All music guide to classical music : the definitive guide to classical music / edited by Chris Woodstra, Gerald Brennan, Allen Schrott. Backbeat Books, c2005. v, 1607 p. ; **016.78026**

1. Music -- Dictionaries. 2. Music -- Discography.
ISBN 9780879308650

LC 2005023988

Includes discographies and index.

Offering comprehensive coverage of classical music, this guide surveys more than eleven thousand albums and presents biographies of five hundred composers and eight hundred performers, as well as twenty-three essays on forms, eras, and genres of classical music.

016.79143 Motion pictures--bibliographies, . . .

Barsanti, Chris

The **sci-fi** movie guide : the universe of film from Alien to Zardoz / Chris Barsanti. Visible Ink Press, 2015. xvii, 510 p. : **016.79143**

1. Science fiction films
ISBN 1578595037

LC 2014017822

"A great book for science fiction cinephiles and novices alike, this is a must for those interested in updating their film guidebook collections." Choice.

016.80883 Bibliographies -- Novels

Dilevko, Juris

Contemporary world fiction : a guide to literature in translation / Juris Dilevko, Keren Dali, and Glenda Garbutt. Libraries Unlimited, c2011. xxvi, 526 p. ; **016.80883**

1. Fiction -- 20th century -- Translations into English -- Bibliography
2. Fiction -- 21st century -- Translations into English -- Bibliography
ISBN 9781591583530

LC 2010052517

This much-needed guide to translated literature offers readers the opportunity to hear from, learn about, and perhaps better understand our shrinking world from the perspective of insiders from many cultures and traditions. --Provided by publisher.

Husband, Janet, 1942-

Sequels : an annotated guide to novels in series / Janet G. Husband & Jonathan F. Husband. American Library Association, 2009. viii, 782 p. ; **016.80883**

1. Fiction -- Bibliography. 2. Sequels (Literature) -- Bibliography.
ISBN 9780838909676

LC 2009016426

Includes index.

A guide to series fiction lists popular series, identifies novels by character, and offers guidance on the order in which to read unnumbered series.

Quillen, C. L.

Read on... romance : reading lists for every taste / C.L. Quillen and Ilene N. Lefkowitz. Libraries Unlimited, 2014 xii, 136 p. ; **016.80883**

1. Romance fiction -- Bibliography 2. Romance fiction -- History and criticism 3. Reading interests 4. Books and reading
ISBN 9781610694001

LC 2014005515

"With thousands of romance novels published each year, librarians--especially those unfamiliar with or indifferent to the genre--can benefit from this well-organized, reference that offers scores of appeals-based read-alike lists for some of the most popular, contemporary romance fiction."-- Provided by publisher

"Each chapter opens with a brief explanation of the specific appeal characteristic and why and how readers may ask for a romance that focuses on a particular element. Lists average about 7 to 10 titles, with solid annotations that capture the essence of each book." Booklist

Ramsdell, Kristin, 1940-

Romance fiction : a guide to the genre / Kristin Ramsdell. Libraries Unlimited, c2012. xxii, 719 p. ; **016.80883**

1. Romance fiction -- Bibliography. 2. Romance fiction -- History and criticism.
ISBN 9781591581772

LC 2011045879

Presents a comprehensive guide for librarians and readers' advisors, provides a brief history of the romance novel, and offers reading lists and subgenre definitions.

016.8093 Bibliographies -- Genre fiction

Niebuhr, Gary Warren

Make mine a mystery II : a reader's guide to mystery and detective fiction / Gary Warren Niebuhr. Libraries Unlimited, c2011. xiv, 292 p. ; **016.8093**

1. Mysteries -- Bibliography. 2. Mysteries -- Stories, plots, etc.
ISBN 9781598845891

LC 2011017226

This valuable reference and collection development tool is designed to assist readers' advisors in helping readers find modern detective mysteries they will enjoy.

"The authors included give a good representation of popular writers today. The bibliographies have also been updated. This is an excellent companion to the original volume and an essential readers advisory tool." Booklist.

016.813 American fiction--1900-1945--bibliographies

Honig, Megan

Urban grit : a guide to street lit / Megan Honig. Libraries Unlimited, 2011. xxiv, 251 p. ; **016.813**

1. Urban fiction, American -- Bibliography. 2. Urban fiction, American -- Stories, plots, etc. 3. Readers' advisory services -- United States. 4. Fiction in libraries.
ISBN 9781591588573

LC 2010041099

Presents annotations for over four hundred titles; provides an overview of the genre, including its history, readership, and defining characteristics; and offers recommendations for titles in a variety of subgenres.

"Recommended for professional reading shelves as well as for researchers who will find value in Honig's defining the genre. This should be the definitive choice on the subject, with Andrew Ratner's practical teaching and classroom guide Street Lit: Teaching and Reading Fiction in Urban Schools as a good complement." Library Journal.

Hooper, Brad

Read on--historical fiction : reading lists for every taste / Brad Hooper. Libraries Unlimited, 2006. xii, 152 p. ; **016.813**

1. Fiction in libraries -- United States. 2. Historical fiction, American -- Bibliography. 3. Historical fiction, English -- Bibliography. 4. Readers' advisory services -- United States.
ISBN 9781591582397

LC 2006003711

Hundreds of popular historical fiction titles are described and categorized according to their underlying appeal features, and under topics not found in the library catalog, such as women with true grit, greatest war stories, royalty rules, quick reads, humor, and others.

Morris, Vanessa Irvin

The **readers'** advisory guide to street literature / Vanessa Irvin Morris ; foreword by Teri Woods. American Library Association, 2012. xxiii, 138 p. : **016.813**

1. Fiction in libraries. 2. Readers' advisory services -- United States. 3. Street life 4. Urban fiction, American
ISBN 0838911102

LC 2011029685

Provides information about the genre of urban fiction, including its appeal to readers, its characteristics and structural elements, its history, and readers' advisory and collection development strategies for librarians.

016.8223 Shakespeare, William, 1564-1616--bibliographies

Collins, Paul, 1969-

★The **book** of William : how Shakespeare's first folio conquered the world / Paul Collins. Bloomsbury USA, c2009. 288 p. **016.8223**

1. Shakespeare, William, 1564-1616. Plays 2. Manuscripts, English. 3. Manuscripts -- Collectors and collecting. 4. Book collecting. 5. Rare books.
ISBN 9781596911956

LC 2009006722

A history of the Bard's competitively pursued First Folio traces the author's travels from the site of a Sotheby auction to regions in Asia, throughout which he investigated the roles played by those who have sought and owned the Folios.

016.92 General collected biographies--bibliographies

Roche, Rick

Read on-- biography : reading lists for every taste / Rick Roche. Libraries Unlimited, c2012. xvi, 163 p. ; **016.92**

1. Autobiography 2. Biography
ISBN 1598847015

LC 2011046293

"Categorizing hundreds of popular biographies according to their primary appeal--character, story, setting, language, and mood--and organizing them into thematic lists, this guide will help readers' advisors more effectively recommend titles". --Provided by publisher.

"Packed with 450 engaging, succinct annotations, this volume is organized by the appeal characteristics of character, story, setting, language, and mood." Booklist

020 Library and information sciences

Woodward, Jeannette A.

The **transformed** library : e-books, expertise, and evolution / Jeannette Woodward. ALA Editions, 2013. xiii, 131 p. ; **020**

1. Librarians -- Effect of technological innovations on. 2. Libraries and electronic publishing. 3. Libraries and society. 4. Libraries and the Internet.
ISBN 9780838911648

LC 2012023767

This wide-ranging survey takes stock of our institutions' strengths, weaknesses, opportunities, and threats, analyzing how libraries and the very concept of librarianship have been comprehensively transformed over the past few decades. --Provided by publisher.

"The goal of this book is to assess the current state of libraries (academic, public, and school); thoughtfully predict future scenarios; and provide suggestions for how librarians can survive these scenarios and, in doing so, create better libraries." Booklist

020.1 Library and information sciences -- Philosophy and theory

Lankes, R. David

The **atlas** of new librarianship / R. David Lankes. MIT Press ; c2011. xv, 408 p. : **020.1**

1. Libraries and community. 2. Libraries and society. 3. Library science -- Forecasting. 4. Library science -- Philosophy.

ISBN 0262015099

LC 2010022788

Includes 1 folded chart in pocket inside back cover.

"Libraries have existed for millennia, but today the library field is searching for solid footing in an increasingly fragmented (and increasingly digital) information environment. What is librarianship when it is unmoored from cataloging, books, buildings, and committees? In The Atlas of New Librarianship, R. David Lankes offers a guide to this new landscape for practitioners. He describes a new librarianship based not on books and artifacts but on knowledge and learning; and he suggests a new mission for librarians: to improve society through facilitating knowledge creation in their communities. The vision for a new librarianship must go beyond finding library-related uses for information technology and the Internet; it must provide a durable foundationfor the field. Lankes recasts librarianship and library practice using the fundamental concept that knowledge is created though conversation. New librarians approach their work as facilitators of conversation; they seek to enrich, capture, store, and disseminate the conversations of their communities. To help librarians navigate this new terrain, Lankes offers a map, a visual representation of the field that can guide explorations of it; more than 140 Agreements, statements about librarianship that rangefrom relevant theories to examples of practice; and Threads, arrangements of Agreements to explain key ideas, covering such topics as conceptual foundations and skills and values. Agreement Supplements at the end of the book offer expanded discussions. Although it touches on theory as well as practice, the Atlas is meant to be a tool: textbook, conversation guide, platform for social networking, and call to action."--M.I.T. Press Web page.

"The author initiates a conversation about librarianship and its future. He builds this conversation using an atlas, or topical mapping, to engage librarians in exploring their profession, their mission, and their future. Grounding the atlas in the why of librarianship, Lankes argues that libraries serve not only as repositories providing access to information but as fertile ground for actively using collections, resources, and information to create knowledge and foster learning via ongoing conversations with our communities. He invites librarians to expand librarianship beyond the support of information seeking, access, and literacy and toward participation in and co-ownership of a community's knowledge-creation processes. Essential for all librarians." Library Journal.

Lankes, R. David, 1970-

The **new** librarianship field guide / R. David Lankes ; with contributions from Wendy Newman, Sue Kowalski, Beck Tench, and Cheryl Gould ; and guidance from the New Librarianship Collaborative: Kimberly Silk, Wendy Newman, and Lauren Britton. The MIT Press, 2016 viii, 226 p. : **020.1**

1. Librarians -- Attitudes. 2. Libraries and community. 3. Libraries and society. 4. Library science -- Philosophy.

ISBN 9780262529082

LC 2015039943

How librarians can be radical positive change agents in their communities, dedicated to learning and making a difference. --Provided by publisher.

"By exploring the mission of the people, the facilities, and the tools required to promote a community-focused profession, the changes in traditional methods of delivering services [Lankes] proposes appear logical and inevitable, rather than radical." Booklist

020.9 History, geographic treatment, biography

Gleick, James

The **information** : a history, a theory, a flood / James Gleick. Pantheon Books, c2011. 416 p. **020.9**

1. Information science -- History. 2. Information society. 3. Technological innovations. 4. Civilization.

ISBN 9780375423727

LC 2010023221

ALA Notable Book, 2012.

Royal Society General Prizes for Science Books, 2012.

National Book Critics Circle Award for Nonfiction finalist, 2011.

Andrew Carnegie Medal for Excellence in Non-Fiction finalist, 2012.

The best-selling author of Chaos analyzes how information has become a defining quality of the modern era, tracing the evolutions of pivotal information technologies while profiling key contributors from Charles Babbage and Ada Byron to Samuel Morse and Claude Shannon.

"As he traces the evolution of intertwined ideas, [Gleick] provides vivid portraits of [Claude] Shannon and other pioneers of our Information Age, including Charles Babbage, whose unbuilt 19th-century Analytical Engine anticipated modern computers, and Alan Turing, whose machines helped the Allies crack German codes during World War II." Wall Street Journal.

020.92 Information scientists, librarians, archivists

Crowley, Bill

Defending professionalism : a resource for librarians, information specialists, knowledge managers, and archivists / Bill Crowley, editor. Libraries Unlimited, an imprint of ABC-CLIO, LLC 2012 xiii, 235 p. ; **020.92**

1. Archivists -- Professional ethics. 2. Archivists -- Training of. 3. Information scientists -- Professional ethics. 4. Information scientists -- Training of.

ISBN 1598848690

LC 2012006410

"This book provides overdue guidance for demonstrating and preserving library, information, knowledge, and archival professionalism in American, British, and Canadian communities and organizations".--Provided by publisher.

021.2 Relationships with the community

Brookover, Sophie, 1975-

Pop goes the library : using pop culture to connect with your whole community / Sophie Brookover and Elizabeth Burns. Information Today, Inc., c2008. xix, 298 p. : **021.2**

1. Libraries -- Special collections -- Popular culture 2. Libraries and community

ISBN 9781573873369

LC 2008019509

Discusses how pop culture can be used to connect with a wider audience at libraries through images, events, collection development, outreach, information technology, and programming.

Damon-Moore, Laura C.

The **artist's** library : a field guide from the Library as Incubator Project / Laura Damon-Moore, Erinn Batykefer. Coffee House Press, 2014. 217 p. : **021.2**

1. Libraries and community. 2. Libraries -- Cultural programs. 3. Libraries -- Social aspects. 4. Arts -- Library resources.
ISBN 9781566893534

LC 2013035168

"Creativity, like information, is free to everyone who steps into a library. The Artist's Library offers the idea that an artist is any person who uses creative tools to make new things, and the guidance and resources to make libraries of all sizes and shapes come alive as spaces for art-making and cultural engagement. Case studies included in the book range from the crafty (pop-up books) to the community-minded (library galleries) to documentary (photo projects) to the technically complex ('listening' to libraries via Dewey decimal frequencies). The Library as Incubator Project was created by Erinn Batykefer, Laura Damon-Moore, and Christina Endres. It highlights the ways that libraries and artists can work together, and works to strengthen these partnerships. By calling attention to one of the many reasons libraries are important to our communities and our culture, it provides a dynamic online forum for sharing ideas. Erinn Batykefer is a librarian, a writer, and a lifelong do-it-yourselfer. She earnedan MFA in writing and a Master of Library and Information Studies from the University of Wisconsin-Madison. Her first poetry collection, Allegheny, Monongahela, won the Benjamin Saltman Poetry Prize. Laura Damon-Moore is a librarian, blogger, and avid art-maker in her spare time. Laura received her master's degree in Library and Information Studies from the University of Wisconsin-Madison in 2012. Jessica Pigza is the assistant curator in the New York Public Library's Rare Book Division. She also writes on handmade material culture, DIY, and handicrafts at Hand-Made Librarian".-- Provided by publisher.

Johnson, Marilyn, 1954-

★**This** book is overdue! : how librarians and cybrarians can save us all / Marilyn Johnson. Harper, c2010. xii, 272 p. ; **021.2**

1. Libraries and society. 2. Knowledge management 3. Librarians -- Anecdotes. 4. Internet -- Library applications
ISBN 9780061431609

LC 2010007860

In This Book Is Overdue! -- a romp through the ranks of information professionals who organize our messy world and offer old-fashioned human help through the maze -- author Marilyn Johnson celebrates libraries and librarians and discovers offbeat and eloquent characters in the quietest corners.

"In an information age full of Google-powered searches, free-by-Bittorrent media downloads and Wiki-powered knowledge databases, the librarian may seem like an antiquated concept. [The author] is here to reverse that notion with a topical, witty study of the vital ways modern librarians uphold their traditional roles as educators, archivists, and curators of a community legacy. Johnson's wry report is a must-read for anyone who's used a library in the past quarter century." Publishers Weekly.

Maddigan, Beth

Community library programs that work : building youth and family literacy / Beth Maddigan and Susan Bloos. Libraries Unlimited, 2014 xiii, 215 p. ; **021.2**

1. Libraries and community -- Canada -- Case studies. 2. Libraries and community -- United States -- Case studies. 3. Family literacy programs -- Canada -- Case studies. 4. Family literacy programs -- United States -- Case studies.
ISBN 9781610692632

LC 2013029493

"A collection of engaging best practices for promoting literacy development by utilizing local community connections in school and public libraries".-- Provided by publisher.

Smallwood, Carol, 1939-

Librarians as community partners : an outreach handbook / edited by Carol Smallwood. American Library Association, 2010. ix, 204 p. ; **021.2**

1. Library outreach programs -- United States -- Case studies. 2. Libraries and community -- United States -- Case studies. 3. Libraries -- Public relations -- United States -- Case studies.
ISBN 9780838910061

LC 2009020359

Including 66 focused snapshots of outreach in action, this resource reflects the creative solutions of librarians searching for new and innovative ways to build programs that meet customer needs while expanding the library's scope into the community. --Provided by publisher.

"Success always requires resources, dedication, and much planning, but even the smallest library with a handful of staff could benefit from this book." Library Journal

021.7 Promotion of libraries, archives, information centers

Phillips, Susan P., 1945-

Great displays for your library step by step / Susan P. Phillips. McFarland & Co., c2008. xiii, 234 p. : **021.7**

1. Library exhibits
ISBN 9780786431649

LC 2007047450

"This volume proves an effective tool for designing unique visual statements for library spaces. Each display includes a brief introduction to the subject; an explanation of the genesis of the idea; specifics regarding the information included and its source; step-by-step instructions for assembly; and ideas on how to customize the display to any available space".--Provided by publisher.

"Phillips' enthusiasm, creativity, and breadth of personal interests are evident throughout this book. . . . This text will inspire readers to locate and showcase the treasures in their own collections." School Library Journal.

Schall, Lucy

Teen talkback with interactive booktalks! / Lucy Schall. Libraries Unlimited, an imprint of ABC-CLIO, LLC, 2013 xviii, 305 p. ; **021.7**

1. Book talks -- United States. 2. Fiction genres 3. Reading promotion -- United States. 4. Teenagers -- Books and reading -- United States.
ISBN 1610692896

LC 2013000241

"Although mostly fiction, there are some nonfiction choices included and the balance of newer titles is respectable. Due to the plethora of topics, detail in descriptions, and variety of related works listed, librarians will be able to locate books for the pickiest of readers." Library Media Connection.

Thenell, Jan

The **library's** crisis communications planner : a PR guide for handling every emergency / Jan Thenell. American Library Association, c2004. vii, 77 p. : 021.7

1. Archives -- Safety measures 2. Archives -- Security measures 3. Crisis management 4. Libraries and mass media

ISBN 9780838908709

LC 2004010891

"Offering advice, firsthand experience, scenarios, and guidelines for communicating effectively before, during, and after a crisis or crisis-producing events ... [the author's] guide is a ready-made workshop on how to establish and maintain relationships with the media, including how to write a press release, how to keep all staff informed and aware of what to do when an emergency occurs, and how to make sure library board members and other community stakeholders are notified and/or involved. Whether or not you have a public relations office or officer, this slim volume is a must for your professional shelf." Library Journal.

023 Personnel management (Human resource management)

Stanley, Mary J.

Managing library employees : a how-to-do-it manual / Mary J. Stanley. Neal-Schuman Publishers, c2008. xi, 247 p. ; **023**

1. Library personnel management

ISBN 9781555706289

LC 2007051961

"Oriented to librarians who do not have a human resources department in the library, Managing Library Employees is for the nonexpert trying to come to terms with managing a library's largest expenditure and assetits employees. The chapters are divided into subtopics posed as questions. The chapters also provide information on writing an effective job description, designing a disciplinary procedure, and identifying potential issues that might lead to a lawsuit. This useful guide for everyday situations should be on any library director or manager's professional reference shelf." Booklist.

Tucker, Dennis C.

Crash course in library supervision : meeting the key players / Dennis C. Tucker and Shelley Elizabeth Mosley. Libraries Unlimited, 2008. ix, 139 p. ; **023**

1. Library personnel management -- Handbooks, manuals, etc. 2. Library administration -- Handbooks, manuals, etc. 3. Supervision of employees -- Handbooks, manuals, etc.

ISBN 9781591585640

LC 2007030131

Provides information on becoming an effective leader in a library, covering such topics as getting to know the staff, evaluating staff, personal laws, hiring and firing employees, finding volunteers, and working with a library board.

025.00285 Libraries--data processing

Bolan, Kimberly

Technology made simple : an improvement guide for small and medium libraries / Kimberly Bolan and Robert Cullin. American Library Association, 2007. ix, 213 p. : **025.00285**

1. Small libraries -- Automation -- Planning 2. Small libraries -- Information technology -- Planning 3. Libraries -- Automation -- Planning 4. Libraries -- Information technology -- Planning

ISBN 9780838909201

LC 2006013191

Provides information on implementing technology services in a small or medium-sized library.

025.04 Information storage and retrieval systems

Brown, Christopher C., 1953-

Librarian's guide to online searching : cultivating database skills for research and instruction / Christopher C. Brown and Suzanne S. Bell. Libraries Unlimited, 2018 xxiii, 374 p. : **025.04**

1. Database searching 2. Electronic information resource searching

ISBN 9781440861567

LC 2018011054

"This book describes the background of how databases work; how they are constructed and in the case of some databases; how they transitioned from the legacy print world to an online environment; how technologies within databases can interact with other products like bibliography citation services, outbound linking to full text content, and social media mentions; and the methods used by libraries to provide access to licensed content from anywhere in the world".-- Provided by publisher.

Seife, Charles

Virtual unreality : just because the Internet told you, how do you know it's true? / Charles Seife. Viking, 2014. 256 p. **025.04**

1. Computer network resources -- Evaluation. 2. Internet -- Safety measures. 3. Internet fraud -- Prevention. 4. Internet literacy.

ISBN 9780670026081

LC 2013047849

The Internet disseminates facts, opinions, and outright fraud, and its questionable reliability has become a significant concern in public discourse. In Virtual Unreality, journalism professor Charles Seife describes in detail how information on the Internet can be falsified, manipulated, and perpetuated. Providing concrete examples of Internet fakery, Seife serves as an engaging and witty guide through the wilderness of digital information, both reliable and fraudulent. Virtual Unreality doesn't suggest that people avoid using the Internet for research, but does provide techniques for identifying the useful and verifiable sites and services -- how to find the wheat amid all that chaff.

"Intense and incisive, Seife's expos of potent tricks on the mesmerizing, overpowering Internet makes us very wary about anything that cannot be verified with our own eyes." Publishers Weekly.

025.0425 Search and retrieval

Devine, Jane, 1947-

Going beyond Google again : strategies for using and teaching the Invisible Web / Jane Devine and Francine Egger-Sider. Neal-Schuman, an imprint of the American Library Association, 2014. xii, 180 p. : **025.0425**

1. Database searching 2. Internet searching 3. Invisible Web -- Study and teaching 4. Invisible Web

ISBN 9781555708986

LC 2013010867

"Chapter summaries and extensive citations make this an attractive choice for students. It should also be of interest to librarians and anyone interested in optimizing their research resources and strategies." Library Journal.

025.06 Information storage and retrieval systems devoted

Modschiedler, Christa,

Guide to reference in medicine and health / Christa Modschiedler and Denise Bennett. ALA Editions, 2014. 468 p. ; **025.06**

ISBN 9780838912218

LC 2014005002

Based on: Guide to reference. 2008-

Drawn from the extensive database of Guide to Reference, this up-to-date resource provides an annotated list of print and electronic biomedical and health-related reference sources, including internet resources and digital image collections. --Provided by publisher.

Sankey, Michael L., 1949-

The **manual** to online public records : the researcher's tool to online resources of public records and public information / Sankey & Hetherington. Facts on Demand Press, 2017 ii, 620 p. : **025.06**

1. Electronic public records -- United States -- Directories 2. Public records -- United States -- Directories

ISBN 9781889150628

LC bl2017002725

Shares strategies for using the Internet to conduct research and access online resources, in a guide that provides the public records available for each state, along with advice on evaluating online data for reliability.

025.1 Administration

Johnson, Doug, 1952-

★The **indispensable** librarian : surviving and thriving in school libraries in the information age / Doug Johnson ; illustrations by Brady Johnson. Linworth, an imprint of ABC-CLIO, LLC, 2013 xix, 207 p. : **025.1**

1. School librarians -- United States. 2. School libraries -- United States -- Administration.

ISBN 161069239X

LC 2012051394

"Johnson offers both theory and practical suggestions on ways to embed [librarians] and [their] jobs into the fabric of a school's culture and curriculum." Library Media Connection.

Landau, Herbert B.

The **small** public library survival guide : thriving on less / Herbert B. Landau. American Library Association, 2008. viii, 159 p. ; **025.1**

1. Libraries and community -- United States. 2. Libraries -- United States -- Marketing. 3. Library finance -- United States. 4. Public libraries -- United States -- Administration.

ISBN 0838935753

LC 2008007425

Details the author's move from the corporate world to running a small rural library, discussing the challenges of dramatic funding cuts and the unorthodox solutions that he used to keep the library afloat.

"This volume covers many topics of interest to staff in small public libraries. Written in a conversational, accessible style, information is presented in short chapters with relevant examples and sample documents. Covering topics from low-budget programming to building non-cash support from the community, this text has something for almost everyone involved in the operations of a small public library. Easy and enjoyable to read." Voice of Youth Advocates.

Larson, Jeanette

★The **public** library policy writer : a guidebook with model policies on CD-ROM / Jeanette C. Larson and Herman L. Totten. Neal-Schuman Publishers, c2008. xxi, 280 p. ; **025.1**

1. Public libraries -- United States -- Handbooks, manuals, etc. 2. Public libraries -- United States -- Administration -- Handbooks, manuals, etc. 3. Library rules and regulations -- United States -- Handbooks, manuals, etc.

ISBN 9781555706036

LC 2008017622

"The guidebook is written mainly for small to medium-sized public library directors who need to analyze current policies, revise or update those still in use, and develop new ones. The book is organized by administrative and service areas such as employment practices, staff and patron conduct, use of materials, collection development, and access to facilities." Booklist

Laughlin, Sara, 1949-

The **quality** library : a guide to staff-driven improvement, better efficiency, and happier customers / Sara Laughlin and Ray W. Wilson. American Library Association, 2008. xiv, 144 p. : **025.1**

1. Library administration -- United States 2. Total quality management -- United States 3. Library planning -- United States 4. Customer services -- United States

ISBN 9780838909522

LC 2007030710

Based on more than 50 years of author expertise in organizational improvement, The Quality Library offers a methodology to pinpoint trouble areas and improve processes. --Provided by publisher.

"This can be a useful guide for libraries whose governing bodies are looking for businesslike solutions and for managers who want to heed input from those who do the job." Booklist

MacKellar, Pamela H

Winning grants : a how-to-do-it manual for librarians / Stephanie K. Gerding and Pamela H. MacKellar ; foreword by Susan Hildreth. ALA Neal-Schuman, 2017 xxi, 224 p. : **025.1**

1. Library fund raising -- United States 2. Proposal writing for grants -- United States 3. Proposal writing in library science -- United States

ISBN 9780838914731

LC 2016025285

Written by two librarians who are experts in grantsmanship, this all-in-one toolkit for winning grants is a must-have for library directors, grant writers, board members, consultants, and anyone else involved in planning library programs and services. --Provided by publisher.

"Overall, the resources are valuable and will facilitate streamlining and refining the process of grant winning while teaching grant seekers how to achieve the results they desire." VOYA

MacKellar, Pamela H.

Writing successful technology grant proposals : a LITA guide / Pamela H. MacKellar. Neal-Schuman Publishers, Inc., 2012 xviii, 227 p. ; **025.1**

1. Libraries -- Automation -- United States -- Finance. 2. Libraries -- Information technology -- United States -- Finance. 3. Proposal writing for grants -- United States. 4. Proposal writing in library science -- United States.

ISBN 1555707637

LC 2011046318

Grants can provide crucial funding to libraries and institutions to implement the latest technology and provide even greater service to visitors. Writing a successful proposal is one step in assuring a technology grant is awarded and this volume covers winning techniques for libraries and grant writers offering best practices and success stories. --Provided by publisher

Smith, G. Stevenson

Cost control for nonprofits in crisis / G. Stevenson Smith. American Library Association, 2011. viii, 133 p. : **025.1**

1. Libraries -- Cost control. 2. Libraries -- Cost effectiveness. 3. Library administration -- Decision making. 4. Library finance -- United States.

ISBN 083891098X

LC 2011025285

Libraries, like many other cultural institutions such as museums, art councils, and theater groups, are looking for answers to the pressing problem of financial stability, and ultimately survival. Cost Control for Nonprofits in Crisis helps managers and directors tackle the harsh realities before them. --Provided by publisher.

"The strategies and methods outlined here will assist managers who want to ensure that the decisions they must make during challenging financial times will keep their organizations vibrant, relevant, and lasting." VOYA

VanDuinkerken, Wyoma

The **challenge** of library management : leading with emotional engagement / Wyoma vanDuinkerken and Pixey Anne Mosley. American Library Association, 2011. 169 p. ; **025.1**

1. Library administration 2. Organizational change -- Management 3. Leadership 4. Library administration -- Problems, exercises, etc

ISBN 9780838911020

LC 2011011349

Peppered with short narratives that use real-life examples of change principles, this book helps managers reassure their staff that change can be an opportunity for reflection and personal growth. --Provided by publisher.

"While the authors tailor the advice to librarians by using example specific to libraries, the advice could be applied to any organizational setting. All in all, the suggestions contained here are helpful when planning change in a library." VOYA

025.17 Administration of collections of special materials

Weir, Ryan O,

Managing electronic resources : a LITA guide / edited by Ryan O. Weir. ALA TechSource, 2012. xii, 179 p. : **025.17**

1. Libraries -- Special collections -- Electronic information resources. 2. Electronic information resources -- Management.

ISBN 9781555707675

LC 2012015102

"Edited by the director of technical services and electronic resources for Murray State University, in Kentucky, this volume will help those working with electronic resources in any type of library. Eight chapters address processes associated with managing electronic collections. Coverage includes the basics, economic issues, acquisition, licensing, staffing, accessibility, and the future." Booklist

025.2 Acquisitions and collection development

Alabaster, Carol

Developing an outstanding core collection : a guide for libraries / Carol Alabaster. American Library Association, 2010. x, 191 p. : **025.2**

1. Public libraries -- Collection development -- United States.

ISBN 0838910408

LC 2009040342

Presents guidelines to developing a high-quality core library collection, and includes discussions on the philosophy behind core collections, strategies for their implementation, and lists containing selection criteria.

"The author suggests that the general public needs materials beyond current best-sellers and ready-reference works; that those materials should be high-quality, enduring pieces; and that librarians are the best persons to decide what constitutes appropriate core collections for their communities. [She also] addresses the technological changes that drastically affect reading habits and our ability to satisfy the needs of the people's university. [This book is] required reading for all those charged with the task of adult collection development." Booklist.

Albitz, Becky,

Rethinking collection development and management / Becky Albitz, Christine Avery, and Diane Zabel, editors. Libraries Unlimited, 2014 xiv, 394 p. ; **025.2**

1. Acquisitions (Libraries) 2. Materials selection (Libraries) 3. Collection management (Libraries) 4. Library materials -- Conservation and restoration.

ISBN 9781610693059

LC 2013038447

"This collection of thought-provoking essays by visionary and innovative library practitioners covers theory, research, and best practices in collection development, examining how it has evolved, identifying how some librarians are creatively responding to these changes, and predicting what is coming next".-- Provided by publisher.

Bartlett, Wendy K.

Floating collections : a collection development model for long-term success / Wendy K. Bartlett. Libraries Unlimited, an imprint of ABC-CLIO, LLC, 2014 xix, 128 p. ; **025.2**

1. Cooperative collection development (Libraries) -- United States. 2. Public libraries -- Collection development -- United States.

ISBN 1598847430

LC 2013033820

"This easy-to-use, comprehensive guide shows how to establish a floating collection in any library--regardless of type or size".-- Provided by publisher.

"Chapters include tips on how to approach the practice with staff, how to ready facilities and collections, and, most importantly, how to manage new collections. Also offered are practical evaluations, FAQs, and a list of larger systems in the United States that offer floating collections." School Library Journal.

Cornog, Martha

Graphic novels beyond the basics : insights and issues for libraries / Martha Cornog and Timothy Perper, editors. Libraries Unlimited/ABC-CLIO, c2009. xxx, 281 p. ; **025.2**

1. Libraries -- Special collections -- Graphic novels. 2. Libraries -- Special collections -- Comic books, strips, etc. 3. Comic books, strips, etc. -- History and criticism. 4. Comics and Graphic novels

ISBN 9781591584780

LC 2009016189

Presents librarians with an introduction to graphic novels, describing such different categories as manga, superhero comics, and graphic nonfiction and explaining how to incorporate the genre in the collection development, purchasing, and cataloging policies of the library.

"Whether you are serious about the genre, interested in the history, or looking for ammunition, this book should be on your shelf. The wealth of knowledge and research that went into these essays is impressive, and reading this book will put you on the road to becoming an expert." Library Media Connection.

Disher, Wayne

Crash course in collection development / Wayne Disher. Libraries Unlimited, 2014 xii, 139 p. ; **025.2**

1. Collection development (Libraries) -- United States. 2. Small libraries -- Collection development -- United States.

ISBN 1610698134

LC 2014018813

"This indispensable resource provides tools for collection management in public libraries, featuring essential strategies for inventory assessment, market analysis, budgeting, marketing, and customer service. This book is a must-have for those just entering the field or professionals in need of a refresher in effective library operations"-- Provided by publisher.

"Disher, a seasoned practitioner and part-time instructor in San Jose State Universitys School of Library and Information Science, speaks primarily to public library staff with little, if any, experience in collection development. Short on theory but long on practicality, the book provides the reader with basic definitions and step-by-step outlines... Recommended for all public library collections." Booklist.

Evans, G. Edward, 1937-

Collection management basics / G. Edward Evans and Margaret Zarnosky Saponaro. Libraries Unlimited, an imprint of ABC-CLIO, LLC, 2012. xvi, 343 p. ; **025.2**

1. Collection management (Libraries). 2. Libraries -- Special collections -- Electronic information resources.

ISBN 1598848631

LC 2012008872

"Now thoroughly revised for today's 21st-century library environment, this title provides a complete update of the classic Developing Library and Information Center Collections--the standard text and authority on collection development for all types of libraries and library school students since 1979".-- Provided by publisher.

Gallaway, Beth, 1975-

Game on! : gaming at the library / Beth Gallaway. Neal-Schuman Publishers, c2009. xiv, 306 p. : **025.2**

1. Libraries -- Special collections -- Electronic games 2. Video games

ISBN 9781555705954

LC 2009014110

"An essential guide for any librarian who plans on embracing the video-game phenomenon, or at the very least, understanding it. . . . [The chapters] are well organized and contain an abundance of practical information. The sections on selection, collection, and circulation of video games include relevant advice on policy, cataloging, marketing, storage, and displays. . . . The annotated list of video games for a core collection is wonderful for selection purposes." School Library Journal.

Goldsmith, Francisca

The **readers'** advisory guide to graphic novels / Francisca Goldsmith. ALA Editions, 2017. xvi, 215 p. ; **025.2**

1. Readers' advisory services -- United States. 2. Graphic novels -- Bibliography.

ISBN 9780838915097

LC 2016042034

"This is a book to spend time with, not flip through, although a strong index and table of contents make it easily consultable for patron interactions as well." Voice of Youth Advocates.

Hughes-Hassell, Sandra

★**Collection** management for youth : equity, inclusion, and learning / Sandra Hughes-Hassell. ALA Editions, 2020. 164 p. **025.2**

1. Constructivism (Education) 2. Educational change. 3. Instructional materials centers -- Collection development. 4. School librarian participation in curriculum planning.

ISBN 9780838947500

LC 2020000768

Previously published under title: Collection management for youth: responding to the needs of learners.

Hughes-Hassell provides models and tools for collection managers that will enable library staff who serve youth to put in place, demonstrate, and create learner-centered collections that are inclusive and provide equitable access to all youth. -- Provided by publisher.

Johnson, Peggy, 1948-

Developing and managing electronic collections : the essentials / Peggy Johnson. ALA Editions, 2013. ix, 186 p. : **025.2**

1. Libraries -- Special collections -- Electronic information resources. 2. Electronic information resources -- Management. 3. Libraries and electronic publishing -- United States.

ISBN 9780838911907

LC 2013005038

As library collections of all types of libraries increasingly become electronic, librarians are faced with coping with rising costs while meeting increasing user expectations; understanding copyright and fair use in the digital environment; and followingrapidly changing technologies. Johnson incorporates current information while providing practical information that will guide librarians in their work with electronic content.

Johnson, Peggy, 1948-

Fundamentals of collection development and management / Peggy Johnson. ALA Editions, 2014. xiv, 554 p. : **025.2**

1. Collection management (Libraries)

ISBN 0838911919

LC 2013049725

Addresses the art of controlling and updating your library's collection. Discussions of the importance and logistics of electronic resources are integrated throughout the book.

Kaplan, Richard, 1954-

Building and managing e-book collections : a how-to-do-it manual for librarians / edited by Richard Kaplan. Neal-Schuman, 2012. xv, 197 p. ; **025.2**

1. Libraries -- Special collections -- Electronic books. 2. Electronic books. 3. Libraries and electronic publishing.

ISBN 9781555707767

LC 2012018143

Offering multiple perspectives from electronic resource professionals at world-renowned libraries such as Harvard, the University of Michigan, Duke, and Northeastern, this book provides a comprehensive and well-rounded e-book education. --Provided by publisher

Kennedy, Marie R.

Marketing your library's electronic resources : a how-to-do-it manual / Marie R. Kennedy & Cheryl LaGuardia. Neal-Schuman, an imprint of the American Library Association, 2013 xxi, 177 p. : **025.2**

1. Libraries -- Special collections -- Electronic information resources 2. Libraries -- Marketing 3. Electronic information resources -- Marketing 4. Libraries -- United States -- Marketing

ISBN 9781555708894

LC 2012028267

Newly expanded and updated, this manual shows library marketing staff how to get the job done from beginning to end and in a variety of library settings. --Provided by publisher

Kovacs, Diane K. (Diane Kaye), 1962-

The **Kovacs** guide to electronic library collection development : essential core subject collections, selection criteria, and guidelines / Diane K. Kovacs. Neal-Schuman Publishers, c2009. xxiii, 303 p. : **025.2**

1. Digital libraries -- Collection development -- United States.
ISBN 1555706649

LC 2009027772

"Chapters cover general collection guidelines and licensing basics; especially useful are individual sections citing specific Web sites for e-collection sources in ready reference, business, medicine, biology, engineering, physical and earth sciences, and the social sciences and humanities. Kovacs . is a very diligent researcher, and her latest title again offers librarians much useful information." Booklist.

Magi, Trina J,

★**Intellectual** freedom manual / Compiled by the Office for Intellectual Freedom of the American Library Association ; Trina Magi, Editor ; Martin Garnar, Assistant Editor . ALA Editions, 2015. xxii, 273 p. ; **025.2**

1. Libraries -- Censorship -- United States -- Handbooks, manuals, etc. 2. Intellectual freedom -- United States -- Handbooks, manuals, etc.
ISBN 9780838912928

LC 2014037437

"All libraries should have a copy of this book to use when writing or revising policies; indispensable." Library Journal.

Pinnell-Stephens, June

★**Protecting** intellectual freedom in your public library : scenarios from the front lines / June Pinnell-Stephens for the Office for Intellectual Freedom. American Library Association, 2012. xi, 148 p. : **025.2**

1. Intellectual freedom -- United States. 2. Public libraries -- Censorship -- United States 3. Public libraries -- Censorship -- United States.
ISBN 0838935834

LC 2011029691

"Packed with current legal information and practical suggestions, this book is a 'must-read' for all levels of library staff." Library Journal.

Pulliam, June Michele

Read on... horror fiction / June Michele Pulliam and Anthony J. Fonseca. Libraries Unlimited, 2006. xvii, 182 p. ; **025.2**

1. Fiction in libraries -- United States 2. Horror tales -- Bibliography 3. Readers' advisory services -- United States 4. Public libraries -- United States -- Book lists
ISBN 9781591581765

LC 2006012719

Provides bibliographic information and brief plot summaries for current and classic horror fiction titles, organized according to their underlying features, such as complex plots, erotic horror, big city horror, and favorite monsters.

Serchay, David S., 1971-

The **librarian's** guide to graphic novels for adults / David S. Serchay. Neal-Schuman Publishers, c2010. xvi, 320 p. : **025.2**

1. Graphic novels -- United States. 2. Libraries -- Special collections -- Graphic novels.
ISBN 1555706622

LC 2009041011

Provides information about how to build and maintain a collection of graphic novels for adults, including such topics as management, cataloging, processing, future development, and display and promotion.

"This book will inspire librarians--and others--with little knowledge of graphic novels (GNs) for adults to pick one up and see what all the buzz is about. Serchay puts forth a complete guide that will enable any librarian, whether a GN novice or seasoned fan, to establish a brand-new collection, fully understanding what GNs are, where to purchase them, how to catalog them, and how to review, promote, and maintain the new collection." Library Journal.

Singer, Carol A.

Fundamentals of Managing Reference Collections / Carol A. Singer. American Library Association, 2012. xii, 167 p. ; **025.2**

1. Collection management (Libraries) -- United States 2. Electronic reference sources -- United States. 3. Libraries -- Special collections -- Reference sources. 4. Reference books -- United States.
ISBN 0838911536

LC 2011044446

This important new book will help librarians make better reference decisions, aligned to customer needs and expectations, especially significant with today's limited budgets.

"Singer's book teaches novices the basics of collection management while helping practicing librarians remember information taught in library school courses and providing additional insights that may not have been previously considered with respect to e-resources. Recommended for public librarians or anyone working with a reference collection, whether novice or experienced." Library Journal

Vnuk, Rebecca

The **weeding** handbook : a shelf-by-shelf guide / Rebecca Vnuk. ALA Editions, 2015. xix, 196 p. : **025.2**

1. Collection development (Libraries) -- United States 2. Discarding of books, periodicals, etc. 3. Public libraries -- Collection development -- United States.
ISBN 083891327X

LC 2015008707

Filled with field-tested, no nonsense strategies, this handbook will enable libraries to bloom by maintaining a collection that users actually use. --Provided by publisher

White, Andrew C. (Andrew Carl), 1966-

★**E-metrics** for library and information professionals : how to use data for managing and evaluating electronic resource collections / Andrew C. White and Eric Djira Kamal. Neal-Schuman Publishers, c2006. xix, 249 p. : **025.2**

1. Digital libraries -- Collection development -- Statistical methods 2. Electronic information resources -- Use studies 3. Web usage mining
ISBN 9781555705145

LC 2004054678

"Chapters cover the capturing and processing of statistics, infrastructure and technical requirements, and staffing needs. With its coherent structure, well-articulated language, and illustrative material (tables, figures, and examples), this book has much to recommend it. The authors are successful in elucidating a subject that may seem daunting and abstract to the uninitiated." Booklist

Wilkinson, Frances C.
The **complete** guide to acquisitions management / Frances C. Wilkinson, Linda K. Lewis, and Rebecca L. Lubas. Libraries Unlimited, 2015 xiv, 200 p. ; **025.2**

1. Acquisitions (Libraries) -- United States.
ISBN 9781610697132

LC 2015007852

Updated and enhanced, the second edition of this text provides both library students and practitioners with a thorough understanding of procedural and philosophical approaches in acquisitions management. --Provided by publisher

025.3 Bibliographic analysis and control

Library of Congress
The **card** catalog : books, cards, and literary treasures / the Library of Congress ; foreword by Carla Hayden. Chronicle Books, 2017. 224 p. **025.3**

1. Library of Congress -- History 2. Library of Congress Catalogs -- History 3. Card catalogs -- United States -- History 4. Librarians 5. Books and reading 6. Cataloging
ISBN 9781452145402

LC 2016017476

A visual celebration of the Library of Congress card catalog system as well as rarely seen treasures in the collection features images of original catalog cards, first edition book covers, and photographs from the library's archives.

"An irresistible treasury for book and library lovers." Booklist.

Maxwell, Robert L., 1957-
Maxwell's handbook for RDA, resource description & access : explaining and illustrating RDA: resource description and access using MARC21 / Robert L. Maxwell. ALA Editions, 2013. x, 900 p. ; **025.3**

1. Resource description & access Handbooks, manuals, etc. 2. Descriptive cataloging -- Standards -- Handbooks, manuals, etc.
ISBN 9780838911723

LC 2013035124

A guided tour of the new standard from a respected authority, this essential handbook will help catalogers, LIS students, and cataloging instructors navigate RDA smoothly and find the information they need efficiently. --Provided by publisher

Mering, Margaret,
The **RDA** workbook : learning the basics of Resource Description and Access / Margaret Mering, editor. Libraries Unlimited, 2014 xviii, 190 p. ; **025.3**

1. Resource description & access. 2. Descriptive cataloging -- Standards. 3. Descriptive cataloging -- Standards -- Problems, exercises, etc.
ISBN 9781610694896

LC 2013042469

Accompanied by a CD-ROM.

"Whether a library catalogs its own materials or not, librarians still need to have some understanding of RDA. Designed to be used by academic, public, and school librarians, this is the perfect introduction"-- Provided by publisher.

025.5 Services for users

Bobick, James E.
Science and technology resources : a guide for information professionals and researchers / James E. Bobick and G. Lynn Berard. Libraries Unlimited, c2011. xiii, 285 p. : **025.5**

1. Science and technology libraries -- Reference services. 2. Science -- Bibliography -- Methodology. 3. Scientific literature -- Bibliography -- Methodology. 4. Technical literature -- Bibliography -- Methodology.
ISBN 159158793X

LC 2011000461

"An indispensible resource for anyone wanting to create, maintain, improve, understand, or use the diverse information resources within a sci-tech library".--Provided by publisher.

"Database descriptions contain annotations, but the listings for websites, dictionaries, handbooks, and other materials do not. A timely resource to add to reference collections and to the library science curriculum." Booklist.

Cords, Sarah Statz, 1974-
The **real** story : a guide to nonfiction reading interests / Sarah Statz Cords ; edited By Robert Burgin. Libraries Unlimited, 2006. xxxii, 460 p. ; **025.5**

1. Readers' advisory services -- United States. 2. Public libraries -- Reference services -- United States. 3. Books and reading -- United States. 4. Reading interests -- United States.
ISBN 9781591582830

LC 2006003712

Explores the genres and sub-genres of nonfiction and provides an annotated bibliography of more than five hundred popular nonfiction titles, organized according to genre with a focus on titles published in the last decade.

"The author describes more than 555 popular nonfiction titles published over the last 15 years, along with classic titles such as Truman Capote's In Cold Blood. . . . Cords has identified 11 broad categories based on subjects, genres, and appeal factors. Among the categories are Biography, Travel, True Adventure, and True Crime. . . . A must-read for any librarian who recommends popular reading titles, it belongs at the reference and readers'-advisory desks of most libraries." Booklist.

Evans, G. Edward, 1937-
Introduction to library public services / G. Edward Evans and Thomas L. Carter. Libraries Unlimited, 2009. xix, 401 p. : **025.5**

1. Public services (Libraries) 2. Reference services (Libraries) 3. Library circulation and loans
ISBN 9781591585961

LC 2008037445

Includes indexes.

This basic text provides a solid, broadly based view of library public service and its functions, marrying the importance of the help ethos with a plethora of technological tools and techniques. --Provided by publisher

Ford, Charlotte
Crash course in reference / Charlotte Ford. Libraries Unlimited, 2008. xi, 143 p. : **025.5**

1. Reference services (Libraries)
ISBN 1591584639

LC 2007052948

Reviews the basics of reference services in public libraries, including information on locating resources, maintaining the collection, the ethics of providing information to all patrons, and joining a network of reference librarians.

Goldsmith, Francisca

Crash course in contemporary reference / Francisca Goldsmith. Libraries Unlimited, 2017 xii, 183 p. ; **025.5**

1. Reference services (Libraries).
ISBN 9781440844812

LC 2016030068

A fresh, detailed, and thoughtful examination of reference services in the context of evolving community information needs and habits, a changing technological landscape, and new search strategies. --Provided by publisher

Hernon, Peter

Assessing service quality : satisfying the expectations of library customers / Peter Hernon + Ellen Altman. American Library Association, 2010. xi, 206 p. : **025.5**

1. Public services (Libraries) -- Evaluation 2. Public services (Libraries) -- United States -- Evaluation
ISBN 9780838910214

LC 2009040332

This classic book is brought fully up to date as Hernon and Altman integrate the use of technology into the customer experience. They offer solid, practical ideas for developing a customer service plan that meets the library's customer-focused mission, vision, and goals, challenging librarians to think about customer service in new ways. --Provided by publisher

Jerrard, Jane, 1961-

Crisis in employment : a librarian's guide to helping job seekers / Jane Jerrard ; foreword by Denise Davis. American Library Association, 2009. vii, 66 p. : **025.5**

1. Job vacancies -- United States -- Information services 2. Libraries and community -- United States 3. Libraries and the unemployed -- United States 4. Public libraries -- Reference services -- United States
ISBN 9780838910139

LC 2009016684

"ALA Editions special reports."

"This special report provides suggestions for providing low-cost assistance to job-seeking unemployed library users. With examples from various public libraries, the report offers advice for planning, how to get the most out of resources at hand, dealing with the need for additional computers, suggestions for community partnerships, and how to best assist users who need to become computer literate for a successful job search." Library Journal.

Kern, M. Kathleen

★**Virtual** reference best practices : tailoring services to your library / M. Kathleen Kern. American Library Association, c2009. viii, 148 p. : **025.5**

1. Electronic reference services (Libraries)
ISBN 9780838909751

LC 2008015379

Outlines available virtual reference services and suggests ways to choose and launch applications to best suit the patrons of a specific library.

"The author offers advice and assistance for libraries considering VR. . . . Kern's guidebook includes useful forms and exercises for every aspect of the VR process from a market assessment of the library's community served to an evaluation of the service. . . . Even those [libraries] which already offer virtual reference will find assistance and suggestions to improve their services." Voice of Youth Advocates.

Kroski, Ellyssa,

The **makerspace** librarian's sourcebook / edited by Ellyssa Kroski. ALA Editions, 2017. xi, 388 p. : **025.5**

1. Makerspaces in libraries. 2. Makerspaces -- Equipment and supplies. 3. Maker movement.
ISBN 9780838915042

LC 2016037887

As useful for those just entering the 'what if' stage as it is for those with makerspaces already up and running, this book will help libraries engage the community in their makerspaces. --Provided by publisher

Lankes, R. David, 1970-

Virtual reference service : from competencies to assessment / R. David Lankes ... [et al.] ; edited by Philip Nast. Neal-Schuman Publishers, c2008 . xv, 206 p. : **025.5**

1. Electronic reference services (Libraries). 2. Reference services (Libraries) -- Information technology. 3. Electronic reference services (Libraries) -- Study and teaching. 4. Reference librarians -- Effect of technological innovations on.
ISBN 9781555705282

LC 2007024104

Provides information about electronic reference services, presenting an overview of seven conferences about the topic and examining problems and solutions.

Moyer, Jessica E.

The **readers'** advisory handbook / edited by Jessica E. Moyer and Kaite Mediatore Stover. American Library Association, c2010. xi, 220 p. ; **025.5**

1. Readers' advisory services -- United States
ISBN 9780838910429

LC 2009045793

Presents guidelines to creating readers' advisory lists for every level of reader in any genre, including such information as how to gain familiarity with one's collection, how to create and market booklists, and how to organize related programs.

"This great generalist title offers guidelines not only on readers' advisory (RA) but on related matters of collection development and marketing books to different reading audiences. . . . [The authors] gather information and instruction from 15 contributing public and school librarians on self-education, managing and improving groups of selectors, making quick but thorough evaluations of different types of materials, writing reviews, and working with book groups as well as other kinds of programming." Library Journal.

Moyer, Jessica E.

Research-based readers' advisory / Jessica E. Moyer ; with contributions by Amanda Blau ... [et al.]. American Library Association, 2008. viii, 278 p. ; **025.5**

1. Readers' advisory services.
ISBN 0838909590

LC 2007049421

Explores research on readers' advisory services and examines the needs of adults, young adults, and children in a public library setting, discussing the practical aspects of each topic.

"Following a survey of the current state of RA, 11 chapters cover topics such as Nonfiction Readers and Nonfiction Advisory, Romance and Genre Readers, and Tools for Readers' Advisory. Each chapter begins with a Research View, in which Moyer summarizes the latest literature. Following the Research View is a Librarian's View, in which an impressive array of contributors talk about practical applications." Booklist.

Mulac, Carolyn
Fundamentals of reference / Carolyn M. Mulac. American Library Association, 2012. xii, 131 p. ; **025.5**
1. Internet in library reference services. 2. Reference services (Libraries) -- United States. 3. Reference sources
ISBN 0838910874
LC 2012010058

An excellent training tool for both new and experienced staff, Fundamentals of Reference will quickly become your fundamental reference! --Provided by publisher

Orr, Cynthia
★**Crash** course in readers' advisory / Cynthia Orr. Libraries Unlimited, an imprint of ABC-CLIO, LLC, 2015 xiv, 173 p. ; **025.5**
1. Readers' advisory services.
ISBN 1610698258
LC 2014027064

"One of the key services librarians provide is helping readers find books they'll enjoy. This "crash course" will furnish you with the basic, practical information you need to excel at readers' advisory (RA) for adults and teens".-- Provided by publisher.

Ross, Catherine Sheldrick
Conducting the reference interview : a how-to-do-it manual for librarians / Catherine Sheldrick Ross, Kirsti Nilsen, and Marie L. Radford. Neal-Schuman Publishers Inc., c2009. xiv, 290 p. : **025.5**
1. Reference services (Libraries) 2. Electronic reference services (Libraries) 3. Interviewing
ISBN 9781555706555
LC 2009017660

"This outstanding work is highly recommended for all libraries and is essential reading for all LIS educators and librarians involved in staff training." Booklist

Saricks, Joyce G.
Readers' advisory service in the public library / Joyce G. Saricks. American Library Association, 2005. xi, 211 p. ; **025.5**
1. Fiction in libraries -- United States. 2. Public libraries -- Reference services -- United States. 3. Readers' advisory services -- United States.
ISBN 0838908977
LC 2004029271

In public libraries, reference librarians are often called on to make recommendations to readers, sometimes in genres that they don't personally read. Learning how to frame a discussion and articulate the appeal of a book, author, or genre marks the essence of a successful readers' advisor.

"In this guide to readers' advisory, online tools for identifying and evaluating titles to suggest to today's new adult leisure readers are described, in addition to tried-and-true print sources. The value of personal reading suggestions from staff and patrons is addressed. Topics for discussion and techniques for marketing good reading material are offered. A priority for all libraries involved in readers' advisory." Booklist.

Wyatt, Neal
The **readers'** advisory guide to nonfiction / Neal Wyatt. American Library Association, 2007. xiv, 318 p. ; **025.5**
1. Readers' advisory services -- United States. 2. Public libraries -- Reference services -- United States. 3. Public libraries -- United States -- Book lists. 4. Books and reading -- United States.
ISBN 9780838909362
LC 2006102318

With a focus on eight catagories including memoir, sports, and true crime, a readers' advisory guide includes coverage of the major authors and works, popularity, and style.

Zabel, Diane
Reference reborn : breathing new life into public services librarianship / Diane Zabel, editor ; preface by Linda C. Smith. Libraries Unlimited, c2011. xx, 401 p. : **025.5**
1. Reference services (Libraries) -- United States. 2. Public services (Libraries) -- United States. 3. Electronic reference services (Libraries) 4. Internet in library reference services.
ISBN 9781591588283
LC 2010041105

More than 30 stellar authors have contributed to these up-to-date essays on public services librarianship, including timely topics such as new service configurations, the impact of e-resources in reference and collection development, and innovative outreach. --Provided by publisher

025.8 Maintenance and preservation of collections

Halsted, Deborah D.
★**Disaster** planning : a how-to-do-it manual for librarians with planning templates on CD-ROM / Deborah D. Halsted, Richard P. Jasper, and Felicia M. Little. Neal-Schuman Publishers, 2005. xx, 267 p. : **025.8**
1. Library buildings -- Safety measures -- Handbooks, manuals, etc. 2. Library materials -- Conservation and restoration -- Handbooks, manuals, etc. 3. Emergency management -- Handbooks, manuals, etc. 4. Library planning -- Handbooks, manuals, etc.
ISBN 9781555704865
LC 2003065152

"Whether a disaster is caused by avalanche, hurricane, computer hackers, explosion, flood, terrorist attack, or other event, this guide will help readers develop a precise, logical, and flexible plan for being prepared." Booklist

Hammer, Joshua, 1957-
★The **bad-ass** librarians of Timbuktu : and their race to save the world's most precious manuscripts / Joshua Hammer. Simon & Schuster, 2016. 278 p. **025.8**
1. Centre de documentation et de recherches "Ahmed Baba." 2. Libraries -- Destruction and pillage -- Mali 3. Manuscripts. 4. Cultural property -- Protection. 5. Islam 6. Mali -- History -- Tuareg Rebellion, 2012- -- Destruction and pillage. 7. Tombouctou, Mali
ISBN 9781476777405
LC 2015030396

Describes how an average, mild-mannered archivist and historian became an expert smuggler when she organized a dangerous operation to sneak 350,000 precious manuscripts out of Timbuktu in the face of the 2012 al Qaeda takeover.

"Hammer's clearly written and engaging chronicle of the achievements of Timbuktu, the risks presented to this area, and the portraits of several brave and dedicated individuals brings to light an important and unfamiliar story." Library Journal.

Lavender, Kenneth

Book repair : a how-to-do-it manual / Kenneth Lavender. Neal-Schuman Publishers Inc., c2011. xiv, 265 p. : **025.8**

1. Books -- Conservation and restoration -- Handbooks, manuals, etc. 2. Bookbinding -- Repairing -- Handbooks, manuals, etc.
ISBN 9781555707477

LC 2011022636

Covering both basic book repair techniques and sound preservation practices, this practical, step-by-step manual offers illustrated sections on cleaning, mending, hinge and spine repair, strengthening paperbacks, and more. --Provided by publisher

026 Specific kinds of institutions

Baker, Jennifer S., 1953-

The **readers'** advisory guide to historical fiction / Jennifer S. Baker. ALA Editions, 2015. xvi, 335 p. ; **026**

1. Fiction in libraries -- United States 2. Libraries -- United States -- Special collections -- Historical fiction 3. Readers' advisory services -- United States 4. Historical fiction -- Bibliography
ISBN 9780838911655

LC 2014018024

Emphasizing an appreciation of historical fiction in its many forms and focusing on what fans enjoy, this guide provides a fresh take on a durable genre. --Provided by publisher

Phoenix, Jack

Maximizing the impact of comics in your library : graphic novels, manga, and more / Jack Phoenix. Libraries Unlimited, 2020 248 p. **026**

1. Libraries -- Special collections -- Comic books, strips, etc. 2. Libraries -- Special collections -- Graphic novels. 3. Libraries -- Activity programs
ISBN 9781440868856

LC 2019056103

"This unique guide offers fresh insights on how graphic novels and comics differ from traditional books and require different treatment in the library-from purchasing, shelving, and cataloging to readers' advisory services, programs, and curriculum".-- Provided by publisher.

Spratford, Becky Siegel

The **readers'** advisory guide to horror / Becky Siegel Spratford. American Library Association, 2012. xi, 170 p. ; **026**

1. Fiction in libraries -- United States. 2. Libraries -- United States -- Special collections -- Horror tales. 3. Readers' advisory services -- United States.
ISBN 9780838911129

LC 2011043954

As both an introductory guide for librarians just dipping their toes into the brackish water of scary fiction, as well as a fount of new ideas for horror-aware reference staff, Spratford's book is infernally appropriate.

"An excellent addition to professional readers' advisory literature authored by a librarian respected in the field, this entry in the ALA Readers' Advisory series summarizes the history of horror writing from the eighteenth century to the present; explains the enduring appeal of horror; and introduces prominent authors in the genre." Voice of Youth Advocates

027 General libraries, archives, information centers

Johnson, Alex, 1969-

Improbable libraries : a visual journey to the world's most unusual libraries / Alex Johnson. The University of Chicago Press, 2015. 240 p. : **027**

1. Libraries -- Miscellanea 2. Library architecture -- Miscellanea 3. Curiosities and wonders 4. Libraries -- Pictorial works
ISBN 9780226263694

LC 2014035714

"The colorful photos--sometimes several per spread--are the attraction in this small, square, browsable tome, which showcases innovative, quirky, and fun ways librarians and others have come up with to display books that are for loan or giveaway." Library Journal

Ryback, Timothy W.

Hitler's private library : the books that shaped his life / Timothy W. Ryback. Alfred A. Knopf, 2008. xx, 278 p. : **027**

1. Hitler, Adolf, 1889-1945 Books and reading. 2. Hitler, Adolf, 1889-1945 Knowledge and learning. 3. Library of Congress catalogs. 4. Books and reading -- Influence. 5. Home libraries. 6. Nazis. 7. Political leadership. 8. Germany -- History -- 1933-1945.
ISBN 9781400042043

LC 2008022010

A study of Hitler's emotional and intellectual world traces the evolution of his life and political philosophy as it examines the books that shaped his life, analyzing key phrases and ideas from his personal books as revealed in his own writings, speeches, conversations, philosophy, and actions.

Rydell, Anders, 1982-

The **book** thieves : the Nazi looting of Europe's libraries and the race to return a literary inheritance / Anders Rydell ; translated from the Swedish by Henning Koch. Viking, 2017, c2015. xiii, 352 pages : **027**

1. Nazis 2. Book thefts 3. Nazi plunder 4. Pillage
ISBN 9780735221222

LC 2016044051

Originally published as Boktjuvarna: Jakten pa de forsvunna biblioteken in 2015 by Norstedts.

An account of the Nazis' systematic pillaging of Europe's libraries, and the heroic efforts of librarians working today to return the books to their owners, explores how stolen books were used as part of a campaign to rewrite history in accordance with Third Reich views.

"An engrossing, haunting journey for bibliophiles and World War II historians." Kirkus.

027.009 History and biography

Kells, Stuart

The **library** : a catalogue of wonders / Stuart Kells. Counterpoint, 2018. xvi, 269 pages ; **027.009**

1. Libraries -- History 2. Books and reading -- History 3. Books -- History 4. Rare books
ISBN 9781640090200

LC 2017055409

Originally published: Melbourne, Vic. : Text Publishing, 2017.

"Kells's revelatory romp through the centuries cues us to the fact that, as has so often been the case, libraries need our passionate attention and support, our advocacy, gratitude, and (given Kells's tales of book-kissing, including Coleridge pressing his lips to his copy of Spinoza) love." Booklist.

027.4 Public libraries

Gunnels, Claire B.
Joint libraries : models that work / Claire B. Gunnels, Susan E. Green, and Patricia M. Butler. American Library Association, 2012. xi, 220 p. : **027.4**

1. Joint-use libraries -- United States.
ISBN 0838911382

LC 2011044057

The joint-use college/public library can be an ideal solution to serving patrons while managing overextended resources, and this illuminating book scrutinizes successes and failures of the joint-use model. --Provided by publisher

Matthews, Joseph R.
Scorecards for results : a guide for developing a library balanced scorecard / Joseph R. Matthews. Libraries Unlimited, 2008. xvii, 112 p. : **027.4**

1. Public libraries -- Evaluation.
ISBN 9781591586982

LC 2008003689

"A balanced scorecard (BSC) is a process and culture for choosing, using, and revising measures to help libraries focus on the success of their mission. . . . [The author] has developed a BSC workbook for public libraries. . . . Individual chapters here detail the six steps in developing and using a balanced scorecard, with sample vision statements, strategic themes, and performance measures." Library Journal.

Orlean, Susan
★The **library** book / Susan Orlean. Simon & Schuster, 2018 319 p. **027.4**

1. Libraries 2. Fires 3. Librarians 4. Arson 5. Los Angeles, California -- History
ISBN 9781476740188

LC 2018022454

The author reopens the unsolved mystery of the most catastrophic library fire in American history, and delivers a dazzling love letter to a beloved institution: our libraries.

"Bibliophiles will love this fact-filled, bookish journey." Kirkus.

027.5 Government libraries

Conaway, James
America's library : the story of the Library of Congress, 1800-2000 / James Conaway ; foreword by James H. Billington ; introduction by Edmund Morris. Yale University Press in association with the Library of Congress, 2000. xiii, 226 p. : **027.5**

1. Library of Congress -- History. 2. National libraries -- Washington (D.C.) -- History -- 19th century. 3. National libraries -- Washington (D.C.) -- History -- 20th century.
ISBN 0300083084

LC 99058751

Traces the history of the Library of Congress under the leadership of each of the men who have been appointed as Librarian of Congress and discusses how the Library's collections have reflected American political and intellectual developments.

"This history of the Library of Congress is organized around that tiny, hardy band of men and women who have used both political acumen and intellectual vision to build the library's collections and establish those services that make the LC library to both Congress and nation. Richly supplemented with photographs, this history reaches out to touch all who love libraries." Booklist.

027.6 Libraries for special groups and organizations

Kowalsky, Michelle
Creating inclusive library environments : a planning guide for serving patrons with disabilities / Michelle Kowalsky, John Woodruff. ALA Editions, 2017. x, 218 p. ; **027.6**

1. Libraries and people with disabilities -- United States
ISBN 9780838914854

LC 2016026241

This planning guide will enable libraries to create and maintain a truly inclusive environment for all patrons. --Provided by publisher

027.62 Libraries for specific age groups

Brown, Amy, 1976-
Let's start the music : programming for primary grades / Amy Brown. ALA Editions, 2014. xiii, 165 p. ; **027.62**

1. Children's libraries -- Activity programs -- United States. 2. Music -- Instruction and study -- United States. 3. School libraries -- Activity programs -- United States.
ISBN 9780838911662

LC 2013010871

"Brown, an experienced programmer in public library settings, makes a solid case for weaving multiple intelligences into primary grade programs." School Library Journal.

Del Negro, Janice
Folktales aloud : practical advice for playful storytelling / Janice M. Del Negro. ALA editions, 2014. x, 212 p. ; **027.62**

1. Children's libraries -- Activity programs 2. Elementary school libraries -- Activity programs 3. Storytelling
ISBN 9780838911358

LC 2013028036

Offers advice for storytelling that promotes reading and fosters the imagination of the listeners.

"Folktales are an integral part of children's literature and are the basis for many classic books librarians use daily in their work. These much loved tales are also the backbone of the art of storytelling...Del Negro leads novice tellers through the nuances of successful storytelling...Advice is offered in a very practical way on how to approach this group and suggestions are made as to how to grab and hold their interest with pacing, movement and suspense. If you have even a passing interest in the art of storytelling, this guide is not to be missed." School Library Journal.

Flowers, Sarah, 1952-
Evaluating teen services and programs / Sarah Flowers. Neal-Schuman, an imprint of the American Library Association, 2012. xv, 119 p. : **027.62**

1. Libraries and teenagers -- United States. 2. Young adults' libraries -- Evaluation -- United States.
ISBN 1555707939

LC 2012015105

Flowers offers guidance for librarians in examining all aspects of teen programming and services to determine where improvement is needed.

"Overall these resources are beneficial to have on hand. We may know that teen services are a valuable and necessary resource, but these materials can help librarians prove and promote the reasons." VOYA

Ghoting, Saroj Nadkarni

STEP into storytime : using StoryTime Effective Practice to strengthen the development of newborns to five-year-olds / Saroj Nadkarni Ghoting and Kathy Fling Klatt. ALA Editions, 2014. xii, 356 p. : **027.62**

1. Children's libraries -- Activity programs -- United States. 2. Storytelling -- United States. 3. Libraries and preschool children -- United States. 4. Libraries and caregivers -- United States.

ISBN 9780838912225

LC 2014004162

"It is a rare volume that could serve as both pleasure reading or as a textbook, but STEP into Storytime walks that fine line...The majority of childrens librarians have studied childhood development and early literacy best practices; consider this book required reading to keep this knowledge fresh while reminding us of the importance--and delightful fun--of our work." Booklist.

Knoll, Debra J.

Engaging babies in the library : putting theory into practice / Debra J. Knoll. ALA Editions, 2016. xvi, 115 p. ; **027.62**

1. Children's libraries. 2. Libraries and families. 3. Libraries and infants. 4. Libraries and toddlers.

ISBN 9780838914342

LC 2015049312

With Knoll's guidance, children's librarians will be informed and inspired to rise to the challenge of providing quality service to babies, toddlers, and care providers. --Provided by publisher

Pattee, Amy

Developing library collections for today's young adults / Amy S. Pattee. The Scarecrow Press, Inc., 2014 xiii, 267 p. ; **027.62**

1. Libraries and teenagers -- United States. 2. Libraries -- Special collections -- Nonbook materials. 3. Multimedia library services -- United States. 4. Young adults' libraries -- Collection development -- United States.

ISBN 0810887347

LC 2013018596

A guide to developing a young adult collection, offers information on assessing, selecting, and maintaining materials.

Reid, Rob, 1955-

★**200+** original and adapted story program activities / Rob Reid. ALA Editions, 2018. xiii, 266 p. ; **027.62**

1. Children's libraries -- Activity programs -- United States. 2. Libraries and preschool children -- United States. 3. Storytelling -- United States.

ISBN 0838917380

LC 2018024987

"200+ Original and Adapted Story Program Activities is Rob Reid's Greatest Hits concept. It gathers over 200 storytime activities (original fingerplays, movement activities, songs and musical activities, poems, and sound effect stories for preschool story programs) from previous ALA Editions books, Upstart books, and LibrarySparks magazine articles and shares them in one package. It also includes a dozen or so new (and previously unpublished) activities".-- Provided by publisher.

"An experienced children's librarian presents storytime activities aimed at preschoolers and early elementary school students: finger plays, movement and sound effects, imagination exercises, felt stories, spoonerisms, raps, and even drama presentations." School Library Journal.

Sweeney, Jennifer

Literacy : a way out for at-risk youth / Jennifer Sweeney. Libraries Unlimited, 2012 xx, 133 p. : **027.62**

1. Juvenile corrections -- United States 2. Juvenile delinquents -- Books and reading -- United States 3. Juvenile delinquents -- Education -- United States 4. Juvenile delinquents -- Rehabilitation -- United States

ISBN 9781598846744

LC 2011042804

"This exploration of juvenile corrections librarianship provides a complete description of these specialized services, addresses unique challenges in this library environment, and promotes intellectual and social growth for at-risk youth".-- Provided by publisher.

027.7 Libraries for educational institutions

Hankins, Rebecca,

Where are all the librarians of color? : the experiences of people of color in academia / coedited by Rebecca Hankins, CA, MLS and Miguel Juarez, MLS, MA. Library Juice Press, 2015. x, 341 p. ; **027.7**

1. Minority librarians -- United States 2. Academic librarians -- United States 3. Minorities in higher education -- United States 4. Diversity in the workplace -- United States

ISBN 9781936117833

LC 2015032617

"This edited volume seeks to address the shared experiences of academic librarians of color, i.e. Hispanic Americans, African Americans, Native Americans and Asian Americans".-- Provided by publisher.

028 Reading and use of other information media

Basbanes, Nicholas A., 1943-

★**Every** book its reader : the power of the printed word to stir the world / Nicholas A. Basbanes. Harper Collins, c2005. xviii, 360 p. : **028**

1. Books and reading.

ISBN 0060593237

LC 2005046164

In celebration of five eventful centuries of the printed word, Basbanes considers of writings that have "made things happen" in the world, works that have both nudged the course of history and fired the imagination of influential people. Basbanes asks what we can know about such figures as Milton, Gibbon, Locke, Newton, Coleridge, John Adams, Frederick Douglass, Abraham Lincoln, Henry James, Thomas Edison, Helen Keller--even the Marquis de Sade and Hitler--by knowing what they read. He shows how books that these people have consulted, in some cases annotated with their marginal notes, can offer clues to the development of their thought. He then profiles some of the most articulate readers of our time, who discuss such concepts as literary canons, classic works in translation, the timelessness of poetry, the formation of sacred texts, and the power of literature to train physicians, nurture children, and rehabilitate criminal offenders.--From publisher description.

"The author focuses on peoples' reading habits and on the books they have read, both obscure and renowned, as well as on the importance of particular books in specific contexts. Basbanes begins by interviewing some of the best-read people alive, among them David McCullough, Harold Bloom, Helen Vendler, and Elaine Pagels; he also mentions a wide variety of contemporary and historical personages. The loosely related stories are often inspirational, making this an engrossing read." Library Journal.

Cole, Natalie, 1971-

★**Transforming** summer programs at your library : outreach and outcomes in action / Natalie Cole, Virginia A. Walter. ALA editions, 2018. xv, 160 p. ; **028**

1. Library outreach programs -- United States. 2. Reading promotion -- United States. 3. Summer reading programs -- United States.
ISBN 9780838916285

LC 2017052415

"Traditional summer reading programs need to be reimagined. Working groups of librarians, in partnership with the California Library Association and the California State Library, have done just that, creating and implementing outcomes- and outreach-basedsummer reading programs that speak directly to diverse and changing communities". -- Provided by publisher.

Dirda, Michael

Browsings : a year of reading, collecting, and living with books / Michael Dirda. Pegasus Books, 2015 246 p. **028**

1. Books and reading 2. Reading 3. Critics. 4. Authors 5. Essays
ISBN 9781605988443

LC 2015298168

A latest volume of writings by the Washington Post columnist shares personal essays on diverse topics ranging from literary pets and cursive writing to book inscriptions and the pleasures of science-fiction conventions.

Manguel, Alberto

A **reader** on reading / Alberto Manguel. Yale University Press, c2010. xi, 308 p. : **028**

1. Manguel, Alberto, 1948- Books and reading. 2. Books and reading. 3. Writing. 4. Essays.
ISBN 9780300159820

LC 2009043719

"Lectures, columns, and other occasional writings are gathered here to form a meditation on the art of reading. Thoughtful interrogations of the value of identity labels like Jewish fiction or gay fiction and the relationship between writers and editors mix with ruminations on the ideal reader and the ideal library. Several autobiographical essays detail a restless life that has taken Manguel from Buenos Aires to Tel Aviv, Canada, and, eventually, France, and an equally restless reading life. Predictable touchstones emerge: Dante and Homer, Shakespeare and Cervantes. Above all, there is Manguel's countryman Borges; he recalls reading aloud to the blind master as a young man in Argentina." The New Yorker.

Mendelsund, Peter

What we see when we read : a phenomenology, with illustrations / Peter Mendelsund. Vintage Contemporaries, 2014. 416 p. : **028**

1. Books and reading. 2. Phenomenology. 3. Visual perception in literature. 4. Literature -- Psychology.
ISBN 9780804171632

LC 2014007896

"An illustrated exploration into the phenomenology of reading".- Provided by publisher.

"This work was written for those who enjoy fully the creative experience of reading, and who read about reading." Library Journal.

Mustich, James

★**1,000** books to read : a life-changing list before you die / James Mustich ; with Margot Greenbaum Mustich, Thomas Meagher, and Karen Templer. Workman Publishing, 2018 xii, 948 p. : **028**

1. Best books. 2. Books and reading -- United States.
ISBN 9781523504459

LC 2018036090

Includes indexes.

A celebration of the reading life presents a cross-genre, historically representative compendium of one thousand works of literature, complemented by essays on each book's particular relevance.

Patrick, Bethanne,

The **books** that changed my life / edited by Bethanne Patrick. Regan Arts, 2016 256 p. **028**

1. Books and reading. 2. Literature -- History and criticism 3. Writing. 4. Essays.
ISBN 9781941393659

LC bl2016012235

Leading authors, politicians, CEOs, actors, and other notables share the books that changed their life, why they love them, and their passion with readers everywhere.

Prose, Francine, 1947-

What to read and why / Francine Prose. HarperCollins, 2018. 336 p. **028**

1. Literature -- History and criticism 2. Books and reading 3. Fiction writing 4. Authors 5. Essays
ISBN 9780062397867

LC 2019296611

In this brilliant collection, the follow-up to her New York Times bestseller Reading Like a Writer, the distinguished novelist, literary critic, and essayist celebrates the pleasures of reading and pays homage to the works and writers she admires above all others, from Jane Austen and Charles Dickens to Jennifer Egan and Roberto Bolano.

Ross, Catherine Sheldrick

★The **pleasures** of reading : a booklover's alphabet / Catherine Sheldrick Ross. Libraries Unlimited, an imprint of ABC-CLIO, LLC, 2014 xi, 270 p. ; **028**

1. Books and reading. 2. Libraries and community. 3. Popular literature. 4. Public services (Libraries).
ISBN 159158695X

LC 2014008161

"Based on years of ground-breaking research, this book supplies a look at the unique relationship between each text and the individual reader that results in a satisfying, pleasurable, and even life-changing reading experience".-- Provided by publisher.

"Librarians who work with RA will not find much new information but will have their experiences validated. Those new to RA will receive a thorough introduction." Library Journal.

Schwalbe, Will

Books for living / Will Schwalbe. Alfred A. Knopf, 2016. 352 p. **028**

1. Books and reading 2. Personal conduct 3. Life change events
ISBN 9780385353540

LC 2016026088

Presents a highly personal celebration of reading, sharing impassioned recommendations for specific books that can offer guidance through daily life.

"In an age when the number of readers is declining, a delightful book like this might just snare a few new recruits." Kirkus.

028.1 Reviews

Naidoo, Jamie Campbell

★**Rainbow** family collections : selecting and using children's books with lesbian, gay, bisexual, transgender, and queer content / Jamie Campbell Naidoo. Libraries Unlimited, an imprint of ABC-CLIO, LLC, 2012 xvii, 260 p. : **028.1**

1. Children of sexual minority parents -- Books and reading -- United States. 2. Children's libraries -- Collection development -- United States. 3. Children's libraries -- Services to minorities -- United States. 4. Libraries and sexual minorities -- United States.

ISBN 1598849603

LC 2012008362

"Rainbow Family Collections examines over 200 children's picture books and chapter books with LGBTQ content from around the world. Highlighting titles for children from infancy to age 12, each entry in Rainbow Family Collections supplies a synopsis of the content, lists awards it has received, cites professional reviews, and provides suggestions for librarians considering acquisition. The book also provides a brief historical overview of LGBTQ children's literature along with the major book awards for this genre and a list of criteria for selecting the best books with this content. Interviews with authors and key individuals in LGBTQ children's book publishing are also featured".-- Provided by publisher.

Szymborska, Wislawa

Nonrequired reading : prose pieces / Wislawa Szymborska ; translated from the Polish by Clare Cavanagh. Harcourt, Inc., c2002. xii, 233 p. ; **028.1**

1. Szymborska, Wislawa 2. Books and reading. 3. Essays.

ISBN 0151006601

LC 2002002440

"The skillful simplicity and lyric quality of these essays make them distinctive. With her poet's gift for compression, Szymborska captures large concepts and brilliantly reduces them to pithy, two-page essays." Library Journal.

028.5 Reading and use of other information media by young people

Keane, Nancy J.

101 great, ready-to-use book lists for teens / Nancy J. Keane. Libraries Unlimited, an imprint of ABC-CLIO, LLC, 2012 xiv, 263 p. ; **028.5**

1. High school libraries 2. Teenagers -- Books and reading -- United States. 3. Young adult literature 4. Young adults' libraries 5. Book lists.

ISBN 9781610691345

LC 2011051428

"The book is meant as an extension to the previous work, The big book of teen reading lists (2006)."

"This is a useful resource for new librarians and may also be helpful to seasoned librarians. The emphasis is on books published within the last ten years, but some older titles are included." Library Media Connection.

028.7 Use of books and other information media as sources of information

Dorr, Christina H.

★**LGBTQAI+** books for children and teens : providing a window for all / Christina Dorr and Liz Deskins ; foreword by Jamie Campbell Naidoo. ALA Editions, 2018. xxix, 132 p. : **028.7**

1. Children -- Books and reading -- United States. 2. Children's literature -- Study and teaching. 3. Libraries -- Special collections -- Sexual minorities. 4. Sexual minorities

ISBN 083891649X

LC 2017052430

"This resource not only surveys the best in LGBTQAI+ lit but, just as importantly, offers guidance on how to share it in ways that encourage understanding and acceptance among parents, school administrators, and the wider community". -- Provided by publisher.

"Despite some limitations, this volume does a superb job on many fronts. An essential purchase for public and school libraries, especially given that few other selections on this topic exist." School Library Journal.

028.9 Reading interests and habits

Dirda, Michael

Book by book : notes on reading and life / Michael Dirda. Henry Holt, 2006, c2005. xvii, 170 p. ; **028.9**

1. Dirda, Michael Books and reading. 2. Critics -- United States -- Books and reading 3. Books and reading -- Influence 4. Reading -- Social aspects. 5. Trivia and miscellaneous facts

ISBN 0805078770

LC 2005055451

Offers a personal meditation on the relationship between books and life and on the role of books in teaching us how to live, drawing on sources ranging from Dr. Seuss to Simone Weil.

"The author writes a guide to reading and its life lessons ranging widely and pithily through the universal themes of learning, school, work, love, childhood and spiritual guidance. Dirda's message is simple: if reading is to be life enhancing, we need to focus our attention on books that are rewarding. For those who enjoy books about reading, and for all those seeking to encourage others to read, Dirda's brief yet suggestive book will inspire." Publishers Weekly.

Maatta, Stephanie L.

A **few** good books : using contemporary readers' advisory strategies to connect readers with books / Stephanie L. Maatta. Neal-Schuman Publishers, c2010. xix, 387 p. ; **028.9**

1. Readers' advisory services -- United States. 2. Readers' advisory services -- Technological innovations. 3. Fiction in libraries -- United States. 4. Books and reading -- United States.

ISBN 9781555706692

LC 2009040999

Offers information for librarians and library students on how to become an effective readers' advisor in a technological and multicultural society.

Spence, Annie

Dear Fahrenheit 451 : love and heartbreak in the stacks

/ Annie Spence. Flatiron Books, 2017. 224 p. **028.9**

1. Books and reading 2. Reading 3. Libraries 4. Books 5. Essays.
ISBN 9781250106490

LC 2017027324

A deeply personal collection of love letters and break-up notes to the books in the librarian author's life explains the complicated reasons why libraries are keeping or removing books that either are no longer checked out by readers or have poor literary value.

"A librarian delivers a charming epistolary volume that begs to be read with pencil in hand." Kirkus.

Young, Damon

The **art** of reading / Damon Young. Scribe, 2018, c2016. 176 p. **028.9**

1. Books and reading. 2. Reading interests. 3. Reading promotion. 4. Popular culture
ISBN 9781947534025

Originally published: Carlton, Vic. : Melbourne University Publishing, 2016.

"This literary study is serious but also witty and fun--a tough balance to strike, but Young nails it." Publishers Weekly.

030 General enclyclopedic works

Janssen, Sarah, 1982-

The **world** almanac and book of facts 2019 / senior editor: Sarah Janssen. World Almanac Books, 2019 1007 p. : **030**

1. Almanacs, American.
ISBN 9781600572203

LC bl2018196272

Includes indexes.

Presents a reference with comprehensive facts and statistics on current events, people, and the countries of the world, along with 2018 sports statistics and original articles on recent issues and topics.

Janssen, Sarah, 1982-

★The **world** almanac and book of facts 2020 / senior editor: Sarah Janssen. World Almanac Books, 2020 1007 p. : **030**

1. Almanacs, American.
ISBN 9781600572289

LC bl2019037434

Includes indexes.

Providing large type sizes and more user-friendly access, a 2020 edition of the best-selling reference features entries in a wide range of subjects, from the launch of Obamacare and iPads to the recent immigration policy debate and the 2020 election.

031 General encyclopedic works in specific languages and

Carlsen, Spike, 1952-

A **walk** around the block : stoplight secrets, mischievous squirrels, manhole mysteries & other stuff you see every day (and know nothing about) / Spike Carlsen. HarperOne, 2020 328 p. **031**

1. Curiosities and wonders. 2. Inventions -- Miscellanea 3. Material culture -- Miscellanea. 4. Everyday life
ISBN 9780062954756

LC 2020025829

On his regular walk one morning, Spike Carlsen realized there was an entire world outside his front door that he knew nothing about. How does that fire hydrant work, he wondered? Why are street lights shining more brightly than ever before? And, on a more personal level, why does an easy stroll around the neighborhood always leave him feeling more creative and spry, better able to take on the day? A simple walk around the block set Carlsen off on an investigative journey to discover everything he could about every thing we take for granted in our everyday life, from manhole covers and recycling bins to pedestrian crossings and bike lanes.

"Writing in the mode of Edward Humes, David Owen, and Mary Roach, Carlsen offers an eye-opening and exuberantly informative walk-around-the-block tour that is made-to-order for this time of necessary at-homeness." Booklist

Guinness World Records Limited,

Guinness world records 2019 / Guinness World Records Guinness World Records Limited, 2018 255 p. : **031**

1. Curiosities and wonders 2. World records
ISBN 9781912286430

LC bl2018116922

Includes index.

Chronicles the evolution of record-breaking while incorporating thousands of new entries and highlights of classic records, as well as "Making History" pages that use LEGOs to illustrate and explain important record-breaking objects.

031.02 Books of miscellaneous facts

Henderson, Caspar

A **new** map of wonders : a journey in search of modern marvels / Caspar Henderson. The University of Chicago Press, 2017. 368 p. ; **031.02**

1. Sense of wonder 2. Curiosity 3. Curiosities and wonders 4. Philosophy of nature
ISBN 9780226291918

LC 2017013309

Sequel to: The Book of Barely Imagined Beings.

Drawing on the form of one of the oldest and most widely known sources of wonder--maps--a sequel to The Book of Barely Imagined Beings explores many realms of the wonderful, in different times and cultures and in the present day, while examining the cognitive basis of wonder and the relationship between wonder and science.

"Part celebration and part meditation, an elegant study of things that should awe and amaze usand why we are capable of awe and amazement in the first place." Kirkus.

Iggulden, Conn

The **double** dangerous book for boys / Conn Iggulden. HarperCollins, 2019. 304 p. **031.02**

1. Boys -- Life skills guides 2. Life skills -- Handbooks, manuals, etc. 3. Amusements. 4. Recreation.
ISBN 9780062857972

LC bl2019032101

This long-awaited sequel to the bestselling Dangerous Book for Boys, which became an instant classic, is designed for boys from eight to eighty and includes more than 70 new chapters and important skills, historical information and essential stories.

National Geographic Society

National Geographic almanac 2019 National Geographic,

2018 398 p. : **031.02**

1. Almanacs.
ISBN 9781426219818

LC bl2018190509

Includes index.

Provides the latest information in exploration, geology, astronomy, biology, medicine, and world views.

032 General encyclopedic works in English

Ayto, John

★**Brewer's** dictionary of modern phrase & fable / [compiled by] John Ayto & Ian Crofton. Brewer's, 2006. ix, 853 p. ; **032**

1. English language -- Terms and phrases 2. Literature -- Dictionaries 3. Mythology -- Dictionaries 4. Allusions 5. Dictionaries
ISBN 9780550105646

LC bl2011025987

Completely updated for the twenty-first century, this reference presents definitions and origins of thousands of words, idioms, catchphrases, slogans, nicknames, and events from TV, literature, music, comic strips, and computer games.

051 General serial publications in specific languages and

Nelson, Jennifer, 1965-

Airbrushed nation : the lure and loathing of women's magazines / Jennifer Nelson. Seal Press, 2012. 256 p. **051**

1. Fashion periodicals 2. Sexism in women's periodicals 3. Women in mass media. 4. Women -- Body image
ISBN 9781580054133

LC 2012012417

Examines the women's magazine business, wonders how it is thriving amid the failing print journalism industry, and asks if the unrealistic body image it portrays is intentional or not.

Peckman, Jodi,

50 years of Rolling stone : the music, politics and people that changed our culture / introduction by Jann S. Wenner ; edited by Jodi Peckman and Joe Levy ; design director, Joseph Hutchinson. Abrams, 2017. 283 p. : **051**

1. Rolling stone (San Francisco, Calif.). 2. Journalism -- United States -- History -- 20th century 3. Journalism -- United States -- History -- 21st century 4. Rock music -- Periodicals -- History 5. Popular culture -- United States -- History -- 20th century
ISBN 9781419724466

LC OC2018146767

"For the past fifty years, Rolling Stone has been a leading voice in journalism, cultural criticism, and--above all--music. This landmark book documents the magazine's rise to prominence as the voice of rock and roll and a leading showcase for era-defining photography. From the 1960s to the present day, the book offers a decade-by-decade exploration of American music and history. Interviews with rock legends--Bob Dylan, Mick Jagger, Kurt Cobain, Bruce Springsteen, and more--appear alongside iconic photographs by Baron Wolman, Annie Leibovitz, Mark Seliger, and other leading image-makers. With feature articles, excerpts, and exposes by such quintessential writers as Hunter S. Thompson, Matt Taibbi, and David Harris, this book is an irresistible and essential keepsake of the magazine that has defined American music for generations of readers". -- provided by publisher.

New York magazine

Highbrow, lowbrow, brilliant, despicable : 50 years of New York / the editors of New York magazine. Simon & Schuster, 2017. 400 p. **051**

1. New York magazine 2. Periodicals 3. Journalism 4. City life 5. Business 6. New York City 7. Anthologies
ISBN 9781501166846

LC bl2017045966

Combines groundbreaking magazine archive pieces with new material in an oversized, full-color celebration of New York magazine's first half century, citing contributions by notables ranging from Nora Ephron and Tom Wolfe to Gloria Steinem and Kurt Anderson while drawing on insider interviews to document the magazine's publication history.

"A great magazine is commemorated with an equally top-flight anthology. History, local and global, unfolds in this fine gathering that represents a half-century and more than 2,300 issues." Kirkus.

060.4 Special topics of general organizations

American Institute of Parliamentarians

American Institute of Parliamentarians standard code of parliamentary procedure / [by American Institute of Parliamentarians]. McGraw-Hill, c2012. x, 326 p. ; **060.4**

1. Parliamentary practice
ISBN 9780071778640

LC 2011048926

Presents a guide to meeting procedure, updated with new motions and protocols pertaining to electronic meetings, discipline, and finance and audit committees.

Robert, Henry M. (Henry Martyn), 1837-1923

Robert's rules of order, newly revised, in brief : updated in accord with the eleventh edition of the complete manual / Henry M. Robert III ... [et al.]. Da Capo Press, c2011. vii, 197 p. ; **060.4**

1. Parliamentary practice.
ISBN 9780306820199

LC 2011932261

Includes index.

An update of the classic parliamentary rules of order presents the protocol behind the orderly conduct of meetings in concise format, offering access to the most important rules.

Robert, Henry M. (Henry Martyn), 1837-1923

Webster's New World Robert's rules of order : simplified and applied / Robert McConnell Productions. Wiley Pub., c2001. xx, 409 p. ; **060.4**

1. Parliamentary practice.
ISBN 0764563998

LC 2001092064

Includes index.

Presents the rules of parliamentary procedure designed to help meetings run smoothly and efficiently.

069 Museology (Museum science)

Conniff, Richard, 1951-

House of lost worlds : dinosaurs, dynasties, and the story of life on earth / Richard Conniff. Yale University Press, 2016 320

p. **069**

1. Peabody Museum of Natural -- History 2. Museums. 3. Natural history museums. 4. Science -- History.

ISBN 9780300211634

LC bl2016013886

Tells the story of how one museum changed ideas about dinosaurs, dynasties, and even the story of life on earth. The Yale Peabody Museum of Natural History, now celebrating its 150th anniversary, has remade the way we see the world.

"Colored, boxed sections highlighting people and events and over 100 illustrations and photos provide a pleasant coffee table-book feel, and 23 pages of footnotes attest to Conniff's exhaustive research." Kirkus.

Wilkins, Robert L.

Long road to hard truth : the 100-year mission to create the National Museum of African American History and Culture / Robert L. Wilkins. Proud Legacy Publishing, [2016] 155 p. **069**

1. National Museum of African American -- History and Culture (U.S.) 2. Museums 3. Race relations. 4. African Americans -- Civil rights -- History 5. African Americans -- Museums -- Washington, D.C.

ISBN 9780997910407

LC 2016950268

In Long Road to Hard Truth: The 100 Year Mission to Create the National Museum of African American History and Culture, Robert L. Wilkins tells the story of how his curiosity about why there wasn't a national museum dedicated to African American history and culture became an obsession-eventually leading him to quit his job as an attorney when his wife was seven months pregnant with their second child, and make it his mission to help the museum become a reality.

"Given all the historical minutiae that Wilkins provides, its a surprisingly gripping historical drama. A delightful, edifying tale written with intelligence and emotional sensitivity." Kirkus.

070.1 Documentary media, educational media, news media

Fager, Jeffrey

Fifty years of 60 minutes : the inside story of television's most influential news broadcast / Jeff Fager. Simon & Schuster, 2017. 320 p. **070.1**

1. 60 minutes (Television program). 2. Broadcast journalism 3. Television news. 4. Television newscasters and commentators. 5. Journalism

ISBN 9781501135804

LC 2017025966

A history of 60 Minutes--the iconic American TV news broadcast--going behind the scenes of the most famous breakthrough stories of its remarkable fifty-year run to reveal the secrets of the program's success.

"This insider perspective gives a behind-the-scenes view of how stories were developed, along with the complex interactions of the talented and competitive staff." Library Journal.

Thompson, Hunter S.

Fear and loathing at Rolling Stone : the essential writing of Hunter S. Thompson / edited and with a foreword by Jann S. Wenner and with an introduction by Paul Scanlon. Simon & Schuster, 2011. 320 p. **070.1**

1. Thompson, Hunter S. Correspondence. 2. Wenner, Jann Correspondence. 3. Rolling Stone Magazine 4. Gonzo journalism 5. Journalism -- Political aspects 6. Periodical writing

ISBN 9781439165959

LC 2011032312

An anthology of "Rolling Stone" articles offers insight into both the late Thompson's early career and the magazine's fledgling years, and includes selected correspondence between Thompson and editor Jann Wenner.

"Thompson published his first article in Rolling Stone in 1970, documenting his campaign for sheriff and the rise of what he called freak power in Aspen, CO. He would continue to be a prolific contributor to the magazine throughout the 1970s from his infamous Fear and Loathing in Las Vegas (1971) to his political journalism beginning with his coverage of the Nixon-McGovern presidential campaign in 1972 and lasting until 2004, a year before his death. Rolling Stone's cofounder and publisher, Wenner, edits this collection of Thompson's Rolling Stone pieces. It includes not only Thompson's writings for the magazine but the two men's correspondence, deepening our understanding of how they worked together. Thompson's iconic voice remains fresh, vibrant, and relevant, also enabling today's readers to gain perspective on over 30 years of political and cultural change." Library Journal.

Wenger, Debora Halpern

Advancing the story : broadcast journalism in a multimedia world / Debora Halpern Wenger and Deborah Potter. CQ Press/SAGE, c2018 xxxi, 380 p. : **070.1**

1. Broadcast journalism

ISBN 9781544332451

LC 2018010986

It's a multimedia world, and today's journalists must develop a multimedia mindset. How does this way of thinking change the newsgathering and news production processes? Having conceived of and written their book in this changed media landscape, broadcast veterans Debora Halpern Wenger and Deborah Potter seamlessly build on the fundamentals of good news reporting while teaching students to use depth, interactivity and immediacy as they maximize the advantages of each platform. --Provided by publisher

Wilkman, Jon

Screening reality : how documentary filmmakers reimagined America / Jon Wilkman. Bloomsbury Publishing, 2020 400 p. **070.1**

1. Documentary films -- History and criticism 2. Filmmaking 3. Historical research 4. Truth 5. United States -- History

ISBN 9781635571035

LC 2019019146

Screening Reality is a widescreen view of the rarely examined relationship between nonfiction movies and American history--how 'reality' has been discovered, defined, projected, televised, and streamed during more than one hundred years of dramatic change, through World Wars I and II, the dawn of mass media, the social and political turmoil of the sixties and seventies, and the communications revolution that led to a twenty-first century of empowered yet divided Americans.

070.4 Journalism

Berkow, Ira

How life imitates sports : a sportswriter recounts, relives, and reckons with 50 years on the sports beat / Ira Berkow. Sports Publishing, 2020 379 p. **070.4**

1. Berkow, Ira 2. Sports -- Social aspects 3. Sportswriters 4. Sports --

History -- 21st century. 5. Sports -- History -- 20th century. 6. Essays
ISBN 9781683583790

For the last half century, Pulitzer Prize-winning sportswriter Ira Berkow has been at the center of some of the most memorable moments in sports history. From the World Series, NBA Finals, and Super Bowl, to Heavyweight Title Fights, the Olympics, and The Masters, he has seen and covered them all. How Life Imitates Sports shares how these events, and their participants, have significantly shaped how we as a nation have come to understand and perceive our culture (and even our politics). They are a historical record of one significant sphere of our life and times: sports.

"A New York Times sports reporter and columnist for more than 25 years and the author of numerous books, Berkow offers a wide-ranging collection of pieces on athletes and sports events from 1970 forward. . . . For those who value sports journalism, Berkow's work is certain to endure." Booklist

Buell, Hal

Moments : the Pulitzer Prize photographs : a visual chronicle of our time / Hal Buell ; foreword by David Halberstam. Black Dog & Leventhal Publishers, 2015 336 p. : **070.4**

1. Photojournalism -- United States -- Awards 2. Pulitzer Prizes
ISBN 9781631910081

LC bl2015036668

Includes index.

Presents dozens of Pulitzer Prize-winning photographs that capture unforgettable moments in twentieth-century history, including the Marines raising the flag at Iwo Jima and Babe Ruth's final salute at Yankee Stadium.

Carr, David, 1956-2015

Final draft : the collected work of David Carr / edited by Jill Carr. Houghton Mifflin Harcourt, 2020. 224 p. **070.4**

1. Journalism -- United States. 2. Mass media -- United States. 3. United States -- Civilization -- 1970- 4. Anthologies
ISBN 9780358206682

LC 2019038033

Presents a career-spanning selection of the legendary reporter David Carr's writing for *The New York Times*, *Washington City Paper*, *New York Magazine*, *The Atlantic* and more.

"Readers will appreciate having this wide-ranging sample of Carr's inimitable perspective on American life." Publishers Weekly

Cronkite, Walter

Cronkite's war : his World War II letters home / Walter Cronkite IV and Maurice Isserman. National Geographic Society, [2013] 352 p. **070.4**

1. Cronkite, Walter Correspondence. 2. Cronkite, Walter Family. 3. Cronkite, Betsy, -2005 Correspondence. 4. United Press International 5. World War II -- Journalists. 6. War correspondents -- United States 7. World War II 8. London, England 9. Love letters 10. Letters
ISBN 9781426210198

LC 2012045334

The iconic American journalist shares the story of his World War II experiences as a then-obscure United Press wire service reporter, tracing his two convoys across the dangerous North Atlantic to assignments in England and North Africa, which he documented in long, detailed letters to his beloved wife, Betsy.

Ferrari, Michelle.

Reporting America at war : an oral history / compiled by Michelle Ferrari with commentary by James Tobin. Hyperion, 2003. viii, 241 p. : **070.4**

1. War in the news media. 2. War in mass media. 3. War correspondents. 4. Oral histories
ISBN 9781401300722

LC 2003049966

A fascinating oral chronicle of journalists on the battlefield shares the personal stories of Peter Arnett, Christianne Amanpour, Walter Cronkite, David Halberstam, Andy Rooney, Morley Safer, and others and includes their reflections on such issues as ethics, censorship, propaganda, the power of the press, and the future of war reporting.

"Beginning with Edward R. Murrow's live reports during the London blitz and ending with an epilogue on the second war in Iraq, this oral history contains transcripts of interviews with 11 top correspondents. . . . Tobin's introductions and transitional and informational interpolations within the transcripts hold this informative volume together." Publishers Weekly.

Friedlander, Edward Jay

Feature writing for newspapers and magazines : the pursuit of excellence / Edward Jay Friedlander, John Lee. Pearson/A&B, c2008. xv, 334 p. ; **070.4**

1. Feature writing
ISBN 9780205484669

LC 2007020885

Includes index.

This book helps the reader cultivate vital journalistic skills with a thorough discussion about creating and refining article ideas, conducting research and interviews, writing, and navigating legal and ethical questions. --Provided by publisher

Fuller, Jack

What is happening to news : the information explosion and the crisis in journalism / Jack Fuller. University of Chicago Press, 2010. xiii, 214 p. ; **070.4**

1. Journalism -- United States. 2. Journalistic ethics. 3. Information society. 4. Newspapers.
ISBN 9780226268989

LC 2009039090

"This worthy addition to the journalism bookshelf will stand the test of time." Choice.

Hankir, Zahra,

Our women on the ground : essays by Arab women reporting from the Arab world / edited by Zahra Hankir ; foreword by Christiane Amanpour. Penguin Books, 2019. xxiv, 278 p. : **070.4**

1. Journalism 2. Women journalists 3. Women -- Arab countries 4. Women in mass media 5. Arab countries 6. Essays.
ISBN 9780143133414

LC 2018052511

"An emotionally resonant and eminently readable anthology of true accounts that will appeal greatly to readers interested in global women's issues, journalism, and the modern Arab world." Library Journal.

Hargreaves, Ian

Journalism : a very short introduction / Ian Hargreaves. Oxford University Press, 2014. xviii, 153 p. : **070.4**

1. Journalism. 2. Mass media. 3. Mass media -- Social aspects.
ISBN 9780199686872

LC 2014937968

Includes index.

First published as Journalism: truth or dare, 2003.

Journalism entered the twenty-first century caught in a paradox. The world had more journalism, across a wider range of media, than at any time since the birth of the western free press in the eighteenth century. Western journalists had found themselves under a cloud of suspicion: from politicians, philosophers, the general public, anti-globalization radicals, religious groups, and even from fellow journalists. Critics argued that the news industry had lost its moral bearings, focusing on high investmentreturns rather than reporting and analysing the political, economic, and social issues of the day. Journalism has a central and profound impact on our worldview; we find it everywhere from newspapers and television, to radio and the Internet. In the new edition of this thought-provoking and provocative Very Short Introduction, Ian Hargreaves examines the world of contemporary journalism. By looking not only at what journalism has been in the past, but also what it is becoming in the digital age, he examines the big issues relating to reportage, warfare, celebrity culture, privacy, and technology worldwide.

Havrilesky, Heather

How to be a person in the world : ask Polly's guide through the paradoxes of modern life / Heather Havrilesky. Doubleday, 2016. 258 p. **070.4**

1. Personal conduct 2. Interpersonal relations 3. Advice 4. Life.
ISBN 9780385540391

LC 2015023592

"A collection of new and prieviously published letters from Ask Polly's advice column, originally featured on The Awl and now on New York Magazine's blog, The Cut."

"Funny, frank advice for people searching for solutions to a myriad of relationship issues." Kirkus.

Kramer, Mark (Mark William), 1944-

Telling true stories : a nonfiction writers' guide from the Nieman Foundation at Harvard University / edited by Mark Kramer and Wendy Call. Plume, c2007. xvii, 317 p. ; **070.4**

1. Reporters and reporting. 2. Journalism -- Authorship.
ISBN 9780452287556

LC 2006026809

Some of the nation's leading journalists and writers offer practical advice, personal anecdotes, and helpful writing techniques and suggestions in a volume that includes essays by Tom Wolfe on the emotional core of the story, Gay Talese on writing about private lives, and other contributions by Malcolm Gladwell, Nora Ephron, Alma Guillermoprieto, and others.

Miller, James A. (James Andrew), 1957-

Those guys have all the fun : inside the world of ESPN / James Andrew Miller and Tom Shales. Little Brown & Co., 2011. 784 p. **070.4**

1. E S P N (Cable television network) 2. Television sports broadcasting. 3. Sports journalism. 4. Sportscasters. 5. Television networks -- History
ISBN 9780316043007

LC 2011925202

Presents the history of sports channel ESPN based on interviews with nearly five hundred current and former employees, featuring announcers and analysts as well as sports stars including LeBron James, Peyton Manning, and Jeff Gordon.

Ritchin, Fred

Magnum photobook : the catalogue raisonne / text by Fred Ritchin & Carole Naggar. Phaidon Press Limited, 2016. 271 p. : **070.4**

1. Magnum Photos. 2. Documentary photography 3. Photobooks 4. Photography, Artistic
ISBN 9780714872117

LC bl2017003952

Includes index.

Surveys over 1,300 photobooks created by Magnum photographers since its founding in 1947, highlighting the cooperative's contributions to documentary photography.

"A valuable reference that will inform and delight those interested in photojournalism, as well as book and graphic design." Library Journal.

Ross, Lillian, 1927-

Reporting always : writing for The New Yorker / Lillian Ross ; foreword by David Remnick. Scribner, 2015. 320 p. **070.4**

1. New Yorker (New York, N.Y. : 1925) 2. Journalism 3. Essays
ISBN 9781501116001

LC 2015013297

Collects the best pieces from a New Yorker journalist's 60-year career, including bringing readers into Robin Williams' living room; Harry Winston's office; the afterschool hangouts of Manhattan private-school children; the hotel rooms of Ernest Hemingway, John Huston and Charlie Chaplin; onto the tennis court with John McEnroe; and much more.

"Readable and rewarding and, though more than a touch old-fashioned, full of exemplary reporting." Kirkus.

Schieffer, Bob

Overload : finding the truth in today's deluge of news / Bob Schieffer, with H. Andrew Schwartz. Rowman & Littlefield, 2017. 204 p. ; **070.4**

1. Journalism -- Political aspects 2. Mass media 3. Press and politics 4. Political journalism
ISBN 9781538107218

LC 2017021959

Includes index.

In Overload, legendary television journalist Bob Schieffer examines today's journalism and those who practice it. Based on interviews with over 40 media leaders from television, print media, and the internet, Schieffer surveys the perils and promises of journalism's rapidly changing landscape.

"Succinct, savvy, and shrewd, this read-in-one-seating treatise on the Fourth Estate provides a crucial tool for critical analysis." Booklist.

Stelter, Brian

Hoax : Donald Trump, Fox News, and the dangerous distortion of truth / Brian Stelter. Signal Press, 2020. 320 p. **070.4**

1. Trump, Donald, 1946- 2. Hannity, Sean, 1961- 3. Fox News 4. Presidents -- United States 5. Television networks 6. Television journalists 7. Mass media bias
ISBN 9781982142445

Brian Stelter, CNN correspondent, subject of the Page One documentary and author of Top of the Morning examines the 45th President's complicated relationship with the media and his controversial relationship with the Fox News network. Over the course of two years, Stelter spoke with over 250 current and former Fox insiders in an effort to understand the inner workings of Rupert Murdoch's multibillion-dollar media empire.

"A deep, dispiriting dive into the nefarious intersection of politics, conspiracy, lies, and money as served up by Donald Trump and Fox News." Kirkus

070.5 Publishing

Pettegree, Andrew

The **book** in the Renaissance / Andrew Pettegree. Yale University Press, c2010. 421 p. **070.5**

1. Book industry and trade -- Europe -- History -- 16th century. 2. Books -- Europe -- History -- 1450-1600. 3. European Renaissance. 4. Reformation. 5. Europe.
ISBN 9780300110098

LC 2009026513

"The author's treatment is both thorough and engaging, ably situating the social, economic, and historical within the stories of individuals involved." Library Journal.

Polanka, Sue

No shelf required 2 : use and management of electronic books / edited by Sue Polanka. American Library Association, 2012. xiv, 254 p. : **070.5**

1. Libraries -- Special collections -- Electronic books. 2. Electronic books. 3. Libraries and electronic publishing.
ISBN 9780838911457

LC 2011040497

Contributors from across the breadth of the e-book world offer their perspectives on what's happening now and what to expect in the coming months and years. --Provided by publisher

Suber, Peter

Open access / Peter Suber. MIT Press, c2012. xii, 242 p. ; **070.5**

1. Open access publishing.
ISBN 0262517639

LC 2011038297

A concise introduction to the basics of open access, describing what it is (and isn't) and showing that it is easy, fast, inexpensive, legal, and beneficial. --Provided by publisher

Yager, Jan, 1948-

★**How** to self publish your book : a complete guide to writing, editing, marketing & selling your own book / Dr. Jan Yager. Square One Publishers, 2019 257 p. : **070.5**

1. Self-publishing -- United States.
ISBN 9780757004650

LC 2018045394

"Choosing to self-publish a book means the author has full control of every step of the process and responsibility for everything. Yager, who has been both traditionally and self-published, breaks it all down in this realistic, accessible, and thorough guide." Booklist

070.92 Biography regardless of area, region, place

Rusbridger, Alan

Breaking news : the remaking of journalism and why it matters now / Alan Rusbridger. Farrar, Straus and Giroux, 2018. 384 p. **070.92**

1. Journalism 2. Mass media 3. Fake news 4. Misinformation
ISBN 9780374279622

An urgent account of the revolution that has upended the news business by the former editor-in-chief of *The Guardian* and author of *Play It Again* shares cautionary recommendations for practicing responsible journalism in today's technology-driven world.

"With social media and myriad blogs, 'vertical' reporting (from newspaper to reader) is being eclipsed by 'horizontal' communications that allow unverified and often wild stories to be accepted and shared in seconds. Rusbridger eloquently describes the dangers of this era." Booklist.

071 Geographic treatment of journalism and newspapers

Baker, Nicholson, 1957-

The **World** on Sunday : graphic art in Joseph Pulitzer's newspaper (1898-1911) / Nicholson Baker and Margaret Brentano. Bulfinch Press, 2005. xii, 131 p. : **071**

1. World (New York, N.Y. : 1860-1931)
ISBN 9780821261934

LC 2005000224

Celebrates the artistry and graphic design that transformed Joseph Pulitzer's New York World at the turn of the twentieth century, presenting a wide array of cartoons, caricatures, typography, photography, drawings, maps, and other artwork from a variety of legendary illustrators.

Burns, Eric

Infamous scribblers : the founding fathers and the rowdy beginnings of American journalism / Eric Burns. Public Affairs, c2006. x, 467 p. ; **071**

1. Journalism -- United States -- 18th century 2. Newspapers -- United States -- History -- 18th century 3. Press -- United States -- History -- 18th century 4. United States -- History -- 18th century 5. United States -- Social life and customs -- 18th century
ISBN 158648334X

LC 2005053542

Discusses the raucous journalism of the Revolutionary era, showing how it helped build a nation that endured and offering new perspectives on today's media wars.

"From the sniping feuds among Boston's first papers to sex scandals involving Alexander Hamilton and Thomas Jefferson, the snappy patter gives clear indication of how much Burns relishes telling his story." Publishers Weekly.

Campbell, W. Joseph

Getting it wrong : ten of the greatest misreported stories in American journalism / W. Joseph Campbell. University of Calif. Press, c2010. xiii, 269 p. : **071**

1. Journalism -- Objectivity -- United States -- History -- 20th century. 2. Journalism -- Social aspects -- United States -- History -- 20th century. 3. Journalistic ethics -- United States -- History -- 20th century. 4. Press and politics -- United States -- History -- 20th century.
ISBN 0520255666

LC 2009047705

"Campbell details how the news media misreported ten major stories over the span of more than a century. The author's case studies include The New York Times's alleged suppression of the US Bay of Pigs invasion in 1961 and The Washington Post's extensive 1972-73 reporting on the Nixon administration, which brought Nixon down." Choice.

Kovach, Bill

The **elements** of journalism : what newspeople should know and the public should expect / Bill Kovach & Tom Rosenstiel.

Three Rivers Press, 2014 xv, 332 p. ; **071**

1. Journalistic ethics. 2. Journalism -- United States.
ISBN 9780804136785

LC 2013049716

The authors outline the main principles of journalism, discussing the ethical and professional issues affecting the work of newspeople, the forces shaping the profession, and the future of journalism.

Michaeli, Ethan

★The **Defender** : how the legendary black newspaper changed America : from the age of the Pullman porters to the age of Obama / Ethan Michaeli. Houghton Mifflin Harcourt, 2016. 320 p. **071**

1. Chicago defender History. 2. African American press 3. Freedom of speech 4. Freedom of the press. 5. African American newspapers
ISBN 9780547560694

LC 2015017437

Founded in 1905 by Georgia native Robert Abbott, Chicago's newspaper--The Defender (now The Chicago Defender)-- served for decades as a prominent voice for African Americans throughout the country, including the Jim Crow South. Author Ethan Michaeli, a former Defender--reporter, provides a riveting account of the newspaper's achievements and of a century of American history in this well-documented and engrossing chronicle.

"Engagingly written and copiously sourced, Michaeli's stimulating read treating central personalities and an iconic institution offers general readers and scholars alike a focused look back at 20th-century battles against America's pervasive racism." Library Journal.

O'Shea, James

The **deal** from hell : how moguls and Wall Street plundered great American newspapers / James O'Shea. PublicAffairs, 2011. 416 p. **071**

1. O'Shea, James. 2. Los Angeles Times. 3. Journalists -- United States 4. Newspaper editors. 5. Newspaper publishers and publishing 6. Press monopolies.
ISBN 9781586487911

LC 2011009204

"The author recounts the events leading to the dissolution of several major American newspapers in this gripping story of a troubled industry. Told from the front-row, O'Shea shows how ill-advised mergers, mismanagement, acquisitive Wall Street execs, and the Tribune Company's eventual bankruptcy filing crippled an industry. For those who want an inside look at what makes American journalism work (and not work), O'Shea offers a unique and valuable perspective." Publishers Weekly.

Ostertag, Bob, 1957-

People's movements, people's press : the journalism of social justice movements / Bob Ostertag. Beacon Press, 2006. 232 p. : **071**

1. Newspapers -- Political aspects -- United States. 2. Underground press publications. 3. Journalism -- Political aspects. 4. Social problems -- United States. 5. United States -- Social life and customs -- 20th century.
ISBN 9780807061640

LC 2005031735

An insightful analysis of five social justice movements and their relationship with the newspapers and journals produced by the activists traces the history of the alternative print media and their influence on the forces of abolition, women's suffrage, environmental awareness, gay liberation, and the Vietnam anti-war movement, as well as on public opinion as a whole.

071.7 Journalism and newspapers in the United States

Cullen, Art

Storm Lake : a chronicle of change, resilience, and hope from a heartland newspaper / Art Cullen. Viking, [2018] 336 p. **071.7**

1. Cullen, Art 2. Storm Lake times History 3. Newspapers 4. Small towns 5. Agribusiness 6. Journalism 7. Iowa
ISBN 9780525558873

LC 2018025006

The Pulitzer Prize-winning owner of a small, twice-weekly Iowa newspaper that took on a big agri-industry corporation for poisoning their local rivers takes a candid look at the changing politics, environment, economics and demographics of his farming and meatpacking town.

080 General collections

McPhee, John, 1931-

★The **patch** / John McPhee. Farrar, Straus and Giroux, 2018. 224 p. **080**

1. Hershey Chocolate Company. 2. Wilderness areas. 3. Social classes. 4. Memories. 5. Fishing. 6. Essays.
ISBN 9780374229481

LC 2018007631

"Earlier versions of most of these essays first appeared in The New Yorker, Time, and Vogue" -- Verso title page.

A collection of essays offers the author's thoughts on sports, including fishing, football, golf, and lacrosse, as well as a visit to Hershey, Pennsylvania and an encounter with Joan Baez.

"McPhee delights in cracking open subjects, both ordinary and esoteric, and making them accessible to the layperson in works that testify to his virtuosity as one of the greatest living American essayists." Publishers Weekly.

081 General collections in American English

Einstein, Albert, 1879-1955

Ideas and opinions / Albert Einstein ; with an introduction by Alan Lightman ; new translations and revisions by Sonja Bargmann. Modern Library, c1994. xix, 418 p. : **081**

1. Physics 2. Science -- Philosophy 3. Peace 4. Science -- Social aspects 5. Essays
ISBN 9780679601050

LC 94002115

"Based on Mein Weltbild, edited by Carl Seelig, and other sources."
Originally published: New York : Crown Publishers, 1954.

A survey of Einstein's scientific achievements follows excerpts from letters, speeches, and interviews that reveal his thoughts on religious, political, cultural, social, and economic issues.

Ferriss, Timothy

Tools of titans : the tactics, routines, and habits of billionaires, icons, and world-class performers / Tim Ferriss ; foreword by Arnold Schwarzenegger ; illustrations by Remie Geoffroi. Houghton Mifflin Harcourt, 2016. xxvii, 673 p. : **081**

1. Change (Psychology) 2. Conduct of life 3. Physical fitness 4. Self-actualization (Psychology) 5. Interviews.
ISBN 9781328683786

LC 2016304630

Fitness, money, and wisdom -- here are the tools. Over the last two years, Tim Ferriss has collected the routines and tools of world-class performers around the globe while interviewing them for his self-titled podcast. Now the distilled notebook of tips and tricks that helped him double his income, flexibility, happiness, and more is available as Tools of Titans.

Scalia, Antonin, 1936-2016

Scalia speaks : reflections on law, faith, and life well lived / Antonin Scalia, Christopher J. Scalia, Edward Whelan ; foreword by Ruth Bader Ginsburg. Crown Forum, 2017. 384 p. **081**

1. Scalia, Antonin, 1936-2016 2. United States. Supreme Court Justices 3. Judicial opinions. 4. Judges -- United States. 5. Judicial system 6. Speeches, addresses, etc.

ISBN 9780525573326

LC 2017034660

"This definitive collection of beloved Supreme Court Justice Antonin Scalia's finest speeches covers topics as varied as the law, faith, virtue, pastimes, and his heroes and friends. Featuring a foreword by longtime friend Ruth Bader Ginsburg and an intimate introduction by his youngest son, this volume includes dozens of speeches, some deeply personal, that have never before been published".-- Provided by publisher.

"This fine representative assemblage of Supreme Court Justice Scalia's speeches pays tribute to his ready wit and facility with language." Library Journal.

082 General collections in English

Brandreth, Gyles Daubeney, 1948-

Oxford dictionary of humorous quotations. / Gyles (EDT) Brandreth. Oxford University Press, 2015. xvii, 465 p. ; **082**

1. Quotations, English 2. Wit and humor

ISBN 9780199681372

LC bl2016035046

Includes indexes.

Furnishes over six thousand quotations, including classic one-liners, quips, and put-downs, from such personalities as Groucho Marx, Oscar Wilde, William Shakespeare, Tom Stoppard, Jane Austen, and Dorothy Parker.

Knowles, Elizabeth (Elizabeth M.)

Oxford dictionary of quotations / edited by Elizabeth Knowles. Oxford University Press, 2014. xxvii, 1126 p. ; **082**

1. Quotations. 2. Quotations, English -- Dictionaries. 3. Quotations -- Translations into English.

ISBN 9780199668700

LC 2014930368

Includes index.

"The new edition of this venerable work has been updated with more than 700 new quotations and 200 new authors. It remains thoroughly cross-referenced, and an exhaustive keyword index makes it easy to trace only partially remembered lines." Booklist

091 Manuscripts

De Hamel, Christopher, 1950-

★**Meetings** with remarkable manuscripts : twelve journeys into the medieval world / Christopher de Hamel. Penguin Press, 2017. 640 p. : **091**

1. Manuscripts 2. Material culture 3. Civilization, Medieval 4. Europe -- History -- 476-1492. 5. Europe -- Social life and customs -- 476-1492.

ISBN 9781594206115

LC 2017031392

In a full-color exploration of the medieval world through 12 manuscripts, a leading expert travels the globe to visit these hand-made treasures and unlocks their mysteries, telling a story of intellectual culture and art over the course of a millennium.

"A rare, erudite, and delightfully entertaining history." Kirkus.

093 Incunabula

Davis, Margaret Leslie

The **lost** Gutenberg : the astounding story of one book's five-hundred-year odyssey / Margaret Leslie Davis. TarcherPerigee, 2019. 304 p. **093**

1. Doheny, Estelle, 1875-1958. 2. Gutenberg Bible 3. Rare books -- Collectors and collecting 4. Book collectors 5. Lost books

ISBN 9781592408672

LC 2018049581

Recounting five centuries in the life of one copy of the extremely rare Gutenberg Bible, a never-before-told story reveals its impact on the lives of the fanatical few who were lucky enough to own it.

"Davis does a fine job telling a fascinating story that touches on the origin of books, the passion of collectors, the unseen world of rare-book dealers, and the lives of the super-rich, past and present." Kirkus.

098 Prohibited works, forgeries, hoaxes

Baez, Fernando

Universal history of the destruction of books : from ancient Sumer to modern-day Iraq / Fernando Baez. W. W. Norton & Co. Inc., 2008. 272 p. **098**

1. Censorship -- History. 2. Book burning. 3. Banned books. 4. Libraries -- History.

ISBN 9781934633014

LC bl2008025448

An investigation into the practice of book destruction and censorship explores such historical examples as the smashed tablets of ancient Sumer, the decimation of the Library of Alexandria, and the looting of libraries in post-war Iraq, in a chronicle that evaluates the political and human motives behind the practice.

"This is a horrific chronicle of the centuries-long assault on human memory. A sobering reminder of just how deep-seated is the instinct to destroy other people's truths." Kirkus.

Bosmajian, Haig A.

Burning books / Haig Bosmajian. McFarland, 2006. 233 p. ; **098**

1. Book burning -- History. 2. Censorship -- History. 3. Arson. 4. Blasphemy.

ISBN 9780786422081

LC 2005035201

"This work provides a detailed account of book burning worldwide over the past 2000 years. The book burners are identified, along with the works they deliberately set aflame".--Provided by publisher.

Tigay, Chanan

The **lost** book of Moses : the hunt for the world's oldest bible

/ Chanan Tigay. Ecco, 2016. 352 p. **098**
1. Shapira, Mozes Vilhelm, 1830?-1884. 2. Bible Manuscripts. 3. Forgers. 4. Forgery. 5. Archaeology.
ISBN 9780062206411
LC bl2016003507

In this combination of biography, memoir, travelogue, and scriptural history, author Chanan Tigay explores the life of a 19th-century antiquities dealer who claimed to have discovered the oldest manuscript of Deuteronomy. The dealer, Moses Shapira, was denounced as a fraud, and the scroll disappeared, but 64 years later the Dead Sea Scrolls were discovered, transforming the field of biblical archaeology. Could Shapira's find have been genuine? In The Lost Book of Moses, Tigay traces his efforts to find the lost manuscript while chronicling Shapira's life. Fans of archaeology and scriptural history won't want to miss this thrilling account.

"A work of broad appeal, for the history buff and mystery lover alike." Kirkus.

100 Philosophy, parapsychology and occultism, psychology

Blackburn, Simon, 1944-
Think : a compelling introduction to philosophy / Simon Blackburn. Oxford University Press, 1999. vii, 312 p. ; **100**
1. Philosophy
ISBN 9780192100245
LC 00265286

An introduction to philosophy explores basic themes and the work of major philosophers

"The author explores such areas as knowledge, mind, free will, identity, God, goodness and justice. His method is to introduce what other philosophers--primarily Plato, Descartes, Locke, Berkeley, Leibniz, Hume, and Kant--have had to say about these themes. Readers new to the subject could very well be captivated." Library Journal.

Ferry, Luc
A **brief** history of thought : a philosophical guide to living / Luc Ferry. Harper Perennial, 2011, c2010. xv, 282 p. ; **100**
1. Philosophy
ISBN 9780062074249
LC bl2011036507

"First published under the title Learning to Live in Great Britain in 2010 by Canongate Books"--T.p verso.

A philosophy professor at the Sorbonne offers a history of Western thought, from the ancient Greeks to the Enlightenment and through the postmodern and deconstructionist periods, describing how religion and philosophy have melded and clashed throughout time.

Gutting, Gary
What philosophy can do / Gary Gutting. W.W. Norton & Company, 2015 320 p. **100**
1. Philosophy. 2. Thought and thinking. 3. Essays
ISBN 9780393242270
LC 2015013783

How can we have meaningful debates with political opponents? How can we distinguish reliable science from over-hyped media reports? How can we talk sensibly about God? In What Philosophy Can Do, Gary Gutting takes a philosopher's scalpel to modern life's biggest questions and the most powerful forces in our society--politics, science, religion, education, and capitalism--to show how we can improve our discussions of contentious contemporary issues.

"While Gutting applies complex philosophical and logical principles in his essays, he does so in an accessible way. The range of essays makes this work appealing to anyone with an interest in philosophy." Library Journal.

Weiner, Eric, 1963-
The **Socrates** express : in search of life lessons from dead philosophers / Eric Weiner. Avid Reader Press, 2020. 352 p. **100**
1. Philosophy 2. Purpose in life
ISBN 9781501129018
LC bl2020019383

The New York Times best-selling author follows in the footsteps of history's greatest thinkers and shows us how each--from Epicurus to Gandhi, Thoreau to Beauvoir--offers practical and spiritual lessons for today's unsettled times.

"Journalist Weiner (The Geography of Bliss) makes a convincing and winningly presented case for the practical applications of philosophy to everyday existence in the 21st century. With humor and thoughtfulness, he distills the wisdom of thinkers from throughout history." Publishers Weekly

101 Theory of philosophy

Ortega Y Gasset, Jose, 1883-1955
What is philosophy? Translated from the Spanish by Mildred Adams. Norton, 1961, c1960 252 p. ; **101**
1. Philosophy
ISBN 9780393001266
LC 61005621

Lectures given in Madrid and Buenos Aires.

A work powerful and pervading in its implications not only for metaphysics but also for art, political science, and the philosophy of history. --Provided by publisher

103 Dictionaries, encyclopedias, concordances of philosophy

Audi, Robert, 1941-
★The **Cambridge** dictionary of philosophy / general editor Robert Audi, university of Notre Dame ; associate editor, Paul Audi, University of Nebraska, Omaha. Cambridge University Press, 2015. xliv, 1161 p. ; **103**
1. Philosophy -- Dictionaries.
ISBN 9781107015050
LC 2014021783

Includes index.

"This is the leading, full-scale comprehensive dictionary of philosophical terms and thinkers to appear in English in more than half a century. Written by a team of more than 550 experts and now widely translated, it contains approximately 5,000 entries ranging from short definitions to longer articles. It is designed to facilitate the understanding of philosophy at all levels and in all fields. Key features of this third edition: 500 new entries covering Eastern as well as Western philosophy, and covering individual countries such as China, France, Germany, Italy, and Spain; Increased coverage of such growing fields as ethics and philosophy of mind; More than 100 new intellectual portraits of leading contemporary thinkers; Wider coverage of Continental philosophy; Dozens of new technical concepts in cognitive science and other areas; Enhanced cross-referencing to add context and increase understanding; Expansions in both text and index to facilitate research and browsing".--Provided by publisher.

Blackburn, Simon, 1944-
The **Oxford** dictionary of philosophy / Simon Blackburn. Oxford University Press, 2005. viii, 407 p. : **103**
1. Philosophy -- Dictionaries
ISBN 9780198610144
LC 2006271895

More than four hundred new entries are contained in the revised and updated edition of this wide-ranging and authoritative reference that covers every aspect of philosophy, from Aristotle to Zen, and contains more than three thousand alphabetical entries that encompasses world philosophical traditions, hundreds of influential philosophers, terms and concepts, and more.

109 History and collected biography

Grayling, A. C.
The **history** of philosophy / A.C. Grayling. Penguin Press, 2019. 704 p. **109**
1. Philosophy -- History. 2. Philosophy 3. Philosophers. 4. Philosophy, Ancient
ISBN 9781984878748
LC 2019035983

"The first authoritative and accessible single-volume history of philosophy to cover both Western and Eastern traditions, from one of the world's most eminent thinkers The story of philosophy is the story of who we are and why. An epic tale, spanning civilizations and continents, it explores some of the most creative minds in history. But not since the long-popular classic Bertrand Russell's A History of Western Philosophy, published in 1945, has there been a comprehensive and entertaining single-volume history of this great, intellectual, world-shaping journey. With characteristic clarity and elegance, A. C. Grayling takes the reader from the worldviews and moralities before the age of the Buddha, Confucius and Socrates through Christianity's capture ofthe European mind, from the Renaissance and Enlightenment on to Mill, Nietzsche, Sartre and, finally, philosophy today. Bringing together these many threads that all too often run parallel, he surveys in tandem the great philosophical traditions of India, China and the Persian-Arabic world".-- Provided by publisher.

Russell, Bertrand, 1872-1970
A **history** of western philosophy, and its connection with political and social circumstances from the earliest times to the present day / Bertrand Russell. Simon and Schuster, 1945 xxiii, 895 p. **109**
1. Philosophy -- History
ISBN 9780671314002
LC 45008884

"Originally designed and partly delivered as lectures at the Barnes foundation in Pennsylvania."--Pref.

Describes and analyzes the major philosophers and philosophical issues from the pre-Socratics to the philosophy of logical analysis.

110 Metaphysics

Hägglund, Martin
This life : secular faith and spiritual freedom / Martin Hägglund. Pantheon Books, 2019. 450 p. **110**
1. Faith 2. Purpose in life 3. Human behavior 4. Philosophers
ISBN 9781101870402
LC 2018029429

Challenging our preconceived notions of faith and freedom, and engaging with great philosphers, the author presents a critique of religion that takes readers to the heart of what it means to mourn our loved ones, be committed and care about a sustainable world.

"In a densely argued critique of religion and capitalism, philosopher Hägglund tackles thorny questions of value, freedom, and responsibility." Kirkus.

Russell, Bertrand, 1872-1970
★The **problems** of philosophy / Bertrand Russell. Gray Cadence, 2011. ix, 189 p. ; **110**
1. Philosophy 2. Intellectual life 3. Ideas (Philosophy)
ISBN 9780983360612
LC 2011926546

Originally published: London : Williams and Norgate, 1912.

"The work is concise, free from technical terms and perfectly clear to the general reader with no prior knowledge of the subject." Booklist.

111 Ontology

Barrow, John D., 1952-
The **infinite** book : a short guide to the boundless, timeless, and endless / John D. Barrow. Pantheon Books, c2005. xvi, 328 p. : **111**
1. Infinity -- Popular works. 2. Infinity -- History 3. Metaphysics -- History 4. Mathematics -- History
ISBN 0375422277
LC 2004060206

Explores the concept of infinity, tracing the history and meaning of infinity from ancient times to the present day, and examining the diverse permutations of the infinite and their influence on the human sense of the world around.

"The author approaches the subject [of infinity] from the viewpoints of mathematics, physics, and scientific cosmology and also delves into philosophers' and theologians' reflections concerning infinity. Well suited to a general audience, this book requires no specialized knowledge of mathematics or science." Library Journal.

Eco, Umberto
History of beauty / edited by Umberto Eco ; translated by Alastair McEwen. Rizzoli, 2005. 438 p. : **111**
1. Aesthetics -- History. 2. Art -- Philosophy. 3. Art and philosophy -- History.
ISBN 0847826465

"The editor traces the protean subject of beauty in art, literature, philosophy, the mass media, and other humanities from ancient times to the present, setting forth various Western cultural aesthetic ideals ranging from ancient Greek to modern American. This is not a quick, one-time coffee-table read but a nearly flawless presentation of the history of a fascinating and elusive idea that will delight and enlighten general readers as well as scholars." Library Journal.

Heidegger, Martin, 1889-1976
★**Being** and time / Martin Heidegger ; translated by John MacQuarrie and Edward Robinson ; foreword by Taylor Carman. Harpercollins, 2008. 589 p. **111**
1. God -- Proof. 2. Existentialism. 3. Religion -- Philosophy. 4. Philosophy.
ISBN 9780061575594
LC 2009293338

The fundamental philosophy of the existentialist movement is revealed in Heidegger's discussion of human existence, nonhuman presence, personal consciousness, and angst.

Sartre, Jean-Paul, 1905-1980
★**Being** and nothingness / Jean-Paul Sartre ; translated and with an introduction by Hazel E. Barnes. Gramercy Books, 1994. lxvii, 636 p. ; **111**
1. Existentialism. 2. Existential psychology.
ISBN 9780517101858
LC 94011808
Includes index.
Originally published: New York : Philosophical Library, 1956.
An informative introduction to Sartre and his philosophy and a key to special terminology enhance a handsome edition of Sartre's classic study of modern existentialism.

Sartre, Jean-Paul, 1905-1980
Existentialism and human emotions. Philosophical Library, 1967. 96 p. **111**
1. Existentialism.
ISBN 0806509023
LC 57004372
"The section on 'Existentialism' is taken from the book of that name, translated by Bernard Frechtman; all other selections are from Being and nothingness, translated by Hazel E. Barnes."
In this provocative philosophical analysis, Jean-Paul Sartre refutes the idea that existentialism drains meaning from human life, by claiming that the philosophy instead gives man total freedom to achieve his own significance. --Provided by publisher

Whitefield-Madrano, Autumn
Face value : the hidden ways that beauty shapes women's lives / Autumn Whitefield-Madrano. Simon & Schuster 2016 288 p. **111**
1. Feminism 2. Feminine beauty (Aesthetics) 3. Women -- Psychology 4. Aesthetics
ISBN 9781476754000
LC 2015038730
Part social commentary, part cultural analysis, part careful investigation and part powerful personal anecdotes, a provocative book explores the relationship between appearance and science, social media, sex, friendship, language and advertising to show how beauty actually affects us day to day.
"This is a valuable addition to contemporary feminist writing, providing much-needed perspective to a pervasive issue that young women and staunch feminists will glean much from, whether they agree with the author's findings or not." Library Journal.

113 Cosmology (Philosophy of nature)

Holt, Jim, 1954-
Why does the world exist? : an existential detective story / Jim Holt. Liveright Pub. Corp., c2012. vi, 309 p. : **113**
1. Cosmology. 2. Philosophy.
ISBN 9780871404091
LC 2012015177
ALA Notable Book, 2013.
National Book Critics Circle Award for Nonfiction finalist, 2012.
Expands the search for the origins of the universe beyond God and the Big Bang theory, exploring more bizarre possibilities inspired by physicists, theologians, mathematicians, and even novelists.

Wilson, Edward O.
★**In** search of nature / Edward O. Wilson. Island Press, c1996. x, 214 p. : **113**
1. Human beings 2. Human ecology -- Philosophy 3. Philosophy of nature
ISBN 9781559632157
LC 96011226
"A Shearwater book."
Focusing on the interrelationship of wild nature and human nature, a collection of short writings and essays explores "Animal Nature, Human Nature," "The Patterns of Nature," and "Nature's Abundance".
"Concerned people of all ages should enjoy the reasoning provided by the dedicated scientific writing presented in this attractive book." Science Books & Films.

121 Epistemology (Theory of knowledge)

Blackburn, Simon, 1944-
On Truth / Simon Blackburn. Profile Books, 2018. 142 p. **121**
1. Truth. 2. Philosophy. 3. Thought and thinking. 4. Language and languages.
ISBN 9780190867218
LC 2017051643
The world's leading thinker on truth explains what it is and why it matters in every important aspect of life.

Dennett, D. C. (Daniel Clement)
Intuition pumps and other tools for thinking / Daniel C. Dennett. W. W. Norton & Company, 2013 xiv, 496 p. : **121**
1. Philosophy 2. Thought and thinking
ISBN 9780393082067
LC 2013000930
A philosophy professor offers exercises and tools to stretch the mind, offering new ways to consider, discuss, and argue positions on dangerous subject matter including evolution, the meaning of life, and free will.

Hecht, Jennifer Michael, 1965-
Doubt : a history : the great doubters and their legacy of innovation, from Socrates and Jesus to Thomas Jefferson and Emily Dickinson / Jennifer Michael Hecht. Harper San Francisco, 2003. xxi, 551 p. : **121**
1. Belief and doubt -- History. 2. Skepticism -- History 3. Religion -- History 4. Reasoning -- Examinations, questions, etc.
ISBN 0060097728
LC 2004266061
In this sweeping history, Jennifer Michael Hecht celebrates doubt as an engine of creativity and as an alternative to the political and intellectual dangers of certainty--just as belief has its own history featuring people whose unique expressions of faith have forever changed the world, doubt has a vibrant story and tradition with its own saints martyrs, and sages.
"The author's brief but splendid study of the great Renaissance skeptic Montaigne is alone worth the price of the book. Hecht's warm prose, lucid insights, and impeccable research combine for a lively, thoughtful, and first-rate study of a neglected idea." Library Journal.

Hoffman, Donald D

The **case** aganist reality : why evolution hid the truth from our eyes / Donald D. Hoffman. W.W. Norton & Company, 2019. 272 p. **121**

1. Reality. 2. Perception 3. Evolution 4. Philosophy of mind.
ISBN 9780393254693

LC 2019006962

Challenging leading scientific theories that claim our senses are objective, a groundbreaking examination of human perception reveals its evolutionary importance and how it is used today in marketing, design, and personal safety.

"A dense, lucid, and often unsettling exploration of how our brains interpret the world." Kirkus.

Locke, John, 1632-1704

An **essay** concerning human understanding / John Locke ; edited by Roger Woolhouse. New York : 1997. xxvii, 784, 1 p. ; **121**

1. Knowledge, Theory of -- Early works to 1800
ISBN 9780140434828

LC 98175907

This new, complete, and unabridged edition represents the very latest in critical thinking on Locke's pioneering work, which set the groundwork for modern philosophy. --Provided by publisher

MacDonald, Hector

Truth : how the many sides to every story shape our reality / Hector MacDonald. Little, Brown and Co., 2018. 346 p. **121**

1. Truth. 2. Ethics. 3. Business communication. 4. Truthfulness and falsehood.
ISBN 9780316510820

LC 2017963338

An exploration of the many ways in which "competing truths" shape opinion, behavior and belief describes how to recognize the gray area between multiple truths and how it is selectively manipulated by businesses, politicians and rivals to promote agendas and initiatives.

"Truth is a fascinating look at how such an abstract concept can be shaped to many purposes, the ethics of bending the truth, and what consumers can do to analyze the innumerable truths presented to us." Booklist.

Schulz, Kathryn

Being wrong : adventures in the margin of error / Kathryn Schulz. Harpercollins, 2010. 416 p. **121**

1. Errors 2. Right and wrong. 3. Human behavior. 4. Misconceptions
ISBN 9780061176043

LC 2010282589

"The author explains what in means to be right or wrong and why it matters so much to people, arguing that humans' tendency to make mistakes is an essential part of our intelligence."

"The author discusses how we make mistakes, how we behave when we find we have been wrong, and how our errors change us. Schulz writes with such lucidity and wit that her philosophical enquiry becomes a page-turner." Publishers Weekly.

Wilson, Edward O.

Consilience : the unity of knowledge / Edward O. Wilson. Knopf, 1998. 332 p. : **121**

1. Philosophy. 2. Order (Philosophy) 3. Philosophy and science. 4. Science and the arts.
ISBN 0679450777

LC 97002816

"As human population burgeons and its environment deteriorates, continued human success depends on making the wise choices that sound knowledge makes possible. Wilson dazzlingly reaffirms the cogency and the power of scientific materialism." Booklist.

123 Determinism and indeterminism

Dennett, D. C. (Daniel Clement)

Freedom evolves / Daniel C. Dennett. Viking, 2003. xiii, 347 p. : **123**

1. Free will and determinism. 2. Decision making.
ISBN 0670031860

LC 2002028085

"Drawing on evolutionary biology, neuroscience, economic game theory, philosophy and Richard Dawkins's meme, the author argues that there is indeed such a thing as free will, but it is not a preexisting feature of our existence, like the law of gravity. This book comprises a kind of toolbox of intellectual exercises favoring cultural evolution, the idea that culture, morality and freedom are as much a result of evolution by natural selection as our physical and genetic attributes. Yet genetic determinism, he argues, does not imply inevitability, as his critics may claim, nor does it cancel out the soul. Dennett clearly relishes pushing other scientists' buttons. Though natural selection itself is still a subject of controversy, the author most certainly is in the vanguard of the philosophy of science." Publishers Weekly.

128 Humankind

Ackerman, Diane, 1948-

Deep play / Diane Ackerman ; illustrations by Peter Sis. Random House, c1999. xiii, 235 p. : **128**

1. Play -- Psychological aspects. 2. Recreation. 3. Outdoor recreation.
ISBN 0679448799

LC 98035067

Provides an exploration of the concept of "deep play"--a psychological state of mind in which we fully engage our faculties--discussing the activities that draw us into this state, the qualities that distinguish deep-play activities, and the ways in which the state can be achieved.

"The author contends that deep play, ecstatic play, transcends practical concerns and grants us passage to the sacred and the holy. Art is deep play, so is religion, the contemplation of nature, and playing sports; in short, pursuits that are all-consuming and inspire feelings of awe and a profound sense of connection with the universe. By turns anecdotal and philosophic, Ackerman vividly recounts her own deep play experiences." Booklist.

Becker, Ernest

★The **denial** of death / Ernest Becker. Free Press 1997, c1973. xxii, 314 p. ; **128**

1. Death -- Psychological aspects. 2. Mortality. 3. Motivation (Psychology) 4. Life
ISBN 9780684832401

LC 73001860

Companion vol.: Escape from evil.
Originally published: New York : Free Press, 1973.
Pulitzer Prize for General Nonfiction, 1974.

Drawing from religion and the human sciences, particularly psychology after Freud, the author attempts to demonstrate that the fear of death is man's central concern.

Cannadine, David, 1950-
The **undivided** past : humanity beyond our differences / David Cannadine. Alfred A. Knopf, 2013. 288 p. **128**
1. Identity (Psychology) 2. Conflict (Psychology) 3. Difference (Psychology) 4. Perception.
ISBN 9780307269072
LC 2012029278
The award-winning author of The Decline and Fall of the British Aristocracy shares a provocative argument against the belief that history is best understood as a chronicle of groups in conflict, investigating six leading categories of human difference while arguing that history must also take into account typically disregarded, positive interactions.

Chittister, Joan
Between the dark and the daylight : embracing the contradictions of life / Joan Chittister. Image, 2015 173 p. ; **128**
1. Life -- Moral and ethical aspects. 2. Life -- Religious aspects. 3. Values.
ISBN 0804140944
LC bl2015006174
Explores the concerns of modern life and argues that readers should embrace the contradictory nature of life in order to live well.

Christian, Brian
The **most** human human : what talking with computers teaches us about what it means to be alive / Brian Christian. Random House, 2011. 320 p. **128**
1. Artificial intelligence. 2. Reasoning. 3. Computers. 4. Humans.
ISBN 9780385533065
LC 2010048572
"In a fast-paced, witty, and thoroughly winning style, Christian documents his experience in the 2009 Turing Test, a competition in which judges engage in five-minute instant-message conversations with unidentified partners, and must then decide whether each interlocutor was a human or a machine. This fabulous book demonstrates that we are capable of experiencing and sharing far deeper thoughts than even the best computersand that too often we fail to achieve the highest level of humanness." Publishers Weekly.

Frayn, Michael
The **human** touch : our part in the creation of a universe / Michael Frayn. Metropolitan Books, 2007. 505 p. ; **128**
1. Philosophical anthropology. 2. Cosmology. 3. Place (Philosophy) 4. Philosophy.
ISBN 9780805081480
"Originally published in the United Kingdom in 2006 by Faber and Faber"--T.p. verso.
"Beginning with a description of the continual traffic between humans and the universe, Frayn shapes a cohesive introduction to philosophy that includes elements of science, determinism, physics, mathematics, psychology, linguistics, and epistemology." Library Journal.

Heath, Chip
The **power** of moments : why certain experiences have extraordinary impact / Chip Heath, and Dan Heath. Simon & Schuster, 2017 288 p. **128**
1. Personal conduct 2. Interpersonal relations 3. Life change events
ISBN 9781501147760
LC bl2017035688
The best-selling authors of Made to Stick explore why certain defining moments can be elevating and transforming, sharing the stories of people who have created and experienced such moments and how readers can facilitate meaningful, powerful moments of positive change themselves.
"Brothers Chip and Dan Heath--coauthors of Decisive and business school professors at, respectively, Stanford and Duke--take on the challenge of teaching readers how to foster memorable moments, for themselves and others, but fail to address the question of authenticity that their prescriptions raise." Publishers Weekly.

Irvine, William Braxton, 1952-
On desire : why we want what we want / William B. Irvine. Oxford University Press, 2006. x, 322 p. ; **128**
1. Desire
ISBN 9780195188622
LC 2005005938
Looks at our impulses, wants, and needs, exploring where these feelings come from and how we can try to rein them in and be content with what we have.
"The author explains how desirereally a multitude of desires, uninvited and unannouncedmanifests itself, how it can be identified and parsed, and how it can be mastered in a way that offers the best chance at self-fulfillment. He uses modern psychology to delineate desire but then shows how the world's great religions--here mainly Christianity and Buddhism, but also Hinduism, Islam, and Judaism--address this phenomenon. He advocates no particular approach, admitting instead that different tacks probably work for different people. And he never lets the reader think that mastering desire will be easy. This is that rare book that should appeal to a wide range of readers without necessarily trying to do so." Booklist.

Louv, Richard
The **nature** principle : human restoration and the end of nature-deficit disorder / Richard Louv. Algonquin Books of Chapel Hill, 2011. 320 p. ; **128**
1. Nature -- Psychological aspects. 2. Health behavior 3. Sustainable societies. 4. Lifestyle change
ISBN 9781565125810
LC 2011003626
Green Prize for Sustainable Literature: Adult Nonfiction, 2012.
Louv reveals how humans are healthier with nature in their lives. The Nature Principle includes seven precepts, including balancing technology excess with time in nature and making a mind/body/nature connection.

Roach, Mary
★**Spook** : science tackles the afterlife / Mary Roach. W.W. Norton, 2005. 311 p. : **129**
1. Life after death. 2. Soul. 3. Religion and science. 4. Near-death experience
ISBN 0393059626
LC 2005014450
Draws on the achievements of scientists, engineers, and mediums to consider the feasibility of life after death, from a reincarnation researcher's experimentation with out-of-body experiences to laboratory investigations into ghosts.
"Roach perfectly balances her skepticism and her boundless curiosity with a sincere desire to know. . . . She is an original who can enliven any subject with wit, keen reporting and a sly intelligence." Publishers Weekly.

Sagan, Carl, 1934-1996
★**Broca's** brain : reflections on the romance of science / Carl Sagan. Presidio Press, [1993], c1979. xiii, 398 p. ; **128**
1. Broca, Paul, 1824-1880. 2. Physicians -- France 3. Intelligence

-- Research. 4. Brain -- Research. 5. Cosmology.
ISBN 0345336895
LC bl 99789926

Originally published: New York : Random House, c1979.

Sagan speculates on the primitive elements of the human mind and the ways the human brain today is coping with new discoveries about the cosmos.

"The author is a lucid, logical writer with a gift for explaining science to the layman and infecting the reader with his own boundless enthusiasm and curiosity." National Review.

Terkel, Studs, 1912-2008

Will the circle be unbroken? : reflections on death, rebirth, and hunger for a faith / Studs Terkel. New Press, 2001. xxiv, 407 p. **128**

1. Death. 2. Death -- Religious aspects. 3. Death -- Psychological aspects. 4. Life after death. 5. Oral histories
ISBN 9781565846920
LC 2001030781

"Terkel talks to 60 people about their encounters with death. His subjects range from emergency room doctors and paramedics to public figures such as author Kurt Vonnegut and guitarist Doc Watson. A stirring celebration of life and exploration of death." Booklist.

Trachtenberg, Peter, 1953-

The **book** of calamities : five questions about suffering and its meaning / Peter Trachtenberg. Little, Brown and Co., 2008. 464 p. **128**

1. Suffering -- Spiritual aspects. 2. Loss (Psychology) 3. Coping. 4. Grief. 5. United States -- Social life and customs.
ISBN 9780316158794
LC 2008013351

The author of 7 Tattoos evaluates the social and spiritual ramifications of human suffering, drawing on classic spiritual texts while sharing the experiences of such individuals as tsunami survivors in Sri Lanka, an innocent death-row inmate, and the family of a September 11 victim.

"This book succeeds because it asks the right questions, calls on the experience of articulate witnesses and--through skillful narrative and trenchant observation--beguiles the reader into facing heartbreaking reality." Publishers Weekly.

Wilson, Edward O.

The **meaning** of human existence / Edward O. Wilson. Liveright Publishing Corporation, a Division of W.W. Norton & Company, [2014] 192 p. **128**

1. Humans. 2. Sociobiology. 3. Social evolution. 4. Human evolution.
ISBN 9780871401007
LC 2014016707

National Book Award for Nonfiction finalist, 2014

A 21st-century philosophical argument against mechanistic views of human life outlines expansive and advanced theories on human behavior to consider how humans are supremely different from all other species. By the Pulitzer Prize-winning author of On Human Nature.

"Wilson's suggested solutions to our paradoxical predicaments are firmly rooted in science and finely crafted with tonic common sense, unusual directness, and no small measure of valor." Booklist.

130 Parapsychology and occultism

Bader, Christopher, 1969-

Paranormal America : ghost encounters, UFO sightings, Bigfoot hunts, and other curiosities in religion and culture / Christopher D. Bader, F. Carson Mencken, and Joseph O. Baker. New York University Press, c2010. viii, 264 p. : **130**

1. Parapsychology -- United States 2. Curiosities and wonders -- United States
ISBN 9780814791349
LC 2010016525

Examines the world of paranormal beliefs in order to understand the people who utilize these beliefs to shape their life.

Dell, Christopher, 1976-

The **occult,** witchcraft & magic : an illustrated history / Christopher Dell. Thames & Hudson, 2016 399 p. : **130**

1. Occultism. 2. Witchcraft. 3. Magic.
ISBN 9780500518885
LC bl2016045815

Shares a history of magic, the occult, witchcraft, and ritual, from their earliest appearances to modern times.

"A stunning treasury for anyone interested in the history of magic." Booklist.

Dickey, Colin

The **unidentified** : mythical monsters, alien encounters, and our obsession with the unexplained / Colin Dickey. Viking, 2020. 307 p. **130**

1. Occultism 2. Paranormal phenomena 3. Curiosities and wonders 4. Belief and doubt
ISBN 9780525557562
LC 2019043380

In a world where rational, scientific explanations are more available than ever, belief in the unprovable and irrational--in fringe--is on the rise. It seems the more our maps of the known world get filled in, the more we crave mysterious locations full of strange creatures. Colin Dickey, co-editor of The Morbid Anatomy Anthology and author of Ghostland, examines the world's most persistent unexplained phenomena, from Atlantis and alien encounters to Flat Earth and the Loch Ness monster, to explore their origins and historical endurance.

"Readers will find this to be a thought-provoking and deliciously unsettling guide into the stranger corners of American culture." Publishers Weekly

Smith, Richard MacLean

Unexplained : real-life supernatural stories for uncertain times / Richard MacLean Smith. Sourcebooks, 2019. xvii, 349 p. **130**

1. Paranormal phenomena 2. Supernatural 3. Curiosities and wonders 4. Perception
ISBN 9781492697718
LC 2019023946

Based on a podcast.

In every corner of this earth there are secrets. They are hidden in the dark edge of the woods, nestled in the cold stars, and staring out from a stranger's eyes. And whether they be demonic possession or an unsolved murder, the unknown has always haunted our dreams. From the hit podcast Unexplained comes a volume perfectly crafted for the curious, the cynical, and the not-easily-frightened. Richard Maclean Smith is the expert in the unknown, and humbly offers up ten tales of real-life events that continue to evade explanation.

131 Parapsychological and occult methods for achieving well-being, happiness, success

Dale, Cyndi
Llewellyn's complete book of chakras : your definitive source of energy center knowledge for health, happiness, and spiritual evolution / Cyndi Dale. Llewellyn Publications, 2016. xl-viii,1006 p. : **131**
1. Chakras
ISBN 9780738739625
LC 2015026134

A comprehensive guide to chakras and energy healing explores the science, history, practices, and structures of energy systems.

Dolnick, Barrie
Luck : understanding luck and improving the odds / Barrie Dolnick and Anthony H. Davidson. Harmony Books, c2007. xiv, 236 p. ; **131**
1. Fortune 2. Superstition
ISBN 9780307347503
LC 2007013235

Looking at the role of luck throughout history, culture, and religion, the authors explain how luck can become opportunity, potential, and a guiding force that can lead to many of life's rewards and offers practical steps designed to improve one's path to fortune.

Mildon, Emma
The **soul** searcher's handbook : a modern girl's guide to the new-age world / Emma Mildon. Beyond Words : 2015 238 p. : **131**
1. Occultism 2. Spiritual life 3. Women
ISBN 9781582705248
LC 2015018843

Filled with tips, tricks and how-tos for incorporating everything from dreamology to alternative healing into everyday life, a lively, tongue-in-cheek guide to everything body-mind-spirit defines New Age practices for a new generation.

"One of the best New Age texts without being preachy." Library Journal.

133 Specific topics in parapsychology and occultism

Goodman, Linda, 1925-1995
Linda Goodman's star signs : the secret codes of the universe: forgotten rainbows and forgotten melodies of ancient wisdom Griffin, 1998 xli, 477 p. : **133**
1. Astrology 2. Self-help psychology
ISBN 9780312192037
LC 87-28375

Discusses a wide variety of matters relating to spiritual and physical well-being, including the Karmic Wheel, reincarnation, holistic health, spiritual advisors, channelers, crystals, and the third eye.

"Goodman explains numerology, lexigrams (secret codes of words, names, and titles), the power of sound, and the power of color. Along with explanations of karma and other modes of spiritual growth, she interweaves her own experiences with avatars and gurus, as well as common folk who are on their own spiritual path." Booklist.

Shermer, Michael
Why people believe weird things : pseudoscience, superstition, and other confusions of our time / Michael Shermer ; foreword by Stephen Jay Gould. A.W.H. Freeman/Owl Book, 2002, c1998. xxvi, 349 p. : **133**
1. Pseudoscience. 2. Creativity in science. 3. Science.
ISBN 0805070893
LC 2002068784

"First Owl Books edition"--T.p. verso.

Argues that the search for meaning and spiritual fulfillment often results in the embracing of extraordinary claims and controversial ideas.

"Dedicated to Carl Sagan, with a foreword by Stephen Jay Gould, this book by the publisher of Skeptic magazine and the Director of the Skeptics Lecture Series at California Institute of Technology, has the pedigree to be accepted as a work of scholarly value. Fortunately, it is also readable, interesting, and well indexed and provides an extensive bibliography." School Library Journal.

Sollee, Kristen J.
Witch hunt : a traveler's guide to the power and persecution of the witch / Kristen J. Sollee. Red Wheel/Weiser 2020 256 p. **133**
1. Witchcraft 2. Trials (Witchcraft)
ISBN 9781578636990

"Part history, part feminist memoir, part travelogue, Witch Hunt provides a personal guide to the witch trials in western Europe and America and explores how their legacy continues to affect women today." Provided by publisher

"This is clearly written for a general audience, but Sollee's judicious use of scholarly sources adds weight to the text and serves as a guide to readers who want to learn more. A valuable resource for planning a magical itinerary--or exploring the landscape of witchcraft from the couch." Kirkus

133.1 Apparitions

Aykroyd, Peter
A **history** of ghosts : the true story of seances, mediums, ghosts, and ghostbusters / Peter Aykroyd, with Angela Narth ; introduction by Dan Aykroyd. Rodale : 2009. 256 p. **133.1**
1. Spiritualism -- History. 2. Ghosts -- History. 3. Paranormal phenomena. 4. Supernatural.
ISBN 9781605298757
LC 2009018360

Introduces the reader to notable mediums while telling the story of the development of spiritualism, interweaving the author's personal history--which includes the inspiration for his son's film Ghostbusters--with a larger narrative about the role the paranormal has played in American culture.

"The author's grandfather was a spiritualist: he believed the human personality survives after bodily death, and practiced regular communication with ghosts--much of which he documented in journals. Aykroyd broadens the discussion with historical figures like Sir Arthur Conan Doyle, creator of Sherlock Holmes, who joined the Society of Psychical Research three weeks after his father's death. This is a smart consideration of the paranormal and a curious artifact of the Aykroyd legacy." Publishers Weekly.

Dickey, Colin
Ghostland : an American history in haunted places / Colin Dickey. Viking, 2016 xiii, 320 p. **133.1**
1. Paranormal phenomena 2. Haunted places. 3. Curiosities and

wonders. 4. Supernatural. 5. United States
ISBN 9781101980194
LC 2016044006

Takes readers on a road trip through some of the United States' most infamously haunted places - and deep into the dark side of American history.

"His book is a fascinating, measured assessment of phenomena more often exploited for sensationalism." Publishers Weekly.

Guiley, Rosemary

★The **encyclopedia** of ghosts and spirits / Rosemary Ellen Guiley ; foreword by Troy Taylor. Facts on File, 2007. xii, 564 p. : **133.1**

1. Ghosts 2. Parapsychology 3. Spirits
ISBN 9780816067374
LC 2006103302

Covers the realm of ghost folklore and mythology with over six hundred entries on historical sightings, paranormal research, and supernatural hauntings.

Jones, Marie D., 1961-

Celebrity ghosts and notorious hauntings / Marie D. Jones. Visible Ink Press, 2019 xi, 388 p. ; **133.1**

1. Celebrities -- Miscellanea 2. Ghosts
ISBN 9781578596898
LC 2019016565

"Stories of fame, death, and ghostly immortality." --Cover.

"Lightly illustrated with photographs and art, Jones's well-researched guide will be a treasure trove for amateur ghost hunters." Publishers Weekly

Norman, Michael, 1947 June 29-

Haunted America / Michael Norman and Beth Scott. Tor, 1995, c1994. xvii, 556 p. ; **133.1**

1. Haunted houses -- United States 2. Ghosts -- United States 3. Haunted houses -- Canada 4. Ghosts -- Canada
ISBN 9780812550542
LC bl 99766422

Authors' names in reverse order in original ed.
Reprint. Originally published: 1994.
"A Tom Doherty Associates book."

A compendium of seventy American true ghost legends includes battlefield specters at Little Big Horn, ghostly apparitions in President Garfield's home in Ohio, and hauntings in the White House.

"This collection of chilling tales of the supernatural includes at least one story from each state and from the English-speaking Canadian provinces. The stories recount sightings of ghostly apparitions and mysterious happenings, and their history and evolution is documented." Library Journal.

Ramsland, Katherine M., 1953-

Ghost : investigating the other side / Katherine Ramsland. Thomas Dunne Books/St. Martin's Press, 2001. xiii, 322 p., 16 p. of plates : **133.1**

1. Ramsland, Katherine M., 1953- 2. Ghosts -- United States
ISBN 9780312261641
LC 2001041725

Takes readers into the world of real-life ghost hunters, revealing their high- and low-tech methods for rooting out spirits.

"Although prepared to dismiss many so-called paranormal occurrences in favor of natural explanations, {the author} nevertheless encounters, experiences, and investigates a variety of inexplicable visual, photographic, and verbal manifestations. Both skeptics and believers will be intrigued by this first-person exploration of ghostly visitations." Booklist.

Robisheaux, Thomas Willard

The **last** witch of Langenburg : murder in a German village / Thomas Robisheaux. W. W. Norton & Co., 2009. 384 p. **133.1**

1. Witchcraft -- Langenburg, Germany -- History. 2. Murder -- Langenburg, Germany -- History. 3. Trials (Witchcraft) 4. Superstition. 5. Germany -- History -- 17th century. 6. Langenburg, Germany -- History -- 17th century.
ISBN 9780393065510
LC 2008043052

"The author gives us the story of one of the last witch hunts in Europe. In 1672, in a German village, a young woman who had just given birth to her second child died after eating a Shrovetide cake made by her neighbor. Stories of witches poisoning innocents were common in the Franconia region. The neighbor was arrested, and the entire family charged with witchcraft. You can't beat a witch hunt for drama. Every childhood nightmare is called to mindthe dark forest on the edge of town, the inaccessibility of God and, worse, our own friends and family. Forget memoir; this is nonfiction." Seattle Times.

Whitmer, Jamie Davis

America's most haunted hotels : checking in with uninvited guests / Jamie Davis Whitmer. Llewellyn Worldwide, 2016. 264 p. **133.1**

1. Haunted hotels. 2. Ghosts -- United States. 3. Ghosts
ISBN 9780738748009
LC 2016024296

"Though readers must decide just how much to believe in Whitmers accounts of ghostly contact, everyone can enjoy the more straightforward travelogue aspects of the book, which provide handy contact information for the hotels and potential itineraries as part of its overview. Perhaps itll help you plan your next trip." Publishers Weekly.

133.3 Divinatory arts

Crispin, Jessa

★The **creative** tarot : a modern guide to an inspired life / Jessa Crispin. Touchstone, 2016 xxi, 327 p. : **133.3**

1. Creative ability -- Miscellanea 2. Tarot
ISBN 9781501120237
LC 2015038927

A reference for artists who would use tarot for guidance adapts readings to promote the creative process and help overcome blocks, sharing engaging anecdotes about how famous artists pursued inspiration.

"Even readers with no previous interest in the tarot will be intrigued and delighted by Crispins ardently researched, spirited, creative, and inspiring elucidation." Booklist.

133.4 Demonology and witchcraft

Abrev, Ileana, 1959-

The **little** big book of white spells / Ileana Abrev. Llewellyn Publications, 2017 ix, 396 p. ; **133.4**

1. Charms 2. Incantations 3. Magic
ISBN 9780738751696
LC bl2017003810

Offers over two hundred spells that will create transformation in the lives of the spell casters.

"For readers wishing to experiment with white magic, this book of mini recipes is a great starting point." Publishers Weekly.

Carlson, Laurie M., 1952-

A **fever** in Salem : a new interpretation of the New England witch trials / Laurie Winn Carlson. I.R. Dee, 1999. xvi, 197 p. ; **133.4**

1. Trials (Witchcraft) -- Salem, Massachusetts -- History 2. Epidemic encephalitis -- Salem, Massachusetts -- 17th century 3. Witchcraft -- Salem, Massachusetts -- History -- 17th century.

ISBN 9781566632539

LC 99027520

"Carlson's compelling narrative begs for assessment by medical experts. A valuable purchase for libraries seeking more than a basic summary of the witch trials." Library Journal.

Copenhaver, Brian P,

The **book** of magic : from antiquity to the Enlightenment / selected and translated with an introduction and notes by Brian Copenhaver. Penguin Books, 2015. xxi, 643 p. : **133.4**

1. Magic -- History.

ISBN 9780241198568

LC bl2016009049

Presents a collection of writings that explore the roots of magical practice, from selections from the Bible to serious studies during the Renaissance.

Feldmann, Erica, 1982-

HausMagick : transform your home with witchcraft / Erica Feldmann. HarperOne, 2019. 254 p. : **133.4**

1. Dwellings -- Miscellanea 2. Households -- Miscellanea 3. Magic 4. Witchcraft

ISBN 9780062906151

LC 2018036758

An illustrated guide from the HausWitch store and brand founder explains how to create a beautiful, healing living space using earth magic, meditation, herbalism, self-awareness, tarot, astrology, feminist spirituality, and interior decoration.

"Blending interior design with tools for spiritual health, the book explores ways that the physical environment can influence and access the magical realm." Publishers Weekly.

Gosden, Chris, 1955-

Magic : a history : from alchemy to witchcraft, from the ice age to the present / Chris Gosden. Farrar, Straus and Giroux, 2020. xix, 482 p. : **133.4**

1. Magic (Occultism) -- Social aspects 2. Magic (Occultism) -- History. 3. Religion. 4. Witchcraft -- History. 5. Illustrated books

ISBN 9780374200121

LC 2020013393

"Originally published in 2020 by Viking, Great Britain, as The History of Magic: From Alchemy to Witchcraft, from the Ice Age to the present."

An Oxford professor of archaeology explores the history of magic and the propaganda campaigns behind the practice's current notoriety while describing the magic-themed traditions of historical cultures and magic's less-recognized role in modern civilization.

"Magic is an authoritative history of humanity's engagement with the supernatural." Booklist

Grimassi, Raven, 1951-2019

What we knew in the night : reawakening the heart of witchcraft / Raven Grimassi. Weiser Books, an imprint of Red Wheel/Weiser, LLC, 2019. xvi, 252 p. ; **133.4**

1. Witchcraft

ISBN 9781578636518

LC 2019021665

"A cohesive and complete system of witchcraft based on traditional sources, assembling and integrating key components from the past and present. Also offers practical instructions and a clear five-step process of empowerment for anyone who wants to walk the path of witchcraft".-- Provided by publisher.

Grossman, Pam

Waking the witch : reflections on women, magic, and power / Pam Grossman. Gallery Books, 2019. 288 p. **133.4**

1. Grossman, Pam 2. Witches 3. Witchcraft 4. Archetype (Psychology) 5. Occultism

ISBN 9781982100704

LC 2018054467

Based on a podcast.

When you think of a witch, what do you picture? Pointy black hat, maybe a broomstick. But witches in various guises have been with us for millennia. In Waking the Witch, Pam Grossman explores the cultural and historical impact of the world's most magical icon. In this fascinating read that is part cultural analysis, part memoir, Pam opens up about her own journey on the path to witchcraft, and how her personal embrace of the witch helped her find strength, self-empowerment, and a deeper purpose.

Guiley, Rosemary

The **encyclopedia** of demons and demonology / Rosemary Ellen Guiley ; foreword by John Zaffis. Facts On File, c2009. xv, 302 p. : **133.4**

1. Demonology -- Encyclopedias. 2. Demonic possession 3. Demons 4. Paranormal phenomena 5. Encyclopedias.

ISBN 9780816073146

LC 2008052488

Brief entries and illustrations introduce topics including individually named demons from a variety of cultures, historical figures, films, and cases of possession.

Guiley, Rosemary

The **encyclopedia** of witches, witchcraft and wicca / Rosemary Ellen Guiley. Facts On File, c2008. xii, 436 p. : **133.4**

1. Wicca 2. Witchcraft 3. Witches

ISBN 9780816071036

LC bl2008030438

Rev. ed. : The encyclopedia of witches and witchcraft. 1999.

More than 480 entries identify famous witches, explains terms dealing with witchcraft, and describes related churches and organizations.

"Spanning centuries and continents, the book defines 480 of witchcraft's and wizardry's major historical events, figures, tools, sites, symbols, and abstract terms. The highly engaging, alphabetically organized entries run several paragraphs in length and deftly clarify a term's etymology as well as its spiritual, historical, or spell-making significance." Library Journal.

Howe, Katherine, 1977-

The **Penguin** book of witches / edited by Katherine Howe. Penguin Books, 2014. xix, 294 p. ; **133.4**

1. Witchcraft -- United States -- History -- Sources. 2. Witchcraft

-- England -- History -- Sources.
ISBN 9780143106180

LC bl2014049676

From a 1597 manual for witch hunters by King James to court papers from the Salem witch trials, primary source documents provide historical accounts of accused witches from medieval Europe to early-nineteenth century America.

Hutton, Ronald

The **triumph** of the moon : a history of modern pagan witchcraft / Ronald Hutton. Oxford University Press, 1999. xv, 486 p. ; **133.4**

1. Witchcraft -- Great Britain -- History -- 19th century. 2. Witchcraft -- Great Britain -- History -- 20th century. 3. Neopaganism -- Great Britain -- History. 4. Great Britain -- Religion -- 19th century. 5. Great Britain -- Religion -- 20th century.
ISBN 0198207441

LC 99031586

"This history of paganism in 19th- and 20th-century Britain centers on Wicca, the system of witchcraft Gerald B. Gardner introduced to a startled public in the 1950s. Hutton's exceptional work is by far the most scholarly, comprehensive and judicious analysis of the subject yet published." Publishers Weekly.

Jones, Marie D., 1961-

Demons, the devil, and fallen angels / Marie D. Jones and Larry Flaxman. Visible Ink, 2017. xv, 368 p. ; **133.4**

1. Demonology 2. Occultism
ISBN 9781578596133

LC 2017022073

"An image-packed compendium on embodiments of evil, this overview incorporates significant historical events and modern phenomena. By salting pages with a portrait of mystic Antoinette Bourignon, photos of Santeria practitioners, and the title page of Malleus Maleficarum, the authors add weight to their entries on the impact of witch hunts in previous eras as well as current strands of the occult, including haunted dolls and the alleged satanic influence on rock and roll." Booklist

Karlsen, Carol F., 1940-

★The **devil** in the shape of a woman : witchcraft in colonial New England / Carol F. Karlsen. Norton, c1987. xvii, 360 p. ; **133.4**

1. Witchcraft -- New England
ISBN 9780393024784

LC 87016615

Includes index.

Analyzes the belief in witchcraft in colonial times, looks at the characteristics of those charged and their accusers, and discusses Puritan attitudess toward women.

Levack, Brian P.

The **Devil** within : possession & exorcism in the Christian West / Brian Levack. Yale University Press, 2013 xii, 346 p. : **133.4**

1. Demoniac possession -- Europe -- History. 2. Exorcism -- Europe -- History.
ISBN 0300114729

LC 2012042933

A fascinating, wide-ranging survey examines the history of possession and exorcism through the ages.

"In this riveting, readable study, Levack... offers readers a comprehensive view of reports of demon possession and efforts to rid victims of it." Publishers Weekly.

Maxwell-Stuart, P. G.

Satan : a biography / P. G. Maxwell-Stuart. Amberley Pub., 2008. 240 p. **133.4**

1. Good and evil. 2. Devil. 3. Demons
ISBN 9781848680821

LC 2009378137

"This history of the papacy provides a good selection of illustrations with a lightweight text." New York Times Book Review.

Rajchel, Diana

Urban magick : a guide for the city witch / Diana Rajchel. Llewellyn Publications, 2020 x, 296 p. **133.4**

1. Witchcraft -- Rites and ceremonies 2. Magic. 3. City life 4. Spirituality
ISBN 9780738752747

LC 2019055224

Engage with the urban landscape around you and harness its boundless possibilities for a thriving magickal practice. Urban Magick shows you how to connect with your city's diverse spiritual ecosystem and channel the powerful energy running through it.

"Presents an informative, socially conscious guide for magic practitioners." Publishers Weekly

Roth, Harold (Authority on plants)

The **witching** herbs : 13 essential plants and herbs for your magical garden / Harold Roth. Weiser Books, 2017. xviii, 263 p. : **133.4**

1. Witchcraft 2. Herbs -- Miscellanea
ISBN 9781578635993

LC 2018137761

"Connecting with plant spirits by growing magical plants yourself is the ultimate in herbal magic, according to this debut. Roth leans heavily on a modernized version of the ancient Doctrine of Signatures that teaches practitioners to look to a plant's morphology to understand its use, adding clues from growth patterns, traditional medicine, and chemistry as well as from traditional lore and personal gnosis." Publishers Weekly

133.43 Magic and witchcraft

Saxena, Jaya

Basic witches : how to summon success, banish drama, and raise hell with your coven / Jaya Saxena and Jess Zimmerman ; illustrated by Camille Chew. Quirk Books, 2017. 206 p. : **133.43**

1. Witchcraft 2. Witches 3. Self-acceptance in women
ISBN 9781594749773

LC 2016961079

Tap into your inner sorceress and channel the dark arts with this magical lifestyle guide for everything from powering up a stylish talisman to banishing terrible tinder dates.

133.5 Astrology

Goodman, Linda, 1925-1995

Linda Goodman's sun signs Taplinger Pub. Co. [1968] xxiii,

549 p. **133.5**

1. Astrology 2. Self-help psychology
ISBN 9780800849009

LC 68031737

"This book is part astrology, part psychology, and always entertaining." Library Journal.

Miller, Susan

Planets and possibilities : explore the worlds beyond your sun sign / Susan Miller. Warner Books, c2001. x, 418 p. : **133.5**

1. Astrology
ISBN 9780446524346

LC 00109235

Provides advice based on how the planets, the sun, and the moon work together to influence lives, with a separate chapter exploring each sun sign.

"The author provides character analysis of each sign. The cosmic gifts, relationship trends, financial tendencies, and career tendencies associated with each sign are all described in detail. The mythology of each sign is included as well, nicely rounding out the book." Library Journal.

Snodgrass, Mary Ellen

Signs of the zodiac : a reference guide to historical, mythological, and cultural associations / Mary Ellen Snodgrass ; illustrated by Raymond Miller Barrett, Jr. Greenwood Press, 1997. xiv, 243 p. : **133.5**

1. Astrology -- History. 2. Astrology. 3. Zodiac.
ISBN 0313302766

LC 97005598

A historical look at astrology examines each zodiac sign, discussing its mythological background and traits associated with those born under it

"After brief descriptions of zodiacal variants from other parts of the world, plus chapters on the historical foundations of astrology and its pervasiveness in the arts and sciences, Snodgrass treats each sign to a full workover: major stars in each, mythological background and symbology, commonly accepted character traits of those born under its influence, and thumbnail biographies of select prominent people who exemplify those traits." School Library Journal.

133.8 Psychic phenomena

Clegg, Brian

Extra sensory : the science and pseudoscience of telepathy and other powers of the mind / Brian Clegg. St. Martin's Press, 2013. 320 p. **133.8**

1. Psychic ability 2. Extrasensory perception 3. Mind and body 4. Paranormal phenomena
ISBN 9781250019066

LC 2013004038

A pop-science tour of legitimate modern studies in the areas of ESP, telekinesis and other seemingly supernatural abilities considers whether they are actual talents or manifestations of fantasy, documenting the question-raising research of serious scientists while assessing the possible physical mechanisms for ESP.

Jacobsen, Annie

Phenomena : the secret history of the U.S. Government's investigations into extrasensory perception and psychokinesis / Annie Jacobsen. Little, Brown & Company, 2017. 544 p. **133.8**

1. CIA 2. Paranormal phenomena 3. Military research 4. Secrecy in government 5. Psychics 6. United States -- Armed Forces 7. United States -- Politics and government
ISBN 9780316349369

LC bl2017003679

The author presents a history of the military's controversial, decades-long investigation into boundary-pushing mental phenomena, sharing inside information about how the program has involved strategic experiments in the name of national security.

133.9 Spiritualism

Blum, Deborah, 1954-

Ghost hunters : William James and the search for scientific proof of life after death / Deborah Blum. Penguin Press, 2006. 370 p. ; **133.9**

1. James, William, 1842-1910. 2. Paranormal phenomena -- History -- 19th century. 3. Spiritualism -- History -- 19th century. 4. Ghosts.
ISBN 1594200904

LC 2006044948

Traces how the respected psychologist brother of Henry James set out to gather scientific data proving the existence of ghosts at the end of the nineteenth century, forming the American Society for Psychical Research.

"In this book, the author examines the Victorian era conflict between science and religion by reviewing the history of the British Society for Psychical Research and its U.S. counterpart, the American Society for Psychical Research, both of which aimed to find scientific proof of the existence of the supernatural. . . . Her clearly written presentation of the history, frauds, and personalities involved in this unique slice of Victorian life is recommended for all history of science collections." Library Journal.

Moody, Raymond A.

★**Life** after life : the investigation of a phenomenon-survival of bodily death / Raymond A. Moody, Jr. ; with a new preface by Melvin Morse and a foreword by Elizabeth Kubler-Ross. HarperSanFrancisco, 2001. xxviii, 175 p. ; **133.9**

1. Future life 2. Near-death experiences
ISBN 9780062517395

LC 00046156

Originally published in 1975 by MBB.Inc. and later published by Bantam Books.

Reports on--and draws careful conclusions from--the out-of-the-body experiences of people who, revived from clinical death or from near-death, regained consciousness, in a twenty-fifth anniversary edition of the pioneering study of the afterlife.

Rasmussen, Christina, 1972-

Where did you go? : a life-changing journey to connect with those we've lost / Christina Rasmussen. HarperOne 2018 229 p. ; **133.9**

1. Future life 2. Spiritualism
ISBN 9780062689627

LC 2018035459

An internationally recognized grief educator reveals how to connect with loved ones who have passed on and provides practical exercises and a step-by-step guide to travel to the other side to find answers and discover peace.

142 Critical philosophy

Barrett, William, 1913-1992
★**Irrational** man : a study in existential philosophy / William Barrett. Anchor Books, Doubleday 1990 305 p. ; **142**
1. Existentialism
ISBN 9780385031387
LC 90033388

Includes index.
Originally published: New York : Doubleday, 1958.
Examines the sources, major proponents, and widespread influence of twentieth-century existentialism.

Kaufmann, Walter Arnold
Existentialism : from Dostoevsky to Sartre / edited, with an introduction, prefaces, and new translations by Walter Kaufmann. Plume, 2004, c1975. 384 p. ; **142**
1. Existentialism 2. Existentialism in literature
ISBN 9780452009301
LC bl2005006739

Originally published: New York : New American Library, [198-], c1975.
Collects philosophical writings by Dostoevsky, Nietzsche, Rilke, Kierkegaard, Kafka, Jaspers, Ortega, Heidegger, Camus, and Sartre, and includes commentary on the philosophers and their work.

146 Naturalism and related systems and doctrines

Dennett, Daniel C.
Darwin's dangerous idea : evolution and the meanings of life / Daniel C. Dennett. Simon & Schuster, 1996, c1995. 586 p. : **146**
1. Darwin, Charles, 1809-1882 2. Natural selection. 3. Evolution -- Philosophy. 4. Human evolution -- Philosophy.
ISBN 068482471X
LC BL 99774686

Reprint. Originally published: c1995.
"A Touchstone book."
Pulitzer Prize for General Nonfiction finalist
National Book Award for Nonfiction finalist, 1995
Offers a wider perspective on Darwin's scientific theory of natural selection, explaining how it extends beyond biology, analyzing current controversies over the origins of life and inherent biases, and challenging popular philosophies.
"Current controversies associated with the origin of life, sociobiology, punctuated equilibrium, the evolution of culture and language, and evolutionary ethics are investigated rigorously within the context of Darwinian science and philosophy. Dennett challenges the ideas of several imminent scientists, including Roger Penrose and Stephen Jay Gould, who, Dennett asserts, tend to limit the power or implications of Darwin's dangerous ideas." Library Journal.

149 Other philosophical systems and doctrines

Rand, Ayn
★The **virtue** of selfishness : a new concept of egoism / Ayn Rand ; with additional articles by Nathaniel Branden. Signet, 2014 xii, 173 p. ; **149**
1. Egoism 2. Objectivism (Philosophy) 3. Selfishness
ISBN 9780451163936
LC bl2017014665

Includes index.
Presents a collection of essays that sets forth the moral principles of the author's philosophy, Objectivism.

150 Psychology

Cordon, Luis A.
★**Popular** psychology : an encyclopedia / Luis A. Cordon. Greenwood Press, 2005. xix, 274 p. : **150**
1. Psychology
ISBN 9780313324574
LC 2004017426

Entries cover a variety of topics in the field of popular psychology, including acupuncture, emotional intelligence, brainwashing, chemical inbalance, and seasonal affective disorder.
"This book provides a concise guide for anyone seeking to understand the true scientific nature of psychology." Library Media Connection.

Glasser, William, 1925-2013
Choice theory : a new psychology of personal freedom / William Glasser. HarperCollinsPublishers, c1998. xii, 340 p. : **150**
1. Psychology.
ISBN 0060191090
LC 97036025

A world-renowned psychiatrist, the author of Reality Therapy, calls for a complete overhaul of traditional psychology based on the goal of strengthening relationships by appealing to each individual's basic needs for love, power, freedom, and pleasure.
"Choice theory helps its users avoid confrontation and ask pertinent questions. It sees conscious or unconscious desire for external control as the main problem in the four major personal relationships: husband-wife, parent-child, teacher-student, and manager-worker. Combining choice theory and reality therapy in his practice, Glasser has been able to shorten the durations of his treatment programs substantially. As he presents them here, his theories and approaches can be applied in education and business as well as for self-help." Booklist.

150.19 Systems, schools, viewpoints

Frankl, Viktor E. (Viktor Emil), 1905-1997
Yes to life : in spite of everything / Viktor E. Frankl ; introduction by Daniel Goleman ; afterword by Franz Vesely ; translated from the German by Joelle Young. Beacon Press, 2020 127 p. ; **150.19**
1. Meaning (Psychology) 2. Resilience (Personality trait)
ISBN 9780807005552
LC 2019059317

"Eleven months after his liberation from Auschwitz, Viktor E. Frankl held a series of public lectures in Vienna, published here for the first time. The psychologist, who was to become world famous, explained his central thoughts on meaning, resilience and the importance of embracing life even in the face of great adversity".-- Provided by publisher.

Freud, Sigmund, 1856-1939
★The **basic** writings of Sigmund Freud : Psychopathology

of Everyday Life/the Interpretation of Dreams/Three Contributions to the Theory of Sex/Wit and translated and edited by A.A. Brill. Modern Library, 1995. xii, 973 p. ; **150.19**

1. Psychoanalysis
ISBN 9780679601661

LC 95013411

Includes index.

Originally published: New York : Modern Library, c1938.

Presents a selection of the important writings of the nineteenth-century psychiatrist, including "Psychopathology of Everyday Life," "The Interpretation of Dreams," and "Totem and Taboo."

Freud, Sigmund, 1856-1939

Civilization and its discontents / Sigmund Freud ; introduction by Christopher Hitchens ; translated and edited by James Strachey ; biographical afterword by Peter Gay. W.W. Norton & Company, c2010. 186 p. ; **150.19**

1. Psychoanalysis. 2. Civilization. 3. Behavior. 4. Human behavior.
ISBN 9780393304510

LC 2004027112

Presents the eminent Austrian psychoanalyst's views on the irreconcilable antagonism between instinctual drives and the repressive attitudes of civilization.

Gay, Peter, 1923-2015

A **Godless** Jew : Freud, atheism, and the making of psychoanalysis / Peter Gay. Yale University Press, c1987. xvii, 182 p. ; **150.19**

1. Freud, Sigmund, 1856-1939 Religion. 2. Psychoanalysis and religion 3. Atheism
ISBN 9780300040081

LC 87008267

Includes index.

Argues that Freud was an atheist and that atheism was an important prerequisite for his development of psychoanalysis.

Judith, Anodea, 1952-

Eastern body, Western mind : psychology and the chakra system as a path to the self / Anodea Judith. Celestial Arts, c2004. xii, 488 p. : **150.19**

1. Chakras -- Miscellanea.
ISBN 9781587612251

LC 2004010256

Revised edition of the groundbreaking New Age book that seamlessly merges Western psychology and science with spirituality, creating a compelling interpretation of the Eastern chakra system and its relevance for Westerners today. --Provided by publisher

Jung, C. G. (Carl Gustav), 1875-1961

★The **basic** writings of C.G. Jung / edited, with an introduction by Violet Staub de Laszlo. Modern Library, 1993. xxxiii, 691 p. ; **150.19**

1. Psychoanalysis
ISBN 9780679600718

LC 93017801

Originally published: New York : Random House, 1959.

Presents selected writings for Jung's major studies on the nature and functioning of the human psyche.

Jung, C. G. (Carl Gustav), 1875-1961

Memories, dreams, reflections / C.G. Jung ; recorded and edited by Aniela Jaffe ; translated from the German by Richard and Clara Winston. Vintage Books, 1989, c1963. xiii, 430 p. ; **150.19**

1. Jung, C. G. (Carl Gustav), 1875-1961. 2. Psychoanalysts -- Switzerland
ISBN 9780679723950

LC 88037040

Translation of: Erinnerungen, Traume, Gedanken.

Includes index.

The Swiss psychologists shares the visions, inner experiences, and dreams that have shaped his work and thought.

May, Rollo, 1909-1994

★The **discovery** of being : writings in existential psychology / Rollo May. Norton, c1983. 192 p. ; **150.19**

1. Existential psychology. 2. Psychotherapy 3. Self-discovery 4. Philosophy, Modern
ISBN 0393017907

LC 83004282

"The author provides the reader with principles of his existential psychotherapy; delineates his view of the cultural-historical context that gave rise to both psychoanalysis and existentialism; and sets forth what he considers to be the contributions to therapy of an existential approach." Choice.

152.1 Sensory perception

Ackerman, Diane, 1948-

A **natural** history of the senses / Diane Ackerman. Random House, 1990. xix, 331p. **152.1**

1. Senses and sensation. 2. Manners and customs. 3. Human behavior. 4. Smell.
ISBN 0394573358

LC 89043416

ALA Notable Book, 1991.

"Ackerman celebrates the senses by examining their biological bases and the various and bizarre ways we have come to indulge them. Her catalog of the senses is itself a sensuous journey, with prose rich in imagery and rhythm. Ackerman's book is a provocative and entertaining treat whose details will bestir the reader's imagination." Library Journal.

Herz, Rachel, 1963-

The **scent** of desire : discovering our enigmatic sense of smell / Rachel Herz. William Morrow, 2007. 288 p. **152.1**

1. Smell. 2. Senses and sensation. 3. Sense organs. 4. Behavior.
ISBN 0060825375

LC 2007033563

A tour of the psychology, biology, and sociology of the olfactory sense explores the function of smell and how it is interconnected with human survival, drawing on extensive research and personal accounts to illuminate the sense's relevance in everyday life.

"This is one of those all-too-rare books that is involving, well written, and solidly grounded in research." Library Journal.

152.109 Sensory perception -- History, geographic treatment, biography

Purnell, Carolyn

The **sensational** past : how the Enlightenment changed the way we use our senses / Carolyn Purnell. W. W. Norton &

Company, 2017. 304 p. **152.109**

1. Senses and sensation 2. Enlightenment (European intellectual movement) 3. Social influence 4. Philosophy, Modern -- 18th century

ISBN 9780393249378

LC 2016031574

A lively exploration of the eccentric ways that human senses were perceived throughout the Enlightenment reveals how the way we think about the senses has dramatically changed throughout history and how today's sensory experiences are representative of the beliefs of earlier times.

152.14 Visual perception

Herman, Amy

Visual intelligence : sharpen your perception, change your life / Amy E. Herman. Houghton Mifflin Harcourt, 2016. xx, 316 p. : **152.14**

1. Visual perception. 2. Visual literacy. 3. Observation (Psychology)

ISBN 9780544381056

LC 2015037245

"An Eamon Dolan Book."

Includes index.

A guide to seeing and communicating more clearly in accordance with the guidelines taught to FBI agents, police officers, CEOs, ER doctors and other professionals draws on the seminars of art historian Amy Herman to explain how to become more observant to recognize and convey important information.

"Sharp and original, this book should alter how readers look at the world." Kirkus.

Hoffman, Donald D.

Visual intelligence : how we create what we see / Donald D. Hoffman. W.W. Norton, c1998. xv, 294 p. : **152.14**

1. Visual perception. 2. Vision. 3. Human information processing. 4. Neuropsychology.

ISBN 0393046699

LC 98006181

Reveals the way the human eye acts on the visual world not just to represent but to actively construct the things we see, outlining the rules of vision and their application in art and technology.

"Not only is this book an outstanding example of creative popular science but, given the many optical illusions it presents, it's also the rare book that, in line with its subject, can be thoroughly enjoyed both right side up and upside down." Publishers Weekly.

152.3 Movements and motor functions

Provine, Robert R.

Curious behavior : yawning, laughing, hiccupping, and beyond / Robert R. Provine. Belknap Press of Harvard University Press, 2012. 246 p. **152.3**

1. Human behavior. 2. Human biology. 3. Neuropsychology. 4. Genetic psychology.

ISBN 9780674048515

LC 2012007754

Explores the quirks of human behavior, looking at why such reflexive acts as yawning, sneezing, and hiccupping can explain how the human brain works and may shed light on the instinctual range of behavior.

Wood, Wendy, 1954 June 17-

Good habits, bad habits : the science of making positive changes that stick / Wendy Wood. Farrar, Straus and Giroux, 2019 303 p. : **152.3**

1. Change (Psychology) 2. Social psychology 3. Cognitive neuroscience. 4. Habit breaking.

ISBN 9781250159076

LC 2018060812

Revealing how a high percentage of everyday life is spent performing unconscious habits, a report based on extensive research into behavioral science reveals how to transition to better habits without exclusive reliance on willpower.

152.4 Emotions

Barrett, Lisa Feldman

★**How** emotions are made : the new science of the mind and brain / Lisa Feldman Barrett. Houghton Mifflin Harcourt, 2017. 304 p. **152.4**

1. Neuroscience 2. Brain -- Research 3. Emotions -- Research 4. Emotions and cognition

ISBN 9780544133310

LC 2016038354

Outlines new theories about how the brain constructs emotions to evaluate a growing potential for revolutionizing psychology, health care, law enforcement and modern understandings about the human mind.

"The book is a challenging read and will offer the most rewards to researchers already familiar with the longstanding and apparently still unresolved arguments about what emotions are." Publishers Weekly.

Beam, Cris

I feel you : the surprising power of extreme empathy / Cris Beam. Houghton Mifflin Harcourt, 2018. 304 p. **152.4**

1. Empathy. 2. Emotions. 3. Caring.

ISBN 9780544558168

LC 2017045815

"A rigorously researched and intensely moving examination of empathy: how it works, how it transforms us, and how our society misunderstands it".-- Provided by publisher.

Brackett, Marc A

Permission to feel : unlocking the power of emotions to help our kids, ourselves, and our society thrive / Marc Brackett, Ph.D., director, Yale Center for Emotional Intelligence, professor, Yale Child Study Center. Celadon Books, 2019. 292 p. ; **152.4**

1. Emotional intelligence.

ISBN 9781250212849

LC bl2019021303

The founding director of the Yale Center for Emotional Intelligence outlines a blueprint for understanding human emotions and using them wisely so that they can help, rather than hinder, personal success and well-being.

Breggin, Peter Roger, 1936-

Guilt, shame, and anxiety : understanding and overcoming negative emotions / Peter R. Breggin, MD. Prometheus Books, 2014. 317 p. ; **152.4**

1. Emotions 2. Guilt 3. Shame 4. Anxiety

ISBN 9781616141493

LC 2014023875

"Breggin conveys empathy and maintains a clear, conversational tone while spelling out his prescriptions for overriding destructive impulses in a variety of real-world situations." Publishers Weekly.

Damasio, Antonio R.

Looking for Spinoza : joy, sorrow, and the feeling brain / Antonio Damasio. Harcourt, 2003. x, 355 p. : **152.4**

1. Spinoza, Benedictus de, 1632-1677. 2. Emotions. 3. Neuropsychology. 4. Joy and sorrow.
ISBN 0151005575

LC 2002011347

"This is a discussion of the difference between emotions (of the body) and feelings (of the mind), various sites in the brain that trigger these states, and the... synthesis of the homeostatic process, memory, sensory input, imagination, and foresight that links the unconscious to consciousness and feelings to reasoning." Booklist.

Fromm, Erich, 1900-1980

★The **art** of loving / Erich Fromm. Continuum, 2000. viii, 130 p. ; **152.4**

1. Love.
ISBN 0826412602

LC 00021030

"An astonishingly simple presentation of an abstract subject." Booklist.

Gardner, Daniel, 1968-

The **science** of fear : why we fear the things we shouldn't-- and put ourselves in greater danger / Daniel Gardner. Dutton, 2008. 320 p. **152.4**

1. Psychology 2. Risk 3. Fear -- Social aspects 4. Fear -- Political aspects
ISBN 9780525950622

LC 2008003024

Reprinted 2015

aOriginally published under the title Risk: the science and politics of fear (Toronto: McClelland & Stewart, 2008).

Science in Society Book Award (Canadian Science Writers' Association), for Adult Nonfiction, 2008.

An analysis of the scientific causes of irrational fear offers insight into the brain's role in causing people to experience and react to fear, in a report that explains how heightened fear in the post-9/11 world is dangerously intersecting with biologically driven responses.

"Gardner analyses everything from the media's predilection for irrational scare stories to the cynical use of fear by politicians pushing a particular agenda. [He] never falls into the trap of becoming frustrated and embittered by the waste and needless worry that he is documenting. A personal anecdote about an unwise foray into a Nigerian slum in search of a stolen wallet disposes of the idea that the author is immune to the foibles he describes. What could easily have been a catalogue of misgovernance and stupidity instead becomes a cheery corrective to modern paranoia." The Economist.

Goleman, Daniel

★**Emotional** intelligence / Daniel Goleman. Bantam Books, 2005. xxiv, 358 p. : **152.4**

1. Emotional intelligence.
ISBN 055338371X

LC 2005282310

Draws on the latest research in psychology and neuroscience to show how the rational and the emotional faculties of the mind work together to shape everything from personal success to physical well-being.

"The author explains how to develop our emotional intelligence in ways that can improve our relationships, our parenting, our classrooms, and our workplaces. Goleman assures us that our temperaments may be determined by neurochemistry, but they can be altered." Booklist.

Havrilesky, Heather

What if this were enough? : essays / Heather Havrilesky. Doubleday, [2018] 240 p. **152.4**

1. Havrilesky, Heather 2. Happiness 3. Everyday life 4. Personal conduct 5. Awareness 6. Essays
ISBN 9780385542883

LC 2018001398

Through her incisive and witty inquiries, Havrilesky urges us to reject the pursuit of a shiny, shallow future that will never come. These timely, provocative, and often hilarious essays suggest an embrace of the flawed, a connection with what already is, who we already are, what we already have. She asks us to consider: What if this were enough? Our salvation, Havrilesky says, can be found right here, right now, in this imperfect moment.

Hone, Lucy

Resilient grieving : finding strength and embracing life after a loss that changes everything / Lucy Hone, PhD ; foreword by Karen Reivich, PhD. the Experiment, 2017, c2016. xii, 240 p. ; **152.4**

1. Hone, Lucy Family. 2. Hone, Abi, d. 2014 Death and burial. 3. Bereavement -- Psychological aspects. 4. Resilience (Personal quality) 5. Traffic accident victims. 6. Control (Psychology)
ISBN 9781615193752

First published as What Abi taught us in 2016.

The first popularization of the science and practice of resilient grieving in a practical guide, urging a more proactive, supportive, mindful, and positive path to recovery that offers an alternative to Kübler-Ross's five stages.

"There is a wealth of empathetic information in this book that will undoubtedly be uplifting to all who are grieving or know of others in the process. Excellent." Library Journal.

Jamison, Kay Redfield

Exuberance : the passion for life / Kay Redfield Jamison. A.A. Knopf, 2004. 405 p. : **152.4**

1. Joy and sorrow. 2. Happiness. 3. Enthusiasm.
ISBN 037540144X

LC 2004046561

"A major creative contribution to positive psychology, this book belongs in every library." Library Journal.

Jeffers, Susan J.

Feel the fear-- and do it anyway / Susan Jeffers. Ballantine Books, 2007. 214 p. : **152.4**

1. Fear
ISBN 9780345487421

LC 2007271292

"20th anniversary edition"--Cover.

A psychotherapist shows how to identify the fears that are inhibiting one's life, ranging from public speaking and intimacy to aging and rejection, and how to transform frustration and helplessness into power to create success in every aspect of life, in a twentieth anniversary edition of the best-selling guide. Reissue.

Leanse, Ellen Petry

The **happiness** hack : how to take charge of your brain and program more happiness into your life / Ellen Petry Leanse. Simple Truths, 2017 xvii, 109 p. : **152.4**

1. Happiness 2. Self-actualization (Psychology)
ISBN 9781492656913

LC 2017047527

"To those who are looking for shortcuts on the road to happiness, TEDx Talk speaker and Stanford University professor Leanse responds with a work about understanding and gaining control over one's brain, asserting that these are the first steps in facing life with clarity and resilience." Library Journal

Lenoir, Frederic

Happiness : a philosopher's guide / Frederic Lenoir ; translated by Andrew Brown. Melville House, 2015 vi, 199 p. ; **152.4**

1. Happiness. 2. Philosophy 3. Social philosophy
ISBN 9781612194394

LC 2014040205

Discusses the idea of everlasting and true happiness, drawing from the writings and teachings of great thinkers across the ages, from Aristotle and Plato to Voltaire and Freud.

"Throughout the book, Lenoir writes economically, devoting only enough words to particular thoughts and approaches as are necessary to stir questions in the minds of readers. A brief though well-considered guide to a wide range of the many schools of thought regarding contentment, joy and happiness." Kirkus.

Lerner, Harriet Goldhor

★The **dance** of anger : a woman's guide to changing the patterns of intimate relationships / Harriet Lerner. Perennial Currents, 2005. xvi, 239 p. : **152.4**

1. Anger. 2. Interpersonal relations. 3. Women -- Psychology.
ISBN 006074104X

LC 2004060074

Originally published: 1st ed. New York : Harper & Row, c1985. With new introd.

Based on the author's clinical experience and workshops she has introduced, a twentieth anniversary edition of the classic guide helps women understand the causes and patterns of their anger while providing specific alternatives for forging more powerful relationships.

Lieberman, David J

Never get angry again : the foolproof way to stay calm and in control in any conversation or situation / David J. Lieberman, Ph.D. St. Martin's Press, 2018. vii, 225 p. ; **152.4**

1. Adjustment (Psychology) 2. Anger 3. Calmness
ISBN 9781250154392

LC 2017037537

A comprehensive, holistic look at the underlying emotional, physical and spiritual causes of anger cites the shortcomings of traditional anger-management techniques while explaining how readers can shift their perspectives to maintain a state of calm and prevent angry feelings.

Lustig, Robert H.

The **hacking** of the American mind : the science behind the corporate takeover of our bodies and brains / Robert H. Lustig. Avery Pub. Group, 2017. 336 p. **152.4**

1. Neuroscience 2. Addiction 3. Depression 4. Anxiety
ISBN 9781101982587

LC 2017031139

The best-selling author of Fat Chance reveals how corporate neuromarketing is triggering imbalances in the body's dopamine and serotonin levels, causing addictions to sugar, social media and other consumer products in high-stress and otherwise susceptible customers.

"This persuasive and eye-opening book reveals the downward spiral of our health and happiness... Well-researched and witty, Lustig's important inquiry will appeal to diverse readers." Booklist.

Manson, Mark

Everything is f*cked : a book about hope / Mark Manson. HarperCollins 2019 224 p. **152.4**

1. Hope 2. Optimism 3. Despair 4. Global warming
ISBN 9780062888433

LC bl2019004875

From the New York Times best-selling author of The Subtle Art of Not Giving a F*ck comes a new unorthodox self-help book.

"The popular blogger and author delivers an entertaining and thought-provoking third book about the importance of being hopeful in terrible times. Clever and accessibly conversational, Manson reminds us to chill out, not sweat the small stuff, and keep hope for a better world alive." Kirkus.

Nettle, Daniel

Happiness : the science behind your smile / Daniel Nettle. Oxford University Press, 2005. vi, 216 p. : **152.4**

1. Happiness. 2. Emotions. 3. Contentment. 4. Smiles and smiling.
ISBN 0192805584

LC 2004030585

Draws on empirical findings in psychology, economics, philosophy, sociology, and evolutionary biology to provide a comprehensive survey of current research and theory on happiness.

"With absolute clarity and admirable brevity, Nettle explores the pursuit of happiness and, happily, makes good sense of it all." Publishers Weekly.

Orloff, Judith

Emotional freedom : liberate yourself from negative emotions and transform your life / Judith Orloff. Harmony Books, c2009. x, 401 p. ; **152.4**

1. Emotions. 2. Negativism. 3. Self-actualization (Psychology).
ISBN 0307338185

LC 2008021482

Shows how to identify the most powerful negative emotions such as depression, anger, worry, and fear and transform them into hope, compassion, and courage to achieve complete emotional freedom.

"In Part 1, Orloff presents four components of emotionbiology, energy, spirituality, and psychologyand provides a 20-question assessment to highlight individuals' strengths and weaknesses. Orloff divides Part 2 into seven chapters, each devoted to a difficult negative emotion. Throughout, Orloff details how one can use the four components of emotion to transform negative emotions into positive ones and become a more centered and emotionally healthy person. This well-written book is full of good advice for anyone who wants to take more control of his or her emotional life." Library Journal.

Owens, Lama Rod, 1979-

Love and rage : the path of liberation through anger / Lama Rod Owens. North Atlantic Books, 2020 xviii, 280 p.; **152.4**

1. Love. 2. Anger. 3. Self-realization. 4. Social change.
ISBN 9781623174095

LC 2020003934

"Reconsidering the power of anger as a positive and necessary tool for achieving spiritual liberation and social change".-- Provided by publisher.

"Highly recommended for Eastern philosophy/Buddhism collections; a wonderful resource for social justice advocates." Library Journal

Ronson, Jon, 1967-

So you've been publicly shamed : a journey through the world of public humiliation / Jon Ronson. Riverhead Hardcover, 2015. 304 p. **152.4**

1. Social control. 2. Shame. 3. Social media. 4. Interpersonal relations.
ISBN 9781594487132

LC 2014038382

We've all seen it happen--someone makes a bad decision in the public eye and people pile on in judgment. His interest piqued by a takeover of his own Twitter account, journalist Jon Ronson dove deep into an exploration of human nature, technology, and humiliation via social media. Interviewing both those famous for being shamed and those doing the shaming, Ronson discusses motivations, consequences, and recoveries.?

Rosenblatt, Roger

The **book** of love : improvisations on a crazy little thing / Roger Rosenblatt. Ecco, 2015 176 p. **152.4**

1. Love 2. Romantic love 3. Husband and wife 4. Marriage
ISBN 9780062349422

LC bl2014055788

Using an innovative format that combines snippets of love-song lyrics, fictional vignettes and notes addressed to his wife of 50 years, the best-selling author of Making Toast and Kayak Morning explores love in all its moods and variations: romance, courtship, battle, mystery, marriage, heartbreak, fury, confusion and more.

"True to its subtitle, this is a collection of improvisations, meandering in a way that allows readers to pick it up and begin from any page in this tiny, precious book." Library Journal.

Saviuc, Luminita D.

15 things you should give up to be happy : an inspiring guide to discovering effortless joy / Luminita D. Saviuc. Perigee Books, 2016. xvii, 188 p. ; **152.4**

1. Happiness. 2. Personal conduct
ISBN 9780399172823

LC 2015032168

"A simple and counterintuitive approach to finding true joy. When PurposeFairy.com founder Luminita Saviuc posted her simple list of things to let go of in order to be happy, she had no idea that it would go viral, shared more than one million times and counting, and be called "the most viral self-development article in the history of the internet." Based on that inspiring post, this heartfelt book gives readers permission to give up--that is, to let go of the bad habits that are holding them back from achieving authentic happiness. Chapters include: Give Up the Past, Give Up Your Limiting Beliefs, Give Up Blaming Others, Give Up the Need to Always Be Right, Give Up Labels, Give Up Attachment. Simple yet wise, and informed by the author's own inspiring personal journey, this is a relatable and fresh take on happiness advice. Author Luminita Saviuc gives readers permission to stop trying so hard and simply let things go".-- Provided by publisher.

"Therapeutic, compassionate prodding for those who feel like they're unable to move forward." Library Journal.

Tallis, Frank

The **incurable** romantic : and other tales of madness and desire / Frank Tallis. Perseus Books Group 2018 304 p. **152.4**

1. Obsession 2. Love -- Psychological aspects 3. Desire -- Psychological aspects 4. People with mental illnesses
ISBN 9781541617551

LC 2017056452

A psychologist describes the amazing stories of patients who were literally crazy in love, including a man who tries to make over 3,000 prostitutes fall in love with him and a woman who stalks her dentist.

Waal, F. B. M. de (Frans B. M.), 1948-

The **age** of empathy : nature's lessons for a kinder society / Frans De Waal. Random House, 2009. x, 291 p. : **152.4**

1. Empathy. 2. Animal behavior 3. Human nature 4. Compassion
ISBN 9780307407764

LC 2009279132

A lighthearted investigation into human and animal empathy shares anecdotal coverage of the ways in which various animals care for one another instinctively and how human biology contributes to our notion of a just society.

153 Conscious mental processes and intelligence

Damasio, Antonio R.

The **feeling** of what happens : body and emotion in the making of consciousness / Antonio R. Damasio. Harcourt Brace, 1999. xii, 386 p. : **153**

1. Consciousness. 2. Consciousness -- Physiological aspects. 3. Emotions -- Physiological aspects. 4. Mind and body.
ISBN 0151003696

LC 99026357

"The author contends that consciousness arises from our ability to map relations between the self and others through our emotions. This bold attempt to mend the classical breach between emotion and reason is all the more compelling for its poetic expression." Publishers Weekly.

Eagleman, David

Incognito : the secret lives of the brain / David Eagleman. Pantheon, 2011. 288 p. **153**

1. Subconsciousness. 2. Brain. 3. Consciousness. 4. Neurology.
ISBN 9780307377333

LC 2010053184

A leading neuroscientist reveals the functions of the unconscious regions of the brain, drawing on up-to-the-minute research to identify the significance of brain areas outside of our awareness and their roles in such areas as mate selection, the perception of beauty and the future of criminal law.

"Eagleman's main theme is that what one calls me, the conscious mind, is only the tip of the iceberg, and that most of the interesting and important things the brain does are inaccessible to the brain's owner. What Eagleman does is explain the idea to the neophyte through discussion of dozens of fascinating, engaging examples. Eagleman's prose is vivid and, more important, accessible." Choice.

Edelman, Shimon

★The **happiness** of pursuit : what neuroscience can teach us about the good life / Shimon Edelman. Basic Books, c2012. x, 237 p. ; **153**

1. Happiness. 2. Thought and thinking. 3. Cognition. 4. Self.
ISBN 9780465022243

LC 2011039326

A Cornell University professor draws on philosophy, literature and brain science to explain why the pursuit of happiness is a more complicated effort than understood by most people, sharing insights into how to apply scientific methods for increasing one's chances of achieving happiness.

"An elegant tour de force that combines neuropsychology with liberal references to Shakespeare and Homer." Kirkus.

Hallinan, Joseph T.

Why we make mistakes : how we look without seeing, forget things in seconds, and are all pretty sure we are way above average / Joseph T. Hallinan. Broadway Books, c2009. 283 p. : **153**

1. Failure (Psychology) 2. Errors. 3. Human behavior. 4. Consequences

ISBN 9780767928052

LC 2008030818

Surveys the workings of the human mind to examine the science behind the brain's ability to see, think, remember, and forget, accompanied by anecdotes, visual puzzles, informational sidebars, and simple solutions for overcoming imperfections.

Hofstadter, Douglas R., 1945-

I am a strange loop / Douglas Hofstadter. Basic Books, 2007. xix, 412 p., 4 p. of plates : **153**

1. Self. 2. Consciousness. 3. Intelligence. 4. Soul.

ISBN 0465030785

LC 2007310563

Argues that the key to understanding selves and consciousness is a special kind of abstract feedback loop inhabiting our brains, which include a network of abstractions that we call "symbols." The most central and complex symbol in our brains is the one we call "I." But how can such a mysterious abstraction be real--or is our "I" merely a convenient fiction?

"The author's model of self is neither spiritual--he's not a religious mannor is it locked into the cold neurological materialism of cellular mechanics. [The book] scales some lofty conceptual heights, but it remains very personal, and it's deeply colored by the facts of Hofstadter's later life." Time

Medina, John, 1956-

Brain rules : 12 principles for surviving and thriving at work, home, and school / John Medina. Pear Press, 2014 i, 288 p. : **153**

1. Human information processing 2. Perception 3. Senses and sensation 4. Knowledge, Theory of

ISBN 9780983263371

LC bl2014015978

Includes index.

Presents twelve scientifically proven facts about how the human brain works and explains how to apply each on a daily basis, discussing such concepts as attention, memory, and sleep.

Pinker, Steven, 1954-

How the mind works / Steven Pinker. Norton, 1997. xii, 660 p. **153**

1. Cognitive neuroscience. 2. Neuropsychology. 3. Natural selection. 4. Human evolution.

ISBN 0393045358

LC 97001855

National Book Critics Circle Award for Nonfiction finalist, 1997.

Pulitzer Prize for General Nonfiction finalist, 1998.

A prominent cognitive scientist explains how the brain evolved to store and use information, allowing our ancestors to control their environment, and why we think and act as we do.

"Pinker has a gift for making enormously complicated mechanisms--and human foibles--accessible." Publishers Weekly.

Sagan, Carl, 1934-1996

The **dragons** of Eden : speculations on the evolution of human intelligence / Carl Sagan. Random House, 1977. 263 p. : **153**

1. Intelligence. 2. Brain. 3. Genetic psychology.

ISBN 0394410459

LC 76053472

Pulitzer Prize for General Nonfiction, 1978.

National Book Critics Circle Award for Nonfiction finalist, 1977.

The well-known astronomer and astrobiologist surveys current knowledge of the development of intelligence on Earth in various forms of life and explains his persuasion that intelligence must have developed along similar paths throughout the universe.

"In this study of human intellect Sagan is principally preoccupied with the neocortex, with its left hemisphere, responsible for language and logic, a right hemisphere in charge of intuition and spatial dimension, and a corpus callosum that mediates and synthesizes the two." The Atlantic.

153.1 Memory and learning

Boser, Ulrich

Learn better : mastering the skills for success in life, business, and school, or, how to become an expert in just about anything / Ulrich Boser. Rodale, 2017 xxvi, 277 p. : **153.1**

1. Learning, Psychology of

ISBN 9781623365264

LC bl2017004372

An education researcher maps out the new science of learning, showing how simple techniques like comprehension check-ins and making material personally relatable can help people gain expertise in dramatically better ways than simple rote memorization.

"This work infuses a sense of fresh excitement and accessibility into a topic sometimes considered stodgy or overly cerebral. Readers will be left craving something new to learn." Publishers Weekly.

Carey, Benedict

How we learn : the surprising truth about when, where, and why it happens / Benedict Carey. Random House, 2014. 272 p. **153.1**

1. Learning. 2. Memory.

ISBN 9780812993882

LC 2013049850

A leading New York Times neuroscientist presents a lighthearted exploration of what is known about learning and memory today that considers how to adapt negative characteristics, like ignorance and laziness, to expand learning potential.

"A totally fascinating look at learning, with helpful insights for students and any reader interested in learning everything from a new language to flying to playing chess." Booklist.

Foer, Joshua

Moonwalking with Einstein : the art and science of remembering everything / Joshua Foer. Penguin Press, 2011. 307 p. ; **153.1**

1. Mnemonics. 2. Memory. 3. Neuroscience. 4. Learning.

ISBN 159420229X

LC 2010030265

Moonwalking with Einstein draws on cutting-edge research, a surprising cultural history of memory, and venerable tricks of the mentalist's trade to transform our understanding of human remembering. Under the tutelage of top "mental athletes," Foer learns ancient techniques once employed by Cicero to memorize his speeches and by medieval scholars to memorize entire books. Using methods that have been largely forgotten, he discovers that we can all dramatically improve our memories.

"Mr. Foer writes in these pages with fresh enthusiasm. His narrative is smart and funny and . it's informed by a humanism that enables its author to place the mysteries of the brain within a larger philosophical and cultural context." New York Times.

Fogler, Janet

Improving your memory : how to remember what you're starting to forget / Janet Fogler and Lynn Stern. Johns Hopkins University Press, 2014. viii, 153 p. : **153.1**

1. Memory in old age 2. Memory -- Age factors 3. Mnemonics
ISBN 9781421415703

LC 2014008681

University of Michigan social workers Janet Fogler and Lynn Stern have completely updated their friendly and usable guide to memory improvement techniques. Recognizing that people worry something is wrong with them when they forget things, Fogler and Stern suggest that the antidote to worry is taking positive actions to help us remember what we want to remember. They provide readers with tools for understanding and improving memory, including sixteen helpful exercises. Simple techniques like writing information down, creating a catch word or phrase, altering something in your environment, and reviewing details in advance can put you actively in charge of retrieving information more easily. --Provided by publisher

Goldman, Bob, 1955-

Brain fitness : anti-aging strategies for achieving super mind power / Robert M. Goldman with Ronald Klatz and Lisa Berger. Main Street Books, 2000, c1999. xiv, 347 p. : **153.1**

1. Aging -- Prevention. 2. Aging. 3. Cognition -- Age factors. 4. Memory -- Age factors.
ISBN 0385488696

LC BL 00004222

"Brain Fitness was originally published in hardcover by Doubleday in 1999"--T.p. verso.

Offers anti-aging strategies designed to keep the brain functioning at peak levels

"This is an exploration of techniques--mental workouts, memory training, physical exercises, and nutrition and dietary supplements--that readers can use to maximize their concentration, memory, imagination, energy, intelligence, and creativity while decreasing fatigue and stress and preventing Alzheimer's disease and other brain diseases." Library Journal.

Malone, Michael S., 1954-

The **guardian** of all things : the epic story of human memory / Michael S. Malone. St Martins Press, 2012. 304 p. **153.1**

1. Memory. 2. Civilization. 3. Brain. 4. Neuroscience.
ISBN 9780312620318

LC 2012010246

An anecdotal exploration of the history of memory and human civilization explores how human ideas, inventions and transformations have been documented in venues ranging from cave drawings and oral histories to libraries and the Internet.

Pink, Daniel H.

Drive : the surprising truth about what motivates us / Daniel H. Pink. Riverhead Books, 2009. 242 p. **153.1**

1. Motivation (Psychology) 2. Growth (Psychology) 3. Goals and objectives. 4. Success (Concept)
ISBN 9781594488849

LC 2009040651

Pink argues that the secret to high performance and satisfaction in today's world is the deeply human need to direct our own lives, to learn and create new things, and to do better by ourselves and our world. Challenges popular misconceptions to reveal what actually motivates people and how to harness that knowledge to promote personal and professional fulfillment.

"The author presents an integral addition to a growing body of literature that argues for a radical shift in how businesses operate in a world dominated by technology, and soon to be led by a generation that doesn't necessarily equate money with happiness.Important reading for frustrated but open-minded business leaders struggling to connect with stressed-out workers." Kirkus.

Schacter, Daniel L.

The **seven** sins of memory : how the mind forgets and remembers / Daniel L. Schacter. Houghton Mifflin, 2001. x, 272 p. : **153.1**

1. Memory disorders. 2. Memory. 3. Memories. 4. Absent-mindedness.
ISBN 9780618040193

LC 00053885

A respected expert on memory describes how the brain stores and recalls information as he describes seven key problems with memory--transience, absent-mindedness, blocking, misattribution, suggestibility, bias, and persistence.

Wiking, Meik

The **art** of making memories : how to create and remember happy moments / Meik Wiking. William Morrow, 2019. 288 p. : **153.1**

1. Happiness. 2. Memory. 3. Neuroscience. 4. Memories.
ISBN 9780062943385

The author shares advice for creating positive memories for overall lasting happiness, drawing on extensive research to explain how to forge positive memories and let go of negative experiences.

"Wiking's focus on the pleasure and solace created by happy memories will make this accessible book great for deep study and casual perusal alike." Publishers Weekly.

153.3 Imagination, imagery, creativity

Bloomston, Carrie, 1972-

The **little** spark : 30 ways to ignite your creativity / Carrie Bloomston. Stash Books, an imprint of C&T Publishing,c 2014 127 p. : **153.3**

1. Creation (Literary, artistic, etc.). 2. Creative ability. 3. Inspiration.
ISBN 1607059606

LC 2014009342

Presents thirty projects designed to enhance creativity, including such tasks as making a vision board, writing down memories, and creating a soulbox.

"Bloomston also offers her own personal anecdotes, as well as stories and tips from numerous others; the extensive list of contributors includes designers, artists and business owners. A sparkling blueprint for stimulating creativity." Kirkus.

Brandt, Anthony K.

The **runaway** species : how human creativity remakes the world / Anthony Brandt and David Eagleman. Catapult, 2017. 200 p. **153.3**

1. Creativity 2. Social psychology.
ISBN 9781936787524

LC bl2017040997

David Eagleman, a neuroscientist and New York Times best-selling author, teams up with composer Anthony Brandt in this powerful, wide-ranging exploration of human creativity. Taking inspiration from the arts, business, education, the space program, architecture, and even hairstyles, Eagleman and Brandt discover the principles guiding human creativity. They incisively explore how individuals, organizations, and education can benefit from increased creativity, and celebrate humanity's spirit and unique ability to remake the world.

"Packed with vivid images, countless examples, and fun facts that will leave readers eager to discuss it with friends, this is a refreshing and thought-provoking book that captures both the wonder of science and the beauty of the human spirit." Booklist.

Csikszentmihalyi, Mihaly

Creativity : flow and the psychology of discovery and invention / Mihaly Csikszentmihalyi. HarperPerennial, 1997, c1996. viii, 456 p. ; **153.3**

1. Creativity 2. Creative thinking.
ISBN 9780062283252

LC BL 99788224

Originally published: New York : HarperCollinsPublishers, c1996.

Explains the creative process and shows how creativity can enrich lives.

Gawain, Shakti, 1948-

★**Creative** visualization : use the power of your imagination to create what you want in your life / Shakti Gawain. Nataraj Pub./New World Library, c2002. xvi, 175 p. : **153.3**

1. Affirmations 2. Self-actualization (Psychology) 3. Visualization
ISBN 9781577312291

LC 2003265316

"25th anniversary edition"--Cover.

Explains how to use mental imagery and affirmations to produce positive change, offering meditation suggestions and exercises designed to strengthen self-esteem, improve health, and promote relaxation.

"The author asserts that people can achieve an ideal existence simply through mental visualization." Library Journal.

Gilbert, Elizabeth, 1969-

★**Big** magic : creative living beyond fear / Elizabeth Gilbert. Riverhead Books, 2015. 276 p. ; **153.3**

1. Conduct of life 2. Confidence 3. Courage 4. Creative ability
ISBN 9781594634710

LC 2015010717

"From the worldwide bestselling author of Eat Pray Love: the path to the vibrant, fulfilling life you've dreamed of. Readers of all ages and walks of life have drawn inspiration and empowerment from Elizabeth Gilbert's books for years. Now this beloved author digs deep into her own generative process to share her wisdom and unique perspective about creativity. With profound empathy and radiant generosity, she offers potent insights into the mysterious nature of inspiration. She asks us to embrace our curiosity and let go of needless suffering. She shows us how to tackle what we most love, and how to face down what we most fear. She discusses the attitudes, approaches, and habits we need in order to live our most creative lives. Balancing between soulfulspirituality and cheerful pragmatism, Gilbert encourages us to uncover the "strange jewels" that are hidden within each of us. Whether we are looking to write a book, make art, find new ways to address challenges in our work, embark on a dream long deferred, or simply infuse our everyday lives with more mindfulness and passion, Big Magic cracks open a world of wonder and joy".-- Provided by publisher.

"Gilbert serves as an enthusiastic coach for readers who want more out of life. Highly recommended." Library Journal.

Godin, Seth

The **practice** : shipping creative work / Seth Godin. Portfolio, 2020 272 p. **153.3**

1. Creativity in business 2. Leadership in business 3. Creation (Literary, artistic, etc.) 4. Entrepreneurship
ISBN 9780593328972

LC 2020025982

Creative work doesn't come with a guarantee. But there is a pattern to who succeeds and who doesn't. And engaging in the consistent practice of its pursuit is the best way forward. Based on the breakthrough Akimbo workshop pioneered by legendary author Seth Godin, The Practice will help you get unstuck and find the courage to make and share creative work. Godin insists that writer's block is a myth, that consistency is far more important than authenticity, and that experiencing the imposter syndrome is a sign that you're a well-adjusted human. Most of all, he shows you what it takes to turn your passion from a private distraction to a productive contribution, the one you've been seeking to share all along.

Grant, Adam M.

Originals : how non-conformists move the world / Adam Grant ; foreword by Sheryl Sandberg. Viking, 2016. 320 p. **153.3**

1. Creative thinking. 2. Creativity in business 3. Creativity 4. Organizational change.
ISBN 9780525429562

LC 2015041287

Examines how provocative thought leaders can champion originality in their organizations, drawing on illustrative studies and stories spanning a range of disciplines to explain how to recognize a good idea, speak up, build allies, choose a time to act and manage doubts.

"No matter whether the reader is an original or a wannabe, this book is enjoyable and full of useful information." Library Journal.

Harford, Tim, 1973-

Messy : the power of disorder to transform our lives / Tim Harford. Riverhead Books, 2016. 288 p. **153.3**

1. Neatness and messiness 2. Chaos 3. Social values 4. Creativity
ISBN 9781594634796

LC bl2016043057

From the award-winning columnist and author of the national best-seller The Undercover Economist comes a provocative big idea book about the genuine benefits of being messy at home, at work, in the classroom and beyond.

"Weaving together lessons from history, art, technology, and social and scientific research, Harfords theories have many potential benefits for individuals and businesses seeking to remain on the creative cutting edge, as well as profound implications for society." Publishers Weekly.

Livio, Mario, 1945-

Why? : an exploration of human curiosity / Mario Livio. Simon & Schuster, 2017. 288 p. **153.3**

1. Curiosity -- History. 2. Learning 3. Neuroscience 4. Knowledge
ISBN 9781476792095

LC 2016040604

An internationally respected astrophysicist explores the science behind curiosity to evaluate its role in human creativity, ambition and culture, drawing on interviews with scientists and students while examining the lives of forefront intellectuals to identify how curiosity manifests in the brain.

"The information presented is accessible to all readers and the tone is engaging, sometimes even playful." Library Journal.

May, Rollo

The **courage** to create / Rollo May. W.W. Norton, 1994. 143 p. ; **153.3**

1. Creative ability 2. Creation (Literary, artistic, etc)
ISBN 9780393311068

LC 93043718

What if imagination and art are not, as many of us might think, the frosting on life but the fountainhead of human experience? What if our logic and science derive from art forms, rather than the other way around? In this trenchant volume, Rollo May helps all of us find those creative impulses that, once liberated, offer new possibilities for achievement. A renowned therapist and inspiring guide, Dr. May draws on his experience to show how we can break out of old patterns in our lives. His insightful book offers us a way through our fears into a fully realized self. --Provided by publisher

Sonenshein, Scott

Stretch : unlock the power of less-- and achieve more than you ever imagined / Scott Sonenshein. HarperBusiness, 2017. xi, 283 p. ; **153.3**

1. Resourcefulness -- Psychological aspects. 2. Creativity 3. Adaptability (Psychology) 4. Success (Concept)
ISBN 9780062457226

LC 2016028800

A guide to driving achievement and promoting creativity and innovation at work explains how to do more with your existing resources through a four-part framework that explains how different mindsets can diversify experiences, act without over-planning and expect positive outcomes.

Zomorodi, Manoush

Bored and brilliant : how spacing out can unlock your most productive and creative self / Manoush Zomorodi. Picador, St. Martin's Press, 2018. ix, 192 p. ; **153.3**

1. Boredom. 2. Creativity 3. Labor productivity.
ISBN 9781250126658

LC bl2018185119

Includes index.

The podcaster and radio host argues that boredom is essential in making lives happier and more productive, and includes exercises for bringing about critical thinking.

"In this age of information, Zomorodi's book seems revolutionary, almost subversive. Sprinkled liberally with research and insights from some of the leading minds in technology and futurism, Bored and Brilliant is an important reminder that we are not beholden to our devices." BookPage.

153.35 Creativity

Lightman, Alan P., 1948-

In praise of wasting time / Alan Lightman. TED Books, 2018. 102 p. : **153.35**

1. Philosophy 2. Creative thinking. 3. Creative ability. 4. Divergent thinking.
ISBN 9781501154362

LC 2018288737

Argues for the value of spending time unplugged from the grid, without scheduled activities or intended tasks, focusing on the benefits that purely idle time can have for creativity, mental replenishment, and exploring the inner self.

153.4 Thought, thinking, reasoning, intuition, value, judgment

Berdik, Chris

Mind over mind : the surprising power of expectations / Chris Berdik. Current, 2012. 272 p. ; **153.4**

1. Expectation (Psychology) 2. Thought and thinking. 3. Cognitive science 4. Psychology
ISBN 9781591845096

LC 2012019144

"How our fast-forward minds make something out of nothing. From a healing placebo to a run on the bank, the self-fulfilling potential of expectations has been observed for years. But now neuroscientists and psychologists are beginning to solve the mysteries of our expectant brain and applying their findings to field ranging from medicine to sports to education. Mind over Mind explores the frontiers of expectations research, revealing how our brains work in the future tense and how our assumptions bend reality. It shows how expectations can sometimes make us healthier, stronger, smarter, and more successful while other times leave us depressed and defeated".-- Provided by publisher.

Brotherton, Rob

Suspicious minds : why we believe conspiracy theories / Rob Brotherton. St. Martin's Press, 2015 288 p. **153.4**

1. Conspiracies 2. Conspiracy theories 3. Belief and doubt 4. Human behavior
ISBN 9781472915610

LC bl2015046771

Looks at the psychology behind conspiracy theories and explains why everyone can be prone to them, revealing the consequences they can have--from discouraging parents from vaccinating their children against deadly diseases to hampering political policies to combat climate change.

"Clearly written and with liberal use of humor and numerous examples from scholarly research, this title provides a valuable look at why conspiracy theories abound and why we should continually assess our thinking." Library Journal.

Christian, Brian, 1984-

Algorithms to live by : the computer science of human decisions / Brian Christian and Tom Griffiths. Henry Holt and Company, 2016 x, 351 p. ; **153.4**

1. Human behavior -- Mathematical models. 2. Computer simulation. 3. Computer algorithms. 4. Problem solving -- Mathematics.
ISBN 9781627790369

LC 2015032177

Explores how computer algorithms can be applied to everyday life, drawing on myriad disciplines to explain how computers have proven adept at making decisions and taking chances.

Dobelli, Rolf, 1966-

The **art** of thinking clearly / Rolf Dobelli ; translated from the German by Nicky Griffin. HarperBusiness, 2013 384 p. **153.4**

1. Cognition. 2. Decision making. 3. Errors -- Psychological aspects. 4. Reasoning (Psychology)

ISBN 0062219707

LC oc2013033342

Translation of the author's Die Kunst des klaren Denkens, published by Hanser in 2012.

This insightful exploration into human reasoning, filled with practical examples and anecdotes, reveals how to recognize and avoid the simple errors we make in our day-to-day thinking so that we can change the way we think and transform our decision-making process.

Gladwell, Malcolm, 1963-

Blink : the power of thinking without thinking / Malcolm Gladwell. Little, Brown and Co., 2005. viii, 277 p. : **153.4**

1. Decision making. 2. Intuition. 3. Thought and thinking. 4. Knowledge.

ISBN 0316172324

Utilizing case studies as diverse as speed dating, pop music, and the shooting of Amadou Diallo, Gladwell reveals that what we think of as decisions made in the blink of an eye are much more complicated than assumed. Drawing on cutting-edge neuroscience and psychology, he shows how the difference between good decision-making and bad has nothing to do with how much information we can process quickly, but on the few particular details on which we focus.

"Gladwell has a dazzling ability to find commonality in disparate fields of study. . . . Each case study is satisfying, and Gladwell imparts his own evident pleasure in delving into a wide range of fields and seeking an underlying truth." Publishers Weekly.

Glei, Jocelyn K,

Manage your day-to-day : build your routine, find your focus, and sharpen your creative mind / edited by Jocelyn K. Glei ; foreward by Scott Belsky. Amazon Publishing, 2013 253 p. ; **153.4**

1. Performance -- Psychological aspects. 2. Work -- Psychological aspects. 3. Mental efficiency. 4. Mental discipline.

ISBN 9781477800676

LC bl2014002802

Offers insights on ways to meet the challenges of the workplace by building a daily routine and finding focus amid chaos.

Gupta, Sanjay, M.D.

★**Keep** sharp : build a better brain at any age / Sanjay Gupta, MD. Simon & Schuster, 2020. 352 p. **153.4**

1. Cognition -- Age factors 2. Human information processing -- Age factors 3. Brain -- Aging 4. Aging -- Prevention

ISBN 9781501166730

LC 2019057039

The Emmy Award-winning CNN chief medical correspondent and best-selling author draws on cutting-edge scientific research to outline strategies for protecting brain function and maintaining cognitive health at any age.

"A genuine source of practical knowledge and sympathy to those struggling with dementia and the family members who are primary caregivers--to whom he tenders a wealth of resources. Inclusive and recognizably sturdy advice on building a healthy brain." Kirk

Herbert, Wray

On second thought : outsmarting your mind's hard-wired habits / Wray Herbert. Crown Publishers, 2010. 289 p. ; **153.4**

1. Thought and thinking. 2. Decision-making. 3. Brain. 4. Cognitive psychology.

ISBN 9780307461636

LC 2010003073

Reveals the evolutionary science behind how and why the human brain makes snap decisions, explaining how biological programming helps and hinders modern lives and how to avoid common mistakes by understanding the factors that prompt biased choices.

"The brain is like a dual processor, [Herbert] argues--one part is logical, deliberate, and cautious, while the other is much older and primitive. The latter is the heuristic brainfast, impressionistic, and sometimes irrational. After years of evolution, the brain has become hardwired with mental shortcuts that help us quickly navigate our daily lives. However, they can also distort our thinking and lead to poor decision making. Heuristics are neither good nor bad; the trick, Herbert says, is in recognizing when to question an instant response." Library Journal.

Jacobs, Alan, 1958-

How to think : a survival guide for a world at odds / Alan Jacobs. Convergent Books, 2017. 192 p. **153.4**

1. Thought and thinking. 2. Reasoning. 3. Decision-making 4. Human behavior.

ISBN 9780451499608

LC 2016052795

A distinguished professor and long-time writer for The Atlantic and Christian Century diagnoses the forces that prevent modern people from thinking, including distraction, social bias and fear of rejection and offers hope and tips to regain our mental lives.

"Witty, engaging, and ultimately hopeful, Jacobss guide is sorely needed in a society where partisanship too often trumps the pursuit of knowledge." Publishers Weekly.

Kahneman, Daniel, 1934-

★**Thinking,** fast and slow / Daniel Kahneman. Farrar, Straus and Giroux, 2011. 499 p. : **153.4**

1. Thought and thinking. 2. Decision making. 3. Intuition. 4. Reasoning.

ISBN 9780374275631

LC 2011027143

ALA Notable Book, 2012.

National Academies Communication Award, 2012.

A Nobel Prize-winning psychologist draws on years of research to introduce his "machinery of the mind" model on human decision making to reveal the faults and capabilities of intuitive versus logical thinking, providing insights into such topics as optimism, the unpredictability of happiness and the psychological pitfalls of risk-taking.

Konnikova, Maria

Mastermind : how to think like Sherlock Holmes / Maria Konnikova. Viking Adult, 2013. 320 p. **153.4**

1. Logic 2. Reasoning 3. Brain 4. Characters and characteristics in literature

ISBN 9780670026579

LC 2012035455

Includes index.

The "Literally Psyched" columnist for Scientific American draws on neuroscience and psychology studies while analyzing the deductive strategies used by the character of Sherlock Holmes to counsel readers on how to promote mental strength, clearer observation and effective problem-solving.

Levitin, Daniel J.

★A **field** guide to lies : critical thinking in the information age / Daniel J. Levitin. Dutton, [2016] 304 p. **153.4**

1. Critical thinking. 2. Misinformation 3. Reasoning. 4. Online journalism

ISBN 9780525955221

LC 2016007356

Updated and reprinted with a new introduction in 2017 as Weaponized lies : how to think critically in the post-truth era. ISBN 9781101983829.

Outlines recommendations for critical thinking practices that meet the challenges of the digital age's misinformation, demonstrating the role of science in information literacy while explaining the importance of skeptical reasoning in making decisions based on online information.

Mudd, Philip

The **HEAD** game : high efficiency analytic decision-making and the art of solving complex problems quickly / Philip Mudd. Liveright Publishing Corporation,, 2015 xix, 266 p. ; **153.4**

1. Decision making 2. Problem solving

ISBN 9780871407887

LC 2015006002

A forefront government analyst and secret intelligence commentator draws on his personal expertise in the area of high-stakes decision-making to outline a groundbreaking approach to effective problem-solving.

"How do you make decisions when the stakes are really, really high? The former deputy director of the CIA's Counterterrorist Center and the FBI's National Security Branch, currently director of enterprise risk at SouthernSun asset management, should know." Library Journal.

Nisbett, Richard E.

Mindware : tools for smart thinking / Richard E. Nisbett. Farrar, Straus and Giroux, 2015. 320 p. **153.4**

1. Reasoning. 2. Thought and thinking.

ISBN 9780374112677

LC 2015005007

A renowned psychology expert offers a tool kit for thinking more clearly and making better decisions, explaining how to reframe problems using simplified concepts from science and statistics including the law of large numbers, statistical regression, cost-benefit analysis and causation and correlation.

"Nisbett's goal is to help us look at problems and choices in new ways, to attack them from new analytic angles, to find clarity out of chaos. No psychological self-help book succeeds completely, but this one comes close." Booklist.

Shermer, Michael

The **believing** brain : from ghosts and gods to politics and conspiracies--how we construct beliefs and reinforce them as truths / Michael Shermer. Times Books, c2011. 400 p. **153.4**

1. Belief and doubt. 2. Knowledge theory. 3. Cognitive neuroscience. 4. Neurology.

ISBN 9780805091250

LC 2010030706

Draws on three decades of research to outline a provocative theory about how humans form beliefs about the world, tracing the ways in which the brain finds patterns in sensory data that are then reinforced with meaning, in a report that explains how the author's findings apply to politics, economics and religion.

Sloman, Steven A.

The **knowledge** illusion : why we never think alone / Steven Sloman and Philip Fernbach. Penguin Group USA, 2017. 304 p. **153.4**

1. Cognition 2. Cognitive science 3. Thought and thinking 4. Cognition and culture

ISBN 9780399184352

LC 2016036297

Two cognitive scientists explain how the human brain relies on the communal nature of intelligence and knowledge, constantly gathering information and expertise stored outside our mind and bodies, to overcome its shortcomings of being error prone, irrational and often ignorant.

"In an increasingly polarized culture where certainty reigns supreme, a book advocating intellectual humility and recognition of the limits of understanding feels both revolutionary and necessary. The fact that its a fun and engaging page-turner is a bonus benefit for the reader." Publishers Weekly.

Trivers, Robert

The **folly** of fools : the logic of deceit and self-deception in human life / Robert Trivers. Basic Books, c2011. 352 p. **153.4**

1. Self-deception. 2. Deception -- Psychological aspects. 3. Dishonesty. 4. Psychology.

ISBN 9780465027552

LC 2011028453

Explores the author's theorized evolutionary basis for self-deception, which he says is tied to group conflict, courtship, neurophysiology, and immunology, but can be negated by awareness of it and its results.

Watts, Duncan J., 1971-

Everything is obvious : once you know the answer / Duncan Watts. Crown Business, c2011. 352 p. **153.4**

1. Thought and thinking. 2. Common sense. 3. Reasoning. 4. Social science research

ISBN 9780385531689

LC 2010031550

Discusses how the concept of common sense is inadequate in an increasingly complex world and draws on multiple disciplines to offer insight into the sources of such topics as popularity, economics, and self-deception.

"The author posits that common sense is a shockingly unreliable guide to truth and yet we rely on it virtually to the exclusion of other methods of reasoning. Mr. Watts, a former sociology professor and physicist who is now a researcher for Yahoo, has written a fascinating book that ranges through psychology, economics, marketing and the science of social networks. He is especially interested in the mistakes we make when we reason about how people influence one anothersuch as our tendency to think of groups in terms of representative or important members rather than as whole entities. The enterprise of prediction-making is another casualty of the limits of common sense. Mr. Watts suggests that the entire field of business strategy suffers from a delusion that the future can be forecast with enough numerical precision to enable accurate planning. One solution he endorses is a systematic process of imagining detailed alternative narratives of the future." Wall Street Journal.

153.43 Reasoning

Levitt, Steven D

Think like a freak : the authors of Freakonomics offer to retrain your brain / Steven D. Levitt & Stephen J. Dubner. William

quickly. Written for a less-experienced audience, the book is clear and nontechnical." Choice.

Dweck, Carol S., 1946-
★**Mindset** : the new psychology of success / Carol S. Dweck. Random House, c2006. x, 276 p. ; **153.8**

1. Belief and doubt. 2. Success (Concept) -- Psychological aspects
ISBN 9781400062751
LC 2005046454

An authority in the fields of motivation and developmental psychology reveals how one's personal mindsets affect one's life, identifying two basic mindsets--the fixed and the growth--and how they control every aspect of one's life and explaining how to use the growth mindset at any stage of life to promote success and personal fulfillment.

Iyengar, Sheena
The **art** of choosing / Sheena Iyengar. Twelve, 2010. xiii, 329 p. : **153.8**

1. Options, alternatives, choices. 2. Decision making. 3. Human behavior. 4. Psychology.
ISBN 9780446504102
LC 2009037664

Discusses the cultural and biological factors that influence free will, addressing such issues as whether the desire for choice is innate or created by culture and how much control people have over their choices.

"In The Art of Choosing, a broad and fascinating survey of current research on the subject, Iyengar stitches together personal anecdotes, examples from popular culture, and scientific evidence to explain the complex calculus that goes into our everyday choices, from picking our favorite soda to choosing our medical insurance. She also writes about the ways in which her blindness (Iyengar lost her sight as a teenager) has given her a unique perspective on the subject." Salon.

Johnson, Steven, 1968-
Farsighted : how we make the decisions that matter the most / Steven Johnson. Riverhead Books, [2018] 272 p. **153.8**

1. Cognition 2. Decision-making 3. Thought and thinking 4. Reason
ISBN 9781594488214
LC 2017060305

Draws on lessons from cognitive science, social psychology, military strategy, and other disciplines to discuss how to take a deliberative approach to making consequential, long-term decisions.

"Science writer Johnson (Wonderland: How Play Made the Modern World) looks at decision-making, on both the individual and collective level, persuasively arguing that it should be approached not intuitively, but deliberately, rationally, and even scientifically." Publishers Weekly.

McGinnis, Patrick J.
Fear of missing out : practical decision-making in a world of overwhelming choice / Patrick J. McGinnis. Sourcebooks, 2020 xvii, 236 p. : **153.8**

1. Fear of missing out. 2. Decision making. 3. Time management 4. Stress management
ISBN 9781492694946
LC 2019053664

A venture capitalist and private equity investor shares the scientific secrets to make any decision simple--while simultaneously eliminating your stress.

"This is a useful one-stop shop for those looking to take a decisive stand against the fear of what could have been." Publishers Weekly

McKeown, Greg
Essentialism : the disciplined pursuit of less / Greg McKeown. Crown Business, 2014 260 p. : **153.8**

1. Choice (Psychology) 2. Decision making 3. Essentialism (Philosophy)
ISBN 9780804137386
LC 2013038729

Outlines a systematic framework for enabling greater productivity without overworking, sharing strategies on how to eliminate unnecessary tasks while streamlining essential employee functions.

"Punctuated with zippy, thoughtful one-liners, this guide to doing 'less but better' offers strategies for determining what is truly necessary, and shedding what is not. Too many people fall for the having-it-all myth, and would benefit from shifting from a non-essentialist mindset (unable to distinguish and parse out the truly important) to an essentialist one (capable of identifying the goal), contends McKeown. Instead of attempting to achieve everything, readers need to figure out how to do the 'right thing the right way at the right time.'" Publishers Weekly.

Partnoy, Frank
Wait : the art and science of delay / Frank Partnoy. PublicAffairs, c2012. 336 p. **153.8**

1. Procrastination. 2. Decision-making. 3. Thought and thinking. 4. Reasoning.
ISBN 9781610390040
LC 2012010970

The renowned financial commentator and author of F.I.A.S.C.O. explains the mysteries and transformative power of the well-time pause to reveal how delay can improve decision making, sharing provocative insights to demonstrate how to assess how long a decision can be delayed and how to avoid making "gut instinct" snap judgments.

Vanderbilt, Tom
You may also like : taste in an age of endless choice / Tom Vanderbilt. Alfred A. Knopf, [2016] 368 p. **153.8**

1. Options, alternatives, choices 2. Consumers' preferences 3. Social media 4. Brand choice
ISBN 9780307958242
LC 2015026997

From the best-selling author of Traffic, a brilliant and entertaining exploration of our personal tastes--why we like the things we like, and what it says about us.

"Essential for readers who are interested in getting a glimpse of the decision-making process at influential online media companies, as well as those who are interested in the processes that govern individual preferences and taste making." Library Journal.

153.9 Intelligence and aptitudes

Beilock, Sian
Choke : what the secrets of the brain reveal about getting it right when you have to / Sian Beilock. Free Press, 2010. viii, 294 p. : **153.9**

1. Failure (Psychology) 2. Performance -- Psychological aspects. 3. Success (Concept) -- Psychological aspects 4. Cognitive neuroscience.
ISBN 9781416596172
LC 2010010595

Includes index.

Explains the brain science behind why some people "choke" under pressure while other people "click," examining how attention and working memory guide human performance; how experience and practice, innate factors and brain development interact to create our abilities; and how these interconnected elements react to stress.

Bloom, Harold, 1930-2019

Genius : a mosaic of one hundred exemplary creative minds / Harold Bloom. Warner Books, 2002. xviii, 814 p. : **153.9**

1. Genius. 2. Gifted persons.

ISBN 0446527173

LC 2002016808

"Although the book is a delight to read, its real value lies in the author's ability to provoke the reader into thinking about literature, genius, and related topics. No similar work discusses literary genius in this way or covers this many writers." Library Journal.

Epstein, David J., 1983-

★**Range** : why generalists triumph in a specialized world / David Epstein. Riverhead Books, 2019. 352 p. **153.9**

1. Success (Concept) 2. Ability 3. Learning 4. Successful people.

ISBN 9780735214484

LC 2018051571

Shares counterintuitive advice on the most effective path to success in any domain while revealing the essential contributions of generalist, not specialist, team members.

"Epstein follows up The Sports Gene, which explored the roots of elite sport performance, with this intriguing analysis of successful artists, musicians, inventors, forecasters, scientists, and athletes. The author's revelation is that generalists, not specialists, are more primed to excel, with generalists often finding their path late and participating in many interests." Library Journal.

Ericsson, K. Anders (Karl Anders), 1947-

Peak : secrets from the new science of expertise / Anders Ericsson and Robert Pool. Houghton Mifflin Harcourt, 2016. xxiii, 307 p. ; **153.9**

1. Ability 2. Expertise 3. Performance -- Psychological aspects

ISBN 9780544456235

LC 2015042796

"An Eamon Dolan book."

Includes index.

Draws on the examples of chess champions, violin virtuosos, star athletes and memory mavens to outline a powerful approach to learning that enables readers to develop proficiency through strategic goal setting, self-motivation and feedback exercises.

Gould, Stephen Jay, 1941-

The **mismeasure** of man / Stephen Jay Gould. Norton, 1981. 352 p. : **153.9**

1. Intelligence tests -- History. 2. Intelligence -- Definition. 3. Ability testing -- History. 4. Personality tests.

ISBN 0393014894

LC 81038430

National Book Critics Circle Award for Non-Fiction, 1981.

Exposes the fatal flaws in the ranking of people according to their supposed gifts and limits by discussing the development of the theory of limits and by reanalyzing the data on which it is based.

Kurzweil, Ray

★The **singularity** is near : when humans transcend biology / Ray Kurzweil. Viking, 2005. xvii, 652 p. : **153.9**

1. Brain -- Evolution. 2. Human evolution. 3. Genetics. 4. Nanotechnology.

ISBN 0670033847

LC 2004061231

A controversial scientific vision predicts a time in which humans and machines will merge and create a new form of non-biological intelligence, explaining how the occurrence will solve such issues as pollution, hunger, and aging.

"Anyone can grasp Mr. Kurzweil's main idea: that mankind's technological knowledge has been snowballing, with dizzying prospects for the future. The basics are clearly expressed. But for those more knowledgeable and inquisitive, the author argues his case in fascinating detail." New York Times.

Murdoch, Stephen, 1968-

IQ : a smart history of a failed idea / Stephen Murdoch. J. Wiley and Sons, 2007. xiv, 269 p. ; **153.9**

1. Intelligence -- History. 2. Intelligence tests -- History. 3. Standardized tests. 4. Educational tests and measurements.

ISBN 9780471699774

LC 2006032488

A thought-provoking study examines the history, politics, and implications of intelligence testing, from its origins to the present day, and discusses its powerful impact on both public policy and private lives, the well-documented shortcomings of testing, and suggestions for developing an entire new model for measuring intelligence.

154.2 The subconscious

Bargh, John A

Before you know it : the unconscious reasons we do what we do / John Bargh. Touchstone, 2017 320 p. **154.2**

1. Subconsciousness. 2. Cognition. 3. Motivation (Psychology). 4. Human behavior.

ISBN 9781501101212

LC 2017008149

A leading expert on the unconscious human mind draws on 20 years of research to present a tour of the influences that shape everyday behavior, combining engaging anecdotes with the stories of remarkable discoveries about the role of science in everything from relationships and parenting to consumer behavior and business.

"In this impressive debut, Bargh, a professor of social psychology at Yale University, dives deep into human behavior and social psychology to unlock the enigmatic human unconscious." Publishers Weekly.

Kandel, Eric R.

The **age** of insight : the quest to understand the unconscious in art, mind, and brain : from Vienna 1900 to the present / Eric R. Kandel. Random House, 2011. 448 p. **154.2**

1. Subconsciousness. 2. Perception. 3. Science and art. 4. Neuroscience. 5. Vienna, Austria -- History -- 20th century.

ISBN 9781400068715

LC 2011025274

A Nobel Prize-winning neuroscientist and author of In Search of Memory documents the work of five leading minds including Sigmund Freud and Gustave Klimt in 1900 Vienna, revealing how their critical breakthroughs in science, medicine and art laid the groundwork for present-day discoveries in brain science.

Mlodinow, Leonard, 1954-

Subliminal : how your unconscious mind rules your behavior /

Leonard Mlodinow. Pantheon Books, c2012. 272 p. **154.2**

1. Subconsciousness. 2. Psychology. 3. Probabilities. 4. Brain.
ISBN 9780307378217

LC 2011048098

An examination of the ways in which the unconscious mind shapes everyday life traces recent scientific advances to reveal the pivotal role of the subliminal mind in influencing experiences and relationships.

Tallis, Frank

Hidden minds : a history of the unconscious / Frank Tallis. Arcade Pub., c2002. xiii, 194 p. ; **154.2**

1. Subconsciousness. 2. Consciousness 3. Brain 4. Psychoanalysis
ISBN 1559706430

LC 2002074566

The author confirms the existence of the unconscious mind and traces its importance, using hypnosis, psychoanalysis, subliminal manipulation, dreams, and hard science to trace the existence of this "hidden mind" within each individual.

154.6 Sleep phenomena

Freud, Sigmund, 1856-1939

★The **interpretation** of dreams / Sigmund Freud ; translated by Joyce Crick ; with an introduction and notes by Ritchie Robertson. Oxford University Press, 2008, c1999. liv, 458 p. : **154.6**

1. Dream interpretation 2. Psychoanalysis
ISBN 9780199537587

LC bl2010001661

Reprint. Originally published: 1999.

Based on the original text, unmodified by Freud's later additions, presents a new translation of his psychoanalytic study of the function, sources, nature, and characteristics of dreams.

155.2 Individual psychology

Bluestein, Jane

The **perfection** deception : why trying to be perfect is sabotaging your relationships, making you sick, and holding your happiness hostage / Jane Bluestein. Health Communications, Inc., 2015 xii, 299 p. ; **155.2**

1. Perfectionism (Personality trait). 2. Psychology. 3. Self-help techniques.
ISBN 0757318258

LC 2015027944

"According to educator and author Bluestein (Creating Emotionally Safe Schools), striving for excellence and striving for perfection are two very different animals. While the former means dedicating oneself to doing one's best, the latter involves being motivated by something artificial and unrealistic." Publishers Weekly

Cain, Susan

Quiet : the power of introverts in a world that can't stop talking / Susan Cain. Crown, 2012. 320 p. **155.2**

1. Interpersonal relations. 2. Introversion. 3. Extroversion. 4. Introverts.
ISBN 9780307352149

LC 2010053204

ALA Notable Book, 2013

Demonstrates how introverted people are misunderstood and undervalued in modern culture, charting the rise of extrovert ideology while sharing anecdotal examples of how to use introvert talents to adapt to various situations.

Crawford, Matthew B.

The **world** beyond your head : on becoming an individual in an age of distraction / Matthew B. Crawford. Farrar Straus & Giroux, 2015. 288 p. **155.2**

1. Skills. 2. Philosophy. 3. Individualism -- Social aspects. 4. Attention.
ISBN 9780374292980

LC 2014043840

Investigates the challenge of mastering one's own mind by showing that our current crisis of attention is only superficially the result of digital technology, and certain assumptions at the root of Western culture are the root of the cause.

"This illuminating work will appeal to students of philosophy and sociology, as well as fans of good cultural analysis." Library Journal.

Dimitrius, Jo-Ellan

Reading people : how to understand people and predict their behavior-- anytime, anyplace / Jo-Ellan Dimitrius and Mark Mazzarella. Random House, c1998. xiv, 281 p. ; **155.2**

1. Body language. 2. Personality assessment 3. Physiognomy.
ISBN 0345425871

LC 98004934

In a New York Times best-seller, the nation's leading jury consultant shows readers how to analyze others' true thoughts and predict their behavior by deciphering the hidden signals they give off.

"Dimitrius shares the people-reading techniques she developed over 15 years as a jury consultant. In so doing, she provides a wealth of tips and strategies for ferreting out people's real viewpoints, motives and character traits." Publishers Weekly.

Ehrenreich, Barbara

★**Bright-sided** : how the relentless promotion of positive thinking has undermined America / Barbara Ehrenreich. Henry Holt and Company, 2009. 256 p. **155.2**

1. Optimism -- United States. 2. Happiness. 3. Self-confidence. 4. Success in business 5. United States -- Social conditions.
ISBN 9780805087499

LC 2009023588

The best-selling author of Bait and Switch exposes the downside of America's penchant for positive thinking, which she believes leads to self-blame and a preoccupation with stamping out "negative" thoughts on a personal level, and, on a national level, has brought on economic disaster.

"The author's tough-minded and convincing broadside raises troubling questions about many aspects of contemporary American life. Bright, incisive, provocative thinking." Kirkus.

Gladwell, Malcolm, 1963-

David and Goliath : underdogs, misfits, and the art of battling giants / Malcolm Gladwell. Little Brown & Co 2013. 304 p. **155.2**

1. Success (Concept) 2. Goals and objectives 3. Strength and weakness
ISBN 9780316204361

LC 2013941807

The best-selling author of Outliers uncovers the hidden rules that shape the balance between the weak and the mighty, the powerful and the dispossessed.

"Gladwell rewards readers with moving stories, surprising insights and consistently provocative ideas." Kirkus.

Goldsmith, Marshall

Triggers : creating behavior that lasts-- becoming the person you want to be / Marshall Goldsmith and Mark Reiter. Crown Business, 2015 xix, 244 p. : **155.2**

1. Adjustment (Psychology). 2. Change (Psychology). 3. Positive psychology.

ISBN 9780804141239

LC bl2015018578

Includes index.

Demonstrates how to recognize and overcome the emotional and psychological triggers that set off a reaction or a behavior that often is detrimental in order to achieve meaningful and sustained change.

Helgoe, Laurie A.

Introvert power : why your inner life is your hidden strength / Laurie Helgoe. Sourcebooks, c2008. xxiv, 256 p. : **155.2**

1. Introversion. 2. Introverts.

ISBN 1402211171

LC 2008004967

Shows readers how to use introversion not as a weakness but as a source of power.

"The author's voice is vivid and engaging, and she skillfully draws real-life examples of awkward scenarios introverts find themselves in when forced to play a role in society or the workplace. Readers will find much insight, as well as a comforting sense of being understood and validated." Publishers Weekly.

Keltner, Dacher

Born to be good : the science of a meaningful life / Dacher Keltner. W. W. Norton, 2009. 352 p. **155.2**

1. Emotions -- Physiological aspects 2. Helpfulness 3. Altruism 4. Cooperation

ISBN 9780393065121

LC 2008042492

"An optimistic assessment of humanity's biological predisposition for goodness draws on scientific findings, personal narrative, and eastern philosophy to explain how positive emotions are a key component of ethical action, the establishment of cooperative societies, and living a happy life."

"A landmark book in the science of emotion and its implications for ethics and human universals, this is essential for all libraries." Library Journal.

McKay, Matthew

★**Self-esteem** : a proven program of cognitive techniques for assessing, improving, & maintaining your self-esteem / Matthew McKay, PHD, Patrick Fanning. New Harbinger Publications, Inc., 2016. vii, 358 p. : **155.2**

1. Self-esteem. 2. Self-help psychology

ISBN 9781626253933

LC 2016461087

The go-to guide for those seeking to increase their sense of self-worth. This fully revised new edition features an innovative application of acceptance and commitment therapy (ACT) to self-esteem and utilizes updated cognitive behavioral therapy (CBT) to help readers create positive change and thrive.

Mischel, Walter

The **marshmallow** test : mastering self-control / Walter Mischel. Little, Brown and Company, 2014. 304 p. **155.2**

1. Self-control 2. Developmental psychology 3. Psychology 4. Decision-making

ISBN 9780316230872

LC 2014018058

A psychologist known for a famous delayed-gratification test discusses whether willpower can be taught and offers tips and strategies for improving and mastering self-control and applying it to everyday challenges like losing weight, quitting smoking and overcoming heartbreak.

Moran, Joe, 1970-

Shrinking violets : the secret life of shyness / Joe Moran. Yale University Press, 2017. 272 p. ; **155.2**

1. Bashfulness. 2. Bashfulness -- Social aspects.

ISBN 9780300222821

LC 2016948565

"First published in the English language in a different form by Profile Books."--Title page verso.

A deeply perceptive and beautifully written cultural history of shyness, from one of our most astute observers of the everyday.

Myers, Isabel Briggs

Gifts differing : understanding personality type / Isabel Briggs Myers with Peter B. Myers. Davies-Black Pub., c1995. xv, 228 p. ; **155.2**

1. Typology (Psychology) 2. Myers-Briggs Type Indicator

ISBN 9780891060741

LC 95004184

Originally published: Palo Alto, CA : Consulting Psychologists Press, c1980.

The classic work on the 16 major personality types as identified in the Myers-Briggs Type Indicator.

Northrup, Christiane

Dodging energy vampires : an empath's guide to evading relationships that drain you and restoring your health and power / Christiane Northrup, M.D. Hay House, Inc., 2018. xii, 230 p. ; **155.2**

1. Empathy 2. Mental health 3. Sensitivity (Personality trait) 4. Well-being

ISBN 9781401954772

LC 2017048779

A guide to identifying and avoiding the most common types of "energy vampires," offers tactics for leaving harmful relationships behind, regaining energy, and becoming happier, wealthier, and more vibrant.

Pinker, Steven, 1954-

The **blank** slate : the modern denial of human nature / Steven Pinker. Viking, 2002. xvi, 509 p. : **155.2**

1. Heredity and environment (Psychology) 2. Human nature. 3. Genetic psychology. 4. Evolution.

ISBN 0670031518

LC 2002022719

Pulitzer Prize for General Nonfiction finalist

"The author attacks the notion that an infant's mind is a blank slate, arguing instead that human beings have an inherited universal structure shaped by the demands made upon the species for survival, albeit with plenty of room for cultural and individual variation." Publishers Weekly.

Rudder, Christian
Dataclysm : who we are (when we think no one's looking) / Christian Rudder. Crown, 2014. 272 p. **155.2**

1. Social psychology 2. Human behavior. 3. Behavioral assessment. 4. Social media.
ISBN 9780385347372
LC 2014007364

An irreverent, provocative, and visually fascinating look at what our online lives reveal about who we really are--and how this deluge of data will transform the science of human behavior. Big Data is used to spy on us, hire and fire us, and sell us things we don't need. In Dataclysm, Christian Rudder puts this flood of information to an entirely different use: understanding human nature. Drawing on terabytes of data from Twitter, Facebook, Reddit, OkCupid, and many other sites, Rudder examines the terrain of human experience. He charts the rise and fall of America's most reviled word through Google Search, examines the new dynamics of collaborative rage on Twitter, and traces human migration over time, showing how groups of people move from certain small towns to the same big cities across the globe. And he grapples with the challenge of maintaining privacy in a world where these explorations are possible. Audacious, entertaining, and illuminating, Dataclysm is a portrait of our essential selves--and a first look at a revolution in the making.

"Demographers, entrepreneurs, students of history and sociology, and ordinary citizens alike will find plenty of provocations and, yes, much data in Rudder's well-argued, revealing pages." Kirkus.

Seligman, Martin E. P.
★**Learned** optimism: how to change your mind and your life / Martin E.P. Seligman. Vintage Books, 2006. x, 319 p. ; **155.2**

1. Optimism. 2. Self-realization.
ISBN 1400078393
LC 2006277713

Originally published: Pocket Books, 1998.

An authority on cognitive psychology and motivation documents the positive effects of optimism on the quality of life and provides a program of specific exercises designed to break the pessimism habit while developing an optimistic outlook.

Shenk, David, 1966-
The **genius** in all of us : why everything you've been told about genetics, talent, and IQ is wrong / David Shenk. Random House Inc., 2010. 288 p. **155.2**

1. Ability. 2. Genetics. 3. Heredity and environment (Psychology) 4. Gifted persons.
ISBN 9780385523653
LC 2009018376

Challenges common beliefs that human potential is largely determined by genetics and other biological factors, drawing on a variety of scientific disciplines to explain how to tap innate abilities that have been influenced by environmental factors.

Storr, Will
Selfie : how we became so self-obsessed and what it's doing to us / Will Storr. Overlook Press, 2018. 416 p. **155.2**

1. Self. 2. Identity (Psychology). 3. Perfectionism. 4. Self-fulfillment.
ISBN 9781468315899
LC bl2017052046

Includes index.

The Amnesty International Award-winning investigative journalist and author of The Unpersuadables examines how our world's establishment of an impossible standard of perfection is leading to unprecedented levels of depression and suicide, tracing the sources of unrealistic human ideals from the ancient world to the present realities of hyper-individualism.

Stout, Martha, 1953-
Outsmarting the sociopath next door : how to protect yourself against a ruthless manipulator / Martha Stout, Ph.D. Harmony Books, 2020 294 p. ; **155.2**

1. Manipulative behavior -- Prevention 2. Psychopaths 3. Control (Psychology)
ISBN 9780307589071
LC 2019024151

"From Dr. Martha Stout's influential work The Sociopath Next Door, we learned how to identify a sociopath. Now she tells us what to actually do about it. Using the many chilling and often heartbreaking emails and letters she has received over the years, Dr. Stout uncovers the psychology behind the sociopath's methods and provides concrete guidelines to help navigate these dangerous interactions".-- Provided by publisher.

Wicks, Robert J
Night call : embracing compassion and hope in a troubled world / Robert J. Wicks Oxford University Press, 2018 xxviii, 248 p. ; **155.2**

1. Resilience (Personality trait). 2. Compassion. 3. Counseling. 4. Social service.
ISBN 9780190669638
LC 2017000502

"Night Call offers important insights into the heaviness of heart that can affect a doctor's psyche when caring for patients who are ill or dying. It opens the philosophical discussion about the need for physician self-care, and provides excellent strategies and suggestions for practicing self-care." Choice

155.3 Sex psychology; psychology of people by gender or sex, by sexual orientation

Chemaly, Soraya L.
Rage becomes her : the power of women's anger / Soraya Chemaly. Atria Books, 2018. 416 p. **155.3**

1. Feminism 2. Social change 3. Anger in women 4. Sexism
ISBN 9781501189555
LC 2018010867

The director of the Women's Media Center Speech Project urges 21st-century women to embrace their anger and harness it as a tool for lasting personal and societal change.

Eldredge, Niles
★**Why** we do it : rethinking sex and the selfish gene / Niles Eldredge. Norton, 2004. 269 p. ; **155.3**

1. Sex (Biology) 2. Sociobiology. 3. Human evolution.
ISBN 0393050823
LC 2003027564

"This book, while written for the lay reader, is appropriate for a scientific audience as well. It could be used as supplementary reading in college courses in animal behavior." Science Books & Films.

Filipovic, Jill
The **H-spot** : the feminist pursuit of happiness / Jill Filipovic. Nation Books, 2017. 288 p. **155.3**

1. Women -- Psychology 2. Feminist theory 3. Happiness 4. Gender

role
ISBN 9781568585475

LC 2016050782

Challenging misperceptions about how today's feminists must work harder or make difficult compromises to achieve fulfillment and happiness, a former Guardian columnist and senior political writer for Cosmopolitan.com identifies irregular cultural and professional expectations that continue to enforce gender divides.

"A timely, enlightening exploration of what American women truly want and need to live purposeful, fulfilling, happy lives." Kirkus.

Fine, Cordelia

Testosterone rex : myths of sex, science, and society / Cordelia Fine. W.W. Norton & Company, [2017] 320 p. **155.3**

1. Brain -- Sex differences. 2. Gender role 3. Sex differences (Psychology) 4. Cognitive science.
ISBN 9780393082081

LC 2016031608

Royal Society General Prizes for Science Books, 2017

The acclaimed author of Delusions of Gender challenges conventional beliefs about evolutionary factors that are used to justify gender politics, outlining lively arguments against cultural stereotypes, in a call for a more equal society that recognizes the potential of both sexes.

Hartley, Gemma, 1988-

Fed up : emotional labor, women, and the way forward / Gemma Hartley. HarperOne, [2018] 272 p. **155.3**

1. Gender role -- Psychological aspects 2. Stress in women 3. Emotions 4. Division of labor
ISBN 9780062855985

LC 2018033285

Asserts that carrying the thankless day-to-day anticipating of needs and solving of problems large and small is adversely affecting women's lives and feeding gender inequality, and shows the way forward for better balancing their lives.

Jamieson, Alexandra, 1975-

Women, food, and desire : embrace your cravings, make peace with food, reclaim your body / Alexandra Jamieson. Gallery Books, 2015 ix, 243 p. ; **155.3**

1. Body image 2. Self-actualization (Psychology) 3. Women -- Nutrition 4. Women -- Psychology
ISBN 9781476765044

LC 2014016467

A transformational health expert and co-star of the documentary Super Size Me describes how actually listening to our body's cravings can help cleanse the nutritional, emotional, physical and mental blocks that are preventing happiness.

Lerner, Harriet Goldhor

The **dance** of deception : pretending and truth-telling in women's lives / Harriet Goldhor Lerner. Harper Collins Publishers, c1993. xvi, 254 p. ; **155.3**

1. Women -- Psychology. 2. Deception. 3. Truthfulness and falsehood.
ISBN 0060168161

LC 92053376

"Patriarchal culture teaches women to pretend and sometimes deceive, Lerner says, and in her study of the role this dissembling plays in women's lives, she shows how 'pretending reflects deep prohibitions, real and imagined, against a more direct and forthright assertion of self.' . She acknowledges that truth telling is not easy, yet her discussion of the many ways women lie and how lying affects them clearly shows the benefits of honesty and makes her prescription appealing." Booklist.

Pincott, J. (Jena)

Do gentlemen really prefer blondes? : bodies, behavior and brains : the science behind sex, love, and attraction / Jena Pincott. Delacorte Press, 2008. xvi, 351 p. : **155.3**

1. Sexual attraction. 2. Sex (Psychology) 3. Dating (Social customs) 4. Mate selection.
ISBN 9780385342155

LC 2008023933

Based on current research in biology, evolutionary psychology, neurology, and cognitive science, author Jena Pincott answers common questions about human sexual behavior and offers advice in understanding successful relationships.

155.4 Psychology of specific ages

Carey, Tanith

What's my child thinking? : practical child psychology for modern parents / Tanith Carey ; contributing editor, Eileen Kennedy-Moore, PhD.. DK, 2019 256 p. : **155.4**

1. Child psychology 2. Parenting 3. Parent and child
ISBN 9781465479372

LC 2018287451

"For ages 2 to 7" -- on cover.

"Find out what your child really means when he says 'Look what I did', 'But I'm not tired,' or 'You're embarrassing me,' and discover what's really going on when he can't express himself at all. Using more than 100 everyday scenarios, the book leads you through each one step by step, explaining not only your child's behavior and the psychology behind it but also your own feelings as a parent. It then gives instant recommendations for what you could say and do in response to best resolve the situation. Covering all your child's developmental milestones from ages 2 to 7 years, What's My Child Thinking? covers important issues, such as temper tantrums, friendships (real and imaginary), sibling rivalry, aggressive behavior, and peer pressure. There's also a bank of practical "survival guides" for critical times, such as traveling in the car, eating out, and going online safely. Rooted in evidence-based clinical psychology and championing positive parenting, What's My Child Thinking? will help you tune in to your child's innermost thoughts and be the parent you want to be."--Amazon.com.

Elkind, David, 1931-

★The **power** of play : how spontaneous, imaginative activities lead to happier, healthier children / David Elkind. Da Capo Lifelong, c2007. xii, 240 p. ; **155.4**

1. Play -- Psychological aspects.
ISBN 0738210536

LC 2006035592

"With clarity and insight, Elkind calls for society to bring back long recesses, encourage imagination and let children develop their minds at a natural pace." Publishers Weekly.

Gopnik, Alison

The **gardener** and the carpenter : what the new science of child development tells us about the relationship between parents and children / Alison Gopnik. Farrar, Straus and Giroux, 2016. 224 p. **155.4**

1. Developmental psychology. 2. Child psychology. 3. Parenting. 4.

Parent and child
ISBN 9780374229702

LC 2015048667

A developmental psychologist uses natural history and the latest scientific research to demonstrate how the modern style of parenting, one of obsessively controlling offspring with goal-oriented labor, is bad for both the child and the parents.

"A highly thoughtful and entertaining treatment of a subject that merits serious consideration." Kirkus.

Gopnik, Alison

The **scientist** in the crib : what early learning tells us about the mind / Alison Gopnik, Andrew N. Meltzoff, Patricia K. Kuhl. Harper Perennial, 2001, c1999. xv, 279 p. ; **155.4**

1. Cognition in children. 2. Cognition. 3. Learning, Psychology of.
ISBN 0688177883

LC bl2007016496

Originally published: New York : William Morrow, c1999.

A exciting review of the newest research on learning and infancy, drawing from hundreds of case studies, shows how children by the age of three are virtual learning machines and discusses how parents can help this learning process.

"The authors examine how children learn to understand and use language, control their emotions and arouse the emotions of others, and establish relationships. Prospective and actual parents stand to learn much that may be helpful to them and their children from this lively book." Booklist.

Kennedy-Moore, Eileen

★**Kid** confidence : help your child make friends, build resilience, and develop real self-esteem / Eileen Kennedy-Moore, PhD. New Harbinger Publications, 2019 ix, 220 p. ; **155.4**

1. Self-esteem in children 2. Self-actualization (Psychology) 3. Interpersonal relations 4. Parenting
ISBN 9781684030491

LC 2018031430

"Help your child cultivate real, lasting confidence! In Kid Confidence, a licensed clinical psychologist and parenting expert offers practical, evidence-based parenting strategies to help kids foster satisfying relationships, develop competence, and make choices that fit who they are and want to become. As parents, it's heartbreaking to hear children say negative things about themselves. But as children grow older and begin thinking about the world in more complex ways, they also become more self-critical. Alarmingly, studies show that self-esteem, for many children, takes a sharp drop starting around age eight, and this decline continues into the early teen years. So, how can you turn the tide on this upsetting trend and help your child build genuine self-esteem? With this guide, you'll learn that self-esteem isn't about telling kids they're 'special.' It's about helping them embrace the freedom that comes with a quiet ego--a way of being in the world that isn'tpreoccupied with self-judgment, and instead embraces a compassionate view of oneself and others that allows for both present awareness and personal growth. When kids are less focused on evaluating and comparing themselves with others, they are freer to empathize with others, embrace learning, and connect with the values that are bigger than themselves. You'll also discover how your child's fundamental needs for connection, competence, and choice are essential for real self-esteem. Connection involves building meaningful and satisfying relationships that create a sense of belonging. Competence means building tangible skills. And choice is about being able to make decisions, figure out what matters, and choose to act in ways that are consistent with personal values. When children are able to fulfill these three basic needs, the question of 'Am I good enough?' is less likely to come up. If your child is suffering from low self-esteem, you need a nuanced parenting approach. Let this book guide you as you help your child create unshakeable confidence and lasting well-being".-- Provided by publisher.

Lancaster, Jen, 1967-

Welcome to the United States of anxiety : observations from a reforming neurotic / Jen Lancaster. Little A, 2020 239 p. **155.4**

1. Lancaster, Jen, 1967- 2. Anxiety 3. Social media 4. Social media -- Psychological aspects. 5. Happiness 6. United States -- Social life and customs
ISBN 9781542007948

LC bl2020033423

Jen Lancaster is here to take a hard look at our elevating anxieties, and with self-deprecating wit and levelheaded wisdom, she charts a path out of the quagmire that keeps us frightened of the future and ashamed of our imperfectly perfect human lives. Take a deep breath,andher advice, and you just might get through a holiday dinner without wanting to disown your uncle.

"Lancaster is very funny, and her insightful, always entertaining critique may motivate readers to back away from social media, if only a little bit." Publishers Weekly

Linn, Susan

The **case** for make believe : saving play in a commercialized world / Susan Linn. New Press, 2008. xi, 258 p. ; **155.4**

1. Play -- Psychological aspects. 2. Play environments 3. Advertising and children.
ISBN 9781565849709

LC 2007042435

Describes the need and desire by children to live and play creatively, and discusses how commercial corporations and branding are curbing creative play to increase profitability.

"Puppeteer and therapist Linn draws on years of work at Boston Children's Hospital to make a thoughtful case for creative play. She distinguishes between children who are familiar with concepts of imagination and make-believe versus those who know only how to play with manufactured toys linked to media campaigns or within the constructs of rule-driven environments. of this will be news to most parents, but Linn seeks to discover what it means for children to no longer spend time pretending to be someone or somewhere else. Her research is comprehensive, her firsthand knowledge is impressive, and her examples are damning in their conclusions." Booklist.

Louv, Richard

Last child in the woods : saving our children from nature-deficit disorder / Richard Louv. Algonquin Books of Chapel Hill, 2008. xii, 390 p. **155.4**

1. Nature -- Psychological aspects. 2. Environment and children. 3. Child development. 4. Outdoor recreation.
ISBN 9781565126053

LC 2007049665

Warning parents about the dangers of allowing children to grow up without contact with natural areas, this provocative study shows how this lack of connection to nature causes obesity, distraction, and depression and offers helpful suggestions on how to develop an environment-based educational program that can enhance children's problem-solving, critical thinking, and decision-making skills.

Seligman, Martin E. P.

The **optimistic** child : a proven program to safeguard children against depression and build lifelong resilience / Martin E.P. Seligman, with Karen Reivich, Lisa Jaycox, and Jane Gillham. Houghton Mifflin Co., c2007. 342 p. : **155.4**

1. Child rearing. 2. Optimism in children. 3. Positive psychology. 4. Resilience (Personality trait) in children.
ISBN 0618918094

LC 2007025480

Originally published: 1995. With new foreword and afterword.

In the face of increasing levels of depression affecting American children, a new edition of the best-selling guide to preventing childhood depression shows parents and educators how to instill optimism, resilience, and confidence in children, enabling them to feel self-reliant, boost self-esteem, and perform better in school.

Shankar, Shalini, 1972-

Beeline : what spelling bees reveal about generation Z's new path to success / Shalini Shankar. Basic Books, [2019] 336 p. **155.4**

1. National Spelling Bee. 2. Generation Z. 3. Spelling bees -- Social aspects. 4. Performance in children. 5. Spelling ability.
ISBN 9780465094523

LC 2018043156

School Library Journal (March 2019)

Uses spelling bees as a window into the diverse traits of Generation Z, arguing that the generation displays a sophisticated understanding of self-promotion, self-direction, and social mobility.

" In this revealing look at how the youngest generation is adapting to face an exceptionally competitive world, Shankar shows that these bright, dedicated competitors give us many reasons to feel hopeful." Booklist.

Siegel, Daniel J., 1957-

★The **yes** brain : how to cultivate courage, curiosity, and resilience in your child / Daniel J. Siegel, M.D. and Tina Payne Bryson, Ph.D. Bantam, 2018 xii, 184 p. : **155.4**

1. Resilience (Personality trait) in children 2. Child rearing 3. Parenting
ISBN 9780399594663

LC 2017037802

The authors counsel caregivers and educators on how to help children reach their full potential by cultivating mental receptivity, sharing scripts, ideas and activities for transitioning resistant children away from reactive states and into mindsets that are more curious, creative and resilient.

Stixrud, William R.

The **self-driven** child : the science and sense of giving your kids more control over their lives / William Stixrud, PhD, and Ned Johnson. Viking, 2018. viii, 367 p. **155.4**

1. Achievement motivation in children 2. Child rearing 3. Parenting 4. Self-reliance in children
ISBN 9780735222519

LC bl2018064074

A clinical psychologist and a test-prep expert combine cutting-edge brain science with insights from their work with families to outline a case for giving children more freedom to unleash their full potential.

Tuck, Shonna L.

Getting from me to we : how to help young children fit in and make friends / Shonna Tuck, M.A., SLP. Woodbine House, 2015 xix, 219 p. ; **155.4**

1. Adjustment (Psychology) in children 2. Child development 3. Friendship in children
ISBN 9781606132692

LC 2015023676

"This book joins Ross W. Greene's The Explosive Child as a helpful tool to aid those who love and work with children with social issues." Library Journal.

155.43 Children by gender or sex

Parker, Kate T.

Strong is the new pretty : a celebration of girls being themselves / Kate T. Parker. Workman Publishing, [2017] v, 250 p. : **155.43**

1. Girls -- Psychology. 2. Self-confidence in girls. 3. Resilience (Personal quality) 4. Creativity.
ISBN 9780761189138

LC 2017007862

"Parker shows how, whether smiling, looking tough, or helping one another out, these girls of various ages, pasts, and abilities are strong. Positively moving and totally glorious." Booklist.

155.44 Children by status and relationships

Wright, Lawrence, 1947-

Twins : and what they tell us about who we are / Lawrence Wright. J. Wiley, 1997. vi, 202 p. **155.44**

1. Twins -- Psychology. 2. Heredity and environment (Psychology) 3. Nature and nurture. 4. Human ecology
ISBN 0471252204

LC 97038827

"Wright does an admirable job of sorting through the differing research in a well-reasoned, clearheaded manner." Publishers Weekly.

155.45 Exceptional children children by social and economic levels, by ethnic or national group

Ruthsatz, Joanne

The **prodigy's** cousin : the family link between autism and extraordinary talent / Joanne Ruthsatz and Kimberly Stephens. Current, 2016. x, 273 p. ; **155.45**

1. Autism 2. Child prodigies 3. Children with autism 4. Heredity and environment (Psychology)
ISBN 9781617230189

In a scientific detective story, the author, along with a reporter, investigates more than 30 child prodigies, all of whom had extraordinary memories and a keen eye for detail, and discovers a genetic link between prodigy and autism, confirming her long-held hunch and an important piece of the puzzle.

"People with an interest in autism or prodigies will be intrigued by the interesting hypothesis posed by this psychologist-journalist duo, who provide a lovely epilogue about what their young prodigies are doing today." Booklist.

Winner, Ellen

Gifted children : myths and realities / Ellen Winner. Basic

Books, c1996. xi, 449 p. : **155.45**

1. Gifted children.
ISBN 9780465017591

LC 95049279

Uses case studies to debunk nine myths of academic, musical, and artistic giftedness.

155.5 Psychology of young people twelve to twenty

Damour, Lisa, 1970-

★**Under** pressure : confronting the epidemic of stress and anxiety in girls / Lisa Damour. Ballantine Books, 2019 xxi, 261 p. ; **155.5**

1. Anxiety in adolescence. 2. Stress in adolescence. 3. Stress management. 4. Teenage girls -- Psychology.
ISBN 9780399180057

LC 2018039456

An urgent guide by the clinical psychologist shares anecdotal reassurance about how to protect today's girls from rising rates of unhealthy anxiety and stress, sharing critical steps for safeguarding against toxic cultural pressure.

"Damour offers practical suggestions for heading off stressful encounters and counteracting their influences. Although aimed at parents, Damour's sensible and empathetic approach will also be reassuring for teens seeking guidance." Booklist.

Siegel, Daniel J., 1957-

Brainstorm : the power and purpose of the teenage brain / Daniel J. Siegel, M.D. Tarcher/Penguin, 2013 321 p. : **155.5**

1. Adolescence 2. Child development. 3. Brain -- Growth.
ISBN 9781585429356

LC 2013029724

Includes index

The best-selling author, drawing on important new research in the field of interpersonal neurobiology, helps parents understand how the brain functions between the ages of 12 and 24 so that they can turn one of the most challenging periods in their children's lives into one of the most rewarding.

Simmons, Rachel, 1974-

★**Enough** as she is : how to help girls move beyond impossible standards of success to live healthy, happy, and fulfilling lives / Rachel Simmons. Harper, 2018 xxiv, 270 p. ; **155.5**

1. Self-confidence in adolescence. 2. Teenage girls -- Psychology.
ISBN 0062438395

LC bl2017051385

Offers advice to help parents guide teenage girls to recognize and reject perfectionist messages that lead to self-doubt, unfulfilling relationships, and fears of failure, and teach them self-compassion, how to take healthy risks, and the importance of finding support.

"A fascinating read that provides ideas for combatting the 'not enough' ideals that are devastating young girls." Library Journal.

155.6 Psychology of adults

Hagerty, Barbara Bradley

Life reimagined : the science, art, and opportunity of midlife / Barbara Bradley Hagerty. Riverhead Books, 2016 400 p. **155.6**

1. Middle-age 2. Middle-aged women 3. Aging 4. Midlife crisis
ISBN 9781594631702

LC 2016006516

An award-winning journalist exposes the myth of the midlife crisis, drawing on emerging information from the fields of neurology, psychology, biology, genetics and sociology and explains that it should instead be about fresh possibilities, transformation and plotting new courses.

"This work is a joyous reminder that the middle years can be satisfying, resilient, and significant." Library Journal.

Lerner, Harriet Goldhor

The **dance** of intimacy : a woman's guide to courageous acts of change in key relationships / Harriet Goldhor Lerner. Perennial Library, 1990, c1989. 25 p. ; **155.6**

1. Women -- Psychology 2. Intimacy (Psychology) 3. Interpersonal relations 4. Change (Psychology)
ISBN 9780060916466

LC BL 99705951

Originally published: New York : Harper & Row, c1989.

Focuses on the anxiety that is born of unhappy relationships--with a loved one, best friend, or family member--and offers advice on how to improve relations.

McConville, Mark

Failure to launch : why your twentysomething hasn't grown up...and what to do about it / Mark McConville, Ph.D. G.P. Putnam's Sons, 2020. 320 p. **155.6**

1. Parent and adult child. 2. Adult children living with parents. 3. Adulthood. 4. Young adults.
ISBN 9780525542186

LC 2019021470

From an expert in adolescent psychology comes a groundbreaking, timely, and necessary guide for parents of the 2.2 million young adults in America who are struggling to find their way in the world.

"A valuable go-to resource for parents and teens alike." Library Journal.

Rauch, Jonathan, 1960-

The **happiness** curve : why life gets better after 50 / Jonathan Rauch. Picador, 2019, c2018. xiv, 257 p. ; **155.6**

1. Middle-age 2. Midlife crisis 3. Depression 4. Anxiety
ISBN 9781250080912

LC 2020304096

Draws on cutting-edge scientific studies to discuss the U-shaped trajectory of happiness, which declines from the optimism of youth before surging upward again after age fifty, and offers ways to endure the slump during midlife.

155.67 People in late adulthood

Applewhite, Ashton

This chair rocks : a manifesto against ageism / Ashton Applewhite. Celadon Books, 2019. 285 p. **155.67**

1. Ageism 2. Aging 3. Seniors -- Public opinion 4. Prejudice
ISBN 9781250311481

LC bl2019001375

An author, activist, and TED-talk speaker has written a manifesto calling for an end to discrimination and prejudice on the basis of age.

"This enjoyable read provides a positive view of aging that is sorely missing in today's popular culture. Appealing to a wide audience, it might even serve as a spark for positive social change." Library Journal.

Cameron, Julia
It's never too late to begin again : discovering creativity and meaning at midlife and beyond / Julia Cameron, with Emma Lively. TarcherPerigee, 2016 xxxii, 265 p. ; **155.67**
1. Creative ability 2. Aging
ISBN 9780399174216
LC 2015050216

"Julia Cameron has inspired millions with her bestseller The Artist's Way. Now at the age of sixty-five, she shows her contemporaries how retirement can be the most creative and fulfilling stage of life yet. For some, retirement is a day to work toward with anticipation. Others approach retirement with greater ambivalence. While the newfound freedom is exciting and filled with possibility, the idea of retirement can also be very daunting. You are in a unique position to explore yourself and your desiresfrom a place of experience. But the line has been drawn in the sand: The life that you have known has changed, and the life to come is yet to be defined. This book is a twelve-week course aimed at defining--and creating--the life you want to have as youredefine--and re-create--yourself. Filled with essays, tools, and exercises to be done alone or in groups, this toolkit will guide and inspire retirees wishing to expand their creativity. This fun, gentle, step-by-step process will help you explore your creative dreams, wishes, and desires--and quickly find that it's never too late to begin anything".-- Provided by publisher.

Moore, Thomas, 1940-
Ageless soul : the lifelong journey toward meaning and joy / Thomas Moore. St. Martins Press, 2017. viii, 294 p. **155.67**
1. Seniors -- Religious life 2. Aging -- Religious aspects 3. Spiritual life 4. Religious psychology.
ISBN 9781250135810
LC 2017018867

Includes index.

Offers advice on how to embrace healthier perspectives on aging through a rich spiritual life, covering subjects ranging from depression and mentorship to sexuality and the spiritual paths that open later in life.

"This gentle book, filled with specific suggestions and thought-provoking examples, will be inspiring to older readers and a comfort to their caregivers." Booklist.

155.7 Evolutionary psychology

Clark, William R., 1938-
Are we hardwired? : the role of genes in human behavior / William R. Clark, Michael Grunstein. Oxford University Press, 2000. ix, 322 p. : **155.7**
1. Behavior genetics. 2. Human behavior -- Genetic aspects
ISBN 9780195138269
LC 99054699

Diving headfirst in the nature-nurture debate, the author brings hard science to bear on the subject, offering readers a nuanced book worthy of th complicated and contentious subject of the role of genetic in human behavior.

"The authors offer an overview of the current evidence supporting genetic causes for general behavioral tendencies, such as aggression, consumption, sexual preferences, and, most controversial, intelligence. Case studies of identical twins separated as infants provide some of the most compelling proofs." Library Journal.

Dunbar, R. I. M. (Robin Ian MacDonald), 1947-
Human evolution : our brains and behavior / Robin Dunbar. Oxford University Press, 2016. 272 p. **155.7**
1. Genetic psychology. 2. Evolution. 3. Cognition. 4. Heredity and environment (Psychology)
ISBN 9780190616786
LC 2016009401

This book covers the psychological aspects of human evolution with a table of contents ranging from prehistoric times to modern days. Dunbar focuses on an aspect of evolution that has typically been overshadowed by the archaeological record: the biological, neurological, and genetic changes that occurred with each "transition" in the evolutionary narrative.

"Readers who pay attention and do not skim the many graphs, tables, and statistics will discover a rich trove of discoveries on how primitive primates became modern humans." Kirkus.

Maestripieri, Dario
Games primates play : an undercover investigation of the evolution and economics of human relationships / Dario Maestripieri. Basic Books, c2012. 288 p. **155.7**
1. Interpersonal relations. 2. Social behavior. 3. Dominance (Psychology) 4. Control (Psychology)
ISBN 9780465020782
LC 2011045523

The primatologist author of Machiavellian Intelligence examines unspoken social customs, from jilting a lover to being competitive on the job, to explain how behavioral complexities are linked to our primate heritage.

Miller, Kenneth R. (Kenneth Raymond), 1948-
The **human** instinct : how we evolved to have reason, consciousness, and free will / Kenneth Miller. Simon & Schuster, [2018] 304 p. **155.7**
1. Human evolution 2. Genetic psychology 3. Consciousness 4. Behavior evolution
ISBN 9781476790268
LC 2017006770

Explores how humans evolved to develop reason, consciousness, and free will, achieving a level of self-awareness and understanding unrivaled by the creatures they evolved alongside.

"Miller's latest work seamlessly crosses between science and philosophy, appealing to readers of both subjects. Those interested in the human condition or wishing to delve into an introspective text on the self and mind will appreciate the depth and thought." Booklist.

Ridley, Matt
The **agile** gene : how nature turns on nurture / Matt Ridley. Harper Perennial, 2004, c2003. 326 p. **155.7**
1. Heredity and environment (Psychology) 2. Human behavior. 3. Human genetics. 4. Genes.
ISBN 9780060006792

Originally published as Nature via nurture: genes, experience, and what makes us human, New York: Harper Collins, 2003.

National Academies Communication Award, 2004.

A historical analysis of the nature-versus-nurture debate documents the 2001 discovery that there are fewer genes in a human genome than previously thought and considers the argument that nurture elements are also largely responsible for human behavior.

155.8 Ethnopsychology and national psychology

Levi-Strauss, Claude

★The **savage** mind. / Claude Levi-Strauss, John (TRN) Weightman, Doreen (TRN) Weightman. University of Chicago Press 1966 xii, 290 p. **155.8**

1. Ethnopsychology
ISBN 9780226474847

LC 66028197

Discusses the significance of totemism among primitive peoples and its interpretation by anthropologists and philosophies.

155.9 Environmental psychology

Aiken, Mary

The **cyber** effect : a pioneering cyber-psychologist explains how human behavior changes online / Mary Aiken. Spiegel & Grau, 2016. 400 p. **155.9**

1. Human behavior. 2. Technology -- Social aspects 3. Social psychology. 4. Interpersonal relations -- Psychological aspects.
ISBN 9780812997859

LC 2016007455

Includes index.

A noted forensic cyberpsychologist explores the impact of technology on human behavior, examining a range of subjects including criminal activity, deviant behavior, the impact of technology on children and teenagers, and online altruism.

"Aiken provides a thoughtful approach to the attractions, distractions, and pitfalls of our digital culture." Kirkus.

Benson, Herbert, 1935-

★The **relaxation** response / Herbert Benson, with Miriam Z. Klipper. Quill, 2001. liv, 179 p. : **155.9**

1. Hypertension -- Prevention 2. Relaxation 3. Stress management
ISBN 9780380815951

LC 2003269877

Originally published: New York, Morrow, 1975.

An updated health handbook outlines techniques of concentration designed to reduce physiological stress and presents scientific data indicating the effectiveness of similar systems of relaxation.

"This guide to relieving stress is recommended for patients suffering from heart conditions, hypertension, chronic pain, and other ailments. A classic." Library Journal.

Bettencourt, Megan Feldman

Triumph of the heart : forgiveness in an unforgiving world / Megan Feldman Bettencourt. Avery, 2015. 304 p. **155.9**

1. Forgiveness. 2. Interpersonal relations 3. Human behavior.
ISBN 9781594632631

LC 2014048570

"The author embarks on a quest to understand the complex idea of forgiveness, drawing on the latest research showing that forgiveness can provide a range of health benefits, from relieving depression to decreasing high blood pressure. Through several remarkable stories of people who have managed to forgive in the toughest of circumstances, she shows us how people are able to do it, where they find the courage, and the profound sense of freedom they feel afterward".-- Provided by publisher.

"This compelling investigation into an important subject may well inspire readers to give the concept of forgiveness a bigger place in their lives." Publishers Weekly.

Cacciatore, Joanne

Bearing the unbearable : love, loss, and the heartbreaking path of grief / Joanne Cacciatore, PhD ; foreword by Jeffrey B. Rubin, PhD. Wisdom Publications, 2017 222 p. ; **155.9**

1. Adjustment (Psychology) 2. Grief 3. Loss (Psychology) 4. Love
ISBN 9781614292968

LC 2016044492

Includes index.

"Cacciatore...has taken a unique, straightforward approach that will enlighten those who have not made this journey, offer guidance to those who are navigating loss, and provide validation for those who failed to meet society's expectations of how they should respond to their lives being forever changed." Choice.

Doka, Kenneth J.

Grief is a journey : finding your path through loss / Dr. Kenneth J. Doka. Atria Books, 2016. ix, 292 p. ; **155.9**

1. Death 2. Grief 3. Loss (Psychology)
ISBN 9781476771489

LC 2015014071

"A new, compassionate way to understand grief as an individual and ongoing journey".-- Provided by publisher.

Dresser, Norine

Saying goodbye to someone you love : your journey through end of life and grief / Norine Dresser, Fredda Wasserman. DemosHealth, c2010. xix, 210 p. ; **155.9**

1. Bereavement 2. Grief 3. Death -- Psychological aspects
ISBN 9781932603859

LC 2010002096

Offers advice to those grieving from the imminent passing or recent loss of a loved one on such topics as hospice, caregiver challenges, funeral preparations, memorials, the stages of grief, and moving on.

Dugdale, Lydia S., 1977-

The **lost** art of dying : reviving forgotten wisdom / L.S. Dugdale ; artwork by Michael W. Dugger. HarperOne, 2020 viii, 259 p.: **155.9**

1. Death. 2. Terminal care. 3. Loss (Psychology)
ISBN 9780062932631

LC 2019031054

"A Yale physician's fascinating and wise exploration of why so many people die poorly and how a medieval bestseller on the art of dying well holds important lessons for today".-- Provided by publisher.

"This illuminating and thought-provoking book will convince many readers to reexamine their assumptions about death and dying." Publishers Weekly.

Edelman, Hope

Motherless daughters : the legacy of loss / Hope Edelman. Da Capo Lifelong, 2014, c1994 400 p. ; **155.9**

1. Mothers and daughters. 2. Mother-separated children. 3. Bereavement. 4. Grief
ISBN 9780738217734

LC 2013044875

Originally published by addison-Wesley in 1994

The author joins with other women whose mothers died when they were young to discuss the lasting effects of this loss on their identity, family, relationships with others, and decisions in life.

"Writing of her own experiences of losing her mother when she was 17, and the grief of hundreds of women she interviewed who lost their mothers through death, abandonment or another form of separation .

Edelman marshals a wealth of anecdotal evidence, supplemented with psychological research about bereavement, that indicates that one's longing for a mother never disappears." Publishers Weekly.

Edelman, Hope

Motherless mothers : how losing a mother shapes the parent you become / Hope Edelman. Harper, 2007 410 p. **155.9**

1. Motherhood 2. Self-help psychology for mothers 3. Mothers -- Psychology. 4. Adult children -- Psychology.

ISBN 9780060532451

LC 2005052812

Examines the effects of maternal loss on the way in which adult daughters parent their own children, blending memoir, interviews, research, and anecdotes to explore what happens to motherless women during the child-rearing years and reveal their parenting choices, styles, patterns, fears, and triumphs, from pregnancy to adulthood.

"Edelman presents emotionally charged concepts in clear, memorable terms (e.g., reaching the neon number of a mother's age of death) to encourage frank, cathartic discussion." Publishers Weekly.

Emswiler, Mary Ann

Guiding your child through grief / Mary Ann Emswiler & James P. Emswiler. Bantam Books, 2000. 286 p. : **155.9**

1. Bereavement in adolescence 2. Bereavement in children 3. Child rearing 4. Children and death

ISBN 9780553380255

LC 00023645

The founders of The Cove, a program for grieving children and their families, offer advice to help children and teenagers cope with the death of a parent or sibling and effective ways to ease family members through a time of difficult transition.

"Thoroughly researched and bolstered with the wisdom of bereavement experts nationwide, this fine guide does those working through the loss of loved ones an enormous service. It should rank amongst the first line of defense and support for those facing a death in the family." Publishers Weekly.

Enayati, Amanda

Seeking serenity : the 10 new rules for health and happiness in the age of anxiety / Amanda Enayati. NAL Hardcover, 2015 viii, 262 p. : **155.9**

1. Mental health 2. Peace of mind 3. Stress (Psychology) 4. Stress management

ISBN 9780451471512

LC 2014029563

Relying on findings of modern science and spirituality, CNN's Health columnist provides relief from the constant and destructive stress of modern lives by offering ten groundbreaking principles to find balance and bliss, including: belong, be happy, be resilient and be creative.

"Enayati's work, while not earth-shattering, provides a positive, inexpensive avenue to inner peace." Library Journal.

Fletcher, Emily

Stress less, accomplish more : meditation for extraordinary performance / Emily Fletcher. William Morrow, 2019 252 p. : **155.9**

1. Meditation 2. Stress management

ISBN 9780062747501

LC bl2019004921

Teaching the powerful trifecta of mindfulness, meditation and manifesting, a leading expert in meditation for high performance shares her 15-minute twice-daily plan called the Z Technique for improving focus and increasing productivity levels.

Gilbert, Sandra M.

★**Death's** door : modern dying and the ways we grieve / Sandra M. Gilbert. W.W. Norton, 2006. xxv, 580 p. : **155.9**

1. Death -- Social aspects. 2. Grief. 3. Mourning customs. 4. Death -- Psychological aspects.

ISBN 0393051315

LC 2004065430

"Those who have experienced the death of a loved one will recognize themselves in this meticulously researched, comprehensively organized, and exceptionally caring examination of society's attitudes about mortality and mourning." Booklist.

Gonzales, Laurence, 1947-

Surviving survival : the art and science of resilience / Laurence Gonzales. W.W. Norton, c2012. 304 p. **155.9**

1. Resourcefulness. 2. Resilience (Personal quality) 3. Disasters -- Psychological aspects. 4. Courage.

ISBN 9780393083187

LC 2012015592

Highlights the survivors of various traumas and describes their lives both before and after and offers a detailed discussion of the fear, courage and the flexibility of the spirit that drives people onward after a life-threatening experience.

Gosling, Sam

Snoop : what your stuff says about you / Sam Gosling. Basic Books, 2008. 272 p. **155.9**

1. Social perception. 2. Personal belongings. 3. Personal property -- Psychological aspects. 4. Personality.

ISBN 9780465027811

LC 2007052071

By exploring our private worlds (desks, bedrooms, even our clothes and our cars), Gosling shows not only how we showcase our personalities in unexpected--and unplanned--ways, but also how we create personality in the first place, communicate it to others, and interpret the world around us.

Greenfield, Susan

Mind change : how digital technologies are leaving their mark on our brains / Susan Greenfield. Random House, 2015 256 p. **155.9**

1. Cognition. 2. Information technology -- Psychological aspects. 3. Information technology -- Social aspects. 4. Cognitive psychology.

ISBN 9780812993820

LC 2014020059

Includes index.

Google. Facebook. Twitter. Repeat. We live in a world unimaginable even a few decades ago, one like no other in human history. It's a parallel world where we can be on the move in the real world, yet always hooked into an alternative time and place. And although it's a two-dimensional world of sight and sound, it offers instant information, connected identities, and constant novelty. In this world, our screen technologies are increasingly where we work, where we unwind, where we relieve our boredom and where we learn. The subsequent transformation in how we live and think is a vitally important issue, perhaps even the most important issue of our time. When toddlers are given iPads, and adults spend ten hours a day staring at a screen, can we afford to assume that our brave new screen technologies are harmless tools? Blending a wide range of scientific studies, news events, and cultural criticism with brio and verve, Mind Change presents an incisive snapshot of the global 'now'.

"While Greenfield is cautious about making definitive statements, she is determined to persuade readers to think about how all our texting, e-mailing, and social networking may be affecting our very brains. Although densely written at times, Mind Change is exceedingly well organized and hits the right balance between academic and provocative. There is no question about the need for us to think more deeply about this topic." Booklist.

James, John W., 1944-

★The **grief** recovery handbook : the action program for moving beyond death, divorce, and other losses including health career, and faith / John W. James and Russell Friedman. Collins Living, c2009. xvi, 208 p. : **155.9**

1. Grief 2. Loss (Psychology) 3. Bereavement -- Psychological aspects

ISBN 9780061686078

LC 2010455458

Presents a step-by-step program for recovering from loss, discussing the concepts of grief and recovery, the extent to which people are prepared to deal with loss, and the active decision to recover.

Johnson, Earl, 1950-

Finding comfort during hard times : a guide to healing after disaster, violence, and other community trauma / Earl Johnson. Rowman & Littlefield, 2020 ix, 166 p. ; **155.9**

1. Disasters -- Psychological aspects 2. Psychic trauma 3. Healing

ISBN 9781538127094

LC 2019046265

"Finding Comfort is about providing emotional and spiritual care following a mass fatality incident like a mass shooting, terrorist act or catastrophic natural disaster. Through examples and practical suggestions, it explores the needs of those who are suffering and how those needs can be met".-- Provided by publisher.

Kerr, Christopher, M.D.

Death is but a dream : finding hope and meaning at life's end / Christopher Kerr, MD, PhD, with Carine Mardorossian, PhD. Avery, 2020. 272 p. **155.9**

1. Dream interpretation 2. Death -- Psychological aspects 3. Mortality 4. Lucid dreams

ISBN 9780525542841

LC 2019038405

Christopher Kerr is a hospice doctor. All of his patients die. Yet he has cared for thousands of patients who, in the face of death, speak of love and grace. Beyond the physical realities of dying are unseen processes that are remarkably life-affirming. These include dreams that are unlike any regular dream. Described as "more real than real," these end-of-life experiences resurrect past relationships, meaningful events and themes of love and forgiveness; they restore life's meaning and mark the transition from distress to comfort and acceptance.

"This comforting guide will reassure the dying and their loved ones while providing instructive portraits of end-of-life patients for those who work in medical and healing professions." Publishers Weekly

Kessler, David, 1959-

Finding meaning : the sixth stage of grief / David Kessler ; written with support of the Elisabeth Kubler-Ross Family and the Elisabeth Kubler-Ross Foundation. Scribner, 2019. 272 p. **155.9**

1. Death -- Psychological aspects. 2. Grief. 3. Meaning (Psychology). 4. Healing

ISBN 9781501192739

LC 2019028917

Drawing on hard-earned experiences, as well as wisdom garnered from decades of work, an expert on grief and the coauthor of the iconic On Grief and Grieving introduces the stages of grief with the same transformative pragmatism and compassion.

Kingma, Daphne Rose

The **ten** things to do when your life falls apart : an emotional and spiritual handbook / Daphne Rose Kingma. New World Library, c2010. xxiv, 214 p. ; **155.9**

1. Adjustment (Psychology). 2. Adjustment (Psychology) -- Religious aspects. 3. Suffering.

ISBN 9781577316985

LC 2010001049

Offers ten strategies for acknowledging, healing, and moving past pain and trauma caused by layoffs, foreclosures, retirement losses, and health insurance problems.

"The author writes for readers whose lives are being wrenched apart by sudden job loss, the death of a loved one, financial ruin, or a dire medical diagnosis. When any of these things happens, either separately or simultaneously, Kingma offers a list of ten ways whereby readers can eventually learn that their difficulties have meaning and purpose. For those lost in the turbulence of life, Kingma offers a genuine hand through." Library Journal.

Kubler-Ross, Elisabeth

★**On** death and dying / Elisabeth Kübler-Ross. Scribner Classics, 1997. 286 p. : **155.9**

1. Death -- Psychological aspects. 2. People with terminal illnesses -- Psychology -- Case studies 3. Grief -- Psychological aspects 4. Coping

ISBN 0684842238

Originally published: New York : Macmillan, 1969.

Explains the attitudes of the dying toward themselves and others and presents a humane approach to relieving the psychological suffering of the terminally ill and their families

Levy, Alexander

The **orphaned** adult : understanding and coping with grief and change after the death of our parents / Alexander Levy. Da Capo Press, 2000, c1999. x, 190 p. ; **155.9**

1. Bereavement -- Psychological aspects. 2. Grief. 3. Loss (Psychology) 4. Parents -- Death -- Psychological aspects.

ISBN 0738203610

LC bl2012030641

Originally published: Reading, Mass. : Perseus Books, 1999.

Offers advice on handling the grief brought on by a parent's death and looks at a parent's continuing influence on their adult children.

"Incorporating his own personal experience with the accounts of others who have lost their parents, psychologist Levy examines this profound life-changing event with compassion and understanding." Library Journal.

Lifton, Robert Jay, 1926-

The **climate** swerve : reflections on mind, hope, and survival / Robert Jay Lifton. New Press, 2017. 144 p. **155.9**

1. Climate change -- Psychological aspects. 2. Nuclear warfare -- Psychological aspects. 3. Global environmental change --

Psychological aspects. 4. Environmental psychology.
ISBN 9781620973479

LC 2017018185

Over his long career as witness to an extreme twentieth century, National Book Award-winning psychiatrist, historian, and public intellectual Robert Jay Lifton has grappled with the profound effects of nuclear war, terrorism, and genocide. Now he shifts to climate change, which, Lifton writes, "presents us with what may be the most demanding and unique psychological task ever required of humankind," what he describes as the task of mobilizing our imaginative resources toward climate sanity.

"In short chapters, this slim title engages readers on everything from the long-term damage to the Marshall Islands from nuclear testing to the ethics of fossil-fuel extraction in our enlightened age. Thoughtful, intelligent, and deeply human, Lifton will not disappoint his fans and will hopefully draw new readers with this deeply informative work." Booklist.

Louv, Richard

Vitamin N : the essential guide to a nature-rich life / Richard Louv. Algonquin Books of Chapel Hill, 2016. xvii, 277 p. : **155.9**

1. Family recreation. 2. Nature study. 3. Nature -- Psychological aspects. 4. Outdoor recreation.
ISBN 1616205784

LC 2015031470

"A companion handbook to Last child in the woods: saving our children from nature-deficit disorder and The nature principle: reconnecting with life in a digital age."

Filled with activities, information websites, down-to-earth advice and provocative essays, a companion to both Last Child in the Woods: Saving Our Children From Nature-Deficit Disorder and The Nature Principle provides an abundance of inspiration for creating a nature-rich life for both kids and adults.

Ripley, Amanda

The **unthinkable** : who survives when disaster strikes and how we can do better / Amanda Ripley. Crown Publishers, 2008. 288 p. **155.9**

1. Resilience (Personal quality) 2. Disasters -- Psychological aspects. 3. Disaster relief. 4. Preparedness.
ISBN 9780307352897

LC 2007040315

Offers a glimpse at disasters and their aftermath, describing the three stages of disaster response, how we react--or do not react--in moments of catastrophe, and how we can train ourselves and other victims to survive in the event of a disaster.

"Ripley offers an elementary discussion of disaster and survival, drawing on both survivors' personal accounts and scientific studies that reveal how the human brain functions under duress. She shows how individuals and groups react when such disasters as shipwrecks, fires, terrorist attacks, and tsunamis occur, detailing the traits survivors demonstrate that help them respond effectively. Offering tips on how we can boost our odds, her self-help approach to survival will attract readers." Library Journal.

Rosenblatt, Roger

★**Kayak** morning : reflections on love, grief, and small boats / Roger Rosenblatt. HarperCollins, 2012. 160 p. **155.9**

1. Grief. 2. Loss (Psychology) 3. Healing -- Psychological aspects. 4. Death.
ISBN 9780062084033

LC 2012374546

"The lyrical nature of the piece, which combines short vignettes, poetic verses, snippets of conversations and meaningful quotations, allows Rosenblatt's masterful writing skills to shine. In one instance, he describes how his two sons still stand as if their deceased sister is between them, and his words connect in a way that conveys his sadness but also affirms the goodness of life." Publishers Weekly.

Rosling, Hans

Factfulness : ten reasons we're wrong about the world--and why things are better than you think / Hans Rosling with Ola Rosling and Anna Rosling Ronnlund. Flatiron Books, 2018. 288 p. **155.9**

1. Decision making. 2. Human behavior. 3. Possibilities 4. Cognition.
ISBN 9781250107817

LC 2018000167

Inspiring and revelatory, this is a book of stories by a late legend, for anyone who wants to really understand the world. It is based on a lifetime trying to teach a fact-based worldview, and of listening to how people misinterpret and overdramatize the facts even when they are right there in front of them. Written by Hans Rosling as he approached death, it features surprising, shocking, funny and poignant stories from Hans' life - from his difficult childhood in Sweden, through his work in Mozambique as a junior doctor, to his later work wowing audiences of millions around the world.

Samuel, Julia

Grief works : stories of life, death and surviving / Julia Samuel. Scribner, 2018. 288 p. **155.9**

1. Grief 2. Death -- Psychological aspects 3. Grief counseling 4. Loss (Psychology)
ISBN 9781501181535

LC bl2017046393

Shares optimistic and compassionate counsel for anyone suffering a loss and shares uplifting case studies from survivors who have journeyed through the process of grief to achieve healing, self-awareness, and confidence.

"As a guide for the newly grieving, the book succeeds on many levels, and the author's compassionate storytelling skills provide even broader appeal. Though often touching on profoundly sad situations, Samuel's stories and reflections consistently hit an authentically inspiring note." Kirkus.

Sandberg, Sheryl

Option B : facing adversity, building resilience, and finding joy / Sheryl Sandberg and Adam Grant. Alfred A. Knopf, 2017. 240 p. **155.9**

1. Coping 2. Psychology 3. Loss (Psychology) 4. Grief
ISBN 9781524732684

LC 2016057738

From the Facebook COO and #1 New York Times best-selling author of Lean In, and the #1 New York Times best-selling author of Originals comes a book about finding resilience and moving forward after life's inevitable setbacks.

"Option B is not simply a self-help book for those who are suffering; rather, it is a richly informed, engaging read that will broaden readers understanding of empathy and reveal the strength of the human spirit." Booklist.

Schuitemaker, Lisette

The **eldest** daughter effect : how firstborn women--like Oprah Winfrey, Sheryl Sandberg, JK Rowling, and Beyonce--harness their strengths / Lisette Schuitemaker & Wies Enthoven. Findhorn Press, 2016. 192 p. ; **155.9**

1. First-born daughters 2. Birth order
ISBN 9781844097074

LC bl2017002540

Analyzes the qualities that characterize first-born daughters and how the responsibility they feel for others can hinder their personal growth, while sharing strategies for how they can find the freedom to become their best selves.

Sife, Wallace

The **loss** of a pet / Wallace Sife. Howell Book House, c2005. xii, 260 p. : **155.9**

1. Bereavement -- Psychological aspects. 2. Pet owners -- Psychology. 3. Pets -- Death -- Psychological aspects.
ISBN 0764579304

LC 2005012603

Includes index.

"The author addresses the pet owner whose grief at a pet's death is largely misunderstood or even ridiculed by friends, associates and society in general. Sife is to be commended for offering information that is not only compassionate but concise, wide-ranging and, above all, practical." Publishers Weekly. {review of 1993 edition}

Warnick, Melody

This is where you belong : the art and science of loving the place you live / Melody Warnick. Viking, 2016 308 p. ; **155.9**

1. Place attachment. 2. Place attachment -- Psychological aspects. 3. Environmental psychology. 4. Neighborhoods -- Psychological aspects.
ISBN 9780525429128

LC 2016285129

Recounts how the author's family moved multiple times throughout the country before she decided to adopt their latest town as a permanent home by identifying reasons to love it, sharing her findings about the psychology of place attachment and the motivations of people dedicated to improving their cities.

Williams, Florence, 1967-

The **nature** fix : why nature makes us happier, healthier, and more creative / Florence Williams. W. W. Norton & Company, 2017. 304 p. **155.9**

1. Nature -- Psychological aspects 2. Humans -- Effect of environment on 3. Environmental psychology 4. Creativity
ISBN 9780393242713

LC 2016040709

An investigation into the restorative benefits of nature draws on cutting-edge research and the author's explorations with international nature therapy programs to examine the relationship between nature and human cognition, mood and creativity.

"This powerful environmental call to arms proposes that for optimal well-being, regular doses of nature are not only recommended but required." Publishers Weekly.

Winch, Guy

★**How** to fix a broken heart / Guy Winch. TED Books, 2018. 120 p. **155.9**

1. Emotions 2. Love 3. Interpersonal relations 4. Coping
ISBN 9781501120121

LC bl2018003809

A licensed psychologist and author explains how heartbreak works, how it impacts the human brain and behavior in dramatic and unexpected ways and offers a toolkit on how to handle the emotion and learn to move on.

"Most importantly, he preaches self-compassion. This tender book reminds readers to be kind to others and themselves." Publishers Weekly.

Yalom, Irvin D., 1931-

Staring at the sun : overcoming the terror of death / Irvin D. Yalom. Jossey-Bass, c2008. viii, 306 p. ; **155.9**

1. Death -- Psychological aspects. 2. Aging -- Psychological aspects. 3. Fear of death. 4. Mortality.
ISBN 9780787996680

LC 2007027048

Irvin D. Yalom is an author whose best-selling trade books and novels tell compelling, dramatic, and illuminating stories with which readers can identify. At 74, Yalom has penned a book that is the climax of his lifework, focusing on the universal human issues of mortality and death. He suggests that what he calls the "awakening experience" can help us acknowledge, accept, and utilize our fear of death in a very positive manner. Such an awakening experience can be as simple as a dream, or quick as a sudden insight. It is often a loss, a trauma, or just plain aging that can prompt an awakening experience that is a turning point for a more meaningful life. He discusses how people can make lasting changes in their lives, rearrange their priorities, communicate more deeply with those they love, eliminate interpersonal fears of rejection, and increase a willingness to take risks for personal fulfillment and a life filled with love.

Zimbardo, Philip G.

The **Lucifer** effect : understanding how good people turn evil / Philip Zimbardo. Random House, c2007. xx, 551 p. : **155.9**

1. Good and evil -- Psychological aspects. 2. Mental health. 3. Situation ethics. 4. Applied psychology.
ISBN 1400064112

LC 2006050388

Discusses why people are susceptible to the power of evil, the ability of group dynamics and situational pressures to transform human behavior, the significance of disobedience, and the true nature of heroism.

"The author masterminded the famous Stanford Prison Experiment, in which college students randomly assigned to be guards or inmates found themselves enacting sadistic abuse or abject submissiveness. In this penetrating investigation, he revisits . . . the SPE study and applies it to historical examples of injustice and atrocity, especially the Abu Ghraib outrages by the U.S. military. Combining a dense but readable and often engrossing exposition of social psychology research with an impassioned moral seriousness, Zimbardo challenges readers to look beyond glib denunciations of evil-doers and ponder our collective responsibility for the world's ills." Publishers Weekly.

156 Comparative psychology

Fouts, Roger

Next of kin : what chimpanzees have taught me about who we are / Roger Fouts with Stephen Tukel Mills ; introduction by Jane Goodall. William Morrow, 1997. xi, 420 p., 16 p. of plates : **156**

1. Fouts, Roger. 2. American Sign Language. 3. Animal communication. 4. Experimental psychologists. 5. Primatologists.
ISBN 9780688148621

LC 97015144

"A living planet book."
ALA Notable Book, 1998.

Presents the story of Roger Fouts, a pioneer in the study of communication with chimpanzees through sign language, and his thirty-year realationship with Washoe, the clever and rambunctious matriarch of a clan of chimpanzees.

"What makes this book an exceptional popularization of scientific research is the authors' ability to charm with a fascinating story while also teaching why the story is so fascinating." Booklist.

Miller, Peter, 1949-

The **smart** swarm : how understanding flocks, herds, and colonies can make us better at communicating, decision making, and getting things done / Peter Miller. Avery, 2010. 304 p. **156**

1. Animal behavior. 2. Human behavior. 3. Decision making. 4. Social networks.

ISBN 9781583333907

LC 2009048619

Draws on the examples of insect colonies and fish schools to demonstrate how ancient animal instincts surpass modern human developments in speed and productivity, revealing how numerous technological breakthroughs were inspired by natural organizations.

"The author examines hives, mounds, colonies, and swarms, whose complex systems of engagement and collective decision making have catalyzed innovations in engineering and can suggest solutions to such problems as climate change. Miller informs, engages, entertains, and even surprises in this thought-provoking study of problem making and problem solving, and through the comparison of human and insect scenarios, shows how social cues and signals can either bring about social cooperation or destruction." Publishers Weekly.

Peterson, Dale

The **moral** lives of animals / Dale Peterson. Bloomsbury Press, 2010. 352 p. **156**

1. Animal behavior. 2. Ethics. 3. Motivation (Psychology) 4. Zoology

ISBN 9781596914247

LC 2010024662

Challenges popular beliefs to reveal the animal kingdom's impulses toward cooperation, generosity and fairness, citing numerous examples of animals who have compromised their own safety to protect each other and what humans can learn from animal codes of behavior.

Suddendorf, Thomas

The **gap** : the science of what separates us from other animals / Thomas Suddendorf. Basic Books, 2013 368 p. **156**

1. Comparative psychology 2. Animal behavior. 3. Human nature. 4. Human behavior

ISBN 9780465030149

LC 2013017538

An award-winning psychologist argues that a capacity for fiction distinguishes humans from animals, explaining how the human mind has a unique ability to imagine, reflect and connect with other minds to consider real and imagined scenarios.

"A reader-friendly examination of the great gap that exists between human beings and the rest of the animal world and an explanation of how our minds came to be unique." Kirkus.

Waal, F. B. M. de (Frans B. M.), 1948-

Our inner ape : a leading primatologist explains why we are who we are / Frans de Waal ; photographs by the author. Riverhead Books, 2005. 274 p. : **156**

1. Chimpanzees -- Behavior. 2. Bonobos -- Behavior. 3. Human behavior. 4. Comparative psychology.

ISBN 1573223123

LC 2005042768

Why we are who we are through vivid, entertaining stories of politics, sex, violence and kindness. An engrossing discourse that proposes thought-provoking and sometimes shocking connections among chimps, bonobos, and those most paradoxical of apes, human beings.

"Readers might be surprised at how much these apes and their stories resonate with their own lives, and may well be left with an urge to spend a few hours watching primates themselves at the local zoo." Publishers Weekly.

158 Applied psychology

Achor, Shawn

Before happiness : the 5 hidden keys to achieving success, spreading happiness, and sustaining positive change / Shawn Achor. Crown Business, 2013 xviii, 252 p. : **158**

1. Change (Psychology) 2. Happiness 3. Positive psychology 4. Success

ISBN 9780770436735

LC 2013022564

Demonstrates the importance of a positive mindset in promoting motivation, engagement, and performance in the workplace, outlining five actionable strategies for reducing the negative effects of stress, finding creative solutions, and identifying opportunities.

Bennett, Michael, 1945-

★**F*ck** feelings : one shrink's practical advice for managing all life's impossible problems / Michael Bennett, MD, Sarah Bennet. Simon & Schuster, 2015 xi, 370 p. ; **158**

1. Interpersonal relations 2. Problem solving therapy 3. Problem solving 4. Self-actualization (Psychology)

ISBN 9781476789996

LC 2014048966

In the title, the [u] is represented by an asterick.

In a book filled with no-nonsense advice, a board-certified, Harvard-educated psychiatrist and his comedy-writer daughter, using humor and common sense, open the shrinks' secret solution manual to show readers how to find a new kind of freedom by working toward realistic goals and doing the best with what one can control.

Bernstein, Gabrielle

Judgment detox : release the beliefs that hold you back from living a better life / Gabrielle Bernstein. North Star Way, 2018 229 p. ; **158**

1. Happiness 2. Judgment 3. Self-actualization (Psychology)

ISBN 9781501168963

LC 2017021778

"From featured 'next-generation thought leader' on Oprah Winfrey's Super Soul 100 and #1 New York Times bestselling author Gabrielle Bernstein comes a clear, proactive, step-by-step program to rid yourself of the tendency to judge yourself and others, and find your way back to true healing and oneness. Judgment--both being judged and judging others--is the core of our discomfort. While it's powerful, judgment isn't complicated. It's simply the separation from oneness. The moment we see ourselves as separate we detour into a false belief system that is out of alignment with our true nature. That separation, often a reflection of our own insecurities projected onto others, keeps us feeling alienated and alone. The Judgment Detox is an interactive processthat calls on spiritual principles from the text A Course in Miracles, Kundalini yoga, meditation, EFT, and metaphysical teachings, allowing us to release the beliefs that hold us back from living a better life. Gabby has demystified these principles to make them easy to apply and commit to. The six steps include: Witness your judgment without judgment Honor the wound Put love on the alter See for the first time Cut the cords Bring your shadows to light. This step-by-step process offers a path to true healing, oneness, and a deeper connection to the universe and those around us".-- Provided by publisher.

"Readers concerned about the downsides of judgementf--or both the judge and the accused--will find relief in Bernstein's comforting words and concrete plans for action." Publishers Weekly.

Brown, Brene

The **gifts** of imperfection : let go of who you think you're supposed to be and embrace who you are / Brene Brown. Random House, 2020, c2010 160 p. **158**

1. Self-acceptance 2. Identity (Psychology) 3. Transformations, Personal. 4. Change (Psychology)

ISBN 9780593133583

LC bl2020033635

Originally published: Center City, MN : Hazelden Publishing, 2010.

"Brown offers exercises for readers to plumb their own emotions and begin to develop the kind of resilience needed to stand up to unrealistic expectations of others and ourselves." Booklist.

Brown, Brene

Rising strong : how the ability to reset transforms the way we live, love, parent, and lead / Brene Brown. Spiegel & Grau, [2015] xxviii, 301 pages ; **158**

1. Purpose in life 2. Growth (Psychology) 3. Coping 4. Transformations, Personal

ISBN 9780812995824

LC 2015010832

Outlines theories about what the author terms the "physics of vulnerability" to explain the role of disappointment, failure and heartbreak in personal strength and achieving a sense of purpose.

"An innovative one-two-three-punch approach to self-help and healing from an author who has helped count less readers change their lives." Kirkus.

Burns, David D.

Feeling good : the new mood therapy / David D. Burns ; preface by Aaron T. Beck. Avon Books, 1999 xxxii, 706 p. : **158**

1. Cognitive therapy. 2. Depression, Mental.

ISBN 0380731762

LC BL 99004455

"Whole care."

A guide to a drug-free cure for anxiety, guilt, pessimism, procrastination, and low self-esteem features information on negative feelings, mood swings, hostility, criticism, and approval addiction.

Canfield, Jack, 1944-

The **success** principles : how to get from where you are to where you want to be / Jack Canfield with Janet Switzer. Harper Resource Book, c2005. xxxiii, 473 p. : **158**

1. Success -- Psychological aspects

ISBN 9780060594886

LC 2004054259

A self-improvement guide for business professionals, teachers, students, parents, or anyone interested in promoting themselves within today's success-oriented culture shares sixty-four practical or inspiring principles on how to reach desired goals.

"The author has an easy style and talks directly to readers, responding to potential what ifs and buts with encouragement and sound advice. The book's layout is superbsmall paragraphs are punctuated by italicized quotes, questions for self-study, and several appropriate cartoons." Library Journal.

Carnegie, Dale, 1888-1955

★**How** to win friends and influence people / Dale Carnegie ; editorial consultant, Dorothy Carnegie, editorial assistance, Arthur R. Pell. Pocket Books, 1982. xxv, 276 p. ; **158**

1. Success

ISBN 9780671723651

LC 94176452

Provides suggestions for successfully dealing with people both in social and business situations

Covey, Stephen R.

The **8th** habit : from effectiveness to greatness / Stephen R. Covey. Free Press, c2004. xvi, 409 p.: **158**

1. Leadership. 2. Self-fulfillment. 3. Success (Concept) 4. Contentment.

ISBN 9780684846651

LC 2004056371

A leading management consultant draws on his seven organizational rules for improving effectiveness to present an eighth principle, voice, that is based on the right balance of talent, need, conscience, and passion.

"Though conceived for individuals, Covey's book will be of tremendous importance to organizations and businesses." Library Journal.

Covey, Stephen R.

First things first : to live, to love, to learn, to leave a legacy / Stephen R. Covey, A. Roger Merrill, Rebecca R. Merrill. Simon & Schuster, 1994. 360 p. : **158**

1. Personal conduct 2. Time management. 3. Priorities. 4. Motivation (Psychology)

ISBN 0671864416

LC 94002305

"The authors offer a 'principle-centered' approach to time management that emphasizes what 'represents our vision, values, principles, mission, conscience, direction--what we feel is important and how we lead our lives.' The authors argue that central to our lives are 'four needs and capacities to live, to love, to learn, to leave a legacy.' The ideas here are not only clearly explained but are reinforced by scenarios from the authors' lives and self-directed activities for the reader." Library Journal.

Covey, Stephen R.

★The **7** habits of highly effective people : powerful lessons in personal change / Stephen R. Covey. Free Press, 2004. 384 p. **158**

1. Success (Concept) -- Psychological aspects. 2. Character. 3. Self-fulfillment. 4. Personal conduct

ISBN 0743272455

LC 2004057494

Includes index.

A leading management consultant outlines seven organizational rules for improving effectiveness and increasing productivity at work and at home.

Duhigg, Charles

Smarter faster better : the secrets of productivity in life and business / Charles Duhigg. Random House, [2016] x, 380 p. : **158**

1. Performance. 2. Motivation (Psychology) 3. Decision making. 4.

Industrial productivity.
ISBN 9780812993394

LC 2015034214

Explores the science of productivity, and why, in today's world, managing how you think--rather than what you think--can transform your life.

"Duhigg shows an uncanny ability to find just the right exciting example of productivity-boosting methods, leaving readers to nod in recognition that they might act in the same way to improve their lives and work." Kirkus.

Fabritius, Friederike

The **leading** brain : powerful science-based strategies for achieving peak performance / Friederike Fabritius, MS, and Hans W. Hagemann, PhD. TarcherPerigee, Book, 2017 xii, 324 p. ; **158**

1. Leadership -- Psychological aspects 2. Performance -- Psychological aspects
ISBN 9780143129356

LC 2016038838

Describes how neuroscience affects leadership and performance in the workplace, discussing how data can be applied in such areas as decision making, focus, teambuilding, and retaining information.

Fisher, Roger, 1922-2012

★**Getting** to yes : negotiating agreement without giving in / Roger Fisher and William Ury, with Bruce Patton, editor. Penguin, 2011. xxix, 204 p. : **158**

1. Negotiation
ISBN 9780143118756

LC 2011006319

"Since it was first published in 1981 Getting to Yes has become a central book in the Business Canon: the key text on the psychology of negotiation. Its message of "principled negotiations"--finding acceptable compromise by determining which needs are fixed and which are flexible for negotiating parties--has influenced generations of businesspeople, lawyers, educators and anyone who has sought to achieve a win-win situation in arriving at an agreement. It has sold over 8 million copies worldwide in 30 languages, and since it was first published by Penguin in 1991 (a reissue of the original addition with Bruce Patton as additional coauthor) has sold over 2.5 million copies--which places it as the #10 bestselling title overall in Penguin Books, and #3 bestselling nonfiction title overall. We have recently relicensed the rights to Getting to Yes, and will be doing a new revised edition--a 30th anniversary of the original publication and 20th of the Penguin edition. The authors will be bringing the book up to date with new material and a assessment of the legacy and achievement of Getting to Yes after three decades".--Provided by publisher.

Fogg, B. J.

Tiny habits : the small changes that change everything / BJ Fogg, PhD. Houghton Mifflin Harcourt, 2019. 320 p. **158**

1. Fogg, B. J. 2. Habit. 3. Change (Psychology). 4. Motivation (Psychology) 5. Behavior
ISBN 9780358003328

LC 2019023920

An expert of habit formation and behavior science describes how to harness the power of transformation, whether it be to lose weight, exercise more or de-stress, through making tiny changes that we can feel good about.

Gilbert, Daniel Todd

★**Stumbling** on happiness / Daniel Gilbert. A.A. Knopf, 2006. xvii, 277 p. : **158**

1. Happiness. 2. Psychology. 3. Decision-making.
ISBN 1400077427

LC 2005044459

Royal Society General Prizes for Science Books, 2007.

A reflection on human nature brilliantly describes all that science has to tell us about the uniquely human ability to envision the future, and how likely we are to enjoy it when we get there.

"The book is a sly, irresistible romp down, or through, memory lanepast, present, and future. It is not only wildly entertaining but also hilarious . and yet full of startling insight, imaginative conclusions, and even bits of wisdom." Booklist.

Hardy, Benjamin

Willpower doesn't work : discover the hidden keys to success / Benjamin Hardy. Hachette Books, 2018. xviii, 235 p. ; **158**

1. Becoming (Philosophy) 2. Identity (Psychology) 3. Proximity spaces 4. Self -- Social aspects
ISBN 9780316441322

LC 2017042668

Includes index.

An organizational psychologist and Medium.com's most-read writer, building on existing research as well as his own experiences, explains how people can change their lives on every level by making small, impactful changes in their environment that will help them to evolve into the person they want to become.

Hay, Louise L.

You can heal your life / Louise L. Hay. Hay House, c1987. viii, 226 p. ; **158**

1. Self-actualization (Psychology) 2. Change (Psychology) 3. Mind and body 4. Holistic medicine
ISBN 9780937611012

LC 88200391

Includes index.

Argues that everyone is responsible for their own experiences, tells how to lead a more creative and fulfilling life, and discusses work, health, success, and personal relationships.

King, Vanessa

10 keys to happier living : a practical handbook for happiness / Vanessa King. Headline, 2016. 336 p. : **158**

1. Happiness. 2. Mental health. 3. Well-being.
ISBN 1472233425

LC bl2018037281

"Action for happiness"--Cover.

A guide to understanding happiness outlines ten ways to be happier in every aspect of life, from connecting with others to self-acceptance.

Langshur, Eric

Start here : master the lifelong habit of wellbeing / Eric Langshur and Nate Klemp, PhD ; foreword by Dr. Richard J. Davidson. North Star Way, 2016. xi, 320 p. ; **158**

1. Happiness. 2. Stress management. 3. Mental health. 4. Contentment.
ISBN 9781501129087

LC 2015043325

"This revolutionary work outlines the first and only cross-training system for mastering the skill of happiness. Think P90x for the soul".--Provided by publisher.

"Personal anecdotes add interest to the nuts-and-bolts format. Other books have touched on these same principles, but this book does an especially good job, walking readers step-by-step through the practices, presenting achievable goals, and encouraging readers to take charge of their emotional lives." Booklist.

Lyubomirsky, Sonja

★The **how** of happiness : a scientific approach to getting the life you want / Sonja Lyubomirsky. Penguin Press, 2008. 366 p. : **158**

1. Happiness.

ISBN 159420148X

LC 2007039942

An easy-to-follow, life-changing approach designed to increase happiness and fulfillment in everyday life furnishes a comprehensive guide that redefines what happiness and what it is not and introduces activities, including exercises in practicing optimism, tips on how to savor life's pleasures, and an emphasis on staying active to achieve a happier life.

McGraw, Phillip C., 1950-

Life strategies : doing what works, doing what matters / Phillip C. McGraw. Hyperion Books, 2000, c1999. xiii, 304 p. : **158**

1. Change (Psychology) 2. Success -- Psychological aspects

ISBN 9780786884599

LC BL 00001109

Reprint. Originally published: 1999.

A behavioral specialist and trail expert explains how to analyze one' life, identify barriers to success, and take practical steps to make life more rewarding, meaningful, and satisfying.

"McGraw claims that people in dire situations have serious problems, including denial and choosing initial assumptions without testing them for accuracy. To create a life strategy that works, McGraw lays out his ten 'Life Laws' along with checklists and 18 assignments." Library Journal.

Palmieri, Jennifer

Dear Madam President : an open letter to the women who will run the world / Jennifer Palmieri. Grand Central Pub., 2018 208 p. **158**

1. Women presidents. 2. Women heads of state 3. Leadership in women. 4. Women politicians.

ISBN 9781538713457

LC bl2018000897

A former Hillary Clinton Communications Director presents an open letter to the future first woman president?and by extension, to all women working to succeed in any field, creating a forward-thinking framework of inspirational and practical advice for all women everywhere who are determined to seize control of their lives, their workplaces and their country.

Peck, M. Scott (Morgan Scott), 1936-2005

Further along the road less traveled : the unending journey toward spiritual growth : the edited lectures / M. Scott Peck. Simon & Schuster, c1993. 255 p. ; **158**

1. Self-fulfillment -- Religious aspects -- Christianity 2. Growth (Psychology) -- Religious aspects -- Christianity 3. Interpersonal relations -- Religious aspects -- Christianity. 4. Spiritual life.

ISBN 9780671781590

LC 93031322

Explores love, relationships, and spiritual growth, covering blame and forgiveness, the New Age movement, death and the meaning of life, and other topics.

"The author discusses 'growing up'becoming self-aware, working through cycles of blame and toward wholesale forgiveness and then the self-examination we each must undergo in order to groom ourselves for the most important step of all: the search for God." Booklist.

Peck, M. Scott (Morgan Scott), 1936-2005

The **road** less traveled and beyond : spiritual growth in an age of anxiety / M. Scott Peck. Simon & Schuster, c1997. 314 p. ; **158**

1. Peck, M. Scott (Morgan Scott), 1936-2005. 2. Spiritual life.

ISBN 0684813149

LC 96043391

The founder of the Foundation for Community Encouragement draws on his counseling experience to lead readers to the spiritual simplicity that lies on the other side of complexity and explains how to cope with the fears and shortcomings of life

"In this volume Peck continues his journey through the existential conflicts and baffling paradoxes on the meandering road of personal development. Through copious detailed references from his previous books, he allows readers unfamiliar with them to understand and enjoy the present work, which completes his Road trilogy." Publishers Weekly.

Roth, Bernard

The **achievement** habit : stop wishing, start doing, and take command of your life / Bernard Roth. HarperBusiness, 2015 273 p. : **158**

1. Achievement motivation 2. Conduct of life 3. Motivation (Psychology) 4. Self-actualization (Psychology)

ISBN 9780062356109

LC bl2015026779

Leads readers through a series of discussions, stories, recommendations, and exercises that will help them gain confidence and achieve goals they never thought possible.

"Roth's excellent advice on how to overcome obstacles and triumph should be of interest to readers college age and up." Library Journal.

Rowling, J. K

Very good lives : the fringe benefits of failure and the importance of imagination / J.K. Rowling. Little, Brown and Company, 2015. 69 p. : **158**

1. Rowling, J. K. Anecdotes. 2. Anxiety 3. Baccalaureate addresses 4. Failure (Psychology) 5. Fear

ISBN 9780316369152

LC 2014959607

In 2008, J.K. Rowling delivered a deeply affecting commencement speech at Harvard University. Now published for the first time in book form, VERY GOOD LIVES presents J.K. Rowling's words of wisdom for anyone at a turning point in life. How can we embrace failure? And how can we use our imagination to better both ourselves and others? Drawing from stories of her own post-graduate years, the world famous author addresses some of life's most important questions with acuity and emotional force.

"Rowling makes neat connections between the challenges of modern life and the tutelary examples of Seneca, Plutarch, and the other ancients. While she discounts the ennobling aspects of poverty and misery, it's also clear that her education provided her with some steel to face those hardships." Kirkus.

Rubin, Gretchen
Outer order, inner calm : declutter & organize to make more room for happiness / Gretchen Rubin. Harmony, 2019. 215 p. ; **158**

1. Self-actualization (Psychology) 2. Happiness 3. Success 4. Orderliness
ISBN 9781984822802

LC 2018029854

"With clarity and humor, bestselling author of The Four Tendencies and The Happiness Project Gretchen Rubin illuminates one of her key realizations about happiness: For most of us, outer order contributes to inner calm. And for most of us, a rigid, one-size-fits-all solution doesn't work. In this easy-to-read but hard-to-put-down book, Gretchen Rubin suggests more than 150 short, concrete clutter-clearing ideas so each reader can choose the ones that resonate most. The fact is, when we tailor our approach to suit our own particular challenges and habits, we're far more likely to be able to create the order that will make our lives happier, healthier, more productive, and more creative. In the context of a happy life, a messy desk or crowded coat closetis a trivial problem--yet Gretchen Rubin has found that getting control of our stuff makes us feel more in control of our lives. By getting rid of things we don't use, don't need, or don't love, as well as things that don't work, don't fit, or don't suit, we free our mind (and our shelves) for what we truly value. In this trim book filled with insights, strategies, and sometimes surprising tips, Gretchen tackles the key challenges of creating outer order, by explaining how to 'Make Choices,' 'Create Order,' 'Know Yourself--and Others,' 'Cultivate Helpful Habits,' and, of course, 'Add Beauty.' At home, at work, and in life, when we get our possessions under control we feel both calmer and more energetic. With a sense of fun, and also a clear idea of what's realistic for most people, Gretchen Rubin suggests dozens of manageable steps for creating a more serene, orderly environment--one that helps us to create the lives we yearn for".-- Provided by publisher.

Schwartz, David Joseph
★The **magic** of thinking big / David Joseph Schwartz. Simon & Schuster, 1987, c1965. 192 p. ; **158**

1. Success
ISBN 9780671646783

LC 87008516

"A Fireside book."
Includes index.
The Magic of Thinking Big gives you useful methods, not empty promises. Dr. Schwartz presents a carefully designed program for getting the most out of your job, your marriage and family life, and your community. He proves that you don't need to be an intellectual or have innate talent to attain great success and satisfaction--but you do need to learn and understand the habit of thinking and behaving in ways that will get you there. This book gives you those secrets! Provided by publisher

Siegel, Bernie S.
Prescriptions for living : inspirational lessons for a joyful, loving life / Bernie S. Siegel. HarperPerennial, 1999, c1998. xxiv, 210 p. ; **158**

1. Self-realization -- Religious aspects. 2. Spiritual life.
ISBN 0060929367

LC BL2001005172

Originally published: New York : HarperCollins, c1998.
A best-selling trendsetter who has helped millions with his explorations of the health connection between body and mind offers a collection of anecdotes, information, and advice for building a more joyful, successful, and fulfilling life.

"Among the topics Siegel covers are how to find peace of mind; how to love, encourage, and forgive other people as well as yourself; and how to thrive in bad times and survive the good times. For those ready to be uplifted by the soothing repetition of time-tested homilies, Siegel delivers the goods." Booklist.

Stutz, Phil
The **tools** : transform your problems into courage, confidence, and creativity / Phil Stutz and Barry Michels. Spiegel & Grau, 2012. 271 p. : **158**

1. Change (Psychology). 2. Self-actualization (Psychology).
ISBN 067964444X

LC 2011044717

A Los Angeles psychotherapist and a Harvard-educated psychiatrist outline specific tools for enabling positive change, explaining how to tap unconscious resources to quickly address a range of persistent psychological issues.

Ury, William
Getting past no : negotiating your way from confrontation to cooperation / William Ury. Bantam Books, 1993. xv, 189 p. : **158**

1. Negotiation
ISBN 9780553371314

LC 94207934

A guide to successful negotiation shows readers how to stay cool under pressure, stand up for themselves without provoking opposition, deal with underhanded tactics, find mutually agreeable options, and more, in a new edition of the classic guide, updated with an all-new introduction. Reissue.

"Ury presents a five-step agenda to deal successfully with opponents, be they unruly teenagers, labor leaders, terrorists or international politicians. Strategies focus on self-discipline, or tactics for defusing the adversary's attacks, and suggestions for developing options designed to lead to a mutually satisfactory agreement." Publishers Weekly.

158.1 Personal improvement and analysis

Allen, Cory
Now is the way : an unconventional approach to modern mindfulness / Cory Allen. A TarcherPerigee Book, 2019 xix, 185 p. ; **158.1**

1. Distraction (Psychology). 2. Mindfulness (Psychology).
ISBN 0525538046

LC 2019010666

"From the popular host of The Astral Hustle, an accessible guide to hacking your mind--and life--to feel more fully present and alive, even if you're not the "the meditating type.""-- Provided by publisher.

Andre, Christophe
Looking at mindfulness : 25 ways to live in the moment through art / Christophe Andre ; translated by Trista Selous. Blue Rider Press, 2014 288 p. : **158.1**

1. Art therapy 2. Meditation -- Therapeutic use 3. Mindfulness-based cognitive therapy
ISBN 9780399175633

LC 2013372471

"Originally published in France as Mediter, jour apres jour by L'Iconoclaste, Paris, in 2011. The English edition was first published in Great Britain as Mindfulness in 2014 by Rider"--Title page verso.

Andre curates a collection of classic and esoteric works, from Rembrandt to Hopper to Magritte, utilizing the paintings as a visual and tangible first step to understanding mindfulness and the benefits of living in the moment.

"A fascinating book, suitable for those who are interested in art or the discipline of mindfulness." Library Journal.

Asprey, Dave

Game changers : what leaders, innovators, and mavericks do to win at life / Dave Asprey. Harper Wave, 2018 xvii, 331 p. : **158.1**

1. Conduct of life 2. Happiness 3. Success

ISBN 9780062652447

LC bl2018188992

The *Bulletproof Radio* podcaster and best-selling author of *The Bulletproof Diet* outlines proven techniques for promoting personal happiness, health and success in accordance with the examples of today's game changers, from David Perlmutter to Arianna Huffington.

Bloomfield, Harold H., 1944-

Making peace with your past : the six essential steps to enjoying a great future / Harold Bloomfield with Philip Goldberg. Quill, 2001, c2000. xvi, 268 p. : **158.1**

1. Autobiographical memory. 2. Self-realization.

ISBN 0060933143

LC BL2001009265

Originally published: New York : HarperCollins, 2000.

Shows readers how confronting, resolving, and releasing the pain of old wounds can open the way to a joy-filled passionate life using a integrative psychospiritual approach.

"The author addresses the syndrome Freud called 'repetition compulsion'humans' tendency to re-create what they have not worked through. With revealing exercises, Bloomfield shows readers how to rediscover 'the passion to live {their} highest destiny.' Library Journal.

Chodron, Pema

Fail, fail again, fail better / Pema Chodron ; foreword by Seth Godin. Sounds True, 2015. xv, 133 p. : **158.1**

1. Failure (Psychology) 2. Uncertainty 3. Self-actualization (Psychology)

ISBN 9781622035311

LC 2015003010

"Wise advice for leaning in to the unknown"--jacket.

Argues that failure is the most direct way to becoming a more complete, loving, and fulfilled human being.

Clearfield, Chris

Meltdown : why our systems fail and what we can do about it / Chris Clearfield, Andras Tilcsik. Penguin, 2018. 352 p. **158.1**

1. Decision-making. 2. Organizational behavior. 3. Business psychology. 4. Industrial psychology.

ISBN 9780735222632

LC 2018285465

Explains how the increasing complexity of our modern systems, gives us new capabilities, but also creates conditions vulnerable for surprising meltdowns, and offers eye-opening and empowering solutions to design better systems and make better decisions at work and at home.

"Though the underlying argument isn't new--the authors draw heavily on the work of social scientist Charles Perrow, particularly his 1984 book Normal Accidents--the authors' body of examples is relatively fresh, if sometimes not so well remembered today.,e.g., the journalistic crimes of Jayson Blair, made possible by a complex accounting system that just begged to be gamed. Programmers, social engineers, and management consultants are among the many audiences for this useful, thought-provoking book." Kirkus.

Cuddy, Amy

Presence : bringing your boldest self to your biggest challenges / Amy Cuddy. Little, Brown & Co., 2015 304 p. **158.1**

1. Self-confidence 2. Influence (Psychology) 3. Human behavior 4. Psychology

ISBN 9780316256575

LC 2015952382

A Harvard psychologist and TED star shares strategic advice on how to live in accordance with one's inner resources to overcome social fears and self-doubt while heightening confidence, productivity and influence.

"Given the popularity of Cuddy's TED Talk, one would expect that this book will be in demand, and readers will not be disappointed." Library Journal.

De la Rosa, Ralph

The **monkey** is the messenger : meditation and what your busy mind is trying to tell you / Ralph De la Rosa ; foreword by Susan Piver. Shambhala, 2018. xx, 261 p. ; **158.1**

1. Meditation 2. Meditation -- Buddhism

ISBN 9781611805840

LC 2018012459

The author uses neuroscience and psychology and his long practice of meditation and yoga to discuss why repetitive thoughts during meditation might actually be a good thing.

Duckworth, Angela

Grit : the power of passion and perseverance / Angela Duckworth. Scribner, 2016. 320 p. **158.1**

1. Success (Concept) 2. Persistence 3. Expectation (Psychology). 4. Diligence.

ISBN 9781501111105

LC 2015042880

Why do some people succeed and others fail? Sharing new insights from her landmark research on grit, MacArthur "genius" Angela Duckworth explains why talent is hardly a guarantor of success. Rather, other factors can be even more crucial such as identifying our passions and following through on our commitments. Drawing on her own powerful story as the daughter of a scientist who frequently bemoaned her lack of smarts, Duckworth describes her winding path through teaching, business consulting, and neuroscience, which led to the hypothesis that what really drives success is not "genius" but a special blend of passion and long-term perseverance. As a professor at the University of Pennsylvania, Duckworth created her own "character lab" and set out to test her theory.

"Not your grandpa's self-help book, but Duckworth's text is oddly encouraging, exhorting us to do better by trying harder, and a pleasure to read." Kirkus.

Duhigg, Charles

★The **power** of habit : why we do what we do in life and business / Charles Duhigg. Random House, c2012. xx, 371 p. : **158.1**

1. Habit. 2. Habit -- Social aspects. 3. Change (Psychology) 4. Social psychology

ISBN 9781400069286

Identifying the neurological processes behind behaviors while explaining that self-control and success are largely driven by habits, a guide by a Yale-educated investigative reporter for The New York Times shares scientifically based guidelines for achieving personal goals and overall well-being by adjusting specific habits.

Dunne, Linnea
Lagom : the Swedish art of balanced living / Linnea Dunne. Running Press, 2017. 160 p. : **158.1**
1. Self-actualization (Psychology) 2. Well-being 3. Work-life balance
ISBN 9780762463756
LC bl2017042018
Includes index.
Explains how to live "lagom," or a balanced life, by cherishing relationships, improving work-life balance, freeing the home from clutter, and savoring good food.

Dyer, Wayne W.
★The **power** of intention : learning to co-create your world your way / Wayne W. Dyer. Hay House, c2004. ix, 259 p. ; **158.1**
1. Intentionalism
ISBN 9781401902155
LC 2003014622
Argues that intention is a force found in the universe that propels an individual into action and includes stories and examples of the prinicples of intention and ways to apply intention to everyday life.
"The author argues that there are seven faces, or energy fields, of intention: creativity, kindness, love, beauty, expansion, abundance and receptivity. Drawing on a variety of spiritual traditions and gurus, Dyer describes how to surmount the barriers that may get in the way of connecting to this power, such as negative thinking, relying on the opinion of others or retaining a controlling ego." Publishers Weekly.

Fredrickson, Barbara
Positivity : groundbreaking research reveals how to embrace the hidden strength of positive emotions, overcome negativity, and thrive / Barbara Fredrickson. Crown Publishers, c2009. 277 p. : **158.1**
1. Positive psychology
ISBN 9780307393739
LC 2008027683
A psychologist explains how to create a richer, healthier, more fulfilling life through a process called the upward spiral that incorporates innovative techniques for using positivity to influence relationships, health, and work.

Harris, Dan, 1971-
Meditation for fidgety skeptics : a 10% happier how-to book / Dan Harris and Jeff Warren, with Carlye Adler. Spiegel & Grau, 2017 xi, 286 p. ; **158.1**
1. Happiness 2. Meditation -- Psychological aspects
ISBN 9780399588945
LC 2017037570
Presents a practical guide to meditation that debunks the myths, misconceptions, and self-deceptions that make many people reluctant to try it, and suggests a range of meditation practices.

Hase, Craig
How not to be a hot mess : a survival guide for modern life / Craig Hase & Devon Hase. Shambhala, 2020 ix, 164 p. ; **158.1**
1. Personal conduct 2. Buddhism 3. Meditation 4. Mindfulness (Psychology)
ISBN 9781611807981
LC 2019022861
"The dumpster fire of life rages on, but you got this. Six good rules to keep you grounded, weather the sh*tstorm, and actually be a decent person. It may seem like the world's going to hell in a handbasket right now. Whether it's the big stuff like politics, family dynamics, and climate change, or the little stuff like paying your bills, getting to work on time, and fending off social media trolls, we can all admit, life's no cakewalk. And yet, we all really want to at least try to show up and do the best we can (even though there's a 100% chance of f*ck-ups along the way). Here are six really good guiding principles, inspired from the ancient wisdom of Buddhism and mindfulness practice, to keep you anchored and steady as the winds of life toss you to and fro".-- Provided by publisher.

Heller, Rick, 1954-
Secular meditation : 32 practices for cultivating inner peace, compassion, and joy / Rick Heller ; foreword by Greg Epstein. New World Library, 2015. xvi, 287 p. ; **158.1**
1. Meditation -- Psychological aspects. 2. Happiness. 3. Relaxation. 4. Secularism
ISBN 9781608683697
LC 2015027201
"A guide from the humanist community at Harvard."
"Many avoid meditation because of its religious trappings. But as bestselling atheist Sam Harris has recently written (in Waking Up), meditation is an age-old secular practice with numerous scientifically verified physical and psychological benefits. As longtime meditation teacher Rick Heller here shows, meditation's benefits extend beyond the personal to enrich relationship with others, with community, and with the world. Step-by-step instructions, personal stories, and provocative questions teach empathy for others, stress reduction and inner peace, and the kind of in-the-moment living that fosters appreciation for life and resilience in the face of adversity. Heller simplifies what is often found mysterious - 'If you have ever loved or even liked another person, you have the prerequisites for learning kindness meditation' - and invites all to partake in 'awe and wonder at the rich experience of being alive.'"-- Provided by publisher.
"This book is an ideal guide for those who want to study meditation and mindfulness but are put off by the focus on Buddhism or religion in general." Library Journal.

Hendricks, Gay
Conscious luck : eight secrets to intentionally change your fortune / Gay Hendricks and Carol Kline. St. Martin's Essentials, 2020. x, 180 p. ; **158.1**
1. Success 2. Fortune 3. Attitude (Psychology)
ISBN 9781250622945
LC 2019054418
"Two New York Times bestselling authors explain how you can Change Your Luck and Create the Life You Want. Many of us believe that luck--that mysterious force that makes life run smoothly--is somehow beyond our control. But what if you could make your own luck? What if luck, like your health and your happiness, is something that you can consciously create for yourself? In Conscious Luck, New York Times bestselling authors Gay Hendricks and Carol Kline share eight secrets-four core shifts and four daily practices-that will allow anyone to intentionally change their fortune. Instead of living at the whim of luck, waiting for the winds of chance to offer opportunities and success, Conscious Luck shows you how to seize control of your destiny, cultivate your own luck, and create the life you want to live. This step-by-step program, which includes practical techniques, inspiring true stories, and the authors' personal journeys, will lead you on the path towards freedom and abundance. From creating a luck mind-set and setting 'luck-worthy' goals to learning how to be in the right place at the right

time, the secrets are insightful and practical. Supported by the authors' many years of experience, this unique and highly effective toolkit offers a revolutionary way to transform your life".-- Provided by publisher.

Holiday, Ryan

Ego is the enemy / Ryan Holiday. Portfolio, Penguin, 2016 xxv, 226 p. ; **158.1**

1. Ambition 2. Conduct of life 3. Egoism 4. Success
ISBN 9781591847816

LC 2016017401

"'While the history books are filled with tales of obsessive visionary geniuses who remade the world in their image with sheer, almost irrational force, I've found that history is also made by individuals who fought their egos at every turn, who eschewedthe spotlight, and who put their higher goals above their desire for recognition.' --from the prologue Many of us insist the main impediment to a full, successful life is the outside world. In fact, the most common enemy lies within: our ego. Early in our careers, it impedes learning and the cultivation of talent. With success, it can blind us to our faults and sow future problems. In failure, it magnifies each blow and makes recovery more difficult. At every stage, ego holds us back. Ego Is the Enemy draws on a vast array of stories and examples, from literature to philosophy to history. We meet fascinating figures such as George Marshall, Jackie Robinson, Katharine Graham, Bill Belichick, and Eleanor Roosevelt, who all reached the highest levels of power and success by conquering their own egos. Their strategies and tactics can be ours as well. In an era that glorifies social media, reality TV, and other forms of shameless self-promotion, the battle against ego must be fought on many fronts. Armed with the lessons in this book, as Holiday writes, 'you will be less invested in the story you tell about your own specialness, and as a result, you will be liberated to accomplish the world-changing work you've set out to achieve.'"-- Provided by publisher.

Hollis, Rachel, (Event planner)

Girl, stop apologizing : a shame-free plan for embracing and achieving your goals / Rachel Hollis. HarperCollins Leadership, 2019. xxv, 216 p. **158.1**

1. Self-fulfillment in women 2. Self-esteem in women. 3. Happiness. 4. Success (Concept)
ISBN 9781400209606

Urges women to stop feeling self-conscious about their ambitions and to start pursuing their dreams with confidence.

"Hollis's writing is beautifully blunt, and she humbly thanks her fans for her success. Her actionable ideas and captivating voice will encourage women to believe in themselves." Publishers Weekly.

Iyer, Pico

The **art** of stillness : adventures in going nowhere / Pico Iyer ; photographs by Eydis Einarsdottir. TED Books/Simon & Schuster, 2014. 74 p. : **158.1**

1. Mind and body 2. Simplicity 3. Spiritual life 4. Spirituality
ISBN 9781476784724

LC bl2014047809

Explores why modern-day technology is making people more likely to retreat into solitude and quiet, with growing numbers of people practicing yoga, meditation and tai chi and even taking an "Internet Sabbath" where online connections are shut down for a day.

"Rather than reading it quickly and filing it, readers will likely slow down to meet its pace and might continue carrying it around as a reminder." Kirkus.

Klauser, Henriette Anne

Write it down, make it happen : knowing what you want-- and getting it! / Henriette Anne Klauser. Simon & Schuster, 2001, c2000. 250 p. ; **158.1**

1. Goal (Psychology) 2. Planning
ISBN 9780684850023

LC BL2001000395

"A Fireside book."

Originally published: New York : Scribner, 2000.

Drawing on compelling, real-life examples of people who have accomplished their goals, a guide to squeezing the most from life advises "writing it down" as a way of bringing dreams to the fore and making them come true.

"The author instructs her readers to write down their most extravagant wishes and, merely by the act of recording them, make them come true. Her technique is intended to clarify goals, increase self-confidence, and dispel self-doubt, and she describes how it has dramatically improved her life and the lives of her friends and acquaintances." Library Journal.

Manson, Mark

The **subtle** art of not giving a f*ck : a counterintuitive approach to living a good life / Mark Manson. HarperOne, 2016. vii, 212 p. ; **158.1**

1. Personal conduct 2. Self-fulfillment 3. Growth (Psychology) 4. Success (Concept)
ISBN 9780062457714

LC 2016011724

Filled with entertaining stories and profane, ruthless humor, a generation-defining self-help guide, written by a blogger who is read by more than 2 million people each month, helps readers figure out the things that they should care about to lead contented, grounded lives.

"This book, full of counterintuitive suggestions that often make great sense, is a pleasure to read and worthy of rereading. A good yardstick by which self-improvement books should be measured." Kirkus.

McHargue, Mike

You're a miracle (and a pain in the ass) : embracing the emotions, habits and mystery that make you you / Mike McHargue. Convergent, 2020 xii, 226 p. : **158.1**

1. Self-acceptance 2. Self-realization 3. Self-management (Psychology)
ISBN 9781984823243

LC 2019048567

"Why is there such a gap between what you want to do and what you actually do? The co-host of The Liturgists Podcast and Ask Science Mike explains why our desires and our real lives are so wildly different--and what you can do to close the gap. For thousands of years, scientists, philosophers, and self-help gurus have wrestled with one of the basic conundrums of human life: why we do the things we do. Or rather, why we so often don't do the things that we want to do. As a podcast host whose voice goes out to millions each month, Mike McHargue gets countless emails from people seeking to understand their own misbehavior--why we binge Netflix when we know taking a walk outside would be better for us, or why we argue politics on Facebook when our real friends live just down the street. Everyone wants to be a good person, but few of us have any idea how to do so, twenty years into the new millennium. In You're a Miracle (and a Pain in the Ass), McHargue addresses why. We like to think we're in control of our thoughts and decisions, he writes, but science has shown that a host of competing impulses, emotions, and environmental factors are at play in every action we undertake. Touching on his listeners' most pressing question topics, from relationships and ethics to stress and mental health, and sharing some of the biggest triumphs and hardships from his own life, McHargue shows readers how some of our qualities that seems most frustrating--including 'negative' emotions like sadness, anger, and anxiety--are actually key to helping humans survive and thrive. In doing so, he invites the reader on a path of self-understanding, and ultimately, self-acceptance. You're a Miracle (and a Pain in the Ass) is a guided tour through the mystery of human consciousness, showing readers how to live more at peace with themselves in a complex world".-- Provided by publisher.

Miller, Caroline Adams, 1961-

★**Creating** your best life : the ultimate life list guide / Caroline Adams Miller and Michael B. Frisch. Sterling, c2009. xi, 276 p. : **158.1**

1. Goal (Psychology) 2. Self-actualization (Psychology) 3. Self-realization 4. Happiness
ISBN 9781402762598

LC 2010275766

Designed to help you understand how to set and achieve clear-cut goals while also learning how and why this process can contribute to greater contentment.

Morin, Amy

13 things mentally strong women don't do : own your power, channel your confidence, and find your authentic voice for a life of meaning and joy / Amy Morin. William Morrow, 2019 335 p. ; **158.1**

1. Fortitude 2. Mental discipline 3. Self-actualization (Psychology) in women
ISBN 9780062847621

LC bl2018197574

Describes how to foster the vital quality of mental toughness by avoiding behaviors such as insisting on perfection, comparing oneself to others, seeing vulnerability as a weakness, and letting self-doubt get in the way of goals.

"More than lists of feelings and behaviors to avoid, each of Morin's points leads into a good examination of the whys and the issues, along with common-sense alternatives " Booklist.

Peck, M. Scott (Morgan Scott), 1936-2005

★The **road** less traveled : a new psychology of love, traditional values, and spiritual growth / M. Scott Peck. Simon & Schuster, 2002, c1978. 315 p. ; **158.1**

1. Self-fulfillment. 2. Growth (Psychology) 3. Interpersonal relations. 4. Love.
ISBN 0743238257

LC 2002075858

"This book proved a smash when it debuted in 1978, selling several million copies. This 25th-anniversary edition includes a new introduction in which the publisher claims the author 'explains the ideas that shaped this book and continue to influence an expanding audience of readers.' That might sound like PR, but this truly was one of the first books dealing with the psychology of spirituality and paved the way for numerous others that followed in its wake."

Prager, Dennis, 1948-

Happiness is a serious problem : a human nature repair manual / Dennis Prager. ReganBooks, 1999, c1998. xii, 179 p. ; **158.1**

1. Happiness
ISBN 9780060987350

LC BL 99000396

Reprint. Originally published: c1998.
Includes index.

Presents insights and techniques to help readers understand, attain, and maintain happiness despite human nature's tendency to be insatiable.

"The author uses the pursuit of happiness as a central motif but generally instructs in the modern art of self-improvement. The 31 short chapters . . . are cogent, complete, and preach a nonreligious yet morally guided moderation that should appeal across a wide range of patron groups." Library Journal.

Rinaldi, Karen

It's great to suck at something : the unexpected joy of wiping out and what it can teach us about patience, resilience, and the stuff that really matters / Karen Rinaldi. Atria Books, c2019. 238 p. **158.1**

1. Failure (Psychology) 2. Resilience (Personal quality) 3. Life skills. 4. Play
ISBN 9781501195761

LC bl2019006313

Citing the inherent shortcomings of today's prioritization of productivity over play, a guide to building resilience through imperfection shares counsel on how to have fun trying new things without the expectation of being good at them.

"For Rinaldi, current trends that elevate hyperspecialization have created a culture of imbalance and stress. To make her points, she brings in ideas of others writers, such as Thich Nhat Hanh, Anthony Bourdain, and Edward Lorenz, to support the suck at something ethos. Rinaldis seductive lessons and embrace of messiness and incompleteness will inspire readers looking to spark personal change." Publishers Weekly.

Robbins, Anthony

Unlimited power : the new science of personal achievement / Anthony Robbins. Simon & Schuster, 1997. xix, 425 p. : **158.1**

1. Neurolinguistic programming 2. Success -- Psychological aspects
ISBN 9780684845777

LC 97035403

Originally published: 1986.

Reveals the secrets of neurolinguistic programming and explains how to master both mind and body while gaining emotional and financial freedom and increasing self-confidence.

Roth, Geneen

This messy magnificent life : a field guide / Geneen Roth. Scribner, 2018. xv, 202 p. ; **158.1**

1. Self-acceptance 2. Self-realization in women
ISBN 9781501182464

LC bl2018001138

Offers inspiration and advice for women to move toward self-acceptance, embrace their power, and begin living with openness, curiosity, and confidence.

" Though hardly groundbreaking, these chapters of simple advice are easily digestible, and reading one per day is a good way to start this practice. Empowering words for women--especially those struggling with body issues--to regain control of their lives." Kirkus.

Roth, Robert, 1950-

Strength in stillness : the power of transcendental meditation / Bob Roth, with Kevin Carr O'Leary. Simon & Schuster, 2018

214 p. ; **158.1**

1. Transcendental Meditation
ISBN 9781501161216

LC 2017035499

A practical guide to meditation by a leading authority shares insights into the scientific principles behind why and how Transcendental Meditation works to reduce stress, access inner power, and build resilience.

" A thorough explanation of what transcendental meditation is and is not that will appeal to readers of mindfulness and seekers of stress reduction and mental composure." Library Journal.

Rubin, Gretchen

Better than before : mastering the habits of our everyday lives / Gretchen Rubin. Crown Publishers, 2015 xii, 298 p. ; **158.1**

1. Change (Psychology). 2. Habit.
ISBN 0385348614

LC 2014031703

"Habits are the invisible architecture of our lives. Rubin provides an analytical and scientific framework from which to understand these habits--as well as change them for good. Infused with her compelling voice and funny stories, she illustrates the core principles of habit formation with dozens of strategies that she uses herself and tests out on others. Rubin provides tools to help readers better understand themselves, and presents a clear, practical menu of strategies so readers can take an individualized approach. She tackles each strategy herself and in doing so shows us the importance of knowing ourselves and our own habit tendencies. Armed with self-knowledge, we can pursue habits in ways that will truly work for us, not against us. Going to thegym can be as easy, effortless, and automatic as putting on a seatbelt. We can file expense reports, take time for fun, or pass up that piece of carrot cake without having to decide. With a foundation of good habits, we can build a life that reflects ourvalues and goals".-- Provided by publisher.

"An exploration of human behavior patterns as viewed through the lens of four specific tendencies." Kirkus.

Shlain, Tiffany

24/6 : the power of unplugging one day a week / Tiffany Shlain. Gallery Books, 2019. 246 p. **158.1**

1. Time management. 2. Technology. 3. Quality of life. 4. Work-life balance.
ISBN 9781982116866

LC 2019943854

The award-winning Internet pioneer and filmmaker chronicles the past, present and future of ideas about time and technology, outlining a strategy for clarity and life-quality based on disconnecting from technology for one restful day of the week.

Siegel, Daniel J., 1957-

Aware : the science and practice of presence : the groundbreaking meditation practice / Daniel J. Siegel, M.D. TarcherPerigee, a imprint of Penguin Random House LLC, 2018 xiii, 379 p. ; **158.1**

1. Meditation 2. Mindfulness (Psychology) 3. Self-actualization (Psychology)
ISBN 9781101993040

LC 2018016987

The *New York Times* best-selling author of *Brainstorm* and *Mindsight* introduces readers to his science-based Wheel of Awareness meditation discipline, demonstrating how a practice of focused attention and kindness can promote brain health and psychological wellness.

Sincero, Jen, 1965-

You are a badass / Jen Sincero. Running Press, 2017. 269 p. ; **158.1**

1. Self-actualization (Psychology). 2. Self-help techniques.
ISBN 0762490543

LC bl2017041242

A special hardcover edition of the #1 New York Times best-selling self-help classic, which empowers readers to create positive changes in their lives, and is filled with unforgettable lessons, features a new foreword from the author, who reflects on the book's almost-five-year span of incredible success.

"Sincero writes with candor about her own struggles, heightening the message's accessibility, particularly among a younger set." Publishers Weekly.

Sincero, Jen, 1965-

You are a badass every day : how to keep your motivation strong, your vibe high, and your quest for transformation unstoppable / Jen Sincero. Viking, 2018 216 p. ; **158.1**

1. Motivation (Psychology) 2. Success
ISBN 9780525561644

LC 2018045770

Includes index.

An empowering collection of edgy, bite-sized daily mantras and meditations counsels readers on how to make the most of personal resources and opportunities while embracing the courage to let go of mistakes, take responsibility and enjoy one's successes.

Stulberg, Brad

Peak performance : elevate your game, avoid burnout, and thrive with the new science of success / Brad Stulberg, Steve Magness. Rodale, 2017. ix, 230 p. ; **158.1**

1. Self-actualization (Psychology) 2. Psychology, Applied
ISBN 9781623367930

LC 2017021865

"A few common principles drive performance, regardless of the field or the task at hand. Whether someone is trying to qualify for the Olympics, break ground in mathematical theory or craft an artistic masterpiece, many of the practices that lead to great success are the same. In Peak Performance, Brad Stulberg, a former McKinsey and Company consultant and writer who covers health and the science of human performance, and Steve Magness, a performance scientist and coach of Olympic athletes, team up to demystify these practices and demonstrate how everyone can achieve their best. The first book of its kind, Peak Performance combines the inspiring stories of top performers across a range of capabilities - from athletic, to intellectual, to artistic - with the latest scientific insights into the cognitive and neurochemical factors that drive performance in all domains. In doing so, Peak Performance uncovers new linkages that hold promise as performance enhancers but have been overlooked in our traditionally-siloed ways of thinking. The result is a life-changing book in which readers learn how to enhance their performance via myriad ways including: optimally alternating between periods of intense work and rest; priming the body and mind for enhanced productivity; and developing and harnessing the power of a self-transcending purpose. In revealing the science of great performance and the stories of great performers across a wide range of capabilities, Peak Performance uncovers the secrets of success, and coaches readers on how to use them. If you want to take your game to the next level, whatever 'your game' may be, Peak Performance will teach you how".-- Provided by publisher.

Suh, Krista

★**DIY** rules for a WTF world : how to speak up, get creative, and change the world / Krista Suh. Grand Central Publishing, 2018 248 p. : **158.1**

1. Creative ability 2. Feminism 3. Self-realization in women
ISBN 9781538712337

LC bl2018000296

Offers advice, personal experiences, and inspiration from the creator of the Pussyhat Project intended to help readers live life purposefully and make the world better though creativity, self confidence, and overcoming obstacles and negativity.

Tierney, John (John Marion)

The **power** of bad : how the negativity effect rules us and how we can rule it / John Tierney and Roy F. Baumeister. Penguin Press, 2019. 304 p. **158.1**

1. Negativism. 2. Interpersonal conflict. 3. Personal conduct. 4. Self-management.
ISBN 9781594205521

LC 2019017303

The best-selling authors present a revelatory analysis of the negativity bias to explain its inherent role in social, political and professional conflicts, sharing recommendations for balancing phobias with rational strategies.

Tippett, Krista

★**Becoming** wise : an inquiry into the mystery and art of living / Krista Tippett. Penguin Group USA, 2016. 384 p. **158.1**

1. Personal conduct. 2. Spirituality 3. Faith. 4. Growth (Psychology)
ISBN 9781594206801

LC bl2016007662

Based on a podcast.

From the best-selling author and host of NPR's On Being comes a master class in living drawn from the inspiring stories of extraordinary individuals who possess what she calls "spiritual genius."

"A hopeful consideration of the human potential for enlightenment." Kirkus.

Viorst, Judith

Imperfect control : our lifelong struggles with power and surrender / Judith Viorst. Simon & Schuster, 1999, c1998. 446 p. ; **158.1**

1. Control (Psychology)
ISBN 9780684848143

LC BL 99002505

"A Fireside book."

Reprint. Originally published: 1998.

A sequel to the best-selling Necessary Losses explores the nature of the need for control, showing how it can keep people in destructive situations, discussing when acquiescence is helpful and when it is not, and the need to sometimes relinquish control.

"Referring to the works of social scientists, psychologists, and philosophers as well as literary examples and personal experiences, Viorst shows how issues of power and surrender confront and affect us throughout our lives. Her book is very readable, with traces of the author's special brand of humor woven throughout." Library Journal.

Wade, Cleo

Heart talk : poetic wisdom for a better life / Cleo Wade. 37INK, Atria, 2018. ix, 212 p. : **158.1**

1. Self-realization. 2. Self-realization 3. Conduct of life. 4. Conduct of life 5. Religious poetry
ISBN 9781501177347

LC bl2018020793

The popular social-media lifestyle personality shares creative inspiration and life lessons in a collection of illustrated poetry, mantras and affirmations, including fan favorites and previously unseen selections that explore how to overcome personal roadblocks to love, happiness and courage while spreading kindness to others.

Wax, Ruby, 1953-

Sane new world : a user's guide to the normal-crazy mind / Ruby Wax. Perigee Books, 2013 247 p. : **158.1**

1. Mind and body. 2. Mindfulness-based cognitive therapy.
ISBN 039917060X

LC 2014016530

A tie-in to the actress and television writer's one-woman show by the same title draws on her Oxford education and personal experiences with depression to counsel readers on mindfulness techniques for overcoming negative cognitive habits.

"Wax's unconventional approach may inspire others to seek help in coping with mental illness." Library Journal.

Wellings, Nigel

Why can't I meditate? : how to get your mindfulness practice on track / Nigel Wellings. TarcherPerigee, 2016. xxviii, 355 p. ; **158.1**

1. Meditation 2. Mindfulness (Psychology)
ISBN 9781101983270

LC 2016007917

"An accessible guide from an expert on Mindfulness on how to get the most out of meditation--and make the practice a permanent part of your daily life. Meditation is supposed to be a practice that's relaxing and beneficial...so why is it so hard to commit to? While many people have taken workshops in meditation, a significant number don't maintain their practice for long after the class is finished. Mindfulness can help us relax and is great for coming to grips with thoughts that make us depressed or anxious, but it can also bring us into a more intimate relationship with ourselves--a prospect that can make some feel uncomfortable. Yes, lots of good things come out of meditation practice, but keeping it up is challenging. This is where Why Can't I Meditate? comes in. Full of practical ways to help our mindfulness practice flourish, it also features guidance from a wide spectrum of secular and Buddhist mindfulness teachers, and personal accounts by new meditators on what they find difficult and what helps them overcome those blocks. It takes what is boring, painful, or downright scary about meditating and shows how these struggles can become an invaluable part of our path. If you have been considering meditating but doubted your ability, if you are having a hard time continuing, or if you've reluctantly stopped, Why Can't I Meditate? will help you get your mindfulness practice back on track".-- Provided by publisher.

"The instructions are clear, easy to follow, and kind, offering readers a path forward while leaving plenty of room for them to decide what works best. New students of mediation would be hard-pressed to find a more patient teacher." Booklist.

Wiking, Meik

The **little** book of hygge : Danish secrets to happy living / Meik Wiking. William Morrow, 2017 ix, 221 p. : **158.1**

1. Conduct of life 2. Happiness -- Denmark 3. Happiness 4. Self-actualization (Psychology)
ISBN 9780062658807

LC bl2016052564

A guide to the Danish philosophy of well-being shares advice and ideas for taking healthy breaks, living in the moment, creating positive atmospheres, building relationships and finding the richness of life in everyday small comforts.

"An exciting and intriguing guide, full of ideas for making everyday life more cozy." Library Journal.

Willink, Jocko

Discipline equals freedom : field manual / Jocko Willink. St. Martin's Press, 2017. 199 p. : **158.1**

1. Discipline 2. Mental discipline 3. Self-control

ISBN 9781250156945

LC bl2017034739

An ex-Navy SEAL presents a guide on how to achieve freedom through discipline, outlining the mental and physical practices that shaped his career and continue to help him reach fulfilling goals while outmaneuvering common pitfalls.

158.2 Interpersonal relations

Botsman, Rachel

Who can you trust? : how technology brought us together and why it might drive us apart / Rachel Botsman. PublicAffairs, 2017. 288 p. **158.2**

1. Trust 2. Technology 3. Networks 4. Persons

ISBN 9781541773677

LC bl2017045890

A new world order is emerging: we might have lost faith in institutions and leaders, but millions of people rent their home to total strangers, exchange digital currencies, or find themselves trusting a bot. This is the age of "distributed trust", a paradigm shift driven by innovative technologies that are rewriting the rules of an all-too-human relationship.

"A sharp, thoughtful, sometimes-surprising account of how we build trust with strangers now." Kirkus.

Dahl, Melissa

Cringeworthy : a theory of awkwardness / Melissa Dahl. Portfolio, 2018. xii, 286 p. ; **158.2**

1. First impressions. 2. Self-perception -- Social aspects. 3. Social phobia. 4. Human behavior.

ISBN 9780735211636

LC 2017052219

The editor of New York magazine's "Science of Us" website explores the compelling psychology of awkwardness, sharing scientific insights into how truly embarrassing moments are actually perceived by others and how learning to accept one's cringe-worthy gaffes can be socially advantageous.

Denworth, Lydia, 1966-

Friendship : the evolution, biology, and extraordinary power of life's fundamental bond / Lydia Denworth. W.W. Norton & Company, [2020] 297 p. **158.2**

1. Friendship 2. Neuropsychology 3. Mind and body 4. Evolution

ISBN 9780393651546

LC 2019032111

The bonds of friendship are universal and elemental. In Friendship, journalist Lydia Denworth visits the front lines of the science of friendship in search of its biological, psychological, and evolutionary foundations. Finding it to be as old as life on the African savannas, she also discovers that friendship is reflected in our brain waves, detectable in our genomes, and capable of strengthening our cardiovascular and immune systems. Its opposite, loneliness, can kill. As a result, social connection is finally being recognized as critical to our physical and emotional well-being. With warmth and compassion, Denworth weaves together past and present, field biology and cutting-edge neuroscience, to show how our bodies and minds are designed to make friends, the process by which social bonds develop, and how a drive for friendship underpins human (and nonhuman) society.

"Denworth's work achieves the best of science writing by making complicated concepts clear. She uses intelligent observation, empathy, and curiosity to offer a friendship manifesto that will absolutely affect readers' own personal approaches to friendship." Booklist.

Fontes, Lisa Aronson

Invisible chains : overcoming coercive control in your intimate relationship / Lisa Aronson Fontes. The Guilford Press, 2015 xvii, 217 p. ; **158.2**

1. Dominance (Psychology). 2. Control (Psychology). 3. Interpersonal relations. 4. Intimate partner violence.

ISBN 9781462520244

LC 2014048835

"When a man showers all of his attention on a woman, it can feel incredibly romantic, and can blind her to hints of problems ahead. But what happens when that attentiveness becomes domination? For certain people, the desire to control leads to jealousy, threats, micromanaging--even physical violence. Lisa Aronson Fontes draws on both professional expertise and personal experience to provide practical guidance and support for readers who find themselves trapped in a web of coercive control. Understanding this destructive pattern and why it occurs is the first step toward repairing or ending a relationship that has become toxic. Readers get vital tools for determining if they are in danger and if their partner can change--and for getting their freedom back".-- Provided by publisher.

Friday, Nancy

My mother/my self: the daughter's search for identity / Nancy Friday. Delta Trade Paperbacks, c1997. xviii, 425 p. ; **158.2**

1. Love, Maternal. 2. Mothers and daughters. 3. Sex (Psychology) 4. Women -- Psychology.

ISBN 0385320159

LC 98115632

"A Delta book"--T.p. verso.

Originally published: New York : Delacorte Press, 1977.

A candid exploration of the mother-daughter relationship probes the private emotions, pains, joys, and secrets and charts the stages of a woman's life.

Goleman, Daniel

★**Social** intelligence : the new science of human relationships / Daniel Goleman. Bantam Books, 2006. 403 p. : **158.2**

1. Interpersonal relations. 2. Intellect -- Social aspects. 3. Emotions -- Social aspects. 4. Social intelligence

ISBN 0558303528

Explores the nature of human relationships, finding that humans are "wired to connect," and bringing together the latest research in biology and neuroscience to reveal how one's daily encounters shape the brain and affect the body.

"The author argues for a new social model of intelligence drawn from the emerging field of social neuroscience. Goleman illuminates new theories about attachment, bonding, and the making and remaking of memory as he examines how our brains are wired for altruism, compassion, concern and rapport." Publishers Weekly.

Goodman, Ellen

I know just what you mean : the power of friendship in women's lives / Ellen Goodman, Patricia O'Brien. Simon & Schuster, 2001, c2000. 300 p. : **158.2**

1. Female friendship 2. Women -- Psychology.
ISBN 074320171X

LC BL2001004221

"A Fireside book."

Reprint. Originally published: 2000.

The authors and friends collect interviews and stories exploring the meaning, importance, and challenges of female relationships.

"Heavy on insight and light on psychological jargon, this book is an intelligent, observant read." Publishers Weekly.

Goulston, Mark

Talking to crazy : how to deal with the irrational and impossible people in your life / Mark Goulston. American Management Association, 2015 259 p. : **158.2**

1. Conflict management. 2. Interpersonal conflict. 3. Interpersonal relations.
ISBN 0814436366

LC 2015012549

Includes index.

Provides a range of techniques for communicating with unreasonable people by empathizing with their "crazy," using this counterintuitive method to change the dynamic of the conversation and become an ally rather than a threat.

Grant, Adam M.

Give and take : a revolutionary approach to success / Adam M. Grant. Viking Press, 2013 320 p. **158.2**

1. Generosity 2. Success (Concept) 3. Goals and objectives. 4. Altruism.
ISBN 9780670026555

LC 2012039995

An award-winning researcher and consultant explains how effective networking, influence and leadership skills are subject to the professional interaction styles of takers, matchers and givers that dramatically shape success rates, citing the essential roles of behind-the-scenes contributors to famous organizations while outlining a revolutionary approach to networking and productivity.

Howes, Molly

A **good** apology : four steps to make things right / Molly Howes. Grand Central Publishing, 2020. 304 p. ; **158.2**

1. Apologizing. 2. Emotions.
ISBN 9781538701317

LC 2019050663

"Those looking for a way to say sorry and mean it will learn much from Howe's approachable demystification of the art of the apology." Publishers Weekly

Murthy, Vivek Hallegere, 1977-

Together : the healing power of human connection in a sometimes lonely world / Vivek H. Murthy, MD. Harper Wave, 2020 352 p. **158.2**

1. Communities. 2. Loneliness. 3. Mental health. 4. Public health.
ISBN 9780062913296

LC 2020002242

"In Together, the former Surgeon General addresses the overlooked epidemic of loneliness as the underpinning to the current crisis in mental wellness and offers solutions to create connection and stresses the importance of community to counteract the forces driving us to depression and isolation".-- Provided by publisher.

"A touch too pat at times but, overall, a well-considered diagnosis of a real and overlooked crisis in public health." Kirkus

Rollag, Keith

What to do when you're new : how to be comfortable, confident, and successful in new situations / Keith Rollag. AMACOM--American Management Association, 2016 x, 230 p. ; **158.2**

1. Interpersonal relations 2. Self-confidence 3. Success
ISBN 9780814434895

LC 2015011043

Provides strategies for becoming more comfortable and achieving success in new situations, explaining how to overcome anxieties in order to make great first impressions, fearlessly perform tasks, and confidently interact with others.

Safer, Jeanne

I love you, but I hate your politics : how to protect your intimate relationships in a poisonous partisan world / Jeanne Safer, Ph.D.. All Points Books, 2019. ix, 228 p. ; **158.2**

1. Interpersonal conflict 2. Interpersonal relations -- Political aspects 3. Partisanship 4. Party affiliation -- Social aspects
ISBN 9781250200396

LC 2019008430

Includes index.

Drawing from interviews with politically-mixed couples and her own experiences as a liberal happily married to a conservative, a psychotherapist offers a practical guide to maintaining respect and intimacy in a strained and increasingly divided world.

"This insightful, well-reasoned book will help readers negotiate the political differences in their relationships with the people they love most." Publishers Weekly.

Schafer, John R., 1954-

The **like** switch : an ex-FBI agent's guide to influencing, attracting, and winning people over / Jack Schafer, Ph.D., with Marvin Karlins, Ph.D. Simon & Schuster, 2015 xv, 270 p. : **158.2**

1. Friendship. 2. Interpersonal attraction. 3. Influence (Psychology). 4. Interpersonal relations.
ISBN 9781476754482

LC 2014009121

Offers advice and strategies for readers to get others to like them, assess truthfulness, and read the body behavior of others.

Stone, Douglas, 1958-

Difficult conversations : how to discuss what matters most / Douglas Stone, Bruce Patton, Sheila Heen. Viking, 1999. xxi, 250 p. : **158.2**

1. Communication 2. Interpersonal relations. 3. Interpersonal communication. 4. Confrontation (Interpersonal relations)
ISBN 0670883395

LC 98033346

Offers advice on working gracefully and effectively through such confrontational situations as ending relationships and asking for a raise, identifying key adjustments necessary to the dialogue process.

Waxman, Jamye

How to break up with anyone : letting go of friends, family, and everyone in-between / Jamye Waxman. Seal Press, 2015 228 p. ; **158.2**

1. Friendship. 2. Conflict resolution 3. Self-fulfillment 4.

Interpersonal relations
ISBN 9781580055970

LC 2015019613

Offers advice to deal with every step of a non-romantic breakup, and provides strategies for disengaging from a friend, family member, or community.

"Sound guidance for those involved in toxic relationships and looking for a way out." Library Journal.

160 Philosophical logic

Copi, Irving M.

★**Introduction** to logic / Irving M. Copi, Carl Cohen. Pearson/Prentice Hall, c2019 xvii, 670 p. : **160**

1. Logic -- Textbooks
ISBN 9781138500860

LC 2018056876

For more than six decades, and for thousands of students, Introduction to Logic has been the gold standard in introductory logic texts. In this 15th Edition, Carl Cohen and Victor Rodych update Irving M. Copi's classic text, improving on its many strengths and introducing new and helpful material that will greatly assist both students and instructors.

169 Analogy

Hofstadter, Douglas R., 1945-

Surfaces and essences / Douglas Hofstadter and Emmanuel Sander. Basic Books, 2010. 512 p. **169**

1. Thought and thinking 2. Psychology 3. Cognitive science. 4. Reasoning.
ISBN 9780465018475

LC bl2010009678

Shows how analogy-making pervades human thought at all levels, choosing our words and phrases for us when we speak, framing how we understand even the most boring everyday situation, guiding us in unfamiliar situations, and giving rise to great acts of imagination.

170 Ethics (Moral philosophy)

Allison, Jay,

This I believe : the personal philosophies of remarkable men and women / edited by Jay Allison and Dan Gediman ; with John Gregory and Viki Merrick ; photographs by Nubar Alexanian ; editorial team, Gladys Chang Hardy ... [et al.]. H. Holt, 2006. xxi, 281 p., 15 p. of plates : **170**

1. Belief and doubt. 2. Personal conduct 3. Life. 4. Celebrities -- Spiritual life. 5. Essays.
ISBN 9780805080872

LC 2006043522

A collection of eighty essays exploring the personal beliefs of a diverse assortment of contributors, both famous and unknown, who reflect on their faith, the evolution of their beliefs, and how they express them.

"This collection of essays from a popular radio series draws transcripts from both the original series and its newer version, including some remarkable statements from the likes of dancer/choreographer Martha Graham, autistic academic Temple Grandin, writer and physicist Alan Lightman, novelist and social critic Thomas Mann, economic historian Arnold Toynbee, and feminist writer Rebecca West. Astonishing to hear and astonishing to read and reread, this work is a wonderful addition to any library." Library Journal.

Allison, Jay,

This I believe II : more personal philosophies of remarkable men and women / edited by Jay Allison and Dan Gediman with John Gregory and Viki Merrick ; additional editing by Emily Botein ... [et al.]. Henry Holt, 2008. 288 p. **170**

1. Belief and doubt. 2. Personal conduct. 3. Life. 4. Celebrities -- Personal conduct 5. Essays.
ISBN 9780805087680

LC 2008010110

Featuring 80 Americans--from the famous to the unknown--this series of insightful observations completes the thought that the book's title introduces. Each piece compels readers to rethink not only how they arrive at their own personal beliefs but also how they share them with others.

Brooks, David, 1961-

The **road** to character / David Brooks. Random House, 2015 xvii, 300 p. ; **170**

1. Character 2. Virtues 3. Ethics 4. Personal conduct
ISBN 9780812993257

The New York Times columnist and best-selling author of The Social Animal evaluates America's transition to a culture that values self-promotion over humility, explaining the importance of an engaged inner life in personal fulfillment.

"Although Brooks goes after the selfie generation, he does so in a fairly nuanced way, noting that it was really the World War II Greatest Generation who started the ball rolling. He is careful to emphasize that no one--even those he profiles--is anywhere near flawless. The author's sincere sermon--at times analytical, at times hortatory--remains a hopeful one." Kirkus.

Catapano, Peter,

Modern ethics in 77 arguments : a Stone reader / edited by Peter Catapano and Simon Critchley. Liveright Publishing Corporation, 2017 xi, 435 p. ; **170**

1. Ethics, Modern -- 21st century 2. Newspapers -- Sections, columns, etc -- Ethics
ISBN 9781631492983

LC 2017018086

The editors of the "New York Times" philosophy column collect seventy-seven essays from its online publications to explore topics ranging from consciousness and religious belief to gun control and drone warfare.

Coles, Robert

★**Lives** of moral leadership / Robert Coles. Random House, c2000. xvii, 247 p. ; **170**

1. Personal conduct -- Case studies. 2. Leadership -- Moral and ethical aspects -- Case studies. 3. Ethics. 4. Role models.
ISBN 9780375501081

LC 00027858

In an incisive study of moral leadership and its implications, the best-selling author of The Moral Life of Children profiles individuals who have had a profound influence on contemporary American life and examines those qualities that allow people to become moral leaders in their homes, communities, and nation.

Covey, Stephen R.

Everyday greatness : inspiration for a meaningful life / insights and commentary by Steven R. Covey ; compiled by David K. Hatch. Rutledge Hill Press, 2006. xvii, 445 p. ; **170**

1. Mormon Church. 2. Personal conduct. 3. Christian life. 4. Spirituality. 5. Christianity.
ISBN 9781401602413

LC 2006019786

"Reader's Digest."

"The stories, which the authors have gleaned from Reader's Digest, illustrate 21 principles such as integrity, gratitude, respect, and perseverance. Covey provides commentary, reflections, and further insights on how readers can apply each principle to their own lives in today's world. Truly inspiring." Library Journal.

Dalai Lama

An **appeal** to the world : the way to peace in a time of division / Dalai Lama XIV William Morrow & Company, 2017. 128 p. **170**

1. Peace-building 2. Political science 3. Philosophy, Buddhist 4. Buddhist doctrines
ISBN 9780062835536

LC 2017278828

A noted religious leader addresses the world's time of division, calling on us to draw upon the innate goodness of our shared humanity to overcome the rancor, mistrust and divisiveness that threaten world peace and sustainability.

"Always inspiring and accessible, this lovely book is, itself, readers will discover, worth meditation and contemplation." Booklist.

Gottlieb, Daniel, 1946-

Learning from the heart : lessons on living, loving, and listening / Daniel Gottlieb. Sterling Pub., c2008. 170 p. ; **170**

1. Conduct of life.
ISBN 1402749996

LC 2007035100

A follow-up to "Letters to Sam" draws on the author's perspective as a quadriplegic to share his thoughts on and insights into what it means to be human, including what divides and unites us, the problems of family life, parental problems, the challengesconfronting the disabled and the aging, and issues of injustice in the modern world.

"Having rebuilt his life after an accident that left him a quadriplegic in his thirties, . [the author] here shares his observations on what makes us human. An uplifting book abounding with encouragement for daily living; recommended for public libraries." Library Journal.

Graham, Lauren

In conclusion, don't worry about it / Lauren Graham. Ballantine Books, 2018. xii, 47 p. : **170**

1. Conduct of life 2. Self-actualization (Psychology) 3. Success -- Psychological aspects
ISBN 9781524799595

LC 2017061314

Expanded version of the author's 2017 commencement speech at her hometown Langley High School (Virginia).

Presents advice about the importance of being curious and compassionate, making life choices that bring personal satisfaction, and accepting the inevitable successes and failures that come with them.

Greene, Joshua David, 1974-

Moral tribes : emotion, reason, and the gap between us and them / Joshua D. Greene. Penguin Press, 2013. 432 p. **170**

1. Ethics. 2. Globalization. 3. Civilization. 4. Emotions.
ISBN 9781594202605

LC 2013007775

A path-breaking neuroscientist explores how globalization has illuminated the deep moral divisions between opposing sides, drawing on pioneering research to reveal the evolutionary sources of morality while outlining recommendations for bridging divided cultures.

Haidt, Jonathan

The **happiness** hypothesis : finding modern truth in ancient wisdom / Jonathan Haidt. Basic Books, c2006. xiii, 297 p. : **170**

1. Happiness. 2. Self-acceptance. 3. Self-perception.
ISBN 0465028012

LC 2005021163

"Why the meaningful life is closer than you think"--Cover.

Explores ten great insights about man, the purpose of life, and happiness selected from diverse traditions and uses current scientific research to question and discuss the ideas.

"Using the wisdom culled from the world's greatest civilizations as a foundation, social psychologist Haidt comes to terms with 10 Great Ideas, viewing them through a contemporary filter to learn which of their lessons may still apply to modern lives. Fascinating stuff, accessibly expressed." Booklist.

Katie, Byron

A **thousand** names for joy : living in harmony with the way things are / Byron Katie with Stephen Mitchell. Harmony Books, c2007. xv, 281 p. ; **170**

1. Laozi. Dao de jing. 2. Personal conduct. 3. Tao. 4. Taoism. 5. Religion.
ISBN 0307339238

LC 2006017754

An in-depth analysis of the classic spiritual guide, the Tao Te Ching, reveals how the wisdom of the ancient texts can be applied to everyday modern life, exploring such important issues as life, death, love, work, and fulfillment in terms of how an awakened mind can attain true freedom.

Kubler-Ross, Elisabeth

★**Life** lessons : two experts on death and dying teach us about the mysteries of life and living / Elisabeth Kubler-Ross and David Kessler. Scribner, c2000. 224 p. ; **170**

1. Personal conduct. 2. Death. 3. Life. 4. Fear.
ISBN 0684870746

LC 00057387

A guide to living life in the moment uses lessons learned from the dying to help the living find the most enjoyment and happiness.

"As in each of their previous individual works, the authors provide useful and accessible information." Library Journal.

McCullough, David

You are not special... and other encouragements : And Other Encouragements / David McCullough, Jr. Ecco, 2014 xxxii, 316 p. ; **170**

1. Conduct of life 2. Success
ISBN 9780062257345

LC bl2014014095

Elaborating on his famous commencement speech, the author takes the pressure off of students to be extraordinary achievers and encourages them to do something useful with their advantages.

"The author tackles big issues, such as gender and race, with searching sincerity, open-heartedness, and a deft, light touch." Kirkus.

Shriver, Maria

I've been thinking ... : reflections, prayers, and meditations for a meaningful life / Maria Shriver. Pamela Dorman Books/ Viking, [2018] xi, 225 p. ; **170**

1. Spiritual life 2. Purpose in life 3. Optimism
ISBN 9780525522607

LC 2018300874

Presents a book of reflections for those seeking wisdom, guidance, encouragement, and inspiration on the road to a meaningful life.

"Among the topics she covers are kindness, mental health, peace, time to reflect, grief, and powerof the mind, of women, of the pause, of empathy. The honesty of this uplifting book will please Shrivers established readership as well as new readers looking for inspiration." Publishers Weekly.

Tutu, Desmond

Made for goodness : and why this makes all the difference / Desmond Tutu and Mpho Tutu. Harpercollins, 2010. 256 p. **170**

1. Hope. 2. Virtue. 3. Common good. 4. Optimism.
ISBN 9780061706592

LC 2010003774

"In his most personal and inspirational book to date, a beloved Nobel Prize-winner joins his daughter, an Anglican minister, to share a powerful vision on why each of us can find hope and joy even in troubled times--because we are all made for goodness."

"The book is founded on the broad notion that we are created with the freedom to choose good or evil but also incline fundamentally to the good. A crucially important book from the Nobel Peace Prize winner; a witness to our tumultuous times." Library Journal.

Viljoen, Edward

Ordinary goodness : the surprisingly effortless path to creating a life of meaning and beauty / Edward Viljoen. TarcherPerigee, 2017 xvii, 215 p. **170**

1. Conduct of life 2. Good and evil 3. Spiritual life
ISBN 9780399183911

LC OC2018139672

Using personal anecdotes, the author discusses how a spiritual practice of faith along with ordinary acts of kindness and compassion can instill a sense of meaning and purpose in life.

Wolfe, Alan, 1942-

Moral freedom : the impossible idea that defines the way we live now / Alan Wolfe. W. W. Norton, 2001. 256 p. **170**

1. Ethics -- United States -- Public opinion. 2. Public opinion -- United States. 3. Loyalty. 4. Honesty.
ISBN 0393048438

LC 00051969

Ventures into the minds and hearts of Americans to determine how we really think about morality in today's age, focusing on traditional values of loyalty, self-restraint, honesty, and forgiveness.

171 Ethical systems

Aristotle

★**Nicomachean** ethics / Aristotle ; translation (with historical introduction) by Christopher Rowe ; philosophical introduction and commentary by Sarah Broadie. Oxford University Press, 2002. x, 468 p. ; **171**

1. Ethics
ISBN 9780198752714

LC 2002283430

This work presents the Nicomachean Ethics in a fresh English translation by Christopher Rowe that strives to be meticulously accurate yet also accessible. The translation is accompanied by Sarah Broadie's detailed line-by-line commentary, which brings out the subtlety of Aristotle's thought as it develops from moment to moment. --Provided by publisher

172 Political ethics

Sandel, Michael J.

Justice : what's the right thing to do? / Michael J. Sandel. Farrar Straus & Giroux, 2009. 288 p. **172**

1. Justice. 2. Values. 3. Ethics. 4. Common good. 5. United States -- Social life and customs -- 21st century
ISBN 9780374180652

LC 2009025438

A Harvard professor assesses the role of justice in modern society as well as the moral responsibilities faced by ordinary citizens, weighing a range of issues from euthanasia and abortion to affirmative action and tax structuring.

"The author has a talent for making the difficult--Kant's categorical imperative or Rawls's difference principle--readily comprehensible, and his relentless, though never oppressive, reason shines throughout the narrative. Sparkling commentary from the professor we all wish we had." Kirkus.

174 Occupational ethics

Callahan, David, 1965-

The **cheating** culture : why more Americans are doing wrong to get ahead / David Callahan. Harcourt, 2004. ix, 366 p. ; **174**

1. Business ethics. 2. Professional ethics. 3. Social ethics. 4. United States -- Moral conditions
ISBN 0156030055

LC bl2005009403

"A Harvest book."

A look at cheating in modern-day society places the blame on the highly competitive economic climate of the past two decades, explaining why an unfettered market and unprecedented economic inequities have eroded American values.

"If all business school students could be required to read one book, this should be it." Choice.

Covey, Stephen M. R.

★**Smart** trust : creating prosperity, energy and joy in a low-trust world / Stephen M.R. Covey and Greg Link ; with Rebecca R. Merrill. Free Press, c2012. xxiii, 296 p.) : **174**

1. Business ethics 2. Ethics 3. Leadership -- Moral and ethical aspects 4. Organizational behavior
ISBN 9781451651454

LC oc2014085095

Builds on the philosophies introduced in the best-selling The Speed of Trust to counsel professionals on how to promote trustworthy relationships in a time of extreme distrust, sharing hundreds of international examples about individuals, teams and organizations that have reaped the benefits of establishing trust in their business dealings.

Gentile, Mary C.
Giving voice to values : how to speak your mind when you know what's right / Mary C. Gentile. Yale University Press, c2010. xliv, 273 p. ; **174**

1. Business ethics 2. Leadership 3. Values
ISBN 9780300161182

LC 2010011905

"Gentile offers a powerful action-oriented manifesto for living with integrity, fighting for one's convictions, and building a more ethical workplace." Publishers Weekly.

Mackey, John, 1954-
Conscious capitalism : liberating the heroic spirit of business / John Mackey & Raj Sisodia. Harvard Business Review Press, c2013. 368 p. **174**

1. Corporate accountability 2. Business ethics 3. Capitalism -- Moral and ethical aspects 4. Corporations -- Moral and ethical aspects
ISBN 9781422144206

LC 2012025305

Profiles the business philosophies of such market leaders as Whole Foods, Costco and Wegmans, revealing how their examples reflect fundamental principles and practices that business managers can adapt to enable conscious leadership and a caring business culture.

Oreskes, Naomi
Merchants of doubt : how a handful of scientists obscured the truth on issues from tobacco smoke to global warming / Naomi Oreskes and Erik M. Conway. Bloomsbury Press, c2010. 368 p. **174**

1. Scientists -- Professional ethics. 2. Democracy and science. 3. Science news -- Moral and ethical aspects. 4. Environmental sciences
ISBN 9781596916104

LC 2009043183

"Documents the troubling influence of a small group of scientists who the author contends misrepresent scientific facts to advance key political and economic agendas, revealing the interests behind their detractions on findings about acid rain, DDT and other hazards."

Sandel, Michael J.
What money can't buy : the moral limits of markets / Michael J. Sandel. Farrar, Straus and Giroux, c2012. 256 p. **174**

1. Economics -- Moral and ethical aspects. 2. Capitalism -- Moral and ethical aspects. 3. Wealth -- Moral and ethical aspects. 4. Value.
ISBN 9780374203030

LC 2011052182

The political philosopher shares a revisionist view of the roles of markets and money in a democratic society, assessing the moral limits of markets in private life and how the market economy has encroached on private and societal values.

Wilmut, Ian
★**After** Dolly : the uses and misuses of human cloning / Ian Wilmut and Roger Highfield. W.W. Norton & Company, 2006. 335 p. ; **174**

1. Dolly (Sheep) 2. Clones and cloning -- Moral and ethical aspects. 3. Humans. 4. Science.
ISBN 0393060667

LC 2006002030

An argument for the benefits of cloning, co-written by a scientist whose team was responsible for a famous cloned sheep, presents the reasons for his opposition to the cloning of humans and explains that cloning technology can be ethically applied to free families from serious hereditary diseases.

"In this account of the program that eventuated in Dolly, . . . [Wilmut] covers a variety of the social, medical, and scientific implications of cloning. . . . Wilmut, aided by science writer Highfield, well explains potentially confusing issues, in the end making a strong enough case to convince us that Dolly neither lived nor died in vain." Booklist.

174.2 Medical and health professions

Dreger, Alice Domurat
Galileo's middle finger : heretics, activists, and the search for justice in science / Alice Dreger. Penguin Press, 2015. 320 p. **174.2**

1. Research -- Moral and ethical aspects. 2. Scientists -- Professional ethics. 3. Science -- Political aspects. 4. Dissenting opinions.
ISBN 9781594206085

LC 2014036659

An advocate for victims of unethical research who also defends the rights of scientists to pursue challenging research into human identities defends intellectual freedom, in this thought-provoking volume told though the ordeals of modern scientists who have been attacked for exploring controversial ideas.

"A crusader in the mold of muckrackers from a century ago, Dreger doesn't try to hide her politics or her agenda. Instead she advocates for change intelligently and passionately. Highly recommended for those interested in academic freedom, controversial issues in academia, and intersex and gender issues." Library Journal.

Tucker, Todd, 1968-
★The **great** starvation experiment : the heroic men who starved so that millions could live / Todd Tucker. Free Press, c2006. xi, 270 p. : **174.2**

1. Keys, Ancel Benjamin, 1904- 2. Hunger -- Physiological effect -- Research -- United States. 3. Human experimentation in medicine -- United States. 4. World War II -- United States. 5. Conscientious objectors 6. United States -- History -- 20th century.
ISBN 9780743270304

LC 2006278255

An account of a six-month, late-World War II experiment on thirty-six American conscientious objectors assigned to the Civilian Public Service corps traces how Dr. Ancel Keys, the inventor of the K-ration, studied the effects of extreme food rationing practices in Europe.

"As WWII neared an end, 36 idealistic conscientious objectors, members of the Civilian Public Service, volunteered to be systematically starved. The project, headed by Dr. Ancel Keys, was designed to develop an understanding of the physiology and psychology of starvation and to provide strategies to manage the mass starvation that might follow the war's end in Europe. Tucker . . . provides a fascinating and moving history of the experiment, centering on the lives and experiences of the volunteers and the formidable obstacles they overcame." Publishers Weekly.

Washington, Harriet A.
Medical apartheid : the dark history of medical experimentation on black Americans from colonial times to the present / Harriet A. Washington. Doubleday, 2006. x, 501 p., 16 p. of

plates : **174.2**

1. Human experimentation in medicine. 2. African Americans -- Medical care -- History. 3. Medical research -- History. 4. Racism in medical care. 5. United States -- History
ISBN 0385509936

LC 2005051873

National Book Critics Circle Award for Non-Fiction, 2007.

The first comprehensive history of medical experimentation on African Americans. Starting with the earliest encounters between Africans and Western medical researchers and the racist pseudoscience that resulted, it details the way both slaves and freedmen were used in hospitals for experiments conducted without a hint of informed consent--a tradition that continues today within some black populations. It shows how the pseudoscience of eugenics and social Darwinism was used to justify experimental exploitation and shoddy medical treatment of blacks, and a view that they were biologically inferior, oversexed, and unfit for adult responsibilities. New details about the government's Tuskegee experiment are revealed, as are similar, less well-known medical atrocities conducted by the government, the armed forces, and private institutions. This book reveals the hidden underbelly of scientific research and makes possible, for the first time, an understanding of the roots of the African American health deficit.--From publisher description.

"The author offers a history of medical experimentation on and mistreatment of black Americans in this stunning work, which is both broad in scope and well documented." Booklist.

176 Ethics of sex and reproduction

Chavez Perez, Inti, 1984-

Respect : everything a guy needs to know about sex, love, and consent / Inti Chavez Perez ; translated from the Swedish by Stuart Tudball. Penguin Books, 2019 206 p. ; **176**

1. Respect 2. Young men 3. Man-woman relationships 4. Interpersonal relations
ISBN 9780143134251

LC 2019018370

Translation of author's book Respekt.

Citing the serious issues revealed by the #MeToo movement, an all-encompassing guide counsels male readers on sex and consent in the 21st century, covering topics ranging from body image and relationships to gender identity and sexual orientation.

Freitas, Donna

The **end** of sex : how hookup culture is leaving a generation unhappy, sexually unfulfilled, and confused about intimacy / Donna Freitas. Basic Books, [2013] 272 p. **176**

1. College students -- Sexuality. 2. Young adults -- Sexuality. 3. Sexual ethics. 4. Dating (Social customs)
ISBN 9780465002153

LC 2012042226

Revealing high levels of social pressure that compel today's college students to engage in casual sex, a report on the consequences of unbalanced sexual lifestyles draws on student testimonies to counsel readers on how to avoid unwanted sex, regard sex from a healthy perspective and pursue meaningful relationships.

Stock, Gregory

Redesigning humans : our inevitable genetic future / Gregory Stock. Houghton Mifflin, 2002. 277 p. ; **176**

1. Human genetics -- Moral and ethical aspects. 2. Human reproductive technology -- Moral and ethical aspects. 3. Genetic engineering -- Moral and ethical aspects.
ISBN 9780618060269

LC 2001051890

"The author gives an overview of the new biotechnology that will allow scientists to delay aging and to insert genes that enhance physical and cognitive performance, combat disease or improve looks into embryos. Stock thoughtfully weighs the ethical dilemmas such advances present, arguing that the real threat is not frivolous abuse of technology but the fact that we don't know the long-term effects of these genetic changes." Publishers Weekly.

177 Ethics of social relations

Ariely, Dan

The **honest** truth about dishonesty : how we lie to everyone--especially ourselves / Dan Ariely. Harper, 2012. xiii, 285 p. ; **177**

1. Dishonesty 2. Truth. 3. Human behavior 4. Behavioral economics
ISBN 9780062183590

LC 2012015990

From Washington to Wall Street, the classroom to the workplace, an award-winning, bestselling author and behavior economist explores the question of dishonesty to help us understand why cheating is so prevalent and what we can do about it.

Armstrong, Karen, 1944-

Twelve steps to a compassionate life / Karen Armstrong. Alfred A. Knopf, 2010. 240 p. **177**

1. Compassion -- Religious aspects -- Christianity. 2. Virtues. 3. Ethics. 4. Christian ethics.
ISBN 9780307595591

LC 2010036870

"A Borzoi book."

The award-winning author shares practical recommendations for promoting world peace by cultivating one's intrinsic tendencies for compassion, outlining a program for achieving mindfulness and engaging in acts of kindness.

Las Comadres para las Americas

★**Count** on me : tales of sisterhoods and fierce friendships / Las Comadres para las Americas. Atria Books, 2012. 336 p. **177**

1. Las Comadres para las Americas. 2. Hispanic American women 3. Female friendship 4. Friendship. 5. Social networks. 6. Essays.
ISBN 9781451642018

LC 2012015552

"A beautiful evocation of love, friendship and community." Kirkus.

Sow, Aminatou

Big friendship : how we keep each other close / Aminatou Sow and Ann Friedman. Simon & Schuster, 2020. 288 p. **177**

1. Sow, Aminatou 2. Friedman, Ann 3. Friendship 4. Female friendship. 5. Interpersonal relations. 6. Long distance friendship
ISBN 9781982111908

LC 2020002283

Includes index.

Based on a podcast.

The feminist hosts of the Call Your Girlfriend podcast argue that close friendship is the most influential and important relationship a human life can have, sharing strategies for creating fulfilling, long-term relationships with friends.

"A soul-searching reflection that delivers an emotional journey to amplify the self-help tips." Kirkus

Velasquez, Lizzie
Dare to be kind : how extraordinary compassion can transform our world / Lizzie Velasquez, with Catherine Avril Morris. Hachette Books, 2017 192 p. ; **177**
1. Bullying 2. Kindness
ISBN 9780316272438
LC 2017002974

A motivational speaker and YouTube sensation shows readers how they can learn to accept all parts of themselves and others, and in doing so create a "culture of kindness" and a more compassionate world.

"This is a wonderful and fast read, full of vitality that captures the luminous spirit of kindness that Velasquez so beautifully embodies." Booklist.

Young, Kevin, 1970-
Bunk : the rise of hoaxes, humbug, plagiarists, phonies, post-facts, and fake news / Kevin Young. Graywolf Press, 2017 480 p. **177**
1. Hoaxes 2. Race (Biology) 3. Stereotypes (Social psychology) 4. Deception
ISBN 9781555977917
LC bl2017037554

Longlisted for the Andrew Carnegie Medal for Excellence in Non-Fiction, 2018.

Longlisted for the National Book Award for Nonfiction, 2017.

The award-winning author traces the history of the hoax as a distinct American phenomenon, exploring the roles of stereotype, suspicion and racism as factors that have shaped fraudulent activities from the heyday of P. T. Barnum through the "fake news" activities of Donald Trump.

"Young presents a rogue's gallery, including Grey Owl, Bernie Madoff, and Lance Armstrong, paying particular attention to the especially heinous frauds of journalists, including Stephen Glass and Jayson Blair. Young closes with an examination of today's constant bombardment of intertwined facts and factoids and the need for each of us to try to suss out the truth. Compelling and eye-opening." Booklist.

179 Other ethical norms

Baur, Gene
Farm Sanctuary : changing hearts and minds about animals and food / Gene Baur. Simon & Schuster, 2008. xv, 286 p. : **179**
1. Livestock factories -- Moral and ethical aspects. 2. Livestock -- Social aspects. 3. Animal industry and trade -- Moral and ethical aspects. 4. Animal welfare.
ISBN 9780743291583
"A Touchstone book."

A founder of an organization dedicated to promoting the compassionate treatment of animals and combating factory farming addresses key questions about the ethics of breeding animals for food, exposing inhumane practices utilized by typical food-production companies.

"Baur's report is not for the faint of heart, but it is critical reading for anyone willing to ask about the origin of their food, and readers are rewarded with tales of animals who have been saved, and the surprising things that have been learned about farm animals from close observation of their habits. A life-altering read." Booklist.

Beers, Diane L.
★**For** the prevention of cruelty : the history and legacy of animal rights activism in the United States / Diane L. Beers. Swallow Press/Ohio University Press, c2006. xvi, 312 p. : **179**
1. Animal rights movement -- United States -- History. 2. Animal welfare -- United States -- History. 3. Animal rights -- United States -- History. 4. Animal rights advocates.
ISBN 0804010870
LC 2006004294

Provides an organized history of advocacy on the behalf of animals in the United States.

Coetzee, J. M., 1940-
The **lives** of animals / J. M. Coetzee ; edited and introduced by Amy Gutmann. Princeton University Press, c1999. 127 p. **179**
1. Animal rights -- Philosophy. 2. Animal welfare -- Moral and ethical aspects.
ISBN 0691004439
LC 98-39591

Discusses animal rights through essays, fiction, and fables from a variety of perspectives in fields such as philosophy, religion, and science.

"This hybrid collection of fiction and essays is a provocative version of Socratic philosophy. It begins with a story about a Doris Lessing-like author who visits her conflicted son and his antagonistic wife while lecturing at the university where they teach. The mother's hobbyhorse, that Animals R Us, embarrasses the academic couple, and her suggestion that they are like Nazis because they eat meat infuriates them. Other distinguished academics carry on this dialogue in playful fiction and sober commentary, in which the most eloquent part may be the descriptions of communication with animals." The New Yorker.

Comte-Sponville, Andre
A **small** treatise on the great virtues : the uses of philosophy in everyday life / Andre Comte-Sponville ; translated from the French by Catherine Temerson. Metropolitan Books, 2001. x, 352 p. ; **179**
1. Virtues. 2. Philosophy.
ISBN 9780805045550
LC 2001030299

"His subject demands a sober seriousness, but Comte-Sponville still manages to avoid taking himself too seriously: humility makes it into his litany of virtues, as does humor. A laudable renewal of the ancient quest for ethical wisdom." Booklist.

Greek, C. Ray
Sacred cows and golden geese : the human cost of experiments on animals / C. Ray Greek and Jean Swingle Greek ; foreword by Jane Goodall. Continuum, 2000. 256 p. ; **179**
1. Animal experimentation. 2. Animal rights. 3. Animals.
ISBN 0826412262
LC 99057157

"This covers the history of animal experimentation, legislation that promulgates it, the real cost to humans, and alternatives. It is a well-written, if disturbing, book." Library Journal.

Hall, Stephen S.
Wisdom : the neuroscience of a timeless virtue / Stephen S. Hall. Knopf, 2010. 352 p. **179**
1. Wisdom. 2. Neuropsychology. 3. Brain. 4. Neurobiology.
ISBN 9780307269102
LC 2009027438

"A Borzoi book."

Explores a range of disciplines to investigate the nature of wisdom, identifying ancient-world views, its role in philosophy, and the scientific findings from the past half century that have offered insight into the characteristics of historical figures.

"Those searching for easy tips on achieving wisdom will not find them here, but diligent readers will be rewarded. A steady stream of insights into the psychology and neurological mechanisms of wise decision-makingand the researchers uncovering them." Kirkus.

Magill, R. Jay (Ronald Jay), 1972-

Sincerity : how a moral ideal born five hundred years ago inspired religious wars, modern art, hipster chic, and the curious notion that we all have something to say (no matter how dull) / R. Jay Magill, Jr. Norton, c2012. 224 p. **179**

1. Sincerity. 2. Honesty. 3. Ethics.
ISBN 9780393080988

LC 2012010360

Explores the history, religion, art and politics behind the history of trying to seem upright, honest and authentic, spanning a timeline dotted with Protestant theology, paintings by the insane, French satire and the anti-hipster movement.

McCain, John, 1936-2018

Why courage matters : the way to a braver life / John McCain with Mark Salter. Random House, c2004. 209 p. : **179**

1. Courage -- Case studies. 2. Personal conduct. 3. Virtues. 4. Toughness (Personal quality)
ISBN 9781400060306

LC 2003058626

A reflection on courage presents a collection of stories of surpassing bravery and selfless devotion to duty and offers portraits of individuals--both famous and unheralded--who confronted adversity and triumphed.

Newkirk, Ingrid

★**Animalkind** : remarkable discoveries about animals and the revolutionary new ways to show them compassion / Ingrid Newkirk and Gene Stone. Simon & Schuster, 2020. 256 p. **179**

1. Animal intelligence 2. Animal behavior. 3. Animal welfare. 4. Animal rights.
ISBN 9781501198540

LC 2019026209

The founder and president of PETA and a bestselling author pair their tour of the astounding lives of animals with a guide to the exciting new tools that allow humans to avoid using or abusing animals as we once did.

"An impassioned plea for preserving animals' lives." Kirkus.

Santi, Jenny

The **giving** way to happiness : stories and science behind the transformative power of giving / Jenny Santi ; foreword by Deepak Chopra. Tarcher, 2015. 336 p. **179**

1. Happiness. 2. Generosity. 3. Self-fulfillment 4. Philanthropy
ISBN 9780399175497

LC 2015027341

"Jenny Santi overturns conventional thinking about what it takes to be happy by revealing how people find purpose and joy in giving".--Provided by publisher.

"Both of these inspiring books will prompt readers to consider and act on making the world a better place." Library Journal.

Shevelow, Kathryn, 1951-

For the love of animals : the rise of the animal protection movement / Kathryn Shevelow. Henry Holt and Company, c2008. 368 p. **179**

1. Animal welfare -- Great Britain -- History -- 18th century. 2. Animal rights advocates -- Great Britain -- History 3. Animal rights -- History 4. Great Britain -- History -- 18th century
ISBN 9780805080902

LC 2007047353

Traces the story of an unlikely group of reformers in eighteenth-century England who worked to raise awareness about animal abuse, from an unconventional duchess who wrote about animal intellect to a gentleman scientist who argued that animals should be treated with compassion.

"This is a fascinating, often disturbing and frequently funny book, a must read for anyone concerned with the treatment of animals and a call to action for the next generation of animal rights activists." Publishers Weekly.

Singer, Peter, 1946-

★**Animal** liberation / Peter Singer. Ecco Book/Harper Perennial, 2009. xiii, 311, 32 p. : **179**

1. Animal rights. 2. Animal welfare. 3. Vegetarianism.
ISBN 9780061711305

LC 2001040903

An updated edition of the groundbreaking study of animal rights describes the shocking abuse of animals--including laboratory experimentation, the fur industry, and product testing procedures--and argues that those who oppose human suffering must also oppose inflicting suffering on animals.

Tillich, Paul, 1886-1965

★The **courage** to be / Paul Tillich ; with an introduction by Peter J. Gomes. Yale University Press, 2000, c1952. 197 p. ; **179**

1. Courage. 2. Ontology. 3. Anxiety. 4. Existentialism.
ISBN 9780300188790

LC 00102364

Includes index.

Originally published: New Haven, CT : Yale University Press, 1952.

Originally published more than fifty years ago, The Courage to Be has become a classic of twentieth-century religious and philosophical thought. The great Christian existentialist thinker Paul Tillich describes the dilemma of modern man and points a way to the conquest of the problem of anxiety. --Provided by publisher

Tutu, Desmond

The **book** of forgiving : the fourfold path for healing ourselves and our world / Desmond Tutu and Mpho A. Tutu ; edited by Douglas C. Abrams. HarperOne, 2014. 240 p. **179**

1. Forgiveness. 2. Revenge 3. Victims 4. Reconciliation -- Religious aspects -- Christianity.
ISBN 9780062203564

LC 2013033890

The Nobel Peace Prize winner and international cultural icon reveals, after much reflection on the process of forgiveness, the four important steps of healing that will allows us to free ourselves of the ties that bind perpetrator to victim in an endless and unyielding cycle of pain and retribution.

"The book is almost entirely practical in focus, geared toward helping people come to grips with issues of anger, grief and loss. It includes meditations, rituals and journal exercises after each chapter." Kirkus.

179.7 Respect and disrespect for human life

Gandhi, Mahatma, 1869-1948
★**Gandhi** on non-violence : selected texts from Mohandas K. Gandhi's non-violence in peace and war / edited with an introduction by Thomas Merton ; preface by Mark Kurlansky. New Directions Pub., c2007. xviii, 101 p. ; **179.7**

1. Nonviolence
ISBN 9780811216869

LC 2007032262

"A New Directions Paperbook."

Originally published: New York : New Directions, 1965.

Originally published in 1965, a compendium of excerpts offers insight into the spiritual leader's beliefs about action as a central component of non-violent resistance, his opposition to the caste system, and legacy as a proponent of spiritual integrity.

Rehm, Diane
★**When** my time comes : conversations about whether those who are dying should have the right to determine when life should end / Diane Rehm ; foreword by John Grisham. Alfred A. Knopf, 2020. 224 p. **179.7**

1. Right to die 2. Assisted suicide 3. Terminal care 4. Terminal care -- Moral and ethical aspects.
ISBN 9780525654759

LC 2019033872

A renowned radio host and best-selling author addresses the hotly contested cause of the right-to-die movement, of which she is one of the strongest voices.

"Rehm and her subjects offer practical information, nuanced perspectives, and poignant stories of peaceful final moments achieved through end-of-life care. Readers faced with similar decisions will cherish this thoughtful account." Publishers Weekly 2019

Sanger, Carol, 1948-
About abortion : terminating pregnancy in twenty-first-century America / Carol Sanger. The Belknap Press of Harvard University Press, 2017. xv, 304 p. ; **179.7**

1. Abortion -- Law and legislation -- United States 2. Abortion -- Moral and ethical aspects -- United States 3. Abortion -- Political aspects -- United States 4. Abortion -- United States -- Psychological aspects
ISBN 9780674737723

LC 2016041934

One of the most private decisions a woman can make, abortion is also one of the most contentious topics in American civic life. Protested at rallies and politicized in party platforms, terminating pregnancy is often characterized as a selfish decision by women who put their own interests above those of the fetus. This background of stigma and hostility has stifled women's willingness to talk about abortion, which in turn distorts public and political discussion. To pry open the silence surrounding this public issue, Sanger distinguishes between abortion privacy, a form of nondisclosure based on a woman's desire to control personal information, and abortion secrecy, a woman's defense against the many harms of disclosure. Laws regulating abortion patients and providers treat abortion not as an acceptable medical decision--let alone a right--but as something disreputable, immoral, and chosen by mistake. Exploiting the emotional power of fetal imagery, laws require women to undergo ultrasound, a practice welcomed in wanted pregnancies but commandeered for use against women with unwanted pregnancies. Sanger takes these prejudicial views of women's abortion decisions into the twenty-first century by uncovering new connections between abortion law and American culture and politics. New medical technologies, women's increasing willingness to talk online and off, and the prospect of tighter judicial reins on state legislatures are shaking up the practice of abortion. As talk becomes more transparent and acceptable, women's decisions about whether or not to become mothers will be treated more like those of other adults making significant personal choices.-- Provided by publisher

Wanzer, Sidney H.
★**To** die well : your right to comfort, calm, and choice in the last days of your life / Sidney H. Wanzer with Joseph Glenmullen. Da Capo Press, 2007. xii, 209 p. ; **179.7**

1. Right to die 2. Assisted suicide 3. Euthanasia
ISBN 9780738210834

LC bl2007006665

Provides clear legal and medical guidelines for the terminally ill and their loved ones who are facing end-of-life decisions, covering such topics as how to appoint a health care proxy, refuse unwanted treatments, and the controversial issue of hasteningthe death of terminally ill patients.

Warraich, Haider
Modern death : how medicine changed the end of life / Haider Warraich. St. Martin's Press, 2017. 336 p. **179.7**

1. Terminal Care. 2. Right to die. 3. Death education 4. Quality of Life.
ISBN 9781250104588

LC 2016038746

A contemporary exploration of death and dying by a young Duke Fellow investigates the hows, whys, wheres and whens of modern death and their cultural significance as they have changed through technological advances and evolving trends.

"An important contribution to a serious discussion of profound life-and-death issues." Kirkus.

Watson, Katie
Scarlet A : the ethics, law, and politics of ordinary abortion / Katie Watson. Oxford University Press, 2018 viii, 280 p. ; **179.7**

1. Abortion -- Moral and ethical aspects -- United States 2. Abortion -- Social aspects -- United States
ISBN 9780190624859

LC 2017018856

In Scarlet A, Watson wisely and respectfully navigates one of the most divisive topics in contemporary life. This book explains the law of abortion, challenges the toxic politics that make it a public football and private secret, offers tools for more productive private exchanges, and leads the way to a more robust public discussion of abortion ethics. --Provided by publisher

179.9 Virtues

Chayka, Kyle
The **longing** for less : living with minimalism / Kyle Chayka. Bloomsbury Publishing, 2020. 258 p. : **179.9**

1. Voluntary simplicity movement 2. Simplicity
ISBN 9781635572100

LC bl2020005914

One of our keenest social observers examines the deep roots--and untapped possibilities--of our newfound, all-consuming drive to reduce. --Provided by publisher

180 History, geographic treatment, biography

Gottlieb, Anthony

The **dream** of reason : a history of western philosophy from the Greeks to the Renaissance / Anthony Gottlieb. W.W. Norton, 2000. ix, 468 p. **180**

1. Philosophy -- History. 2. Philosophy, Western -- History. 3. Philosophy, Ancient. 4. Renaissance philosophy.
ISBN 0393049515

LC 00049012

"This eloquent book offers a lively chronicle of the evolution of Western philosophy." Publishers Weekly.

181 Eastern philosophy

Pacheco, Rebecca

Do your om thing : bending yoga tradition to fit your modern life / Rebecca Pacheco. HarperWave, 2015 xv, 264 p. : **181**

1. Yoga 2. Spirituality 3. Spiritual life 4. Well-being
ISBN 9780062273376

LC 2014044390

The yoga teacher and creator of OmGal.com presents a modern guide to the full mind-body practice that demonstrates how to benefit from the ancient wisdom and philosophy of yoga and provides simple poses and sequences for daily balance and helpful meditation tips.

183 Sophistic, Socratic, related Greek philosophies

Kreeft, Peter

★**Philosophy** 101 by Socrates : an introduction to philosophy via Plato's apology : forty things philosophy is according to history's first and wisest philosopher / Peter Kreeft. Ignatius Press, c2002. 149 p. ; **183**

1. Plato. Apology. 2. Socrates. 3. Philosophy
ISBN 9780898709254

LC 2001098029

Philosophy means "the love of wisdom." Kreeft uses the dialogues of Socrates to help the reader grow in that love. He says that no master of the art of philosophizing has ever been more simple, clear, and accessible to beginners as has Socrates. He focuses on Plato's dialogues, the Apology of Socrates, as a lively example to imitate, and a model partner for the reader for dialogue.

Stone, I. F. (Isidor Feinstein), 1907-1989

The **trial** of Socrates / I.F. Stone. Little, Brown, c1988. xi, 282 p. ; **183**

1. Socrates, 469-399 B.C. 2. Socrates, 469-399 B.C. Trials, litigation, etc. 3. Civilization, Ancient. 4. Philosophers -- Ancient Greece 5. Trials (Blasphemy) 6. Trials (Sedition) 7. Athens, Ancient Greece -- Social life and customs. 8. Athens, Ancient Greece -- Civilization.
ISBN 0316817589

LC 87022855

Includes index.

Combines classical scholarship with techniques of modern investigative journalism in an attempt to unravel the mystery behind the trial and conviction of Athens' most prominent philosopher.

184 Platonic philosophy

Hare, R. M. (Richard Mervyn)

Plato / R.M. Hare. Oxford University Press, 1982. vi, 82 p. ; **184**

1. Plato, 428-347 B.C. 2. Philosophy, Ancient.
ISBN 9780192875853

LC 83159441

Offers a look at Plato's life and discusses his philosophy and teachings.

Plato, 428-347 B.C.

The **collected** dialogues of Plato, including the letters / edited by Edith Hamilton and Huntington Cairns. With introd. and prefatory notes. [Translators: Lane Cooper and others]. Pantheon Books, 1961 xxv, 1743 p. **184**

1. Philosophy, Ancient.
ISBN 9780691097183

LC 61011758

Presents outstanding translations of the Greek philosopher's works by leading British and American scholars of the last century.

185 Aristotelian philosophy

Adler, Mortimer Jerome, 1902-2001

Aristotle for everybody : difficult thought made easy / Mortimer J. Adler. Simon & Schuster, 1997. xiv, 206 p. ; **185**

1. Aristotle. 2. Aristoteles.
ISBN 9780684838236

LC oc2007014723

"A Touchstone book."

Originally published: New York : Macmillan, c1978.

Offers an imaginative perspective on Aristotelian logic, presenting an exploration of nature, society, and man in light of commonplace events and reexamining concepts of body, mind, change, cause, part, whole, one, and many.

Aristotle

★The **basic** works of Aristotle / edited by Richard McKeon ; introduction by C.D.C. Reeve. Modern Library, 2001. xxi, 1487 p. ; The Modern Library classics **185**

1. Philosophy
ISBN 9780375757990

LC 2001030607

Originally published: New York : Random House, c1941. With new introd.

Examines the pervading influence of this eminent Greek philosopher through a collection of his major works.

Shields, Christopher John

Aristotle / Christopher Shields. Routledge, Taylor & Francis Group, 2014. xviii, 505 p. ; **185**

1. Aristotle.
ISBN 9780415622493

LC 2013021013

In this extensively revised new edition of his excellent guidebook, Christopher Shields introduces the whole of Aristotle's philosophy, showing how his powerful conception of human nature shaped much of his thinking on the nature of the soul and the mind, ethics, politics, and the arts. --Provided by publisher

187 Epicurean philosophy

Lucretius Carus, Titus

On the nature of things = : De rerum natura / Lucretius ; edited and translated by Anthony M. Esolen. Johns Hopkins University Press, c1995. ix, 296 p. ; **187**

1. Didactic poetry, Latin -- Translations into English 2. Philosophy, Ancient -- Poetry
ISBN 9780801850554

LC 94025165

"Ensolen has focused on the poet, translating the Latin hexameters into accented pentameter in order to capture the dynamics, rhythms, and syntax of the original. The results are both satisfying and readable. Ensolen includes an elegant introduction on Lucretius, as well as useful notes. A valuable contribution to students of literature as well as philosophy." Library Journal.

188 Stoic philosophy

Holiday, Ryan

Lives of the stoics : the art of living from Zeno to Marcus Aurelius / Ryan Holiday and Stephen Hanselman, authors of The daily stoic. Portfolio/Penguin, 2020 xv, 329 p. : **188**

1. Stoics. 2. Philosophy
ISBN 9780525541875

LC 2020011797

"From the bestselling authors of The Daily Stoic comes an inspiring guide to the lives of the Stoics, and what the ancients can teach us about happiness, success, resilience and virtue. Nearly 2,300 years after a ruined merchant named Zeno first established a school on the Stoa Poikile of Athens, Stoicism has found a new audience among those who seek greatness, from athletes to politicians and everyone in between. It's no wonder; the philosophy and its embrace of self-mastery, virtue, and indifference tothat which we cannot control is as urgent today as it was in the chaos of the Roman Empire. In Lives of the Stoics, Holiday and Hanselman present the fascinating lives of the men and women who strove to live by the timeless Stoic virtues of Courage. Justice. Temperance. Wisdom. Organized in digestible, mini-biographies of all the well-known--and not so well-known--Stoics, this book vividly brings home what Stoicism was like for the people who loved it and lived it, dusting off powerful lessons to be learned from their struggles and successes. More than a mere history book, every example in these pages, from Epictetus to Marcus Aurelius--slaves to emperors--is designed to help the reader apply philosophy in their own lives. Holiday and Hanselman unveil the core values and ideas that unite figures from Seneca to Cato to Cicero across the centuries. Among them are the idea that self-rule is the greatest empire, that character is fate; how Stoics benefit from preparing not only for success, but failure; and learn to love, not merely accept, the hand they are dealt in life. A treasure of valuable insights and stories, this book can be visited again and again by any reader in search of inspiration from the past." Provided by publisher.

"This illuminating collection of biographies makes great use of Stoic wisdom to demonstrate the tradition's values for any reader interested in ancient philosophy." Publishers Weekly

Marcus Aurelius, Emperor of Rome, 121-180

★**Meditations** / Marcus Aurelius ; a new translation, with an introduction, by Gregory Hays. Modern Library, 2002. lvii, 191 p. ; **188**

1. Ethics 2. Life 3. Stoics
ISBN 9780679642602

LC 2001057947

An incisive introduction to the life and times of the Roman philosopher and emperor, the fundamental principles and concepts of Stoicism, the recurring themes and structure of The Meditations, and the work's impact preface a new translation of the influential and admired journal.

189 Medieval western philosophy

Rubenstein, Richard E.

Aristotle's children : how Christians, Muslims, and Jews rediscovered ancient wisdom and illuminated the Dark Ages / Richard E. Rubenstein. Harcourt, c2003. xii, 368 p. ; **189**

1. Aristotle Influence. 2. Scholasticism. 3. Faith and reason -- Christianity -- History of doctrines. 4. Intellectual life. 5. Philosophers.
ISBN 9780151007202

LC 2003006582

Traces the rediscovery and translation of the works of Aristotle at the height of the Dark Ages, chronicling the rapid spread of the intellectual's philosophies and the ensuing backlash on the part of the Catholic Church.

"Although the book purports to trace Aristotle's influence on Christianity, Islam and Judaism, it devotes more attention to Christianity. Even so, Rubenstein's lively prose, his lucid insights and his crystal-clear historical analyses make this a first-rate study in the history of ideas." Publishers Weekly.

190 Modern western and other noneastern philosophy

Durant, Will, 1885-1981

★The **story** of philosophy : the lives and opinions of the great philosophers of the Western world / Will Durant. Simon and Schuster, 1983? c1933. xvi, 412 p. ; **190**

1. Philosophy 2. Philosophers
ISBN 9780671201593

LC 83171619

Includes index.

Examines the history of speculative thought by focusing on such dominant personalities as Plato, Bacon, Spinoza, Kant, Schopenhauer, and Nietzsche

Gay, Peter, 1923-2015

The **enlightenment** : an interpretation : the science of freedom / Peter Gay. W.W. Norton, 1996, c1969. xviii, 705, xviii p. ; **190**

1. Enlightenment -- Europe 2. Philosophy -- History -- 18th century 3. Europe -- Intellectual life -- History -- 18th century.
ISBN 9780393313666

LC BL 99780253

Originally published: The enlightenment: an interpretation. Volume 2: The science of freedom. New York : Knopf, 1966-69.

The Science of Freedom completes Peter Gay's brilliant reinterpretation begun in The Enlightenment: The Rise of Modern Paganism. In the present book, he describes the philosophes' program and their views of society. His masterful appraisal opens a new range of insights into the Enlightenment's critical method and its humane and libertarian vision. --Provided by publisher

Gay, Peter, 1923-

The **enlightenment** : the rise of modern paganism / Peter Gay. W.W. Norton, 1995- , c1966. 2 vol. **190**

1. Enlightenment -- Europe 2. Philosophy -- History -- 18th century 3. Europe -- Intellectual life -- History -- 18th century.
ISBN 9780393313024

LC BL 99766232

Originally published: New York : Knopf, c1966.

The eighteenth-century Enlightenment marks the beginning of the modern age, when the scientific method and belief in reason and progress came to hold sway over the Western world. In the twentieth century, however, the Enlightenment has often been judged harshly for its apparently simplistic optimism. Now a master historian goes back to the sources to give a fully rounded account of its true accomplishments. --Provided by publisher

Gottlieb, Anthony

★The **dream** of enlightenment : the rise of modern philosophy / Anthony Gottlieb. Liveright Publishing Corporation, a division of W. W. Norton & Company, [2016] 384 p. **190**

1. Philosophy -- History. 2. Intellectual life -- History. 3. Enlightenment (European intellectual movement) 4. Philosophy, Modern -- History.
ISBN 9780871404435

LC 2016015063

Presents a chronicle of modern thought from Descartes to Rousseau, detailing the role of then-amateur philosophers in shaping Western intellectual pursuits against a backdrop of religious upheaval and the rise of Galilean science.

" Accessibly written philosophical studies can be surprisingly popular as evidenced by the current success of Sarah Bakewell's At the Existentialist Cafe. Don't miss." Library Journal.

Himmelfarb, Gertrude

The **roads** to modernity : the British, French, and American enlightenments / Gertrude Himmelfarb. Knopf, 2004. xii, 284 p. ; **190**

1. Enlightenment (European intellectual movement) -- Great Britain 2. Enlightenment (European intellectual movement) -- France. 3. Enlightenment (European intellectual movement) -- United States. 4. Intellectual life -- History. 5. Great Britain -- History -- 18th century. 6. France -- History -- 18th century. 7. United States -- History -- 18th century.
ISBN 1400042364

LC 2003060576

Contrasting the Enlightenments in the three nations of France, England, and America, a distinguished intellectual historian demonstrates the primacy of the British Enlightenment, arguing that the moral and social philosophy it created still resonates strongly today.

"This is a book with important ideological implications that deserves to be read and debated across the political spectrum." Publishers Weekly.

Magee, Bryan

The **story** of philosophy / Bryan Magee. DK Pub., 1998. 240 p. : **190**

1. Philosophy -- History.
ISBN 078943511X

LC 98003780

"Writing with a clear and lively style, Magee provides an excellent introduction to the topic." School Library Journal.

191 Philosophy of United States and Canada

Rand, Ayn

The **voice** of reason : essays in objectivist thought / Ayn Rand ; edited and with an introduction by Leonard Peikoff ; and with additional essays by Leonard Peikoff and Peter Schwartz. New American Library, 1989, c1988. xii, 353 p. ; **191**

1. Rand, Ayn Philosophy. 2. Philosophy 3. Political science -- Philosophy 4. Civilization, Modern -- 1950-
ISBN 9780453006347

LC 88018192

Essays discuss Objectivism, Apollo II, the quota system, public TV, foreign aid, socialized medicine, religion, and Vietnam.

Romano, Carlin

America the philosophical / Carlin Romano. Knopf, 2012. 672 p. **191**

1. Philosophy -- United States. 2. Intellectual life. 3. Philosophy, Modern.
ISBN 9780679434702

LC 2011034753

A former president of the National Book Critics Circle and finalist for the Pulitzer Prize in criticism argues that America is a leading philosophical culture in the history of the world, outlining a rich overview of thought to explain that Americans demonstrate a high capacity for intellectual enterprises in the spirit of the less-remembered Greek philosopher, Isocrates.

192 Philosophy of British Isles

Edmonds, David, 1964-

Wittgenstein's poker : the story of a ten-minute argument between two great philosophers / David Edmonds and John Eidinow. Ecco, 2001. x, 340 p. : **192**

1. Wittgenstein, Ludwig, 1889-1951. 2. Popper, Karl, 1902-1994. 3. Philosophers, Austrian. 4. Debates and debating. 5. College teachers.
ISBN 0066212448

LC 2002276301

"On the Cambridge University campus in 1946, two of the twentieth-century's most notable philosophers, Ludwig Wittgenstein and Karl Popper, squared off in an intense 10-minute clash rumored to have culminated with Wittgenstein brandishing a red-hot poker. The authors explain what the fight was about and how it reflects the development of philosophy. Ivory-tower drama at its crackling best." Booklist.

193 Philosophy of Germany and Austria

Heidegger, Martin, 1889-1976

Basic writings : from Being and time (1927) to The task of thinking (1964) / Martin Heidegger ; edited, with general introduction and introductions to each selection by David Farrell Krell. HarperSanFrancisco, c1993. xii, 452 p. ; **193**

1. Society and culture -- Philosophy. 2. Spirituality and Religion
ISBN 9780060637637

LC 91058187

Heidegger's most popular collection of essential writings--now revised and expanded -- includes the 10 key essays plus the introduction to Being and Time. --Provided by publisher

Kant, Immanuel, 1724-1804
★**Basic** writings of Kant / edited and with an introduction by Allen W. Wood. Modern Library, 2001. xxv, 478 p. ; The Modern Library classics **193**
1. Philosophy
ISBN 9780375757334
LC 2001018303

Presents the essential works of the philosopher, including "Critique of Pure Reason" and "Eternal Peace."

Nietzsche, Friedrich Wilhelm, 1844-1900
★**Basic** writings of Nietzsche / introduction by Peter Gay ; translated and edited by Walter Kaufmann. Modern Library, 2000. xxiv, 862 p. ; **193**
1. Philosophy
ISBN 9780679783398
LC 00064578

Includes indexes.

Originally published: New York : Modern Library, 1968. With new commentary.

Six works selected from Nietzsche's writings, including "The Birth of Tragedy," "Beyond Good and Evil," and "On the Genealogy of Morals" reflect the philosopher's critique of Western morality and insights into Christianity and art.

Nietzsche, Friedrich Wilhelm, 1844-1900
★**Thus** spoke Zarathustra : a book for everyone and nobody / Friedrich Nietzsche ; translated with an introduction and notes by Graham Parkes. Oxford University Press, c2005. xliii, 335 p. ; 20 **193**
1. Philosophy 2. Superman (Philosophical concept)
ISBN 9780192805836
LC 2005019431

Thus Spake Zarathustra is a masterpiece of literature as well as philosophy. It was Nietzsche's own favorite and has proved to be his most popular. In this book he addresses the problem of how to live a fulfilling life in a world without meaning, in the aftermath of 'the death of God.' His solution lies in the idea of eternal recurrence, which he calls 'the highest formula of affirmation that can ever be attained.' A successful engagement with this profoundly Dionysian idea enables us to choose clearly among the myriad possibilities that existence offers, and thereby to affirm every moment of our lives with others on this 'sacred' earth. --Provided by publisher

Nietzsche, Friedrich Wilhelm, 1844-1900
The **will** to power / a new translation by Walter Kaufmann and R. J. Hollingdale ; edited, with commentary, by Walter Kaufmann, with facsims. of the original manuscript. Random House 1967 xxxii, 576 p. **193**
ISBN 9780394704371
LC 66021465

Translation of Der Wille zur Macht.

Offers a selection from the author's notebooks, chosen by his sister, that reveals his views on nihilism, art, morality, religion, the theory of knowledge, and other subjects.

Sherratt, Yvonne, 1966-
Hitler's philosophers / Yvonne Sherratt. Yale University Press, c2013. xx, 302 p., 8 p. of plates : **193**
1. Hitler, Adolf, 1889-1945. 2. Philosophers -- Germany -- 20th century 3. Philosophy, German -- 20th century. 4. Political leadership. 5. Nazism. 6. Germany.
ISBN 9780300151930
LC 2012026930

Offers an account of the philosophers who supported Hitler's rise to power and those whose lives were wrecked by his regime.

194 Philosophy of France

Descartes, Rene, 1596-1650
★**Descartes** : selected philosophical writings / translated by John Cottingham, Robert Stoothoff, Dugald Murdoch ; with an introduction by John Cottingham. Cambridge University Press, 1988. xii, 249 p. : **194**
1. Descartes, Rene, 1596-1650 2. Philosophy. 3. Philosophy, French -- 17th century
ISBN 9780521352642
LC 87026799

Includes index.

Based on the new and much acclaimed two volume Cambridge edition of The Philosophical Writings of Descartes by Cottingham, Stoothoff, and Murdoch, this anthology of essential texts contains the most important and widely studied of those writings, including the Discourse and Meditations and substantial extracts from the Regulae, Optics, Principles, Objections and Replies, Comments on a Broadsheet, and Passions of the Soul. --Provided by publisher

200 Religion

Ahlstrom, Sydney E.
A **religious** history of the American people / Sydney E. Ahlstrom. Yale University Press, 2004, c1972. xxiv, 1192 p. ; **200**
1. United States -- Religion. 2. United States -- Church history.
ISBN 0300100124
LC 2003116918

Originally published: New Haven, CT : Yale University Press, 1972.

Provides a comprehensive survey of religious beliefs, practices, and trends in America and includes background information on secular movements and influences.

Almond, Gabriel A. (Gabriel Abraham), 1911-2002
★**Strong** religion : the rise of fundamentalisms around the world / Gabriel A. Almond, R. Scott Appleby, and Emmanuel Sivan. University of Chicago Press, c2003. ix, 281 p. ; **200**
1. Fundamentalism. 2. Philosophy and religion 3. Religion -- Social aspects -- United States 4. United States -- Religious life and customs -- 21st century
ISBN 0226014975
LC 2002013665

"This may be the single most cogent sociohistorical analysis of the modern religious phenomenon called fundamentalism. This foundational work is essential for academic and major public libraries." Library Journal.

Armstrong, Karen, 1944-
★The **battle** for God / Karen Armstrong. Alfred A. Knopf, 2000. xvi, 442 p. **200**
1. God 2. Fundamentalism 3. Orthodox Judaism -- Israel -- History.

4. Christianity.
ISBN 9780679435976
LC 99034022

Focusing on the rise of fundamentalism in three major religions reveals how these movements in Christianity, Judaism, and Islam were born out of a dread of modernity.

"The author is sympathetic to the human need for spiritual meaning, but she points out that the intellectual flaws of fundamentalist beliefs are customarily accompanied by paranoia, anger, and aggression--which, in turn, frequently betray the message of the faith." The New Yorker.

Barbour, Ian G.

When science meets religion : enemies, strangers, or partners? / Ian G. Barbour. HarperSanFrancisco, 2000. xiv, 205 p. ; **200**

1. Religion and science. 2. Theologians. 3. Scientists.
ISBN 006060381X
LC 99055579

"The author guides readers through a four-fold typology of the science/religion relationship: Conflict, Independence, Dialogue and Integration. Barbour's own sympathies are markedly on the side of dialogue and integration, but he makes an unusually sucessful effort to represent other perspectives in a fair light." Publishers Weekly.

Chittister, Joan

The **gift** of years : growing older gracefully / Joan Chittister. BlueBridge, 2008. xvi, 222 p. **200**

1. Seniors -- Psychology. 2. Aging -- Psychological aspects. 3. Aging -- Religious aspects -- Christianity. 4. Personal conduct
ISBN 9781933346106
LC 2008000332

Author Joan Chittister examines the aging process from a Christian perspective. Urging listeners to celebrate their growing older, Chittister highlights the rewards of old age and also addresses key issues facing the elderly.

"This collection of inspirational reflections, not meant to be read in one sitting, or even in order, but one topic at a time, abounds in gentle insights and arresting aphorisms." Publishers Weekly.

Cooke, Tim

Concise history of world religions : an illustrated time line / edited by Tim Cooke. National Geographic, c2011. 352 p. **200**

1. Religions -- History. 2. World history.
ISBN 9781426206986
LC bl2011032086

Presents a comprehensive guide to religions throughout history, from the origins of spiritual belief to modern organized religions and churches, and discusses how religion has affected and helped shape the history of the world.

De Botton, Alain

Religion for atheists : a non-believer's guide to the uses of religion / Alain de Botton. Pantheon Books, c2012. 320 p. **200**

1. Atheists. 2. Religious life. 3. Atheism
ISBN 9780307379108
LC 2011021286

An atheist's provocative argument for how everyone can benefit from the wisdom and power of religion regardless of beliefs explains how the secular world can glean insights from religious stories about how to live, structure societies and achieve a greater appreciation for culture.

Dennett, D. C. (Daniel Clement)

Breaking the spell : religion as a natural phenomenon / Daniel C. Dennett. Viking, c2006. xvi, 448 p. ; **200**

1. Religion -- Controversial literature. 2. Spirituality. 3. Faith.
ISBN 067003472X
LC 2005042415

Explores the nature of faith and how religion shapes everyday life, addressing controversial issues about the relevance of faith, while tracing the history of organized religion from its roots in folk beliefs to its key role in modern issues.

Gaustad, Edwin Scott, 1923-

The **religious** history of America : the heart of the American story from Colonial times to today / Edwin S. Gaustad and Leigh E. Schmidt. Harper San Francisco, 2002. x, 454 p. : **200**

1. African Americans -- Religion -- History 2. Native Americans -- Religion -- History 3. Eastern religions -- History 4. Spiritual journeys 5. United States -- Church history. 6. United States -- Social life and customs -- 21st century
ISBN 9780060630577
LC 2002190208

A revised edition of the classic text covers the religious dimensions of American history, offering increased discussion of African American and Native American religious life, Eastern religions, and spiritual seeking.

"The overall result is a well-balanced enhancement of an excellent work." Library Journal.

Hexham, Irving

Understanding world religions : An Interdisciplinary Approach / Irving Hexham. Zondervan, c2011. 512 p. : **200**

1. Religions.
ISBN 0310259444
LC 2010013103

Cover subtitle: An interdisciplinary approach.

Irving Hexham's introductory world religions text explores various religions under the broad categories of African Religions, the Yogic Traditions (including Buddhism), and the Abrahamic traditions. He presents an appreciative yet realistic approach, noting both the strengths and inherent problems of various world religions. --Provided by publisher

Hitchens, Christopher 1949-2011

God is not great : how religion poisons everything / Christopher Hitchens. Twelve, 2007. 307 p. ; **200**

1. Religion -- Controversial literature. 2. Religion and culture. 3. Atheism. 4. Religion and science.
ISBN 0446579807
LC 2006023039

National Book Award for Nonfiction finalist, 2007

"A case against religion and a description of the ways in which religion is man-made"--Provided by the publisher.

"Hitchens has outfoxed the Hitchens watchers by writing a serious and deeply felt book, totally consistent with his beliefs of a lifetime. And God should be flattered: unlike most of those clamoring for his attention, Hitchens treats him like an adult." New York Times Book Review.

Lewis, James R.

The **encyclopedia** of cults, sects, and new religions / [edited by] James R. Lewis. Prometheus Books, 2002. 951 p. : **200**

1. Cults -- United States -- Encyclopedias. 2. Sects -- United States -- Encyclopedias. 3. United States -- Religion Encyclopedias.
ISBN 9781573928885
LC 2002019180

Provides brief introductions to more than one thousand religious movements that fall outside the American mainstream, with lengthier treatment of those that are controversial or have received media attention.

Lewis, James R.

★**Legitimating** new religions / James R. Lewis. Rutgers University Press, c2003. viii, 272 p. : **200**

1. Cults -- Psychological aspects. 2. Religious psychology. 3. Authority -- Religious aspects. 4. Religious pluralism.
ISBN 9780813533230

LC 2003005987

"Lewis's work is a valuable contribution. Recommended for academic libraries with religious studies collections." Library Journal

Marty, Martin E., 1928-

Pilgrims in their own land : 500 years of religion in America / Martin E. Marty. Little, Brown, 1984. xii, 500 p. : **200**

1. Christianity -- United States. 2. Religion -- History. 3. United States -- Church history. 4. United States -- Religion.
ISBN 9780316548670

LC 84000821

An eminent historian of religion offers candid accounts of the lives of America's leading religious leaders and of the movements, spiritual forces, and groups that shaped religion in the United States.

Minois, Georges, 1946-

The **atheist's** Bible : the most dangerous book that never existed / Georges Minois ; translated by Lys Ann Weiss. The University of Chicago Press, 2012. xii, 249 p. : **200**

1. De tribus impostoribus. 2. Rationalism -- History. 3. Books 4. Heresy. 5. Popes
ISBN 9780226530291

LC 2012011212

Like a lot of good stories, this one begins with a rumor: in 1239, Pope Gregory IX accused Frederick II, the Holy Roman Emperor, of heresy. Without disclosing evidence of any kind, Gregory announced that Frederick had written a supremely blasphemous book--De tribus impostoribus, or the Treatise of the Three Impostors--in which Frederick denounced Moses, Jesus, and Muhammad as impostors. Of course, Frederick denied the charge, and over the following centuries the story played out across Europe, with libertines, freethinkers, and other 'strong minds' seeking a copy of the scandalous text. --Provided by publisher

Prothero, Stephen R.

God is not one : the eight rival religions that run the world--and why their differences matter / Stephen Prothero. HarperOne, 2010. 400 p. **200**

1. Religions. 2. Religion -- Social aspects
ISBN 9780061571275

LC 2009053372

Argues that the differences between the world's religions are far greater than previously acknowledged, and presents cautionary advice against underestimating these differences.

"Provocative, thoughtful, fiercely intelligent and, for both believing and nonbelieving, formal and informal students of religion, a must-read." Booklist.

Williams, Juan

This far by faith : stories from the African-American religious experience / Juan Williams and Quinton Dixie. William Morrow, c2003. 326 p. : **200**

1. African Americans -- Religion 2. African Americans -- History
ISBN 9780060188634

LC 2002071884

A detailed examination of African-American religious life and its relationship with the black American experience brings together historical research, photographs, contemporary interviews, and commentary by top clergy.

200.71 Education

Prothero, Stephen R.

Religious literacy : what every American needs to know--and doesn't / Stephen Prothero. Harper San Francisco, 2007. viii, 296 p. ; **200.71**

1. Religious education. 2. Religions. 3. Religion in the public schools.
ISBN 0060846704

LC 2006041310

A religious primer serves as an argument for why religion should become a mandatory subject in American public schools, contending that most Americans are not able to identify basic tenets of their faith and that key political challenges can be better met with faith-based resolutions.

"In this book, the author combines a lively history of the rise and fall of American religious literacy with a set of proposed remedies based on his hope that the Fall into religious ignorance is reversible. He also includes a useful multicultural glossary of religious definitions and allusions, in which religious illiterates can find the prodigal son, the promised land, the Quakers and the Koran." Washington Post Book World.

200.8 Groups of people

Coles, Robert

★The **spiritual** life of children / Robert Coles. Houghton Mifflin, 1990. xix, 358 p. : **200.8**

1. Children -- Religious life. 2. Children -- Spiritual life.
ISBN 0395559995

LC 90040097

"A Peter Davison book."

Addresses the religious and spiritual lives of children of various faiths, detailing, in youngsters' own words and pictures, their views on God, salvation, and the meaning of life.

"One of the delights of his presentation is the combination of the children's searching comments and the struggle the author makes to hear beyond his own conceptions." Journal of Youth Services in Libraries.

Reed, Wendy, 1966-

Circling faith : Southern women on spirituality / edited by Wendy Reed and Jennifer Horne. University of Alabama Press, c2012. xiv, 230 p. ; **200.8**

1. Faith in women. 2. Women authors. 3. Spirituality. 4. Southern States -- Religion. 5. Essays. 6. Anthologies.
ISBN 9780817317676

LC 2011034803

Circling Faith is a collection of essays by southern women thatencompasses spirituality and the experience of winding through the religiously charged environment of the American South. --Provided by publisher

200.9 History, geographic treatment, biography

Armstrong, Karen, 1944-

★The **great** transformation : the beginning of our religious traditions / Karen Armstrong. Knopf, 2006. xviii, 469 p. : **200.9**

1. Religion -- History. 2. Monotheism. 3. Philosophy, Ancient. 4. Ancient history. 5. China -- Religion -- History. 6. India -- Religion -- History. 7. Israel -- Religion -- History. 8. Greece -- Religion -- History.

ISBN 0375413170

LC 2005047536

Examines the origins of the religious traditions of the world during the ninth century B.C.E. in four distinct regions--Confucianism and Daoism in China, Hinduism and Buddhism in India, monotheism in Israel, and philosophical rationalism in Greece.

"This could very possibly be one of the greatest intellectual histories ever written." Library Journal.

Miles, Jack, 1942-

Religion as we know it : an origin story / Jack Miles. W. W. Norton & Company, Inc., [2020] 128 p. **200.9**

1. Religion -- History 2. Civilization, Western. 3. Western religions. 4. Christianity -- Influence. 5. Western Hemisphere -- Religion

ISBN 9781324002789

LC 2019026444

In his new book, acclaimed scholar Jack Miles poses a question: How did our forebears begin to think about religion as a distinct domain, separate from other activities that were once inseparable from it? Starting at the birth of Christianity - a religion inextricably bound to Western thought - Miles reveals how we in the West have come to isolate religion as an object of study, and how drastically our perception has changed over time and across societies.

200.951 Religion -- China

Johnson, Ian, 1962 July 27-

The **souls** of China : the return of religion after Mao / Ian Johnson. Pantheon Books, 2017 384 p. **200.951**

1. Communism and Christianity. 2. Communism and religion. 3. China -- Religion.

ISBN 9781101870051

LC 2016036412

A Pulitzer Prize-winning journalist--who lived for extended periods with underground church members, rural Daoists and Buddhist pilgrims--uses his experiences to paint a revelatory portrait of religion in China today: its history, the spiritual traditions of its Eastern and Western faiths and the ways in which it is influencing China's future.

"Johnson provides a fascinating account of how traditional activities recovered after enduring severe repression during China's Cultural Revolution (1966-1976)." Library Journal.

200.973 Religion -- United States

Hutchison, William R.

Religious pluralism in America : the contentious history of a founding ideal / William R. Hutchison. Yale University Press, 2003. xi, 276 p. : **200.973**

1. Religious pluralism -- United States -- History. 2. United States -- Religion.

ISBN 0300098138

LC 2002151893

Offers a history of the idea of religious pluralism in America, exploring the need to balance the inclusion of an ever-multiplying cast of new and different religions with the desire for a consensus vision of America's religious landscape.

"The author illuminates the cultural transformations that enabled twentieth-century Americans to embrace belatedly the religious diversity that emerged in the nineteenth-century influx of Catholic and Jewish immigrants and in the rise of new American-born faiths such as Mormonism and Transcendentalism. Though he acknowledges the concerns of critics worried about the moral balkanization of a society lacking shared religious premises, Hutchison hails America's new religious pluralism as a great achievement. A balanced and informative narrative." Booklist.

Olson, Roger E.

★**Handbook** of denominations in the United States / Roger E. Olson, Frank S. Mead, Samuel S. Hill & Craig D. Atwood. Abingdon Press, c2018 384 p. : **200.973**

1. Sects -- United States 2. Christian sects -- United States 3. United States -- Religion.

ISBN 9781501822513

LC 2010007092

The 14th edition is completely updated with current statistics, new denominations, and recent trends. The book has been made more useful and manageable by moving very small groups into broader articles while giving more detail and description to the large and influential denominations. --Provided by publisher

Ozment, Katherine

Grace without God : the search for meaning, purpose, and belonging in a secular age / Katherine Ozment. Harper Wave, HarperCollins Publishers, 2016. 256 p. **200.973**

1. Religion. 2. Irreligion. 3. Spirituality. 4. Spiritual life.

ISBN 9780062305114

LC 2016004086

Looks at the trends and ramifications of a country increasingly leaving organized religion behind, focusing on how this growing number of nonreligious Americans find meaning, purpose, and community.

"Ozment successfully writes an informative and relatable discussion on the changing landscape of religion, society, and identity." Library Journal.

Sharlet, Jeff,

Believer, beware : first person dispatches from the margins of faith / selected by Jeff Sharlet, Peter Manseau, and the editors of Killing the Buddha. Beacon Press, 2009. xv, 263 p. **200.973**

1. Faith. 2. Religion. 3. United States -- Religion. 4. Essays.

ISBN 9780807077399

LC 2008047403

Collects ambivalent confessions, skeptical testimonies, and accounts of faith lost and found and lost again from Americans who have floundered in their search for an authentic spiritual life.

"The editors are among the smart, candid, and insightful authors whose personal narratives form the book's 35 brief chapters. The selections represent a wide range of experiences from cheating on bar mitzvah prep to discovering hunger as spiritual food in a Ramadan fast, from sabotaging Bible camp to stumbling upon barbershop theology. Contributions reflect the scope of religious diversity, including orthodox Judaism, Roman Catholicism, Islam, Zen Buddhism and even a meditation on agnosticism. Some are funny, others heartbreaking, and some are simply revelatory." Publishers Weekly.

201 Specific aspects of religion

Armstrong, Karen, 1944-
★**Fields** of blood : religion and the history of violence / Karen Armstrong. Knopf, 2014. 512 p. **201**
1. Violence -- Religious aspects. 2. Religious terrorism -- History 3. Ethics 4. Religion -- Social aspects -- History.
ISBN 9780307957047
LC 2014011057

Provides a sweeping exploration of religion's connection to violence, from the agrarian societies of early civilized man to the growing post-9/11 disillusionment with religion.

Armstrong, Karen, 1944-
★A **short** history of myth / Karen Armstrong. Canongate, 2006, c2005. 159 p. ; **201**
1. Mythology -- History. 2. Folklore -- History 3. Civilization, Stone age -- History 4. Civilization, Western -- History
ISBN 9781841958002
LC bl2006026966

Reprint. Originally published: 2005.

The author of The History of God and In the Beginning: A New Reading of Genesis offers a useful, well-written introduction to mythology from the Paleolithic period to the "Great Western Transformation" that used science to discredit myth.

"This is an overview of the ever-evolving partnership betweeh myth and man from Paleolithic times to the present. Succinct and cleanly written, it is hugely readable and, in its journey across the epochs of human experience, often moving. . . . Armstrong's exposition is streamlined and uncluttered without being simplistic. " New York Times Book Review.

Carroll, Georgie
The **mythology** book / Philip Wilkinson, consultant ; contributors Georgie Carroll, Dr. Mark Faulkner, Dr. Jacob F. Field, Dr. John Haywood, Michael Kerrigan, Neil Philip, Dr. Nicholaus Pumphrey, Juliette Tocino-Smith. DK, 2018. 351 p. : **201**
1. Mythology.
ISBN 9781465473370
LC bl2018080006

Includes index.

Explores the mythology of different cultures throughout history and around the world, through retellings and explanations of over eighty traditional stories, presented in an accessible, visual style.

Frank, Adam, 1962-
The **constant** fire : beyond the science vs. religion debate / Adam Frank. University of California Press, c2009. xi, 288 p. ; **201**
1. Religion and science -- History. 2. Science -- Philosophy 3. Christian doctrines 4. Spirituality
ISBN 9780520254121
LC 2008025402

Looks at the shared connections between science and religion, citing the great scholars of philosophy, mythology, and religion.

Grant, Edward, 1926-
★**Science** and religion, 400 B.C. to A.D. 1550 : from Aristotle to Copernicus / Edward Grant. Greenwood Press, 2004. xxvi, 307 p. : **201**
1. Religion and science -- History.
ISBN 0313328587
LC 2004017429

Explores the relationship between science and religion during the Middle Ages and argues that theologians did not discourage science, but embraced it, which ultimately led to the Scientific Revolution.

Haidt, Jonathan
★The **righteous** mind : why good people are divided by politics and religion / Jonathan Haidt. Pantheon Books, c2012. 384 p. **201**
1. Ethics. 2. Social psychology. 3. Political psychology. 4. Religious psychology
ISBN 9780307377906
LC 2011032036

Presents a groundbreaking investigation into the origins of morality at the core of religion and politics, offering scholarly insight into the motivations behind cultural clashes that are polarizing America.

Harman, Oren Solomon
Evolutions : fifteen myths that explain our world / Oren Harman. Farrar, Straus and Giroux, 2018. 240 p. **201**
1. Myth. 2. Evolution 3. Science. 4. Philosophy
ISBN 9780374150709
LC 2017047954

A lyrical exploration of how modern science illuminates what it means to be human shares the latest understandings about the birth of the universe and the evolution of the mind to create new mythologies connecting science to our existential questions.

Karabell, Zachary
Peace be upon you : the story of Muslim, Christian, and Jewish coexistence / Zachary Karabell. Alfred A. Knopf, 2007. 343 p. : **201**
1. Interfaith relations 2. Judaism -- Relations -- Christianity. 3. Christianity -- Relations -- Judaism. 4. Judaism -- Relations -- Islam.
ISBN 1400043689
LC 2006031501

Ranging from the advent of Islam in the seventh century to the present day, the author of The Last Campaign looks at the legacy of cooperation and coexistence among the three great religions--Christianity, Judaism, and Islam--from the Baghdad court of the caliphs, to medieval Spain, to the religious autonomy of the Ottoman Empire.

"This outstanding book . . . combines in a single volume centuries of interaction among the three great monotheistic religions." Choice.

Lombard, Jay
The **mind** of God : neuroscience, faith, and a search for the soul / Dr. Jay Lombard ; foreword by Patrick J. Kennedy. Harmony Books, 2017 xxi, 197 p. ; **201**
1. God -- Proof 2. Neuroscience -- Religious aspects. 3. Religion and science. 4. Christian life.
ISBN 9780553418675
LC bl2017023451

Is there a God? It's a question billions of people have asked since the dawn of time. You would think by now we'd have a satisfactory, universal answer. No such luck. Or maybe we do and we just need to look in the right place. For Dr. Jay Lombard that place is the brain, and more importantly the mind, that center of awareness and consciousness that creates reality. In The Mind of God, Dr. Lombard employs case studies from his own behavioral neurology practice to explore the spiritual conundrums that we all ask ourselves: What is the nature of God? Does my life have purpose? What's the meaning of our existence? Are we free? What happens to us when we die?

"Along the path carrying him from early years as an aimless druggie to professional maturity as an esteemed neurologist, Lombard has learned a great deal about the science of the brain. Surprisingly, he has also learned much about faith, especially as it manifests itself as a formative mental force." Booklist.

Niebuhr, Gustav

Beyond tolerance : searching for interfaith understanding in America / Gustav Niebuhr. Viking, 2008. 208 p. **201**

1. Interfaith relations 2. Religious tolerance. 3. Freedom of religion -- United States -- History 4. Religion and politics -- United States -- History. 5. United States -- Church history.

ISBN 9780670019564

LC 2007040479

"Niebuhr brings his reporter's eye for detail to this work, which he populates with people and organizations who strive to find religious meaning in our diverse lives. This is no dry, academic exposition. Written for a general audience, it is also valuable for scholars wishing to see an America many might have thought was calcifying into an insular continent, worshipping hard gods or God." Library Journal.

Sacks, Jonathan, 1948-

★The **great** partnership: God, science and the search for meaning / Jonathan Sacks. Schocken Books, c2012. 384 p. **201**

1. Religion and science 2. Meaning (Psychology) -- Religious aspects 3. Purpose in life 4. Science -- Religious aspects

ISBN 9780805243017

LC 2012006601

A renowned author and rabbi discusses the relationship between science and religion and the importance of the coexistence of both in that religion is the search for meaning and science is the search for explanation.

Sacks, Jonathan, 1948-

Not in God's name : confronting religious violence / Jonathan Sacks. Schocken Books, 2015 ix, 305 p. ; **201**

1. Bible. Genesis 2. Violence -- Religious aspects 3. Abrahamic religions 4. Religious tolerance 5. Religions

ISBN 9780805243345

"While Sacks has no recipe to cure religious violence, he successfully illustrates the roots of responsibility in this terrible dynamic. A worthy read that is sure to spur conversation." Library Journal.

201.3 Mythology and mythological foundations

Campbell, Joseph, 1904-1987

The **masks** of God / Joseph Campbell. Arkana, 1991, c1959. 4 v. : **201.3**

1. Mythology -- History and criticism 2. Heroes and heroines. 3. Gods and goddesses. 4. Human behavior.

ISBN 0140194436

LC 91214960

Originally published: New York : Viking Press, 1959.

Studies the development of man's philosophical views of supreme beings in primitive, Eastern, and Western culture.

Campbell, Joseph, 1904-1987

★The **power** of myth / Joseph Campbell, with Bill Moyers ; Betty Sue Flowers, editor. Doubleday, 1988. xix, 231 p., 16 p. of plates : **201.3**

1. Campbell, Joseph, 1904-1987 Interviews. 2. Mythology -- History and criticism 3. Heroes and heroines. 4. Human behavior. 5. Religion -- Social aspects.

ISBN 0385247745

LC 88004218

Explores the common themes that underlie diverse religions of Eastern and Western cultures.

"Campbell is the hero on his own voyage of discovery. This well-bound book on lovely paper with helpful illustrations from art is highly recommended for all libraries." Choice.

201.723 Civil rights

Nussbaum, Martha Craven, 1947-

★The **new** religious intolerance : overcoming the politics of fear in an anxious age / Martha C. Nussbaum. Belknap Press of Harvard University Press, 2012. 304 p. **201.723**

1. Freedom of religion 2. Religious tolerance. 3. Religious discrimination. 4. Fear -- Religious aspects.

ISBN 9780674065901

LC 2011051712

"This powerful and profound book is useful to anyone seriously concerned with religious pluralism and civil liberty." Library Journal

202 Doctrines

Armstrong, Karen, 1944-

A **history** of God : the 4000-year quest of Judaism, Christianity, and Islam / Karen Armstrong. Gramercy Books, 2004, c1993. xxiii, 460 p. : **202**

1. God -- Comparative studies 2. God -- Biblical teaching 3. God (Christianity) -- History of doctrines. 4. God (Islam) -- History of doctrines.

ISBN 0517223120

LC 2003062755

Originally published: New York : Ballantine Books, 1993.

"Public librarians should be aware that conservative readers may be offended by this book, and even religious scholars may find Armstrong's rather one-sided death of God optimism about humanity a bit passé. Otherwise, this is an excellent and informative book." Library Journal.

Bartlett, Sarah

A **brief** history of angels and demons / Sarah Bartlett. Running Press, 2011. xii, 259 p. ; **202**

1. Angels 2. Demons 3. Spirituality -- History

ISBN 9780762442782

LC bl2012029693

Looks at the history of angels and demons and their depiction in literature, myth, religion, and art through the ages.

Holloway, Richard, 1933-

Waiting for the last bus : reflections on life and death / Richard Holloway. Canongate Books, 2018. 165 pages ; **202**

1. Death 2. Coping 3. Spiritual life 4. Loss (Psychology)

ISBN 9781786890214

LC bl2018053415

Now in his ninth decade, former Bishop of Edinburgh Richard Holloway has spent a lifetime at the bedsides of the dying, guiding countless men and women towards peaceful deaths. In The Last Bus, he presents a positive, meditative and profound exploration of the many important lessons we can learn from death: facing up to the limitations of our bodies as they falter, reflecting on our failings, and forgiving ourselves and others.

"This powerful volume abounds with thoughtful guidance for soothing the dying, comforting the grieving, and preparing for ones own death." Publishers Weekly.

Jordan, Michael, 1941-

Dictionary of gods and goddesses / Michael Jordan. Facts on File, c2004. xi, 402 p. : **202**

1. Goddesses 2. Gods
ISBN 9780816059232

LC 2004013028

Rev. ed. of: Encyclopedia of gods. c1993.

Provides information on both significant and minor deities of cultures from around the world, discussing the role of the god in each culture and the characteristics and symbols associated with each god.

"The author's alphabetical list includes gods and goddesses from a variety of religions. Each entry provides a brief description with cross-references where appropriate; some supply translations of the names. Longer entries include origin, dates of observance, synonyms, geographic location of the cult center, art references by type (e.g., stone carvings), and literary sources. This [is] a usable, well-written resource for short descriptions of cross-cultural deities." Choice.

Miller, Lisa

Heaven : our 2000-year-old fascination with the afterlife / Lisa Miller. Harper, 2010. 320 p. **202**

1. Heaven. 2. Life after death. 3. Hope. 4. Salvation (Christianity)
ISBN 9780060554750

LC 2009026063

Drawing from history and popular culture, biblical research and the beliefs of everyday people, Newsweek's religion editor offers a new understanding of one of the most cherished and shared ideals of spiritual life.

"In this sweeping historical and literary geography of heaven . [Miller] talks to priests, a Dominican monk, Muslim clerics, rabbis, and professors (and even visits a psychic, who channels a balding Ed Asner look-alike--no one she knows, though she racks her brain). She doesn't ignore pop culture, either, touching on everything from The Lovely Bones to the hugely popular Left Behind series. But once she has finished reporting and researching, Miller's book loses its hard journalistic edge and becomes something else: a memoir. Her own qualms about faith have danced around the edges of the story, but finally they come front and center. What Miller ultimately concludes may surprise you. It certainly surprised her." Entertainment Weekly.

Speerstra, Karen

The **divine** art of dying : how to live well while dying / Karen Speerstra + Herbert Anderson ; foreword by Ira Byock, MD. DIVINE ARTS, 2014 xviii, 268 p. ; **202**

1. Death -- Religious aspects. 2. Death -- Psychological aspects 3. Palliative treatment 4. Hospice care.
ISBN 9781611250237

LC 2013047709

A guide to end-of-life decisions combines personal stories with research on palliative and hospice care.

"A valuable resource; this books brims with wisdom and grace." Publishers Weekly.

203 Public worship and other practices

Salamone, Frank A.

★**Encyclopedia** of religious rites, rituals, and festivals / Frank A. Salamone, editor. Routledge, 2004. xiii, 487 p. : **203**

1. Religions -- Encyclopedias. 2. Rites and ceremonies -- Encyclopedias.
ISBN 9780415941808

LC 2003020389

"A Berkshire Reference work."

"Haircutting, identity, satanic, marriage, death these are just a few of the rituals crossing religious boundaries explained in this wonderful new addition to Routledge's 'Religion and Society' series. Its topic is vast, and no one work, certainly not one volume, could comprehensively cover it all. But the selections here are broad and provide an excellent introduction to viewing our world through rites and rituals." Library Journal

204 Religious experience, life, practice

Chopra, Deepak

Metahuman : unleashing your infinite potential / Deepak Chopra, M.D. Harmony Books, 2019 354 p. ; **204**

1. Mind and body 2. Self-realization 3. Spiritual life
ISBN 9780307338334

LC 2019004165

The best-selling author of You Are the Universe draws on wisdom traditions and the latest research into the human brain, artificial intelligence and biometrics to explain what higher consciousness is and its role in health and spirituality. Illustrations.

James, William, 1842-1910

★The **varieties** of religious experience : a study in human nature / William James ; introduction by Reinhold Niebuhr. Simon & Schuster, 2004. xiii, 398 p. ; **204**

1. Experience (Religion) 2. Religious psychology. 3. Religion. 4. Religious conversion
ISBN 9780743257879

LC 2004042870

"A Touchstone book."

In a series of twenty lectures, the philosopher explores conversion, mysticism, repentence, prayer, saintliness, hopes of reward, and fears of punishment with sympathy and boldness. Religious phenomena are documented by various case histories. Both the believer and the nonbeliever will find a great deal of food for thought.

Salzberg, Sharon

Real happiness : the power of meditation : a 28-day program / Sharon Salzberg. Workman Pub., c2011. 208 p. : **204**

1. Meditation
ISBN 9780761159254

LC 2010052087

"Book includes a CD with four guided meditations"--Cover.

Presents instructions for a twenty-eight day program that teaches readers how to meditate, using three main skills concentration, mindfullness, and loving kindness.

Tolle, Eckhart, 1948-

A **new** Earth : awakening to your life's purpose / Eckhart

Tolle. Dutton/Penguin Group, 2005. 315 p. **204**

1. Consciousness. 2. Spiritual life. 3. Kindness. 4. Altruism.
ISBN 0525948023

LC 2005023358

Explaining that the current state of humanity is erroneously and dangerously ego-centric, an argument for a shift in consciousness reveals how the modern world can become more sane and loving, in a spiritual exploration that offers practical advice on how to promote kindness, freedom, and a realization of humanity's potential.

"According to Tolle, ... humans are on the verge of creating a new world by a personal transformation that shifts our attention away from our ever-expanding egos." Publishers Weekly.

Wathey, John C., 1953-

The **illusion** of God's presence : the biological origins of spiritual longing / John C. Wathey. Prometheus Books, 2016. 445 p. **204**

1. Experience (Religion). 2. Religion and science. 3. Biology -- Religious aspects -- Christianity. 4. God
ISBN 9781633880740

LC 2015030319

An essential feature of religious experience across many cultures is the intuitive feeling of God's presence. More than any rituals or doctrines, it is this experience that anchors religious faith, yet it has been largely ignored in the scientific literature on religion. This book delves into the biological origins of this compelling feeling, attributing it to innate neural circuitry that evolved to promote the mother-child bond.

204.4 Religious life and practice

Tolle, Eckhart, 1948-

The **power** of now : a guide to spiritual enlightenment / Eckhart Tolle. New World Library, 1999, c1997 xxiii, 193 p. ; **204.4**

1. Spiritual life. 2. Consciousness. 3. Self-fulfillment. 4. Spirituality.
ISBN 1577311523

LC 99042366

Originally published in Canada by Namaste Publishing Inc. in 1997.

A counselor and spiritual teacher shares the secret of his own self-realization and the philosophy for living in the present he has developed.

208 Sources

Armstrong, Karen, 1944-

The **lost** art of Scripture : rescuing the sacred texts / Karen Armstrong. Alfred A. Knopf, 2019. 448 p. **208**

1. Bible Criticism and interpretation 2. Qur'an Criticism and interpretation 3. Bible. Pentateuch Criticism and interpretation 4. Sacred books 5. Religion and culture 6. Semantics (Philosophy) 7. Fundamentalism
ISBN 9780451494863

LC 2019009391

A history of the holy texts from a number of the world's religions and how in our secular world they are at best seen as irrelevant and at worst as a reason to incite violence, hatred, and division.

Brown, Brian Arthur,

Three testaments: Torah, Gospel, and Quran / Brian Arthur Brown. Rowman & Littlefield Publishers, c2012. 635 p. **208**

1. Bible. Pentateuch Criticism and interpretation. 2. Bible. New Testament Criticism and interpretation. 3. Qur'an Criticism and interpretation 4. Interfaith relations 5. Abrahamic religions. 6. Sacred books -- Comparative studies.
ISBN 9781442214927

LC 2012009166

Presents the full text of the Torah, the New Testament, and the Quran as well as commentaries from religious scholars that explore the connections and points of departure of the three faiths.

209.0973 New religious movements--United States

Weiss, Mitch

Broken faith : inside the Word of Faith Fellowship, one of America's most dangerous cults / Mitch Weiss and Holbrook Mohr. Hanover Square Press, 2020. 416 p. **209.0973**

1. Cults 2. Cult leaders 3. Families 4. Former cult members 5. North Carolina 6. United States
ISBN 9781335145239

LC bl2019037008

Investigates Jane Whaley's Word of Faith Fellowship--a secretive evangelic cult that destroyed the lives of its congregants through a combination of manipulation, blackmail and violence--and provides a dramatic portrait of those who escaped.

"A compelling examination of a Christianist cabal whose crimes are evident but whose power seems, for the moment, unbreakable." Kirkus

210 Philosophy and theory of religion

Gutting, Gary,

Talking God : philosophers on belief / edited by Gary Gutting. W.W. Norton & Company, 2016. xii, 219 p. **210**

1. Religions. 2. Belief and doubt. 3. Faith 4. Atheism.
ISBN 9780393352818

LC 2016023255

Conversations with 12 skeptics, atheists, agnostics and believers from Alvin Plantinga and Philip Kitcher to Michael Ruse and John Caputo explore current debates about the origins of faith and atheism while tracing the role of secular humanism and faith in the modern world.

Huxley, Aldous, 1894-1963

★The **perennial** philosophy / Aldous Huxley. Harper Perennial Modern Classics, 2009, c1945. xi, 312 p. ; **210**

1. Religion -- Philosophy. 2. Spirituality. 3. Philosophy and religion. 4. Faith.
ISBN 9780061724947

LC bl2012017927

Originally published: New York: Harper & Brothers, 1945.

Examines well-known works on Western mysticism and the writings of Oriental and Mohammedan mystics to provide an overview of the "Philosophia Perennis."

211 Concepts of God

Armstrong, Karen, 1944-

The **case** for God / Karen Armstrong. Knopf, 2009. 432 p. **211**

1. God -- History of doctrines 2. God (Christianity) -- History of

doctrines 3. Religious life -- History. 4. Monotheism.
ISBN 9780307269188

LC 2009014044

"Magisterial is the adjective of choice to describe Armstrong's work; her usual confident sweep across times and cultures rises above the answer-the-atheists tired angle to make a passionate footnoted argument for the human need for a God." Publishers Weekly.

Aslan, Reza

God : a human history / Reza Aslan. Random House, 2017. 240 p. **211**

1. God 2. Religion -- Origin 3. Monotheism -- History 4. Philosophy and religion
ISBN 9780553394726

LC 2017034711

The best-selling author of Zealot and host of Believer explores how different ideas about religion have united, divided and propelled humanity forward for millennia.

Dawkins, Richard, 1941-

★The **God** delusion / Richard Dawkins. Houghton Mifflin, 2006. x, 406 p. ; **211**

1. God 2. Atheism. 3. Religion -- Social aspects 4. Irreligion
ISBN 0618680004

LC 2006015506

Argues that belief in God is irrational, and describes examples of religion's negative influences on society throughout the centuries, such as war, bigotry, child abuse, and violence.

"Both fans of Dawkins and his many opponents will want to read this book." Library Journal.

Hazleton, Lesley, 1945-

Agnostic : a spirited manifesto / Lesley Hazleton. Riverhead Books, 2016. 240 p. **211**

1. Agnostics. 2. Belief and doubt 3. Agnosticism
ISBN 9781594634130

LC 2016006449

One in four Americans reject any affiliation with organized religion, and nearly half of those under thirty describe themselves as "spiritual but not religious." But as the airwaves resound with the haranguing of preachers and pundits, who speaks for the millions who find no joy in whittling the wonder of existence to a simple yes/no choice?

"This engaging and highly accessible read will satisfy those who puzzle over the idea of infinity, question theological truth or what death means for the mind and body, and who wish to delve deeper into our belief system." Library Journal.

Hitchens, Christopher, 1949-2011

The **four** horsemen : the conversation that sparked an atheist revolution / Christopher Hitchens, Richard Dawkins, Sam Harris, Daniel Dennett ; foreword by Stephen Fry. Random House, [2019] xix, 134 pages ; **211**

1. Atheism. 2. Belief and doubt. 3. Existentialism. 4. Faith. 5. Essays.
ISBN 9780525511953

LC 2019004626

A transcript of the 2007 viral documentary features intellectual responses to the fundamental questions of faith, human existence and the new atheism, in a volume that is complemented by new, contextualized essays by the group's three surviving members.

"Spanning religion and philosophy, this work will appeal to readers of both, especially those interested in atheism and apologetics." Library Journal.

Moore, R. Laurence (Robert Laurence), 1940-

Godless citizens in a godly republic : atheists in American public life / R. Laurence Moore and Isaac Kramnick. W. W. Norton & Company, 2018 xx, 236 p. ; **211**

1. Atheists 2. Religion and state 3. Religion and politics 4. Freedom of religion 5. United States -- Religion
ISBN 9780393254969

LC 2018001550

Two Cornell University professors examine the stigma that has caused atheists to be marginalized by First Amendment protections, the dramatic rise of atheism in America and the inherent prejudices of a non-secular Constitution that accepts religion as proof of integrity.

"This work provides important historical insights into a contentious contemporary issue. Highly recommended for readers interested in history, law, and political science, as well as those seeking positive approaches to expanding religious liberty." Library Journal.

Zuckerman, Phil

Living the secular life : new answers to old questions / Phil Zuckerman. Penguin Press, 2014. 240 p. **211**

1. Secularism. 2. Irreligion. 3. Ethics. 4. Atheism. 5. United States -- Religion.
ISBN 9781594205088

LC 2014009785

A sociology professor examines the demographic shift that has led more Americans than ever before to embrace a nonreligious life and highlights the inspirational stories and beliefs that empower modern-day secular culture.

"Highly recommended for all readers, both religious and nonreligious, seeking a more accurate understanding of this ever-growing segment of the American population." Library Journal.

212 Existence of God, ways of knowing God, attributes of God

Overman, Dean L.

A **case** for the existence of God / Dean L. Overman ; foreword by RObert Kaita ; afterword by Armand Nicholi. Rowman & Littlefield, c2009. xxxii, 229 p. ; **212**

1. God -- Proof, Cosmological. 2. Religion and science.
ISBN 074256312X

LC 2008021731

Argues that theism, rather than atheism, offers the best answers to life's most difficult questions and examines the existence of God within the framework of the latest theories of the origin of the universe.

"Drawing on modern cosmology and information theory, Overman exposes fallacies that have infested skeptics' thinking since Hume and Kant. Clearer reasoning establishes an astonishing harmony between quantum physics and religious orthodoxy, so providing a credible defense for free will and moral judgment. Still, readers looking for certainty will not find it here: Overman acknowledges that the believer must make a leap of faith. The intensely personal character of spiritual conversion emerges in the lives of the nine remarkable believers--including St. Augustine and Pascal, Dostoyevsky and Weil--whose testimonies resonate with passionate conviction. A book for readers willing to wrestle with the largest questions." Booklist.

215 Science and religion

Collins, Francis S.

The **language** of God : a scientist presents evidence for belief / Francis S. Collins. Free Press, c2006. viii, 294 p. : **215**

1. Religion and science. 2. Christian apologetics. 3. Religion.
ISBN 0743286391

LC 2006045316

A head of the Human Genome Project and former atheist presents a scientific argument for the existence of God, revealing how science can support faith by citing the areas of nature that can and cannot be fully explained by Darwinian evolution.

"The author entertains propositions both for and against the existence of God and biblical authority, as well as the moral implications of bioethics. He personalizes the narrative by recounting his own journey from atheism to faith, portraying it as much an intellectual quest as a spiritual one. . . . An essential read, equally for readers of religious or secular persuasions." Library Journal.

Ecklund, Elaine Howard

Science vs. religion : what scientists really think / Elaine Howard Ecklund. Oxford University Press, 2010. xi, 228 p. ; **215**

1. Religion and science. 2. Scientists. 3. Science. 4. Social scientists.
ISBN 9780195392982

LC 2009034731

"Ecklund's outstanding research, articulately presented, and judicious recommendations make this a valuable work for all who care about the subject of science and religion." Library Journal.

215.3 Physics

Barr, Stephen M., 1953-

★**Modern** physics and ancient faith / Stephen M. Barr. University of Notre Dame Press, c2003. ix, 312 p. : **215.3**

1. Physics -- Religious aspects -- Christianity. 2. Christianity and science. 3. Faith (Christianity) 4. Christianity -- History.
ISBN 0268034710

LC 2002151565

"Often invoked as justification for unbelief, modern science here provides the basis for an unusual and provocative affirmation of religious faith. A physicist at the University of Delaware, Barr deploys his scientific expertise to challenge the dogmas of materialism and to assert his belief that nothing explains the order of the galaxies better than divine design." Booklist

220.09 History, geographic treatment, biography

Barton, John, 1948-

A **history** of the Bible : the story of the world's most influential book / John Barton. Viking, 2019 xix, 613 p. : **220.09**

1. Bible. Old Testament History of Biblical events 2. Bible. New Testament History of Biblical events. 3. Judaism -- History 4. Christianity -- History 5. Jews -- History -- To 70 A.D.
ISBN 9780525428770

LC 2019022727

An Oxford scholar and Anglican priest discusses the bible in its historical context, from its beginnings as myth and folklore through the additions of narratives, laws, proverbs, prophesies, poems and letters to its interpretations through the centuries.

220.3 Encyclopedias and topical dictionaries

Douglas, J. D. (James Dixon)

Zondervan illustrated Bible dictionary / [edited by] J.D. Douglas and Merrill C. Tenney ; revised by Moises Silva. Zondervan, c2011. xii, 1571 p. : **220.3**

1. Bible Dictionaries.
ISBN 9780310229834

LC 2010034210

Rev. ed. of: New international dictionary of the Bible. Grand Rapids, MI, U.S.A. : Regency Reference Library, Zondervan Pub. House, c1987.

More than seven thousand entries present information on the Old and New Testaments, with maps, images, charts, and illustrations.

Freedman, David Noel, 1922-

Eerdmans dictionary of the Bible / David Noel Freedman, editor-in-chief; Allen C. Myers, associate editor; Astrid B. Beck, managing editor. W.B. Eerdmans, 2000. xxxiii, 1425 p. : **220.3**

1. Bible Dictionaries.
ISBN 9780802824004

LC 00056124

The most comprehensive and current single volume bible dictionary on the market features 5,000 articles on books, persons, and locales, compiled by more than 600 experts.

Metzger, Bruce M. (Bruce Manning), 1914-2007

The **Oxford** companion to the Bible / edited by Bruce M. Metzger, Michael D. Coogan. Oxford University Press, 1993. xxi, 874 p. : **220.3**

1. Bible Dictionaries.
ISBN 9780195046458

LC 93019315

Features interpretive articles on the Bible's impact on the Western world and its influence on literature, music, art, and law, as well as entries on each book of the Bible, the major figures, important events, and life in biblical times. $50,000 ad/promo.

Powell, Mark Allan, 1953-

The **HarperCollins** Bible dictionary HarperCollins, 2011. xxiii, 1142 p., 32 p. of plates : **220.3**

1. Bible Dictionaries. 2. Dictionaries
ISBN 9780061469060

LC 2010007897

More than four thousand entries present information on the Old Testament, Apocrypha, and New Testament.

220.5 Modern versions and translations

Carroll, Robert P.

★The **Bible** : Authorized King James Version / with an introduction and notes by Robert Carroll and Stephen Prickett. Oxford University Press, 2008. lxxiv, 1039, 248, 445 p. : **220.5**

ISBN 9780199535941

LC 2008273825

Originally published: Oxford ; New York : Oxford University Press, 1997.

This unique edition offers an exciting new approach to the most influential of all English biblical texts--the Authorized King James Version, complete with the Apocrypha. Its wide-ranging Introduction and the substantial notes to each book of the Bible guide the reader through the labyrinth of literary, textual, and theological issues, using the most up-to-date scholarship to demonstrate how and why the Bible has affected the literature, art and general culture of the English-speaking world. -- From publisher description

Ferrell, Lori Anne, 1957-

The **Bible** and the people / Lori Anne Ferrell. Yale University Press, 2009. 288 p. **220.5**

1. Bible History. 2. Bible Translating 3. Christianity -- History
ISBN 9780300114249

LC 2008026769

"Written for a general audience, this is an engaging and accessible overview of the history of the English Bible." Library Journal.

★The **New** Jerusalem Bible : reader's edition Doubleday, c1990. viii, 1463 p., 8 p. of plates : **220.5**

ISBN 9780385248334

LC 89039911

Includes indexes.

Encompasses the complete, unabridged biblical text, condensed section introductions, and concise tabular introductions to each book that outline themes and sections.

Ruden, Sarah

The **face** of water : a translator on beauty and meaning in the Bible / Sarah Ruden. Pantheon Books, 2017 xxxviii, 232 p. ; **220.5**

1. Bible Criticism, interpretation, etc. 2. Bible Translating. 3. Bible. English Versions Authorized.
ISBN 9780307908568

LC 2016014872

Offers an exploration of the original languages and texts of the Bible, with examinations and retranslations of some of its most famous passages as well as inquiries into the historical development of the work and the purposes of translation.

"This combination of casual ease and serious scholarship allows Ruden to bring fresh insights into even the most familiar stories and will make the book a true pleasure for anyone with an interest in translation or the Bible." Publishers Weekly.

Strong, James, 1822-1894

The **new** Strong's expanded exhaustive concordance of the Bible / James Strong. Thomas Nelson, c2010. 1 volume (various pagings) **220.5**

1. Bible 2. Hebrew language 3. Greek language, Biblical
ISBN 9781418541682

LC bl2010015608

"Expanded with the best of Vine's dictionary of Old & New Testament words."

An index to every word of the King James Version of the Bible includes a dictionary of Greek and Hebrew words, Strong's numbering system, and the words of Christ emphasized.

220.5205 Confraternity Bible and New American Bible

Confraternity of Christian Doctrine

★The **new** American Bible : translated from the original languages with critical use of all the ancient sources including the revised Psalms and the revised New Testament / authorized by the Board of Trustees of the Confraternity of Christian Doctrine and approved by the Administrative Committee Board of the National Conference of Catholic Bishops and the United States Catholic Conference. Oxford University Press, 2005 xxiii, 1514 p. ; **220.5205**

1. Bible. English. Catholic Biblical Association. 2005.
ISBN 9780195289046

This edition is perfect for anyone needing a straightforward text of the New American Bible, whether for reading or personal devotions. It includes a presentation section, prayers and devotions of the Church, the Dogmatic Constitution on Divine Revelation (Dei Verbum), a select NAB concordance, an essay on using the lectionary, and weekday and Sunday lectionary readings. -- From publisher description

220.6 Interpretation and criticism (Exegesis)

Levine, Amy-Jill, 1956-

The **Bible** with and without Jesus : how Jews and Christians read the same stories differently / Amy-Jill Levine, Marc Zvi Brettler. HarperOne, 2020. 448 p. **220.6**

1. Bible. Old Testament Criticism and interpretation 2. Bible. New Testament 3. Bible Criticism and interpretation 4. Bible 5. Judaism -- Relations -- Christianity. 6. Christianity -- Relations -- Judaism. 7. Theology 8. Interfaith relations.
ISBN 9780062560155

LC 2020003441

The editors of The Jewish Annotated New Testament, Amy-Jill Levine and Marc Brettler, explore how Jews and Christians can learn from and understand each other better by exploring how they read many of the same Bible stories through different lens.

"The chapter on the original meanings of sections of the Sermon on the Mount is alone worth the price of admission. A rich and important offering." Booklist

Loveday, Simon, 1949-

The **Bible** for grown-ups : a new look at the good book / Simon Loveday. Icon Books, 2017. 285 p. **220.6**

1. Bible. Old Testament Criticism and interpretation 2. Bible. New Testament Criticism and interpretation 3. Sacred books 4. Literature -- History and criticism 5. Christian doctrines
ISBN 9781785781315

LC bl2017033852

A startling new look at the Bible that is 'fascinating and persuasive' (Matthew Parris)

"After first setting aside belief, the late Loveday intelligently and successfully assesses the Bible in ways that are accessible and useful for those with open, inquiring minds." Publishers Weekly.

Wray, T. J.

What the Bible really tells us : the essential guide to biblical literacy / T.J. Wray. Rowman & Littlefield, c2011. xi, 249 p. ; **220.6**

1. Bible Criticism, interpretation, etc.
ISBN 9780742562530

LC 2011011778

Explores what the Bible really says about key issues today--including heaven & hell, wealth & money, and sexuality--then encourages readers to pursue Bible reading on their own.

"This volume is not an introduction in the usual sense (i.e., a discussion of the individual books in the Bible), but instead an introduction to the basic issues for human readers, and to the Bible's overall take on those issues. With her fresh approach to 'Introducing' the Bible, Wray succeeds in broaching issues without trivializing them." Choice.

220.8 Nonreligious subjects treated in Bible

Murphy, Cullen
The **Word** according to Eve : women and the Bible in ancient times and our own / Cullen Murphy ; foreword by Karen Armstrong. Houghton Mifflin, 1999. xxv, 302 p. ; **220.8**
1. Bible and feminism.
ISBN 0618001921
LC 99040646

"A Mariner book."
"A Peter Davison book."
Originally published: Boston : Houghton Mifflin, 1998. With new foreword.
"This is an examination of feminist Biblical scholarship. Murphy divides his study into Old Testament scholarship and New Testament and early church history." New York Times Book Review.

220.9 Geography, history, chronology, persons of Bible lands in Bible times

Chilton, Bruce
The **Cambridge** companion to the Bible / Bruce Chilton, general editor ; Howard Clark Kee ... [et al.]. Cambridge University Press, 2008. x, 724 p. 4 p. of plates : **220.9**
1. Bible Introductions. 2. Bible History of contemporary events. 3. Bible History of Biblical events.
ISBN 9780521691406
LC 2008270190

Provides information about the changing historical, social, and cultural contexts in which the Biblical writers and their original readers thought and lived, including writers of Jewish and Christian apocryphal works.

Currie, Robin, 1948-
The **letter** and the scroll : what archaeology tells us about the Bible / Robin Currie and Stephen G. Hyslop. National Geographic, c2009. 335 p. : **220.9**
1. Bible Antiquities. 2. Archaeology.
ISBN 9781426205149
LC 2009008572

A lavishly illustrated survey of archaeological finds that augment our understandings of biblical cultures features profiles of ancient cities, captioned photographs of important relics and descriptions of archaeological discoveries that reflect historical events and people.

Curtis, Adrian
Oxford Bible atlas / edited by Adrian Curtis. Oxford University Press, c2007. x, 229 p. : **220.9**
1. Bible Geography. 2. Bible Geography Maps.
ISBN 9780191001581
LC bl2007009916

Photographs accent maps and archaeological data pertaining to the Holy Land during biblical times.

221 Old Testament (Tanakh)

Jewish Publication Society
The **Jewish** Bible. A JPS Guide / Jewish Publication Society The Jewish Publication Society, 2008. ix, 291 p. : **221**
1. Bible. Old Testament
ISBN 9780827608511
LC 2008010794

A companion reference to the Jewish Bible instructs beginner through advanced students on basic biblical facts, including the Bible's origins and organization, the histories of its translations and popular methods of study, providing supplemental summaries of biblical books and a glossary of terms.

Kugel, James L.
How to read the Bible : a guide to Scripture, then and now / James L. Kugel. Free Press, 2007. xiv, 819 p. : **221**
1. Bible. Old Testament Criticism and interpretation 2. Religion. 3. Theology. 4. Judaism.
ISBN 9780743235860
LC 2007023466

A reader's companion to the Bible draws on classic interpretations as well as modern scholarship to explain how the Bible may also be a metaphorical reflection of anthropological history, in a guide that covers such topics as the fates of Israelites who remained behind in Canaan and the correlation between the commandments and the Code of Hammurabi.

Telushkin, Joseph, 1948-
Biblical literacy : the most important people, events, and ideas of the Hebrew Bible / Joseph Telushkin. William Morrow, c1997. xxviii, 628 p. ; **221**
1. Bible. Old Testament Introductions. 2. Jewish law.
ISBN 0688142974
LC 97006645

All the Bible's timeless stories of love, greed, and the human condition are arranged in one volume, providing a complete education in the books of the Hebrew Bible and conveying their psychological and emotional truths as well

"Biblical truths that many a reader may have glossed over before stand out, thanks to this superb book, and, more important, misunderstandings are cleared up and previously mistranslated words correctly rendered." Booklist.

222 Historical books of Old Testament

Alter, Robert,
★The **five** books of Moses : a translation with commentary / Robert Alter. W.W. Norton & Co., 2004. l, 1064 p. : **222**
1. Bible. Pentateuch Commentaries
ISBN 0393019551
LC 2004014067

"In this new translation of the first five books of the Bible {Alter} . seeks to reproduce as faithfully as possible in standard English the nuances, literary devices, and metaphors of the original Hebrew text. In doing so, he aims to show where many modern translations (including the King James Bible) have failed to represent the original Hebrew's varied nuances. In his commentary, found in the introductions to each book and on many individual verses, Alter expounds the theological meaning of the text's narrative in its larger biblical context." Library Journal.

Crumb, R.,
The **book** of Genesis / illustrated by R. Crumb. W.W. Norton, c2009. 224 p. **222**
1. Bible. Genesis 2. Creation (Bible) 3. The Flood. 4. Comics and Graphic novels
ISBN 9780393061024
LC 2009014303

Four years in the making, a graphic translation of the first book of the Bible uses actual word-for-word text as a basis for its dramatic presentations and includes intricately detailed depictions of the stories of Adam and Eve, and Noah's ark.

"This is the Bible that distressed 19th-century English philanthropist and man of letters Thomas Bowdler: not stories for sweet-faced kiddies, but sex and blood. We could not expect less from the patriarch of underground comix--themselves notorious for sex and violence and deals gone sour. Indeed, Crumb's muscular, detailed black-and-white seems ideally suited to Old Testament scuffles and seaminess." Library Journal.

Feiler, Bruce, 1964-
The **first** love story : Adam, Eve, and us / Bruce Feiler. Penguin Group USA, 2017. 368 p. **222**
1. Adam (Biblical figure) 2. Eve (Biblical figure) 3. Men/women relations 4. Interpersonal relations 5. Gender wars 6. Love
ISBN 9781594206818
LC 2016043490

The PBS host and best-selling author of Walking the Bible and Abraham presents a revelatory account of Adam and Eve's symbolism as central figures in Western imagination and their role in shaping humanity's deepest feelings about relationships, family and togetherness.

"Part travelogue, part historical survey, the book presents an impressive array of perspectives and a broad archive." Booklist.

Fox, Everett
The **five** books of Moses : Genesis, Exodus, Leviticus, Numbers, Deuteronomy : a new translation with introductions, commentary, and notes / Everett Fox ; illustrations by Schwebel. Schocken Books, 2000, c1995. xxxi, 1024 p. : **222**
1. Bible. O.T. Pentateuch Commentaries.
ISBN 9780805211191
LC BL 00007461

Offers a translation of and commentary on the first five books of the Hebrew Bible.

Kass, Leon
The **beginning** of wisdom : reading Genesis / Leon R. Kass. Free Press, c2003. xv, 700 p. : **222**
1. Bible. Genesis Commentaries.
ISBN 0743242998
LC 2002045593

Looks at the wisdom of nature and of man as seen through an interpreation of the book of Genesis.

Moyers, Bill D.
Genesis : a living conversation / Bill Moyers ; Betty Sue Flowers, editor ; Judith Davidson Moyers, executive editor ; Elizabeth Meryman-Brunner, art research. Doubleday, 1997, c1996. xxxvii, 361 p. : **222**
1. Bible. O.T. Genesis Criticism, interpretation, etc. 2. United States -- Interviews.
ISBN 0385490437
LC BL 99792848

Main Street Books imprint on spine.

Reprint. Originally published: 1996.

In the profusely illustrated companion book to his ten-part PBS series, the acclaimed television journalist brings together more than fifty writers, theologians, artists, and intellectuals to discuss the themes and teachings of Genesis.

Stein, David E. S., 1957-
The **contemporary** Torah : a gender-sensitive adaptation of the JPS translation / revising editor, David E.S. Stein ; consulting editors, Adele Berlin, Ellen Frankel, and Carol L. Meyers. Jewish Publication Society, c2006. xlii, 412 p. ; **222**
ISBN 9780827607965
LC 2006040608

This adaptation of the JPS translation of the Torah (1962) will appeal to readers who are interested in a historically based picture of social gender roles in the Bible as well as those who have become accustomed to gender-sensitive English in other aspects of their lives. --Provided by publisher

223 Poetic books of Old Testament

Greenstein, Edward L.
Job : a new translation / Edward L. Greenstein. Yale University Press, 2019 xxxvii, 206 p. ; **223**
1. Bible. Job Commentaries. 2. Bible. Job Translations into English.
ISBN 0300162340
LC bl2019023158

This revelatory new translation of Job by one of the world's leading biblical scholars will reshape the way we read this canonical text. --Provided by publisher

Kushner, Harold S.
The **book** of Job : when bad things happened to a good person / Harold S. Kushner. Nextbook : Schocken, c2012. 224 p. **223**
1. Bible. Job Commentaries. 2. Suffering -- Religious aspects -- Judaism. 3. Fairness -- Religious aspects 4. Judaism
ISBN 9780805242928
LC 2011051531

Draws on lessons from the Book of Job to offer advice on how to retain faith in the face of adversity and explains how to recognize controllable and uncontrollable factors.

225 New Testament

Borg, Marcus J.
Evolution of the Word : reading the New Testament in the order it was written / Marcus J. Borg. HarperOne, c2012. 592 p. **225**
1. Bible. New Testament 2. Christianity. 3. Theology.
ISBN 9780062082107
LC 2012001947

Analyzes the New Testament chronologically through each book of the Bible, detailing how the core values of Christianity took shape and developed over time.

Brown, Raymond Edward
An **introduction** to the New Testament / Raymond E. Brown. Yale University Press, 2010. xxxvii, 878 p. : **225**
1. New Testament Introductions. 2. New Testament Canon. 3. New

Testament Theology.
ISBN 0300140169

LC oc2012538238

Originally published: London: Doubleday, 1997.

From the experience of a lifetime of scholarship, preaching, teaching, and writing, Raymond E. Brown covers the entire scope of the New Testament with ease and clarity. He walks readers book by book through the basic content and issues of the New Testament. --Provided by publisher

225.9 Geography, history, chronology, persons of New Testament lands in New Testament times

Ruden, Sarah

Paul among the people : the Apostle reinterpreted and reimagined in his own time / Sarah Ruden. Pantheon Books, 2010. xix, 214 p. ; **225.9**

1. Paul, the Apostle, Saint 2. Bible. Epistles of Paul 3. Religion -- History 4. Christianity -- History
ISBN 9780375425011

LC 2009020969

An assessment of the Apostle Paul explores the ways in which his edicts may have been misinterpreted, in an account that translates Paul's writings from Koine Greek to assess how he may have been wrongly perceived as a misogynist and social conformist.

"In reimagining Paul with the aid of her intimate knowledge of classical literature, Ruden hasn't only helped us to better understand him and his message in the context of his time (as indispensable as that service is). She has also brought Paul to us, to our time. In an uncanny way, her book is animated by the apostle's style: his urgency, his argumentative agility, his bluntness, his exasperation, his vision of great felicity." National Review.

226 Gospels and Acts

Kloppenborg, John S., 1951-

Q, the earliest Gospel : an introduction to the original stories and sayings of Jesus / John S. Kloppenborg. Westminster John Knox Press, c2008. x, 170 p. : **226**

1. Q hypothesis (Synoptics criticism) 2. Two source hypothesis (Synoptics criticism)
ISBN 0664232221

LC 2008008394

"The author is an authority on the Q Gospel, a sayings gospel that is thought to be a source (from the German Quelle for source) for the Gospels of Matthew and Luke. No copy of Q has been found, but scholars have recreated it through analysis of the three synoptic Gospels, looking for common elements and focusing on the sayings of Jesus. This book is a succinct introduction to Q, addressing questions about its composition and importance. A complete reconstruction of Q is included as well as notes and a bibliography." Library Journal.

226.2 Specific Gospels

Spong, John Shelby, 1931-

Biblical literalism : a gentile heresy : a journey into a new Christianity through the doorway of Matthew's gospel / John Shelby Spong. HarperOne, 2016. 400 p. **226.2**

1. Bible. Matthew Criticism and interpretation 2. Bible. Gospels. 3. Christianity
ISBN 9780062362308

LC 2015018099

Includes index.

Using the Gospel of Matthew as a guide, Spong explores the Bible's literary and liturgical roots--its grounding in Jewish culture, symbols, icons, and storytelling tradition--to explain how the events of Jesus' life, including the virgin birth, the miracles, the details of the passion story, and the resurrection and ascension, would have been understood by both the Jewish authors of the various gospels and by the Jewish audiences for which they were originally written. Spong makes clear that it was only after the church became fully Gentile that readers of the Gospels took these stories to be factual, distorting their original meaning.

"A worthwhile read for the progressive layperson concerned with living out one's faith and applying the Bible as a touchstone." Library Journal.

226.3 Mark

Price, Reynolds, 1933-2011

The **three** Gospels / Reynolds Price. Scribner, 1996. 288 p. **226.3**

1. Jesus Christ Person and offices. 2. Bible. New Testament. Gospels History of Biblical events. 3. Bible. Gospels Criticism and interpretation
ISBN 0684803364

LC 95039948

"Although there is so much to appreciate in these commentaries and in the translated texts, the best part of the book . . . is left to last: Price's own joyously written account of Jesus' life." Booklist.

226.8 Parables

Levine, Amy-Jill, 1956-

Short stories by Jesus : the enigmatic parables of a controversial rabbi / Amy-Jill Levine. HarperOne, 2014. 320 p. **226.8**

1. Jesus Christ Parables. 2. Christianity. 3. Parables -- History and criticism. 4. Philosophy, Jewish.
ISBN 9780061561016

LC 2014012012

Examines Jesus' most popular parables and looks at how they have been misinterpreted and misunderstood, seeking to make them more relevant to today's readers.

229 Apocrypha, pseudepigrapha, intertestamental works

Pagels, Elaine H., 1943-

★ **Beyond** belief : the secret Gospel of Thomas / Elaine Pagels. Random House, 2003. 241 p. **229**

1. Jesus Christ Person and offices. 2. Gospel of Thomas Criticism and interpretation. 3. Bible. John Criticism and interpretation 4. Christianity -- Essence, genius, nature. 5. Gnosticism
ISBN 0375501568

LC 2002036840

Spurred by personal tragedy, Elaine Pagels turns to a consideration of the Gnostic Gospels--in particular, the Gospel of Thomas. Pagels believes that Thomas's words lead to a more open, welcoming, and equitable kind of Christianity. If Beyond belief is at odds with conservative theological certainties, it nonetheless speaks to Jesus's humanity--and to our own.

"Even those who possess only a nodding acquaintance with Gnostic writings will find themselves stimulated by the author's arguments and perhaps transformed by her conclusions. A fresh and exciting work of theology and spirituality." Booklist.

230 Christianity

Dark, David, 1969-

Life's too short to pretend you're not religious / David Dark. InterVarsity Press, 2016. 192 p. **230**

1. Philosophical theology. 2. Christian apologetics 3. Religious life 4. Religions

ISBN 9780830844463

LC 2015036062

"Dark's argument couched in a memoir is a persuasive, well-grounded case for religion's place in modern society." Publishers Weekly.

Davies, Brian, 1951-

The **thought** of Thomas Aquinas / Brian Davies. Oxford University Press, 1992. xv, 391 p. ; **230**

1. Thomas, Aquinas, Saint, 1225?-1274 2. Catholic Church. 3. Catholic theology -- History. 4. Theology, Doctrinal -- History -- Middle Ages, 600-1500.

ISBN 0198264585

LC 91035671

"Davies aims to cover the whole programme of the Summa in 370 pages. This necessarily means that, though his writing is admirably clear and never cryptic, much of what he says is extremely concise, and some topics get less airing than others." Times Literary Supplement.

Edman, Elizabeth M., 1962-

Queer virtue : what LGBTQ people know about life and love and how it can revitalize Christianity / The Reverend Elizabeth M. Edman. Beacon Press, 2016. 216 p. **230**

1. Queer theology. 2. Christianity and sexuality. 3. Queer theory. 4. Christianity.

ISBN 9780807061343

LC 2015027701

Frustrated by the notion that "Christian love = tolerance," Edman argues that Christianity, at its scriptural core, is not a tradition that is hostile to queer people but is, in fact, itself inherently queer. Edman reveals how "queering" Christianity--that is, disrupting simplistic ways of thinking about gender and sexuality--can illuminate contemporary Christian faith and shows why queer Christians are gifts to the Church.

"An intellectual and provocative perspective challenging Christians and others to reconsider the confines of spiritual interconnection, harmony, and progressive inclusion in modern religion." Kirkus.

Hastings, Adrian

The **Oxford** companion to Christian thought / edited by Adrian Hastings, Alistair Mason, and Hugh Pyper ; with Ingrid Lawrie and Cecily Bennett. Oxford University Press, 2000. xxviii, 777 p. ; **230**

1. Theology -- Dictionaries.

ISBN 9780198600244

LC 2001267818

Encompassing the perspectives of Catholic, Protestant, and Orthodox theologians, this comprehensive overview of Christian thought and teaching presents six hundred alphabetically organized entries that explore the history of Christian thought, national and regional traditions, various denominations, major theological topics, symbolism, and controversial issues.

Holifield, E. Brooks

★**Theology** in America : Christian thought from the age of the Puritans to the Civil War / E. Brooks Holifield. Yale University Press, c2003. ix, 617 p. ; **230**

1. Theology, Doctrinal -- United States -- History. 2. Christianity -- History. 3. Religion. 4. United States -- Religion -- To 1800. 5. United States -- Religion -- 19th century.

ISBN 0300095740

LC 2003042289

"In this majestic achievement, Holifield provides a first-rate, richly evocative and unrivaled history of theology in America. This masterfully narrated, splendid book will become the definitive study of the development of American theology." Publishers Weekly.

Kung, Hans, 1928-

Great Christian thinkers : Paul, Origen, Augustine, Aquinas, Luther, Schleiermacher, Barth / Hans Kung. Continuum, 1995, c1994. 235 p. ; **230**

1. Theologians. 2. Theology -- Introductions.

ISBN 0826408486

LC bl 99779007

Reprint. Originally published: c1994.

An introduction to theologians who greatly affected Christian thought includes portraits of Paul, Origen, Augustine, Thomas Aquinas, Martin Luther, Friedrich Schleiermacher, and Karl Barth.

Lewis, C. S. (Clive Staples), 1898-1963

★**Mere** Christianity : a revised and amplified edition, with a new introduction, of the three books, Broadcast talks, Christian behaviour, and Beyond personality / C.S. Lewis. Harper San Francisco, 2001, c1952. xx, 227 p. ; **230**

1. Theology, Doctrinal. 2. Christian apologetics. 3. Christian ethics -- Anglican authors. 4. Christianity.

ISBN 9780060652883

LC 00049862

Originally published: London : G. Bles, 1952.

Discusses the essence of Christian faith and the doctrine of the Trinity.

Thomas, Aquinas, Saint, 1225?-1274

Selected writings / Thomas Aquinas ; edited and translated with an introduction and notes by Ralph McInerny. Penguin Books, 1998. xxxviii, 841 p. ; **230**

1. Catholic Church Doctrines Early works to 1800. 2. Theology, doctrinal -- Early works to 1800

ISBN 9780140436327

LC 99180304

Brings together sermons, commentary responses to criticism, and substantial extracts from the "Summa Theologiae," arranged chronologically.

231 Christian doctrinal theology

Bass, Diana Butler, 1959-

Grounded : finding God in the world--a spiritual revolution

/ Diana Butler Bass. HarperOne, 2015. 304 p. **231**

1. God (Christianity). 2. Spiritual life -- Christianity 3. Faith (Christianity) 4. Christianity -- 21st century.

ISBN 9780062328540

LC 2015018071

Argues that the apparent shift away from traditional religion in today's culture actually signals an ongoing change in how people understand God, as people replace old ideas of a distant god with an intimate understanding that is transforming religion and society.

"Its a deeply theological book, but also a practical one; a book that causes one to ponder the spiritual implications of farmers' markets in altogether new ways." Booklist.

231.7 Relation to the world

Lewis, C. S. (Clive Staples), 1898-1963

Miracles : a preliminary study / C.S. Lewis. Harper San Francisco, 2001, c1947. 294 p. ; **231.7**

1. Miracles. 2. Christianity. 3. Spirituality. 4. Faith in men.

ISBN 0060653019

LC 00049863

Originally published: London : G. Bles, 1947.

British author C. S. Lewis discusses the possibility that supernatural occurrences have taken place throughout history. Centering his argument on The Incarnation, the moment where God and man became one, Lewis challenges skeptics and non-believers with sound evidence.

"Mr. Lewis casts his net fairly wide and, under the guise of a book on miracles, offers a rational justification both of theism and of doctrinal Christianity." Times Literary Supplement.

McKnight, Scot

Kingdom conspiracy : returning to the radical mission of the local church / Scot McKnight. Brazos Press, 2014 289 p. ; **231.7**

1. Jesus Christ Kingdom. 2. Kingdom of God 3. Mission of the church

ISBN 9781587433603

LC 2014015580

Includes index.

"This is a must-read for church leaders today." Publishers Weekly.

Winner, Lauren F.

Wearing God : clothing, laughter, fire, and other overlooked ways of meeting God / Lauren F. Winner. HarperCollins 2015 256 p. **231.7**

1. Spiritual life 2. Christianity 3. Spirituality 4. Faith (Christianity)

ISBN 9780061768125

LC 2015001455

A teacher at Duke Divinity School explores both familiar and unfamiliar metaphors for God, going past that of the Lord as a father, savior, creator and judge and viewing God as a comedian, a garment or as a vintner making fine wine. Reading-group guide available. By the author of Still: Notes on a Mid-faith Crisis.

"Winner's honest, charming reflections stir the imagination and invite the reader to explore not just the metaphors she has chosen, but the treasure trove the Bible provides. Prayers and quotations promote further contemplation." Publishers Weekly.

Wintz, Jack

Will I see my dog in heaven? : God's saving love for the whole family of creation / Jack Wintz. Paraclete Press, 2009. 153 p. **231.7**

1. Animals -- Religious aspects -- Christianity. 2. Life after death -- Religious aspects -- Christianity. 3. Catholic theology 4. Religion.

ISBN 9781557255686

LC 2009000259

"The author, a Franciscan friar, argues that God's promise of a new creation at the end of time extends to the animal companions we have known and loved in this life. Strongly recommended." Library Journal.

Woodward, Kenneth L.

The **book** of miracles : the meaning of the miracle stories in Christianity, Judaism, Buddhism, Hinduism, Islam / Kenneth L. Woodward. Simon & Schuster, 2001, c2000. 429 p. ; **231.7**

1. Miracles

ISBN 9780743200295

LC BL2001011232

"A Touchstone book."

Originally published: 2000.

A collection of stories about miracle workers explores scriptural contexts of each religious tradition and discusses traditions relating to the Sufi mystics, Hindu and Buddhist saints, Christian hermits, Talmudic wonder-workers, and Muslim ascetics.

"A great resource for studies in comparative religions and interfaith dialog." Library Journal.

232 Jesus Christ and his family

Blum, Edward J.

The **color** of Christ : the Son of God and the saga of race in America / Edward J. Blum and Paul Harvey. University of North Carolina Press, c2012. 336 p. **232**

1. Jesus Christ. 2. Racism -- Religious aspects -- Christianity. 3. Race relations. 4. Interethnic relations. 5. African Americans -- Religion. 6. United States -- Church history.

ISBN 9780807835722

LC 2012004088

"A must-read for those interested in American religious history, this book will forever change the way you look at images of Jesus." Publishers Weekly.

Gordon, Mary, 1949-

Reading Jesus : a writer's encounter with the Gospels / Mary Gordon. Pantheon Books, c2009. 240 p. **232**

1. Jesus Christ Person and offices. 2. Bible. Gospels Criticism and interpretation 3. Faith (Christianity) 4. Spiritual life. 5. Christianity. 6. Religion.

ISBN 9780375424571

LC 2009004975

In this impassioned and eye-opening book, Gordon takes us through all the fundamental stories--the Prodigal Son, the Temptation in the Desert, the parable of Lazarus, the Agony in the Garden--pondering the intense strangeness of a deity in human form, the unresolved more ambiguities, the problem posed to her as an enlightened reader by the miracle of the Resurrection. What she rediscovers--and reinterprets with her signature candor, intelligence, and straightforwardness--is a rich store of overlapping, sometimes conflicting teachings that feel both familiar and tantalizingly elusive. It is this unsolvable conundrum that rests at the heart of Reading Jesus.

"Gordon examines her faith by closely reading, in a kind of literary lectio divina (sacred reading), the four Christian gospels that recount the life of Christ. The accounts by evangelists Matthew, Mark, Luke and John of the life of Jesus have a common subject and amazingly different treatments. Gordon tackles the power and puzzle of the Christian gospels with measure and imagination, providing welcome relief for those left cold by scholarly or fundamentalist parsing." Publishers Weekly.

Rohr, Richard

The **universal** Christ : how a forgotten reality can change everything we see, hope for, and believe / Richard Rohr. Convergent Books, 2019. 240 p. **232**

1. Jesus Christ Person and offices. 2. Faith (Christianity) 3. Christian life. 4. Religion and culture. 5. Spirituality.
ISBN 9781524762094

LC 2018056812

From one of the world's most influential spiritual thinkers, a long-awaited book exploring what it means that Jesus was called "Christ," and how this forgotten truth can restore hope and meaning to our lives.

232.9 Family and life of Jesus

Girzone, Joseph F.

A **portrait** of Jesus / Joseph F. Girzone. Image Books, 1999, c1998. 179 p. ; **232.9**

1. Jesus Christ Biography Devotional literature. 2. Christian life -- Catholic authors.
ISBN 0385484771

LC BL 99012297

Originally published: New York : Doubleday, 1998.

An acclaimed religious author offers a study of Jesus as he was perceived by those around him, in an effort to place the man in the historical context of his time and to make him palpably real.

"This is popular liberal Catholic theology, more filled with forgiveness and fellowship than shaming and hierarchy. Many a non-Catholic and even non-Christian may embrace it, too." Booklist.

Meier, John P.

A **marginal** Jew: rethinking the historical Jesus, volume 1 : the roots of the problem and the person / John P. Meier. Doubleday, 1991 496 p. **232.9**

1. Jesus Christ Historicity. 2. Jesus Christ Jewishness. 3. Bible. New Testament Criticism and interpretation 4. Judaism -- Relations -- Christianity. 5. Christianity -- Relations -- Judaism. 6. Jews in the New Testament. 7. Judaism (Christian theology) 8. Palestine.
ISBN 0385264259

LC 91010538

"The author summarizes the first two volumes of A Marginal Jew and forecasts the next while meticulously documenting his understanding of the relations between the historical Jesus, his historical companions, and his historical competitors: Pharisees, Sadducces, Essenes, and others. The only thing common about Meier's project is fascination with the character of Jesus. Those who share that will find this dense, academic work worth their effort." Booklist. {review of volume 3}

232.91 Mary, mother of Jesus

Pelikan, Jaroslav, 1923-2006

Mary through the centuries : her place in the history of culture / Jaroslav Pelikan. Yale University Press, c1996. x, 267 p., 16 p. of plates : **232.91**

1. Mary, Blessed Virgin, Saint History of doctrines. 2. Mary, Blessed Virgin, Saint Theology.
ISBN 9780300069518

LC 96024726

Explores how Mary has been represented in theology, art, music, and literature throughout the ages.

"Although volumes have been written about the Virgin Mary from a wide variety of perspectives, it is rare to find a scholarly work that is easily accessible to the general, educated reader." Choice.

232.96 Passion and death of Jesus

Wright, N. T. (Nicholas Thomas)

The **day** the revolution began : reconsidering the meaning of Jesus's crucifixion / N.T. Wright. HarperOne, an imprint of HarperCollinsPublishers, 2016 viii, 440 p. : **232.96**

1. Jesus Christ Crucifixion. 2. Redemption (Christianity) 3. Salvation (Christianity) 4. Faith (Christianity) 5. Crosses (Christianity)
ISBN 9780062334381

LC 2016028318

Includes index.

Argues that the Protestant Reformation did not go far enough in reconsidering the meaning of Jesus's crucifixion and claims that his death on the cross was actually a calling for the faithful to restore and reconcile all of God's creation.

233 Humankind

Greenblatt, Stephen, 1943-

★The **rise** and fall of Adam and Eve / Stephen Greenblatt. W. W. Norton & Company, 2017. 719 p. ; **233**

1. Adam (Biblical figure) 2. Eve (Biblical figure) 3. Bible Genesis 4. Parents 5. Humans -- Origin 6. Creation 7. Garden of Eden (Biblical place)
ISBN 9780393240801

Longlisted for the Andrew Carnegie Medal for Excellence in Non-Fiction, 2018.

Explores the biblical story of human origins, drawing on theological, artistic, and cultural influences to discuss how the story of Adam and Eve reflects the fears, desires, and problems of humanity through the ages.

"Greenblatt has shaped an enjoyable and well-paced narrative that effectively draws from many disciplines." Library Journal.

Jacobs, Alan, 1958-

Original sin : a cultural history / Alan Jacobs. Harper Collins, 2008. 304 p. **233**

1. Sin. 2. Original sin (Christian theology) 3. Good and evil. 4. Free will and determinism.
ISBN 0060783400

LC 2008006582

A cultural history of the controversial idea that people are born with a predisposition to evil shares the stories of the philosophy's proponents and disclaimers, in an account that cites the contributions of such figures as St. Augustine, G. K. Chesterton, and Blaise Pascal.

Kierkegaard, Søren, 1813-1855

The **concept** of anxiety : a simple psychologically oriented deliberation in view of the dogmatic problem of hereditary sin / Søren Kierkegaard ; edited and translated with introduction and notes by Alastair Hannay. Liveright Publishing Corporation,

2014. 288 p. 233

1. Anxiety -- Religious aspects -- Christianity. 2. Original sin (Christian theology) 3. Religious psychology
ISBN 9780871407191
LC 2013037399

"Almost as valuable as the translation is Hannay's introduction in which he provides the background necessary to grapple with Kierkegaard and a heartfelt argument for the value of studying this fountainhead of existentialism in general and Anxiety in particular." Library Journal.

Teilhard de Chardin, Pierre, 1881-1955

★The **divine** Milieu / Pierre Teilhard de Chardin. Perennial, 2001. xlvii, 140 p. ; 233

1. Christian philosophy. 2. Spiritual life -- Christianity 3. Philosophy and religion
ISBN 0060937254
LC 2001039440

Includes index.

Teilhard de Chardin -- geologist, priest, and major voice in twentieth-century Christianity -- probes the ultimate meaning of all physical exploration and the fruit of his own inner life. The Divine Milieu is a spiritual treasure for every religion bookshelf. --Provided by publisher

234 Salvation and grace

Carter, Jimmy, 1924-

Faith : a journey for all / Jimmy Carter. Simon & Schuster, 2018. 208 p. 234

1. Faith 2. Christianity and culture 3. History -- Religious aspects -- Christianity 4. Faith (Christianity)
ISBN 9781501184413
LC 2018003986

Includes index.

Explores the meaning of faith and its profound effects on people's lives and the world, as well as how the author's own religious faith has guided, sustained, and challenged him throughout his life.

Eldredge, John, 1960-

All things new : heaven, Earth, and the restoration of everything you love / John Eldredge. Nelson Books, 2017 xii, 224 p. ; 234

1. Heaven -- Christianity. 2. Paradise. 3. Redemption.
ISBN 0718037995
LC 2017011696

Offers hope to believers by outlining the coming afterlife on a New Earth, with all the joys people know in this life, that God will soon establish, and that, rather than a Heaven in the clouds, will be the eternal home of the faithful.

Teresa, Mother, 1910-1997

A **call** to mercy : hearts to love, hands to serve / Mother Teresa. Image, [2016] xx, 364 p. ; 234

1. Spiritual life. 2. Compassion 3. Spirituality. 4. Faith.
ISBN 9780451498205
LC bl2016027911

A collection of unpublished material from the Nobel Peace Prize-winning holy woman who was canonized as a Saint by the Vatican in September 2016 offers her wisdom on showing compassion in our daily lives and working to create a heaven on earth.

"These reflections, stories, and testimonials will challenge and inspire readers to bear witness to a venerable spiritual legacy." Publishers Weekly.

235 Spiritual beings

McCarthy, David Matzko

Sharing God's good company : a theology of the Communion of Saints / David Matzko McCarthy. William B. Eerdmans Pub. Co., 2012. viii, 174 p. ; 235

1. Christian saints -- Biography -- History and criticism.
ISBN 080286709X
LC 2011049265

In Sharing God's Good Company David Matzko McCarthy explores the role and significance of the saints in Christians' lives today. While examining the lives of specific saints like Martin de Porres, Therese de Lisieux, and Mother Teresa, McCarthy especially focuses on such topics as the veneration of martyrs, realism and hagiography, science and miracles, images and pilgrimage, and why the saints continue to captivate Christians and inspire devotion. --Provided by publisher

Pagels, Elaine H., 1943-

The **origin** of Satan / Elaine Pagels. Random House, c1995. xxiii, 214 p. ; 235

1. Bible. Gospels Criticism and interpretation 2. Devil -- Biblical teaching. 3. Antisemitism in Christianity. 4. Paganism.
ISBN 9780679401407
LC 95007983

A study of the role of the devil in biblical and modern times theorizes that dissident social groups that resisted Christianity were typically portrayed as demons and therefore established as threats.

"Pagels shows herself to be a masterful guide through the risk-laden complexities of biblical studies." Publishers Weekly.

Wray, T. J.

The **birth** of Satan : tracing the devil's biblical roots / T.J. Wray, Gregory Mobley. Palgrave Macmillan, 2005. xix, 211 p. ; 235

1. Bible 2. Devil -- Biblical teaching. 3. Good and evil. 4. Religion. 5. Faith.
ISBN 9781403969330
LC 2005043046

A groundbreaking search for the origins of the Prince of Darkness. --Provided by publisher

235.24 Beatification and canonization

Woodward, Kenneth L.

Making saints : how the Catholic Church determines who becomes a saint, who doesn't, and why / Kenneth L. Woodward. Simon & Schuster, c1996. xv, 462 p. : 235.24

1. Catholic Church Customs and practices 2. Canonization -- History -- 20th century. 3. Christian saints. 4. Catholic theology -- 20th century
ISBN 9780684815305
LC 97126222

"A Touchstone book."

A pioneering work of investigative journalism penetrates the Vatican to explain the canonization process and describes the political in-fighting, the medical questions, and the costs of canonization.

"This is the most comprehensive, critical and up-to-date look at saint making so far written." New York Times Book Review.

236 Eschatology

Brown, Samuel Morris

In heaven as it is on earth : Joseph Smith and the early Mormon conquest of death / Samuel Morris Brown. Oxford University Press, 2011. 400 p. **236**

1. Smith, Joseph, 1805-1844. 2. Mormon Church. 3. Death -- Religious aspects. 4. Mormon theology. 5. Theology.
ISBN 9780199793570

LC 2011002848

Discusses the foundational beliefs of the Mormon Church by focusing on early Mormon conceptions of death.

Eire, Carlos M. N.

A **very** brief history of eternity / Carlos Eire. Princeton University Press, 2010. xv, 268 p. : **236**

1. Eternity. 2. Theology. 3. Christian doctrines. 4. Christianity.
ISBN 9780691133577

LC 2009022951

"The author's skill at engaging readers conceals the rigorous, thoughtful research and methodology that went into this volume. This thought-provoking book is sure to be a classic." Choice.

Spong, John Shelby, 1931-

Eternal life : pious dream or realistic hope? / John Shelby Spong. Harper One, c2009. 288 p. **236**

1. Death -- Religious aspects -- Christianity. 2. Life after death -- Religious aspects -- Christianity. 3. Fear of death -- Religious aspects -- Christianity 4. Eternity.
ISBN 9780060762063

LC 2008051443

A best-selling author and controversial bishop continues to challenge traditional Christian theology with his thoughts on one of the most profound issues of all: God and life after death.

Turner, Alice K.

The **history** of hell / Alice K. Turner. Harcourt Brace, 1993. vi, 275 p., 22 p. of plates : **202.3**

1. Hell -- Comparative studies 2. Hell -- History. 3. Life after death.
ISBN 015140934X

LC 93009909

"Belief in a hell or some sort of afterlife has been intrinsic to the religions of the world ever since the first stories were shared aloud and incised in clay tablets. Turner's richly illustrated history surveys the myriad forms hell has taken in the West from Sumer to Rome and beyond." Booklist.

Weber, Eugen, 1925-2007

Apocalypses : prophecies, cults, and millennial beliefs through the ages / Eugen Weber. Harvard University Press, 1999. 294 p. ; **236**

1. End of the world -- History of doctrines. 2. Millennialism -- History 3. Eschatology, Christian -- History of doctrines 4. Religion -- History 5. Apocalyptic literature
ISBN 0674040805

LC 99018001

"Weber traces millennial beliefs as professed through the ages. From ancient and pre-Christian times to the present day, humankind has had an unshakable belief that the end is at hand. Weber has an excellent grasp of his subject, an accessible style, and an understated sense of humor." Booklist.

Wright, N. T. (Nicholas Thomas)

Surprised by hope : rethinking Heaven, the resurrection, and the mission of the church / N.T. Wright. HarperOne, 2008. xiv, 332 p. ; **236**

1. Resurrection. 2. Church and the world. 3. Christian doctrines. 4. Intersectionality
ISBN 0061551821

LC bl2008002874

Offers a reinterpretation of biblical teaching on what happens after death, arguing that literal bodily resurrection is at the heart of Christianity and exploring the implications of this for the church's work in the world.

"Readers will need a Bible handy to appreciate this work fully, as Wright prefers to cite rather than print Scripture. His prose, deep but not murky, is lightened by glints of humor. For any library serving patrons who are willing to think a bit about religion." Library Journal.

239 Apologetics and polemics

Augustine, Saint, Bishop of Hippo

Concerning the city of God against the pagans / St. Augustine ; translated by Henry Bettenson ; with a new introduction by G.R. Evans. Penguin Books, 2003. lxxi, 1097 p. ; **239**

1. Christian apologetics 2. Kingdom of God
ISBN 9780140448948

LC 2004269353

Originally published: 1972.

St Augustine, bishop of Hippo, was one of the central figures in the history of Christianity, and City of God is one of his greatest theological works. Written as an eloquent defence of the faith at a time when the Roman Empire was on the brink of collapse, it examines the ancient pagan religions of Rome, the arguments of the Greek philosophers and the revelations of the Bible. Pointing the way forward to a citizenship that transcends the best political experiences of the world and offers citizenship that will last for eternity, City of God is one of the most influential documents in the development of Christianity. --Provided by publisher

Keller, Timothy J., 1950-

The **reason** for God : belief in an age of skepticism / Timothy Keller. Dutton, 2008. 320 p. **239**

1. Christian apologetics. 2. Christianity. 3. Faith. 4. Skepticism.
ISBN 9780525950493

LC 2007043745

Arguing that most Americans are members of the Christian faith, a response to promoters of science and secularism addresses key questions about suffering, exclusivity, and the belief that Christianity is the only true religion.

"Using literature, philosophy, and pop culture, the author gives convincing reasons for a strong belief in God. [The author] presents a religious view without being overly critical of the secular side presented in other books. This book presents a valid, well-written, and well-researched argument." Library Journal.

241 Christian ethics

Bass, Diana Butler, 1959-

Grateful : the transformative power of giving thanks

/ Diana Butler Bass. HarperCollins, 2018 256 p. **241**

1. Gratitude 2. Personal conduct 3. Faith (Christianity)
ISBN 9780062659477

LC 2017047233

The author of the multiple award-winning Grounded and leading trend spotter in contemporary Christianity explores why gratitude is missing as a modern spiritual practice, offers practical suggestions for reclaiming it, and illuminates how the shared practice of gratitude can lead to greater connection with God, our world, and our own souls.

Becker, Joshua

The **minimalist** home : a room-by-room guide to a decluttered, refocused life / Joshua Becker, with Eric Stanford. WaterBrook, 2018 xii, 239 p. ; **241**

1. House cleaning. 2. Orderliness. 3. Personal belongings. 4. Simplicity -- Religious aspects -- Christianity.
ISBN 1601427999

LC 2018014041

The popular blogger and author of <I>The More of Less</I> outlines practical guidelines for simplifying a home lifestyle and rendering spaces both peaceful and purposeful while addressing the underlying issues that contribute to home clutter problems.

"For readers seeking a no excuses approach to minimizing their living spaces." Booklist.

Becker, Joshua

The **more** of less : finding the life you want under everything you own / Joshua Becker. WaterBrook Press, 2016. 230 p. ; **241**

1. Consumption (Economics) -- Religious aspects -- Christianity 2. Simplicity -- Religious aspects -- Christianity
ISBN 9781601427960

LC 2015042586

Offers a guide to adopting a minimalist lifestyle, offering practical advice and encouraging readers to find contentment by divesting themselves of nonessential possessions.

"With action plans, lists, and appeals to the reader's quiet nature, Becker successfully presents a well-rounded argument that a journey toward minimalism is possible and even enjoyable." Publishers Weekly.

Chapman, Gary D., 1938-

Love as a way of life : seven keys to transforming every aspect of your life / Gary Chapman. Doubleday, c2008. xiv, 239 p. ; **241**

1. Interpersonal relations -- Religious aspects -- Christianity. 2. Love -- Religious aspects -- Christianity.
ISBN 0385518587

LC 2007050546

A follow-up to the best-selling The Five Love Languages reveals the seminal role of spiritual insight and understanding in our daily lives and sheds new light on the qualities that help us express and respond to love--kindness, patience, forgiveness, humility, courtesy, giving, and honesty--as well as the obstacles and misunderstandings that undermine relationships.

"All self-help books run the risk of cliché, but Chapman manages to make tried-and-true material feel fresh through carefully chosen examples from his pastoral counseling practice and his own life. Although Christian faith provides the scaffolding for his program and a concluding chapter makes the need for God's help explicit, Chapman's judicious counsel can be implemented by people of many religious traditions." Publishers Weekly.

Davis, Will, 1962-

Enough : finding more by living with less / Will Davis, Jr. Revell, c2012. 232 p. ; **241**

1. Christian life. 2. Contentment -- Religious aspects -- Christianity. 3. Simplicity -- Religious aspects -- Christianity.
ISBN 0800720024

LC 2012003547

Uses a Christian perspective to discuss contentment with life and compassion for others.

Lamott, Anne

★**Hallelujah** anyway : rediscovering mercy / Anne Lamott. Riverhead Books, 2017. 176 p. **241**

1. Mercy 2. Kindness 3. Compassion 4. Faith (Christianity)
ISBN 9780735213586

LC 2016036301

An impassioned exploration of mercy, its elusive presence and why people ignore or embrace it shares advice for forging deeper self-understanding and how to pursue an honest, meaningful life that involves kindness to others.

"As in previous works, Lamotts courageous honesty and humility, laced with wit and compassion, offer wisdom and hope for difficult times." Publishers Weekly.

Price, Reynolds, 1933-2011

A **serious** way of wondering : the ethics of Jesus imagined / Reynolds Price. Scribner, c2003. 146 p. ; **241**

1. Jesus Christ Ethics. 2. Ethics. 3. Christian ethics. 4. Religious ethics. 5. Homosexuality.
ISBN 0743230086

LC 2003041506

A collection of literary and analytical writings, based on the author's lectures at the National Cathedral and Auburn Seminary, considers the ethics of Jesus Christ and presents fictional situations where He confronts such issues as suicide, homosexuality, and misogyny.

"In three brilliant and moving apocryphal gospel stories, Price's Jesus engages in conversations about homosexuality, suicide and the plight of women in male-dominated societies. Elegant and passionate, Price's provocative parables provide no simple answers to the saccharine question What would Jesus do? Rather, they compel us to imagine creatively our engagements with Jesus' teachings and the impact of those teachings on our lives." Publishers Weekly.

241.5 Codes of conduct

Bonhoeffer, Dietrich, 1906-1945

The **cost** of discipleship / Dietrich Bonhoeffer. Touchstone, 1995, c1948. 316 p. ; **241.5**

1. Sermon on the Mount -- Criticism and interpretation. 2. Christian life. 3. Grace (Christian theology) 4. Christianity.
ISBN 0684815001

LC 95022223

Includes indexes.

Originally published in English: London : SCM Press, 1948.

What can the call to discipleship--the adherence to the word of Jesus--mean today to the businessman, the soldier, the laborer, or the aristocrat? What did Jesus mean to say to us? What is His will for us today? Drawing on the Sermon on the Mount, Bonhoeffer answers these timeless questions by providing a seminal reading of the dichotomy between "cheap grace" and "costly grace."

242 Devotional literature

King, Martin Luther, Jr., 1929-1968

"Thou, dear God" : prayers that open hearts and spirits / Martin Luther King, Jr. ; foreword by the Julius R. Scruggs ; edited and introduced by Lewis V. Baldwin. Beacon Press, c2012. 245 p. ; **242**

1. Prayers.

ISBN 9780807086032

LC 2011031431

Collects sixty-eight prayers by Martin Luther King, Jr., covering such situations as spiritual guidance, special occasions, times of adversity, times of trial, uncertain times, and social justice.

Lewis, C. S. (Clive Staples), 1898-1963

★A **grief** observed / C.S. Lewis. Harper San Francisco, 2001, c1961. xxxi, 76 p. ; **242**

1. Davidman, Joy, 1915-1960. 2. Lewis, C. S. (Clive Staples), 1898-1963 Religion. 3. Consolation. 4. Bereavement -- Religious aspects -- Christianity. 5. Grief. 6. Faith in men.

ISBN 0060652381

LC 00063227

Originally published: 1961.

The author recounts his grief over the death of his wife, and explains how he reexamined his religious beliefs.

Thomas, a Kempis, 1380-1471

The **imitation** of Christ in four books / Thomas a Kempis ; a translation from the Latin by Joseph N. Tylenda. Vintage Books, 1998. xliii, 242 p. ; **242**

1. Catholic Church Doctrines Early works to 1800. 2. Meditations -- Early works to 1800. 3. Spiritual life -- Catholic Church -- Early works to 1800.

ISBN 9780375700187

LC 97046369

A classic fifteenth-century meditation on the spiritual life features hundreds of inspirational and moral aphorisms that extol the humble lifestyle of Jesus Christ, offering instructions for renouncing worldly vanities in favor of eternal truths.

248 Christian experience, practice, life

Scorgie, Glen G.

Dictionary of Christian spirituality / general editor, Glen G. Scorgie ; consulting editors: Simon Chan, Gordon T. Smith, James D. Smith III. Zondervan, c2011. ii, 852 p. ; **248**

1. Spirituality.

ISBN 9780310290667

LC 2010037314

Collects entries that discuss the global, biographical, historical, and biblical understanding of contemporary Christian spirituality.

248.2 Religious experience

Armstrong, Karen, 1944-

Visions of God : four medieval mystics and their writings / translated by Karen Armstrong. Bantam Books, 1994. 228 p. **248.2**

1. Mystics -- England -- History -- 476-1492. 2. Mysticism -- History -- Middle Ages, 600-1500. 3. Religious thought -- England -- History -- 14th century. 4. Spirituality. 5. England -- Religion -- 14th century

ISBN 9780553351996

LC 94020217

"The collection is eminently readable and should serve to make these important sources more accessible to a general audience. The selections are arranged chronologically, but Armstrong's reflections also place them in a 'developmental sequence.' " Booklist.

248.3 Worship

Lewis, C. S. (Clive Staples), 1898-1963

Letters to Malcolm : chiefly on prayer : reflections on the intimate dialogue between man and God / C.S. Lewis. Harcourt, 1992, c1964. 124 p. ; **248.3**

1. Prayer -- Christianity 2. Christian life

ISBN 9780156027663

LC bl2012030463

"A Harvest book."

The British scholar discusses many aspects of the private dialogue between man and God in these informal letters to a close friend.

Lucado, Max

Before amen : the power of a simple prayer / Max Lucado. Thomas Nelson, 2014. 192 p. **248.3**

1. Prayer (Christianity) 2. Christian life 3. Faith (Christianity) 4. Christianity

ISBN 9780849948480

LC 2014007855

Distilling prayers in the Bible down to one pocket-sized prayer, a best-selling author reminds readers that prayer is not a privilege for the pious nor the art of a chosen few but simply a heartfelt conversation between God and his child.

"The concept that there is power in a simple prayer normally wouldn't take a whole book to convey, but Lucado (You'll Get Through This), a prolific author with 92 million books in print, succeeds in getting readers to approach communication with God in a whole new way." Publishers Weekly.

248.4 Christian life and practice

Carter, Jimmy, 1924-

Sources of strength : meditations on Scripture for a living faith / Jimmy Carter. Times Books, c1999. xvii, 252 p. ; **248.4**

1. Bible Meditations. 2. Christian life -- Baptist authors. 3. Christian life -- Biblical teaching -- Meditations.

ISBN 0812932366

LC BL 99012849

Includes indexes.

"Originally published in hardcover by Times Books, in 1977 [i.e. 1997]"--T.p. verso.

In the sequel to Living Faith, the former president shares his favorite readings from the Bible, presenting scriptural texts, dealing with themes ranging from family to reconciliation to the transforming power of God's love, accompanied by his personal reflections on their meaning in terms of the challenges of modern life.

"This is a collection of 52 brief Bible lessons--one for each week of the year--written by former president Jimmy Carter. All were used in adult Sunday school classes he taught himself. Carter's lessons are open-minded and socially progressive while remaining unapologetically conservative and Christian theologically. The lessons are grouped in nine categories, such as 'What We Believe' and 'Christians in the World,' but each lesson stands well on its own." Library Journal.

Cron, Ian Morgan, 1960-

The **road** back to you : an Enneagram journey to self-discovery / Ian Morgan Cron and Suzanne Stabile. IVP Books, an imprint of InterVarsity Press, 2016 238 p. ; **248.4**

1. Enneagram. 2. Personality -- Religious aspects -- Christianity. 3. Typology (Psychology) -- Religious aspects -- Christianity.
ISBN 0830846190

LC 2016036470

Explores Enneagram's connections with Christian spirituality, guiding readers to discover their true selves in discovering God, allowing oneself to become wiser and more compassionate.

Francis, Pope, 1936-

Happiness in this life : a passionate meditation on earthly existence / Pope Francis ; translated from the Italian by Oonagh Stransky. Random House, [2017] 272 p. **248.4**

1. Christian life. 2. Happiness -- Religious aspects -- Christianity. 3. Joy -- Religious aspects -- Christianity. 4. Civil rights -- Religious aspects -- Christianity.
ISBN 9780525510970

Presents a collection of homilies, speeches and "messages of the day" that brings together Pope Francis' wisdom on finding happiness in the here and now.

Girzone, Joseph F.

Never alone : a personal way to God by the author of Joshua / Joseph F. Girzone. Image Books, 1995, c1994. 115 p. : **248.4**

1. Girzone, Joseph F. 2. Catholic Church Membership. 3. Spiritual life -- Christianity -- Catholic views 4. Love (Christianity) 5. Forgiveness. 6. Christian life -- United States 7. United States -- Religious life and customs -- 20th century
ISBN 0385476833

LC BL 99760988

Originally published: New York : Doubleday, 1994.

The author unveils his personal way to God, describing a God who is neither silent nor condemning with words of wisdom, sympathy, and generosity.

"Girzone's empathy for the loneliness and insecurity of being human guides readers toward a more satisfying religious experience than that provided by organized religions, which he continues to criticize for not sufficiently following the living message of Jesus' life." Booklist.

Jakes, T. D

Destiny : step into your purpose / T.D. Jakes. Faithwords Large Print, 2015. xiii, 349 p. ; **248.4**

1. Christian life. 2. Fate and fatalism -- Religious aspects -- Christianity. 3. Vocation -- Christianity. 4. Large type books.
ISBN 9781455589630

LC bl2015030474

The #1 New York Times best-selling author of Instinct outlines steps for recognizing and accepting one's personal destiny in the face of apparent setbacks.

Jakes, T. D.

Instinct : the power to unleash your inborn drive / T.D. Jakes. Faith Words, 2014. viii, 271 p. ; **248.4**

1. Christian life. 2. Instinct.
ISBN 1455554049

LC 2014007406

Outlines how to re-discover one's natural aptitudes and re-claim the wisdom of past experiences to become in sync with the opportunities life offers.

"This positive book encourages readers to get in touch with their instincts, trust them, and rely on them." Publishers Weekly.

Lentz, Carl

Own the moment / Carl Lentz. Simon & Schuster, 2017 xxix, 321 p. ; **248.4**

1. Christian life
ISBN 9781501177002

LC 2017049418

Shares the story of how the author went from an average adolescent to being the stylish leader of a thriving congregation and ministering to celebrities, along with advice for Christians to maintain their faith in an often ungodly world.

Lucado, Max

Unshakable hope : building our lives on the promises of God / Max Lucado. Thomas Nelson, 2018 xiv, 216 p. ; **248.4**

1. Christian life.
ISBN 0718096142

LC bl2018100083

Citing a dramatic rise in suicide in the past 20 years, a <I>New York Times<I> best-selling author draws on favorite scriptural passages to inspire readers to find encouragement in the promises of God and the Christian faith.

Lucado, Max

You are never alone : trust in the miracle of God's presence and power / Max Lucado. Thomas Nelson, 2020 xii, 219 p. ; **248.4**

1. Christian life. 2. Faith development.
ISBN 9781400217342

LC bl2020018068

Offers a guide to finding biblical inspiration, strength, and comfort in the face of life's more daunting challenges.

"Christians looking for strength and direction in prayer will love this faith-affirming, impassioned work." Publishers Weekly

Martin, James, S.J.

The **Jesuit** guide to (almost) everything : a spirituality for real life / James Martin. HarperCollins Publishers, c2010. vii, 420 p. : **248.4**

1. Ignatius, of Loyola, Saint, 1491-1556. 2. Jesuits Spiritual life. 3. Spiritual life -- Catholic Church.
ISBN 0061981400

LC oc2012193217

A practical, spiritual guidebook based on the life and teachings of St. Ignatius of Loyola shows readers how to manage relationships, money, work, prayer and decision making, while keeping a sense of humor about it all.

"In this digestible account of all things Jesuit, James Martin, S.J., encapsulates the uniquely Ignatian concept of spirituality. Translating the essence of the Jesuit philosophy into layman's terms, he uses both traditional stories and personal anecdotes to vividly illustrate the Jesuit approach to God, friendship, social justice, decision-making, prayer, simplicity, obedience, and self-actualization. Martin's engaging, intimate tone will appeal to anyone interested in understanding the history, the efficacy, and the universality of the Jesuit mission and way of life." Booklist.

Meyer, Joyce, 1943-

Seize the day : living on purpose and making every day count / Joyce Meyer. Faith Words, 2016. 234 p. ; **248.4**

1. Christian life. 2. Older people -- Religious life.
ISBN 145555989X

LC 2016015536

A guide to living a purposeful, urgent life spent in daily commitment to God shares personal stories and biblical insights to explain how to discover one's purpose in order to achieve greater happiness and blessings.

"Meyer advocates seizing control of one's schedule to focus on life's purpose, but also recommends being flexible, finding a system that fits one's style, and taking time to laugh." Publishers Weekly.

Nouwen, Henri J. M.

Discernment : reading the signs of daily life / Henri J.M. Nouwen ; with Michael J. Christensen and Rebecca J. Laird. HarperOne, 2013 xxix, 223 p. ; **248.4**

1. Discernment (Christian theology).
ISBN 0061686166

LC 2013004593

In this third installment of the practical spirituality series, two of the late world-renowned spiritual guide and counselor's longtime students present his principles of discernment, which will teach readers how to read the signs of the times in daily life in order to know what next to do.

Osteen, Joel

The **power** of I am : two words that will change your life today / Joel Osteen. Faith Words, 2015. x, 269 p. ; **248.4**

1. Affirmations. 2. Self-confidence -- Religious aspects -- Christianity. 3. Self-talk -- Religious aspects -- Christianity.
ISBN 0892969962

LC 2015025973

A #1 New York Times best-selling author shares a principle that he hopes will give the readers the confidence they need to face life's challenges.

"Directing believers to look beyond their own needs and wants, Osteen advances his message to a higher plane, advocating a life of reaching out and sharing your blessings." Publishers Weekly.

Osteen, Joel

Think better, live better : a victorious life begins in your mind / Joel Osteen. FaithWords, 2016 vi, 212 p. ; **248.4**

1. Attitude (Psychology) -- Religious aspects -- Christianity. 2. Thought and thinking -- Religious aspects -- Christianity.
ISBN 0892969679

LC 2016022264

A #1 New York Times best-selling author shares how reprogramming one's thoughts to remove negativity will lead to a more blessed, fulfilled life.

"Osteen writes in this uplifting call to action that, one way or another, you are going to become what you think." Publishers Weekly.

Peale, Norman Vincent, 1898-1993

★The **power** of positive living / Norman Vincent Peale. Fawcett Columbine, 1996. xii, 258 p. ; **248.4**

1. Peace of mind -- Religious aspects -- Christianity. 2. Success (Concept) -- Religious aspects -- Christianity 3. Spiritual life -- Christianity 4. Motivation (Psychology)
ISBN 0449911667

LC 96096721

Includes index.

"In this volume Peale strings together dozens of personal success stories (success is always materialistic) that make readers feel good. Believing (in yourself, others, values, God) is all-important, and the stories of wealthy business executives who made it on their own grab center stage." Library Journal.

Schuller, Bobby, 1981-

Change your thoughts, change your world : how life-giving thoughts can unlock your destiny / Bobby Schuller. Nelson Books, 2019 xiii, 209 p. : **248.4**

1. Christian life. 2. Thought and thinking -- Religious aspects -- Christianity.
ISBN 1400201705

LC bl2019015926

"Any Christians looking for ways to deepen their Bible study will be enlightened by Schuller's persuasive techniques for pondering scripture." Publishers Weekly.

Smith, Myquillyn

The **nesting** place : it doesn't have to be perfect to be beautiful / Myquillyn Smith. Zondervan, 2014 199 p. : **248.4**

1. Home economics 2. Home -- Religious aspects -- Christianity 3. Rental housing
ISBN 9780310337904

LC 2013034145

Revealing the secret to decorating for real people, a popular blogger and self-taught decorator shows readers how to find the beauty in imperfection and build a home that welcomes everyone.

Villodas, Rich

The **deeply** formed life : five transformative values to root us in the way of Jesus / Rich Villodas ; foreword by Pete Scazzero. WaterBrook, 2020 xxviii, 230 p. ; **248.4**

1. Spiritual life -- Christianity. 2. Christian life. 3. Spiritual growth.
ISBN 9780525654384

LC 2020010606

"The world is faster and busier than it's ever been, with more noise and distraction unsettling our already restless souls. We are a people out of rhythm. For Christians who are frustrated with churches that only add to the hustle and bustle, there must be an answer in our interior spiritual life. We long for deeper, more meaningful faith. Author and pastor Rich Villodas's The Deeply Formed Life offers an expansive, interconnected vision of spiritual formation comprised of five key pathways." Provided by publisher.

"Christians looking to bring more intention and emotion into their religious life will love this." Publishers Weekly

248.8 Guides to Christian life for specific groups of people

Brizendine, Judy

Stunned by grief : remapping your life when loss changes everything / Judy Brizendine. BennettKnepp Publishing, 2011 xvii, 274 p. : **248.8**

1. Grief -- Religious aspects. 2. Grief -- Psychological aspects. 3. Bereavement -- Religious aspects. 4. Bereavement -- Psychological

aspects.
ISBN 9780983168812
LC bl2014010214

Provides advice to aid those who are dealing with death and other tragic losses, including what to expect and how to thrive again, strategies to enhance healing, and allowing God to transform grief.

"A former market analyst and interior designer, ... [the author] found her world turned upside down when her husband died. She uses her own experience combined with the advice of psychologists, grief counselors, the Bible, and fellow mourners to provide a sort of roadmap for the unwelcome journey of grief. ... This book will comfort and support anyone new to grief and will serve as a companion in times of loneliness. Realistic, practical, and highly recommended." Library Journal.

Brownback, Lydia, 1963-
Finding God in my loneliness / Lydia Brownback. Crossway, 2017 174 p. ; **248.8**

1. Christian women -- Prayers and devotions 2. Loneliness -- Religious aspects -- Christianity. 3. Loneliness -- Biblical teaching -- Meditations. 4. Encouragement -- Religious aspects -- Christianity.
ISBN 9781433553936
LC 2016031222

"Brownback's encouraging book is a sharp, thoroughly readable entreaty to readers looking for grace in loneliness." Publishers Weekly. Annex.

Hatmaker, Jen
Of mess and moxie : wrangling delight out of this wild and glorious life / Jen Hatmaker. Thomas Nelson, 2017. 224 p. **248.8**

1. Resilience (Personal quality) 2. Christian life 3. Gender role 4. Faith (Christianity)
ISBN 9780718031848
LC bl2017028740

Author Jen Hatmaker, with playful hilarity, shameless honesty, and refreshing insight, assures readers they have all the pluck they need for vibrant, courageous, grace-filled lives.

"Hatmaker shares the importance of reaching beyond comfort zones and extending welcomes. She owns the moxie she's writing about." Booklist.

Hendey, Lisa M.
A **book** of saints for Catholic moms : 52 companions for your heart, mind, body, and soul / Lisa M. Hendey. Ave Maria Press, c2011. xiv, 334 p. : **248.8**

1. Catholic Church Prayers and devotions. 2. Christian saints 3. Mothers 4. Prayers and devotions.
ISBN 1594712735
LC 2011025284

Guided by the example of the saints, Hendey eloquently links personal stories, scripture, prayer, and soul-strengthening exercises into a spiritually rich and deeply practical resource for Catholic women. This edition includes a new preface and cover and is updated with information about saints canonized since the first edition. --Provided by publisher

Jaynes, Sharon
Enough : silencing the lies that steal your confidence / Sharon Jaynes. Harvest House Publishers, 2018 270 p. ; **248.8**

1. Christian women -- Religious life. 2. Self-esteem -- Religious aspects -- Christianity. 3. Self-perception -- Religious aspects -- Christianity. 4. Women -- Religious aspects -- Christianity.
ISBN 0736973540
LC 2017039262

Originally published under title: I'm not good enough--and other lies women tell themselves, c2009.

Sharon Jaynes exposes the lies that keep women bogged down in guilt and shame. Learn to recognize and replace the lies you've told yourself and find confidence and rest in your identity as an imperfect--but wholly redeemed--woman of value. --Provided by publisher

Lucado, Max
Anxious for nothing : finding calm in a chaotic world / Max Lucado. Thomas Nelson, 2017. 240 p. **248.8**

1. Bible. Epistles of Paul Criticism and interpretation 2. Bible. Philippians Criticism and interpretation 3. Anxiety -- Religious aspects -- Christianity 4. Coping -- Religious aspects -- Christianity. 5. Trust in God -- Christianity. 6. Faith (Christianity)
ISBN 9780718096120
LC bl2017037014

Anxiety is at an all time high, but there's a prescription for dealing with it. Max Lucado invites readers into a study of Philippians 4:6-7 where the Apostle Paul admonishes the followers of Christ, 'Do not be anxious about anything . . .'

"A compulsively readable book focused on an aspect of Christian living that many find challenging: overcoming guilt to find peace in life." Publishers Weekly.

Lucado, Max
Fearless : imagine your life without fear / Max Lucado. Thomas Nelson, c2009. xii, 221 p. ; **248.8**

1. Fear -- Religious aspects -- Christianity
ISBN 9780849921391
LC 2009000707

Includes discussion guide.

Invites readers to envision their lives untouched by fear and encourages to trust more, at a time when people are losing their jobs, the economy is slowing down, and terrorism plagues the world.

Miller, Donald, 1971-
Scary close : dropping the act and finding true intimacy / Donald Miller. Thomas Nelson Inc., 2015. 256 p. **248.8**

1. Intimacy (Psychology) 2. Courtship. 3. Christian couples. 4. Dating (Social customs)
ISBN 9780785213185
LC bl2015003255

"Older, married readers might chuckle at the authors description of Betsy as near perfect, but younger readers will relate to the frankly expressed concerns about pressure to fit in, difficulties in the dating scene, and hard lessons learned, some with the help of counseling." Publishers Weekly.

Norris, Kathleen, 1947-
Acedia & me : a marriage, monks, and a writer's life / Kathleen Norris. Riverhead Books, 2008. 352 p. **248.8**

1. Norris, Kathleen, 1947- 2. Soul (Christianity) 3. Melancholy -- Religious aspects -- Christianity. 4. Unhappiness -- Religious aspects -- Christianity. 5. Depression -- Religious aspects -- Christianity.
ISBN 9781594489969
LC 2008010150

Discusses the ancient concept of "soul weariness" and explores the phenomenon's relevance in modern culture, meditating on the ways in which depression-like acedia influenced the author's experiences as a writer, a family member, and a patient.

Shankle, Melanie
Church of the small things : the million little pieces that make up a life / Melanie Shankle ; foreword by Ree Drummond. Zondervan, 2017. 224 p. **248.8**

1. Shankle, Melanie 2. Everyday life 3. Purpose in life 4. Family relationships 5. Simplicity 6. Essays
ISBN 9780310348870

LC 2017003557

In Church of the Small Things, New York Times bestselling author Melanie Shankle celebrates, with her trademark stories and humor, the wonder of the many small moments in life that add up to make a big difference and ultimately shape the person we become.

"Shankle's winsome book will be well-received by Christian readers looking to be more conscientious in everyday life." Publishers Weekly.

TerKeurst, Lysa
It's not supposed to be this way : finding unexpected strength when disappointments leave you shattered / Lysa TerKeurst. Nelson Books, 2018 xvii, 264 p. ; **248.8**

1. Disappointment -- Religious aspects -- Christianity. 2. Expectation (Psychology) -- Religious aspects -- Christianity. 3. Self-help psychology for Christians
ISBN 9780718039851

LC 2018021939

Offering fresh biblical insight and life-giving perspectives, the president of Proverbs 31 Ministries draws on her own experiences to present this guide that shows us how to live assured when life doesn't turn out the way we expected.

Yoder, Brenda L.
Fledge : launching your kids without losing your mind / Brenda L. Yoder. Herald Press, 2018 239 p. ; **248.8**

1. Child rearing -- Religious aspects -- Christianity. 2. Parenting -- Religious aspects -- Christianity.
ISBN 1513802364

LC 2017038550

In Fledge, counselor, educator, and mother Brenda L. Yoder helps Christian parents navigate the many transitions of the launching years. --Provided by publisher

"To help parents prepare for the process of enabling children to mature and eventually leave home, Yoder concentrates on five phases: giving up control, setting boundaries, building family ties, accepting mid-life with grace, and preparing for the transition to an empty nest marriage." Publishers Weekly

252 Texts of sermons

American sermons : the pilgrims to Martin Luther King, Jr. Library of America, c1999. xv, 939 p. ; The Library of America ; **252**

1. Sermons, American.
ISBN 9781883011659

LC 98034295

A comprehensive anthology collects fifty-eight sermons from each period of American history, showing the development of this neglected literary form from Colonial times to powerful sermons of the Civil Rights Movement

Francis, Pope, 1936-
★The **Church** of mercy / Pope Francis. Loyola Press, 2014. 200 p. **252**

1. Catholic Church 2. Mercy 3. Charity 4. Hope 5. Catholic Church renewal. 6. Essays.
ISBN 9780829441680

LC 2014934036

Designed for a broad readership, The Church of Mercy is a compilation of essays, speeches, and homilies by Pope Francis since his election on being a church that exists among and for the people, solidarity with the poor, and the need to demolish the idols of power and money.

"Refreshingly humane, focusing on people rather than institutions. Admirers of Francis and students of church history alike will find this a useful introduction to the pontiff's thought." Kirkus.

253 Pastoral office and work (Pastoral theology)

Smith, C. Christopher
Slow church : cultivating community in the patient way of Jesus / C. Christopher Smith and John Pattison. IVP Books, 2014 246 p. ; **253**

1. Church 2. Communities -- Religious aspects -- Christianity
ISBN 9780830841141

LC 2014011067

Suggests that modern religion is too fast paced and that a slower approach should be used so that parishioners get a more fulfilling experience.

"Though primarily focused upon church communities, the ideas presented here may appeal to other types of religious or intentional communities. Individuals who are attempting to bring their own lives into line with their ethics and values will also find help." Publishers Weekly.

255 Religious congregations and orders

Norris, Kathleen, 1947-
The **cloister** walk / Kathleen Norris. Riverhead Books, 1996. xv, 384 p. **255**

1. Norris, Kathleen, 1947- 2. Catholic Church. Liturgy 3. Monasticism and religious orders. 4. Spiritual life -- Christianity -- Catholic views 5. Faith in women. 6. Monasteries.
ISBN 1573220280

LC 96000863

A reverent study of the monastic world assesses the meaning of the cloistered life in modern times, journeying through a liturgical year to capture the relevance and spiritual significance of the religious life.

261 Social theology and interreligious relations and attitudes

Carroll, James, 1943-
Constantine's sword : the church and the Jews : a history / James Carroll. Houghton Mifflin, 2001. xii, 756 p. **261**

1. Catholic Church Relations Judaism. 2. Former priests -- United States 3. Antisemitism in Christianity. 4. Judaism -- Relations -- Catholic Church.
ISBN 0395779278

LC 00061329

National Jewish Book Award, 2001.

Examines the two-thousand-year relationship between Christianity and Judaism, examining the long entrenched tradition of anti-Semitism that culminated in the Church's failure to protest the Holocaust during World War II.

"This magisterial work will satisfy Jewish and Christians readers alike, challenging both to a renewed conversation with one another." Publishers Weekly.

Holland, Tom

Dominion : how the Christian revolution remade the world / Tom Holland. Basic Books, 2019. 496 p. **261**

1. Civilization, Christian. 2. Civilization, Western -- Christian influences. 3. Religion and culture. 4. Christianity -- History.
ISBN 9780465093502

LC bl2019024758

Shows how the Christian Revolution forged the Western imagination.

261.2 Christianity and other systems of belief

Bidwell, Duane R.

When one religion isn't enough : the lives of spiritually fluid people / Duane R. Bidwell. Beacon Press, 2018. 200 p. **261.2**

1. Religion 2. Identity (Religion) 3. Social change 4. Faith
ISBN 9780807091241

LC 2018018026

Through in-depth conversations with spiritually fluid people, renowned scholar Duane Bidwell explores how people come to claim and be claimed by multiple religious traditions, how spiritually fluid people engage radically opposed truth claims, and what this growing population tells us about change within our communities.

"Will appeal to spiritual readers seeking an understanding and affirmation of the growing multireligious movement. Strongly recommended for libraries of all types." Library Journal.

Kertzer, David I., 1948-

The **popes** against the Jews : the Vatican's role in the rise of modern anti-Semitism / David I. Kertzer. Alfred A. Knopf, 2001. vii, 355 p. ; **261.2**

1. Catholic Church Relations Judaism. 2. Judaism -- Relations -- Catholic Church. 3. Popes -- History. 4. Antisemitism.
ISBN 0375406239

LC 2001033728

Drawing on previously hidden Vatican sources and archival materials, a provovative historical study traces the evolution of anti-Semitism in the Catholic Church from the French Revolution to World War II and assesses the Church's role in promoting and disseminating a centuries-long demonization of the Jews throughout Europe that led to the Holocaust.

"This is a devastating indictment, and fair-minded critics will find flaws in Kertzer's methodology and sweeping conclusions. Nevertheless, he has opened a window that should be opened." Booklist.

261.55 Christianity and science

Wilson, D. K.

A **magical** world : superstition and science from the Renaissance to the Enlightenment / Derek K. Wilson. Pegasus Books, [2018] x, 310 pages ; **261.55**

1. Religion and science 2. Science -- Philosophy 3. Ideas (Philosophy) 4. Superstition 5. Europe -- History
ISBN 9781681776453

LC 2018303384

A rich and multi-faceted history of heroes and villains interwoven with the profound changes in human knowledge that took place between the Renaissance and the Enlightenment.

"A dazzling chronicle, a bracing challenge to modernitys smug assumptions." Booklist.

261.7 Christianity and political affairs

Volf, Miroslav

Public faith in action : how to think carefully, engage wisely, and vote with integrity / Miroslav Volf and Ryan McAnnally-Linz. Brazos Press, 2016. xiii, 240 p. ; **261.7**

1. Christianity and politics. 2. Christians -- Political activity. 3. Church and social problems.
ISBN 1587433842

LC 2016003425

Includes index.

This nonpartisan handbook offers Christians practical guidance for thinking through complicated public issues and faithfully following Jesus as citizens of their countries. --Provided by publisher

"Working on the premise that Christian faith must naturally spill over into public discussion, they offer insight into making informed decisions around candidates and political issues. Aptly subtitled, the book asks readers to consider issues from a biblical perspective and then to take action in a courageous but respectful and humble manner, working to influence society while representing Christ well." Publishers Weekly

261.8 Christianity and socioeconomic problems

Betrayal : the crisis in the Catholic Church / the investigative staff of the Boston Globe. Back Bay Books, 2015. ix, 282 p. : **261.8**

1. Catholic Church Clergy Sexual behavior. 2. Catholic Church Discipline. 3. Child sexual abuse by clergy.
ISBN 9780316271530

LC bl2016000753

Presents an account of sexual abuse of children by priests in the Catholic Church and how these crimes were covered-up by senior church officials.

Bolz-Weber, Nadia

Shameless : a sexual reformation / Nadia Bolz-Weber. Convergent, [2019] 224 p. **261.8**

1. Bolz-Weber, Nadia 2. Bible 3. Sexuality -- Religious aspects 4. Christianity and sexuality 5. Shame 6. Judgment
ISBN 9781601427588

LC 2018021697

Christians are obsessed with sex. But not in a good way. For generations countless people have suffered pain, guilt, and judgment as a result of this toxic fixation on sex, the body, and physical pleasure. In the follow-up to her celebrated New York Times bestseller Accidental Saints, Bolz-Weber unleashes her critical eye, her sharp pen, and her vulnerable but hopeful soul on the caustic, fear-riddled, and religiously inspired messages about sex that have fed our shame.

D'Antonio, Michael

★**Mortal** sins : sex, crime, and the era of Catholic scandal / Michael D'Antonio. Thomas Dunne Books, 2013. viii, 400 p.

; **261.8**

1. Catholic Church Clergy Sexuality 2. Sex crimes 3. Pedophilia 4. Religious cover-ups. 5. Scandals.

ISBN 9780312594893

Presents an account of the Catholic Church's pedophile scandal that traces the efforts of a young lawyer who uncovered thousands of complaints that were systematically dismissed and covered up by Church officials.

Gilliard, Dominique Dubois

Rethinking incarceration : advocating for justice that restores / Dominique Dubois Gilliard. InterVarsity Press, 2018. 240 p. **261.8**

1. Prisons. 2. Imprisonment -- Social aspects 3. Criminal justice system. 4. Christian life Social aspects

ISBN 9780830845293

LC 2018005769

The United States has more people locked up in jails, prisons, and detention centers than any other country in the history of the world. Exploring the history and foundations of mass incarceration, Dominique Gilliard examines Christianity's role in its evolution and expansion, assessing justice in light of Scripture, and showing how Christians can pursue justice that restores and reconciles.

"In his debut, Gilliard, an Evangelical Covenant Church pastor, builds on the work of Michelle Alexander (The New Jim Crow), Bryan Stevenson (Just Mercy), and Christopher D. Marshall (Compassionate Justice) to create a readable narrative history of racialized incarceration in the U.S." Publishers Weekly.

Griffith, R. Marie (Ruth Marie), 1967-

Moral combat : how sex divided American Christians and fractured American politics / R. Marie Griffith. Basic Books, 2017. 384 p. **261.8**

1. Catholic Church Relations Protestant churches. 2. Religion and politics. 3. Christianity and politics. 4. Fundamentalism. 5. Gender role. 6. United States -- Religion -- History.

ISBN 9780465094752

LC 2017037768

A scholar of American religion and sexuality chronicles the century of religious conflict behind many of today's most contentious issues, exploring how the Christian consensus about gender roles and sexual morality has changed throughout recent decades.

"Griffith's remarkably comprehensive book will be of interest to scholars and lay readers alike." Publishers Weekly.

Lehmann, Chris

The **money** cult : capitalism, Christianity, and the unmaking of the American dream / Chris Lehmann. Melville House, 2016. 368 p. **261.8**

1. Christianity and capitalism 2. Capitalism 3. Christianity 4. Money 5. United States

ISBN 9781612195087

LC 2016001439

"This book is unlikely to embarrass believers into a social conscience or different political allegiance, but Lehmann does reveal the modern evangelical right as deeply faithful to an American economic model--one focused on industrial production--that no longer exists." Publishers Weekly.

262 Ecclesiology

Chaves, Mark

Ordaining women : culture and conflict in religious organizations / Mark Chaves. Harvard University Press, 1999, c1997. x, 237 p. : **262**

1. Ordination of women -- United States. 2. Christianity and women 3. Religious sociology 4. Clergywomen 5. United States -- Church history -- 20th century. 6. United States -- Religious life and customs -- 20th century

ISBN 9780674641464

LC BL 99006819

Reprint. Originally published: 1997.

Combining historical and sociological perspectives, Mark Chaves deftly shows that formal institutional rules about ordination often diverge from the actual roles of women and are best understood as symbolic gestures in favor of--or in opposition to--gender equality. Ordaining Women concludes that external pressures from the women's movement and ecumenical pressure expressed through interdenominational organizations such as the National Council of Churches influence ordination practices. At the same time, internal factors such as having a source of religious authority that is considered superior to modern principles of equal rights also explain why some denominations ordain women much earlier than others.

"The author provides a study of the 19th- and 20th-century ordination policies and practices of many Christian groups in the United States, including the Roman Catholic Church." Library Journal.

Duffy, Eamon

Saints & sinners : a history of the Popes / Eamon Duffy. Yale University Press, in association with S4C, c1997, c2015. 326 p. : **262**

1. Catholic Church 2. Papacy -- History. 3. Popes.

ISBN 9780300206128

LC 97060897

Published in conjunction with the TV production of the same title.

Traces the history of the Papacy from its development after the execution of Peter to the reign of Pope John Paul II. This 4th edition also covers the unprecedented resignation of Benedict XVI and the election of the first Argentinian pope.

263 Days, times, places of religious observance

Egan, Timothy

A **pilgrimage** to eternity : from Canterbury to Rome in search of a faith / Timothy Egan. Viking, 2019. 384 p. **263**

1. Pilgrims and pilgrimages 2. Faith (Christianity) 3. Walking 4. Catholic families 5. Europe -- Description and travel

ISBN 9780735225237

LC 2019015599

The Pulitzer Prize-winning reporter and author traces an ancient pilgrimage route from Canterbury to Rome, visiting some of Christianity's most important shrines to explore the faith's past, present and future.

Mullins, Edwin, 1933-

The **four** roads to Heaven : France and the Santiago pilgrimage / Edwin Mullins. Interlink Books, 2018, c2017. x, 254 p., 12 unnumbered p. of plates : **263**

1. Pilgrims and pilgrimages 2. Walking 3. Voyages and travels 4. Travelers 5. Camino de Santiago de Compostela 6. Spain --

Description and travel
ISBN 9781623719913
Originally published: Oxford, UK : Signal Books, 2017.
"Essential for potential pilgrims and an excellent European history for others." Library Journal.

270 History, geographic treatment, biography of Christianity; Church history; Christian denominations and sects

MacCulloch, Diarmaid
★**Christianity** : the first three thousand years / Diarmaid MacCulloch. Viking, 2010, c2009. xvii, 1161 p., 32 p. of plates : **270**
1. Bible. New Testament 2. Church history. 3. Christianity -- History. 4. Evangelicalism. 5. Christians.
ISBN 9780670021260
LC 2009040184
Originally published as: A history of Christianity: the first three thousand years. London : Allen Lane, 2009.
Cundill Prize in History, 2010.
Conveyed with compelling skill and scholarship, this groundbreaking work ranges back to the origins of the Hebrew Bible and follows the three mains strands of the Christian faith.
"It is difficult to imagine a more comprehensive and surprisingly accessible volume on the subject than MacCulloch's. Want a refresher on the rise of the papacy? It is here. On Charlemagne and Carolingians? That is here, too. On the Fourth Crusade and its aftermath? Look no farther." New York Times Book Review.

270.1 Historical periods

Ehrman, Bart D.
The **triumph** of Christianity : how a forbidden religion swept the world / Bart D. Ehrman. Simon & Schuster, 2018. 352 p. **270.1**
1. Constantine I, Emperor of Rome, died 337 Influence. 2. Church history -- Primitive and early church, ca. 30-600. 3. Christianity. 4. Religions.
ISBN 9781501136702
LC 2016056895
Looks at how Christianity went from being an obscure sect of Judaism followed by a small group of rural peasants to being the dominant religion in the west in less than four hundred years.
"The author maps out the early growth of Christianity against a detailed background of Roman society and history . . . He not only brings a clear presentation of his own views but also gives alternative interpretations a fair hearing." Library Journal.

Kaatz, Kevin
Voices of early Christianity : documents from the origins of Christianity / Kevin W. Kaatz, editor. Greenwood, 2013 xxii, 277 p. : **270.1**
1. Church history -- Primitive and early church, ca. 30-600 -- Sources.
ISBN 9781598849523
LC 2012041162
This fascinating resource examines the day-to-day lives of early Christians--as depicted through documented accounts of the period--from the beginning of Christianity through 325 CE. --Provided by publisher
"The issues that Kaatz discusses resonate strongly today just as they did when they were first created. Kaatz cuts to the heart of what could be an unwieldy subject and provides excellent context and explanations on all the issues he discusses." Library Journal

Riley, Gregory J. 1947-
The **river** of God : a new history of Christian origins / Gregory J. Riley. Harper San Francisco, c2001. iii, 252 p. ; **270.1**
1. Christianity -- Origin.
ISBN 0060669799
LC 2001016888
Argues that true Christianity is pluralistic and receptive to diverse beliefs, presents a new understanding of the early churches, and communicates a critical message regarding the true nature of Christian faith in today's society.
"This volume will become one of the most important books on the subject." Library Journal.

270.2 Period of ecumenical councils, 325-787

Brown, Peter, 1935-
Through the eye of a needle : wealth, the fall of Rome, and the making of Christianity in the West, 350-550 AD / Peter Brown. Princeton University Press, c2012. xxx, 759 p., 16 p. of plates : **270.2**
1. Church history -- Primitive and early church, ca. 30-600. 2. Wealth -- Religious aspects -- Christianity -- History. 3. Rome -- History -- Empire, 284-476.
ISBN 9780691152905
LC 2011045697
Map on lining papers.
Traces the intellectual and social history of wealth in the early Christian church, examining the financial rise of the church and its effects on the waning Roman empire as well as the church's own beliefs on poverty.

270.6 Period of Reformation and Counter-Reformation, 1517-1648

MacCulloch, Diarmaid
The **Reformation** / Diarmaid MacCulloch. Viking, 2004. xxiv, 792 p. : **270.6**
1. Catholic Church -- History 16th century. 2. Reformation. 3. Protestantism. 4. Christianity -- History.
ISBN 9780670032969
LC 2003061607
National Book Critics Circle Award for Non-Fiction, 2004.
"The author has produced the definitive survey for this generation. This well-written book is a joy to read, with new facts and interpretations on nearly every page." Library Journal.

270.8 Modern period, 1789-

Jenkins, Philip, 1952-
The **new** faces of Christianity : believing the Bible in the global south / Philip Jenkins. Oxford University Press, c2006. x,

252 p. ; **270.8**

1. Christianity -- Forecasts 2. Theocracy. 3. Religion and culture. 4. Religion and politics.

ISBN 9780195300659

LC 2006015490

The best-sellling author of The New Christendom continues his study of the growth of Christianity in the southern regions of the world, examining the influence of the Bible on the peoples of Africa, Asia, and Latin America, including the impact on growing liberation movements and the rise of women's rights.

"Those interested in religious trends across the globe, the Muslim-Christian friction, and world politics will benefit from this resource." Library Journal.

Stanley, Brian, 1953-

★**Christianity** in the twentieth century : a world history / Brian Stanley. Princeton University Press, 2018. 472 p. **270.8**

1. Church history -- 20th century. 2. Christianity. 3. Christianity and culture. 4. Political change.

ISBN 9780691157108

LC 2017039619

Offers a history of world Christianity in the twentieth century, documenting its profound transformation during a period of political and cultural upheavals, accompanied by case studies intended to shed light on themes important for understanding modern Christianity.

"A finely crafted exploration of Christianity in the 20th century." Kirkus.

Tickle, Phyllis

The **great** emergence : how Christianity is changing and why / Phyllis Tickle. Baker Books, c2008. 172 p. **270.8**

1. Christianity -- 21st century. 2. Religion. 3. Church history. 4. Religions. 5. United States -- Religion.

ISBN 9780801013133

LC 2008021706

"From the church's birth to the reign of St. Gregory the great, to the Great Schism and through the Reformation, Phyllis Tickle notes that every 500 years the church has been rocked by massive transitions. Remarkably enough, Tickle suggests to us that we live in such a time right now. The Great Emergence examines history, social upheaval, and current events, showing how a new form of Christianity is rising within postmodern culture. Anyone interested in the future of the church in America, no matter what their personal affiliation, will find this book a fascinating exploration".--from publisher's web site.

"This is a must-read for anyone seeking to understand the face and future of Christianity." Publishers Weekly.

271 Religious congregations and orders in church history

Jones, Dan, 1981-

The **Templars** : the rise and spectacular fall of God's holy warriors / Dan Jones. Viking Press, 2017 384 p. **271**

1. Knights Templar (Masonic order) 2. Catholic Church 3. Crusades -- History 4. Heresy 5. Military religious orders 6. Armies

ISBN 9780525428305

LC 2017025385

A narrative history of the Knights Templar draws on extensive original sources to separate fact from myth, exploring their actual work and influence, the reasons they fell out of favor, and whether or not they were guilty of heresy.

"This is an engrossing examination of a period whose conflicts are still reverberating today." Publishers Weekly.

Sweeney, Jon M., 1967-

What I am living for : lessons from the life and writings of Thomas Merton / edited by Jon M. Sweeney, James Martin, Robert Ellsberg, Daniel P. Horan, Kaya Oakes. Ave Maria Pr 2018 224 p. **271**

1. Merton, Thomas, 1915-1968 2. Trappists 3. Monks 4. Christianity 5. Christian life 6. Spiritual life 7. Essays

ISBN 9781594717413

LC 2017044813

"Many of the writers list Merton's 1948 autobiography The Seven Storey Mountain as an influence when deciding to write about their spiritual inner life and discuss topics such as spiritual identity, sexual relationships, interfaith dialogue, and expansive (as opposed to constrictive) theology. A time line of Merton's life and world events that happened during his life (1915-1968) is also helpfully included in Sweeney's well-rounded collection." Publishers Weekly.

271.7913 Knights Templars

Haag, Michael, 1943-

The **tragedy** of the Templars : the rise and fall of the Crusader states / Michael Haag. Harper, 2013, c2012. 433 p., 16 unnumbered p. of plates : **271.7913**

1. Saladin, Sultan of Egypt and Syria, 1137-1193. 2. Knights Templar (Masonic order) -- History. 3. Military religious orders -- History. 4. Crusades. 5. Secret societies. 6. Civilization, Medieval 7. Islamic Empire -- History -- 750-1258.

ISBN 9780062059758

LC 2014397588

Originally published: London : Profile, 2012.

In this companion to The Templars: The History & the Myth, a noted historian expertly recounts the clashes and crashes that sent the religious order of fighter knights, who were dedicated to defending the Holy Land and Christian pilgrims, from domination and power to condemnation.

272 Persecutions in general church history

Kamen, Henry

The **Spanish** Inquisition : a historical revision / Henry Kamen. Yale University Press, 1998. xii, 369 p. : **272**

1. Inquisition -- Spain. 2. Church and state -- Spain. 3. Spain -- Church history. 4. Spain -- Religion.

ISBN 0300075227

LC 97032451

"In this revision of his 1965 study, the author restates his original argument. He reaffirms his contention that an all-powerful, torture-mad Inquisition is largely a 19th-century myth. In its place he portrays a poor, understaffed institution whose scattered tribunals had only a limited reach and whose methods were more humane than those of most secular courts. As for the Inquisition's much-vaunted role as Big Brother and its responsibility for intellectual decline, Kamen rejects this hypothesis out of hand. {He} also dismisses the notion that the Inquisition enjoyed widespread popular support." New York Times Book Review.

Perez, Joseph

★The **Spanish** Inquisition : a history / Joseph Perez ; translated from the French by Janet Lloyd. Yale University Press, 2005. vii, 248 p. ; **272**

1. Catholic Church Spain -- History. 2. Inquisition -- Spain --

History. 3. Spain -- Religious life and customs.
ISBN 9780300107906
LC 2004114614

A new history of the Spanish Inquisition--a terrifying battle for a unified faith.

"Perez, a noted historian of early modern Spain (emer., Univ. of Bordeaux), has produced an objective, scholarly, and eminently usable overview of the origins, administration, operations, and impact of the Spanish Inquisition." Choice.

Rounding, Virginia

The **burning** time : Henry VIII, Bloody Mary, and the Protestant martyrs of London / Virginia Rounding. St. Martin's Press, 2017. 432 p. **272**

1. Mary I, Queen of England, 1516-1558. 2. Henry VIII, King of England, 1491-1547. 3. Edward VI, King of England, 1537-1553 4. Religious persecution -- History -- 16th century. 5. Church and state -- England. 6. Christian martyrs -- England -- 16th century. 7. Christian heretics -- History -- 16th century. 8. Great Britain -- History -- Mary I, 1553-1558. 9. Great Britain -- History -- Henry VIII, 1509-1547. 10. Great Britain -- History -- Edward VI, 1547-1553. 11. England -- Church history -- 16th century. 12. Great Britain -- History -- Tudors, 1485-1603.
ISBN 9781250040640
LC 2017023617

Offers an account of the religious persecutions in England under Henry VIII and his daughter, Mary, with a focus on the lives of Baron Richard Rich, who played a role in the persecutions, and John Deane, who managed to avoid them throughout the period.

"An excellent account of 16th-century religious persecution and martyrdom." Publishers Weekly.

273 Doctrinal controversies and heresies in general church history

Pagels, Elaine H., 1943-

★The **Gnostic** gospels / Elaine Pagels. Vintage Books, 1989, c1979. xxxvi, 182 p. ; **273**

1. Nag Hammadi manuscripts. 2. Gnosticism 3. Chenoboskion manuscripts 4. Christianity -- Essence, genius, nature. 5. Apocryphal Gospels -- Criticism and interpretation
ISBN 9780679724537
LC 79004764

Originally published: New York : Random House, 1979.

A study of the Gnostic texts, which describe the same people and events portrayed in the New Testament but from a different perspective, reveals why their suppression was essential to the development of the Christian church.

"Pagels writes for the layman, which is refreshing, and she does so lucidly, which is a challenge, especially when gnosticism was regarded by its own adherents to be for the initiated only." Christian Science Monitor.

275 Christianity in Asia

Liao, Yiwu, 1958-

God is red : the secret story of how Christianity survived and flourished in Communist China / Liao Yiwu ; translated by Wen Huang. HarperOne, c2011. 256 p. **275**

1. Communism and Christianity. 2. Communism and religion. 3. Christianity and politics. 4. Communism. 5. China -- Religion -- History.
ISBN 9780062078469
LC 2010051154

Profiling the remarkable lives of ordinary Chinese believers, the author, a celebrated Chinese dissident who was imprisoned, provides a rare glimpse into the thriving--and secret--underground Christian movement in China.

"The author examines Christianity, which survived under China's Cultural Revolution despite attempts to eradicate it as a lackey of the imperialists. In an attempt to understand why a foreign religion gained such popularity, Liao interviews a wide range of Chinese Christians, from an elderly nun who witnessed both the closing and eventual reopening of her church by the Communist regime, to a missionary doctor treating impoverished villagers in lieu of working in a government-run hospital, to a dying tailor who finds meaning in his recent conversion to the faith. Will appeal to both Christian and secular readers interested in the cultural realities of China's Great Leap Forward." Kirkus.

277 Christianity in North America

Boyle, Greg

Tattoos on the heart : the power of boundless compassion / Gregory Boyle. Free Press, 2010. xv, 217 p. ; **277**

1. Boyle, Greg. 2. Christian life -- Anecdotes. 3. Church work. 4. Christian men.
ISBN 9781439153024
LC 2009032970

A Jesuit priest shares anecdotes from his life of working in broken-down urban areas with underprivileged children, describing how he helped them to find faith and embrace such values as patience, self-worth, and kinship.

Dochuk, Darren

From Bible belt to sunbelt : plain-folk religion, grassroots politics, and the rise of evangelical conservatism / Darren Dochuk. W.W. Norton, 2011. 416 p. **277**

1. Christian conservatism. 2. Evangelicalism. 3. Conservatism. 4. Religion and politics. 5. Southern California.
ISBN 9780393066821
LC 2010032740

A five-decade history of the evangelical movement in southern California explains how the influx of migrants from the Bible Belt during the Great Depression ultimately led to the rise of the New Right and modern conservatism in the late twentieth century.

"Well-written and documented, a supremely helpful guide in sorting out how we arrived at that odd state of affairs." Kirkus.

FitzGerald, Frances, 1940-

★The **Evangelicals** : the struggle to shape America / Frances FitzGerald. Simon & Schuster, 2017. 848 p. **277**

1. Fundamentalism 2. Evangelicalism -- United States -- History 3. Christianity and politics -- United States -- History 4. Religion and politics 5. United States -- Church history
ISBN 9781439131336
LC 2016025851

National Book Critics Circle Award for Non-Fiction, 2017.
National Book Award for Nonfiction finalist, 2017

A dramatic history of the Evangelical movement in America traces the revivals of the 18th and 19th centuries that rendered evangelism a dominant religious force, describing the rise and fall of denominations and how they influenced American agendas ranging from civil rights and gender equality to climate change and immigration reform.

"This is a timely and accessible contribution to the rapidly growing body of literature on Christianity in modern America." Publishers Weekly.

Jones, Robert P. (Robert Patrick)

White too long : the legacy of white supremacy in American Christianity / Robert P. Jones. Simon & Schuster, 2020. 288 p. **277**

1. Jones, Robert P. (Robert Patrick) 2. Christians -- United States 3. Whiteness (Concept) 4. Racism -- Religious aspects -- Christianity. 5. Christian church and race relations 6. United States -- Church history.

ISBN 9781982122867

LC 2019049393

White too long draws on history, statistics, and memoir to urge that white Christians reckon with the racism of the past and the amnesia of the present to restore a Christian identity free of the taint of white supremacy.

"An indispensable study of Christianity in America. . . . a concise yet comprehensive combination of deeply documented religious history, social science research about contemporary religion, and heartfelt memoir." Kirkus

Manseau, Peter

Objects of devotion : religion in early America / Peter Manseau. Smithsonian Books, 2017 vii, 251 p. ; **277**

1. Material culture -- Religious aspects -- Christianity. 2. Material culture -- Religious aspects. 3. Material culture -- United States. 4. United States -- Church history. 5. United States -- Religion.

ISBN 1588345920

LC 2016038040

Explores the wide range of religions vying for a prominent place in the early American public square, focusing on such Christian sects as Anglicans, Baptists, and Methodists, as well as faiths ranging from Judaism to Native American beliefs.

"This landmark study of the role of religion in the early history of the U.S.from the mid-17th century to the mid-19th centurydemonstrates how deeply religion influenced Americas founders and their descendants." Publishers Weekly.

Sutton, Matthew Avery, 1975-

American apocalypse : a history of modern evangelicalism / Matthew Avery Sutton. Belknap Press of Harvard University Press, 2014. 420 p. **277**

1. Evangelicalism -- History. 2. Evangelists 3. Fundamentalists 4. Christianity 5. United States -- Church history -- 20th century.

ISBN 9780674048362

LC 2014014034

In the first comprehensive history of American evangelicalism to appear in a generation, Matthew Sutton shows how charismatic Protestant preachers, anticipating the end of the world, paradoxically transformed it. Narrating the story from the perspective of the faithful, he shows how apocalyptic thinking influences the American mainstream today. --Provided by publisher

277.308 Christianity -- United States

Du Mez, Kristin Kobes

Jesus and John Wayne : how white evangelicals corrupted a faith and fractured a nation / Kristin Kobes Du Mez. Liveright Publishing Corporation, 2020 365 p. **277.308**

1. Trump, Donald, 1946- 2. Christianity and politics. 3. Evangelicalism 4. New Right 5. Ideology -- United States 6. United States -- Religion -- 21st century

ISBN 9781631495731

LC 2019059451

A scholar of American Christianity presents a seventy-five-year history of evangelicalism that identifies the forces that have turned Donald Trump into a hero of the Religious Right.

"This lucid, potent history adds a much needed religious dimension to understanding the current American right and the rise of Trump." Publishers Weekly

280 Denominations and sects of Christian church

Ryrie, Alec

Protestants : the faith that made the modern world / Alec Ryrie. Viking Press, 2017. 464 p. **280**

1. Protestantism 2. Reformation 3. Fundamentalism 4. Christianity

ISBN 9780670026166

LC 2016056692

Five hundred years ago an obscure monk challenged the authority of the pope with a radical vision of what Christianity could be. The revolution he set in motion inspired one of the most creative and destructive movements in human history. In this global history that charts five centuries of innovation and change, Alec Ryrie makes the case that Protestants made the modern world.

"Rarely has an author of such deep faith offered such a tolerant, engaging history of any religion." Kirkus.

281.9 Orthodox churches

Mathewes-Green, Frederica

Welcome to the Orthodox Church : an introduction to Eastern Christianity / Frederica Mathewes-Green. Paraclete Press, 2015 xviii, 361 p. ; **281.9**

1. Orthodox Eastern Church. 2. RELIGION / Christianity / Orthodox.

ISBN 1557259216

LC 2014041905

"There are other introductory books about Orthodoxy, but they are all somewhat academic. This one comprehensively covers the history, theology, and practice without talking over your head. Mathewes-Green takes the original approach of bringing you into a typical church for a series of visits. That is how Christians learned the faith for most of history, by coming into a community and keeping their eyes and ears open. Designed primarily for newcomers to come to understand Orthodoxy and Orthodox Christians, this guide to the faith is also a non-threatening and accessible introduction to people already 'in the pews.' Inviting rather than argumentative, Orthodox Christians will be giving this to their friends".-- Provided by publisher.

281.909 Orthodox churches--History, geographic treatment, biography

McGuckin, John Anthony

The **Eastern** Orthodox Church : a new history / John Anthony McGuckin. Yale University Press, 2020. 352 p. **281.909**

1. Orthodox Eastern Church -- History 2. Christian sects 3. Faith

(Christianity) 4. Theology 5. Orthodox Eastern Church doctrines
ISBN 9780300218763

LC 2019948578

In this short, accessible account of the Eastern Orthodox Church, John McGuckin begins by tackling the question "What is the Church?" His answer is a clear, historically and theologically rooted portrait of what the Church is for Orthodox Christianity and how it differs from Western Christians' expectations.

"McGuckin presents another well-written and well-researched work in this fantastic introduction to the Eastern Orthodox Church." Library Journal

282 Roman Catholic Church

Allen, John L., 1965-

The **Catholic** church : what everyone needs to know / John L. Allen. Oxford University Press, c2013. 336 p. **282**

1. Catholic Church 2. Catholic theology 3. Church history 4. Church history
ISBN 9780199975105

LC 2012038594

A guide to the past, present, and future of the Catholic Church looks at the internal and external challenges the institution faces and how it can make itself relevant and improve its moral standing in light of recent crises.

John Paul

Crossing the threshold of hope / John Paul II ; edited by Vittorio Messori ; translated from the Italian by Jenny McPhee and Martha McPhee. Knopf, 1995, c1994. ix, 244 p. ; **282**

1. John Paul II, Pope, 1920- Interviews. 2. Catholic Church Doctrines Papal documents. 3. Spiritual life -- Catholic Church -- Papal documents.
ISBN 0679765611

LC bl 99766484

Includes indexes.

Reprint. Originally published: 1994.

Pope John Paul II speaks out on some of the major issues confronting humankind at the dawn of the twenty-first century

282.09 Roman Catholic Church--History, geographic treatment, biography

Francis, Pope, 1936-

Walking with Jesus : a way forward for the Church / Pope Francis. Loyola Press, 2015. 160 p. **282.09**

1. Jesus Christ. 2. Catholic Church. 3. Christian doctrines 4. Sacraments 5. Catholics
ISBN 9780829442489

LC bl2015028437

Two thousand years ago Jesus said, "Follow me." Whatif the twenty-first-century church actually heeded that call? What would theworld look like if the church were truly on the move? Simply put, very different. But these ponderings beg one more critical question: What exactly should the church be moving toward? In Walking with Jesus: A Way Forward for the Church With a foreword by Archbishop of Chicago, Blase J.Cupich, Pope Francis' first major appointment in the United States, Walking with Jesus offers the church a much-needed way forward, past its inner and outer walls, as it fearlessly follows Christ toward the future.

"Perhaps no one has as much potential to buoy the human spirit through his words as Francis, whose life and public speeches are closely watched by so many. The book's foreword is by Archbishop Blase J. Cupich of Chicago, the pope's first major U.S. appointment." Publishers Weekly.

Weigel, George, 1951-

The **irony** of modern Catholic history : how the Church rediscovered itself and challenged the modern world to reform / George Weigel. Basic Books, 2019. 336 p. **282.09**

1. Catholic Church -- History 19th century. 2. Catholic Church -- History 20th century. 3. Catholic Church -- History 21st century. 4. Catholics. 5. Catholic theology. 6. Modernization (Social sciences)
ISBN 9780465094332

LC 2019013176

An account of two centuries of profound change in the church and the world.

Wills, Garry, 1934-

The **future** of the Catholic Church with Pope Francis / Garry Wills. Viking, 2015. xxi, 263 p. ; **282.09**

1. Francis, Pope, 1936- 2. Catholic Church Infallibility. 3. Popes. 4. Church history. 5. Christian doctrines. 6. Change.
ISBN 9780525426967

Includes index.

The Pulitzer Prize-winning historian considers Pope Francis' potential for enabling change in the Catholic Church, analyzing seven key examples of profound change within the past century that have not been advanced by the papacy.

"Highly recommended for all interested in a fact-based study of the church's evolution." Library Journal.

282.092 Roman Catholics -- Biography

Eisner, Peter

The **pope's** last crusade : how an American Jesuit helped Pope Pius XI's campaign to stop Hitler / Peter Eisner. William Morrow, 2013. 292 p. : **282.092**

1. Pius XI, Pope, 1857-1939. 2. Hitler, Adolf, 1889-1945. 3. Jesuits. 4. Nazism. 5. Catholic Church and Nazism. 6. Popes -- History -- 20th century. 7. Ideology. 8. Germany -- Politics and government -- 1933-1945.
ISBN 9780062049148

In 1939, American Jesuit priest, John LaFarge, worked with Pope Pius XI on an encyclical (a formally stated Vatican policy) that condemned anti-Semitism in general and Nazi oppression in particular. Sadly, Pius XI died before its completion, and his successor (Pope Pius XII) saw Communism as more dangerous than Nazism and took a course that tended toward anti-Semitism. The Pope's Last Crusade reveals LaFarge's draft encyclical and explores the forces that prevented its release -- begging the poignant question: how might this have changed history, had it been released?

Kertzer, David I., 1948-

The **pope** who would be king : the exile of Pius IX and the emergence of modern Europe / David I. Kertzer. Random House, 2018. 304 p. **282.092**

1. Pius IX, Pope, 1792-1878 2. Catholic Church Political activity 3. Popes 4. Church history 5. Power (Social sciences) 6. Exiles 7.

Europe -- Politics and government
ISBN 9780812989915

LC 2017038825

The Pulitzer Prize-winning author documents the lesser-known story of the violent revolution that established the end of the papacy as a political power and signaled the birth of modern Europe.

"A consummate storyteller, Kertzer blends academic rigor with fluid, energetic prose, and the result will satisfy specialists while entertaining those who might otherwise expect to be bored stiff by a volume of church history." Publishers Weekly.

Nouwen, Henri J. M

Love, Henri : letters on the spiritual life / Henri J.M. Nouwen ; edited and with a preface by Gabrielle Earnshaw ; foreword by Brene Brown. Convergent, 2016 xxiv, 351 p. ; **282.092**

1. Nouwen, Henri J. M. Correspondence.
ISBN 9781101906354

LC 2016034448

Presents over one hundred letters throughout Nouwen's career, highlighting such themes in his work and life as vocation, solitude, prayer, suffering, and perseverance in difficult times.

289 Other denominations and sects

Stein, Stephen J., 1940-

The **Shaker** experience in America : a history of the United Society of Believers / Stephen J. Stein. Yale University Press, c1992. xx, 554 p. : **289**

1. Shakers United States -- History.
ISBN 0300051395

LC 91030836

Draws on oral and written testimony to trace the history and evolution of the Shakers, set within the broader context of American life.

289.3 Latter-Day Saints (Mormons)

Bushman, Richard L.

Joseph Smith and the beginnings of Mormonism / Richard L. Bushman. University of Illinois Press, c1984. 262 p. ; **289.3**

1. Smith, Joseph, Jr., 1805-1844. 2. Mormon Church -- History -- 19th century
ISBN 9780252060120

LC 84002451

Includes index.

Focuses on the first twenty-five years of Smith's life, describes his visions, and recounts how he established the Church of the Latter-day Saints

Bushman, Richard L.

Mormonism : a very short introduction / Richard Lyman Bushman. Oxford University Press, 2008. 144 p. **289.3**

1. Mormon Church -- History. 2. Mormon theology.
ISBN 0195310306

LC 2007044444

Looks at the history and teachings of the Church of Jesus Christ of Latter-day Saints.

Gutjahr, Paul C.

★The **Book** of Mormon : a biography / Paul C. Gutjahr. Princeton University Press, 2012. xix, 255 p. : **289.3**

1. Smith, Joseph, 1805-1844. 2. Mormon Church. 3. Book of Mormon History. 4. Mormons
ISBN 9780691144801

LC 2011044063

Shows how Joseph Smith, Jr.'s influential Book of Mormon launched one of the fastest growing new religions on the planet.

Hardy, Grant, 1961-

★**Understanding** the Book of Mormon : a reader's guide / Grant Hardy. Oxford University Press, 2010. xxi, 346 p. ; **289.3**

1. Book of Mormon Criticism, Narrative.
ISBN 0199731705

LC 2009026675

Examines the Book of Mormon not as scripture or fraud, but as a highly influential work of literature, with an emphasis on the distinctive voices of its three main narrators, Nephi, Mormon, and Moroni.

289.6 Society of Friends (Quakers)

Hamm, Thomas D.

★The **Quakers** in America / Thomas D. Hamm. Columbia University Press, 2003. viii, 293 p. : **289.6**

1. Society of Friends. 2. Quakers.
ISBN 0231123620

LC 2002041422

"The author provides an introduction to Quaker origins abroad, their influences on American politics and culture, as well as their beliefs and traditions as they are played out on American soil. Though this is a serious history with a glossary, chronology, and 40 pages of notes, cartoons and anecdotes leaven the text. For both public and academic libraries." Library Journal.

289.7 Mennonite churches

Kraybill, Donald B.

Concise encyclopedia of Amish, Brethren, Hutterites, and Mennonites / Donald B. Kraybill. Johns Hopkins University Press, 2010. xvii, 302 p. : **289.7**

1. Anabaptists
ISBN 0801896576

LC 2009046015

Donald B. Kraybill has spent his career among Anabaptist groups, gaining an unparalleled understanding of these traditionally private people. Kraybill shares that deep knowledge in this succinct overview of the beliefs and cultural practices of Amish, Brethren, Hutterites, and Mennonites in North America. Found throughout Canada, Central America, Mexico, and the United States, these religious communities include more than 200 different groups with 800,000 members in 17 countries. Through 340 short entries, Kraybill offers readers information on a wide range of topics related to religious views and social practices. With thoughtful consideration of how the diverse communities are related, this compact reference provides a brief and accurate synopsis of these groups in the twenty-first century. No other single volume provides such a broad overview of Amish, Brethren, Huterites, and Mennonites in North America. Organized for ease of searching--with a list of entries, a topic finder, an index of names, and ample cross-references--the volume also includes abundant resources for accessing additional information. Wide in scope, succinct in content, with directional markers along the way, the Concise Encyclopedia of Amish, Brethren, Hutterites, and Mennonites isa must-have reference for anyone interested in Anabaptist groups.--Book Jacket.

Kraybill, Donald B.

★**On** the backroad to heaven : Old Order Hutterites, Mennonites, Amish, and Brethren / Donald B. Kraybill, Carl F. Bowman. Johns Hopkins University Press, c2001. xvi, 330 p. : **289.7**

1. Hutterite Brethren. 2. Old German Baptist Brethren. 3. Old Order Mennonites. 4. Amish. 5. Plain People -- Comparative studies.
ISBN 0801865654

LC 00010406

"The authors give the general reader an excellent basic understanding of the beliefs and practices shared by all of these separatists while making the uniqueness of each group clear. One of the best single-volume works on this subject; highly recommended for academic and public libraries." Library Journal

Mackall, Joe

Plain secrets : an outsider among the Amish / Joe Mackall. Beacon Press, c2007. xxxiv, 208 p. ; **289.7**

1. Amish -- Ohio. 2. Religion. 3. Rumspringa 4. Ohio -- Religious life and customs.
ISBN 0807010642

LC oc2007129864

The author describes his relationship with a neighboring Swartzentruber Amish family, the Shetlers, over sixteen years, using the example of the Shetlers to look at the lives and customs of the Swartzentruber Amish in general.

"This is a loving portrait, warts and all, of an often-misunderstood people." Booklist.

292 Classical religion (Greek and Roman religion)

Hughes, Bettany

Venus and Aphrodite : a biography of desire / Bettany Hughes. Basic Books, 2020 224 p. **292**

1. Aphrodite (Greek deity) 2. Venus (Roman deity) 3. Gods and goddesses 4. Women warriors
ISBN 9781541674233

LC 2020013390

Aphrodite was said to have been born from the sea, rising out of a froth of white foam. But long before the Ancient Greeks conceived of this voluptuous blonde, she existed as an early spirit of fertility on the shores of Cyprus -- and thousands of years before that, as a ferocious warrior-goddess in the Middle East. Proving that this fabled figure is so much more than an avatar of commercialized romance, historian Bettany Hughes reveals the remarkable lifestory of one of antiquity's most potent myths.

"British historian Hughes (Istanbul: A Tale of Three Cities) presents a brisk and incisive cultural history of the mythological goddess of sexual love." Publishers Weekly

292.1 Specific elements

Hamilton, Edith, 1867-1963

Mythology : timeless tales of gods and heroes / Edith Hamilton ; illustrated by Jim Tierney. Black Dog & Leventhal Publishers, 2017. 371 p. : **292.1**

1. Gods and goddesses. 2. Heroes and heroines in mythology.
ISBN 9780316438520

LC bl2017036579

Includes index.

A collection of Greek and Roman myths arranged in sections on the gods and early heroes, love and adventure stories, the Trojan War, and a brief section on Norse mythology.

293 Germanic religion

Larrington, Carolyne

The **Norse** myths : a guide to the gods and heroes / Carolyne Larrington. Thames & Hudson, 2017. 208 p. **293**

1. Mythology, Norse 2. Gods and goddesses, Norse 3. Characters and characteristics in mythology. 4. Odin (Norse deity) 5. Scandinavia 6. Northern Europe
ISBN 9780500251966

LC 2016941839

Introduces the gods and goddesses of the Norse tradition and describes the cosmos they inhabit, their escapades, and their cultural legacy.

294 Religions of Indic origin

Dalrymple, William

Nine lives : in search of the sacred in modern India / William Dalrymple. Alfred A. Knopf, 2010, c2009. xvii, 275 p. : **294**

1. India -- Religious life and customs 2. India -- Social life and customs
ISBN 9780307272829

First published: London : Bloomsbury, 2009.

A study of the ways in which traditional forms of religious life in India have been transformed in the vortex of the region's rapid change.

"Throughout the book, Dalrymple showcases his knowledge of the breadth of India and his fearless willingness to penetrate its sometimes unsavory nooks and crannies, rendering this a truly heartfelt work for readers craving a deeper connection to India and its rich spiritual heritage. A remarkable feat of journalism." Kirkus.

294.3 Buddhism

Chodron, Pema

How to meditate : a practical guide to making friends with your mind / Pema Chodron. Sounds True, 2013. viii, 175 p. ; **294.3**

1. Meditation -- Buddhism
ISBN 9781604079333

LC 2012046126

An American-born Tibetan Buddhist nun offers her own unique explanation of meditation and guides readers through practicing this calming ritual.

"At all times Chodron is careful not to overwhelm readers or make meditation feel like an Everest expedition, and she features her own practice as an example of challenges and successes." Library Journal.

Chodron, Pema

Practicing peace / Pema Chodron ; based on talks edited

by Sandy Boucher. Shambhala, 2018. x, 88 p. ; **294.3**

1. Dharma (Buddhism) 2. Peace of mind 3. Peace -- Religious aspects -- Buddhism 4. Spiritual life -- Buddhism
ISBN 9781611806137

LC bl2018180023

Draws on Buddhist teachings to explore the origins of anger, aggression, hatred, and war, and offers practical techniques that are used to find genuine, lasting peace.

"Chodron teaches readers how to pause and let experiences pierce the heart so that the sparks of aggression may burn themselves out, leaving a positive sense of groundlessness and insecurity. These are familiar teachings to those acquainted with her work, but her approach remains invaluable for guidance on working with hatred and anger." Publishers Weekly.

Chodron, Pema

Taking the leap : freeing ourselves from old habits and fears / Pema Chodron ; edited by Sandy Boucher. Shambhala, 2012, c2009. vii, 111 p. ; **294.3**

1. Spiritual life -- Buddhism. 2. Buddhism 3. Buddhist doctrines 4. Shenpa
ISBN 9781590309810

LC bl2012031965

Discusses the Buddhist concept of shenpa to explain how to free oneself from destructive energy experienced as a sensation of tightening and negativity at moments of conflict, explaining how to replace angry or addictive responses with courage and compassion.

Connelly, Ben

Inside Vasubandhu's Yogacara : a practitioner's guide / Ben Connelly ; with a new translation from Sanskrit by Ben Connelly and Weijen Teng ; foreword by Norman Fischer. Wisdom Publications, 2016 xi, 231 p. ; **294.3**

1. Vasubandhu. Triikvijñaptimtratsiddhi. 2. Yogcra (Buddhism).
ISBN 9781614292845

LC 2016008752

"A practical, down-to-earth guide to Vasubandhu's classic work 'Thirty Verses of Consciousness Only' that can transform modern life and change how you see the world. In this down-to-earth book, Ben Connelly sure-handedly guides us through the intricaciesof Yogacara and the richness of the 'Thirty Verses.' Dedicating a chapter of the book to each line of the poem, he lets us thoroughly lose ourselves in its depths. His warm and wise voice unpacks and contextualizes its wisdom, showing us how we can apply its ancient insights to our own modern lives, to create a life of engaged peace, harmony, compassion, and joy. In fourth-century India one of the great geniuses of Buddhism, Vasubandhu, sought to reconcile the diverse ideas and forms of Buddhism practiced at the time and demonstrate how they could be effectively integrated into a single system. This was the Yogacara movement, and it continues to have great influence in modern Tibetan and Zen Buddhism. 'Thirty Verses on Consciousness Only,' or 'Trimshika,' is the most concise, comprehensive, and accessible work by this revered figure. Vasubandhu's 'Thirty Verses' lay out a path of practice that integrates the most powerful of Buddhism's psychological and mystical possibilities: Early Buddhism's practices for shedding afflictive emotional habit and the Mahayana emphasis on shedding divisive concepts, the path of individual liberation and the path of freeing all beings, the path to nirvana and the path of enlightenment as the very ground of being right now. Although Yogacara has a reputation for being extremely complex, the 'Thirty Verses' distills the principles of these traditions to their most practical forms, and this book follows that sense of focus; it goes to the heart of the matter--how do we alleviate suffering through shedding our emotional knots and our sense of alienation? This is a great introduction to a philosophy, a master, and a work whose influence reverberates throughout modern Buddhism".-- Provided by publisher.

"Newcomers and adherents to this lesser-known Buddhist school alike are lucky to have Connelly as an exceptional guide to the central themes of Yogacara." Publishers Weekly.

Dalai Lama

Approaching the Buddhist path / the Dalai Lama and Thubten Chodron. Wisdom Publications, 2017. 384 p. **294.3**

1. Gautama Buddha 2. Buddhism 3. Spiritual life -- Buddhism 4. Enlightenment (Buddhism) 5. Spiritual growth
ISBN 9781614294412

LC 2016053409

The Dalai Lama has been publicly teaching Buddhism for decades. This series collects his presentations of every step of the path to enlightenment.

"An excellent and intellectually stimulating introduction to the Buddhist way of life." Publishers Weekly.

Dalai Lama

The **book** of joy : lasting happiness in a changing world / His Holiness the Dalai Lama and Archbishop Desmond Tutu, with Douglas Abrams. Avery, 2016. 288 p. **294.3**

1. Happiness -- Religious aspects. 2. Joy -- Religious aspects. 3. Spiritual life. 4. Spiritual growth.
ISBN 9780399185045

LC 2016026669

Two leading spiritual masters share their hard-won wisdom about living with joy even in the face of adversity, sharing personal stories and teachings about the science of profound happiness and the daily practices that anchor their emotional and spiritual lives.

Dalai Lama

★**How** to be compassionate : a handbook for creating inner peace and a happier world / Dalai Lama XIV, translated and edited by Jeffrey Hopkins. Atria Books, 2011. 224 p. **294.3**

1. Compassion -- Religious aspects -- Buddhism 2. Happiness -- Religious aspects -- Buddhism 3. Transformations, Personal -- Religious aspects -- Buddhism 4. Spirituality
ISBN 9781451623901

LC bl2011001885

Through practical exercises and personal anecdotes, a revered spiritual leader shows how individuals' compassion can lead to global changes.

"Light on politics and even lighter on the more abstruse points of Tibetan Buddhism, this is a fine and accessible book for the everyday reader." Library Journal.

Dalai Lama

Violence and compassion / the Dalai Lama and Jean-Claude Carriere. Doubleday, 1996. 248 p. ; **294.3**

1. Compassion (Buddhism) 2. Violence -- Religious aspects -- Buddhism 3. Compassion -- Religious aspects -- Buddhism 4. Toleration. 5. Tibet -- Religious life and customs 6. India -- Religious life and customs
ISBN 0385479603

LC 95030694

Originally published in France as Le force du bouddhisme by Editions Robert Laffont-Fixott.

Addressing the problems our world currently faces, including terrorism, environmental dangers, and overpopulation, the Dalai Lama offers direct guidance and gentle wisdom on how to overcome such major issues.

"This is a rich and invigorating volume, full of ponderable wisdom." Booklist.

Dge-'dun-rgya-mtsho, Dalai Lama II, 1476-1542

The **second** Dalai Lama : his life and teachings / translated, edited, introduced, and annotated by Glenn H. Mullin. Snow Lion Publications, 2005. xvii, 270 p. ; **294.3**

1. Dge-dun-rgya-mtsho, Dalai Lama II, 1476-1542. 2. Dge-lugs-pa doctrines -- Early works to 1800. 3. Religion. 4. Buddhism. 5. Dalai lamas

ISBN 1559392339

LC 2005281580

Previously published under the title: Mystical verses of a mad Dalai Lama. Wheaton, Ill. : Theosophical Pub. House, 1994.

Illuminating one of the great Lamas in the Tibetan Buddhist tradition, the author offers a rare look at the life and work of teachers who influenced the current Dalai Lama.

Emet, Joseph

Finding the blue sky : a mindful approach to choosing happiness here and now / Joseph Emet. TarcherPerigee., LLC, 2016 xiii, 193 p. ; **294.3**

1. Happiness -- Religious aspects -- Buddhism 2. Spiritual life -- Buddhism

ISBN 9780143109631

LC 2016022074

Examines the principles of Buddhism and discusses how they correlate with the latest research into happiness outlined in positive psychology.

Gunaratana, Henepola, 1927-

Start here, start now : a short guide to mindfulness meditation / Bhante Gunaratana. Wisdom Publications, 2019 vi, 155 p. ; **294.3**

1. Vipayan (Buddhism). 2. Meditation -- Buddhism.

ISBN 9781614296270

LC 2019014015

"Gunaratana (Mindfulness in Plain English) offers a straightforward and informative introduction to mindfulness meditation, walking a fine line between familiar secularized instructions and careful guidance through difficult experiences that may challenge one's worldview." Publishers Weekly

Keown, Damien, 1951-

★A **dictionary** of Buddhism / Damien Keown ; contributors, Stephen Hodge, Charles Jones, Paoli Tinti. Oxford University Press, 2003. viii, 357 p. : **294.3**

1. Buddhism

ISBN 0198605609

LC 2003276701

A wide-ranging, comprehensive, and accessible guide to Buddhism includes more than two thousand entries covering the history, beliefs, and practices of Buddhists worldwide. (World Religion)

"The entries are short . . . but such accessibility is the very reason why this should be on the bookshelf of every student of Buddhism." Publishers Weekly.

Kerouac, Jack, 1922-1969

Some of the dharma / Jack Kerouac. Penguin Books, 1999, c1997. 419 p. ; **294.3**

1. Buddhism

ISBN 9780140287073

LC BL 00001221

Originally published: New York : Viking, 1997.

Jack Kerouac's earliest foray into Buddhism is captured in a volume that includes poems, haiku, prayers, journal entries, meditations, letter fragments, ideas, and much more, all assembled in the visually daring format Kerouac originally envisioned.

"Begun in December 1951 as a notebook for his Buddhist studies, this work records Kerouac's reactions to a variety of Buddhist texts. Over the course of five years, it grew to include poems, prayers, dialogs, meditations, and notes on his reading, as well as commentary on family, friends, and meaningful concerns in his life. Long anticipated by Kerouac scholars, this major work belongs in all literature collections." Library Journal.

Kornfield, Jack, 1945-

The **wise** heart : a guide to the universal teachings of Buddhist psychology / Jack Kornfield. Bantam Books, 2008. x, 429 p. ; **294.3**

1. Buddhism -- Psychology

ISBN 9780553803471

LC 2008005916

Presents a guide to Buddhist psychology, concepts, and practices, offering techniques for healing, training, and transforming the mind.

Masuno, Shunmy

The **art** of simple living : 100 daily practices from a Japanese Zen monk for a lifetime of calm and joy / Shunmy Masuno ; translated by Allison Markin Powell ; artwork by Harriet Lee-Merrion. Penguin Books, 2019 xvi, 207 p. : **294.3**

1. Religious life -- Zen Buddhism 2. Simplicity -- Religious aspects -- Zen Buddhism 3. Spiritual life -- Zen Buddhism

ISBN 9780143134046

LC 2018051572

Relax and find happiness amid the swirl of the modern world with this internationally best-selling guide to simplifying your life by a Japanese monk who embodies the wisdom of Zen. Illustrations.

Nhat Hanh, Thich

The **art** of living : peace and freedom in the here and now / Thich Nhat Hanh. HarperOne, 2017. ix; 206 p. **294.3**

1. Nhat Hanh, Thich 2. Spiritual life -- Buddhism 3. Meditation 4. Everyday life 5. Awareness -- Religious aspects -- Buddhism

ISBN 9780062434661

LC 2017013611

Offers a guide to the art of living in mindfulness, consisting of seven meditations intended to help readers live lives that are happy, peaceful, active, and free of fear in the face of death.

Nhat Hanh, Thich

Living Buddha, living Christ / Thich Nhat Hanh ; introduction by Elaine Pagels ; foreword by David Steindl-Rast. Riverhead Books, 1995. xxvii, 208 p. ; **294.3**

1. Buddhism. 2. Christianity 3. Buddhist meditations. 4. Christianity -- Relations -- Buddhism. 5. Vietnam -- Religious life and customs

ISBN 1573220183

LC 95024014

Exploring the spiritual connection between Christianity and Buddhism, the Vietnamese monk and Buddhist teacher reawakens an understanding of both religions and offers simple yet meaningful ways to enhance our daily lives, in a tenth anniversary edition of the classic spiritual text. Reissue.

"The author offers insights into his own spiritual heritage and beckons readers to find meaning and peace within Buddhismwithout abandoning their own belief system. Nh'at Hanh observes many intersections of faith and belief between Buddhism and the Judeo-Christian faiths. He does, however, clearly delineate differences." School Library Journal.

Nhat Hanh, Thich

Peace is every step : the path of mindfulness in everyday life / Thich Nhat Hanh ; edited by Arnold Kotler. Bantam Books, 1992, c1991. xv, 134 p. ; **294.3**

1. Religious life -- Buddhism. 2. Buddhism and peace. 3. Peace. 4. Awareness.

ISBN 0553351397

LC BL 99725027

Originally published: New York : Bantam, 1991.

"Emphasizing that all things are interconnected on personal and political levels, he notes, for example, that the wealth of one society is based on the poverty of others. This book of illuminating reminders bids us to reorient the way we look at the world, turning away from a goal-driven, me-first modality toward a humanitarian perspective." Publishers Weekly.

Nichtern, David

Creativity, spirituality & making a buck / David Nichtern. Wisdom Publications, 2019 xviii, 225 p. ; **294.3**

1. Spiritual life 2. Creative ability -- Religious aspects 3. Creation (Literary, artistic, etc) -- Religious aspects 4. Success in business -- Religious aspects

ISBN 9781614294986

LC 2019016594

"In this profound, delightful work, Nichtern (Awakening from the Daydream), a Buddhist teacher and professional guitarist, humorously explores balancing one's spirituality with earning a living." Publishers Weekly

Nichtern, Ethan

The **road** home : a contemporary exploration of the Buddhist path / Ethan Nichtern. North Point Press, 2015 240 p. **294.3**

1. Buddhism. 2. Spirituality 3. Buddhist doctrines 4. Enlightenment (Buddhism)

ISBN 9780374251932

LC 2014030912

In The Road Home, Ethan Nichtern, a senior teacher in the Shambhala Buddhist tradition, investigates the journey each of us takes to find where we belong. Drawing from contemporary research on meditation and mindfulness and his experience as a Buddhist teacher and practitioner, Nichtern describes in fresh and deeply resonant terms the basic existential experience that gives rise to spiritual seeking?and also to its potentially dangerous counterpart, spiritual materialism.

"Valuable for readers looking for an introduction to Buddhist teachings as they relate to meditation practice or for those searching for ways to live their lives in the here and now." Library Journal.

Oliver, Joan Duncan

Buddhism : an introduction to the Buddha's life, teachings, and practices / Joan Duncan Oliver. St. Martins Essentials, 2019. 205 p. **294.3**

1. Gautama Buddha 2. Buddhism 3. Buddhist doctrines 4. Buddhist meditation

ISBN 9781250313683

LC 2018050710

Buddhism: An Introduction to the Buddha's Life, Teachings, and Practices is an indispensable guide to a 2,600-year-old wisdom tradition that has transformed the lives of millions across centuries and around the world. Readers will learn how Siddhartha Gautama became the Buddha, one of the most influential spiritual leaders of all time, and discover how they too can follow his revolutionary methods to attain happiness and inner freedom.

"She begins her guidance with a biography of the Buddha, followed by a history of the evolution of Buddhism and its teachings after the Buddhas death, bringing her coverage up to the current day to include the presence of cyber-sanghas (communities of followers) using such new methods of delivery of the Dharma (teachings and practices taught by the Buddha) as podcasts and social media." Booklist.

Olson, Carl

Historical dictionary of Buddhism / Carl Olson. Scarecrow Press, 2009. xxix, 327 p., 11 p. of plates : **294.3**

1. Buddhism -- History

ISBN 9780810857711

LC 2009007383

Rev. ed. of: Historical dictionary of Buddhism / Charles S. Prebish. 1993.

The Historical Dictionary of Buddhism covers and clarifies Buddhist concepts, significant figures, movements, schools, places, activities, and periods. This is done through a chronology, an introductory essay, a bibliography, and over 700 cross-referenced dictionary entries. --Provided by publisher

Rinzler, Lodro

The **Buddha** walks into a bar : a guide to life for a new generation / Lodro Rinzler. Shambhala, 2012. 211 p. **294.3**

1. Spiritual life. 2. Buddhism. 3. Buddhists. 4. Spirituality.

ISBN 9781590309377

LC 2011014498

"A fine beginning resource for younger adults ready to try the approaches of Buddhism; this is Eastern spirituality for the Harry Potter generation." Library Journal.

Rinzler, Lodro

Love hurts : Buddhist advice for the heartbroken / Lodro Rinzler. Shambhala, 2016 xii, 170 p. ; **294.3**

1. Consolation. 2. Suffering -- Religious aspects -- Buddhism. 3. Suffering -- Religious aspects.

ISBN 1611803543

LC 2016013202

Shares Buddhist wisdom on how to deal with emotional suffering, and includes practical advice for self-care.

"Rinzler melds his Shambhala training with sharp humor, an eye for detail, and deep empathy in this superb book for any heartbroken reader." Publishers Weekly.

Sawaki, Kodo, 1880-1965

Discovering the true self : Kodo Sawaki's art of Zen meditation / translated, edited, and with an introduction by Arthur Braverman. Counterpoint Press, 2020 272 p. **294.3**

1. Sawaki, Kodo, 1880-1965 2. Sawaki, Kodo, 1880-1965 Teachings 3. Zen priests 4. Orphans 5. Men -- Japan 6. Spiritual life -- Zen Buddhism

ISBN 9781640093775

LC 2020000997

Having come of age as an orphan in the slums of Tsu City, Japan, Kodo Sawaki had to fight his way to adulthood, and became one of the most respected Zen masters of the 20th century. He had a great understanding of Dogen Zenji's teaching and he knew how to express Dogen's philosophy in clear, easily-understood language. Sawaki's primary mission was to bring all people to an awareness of the Self, which he believed came through Zen meditation. One of a few collections of Sawaki's teachings published in English, this anthology of his life and work brackets the most intriguing and influential period of modern Zen practice in Japan and America.

"This is an essential resource for those interested in Zen meditation." Publishers Weekly

Siff, Jason

Thoughts are not the enemy : an innovative approach to meditation practice / Jason Siff. Shambhala, 2014. x, 212 p. ; **294.3**

1. Meditation -- Buddhism 2. Meditation

ISBN 9781611800432

LC 2013046153

"A revolutionary new approach to meditation: a mindfulness of thinking that accepts and investigates the thoughts that arise as you meditate--from the author of Unlearning Meditation. In most forms of meditation, the meditator is instructed to let go of thoughts as they arise. As a result, thinking is often taken, unnecessarily, to be something misguided or evil. This approach is misguided, says Jason Siff. In fact, if we allow thoughts to arise and become mindful of the thoughts themselves, we gain tranquillity and insight just as in other methods without having to reject our natural mental processes. And by observing the thoughts themselves with mindfulness and curiosity, we can learn a good deal about ourselves in the process".-- Provided by publisher.

"Though Siff emphasizes open and unstructured exploration, some instructions veer toward technical, which may leave inexperienced meditators behind. Meditation scenarios, in which he presents fictionalized accounts of practitioners using different methods, often serve as awkward detours in this otherwise excellent work. Unafraid to go against the grain, Siff teaches readers how to adequately approach conceptual thought, the everyday state of existence, in all of its messiness." Publishers Weekly.

Sogyal, Rinpoche

The **Tibetan** book of living and dying / Sogyal Rinpoche ; edited by Patrick Gaffney and Andrew Harvey. Harper San Francisco, c1992. xiv, 425 p. : **294.3**

1. Buddhism -- China -- Tibet Autonomous Region -- Doctrines. 2. Religious life -- Buddhism. 3. Death -- Religious aspects -- Buddhism. 4. Intermediate state -- Buddhism.

ISBN 9780062507938

LC 90056214

A discussion of the age-old techniques on which the classic "Tibetan Book of the Dead" is based examines the possibility for healing that can be released when people begin to view death as another chapter of life.

"The author is well qualified to pass on his tradition. He does this beautifully, in limpid prose free of the scholastic list making that deadens many Tibetan Buddhist primers." New York Times Book Review.

Thondup, Tulku

Enlightened journey : Buddhist practice as daily life / Tulku Thondup ; edited by Harold Talbott. Shambhala ; 1995. xix, 268 p. ; **294.3**

1. Spiritual life -- Rnying-ma-pa (Sect) 2. Rdzogs-chen

ISBN 9781570620218

LC 94036154

Collects fifteen articles and talks by a Tibetan Buddhist scholar on the principles of Buddhism, the Buddhist way of life, and Buddhist forms of meditation.

Thubten Zopa, Rinpoche, 1945-

The **Four** Noble Truths : a guide for everyday life / Lama Zopa Rinpoche ; edited by Yeo Puay Huei. Wisdom, 2018 viii, 293 p. **294.3**

1. Four Noble Truths

ISBN 9781614293941

LC 2017048508

Includes index.

The Buddha's profound teachings on the four noble truths are illuminated by a Tibetan master simply and directly, so that readers gain an immediate and personal understanding of the causes and conditions that give rise to suffering as well as the spiritual life as the path to liberation. --Provided by publisher

"Using a mix of personal stories, familiar fables, simple analogies, and a touch of gentle humor, Zopa (How to Enjoy Death), a Tibetan Buddhist scholar, skillfully explains how Buddhism's four noble truths (suffering, the cause of suffering, the cessation of suffering, and the path to end suffering) offer hope for genuine happiness." Publishers Weekly

Van Buren, Mark

A **fool's** guide to actual happiness / Mark Van Buren. Wisdom, 2018 xiii, 244 p. ; **294.3**

1. Buddhism -- Psychology 2. Happiness -- Religious aspects -- Buddhism

ISBN 9781614294481

LC 2017048415

Presents advice on cultivating empathy, self-acceptance, and wisdom in facing life's challenges and finding inner peace through a practice of mindfulness.

Watts, Alan, 1915-1973

The **way** of Zen / Alan Watts. Vintage Books, 1999, c1957. xv, 236 p. : **294.3**

1. Zen Buddhism

ISBN 9780375705106

LC bl2012026394

Originally published: New York : Pantheon, 1957.

Traces the origin of Zen and discusses the Zen way of life against its historical and cultural background.

Wright, Robert, 1957-

Why Buddhism is true : the science and philosophy of meditation and enlightenment / Robert Wright. Simon & Schuster, 2017 336 p. **294.3**

1. Philosophy, Buddhist. 2. Cognitive psychology. 3. Personal conduct 4. Buddhism

ISBN 9781439195451

LC 2016041766

The best-selling author of The Evolution of God philosophically explains how the human mind evolved to channel anxiety, depression, anger and greed and how a healthy practice of Buddhist meditation can promote clarity and alleviate suffering.

"Wrights joyful and insightful book is both entertaining and informative, equally accessible to general audiences and more experienced practitioners." Publishers Weekly.

294.309 Buddhist fundamentalism -- History, geographic treatment, biography

Sutin, Lawrence, 1951-

★**All** is change : the two-thousand-year journey of Buddhism to the West / Lawrence Sutin. Little, Brown and Co., c2006. x, 403 p. : **294.309**

1. Buddhism -- Western countries -- History. 2. Buddhism -- Relations. 3. Buddhism -- Influence.
ISBN 0316741566

LC 2006040824

A history of Buddhism's journey and entry into the western world explores such topics as the early exchanges between the classical Greeks and the Buddhists of India, the influence of Buddhism on western philosophers, and the current fascination with the Dalai Lama.

"Greeks and Buddhists in India found common metaphysical ground 2,000 years ago, and Sutin also documents parallels between Buddist and Gnostic teachings in this vital study of a remarkable spiritual migration." Booklist.

294.5 Hinduism

Calasso, Roberto

Ardor / Roberto Calasso ; translated from the Italian by Richard Dixon. Farrar, Straus and Giroux, 2014. 420 p. : **294.5**

1. Vedas Criticism, interpretation, etc. 2. RELIGION / Hinduism / Sacred Writings
ISBN 9780374182311

LC 2013044345

"A meditation on the ancient wisdom of the Vedas, in which Calasso brings ritual and sacrifice to bear on the modern world".-- Provided by publisher.

"Richard Dixons supple and elegant translation brings Calasso's poetic meditations to life. Readers will return again and again for wisdom and insight." Publishers Weekly.

Das, Gaur Gopal

The **way** of the monk : how to find purpose, balance, and lasting happiness / Gaur Gopal Das. Sounds True, 2020. xi, 209 p. : **294.5**

1. Hare Krishna Movement 2. Spiritual life 3. Spiritual life -- Hinduism.
ISBN 9781683646624

LC 2019052848

"In The Way of the Monk, Gopal Das presents a guide to navigating some of the contemporary world's most fundamental questions. How can we achieve peace when the world is so full of noise and conflict? How do we learn to let go of attachment when consumerculture constantly tells us that we are unfulfilled? How can we embody love when our interactions with others are so fraught with old wounds and misunderstanding?"-- Provided by publisher.

"Krishna monk Das follows up Life's Amazing Secrets with this delightful collection of spiritual and life tools. . . . Das's sharp methods for discovering one's purpose will be appreciated by readers who enjoyed Zen and the Art of Motorcycle Maintenance." Publishers Weekly

Davis, Richard H., 1951-

The **Bhagavad** Gita : a biography / Richard H. Davis. Princeton University Press, [2015] x, 243 p. : **294.5**

1. Bhagavadgita History. 2. Hinduism
ISBN 9780691139968

LC 2014023890

An essential biography of a timeless masterpiece, this book is an ideal introduction to the Gita and its insights into the struggle for self-mastery that we all must wage.

"Davis neatly organizes a great deal of material, and he presents it in utterly accessible prose." Choice.

Doniger, Wendy

On Hinduism / Wendy Doniger. Oxford University Press, 2014. 680 p. **294.5**

1. Hinduism. 2. Worship (Hinduism) 3. Religion 4. Polytheism. 5. Essays
ISBN 9780199360079

LC 2013038952

On Hinduism is a penetrating analysis of many of the most crucial and contested issues in Hinduism, from the Vedas to the present day. In a series of 63 connected essays, it discusses Hindu concepts of polytheism, death, gender, art, contemporary puritanism, non-violence, and much more.

"This book assumes some basic knowledge of the subject, but [Doniger's] writing is clear and direct and will be intelligible to readers unacquainted with the technicalities of Hindu doctrine and literature." Library Journal.

Iyengar, B. K. S., 1918-2014

Light on life : the yoga journey to wholeness, inner peace, and ultimate freedom / B.K.S. Iyengar, with John J. Evans and Douglas Abrams. Rodale, c2005. xxii, 282 p. : **294.5**

1. Hatha yoga. 2. Spiritual life.
ISBN 9781594862489

LC 2005015700

Includes index.

A leading yoga instructor demonstrates how practitioners can apply yogic principles to all aspects of daily living for improved mental and physical health, in a guide that features personal stories and explains how yoga can integrate different parts of the self and assist the progression of a spiritual path.

Majmudar, Amit,

★**Godsong** : a verse translation of the Bhagavad Gita, with commentary / Amit Majmudar. Alfred A. Knopf, 2018 210 p. ; **294.5**

1. Religious poetry 2. Epic poetry
ISBN 9781524733476

LC 2017025404

"This is a Borzoi book"

A fresh, strikingly immediate and elegant verse translation of the classic, with an introduction and helpful guides to each section, by the rising American poet. --Provided by publisher

"This is a well-crafted and exceptional translation of a spiritual and cultural masterpiece." Library Journal

Narayan, R. K., 1906-2001

★The **Ramayana** : a shortened modern prose version of the Indian epic (suggested by the Tamil version of Kamban) / R.K. Narayan ; introduction by Pankaj Mishra. Penguin Books, 2006, c1972. xviii, 157 p. ; **294.5**

1. Rama (Hindu deity) 2. Kidnapping 3. Courtship
ISBN 9780143039679

LC 2006045201

A sweeping tale of abduction, battle, and courtship played out in a universe of deities and demons.

Sengupta, Hindol

Being Hindu : understanding a peaceful path in a violent world / Hindol Sengupta. Rowman & Littlefield, 2017, c2015 ix, 189

p. ; **294.5**
1. Hinduism 2. Hindus 3. Religion
ISBN 9781442267459

LC 2017023126

Originally published: Haryana, India : Penguin Books, 2015.

Told from the frank and refreshing perspective of a practicing Hindu, this book analyses the importance of Hinduism as the secular, plural middle path in the battle between Islam and Christianity that is playing out across the globe. Being Hindu presents a faith of peace, liberation, and understanding in an increasingly violent world.

"Sengupta's enlightening elucidation is invaluable for understanding Hinduism, India, and the growing Hindu community in the U.S." Booklist.

294.509 History, geographic treatment, biography

Goldberg, Philip, 1944-

American Veda : from Emerson and the Beatles to yoga and meditation : how Indian spirituality changed the West / Philip Goldberg. Harmony Books, c2010. xv, 398 p., 8 p. of plates : **294.509**
1. Hinduism -- United States -- History. 2. Vedanta -- History. 3. Yoga -- History. 4. United States -- Religion.
ISBN 9780385521345

LC 2010011040

Traces the history and influence of Indian spirituality in the United States while explaining how Hinduism and Vedic tradition have shaped American practices, ranging from prayer and pop culture to relationships and meditation.

"From meditating movie stars, scandalous gurus, and psychedelic drugs to genuine spiritual breakthroughs and devotion to helping others, Goldberg's history of American Veda takes measure of a powerful, if underappreciated, force." Booklist.

294.592 Sacred books and scriptures

DK Publishing, Inc,

The **illustrated** Mahabharata : a definitive guide to India's greatest epic DK Publishing, 2017. 509 p. : **294.592**
1. Mahbhrata Criticism, interpretation, etc. 2. Mahbhrata Pictorial works. 3. Mythology, Indic -- Pictorial works. 4. Folklore -- India -- Pictorial works.
ISBN 9781465462916

LC bl2017030780

Includes index.

Presents an illustrated guide to India's greatest epic, including discussions of all eighteen chapters, the Bhagavad Gita, and the Harivamsa.

296 Judaism

Berlin, Adele

★The **Oxford** dictionary of the Jewish religion / editor in chief, Adele Berlin. Oxford University Press, c2011. xxiv, 934 p. ; **296**
1. Judaism -- Dictionaries 2. Encyclopedias 3. Dictionaries
ISBN 9780199730049

LC 2010035774

Under the editorship of Adele Berlin, nearly 200 internationally renowned scholars have created a new edition that incorporates updated bibliographies, biographies of 20th-century individuals who have shaped the recent thought and history of Judaism, and an index with alternate spellings of Hebrew terms. Entries from the previous edition have been be revised, new entries commissioned, and cross-references added, all to increase ease of navigation research. --Provided by publisher

Bronfman, Edgar M., 1929-

Why be Jewish? : a testament / Edgar M. Bronfman. Twelve, 2016. 256 p. **296**
1. Judaism -- Essence, genius, nature. 2. Jewish way of life. 3. Jews -- Identity.
ISBN 9781455562893

LC 2015039135

A former CEO of the Seagram Company and a renowned philanthropist offers a passionate testimonial to his own personal Jewish journey and the story of the Jewish people.

"Excellent for nontheistic and unaffiliated readers, Jewish or not, who want to better understand this religion." Library Journal.

Davies, W. D. (William David), 1911-

The **Cambridge** history of Judaism. edited by William Horbury, W.D. Davies, John Sturdy. Cambridge University Press, 2000. 1346 p. ; **296**
1. Judaism -- History.
ISBN 9780521243773

LC 77085704

Includes index.

This third volume of The Cambridge History of Judaism focuses on the early Roman period. --Provided by publisher

Freedman, Samuel G.

Jew vs. Jew : the struggle for the soul of American Jewry / Samuel G. Freedman. Simon & Schuster, 2000. 397 p. **296**
1. Judaism -- United States. 2. Judaism -- History -- 20th century. 3. Jewish Americans -- Social conditions. 4. Orthodox Judaism. 5. United States -- Interethnic relations.
ISBN 0684859440

LC 00033907

"The author describes the paradoxical situation faced by today's American Jews, living in a country where religious freedom has yielded unreconcilable devisiveness. This is a helpful guide for anyone seeking an understanding of intra-Jewish conflicts in contemporary America." Library Journal.

Sarna, Jonathan D.

★**American** Judaism : a history / Jonathan D. Sarna. Yale University Press, c2004. xx, 490 p. : **296**
1. Judaism -- United States -- History. 2. Jewish Americans -- History. 3. Religion. 4. United States -- Interethnic relations.
ISBN 030010197X

LC 2003014464

"This comprehensive and insightful study of the American Jewish experience is much more than just a record of events. It is an account of how people shaped events: establishing and maintaining communities, responding to challenges, and working for change. It is compelling reading for Jews and non-Jews alike." Booklist.

Terry, Michael, 1957-

Reader's guide to Judaism / editor, Michael Terry. Fitzroy

Dearborn, 2000. xxv, 718 p. ; **296**
1. Judaism -- Encyclopedias.
ISBN 9781579581398
LC 2001274119

"An oversize volume with double-column pages, this massive work covers over 400 topics, including interfaith relations, historical periods, philosophical and mystical movements, important figures, and more. Preceding each essay is a bibliography of five to ten English-language titles, though bigger topics may have more; these titles are mainly books, though articles are also included." Library Journal

Wigoder, Geoffrey, 1922-
★The **new** encyclopedia of Judaism / editor-in-chief, Geoffrey Wigoder ; coeditors, Fred Skolnik and Shmuel Himelstein. New York University Press, c2002. xv, 856 p. : **296**
1. Judaism -- Dictionaries.
ISBN 9780814793886
LC 2002016614

Updated ed. of: The encyclopedia of Judaism.

An updated edition of the classic reference work adds nearly 250 new entries, with contributors from Israel, England, and the United States representing current thinking in the Reform, Conservative, and Orthodox movements.

296.09 History, geographic treatment, biography

Goodman, Martin, 1953-
★A **history** of Judaism : from its origins to the present / Martin Goodman. Princeton University Press, 2018. xxix, 623 pages : **296.09**
1. Judaism -- History 2. Religion -- History 3. Judaic doctrines.
ISBN 9780691181271
LC 2017957814

A spellbinding chronicle of a vibrant and multifaceted religious tradition that has shaped the spiritual heritage of humankind like no other.

"While dense and detailed, this volume is ideal for anyone looking for a comprehensive history of Judaism. Even experts will find something new to consider." Library Journal.

Hoffman, Adina
★**Sacred** trash : the lost and found world of the Cairo Geniza / Adina Hoffman and Peter Cole. Schocken, c2010. 288 p. **296.09**
1. Judaism -- History -- Medieval and early modern period -- 425-1789. 2. Jews -- History -- 70-1789. 3. Manuscripts. 4. Intellectual life.
ISBN 9780805242584
LC 2010016751

Sophie Brody Medal, 2012.

Traces the efforts of two women scholars who in 1896 traveled throughout multiple countries to recover what has become the most vital cache of Hebrew manuscripts ever discovered, in an account that profiles key contributors and explains what the findings reveal about Mediterranean Judaism throughout the past millennium.

"An accessible, neatly narrated story of hallowed detritus and the resurrection of nearly 1,000 years of culture and learning." Kirkus.

296.0973 Judaism--United States

Weisman, Steven R.
The **chosen** wars : how Judaism became an American religion / Steven R. Weisman. Simon & Schuster, 2018. 368 p. **296.0973**
1. Judaism -- United States 2. Religion and culture -- United States -- History 3. Jewish Americans 4. Social history 5. United States -- Religion
ISBN 9781416573265
LC 2017058478

The award-winning author traces the redefinition of Judaism throughout the 18th and 19th centuries, citing the roles of key contributors and the dynamic influence of western culture.

296.1 Sources

Freedman, H. (Harry)
The **Talmud** : a biography : banned, censored and burned, the book they couldn't suppress / Harry Freedman. Bloomsbury, 2014. x, 243 p. ; **296.1**
1. Talmud History. 2. Judaism -- Study and teaching. 3. Judaic doctrines. 4. Judaic law -- Sources. 5. Tradition (Judaism)
ISBN 9781472905949
LC bl2014033550

Discusses the history of the Talmud, tracing its path from a record of discussions among scholars in towns and villages close to modern-day Baghdad, its role during the Enlightenment, and its influence over traditional Judaism.

"Freedman (independent scholar) makes clear that this is no academic volume; his goal is to make the Talmud's story interesting and perhaps even inspiring to the unacquainted reader." Choice.

Schiffman, Lawrence H.
Reclaiming the Dead Sea scrolls : the history of Judaism, the background of Christianity, the lost library of Qumran / Lawrence H. Schiffman ; with a foreword by Chaim Potok. Doubleday, 1995. xxvii, 529 p. : The Anchor Bible reference library **296.1**
1. Dead Sea scrolls 2. Qumran community.
ISBN 0385481217
LC 95017280

Previously published: 1st ed. Philadelphia : Jewish Publication Society, 1994.

"Schiffman provides a description and evaluation of the scrolls, the archeology of Qumran (the site near the Dead Sea from which the scrolls originated), the history and nature of the Jewish community that lived at Qumran and the setting of the scrolls in Jewish history and thought from the second century B.C. through the first century A.D." New York Times Book Review.

296.3 Theology, ethics, views of social issues

Epstein, Lawrence J. (Lawrence Jeffrey)
The **basic** beliefs of Judaism : a twenty-first-century guide to a timeless tradition / Lawrence J. Epstein. Jason Aronson, 2013 xxii, 201 p. ; **296.3**
1. Jewish way of life. 2. Judaism.
ISBN 0765709694
LC 2013015985

One of the oldest monotheistic religions known to humankind, Judaism has withstood the tests of time. So what exactly are the tenets of this ancient faith that have been passed down over the millennia, and how do they apply to our lives in the 21st century? The Basic Beliefs of Judaism gives an updated overview of the belief system on which the Jewish faith is based. --Provided by publisher

Kugel, James L.
The **great** shift : encountering God in Biblical times / James L. Kugel. Houghton Mifflin Harcourt, 2017. xvi, 476 pages ; **296.3**
1. Bible Criticism and interpretation 2. Belief and doubt 3. Religion 4. Religion and culture 5. Theology.
ISBN 9780544520554
LC 2017019809

One of the world's leading Bible scholars summarizes a career of study to ask the biggest questions: how has the nature of God changed over time? What are the origins of belief and religion? Why is the modern West so unusual in its worldview?

"Biblical exegesis at its best: a brilliant and sensitive reading of ancient texts, all with an eye to making them meaningful to our time by making sense of what they meant in their own." Kirkus.

Kushner, Harold S.
★**When** bad things happen to good people / Harold S. Kushner. Schocken Books, 2001, c1981. vii, 202 p. ; **296.3**
1. Providence and government of God (Judaism) 2. Theodicy. 3. Suffering. 4. Pastoral counseling (Judaism)
ISBN 9780805241938
LC 81040411

A twentieth anniversary edition of the classic self-help guide by the respected rabbi explains how to find comfort and strength in the face of tragedy and the challenges of life and how to understand God's role in recovery.

"A bright and happy infant, Rabbi Kushner's first-born son gradually succumbed to progeria, 'rapid aging': he never grew beyond three feet tall, looked like a hairless, wizened old man, and died in his teens. This book is his father's attempt to make sense out of his son's fate, his own pain, and the pain of others enduring undeserved misfortunes." Library Journal.

Telushkin, Joseph, 1948-
Jewish wisdom : ethical, spiritual, and historical lessons from the great works and thinkers / Rabbi Joseph Telushkin. W. Morrow, c1994. xxiv, 663 p. ; **296.3**
1. Jewish ethics. 2. Jews -- Quotations. 3. Judaism -- Essence, genius, nature. 4. Judaism -- Quotations, Maxims, etc.
ISBN 0688129587
LC 94009186

A companion volume to Jewish Literacy sets texts from chosen Jewish passages, ranging from the Talmud to modern writings, in a historical perspective while explaining why they are vital and challenging to contemporary Jews.

"Organized by subject, this is a collection of teachings and quotations from the Talmud, the Bible, rabbinical commentaries, and ancient and modern religious and secular writings. Writers include Elie Wiesel, Isaac Bashevis Singer, Hebrew poet Hayim Bialik, Cynthia Ozick, Emile Zola, Albert Einstein, Bruno Bettelheim, Gertrude Stein, Irving Howe, and Maimonides. Jewsand even non-Jews will find the book a treasure." Booklist.

296.4 Traditions, rites, public services

Ashton, Dianne
Hanukkah in America : a history / Dianne Ashton. New York University Press, 2013. 368 p. **296.4**
1. Hanukkah. 2. Judaism. 3. Jewish Americans
ISBN 9780814707395
LC 2013014009

Provides a comprehensive history of the Jewish holiday, from its roots in ancient history through its rise to prominence in the United States.

Axelrod, Matt, 1966-
Your guide to the Jewish holidays : from shofar to Seder / cantor Matt Axelrod. Jason Aronson, 2014 203 p. ; **296.4**
1. Fasts and feasts -- Judaism.
ISBN 0765709899
LC 2013033886

Includes index.

Presents a light-hearted look at eleven of the most important Jewish holidays, including Yom Kippur, Purim, and Passover, describing each holiday's rituals in a historical context.

Bolsta, Hyla Shifra
The **illuminated** Kaddish : interpretations of the Mourner's Prayer / paintings, calligraphy, and interpretations by Hyla Shifra Bolsta. KTAV Pub. House, Inc., c2012. 108 p. : **296.4**
1. Kaddish 2. Judaism -- Prayers and devotions. 3. Judaism -- Rites and ceremonies
ISBN 9781602801912
LC 2011033483

"The kaddish is the Jewish prayer of mourning, though the word death is never mentioned. In fact, the prayer is a sanctification of God's name, spoken even (or especially) in the midst of grief. This compelling illustrated volume looks at the kaddish from many different angles." Booklist

Diamant, Anita
The **Jewish** wedding now / Anita Diamant. Scribner, 2017. xxi, 224 p. : **296.4**
1. Jewish marriage customs and rites. 2. Weddings -- Planning.
ISBN 9781501153945
LC bl2017051420

Presents suggestions for ceremonies and celebrations that are true to contemporary values as well as time-honored Jewish customs.

Goldman, Ari L., 1949-
Being Jewish : the spiritual and cultural practice of Judaism today / Ari L. Goldman. Simon & Schuster, c2000. 286 p. : **296.4**
1. Judaism -- Rites and ceremonies 2. Religious holidays. 3. Jewish way of life.
ISBN 0684823896
LC 00044047

Discussing the practice of Judaism from both a contemporary and a historical perspective, an exploration of the nature of Judaism, its spiritual heritage, and its rituals offers a non-ideological framework for its viewpoint.

"An excellent resource." Booklist.

Shulevitz, Judith, 1963-
The **Sabbath** world : glimpses of a different order of time

/ Judith Shulevitz. Random House, 2010. 352 p. **296.4**

1. Shulevitz, Judith, 1963- 2. Sabbath. 3. Sunday. 4. Rest -- Religious aspects -- Judaism. 5. Time -- Religious aspects -- Judaism.
ISBN 9781400062003
LC 2009026417

Sophie Brody Medal, 2011.

Questions the origin, meaning and cultural importance of keeping one day a week holy through an exploration of ritual, religious law and the communitarian way of life in our modern, workaholic, increasingly secular world.

"In personal terms, and without sanctimony, [the author] explores the history of the Sabbath, its philosophical foundations, its consolations, its purposes, and, in doing so, writes a swift, penetrating book intent on shattering the habits of mindless workaholism and the inability to recognize the blessings of rest, reflection, spirit, and family." The New Yorker.

Wagner, Jordan Lee

The **synagogue** survival kit : A Guide to Understanding Jewish Religious Services / Jordan Lee Wagner. Rowman & Liittlefield Publishers, Inc., 2013. xviii, 347 p. : **296.4**

1. Siddur. 2. Judaism -- Customs and practices. 3. Judaism -- Liturgy. 4. Prayer -- Judaism. 5. Synagogue etiquette.
ISBN 0765709686
LC bl2014000876

"A guide to understanding Jewish religious services"--Cover.

"A Jason Aronson book."

Includes index.

Explains synagogue services, etiquette, and the prayer cycle, including Orthodox, Conservative, Reform, and Reconstructionist traditions.

"Extensive notes follow each chapter, and a cross-reference to selections in the most commonly used prayer books fleshes out this carefully crafted primer, which is perfect for Jews rediscovering their own traditions, Jews by choice and others who wish to participate in Jewish events." Publishers Weekly.

Wieseltier, Leon

Kaddish / Leon Wieseltier. Knopf, 1998. xi, 588 p. **296.4**

1. Wieseltier, Leon Religion. 2. Kaddish. 3. Judaism -- Rites and ceremonies. 4. Jewish mourning customs. 5. Fathers -- Death.
ISBN 0375403892
LC 98015881

"When his father died in 1996 . Wieseltier began to observe the Jewish rituals of the traditional year of mourning. His own mourning led him to an in-depth study of the history and meaning of Kaddish in Judaism. Wieseltier provides a work of history, philosophy and spiritual memoir that demonstrates how the practice of religion meets the needs of a troubled soul." Publishers Weekly.

296.7 Religious experience, life, practice

Isaacs, Ronald H.

★**Kosher** living : it's more than just the food / Ron Isaacs. Jossey-Bass, c2005. xlvii, 286 p. ; **296.7**

1. Jewish ethics 2. Jewish law 3. Jewish way of life 4. Judaism -- Customs and practices
ISBN 0787976423
LC 2004026727

"An Arthur Kurzweil book."

"The book not only covers the expected Jewish topics circumcision, marriage, prayer, Shabbat, synagogue behavior and morebut also intriguing items of general interest such as employer-employee relations, shopping and even war. This resource offers timeless wisdom through a contemporary lens." Publishers Weekly.

Kushner, Harold S.

How good do we have to be? : a new understanding of guilt and forgiveness / Harold S. Kushner. Little, Brown & Co., 1996. ix, 181 p. ; **296.7**

1. Bible. Genesis I-IV Criticism and interpretation 2. Good and evil. 3. Eden. 4. Self-esteem -- Religious aspects. 5. Perfection -- Religious aspects.
ISBN 9780316507417
LC 95025350

Drawing on the Bible, modern literature, psychology, theology, and his own thirty years as a congregational rabbi, Harold Kushner reveals why we should not fear the loss of God's love when we make mistakes and shows how acceptance and forgiveness can enhance our lives.

"This is one psychological self-help book that deserves the popularity it is likely to achieve." Booklist.

Kushner, Harold S.

Who needs God / Harold Kushner. Summit Books, 1989. 208 p. ; **296.7**

1. God (Judaism) -- Worship and love 2. God -- Worship and love 3. Jewish way of life. 4. Spiritual life.
ISBN 0671680269
LC 89035140

The author calls for a return to religious commitment in people's lives in order to fulfill a need for connection, joy, and community, and explains what religion can offer.

Levy, Naomi

To begin again : the journey toward comfort, strength, and faith in difficult times / Naomi Levy. Ballantine Books, 1999, c1998. xii, 267 p. ; **296.7**

1. Levy, Naomi. 2. Bereavement -- Religious aspects -- Judaism. 3. Consolation (Judaism) 4. Jewish way of life.
ISBN 0345413830
LC BL 99014171

Originally published: New York : Alfred A. Knopf, 1998.

A woman who lost her father to a violent crime when she was just fifteen years old describes the process of spiritual healing from suffering, the secret to rekindling hope and regaining faith in face of difficult times.

"A wise and practical guide for readers of any religious persuasion." Library Journal.

Reuben, Steven Carr

★**Becoming** Jewish : the challenges, rewards, and paths to conversion / Steven Carr Reuben and Jennifer S. Hanin. Rowman & Littlefield, c2011. xvi, 256 p. ; **296.7**

1. Conversion to Judaism 2. Converts to Judaism
ISBN 9781442208483
LC 2011014083

Includes index.

"Converting to Judaism is a long, involved process. This guide by a Reconstructionist rabbi and a freelance writer who converted is a welcome resource. The authors explain such details as finding the right denomination, choosing a rabbi, selecting a Hebrew name, and the need to learn Hebrew." Booklist

297 Islam, Babism, Bahai Faith

Abdul-Ghafur, Saleemah,

Living Islam out loud : American Muslim women speak / edited by Saleemah Abdul-Ghafur. Beacon Press, 2005. 209 p. ; **297**

1. Muslim women -- United States 2. Muslim women -- Religious life -- United States. 3. Islam and women. 4. Essays.
ISBN 0807083836

LC 2004028161

The first collection of writing from American Muslim women under the age of forty includes essays on a wide variety of topics, including the hijab, sex, activism, spirituality, relationships, and much more.

"Although the contributions are uneven, this anthology opens the door for other writers to explore the important and understudied topic of Muslim American women." Publishers Weekly.

Abdul Rauf, Feisal, 1948-

Moving the mountain : beyond ground zero to a new vision of Islam in America / Feisal Abdul Rauf. Free Press, c2012. 240 p. **297**

1. Religion and culture -- United States 2. Islam -- United States. 3. Muslims -- United States. 4. Interfaith relations 5. United States -- Religion.
ISBN 9781451656008

LC 2011050797

The Muslim leader best known for his contributions to the establishment of an interfaith community center near Manhattan's Ground Zero offers insight into his progressive beliefs, ambassador service and advocacy of tolerance and equal rights.

Armstrong, Karen, 1944-

★**Islam** : a short history / Karen Armstrong. Modern Library, 2000. xxxiv, 222 p. : **297**

1. Islam -- History. 2. Muslims. 3. Religion -- History. 4. Monotheism. 5. Islamic Empire -- History.
ISBN 0679640401

LC 00025285

A concise summation of years of thinking and writing about the world's fastest growing religion, by one of the foremost international scholars on religious affairs.

"The author does an admirable job of presenting Islamic history from an objective, unbiased point of view." Library Journal.

Aslan, Reza

★**No** god but God : the origins, evolution, and future of Islam / Reza Aslan. Random House, 2005. xxxii, 310 p. ; **297**

1. Islam. 2. Islam -- Customs and practices. 3. Islam -- History.
ISBN 9781400062133

LC 2006272556

Originally published: New York : Random House, 2005. With new introd. by the author.

An authoritative study of the Islamic faith in relation to the other world religions sheds new light on its origins and history, from the social reformation role of Muhammad to the impact of fundamentalism and terrorism on Islam.

"Beginning with an exploration of the religious climate in the years before the Prophet's Revelation, Aslan traces the story of Islam from the Prophet's life and the so-called golden age of the first four caliphs all the way through European colonization and subsequent independence. This is an excellent overview that doubles as an impassioned call to reform." Booklist.

Barrett, Paul (Paul M.)

American Islam : the struggle for the soul of a religion / Paul M. Barrett. Farrar, Straus and Giroux, 2007. 304 p. ; **297**

1. Muslims -- United States. 2. Islam -- United States. 3. Muslims -- United States -- Social conditions. 4. Muslim families -- United States. 5. United States -- Interethnic relations.
ISBN 0374104239

LC 2006011404

An intricate mixture of ideologies and cultures, American Muslims include immigrants and native born, black and white converts, those who are well integrated into the larger society and those who are alienated and extreme in their political views. Even as many American Muslims succeed in material terms and enrich our society, Islam is enmeshed in controversy in the United States, as thousands of American Muslims have been investigated and interrogated in the wake of 9/11. -- From publisher description.

"The heated debates among Muslims themselves about violence committed under the banner of Islam are often drowned out in the fray. Paul M. Barrett's... engaging book brings some of those voices in the United States to life." New York Times.

Dardess, George

Meeting Islam : a guide for Christians / George Dardess. Paraclete Press, c2005. xiv, 242 p. ; **297**

1. Christianity and other religions -- Islam. 2. Islam -- Doctrines. 3. Islam -- Relations -- Christianity.
ISBN 1557254338

LC 2005013504

Islam's key facts, chief concepts, and practices are shared through the author's own failings and successes in a guide that explores the rewards and dangers of venturing outside the boundaries of one's faith.

Ende, Werner, 1937-

★**Islam** in the world today : a handbook of politics, religion, culture, and society / edited by Werner Ende and Udo Steinbach. Cornell University Press, 2010. xviii, 1114 p. : **297**

1. Islam -- 20th century 2. Islam -- 21st century 3. Islam -- History 4. Islam and state
ISBN 9780801445712

LC 2009039910

Provides authoritative information on the religious, political, social, and cultural life of Islamic nations and of Islamic communities, detailing the history of Islam, Islam in diaspora, and women in Islam.

Esposito, John L.

What everyone needs to know about Islam / John L. Esposito. Oxford University Press, 2002. xviii, 204 p. ; **297**

1. Islam -- Essence, genius, nature. 2. Religions. 3. Muslims. 4. Religion.
ISBN 9780195157130

LC 2002008387

Uses a question and answer format to present information on topics including faith and practice, Islam and other religions, customs and culture, and Muslims in the West.

"In question-and-answer format the author presents information on a variety of aspects of Islam... In his answers, which are anywhere from a paragraph to several pages long, Esposito elegantly educates the reader through what the Qur'an says, how Muslims are influenced by their local cultures, and how the unique politics of Islamic countries affects Muslims' views." Publishers Weekly.

Grieve, Paul

★A **brief** guide to Islam : history, faith and politics : the complete introduction / Paul Grieve. Carroll and Graf Publishers, 2006. ix, 433 p. : **297**

1. Islam -- 21st century. 2. Christianity -- Relations -- Islam. 3. Judaism -- Relations -- Islam. 4. Islam -- History.

ISBN 9780786718047

LC 2006282191

Includes index.

Originally published: London : Robinson, 2006.

Looks at the similarities and differences among the three major world religions--Judaism, Christianity, and Islam-- and explores the history of Islam and the foundations of the culture that grew out of the Islamic faith.

Husain, Ed

The **house** of Islam : a global history / Ed Husain. Bloomsbury USA, 2018. 320 p. **297**

1. Qur'an. 2. Islam. 3. Muslims. 4. Ethics. 5. Faith.

ISBN 9781632866394

LC 2018023581

Authoritative and engaging, Ed Husain leads us clearly and carefully through the nuances of Islam and its people, taking us back to basics to contend that the Muslim world need not be a stranger to the West, nor our enemy, but our peaceable allies.

"By explaining the contours of global Islam, Husain ends up making a strong case against Koranic textual literalism that readers of all backgrounds will appreciate." Publishers Weekly.

Jelloun, Tahar ben, 1944-

Islam explained / Tahar Ben Jelloun. New Press, 2002, c2002. 120 p. **297**

1. Muhammad, Prophet, d. 632. 2. Qur'an 3. Islamic doctrines 4. Islamic apologetics. 5. Islam -- History. 6. Questions and answers.

ISBN 9781565847811

LC 2002030500

Includes index.

Originally published in French as Islam explique aux enfants: New York : New Press, 2002.

"Cast in the form of an extended conversation between Ben Jelloun and his young daughter. Father and child discuss the history of Islam, what it means to be a Muslim today, the challenges facing the Islamic world, and terrorism. Its openness and emotional honesty, particularly when discussing the tragedy of 9/11, make it a valuable addition to a growing public discourse. As an introduction to the religion, it is spotty, but as a liberal Muslim voice of reconciliation, heartbreak, and compassion, it is priceless." Booklist.

Kugle, Scott Alan, 1969-

Living out Islam : voices of gay, lesbian, and transgender Muslims / Scott Siraj al-Haqq Kugle. NYU Press, [2014] x, 265 p. ; **297**

1. Homosexuality -- Religious aspects -- Islam. 2. Muslims 3. Gay activists 4. Lesbian activists

ISBN 9780814744482

LC 2013023734

Stonewall Book Awards: Israel Fishman Non-fiction Award, 2015.

"Living Out Islam documents the rarely-heard voices of Muslims who live in secular democratic countries and who are gay, lesbian, and transgender. It weaves original interviews with Muslim activists into a compelling composite picture which showcases the importance of the solidarity of support groups in the effort to change social relationships and achieve justice. This nascent movement is not about being "out" as opposed to being "in the closet." Rather, as the voices of these activists demonstrate, it is about finding ways to live out Islam with dignity and integrity, reconciling their sexuality and gender with their faith and reclaiming Islam as their own."-- Provided by publisher.

Nasr, Seyyed Hossein

Islam : religion, history, and civilization / Seyyed Hossein Nasr. HarperSanFrancisco, 2003. xxv, 198 p. ; **297**

1. Islam -- Essence, genius, nature. 2. Religion and culture. 3. Civilization, Islamic. 4. Islam -- History.

ISBN 9780060507145

LC 2002032810

Explores the doctrines and beliefs of Islam, its practices and institutions, the history of the religion, schools of thought, its place in contemporary society, its relationship to other religions, and its spiritual significance.

"Provides compelling analysis of contemporary Islam and its conflicts without overwhelming the reader with information." Booklist.

Pickthall, Marmaduke William, 1875-1936

★The **meaning** of the glorious Koran / an explanatory translation by Marmaduke Pickthall ; with an introduction by William Montgomery Watt. A.A. Knopf, 1992. xxviii, 693 p., 6 p. of plates : **297**

1. Qur'an

ISBN 0679417362

LC 92052928

While in the service of India's Nizam of Hyderabad, Marmaduke Pickthall converted to Islam and, with the help of Muslim theologians and linguists, produced this clear and lovingly precise English interpretation of the Holy Koran. His work is honored by believer and nonbeliever alike for its unique combination of piety, scholarly rigor in its translation and explanatory notes, and deep feeling for the poetic beauty and moral grandeur of its Arabic original. -- From publisher description

Ramadan, Tariq

Introduction to Islam / Tariq Ramadan. Oxford University Press, 2017. 256 p. **297**

1. Islam 2. Muslims 3. Pillars of Islam 4. Faith (Islam)

ISBN 9780190467487

LC 2017004515

Whether the issue is violence, terrorism, women's rights, or slavery, Muslims today are expected to provide answers and to justify what Islam is-or is not. But little opportunity exists, either in the media or in society as a whole, to describe Islam. In simple, direct language, An Introduction to Islam introduces readers to Islam and to its principles, rituals, diversity, and evolution.

"For non-Muslims, it is an invitation to understand the basics of Islam as well as to dive a bit deeper into its history, theology, and various manifestations over time and across the globe." Publishers Weekly.

Rejwan, Nissim

The **many** faces of Islam : perspectives on a resurgent civilization / Nissim Rejwan [editor]. University Press of Florida, 2000. xii, 282 p. ; **297**

1. Islam -- Appreciation. 2. Islam -- Essence, genius, nature. 3. Islam and world politics. 4. Islam -- 20th century. 5. Islamic countries -- politics and government.

ISBN 9780813018072

LC 00032587

Written in a style easily accessible to both students and general readers, The Many Faces of Islam offers a wide range of perspectives on modern Islamic culture and religious practice. --Provided by publisher

Renard, John, 1944-

The **handy** Islam answer book / John Renard, Ph.D. Visible Ink Press, 2015 xii, 435 p. : **297**

1. Islam
ISBN 9781578595105

LC 2014033780

A comprehensive set of questions and answers regarding Islam includes such topics as history, beliefs, symbols, rituals, art and literature, customs, leadership, traditions, and ethnic diversity.

Smith, Jane I.

Islam in America / Jane I. Smith. Columbia University Press, c1999. xvi, 251 p. : **297**

1. Islam -- United States.
ISBN 0231109660

LC 98031943

"Islam in America outlines the influences of a secular and materialistic Western culture, the keenly felt prejudices on the part of non-Muslims, and the misunderstandings between Muslims that often arise when they try to balance cultural expectations with the value system of the conservative Middle East." Library Journal

Zafar, Harris, 1979-

Demystifying Islam : tackling the tough questions / Harris Zafar. Rowman & Littlefied, 2014. 248 p. **297**

1. Muhammad, Prophet, d. 632. 2. Qur'an 3. Islam 4. Islamic doctrines
ISBN 9781442223271

LC 2014004827

Includes index.

A concise guide to what Islam really teaches about provocative topics, from the burqa to Shariah law.

297.03 Islam--Dictionaries, encyclopedias, concordances

Glasse, Cyril

The **new** encyclopedia of Islam / Cyril Glasse. Rowman & Littlefield, 2013 viii, 736 p. : **297.03**

1. Islam
ISBN 9781442223486

LC bl2013055985

A comprehensive reference work covering the different aspects of Islamic civilization, with maps showing the faith's spread over the centuries, and charts of the different branches of Islam.

"This beautifully illustrated and clearly written book provides a myriad of facts and insights about Islam that many readers--novices and scholars alike--will find informative, interesting, and enlightening." Choice.

297.09 History, geographic treatment, biography

Abou El Fadl, Khaled, 1963-

The **great** theft : wrestling Islam from the extremists / Khaled Abou El Fadl. Harper San Francisco, 2005. viii, 308 p. ; **297.09**

1. Islamic doctrines. 2. Wahhabiyah. 3. Fundamentalism 4. Islam
ISBN 9780060563394

LC 2005283877

A passionate defense of Islam against the influence of fundamentalism defines moderate Islam as a religion that opposes extremism and is based on moral tradition, in a volume that discusses the importance of reconnecting with past beliefs in order to safeguard the faith from radical practices.

"This book is a fulfilling read for moderate Muslims concerned about conservative leadership and any non-Muslims who want to inform themselves about the extremists' misuse of Islam." Publishers Weekly.

Fuller, Graham E., 1939-

A **world** without Islam / Graham E. Fuller. Little Brown & Co., 2010. 352 p. **297.09**

1. Islam and politics. 2. Religion and politics. 3. Geopolitics. 4. Ethnic groups. 5. Middle East.
ISBN 9780316041195

LC 2009054078

"A cogent argument demonstrating that a knowledgeable awareness of the rich dynamics that drive societies will better help diffuse tensions." Kirkus.

Ghobash, Omar Saif, 1971-

Letters to a young Muslim / Omar Saif Ghobash. Picador, 2017. 272 p. **297.09**

1. Ghobash, Omar Saif, 1971- 2. Islam -- 21st century 3. Advice 4. Muslim youth 5. Fundamentalism 6. Letters
ISBN 9781250119841

LC 2016039168

In a series of personal letters to his sons, Omar Saif Ghobash offers a short and highly readable manifesto that tackles our current global crisis with the training of an experienced diplomat and the personal responsibility of a father.

"He urges them to pursue a middle path that is simultaneously true to Islam and yet effectively and energetically engaged in the modern world. This is a fantastic book for Muslims and non-Muslims alike." Publishers Weekly.

Kennedy, Hugh (Hugh N.)

★The **great** Arab conquests : how the spread of Islam changed the world we live in / Hugh Kennedy. Da Capo Press, 2007. viii, 421 p. : **297.09**

1. Conquerors. 2. Islam -- History. 3. Conversion to Islam. 4. Religion and culture. 5. Islamic Empire -- History. 6. Middle East -- History.
ISBN 0306815850

LC bl2007021158

Originally published: London : Weidenfeld & Nicolson, 2007.

Examines the history of the great Islamic expansion, reveals how the Arab armies were able to overcome almost everything in their path, and brings to light the unique characteristics of Islamic settlement in new lands and the conversion to Islam of vast populations.

"The author has produced an extremely readable work chronicling the early Arab conquests to 750 CE. In the flowing narrative style for which he has become known, Kennedy brings together Arab, Byzantine, Armenian, Coptic, and Persian histories, legends, and anecdotes related to Arab expansion into the lands stretching from the Iberian Peninsula to the Sind. Each chapter details the conquest of a given region, intertwining historic reality with legendary tales to provide for very colorful reading." Choice.

297.092 Biography

Ali, Wajahat,

All-American : 45 American men on being Muslim / co-editors Wajahat M. Ali and Zahra T. Suratwala ; foreword by Congressman Keith Ellison. White Cloud Press, 2012. 256 p. **297.092**

1. Muslim men. 2. Muslim-American men. 3. Muslims. 4. Islam. 5. Essays.

ISBN 9781935952596

LC 2012014744

Collects essays by American Muslim men, examining their lives and how their beliefs impact others inside and outside of the Muslim community.

297.1 Sources of Islam

Cook, M. A.

The **Koran** : a very short introduction / Michael Cook. Oxford University Press, 2000. 162 p. : **297.1**

1. Qur'an Criticism and interpretation 2. Islam. 3. Islamic literature.

ISBN 0192853449

LC 99057686

The Koran has constituted a remarkably resilient core of identity and continuity for a religious tradition that is now in its fifteenth century. In this Very Short Introduction, Michael Cook provides a lucid and direct account of the significance of the Koran both in the modern world and in that of traditional Islam. He gives vivid accounts of its role in Muslim civilization, illustrates the diversity of interpretations championed by traditional and modern commentators, discusses the processes by which the book took shape, and compares it to other scriptures and classics of the historic cultures of Eurasia. --Provided by publisher

Haleem, M. A. S. Abdel

The **Qur'an** : English translation and parallel Arabic text / translated with an introduction and notes by M.A.S. Abdel Haleem. Oxford University Press, 2010. xxxix, 624 p. : **297.1**

1. Qur'an.

ISBN 019957071X

LC 2010281328

"Approved by Al-Azhar"--P. [4] of cover.

Edition statement from front jacket flap.

Prev. ed. published in 2004.

One of the most influential books in the history of literature, recognized as the greatest literary masterpiece in Arabic, the Qur'an is the supreme authority and living source of all Islamic teaching, the sacred text that sets out the creed, rituals, ethics, and laws of Islam. First published in 2004, M. A. S. Abdel Haleem's superb English translation has been acclaimed for both its faithfulness to the original and its supreme clarity. Now Haleem's translation is published side-by-side with the original Arabic text, to give readers a greater appreciation and understanding of the holy book. --Provided by publisher

Mattson, Ingrid

★The **story** of the Qur'an : its history and place in Muslim life / Ingrid Mattson. Wiley-Blackwell, 2013. xiii, 298 p. : **297.1**

1. Qur'an 2. Islamic values 3. Islamic doctrines 4. Muslims. 5. Islamic law

ISBN 9780470673492

LC 2012042779

"An excellent companion resource for study and understanding of the Qur'an." Library Journal.

Wagner, Walter H., 1935-

Opening the Qur'an : introducing Islam's holy book / Walter H. Wagner. University of Notre Dame Press, c2008. xix, 547 p. ; **297.1**

1. Qur'an Criticism, interpretation, etc. 2. Qur'an Hermeneutics. 3. Qur'an History. 4. Qur'an Reading.

ISBN 0268044155

LC 2008027221

"This work, premised on the conviction that understanding the Qur'an is the key to understanding Islam, insists on the importance of approaching the Qur'an in an open, critically informed manner, yet one that is sensitive to Muslim perspectives." Choice

Wills, Garry, 1934-

What the Qur'an meant and why it matters : And Why It Matters / Garry Wills. Viking, 2017. 240 p. **297.1**

1. Qur'an Criticism, interpretation, etc. 2. Islamic doctrines. 3. Islam 4. Islam and women 5. Islam and politics

ISBN 9781101981023

LC 2017025389

Includes index.

A Pulitzer Prize-winning historian and religious scholar redirects his lifelong focus on Christianity and takes open-minded look at the Qur'an, finding the original meaning of the sacred text and showing numerous parallels between it and the Old and New Testaments.

297.2 Islamic doctrinal theology Islam and secular disciplines Islam and other

Akyol, Mustafa, 1972-

The **Islamic** Jesus : how the king of the Jews became a prophet of the Muslims / Mustafa Akyol. St. Martins Press, 2017. 256 p. **297.2**

1. Jesus Christ Islamic interpretations. 2. Interfaith relations. 3. Prophets. 4. Religions. 5. Faith.

ISBN 9781250088697

LC 2016038747

An exploration of the connection between Christianity and Islam through the lost "heresy" of Jewish Christianity reveals new truths about Islam in the context of the first Muslims and the early origins of Christianity, explaining how key differences in early beliefs diverged and evolved.

"A fascinating bridge text between Islam and Christianity." Kirkus.

Al-Hassani, Salim T. S.,

1001 inventions : the enduring legacy of Muslim civilization / Salim T. S. Al-Hassani, chief editor. National Geographic, c2012, c2007. 352 p. : **297.2**

1. Islam and science. 2. Inventions -- History. 3. Technological innovations. 4. Muslims.

ISBN 9781426209345

LC 2011294410

Previously published as 1001 Inventions: Muslim heritage in our World in Manchester, Great Britain : Foundation for Science Technology and Civilisation, 2007.

Shows one thousand scientific and technological inventions with Islamic roots that are still being used in the world today.

Bhutto, Benazir, 1953-2007

★**Reconciliation** : Islam, democracy, and the West / Benazir Bhutto. Harper Collins, 2008 viii, 328 p. ; **297.2**

1. Bhutto, Benazir, 1953-2007 2. Women prime ministers -- Pakistan 3. Islam -- Middle East 4. International relations 5. Islam and politics -- Pakistan 6. United States -- Foreign relations Pakistan 7. Pakistan -- Foreign relations United States 8. Pakistan -- Politics and government -- 1988- 9. Pakistan -- Religious life and customs -- 21st century 10. United States -- Politics and government -- 21st century 11. United States -- Politics and government -- 21st century 12. Asia -- Politics and government -- 21st century

ISBN 0061567582

LC 2008273737

A former prime minister of Pakistan offers a provocative assessment of the growing tensions between Islam and the western world, in an account that shares historical information that traces the roots of international terrorism to American support for former dictator Zia ul Haq and reveals how democracy and Islam can be compatible.

"This is a book of enormous intelligence, courage and clarity. Washington should arrange to have the portions of the book about Islam republished as a separate volume and translated into several languages. It would do more to win the battle of ideas within Islam than anything an American president could ever say." New York Times Book Review.

Griswold, Eliza, 1973-

The **tenth** parallel : dispatches from the fault line between Christianity and Islam / Eliza Griswold. Farrar, Straus and Giroux, 2010. xi, 317 p. : **297.2**

1. Islam -- Relations -- Christianity. 2. Christianity -- Relations -- Islam. 3. Religion -- Social aspects 4. Faith

ISBN 9780374273187

LC 2010001480

J. Anthony Lukas Book Prize, 2011.

Uses stories about the region where Islam and Christianity collide to examine the complex relationships of religion, land, and oil, among other resources; local conflicts and global ideology; and politics and contemporary martyrdom, both Islamic and Christian.

"This is a beautifully written book, full of arresting stories woven around a provocative issuewhether fundamentalism leads to violence-which Griswold investigates through individual lives rather than caricatures or abstractions." New York Times Book Review.

Harris, Sam, 1967-

Islam and the future of tolerance : a dialogue / Sam Harris, Maajid Nawaz. Harvard University Press, 2015 120 p. **297.2**

1. Toleration -- Religious aspects -- Islam 2. Dialogue -- Religious aspects 3. Islam 4. Extremism

ISBN 9780674088702

LC 2015009535

A famous atheist and a former radical discuss the nature of Islam as it relates to tolerance, including such topics as why so many Muslims are drawn to extremism and if reformation of the religion is possible.

Miles, Jack, 1942-

God in the Qur'an / Jack Miles. Alfred A. Knopf, 2018. 256 p. **297.2**

1. Qur'an 2. Bible 3. God (Islam) 4. Islam 5. Religions 6. Comparisons

ISBN 9780307269577

LC 2018005105

Who is Allah? What makes Him unique? And what does He ask of those who submit to His teachings? In the spirit of his Pulitzer Prize-winning God, a trailblazing "biography" of the protagonist of the Old Testament, and Christ, his brilliant portrait of biblical Jesus, acclaimed religious scholar Jack Miles undertakes to answer these questions with his characteristic perspicacity, intelligence, and command of the subject.

"Readers will discover that writings in the Qur'an have less literary complexity but consistently show God (Allah) as full of forgiveness and compassion. Miles concludes by urging Christians to rethink their ideas about Islam and to respond with charity and tolerance." Library Journal.

297.272 Islam and politics

Hirsi Ali, Ayaan, 1969-

Heretic: why Islam needs a reformation now / Ayaan Hiris Ali. HarperCollins, 2015. 256 p. **297.272**

1. Islam 2. Muslim women's rights. 3. Religion and culture. 4. Religious minorities -- Legal status, laws, etc. -- Islamic countries. 5. Islamic countries -- Social conditions. 6. Middle East -- Religion -- 21st century

ISBN 9780062333933

LC 2015385062

An impassioned plea for an Islamic Reformation by the award-winning author of Infidel explores how Islam can be reconciled with modernity to end terrorism, sectarian warfare and the repression of women and minorities.

"This an urgent, complicated, risky subject, and Hirsi Ali, valiant, indomitable, and controversial, offers a potent indictment, idealistic blueprint, and galvanizing appeal to both conscience and reason." Booklist.

297.3 Islamic worship

Morrow, John A. (John Andrew), 1971-

Islamic images and ideas : essays on sacred symbolism / edited by John Andrew Morrow. McFarland & Company, 2014 x, 277 p. **297.3**

1. Islam. 2. Islamic art and symbolism. 3. Symbolism.

ISBN 9780786458486

LC oc2014086432

"These 24 studies on specific symbols, images and icons from the Muslim tradition authored by scholars from around the world. Divided into four sections, the Divine, the Spiritual, the Physical, and the Societal".-- Provided by publisher.

297.4 Sufism (Islamic mysticism)

Ernst, Carl W., 1950-

The **Shambhala** guide to Sufism / Carl W. Ernst. Shambhala, 1997. xxi, 264 p. : **297.4**

1. Sufism.

ISBN 1570621802

LC 97010189

"This guide to Sufism covers its beginnings, its basic philosophies, and its place in Islam." Library Journal.

297.7 Protection and propagation of Islam

Lewis, Bernard, 1916-

★The **crisis** of Islam : holy war and unholy terror / Bernard Lewis. Modern Library, 2003. xxxii, 184 p. : **297.7**

1. Jihad 2. Terrorism -- Religious aspects -- Islam. 3. Islam and

politics. 4. War -- Religious aspects -- Islam. 5. Islamic countries.
ISBN 9780679642817

LC 2002045219

Traces the history of conflict between Islam and the West, exploring the meaning of the Islamic doctrine of jihad, the rise of militant Islam, and the impact of Saudi proselytizing and oil money on the rest of the Islamic world.

297.8 Islamic sects and reform movements

Hazleton, Lesley, 1945-

After the prophet : the epic story of the Shia-Sunni split in Islam / Lesley Hazleton. Doubleday, 2009. 239 p. : **297.8**

1. Muhammad, Prophet, d. 632 2. Aishah, ca. 614-678. 3. Ali ibn Abi Talib, Caliph, ca. 600-661 4. Islam -- History 5. Caliphate 6. Shiah Islam 7. Sunni Islam.
ISBN 9780385523936

LC 2009006498

A narrative history of the origins of the Shia and Sunni conflict describes how a seventh-century struggle between the supporters of the late Muhammad's surviving family members erupted in a massacre at Karbala that would become a central component of Shia Islam.

Nasr, Seyyed Vali Reza, 1960-

★The **Shia** revival : how conflicts within Islam will shape the future / Vali Nasr. W. W. Norton, 2006. 287 p. : **297.8**

1. Shiah Islam -- Political aspects -- Middle East. 2. Sunni Islam. 3. Islam and politics -- Middle East -- History -- 20th century. 4. Social conflict -- Religious aspects. 5. Middle East -- Politics and government -- 1979-
ISBN 9780393062113

LC 2006012361

Considers the ways in which struggles between the Shia and Sunni in the Middle East will affect the region's future, offering insight into the power conflicts between Iran and Saudi Arabia for political and spiritual leadership of the Muslim world.

299 Religions not provided for elsewhere

Adler, Margot, 1946-

Drawing down the moon : witches, druids, Goddess-worshippers, and other pagans / Margot Adler. Penguin, 2006. 672 p. **299**

1. Neopaganism 2. Witchcraft 3. Paganism 4. United States
ISBN 9780143038191

LC 2006043786

"Despite its clear anti-Judaic and anti-Christian bias, this book is recommended for general and college audiences interested in religion, the occult, and modern social phenomena." Choice. {review of 1979 edition}

Barnstone, Willis, 1927-

★The **Gnostic** Bible / edited by Willis Barnstone and Marvin Meyer. New Seeds, 2006, c2003. ix, 860 p. ; **299**

1. Gnosticism 2. Religion.
ISBN 1590301994

LC 2005018190

Originally published: Boston, Mass. : Shambhala, 2003.

"The book provides Gnostic texts from their Jewish origins, into early Christianities, on into the medieval world. Though it concentrates on the early Jewish-Christian matrix of early Gnosticism, the collection . manifests the breadth and depth of Gnostic variations in neo-Platonist, Manichean, Mandean, Islam, and Cathar movements." Choice.

Castaneda, Carlos, 1931-1998

The **teachings** of Don Juan; a Yaqui way of knowledge. / Carlos Castaneda. University of California Press, 1968. viii, 196 p. **299**

1. Juan, Don, 1891- 2. Yaqui Indians -- Religion 3. Hallucinogenic drugs and religious experience
ISBN 9780520217553

LC 68017303

An anthropologist records his corversations with the Yaqui Indian sorcerer and offers a structural analysis of Don Juan's teachings

Chevannes, Barry

Rastafari : roots and ideology / Barry Chevannes. Syracuse University Press, 1994. xiv, 298 p. ; **299**

1. Rastafarians. 2. Dreadlocks. 3. Kingston, Jamaica -- Religion.
ISBN 081562638X

LC 94018608

"Vital for students of African American religions and Caribbean religions, but also of interest to anthropologists, sociologists, and historians." Choice.

Crosson, Monica

The **magikal** family : pagan living in harmony with nature / Monica Crosson. Llewellyn Worldwide, Ltd., 2017. xv, 300 p. : **299**

1. Families 2. Magic
ISBN 9780738750934

LC 2017025403

"In this delightful mix of memoir and Wiccan ritual advice guide, Crosson (Summer Sage) relates anecdotes of her children's spiritual awakening and celebrations of the pagan lifestyle. Crosson, a resident of the Pacific Northwest and member of the Blue Moon Coven, explores how families can live holistically and spiritually year-round by following the Goddess's teachings." Publishers Weekly

Mar, Alex

Witches of America / Alex Mar. Sarah Crichton Books- Farrar, Straus and Giroux, 2015. 368 p. **299**

1. Neopaganism 2. Witchcraft 3. Paganism 4. United States
ISBN 9780374291372

LC 2015010897

"A top-notch read for pagans and open-minded seekers curious about the fascinating beginnings of American witchcraft and some of the various directions its form is taking." Library Journal.

Reitman, Janet

★**Inside** scientology : the story of America's most secretive religion / Janet Reitman. Houghton Mifflin Harcourt, 2011. 400 p. **299**

1. Scientology. 2. Dianetics. 3. Secrets. 4. Western religions. 5. United States -- Religion.
ISBN 9780618883028

LC 2010049837

ALA Notable Book, 2012.

Traces the story of the fast-growing religion while addressing such controversies as the organization's attacks on psychiatry, its celebrity support, and its steep tithing requirements.

"An exposé culled from hundreds of interviews with active Scientologists and defectors alike. Reitman brings an almost clinical detachment to the religion's story, from its birth in the sci-fi imagination of founder L. Ron Hubbard to its current Hollywood heyday. Her revelations--including abuse allegations against church leader David Miscavige and details about the organization's aggressive courtship of Tom Cruise--come with impressive backup." Entertaiment Weekly.

Wilkinson, Richard H.

★The **complete** gods and goddesses of ancient Egypt / Richard H. Wilkinson. Thames & Hudson, 2003. 256 p. : **299**

1. Gods, Egyptian. 2. Goddesses, Egyptian. 3. Mythology, Egyptian. 4. Egypt -- Religion.

ISBN 9780500051207

LC 2002110321

A guide to Egyptian religion describes the mythology, iconography, and forms of worship associated with each god and goddess.

Wilkinson, Richard H.

The **complete** temples of ancient Egypt / Richard H. Wilkinson. Thames & Hudson, 2000. 256 p. ; **299**

1. Temples -- Egypt 2. Egypt -- Religion. 3. Egypt -- Antiquities.

ISBN 9780500051009

LC 99066106

A lavishly illustrated study of ancient Egyptian temples traces the history of the largest religious monuments ever known, from the earliest times through their period of glory and ultimate decline to their rediscovery and study in modern times.

"An indispensable work for a student of Egyptian life or architecture." Library Journal.

Williamson, Marianne, 1952-

Tears to triumph : the spiritual journey from suffering to enlightenment / Marianne Williamson. HarperLuxe, 2016 xx, 275 p. ; **299**

1. Suffering -- Religious aspects.

ISBN 0062441590

LC bl2016024499

Argues that avoiding pain and hurt denies people opportunities to gain wisdom, personal growth, and enlightenment and encourages readers to face pain and become aware of what it can teach.

Wright, Lawrence, 1947-

★**Going** clear : Scientology, Hollywood, and the prison of belief / Lawrence Wright. Alfred A. Knopf, 2013. xiii, 430 p. : **299**

1. Hubbard, L. Ron (La Fayette Ron), 1911-1986 2. Scientology. 3. Authors, American -- 20th century 4. Scientologists 5. Philosophy and religion 6. Scientology -- History 7. United States -- Religion. 8. United States -- Religious life and customs -- 20th century

ISBN 9780307700667

National Book Award for Nonfiction finalist, 2013

National Book Critics Circle Award for Nonfiction finalist, 2013.

Examines the Church of Scientology; discusses the esoteric cosmology, the auditing process for determining an inductee's state of being, and the Bridge for Total Freedom; and details how the church pursues celebrities.

299.5 Religions of East and Southeast Asian origin

Hardacre, Helen, 1949-

Shinto : a history / Helen Hardacre. Oxford University Press, 2016. 720 p. **299.5**

1. Shinto -- Customs and practices 2. Shinto -- History 3. Rites and ceremonies 4. Religion 5. Japan -- History 6. Japan -- Politics and government 7. Japan -- Social life and customs

ISBN 9780190621711

LC 2016021265

Often called "the indigenous religion of Japan," Shinto's institutions, rituals, and symbols are omnipresent throughout the island nation. But, perhaps surprisingly, both its religiosity and its Japanese origins have been questioned. Hardacre investigates the claims about Shinto as the embodiment of indigenous tradition, and about its rightful place in the public realm.

"Hardacre, a professor of Japanese religions and society at Harvard, surveys the history of Shinto from ancient Japan to the present in this even-handed and detailed treatment of the topic." Publishers Weekly.

Yang, Lihui

★**Handbook** of Chinese mythology / Lihui Yang and Deming An, with Jessica Anderson Turner. ABC-CLIO, c2005. xiii, 293 p. : **299.5**

1. Mythology, Chinese -- Handbooks, Manuals, etc

ISBN 9781576078068

LC 2005013851

An informative work of historical and contemporary Chinese myths, including a useful collection of historical documents, detailing myths as they live and change in China today. --Provided by publisher

299.7 Religions of North American native origin

Nabokov, Peter

Where the lightning strikes : the lives of American Indian sacred places / Peter Nabokov. Viking, 2006. xvii, 350 p. ; **299.7**

1. Indians of North America -- Religion. 2. Sacred space -- United States. 3. Geographical perception -- United States. 4. Mythology -- History and criticism 5. United States -- History.

ISBN 0670034320

LC 2005042227

Profiles sixteen locations of sacred relevance to Native Americans, explaining how each site reflects the diversity of a unique Native American culture, including the Rainbow Canyon in Arizona and the high country of northwestern California.

"The author's careful documentation of unbroken reverence for these sacred places powerfully illuminates Native American attachment to the earth itself." Booklist.

300 Social sciences

Calhoun, Craig J., 1952-

★**Dictionary** of the social sciences / edited by Craig Calhoun. Oxford University Press, 2002. xvi 563 p. ; **300**

1. Social sciences -- Dictionaries.

ISBN 9780195123715

LC 00068151

Defines key terms in such areas as anthropology, sociology, political science, economics, human geography, cultural studies, and Marxism, and covers concepts, theories, schools of thought, methodologies, issues, and controversies.

301 Sociology and anthropology

Palmisano, Joseph M.

World of sociology / Joseph M. Palmisano, editor. Gale Group, 2001. 2 volumes : **301**

1. Sociology 2. Encyclopedias
ISBN 9780787649654

LC 00048399

More than twelve hundred entries describe the ideas, discoveries, and developments in sociology and related areas of psychology, history, geography, and other fields, along with profiles of individuals and a timeline.

Underdown, Simon,

Know-it-all anthropology : the 50 most important ideas in anthropology, each explained in under a minute / editor, Simon Underdown ; contributors, Russell Adams, Sue Black, Brad K. Blitz, Jason Danely, Ken Dark, Jan Freedman, Charlotte Houldcroft, Marta Mirazon Lahr, Michael Bang Petersen, Joshia Pollard [and 3 others]. Wellfleet Press, 2018. 160 p. : **301**

1. Anthropology.
ISBN 9781577151739

LC bl2018184447

Provides information about anthropology through short entries that each thoroughly explain a single topic.

301.092 Sociology and anthropology--Biography

Cottom, Tressie McMillan

★**Thick** : and other essays / Tressie Mcmillan Cottom. The New Press, 2019. 224 p. **301.092**

1. Cottom, Tressie McMillan 2. African American women college teachers 3. Political culture -- United States 4. Feminism 5. Beauty 6. United States -- Social life and customs -- 21st century 7. Essays
ISBN 9781620974360

LC 2018042930

ALA Notable Book, 2020.

National Book Award for Nonfiction finalist, 2019.

In these eight piercing explorations on beauty, media, money, and more, Tressie McMillan Cottom--award-winning professor and acclaimed author of Lower Ed--embraces her venerated role as a purveyor of wit, wisdom, and Black Twitter snark about all that is right and much that is wrong with this thing we call society.

"Sociology and personal experience blend in a concise collection of essays about contemporary black American women." Kirkus.

302 Specific topics in sociology and anthropology

Abramsky, Sasha

Jumping at shadows : the triumph of fear and the end of the American dream / Sasha Abramsky. Nation Books, 2017. 336 p. **302**

1. Fear 2. Panic 3. Social problems 4. Risk
ISBN 9781568585192

LC 2017012751

Sasha Abramsky's searing account of America's most dangerous epidemic: irrational fear. Taking readers on a dramatic journey through a divided nation, where everything from immigration to disease, gun control to health care has become fodder for fearmongers and conspiracists, he delivers an eye-popping analysis of our misconceptions about risk and threats.

"In this fascinating examination of fear, journalist Abramsky (The American Way of Poverty) reveals how it has infected the collective American psyche, influencing everything from child rearing to government." Library Journal.

Brooks, David, 1961-

★The **second** mountain : the quest for a moral life / David Brooks Random House, 2019. 240 p. **302**

1. Commitment (Psychology) 2. Happiness 3. Responsibility 4. Purpose in life
ISBN 9780812993264

LC 2019004624

In The Second Mountain, David Brooks explores the four commitments that define a life of meaning and purpose: to a spouse and family, to a vocation, to a philosophy or faith, and to a community. Our personal fulfillment depends on how well we choose and execute these commitments. In The Second Mountain, Brooks looks at a range of people who have lived joyous, committed lives, and who have embraced the necessity of dependence. He gathers their wisdom on how to choose a partner, how to pick a vocation, how to live out a philosophy, and how we can begin to integrate our commitments into one overriding purpose.

"A thoughtful work that offers an uplifting message to those struggling in the wilderness of career and existential challenge." Kirkus.

Gladwell, Malcolm, 1963-

Outliers : the story of success / Malcolm Gladwell. Little, Brown and Co., 2008. 320 p. **302**

1. Successful people. 2. Success (Concept) 3. Success in business 4. High achievement.
ISBN 9780316017923

LC 2008032824

Identifies the qualities of successful people, posing theories about the cultural, family, and idiosyncratic factors that shape high achievers, in a resource that covers such topics as the secrets of software billionaires and why the Beatles earned their fame.

"Gladwell's subject is success--an outlier is a superachiever, like Bill Gates or the four Beatles, and Gladwell wants to know what sets these titans apart. It's not mere talent, he insists, offering up instead one thrilling, exquisitely unfurled counterargument after another. There are both brilliant yarns and life lessons here: Outliers is riveting science, self-help, and entertainment, all in one book." Entertainment Weekly.

Gladwell, Malcolm, 1963-

★**Talking** to strangers : what we should know about the people we don't know / Malcolm Gladwell. Little, Brown & Company, 2019. 304 p. **302**

1. Interpersonal relations 2. Interpersonal communication 3. Mass media -- Social aspects 4. Strangers
ISBN 9780316478526

LC 2019935109

Talking to Strangers is a classically Gladwellian intellectual adventure, a challenging and controversial excursion through history, psychology, and scandals taken straight from the news. Something is very wrong, Gladwell argues, with the tools and strategies we use to make sense of people we don't know. And because we don't know how to talk to strangers, we are inviting conflict and misunderstanding in ways that have a profound effect on our lives and our world.

"This work should stimulate further research that could serve as control for these variables and more directly link how the factor of strangeness might influence certain reactions, providing a valuable contribution to psychology and psychiatry collections in larger university libraries." Library Journal.

Gladwell, Malcolm, 1963-

The **tipping** point : how little things can make a big difference / Malcolm Gladwell. Little, Brown, 2000. viii, 279 p. **302**

1. Social psychology. 2. Contagion (Social psychology) 3. Causation. 4. Human behavior.
ISBN 0316316962

LC 99047576

Explains why major changes in society often happen suddenly and unexpectedly. Also describes the personality types who are natural originators of new ideas and trends.

Hertz, Noreena

The **lonely** century : how to restore human connection in a world that's pulling apart / Noreena Hertz. Currency, 2020. 352 p. ; **302**

1. Loneliness -- Psychological aspects 2. Social isolation. 3. Alienation (Social psychology) 4. Quality of life.
ISBN 9780593135839

LC 2020028384

Also published: London : Hodder & Stoughton, 2020.

An economist, strategist, and advisor to business and political figures examines modern loneliness and the unraveling of the community, brought on, not by technology, but on the dismantling of civic institutions, urban migration and the reorganization of the workplace.

"An alternately dispiriting and bracing dissection of loneliness and how to build community from the ground up." Kirkus

Kaufman, Sarah L.

The **art** of grace : on moving well through life / Sarah L. Kaufman. W. W. Norton & Company, [2016] xxvi, 310 p. : **302**

1. Personal conduct 2. Self-control 3. Movement (Aesthetics) 4. Dignity
ISBN 9780393243956

LC 2015028036

A Pulitzer Prize-winning culture writer and dance critic describes how to see elegance and grace in the everyday, finding examples in the most unlikely of places, from the bustling kitchen of a high-end restaurant to strippers in a basement go-go bar.

Lieberman, Matthew D.

Social : why our brains are wired to connect Matthew D. Lieberman. Crown Publishers, 2013. 288 p. **302**

1. Social psychology. 2. Cognitive neuroscience. 3. Social networks. 4. Social interaction.
ISBN 9780307889096

LC 2013006226

Draws on original neuro research to reveal the human brain's powerful capacity for social networking, sharing arguments about the importance of social relationships for happiness and how the brain is innately conditioned to promote human connections.

"A fascinating explanation of why 'a broken heart can feel as painful as a broken leg' and social recognition is frequently prized above money." Kirkus.

Pinker, Susan, 1957-

The **village** effect : how face-to-face contact can make us healthier, happier, and smarter / Susan Pinker. Spiegel & Grau, 2014. 224 p. **302**

1. Social interaction 2. Interpersonal relations 3. Interpersonal communication 4. Social psychology.
ISBN 9781400069576

LC 2014008307

A developmental psychologist and award-winning author of The Sexual Paradox shares scientific insights and examples from real life to explain the importance of face-to-face social interactions in relationships, arguing that in-person human contact promotes health and happiness.

Stryker, Kitty, 1984-

Ask : building consent culture / Kitty Stryker ; afterword by Carol Queen ; foreword by Laurie Penny. Thorntree Press, 2017. 224 p. **302**

1. Feminism. 2. Power (Social sciences) 3. Feminist theory. 4. Boundaries (Interpersonal relations)
ISBN 9781944934255

LC 2017022470

Assembles writers, journalists, and activists to examine how a culture based on consent can empower us outside the bedroom, from the doctor's office to the justice system to schools and families.

"A vibrant treatise from the very first page, this radical collection provides a multifaceted view of consent as an essential concept in not only the bedroom but in the realms of politics, technology, education, and society overall." Library Journal.

Tannen, Deborah

You just don't understand : women and men in conversation / Deborah Tannen. Quill, 2001, c1990. 342 p. ; **302**

1. Sex differences (Psychology) 2. Communication -- Sex differences. 3. Communication in marriage. 4. Interpersonal communication.
ISBN 9780060959623

LC 89049000

Originally published: New York : Morrow, c1990.

A critique of male/female relationships stresses the importance of the language barrier that separates the genders and offers ways to improve relationships between the sexes.

"[A] refreshing and readable account of the complexities of communication between men and women [with] vivid examples and lively prose." New York Times Book Review.

302.02 Social interaction--Miscellany

Wright, Jennifer Ashley, 1986-

It ended badly : thirteen of the worst breakups in history / Jennifer Wright. Henry Holt and Co., 2015. 256 p. **302.02**

1. Men/women relations. 2. Interpersonal relations 3. Interpersonal conflict 4. Dating (Social customs)
ISBN 9781627792868

LC 2015004347

In It Ended Badly, New York Observer columnist Jennifer Wright guides you through thirteen of the worst breakups of notable figures in history--from Emperor Nero (sadist, murderer several times over), to Viennese artist Oskar Kokoschka (he of the aforementioned sex doll), to Norman Mailer (public stabbing). It's fun, pop history that educates, entertains, and really puts your own bad breakup behavior into perspective.

"Wright's ability to blend historical facts with humor will make this book attractive to readers looking for a delightful page-turner, as well as those who enjoy the dynamic people who have been peppered throughout history." Library Journal.

302.13 Social choice

Berger, Jonah

Invisible influence : the hidden forces that shape behavior / Jonah Berger. Simon & Schuster, 2016. 256 p. **302.13**

1. Social influence 2. Culture 3. Behavior 4. Behavior and culture
ISBN 9781476759692

LC 2016287170

The best-selling author of Contagious explores the subtle social influences that affect everyday and long-term decisions, drawing on research from various disciplines to raise reader awareness of social influence and how to embrace or resist it to make healthier choices.

302.2 Communication

Cairo, Alberto, 1974-

How charts lie : getting smarter about visual information / Alberto Cairo. W.W. Norton & Company, 2019. 221 p. **302.2**

1. Charts 2. Visual communication 3. Misinformation 4. Information visualization
ISBN 9781324001560

LC bl2019027913

We've all heard that a picture is worth a thousand words, but what if we don't understand what we're looking at? Social media has made charts, infographics, and diagrams ubiquitous?and easier to share than ever. We associate charts with science and reason; the flashy visuals are both appealing and persuasive. However, they can also lead us astray. Charts lie in a variety of ways--displaying incomplete or inaccurate data, suggesting misleading patterns, and concealing uncertainty--or are frequently misunderstood. To make matters worse, many of us are ill-equipped to interpret the visuals that politicians, journalists, advertisers, and even our employers present each day, enabling bad actors to easily manipulate them to promote their own agendas.

Colier, Nancy

The **power** of off : the mindful way to stay sane in a virtual world / Nancy Colier. Sounds True, 2017 xxii, 229 p. ; **302.2**

1. Information technology -- Psychological aspects 2. Information technology -- Social aspects 3. Attention 4. Self-control
ISBN 9781622037957

LC 2016022006

Describes how an immersion in digital technolgy can have an adverse effect on individual well-being and relationships and that using meditation to connect with the present moment can be a means of healing.

Kinzler, Katherine D.

How you say it : why you talk the way you do and what it says about you / Katherine D. Kinzler. Houghton Mifflin Harcourt, 2020. 272 p. **302.2**

1. Language and languages 2. Linguistic change 3. Languages in contact 4. Second language acquisition.
ISBN 9780544986558

LC 2019049915

A pioneering psychology professor explains how we are hardwired to prejudge others by the way they speak and discusses how accents can even determine the economic opportunity and discrimination one might face in life.

"Writing informally and concisely, Kinzler aims to raise our awareness of this unnoticed prejudice so that we can put an end to it. An articulate examination of an underrecognized aspect of human communication." Kirkus

Postman, Neil

Amusing ourselves to death : public discourse in the age of show business / Neil Postman ; new introduction by Andrew Postman. Penguin Books, 2006. xx, 184 p. ; **302.2**

1. Mass media -- Influence. 2. Mass media -- United States. 3. Television -- Social aspects.
ISBN 014303653X

LC 2006275381

Examines the ways in which television has transformed public discourse--in politics, education, religion, science, and elsewhere--into a form of entertainment that undermines exposition, explanation and knowledge.

"A sustained, withering and thought-provoking attack on television and what it is doing to us." Publishers Weekly.

Schein, Edgar H.

★**Humble** inquiry : the gentle art of asking instead of telling / Edgar H Schein. Berrett-Koehler Publishers, Inc., 2013 123 p. : **302.2**

1. Humility 2. Interpersonal communication 3. Interpersonal relations 4. Organizational behavior
ISBN 9781609949815

LC 2013016855

"From one of the true giants in organizational development, career development and organizational psychology comes a simple and effective technique for building more positive relationships--particularly between people of different status--that will lead to more honest and open interactions and stronger organizations".-- Provided by publisher.

Von Petzinger, Genevieve

The **first** signs : my quest to unlock the mysteries of the world's oldest symbols / Genevieve von Petzinger. Atria, 2016. 240 p. **302.2**

1. Stone age. 2. Ice age (Geology) 3. Signs and symbols 4. Symbolism in art -- History. 5. Europe -- Antiquities.
ISBN 9781476785493

LC 2015051281

"Archaeologist Genevieve von Petzinger looks past the horses, bison, ibex, and faceless humans in the ancient paintings and instead focuses on the abstract geometric images that accompany them. She offers her research on the terse symbols that appear more often than any other kinds of figures--signs that have never really been studied or explained until now".-- Provided by publisher.

"An exceptional read that should capture the imagination of anyone fascinated by time, humanity, and prehistory." Library Journal.

302.23 Media (Means of communication)

Alter, Adam L., 1980-

Irresistible : the rise of addictive technology and the business of keeping us hooked / Adam Alter. Penguin Press, 2017. 256 p. **302.23**

1. Digital media 2. Applied psychology 3. Technology -- Psychological aspects 4. Computers -- Psychological aspects
ISBN 9781594206641

LC 2016043481

Presents an urgent and expert investigation into behavioral addiction, the insidious flipside to today's unavoidable digital technologies and how we can turn the tide to regain control. By the New York Times best-selling author of Drunk Tank Pink.

"An excellent offering for those interested in technology, especially those grappling with the topic themselves." Library Journal.

Clark, Lynn Schofield

The **parent** app : understanding families in the digital age / Lynn Schofield Clark. Oxford University Press, c2013. xx, 299 p. ; **302.23**

1. Internet -- Social aspects. 2. Parent and child. 3. Parenting 4. Internet and children.

ISBN 9780199899616

LC 2012006687

Offers parents strategies for coping with the increasing presence of digital and mobile media and for managing new technology for their children, and examines how approaches differ among families according to income.

Fertik, Michael

The **reputation** economy : how to optimize your digital footprint in a world where your reputation is your most valuable asset / Michael Fertik and David C. Thompson. Crown Business, 2015 244 p. ; **302.23**

1. Internet in publicity 2. Online identities -- Social aspects 3. Online social networks 4. Public relations

ISBN 9780385347594

LC bl2014055342

The founder and CEO of a large privacy-management firm offers tips, techniques and strategies for managing and enhancing your digital reputation to improve your potential standings with future employers, banks, investors and romantic partners.

"Full of invaluable information that readers will be very grateful to have when they need it, this book explains the rules and provides the tools for overcoming online attacks and regaining a positive reputation." Publishers Weekly.

Gladstone, Brooke

★The **influencing** machine : Brooke Gladstone on the media / Brooke Gladstone ; illustrated by Josh Neufeld ; with additional penciling by Randy Jones and Susann Ferris-Jones. W. W. Norton, 2011. xxii, 170 p. : **302.23**

1. Mass media. 2. Newspapers. 3. Broadcast journalism 4. Television. 5. Comics and Graphic novels

ISBN 9780393077797

LC 2011009820

The cohost of NPR's "On the Media" narrates, in cartoon form, two millennia of history of the influence of the media on the populace, from newspapers in Caesar's Rome to the penny press of the American Revolution to today.

Gonzalez, Juan, 1947-

News for all the people : the epic story of race and the American media / Juan Gonzalez and Joseph Torres. Verso, 2011. 453 p., 16 p. of plates : **302.23**

1. Racism in mass media 2. Mass media bias 3. Press and politics 4. Mass media and minorities 5. United States -- Race relations

ISBN 9781844676873

LC 2011501351

Offers a sweeping account of the class and racial conflicts in the American news media, from the first colonial newspaper to the Internet age.

Hajdu, David

The **ten-cent** plague : the great comic-book scare and how it changed America / David Hajdu. Farrar, Straus and Giroux, 2008. 434 p., [8] p. of plates : **302.23**

1. Comic books, strips, etc. -- History and criticism. 2. Banned books. 3. Conservatism. 4. Popular culture -- History -- 1950-1959. 5. United States -- Popular culture -- History -- 20th century.

ISBN 0374187673

LC 2007025024

The author examines the influence of comic books on the evolution of American popular culture in the years between World War II and the emergence of television, focusing on the battle against comic books by church groups, community elite, and a right-wing Congress.

"Hajdu offers captivating insights into America's early bluestocking-versus-blue-collar culture wars, and the later tensions between wary parents and the first generation of kids with the buying power to mold mass entertainment." Village Voice.

Harris, Michael, 1980-

The **end** of absence : reclaiming what we've lost in a world of constant connection / Michael Harris. Current, 2014. 256 p. **302.23**

1. Information society. 2. Social media 3. Internet 4. Information technology -- Social aspects.

ISBN 9781591846932

LC 2014009772

Governor General's Literary Award for English-Language Nonfiction, 2014.

Citing the current generation's unique experience of life on and without the Internet, a chronicle of the modern world's massive shift to an information-driven, online existence evaluates the connected world's potentially costly absence of silence, contemplation and solitude.

"Harris's core argument regarding the values of technological disengagement feels valid, and his prose is graceful, but as a social narrative, the book becomes repetitive and less focused as it proceeds.A thoughtful addition to the bookshelf addressing the unintended consequences of a wired world." Kirkus.

Heitner, Devorah, 1975-

Screenwise : helping kids thrive (and survive) in their digital world / Devorah Heitner, PhD. Bibliomotion, Inc., 2016 x, 244 p. ; **302.23**

1. Internet and children 2. Internet -- Social aspects 3. Internet -- Moral and ethical aspects 4. Parenting

ISBN 9781629561455

LC 2016024745

Offers strategies and hacks for mentoring children in the digital age and navigating the unique parenting challenges it presents.

Keen, Andrew

The **Internet** is not the answer / Andrew Keen. Atlantic Monthly Press, 2015. 288 p. **302.23**

1. Internet -- Social aspects. 2. Computers and civilization. 3. Technological innovations -- Social aspects. 4. Electronic commerce -- Social aspects.

ISBN 9780802123138

LC 2015452746

A former Internet entrepreneur and chat show host on Techcrunch discusses the negative effects the internet has on human psychology, the economy and culture and shows how big data companies are trying to monetize every normal human function.

"A must-read for technophiles and business leaders, or those curious about technology's societal effects." Library Journal.

McChesney, Robert Waterman, 1952-
Digital disconnect : how capitalism is turning the Internet against democracy / Robert W. McChesney. The New Press, 2013. 299 p. **302.23**

1. Internet -- Political aspects. 2. Capitalism. 3. Democracy.
ISBN 9781595588678

LC 2012035748

Looks at the relationship between economic power and the digital world, encouraging readers to fight back against the monopolies that are making the Internet less democratic.

McLuhan, Marshall, 1911-1980
Understanding media : the extensions of man / Marshall McLuhan ; edited by W. Terrence Gordon. Gingko Press, 2003. xxi, 611 p. : **302.23**

1. Mass media
ISBN 9781584230731

LC 2003012174

When first published, Marshall McLuhan's Understanding Media made history with its radical view of the effects of electronic communications upon man and life in the twentieth century. This edition of McLuhan's best-known book both enhances its accessibility to a general audience and provides the full critical apparatus necessary for scholars. This critical edition makes available for the first time the core of the research project that spawned the book. --Provided by publisher

Palfrey, John
Born digital : understanding the first generation of digital natives / John Palfrey and Urs Gasser. Basic Books, 2008. 288 p. **302.23**

1. Information society -- Social aspects. 2. Information technology -- Social aspects. 3. Technological innovations -- Social aspects. 4. Internet and children.
ISBN 9780465005154

LC 2008021538

Examines the impact that the first generation born into an entirely digital world will have on society as a whole with regard to innovation, privacy, safety, and the digital future itself.

"The authors document the myriad ways downloading, text-messaging, Massively Multiplayer Online Games-playing, YouTube-watching youth are transforming society. Energetic, expert, and forward-looking, the authors serve as envoys between the generations, addressing issues that worry parents and educators, from privacy and safety concerns to the quality of digital information, the psychological and physical effects of information overload and excessive online time, and legal and ethical issues, all the while stressing the need for digital literacy and critical thinking." Booklist.

Singer, P. W. (Peter Warren)
Likewar : the weaponization of social media / P. W. Singer, Emerson T. Brooking. Houghton Mifflin Harcourt 2018. 400 p. **302.23**

1. Social media -- Political aspects 2. Internet -- Political aspects 3. Cyberterrorism 4. Propaganda -- Technological innovations.
ISBN 9781328695741

LC 2018017519

Two defense experts explore the collision of war, politics, and social media, discussing how the online world affects and is affected by war and the role that ordinary people can play in international conflicts.

Standage, Tom
Writing on the wall : social media - the first 2,000 years / Tom Standage. Bloomsbury, 2013. viii, 278 p. : **302.23**

1. Mass media 2. Communication 3. Social networks 4. Social media
ISBN 9781620402832

LC 2018276958

Chronicles social media over two millennia, from papyrus letters that Cicero used to exchange news across the Empire to today, reminding us how modern behavior echoes that of prior centuries and encouraging debate and discussion about how we'll communicate in the future.

"Standage offers historical perspective on such concerns about evolving social media as faddishness, coarsening of discourse, distraction from serious work, and erosion of social skills." Booklist.

Stephens-Davidowitz, Seth
Everybody lies : big data, new data, and what the internet can tell us about who we really are / Seth Stephens-Davidowitz. HarperCollins 2017 288 p. **302.23**

1. Big data 2. Statistics 3. Human behavior 4. Deception
ISBN 9780062390851

LC bl2017013861

The New York Times op-ed columnist and former Google data scientist presents an insider's look at what today's vast, instantly available amounts of information can reveal about our world.

Turkle, Sherry
Reclaiming conversation : the power of talk in a digital age / Sherry Turkle. Penguin Group USA, 2015 352 p. **302.23**

1. Conversation. 2. Text messaging 3. Interpersonal relations. 4. Communication technology.
ISBN 9781594205552

LC bl2015038669

A renowned media scholar investigates how a flight from conversation undermines our relationships, creativity and productivity?and why reclaiming face-to-face conversation can help us regain lost ground.

"A timely wake-up call urging us to cherish the intimacy of direct, unscripted communication." Kirkus.

Zuckerman, Ethan
Rewire : digital cosmopolitans in the age of connection / Ethan Zuckerman. W. W. Norton & Company, 2013 312 p. **302.23**

1. Virtual community. 2. Social media. 3. Internet -- Social aspects. 4. User-generated content.
ISBN 9780393082838

LC 2013007124

A media scholar discusses the challenges that still need to be met to achieve a truly online global experience, including needed advances in language translation and cross-cultural inspiration which will lead to increased connectivity between people.

302.230973 Media--United States

Taibbi, Matt
Hate Inc. : why today's media makes us despise one another / Matt Taibbi. OR Books, 2019. 294 p. **302.230973**

1. News media 2. Political culture -- United States 3. Political parties 4. Political journalism
ISBN 9781949017250

LC bl2019023828

In this characteristically turbocharged new book, Rolling Stone journalist Matt Taibbi provides an insider's guide to the variety of ways today's mainstream media tells us lies. Part tirade, part confessional, it reveals that what most people think of as "the news" is, in fact, a twisted wing of the entertainment business.

302.3 Social interaction within groups

Christakis, Nicholas A.

Connected : the surprising power of our social networks and how they shape our lives / Nicholas A. Christakis and James H. Fowler. Little, Brown and Co., 2009. xiii, 338 p., 8 p. of plates : **302.3**

1. Social networks
ISBN 9780316036146

LC 2009018349

Suggests that people within three degrees of influence can have a profound impact on those they have never met and that individual acts like voting and suicide may be directly tied to the actions of a friend of a friend.

Elsesser, Kim

Sex and the office : women, men, and the sex partition that's dividing the workplace / Kim Elsesser. Taylor Trade Publishing, 2015 256 p. **302.3**

1. Women -- Employment. 2. Sex discrimination 3. Gender role in the work environment 4. Gender role
ISBN 9781493007943

LC 2015006762

Explains how such issues as sexual harassment, workplace romance, spousal jealousy, and communication styles create barriers between the sexes at work and argues that these walls tend to have the greatest impact on the careers of women.

Fisher, Helen E.

Anatomy of love : a natural history of mating, marriage, and why we stray / Helen Fisher. W. W. Norton & Company, 2016, c1992. 400 p. **302.3**

1. Extramarital affairs 2. Sex customs. 3. Interpersonal relations. 4. Marriage.
ISBN 9780393285222

LC 2015037510

Revised edition of the author's Anatomy of love: the natural history of monogamy, adultery, and divorce, 1992.

Lust; romance; attachment . . . is monogamy natural? Why him? Why her? Love addictions. Hooking up. Why adultery? Future sex. In this completely revised edition, anthropologist Helen Fisher adds a host of new data on the brain in love, and on courtship in our digital age. She casts an original (and optimistic) lens on modern love--proposing that we are returning to patterns of romance that evolved in our primordial past.

"This work remains a solid introduction to the nature of sex and relationships, albeit cursory in depth of coverage. Highly recommended to readers interested in human sexuality." Library Journal.

Fisher, Len

The **perfect** swarm : the science of complexity in everyday life / Len Fisher. Basic Books, c2009. xx, 260 p. : **302.3**

1. Swarm intelligence -- Social aspects 2. Group decision making 3. Group problem solving 4. Social groups -- Psychological aspects
ISBN 9780465018840

LC 2009031018

Examines how science-based solutions can be applied to the everyday challenges of an increasingly chaotic world, covering topics ranging from "swarm intelligence" and the science of parties to the best ways to start a fad and the utility of complexity theory.

Lyons, Daniel, 1960-

Lab rats : how Silicon Valley made work miserable for the rest of us / Dan Lyons. Hachette Books 2018 304 p. **302.3**

1. Corporate culture 2. Job satisfaction 3. Quality of work life 4. Work 5. Silicon Valley, California
ISBN 9780316561860

LC 2018948927

Examines how the half-baked ideas of Silicon Valley and its "new oligarchs" have changed the way we work, damaged our brains and left us poorer and insecure.

O'Connor, Rory, 1951-

Friends, followers, and the future : how social media are changing politics, threatening big brands, and killing traditional media / Rory O'Connor. City Lights Books, c2012. 184 p. **302.3**

1. Social media. 2. Information technology. 3. Press and politics. 4. Mass media -- Social aspects.
ISBN 9780872865563

LC 2012005506

Discusses the impact online social networking has had on business, politics, media, and culture, and how it will affect the future.

Sciolino, Elaine

La seduction : how the French play the game of life / Elaine Sciolino. Times Books, 2011. 384 p. **302.3**

1. Seduction -- France. 2. National characteristics, French. 3. Cultural differences. 4. Culture. 5. France -- Social life and customs.
ISBN 9780805091151

LC 2010049572

The Paris correspondent and author reveals the role of seduction in French culture while explaining how crucial the game of seduction is to understanding France, identifying seduction as a key ideology that shapes how the French conduct business, politics and relationships.

302.30285 Computer applications

Harrison, Guy P.

Think before you like : social media's effect on the brain and the tools you need to navigate your newsfeed / Guy P. Harrison. Prometheus Books, [2017] 380 p. **302.30285**

1. Social media 2. Brain 3. Online social networks 4. News media
ISBN 9781633883512

LC 2017022168

An award-winning journalist, who is an upbeat advocate of scientific literacy and positive skepticism, shows readers how critical thinking can enhance the benefits of social media while giving users the skills they need to guard against its dangers.

"In this skillfully written and researched survey, journalist Harrison (Good Thinking) makes an argument for appreciating social medias good points while exercising prudence to avoid its downside." Publishers Weekly.

Martinez, Antonio Garcia

★**Chaos** monkeys : obscene fortune and random failure in Silicon Valley / Antonio Garcia Martinez. HarperCollins, 2016

320 p. **302.30285**

1. Social media. 2. Internet marketing. 3. Internet advertising.
ISBN 9780062458193

LC 2017304446

The industry provocateur behind such companies as Twitter and a nascent Facebook presents an irreverent expose of life inside the tech bubble that traces his hedonist lifestyle against a backdrop of early social media and online marketing, sharing critical insights into how they are shaping today's world.

Van Susteren, Greta, 1954-

Everything you need to know about social media : (without calling a kid) / Greta Van Susteren. Simon & Schuster Paperbacks, 2017 305 p. ; **302.30285**

1. Social media.
ISBN 150113244X

LC 2017014973

Includes index.

A step-by-step guide intended to help readers understand the major social platforms, including Facebook, Twitter, LinkedIn, Instagram, and Snapchat, addresses important moral and behavioral issues.

"Readers who are curious about (but are still hesitant to use) social media will likely find Van Susterens advice helpful." Publishers Weekly.

302.309 Social interaction within groups--History

Ferguson, Niall

The **square** and the tower : networks and power, from the Freemasons to Facebook / Niall Ferguson. Penguin Press, 2018. 480 p. **302.309**

1. Social networks -- History. 2. Networks 3. Social change 4. Power (Social sciences)
ISBN 9780735222915

LC bl2017046053

A reevaluation of history's turning points as collisions between old power hierarchies and new social networks explains how networks have always existed and have been responsible for key innovations and revolutionary ideas, from clustering and degrees of separation to contagions and phase transitions.

"Making profitable use of information science, Ferguson offers a novel way of examining data that will be highly intriguing to students of history and current affairs." Kirkus.

302.34 Social interaction in primary groups

Bazelon, Emily

★**Sticks** and stones : defeating the culture of bullying and rediscovering the power of character and empathy / Emily Bazelon. Random House, c2013. 256 p. **302.34**

1. Bullying and bullies -- Prevention 2. Schools 3. Aggressiveness (Psychology) 4. Interpersonal relations.
ISBN 9780812992809

LC 2012022773

Offers insights into teen bullying in the Internet era, counseling parents, educators, advocates, and kids on how to understand its dynamics and consequences and take appropriate protective measures.

"While less prescriptive than other books on the topic, very useful FAQs are included, as are resource lists for readers. Masterfully written, Bazelon's book will increase understanding, awareness, and action." Publishers Weekly.

Hitchcock, Jayne A

Cyberbullying and the wild, wild web : what everyone need to know / J. A. Hitchcock. Rowman & Littlefield, 2017 xi, 128 p. : **302.34**

1. Cyberbullying -- Prevention. 2. Cyberbullying.
ISBN 1442251174

LC 2016042062

Using real-life examples, explains how anyone can become a victim of cyberbulling or cyberstalking, and shares tips for staying safe online.

"This book will be a useful resource for anyone who wants to know how to deal with cyberbullying." Booklist.

McKee, Jonathan R. (Jonathan Ray), 1970-

The **bullying** breakthrough : real help for parents and teachers of the bullied, bystanders, and the bullies / Jonathan McKee. Shiloh Run Press, an imprint of Barbour Publishing, Inc., 2018 181 p. ; **302.34**

1. Bullying 2. Bullying in schools
ISBN 9781683226888

LC bl2018191559

Provides readers ways to offer open dialogue, encouragement, and validation for those being bullied, the bystanders, and the bullies themselves.

Scheff, Sue

Shame nation : the global epidemic of online hate / Sue Scheff with Melissa Schorr ; with a foreword from Monica Lewinksy. Sourcebooks, 2017. 356 p. **302.34**

1. Cyberbullying 2. Online trolling 3. Shame. 4. Social media.
ISBN 9781492648994

LC 2017013493

"Parents will find the book's advice useful in protecting their children from danger as they explore online, as will anyone who has made a hasty comment or tweet and lived to regret it. Shame Nation is a strong addition to any collection." Booklist.

Strauss, Susan, 1946-

★**Sexual** harassment and bullying : a guide to keeping kids safe and holding schools accountable / Susan L. Strauss. Rowman & Littlefield Publishers, c2012. xii, 290 p. ; **302.34**

1. Bullying -- Prevention 2. Bullying 3. Sexual harassment in education 4. Sexual harassment -- Prevention
ISBN 9781442201620

LC 2011031731

Despite headlines that label all harassment among youth as bullying, there is in fact a difference between sexual harassment and bullying. This book discusses the similarities and important differences between the two, offering firsthand accounts from victims and others involved in combating the activities that victimize students. It provides parents, youth advocates, scout leaders, and other concerned adults with practical steps to partner with schools to prevent and intervene on the behaviors to help keep kids safe. The book clearly identifies the steps to take to hold schools accountable when a student has been harassed or bullied, even when the school is not stopping the behavior. Providing examples throughout the work, Strauss helps readers become better acquainted with the various activities that constitute sexual harassment and bullying and what they can do to combat the problem.

Whitson, Signe

8 keys to end bullying : strategies for parents & schools / Signe Whitson ; foreword by Babette Rothschild. W.W. Norton & Company, 2014 xvii, 218 p. ; 8 Keys to Mental Health **302.34**

1. Bullying -- Prevention. 2. Bullying in schools -- Prevention. 3. Aggressiveness in children.

ISBN 9780393709285

LC 2014001241

Featuring example scenarios and exercises, equips educators and parents with eight strategies for addressing the issue of bullying in schools and online, and discusses the psychology behind why children bully.

"Complete with example scenarios, exercises for readers, and sample responses, the author does a convincing job of helping adults feel empowered to address this important issue." Library Journal.

302.34082 Women--Friendship

Schaefer, Kayleen

Text me when you get home : the evolution and triumph of modern female friendship / Kayleen Schaefer. E.P. Dutton, 2018. 224 p. **302.34082**

1. Female friendship 2. Interpersonal relations 3. Sociology. 4. Gender role

ISBN 9781101986127

LC 2017041842

A personal and sociological examination of the evolution of female friendship in pop culture and modern society draws on the experiences of diverse women and the author's own life to celebrate how the bonds between women have evolved to have as much significance as relationships with romantic partners and family members.

"Schaefer provides an engaging, deeply researched sociological perspective into the evolution of female friendships. Consider purchasing where women's studies topics circulate well." Library Journal.

Tannen, Deborah

You're the only one I can tell : women, friendship, and the power of conversation / Deborah Tannen. Ballantine Books, 2017 288 p. **302.34082**

1. Female friendship 2. Interpersonal communication 3. Conversation 4. Interpersonal relations

ISBN 9781101885802

LC bl2017011922

Through research into the unique way women talk to one another, this validating and illuminating analysis of female friendship will help women lean into the comfort these powerful relationships offer and avoid the hurt feelings that come from common miscommunications.

"Tannen sets out to help women make friendships stronger, accomplishing this in a highly accessible manner with both scientific research and a warm heart." Library Journal.

302.5 Relation of individual to society

Appiah, Anthony

The **lies** that bind : rethinking identity / Kwame Anthony Appiah. W W Norton & Co Inc 2018 256 p. **302.5**

1. Identity (Psychology) 2. Intersectionality 3. Misconceptions 4. Human behavior

ISBN 9781631493836

LC 2018023080

The author of *Cosmopolitanism* draws on historical events to reveal how the collective identities that shape our polarized world are inherently contradictory, subject to cycles of conflict and based on illusory misconceptions.

"Written in a clear, nontechnical style, this book by an outstanding contemporary philosopher presents critical thinking about public issues at its best and should appeal widely to anyone interested in serious thought." Library Journal.

Putnam, Robert D.

The **upswing** : how America came together a century ago and how we can do it again / Robert D. Putnam ; with Shaylyn Romney Garrett. Simon & Schuster, 2020. 304 p. **302.5**

1. Individualism -- United States -- History -- 20th century. 2. Communitarianism. 3. Polarization (Social sciences) 4. Political culture -- United States -- History -- 20th century. 5. United States -- Social conditions -- 20th century 6. United States -- Social conditions -- 21st century

ISBN 9781982129149

LC 2020001227

An eminent political scientist's brilliant synthesis of social and political trends over the past century that shows how we have gone from an individualistic society to a more communitarian society and then back again -- and how we can use that experience to overcome once again the individualism that currently weakens our country.

"A tour de force exploration of why America got better and then went into reverse." Kirkus

Simmons, Rachel, 1966-

★**Odd** girl out : the hidden culture of aggression in girls / Rachel Simmons. Mariner Books, 2011. xix, 412 p. ; **302.5**

1. Aggressiveness in children 2. Girls -- Psychology

ISBN 9780547520193

LC bl2011020952

Identifies the subtle means by which girls behave aggressively toward one another and examines specific behaviors while explaining the importance of enabling girls to express anger and resolve conflicts.

303.3 Coordination and control

Brown, Archie, 1938-

The **myth** of the strong leader : political leadership in the modern age / Archie Brown Basic Books, 2014. 512 p. **303.3**

1. Political leadership. 2. Politicians 3. Leadership. 4. Charismatic political leadership.

ISBN 9780465027668

LC 2014931301

All too frequently, leadership is reduced to a simple dichotomy: the strong versus the weak. Yet, there are myriad ways to exercise effective political leadership -- as well as different ways to fail. In this magisterial and wide-ranging survey of political leadership over the past hundred years, renowned Oxford politics professor Archie Brown challenges the widespread belief that strong leaders -- meaning those who dominate their colleagues and the policy-making process -- are the most successful and admirable.

Bueno de Mesquita, Bruce, 1946-

The **dictator's** handbook : why bad behavior is almost always good politics / Bruce Bueno de Mesquita and Alastair Smith. PublicAffairs, 2011. xxv, 319 p. ; **303.3**

1. Political leadership -- Philosophy. 2. Power (Social sciences) 3. Political corruption. 4. Dictatorship.

ISBN 9781610390446

LC 2011024164

Explains the theory of political survival, particularly in cases of dictators and despotic governments, arguing that political leaders seek to stay in power using any means necessary, most commonly by attending to the interests of certain coalitions.

Eberhardt, Jennifer L. (Jennifer Lynn)

★**Biased** : uncovering the hidden prejudice that shapes what we see, think, and do / Jennifer L. Eberhardt. PhD. Viking, [2019] 352 p. **303.3**

1. Prejudice 2. Discrimination. 3. Race relations. 4. Racism.
ISBN 9780735224933

LC 2018051011

Includes index.

A leading expert on unconscious racial bias examines the manifestations of automatic racism in contemporary society and how they influence race relations and criminal justice.

"Though there's no easy answer, Eberhardt posits the key to change is confronting bias head-on rather than trying to pretend it doesnt exist, and to question and challenge our own snap judgments and their sources. This is a seminal work on a topic that necessitates wide and frank discussion." Booklist.

Naim, Moises

The **end** of power : from boardrooms to battlefields and churches to states, why being in charge isn't what it used to be / Moises Naim. Basic Books, 2013. 304 p. **303.3**

1. Social change. 2. Power (Social sciences) 3. Hierarchy (Social sciences) 4. Globalization -- Social aspects.
ISBN 9780465031566

LC 2012049642

Based on an examination of global affairs and world history, a scholar and columnist discusses the changing nature of being in charge and the modern dynamics of power and argues that current leaders actually have less power than ever before.

Robbins, Alexandra, 1976-

The **geeks** shall inherit the Earth : quirk theory and why outsiders thrive after high school / Alexandra Robbins. Hyperion, 2011. 256 p. **303.3**

1. Group identity. 2. Conformity. 3. Social isolation. 4. Popularity.
ISBN 9781401302023

LC 2011002181

"In her new book, Alexandra Robbins explores the ways group identity theories play out among cliques - and the students they exclude. She reveals the new labels students stick onto each other today, the long-term effects of this marginalization, and the reasons students falling under these categories are often shunned. And then she will celebrate them. In this ever-conformist, cookie-cutter, magazine-celebrity-worshipping, creativity-stifling society, the innovation, courage, and differences of outcasts - nerds, freaks, weirdos, punks, Goths, etc. - are crucial to America's progress. No Child Left Behind and the homogenization of the US education system have made outcasts bolder and more important than ever. Robbins intertwines psychology with science inentertaining, illuminating prose, addressing questions such as 'Why are popular people mean?' 'Why is seventh grade the worst?' 'Why do social labels stick?' and "Are students better off popular or unpopular?" As in Pledged and The Overachievers, Robbins follows students throughout the course of a year to present compelling narratives that thread investigative discussions about of-the-moment issues. In her other books, however, Robbins merely observed students. This time, Robbins crosses the line. She forces the students to examine who they are and how other students perceive them. And then she dares them to step outside of their comfort zone. She challenges some of these students to attempt social experiments at their schools - experiments that end up changing their lives".-- Provided by publisher.

"At the heart of Geeks is quirk theory, which hypothesizes that the very characteristics that exclude the cafeteria fringe in school are the same traits that will make them successful as adults and outside the school setting: creativity/originality, freethinking/vision, resilience, authenticity/self-awareness, integrity/candor, curiosity/love of learning/passion, and courage. Robbins' breezy writing style allows her to effortlessly wade through compelling psychological data, pop culture trends and interviews with high school students, but her narrative masterstroke lies in the decision to follow seven individuals who exemplify the cafeteria fringe. These characters are the heart and soul of the book." Chicago Sun-Times.

Salvanto, Anthony

Where did you get this number? : a pollster's guide to making sense of the world / Anthony Salvanto. Simon & Schuster 2018 288 p. **303.3**

1. Demography 2. Voting research 3. Public opinion polls 4. Presidential election, 2016 5. United States -- Politics and government -- 21st century
ISBN 9781501174834

LC 2018013690

The elections and surveys director for CBS News presents a fast-paced, illuminating tour through the world of polling and elections to reveal what they actually say about today's America.

"General interest readers and news junkies alike will come away with a greater appreciation of how polls and surveys are conducted, as well as a much clearer sense of what they mean." Publishers Weekly.

Solnit, Rebecca

★**Call** them by their true names : American crises (and essays) / Rebecca Solnit. Haymarket Books, 2018. 188 p. **303.3**

1. Feminism 2. Environmentalism 3. Political culture -- United States 4. Social problems -- United States 5. Essays
ISBN 9781608463299

LC bl2018184189

Kirkus Prize for Nonfiction, 2018.

Rebecca Solnit unearths the roots of our contemporary crises, countering the despair of our age with a dose of solidarity, creativity, and hope.

"Solnit is careful with her words (she always is) but never so much that she mutes the infuriated spirit that drives these essays." Kirkus.

Surowiecki, James, 1967-

The **wisdom** of crowds : why the many are smarter than the few and how collective wisdom shapes business, economies, societies, and nations / James Surowiecki. Doubleday : 2004. xxi, 296 p. **303.3**

1. Consensus (Social sciences) 2. Common good. 3. Group decision making. 4. Crowds -- Psychology.
ISBN 0385503865

LC 2003070095

An analysis of how to understand the workings of the world as it is reflected by groups contends that large groups have more collective intelligence than a smaller number of experts, drawing on a wide range of disciplines to offer insight into such topics as politics, business, and the environment.

"The author analyzes the concept of collective wisdom and applies it to various areas of the social sciences, including economics and politics. This work is an intriguing study of collective intelligence and how it works in contemporary society." Library Journal.

Taibbi, Matt

The **divide** : American injustice in the age of the wealth gap / Matt Taibbi. Spiegel & Grau, 2014. 288 p. **303.3**

1. Injustice. 2. Income distribution. 3. Imprisonment -- United States. 4. Wealth -- Moral and ethical aspects. 5. United States -- Social conditions.

ISBN 9780812993424

LC 2013024907

The investigative journalist analyzes the emotionally galvanizing wealth gap in America and how it is transforming the meaning of rights, justice, and basic citizenship.

"Taibbi's chapters are high-definition photographs contrasting the ways we pursue small-time corruption and essentially reward high-level versions of the same thing. [He mixes] case studies, interviews and anecdotes with comprehensive research on his topics." Kirkus.

Viroli, Maurizio

How to choose a leader : Machiavelli's advice to citizens / Maurizio Viroli. Princeton University Press, 2016. xviii, 116 p. ; **303.3**

1. Machiavelli, Niccolo, 1469-1527. 2. Political leadership -- Philosophy 3. Political participation -- Philosophy

ISBN 9780691170145

LC 2015043592

"One of the greatest political advisers of all time, Niccolo Machiavelli thought long and hard about how citizens could identify great leaders--ones capable of defending and enhancing the liberty, honor, and prosperity of their countries. Drawing on thefull range of the Florentine's writings, acclaimed Machiavelli biographer Maurizio Viroli gathers and interprets Machiavelli's timeless wisdom about choosing leaders. The brief and engaging result is a new kind of Prince--one addressed to citizens ratherthan rulers and designed to make you a better voter. Demolishing popular misconceptions that Machiavelli is a cynical realist, the book shows that he believes republics can't survive, let alone thrive, without leaders who are virtuous as well as effective. Among much other valuable advice, Machiavelli says that voters should pick leaders who put the common good above narrower interests and who make fighting corruption a priority, and he explains why the best way to recognize true leaders is to carefully examine their past actions and words. On display throughout are the special insights that Machiavelli gained from long, direct knowledge of real political life, the study of history, and reflection on the great political thinkers of antiquity. Recognizing the difference between great and mediocre political leaders is difficult but not at all impossible--with Machiavelli's help. So do your country a favor. Read this book, then vote like Machiavelli would".-- Provided by publisher.

Wills, Garry, 1934-

Certain trumpets : the call of leaders / Garry Wills. Simon & Schuster, 1994. 336 p. : **303.3**

1. Leadership -- Case studies. 2. Power (Social sciences) -- Case studies. 3. Social participation. 4. Essays.

ISBN 067165702X

LC 94006526

"A wise, witty, entertaining look at the psychology of leaders and their followers." Publishers Weekly.

303.4 Social change

Colvile, Robert

The **great** acceleration : how the world is getting faster, faster / Robert Colvile. Bloomsbury USA, 2016. 390 p. **303.4**

1. Technology and civilization 2. Human behavior

ISBN 9781632864550

LC bl2016020056

Colvile inspects the various ways in which the pace of life in our society is increasing and examines the evolutionary science behind our need for constant acceleration, as well as why it's unlikely we'll be able to slow down--or even want to.

"Anyone worried about our increasingly frenetic lives will find food for thought". Booklist.

Diamond, Jared M.

★**Guns,** germs, and steel : the fates of human societies / Jared Diamond. Norton, 2005, c1997. 518 p. : **303.4**

1. Social evolution. 2. Civilization -- History. 3. Ethnology. 4. Humans -- Effect of environment on

ISBN 9780393061314

LC 2005284261

Originally published: New York : W.W. Norton, 1997.

Pulitzer Prize for General Nonfiction, 1998.

Royal Society General Prizes for Science Books, 1998.

"This book poses a simple but profound question about the distribution of wealth and power in the modern world: Why weren't Native Americans, Africans, and Aboriginal Australians the ones who decimated, subjugated, or exterminated Europeans and Asians?. . . To explore the discrepancies in technological and cultural development he looks not at peoples but at places, and at the natural resources available to different indigenous populations since 11,000 B.C. The scope and the explanatory power of this book are astounding." The New Yorker.

Gore, Albert, 1948-

The **future** : six drivers of global change / Albert Gore. Random House, 2013. 512 p. **303.4**

1. Globalization 2. World economy. 3. World politics. 4. Economics

ISBN 9780812992946

LC 2012039890

The former vice president and #1 best-selling author of An Inconvenient Truth offers a frank assessment of six critical drivers of global change in the decades to come--economic globalization, worldwide digital communications, a growing balance of global power, unsustainable population growth, scientific revolution and disruption of ecosystems.

"Gore's strengths lie in his passion for the subject and in his ability to take the long view by putting current events and trends in historical context." Publishers Weekly.

Heath, Chip

Switch : how to change things when change is hard / Chip Heath and Dan Heath. Broadway Books, 2010. 304 p. **303.4**

1. Change (Psychology) 2. Identity (Psychology) 3. Life change events.

ISBN 9780385528757

LC 2009027814

Offers insight into the difficult nature of lasting change, presenting metaphorical illustrations of the conflict between the instinctual and the intellectual areas of the brain while sharing case stories of successful individuals and organizations.

"The authors analyze what must be addressed if societal, organizational, and personal habits and practices are to be instilled with new ideas. They draw upon numerous behavioral studies, business case studies, and hypothetical examples to illustrate their principles." Library Journal.

Pagel, Mark D.
Wired for culture : origins of the human social mind / Mark Pagel. W. W. Norton & Company, c2012. 384 p. **303.4**
1. Human evolution. 2. Social evolution. 3. Evolution 4. Evolutionary genetics.
ISBN 9780393065879
LC 2011044465

An evolutionary biologist explores the concept of culture and how it influenced our collective human behaviors from the beginning of evolution through modern times and offers new insights on how art, morality and altruism and self-interest define being human.

Pipher, Mary Bray
The **green** boat : reviving ourselves in our capsized culture / Mary Pipher. Riverhead Books, 2013. 224 p. **303.4**
1. Social change -- Psychological aspects. 2. Social problems -- Psychological aspects. 3. Environmentalism. 4. Culture shock.
ISBN 9781594485855
LC 2012043406

Offers guidance for transforming fears about environmental issues into useful forces in individual lives, advocating the taking of small, constructive steps toward handling problems that seem beyond our control, and maintaining hope.

Toffler, Alvin
★**Future** shock / Alvin Toffler. Random House, 1970. xii, 505 p. **303.4**
1. Social history -- 1945- 2. Social change. 3. Civilization, Western -- 1950- 4. Regression (Civilization)

LC 67012744

"According to the author, future shock is the dizzying disorientation brought on by the premature arrival of the future. Toffler outlines some interesting strategies for survival, writing in a clear popular style." Publishers Weekly.

303.40973 Social change--United States

Giridharadas, Anand
Winners take all : the elite charade of changing the world / Anand Giridharadas. Random House Inc 2018 304 p. **303.40973**
1. World politics 2. Elite (Social sciences) 3. Power (Social sciences) 4. Wealth
ISBN 9780451493248
LC 2017045477

The author of *The True American* presents a scathing insider's report on the realities of the global elite's efforts to tackle important world issues through philanthropy and free enterprise while ignoring their direct role in creating the problems.

Klineberg, Stephen L., 1940-
Prophetic city : Houston on the cusp of a changing America / Stephen L. Klineberg. Avid Reader Press, 2020. ix, 319 p. : **303.40973**
1. Cities and towns 2. Social change 3. Urban sociology 4. Sociology 5. Houston, Texas
ISBN 9781501177910

A sociologist uses a longitudinal study of the ethnically and culturally diverse city of Houston to demonstrate how American society is going to change in the next century, cataloging ongoing changes in attitudes, beliefs and life experiences.

"A must-read, highly recommended sociological perspective of America's future." Library Journal

303.44 Growth and development

Pinker, Steven, 1954-
★**Enlightenment** now : the case for reason, science, humanism, and progress / Steven Pinker. Viking Press, 2018. 528 p. **303.44**
1. Quality of life 2. Social indicators 3. Social behavior 4. Social psychology
ISBN 9780525427575
LC 2017301147

A follow-up to The Better Angels of Our Nature challenges the doom-and-gloom outlooks of today's media to present dozens of graphs and charts demonstrating that life quality, health, prosperity, safety, peace, knowledge and happiness are actually on the rise throughout the world as a result of the philosophies about an Enlightenment era that uses science to improve human existence.

"Pinker's sober, lucid, and meticulously researched vision of human progress is heartening and important." Publishers Weekly.

West, Geoffrey B.
Scale : the universal laws of growth, innovation, sustainability, and the pace of life, in organisms, cities, economies, and companies / Geoffrey West. Penguin Press, 2017. 496 p. **303.44**
1. Size 2. Longevity 3. Evolution 4. Complexity (Philosophy)
ISBN 9781594205583
LC 2016056756

A theoretical physicist and pioneer in complexity science uncovers interesting details about the body's use of energy and its metabolism while investigating the human lifespan, and uncovers even more surprising results when applying the same investigative principles towards cities and companies.

"Illuminating and entertaining--heady science written for a lay readership, bringing scaling theory and kindred ideas to a large audience." Kirkus.

303.48 Causes of change

Albert, Daniel M. (Daniel Marc)
Are we there yet? : the American automobile, past, present, and driverless / Dan Albert. W. W. Norton & Company, [2019] 304 p. **303.48**
1. Automobile driving 2. Automobiles -- Social aspects 3. Automobiles -- History 4. Automobiles -- Technological innovations
ISBN 9780393292749
LC 2019014088

"Tech giants and automakers have been teaching robots to drive. In Are We There Yet?, Dan Albert combines historical scholarship with personal narrative to explore how car culture has suffused America's DNA. The plain, old-fashioned, human-driven car built our economy, won our wars, and shaped our democratic creed as it moved us about. Since the 1980s, the car culture has triumphed and we now drive more miles than ever before. Have we reached the end of the road this time?"--Provided by publisher.

Arbesman, Samuel
Overcomplicated : technology at the limits of comprehension

/ Samuel Arbesman. Current, 2016. x, 244 p. ; **303.48**

1. Technology and civilization. 2. Technological complexity 3. Complexity (Philosophy) 4. Systems theory
ISBN 9781591847762

LC 2016286046

A complexity scientist describes how our computer and technological systems have become too complex and interconnected for humans to fully understand or predict how they will function anymore and argues for a new framework that will make them simpler.

Bingham, Clara

Witness to the revolution : radicals, resisters, vets, hippies, and the year America lost its mind and found its soul / Clara Bingham. Random House, 2016. 384 p. **303.48**

1. Social movements. 2. Student movements. 3. Vietnam War, 1961-1975 -- Protest movements. 4. Radicalism. 5. United States -- Social conditions -- 1960-1980. 6. Oral histories
ISBN 9780812993189

LC 2015046134

Includes index.

Offers a riveting oral history of American society in the turbulent years of the Vietnam War as told by the people in the thick of it, including Jane Fonda, Daniel Ellsberg, Bill Ayers, and many more.

"While Bingham's is one of many retrospective looks at that period, it is one of the most immediate and personal." Booklist.

Brooks, Mike, 1968-

Tech generation : raising balanced kids in a hyper-connected world / Mike Brooks, PH.D. and Jon Lasser, Ph.D.. Oxford University Press, 2018 xii, 314 p. ; **303.48**

1. Technology and children 2. Computers and families 3. Internet and families 4. Child rearing
ISBN 9780190665296

LC 2017047898

"Tech Generation: Raising Balanced Kids in a Hyper-Connected World guides parents in teaching their children how to reap the benefits of living in a digital world while also preventing its negative effects. Mike Brooks and Jon Lasser, psychologists with extensive experience working with kids, parents, and teachers, combine cutting-edge research and expertise to create an engaging and helpful guide that emphasizes the importance of the parent-child relationship".-- Provided by publisher.

Brynjolfsson, Erik

★The **second** machine age : work, progress, and prosperity in the time of brilliant technologies / Erik Brynjolfsson and Andrew McAfee. W W Norton & Co Inc 2014. 304 p. **303.48**

1. Forecasting. 2. Technology -- Social aspects 3. Technological innovations 4. Information technology
ISBN 9780393239355

LC 2013041204

A pair of technology experts describe how humans will have to keep pace with machines in order to become prosperous in the future and identify strategies and policies for business and individuals to use to combine digital processing power with human ingenuity.

Burrough, Bryan, 1961-

Days of rage : America's radical underground, the FBI, and the forgotten age of revolutionary violence / Bryan Burrough. Penguin, 2015 464 p. **303.48**

1. FBI -- History 2. Weather Underground Organization 3. Symbionese Liberation Army. 4. Black Liberation Army 5. Guerrillas. 6. Political violence. 7. Radical organizations -- United States -- History. 8. Radicalism -- United States -- History.
ISBN 9781594204296

LC 2014036663

An account of the decade-long battle between the FBI and America's revolutionary counterculture documents terrorist activities stemming from radical period beliefs, tracing the stories of such groups as the Weathermen and the Black Liberation Army.

"The author's history is thoroughgoing and fascinating, though with a couple of curious notes--e.g., the likening of the Weathermen et al. to the Nazi Werewolf guerrillas 'who briefly attempted to resist Allied forces after the end of World War II.' A superb chronicle, long--but no longer than needed--and detailed, that sheds light on how the war on terror is being waged today." Kirkus.

Carr, Nicholas G., 1959-

The **big** switch : rewiring the world, from Edison to Google / Nicholas Carr. W. W. Norton & Co., 2008. vii, 278 p. ; **303.48**

1. Computers and civilization. 2. Information technology -- Social aspects. 3. Computer technology -- Business applications. 4. Technological innovations.
ISBN 9780393062281

LC 2007038084

A hundred years ago, companies stopped producing their own power with steam engines and plugged into the newly built electric grid. The cheap power pumped out by electric utilities not only changed how businesses operated but also brought the modern world into existence. Today a similar revolution is under way. Companies are dismantling their private computer systems and tapping into rich services delivered over the Internet. This time it's computing that's turning into a utility. The shift is already remaking the computer industry, bringing new competitors like Google to the fore and threatening traditional stalwarts like Microsoft and Dell. But the effects will reach much further. Cheap computing will ultimately change society as profoundly as cheap electricity did. Here, business journalist Carr weaves together history, economics, and technology to explain why computing is changing--and what it means for all of us.--From publisher description.

"The author examines the future of the Internet, which he says may one day completely replace the desktop PC as all computing services are delivered over the Net as a utility, the Internet morphing into one giant World Wide Computer." Booklist.

Carr, Nicholas G., 1959-

Utopia is creepy : and other provocations / Nicholas Carr. W. W. Norton & Co., 2016 320 p. **303.48**

1. Technology 2. Computers 3. Essays
ISBN 9780393254549

LC 2016018920

An alternative history of the digital age chronicles its roller-coaster crazes and crashes through a series of incisive essays including, "Is Google Making Us Stupid?" and "Life, Liberty, and the Pursuit of Privacy."

"A collection that reminds us that critical thinking is the best way to view the mixed blessings of rampant technology." Kirkus.

Dear, Brian, 1961-

The **friendly** orange glow : the story of the PLATO system and the dawn of cyberculture / Brian Dear. Pantheon Books, [2017] 384 p. **303.48**

1. PLATO (Electronic computer system) -- History 2. Computers 3. Cyberspace 4. Computer networks
ISBN 9781101871553

LC 2017013007

Documents the lesser-known story of the 1960s computer program and platform that the author argues marked the true beginning of cyberculture, revealing the role of PLATO ideas in inspiring countless technological innovations, from flat-panel wall TVs to multiplayer games.

"An exploration of the computer system that was too far ahead of its time to succeed but whose legacy quietly endures." Kirkus.

Diamandis, Peter H.

Abundance : the future is better than you think / Peter H. Diamandis and Steven Kotler. Free Press, 2012. 256 p. **303.48**

1. Technological innovations. 2. Technological forecasting. 3. Abundance. 4. Technology -- Social aspects.

ISBN 9781451614213

LC 2011039926

Proposes that the current exponential progress of technology in certain fields will allow us to easily provide for the needs of all people within the near future, and profiles some of today's most promising advances toward that end.

Diamond, Jared M.

★**Upheaval** : Turning Points for Nations in Crisis / Jared Diamond. Little Brown & Co, 2019. 512 p. **303.48**

1. Social evolution. 2. Crisis management 3. Sociocultural anthropology. 4. Psychic trauma

ISBN 9780316409131

LC 2018952825

The Pulitzer Prize-winning author of Guns, Germs, and Steel and Collapse offers a new theory of how and why some nations recover from national trauma and others don't.

"Diamond is a master at explicating matters of pressing importance. His earlier books garnered a vast readership, and there will be equal demand for this one, too. " Library Journal.

Ernst, Carl W., 1950-

Following Muhammad : rethinking Islam in the contemporary world / Carl W. Ernst. University of North Carolina Press, 2003. xxv, 244 p. : **303.48**

1. Islam -- 21st century. 2. Religion and culture. 3. Civilization, Islamic. 4. Muslims.

ISBN 9780807828373

LC 2003011162

The author departs from the Middle Eastern-focused orientation of many guides to Islam, focusing on the religion as a worldwide phenomenon that is practiced by twenty percent of the world's population, covering the various movements within the religion that affect the modern world. (Religion--Islam)

"The author informs readers of the roles played by colonialism, Christian missionary efforts, and Western conceptions of just what religion is, all in relation to American conceptions of Islam." Library Journal.

Freeberg, Ernest

The **age** of Edison : electric light and the invention of modern America / Ernest Freeberg. Penguin, 2013. 368 p. **303.48**

1. Edison, Thomas A. (Thomas Alva), 1847-1931 2. Electrical engineering -- History. 3. Electricity -- History.

ISBN 9781594204265

LC 2012039513

A history of the culture of invention as epitomized by Thomas Edison demonstrates how America's lead in the electric light revolution of the late-19th century transformed the country, explaining how electric light served as a catalyst for a profound shift from rural to urban-dominated culture and prompted the migration of millions of workers to urban centers while shifting priorities to science, technology and patent law.

Friedman, Thomas L.

★**Thank** you for being late : an optimist's guide to thriving in the age of accelerations / Thomas L. Friedman. Farrar Straus & Giroux 2016 320 p. **303.48**

1. Information technology 2. Globalization. 3. Climate change 4. Human/computer interaction 5. United States -- Politics and government.

ISBN 9780374273538

LC 2016034910

A field guide to the 21st century by a three-time Pulitzer Prize recipient and author of The World Is Flat shares strategies for surviving today's hectic technological, environmental and economic challenges, contrasting present-day environments with the working model of an earlier generation.

"Required reading for a generation that's 'going to be asked to dance in a hurricane.'" Kirkus.

Fry, Hannah

Hello world : being human in the age of algorithms / Hannah Fry. W.W. Norton & Company, 2018. 272 p. **303.48**

1. Human/computer interaction 2. Algorithms 3. Options, alternatives, choices 4. Computer programs

ISBN 9780393634990

LC 2018029663

A mathematician takes readers on a tour of the algorithms that automate our modern decisions, telling us what to watch and where to go and describes their inner workings, their limitations and the ways they can improve human systems.

Gray, Emma

A **girl's** guide to joining the resistance : a feminist handbook on fighting for good / Emma Gray ; illustrated by Eva Hill. William Morrow, 2018 xiii, 130 p. : **303.48**

1. Social action -- United States. 2. Social change -- United States. 3. Women -- Political activity -- United States. 4. Women social reformers -- United States.

ISBN 9780062748089

LC bl2018028853

Ideally suited to gift-giving, a guide for prospective activists by the Executive Women's Editor at HuffPost shares background information on key issues affecting today's women, insights into how to recognize bogus news, advice for navigating critical friends and practical guidelines for how to get and stay involved.

Hedges, Chris

Wages of rebellion / Chris Hedges. Nation Books, 2015 304 p. **303.48**

1. Revolutions -- Social aspects. 2. Social movements. 3. Protest movements.

ISBN 9781568589664

LC 2014044940

"Revolutions come in waves and cycles. We are again riding the crest of a revolutionary epic, much like 1848 or 1917, from the Arab Spring to movements against austerity in Greece to the Occupy movement. In Wages of Rebellion, Chris Hedges--who has chronicled the malaise and sickness of a society in terminal moral decline in his books Empire of Illusion and Death of the Liberal Class--investigates what social and psychological factors cause revolution, rebellion, and resistance. Drawing on an ambitious overview of prominent philosophers, historians, and literary figures he shows not only the harbingers of a coming crisis but also the nascent seeds of rebellion. Hedges' message is clear: popular uprisings in the United States and around the world are inevitable in the face of environmental destruction and wealth polarization".-- Provided by publisher.

"People tend to either love or hate Hedges, but librarians in public, academic, and relevant special libraries will want this book because, even if the revolution isn't about to happen, Hedges's voice is an important one." Library Journal.

Heffernan, Virginia

Magic and loss : the pleasures of the internet / Virginia Heffernan. Simon & Schuster, 2016 256 p. **303.48**

1. Internet 2. Culture 3. Digital media

ISBN 9781439191705

LC 2016288052

A digital-culture expert who writes for The New York Times Magazine discusses the logic, aesthetics, cultural potential and societal impact of the Internet, a medium that favors speed, accuracy, wit, prolificacy and versatility.

"A thoroughly engrossing examination of the Internet's past, present, and future." Kirkus.

Hessler, Peter, 1969-

Country driving : a journey from farm to factory / Peter Hessler. Harper, 2010. 448 p. **303.48**

1. Modernization (Social sciences) 2. Industrialization. 3. Transportation, Automotive. 4. Voyages and travels. 5. China -- Description and travel.

ISBN 9780061804090

LC 2009027502

"Narrative account of how the development and diffusion of cars and roads have changed China".--Provided by publisher.

"Full of exotic detail, solid reporting, and ironic observation, Country Driving offers a personal snapshot of the world's second superpower hurtling through the 21st century." Boston Globe.

Ito, Joichi, 1966-

Whiplash : how to survive our faster future / Joi Ito and Jeff Howe. Grand Central Publishing, 2016. 320 p. **303.48**

1. Massachusetts Institute of Technology. Media Laboratory. 2. Technology and civilization. 3. Digital communications. 4. Technological innovations -- Social aspects. 5. Forecasting.

ISBN 9781455544592

LC 2016032313

"A standout among titles on technology and innovation, it will repay readingand rereadingby leaders in all fields." Kirkus.

Kaku, Michio

Physics of the future : how science will shape human destiny and our daily Lives by the year 2100 / Michio Kaku. Random House Inc 2011 352 p. **303.48**

1. Forecasting. 2. Physics -- Miscellanea. 3. Science -- Miscellanea. 4. Mathematical physics

ISBN 9780385530804

LC 2010026569

Outlines a provocative vision of the role of science in daily life at the beginning of the next century, describing such technologies as mind-controlled computers, sensor-based health care, and laser-propulsion spaceships.

Kelly, Kevin, 1952-

The **inevitable** : understanding the 12 technological forces that will shape our future / Kevin Kelly. Viking Press, 2016. 336 p. **303.48**

1. Technology -- Social aspects. 2. Technology and civilization. 3. Information society 4. High technology -- Influence.

ISBN 9780525428084

LC bl2016020837

In expert tech writer discusses the forces and trends--including flowing, screening, accessing, sharing, filtering, remixing, tracking and questioning--that will revolutionize our daily lives through the upcoming technological advances of the next 30 years.

"Kelly's arguments ring true, and his enthusiasm is contagious." Kirkus.

Khalidi, Rashid

Resurrecting Empire : western footprints and America's perilous path in the Middle East / Rashid Khalidi. Beacon Press, c2004. xiv, 223 p. ; **303.48**

1. Democracy -- Middle East. 2. Arab-Israeli conflict. 3. Middle East -- Foreign relations United States. 4. United States -- Foreign relations Middle East.

ISBN 0807002348

LC 2003023161

Describes the history of Western involvement in the Middle East and argues that the United States ignores history and is blindly committed to a path that is doomed for failure.

Ladd, Brian, 1957-

Autophobia : love and hate in the automotive age / Brian Ladd. University of Chicago Press, 2008. 236 p. **303.48**

1. Automobiles -- Social aspects. 2. Transportation, Automotive -- Social aspects -- History 3. Environmental degradation. 4. Automobile ownership -- Social aspects. 5. United States -- Social life and customs 6. United States -- Social life and customs -- 20th century 7. United States -- Social life and customs -- 20th century

ISBN 9780226467412

LC 2008014520

"Increases in oil prices have driven gasoline costs into the psyche of every American. Ladd (The Ghosts of Berlin) documents a century of expanding U.S. reliance on vehicles powered by oil, most of which has to be imported. He frames his analysis in familiar concepts: the automotive industry as employer, urban migration from cities by families relying on automobiles for transportation, traffic/congestion/roadways, and damage to the environment from burning fossil fuels." Library Journal

Lanier, Jaron

★**You** are not a gadget : a manifesto / Jaron Lanier. Alfred A. Knopf, 2010. 209 p. ; **303.48**

1. Internet. 2. Internet and identity. 3. Technology and civilization. 4. Web 2.0.

ISBN 9780307269645

LC 2009020298

"In the nineteen-eighties, Lanier belonged to what he calls a merry band of Internet pioneers who believed that the digital revolution would mean a groundswell of creativity. But, he argues in this manifesto, around the turn of this century the dream was hijacked by digital Maoists, who value the crowd above the individual. Their influence, he writes, has led to an online culture of mashups, pervasive anonymity (which encourages bullying and moblike behavior), open access (so that individual ownership is devalued or lost), and social-networking sites that reduce the deep meaning of personhood. He fears that these characteristics are perilously close to lock-in: becoming permanent features of the Web. Lanier's detractors have accused him of Ludditism, but his argument will make intuitive sense to anyone concerned with questions of propriety, responsibility, and authenticity." The New Yorker.

Marantz, Andrew

Antisocial : online extremists, techno-utopians, and the hijacking of the American conversation / Andrew Marantz. Viking, 2019. 380 p. ; **303.48**

1. Social media 2. Extremism 3. Political culture -- United States 4. High technology industry and trade

ISBN 9780525522263

A New Yorker staff writer presents a deeply immersive chronicle of how well-intentioned entrepreneurs of Silicon Valley created a democratic internet where freedoms have been exploited by propagandists who have shifted extreme ideologies into the mainstream.

McAfee, Andrew

Machine, platform, crowd : harnessing the digital revolution / Andrew McAfee and Erik Brynjolfsson. W W Norton & Co Inc., 2017. 288 p. **303.48**

1. Technological innovations 2. Leadership in business 3. Change 4. Management

ISBN 9780393254297

LC 2017016682

The authors of the best-selling The Second Machine Age present a guide to leadership success in today's dynamic, counter-intuitive economy, explaining the importance of rebalancing organizations away from traditional models in favor of the actual sources of profitable innovation.

"Provocative reading for futurists, investors, and inventors." Kirkus.

Otto, Shawn Lawrence

Fool me twice : fighting the assault on science in America / Shawn Lawrence Otto. Rodale ; c2011. 376 p. ; **303.48**

1. Science -- Political aspects. 2. Science policy. 3. Knowledge -- Social aspects. 4. Learning and scholarship.

ISBN 9781605292175

LC 2011033902

Reveals how social and policy changes are failing to support scientific research in such key areas as climate change, energy and genetics, counseling readers on how to overcome such challenges as political denials and a lack of scientific government expertise. By the writer of the Academy Award-nominated House of Sand and Fog.

"The author explores the devaluation of science in America. His exhaustively researched text explains the three-pronged attack on science: how right-wing Christian fervor discredits evolution; how post-modernism and cultural sensitivity makes people believe that objective truth doesn't exist; and how corporations discredit scientists in order to further economic agendas. The accessible book will inform scientists about what has happened to their field, provide an overview for laypeople, and allow educators to equip themselves to address these issues for the next generation and reverse this troubling trend." Publishers Weekly.

The **war** on science : who's waging it, why it matters, what we can do about it / Shawn Otto Milkweed Editions, 2016 x, 514 p. **303.48**

1. Science -- Political aspects 2. Science policy. 3. Climate change 4. Politicians

ISBN 9781571313539

LC 2016002797

Includes index

Examines the current state of science in the political sphere, looking at how strategies for alleviating global warming are resisted by powerful interests and faith-based objections to the teaching of evolution erupt from the public.

Preston, Diana, 1952-

Before the fallout : from Marie Curie to Hiroshima / Diana Preston. Walker & Co., 2005. xiv, 400 p. : **303.48**

1. Nuclear weapons development -- Moral and ethical aspects. 2. Science -- Moral and ethical aspects. 3. Atomic bomb -- Human effects. 4. Weapons of mass destruction -- Moral and ethical aspects. 5. Hiroshima, Japan -- Atomic bombing, 1945.

ISBN 0802714455

LC 2004061953

"Avidly researched and gracefully constructed, Preston's revelatory history is rich in telling moments, powerful personalities, intense confrontations, and indelible images of the devastation delivered by nuclear weapons, our Damoclean sword." Booklist.

Ramo, Joshua Cooper

The **seventh** sense : power, fortune, and survival in the age of networks / Joshua Cooper Ramo. Little, Brown and Co., 2016. 352 p. **303.48**

1. Internet -- Social aspects. 2. Computer networks. 3. Social networks. 4. Technology and civilization.

ISBN 9780316285063

LC 2015960065

A director of the Starbucks and FedEx corporations and policy expert--drawing on examples from business, science and politics--sheds new light on our transformative world, explaining how to understand and survive the modern digital age. By the author of the international best-seller The Age of the Unthinkable.

Razsa, Maple

Bastards of utopia : living radical politics after socialism / Maple Razsa. Indiana University Press, 2015 296 p. **303.48**

1. Radicalism 2. Post-communism 3. Anti-globalization movement 4. Occupy movement 5. Croatia

ISBN 9780253015839

LC 2014044169

"In this novel work of ethnography, Razsa takes readers into the intimate world of protest shared by Balkan activists in the alter-globalization movement." Publishers Weekly

Rid, Thomas, 1975-

Rise of the machines : a cybernetic history / Thomas Rid. W. W. Norton & Co., 2016 xvi, 414 p. ; **303.48**

1. Cybernetics 2. Social history. 3. Technology and civilization. 4. Computers and civilization

ISBN 9780393286007

A sweeping history of cybernetics explores the discipline's early myths and wide-ranging influence after World War II, illuminating specific examples of cybernetics applications as utopian technologies, political tools and military weapons.

Ridley, Matt

The **evolution** of everything : how new ideas emerge / Matt Ridley. Harper, 2015. 400 p. **303.48**

1. Evolution. 2. Diffusion of innovations. 3. Technology and civilization. 4. Civilization, Western

ISBN 9780062296009

LC 2015026886

"A book that makes the case for evolution over design and skewers a widespread but dangerous myth: that we have ultimate control over our world".-- Provided by publisher.

How innovation works : and why it flourishes in freedom /

Matt Ridley. Harper, 2020. 320 p. **303.48**
1. Diffusion of innovations 2. Technological innovations
ISBN 9780062916594
LC bl2020010770

The author describes the history of innovation and how it differs from invention through lively stories about steam engines, jet engines, search engines, airships, coffee, potatoes, vaping, antibiotics and mosquito nets.

"An enthusiastic history of human technical innovation. . . . Opinionated, often counterintuitive, full of delicious stories, always provocative." Kirkus

Rushkoff, Douglas

Present shock : when everything happens now / Douglas Rushkoff. Current, 2013. 240 p. **303.48**
1. Technology -- Philosophy. 2. Mass media and culture. 3. Time -- Social aspects. 4. Forecasting. 5. United States -- Social conditions -- 21st century -- Forecasts.
ISBN 9781591844761
LC 2012039915

Examines the pros and cons of today's digitally driven, real-time world, explaining how to safeguard against the vulnerabilities of instant-experience media while maximizing its benefits.

Solnit, Rebecca

A **paradise** built in hell : the extraordinary communities and strange joys that arise in disasters / Rebecca Solnit. Viking, 2009. 432 p. **303.48**
1. Disasters -- Social aspects. 2. Altruism 3. Solidarity. 4. Disasters -- Psychological aspects.
ISBN 9780670021079
LC 2009004101

Explores the phenomenon through which people become resourceful and altruistic after a disaster and communities often reflect a shared sense of purpose, analyzing such events as the 1906 San Francisco earthquake, the September 11 attacks, and Hurricane Katrina.

Steiner-Adair, Catherine

The **big** disconnect : protecting childhood and family relationships in the digital age / Catherine Steiner-Adair, Ed. D. ; with Teresa H. Barker. Harper, 2013 374 p. ; **303.48**
1. Internet and families -- Social aspects -- United States 2. Technology and children -- Social aspects -- United States 3. Computers and families -- Social aspects -- United States 4. Digital media -- Social aspects -- United States
ISBN 9780062082428
LC 2013372439

In this book the author offers insights and advice that can help parents achieve greater understanding, authority, and confidence as they come up against the tech revolution and how families can combat the disconnection we are experiencing from our extreme device dependence.

Sumpter, David

Outnumbered : from Facebook and Google to fake news and filter-bubbles - the algorithms that control our lives / David Sumpter. Bloomsbury Sigma, 2018. 272 p. : **303.48**
1. Google (Firm) 2. Facebook (Firm) 3. Data mining. 4. Algorithms. 5. Computers and civilization. 6. Mathematics.
ISBN 9781472947413
LC bl2018134735

The surprising--and terrifying--story of how math and stats work in the real world.

"In his clear account of how algorithms work, Sumpter provides comfort to those who fear them as an insidious form of mind control, concluding that the real work is to address human biases." Publishers Weekly.

Tenner, Edward

Our own devices : the past and future of body technology / Edward Tenner. Alfred A. Knopf, 2003. xviii, 314 p. **303.48**
1. Technology -- Social aspects. 2. Technological innovations -- Social aspects. 3. Human body -- Social aspects. 4. Human body
ISBN 9780375407222
LC 2002040694

Looks at how the inventions we have created to help, protect, and ease our lives dramatically affect the human body and human life, examining the sometimes surprising ways in which technology has transformed the world.

Thompson, Clive, 1968-

Smarter than you think : how technology is changing our minds for the better / Clive Thompson. The Penguin Press, 2013 341 p. ; **303.48**
1. Technology. 2. Internet 3. Information technology. 4. Knowledge management.
ISBN 9781594204456
LC 2013017155

Shows how every technological advance, from the printing press to the Internet, has been disparaged, caused hand-wringing, and has generated anxious predictions of doom, but actually has augmented human life for the better.

"A well-framed celebration of how the digital world will make us bigger, rather than diminish us." Kirkus.

Turkle, Sherry

Alone together : why we expect more from technology and less from each other / Sherry Turkle. Basic Books, 2017. xxvi, 361 p. ; **303.48**
1. Information technology -- Social aspects. 2. Interpersonal relations. 3. Human-computer interaction. 4. Technological innovations.
ISBN 9780465093656
LC 2010030614

Argues that social-networking sites, companion robots, and other technology are fueling disturbing levels of isolation and are causing humans to mistake digital communication for actual human connection.

"Turkle's prescient book makes a strong case that what was meant to be a way to facilitate communications has pushed people closer to their machines and further away from each other." Publishers Weekly.

Venter, J. Craig

Life at the speed of light : from the double helix to the dawn of digital life / J. Craig Venter. Viking, 2013 240 p. **303.48**
1. Science -- Social aspects. 2. Biology -- Philosophy. 3. Genetics 4. Genomes.
ISBN 9780670025404
LC 2013017049

The author of A Life Decoded explains how his team's achievement with sequencing the human genome has launched an important age of biological research, revealing a growing potential for enabling humans to adapt and evolve for long-term survival and environmental improvement.

Wachter-Boettcher, Sara

Technically wrong : sexist apps, biased algorithms, and other threats of toxic tech / Sara Wachter-Boettcher. W. W. Norton &

Company, 2017 232 p. **303.48**

1. System failures (Engineering) 2. Business failures 3. Technology -- Social aspects. 4. Ethics.

ISBN 9780393634631

Explores the ways in which technology can fail its users by returning unethical, inaccurate, and biased information and argues that technology design needs to be modified to be of better service.

"In straightforward prose, Wachter-Boettcher lays out a convincing and damning argument about the small daily failures and large systemic issues that stem from Silicon Valley's diversity problem." School Library Journal.

Weinberger, David, 1950-

Too big to know : rethinking knowledge now that the facts aren't the facts, experts are everywhere, and the smartest person in the room is the room / David Weinberger. Basic Books, c2011. xiv, 231 p. ; **303.48**

1. Information technology -- Social aspects. 2. Internet -- Social aspects. 3. Knowledge. 4. Computers and civilization.

ISBN 9780465021420

LC 2011034727

Reveals how business, science, education, and the government are learning to use networked knowledge to make better decisions, offering insight into how the Internet age has enabled greater access to information from various perspectives.

Young, Ralph F.

Dissent : the history of an American idea / Ralph Young. New York University Press, 2015. xi, 603 p. ; **303.48**

1. Dissenters -- United States -- History. 2. Protest movements 3. Social reformers -- United States -- History. 4. Democracy -- United States -- History. 5. United States -- Politics and government. 6. United States -- Social conditions.

ISBN 9781479806652

Examines the key role dissent has played in shaping the United States, focusing on those who, from colonial times to the present, dissented against the ruling paradigm of their time, responding to what they saw as the injustices that prevented them from fully experiencing their vision of America.

Zarkadakis, George

In our own image : savior or destroyer? the history and future of artificial intelligence / George Zarkadakis. Pegasus Books, 2016 384 p. **303.48**

1. Artificial intelligence 2. Human/computer interaction. 3. Machine theory. 4. Intelligence.

ISBN 9781605989648

LC bl2016009645

Exploring the history and future, as well as the societal and ethical implications, of Artificial Intelligence (AI), the author, who has a PhD in AI, explains its history, technology and potential; its manifestations in intelligent machines; its connections to neurology and conscious; and what AI reveals about us human beings.

"A delightfully lucid combination of the history, philosophy, and science behind thinking machines." Kirkus.

303.482 Contact between cultures

Linden, Eugene, 1947-

The **ragged** edge of the world : encounters at the frontier where modernity, wildlands, and indigenous peoples meet / Eugene Linden. Viking, 2011. 272 p. **303.482**

1. Indigenous peoples -- Social conditions 2. First contact of indigenous peoples with Europeans 3. Anthropology 4. Kinship-based society

ISBN 9780670022519

LC 2010043578

Includes index.

A noted environmental writer shares his observations about natural regions of the world that have been dramatically changed by modern influences, describing cultural and climate transformations in such areas as Vietnam, Cuba, and the Antarctic.

"Traveling to the rain forests of Borneo and to the Amazon, the Antarctic, and Africa, Linden provides firsthand accounts of cargo cults in New Guinea, practices of Pygmy tribes in Africa, and conservation efforts in Cuba--some of which show positive responses to deforestation and loss of habitat for wildlife, while others reveal the downward spiral to extinction for rain forests and many animal species. He highlights cultural extinction as much as environmental devastation to habitats. Linden provides an original look at globalization and its impact on various cultures and species throughout the world. Anyone interested in global environmental issues will find this book informative." Library Journal.

303.4833 Development of science and technology -- Communication

Johnson, Clay A.

The **information** diet : a case for conscious consumption / Clay A. Johnson. O'Reilly Media, c2012. ix, 150 p. ; **303.4833**

1. Personal information management. 2. Information management. 3. Information technology -- Management. 4. Information.

ISBN 9781449304683

"The modern human animal spends upwards of 11 hours out of every 24 in a state of constant consumption. Not eating, but gorging on information ceaselessly spewed from the screens and speakers we hold dear. Just as we have grown morbidly obese on sugar, fat, and flour--so, too, have we become gluttons for texts, instant messages, emails, RSS feeds, downloads, videos, status updates, and tweets.We're all battling a storm of distractions, buffeted with notifications and tempted by tasty tidbits of information. And just as too much junk food can lead to obesity, too much junk information can lead to cluelessness." -- Publisher's blurb.

303.484 Purposefully induced change

McCarthy, Timothy Patrick

The **radical** reader : a documentary history of the American radical tradition / edited by Timothy Patrick McCarthy and John McMillian ; foreword by Eric Foner. New Press, 2003. xvi, 688 p. ; **303.484**

1. Radicalism -- United States -- History

ISBN 9781565846821

LC 2002041051

"For this collection, McCarthy and McMillian (both history & literature, Harvard) selected more than 200 primary documents representing American progressive radical traditions." Library Journal

303.49 Social forecasts

Khanna, Parag

Connectography : mapping the future of global civilization

/ Parag Khanna. Random House, 2016 320 p. **303.49**

1. Human geography. 2. Geopolitics. 3. International economic relations. 4. International relations.
ISBN 9780812988550

LC 2015041766

Argues that control of highways, railways, canals, Internet cables and electricity grids is the key to nations' power in the future, in a book that explores which countries have, and will have in the future, the strongest hold on the world's supply chains and trade routes.

303.4909 Social forecasts--History and biography

Brockman, John, 1941-,

This will change everything : ideas that will shape the future / edited by John Brockman. Harper Perennial, c2010. xxiii, 390 p. **303.4909**

1. Scientific discoveries. 2. Social prediction. 3. Inventions.
ISBN 9780061899676

LC bl2011021495

"Edge.org presents 125 of today's leading thinkers ... [responding to the question,] 'What game-changing scientific ideas and developments do you expect to live to see?'"--Cover.

Collects the perspectives of more than 150 leading intellectuals on scientific ideas and developments that are expected to change the world in the near future, from Ian McEwan's thoughts on the flourishing of solar power to Chris Anderson's views on how the Internet will revolutionize education.

303.6 Conflict and conflict resolution

Camus, Albert, 1913-1960

★The **rebel** : an essay on man in revolt / Albert Camus ; with a foreword by Herbert Read ; a revised and complete translation of L'Homme revolte by Anthony Bower. Vintage Books, 1991. xii, 306 p. ; **303.6**

1. Revolutions. 2. Essays
ISBN 9780679733843

LC 91050022

The author traces the ways in which the theories of philosophers such as Rousseau, Hegel and Marx have been misused.

Carr, Caleb, 1955-

The **lessons** of terror : a history of warfare against civilians / Caleb Carr. Random House Trade Paperbacks, 2003, c2002. xiv, 302 p. **303.6**

1. Terrorism -- History. 2. Essays.
ISBN 9780375760747

LC 2003269876

Originally published: New York : Random House, 2002.

"The author argues that terrorism must be viewed in terms of military history, rather than political science or sociology, and that the refusal to label terrorists as soldiers, rather than criminals, is a mistake. This often fascinating, accessible tome skillfully contends that the terrorizing of civilians has a long and controversial history but, as an inferior method, is prone to failure." Publishers Weekly.

Junger, Sebastian

Tribe : on homecoming and belonging / Sebastian Junger. Twleve, 2016. 160 p. **303.6**

1. Veterans 2. Homecomings 3. Psychic trauma 4. Belonging
ISBN 9781455566389

LC 2016933855

Takes readers on an investigation of how we overcome trauma and seek something bigger than ourselves.

"Junger uses every word in this slim volume to make a passionate, compelling case for a more egalitarian society." Booklist.

Morris, Ian, 1960-

War! what is it good for? : conflict and the progress of civilization from primates to robots / Ian Morris. Farrar, Straus and Giroux, 2014 512 p. **303.6**

1. War and civilization. 2. War. 3. Military history. 4. War -- Influence.
ISBN 9780374286002

LC 2013038722

A powerful and provocative exploration of how war has changed our society--for the better "War! What is it good for? Absolutely nothing," says the famous song--but archaeology, history, and biology show that war in fact has been good for something. Surprising as it sounds, war has made humanity safer and richer. In War! What Is It Good For? the renowned historian and archaeologist Ian Morris tells the gruesome, gripping story of fifteen thousand years of war, going behind the battles and brutality to reveal what war has really done to and for the world. War has been history's greatest paradox, but this searching study of fifteen centuries of violence suggests that the next half century is going to be the most dangerous of all time. If we can survive it, the age-old dream of ending war may yet come to pass. But, Morris argues, only if we understand what war has been good for can we know where it will take us next.

"A profoundly uncomfortable but provocative argument that 'productive war' promotes greater safety, a decrease in violence and economic growth." Kirkus.

Popovi, Srdja

★**Blueprint** for revolution : how to use rice pudding, Lego men, and other nonviolent techniques to galvanize communities, overthrow dictators, or simply change the world / Srdja Popovic ; with Matthew Miller. Spiegel & Grau, 2015. xv, 282 p. : **303.6**

1. Civil disobedience. 2. Nonviolence. 3. Pacifism -- Political aspects. 4. Protest movements -- Philosophy.
ISBN 9780812995305

LC 2014005583

"In Blueprint for Revolution, Srdja Popovic outlines his philosophy for implementing peaceful world change and provides a model for activists everywhere through stories of his own experience toppling dictatorships (peacefully) and of smaller examples of social change (like Occupy Wall Street or fighting for gay rights or zoning changes). Through examples of using laughter and music (e.g., Pussy Riot) to disarm the opposition and gather supporters, to staging a protest of Lego Men in Siberia (when flesh-and-blood people would have been shot), to a boycott of Cottage cheese in Israel to challenge price inflation while organizing around rice pudding to overthrow the dictator of the Maldives, Popovic uses true and sometimes outrageously clever examples of the ways in which non-violent resistance has achieved its means. Popovic argues in favor of non-violent resistance not for ideological reasons (as persuasive as those are) but because non-violence actually works better than violence. An inspiring (and useful!) guide for any activist--and a thoroughly entertaining read for any armchair politico".-- Provided by publisher.

Rees, Martin J., 1942-

On the future : prospects for humanity / Martin Rees. Princeton University Press, 2018. 136 p. **303.6**

1. Humans 2. Survival 3. Forecasting 4. Technological forecasting
ISBN 9780691180441

LC bl2018189959

A world-renowned scientist and the author of Our Final Hour offers a provocative and inspiring look at the future of humanity and science, arguing that humans must think differently and harness technologies in the correct way to ensure their survival.

"An impassioned call to action from one of the world's foremost scientists. A book to be read by anyone on Earth who cares about its future." Kirkus.

Sontag, Susan, 1933-2004

Regarding the pain of others / Susan Sontag. Farrar, Straus and Giroux, 2003. 131 p. **303.6**

1. War and society. 2. War photography -- Social aspects. 3. War in art -- Social aspects. 4. Photojournalism -- Social aspects. 5. Essays
ISBN 9780374248581

LC 2002192527

An examination of the role of imagery in modern culture considers how depictions of violence, from wartime photographs to footage of the September 11 attacks, are used and how they impact the world.

"All libraries, regardless of type, size, or demographics, should own this book." Library Journal.

303.6083 Children--Social conflict

Canada, Geoffrey

Fist, stick, knife, gun : a personal history of violence in America / Geoffrey Canada. Beacon Press, 1995. xi, 179 p. ; **303.6083**

1. Children and violence. 2. Inner city. 3. Urban violence. 4. Violence. 5. New York City. 6. Bronx, New York City.
ISBN 0807004227

LC 94041357

"The author explains what is happening to poor, mostly black and brown youth in this country, as guns have replaced fist, stick, and knife as aggressive and protective weapons of choice. Canada's own battles for survival as a youth in the South Bronx punctuate and shape his argument." Library Journal.

303.60835 Adolescents--Social conflict

Younge, Gary

Another day in the death of America : a chronicle of ten short lives / Gary Younge. Nation Books, [2016] 256 p. **303.60835**

1. Gunshot victims 2. Violence -- United States. 3. Gun control 4. Violent crimes -- United States. 5. United States -- Social conditions -- 1980-
ISBN 9781568589756

LC 2016014076

J. Anthony Lukas Book Prize, 2017.

Tells the stories of the lives lost on November 23, 2013, profiling ten victims whose deaths exemplify the statistic that on an average day in America, seven young people aged nineteen or under will be shot dead.

"Younge provides nuance and context to a polarizing issue. The personal touches, however, are most affecting, as Younge pieces together each story from news reports and interviews with friends and family, weaving a tragic narrative of wasted potential." Publishers Weekly.

303.609 Conflict and conflict resolution--History, geographic treatment, biography

Pinker, Steven, 1954-

The **better** angels of our nature : why violence has declined / Steven Pinker. Viking, 2011. 848 p. **303.609**

1. Violence -- Psychological aspects. 2. Violence -- Social aspects. 3. Conscience. 4. Human nature.
ISBN 9780670022953

LC 2011015201

Cundill Prize in Historical Literature finalist

A controversial history of violence argues that today's world is the most peaceful time in human existence, drawing on psychological insights into intrinsic values that are causing people to condemn violence as an acceptable measure.

"This long, well-researched, comprehensive tour-de-force provides a helpful look at the human condition." Booklist.

303.60973 Social conflict--United States

Murphy, Chris (Christopher Scott), 1973-

★The **violence** inside us : a brief history of an ongoing American tragedy / Chris Murphy. Random House, [2020] 256 p. **303.60973**

1. Violence 2. Violence and guns 3. Gun control 4. Violence -- United States -- History. 5. United States -- Social conditions. 6. United States -- Politics and government.
ISBN 9781984854575

LC 2019030481

The youngest-elected U.S. Senator presents a sweeping history of the origins of humanity's violent impulses and obsession with firearms while exposing the national mythologies that block action against violence in today's America.

"Murphy's clear-eyed assessment of the nature of violence in America is destined to provoke meaningful, urgently needed discussions." Booklist.

304 Factors affecting social behavior

Davies, William, 1976-

The **happiness** industry : how the government and big business sold us well-being / William Davies. Verso, 2015. 314 p. ; **304**

1. Happiness. 2. Consumerism. 3. Emotions -- Economic aspects. 4. Marketing.
ISBN 9781781688458

LC 2014041594

"When Jeremy Bentham proposed that government should run 'for the greatest benefit of the greatest number,' he posed two problems: what is happiness and how can we measure it? With the rise of positive psychology, freakonimics, behavioural economics, endless TED talks, the happiness manifesto, the Happiness Index, the tyranny of customer service, the emergence of the quantified self movement, we have become a culture obsessed with measuring our supposed satisfaction. In anecdotes that include the Buddhist monk who lectured the business leaders of the world at Davos, why the Nike Fuel band makes us more worried about our fitness, how parts of our city are being rebuilt in response to scientific studies of oxytocin levels in our brain, and what a survey from Radisson hotels--that proves that 62% of us believe that well-being is a luxury worth more than work or a good relationship--really tells us about the way we measure ourselves, and continually find ourselves wanting".-- Provided by publisher.

304.2 Human ecology

Ackerman, Diane, 1948-

★The **human** age : the world shaped by us / Diane Ackerman. W.W. Norton & Company, 2014 352 p. **304.2**

1. Humans -- Effect of environment on 2. Environmental engineering 3. Environmental ethics. 4. Environmental degradation.
ISBN 9780393240740

LC 2014027691

National Outdoor Book Award for Natural History Literature, 2015.

Explores how human beings have become the dominant force shaping Earth's future by subduing three-quarters of the planet's surface, tinkering with nature, and altering the climate.

Barnosky, Anthony D.

Tipping point for planet earth : how close are we to the edge? / Anthony D. Barnosky and Elizabeth A. Hadly. Thomas Dunne Books, 2016. 272 p. **304.2**

1. Global environmental change. 2. Nature -- Effect of humans on 3. Conservation of natural resources. 4. Climate change
ISBN 9781250051158

LC 2015045236

Tipping Point for Planet Earth explains why Earth is headed for a tipping point, a change so fast, dramatic, and unexpected that humanity will reel at the consequences. Midway through this century, there will be more than nine billion people on the planet. Already we are using most of the arable land that exists and overfishing the oceans. Water, too, is becoming scarce in many places. The services that humans depend upon--like a supply of clean water, food production, and protection from disease--are subject to dangerous threats as well. We can still keep humanity moving forward by ensuring that the negative changes that are accumulating do not outweigh the positive ones.vided by publisher.

"Frequently unsettling, often surprising, yet not without a modicum of hope, the authors cogent and articulate analysis of our past and present offers an urgent view of the steps required to ensure a livable future." Booklist.

Busch, Akiko

How to disappear : notes on invisibility in a time of transparency / Akiko Busch. Penguin Press, 2019. 207 p. ; **304.2**

1. Invisibility 2. Camouflage (Biology) 3. Self 4. Privacy
ISBN 9781101980415

LC 2018029070

The author of Nine Ways to Cross a River explores the idea of invisibility in nature, art and science as part of the search for a more joyful and peaceful way of life in today's increasingly surveilled and publicity-obsessed world.

Diamond, Jared M.

★**Collapse** : how societies choose to fail or succeed / Jared Diamond. Viking, 2005. xi, 575 p., 24 p. of plates : **304.2**

1. Social history -- Case studies. 2. Social change -- Case studies. 3. Environmental policy -- Cases. 4. Environmental degradation.
ISBN 0670033375

LC 2004057152

ALA Notable Book, 2006.

"The author ... explores patterns of population growth, overfarming, overgrazing and overhunting, often abetted by drought, cold, rigid social mores and warfare, that lead inexorably to vicious circles of deforestation, erosion and starvation prompted by the disappearance of plant and animal food sources. . . . Readers will find his book an enthralling, and disturbing, reminder of the indissoluble links that bind humans to nature." Publishers Weekly.

Florida, Richard L.

Who's your city? : how the creative economy is making where to live the most important decision of your life / Richard Florida. Basic Books, 2008. viii, 374 p. : **304.2**

1. Human geography. 2. Human geography -- Economic aspects. 3. Cities and towns -- United States -- Rankings. 4. Cities and towns -- United States -- Ratings.
ISBN 9780465003525

LC 2008000134

Published in Canada by Random House Canada, 2008.

Examines the significance of place in terms of the global economy and our individual lives, careers, and social networks and includes city rankings by life stage that reveal the best places for singles, families, and empty-nesters to live.

Gessner, David, 1961-

My green manifesto : down the Charles River in pursuit of a new environmentalism / David Gessner. Milkweed Editions, 2011. 225 p. ; **304.2**

1. Environmentalism -- Psychological aspects 2. Environmental protection 3. River travel 4. Charles River, Massachusetts -- Description and travel
ISBN 9781571313249

LC 2011012994

A frank and lighthearted argument for a new environmentalism, inspired by the author's rough-and-tumble cross-country and down-river travels, explains how a previous working environmental movement has given way to extremism and capitalist ventures, calling for a refocus on local issues grounded in holistic and more effective defenses.

Hertsgaard, Mark, 1956-

Hot : living through the next fifty years on earth / Mark Hertsgaard. Houghton Mifflin Harcourt, 2010. 288 p. **304.2**

1. Global warming. 2. Climate change 3. Global environmental change. 4. Sustainable societies.
ISBN 9780618826124

LC 2010012416

Includes index.

"The author notes that we have entered the second era of global warming. Even if greenhouse-gas emissions ceased today, the consequences would continue for hundreds of years. Consequently, the author persuasively argues that we need to begin adapting to those changes, which does not mean that mitigating global warming is no longer important; in fact, it grows more urgent every day. Starkly clear and of utmost importance." Kirkus.

Jensen, Derrick, 1960-

What we leave behind / Derrick Jensen and Aric McBay. Seven Stories Press, c2009. x, 453 p. ; **304.2**

1. Solid waste disposal. 2. Nature -- Effect of humans on 3. Pollution 4. Environmental degradation
ISBN 9781583228678

LC 2008047287

This compelling book has a refreshing style, at once very personal and very passionate. It is also thorough, with historical, scientific, statistical, and anecdotal evidence filtered through a lot of anger and some quirky humor." Library Journal.

Kimmerer, Robin Wall

★**Braiding** sweetgrass : indigenous wisdom, scientific knowledge and the teachings of plants / Robin Wall Kimmerer. Milkweed Editions, 2013. 320 p. **304.2**

1. Kimmerer, Robin Wall. 2. Philosophy, Native American 3. Indigenous peoples -- Ecology. 4. Nature 5. Philosophy of nature. 6. Essays

ISBN 9781571311771

LC 2013012563

"As a botanist, Robin Wall Kimmerer has been trained to ask questions of nature with the tools of science. As a member of the Citizen Potawatomi Nation, she embraces the notion that plants and animals are our oldest teachers. In Braiding Sweetgrass, Kimmerer brings these two lenses of knowledge together to take us on "a journey that is every bit as mythic as it is scientific, as sacred as it is historical, as clever as it is wise.""-- Provided by publisher.

"Anyone who enjoys reading about natural history, botany, protecting nature, or Native American culture will love this book." Library Journal

McKibben, Bill

Eaarth : a survivor's guide / Bill McKibben. Time Books, c2010. 272 p. **304.2**

1. Climate change 2. Global warming. 3. Environmental degradation. 4. Greenhouse effect, Atmospheric.

ISBN 9780805090567

LC 2009030040

Also subtitled: Making a life on a tough new planet.

Green Prize for Sustainable Literature: Adult Nonfiction, 2011.

Argues that a large-scale shift in Earth's climate is unavoidable and explains how humans should live if they are going to sustain themselves on the new planet that their mistakes have created.

"The author demonstrates how global warming has already occurred and is irreversible. He describes a new Eaarth, where the cumulative effects of the release of carbon dioxide in the atmosphere have already changed the planet. McKibben envisions a future in which humanity transitions from unfettered growth and a dependence on external markets for sustenance and fossil-fuel-driven energy, to smaller, self-contained communities, growing food locally and generating sustainable distributed electricity. An absolute must-read." Kirkus.

The **end** of nature / Bill McKibben. Random House Trade Paperbacks, 2006, c1989. xxiv, 195 p. **304.2**

1. Nature -- Effect of humans on 2. Global warming. 3. Environmental protection. 4. Environmentalism.

ISBN 0812976088

LC 2006283925

Includes index.

Originally published: New York : Random House, 1989. With new introd.

Addressing the moral and practical aspects of dealing with environmental issues, this study spells out the tragic consequences of the greenhouse effect and discusses options for avoiding ecological calamity.

"McKibben urges us to see the horror of life beyond nature , ending with a call for a new humility that would allow us to help bring it back. An extraordinary, eye-opening plea, as important--and as likely to have as great an impact--as Silent Spring or The Fate of the Earth." Kirkus.

McPhee, John, 1931-

The **control** of nature / John McPhee. Farrar, Straus, Giroux, 1989. 272 p. ; **304.2**

1. Environmental protection. 2. Environmentalism. 3. Nature -- Effect of humans on 4. Geology

ISBN 0374128901

LC 89001052

"The text of this book originally appeared in the New Yorker"-- T.p. verso.

Profiles various effects by humankind to thwart the course of nature, detailing the changing physical landscapes, as well as the political, economic, and legal battles that have arisen from these struggles.

Raygorodetsky, Gleb

The **archipelago** of hope : wisdom and resilience from the edge of climate change / Gleb Raygorodetsky. Pegasus Books, 2017. 336 p. **304.2**

1. Climate change 2. Environmentalists 3. Environmental movement 4. Global warming

ISBN 9781681775326

LC bl2017047423

One cannot turn on the news today without a report on an extreme weather event or the latest update on Antarctica. But while our politicians argue, the truth is that climate change is already here. Nobody knows this better than Indigenous peoples who, having developed an intimate relationship with ecosystems over generations, have observed these changes for decades. For them, climate change is not an abstract concept or policy issue, but the reality of daily life. After two decades of working with indigenous communities, Gleb Raygorodetsky shows how these communities are actually islands of biological and cultural diversity in the ever-rising sea of development and urbanization.

" Filled with admiration for those at the center of his study, Raygorodetsky delivers a valuable addition for all environmental collections and readers interested in cultural studies and international relations." Library Journal.

Wallace-Wells, David

The **uninhabitable** Earth : life after warming / David Wallace-Wells. Tim Duggan Books, 2019. 256 p. **304.2**

1. Global warming 2. Climate change 3. Forecasting 4. Global environmental change

ISBN 9780525576709

LC 2018051268

ALA Notable Book, 2020.

"A well-organized, fully sourced, powerfully composed survey of the planetary changes happening now at shockingly rapid rates and their dire human consequences." Booklist

Weisman, Alan

Countdown : our last, best hope for a future on earth? / Alan Weisman. Little, Brown and Company, 2013. 420 p. **304.2**

1. Nature -- Effect of humans on 2. Overpopulation. 3. Population control 4. Sustainability

ISBN 9780316097758

LC 2013017113

The author visits twenty countries around the world to get their take on the sustainability of human life on the planet, discussing optimum population and how to prosper without endless growth.

"Provocative and sobering, this vividly reported book raises profound concerns about our future." Publishers Weekly.

The **world** without us / Alan Weisman. Thomas Dunne Books, 2007. viii, 324 p. : **304.2**

1. Nature -- Effect of humans on 2. Material culture. 3. Humans and

plants. 4. Human/animal relationships
ISBN 0312347294

LC 2007011565

ALA Notable Book, 2008.

National Book Critics Circle Award for Nonfiction finalist, 2007.

A study of what would happen to Earth if the human presence was removed examines our legacy for the planet, from the objects that would vanish without human intervention to those that would become long-lasting remnants of humankind.

"Weisman is a thoroughly engaging and clarion writer fueled by curiosity and determined to cast light rather than spread despair. His superbly well researched and skillfully crafted stop-you-in-your-tracks report stresses the underappreciated fact that humankind's actions create a ripple effect across the web of life." Booklist..

304.209 Human ecology--History, geographic treatment, biography

Smith, Laurence C.

The **world** in 2050 : four forces shaping civilization's northern future / Laurence C. Smith. Penguin Group USA, 2010. 336 p. **304.209**

1. Scientific forecasting. 2. Social indicators. 3. Forecasting. 4. Possibilities.
ISBN 9780525951810

LC 2010029553

"This thought experiment predicts that four mega--trends--more people, fewer resources, globalization, and climate change will utterly transform the world in the next 40 years. Mother Jones Smith demonstrates the breadth of geography and emerges as a champion of the discipline. His engaging style and understandable prose will appeal to a wide range of readers interested in social and environmental sciences." Library Journal.

304.2091732 Human ecology--Urban areas

Owen, David, 1955-

Green metropolis : why living smaller, living closer, and driving less are the keys to sustainability / David Owen. Riverhead Books, c2009. 368 p. **304.2091732**

1. Human ecology -- New York City 2. Urban ecology -- New York City 3. Sustainable living -- New York City 4. Landscape architecture -- Environmental aspects 5. New York City -- Environmental conditions.
ISBN 9781594488825

LC 2009017116

Green Prize for Sustainable Literature: Adult Nonfiction, 2010.

Upending the environmentalist viewpoint that urban areas are "anti-green," New Yorker staff writer David Owen argues that sustainability is achieved in areas like New York City, while open space, backyard compost heaps, locavorism and high-tech gadgetry like solar panels and triple-paned windows are formulas for wasteful sprawl and green-washed consumerism.

304.2097 Human ecology--North America

Worster, Donald, 1941-

Shrinking the Earth : the rise and decline of American abundance / Donald Worster. Oxford University Press, 2016 288 p. **304.2097**

1. Power (Social sciences) 2. Discoveries in geography. 3. Natural history 4. Environmentalism. 5. United States
ISBN 9780199844951

LC 2016301463

Green Prize for Sustainable Literature: Adult Nonfiction, 2017.

Acknowledging the earth's agency throughout human history,Shrinking the Earth offers a compelling explanation of how we have arrived where we are and a hopeful way forward on a planet that is no longer as large as it once was.

"A bracing, intelligent survey of wealth become immiseration, essential for students of environmental history." Kirkus.

304.20973 Human ecology--United States

Hohn, Donovan

The **inner** coast : essays / Donovan Hohn. W W Norton & Co Inc 2020 256 p. **304.20973**

1. Human ecology. 2. Coastal towns 3. Nature -- Effect of humans on 4. Essays
ISBN 9781324005971

LC 2020008292

Prize-winning essays on our changing place in the natural world by the best-selling author of Moby-Duck.

"Settle in and savor a keen mind with a laudable moral compass." Kirkus

304.209798 Human ecology--Alaska

Wohlforth, Charles P.

The **fate** of nature : rediscovering our ability to rescue the earth / Charles Wohlforth. St. Martin's Press, 2010. 434 p. : **304.209798**

1. Human ecology. 2. Human ecology -- Alaska. 3. Natural history -- Alaska. 4. Conservation of natural resources -- Alaska. 5. Alaska -- Environmental conditions.
ISBN 9780312377373

LC 2009045779

"Thomas Dunne Books."

"The author considers the consequences of Captain John Cook's hasty visit to the gulf in 1778, the Russian conquest of coastal Alaska, . . . the crash of the herring fisheries, and the cruel fates of the region's indigenous peoples. But Wohlforth believes that our consuming nature is balanced by the impulse to understand and cherish the living world, which is borne out in his compelling profiles of whale biologist Eva Saulitis; Geerat Vermeij, a blind evolutionary scientist who discovered an arms race among crustaceans; and various environmental heroes. . . . By analyzing competition and evolution, culture and economics, habits of living and of mind, science and suffering, Wohlforth brings a truly ecological perspective to the global debate over how to protect the biosphere." Booklist.

304.5 Genetic factors

Taylor, Shelley E.

The **tending** instinct : how nurturing is essential for who we are and how we live / Shelley E. Taylor. Times Books, 2002.

vii, 290 p. ; **304.5**

1. Sociobiology. 2. Sex differences. 3. Nurturing behavior. 4. Stress.
ISBN 9780805068375

LC 2002019879

"The author launched a series of innovative experiments that led her to believe that humans are biologically wired to nurture. She thus devised no less than a whole new psychology of women, presented in this accessible and well-grounded work." Library Journal.

304.6 Population

Mannix, Kathryn

With the end in mind : dying, death, and wisdom in an age of denial / Kathryn Mannix. Little, Brown and Company, 2018. 304 p. **304.6**

1. Physician and patient 2. Death. 3. Terminal care. 4. Physicians
ISBN 9780316504485

LC bl2017046529

A palliative care physician draws on stories from her own practice to explain how to enable a gentle and peaceful death and how modern medicine, augmented by traditional palliative approaches, can restore dignity, humanity, and meaning to the end of life.

"Using case histories, Mannix provides poignant insight into the way people live when they know they are dying, and what those around them may be thinking and wishing to say." Library Journal.

304.8 Movement of people

Caldwell, Christopher

Reflections on the revolution in Europe : immigration, Islam, and the West / Christopher Caldwell. Doubleday, c2009. 416 p. **304.8**

1. Muslims -- Europe. 2. Islam -- Europe. 3. Culture conflict -- Europe. 4. Multiculturalism -- Europe. 5. Europe -- Immigration and emigration. 6. Islamic countries -- Immigration and emigration. 7. Europe -- Race relations -- Religious aspects. 8. Europe -- Civilization -- 21st century. 9. Europe -- Civilization -- Islamic influences.
ISBN 9780385518260

LC 2008051563

Examines the effect of immigration in Europe, caught in a demographic revolution it never expected, and discusses the increasingly assertive Muslim population shaping the continent's future.

Chung, Nicole,

A **map** is only one story : twenty writers on immigration, family, and the meaning of home / edited by Nicole Chung and Mensah Demary. Catapult, 2020. 256 p. **304.8**

1. Immigration and emigration 2. Families 3. Home (Concept) 4. Identity (Psychology) 5. Essays 6. Anthologies
ISBN 9781948226783

LC bl2020008444

In the first published anthology of writing from Catapult magazine, twenty writers share stories of migration, family, the search for home and belonging, and what it means to exist between languages and cultures.

"Fierce and diverse, these essays tell personal stories that humanize immigration in unique, necessary ways. A provocatively intelligent collection." Kirkus

Khakpour, Porochista

Brown album : essays on exile and identity / Porochista Khakpour. Vintage, 2020. 226 p. **304.8**

1. Khakpour, Porochista 2. Iranian American women 3. Immigrants -- United States 4. Identity (Psychology) 5. Women authors 6. United States 7. Essays
ISBN 9780525564713

The award-winning author presents a collection of essays that draws on his personal experiences to explore the realities of the Iranian-American immigration experience in the post-9/11 era of Donald Trump.

"A triumphant entry in the personal essay canon." Library Journal

Urrea, Luis Alberto

The **devil's** highway : a true story / Luis Alberto Urrea. Little, Brown, c2004. xii, 239 p. ; **304.8**

1. Human smuggling -- Mexican-American Border Region 2. Desert survival 3. Undocumented immigrants. 4. Undocumented workers -- Mexican-American Border Region 5. Mexican-American Border Region -- Social conditions 6. United States -- Immigration and emigration -- Social aspects. 7. Mexico -- Immigration and emigration -- Social aspects.
ISBN 0316746711

LC 2003058930

Includes index.

Pulitzer Prize for General Nonfiction finalist

Describes the attempt of twenty-six men to cross the Mexican border into the desert of southern Arizona, a region known as the Devil's Highway, detailing their harrowing ordeal and battle for survival against impossible odds.

Vollmann, William T.

Imperial / William T. Vollmann. Viking, 2009. 1344 p. **304.8**

1. Immigrants, Mexican -- California. 2. Mexicans in California -- History. 3. Mexicans in California -- Social conditions. 4. Immigrants -- Imperial County, California -- History. 5. Imperial County, California -- Social conditions.
ISBN 9780670020614

LC 2008029532

National Book Critics Circle Award for Nonfiction finalist, 2009.

A report on the emblematic county in southeast California by the National Book Award-winning author of Europe Central explores the ways in which the author believes the region reflects the darker side of American imperialism, in an account that considers such topics as immigration, agribusiness, and corporate exploitation.

Yans-McLaughlin, Virginia, 1943-

Ellis Island and the peopling of America : the official guide / Virginia Yans-McLaughlin and Marjorie Lightman, with the Statue of Liberty-Ellis Island Foundation. New Press, c1997. 209 p. : **304.8**

1. Ellis Island Immigration Station (NY and NJ) 2. United States -- Emigration and immigration -- History -- Sources.
ISBN 9781439504628

LC 96054713

"[The authors] offer a well-documented, easy-to-read guide to the museum at Ellis Island in New York Harbor for parents and teachers." Library Journal

304.80973 Movement of people--United States

Wilkerson, Isabel

★The **warmth** of other suns : the epic story of America's great migration / Isabel Wilkerson. Random House, 2010. 720 p. **304.80973**

1. African Americans -- Migrations -- History -- 20th century. 2. Migration, Internal -- United States -- History -- 20th century. 3. Rural-urban migration -- United States -- History -- 20th century. 4. African Americans -- History -- 1877-1964. 5. United States -- Civilization -- African American influences. 6. United States -- Immigration and emigration -- History -- 20th century
ISBN 9780679444329

LC 2009049753

ALA Notable Book, 2011.
Hurston/Wright Legacy Award: Nonfiction, 2011.
Mark Lynton History Prize, 2011.
National Book Critics Circle Award for Non-Fiction, 2010.

In this epic, beautifully written masterwork, Pulitzer Prize-winning author Isabel Wilkerson chronicles one of the great untold stories of American history: the decades-long migration of black citizens who fled the South for northern and western cities, in search of a better life. From 1915 to 1970, this exodus of almost six million people changed the face of America.

"An account of the Great Migration, the 55-year stretch (1915-1970) during which 6 million black Americans fled the Jim Crow South. Wilkerson, a Pulitzer Prize-winning journalist, uses the journeys of three of them -- a Mississippi sharecropper, a Louisiana doctor, and a Florida laborer -- to etch an indelible and compulsively readable portrait of race, class, and politics in 20th-century America. History is rarely distilled so finely." Entertainment Weekly.

305 Groups of people

Payne, Keith

★The **broken** ladder : how inequality affects the way we think, live, and die / Keith Payne. Viking Press, 2017 288 p. **305**

1. Equality 2. Poverty 3. Wealth 4. Racism
ISBN 9780525429814

LC 2016056838

A leading social scientist presents a timely examination of the physical, psychological and moral effects of inequality that explains how inequality is attributed to factors identified by both conservatives and progressives and has a profound impact on health and value systems.

"Interspersed with personal experiences and written in an engaging style, the book is a must read for any individual interested in the psychological effects of inequality." Choice.

Piketty, Thomas, 1971-

★**Capital** and ideology / Thomas Piketty, translated from the French by Arthur Goldhammer. Harvard University Press, 2020, c2019. ix, 1093 p. **305**

1. Equality 2. Socialism 3. Ideology 4. Capitalism -- History
ISBN 9780674980822

LC 2019040839

Originally published: Paris : Editions du Seuil, 2019.

The successor to the *Capital in the Twenty-First Century* is at once a retelling of global history, a scathing critique of contemporary politics and a bold proposal for a new and fairer economic system.

"A deftly argued case for a new kind of socialism that, while sure to inspire controversy, bears widespread discussion." Kirkus

305.23 Young people

Clinton, Hillary Rodham

It takes a village : and other lessons children teach us / Hillary Rodham Clinton. Simon & Schuster, c1996. 318 p. : **305.23**

1. Clinton, Hillary Rodham. 2. Child development -- United States 3. Child welfare -- United States 4. Families -- United States 5. Parenting -- United States
ISBN 9780684818436

LC OC2014040133

The First Lady shares her observations on the needs of children and families in the modern, fragmented, fast-paced world and explores diverse ways in which we can improve family and community life.

Griffiths, Jay

A **country** called childhood : children and the exuberant world / Jay Griffiths. Counterpoint Press, 2014 432 p. **305.23**

1. Children -- Cross-cultural studies. 2. Humans -- Effect of environment on 3. Childhood.
ISBN 9781619024298

LC 2014022401

In A Country Called Childhood, Griffiths seeks to discover why we deny our children the freedoms of space, time and the natural world. Visiting communities as far apart as West Papua and the Arctic as well as the UK, and delving into history, philosophy, language and literature, she explores how children's affinity for nature is an essential and universal element of childhood. It is a journey deep into the heart of what it means to be a child, and it is central to all our experiences, young and old.

Kozol, Jonathan

Ordinary resurrections : children in the years of hope / Jonathan Kozol. Crown Publishers, 2000. ix, 388 p. **305.23**

1. Children -- New York City -- Social conditions. 2. Children with social disabilities -- New York City. 3. Developmental psychology. 4. Mott Haven, New York City -- Social conditions.
ISBN 9780517700006

LC 99059808

The author examines America's poverty-stricken urban neighborhoods, recalling the lessons he has learned from time spent among the nation's poorest people.

"Kozol tells of his continued visits with the children who attend the afterschool program at St. Ann's Episcopal Church in the racially segregated, impoverished South Bronx." School Library Journal.

Mintz, Steven, 1953-

★**Huck's** raft : a history of American childhood / Steven Mintz. Belknap Press of Harvard University Press, 2004. xi, 445 p. : **305.23**

1. Childhood -- United States -- History. 2. Child rearing -- United States -- History. 3. Children -- United States -- Social conditions. 4. United States -- Social life and customs.
ISBN 0674015088

LC 2004042220

"Mintz's thorough yet accessibly written study delves into the external forces that have shaped the lives of our young while also probing the internal developments in their collective consciousness." Library Journal.

305.23082 Girls

Durham, M. Gigi

The **Lolita** effect : the media sexualization of young girls and what we can do about it / M. Gigi Durham. Overlook Press, 2008. 320 p. ; **305.23082**

1. Girls -- United States. 2. Mass media and girls -- United States. 3. Girls in popular culture -- United States. 4. Self-perception in girls 5. United States -- Social life and customs -- 20th century
ISBN 9781590200636

LC bl2008006320

Evaluates media messages that promote the early maturation and sexualization of pre-adolescent girls, revealing the detrimental and restrictive definitions of sexuality in media while counseling parents on how to raise sexually healthy young women.

"In this exploration of the media's exploitation of girls, Durham exposes the links between destructive teenage self-images and the popular, highly sexed, and negative representations of girls in magazines, television programs, and movies. [Her] provocative and erudite study of the demeaning way society views girls serves to both alarm and educate; consider it required reading for parents and their daughters." Booklist.

Orenstein, Peggy

Cinderella ate my daughter : dispatches from the frontlines of the new girlie-girl culture / Peggy Orenstein. HarperCollins, c2011. 288 p. **305.23082**

1. Girls -- Psychology. 2. Femininity 3. Mothers and daughters 4. Popular culture.
ISBN 9780061711527

LC 2010028724

"The author finds today's pink and princess-obsessed girl culture grating when it threatens to lure her own young daughter, Daisy. In her quest to determine whether princess mania is merely a passing phase or a more sinister marketing plot with long-term negative impact, Orenstein travels to Disneyland, American Girl Place, the American International Toy Fair; visits a children's beauty pageant; attends a Miley Cyrus concert; tools around the Internet; and interviews parents, historians, psychologists, marketers, and others. With insight and biting humor, the author explores her own conflicting feelings as a mother as she protects her offspring and probes the roots and tendrils of the girlie-girl movement." Publishers Weekly.

Sax, Leonard

Girls on the edge : the four factors driving the new crisis for girls : sexual identity, the cyberbubble, obsessions, environmental toxins / Leonard Sax. Basic Books, c2010. 272 p. **305.23082**

1. Girls -- Psychology. 2. Girls -- Health 3. Gender role 4. Girls -- Identity.
ISBN 9780465015610

LC 2010003800

"Psychologist and physician Leonard Sax's work with young people reveals that girls today have an incredibly brittle sense of self. Though they may look confident on the outside, teens and tweens are fragile inside, obsessed with grades, sports, networking sites, and appearances. They are confused about their sexual identity, as environmental toxins are accelerating physical maturity faster than their emotional maturity. Now, Sax gives us the tools we need to help girls become independent and confident women. He provides parents with practical tips on everything from helping their daughter make decisions to nurturing her spirit through female-centered activities to getting her involved in communities of female role models, which give young women pride and allow them to grow in a safe environment that nurtures curiosity and confidence".--Publisher's description.

305.23086 Children by miscellaneous social attributes

Luiselli, Valeria, 1983-

★**Tell** me how it ends : an essay in 40 questions / Valeria Luiselli. Coffee House Press, 2017. 119 p. **305.23086**

1. Undocumented immigrants. 2. Child immigrants 3. Deportation 4. Citizenship 5. United States -- Immigration and emigration 6. Essays
ISBN 9781566894951

LC 2017000414

Kirkus Prize for Nonfiction finalist, 2017.

"Structured around the forty questions Luiselli translates and asks undocumented Latin-American children facing deportation, Tell Me How It Ends (an expansion of her 2016 Freeman's essay of the same name) humanizes these young migrants and highlights the contradiction of the idea of America as a fiction for immigrants with the reality of racism and fear--both here and back home".--Provided by publisher.

305.231 Child development

Brazelton, T. Berry, 1918-2018

Touchpoints : birth to 3 : your child's emotional and behavioral development / T. Berry Brazelton ; revised with Joshua Sparrow. Da Capo Lifelong Books, c2006. xxvi, 500 p. : **305.231**

1. Child development -- United States 2. Infants -- Development -- United States 3. Child psychology -- United States 4. Infant psychology -- United States
ISBN 9780738210490

LC 2008274711

"A Merloyd Lawrence book."

A pediatrician and a child psychiatrist examine the cognitive, behavioral, and emotional development of children from birth to age three.

305.232 Infants

Hamilton, Robert C.

7 secrets of the newborn : Secrets and (Happy) Surprises of the First Year / Robert C. Hamilton, M.D. with Sally Collings. St. Martin's Press, 2018 xi, 323 p. ; **305.232**

1. Child rearing 2. Infants -- Care 3. Infants -- Health and hygiene
ISBN 9781250114426

LC 2018022132

Includes index.

An experienced pediatrician and father provides new parents with clear, sensible and warm advice about sleeping, vaccinations, breast feeding, eating, crying, clothes, toys and screen time during the first year of their baby's life.

Klein, Tovah P.

★**How** toddlers thrive : what parents can do today for children ages 2-5 to plant the seeds of lifelong success / Tovah P. Klein, PhD. Simon & Schuster, 2014. xxii, 280 p. ; **305.232**

1. Child rearing. 2. Toddlers -- Care. 3. Toddlers -- Development.
ISBN 1476735131

LC 2013032839

"A Touchstone Book."

A Sesame Street advisor and expert in toddler psychology argues that adult success is often established in the developmental preschool years, sharing advice for parents on how to promote such success-driving positive attributes as resilience, self-regulation and empathy.

Murkoff, Heidi Eisenberg

★**What** to expect the first year / Heidi Murkoff and Sharon Mazel ; foreword by Mark D. Widome, M.D., M.P.H., Professor of Pediatrics, Penn State Hershey Children's Hospital, Hershey, Pennsylvania. Workman Publishing, 2014 xxv, 678 p. : **305.232**

1. Infants 2. Child rearing 3. Infants -- Care
ISBN 9780761181507

LC 2014004520

An infant care guide describes monthly growth and development from infancy to toddler, discussing such topics as common childhood ailments, feeding, allergies, vaccinations, sleep strategies, and decoding crying.

305.233 Children three to five

Santomero, Angela C

Preschool clues : raising smart, inspired, and engaged kids in a screen-filled world / Angela C. Santomero, M.A. with Deborah Reber. Touchstone, 2018 xviii, 298 p. : **305.233**

1. Blue's clues (Television program). 2. Preschool children 3. Toddlers 4. Child development 5. Child rearing
ISBN 9781501174339

LC 2017030842

"The award-winning creator of Blue's Clues, Super Why!, and Daniel Tiger's Neighborhood shares the secret sauce behind her shows' powerful, transformative results in the form of eleven research-based, foundational 'clues' to ensure that preschoolers flourish academically, socially, and emotionally during this critical time".-- Provided by publisher.

305.235 Young people twelve to twenty

Damour, Lisa, 1970-

Untangled : guiding teenage girls through the seven transitions into adulthood / Lisa Damour, Ph.D.. Ballantine Books, 2016 xix, 326 p. ; **305.235**

1. Adolescence. 2. Adolescent psychology. 3. Adulthood. 4. Teenage girls -- Psychology.
ISBN 0553393057

LC 2015040046

A clinical psychologist offers guidance to parents of teenage girls, helping to demystify their erratic behavior and mood swings by describing the seven developmental passages that all girls go through as they transition to adulthood.

Hine, Thomas, 1947-

The **rise** and fall of the American teenager / Thomas Hine. Bard, 1999. viii, 322 p. **305.235**

1. Teenagers -- United States 2. Preteens. 3. Youth culture -- United States. 4. United States -- History.
ISBN 0380973588

LC 99024381

"An Avon book."

"In this social history Hine writes about ways the culture has affected what teenage has meant for youth and how youth have been perceived, as in World War II when teenagers readily took on roles supporting the war effort. Interesting, enjoyable, and multifaceted, Hine's work defies pigeonholing by covering anthropology, psychology, communications, and sociology." Library Journal.

Orenstein, Peggy

★**Boys** & sex : young men on hookups, love, porn, consent, and navigating the new masculinity / Peggy Orenstein. Harper, 2020 320 p. **305.235**

1. Teenage boys -- Sexuality 2. Teenage boys -- Attitudes. 3. Young men -- Sexuality 4. Sexuality.
ISBN 9780062666970

LC 2019040572

The author of the groundbreaking, best-selling Girls & Sex turns her attention to young men, discussing and revealing how modern young men understand and navigate the new rules of physical and emotional intimacy.

"A highly constructive analysis that provides many topics for exploration and discussion by parents and others who interact with boys." Kirkus.

Shachtman, Tom, 1942-

★**Rumspringa** : to be or not to be Amish / Tom Shachtman. North Point Press, 2006. 286 p. ; **305.235**

1. Personal conduct. 2. Amish teenagers -- Personal conduct. 3. Amish teenagers -- Religious life. 4. Amish teenagers -- Social life and customs.
ISBN 086547687X

LC 2006004329

"This book is based, in part, on research done for the Stick Figure Productions documentary The Devil's Playground"--P. opposite tp.

An analysis of Amish youth culture profiles the coming-of-age ritual known as the rumspringa, during which sixteen-year-old Amish adolescents are permitted to venture outside of the bounds of their faith, experiment with alcohol and smoking, wear trendy clothes, and ultimately decide if they want to remain detached from the outside world.

"Shachtman is like a maestro, masterfully conducting an orchestra of history, anthropology, psychology, sociology, and journalism together in a harmonious and evocative symphony of all things Amish." Christian Science Monitor.

Tanenbaum, Leora, 1969-

I am not a slut : slut-shaming in the age of the Internet / Leora Tanenbaum. Perennial, 2015 304 p. **305.235**

1. Sexism -- United States. 2. Girls -- United States -- Social conditions. 3. Stereotypes (Social psychology) 4. Teenage girls -- United States -- Social conditions.
ISBN 9780062282590

LC bl2015006824

Explains the concept of slut-shaming and analyzes how young women cope with it both on and offline.

"This brilliant, thoughtful, and compelling investigation of young womanhood commands the readers attention from beginning to end." Booklist.

Wiseman, Rosalind, 1969-

Masterminds & wingmen : helping our boys cope with schoolyard power, locker-room tests, girlfriends, and the new rules of Boy World / Rosalind Wiseman. Harmony Books, 2013 377 p. : **305.235**

1. Parent and teenager 2. Teenage boys -- Psychology
ISBN 9780307986658

LC 2013372427

Here is a landmark book that reveals how boys think, showing parents, educators, and coaches how to reach out and help boys overcome their most common yet difficult challenges. Do you constantly struggle to pull information from your son, student, or athlete, only to encounter evasive assurances like "It's nothing"? Do you sense that the boy you care about is being bullied, but that he'll do anything to avoid your "help?" Have you watched with frustration as your boy flounders with girls? Welcome to Boy World: a place where asking for help or showing emotional pain often feels impossible. Where sports and video games can mean everything, but working hard in school frequently earns ridicule. Where hiding problems from adults is the ironclad rule. Boy World is governed by social hierarchies and a powerful set of unwritten rules that have huge implications for your boy's relationships, his interactions with you, and the man he'll become. If you want what's best for him, you need to know what these rules areand how to work with them effectively.--From publisher description.

"Wiseman's sound and steady assistance provides a calm response to every twist and turn on the multifaceted road of parenthood. A wealth of sensible information for parents of boys." Kirkus.

305.2350973 Young people twelve to twenty--United States

Kim, Anne (Journalist)

★**Abandoned** : America's lost youth and the crisis of disconnection / Anne Kim. The New Press, 2019. 208 p. **305.2350973**

1. Young adults 2. Problem youth 3. Adulthood 4. Teenagers 5. United States -- Social conditions

ISBN 9781620975008

LC 2019034594

The director of domestic and social policy at the Progressive Policy Institute examines the 11.5 percent of sixteen- to twenty-four-year-olds who age out of foster care and the justice system and are forced to navigate early adulthood alone and impoverished.

"An outstanding book for policymakers and people who work with adrift young people." Kirkus

305.24 Adults

Sheehy, Gail, 1937-2020

New passages : mapping your life across time / Gail Sheehy. Ballantine Books, 1996, c1995. xxv, 498 p. : **305.24**

1. Adulthood 2. Maturation (Psychology) 3. Middle aged persons -- Psychology 4. Socialization 5. United States -- Social conditions -- 1980-

ISBN 9780345404459

LC BL 99773709

Originally published: New York : Random, 1995.

Explores radical changes that occur at every stage in one's life, describes the Second Adulthood that takes place during middle age, and explains how to make the most of this time of life.

305.240973 Adults--United States

Caldwell, Christopher

The **age** of entitlement : America since the sixties / Christopher Caldwell. Simon & Schuster, 2020. 352 p. **305.240973**

1. Political culture -- United States 2. Progressivism (United States politics) 3. Right and left (Political science) 4. Polarization (Social sciences) 5. United States -- Politics and government 6. United States -- Social conditions

ISBN 9781501106897

LC 2019012957

An American intellectual argues that the reforms of the 1960s, reforms intended to make the nation more just and humane, instead left many Americans feeling alienated, despised, misled|and ready to put an adventurer in the White House.

"Liberals will find much to dispute, but Caldwell delivers the sharpest and most insightful conservative critique of mainstream politics in years." Publishers Weekly.

Sasse, Benjamin E.

The **vanishing** American adult : our coming-of-age crisis--and how to rebuild a culture of self-reliance / Ben Sasse. St Martin's Press, 2017 352 p. **305.240973**

1. Overprotectiveness in parents 2. Adulthood. 3. Young adults 4. Self-reliance

ISBN 9781250114402

LC 2017005552

In The Vanishing American Adult, Sasse diagnoses the causes of a generation that can't grow up and offers a path for raising children to become active and engaged citizens. He identifies core formative experiences that all young people should pursue: hard work to appreciate the benefits of labor, travel to understand deprivation and want, the power of reading, the importance of nurturing your body--and explains how parents can encourage them.

"Deeply thoughtful, delightfully personal, and bravely ecumenical in scope, Sasse's guide for stemming the tide of delayed responsibility showcases what is both practical and possible." Booklist.

305.242 People in early adulthood

Burge, Kimberly

The **born** frees : writing with the girls of Gugulethu / Kimberly Burge. W.W. Norton & Company, 2015 288 p. **305.242**

1. Teenage girls. 2. Writing -- Study and teaching. 3. Self-fulfillment in teenage girls. 4. Post-apartheid era -- South Africa. 5. South Africa.

ISBN 9780393239164

LC 2015010037

Forming a creative writing group in the township of Gugulethu, South Africa, a journalist inspires young women, some of whom have been ravaged by poverty, violence, sexual abuse and AIDS, to find reassurance, courage and a temporary escape from their lives as they claim their own voices and define themselves.

Yancy, George,

Our black sons matter : mothers talk about fears, sorrows, and hopes / edited by George Yancy, Maria del Guadalupe Davidson, and Susan Hadley. Rowman & Littlefield, 2016 xii, 227 p. ; **305.242**

1. African American young men. 2. African American boys. 3. Mothers and sons -- United States. 4. African Americans -- Family relationships.

ISBN 9781442269118

LC 2016023174

"Our Black Sons Matter is a powerful collection of original essays, letters, and poems that addresses both the deep joys and the very real challenges of raising black boys today. From Trayvon Martin to Tamir Rice, the list of young black men who have suffered racial violence continues to grow. Young black people also deal with profound stereotypes and structural barriers. And yet, young black men are often paradoxically revered as icons of cultural cool. Our Black Sons Matter features contributions from women across the racial spectrum who are raising or have raised black sons--whether biologically theirs or not. The book courageously addresses painful trauma, challenges assumptions, and offers insights and hope through the deep bonds between mothers and their children. Both a collective testimony and a collective love letter, Our Black Sons Matter sends the message that black lives matter and speaks with the universal love of all mothers who fear for the lives of their children."--Provided by publisher.

305.2420973 Young adults--United States

Petersen, Anne Helen

Can't even : how millennials became the burnout generation / Anne Helen Petersen. Houghton Mifflin Harcourt, 2020. xxvi, 276 p. **305.2420973**

1. Burn out (Psychology) 2. Mental fatigue. 3. Group identity 4. Millennials

ISBN 9780358315070

LC 2020022439

An incendiary examination of burnout in millennials-the cultural shifts that got us here, the pressures that sustain it, and the need for drastic change.

"Petersen is more focused on bluntly describing her generation's many obstacles than offering solutions to burnout. By turns exasperated, indignant, and empathetic, she supports her claims with strong evidence and calls on millennials to be a force for widespread social change. The result is an incisive portrait of a generation primed for revolt." Publishers Weekly

305.2440973 Middle-aged people--United States

Calhoun, Ada

Why we can't sleep : women's new midlife crisis / Ada Calhoun. Grove Press, 2020. 288 p. **305.2440973**

1. Middle-aged women -- Psychology 2. Midlife crisis 3. Generation X 4. Anxiety in women

ISBN 9780802147851

LC 2019040577

The award-winning author presents a generation-defining exploration of the impossible standards being imposed on middle-aged Generation X women and what the author recommends to avoid burnout.

"Women of every generation will find much to relate to in this humorous yet pragmatic account." Publishers Weekly.

305.26 People in late adulthood

Jenkins, Jo Ann

Disrupt aging : a bold new path to living your best life at every age / Jo Ann Jenkins, CEO, AARP with Boe Workman. PublicAffairs, 2016. 240 p. **305.26**

1. Seniors 2. Aging. 3. Self-fulfillment in seniors. 4. Self-fulfillment

ISBN 9781610396769

LC 2016002025

Includes index.

Offers advice for people to remain, or become, active, healthy, and happy as they advance past the age of fifty, touching on strategies for handling issues related to health, wealth, and self.

"With a positive outlook and many creative suggestions, this straightforward book will be an inspiration to boomers and millennials." Booklist.

Leland, John, 1959-

Happiness is a choice you make : lessons from a year among the oldest old / John Leland. Sarah Crichton Books, Farrar, Straus and Giroux, 2018. 242 p.: **305.26**

1. Conduct of life. 2. Happiness in old age. 3. Older people. 4. Wisdom.

ISBN 0374168180

LC 2017028940

A reporter recounts his time spent with six of New York's oldest inhabitants, all eighty-five and older, who share their wisdom about aging, life quality, and the art of living.

"Leland entertains and intrigues readers as six unique personalities emerge, sharing their reminiscences about love, heartache, aches and pains, and joy. This is a sympathetic and honest look at growing old." Booklist.

Manly, Carla Marie

Aging joyfully : a woman's guide to optimal health, relationships, and fulfillment for her 50s and beyond / Carla Marie Manly, PhD. Familius LLC, 2019 254 p. ; **305.26**

1. Older women -- Psychology. 2. Aging -- Psychological aspects. 3. Aging -- Social aspects. 4. Women -- Identity.

ISBN 9781641701419

LC bl2020000982

"Psychologist Manly (Joy from Fear) guides women into their later years with wisdom and empathy in this touching work. Manly encourages those 50 and older to look at their life's experiences and celebrate them rather than to look back with regret about dreams not achieved." Publishers Weekly

Pipher, Mary Bray

Women rowing north : navigating the challenges to our selves as we age / Mary Pipher. Bloomsbury Publishing, 2019. 320 p. **305.26**

1. Senior women -- Psychology 2. Aging -- Psychological aspects 3. Women -- Identity 4. Aging -- Social aspects

ISBN 9781632869609

LC 2018015192

The best-selling author of Reviving Ophelia presents a guide to wisdom, authenticity and bliss for women as they age, exploring how the myriad roles and challenges of women can help promote balance and a transcendent sense of well-being.

"Attentive to varying experiences of class, race, gender, health, and marital status, even as she considers the deep 'challenges of aging, including ageism and lookism, caregiving, loss, and loneliness,' Pipher offers practical, specific advice." Publishers Weekly.

305.260973 Aging--Social aspects--United States

Jacoby, Susan, 1945-

Never say die : the myth and marketing of the new old age / Susan Jacoby. Pantheon Books, c2011. 336 p. **305.260973**

1. Aging -- United States. 2. Seniors 3. Age.

ISBN 9780307377944

LC 2010017123

In a narrative that combines the intensely personal with social, economic, and historical analysis, Susan Jacoby turns an unsparing eye on the pharmaceutical companies, lifestyle gurus, and scientific businessmen who suggest that there will soon be a 'cure' for the 'disease' of aging. She separates wishful hype from realistic hope in a wide-ranging appraisal of subjects that include the explosion of Alzheimer's cases and the impact of possible cuts in Social Security.

"The author offers an important reality check for Americans enamored of the images of healthy, active seniors featured in advertisements." Booklist.

Lawrence-Lightfoot, Sara, 1944-

The **third** chapter : passion, risk, and adventure in the twenty-five years after fifty / By Sara Lawrence-Lightfoot. Farrar, Straus and Giroux, 2009. 260 p. ; **305.260973**

1. Seniors -- United States -- Interviews 2. Adulthood -- Psychological aspects 3. Aging -- Psychological aspects. 4. Fifties (Age) 5. United States -- Social life and customs -- 21st century

ISBN 9780374275495

LC 2008029147

Citing a growing population of middle-aged citizens and a mainstream perspective that its members are neither young nor old, a demographic assessment explores the ways in which people between the ages of fifty and seventy-five are redefining beliefs about maturity, power, and sexuality.

"New opportunities for creativity and self-fulfillment await men and women between the ages of 50 and 75. [The author] coins the term Third Chapter to describe the rich possibilities as illustrated in her extended interviews with 40 well-educated, affluent Americans. Founding her thesis on classic formulations of life-stage development, particularly that of Erik Erikson, the author offers a wide range of models for people who feel burned out, restless or dissatisfied with their lives, describing how each of her subjects became a different person. Readers feeling that something is missing from their lives, that there is something more they can contribute, will find this book a helpful guide." Publishers Weekly.

Pillemer, Karl A.

30 lessons for living : tried and true advice from the wisest Americans / Karl Pillemer. Hudson Street Press, c2011. xiii, 271 p. ; **305.260973**

1. Aging. 2. Conduct of life. 3. Happiness. 4. Old age.

ISBN 1594630844

LC 2011017113

Draws on a renowned gerontologist's extensive discussions with hundreds of senior-aged Americans to reveal wisdom gleaned from their experiences on topics ranging from families and finances to careers and aging.

"Who better to teach lessons on living . . . than the thousands of Americans over the age of 65 who have successfully navigated the territories of marriage, career, money, and aging? By conducting innumerable interviews, Pillemer found that their advice upends contemporary wisdom: they suggest marrying a person like oneself, choosing a career for intrinsic rewards, and spending more time with one's children. The author skillfully weaves a prevailing theme (e.g., parenting, aging fearlessly) with self-disclosing statements from interviewees to create a compelling, inspirational book. One of the best of its kind." Library Journal.

305.3 People by gender or sex

Airton, Lee

★**Gender** : your guide : a gender-friendly primer on what to know, what to say, and what to do in the new gender culture / Lee Airton, PHD. Adams Media, 2018. 239 p. ; **305.3**

1. Gender identity. 2. Parent and child. 3. Parenting.

ISBN 1507209002

LC 2018023274

"An authentic and accessible guide to understanding--and engaging in--today's gender conversation. The days of two genders--male, female; boy, girl; blue, pink--are over, if they ever existed at all. Gender is now a global conversation, and one that is constantly evolving. More people than ever before are openly living their lives as transgender men or women, and many transgender people are coming out as neither men or women, instead living outside of the binary. Gender is changing, and this change is gaining momentum. We all want to do and say the right things in relation to gender diversity--whether at a job interview, at parent/teacher night, and around the table at family dinners. But where do we begin? From the differences among gender identity, gender expression, and sex, to the use of gender-neutral pronouns like singular they/them, to thinking about your own participation in gender, Gender: Your Guide serves as a complete primer to all things gender. Guided by professor and gender diversity advocate Lee Airton, PhD, you will learn how gender works in everyday life, how to use accurate terminology to refer to transgender, non-binary, and/or gender non-conforming individuals, and how to ask when you aren't sure what to do or say. It provides you with the information you need to talk confidently and compassionately about gender diversity, whether simply having a conversation or going to bat as an advocate. Just like gender itself, being gender-friendly is a process for all of us. As revolutionary a resource as Our Bodies, Ourselves, Gender: Your Guide invites everyone on board to make gender more flexible and less constricting: a source of more joy, and less harm, for everyone. Let's get started".-- Provided by publisher.

"This guide is unlike anything else available today, and an obvious and necessary item for collections of all kinds." Library Journal.

Browning, Frank, 1946-

The **fate** of gender : nature, nurture, and the human future / Frank Browning. Bloomsbury USA, 2016. 304 p. **305.3**

1. Gender role 2. Sex differences (Psychology). 3. Gender identity. 4. Sex (Psychology).

ISBN 9781620406199

LC 2015050790

Browning takes us into human gender geographies around the world, from gender-neutral kindergartens in Chicago and Oslo to femminielli weather casters in Naples, from conservative Catholics in Paris fearful of God and Nature to transsexual Mormon parents in Utah. Along the way he elucidates the neuroscience that distinguishes male and female biology, shows us how all parents' brains change during the first weeks of parenthood, and finally how men's and women's responses to age differ worldwide based not on biology but on their earlier life habits.

"Although the author sacrifices depth for range, this account provides a solid overview of the shifting landscape of gender issues today." Library Journal.

Gottlieb, Iris

Seeing gender : an illustrated guide to identity and expression / Iris Gottlieb ; foreword by Meredith Talusan. Chronicle Books, 2019. 208 p. **305.3**

1. Gender identity 2. Gender expression 3. Identity (Psychology) 4. Sexual orientation

ISBN 9781452176611

LC 2018058585

Meticulously researched and fully illustrated, this examination into how we express and understand the complexities of gender today brings clarity and reassurance to the sometimes confusing process of navigating one’s identity.

"Gottlieb takes on the complexities of gender in the modern world through easy-to-digest writing, humor, and powerful illustrations. It's like a series of informative Twitter threads compressed into a book. Highly recommended for school and public libraries." School Library Journal.

305.309581 Gender roles--Afghanistan

Nordberg, Jenny

★The **underground** girls of Kabul : in search of a hidden resistance in Afghanistan / Jenny Nordberg. Crown, [2014] 288 p. **305.309581**

1. Gender Identity 2. Gender role 3. Male impersonators 4. Disguises 5. Afghanistan

ISBN 9780307952493

LC 2014000295

J. Anthony Lukas Book Prize, 2015.

In Afghanistan, a culture ruled almost entirely by men, the birth of a son is cause for celebration and the arrival of a daughter is often mourned as misfortune. A bacha posh (literally translated from Dari as "dressed up like a boy") is a third kind of child ' a girl temporarily raised as a boy and presented as such to the outside world. Jenny Nordberg, the reporter who broke the story of this phenomenon for the New York Times, constructs a powerful and moving account of those secretly living on the other side of a deeply segregated society where women have almost no rights and little freedom.

"Nordbergs subtle, sympathetic reportage makes this one of the most convincing portraits of Afghan culture in print; through a small breach in the wall of gender apartheid, she reveals the harsh ironies of a system that so devalues women that it forces them to become men." Publishers Weekly.

305.30973 Sex role -- United States

Lipman, Joanne

That's what she said : what men need to know and women need to tell them about working together / Joanne Lipman. William Morrow & Company, 2018. 320 p. **305.30973**

1. Gender gap 2. Women executives 3. Inequality 4. Businesspeople

ISBN 9780062437211

LC bl2017050883

An award-winning journalist and publisher outlines anecdotal solutions for harmonious working relationships between the sexes, citing the unique contributions of professional women and how their male counterparts can implement a healthier business culture that bridges gender gaps.

"A solid start to an essential, gender-inclusive conversation." Kirkus.

305.310973 Men--United States

Bly, Robert

★**Iron** John : a book about men / Robert Bly. Da Capo Press, 2015, c1990. xii, 292 p. ; **305.310973**

1. Men -- United States. 2. Masculinity 3. Men -- United States -- Psychology.

ISBN 9780306824265

LC 2004056137

Originally published: Reading, Mass. : Addison-Wesley, 1990.

"In this timeless and deeply learned classic, poet and translator Robert Bly offers nothing less than a new vision of what it means to be a man. Bly's vision is based on his ongoing work with men, as well as on reflections on his own life. He addresses the devastating effects of remote fathers and mourns the disappearance of male initiation rites in our culture. Finding rich meaning in ancient stories and legends, Bly uses the Grimm fairy tale "Iron John"-in which a mentor or "Wild Man" guides a young man through eight stages of male growth-to remind us of ways of knowing long forgotten, images of deep and vigorous masculinity centered in feeling and protective of the young. At once down-to-earth and elevated, combining the grandeur of myth with the practical and often painful lessons of our own histories, Iron John is an astonishing work that will continue to guide and inspire men-and women-for years to come".-- Provided by publisher.

305.4 Women

Beauvoir, Simone de, 1908-1986

★The **second** sex / Simone de Beauvoir ; translated and edited by H.M. Parshley ; with an introduction by Margaret Crosland. Alfred A. Knopf, 1993. lv, 786 p. ; **305.4**

1. Women. 2. Gender role 3. Feminism. 4. Feminists.

ISBN 9780679420163

LC 92054303

Originally published: New York : Knopf, 1953.

Woman's past and contemporary situation in Western culture is the focus of a detailed and uninhibited analysis of womanhood.

Grunwald, Lisa,

★**Women's** letters : America from the Revolutionary War to the present / edited by Lisa Grunwald & Stephen J. Adler. Dial Press, 2005. 824 p. ; **305.4**

1. Women -- United States -- History. 2. Women -- United States -- Correspondence. 3. Women -- United States -- History -- Pictorial works. 4. Women -- Literary collections 5. United States -- History. 6. United States -- Social conditions. 7. United States -- Social life and customs. 8. First person narratives. 9. Letters

ISBN 9780385335539

LC 2005041446

A survey of American history collects more than four hundred letters, arranged chronologically by era, that document the experiences of women representing all walks of life from the eighteenth century to the present.

"This collection of more than 400 entries begins with a letter written by Abigail Grant, accusing her husband of cowardice in battle, and ends with an e-mail by Wall Street Journal correspondent Farnaz Fassihi on the stark state of affairs in war-torn Iraq. In between, a wide variety of compelling subjects is covered. . . . The letters are accompanied by information about the topics included, biographical details about the author and the recipient, and other interesting facts." School Library Journal.

Saini, Angela, 1980-

Inferior : how science got women wrong and the new research that's rewriting the story / Angela Saini. Beacon Press, 2017. 224 p. **305.4**

1. Women's studies 2. Science -- History 3. Sexism in science 4. Research

ISBN 9780807071700

LC 2016048808

What science has gotten so shamefully wrong about women, and the fight, by both female and male scientists, to rewrite what we thought we knew.

"In admirably subtle prose, Saini questions, considers, and refuses to accept traditional generalizations. A brilliant approach to a long overlooked topic, Inferior is impossible to ignore and invaluable." Booklist.

Stratton, Joanna L.

Pioneer women : voices from the Kansas frontier / Joanna L. Stratton ; introduction by Arthur M. Schlesinger, Jr. Simon and Schuster, 1982, c1981. 319 p., 32 p. of plates : **305.4**

1. Pioneers -- Kansas -- History. 2. Pioneer women. 3. Frontier and pioneer life -- Kansas. 4. Women -- Kansas -- History. 5. Kansas -- History. 6. Anthologies.
ISBN 0671447483

LC BL 99928171

Reprint. Originally published: 1981.

A collection of firsthand accounts by pioneer women portrays the hardiness, perseverance, devotion, and ingenuity they displayed in the face of a lonely, dangerous, and exciting life.

"A unique book based on the memoirs of nearly 800 pioneer women who lived in Kansas between 1854 and 1890. The book presents personal and detailed accounts of life inside homes, the schools, and the social organizations of early Kansas." Choice.

305.409 History, geographic treatment, biography

Beard, Mary, 1955-

★**Women** & power : a manifesto / Mary Beard. Liveright, 2017. 128 p. **305.409**

1. Power (Social sciences) 2. Literature and society 3. Women in literature 4. Misogyny
ISBN 9781631494758

LC 2017054169

At long last, Mary Beard addresses in one brave book the misogynists and trolls who mercilessly attack and demean women the world over, including, very often, Mary herself. In Women & Power, she traces the origins of this misogyny to its ancient roots, examining the pitfalls of gender and the ways that history has mistreated strong women since time immemorial.

"This slim and timely volume leaves readers to contemplate how women can reconfigure societys current perceptions of power." Publishers Weekly.

Davis, Lisa Selin

Tomboy : the surprising history and future of girls who dare to be different / Lisa Selin Davis. Hachette Go, 2020. 336 p. **305.409**

1. Tomboys 2. Gender identity 3. Gender nonconformity 4. Girls
ISBN 9780316458313

LC bl2020017407

Inspired by her thought-provoking op-ed for the New York Times, Lisa Selin Davis's Tomboy explores the history and imagines the future of girls who defy societal expectations based on their gender. Tomboy is a revealing dive into the forces that have shifted and narrowed our ideas of what's normal for boys and girls, and for kids who don't fall neatly into either category. Davis talks to experts from clothing designers to psychologists, historians to neuroscientists, and tomboys from eight to eighty, to illuminate debates about what is masculine and feminine; what is biological versus socially constructed; what constitutes the categories of boy and girl; and the connection between tomboyism, gender identity, and sexuality.

"Davis's persuasive and deeply personal argument for moving beyond the gender binary will resonate with those curious about child rearing free of normative expectations." Publishers Weekly

Jewell, Hannah

She caused a riot : 100 unknown women who built cities, sparked revolutions, and massively crushed it / Hannah Jewell. Sourcebooks, Inc., 2018 324 p. **305.409**

1. Women -- History. 2. Social history.
ISBN 9781492662921

LC 2017046004

From writer Hannah Jewell, She Caused a Riot is an empowering, no-holds-barred look into the epic adventures and dangerous exploits of 100 inspiring women who were too brave, too brilliant, too unconventional, too political, too poor, not ladylike enough and not white enough to be recognized by their contemporaries.

305.40944 Women--France

Sebba, Anne

Les Parisiennes : how the women of Paris lived, loved, and died under Nazi occupation / Anne Sebba. St. Martin's Press, 2016. 368 p. **305.40944**

1. Women. 2. Women and war. 3. World War II -- Social aspects. 4. France -- History -- German occupation, 1914-1918 5. Paris, France -- History -- German occupation, 1940-1944.
ISBN 9781250048592

LC 2016020685

"First published in Great Britain by Weidenfeld & Nicolson"--Title page verso.

Traces the experiences of women in Nazi-occupied Paris, detailing how, while men were fighting in the war or forced to work in German factories, women worked desperately to care for their families and survive while enduring daily contact with occupying forces.

"Paris history buffs will enjoy a new look at the city during World War II." Library Journal.

305.40952 Women--Japan

Johnson, Akemi

Night in the American village : women in the shadow of the U.S. military bases in Okinawa / Akemi Johnson. The New Press, [2019] 224 p. **305.40952**

1. Military bases, American 2. Women and the military 3. Women -- Japan -- Social conditions 4. Soldiers -- United States 5. Okinawa 6. Japan 7. United States -- Military relations
ISBN 9781620973318

LC 2019004697

"An examination of the complex relationship between the women living near the U.S. base in Okinawa and the servicemen who are stationed there." --Provided by publisher.

"Johnson masterfully weaves historical details and current events into the interviews with her subjects, with each aspect enriching the broader tale. Highly recommended to readers with an interest in military history, women's studies, women's history, and Japanese-U.S. relations." Library Journal.

305.409581 Women--Afghanistan

Badkhen, Anna, 1976-

★The **world** is a carpet : four seasons in an Afghan village / Anna Badkhen. Penguin Group USA, 2013. 288 p. **305.409581**

1. Villages -- Afghanistan. 2. Rural families -- Afghanistan. 3. Tradition (Phiosophy) 4. Families -- Afghanistan. 5. Afghanistan -- Social conditions. 6. Central Asia -- Social conditions. 7. Islamic countries -- Social conditions.

ISBN 9781594488320

LC 2013003827

Despite war and invasion, Turkoman weavers have created gorgeous carpets for centuries. In the tiny desert village of Oqa, Afghanistan, people still believe the world is flat; American fighter planes fly overheard, and hunger is common. An award-winning journalist traces the path of one beautifully intricate carpet woven here--from the purchase of its yarn, through months of intricate weavings that reflect the village's life, to its journey to market. This compelling read portrays fascinating people you won't soon forget, in a community bonded by rich traditions and tremendous hardships.

305.40973 Women--United States

Collins, Gail

When everything changed : the amazing journey of American women from 1960 to the present / Gail Collins. Little, Brown and Co, 2009. 480 p. **305.40973**

1. Women -- United States -- History. 2. Gender role 3. Women's role. 4. Civil rights. 5. United States -- History.

ISBN 9780316059541

LC 2008054933

A follow-up to America's Women by a former New York Times editorial page editor chronicles the revolution of women's civil rights throughout the past half century, drawing on oral history and research in a variety of disciplines while celebrating Hillary Clinton's 2008 presidential campaign.

"Collins can be deadly serious and great fun to read at the same time. A revelatory book for readers of both sexes, and sure to become required reading for any American women's-studies course." Kirkus.

Doyle, Sady

Trainwreck : the women we love to hate, mock, and fear... and why / Sady Doyle. Melville House, [2016] 288 p. **305.40973**

1. Women in mass media. 2. Celebrities -- Personal conduct. 3. Sexism 4. Women in public life.

ISBN 9781612195636

LC 2016015117

"With compassion for its subjects and a vibrantly satirical tone, Doyle's debut book places her on the A-list of contemporary feminist writers." Publishers Weekly.

Petersen, Anne Helen

Too fat, too slutty, too loud : the rise and reign of the unruly woman / Anne Helen Petersen. Plume Books, 2017. 304 p. **305.40973**

1. Women celebrities 2. Personal conduct 3. Self-confidence in women 4. Assertiveness in women

ISBN 9780399576850

LC 2016058237

A popular BuzzFeed columnist examines the phenomenon of popular provocative womanhood to discuss the rise of such counterculture stars as Amy Schumer, Nicki Minaj and Caitlyn Jenner, exploring why they are popular in spite of negative behaviors and what makes and breaks today's divas.

"Media studies scholar Petersen (BuzzFeed News) offers a trenchant and intersectional analysis of the celebrity narratives we create around famous women who, in some way, defy the cultural scripts of classed and raced femininity." Library Journal.

305.42 Social role and status of women

Adichie, Chimamanda Ngozi, 1977-

We should all be feminists / Chimamanda Ngozi Adichie. Random House, 2015. 64 p. **305.42**

1. Gender equity. 2. Sex discrimination. 3. Social change. 4. Feminism. 5. Essays.

ISBN 9781101911761

LC bl2015005730

Based on the 2012 TED talk given by the author.

"An eloquent, stirring must-read for budding and reluctant feminists." School Library Journal.

Anderson, Gillian, 1968-

We : a manifesto for women everywhere / Gillian Anderson and Jennifer Nadel. Atria Books, 2017 xxiii, 360 p. ; **305.42**

1. Women -- Personal conduct 2. Women -- Psychology 3. Spiritual life 4. Self-realization

ISBN 9781501126277

LC 2016052691

Inspires women to use practical, psychological, and spiritual tools to create a more fulfilling way of life and to attain happiness and freedom from the have-it-all superwoman culture.

Brownmiller, Susan

In our time : memoir of a revolution / Susan Brownmiller. Dial Press, 1999. 360 p. : **305.42**

1. Brownmiller, Susan. 2. Feminism -- United States -- History -- 20th century. 3. Women's rights -- History -- 20th century. 4. Feminists -- United States. 5. Women's Movement.

ISBN 0385314868

LC 99039344

"A riveting blend of eyewitness accounts and keen analysis, this is history at its most vital and a stirring testament to our ability to come together to combat social injustice, no matter how deeply entrenched it has become." Booklist.

Conde Nast Publications,

Together we rise : the Women's March : behind the scenes at the protest heard round the world / the Women's March organizers and Conde Nast. Dey Street Books, 2018. 304 p. **305.42**

1. Women's March on Washington (2017) 2. Women's rights -- History -- 21st century. 3. Protests, demonstrations, vigils, etc. 4. Feminism 5. Protest movements 6. United States -- Politics and government 7. Interviews 8. Essays

ISBN 9780062843432

LC bl2017046276

With essays by: Rowan Blanchard, Senator Tammy Duckworth, America Ferrera, Roxane Gay, Ilana Glazer, Ashley Judd, Valarie Kaur, David Remnick, Yara Shahidi, Jill Soloway, Jia Tolentino, Congresswoman Maxine Waters, and Elaine Welteroth, Jose Antionio Vargas, and more.

A celebration of the one-year anniversary of the Womens March presents exclusive interviews with Womens March organizers, never-before-seen photographs, and essays by feminist activists.

"Interspersed between the organizers narratives are accounts of the day from women all over the world, explaining how that show of dissent impacted their lives, and notes from celebrities like America Ferrera, Roxane Gay, and Jill Solloway detailing their own views of the march. Large and plentiful photos show many shades of hope and inclusion in this energizing and emotional trip through the movement." Booklist.

Conger, Cristen

Unladylike : a field guide to smashing the patriarchy and claiming your space / Cristen Conger and Caroline Ervin ; illustrated by Tyler Feder. Ten Speed Press, 2018 281 p. : **305.42**

1. Feminism 2. Sexism 3. Self-esteem in women
ISBN 9780399580451

LC 2018006581

Combines histories, statistics, and social justice principles to connect the personal and the political in this field guide to intersectional feminism and practical hell-raising.

Dorr, Luisa

Firsts : women who are changing the world : interviews, photographs, breakthroughs / portraits by Luisa Dorr. Liberty Street, 2017 188 p. : **305.42**

1. Leadership in women 2. Role models 3. Leadership 4. Women -- Interviews
ISBN 9781683300687

LC 2017941458

"This groundbreaking collection profiles nearly 50 women across a range of endeavors: business, politics, science, technology, sports, entertainment and more. A companion to TIME's multi-platform documentary, the book includes 15 first person deep-dives into the lives of influential women such as General Lori Robinson, the first woman to lead troops into combat, Kathryn Sullivan, the first woman to walk in space, and Aretha Franklin, the first woman inducted into the Rock and Roll Hall of Fame. Many others, including Oprah Winfrey, Madeline Albright, and Sheryl Sandburg offer their own personal reflections, thematic quotes and perspectives on balance, perseverance and strength. Each first-person piece or quote is accompanied by a distinctive portrait by photographer Luisa Dorr - set up and taken on her iPhone. Others included in this unforgettable volume: Serena Williams, Ellen Degeneres, Loretta Lynch, Shonda Rimes, Nancy Pelosi, Rita Moreno, Cindy Sherman and Mo'Ne Davis."--Publisher's description.

Eltahawy, Mona, 1967-

The **seven** necessary sins for women and girls / Mona Eltahawy. Beacon Press, 2019. 208 p. **305.42**

1. Feminism 2. Women's rights 3. Anger in women 4. Leadership in women
ISBN 9780807013816

LC 2019006195

A bold and uncompromising feminist manifesto that shows women and girls how to defy, disrupt, and destroy the patriarchy by embracing the qualities they've been trained to avoid. Seizing upon the energy of the #MeToo movement, feminist activist Mona Eltahawy advocates a muscular, out-loud approach to teaching women and girls to harness their power through what she calls the "seven necessary sins" that women and girls are not supposed to commit: to be angry, ambitious, profane, violent, attention-seeking, lustful, and powerful. All the necessary "sins" that women and girls require to erupt.

Friedan, Betty, 1921-

★The **feminine** mystique / Betty Friedan ; introduction by Anna Quindlen. Norton, 2001, c1963. xxxiv, 430 p. ; **305.42**

1. Feminism -- United States. 2. Gender role 3. Sexism 4. Power (Social sciences)
ISBN 0393322572

LC 2001044231

Views the distorted image of women that prevailed from the end of the Second World War through the early sixties and relects upon changes.

Friedman, Jaclyn,

Believe me : how trusting women can change the world / edited by Jessica Valenti and Jaclyn Friedman; essays by various contributors. Seal Press, 2020. 288 p. **305.42**

1. Sexism 2. Sexual harassment of women 3. Women's rights 4. Feminism 5. Essays 6. Anthologies
ISBN 9781580058797

LC 2019013503

In an anthology that draws readers into the evolving landscape of the movement against sexual violence, the contributors ask and answer the crucial question: What would happen if we didn?t just believe women, but acted as though they matter?

"Consistently well-written and soundly reasoned, these essays persuasively cast the tendency to doubt women as one of America's greatest social ills." Publishers Weekly.

Gates, Melinda, 1964-

★The **moment** of lift : how empowering women changes the world / Melinda Gates. Flatiron Books, [2019] 224 p. **305.42**

1. Feminism. 2. Women -- Social conditions. 3. Women -- Economic conditions. 4. Equality.
ISBN 9781250313577

LC 2018051054

A timely call to action for women's empowerment by the influential co-chair of the Bill & Melinda Gates Foundation identifies the link between women's equality and societal health, sharing uplifting insights by international advocates in the fight against gender bias.

"At a time when beneficial globalization is being threatened by nationalism, and women's rights are in danger of being rolled back to nineteenth-century norms, Gates offers urgent reminders of why it's necessary to help women everywhere achieve their full potential." Booklist.

Hay, Carol, 1977-

Think like a feminist : the philosophy behind the revolution / Carol Hay. W.W. Norton & Company, 2020 xvi, 222 p. **305.42**

1. Feminist theory. 2. Feminism. 3. Intersectionality 4. Gender role
ISBN 9781324003090

LC 2020010917

Think Like a Feminist is an irreverent yet rigorous primer that unpacks two hundred years of feminist ideas. Professor Carol Hay takes the long view on our current moment, framing it within the philosophical thinking that underlies the organization and activism that has transformed women's roles and lives. She delves into topics such as the role of oppression, gender roles, sexual violence, what it means to identify as a woman, and the intersections of sexism, racism, classism, and homophobia. Hay shatters common misconceptions about feminism as she sheds light on the social structures that continue to restrict women.

"Hay succeeds in clarifying abstract--and often sobering--concepts with straightforward terminology and a dash of irreverent humor. This crisp, well-informed primer on feminist theory will resonate with young women and experienced activists alike." Publishers Weekly

Orenstein, Peggy

Don't call me princess : essays on girls, women, sex, and life / Peggy Orenstein. HarperCollins, 2018 336 p. **305.42**

1. Women in popular culture 2. Feminism 3. Sexuality 4. Women 5. Essays

ISBN 9780062834058

LC bl2017052008

The best-selling author of Girls & Sex presents a first collection of essays, drawn from three decades of writing, that traces the progress and setbacks of feminism as reflected in areas ranging from princess culture and miscarriage to breast cancer and motherhood.

"Compelling and intelligent, Orenstein's book offers a powerful vision of the challenges of modern womanhood and of what it means to be female in 21st-century America. A sharp, timely collection of essays." Kirkus.

Paglia, Camille, 1947-

Free women, free men : sex, gender, feminism / Camille Paglia. Pantheon, 2017. 160 p. **305.42**

1. Feminism 2. Feminists 3. Gender identity 4. Popular culture 5. United States -- Social conditions 6. Essays

ISBN 9780375424779

LC 2016034574

A collection of essays from the social critic and intellectual provocateur behind 1990's best-selling Sexual Personae challenges modern feminism in musings that declare Madonna the future of feminism and question if men are obsolete.

"Intriguing and thought provoking for readers interested in different perspectives of feminism." Library Journal.

Palmieri, Jennifer

She proclaims : our declaration of independence from a man's world / Jennifer Palmieri. Grand Central Publishing, 2020. xi, 193 p. ; **305.42**

1. Feminism. 2. Self-fulfillment in women 3. Political participation 4. Women -- Political activity

ISBN 9781538750650

LC 2020005491

An empowering guide to feminism by the best-selling author of Dear Madam President outlines a blueprint for activism while sharing lessons from her personal choice to live on her own terms instead of embracing toxic patriarchal norms.

"Feminists will be heartened by this inspirational guide to fighting for gender equality." Publishers Weekly

Romm, Robin,

Double bind : women on ambition / edited by Robin Romm. W W Norton & Co Inc., 2017. 336 p. **305.42**

1. Ambition in women 2. Social norms 3. Gender gap 4. Taboo 5. Essays

ISBN 9781631491214

LC 2016054987

The author of The Mother Garden presents an urgent exploration of why today's feminists still dissociate themselves from healthy ambition, sharing the views of such contributors as Ayana Mathis, Molly Ringwald and Roxane Gay to illuminate why ambition remains a taboo in gender equality.

Rosin, Hanna

The **end** of men : and the rise of women / Hanna Rosin. Riverhead Books, 2012. 320 p. **305.42**

1. Women -- Social conditions -- 21st century. 2. Power (Social sciences) 3. Feminism. 4. Gender equity

ISBN 9781594488047

LC 2012018005

A full-length report based on the author's Atlantic cover story argues that a radical shift in power dynamics between men and women at every level of society is having profound implications for marriage, sex, children, work and more, demonstrating the radically different and promising ways today's men and women become educated, earn money and conduct relationships.

Rowe-Finkbeiner, Kristin

Keep marching : how every woman can take action and change our world / Kristin Rowe-Finkbeiner. Hachette Books, 2018. xii, 323 p. : **305.42**

1. Women -- Political activity 2. Feminism 3. Social action 4. Women's rights

ISBN 9780316515566

LC 2017054730

The cofounder and CEO of a national women's organization examines the political, economic and institutional barriers that hold women back from achieving their goals and offers solutions and strategies for clearing these hurdles.

"A crucial resource for women interested in beginning political advocacy work." Library Journal.

Solnit, Rebecca

★**Men** explain things to me / Rebecca Solnit. Haymarket Books, 2014. 160 p. **305.42**

1. Men/women relations 2. Feminism 3. Control (Psychology) 4. Gender equity. 5. Essays

ISBN 9781608464968

LC 2013427537

In her comic, scathing essay "Men Explain Things to Me," Rebecca Solnit took on what often goes wrong in conversations between men and women. This book features that now-classic essay with six perfect complements, including an examination of the great feminist writer Virginia Woolf's embrace of mystery, of not knowing, of doubt and ambiguity, a highly original inquiry into marriage equality, and a terrifying survey of the scope of contemporary violence against women.

"Sharp narratives that illuminate and challenge the status quo of women's roles in the world. Slim in scope, but yet another good book by Solnit." Kirkus.

The **mother** of all questions : further reports from the feminist revolutions / Rebecca Solnit. Haymarket Books, 2017. 180 p. **305.42**

1. Feminism 2. Gender wars 3. Gender gap 4. Social justice 5. Essays

ISBN 9781608467402

LC 2018418036

"Solnit's voice is calm, clear, and unapologetic; each essay balances a warm wit with confident, thoughtful analysis, resulting in a collection that is as enjoyable and accessible as it is incisive." Booklist.

Spar, Debora L.

Wonder women : sex, power, and the quest for perfection / Debora Spar. Sarah Crichton Books/Farrar, Straus and Giroux, 2013. 288 p. **305.42**

1. Women 2. Gender role 3. Success (Concept) 4. Feminism.

ISBN 9780374298753

LC 2013941741

One of the first women professors at Harvard Business School and the current president of Barnard College, the most important all-women school in the country, examines how women's lives have--and have not--changed over the past 40 years.

Spruill, Marjorie Julian, 1951-

Divided we stand : the battle over women's rights and family values that polarized American politics / Marjorie J. Spruill. Bloomsbury, 2017. 368 p. **305.42**

1. Women's rights. 2. Feminism. 3. Women social advocates 4. Liberals. 5. United States -- Politics and government

ISBN 9781632863140

LC bl2017007810

Forty years ago, two women's movements drew a line in the sand between liberals and conservatives. The legacy of that rift is still evident today in American politics and social policies.

"There are countless kernels of amazing achievement and courage throughout this jam-packed, engaging history." Kirkus.

Steinem, Gloria, 1934-

Outrageous acts and everyday rebellions / Gloria Steinem ; with a new foreword by Emma Watson and new material by the author Picador, 2019, c1983. xxii, 406 p. ; **305.42**

1. Steinem, Gloria, 1934- 2. Feminists -- United States 3. Feminism -- United States. 4. Essays

ISBN 9781250204868

LC 95031711

An updated, third edition of the renowned feminist's most diverse and timeless collection of essays.

The **truth** will set you free, but first it will piss you off : thoughts on life, love, and rebellion / Gloria Steinem ; illustrations by Samantha Dion Baker. Random House, 2019. 304 p. **305.42**

1. Steinem, Gloria, 1934- 2. Life 3. Feminism 4. Inspiration -- Quotations 5. Quotations 6. Essays

ISBN 9780593132685

LC 2019029832

An illustrated collection of Gloria Steinem's most inspirational and outrageous quotes, with an introduction and essays by the feminist activist herself.

Ulrich, Laurel

Well-behaved women seldom make history / Laurel Thatcher Ulrich. Alfred A. Knopf, 2007. xxxiv, 284 p. : **305.42**

1. Christine, de Pisan, ca. 1364-ca. 1431. Livre de la cite des dames 2. Stanton, Elizabeth Cady, 1815-1902. Eighty years and more. 3. Woolf, Virginia, 1882-1941. Room of one's own. 4. Women -- History. 5. Women in literature. 6. Feminism.

ISBN 1400041597

LC 2006100581

Examines three key works by women--the fifteenth-century "Book of the City of Ladies" by Christine de Pizan, Elizabeth Cady Stanton's memoirs, and Virginia Woolf's "A Room of One's Own," to explore the making of history from a woman's perspective.

"This book is by no means jargon-ridden or academic in tone. Ulrich's style is plain and direct, agreeable but without frills, and she moves efficiently right along. The book is a pleasure to read." Washington Post Book World.

Valenti, Jessica

Full frontal feminism : a young woman's guide to why feminism matters / Jessica Valenti. Seal Press, 2014, c2007. 279 p. : **305.42**

1. Feminism. 2. Feminists. 3. Women -- Social conditions -- 21st century. 4. Popular culture -- Social aspects 5. United States -- Social life and customs -- 21st century

ISBN 9781580055611

LC 2006038573

The creator of Feministing.com presents evidence of the ongoing spirit of feminism that considers a wide range of topics from health and reproductive rights to violence and education, in a volume that challenges modern criticisms of today's young women and invites the newest generation to become comfortable with feminist activism.

"These are lessons we already know; little in this book will prove useful to most women. Most public libraries will want the Siegel book; a few may want Valenti's." Library Journal.

Worden, Minky,

The **unfinished** revolution : voices from the global fight for women's rights / edited by Minky Worden. Seven Stories Press, 2012. 361 p. **305.42**

1. Women's rights. 2. Human rights. 3. Violence against women. 4. Essays.

ISBN 9781609803872

LC 2011052738

Presents a collection of thirty essays by prominent women's rights activists reflecting on the global struggle waged for women's rights.

"Diverse voices of hopeless, hopeful, and boldly determined women from around the world constitute a compelling, multicultural resource supplemented by copious endnotes, a reading list, and an index." Booklist.

Zoepf, Katherine

Excellent daughters : the secret lives of young women who are transforming the Arab world / Katherine Zoepf. Penguin Press, 2016 288 p. **305.42**

1. Women -- Arab countries 2. Young women 3. Muslim women 4. Social change. 5. Arab countries 6. Middle East

ISBN 9781594203886

LC 2015043395

A first-of-its-kind exploration of a new generation of Arab women who are questioning authority, changing societies and leading revolutions brings a new understanding of the changing Arab societies, from 9/11 to Tahrir Square to the rise of ISIS, and gives voice to the extraordinary women at the forefront of this change.

"In her absorbing, window-opening book, Zoepf reveals the variety of womens lives and interests away from political headlines and conventional stereotypes, and their power, often by small steps, to transform their world." Publishers Weekly.

305.4209 Feminism--History

Chocano, Carina

You play the girl : on Playboy bunnies, Stepford wives, trainwrecks, & other mixed messages / Carina Chocano. Mariner Books, 2017 272 p. **305.4209**

1. Popular culture 2. Women in mass media 3. Women's role 4. Expectation (Psychology) 5. Essays

ISBN 9780544648944

LC 2017289231

From *Pretty Woman to Frozen*, Carina Chocano (a staff writer for Salon) digs into portrayals of women in popular culture over the last 50 years. In addition to her insightful analysis of topics such as sexuality, motherhood, and women in the workplace, Chocano offers personal anecdotes from her own childhood (when she was unmoved by the Disney princesses popular among her peers) as well as her current efforts to raise a confident daughter.

"A sharply perceptive look at the myths that constrain women." Kirkus.

Coontz, Stephanie

A **strange** stirring : the Feminine mystique and American women at the dawn of the 1960s / Stephanie Coontz. Basic Books, c2010. 224 p. **305.4209**

1. Friedan, Betty, 1921- Feminine mystique. 2. Feminism -- United States -- History -- 20th century. 3. Women -- United States -- Social conditions -- 20th century. 4. Gender role 5. United States -- Social life and customs -- 20th century

ISBN 9780465002009

LC 2010022163

The author of Marriage, a History chronicles the impact of Betty Friedan's landmark feminist book Feminine Mystique on stay-at-home married women of the early 1960s, who had become dissatisfied with domestic life.

Freedman, Estelle B., 1947-

The **essential** feminist reader / edited and with an introduction by Estelle B. Freedman. Modern Library, 2007. xviii, 472 p. ; **305.4209**

1. Feminism -- History. 2. Feminist theory -- History. 3. Women -- Literary collections 4. Essays.

ISBN 9780812974607

LC 2007299488

An in-depth anthology of feminist writing ranges from the origins of feminist ideas to the global feminism and Third Wave movements of the late 1990s in a collection that includes works by Betty Friedan, Virginia Woolf, Emma Goldman, Eve Ensler, the Guerrilla Girls, and John Stuart Mill, along with lively commentary on each piece's context and meaning.

"Embracing a daunting but necessary task, Freedman has compiled some 600 years of feminist thought into one all-inclusive volume that examines and extols the movement's essential tenets from its inception in the fifteenth century to its rebirth in the twenty-first." Booklist.

Morris, Bonnie J., 1961-

★The **feminist** revolution : the struggle for women's liberation / Bonnie J. Morris, D-M Withers. Smithsonian Books, 2018. 224 p. **305.4209**

1. Feminism -- History. 2. Women's rights. 3. Women's studies.

ISBN 9781588346124

LC 2017039814

Describes the political campaigns, protests, formation of women's publishing houses, groundbreaking magazines and other contributions that helped women around the world mobilize into the feminist revolution that began in 1966.

"Much like a museum exhibition, this collection uses accessible text and rich visual materials that invite readers to explore in a nonlinear fashion. It will appeal to both those deeply familiar with the topic as well as beginners of this influential moment in feminist history." Library Journal.

Woo, Ilyon

The **great** divorce : a nineteenth-century mother's extraordinary fight against her husband, the Shakers, and her times / Ilyon Woo. Atlantic Monthly Press, 2010 416 p. **305.4209**

1. Shakers 2. Divorced women. 3. Child custody. 4. Parents' rights. 5. Trials (Child custody) 6. New York (State)

ISBN 9780802119469

LC 2011293155

"Both Eunice's struggle and the Shakers' story fascinate equally while dispelling romanticized myths of utopian societies in the tumultuous postrevolutionary period." Publishers Weekly.

305.420973 Feminism--United States

Hanauer, Cathi,

The **bitch** is back : older, wiser, and getting happier / edited by Cathi Hanauer. William Morrow & Company, 2016. 304 p. **305.420973**

1. Women 2. Feminism 3. Motherhood 4. Essays

ISBN 9780062389510

LC bl2016041569

Nine of the original contributors to The Bitch in the House have returned for this second collection of essays to reveal how their lives have changed since the first volume and discuss their unique views on womanhood and feminism today.

"Like an all-night gab session with ones best friend, these essays shed sincere and searing light on subjects that are often hard for women to face. In doing so, Hanauer and company give voice to topics all too frequently hidden under a damaging cone of silence." Booklist.

Hirshman, Linda R

Reckoning : the epic battle against sexual abuse and harassment / Linda Hirshman. Houghton Mifflin Harcourt, 2019. 304 p. **305.420973**

1. Sexual harassment of women 2. Trials (Sex crimes) 3. Sex crimes 4. Feminism 5. United States -- Social conditions

ISBN 9781328566447

LC 2018051341

The best-selling author of Sisters in Law chronicles America's ongoing fight against sexual harassment, from the pivotal civil rights battles of the 1970s through the headline events of the #MeToo movement.

"An intense, harsh view of a long struggle; well worth a look for anyone curious about where #MeToo came fromand where it should go next." Library Journal.

Kendall, Mikki

Hood feminism : notes from the women that a movement forgot / Mikki Kendall. Viking Press, 2020. 288 p. **305.420973**

1. Feminism 2. Minority women. 3. Feminism 4. Intersectionality 5. Essays.

ISBN 9780525560548

LC 2019033697

Insightful, incendiary and ultimately hopeful, Hood Feminism is both an irrefutable indictment of a movement in flux and also clear-eyed assessment of how to save it.

"This hard-hitting guide delivers crucial insights for those looking to build a more inclusive movement." Publishers Weekly

Mukhopadhyay, Samhita,

Nasty women : feminism, resistance, and revolution in Trump's America / edited by Samhita Mukhopadhyay and Kate Harding. Picador, [2017] 256 p. **305.420973**

1. Feminism -- United States. 2. Women -- Political activity -- United States 3. Women radicals 4. Women's rights 5. United States -- Politics and government -- 21st century 6. United States -- Social

conditions -- 21st century 7. Essays 8. Anthologies
ISBN 9781250155504

LC 2017027142

This collection of essays from leading feminist writers, including Cheryl Strayed, Rebecca Solnit and Jessica Valenti describe how liberals, progressives and marginalized people around the United States can persist, resist and enact lasting change despite Donald Trump's presidency.

"The writers are emotionally generous as they meditate on this pivotal moment in American history. This book invites readers to converse, comfort, and hold one another accountable in the hope of igniting radical, intersectional change." Booklist.

Traister, Rebecca

Good and mad : the revolutionary power of women's anger / Rebecca Traister. Simon & Schuster 2018 352 p. **305.420973**

1. Feminism -- History. 2. Women -- Political activity. 3. Social change. 4. Women's rights
ISBN 9781501181795

LC 2018035975

The New York Times best-selling author explores the transformative power of female anger and its ability to transcend into a political movement.

West, Lindy

★The **witches** are coming / Lindy West. Hachette Books, 2019. 272 p. **305.420973**

1. Women -- Public opinion 2. Women in popular culture 3. Women in mass media 4. Women in films 5. United States -- Social conditions 6. Essays
ISBN 9780316449885

LC bl2019030022

West unpacks the complicated, and sometimes tragic, journey and politics of not being a white man in the 21st century.

"Covering everything from the 2016 election and #metoo to abortion rights and fat-positive body representation to the climate crisis, West's latest will have progressive readers, especially longtime followers of her work, nodding along, quoting passages to friends. Hand to fans of Rebecca Traister, Ijeoma Oluo, and Roxane Gay." Library Journal.

305.48 Specific groups of women

Abu-Lughod, Lila

Do Muslim women need saving? / Lila Abu-Lughod. Harvard University Press, 2013. 336 p. **305.48**

1. Muslim women. 2. Women -- Islamic countries. 3. Stereotypes (Social psychology) 4. Women's rights -- Islamic countries. 5. Middle East -- Social life and customs. 6. Islamic countries -- Social life and customs.
ISBN 9780674725164

LC 2013005846

"While offering no easy solution, the author recommends observation over moral crusades, stating: "Anyone seriously interested in Muslim women's rights must follow them as they move." This book is an excellent place to begin." Publishers Weekly.

Berry, Daina Ramey

★A **Black** women's history of the United States / Daina Ramey Berry and Kali Nicole Gross. Beacon Press, 2020 288 p. **305.48**

1. African American women -- History 2. Intersectionality 3. Racism 4. Sexism 5. United States -- History 6. United States -- Race relations
ISBN 9780807033555

LC 2019026852

In centering Black women's stories, two award-winning historians seek both to empower African American women and to show their allies that Black women's unique ability to make their own communities while combatting centuries of oppression is an essential component in our continued resistance to systemic racism and sexism. Daina Ramey Berry and Kali Nicole Gross offer an examination and celebration of Black womanhood, beginning with the first African women who arrived in what became the United States to African American women of today.

"For anyone hoping to topple the remaining barriers, this book is a font of inspiration. A vital book for any library or classroom?and for foot soldiers in the fight for racial justice." Kirkus

Bond, Beverly,

Black girls rock! : owning our magic, rocking our truth / edited by Beverly Bond. 37 INK, Atria, 2018. xxi, 227 p. : **305.48**

1. African American women. 2. Women, Black. 3. African American women -- Portraits. 4. Women, Black -- Portraits.
ISBN 9781501157929

LC bl2017052882

A tribute to the achievements of black women throughout the world shares anecdotes, affirmations, and inspirational essays from a diverse range of contributors, including Kerry Washington, Serena Williams, and Michelle Obama.

Brooks, Geraldine

Nine parts of desire : the hidden world of Islamic women / Geraldine Brooks. Anchor Books, 1995. 255 p. **305.48**

1. Muslim women -- Middle East -- Social conditions. 2. Islam and women 3. Women's role 4. Sexism 5. Middle East -- Religion
ISBN 0385475764

LC 94017496

ALA Notable Book, 1996.

An intimate portrait of the lives of modern Muslim women reveals how male pride and power have distorted the message of Islam to justify the subjugation of women and how a feminism of sorts has flowered in spite of repression.

"The author's revelations about these women's lives behind the veil are frank, enraging, and captivating." The New Yorker.

Hartman, Saidiya V.

Wayward lives, beautiful experiments : intimate histories of riotous black girls, troublesome women, and queer radicals / Saidiya Hartman. W.W. Norton & Company, 2020, c2019 xxi, 441 p. **305.48**

1. African American women. 2. Gender role. 3. Social change. 4. African Americans. 5. Philadelphia, Pennsylvania. 6. New York City.
ISBN 9780393357622

LC bl2020045518

Finalist for the Hurston/Wright Legacy Awards for Nonfiction, 2020.

Traces a lesser-known time of radical transformation of black life in early 20th-century America, revealing how a large number of black women forged relationships, families and jobs that were more empowered and typically indifferent to moral dictates.

"This passionate, poetic retrieval of women from the footnotes of history is a superb literary achievement." Publishers Weekly.

Scroggins, Deborah

Wanted women : faith, lies, and the war on terror: the lives of Ayaan Hirsi Ali and Aafia Siddiqui / Deborah Scroggins. Harpercollins, 2011. 256 p. **305.48**

1. Muslim women. 2. Women's rights. 3. Islam and politics. 4. Terrorism.

ISBN 9780060898977

LC 2011022153

The journalist highlights the lives of two champions of Muslim women's rights, Islam critic Ayaan Hirsi Ali and neuroscientist Aafia Siddiqui, to examine the role women have played in the conflict between radical Islam and the West.

305.5 People by social and economic levels

Boo, Katherine

★**Behind** the beautiful forevers : life, death, and hope in a Mumbai undercity / Katherine Boo. Random House, c2011. 256 p. **305.5**

1. Urban poor people. 2. Inequality. 3. Poverty. 4. Poor people. 5. Mumbai, India

ISBN 9781400067558

LC 2011019555

ALA Notable Book, 2013

National Book Award for Nonfiction, 2012.

National Book Critics Circle Award for Nonfiction finalist, 2012.

Pulitzer Prize for General Nonfiction finalist, 2013.

Profiles everyday life in the settlement of Annawadi as experienced by a Muslim teen, an ambitious rural mother, and a young scrap metal thief, illuminating how their efforts to build better lives are challenged by religious, caste, and economic tensions.

Brooks, David, 1961-

The **social** animal : a story of love, character, and achievement / David Brooks. Random House, 2011. 224 p. **305.5**

1. Men/women relations 2. Social mobility 3. Social status 4. Elite (Social sciences)

ISBN 9781400067602

LC 2010045785

Looks at current research from a variety of disciplines by following the lives and unconscious motivations of a hypothetical American couple as they grow, meet, and change throughout their lives.

"Brooks offers fictional characters Harold and Erica to illustrate how humans communicate, are educated, and succeed--or don't. Synthesizing research on human unconsciousness, Brooks meshes sociology, psychology, and economics to show how character is formed and how we strive for happiness and success. [The author] offers a new look at the assumptions we make about life and a close, deep examination of the failure of social and economic policies that do not take into account the complexities of human behavior, treating us as if we were totally rational and guided by our thoughts rather than some combination of intellect and emotion." Booklist.

Cowen, Tyler

The **complacent** class : the self-defeating quest for the American dream / Tyler Cowen. St. Martin's Press, 2017. 272 p. **305.5**

1. Social classes. 2. American dream 3. Social change. 4. Quality of life

ISBN 9781250108692

LC 2016049031

An economics professor and best-selling author of The Great Stagnation describes how the modern American "matching culture" and quest for comfort ultimately has created greater inequality and segregation and decreased innovation and creativity.

"A book that will undoubtedly stir discussion--as many of Cowen's books do--with readers divided about how they stand based on where they currently sit." Kirkus.

Epstein, Joseph, 1937-

Snobbery : the American version / Joseph Epstein. Houghton Mifflin, 2002. xii, 274 p. **305.5**

1. Social status -- United States. 2. Snobs and snobbishness. 3. Essays.

ISBN 0395944171

LC 2001051623

A look at snobbery in modern-day America after the fall of the old culture of prep schools, the Ivy League, and the Social Register examines new outlets for snobbery, including food and wine, fashion, schools, and high-achieving children.

"Every bracing page is a mirror in which readers can't help but recognize themselves, and each offers a quotable quip . . . and much to think about." Booklist.

Freeland, Chrystia, 1968-

Plutocrats : the rise of the new global super-rich and the fall of everyone else / Chrystia Freeland. Penguin Press, 2012. 304 p. **305.5**

1. Rich people -- Personal conduct 2. Poverty 3. Poor people 4. Social classes

ISBN 9781594204098

LC 2012015119

Includes index.

Lionel Gelber Prize (Canada), 2013.

A journalist and industry specialist for Reuters examines the growing disparity between the rich and the poor, taking a non-partisan look into the businesspeople who are amassing colossal fortunes and preferring the company of similar people around the world.

Hayes, Christopher, 1979-

Twilight of the elites : America after meritocracy / Christopher Hayes. Crown, 2012. 320 p. **305.5**

1. Business and politics 2. Corporate power 3. Business -- Corrupt practices 4. Scandals 5. United States -- Politics and government -- 21st century. 6. United States -- Economic conditions -- 21st century. 7. United States -- Social conditions -- 21st century.

ISBN 9780307720450

LC 2012002435

Analyzes scandals in high-profile institutions, from Wall Street and the Catholic Church to Major League Baseball, while evaluating how an elite American meritocracy rose throughout the past half-century before succumbing to corruption and failure.

Hedges, Chris

Days of destruction, days of revolt / Chris Hedges and Joe Sacco. Nation Books, 2012. 304 p. : **305.5**

1. Poor people -- United States 2. Social classes -- United States. 3. Crime -- United States. 4. United States -- Social conditions -- 20th century. 5. Comics and Graphic novels

ISBN 9781568586434

LC 2012004701

An award-winning cartoonist presents a scathing graphic report on the crises facing America's poor as reflected in the city of Camden, New Jersey, tracing its descent from an industrial giant to a region torn by unemployment, open-air drug markets and budget cuts.

Isenberg, Nancy

★**White** trash : the 400--year untold history of class in America / Nancy Isenberg. Viking, 2016 480 p. **305.5**

1. Social classes 2. Poor people 3. European Americans 4. Working class

ISBN 9780670785971

LC 2016302095

A history of the class system in America from Colonial times to the present illuminates the crucial legacy of the underprivileged white demographic, challenging popular notions about equality while citing the pivotal contributions of lower-class white workers in wartime, social policy and the rise of the Republican party. By the author of Fallen Founder.

"A riveting thesis supported by staggering research." Kirkus.

Markovits, Daniel, 1969-

The **meritocracy** trap : how America's foundational myth feeds inequality, dismantles the middle class, and devours the elite / Daniel Markovits. Penguin Press, 2019. 336 p. **305.5**

1. Middle class 2. Intellectuals 3. Elite (Social sciences) 4. Inequality 5. United States -- Social conditions -- 21st century

ISBN 9780735221994

LC 2019007519

An eminent Yale law professor challenges the myth of meritocracy to reveal its direct role in today's political, economic and psychological crises, outlining recommendations for ending and reversing the damage of current fraudulent practices.

"Bold proposals for a radical revision of contemporary society." Kirkus.

Putnam, Robert D.

★**Our** kids : the American dream in crisis / Robert D. Putnam. Simon & Schuster 2015 416 p. **305.5**

1. American Dream 2. Social mobility 3. Middle class -- United States. 4. Social policy. 5. United States -- Economic conditions

ISBN 9781476769899

LC 2015001534

In an authoritative, yet personal, examination of the growing inequality gap, a leading humanist and renowned scientist who has consulted for the last four U.S. Presidents, drawing on poignant life stories of rich and poor kids across the country, provides a disturbing account of the American dream. By the author of Bowling Alone. Includes 30 charts and graphs.

Quart, Alissa

Squeezed : why our families can't afford America / Alissa Quart. Ecco, 2018. 272 p. **305.5**

1. Middle class 2. Household finances 3. Cost and standard of living 4. Personal finance 5. United States -- Economic conditions

ISBN 9780062412256

LC 2017056972

The executive editor of the journalism nonprofit, Economic Hardship Reporting Project, outlines counter-intuitive recommendations for meeting the challenges of today's high parenting costs and unstable job markets that are imposing difficult hardships on the middle class.

"Quart details sound policy-related solutions an adjunct rights movement; free preschool; welfare-type assistance for elder care and childcare; an end to federal funding for sketchy, for-profit schools; and universal basic income. Her ambitious, top-tier reportage tells a powerful story of America today." Publishers Weekly.

Reeves, Richard V.

Dream hoarders : how the American upper middle class is leaving everyone else in the dust, why that is a problem, and what to do about it / Richard V. Reeves. Brookings Institution Press, 2017. 180 p. **305.5**

1. Middle class 2. Social mobility 3. Wealth -- United States 4. Income distribution.

ISBN 9780815729129

LC 2017010289

Shows how American society has become the very class-defined society that earlier Americans rebelled against, discussing how Americans can take effective action to reduce opportunity hoarding and thus provide ways to restore a more equitable society

Smith, Douglas, 1962-

Former people : the final days of the Russian aristocracy / Douglas Smith. Farrar, Straus and Giroux, 2012. 496 p. **305.5**

1. Sheremetev family History -- 20th century. 2. Golitsyn family History -- 20th century. 3. Aristocracy -- Russia. 4. Peasant uprisings. 5. Revolutions. 6. Nobility -- Russia. 7. Soviet Union -- History -- Revolution, 1917-1921.

ISBN 9780374157616

LC 2012003819

A book that includes illustrations, maps and family trees focuses on the fate of two Russian aristocratic families in a detailed account of the Bolshevik Revolution's effect on the upper class, which looks at the relentless lootings, harrowing escapes, humbling exile and imprisonment and summary executions that took place during this violent time of transition.

Veblen, Thorstein, 1857-1929

★The **theory** of the leisure class / Theodore Veblen ; edited with an Introduction and notes by Martha Banta. Oxford University Press, 2007. xxxv, 263 p. ; **305.5**

1. Leisure class.

ISBN 9780192806840

LC 2007008544

Originally published: New York : Macmillan, 1899.

In his scathing The Theory of the Leisure Class, Thorstein Veblen produced a landmark study of affluent American society that exposes, with brilliant ruthlessness, the habits of production and waste that link invidious business tactics and barbaric social behavior. --Provided by publisher

Warren, Elizabeth

This fight is our fight : the battle to save America's middle class / Elizabeth Warren. Henry Holt & Company, 2017 337 p. **305.5**

1. Middle class 2. Fiscal policy. 3. Economic policy. 4. Social policy 5. United States -- Politics and government

ISBN 9781250120618

LC 2017007458

The senator shares stories of her battles in the Senate fighting for the working class, describing the experiences of middle class Americans struggling to survive.

"Warren's education in maneuvering through the powers that be is eye-opening, and she shares her experiences with grim frankness." Kirkus.

Wilkerson, Isabel

★**Caste** : the origins of our discontents / Isabel Wilkerson. Random House, [2020] 400 p. **305.5**

1. Caste 2. Social classes 3. Ethnicity 4. Race relations 5. United

States
ISBN 9780593230251

LC 2020012794

The Pulitzer Prize-winning author of The Warmth of Other Suns identifies the qualifying characteristics of historical caste systems to reveal how a rigid hierarchy of human rankings, enforced by religious views, heritage and stigma, impact everyday American lives.

"In this outstanding work of social history, she explains how a rigid social order, or caste, is about power. . . . Similar to her previous book, the latest by Wilkerson is destined to become a classic, and is urgent, essential reading for all." Library Journal

305.50973 Class--United States

Bageant, Joe

Deer hunting with Jesus : dispatches from America's class war / Joe Bageant. Crown Publishers, c2007. 273 p. ; **305.50973**

1. Social classes -- United States. 2. Working poor people -- Political activity. 3. United States -- Social conditions -- 1980- 4. Winchester, Virginia -- Social conditions -- 1980-
ISBN 030733936X

LC 2007001343

A Web columnist describes the permanent and largely invisible underclass that resides in many American small towns, examining a section of society that exists in a world of taverns, churches, and double-wide trailers.

Postel, Charles

Equality : an American dilemma, 1866-1896 / Charles Postel. Farrar, Straus and Giroux, [2019] 464 p. **305.50973**

1. Equality -- United States -- History -- 19th century. 2. Social movements -- United States -- History -- 19th century. 3. Reconstruction (United States history) 4. Working class. 5. United States -- Social conditions -- 19th century. 6. United States -- History -- 1865-1898. 7. United States -- History -- Civil War, 1861-1865 -- Influence.
ISBN 9780809079636

LC 2019000171

Presents an in-depth study of the American social movements of the post-Civil War period, demonstrating their pivotal role in establishing anti-discrimination laws and informing today's world about approaches to inequality.

"With deep research and clear prose, Postel ably demonstrates that African-Americans were consistently excluded from these reformer's visions of a more equal America. Postel's broad and valuable study ably illuminates the era." Publishers Weekly.

Stiglitz, Joseph E.

★The **price** of inequality : how today's divided society endangers our future / Joseph E. Stiglitz. W.W. Norton & Co., c2012. 448 p. **305.50973**

1. Income distribution. 2. Inequality -- United States. 3. Social problems -- United States. 4. Prosperity. 5. United States -- Economic conditions -- 21st century. 6. United States -- Social conditions -- 21st century.
ISBN 9780393088694

LC 2012014811

Robert F. Kennedy Book Award, 2013.

Examines how the wealthy classes have contributed to growing inequality in society and explains how the quest to increase wealth has hindered the country's economic growth as well as its efforts to solve its most pressing economic problems.

305.6 Religious groups

Curtis, Edward E., 1970-

Muslims in America : a short history / Edward E. Curtis IV. Oxford University Press, 2009. 168 p. **305.6**

1. Muslims -- United States -- History. 2. Islam -- United States -- History. 3. Religions. 4. Muslims -- United States -- Social conditions. 5. United States -- Interethnic relations. 6. United States -- Religious life and customs.
ISBN 9780195367560

LC 2008047566

A history of the Muslim presence in the United States from slaves who managed to keep their religion to the varied communities of the twenty-first century covers the role of converts and immigrants in every stage of American history.

305.8 Ethnic and national groups

Baldwin, James, 1924-1987

★**Notes** of a native son / James Baldwin. Beacon Press, 2012, c1963. 179 p. **305.8**

1. Baldwin, James, 1924-1987. 2. African Americans -- Civil rights. 3. Civil rights 4. Race relations 5. Racism 6. United States -- Race relations. 7. Essays.
ISBN 9780807006115

LC 90052598

Originally published: New York : Dial Press, 1963.

A Black writer records his response to the conditions of Black life and white racism.

"The expression of so many insights enriches rather than clarifies, and behind every page stalks a man, an everyman, seeking his identity... and ours. Exceptional writing." Kirkus.

Brown, Brene

Braving the wilderness : the quest for true belonging and the courage to stand alone / Brene Brown. Random House, 2017. 208 p. **305.8**

1. Belonging 2. Identity (Psychology) 3. Communities 4. Group identity.
ISBN 9780812995848

LC 2017030221

The influential TED speaker and best-selling author of The Gifts of Imperfection draws on new research to challenge conventional beliefs about fitting in to counsel readers on the skills required to achieve actual belonging while being true to oneself.

"Grounded by moving interviews, case studies, her experience spearheading four educational companies, and a winning combination of perceptiveness and humor, Brown's enthusiastic narrative urges readers to discover their own 'wilderness' by culling the strength and determination (and risk) necessary to truly live 'from our wild heart rather than our weary hurt.' Nothing truly groundbreaking, but an enthusiastic, practical guide to achieving a healthy sense of interconnectedness within one's culture and community." Kirkus.

Davis, Wade

The **wayfinders** : why ancient wisdom matters in the modern world / Wade Davis. House of Anansi Press, 2009. 262

p. **305.8**

1. Acculturation. 2. Language and culture. 3. Endangered languages. 4. Indigenous peoples -- Languages.
ISBN 9780887848421
LC 2009929674

Every culture has a unique answer to the question of what it is to be alive and human. Wade Davis, Anthropologist and National Geographic Explorer in Residence, leads us on an exciting journey to celebrate the wisdom of the world's indigenous cultures. Ten centuries before Christ in Polynesia, we set sail with navigators whose ancestors settled the Pacific. We meet the descendants of a true Lost Civilization in Amazon who are called the people of the Anaconda. We discover the Earth is really alive in the Andes, and in the far reaches of Australia we experience Dreamtime, the philosophy of the first humans to walk out of Africa. The Wayfinders is a vast archive of knowledge and expertise; a catalogue of the imagination that rediscovers a new appreciation for the diversity of the human spirit which is expressed through culture.

DiAngelo, Robin J.

★**White** fragility : why it's so hard for white people to talk about racism / Robin DiAngelo ; foreword by Michael Eric Dyson. Beacon Press, 2018. 192 p. **305.8**

1. Racism 2. European Americans 3. Race relations 4. Interpersonal relations
ISBN 9780807047415
LC 2018003562

Groundbreaking book exploring the counterproductive reactions white people have when discussing racism that serve to protect their positions and maintain racial inequality.

"While especially helpful for those new to the critical analysis of whiteness, this work also offers a useful refresher to anyone committed to the ongoing process of self-assessment and antioppression work." Library Journal.

Eddo-Lodge, Reni

Why I'm no longer talking to white people about race / Reni Eddo-Lodge. Bloomsbury Circus, 2017. xvii, 249 p. ; **305.8**

1. Racism -- Great Britain 2. Social classes 3. Race relations 4. Multiculturalism 5. Great Britain
ISBN 9781408870556
LC 2017431364

Exploring issues from eradicated black history to the inextricable link between class and race, Reni Eddo-Lodge has written a searing, illuminating, absolutely necessary examination of what it is to be a person of colour in Britain today .

"With this thoughtful and direct book, Eddo-Lodge stokes the very conversation that the title rejects." Publishers Weekly.

Hamad, Ruby

White tears/brown scars : how white feminism betrays women of color / Ruby Hamad. Catapult, 2020, c2019. xvii, 284 p. **305.8**

1. Antiracism 2. Sexism 3. Entitlement attitudes 4. Minority women
ISBN 9781948226745
LC 2020931161

Originally published: Carlton, Victoria : Melbourne University Publishing, 2019.

Tells a charged story of white women's active participation in campaigns of oppression. It offers a long overdue validation of the experiences of women of color.

"This insistent and incisive call for change belongs in the contemporary feminist canon." Publishers Weekly

King, Martin Luther, Jr., 1929-1968

Why we can't wait / Martin Luther King, Jr. ; introduction by Dorothy Cotton. Harper & Row, 1964. xii, 178 p. : **305.8**

1. African Americans -- Civil rights. 2. Civil Rights Movement 3. Social justice 4. Nonviolence
ISBN 0451527534
LC 64019514

An impassioned work by Dr. Martin Luther King, Jr., shares a heartfelt argument for equality and an end to racial discrimination that explains why the civil rights struggle is vital to the United States.

Murray, Charles A.

Coming apart : the state of white America, 1960-2010 / Charles Murray. Crown, 2012. 416 p. **305.8**

1. Social classes -- United States 2. European Americans -- Attitudes 3. Social mobility -- United States
ISBN 9780307453426
LC 2011501987

A critique of the white American class structure argues that the paths of social mobility that once advanced the nation are now serving to further isolate an elite upper class while enforcing a growing and resentful white underclass.

"Though it provides much to argue with, the book is a timely investigation into a worsening class divide no one can afford to ignore." Publishers Weekly.

Phillips, Patrick, 1970-

★**Blood** at the root : a racial cleansing in America / Patrick Phillips. W.W. Norton & Company, 2016. 320 p. **305.8**

1. Hate crimes 2. Racism 3. Race relations 4. Domestic terrorism 5. Forsyth County, Georgia -- Race relations -- History. 6. Georgia -- Race relations
ISBN 9780393293012
LC 2016018237

ALA Notable Book, 2017.

Andrew Carnegie Medal for Excellence in Non-Fiction Finalist, 2017

A harrowing testament to the deep roots of racial violence in America chronicles acts of racial cleansing in early 20th-century Forsyth County, Georgia, where the murder of a young girl led to mob lynchings, acts of terror against black workers and violent protests by night riders who would enforce whites-only citizenship.

"This is a gripping, timely, and important examination of American racism, and Phillips tells it with rare clarity and power." Publishers Weekly.

Roberts, Dorothy E., 1956-

Fatal invention : how science, politics, and big business recreate race in the twenty-first century / Dorothy Roberts. New Press, c2011. 512 p. **305.8**

1. Race -- Social aspects. 2. Physical anthropology. 3. Human population genetics. 4. Genomics.
ISBN 9781595584953
LC 2011012830

Explores the ways science, politics, and large corporations affect race in the twenty-first century, discussing the efforts and results of the Human Genome Project, and describing how technology-driven science researchers are developing a genetic definition of race.

Sokol, Jason

★**There** goes my everything : white Southerners in the age of civil rights, 1945-1975 / Jason Sokol. Alfred A. Knopf, 2006.

433 p. : **305.8**

1. European Americans -- Southern States -- Attitudes -- History -- 20th century. 2. European Americans -- Southern States -- Social conditions -- 20th century. 3. Civil Rights Movement 4. African Americans -- Civil rights -- Southern States -- History -- 20th century. 5. Southern States -- Race relations -- History -- 20th century. 6. Southern States -- Social conditions -- 1945-
ISBN 0307263568

LC 2005044488

A history of race and class in diverse areas in the South explores the experiences and attitudes of white Southerners during the civil rights era, as their relationships with blacks were changed forever.

Wise, Tim J.

White like me / Tim Wise. Soft Skull Press, 2005. xii, 155 p. ; **305.8**

1. Wise, Tim J. 2. Racism -- United States. 3. European Americans -- Social life and customs 4. United States -- Race relations.
ISBN 1932360689

A memoir of white privilege explores the various ways in which white skin constitutes an advantage in American society in education, employment, housing, criminal justice, and health care.

"Activist, lecturer and director of the new Association for White Anti-Racist Education (AWARE), Wise works from anecdote rather than academic argument to recount his path to greater cultural awareness in a colloquial, matter-of-fact quasi-memoir that urges white people to fight racism 'for our own sake.'" Publishers Weekly

305.800973 Ethnic groups--United States

Anderson, Carol (Carol Elaine)

★**White** rage : the unspoken truth of our racial divide / Carol Anderson. Bloomsbury, 2016. 272 p. **305.800973**

1. Racism 2. Race (Social sciences) 3. African Americans -- Civil rights 4. Civil rights 5. United States -- Race relations
ISBN 9781632864123

LC 2015049398

From the end of the Civil War to the tumultuous issues in America today, an acclaimed historian reframes the conversation about race, chronicling the powerful forces opposed to black progress in America.

"Fitting together historical flash points from the aftermath of the Civil War to the current Black Lives Matter movement, historian Anderson (African American studies, Emory Univ.; Bourgeois Radicals) displays how public policies have systematically discarded all attempts at a colorblind U.S. democracy." Library Journal

Bailey, Issac J.

Why didn't we riot? : a black man in Trumpland / Issac J. Bailey. Other Press, 2020. xi, 173 p. **305.800973**

1. Racism -- United States -- History 2. African Americans -- Social conditions -- 21st century 3. Discrimination in law enforcement 4. Police brutality 5. United States -- Race relations -- History -- 21st century 6. Essays
ISBN 9781635420289

LC 2020008891

South Carolina-based journalist Issac J. Bailey reflects on a wide range of complex, divisive topics - from police brutality and Confederate symbols to respectability politics and white discomfort - which have taken on a fresh urgency with the protest movement sparked by George Floyd's killing. Why Didn't We Riot? speaks to and for the millions of black and brown people throughout the United States who were effectively pushed to the back of the bus in the Trump era by a media that prioritized the concerns and feelings of the white working class and an administration that made white supremacists giddy, and explains why the country's fate in 2020 and beyond is largely in their hands.

"By no fault of Bailey's, die-hard Trumplandians aren't likely to be swayed; conscientious Americans will come away from this book further enraged by the pernicious, persistent pattern of racial injustice in this country. Brilliant, searing, and surprisingly vulnerable." Kirkus

Baker, Calvin, 1972-

A **more** perfect reunion : race, integration, and the future of America / Calvin Baker. Bold Type Books, 2020 304 p. **305.800973**

1. Racism -- United States 2. African Americans -- Civil rights -- History 3. Social integration 4. Democracy 5. United States -- Race relations 6. United States -- History
ISBN 9781568589237

LC 2019058186

A provocative case for integration as the single most radical, discomfiting idea in America, yet the only enduring solution to the racism that threatens our democracy. Americans have prided ourselves on how far we've come from slavery, lynching, and legal segregation--measuring ourselves by incremental progress instead of by how far we have to go. But fifty years after the last meaningful effort toward civil rights, the US remains overwhelmingly segregated and unjust. Our current solutions--diversity, representation, and desegregation--are not enough. At once a profound, masterful reading of US history from the colonial era forward and a trenchant critique of the obstacles in our current political and cultural moment, A More Perfect Reunion is also a call to action.

"Required reading for any American serious about dismantling systemic racism." Kirkus

Bishop, Bill, 1953-

The **big** sort : why the clustering of like-minded America is tearing us apart / Bill Bishop ; with Robert G. Cushing. Houghton Mifflin, 2008. viii, 370 p. : **305.800973**

1. Group identity -- Political aspects -- United States. 2. Segregation -- Political aspects -- United States. 3. Polarization (Social sciences) 4. Minorities -- United States. 5. United States -- Politics and government -- 1989- 6. United States -- Social conditions -- 1980-
ISBN 9780618689354

LC 2007043907

Drawing on intensive research and extensive demographic data, a noted journalist reveals how Americans have been sorting themselves into homogeneous communities over the past three decades, and analyzes the implications of this way-of-life segregation in terms of the cultural, political, and ideological divisiveness and polarization that exists in America today.

Chang, Jeff

We gon' be alright : notes on race and resegregation / Jeff Chang. Picador, 2016. 192 p. **305.800973**

1. African Americans -- Social conditions -- 21st century. 2. Race relations 3. Social change -- United States. 4. Political culture -- United States. 5. Essays
ISBN 9780312429485

LC 2016038855

A collection of essays from a celebrated hip-hop journalist examines the rise of the Black Lives Matter movement in the wake of the death of Michael Brown in Ferguson, Missouri, and discusses America's increasing racial and economic divides.

Cooper, Marianne, 1973-

Cut adrift : families in insecure times / Marianne Cooper. University of California Press, 2014. 297 p. **305.800973**

1. Equality -- United States. 2. Recession (Economics) 3. Financial security 4. Economic security 5. United States -- Social conditions -- 21st century.

ISBN 9780520277670

LC 2013041571

Includes index.

Cut Adrift makes an important and original contribution to the national conversation about inequality and risk in American society. Set against the backdrop of rising economic insecurity and rolled up safety nets, Marianne Cooper explores what keeps Americans up at night. Through poignant case studies, she reveals what families are concerned about, how they manage their anxiety, whose job it is to worry, and how social class shapes all of these dynamics, including what is even worth worrying about in the first place. This powerful study is packed with intriguing discoveries ranging from the surprising anxieties of the rich, to the critical role of women in keeping struggling families afloat. Through tales of stalwart stoicism, heart-wrenching worry, marital angst, and religious conviction, Cut Adrift deepens our understanding about how families are coping in a go-it-alone age -- and how the different strategies affluent, middle-class, and poor families rely upon not only reflect inequality, but also fuel it.

Currie, Elliott

A **peculiar** indifference : the neglected toll of violence on black America / Elliott Currie. Metropolitan Books, 2020. 304 p. **305.800973**

1. Violence against African Americans. 2. Crimes against African Americans. 3. African Americans -- Social conditions. 4. Racism -- United States -- History. 5. United States -- Race relations -- History -- 21st century.

ISBN 9781250769930

LC 2020013956

Offers a devastating exploration of the racial disparities in violent death and injury in America and a blueprint for ending this fundamental social injustice.

"Meticulously researched and densely packed with stats and studies, Currie's book paints a heartbreaking picture, but it also makes an urgent case for bold measures to turn the tide in Black communities. A damning examination of violence in Black America and a call for intervention that is long overdue." Kirkus

Darby, Seyward

★**Sisters** in hate : American women on the front lines of white nationalism / Seyward Darby. Little, Brown & Company, 2020. vii, 309 p. **305.800973**

1. Women white supremacists 2. White supremacy movements 3. Racism 4. European American women 5. United States -- Race relations

ISBN 9780316487771

LC bl2020016280

After the election of Donald J. Trump, journalist Seyward Darby went looking for the women of the so-called "alt-right" -- really just white nationalism with a new label. The mainstream media depicted the alt-right as a bastion of angry white men, but was it? As women headlined resistance to the Trump administration's bigotry and sexism, Darby wanted to know why others were joining a movement espousing racism and anti-feminism. Darby researched dozens of women across the country before settling on three -- Corinna Olsen, Ayla Stewart, and Lana Lokteff. Each was born in 1979, and became a white nationalist in the post-9/11 era. Their respective stories of radicalization upend much of what we assume about women, politics, and political extremism.

"Atavist editor-in-chief Darby describes women as a 'sustaining feature' of white nationalism in her revelatory and harrowing debut focused on three women with ties to the 'alt-right' movement. . . . The result is a disturbing and informative must-read." Publishers Weekly

Dyson, Michael Eric

★The **Black** presidency : Barack Obama and the politics of race in America / Michael Eric Dyson. Houghton Mifflin Harcourt, 2016. 288 p. **305.800973**

1. Obama, Barack 2. Racism -- Political aspects 3. Race relations -- Political aspects. 4. Presidents -- United States -- Messages. 5. Race (Social sciences) 6. United States -- Race relations -- Political aspects.

ISBN 9780544387669

LC 2015037026

Kirkus Prize for Nonfiction finalist, 2016.

Offers a deep-dive into the meaning of America's first black presidency, and an analysis of how race and blackness shape our understanding of Barack Obama's achievements, failures?and America's racial future.

★**Tears** we cannot stop : a sermon to white America / Michael Eric Dyson. St. Martin's Press, 2017. 160 p. **305.800973**

1. Racism 2. Race relations 3. Police brutality 4. African Americans -- Social conditions 5. United States -- Race relations

ISBN 9781250135995

LC 2016049919

A call for change in the United States argues that racial progress can only be achieved after facing difficult truths, including being honest about how black grievance has been ignored, dismissed, and discounted.

"With a reading list to encourage further learning, Dyson offers an intellectual framework for everyone to adopt in order to understand and embrace each other's struggles to be united." Booklist.

What truth sounds like : Robert F. Kennedy, James Baldwin, and our unfinished conversation about race in America / Michael Eric Dyson. St Martins Pr 2018 288 p. **305.800973**

1. Baldwin, James, 1924-1987 2. Kennedy, Robert Francis, 1925-1968 3. Racism 4. Race relations 5. African Americans -- Social conditions 6. Social change 7. United States -- Race relations

ISBN 9781250199416

LC 2018017174

Examines the sources of America's torturous racial politics, tracing the 1963 meeting that included James Baldwin, Robert Kennedy, and a host of expert activists, who transformed racial and political understandings and set the stage for national disputes that are still raging today.

"Dyson's much-recommended work puts forth the artists and activists who continue to celebrate blackness, offering a welcome reminder of the power of art to maintain dialog with and within America." Library Journal.

Fleming, Crystal Marie, 1981-

How to be less stupid about race : on racism, white supremacy and the racial divide / Crystal M. Fleming. Beacon Press, [2018] 256 p. **305.800973**

1. Race awareness 2. Racism 3. Ignorance 4. Intersectionality 5. United States -- Race relations

ISBN 9780807050774

LC 2018009257

Combining no-holds-barred social critique, humorous personal anecdotes, and analysis of the latest interdisciplinary scholarship on systemic racism, sociologist Crystal M. Fleming provides a fresh, accessible, and irreverent take on everything that's wrong with our "national conversation about race." Drawing upon critical race theory, as well as her own experiences as a queer black millennial college professor and researcher, Fleming unveils how systemic racism exposes us all to racial ignorance--and provides a road map for transforming our knowledge into concrete social change.

"In this insightful and irreverent text, Fleming, a sociologist and self-described 'black bi girl from Tennessee,' attempts to simplify critical race theory for the masses." Publishers Weekly

Guo, Winona

Tell me who you are : sharing our stories of race, culture, & identity / Winona Guo and Priya Vulchi. TarcherPerigee, 2019 400 p. **305.800973**

1. Race (Social sciences) 2. Race relations 3. Racism 4. Inequality 5. United States -- Race relations 6. Interviews

ISBN 9780525541127

LC 2018050286

An exploration of race in America features one hundred fifty interviews that reveal the lines that separate people based on perceived differences and how listening to the stories of others can be the first step toward negating racial inequality.

Kendi, Ibram X.

★**Stamped** from the beginning : the definitive history of racist ideas in America / Ibram X. Kendi. Nation Books, 2016. 464 p. **305.800973**

1. Racism -- United States -- History. 2. Race relations 3. Discrimination 4. Antiracism 5. United States -- Race relations.

ISBN 9781568584638

LC 2015033671

National Book Award for Nonfiction, 2016.

National Book Critics Circle Award for Nonfiction finalist, 2016

A comprehensive history of anti-black racism focuses on the lives of five major players in American history, including Cotton Mather and Thomas Jefferson, and highlights the debates that took place between assimilationists and segregationists and between racists and antiracists.

"Kendi's provocative egalitarian argument combines prodigious reading and research with keen insights into the manipulative power of racist ideologies that suppress the recognition of diversity." Library Journal.

Lee, Erika

America for Americans : a history of xenophobia in the United States / Erika Lee. Basic Books, 2019. vii, 416 p. **305.800973**

1. Xenophobia 2. Immigrants -- United States -- History 3. Minorities -- United States -- History 4. Racism 5. United States -- Race relations -- History 6. United States -- Immigration and emigration -- History

ISBN 9781541672604

LC 2019016168

The United States is known as a nation of immigrants. But it is also a nation of xenophobia. In America for Americans, Erika Lee shows that an irrational fear, hatred, and hostility toward immigrants has been a defining feature of our nation from the colonial era to the Trump era. Forcing us to confront this history, America for Americans explains how xenophobia works, why it has endured, and how it threatens America. It is a necessary corrective and spur to action for any concerned citizen.

Lehr, Dick

★The **Birth** of a Nation : how a legendary director and a crusading editor reignited America's Civil War / Dick Lehr. PublicAffairs, a member of the Perseus Books Group, 2014. 336 p. **305.800973**

1. Griffith, D. W. (David Wark), 1875-1948. 2. Trotter, William Monroe, 1872-1934. 3. Birth of a nation (Film) 4. Civil War films 5. Race relations 6. Racism 7. Journalists 8. United States -- Race relations -- History -- 20th century.

ISBN 9781586489878

LC 2014029679

Documents the 1915 rivalry between a journalist agitator and a controversial filmmaker whose respective political views about a Civil War photoplay villainizing free slaves reignited the American debate between free speech and civil rights.

"The book culminates, as expected, with the highly publicized battle in Boston over the censorship of Griffith's film. However, the larger story for the reader is Lehr's fascinating portrait of simmering American racial tensions moving into the early 20th century, and his spotlight on men and women who, intentionally or not, helped galvanize painful and necessary conversations about civil rights, race relations, and the power of mass media for decades to come." Library Journal.

Oluo, Ijeoma

★**So** you want to talk about race / Ijeoma Oluo. Seal Press, 2018. v, 248 p. ; **305.800973**

1. Intercultural communication 2. Race relations 3. Racism 4. Prejudice 5. United States -- Race relations

ISBN 9781580056779

LC 2017041919

School Library Journal (May 2018)

A Seattle-based writer, editor and speaker tackles the sensitive, hyper-charged racial landscape in current America, discussing the issues of privilege, police brutality, intersectionality, micro-aggressions, the Black Lives Matter movement, and the "N" word.

"A clear and candid contribution to an essential conversation." Kirkus.

Ortiz, Paul, 1964-

An **African** American and Latinx history of the United States / Paul Ortiz. Beacon Press, 2018 xi, 276 p. ; **305.800973**

1. Hispanic Americans -- History. 2. African Americans -- History. 3. Anti-imperialist movements. 4. Working class. 5. United States -- Race relations. 6. United States -- Interethnic relations 7. United States -- Foreign relations Latin America. 8. Latin America -- Foreign relations United States.

ISBN 9780807013106

LC 2017020565

"Paul Ortiz delivers us the history of the United States from the viewpoint of black and brown people, from Crispus Attucks and Jos Maria Morelos to CŠar Chv̀ez and Martin Luther King Jr. The result is simultaneously invigorating, embarrassing, and essential to anyone interested in what the revolutionaries of years past can teach us about struggles for freedom, equality, and democracy today.| |William P. Jones, author of The March on Washington: Jobs, Freedom, and the Forgotten History of Civil Rights

"A sleek, vital history that effectively shows how, 'from the outset, inequality was enforced with the whip, the gun, and the United States Constitution.'" Kirkus.

Painter, Nell Irvin

The **history** of white people / Nell Irvin Painter. W.W. Norton, c2010. 448 p. **305.800973**

1. European Americans -- History 2. European Americans -- Identity 3. Identity (Psychology) 4. Race relations. 5. United States -- Race relations.

ISBN 9780393049343

LC 2009034515

"The author examines the history of whiteness as a racial category and rhetorical weapon: who is considered to be white, who is not, what such distinctions mean, and how notions of whiteness have morphed over time in response to shifting demographics, aesthetic tastes, and political exigencies. Painter's narrative succeeds as an engaging and sophisticated intellectual history, as well as an eloquent reminder of the fluidity (and perhaps futility) of racial categories." Booklist.

Pinckney, Darryl, 1953-

Busted in New York and other essays / Darryl Pinckney ; foreword by Zadie Smith. Farrar, Straus and Giroux, 2019. 304 p. **305.800973**

1. Social history 2. Racism 3. Race (Social sciences) 4. African Americans -- Social conditions. 5. United States -- Race relations. 6. Essays

ISBN 9780374117443

LC 2019020214

A collection of 25 essays from the celebrated literary critic and novelist provides a view of our recent racial history that blends the social and personal and wonders how we arrived at our current moment.

"A deeply satisfying, beautifully crafted collection of work by a writer of uncommon excellence and humanity." Kirkus.

Porter, Eduardo

American poison : how racial hostility destroyed our promise / Eduardo Porter. Alfred A. Knopf, 2020. 272 p. **305.800973**

1. Racism -- United States -- History 2. Race awareness 3. Social policy 4. Inequality 5. United States -- Race relations

ISBN 9780451494887

LC 2019030765

An economics reporter for The New York Times discusses how America's racism has stunted the country's development in organized labor, public education and the social safety net and offers a path towards hope, change and a better future.

"American Poison is a work for our times from a writer who has found his subject." Booklist

Rothstein, Richard

★The **color** of law : a forgotten history of how our government segregated America / Richard Rothstein. Liveright Publishing Corporation, 2017. 336 p. **305.800973**

1. Segregation. 2. Discrimination 3. Racism 4. African Americans 5. United States -- Social conditions -- 1945-

ISBN 9781631492853

LC 2017004962

Longlisted for the National Book Award for Nonfiction, 2017.

Richard Rothstein has painstakingly documented how American cities, from San Francisco to Boston, became so racially divided. Rothstein describes how federal, state, and local governments systematically imposed residential segregation: with undisguised racial zoning, public housing that purposefully segregated previously mixed communities, subsidies for builders to create whites-only suburbs, tax exemptions for institutions that enforced segregation, and support for violent resistance to African Americans in white neighborhoods. He demonstrates that such policies still influence tragedies in places like Ferguson and Baltimore.

"This is essential reading for anyone interested in social justice, poverty, American history, and race relations, and its narrative nonfiction style will also draw general readers." Booklist.

Shukla, Nikesh,

The **good** immigrant : 26 writers reflect on America / edited by Nikesh Shukla and Chimene Suleyman. Little Brown & Co, 2019. 320 p. **305.80097309**

1. Immigrants 2. Children of immigrants 3. Immigration and emigration 4. Cultural differences 5. United States -- Immigration and emigration. 6. Essays

ISBN 9780316524285

LC bl2018196366

An urgent collection of essays by first and second-generation immigrants, exploring what it's like to be othered in an increasingly divided America.

"This anthology adds an intriguing component to the complicated kaleidoscope that is the modern immigrant debate." Booklist.

Signer, Michael

Cry havoc : Charlottesville and American democracy under siege / Michael Signer. Public Affairs, 2020. 383 p. **305.800973**

1. Signer, Michael. 2. Unite the Right Rally (2017 : Charlottesville, Virginia) 3. Protests, demonstrations, vigils, etc. 4. Racism -- History 5. Public safety 6. White nationalism. 7. Virginia -- Race relations. 8. Charlottesville, Virginia -- Politics and government -- 21st century. 9. Virginia -- Race relations. 10. United States -- Politics and government

ISBN 9781541736153

LC bl2020006703

The former mayor of Charlottesville, Virginia, describes the events of the August 2017 "Unite the Right" white supremacist rally that turned violent after protestors clashed with counter-protestors and calls for optimism and opportunities to bolster democracy

"A complex, disturbing, valuable tale of racial disharmony, government failure, and one man's frantic attempts to save the day." Kirkus

Tatum, Beverly Daniel

★**"Why** are all the black kids sitting together in the cafeteria?" : and other conversations about race / Beverly Daniel Tatum. Basic Books, 2017. vi, 453 p. ; **305.800973**

1. African Americans 2. Race relations 3. Identity (Psychology) 4. African American children 5. United States -- Race relations.

ISBN 9780465060689

LC 2017014766

"Fully revised and updated"--Provided by publisher.

"Originally published in hardcover and ebook by Basic Books in September 1997"--title page verso.

"Walk into any racially mixed high school and you will see Black, White, and Latino youth clustered in their own groups. Is this self-segregation a problem to address or a coping strategy we should support? How can we get past our reluctance to discuss racial issues? Beverly Daniel Tatum, a renowned authority on the psychology of racism, argues that straight talk about our racial identities is essential if we are serious about enabling communication across racial and ethnic divides. These topics have only become more urgent as the national conversation about race is increasingly acrimonious. This fully revised and updated edition is essential reading for anyone seeking to understand the dynamics of race in America".-- Provided by publisher.

"In balanced sections, she considers understanding blackness in a white context and the development of a white identity itself. There is also an examination of critical issues in Latino, American Indian, and Asian-Pacific American identity development." School Library Journal

Trillin, Calvin

Jackson, 1964 : and other dispatches from fifty years of reporting on race in America / Calvin Trillin. Random House, 2016 304 p. **305.80097309**

1. Racism -- United States -- History -- 20th century. 2. Minorities -- United States -- Social conditions -- 20th century. 3. African Americans -- Social conditions -- 20th century. 4. United States -- Race relations -- History -- 20th century. 5. Essays

ISBN 9780399588242

LC 2015045274

An anthology of previously uncollected essays, originally published in The New Yorker, reflects the work of the eminent journalist's early career and traces his witness to the fledgling years of desegregation in Georgia.

305.800975 Ethnic groups--South Atlantic states

Thompson, Tracy

★The **new** mind of the South : an unconventional portrait for the Twenty-first Century Tracy Thompson. Simon & Schuster, 2013. 320 p. **305.800975**

1. Group identity 2. Race relations 3. Identity (Psychology) 4. Ethnic identity 5. Southern States -- History 6. Southern States -- Race relations.

ISBN 9781439158036

LC 2012021581

"Highly recommended for libraries of all types, especially those with Southern history collections and readers in American studies." Library Journal.

305.8009753 Ethnic groups--Washington D.C.

Asch, Chris Myers

Chocolate City : a history of race and democracy in the nation's capital / Chris Myers Asch and George Derek Musgrove. The University of North Carolina Press, 2017 512 p. **305.8009753**

1. African Americans. 2. Race relations. 3. Washington, D.C.

ISBN 9781469635866

LC 2017026934

Telling the four-century story of race and democracy in our nation's capital, a meticulously researched and detailed history traces D.C.'s massive transformations, from a sparsely inhabited plantation society to the nation's first black-majority city, introducing an unforgettable cast of characters.

305.8009756 Ethnic groups--North Carolina

Zucchino, David

Wilmington's lie : the murderous coup of 1898 and the rise of white supremacy / David Zucchino. Atlantic Monthly Press, 2020. 336 p. **305.8009756**

1. African Americans -- Civil rights 2. Coups d'etat 3. Violence against African Americans 4. White supremacy movements 5. Wilmington, North Carolina 6. North Carolina -- Race relations -- History -- 19th century. 7. North Carolina -- Politics and government -- 19th century.

ISBN 9780802128386

LC 2019040587

The Pulitzer Prize-winning journalist documents the events of the 1898 Wilmington Insurrection and its unrecognized role in reversing the city's mixed-race advances, overthrowing local government and promoting white-supremacist agendas.

305.8009757 Ethnic groups--South Carolina

Hargrave, Courtney

Burden / Courtney Hargrave. Random House Inc., 2018 320 p. **305.8009757**

1. Burden, Michael (Michael Eugene) 2. Kennedy, David (David E.) 3. Ku-Klux Klan 4. White supremacists 5. African American clergy 6. Transformations, Personal 7. Race relations 8. South Carolina 9. Southern States -- Race relations

ISBN 9781984823335

LC 2018013781

Tells the true story of a man who started a controversial museum honoring the Ku Klux Klan and the African-American family who took him in after he had changed his ways and ended up broke and homeless.

305.8009763 Ethnic groups--Louisiana

Brook, Daniel

The **accident** of color : a story of race in Reconstruction / Daniel Brook. W.W. Norton & Company, 2019. 336 p. **305.8009763**

1. Multiracial persons -- Identity 2. Race (Social sciences) 3. Segregation 4. Racism -- Southern States 5. United States -- Social conditions -- 1865-1918 6. United States -- Race relations -- History -- 19th century.

ISBN 9780393247442

LC 2019001184

In The Accident of Color, Daniel Brook journeys to nineteenth-century New Orleans and Charleston and introduces us to cosmopolitan residents who elude the racial categories the rest of America takes for granted. Before the Civil War, these free, openly mixed-race urbanites enjoyed some rights of citizenship and the privileges of wealth and social status. But after Emancipation, as former slaves move to assert their rights, the black-white binary that rules the rest of the nation begins to intrude. During Reconstruction, a movement arises as mixed-race elites make common cause with the formerly enslaved and allies at the fringes of whiteness in a bid to achieve political and social equality for all.

"This poignant and powerful book shows us that decisions and laws surrounding racial identity and interest were deliberate." Library Journal.

305.800977 Ethnic groups--North central United States

Johnson, Walter, 1967-

River of dark dreams : slavery and empire in the cotton kingdom / Walter Johnson. Belknap Press of Harvard University Press, 2013. 524 p. **305.800977**

1. Slavery -- Southern States -- History -- 19th century. 2. Capitalism -- Southern States -- History -- 19th century. 3. Slave trade -- History -- 19th century. 4. Social change -- Southern States -- History -- 19th century. 5. Southern states -- Race relations -- History -- 19th century. 6. Mississippi River Valley -- Commerce -- History -- 19th

century. 7. United States -- Territorial expansion -- History -- 19th century.
ISBN 9780674045552

LC 2012030065

Looks at the history of the Mississippi River Valley in the nineteenth century and the economy that developed there, powered by steam engines and slave labor.

305.8009773 Ethnic groups--Illinois

Moore, Natalie Y.

The **South** Side : a portrait of Chicago and American segregation / Natalie Y. Moore. St. Martin's Press, 2016 272 p. **305.8009773**

1. Moore, Natalie Y. 2. African Americans -- Segregation -- Chicago, Illinois -- History. 3. Segregation -- Chicago, Illinois -- History -- 20th century. 4. Discrimination in housing -- Chicago, Illinois -- History. 5. Racism -- Chicago, Illinois -- History. 6. Chicago, Illinois -- Race relations -- History.
ISBN 9781137280152

LC 2015033955

In this intelligent and highly important narrative, Chicago-native Natalie Moore shines a light on contemporary segregation on the South Side of Chicago through reported essays, showing the life of these communities through the stories of people who live in them. The South Side shows the important impact of Chicago's historic segregation - and the ongoing policies that keep it that way.

305.8009794 Ethnic groups--California

Miranda, Deborah A.

Bad Indians : a tribal memoir / Deborah A. Miranda. Heyday, c2013. xx, 217 p. : **305.8009794**

1. Indians of North America -- California -- History. 2. Indians of North America, Treatment of 3. Race relations. 4. Indians of North America -- Missions -- California. 5. California -- Social conditions. 6. California -- Race relations.
ISBN 9781597142014

LC 2012025266

This beautiful and devastating book--part tribal history, part lyric and intimate memoir--should be required reading for anyone seeking to learn about California Indian history, past and present. Deborah A. Miranda tells stories of her Ohlone Costanoan Esselen family as well as the experience of California Indians as a whole through oral histories, newspaper clippings, anthropological recordings, personal reflections, and poems. The result is a work of literary art that is wise, angry, and playful all at once, a compilation that will break your heart and teach you to see the world anew. --Provided by publisher

305.809 Caucasian people

Saad, Layla F.

★**Me** and white supremacy : combat racism, change the world, and become a good ancestor / Layla F. Saad. Sourcebooks, [2020] 241 p. **305.809**

1. European Americans 2. Racism 3. Prejudice 4. Equality
ISBN 9781728209807

LC 2019031113

When Layla Saad began an Instagram challenge called #meandwhitesupremacy, she never predicted it would become a cultural movement. She encouraged people to own up and share their racist behaviors, big and small. Updated and expanded from the original edition, Me and White Supremacy teaches readers how to dismantle the privilege within themselves so that they can stop (often unconsciously) inflicting damage on people of color, and in turn, help other white people do better, too.

"This groundbreaking book should be required reading for people ready to acknowledge their behaviors, whether intentional or not. It will make a strong addition to both public and university libraries where it will equip scholars, activists, and allies with real tools to promote systemic change." Library Journal

305.868 Spanish Americans

Gomez, Laura E., 1964-

★**Inventing** Latinos : a new story of American racism / Laura E. Gomez. The New Press, 2020. 336 p. **305.868**

1. Hispanic Americans -- Identity 2. Hispanic Americans -- Government policy. 3. Hispanic Americans -- Social conditions. 4. Racism -- United States -- History. 5. Latin America -- Immigration and emigration -- History 6. United States -- Race relations -- History. 7. United States -- Foreign relations Latin America
ISBN 9781595589170

LC 2020010659

Part history, part guide for the future, the author, a professor of law, sociology and Chicana/Chicano studies at UCLA, presents a groundbreaking examination of how Latinos' new collective racial identity has changed the way race functions in this country.

"While not all Latinos agree with Gomez's call for censuses to treat 'Latino' as a race and not an ethnicity, she delivers a rigorous and provocative study of the liminal zone Latino/as inhabit in America's racial continuum. Required reading." Library Journal

Grande, Reyna

A **dream** called home : a memoir / Reyna Grande. Atria Books, [2018] 336 p. **305.868**

1. Grande, Reyna. 2. First-generation college students 3. Creative writing -- Study and teaching 4. Immigrants -- California 5. Women teachers 6. Mexico -- Emigration and immigration -- Social aspects. 7. United States -- Emigration and immigration -- Social aspects.
ISBN 9781501171420

LC 2017053844

Describes the author's early experiences as a first-generation Latina university student and aspiring writer who navigated racism and poverty to build a life for her family.

Thorpe, Helen, 1965-

Just like us : the true story of four Mexican girls coming of age in America / Helen Thorpe. Scribner, 2009. 388 p. **305.868**

1. Mexican American girls -- Denver, Colorado -- Social conditions 2. Immigrants -- Social conditions 3. Citizenship 4. Undocumented immigrants. 5. Denver, Colorado -- Social conditions 6. Denver, Colorado -- Social life and customs
ISBN 9781416538936

LC 2009022722

Traces the journeys of four young Mexican women coming of age in Denver whose prospects for college and careers are shaped by their immigration statuses, a shooting involving a Mexican immigrant and a police officer, and heated debates about the rights of legal and illegal immigrants.

305.892 Semites

Aly, Götz, 1947-

Europe against the Jews : 1880-1945 / Götz Aly ; translated by Jefferson Chase. Metropolitan Books ; 2019. 432 p. **305.892**

1. Antisemitism -- Europe 2. Jews -- Persecutions 3. Racism 4. Genocide 5. Europe -- History -- 19th century 6. Europe -- History -- 20th century

ISBN 9781250170170

LC 2019038047

Originally published: Bonn : Bundeszentrale fur politische Bildung, 2017.

The Holocaust was perpetrated by the Germans, but it would not have been possible without the assistance of thousands of helpers in other countries: state officials, police, and civilians who eagerly supported the genocide. If we are to fully understand how and why the Holocaust happened, Götz Aly argues in this groundbreaking study, we must examine its prehistory throughout Europe. We must look at countries as far-flung as Romania and France, Russia and Greece, where, decades before the Nazis came to power, a deadly combination of envy, competition, nationalism, and social upheaval fueled a surge of anti-Semitism, creating the preconditions for the deportations and murder to come.

"This expertly researched account is destined to influence future histories of the Holocaust." Publishers Weekly

Bayoumi, Moustafa

How does it feel to be a problem? : being young and Arab in America / Moustafa Bayoumi. Penguin Press, 2008. 304 p. **305.892**

1. Arab Americans 2. Ethnic identity. 3. Young adults. 4. Teenagers. 5. United States -- Race relations -- History -- 21st century

ISBN 9781594201769

LC 2007049272

A study of the Arab- and Muslim-American experience as reflected by the lives of seven young men and women in Brooklyn evaluates their daily encounters with such factors as prejudice, the Christian faith, and their relationships with friends and family members in the Middle East.

Chesler, Phyllis, 1941-

The **new** anti-semitism : the current crisis and what we must do about it / Phyllis Chesler. Jossey-Bass, c2003. ix, 307 p. ; **305.892**

1. Antisemitism -- History -- 20th century. 2. Zionism -- Public opinion. 3. Jews -- Public opinion. 4. Public opinion -- Arab countries. 5. Israel -- Public opinion, Arab.

ISBN 078796851X

LC 2003006448

"A Wiley imprint".

Argues that the re-emergence of anti-Jewish hatred, disguised as political correctness, threatens Jews and all of Western civilization, unless this anti-Zionist movement is stopped.

"The author addresses what she sees as a re-emergence of virulent anti-Jewish hatred cloaked in political correctness, closely linked to anti-American attitudes, sustained by many liberal feminists, intellectuals and Jewish leftists, acted upon by Islamic terrorists and jihadists, and fueled by a demonization of Jews in the media. One of the main thrusts of Chesler's argument is that in our contemporary world anti-Zionism is nearly inseparable from anti-Semitism, and that while there are valid criticisms to be made of Israeli policies for instance, she sees the West Bank settlements as an impediment to peacemany of these critiques are, she contends, rooted in a profound and soci ally accepted anti-Semitism." Publishers Weekly.

Goldhagen, Daniel Jonah

The **devil** that never dies : the rise and threat of global anti-semitism / Daniel Jonah Goldhagen. Little Brown & Co, 2013. 432 p. **305.892**

1. Antisemitism 2. Prejudice 3. Antisemites 4. Violence against minorities

ISBN 9780316097871

LC 2013941806

"Goldhagen . . . comes out swinging in this frontal assault on anti-Semitism and its practitioners . A frightening photograph of a mutable demon so many fail to recognize and continue to embrace." Kirkus.

Keinan, Tal

God is in the crowd : Twenty-first-century Judaism / Tal Keinan. Spiegel & Grau, 2018. 240 p. **305.892**

1. Jews -- Identity 2. Jewish way of life 3. Judaism -- 21st century 4. Judaism and state -- Israel

ISBN 9780525511168

LC 2018000337

Argues that the concentration of Jewish people into two hubs, America and Israel, has threatened Jewish continuity by robbing it of the subtle code of governance of the diaspora, and argues for resurrecting this code through a virtual diaspora.

Rosenbaum, Ron

Those who forget the past : the question of anti-Semitism / edited and with an introduction by Ron Rosenbaum ; afterword by Cynthia Ozick. Random House Trade Paperbacks, 2004. lxix, 649 p. ; **305.892**

1. Antisemitism -- History -- 21st century. 2. Jews -- Public opinion. 3. Prejudice. 4. Israel -- Public opinion. 5. Essays.

ISBN 0812972031

LC 2003065542

Presents a series of essays on the rise of new forms of anti-Semitism, with an analysis of how the current political situation in Europe, Israel and the Middle East is contributing to this rise.

"This is an important and vital contribution to efforts to comprehend what is new and what is the same in this ancient virus of ignorance and hatred." Booklist.

Thornhill, Teresa

Hara Hotel : a tale of Syrian refugees in Greece / Teresa Thornhill. Verso, 2018. viii, 341 pages : **305.892**

1. Refugees 2. Refugee camps 3. Refugee services 4. Refugees, Syrian 5. Syria -- Social conditions 6. Greece -- Social conditions

ISBN 9781786635198

LC 2017046461

A firsthand account of a Greek refugee camp--and the stories of the refugees staying in them.

Wasserstein, Bernard

On the eve : the Jews of Europe before the Second World War / Bernard Wasserstein. Simon & Schuster, 2012. xxi, 552 p., [16] p. of plates : **305.892**

1. Jews, European. 2. Jewish way of life. 3. Interethnic relations. 4. World War II -- Causes. 5. Europe -- Interethnic relations -- History -- 1900-1933.

ISBN 9781416594277

LC 2011020529

Explores the political and social realities endured by private Jewish citizens in the years before World War II to demonstrate how Jewish individuals and families suffered as much from hidden cultural breakdowns as from external attacks.

Weisman, Jonathan

Semitism : being Jewish in America in the age of Trump / Jonathan Weisman. St. Martin's Press, 2018 240 p. **305.892**

1. Trump, Donald, 1946- 2. Antisemitism. 3. New Right 4. Jews. 5. United States -- Politics and government -- 21st century.

ISBN 9781250169938

LC 2017043692

Includes index.

A literary assessment of how Jewish people are regarded in America in the aftermath of Trump's election reveals the upsurge of threats to Jewish communities throughout the administration's first year, relating the author's direct experience with anti-Semitic attacks on social media while sharing recommendations for reversing hate trends.

" An urgent and compelling report on the clear and present danger of proto-fascism in the U.S." Kirkus.

305.896 Africans and people of African descent

Asim, Jabari, 1962-

We can't breathe : on Black lives, white lies, and the art of survival / Jabari Asim. Picador, 2018. 208 p. **305.896**

1. African Americans 2. Survival 3. Resilience (Personal quality) 4. Racism 5. United States -- History 6. United States -- Race relations 7. Essays

ISBN 9781250174536

LC 2018022983

A critically acclaimed writer presents eight wide-ranging and powerful essays that tell the story of black survival and persistence through art and community in the face of centuries of racism.

"A sharp vision that challenges readers to shift perspective and examine conventional narratives." Kirkus.

Baldwin, James, 1924-1987

★The **fire** next time / James Baldwin ; with connections. Holt, Rinehart and Winston, 2000, c1963. 167 p. ; **305.896**

1. African Americans 2. Racism 3. Civil rights 4. Black Muslims. 5. United States -- Race relations.

ISBN 003055442X

LC 2001265860

Originally published: New York : Dial Press, 1963.

A plea and a warning to citizens to examine the actual state of America after a century of emancipation.

Bennett, Michael, 1985-

Things that make white people uncomfortable / Michael Bennett and Dave Zirin ; foreword by Martellus Bennett. Haymarket Books, 2018. 220 p. **305.896**

1. Professional athletes 2. Football players 3. Social justice 4. Racism 5. United States -- Social conditions

ISBN 9781608468935

LC bl2018052748

Bennett adds his voice to discussions of racism and police violence, Black athletes and their relationship to powerful institutions like the NCAA and the NFL, the role of protest in history, and the responsibilities of athletes as role models to speak out against injustice. Following in the footsteps of activist-athletes from Muhammad Ali to Colin Kaepernick, Bennett demonstrates his outspoken leadership both on and off the field. --From publisher description.

Blackmon, Douglas A.

Slavery by another name : the re-enslavement of Black people in America from the Civil War to World War II / Douglas A. Blackmon. Doubleday, c2008. 304 p. **305.896**

1. African Americans -- Civil rights -- History -- 19th century. 2. African Americans -- Civil rights -- History -- 20th century. 3. African Americans -- Employment -- History. 4. Crimes against African-Americans -- History. 5. United States -- Race relations -- History -- 19th century. 6. United States -- Race relations -- History -- 20th century.

ISBN 0385506252

LC 2007034500

Pulitzer Prize for General Nonfiction, 2009.

Bringing to light a shameful chapter in American history, a shocking study reveals how, from the late 1870s through the mid-twentieth century, thousands of African-American men were arrested and forced to work off the outrageous fines by serving as unpaid labor to small-town businesses, provincial farmers, and even large corporations.

"The author gives a groundbreaking and disturbing account of a sordid chapter in American history the lease (essentially the sale) of convicts to commercial interests between the end of the 19th century and well into the 20th. [The] book reveals in devastating detail the legal and commercial forces that created this neoslavery along with deeply moving and totally appalling personal testimonies of survivors." Publishers Weekly.

Chafe, William Henry,

★**Remembering** Jim Crow : African Americans tell about life in the segregated South / edited by William H. Chafe ... [et al.]. New Press, 2001. xxxv, 346 p. : **305.896**

1. African Americans -- Segregation -- Southern States -- History. 2. Race relations. 3. African Americans -- Civil rights -- Southern States -- History. 4. African Americans -- Southern States -- Interviews. 5. Southern States -- Race relations. 6. Oral histories

ISBN 1565846974

LC 2001031224

Recollections taken from interviews compiled by the Behind the Veil Project at the Center for Documentary Studies at Duke University.

Accompanying sound recordings contain the complete American RadioWorks documentary and additional selections from the Behind the Veil Project.

Compiles interviews taken of survivors of the Jim Crow laws as they speak of their lives during segregation and share how they fought against the injustices of racism while building communities and raising their children.

"This work offers views into the thoughts, activities, and anxieties of black Americans. . . . Included are two one-hour CDs of the radio documentary produced by American Radio Works, a transcript of the audio program, 50 rare segregation-era photographs, biographical information, and suggestions for further reading. This [is a] superb primary source." Library Journal.

Coates, Ta-Nehisi

★**We** were eight years in power : an American tragedy / Ta-Nehisi Coates. One World, 2017. 256 p. **305.896**

1. Obama, Barack 2. Racism. 3. Race relations 4. Race (Social sciences) 5. United States -- Politics and government -- 2001-2009. 6. United States -- Race relations. 7. Essays

ISBN 9780399590566

LC 2017039343

Longlisted for the Andrew Carnegie Medal for Excellence in Non-Fiction, 2018.

A compelling portrait of the historic Barack Obama era, combining new and annotated essays from the National Book Award-winning author of Between the World and Me, includes the articles, "Fear of a Black President" and "The Case for Reparations" as well as two new pieces on the Obama administration and what is coming next.

"Biting cultural and political analysis from the award-winning journalist. Emotionally charged, deftly crafted, and urgently relevant essays." Kirkus.

Du Bois, W. E. B. (William Edward Burghardt), 1868-1963
The **Oxford** W.E.B. Du Bois reader / edited by Eric J. Sundquist. Oxford University Press, 1996. ix, 680 p. ; **305.896**

1. African Americans 2. United States -- Race relations.
ISBN 9780195091786

LC 95021307

The Oxford W.E.B. Du Bois Reader encompasses the whole of Du Bois's long and multifaceted writing career, from the 1890s through the early 1960s. The volume selects key essays and longer works that portray the range of Du Bois's thought on such subjects as African American culture, the politics and sociology of American race relations, art and music, black leadership, gender and women's rights, Pan-Africanism and anti-colonialism, and Communism in the U.S. and abroad. --Provided by publisher

Gates, Henry Louis, 1950-
And still I rise : Black America since MLK / Henry Louis Gates Jr. and Kevin M. Burke. Ecco, 2015 304 p. **305.896**

1. African Americans. 2. Racism. 3. Race awareness -- United States. 4. Civil Rights Movement. 5. United States -- Race relations.
ISBN 9780062427007

LC bl2015035373

This companion book to the PBS series examines black history from the passage of the Civil Rights Act to the election of Barack Obama and describes the contradictions in the modern African-American community.

"This is an amazing collection of images of achievement on the long road to equality in the U.S." Booklist.

The **future** of the race / Henry Louis Gates, Jr. and Cornel West. A. A. Knopf, 1996. xvii, 196 p. ; **305.896**

1. African Americans -- Social conditions -- 1975- 2. African American leadership. 3. African American intellectuals 4. Upper class -- United States. 5. United States -- Race relations.
ISBN 067944405X

LC 96014450

"Gates and West explore the challenge of W.E.B. DuBois's famous essay The Talented Tenth and consider the future of African American society in light of it. The authors examine the responsibility of the successful and talented black middle and upper classes to uplift the impoverished. The text includes DuBois's The Talented Tenth and, reprinted for the first time, his 1948 critique of it." Library Journal.

Hill, Anita
Reimagining equality : stories of gender, race, and finding home / Anita Hill. Beacon Press, c2011. 224 p. **305.896**

1. Home ownership. 2. Equality -- United States. 3. African American women -- Social conditions. 4. African Americans -- Social conditions.
ISBN 9780807014370

LC 2011020232

Anita Hill's bravery, intellect and commitment to justice galvanized a generation of women. If that weren't enough, it turns out she's also a wonderful storyteller. Reimagining Equality will change your ideas about home, race and gender--and it's also great fun to read.

"Serious readers of all kinds, especially those interested in current affairs and social policy, will appreciate a book that is both highly readable and deeply analytical." Library Journal.

Johnson, Yvette
The **song** and the silence : a story about family, race, and what was revealed in a small town in the Mississippi Delta While searching for Booker Wright / Yvette Johnson. Atria Books, 2017. 320 p. **305.896**

1. Johnson, Yvette 2. Wright, Booker 3. Civil Rights Movement. 4. Identity (Psychology) 5. Race (Social sciences) 6. Racism 7. Mississippi
ISBN 9781476754949

LC 2016055229

The granddaughter of Booker Wright ?an unwitting icon of the Civil Rights Movement, whose murder was the basis for the documentary Booker's Place: A Mississippi Story?compelled to learn about her roots, travels back to Greenwood, Mississippi, where she confronts her own feelings surrounding race, family, forgiveness and faith.

"Johnson brilliantly constructs a complex and empathetic look at racism in the South." Publishers Weekly.

Kelly, Joseph, 1962-
America's longest siege : Charleston, slavery, and the slow march toward Civil War / Joseph Kelly. Overlook Duckworth, 2013. 368 p. **305.896**

1. Slavery -- Charleston, South Carolina -- History. 2. Slaves -- South Carolina 3. Sieges 4. African Americans -- Charleston, South Carolina -- Social conditions. 5. Charleston, South Carolina -- Race relations -- History. 6. Charleston, South Carolina -- History -- 1775-1865.
ISBN 9781590207192

LC 2013015841

An account of the 200-year practice of slavery in Charleston examines its hotly contested debates and early slave rebellions through the Nullification crisis and the secession that sparked the Civil War, offering insight into how Charleston became a focal point for nationwide slavery disputes while examining the roles of key contributors.

King, Gilbert
★**Devil** in the grove : Thurgood Marshall, the Groveland Boys, and the dawn of a new America / Gilbert King. Harper, c2012. 352 p. **305.896**

1. Marshall, Thurgood, 1908-1993. 2. National Association for the Advancement of Colored People. 3. Ku-Klux Klan 4. Racism in the criminal justice system 5. Rape 6. African Americans -- Civil rights 7. Innocence (Law) 8. Florida -- Race relations 9. Groveland, Florida
ISBN 9780061792281

LC 2011033757

Pulitzer Prize for General Nonfiction, 2013.

Chronicles a little-known court case in which Thurgood Marshall successfully saved a black citrus worker from the electric chair after the worker was accused of raping a white woman with three other black men.

Lebron, Christopher J
The **making** of Black lives matter : a brief history of an idea / Christopher J. Lebron. Oxford University Press, 2017. xxii, 187 p. **305.896**

1. Black Lives Matter movement 2. Protest movements. 3. African

Americans -- Social conditions -- 21st century. 4. African Americans -- Politics and government -- 21st century. 5. United States -- Race relations.
ISBN 9780190601348

LC 2016042413

Started in the wake of George Zimmerman's 2013 acquittal in the death of Trayvon Martin, the #BlackLivesMatter movement has become a powerful and uncompromising campaign demanding redress for the brutal and unjustified treatment of black bodies by law enforcement in the United States. The movement is only a few years old, but as Christopher J. Lebron argues in this book, the sentiment behind it is not; the plea and demand that "Black Lives Matter" comes out of a much older and richer tradition arguing for the equal dignity -- and not just equal rights -- of black people.

"Throughout five brief essays, an introduction, and an afterword, black scholars consider the persistent failure of the U.S. justice system to redress or remedy the white terrorism responsible for harming black lives." Library Journal.

McWhorter, John H.

Losing the race : self-sabotage in Black America / John H. McWhorter ; [with a new afterword by the author]. Perennial, 2001, c2000. xv, 299 p. ; **305.896**

1. African Americans -- Psychology. 2. Success (Concept) -- Psychological aspects 3. Self-defeating behavior. 4. African Americans -- Social conditions -- 1975- 5. United States -- Social life and customs -- 21st century
ISBN 9780060935931

LC 2001024092

Originally published: New York : The Free Press, 2000.

A professor of linguistics paints a controversial portrait of defeatism and pessimism in black America that threatens to hold young African Americans back.

Raboteau, Emily

Searching for Zion : the perpetual quest for home in the wake of the African Diaspora / Emily Raboteau. Atlantic Monthly Press, 2013. 320 p. **305.896**

1. Ethnic identity 2. Multiracial women 3. African diaspora 4. Identity (Psychology)
ISBN 9780802120038

LC 2013474601

Documents the author's decade-long search for identity and a place of belonging as inspired by African-American and Jewish history as well as the exoduses of black communities that left ancestral homes in search of "promised lands," in an account that describes the author's visits to regions where Black Zionists imparted the stories of their own cultural migrations.

Rankine, Claudia, 1963-

★**Just** us : an American conversation / Claudia Rankine Graywolf Press, 2020 342 p. : **305.896**

1. Racism 2. Identity (Psychology) 3. Justice 4. African Americans 5. United States -- Race relations. 6. Essays
ISBN 9781644450215

LC 2019956891

As everyday white supremacy becomes increasingly vocalized with no clear answers at hand, how best might we approach one another? Claudia Rankine, without telling us what to do, urges us to begin the discussions that might open pathways through this divisive and stuck moment in American history. Just Us is an invitation to discover what it takes to stay in the room together, even and especially in breaching the silence, guilt, and violence that follow direct addresses of whiteness. Rankine's questions disrupt the false comfort of our culture's liminal and private spaces--the airport, the theater, the dinner party, the voting booth--where neutrality and politeness live on the surface of differing commitments, beliefs, and prejudices as our public and private lives intersect.

"Rankine presents another arresting blend of essays and images, perfectly attuned to this long-overdue moment of racial reckoning. In language all the more devastating for its simplicity, Rankine analyzes the overwhelming power of whiteness in everyday interactions." Booklist.

Robinson, Eugene, 1954-

Disintegration : the splintering of Black America / Eugene Robinson. Doubleday, 2010. 208 p. **305.896**

1. African Americans -- Social conditions -- 21st century. 2. Identity (Psychology) 3. Group identity 4. Social classes -- United States. 5. United States -- Social conditions -- 21st century. 6. United States -- Race relations.
ISBN 9780385526548

LC 2010020405

Eugene Robinson shines light on crucial debates about affirmative action, the importance of race versus social class, and the ultimate questions of whether and in what form racism and the black community endure.

Toure, 1971-

Who's afraid of post-blackness? : what it means to be Black now / Toure ; foreword by Michael Eric Dyson. Free Press, 2011. xviii, 251 p. : **305.896**

1. African Americans -- Identity 2. African Americans -- Psychology. 3. United States -- Race relations.
ISBN 9781439177556

LC 2010042788

Drawing on his own experience, as well as interviews with more than 100 black Americans--including Henry Louis Gates Jr., Malcolm Gladwell, Chuck D, Soledad O-Brien, the Reverend Jesse Jackson, Aaron McGruder and more--the author explores what it means to be black in a post-2008 United States. By the author of Never Drank the Kool-Aid

Walker, Anders

The **burning** house : Jim Crow and the making of modern America / Anders Walker. Yale University Press, 2018. 288 p. **305.896**

1. Racism -- Southern States 2. Race relations 3. Segregation 4. African Americans -- Segregation 5. Southern States -- Social conditions -- 20th century
ISBN 9780300223989

LC bl2018071640

A startling and gripping reexamination of the Jim Crow era, as seen through the eyes of some of the most important American writers.

"Readers unfamiliar with the anti-integration culture might find some of the invective difficult to process, but Walker skillfully presents his interpretations of his subjects' writing." Kirkus.

Walker, Jerald

How to make a slave and other essays / Jerald Walker. Mad Creek Books/The Ohio State University Press, 2020 152 p. **305.896**

1. Walker, Jerald 2. African American Authors 3. African American families 4. College teachers 5. African Americans -- Social conditions 6. Essays
ISBN 9780814255995

LC 2020007415

"Personal essays exploring identity, family, and community through the prism of race and black culture. Confronts the medical profession's racial biases, shopping while black at Whole Foods, the legacy of Michael Jackson, raising black boys, haircuts that scare white people, racial profiling, and growing up in Southside Chicago".-- Provided by publisher.

"Walker's rich compilation adds up to a rewardingly insightful self-portrait that reveals how one man relates to various aspects of his identity." Publishers Weekly

Ward, Jesmyn

★The **fire** this time : a new generation speaks about race / Jesmyn Ward. Scribner, 2016 288 p. **305.896**

1. African Americans 2. Racism 3. Civil rights 4. Race relations 5. United States -- Race relations. 6. Anthologies
ISBN 9781501126345

LC 2016005371

The National Book Award-winning author of Salvage the Bones presents a continuation of James Baldwin's 1963The Fire Next Time that examines race issues from the past half century through essays, poems and memoir pieces by some of her generation's most original thinkers and writers.

"Wards remarkable achievement is the gift of freshly minted perspectives on a tale that may seem old and twice-told. Readers in search of conversations about race in America should start here." Publishers Weekly.

Whitaker, Mark

Smoketown : the untold story of the other great Black Renaissance / Mark Whitaker. Simon & Schuster, [2018] 432 p. **305.896**

1. African Americans 2. Intellectual life. 3. African American athletes 4. Jazz musicians 5. Pittsburgh, Pennsylvania
ISBN 9781501122392

LC 2017019428

Chronicles the lesser-known African-American renaissance in Pittsburgh from the 1920s through the 1950s, assessing how it rivaled Harlem and Chicago as the site of the most widely read black newspaper in the nation, the two leading Negro Leagues baseball teams and the childhood homes of forefront jazz pioneers.

"An expansive, prodigiously researched, and masterfully told history." Kirkus.

Winters, Mary-Frances

Black fatigue : how racism erodes the mind, body, and spirit / Mary-Frances Winters. Berrett-Koehler Publishers, 2020 xv, 234 p. **305.896**

1. Winters, Mary-Frances 2. Social justice 3. African Americans 4. Racism 5. Fatigue
ISBN 9781523091300

LC 2020941572

Presents information about the intergenerational impact of systemic racism on the physical and psychological health of African Americans and explains why and how society needs to collectively do more to combat its pernicious effects.

"An excellent entry-level resource on antiracism for anyone looking to begin but unsure of how to get started." Library Journal.

Woodward, C. Vann, 1908-1999

The **strange** career of Jim Crow / C. Vann Woodward ; with a new afterword by William S. McFeely. Oxford University Press, 2002, c1955. xvii, 245 p. ; **305.896**

1. African Americans -- Segregation -- History. 2. Reconstruction (United States history) 3. Racism -- Southern States. 4. African Americans -- History -- 1863-1877. 5. United States -- Race relations. 6. Southern States -- Race relations. 7. United States -- Politics and government -- 1865-1877.
ISBN 0195146891

LC 2001021668

Originally published: New York : Oxford University Press, 1955.

Surveys the history of segregation in the United States, citing the changes, controversies, and leaders that have emerged from the Civil Rights movement.

305.897 North American native peoples

Fenn, Elizabeth A. (Elizabeth Anne), 1959-

Encounters at the heart of the world : a history of the Mandan people / Elizabeth A. Fenn. Hill and Wang, 2014. 512 p. **305.897**

1. Mandan Indians -- History. 2. Indians of North America 3. Mandan Indians 4. Government relations with indigenous peoples 5. Missouri Valley 6. North Dakota
ISBN 9780809042395

LC 2013032994

Includes index.

Pulitzer Prize for History, 2015.

Draws on important new discoveries in a range of disciplines to chronicle the history of the Mandan Native Americans while sharing revisionist perspectives about their thriving commercial and agricultural practices before European diseases decimated their culture.

"A nonpolemical, engaging study of a once-thriving Indian nation of the American heartland whose origins and demise tell us much about ourselves." Kirkus.

Talaga, Tanya

Seven fallen feathers : racism, death, and hard truths in a northern city / Tanya Talaga Anansi Nonfiction, 2017 304 p. **305.897**

1. First Nations (Canada) 2. Race relations 3. Government relations with indigenous peoples 4. Children -- Death 5. Thunder Bay, Ontario. 6. Canada -- Race relations
ISBN 9781487002268

LC 2019401136

Includes index.

Charles Taylor Prize for Literary Non-Fiction (Canada), 2018.

Shaughnessy Cohen Prize for Political Writing (Canada), 2017.

Hilary Weston Writers' Trust Prize for Nonfiction finalist, 2017.

Presents the story of seven Indigenous high school students who died in Thunder Bay, Ontario from 2010 to 2011. They were sent hundreds of kilometres away from their families because there was no sufficient high school on their reserves.

"Talaga's incisive research and breathtaking storytelling could bring this community one step closer to the healing it deserves." Booklist.

305.898 South American native peoples

Everett, Daniel Leonard

Don't sleep, there are snakes : life and language in the Amazonian jungle / Daniel L. Everett. Pantheon Books, c2008. 304 p. **305.898**

1. Everett, Daniel Leonard Travel Amazon Valley.. 2. Indians of South America -- Amazon Valley -- Social life and customs 3.

Jungles -- Amazon Valley. 4. Language and languages 5. Piraha Indians -- Amazon Valley -- Social life and customs. 6. Amazon Valley -- Social life and customs. 7. Brazil -- Social life and customs.
ISBN 9780375425028

LC 2008016306

"A linguist offers a thought-provoking account of his experiences and discoveries while living with the Pirah, a small tribe of Amazonian Indians living in central Brazil and a people possessing a language that defies accepted linguistic theories and reflects a culture that has no counting system, concept of war, or personal property, and lives entirely in the present.

"The author has crafted a fascinating account of his 30 years of linguistics work among the Pirah (pronounced pee-da-HAN) Indians, a tribal group living along the Maici and Marmelos Rivers in a remote area of western Brazil. With a clear, detail-rich writing style, Everett provides evocative ethnographic descriptions of Pirah life and culture as well as perceptive linguistic analysis." Library Journal.

305.899 Oceanian native peoples

DeParle, Jason

★A **good** provider is one who leaves : one family and migration in the 21st century / Jason DeParle. Viking, 2019. 352 p. **305.899**

1. Comodas, Rosalie Family 2. Immigrants -- United States 3. Filipinos 4. Immigrant workers 5. Extended families 6. United States -- Immigration and emigration -- History -- 21st century
ISBN 9780670785926

LC 2019011071

ALA Notable Book, 2020.

An investigative reporter describes the lives of the Comodas family over several decades and three generations and shows the impact of global migration and how it has reordered economics, politics and culture around the world.

"A gorgeously written, uniquely insightful, and evenly critical volume that hits every talking point on immigration today." Kirkus.

305.8994 Polynesian native peoples

Thompson, Christina, 1959-

★**Sea** people : the puzzle of Polynesia / Christina Thompson. Harper, 2019. xvi, 365 p., 8 unnumbered p. of plates : **305.8994**

1. Polynesians 2. Maori (New Zealand people) 3. Polynesia 4. Islands of the Pacific. 5. South Pacific Ocean. 6. Polynesia -- Exploration 7. Oceania 8. Pacific Ocean
ISBN 9780062060877

NSW Premier's History Awards, General History Prize, 2019.

Explores the origins of the Polynesian people, attempting to answer the questions about who founded and settled these remote Pacific islands in an era before writing or metal tools.

"A superb chronicler of the intellectual explorers of Polynesian history, Thompson writes with command and insight, enhancing this fascinating books rich appeal." Booklist.

305.9 People by occupation and miscellaneous social statuses; people with disabilities and illnesses, gifted people

Malone, John Williams

21st century gay / John Malone. M. Evans, c2000. 198 p. ; **305.9**

1. Gay men -- United States -- Social conditions. 2. Lesbians -- United States -- Social conditions. 3. Same-sex marriage -- United States. 4. LGBTQIA rights -- United States 5. United States -- History -- 20th century 6. United States -- History -- 21st century 7. United States -- Social life and customs -- 21st century
ISBN 087131911X

LC 00041063

Looks at sexuality in history and the events that have influenced the gay movement.

Martinez, Oscar (Oscar Enrique)

★The **beast** : riding the rails and dodging narcos on the migrant trail / Oscar Martinez ; translated by Daniela Maria Ugaz and John Washington. Verso, 2013, c2010. 224 p. **305.9**

1. Undocumented immigrants. 2. Drug cartels 3. Kidnapping 4. Central Americans 5. Mexico -- Immigration and emigration 6. Central America -- Immigration and emigration 7. United States -- Immigration and emigration
ISBN 9781781681329

LC 2013020580

"First published as Los migrantes que no importan, Icaria Editorial 2010."

An El Salvadoran investigative journalist for the Latin American gang violence project, El Faro, documents the recent abduction of 300 migrant workers from the border towns between Mexico and Arizona and how their disappearances reflect the increasing dangers facing migrants.

Martinez, Ruben

★The **new** Americans / Ruben Martinez ; photographs by Joseph Rodriguez. New Press, c2004. viii, 251 p. : **305.9**

1. Immigrants -- History -- 21st century -- Case studies. 2. Immigration and emigration. 3. United States -- Immigration and emigration -- History -- 21st century Case studies.
ISBN 156584792X

LC 2003070621

A companion to the PBS television mini-series tells the story of five different families as they arrive and settle in the United States, offering a personal look at the modern generation of American immigrants and the challenges and triumphs they experience.

"Masterfully evoking such diverse settings as a Palestinian wedding in Chicago, a raucous ball game in Guatemala City and a torpid migrant trailer camp in California, Martnez's writing is clear-eyed and incisive--and sometimes heartbreaking and hilarious." Publishers Weekly.

McDonald-Gibson, Charlotte

Cast away : true stories of survival from Europe's refugee crisis / Charlotte McDonald-Gibson. New Press, 2016. 256 p. **305.9**

1. Refugees -- Legal status, laws, etc.. 2. Immigration and emigration 3. Immigration policy. 4. Immigrants. 5. Europe -- Emigration and immigration -- History -- 21st century. 6. Mediterranean Region -- Emigration and immigration -- History -- 21st century.
ISBN 9781620972632

LC 2016019359

Examines the refugee crisis in Europe as droves of people try to escape turmoil in the Middle East and Africa, describing the agonizing stories and terrible decisions that migrants have to make as they head toward what they believe is a better life.

"A powerfully written, well-documented account of a humanitarian crisis of epic proportions." Kirkus.

Nugent, Benjamin

American nerd : the story of my people / Benjamin Nugent. Simon & Schuster, 2008. 192 p. **305.9**

1. Misfits (Persons) -- United States 2. Subcultures -- United States 3. Popular culture 4. Stereotypes (Social psychology) -- Social aspects 5. United States -- Social life and customs -- 21st century
ISBN 9780743288019

LC 2008274215

A social exploration of the concept of the intellectual misfit presents a tour of nerd subcultures while tracing the personality's evolution in the media, literature, and society, in a report that reveals lesser-known common traits and interests among various subcultures.

"In a lighthearted, often laugh-out-loud manner, Nugent challenges us to reexamine our long-held belief of what it means to be a nerd and to reposition the nerd as, if not an American hero, at least an American antihero. Great fun and remarkably insightful between the laughs." Booklist.

Pipher, Mary Bray

The **middle** of everywhere : the world's refugees come to our town / Mary Pipher. Harcourt, c2002. 390 p. ; **305.9**

1. Refugees -- United States. 2. Immigrants -- United States. 3. Immigrants -- United States -- Social conditions. 4. Assimilation (Sociology). 5. Lincoln, Nebraska. 6. Nebraska. 7. United States -- Immigration and emigration -- History -- 20th century 8. United States -- Immigration and emigration -- History -- 21st century
ISBN 0151006008

LC 2001005863

"The author writes in rich, empathetic language and with a keen, observant eye for detail and nuance." Publishers Weekly.

Sacks, Oliver, 1933-2015

Seeing voices : a journey into the world of the deaf / Oliver Sacks. University of California Press, c1989. xv, 180 p. : **305.9**

1. Gallaudet University Strike, 1988. 2. People who are deaf -- History. 3. Children who are deaf. 4. Deaf culture. 5. Teenagers who are deaf.
ISBN 9780520060838

LC 89004817

Includes index.

A neurologist investigates the world of the deaf, examining their past and present treatment at the hands of society, and assesses the value and significance of sign language.

"With his philosopher's penchant for profound discovery and his neurologist's knowledge of biology and the brain, Sacks offers provocative connections and acute observations about the nature of language and culture." Booklist.

Stephenson, Michael, 1946-

The **last** full measure : how soldiers die in battle / Michael Stephenson. Crown Publishers, c2012. xvi, 464 p. ; **305.9**

1. Battle casualties. 2. Military history. 3. Soldiers. 4. Death.
ISBN 9780307395849

LC 2011005874

Considers how soldiers through the ages have met their deaths in times of war, covering such subjects as weapons and battlefield strategies while offering insight into cultural differences and the nature of military combat.

Nguyen, Viet Thanh,

The **displaced** : refugee writers on refugee lives / edited by Viet Thanh Nguyen. Harry N Abrams, 2018. 240 p. **305.9**

1. Refugees 2. Human rights 3. Immigration and emigration 4. Essays
ISBN 9781419729485

LC 2017949746

Published in support of the International Rescue Committee and edited by the Pulitzer Prize-winning author of The Sympathizer, a collection of searing personal essays by prominent international refugees shares candid reflections on the Trump administration's 2017 executive order to limit or ban Muslim refugees from America.

306 Culture and institutions

Flanders, Judith

Inside the Victorian home : a portrait of domestic life in Victorian England / Judith Flanders. W.W. Norton, 2004, c2003. xxviii, 499 p. : **306**

1. Families -- England -- History -- 19th century. 2. Homemaking -- England -- History -- 19th century. 3. Middle class -- England -- History -- 19th century. 4. England -- Social life and customs -- 19th century. 5. England -- Social conditions -- 19th century.
ISBN 0393052095

LC 2003027693

Originally published under the title: The Victorian house : domestic life from childbirth to deathbed. London : HarperCollins, 2003.

Takes readers through daily life in a Victorian house on a room-by-room basis, providing detailed descriptions of each area's furnishings and decorations while recounting events that may have transpired in the parlor, master bedroom, scullery, sickroom, and more. By the author of A Circle of Sisters.

"Room by room, Flanders walks us through the typical home of upper-middle-class Britain, explaining its use, its dcor, the habits of occupants, and more. The result is a genteel yet absorbing and thoroughly researched book. Fearsomely entertaining and yet a wonderful addition to academic literature, this book is sure to become a classic." Library Journal.

Francis, Gavin

Shapeshifters : a journey through the changing human body / Gavin Francis. Basic Books, 2018. 282 p. : **306**

1. Human biology 2. Humans 3. Identity (Psychology) 4. Biology
ISBN 9781541697522

LC 2018938201

A physician and award-winning author discusses the transitions and experiences the human body goes through during a lifetime, including puberty, childbirth and getting a tattoo and discusses the biological, psychological and philosophical natures of identity.

Gies, Frances

Life in a medieval village / Frances and Joseph Gies. Harper Perennial, 1991, c1990. ix, 257 p. : **306**

1. Peasantry -- Great Britain -- History 2. Elton, England -- Social conditions -- Medieval period, 1066-1485. 3. Elton, England -- Rural conditions. 4. England -- Social life and customs -- Medieval period, 1066-1485.
ISBN 0060920467

LC BL 99714619

Originally published: New York : Harper & Row, 1990.

Focusing on the village of Elton, in the English East Midlands, this book describes the food and housing of the peasants, the tension between them and the lord of the manor, and the place of the Church in their lives

"Elton, England, is the focal point of the authors' efforts to portray the everyday life and social structure of the High Middle Ages. After giving a brief summary of Elton's origins and development in the Roman and Anglo-Saxon periods, the book examines just how the residents lived and worked within the feudal structure at the beginning of the fourteenth century." Booklist.

Klosterman, Chuck, 1972-

Sex, drugs, and cocoa puffs : a low culture manifesto / Chuck Klosterman. Scribner, c2003. 244 p. ; **306**

1. Popular culture. 2. National characteristics, American. 3. United States -- Civilization -- 1970-
ISBN 0743236009

LC 2003045535

Includes index.

Explores a range of modern cultural phenomenon, including Internet pornography, tribute bands, baseball rivalries, and reality television.

Lasch, Christopher

The **revolt** of the elites : and the betrayal of democracy / Christopher Lasch. W.W. Norton, c1995. x, 276 p. ; **306**

1. Democracy -- United States. 2. Elite (Social sciences) -- United States. 3. Polarization (Social sciences) -- United States. 4. Populism -- United States. 5. United States -- Politics and government -- 20th century. 6. United States -- Social conditions -- 1945-
ISBN 0393036995

LC 94037270

Argues that global mobility and a refusal to identify with one nation have caused America's professional and managerial elites to betray the ideal of democracy.

Mead, Margaret, 1901-1978

★**Coming** of age in Samoa : a psychological study of primitive youth for western civilisation / Margaret Mead. Perennial Classics, 2001. xxviii, 223 p. ; **306**

1. Samoans -- Psychology 2. Girls -- Samoan Islands 3. Children -- Samoan Islands 4. Women, Samoan -- Social life and customs 5. Samoan Islands -- Social life and customs.
ISBN 9780688050337

LC 00057528

Includes index.

Originally published: William Morrow and Co., 1930.

The classic anthropological study describes what it was like in the 1920s for girls growing up in the primitive culture of the Samoan Islands, offering provocative insights into such topics as childhood, gender roles, and culture.

Paz, Octavio, 1914-1998

★The **labyrinth** of solitude : life and thought in Mexico / Octavio Paz ; translated from the Spanish by Lysander Kemp. Grove Press, 1985. 199 p. ; **306**

1. National characteristics, Mexican. 2. Identity (Philosophical concept) 3. Culture -- Mexico 4. Aztec women -- Mexico -- History -- 16th century. 5. Mexico -- Civilization. 6. Mexico -- History -- Conquest, 1519-1540.
ISBN 0140080767

Penny, Laurie

Bitch doctrine : essays for dissenting adults / Laurie Penny. St. Martins Press, 2017. 288 p. **306**

1. Feminism. 2. Gender equity. 3. Women's rights. 4. Sexism.
ISBN 9781632867537

LC 2017301123

The author of Unspeakable Things argues that feminism, in this day and age, is still a true liberation struggle, one connected to all struggles for equal rights and freedom.

"Thought at times self-righteous, the author wears the trademark fearlessness that has earned her the name of "bitch" with an admirable lack of apology. Intelligent and defiant, Penny probes the current antifeminist backlash while exploring zones of social discomfort, all in the name of "imagining a society beyond patriarchy." Polemical writing at its thoughtful best." Kirkus.

Said, Edward W., 1935-2003

The **selected** works of Edward Said, 1966 - 2006 / Edward W. Said ; edited by Moustafa Bayoumi and Andrew Rubin. Vintage, 2019. 544 p. **306**

1. Said, Edward W. 1935-2003 2. Critics 3. Arab Americans 4. Literature -- History and criticism 5. Palestinians 6. Essays
ISBN 9780525565314

LC 2019285000

Originally published as The Edward Said reader-- newly expanded to represent the full scope of his career-- cover.

The renowned literary and cultural critic Edward Said was one of our era's most provocative and important thinkers. The Selected Works includes key sections from all of Said's books, including his groundbreaking Orientalism; his memoir, Out of Place; and his last book, On Late Style. Whether writing of Zionism or Palestinian self-determination, Jane Austen or Yeats, or of music or the media, Said's uncompromising intelligence casts urgent light on every subject he undertakes.

"This quasi--anthology will appeal to general readers but also serves as an indispensable resource for scholars of cultural studies, history and politics, literature, sociology, anthropology, Western classical music, and the arts." Library Journal.

306.01 Culture--Philosophy

Wilkinson, Richard G.

The **spirit** level : why greater equality makes societies stronger / Richard Wilkinson and Kate Pickett. Bloomsbury Press, 2009. 352 p. **306.01**

1. Equality. 2. Social mobility. 3. Quality of life. 4. Social policy.
ISBN 9781608190362

LC 2009030428

Shows that there is one common factor that links the healthiest and happiest societies--the degree of equality among their members--and offers a way toward a new political outlook, shifting from self-interested consumerism to friendlier, more sustainable societies.

"The authors make an eloquent case that the income gap between a nation's richest and poorest is the most powerful indicator of a functioning and healthy society. Felicitous prose and fascinating findings make this essential reading." Publishers Weekly.

306.09 Social history

Easterbrook, Gregg

It's better than it looks : reasons for optimism in an age of fear / Gregg Easterbrook. PublicAffairs, 2018. xx, 330 pages

; 306.09

1. Optimism 2. Civilization 3. Progress 4. Forecasting
ISBN 9781610397414

LC 2017048518

It's not a coincidence that we're confused--our perspectives on the world are blurred by the rise of social media, the machinations of politicians, and our own biases. Meanwhile, political reforms like the Clean Air Act and technological innovations like the hybridization of wheat have saved huge numbers of lives. In that optimistic spirit, Easterbrook offers specific policy reforms to address climate change, inequality, and other problems, and reminds us that there is real hope in conquering such challenges. In an age of discord and fear-mongering, It's Better Than It Looks will profoundly change your perspective on who we are, where we're headed, and what we're capable of.

306.0948 Culture--Scandinavia

Partanen, Anu

The **Nordic** theory of everything : in search of a better life / Anu Partanen. HarperCollins, 2016 432 p. **306.0948**

1. Culture shock 2. Finnish Americans 3. National characteristics, American 4. Welfare 5. Finland -- Social life and customs
ISBN 9780062316547

LC bl2016016859

A Finnish journalist and naturalized American citizen examines four key human relationships to encourage Americans to draw on practices from the Nordic way of life to create a fairer, happier, more secure and less stressful society for themselves and future generations.

"An earnest, well-written work worth heeding, especially in our current toxic political climate." Kirkus.

306.0956 Culture--Middle East

Shadid, Anthony

★**House** of stone : a saga of home, family, and a lost Middle East / Anthony Shadid. Houghton Mifflin Harcourt, 2012. 256 p. **306.0956**

1. Home (Concept) 2. Houses -- Conservation and restoration. 3. Immigrants. 4. Identity (Psychology) 5. Lebanon -- Emigration and immigration -- Social aspects. 6. Middle East -- Social conditions.
ISBN 9780547134666

LC 2011036906

National Book Critics Circle Award for Autobiography/ Memoir finalist

National Book Award for Nonfiction finalist, 2012

A two-time Pulitzer Prize winner who was one of the four New York Times reporters to be captured and freed in Libya traces the story of his family's effort to rebuild an ancestral home in Lebanon amid political strife and how the work enabled a greater understanding of the emotions behind Middle East turbulence.

306.0973 Culture--United States

Brill, Steven, 1950-

★**Tailspin** : the people and forces behind America's fifty-year fall--and those fighting to reverse it / Steven Brill. Alfred A. Knopf, 2018. 352 p. **306.0973**

1. Social change. 2. Political culture. 3. Equality. 4. Democracy. 5. United States -- Politics and government -- 1989-
ISBN 9781524731632

LC 2017051857

The award-winning journalist and best-selling author of America's Bitter Pill explores the reasons why major American institutions are no longer able to function as intended and are triggering deep economic divides, in a sobering report that also traces the stories of individuals and organizations who are laying the foundations for sustainable change.

"He brings both detailed reporting and wide-ranging perspective to this insightful account of how America reached its current state." Publishers Weekly.

Fallows, James M., 1949-

★**Our** towns : a 100,000-mile journey into the heart of America / James Fallows and Deborah Fallows. Pantheon, 2018. 320 p. **306.0973**

1. Fallows, James M., 1949- 2. Fallows, Deborah. 3. Public opinion. 4. Social surveys. 5. Voyages and travels 6. United State -- Social conditions -- Public opinon. 7. United States -- Politics and government -- Public opinion.
ISBN 9781101871843

LC 2017052007

A portrait of the civil and economic renewal currently underway in American towns and under the radar of the media draws on the authors' visits with the nation's civic leaders, factory workers, recent immigrants and young entrepreneurs, who are observing and understanding the beginnings of important transitional dynamics and opportunities.

"With a commitment to observation and a sincere desire to understand each place on their journey, they offer a fascinating review of the many economic, environmental, educational, and cultural efforts taking place all over America. Far from the national narrative of crisis and decay, the authors suggest that a more hopeful renewal may be under way." Booklist.

Hill, Marc Lamont

★**Nobody** : casualties of America's war on the vulnerable, from Ferguson to Flint and beyond / Marc Lamont Hill. Atria Books, 2016 320 p. **306.0973**

1. Brown, Michael, Jr. 1996-2014 2. Garner, Eric, died 2014 3. Gray, Freddie 1989-2015. 4. Police brutality 5. Police and minorities. 6. Racism in law enforcement 7. Racism in the judicial system.
ISBN 9781501124945

LC 2016023107

The award-winning journalist, BET News host and CNN political contributor presents an analysis of the high-profile deaths of such unarmed citizens as Michael Brown, Eric Garner and Freddie Gray to lend essential insights into the intersection of race and class in America today.

"A thought-provoking and important analysis of oppression, recommended for those seeking clarity on current events." Library Journal.

Klein, Ezra

★**Why** we're polarized / Ezra Klein. Avid Reader Press, 2020. 384 p. **306.0973**

1. Polarization (Social sciences) 2. Right and left (Political science) 3. Identity (Psychology) -- Political aspects 4. Political culture -- United States 5. United States -- Politics and government -- 21st century.
ISBN 9781476700328

LC bl2019037462

A journalist, political commentator and cofounder of Vox explains how today's rigidly partisan politics came to be, why we all participate in it and what it means for America's future.

"With YA crossover appeal, Klein's accessible work is for anyone wondering how we got here; it shows how understanding history can help us plan for the future." Library Journal

Kristof, Nicholas D., 1959-

★**Tightrope** : Americans reaching for hope / Nicholas D. Kristof, Sheryl Wudunn. Alfred A. Knopf, 2020. 304 p. : **306.0973**

1. Working class 2. Blue collar workers 3. Communities 4. Life expectancy 5. United States -- Social conditions -- 21st century

ISBN 9780525655084

LC 2019014592

The Pulitzer Prize-winning authors draw on the true experiences of working-class Americans to outline possible solutions to governmental failures behind rising unemployment, poverty and opioid addiction.

"This essential, clear-eyed account provides worthy solutions to some of America's most complex socioeconomic problems." Publishers Weekly.

LeDuff, Charlie

Sh*tshow! : the country's collapsing . . . and the ratings are great / Charlie LeDuff. Penguin Press, [2018] 276 pages ; **306.0973**

1. The Americans (TV series) 2. Social classes 3. Drug use 4. Race relations 5. Immigration and emigration 6. United States -- Social conditions

ISBN 9780525522027

LC 2018006192

Presents an assessment of today's America based on his experiences while recording the television series, The Americans, to reveal how technology, social media, opioid addiction, economic imbalance and other hot-button issues are inflicting real-world harm on a mass scale.

"This timely portrait of America is a superb example of contemporary gonzo journalism." Publishers Weekly.

Quinn, Colin, 1959-

Overstated : a coast-to-coast roast of the 50 states / Colin Quinn. St. Martin's Press, 2020 x, 243 p. ; **306.0973**

1. States 2. Regionalism 3. Political culture 4. National characteristics, American 5. United States -- Geography 6. United States -- History 7. United States -- Politics and government

ISBN 9781250268440

The comedian star of the one-man Broadway show Red State, Blue State lampoons the idiosyncrasies of the 50 United States, sharing sharp-witted observations about their contradictory interpretations of the Constitution and a representative government.

"For all 50 states Quinn pulls off the remarkable feat of being both very informative and thoroughly entertaining. This delightful read is highly recommended." Booklist

Wann, David

The **new** normal : an agenda for responsible living / David Wann. St. Martin's Griffin, 2011. x, 274 p. : **306.0973**

1. Social values -- United States. 2. Sustainable living -- United States. 3. Lifestyles -- United States. 4. Quality of life.

ISBN 9780312575434

LC 2010037913

The author of Simple Prosperity urges readers to promote environmental health by lobbying for sustainable lifestyle habits, covering such practices as buying locally, using natural chemicals and conserving water.

"Wann pulls from the disciplines of biology, anthropology, history, and psychology to make his case that the current paradigm of bigger and more is not working. He proposes the Era of Emerging Restoration, in which healthy families, communities, and ecosystems are the best measures of wealth. This is one of the best approaches to promoting a sustainable world." Library Journal.

306.09747 Culture--New York

Helmreich, William B., 1945-2020

The **New** York nobody knows : walking 6,000 miles in the city / William B. Helmreich. Princeton University Press, 2013 480 p. **306.09747**

1. City life. 2. City dwellers -- New York City. 3. Urban sociology. 4. Communities. 5. New York City

ISBN 9780691144054

LC 2013017223

As a child growing up in Manhattan, William Helmreich played a game with his father called 'Last Stop.' They would pick a subway line, ride it to its final destination, and explore the neighborhood. Decades later, his love for exploring the city was as strong as ever. Putting his feet to the test, he decided that the only way to truly understand New York was to walk virtually every block of all five boroughs--an astonishing 6,000 miles. --Provided by publisher

306.09794 Culture--California

Talbot, David, 1951-

Season of the witch : enchantment, terror, and deliverance in the city of love / David Talbot. Free Press, 2012. xvii, 452 p. : **306.09794**

1. City and town life -- California -- San Francisco -- History -- 20th century. 2. Counterculture -- California -- San Francisco -- History -- 20th century. 3. Culture conflict -- California -- San Francisco -- History -- 20th century. 4. Political culture -- California -- San Francisco -- History -- 20th century. 5. San Francisco (Calif.) 6. San Francisco (Calif.) -- History -- 20th century. 7. San Francisco (Calif.) -- Social conditions -- 20th century. 8. San Francisco (Calif.) -- Social life and customs -- 20th century.

ISBN 1439108218

LC 2011032082

A founder of the web magazine Salon traces the story of San Francisco in the latter half of the 20th century, covering topics ranging from the civil rights movement and pop culture to the 49ers and famous crime cases.

306.2 Cultural institutions

Bakken, Tim

The **cost** of loyalty : dishonesty, hubris, and failure in the U.S. Military / Tim Bakken. Bloomsbury Publishing, 2020. 320 p. **306.2**

1. Dishonesty 2. Corruption 3. Incompetence 4. Military education 5. United States -- Armed Forces

ISBN 9781632868985

LC bl2020000233

A West Point professor of law argues that much destruction has been wrought by the arrogance, incompetence and duplicity he sees as prevalent in the U.S. military.

"A provocative, disturbing argument that a democracy is in trouble when it venerates the military unconditionally." Kirkus

Maddow, Rachel
Drift : the unmooring of American military power / Rachel Maddow. Crown, 2012. 304 p. **306.2**

1. United States. Department of Defense Appropriations and expenditures 2. National security -- United States 3. Militarism -- United States 4. Political culture -- United States 5. Military policy 6. United States -- Politics and government -- 1989- 7. United States -- Foreign relations -- 1989-
ISBN 9780307460981

LC 2012000998

Explains how the focus on national security is actually compromising national stability, tracing the historical events and contributing factors that have promoted a deeply militarized American culture.

306.20951 Politics--China

Pan, Philip P.
★**Out** of Mao's shadow / Philip P. Pan. Simon & Schuster, 2008. 368 p. **306.20951**

1. Politics and culture -- China 2. Democracy -- China. 3. International relations -- China 4. Capitalism -- China 5. China -- Social conditions -- 1976-2000. 6. China -- Social conditions -- 2000- 7. China -- History -- 1949-
ISBN 9781416537052

LC 2008011550

A vivid chronicle of the world's most successful authoritarian state. Pan, who reported from China for seven years, eluded the police and succeeded in going where few Western journalists have dared. From the rusting factories in the industrial northeast to a tabloid newsroom in the booming south, from a small-town courtroom to the plush offices of the nation's wealthiest tycoons, he takes us inside the battle for China's soul and into the lives of individuals struggling to come to terms with their nation's past and to take control of its future.

306.20973 Politics--United States

Bryant, Howard, 1968-
Full dissidence : notes from an uneven playing field / Howard Bryant. Beacon Press, 2020. 192 p. **306.20973**

1. Political culture 2. Civil rights 3. Power (Social sciences) 4. Political corruption 5. United States -- Politics and government -- 2017- 6. Essays
ISBN 9780807019559

LC 2019026263

An impassioned meditation on injustice in America examines the fundamental inequities behind the country's most divisive issues, explaining how a normalizing of authoritarianism in today's political arenas is undermining freedom and democracy for everyday people.

"Bryant is a masterful writer and a voice of this generation. His passion and analysis on important topics is unparalleled." Library Journal.

Frank, Thomas, 1965-
Rendezvous with oblivion : reports from a sinking society / Thomas Frank. Metropolitan Books, Henry Holt and Company, 2018. 224 p. **306.20973**

1. Political culture -- United States. 2. Polarization (Social sciences) 3. Social classes 4. Divided government 5. United States -- Politics and government -- 21st century. 6. Essays
ISBN 9781250293664

LC 2017060877

A collection of interlocking essays denounces the four-decade economic battle in America that has culminated in today's devastating levels of financial inequality.

Hetherington, Marc J., 1968-
Prius or pickup? : how the answers to four simple questions explain America's great divide / Marc Hetherington & Jonathan Weiler. Houghton Mifflin Harcourt, 2018. 304 p. **306.20973**

1. Political culture -- United States. 2. Polarization (Social sciences) 3. Political psychology 4. Liberals 5. United States -- Politics and government -- 21st century
ISBN 9781328866783

LC 2018012316

Two award-winning political scientists provide the psychological key to America's deadlocked politics, showing that we are divided not by ideologies but something deeper: personality differences that appear in everything from politics to parenting to the workplace to TV preferences.

Kakutani, Michiko
The **death** of truth : notes on falsehood in the age of Trump / Michiko Kakutani. Tim Duggan Books, 2018. 208 p. **306.20973**

1. Truth 2. Information 3. Dishonesty 4. Politics and culture
ISBN 9780525574828

LC 2018010263

A Pulitzer Prize-winning critic offers an analysis of our current condition--a world where truth has become an endangered species?and presents a new way forward for our truth-challenged times.

Kornacki, Steve
The **red** and the blue : the 1990s and the birth of political tribalism / Steve Kornacki. Ecco Press, 2018. 288 p. **306.20973**

1. Clinton, Bill, 1946- 2. Politicians 3. Political science 4. Political parties 5. Popular culture 6. United States -- Politics and government -- 1989-
ISBN 9780062438980

LC 2018016635

An MSNBC and NBC News national political correspondent presents a history of the 1990s twin paths of Bill Clinton and Newt Gingrich to argue that their rivalry triggered massive policy shifts that reverberate in today's political landscape.

"Now his journalistic prowess is on display in this sharp narrative tracking the steps and missteps over the last quarter-century that brought us to today's combative political stasis." Booklist.

Nussbaum, Martha Craven, 1947-
The **monarchy** of fear : a philosopher looks at our political crisis / Martha C. Nussbaum. Simon & Schuster, 2018. xviii, 249 p. ; **306.20973**

1. Presidential election, 2016 2. Divided government 3. Fear 4. Political parties 5. United States -- Politics and government -- 21st century
ISBN 9781501172496

The award-winning moral philosopher and author of Upheavals of Thought presents an examination of America's turbulent political environment since the 2016 election, outlining recommendations for how to mend partisan divides.

"Nussbaum's erudite but very readable investigation engages figures from Aristotle to Donald Trump in lucid and engaging prose, though some readers may feel she psychologizes politics without grappling sufficiently with positions substance. Still, Nussbaum offers fresh, worthwhile insights into the animosities that roil contemporary public life." Publishers Weekly.

Posner, Eric A., 1965-

The **demagogue's** playbook : the battle for American democracy from the founders to Trump / Eric A. Posner. All Points Books, 2020. 256 p. **306.20973**

1. Trump, Donald, 1946- 2. Political leadership 3. Political culture 4. Populism 5. Democracy 6. United States -- Politics and government. 7. United States -- Politics and government -- 2017-

ISBN 9781250303035

LC 2020002693

Includes index.

In The Demagogue's Playbook, acclaimed legal scholar Eric A. Posner offers a blueprint for how America can prevent the rise of another demagogue and protect the features of a democracy that help it thrive?and restore national greatness, for one and all.

"Though Posner's prose tends to be more dry and technical than vivid, he delivers a powerful argument for the need to restore constitutional safeguards against demagoguery." Publishers Weekly

Wilentz, Sean

The **politicians** & the egalitarians : the hidden history of American politics / Sean Wilentz. W.W. Norton & Company, 2016. 400 p. **306.20973**

1. Equality -- United States -- History. 2. Political culture -- United States -- History. 3. Politicians -- United States 4. Political activists -- United States 5. United States -- Politics and government.

ISBN 9780393285024

The author of the Bancroft Prize-winning The Rise of American Democracy reminds readers of the commanding role party politics has played in America's enduring struggle against economic inequality.

"In other hands, this would seem silly and lacking force; in Wilentzs, it's authoritative and telling. The result is wonderfully readable and the best kind of serious, sharp argumentation from one of the leading historians of the United States." Publishers Weekly.

306.3 Economic institutions

Atwood, Margaret, 1939-

Payback : debt and the shadow side of wealth / Margaret Atwood. Anansi, 2008. 280 p. **306.3**

1. Debt. 2. Money -- Social aspects. 3. Debtor and creditor. 4. Wealth -- Social aspects. 5. Essays.

ISBN 9781487006976

LC 2008924729

"Delivered with . [Atwood's] trademark wit and imagination, this is a meditation that challenges conventional thinking on one of the most morally pressing issues we face." Booklist.

Bales, Kevin

Blood and earth : modern slavery, ecocide, and the secret to saving the world / Kevin Bales. Spiegel & Grau, 2016. 304 p. **306.3**

1. Slavery -- Environmental aspects -- Developing countries -- History -- 21st century. 2. Slave labor -- Environmental aspects -- Developing countries. 3. Environmental degradation -- Developing countries. 4. Consumer economics

ISBN 9780812995763

LC 2015008438

Green Prize for Sustainable Literature: Adult Nonfiction, 2017.

The co-founder of the largest abolitionist organization in the world identifies key links between environmental destruction and human trafficking while outlining new approaches to solving both crises.

"Readers will be deeply disturbed to learn how the links connecting slavery, environmental issues, and modern convenience are forged." Publishers Weekly.

Baptist, Edward E.

★The **half** has never been told : slavery and the making of American capitalism / Edward E. Baptist. Basic Books, 2014 528 p. **306.3**

1. Slavery -- History. 2. African Americans -- Social conditions -- 19th century 3. United States -- Economic conditions -- 19th century.

ISBN 9780465002962

LC 2014012546

As historian Edward Baptist reveals in The Half Has Never Been Told, the expansion of slavery in the first eight decades after American independence drove the evolution and modernization of the United States. In the span of a single lifetime, the South grew from a narrow coastal strip of worn-out tobacco plantations to a continental cotton empire, and the United States grew into a modern, industrial, and capitalist economy. Until the Civil War, Baptist explains, the most important American economic innovations were ways to make slavery ever more profitable. The Half Has Never Been Told offers a radical new interpretation of American history. It forces readers to reckon with the violence at the root of American supremacy, but also with the survival and resistance that brought about slavery's end - and created a culture that sustains America's deepest dreams of freedom.

"Through an incredible amount of detail and the use of an array of primary sources, the author argues that the South's use of slave labor in cotton production was the primary factor in the United States becoming a leading modern industrial nation." Library Journal.

Berlin, Ira, 1941-

Remembering slavery : African Americans talk about their personal experiences of slavery and freedom / edited by Ira Berlin, Marc Favreau, and Steven F. Miller. New Press, 1998. lii, 355 p. : **306.3**

1. Slaves -- Southern States -- Interviews. 2. Slaves -- Southern States -- Social conditions 3. African Americans -- Southern States -- Social conditions -- 19th century -- Sources. 4. Freed slaves 5. Southern States -- History -- 19th century. 6. Interviews

ISBN 1565844254

LC 2003389301

Includes live recordings of interviews with former slaves and dramatic readings from written interviews.

"This book-and-tapes collection of slave narratives, drawn from slave narratives and audio recordings of former slaves collected by the Federal Writers' Project (FWP) during the 1930s and 1940s (some of which have been remastered and included in two 60-minute cassettes with the book), brings slavery to life as few recent books have done." Library Journal.

Berry, Daina Ramey

The **price** for their pound of flesh : the value of the enslaved, from womb to grave, in the building of a nation / Daina Ramey Berry. Beacon Press, 2017. 256 p. **306.3**

1. Slavery 2. Slave-trade -- United States -- History 3. Slaves -- Social conditions 4. Capitalism and slavery 5. Southern States -- History -- 19th century 6. United States -- History -- 19th century

ISBN 9780807047620

LC 2016014894

The first book to explore the economic value of enslaved people through every phase of their lives--including from before birth to after death--in the American domestic slave trades. Covering the full "life cycle" (including preconception, infancy, childhood, adolescence, adulthood, the senior years, and death), historian Daina Berry shows the lengths to which slaveholders would go to maximize profits.

"Berry's groundbreaking work in the historiography of American slavery deserves a wide readership beyond academia." Publishers Weekly

Biss, Eula

Having and being had / Eula Biss. Riverhead Books, 2020 176 p. **306.3**

1. Leisure -- Social aspects. 2. Work -- Social aspects. 3. Quality of life. 4. Social classes 5. Essays

ISBN 9780525537458

LC 2020010815

"Having just purchased her first home, the author embarks on a self-audit of the value system she has bought into. The essays in this volume offer an interrogation of work, leisure, and the lived experience of capitalism".-- Provided by publisher.

"A typically thoughtful set of Biss essays: searching, serious, and determined to go beyond the surface." Kirkus

Brody, Lauren Smith

The **fifth** trimester : the working mom's guide to style, sanity, and big success after baby / Lauren Smith Brody. Doubleday, 2017 xxvi, 319 p.; **306.3**

1. Work and family 2. Working mothers 3. Work-life balance

ISBN 9780385541411

LC 2016019667

An award-winning Glamour executive editor presents a tell-it-like-it-is guide for new moms coping with the demands of the real world after childbirth, offering advice on everything from returning to work and maintaining a work/life balance to breastfeeding and obtaining childcare.

Davies, Richard (Economics adviser)

Extreme economies : what life at the world's margins can teach us about our own future / Richard Davies. Farrar, Straus & Giroux, 2020. 304 p. **306.3**

1. Economics -- Social aspects 2. Microeconomics 3. Economic forecasting 4. Alternative economics

ISBN 9781250170484

LC bl2020001098

To predict our future, we must look to the extremes. So argues the economist Richard Davies, who takes readers to the margins of the modern economy and beyond in his globe-trotting book. From a prison in rural Louisiana where inmates purchase drugs with prepaid cash cards to the poorest major city on earth, where residents buy clean water in plastic bags, from the world's first digital state to a prefecture in Japan whose population is the oldest in the world, how these extreme economies function--most often well outside any official oversight--offers a glimpse of the forces that underlie human resilience, drive societies to failure, and will come to shape our collective future.

"Highly recommended, sobering reading for anyone interested in the economic future, for good and bad." Kirkus.

Davis, David Brion

★The **problem** of slavery in the age of emancipation / David Brion Davis. Knopf, 2014. 352 p. **306.3**

1. American Colonization Society. 2. Slavery -- History -- 19th century. 3. Slaves -- Emancipation 4. Anti-slavery movements -- History -- 19th century 5. Free African Americans -- History -- 19th century. 6. United States -- History -- 19th century

ISBN 9780307269096

LC 2013032893

National Book Critics Circle Award for Non-Fiction, 2014.

A conclusion to the award-winning historian's three-volume history of slavery in Western culture includes coverage of the influential Haitian revolution, the complex significance of colonization and the less-recognized importance of freed slaves to abolition.

"This is a well-researched and broad historical and global analysis of the complex motives and actions on all fronts, highlighting the transcontinental tension between efforts by white society to dehumanize and the fight by freedmen and slaves for freedom, full humanity, and citizenship." Booklist.

De Botton, Alain

The **pleasures** and sorrows of work / Alain de Botton. Pantheon Books, 2009. 336 p. **306.3**

1. Work -- Miscellanea. 2. Occupations. 3. Human behavior. 4. Personal conduct.

ISBN 9780375424441

LC 2008046060

"De Botton's sprightly mix of reportage and rumination expands beyond the workplace to investigate the broader meaning of life." Publishers Weekly.

Dewitt, David

Precious cargo : how foods from the Americas changed the world / David Dewitt. Counterpoint 2014 256 p. **306.3**

1. Food 2. International trade 3. Exports

ISBN 9781619023093

LC bl2014023965

Chronicles the story of how western-hemisphere foods spread throughout the world and helped prevent mass starvation, tracing the science and rise of everyday crops into commodities while examining the roles of pioneering individuals responsible for western food dominance.

"Both public and academic libraries will find this a welcome addition to sociological, anthropological, and culinary collections." Library Journal.

Grandin, Greg, 1962-

The **empire** of necessity : slavery, freedom, and deception in the new world / Greg Grandin. Metropolitan Books, 2014. 384 p. **306.3**

1. Delano, Amasa, 1763-1823. 2. Slavery -- South America -- History 3. Slave resistance and revolts. 4. Slave trade 5. Mutiny

ISBN 9780805094534

LC 2013014309

Includes index.

The institution of slavery dominated many aspects of the U.S. economy well into the 19th century (including in "free" states), and even abolitionists often believed that Africans were intellectually inferior to Europeans. Amasa Delano, captain of a sealing ship, was one such abolitionist. When his crew boarded another ship in the South Pacific to offer aid, Delano horrendously overreacted after he discovered that West Africans were in control. In his carefully researched and accessible -- if disturbing -- book, historian Greg Grandin explains Delano's actions and their context. He also details the nature of the slave trade.

Hartman, Saidiya V.

Lose your mother : a journey along the Atlantic slave route / Saidiya Hartman. Farrar, Straus and Giroux, 2007. xi, 270 p.

: 306.3

1. Hartman, Saidiya V. Travel Ghana. 2. Slave trade -- Ghana -- History. 3. Historic sites -- Ghana. 4. Slavery. 5. Ghana -- Description and travel. 6. Ghana -- History

ISBN 9780374270827

LC 2006029407

Saidiya Hartman traces the history of the Atlantic slave trade by recounting a journey she took along a slave route in Ghana. Following the trail of captives from the hinterland to the Atlantic coast, Hartman reckons with the blank slate of her own genealogy and vividly dramatizes the effects of slavery on three centuries of African and African-American history.

Kars, Marjoleine

Blood on the river : the untold story of the Berbice slave rebellion: a chronicle of mutiny and freedom on the Wild Coast / Marjoleine Kars. The New Press, [2020] 336 p. **306.3**

1. Slave resistance and revolts 2. Guerrilla warfare 3. Colonialism 4. Slave trade 5. Guyana -- History 6. South American -- History

ISBN 9781620974599

LC 2019053892

On Sunday, February 27, 1763, thousands of slaves in the Dutch colony of Berbice -- in present-day Guyana -- launched a massive rebellion which came amazingly close to succeeding. Surrounded by jungle and savannah, the revolutionaries (many of them African-born) and Europeans struck and parried for an entire year. In the end, the Dutch prevailed because of one unique advantage -- their ability to get soldiers and supplies from neighboring colonies and from Europe. Blood on the River is the explosive story of this little-known revolution, one that almost changed the face of the Americas.

"A must-read for anyone interested in slave revolts and the history of Atlantic slavery." Library Journal

Levs, Josh

All in : how our work-first culture fails dads, families, and business and how we can fix it together / Josh Levs. HarperOne, 2015 272 p. **306.3**

1. Family and work 2. Father and child 3. Families 4. Parental leave 5. United States -- Social conditions.

ISBN 9780062349613

LC 2014042031

A "Parenting" columnist for CNN.com who wrote the highly publicized essay on the EEOC charge against Time Warner for discrimination against fathers explores the changing face of fatherhood and how it is reshaping families, business and society.

"Lev's thoughtful plea for men and women to work together is more persuasive, providing a useful guide for those looking to effect change in their own workplaces and communities." Publisher's Weekly.

Postma, Johannes

The **Atlantic** slave trade / Johannes Postma. Greenwood Press, 2003. xxii, 177 p., 7 p. of plates : **306.3**

1. Slave trade -- Africa -- History. 2. Slave trade -- America -- History. 3. Slave trade -- Europe -- History.

ISBN 031331862X

LC 2002035338

Drawing on surviving firsthand accounts, the author explains the context of the slave trade from the moment of enslavement in Africa to the sale of the slaves in American markets.

"The author covers the entire Atlantic slave trade era, from the 1400s to the final abolition of chattel slavery in the New World in 1888. The focus is on Africa and the entire New World. While he describes the many horrors of the Middle Passage, he also examines how the slave trade contributed to the development of the modern international economy. The last chapters discuss the efforts to abolish the slave trade and its legacy." School Library Journal

Rae, Noel (Noel Martin Douglas)

★The **great** stain : witnessing American slavery / Noel Rae. The Overlook Press, 2018. 591 pages : **306.3**

1. Slaves 2. Slaveholders 3. Slavery 4. Slave trade 5. United States -- History -- 19th century

ISBN 9781468315134

LC bl2017051090

Comprising personal accounts from an intensely consequential chapter in human history, the transatlantic slave trade, The Great Stain takes readers from the depths of suffering to the heights of human dignity.

"Highly recommended for U.S. colonial, middle period, and Civil War scholars, and general readers." Library Journal.

Resendez, Andres

★The **other** slavery : the uncovered story of Indian enslavement in America / Andres Resendez. Houghton Mifflin Harcourt, 2016 448 p. **306.3**

1. Native American slaves -- United States -- History 2. Slave trade -- United States -- History. 3. Indians of North America, Treatment of -- United States -- History 4. Indians of North America -- History. 5. United States

ISBN 9780547640983

LC 2015037557

Draws on new evidence to reveal the massive enslavement of tens of thousands of Native Americans from the 16th through the 19th centuries, describing how kidnapping and forced labor played a key role in the decimations of Indian populations across North America.

"This eye-opening exposure of the abuse of the indigenous peoples of America is staggering; that the mistreatment continued into the 20th century is beyond disturbing." Kirkus.

Sax, David

The **revenge** of analog : real things and why they matter / David Sax. PublicAffairs, 2016. 336 p. **306.3**

1. Records, Phonograph 2. Entrepreneurship -- History. 3. Electronic commerce -- History. 4. Marketing.

ISBN 9781610395717

LC 2016012413

A lighthearted tribute to the historical and future role of analog technologies traces the renewal of interest in tangible goods from books to vinyl records, exploring how underreported trends in analog consumerism are reflecting how today's people think, shop and do business.

"This book has a calming effect, telling readers, one analog page at a time, that tangible goods, in all their reassuring solidity, are back and are not going anywhere." Publishers Weekly.

Siler, Julia Flynn

★The **white** devil's daughters : the fight against slavery in San Francisco's Chinatown / Julia Flynn Siler. Alfred A. Knopf, 2019. 352 p. **306.3**

1. Occidental Mission Home -- History. 2. Human trafficking -- San Francisco, California 3. Immigration and emigration 4. Social work 5. Chinese in California. 6. San Francisco, California 7. United States -- Immigration and emigration

ISBN 9781101875261

LC 2018039985

"This is a Borzoi Book."

A revelatory history of the trafficking of young Asian girls throughout the first century of Chinese immigration in San Francisco shares insights into the activities of the Occidental Mission Home and its work as a refuge for freedom-seeking victims.

"An accessible, well-written, riveting tale of a dismal, little-known corner of American history." Kirkus.

Stromberg, Lisen

Work pause thrive : how to pause for parenthood without killing your career / Lisen Stromberg. BenBella Books, Inc., [2017] 288 p. **306.3**

1. Working mothers. 2. Family and work. 3. Success (Concept) 4. Work-life balance.

ISBN 9781942952732

LC 2016034628

"Stuffed with realistic but inspiring stories and concrete advice, this is a healthy reminder that those who pause to place the personal before the professional are not failures." Publishers Weekly.

Thompson, Derek

Hit makers : the science of popularity in an age of distraction / Derek Thompson. Penguin Press, 2017. 352 p. **306.3**

1. Popular culture 2. Mass media 3. Culture. 4. Human behavior.

ISBN 9781101980323

LC 2016043453

An Atlantic senior editor presents an investigation into the lucrative quality of popularity in the 21st century to share economic insights into what makes ideas, productions and products successful.

"Good reading for anyone who aspires to understand the machinery of pop cultureand perhaps even craft a hit of his or her own." Kirkus.

Underhill, Paco

The **call** of the mall : the geography of shopping / Paco Underhill. Simon & Schuster, 2004. 227 p. **306.3**

1. Shoppers. 2. Shopping malls. 3. Consumer economics. 4. Consumers -- Attitudes.

ISBN 0743235916

LC 2003064960

Includes index.

"The author takes readers on a tour of a typical Saturday at a large, regional mall. He examines the routes there, the shopping center itself, the stores, food, entertainment, ambience, and the customers. He shows why the mall is the way it is and how it could be improved. He provides insight into how the stores are arranged, how they display merchandise. and the different ways that men and women respond to this environment." School Library Journal.

Warren, Wendy

★**New** England bound : slavery and colonization in early America / Wendy Warren. Liveright Publishing Corporation, 2016 352 p. **306.3**

1. Slavery 2. New England -- History

ISBN 9780871406729

LC 2016007276

Pulitzer Prize for History finalist, 2017.

Based on new evidence, an important work on 17th-century New England reclaims the lives of so many long-forgotten enslaved Africans and Native Americans, forcefully demonstrating that the history of American slavery can no longer confine itself to the 19th-century South.

Williams, Heather Andrea

Help me to find my people : the African American search for family lost in slavery / Heather Andrea Williams. University of North Carolina Press, c2012. 251 p. : **306.3**

1. Slavery -- History. 2. African American families -- History. 3. Slaves. 4. Family relationships.

ISBN 9780807835548

LC 2011050216

Utilizes narratives, letters, interviews, public records, and diaries to explore the stories of separation of former slave families and their quest for reunification.

306.36 Systems of labor

Hurston, Zora Neale

★**Barracoon** : the story of the last 'black cargo' / Zora Neale Hurston, edited and with an introduction by Deborah G. Plant. Amistad Press, 2018. 208 p. **306.36**

1. Lewis, Cudjo 2. Slave trade 3. Slaves 4. Slavery 5. Slaveholders

ISBN 9780062748201

LC 2018466206

Presents a never-before-published work that illuminates the horror and injustices of slavery as it tells the true story of one of the last known survivors of the Atlantic slave trade--abducted from Africa on the last "Black Cargo" ship to arrive in the United States.

"This is a fascinating look at the journey of one man, reflective of the African American experience. It also attests to Hurston's development as an author and ethnographer, and stands as a work of profound relevance, its illumination of slavery, freedom, and race as timely as ever." Booklist.

306.4 Specific aspects of culture

Burr, Ty

Gods like us : on movie stardom and modern fame / Ty Burr. Pantheon, 2012. 304 p. **306.4**

1. Celebrities in mass media. 2. Fame -- Social aspects. 3. Popular culture. 4. Celebrities.

ISBN 9780307377661

LC 2012000618

"How--and why--do we focus on those individuals we come to call stars? How does stardom both reflect and mask the person behind it? How have the image of stardom and our stars' images changed over the past hundred years? What does celebrity mean if people can become famous simply for being famous? Ty Burr answers these questions in this lively, wonderfully anecdotal history of stardom--both its blessings and its curses, for the star and the stargazer alike. From Florence Lawrence, Mary Pickford, and Charlie Chaplin, to Archie Leach (a.k.a. Cary Grant), Ruby Stevens (a.k.a. Barbara Stanwyck), and Marion Morrison (a.k.a. John Wayne), to Jim Belushi, Tom Cruise, and Julia Roberts, to such no-cal stars of today as the Kardashians and the new online celebrity(i.e., you and me), Burr takes us on a brilliantly insightful and entertaining journey through the modern fame game at its flashiest, its most indulgent, occasionally its most tragic and, ultimately, its most culturally revealing".-- Provided by publisher.

Chang, Jeff

Can't stop, won't stop : a history of the hip-hop generation / Jeff Chang ; introduction by DJ Kool Herc. Picador, 2006, c2005. xiii, 546 p. : **306.4**

1. Rap music -- History and criticism 2. Hip-hop culture 3. Music

and society
ISBN 0312425791

LC bl2006001087

Originally published: New York : St. Martin's Press, 2005.

A history of hip-hop cites its origins in the post-civil rights Bronx and Jamaica, drawing on interviews with performers, activists, gang members, DJs, and others to document how the movement has influenced politics and culture.

"A fascinating, far-reaching must for pop-music and pop-culture collections." Booklist.

Charnas, Dan

The **big** payback : the history of the business of hip-hop / Dan Charnas. New American Library, 2010. 352 p. **306.4**

1. Rap (Music) -- Social aspects. 2. Hip-hop. 3. Sound recording industry and trade. 4. Rap music industry and trade
ISBN 9780451229298

LC 2010016062

Includes index.

Draws on the stories of three hundred industry veterans to chronicle hip-hop's rise from street culture to global industry, tallying who won, who lost, and who was on the cutting edge.

Ekirch, A. Roger, 1950-

★**At** day's close : night in times past / A. Roger Ekirch. Norton, 2005. xxxii, 447 p. : **306.4**

1. Social history. 2. Night -- History. 3. Night -- Social aspects.
ISBN 0393050890

LC 2005002784

"This history finds Ekirch reminding us of how preindustrial Westerners lived during the nocturnal hours, when most were plunged into almost total darkness. A rich weave of citation and archival evidence, Ekirch's narrative is rooted in the material realities of the past, evoking a bygone world of extreme physicality and preindustrial survival stratagems." Publishers Weekly.

Fadiman, Anne, 1953-

★The **spirit** catches you and you fall down : a Hmong child, her American doctors, and the collision of two cultures / Anne Fadiman. Farrar, Straus, and Giroux, 1997. xi, 339 p. **306.4**

1. Cross-cultural medical care -- Case studies. 2. Cultural differences. 3. Hmong American girls 4. Hmong Americans -- Medical care. 5. California.
ISBN 0374267812

LC 97005175

National Book Critics Circle Award for Non-Fiction, 1997.

A study in the collision between Western medicine and the beliefs of a traditional culture focuses on a hospitalized child of Laotian immigrants, members of the Hmong tribe, whose belief that illness is a spiritual matter came into conflict with doctors' methods.

"Fadiman reveals the rigidity and weaknesses of these two ethnographically separated cultures. In a shrinking world, this painstakingly researched account of cultural dislocation has a haunting lesson for every healthcare provider." Library Journal.

Helfand, Jessica

Scrapbooks : an American history / Jessica Helfand. Yale University Press, 2008. 190 p. : **306.4**

1. Scrapbooks. 2. Photograph albums. 3. Photographs -- Conservation and restoration 4. Hobbies 5. United States -- History 6. United States -- History -- 19th century 7. United States -- History -- 20th century 8. United States -- History -- 21st century
ISBN 9780300126358

LC 2008923233

The author examines the evolution of scrapbooks from the beginning of the nineteenth century to the present, including their origins, their makers, their diverse forms, the reasons for their popularity, and their place in American cultural life.

"The author offers both an overview of the history of the creation of scrapbooks and a visual feast for readers via the integration of texts, images, and memorabilia of all types. Helfand has made a brilliant selection of unusual examples by visiting numerous archives, and she weaves a narrative based on examples that she found . . . The book is sumptuous, a superb marriage in fine design, paper, and print." Choice.

Kugel, Seth

Rediscovering travel : a guide for the globally curious / Seth Kugel. Liveright Publishing Corporation, [2018] 320 p. **306.4**

1. Kugel, Seth Travel. 2. Tourism. 3. Vacations. 4. Misadventures. 5. Adventurers.
ISBN 9780871408501

The former New York Times "Frugal Traveler" columnist and host of "Amigo Gringo" challenges the practices of the modern travel industry while sharing stories of memorable discoveries and misadventures that demonstrate how to enjoy a technology-balanced vacation.

Langlands, Alex

Craeft : an inquiry into the origins and true meaning of traditional crafts / Alexander Langlands. W. W. Norton & Company, 2018. 336 p. **306.4**

1. Material culture 2. Artisans 3. Handicraft 4. Consumerism.
ISBN 9780393635904

LC 2017047723

Includes index.

An archaeologist takes us into the ancient world of traditional crafts to uncover their deep, original histories.

"Langlands offers a fascinating history of what's setting trends today." Booklist.

Leonard, Annie

The **story** of stuff : how our obsession with stuff is trashing the planet, our communities, and our health--and a vision for change / Annie Leonard with Ariane Conrad. Free Press, 2010. 272 p. **306.4**

1. Material culture. 2. Personal belongings. 3. Consumerism. 4. Acquisitiveness.
ISBN 9781439125663

LC 2009042207

Green Prize for Sustainable Literature, 2011.

Leonard traces the life cycle of the things we use every day--from their creation to their eventual end in a landfill or otherwise--to illustrate how this cycle affects our environment.

"Leonard explains that our consumer goods undergo extraction, production, distribution, consumption, and disposal processes that are trashing the planet, diminishing our resources, exploiting workers, and contributing to high levels of disease and death. She advocates an international cooperative effort to develop domestic and international policies and laws that will reverse our planet's ecological decline and leave a sustainable world for future generations. An important work for consumers of all ages." Library Journal.

McGonigal, Jane

Reality is broken : why games make us better and how they can change the world / Jane McGonigal. Penguin Press, 2011. 400 p. **306.4**

1. Video games -- Social aspects. 2. Alternate reality games 3. Quality of life 4. Computer games -- Social aspects.
ISBN 9781594202858

LC 2010029619

A visionary game designer explains how video games are increasingly fulfilling genuine human needs, revealing how to use the lessons of game design to address pressing real-world issues, from mental illness to social disparities.

"If the world of gaming seems alien to you, this book will crack it wide open. For experienced gamers, it will likely inspire you to play or even invent better, more meaningful games. Despite her expertise, McGonigal's book is never overly technical, and as with a good computer game, anyone, regardless of gaming experience, is likely to get sucked in." The New Scientist.

Mohr, Tim

Burning down the Haus : punk rock, revolution, and the fall of the Berlin Wall / Tim Mohr. Algonquin Books of Chapel Hill, 2018. 320 p. **306.4**

1. Bergmann, Britta 2. Punk culture 3. Punk rock music 4. Punk rock musicians 5. Counterculture 6. East Germany -- History -- 20th century 7. Berlin, Germany -- History -- 20th century
ISBN 9781616208431

LC 2018010846

Traces how East German fans of punk rock found enough inspiration in punk's revolutionary philosophy to launch underground movements that helped bring down the Berlin Wall in spite of violent targeting by the Stasi secret police.

"Mohr tells a frantic and exciting true story of music versus dictatorship, and the infamous wall it helped bring down." Booklist.

Pollan, Michael

The **botany** of desire : a plant's eye view of the world / Michael Pollan. Random House, 2001. xxv, 271 p. **306.4**

1. Humans and plants. 2. Coevolution. 3. Plants -- Development. 4. Men and nature.
ISBN 0375501290

LC 00066479

Focusing on the human relationship with plants, uses botany to explore four basic human desires--sweetness, beauty, intoxication, and control--through four plants that embody them: the apple, tulip, marijuana, and potato.

"Pollan intertwines history, anecdote, and revelation as he investigates the connection between four plants that have thrived under human care--apples, tulips, marijuana, and potatoes--and the four human desires they satisfy in return: sweetness, beauty, intoxication, and control. Pollan's dynamic, intelligent, and intrepid parsing of the wondrous dialogue between plants and humans is positively paradigm-altering." Booklist.

Rose, Frank

The **art** of immersion : how the digital generation is remaking Hollywood, Madison Avenue, and the way we tell stories / Frank Rose. W.W. Norton & Co., 2011. 256 p. **306.4**

1. Internet entertainment industry and trade -- Social aspects. 2. Internet entertainment -- Social aspects. 3. Internet marketing -- Social aspects. 4. Entertainment industry and trade
ISBN 9780393076011

LC 2010038676

A contributing editor at Wired examines the way entertainment has shifted in the face of new media and discusses the way that people like Will Wright, James Cameron and Damon Lindelof are changing how we play, relax and think.

"The author theorizes that we are encountering a profound shift in the way we play, consume, and communicate. He explains that our experiences with television, movies, games, and advertisements are becoming increasingly more immersive and consumer-driven. This engrossing study of how new media is reshaping the entertainment, advertising, and communication industries is an essential read for professionals in the fields of digital communications, marketing, and advertising, as well as for fans of gaming and pop culture." Library Journal.

Trumble, Angus

The **finger** : a handbook / Angus Trumble. Farrar, Straus and Giroux, 2010. xx, 300 p. : **306.4**

1. Fingers -- Social aspects. 2. Fingers in art.
ISBN 9780374154981

LC 2009042220

An acclaimed art historian examines the finger from every angle, whether it be its portrayal in great works of art, its varied roles in history and pop culture or what science has revealed to us about it. By the author of A Brief History of the Smile.

306.7 Sexual relations

Ackerman, Diane, 1948-

A **natural** history of love / Diane Ackerman. Random House, c1994. xxiii, 358 ; **306.7**

1. Love -- History. 2. Romantic love. 3. Love of animals. 4. Familial love.
ISBN 0679403477

LC 94171385

The author explores the diverse faces and forms of love from a scientific, psychological, and philosophical perspective.

"Ackerman sets out on her exploration by reviewing the lessons provided across time by such lovers as Antony and Cleopatra, Orpheus and Eurydice, Dido and Aeneas, Abelard and Heloise, and Romeo and Juliet. During this journey, she explores the neurophysiology of love. With dazzling poetic charm and insight, she uses history, literature, science, psychology, and personal experience as tools to illuminate the vigor and vehemence of the thrilling, devastating, and comforting phenomenon of love." Library Journal.

Berkowitz, Eric

The **boundaries** of desire : bad laws, good sex, and changing identities / Eric Berkowitz. Counterpoint, 2015. 304 p. **306.7**

1. Sexuality -- Social aspects. 2. Sex customs -- History. 3. Sex laws. 4. Homosexuality
ISBN 9781619025295

LC 2015005123

Explores the changing aspects of sexual morality in the Western world, from when it was acceptable for husbands to rape their wives, to the sexual revolution, and the fight for gay rights and discusses how the laws always lag behind popular acceptance.

"A bracing look at the often-strange relationship between sexuality and the legal system over six tumultuous decades." Booklist.

Chen, Angela, 1991-

Ace : what asexuality reveals about desire, society, and the meaning of sex / Angela Chen. Beacon Press, 2020. 224

p. **306.7**

1. Sexuality 2. Asexuality 3. Desire. 4. Sexual attraction.
ISBN 9780807013793

LC 2020002390

A journalist, using her own perspective along with those of a diverse group of asexual people, presents a careful cultural analysis that explores how societal norms limit understanding of sex and relationships and celebrates the breadth of sexuality and queerness.

"Writing as an asexual woman of color, journalist and editor Chen has produced a thoughtful if occasionally unfocused look at what it means not to experience sexual attraction. . . . Most likely to appeal readers of any orientation seeking a general text about asexuality and its place on the wider spectrum of human sexuality." Library Journal

Coles, Joanna

Love rules : how to find a real relationship in a digital world / Joanna Coles. Harper, 2018 xii, 235 p. ; **306.7**

1. Dating (Social customs). 2. Man-woman relationships. 3. Online dating. 4. Women -- Conduct of life.
ISBN 0062652583

LC bl2018003955

Shares advice for women on how to find meaningful relationships in a complicated, largely digital, romantic landscape, offering recommendations for recognizing and connecting with prospective quality partners who are capable of intimate, long-term commitments.

McConnachie, James

The **book** of love : the story of the kamasutra / James McConnachie. Metropolitan Books, 2008. xviii, 267 p. ; **306.7**

1. Vatsyayana. Kamasutra. 2. Kamasutra 3. Love. 4. Sex manuals -- India 5. Sexuality -- History 6. India -- History 7. Europe -- History
ISBN 9780805088182

LC 2007047172

Traces the history of the famous text typically associated with its instruction for ambitious sexual techniques, tracing its origins to third-century India, where it began as a primer on urbane sophistication that counseled early readers about friendship and home decor, until a western adventurer launched the text into fame in Victorian society.

"In an impressively researched, charming volume, McConnachie traces the Kamasutra's history from its creation by the third-century sage Vatsyayana as a guide to the good life for urbane dandies. Since not a single posture is described, consider it G-rated." Booklist.

Shlain, Leonard

Sex, time, and power : how women's sexuality shaped human evolution / Leonard Shlain. Viking, c2003. xx, 420 p. : **306.7**

1. Sexual attraction. 2. Mate selection. 3. Human evolution. 4. Social evolution.
ISBN 0670032336

LC 2002041186

Theorizes about a profound change in prehistoric female sexuality that gave way to the emergence of Homo sapiens 150,000 years ago, citing evolutionary circumstances that led to the development of religion, death awareness, patriarchal culture, and human love.

"The author takes an evolutionary approach to solving the conundrums of misogyny and patriarchy, guiding his . . . readers through . . . speculations about the purpose of such seemingly impractical, even dangerous traits as bipedalism, menstruation, the perils of childbirth, and the helplessness of infants. Lucid and compelling, Shlain asks startling and crucial questions about human nature and presents truly imaginative and mind-stretching answers." Booklist.

Spiegel, Amy Rose

Action : a book about sex / Amy Rose Spiegel. Grand Central Publishing, 2016. xvii, 217 p. : **306.7**

1. Sex education for adults 2. Sexuality 3. Sexual excitement. 4. Sex manuals.
ISBN 1455534498

LC 2015050562

"With whip-smart prose, reminiscent of Roxane Gay and Meghan Daum, ACTION interweaves Spiegel's own sexual autobiography with loving advice on one-night stands, relationships, and everything in between. ACTION is a book about sex that people won't feel embarrassed about owning. There are absolutely zero provocatively shaped fruit on the cover, for one. In ACTION, Amy Rose Spiegel exhorts you to trust yourself and be respectful of others--and to have the best possible time doing the things you search for on the Internet, except in reality. The book covers consent, safety, group sex, gender, and the best breakfast to make for a one-night stand. Spiegel also includes dissections of threesomes, how to pick people up without being a skeezer, celibacy as a display of autonomy, and, of course, how to clean your room in 10 minutes if a devastatingly lovely side-piece is about to stop by. All told, ACTION totally doesn't think it's weird that you want to try that thing together. In fact, ACTION is very into it".-- Provided by publisher.

306.7082 Women--Sexual relations

Alptraum, Lux

Faking it : the lies women tell about sex--and the truths they reveal / Lux Alptraum. Seal Press, 2018. 237 p. **306.7082**

1. Women -- Sexuality 2. Orgasm, Female 3. Deception 4. Dishonesty
ISBN 9781580057653

LC 2018014655

From Out of the Binders co-founder Lux Alptraum, a controversial look at women, sex, and lying--why myths about women's deceit persist, how they came to be, and ultimately why we must trust women.

Bergner, Daniel

★What do women want? : adventures in the science of female desire / / Daniel Bergner. Ecco, 2013. 240 p. **306.7082**

1. Women -- Sexuality 2. Sexual excitement 3. Lust 4. Sexuality
ISBN 9780061906084

LC 2013431147

Going behind the scenes of some of the most revolutionary experiments on sexuality today, this stimulating exploration of female desire answers a vast array of thought-provoking questions that shed new light on women and sex.

"Stylishly written and cogently organized, making it easy and rewarding for lay readers to understand and appreciate some fairly complex science." Kirkus.

Koenig, Emma,

Moan : anonymous essays on female orgasm / collected by Emma Koenig ; foreword by Rachel Bloom. Grand Central Publishing, 2018. xi, 226 p. ; **306.7082**

1. Orgasm, Female. 2. Women -- Sexuality 3. Sexual intercourse. 4. Sexual excitement.
ISBN 9781455540556

LC 2017025281

Tackling the elusive orgasm head on, a series of essays aim to empower women to embark on their own journey of sexual exploration to find out what they want or don't want in the bedroom.

Friedman, Jaclyn,

Yes means yes! : visions of female sexual power & a world without rape / Jaclyn Friedman & Jessica Valenti [editors] ; foreword by Margaret Cho. Seal Press, c2008. 361 p. ; **306.7082**

1. Violence against women. 2. Sexism. 3. Rape. 4. Body image. 5. Essays.

ISBN 9781580052573

LC 2008020989

A modern analysis of rape by the activist author of Full Frontal Feminism calls for a greater understanding of and respect for female sexual pleasure as part of a societal effort to end rape by having men see women as equal collaborators instead of sexual conquests.

"The editors present an extraordinary, eye-opening essay collection that focuses on the importance of sexual identity and ownership in the struggle against rape in the U.S., as well as a number of related issues, including sexual pleasure, self-esteem and the mixed societal messages that turn nice guys bad." Publishers Weekly.

McLaughlin, August, 1978-

Girl boner : the good girl's guide to sexual empowerment / August McLaughlin. Amberjack Publishing, 2018 xii, 353 p. : **306.7082**

1. Women -- Sexual behavior.

ISBN 9781944995713

LC 2018002591

Offers practical advice and personal anecdotes for women on sexual health, discussing body image, relationships, gender identity, birth control, safe sex, eating disorders, and the role of self-acceptance in feelings of empowerment.

Rowland, Katherine

The **pleasure** gap : American women and the unfinished sexual revolution / Katherine Rowland. Seal Press, 2020. 304 p. **306.7082**

1. Women -- Sexuality 2. Sexuality 3. Sexual freedom 4. Sexual excitement

ISBN 9781580058360

LC 2019032150

American culture is more sexually liberal than ever. But compared to men, women's sexual pleasure has not grown: Up to 40 percent of American women experience the sexual malaise clinically known as low sexual desire. Between this low desire, muted pleasure, and experiencing sex in terms of labor rather than of lust, women by the millions are dissatisfied with their erotic lives. Katherine Rowland rejects the idea that women should settle for diminished pleasure; instead, she argues women should take inequality in the bedroom as seriously as we take it in the workplace and understand its causes and effects.

"Rowland skillfully synthesizes many different ideas and approaches, and encourages women to embrace a broader understanding of their own sexual desire as an ongoing process of self-discovery and self-assertion. Readers interested in feminism, women's issues, and contemporary sexual mores will find this to be an edifying and comprehensive study." Publishers Weekly

Taddeo, Lisa

★**Three** women / Lisa Taddeo. Avid Reader Press, 2019 306 p. **306.7082**

1. Desire 2. Intimacy (Psychology) 3. Sexuality 4. Women -- Sexuality 5. United States -- Social life and customs

ISBN 9781451642292

LC 2018045846

An account based on nearly a decade of reporting examines the sex lives of three American women, exploring the complexity and fragility of female desire.

"Dramatic, immersive, and wanting--much like desire itself." Kirkus.

306.70835 Adolescents--Sexual relations

Orenstein, Peggy

★**Girls** & sex : navigating the complicated new landscape / Peggy Orenstein. HarperCollins, 2016. 320 p. **306.70835**

1. Teenage girls -- Sexuality. 2. Sexuality. 3. Sex education for children

ISBN 9780062209726

LC 2016304590

The New York Times best-selling author of Cinderella Ate My Daughter presents an analysis of the new sexual landscape faced by girls in today's high schools and colleges, revealing hidden truths, hard lessons and important possibilities in girls' modern-world sex lives.

"Ample, valuable information on the way young women in America perceive and react to their sexual environment." Kirkus.

306.70944 France--Sexual relations

Yalom, Marilyn

How the French invented love : nine hundred years of passion and romance / Marilyn Yalom. HarperCollins, 2012. 320 p. **306.70944**

1. Culture. 2. Love. 3. France.

ISBN 9780062048318

LC bl2012038461

Interweaving readings of French literary works with memories of her experiences in France, an acclaimed scholar explores a love-obsessed culture, from the Middle Ages to the present, documenting how the French concept and practice of love has evolved throughout history.

306.70973 United States--Sexual relations

Wade, Lisa (Professor)

American hookup : the new culture of sex on campus / Lisa Wade. W W Norton & Company, 2017 288 p. **306.70973**

1. Rape in universities and colleges. 2. College students. 3. Sexuality 4. Sexual violence

ISBN 9780393285093

LC 2016035704

A revelatory account of the new culture of sex at today's colleges profiles how students are navigating a harrowing emotional landscape marked by one-sidedness, status competition and sexual violence that is particularly challenging to minorities and women.

"An eye-opening, conversation-starting examination of sex on the American college campus." Kirkus.

306.73 General institutions

Martin, Wednesday

Untrue : why nearly everything we believe about women, lust, and infidelity is wrong and how the new science can set us free /

Wednesday Martin. Little Brown & Co., 2018. 288 p. **306.73**

1. Women -- Sexuality 2. Sexuality -- Social aspects 3. Cheating (Interpersonal relations) 4. Monogamy
ISBN 9780316463614

LC 2018941914

Reveals sanctioned practices of infidelity in diverse cultures and historical periods to assert that female sexual autonomy is an ultimate metric of gender equality.

"An indispensable work of popular psychology and sociology." Kirkus.

Perel, Esther

The **state** of affairs : rethinking infidelity / Esther Perel. HarperCollins, 2017 272 p. **306.73**

1. Men/women relations 2. Cheating (Interpersonal relations) 3. Extramarital affairs 4. Betrayal
ISBN 9780062322586

LC bl2017041564

A couples therapist and best-selling author describes her findings after spending a decade working with couples whose lives were shattered by infidelity and discusses how individuals can grow and heal after a betrayal, either together or apart.

"This is a thought-provoking take on relationships and essential reading for couples dealing with infidelity." Publishers Weekly.

Weigel, Moira, 1984-

Labor of love : the invention of dating / Moira Weigel. Farrar, Straus and Giroux, 2016. 336 p. **306.73**

1. Dating (Social customs). 2. Courtship. 3. Mate selection. 4. United States
ISBN 9780374182533

LC 2015041606

"A brilliant and surprising investigation into why we date the way we do".-- Provided by publisher.

306.7409773 Prostitution--Illinois

Abbott, Karen, 1973-

Sin in the Second City : madams, ministers, playboys, and the battle for America's soul / Karen Abbott. Random House, c2007. xxiv, 356 p. : **306.7409773**

1. Everleigh, Ada. 2. Everleigh, Minna. 3. Everleigh Club. 4. Prostitution 5. Brothels 6. Chicago, Illinois -- History. 7. Illinois -- History.
ISBN 1400065305

LC 2006051878

A history of America's most famous brothel, Chicago's Everleigh Club, which catered to some of America's leading moguls, actors, and writers from 1900 to 1911, profiles its aristocratic proprietors and their efforts to elevate the industry to new heights.

"Lavish in her details, nicely detached in her point of view, [and with] scrupulous concern for historical accuracy, Ms. Abbott has written an immensely readable book. Sin in the Second City offers much in the way of reflection for those interested in the unending puzzle that goes by the name of human nature." Wall Street Journal

306.76 Sexual orientation, transgenderism, intersexuality

Beachy, Robert

Gay Berlin : birthplace of a modern identity / Robert Beachy. Knopf, 2014. 304 p. **306.76**

1. Gay men -- Berlin, Germany -- Identity. 2. Gay culture -- Berlin, Germany. 3. Homosexuality -- Berlin, Germany. 4. Gender identity -- Berlin, Germany. 5. Berlin, Germany
ISBN 9780307272102

LC 2014004986

"A detailed historical look at the surprising ways in which the uninhibited urban sexuality, sexual experimentation and medical advances of pre-Weimar Berlin created and molded our modern understanding of sexual orientation and gay identity".-- Provided by publisher.

Blank, Hanne

Straight : the surprisingly short history of heterosexuality / Hanne Blank. Beacon Press, c2012. 264 p. **306.76**

1. Heterosexuality -- History. 2. Homosexuality -- History. 3. Sexual orientation.
ISBN 9780807044438

LC 2011031432

Presents a history of heterosexuality, explores the contemporary psyche of sexual orientation, and shows how culture creates and manipulates thoughts and experiences of desire, love, and relationships.

Bronski, Michael

★A **queer** history of the United States / Michael Bronski. Beacon Press, 2011. 288 p. **306.76**

1. Homosexuality -- United States -- History. 2. Gay men -- United States -- History. 3. Lesbians -- United States -- History. 4. Homosexuality -- United States -- Miscellanea 5. United States -- Social life and customs.
ISBN 9780807044391

LC 2010050225

Lambda Literary Award, 2011.

Stonewall Book Award for the Israel Fishman Non-fiction Award, 2012.

"A Queer History of the United States is groundbreaking and accessible. It looks at how American culture has shaped the LGBT, or queer, experience, while simultaneously arguing that LGBT people not only shaped but were pivotal in creating our country. Using numerous primary documents and literature, as well as social histories, Bronski's book takes the reader through the centuries--from Columbus' arrival and the brutal treatment the Native peoples received, through the American Revolution's radical challenging of sex and gender roles--to the violent, and liberating, 19th century--and the transformative social justice movements of the 20th. Bronski's book is filled with startling examples of often ignored or unknown aspects of American history: the ineffectiveness of sodomy laws in the colonies, the prevalence of cross-dressing women soldiers in the Civil War, the effect of new technologies on LGBT life in the 19th century, and how rock music and popular culture were, in large part, responsible for the great backlash against gay rights in the late 1970s. More than anything, A Queer History of the United States is not so much about queer history as it is about all American history--and why it should matter to both LGBT people and heterosexuals alike".-- Provided by publisher.

"This enthralling history spans 500 years of evolving perspectives on sexuality in America--from the European setters' violent responses to the more fluid gender roles of Native Americans to how the birth control pill, which separated sex from reproduction, contributed to the cause of LGBT liberation. A savvy political, legal, literary (and even fashion) history, Bronski's narrative is as intellectually rigorous as it is entertaining." Publishers Weekly.

Carter, David

Stonewall : the riots that sparked the gay revolution / David

Carter. St. Martin's Griffin, 2010, c2004. 336 p. : **306.76**

1. Stonewall Riots, New York, N.Y., 1969 2. Gay and Lesbian Movement 3. Gay men -- United States -- History -- 20th century. 4. Lesbians -- United States -- History -- 20th century. 5. Greenwich Village, New York City -- History -- 20th century. 6. United States -- History -- 20th century.

ISBN 9780312671938

Originally published: New York : St. Martin's Press, 2004.

An examination of the 1969 series of riots over police action against The Stonewall Inn provides a background of the mob-controlled Greenwich Village gay bar, the political and social elements that contributed to the riots, and the event's impact on subsequent attitudes.

"The author depicts the Stonewall riots as a unique convergence of time, place, and circumstance and performs some gentle revisionism on the received version of events, emphasizing the contributions of lesbians and street youth while downplaying, but not discounting, the role of drag queens." Library Journal.

Craggs, Charlie,

To my trans sisters / edited by Charlie Craggs. Jessica Kingsley Publishers, 2017 344 p. **306.76**

1. Transgenderism 2. Transgender persons 3. Anthologies 4. Essays

ISBN 9781785923432

LC 2017026096

"This invigorating anthology, written by trans women for trans women, is a welcome departure from the established genre of texts about trans individuals that seek to explain their lives and experiences for a presumed audience of primarily cisgendered individuals." Publishers Weekly.

Davis, Heath Fogg

★**Beyond** trans : does gender matter? / Heath Fogg Davis. New York Univeristy Press, 2017 208 p. **306.76**

1. Transgender persons 2. Gender identity 3. Gender role 4. Sexism

ISBN 9781479855407

LC 2017003478

Beyond Trans pushes the conversation on gender identity to its limits: questioning the need for gender categories in the first place. Whether on birth certificates or college admissions applications or on bathroom doors, why do we need to mark people and places with sex categories? Do they serve a real purpose or are these places and forms just mechanisms of exclusion?

"This book is a rare example of a text that speaks fluently to experts and novices alike. Indispensable for all libraries and readership levels." Choice.

Deschamps, David

LGBTQ stats : lesbian, gay, bisexual, transgender, and queer people by the numbers / David Deschamps and Bennett Singer. The New Press, 2017. 339 p. : **306.76**

1. Gays -- United States -- Statistics 2. Sexual minorities -- United States -- Statistics

ISBN 9781620972441

LC 2016032471

Provides current statistics and data on lesbian, gay, bisexual, transgender, and queer people, including LGBTQ characters on television, same-sex parenting, LGBTQ health objectives, and federal employment laws involving sexuality and gender.

Duberman, Martin B.

★**Has** the gay movement failed? / Martin Duberman. University of California Press, [2018] 247 p. **306.76**

1. Gay Liberation Front (New York, N.Y.). 2. Gay and Lesbian Movement 3. LGBTQIA rights 4. Social movements 5. Homosexuality 6. United States -- Social conditions -- 21st century

ISBN 9780520298866

LC 2017056078

A founder of the Center for Lesbian and Gay Studies at City University of New York discusses the successes of the acceptance of LGBTQ people in the past 50 years but also highlights the failures.

"Duberman challenges gay readers and their allies to become active within a complex caucus he feels has become unfocused and misled. A relevant, fiery, and dizzying treatise certain to provoke debate and discussion." Kirkus.

The **Martin** Duberman reader : the essential historical, biographical, and autobiographical writings / Martin Duberman. The New Press, 2013 336 p. **306.76**

1. Duberman, Martin B. 2. LGBTQIA rights -- United States 3. Gay men -- United States -- History 4. United States -- History. 5. United States -- Social conditions. 6. United States -- Politics and government.

ISBN 9781595586797

LC 2012041856

The Martin Duberman Reader assembles the core of Duberman's most important writings, offering a wonderfully comprehensive overview of our lives and times--and giving us a crucial touchstone for a new generation of activists, scholars, and readers. --Provided by publisher

Eisner, Shiri

Bi : notes for a bisexual revolution / Shiri Eisner. Seal Press, 2013 345 p. ; **306.76**

1. Bisexuality.

ISBN 9781580054744

LC 2012047200

In this forward-thinking and eye-opening book, feminist bisexual and genderqueer activist Shiri Eisner takes readers on a journey through the many aspects of the meanings and politics of bisexuality, specifically highlighting how bisexuality can open up new and exciting ways of challenging social convention. --Provided by publisher

Erickson-Schroth, Laura

Trans bodies, trans selves : a resource for the transgender community / edited by Laura Erickson-Schroth. Oxford University Press, USA, 2014. xxi, 649 p. : **306.76**

1. Transgender people 2. Transgenderism 3. Gender identity

ISBN 9780199325351

LC 2014007921

"There is no one way to be transgender. Transgender and gender non-conforming people have many different ways of understanding their gender identities. Only recently have sex and gender been thought of as separate concepts, and we have learned that sex (traditionally thought of as physical or biological) is as variable as gender (traditionally thought of as social). While trans people share many common experiences, there is immense diversity within trans communities. There are an estimated 700,000 transgendered individuals in the US and 15 million worldwide. Even still, there's been a notable lack of organized information for this sizable group. Trans Bodies, Trans Selves is a revolutionary resource-a comprehensive, reader-friendly guide for transgender people, with each chapter written by transgender or genderqueer authors. Inspired by Our Bodies, Ourselves, the classic and powerful compendium written for and by women, Trans Bodies, Trans Selves is widely accessible to the transgender population, providing authoritative information in an inclusive and respectful way and representing the collective knowledge base of dozens of influential experts. Each chapter takes the reader through an important transgender issue, such as race, religion, employment, medical and surgical transition, mental health topics, relationships, sexuality, parenthood, arts and culture, and many more. Anonymous quotes and testimonials from transgender people who have been surveyed about their experiences are woven throughout, adding compelling, personal voices to every page. In this unique way, hundreds of viewpoints from throughout the community have united to create this strong and pioneering book. It is a welcoming place for transgender and gender-questioning people, their partners and families, students, professors, guidance counselors, and others to look for up-to-date information on transgender life"-- Provided by publisher.

★**"You're** in the wrong bathroom!" : and 20 other myths and misconceptions about transgender and gender nonconforming people / Laura Erickson-Schroth, MD, Laura A. Jacobs, LCSW-R. Beacon Press, [2017] 200 p. **306.76**

1. Transgender persons. 2. Transgenderism. 3. LGBTQIA persons 4. Gender role.
ISBN 9780807033890

LC 2016055090

Describes the twenty-one most common myths and misconceptions about transgender and gender-nonconforming people, bringing together the medical, social, psychological, and political aspects of being trans in the United States today.

"A timely and worthwhile purchase for libraries as well as middle- and high-school counseling offices, community centers, and places of worship." Booklist.

Faderman, Lillian

The **gay** revolution : the story of the struggle / Lillian Faderman. Simon & Schuster, 2015 512 p. **306.76**

1. LGBTQIA rights -- United States 2. Gay and Lesbian Movement. 3. Transgender persons -- Rights. 4. Gay men -- Rights.
ISBN 9781451694116

LC 2015007285

ALA Notable Book, 2016.
Stonewall Non-Fiction Honor Book, 2016

A chronicle of the modern struggle for gay, lesbian and transgender rights draws on interviews with politicians, military figures, legal activists and members of the LGBT community to document the cause's struggles since the 1950s.

"Throughout this engaging and extremely well-documented book, Faderman clearly shows that for the LGBT community, equality is not a completed goal. Yet the ideal of fully integrated citizenship is closer to becoming reality than ever before. Inspiring and necessary reading for all Americans interested in social justice." Kirkus.

Fleishman, Jane, 1954-

The **Stonewall** generation : LGBTQ elders on sex, activism, and aging / Jane Fleishman ; foreword by Kate Bornstein and Barbara Carrellas. Skinner House Books, 2020 264 p. **306.76**

1. LGBTQIA persons 2. Seniors 3. LGBTQIA rights 4. Transgender persons
ISBN 9781558968530

LC 2020001469

Sexuality researcher Jane Fleishman shares the stories of fearless elders in the LGBTQ community who came of age around the time of the Stonewall Riots of 1969. In candid interviews, they lay bare their struggles, strengths, activism, and sexual liberation in the context of the political movements of the 1960s and 1970s and today. These are the stories of those whose lives were changed forever by Stonewall and who in turn became agents of change themselves.

"Though this inspirational volume represents just a small sampling of the community's movers and shakers, it deserves prominent placement on LGBTQ history bookshelves. . . . An indelible collection of wise voices resonating with experience, pride, resilience, and revolution." Kirkus

Gevisser, Mark

The **pink** line : journeys across the world's queer frontiers / Mark Gevisser. Farrar, Straus & Giroux, 2020. 528 p. **306.76**

1. Homosexuality 2. Gender nonconformity 3. LGBTQIA rights 4. Gender identity
ISBN 9780374279967

LC 2019056416

More than five years in the making, Mark Gevisser's The Pink Line: Journeys Across the World's Queer Frontiers is a globetrotting exploration of how the human rights frontier around sexual orientation and gender identity has come to divide--and describe--the world in an entirely new way over the first two decades of the twenty-first century. No social movement has brought change so quickly and with such dramatically mixed results. While same-sex marriage and gender transition is celebrated in some parts of the world, laws are being strengthened to criminalize homosexuality and gender nonconformity in others. A new Pink Line, Gevisser argues, has been drawn across the world, and he takes readers to its frontiers.

"This necessary, timely, intelligent book belongs in every library, the world over." Booklist

Hirshman, Linda R.

Victory : the triumphant gay revolution / Linda Hirshman. HarperCollins, 2012. 464 p. **306.76**

1. LGBTQIA rights 2. Gay and Lesbian Movement -- United States -- History. 3. People with AIDS -- Care -- Government policy. 4. Gay men -- Legal status, laws, etc. 5. United States -- Social conditions -- 21st century
ISBN 9780061965500

LC 2012406399

Drawing on rich archival material and in-depth interviews, a Supreme Court lawyer and political pundit chronicles the gay rights movement, revealing how the fight for gay rights has changed the American landscape for all citizens, blurring rigid gender lines and redefining the definition of family.

Nealy, Elijah C.

★**Transgender** children and youth : cultivating pride and joy with families in transition / Elijah C. Nealy. W.W Norton & Company, 2017. xxii, 423 p. : **306.76**

1. Gender nonconformity. 2. Transgender children -- Mental health. 3. Transgender people -- Family relationships. 4. Transgender people -- Identity.
ISBN 0393711390

LC 2016036762

"A must-read for anyone who wants to help trans youth." Booklist.

Odets, Walt

Out of the shadows : reimagining gay men's lives / Walt Odets. Farrar, Straus and Giroux, [2019] 352 p. **306.76**

1. Gay men -- Identity. 2. AIDS (Disease) 3. Gay men -- United States. 4. Self acceptance
ISBN 9780374285852

LC 2018050164

National Book Critics Circle Award for Nonfiction finalist, 2019

A clinical psychologist, writer and gay activist reflects on what it means to be gay today through moving stories of friends and patients in the aftermath of the AIDS epidemic and shifting social values.

"The stated primary audience is gay men, but Odets believes that all can profit from and recognize themselves in the emotional contentand he's right. Nearly anyone interested in how much people are alike, despite differences in sexual orientation, will find much to appreciate." Library Journal.

Parkinson, R. B.

A **little** gay history : desire and diversity across the world / R. B. Parkinson. Columbia University Press, 2013. 128 p. : **306.76**

1. Homosexuality -- History 2. Art 3. Censorship 4. Homosexuality in art

ISBN 9780231166638

LC 2013001699

"This little gay history is a little terrific book. Parkinson ... explore[s] the subject of homosexual desire throughout history; he discusses artistic movements, ordinary material culture, facades of conventional life, warrior traditions, legal persecutions, and definitions of the sacred." Library Journal.

Robb, Graham, 1958-

Strangers : homosexual love in the nineteenth century / Graham Robb. W. W. Norton, 2004. viii, 341 p. : **306.76**

1. Homosexuality -- Europe -- History. 2. Homosexuality -- United States -- History. 3. Gay men -- Europe -- History. 4. Gay men -- United States -- History.

ISBN 9780393020380

LC 2003066239

A fresh examination of the development of homosexual culture during the nineteenth century in Europe and America describes the lives of gay men and women, how they discovered their sexuality, how they made contact with like-minded people, the relationship of gay culture to religion, and how homosexuals were treated by society.

"The author has produced a brilliant work of social archaeology. In excavating the long-buried lives of our gay great-great-granduncles and lesbian great-great-grandaunts, Robb has done more than make a major historical contribution. He has, as it were, provided their distant nieces and nephews, gay and straight, with a family tree that we have never had before." New York Times Book Review.

Schwenke, Chloe

★**Self-ish** : a transgender journey toward wholeness / Chloe Schwenke. Red Hen Press, [2018] 256 p. **306.76**

1. Schwenke, Chloe 2. Trans women 3. Transgender persons 4. Transitioning (Gender identity) 5. Quakers

ISBN 9781597096089

LC 2017054802

" It is a fascinating, illuminating story of an exemplary life and an essential book in helping people understand the condition of being a transgender person." Booklist.

Stein, Arlene

Unbound : transgender men and the remaking of identity / Arlene Stein. Pantheon Books, [2018] 288 p. **306.76**

1. Transgender persons -- Identity 2. Trans men 3. Gender nonconformity. 4. Transitioning (Gender identity) 5. Interviews

ISBN 9781524747459

LC 2017046998

Drawn from interviews with transgender people, medical and psychological experts, as well as activists, an award-winning sociologist reveals how a younger generation of trans men are changing our perceptions about gender.

"Stein posits that trans identity as it exists right now in younger people is less an act of survival and more an act of self-reinvention. Though Stein finds no tidy conclusions, her book succeeds in documenting what it means to be trans today." Publishers Weekly.

Testa, Rylan Jay

The **gender** quest workbook : a guide for teens and young adults exploring gender identity / Rylan Jay Testa, Deborah Coolhart, and Jayme Peta. Instant Help, [2015] 168 p. Instant help solutions series **306.76**

1. Gender identity 2. Sex differences (Psychology) 3. Sexuality 4. Transgenderism

ISBN 9781626252974

LC 2015032696

"From inconspicuous activities such as people watching to more task-oriented ideas for encouraging young people to broach their concerns to family members, this volume serves as a valuable resource. While this isn't the best acquisition for libraries (it is truly a workbook), librarians would do well to be informed of its availability" Library Journal.

Tobin, Kay,

Love and resistance : out of the closet into the Stonewall era / photographs by Kay Tobin Lahusen and Diana Davies ; from the New York Public Library Archives ; edited by Jason Baumann ; with an Introduction by Roxane Gay. W. W. Norton & Company, 2019 xvi, 173 p. ; **306.76**

1. Gay liberation movement -- United States -- History.

ISBN 9781324002062

LC 2018057897

Selected from the New York Public Library archives, a powerful collection featuring the images of two pioneering civil-rights photojournalists captures the energy, humor and humanity of the groundbreaking LGBTQ equality protests that surrounded the Stonewall Riots.

306.77 Sexual and related practices

Bader, Michael J.

Arousal : the secret logic of sexual fantasies / Michael J. Bader. Thomas Dunne Books, 2002. x, 293 p. ; **306.77**

1. Sex (Psychology) 2. Sexual fantasies.

ISBN 0312269331

LC 2001051290

Based on his twenty-five years of experience as a psychotherapist, a renowned doctor furnishes a new theory of sexual desire that allows readers to comprehend their own sexual preferences and fantasises, and those of their partners.

306.770973 Sexual and related practices--United States

Talese, Gay

★The **voyeur's** motel / Gay Talese. Grove Press, 2016 240 p. **306.770973**

1. Voyeurism 2. Sexuality. 3. Motels. 4. Deception. 5. United States -- Moral conditions. 6. Colorado

ISBN 9780802125811

LC bl2016024869

The author of Thy Neighbor's Wife presents an exposé 35 years in the making, in which a man from Colorado reveals a secret so shocking that the author traveled across the country to verify it himself--and now, the man has finally decided to go public.

306.81 Marriage and marital status

Carroll, Elizabeth, 1956-
Marriage boot camp : defeat the top ten marriage killers and build a rock-solid relationship / Elizabeth and Jim Carroll. New American Library, 2016. vi, 276 p. ; **306.81**

1. Interpersonal conflict 2. Interpersonal relations 3. Marital quality 4. Marriage
ISBN 9780451476777

Drawing on 20 years of experience, relationship experts and the stars of WeTV's Marriage Boot Camp present a "do-it-yourself" relationship bible that will help fix marriages, revive relationships and make the happily-ever-afters come true.

Flock, Elizabeth
The **heart** is a shifting sea : love and marriage in Mumbai / Elizabeth Flock. HarperCollins 2018 352 p. **306.81**

1. Couples 2. Marriage 3. Gender role 4. Culture 5. Mumbai, India 6. India -- Social life and customs
ISBN 9780062456489

LC 2017278212

A deeply reported and revelatory examination of love, marriage and the state of modern India traces the experiences of three very different Mumbai couples whose realities are shaped by disparate views regarding independence, parenthood, gender roles and religion.

"Flock writes about these sensitive topics with generosity and empathy in this beautifully rendered, intricate, and human exploration of love and marriage in Mumbai." Library Journal.

Klinenberg, Eric
Going solo : the extraordinary rise and surprising appeal of living alone / Eric Klinenberg. Penguin Press, 2012. 288 p. **306.81**

1. Living alone. 2. Single people -- United States. 3. Lifestyles 4. Demography 5. United States -- Social life and customs
ISBN 9781594203220

LC 2011031522

With eye-opening statistics, original data, and vivid portraits of people who go solo, Klinenberg upends the conventional wisdom to deliver the definitive take on how the rise of living alone is transforming the American experience.

Thomas, Marlo
★**What** makes a marriage last : 40 celebrated couples share the secrets to a happy life together / Marlo Thomas and Phil Donahue ; edited by Bruce Kluger. HarperOne, 2020. 336 p. **306.81**

1. Married people 2. Marriage 3. Romantic love 4. Celebrities
ISBN 9780062982582

LC 2019060252

Long-married icons Marlo Thomas and Phil Donahue offer a collection of intimate conversations with famous couples about their long marriages and how they have made their partnerships last.

"Love and understanding shine through in this inspiring collection. . . . delightful and instructive." Publishers Weekly

Traister, Rebecca
★**All** the single ladies : unmarried women and the rise of an independent nation / Rebecca Traister. Simon & Schuster, 2016. 352 p. **306.81**

1. Single women. 2. Feminism -- History. 3. Women -- Political activity. 4. Independence in single women.
ISBN 9781476716565

LC 2015045131

A National Magazine Award-finalist and outspoken feminist reveals that the concept of a powerful single woman, often perceived as a modern phenomenon, is not a new idea and explores the options, besides traditional marriage, that were historically available to women.

"Traister is funny and fair in how she deals with the prevalent stereotypes and remaining stigmas attached to being an unmarried woman in society. She sticks to her central argument that the world is changing and policies need to catch up to the social reality. The result is an invigorating study of single women in America with refreshing insight into the real life of the so-called spinster." Publishers Weekly.

306.84 Types of marriage and relationships

Cleves, Rachel Hope, 1975-
Charity and Sylvia : a same-sex marriage in early America / Rachel Hope Cleves. Oxford University Press, 2014. 336 p. **306.84**

1. Bryant, Charity. 2. Drake, Sylvia, 1784-1868. 3. Same-sex marriage. 4. Lesbian couples 5. Homosexuality 6. Independence in women
ISBN 9780199335428

LC 2013050416

Conventional wisdom holds that same-sex marriage is a purely modern innovation, a concept born of an overtly modern lifestyle that was unheard of in nineteenth century America. But as Rachel Hope Cleves demonstrates in this eye-opening book, same-sex marriage is hardly new.

"This volume provides an exhaustive and valuable look into a relatively unknown lesbian relationship in Colonial America, proving that Puritans could be accepting in their own way of 'marriages' between women." Library Journal.

Sheff, Elisabeth,
Stories from the polycule : real life in polyamorous families / edited by Dr. Elisabeth Sheff. Thorntree Press, 2015 288 p. **306.84**

1. Non-monogamous relationships 2. Polyamory 3. Families 4. Nontraditional families
ISBN 9780991399772

LC 2016449048

"Readers engaged in or curious about polyamorous families will find plenty to ponder in this eclectic and enlightening collection." Publishers Weekly.

Solomon, Marc, 1966-
Winning marriage : the inside story of how same-sex couples took on the politicians and pundits and won / Marc Solomon ; with a foreward by governor Deval Patrick. University Press of New England 2014 368 p. **306.84**

1. Same-sex marriage 2. Marriage law 3. Marriage 4. Homosexuality
ISBN 9781611684018

LC 2014936578

Ten years ago no state allowed same-sex couples to marry, support for gay marriage nationwide hovered around 30 percent, and politicians everywhere thought of it as the third rail of American politics -- draw near at your peril. Today, same-sex couples can marry in seventeen states, polls consistently show majority support, and nearly three-quarters of Americans believe legalization is inevitable. In Winning Marriage Marc Solomon, a veteran leader in the movement for marriage equality, gives the reader aseat at the strategy-setting and decision-making table in the campaign to win and protect the freedom to marry. With depth and grace he reveals the inner workings of the advocacy movement that has championed and protected advances won in legislative, court, and electoral battles over the decade since the landmark Massachusetts ruling guaranteeing marriage for same-sex couples for the first time. From the gritty battles in the state legislatures of Massachusetts and New York to the devastating loss at theballot box in California in 2008 and subsequent ballot wins in 2012 to the joyous victories of securing President Obama's support and prevailing in the Supreme Court, Marc Solomon has been at the center of one of the great civil and human rights movements of our time. Winning Marriage recounts the struggle with some of the world's most powerful forces -- the Catholic hierarchy, the religious right, and cynical ultraconservative political operatives -- and the movement's eventual triumph.

306.85 Family

Barry, Dave

You can date boys when you're forty : Dave Barry on parenting and other topics he knows very little about / Dave Barry. G.P. Putnam's Sons, 2014 256 p. **306.85**

1. Families -- Humor. 2. Parenting -- Humor. 3. Fathers and daughters 4. Family relationships
ISBN 9780399165948

LC 2013037714

"In uproarious, brand-new pieces, Barry tackles everything from family trips, bat mitzvah parties and dating (he's serious about that title: "When my daughter can legally commence dating--February 24, 2040--I intend to monitor her closely, even if I am deceased") to funeral instructions ("I would like my eulogy to be given by William Shatner"), the differences between male and female friendships, the deeper meaning of Fifty Shades of Grey, and a father's ultimate sacrifice: accompanying his daughter to a Justin Bieber concert ("It turns out that the noise teenaged girls make to express happiness is the same noise they would make if their feet were being gnawed off by badgers")."-- Provided by publisher.

"A mishmash, but even those who don't have children and have never lived in Miami or searched for a Wi-Fi connection in the Israeli desert will appreciate Barry's lighthearted absurdity." Kirkus.

Janning, Michelle Yvonne

The **stuff** of family life : how our homes reflect our lives / Michelle Janning. Rowman & Littlefield, 2017. xii, 225 p. **306.85**

1. Families. 2. Domestic space. 3. House furnishings -- Psychological aspects. 4. Personal belongings -- Psychological aspects.
ISBN 9781442254794

LC 2016058386

Does putting your phone on the dinner table impact your relationships? How does the TV placement in your home affect your family? The Stuff of Family Life looks at the changing world of families through a unique examination of their stuff. The book takes readers through phases of family life, examining our choices about spaces and objects.

"Whether familiar with sociological methods or not, readers will be fascinated by Janning's ideas and the connections she draws between household items and family life." Booklist.

306.850942 Family--England and Wales

Worsley, Lucy

If walls could talk : an intimate history of the home / Lucy Worsley. Walker & Co., 2012, c2011. xv, 351 p. : **306.850942**

1. Home (Concept) -- England -- History 2. Houses -- England -- History 3. Social classes -- England -- History 4. Fashion -- England -- History 5. England -- Social life and customs 6. England -- History
ISBN 9780802779953

LC 2011038759

Originally published: London : Faber & Faber, 2011.

An architectural and cultural history of home life in England covers a wide range of topics from cooking and oral hygiene to sex and marriage, describing such subjects as why medieval people slept sitting up and why people feared fruit for centuries.

306.850947 Family--Russia

Figes, Orlando

★The **whisperers** : private life in Stalin's Russia / Orlando Figes. Metropolitan Books, 2007. 784 p. **306.850947**

1. Communism -- Soviet Union -- History 2. Stalinism -- Soviet Union 3. Informers 4. Nationalism. 5. Soviet Union -- Social conditions. 6. Soviet Union -- History -- 1925-1953.
ISBN 0805074619

LC 2007024223

Provides a portrait of everyday Russian life during the repression of the Stalin years, analyzing the regime's effect on people's personal lives as they struggled to survive in the middle of the fear, mistrust, betrayal, and compromise of the world in which they lived.

"This is a humbling monument to the evil and endurance of Russia's Soviet past and, implicitly, a guide to its present." The Economist.

306.850973 Family--United States

Carbone, June

Marriage markets : how inequality is remaking the American family / June Carbone, Naomi Cahn. Oxford University Press, 2014 vii, 258 p. : **306.850973**

1. Families -- Economic aspects 2. Marriage -- Economic aspects 3. Equality 4. Family relationships 5. United States -- Social conditions
ISBN 9780199916580

LC 2013045704

"This book is a methodical and skillful discussion of how the American family has changed and what needs to happen to rescue it. Social scientists, family advocates, and policymakers will find it thought provoking." Library Journal.

306.87 Intrafamily relationships

Tannen, Deborah

I only say this because I love you : how the way we talk can make or break family relationships throughout our lives / Deborah Tannen. Random House, 2001. xxvii, 336 p. ; **306.87**

1. Communication in families. 2. Families 3. Communication. 4. Conversation.
ISBN 9780679456018

LC 00068851

A guide to communicating better within families explains how to untie the knots that often hamper important discussions and how to enhance personal relationships among family members by understanding the art of conversation and listening.

"With lively prose and genuine concern for people, Tannen brings linguistic concepts--metamessage, re-framing, indirect request--to bear on dozens of situations to help lay readers strenghten family ties." Library Journal.

306.872 Spousal relationship

Yalom, Marilyn

A **history** of the wife / Marilyn Yalom. Harper Collins, c2001. xix, 441 p. : **306.872**

1. Married women -- History. 2. Homemakers -- History. 3. Marriage -- History. 4. Women -- History.

ISBN 0060193387

LC 00058153

Using the modern marriage as a focal point, a study of how marriage in the Judeo-Christian world has affected the lives of women ranges from the earliest days of civilization to the twenty-first century and speculates about what is to come in the future.

"Yalom has apparently written the first truly comprehensive history of the Western female spousal experience; indeed, there are precious few long views of either marriage or the family to which this book can be compared." Library Journal.

306.874 Parent-child relationship

Babul, Denna D.

The **fatherless** daughter project : understanding our losses and reclaiming our lives / Denna D. Babul, RN, and Karin Luise, PhD. Avery, [2015] 304 p. **306.874**

1. Fathers and daughters. 2. Children of single parents. 3. Parent and adult child. 4. Loss (Psychology).

ISBN 9781594633690

LC 2015025161

"With interesting personal stories woven throughout, fatherless daughters will find this to be a supportive and encouraging guidebook to reclaiming their lives and healing their wounds." Publishers Weekly.

Blackstone, Amy

Childfree by choice : the movement redefining family and creating a new age of independence / Dr. Amy Blackstone. Dutton, 2019. 304 p. **306.874**

1. Childlessness 2. Child-free lifestyle 3. Self-fulfillment 4. Family relationships

ISBN 9781524744090

LC 2018039378

The co-creator of the "We're (Not) Having a Baby" blog shares expert insights into the history and growing movement of adults choosing to forego parenthood, exploring its cultural, economic, and environmental significance.

"Though this book's offerings are much more substantial than mere peer support, childfree readers will certainly feel affirmed, and possibly inspired to pass copies along to those who doubt their choices." Publishers Weekly.

Bradley, Michael J., 1951-

Crazy-stressed : saving today's overwhelmed teens with love, laughter, and the science of resilience by / Michael J. Bradley, Ed.D. AMACOM, 2017 288 p. **306.874**

1. Parent and teenager. 2. Parenting. 3. Stress management for teenagers. 4. Resilience (Personal quality)

ISBN 9780814438046

LC 2017000499

"Bradley's book is aimed at teaching parents to help teens develop resilience. It is also a useful and important book for those who work with teens." Voice of Youth Advocates.

Brott, Armin A.

The **expectant** father : the ultimate guide for dads-to-be / Armin A. Brott and Jennifer Ash. Abbeville Press, 2015. 333 p. : **306.874**

1. Fathers. 2. Pregnancy

ISBN 0789212129

LC 2015009011

Revised edition of the authors' The expectant father, 2010.

"An expanded and updated month-to-month guide to the emotional, financial, and physical changes the father-to-be may experience during his partner's pregnancy".-- Provided by publisher.

Cusk, Rachel, 1967-

A **life's** work : on becoming a mother / Rachel Cusk. Picador USA, 2002, c2001 213 p. **306.874**

1. Motherhood. 2. Parenting. 3. New mothers. 4. Mothers.

ISBN 0312269870

LC 2001054894

Originally published: Great Britain : Fourth Estate, 2001.

An account of a year of modern motherhood, set against the backdrop of sexual equality, details the author's many experiences during and after her transformation into a mother, all of which have taught her valuable lessons in life.

"This is not a happy guide; instead, it is a penetrating, sometimes joyful and amusing, sometimes frightening and disturbing look at pregnancy and motherhood." Booklist.

DeGarmo, John, 1969-

The **foster** parenting manual : a practical guide to creating a loving, safe and stable home / John DeGarmo ; foreword by Mary Perdue. Jessica Kingsley Publishers, 2013. 160 p. ; **306.874**

1. Foster children. 2. Foster parents. 3. Parenting.

ISBN 184905956X

LC 2013012292

"DeGarmo includes both big-picture ideas about child development and nuts-and-bolts considerations for fostering, such as how often a caseworker must visit a home, what foster families are reimbursed for, and what training is required." Library Journal.

Dell'Antonia, K. J

How to be a happier parent : raising a family, having a life, and loving (almost) every minute / KJ Dell'Antonia. Avery, 2018 311 p. ; **306.874**

1. Parenthood. 2. Parent and child. 3. Stress management.

ISBN 9780735210479

LC 2017301186

A former lead editor of the *New York Times* Motherlode blog presents a guide for overwhelmed parents on how to achieve greater happiness in everyday family life, drawing on the latest research to outline common missteps and practical solutions.

Gallagher, Shaun
Experimenting with babies : 50 amazing science projects you can perform on your kid / Shaun Gallagher. Perigee Book, 2013. xvi, 205 p. : **306.874**
1. Parent and child
ISBN 9780399162466
LC 2013021018

"Babies can be a joy-and hard work. Now, they can also be a 50-in-1 science project kit! This fascinating and hands-on guide shows you how to re-create landmark scientific studies on cognitive, motor, language, and behavioral development--using your own bundle of joy as the research subject. Simple, engaging, and fun for both baby and parent, each project sheds light on how your baby is acquiring new skills--everything from recognizing faces, voices, and shapes to understanding new words, learning to walk, and even distinguishing between right and wrong. Whether your little research subject is a newborn, a few months old, or a toddler, these simple, surprising projects will help you see the world through your baby's eyes--and discover ways to strengthen newly acquired skills during your everyday interactions".-- Provided by publisher.

"This is a unique work that presents an enjoyable and intelligent look at child development." Library Journal.

Glowacki, Jamie
Oh crap! I have a toddler : tackling these crazy awesome years--no time-outs needed / Jamie Glowacki. Gallery Book, 2019 viii, 292 p. ; **306.874**
1. Toddlers 2. Parenting 3. Child rearing
ISBN 9781982109738
LC 2018061341

Describes the avid curiosity that marks toddlerhood and its often-misunderstood behaviors, sharing strategies for promoting child potential in age-appropriate ways.

Graham, Barbara, 1947-
Eye of my heart : 27 writers reveal the hidden pleasures and perils of being a grandmother / edited by Barbara Graham; introduction by Mary Pipher. Harpercollins, 2009. 304 p. **306.874**
1. Grandmothers 2. Grandparenting 3. Parenting. 4. Grandparent and child 5. Essays
ISBN 9780061474156
LC bl2009013733

Twenty-five forefront women novelists, essayists, and journalists share unsentimental perspectives on the experiences of today's grandmothers, in a volume that features pieces by such writers as Elizabeth Berg, Bharati Mukherjee, and Judith Viorst.

Greene, Ross W
Raising human beings : creating a collaborative partnership with your child / Ross W. Greene, PhD. Scribner, 2016. xv, 281 p. ; **306.874**
1. Child rearing 2. Parent and child 3. Parenting
ISBN 9781476723747
LC 2016021664

The renowned child psychologist and best-selling author of The Explosive Child explains how to cultivate a better parent-child relationship while nurturing empathy, honesty, resilience and independence through balanced, non-adversarial parenting approaches.

"This book is a game-changer for parents, teachers, and other caregivers of children. Its advice is reasonable and empathetic, and readers will feel ready to start creating a better relationship with the children in their lives." Publishers Weekly.

Gresko, Brian,
When I first held you : 22 critically acclaimed writers talk about the triumphs, challenges, and transformative experience of fatherhood / edited by Brian Gresko. Berkley, 2014. 304 p. **306.874**
1. Fatherhood. 2. Fathers. 3. Parenting 4. Parents 5. Essays
ISBN 9780425269244
LC 2013050514

"This impressive collection deeply probes both the exterior and interior changes that come with fatherhood." Publishers Weekly.

Holroyd, Michael
A **book** of secrets : illegitimate daughters, absent fathers / Michael Holroyd. Farrar, Straus and Giroux, 2011. 272 p. **306.874**
1. Keppel, Alice, 1869-1947. 2. Fairfax, Evelyn Constance, 1871-1978. 3. Trefusis, Violet Keppel, 1894-1972 4. Illegitimacy 5. Child-separated fathers. 6. Single mothers. 7. Gifted women. 8. Italy.
ISBN 9780374115586
LC 2011003839

The award-winning author shares the stories of unknown women who played significant roles in the lives of prominent figures, including a mistress shared by the second Lord Grimthorpe and the Prince of Wales, a creative muse of Auguste Rodin and a novelist lover of Vita Sackville-West.

Hurley, Katie
No more mean girls : the secret to raising strong, confident, and compassionate girls / Katie Hurley, LCSW. TarcherPerigee, [2018] 320 p. **306.874**
1. Daughters. 2. Parenting. 3. Female friendship. 4. Compassion.
ISBN 9780143130864
LC 2017031973

A child and adolescent psychotherapist presents a guide for parents of young daughters in which they will learn how to help them navigate tricky territories such as friendship building, creating an authentic self, standing up for themselves and others and expressing themselves in a healthy way.

"Hurleys user-friendly layout and compassionate advice ensure that her book will be a useful workbook not just for parents, but also for youth counselors, teachers, and other caregivers." Publishers Weekly.

Isay, Jane
Unconditional love : a guide to navigating the joys and challenges of being a grandparent today / Jane Isay. Harper, 2018 x, 226 p. **306.874**
1. Grandparent and child. 2. Grandparenting.
ISBN 9780062427168
LC oc2018120130

"Isay... shares what it is to be a grandparent and how to keep family conflicts to a minimum and joy at the maximum in this lovely treatment of a widely shared experience." Publishers Weekly.

Leap, Jorja, 1955-
Project Fatherhood : a story of courage and healing in one of America's toughest communities / Jorja Leap. Beacon Press, 2015. 256 p. **306.874**
1. Leap, Jorja, 1955- 2. Former criminals 3. Fatherhood. 4. Father and child. 5. Parenting. 6. Los Angeles, California
ISBN 9780807014523
LC 2014043792

A reformed gang member who became a community activist describes his experiences working with a group of young men in South

Los Angeles, helping them to become better fathers despite their daily struggles and lacking of their own positive father figures.

"Leap observes and captures, in the member's own words, the group's development and its members four years of progress toward healing their families and, perhaps, their community." Publishers Weekly.

Lenz, Lyz

Belabored : a vindication of the rights of pregnant women / Lyz Lenz. Bold Type Books, 2020 224 p. **306.874**

1. Reproductive rights 2. Motherhood -- United States. 3. Pregnant women 4. Pregnancy 5. United States

ISBN 9781541762831

LC 2020001916

Journalist Lyz Lenz lays bare the misogynistic logic of U.S. cultural narratives about pregnancy, tracing them back to our murky, potent cultural soup of myths, from the religious to the historical. She details how sexist assumptions inform our expectations for pregnant people. An urgent call for us to embrace new narratives around pregnancy and the choice whether or not to have children, emphasizing wholeness and agency, and to reflect those values in our laws, medicine, and interactions with each other.

"By using her experiences to explore wide-ranging questions relating to motherhood, Lenz has joined the ranks of Jessica Valenti and others as a reframer (and hopefully reformer) of the politics of motherhood. A strong addition to courses in women's, gender, and sexuality studies." Library Journal

Lythcott-Haims, Julie

How to raise an adult : break free of the overparenting trap and prepare your kid for success / Julie Lythcott-Haims. Henry Holt and Co., 2015. 256 p. **306.874**

1. Parenting. 2. Overprotectiveness in parents 3. Parent and child. 4. Overprotection.

ISBN 9781627791779

LC 2014044394

A provocative manifesto exposes the detrimental effects of helicopter parenting and puts forth an alternative philosophy for raising self-sufficient young adults.

"Well-presented, solid facts that address the many detriments of helicopter parenting." Kirkus.

McConville, Brigid, 1956-

On becoming a mother : welcoming your new baby & your new life with wisdom from around the world / Brigid McConville. Oneworld, 2014. 291 p. : **306.874**

1. Childbirth. 2. Motherhood. 3. Pregnancy.

ISBN 1780743890

LC oc2014018252

Includes index.

An international celebration of pregnancy, childbirth, and the first months of a new baby's life.

"The American baby shower, Islamic naming ceremonies, and first birthdays in Korea sit comfortably next to each other in this global celebration of motherhood." Publishers Weekly.

Meeker, Margaret J.

★**Strong** mothers, strong sons : lessons mothers need to raise extraordinary men / Meg Meeker, M.D. Ballantine Books, 2014 xix, 341 p. ; **306.874**

1. Interpersonal relations. 2. Motherhood. 3. Mothers and sons. 4. Parenting.

ISBN 0345518098

LC 2014002148

Builds on the techniques introduced in Strong Fathers, Strong Daughters to counsel moms on how to promote health and success in boys, sharing related advice on rebuilding positive mother-son bonds.

Millwood, Molly

To have and to hold : motherhood, marriage, and the modern dilemma / Molly Millwood. HarperCollins 2019 288 p. **306.874**

1. Motherhood 2. New mothers 3. Mothers -- Psychology 4. Marriage

ISBN 9780062838650

LC bl2019008534

A clinical therapist and founding member of Vermont's Postpartum Wellness Project outlines practical recommendations for navigating the physical, professional and emotional complexities of early motherhood, including its impact on a marriage.

"Miller's resonant message is that everyone should acknowledge all facets of motherhood, including the negative. Mothers-to-be and parents of babies and young children may find it reassuring that it's typical to feel conflicted and even angry owing to the upheaval and transformation of their lives." Library Journal.

Pearlman, Catherine

Ignore it! : how selectively looking the other way can decrease behavioral problems and increase parenting satisfaction / Catherine Pearlman, PhD, LCSW. TarcherPerigee, 2017 256 p. **306.874**

1. Children -- Family relationships 2. Conflict management 3. Parenting

ISBN 9780143130338

LC oc2018142239

The founder of The Family Coach, a private practice that helps families resolve everyday problems, presents a groundbreaking parenting book that shows parents that, by "selectively ignoring" their kids' misbehavior, they allow their children the space they need to actually absorb the real-life consequences of negative behavior.

"Fun to read and written in a parent-to-parent voice, this is a welcome reintroduction of well-tested child-raising methods and should be required reading for all parents." Publishers Weekly.

Peri, Camille,

Because I said so : 33 mothers write about children, sex, men, aging, faith, race, & themselves / from the editors of Mothers who think, Camille Peri & Kate Moses. HarperCollins, 2005. xxi, 372 p. ; **306.874**

1. Motherhood. 2. Child rearing. 3. Families 4. Mothers -- Social conditions. 5. Essays

ISBN 9780060598785

LC bl2006012347

A collection of essays culled by the editors of Mothers Who Think explores the issues faced by twenty-first-century mothers, from raising kids in a pervasively sexualized culture and surviving illness, to managing racial and religious intolerance and struggling with custody battles.

"Women will appreciate the humor and candor, and men will gain insight into the stunning challenges of motherhood." Booklist.

Pipher, Mary Bray

Another country : navigating the emotional terrain of our elders / Mary Pipher. Riverhead Books, 1999. xx, 328 p. ; **306.874**

1. Aging parents -- United States -- Psychology. 2. Aging parents -- Family relationships -- United States. 3. Aging parents -- Care

-- United States. 4. Children of aging parents -- Family relationships -- United States.
ISBN 9781573221290

LC 98031877

An exploration into the period of transition that marks the beginnings of old age offers a compassionate view of ways to build communication between generations.

"The author is interested in studying the aging process in order to promote meaningful connections between the generations and more cultural support for pursuing them. Pipher describes strategies for dealing with illness, physical decline, the death of a husband or wife and the emotional problems that arise for both the elderly and their families. One of the strengths of this excellent study is that Pipher includes examples of troubled as well as rewarding marital and parent/child relationships." Publishers Weekly.

Sandler, Lauren

One and only : the freedom of having an only child, and the joy of being one / Lauren Sandler. Simon & Schuster, [2013] 256 p. **306.874**

1. Only child. 2. Family size. 3. Stereotypes (Social psychology) 4. Family relationships.
ISBN 9781451626957

LC 2013000707

"A prominent journalist, only child and mother of an only child presents an unstinting case in support of the benefits of one-child family life, challenging popular beliefs while offering perspectives on how single-child families can benefit the economy and environment while promoting child and parent autonomy."

Senior, Jennifer

All joy and no fun : the paradox of modern parenthood / Jennifer Senior. Ecco Press, 2014 384 p **306.874**

1. Parenting 2. Parent and child 3. Unhappiness 4. Child care
ISBN 9780062072221

LC 2013498720

Drawing on a vast array of sources in history, sociology, economics, psychology, philosophy and anthropology, an award-winning journalist challenges our culture's most basic beliefs about parenthood, while revealing the profound ways children deepen and add purpose to our lives.

"Full of fascinating ideas and information about the family structure and its history, this work is sure to be of strong interest to parents, in particular, as they look for meaning beyond the day to day." Library Journal.

Settersten, Richard A.

Not quite adults : why 20-somethings are choosing a slower path to adulthood, and why it's good for everyone / Rick Settersten and Barbara Ray. Delacorte Press, 2010. 256 p. **306.874**

1. Young adults. 2. Twenties (Age) 3. Adulthood. 4. Adults. 5. United States -- Social life and customs.
ISBN 9780553807400

LC 2010027109

"Drawing on eight years of data and more than 500 interviews with young people between 18 and 34, Richard Settersten and Barbara Ray dismantle the common belief that this generation has been coddled into laziness. Rather, these young adults have come of age at a particularly merciless moment. Not Quite Adults offers a valuable portrait of the diverging destinies of young people today." The Economist.

Traig, Jennifer

Act natural : a cultural history of misadventures in parenting / Jennifer Traig. Ecco, 2019. 320 p. **306.874**

1. Parenting -- History 2. Child rearing 3. Social history.
ISBN 9780062469809

LC 2018022056

From ancient Rome to Puritan New England to the Dr. Spock craze of mid-century America, the author, in this entertaining history of Western parenting, explores parenting techniques ranging from the misguided, to the nonsensical, to the truly horrifying.

Tsabary, Shefali, 1972-

★The **awakened** family : a revolution in parenting / Shefali Tsabary, Ph.D. Viking, 2016 xii, 348 p. ; **306.874**

1. Parenting 2. Parent and child 3. Families
ISBN 9780399563966

LC 2016003716

Explains how parents can raise children to be their best, most authentic selves without harmful competition, challenging popular parenting beliefs while discussing how to minimize anxiety and let go of impossible societal ideals.

Uhls, Yalda T.

Media moms & digital dads : a fact-not-fear approach to parenting in the digital age / Yalda T. Uhls, PhD. Bibliomotion, 2015. xxiv, 238 p. : **306.874**

1. Child rearing. 2. Parenting -- Social aspects. 3. Social media.
ISBN 1629560847

LC 2015021252

"A new media was unleashed upon the world and children took to it like ducks to water. Young people everywhere devoured its content, spending hours upon end immersed in it, while simultaneously ignoring the adults in their lives. Parents were understandably alarmed and worried that this new media was ruining young minds. It may surprise you to know that this new media was not the Internet, radio, or television but rather the 19th-century novel. Yes, parents were concerned that reading too much Jane Austin was going to ruin their children. Fast forward to today and we are still having the same conversation. Will digital media, in its various forms, ruin our children? In Media Moms & Digital Dads, former film producer turned child psychologist Yalda Uhls cautions parents not to be afraid of the changing state of media but to deal with the realities of how our kids engage with it. The truth is children today spend more time with media than they do with parents or in schools. And as parents, many of us did not have early exposure to the Internet, mobile phones, and gaming, making the world of our children somewhat foreign to us. The key, says Uhls, is to understand the pros and cons of media so that parents can make informed decisions about cause and effect, boundaries and exposure. Uhls debunks the myths around media by delving into the extensive body of social science research, proving that our kids are all right, and that parents can and must adapt to help their children thrive in the digital age. The author explores critical questions: Do kids learn better from paper versus screens? Why do tween girls post videos of themselves online asking if they are ugly? Do children really learn from video games? Is the era of the selfie creating self-obsessed children? Does the endless stream of information and multitasking lead to distraction? Do kids learn the same things about the world when they look at faces on screens versus in real life? Is the brain changing? This ground-breaking book will draw back the curtain and reveal the truth - often surprising and counterintuitive, and other times reassuring - in order to help guide the conversation about our digital age and the future of childhood".-- Provided by publisher.

"Research-based information, common sense, and opinion drive the discussion as questions are raised concerning when, where, and how the use of digital media is appropriate." ForeWord.

Warner, Judith, 1965-

And then they stopped talking to me : making sense of middle school / Judith Warner. Crown, 2020. 272 p. **306.874**

1. Middle school students 2. Middle schools 3. Parent and child 4. Social pressure

ISBN 9781101905883

LC 2019030216

Citing the convergence of developmental changes that often render the middle-school years difficult, a compassionate guide draws on student testimonies and professional insights to counsel parents on how to help middle-school children thrive.

"This readable, relatable, and well-documented account makes sense, and should help families survive the middle school years." Booklist

Warner, Judith

★**Perfect** madness : motherhood in the age of anxiety / Judith Warner. Riverhead Books, 2005. 327 p. **306.874**

1. Motherhood -- United States. 2. Mothers -- United States -- Social conditions. 3. Mothers -- Psychology. 4. Guilt.

ISBN 1573223042

LC 2004056615

"Writing from the perspective of her first few years of motherhood spent in France and her subsequent return to the U.S., Warner ponders the cultural factors driving the madness of pursuing perfect motherhood and the toll it is taking on American women." Booklist

The **strength** switch : how the new science of strength-based parenting can help you and your child flourish / Lea Waters, PhD. Avery, 2017 352 p. **306.874**

1. Parent and child. 2. Parenting.

ISBN 1101983663

LC 2017012619

Explains how making small shifts in one's parenting style can yield big results by uncovering a child's strengths, rather than focusing on his or her weaknesses. Includes diagrams.

"Waters's clearly presented, easily implemented ideas will make sense to parents looking to escape the corrective mind-set ." Publishers Weekly.

Xinran, 1958-

Message from an unknown Chinese mother : stories of loss and love / Xinran. Simon & Schuster, 2011, c2010. 240 p. **306.874**

1. Motherhood. 2. Abandoned girls. 3. Coping in women. 4. Infanticide. 5. China -- History -- 20th century.

ISBN 9781451610895

LC bl2011005837

Translated from the Chinese by Nicky Harman.

Originally published: London : Chatto & Windus, 2010.

Xinran has gained entrance to the most pained, secret chambers in the hearts of Chinese mothers--students, successful businesswomen, midwives, peasants--who have given up their daughters. Whether as a consequence of the single-child policy, destructive age-old traditions, or hideous economic necessity, these women had to give up their daughters for adoption; others even had to watch as their baby daughters were taken away at birth and drowned. Xinran beautifully portrays the "extra-birth guerrillas" who travel the roads and the railways, evading the system, trying to hold on to more than one baby; naive young girl students who have made life-wrecking mistakes; the "pebble mother" on the banks of the Yangzte River still looking into the depths for her stolen daughter; peasant women rejected by their families because they can't produce a male heir; and Little Snow, the orphaned baby fostered by Xinran but confiscated by the state.--Publisher.

"The author collects the heartbreaking stories of Chinese women forced to give up their baby girls because of the one-child-only policy or feudal traditions that prefer boys, in an oral history written for those abandoned daughters. This is a brutally honest book written for those relinquished children, so that they will know how much their birth mothers loved them and how--in the words of one mother who gave up her daughter--they paid for that love with an endless stream of bitter tears." Publishers Weekly.

306.874084 Aging parents

Morris, Virginia

How to care for aging parents : a one-step resource for all your medical, financial, housing, and emotional issues ; foreword by Jennie Chin Hansen / Virginia Morris. Workman Pub., 2014 xvi, 671 p. ; **306.874084**

1. Aging parents -- Family relationships -- Handbooks, manuals, etc. 2. Aging parents -- Care -- Handbooks, manuals, etc.

ISBN 9780761166764

LC 2014003071

Includes index.

Completely revised and updated, this comforting and authoritative guide offers support and advice for those caring for an elderly relative or friend, incorporating recent medical findings, information on fraud, helpful online resources and |aging in place| technologies.

Newman, Katherine S., 1953-

The **accordion** family : boomerang kids, anxious parents, and the private toll of global competition / Katherine S. Newman. Beacon Press, c2012. 288 p. **306.874084**

1. Parent and adult child. 2. Adult children -- Family relationships 3. International competition 4. Globalization

ISBN 9780807007433

LC 2011027846

Why are adults in their twenties and thirties boomeranging back to or never leaving their parents' homes in the world's wealthiest countries? Acclaimed sociologist Newman addresses this phenomenon in this timely and original book that uncovers fascinating links between globalization and the failure-to-launch trend.

Waichler, Iris

Role reversal : how to take care of yourself and your aging parents / Iris Waichler, MSW, LCSW. She Writes Press, 2016. xvii, 283 p. : **306.874084**

1. Aging parents -- Family relationships -- United States 2. Adult children of aging parents -- United States 3. Aging parents -- Care 4. Caregivers -- Family relationships

ISBN 9781631520914

LC bl2018086733

"Waichler, a medical social worker, delivers an intensely personal story of observing her parents' struggles with aging and shares plenty of lessons and strategies for people who find themselves in similar caregiver roles for their aging parents." Publishers Weekly

306.874086 LGBTQ parents

Rosswood, Eric

Journey to same-sex parenthood : firsthand advice, tips, and stories from lesbian and gay couples / Eric Rosswood ; foreword by Melissa Gilbert ; introduction by Charlie Condou. New Horizon Press, 2016 xix, 231 p. ; **306.874086**

1. Gay adoption. 2. Gay parents 3. Gay parents. 4. Lesbian couples as parents.

ISBN 0882825143

LC bl2016025055

Shares advice and firsthand accounts for same-sex couples that provide insight into the process of becoming parents, discussing five family-building paths and the unique challenges each presents.

306.8745 Grandparent-child relationship

Day, Marianne Waggoner

Camp Grandma : next-generation grandparenting -- beyond babysitting / Marianne Waggoner Day. She Writes Press, 2019. xxiii, 228 p. : **306.8745**

1. Grandparenting 2. Grandparent and child 3. Child development

ISBN 9781631525117

LC 2018958906

Includes index.

Camp Grandma reveals how a successful businesswoman merged her working career with her role as grandmother--and offers grandparents fun and creative ideas for enriching their relationships with their grandchildren while teaching the children valuable life skills that will help them grow strong and think critically. Readers will be introduced to a compelling, sometimes humorous, and totally unexpected twist on a role people often take for granted--as well as enter into the larger societal conversation we should be having about the possibilities and value of grandparenting, and how the women's movement has reinvigorated and reshaped not only women's approach to being grandmothers but also men's approach to the grandfather role. Warm cookies and milk are still okay, but what if they came with a workshop on goal setting or writing a business plan for the school year? Babysitting? Not even close.

306.88 Alteration of family arrangements

Meekhof, Kristin

A **widow's** guide to healing : gentle support and advice for the first 5 years / Kristin Meekhof, L MSW, James Windell, MA. Sourcebooks, Inc., 2015 xii, 244 p. ; **306.88**

1. Adjustment (Psychology) 2. Widowhood 3. Widows 4. Life skills guides.

ISBN 9781492620594

LC 2015013013

Focusing on the first five years of widowhood, a guide for women on how to manage the loss of a life partner shares advice on everything from estates and medical bills to single parenthood and navigating social situations.

306.89 Separation and divorce

Blackstone-Ford, Jann

Co-parenting through separation and divorce : putting your children first / Jann Blackstone, PsyD ; David L. Hill, MD, FAAP. American Academy of Pediatrics, 2020 xx, 260 p. : **306.89**

1. Children of divorced parents. 2. Parenting, Part-time. 3. Divorce.

ISBN 9781610023801

LC bl2020045694

Includes index.

"Parents going through separation or divorce are understandably worried about how the change in the family will affect their children. This guide walks parents through all the factors they should consider and offers step-by-step guidance on how to work together to put their children first. From sharing the news with children in an age-appropriate way to handling the issue of custody, from concerns about affairs or abuse to embarking on remarriage and blending families, Co-Parenting Through Separation and Divorce offers a roadmap through one of life's most difficult challenges with the goal of healthy, happy kids informing every decision along the way."-- Provided by publisher.

Emery, Robert E.

Two homes, one childhood : a parenting plan to last a lifetime / Robert E. Emery, PhD. Avery, 2016. 325 p. ; **306.89**

1. Children of divorced parents. 2. Parent and child. 3. Parenting.

ISBN 1594634157

LC 2016010866

A paradigm-shifting approach to sharing custody builds on the author's philosophies in The Truth About Children and Divorce to outline a long-term, customizable plan that provides for the developing needs of families in more than one home.

Green, Janice, 1948-

★**Divorce** after 50 : your guide to the unique legal & financial challenges of a gray divorce / Attorney Janice Green. Nolo, 2019. 370 p. ; **306.89**

1. Divorce -- Law and legislation -- United States 2. Middle-aged persons -- United States

ISBN 9781413325935

LC 2018037647

Includes index.

Discusses the emotional, social, legal, and financial effects of late-life divorce.

Moffett, Kay

Not your mother's divorce : a practical, girlfriend-to-girlfriend guide to surviving the end of an early marriage / Kay Moffett and Sarah Touborg. Broadway Books, 2003. 259 p. ; **306.89**

1. Divorce -- Psychological aspects. 2. Young women 3. Young women -- Conduct of life. 4. Young women -- Psychology. 5. Life skills guides.

ISBN 0767913507

LC 2003058531

An empowering guide to divorce for young women without children addresses the challenges of young women who divorce early in life, sharing legal and practical advice for such areas as breaking the news to others, changing one's name, protecting oneself financially, and reentering the dating scene.

"The authors help young divorce's tackle both legal and emotional problems. Overwhelming issues like mutual photographs, wedding rings, and family, as well as legal console, mediators, and even Internet divorce, are discussed with authority and sensitivity. The authors realize that each person is different and comes out her relationship with a different set of circumstances, so they also provide many personal stories--including their own." Library Journal.

Riss, Suzanne

The **optimist's** guide to divorce : how to get through your breakup and create a new life you love / Suzanne Riss & Jill Sockwell. Workman Publishing, 2016. x, 278 p. : **306.89**

1. Divorce -- Psychological aspects. 2. Divorce. 3. Divorced women 4. Life skills guides.

ISBN 0761187421

LC 2016053408

"Close to 50 percent of marriages in America fail, leading to about 1.5 million divorces a year. But for Suzanne Riss and Jill Sockwell, who've been there and done that, there's no comfort in statics, only community. Community is the one thing that can turn the shattering experience of divorce into a tolerable one--and, finally, a positive one. And community is what the authors offer in their inspiring and brilliantly helpful book, The Optimist's Guide to Divorce. This is the girlfriend-to-girlfriend guide that belongs in the hands of every one of those 1.5 million divorcing women. It's the book that draws on real women's experiences--not only the authors' but ten other women from the support group the authors started who all share their stories, insights,and wisdom. It's the book that gets into the trenches at the beginning of the process, in the section called Deal, which focuses on what readers need to know right away -- including how to tell the kids, confront the financial issues, figure out where to live, find legal help, and emotionally get through the day. From there it moves to Heal, which helps readers work through their anger, loss, and sadness and develop an action plan for the future. And, finally, Reveal, when it's time to celebrate the hard work and a new, stronger self. Because--in the succinct words of the book's underlying promise--the best time to find yourself is after losing him. Direct, warm, friendly, humorous, it's the book that will get every reader into a better relationship with the one person she'll be with for the rest of her life-herself".-- Provided by publisher.

"From varying backgrounds and portrayed with their identifying details obscured, they've left passionless, abusive, or faithless unions, or been left themselves. The overall effect is a chorus of relatable, emotional, and true-feeling stories about the many facets of divorce that will have newly single advice-seekers feeling less alone and more sure theyll get through it, too." Booklist.

Sexton, James J.

If you're in my office, it's already too late : a divorce lawyer's guide to staying together / James J. Sexton, Esq. Henry Holt and Company, 2018 xix, 262 p. : **306.89**

1. Married people 2. Marriage. 3. Advice 4. Interpersonal conflict.

ISBN 9781250130778

LC 2017042566

A divorce lawyer offers advice on how to maintain a lasting, fulfilling, and loving marriage.

Wallerstein, Judith S.

The **unexpected** legacy of divorce : a 25 year landmark study / Judith Wallerstein, Julia Lewis and Sandra Blakeslee. Hyperion, 2000. xxxv, 347 p. **306.89**

1. Children of divorced parents -- Longitudinal studies. 2. Divorce -- Longitudinal studies. 3. Families -- United States. 4. Marriage.

ISBN 0786863943

LC 00035071

A landmark cultural event that changed the way all of us view divorce. More than a quarter century ago, Judith Wallerstein began talking to a group of 131 children whose parents were all going through a divorce. From those conversations have come two bestsellers: Surviving the Breakup and Second Chances. This third volume of the longitudinal study, The Unexpected Legacy of Divorce, brings all of her research up to the present and shows for the first time how children are affected by divorce long into adulthood. Using a comparison group of adults who grew up in the same communities but whose parents never divorced, Wallerstein shows how adult children of divorce essentially view life differently from their peers in intact homes, and also sheds light on the question that so many parents confront--whether to stay unhappily married or to divorce. This book is a landmark cultural event that changes the way all of us view divorce.

"The author follows her two studies on the effects of divorce on children (Surviving the Breakup, 1980; Second Chances, 1989) with this third study of 93 adults whom she first interviewed as children 25 years ago. Her findings are presented through five very readable case studies interwoven with other data." Library Journal.

306.9 Institutions pertaining to death

Doughty, Caitlin

Will my cat eat my eyeballs? : big questions from tiny mortals about death / Caitlin Doughty ; illustrated by Diann Ruz. W. W. Norton & Co., 2019. 208 p. **306.9**

1. Dead 2. Death 3. Undertakers 4. Biodegradation

ISBN 9780393652703

The creator of the "Ask a Mortician" web series and best-selling author provides comprehensive, science based answers to common questions about death, dead bodies and decomposition.

"An entertaining read, straightforward without being morbid. Of interest to anyone, young or old, who is curious about what happens to our bodies after we die." Library Journal.

Lovejoy, Bess

Rest in pieces : the curious fates of famous corpses / Bess Lovejoy. Simon & Schuster, 2013. 256 p. **306.9**

1. Dead -- Miscellanea. 2. Celebrities' gravesites. 3. Celebrities -- Miscellanea. 4. Death -- Humor.

ISBN 9781451654981

LC 2012034706

The writer and researcher behind the best-selling Schott's Almanac presents a whimsically macabre collection of tales about the posthumous adventures of famous remains, from the dynasty founded by Alexander the Great's corpse to the American road trip taken by Einstein's brain.

Sacks, Oliver, 1933-2015

Gratitude / Oliver Sacks. Alfred A. Knopf, 2015. 45 p. **306.9**

1. Sacks, Oliver, 1933-2015 2. Death 3. Neurologists 4. Authors 5. Sick persons 6. Essays

ISBN 9780451492937

LC bl2015052034

No writer has succeeded in capturing the medical and human drama of illness as honestly and as eloquently as Oliver Sacks. During the last few months of his life, he wrote a set of essays in which he movingly explored his feelings about completing a life and coming to terms with his own death.

Schechter, Harold

The **whole** death catalog : a lively guide to the bitter end / Harold Schechter. Ballantine Books, c2009. xiv, 304 p. : **306.9**

1. Death. 2. Mortality.

ISBN 9780345499646

LC 2009013779

Includes index.

Explores all facets of death with a variety of facts, anecdotes, practical information, and wisdom in an irreverent yet meticulously researched sourcebook.

"The author offers readers a scholarly yet wildly hilarious romp through the cultural history of death and dying. It is not only rollicking entertainment but also provides a wealth of practical and historical information about death." Library Journal.

307.1 Planning and development

Binelli, Mark

Detroit City is the place to be : the afterlife of an American metropolis / Mark Binelli. Metropolitan Books, 2012. 336 p. **307.1**

1. Urban beautification. 2. Environmental planning. 3. Urban planning -- United States -- Case studies. 4. Architecture. 5. Detroit, Michigan.

ISBN 9780805092295

LC 2012016123

Includes index.

Once America's capitalist dream town, Detroit is our country's greatest urban failure, having fallen the longest and the farthest. But the city's worst crisis yet (and that's saying something) has managed to do the unthinkable: turn the end of days into a laboratory for the future. Urban planners, land speculators, neo-pastoral agriculturalists, and utopian environmentalists all have been drawn to Detroit's baroquely decaying, nothing-left-to-lose frontier.--Publisher's description.

Cornett, Mick

The **next** American city : the big promise of our midsize metros / Mick Cornett, with Jayson White. G.P. Putnam's Sons, 2018. 288 p. **307.1**

1. Urban planning 2. Cities and towns -- Growth 3. Urban sociology 4. Urban policy 5. United States

ISBN 9780399575099

LC 2018022150

Includes index.

From the four-term Oklahoma City mayor comes a hopeful and illuminating look at the dynamic and inventive urban centers that will lead the United States in coming years.

Graham, Wade

Dream cities : seven urban ideas that shape the world / Wade Graham. HarperCollins, 2016 320 p. **307.1**

1. Urban planning 2. Cities and towns 3. Architecture 4. City life

ISBN 9780062196316

LC bl2015053772

A California-based garden designer, historian and writer presents a highly accessible and entertaining cultural history of modern cities as told through the eyes of the pivotal dreamers and brilliant, obsessed and sometimes megalomaniacal designers behind the concepts.

307.121609 City planning--History, geographic treatment, biography

Sudjic, Deyan

The **language** of cities / Deyan Sudjic. Allen Lane, 2016. 230 p. : **307.121609**

1. Cities and towns 2. City life 3. City dwellers 4. Urban planning

ISBN 9780241188040

We live in a world that is now predominantly urban. So how do we define the city as it evolves in the 21st century? Drawing examples from across the globe, Deyan Sudjic decodes the underlying forces that shape our cities, such as resources and land, to the ideas that shape conscious elements of design, whether of buildings or of space. Erudite and entertaining, he considers the differences between capital cities and the rest to understand why it is that we often feel more comfortable in our identities as Londoners, Muscovites, or Mumbaikars than in our national identities.

"This title by design historian . . . and director of London's Design Museum, Sudjic's is the most celebratory book about cities to come along for years." Library Journal.

307.3 Structure

Duneier, Mitchell

★**Ghetto** : the invention of a place, the history of an idea / Mitchell Duneier. Farrar, Straus and Giroux, 2016 224 p. **307.3**

1. Inner city -- United States 2. Segregation -- History. 3. Ghettoes 4. Ghettoes, Jewish

ISBN 9780374161804

LC 2015036373

Chronicles the history of the ghetto, from its beginnings in the 16th century as a Venetian edict forcing Jewish citizens to live in a closed quarter, to its revival by the Nazis in the 20th century, to its urban manifestations in the present-day world.

"Americans did not create the ghetto, but in this well-documented study, we see clearly how those urban areas have come to embody so many of our shortcomings when it comes to matters of race." Kirkus.

Moss, Jeremiah

Vanishing New York : how a great city lost its soul / Jeremiah Moss. Dey Street Books, 2017. 352 p. **307.3**

1. Urban renewal 2. Gentrification of cities 3. Community life. 4. City life. 5. New York City

ISBN 9780062439697

LC bl2017030665

The writer behind the popular blog, "Vanishing New York," discusses the unwelcome shift to gentrification taking root around Manhattan and provides a sad tour through beloved neighborhoods that have lost their treasured and unofficial landmarks.

"New York, he argues in a brilliantly written and well-informed account, is losing its bohemian flair and often raffish charm." Booklist.

Philp, Drew

A **$500** house in Detroit : rebuilding an abandoned home and an American city / Drew Philp. Scribner, 2017 256 p. **307.3**

1. Philp, Drew Homes and haunts. 2. Houses -- Remodeling. 3. Urban renewal. 4. Gentrification of cities. 5. Houses -- Conservation and restoration. 6. Detroit, Michigan.

ISBN 9781476797984

LC 2016046283

A man describes his experiences buying a house in Detroit in 2009 for $500 and rebuilding it himself and shares the struggles, pain and joy of being part of the rebirth of a city in massive decline.

"Philp ably outlines the broad issues of race and class in the city, but it is the warmth and liveliness of his storytelling that will win many readers." Kirkus.

307.76 Urban communities

Badkhen, Anna, 1976-

Fisherman's blues : a West African community at sea / Anna Badkhen. Riverhead Books, 2018. 256 p. **307.76**

1. Fishing villages 2. Fishers 3. Sociocultural anthropology 4. Coastal towns 5. Joal-Fadiout, Senegal -- Social conditions. 6. Senegal -- Social conditions.

ISBN 9781594634864

LC 2017030225

"An intimate and unexpected account of life in the largest artisanal fishing village in West Africa, caught between the ancient and the modern, and dependent on an ocean that is being radically transformed".--Provided by publisher.

"Badkhen is a spellbinding writer, her observations at once hypnotic and elegiac, witnessing a fragile community just barely getting by." Booklist.

Duany, Andres

Suburban nation : the rise of sprawl and the decline of the American Dream / Andres Duany, Elizabeth Plater-Zyberk, and Jeff Speck. North Point Press, c2000. xiv, [290] p. : **307.76**

1. Urbanization -- United States. 2. Suburbs -- United States. 3. Community development -- United States. 4. Urban planning -- United States. 5. United States.

ISBN 0865475571

LC 99052186

Three members of the Founders of the Congress for the New Urbanism give voice to a growing movement in North America to put an end to suburban sprawl and to replace the automobile-based settlement patterns of the past fifty years with a return to traditional planning principles.

Glaeser, Edward L. (Edward Ludwig), 1967-

Triumph of the city : how our greatest invention makes us richer, smarter, greener, healthier, and happier / Edward L. Glaeser. Penguin Press, 2011. 400 p. **307.76**

1. Urbanization. 2. Cities and towns -- Growth. 3. Urban economics. 4. Urban sociology.

ISBN 9781594202773

LC 2010034609

A pioneering urban economist poses arguments for the city's potential for securing the world's future, challenging common perceptions to reveal why cities are actually more environmentally sound and are comprised of healthier and wealthier populations.

Grandin, Greg, 1962-

Fordlandia : the rise and fall of Henry Ford's forgotten jungle city / Greg Grandin. Metropolitan Books, 2009. xii, 416 p. : **307.76**

1. Ford, Henry, 1863-1947 Political and social views. 2. Ford Motor Company -- History. 3. Planned communities. 4. Rubber plantations. 5. Culture conflict. 6. Capitalism and imperialism. 7. Fordlandia, Brazil -- History. 8. Brazil -- Civilization. 9. Amazon Valley -- Social conditions.

ISBN 9780805082364

LC 2008049642

National Book Award for Nonfiction finalist, 2009

National Book Critics Circle Award for Nonfiction finalist, 2009.

Pulitzer Prize for History finalist, 2010.

Shortlisted for the James Tait Black Memorial Prize for Biography, 2010

This never-before-told story of the auto magnate's attempt to recreate small-town America, along with a rubber plantation, in the heart of the Amazon details the epic clash between Ford and the jungle and its inhabitants, as the tycoon attempted to force his will on the natural world.

Green, Hardy

The **company** town : the industrial Edens and satanic mills that shaped the American economy / Hardy Green. Basic Books, 2010. 264 p. **307.76**

1. Company towns. 2. Industries -- History. 3. Labor-management relations. 4. Capitalism.

ISBN 9780465018260

LC 2010013434

A history of how companies have created communities for their workers explores both the positive and negative effects the institution of "the company town" has had--on the one hand, companies have tried to take care of their workers and their families; on the other, they have also exploited the workers and tried to extract as much labor for as little compensation possible.

Knox, Paul L,

Atlas of cities / edited by Paul Knox. Princeton University Press, 2014. 256 p. : **307.76**

1. Urbanization. 2. Cities and towns -- Growth.

ISBN 9780691157818

LC bl2014039639

Examines different cities from all over the world and looks at their physical, economic, social, and political structure, as well as their relationships to each other and where future urbanization might be headed.

Mumford, Lewis, 1895-1990

The **city** in history : its origins, its transformations, and its prospects / Lewis Mumford. Harcourt, Brace & Co., 1989, c1961. xi, 657 p., 64 p. of plates : **307.76**

1. Cities and towns -- History. 2. City life -- History.

ISBN 9780156180351

LC 61007689

National Book Award for Nonfiction, 1962.

An examination of cities of the Western world tracing their development from Egypt through the Middle Ages to the present.

Smith, Peter D. (Peter Daniel), 1965-

City : a guidebook for the urban age / P.D. Smith. Bloomsbury, 2012. 352 p. **307.76**

1. Cities and towns -- History. 2. City life -- History. 3. Urban sociology.

ISBN 9781608196760

LC 2011051430

A sumptuously illustrated tribute to city dwelling surveys thousands of years of history to trace urban languages, customs, economies and more, comparing examples from ancient through modern times while providing mini essays on such topics as the Tower of Babel and SimCity. By the author of Doomsday Men.

Wilson, David Sloan

The **neighborhood** project : using evolution to improve my city, one block at a time / David Sloan Wilson. Little, Brown and Company, 2011. 448 p. **307.76**

1. Cities and towns -- Growth. 2. Urban planning 3. Environmentalism 4. Civic improvement.

ISBN 9780316037679

LC 2011002752

An evolutionary biologist applies the ideas of evolutionary science to his post-industrial hometown and uses the traits he discovers, including what bullying feeds on and how neighborhood quality affects test scores, to improve the lives of his fellow citizens.

"Although the book meanders, Wilson gives a vivid, in-depth description of several scientific studies, and offers a biography for each scientist he cites; the tangents are mostly pleasurable and provide more evidence for how lives, like ideas, intersect in fascinating ways." Publishers Weekly.

307.760973 Cities--United States

Ehrenhalt, Alan, 1947-

The **great** inversion and the future of the American city / Alan Ehrenhalt. Knopf, 2012. 272 p. **307.760973**

1. Cities and towns. 2. Gentrification of cities. 3. Urban sociology. 4. Urban planning.
ISBN 9780307272744

LC 2011035139

"This is a Borzoi book."

"Alan Ehrenhalt, one of our leading urbanologists, takes us to cities across the country to reveal how the roles of America's cities and suburbs are changing places--young adults and affluent retirees moving in, while immigrants and the less affluent aremoving out--and the implications for the future of our society. How will our nation be changed by the populations shifting in and out of the cities? Why are these shifts taking place? Ehrenhalt answers these and other questions in this illuminating study. He shows us how mass transit has revitalized inner-city communities in Chicago and Brooklyn, New York, while inner suburbs like Cleveland Heights struggle to replace the earlier generation of affluent tax-paying residents who left for more distant suburbs; how the sprawl of Phoenix has frustrated attempts to create downtown retail spaces that can attract large crowds; and how numerous suburban communities have created downtown areas to appeal to the increasing demand for walkable commercial zones. Finally, he explains what cities need to do to keep the affluent and educated attracted to and satisfied with downtown life. An eye-opening and thoroughly engaging look at American urban/suburban society and its future".-- Provided by publisher.

Klinenberg, Eric

Palaces for the people : how social infrastructure can help fight inequality, polarization, and the decline of civic life / Eric Klinenberg. Crown, 2018. 336 p. **307.760973**

1. Infrastructure 2. Urban planning 3. Equality 4. Quality of life 5. United States -- Social conditions
ISBN 9781524761165

LC 2018002837

Explains how the resilience of communities can be found not only in shared values but in such shared spaces as libraries, child-care centers, and gardens that enable life-transforming human connections.

307.77 Self-contained communities

Wayland-Smith, Ellen, 1966-

Oneida : from free love utopia to the well-set table / Ellen Wayland-Smith. Picado USA, 2016. 336 p. **307.77**

1. Sexual freedom 2. Religious communities 3. Spiritual life 4. Gender equity 5. New York (State)
ISBN 9781250043085

LC 2015044336

Tells the uniquely American story of a community whose radical notions of equality, sex and religion transformed into a symbol of American middle-class respectability.

"This book is a fascinating look into the strange history of Oneida silverware and how its origins reflect an exhilarating period of American history." Publishers Weekly.

320 Political science (Politics and government)

Aristotle

Politics / Aristotle ; translated by Ernest Barker; revised with an introduction and notes by R.F. Stalley. Oxford University Press, c1998. xlvii, 423 p. : **320**

1. Political science -- Early works to 1800
ISBN 9780192833938

LC 98215869

The Politics is one of the most influential texts in the history of political thought, and it raises issues which still confront anyone who wants to think seriously about the ways in which human societies are organized and governed. By examining the way societies are run--from households to city states--Aristotle establishes how successful constitutions can best be initiated and upheld. --Provided by publisher

Cohen, Richard E.

The **almanac** of American politics 2020 : members of Congress and governors: their profiles and election results, their states and districts / Richard E. Cohen, Charlie Cook ; senior authors, Louis Jacobson, Louis Peck ; [Abby Livingston, Jessica Taylor, Cameron Joseph] ; founding author, Michael Barone. Columbia Books & Information Services, National Journal, 2019. xx, 2043 p. : **320**

1. United States. Congress 2. United States. Congress Committees. 3. Election districts -- United States 4. Almanacs.
ISBN 9781938939891

The 2020 edition includes: In-depth profile of every governor, Senator, and House member. Updated demographic information for every state and district, including information from the Census Bureau's American Community Survey, with new categories of economic, occupational, social and geographic data.

Jay, Antony, 1930-2016

Lend me your ears : Oxford dictionary of political quotations / edited by Sir Antony Jay. Oxford University Press, 2010. xxv, 446 p. ; **320**

1. Political science -- Quotations, maxims, etc. 2. Politicians -- Quotations.
ISBN 9780199572670

LC 2010923325

"Previous editions published as Oxford dictionary of political quotations"--T.p. verso.

Includes index.

"Caligula, William Shakespeare, Crazy Horse, and 1,500 other commentators from ancient Greek philosophers to Sarah Palin trade remarks profound, caustic, trenchant, and humorous in this entertaining omnibus." Choice

Reid-Henry, Simon

Empire of democracy : the remaking of the West since the Cold War, 1971-2017 / Simon Reid-Henry. Simon & Schuster,

2019. 880 p. **320**

1. Democracy -- History 2. Liberalism 3. Cold War 4. Social change 5. Western bloc
ISBN 9781451684964

LC 2019013544

Describes the new political-economic order that took hold after the Cold War ended and how the emerging politicians, Thatcher, Reagan, Mitterand and Kohl affected the economic boom that eventually led to the fiasco in Iraq and the 2008 financial crisis.

"One of the important books of the current dialog on Western democracy. All serious scholars and informed political science and history readers should find it worth the effort." Library Journal.

320.01 Philosophy and theory

Acemoglu, Daron

The **narrow** corridor : states, societies, and the fate of liberty / Daron Acemoglu, James A. Robinson. Penguin Press, 2019. 496 p. **320.01**

1. Freedom 2. State (Political science) 3. Power (Social sciences) -- Political aspects 4. Democracy
ISBN 9780735224384

LC 2019009146

"A crucial new big-picture framework that answers the question of how liberty flourishes in some states but falls to authoritarianism or anarchy in others--and explains how it can continue to thrive despite new threats".-- Provided by publisher.

Hobbes, Thomas, 1588-1679

Leviathan / Thomas Hobbes ; edited by J.C.A. Gaskin. Oxford University Press, 2008. 508 p. **320.01**

1. Political science -- Philosophy
ISBN 9780199537280

LC oc2008095159

Leviathan is both a magnificent literary achievement and the greatest work of political philosophy in the English language. Permanently challenging, it has found new applications and new refutations in every generation. This new edition reproduces the first printed text, retaining the original punctuation but modernizing the spelling. It offers exceptionally thorough and useful annotation, an introduction that guides the reader through the complexities of Hobbes's arguments, and a substantial index. --Provided by publisher

Ryan, Alan, 1940-

On politics : a history of political thought from Herodotus to the present / Alan Ryan. W. W. Norton & Co., 2012. 2 v. (1120 p.) **320.01**

1. Political science -- Philosophy -- History. 2. Political scientists -- History. 3. Thought and thinking -- Political aspects 4. Ideology
ISBN 9780871404657

LC 2012012351

Traces the origins of political philosophy and the lives of the great thinkers from the ancient Greeks to Machiavelli to Hobbes and to the present and illuminates the ideas and beliefs that helped shape each era.

320.082 Women in politics

Moscatello, Caitlin

See Jane win : the inspiring story of the women changing American politics / Caitlin Moscatello. E.P. Dutton, 2019. 336 p. **320.082**

1. Women politicians 2. Women legislators 3. Women political activists 4. Political participation -- United States 5. United States -- Politics and government -- 21st century
ISBN 9781524742928

LC 2019011447

The award-winning journalist best known for New York magazine's "The Cut" shares insider perspectives into the female candidates who fought back and won crucial elections in 2018, from Abigail Spanberger and Catalina Cruz to Anna Eskamani and London Lamar.

"While the percent of women in office has been relatively static prior to the recent influx, Moscatello optimistically and realistically balances a blend of demographics and anecdotes from the candidates and politicians, painting a provocative picture about the impact of equalizing representation in the American political world. Memorable stories and illustrative data combine in a pertinent political and cultural analysis." Kirkus.

Steinhauer, Jennifer

The **firsts** : the inside story of the women reshaping Congress / Jennifer Steinhauer. Algonquin Books of Chapel Hill, 2020. 262 p. **320.082**

1. United States. Congress. 2. Women legislators -- United States. 3. Women -- Political activity -- United States. 4. United States -- Politics and government -- 21st century.
ISBN 9781616209995

A lively, behind-the-scenes look at the historic cohort of diverse, young, and groundbreaking women newly elected to the House of Representatives in 2018 as they arrive in Washington, DC, and start working for change.

"A fine lesson in civics and political journalism and must reading for anyone contemplating working in electoral politics." Kirkus.

320.1 The state

Cicero, Marcus Tullius

The **republic** : and the laws / Cicero; a new translation by Niall Rudd. Oxford University Press, 2008, c1998. 288 p. **320.1**

1. Political science -- Early works to 1800 2. Utopias. 3. Natural law 4. State (Political science) -- Early works to 1800 5. Rome -- Politics and government -- 265-30 B.C.
ISBN 9780199540112

LC oc2008018000

This translation originally published: 1998.

Cicero's The Republic is an impassioned plea for responsible government written just before the civil war that ended the Roman Republic in a dialogue following Plato. Drawing on Greek political theory, the work embodies the mature reflections of a Roman ex-consul on the nature of political organization, on justice in society, and on the qualities needed in a statesman. Its sequel, The Laws, expounds the influential doctrine of Natural Law, which applies to all mankind, and sets out an ideal code for a reformed Roman Republic, already half in the realm of utopia. --Provided by publisher

Fukuyama, Francis

Political order and political decay : from the industrial revolution to the globalization of democracy / Francis Fukuyama. Farrar, Straus and Giroux, 2014. 672 p. **320.1**

1. State (Political science) -- History 2. Comparative government

-- History. 3. Democracy -- History. 4. Order (Philosophy)
ISBN 9780374227357

LC 2014016973

Sequel to: The origins of political order : from prehuman times to the French Revolution

Taking up the essential question of how societies develop strong, impersonal, and accountable political institutions, Fukuyama follows the story from the French Revolution to the so-called Arab Spring and the deep dysfunctions of contemporary American politics. He examines the effects of corruption on governance, and why some societies have been successful at rooting it out. He explores the different legacies of colonialism in Latin America, Africa, and Asia, and offers a clear-eyed account of why some regions have thrived and developed more quickly than others. And he boldly reckons with the future of democracy in the face of a rising global middle class and entrenched political paralysis in the West. A sweeping, masterful account of the struggle to create a well-functioning modern state, Political Order and Political Decay is destined to be a classic.

"A compelling historical overview of a useful template for the retooling of institutions in the modern state. Systematic, thorough and even hopeful fodder for reform-minded political observers." Kirkus.

Machiavelli, Niccolo, 1469-1527

★The **prince** / Niccolo Machiavelli ; translated by W.K. Marriott ; with an introduction by Dominic Baker-Smith. Knopf, c1992. xxxi, 190 p. ; **320.1**

1. Political science -- Early works to 1800. 2. Political ethics -- Early works to 1800.
ISBN 9780679410447

Translation of: Principe, first published in 1532.

"This translation first published in Penguin Classics 1961"-- T.p. verso.

Records the Italian statesman's classic statement on the nature of government and the means by which political power is obtained.

Rousseau, Jean-Jacques, 1712-1778

The **social** contract / Jean-Jacques Rousseau ; translated by Maurice Cranston. Penguin Books, 2006. 167 p. ; **320.1**

1. Political science -- Early works to 1800 2. Social contract. 3. Philosophy. 4. Freedom.
ISBN 0143037498

LC 2006043772

Translation of : Du contrat social.

Originally published in France in 1762.

Rousseau sought to ground his political theory in an understanding of human nature, which he believed to be basically good but corrupted by the conflicting interests within society. Here self-interest degenerated into a state of war from which humanity could only be extricated by the imposition of a contract. As a party to the compact, each individual would find his true interest served within the political expression of the community of man, or the general will.

320.473 Structure and functions of government -- United States

Moss, David A., 1964-

Democracy : a case study / David A. Moss. The Belknap Press of Harvard University Press, 2017. 690 p. **320.473**

1. Democracy -- United States 2. Social conflict 3. Social change 4. Political science 5. United States -- Politics and government Case studies.
ISBN 9780674971455

LC 2016020796

Historian David Moss adapts the case study method made famous by Harvard Business School to revitalize our conversations about governance and democracy and show how the United States has often thrived on political conflict. These 19 cases ask us to weigh choices and consequences, wrestle with momentous decisions, and come to our own conclusions.-- Provided by publisher

Sunstein, Cass R.,

Can it happen here? : authoritarianism in America / edited by Cass R. Sunstein. Dey Street Books, 2018. 272 p. **320.473**

1. Fascism 2. Authoritarianism 3. Democracy 4. Political participation 5. United States -- Politics and government -- 21st century 6. Essays
ISBN 9780062696199

LC 2018275323

The Harvard professor and best-selling author of The World According to Star Wars presents a collection of essays by some of today's brightest minds on the vulnerability of America to authoritarianism and how the election of Donald Trump, the rise of propaganda and the shortcomings of our elections processes are curtailing democratic freedoms.

"While the contributors express a healthy variety of opinions about the direction the country is heading, they do agree that we must be vigilant against authoritarian figures exploiting our open society to aggregate power. History has shown that it is possible to irrevocably damage a democracy." Booklist.

320.51 Liberalism

Brennan, Jason, 1979-

Libertarianism : what everyone needs to know / Jason Brennan. Oxford University Press, 2012. xvi, 213 p. ; What everyone needs to know **320.51**

1. Libertarianism -- United States. 2. United States -- Politics and government.
ISBN 9780199933891

LC 2012020049

Presents an introduction to libertarianism, describing how libertarians view such topics as human nature, government, democracy, civil rights, economics, social justice, and contemporary problems, including immigration, health care, and education.

Maxwell, Zerlina

The **end** of white politics : how to heal our liberal divide / Zerlina Maxwell. Hachette Books, 2020 256 p. **320.51**

1. Democratic Party. 2. Whiteness (Concept) 3. Progressivism (United States politics) 4. Democrats 5. Race awareness -- Political aspects 6. United States -- Politics and government
ISBN 9780306873614

LC bl2020016199

A political analyst discusses how Donald Trump tapped into white male angst in his winning campaign and what progressives can do to help forge a new coalition that more accurately reflects the diversity of the American electorate.

"With a style that is as infectious as it is cogent and accessible, the author outlines and defends her recommendations and strategies so thoroughly that the only possible dissent is a willful disregard for the future of not just the Democratic Party, but the future of all but the most privileged Americans." Kirkus

320.520973 Conservatism--United States

Allitt, Patrick

★The **conservatives** : ideas and personalities throughout American history / Patrick Allitt. Yale University Press, c2009. x, 325 p. ; **320.520973**

1. Conservatism -- United States -- History. 2. Conservatives. 3. Politicians. 4. Political science. 5. United States -- Politics and government.

ISBN 9780300118940

LC 2008042559

"From present-day questions of taxation and big government, Allitt traces conservative principles to the earliest days of the republic. Cutting across the stereotypes of present-day conservatism, this nuanced, thoughtful history should educate the unaffiliated and help the disillusioned recover." Publishers Weekly.

Dionne, E. J.

Why the right went wrong : conservatism-- from Goldwater to the Tea Party and beyond / E.J. Dionne, Jr. Simon & Schuster, 2016 384 p. **320.520973**

1. Conservatism -- United States -- History. 2. Political parties 3. Conservatives 4. Politicians

ISBN 9781476763798

LC 2015027336

A best-selling author and syndicated columnist for The Washington Post describes the history of the conservative right since the 1960s and discusses his belief that the Tea Party is the direct ideological descendant of the Goldwater movement.

Flake, Jeff, 1962-

Conscience of a conservative : a rejection of destructive politics and a return to principle / Jeff Flake. Random House, 2017. 160 p. **320.520973**

1. Conservatism 2. Ideology 3. Political science 4. Populism 5. United States -- Politics and government -- 2009-2017

ISBN 9780399592911

LC bl2017031615

In a bold act of conscience, Republican Senator Jeff Flake takes his party to task for embracing nationalism, populism, xenophobia, and the anomalous Trump presidency. The book is an urgent call for a return to bedrock conservative principle and a cry to once again put country before party.

"The junior senator from Arizona offers a critical (in both senses of the word) look at the Republican Party." Booklist.

Hacker, Jacob S.

Let them eat tweets : how the right rules in an age of extreme inequality / Jacob S. Hacker and Paul Pierson. Liveright Publishing, 2020. 288 p. **320.520973**

1. Republican Party 2. Conservatism -- United States 3. Plutocracy 4. Polarization (Social sciences) 5. Populism 6. United States -- Politics and government -- 2017-

ISBN 9781631496844

LC 2019057133

The authors of Winner-Take-All Politics present a groundbreaking account of how the current alliance between right-wing plutocrats and populists is reversing policies that support the working and middle classes, triggering devastating economic consequences.

"A cogent and dispiriting contribution to the growing number of analyses of the ailing American democracy." Kirkus

Hochschild, Arlie Russell, 1940-

★**Strangers** in their own land : anger and mourning on the American Right / Arlie Russell Hochschild. New Press, 2016. 288 p. **320.520973**

1. Republican Party. 2. Conservatism -- United States. 3. Tea Party movement. 4. Politics and culture. 5. Conservatives.

ISBN 9781620972250

LC 2016017892

In Strangers in Their Own Land, the renowned sociologist Arlie Hochschild embarks on a thought-provoking journey from her liberal hometown of Berkeley, California, deep into the heart of the bayou of Lake Charles, Louisiana, a stronghold of the conservative Right.

"A well-told chronicle of an ambitious sociological project of significant current importance." Kirkus.

Nelson, Anne, 1954-

Shadow network : media, money, and the secret hub of the radical Right / Anne Nelson. Bloomsbury USA, 2019. 416 p. **320.520973**

1. Council for National Policy (U.S.) 2. Conservatism 3. Right and left (Political science) 4. Political culture -- United States 5. News media 6. United States -- Politics and government

ISBN 9781635573190

LC 2019950898

The journalist and author of Red Orchestra documents the four-decade activities of the Council for National Policy, a coalition of Republican operatives, evangelicals, oil barons and gun lobbyists who finance media campaigns and colleges to promote extremist ideas.

Seib, Gerald F. 1956-

We should have seen it coming : from Reagan to Trump -- a front-row seat to a political revolution / Gerald F. Seib. Random House, 2020 288 p. **320.520973**

1. Republican Party 2. Conservatism -- United States 3. Presidents -- United States 4. Populism 5. Conservatives

ISBN 9780593135150

LC bl2020016084

Chronicles the forty-year rise and decline of the conservative movement in America, sharing insights into the roles of such contributors as the Federalist Society, the NRA, and Fox News, and demonstrating how it evolved into the populist movement that elected Donald Trump.

"Although much of the information detailed is not new, Seib's accessible, well-written account will allow all readers to understand better the shifting political environment, especially the popularity of Reagan's conservative ideology in the decades after he left office." Library Journal

Sykes, Charles J., 1954-

How the right lost its mind / Charles J. Sykes. St. Martin's Press, 2017 288 p. **320.520973**

1. Conservatism. 2. Right and left (Political science). 3. Political culture. 4. United States -- Politics and government.

ISBN 9781250147172

LC 2017018870

An impassioned analysis of how the author believes America's conservative movement has lost its values traces his March 2016 challenge to then-candidate Donald Trump and his ongoing efforts to discredit the Obama administration, identifying specific recommendations for how mainstream conservatives can reconnect with core principles.

"Exceedingly readable, Syke's voice comes across as clearly as if over the airwaves." Library Journal.

Will, George F.
The **conservative** sensibility / George F. Will. Hachette Books, 2019. 736 p. **320.520973**

1. Republican Party 2. Conservatism -- United States -- History. 3. Founding Fathers of the United States. 4. Constitutional history. 5. Civics 6. United States -- Politics and government

ISBN 9780316480932

LC 2018048055

"A reflection on American conservatism, examining how the Founders' belief in natural rights created a great American political tradition--one that now finds itself under threat, both from progressives and elements inside the Republican Party".-- Provided by publisher.

"This is a timely and important book by one of the foremost contemporary conservative thinkers and writers. Recommended for most collections." Library Journal.

320.53 Collectivism and fascism

Albright, Madeleine Korbel
Fascism : a warning / Madeleine Albright. Harper, 2018. 304 p. **320.53**

1. Fascism 2. Political science -- Philosophy 3. Social movements 4. Authoritarianism

ISBN 9780062802187

LC 2018404338

A former U.S. secretary of state and New York Times best-selling author presents a timely, considered and personal look at the history and current resurgence of fascism today and the virulent threat it poses to international freedom, prosperity and peace.

Arendt, Hannah, 1906-1975
★The **origins** of totalitarianism / Hannah Arendt ; intoduction by Samantha Power. Schocken Books, 2004, c1951. xxvii, 674 p. ; **320.53**

1. Totalitarianism. 2. Imperialism. 3. Antisemitism. 4. Politics and culture.

ISBN 0805242252

LC 2003060749

Originally published: 1st ed. New York : Harcourt, Brace, 1951.

A political analysis of totalitarian societies traces the nineteenth-century rise of anti-Semitism in central and western Europe and considers the institutions and operations of Nazi Germany and Stalinist Russia, examining such phenomena as the transformation of classes into masses, the applications of propaganda, and the use of terror.

Brown, Archie, 1938-
★The **rise** and fall of communism / Archie Brown. Ecco, 2009. 800 p. **320.53**

1. Communism -- History 2. Ideology 3. Political science -- Philosophy 4. Marxism -- History

ISBN 9780061138799

LC bl2009012711

An in-depth history by the prize-winning Oxford professor author of The Gorbachev Factor traces the origins of the communist ideology through its collapse in many nations following perestroika, in an extensively researched volume that also explores communism's current incarnations.

"A seminal work from a distinguished scholar; highly recommended." Library Journal

Paxton, Robert O.
★The **anatomy** of fascism / Robert O. Paxton. Alfred A. Knopf, 2004. xii, 321 p. ; **320.53**

1. Fascism. 2. Fascism -- Europe.

ISBN 1400040949

LC 2004100489

"While there are countless studies on fascism, readers will be hard pressed to find anything more in-depth from a scholar with Paxton's credentials." Library Journal.

Riemen, Rob, 1962-
To fight against this age : on fascism and humanism / Rob Riemen. W.W. Norton & Company, 2018. 160 p. **320.53**

1. Fascism. 2. Humanism. 3. Political ethics. 4. World politics -- 21st century.

ISBN 9780393635867

LC 2017043652

Collects two essays: "The Eternal Return of Fascism," which explores the theoretical weakness of fascism--which depends on resentment, anger and fear, xenophobia, scapegoats, and its hatred of the life of the mind--and "The Return of Europa," which discusses European humanism and its democratic values of truth, beauty, justice, and love for life. An international best-seller.

"His erudite essays add an enriching element to the ongoing conversation of a contentious political moment." Publishers Weekly.

320.53094 Collectivism and fascism--Russia

Snyder, Timothy
The **road** to unfreedom : Russia, Europe, America / Timothy Snyder. Tim Duggan Books, 2018 359 p. : **320.53094**

1. Putin, Vladimir Vladimirovich, 1952- 2. Power (Social sciences) 3. Cold War -- Influence 4. Authoritarianism 5. Despotism 6. Russia -- Politics and government 7. Europe -- Politics and government 8. United States -- Politics and government

ISBN 9780525574460

Kirkus Prize for Nonfiction finalist, 2018.

Chronicles the rise of authoritarianism from Russia to Europe and America in the post-Cold War years, tracing how, in the aftermath of celebrations predicting a peaceful and globalized future, Putin developed a power-consolidating political system that has spread throughout the west, triggering inflammatory elections and uprisings.

320.530973 Collectivism and fascism--United States

MacLean, Nancy
Democracy in chains : the deep history of the radical Right's stealth Plan for America / Nancy MacLean. Viking Press, 2017 400 p. **320.530973**

1. Conservatism. 2. Democracy. 3. Right-wing extremists. 4. Voting. 5. United States -- Politics and government

ISBN 9781101980965

LC 2017009048

National Book Award for Nonfiction finalist, 2017

In this well-researched biographical study, acclaimed historian Nancy MacLean offers a sobering analysis of the radical Libertarians' rise to political power in the U.S. Focusing on the late James Buchanan, a Nobel Prize-winning economist, she explores his plan to inject his views into the operations of every branch of government. Funded in part by multibillionaire Charles Koch, Buchanan's ideas have been carried out by like-minded political operatives. Here's an unprecedented explanation of the origins of America's current political rift.

"MacLean's intense and extensive examination of the right-wing's rise to power is perhaps the best explanation to date of the roots of the political divide that threatens to irrevocably alter American government." Booklist.

320.55 Religiously oriented ideologies

Hamid, Shadi, 1983-

Islamic exceptionalism : how the struggle over Islam is reshaping the Middle East / Shadi Hamid. St. Martin's Press, 2016. 256 p. **320.55**

1. Islam and politics. 2. Middle East -- Politics and government. 3. Arab countries -- Politics and government.

ISBN 9781250061010

LC 2015049286

"From the founding of Islam in the seventh century, there had always been a dominant Muslim empire, or "caliphate." But in 1924, the Ottoman Caliphate was formally abolished. Since then, there has been an ongoing struggle to establish a legitimate political order in the Middle East. At the center of that struggle is the vexing problem of religion and its role in political life. In Islamic Exceptionalism, Brookings Institution scholar and acclaimed author Shadi Hamid offers a novel and provocative argument on how Islam is, in fact, "exceptional" in how it relates to politics, with profound implications for how we understand the future of the Middle East.

320.56 Ideologies based on groups of people

Frank, Thomas, 1965-

The **people,** no : a brief history of anti-populism / Thomas Frank. Metropolitan Books, 2020. 307 p. **320.56**

1. Populism -- United States -- History 2. Political culture 3. Social movements 4. Democracy -- United States 5. United States -- History 6. United States -- Politics and government

ISBN 9781250220110

LC 2020009048

Published in Australia under the title, "People without power: the war on populism and the fight for democracy," Scribe, 2020.

Today "populism" is seen as a frightening thing, a term pundits use to describe the racist philosophy of Donald Trump and European extremists. But this is a mistake. The real story of populism is an account of enlightenment and liberation; it is the story of American democracy itself, of its ever-widening promise of a decent life for all. Taking us from the tumultuous 1890s, when the radical left-wing Populist Party--the biggest mass movement in American history--fought Gilded Age plutocrats to the reformers' great triumphs under Franklin Roosevelt and Harry Truman, Frank reminds us how much we owe to the populist ethos.

"Frank's writing is notable for its clarity and its ability to make connections. His provocative conclusions, about elites and the people, sometimes turn common assumptions upside down--all the better for making readers think." Booklist

320.943 Germany--Politics

Feigel, Lara

The **bitter** taste of victory : in the ruins of the Reich / Lara Feigel. Bloomsbury USA, 2016 384 p. **320.943**

1. World War II -- Post-war aspects 2. Denazification -- History. 3. Reconstruction (1939-1951) -- Germany. 4. Postwar life 5. Germany -- History -- 1945-1955.

ISBN 9781632865519

LC bl2016020710

When Germany surrendered in May 1945 it was a nation reduced to rubble. Immediately, America, Britain, Soviet Russia, and France set about rebuilding in their zones of occupation. Most urgent were physical needs--food, water, and sanitation--but from the start the Allies were also anxious to indoctrinate the German people in the ideas of peace and civilization.

"Many individuals had to come to terms with the evil they saw and with themselves, and Feigel does a masterful job in sorting it out. This is uniquely nuanced history." Booklist.

320.956 Politics--Middle East

Bergman, Ronen

Rise and kill first : the secret history of Israel's targeted assassinations / Ronen Bergman. Random House, 2018 736 p. **320.956**

1. Targeted killing. 2. Assassination 3. Arab-Israeli conflict. 4. Arab-Israeli relations. 5. Israel -- Politics and government -- 21st century.

ISBN 9781400069712

LC bl2017046042

National Jewish Book Award, 2018.

A political and military analyst for Israel's daily newspaper, Yedioth Ahronoth, presents an assessment of Israel's state-sponsored assassination programs that evaluates the protective beliefs that are instituted into every Israeli citizen, the role of assassination in the state's history and the ethical challenges of Israel's policies on targeted killings.

"The senior political and military analyst for Israel's largest daily newspaper, Yedioth Ahronoth, Bergman interviewed dozens of current and former government officials in Israel to tell the story of its state-sponsored assassination programs. Billed as news-breaking." Library Journal.

320.973 Politics -- United States

Achen, Christopher H.

Democracy for realists : why elections do not produce responsive government / Christopher H. Achen, Larry M. Bartels. Princeton University Press, 2016. 432 p. **320.973**

1. Democracy 2. Inequality 3. Political participation 4. Corruption

ISBN 9780691169446

LC 2016930927

Achen and Bartels argue that democratic theory needs to be founded on identity groups and political parties, not on the preferences of individual voters. Democracy for Realists provides a powerful challenge to conventional thinking, pointing the way toward a fundamentally different understanding of the realities and potential of democratic government.

"A comprehensive analysis that lays the foundation for a discussion of necessary reforms and how they can be achieved." Kirkus.

Edwards, Mickey, 1937-

The **parties** versus the people : how to turn Republicans and Democrats into Americans / Mickey Edwards. Yale University Press, 2012. 256 p. **320.973**

1. Political parties -- United States. 2. Democracy -- United States. 3.

Polarization (Social sciences) -- United States. 4. Two-party systems -- United States.
ISBN 9780300184563

LC 2012013008

To banish the negative effects of partisan warfare from our political system, a former congressman, drawing on his first-hand experience with legislative battles, presents a solution-based, practical way to break the stranglehold of the political party system.

Hennessey, Jonathan, 1971-

The **United** States Constitution : a graphic adaptation / written by Jonathan Hennessey ; art by Aaron McConnell. Hill and Wang, 2008. 149 p. : **320.973**

1. United States. Constitution. 2. Constitution. 3. Constitutional history. 4. United States -- History. 5. United States -- Politics and government. 6. Comics and Graphic novels
ISBN 9780809094875

LC 2008017927

An illustrated account of the American Constitution covers each article and amendment in a graphic format designed to render its meanings more relevant and accessible to modern readers, in a volume that addresses such topics as the separation of church and state, the break from the monarchy, and the limits imposed on presidential power.

Lepore, Jill, 1966-

This America : the case for the nation / Jill Lepore. Liveright Publishing, 2019. 128 p. **320.973**

1. Nationalism -- United States 2. National characteristics, American 3. Patriotism 4. Political science 5. United States -- History 6. United States -- Race relations -- History
ISBN 9781631496417

LC 2019013594

At a time of much despair over the future of liberal democracy, Harvard historian Jill Lepore makes a stirring case for the nation in This America. Since the end of the Cold War, Lepore writes, American historians have largely retreated from the idea of "the nation," in part because postmodernism has corroded faith in grand narratives, and in part because the rise of political nationalism has rendered it suspect and unpalatable. A trenchant work of political philosophy as well as a reclamation of America's national history, This America asks us to look our nation's sovereign past square in the eye to reveal not only a history of contradictions, but a path of promise for the future.

" A frank, well-written look at the dangers we face. We ignore them at our peril. " Kirkus.

Lewis, Michael (Michael M.)

★The **fifth** risk : undoing democracy / Michael Lewis. W W Norton & Co Inc 2018 256 p. **320.973**

1. Political science 2. Administrative agencies 3. Incompetence 4. Politicians 5. United States -- Politics and government -- 21st century 6. United States -- Officials and employees -- Selection and appointment
ISBN 9781324002642

LC 2018038204

What are the consequences if the people given control over our government have no idea how it works?

"Lewis persuasively documents the dangers that result from placing people without the necessary skills in charge of these departments and from cutting funding. This is an illuminating primer on some of the government projects most crucial to the well-being of the populace, and its relevance to readers won't end with the Trump era." Publishers Weekly.

Morone, James A., 1951-

Republic of wrath : how American politics turned tribal, from George Washington to Donald Trump / James A. Morone. Basic Books, 2020. 423 p. **320.973**

1. Nativism 2. Polarization (Social sciences) 3. Political parties -- United States -- History 4. Political culture -- United States -- History 5. United States -- Politics and government
ISBN 9780465002443

LC 2020938784

A prize-winning political scientist, in this revelatory work of political history that untangles the deep roots of tribalism in America, explains the origins of our fractious times and suggests how we might build a more robust republic.

"A brilliant expose of the uglier undercurrents of American political history." Kirkus

Muirhead, Russell, 1965-

A **lot** of people are saying : the new conspiracism and the assault on democracy / Russell Muirhead, Nancy L. Rosenblum. Princeton University Press, 2019. 211 p. **320.973**

1. Democracy. 2. Conspiracies. 3. Conspiracy theories. 4. Government and politics. 5. United States -- Politics and government -- 21st century.
ISBN 9780691188836

LC 2018957712

Explains how the New Conspiracists are undermining democracy--and what can be done about it.

Pfeiffer, Dan

Yes we (still) can : politics in the age of Obama, Twitter, and Trump / Dan Pfeiffer. Twelve Books, 2018. 304 p. **320.973**

1. Pfeiffer, Dan 2. Political consultants 3. Political culture 4. Political parties 5. Presidential election, 2008
ISBN 9781538711712

LC 2018932320

Based on a podcast.

A former White House director of communications and current co-host of Pod Save America explores how politics, the media and the internet changed during the Obama administration and how Democrats can fight back in the Trump era.

"Those who share Pfeiffer's admiration of Obama and his hopes for a Democratic resurgence--and, of course, fans of his podcast--will love both the chatty insider anecdotes and the advice." Publishers Weekly.

Tocqueville, Alexis de, 1805-1859

★**Democracy** in America / Alexis de Tocqueville ; translated from the French by Arthur Goldhammer. Library of America, c2004. xvi, 941 p. : **320.973**

1. Americans. 2. Democracy -- United States. 3. Political science -- United States -- History. 4. Political parties. 5. United States -- Politics and government. 6. United States -- Social conditions -- To 1865.
ISBN 1931082545

LC 2003061885

Translation of: De la democratie en Amerique (1835).

A study of our national government and character follows the author's concern about the effect of majority rule on the rights of individuals and provides insight into the rewards and responsibilities of a democratic government.

Tomasky, Michael, 1960-

If we can keep it : how the republic collapsed and how it might be saved / Michael Tomasky. Liveright Publishing, 2019. 288 p. **320.973**

1. Political culture -- United States. 2. Polarization (Social sciences) 3. Political participation -- United States. 4. United States -- Politics and government -- 21st century. 5. United States -- History
ISBN 9781631494086

LC 2018043229

The Daily Beast columnist and editor of Democracy: A Journal of Ideas assesses the origins of political polarization in America that outlines ambitious recommendations in the areas of ranked-choice voting, at-large congressional elections and civics education.

"This timely and sophisticated analysis is recommended for all collections and nicely complements Jon Meacham's The Soul of America, which provides a similar mature assessment of modern America." Library Journal.

320.9775 Politics--Wisconsin

Kaufman, Dan, 1970-

The **fall** of Wisconsin : the conservative conquest of a progressive bastion and the future of American politics / Dan Kaufman. W. W. Norton & Company, [2018] 319 pages ; **320.9775**

1. Walker, Scott, 1967- 2. Republican Party 3. Conservatism 4. Political science 5. Right and left (Political science) 6. Progressivism (United States politics) -- Wisconsin 7. Wisconsin
ISBN 9780393635201

LC 2018016668

Evaluates the deconstruction of state laws protecting voting rights, public health, the environment and education in the once-progressive state of Wisconsin, tracing the contributions of key leaders and activists in galvanizing resistance to the Trump administration.

"Still, the author's vivid reportage and trenchant insights illuminate America's changing political landscape." Publishers Weekly.

321 Systems of governments and states

Plato

★The **republic** / Plato ; edited by G.R.F. Ferrari ; translated by Tom Griffith. Cambridge University Press, 2000. xlviii, 382 p. ; **321**

1. Justice 2. Political science 3. Utopias
ISBN 9780521484435

LC 00024471

Presents the most important of the Socratic dialogues as if it were a conversation; deals with the creation of an ideal commonwealth and ranks as one of the earliest Utopian works.

"Griffith's aim was to translate the Greek text as if it were a conversation, and he has succeeded admirably. The text does indeed flow like a conversation, with the entire back-and-forth interaction that such exchanges involve. [He] has also written a very useful introduction that places the work in a historical context and provides a glossary that will help readers identify individuals and places mentioned in the work." Library Journal.

321.8 Democratic government

Cartledge, Paul

Democracy : a life / Paul Cartledge. Oxford University Press, 2016 312 p. **321.8**

1. Democracy -- History. 2. Political science. 3. World politics. 4. Ancient Greece
ISBN 9780199837458

LC 2015034058

In ancient Greece there can be traced not only the rudiments of modern democratic society but the entire Western tradition of anti-democratic thought. In Democracy: A Life, Paul Cartledge provides a detailed history of this ancient political system. In addition, by drawing out the salient differences between ancient and modern forms of democracy he enables a richer understanding of both.

"No library should be without this wonderful book, in which Cartledge has abundantly shared his love and knowledge of ancient Greece with us." Kirkus.

Greenberg, Leah

★**We** are indivisible : a blueprint for democracy after Trump / Leah Greenberg, Ezra Levin. One Signal Publishers/Atria, 2019. xv, 347 pages ; **321.8**

1. Trump, Donald, 1946- 2. Social advocates 3. Social reformers 4. Democracy 5. Voting 6. United States -- Politics and government
ISBN 9781982129972

LC bl2019034562

The co-executive directors of Indivisible tell the story of their anti-Trump movement, offering a behind-the-scenes look at how change comes to Washington and explaining how we'll win the coming fight for the future of American democracy.

Levitsky, Steven

★**How** democracies die / Steven Levitsky and Daniel Ziblatt. Crown Publishing, 2018. 312 p. ; **321.8**

1. Democracy. 2. Political culture. 3. Totalitarianism 4. Civil rights 5. United States -- Politics and government -- 2017-
ISBN 9781524762933

LC 2017045872

A cautionary assessment of the demise of history's liberal democracies identifies such factors as the steady weakening of critical institutions, from the judiciary to the press, while sharing optimistic recommendations for how America's democratic system can be saved.

"A provocative analysis of the parallels between Donald Trump's ascent and the fall of other democracies." Kirkus.

Litt, David, 1986-

Democracy in one book or less : how it works, why it doesn't, and why fixing it is easier than you think / David Litt. Ecco, 2020 320 p. **321.8**

1. Democracy -- United States 2. Political science 3. Voting 4. Political participation -- United States. 5. United States -- Politics and government
ISBN 9780062879363

LC bl2020013829

What explains the gap between what We, the People want and what our elected leaders do? How can we fix our politics before it's too late? And how can we truly understand the state of our democracy without wanting to crawl under a rock? That's what former Obama speechwriter David Litt set out to answer. Citing the increased voting restrictions and fall in competitive Congressional districts behind major changes to democracy in America, the former White House speechwriter outlines strategies for reclaiming representation for all citizens.

"Both optimistic and clear-eyed, this quip-filled call to action will resonate strongly with young progressives." Publishers Weekly

Miller, Jim, 1947-

Can democracy work? : a short history of a radical idea, from ancient Athens to our world / James Miller. Farrar, Straus and Giroux, 2018. 320 p. **321.8**

1. Democracy -- History. 2. Democracy -- Philosophy. 3. Political science 4. Citizen participation in government

ISBN 9780374137649

LC 2018002536

The critically acclaimed author of Examined Lives presents an urgent history of democracy to explain how it has become history's most widely accepted political system in spite of conflicting interpretations, war and corruption.

Rice, Condoleezza, 1954-

Democracy : stories from the long road to freedom / Condoleezza Rice. Grand Central Pub., 2017. 512 p. **321.8**

1. Democracy 2. Political science 3. Democratization 4. Change 5. United States -- Politics and government

ISBN 9781455540181

LC 2016056710

The controversial former Secretary of State traces her witness to key events throughout the past half century while assessing the evolution of global democracy and how it is under attack in all world regions.

"George W. Bush's secretary of state returns to her academic roots with this accessibly written study of that imperfect but ideal form of government." Kirkus.

321.9 Authoritarian government

Applebaum, Anne, 1964-

★**Twilight** of democracy : the seductive lure of authoritarianism / Anne Applebaum. Doubleday, 2020. 208 p. **321.9**

1. Authoritarianism. 2. Democracy. 3. Nationalism. 4. One-party systems.

ISBN 9780385545808

LC 2020012450

A Pulitzer Prize-winning historian and journalist examines the current world-wide rise of authoritarianism and explains how it appeals to citizens by using conspiracy theory, political polarization, social media and nostalgia.

"Equal parts memoir, reportage, and history, this sobering account of the roots and forms of today's authoritarianism, by one of its most accomplished observers, is meant as a warning to everyone." Kirkus

Kalder, Daniel, 1974-

★The **infernal** library : on dictators, their books, and other catastrophes of literacy / Daniel Kalder. Henry Holt and Company, 2018. 464 p. **321.9**

1. Dictatorship 2. Dictators 3. Propaganda 4. Language and power (Social sciences)

ISBN 9781627793421

LC 2017009633

Includes index.

A harrowing tour of "dictator literature" in the twentieth-century, featuring the soul-killing prose and poetry of Hitler, Mao, and many more, which shows how books have sometimes shaped the world for the worse.

"The author renders his highly compelling narrative in a cheeky yet erudite tone that will keep readers smirking despite the monstrousness of the book's protagonists. Dictators have never looked so educated." Kirkus.

Stanley, Jason

How fascism works : the politics of us and them / Jason Stanley. Random House, [2018] 208 p. **321.9**

1. Fascism 2. Polarization (Social sciences) 3. Political science -- Philosophy 4. Nationalism

ISBN 9780525511830

LC 2018013266

The Yale philosopher reveals the fascist politics behind today's ethnic, racial, and religious divides, identifying ten key examples of fascist politics that are used by political leaders to hold onto power.

322 Relation of the state to organized groups and their members

Preston, Andrew, 1973-

Sword of the spirit, shield of faith : religion in American war and diplomacy / Andrew Preston. Alfred A. Knopf, 2012. 816 p. **322**

1. Religion and politics -- United States -- History 2. Religion and state -- United States -- History 3. United States -- History, Military -- Religious aspects 4. United States -- Foreign relations -- Religious aspects 5. United States -- Military policy -- Religious aspects

ISBN 9781400043231

LC 2011035138

Charles Taylor Prize for Literary Non-Fiction (Canada), 2013.

Cundill Prize in Historical Literature finalist

An analysis of the pivotal role of religion in American foreign policy from the nation's beginnings through the end of the Cold War demonstrates how the beliefs of leaders and everyday citizens have shaped their views on America's place in the world.

Reich, Robert B., 1946-

The **system** : who rigged it, how we fix it / Robert B. Reich. Alfred A. Knopf, 2020. 224 p. **322**

1. Inequality 2. Wealth 3. Elite (Social sciences) 4. Power (Social sciences) 5. United States -- Politics and government 6. United States -- Social conditions

ISBN 9780525659044

LC 2019044129

"A Borzoi Book."

Millions of Americans have lost confidence in our political and economic system. After years of stagnant wages, volatile job markets, and an unwillingness by those in power to deal with profound threats such as climate change, there is a mounting sense that the system is fixed, serving only those select few with enough money to secure a controlling stake. With the characteristic clarity and passion that has made him a central civil voice, Robert B. Reich shows how wealth and power have interacted to install an elite oligarchy, eviscerate the middle class, and undermine democracy. Reich's objective is not to foster cynicism, but rather to demystify the system so that we might instill fundamental change and demand that democracy works for the majority once again.

"Much-needed, readably concise political and economic analysis." Kirkus

322.4 Political action groups

Chalmers, David Mark

Hooded Americanism : the history of the Ku Klux Klan / David M. Chalmers. Duke University Press, 1987, c1981. xii, 477

p., 16 p. of plates : **322.4**

1. Ku Klux Klan -- History. 2. Hate groups
ISBN 9780822307723

LC 86029133

Includes index.

Reprint. Originally published: New York : F. Watts, c1981.

The nature and objectives of the Ku Klux Klan are revealed in a study of its development and members over one hundred years

O'Neill, Connor Towne, 1989-

★**Down** along with that devil's bones : a reckoning with monuments, memory, and the legacy of white supremacy / Connor Towne O'Neill. Algonquin Books of Chapel Hill, 2020. 262 p. **322.4**

1. Forrest, Nathan Bedford, 1821-1877. 2. Ku-Klux Klan 3. Generals -- Confederate States of America 4. Soldiers' monuments 5. Whiteness (Concept) 6. Racism 7. Southern States 8. United States
ISBN 9781616209100

LC 2020016840

A journalist's memoir-plus-reporting about modern-day conflicts over Southern monuments to Nathan Bedford Forrest, a Confederate hero and original leader of the Ku Klux Klan, as well as a personal examination of the legacy of white supremacy through the US today, tracing the throughline from Appomattox to Charlottesville.

"A personal examination of one of the great divides in our country today. O'Neill's NPR podcast, White Lies, was a finalist for the Pulitzer Prize in audio recording. In his first book, the author widens his inquiry into race and violence with an urgent and eye-opening look at Confederate monuments in the South." Kirkus

Yassin-Kassab, Robin

Burning country : Syrians in revolution and war / Robin Yassin-Kassab and Leila Al-Shami. Pluto Press, 2016. xii, 262 p. : **322.4**

1. Assad, Bashar, 1965- 2. Assad, Bashar, 1965- fast (OCoLC) fst01578713 3. Civil War (Syria : 2011-). fast (OCoLC)fst01907471 4. Syria -- History -- Civil War, 2011- 5. Syria -- Politics and government -- 2000- 6. Syria. fast (OCoLC)fst01208757
ISBN 9780745336275

LC 2017286184

In 2011, Syrians took to the streets to demand the overthrow of the regime of Bashar al-Assad. Today, much of Syria has become a warzone where foreign journalists find it almost impossible to go. Burning Country explores the reality of life in present-day Syria. Drawn from over fifteen years of work with the people of Syria, it reveals the stories of opposition fighters, exiles lost in an archipelago of refugee camps, and many others. Examining new grassroots revolutionary organisations, the rise of ISIS and Islamism, and the emergence of the worst refugee crisis since World War Two, Burning Country is a vivid account of a modern-day political and humanitarian nightmare. -- from back cover.

323 Civil and political rights

Arsenault, Raymond

Freedom riders : 1961 and the struggle for racial justice / Raymond Arsenault. Oxford University Press, 2006. 690 p. **323**

1. African American civil rights workers -- History -- 20th century. 2. Civil rights workers -- United States -- History -- 20th century. 3. African Americans -- Segregation -- Southern States -- History -- 20th century. 4. Segregation in transportation -- Southern States -- History -- 20th century. 5. Southern States -- Race relations -- History -- 20th century. 6. United States -- Race relations -- History -- 20th century.
ISBN 0195136748

LC 2005018108

Relives a critical episode in American history that transformed the Civil Rights Movement when a group of volunteers traveled by bus in 1961 from Washington, D.C., through the deep South, defying Jim Crow laws and putting their lives on the line for racial justice.

Dershowitz, Alan M.

★**Rights** from wrongs : a secular theory of the origin of rights / Alan Dershowitz. Basic Books, 2005. 261 p. **323**

1. Human rights. 2. Civil rights. 3. Injustice. 4. Justice.
ISBN 0465017134

LC 2004020006

"Whether conservative or liberal, absolutist or relativist, readers will find areas of disagreement, but most will concur that a talented and creative legal mind is at work." Publishers Weekly.

Kirby, David, 1960-

When they come for you : how police and government are trampling our liberties--and how to take them back / David Kirby. St. Martin's Press, 2019. 400 p. **323**

1. Freedom 2. Civil rights 3. Corruption 4. Law enforcement
ISBN 9781250064363

LC 2019024265

Liberty and justice for all is the bedrock of American democracy, but has America betrayed our founders' vision for the nation? Author David Kirby exposes federal, state, and local violations of basic constitutional rights that should trouble every American, whether liberal, conservative, or libertarian. Free speech, privacy, protection from unreasonable search and seizure, due process, and equal protection under the law are rights that belong to every American citizen, but are being shredded at an alarming rate all across the country.

Kotz, Nick

★**Judgment** days : Lyndon Baines Johnson, Martin Luther King, Jr., and the laws that changed America / Nick Kotz. Houghton Mifflin, 2005. xix, 522 p. : **323**

1. Johnson, Lyndon B., 1908-1973 Friends and associates. 2. King, Martin Luther, Jr., 1929-1968 Friends and associates. 3. Johnson, Lyndon B., 1908-1973 Relations with African-Americans. 4. Civil Rights Act of 1964. 5. Voting Rights Act of 1965. 6. African Americans -- Civil rights -- History -- 20th century. 7. African Americans -- Legal status, laws, etc. 8. United States -- Politics and government -- 1963-1969. 9. United States -- Race relations -- Political aspects.
ISBN 0618088253

LC 2004059852

The first comprehensive account of the relationship between President Johnson and Martin Luther King uses FBI wiretaps, Johnson's taped telephone conversations, and previously undisclosed communications between the two to paint a fascinating portrait of this important relationship.

"This book is an informed political investigation of these two civil rights warriors and the cause for which they fought and, in King's case, died." Library Journal.

Pepper, William F., 1937-

An **act** of state : the execution of Martin Luther King / William

F. Pepper. Verso, 2003. ix, 334 p. ; 323

1. King, Martin Luther, Jr., 1929-1968 Assassination. 2. African Americans 3. Race relations. 4. Assassination. 5. Conspiracies. 6. United States -- History -- 20th century.

ISBN 1859846955

LC BL2003000155

Reprinted in 2018

Recounts the death of Martin Luther King, Jr., argues that the events represent a government conspiracy to assassinate him, and discusses his proposed run for president, media cover-ups, and the role of contributing corporations.

"Forget everything you think you know, Pepper insists. James Earl Ray did not pull the trigger. Pepper gradually introduces the vast cast of characters in a dizzying murder conspiracy that winds from a Memphis bar through the shadows of organized crime to the far reaches of national government. He carefully maps each player's place and role in the tangled web and doggedly tries to stick to a straightforward narrative. Pepper attempts nothing less than a rewrite of history, and a spurring of further investigation." Publishers Weekly.

Chabon, Michael,

★**Fight** of the century : writers reflect on 100 years of landmark ACLU cases/edited by Michael Chabon and Ayelet Waldman; foreword by David Cole. Avid Reader Press, 2020. 288 p. 323

1. American Civil Liberties Union -- History 2. United States. Supreme Court Cases 3. Civil rights 4. Constitutional law 5. Discrimination 6. Courts 7. Essays 8. Anthologies

ISBN 9781501190407

LC bl2019037404

In collaboration with the ACLU, prize-winning authors Michael Chabon and Ayelet Waldman have curated an anthology of essays about landmark cases in the ACLU's 100-year history. Bestselling and award-winning authors present unique literary takes on historic decisions like Brown v. Board of Education, the Scopes trial, and Roe v. Wade. Contributors include Geraldine Brooks, Michael Cunningham, Jennifer Egan, Dave Eggers, Louise Erdrich, Neil Gaiman, Lauren Groff, Marlon James, Viet Thanh Nguyen, Morgan Parker, Ann Patchett, Salman Rushdie, George Saunders, Elizabeth Strout, Jesmyn Ward, Meg Wolitzer, and more.

"Vigorous, informative, and well-organized, this outstanding collection befits the ACLU's substantial impact on American law and society." Publishers Weekly.

323.0420973 Citizen participation--United States

Newman, Dan (Dan G.)

Unrig : how to fix our broken democracy / written by Daniel G. Newman ; art by George O'Connor ; color by Frank Reynoso. First Second, 2020 280 p. : 323.0420973

1. Wealth -- Political aspects 2. Democracy -- United States 3. Inequality 4. Political reform 5. United States -- Politics and government

ISBN 9781250295309

LC 2019930675

An intriguing and accessible nonfiction graphic novel about the role wealth and influence play in American democracy.

"This cogent plea for democracy is fueled with an urgency that should initiate debate and inspire action." Publishers Weekly

323.092 Civil rights leaders

Burns, Rebecca, 1966-

Burial for a King : Martin Luther King Jr.'s funeral and the week that transformed Atlanta and rocked the nation / Rebecca Burns. Scribner, 2011. 208 p. 323.092

1. King, Martin Luther, Jr., 1929-1968 Death and burial. 2. Race relations. 3. Civil Rights Movement. 4. Funerals 5. Grief. 6. United States -- Race relations -- History -- 20th century. 7. Atlanta, Georgia -- Race relations -- History -- 20th century.

ISBN 9781439130544

LC 2010029980

"This is a recreation of the aftermath of Martin Luther King Jr.'s assassination. [The author] provides a snapshot of a still-segregated nation poised between uneasy reconciliation and violent chaos. Using terse language and precise, straightforward description . . . she views the crisis and aftermath of King's death in Memphis through multiple points of view, beginning with the traumatic center of his family and closest associates in Atlanta. A pertinent, you-are-there historical page-turner with a strong moral message." Kirkus.

King, Martin Luther, Jr., 1929-1968

The **radical** King / Martin Luther King, Jr. ; edited and introduced by Cornel West. Beacon Press, 2014. 320 p. 323.092

1. King, Martin Luther, Jr., 1929-1968 Political and social views. 2. King, Martin Luther, Jr., 1929-1968 Philosophy. 3. Poverty 4. Civil rights 5. Social justice 6. Race relations

ISBN 9780807012826

LC 2014022515

"This volume features a popularly referenced spiritual giant too seldom recognized in his true dimensions. Readers looking to discover the 'real' Martin Luther King Jr., revolutionary Christianity, social justice, or the state of contemporary America will enjoy West's provocative and pithy work as it calls on King to speak again about America, the world, and 'where we go from here.'" Library Journal.

Mckesson, Deray

On the other side of freedom : the case for hope / Deray Mckesson. Penguin Group USA, 2018 256 p. 323.092

1. Social advocacy 2. Civil rights workers 3. African American social advocates 4. Social justice

ISBN 9780525560326

LC 2018030658

Based on a podcast.

The internationally recognized civil rights activist and popular host of Pod Save the People presents a meditative call to action on resistance, justice and freedom on the front lines of the Black Lives Matter movement.

Rieder, Jonathan

Gospel of freedom : Martin Luther King, Jr.'s letter from Birmingham Jail and the struggle that changed a nation / Jonathan Rieder. Bloomsbury Press, 2013. 224 p. 323.092

1. King, Martin Luther, Jr., 1929-1968. Letter from Birmingham jail. 2. Civil Rights Movement -- Birmingham, Alabama 3. African Americans -- Civil rights -- Birmingham, Alabama 4. Civil disobedience -- Birmingham, Alabama -- History -- 20th century. 5. Nonviolence. 6. Birmingham, Alabama -- Race relations.

ISBN 9781620400586

LC 2012044387

Published to commemorate the 50th anniversary of the Civil Rights leader's famous "Letter from Birmingham Jail," an account of the story behind its creation and the related protest march on Washington offers insight into its timeless message and crucial position in the history of human rights.

"Rieder's trenchant comments approach the letter on historical and literary grounds but also as a way to better understand the often elusive King. Several chapters offer a close analysis of the letter, while later chapters trace the impact it had on subsequent events." Booklist.

323.0973 Civil rights--United States

Cose, Ellis

Democracy, if we can keep it : the ACLU's 100-year fight for rights in America / Ellis Cose. The New Press, 2020. 480 p. **323.0973**

1. American Civil Liberties Union -- History. 2. Democracy 3. Civil rights -- United States -- History. 4. Civil rights organizations 5. Civil rights workers 6. United States -- Politics and government
ISBN 9781620973837

LC 2020010660

A vivid work of history and journalism, Democracy, If We Can Keep It is not just the definitive story of the ACLU but also an essential account of America's rediscovery of rights it had granted but long denied. A chronicle of America's most difficult ethical quandaries from the Red Scare, the Scottsboro Boys' trials, Japanese American internment, McCarthyism, and Vietnam, Democracy, If We Can Keep It weaves these accounts into a deeper story of American freedom--one that is profoundly relevant to our present moment.

"Cose's book is an excellent choice for anyone seeking to understand the ACLU as an organization and for those wanting to explore how the fight for civil liberties has evolved and helped to shape the society we have today." Library Journal

323.1 Civil and political rights of nondominant groups

Halberstam, David

★The **children** / David Halberstam. Random House, 1998. 783 p., 16 p. of plates : **323.1**

1. African American students 2. Nonviolence -- Nashville, Tennessee. 3. Civil Rights Movement 4. African Americans -- Civil rights -- History -- 20th century. 5. Nashville, Tennessee -- Race relations -- History -- 20th century. 6. United States -- Race relations.
ISBN 0679415610

LC 97019974

The Children is David Halberstam's brilliant and moving evocation of the early days of the civil rights movement, as seen through the story of the young people--the Children--who met in the 1960s and went on to lead the revolution. The Children is a story one of America's preeminent journalists has waited years to write, a powerful book about one of the most dramatic movements in American history.

"This is a recreation of the early days of the civil rights movement. The author focuses on a small group of young African Americans who attended the Reverend James Lawson's workshop for nonviolent demonstrators in Nashville in 1959, then went on to play active roles in the movement. A masterful achievement in reporting, research and understanding." Publishers Weekly.

King, Martin Luther, Jr., 1929-1968

★A **testament** of hope : the essential writings and speeches of Martin Luther King, Jr. / edited by James Melvin Washington. HarperSanFrancisco, 1991. xxvii, 702 p. ; **323.1**

1. African Americans -- Civil rights 2. United States -- Race relations.
ISBN 9780060646912

LC 90048203

Collects the civil rights leader's writings on nonviolence, social policy, integration, black nationalism, and more.

323.1196 Blacks (African origin) -- Civil and human rights

Abu-Jamal, Mumia, 1954-

Have black lives ever mattered? / Mumia Abu-Jamal. City Lights Books, 2017. 144 p. **323.1196**

1. Racism 2. Police misconduct 3. Racism in law enforcement 4. Violence against African-Americans 5. Essays
ISBN 9780872867383

LC 2017013442

A powerful indictment on the history of police violence against people of color, from slavery to today's Black Lives Matter.

"A must-read for anyone interested in social justice and inequalities, social movements, the criminal justice system, and African American history." Library Journal

Baldwin, James, 1924-1987

I am not your negro : a major motion picture directed by Raoul Peck / from texts by James Baldwin ; compiled and edited by Raoul Peck. Vintage International, [2017] 118 p. **323.1196**

1. African Americans -- Civil rights 2. Race relations 3. Racism 4. Social justice 5. United States -- Race relations 6. Interviews 7. Essays
ISBN 9780525434696

LC 2016053419

Transcript of the documentary film, I Am Not Your Negro, by Raoul Peck composed of unpublished and published writings, interviews, and letters by James Baldwin on the subject of racism in America.

Boyd, Herb, 1938-

★**We** shall overcome / Herb Boyd ; narrated by Ossie Davis & Ruby Dee. Sourcebooks, c2004. 263 p. : **323.1196**

1. King, Martin Luther, Jr., 1929-1968 2. Till, Emmett, 1941-1955 3. Civil Rights Movement 4. Civil rights 5. Racism 6. Race relations 7. United States -- History -- 20th century
ISBN 9781402202131

LC 2004012509

Chronicles the significant events and key figures from the civil right movement, including the assassination of Martin Luther King Jr., the murder of Emmet Till, and the Watts riots, with archival audio recordings on the accompanying CDs.

"Through text, images, and actual recordings (found on 2 CDs), Boyd . . . presents some of the major events in the Civil Rights Movement, including the murder of Emmett Till, the march on Washington, and the life and death of Martin Luther King Jr." Library Journal.

Gergel, Richard

Unexampled courage : the blinding of Sgt. Isaac Woodard and the awakening of President Harry S. Truman and Judge J. Waties Waring / Richard Gergel. Sarah Crichton Books ; 2019. 336 p. **323.1196**

1. Waring, Julius Waties, 1880-1968 2. Woodard, Isaac, 1919-1992 3. Violence against African Americans 4. African Americans -- Civil

rights 5. Police brutality 6. Hate crimes
ISBN 9780374107895

LC 2018021690

Documents the 1946 case of decorated African-American veteran Isaac Woodard, whose victimization by police brutality prompted Harry Truman to establish the first presidential commission on civil rights and order the desegregation in the U.S. armed forces.

Jones, Doug (G. Douglas), 1954-

Bending toward justice : the Birmingham church bombing that changed the course of civil rights / U.S. Senator Doug Jones with Greg Truman. All Points Books, 2019. 400 p. **323.1196**

1. Jones, Doug (G. Douglas), 1954- 2. 16th Street Baptist Church (Birmingham, Ala.) 3. Trials (Murder) 4. Bombings 5. Terrorism 6. Racism 7. Birmingham, Alabama -- Race relations 8. Alabama -- Race relations -- History.
ISBN 9781250201447

LC 2018039980

Includes index.

The story of the decades-long fight to bring justice to the victims of the 16th Street Baptist Church bombing, culminating in Sen. Doug Jones' prosecution of the last living bombers.

"This poignant and powerful story tracks changes in Southern life since the 1960s, uncovering hard truths to correct America's moral compass with an understanding of the need for activism and political discourse to achieve social justice." Library Journal.

Joseph, Peniel E.

Waiting 'til the midnight hour : a narrative history of Black power in America / Peniel E. Joseph. Henry Holt and Co., 2006. 399 p. : **323.1196**

1. Black power -- United States -- History -- 20th century. 2. African Americans -- Civil rights -- History -- 20th century. 3. Civil Rights Movement 4. African Americans -- Political activity -- History -- 20th century 5. United States -- Race relations.
ISBN 0805075399

LC 2005046765

A history of the Black Power movement in the United States traces the origins and evolution of the influential movement and examines the ways in which Black Power redefined racial identity and culture.

"Rather than simply detailing the history of radical organizations, Joseph . . . also profiles several famous leaders and uses their stories to spearhead a discussion of the intellectual and practical history of Black Power as a political movement. Enthusiastically recommended for public and academic libraries." Library Journal.

Katznelson, Ira

When affirmative action was white : an untold history of racial inequality in twentieth-century America / Ira Katznelson. W.W. Norton, c2005. xv, 238 p. ; **323.1196**

1. Johnson, Lyndon B., 1908-1973 Political and social views. 2. African Americans -- Civil rights -- History -- 20th century. 3. Affirmative action -- United States -- History -- 20th century. 4. African Americans -- Legal status, laws, etc. -- History -- 20th century. 5. African Americans -- Economic conditions -- 20th century. 6. United States -- Race relations. 7. United States -- Politics and government -- 1945-1989.
ISBN 0393052133

LC 2004024359

A study on the lesser-known origins of affirmative action argues that key programs passed during the New Deal and Fair Deal era of the 1930s and 1940s were purposefully discriminatory, revealing how Southern democrats widened the gap between black and white Americans through specific restrictions in social security, the GI bill, and landmark labor laws.

King, Martin Luther, Jr., 1929-1968

The **trumpet** of conscience / Martin Luther, Jr. King ; foreword by Coretta Scott King ; new foreword by Marian Wright Edelman. Beacon Press, 2010. xiv, 80 p. ; **323.1196**

1. Nonviolence 2. Social justice 3. Civil Rights Movement 4. Speeches, addresses, etc.
ISBN 9780807000717

LC 2010007881

Five lectures delivered for the renowned Canadian Broadcasting Corporation Massey Lecture Series in 1967 encompass distinct themes and speak prophetically to today's perils, addressing issues of racial equality, conscience and war; the mobilization of young people; and nonviolence.

King, Martin Luther, Jr., 1929-1968

Where do we go from here : chaos or community? / Martin Luther King, Jr. ; [foreword by Coretta Scott King ; introduction by Vincent Harding]. Beacon Press, c2010. xxiv, 223 p. ; **323.1196**

1. African Americans -- History -- 1964- 2. Civil Rights Movement 3. Social justice 4. Race relations
ISBN 9780807000670

LC 2009035950

Originally published: 1968.

The celebrated civil rights leader outlines the trends in the African American struggle during the sixties, and pleads for peaceful coexistence between the African American and white communities.

Sokol, Jason

All eyes are upon us : race and politics from Boston to Brooklyn / Jason Sokol. Basic Books, 2014 416 p. **323.1196**

1. Racism 2. Segregation. 3. Race relations 4. Northeastern States.
ISBN 9780465022267

LC 2014023616

A revelatory account of the tumultuous modern history of race and politics in the Northeast, All Eyes Are Upon Us presents the Northeast as a microcosm of America as a whole: outwardly democratic, inwardly conflicted, but always striving to live up to its highest ideals.

"Sokol provides some of the participants' previously unavailable recollections, based on interviews conducted for this history. Ultimately, the book provides a much-needed reminder of the difficult battles discrimination's enemies faced, even in the heart of what was supposed to be an already color-blind society." Choice.

Solomon, Akiba,

★**How** we fight white supremacy : a field guide to Black resistance / [edited by] Akiba Solomon + Kenrya Rankin. Nation Books, 2019. 368 p. **323.1196**

1. African Americans -- Civil rights. 2. Social justice. 3. Civil rights. 4. African Americans -- Politics and government -- 21st century. 5. United States -- Race relations.
ISBN 9781568588490

LC 2018032817

In this must-read for anyone new to resistance work, the authors celebrate the Black Resistance, from protests to art to sermons to joy, and provide a blueprint for the fight for freedom and justice--and ideas for how each of us can contribute.

"A powerful anthology that might indeed fulfill the wish of the co-authors that readers craft potent strategies to resist white supremacy." Kirkus.

Sorin, Gretchen Sullivan

Driving while black : African American travel and the road to civil rights / Gretchen Sorin. Liveright Publishing, [2020] 352 p. **323.1196**

1. African Americans 2. Tourism 3. Segregation in transportation 4. Automobile travel -- United States -- History -- 20th century 5. United States -- Race relations -- History -- 20th century

ISBN 9781631495694

LC 2019036574

The true story behind the award-winning film of the same name explores the role of travel in civil rights, the specific impact of the automobile on African-American life and the cultural importance of Victor and Alma Green's famous Green Book.

"The author also discusses how the car became a vehicle integral to the civil rights movement. A pleasing combination of terrific research and storytelling and engaging period visuals." Kirkus

Theoharis, Jeanne

A **more** beautiful and terrible history : the uses and misuses of civil rights history / Jeanne Theoharis. Beacon Press, 2018. 288 p. **323.1196**

1. African Americans -- Civil rights -- History -- 20th century 2. Civil Rights Movement 3. Social movements 4. Historiography 5. United States -- Race relations -- History -- 20th century

ISBN 9780807075876

LC 2017030979

Examines the accepted narrative of the civil rights movement to reveal the myths and fables that diminish its scope, and reveals the diversity of activists and the immense barriers and repression they faced.

"Chronicling the efforts of many activists, the author underscores her message that reform requires courage and hard work. An impassioned call for continued efforts for change." Kirkus.

Watson, Bruce, 1953-

Freedom summer : the savage summer that made Mississippi burn and made America a democracy / Bruce Watson. Viking, c2010. 384 p. **323.1196**

1. Race relations 2. Civil rights. 3. African Americans -- Suffrage -- Mississippi -- History -- 20th century. 4. Civil Rights Movement -- Mississippi 5. Mississippi -- Race relations -- History -- 20th century.

ISBN 9780670021703

LC 2009047211

Analyzes a critical shift in American race relations during the summer of 1964, documenting how civil rights demonstrations by hundreds of college students triggered African-American voter registries and violent uprisings.

323.1197 Native Americans--Civil rights

Hendricks, Steve

The **unquiet** grave : the FBI and the struggle for the soul of Indian country / Steve Hendricks. Thunder Mouth Press, 2006. 544 p. **323.1197**

1. FBI. 2. American Indian Movement. 3. Indians of North America -- History. 4. Native American organizations. 5. Red Power. 6. Native American resistance and revolts.

ISBN 1560257350

LC bl2006023860

Citing the 1976 murder of Native American activist Anna Mae Aquash, a history of the adversarial relationship between the FBI and Native Americans draws on the author's archival research into previously unreleased documents to reveal murderous conspiracies and cover-ups on both sides of the unofficial conflict.

Saunt, Claudio

Unworthy republic : the dispossession of Native Americans and the road to Indian Territory / Claudio Saunt. W. W. Norton & Co., 2020. 288 p. **323.1197**

1. Indian Removal, 1813-1903 2. Indians of North America -- Land tenure. 3. Forced relocations -- History 4. Indians of North America -- Relocation. 5. United States -- History -- 19th century

ISBN 9780393609844

A history of the 1830s forced migration of indigenous populations to territories west of the Mississippi describes the government-driven fraud, intimidation and murder that were used to confiscate Native American homelands and property.

"This valuable addition to the scholarship of Native American dispossession and extermination should be read by scholars and general readers alike." Library Journal

323.173 Minority rights--United States

Sanders, Symone D.

No, you shut up : speaking truth to power and reclaiming America / Symone D. Sanders. HarperCollins, 2020. 228 p. **323.173**

1. Sanders, Symone D. 2. Women political consultants 3. Political activists 4. Political participation 5. African American women 6. United States -- Politics and government -- 21st century

ISBN 9780062942685

LC bl2020012141

A senior advisor for former Vice President Joe Biden's 2020 presidential campaign and self-described millennial spokesperson offers an inspiring call-to-action for finding your authentic voice and effectively fighting ideological battles through stories from her own life.

"A black woman opens up about her journey to the forefront of American politics. . . . Provocative, galvanizing words that should inspire others to take action against the status quo." Kirkus

323.4 Specific civil rights limitation and suspension of

McCoy, Alfred W.

A **question** of torture : CIA interrogation, from the Cold War to the War on Terror / Alfred W. McCoy. Metropolitan Books/ Henry Holt and Co., 2006. 290 p. : **323.4**

1. CIA. 2. Torture -- United States -- History. 3. Military interrogation -- United States -- History. 4. Intelligence service -- United States -- History. 5. United States -- Politics and government.

ISBN 0805080414

LC 2005051124

Describes the CIA's use of psychological torture, from the Cold War to the post-September 11th era, detailing the use of isolation, extremes of temperature, the manipulation of time, and assessing the implications of such inhumane practices.

"The author shows how, since 1950, the CIA and various nations have augmented traditional physical torture with psychological abuse techniques of sensory disorientation and self-inflicted pain, which he documents with some gruesome first-person accounts by victims and with stories of doctors who conducted horrific experiments." Library Journal.

Williams, Juan

Eyes on the prize : America's civil rights years, 1954-1965 / Juan Williams ; with the Eyes on the prize production team ; introduction by Julian Bond. Viking, 1987. xv, 300 p. : **323.4**

1. African Americans -- Civil rights -- History -- 20th century. 2. Civil Rights Movement 3. Race relations. 4. United States -- Race relations.
ISBN 0670814121
LC 86040271

Includes index.

"Highly recommended both as a socio-historical document and as a heartfelt, poignant remembrance of a movement and its activists." Booklist.

323.44 Freedom of action (Liberty)

Nossel, Suzanne, 1969-

Dare to speak : defending free speech for all / Suzanne Nossel. Dey Street Books, 2020. 208 p. **323.44**

1. United States. Constitution. 1st Amendment. 2. Freedom of speech. 3. Human rights 4. Civil rights 5. Democracy
ISBN 9780062966032
LC 2019054636

The CEO of PEN America and former executive director of Amnesty International USA outlines vital steps for maintaining open democratic debates that respect diversity while defending free speech and cultivating a more inclusive society.

Nussbaum, Martha Craven, 1947-

Liberty of conscience : in defense of America's tradition of religious equality / Martha C. Nussbaum. Basic Books, c2008. viii, 406 p. ; **323.44**

1. United States. Constitution. 1st Amendment 2. Freedom of religion -- United States 3. Religion and politics. 4. Church and state -- United States. 5. Religion. 6. United States -- Religion.
ISBN 9780465051649
LC 2007038176

"The author plumbs the historical, political, philosophical, and legal debates surrounding religious freedom." Booklist.

Shipler, David K., 1942-

Freedom of speech : mightier than the sword / David K. Shipler. Knopf, 2015. 384 p. **323.44**

1. United States. Constitution. 1st Amendment. 2. Freedom of speech. 3. Censorship. 4. Civil rights
ISBN 9780307957320
LC 2014032127

Presents an expansive assessment of the state of free speech in America as reflected by current events and personal stories.

"This book addresses a timely subject and is written by someone with a deep interest in the controversies and difficulties surrounding freedom of speech." Library Journal.

Stone, Geoffrey R.

★**Perilous** times : free speech in wartime from the Sedition Act of 1798 to the war on terrorism / Geoffrey R. Stone. W.W. Norton & Co., 2004. xx, 730 p. : **323.44**

1. Freedom of speech -- History. 2. Political persecution 3. Civil rights. 4. Dissenting opinions -- United States. 5. United States -- History.
ISBN 0393058808
LC 2004017871

Robert F. Kennedy Book Award, 2005.

"The author delivers rich material in an engaging, character-based narrative. Stone offers deep insight into rhetorical history and the men and women who made it--resisters like Clement Vallandingham, Emma Goldman, Fred Korematsu and Daniel Ellsberg; presidents faced with wartime dilemmas; and the prosecutors, defenders and Supreme Court justices who shaped our understanding of the First Amendment today." Publishers Weekly.

Strittmatter, Kai

We have been harmonized : life in China's surveillance state / Kai Strittmatter. Custom House, [2020] vi, 360 p. ; **323.44**

1. Xi Jinping 2. Communist Party of China. 3. Authoritarianism 4. Electronic surveillance -- China. 5. Technology -- Political aspects 6. Censorship 7. China -- Politics and government. 8. China -- Social conditions.
ISBN 9780063027299
LC bl2020052315

"Originally published in Germany in 2018 by Piper Verlag GmbH."

"First English publication in Great Britain in 2019 by Old Street Publishing."

The China correspondent for Germany's Sueddeutsche Zeitung national newspaper draws on in-depth investigative reporting to reveal how the chilling vision of authoritarianism in George Orwell's 1984 has come true in China's high-tech surveillance state.

"Strittmatter's accessible yet hard-hitting narrative will find an audience with policymakers and general readers alike." Kirkus

Waldman, Steven

Founding faith : the birth of religious freedom in America / Steven Waldman. Random House, 2008. 277 p. **323.44**

1. Freedom of religion -- United States 2. Religion and state. 3. Civil religion. 4. Church and state. 5. United States -- Religion -- History.
ISBN 1400064376
LC 2007021710

The co-founder of Beliefnet.com traces the origins and history of religious freedom in America, looking at the role of religion in the early republic, the ways religion promoted the American Revolution, the separation of church and state, and how the religious beliefs of the Founding Fathers affected the battle for religious freedom.

"This is an excellent book about an important subject: the inescapable--but manageable--intersection of religious belief and public life. With a grasp of history and an understanding of the exigencies of the moment, Waldman finds a middle ground between those who think of the Founders as apostles in powdered wigs and those who assert, equally inaccurately, that the Founders believed religion had no place in politics." Newsweek.

Weatherford, J. McIver

Genghis Khan and the quest for God : how the world's greatest conqueror gave us religious freedom / Jack Weatherford. Penguin Group USA, 2016. 304 p. **323.44**

1. Genghis Khan, 1162-1227 2. Conquerors 3. Religious tolerance 4. Religion and culture 5. Civilization 6. Mongolia -- Rulers
ISBN 9780735221154
LC 2016039793

Reveals how Genghis Khan harnessed the power of religion to rule the largest empire the world has ever known. By the New York Times best-selling author of Genghis Khan and the Making of the Modern World.

"This sound examination of Khan, his methods of rule, and his views on religious tolerance presents a valid and welcome addition to scholarship on the subject." Library Journal.

323.440973 Liberty--United States

Metaxas, Eric

If you can keep it : the forgotten promise of American liberty / Eric Metaxas. Viking Press, 2016 260 p. **323.440973**

1. Power (Social sciences) 2. National characteristics, American 3. Religion and politics 4. Patriotism 5. United States

ISBN 9781101979983

LC 2017449517

Presents a critical analysis of the Founding Fathers' original intentions that argues that America is a nation bound by a radical and unprecedented idea about liberty and freedom that must be upheld by every citizen.

323.6 Citizenship and related topics

Rather, Dan

What unites us : reflections on patriotism / Dan Rather & Elliot Kirschner. Algonquin Books, 2017. 176 p. **323.6**

1. National characteristics, American 2. Patriotism 3. Citizenship 4. United States 5. Essays

ISBN 9781616207823

LC 2017028401

The Emmy Award-winning veteran journalist shares passionate essays about what it means to be an American and the relevance of patriotism in today's world, exploring subjects ranging from the institutions that support the nation, major events from that past half century and how the country can better unite to secure a collective future.

"Rather has issued a stirring call for overcoming todays strident partisanship." Publishers Weekly.

324.0973 Political process--United States

Plouffe, David

A **citizen's** guide to beating Donald Trump / David Plouffe. Viking, 2020. xxiii, 228 p. ; **324.0973**

1. Democratic Party. 2. Political campaigns. 3. Elections -- United States 4. Presidential election, 2020 5. Citizen participation in government 6. United States -- Politics and government -- Citizen participation.

ISBN 9781984879493

LC 2019052889

A voter's playbook on making a difference in the 2020 election and beyond, written by Barack Obama's campaign manager, outlines practical activities that everyday citizens can use to counter misinformation and garner voter support.

"For Democrats, liberals, and progressives . . . this is an invaluable map for political engagement." Booklist

324.2 Political parties

Sassoon, Donald

One hundred years of socialism : the West European left in the twentieth century / Donald Sassoon. New Press, 1996. xxv, 965 p. : **324.2**

1. Socialism -- Western Europe -- History -- 20th century. 2. Communism -- Europe -- History. 3. Socialist parties -- Western Europe. 4. Western Europe -- Politics and government.

ISBN 1565844866

LC 2003389177

"Sassoon's knowledge of the minutiae of history and his respect for the image drive the narrative. {This work is} thoroughly researched and highly readable." Library Journal.

324.2734 Republican Party

Bordewich, Fergus M.

Congress at war : how Republican reformers fought the Civil War, defied Lincoln, ended slavery, and remade America / Fergus M. Bordewich. Alfred A. Knopf, 2020. 464 p. **324.2734**

1. Republican Party -- History 2. United States. Congress -- History 19th century 3. Legislators -- United States 4. War -- Economic aspects 5. Slavery 6. Social change 7. United States -- Politics and government -- 1861-1865 8. United States -- History -- Civil War, 1861-1865

ISBN 9780451494443

LC 2019015354

"A Borzoi Book."

Explains how Congress helped win the Civil War--a new perspective that puts the House and Senate, rather than Lincoln, at the center of the conflict.

"Bordewich contributes an entertaining, fresh perspective to our ever-evolving understanding and discussion of the Civil War. An important addition for both general readers of American history and scholars of the growing interpretations of Civil War studies." Library Journal

Gould, Lewis L.

Grand Old Party : a history of the Republicans / Lewis L. Gould. Random House, 2003. xv, 597 p., 16 p. of plates : **324.2734**

1. Republican Party -- History.

ISBN 0375507418

LC 2003046604

A narrative history of the Republican party ranges from its emergence as the antislavery party during the 1850s to its current role as the champion of political conservatism.

"This is an account of the Grand Old Party that spans its earliest days under Abraham Lincoln to its conservative bent today. Much of the book documents the shifts of its platform. Gould also discusses the leadership qualities, farsighted policies, conservative federal spending, and willingness to provide social programs at the cost of future generations of four Republican presidents: Lincoln, Theodore Roosevelt, Eisenhower, and Reagan." Library Journal.

Stevens, Stuart

It was all a lie : how the Republican Party became Donald Trump / Stuart Stevens. Alfred A. Knopf, 2020. 256 p. **324.2734**

1. Trump, Donald, 1946- 2. Goldwater, Barry M. 1909-1998 3. Reagan, Ronald 4. Republican Party 5. Conservatism -- United States 6. Political culture -- United States 7. Nationalism -- United States 8. Political parties -- United States 9. United States -- Politics

and government 10. United States -- Race relations.
ISBN 9780525658450

LC 2019048755

"This is a Borzoi book published by Alfred A. Knopf."

A leading Republican political operative presents an unflinching exposé of today's Republican party that argues that the Trump administration is a logical outcome for a morally bankrupt party still largely motivated by racism, political grandstanding and fiscal inequality.

"A one-time Republican operative recounts the transformation of the big-tent GOP into an organ of white nationalism. . . . [O]f interest to all politics junkies, for a formerly venerable party by a champion-turned-gravedigger." Kirkus

324.2734089 Republican Party--Ethnic groups

Cadava, Geraldo L., 1977-

The **Hispanic** Republican : the shaping of an American political identity, from Nixon to Trump / Geraldo Cadava. Ecco Press, 2020. 272 p. **324.2734089**

1. Republican Party 2. Hispanic Americans -- Political activity 3. Political participation 4. Conservatism
ISBN 9780062946348

LC bl2020010968

A history of the growth of Hispanic-American Republican voters throughout the past half century discusses how the unlikely partnership between Latino voters and the Republican party has had a surprising impact on U.S. politics.

"A necessary acquisition for every nonfiction collection during this election year." Booklist

324.273409 Republican Party--History

Alberta, Tim

American carnage : on the front lines of the Republican civil war and the rise of President Trump / Tim Alberta. HarperCollins, 2019. 352 p. **324.273409**

1. Trump, Donald, 1946- 2. Republican Party 3. Political culture -- United States -- History -- 21st century 4. Presidential election, 2016 5. Polarization (Social sciences) 6. Republicans 7. United States -- Politics and government -- 21st century
ISBN 9780062896445

LC bl2019014945

The *Politico Magazine* chief political correspondent reveals how a decade of cultural upheaval, populist outrage and ideological warfare made the GOP vulnerable to a hostile takeover by an unlikely presidential candidate.

324.6 Election systems and procedures; suffrage

American women's suffrage : voices from the long struggle for the vote 1776-1965 / edited by Susan Ware. Library of America, 2020. 731 p. Library of America **324.6**

1. Suffragist movement 2. Women -- Suffrage 3. Suffragists 4. Anti-suffragists 5. Essays 6. Speeches, addresses, etc. 7. Anthologies
ISBN 9781598536645

LC bl2020045836

The full, definitive story of the movement for voting rights for American women, of every race, told through the voices of the women and men who lived it. Here are the most recognizable figures in the campaign for women's suffrage, like Elizabeth Cady Stanton and Susan B. Anthony, but also the black, Chinese, and American Indian women and men who were not only essential to the movement but expanded its directions and aims. Expertly curated and introduced by scholar Susan Ware, each piece is prefaced by a headnote so that together these 100 selections by over 80 writers tell the full history of the movement.

"An unusually diverse mix of top-down and bottom-up views of the fight for votes for women." Kirkus

Anderson, Carol (Carol Elaine)

★**One** person, no vote : how voter suppression is destroying our democracy / Carol Anderson ; foreword by Senator Dick Durbin. Bloomsbury Publishing, 2018. 256 p. **324.6**

1. Voting Rights Act of 1965. 2. African Americans -- Suffrage. 3. Suffrage -- United States. 4. Civil rights. 5. Racism -- Political aspects. 6. United States -- Politics and government.
ISBN 9781635571370

LC 2018015633

The *New York Times* best-selling author of *White Rage* presents a timely history of voter suppression that exposes America's insidious history of policies that have blocked African-American voting participation, placing particular focus on the Supreme Court's 2013 <I>Shelby</I> ruling.

Berman, Ari

Give us the ballot : the modern struggle for voting rights in America / Ari Berman. Farrar, Straus and Giroux, 2015. 320 p. **324.6**

1. Voting Rights Act of 1965 2. Civil rights. 3. Suffrage -- United States. 4. Election law 5. Race relations.
ISBN 9780374158279

LC 2015004989

Includes index.

ALA Notable Book, 2016.

National Book Critics Circle Award for Nonfiction finalist

In 1965, the Voting Rights Act transformed election demographics in the United States. African Americans in the South began voting, running for office, and being elected for the first time since the Reconstruction period after the Civil War. Journalist Ari Berman compellingly details the act's history and also describes the recent "counterrevolution" against the VRA, in which dozens of state legislatures have passed measures making it more difficult to register and vote. Including views from different sides of the debate on voting restrictions, he presents a balanced but still revealing report on a wide variety of measures that have the potential to influence election results.

"General readers will appreciate the panoramic survey of the cases in which the VRA has been challenged and defended in federal and state courts and legislatures, and the fair inclusion of voices from both sides of the arguments. A timely and needed addition to the voting rights debate." Library Journal.

Cross, Tiffany D.

★**Say** it louder! : Black voters, white narratives, and saving our democracy / Tiffany Cross. Amistad, 2020. 176 p. **324.6**

1. African Americans. 2. Elections. 3. Democracy. 4. Women journalists. 5. United States.
ISBN 9780062976772

LC bl2020016123

A political analyst discusses American Democracy and the role that African Americans have played in its shaping while exposing political forces aligned to subvert and suppress black voters.

"An urgent plea for black involvement in the political process, essential in this election year." Kirkus

DuBois, Ellen Carol, 1947-

Suffrage : women's long battle for the vote / Ellen Carol Dubois. Simon & Schuster, 2020. 256 p. **324.6**

1. United States. Constitution. 19th Amendment 2. Suffrage -- United States 3. Voting 4. Women -- Suffrage 5. African American women -- Suffrage 6. United States -- Politics and government -- 20th century

ISBN 9781501165160

LC bl2020000218

Honoring the 100th anniversary of the 19th amendment to the Constitution, this exciting history explores the full scope of the movement to win the vote for women through portraits of its bold leaders and devoted activists.

"An authoritative, brisk, and sharply drawn history." Kirkus

Jenkins, Jessica D.

Exploring women's suffrage through 50 historic treasures / Jessica D. Jenkins. Rowman & Littlefield, 2020 xxxvi, 305 p. : **324.6**

1. United States. Constitution. 19th Amendment. 2. Women -- Suffrage -- United States -- History.

ISBN 9781538112793

LC 2019057194

Includes index.

"Jenkins brings together a wide selection of cultural objects representing the milestones and legacy of the long fight for women's voting rights. Color photos and essays detailing each object's story placed readers in the action of a groundbreaking movement and transports them to the sites that are the keepers of our country's past".-- Provided by publisher.

Lichtman, Allan J.

The **embattled** vote in America : from the founding to the present / Allan J. Lichtman. Harvard University Press, 2018. 336 p. **324.6**

1. Suffrage -- United States -- History 2. Voting 3. Inequality 4. Elections 5. United States -- Politics and government

ISBN 9780674972360

LC 2018006882

Americans have died for the right to vote. Yet our democratic system guarantees no one, not even citizens, the opportunity to elect a government. Allan Lichtman calls attention to the founders' greatest error--leaving the franchise to the discretion of individual states--and explains why it has triggered an unending struggle over voting rights.-- Provided by publisher

Quinn, Bridget

She votes : how U.S. women won suffrage, and what happened next / Bridget Quinn ; with a foreword by Nell Painter ; with illustrations by 100 women artists. Chronicle Books, 2020. 240 p. **324.6**

1. Women -- Suffrage -- United States -- History 2. Suffragists -- United States 3. Gender equity. 4. Intersectionality 5. Illustrated books

ISBN 9781452173160

LC 2019047183

She Votes is an intersectional story of the women who won suffrage, and those who have continued to raise their voices for equality ever since. From the first female Principal Chief of the Cherokee Nation to the first woman to wear pants on the Senate floor, author Bridget Quinn shines a spotlight on the women who broke down barriers.

"Art historian Quinn (Broad Strokes) commemorates the 100th anniversary of the ratification of the 19th Amendment in this vibrant and witty chronicle of women's rights in America. In 19 chapters illustrated by 100 female artists, Quinn profiles leaders of the women's suffrage and feminist movements, as well as groundbreaking women in the fields of art, politics, sports, and music. . . . This soaring movement history has something for neophytes and experts alike." Publishers Weekly

Wagner, Sally Roesch,

The **women's** suffrage movement / edited by Sally Roesch Wagner ; foreword by Gloria Steinem. Penguin Classics, 2019 368 p. **324.6**

1. Suffragists 2. Social history 3. Intersectionality 4. Suffragist movement 5. United States -- Social conditions -- 19th century 6. Anthologies

ISBN 9780143132431

LC 2018050035

Covers the major issues and figures involved in the women's suffrage movement with a special focus on diversity, incorporating race, class, and gender. The writings of such figures as Elizabeth Cady Stanton and Susan B. Anthony are featured alongside accounts of Native American women and African American suffragists such as Sarah Mapps Douglas and Harriet Purvis.

"Abundantly useful for aspiring scholars, while those with a casual interest in the subject will be struck by its surprising complexity." Kirkus.

Waldman, Michael, 1960-

The **fight** to vote / Michael Waldman. Simon & Schuster, 2016. 288 p. **324.6**

1. Suffrage. 2. Voting. 3. Political rights, Loss of 4. Political participation 5. United States -- Politics and government

ISBN 9781501116483

LC 2015030899

The president of a nonpartisan law and policy institute at NYU describes the fight for the right to vote and the historical, and ongoing, efforts by some to making voting difficult for the elderly, the poor and the young.

"Waldman urges citizens to find a way to celebrate democracy and reinvigorate political engagement for all. A timely contribution to the discussion of a crucial issue." Kirkus.

Weiss, Elaine F., 1952-

★The **woman's** hour : the great fight to win the vote / Elaine F. Weiss. Viking Press, 2018. 352 p. **324.6**

1. United States. Constitution. 19th Amendment. 2. Equal Rights Amendment (Proposed) 3. Suffragists. 4. Women's rights. 5. Suffragist movement. 6. Women -- Suffrage.

ISBN 9780525429722

LC 2018006746

An uplifting account of the 1920 ratification of the constitutional amendment that granted voting rights to women traces the culmination of seven decades of legal battles and cites the pivotal contributions of famous suffragists and political leaders.

"Weiss brings to life the fascinating characters at the heart of one of the most pivotal events in U.S. history with striking similarity to the social and political tensions of today." Booklist.

324.60973 Election systems and procedures--United States

Abrams, Stacey

Our time is now : power, purpose, and the fight for a fair America / Stacey Abrams. Henry Holt and Company, 2020. 272 p. **324.60973**

1. Abrams, Stacey. 2. Elections -- United States -- Corrupt practices. 3. Democracy. 4. Political participation. 5. Voter suppression. 6. United States -- Politics and government -- 2017-
ISBN 9781250257703

LC 2020005940

The award-winning House Democratic Leader and best-selling author draws on extensive national research to outline an empowering blueprint for ending voter suppression, reclaiming identity and reshaping progressive politics in America.

"If you are feeling hopeless about politics, this well-informed blueprint for change may begin to restore your faith." Kirkus

Shimer, David

Rigged : America, Russia, and one hundred years of covert electoral interference / David Shimer. Alfred A. Knopf, 2020. 367 p. ; **324.60973**

1. Trump, Donald, 1946- 2. Elections -- Corrupt practices. 3. Diplomatic and consular service 4. Political corruption 5. Foreign election influence 6. Russia -- Foreign relations United States 7. United States -- Politics and government -- 2017- 8. United States -- Foreign relations Russia
ISBN 9780525659006

LC bl2020013190

"A Borzoi Book"--Title page verso.

Presents a judicious history of covert foreign interference in world elections since the Cold War that discusses Russia's role in America's 2016 presidential election and why the threat is greater than ever in 2020.

"This incisive treatise lays bare the monumental task of countering foreign interference in the 2020 election." Publishers Weekly

Wehle, Kim

What you need to know about voting and why / Kim Wehle. HarperCollins, 2020. 304 p. **324.60973**

1. Voting 2. Elections -- United States 3. Suffrage 4. Voter registration 5. United States -- Politics and government
ISBN 9780062974785

LC bl2020013672

Law professor and constitutional scholar Kimberly Wehle offers practical, useful advice on the mechanics of voting and an enlightening survey of its history and future. For new voters, would-be voters, young people and all of us looking ahead to the next election, here is a timely and informative guide, providing the background you need in order to make informed choices that will shape our shared destiny for decades to come.

"A probing and limpid explanation of an often misunderstood patchwork of systems, requirements, and mechanisms." Kirkus

324.7 Conduct of election campaigns

Poniewozik, James

Audience of one : Donald Trump, television, and the fracturing of America / James Poniewozik. Liveright Publishing, 2019. xxiii, 325 p. **324.7**

1. Trump, Donald, 1946- 2. Television -- History 3. Presidents -- United States 4. Mass media -- Political aspects 5. Fame
ISBN 9781631494420

LC 2019021970

The New York Times chief television critic documents the history of mass media from the early 1980s through today, revealing how Donald Trump merged with America's most powerful medium to orchestrate his reinvention as a world leader.

324.70973 Election campaigns--United States

Harding, Luke, 1968-

Collusion : secret meetings, dirty money, and how Russia helped Donald Trump win / Luke Harding. Vintage Books, 2017 354 p. **324.70973**

1. Trump, Donald, 1946- 2. Political culture. 3. Political corruption 4. Presidential election, 2016 5. United States -- Politics and government -- 2017- 6. United States -- Foreign relations Russia 7. Russia -- Foreign relations United States
ISBN 9780525562511

LC 2017470511

"One point not in dispute is Harding's ability to bring together diverse strands of a complicated story to make a book that is informative, accessible, and hard to put down." Publishers Weekly

324.973 Elections--United States

Allen, Jonathan (Jonathan J. M.)

Shattered : inside Hillary Clinton's doomed campaign / Jonathan Allen and Amie Parnes. Crown, 2017. 288 p. **324.973**

1. Clinton, Hillary Rodham 2. Presidential election, 2016 3. Elections 4. Presidential candidates. 5. Political campaigns 6. United States -- Politics and government -- 21st century
ISBN 9780553447088

LC 2017010338

A dramatic analysis of the bitter 2016 election, told from the viewpoints of Hilary Clinton campaign insiders, reconstructs key decisions and missed opportunities that are being cited as the cause of the election upset.

"A top-notch campaign examination." Kirkus.

Davis, Lanny J.

The **unmaking** of the president 2016 : how FBI director James Comey cost Hillary Clinton the presidency / Lanny J. Davis. Scribner, 2018. 224 p. **324.973**

1. Comey, James B., Jr., 1960- 2. Clinton, Hillary Rodham 3. Presidential election, 2016 4. Elections 5. Presidential candidates. 6. Political campaigns 7. United States -- Politics and government -- 21st century
ISBN 9781501177729

LC bl2017051690

A longtime Washington insider argues that FBI Director James Comey's fateful letter to Congress, sent in the crucial days leading up to the presidential election, was an ultimate factor in how the election shifted to a Trump victory, revealing how the letter violated long-standing justice department policies.

"Lapsed Trump supporters might well open their minds to this attorney's scholarly, entirely convincing proof of the damage done." Kirkus.

Dickerson, John, 1968-

Whistlestop : my favorite stories from presidential campaign history / John Dickerson. Twelve, 2016. xxi, 439 p. : **324.973**

1. Presidential elections 2. Political campaigns. 3. Elections. 4. Politicians. 5. United States -- Politics and government
ISBN 9781455540488

LC bl2016031374

Collects insider stories from campaign aides and reporters about presdiental campaigns, from "Dukakis in the tank" to "Cuomo's plane to New Hampshire."

"A politically astute, timely book that will also have great historical value for future campaigns." Kirkus.

Farris, Scott

Almost president : the men who lost the race but changed the nation / Scott Farris. Lyons Press, 2012. 336 p. **324.973**

1. Presidential candidates -- United States 2. Presidential elections -- History. 3. Politicians. 4. United States -- Politics and government.
ISBN 9780762763788

LC 2011033001

"When the author lost a 1998 race for Wyoming's at-large congressional district, he was prompted to examine the role losers play in democracy. Farris notes that some unsuccessful White House aspirants have had a far greater impact on American history than many who became president. . . . Documenting changes in the face of America and the impact of such issues as race, religion, and workplace reform on elections, Farris writes with a lively flair, skillfully illustrating his solid historical research with revelatory anecdotes and facts." Publishers Weekly.

Fountain, Ben

Beautiful country burn again : democracy, rebellion, and revolution / Ben Fountain. Ecco Press, 2018. 448 p. **324.973**

1. Presidential election, 2016 2. Elections 3. Political parties 4. Social change 5. United States -- Politics and government -- 21st century 6. United States -- Social conditions -- 21st century 7. United States -- History 8. Essays
ISBN 9780062688842

LC 2018022055

The author of Billy Lynn's Long Halftime Walk presents a cautionary work of reportage that ties 2016's complicated political events to two other periods of American existential crises.

"Month by month, Fountain recaps campaign absurdities and national and international tragedies. Interspersed are essays pinpointing relevant historic events that have influenced the current political climate. Marry the two, and the result is a chronicle of past existential threats to our democracy and a warning-cum-prediction of what most probably lies ahead." Booklist.

Halperin, Mark

Double down : game change 2012 / Mark Halperin and John Heilemann. Penguin Group USA, 2013. 512 p. **324.973**

1. Presidential election, 2012 2. Presidential candidates. 3. Vice-Presidential candidates. 4. Politicians -- United States. 5. United States -- Politics and government
ISBN 9781594204401

LC 2013431166

An account of the 2012 presidential election draws on insider interviews to illuminate what the election meant to both parties, covering the dramatic Republican nomination fight, the rise and fall of Mitt Romney, and Barack Obama's Election Day triumph.

"The well-connected authors have worked their sources thoroughly to give readers a warts-and-all look at what went on behind the scenes." Booklist.

Hasen, Richard L.

Election meltdown : dirty tricks, distrust, and the threat to American democracy / Richard L. Hasen. Yale University Press, 2020 xi, 187 p. : **324.973**

1. Elections -- United States. 2. Manipulation (Social sciences) 3. Voting 4. Elections -- Corrupt practices. 5. United States -- Politics and government -- 2017-
ISBN 9780300248197

LC 2019945878

From the nation's leading expert, an indispensable analysis of key threats to the integrity of the 2020 American presidential election.

"A hard-hitting critique of the American election process as timely as it is frightening. . . . Required reading for legislators and voters." Kirkus

Ingraham, Laura

Billionaire at the barricades : the populists vs. the establishment from Reagan to Trump / Laura Ingraham. St Martin's Press, 2017 272 p. **324.973**

1. Trump, Donald, 1946- 2. Republican Party 3. Conservatism. 4. Populism 5. Political participation 6. Political culture 7. United States -- Politics and government -- 2009-2017
ISBN 9781250150646

LC 2017036170

The best-selling author of The Obama Diaries traces the 45th President's unexpected election at the head of a misunderstood populist revolt, arguing that Trump has reinvented the Reagan years in his own image by attracting a new coalition of voters who disagree with GOP elitism.

Rehnquist, William H., 1924-2005

Centennial crisis : the disputed election of 1876 / William H. Rehnquist. Alfred A. Knopf, 2004. ix, 274 p. : **324.973**

1. Hayes, Rutherford B., 1822-1893. 2. Tilden, Samuel J. (Samuel Jones), 1814-1886. 3. Bradley, Joseph P., 1813-1892. 4. Presidential election, 1876 5. Contested elections -- United States -- History -- 19th century. 6. Elections -- Corrupt practices -- United States -- History -- 19th century. 7. Political corruption -- History -- 19th century. 8. United States -- Politics and government -- 1869-1877.
ISBN 0375413871

LC 2003059630

Documents the contested presidential election campaign between Samuel Tilden and Rutherford B. Hayes, covering the five-month electoral dispute in multiple states, the corruption and turmoil that contributed to the outcome, and the endeavors of Justice Joseph Bradley and the Electoral Commission to cast the deciding vote.

"This is Supreme Court Chief Justice Rehnquist's narrative of the conflict between civil liberties and military necessity. Fully two-thirds of the book covers Civil War issues. One chapter discusses World War I espionage and draft resistance cases; three, the World War II internment of Japanese Americans and the imposition of martial law in Hawaii. Far from a complete survey of wartime civil liberties--reviewing only cases that reached the Supreme Court before 1950--this is nonetheless both enlightening and entertaining." Booklist.

Smith, Erin Geiger

★**Thank** you for voting : the maddening, enlightening, inspiring truth about voting in America / Erin Geiger Smith. HarperCollins, 2020 208 p. **324.973**

1. Voting 2. Civics 3. Voter registration 4. Citizen participation in government 5. United States -- Politics and government -- Citizen

participation
ISBN 9780062934826

LC bl2020046592

A journalistic examination of the ongoing fight for voting equality shares insights into why so few Americans vote, citing the role of corporations in encouraging voter turnout while outlining innovative approaches to voter education and motivation.

"This is an excellent resource for first-time voters and activists hoping to motivate young people to get to the polls." Publishers Weekly

325.73 International migration -- United States

Cannato, Vincent, 1967-

American passage : the history of Ellis Island / Vincent J. Cannato. Harper, c2009. 496 p. **325.73**

1. Ellis Island Immigration Station, New York -- History 2. Immigrants -- New York City -- History. 3. Immigration and emigration. 4. Immigrants -- United States -- History. 5. Ellis Island, New York -- History 6. United States -- Immigration and emigration -- History. 7. New York City -- Immigration and emigration -- History.
ISBN 9780060742737

LC 2008052245

A chronicle of the landmark port of entry's history documents its role as an execution site, immigration post, and deportation center that was profoundly shaped by evolving politics and ideologies.

"The author reaches back to the island's beginnings in the early 19th century, when, then named Gibbet Island, it served as a venue for hanging convicted pirates. Cannato then chronicles the many different people--immigrants, immigration officials, politicians and others--who made Ellis Island what it was in the early 20th century. Ambitious in scope and rooted in solid storytelling." Kirkus.

Soboroff, Jacob

★**Separated** : inside an American tragedy / Jacob Soboroff. Custom House, 2020. xxii, 388 p. **325.73**

1. Immigrants 2. Parent-separated children 3. Immigration policy 4. Undocumented immigrants 5. Mexican-American Border Region 6. United States -- Immigration and emigration
ISBN 9780062992192

LC 2020014644

An NBC News correspondent lays bare the full truth behind the Trump administration's systematic separation of desperate migrant families at the US-Mexico border. In June 2018, Donald Trump's most notorious decision as president had secretly been in effect for months before most Americans became aware of the astonishing inhumanity being perpetrated by their own government. Jacob Soboroff was among the first journalists to expose this reality after seeing firsthand the living conditions of the children in custody.

"Soboroff's thoroughly engaging expose of the inner workings of a corrupt and unfeeling government is essential to understanding America's current immigration misery." Booklist

Yang, Jia Lynn

★**One** mighty and irresistible tide : the epic struggle over American immigration, 1924-1965 / Jia Lynn Yang. W.W. Norton & Company, 2020 384 p. **325.73**

1. Immigration and emigration law -- History 2. Immigrants -- United States -- History -- 20th century. 3. Immigration and emigration law reform 4. Immigration enforcement 5. United States -- Immigration and emigration -- History -- 20th century.
ISBN 9780393635843

LC 2019050475

A history of the 20th-century battle to reform the American immigration laws behind today's most contentious debates discusses the Congressional immigration restrictions of 1924, the 1965 Immigration and Nationality Act and the impact of transformative laws on nonwhite migration.

"The combination of meticulous research and captivating writing creates a beautiful surprise; a dark history that gleams under the spotlight of unvarnished truthtelling. Expect a lot of reader requests and award attention for this significant title." Booklist

326 Slavery and emancipation

Hochschild, Adam

Bury the chains : prophets and rebels in the fight to free an empire's slaves / Adam Hochschild. Houghton Mifflin, 2005. viii, 468 p. : **326**

1. Clarkson, Thomas 1760-1846. 2. Anti-slavery movements -- Great Britain -- History -- 18th century. 3. Anti-slavery movements -- Great Britain -- History -- 19th century. 4. Slavery 5. Slave trade -- Great Britain -- History. 6. Great Britain -- History -- 18th century. 7. Great Britain -- History -- 19th century.
ISBN 0618104690

LC 2004054091

Lionel Gelber Prize (Canada), 2006.
National Book Award for Nonfiction finalist, 2005

"The author brings drama and incredible research to this thrilling look at the little-celebrated abolition movement in Britain and its reverberations throughout modern democracies." Booklist.

Sinha, Manisha

The **Slave's** cause : a history of abolition / Manisha Sinha. Yale University Press, 2016. 784 p. **326**

1. Abolitionists 2. Slavery 3. Anti-slavery movements -- History 4. African Americans
ISBN 9780300181371

LC 2015948091

A groundbreaking history of abolition that recovers the largely forgotten role of African Americans in the long march toward emancipation from the American Revolution through the Civil War.

"Sinha's book is a tour de force that surpasses all previous works in scope, scale, and scholarship." Library Journal.

326.0973 Slavery and emancipation--United States

Rediker, Marcus

★The **Amistad** rebellion : an Atlantic odyssey of slavery and freedom / Marcus Rediker. Viking, 2012. 304 p. **326.0973**

1. Amistad (Schooner) 2. Slave trade -- United States -- History 3. Slaves -- United States -- History 4. Slavery 5. Trials (Mutiny) -- United States -- History -- 19th century 6. United States -- History -- 19th century
ISBN 9780670025046

LC 2012014810

A scholarly account of the 19th-century slave ship rebellion is presented from the perspectives of the slaves and discusses their shared culture on another continent and their harrowing fight for freedom while placing their victory in a context of the great chain of resistance spanning the earliest slave revolts through the Civil Rights era.

"Spectacularly researched and fluidly composed, this latest study offers some much needed perspective on a critical yet oft-overlooked event in America's history." Publishers Weekly.

327 International relations

Kissinger, Henry, 1923-
World order / Henry Kissinger. Penguin Group USA, 2014 432 p. **327**

1. Great powers. 2. Diplomacy. 3. Rulers. 4. History.
ISBN 9781594206146

LC 2014028152

Grounded in Kissinger's deep study of history and experience as national security advisor and secretary of state, World Order guides readers on a tour of the globe. It examines the events and ideas that formed the historic concepts of order, their manifestations in contemporary controversies, and the ways in which they might ultimately be reconciled.

"Critics are unlikely to find much interest in this volume as it largely summarizes Kissinger's thinking, but students and historians of political science may appreciate his suggestion that both realism and idealism are necessary in modern times." Library Journal.

327.0285 International relations--Computer applications

Klimburg, Alexander, 1976-
The **darkening** web : the war for cyberspace / Alexander Klimburg. Penguin Press, [2017] 400 p. **327.0285**

1. International relations 2. Information society -- Political aspects. 3. Cyberspace -- Government policy. 4. Information warfare -- Risk assessment.
ISBN 9781594206665

LC 2017008579

A cybersecurity expert explores how the Internet has become a tool of warfare and exploitation, sharing cautionary insights into how global powers are creating and disseminating distorted versions of reality to advance national interests.

"The dark side of cyberspace is a daunting subject, but Klimburgs narrative is very accessible, and frankly, this is all far too important to ignore." Booklist.

327.09 International relations--History

Reynolds, David, 1952-
Summits : six meetings that shaped the twentieth century / David Reynolds. Basic Books, 2007. 544 p. **327.09**

1. Summit meetings -- History 2. Summit meetings (Soviet-American relations) -- History 3. Diplomacy -- History 4. World politics -- 20th century 5. United States -- Social life and customs -- 20th century.
ISBN 9780465069040

LC 2009281197

Drawing on extensive archival material, the historian-author of In Command of History traces the history of the twentieth century through six fateful summit meetings and the remarkable personalities who took part, ranging from Neville Chamberlain's disastrous appeasement policy in 1938 Munich to Reagan and Gorbachev's successful encounter in 1985 Geneva.

"The author's thorough mastery of his subject is reflected in the fluency and assurance of the writing." Publishers Weekly.

327.1 Foreign policy and specific topics in international

Foer, Franklin
How soccer explains the world : an unlikely theory of globalization / Franklin Foer. Harper Collins, c2004. 261 p. ; **327.1**

1. Globalization (Economics) 2. Soccer. 3. World politics.
ISBN 0066212340

LC bl2005003423

Provides an analysis of the sport's reflection of history as well as its modern influence and identifies commonalities between tribalism and globalization, explaining how such factors as terrorism, poverty, racism, and religion contribute to how the gameis played today.

"Though the globalism thread sometimes disappears, the author is unfailingly interesting. Lively and provocative-even for those who just don't get what FIFA is all about." Kirkus.

327.12 Espionage and subversion

Anderson, Scott, 1959-
★The **quiet** Americans : four CIA spies at the dawn of the Cold War -- a tragedy in three acts / Scott Anderson. Doubleday, 2020 448 p. **327.12730092**

1. Burke, Michael, 1918- 2. Wisner, Frank, 1909-1965. 3. Sichel, Peter M. F. 4. Lansdale, Edward Geary, 1908-1987. 5. United States. Central Intelligence Agency Officials and employees 6. Cold War. 7. Espionage 8. Intelligence officers -- United States 9. Spies -- United States
ISBN 9780385540452

LC 2019054799

From the best-selling author of Lawrence in Arabia, a gripping history of the early years of the Cold War, the CIA's covert battles against communism, and the tragic consequences which still affect America and the world toda

"The roots of America's decline in international reputation since WWII lie in the government's confused and hypocritical actions during the first decade of the Cold War, according to this fascinating history by journalist Anderson (Fractured Lands). . . . Laced with vivid character sketches and vital insights into 20th-century geopolitics, this stand-out chronicle helps to make sense of the world today." Publishers Weekly

Friedman, Matti
Spies of no country : secret lives at the birth of Israel / Matti Friedman. Algonquin Books of Chapel Hill, 2019. 224 p. **327.12095694**

1. Mossad. 2. Palmach. 3. Haganah (Organization) 4. Spies. 5. Espionage. 6. Undercover operations. 7. Mossad agents. 8. Palestine -- History -- 1929-1948. 9. Beirut, Lebanon -- History. 10. Israel -- History -- 1948-1949.
ISBN 9781616207229

LC 2018026756

Canadian Jewish Book Award, 2019.

A meticulously researched chronicle of the Arab Section, Israel's first spy organization, details how undercover intelligence operatives in 1948 Beirut risked or lost their lives in support of Israeli statehood.

Gellman, Barton, 1960-
★**Dark** mirror : Edward Snowden and the American sur-

veillance state / Barton Gellman. Penguin Press, 2020. 400 p. **327.12730092**

1. Snowden, Edward J., 1983- 2. Gellman, Barton, 1960- 3. United States. National Security Agency. 4. Investigative journalists 5. Secrecy in government 6. Electronic surveillance 7. Government information 8. United States -- Politics and government
ISBN 9781594206016

LC 2019049573

An inside account of the surveillance-industrial revolution and its discontents, fighting back against state and corporate intrusions into our most private spheres.

"A riveting, timely book sure to be one of the most significant of the year." Kirkus

Greenwald, Glenn

★**No** place to hide : Edward Snowden, the NSA, and the U.S. surveillance state / Glenn Greenwald. Henry Holt and Company, 2014. 320 p. **327.12**

1. Snowden, Edward J., 1983- 2. United States. National Security Agency. 3. Leaks (Disclosure of information) 4. National security -- United States 5. Privacy.
ISBN 9781627790734

LC 2014932888

ALA Notable Book, 2015.

An investigative reporter for The Guardian and best-selling author of With Liberty and Justice for Some presents an assessment of the NSA surveillance scandal that has triggered debates over national security and information privacy to explore its alliances and consequences.

"In his analysis, the author breaks down the dense NSA subject matter and uses excerpts and slides from the documents to illustrate his points, making this work readable for even those unfamiliar with the technical concepts." Library Journal.

327.1209 Espionage and subversion--History

Andrew, Christopher M.

The **secret** world : a history of intelligence / Christopher Andrew. Yale University Press, 2018. 900 p. **327.1209**

1. Espionage -- History 2. Intelligence service 3. Spies 4. Military intelligence
ISBN 9780300238440

LC 2018947154

The first-ever detailed, comprehensive history of intelligence, from Moses and Sun Tzu to the present day.

327.125694 Espionage--Israel and Palestine

Berg, Raffi

Red Sea spies : the true story of Mossad's fake diving resort / Raffi Berg. Icon Books, 2020. xxvii, 324 p., 16 unnumbered p. of plates : **327.125694**

1. Israel. Mosad le-modiʻin ṿe-tafḳidim meyuḥadim. 2. Intelligence service -- Israel -- History -- 20th century. 3. Espionage -- Sudan. 4. Jews, Ethiopian -- Sudan -- History -- 20th century. 5. Jews, Ethiopian -- Israel -- History -- 20th century.
ISBN 9781785786006

LC 2019467991

"The little-known story of a daring Mossad operation and the holiday resort run by spies."-- Provided by publisher.

327.1273 Espionage--United States

Hanson, Jason (Security specialist)

Survive like a spy : real CIA operatives reveal how they stay safe in a dangerous world and how you can too / Jason Hanson. TarcherPerigee, 2017. xii, 241 p. ; **327.1273**

1. Spies -- United States -- Anecdotes. 2. Survival. 3. Life skills.
ISBN 9780143131595

LC 2017058350

A follow-up to the best-selling Spy Secrets That Can Save Your Life reveals high-stakes techniques and survival tactics from real intelligence officers who have employed the same measures in life-or-death situations throughout the world.

Jacobsen, Annie

Surprise, kill, vanish : the secret history of CIA paramilitary armies, operators, and assassins / Annie Jacobsen. Little, Brown & Company, 2019. 560 p. **327.1273**

1. CIA -- History 2. Elite operatives 3. Paramilitary forces 4. Undercover operations 5. Intelligence service 6. United States -- Foreign relations 7. United States -- Covert operations
ISBN 9780316441438

LC bl2019008459

Tells the untold story of the CIA's Special Activities Division, a highly-classified branch of the CIA and the most effective black-operations force in the world.

"Similar to her previous treatments of the Pentagon's research division (The Pentagon's Brain) and paranormal activity (Phenomena), Jacobsen here presents a tour de force exploring the CIA's paramilitary activities. Highly recommended for those seeking a better understanding of American foreign policy in action." Library Journal.

327.1273009 Espionage--United States--History

Weiner, Tim

Legacy of ashes : the history of the CIA / Tim Weiner. Doubleday, 2007. 702 p., [8] p. of plates : **327.1273009**

1. CIA -- History. 2. Intelligence service -- United States -- History. 3. Intelligence officers 4. Secrecy in government 5. Spies 6. United States -- History -- 1945-
ISBN 038551445X

National Book Award for Nonfiction, 2007.

National Book Critics Circle Award for Nonfiction finalist, 2007.

Traces the history of the CIA from the end of World War II to Iraq, in a study that condemns the organization for its record, its inability to understand world affairs, the violence it has unleashed, and its undermining of American politics.

327.1273043 Espionage--United States and Germany

Vogel, Steve, 1960-

Betrayal in Berlin : the true story of the Cold War's most audacious espionage operation / Steve Vogel. Custom House, 2019. 464 p. **327.1273043**

1. Blake, George, 1922- 2. KGB 3. Tunnels 4. Cold War 5. Moles (Spies) 6. Surveillance 7. Berlin, Germany -- History -- 1945-1990 8. East Berlin, Germany 9. West Berlin, Germany 10. Soviet Union
ISBN 9780062449627

LC bl2019021002

Its code name was "Operation Gold," a wildly audacious CIA plan to construct a clandestine tunnel into East Berlin to tap into critical KGB and Soviet military telecommunication lines. Success would provide the CIA and the British Secret Intelligence Service access to a vast treasure of intelligence. Exposure might spark a dangerous confrontation with the Soviets. Yet as the Allies were burrowing into the German soil, a traitor, code-named Agent Diamond by his Soviet handlers, was burrowing into the operation itself. . .

327.41043 International relations--United Kingdom and Germany

Bouverie, Tim, 1987-

Appeasement : Chamberlain, Hitler, Churchill, and the road to war / Tim Bouverie. Tim Duggan Books, 2019. 416 p. **327.41043**

1. Chamberlain, Neville, 1869-1940. 2. Churchill, Winston, 1874-1965. 3. Hitler, Adolf, 1889-1945. 4. World War II -- Causes. 5. World War II -- Diplomatic history. 6. Great Britain -- Foreign relations Germany. 7. Great Britain -- Politics and government -- 1936-1945. 8. Great Britain -- Foreign relations -- 1936-1945.
ISBN 9780451499844

LC 2019000625

A narrative history of the British appeasement of the Third Reich before World War II draws on previously unseen archival resources to identify the indecision, failed diplomacy and parliamentary infighting that enabled Hitler's domination of Europe.

Phillips, Adrian (Historian)

Fighting Churchill, appeasing Hitler : Neville Chamberlain, Sir Horace Wilson, & Britain's plight of appeasement, 1937-1939 / Adrian Phillips. Pegasus Books, 2019. xxxi, 448 p., 8 unnumbered p. of plates : **327.41043**

1. Chamberlain, Neville, 1869-1940. 2. Churchill, Winston, 1874-1965. 3. Wilson, Horace, 1882-1972 4. Hitler, Adolf, 1889-1945. 5. Political culture 6. World War II -- Causes. 7. Aggression (International relations) 8. Political science -- History. 9. Great Britain -- Foreign relations Germany. 10. Germany -- Foreign relations Great Britain. 11. Great Britain -- Politics and government -- 1936-1945. 12. Great Britain -- Foreign relations -- 1936-1945.
ISBN 9781643132211

LC bl2019032886

The author presents a controversial revisionist examination of the British policy of appeasement in the late 1930s to identify key miscalculations and fateful concessions that rendered World War II inevitable.

327.73 Foreign relations--United States

Chomsky, Noam

Who rules the world? / Noam Chomsky. Metropolitan Books 2016 320 p. **327.73**

1. September 11 Terrorist Attacks, 2001 -- Influence 2. Military power. 3. Democracy 4. United States -- Politics and government. 5. Essays
ISBN 9781627793810

LC 2016010018

Presents an examination of the waning American Century, the nature of U.S. policies in the post-9/11 world, and the dangers of prioritizing military power over democracy and human rights.

"Chomsky, fierce and unapologetic, has a strong fan base and continues to be an important voice." Booklist.

Farrow, Ronan, 1987-

War on peace : the end of diplomacy and the decline of American influence / Ronan Farrow. W W Norton & Company, 2018 384 p. **327.73**

1. United States. Department of State 2. Diplomacy 3. United States -- Foreign relations administration
ISBN 9780393652109

LC 2018006827

Includes index.

American diplomacy is under siege. Offices across the State Department sit empty, while abroad the military-industrial complex has assumed the work once undertaken by peacemakers. We're becoming a nation that shoots first and asks questions later. In an astonishing account ranging from Washington, D.C., to Afghanistan, Pakistan, and North Korea in the years since 9/11, acclaimed journalist and former diplomat Ronan Farrow illuminates one of the most consequential and poorly understood changes in American history.

"Excellent, wide-ranging reporting and sharp-edged analysis make this a book that's sure to be talked about inside the Beltwayand that deserves a wide audience beyond." Kirkus. Reviews

Ferreiro, Larrie D.

Brothers at arms : American independence and the men of France and Spain who saved it / Larrie D. Ferreiro. Knopf, 2016. 416 p. **327.73**

1. American Revolution, 1775-1783 2. Alliances 3. International relations -- History 4. United States -- Foreign relations 5. United States -- History -- Revolution, 1775-1783 -- French participation 6. United States -- History -- Revolution, 1775-1783 -- Spanish participation 7. Great Britain -- Foreign relations 8. France -- Foreign relations Great Britain. 9. Great Britain -- Foreign relations France. 10. Spain -- Foreign relations Great Britain. 11. Great Britain -- Foreign relations Spain.
ISBN 9781101875247

LC 2016007136

Pulitzer Prize for History finalist, 2017.

"The remarkable untold story of how the American Revolution's success depended on substantial military and financial assistance provided by France and Spain, and places the Revolution in the context of the global strategic interests of those nations in their fight against Great Britain".-- Provided by publisher.

"A largely untold, engrossing history of our nations fraught, and unlikely, path to liberty." Kirkus.

Kagan, Robert

The **jungle** grows back : the case for American power / Robert Kagan. Alfred A. Knopf, 2018. 192 p. **327.73**

1. Geopolitics 2. International security 3. International relations 4. Power (Social sciences 5. United States -- Foreign relations -- 1945-1989. 6. United States -- Foreign relations -- 1989- 7. United States -- History -- 21st century
ISBN 9780525521655

LC 2018011882

"A brilliant and visionary argument for America's role as an enforcer of peace and order throughout the world--and what is likely to happen if we withdraw and focus our attention inward".-- Provided by publisher.

Kennedy, Robert F., 1925-1968

Thirteen days : a memoir of the Cuban Missile Crisis / Robert

F. Kennedy ; foreword by Arthur Schlesinger, Jr. W.W. Norton, 1999, c1969. 185 p. ; **327.73**

1. Military bases, Soviet -- Cuba 2. United States -- Foreign relations Soviet Union. 3. Soviet Union -- Foreign relations United States.
ISBN 9780393318340

LC BL 00004822

Reprint. Originally published: 1969. With a new foreword.

Kennedy describes the moral dilemma the crisis posed and describes the attitudes and actions of President Kennedy and his advisory staff.

Kinzer, Stephen

★The **true** flag : Theodore Roosevelt, Mark Twain, and the birth of American empire / Stephen Kinzer. Henry Holt and Company, 2016. 320 p. **327.73**

1. Roosevelt, Theodore, 1858-1919 2. Lodge, Henry Cabot, 1902-1985 3. Twain, Mark, 1835-1910 4. Spanish-American War, 1898 -- Influence. 5. Imperialism -- History 6. Imperialism, American 7. International relations -- History 8. United States -- Foreign relations 9. United States -- Politics and government 10. United States -- Territorial expansion.
ISBN 9781627792165

LC 2016019840

The author of All the Shah's Men and The Brothers brings to life the forgotten political debate that set America's interventionist course in the world for the 20th century and beyond.

"A tremendously elucidating book that should be required reading for civics courses." Kirkus.

Walt, Stephen M., 1955-

The **Hell** of good intentions : America's foreign policy elite and the decline of U.S. primacy / Stephen M. Walt. Farrar, Straus and Giroux, 2018. 378 p. **327.73**

1. Political consultants 2. International relations 3. Peace-building 4. Nation-building 5. United States -- Foreign relations
ISBN 9780374280031

LC 2018007639

An International Affairs professor at Harvard University discusses the failures of the foreign policy elite since the Bush administration and makes suggestions for a fresh approach to improve global relations and stop violent extremism.

Woodward, Bob, 1943-

The **commanders** / Bob Woodward. Simon & Schuster, 2002, c1991. 398 p. : **327.73**

1. Bush, George, 1924-2018 Military leadership. 2. Persian Gulf War, 1991. 3. Persian Gulf Crisis, 1990-1991. 4. Command of troops. 5. Leadership in men. 6. United States -- Foreign relations -- 1989-1993 -- Decision making. 7. United States -- Military policy -- Decision making.
ISBN 0743234758

LC oc2010004431

Includes index.

Originally published in 1991.

"This book discusses top-level White House [and] Pentagon decisionmaking, first in the attack on Panama, and then in the 5 months of diplomatic and especially military maneuvering that preceded the [1991] war with Iraq." Christian Science Monitor.

327.73017 Foreign relations--United States--Socioeconomic regions

Richter, Paul

The **ambassadors** : America's diplomats on the front lines / Paul Richter. Simon & Schuster, 2019. xxv, 322 p. : **327.73017**

1. Crocker, Ryan C. (Ryan Clark), 1949- 2. Ford, Robert Stephen 3. Stevens, John Christopher, 1960-2012 4. Patterson, Anne Woods, 1949- 5. Ambassadors 6. International relations 7. Diplomats 8. Ambassadors -- United States 9. Islamic countries -- Foreign relations United States. 10. United States -- Foreign relations Islamic countries. 11. Middle East -- Foreign relations United States. 12. United States -- Foreign relations Middle East.
ISBN 9781501172410

LC 2019287191

A veteran diplomatic correspondent shares behind-the-headlines insights into the significant contributions of American ambassadors in the Middle East who are risking their lives to help direct government, organize defenses and broker agreements.

327.73047 Foreign relations--United States and Russia

Budiansky, Stephen

Code warriors : NSA's codebreakers and the secret intelligence war against the Soviet Union / Stephen Budiansky. Alfred A. Knopf, 2016. 384 p. **327.73047**

1. United States. National Security Agency -- History. 2. Cryptography. 3. Codes (Communication) 4. Cold War 5. United States -- Foreign relations Soviet Union. 6. Soviet Union -- Foreign relations United States.
ISBN 9780385352666

LC 2015045330

A sweeping history of the NSA and its codebreaking achievements from World War II through the Cold War shares insights into the challenges faced by cryptanalysts and their role in some of the most complicated events of the twentieth century.

McFaul, Michael, 1963-

From Cold War to hot peace : the inside story of Russia and America / Michael McFaul. Houghton Mifflin Harcourt, 2018. 496 p. **327.73047**

1. McFaul, Michael, 1963- 2. Ambassadors 3. International relations 4. Cold War 5. Diplomacy 6. United States -- Foreign relations Russia 7. Russia -- Foreign relations United States. 8. United States -- Foreign relations -- 1989- 9. United States -- Foreign relations -- 2009-2017.
ISBN 9780544716247

LC 2017045603

A former ambassador to Russia during the Obama administration describes how the progress made between the two countries was destroyed when Vladimir Putin returned to power and recounts how the Kremlin actively sought to discredit and undermine him.

Weiner, Tim

The **folly** and the glory : America, Russia, and political warfare, 1945-2020 / Tim Weiner. Henry Holt and Company, 2020. 320 p. **327.73047**

1. Trump, Donald, 1946- 2. Putin, Vladimir Vladimirovich, 1952- 3. Cold War. 4. Intelligence service -- United States -- History. 5. Intelligence service -- Soviet Union -- History. 6. Secrecy in government 7. United States -- Foreign relations Russia 8. Russia

-- Foreign relations United States
ISBN 9781627790857

LC 2019057823

The Pulitzer Prize and National Book Award-winning author presents a contextual history of the development of political warfare between the U.S. and Russia from the Stalin era to today.

"Weiner offers a significant contribution to the literature of U.S.-Russia relations with a book that emphasizes the asymmetry of American capacity for political warfare, currently consisting of effective cyber counterespionage." Library Journal

327.73051 Foreign relations--United States and China

Allison, Graham T., 1940-

Destined for war : America, China, and Thucydides's trap / Graham Allison. Houghton Mifflin Harcourt, 2017. xx, 364 pages ; **327.73051**

1. War -- Causes 2. East and West 3. International competition 4. Geopolitics 5. China -- Military relations United States 6. United States -- Military relations China
ISBN 9780544935273

LC 2017005351

A cautionary assessment of the modern state of China summarizes key historical events that have led to today's state, citing the growing breakdown in U.S.-China relations while outlining several scenarios in which both nations could slide into war in accordance with the examples of earlier conflicts.

"A timely, reasoned treatise by a keen observer and historian." Kirkus.

327.73055 Foreign relations--United States and Iran

Crist, David

The **twilight** war : the secret history of America's thirty-year conflict with Iran / David Crist. Penguin Press, 2012. 656 p. **327.73055**

1. CIA 2. Espionage -- History 3. National security 4. International relations -- History 5. Iran -- Foreign relations United States. 6. United States -- Foreign relations Iran. 7. United States -- Military relations Iran. 8. Iran -- Military relations United States. 9. United States -- Politics and government -- 1981-1989. 10. United States -- Politics and government -- 1989-
ISBN 9781594203411

LC 2011050573

A senior historian for the federal government reveals the covert operations that have brought the United States and Iran on the brink of open war--including, Iran's grand proposal for peace after 9/11, which was rejected by President Bush; Iran's secret army in post-U.S. invasion Iraq; and more.

328.73 Legislative process--United States

Congressional Quarterly, inc

Congress A to Z CQ Press, c2008. xxxiv, 704 p. : **328.73**

1. United States. Congress Dictionaries.
ISBN 9780872895584

LC 2008011284

Present alphabetically arranged entries on the history of Congress, some of its influental members, terms and concepts, scandals, the legislative process, appointments, and appropriations.

MacNeil, Neil, 1923-2008

The **American** Senate : an insider's history / Neil MacNeil and Richard A. Baker. Oxford University Press, Inc., 2013. 384 p. **328.73**

1. United States. Congress. Senate -- History.
ISBN 9780195367614

LC 2012046807

Shares the history of the United States Senate, including its struggles with the presidency, its investigative power, and how filibustering became a common practice.

Zelizer, Julian E

Burning down the house : Newt Gingrich, the fall of a speaker, and the rise of the new Republican Party / Julian E. Zelizer. Penguin Press, 2020. 352 p. **328.73**

1. Gingrich, Newt. 2. United States. Congress. House Speakers. 3. Republican Party 4. Communication in politics -- United States. 5. Political culture -- United States. 6. Partisanship -- Political aspects -- United States. 7. Rhetoric -- Political aspects. 8. United States -- Politics and government -- 1989-
ISBN 9781594206658

LC 2019044440

Traces the story of how the former Speaker of the House and his allies orchestrated an era of ruthless GOP initiatives directly responsible for today's partisan divides.

"A masterfully written political road map for anyone wondering how we got to where we are." Kirkus

330 Economics

Acemoglu, Daron

Why nations fail : the origins of power, prosperity and poverty / Daron Acemoglu, James A. Robinson. Crown Business, c2012. 448 p. **330**

1. Economic development -- Developing countries. 2. Economic history. 3. Economic policy -- Developing countries. 4. Economics -- Political aspects. 5. Developing countries.
ISBN 9780307719218

LC 2011023538

An award-winning professor of economics at MIT and a Harvard University political scientist and economist evaluate the reasons that some nations are poor while others succeed, outlining provocative perspectives that support theories about the importance of institutions.

"The authors make what could be a weighty topic both engaging and accessible. It will appeal not only to students of economics and political science but also to anyone looking to gain insight into the current state of our global economy, its origins, and the kind of transformations that might level the playing field." Library Journal.

Chang, Ha-Joon

Economics : the user's guide / Ha-Joon Chang Bloomsbury, 2014. 384 p. **330**

1. Economics 2. Economic policy. 3. Capitalism.
ISBN 9781620408124

LC 2014498623

The award-winning author of 23 Things They Don't Tell You About Capitalism outlines the real-world processes of the global economy while explaining how to better understand the strengths and weaknesses of key economics theories to better navigate today's interconnected world.

"A solid choice for those who want to learn more about economics without feeling like they are back in the classroom." Library Journal.

Kwak, James

Economism : bad economics and the rise of inequality / James Kwak. Pantheon Books, 2016 192 p. **330**

1. Economics -- Sociological aspects. 2. Economic policy. 3. United States -- Economic policy.

ISBN 9781101871195

LC 2016024099

Outlines a deconstruction of the framework for understanding the world of classroom economics, clarifying assumptions and misleading teachings while sharing historical insights into how economism became a prevalent influence in the U.S.

"It should be companion reading to every introductory economics text." Publishers Weekly.

Levitt, Steven D.

★**Freakonomics** : a rogue economist explores the hidden side of everything / Steven D. Levitt and Stephen J. Dubner. William Morrow, 2005. xii, 242 p. **330**

1. Economics -- Social aspects. 2. Regression analysis. 3. Causation. 4. Economics -- Psychological aspects. 5. United States -- Social life and customs. 6. United States -- Economic conditions.

ISBN 9780060731328

LC 2004065478

"This excellent, readable book will enlighten many library patrons." Booklist.

Superfreakonomics : global cooling, patriotic prostitutes, and why suicide bombers should buy life insurance / Steven D. Levitt and Stephen J. Dubner. William Morrow, 2009. xvii, 270 p. ; **330**

1. Economics -- Social aspects. 2. Regression analysis. 3. Causation. 4. Economics -- Psychological aspects. 5. United States -- Social life and customs. 6. United States -- Economic conditions.

ISBN 9780060889579

LC 2009035852

In a follow-up to "Freakonomics," the authors offer a new analysis of how the economy really works.

"The authors assert that the unifying principle in the various topics they address is people responding to incentives in ways that are not necessarily predictable or manifest. Major themes are explored using a wide range of examples, e.g., life and death issues, terrorism, altruism, medical care, crime, and the environment. Levitt and Dubner succeed in applying economic analysis to timely topics with stimulation, wit, and humor. Best of all, their book will appeal to a broad segment of the population." Choice.

When to rob a bank : and 131 more warped suggestions and well-intended rants from the Freakonomics guys / Steven D. Levitt and Stephen J. Dubner. William Morrow, 2015. 387 p. ; **330**

1. Economics -- Social aspects. 2. Essays.

ISBN 9780062385321

The best-selling authors of Freakonomics present a 10th anniversary, curated collection of blog posts from Freakanomics.com to share insights into the role of luck in making money, the unpredictable nature of winning and more.

Schumacher, E. F. (Ernst Friedrich), 1911-1977

Small is beautiful : economics as if people mattered / E.F. Schumacher ; foreword by Bill McKibben. Harper Perennial, 2010. xvi, 324 p. ; **330**

1. Economics.

ISBN 9780061997761

LC 2019300265

"This book was originally published by Blond & Briggs Ltd., London, in 1973"--Title page verso.

"Small is Beautiful is Oxford-trained economist E.F. Schumacher's classic call for the end of excessive consumption. Schumacher inspired such movements as "Buy Locally" and "Fair Trade", while voicing strong opposition to "casino capitalism" and wasteful corporate behemoths. ... [It] presents eminently logical arguments for building our economies around the needs of communities, not corporations."--Back cover.

Sowell, Thomas, 1930-

Basic economics : a common sense guide to the economy / Thomas Sowell. Basic Books, 2015. ix, 689 p. ; **330**

1. Economics. 2. Finance. 3. Banks and banking. 4. Commerce. 5. United States -- Economic conditions.

ISBN 9780465060733

An accessible, jargon-free resource outlines the principles behind each major type of economy including capitalist, socialist, and feudal, in terms of the incentives each creates.

"Sowell's volume does a fantastic job in cultivating the reader's economic imagination." Choice.

Taylor, Timothy, 1960-

The **instant** economist : everything you need to know to about how the economy works / Timothy Taylor. Plume, c2012. 272 p. **330**

1. Economics. 2. Microeconomics. 3. Macroeconomics.

ISBN 9780452297524

LC 2011033416

Provides the key principles of both macro and microeconomics in an accessible and easily understood way, including explanations about why budget deficits matter, what the Federal Reserve actually does and why health insurance is so expensive.

Varoufakis, Yanis

Talking to my daughter about the economy, or, how capitalism works-- and how it fails / Yanis Varoufakis ; translated from the Greek by Jacob Moe and Yanis Varoufakis. Farrar, Straus and Giroux, [2018] 224 p. **330**

1. Economics. 2. Capitalism. 3. World economy 4. Economic policy. 5. Letters

ISBN 9780374272364

LC 2017054137

Includes index.

Greece's former finance minister, through a series of letters written to his young daughter, explains the workings of the world economic system, discusses the historical origins of inequality among and within nations, shows why economic instability is a chronic risk and addresses the rapidly declining health of the planet.

Wheelan, Charles J.

Naked economics : undressing the dismal science / Charles Wheelan ; foreword by Burton G. Malkiel. Norton, c2002. 260

p. ; **330**

1. Board of Governors of the Federal Reserve System (U.S.) 2. World economy. 3. Economic policy. 4. Economics -- Humor. 5. Capitalism.
ISBN 0393049825

LC 2002023580

In Naked Economics, journalist Charles Wheelan does 'the impossible" he makes economic principles relevant, interesting and fun. Brimming with scores of down-to-earth examples and sprinkled with humorous anecdotes, this comprehensive overview will keep listeners smiling and wide awake.

"The author explains the essentials of economics, defining terms like GDP and inflation, explaining how they work and what the short- and long-term impact might be. This is a thoughtful, well-written introduction to economics, with the author projecting a genuine excitement for his material." Library Journal.

Yunus, Muhammad, 1940-

A **world** of three zeros : the new economics of zero poverty, zero unemployment, and zero net carbon emissions / Muhammad Yunus, with Karl Weber. PublicAffairs, 2017. 304 p. **330**

1. Capitalism 2. Free enterprise 3. Altruism 4. Entrepreneurship
ISBN 9781610397575

LC 2017017988

The co-winner of the 2006 Nobel Peace Prize describes why he feels that current capitalism is broken and leads to inequality, unemployment and environmental destruction and presents his ideas for a new capitalism that serves human needs in innovative ways.

330.01 Philosophy and theory

Roth, Alvin E., 1951-

Who gets what--and why : the new economics of matchmaking and market design / Alvin E. Roth. Eamon Dolan/Houghton Mifflin Harcourt, 2015. 320 p. **330.01**

1. Economics. 2. Matching theory. 3. Game theory. 4. Markets.
ISBN 9780544291133

LC 2015010771

A Nobel laureate reveals the often surprising rules that govern a vast array of activities -- both mundane and life-changing -- where money plays little or no role.

Thaler, Richard H., 1945-

Misbehaving : the making of behavioral economics / Richard H. Thaler. W.W. Norton & Company, 2015 336 p. **330.01**

1. Economics -- Psychological aspects. 2. Human behavior. 3. Decision-making
ISBN 9780393080940

LC 2015004600

Argues that economical trends cannot be predicted as much as thought, mainly because humans are so unpredictable, and reveals how behavioral economic analysis opens up new ways to look at everything from household finance to assigning faculty offices in a new building. By the best-selling co-author of Nudge.

"Misbehaving chronicles Thaler's participation in the development of behavioral economics, describes how it happened, and details some of what he and his colleagues learned along the way. This challenging book is written in an understandable manner and contains valuable insight for those interested in economics, psychology, other social sciences, public policy, and business." Booklist.

Nudge : improving decisions about health, wealth, and happiness / Richard H. Thaler, Cass R. Sunstein. Yale University Press, 2008. x, 293 p. : **330.01**

1. Economics -- Psychological aspects. 2. Choice (Psychology) -- Economic aspects. 3. Decision making -- Psychological aspects. 4. Consumer behavior.
ISBN 9780300122237

"A Caravan book"--T.p. verso.

Offering a study of the application of the science of choice, a guide that uses examples from all aspects of life demonstrates how it is possible to design environments that make it more likely for us to act in our own interests.

330.1 Systems, schools, theories

Lanchester, John

How to speak money : what the money people say--and what It really means / John Lanchester. W W Norton & Co Inc., 2014. 256 p. **330.1**

1. Economics. 2. Personal finance. 3. Banks and banking. 4. Money.
ISBN 9780393243376

LC 2014028529

The award-winning author of I.O.U. presents a comprehensive and upbeat explanation of how the world of finance and economics really works, from the terms and conditions of personal checking accounts to the deliberate concealments of bankers.

"This entertaining, informative, useful reference, written in a lively style, is suitable for both practitioners and newcomers to the subject of economics." Choice.

Sowell, Thomas, 1930-

★**Wealth,** poverty and politics : an international perspective / Thomas Sowell. Basic Books, 2015. 320 p. **330.1**

1. Economics. 2. Income distribution. 3. Income. 4. Wealth
ISBN 9780465082933

LC bl2015035525

Drawing on accurate, empirical data, one of the foremost conservative public intellectuals in the U.S. argues that political and ideological struggles have led to dangerous confusion about income inequality in America.

330.12 Systems

King, Mervyn

The **end** of alchemy : money, banking, and the future of the global economy / Mervyn King. W W Norton & Co Inc, 2016 368 p. **330.12**

1. Global Financial Crisis, 2008-2009. 2. Banks and banking 3. Monetary policy. 4. Money.
ISBN 9780393247022

LC 2015048306

The former governor of the Bank of England recounts his country's experiences throughout the Great Recession while outlining a blueprint for recovery-era capitalism that is more resilient to modern-world boom-and-bust cycles.

"King provides a terrific analysis of what went wrong in the global financial system and with economics in general." Library Journal.

McMillan, John, 1951-
Reinventing the bazaar : a natural history of markets / John McMillan. Norton, 2002. x, 278 p. **330.12**

1. Capitalism. 2. Economic history. 3. Capitalism -- History. 4. Free enterprise.

ISBN 0393050211

LC 2002000521

"The author examines how markets in ancient times evolved and shows how countries experimented with markets, some successfully and some not. He takes a refreshingly commonsense approach to his subject, doesn't talk down to his readers, and refrains from excessive economic jargon." Library Journal.

330.15 Schools of economic thought

Keynes, John Maynard, 1883-1946
★The **general** theory of employment, interest, and money / John Maynard Keynes. Harcourt, Brace, Jovanovich, 1964 1991 printing xii, 403 p. : **330.15**

1. Economics 2. Money 3. Monetary policy 4. Interest

ISBN 9780156347112

LC 91006533

"A Harvest/HBJ book."

Originally published: 1953.

Keynes profoundly influenced the New Deal and created the basis for classic economic theory. --Provided by publisher

Smith, Adam, 1723-1790
★The **wealth** of nations : Adam Smith ; Introduction by Robert Reich ; Edited, With Notes, Marginal Summary, and Enlarged Index by Edwin Cannan / Adam Smith ; introduction by Robert Reich ; edited, with notes, marginal summary, and enlarged index by Edwin Cannan. Modern Library, 2000. xxvi, 1154 p. ; **330.15**

1. Economics

ISBN 9780679783367

LC 00064573

Originally published: An inquiry into the nature and causes of the wealth of nations / Adam Smith ; edited ... by Edwin Cannan. 1994. With new introd. by Robert Reich.

Presents the classic eighteenth-century treatise on political economics.

330.9 Economic situation and conditions

Davidson, Adam
The **passion** economy : the new rules for thriving in the twenty-first century / Adam Davidson. Alfred A. Knopf, 2020. 240 p. **330.9**

1. Economics 2. Businesspeople -- Case studies. 3. Economic forecasting. 4. Goals and objectives

ISBN 9780385353526

LC 2019022771

Includes index.

The award-winning New Yorker staff writer and creator of NPR's Planet Money podcast explains the internal logic of today's dynamic economy while revealing its transformative potential for enabling millions to thrive.

"Fine inspiration for entrepreneurs that should be required reading in any business school curriculum." Kirkus.

Hickel, Jason, 1982-
The **divide** : global inequality from conquest to free markets / Jason Hickel. W. W. Norton & Company, 2018, c2017 344 p. **330.9**

1. Equality. 2. Globalization. 3. Poverty.

ISBN 9780393651362

LC 2017052787

"First published [in 2017] by The Random House Group Ltd in Great Britain under the title THE DIVIDE: A Brief Guide to Global Inequality and its Solutions."

An award-winning professor of anthropology examines global poverty and the growing divide between developed and developing countries as it relates to the global economy that has resulted from hundreds of years of conquest, colonialism, regime change, debt and trade deals.

"A sharply argued analysis of the traditional explanations for wealth and poverty in the world, offering a program for easing misery while addressing structural inequalities." Kirkus.

Lanchester, John
★**I.O.U.** : why everyone owes everyone and no one can pay / John Lanchester. Simon & Schuster, 2010. 260 p. **330.9**

1. Global financial crisis, 2008-2009. 2. Capitalism. 3. Debt. 4. Debtor and creditor.

ISBN 9781439169841

LC 2009036465

Published in Canada by McClelland & Stewart, 2010.

Lanchester's survey of the current financial crisis explains how the booming global economy collapsed seemingly overnight.

Sharma, Ruchir
The **rise** and fall of nations : forces of change in the post-crisis world. / Ruchir Sharma. W.W. Norton & Company, 2016. xii, 466 p. ; **330.9**

1. Economic forecasting. 2. Economic history -- 21st century. 3. Social change 4. World economy. 5. Developing countries -- Economic conditions.

ISBN 9780393248890

A reevaluation of economics as a practical art form by the Morgan Stanley economist and author of the best-selling Breakout Nations distills economics into 10 succinct rules while counseling readers on how to recognize political, economic and social changes that affect everyday life.

Taplin, Jonathan
Move fast and break things : how Facebook, Google, and Amazon cornered culture and undermined democracy / Jonathan Taplin. Little, Brown & Company, 2017. 320 p. **330.9**

1. Google (Firm) 2. Facebook (Firm) 3. Amazon.com (Firm) 4. Internet 5. Monopolies 6. Intellectual property 7. Culture

ISBN 9780316275774

LC bl2017013605

Describes the history of Facebook, Amazon and Google and the shift in power they presided over wherein more creative content is being devoured than ever before, but with less revenue flowing to the creators and owners of that content.

330.9172 Socioeconomic regions by degree of economic development

Sharma, Ruchir

★**Breakout** nations : in pursuit of the next economic miracles / Ruchir Sharma. W.W. Norton, c2012. x, 292 p. : **330.9172**

1. Economic forecasting. 2. Economic history -- 21st century. 3. World economy. 4. Developing countries -- Economic conditions.
ISBN 9780393080261

LC 2012005810

Discusses how the global economy will be shaped in the future by focusing on Nigeria, Indonesia, and Poland instead of the superstars of the last decade, China, Russia, and Brazil.

330.941 Economic conditions--British Isles

Satia, Priya

Empire of guns : the violent making of the Industrial Revolution / Priya Satia. Penguin Group USA, 2018 512 p. **330.941**

1. Gun ownership 2. Industrial Revolution 3. Weapons 4. Gun control 5. Great Britain -- History -- 18th century.
ISBN 9780735221864

LC 2018006181

A prizewinning historian's reframing of the Industrial Revolution, the expansion of British empire and the emergence of industrial capitalism presents them as inextricable from the gun trade and the story of disgraced Quaker gunmaker Samuel Galton, sharing insights into modern debates about gun control and the complex partnerships of government, the economy and the military.

330.973 Economic conditions--United States

Alexander, Brian, 1959-

Glass house : the 1% economy and the shattering of the all-American town / Brian Alexander. St Martins Press, 2017. 304 p. **330.973**

1. Anchor-Hocking (Firm) 2. Company towns. 3. Capitalism and inequality. 4. Working class. 5. Factories. 6. United States -- History -- 20th century. 7. Lancaster, Ohio.
ISBN 9781250085801

LC 2016044045

Traces the downfall of once-idyllic Lancaster, Ohio, exploring how the financial problems of primary employer Anchor Hocking Glass Company and the challenges of local corruption, the drug trade and evolving technologies have illuminated the vulnerabilities of inequality in rural America.

"This is a particularly timely read for our tumultuous and divisive era." Publishers Weekly.

Barlett, Donald L., 1936-

The **betrayal** of the American dream : what went wrong / Donald L. Barlett and James B. Steele. PublicAffairs, c2012. 256 p. **330.973**

1. Middle class -- United States -- Economic conditions 2. Working class -- United States -- Economic conditions 3. Economic policy -- 2001- 4. United States -- Economic conditions -- 21st century
ISBN 9781586489694

LC 2012012879

The Pulitzer Prize-winning authors present a scathing indictment of the formidable challenges facing the middle class, calling for fundamental changes while surveying the extent of the problem and identifying the people and agencies they believe to be responsible.

Bartiromo, Maria

The **weekend** that changed Wall Street : an eyewitness account / Maria Bartiromo, with Catherine Whitney. Portfolio/ Penguin, 2010. viii, 232 p. ; **330.973**

1. Financial crises. 2. Investment banking. 3. Financial institutions. 4. Economics. 5. Wall Street, New York City.
ISBN 9781591843511

A noted business reporter from CNBC draws on her network of high-level sources to give her unique perspective on the white-knuckled weekend that brought Wall Street to its knees, the three day period in September 2008 when Lehman Brothers failed, Merrill Lynch barely survived and AIG became a ward of the government.

"Bartiromo lays out the facts of the Lehman Brothers downfall using both her own account and those of the most powerful people on Wall Street. The most fascinating aspects of . . . [this book] were not so much the details of the collapse . . . but the book's early focus on the lavish lives of those involved in the Wall Street game; Bartiromo details the parties they threw, the apartments they owned that resembled art galleries and the confidence they exuded, which came across not only in their business conversations, but also in the casual talks between the author and her trusting subjects. " Risk Management.

Blinder, Alan S.

After the music stopped : the financial crisis, the response, and the work ahead / Alan S. Blinder. Penguin Press, 2013. 400 p. **330.973**

1. Global Financial Crisis, 2008-2009. 2. Financial crises -- United States. 3. Finance -- United States. 4. United States -- Economic conditions -- 2009- 5. United States -- Economic policy -- 2009-
ISBN 9781594205309

LC 2012031025

A narrative assessment of the U.S. financial crisis and its lessons explores its complex contributing factors while revealing some of its more devastating but lesser-known consequences, outlining potentially divisive solutions that the author believes may be necessary for recovery.

Dayen, David

Chain of title : how three ordinary Americans uncovered Wall Street's great foreclosure fraud / David Dayen. New Press, 2016. 320 p. **330.973**

1. Financial crises -- United States -- History -- 21st century. 2. Foreclosure 3. Global Financial Crisis, 2008-2009 4. Banks and banking -- United States -- History -- 21st century. 5. United States -- History -- 21st century
ISBN 9781620971581

LC 2016005544

"In the depths of the Great Recession, a cancer nurse, a car dealership worker, and an insurance fraud specialist helped uncover the largest consumer crime in American history--a scandal that implicated dozens of major executives on Wall Street. They called it foreclosure fraud: millions of families were kicked out of their homes based on false evidence by mortgage companies that had no legal right to foreclose. Lisa Epstein, Michael Redman, and Lynn Szymoniak did not work in government or law enforcement. They had no history of anticorporate activism. Instead they were all foreclosure victims, and while struggling with their shame and isolation they committed a revolutionary act: closely reading their mortgage documents, discovering the deceit behind them, and building a movement to expose it. Fiscal Times columnist David Dayen recounts how these ordinary Floridians challenged the most powerful institutions in America armed only with the truth--and for a brief moment they brought the corrupt financial industry to its knees"-- Provided by publisher.

"Dayen relates how prosecutors, judges, and the Department of Justice have caved to powerful mortgage industry donors while illegal foreclosures continue. An inspiring, well-rendered, deeply reported, and often infuriating account." Kirkus.

De Graaf, John

What's the economy for, anyway? : why it's time to stop chasing growth and start pursuing happiness / John de Graaf and David K. Batker. Bloomsbury Press, 2011. 288 p. **330.973**

1. Economic development. 2. Happiness. 3. Economics. 4. Economic policy. 5. United States -- Economic conditions.

ISBN 9781608195107

LC 2011017438

"What's The Economy For, Anyway? is a thought-provoking, funny, readable, anti-ideological book based on the cult hit film of the same name. Here, scholars John de Graaf (author of Affluenza) and David Batker tackle thirteen touchstone economic issues and challenge readers to consider just what the point of our economy is. Emphasizing powerful American ideals such as working together, pragmatism, and equality for all, de Graaf and Batker set forth a simple, powerful goal for any economic system: the greatest good for the greatest number, over the longest run. Their vision will appeal to a wide array of readers across traditional silos. Drawing from this nation's rich economic history, the book shows that the good life in America is achieved when people and markets work together with an active government to create a better economy, one that works for everyone, not just the privileged few. Beginning by taking our fetish for GDP and shattering it, the chapters touch on quality of life, health, security, time management, worklife, leisure, social justice, and perhaps most important, sustainability. This sparkling, message-driven book is exactly what we need: a guide to what really matters, and how we can use the resources of our economy to make the world a better place".-- Provided by publisher.

"De Graaf and Batker examine new ways to think about economic processes, specifically as they relate to human happiness and well-being. The authors show that the indicators of performance developed during World War II--the Gross National Product--have become both obscurantist and counterproductive. They argue that human purposes and needs ought to provide the basis for much more broadly based measures of performance, which would consider what is the greatest good and benefit for the greatest number of people over the longest period of time. An entertaining presentation of important ideas and information about how lives could be improved." Kirkus.

Ferguson, Charles H.

Predator nation : corporate criminals, political corruption, and the hijacking of America / Charles Ferguson. Crown Business, c2012. 288 p. **330.973**

1. Financial crises -- United States. 2. Banks and banking -- United States. 3. White collar crime 4. Global Financial Crisis, 2008-2009. 5. United States -- Economic conditions -- 21st century 6. United States -- Politics and government.

ISBN 9780307952554

LC 2011052366

A continuation of the Academy Award-nominated documentary, No End in Sight, draws on new interviews to present controversial arguments that the financial crisis occurred because of decades of deregulation that enabled the financial sector to commit industrial-scale fraud..

Greenspan, Alan, 1926-

Capitalism in America : a history / Alan Greenspan, Adrian Wooldridge. Penguin Group USA, 2018. 512 p. **330.973**

1. Economics -- History 2. Capitalism 3. Entrepreneurship 4. Business innovations 5. United States -- History

ISBN 9780735222441

LC 2018020397

The former Federal Reserve Chairman and the acclaimed Economist historian trace the epic story of America's evolution from a small patchwork of threadbare colonies to the world's most powerful engine of wealth and innovation.

Krugman, Paul R.

Arguing with zombies : economics, politics, and the fight for a better future / Paul Krugman. W. W. Norton & Company, 2020 480 p. **330.973**

1. Economics 2. Economic policy 3. Misconceptions 4. Economic history 5. United States -- Economic conditions -- 21st century 6. United States -- Politics and government.

ISBN 9781324005018

LC 2019032129

Includes index.

An introduction to today's major policy issues by the Nobel Prize-winning columnist clarifies widespread misunderstandings in basic economics while providing thematic explanations of subjects ranging from health care and housing bubbles to tax reform and social security.

"While Krugman's rousing, jargon-free writings will please progressive readers, they will be disconcerting to many conservative ones. An informative and controversial study combining business and political science." Library Journal.

★**End** this depression now! / Paul Krugman. W. W. Norton, c2012. 259 p. **330.973**

1. Financial crises 2. Recession (Economics) 3. Unemployment 4. Economic policy 5. United States -- Politics and government -- 21st century

ISBN 9780393088779

LC 2012009067

Includes index.

"Krugman's forceful jargon-free criticisms and solutions directed at a general audience are a thoughtful contribution to both economic and political discourse in this election year. Highly recommended for a broad readership." Library Journal.

Lemann, Nicholas

Transaction man : the rise of the deal and the decline of the American dream / Nicholas Lemann. Farrar, Straus and Giroux, [2019] 304 p. **330.973**

1. Corporations 2. Economic policy 3. Inequality 4. Economists 5. United States -- Economic conditions -- 20th century 6. United States -- Politics and government -- 1945-1989

ISBN 9780374277888

LC 2019020255

Includes index.

The New Yorker writer chronicles how American strategists, financiers and politicians have influenced the perception of disruption strategies, creating a damaging culture of inequality and polarization that victimizes working-class families.

Lewis, Michael (Michael M.)

The **big** short : inside the doomsday machine / Michael Lewis. W. W. Norton, 2010. 320 p. **330.973**

1. Financial crises 2. Economics -- History -- United States 3. World

economy. 4. United States -- Economic conditions -- 21st century
ISBN 9780393072235

Robert F. Kennedy Book Award, 2011.

Lewis examines the American economic collapse of the early 21st century, profiling very few heroes, numerous villains and several people who just should have known better. Lewis offers a biting rebuke to this motley band of financial "experts" with keen research and a sharp pen.

"The Big Short manages to give us the truest picture yet of what went wrong on Wall Street--and why. At times, it reads like a morality play, at other times like a modern-day farce. But as with any good play, its value lies in the way it reveals character and motive and explores the cultural context in which the plot unfolds." Washington Post.

Lind, Michael, 1962-

Land of promise : an economic history of the United States / Michael Lind. Broadside Books, 2012. 304 p. **330.973**

1. Economics -- History -- United States 2. Monetary policy. 3. Finance. 4. Economic policy. 5. United States -- Economic conditions.
ISBN 9780061834806

LC 2011047794

The author of The Next American Nation and Up from Conservatism presents a much-needed historical perspective on the relationship between economic, technological and political change by analyzing America's economic growth over the course of two centuries.

Liveris, Andrew

Make it in America : the case for re-inventing the economy / Andrew Liveris. Wiley, c2011. xxi, 208 p. : **330.973**

1. Industrial policy. 2. Manufacturers. 3. Economic forecasting. 4. Mass production. 5. United States -- Economic conditions -- 2009-
ISBN 9780470930229

LC 2010045654

Presents a powerful case for the importance of manufacturing to the American economy-and offers a plan to take back our future before it's too late.

"The author calls for a national strategy to revive manufacturing. We need manufacturing jobs, he says, if we are to keep a growing population busy and start paying off our debts to the rest of the world." Wall Street Journal.

Madrick, Jeffrey G.

Age of greed : the triumph of finance and the decline of America, 1970 to the present / Jeff Madrick. Alfred A. Knopf, 2011. 480 p. **330.973**

1. Wealth -- Moral and ethical aspects. 2. Financial crises -- United States -- History. 3. Greed 4. Capitalism -- United States. 5. United States -- Politics and government -- 20th century. 6. United States -- Politics and government -- 21st century.
ISBN 9781400041718

LC 2011003399

Includes index.

A vivid chronicle of the events that led to today's economic troubles cites the promotion of the idea that self-interest guides society more effectively than community concerns, in a report that traces the roles played by such figures as Citicorp head Walter Wriston, economist Milton Friedman and President Richard Nixon.

"This book is a fascinating and deeply disturbing tale of hypocrisy, corruption, and insatiable greed. But more than that, it's a much-needed reminder of just how we got into the mess we're in--a reminder that is greatly needed when we are still being told that greed is good". New York Rev Books

McCraw, Thomas K.

★The **founders** and finance : how Hamilton, Gallatin, and other immigrants forged a new economy / Thomas K. McCraw. Belknap Press of Harvard University Press, 2012. viii, 485 p. : **330.973**

1. Hamilton, Alexander, 1757-1804. 2. Gallatin, Albert, 1761-1849. 3. United States. Department of the Treasury -- History. 4. Public finance -- United States -- History. 5. Monetary policy -- United States -- History. 6. Economic policy. 7. Revolutions 8. United States -- Economic policy. 9. United States -- History -- Revolution, 1775-1783. 10. United States -- History -- 1783-1865. 11. United States -- Politics and government -- 1783-1865.
ISBN 9780674066922

LC 2012014006

Discusses how such immigrant founders as Alexander Hamilton, Albert Gallatin, and others were more financially savvy than native-born plantation owners Washington, Jefferson, and Madison, and how they carried the nation to prosperity.

"McCraw is a talented storyteller. His highly readable and fascinating work portrays the brilliance of Hamilton and Gallatin against the difficulty of their time and is strongly recommended to all readers interested in American and financial history." Library Journal.

McLean, Bethany

All the devils are here : the hidden history of the financial crisis / Bethany McLean and Joe Nocera. Portfolio Penguin, 2010. 496 p. **330.973**

1. Global Financial Crisis, 2008-2009. 2. Financial crises. 3. Mortgage backed securities. 4. Financial institutions. 5. United States -- Economic conditions.
ISBN 9781591843634

LC 2010032893

Before the dust even settled, competing theories emerged to explain the financial crisis. Should the blame fall on Wall Street, Main Street, or Pennsylvania Avenue? Bethany McLean and Joe Nocera, two of America's most acclaimed business journalists, offer the definitive answer. This surprising narrative goes back more than twenty years to reveal how Wall Street, the mortgage industry, and the government conspired to change the way Americans bought their homes.

"This is an account of the late financial meltdown, when, in the words of one analyst, we went from a collective belief in soundness to a collective belief in insolvency. Hard-hitting reporting and fluent writing bring the utter devastation of the Great Recession to life." Kirkus.

Paulson, Henry M., 1946-

★**On** the brink : inside the race to stop the collapse of the global financial system / Henry M. Paulson. Grand Central Pub, 2010. 288 p. **330.973**

1. Financial crises. 2. Economic policy. 3. Credit management. 4. Financial institutions. 5. United States -- Economic conditions -- 2001-
ISBN 9780446561938

LC 2009939043

The Secretary of the Treasury during the final years of George W. Bush's presidency presents his side of the economic collapse that occurred in the waning days of his watch over America's banking system.

"This is the ultimate insider's account of the crisis, and, owing to its even-handed tone and penetrating insights into government actions, it will also remain an important contribution to the historical record of the crisis, essential reading for everyone interested in knowing what happened." Library Journal.

Perino, Michael A.

The **hellhound** of Wall Street : how Ferdinand Pecora's investigation of the Great Crash forever changed American finance / Michael Perino. Penguin Press, 2010. 352 p. **330.973**

1. Pecora, Ferdinand, 1882-1971 2. Stock market crash, October 1929. 3. Stock market. 4. Financial crises -- United States -- History 5. Business -- Corrupt practices.

ISBN 9781594202728

LC 2010019157

Chronicles the 1933 Senate committee hearings into the causes of the stock market crash of 1929, describing the rigorous questioning by former New York prosecutor Ferdinand Pecora that revealed shocking financial abuses and led to the economic reforms ofthe New Deal.

"The author recounts the 1933 investigation into Wall Street abuses by the Senate Committee on Banking and Currency, focusing on the 10-day interrogation by chief counsel Ferdinand Pecora of executives of National City Bank (precursor to Citigroup). Perino's book is a trenchant, entertaining study of the New Deal's heroic beginnings, one with obvious relevance to latter-day efforts to rein in Wall Street's excesses." Publishers Weekly.

Reich, Robert B., 1946-

Aftershock : the next economy and America's future / Robert B. Reich. Alfred A. Knopf, 2010. 192 p. **330.973**

1. Financial crises. 2. Social classes. 3. Economic policy. 4. Speculation. 5. United States -- Economic conditions. 6. United States -- Social conditions -- 21st century -- Forecasting.

ISBN 9780307592811

LC 2010004134

A former Secretary of Labor analyzes the economic crisis while making recommendations for responsibly navigating its aftermath, suggesting that the downturn actually resulted from a disproportionate concentration of wealth at the expense of a debt-burdened middle class.

"Reich argues that America will not have a sustained economic recovery until the middle class has more buying power. In this call for reform, the author writes that the increasing concentration of wealth among a small percentage of Americans was the main culprit in the destabilization of the U.S. economy in 2008. Lucid and cogent." Kirkus.

Saving capitalism : for the many, not the few / Robert B. Reich. Alfred A. Knopf, 2015. 240 p. **330.973**

1. Capitalism -- United States. 2. Democracy -- Economic aspects -- United States. 3. Income distribution -- United States. 4. Middle class 5. United States -- Economic conditions. 6. United States -- Social conditions -- 21st century -- Forecasting.

ISBN 9780385350570

LC 2015001873

Outlines how the American economic system is failing, with increasing income inequality and a shrinking middle class, and reveals how a market designed for broad prosperity can reverse the trend toward diminished opportunity.

"Reich's overriding message is that we don't have to put up with things as they are. It's a useful and necessary one, if not likely to sway the powers that be to become more generous of their own volition." Kirkus.

Sachs, Jeffrey

The **price** of civilization : American values and the return to prosperity / Jeffrey D. Sachs. Random House, c2011. 336 p. **330.973**

1. Corporate accountability. 2. Environmental responsibility -- United States. 3. Social responsibility -- Economic aspects 4. Economic policy. 5. United States -- Economic conditions -- 2009- 6. United States -- Politics and government -- 21st century.

ISBN 9781400068418

LC 2011014631

Offers a diagnosis of the country's economic ills and argues that Americans can restore the virtues of fairness, honesty, and foresight as the foundations of national prosperity.

"The author explores the economic, political, social, and psychological roots of the U.S.'s 30-year journey from decades of consensus and high achievement to an era of deep division and growing crisis. He indicts America's elites for abandoning social responsibility, politicians for giving up on solving problems, the media for distraction and hyper-commercialization, and citizens for surrendering to that distraction. He urges mindfulness, clear goals for political reform, and significant tax changes, and he suggests that the millennial generation will lead the way to a restoration of the nation's highest aspirations " Booklist.

Sorkin, Andrew Ross

Too big to fail : the inside story of how Wall Street and Washington fought to save the financial system from crisis--and themselves / Andrew Ross Sorkin. Viking, 2009. xx, 600 p., [16] p. of plates : **330.973**

1. Financial crises -- United States -- History -- 21st century. 2. Economics -- Political aspects 3. Business losses 4. World economy 5. United States -- History -- 21st century.

ISBN 9780670021253

LC 2009036494

Presents a moment-by-moment account of the recent financial collapse that documents state efforts to prevent an economic disaster, offering insight into the pivotal consequences of decisions made throughout the past decade.

"Sorkin boasts of the hours spent interviewing, emailing, inspecting telephone call logs, billing time sheets and even expense reports [for this book], and his reward is the fullest and most convincing account of the Lehman debacle. Conversations are reconstructed, and an air of authenticity created by the accumulation of thousands of small facts." Times Literary Supplement.

Stone, James Martin

Five easy theses : common-sense solutions to America's greatest economic challenges / James M. Stone. Houghton Mifflin Harcourt, 2016. 224 p. **330.973**

1. Fiscal balance 2. Inequality 3. Education 4. Right to medical care 5. United States -- Economic conditions -- 2009- 6. United States -- Economic policy -- 2009- 7. United States -- Social conditions -- 1980- 8. United States -- Social policy -- 1993-

ISBN 9780544749009

LC 2015037880

A business leader and esteemed economic thinker outlines simple solutions to America's five most pressing public policy issues, from healthcare to education to inequality.

Waterhouse, Benjamin C., 1978-

The **land** of enterprise : a business history of the United States / Benjamin C. Waterhouse. Simon & Schuster, 2017 304 p. **330.973**

1. Economic history 2. Economic development 3. Entrepreneurship -- History. 4. Commerce -- History.

ISBN 9781476766645

LC bl2017013978

A prominent historian of American politics, business and capitalism charts the development of American business from the colonial period to the present, exploring the nation's evolving economic, social and political landscape, paying tribute the unnamed millions who traded their labor and offering clues as to how to confront the challenges of today's world.

"A historian makes his case that the story of private enterprise has been undervalued as a window into the history of the United States." Kirkus.

330.9747 Economic conditions--New York

Phillips-Fein, Kim

★**Fear** city : New York's fiscal crisis and the rise of austerity politics / Kimberly Phillips-Fein. Metropolitan Books, 2017. 384 p. **330.9747**

1. Fiscal policy 2. Financial crises 3. Municipal budgets 4. Social policy 5. New York City -- Economic conditions -- 20th century 6. New York (State) -- History -- 20th century

ISBN 9780805095258

LC 2016033559

Pulitzer Prize for History finalist, 2018.

The author of Invisible Hands presents a history of an imperiled New York City while analyzing what the author terms the politics of austerity and how they are continuing to shape the world today.

"Paced like a thriller and extremely well written, the book chronicles the slow descent of the city into a fiscal abyss and its unlikely rescue by a group of hardened bureaucrats, altruistic investment bankers, and political power players ." Publishers Weekly. Annex

330.9775 Economic conditions--Wisconsin

Goldstein, Amy, 1957-

Janesville : an American story / Amy Goldstein. Simon & Schuster, 2017 xiii, 351 p. ; **330.9775**

1. Automobile industry and trade 2. Plant closings 3. Blue collar workers 4. Automobile assembly lines. 5. Janesville, Wisconsin 6. Wisconsin 7. United States -- Economic conditions 8. Middle West

ISBN 9781501102233

J. Anthony Lukas Book Prize, 2018.

A Washington Post reporter provides an intimate account of the fallout from the closing of a General Motors' assembly plant in Janesville, Wisconsin--Paul Ryan's hometown--and a larger story of the hollowing of the American middle class.

"A simultaneously enlightening and disturbing look at working-class lives in America's heartland." Kirkus.

330.9794 Economic conditions--California

Piscione, Deborah Perry

Secrets of Silicon Valley : what everyone else can learn from the innovation capital of the world / Deborah Perry Piscione. Palgrave Macmillan, 2013 256 p. **330.9794**

1. Technological innovations 2. Business innovations 3. Business -- Growth. 4. Entrepreneurship. 5. Silicon Valley, California

ISBN 9780230342118

LC 2012038481

Offers Silicon Valley as a productive example of entrepreneurship and innovation, noting how the region has demonstrated continued growth and investor interest in spite of economic setbacks elsewhere in the world.

331 Economics of labor, finance, land, energy

Crawford, Matthew B.

Shop class as soulcraft : an inquiry into the value of work / Matthew B. Crawford. Penguin Press, c2009. 320 p. **331**

1. Work. 2. Purpose in life 3. Job satisfaction 4. Quality of work life.

ISBN 9781594202230

LC 2009001789

"The author extols the value of making and fixing things in this masterful paean to what he calls manual competence, the ability to work with one's hands. With wit and humor, the author deftly mixes the details of his own experience as a tradesman and then proprietor of a motorcycle repair shop with more philosophical considerations." Publishers Weekly.

Murolo, Priscilla, 1949-

From the folks who brought you the weekend : a short, illustrated history of labor in the United States / Priscilla Murolo and A.B. Chitty ; illustrations by Joe Sacco. New Press : 2001. xx, 364 p. : **331**

1. Labor -- United States -- History 2. Working class -- United States -- History 3. Labor movement -- United States -- History

ISBN 9781565847767

LC 2001030978

A history of labor in the United States explores the efforts of working people to win the rights one takes for granted--basic health and safety standards, fair on-the-job treatment, minimum wage, and weekend leisure.

331.0973 Labor--United States

Guendelsberger, Emily

On the clock : what low-wage work did to me and how it drives America insane / Emily Guendelsberger. Little, Brown and Company, 2019. xi, 335 pages : **331.0973**

1. Minimum wage 2. Employees -- Psychology 3. Work -- Psychological aspects 4. Working class -- United States -- Economic conditions

ISBN 9780316509008

LC 2019930997

A college-educated young professional details his struggles to find a qualitative job, detailing the grueling realities of hourly labor for the fastest-growing segment of the American workforce while outlining strategies for more humane employment practices.

"This is a riveting window into minimum-wage work and the subsistence living it engenders." Publishers Weekly.

Reef, Catherine

Working in America / Catherine Reef. Facts On File, c2007. xxviii, 484 p. : **331.0973**

1. Labor -- North America -- History.

ISBN 9780816062393

LC 2006031191

Traces the history of the American working experience from the colonial era to the present, describing the lives of farmers, slaves, factory workers, miners, cowboys, child and female laborers, and migrant farmworkers.

331.12 Labor market

Bolles, Richard Nelson

★**What** color is your parachute? : a practical manual for job-hunters and career-changers / Richard N. Bolles. Ten Speed Press, 2016 355 p. : **331.12**

1. Applications for positions. 2. Career changes. 3. Job hunting. 4. Vocational guidance.

ISBN 0399578218

LC bl2016033851

Explains how to identify personal goals and interests and reveals how to apply that information toward obtaining satisfying employment, with tips on interviews, salary-negotiation techniques, and career searching online.

331.13 Discrimination in employment, labor shortages, unemployment

Ford, Martin (Martin R.)

Rise of the robots : technology and the threat of a jobless future / Martin Ford. Basic Books, [2015] 288 p. **331.13**

1. Employment forecasting. 2. Technological innovations -- Economic aspects. 3. Labor supply 4. Automation

ISBN 9780465059997

LC 2014041327

Examines the effects of accelerating technology on the economic system.

Taylor, Nick, 1945-

★**American** made : the enduring legacy of the WPA : when FDR put the nation to work / Nick Taylor. Bantam Book, 2008. 640 p. **331.13**

1. United States. Works Progress Administration. 2. Job creation -- United States -- History -- 20th century. 3. United States -- Politics and government -- 20th century.

ISBN 0553802356

LC 2007034563

ALA Notable Book, 2009.

A history of FDR's New Deal looks at the origins of the Works Progress Administration in the dark days of the Great Depression, examining the politics and development of the WPA from 1935 to 1943 and assessing the legacy of the controversial program.

"Lavishly illustrated, the book also has a list of New Deal organizations, a partial list of construction projects, a New Deal chronology, and endnotes. It will be a boon to all 20th-century history collections." Library Journal.

Urofsky, Melvin I.

The **affirmative** action puzzle : a living history from reconstruction to today / Melvin I. Urofsky. Pantheon Books, 2020. 576 p. **331.13**

1. United States. Supreme Court Cases. 2. Affirmative action 3. Higher education 4. Civil rights 5. Minorities 6. United States

ISBN 9781101870877

LC 2019016086

The legal historian examines the Supreme Court cases that upheld or struck down affirmative-action plans, exploring their impact on employment, education and the ongoing debates of today's world.

"A must-read for anyone interested in the history of affirmative action and its associated legal conundrums." Kirkus.

331.2 Conditions of employment

Clifford, Steven

The **CEO** pay machine : how it trashes America and how to stop it / Steven Clifford. Penguin Group USA, 2017. 240 p. **331.2**

1. Corruption 2. Income distribution 3. Chief executive officers 4. Business -- Corrupt practices

ISBN 9780735212398

LC 2016052097

A former top CEO examines the scandalous and corrupt reasons behind why corporate executives receive lucrative pay packages at the expense of the rest of the working force, outlining strategic approaches to understanding how the process works, why it hurts and how it can be stopped.

"Clifford . takes an enlightening and refreshingly candid look at the contentious topic of chief executive compensation." Publishers Weekly.

331.25 Other conditions of employment

Chertavian, Gerald

A **Year** Up : how a pioneering program that teaches young adults real skills for real jobs- - with real success / Gerald Chertavian. Viking, 2012. 320 p. **331.25**

1. Year Up (Organization) 2. Occupational training. 3. Vocational education. 4. Young adults -- Employment. 5. Internship programs.

ISBN 9780670023776

LC 2012000606

Includes index.

Shares the uplifting story of a pioneering program that offers low-income young adults training, mentorship, internships and jobs with leading companies, tracing the progress of a Year Up class from admissions through graduation to illuminate student challenges, failures and successes.

Schultz, Ellen

Retirement heist : how companies plunder and profit from the nest eggs of American workers / Ellen E. Schultz. Portfolio Hardcover, 2011. 256 p. **331.25**

1. Pensions 2. Corporations -- Moral and ethical aspects 3. Life insurance 4. Retirement benefits

ISBN 9781591843337

LC 2011015064

"An exposé of the ways corporations manipulate retirement plans at employee expense. It's no secret that hundreds of companies, from GM to IBM, have been slashing pensions and health coverage for millions of retirees. Employers blame an aging workforce, stock market losses, and spiraling costs. But the so-called retirement crisis is no demographic accident-- and large corporations have played a significant and hidden role in creating it. Award-winning Wall Street Journal reporter Ellen E. Schultz draws back the curtain on one of the biggest and least understood scandals in decades. She shows how companies: created the pension crisis by plundering billions from their pension plans; cut pensions for millions of midlevel, middle aged workers, but used the savings to boost special executive pensions; purchase life insurance policies on employees and collect death benefits when they die-- without telling them or their families This is a must read for all who are concerned about their financial future and that of the whole country".-- Provided by publisher.

"Readers are no stranger to the grumblings of their corporate overlords: Pensions are untenable; health-care costs too high; retiree benefits hurt competitiveness. But according to . Schultz, employee pensions actually make money for corporations, and the funds diverted from them help feather the beds of multimillionaire executives. She exposes all this and more in a rapid-fire narrative. Individual stories of retired men and women (some with more than 40 years of service) robbed of their nest eggs put a human face on the proceedings. Essential reading for anyone who works for a living." Kirkus.

331.3 Labor force by personal attributes

Bruder, Jessica

★**Nomadland**: surviving America in the twenty-first century / Jessica Bruder. W W Norton & Co Inc 2017 320 p. **331.3**

1. Migrant workers 2. Seniors 3. Retirement 4. Economic security 5. United States -- Economic conditions.

ISBN 9780393249316

LC 2017018056

Author Jessica Bruder, who teaches at the Columbia School of Journalism, spent several years traveling with older Americans who have become itinerant workers in order to make ends meet. In Nomadland, she describes how they assume a "wheel estate" (instead of "real estate") existence as they travel from one seasonal job to the next, exchanging information on safe camping sites and enjoying the camaraderie of the road. Bruder vividly and sympathetically characterizes these "workampers" as she critiques the financial systems that have led them to adopt this solution.

"Engaging, highly relevant immersion journalism." Kirkus.

Fideler, Elizabeth F.

Men still at work: professionals over sixty and on the job / Elizabeth F. Fideler. Rowman & Littlefield, 2014. 232 p. **331.3**

1. Senior men 2. Age and employment. 3. Professional employees 4. Women employees 5. United States -- Social life and customs -- 21st century.

ISBN 9781442222755

LC 2013040402

"Overall, an engaging, accessible overview of what the future holds for many younger men who will undoubtedly work into their 60s ... and beyond." Choice.

331.4 Women workers

Bohnet, Iris

What works: gender equality by design / Iris Bohnet. The Belknap Press of Harvard University Press, 2016. 320 p. **331.4**

1. Sex discrimination in employment. 2. Gender mainstreaming. 3. Organizational behavior. 4. Sex discrimination

ISBN 9780674089037

LC 2015039199

"Gender equality is a moral and a business imperative. But unconscious bias holds us back and de-biasing minds has proven to be difficult and expensive. Behavioral design offers a new solution. Iris Bohnet shows that by de-biasing organizations instead of individuals, we can make smart changes that have big impacts--often at low cost and high speed."--Provided by publisher

Chang, Emily

Brotopia : breaking up the boys' club of Silicon Valley / Emily Chang. Portfolio, 2018. 288 p. **331.4**

1. Internet industry and trade 2. Sex discrimination in employment 3. Sex discrimination against women. 4. Sexism in employment. 5. Santa Clara County, California -- Social conditions. 6. Silicon Valley, California.

ISBN 9780735213531

LC bl2017050241

Reveals how male-dominated Silicon Valley became sexist despite its utopian ideals and decades of companies claiming the moral high ground, and how women are finally starting to fight back against toxic workplaces and sexual harrassment.

Chang, Leslie

Factory girls : from village to city in a changing China / Leslie T. Chang. Spiegel & Grau, 2008. 420 p. : **331.4**

1. Manufacturing industry and trade -- Employees -- China. 2. Women migrant workers. 3. Migrant workers. 4. Blue collar women. 5. China -- Social conditions. 6. China -- Economic conditions.

ISBN 9780385520171

LC 2008012880

Explores the world of the millions of female Chinese migrant workers who have left their homes in rural towns to find jobs in China's cities, as revealed through a two-year study of the lives of two young women.

"This is an exceptionally vivid and compassionate depiction of the day-to-day dramas, and the fears and aspirations, of the real people who are powering China's economic boom." New York Times Book Review.

Farrow, Ronan, 1987-

★**Catch** and kill : lies, spies and a conspiracy to protect predators / Ronan Farrow. Little, Brown and Company 2019 448 p. ; **331.4**

1. Farrow, Ronan, 1987- 2. Lauer, Matt, 1957- 3. Weinstein, Harvey, 1952- 4. Sexual harassment 5. Threat (Psychology) 6. Investigative journalism 7. Surveillance 8. Hollywood, California

ISBN 9780316486637

National Book Critics Circle Award for Autobiography/Memoir finalist, 2019

Describes the author's investigation of sexual assault, sexual harassment, and rape accusations against Harvey Weinstein and Matt Lauer, and the many obstacles he faced, not only from Weinstein but also from his own employer, NBC.

Fideler, Elizabeth F.

Women still at work : professionals over sixty and on the job / Elizabeth S. Fideler. Rowman & Littlefield Publishers, c2012. 220 p. **331.4**

1. Senior women -- Employment. 2. Age and employment. 3. Professional employees 4. Women employees 5. United States -- Social life and customs -- 21st century.

ISBN 9781442215504

LC 2012017802

The fastest growing segment of the workforce is women age sixty-five and older. Women Still at Work draws on national survey data and in-depth interviews to show the many reasons why women are working well past the traditional retirement age. The book is filled with profiles of real working women, with a focus on women in the professional workforce. --Provided by publisher

Kessler-Harris, Alice

★**Out** to work : a history of wage-earning women in the United States / Alice Kessler-Harris. Oxford University Press, 2003, c1982. xvi, 414 p. : **331.4**

1. Women -- Employment -- United States -- History. 2. Working class women -- United States -- History. 3. Working class -- United

States -- History.
ISBN 0195157095

LC 2003267644

Originally published: New York : Oxford University Press, 1982.

"This work remains a landmark in the field of analyzing the history of women's work in the United States from Colonial times to the Reagan era." Library Journal.

Lacy, Sarah, 1975-

A **uterus** is a feature, not a bug : the working woman's guide to overthrowing the patriarchy / Sarah Lacy. Harper Business, 2017. x, 306 p. ; **331.4**

1. Working mothers 2. Maternity leave 3. Discrimination 4. Women's role
ISBN 9780062641816

Seeks to reverse negative stereotypes about how female employees with families are weak, emotional, or distracted, counseling women to rethink their identities after giving birth while arguing in favor of fairer wages, equal opportunities, and more flexible maternity leave.

"A fierce and persuasive call to action that demands women, especially millennials, rethink the relationship b e tween maternity and career ambitions." Kirkus.

Povich, Lynn

★The **good** girls revolt : how the women of Newsweek sued their bosses and changed the workplace / Lynn Povich. PublicAffairs, c2012. 256 p. **331.4**

1. Newsweek 2. Gender role in the work environment 3. Sexism in employment 4. Sex discrimination 5. Women journalists -- United States -- History -- 20th century 6. United States -- Social life and customs -- 20th century
ISBN 9781610391733

LC 2012006936

The untold story of an uprising that transformed the Mad Men office culture: its bittersweet impact on the women involved, and what has--and hasn't--changed

Ryckman, Pamela

Stiletto network : inside the women's power circles that are changing the face of business / Pamela Ryckman. American Management Association, 2013. 256 p. **331.4**

1. Businesspeople 2. Women executives 3. Women professional employees 4. Business networks
ISBN 9780814432532

LC 2012051563

Includes index.

Discusses the women's networks forming in and changing the business world.

Zahidi, Saadia

Fifty million rising : the new generation of working women revolutionizing the Muslim world / Saadia Zahidi. Nation Books, [2018] 288 p. **331.4**

1. Muslim women 2. Women employees 3. Gender role 4. Feminism
ISBN 9781568585901

LC 2017029076

An award-winning economist and the head of Education, Gender and Work describes a shift in the Muslim world created by more than 50 million women joining the workforce and discusses how they are challenging and changing familial norms and social conventions.

"In this fascinating look at a monumental shift, Zahidi elevates the voices of women across the world who speak about their motivations, successes, and challenges in forging new paths." Booklist.

331.5 Workers by personal attributes other than age

Browne, John

The **glass** closet : why coming out is good business / John Browne. Harperbusiness, 2014. 224 p. **331.5**

1. Homosexuality 2. Homophobia 3. Corporate culture 4. Businesspeople
ISBN 9780062316974

LC bl2014024653

"Brown's rhetoric is businesslike and a little dry but also to the point, supported by research, and culturally significant. He has taken pains to provide strikingly honest personal narratives and uses them to put a face on the problems at hand." Booklist.

331.6 Workers by ethnic and national origin

Chang, Gordon H.

Ghosts of Gold Mountain : the epic story of the Chinese who built the transcontinental railroad / Gordon H. Chang. Houghton Mifflin Harcourt, 2019 304 p. **331.6**

1. Central Pacific Railroad -- History 19th century 2. Railroad construction workers 3. Chinese in the United States 4. Immigrant workers 5. Labor exploitation 6. China -- Immigration and emigration -- History -- 19th century 7. The West (United States) -- History -- 19th century
ISBN 9781328618573

LC 2018042558

Asian Pacific American Award for Literature: Adult Nonfiction, 2020.

A history of the Chinese laborers who were pivotal to the construction of the American Transcontinental Railroad details the construction perils that cost innumerable lives before survivors were almost instantly lost to public memory.

"Successfully shedding light on the fascinating lives of the workers who completed a monumental task in the mountainous west, this is an essential read for anyone interested in the history of Chinese Americans, the American West, or the Transcontinental Railroad." Library Journal.

331.7 Labor by industry and occupation

Fisher, James T.

On the Irish waterfront : the crusader, the movie, and the soul of the port of New York / James T. Fisher. Cornell University Press, 2009. xiv, 370 p. : **331.7**

1. Catholic Church Missions. 2. On the waterfront (Motion picture) 3. Stevedores 4. Irish Americans -- New York City -- History. 5. Harbors -- Hudson River. 6. Immigrants, Irish 7. Hudson River. 8. New York City.
ISBN 9780801448041

LC 2009013058

"The author presents a history of the New York-New Jersey waterfront depicted in Elia Kazan's Oscar-winning 1954 film, On the Waterfront. Fischer's impeccable research delves into the real-life stories behind the characters. This engaging narrative is essential reading for both labor historians and cinema buffs, plus anyone studying the waterfront, working-class and immigrant history, anticommunism, blacklisting, and the House Un-American Activities Committee." Library Journal.

Nagle, Robin

Picking up : on the streets and behind the trucks with the sanitation workers of New York City / Robin Nagle. Farrar, Straus and Giroux, 2013. 288 p. **331.7**

1. Garbage collectors 2. Solid waste 3. Solid waste disposal 4. Garbage collection 5. New York City
ISBN 9780374299293

LC 2012028941

Charting New York's 400-year struggle with trash, an anthropologist, spending 10 years with sanitation workers of all ranks, takes readers inside New York City's Department of Sanitation where she reveals what it really takes to manage Gotham's garbage.

331.700973 Occupations--United States

Wartzman, Rick

The **end** of loyalty : the rise and fall of good jobs in America / Rick Wartzman. PublicAffairs, 2017. 432 p. **331.700973**

1. Labor-management relations 2. Corporations 3. Labor policy 4. Industrial policy 5. United States -- Economic conditions -- 1945-
ISBN 9781586489144

LC 2017006668

Tracing the history of the social contract between companies and their employees, and showing how it has been ripped apart, a senior advisor at the Drucker Institute discusses four iconic American companies over 70 years, bringing to light the many acts that have comprised a kind of biography of the American Dream gone sideways.

"A sharp-edged examination of why large American employers shifted from loyalty to their workers to loyalty focused primarily on stockholders." Kirkus.

331.702 Choice of vocation

Morgan, Genevieve

Undecided : navigating life and learning after high school / Genevieve Morgan. Zest Books, 2020, c2014. 247 p. **331.702**

1. Vocational guidance for high school students. 2. Vocational interests. 3. Educational guidance. 4. Teenagers -- Career aspirations.
ISBN 9781541597785

LC bl2014012501

Originally published: San Francisco, CA : Zest Books, 2014.

A comprehensive handbook for high school teens who have not yet established their post-graduation path outlines options ranging from training programs and the military to community colleges and universities to help students decide which course is best for them.

"A helpful guide full of good, sensible advice to teens feeling overwhelmed by the prospect of major life transitions." Kirkus.

331.880973 Labor unions--United States

Dray, Philip

There is power in a union : the epic story of labor in America / Philip Dray. Doubleday, 2010. 368 p. **331.880973**

1. Labor unions -- United States -- History. 2. Labor movement -- United States -- History. 3. Industrialization -- United States -- History. 4. Employees -- Empowerment 5. United States -- Social conditions.
ISBN 9780385526296

LC 2010002357

The Pulitzer Prize finalist author presents a narrative chronicle of American organized labor from the origins of the industrial age to the present, documenting the rise and fall of unions and the ongoing fight for workplace equality.

Dubofsky, Melvyn, 1934-

★**Labor** in America : a history / Melvyn Dubofsky, Distinguished Professor Emeritus of History & Sociology, Binghamton University and Joseph A. McCartin, Professor of History, Georgetown University. Wiley Blackwell, 2017 xix, 469 p. ; **331.880973**

1. Labor -- United States -- History 2. Working class -- United States -- History 3. Labor unions -- United States -- History
ISBN 9781118976852

LC 2016043343

This book, designed to give a survey history of American labor from colonial times to the present, is uniquely well suited to speak to the concerns of today's teachers and students. As issues of growing inequality, stagnating incomes, declining unionization, and exacerbated job insecurity have increasingly come to define working life over the last 20 years, a new generation of students and teachers is beginning to seek to understand labor and its place and ponder seriously its future in American life. Like its predecessors, this ninth edition of our classic survey of American labor is designed to introduce readers to the subject in an engaging, accessible way. --Provided by publisher

Greenwald, Richard A.,

Labor rising : the past and future of working people in America / edited by Richard A. Greenwald, Daniel Katz. New Press, The, 2012. 256 p. **331.880973**

1. Labor movement -- United States -- History. 2. Working class -- United States -- History. 3. Protests, demonstrations, vigils, etc. 4. Labor unions. 5. Essays.
ISBN 9781595585189

LC 2012001464

"When Wisconsin Governor Scott Walker threatened the collective bargaining rights of the state's public-sector employees in early 2011, the huge protests that erupted in response put the labor movement back on the nation's front pages. It was a fleeting reminder of a not-so-distant past when the "labor question"--and the power of organized labor--was part and parcel of a century-long struggle for justice and equality in America. Now, on the heels of the expansive "Occupy Wall Street" movement, the lessons of history--in seemingly short supply--are a vital handhold for the thousands of activists and citizens everywhere who sense that something has gone terribly wrong. This pithy but accessible volume provides readers with an understanding of the history that is directly relevant to the economic and political crises working people face today, and points the way to a revitalized twenty-first-century labor movement. With original contributions from leading labor historians, social critics, and activists, LaborRising makes crucial connections between the past and present, and then looks forward, asking how we might imagine a different future for all Americans".-- Provided by publisher.

331.890973 Collective bargaining--United States

McAlevey, Jane

A **collective** bargain : unions, organizing, and the fight for democracy / Jane McAlevey. Ecco, 2019 256 p. **331.890973**

1. Labor unions 2. Collective bargaining 3. Strikes 4. Democracy 5.

United States -- Social conditions -- 21st century.
ISBN 9780062908599

LC 2019028863

Includes index.

A longtime labor, environmental and political organizer argues that unions are the only institution capable of fighting back against today's super-rich corporate class.

"After calling out Silicon Valley, with all its progressive veneer, for its anti-labor actions, McAlevey finishes with keen insights into creating a union and rebuilding a union from within. Another most-valuable book from McAlevey." Booklist.

331.892 Strikes

Loomis, Erik

A **history** of America in ten strikes / Erik Loomis. The New Press, 2018. 288 p. **331.892**

1. Strikes 2. Labor disputes 3. Labor movement 4. Labor unions
ISBN 9781620971611

LC 2018017580

"This concise history, seen through the lens of 10 labor strikes from the nineteenth century on, uses those encounters between capitalists and workers to tell a broader and very sad story." Booklist.

332 Financial economics

Gasparino, Charles

The **sellout** : how three decades of Wall Street's greed and government mismanagement destroyed the global financial system / Charles Gasparino. Wiley, 2009. 576 p. **332**

1. Financial crises -- United States -- History. 2. Greed -- History. 3. Investment banking. 4. Brokers. 5. Wall Street, New York City -- History.
ISBN 9780061697166

LC 2009028097

The author of Blood on the Street offers an account of the most dramatic and anxiety-ridden era in national socioeconomic history--not merely a recounting of the collapse of Wall Street's legendary firms, but a broad examination of the people and the forces who killed Wall Street.

"Of all the books documenting the financial crisis . The Sellout tells it better than most. Filled with very little of the boring, complex financial jargon that comprises many books of the genre, this tome makes for a surprisingly entertaining and easy read." Risk Management.

O'Rourke, P. J.

None of my business / P. J. O'Rourke. Atlantic Monthly, 2018 304 p. **332**

1. Finance 2. Social change 3. Technology and civilization 4. Economics 5. Wall Street, New York City
ISBN 9780802128485

LC 2018026530

In his latest book, P.J. O'Rourke takes forty-five years of experience making fun of terrible things in the most awful places in the world and applies it to a place that's even worse--Wall Street, and the whole wide world of finance.

Piketty, Thomas, 1971-

★**Capital** in the twenty-first century / Thomas Piketty ; translated from the French by Arthur Goldhammer. The Belknap Press of Harvard University Press, 2014, 2013. viii, 685 p. : **332**

1. Income distribution. 2. Wealth. 3. Capitalism and inequality. 4. Labor economics.
ISBN 9780674430006

LC 2013036024

Translation from the French of: Le capital au XXIe siecle.

Originally published: Paris : Editions du Seuil, 2013.

Kirkus Prize for Nonfiction finalist, 2014.

National Book Critics Circle Award for Nonfiction finalist, 2014.

Analyzes a collection of data from twenty countries, ranging as far back as the eighteenth century, to uncover key economic and social patterns, transform debate, and set the agenda for the next generation of thought about wealth and inequality.

"Shows that plain language can be put to work explaining the most complex of ideas, foremost among them the fact that economic inequality is at an all-time high--and is only bound to grow worse." Kirkus.

332.024 Personal finance

Ariely, Dan

★**Dollars** and sense : how we misthink money and how to spend smarter / Dan Ariely and Jeff Kreisler. Harper, an imprint of HarperCollinsPublishers, 2017. 256 p. **332.024**

1. Personal finance 2. Money -- Psychological aspects 3. Credit cards 4. Budget
ISBN 9780062651204

LC bl2017036961

Shares anecdotal insight into the illogical influences behind poor financial decisions and how to outmaneuver them, covering topics ranging from credit-card debt and household budgeting to holiday spending and real estate sales.

"A user-friendly and often entertaining treatise on how to be a more discerning, vastly more aware handler of money." Kirkus.

Choudhri, Nihara K.

Preparing for baby : all the legal, financial, tax, and insurance information new and expectant parents need / Nihara K. Choudhri. American Bar Association, 2015 xii, 320 p. : **332.024**

1. Domestic relations -- United States 2. Children -- Legal status, laws, etc -- United States 3. Parent and child (Law) -- United States 4. Pregnant women -- Legal status, laws, etc -- United States
ISBN 9781634251877

LC 2015034391

Includes index.

A baby book unlike any other, this resource deals with the important legal and financial matters of your new baby. The book contains easy-to-understand information about the basic legal and financial issues most new parents face, broken down into an easy to digest and reference Q&A format for parents busy with the day. It's a book every new parent needs on their shelf next to the more traditional tomes. --Provided by publisher

"This is a valuable resource for making valuable decisions. It provides the legal details and definitions parents need to make challenging decisions, and the Q&A format is a road map for people who don't know where--or how--to start." Booklist

Cramer, Jim

Jim Cramer's get rich carefully / James J. Cramer. Blue Rider Press, 2013 xiv, 433 p. : **332.024**

1. Investment analysis -- United States. 2. Investments -- United States. 3. Personal finance -- United States. 4. Stocks -- United

States.
ISBN 0399168184

LC 2013042642

Includes index.

"Tired of phony promises about getting rich quickly, promises that lead to reckless decisions (the stepping stones to the poor house)? How about trying something different? How about going for lasting wealth-and doing it the cautious way? In Get Rich Carefully, Jim Cramer uses his thirty-five years of experience as a Wall Street veteran and host of CNBC's Mad Money to create a guide to high-yield, low-risk investing. In our recovering economy, this is the plan you need to make big money without taking big risks. Drawing on his unparalleled knowledge of the stock market and on the mistakes and successes he's made on the way to his own fortune, Cramer explains-in plain English-why you can get rich in a prudent, methodical way, as long as you start now. In his own inimitable style, Cramer lays it on the line, no waffling, no on-the-one-hand-or-the-other hedging, just the straight stuff you need to accumulate wealth. This is a book of wisdom as well as specifics. Cramer names names, highlights individual and sector plays, and identifies the best long-term investing themes--and shows you how to develop the disciplines you need to exploit them. The personal finance book of the year, Get Rich Carefully is the invaluable guide to turning your savings into real, lasting wealth in a practical, and yes-because this is, after all, a book by Jim Cramer-highly readable and entertaining way".-- Provided by publisher.

Economides, Steve

The **moneysmart** family system : teaching financial independence to children of every age / Steve and Annette Economides. Thomas Nelson, c2012. ix, 261 p. : **332.024**

1. Children -- Finance, Personal. 2. Families -- Economic aspects. 3. Personal finance
ISBN 1400202841

LC 2012941594

"Learn how to: get the kids out the door for school with less stress; end the battle over clothing--forever; teach your children to be grateful and generous; inspire your kids to help with chores as a member of a winning team; prepare your kids for theirfirst paying job; help your kids pay for their own auto insurance, and even pay cash for their own cars; employ strategies for debt-free college educations; truly help your adult children when they want to move back home; be prepared to deal with your adult children when they ask for bailouts"--P. [4] of cover.

Includes index.

The system will show you how to teach your children to manage money and have a good attitude while they're learning to earn, budget, and spend wisely.

Fagan, Chelsea

The **financial** diet : a total beginner's guide to getting good with money / Chelsea Fagan ; designed by Lauren Ver Hage ; illustrations by Eve Mobley. Henry Holt and Company, 2018 196 p. : **332.024**

1. Personal finance 2. Women -- Finance, Personal
ISBN 9781250176165

LC 2017027973

"A Holt Paperback."

Offers guidance on personal finance for readers who might be reluctant to bother with the subject, with easy-to-follow advice for budgeting, investing, handling credit, and living a satisfying lifestyle that is still budget conscious.

"The breezy lifestyle-magazine-like writing style and easy-to-digest layout make this guide a useful and readable resource." Publishers Weekly.

Kessel, Brent

It's not about the money : unlock your money type to achieve spiritual and financial abundance / Brent Kessel. HarperOne, c2008. 299 p. **332.024**

1. Personal finance -- Psychological aspects. 2. Typology (Psychology) 3. Self-perception. 4. Money -- Psychological aspects.
ISBN 9780061234064

LC 2007018380

"The author offers holistic financial advice in this Buddhist-influenced debut promising both a better financial strategy and greater fulfillment and happiness. Readers interested in an Eastern-influenced approach will find useful advice on how to think about money, as well as insight into what makes us tick." Publishers Weekly.

Kiyosaki, Robert T., 1947-

★**Rich** dad, poor dad : with updates for today's world--and 9 new study session sections / Robert T. Kiyosaki. Plata Publishing, 2017. xi, 352 p. : **332.024**

1. Personal finance 2. Investments. 3. Rich people.
ISBN 9781612680194

LC bl2017014790

"What the rich teach their kids about money--that the poor and middle class do not!"--Cover.

Argues that a good education and a secure job are not guarantees for financial success, and describes guidelines for making money work for oneself.

Why "A" students work for "C" students : and "B" students work for the government / [Robert T. Kiyosaki]. Plata Pub., 2013. 453 p. : **332.024**

1. Child rearing 2. Personal finance
ISBN 9781612680767

LC bl2013013725

"Rich Dad's guide to financial education for parents. How to give your child a financial headstart-- without giving them money"--Cover.

A best-selling personal finance author encourages parents to not put so much emphasis on letter grades, arguing that many C students grow up to become CEOs and successful entrepreneurs.

Kobliner, Beth, 1965-

Make your kid a money genius (even if you're not) : a parents' guide for kids 3 to 23 / Beth Kobliner. Simon & Schuster, 2017. 256 p. : **332.024**

1. Children -- Finance, Personal. 2. Parenting. 3. Personal finance
ISBN 1476766819

LC 2016021573

From Beth Kobliner, the author of the bestselling personal finance bible Get a Financial Life--a new, must-have guide showing parents how to teach their children (from toddlers to young adults) to manage money in a smart way.

"Best-selling financial author Kobliner (Get a Financial Life) here provides a step-by-step look at developing financial literacy skills throughout childhood." Library Journal.

Mecham, Jesse

You need a budget : the proven system for breaking the paycheck-to-paycheck cycle, getting out of debt, and living the life you want / Jesse Mecham. HarperBusiness, 2017 207 p. : **332.024**

1. Budgets, Personal. 2. Personal finance
ISBN 0062567586

LC bl2017041802

Includes index.

A guide based on the tenets of the "You Need a Budget" financial platform argues that a well-planned budget can help to prioritize financial goals, reduce stress through strategic cash flow allocations, and meet the challenges of unplanned expenses.

"Mecham's book is a handy guide for readers looking to increase their financial literacy and manage their money carefully and successfully." Booklist.

Morduch, Jonathan

The **financial** diaries : how American families cope in a world of uncertainty / Jonathan Morduch and Rachel Schneider. Princeton University Press, [2017] xii, 233 pages : **332.024**

1. Family income 2. Personal finance 3. Household finances 4. Survival (Economics)
ISBN 9780691172989

LC 2016955128

Combining hard facts with the personal stories of 235 low- and middle-income families as they navigate through a year, the authors examine the economic stresses of today's families and offer fresh ideas for solving them.

"This is a must-read for anyone interested in causes ofand potential solutions toAmerican poverty." Publishers Weekly.

Orman, Suze

The **money** class : learn to create your new American dream / Suze Orman. Spiegel & Grau, 2011. xiv, 281 p. ; **332.024**

1. Personal finance -- United States. 2. Wealth -- United States.
ISBN 1400069734

LC 2011001394

From a popular financial guru who has appeared on the Oprah Winfrey Show comes a new no-nonsense guide to personal finance.

Palmer, Kimberly

Smart mom, rich mom : how to build wealth while raising a family / Kimberly Palmer. AMACOM, American Management Association, 2016 x, 246 p. ; **332.024**

1. Women -- Personal finance 2. Working mothers -- Self-help materials 3. Families -- Economic aspects. 4. Family and work
ISBN 9780814436806

LC 2015050487

Provides mothers with strategies for building wealth while attending to their family's financial needs in the present.

Quinn, Jane Bryant

Making the most of your money now : The Classic Bestseller Completely Revised for the New Economy / Jane Bryant Quinn. Simon & Schuster, 2010. xviii, 1242 p. ; **332.024**

1. Investments. 2. Personal finance
ISBN 0743269969

LC 2009032610

Includes index.

Rev. ed. of: Making the most of your money. 1997.

An updated edition of a popular personal financial reference shares a blueprint for overcoming such challenges as debt and high mortgage rates while saving money on a budget and achieving financial security.

"This is an excellent primer, especially for those new to managing their money." Library Journal.

Ramsey, Dave

★The **total** money makeover : a proven plan for financial fitness / Dave Ramsey. Nelson Books, 2013 xxvii, 237 p. : **332.024**

1. Personal finance 2. Debt.
ISBN 9781595555274

LC 2013431148

Includes index.

A strategy for changing attitudes about personal finances covers such topics as getting out of debt, the dangers of cash advances and keeping spending within income limits.

Robbins, Anthony

Money : master the game : 7 simple steps to financial freedom / Tony Robbins. Simon & Schuster, 2014. xxviii, 656 p. : **332.024**

1. Personal finance
ISBN 9781476757803

LC bl2014048627

Includes index.

Based on extensive research and one-on-one interviews with more than 50 of the most legendary financial experts in the world--from Carl Icahn and Warren Buffett to Ray Dalio and Steve Forbes--a popular motivational speaker has created a simple seven-step blueprint that anyone can use for financial freedom. Includes more than 60 charts. Illustrations.

Robin, Vicki

★**Your** money or your life : 9 steps to transforming your relationship with money and achieving financial independence / Vicki Robin and Joe Dominguez. Penguin Books, 2008. xxxvii, 325, 11-27 p. : **332.024**

1. Personal finance
ISBN 9780143115762

LC 2008044048

Offers a nine-step program for living a more meaningful life by taking control of one's finances, showing readers how to get out of debt, save money, reorder priorities, live well for less, and convert problems into opportunities.

Sabatier, Grant

Financial freedom : a proven path to all the money you will ever need / Grant Sabatier ; foreword by Vicki Robin. Avery, 2019 342 p. : **332.024**

1. Personal finance
ISBN 9780525534594

LC 2018049617

"Money is unlimited. Time is not. Become financially independent as fast as possible".-- Provided by publisher.

Sethi, Ramit

I will teach you to be rich / Ramit Sethi. Workman Pub., c2009. vi, 266 p. : **332.024**

1. Investments. 2. Personal finance 3. Wealth.
ISBN 0761147489

LC 2008056014

Includes index.

Presents a six-week program that introduces the principles and practices of personal finance for twenty to thirty-five year olds, covering four key elements--banking, saving, budgeting, and investing--as well as tips on personal entrepreneurship, the art of managing money, taxes, and other aspects of building wealth and personal security.

Stanley, Thomas J.

★The **next** millionaire next door : enduring strategies for building wealth / Thomas J. Stanley, PhD, and Sarah Stanley Fallaw, PhD. Lyons Press, 2018 xii, 260 p. : **332.024**

1. Wealth -- United States. 2. Personal finance -- United States.
ISBN 9781493035359

LC 2018030576

Twenty years after Thomas J. Stanley's groundbreaking work on self-made affluence, he and his daughter examine the changes in specific decisions, behaviors and characteristics, along with consumption, budgeting, careers and investing that have changed wealth-building in more recent years.

Tobias, Andrew P.

★The **only** investment guide you'll ever need / Andrew Tobias. Mariner Books/Houghton Mifflin Harcourt, 2016. xxi, 296 p. : **332.024**

1. Investments 2. Personal finance
ISBN 9780544781931

LC 2016304579

Presents financial advice on such topics as the stock market, savings accounts, taxes, Social Security, wills, college funds, life insurance, and mutual funds.

Yeager, Jeff

The **cheapskate** next door : the surprising secrets of Americans living happily below their means / Jeff Yeager. Broadway Books, c2010. xix, 231 p. ; **332.024**

1. Personal finance 2. Saving and thrift 3. Money -- Philosophy. 4. Americans -- Interviews.
ISBN 9780767931328

"The amazing fact about this book is that in addition to his instructions making perfect sense, like no other book of its kind, this one can be read simply for the humor of the author's prose." Booklist.

332.0240082 Women--Personal finance

Orman, Suze

Women & money / Suze Orman. Spiegel & Grau, 2018 xiii, 206 p. ; **332.0240082**

1. Women -- United States -- Personal finance 2. Personal finance -- United States. 3. Wealth -- Psychological aspects.
ISBN 9780812987614

LC 2018019618

Revised edition of the author's Women & money, c2007.

Includes index.

In a book that includes up-to-date tax information and economic data, a renowned personal-finance expert, TV host and best-selling author offers insights and compassion along with a clear and streamlined plan for women to attain durable financial security.

332.0240083 Young people--Personal finance

Lieber, Ron

The **opposite** of spoiled : raising kids who are grounded, generous, and smart about money / Ron Lieber. HarperCollins, 2015. 320 p. **332.0240083**

1. Parenting 2. Personal finance 3. Generosity 4. Money
ISBN 9780062247018

LC 2014035600

A New York Times personal-finance columnist challenges popular taboos to explain how talking openly to children about money can help parents raise grounded, financially responsible young adults.

"Humble stories of kids raising money for Down syndrome research or creating kit bags to give to people living on the street offer inspiration for those who do have money to spend it wisely in the world and to teach their children to do the same. Sound advice on managing family finances but only if you have sufficient finances to manage." Kirkus.

332.09 Finance--History

Ferguson, Niall

★The **ascent** of money : a financial history of the world / Niall Ferguson. Penguin Books, 2008. 432 p. **332.09**

1. Economics. 2. World economy. 3. Finance. 4. History.
ISBN 9781594201929

LC bl2008023250

Chronicles the human drama behind the evolution of finance from its origins in Mesopotamia to the modern world's most recent upheavals, in an account that covers such topics as the stock market bubble that prompted the French Revolution, the theories behind common investment vehicles, and the reasons why the free market is failing to protect Hurricane Katrina victims.

"The author presents the history of money within these contexts: the rise of money and the history of credit, and the histories of the bond market, the stock market, insurance, the real-estate market, and international finance. There is an ease to his prose that leaves this complicated subject interesting to and approachable by any general reader." Booklist.

332.1 Banks

Enrich, David, 1979-

Dark towers : Deutsche Bank, Donald Trump, and an epic trail of destruction / David Enrich. Custom House, 2020. 384 p. **332.1**

1. Trump, Donald, 1946- 2. Deutsche Bank. 3. Banks and banking -- Corrupt practices. 4. Investment banking -- Corrupt practices. 5. Corruption 6. International banking
ISBN 9780062878816

LC 2019034196

Presents a journalistic expose of the scandalous activities of Deutsche Bank and its shadowy ties to Donald Trump's business empire.

"Part exposé, part mystery, Enrich's account is important because it illuminates Deutsche Bank's excesses and Trump's business practices. Readers of Andrew Sorkin's Too Big To Fail, which unveiled vulnerabilities in the financial industry, will find Enrich's more focused account equally compelling." Library Journal

Lowenstein, Roger

America's bank : the epic struggle to create the Federal Reserve / Roger Lowenstein. Penguin Group USA, 2015 368 p. **332.1**

1. Board of Governors of the Federal Reserve System (U.S.) -- History. 2. Federal Reserve banks. 3. Banks and banking. 4. Central banking.
ISBN 9781594205491

LC 2015373201

Chronicles the tumultuous era and remarkable personalities that created the Federal Reserve, tracing the financial panic and widespread distrust of bankers that prompted the landmark 1913 Federal Reserve Act and launched America's first steps onto the world financial stage.

"Readers seeking a comprehensive history of the Federal Reserve from its conception to modern times will find this work especially appealing." Library Journal.

Meltzer, Allan H.

★A **history** of the Federal Reserve : 1913-1951 / Allan H. Meltzer ; with a foreword by Alan Greenspan. University of Chicago, Ill. :Press, c2003-<c2009 > 848 p. ; **332.1**

1. Board of Governors of the Federal Reserve System (U.S.). 2. Federal Reserve banks

ISBN 9780226519999

LC 2002072007

"The author provides a definitive history of the U.S. Federal Reserve from its founding in 1913 to its establishment as a separate, independent entity in 1951. Using meeting minutes, correspondence, and internal Federal Reserve documents, he traces the reasons behind Federal Reserves policy decisions, highlights the impact that individuals and events had on the Fed, and examines the Fed's influence on international affairs. This well-written and thoroughgoing account is recommended for academic, business, and public libraries." Library Journal.

Prins, Nomi

Collusion : how central bankers rigged the world / Nomi Prins. Nation Books, 2018. 368 p. **332.1**

1. World Bank 2. International Monetary Fund 3. Financial institutions 4. Banks and banking -- Corrupt practices 5. Central banking 6. World economy

ISBN 9781568585628

LC 2017044122

A journalist and former Wall Street executive exposes the collusion between central bankers as they control the global markets and dictate economic policy, casting an unflinching spotlight on the dark conspiracies and unsavory connections within the halls of power.

Wessel, David

★**In** Fed we trust : Ben Bernanke's war on the great panic / David Wessel. Crown Business, c2009. xii, 323 p. ; **332.1**

1. Bernanke, Ben. 2. Board of Governors of the Federal Reserve System (U.S.) 3. Central banking. 4. Financial crises. 5. Monetary policy. 6. Banks and banking. 7. United States -- Economic conditions.

ISBN 9780307459688

"How the federal reserve became the fourth branch of government"--Dust jkt.

"The author has written a gripping blow-by-blow account of how the top brass at the Federal Reserve and Treasury flailed against financial collapse. [The story] is a thrilling one, deftly told by a veteran journalist with access to those involved. Mr Wessel has an eye for enlivening detail . . . and he has a knack for making finance accessible to the layman without boring the specialist." The Economist.

332.10973 Banks (Finance)--United States

Farrell, Greg

Crash of the titans : greed, hubris, the fall of Merrill Lynch, and the near-collapse of Bank of America / Greg Farrell. Crown Business, 2010. 471 p. ; **332.10973**

1. Merrill Lynch and Co. 2. Bank of America. 3. Bank mergers. 4. Bank failures. 5. Banks and banking. 6. Investment banking. 7. Wall Street, New York City.

ISBN 9780307717863

LC bl2010029443

The "Financial Times" reporter who revealed key controversies pertaining to the merger of Merrill Lynch and Bank of America presents a dual portrait of John Thain and Ken Lewis that reveals their roles in costing shareholders billions in investments.

Johnson, Simon, 1963-

13 bankers : the Wall Street takeover and the next financial meltdown / Simon Johnson and James Kwak. Pantheon Books, 2010. 240 p. **332.10973**

1. Banks and banking -- United States. 2. Bank failures. 3. Financial crises. 4. Finance -- United States. 5. Wall Street, New York City. 6. United States -- Economic conditions.

ISBN 9780307379054

LC 2010000168

Provides historical context for the 2008 financial crisis and proposes a radical solution--the megabanks deemed "too big to fail" must be made smaller.

"The book is a thoughtful, stimulating read on a topic of much ongoing debate and concern." Choice.

Servon, Lisa

The **unbanking** of America : how the new middle class survives / Lisa Servon. Houghton Mifflin Harcourt 2017. 288 p. **332.10973**

1. Middle class 2. Banks and banking 3. Personal finance 4. Bank regulation 5. United States -- Economic conditions.

ISBN 9780544602311

LC bl2016055430

A gripping and incisive exposé of our broken banking system--why so many Americans on many rungs of the economic ladder are unable to efficiently get at their money, pay bills, or save for emergency expenses.

"This well-written book offers a fascinating read." Library Journal.

332.3 Credit and loan institutions

Grind, Kirsten

The **lost** bank : the story of Washington Mutual--the biggest bank failure in American history / Kirsten Grind. Simon & Schuster, c2012. 384 p. **332.3**

1. Washington Mutual, Inc. 2. Savings and loan association failures -- United States -- History. 3. Bank failures -- United States -- History. 4. Savings and loan associations -- Seattle, Washington -- History. 5. Banks and banking -- Seattle, Washington -- History. 6. Seattle, Washington -- History.

ISBN 9781451617924

LC 2011048587

An award-winning journalist best known for her coverage of the failure of Washington Mutual offers insight into the failings at the root of the recession, exploring how the bank was rendered vulnerable by destructive financial instruments and the well-intentioned practices of executives, customers, shareholders and regulators.

332.4 Money

Goldstein, Jacob

Money : the true story of a made-up thing / Jacob Goldstein.

Hachette Books, 2020. xiii, 257 p. **332.4**

1. Money -- History. 2. Monetary policy 3. Economic policy 4. Finance

ISBN 9780316417198

LC 2020011586

Money only works because we all agree to believe in it. In Money, Jacob Goldstein shows how money is a useful fiction that has shaped societies for thousands of years, from the rise of coins in ancient Greece to the first stock market in Amsterdam to the emergence of shadow banking in the 21st century.

"An informative primer from a genial guide." Kirkus

Ledbetter, James

One nation under gold : how one precious metal has dominated the American imagination for four centuries / James Ledbetter. Liveright Pub Corp., 2017. 384 p. **332.4**

1. Gold 2. Gold standard 3. Monetary policy 4. Political science 5. United States -- Economic conditions

ISBN 9780871406835

LC 2017005139

An account of America's historical obsession with gold documents events ranging from the search for El Dorado to FDR's ban on private gold ownership, sharing insights into its current influences on the economy and human psyche.

"A vibrant and fascinating account of monetary golds volatile fortunes in the U.S." Booklist.

Popper, Nathaniel

Digital gold : bitcoin and the inside story of the misfits and millionaires trying to reinvent money / Nathaniel Popper. Harper, 2015. 352 p. **332.4**

1. Digital currency 2. Bitcoin 3. Money. 4. Credit.

ISBN 9780062362490

LC 2015002576

Digital Gold is New York Times reporter Nathaniel Popper's brilliant and engrossing history of Bitcoin, the landmark digital money and financial technology that has spawned a global social movement.The notion of a new currency, maintained by the computers of users around the world, has been the butt of many jokes, but that has not stopped it from growing into a technology worth billions of dollars, supported by the hordes of followers who have come to view it as the most important new idea since the creation of the Internet. Believers from Beijing to Buenos Aires see the potential for a financial system free from banks and governments. More than just a tech industry fad, Bitcoin has threatened to decentralize some of society's most basic institutions.An unusual tale of group invention, Digital Gold charts the rise of the Bitcoin technology through the eyes of the movement's colorful central characters.

Rickards, James

Currency wars : the making of the next global crisis / James Rickards. Portfolio/Penguin, c2011. 304 p. **332.4**

1. Currency crises. 2. Foreign exchange. 3. National security 4. Financial crises.

ISBN 9781591844495

LC 2011026906

Sequel: The death of money.

"The author tells us we are in a new currency war that could destroy faith in the U.S. dollar; he examines that war through the lens of economic policy, national security, and historical precedent. As a national security issue, he tells a fascinating story of his involvement with the Pentagon and other agencies in designing and participating in a war game using currencies and capital markets, instead of ships and planes, to gain early warning of attacks on the U.S. dollar. He presents a compelling case for his views and offers thought-provoking information for library patrons. This is a must-read book." Booklist.

Wheelan, Charles J.

Naked money : a revealing look at what it is and why it matters / Charles Wheelan. W.W. Norton & Company, 2016. xx, 348 p. ; **332.4**

1. Money. 2. Monetary policy. 3. Banks and banking -- United States. 4. Recession (Economics) 5. United States -- Economic conditions.

ISBN 9780393069020

The best-selling author explores the colorful world of money and banking to answer such questions as how money creation is used to counter financial crises, why the shared European currency has caused so much trouble and how Bitcoin will impact the future.

332.401 Philosophy and theory

Hammond, Claudia

Mind over money : the psychology of money and how to use it / Claudia Hammond. Harper Perennial, [2016] 372 p. **332.401**

1. Money -- Psychological aspects. 2. Personal finance -- Psychological aspects. 3. Wealth -- Psychological aspects. 4. Applied psychology.

ISBN 9780062317001

LC 2017448126

An award-winning BBC Radio 4 host delves into the latest research in the fields of neuroscience, psychology and biology to show us that our relationship with money is more complex than we might think and reveals some simple and effective tricks that will help us use and save money better.

"Part history, part anecdotes, part research, part tips, Hammonds deep look into our conflicted, world-shaping involvement with money provides striking insights, sage advice, humor, and much food for thought." Booklist.

332.6 Investment

Bernstein, William J.

The **investor's** manifesto : preparing for prosperity, Armageddon, and everything in between / William J. Bernstein. Wiley, c2010. xxii, 201 p. : **332.6**

1. Investments 2. Risk 3. Securities 4. Stocks

ISBN 9780470505144

LC 2009020116

By focusing on the concept of Pascal's Wager--identifying and avoiding worst-case scenarios and planning investment decisions on that basis--a valuable guide is filled with a wealth of practical advice and indepth insights, showing readers how to invest wisely and safely during these turbulent times.

"Touching on lessons from the dot.com and 2008 market sell-offs, [the author] discusses market and investor psychology, asset allocation, the unpredictability of returns, how to keep costs low, and, ultimately, how to avoid dying poor." Library Journal.

Bogle, John C.

The **clash** of the cultures : investment vs. speculation / John C. Bogle. John Wiley & Sons, c2012. xxv, 353 p. : **332.6**

1. Capital gains 2. Investments 3. Speculation

ISBN 9781118122778

LC 2012026770

Examines the financial world's shift from healthy long-term investment to damaging speculation, and outlines helpful hints for investors to avoid common hazards.

Cortese, Amy, 1961-

Locavesting : the revolution in local investing and how to profit from it / Amy Cortese. John Wiley & Sons, Inc., c2011. 288 p. **332.6**

1. Small business -- Finance. 2. Investments. 3. Community development. 4. Economics

ISBN 9780470911389

LC 2011005647

Includes index.

Explores the local investing movement, whereby investing in local businesses rather than giant conglomerates helps earn profits while building healthy, self-reliant communities, and introduces the ideas and pioneers behind the movement and offers investment strategies.

"With the recent crash of the financial markets, many investors are looking for new places to put their money. At the same time, many small businesses are finding it ever more difficult to get credit. Cortese . . . covers this current confluence, providing examples of how investing in local small businesses can be beneficial to all parties. Various types of funding methods are discussed, including cooperatives, credit unions, local stock exchanges, community development funds, public venture capital, and raising money through social networking. Timely and easy to read, this is a nice introduction to something many of us have never considered. A good choice for public libraries and fruitful reading for small businesses and investors." Library Journal.

Ellis, Charles D.

Winning the loser's game : timeless strategies for successful investing / Charles D. Ellis. McGraw/Hill, c2010. xix, 234 p. : **332.6**

1. Investment analysis 2. Investments 3. Portfolio management

ISBN 9780071545495

LC 2010485624

The new edition of this best-selling guide has been updated to reflect the unique trends in today's stock market and presents investors with common-sense strategies to build big profits over the long run.

Fox, Justin, 1964-

★The **myth** of the rational market : a history of risk, reward, and delusion on Wall Street / Justin Fox. Harper Business, 2009. xvi, 382 p. **332.6**

1. Efficient market theory. 2. Finance. 3. Behavioral economics. 4. Investments. 5. Wall Street, New York City.

ISBN 9780060598990

LC 2008052718

Examines the rise and fall of the efficient markets theory, the development of modern finance, and the rise of behavioral economics, in an account that draws on interviews with top thinkers while demystifying the ideas that forged the modern market.

Lewis, Michael (Michael M.)

Flash boys : a Wall Street revolt / Michael Lewis. W.W. Norton & Company, 2014 274 p. ; **332.6**

1. Brokers. 2. Finance. 3. Money. 4. Corruption 5. Wall Street, New York City.

ISBN 9780393244663

LC 2014003208

Argues that post-crisis Wall Street continues to be controlled by large banks and explains how a small, diverse group of Wall Street men have banded together to reform the financial markets.

"An engrossing true-life morality play that unmasks the devil in the details of high finance." Publishers Weekly.

Town, Danielle

Invested : how Warren Buffett and Charlie Munger taught me to master my mind, my emotions, and my money--with a little help from my dad / Danielle Town, Phil Town. William Morrow & Co., 2018. 256 p. **332.6**

1. Personal finance 2. Investments 3. Wealth

ISBN 9780062672650

LC bl2018000864

Based on a podcast.

The co-hosts of the popular "InvestED" podcast describe Danielle Town's year-long journey learning to invest in accordance with the practices and strategies of her father, hedge fund manager and best-selling author Phil Town, in a guide that outlines 12 lessons for profitably investing in companies with missions that match personal values.

332.601 Investment -- Philosophy and theory

Dreman, David

Contrarian investment strategies : the psychological edge / David Dreman. Free Press, 2012. 496 p. **332.601**

1. Investment analysis. 2. Investments -- Psychological aspects. 3. Securities 4. Financial analysis.

ISBN 9780743297967

LC 2011023716

"In this major revision of his investment classic, one of the premier investment managers introduces vitally important new findings in psychology that show why most investment strategies are fatally flawed and his contrarian strategies are the best way to beat the market. The need to switch to a new approach for investing has never been more urgent. The Crash of 2007 revealed in dramatic fashion that there are glaring flaws in the theory that underlies all of the prevailing investment strategies-efficient market theory. This theory, and all of the most popular investing strategies, fail to account for major, systematic errors in human judgment that the powerful new research in psychology David Dreman introduces has revealed, such as emotional over-reactions and a host of mental shortcuts in judgment that lead to wild over and under-valuations of stocks, bonds, and commodities and to bubbles and crashes. It also leads to horribly flawed assessments of risk. Dreman shows exactly how the new psychological findings definitively refute those strategies and reveals how his alternative contrarian strategies do a powerful job of accounting for them. He shows readers how by being aware of these new findings, they can become saavy psychological investors, crash-proofing their portfolios and earning market beating long-term returns. He also introduces a new theory of risk and substantially updates his core contrarian strategies with a number of highly effective methods for facing the most pressing challenges in the coming years, such as greatly increased volatility and the prospect of inflation. This is every investor's essential guide to optimal investing".-- Provided by publisher.

Malkiel, Burton Gordon

★A **random** walk down Wall Street : the time-tested strategy for successful investing / Burton G. Malkiel. W.W. Norton &

Co., c2011. 445 p. : **332.601**

1. Investments. 2. Random walks (Mathematics) 3. Stocks.
ISBN 0393081435

LC 2010041866

Edition statement from jacket.
Includes index.

An informative, timely and irreverent guide to financial investment offers a close-up look at the current high-tech boom, explains how to maximize gains and minimize losses and examines a broad spectrum of financial opportunities, from mutual funds to real estate to gold, especially in light of the recent financial crisis.

"The author argues that it is extremely rare for an individual investor to consistently beat the stock-market averages. Investors are better off buying and holding an index fund than attempting to buy and sell individual securities or actively managed mutual funds. This readable investment guide for individuals offers information on the full range of new investment products available, the results of current research by academics and other marketplace professionals, and a section on investment strategies for retired investors or those anticipating retirement. This excellent book offers important information for individual investors and is a valuable resource for library patrons." Booklist.

332.62 Securities brokers

Lutnick, Howard, 1961-

On top of the world : Cantor Fitzgerald, Howard Lutnick, and 9/11 : a story of loss and renewal / Tom Barbash. HarperCollins, 2003. 282 p., 32 p. of plates : **332.62**

1. Cantor Fitzgerald (Firm) -- History. 2. World Trade Center (New York City) 3. Brokers -- New York City -- History. 4. September 11 Terrorist Attacks, 2001. 5. Terrorism -- New York City. 6. New York City -- History -- 21st century.
ISBN 9780060510299

LC 2002027550

"The bond-trading firm Cantor Fitzgerald lost 658 employees on September 11, 2001. On Top of the World sets out to tell the story of Cantor Fitzgerald's tragedy, and its survival, largely from its chairman's point of view; the book is interspersed with . . . passages in {Howard} Lutnick's own voice." New York Times Book Review.

332.63 Specific forms of investment

Bogle, John C.

The **little** book of common sense investing : the only way to guarantee your fair share of stock market returns / John C. Bogle. Wiley, 2017 xxxi, 270 p. : **332.63**

1. Index funds. 2. Investments.
ISBN 9781119404507

LC bl2017052731

Presents an investment strategy for building wealth over the long term by buying and holding very low cost index mutual funds, and includes new chapters on asset allocation and retirement investing.

Fisher, Philip A.

Common stocks and uncommon profits and other writings / Philip A. Fisher. John Wiley & Sons, 2003, c1958. 292 p. **332.63**

1. Stocks. 2. Investments.
ISBN 9780471445500

Gathers the investment philosophies of Philip A. Fisher, a securities analyst who founded an investment counseling business.

Hudson, Michael W.

The **monster** : how a gang of predatory lenders and Wall Street bankers fleeced America--and spawned a global crisis / Michael W. Hudson. Times Books, 2010. 320 p. **332.63**

1. Mortgages. 2. Loans. 3. Mortgage backed securities. 4. Investment banking -- Corrupt practices.
ISBN 9780805090468

LC 2010003223

An award-winning former staff reporter for The Wall Street Journal presents an inflammatory critique of the subprime-mortgage industry and its relationship with Wall Street that charges a group of maverick entrepreneurs with using high-pressure sales tactics and triggering the current economic crisis.

"The author exposes the source of the so-called toxic subprime mortgages that led to the 2008 financial crisis. He picks his way through a warren of mortgage brokers and lending companies that sat just outside banking regulations in the years following the savings and loan crisis. The book concentrates on the practices of mortgage lenders FAMCO and Ameriquest Mortgage, at one point the largest U.S. subprime lender. This is essential reading for anyone concerned with the mortgage crisis." Library Journal.

Lynch, Peter (Peter S.)

One up on Wall Street : how to use what you already know to make money in the market / Peter Lynch with John Rothchild. Simon & Schuster, 2000. 304 p. : **332.63**

1. Investments. 2. Stocks. 3. Speculation.
ISBN 9780743200400

LC 00025839

"A Fireside book."
"With a new introduction by the author" -- Cover.
Includes index.

The manager of a top investment fund discusses how individuals can make a killing in the market through research and investment techniques that confound conventional market wisdom.

Shiller, Robert J.

Irrational exuberance / Robert J. Shiller. Princeton University Press, 2015, c2000 376 p. **332.63**

1. Stocks 2. Stock market 3. Real estate -- Prices 4. Stocks -- Prices 5. United States -- Economic conditions
ISBN 9780691166261

LC 2014036705

The author argues that investor euphoria and discouragement can cause extreme fluctuations in the stock, bond, and housing markets and presents advice for investors on protecting themselves from future bubbles.

Siegel, Jeremy J.

Stocks for the long run : the definitive guide to financial market returns & long-term investment strategies / Jeremy J. Siegel. McGraw-Hill Education, 2014 xxiii, 422 p. : **332.63**

1. Rate of return 2. Stocks -- History 3. Stocks -- Rate of return 4. Stocks
ISBN 9780071800518

LC 2013037218

"Provides investors with strategies and financial market return information, recapping the global financial crisis, emerging markets, and international investing. -- Provided by publisher.

Turner, Brandon

The **book** on rental property investing : how to create wealth and passive Income through smart buy & hold real estate investing / Brandon Turner. BiggerPockets, 2016 347 p. : **332.63**

1. Investments 2. Real estate investment
ISBN 9780990711797

LC bl2019029683

At head of cover title: BiggerPockets presents...

"A detailed, step-by-step manual focuses on investing in rental properties and becoming a landlord." Kirkus

Weatherall, James Owen

The **physics** of Wall Street : a brief history of predicting the unpredictable / James Owen Weatherall. Houghton Mifflin Harcourt, 2013. 320 p. **332.63**

1. Securities industry and trade 2. Physics 3. Financial forecasting 4. Economics 5. Wall Street, New York City
ISBN 9780547317274

LC 2012017323

A Harvard scholar challenges popular beliefs to argue that mathematical models can provide solutions to current economic challenges, citing the pivotal historical contributions of physicists to Wall Street while explaining that the economic meltdown of 2008 was based on a misunderstanding of scientific models rather than on the models themselves.

332.64 Exchange of securities and commodities; speculation

Henriques, Diana B.

A **first-class** catastrophe : the road to Black Monday, the worst day in Wall Street history / Diana B. Henriques. Henry Holt & Company, [2017] 416 p. **332.64**

1. Stock market crash, October 1987. 2. Financial crises -- United States 3. Banks and banking 4. Stock market
ISBN 9781627791649

LC 2017002890

On Monday, October 19, 1987 the financial market fell 22.6 percent, making "Black Monday" the worst day in Wall Street history. In accessible, jargon-free prose, author Diana Henriques explains why regulatory agencies were caught unprepared as financial disaster loomed. She explores its influence on silver trading; the increased significance of financial futures trading; and the introduction of both institutional investors and computer-driven trades.

"Its a must-read for anyone who wants to understand why financial markets lurch from crisis to crisis and are still so frighteningly susceptible to crashes today." Publishers Weekly.

Lowenstein, Roger

The **end** of Wall Street / Roger Lowenstein. Penguin Group USA, 2010. 288 p. **332.64**

1. Investments. 2. Financial crises. 3. Free enterprise. 4. Loans. 5. Wall Street, New York City.
ISBN 9781594202391

LC 2009050864

A Bloomberg columnist and former Wall Street Journal reporter draws on 180 interviews to trace the origins of the mortgage bubble and the Wall Street collapse of 2008 while offering insight into the government's response.

Mahar, Maggie

★**Bull!** : a history of the boom, 1982-1999 : what drove the breakneck market-- and what every investor needs to know about financial cycles / Maggie Mahar. HarperBusiness, c2003. xxii, 486 p. : **332.64**

1. Stock market -- United States -- History -- 20th century. 2. Business cycles. 3. Bull markets 4. Wall Street, New York City -- History -- 20th century.
ISBN 006056413X

LC 2003051131

A history of the "bull market" at the end of the twentieth century identifies the factors that contributed to an unprecedented rise in market values, linking the period to a longer cycle that governs the stock market.

"This is a history of the 1982-99 bull market in U.S. stocks. {The author} explains that this bull market got its initial impetus from both the undervaluation of equities during the 1970s and the end of the Cold War. Mahar concludes by summarizing how investors who haven't seen a bear market for 17 years might plan their investing strategies. Mahar takes complicated topics and explains them clearly for the average reader. Her exceptional book is most highly recommended to even the smallest public or academic library." Library Journal.

Schwed, Fred, 1901 or 1902-1966

Where are the customers' yachts?, or, A good hard look at Wall Street / Fred Schwed, Jr. ; illustrated by Peter Arno, introduction by Jason Zweig. John Wiley, 2006, c1940 xxxv, 170 p. : **332.64**

1. Stocks. 2. Investments. 3. Wall Street, New York City
ISBN 9780471770893

LC 2005043670

Originally published: New York : Simon & Schuster, 1940.

Humorous and entertaining, this book exposes the folly and hypocrisy of Wall Street. The title refers to a story about a visitor to New York who admired the yachts of the bankers and brokers. Naively, he asked where all the customers' yachts were? Of course, none of the customers could afford yachts, even though they dutifully followed the advice of their bankers and brokers. Full of wise contrarian advice and offering a true look at the world of investing, in which brokers get rich while their customers go broke, this book continues to open the eyes of investors to the reality of Wall Street. --Provided by publisher

332.645 Speculation

Buffett, Mary

Warren Buffett and the art of stock arbitrage : proven strategies for arbitrage and other special investment situations / Mary Buffett & David Clark. Scribner, c2010. xviii, 153 p. ; **332.645**

1. Buffett, Warren. 2. Arbitrage 3. Investments
ISBN 9781439198827

LC 2011280299

Includes glossary and index.

Analyzes Buffett's techniques for arbitrage and special situations investing and offers step-by-step instructions on how to take advantage of such events as spin-offs, liquidations, recapitalizations, and tender offers.

332.660973 Investment banks--United States

Cohan, William D.

Money and power : how Goldman Sachs came to rule the world / William D. Cohan. Doubleday, 2011. 672 p. **332.660973**

1. Goldman, Sachs and Company. 2. Investment banking. 3. Financial crises. 4. Banks and banking. 5. Business -- Corrupt practices.
ISBN 9780385523844

LC 2011290548

A revelatory history of Goldman Sachs.

"The book offers the best analysis yet of Goldman's increasingly tangled web of conflicts. The writing is crisp and the research meticulous, drawing on reams of documents made publicly available by congressional committees and the Financial Crisis Inquiry Commission." The Economist.

Kelly, Kate, 1975-

Street fighters : the last 72 hours of Bear Stearns, the toughest firm on Wall Street / Kate Kelly. Viking, 2009. 256 p. **332.660973**

1. Bear, Stearns & Co., Inc. 2. Investment banking. 3. Bank failures. 4. Financial crises. 5. Investments. 6. Wall Street, New York City.
ISBN 9781591842736

LC 2009007694

Includes index.

"Enlivened by graphic descriptions of executive disarray and cameo profiles of scrambling financiers as they come to appreciate the magnitude of the disaster they unleashed . . . this riveting account puts the ensuing worldwide financial crises in stark perspective." Publishers Weekly.

McGee, Suzanne

Chasing Goldman Sachs : how the masters of the universe melted Wall Street down... and why they'll take us to the brink again / Suzanne McGee. Crown Publishers, c2010. 320 p. **332.660973**

1. Goldman, Sachs and Company 2. Investment banking -- United States 3. Financial crises -- United States -- History 4. Economics -- History -- 21st century. 5. Finance -- United States -- History -- 21st century. 6. United States -- History -- 21st century
ISBN 9780307460110

LC 2009053440

Shares the author's sobering views on Wall Street's role in the recent economic crisis while arguing that practices in proprietary trading and insider deals caused heavy losses for mainstream investors.

Tett, Gillian

Fool's gold : how the bold dream of a small tribe at J.P. Morgan was corrupted by Wall Street greed and unleashed a catastrophe / Gillian Tett. Free Press, 2009. 304 p. **332.660973**

1. J.P. Morgan & Co. 2. Derivative securities. 3. Securities. 4. Credit derivatives -- United States -- History. 5. Housing -- United States -- Finance. 6. Wall Street, New York City.
ISBN 9781416598572

LC 2009005127

Traces the relationship between a team of JP Morgan banking gurus and the current financial crisis, documenting their invention of a bold variety of allegedly risk-free investments that sparked a frenzy in the banking world.

"Tett deploys a remarkable sense of pacing, generating real suspense over rapidly inflating debt on bank balance sheets; by the time Lehman Brothers fails, the book has become a bonafide page-turner. Tett's explosive, illuminating narrative is the one to read for anyone confused by the present financial mess." Publishers Weekly.

332.67 Investments in specific industries, in specific kinds of enterprise, by specific kinds of investors international

Graham, Benjamin, 1894-1976

★The **intelligent** investor : the classic text on value investing / Benjamin Graham. HarperBusiness, c2005. xxvii, 269 p. : **332.67**

1. Securities. 2. Investments.
ISBN 9780060752613

LC 2005282229

Originally published: New York : Harper, 1949. Featuring a new foreword from John C. Bogle.

Analyzes the principles of stock selection and various approaches to investing, and compares the patterns and behavior of specific securities under diverse economic conditions.

332.7 Credit

Acharya, Viral V.,

Guaranteed to fail : Fannie Mae, Freddie Mac, and the debacle of mortgage finance / Viral V. Acharya ... [et al.]. Princeton University Press, c2011. x, 222 p. : **332.7**

1. Freddie Mac (Firm) 2. Federal National Mortgage Association. 3. Business failures. 4. Financial crises. 5. Mortgages. 6. Housing -- United States -- Finance.
ISBN 9780691150789

LC 2011000247

"The authors of Guaranteed to Fail are specialists in applied financial and housing economics. They believe in the necessity of choosing among three options: should Fannie Mae and Freddie Mac exist? Should there be a private-public partnership of mortgage guarantees? Should government end housing subsidies? . . . The authors argue that overextension in housing came from the private sector, Congress, and government-sponsored enterprises." Choice.

Davenport, Anthony

Your score : an insider's secrets to understanding, controlling, and protecting your credit score / Anthony Davenport with Matthew Rudy. Houghton Mifflin Harcourt, 2018. xvi, 202 p. ; **332.7**

1. Consumer credit -- United States. 2. Personal finance -- United States.
ISBN 1328695271

LC 2017044246

"A road map for how to navigate the confusing, secretive world of consumer credit, and how to upgrade and correct your score".-- Provided by publisher.

"All readers who seek to better their knowledge of financial literacy, personal finance, and banking will find this a valuable resource." Booklist.

Howard, Timothy (Business writer)

The **mortgage** wars : inside Fannie Mae, big-money politics, and the collapse of the American dream / Timothy Howard. McGraw-Hill, 2013. xvi, 288 p. **332.7**

1. Federal National Mortgage Association. 2. Mortgages 3. Global Financial Crisis, 2008-2009. 4. Banks and banking -- United States. 5. Housing -- United States.
ISBN 9780071821094

LC 2013033450

The former Fannie Mae CFO's inside look at the war between the financial giants and government regulators. A provocative true-life thriller about the all-out fight for dominance of the mortgage industry -- and how it nearly destroyed the global financial system.

Leonard, Robin

★**Credit** repair : make a plan, improve your credit, avoid scams / Robin Leonard, J.D. ; updated by Attorney Amy Loftsgordon Nolo, 2015. 394 p. ; **332.7**

1. Consumer credit -- United States -- Handbooks, manuals, etc. 2. Personal finance -- United States -- Handbooks, manuals, etc. 3. Consumer credit -- Law and legislation -- United States
ISBN 9781413321548

LC 2014043496

Includes index.

Presents information on credit repair, covering such topics as cleaning up credit reports, improving credit scores, paying debt, considering bankruptcy, dealing with collection agencies, and the best ways to build credit for the future.

Morgenson, Gretchen

Reckless endangerment : how outsized ambition, greed, and corruption led to economic armageddon / Gretchen Morgenson, Joshua Rosner. Times Books, 2011. 352 p. **332.7**

1. Federal National Mortgage Association. 2. Financial crises -- United States -- History -- 21st century. 3. Economics. 4. Mortgages 5. Global Financial Crisis, 2008-2009.
ISBN 9780805091205

LC 2010047594

Includes index.

Exposes how the watchdogs who were supposed to protect the country from financial harm were actually complicit in the actions that finally blew up the American economy in 2008-2009.

"A sobering account of some sordid recent history that's so clear and detailed that pros and novices will find its account rich and informative, and deeply depressing." Publishers Weekly.

332.70973 Credit--United States

Halpern, Jake

Bad paper : chasing debt from Wall Street to the underworld / Jake Halpern. Farrar, Straus and Giroux, 2014. 256 p. **332.70973**

1. Personal finance 2. Debt 3. Consumer credit. 4. Bill collecting
ISBN 9780374108236

LC 2014013576

"Frequent New Yorker contributor Jake Halpern investigates the shadowy, unregulated world of consumer debt collection, focusing on an unlikely friendship between a former banking executive and former armed robber who go in search of "paper," spreadsheets of uncollected debt sold off by banks for pennies on the dollar".-- Provided by publisher.

"Colorful and chilling, this work is an important peek into the dark corner of consumer finance and recommended for all consumers and true crime aficionados." Library Journal.

332.8 Interest

Mayer, Robert, 1960-

Quick cash : the story of the loan shark / Robert Mayer. Northern Illinois University Press, c2010. 293 p. **332.8**

1. Interest rates. 2. Loans. 3. Finance.
ISBN 9780875804309

LC 2010014718

"While popular culture has portrayed the loan shark as a Mafia associate using strong-arm tactics on his clients, Mayer's book gives us a historical portrait of these predatory lenders, who were at work long before the Mafia was involved. Mayer (political science, Loyola Univ.) traces high-interest lending from the late 19th century through the latest financial crisis." Library Journal

333.3 Private ownership of land

Linklater, Andro

Owning the earth : the transforming history of land ownership / Andro Linklater. Bloomsbury, 2013. viii, 482 p., 16 p. of unnumbered plates : **333.3**

1. Property rights. 2. Private property. 3. Land tenure -- History. 4. Landowners.
ISBN 9781620402894

LC 2013011970

Exploring the history and evolution of landownership, the author of Measuring America focuses on the idea of individual, exclusive ownership of land - a creative, yet destructive, cultural force that brought about the concept of individual freedom and a distinct form of democratic government.

"Many aspire to land ownership, taking the concept--that individuals may obtain a sliver of our planet as their own--for granted. Linklater's global study looks at land ownership--feudal, private, communal--through the lens of history and politics, rather than as merely a matter for economic study. The results are enlightening for our understanding not only of the past but of our future." Library Journal.

333.330973 Real estate--United States

Ilgunas, Ken

This land is our land : how we lost the right to roam and how to take it back / Ken Ilgunas. Plume, an imprint of Penguin Random House, LLC, [2018] 208 p. **333.330973**

1. Land use 2. Public lands 3. Property rights 4. Land tenure
ISBN 9780735217843

LC 2017036689

"A Plume Book."

Inspired by the United States' history of roaming, and taking guidance from present-day Europe, Ilgunas calls into question our entrenched understanding of private property and provocatively proposes something unheard of: opening up American private property for public recreation. He imagines a future in which folks everywhere will have the right to walk safely, explore freely, and roam boldly--from California to the New York island, from the Redwood Forest to the Gulf Stream waters.

333.7 Natural resources and energy

Goleman, Daniel

Ecological intelligence : how knowing the hidden impacts of what we buy can change everything / Daniel Goleman. Broadway Books, c2009. x, 276 p. ; **333.7**

1. Consumer behavior -- Environmental aspects 2. Environmental responsibility -- Economic aspects 3. Environmentalism -- Economic aspects 4. Industries -- Environmental aspects
ISBN 9780385527828

LC 2008041811

Reveals the hidden environmental consequences of what societies make and buy, and how that knowledge can drive the changes necessary to save the planet.

333.703 Natural resources--Dictionaries, encyclopedias, concordances

Park, Chris C.

A **dictionary** of environment and conservation / Chris Park, Michael Allaby. Oxford University Press, 2013. 504 p. : **333.703**

1. Environmental sciences -- Dictionaries 2. Conservation of natural resources -- Dictionaries 3. Dictionaries

ISBN 9780199641666

LC 2013387302

Thoroughly revised and updated to include the latest research in the field, A Dictionary of Environment and Conservation provides over 9,000 alphabetically arranged entries on scientific and social aspects of the environment, including concise and authoritative information on key thinkers, treaties, movements, organizations, concepts, and theories. --Provided by publisher

333.72 Conservation and protection

Freeman, Scott

Saving Tarboo Creek : one family's quest to heal the land / Scott Freeman, with illustrations by Susan Leopold Freeman. Timber Press, 2018 256 p.

1. Freeman family. 2. Leopold, Aldo, 1886-1948 Sand County almanac 3. Conservation of natural resources. 4. Environmentalists 5. Nature -- Effect of humans on 6. Streams. 7. Washington (State) 8. Autobiographies and memoirs

ISBN 9781604697940

LC 2016055648

Examine the most pressing environmental issues of our time through one family's detailed account of creek restoration.

"Thought-provoking and unsettling, this highly readable book is made lovely by homey drawings sprinkled throughout." Booklist.

McDaniel, Carl N., 1942-

Wisdom for a livable planet : the visionary work of Terri Swearingen, Dave Foreman, Wes Jackson, Helena Norberg-Hodge, Werner Fornos, Herman Daly, Stephen Schneider, and David Orr / Carl N. McDaniel. Trinity University Press, c2005. x, 277 p. ; **333.72**

1. Environmental sciences. 2. Nature. 3. Environmentalism. 4. Ecology.

ISBN 1595340084

LC 2004019081

"The author personalizes critical environmental issues via profiles of eight visionaries agitating for a more livable planet. . . . His subjects are prominent in the areas of hazardous waste incineration, biodiversity, sustainable agriculture, appropriate technology, population control, rational economic planning, climate concerns and environmental education. . . . The stories of these eight ecological warriors are profoundly appealing in that they show the diverse ways that people can commit to a common cause." Publishers Weekly.

McKibben, Bill

★The **Bill** Mckibben reader : pieces from an active life / Bill McKibben. Henry Holt, 2008. 442 p. **333.72**

1. Environmental protection -- Citizen participation. 2. Environmental movement. 3. Environmentalism. 4. Essays.

ISBN 0805076271

LC 2007039609

Includes index.

A powerful compilation of incisive, groundbreaking essays by the author of The End of Nature explores the human relationship with the world around us in a collection that meditates on today's golden age of radio, the natural role of biting black flies, and a patriotic grandmother battling to remove corporate money from politics.

"This is a collection of essays gleaned from books and periodicals published between 1982 and 2007. Most of the 44 essays come from a diverse array of magazines, including The New Yorker, Mother Jones, Outside, Gourmet, and Christian Century. Essays are loosely divided into categories that include consumerism, activism, the changing planet, the meaning of community, and the sufficiency of nature. Readers new to McKibben will be entertained, informed, and perhaps even inspired to make the positive changes that McKibben desires for the world." Library Journal.

333.7209798 Conservation--Alaska

Brinkley, Douglas

The **quiet** world : saving Alaska's wilderness kingdom, 1910-1960 / Douglas Brinkley. Harper, 2011. 480 p. **333.7209798**

1. Nature conservation 2. Wildlife. 3. Environmentalism. 4. Wildlife conservationists. 5. Alaska.

ISBN 9780062005960

LC bl2010032069

Brinkley examines a decades-long struggle to preserve the Alaskan wilderness.

"This book brims over with information and insight, passion and insistence and some carelessness. In fact, it's a bit like Alaska itself: large, formidable, raw and ultimately unforgettable." Washington Post.

333.73 Land

Biggers, Jeff 1963-

Reckoning at Eagle Creek : the secret legacy of coal in the heartland / Jeff Biggers. Nation Books, 2010. 336 p. **333.73**

1. Coal mines and mining. 2. Strip mining. 3. Mountain life. 4. Small town life. 5. Shawnee National Forest Region, Illinois -- History. 6. Eagle Creek Region, Illinois.

ISBN 9781568584218

LC 2009032686

"Biggers takes a look at coal and its role in the history of southern Illinois as well as its human and environmental costs. Biggers also tells a personal story as he chronicles the saga of his family's strip-mined homestead in an area that one day would be a part of the Shawnee National Forest. A lot of history is presented here in a personal style by a cultural historian with a keen eye. A valuable read for followers of environmental history." Library Journal.

333.730978 Land--American West

Ketcham, Christopher, 1973-

This land : how cowboys, capitalism, and corruption are ruining the American West / Christopher Ketcham. Viking, [2019] 416 p. **333.730978**

1. Ketcham, Christopher, 1973- 2. Public lands 3. Environmental degradation 4. Capitalism -- Environmental aspects 5. Deregulation 6. The West (United States) -- Environmental conditions

ISBN 9780735220980

LC 2019002212

Presents an urgent report on the present-day battle for the fate of public lands in the American West, citing the rampant environmental destruction being caused by relaxed regulations, corruption and special interests.

333.75 Forest lands

Quammen, David, 1948-

Yellowstone : a journey through America's wild heart / David Quammen. National Geographic, [2016] 240 p. **333.75**

1. National parks and reserves. 2. Nature conservation -- Yellowstone National Park. 3. Outdoor recreation. 4. Natural history. 5. The West (United States) 6. Yellowstone National Park. 7. Old Faithful Geyser.
ISBN 9781426217548

LC 2016014893

Blending history, science and field research, a visual tour depicts the storied past, dynamic landscape and rich ecosystem that makes up Yellowstone National Park, from Old Faithful to the lone gray wolf and from misty mountain tops to fields of wild blooms.

333.78 Recreational and wilderness areas

Duncan, Dayton

The **national** parks : America's best idea : an illustrated history / Dayton Duncan, Ken Burns. Alfred A. Knopf, 2009. 400 p. **333.78**

1. United States. National Park Service -- History 2. National parks and reserves -- United States -- History 3. Nature conservation -- United States -- History 4. Natural areas 5. Parks -- United States -- History 6. United States -- History, Local
ISBN 9780307268969

LC 2009020880

Presents a narrative history of the American national park system, examining the events and political battles that led to the establishment of each park while profiling each for its unique attributes.

Diamant, Rolf,

A **thinking** person's guide to America's national parks / edited by Robert Manning, Rolf Diamant, Nora Mitchell, David Harmon. George Braziller Publishers, 2016. 304 p. : **333.78**

1. Landscape protection -- United States 2. National parks and reserves -- Conservation and restoration -- United States 3. National parks and reserves -- Study and teaching -- United States 4. National parks and reserves -- United States -- History
ISBN 9780807600191

LC 2015038434

"Contributors of essays: Brenda Barrett, Leah Bremer, Jessica Brown, Megan Camp, Joseph Corn, Jennifer Cirillo, Michael Creasey, Rolf Diamant, David Graber, David Harmon, Thomas Hudspeth, Melia Lane-Kamehele, Edward Linenthal, Robert Manning, John Maounis, Rebecca Stanfield McCown, Robert McIntosh, Ben Minteer, Brent Mitchell, Nora Mitchell, Dwight Pitcaithley, John Reynolds, Taylor Ricketts, Michael Soukup, Vanessa Torres, Karen Treviøo, and William Tweed"--Title page verso.

A visually stunning exploration of America's national park system contains 23 essays from contributing authors with deep personal and professional connections to the national parks that delve into issues affecting such parks as Yellowstone, Statue of Liberty National Monument and Mesa Verde National Park.

333.780973 Recreational and wilderness areas--United States

Williams, Terry Tempest

★The **hour** of land : a personal topography of America's national parks / Terry Tempest Williams. Sarah Crichton Books/Farrar, Straus and Giroux, 2016. 368 p. **333.780973**

1. Williams, Terry Tempest. 2. National parks and reserves -- United States. 3. Natural history. 4. Human ecology. 5. Landscapes. 6. United States -- Environmental conditions.
ISBN 9780374280093

LC 2015042477

Green Prize for Sustainable Literature: Adult Nonfiction, 2017.

In honor of the United States National Park Service's centennial this year, naturalist and author Terry Tempest Williams reflects on 12 of the 400+ parks, seashores, monuments, and recreation areas that are, as she so elegantly puts it, "portals and thresholds of wonder." Visiting Gettysburg, Alcatraz Island, Grand Teton, Acadia, Gates of the Arctic, and more, she reflects on her trips and her own past as well as the history of the parks, how politics and people have shaped them and continue to shape them, and the environmental issues they face. Gorgeously illustrated with selections from several accomplished photographers, The Hour of Land is a fascinating book that nature lovers will cherish.

333.79 Energy

Bittle, Scott

Who turned out the lights? : your guided tour to the energy crisis / Scott Bittle & Jean Johnson. Harper, c2009. xxii, 339 p. : **333.79**

1. Energy resources 2. Energy conservation 3. Natural resources. 4. Energy consumption
ISBN 9780061715648

LC 2009018884

Presents an entertaining and nonpartisan view of the energy crisis, examining the politics behind energy consumption and conservation and explaining alternatives in easy-to-understand terms.

Helm, Dieter

The **carbon** crunch : how we're getting climate change wrong--and how to fix it / Dieter Helm. Yale University Press, 2012. 273 p. **333.79**

1. Energy policy. 2. Renewable energy sources. 3. Energy conservation. 4. Climate change
ISBN 9780300186598

LC 2012017386

"Despite commitments to renewable energy and two decades of international negotiations, global emissions continue to rise. Coal, the most damaging of all fossil fuels, has actually risen from 25% to almost 30% of world energy use. And while European countries have congratulated themselves on reducing emissions, they have increased their carbon imports from China and other developing nations, who continue to expand their coal use. As standards of living increase in developing countries, coal use can only increase as well--and global temperatures along with it.In this hard-hitting book, Dieter Helm looks at how and why we have failed to tackle the issue of global warming and argues for a new, pragmatic rethinking of energy policy--from transitioning from coal to gas and eventually to electrification of transport, to carbon pricing and a focus on new technologies. Lucid, compelling and rigorously researched, this book will have a lasting impact on how we think about climate change".-- Provided by publisher.

Muller, R. (Richard)

Energy for future presidents : the science behind the headlines / Richard A. Muller. W. W. Norton, 2012. 288 p. **333.79**

1. Energy resources. 2. Energy policy. 3. Technology policy.
ISBN 9780393081619

LC 2012015586

The author of Physics for Future Presidents provides answers to the big energy questions that will be asked over the next century, covering such topics as whether natural gas deposits hold promise, whether solar and wind power is viable and whether nuclear power will ever be safe.

Vollmann, William T.

No immediate danger : volume one of carbon ideologies / William T. Vollmann. Viking Press, 2018. 704 p. Carbon ideologies ; **333.79**

1. Fukushima Nuclear Disaster, Japan, 2011. 2. Nuclear accidents 3. Nuclear reactor accidents 4. Climate change
ISBN 9780399563492

LC 2018013155

A National Book Award-winning author presents a timely, eye-opening book about climate change and energy generation that focuses on the consequences of nuclear-power production.

Yergin, Daniel

The **new** map : energy, climate, and the clash of nations / Daniel Yergin. Penguin Press, 2020. xx, 492 p. **333.79**

1. Energy policy. 2. Climate change 3. Geopolitics 4. Renewable energy sources.
ISBN 9781594206436

LC 2020002299

The global energy expert and Pulitzer Prize-winning author shares revelatory insights into how energy revolutions, climate battles and geopolitics are mapping a near future already complicated by the coronavirus pandemic and related economic fallout.

"Pulitzer Prize-winning energy expert Yergin shows us how the world has been remapped because of these major energy and geopolitical changes, even as climate change threatens further transformation." Library Journal

The **quest** : energy, security and the remaking of the modern world / Daniel Yergin. Penguin Press, 2011. 704 p. **333.79**

1. Energy resources 2. Money -- Political aspects. 3. Oil industry and trade -- Political aspects. 4. Oil industry and trade -- Military aspects.
ISBN 9781594202834

LC 2011013100

"This book is a masterly piece of work and, as a comprehensive guide to the world's great energy needs and dilemmas, it will be hard to beat." The Economist.

333.7909 Energy--History, geographic treatment, biography

Rhodes, Richard, 1937-

★**Energy** : a human history / Richard Rhodes. Simon & Schuster, 2018. xiv, 464 pages : **333.7909**

1. Energy development 2. Energy resources 3. Energy production 4. Energy
ISBN 9781501105357

LC bl2018045157

Describes five centuries of progress through the history of energy sources, from wood to coal to oil to electricity and beyond and highlights the successes and failures that led to each innovation.

"Pulitzer Prize-winning historian and author Rhodes ... takes on entangled issues around the use of science and technology and makes complicated matters more approachable." Library Journal.

333.790973 Energy--United States

Koerth-Baker, Maggie, 1981-

Before the lights go out : conquering the energy crisis before it conquers us / Maggie Koerth-Baker. John Wiley & Sons, 2012. 320 p. **333.790973**

1. Renewable energy sources. 2. Energy development. 3. Energy conservation. 4. Energy consumption.
ISBN 9780470876251

LC 2011043334

"This text argues we're not going to solve the energy problem by convincing everyone to live like it's 1900 because that's not a good thing. Instead of reverting to the past, we have to build a future where we get energy from new places, use it in new ways, and do more with less. Clean coal? Natural gas? Nuclear? Electric cars? We'll need them all. When you look at the numbers, you'll find that we'll still be using fossil fuels, nuclear, and renewables for decades to come. Looks at new battery technology, smart grids, passive buildings, decentralized generation, clean coal, and carbon sequestration. These are buzzwords now, but they'll be a part of your world soon. For many people, they already are".-- Provided by publisher.

333.7909748 Energy--Pennsylvania

Mcgraw, Seamus

The **end** of country : imagine a small farming town where everybody has shared hard luck for as long as they can remember, scratching out a living from the rocky earth / Seamus Mcgraw. Random House Inc, 2011. 224 p. **333.7909748**

1. Natural gas supply. 2. Small towns. 3. Greed. 4. Natural gas. 5. Pennsylvania.
ISBN 9781400068531

LC bl2012026563

Green Prize for Sustainable Literature: Adult Nonfiction, 2012.

Traces the 2007 rush to prospect Pennsylvania's Marcellus Shale natural gas deposits, drawing on the experiences of the author's mother and her neighbors to trace their efforts to defend their community and characters against the gas companies that would take over their lands.

"In 2006, in a hardscrabble part of Pennsylvania that had long lost its allure as a farming and industrial area, geologists began investigating the Marcellus Shale. It turned out to be the richest deposit of natural gas ever discovered anywhere. When his widowed mother was approached about permitting natural-gas exploration on their farm, journalist McGraw had to weigh their need for money against the future prospects of the farmland. Chronicling the impact of the find on his mother and her neighbors, McGraw's research led to this impressively detailed, highly engaging look at issues of energy policy, economics, and sociology that arose when a bucolic town was suddenly faced with the traveling circus of energy exploration. A completely engaging look at how energy policy affected a quiet, rural town." Booklist.

333.792 Primary forms of energy

Barnham, Keith

The **burning** answer: the solar revolution: a quest for sustainable power / Keith Barnham. Pegasus, 2015 400 p. **333.792**

1. Solar energy 2. Energy industry and trade. 3. Renewable energy sources
ISBN 9781605987767

LC bl2015016332

"The author makes some big claims about the viability (and necessity) of solar energy, and while he seems oblivious to the strength of NIMBYism (Not In My Backyard), many readers will be inclined to agree with him. He persuades not with charts and graphs but with the power of his storytelling and his passion for science." Library Journal.

Ferguson, Charles D.

Nuclear energy : what everyone needs to know / Charles D. Ferguson. Oxford University Press, c2011. xvii, 222 p. ; **333.792**

1. Nuclear energy
ISBN 9780199759460

LC 2010044449

"This compelling assembly of historical and scientific information deftly steps through the essential discoveries, definitions, and theory that led to the development of nuclear reactors and nuclear bombs. [F]ollowing chapters . . . cover safety, climate change, nuclear proliferation concerns, security, and the politically charged options for disposal of radioactive waste." Choice.

Mahaffey, James A.

Atomic adventures: secret islands, forgotten N-rays, and isotopic murder: a journey into the wild world of nuclear science / James Mahaffey. W W Norton & Co Inc., 2017. 464 p. **333.792**

1. Nuclear physics 2. Science 3. Atoms 4. Scientists
ISBN 9781681774213

LC bl2017022514

The latest investigation from acclaimed nuclear engineer and author James Mahaffey unearths forgotten nuclear endeavors throughout history that were sometimes hair-brained, often risky, and always fascinating.

"His expertise and astonishing stories are matched by his writing skills, creating a sometimes humorous book that offers a valuable history of a deadly modern force and uncommonly clear, enjoyable explanations of related physics." Booklist.

333.793 Secondary forms of energy

Bakke, Gretchen Anna

The **grid** : the fraying wires between Americans and our energy future / Gretchen Bakke. Bloomsbury USA, 2016. 288 p. **333.793**

1. Electric power distribution. 2. Clean energy. 3. Power failures. 4. Energy policy -- Social aspects.
ISBN 9781608196104

LC 2016001376

A revelatory examination of America's national power grid traces how it developed while exposing its current vulnerabilities, making strategic recommendations for how it can be improved to meet the challenges of instability, security and sustainability.

"A lively analysis of the challenges renewables present to the production and distribution of electricity." Kirkus.

333.8 Subsurface resources

Wilber, Tom, 1958-

Under the surface : fracking, fortunes and the fate of the Marcellus Shale / Tom Wilber. Cornell University Press, 2012. 272 p. **333.8**

1. Natural gas. 2. Natural gas industry and trade 3. Natural resources. 4. Shale gas industry. 5. Marcellus Shale.
ISBN 9780801450167

LC 2011047166

Describes the history, process, and effect of the search and extraction of natural gas from the Marcellus Shale along the New York and Pennsylvania border.

333.91 Water and lands adjoining bodies of water

Dean, Cornelia

Against the tide : the battle for America's beaches / Cornelia Dean. Columbia University Press, 1999. xiv, 279 p. : **333.91**

1. Coast changes. 2. Shore protection. 3. Erosion. 4. Coastal towns.
ISBN 0231084188

LC 98050755

"This thoroughly researched and thoughtful book is destined to become a classic of environmental science writing." Library Journal.

Doyle, Martin

The **source** : how rivers made America and America remade its rivers / Martin Doyle. W W Norton & Company, 2018 352 p. **333.91**

1. Rivers -- History. 2. Humans -- Effect of environment on 3. River life. 4. United States -- History
ISBN 9780393242355

LC 2017051192

An environmental history of the role of rivers in shaping American politics, economics and society touches on subjects ranging from conservation and the New Deal to the Hoover Dam and Hurricane Katrina, drawing on experts from diverse backgrounds to explore how the natural and human transformations of rivers have made a significant impact on the nation.

"Doyle tackles the shifts in how America has viewed and used its extensive waterways, producing a comprehensive and enjoyable account." Publishers Weekly.

Fishman, Charles, 1961-

The **big** thirst : the secret life and turbulent future of water / Charles Fishman. Simon & Schuster, 2011. 288 p. **333.91**

1. Water. 2. Water conservation. 3. Water-supply. 4. Water resources development.
ISBN 9781439102077

Explores every facet of water and examines the issues surrounding water scarcity and what can be done to ensure that humans have plenty of clean water in the future. By the best-selling author of The Wal-Mart Effect.

Rothfeder, Jeffrey

Every drop for sale : our desperate battle over water in a world about to run out / Jeffrey Rothfeder. Jeremy P Tarcher/Penguin, 2004, c2001. xiii, 205 p. **333.91**

1. Water-supply -- Economic aspects. 2. Drinking water.
ISBN 158542367X

LC bl2005007411

Originally published: New York : Jeremy P. Tarcher/Putnam, 2001. With a new pref.

An investigative journalist probes the startling gap between supply and demand of safe drinking water in the world, speculating that a water crisis looms on the horizon.

"Like the drip of water on stone, Rothfeder's steady exposition of horrors will wear down any reader's doubts that water is the next flashpoint of global politics, human rights and health issues." Publishers Weekly.

333.95 Biological resources

Barrow, Mark V., 1960-

Nature's ghosts : confronting extinction from the age of Jefferson to the age of ecology / Mark V. Barrow, Jr. The University of Chicago Press, 2009. 512 p. **333.95**

1. Wildlife conservation -- United States -- History. 2. Rare and endangered animals -- Law and legislation -- United States -- History. 3. Extinction (Biology) 4. Rare and endangered plants.
ISBN 9780226038148

LC 2008049085

"The author retraces the history of the earliest European and North American naturalists, from those who refused to believe that species comprising a perfect, stable world could go extinct, to the acceptance of extinction at the hands of humans and the legal mechanisms created to halt it. Professionals in ecology, conservation biology, and wildlife management and readers interested in natural history will find this book hard to put down." Choice.

Ellis, Richard, 1938-

Tuna : a love story / Richard Ellis. Knopf, 2008. xi, 334 p. : **333.95**

1. Tuna 2. Rare and endangered fishes 3. Overfishing. 4. Bluefin tuna fisheries. 5. Japan -- Social life and customs -- 21st century
ISBN 9780307267153

LC 2007052253

Examines the natural history of the tuna, one of the world's most endangered marine animals, revealing how the increasing demand for sushi has caused a devastating overfishing of the tuna and detailing the implications of its potential extinction.

Flach, Tim

Endangered / Tim Flach ; text by Professor Jonathan Baillie, Sam Wells. Abrams, in association with Blackwell & Ruth, 2017 335 p. : **333.95**

1. Rare and endangered animals 2. Photography of animals.
ISBN 9781419726514

LC 2016960608

A photographic tribute to endangered animals around the world highlights primates coping with habitat loss, big cats losing their battle with human settlements, elephants hunted for their ivory, and numerous bird species taken as pets.

Fraser, Caroline

Rewilding the world : dispatches from the conservation revolution / Caroline Fraser. Metropolitan Books, 2009. 416 p. **333.95**

1. Genetic resources conservation. 2. Rare and endangered animals. 3. Restoration ecology. 4. Biodiversity
ISBN 9780805078268

LC 2009032989

Citing dire predictions about the losses of survival-level resources, a dramatic account of a visionary campaign to save endangered species and landscapes documents the contributions of wildlife biologists and conservationists at key strategic locations.

"Heavily researched with endnotes for those looking for more information, this truly is an essential read for conservationists, biologists, and anyone interested in the natural world." Library Journal.

Goldfarb, Ben (Environmental journalist)

Eager : the surprising, secret life of beavers and why they matter / Ben Goldfarb ; foreword by Dan Flores. Chelsea Green Publishing, 2018. 240 p. **333.95**

1. Beavers -- Ecology. 2. Wildlife conservation. 3. Ecology. 4. Ecosystem management. 5. North America -- Environmental conditions.
ISBN 9781603587396

LC 2018004621

An environmental journalist discusses why beavers are so important to the ecosystem and follows a growing number of passionate "Beaver Believers," including scientists, ranchers and regular citizens, who are working to help restore the helpful rodent to its habitat.

"Goldfarb traveled the country to observe researchers, beaver damage mitigators, county engineers, hydrologists, and wildlife biologists, all working with beavers and studying their positive effects on ecosystems from the western deserts to the replenishing forests of the east. Beavers are kind of magical, Goldfarb tells us: they can make wetlands appear." Booklist.

Goodall, Jane, 1934-

★The **ten** trusts : what we must do to care for the animals we love / Jane Goodall and Marc Bekoff. Harper San Francisco, 2002. xx, 200 p. ; **333.95**

1. Human/animal relationships 2. Animal rights. 3. Animal welfare. 4. Wildlife conservation.
ISBN 0062517570

LC 2002068717

The scientist who documented the lives of chimpanzees joins an animal behaviorist to present ten fundamental principles designed to show readers how to live in harmony with the animal kingdom.

"An accessible, compelling, and important expose." Booklist.

Greenberg, Paul, 1967-

American catch : the fight for our local seafood / Paul Greenberg. The Penguin Press, 2014. 320 p. **333.95**

1. Seafood. 2. Seafood industry and trade 3. Food habits. 4. Imports -- United States.
ISBN 9781594204487

LC 2014005395

In 2005, the United States imported twelve billion dollars worth of seafood, nearly double what we had imported ten years earlier. During that same period, our seafood exports rose by a third. In American Catch, our foremost fish expert Paul Greenberg looks to New York oysters, gulf shrimp, and Alaskan salmon to reveal how it came to be that 91 percent of the seafood Americans eat is foreign.

Four fish : the future of the last wild food / Paul Greenberg. Penguin Press, 2010. 284 p. ; **333.95**

1. Fish farming. 2. Fishery management. 3. Fishing. 4. Fishing

industry and trade.
ISBN 9781594202568

LC 2010001276

Includes index.

James Beard Foundation Book Awards, Writing and Literature, 2011.

"Award-winning writer and lifelong fisherman Paul Greenberg takes us on a culinary journey, exploring the history of the fish that dominate our menus -- salmon, sea bass, cod, and tuna -- and investigating where each stands at this critical moment in time." -- Dust jacket.

"The narrative is grounded in common sense and anchored by first-rate, on-scene reporting from the Yukon and Mekong Rivers, Lake Bardawil in the Sinai Peninsula and the waters off the coasts of Long Island, Greece, Hawaii and the Shetland Islands. Hugely informative, sincere and infectiously curious and enthusiastic." Kirkus.

Hanes, Stephanie

White man's game : saving animals, rebuilding Eden, and other myths of conservation in Africa / Stephanie Hanes. Metropolitan Books, Henry Holt and Company, [2017] 288 p. **333.95**

1. Philanthropy: 2. Culture conflict 3. Wildlife conservation -- Social aspects. 4. environmentalists 5. Parque Nacional da Gorongosa (Mozambique). 6. Mozambique 7. Southern Africa
ISBN 9780805097160

LC 2016034296

A behind-the-scenes account of the celebrated but troubled Gorongosa wildlife preserve cites the revival work of millionaire philanthropist Greg Carr and how Western conservation efforts are colliding with African culture.

"In straightforward and fervent prose, Hanes gives readers 'a new way of thinking about nature, conservation, and the pitfalls of best intentions.' " Publishers Weekly.

Horwitz, Josh

War of the whales : a true story / Joshua Horwitz. Simon & Schuster 2014 448 p. **333.95**

1. Reynolds, Joel 2. Balcolm, Ken 3. Military secrets 4. Whales 5. Military cover-ups
ISBN 9781451645019

LC 2015301075

Green Prize for Sustainable Literature: Adult Nonfiction, 2015.

Documents the efforts of crusading lawyer Joel Reynolds and marine biologist Ken Balcolm to expose a covert U.S. Navy sub detection system that caused whales to beach themselves, an effort that challenged Ken's loyalties and pitted them against powerful military adversaries.

"Based on years of interviews and research, Horwitz delivers a powerful, engrossing narrative that raises serious questions about the unchecked use of secrecy by the military to advance its institutional power." Kirkus.

Kurlansky, Mark

Cod : a biography of the fish that changed the world / Mark Kurlansky. Walker and Co., 1997. viii, 294 p. : **333.95**

1. Cod. 2. Fisheries -- North Atlantic Ocean. 3. Cod fisheries -- History. 4. Cod fishing.
ISBN 0802713262

LC 97012165

Colored maps on endpapers.

A history of the fish that has led to wars, stirred revolutions, sustained economies and diets, and helped in the settlement of North America features photographs, drawings, and recipes, as well as the natural history of this much sought after fish.

"This book offers maximum readability, plenty of handsome illustrations, and a 40-page appendix of superlatively annotated recipes." Booklist.

Lebbin, Daniel J. (Daniel Jason), 1978-

The **American** Bird Conservancy guide to bird conservation / Daniel J. Lebbin, Michael J. Parr, and George H. Fenwick ; with a foreword by Jonathan Franzen. University of Chicago Press, 2010. ix, 446 p. : **333.95**

1. Birds -- Conservation -- United States 2. Birds -- Habitat -- United States 3. Birds -- Conservation -- North America 4. Birds -- Habitat -- North America
ISBN 9780226647272

LC 2010007646

The Guide presents for the first time anywhere a classification system and threat analysis for bird habitats in the United States, the most thorough and scientifically credible assessment of threats to birds published to date, as well as a new list of birds of conservation concern. --Provided by publisher

"A beautiful production visually, the book is inviting as well as an unprecedented, rewarding conservation reference source." Choice.

MacDonald, Cameron

The **endangered** species road trip : a summer's worth of dingy motels, poison oak, ravenous insects, and the rarest species in North America / Cameron MacDonald. Greystone Books, 2013 216 p. : **333.95**

1. MacDonald, Cameron Travel North America. 2. Rare and endangered animals -- North America. 3. Automobile travel 4. Voyages and travels. 5. North America
ISBN 9781553659358

LC bl2013032317

Details the author's four-month road trip across the U.S. and Canada to spot some of the endangered species that call North America home, a trip on which he was accompanied by his wife, two children, and the family dog.

"Documenting the ongoing simplification of North America's ecologies could be grim work--but MacDonald's comedic sense and his engaging style are addictive and the resulting tale is intensely charming." Publishers Weekly.

McNamee, Thomas, 1947-

The **return** of the wolf to Yellowstone / Thomas McNamee. Henry Holt, 1997. xi, 354 p. : **333.95**

1. Animal conservation. 2. Wolves -- Yellowstone National Park. 3. Wolves -- Conservation -- Yellowstone National Park. 4. Yellowstone National Park.
ISBN 9780805031010

LC 96039702

Maps of Greater Yellowstone ecosystem on endpapers.

Chronicles the reintroduction of wolves to Yellowstone National Park, the political machinations behind it, and the stories of the wolves themselves.

"An advocate for the reintroduction of the gray wolf to Yellowstone National Park, McNamee kept careful watch over the legal wrangling that accompanied this controversial endeavor, the challenges of its execution, and the complex questions it has raised, then recorded the entire story in this vivid day-by-day chronicle." Booklist.

Mooallem, Jon

Wild ones : a sometimes dismaying, weirdly reassuring story about looking at people looking at animals in America / Jon

Mooallem. The Penguin Press, 2013 339 p. ; **333.95**

1. Mooallem, Jon Travel United States. 2. Cultural property 3. Wildlife 4. Wildlife conservation 5. Animals

ISBN 9781594204425

LC bl2013021689

Tracks the dynamic relevance of America's animals throughout history to illuminate current extinction threats, tracing the author's tour of environmental regions with his young daughter to examine the conservation efforts for such species as the polar bear and the whooping crane.

Orenstein, Ronald I. (Ronald Isaac), 1946-

Ivory, horn and blood : behind the elephant and rhinoceros poaching crisis / Ronald Orenstein. Firefly Books, 2013. 216 p. : **333.95**

1. Poaching. 2. Elephants -- Effect of poaching on -- Africa. 3. Rhinoceros -- Effect of poaching on -- Vietnam. 4. Rare and endangered animals.

ISBN 1770852271

An in-depth look at the illegal ivory trade and the poaching crisis of African elephants and Vietnamese rhinoceroses.

Wilson, Edward O.

The **diversity** of life / Edward O. Wilson. W. W. Norton, 1999, c1992. 424 p. : **333.95**

1. Biodiversity 2. Genetic resources conservation. 3. Conservation of natural resources. 4. Environmentalism.

ISBN 0393319407

LC 00265625

Originally published: Cambridge, MA : Belknap Press of Harvard University Press, 1992.

National Book Critics Circle Award for Nonfiction finalist, 1992.

"Identifying five natural events that have disrupted evolution and global diversity (climatic changes, meteorite strikes), Wilson maintains that the present sixth great extinction is being caused by human neglect and ignorance. This important book is highly recommended." Library Journal.

★The **future** of life / Edward O. Wilson. Alfred A. Knopf, 2002. xxiv, 229 p. : **333.95**

1. Rare and endangered animals. 2. Rare and endangered plants. 3. Extinction (Biology) 4. Nature conservation.

ISBN 0679450785

LC 2001038316

ALA Notable Book, 2003.

"Wilson proposes that there is yet time to avoid a grand planetary environmental crash provided we get serious, acknowledge a duty of stewardship and recognize an emotional affiliation . . .with other kinds of life." New York Times Book Review.

Half-earth : our planet's fight for life / Edward O. Wilson. Liveright Publishing Corporation, a division of W. W. Norton & Company, 2016 256 p. **333.95**

1. Social evolution 2. Human evolution -- Philosophy. 3. Evolution -- Philosophy. 4. Biodiversity conservation.

ISBN 9781631490828

LC 2015041784

A conclusion to the trilogy by the Pulitzer Prize-winning author of the National Book Award-finalistThe Meaning of Human Existence argues that humanity must consider the histories of millions of other Earth species and increase the planet's regions of natural reserves in order to prevent future mass extinctions.

"This startling, courageous, many will say wildly quixotic vision of a truly global preservation effort is guaranteed to stoke the fires of environmental debate." Booklist.

A **window** on eternity : Gorongosa and biodiversity / Edward O. Wilson ; photographs by Piotr Naskrecki. Simon & Schuster, 2014. 228 p. **333.95**

1. Biodiversity. 2. Nature conservation. 3. Natural history. 4. Restoration ecology. 5. Parque Nacional da Gorongosa (Mozambique) 6. Mozambique

ISBN 9781476747415

LC 2013032607

"Simon & Schuster nonfiction original hardcover"--Title page verso.

Includes index.

Featuring beautiful full-color photographs by two of the world's best wildlife photographers, a world-renowned biologist and Pulitzer Prize-winner tells the extraordinary story of how Gorongosa National Park in Mozambique was destroyed, restored and continues to evolve.

"Wilson . . . presents a lyrical ode to biodiversity within the framework of a memoir of his work in Mozambique's Gorongosa National Park, helping to rebuild it from the loss of nearly all of its megafauna as it was neglected, repurposed as a battleground, and destroyed by poachers during the 16-year civil war." Publishers Weekly.

Chivian, Eric,

★**Sustaining** life : how human health depends on biodiversity / edited by Eric Chivian and Aaron Bernstein. Oxford University Press, c2008. 568 p. **333.95**

1. Biodiversity 2. Environmental health. 3. Humans -- Effect of environment on

ISBN 9780195175097

LC 2007020609

Examines the relationship between the animals, plants, and insects on land and in the water and how they have provided health benefits to society.

"A collaborative survey of biodiversity issues written and/or reviewed for accuracy by more than 100 scientists... ... Criticizing modern, industrial-scale marine fishing and agricultural practices, this volume holds forth organic farming as a viable alternative and offers readers an action list of things to do and organizations to join. Abundantly illustrated, this is a valuable, urgent resource suited to any general-interest library." Booklist.

Hoekstra, Jonathan M.

The **atlas** of global conservation : changes, challenges and opportunities to make a difference / Jonathan Hoekstra ... [et al.] ; edited by Jennifer L. Molnar. University of California Press, c2010. xv, 234 p. : **333.95**

1. Conservation of natural resources. 2. Environmental protection. 3. Globalization.

ISBN 9780520262560

LC 2009023617

"The Atlas of Global Conservation is a premier resource for everyone concerned about the natural world. Top scientists at The Nature Conservancy have joined forces to create this guide to the state of the planet today. With over 80 full-color maps and other graphics contextualized with clear, informative discussion, this book offers an unprecedented view of trends across the world's terrestrial, marine, and freshwater environments. Interspersed throughout, essays by noted international authorities point the way forward in confronting some of our greatest conservation challenges."--BOOK JACKET.

333.95822 Rare and endangered birds

Hirschfeld, Erik

The **world's** rarest birds / Erik Hirschfeld, Andy Swash & Robert Still ; with contributions by Nick Langley ... [et al.] ; and illustrations by Tomasz Cofta. Princeton University Press, c2013. 360 p. : **333.95822**

1. Rare birds 2. Rare birds -- Identification 3. Rare birds -- Geographical distribution 4. Extinct birds
ISBN 9780691155968

LC 2012945960

Includes index.

"This illustrated book vividly depicts the most threatened birds on Earth. It provides up-to-date information from BirdLife International on the threats each species faces, and the measures being taken to save them. Today, 590 birds species are classified as Endangered or Critically Endangered, or now only exist in captivity. This landmark publication features stunning photographs of 515 of these species--including the results of a prestigious international photographic competition organized specifically for this book. This is the first time that images of many of these birds have been published. It also showcases meticulously accurate illustrations by acclaimed wildlife artist Tomasz Cofta for the 75 species of which no photographs are known to exist.

335 Socialism and related systems

Bregman, Rutger, 1988-

Utopia for realists : how we can build the ideal world / Rutger Bregman. Little, Brown & Company, 2017. 272 p. **335**

1. Utopias 2. Social forecasting 3. Wealth 4. Income
ISBN 9780316471893

LC bl2017009661

A noted Dutch journalist and economist proposes an outline for a new worldwide Utopia, with central tenets including a shortened work week, a guaranteed basic income for all, wealth redistribution, and open borders everywhere.

"A provocative pleasure to contemplate." Kirkus.

Butterworth, Alex

The **world** that never was : a true story of dreamers, schemers, anarchists & secret agents / Alex Butterworth. Pantheon Books, c2010. 528 p. **335**

1. Anarchism -- History. 2. Anarchists -- History. 3. Radicalism -- History. 4. Revolutionaries -- History -- 19th century.
ISBN 9780375425110

LC 2009048115

A history of anarchism in the late 19th century is presented through the stories of violent revolutionaries, the secret police who tracked them and famous figures who played lesser-known roles, in a chronicle that traces the Paris Commune of 1871 through the 1905 Russian Revolution.

335.4 Marxian systems

Marx, Karl, 1818-1883

★**Capital** : an abridged edition / Karl Marx ; edited with an introduction and notes by David McLellan. Oxford University Press, 2008. xxxii, 499 p. ; **335.4**

1. Capital 2. Economics
ISBN 9780199535705

LC 2008274361

"First issued as a World's Classic paperback 1995, reissued as an Oxford World's Classic paperback in 1999, reissued in 2008"--T.p. verso.

Includes indexes.

A classic of early modernism, Capital combines vivid historical detail with economic analysis to produce a bitter denunciation of mid-Victorian capitalist society. It has proved to be the most influential work in twentieth-century social science; Marx did for social science what Darwin had done for biology. This is the only abridged edition to take into account the whole of Capital. --Provided by publisher

335.43 Communism (Marxism-Leninism)

Pipes, Richard

★**Communism** : a history / Richard Pipes. Modern Library, 2001. xi, 175 p. ; **335.43**

1. Marxism. 2. Communism -- History.
ISBN 0679640509

LC 2001275458

Here is an exploration of a promising theory that, when put into practice, wreaked havoc on the world. An expert on communism, Richard Pipes follows the history of the Soviet Union from the 1917 revolution to the Cold War, and finally, to its deterioration and collapse.

"As a brief, polemical diatribe...this short account of communism should provoke and instruct." Library Journal.

336.200973 Taxes--United States

Burman, Leonard

Taxes in America : what everyone needs to know / Leonard E. Burman, Joel Slemrod. Oxford University Press, c2020 337 p. : **336.200973**

1. Taxation -- United States
ISBN 9780190920852

Arguments about taxation are among the most heated- no other topic is as influential to the role of government and the distribution of costs and benefits in America. But while understanding of our tax system is of vital importance, the complexity can create confusion. Two of America's leading authorities on taxes, Leonard E. Burman and Joel Slemrod, bring clarity in this concise explanation of how our tax system works, how it affects people and businesses, and how it might be improved. --Provided by publisher

Reid, T. R.

A **fine** mess : a global quest for a simpler, fairer, and more efficient tax system / T.R. Reid. Penguin Group USA, 2017. 256 p. **336.200973**

1. Taxation 2. Tax policy 3. Public finance 4. Government spending policy 5. United States -- Economic conditions -- 21st century
ISBN 9781594205514

LC 2017301115

The Washington Post correspondent and best-selling author of The Healing of America presents an international investigation into America's failing tax code to share plainspoken assessments of current problems and what the author believes can be learned from other democratic nations.

"Washington Post correspondent Reid...examines taxation in countries around the world to find alternatives to the American system in this highly readable and informative book." Publishers Weekly.

336.3 Public debt and expenditures

Kirshner, Jodie Adams

Broke : hardship and resilience in a city of broken promises / Jodie Adams Kirshner. St. Martin's Press, [2019] 352 p. **336.3**

1. Bankruptcy 2. Urban problems 3. Urban poor people 4. Urban economics 5. Michigan 6. Detroit, Michigan 7. United States -- Economic conditions.

ISBN 9781250220639

LC 2019024268

Traces the experiences of seven Detroit residents throughout the city's 2013 bankruptcy, revealing the larger human ramifications of poor urban policies, restorative negligence and municipal distress for hundreds of thousands living below the poverty line.

337 International economics

Friedman, Thomas L.

The **Lexus** and the olive tree / Thomas L. Friedman. Farrar, Straus, Giroux, 1999. xix, 394 p. : **337**

1. International economic relations. 2. Free trade. 3. Capitalism -- Social aspects. 4. Technological innovations -- Economic aspects. 5. United States -- Foreign economic relations.

ISBN 9780374192037

LC 99010742

Includes index.

Looks at globalization from a social, economic, political, and cultural perspective and assesses the impact of this trend both at home and abroad.

"Friedman explains, with anecdotes as well as analyses, what the instant electronic global economy is and what it may take to live there." New York Times Book Review.

Stiglitz, Joseph E.

Globalization and its discontents / Joseph E. Stiglitz. W. W. Norton, c2002 xxii, 282 p. ; **337**

1. International Monetary Fund Developing countries' operations 2. International economic integration. 3. International trade regulation. 4. International finance. 5. Globalization (Economics) -- Developing countries 6. United States -- Politics and government.

ISBN 0393051242

LC 2002023148

Examines the effects of global economic policies on developing nations, discussing agencies and concepts including the International Monetary Fund, the East Asia crisis, trade laws, fair markets, and privatization.

"This smart, provocative study contributes significantly to the ongoing globalization debate." Publishers Weekly.

337.09 International economics--History

Conway, Ed

The **summit** : Bretton Woods, 1944: J. M. Keynes and the reshaping of the global economy / Ed Conway. Pegasus Books, 2015. 480 p. **337.09**

1. Keynes, John Maynard, 1883-1946. 2. White, Harry Dexter, 1892-1948. 3. International Monetary Fund. 4. World Bank. 5. International economic relations. 6. Economic development. 7. Bretton Woods Conference, July 1944. 8. Financial crises.

ISBN 9781605986814

A narrative history of the World War II-era economic summit offers insight into its dramas and achievements, discussing such topics as John Maynard Keynes' heart attack, the corruption of Harry Dexter White and the machinations of the Russians and French.

"This is a gripping story for both general readers and scholars interested in World War II, the Cold War, and domestic and international political economy. The author knows how to write for those who are less informed about economics while telling the history of the turbulent conference through its leading characters and updating its legacy today. An essential purchase on this topic." Library Journal.

338 Production

Clark, Taylor, 1979-

Starbucked : a double tall tale of caffeine, commerce, and culture / Taylor Clark. Little, Brown, 2007. 297 p. ; **338**

1. Starbucks Coffee Company. 2. Coffee industry and trade -- History. 3. Coffee -- Social aspects. 4. Coffee shops -- Social aspects. 5. Corporate culture -- Case studies. 6. United States -- Social life and customs -- 20th century 7. United States -- Social life and customs -- 21st century 8. United States -- History -- 20th century 9. United States -- History -- 21st century 10. Pacific Northwest literature

ISBN 031601348X

LC 2007013074

Traces the meteoric rise of the Starbucks chain while evaluating the myriad ways in which the coffeehouse movement has impacted everyday life, in an investigative account that credits specific societal groups with the corporation's success.

"This is a breezily written business yarn with plenty of big-picture punch." Christian Science Monitor.

O'Reilly, Tim

WTF? : what's the future and why it's up to us / Tim O'Reilly. HarperCollins, 2017. 320 p. **338**

1. Business 2. Technology 3. Forecasting 4. Business ethics

ISBN 9780062565716

LC 2017277455

The Silicon Valley intellectual and founder of O'Reilly Media surveys the positive and negative world-changing potential of emerging technologies, drawing on the insights of an unlikely coalition of experts to explore how AI, algorithms and new approaches to business organization will change life in the near future.

338.0973 Industry--United States

Dauch, Richard E.

American drive : the road to more jobs, a stronger economy, and renewed industrial dominance in America / Richard Dauch with Hank H. Cox. St. Martins Press, 2012. 352 p. **338.0973**

1. Products 2. Economics 3. Occupations -- United States 4. Business -- United States 5. United States -- Economic conditions -- 21st century

ISBN 9781250010827

LC 2012028235

A Detroit automobile industry veteran describes how he transformed a lagging supply and parts business into a world-class manufacturer that achieved $60 million in profit its first year, offering insight into historical events, the recent financial crisis and how the company's examples can provide a blueprint for job creation and economic growth.

Folsom, W. Davis

★**Encyclopedia** of American business / general editor, W. Davis Folsom ; associate editor, Stacia N. VanDyne. Facts On File, c2011. 2 v. (xvii, 844 p.) ; **338.0973**

1. Business -- United States -- Encyclopedias. 2. Finance -- United States -- Encyclopedias. 3. Industries -- United States -- Encyclopedias. 4. United States -- Commerce Encyclopedias. 5. Encyclopedias
ISBN 9780816081127

LC 2010028372

"This plain-language work will help beginners learn how businesses operate, the environment most operate in, what different features of specific business-related functions mean, and how they are evaluated." Booklist.

338.1 Specific kinds of industries

Ackerman-Leist, Philip, 1963-

Rebuilding the foodshed : how to create local, sustainable, and secure food systems / Philip Ackerman-Leist. Post Carbon Institute ; 2013. 304 p. **338.1**

1. Food supply. 2. Local foods. 3. Food security. 4. Agriculture
ISBN 9781603584234

LC 2012043955

Showcasing some of the most promising, replicable models for growing, processing, and distributing sustainably grown food, this book points the reader toward the next stages of the food revolution. It also covers the full landscape of the burgeoning local-food movement, from rural to suburban to urban, and from backyard gardens to large-scale food enterprises. --Provided by publisher

"Dense with information and studded with numerous graphs and charts, this book provides a deeper understanding of what principles need to change in order to create local food environments." Kirkus

Faruqi, Sonia

Project animal farm : an accidental journey into the secret world of farming and the truth about ... our food. / Sonia Faruqi. Pegasus Books, 2015. 336 p. **338.1**

1. Farms 2. Animal welfare 3. Organic farming 4. Factory farming
ISBN 9781605987989

LC bl2015024464

Traces the author's covert and sometimes life-risking tour of animal farms throughout the world to expose animal cruelty and identify ways to farm compassionately while promoting human health, economics, and environmental consciousness.

"Not for the fainthearted, but a good wake-up call for those concerned with decent treatment of animals and healthy food on the table." Kirkus.

Hesterman, Oran B.

Fair food : growing a healthy, sustainable food system for all / Oran B. Hesterman. PublicAffairs, c2011. xvi, 302 p. ; **338.1**

1. Food supply -- United States. 2. Agricultural products. 3. Food industry and trade. 4. Organic farming.
ISBN 9781610390064

LC 2010053129

Describes the dysfunctions in the current food system, from chemical runoff to inhumane treatment of animals, and presents new principles and concrete steps to restructure how food is grown, packaged, delivered, marketed, and sold.

Hewitt, Ben, 1971-

The **town** that food saved : how one community found vitality in local food / Ben Hewitt. Rodale, 2009. 256 p. **338.1**

1. Food supply -- Social aspects. 2. Food industry and trade 3. Sustainable agriculture 4. Entrepreneurship. 5. Hardwick, Vermont -- Economic conditions -- 21st century.
ISBN 9781605296869

LC 2009034294

Relates how the farming community of Hardwick, Vermont, developed a sustainable, local food system with its own support network where entrepreneurs share advice, equipment, and business plans, and shows how the town is becoming a model for other communities.

"Adroitly balancing professional neutrality with personal commitment, Hewitt engagingly examines this paradigm shift in the way a community feeds its citizens." Booklist.

Rude, Emelyn

Tastes like chicken : a history of America's favorite Bird / Emelyn Rude. Pegasus, 2016. 272 p. **338.1**

1. Chickens 2. Domestic animals 3. Livestock 4. Food -- History
ISBN 9781681771632

LC bl2016031510

From the domestication of the bird nearly ten thousand years ago to its current status as our go-to meat, the history of this seemingly commonplace bird is anything but ordinary.

"Readers of food histories such as Mark Kurlansky's Cod will appreciate this engaging, well-researched, and thorough history of America's changing food preferences." Library Journal.

Stuart, Andrea

Sugar in the blood : a family's story of slavery and empire / Andrea Stuart. Knopf, 2013. 448 p. **338.1**

1. Slavery 2. Families -- History 3. Slaves 4. Sugar 5. Barbados -- History -- 17th century
ISBN 9780307272836

LC 2012034259

Presents a history of the interdependence of sugar, slavery and colonial settlement in the New World through the story of the author's ancestors, exploring the myriad connections between sugar cultivation and her family's identity, genealogy and financial stability.

338.10973 Agricultural industries--United States

Berry, Wendell, 1934-

The **art** of loading brush : last agrarian writings / Wendell Berry. Counterpoint, 2017. 240 p. **338.10973**

1. Political science. 2. Agriculture. 3. Farm management. 4. Environmentalism 5. Essays
ISBN 9781619020382

LC 2017034645

Wendell Berry's profound critique of American culture has entered its sixth decade, and in this new gathering he reaches with deep devotion toward a long view of Agrarian philosophy. Mr. Berry believes that

American cultural problems are nearly always aligned with their agricultural problems, and recent events have shone a terrible spotlight on the divides between our urban and rural citizens. Our communities are as endangered as our landscapes. There is, as Berry outlines, still much work to do, and our daily lives--in hope and affection--must triumph over despair.

"About everything he loves and everything he regrets, he has never written better." Booklist.

Bittman, Mark

A **bone** to pick : the good and bad news about food, along with wisdom, insights, and advice on diets, food safety, GMOs policy, farming, and more / Mark Bittman. Clarkson Potter, 2015. 256 p. **338.10973**

1. Food industry and trade 2. Agricultural policy 3. Nutrition -- Political aspects 4. Diet -- United States. 5. Essays.

ISBN 9780804186544

LC 2014044874

Collection of articles published in the New York times.

Includes index.

"Mark Bittman made headlines three years ago when it was revealed that, for the first time, the New York Times opinion page would feature a food writer to help us make sense of the tangled webs of food, health, environment, politics, and culture. As an opinion columnist, Mark has delighted us, enraged us, and inspired us to do more for ourselves and our world with the same no-nonsense style. In the tradition of his NYT bestselling Food Matters, this book collects the best of his columns, updated to reflect the latest research, and tied together with new material to give context and show how far we've come in just a few years. What emerges is a collection that shows us the story of who we are as a nation of cooks, eaters, and voters right now".-- Provided by publisher.

"The author's keen analysis of the weakness of the Food and Drug Administration and its failures regarding food safety proves especially informative and enraging. Bittman successfully links a sound food system not just to the tastes of foodies (a word the author dislikes), but also to larger public health issues. An intelligent rallying cry for anyone seeking a safe and healthy food supply, and all that entails." Kirkus.

Hamilton, Lisa M.

Deeply rooted : unconventional farmers in the age of agribusiness / Lisa M. Hamilton. Counterpoint, c2009. 230 p. **338.10973**

1. Farmers -- Sulphur Springs, Texas -- Case studies. 2. Agribusiness 3. Agriculture -- Economic aspects. 4. Farmers -- Abiquiu, New Mexico -- Case studies. 5. Sulphur Springs, Texas -- Social life and customs 6. La Moure, North Dakota -- Social life and customs 7. Abiquiu, New Mexico -- Social life and customs

ISBN 9781593761806

LC 2008050526

A narrative report adds a critical perspective to the national discussion about where our food comes from, exploring key issues as perceived by everyday food growers from a Texas dairyman who battles agribusiness corporations to a tenth-generation rancher in New Mexico who struggles to restore his community's agriculture.

"Hamilton profiles farmers and ranchers who believe that agriculture is not an industry but, rather, a fundamental act that determines whether we as a society will live or die.. Hamilton's in-depth portraits of independent farmers offer invaluable perspectives on American agriculture, past and present, while offering hope for a life-sustaining future." Booklist.

Logsdon, Gene

Letter to a young farmer : how to live richly without wealth on the new garden farm / Gene Logsdon. Chelsea Green Publishing, [2017] 224 p. **338.10973**

1. Farm life 2. Agriculture 3. Sustainable agriculture 4. Sustainable living

ISBN 9781603587259

LC 2016050357

"This work serves as a guiding light and lodestar for farmers facing the modern challenges of any farming operation, large or small." Publishers Weekly. Annex.

338.2 Extraction of minerals

Burgis, Tom

The **looting** machine : warlords, oligarchs, corporations, smugglers, and the theft of Africa's wealth / Tom Burgis. Public Affairs, 2015. 320 p. **338.2**

1. Economic development -- Africa. 2. Business. 3. Africa -- Economic conditions -- 1960- 4. Africa -- Commerce.

ISBN 9781610394390

LC bl2015011101

In his first book, The Looting Machine, Tom Burgis exposes the truth about the African development miracle: for the resource states, it's a mirage. The oil, copper, diamonds, gold and coltan deposits attract a global network of traders, bankers, corporate extractors and investors who combine with venal political cabals to loot the states' value. And the vagaries of resource-dependent economies could pitch Africa's new middle class back into destitution just as quickly as they climbed out of it. The ground beneath their feet is as precarious as a Congolese mine shaft; their prosperity could spill away like crude from a busted pipeline.

"Essential for understanding the colonial Africa of the past and, even more so, the diverse Africa of today." Library Journal.

Burrough, Bryan, 1961-

The **big** rich : the rise and fall of the greatest Texas oil fortunes / Bryan Burrough. Penguin Press, 2008. 464 p. **338.2**

1. Oil industry and trade -- Texas. 2. Capitalism. 3. Business. 4. Money. 5. Texas -- History.

ISBN 9781594201998

LC 2008027043

An account of how Texas oil transformed wealth and power in America is presented through the stories of the state's four most influential oil families, tracing how they rose from modest backgrounds, shaped the government, and bankrolled the nation's largest rise of modern conservatism.

LeCain, Timothy J., 1960-

Mass destruction : the men and giant mines that wired America and scarred the planet / Timothy J. LeCain. Rutgers University Press, c2009. xii, 273 p. : **338.2**

1. Copper industry and trade -- West (US) -- History 2. Copper mines and mining -- Environmental aspects -- West (US) -- History 3. Copper mines and mining -- Health aspects -- West (US) -- History 4. Copper mines and mining -- West (US) -- History

ISBN 9780813545295

LC 2008035434

"The author writes about the history, the engineering challenges, the successes of production and resulting consumption, and the environmental consequences of open-pit copper mining, mainly in the first half of the 20th century. This book provokes serious second thoughts about the future of the exploitation of nature's bounty, and it should appeal to a wide audience." Choice.

Maass, Peter, 1960-
Crude world : the violent twilight of oil / Peter Maass. Alfred A. Knopf, 2009. 288 p. **338.2**

1. Oil industry and trade -- History 2. Oil production. 3. Energy production. 4. Oil supply.
ISBN 9781400041695

LC 2009012303

"This is a Borzoi book."

A stunning and revealing examination of oil's indelible impact on the countries that produce it and the people who possess it, of the power of oil to exacerbate existing problems and create new ones.

Maddow, Rachel
Blowout : corrupted democracy, rogue state Russia, and the richest, most destructive industry on Earth / Rachel Maddow. Crown, [2019] 304 p. **338.2**

1. Oil industry and trade 2. Oil executives 3. Business -- Corrupt practices 4. Business and politics
ISBN 9780525575474

LC 2019026915

Includes index.

The author explains how Big Oil and Gas adversely affect democracy.

Margonelli, Lisa
Oil on the brain : adventures from the pump to the pipeline / Lisa Margonelli. Nan A. Talese, Doubleday, c2007. 324 p. ; **338.2**

1. Oil industry and trade 2. Oil -- Prices 3. Energy consumption -- United States 4. United States -- Social life and customs -- 21st century
ISBN 0385511450

LC 2006020789

ALA Notable Book, 2008.

Looks at the economics of the petroleum industry and traces how crude oil from fields around the world eventually becomes the gasoline for automobiles.

"By giving voice to the people who are the links in the global oil chain, Margonelli invites us to leapfrog all the rhetoric, dry statistics, and dire pronouncements about oil in order to truly understand it." Fast Company.

Rao, Maya, 1984-
Great American outpost : dreamers, mavericks, and the making of an oil frontier / Maya Rao. PublicAffairs, 2018. vii, 324 pages: **338.2**

1. Oil industry and trade 2. Oil workers
ISBN 9781610396462

LC 2017044028

A journalist, in response to an ad that you could earn $17,000 a month in the Bakken Oilfield of North Dakota, sets out in steel-toed boots to chronicle the largest oil boom since the 1968 discovery of oil in Prudhoe Bay, Alaska, and introduces the colorful cast of characters she encountered who would do just about anything to cash in.

Yergin, Daniel
★The **prize** : the epic quest for oil, money, and power / Daniel Yergin. Simon & Schuster, 1991. 877 p., 32 p. of plates : **338.2**

1. Oil industry and trade -- Political aspects. 2. Oil industry and trade -- Military aspects. 3. Oil industry and trade -- History. 4. World War I -- Causes.
ISBN 0671502484

LC 90047575

Pulitzer Prize for General Nonfiction, 1992.

Oil is the dominant player in world politics in this century. Yergin shows how and why oil is the biggest industry in the world and why it caused the two world wars.

"This is a history of the oil industry, from the first oil well ever drilled (near Titusville, Pennsylvania, in 1859) to the Iraqi invasion of Kuwait. It recalls advances in technology, innovations in salesmanship, and wars and truces among corporations and nations." The New Yorker.

338.3 Other extractive industries

Fagan, Brian M.
Fishing : how the sea fed civilization / Brian Fagan. Yale University Press, 2017. 352 p. **338.3**

1. Fishing 2. Humans and fish 3. Civilization 4. Fishing equipment
ISBN 9780300215342

LC 2017934016

Humanity's last major source of food from the wild, and how it enabled and shaped the growth of civilization.

"A much-needed volume for serious students of world history. Highly recommended for readers interested in archaeology, anthropology, ecology, and environmental science." Library Journal.

Hilborn, Ray, 1947-
Overfishing : what everyone needs to know / Ray Hilborn with Ulrike Hilborn. Oxford University Press, c2012. xviii, 150 p. ; What everyone needs to know **338.3**

1. Overfishing. 2. Sustainable fisheries. 3. Fisheries -- Environmental aspects. 4. Environmental Policy
ISBN 9780199798148

LC 2011031308

A discussion of overfishing explores the scientific, political, ethical, and economic issues associated with harvesting the ocean's fish, using case studies of fisheries from around the world to answer the issue's most pressing questions.

Strøksnes, Morten Andreas, 1965-
Shark drunk : the art of catching a large shark from a tiny rubber dinghy in a big ocean through four seasons / Morten Strøksnes ; translated by Tiina Nunnally. Alfred A. Knopf, 2017. 320 p. **338.3**

1. Shark fishing 2. Greenland shark 3. Fishing 4. Sailing 5. Norway
ISBN 9780451493484

LC 2016044185

Fishing trip! Topically wide-ranging, Shark Drunk documents the quest of award-winning journalist Morten Strøksnes and artist Hugo Aasjord to catch a massive Greenland Shark in the frigid waters near Norway's Lofoten islands. In a rubber dinghy over the course of four seasons, the two friends baited hooks in order to entice the massive shark while they sat, occasionally got wet, reeled in cod, ruminated, and talked. Covering ocean life, poetry, mythology, science, history, and more, this lyrical book reads like a novel and will hook fans of philosophical stories.

"Strøksnes's erudition, salty humor, and unfussy prose yield a fresh, engrossing natural history." Publishers Weekly.

338.4 Secondary industries and services

Almond, Steve
★**Candyfreak** : a journey through the chocolate underbelly

of America / Steve Almond. Algonquin Books of Chapel Hill, 2004. 266 p. **338.4**

1. Almond, Steve 2. Hershey Chocolate Company. 3. Nestle Corporation. 4. Candy industry and trade. 5. Candy. 6. Chocolate.
ISBN 9781565124219
LC 2003070801

Perhaps you remember The Marathon, Oompahs, Bit-O-Choc, or Kit Kat Dark. Where did they go? Driven by his obsession, stubborn idealism, and the promise of free candy, self-confessed candyfreak Steve Almond takes off on a quest to discover candy's origins in America, to explore little companies that continue to get by on pluck and perseverance, and to witness the glorious excess of candy manufacturing. Part candy porn, part candy polemic, part social history, part confession, Candyfreak explores the role candy plays in our lives as both source of pleasure and escape from pain. By turns ecstatic, comic, and bittersweet, Candyfreak is the story of how Steve Almond grew up on candy--and how, for better and worse, candy has grown up too.

"The author tells how candy shaped his childhood and continues to define his life in ways large and small. Once hundreds of American confectioners delivered regional favorites to consumers, but now the big three of candy--Hershey, Mars, and Nestlé--control the market. To find out what happened to those candies of yesteryear, Almond talks to candy collectors and historians and visits a few of the remaining independent candy companies. Flavored with the author's amusingly tart sense of humor, Candyfreak is an intriguing chronicle of the passions that candy inspires and the pleasures it offers." Library Journal.

Becker, Elizabeth

Overbooked : the exploding business of travel and tourism / Elizabeth Becker. Simon & Schuster, 2013. 320 p. **338.4**

1. Tourism -- Political aspects 2. Tourism -- Environmental aspects 3. Recreation industry and trade 4. International relations
ISBN 9781439160992
LC 2012032848

Though the travel industry is relatively new, it's a trillion-dollar business, one of the largest in the world. Pulitzer Prize-winning journalist Elizabeth Becker presents a sobering assessment of what that means for the world economy, the environment, local cultures, historical sites, and individuals. From cruises to safaris -- and traveling everywhere from Costa Rica to France -- she unveils how the industry's shiny surfaces sometimes hide seedy underpinnings, including government corruption and sex trafficking.

Beckert, Sven

Empire of cotton : a global history / Sven Beckert. Knopf, 2014. 512 p. **338.4**

1. Cotton manufacture 2. Cotton fabrics 3. Cotton industry and trade 4. Cotton textile industry and trade
ISBN 9780375414145
LC 2014009320

Pulitzer Prize for History finalist, 2015.

Cundill Prize in Historical Literature finalist

The epic story of the rise and fall of the empire of cotton, its centrality in the world economy, and its making and remaking of global capitalism. Sven Beckert's book tells the story of how, in a remarkably brief period, European entrepreneurs and powerful statesmen recast the world's most significant manufacturing industry combining imperial expansion and slave labor with new machines and wage workers to change the world.

"Both chronologically and geographically, this is a wide-ranging saga that examines the role of nation-states, politicians, entrepreneurs, and laborers on every continent. This is not a pretty story, since Beckert shows that this empire often depended upon coercion and violence for its growth and maintenance. This is a highly detailed, provocative work that combines history, economics, and sociology in an effort to show how cotton shaped the modern world." Booklist.

Campbell-Kelly, Martin

From airline reservations to Sonic the Hedgehog : a history of the software industry / Martin Campbell-Kelly. MIT Press, c2003. xiv, 372 p. : **338.4**

1. Computer software industry and trade -- History 2. Computers. 3. Technology. 4. Technological innovations.
ISBN 9780262033039
LC 2002075351

Chronicles the software history's rise from its beginnings in the 1950s to America's fourth largest industrial sector, describing the different kinds of software, products, and markets that have developed.

"The author presents a history of the software industry from the 1950s to 1995. Dividing the business into three sectors (software contracting, corporate software precuts, and mass-market software products), he examines the key products and players in each. The result is a well-rounded look at the software industry from a business perspective." Library Journal.

DeBord, Matthew

Return to glory : the story of Ford's revival and victory in the toughest race in the world / Matthew Debord. Atlantic Monthly Press, 2017. 272 p. **338.4**

1. Mulally, Alan R. 2. Ford Motor Company 3. 24 Heures du Mans (Automobile race) 4. Automobile racing 5. Automobile industry and trade 6. Success in business 7. Business competition
ISBN 9780802126504
LC 2016046214

A veteran transportation journalist chronicles the development and racing achievement of the new 2015 Ford GT, exploring how the company has been returning to an era of success after implementing the decade-long "One Ford" plan of CEO Alan Mulally.

"DeBord, a senior correspondent for Business Insider, takes readers inside Ford before, during and after the 2016 Le Mans race and emerges with an upbeat, feel-good business story." Publishers Weekly.

Diaz, Tom

The **last** gun : how changes in the gun industry are killing Americans and what it will take to stop it / Tom Diaz. The New Press, [2013] 319 p. **338.4**

1. Gun industry and trade -- United States 2. Guns -- Social aspects 3. Gun control 4. Gun ownership
ISBN 9781595588302
LC 2012047230

Explores how the gun industry has changed and how the nature of gun violence has changed in step with industry trends and argues that a renewed political effort is necessary.

Fine, Doug

Too high to fail : cannabis and the new green economic revolution / Doug Fine. Gotham Books, c2012. 368 p. **338.4**

1. Marijuana traffic. 2. Drug industry and trade. 3. Hemp industry and trade. 4. Hemp growing.
ISBN 9781592407095
LC 2012014437

An in-depth assessment of the legal cannabis industry and its potential role in today's evolving economy cites the lucrative proceeds generated by a small number of registered users and the underground revenues of illegal uses, providing a concise history of hemp and insider perspectives on a profitable growing season in Mendocino County.

Goldstone, Lawrence, 1947-

Drive! : Henry Ford, George Selden, and the race to invent the auto age / Lawrence Goldstone. Ballantine Books, 2016. 400 p. **338.4**

1. Ford, Henry, 1863-1947 2. Selden, George Baldwin, 1846-1922 3. Ford Motor Company 4. Automobile industry and trade. 5. Automobiles -- History

ISBN 9780553394184

LC 2016002581

From the acclaimed author of Birdmen comes another hidden history of entrepreneurship--a true tale of invention and competition that will forever change the way readers view the creation of the vehicle that forever changed America, and sets the record straight on Henry Ford.

"A splendid dissection of the Selden/Ford patent face-off and its place in automotive historiography." Library Journal.

Haag, Pamela

★The **gunning** of America : business and the making of American gun culture / Pamela Haag. Basic Books, 2016. 368 p. **338.4**

1. Winchester Repeating Arms Company -- History. 2. Guns -- United States -- History. 3. Gun industry and trade. 4. Social history. 5. Winchester guns.

ISBN 9780465048953

LC 2015036679

An acclaimed historian explodes the myth about the 'special relationship' between Americans and their guns, revealing that savvy 19th century businessmen--not gun lovers--created American gun culture

Lenzer, Jeanne

The **danger** within us : America's untested, unregulated medical device industry and one man's battle to survive it / Jeanne Lenzer. Little, Brown and Company, 2017 320 p. **338.4**

1. Medical equipment industry and trade 2. Medical equipment 3. Corruption 4. Medical ethics.

ISBN 9780316343763

LC 2017954610

An award-winning medical investigative journalist presents an unsettling exposé of the under-regulated medical-device industry, revealing the corruption, greed and deceit that have combined to render medical interventions a leading cause of death in America.

" An impassioned exposé that uncovers a significant danger within the contemporary health care industry." Kirkus.

McMillan, Tracie

★The **American** way of eating : undercover at Walmart, Applebee's, farm fields and the dinner table / Tracie McMillan. Simon & Schuster, 2012. x, 319 p. **338.4**

1. Food habits -- United States 2. Poverty 3. Investigative journalism -- United States. 4. Nutrition -- United States 5. California 6. Detroit, Michigan 7. New York City

ISBN 9781439171950

An award-winning journalist traces her 2009 immersion into the national food system to explore issues about how working-class Americans can afford to eat as they should, describing how she worked as a farm laborer, Wal-Mart grocery clerk and Applebee's expediter while living within the means of each job.

"Full of personal stories of the daily struggle to put food of any kind on the table in today's economy, McMillan's book will force readers to question their own methods of purchasing and preparing food." Kirkus.

McNish, Jacquie

Losing the signal : the untold story behind the extraordinary rise and spectacular fall of Blackberry / Jacquie McNish and Sean Silcoff. Flatiron Books, 2015. 288 p. **338.4**

1. BlackBerry Limited. 2. BlackBerry (Smartphone) 3. Cell phones 4. Smartphones 5. Technology

ISBN 9781250060174

LC 2015012152

An inside account of the dramatic rise and fall of BlackBerry traces the partnership between engineer Mike Lazaridis and Harvard Business School graduate Jim Balsillie and how their innovation succumbed to mobile phone competition at the height of its influence.

Mitford, Jessica, 1917-1996

★The **American** way of death revisited / Jessica Mitford. Alfred A. Knopf, 1998, c1963. xix, 296 p. ; **338.4**

1. Mitford, Jessica, 1917-1996. American Way of death. 2. Undertakers 3. Funerals -- Economic aspects 4. Death. 5. United States -- Economic conditions -- 20th century

ISBN 0679450378

LC 97049349

Originally published: New York : Simon and Schuster, 1963.

A revised version of an exposé of the funeral industry includes new chapters on the practice of prepayment for funerals and other issues.

"Very interesting, informative, and easy to read, this book is written with wit, solid information, and refreshing bluntness." Library Journal.

Noonan, Meg

The **coat** route : craft, luxury, and obsession on the trail of a $50,000 coat / Meg Lukens Noonan. Spiegel & Grau, 2013. 288 p. **338.4**

1. Luxury. 2. Couture clothing 3. Coats 4. Dressmaking

ISBN 9781400069934

LC 2012042994

"The journalist co-author of Albatross recounts her international travels to sites where the rare materials for a luxury hand-crafted coat are gathered and created, from a vicuna shearing festival in the Peruvian Andes to the elite silk boutiques of Florence, where she witnessed the struggles of elite artisans against the forces of globalization and mass production."

Pein, Corey

Live work work work die : a journey into the savage heart of Silicon Valley / Corey Pein. Metropolitan Books, 2018. 320 p. **338.4**

1. Internet industry and trade 2. High-technology industry and trade 3. Business competition 4. Technological innovations 5. Silicon Valley, California

ISBN 9781627794855

LC 2017040258

A journalist explores the true heart of Silicon Valley by becoming an entrepreneur and describes first-hand his experiences at gimmicky tech conferences, pitching his insane business ideas to investors and through interviews with quirky and outrageous characters including con artists, hackers and naive programmers.

Posner, Gerald L.

Pharma : greed, lies, and the poisoning of America / Gerald Posner. Avid Reader Press, 2020. xi, 802 p. **338.4**

1. Drug industry and trade 2. Corruption 3. Corporate power 4. Corporations

ISBN 9781501151897

LC bl2020004435

The award-winning author of God's Bankers traces the rise of the Salker family and the role of opioid addiction and soaring drug prices on healthcare, exposing the deadly consequences of industry corruption and profiteering.

"Explosively, even addictively, readable, Posner's meticulously documented investigation of the historical roots and contemporary state of Big Pharma examines everything from aspirin to Zantac." Booklist

Quigley, Fran, 1962-

Prescription for the people : an activist's guide to making medicine affordable for all / Fran Quigley. ILR Press, an imprint of Cornell University Press, 2017. 341 p. **338.4**

1. Drug industry and trade 2. Health policy 3. Drug Prices 4. Prescription pricing

ISBN 9781501713750

LC 2017020499

In Prescription for the People, Fran Quigley diagnoses our inability to get medicines to the people who need them and then prescribes the cure. He delivers a clear and convincing argument for a complete shift in the global and U.S. approach to developing and providing essential medicines--and a primer on how to make that change happen.

"Quigley offers a focused analysis of the problem and advice for those who wish to help change the system." Library Journal.

Rudacille, Deborah

Roots of steel : the boom and bust of an American mill town / Deborah Rudacille. Pantheon Books, 2010. 304 p. **338.4**

1. Steel industry and trade. 2. Mill towns. 3. Small town life. 4. Metal industry and trade 5. Maryland -- History. 6. Sparrows Point, Maryland -- Economic conditions. 7. Sparrows Point, Maryland -- History.

ISBN 9780375423680

LC 2009020962

"The author of The Riddle of Gender traces the history of a Maryland steel mill town where she grew up as the daughter of a steelworker, a childhood during which she witnessed how the industry's decline and complicated social disputes put tens of thousands out of work."

Sedgewick, Augustine

Coffeeland : one man's dark empire and the making of our favorite drug / Augustine Sedgewick. Penguin Press, 2020. 432 p. **338.4**

1. Coffee industry and trade 2. Colonialism 3. Consumerism -- United States 4. Coffee plantations 5. El Salvador -- History 6. United States -- History -- 20th century

ISBN 9781594206153

LC 2019031332

The epic story of the rise of coffee in the Americas, and how it connected and divided the modern world. Sedgewick reveals how the growth of coffee production, trade, and consumption went hand in hand with the rise of the scientific idea of energy as a universal force, which transformed thinking about how the human body works as well as ideas about the relationship of one person's work to another's. In the process, both El Salvador and the United States earned the nickname "Coffeeland," though for radically different reasons, and with consequences that reach into the present. This history of how coffee came to be produced by the world's poorest people and consumed by its richest opens up a unique perspective on how the modern globalized world works, ultimately provoking a reconsideration of what it means to be connected to far-away people and places through the familiar things that make up our everyday lives.

"The breadth of Sedgewick's analysis of coffee's place in the world economy astonishes, as does his ability to bring historical figures to life. Coffee connoisseurs will relish this eye-opening history." Publishers Weekly

Vlasic, Bill

Once upon a car : the fall and revival of America's big three auto makers -- GM, Ford, and Chrysler / Bill Vlasic. Harpercollins, 2011. 352 p. **338.4**

1. General Motors Corporation. 2. Ford Motor Company. 3. Chrysler Corporation. 4. Automobile industry and trade. 5. Business. 6. Financial crises. 7. Automobiles.

ISBN 9780061845628

LC 2011020572

In this uniquely American story of success, failure and redemption, the Detroit bureau chief for the New York Times, covering events from 2005 to the present, documents the crumbling of the once-mighty car industry, revealing the impact of this crisis on workers and communities.

338.47796 Sports industry

Futterman, Matthew

Players : the story of sports and money--and the visionaries who fought to create a revolution / Matthew Futterman. Simon and Schuster, 2016 336 p. **338.47796**

1. Sports -- Economic aspects. 2. Athletes -- Salaries, etc. -- United States. 3. Wealth 4. Business

ISBN 9781476716954

LC 2015025635

Traces the single-generation transformation of sports from a cottage industry to a massive global business, reflecting on how elite athletes, agents, TV executives, coaches, owners and athletes who once had to take second jobs worked together to create the dominating, big-ticket industry of today.

"This lively take on the money game in contemporary sports should be read widely." Library Journal.

338.5 General production economics

Derks, Scott

The **value** of a dollar : colonial era to the Civil War, 1600-1865 / Scott Derks and Tony Smith. Grey House Pub., 2005. 436, 21 p. : **338.5**

1. Cost and standard of living -- United States -- History 2. Prices -- United States -- History 3. Purchasing power -- United States -- History 4. Wages -- United States -- History

ISBN 9781592370948

LC 2006275331

"[This is] the first edition of The Value of a Dollar, 1600-1865. This book both parallels and compliments its popular older brother The Value of a Dollar, 1860-2004"--P. [i].

"A Universal Reference Book."

"This source is an engaging statistical summary that looks at the history of the American people through the eyes of everyday workers and consumers. The 265 years it covers are presented in six chronological chapters: 1600-1749: The Development of the Colonies, 1750-1774: The Run up to the War of American Independence, and so on, ending with the close of the Civil War in 1865. [This book] will find a happy audience among students, researchers, and general browsers. It offers a fascinating and detailed look at early American history from the viewpoint of everyday people trying to make ends meet." Booklist.

The **value** of a dollar : prices and incomes in the United States, 1860-2009 / Scott Derks. Grey House Pub., 2009. xix, 690 p. : **338.5**

1. Cost and standard of living -- United States -- History 2. Prices -- United States -- History 3. Purchasing power -- United States -- History 4. Wages -- United States -- History
ISBN 9781592374038

LC 2010286212

"A universal reference book"--Cover.

"Both great-grandparents and serious students in historical research will benefit from this book. It will be an especially valuable study to students of American history, economics, and even mathematics." Library Journal.

Galbraith, John Kenneth, 1908-2006
★The **great** crash, 1929 / John Kenneth Galbraith ; with a new introduction by the author. Houghton Mifflin Co., c1997. xiv, 206 p. : **338.5**

1. Depressions -- 1929-1941. 2. Stock market crash, October 1929.
ISBN 9780395859995

LC 97022051

"A Mariner book."

A study of the stock market crash of 1929 reveals the influential role of Wall Street on the economic growth of America

Lewis, Michael (Michael M.),
Panic : the story of modern financial insanity / Michael Lewis. W. W. Norton & Company, 2008. 352 p. **338.5**

1. Financial crises -- History -- 20th century. 2. Finance -- Psychological aspects. 3. Investments -- Psychological aspects. 4. Financial crises -- History -- 21st century.
ISBN 9780393065145

LC 2008039523

An analysis of five financial upheavals in recent history includes coverage of the 1987 stock market crash, the Internet bubble, and the sub-prime mortgage crisis, in a report that reveals how public knowledge differed from what was actually taking place.

"The editor has compiled an anthology of articles related to five major financial crises in recent decades: the 1987 stock market crash, the Russian default, the Asian currency crisis, the Internet bubble and most recently the subprime mortgage collapse (the final article included is from January 2008). For each crisis, Lewis offers articles from journals, books, transcripts, and newspapers, all written immediately before, during, or after the event. Timely and highly readable, this work includes in one accessible source two decades' worth of some of the best writing on the various crises and panics." Library Journal.

Mullainathan, Sendhil
Scarcity : why having too little means so much / Sendhil Mullainathan and Eldar Shafir. Times Books, Henry Holt and Company, 2013 304 p. **338.5**

1. Supply and demand. 2. Scarcity. 3. Decision making. 4. Psychology.
ISBN 9780805092646

LC 2013004167

An examination of how scarcity--and our flawed responses to it--shapes our lives, our society, and our culture.

Nations, Scott
A **history** of the United States in five crashes : stock market meltdowns that defined a nation / Scott Nations. William Morrow & Company, 2017. 304 p. **338.5**

1. Stock market. 2. Financial crises 3. Recession (Economics) 4. Market indicators.
ISBN 9780062467270

LC 2017033698

A financial executive and CNBC contributor examines the five most significant stock market crashes over the past century to reveal how they happened and shaped the present-day United States.

"An eye-opening examination of the many ways money can be made--and disappear." Kirkus.

Reinhart, Carmen M.
This time is different : eight centuries of financial folly / Carmen M. Reinhart, Kenneth S. Rogoff. Princeton University Press, 2009. 496 p. **338.5**

1. Financial crises. 2. Fiscal policy. 3. Business cycles. 4. Economic history.
ISBN 9780691142166

LC 2009022616

"The authors have compiled an impressive database, which covers eight centuries of government debt defaults from around the world. They have also collected statistics on inflation rates from every country where information is available and on banking crises and international capital flows over the past couple of centuries. This lengthy historical study gives what they call a panoramic view of the unending cycle of boom and bust, showing how claims that this time is different are invariably proven wrong. [This] is an important addition to the literature of financial history." Wall Street Journal.

338.6 Organization of production

Freeman, Joshua Benjamin
★**Behemoth** : a history of the factory and the making of the modern world / Joshua B. Freeman. W W Norton & Co, 2018 464 p. **338.6**

1. Factories. 2. Factory system -- History. 3. Technology and civilization. 4. Industrialization -- History.
ISBN 9780393246315

LC 2017051960

A global history of the rise of the factory and its positive and negative effects on society traces the Industrial Revolution textile mills, through the massive steel and car plants of the 20th century, to the massive retail producers of today's world, offering insights into the views, debates and innovations of Alexander Hamilton, Henry Ford, Charlie Chaplin and others.

" Freeman has provided an ambitious, sweeping, and well-researched history of factories, which remains accessible and relevant to general readers." Library Journal.

338.7 Business enterprises

Acitelli, Tom
Pilsner : how the beer of kings changed the world / Tom Acitelli. Chicago Review Press, 2020. 320 p. **338.7**

1. Busch family 2. Anheuser-Busch, Inc. -- History. 3. Brewing industry and trade -- United States -- History 4. Beer 5. Brewing 6.

Alcoholic beverages.
ISBN 9781641601825

LC 2020007838

"The remarkable story of the world's most popular style of beer, from its humble birth in a far corner of the Austrian Empire in 1842 to its present dominance worldwide. Shattering myths about the style's origins and immediate parentage, this book shows how pilsner influenced everything from modern-day advertising and marketing to today's craft beer movement".-- Provided by publisher.

"Journalist Acitelli (The Audacity of Hops) recounts the history of one of the world's most popular beers in this effervescent and informative take. . . . will intoxicate both beer nerds and history buffs." Publishers Weekly

Auletta, Ken

Googled : the end of the world as we know it / Ken Auletta. Penguin Press, 2009. 400 p. **338.7**

1. Google (Firm) 2. Internet industry and trade -- United States 3. Web search engines 4. Internet searching. 5. Computers.
ISBN 9781594202353

LC 2009024770

Critically examines the influence of Google on today's dynamic media landscape, profiling company founders Larry Page and Sergey Brin while offering insight into their lucrative business processes and assessing the internal and external threats that may inhibit the company's future prospects.

"The author's thorough reporting and declarative writing provide a crisp, informative read. Auletta displays the skill of a responsible journalist in both researching and crafting this snapshot of today's technological landscape." Christian Science Monitor.

Bissonnette, Zac

The **great** Beanie Baby bubble : mass delusion and the dark side of cute / Zac Bissonnette. Portfolio, 2015. 272 p. **338.7**

1. Warner, Ty, 1944- 2. Ty, Inc. -- History 3. Beanie Babies (Trademark) 4. Toy industry and trade
ISBN 9781591846024

LC 2014038639

A classic American story of people winning and losing vast fortunes chasing what one dealer remembers as the most spectacular dream ever sold.

Brenner, Joel Glenn

The **emperors** of chocolate : inside the secret world of Hershey and Mars / Joel Glenn Brenner. Random House, 1999. xiv, 366 p. : **338.7**

1. Hershey, Milton Snavely, 1857-1945. 2. Mars, Forrest, 1904-1999. 3. Hershey Foods Corporation -- History. 4. Mars, Inc -- History. 5. Chocolate industry and trade -- History 6. Candy industry and trade. 7. Chocolate candy -- History. 8. Business competition.
ISBN 0679421904

LC 98021610

"Brenner examines the candy industry, focusing on the rivalry between Hershey and Mars. Milton Hersey was and Forrest Mars is highly secretive and eccentric, and they both amassed huge fortunes. A wonderful inside look at successful businessmen." Booklist.

Carreyrou, John

★**Bad** blood : secrets and lies in a Silicon Valley startup / John Carreyrou. Knopf, 2018. 352 p. **338.7**

1. Theranos (Firm) 2. New businesses. 3. Fraud 4. Biotechnology. 5. Business -- Corrupt practices
ISBN 9781524731656

LC 2018000263

Recounts the story behind Theranos, the medical equipment company that misled investors to believe they developed a revolutionary blood testing machine, detailing how its CEO, Elizabeth Holmes, perpetuated the lie to bolster the value of the company by billions.

"Crime thriller authors have nothing on Carreyrou's exquisite sense of suspenseful pacing and multifaceted character development in this riveting, read-in-one-sitting tour de force. Investigative journalists are perhaps the country's last true protectors of truth and justice, and Carreyrou's commitment to unraveling Holmes crimes has been literally of life-saving value." Booklist.

Coll, Steve

★**Private** empire : ExxonMobil and American power / Steve Coll. Penguin Press, 2012. 688 p. **338.7**

1. Exxon Corporation. 2. Oil industry and trade -- Political aspects -- United States 3. Corporate power 4. Big business -- United States. 5. United States -- Politics and government -- 21st century
ISBN 9781594203350

LC 2011044722

National Book Critics Circle Award for Nonfiction finalist, 2012.

An investigation into the influential and fiercely private corporation traces the period between the Exxon Valdez accident and the Deepwater Horizion spill to profile chief executives Lee Raymond and Rex Tillerson as well as the company's role in violent international incidents. By the Pulitzer Prize-winning author of The Bin Ladens.

"Highly recommended for students of the energy economy as well as for motivated general readers." Library Journal.

Doran, Peter B.

Breaking Rockefeller : the incredible story of the ambitious rivals who toppled an oil empire / Peter B. Doran. Viking Press, 2016 352 p. **338.7**

1. Rockefeller, John D. (John Davison), 1839-1937 2. Samuel, Marcus, 1853-1927 3. Deterding, Henri, 1866-1939 4. Standard Oil Company -- History. 5. Royal Dutch Shell plc 6. Oil industry and trade. 7. Monopolies. 8. Businesspeople.
ISBN 9780525427391

LC bl2016012688

Based on a podcast.

The author of the popular History of Oil podcast traces the early-20th-century rivalry between John D. Rockefeller's Standard Oil and Royal Dutch Shell, describing the origins of partners Marcus Samuel, Jr. and Henri Deterding and how they used respective talents to break Rockefeller's daunting monopoly.

"A readable popular history told largely through the actions of swashbuckling tycoons." Kirkus.

Elmore, Bartow J.

Citizen Coke : the making of Coca-Cola capitalism / Bartow J. Elmore. W.W. Norton & Company, 2014 304 p. **338.7**

1. Coca-Cola Company. 2. Soft drink industry and trade 3. International businesses. 4. Soft drinks. 5. Sustainable development.
ISBN 9780393241129

LC 2014022329

A critical history of Coca-Cola's business successes outlines the company's particularly effective strategies for production, cost control and franchising while citing Coke's role in world resource depletion and the obesity crisis.

"Without a doubt, Coke has been a good public citizen that stimulates economies and improves lives, writes the author, but the costs to taxpayers--for recycling systems, public pipes and subsidized farms--and the environment call into question how such unsustainable practices can continue in an age of scarcity. A superb, quietly devastating environmental and business history." Kirkus.

Ewing, Jack (Economics correspondent)

Faster, higher, farther : the Volkswagen scandal / Jack Ewing. W. W. Norton & Co Inc, 2017 320 p. **338.7**

1. Volkswagen of America, Inc. 2. Automobile industry and trade. 3. Business -- Corrupt practices. 4. Greenhouse gas mitigation. 5. Energy policy -- Environmental aspects.
ISBN 9780393254501

LC 2017012672

In 2015, Volkswagen proudly reached its goal of surpassing Toyota as the world's largest automaker. Two months later, the EPA disclosed that Volkswagen had installed software that deceived emissions-testing mechanisms in 11 million cars. By August 2016, VW had settled with American regulators and car owners for $15 billion, with additional fines and suits still looming. In Faster, Higher, Farther, Jack Ewing rips the lid off the conspiracy.

"Capturing the public fascination with craven financial scandals, and with a movie in the works, Ewings sordid saga is the latest addition to the history of corporate fraud." Booklist.

Galloway, Scott

The **four** : the hidden DNA of Amazon, Apple, Facebook, and Google / Scott Galloway. Penguin, 2017. 288 p. **338.7**

1. Apple Computer, Inc. 2. Amazon.com (Firm) 3. Google (Firm) 4. Facebook (Firm) 5. Success in business -- United States -- Case studies. 6. Internet. 7. Computers and civilization. 8. Digital media.
ISBN 9780735213654

LC 2017037152

An acclaimed NYU business professor examines the rise and influence of technology titans Apple, Amazon, Google and Facebook to reveal how they became successful by adapting the ideas of others in ways that reflect evolutionary psychology, outlining the likely path of a next possible major contender.

"Readers interested in innovation and strategies in technology and business management will find this book to be a provocative and insightful look at four powerful forces that dominate our social, psychological, and economic states today." Booklist.

Genoways, Ted

The **chain** : farm, factory, and the fate of our food / Ted Genoways. Harper, 2014. 320 p. **338.7**

1. Hormel Foods Corporation. 2. Meat industry and trade. 3. Food processing plants. 4. Factory farming. 5. Occupational health and safety
ISBN 9780062288752

LC 2014019018

An acclaimed journalist uses the story of Hormel Foods and soaring recession-era demand for its most famous product, Spam, to probe the state of the meatpacking industry, including the expansion of agribusiness and the effects of immigrant labor on Middle America, and expose such alarming trends as pollution, abused animals and more.

"Readers curious about meatpacking and agriculture as well as the social, economic, and environmental impacts of the food industry will find Genoways's nonfiction debut a valuable and stimulating read." Library Journal.

Goldman, Seth

Mission in a bottle : the honest guide to doing business differently--and succeeding / Seth Goldman and Barry Nalebuff; illustrated by Sungyoon Choi. Crown Business, 2013. 278 p. : **338.7**

1. Honest Tea (Firm) -- History 2. Tea industry and trade 3. Soft drink industry and trade 4. Tea 5. Comics and Graphic novels
ISBN 9780770437497

LC 2013004799

Chiefly illustrations.

In graphic novel format, the cofounders of Honest Tea present the history of the company and provide practical advice on launching a successful business, perseverance, and creative problem-solving.

Gryta, Thomas

Lights out : pride, delusion, and the fall of General Electric / Thomas Gryta and Ted Mann. Houghton Mifflin Harcourt, 2020. ix, 353 p. ; **338.7**

1. General Electric Company. 2. Electric industries -- United States -- History
ISBN 9780358250418

LC 2020005518

"How could General Electric--perhaps America's most iconic corporation-suffer such a swift and sudden fall from grace?"-- Provided by publisher.

Harris, Blake J.

Console wars : Sega, Nintendo, and the battle that defined a generation / Blake J. Harris. It Books, 2014. 320 p. **338.7**

1. Nintendo Company, Ltd. 2. Video games industry and trade 3. Video games. 4. Nintendo video games. 5. Sega Genesis games.
ISBN 9780062276698

LC 2013050668

Chronicles how Sega--a small, scrappy gaming company led by an unlikely visionary and a team of rebels--took on the juggernaut Nintendo and revolutionized the video game industry.

"Harris defines the players immediately, honing in on their most notable characteristics, and puts the reader in the thick of the meetings and deal-making with a confidence stemming from hundreds of interviews." Booklist.

Hart, Matt

Win at all costs : inside Nike running and its culture of deception / Matt Hart. Dey Street Books, 2020. 416 p. **338.7**

1. Salazar, Alberto, 1958- 2. Nike (Firm) Corrupt practices. 3. Nike (Firm). Oregon Project. 4. Runners 5. Doping in sports 6. Sports equipment industry and trade 7. Track and field 8. United States
ISBN 9780062917775

LC 2020021183

A behind-the-scenes journalistic exposé of the illicit activities of the Nike Oregon Project reveals how a company insider and two Olympic athletes risked their careers to expose cheating by Nike-sponsored runners, including top world athletes.

“A touch overlong, but a deeply reported and revealing look at the dire commercialization of American sports.” Kirkus

Kealing, Bob

Tupperware, unsealed : Brownie Wise, Earl Tupper, and the home party pioneers / Bob Kealing. University Press of Florida, c2008. x, 250 p. : **338.7**

1. Tupper, Earl Silas. 2. Wise, Brownie. 3. Tupperware Corporation -- History. 4. Tupperware Home Parties -- History. 5. Home parties (Marketing) -- United States -- History 6. Plastic container industry -- United States -- History 7. Plastic tableware -- United States --

History
ISBN 9780813032276

LC 2007047539

Traces the career of pioneering businesswoman Brownie Wise, the driving force behind making Tupperware a household name in the 1950s, who invented the concept of marketing through in-home sales, before being unceremoniously fired from the company by owner Earl Tupper at the height of her national celebrity.

"The author explores the origins of the Tupperware industry as seen through the insightful genius of Brownie Wise, the impetus behind the home party craze that catapulted Tupperware revenues into the millions. This work proves to be a valuable contribution to the growing body of literature that focuses on the individual contributions of women to US business and industry." Choice.

Kirkpatrick, David, 1953 June 14-

The **Facebook** effect : the inside story of the company that is connecting the world / David Kirkpatrick. Simon & Schuster, 2010. 320 p. **338.7**

1. Facebook (Firm) 2. Internet industry and trade -- United States 3. Online social networks. 4. Social networks. 5. Electronic commerce.
ISBN 9781439102114

LC 2009051983

"An insider's history of the online social network traces the collaborations and conflicts among its founders, the personalities that shaped its development and the ways in which the site has become an integral part of today's culture."

"The author was encouraged by Mark Zuckerberg, the founder and chief executive of Facebook.com, to write this book and was granted extensive access to him and his associates. Their cooperation has resulted in a mostly sympathetic--at times, gushingly laudatory--account of the company, though Mr. Kirkpatrick does not shy away from dissecting its missteps and successive disputes over privacy. He gives the reader a detailed understanding of how the company grew from a 2004 Harvard dorm-room project into the world's second-most-visited site after Google." New York Times.

Knoedelseder, William, 1947-

Bitter brew : the rise and fall of Anheuser-Busch and America's kings of beer / William Knoedelseder. HarperBusiness, c2012. 400 p. **338.7**

1. Busch family 2. Anheuser-Busch, Inc. -- History 3. Brewing industry and trade 4. Name-brand products 5. Corporate mergers 6. Beer
ISBN 9780062009265

LC 2012026942

Part cautionary tale, part business manual, this engrossing book, spanning three centuries, tells the story of how five generations of men took a small, bankrupt brewery on the banks of the Mississippi and turned it into an international empire until its downfall.

Lashinsky, Adam

Inside Apple : how America's most admired--and secretive--company really works / Adam Lashinsky. Business Plus, c2012. 256 p. **338.7**

1. Apple Computer, Inc. 2. Computer industry and trade -- Management 3. Corporate culture -- United States. 4. Success in business
ISBN 9781455512157

LC 2011044773

An analysis of the systems, tactics, and leadership strategies that have contributed to Apple's successes profiles such practices as the direct accountability of employees and shares insider perspectives on Apple's plans after the loss of Steve Jobs.

Leonard, Christopher, 1975-

Kochland : the secret history of Koch Industries and corporate power in America / Christopher Leonard. Simon & Schuster, 2019. x, 687 p. : **338.7**

1. Koch, Charles G. (Charles de Ganahl), 1935- 2. Koch Industries 3. Executives 4. Corporations -- Political activity 5. Corporate power 6. Business and politics
ISBN 9781476775388

A history of modern corporate America is presented through the story of the rise of Koch Industries, revealing how the Koch brothers operated as master disruptors and anti-union strategists for decades to become global billionaires.

"Based on six years of research and with a fast-paced writing style that interweaves multiple stories, this illuminating work on the exceedingly influential Koch and his company will be welcomed by all readers of business or politics. Leonard does for Koch what Andrew Sorkin's Too Big To Fail did for the 2008 financial crisis." Library Journal.

Levy, Steven

In the plex : how Google thinks, works, and shapes our lives / Steven Levy. Simon & Schuster 2011. 352 p. **338.7**

1. Google (Firm) 2. Google. 3. Internet industry and trade 4. Internet programming 5. Web search engines 6. Internet searching.
ISBN 9781416596585

LC 2010049964

The world according to Google: biography of a search engine -- Googlenomics: cracking the code on internet profits -- Don't be evil: how Google built its culture -- Google's cloud: how Google built data centers and killed the hard drive -- Outside the box: the Google phone company. and the Google t.v. company -- Guge: Google moral dilemma in China -- Google.gov: is what's good for Google, good for government or the public? -- Epilogue: chasing tail lights: trying to crack the social code.

"This is the most comprehensive, intelligent and readable analysis of Google to date. Levy is particularly good on how those behind Google think and work. [This work] teems with original insight into Google's most controversial affairs." The New Scientist.

Macy, Beth

★**Factory** man : how one furniture maker battled offshoring, stayed local--and helped save an American town / Beth Macy. Little Brown & Co., 2014. 368 p. **338.7**

1. Bassett Furniture Industries. 2. Globalization (Economics) -- Employment effects. 3. Furniture industry and trade. 4. Labor costs. 5. Family businesses. 6. Virginia -- Economic conditions. 7. China -- Foreign relations United States. 8. United States -- Foreign relations China.
ISBN 9780316231435

LC 2014937343

ALA Notable Book, 2015.

Describes how the chairman of Vaughan-Bassett Furniture fought for his more than 700 employees in a small Virginia town using legal maneuvers, factory efficiencies and his wits and determination in the wake of sales losses to cheap Asian furniture imports.

"Macy's down-to-earth writing style and abundance of personal stories from manufacturing's beleaguered front lines make her work a stirring critique of globalization." Booklist.

Magner, Mike

Poisoned legacy : the human cost of BP's rise to power

/ Mike Magner. St. Martin's Press, c2011. 384 p. **338.7**

1. British Petroleum Company. 2. Oil industry and trade -- Moral and ethical aspects. 3. Oil -- Refining. 4. Oil workers -- Health and hygiene -- United States. 5. Corporations.
ISBN 9780312554941

LC 2010054461

An exposé on British oil giant BP not only looks at the massive Deepwater Horizon explosion and oil spill but also the company's ongoing history of environmental and safety violations.

Maxfield, Katherine

Starting up Silicon Valley : how ROLM became a cultural icon and Fortune 500 company / Katherine Maxfield. Emerald Book Co., 2014 350 p. **338.7**

1. ROLM Corporation 2. Computer industry and trade 3. Corporate culture 4. Success in business 5. Technological innovations 6. Santa Clara Valley, California
ISBN 9781937110628

LC 2013955281

"Few authors have Maxfield's knack for describing both the forest and the trees, which makes her history of ROLM a worthy model for other histories of Silicon Valley companies. Corporate history with enough drama for a movie." Kirkus.

Mazzeo, Tilar J.

The **secret** of Chanel No. 5 : the intimate history of the world's most famous perfume / Tilar J. Mazzeo. Harper, 2010. 304 p. **338.7**

1. Chanel, Coco, 1883-1971. 2. Parfums Chanel (Firm) 3. Perfumes industry and trade 4. Perfumes. 5. Fashion designers. 6. Odors. 7. France.
ISBN 9780061791017

LC 2010015284

Tilar Mazzeo shares her journey to discover the secret behind the creation, iconic status, and extraordinary success of Chanel No. 5, the world's most famous perfume.

"This unauthorized biography of a scent unearths the roots of the creation and fame of Coco Chanel's famous perfume. Mazzeo's lush prose covers relevant aspects of Coco Chanel's life, from the stark beauty of the orphanage where she was raised to the glamour and luxury of her adulthood, to the scents that wove through her life and shaped the development of her signature perfume. However, the book never bogs down in the details--despite the extensive research showcased in the bibliography--and a smooth pacing keeps it moving along at a fast clip." Library Journal.

Micklethwait, John

The **company** : a short history of a revolutionary idea / John Micklethwait and Adrian Wooldridge. Modern Library, 2003. xxiii, 227 p. **338.7**

1. Corporations -- History. 2. Incorporation. 3. Entrepreneurship -- History. 4. Business -- History.
ISBN 0679642498

LC 2002026429

In The Company, the largely unknown history of the joint-stock company is presented by the editors of The Economist.

"In this history of the joint-stock company, Micklethwait and Wooldridge trace its progress from Assyrian partnership agreements through the 16th- and 17th-century European charter companies that opened trade with distant parts of the world, to today's multinationals. The authors' breadth of knowledge is impressive. They infuse their engaging prose with a wide range of cultural, historical and literary references, with quotes from poets to presidents. Moreover, the authors argue that for all the change companies have engendered over time, their force has been for an aggregate good." Publishers Weekly.

Robertson, David C. (David Chandler)

Brick by brick : how LEGO rewrote the rules of innovation and conquered the global toy industry / David C. Robertson and Bill Breen. Crown Business, 2013. 304 p. **338.7**

1. LEGO koncernen (Denmark) 2. LEGO toys. 3. Toy industry and trade 4. Toys
ISBN 9780307951601

LC 2013004798

The authors take you inside the LEGO you've never seen. By following the teams that are inventing some of the world's best-loved toys, it spotlights the company's disciplined approach to harnessing creativity and recounts one of the most remarkable business transformations in recent memory.

Taulbert, Clifton L.

Who owns the ice house? : eight life lessons from an unlikely entrepreneur / Clifton L. Taulbert and Gary G. Schoeniger. ELI Press, [2010] 178 p. ; **338.7**

1. Taulbert, Clifton L. 2. Success in business 3. Entrepreneurship 4. New businesses 5. Advice 6. Mississippi
ISBN 9780971305915

LC bl2014054716

Drawing on the life lessons that Clifton Taulbert learned from his Uncle Cleve, chronicles Taulbert's journey from life in the Mississippi Delta at the height of legal segregation to being recognized as one of our nation's most outstanding emerging entrepreneurs.

338.7092 Business enterprises--Biography

Cabot, Heather

Geek girl rising : inside the sisterhood shaking up tech / Heather Cabot and Samantha Walravens. St Martins Pr., 2017. 256 p. **338.7092**

1. Technology 2. Women entrepreneurs 3. Technological innovations 4. Gender wars
ISBN 9781250112262

LC 2017001937

A former ABC News correspondent and the editor of the New York Times-acclaimed anthology Torn counsel today's women on how to use technology to start their own businesses, invest in women's ventures and challenge male hacker stereotypes, sharing the examples of such innovators as Debbie Sterling and Michelle Phan.

"This enlightening read reveals many problems embedded in start-up culture, but, more importantly, it is an invigorating call to action and testament to the wide-ranging successes of women in this field." Booklist.

338.8 Combinations

Bown, Stephen R.

Merchant kings : when companies ruled the world, 1600-1900 / Stephen R. Bown. Thomas Dunne Books, 2010, c2009. 314 p. : **338.8**

1. Merchants -- Europe 2. Monopolies -- History. 3. International businesses. 4. Merchant ships. 5. Europe -- Commerce. 6. Europe

-- History.
ISBN 9780312616113

Originally published: Vancouver, B.C. : Douglas & McIntyre, 2009.

Traces the historically relevant contributions of six notorious merchant-adventurers who expanded their commercial enterprises to establish the world's first global monopolies, in a series of vignettes that includes profiles of such figures as Jan Pieterszoon Coen of the Dutch East India Company.

"The author has produced a magnificent description of the six great companies, and their leaders, that dominated the Heroic Age of Commerce. Bown demonstrates how the corporations served as stalking horses for kings and parliaments while enriching shareholders and the powerful managers themselves. Bown presents a fascinating look at the men who exploited resources and native peoples while laying the foundations of empires." Publishers Weekly.

Dayen, David

Monopolized : life in the age of corporate power / David Dayen. The New Press, 2020. 336 p. **338.8**

1. Antitrust law 2. Corporations -- Moral and ethical aspects. 3. Business ethics. 4. Corporate power.
ISBN 9781620975411

LC 2019055148

Through vignettes and case studies, the editor of the American Prospect shows what it means to live in this new age of monopoly and how we might resist this corporate hegemony.

"A powerful, necessary call to arms to strengthen the antitrust movement and fight a system whose goal is complete control." Kirkus

MacIntosh, Julie

Dethroning the king : the hostile takeover of Anheuser-Busch, an American icon / Julie MacIntosh. Wiley, 2010. 256 p. **338.8**

1. Busch family 2. Anheuser-Busch, inc. 3. Corporate mergers. 4. Brewing industry and trade 5. Name-brand products. 6. Beer.
ISBN 9780470592700

LC 2010032279

Includes index.

Describes the corporate drama that unfolded behind the scenes when American company Anheuser-Busch was taken over by Belgian company InBev and discusses whether or not this buyout is indicative of America's dwindling financial and political dominance.

"In a narrative that reads as fast as any fiction thriller, . . . MacIntosh details the 2008 takeover of the iconic Anheuser-Busch brewing company by Belgian corporation InBev, focusing particularly on the company's importance to the St. Louis region; its management, or lack thereof, by the Busch family (particularly the August Busches III and IV); and the broader unsettled economic climate of 2008." Library Journal.

Teachout, Zephyr

Break 'em up : recovering our freedom from big ag, big tech, and big money / Zephyr Teachout ; foreword by Senator Bernie Sanders. All Points Books, 2020 320 p. **338.8**

1. Monopolies. 2. Antitrust law 3. Corporations -- Moral and ethical aspects. 4. Wealth
ISBN 125020089X

LC 2019058373

Teachout makes a compelling case that monopolies are the root cause of many of the issues that today's progressives care about; they drive economic inequality, harm the planet, limit the political power of average citizens,and historically-disenfranchised groups bear the brunt of their shameful and irresponsible business practices. In order to build a better future, we must eradicate monopolies from the private sector and create new safeguards that prevent new ones from seizing power. Through her expert analysis of monopolies in several sectors and their impact on courts, journalism, inequality, and politics, Teachout offers a concrete path toward thwarting these enemies of working Americans and reclaiming our democracy before it's too late.

"Attorney and political activist Teachout (Corruption in America) makes a passionate and persuasive case for a revitalized antitrust movement to strengthen democracy and improve the lives of middle- and working-class Americans ... Teachout delivers a forceful, clearly articulated vision of 'moral markets' built on freedom, choice, and human dignity. Progressives will heed this clarion call for reform." Publishers Weekly

338.9 Economic development and growth

Byrd, Rosaly, 1988-

Sustainability made simple : small changes for big impact / Rosaly Byrd and Laurn DeMates. Rowman & Littlefield, 2017 x, 203 p. : **338.9**

1. Sustainability 2. Sustainable living
ISBN 9781442269095

LC 2016032731

Sustainability Made Simple explores the relationship between everyday life and the intricate global environmental issues of today, illustrating how small changes in daily routines and mentalities can add up to a big impact. --Provided by publisher

"Looking at such regular activities as grocery shopping, household cleaning, gardening, and traveling, the authors offer practical advice regarding small but essential changes that can be easily adopted. Helpful sidebars list environmentally sound companies and products, pinpoint specific behaviors, and highlight current trends." Booklist

Hayek, Friedrich A. von (Friedrich August), 1899-1992

The **road** to serfdom : text and documents / F.A. Hayek ; edited by Bruce Caldwell. University of Chicago Press, 2007, c1944. xi, 283 p. ; **338.9**

1. Economic policy. 2. Totalitarianism. 3. Political science -- Philosophy. 4. Production control. 5. United States -- Economic conditions -- 20th century 6. United States -- Politics and government -- 20th century.
ISBN 9780226320540

Originally published in 1944, this book offers persuasive warnings against the dangers of central planning, along with what Orwell described as "an eloquent defense of laissez-faire capitalism." Hayek shows that the idea that "under a dictatorial government you can be free inside," is nothing less than a grievous fallacy. Such dictatorial governments prevent individual freedoms and they often use psychological measures to perform "an alteration of the character of the people." Gradually, the people yield their individuality to the point where they become part of the collectivist mass.

Sachs, Jeffrey

The **age** of sustainable development / Jeffrey D. Sachs. Columbia University Press, 2015. xvi, 543 p. : **338.9**

1. Sustainable development 2. Energy consumption. 3. Economics -- Social aspects. 4. Renewable energy sources.
ISBN 9780231173148

LC 2014034070

Presents a practical framework to address the seemingly intractable worldwide problems of persistent extreme poverty, environmental degradation, and political-economic injustice: sustainable development.

Sachs explains how modern societies can develop economically, equitably, and sustainably.

"Overall, Sachs's book provides a basic but ambitious argument: to reverse current unsustainable trends, global warming must be mitigated, extreme poverty must end, gender imbalance must be corrected, and access to basic health care and education must be granted to all." Choice.

338.91 International development and growth

Steil, Benn

★The **Marshall** Plan : dawn of the Cold War / Benn Steil. Simon & Schuster, 2018 592 p. **338.91**

1. Marshall Plan, 1948-1952 2. Economic assistance, American 3. Economic assistance. 4. World politics 5. Europe -- Economic conditions -- 1945- 6. United States -- Foreign economic relations Europe. 7. Europe -- Foreign economic relations United States.

ISBN 9781501102370

LC 2017301149

American History Book Prize, 2018.

The award-winning author of The Battle of Bretton Woods traces the dramatic history of the Marshall Plan and the ambitious efforts of Secretary of State George C. Marshall to reconstruct western Europe as a bulwark against communist authoritarianism, tracing a two-year period that shaped the collapse of postwar U.S.-Soviet relations and the beginning of the Cold War.

"Political history is often a tough slog, but Steil writes a vivid, opinionated narrative full of colorful characters, dramatic scenarios, villains, and genuine heroes, and the good guys won. It will be the definitive account for years to come." Kirkus.

339.2 Distribution of income and wealth

Milanovic, Branko

The **have** and the have-nots : a short and idiosyncratic history of global inequality / Branko Milanovic. Basic Books, 2010. 236 p. **339.2**

1. Income distribution -- History. 2. Economic assistance. 3. Wealth -- History. 4. Poverty -- History.

ISBN 9780465019748

LC 2010029295

A leading economist at the World Bank's research division traces the history of financial inequality as reflected in famous stories, analyzing such examples as the monetary disparities between Elizabeth Bennet and Mr. Darcy and the assets of wealthy ancient Romans compared to today's super-rich.

Noah, Timothy

The **great** divergence : America's growing inequality crisis and what we can do about it / Timothy Noah. Bloomsbury, c2012. 264 p. : **339.2**

1. Income distribution -- United States. 2. Inequality -- United States. 3. Wealth -- United States. 4. Poverty -- United States. 5. United States -- Economic conditions.

ISBN 9781608196333

LC 2011048447

Critically assesses income inequality in America and the ways it threatens democracy, tracing disturbing income ratio trends throughout the past three decades while outlining an urgent call for nonpartisan solutions.

Piketty, Thomas, 1971-

The **economics** of inequality / Thomas Piketty, translated by Arthur Goldhammer. Belknap Press of Harvard University Press, 2015, c1997 144 p. **339.2**

1. Income distribution 2. Capitalism and inequality. 3. Equality -- Economic aspects. 4. Resource allocation.

ISBN 9780674504806

LC 2015008813

Originally published in French as Economie des inegalites, 1997

Thomas Piketty--whose Capital in the Twenty-First Century pushed inequality to the forefront of public debate--wroteThe Economics of Inequality as an introduction to the conceptual and factual background necessary for interpreting changes in economic inequality over time. This concise text has established itself as an indispensable guide for students and general readers in France, where it has been regularly updated and revised. Translated by Arthur Goldhammer, The Economics of Inequality now appears in English for the first time.

"Most readers will be better served by Capital in the Twenty-First Century, leaving students and economists as the likeliest audience for this title." Library Journal.

Ridley, Matt

The **rational** optimist : how prosperity evolves / Matt Ridley. Harper, 2010. 438 p. : **339.2**

1. Practical reason. 2. Optimism. 3. Prosperity. 4. Wealth.

ISBN 9780061452055

LC 2010004907

By looking at human history from its very beginning, the author argues disasters, downturns and setbacks are just part of a millenia-long cycle of increasing prosperity that will continue through the 21st century and beyond.

"The author posits that as long as civilization engages in exchange and specialization, we will be able to reinvent ourselves and responsibly use earthly resources ad infinitum. Ridley puts current perceptions about violence, wealth, and the environment into historical perspective, reaching back thousands of years to advocate global free trade, smaller government, and the use of fossil fuels. He confidently takes on the experts, from modern sociologists who fret over the current level of violence in the world to environmentalists who disdain genetically modified crops. An ambitious and sunny paean to human ingenuity, this is an argument for why ambitious optimism is morally mandatory." Publishers Weekly.

Schwartz, Nelson

The **velvet** rope economy : how inequality became big business / Nelson Schwartz. Doubleday, 2020 304 p. **339.2**

1. Income distribution -- United States. 2. Classism -- United States. 3. Inequality 4. Consumerism 5. United States -- Economic conditions -- 21st century.

ISBN 9780385543088

LC 2019021223

A New York Times business reporter investigates the invisible velvet rope that separates the rich from the middle- and working-class in America and how business innovators have exploited this divide catering to the wealthy while creating obstacles for everyone else.

"Economists and business professionals will be well-served by this insightful analysis, as will social activists and all those concerned by the growing separation between rich and poor." Library Journal

339.4 Factors affecting income and wealth

Banerjee, Abhijit V.
Poor economics : a radical rethinking of the way to fight global poverty / Abhijit V. Banerjee and Esther Duflo. PublicAffairs, c2011. xi, 303 p. ; **339.4**

1. Economic assistance -- Developing countries. 2. Poverty -- Prevention. 3. Poor people.
ISBN 9781586487980

LC 2010050938

"Billions of government dollars, and thousands of charitable organizations and NGOs, are dedicated to helping the world's poor. But much of the work they do is based on assumptions that are untested generalizations at best, flat out harmful misperceptions at worst. Banerjee and Duflo have pioneered the use of randomized control trials in development economics. Work based on these principles, supervised by the Poverty Action Lab at MIT, is being carried out in dozens of countries. Their work transforms certain presumptions: that microfinance is a cure-all, that schooling equals learning, that poverty at the level of 99 cents a day is just a more extreme version of the experience any of us have when our income falls uncomfortably low. Throughout, the authors emphasize that life for the poor is simply not like life for everyone else: it is a much more perilous adventure, denied many of the cushions and advantages that are routinely provided to the more affluent".-- Provided by publisher.

"This book draws on a variety of evidence, not limiting itself to the results of randomised trials, as if they are the only route to truth. And the authors' interest is not confined to what works, but also to how and why it works. Indeed, Ms Duflo and Mr Banerjee, perhaps more than some of their disciples, are able theorists as well as thoroughgoing empiricists." The Economist.

Cohen, Lizabeth
A **consumers'** republic : the politics of mass consumption in postwar America / Lizabeth Cohen. Knopf, 2003. 567 p. : **339.4**

1. Consumer economics. 2. Consumer behavior -- United States. 3. Equality. 4. United States -- Social conditions -- 1980- 5. United States -- Economic conditions -- 1933-1945. 6. United States -- Economic conditions -- 1945-
ISBN 0375407502

LC 2002141599

An illuminating social and political history describes how mass consumption and the pursuit of prosperity transformed American life during the second half of the twentieth century, detailing the rise of political activism through the civil rights and consumer movements, the suburbanization of metropolitan areas, the changing relationship of Americans with government, and more.

"Without question, this is a difficult, demanding, and dense bookbut it is also a greatly significant contribution to business literature. Cohen submits a copiously researched, brilliantly conceived, and ultimately quite instructive study of American economics since the Depression." Booklist.

Desmond, Matthew
★**Evicted** : poverty and profit in the American city / Matthew Desmond. Crown, 2016. 432 p. **339.4**

1. Low-income housing 2. Eviction 3. Poverty -- United States. 4. Poor families
ISBN 9780553447439

LC 2015027374

ALA Notable Book, 2017.
Andrew Carnegie Medal for Excellence in Non-Fiction, 2017.
National Book Critics Circle Award for Non-Fiction, 2016.
Pulitzer Prize for General Nonfiction, 2017.
Robert F. Kennedy Book Award, 2017.
Kirkus Prize for Nonfiction finalist, 2016.

A Harvard sociologist examines the under-represented challenge of eviction as a formidable cause of poverty in America, revealing how millions of people are wrongly forced from their homes and reduced to cycles of extreme disadvantage that are reinforced by dysfunctional legal systems.

Edin, Kathryn J.
$2.00 a day : living on almost nothing in America / Kathryn J. Edin, H. Luke Shaefer. Houghton Mifflin Harcourt 2015. 288 p. **339.4**

1. Poverty 2. Welfare 3. Poor people 4. Income distribution
ISBN 9780544303188

LC 2015004337

A revelatory assessment of poverty in America examines the survival methods employed by households with virtually no income to illuminate disturbing trends in low-wage labor and income inequality.

"An eye-opening account of the lives ensnared in the new poverty cycle." Kirkus.

Gerth, Karl
As China goes, so goes the world : how Chinese consumers are transforming everything / Karl Gerth. Hill and Wang, 2011. 272 p. **339.4**

1. Consumerism -- China 2. Consumer economics 3. Consumer behavior -- China 4. Economic history -- 21st century. 5. China -- Economic conditions
ISBN 9780809026890

LC bl2013023456

Shares cautionary predictions about China's evolving consumer society and economy, revealing how the country's rapid development of a western-influenced consumer culture is resulting in a Chinese customer base that makes profoundly relevant, modern-world lifestyle choices.

Gordon, Robert J. (Robert James), 1940-
★The **rise** and fall of American growth : the U.S. standard of living since the Civil War / Robert J. Gordon. Princeton University Press, 2016 776 p. **339.4**

1. Cost and standard of living -- United States -- History. 2. Economics 3. Economic history 4. United States -- Economic conditions -- 1865-1918. 5. United States -- Economic conditions -- 1918-1945. 6. United States -- Economic conditions -- 1945-
ISBN 9780691147727

LC 2015027560

Discusses how the era of growth and innovations, which included the widespread affordability of amazing advances, from electricity to air travel, has ended and warns that the younger generation may be the first ever not to exceed their parents' standard of living.

"A masterful study to be read and reread by anyone interested in today's political economy." Kirkus.

Miller, Geoffrey, 1965-
Spent : sex, status, and the secrets of consumerism / Geoffrey Miller. Viking, 2009. 384 p. **339.4**

1. Consumer economics 2. Consumer behavior. 3. Behavioral economics 4. Human nature
ISBN 9780670020621

LC 2008051554

"Since evolutionary psychology seeks to examine how natural selection acts on psychological and mental traits, Miller applies this knowledge to help us understand what actually motivates us to buy. He pokes fun at popular culture and at the things we buy and flaunt to inflate our self-esteem and try to make ourselves more attractive. Personality research can inform the study of consumer behavior, and Miller shows us how having a better understanding of our own personalities will help us avoid the pitfalls of runaway consumerism." Library Journal.

Novogratz, Jacqueline

The **blue** sweater : bridging the gap between rich and poor in an interconnected world / Jacqueline Novogratz. Rodale, 2009. 272 p. **339.4**

1. Poverty. 2. Economic assistance. 3. Charities. 4. Microlending
ISBN 9781594869150
LC 2008043621

Includes index.

A narrative account of the author's investigation into the world's economic gap describes her rediscovery of a blue sweater she had given away to Goodwill and found on a child in Rwanda, in a passionate call to action that relates her work as a venture capitalist on behalf of impoverished nations.

Rivlin, Gary

Broke, USA : from pawnshops to Poverty, Inc. : how the working poor became big business / Gary Rivlin. Harper, 2010. 358 p. **339.4**

1. Poor people. 2. Poverty. 3. Income. 4. Social classes -- United States 5. United States -- Economic conditions -- 21st century.
ISBN 9780061733215
LC 2010002874

Delivers a shocking look at the under-reported poverty industry, which aims to mine the thin wallets of the country's poor through such ventures as subprime loans, pawn shops, check-cashing businesses, instant tax refunds, payday loans and more.

"A timely, important, and deeply disturbing look at the cycle of debt of the nation's most vulnerable." Publishers Weekly.

Roberts, James A. (James Andrew)

Shiny objects : why we spend money we don't have in search of happiness we can't buy / James A. Roberts. HarperOne, c2011. 368 p. **339.4**

1. Consumer economics 2. American Dream. 3. Materialism -- United States.
ISBN 9780062093608
LC 2010005086

A leading expert on consumer behavior delves into the American obsession with consumerism, exploring the evolution of the American Dream, revealing a direct link between how much we spend and the negative impact on our happiness, and offering practical advice for correcting this materialistic trend.

339.5 Macroeconomic policy

Steil, Benn

The **battle** of Bretton Woods : John Maynard Keynes, Harry Dexter White, and the making of a new world order / Benn Steil. Princeton University Press, c2013. 456 p. **339.5**

1. Keynes, John Maynard, 1883-1946. 2. White, Harry Dexter, 1892-1948. 3. United Nations Monetary and Financial Conference (1944 : Bretton Woods, N.H.) 4. Monetary policy -- History -- 20th century 5. International finance -- History -- 20th century. 6. Economics 7. Bretton Woods Conference, July 1944.
ISBN 9780691149097
LC 2012035709

"A Council on Foreign Relations Book."

Reveals how the blueprint for the post-World War II economic order was actually drawn.

340 Law

Garner, Bryan A,

Black's law dictionary / Bryan A. Garner, editor in chief. Thomson Reuters, 2014 xxxv, 2016 p. ; **340**

1. Law -- United States -- Dictionaries. 2. Law -- Dictionaries.
ISBN 9780314621306
LC 2015372206

Provides definitions of legal terms and phrases used in various branches of law, in a new edition that includes a more extensive dating of terms, over 7,500 new entries, and increased bibliographic coverage.

Kritzer, Herbert M., 1947-

Legal systems of the world : a political, social, and cultural encyclopedia / edited by Herbert M. Kritzer. ABC-CLIO, c2002. 4 v. (x, 1883 p.) : **340**

1. Law -- Encyclopedias.
ISBN 9781576072318
LC 2002002659

"Written by an international team of more than 350 legal scholars, the more than 400 signed entries cover legal systems of countries from around the world, Australia, and the provinces of Canada; transnational systems (International Court of Justice); general systems (Islamlic law, indigenous, and folk legal systems); and key concepts. Each country profile includes a map with an inset of its location on the globe, general information about the country, its history, diagrams of its court structure, the evolution of its legal framework, its current structure, staffing or how judges are appointed, any specialized judicial bodies (i.e. military court), and the impact that the legal system has had on the country. Articles conclude with references and a bibliography. Academic and public libraries will find this source invaluable for comparative studies in legal and judicial systems."--"The Best of the Best Reference Sources," American Libraries, May 2003.

340.071 Law schools

Tamanaha, Brian Z.

Failing law schools / Brian Z. Tamanaha. The University of Chicago, Ill. :Press, 2012. xvi, 235 p. ; **340.071**

1. American Bar Association. 2. Law schools -- United States -- Finance 3. Law -- Study and teaching -- United States
ISBN 9780226923611
LC 2012006829

"Why does law school cost so much, and is it worth it? Tamanaha . . . takes up these questions, recently subject to vigorous debate in the press and online." Library Journal

340.072 Law--Research

Tucker, Virginia, 1953-

Finding the answers to legal questions / Virginia M. Tucker, Marc Lampson. ALA Neal-Schuman, 2018 xxiv, 232 p. : **340.072**

1. Law -- United States 2. Legal research -- United States
ISBN 9780838915691

LC 2017056093

"This timely, clearly organized, and easy-to-use resource is an ideal text for LIS students preparing for careers as librarians. It provides an overview of the basic structure of the U.S. legal system; how-to instructions for finding primary law in printsources, free websites and pay-for-view databases; information on how to evaluate the trustworthiness of online and print resources; tips for conducting a legal reference interview; and guidance for handling common legal questions, such as lawsuits, family law, landlord-tenant disputes, and wills".-- Provided by publisher.

340.09 History, geographic treatment, biography of law

Roffer, Michael H.

The **law** book : from Hammurabi to the international criminal court, 250 milestones in the history of law / Michael H. Roffer. Sterling, 2015 528 p. : **340.09**

1. Law -- History
ISBN 9781454901686

LC bl2015050164

A visually stunning guide that is organized chronologically explores 250 of the most fundamental, far-reaching and often-controversial cases, laws and trials that have profoundly changed the world--for good or bad--presenting a comprehensive look at the rules by which people live their lives.

"This high quality and engaging book is recommended for most public libraries, where it will be appreciated more in a browsing collection than on a reference shelf." Booklist.

340.5 Legal systems

Ali-Karamali, Sumbul, 1964-

Demystifying Shariah : what it is, how it works, and why it's not taking over our country / Sumbul Ali-Karamali. Beacon Press, 2020. 256 p. **340.5**

1. Islamic law 2. Stereotypes (Social psychology) 3. Islamophobia 4. Sharia (Islamic religious practice) 5. United States -- Religion
ISBN 9780807038000

LC 2019037396

A direct counterpoint to fear mongering headlines about shariah law tells the real story, eliminating stereotypes and assumptions with compassion, irony, and humor. Introducing us to the basic principles, goals and general development of shariah law, a Muslim American legal expert explains that shariah is religious rules and recommendations that provide Muslims with guidance in various aspects of life and describes the key lies and misunderstandings about shariah circulating in our public discourse.

"Taking something as complex as the Sharia and exploring it succinctly, lucidly, and without oversimplification is where this book excels. While a background in Islam is not required, some basic understanding of the faith will help readers. Well-suited--and highly recommended--for general readers (both Muslim and non-Muslim) with an interest in Sharia." Booklist

341.23 United Nations

Fasulo, Linda M.

★An **insider's** guide to the UN / Linda Fasulo. Yale University Press, c2015. 272 p. **341.23**

1. United Nations Popular works. 2. United Nations -- History. 3. United Nations Management. 4. United Nations Officials and employees. 5. Diplomats. 6. International relations. 7. World politics.
ISBN 9780300203653

LC 2003010668

Termed "the indispensable source on the United Nations" by Joseph S. Nye of Harvard's Kennedy School of Government, this book is now fully revised and updated to include new material on fragile states, R2P (responsibility to protect), recent Security Council issues such as the revolts in Libya and Syria, and a greatly expanded section on understanding and participating in a Model UN. -- Provided by publisher.

341.23092 United Nations--Biography

Somaiya, Ravi

The **golden** thread : the Cold War mystery surrounding the death of Dag Hammarskjold / Ravi Somaiya. Twelve, 2020. 320 p. **341.23092**

1. Hammarskjold, Dag, 1905-1961 2. Secretaries-General (United Nations) 3. United Nations. 4. United Nations Operation in the Congo 5. Espionage 6. International intrigue. 7. Assassination. 8. Airplane accidents. 9. Congo, Democratic Republic -- History -- Civil War, 1960-1965. 10. Africa -- Foreign relations -- 1945-1960. 11. Congo (Democratic Republic) -- History -- Civil War, 1960-1965 12. Africa. 13. Africa -- Foreign relations -- 1960-
ISBN 9781455536542

LC 2019058754

Investigates the mystery behind the 1961 death of UN Secretary General Dag Hammarskjold, drawing on previously undisclosed evidence, recently revealed firsthand accounts and groundbreaking interviews to identify the powerful international cabal behind his death.

"Equal parts true crime, spy thriller, and work of international political intrigue, this thought-provoking work explores the death of Dag Hammarskjold, a Swedish diplomat and the second secretary general of the United Nations." Library Journal

341.4 Jurisdiction over physical space human rights

Waldman, Steven

Sacred liberty : America's long, bloody, and ongoing struggle for religious freedom / Steve Waldman. HarperOne, 2019. 288 p. **341.4**

1. United States. Constitution. 1st Amendment. 2. Freedom of religion -- History. 3. Freedom of religion -- United States. 4. Religion 5. Church and state 6. United States -- Religion 7. United States -- History
ISBN 9780062743145

LC bl2019006229

Argues that religious liberty is America's greatest innovation and the protection of religious minorities and the separation of church and state are at risk today.

341.5 Disputes and conflicts between states

Bass, Gary Jonathan, 1969-

Freedom's battle : the origins of humanitarian intervention / Gary J. Bass. Alfred A. Knopf, 2008. 528 p. **341.5**

1. Intervention (International relations) -- History. 2. Intervention (International law) 3. Humanitarian assistance. 4. Human rights policy.

ISBN 9780307266484

LC 2007052252

Traces the history of international humanitarian intervention, looking back over more than two hundred years to reveal the cultural and political factors that spawned early human rights activists and the role of a free press that exposed atrocities, from Greek oppression by the Ottoman Empire to the U.S. campaign against the 1915 Armenian genocide.

"This history of nineteenth-century campaigns to stop atrocities in Greece, Syria, and Bulgaria is a corrective to the idea that humanitarian interventions are a product of the dreamy interlude between 1989 and 9/11. The compelling narrative, rich with accounts of parliamentary debate and battlefield confrontation, presents a world of familiar political and military concerns, from the pressure of nonstop media coverage to the importance of a clear exit strategy. Bass's thesis that humanitarianism long preceded the crises of Bosnia and Rwanda is persuasive." The New Yorker.

341.6 Law of war

Lamb, Christina

Our bodies, their battlefields : war through the lives of women / Christina Lamb. Scribner, 2020 320 p. **341.6**

1. Women and war 2. Violence against women 3. Rape 4. War

ISBN 9781501199172

LC bl2020052300

Lamb chronicles extraordinary tragedy and challenges in the lives of women in wartime. And none is more devastating than the increase of the use of rape as a weapon of war. Told as a journey, and structured by country, Our Bodies, Their Battlefields gives these women voice.

"A searing, absolutely necessary expose of the uses of rape in recent wars and of global injustices to the survivors." Kirkus

341.69 War crimes

Rashke, Richard

★**Useful** enemies : John Demanjuk and America's open-door policy for Nazi war criminals / Richard Rashke. HarperCollins, 2013. xvii, 621 p. **341.69**

1. Nazis. 2. War crimes. 3. Immigration and emigration.

ISBN 9781883285517

LC 2012285813

"A richly researched, gripping narrative about war, suffering, survival, corruption, injustice and morality." Kirkus.

342.42 Law--England

Wise, Steven M.

Though the heavens may fall : the landmark trial that led to the end of human slavery / Steven M. Wise. Da Capo Press, 2005. xvi, 282 p. : **342.42**

1. Sommersett, James Trials, litigation, etc. 2. Slavery -- Law and legislation -- England -- History -- 18th century. 3. Trials. 4. Escapes. 5. Politicians. 6. England -- History -- 18th century.

ISBN 9780738206950

LC 2004025346

"A Merloyd Lawrence book."

Describes one of the most important and significant legal cases in history, the trial of James Somerset, which featured an incredible array of colorful figures fighting a landmark battle that would eventually lead to the end of slavery in the western world. 50,000 first prinitng.

"The author has an eye for evocative detail and an interest in the trappings and procedures of an 18th-century courtroom that do as much to engage the reader as the drama of the trials themselves." New York Times Book Review.

342.73 Constitutional law--United States

Amar, Akhil Reed

The **constitution** today : timeless lessons for the issues of our era / Akhil Reed Amar. Basic Books, 2016. 464 p. **342.73**

1. United States. Supreme Court -- History. 2. Constitutional history. 3. Constitutional law. 4. Essays

ISBN 9780465096336

LC 2016023102

The Sterling Professor of Law and Political Science at Yale University considers the most bitterly contested debates of the last two decades--from gun control to gay marriage, affirmative action to criminal procedure, Bill Clinton's impeachment to Obamacare--helping readers to understand America's Constitution and its relevance today.

Barron, David J.

Waging war : the clash between presidents and Congress, 1776 to ISIS / David J. Barron. Simon & Schuster, 2016. 496 p. **342.73**

1. United States. Congress -- History. 2. War and emergency powers. 3. War, Declaration of. 4. Executive power -- United States -- History. 5. Legislative power -- United States -- History. 6. United States -- Politics and government.

ISBN 9781451681970

A United States Circuit Judge describes the historical struggles that took place between sitting presidents and Congress over who has the power to start wars, including the American Revolution, the War of 1812 and the Civil War, all the way up through the fight against ISIS.

Brettschneider, Corey Lang

The **oath** and the office : a guide to the Constitution for future presidents / Corey Brettschneider. W.W. Norton & Company, 2018. 224 p. **342.73**

1. United States. Constitution. 2. United States. Constitution. 1st-10th Amendments. 3. United States. Congress Powers and duties. 4. Presidents -- Legal status, laws, etc. -- United States. 5. Executive power -- United States. 6. Constitutional law -- United States. 7. Constitutional history -- United States. 8. United States -- Politics and government.

ISBN 9780393652123

LC 2018016664

An essential guide to the presidential powers and limits of the Constitution answers timely questions about the checks and balances of government power and how the people of today's America can make informed voting and running decisions.

"The author offers a clear explanation of many complex issues, such as the provisions of the 14th Amendment, which guarantees equal protection under the law; and the process involved in impeachment, including the question of whether obstruction of justice is an impeachable offense. A clear-eyed, accessible, and informative primer: vital reading for all Americans." Kirkus.

Engel, Jeffrey A.,

Impeachment : an American history / Jeffrey A. Engel, Jon Meacham, Timoth Naftali, Peter Baker. Modern Library, 2018. 160 p. **342.73**

1. Nixon, Richard M. (Richard Milhous), 1913-1994 Impeachment 2. Johnson, Andrew, 1808-1875 Impeachment 3. Clinton, Bill, 1946- Impeachment 4. Impeachments -- United States 5. Politicians 6. Presidents -- United States 7. Constitutional law 8. United States -- Politics and government

ISBN 9781984853783

LC 2018034718

Includes index.

Four experts on the American presidency review the only three impeachment cases from history--against Andrew Johnson, Richard Nixon and Bill Clinton--and explore its power and meaning for today.

Foner, Eric, 1943-

The **second** founding : how the Civil War and Reconstruction remade the Constitution / Eric Foner. W.W. Norton & Company, 2019. 288 p. **342.73**

1. United States. Constitution. 13th-15th Amendments 2. Constitutional history 3. Reconstruction (United States history) 4. Constitutional law 5. Judicial process 6. United States -- History -- Civil War, 1861-1865 -- Law and legislation 7. United States -- Race relations -- Political aspects

ISBN 9780393652574

LC 2019014793

The Declaration of Independence announced equality as an American ideal, but it took the Civil War and the subsequent adoption of three constitutional amendments to establish that ideal as American law. The author of The Fiery Trial presents a timely history of the constitutional changes that built or compromised equality within America's foundation, documenting alarming parallels between the Jim Crow era and the present day.

"Readers invested in social equality will find Foners guarded optimism about the possibility of judicial activism in this area inspiring, and both casual readers and those well-versed in American legal history will benefit from his clear prose and insightful exploration of constitutional history." Publishers Weekly.

Hall, Kermit L., 1934-2006

The **Oxford** guide to United States Supreme Court decisions / edited by Kermit L. Hall, James W. Ely, Jr. Oxford University Press, 2009. xvi, 499 p. ; **342.73002643**

1. Constitutional law -- United States -- Encyclopedias 2. Constitutional law -- United States -- Digests 3. Encyclopedias

ISBN 9780195379396

LC 2008023763

Rev. ed. of: The Oxford guide to United States Supreme Court decisions / edited by Kermit L. Hall. 1999.

This new edition of the Guide contains more than 450 entries on major Supreme Court cases, including 53 new entries on the latest landmark rulings. --Provided by publisher

“An outstanding single-volume reference.” Library Journal

Rabban, David M., 1949-

Free speech in its forgotten years / David M. Rabban. Cambridge University Press, 1997. xi, 404 p. : **342.73**

1. Freedom of speech -- History. 2. United States -- History.

ISBN 0521620139

LC 97015281

"The author focuses on free speech issues between the Civil War and World War I. Through an impressive marshaling of controversies, cases, and litigants, he persuasively argues that libertarian radicalism and the Free Speech League . . . deserves much of the credit for pushing valuable First Amendment issues to the forefront of American social, political, and legal circles. This enlightening work fills a void in First Amendment civil liberties studies." Library Journal.

Simon, James F.

What kind of nation : Thomas Jefferson, John Marshall, and the epic struggle to create a United States / James F. Simon. Simon & Schuster, 2002. 348 p. **342.73**

1. Jefferson, Thomas, 1743-1826. 2. Marshall, John, 1755-1835. 3. United States. Supreme Court -- History. 4. Constitutional history. 5. State rights (United States constitutional law) 6. Federal government -- United States -- History. 7. Political questions and judicial power -- United States -- History. 8. United States -- Politics and government -- 1783-1809.

ISBN 9780684848709

LC 2001055027

A re-creation of the battle between a President and a Chief Justice reveals how John Marshall's view that a strong federal government and an independent judiciary provide the best protection for the Constitution and the people still exists today.

"Simon's enlivening account proves that writing about constitutional law needn't be the dry preserve of academics." Booklist.

Sullivan, Kevin, 1959-

★**Trump** on trial : the investigation, impeachment, acquittal and aftermath / Kevin Sullivan and Mary Jordan. Scribner, 2020 xxvi, 532 p. **342.73**

1. Trump, Donald, 1946- Impeachment 2. Presidents -- United States -- Impeachment 3. Trials (Impeachment) -- United States 4. Abuse of administrative power 5. Politicians 6. United States -- Politics and government -- 2017- 7. United States -- Foreign relations Ukraine 8. Ukraine -- Foreign relations United States

ISBN 9781982152994

LC bl2020019453

In the spring of 2019, Speaker of the House Nancy Pelosi did not favor pursuing President Trump's impeachment. Her view was: "He's just not worth it." But by September, after a whistleblower complaint suggesting that Trump had used his office for his political benefit, Pelosi decided to risk it. The impeachment inquiry led to charges of abuse of power and obstruction of Congress, a gamble that ultimately meant Trump would be the first impeached president on the ballot in US history. Kevin Sullivan and Mary Jordan deftly illuminate the aims and calculations of key figures.

"Including 45 pages of footnotes and an exhaustive index, the granular detail of this history makes it a gift to posterity--and to news junkies--but any reader who does not support Trump will find plenty of useful material. Sets a standard for political storytelling with impeccable research and lively writing." Kirkus

Sunstein, Cass R.

★**Impeachment** : a citizen's guide / Cass R. Sunstein. Harvard University Press, 2017. 199 p. ; **342.73**

1. Impeachments -- United States 2. Political obligation 3. Responsibility 4. Trials (Impeachment) -- United States
ISBN 9780674983793

Cass Sunstein considers actual and imaginable arguments for a president's removal, explaining why some cases are easy and others hard, why some arguments for impeachment are judicious and others not. In direct and approachable terms, he dispels the fog surrounding impeachment so that all Americans may use their ultimate civic authority wisely.

"The resulting book is an essential guide to understanding impeachments function within the 'constitutional system as a whole' and a persuasive argument that the impeachment clause places 'the fate of the republic' in the hands of its citizenry." Publishers Weekly.

Tribe, Laurence H.

Uncertain justice : the Roberts court and the constitution / Laurence Tribe, Joshua Matz. Henry Holt and Co., 2014. 352 p. **342.73**

1. United States. Supreme Court 2. Constitutional law 3. Constitutional law -- Social aspects -- United States. 4. United States -- Politics and government
ISBN 9780805099096
LC 2014002845

Includes index.

An assessment of how the Supreme Court under Chief Justice John Roberts is significantly influencing the nation's laws and reinterpreting the Constitution includes in-depth analysis of recent rulings and their implications.

"A well-researched, unsettling investigation of recent trends in the nation's highest court." Kirkus.

United States

The **Mueller** report : the final report of the Special Counsel into Donald Trump, Russia, and collusion / as issued by the Department of Justice ; with an introduction by Alan Dershowitz. Skyhorse Publishing, 2019. 960 p. **342.73**

1. Trump, Donald, 1946- 2. Presidential election, 2016 3. Criminal investigation 4. Elections -- Corrupt practices 5. Corruption investigation 6. United States -- Foreign relations Russia
ISBN 9781510750166
LC bl2019011751

The wait is over. Robert Mueller, a lifelong Republican, has concluded his investigation and submitted its findings to Attorney General William Barr. Special Counsel Robert Mueller III's probe into Russian influence on the 2016 election of Donald Trump--including links between the campaign and Russian interests, obstruction of justice by President Trump, and any other matters that may have arisen in the course of the investigation--has been the focal point of American politics since its inception in May 2017.

"An essential document for anyone concerned with the unfolding constitutional crisis of the Trump presidency and one that helps make sense of current headlines." Kirkus.

342.7302 Constitutions--United States

Amar, Akhil Reed

★**America's** constitution : a biography / Akhil Reed Amar. Random House, c2005. xii, 657 p. : **342.7302**

1. United States. Constitution. 2. Constitution. 3. Constitutional history. 4. Constitutional law. 5. United States -- Politics and government. 6. United States -- History.
ISBN 1400062624
LC 2004061464

Offers an analysis of the history and tenets of the U.S. Constitution, detailing the original intent of the creators of the document, answering questions about the text, and critically assessing the evolution of the Bill of Rights and all other amendments.

"Only rarely do you find a book that embodies scholarship at its most solid and invigorating; this is such a book." Publishers Weekly.

Beeman, Richard R.

★**Plain,** honest men : the making of the American Constitution / Richard Beeman. Random House, 2009. 544 p. **342.7302**

1. United States. Constitutional Convention (1787) 2. Constitutional history 3. Conflict resolution 4. Common good -- History -- 18th century 5. Separation of powers 6. United States -- History -- 18th century
ISBN 9781400065707
LC 2008028841

Demonstrates how the American Constitution was forged through conflict, compromise, and eventually fragile consensus as James Madison and his cohorts devised a plan to radically alter the balance of governmental power.

Ellis, Joseph J.

The **quartet** : orchestrating the second American Revolution, 1783-1789 / Joseph J. Ellis. Alfred A. Knopf, 2015 320 p. **342.7302**

1. Washington, George, 1732-1799 2. Hamilton, Alexander, 1757-1804 3. Jay, John, 1745-1829. 4. Madison, James, 1751-1836. 5. Founding Fathers of the United States. 6. Revolutions -- United States 7. American Revolution, 1775-1783 8. United States -- History -- Revolution, 1775-1783. 9. United States -- Politics and government -- 1783-1789.
ISBN 9780385353403
LC 2014034503

The Pulitzer Prize-winning author of Founding Brothers shares historical insights into America's post-Revolution efforts for independence, citing key debates over the creations of the Articles of Confederation and the Bill of Rights.

"Ellis's approach employs deft characterizations and insights into these politicians and philosophers. With his usual skill, Ellis brings alive what otherwise might seem dry constitutional debates, with apt quotations and bright style." Publishers Weekly.

Klarman, Michael J.

The **framers'** coup : the making of the United States Constitution / Michael J. Klarman. Oxford University Press, 2016. 840 p. **342.7302**

1. United States. Constitution. 2. United States. Constitution. Signers 3. Constitutional history 4. Historic documents 5. Constitutions 6. Founding Fathers of the United States
ISBN 9780199942039
LC 2016009496

"A monumental project carried off to a high degree of excellence." Kirkus.

Madison, James, 1751-1836

★The **Constitutional** Convention : a narrative history : from the notes of James Madison / Edward J. Larson and Michael P. Winship. Modern Library, 2005. x, 229 p. ; **342.7302**

1. United States. Constitutional Convention (1787) 2. United States.

Constitution. 3. Constitutional history -- United States
ISBN 9780812975178

LC 2005041649

Authoritative editions of great classics of world literature feature introductions by acclaimed writers, meticulous translations of foreign literature, commentary by distinguished writers and critics, biographical notes, and a comprehensive Reading Group Guide bound into each volume.

Maier, Pauline, 1938-

Ratification : the people debate the constitution, 1787-1788 / Pauline Maier. Simon & Schuster, 2010. 544 p. **342.7302**

1. Constitution. 2. Constitutional history. 3. Founding fathers of the United States. 4. Civil rights. 5. United States -- Politics and government -- 18th century.
ISBN 9780684868547

LC 2010027709

Draws on the speeches and letters of the United States' founders to recount the dramatic period after the Constitutional Convention and before the Constitution was finally ratified, describing the debates that took place in homes, taverns, and convention halls throughout the colonies.

"On Sept. 17, 1787, the convention that had been sitting in Philadelphia for four months to design a new form of government for the United States adjourned, offering its handiwork to the nation. Almost a year later, on Sept. 13, 1788, Congress declared that the Constitution had been duly ratified, and prescribed the rules for the first presidential election the following year. [This] book shows how America got from the first date to the secondand ultimately to today, since we still live with the same document, however modified." New York Times Book Review.

Meyerson, Michael

Liberty's blueprint : how Madison and Hamilton wrote the federalist papers, defined the constitution, and made democracy safe for the world / Michael I. Meyerson. Basic Books, c2008. 272 p. **342.7302**

1. Hamilton, Alexander, 1757-1804 2. Madison, James, 1751-1836 3. Federalist. 4. Founding fathers of the United States. 5. Constitutional history. 6. Constitutional law. 7. Intellectuals.
ISBN 0465002641

LC 2007035376

Examines how the Federalist Papers were written and the philosophical thinking that shaped the Constitution, and explores how the wisdom of the Papers' main authors can illuminate current discussions of controversial issues.

Paulsen, Michael Stokes

The **Constitution** : an introduction / Michael Stokes Paulsen and Luke Paulsen. Basic Books, 2015. 448 p. **342.7302**

1. United States. Constitution. 2. Constitutional history 3. Constitutional law 4. Political science -- History -- United States 5. United States -- Politics and government
ISBN 9780465053728

LC 2014041943

Offers a lively introduction to the supreme law of the United States, covering the Constitution's history and meaning in clear, accessible terms.

"This is a highly accessible and scholarly but lively look at the nations guiding document." Booklist.

Rakove, Jack N., 1947-

The **annotated** U.S. Constitution and Declaration of Independence / edited by Jack N. Rakove. Belknap Press, 2009. xii, 354 p. : **342.7302**

1. United States. Constitution. 2. United States. Constitution. 1st-27th Amendments. 3. United States. Declaration of Independence. 4. Constitutional law 5. Constitutional history 6. Political science -- History -- United States 7. United States -- History 8. United States -- Politics and government
ISBN 9780674036062

LC 2009022907

The complete text of the US Constitution and Declaration of Independence, including a timeline of key events from 1607 through 2008 and notes by a Pulitzer-prize winning historian providing historical contexts and interpretive commentary.

"The author presents both the Declaration and the Constitution with carefully laid out annotation that's accessible to general readers as well as high school and college students. His extended introduction provides a readable and instructive analysis of how the writing of the Constitution progressed, especially on matters concerning representation, executive power, and creation of the amendments. His annotations often rely upon contemporary usage and meaning from the time of the Declaration of Independence and Constitution . . . and he compares such usage to other documents of the time." Library Journal.

Raphael, Ray

Constitutional myths : what we get wrong and how to get it right / Ray Raphael. The New Press, 2013. 316 p. **342.7302**

1. Constitutional history -- 18th century 2. Political science 3. Democracy. 4. United States -- History -- 1783-1815.
ISBN 9781595588326

LC 2012041849

Aims to dispel myths about the Constitution propagated by both the left and the right.

Urofsky, Melvin I.

Dissent and the Supreme Court : its role in the Court's history and nation's constitutional dialogue / Melvin I. Urofsky. Pantheon Books, 2015. xiii, 528 p. : **342.7302**

1. United States. Supreme Court -- History. 2. Dissenting opinions. 3. Judges. 4. Constitutional law -- Interpretation and construction. 5. Law -- History and criticism. 6. United States -- Politics and government
ISBN 9780307379405

LC 2014048245

An examination of the role of dissent in the Supreme Court and interpretations of the Constitution examines key events throughout the Court's more than two-century history.

"This is an insightful look at dissents as dialogues between the justices that reflect broader dialogues among citizens on the controversial issues of our time." Kirkus.

342.730203 Constitutions--United States--Dictionaries and encyclopedias

Maddex, Robert L., 1942-

The **U.S.** Constitution A to Z / Robert L. Maddex. CQ Press, c2008. xxix, 736 p. : **342.730203**

1. Constitutional law -- United States -- Encyclopedias 2. Constitutional history -- United States -- Encyclopedias 3. Encyclopedias
ISBN 9780872897649

LC 2008021902

Presents alphabetically arranged entries on topics related to the U.S. Constitution, ranging from abortion to zoning, and highlights current controversies and debates.

Schultz, David A. (David Andrew), 1958-

Encyclopedia of the United States Constitution / David Schultz. Facts On File, c2009. 2 v. (xvii, 904 p.) : **342.730203**

1. Constitutional law -- United States

ISBN 0816067635

LC 2008023349

Presents more than seven hundred alphabetically arranged entries on topics related to the U.S. Constitution, covering such areas as affirmative action, freedom of speech, privacy, and environmental regulations.

"This reference source can help high-school students, the general public, and other interested parties comprehend the fundamental concepts, evolutionary character, and historic people and events that have shaped the [Constitution]. . . . The alphabetically arranged entries cover terms, events, people, landmark cases, and issues that help explain the Constitution's history. The appendix provides the Declaration of Independence, the Articles of Confederation, the Constitution, and the Bill of Rights as well as Other Amendments to the Constitution, a U.S. Constitution Time Line, and instructions on locating court cases." Booklist.

342.7303 Constitutional amendments--United States

Vile, John R.

Encyclopedia of constitutional amendments, proposed amendments, and amending issues, 1789-2010 / John R. Vile. ABC-CLIO, c2010. 2 v. (xxxiv, 628, xiv, 28 p.) ; **342.7303**

1. Constitutional amendments -- United States. 2. Constitutional history 3. Encyclopedias

ISBN 1598843168

LC 2010002113

"The author discusses the Constitution, its 27 ratified amendments, and the approximately 11,700 amendments proposed within the titular time frame to present a unique window into American history and politics. The alphabetical format and detailed index make information access a breeze, and the six appendixes provide a reprint of the Constitution along with charts of the number of proposals by decade, key events, and names of individuals submitting the proposals." Library Journal.

342.7308 Constitutional law -- United States -- Groups of people

Bray, Ilona M., 1962-

How to get a green card / Ilona Bray, J.D., and Loida Nicolas Lewis, J.D., ; updated by attorney Kristina Gasson. Nolo, 2016. 402 p. : **342.7308**

1. Aliens -- United States 2. Emigration and immigration law -- United States 3. Green cards

ISBN 9781413322552

LC bl2016032677

Includes index.

A step-by-step guide to obtaining U.S. residency by various nonwork related means, such as political asylum, the visa lottery, or a family member.

★**U.S.** immigration made easy / Ilona Bray, J.D. ; updated by Attorney Richard Link. Nolo, 2017. 670 p. : **342.7308**

1. Emigration and immigration law -- United States

ISBN 9781413323672

LC bl2017004167

Includes index.

Provides a thorough overview of U.S. immigration law, clearly explaining the steps needed to live in the country legally.

Carpenter, Dale, 1966-

Flagrant conduct : the story of Lawrence v. Texas : how a bedroom arrest decriminalized gay Americans / Dale Carpenter. W. W. Norton & Company, 2012. 352 p. **342.7308**

1. Lawrence, John Geddes Trials, litigation, etc. 2. Sodomy (Law) -- Cases 3. Homosexuality -- Law and legislation -- Texas -- Criminal provisions. 4. LGBTQIA rights 5. Gay men -- Rights 6. Lawrence v. Texas, 539 U.S. 558 (2003)

ISBN 9780393062083

LC 2011047245

Lambda Literary Award for LGBT Nonfiction

Provides a detailed legal history and examines the motives of all players involved with the landmark Supreme Court gay rights case that protected consenting adults' rights, regardless of sexual preference, in the bedroom.

Davis, Lennard J., 1949-

Enabling acts : the hidden story of how the Americans with Disabilities Act gave the largest us minority its rights / Lennard Davis. Beacon Press, 2015. 296 p. **342.7308**

1. Americans with Disabilities Act of 1990 2. People with disabilities -- Legal status, laws, etc. 3. Discrimination 4. Services for people with disabilities 5. People with disabilities -- Social conditions

ISBN 9780807071564

LC 2014046510

Published to coincide with the 25th anniversary of the Americans with Disabilities Act (ADA), an acclaimed disability scholar tells the untold story of how a group of leftist Berkeley hippies managed to make an alliance with conservative Republicans to bring about a truly bipartisan bill.

"A lively and well-researched legal saga suited to general readers interested in current events and disability issues." Library Journal.

Davis, Thomas J. (Thomas Joseph)

Plessy v. Ferguson / Thomas J. Davis. Greenwood, c2012. xx, 238 p. ; **342.7308**

1. Plessy, Homer Adolph Trials, litigation, etc. 2. Segregation in transportation -- Law and legislation -- Louisiana -- History. 3. Segregation -- Law and legislation -- United States -- History. 4. Trial and arbitral proceedings. 5. United States -- Race relations -- History. 6. Plessy v. Ferguson, 163 U.S. 537 (1896)

ISBN 0313391874

LC 2012011735

"More than the story of one man's case, this book tells the story of entire generations of people marked as 'mixed race' in America amid slavery and its aftermath, and being officially denied their multicultural identity and personal rights as a result." --Provided by publisher.

"This book on a landmark court case goes beyond legal discussion and examines the larger questions of race, social status, and class status... This is an excellent introduction not merely to the case itself but to the many issues surrounding it. Designed as a high school teaching tool, with glossary, time line, and biographies of principal players, it is highly recommended not only to its intended readers but any reader wanting a sound introduction to the world that created and responded to Plessy." Library Journal Express

Ford, Richard T. (Richard Thompson)

Rights gone wrong : how law corrupts the struggle for equality / Richard Thompson Ford. Farrar, Straus and Giroux, 2011. 288 p. **342.7308**

1. Civil rights -- United States. 2. Racism. 3. Social justice.
ISBN 9780374250355

LC 2011010705

Argues that civil rights laws do very little to combat less-overt forms of discrimination and prejudice.

Goldstone, Lawrence, 1947-

On account of race : the Supreme Court, white supremacy, and the ravaging of African American voting rights / Lawrence Goldstone. Counterpoint Press, 2020. xii, 283 p. ; **342.7308**

1. Race discrimination -- Law and legislation -- United States -- History -- 19th century. 2. Race discrimination -- Law and legislation -- United States -- History -- 20th century. 3. African Americans -- Suffrage -- History -- 19th century. 4. African Americans -- Suffage -- History -- 20th century.
ISBN 9781640093928

LC 2019037734

The award-winning Constitutional Law historian and author of Inherently Unequal examines case-based evidence to reveal the Supreme Court's long-standing support of white supremacy in the form of "state rights" and how bias has enabled imbalances in key judicial powers.

"This well-sourced and accessible account makes a convincing case that America's highest court played a key role in stalling black progress for a century." Publishers Weekly

Healy, Thomas

The **great** dissent : how Oliver Wendell Holmes changed his mind and changed the history of free speech in America / Thomas Healy. Henry Holt and Company, 2013. 320 p. **342.7308**

1. Abrams, J., 1886-1953 Trials, litigation, etc. 2. Holmes, Oliver Wendell, 1841-1935. 3. Trials (Anarchy) -- New York City 4. Freedom of speech 5. Change (Psychology) 6. Abrams v. United States, 250 U.S. 616 (1919)
ISBN 9780805094565

LC 2012047539

Robert F. Kennedy Book Award, 2014.

Based on newly discovered letters and memos, this riveting scholarly history of the conservative justice who became a free-speech advocate and established the modern understanding of the First Amendment reconstructs his journey from free-speech skeptic to First Amendment hero.

Hull, N. E. H., 1949-

★**Roe** v. Wade : the abortion rights controversy in American history / N.E.H. Hull and Peter Charles Hoffer. University Press of Kansas, c2010. xiii, 370 p. ; **342.7308**

1. Roe, Jane, 1947-2017 Trials, litigation, etc. 2. Wade, Henry Trials, litigation, etc. 3. Trials (Abortion) -- Washington (DC) 4. Abortion -- Law and legislation -- United States -- History
ISBN 9780700617531

LC 2010021294

This up-to-date history of Roe v. Wade covers the complete social and legal context of the case that remains the touchstone for America's culture wars. --Provided by publisher

Luxenberg, Steve

Separate : the story of Plessy v. Ferguson, and America's journey from slavery to segregation / Steve Luxenberg. W. W. Norton & Company, 2019. 560 p. **342.7308**

1. Plessy, Homer Adolph Trials, litigation, etc. 2. Harlan, John Marshall, 1833-1911 3. Tourgee, Albion W., 1838-1905 4. Brown, Henry Billings, 1836-1913 5. Martinet, Louis A., 1849-1917 6. Segregation 7. Segregation in transportation 8. African Americans -- Civil rights -- History -- 19th century 9. Civil rights workers 10. United States -- Race relations -- History -- 19th century 11. Plessy v. Ferguson, 163 U.S. 537 (1896)
ISBN 9780393239379

LC 2018043111

The award-winning author of Annie's Ghosts documents the story of the infamous 19th-century Supreme Court ruling in favor of segregation, tracing the half-century of history that shaped the ruling and the reverberations that are still being felt today.

"This engrossing work builds to the courtroom drama in which Tourgee argues passionately but unsuccessfully on behalf of Homer Plessy to a Supreme Court, including, Brown, who wrote the majority opinion, and Harlan, the onetime slave owner, whose only dissenting vote revealed separate but equal hypocrisy." Library Journal.

Purdum, Todd S.

An **idea** whose time has come : two presidents, two parties, and the battle for the Civil Rights Act of 1964 / Todd S. Purdum. Henry Holt and Co., 2014. 400 p. **342.7308**

1. Civil Rights Act of 1964 History 2. Political culture -- United States -- History -- 20th century. 3. Civil Rights Movement. 4. Legislative histories. 5. Civil rights -- United States -- History -- 20th century. 6. United States -- Politics and government -- 1961-1969.
ISBN 9780805096729

LC 2013038545

A top Washington journalist recounts the dramatic political battle to pass the Civil Rights Act of 1964.

"Those battling the neo-Confederates and nullificationists of today will want this book to see how it's done. Readers with an interest in American history and the American promise will find it a must-read as well." Kirkus.

Richards, Leonard L.

Who freed the slaves? : the fight over the Thirteenth Amendment / Leonard L. Richards. 322 p. **342.7308**

1. Ashley, James Mitchell, 1824-1896. 2. United States. Constitution. 13th Amendment. 3. Emancipation Proclamation. 4. Slaves -- Emancipation 5. Slavery -- Law and legislation. 6. Legislation -- United States. 7. Politicians -- United States. 8. United States -- History -- Civil War, 1861-1865 -- Law and legislation.
ISBN 9780226178202

LC 2014023200

"It... provides a perceptive explanation as to how and why the promise of the 13th Amendment as an instrument for civil rights never came to fruition. In doing so, it reminds us that freedom is not a given; principled, pragmatic, and persistent advocates must work to realize and secure it." Library Journal.

Risen, Clay

The **bill** of the century : the epic battle for the Civil Rights Act / Clay Risen. St Martins Press, 2014. 320 p. **342.7308**

1. Civil Rights Act of 1964. 2. African Americans -- Civil rights -- History -- 20th century. 3. Segregation 4. Racism 5. African Americans -- Legal status, laws, etc. 6. United States -- Politics

and government -- 1963-1969. 7. United States -- Race relations -- Political aspects. 8. United States -- History -- 1961-1969. 9. United States -- Race relations -- History -- 20th century.
ISBN 9781608198245

LC 2014004662

Offers a full acount of the complex battle to get the Civil Rights bill passed.

"A work of high academic quality written with a journalist's flair for telling a tale." Choice.

Strossen, Nadine

Hate : why we should resist it with free speech, not censorship / Nadine Strossen. Oxford University Press, 2018. 208 p. **342.7308**

1. United States. Constitution. 1st Amendment 2. Hate speech 3. Freedom of speech 4. Censorship 5. Constitutional law
ISBN 9780190859121

LC 2017054213

"Dispelling rampant confusion about "hate speech," this book explains how U.S. law appropriately distinguishes between punishable and protected discriminatory speech. It shows that more speech-restrictive laws consistently have suppressed vital expression about public issues, targeting minority viewpoints and speakers; and that "counterspeech" has more effectively promoted equality and societal harmony".-- Provided by publisher.

"Strossen succeeds in lucidly explaining the relevant legal issues in a way that benefits both professional and lay readers." Library Journal.

Weiner, Mark Stuart

Black trials : citizenship from the beginnings of slavery to the end of caste / Mark S. Weiner. Alfred A. Knopf, 2004 xvii, 421 p. ; **342.7308**

1. Slavery. 2. Race relations. 3. African Americans -- Legal status, laws, etc. -- History.
ISBN 9780375409813

LC 2004040860

Examines how the role of blacks in America has evolved from the colonial period to the present day as exemplified in American courts of laws, providing an insightful analysis of fourteen key legal cases that transformed American civic identity.

"This book is the best of its' kind--a serious, deeply felt reflection on the weight of history on contemporary affairs." Publishers Weekly.

Wexler, Jay, 1969-

Holy hullabaloos : a road trip to the battlegrounds of the church/state wars / Jay Wexler. Beacon Press, 2009. 272p. **342.7308**

1. Church and state -- United States. 2. Freedom of religion -- United States 3. Religious minorities -- Legal status, laws, etc. -- United States. 4. Automobile travel. 5. United States -- Description and travel.
ISBN 9780807000441

LC 2008047405

A lighthearted account of a church-and-state law professor's cross-country visits to the places and people responsible for some of today's most hotly contested Supreme Court cases includes the author's encounters with a Cambridge bar whose liquor license was challenged by a nearby church and the Austin Capitol site where the Ten Commandments are controversially posted.

"This is a rare treat, a combination of thoughtful analysis and quirky humor that illuminates an issue that rarely elicits a laughand that is central to the American body politic." Publishers Weekly.

343.0526 Income taxes by incidence

Fishman, Stephen

Working for yourself : law & taxes for independent contractors, freelancers & gig workers of all types / Stephen Fishman, J.D. Nolo, 2019 529 p. : **343.0526**

1. Independent contractors -- Legal status, laws, etc. -- United States -- Popular works. 2. Independent contractors -- Taxation -- United States -- Popular works. 3. Self-employed persons -- Taxation -- Law and legislation -- United States -- Popular works. 4. Self-employed persons -- Self-help materials
ISBN 9781413325812

LC 2018299299

"Covers the new tax law"--Cover.

Includes index.

Whether you're starting a full-scale consulting business or booking gigs on the side, Working for Yourself provides all the legal and tax information you need in one place. This eleventh edition has been thoroughly updated to reflect all the changes under the Tax Cuts and Jobs Act--changes that are largely beneficial to the self-employed.

"There's a good chance having a side business will mean being an independent contractor, a freelancer, or a consultant. This thorough and well-organized volume will guide individuals through the legal and tax issues that come with the territory. From deciding on legal structures to drafting contracts to collecting payment from deadbeat clients, this is excellent information." Library Journal.

343.73 Military, defense, public property, public finance, tax, commerce (trade), industrial law -- United States

Bray, Chris (Historian)

Court- martial : how military justice has shaped America from the revolution to 9/11 and beyond / Chris Bray. W.W.Norton & Company, 2016. 400 p. **343.73**

1. Courts-martial and courts of inquiry 2. Military history 3. Military law 4. United States -- History
ISBN 9780393243406

LC 2016002824

Tells the sweeping story of military justice, from the institution of the court martial in the earliest days of the Republic to contemporary arguments over how to use military courts to try foreign terrorists or soldiers accused of sexual assault.

Witt, John Fabian

Lincoln's code : the laws of war in American history / John Fabian Witt. Free Press, 2012. 240 p. **343.73**

1. Lincoln, Abraham, 1809-1865 Military leadership. 2. Military law. 3. War and emergency legislation. 4. War (International law) 5. War -- History. 6. United States -- History -- Civil War, 1861-1865.
ISBN 9781416569831

LC 2012006187

Pulitzer Prize for History finalist, 2013.

A Yale historian and author of The Accidental Republic presents the story of the pioneering American role in establishing modern laws of war, recounting decades of controversy and debate that resulted in a code of conduct adopted by the 16th President in the final years of the Civil War that influenced subsequent military conflicts.

343.7309 Public utilities--United States

Chertoff, Michael, 1953-

Exploding data : reclaiming our cybersecurity in the digital age / Michael Chertoff. Atlantic Monthly Press, [2018] 288 p. **343.7309**

1. Data protection -- Law and legislation 2. Internet -- Law and legislation 3. Privacy rights 4. Conflict of laws 5. United States -- Politics and government -- 21st century

ISBN 9780802127938

LC 2018012763

The former Secretary of Homeland Security and author of <I>Homeland Security: Assessing the First Five Years</I> outlines powerful arguments for new laws and policies to protect society and individual autonomy from cyber-security threats.

"A tremendous resource for any reader about ever-shifting threats embedded in data collection and control." Library Journal.

343.746 Law--Connecticut

Benedict, Jeff

Little pink house : a true story of defiance and courage / Jeff Benedict. Grand Central Pub, 2009. 416 p. **343.746**

1. Kelo, Susette Trials, litigation ,etc. 2. United States. Supreme Court Cases 3. Eminent domain -- Connecticut -- Cases. 4. Property rights -- History 5. Land use -- Laws, statutes, etc. 6. Homeowners -- Legal status, laws, etc. 7. United States -- Laws, statutes, etc. 8. United States -- Social life and customs -- 20th century 9. United States -- Social life and customs -- 21st century 10. Connecticut -- Social life and customs -- 20th century

ISBN 9780446508629

LC 2008017650

In Little Pink House, award-winning investigative journalist Jeff Benedict takes readers behind the scenes of the Suzatte Kelso case (a case that ultimately reached the United States Supreme Court) in which Kelso led the charge to take on corporate America to save her home.

"Benedict has pieced together a fascinating narrative, using e-mail messages, planning documents, interviews and personal diaries to produce a sordid account of ruthless local politicians working hand-in-medical-glove with big business to drive hardworking Americans from their homes." New York Times Book Review.

344.04 Miscellaneous social problems and services

Bilott, Robert, 1965-

Exposure : poisoned water, corporate greed, and one lawyer's twenty-year battle against DuPont / Robert Bilott, with Tom Shroder. Atria Books,. 2019 xii, 386 p. **344.04**

1. Bilott, Robert, 1965- 2. DuPont de Nemours (E. I.) and Company 3. Lawyers 4. Corporations 5. Corporate cover-ups 6. Hazardous waste 7. West Virginia

ISBN 9781501172816

LC bl2019027138

Includes index.

Inspiration for the movie Dark waters.

Green Prize for Sustainable Literature: Adult Nonfiction, 2020.

In 1988, Rob Bilott began a legal battle against DuPont that would consume the next twenty years of his life, uncovering the worst case of environmental contamination in modern history and a corporate cover-up that put the health of hundreds of thousands of people at risk. Representing a single farmer who was convinced the creek on his property had been poisoned by runoff from a nearby DuPont landfill, Rob ultimately discovers the truth about PFAS--unregulated, toxic chemicals used in the manufacturing of Teflon and a host of other household goods.

344.73 Labor, social service, education, cultural law--United States

Driver, Justin

The **schoolhouse** gate : public education, the Supreme Court, and the battle for the American mind / Justin Driver. Pantheon, 2018. 576 p. **344.73**

1. United States. Supreme Court 2. Students 3. Public schools 4. Civil rights 5. Educational law and legislation 6. United States -- Politics and government

ISBN 9781101871652

LC 2017058167

Includes index.

An constitutional law scholar and clerk to such justices as Stephen Breyer and Sandra Day O'Connor presents a cautionary assessment of public schools to reveal how Supreme Court rulings in recent decades are undermining the constitutional rights of students.

"Readers with the ability to grapple with complex constitutional issues will find much to learn from Driver's independent thinking and unique insights." Publishers Weekly.

Okrent, Daniel, 1948-

The **guarded** gate : bigotry, eugenics, and the law that kept two generations of Jews, Italians, and other European immigrants out of America / Daniel Okrent. Scribner, 2019. xvi, 478 p. : **344.73**

1. Eugenics 2. Immigration policy. 3. Xenophobia 4. Prejudice. 5. United States -- Race relations -- History

ISBN 9781476798035

LC 2019006830

National Jewish Book Award, 2019.

The author of the Pulitzer finalist, *Great Fortune*, examines how eugenics and government-supported anti-immigration initiatives in the 1920s changed policies to ban discriminated-against groups from the U.S. for more than 40 years.

"A frighteningly timely book about a particularly ugly period in American history, a bigotry-riddled chapter many thought was closed but that shows recent signs of reopening. In his latest book, Okrent, the former managing editor of Life magazine and editor at large at Time Inc., chronicles a time when white-supremacist policymakers joined forces with pseudo-scientists promoting eugenics, creating widespread anti-immigration sentiment throughout the country." Kirkus.

344.7301 Labor law--United States

Sack, Steven Mitchell, 1954-

The **employee** rights handbook : effective legal strategies to protect your job from interview to pink slip / Steven Mitchell Sack. Legal Strategies Publications, c2010 xvii, 620 p. : **344.7301**

1. Employee rights -- United States 2. Labor laws and legislation -- United States

ISBN 9780963630674

LC 2010926886

Includes index.

"The author advises readers on topics from avoiding prehiring abuses and protecting on-the-job rights through postemployment litigation and finding and hiring a lawyer. Readers looking for an all-in-one employee legal primer or layperson's quick reference should find this a useful tool." Library Journal.

Steingold, Fred S., 1936-

The **employer's** legal handbook / Attorney Fred S. Steingold. Nolo, 2017. 482 p. ; **344.7301**

1. Labor laws and legislation -- United States
ISBN 9781413323993

LC bl2017026668

Includes index.

Provides the information for employers on the most common and current employment law issues, including hiring, wage and hour laws, employee discipline and performance reviews, benefits, and family and medical leave, employee privacy, and layoffs.

Thomas, Gillian, (lawyer)

Because of sex : one law, ten cases, and fifty years that changed American women's lives at work / Gillian Thomas. St. Martin's Press, 2016. 272 p. **344.7301**

1. Sex discrimination in employment. 2. Sexism in employment. 3. Sex discrimination against women. 4. Women's rights.
ISBN 9781137280053

LC 2015033086

The 1964 Civil Rights Act is best known as a monumental achievement of the civil rights movement, but it also revolutionized the lives of American women. Title VII of the law made it illegal to discriminate "because of sex." But Congress did not specify how that would affect a "Mad Men" world where women played mainly supporting roles. The Supreme Court had to endow the phrase with meaning, and its decisions dramatically changed how the nation sees working women -- women like Ida Phillips, denied an assembly line job because having small children deemed her unreliable; or Kim Rawlinson, who fought to be a prison guard because she believed that being 5'3" and 115 pounds didn't mean she couldn't do a "man's job"; or Ann Hopkins, who refused a partnership at Price Waterhouse because the men in charge thought she needed "a course at charm school."

"The author merges the personal stories with the legal intricacies of the litigation, and crafts a moving and informative account of a struggle for equality that remains incomplete." Publishers Weekly.

344.7304 Miscellaneous social problems and services--United States

Ball, Howard, 1937-

At liberty to die : the battle for death with dignity in America / Howard Ball. New York University Press, c2012. ix, 229 p. ; **344.7304**

1. Right to die. 2. Assisted suicide. 3. Euthanasia. 4. Terminal illness.
ISBN 9780814791042

LC 2011052258

A legal history of euthanasia in America offers a state-by-state comparison of legislation in support of and in opposition to physician-assisted death, following battles to legalize the practice in such states as Oregon and Vermont.

Cohen, Adam (Adam Seth)

★**Imbeciles** : the Supreme Court, American eugenics, and the sterilization of Carrie Buck / Adam Cohen. Penguin Press, 2016. 400 p. **344.7304**

1. Buck, Carrie, 1906-1983 Trials, litigation, etc. 2. Taft, William H. (William Howard), 1857-1930 3. Holmes, Oliver Wendell, 1841-1935. 4. Brandeis, Louis Dembitz, 1856-1941 5. Involuntary sterilization -- Law and legislation -- United States. 6. Eugenics -- Law and legislation -- United States. 7. Discrimination. 8. Prejudice. 9. Buck v. Bell, 274 U.S. 200 (1927)
ISBN 9781594204180

LC 2015044207

Describes a dark moment in American history, when the Supreme Court agreed, in 1927, to support eugenic sterilization for "undesirables," including epileptics and the "feebleminded," resulting in the sterilization of 70,000 Americans.

"A shocking tale about science and law gone horribly wrong, an almost forgotten case that deserves to be ranked with Dred Scott, Plessy, and Korematsu as among the Supreme Court's worst decisions." Kirkus.

Nourse, Victoria F.

In reckless hands : Skinner v. Oklahoma and the near triumph of American eugenics / Victoria F. Nourse. W. W. Norton & Co., 2008. 256 p. **344.7304**

1. Skinner, Jack T., d.1977 Trials, litigation, etc. 2. Trials (Involuntary sterilization) -- Oklahoma. 3. Trials (Involuntary sterilization) -- United States. 4. Eugenics -- United States -- History -- 20th century. 5. Oklahoma -- History -- 20th century 6. United States -- History -- 20th century
ISBN 9780393065299

LC 2008013140

An account of the controversial early twentieth-century effort to sterilize criminals and the mentally ill profiles the activities at Oklahoma's McAlester prison, the trial of Jack Skinner, and the influence of Nazi Germany's eugenics practices on the outcome of an ensuing Supreme Court case.

"The author provides a legal history of the Supreme Court case that served to increase the recognition of individual rights, although it fell short of ending the practice and debate of eugenics in the US. This book deserves attention from those interested in the history and politics of the legal system." Choice.

344.7305 Social law -- United States -- Public safety and morals

Friedman, Barry, 1958-

★**Unwarranted** : policing without permission / Barry Friedman. Farrar, Straus and Giroux, 2017. 416 p. **344.7305**

1. United States. Constitution. 4th Amendment. 2. Electronic surveillance -- Law and legislation. 3. Privacy rights. 4. Searches and seizures. 5. Intelligence service. 6. United States -- Politics and government.
ISBN 9780374280451

LC 2016033246

Includes index.

As the debate about out-of-control policing heats up, an authority on constitutional law offers a provocative account of how our rights have been eroded.

345 Criminal law

George, Cherian

Hate spin : the manufacture of religious offense and its threat to democracy / Cherian George. The MIT Press, 2016 xviii, 308 p. ; **345**

1. Freedom of speech. 2. Hate speech -- Law and legislation. 3. Offenses against religion -- Law and legislation. 4. Offenses against religion -- Political aspects.
ISBN 0262035308

LC 2016014335

"This timely work provides an essential warning against the misuse of perceived religious-based bias and an unmasking of the real motives of those who incite manufactured offense." Publishers Weekly.

Kadri, Sadakat

The **trial** : a history, from Socrates to O.J. Simpson / Sadakat Kadri. Random House, c2005. xviii, 459 p. : **345**

1. Trials -- History. 2. Criminal justice system.
ISBN 0375505504

LC 2005042925

Ranging from ancient Greece to the present day, a history of the criminal trial begins with the trial of Socrates and continues over the course of more than two thousand years, detailing the events, outcomes, and implications of the changing world of criminal justice.

"This history of the trial from ancient times to the present provides . [a] history of the various forms and purposes of trials throughout Western civilization. The result is a magnificent book suitable for all sorts of people, from inquisitive high school students to blue-chip lawyers." Choice.

Minow, Martha, 1954-

When should law forgive? / Martha Minow. W.W. Norton & Company, [2019] 252 p. **345**

1. Pardon 2. Forgiveness 3. Law 4. Clemency
ISBN 9780393081763

LC 2019014868

The former Harvard Law School dean and Pro Bono Task Force chair of the Legal Services Corporation explores contradictions in how criminal acts and financial debts are forgiven and how offering pardon for justified grievances can render laws more just.

Sands, Philippe, 1960-

East West Street : on the origins of genocide and crimes against humanity / Philippe Sands. Alfred A. Knopf, 2016. 464 p. **345**

1. Lauterpacht, Hersch, 1897-1960 2. Lemkin, Raphael, 1900-1959 3. Genocide. 4. Crimes against humanity 5. Nuremberg war crime trials, 1946-1949 6. Trials (Crimes against humanity)
ISBN 9780385350716

LC 2016933268

Baillie Gifford Prize for Non-Fiction, 2016.

Pieces together how the lives of humanitarian-law professors Rafael Lemkin and Hersch Lauterpacht--as well as the life of Hitler's personal lawyer, who ordered the death of more than a million Jews and Poles, including the families of Lemkin and Lauterpacht--converged in October 1946 at the International Military Tribunals at Nuremberg.

"Readers interested in history, political science, and/or religion shouldn't miss this compelling work with unforgettable characters." Library Journal.

Schiff, Stacy

★The **witches** : Salem, 1692 / Stacy Schiff. Little, Brown, 2015. xiv, 498 p., 16 unnumbered p. of plates : **345**

1. Trials (Witchcraft) -- Salem, Massachusetts. 2. Witchcraft. 3. Puritanism. 4. Puritans. 5. Salem, Massachusetts -- History -- Colonial period, 1626-1775. 6. Massachusetts -- History -- Colonial period, 1600-1775.
ISBN 9780316200608

The Pulitzer Prize-winning author of Cleopatra analyzes the Salem Witch Trials to offer key insights into the role of women in its events while explaining how its tragedies became possible.

"This fully documented narrative, if a bit exhausting and disorganized, will find a welcome audience among readers of witchcraft or colonial histories as well as Schiff's legion of fans." Library Journal.

Schneps, Leila

Math on trial : how numbers get used and abused in the courtroom / Leila Schneps and Coralie Colmez. Basic Books, 2013. 272 p. **345**

1. Statistics 2. Probabilities 3. Trials 4. Judicial error
ISBN 9780465032921

LC 2012040624

Mother and daughter mathematicians describe the harm that can be done when mathematical arguments are improperly used and discuss ten trials where they were misused as evidence, including the Dreyfus Affair, the Amanda Knox Case and Charles Ponzi's original scheme.

345.43 Criminal law--Germany

King, David, 1970-

The **trial** of Adolf Hitler : the beer hall putsch and the rise of Nazi Germany / David King. W. W. Norton & Company, 2017. 336 p. **345.43**

1. Hitler, Adolf, 1889-1945 2. Nazi Party (Germany) 3. Politicians 4. Trials (Treason) 5. Coups d'etat 6. Prisoners 7. Germany -- History -- Beer Hall Putsch, 1923
ISBN 9780393241693

LC 2017008985

Documents the lesser-known story of the scandalous courtroom drama that paved the way for the rise of the Nazi Party, recounting the 1924 trial of Hitler and nine associates who successfully threw off charges of high treason and used the trial to gain international attention and launch an improbable path to power.

"King . . . affirms his reputation as a first-rate narrative historian in this well-researched analysis of Adolf Hitler's trial for treason in the aftermath of the 1923 Beer Hall Putsch." Publishers Weekly.

345.567 Criminal law--Iraq

Newton, Michael A.

Enemy of the state : the trial and execution of Saddam Hussein / Michael A. Newton & Michael P. Scharf. St. Martin's Press, 2008. 320 p. **345.567**

1. Hussein, Saddam, 1937-2006 Trials, litigation, etc. 2. Trials (Crimes against humanity) 3. Trials (Murder) 4. Crimes against humanity. 5. Political leadership. 6. Iraq -- Politics and government. 7. Baghdad, Iraq -- Politics and government.
ISBN 9780312385569

LC 2008021087

A behind-the-scenes account documents the events surrounding the executed Iraqi dictator's capture and the assemblage of the High Tribunal, describing how its team of judges and prosecutors was prepared to run a fair trial in the face of such obstacles as international upheavals and the disapprovals of the U.K. and the U.N.

345.5694 Criminal law--Israel and Palestine

Lipstadt, Deborah E., 1947-

The **Eichmann** trial / Deborah E. Lipstadt. Nextbook Schocken, c2010. 256 p. **345.5694**

1. Eichmann, Adolf, 1906-1962 Trials, litigation, etc. 2. War crime trials -- Jerusalem, Israel. 3. Holocaust (1933-1945) 4. War crimes.
ISBN 9780805242607

LC 2010028620

The National Jewish Book Award-winning author of History on Trial presents a reassessment of the groundbreaking 1960 trial of Nazi SS Lieutenant Colonel Adolf Eichmann by an Israeli court while exploring the controversial processes it introduced and its reflection of world views on genocide.

"Lipstadt has done a great service by untethering the trial from [Hannah] Arendt's polarizing presence, recovering the event as a gripping legal drama, as well as a hinge moment in Israel's history and in the world's delayed awakening to the magnitude of the Holocaust." New York Times Book Review.

345.73 Criminal law--United States

Abrams, Dan, 1966-

Theodore Roosevelt for the defense : the courtroom battle to save his legacy / Dan Abrams and David Fisher. Hanover Square Press, 2019. 400 p. **345.73**

1. Roosevelt, Theodore, 1858-1919 2. Former presidents -- United States 3. Trials (Libel) 4. Politicians 5. Political corruption
ISBN 9781335016447

LC bl2019008611

Chronicles the epic 1915 libel case in which Theodore Roosevelt, weighing a last presidential run, turned on former allies to challenge corruption in the political party that made him.

"Many of the questions the trial raised about the effects of money in politics, the dangers of blind allegiance to party politics, and oversize corporate political influence will resonate with contemporary readers. Legal eagles and history buffs will enjoy this one." Publishers Weekly.

Bazelon, Emily

★**Charged** : the new movement to transform American prosecution and end mass incarceration / Emily Bazelon Random House, 2019. xxxi, 409 p. : **345.73**

1. Criminal justice system 2. Imprisonment -- United States 3. Injustice 4. Punishment -- United States.
ISBN 9780399590016

An investigative journalist exposes the unchecked power of the prosecutor as a driving force in America's mass incarceration crisis, offering strategic recommendations for reversing discriminatory practices without changing the law.

"A vitally important new entry in the continued heated debates about criminal justice." Kirkus.

Boyle, Kevin, 1960-

Arc of justice : a saga of race, civil rights, and murder in the Jazz Age / Kevin Boyle. H. Holt, 2004. 415 p., 8 p. of plates : **345.73**

1. Sweet, Ossian, 1895-1960 Trials, litigation, etc. 2. Darrow, Clarence, 1857-1938. 3. Trials (Murder) -- Detroit, Michigan. 4. African Americans -- Detroit, Michigan. 5. African Americans -- Civil rights -- History -- 20th century. 6. Racism -- Detroit, Michigan. 7. Detroit, Michigan -- Race relations. 8. United States -- Race relations.
ISBN 0805071458

LC 2004047352

National Book Award for Nonfiction, 2004.
National Book Critics Circle Award for Nonfiction finalist, 2004.
Pulitzer Prize for History finalist, 2005.

The grandson of a slave, Dr. Ossian Sweet moved his family to an all-white Detroit neighborhood in 1925. When his neighbors attempted to drive him out, Sweet defended himself--resulting in the death of a white man and a murder trial for Sweet. There followed one of the most important (and shockingly unknown) cases in Civil Rights history. Also caught up in the intense courtroom drama were legal giant Clarence Darrow and the newly formed National Association for the Advancement of Colored People (NAACP).

"Boyle has brilliantly rescued from obscurity a fascinating chapter in American history that had profound implications for the rise of the Civil Rights movement." Publishers Weekly.

Garrett, Brandon

Too big to jail : how prosecutors compromise with corporations / Brandon L. Garrett. Belknap Press, 2014. 340 p. **345.73**

1. Corporate crime 2. Corporation law -- Criminal provisions 3. Legal malpractice 4. Corporate governance -- Law and legislation
ISBN 9780674368316

LC 2014013351

American courts routinely hand down harsh sentences to individuals, but a very different standard of justice applies to corporations. Too Big to Jail takes readers into a complex, compromised world of backroom deals, for an unprecedented look at what happens when criminal charges are brought against a major company in the United States.

"A well-written, detailed exposé for all audiences." Library Journal.

Houppert, Karen, 1962-

Chasing Gideon : the elusive quest for poor people's justice / Karen Houppert. The New Press, 2013. 288 p. **345.73**

1. Legal assistance to poor people 2. Right to counsel 3. Poor people 4. Civil rights.
ISBN 9781595588692

LC 2012047464

"Earlier and shorter versions of the chapters "A Perfect Storm" and "Death in Georgia" were first published in The Nation."

On the 50th anniversary of Gideon v. Wainwright, the landmark case that led to free legal counsel for those who needed it, a veteran journalist investigates the way justice is delivered to the poor--and discovers a crisis in our nation's courts.

Lewis, Anthony, 1927-

Gideon's trumpet / Anthony Lewis. Vintage Books, 1989, c1964. 277 p. **345.73**

1. Gideon, Clarence Earl Trials, litigation, etc. 2. Wainwright, Louie L. Trials, litigation, etc. 3. United States. Supreme Court. 4. Right to counsel.
ISBN 0679723129

LC 88040504

Originally published: New York : Random House, 1964.
Edgar Allan Poe Award for Best Fact Crime, 1965.

The story of a convict's defense of his contention that a person on trial should not be denied the assistance of counsel.

"His description of procedures, and his explication of the way new interpretations of law evolve, humanize the Supreme Court without lessening its majesty." Kirkus.

Mandery, Evan J.

A **wild** justice : the death and resurrection of capital punishment in America / Evan J. Mandery. W. W. Norton & Company, 2013. 496 p. **345.73**

1. Capital punishment -- United States. -- History -- 20th century 2. Capital punishment -- Law and legislation

ISBN 9780393239584

LC 2013010126

A professor and former capital defense attorney discusses the history of the two Supreme Court cases that were responsible for changing the laws regarding the death penalty in America and polarizing the nation.

Rabinowitz, Dorothy

★**No** crueler tyrannies : accusation, false witness, and other terrors of our times / Dorothy Rabinowitz. Free Press, 2003. xi, 239 p. ; **345.73**

1. Fells Acres Day Care (Firm) Trials, litigation, etc. 2. Child sexual abuse investigation 3. Trials (Child sexual abuse) 4. False testimony. 5. Child witnesses. 6. Essays.

ISBN 0743228340

LC 2002044670

"These articles were previously published individually in The Wall Street journal"--T.p. verso.

Includes index.

"This book reexamines high-profile cases of the 1980s and 1990s involving mass sexual abuse. Demonstrating that overzealous prosecutors and indifferent courts led to the prosecution of many innocents, Rabinowitz provides in-depth analyses of the major cases, especially those that involved child-care workers. This gripping, well-written book about social injustice and public hysteria is recommended for social science and law collections." Library Journal.

Temkin, Moshik, 1971-

The **Sacco-Vanzetti** Affair : America on trial / Moshik Temkin. Yale University Press, c2009. xii, 316 p., 12 p. of plates : **345.73**

1. Sacco-Vanzetti case 2. Trials (Murder) -- Dedham, Massachusetts. 3. Murderers. 4. International relations. 5. United States -- History -- 20th century.

ISBN 9780300124842

LC 2008045606

"This study of the trial and appeals of these two condemned murderers and of the life and times of the country, which feared foreign contamination, surpasses all prior analyses of this subject in terms of scope, erudition, and objectivity. This book discusses many fascinating elements of controversy, not least the long-term views held by Sacco and Vanzetti's defenders and accusers and how their participation in the search for justice was perceived by their peers." Library Journal.

Toobin, Jeffrey

The **run** of his life : the people v. O.J. Simpson / Jeffrey Toobin. Random House, 1996. 466 p. ; **345.73**

1. Simpson, O. J., 1947- Trials, litigation, etc. 2. Trials (Murder) -- Los Angeles, California. 3. Mass media and criminal justice. 4. Prosecution -- Los Angeles, California. 5. Criminal justice system. 6. Los Angeles, California.

ISBN 9780679441700

LC 96210907

A behind-the-scenes look at the "crime of the century" and the legal proceedings that followed sheds new light on the arrest and trial of O.J. Simpson, the evidence in the case, and the role of the prosecution and defense.

Trainum, James L.

How the police generate false confessions : an inside look at the interrogation room / James L. Trainum. Rowman & Littlefield, 2016 xix, 308 p. : **345.73**

1. Confession (Law) -- United States. 2. Police questioning -- United States. 3. Self-incrimination -- United States.

ISBN 144224464X

LC 2017478440

Despite the rising number of confirmed false confession cases, most people have a hard time grasping why someone would confess to a crime they did not commit, or even why a guilty person would admit to something that could put them in jail for life. How the Police Generate False Confessions takes you inside the interrogation room, exposing the tactics that law enforcement uses to make confessions happen. James L. Trainum reveals how innocent people can become suspects and then confessed criminals even when they have not committed a crime. Using real stories, he looks at the inherent coerciveness of the interrogation process and why so many false confessions contain so many of the details that only the true perpetrator would know. More disturbingly, the book examines how these same processes corrupt witness and victim statements, create lying informants and cooperators, and induce innocent people to plead guilty. Trainum also offers recommendations for change in the U.S. by looking at how other countries are changing the process to prevent such miscarriages of justice. The reasons that people falsely confess can be complex and varied; throughout How the Police Generate False Confessions Trainum encourages readers to critically evaluate confessions on their own by gaining a better understanding of the interrogation process.--Publisher description.

"Using numerous examples and backed by persuasive academic research, Trainum proposes a better way that is already at work in countries with similar criminal justice systems. His book will hit a nerve with a public newly concerned with abuses of police power, and hopefully will influence those tasked with law enforcement and public policy as well." Publishers Weekly.

Turow, Scott

★**Ultimate** punishment : a lawyer's reflections on dealing with the death penalty / Scott Turow. Farrar, Straus, and Giroux, 2003. 164 p. ; **345.73**

1. Ryan, George H. 2. Criminal justice system 3. Innocence (Law) 4. Capital punishment -- United States. 5. Capital punishment -- History.

ISBN 0374128731

LC 2003007873

Robert F. Kennedy Book Award, 2004.

Explores America's uneasy relationshsip with capital punishment from colonial days through Illinois Governor George Ryan's commutation of the sentences of 164 death row inmates before he left office in 2003.

Watson, Bruce, 1953-

★**Sacco** and Vanzetti : the judgment of mankind / Bruce Watson. Viking, 2007. 448 p. **345.73**

1. Sacco, Nicola, 1891-1927 Trials, litigation, etc. 2. Vanzetti, Bartolomeo, 1888-1927 Trials, litigation, etc. 3. Sacco-Vanzetti case. 4. Trials (Murder) -- Massachusetts. 5. Massachusetts -- Social life and customs.

ISBN 0670063533

LC 2006103092

Documents the infamous 1927 trial and execution of Nicola Sacco and Bartolomeo Vanzetti, from the anarchist bombings in Washington, D.C., for which they may have been wrongfully convicted to the fierce public debates that occurred as a result of the case.

"The author has written a well-researched page-turner. Highly recommended." Library Journal.

345.7302 Organized crime--Law--United States

Stone, Geoffrey R.

★**Sex** and the constitution : sex, religion, and law from America's origins to the twenty-first century / Geoffrey R. Stone. Liveright Publishing Corporation, 2017. 704 p. **345.7302**

1. Sexuality 2. Law -- United States 3. Constitutional law. 4. Sex laws -- United States -- History.
ISBN 9780871404695

LC 2016047264

A monumental work of scholarship, Sex and the Constitution illuminates how the clash between sex and religion has defined our nation's history.

"This title is a commanding synthesis of scholarship on over two centuries of American legal debate and practice regarding these issues, and would work well as the core text for a course of the subject." Publishers Weekly.

345.744 Criminal law--Massachusetts

Hoffer, Peter Charles, 1944-

The **Salem** witchcraft trials : a legal history / Peter Charles Hoffer. University Press of Kansas, c1997. xi, 165 p. ; **345.744**

1. Trials (Witchcraft) -- Salem, Massachusetts 2. Salem, Massachusetts -- History -- Colonial period, ca. 1600-1775.
ISBN 9780700608584

LC 97019986

Peter Charles Hoffer tells the real story of how religious beliefs, superstitions, clan disputes, and Anglo-American law and custom created an epidemic of accusations that resulted in the investigation of nearly two hundred colonists and, for many, the ordeal of trial and incarceration. Along the way, he shows how many rights we take for granted today -- such as rules of evidence and a defendant's right to legal counsel -- did not apply in colonial times.

"Hoffer offers little that is new in terms of interpretation, but he presents it well and in a manner easily grasped by the general reader." Choice.

Robertson, Cara

The **trial** of Lizzie Borden : a true story / Cara Robertson. Simon & Schuster, 2019. 288 p. **345.744**

1. Borden, Lizzie, 1860-1927 Trials, litigation, etc. 2. Trials (Murder) 3. Murder -- Fall River, Massachusetts. 4. Murder suspects 5. Massachusetts.
ISBN 9781501168376

LC 2018037560

Drawing on 20 years of research and recently discovered evidence, an account of the infamous Lizzie Borden trial explores professional and public opinions while considering how Gilded Age values and fears influenced the case.

"Robertson methodically rebuts the numerous theories advanced at the time and since, some of which pointed to other members of the household. The end result is a superior, page-turning true crime narrative that will leave most readers believing that the jury got it wrong." Publishers Weekly.

345.747 Criminal law -- New York

Davis, Kevin (Kevin A.)

The **brain** defense : murder in Manhattan and the dawn of neuroscience in America's courtrooms / Kevin Davis. Penguin Press, 2017. 384 p. **345.747**

1. Weinstein, Herbert Trials, litigation, etc. 2. Trials (Murder). 3. Insanity defense. 4. Insanity (Law). 5. Forensic neurology.
ISBN 9781594206337

LC 2016043485

In 1991, the police were called to East 72nd St. in Manhattan, where a woman's body had fallen from a twelfth-story window. The woman's husband, Herbert Weinstein, soon confessed to having hit and strangled his wife after an argument, then dropping her body out of their apartment window to make it look like a suicide. The 65-year-old Weinstein, a quiet, unassuming retired advertising executive, had no criminal record, no history of violent behavior--not even a short temper. How, then, to explain this horrific act? Journalist Kevin Davis uses the perplexing story of the Weinstein murder to present a riveting, deeply researched exploration of the intersection of neuroscience and criminal justice.

"A thoroughly researched, clearly presented book that suggests that imprecise brain science will become increasingly more common as evidence in criminal cases." Kirkus.

Malcolm, Janet

Iphigenia in Forest Hills : anatomy of a murder trial / Janet Malcolm. Yale University Press, c2011. 168 p. **345.747**

1. Borukhova, Mazoltuv Trials, litigation, etc. 2. Mallayev, Mikhail Trials, litigation, etc. 3. Malakov, Daniel Death and burial. 4. Trials (Murder) 5. Murder for hire. 6. Husband-killing. 7. Family violence. 8. Queens, New York City.
ISBN 9780300167467

LC 2010035851

"Malcolm's book chronicles the fate of Mazoltuv Borukhova, a 35-year-old doctor and a member of the Bukharan Jewish sect who stands accused of hiring an assassin to kill her ex-husband, Daniel Malakov. On the morning of Oct. 28, 2007, Malakov was shot to death in a park in Queens, N.Y., in front of his and Borukhova's 4-year-old daughter. Malcolm shows us what happens when the abstract ideals of the law are applied, as they always are, by human beings. We meet one judge who, acting out of incompetence or malice, makes an inexplicable and terrible child-custody decision. Another proves less interested in serving justice than in wrapping up proceedings in time for his Caribbean vacation. A lawyer who, on the stand, appears to be intelligent and well-spoken turns out to be both negligent and delusional. All told, it's such a damning portrait of American jurisprudence that Malcolm scarcely need editorialize. As lawyers would say, res ipsa loquitur: the thing speaks for itself." Boston Globe.

345.759 Criminal law--Florida

Smith, Clive Stafford

The **injustice** system : a murder in Miami and a trial gone wrong / Clive Stafford Smith. Viking, 2012. 352 p. **345.759**

1. Maharaj, Kris Trials, litigation, etc. 2. Judicial error 3. Trials (Murder) 4. Criminal justice system 5. Businesspeople
ISBN 9780670023707

LC 2012019068

The award-winning criminal lawyer and author of Eight O'Clock Ferry to the Windward Side shares the story of the most discouraging case of his career, during which he defended an innocent Miami businessman whose murder conviction reflects disturbing and fundamental flaws in today's legal system.

345.761 Criminal law -- Alabama

Morrison, Melanie, 1949-
Murder on Shades Mountain : the legal lynching of Willie Peterson and the struggle for justice in Jim Crow Birmingham / Melanie S. Morrison. Duke University Press, 2018. 264 p. **345.761**

1. Peterson, Willie, 1896-1940 Trials, litigation, etc. 2. Trials (Rape) -- Alabama 3. Lynching. 4. Hate crimes. 5. Racism. 6. Southern States -- Race relations. 7. Birmingham, Alabama -- Race relations -- History -- 20th century 8. United States -- Race relations -- History -- 20th century
ISBN 9780822371175

LC 2017039036

Melanie S. Morrison tells the tragic story of the murder and attempted murder of three young women in 1930s Birmingham, Alabama, and the aftermath, which saw a reign of terror unleashed on the town's black community, the wrongful conviction and death sentencing of Willie Peterson, and a black-led effort to free Peterson.

345.763 Criminal law--Louisiana

Van Meter, Matthew
Deep Delta justice : a black teen, his lawyer, and their groundbreaking battle for civil rights in the South / Matthew Van Meter. Little, Brown & Company, 2020 290 p. **345.763**

1. Sobol, Richard B. 2. Duncan, Gary 3. United States. Supreme Court Cases 4. African Americans -- Civil rights -- History. 5. Trials. 6. Judicial system. 7. African American defendants. 8. Louisiana.
ISBN 9780316435031

LC bl2020015425

In 1966 in a small town in Louisiana, a 19-year-old black man named Gary Duncan pulled his car off the road to stop a fight between a group of four white kids and two of Gary's own cousins. After putting his hand on the arm of one of the white children, Duncan was arrested for assault. A member of the local branch of the NAACP, Duncan used his contacts to reach Richard Sobol, a 29-year-old born and bred New Yorker working that summer in a black firm ("the most radical law firm") in New Orleans, to represent him. In this powerful work of character-driven history, Van Meter brings alive how one court case changed the course of justice in the South, and eventually the entire country.

"This deeply researched and vividly written chronicle is the definitive account of one of the civil rights movement's most unheralded victories." Publishers Weekly

345.773 Criminal law--Illinois

Bogira, Steve
Courtroom 302 : a year behind the scenes in an American criminal courthouse / Steve Bogira. Vintage Books, 2006, c2005. 401 p. ; **345.773**

1. Criminal courts -- Chicago, Illinois. 2. Criminal justice system -- Chicago, Illinois. 3. Criminal justice personnel -- Chicago, Illinois. 4. Criminals -- Chicago, Illinois.
ISBN 0679752064

LC bl2006004313

Originally published: New York : A. Knopf, 2005.

Follows a year in the events of a felony courthouse and the lives of men and women on both sides of the law, chronicling cases from the point-of-view of the prisoners' lockup, the jury room, the spectators' gallery, and the judge's chambers.

"Bogira provides a balanced view of the realities of the day-to-day, assembly-line grind that marks so much of the process from arrest to final disposition. The brilliance of Bogira's insights will lead many to hope that he will follow this debut with proposals to cure the many ills he has diagnosed." Publishers Weekly.

345.775 Criminal law--Wisconsin

Strang, Dean A.
Worse than the devil : anarchists, Clarence Darrow, and justice in a time of terror / Dean A. Strang. The University of Wisconsin Press, c2013. 268 p. **345.775**

1. Darrow, Clarence, 1857-1938. 2. Trials -- Milwaukee, Wisconsin -- History -- 20th century. 3. Judicial corruption -- Milwaukee, Wisconsin -- History -- 20th century. 4. Anarchists -- Milwaukee, Wisconsin -- History -- 20th century. 5. Italian Americans -- Milwaukee, Wisconsin -- History -- 20th century. 6. Milwaukee, Wisconsin -- History -- 20th century. 7. Bay View (Milwaukee, Wis.) -- History -- 20th century.
ISBN 9780299293949

LC 2012032689

"Strang, a criminal defense lawyer and professor of law, examines the dramatic case of the Bay View Eleven, a group of Italian immigrants arrested after a Milwaukee riot in 1917. In this in-depth study, he analyzes how their trial, coming on the heels of a police station bombing, was grossly mismanaged and sensationalized--essentially acting as proxy for the other tragedy." Publishers Weekly

346.04 Property

Cass, Ronald A.
Laws of creation : property rights in the world of ideas / Ronald A. Cass and Keith N. Hylton. Harvard University Press, 2013. 275 p. : **346.04**

1. Intellectual property 2. Copyright
ISBN 9780674066458

LC 2012011488

Cass and Hylton explain how technological advances strengthen the case for intellectual property laws, and argue convincingly that IP laws help create a wealthier, more successful, more innovative society than alternative legal systems. Ignoring the social value of IP rights and making what others create 'free' would be a costly mistake indeed. --Provided by publisher

Lessig, Lawrence
The **future** of ideas : the fate of the commons in a connected world / Lawrence Lessig. Random House, 2001. xiii, 352 p. ; **346.04**

1. Intellectual property. 2. Copyright and electronic data processing. 3. Internet -- Law and legislation. 4. Information society.
ISBN 0375505784

LC 2001031968

Explores the meaning of intellectual property in the new high-tech digital age, addressing the legal, social, and economic factors at work and provides a thought-provoking argument that those qualities that have made the Internet a dynamic force for creativity, freedom, and innovation could destroy the Intenet's potential.

Norwick, Kenneth P.

The **legal** guide for writers, artists and other creative people : protect your work and understand the law / Kenneth P. Norwick with Cooper Knowlton. Pate Street Publishing Co., 2017. 288 p. ; **346.04**

1. Artists -- Legal status, laws, etc -- United States 2. Authors -- Legal status, laws, etc -- United States 3. Copyright 4. Intellectual property

ISBN 9781624144493

LC bl2017041447

Includes index.

Enables creators to understand their legal rights and safeguard their work from risks in both cyberspace and traditional media.

346.73 Private law -- United States

American Bar Association

★The **American** Bar Association legal guide for small business : everything you need to know about small business, from start-up to employment laws to financing and selling. / American Bar Association (COR). American Bar Association ; c2010. xvii, 472 p. ; **346.73**

1. Small business -- Law and legislation -- United States

ISBN 9780375723032

LC 2009049394

Includes index.

A comprehensive updated edition includes an appendix of resources and covers everything from an initial idea, to deciding what form a firm should take, to financing, hiring, working with customers, dealing with liabilities, intellectual property, taxes, selling a business and much more.

"Topics covered include legal forms of operating businesses, buying an existing business or a franchise, hiring and firing employees, managing temps and independent contractors, dealing with contracts and scams, taxes of all types, and, finally, closing, selling, or bequeathing the business." Library Journal. [review of 2000 edition]

Kaiser, Robert G., 1943-

Act of Congress : how America's essential institution works, and how it doesn't / Robert G. Kaiser. Alfred A. Knopf, 2013. 304 p. **346.73**

1. United States. Congress. 2. United States. Dodd-Frank Wall Street Reform and Consumer Protection Act. 3. Financial services industry and trade 4. Global Financial Crisis, 2008-2009. 5. United States -- Politics and government.

ISBN 9780307700162

LC 2012038245

Documents the journey of a financial reform bill in the wake of the 2008 economic collapse by focusing on two of the major players behind the legislation--Congressman Barney Frank and Senator Christopher Dodd.

Oller, John

White shoe : how a new breed of Wall Street lawyers changed big business and the American century / John Oller. E.P. Dutton, 2019. 448 p. **346.73**

1. Corporate lawyers 2. Corporations 3. Big business 4. Wealth 5. Wall Street, New York City 6. New York City

ISBN 9781524743253

LC 2018029007

A former Manhattan lawyer presents a rollicking account of how an ambitious new class of attorneys in the 20th century devised and implemented the strategies that launched the era of American big business and international Wall Street prominence.

"Oller doesn't shy away from detailing early corporate lawyers role as tools of monopolistic robber barons, or the endemic prejudice against Jewish lawyers. That balance makes this a valuable addition to the literature on Americas transformation during the Gilded Age." Publishers Weekly.

Pakroo, Peri

★The **small** business start-up kit : a step-by-step legal guide / Peri H. Pakroo, J.D. ; edited by Marcia Stewart. Nolo, 2018. 343 p. ; **346.73**

1. Small business -- Law and legislation -- United States 2. New business enterprises -- Law and legislation -- United States

ISBN 9781413324747

LC bl2018029341

Includes index.

Shows how to launch a business quickly and efficiently, explaining how to write an effective business plan; get the proper licenses and permits; price, bid, and bill projects; manage finances and taxes; and create a business website.

Winkler, Adam

We the corporations : how American businesses won their civil rights / Adam Winkler. Liveright Publishing Corporation, 2018. xxiv, 471 p. : **346.73**

1. United States. Supreme Court Cases 2. Lobbying -- Corrupt practices. 3. Business and politics. 4. Business -- Lobbying. 5. Civil rights of corporations.

ISBN 9780871407122

LC 2017051893

National Book Critics Circle Award for Nonfiction finalist, 2018

Traces the two-hundred-year history of corporate America's battle to achieve constitutional freedom from federal control, examining the civil rights debates and key events that shaped the controversial 2010 Supreme Court decision to extend constitutional protections to businesses.

"Winkler employs an evocative, fast-paced storytelling style, making for an entertaining and enlightening book that will likely complicate the views of partisans on both sides of the issue." Publishers Weekly.

346.7301 Private law--United States--Persons and domestic relations

Cathcart, Kevin,

Love unites us : winning the freedom to marry in America / edited by Kevin M. Cathcart, Leslie J. Gabel-Brett ; foreword by Eric Holder. New Press, 2016. 352 p. **346.7301**

1. United States. Defense of Marriage Act 2. Same-sex marriage -- Law and legislation -- United States 3. Gay couples -- Legal status, laws, etc. 4. LGBTQIA rights -- United States 5. Equality

ISBN 9781595585509

LC 2016006203

Telling the stories of people who loved and cared for one another, in sickness and in health, cut through the antigay noise and moved people, a history of activists? passion and persistence in the struggle for marriage rights for same-sex couples in the United States is told in the words of those who waged the battle.

"As a core text about one of our societys most significant developments, this volume belongs in every library." Booklist.

Cenziper, Debbie

★**Love** wins : the lovers and lawyers who fought the landmark case for marriage equality / Debbie Cenziper & Jim Obergefell. William Morrow, 2016. 304 p. **346.7301**

1. United States. Supreme Court Cases 2. Same sex marriage -- Law and legislation 3. Civil rights 4. LGBTQIA rights -- United States 5. Gay men -- Rights 6. United States -- History -- 21st century

ISBN 9780062456083

LC 2016014548

Documents the inspirational story of the partners, lawyers, judges, and activists behind the groundbreaking Supreme Court case that legalized same-sex marriage in all fifty states.

"Uplifting, well-written story of personal courage and political empowerment." Kirkus.

Doskow, Emily

★**Nolo's** essential guide to divorce / attorney Emily Doskow. Nolo, 2018. 497 p. : **346.7301**

1. Divorce -- Law and legislation -- United States

ISBN 1413325319

LC bl2018094567

Includes index.

Presents a step-by-step guide through every aspect of the divorce process and includes updated information on foreclosure and debt issues.

"The author covers the before, during, and after of divorce, counseling readers on the types of divorces, how to make decisions about living arrangements and the division of property, and how custody decisions are made. She advocates minimizing conflict but includes sections on domestic violence and kidnapping if the worst happens. Appendixes contain state-to-state grounds for divorce and financial inventory forms." Library Journal.

Doskow, Emily

The **legal** answer book for families / Emily Doskow and Marcia Stewart. Nolo, 2011. 386 p. ; **346.7301**

1. Domestic relations -- United States 2. Domestic relations -- United States -- States

ISBN 9781413313734

LC 2010042816

"Provides a clear and concise overview of laws that affect personal relationships and families and answers everyday legal questions that nearly every family encounters at some point. This book includes a quick-reference glossary of legal terms and an appendix of detailed information for all 50 states"--Provided by publisher.

Hertz, Frederick

A **legal** guide for lesbian and gay couples / attorneys Frederick Hertz and Emily Doskow. Nolo, 2016. 418 p. ; **346.7301**

1. Gay couples -- Legal status, laws, etc -- United States

ISBN 9781413322798

LC 2016019762

Includes index.

Provides legal information to help same-sex couples exercise their rights and make sound decisions together.

Kaplan, Roberta A.

Then comes marriage : United States v. Windsor and the defeat of DOMA / Roberta Kaplan with Lisa Dickey ; Foreword by Edie Windsor. W. W. Norton & Company, 2015. 320 p. **346.7301**

1. Windsor, Edie Trials, litigation, etc. 2. United States. Defense of Marriage Act 3. Marriage law. 4. Same-sex marriage. 5. LGBTQIA rights 6. Lesbian couples -- Legal status, laws, etc.

ISBN 9780393248678

LC 2015023636

Includes index.

"Readers with an interest in constitutional law and Supreme Court politics, as well as the road to marriage equality, will find this account deliciously gripping." Library Journal.

Lapidus, Lenora M.

★The **rights** of women : the authoritative ACLU guide to women's rights / Lenora M. Lapidus, Emily J. Martin, Namita Luthra. New York University Press, c2009. xvii, 412 p. ; **346.7301**

1. Women -- Legal status, laws, etc -- United States

ISBN 9780814752296

LC 2008047033

Rev. ed. of: The rights of women / Susan Deller Ross ... [et al.]. 3rd ed., completely rev. and up-to-date. c1993.

The Rights of Women is a comprehensive guide that explains in detail the rights of women under present U.S. law, and how these laws can be used in the continuing struggle to achieve full gender equality at home, in the workplace, at school, and in society at large. --Provided by publisher

National Association of the Deaf

★**Legal** rights : the guide for deaf and hard of hearing people / National Association of the Deaf. Gallaudet University Press, 2015. xiii, 283 p. ; **346.7301**

1. Deaf -- Legal status, laws, etc. -- United States. 2. Hearing impaired -- Legal status, laws, etc. -- United States. 3. Reference books

ISBN 9781563686443

LC 2015005783

"Highly recommended for those with hearing impairments and their loved ones, along with students and practitioners of law, education, medicine, and politics. A necessity for all public library collections." Library Journal.

346.7302 Private law--United States--Juristic acts, contracts, agency

Leamer, Laurence

The **price** of justice : a true story of greed and corruption / Laurence Leamer. Times Books, 2013. 384 p. **346.7302**

1. Caperton, Hugh Trials, litigation, etc. 2. Blankenship, Donald Leon. 3. Massey Energy (Firm) Trials, litigation, etc. 4. Coal mines and mining -- Appalachian Region. 5. Business -- Corrupt practices 6. Coal industry and trade -- Corrupt practices -- West Virginia. 7. Judicial corruption. 8. Caperton v. A. T. Massey Coal Co., 129 S. Ct. 2252 (2009)

ISBN 9780805094718

LC 2012041537

Describes how the tyrannical head of a large energy conglomerate bought judges, disregarded safety standards for mine workers, and polluted drinking water until challenged by two lawyers who brought him to justice.

Lindner, Dan, 1955-
★A **guide** to federal contracting : principles and practices / Dan Lindner. Bernan Press, 2017 x, 622 p. ; **346.7302**

1. Government purchasing -- Law and legislation -- United States 2. Letting of contracts -- United States 3. Public contracts -- United States
ISBN 9781598889659

LC 2017046917

"There are other, less-expensive guides, but none are as complete or authoritative. This is an essential resource for large public and academic libraries where federal contracts play an important role." Booklist.

346.7304 Property law--United States

Butler, Rebecca P.
★**Copyright** for teachers & librarians in the 21st century / Rebecca P. Butler. Neal-Schuman Publishers, c2011. xvii, 276 p. : **346.7304**

1. Copyright -- United States. 2. Fair use (Copyright) -- United States. 3. Teachers -- Legal status, laws, etc. -- United States.
ISBN 1555707386

LC 2011012600

Here is a practical copyright handbook designed to help librarians, media specialists, technology coordinators and specialists, and teachers stay within copyright law while making copyrighted print, non-print, and Web sources available to students and others.

Crews, Kenneth D.
★**Copyright** law for librarians and educators : creative strategies and practical solutions / Kenneth D. Crews. ALA Editions, 2020. 308 p. **346.7304**

1. Copyright -- United States. 2. Fair use (Copyright) -- United States. 3. Librarians -- United States -- Handbooks, manuals, etc. 4. Teachers -- United States -- Handbooks, manuals, etc.
ISBN 9780838916292

LC 2019051377

"This newly revised and updated edition by respected copyright authority Crews offers timely insights and succinct guidance for LIS students, librarians, and educators alike".-- Provided by publisher.

Decherney, Peter
Hollywood's copyright wars : from Edison to the internet / Peter Decherney. Columbia University Press, c2012. xii, 287 p. : **346.7304**

1. Copyright -- Broadcasting rights -- United States -- History. 2. Copyright -- Motion pictures -- United States -- History.
ISBN 0231159463

LC 2011041745

Beginning with Thomas Edison's aggressive copyright disputes and concluding with recent lawsuits against YouTube, Hollywood's Copyright Wars follows the struggle of the film, television, and digital media industries to influence and adapt to copyright law. --Provided by publisher

Elias, Stephen
The **foreclosure** survival guide : keep your house or walk away with money in your pocket / Attorneys Stephen Elias and Amy Loftsgordon ; with bankruptcy updates by Attorney Leon Bayer. Nolo, 2015. 346 p. ; **346.7304**

1. Foreclosure -- United States
ISBN 9781413321845

LC 2015009962

Offers options to help homeowners make the best decisions when faced with foreclosure, detailing federal programs, nonprofit help, and common scams.

Fishman, Stephen
★The **copyright** handbook : what every writer needs to know / Stephen Fishman, J.D.. Nolo, 2014. 458 p. ; **346.7304**

1. Copyright -- United States
ISBN 9781413320480

LC bl2014048732

Introduces the principles of copyright; discusses notice, registration, what is and is not protected, authorship, transfer, fair use, infringement, and international protection; and provides detailed instructions on how to fill out the registration forms.

The **public** domain : find and use free content for your website, book, app, music, video, art, and more / Stephen Fishman, J.D.. Nolo, 2017. 433 p. : **346.7304**

1. Public domain (Copyright law) -- United States
ISBN 9781413324013

LC bl2017026781

Includes index.

Offers advice on finding creative works in the public domain, including music, writings, art, architecture, maps, photography, movies, and software.

Gasaway, Laura N.
Copyright questions and answers for information professionals : from the columns of Against the Grain / Laura N. Gasaway. Purdue University Press, c2013. 298 p. **346.7304**

1. Fair use (Copyright) 2. Copyright 3. Photocopying processes -- Fair use (Copyright)
ISBN 9781557536396

LC oc2013003292

Includes index.

"All in all, there are answers to well over 300 questions concerning copyright, fair use, and related issues. The appendix provides a chart to assist in knowing when a book passes into public domain." Library Journal

Harris, Lesley Ellen
Licensing digital content : a practical guide for librarians / Lesley Ellen Harris. ALA Editions, 2018. xviii, 181 p. ; **346.7304**

1. Copyright -- Electronic information resources -- United States. 2. Copyright -- Electronic information resources. 3. License agreements -- United States. 4. Libraries and electronic publishing -- United States.
ISBN 9780838916308

LC 2017044800

In its new edition, this resource remains a must-have for all information professionals who deal with licenses for electronic resources. --Provided by publisher

"The revised version of this book is well organized and updated to help professionals with the licensing process. The book includes detailed chapters, analysis, terminology, a thorough index, and examples of copyright law, all compiled by an expert in the field." Booklist

Lessig, Lawrence
Remix : making art and commerce thrive in the hybrid economy

/ Lawrence Lessig. Penguin Press, 2008. 256 p. **346.7304**

1. Copyright -- Neighboring rights -- United States. 2. Copyright and electronic data processing -- United States. 3. Cultural industry and trade -- Law and legislation -- United States. 4. Creativity -- Economic aspects. 5. United States -- Social life and customs -- 20th century. 6. United States -- Social life and customs -- 21st century.
ISBN 9781594201721

LC 2008032392

Argues that future generations are being harmed by a restrictive copyright system that protects corporate interests, in a report that calls for an end of the practice of criminalizing artists who build on the creative works of others and for implementing a collaborative and profitable "hybrid economy" that protects both creative and ethical needs.

"As Lessig sees it, if intellectual-property law is left as it is an entire generation will be criminalized. He argues that the ways in which young people break copyright laws help them to become the sort of people we want them to be: creative and collaborative. Kids today are simply not going to give up downloading music and using copyrighted material in YouTube videos: they belong to a culture for which remix is the essential art. Lessig's proposals for revising copyright are compelling, because they rethink intellectual-property rights without abandoning them." The New Yorker.

Lobel, Orly

You don't own me : how Mattel v. MGA entertainment exposed Barbie's dark side / Orly Lobel. W. W. Norton & Company, 2018. 320 p. **346.7304**

1. Bryant, Carter Trials, litigation, etc. 2. MGA Entertainment (Firm) Trials, litigation, etc. 3. Mattel, Inc. Trials, litigation, etc. 4. Trials 5. Intellectual property 6. Labor disputes 7. Intellectual property infringement
ISBN 9780393254075

LC 2017027183

"The end result is a thoroughly researched book that explains the legalese of patent, property, and copyright law in laymans terms while providing an entertaining narrative." Publishers Weekly.

Pressman, David, 1937-

Patent it yourself : your step-by-step guide to filing at the U.S. Patent Office / Patent attorneys David Pressman and David E. Blau. Nolo, 2018. 656 p. : **346.7304**

1. Patent practice -- United States 2. Patent laws and legislation -- United States
ISBN 9781413325393

LC bl2018187564

Includes index.

Presents an introduction to the patenting process for inventors, covering documentation, searching, commercial potential, specifications, drawings, claims, applications, marketing, patent infringement, and licensing.

Stewart, Marcia

★**Every** landlord's legal guide / Marcia Stewart & attorney Janet Portman. Nolo, 2018. 489 p. : **346.7304**

1. Landlord and tenant -- United States 2. Landlords -- United States -- Handbooks, manuals, etc.
ISBN 9781413325171

LC bl2018095007

A reference for residential landlords shares comprehensive guidelines for saving money and maintaining legal requirements, providing coverage of everything from screening tenants to hiring a property manager.

346.7305 Inheritance, succession, and trusts--United States

Clifford, Denis

★**Plan** your estate / Attorney Denis Clifford. Nolo, 2018. 511 p. : **346.7305**

1. Estate planning -- United States
ISBN 1413325114

LC bl2018072204

Presents a guide on estate planning that covers property ownership laws, beneficiaries, probate avoidance, living trusts, joint tenancy, health care directives, life insurance, estate taxes, wills, business ownership, and pensions.

Hanks, Liza Weiman, 1961-

The **trustee's** legal companion / Lisa [i.e. Liza] Hanks and Carol Elias Zolla. Nolo, 2019 395 p. : **346.7305**

1. Living trusts -- United States 2. Executors and administrators -- United States
ISBN 9781413325973

LC 2018042915

Includes index.

Explains how to administer a living trust, including investing trust assets, handling taxes, and distributing trust property.

346.7307 Commercial law--United States

Leonard, Robin

★**Solve** your money troubles / Robin Leonard, J.D.. Nolo, 2015. 375 p. ; **346.7307**

1. Debtor and creditor -- United States 2. Credit -- Law and legislation -- United States
ISBN 9781413321708

LC bl2015033768

Includes index.

Shares practical guidelines for debt prioritizing and budgeting, offering sample letters for creditors while providing advice on such topics as stopping collector harassment, rebuilding credit, and qualifying for a mortgage.

O'Neill, Cara

★**How** to file for Chapter 7 bankruptcy / Attorney Cara O'Neill & Albin Renauer, J.D. Nolo, 2017. 452 p. ; **346.7307**

1. Bankruptcy -- United States
ISBN 9781413324327

LC bl2017046487

Includes index.

Provides advice, explanations, and sample forms, including how to complete required paperwork, schedule repayment plans, and arrange redemption agreements.

Chapter 13 bankruptcy : keep your property & repay debts over time / attorney Cara O'Neill. Nolo, 2018. 394 p. : **346.7307**

1. United States. Bankruptcy. Chapter 13, Adjustment of debts of an individual with regular income 2. Bankruptcy -- United States
ISBN 9781413325157

LC bl2018095009

Includes index.

Answers questions about bankruptcy that range from how to face the reality of being in debt and possible alternatives to filing procedures and strategies for rebuilding credit after the process is complete.

346.79401 Private law--California--Persons and domestic relations

Becker, Jo

★**Forcing** the spring : inside the fight for marriage equality / Jo Becker. Penguin Press, 2014. 480 p. **346.79401**

1. United States. Defense of Marriage Act 2. Civil rights -- United States. 3. Gay and Lesbian Movement. 4. LGBTQIA rights -- United States. 5. Gay marriage
ISBN 9781594204449

LC 2014005342

Draws on interviews and in-depth reporting to present an insider's account of a national civil rights struggle to stop Proposition 8, which removed the right of gay men and women to marry, and the campaign to undermine the Defense of Marriage Act.

"Becker's chronicle of a legal battle reveals deeper changes in the cultural and political landscape of a nation grappling with old prejudices and changing public opinion that continue to resonate." Booklist.

Yoshino, Kenji

Speak now : marriage equality on trial / Kenji Yoshino. Crown, 2015. 376 p. **346.79401**

1. Hollingsworth, Dennis, 1967- Trials, litigation, etc. 2. Perry, Kristin Trials, litigation, etc. 3. United States. Defense of Marriage Act. 4. California. Proposition 8 (2008) 5. Gay marriage 6. Civil rights -- United States. 7. Gay and Lesbian Movement. 8. LGBTQIA rights -- United States.
ISBN 9780385348805

LC 2014042967

Stonewall Book Awards: Israel Fishman Non-fiction Award, 2016.

Drawing on interviews with lawyers and witnesses on both sides of the case, a prominent legal scholar?and newly married gay man?takes readers deep inside the groundbreaking federal suit against Proposition 8, which rescinded the right of same-sex couples to marry in the state of California.

"This is the well-told story of one of the most important civil trials in recent American history, Hollingsworth v. Perry, the 12-day trial challenging the constitutionality of California's Proposition 8. Because this case was tried in federal court, most of America was aware that it might end up being argued before the US Supreme Court. Yoshino takes the reader behind the scenes of both sides of this civil trial. Well beyond its outcome, however, this case is all about why trials can be crucial to the American system of justice." Choice.

347.73 Civil procedure and courts of the United States

Bharara, Preet, 1968-

Doing justice : a prosecutor's thoughts on crime, punishment, and the rule of law / Preet Bharara. Alfred A. Knopf, 2019. 368 p. **347.73**

1. Criminal justice system 2. Social justice 3. Law 4. Fairness 5. United States -- Politics and government
ISBN 9780525521129

LC 2018053931

From a one-time federal prosecutor for the Southern District of New York comes an important overview of the way the American justice system works, and why the rule of law is essential to U.S. society, in a book that uses case histories, personal experiences and more.

"The former federal prosecutor for the Southern District of New York skillfully explains how he approached his job, offering a mixture of guiding principles and compelling anecdotes." Kirkus.

Breyer, Stephen G., 1938-

Making our democracy work : a judge's view / Stephen Breyer. Alfred A. Knopf, 2010. 336 p. **347.73**

1. United States. Supreme Court. 2. Judicial review. 3. Political questions and judicial power -- United States. 4. Separation of powers. 5. Judicial power.
ISBN 9780307269911

LC 2010016839

A Supreme Court justice outlines an accessible profile of the legislative branch's duties that explains its responsibility to safeguard the public while ensuring the cooperation of other government branches, sharing the stories behind key historical decisions.

Chemerinsky, Erwin

Closing the courthouse door : how your constitutional rights became unenforceable / Erwin Chemerinsky. Yale University Press, 2017 256 p. **347.73**

1. United States. Supreme Court Cases. 2. Freedom. 3. Political rights. 4. Civil rights 5. State (Political science)
ISBN 9780300211580

LC 2016941955

A leading legal scholar, using many stories of people whose rights have been trampled yet had no legal recourse, explores how the constitutional right to seek justice has been restricted by the Supreme Court.

"A dramatic challenge to understand the shakiness of the foundations we take for granted and where energies committed to redress should be directed." Kirkus.

Cohen, Adam (Adam Seth)

★**Supreme** inequality : the Supreme Court's fifty-year battle for a more unjust America / Adam Cohen. Penguin Press, 2020. 448 p. **347.73**

1. United States. Supreme Court -- History 2. Judicial power 3. Equality 4. Equality before the law 5. Political questions and judicial power 6. United States -- Politics and government
ISBN 9780735221505

LC 2019031002

The Time senior writer and author of Imbeciles traces the increasingly conservative direction of the Supreme Court throughout the past half-century, exploring the appointments and rulings of Justices who have supported the reversals of egalitarian law. As the nation comes to grips with two new Trump-appointed justices, Cohen proves beyond doubt that the modern Court has been one of the leading forces behind the nation's soaring level of economic inequality, and that an institution revered as a source of fairness has been systematically making America less fair.

"Weaving legal, political, and social history, Cohen creates a richly detailed, but accessible, account for all interested in the personalities and politics that have shaped and are continuing to shape not only the U.S. criminal justice system but also the fabric of American life. A must-read." Library Journal

Coyle, Marcia

★The **Roberts** court : the struggle for the constitution / Marcia Coyle. Simon & Schuster, 2013. 384 p. **347.73**

1. Roberts, John G., 1955- 2. United States. Supreme Court -- History 21st century. 3. United States. Supreme Court -- Political aspects 4. United States. Patient Protection and Affordable Care Act 5. Judicial review 6. Judges. 7. Law and politics 8. Conservatism -- United States. 9. United States -- Social life and customs -- 21st

century
ISBN 9781451627510

LC 2012051637

A National Law Journal correspondent and forefront expert on the Supreme Court traces the first seven years of the Roberts Court to report on its direction and the resolutions of five landmark cases on race, guns, immigration, campaign finance and health care.

"In this insightful, important look at the Roberts court, Coyle also explores the broader implications for American politics and justice." Booklist.

Finkelman, Paul, 1949-

★**Landmark** decisions of the United States Supreme Court / Paul Finkelman, Melvin I. Urofsky. CQ Press, c2008. xix, 791p.; **347.73**

1. Constitutional law -- United States -- Cases
ISBN 9780872894099

LC 2007042588

An important reference that provides the historical context and constitutional perspective of more than 1,000 of the most important Supreme Court cases. Landmark Decisions of the United States Supreme Court offers an unparalleled history of the Supreme Court and its impact on American democracy and society. --Provided by publisher

Friedman, Barry, 1958-

The **will** of the people : how public opinion has influenced the Supreme Court and shaped the meaning of the Constitution / Barry Friedman. Farrar, Straus and Giroux, 2009. 688 p. **347.73**

1. United States. Supreme Court Public opinion. 2. Judicial process -- United States -- Public opinion. 3. Public opinion -- United States. 4. Judicial system. 5. United States -- Politics and government.
ISBN 9780374220341

LC 2008054247

An account of the relationship between the public and the Supreme Court challenges complaints about the legitimacy of an appointed judicial authority, citing historical precedents that demonstrate how and why the rulings of justices have not overly strayed from public opinion.

"This book is a thought-provoking and authoritative history of the Supreme Court's relationship to popular opinion. Friedman's contribution to [the] discussion is the breadth and detail of his historical canvas, and it's a significant one." New York Times Book Review.

Graetz, Michael J.

The **Burger** court and the rise of the judicial right / Michael J. Graetz and Linda Greenhouse. Simon & Schuster, 2016. 512 p. **347.73**

1. Burger, Warren Earl, 1907-1995. 2. United States. Supreme Court -- History 20th century. 3. Political questions and judicial power -- United States -- History -- 20th century 4. Judges -- United States 5. Constitutional law. 6. Judicial system
ISBN 9781476732503

LC 2015031713

Drawing on the personal papers of justices as well as other archives, a first-of-its-kind book provides a fresh perspective at the Warren Burger Supreme Court, digging down to the roots of its most significant decisions and shows how their legacy affects us today.

"Two powerhouse law historians/journalists deliver a major contribution to the history of the Supreme Court." Kirkus.

Jost, Kenneth

★The **Supreme** Court A to Z / Kenneth Jost. CQ Press, c2012. xvii, 668 p. American government A to Z **347.73**

1. United States. Supreme Court. 2. United States. Supreme Court Justices 3. Civics.
ISBN 9781608717446

LC 2006038701

Provides information on the US Supreme Court, including its history, traditions, organization, biographies of past and present justices, cases, constitutional principles, legal concepts, and the Court's relationships to the government, public, and media.

Kaplan, David A., 1956-

The **most** dangerous branch : inside the Supreme Court's assault on the Constitution / David A. Kaplan. Crown Publishing, 2018. 446 p. **347.73**

1. United States. Supreme Court 2. United States. Supreme Court Justices 3. Judges 4. Judicial power 5. Constitutional law 6. Political parties
ISBN 9781524759902

LC 2018004533

Kaplan presents a sweeping narrative of the justices' aggrandizement of power over the decades -- from Roe v. Wade to Bush v. Gore to Citizens United, to rulings during the 2017-18 term. But the arrogance of the Court isn't partisan: Conservative and liberal justices alike are guilty of overreach. Challenging conventional wisdom about the Court's transcendent power, The Most Dangerous Branch is sure to rile both sides of the political aisle.

"In his penetrating if anxious analysis of Supreme Court jurisprudence, Kaplan laments recent decisions lacking judicial restraint and pleads for narrow exercise of the courts power despite public pressure and ample temptation to rule broadly on controversial matters." Booklist.

O'Brien, David M

Storm center : the Supreme Court in American politics / David M. O'Brien, University of Virginia. W.W. Norton & Company, 2017 xxi, 456 p. : **347.73**

1. United States. Supreme Court. 2. Judicial process -- United States 3. Political questions and judicial power -- United States
ISBN 9780393603538

LC 2016059480

An inside look at the workings of the Supreme Court. --Provided by publisher

O'Connor, Sandra Day, 1930-

★**Out** of order : stories from the history of the Supreme Court / Sandra Day O'Connor. Random House, 2013. 160 p. **347.73**

1. United States. Supreme Court -- History 2. Courts of last resort -- United States -- History 3. Judicial system -- United States -- History. 4. Trials. 5. Courts.
ISBN 9780812993929

LC 2012025708

The former Supreme Court Justice and author of Lazy B shares stories about the history and evolution of the Supreme Court that traces the roles of key contributors while sharing the events behind important transformations.

Shesol, Jeff, 1969-

★**Supreme** power : Franklin Roosevelt vs. the Supreme Court / Jeff Shesol. W.W. Norton, c2010. 512 p. **347.73**

1. Roosevelt, Franklin D. (Franklin Delano), 1882-1945 Political and social views. 2. United States. Supreme Court -- History 20th century. 3. Political questions and judicial power -- United States

-- History -- 20th century. 4. Judicial system. 5. Political leadership. 6. Presidents. 7. United States -- Politics and government -- 20th century.
ISBN 9780393064742

LC 2009046365

Chronicles Franklin Roosevelt's battle with the Supreme Court, which culminated in him trying to suppress its conservative justices by expanding the size of the court, an attempt which failed and divided the Democratic party.

"This is an impressive and engaging book--an excellent work of narrative history. It is deeply researched and beautifully written. Even readers who already know the outcome will find it hard not to feel the suspense that surrounded the battle, so successfully does Shesol recreate the atmosphere of this great controversy." New York Times Book Review.

Simon, James F.

Eisenhower vs. Warren : the battle for civil rights and liberties / James F. Simon. Liveright Publishing Corporation, 2018. 464 p. **347.73**

1. Warren, Earl, 1891-1974. 2. Eisenhower, Dwight D. (Dwight David), 1890-1969. 3. School integration. 4. Civil Rights Movement. 5. Social change. 6. Civil rights 7. United States -- Politics and government -- 1953-1961.
ISBN 9780871407559

LC bl2018003663

Traces the bitter 1950s rivalry between President Eisenhower and Chief Justice Earl Warren and how it framed the tumultuous future of the modern civil rights movement.

"This is a cogently written book, especially given the complexity of many of the issues. Simon does great justice to an important segment of a critical period in American history." Booklist.

Toobin, Jeffrey

The **oath** : the Obama White House and the Supreme Court / Jeffrey Toobin. Doubleday, 2012. 368 p. **347.73**

1. Obama, Barack. 2. Roberts, John G., 1955- 3. United States. Supreme Court Political aspects 4. Political questions and judicial power -- United States. 5. Judicial review 6. Judges. 7. Conservatism -- United States. 8. United States -- Social life and customs -- 20th century 9. United States -- Social life and customs -- 21st century
ISBN 9780385527200

LC 2012029205

A dramatic insider's account of what is identified as an ideological war between the John Roberts Supreme Court and the Obama administration, tracing several landmark cases and the strong views that will be shaping the Court of the near future.

★The **nine** : inside the secret world of the Supreme Court / Jeffrey Toobin. Doubleday, c2007. viii, 369 p. : **347.73**

1. United States. Supreme Court. 2. Political questions and judicial power -- United States. 3. Judicial review 4. Judges. 5. Conservatism -- United States. 6. United States -- Social life and customs -- 20th century 7. United States -- Social life and customs -- 21st century
ISBN 0385516401

LC 2007020287

J. Anthony Lukas Book Prize, 2008.

Drawing on interviews with the Supreme Court justices and other insiders, a look at the powerful, often secretive world of the Supreme Court offers profiles of each justice and how their individual styles affect the way in which they wield their power.

"Beautifully written, this is an essential purchase for all libraries interested in the contemporary Supreme Court." Library Journal.

Tushnet, Mark V., 1945-

In the balance : law and politics on the Roberts Court / Mark Tushnet. W. W. Norton & Company, 2013 352 p. **347.73**

1. Roberts, John G., 1955- 2. United States. Supreme Court. 3. United States. Patient Protection and Affordable Care Act. 4. Judges. 5. Debates and debating. 6. Judicial system. 7. Law.
ISBN 9780393073447

LC 2013012744

A constitutional law expert examines the initial years of the Roberts Court, covering the legal philosophies that have informed decisions on such major cases as the Affordable Care Act, the political structures behind Court appointments and the struggle for intellectual dominance of the Court.

348.73 Federal laws, regulations, cases of the United States

Stathis, Stephen W.

Landmark legislation 1774-2012 : major U.S. acts and treaties / Stephen W. Stathis. CQ Press, 2014 517 p. ; **348.73**

1. United States. Congress -- History. 2. Legislation -- United States -- History
ISBN 9781452292304

LC 2013029374

The Second Edition of this renowned treasure trove of information about the most important laws and treaties enacted by the U.S. Congress now deepens its historical coverage and examines an entire decade of new legislation. Landmark Legislation 1774-2012 includes additional acts and treaties chosen for their historical significance or their precedential importance for later areas of major federal legislative activity in the over 200 years since the convocation of the Continental Congress. --Provided by publisher

349.73 Federal law--United States

Friedman, Lawrence M. (Lawrence Meir), 1930-

American law in the 20th century / Lawrence M. Friedman. Yale University Press, c2002. xii, 722 p. ; **349.73**

1. Law -- United States -- History -- 20th century
ISBN 9780300091373

LC 2001003332

"The author examines the American legal system as an integral part of the larger society, both reflecting and causing changes therein. By adopting such a focus, the author makes his book accessible to readers who are not legal scholars." Booklist.

351.73 Public administration--United States

Nelson, Michael, 1949-

Guide to the presidency and the executive branch / Michael Nelson, editor. CQ Press, c2013. 2 v. (xix, 2141 p.) : **351.73**

1. Presidents -- United States.
ISBN 9781608719068

LC 2012023291

Rev. ed. of: Guide to the presidency.

This comprehensive guide provides a wealth of facts and analysis and is the definitive source for researchers seeking an understanding of those who have occupied the White House and on the institution of the U.S. presidency. --Provided by publisher

352.23 Chief executives

Kalb, Deborah
State of the union : presidential rhetoric from Woodrow Wilson to George W. Bush / edited by Deborah Kalb, Gerhard Peters and John T. Woolley. / Deborah (EDT) Kalb. CQ Press, c2007. xii, 1185 p. : **352.23**

1. Presidents -- United States -- Messages. 2. Presidents -- United States -- Inaugural addresses. 3. Rhetoric -- Political aspects -- History -- 20th century -- Sources. 4. Rhetoric -- Political aspects -- History -- 21st century -- Sources. 5. United States -- Politics and government -- 20th century Sources. 6. United States -- Politics and government -- 2001-2009 Sources.
ISBN 9780872894334

LC 2006035973

Presents one hundred State of the Union addresses in their entirety, covering 1913 to 2006, with introductory notes on the historical and political context of each speech and the reaction to it.

Emanuel, Rahm, 1959-
The **nation** city : why mayors are now running the world / Rahm Emanuel. Alfred A. Knopf, 2020. 240 p. **352.23**

1. Emanuel, Rahm, 1959- 2. Mayors 3. Municipal government 4. Political leadership -- United States 5. Cities and towns 6. United States -- Politics and government -- 21st century
ISBN 9780525656388

LC 2019024936

At a time of anxiety about the effectiveness of our national government, Rahm Emanuel provides a clear vision, for both progressives and centrists, of how to get things done in America today--a bracing, optimistic vision of America's future from one of our most experienced and original political minds.

"At its best, Emanuel's chronicle offers a revelatory view into how mayors run cities, and provokes readers to ponder whether cities really might save the world." Booklist

352.230973 Presidents--United States

Raphael, Ray
Mr. president : how and why the founders created a chief executive / Ray Raphael. Alfred A. Knopf, 2012. 324 p. ; **352.230973**

1. Executive power. 2. Political leadership. 3. Presidents -- United States -- History -- 18th century. 4. Reasoning. 5. United States -- Politics and government -- 1783-1809.
ISBN 9780307595270

LC 2011033471

Offers the exciting story of how the American presidency was shaped during the Constitutional Convention, in a history that includes Gouverneur Morris, James Madison, Alexander Hamilton, Benjamin Franklin and George Washington, each jockeying for position and trying to see his vision for the office of the president realized.

"Raphael here delves into the Constitutional Convention of 1787 to elucidate compromises that created the presidency. Saving readers the tedium of digesting Madison?s secret journal of the proceedings, Raphael converts it and supplementary sources into a dramatized narrative that emphasizes how differently the office could have been framed." Booklist.

Young, Nancy Beck
Encyclopedia of the U.S. presidency : a historical reference / edited by Nancy Beck Young. Facts On File, c2013. 6 v. : **352.230973**

1. Presidents -- United States 2. Presidents -- United States -- History 3. United States -- Politics and government Encyclopedias, Juvenile.
ISBN 9780816067442

LC 2010020746

Profiles each president, providing articles on the campaigns, administrations, and every major event, law, incident, and action that took place during their term in office.

352.3 Executive management

Moynihan, Daniel Patrick, 1927-
Secrecy : the American experience / Daniel Patrick Moynihan ; introduction by Richard Gid Powers. Yale University Press, 1998. ix, 262 p. : **352.3**

1. Information access. 2. Secrecy in government. 3. Executive privilege (Government information) 4. Security classification (Government documents) 5. United States -- Politics and government.
ISBN 9780300077568

LC 98008144

Traces the development of secrecy as a government policy over the twentieth century, demonstrates its adverse effects on Cold War policy making, and offers recommendations on curtailing its exploitation by government agencies.

355 Military science

Bacevich, Andrew J.
Washington rules : America's path to permanent war / Andrew J. Bacevich. Metropolitan Books, 2010. 224 p. **355**

1. Military policy -- United States 2. National security. 3. Intervention (International relations) 4. Aggression (International relations) 5. United States -- Foreign relations -- Decision making.
ISBN 9780805091410

LC 2010006302

Bacevich offers a critical analysis of U.S. policies concerning a continuing military vigilance, even as maintaining a global military presence becomes increasingly expensive and challenging to maintain.

"The U.S. spends more on the military than the entire rest of the world combined and maintains 300,000 troops abroad in an empire of bases, all part of a credo of global leadership and a consensus that the U.S. must maintain a state of semiwar. [The author offers an] analysis of the assumptions behind the credo of global leadership and eternal military vigilance that has become increasingly expensive and unsustainable." Booklist.

Belfiore, Michael P., 1969-
★The **department** of mad scientists : DARPA, its influence, and why it matters to you / Michael Belfiore. Smithsonian Books ; 2009. 320 p. **355**

1. United States. Defense Advanced Research Projects Agency. 2. Science policy. 3. Inventions. 4. Technological innovations. 5. Technology.
ISBN 9780061577932

LC 2009018015

"Founded by Eisenhower in response to Sputnik and the Soviet space program, DARPA [Defense Advanced Research Projects Agency] mixes military officers with sneaker-wearing scientists, seeking paradigm-shifting ideas in varied fieldsfrom energy, robotics, and rockets to peopleless operating rooms, driverless cars, and planes that can fly halfway around the world in just hours. DARPA gave birth to the Internet, GPS, and mind-controlled robotic arms. Michael Belfiore was given unprecedented access to write this first-ever popular account of DARPA." Bookmarks.

Brooks, Rosa

★**How** everything became war and the military became everything : tales from the Pentagon / Rosa Brooks. Simon & Schuster, 2016 448 p. **355**

1. National security. 2. Militarism -- United States. 3. Military policy. 4. Strategic culture -- United States. 5. United States -- History, Military.

ISBN 9781476777863

LC 2016005348

A former top Pentagon official, daughter of anti-war activists, wife of an Army Green Beret and human rights activist presents a scholarly examination of how a constant state of war is contrary to America's founding values, undermines international rules and compromises future security.

Buckley, Gail Lumet, 1937-

★**American** patriots : the story of blacks in the military from the Revolution to Desert Storm / Gail Buckley. Random House Trade Paperbacks, 2001. xxviii, 541 p. : **355**

1. African American soldiers 2. African American soldiers -- History. 3. United States -- Armed Forces -- History. 4. United States -- History, Military. 5. United States -- Race relations.

ISBN 0375760091

LC 2002069924

Robert F. Kennedy Book Award, 2002.

Profiles black soldiers, such as Crispus Attacks and Colin Powell, and the roles they and others played throughout American history from the time of the Revolution to the modern day.

"This is an account of blacks in the U.S. military, both at home and abroad, from the 1770s to the 1990s. This readable, spirited story deserves a place in every U.S. history collection, as well as in the black or military collections." Library Journal.

Capozzola, Christopher

Bound by war : how the United States and the Philippines built America's first Pacific century / Christopher Capozzola. Basic Books, 2020. 496 p. **355**

1. International relations 2. Alliances 3. Colonialism 4. Geopolitics 5. United States -- Military relations Philippines 6. Philippines -- Foreign relations United States 7. Pacific Area

ISBN 9781541618275

LC 2019057160

Ever since US troops occupied the Philippines in 1898, generations of Filipinos have served in and alongside the US armed forces. In Bound by War, historian Christopher Capozzola reveals this forgotten history, showing how war and military service forged an enduring, yet fraught, alliance between Americans and Filipinos. Telling the epic story of a century of conflict and migration, Bound by War is a fresh, definitive portrait of this uneven partnership and the two nations it transformed.

"Readers will savor this detailed study of an underexamined aspect of American foreign policy." Publishers Weekly

Carroll, James, 1943-

House of war : the Pentagon and the disastrous rise of American power / James Carroll. Houghton Mifflin Co., 2006. xiv, 657 p., 16 p. of plates : **355**

1. United States. Department of Defense 2. Pentagon (Va.) -- History. 3. Militarism -- United States -- History -- 20th century. 4. Militarism -- United States -- History -- 21st century. 5. Arms race -- History -- 20th century. 6. Arms race -- History -- 21st century. 7. United States -- Military policy.

ISBN 0618187804

LC 2005024014

An analysis of the Pentagon, the military, and their vast, frequently hidden influence on American life argues that the Pentagon has, since its inception, operated beyond the control of any force in government or society.

Daalder, Ivo H.

In the shadow of the Oval Office : profiles of the national security advisers and the presidents they served / Ivo H. Daalder and I.M. Destler. Simon & Schuster, c2009. 336 p. **355**

1. United States. Special Assistant to the President for National Security Affairs -- History. 2. Presidents -- United States -- Staff. 3. National security -- United States. 4. International relations. 5. Political leadership. 6. United States -- Politics and government. 7. United States -- Foreign relations.

ISBN 9781416553199

LC 2008040699

Traces the inside stories of how national security advisors throughout history have enabled the presidents who appointed them to exert greater control over American foreign policy, in a cautionary report that explores what the authors believe to be their roles in promoting White House secrecy and reducing its accountability.

"A revealing, unsettling look at how our presidents receive advice on foreign policy." Kirkus.

France, John

Perilous glory : the rise of western military power / John France. Yale University Press, c2011. 438 p. **355**

1. Military history. 2. Military art and science -- History. 3. Military strategy.

ISBN 9780300120745

LC 2011006437

Looks at the history of warfare from ancient Mesopotamia to the Gulf War.

Gans, John (John A.)

White House warriors : how the National Security Council transformed the American way of war / John Gans. Liveright Publishing Corporation, [2019] 272 p. **355**

1. United States. National Security Council. 2. International relations 3. Defense planning. 4. National security -- United States -- Decision making. 5. Strategic culture -- United States. 6. United States -- Military policy 7. United States -- Foreign relations -- 1945-

ISBN 9781631494567

LC 2018054255

A revelatory history of the elusive National Security Council reveals how staffers operating in the shadows have driven foreign policy clandestinely for decades and is partially responsible for present-day escalations of hostility and polarization in American government.

"This book is essential reading for all interested in politics, government, and contemporary U.S. history." Booklist.

Hagedorn, Ann

The **invisible** soldiers : how America outsourced our security

/ Ann Hagedorn. Simon & Schuster, 2014. 320 p. **355**

1. Defense industry and trade 2. Military policy -- United States. 3. Private security services. 4. National security -- United States. 5. United States -- Politics and government.
ISBN 9781416598800

LC 2014015007

During the past three decades, the U.S. government has increasingly come to rely on private security and military contractors (PSMCs) to handle everything from police work to combat support. As a result, U.S. operations, in addition to relations with allies on the ground, are often complicated by the fact that contractors -- rather than government personnel -- handle training, drone operations, embassy security, and many other functions. Author Ann Hagedorn employs a neutral tone to expose problems and describe success stories in this absorbing analysis of PSMCs.

"A brisk, disturbing account that adds to the sense that liberties taken in the war on terror have created long-term liabilities for American society." Kirkus.

Hanson, Victor Davis

The **soul** of battle : from ancient times to the present day, how three great liberators vanquished tyranny / Victor Davis Hanson. Anchor Books, 2001, c1999. 480 p. **355**

1. Epaminondas, b. ca. 420 B.C. Military leadership 2. Sherman, William Tecumseh, 1820-1891 Military leadership. 3. Patton, George S., 1885-1945 Military leadership. 4. Military history. 5. Motivation (Psychology) 6. Military tactics. 7. Command of troops
ISBN 0385720599

LC 00063979

Originally published: New York : Free Press, 1999.

Argues that American generals Sherman and Patton, as well as Athenian general Epaminondas, were the greatest military leaders in history.

"Hanson narrates the success of three military campaigns-Epaminondas defeat of the Spartans in the fourth century B.C., Sherman's march through Georgia and the Carolinas during the Civil War, and Patton's race into Germany at the head of the Third Army in 1944-45. In Hanson's view, the individual traits of spontaneity and creativity that are nourished in a free society are assets, not hindrances, in warfare." Booklist.

Hastings, Max

Warriors : portraits from the battlefield / Max Hastings. Knopf, 2005. xxiii, 354 p. : **355**

1. Soldiers 2. War. 3. Combat.
ISBN 1400044413

LC 2005044302

Assessing the experiences of thirteen soldiers, airmen, and sailors, a military historian explores what it meant to be a warrior during the wars of the nineteenth and twentieth centuries, examining their triumphs, tragedies, and motivations.

Jacobsen, Annie

The **Pentagon's** brain : an uncensored history of DARPA, America's top-secret military research agency / Annie Jacobsen. Little Brown & Company, 2015 viii, 552 p., 16 unnumbered p. of plates : **355**

1. United States. Defense Advanced Research Projects Agency. 2. Military-industrial complex. 3. Military research. 4. United States -- History, Military.
ISBN 9780316371766
Pulitzer Prize for History finalist, 2016.

No one has ever written the history of the Defense Department's most secret, most powerful, and most controversial military science R&D agency. In the first-ever history about the organization,New York Times bestselling author Annie Jacobsen draws on inside sources, exclusive interviews, private documents, and declassified memos to paint a picture of DARPA, or "the Pentagon's brain," from its Cold War inception in 1958 to the present.

"This engrossing, conversation-starting read is highly recommended for policymakers, historians, scientists, and others who study technology's implications. It will complement Jonathon Moreno's Mind Wars and Sarah Bridger's Scientists at War." Library Journal.

Keegan, John, 1934-

The **book** of war / edited by John Keegan. Viking, 1999. xix, 492 p. ; **355**

1. Military history. 2. War. 3. Essays.
ISBN 9780670888047

LC 99042660

"This is an anthology of eyewitness and participant writing covering 25 centuries, from Thucydides' history of the Peloponnesian War to a small-unit engagement between British and Iraqi infantry in the Persian Gulf war." New York Times Book Review.

Kindsvatter, Peter S.

American soldiers : ground combat in the World Wars, Korea, and Vietnam / Peter S. Kindsvatter ; foreword by Russell F. Weigley. University Press of Kansas, 2003. xxiii, 432 p., 16 p. of plates : **355**

1. United States. Army. Infantry -- History 20th century. 2. United States. Marine Corps -- History 20th century. 3. Combat -- History. 4. Marines 5. Soldiers -- United States
ISBN 0700612297

LC 2002012957

By capturing the core 'band of brothers' experience across several generations of warfare, Kindsvatter celebrates the American soldier while helping us to better understand war's lethal reality, and why soldiers persevere in the face of its horrors.

"Mining twentieth-century foot soldiers' memoirs and novels, Kindsvatter integrates this literature of personal experience into a generalized assessment of what combat was like and how men reacted to it. Kindsvatter's illuminating work is about coping with fear at the foxhole level, and it powerfully conveys the psychology and military sociology of combat in the draft-era armies." Booklist.

Pennington, Reina, 1956-

★**Amazons** to fighter pilots : a biographical dictionary of military women / Reina Pennington, editor ; Robin Higham, advisory editor ; foreword by Gerhard Weinberg. Greenwood Press, 2003. 2 v. (lxviii, 760 p.) : **355**

1. Women sailors 2. Women soldiers
ISBN 9780313291975

LC 2002044777

Presents profiles of more than three hundred women in the military, from antiquity to the present day.

"This peerless work, situated at the nexus of military history and women's studies, is an essential companion to more male-biased biographical resources." Choice.

Roach, Mary

★**Grunt** : the curious science of humans at war / Mary Roach. W. W. Norton & Co., 2016. 256 p. **355**

1. Military art and science -- United States -- Technological

innovations. 2. Military research -- United States. 3. War and civilization 4. Technology and war
ISBN 9780393245448
LC 2016008754

Explores the science of keeping humans healthy and focused in the extreme environments of war, drawing on interviews with doctors, uniform designers, trainers and weapons testers to illuminate how soldiers are conditioned to survive traumas ranging from heat and panic to exhaustion and noise.

"Roach's book is not for the squeamish or those who envision war as a glorious enterprise; it is a captivating look at the lengths scientists go to in order to reduce the horrors of war." Publishers Weekly.

Wiener, Tom,

★**Voices** of war : stories of service from the home front and the front lines / edited by Tom Wiener. National Geographic Society, c2004. 336 p. : **355**

1. Veterans -- United States 2. Armed forces. 3. War. 4. Military history. 5. United States -- Armed Forces 6. United States -- History, Military -- 20th century. 7. Oral histories.
ISBN 9780792278382
LC 2004049986

"Library of Congress Veterans History Project."
Includes index.

An oral history of the themes of war provides letters, photographs, and sketches from from U.S. veterans' who fought in World War I and II, Korea, Vietnam, and the Persian Gulf.

"This book showcases the oral histories collected by the Veteran's History Project, the Library of Congress's nationwide effort to collect and preserve the stories not only of war veterans, but also of those who served in support of the frontline troops. The personal accounts cover the major conflicts of the 20th century, from World War I to the Persian Gulf War, and include letters, diaries, and journals. The chapters are nicely arranged to show the commonalities of military experience, e.g., basic training, daily life, combat, the home front, and returning home." Library Journal.

355.001 Philosophy and theory

Tyson, Neil deGrasse

★**Accessory** to war : the unspoken alliance between astrophysics and the military / Neil deGrasse Tyson, Avis Lang. W W Norton, 2018. 448 p. **355.001**

1. Astrophysics. 2. Technological innovations. 3. Military engineering. 4. Military art and science.
ISBN 9780393064445
LC 2018019206

From early celestial navigation to satellite-enabled warfare, a well-researched book provides a thought-provoking exploration of the centuries-old relationship between science and military power.

"Well paced and skillfully written, the narrative seamlessly integrates science lessons, military strategy, and world history--surely suiting military and science buffs alike." Publishers Weekly.

355.0071 Military service academies

Dobson, Michael Singer

How to get Into a military service academy : a step-by-step guide to getting qualified, nominated, and appointed / Michael Singer Dobson. Rowman & Littlefield, 2015 xxi, 192 p. ; **355.0071**

1. United States Military Academy Admission. 2. United States Air Force Academy Admission. 3. United States Naval Academy Admission.
ISBN 9781442243149
LC 2015019469

The process for getting into a military service academy is not the same as that for getting accepted to a private or public university. This book walks prospective students and their families through the process and procedures, provides information on available resources, and uses a step by step approach that is easy to follow. --Provided by publisher

355.0086 Military science--People by miscellaneous social attributes

Nicholson, Alexander

Fighting to serve : behind the scenes in the war to repeal "don't ask, don't tell" / Alexander Nicholson. Chicago Review Press, c2012. 288 p. **355.0086**

1. Servicemembers United (United States) 2. United States. Army. 3. Nicholson, Alexander. 4. Gay soldiers. 5. Lesbian soldiers. 6. LGBTQIA rights
ISBN 9781613743720
LC 2012021821

Includes index.

Describes the formation, mission, and history of Servicemembers United, an organization for gay and lesbian servicemembers discharged under the "Don't Ask, Don't Tell" provision and successfully fought for its repeal.

355.0089 Military science--Ethnic and national groups

National Museum of African American History and Culture (U.S.),

Fighting for freedom : photographs from the National Museum of African American History and Culture / National Museum of African American History and Culture ; Earl W. and Amanda Stafford Center for African American Media Arts. National Museum of African American History and Culture, Smithsonian Institution, 2017. 80 p. : **355.0089**

1. United States. Army African American troops -- History Pictorial works. 2. African American soldiers -- History -- Pictorial works. 3. African American soldiers -- Portraits. 4. African Americans -- History
ISBN 9781911282013
LC 2017465186

Some pages fold out.

"'Double Exposure,' is a major new multi-volume series based on the Smithsonian's National Museum of African American History and Culture (NMAAHC)'s photography collection."--Provided by publisher.

"Volume 5 of Double Exposure presents 50 images of African Americans in uniform, from the Civil War to the War in Iraq" -- publisher's catalogue.

"The fifth volume in the Double Exposure series ... is a short yet powerful pictorial history of black men and women who served in the United States Armed Forces, from the Civil War to today." Publishers Weekly.

355.009 History, geographic treatment, biography

Chamberlin, Paul Thomas

The **Cold** War's killing fields : rethinking the long peace / Paul Thomas Chamberlin. HarperCollins, 2018 592 p. **355.009**

1. Cold War 2. Military history 3. War casualties 4. World politics
ISBN 9780062367204

LC bl2018080039

Offers an international military history of the Cold War arguing that the decade-long superpower struggles were one of the three great conflicts of the 20th century alongside the two World Wars, and reveals how bloody the "Long Peace" actually was.

Matloff, Judith

No friends but the mountains : dispatches from the world's violent highlands / Judith Matloff. Basic Books, 2017. 272 p. **355.009**

1. Mountains 2. Violence 3. Social conflict 4. Mountain life
ISBN 9780465097883

LC 2016043569

A veteran war correspondent travels to different conflict zones around the world, from Albania to Nepal and to Mexico, to investigate why a disproportionate amount of conflicts occur in remote mountain communities and how the drugs, terrorism and instability there affects us all.

"A tightly focused study of mountain societies that hints at future conflicts." Kirkus.

355.0092 Military science--Biography

Sites, Kevin

The **things** they cannot say : stories soldiers won't tell you about what they've seen, done or failed to do in war / Kevin Sites. Perennial, 2013. 384 p. **355.0092**

1. War 2. Journalists 3. War correspondents 4. Soldiers
ISBN 9780061990526

LC 2013409076

Compiling the accounts of soldiers, Marines, their families and friends as well as an unsettling narrative of his own failures during war, an award-winning journalist, presenting real stories of battle, learns that war both gives and takes from those most intimately involved in it.

Toler, Pamela D.

Women warriors : an unexpected history / Pamela D. Toler. Beacon Press, 2019. 240 p. **355.0092**

1. Women and war. 2. Women soldiers 3. Women warriors 4. Courage in women
ISBN 9780807064320

LC 2018028811

From Vikings and African queens to cross-dressing military doctors and WWII Russian fighter pilots, Women Warrior reclaims lost stories of women for whom battle was not a metaphor, debunking the pervasive claim that women do not, and should not, fight.

"Toler blows past all expectations with this thoroughly delightful, personable, and crucially important history of women warriors... Her captivating writing style, which is marked by disarmingly cheeky footnotes, makes this trip through so much forgotten history an exceedingly pleasurable reading experience, and her subjects, from the famous (Joan of Arc) to the criminally overlooked (Buffalo Calf Road Woman, who likely killed Custer) are a treat to learn about. An absolute research gem, Women Warriors is a historians roar all libraries should welcome." Booklist.

355.009437 Military history--Czech Republic and Slovakia

McNamara, Kevin J.

Dreams of a great small nation : the mutinous army that threatened a revolution, destroyed an empire, founded a republic, and remade the map of Europe / Kevin J. McNamara. PublicAffairs, 2016. 464 p. **355.009437**

1. Murder 2. International relations 3. Czech Republic 4. Slovakia 5. Czechoslovakia -- History -- 1918-1938 6. Soviet Union -- History -- Allied intervention, 1918-1920
ISBN 9781610394840

LC 2016930908

Documents the history-shaping murder of an Austrian by a Czech soldier in 1918 Chelyabinsk during a railway brawl, detailing how the event sparked violent reactions, massive military engagements and a plan by fugitive philosophy professor Tomas Masaryk to reclaim and establish the Czechoslovakia homeland.

"McNamara's work presents a vital first entry that opens the doors on this integral part of World War I history and the shaping of the Soviet-influenced Eastern European political and social fabric." Library Journal.

355.00973 Military history--United States

Beschloss, Michael R.

★**Presidents** of war / Michael Beschloss. Crown, [2018] 752 p. **355.00973**

1. Presidents -- United States -- History. 2. Political leadership -- United States -- History. 3. Military strategy. 4. Executive power -- United States -- History. 5. United States -- History, Military.
ISBN 9780307409607

LC 2018007697

The best-selling author of The Conquerors charts the controversial leadership, public reputations and evolving political powers of American wartime presidents from the War of 1812 through Vietnam, including Lincoln, Wilson and LBJ.

"With ample detail and enticing storytelling, this readable work will be enjoyed by students and American history buffs." Publishers Weekly.

Dower, John W.

Cultures of war : Pearl Harbor : Hiroshima : 9-11 : Iraq / John W. Dower. W.W. Norton : 2010. 576 p. **355.00973**

1. War and society -- United States. 2. World War II. 3. September 11 Terrorist Attacks, 2001. 4. Iraq War, 2003-2011 5. United States -- History, Military -- 20th century. 6. United States -- History, Military -- 21st century. 7. United States -- Military policy.
ISBN 9780393061505

LC 2010020395

National Book Award for Nonfiction finalist, 2010

Presents a comparative analysis of September 11 and the subsequent War on Terror with Pearl Harbor and World War II, addressing institutional failures of intelligence and imagination and the driving forces behind Pan-Asian and Pan-Islam movements.

"The author draws astute ironies between Pearl Harbor and 9/11 in terms of the overweening arrogance of military superpowers. The author moves back and forth between these two definitive eras in history, providing a brilliant examination of the willful self-delusion and selective reasoning involved in the highest levels of decision making--from

Japan's spectacularly ill-advised bombing of Pearl Harbor to the Bush Administration's bundling of weapons of mass destruction and Osama bin Laden as justification for invasion of Iraq. An unrelenting, incisive, masterly comparative study." Kirkus.

Glatthaar, Joseph T., 1956-

The American military : a concise history / Joseph T. Glatthaar. Oxford University Press, [2018] x, 142 p. : **355.00973**

1. Military history 2. Military life 3. Military engineering 4. United States -- Armed Forces -- History 5. United States -- History, Military
ISBN 9780190692810

LC 2018000396

Explores the origins of the U.S. military, from the 13 colonies to today's ongoing conflicts in the Middle East, examining the challenges of unconventional warfare, including terrorism and cyberwar, and looking to the future of the U.S. military.

"Glatthaar (UNC Chapel Hill) delivers a masterpiece of compression, covering US arms from the colonial beginnings to yesterday in four chapters and 127 pages." Choice.

Rose, Gideon

How wars end : why we always fight the last battle / Gideon Rose. Simon & Schuster, 2010. 432 p. **355.00973**

1. Military planning. 2. Politics and war 3. War -- History 4. Military art and science 5. United States -- History, Military -- 20th century 6. United States -- History, Military -- 21st century
ISBN 9781416590538

LC 2010034817

"Surveying the settlements of America's wars since WWI, Rose analyzes reasons for the manner and substance of their conclusions. Public spirited and accessible, Rose's presentation should impress anyone hoping for better management of war and peace by Washington." Booklist.

Scahill, Jeremy

Dirty wars : the world is a battlefield / Jeremy Scahill. Nation Books, [2013] 384 p. **355.00973**

1. Special operations (Military science) -- United States -- History -- 21st century 2. Terrorism -- Prevention -- United States -- Government policy -- History -- 21st century 3. Assassination -- United States -- History -- 21st century 4. Intelligence service -- United States -- History -- 21st century 5. United States -- History, Military -- 21st century 6. United States -- Military policy -- History -- 21st century
ISBN 9781568586717

LC 2012051769

A sobering exposé of secret war programs currently being conducted behind the scenes of the War on Terror, drawing on interviews with CIA agents, mercenaries and other operators to reveal the human consequences of night raids, drone strikes and other unofficial "dirty-war" tactics.

355.009747 Military history--New York

Cohen, Eliot A.

Conquered into liberty : two centuries of battles along the great warpath that made the American way of war / Eliot A. Cohen. Free Press, 2011. 416 p. **355.009747**

1. Military history. 2. War. 3. Military strategy. 4. New York (State) -- History, Military. 5. Canada -- History, Military
ISBN 9780743249904

LC 2011023717

The author of Supreme Command documents the turbulent history of a contested corridor between Albany and Montreal, offering analyses of a series of pivotal battles to explain how they shaped American military culture for more than a century.

"This is an engaging account of the wars fought on the Great Warpath. [ʃr A delightful-to-read piece of American history." Kirkus.

355.02 War and warfare

Armitage, David, 1965-

Civil wars : a history in ideas / David Armitage. Alfred A. Knopf, 2017. 320 p. **355.02**

1. Civil war 2. Military history 3. War and civilization
ISBN 9780307271136

LC 2016023404

"A highly original history, tracing civil war, the least understood and most intractable form of organized human aggression, from Ancient Rome through the centuries to present day."--Provided by publisher.

Arnold, James R., 1952-

Jungle of snakes : a century of counterinsurgency warfare from the Philippines to Iraq / James R. Arnold. Bloomsbury Press, c2009. 304 p. **355.02**

1. Unconventional warfare. 2. Military history -- 20th century. 3. World politics. 4. War. 5. United States -- History, Military -- 20th century. 6. Great Britain -- History, Military -- 20th century. 7. France -- History, Military -- 20th century.
ISBN 9781596915039

LC 2008054018

A former central intelligence agency director presents a history of modern warfare that evaluates how the post-cold war era has been fraught by such challenges as terrorism, insurgency, and guerilla tactics, in an account that also discusses America's struggles for civilian support and the nation's failure to learn from past mistakes throughout the occupation of Iraq.

Boot, Max, 1968-

Invisible armies : an epic history of guerrilla warfare from ancient times to the present / Max Boot. Liveright Pub. Corporation, 2012. 576 p. **355.02**

1. Guerrilla warfare -- History 2. Unconventional warfare 3. Military strategy 4. Insurgency
ISBN 9780871404244

LC 2012028522

Describes the history of unconventional and nontraditional warfare from the nomads used by Alexander the Great to the shadowy modern battlefields of the post-9/11 era and featuring a diverse cast of historical tacticians and revolutionaries from Mao Zedong to Edward Lansdale.

Gordin, Michael D.

Red cloud at dawn : Truman, Stalin, and the end of the atomic monopoly / Michael D. Gordin. Farrar, Straus and Giroux, 2009. 416 p. **355.02**

1. Truman, Harry S., 1884-1972. 2. Stalin, Joseph, 1879-1953. 3. Nuclear weapons -- History -- 20th century. 4. Arms race -- History -- 20th century. 5. Cold War. 6. World politics -- 1945-1955. 7. United States -- Foreign relations Soviet Union. 8. Soviet Union -- Foreign relations United States. 9. United States -- Foreign relations -- 1945-1953. 10. Soviet Union -- Foreign relations -- 1945-1991.
ISBN 9780374256821

LC 2009001424

The author of Five Days in August explores the covert process through which nations develop and hide their weapons programs and how other states detect nuclear proliferation, examining the role of intelligence in arms development and political decision-making.

Hedges, Chris

War is a force that gives us meaning / Chris Hedges. PublicAffairs, 2002. 211 p. **355.02**

1. Hedges, Chris. 2. War -- Psychological aspects. 3. Nationalism. 4. Military history -- 20th century.
ISBN 1586480499

LC 2002068136

National Book Critics Circle Award for Nonfiction finalist, 2002.

Looks at the appeal of war, arguing that the ideas of combat are noble and glorious, providing a purpose for living for some people.

"This should be required reading in this post-9/11 world." Library Journal.

Langewiesche, William

The **atomic** bazaar : the rise of the nuclear poor / William Langewiesche. Farrar, Straus and Giroux, 2007. 179 p. : **355.02**

1. Nuclear weapons. 2. Nuclear weapons -- Pakistan. 3. Nuclear nonproliferation. 4. World politics -- 21st century. 5. Pakistan -- Politics and government.
ISBN 0374106789

LC 2006102539

In his shocking and revelatory new work, celebrated journalist William Langewiesche investigates the burgeoning threat of nuclear-weapons production and the inexorable drift of nuclear-weapons technology from the hands of the rich into the hands of the poor. As more unstazble and undeveloped nations acquire the ultimate arms, the stakes of state-sponsored nuclear activity have soared to frightening heights...

"Langewiesche's bracing expose of nuclear criminality blasts away the ubiquitous misinformation usually attendant on this alarming subject." Booklist.

Latiff, Robert H.

Future war : preparing for the new global battlefield / Robert H. Latiff. Alfred A. Knopf, 2017. 192 p. **355.02**

1. Military art and science 2. National security 3. Technology and war. 4. Geopolitics
ISBN 9781101947609

LC 2017002411

"A Borzoi book."

A retired U.S. Air Force major general presents an expert assessment of how evolving technologies will change virtually every aspect of war as it is known, outlining urgent recommendations for how to best prepare for imminent national security challenges.

"This is a quick and stimulating read, and its focus on ethics makes it an important part of the growing literature related to managing the continuing acceleration of technological development." Publishers Weekly.

Rhodes, Richard, 1937-

Arsenals of folly : the making of the nuclear arms race / Richard Rhodes. Alfred A. Knopf, 2007. 386 p. : Making of the nuclear age ; **355.02**

1. Gorbachev, Mikhail, 1931- 2. Reagan, Ronald. 3. Nuclear weapons. 4. Arms race. 5. Disarmament. 6. Cold War. 7. United States -- History -- 1961-
ISBN 9780375414138

LC 2007017613

The story of the postwar superpower arms race, climaxing during the Reagan-Gorbachev decade. Drawing on a wealth of new documentation, Rhodes reveals how the Reagan administration's unprecedented arms buildup in the early 1980s led Soviet leader Andropov to conclude that Reagan must be preparing for a nuclear war.

"This historical record, drawing upon many firsthand accounts and interviews, details pivotal events in world history and should be necessary reading for anyone interested in 20th-century history." Library Journal.

Ruane, Kevin

Churchill and the bomb in war and Cold War / Kevin Ruane. Bloomsbury Academic, 2016. xxi, 402 p. : **355.02**

1. Churchill, Winston, 1874-1965 2. Nuclear weapons 3. Politicians 4. Atomic bomb 5. Cold War 6. Great Britain -- History -- 20th century
ISBN 9781472523389

LC 2016000484

Moving from the development of the atomic bomb during the Second World War to the Cold War and the advent of the hydrogen bomb, Churchill and the Bomb explores Winston Churchill's changing relationship with and views on nuclear weapons.

"An important story very well told." Choice.

Singer, P. W. (Peter Warren)

Wired for war : the robotics revolution and conflict in the twenty-first century / P.W. Singer. Penguin Group, 2009. 499 p., 16 p. of plates : **355.02**

1. Military art and science -- Forecasts 2. Technological innovations -- Social aspects. 3. Robotics. 4. Ordnance.
ISBN 9781594201981

LC 2009290632

A military expert reveals how science fiction is fast becoming reality on the battlefield, changing not just how wars are fought, but also the politics, economics, laws, and ethics that surround war itself.

Sun-tzu, 6th cent. B.C.

★The **illustrated** art of war / Sun Tzu ; the definitive English translation by Samuel B. Griffith. Oxford University Press, 2005. 272 p. : **355.02**

1. Military art and science -- Early works to 1800. 2. Leadership 3. Military tactics
ISBN 9780195189995

LC 2005010651

Seventy-five color and black-and-white images are featured in this striking illustrated edition of the classic, two-thousand-year-old work on combat, military strategy, and leadership.

Wilson, Ward

Five myths about nuclear weapons / Ward Wilson. Houghton Mifflin Harcourt, 2013. 176 p. **355.02**

1. Nuclear warfare. 2. Nuclear weapons. 3. Nuclear deterrence strategy. 4. Strategy.
ISBN 9780547857879

LC 2012017322

Expanded from a controversial article, an argument against the necessity of nuclear weapons challenges common beliefs that they overcome opposition, provide deterrence and maintain peace, drawing on new facts and historical research to consider how the world could be peaceful without nuclear weaponry.

355.020285 War and warfare--Computer applications

Watts, Clint

Messing with the enemy / Clint Watts. HarperCollins, 2018. 304 p. **355.020285**

1. Online social networks 2. Misinformation 3. National security 4. Computer security

ISBN 9780062795984

LC bl2018001174

A former FBI Special Agent and leading cyber-security expert presents a sobering and essential look at the misinformation campaigns, bogus news and electronic espionage operations that have become the cutting-edge of modern warfare, offering urgent recommendations for strategic protections at individual and national levels.

355.0209 War and warfare--History, geographic treatment, biography

Boot, Max, 1968-

★**War** made new : technology, warfare, and the course of history, 1500 to today / Max Boot. Gotham Books, c2006. 624 p., 16 p. of plates : **355.0209**

1. Military history. 2. War. 3. Military art and science -- Technological innovations.

ISBN 1592402224

LC 2006015518

"A Council on Foreign Relations book"--Jacket.

An analysis of the pivotal role of technology in modern warfare focuses on four historical periods that shaped the rise and fall of empires, in a narrative account that covers such topics as gunpowder, the Industrial Revolution, and stealth aircraft.

David, Saul, 1966-

★**War** : from ancient Egypt to Iraq / editorial consultant, Saul David. DK Pub., 2009. 512 p. : **355.0209**

1. Military history -- Pictorial works 2. War -- History -- Pictorial works 3. Battles -- History -- Pictorial works 4. Military art and science -- History -- Pictorial works

ISBN 9780756655723

LC 2010278612

"The definitive visual history, from Bronze-Age battles to 21st-century conflict"--Cover.

Includes index.

"War" combines a coherent and compelling historical narrative with a wealth of supporting features on weapons and technology, strategy and tactics, the experience of war, and history's fighting elites to recount the epic 5,000-year story of warfare and combat through the ages.

Hanson, Victor Davis

The **father** of us all : war and history, ancient and modern / Victor Davis Hanson. Bloomsbury Press, 2010. 259 p. **355.0209**

1. War -- History. 2. Military history. 3. War and society. 4. Ancient history. 5. Essays.

ISBN 9781608191659

LC 2009041714

A sweeping survey on how war has shaped historical societies evaluates conflicts from Ancient Greece to the present while sharing essays that impart lessons on how to draw from past examples to address modern challenges. By the best-selling author of A War Like No Other.

"This anthology brings together 13 of Hanson's essays and reviews, revised and re-edited. They have appeared over the past decade in periodicals from the American Spectator to the New York Times. Hanson's introductory generalization that war is a human enterprise that seems inseparable from the human condition structures such subjects as an eloquent answer to the question Why Study War?, a defense of the historicity of the film 300, about the Persian Wars, in a masterpiece of envelope pushing, and a comprehensive and dazzling analysis of why America fights as she does. The pieces are well written, sometimes elegantly so, and closely reasoned." Publishers Weekly.

MacMillan, Margaret, 1943-

War : how conflict shaped us / Margaret MacMillan. Random House, 2020 336 p. **355.0209**

1. War and society. 2. Military history 3. War -- History. 4. War -- Economic aspects

ISBN 9781984856135

LC 2020014498

From the internationally renowned historian and bestselling author of Paris 1919 comes a provocative argument that war is an essential aspect of human nature, and that peace is an aberration in history.

"Like a great general, MacMillan marshals strands of culture, economics, technology, strategy, tactics, and even music, art, literature, and movies, clearing away the smoke of battle to reveal war's inner structure and impact. This is an erudite yet clearly written synthesis, sure to appeal to many readers." Booklist

355.1 Military life and customs

Farley, Janet I.

Military 101 : basic training for new military families / Janet I. Farley. Rowan & Littlefield, 2016 xx, 207 p. ; **355.1**

1. Military spouses -- United States -- Handbooks, manuals, etc. 2. Families of military personnel -- United States -- Handbooks, manuals, etc. 3. United States -- Armed Forces -- Military life Handbooks, manuals, etc.. 4. Reference books

ISBN 9781442256019

LC 2015050849

"Farley... has created an accessible and important guide, suitable for most public librariesessential for base libraries and libraries in military-service areas." Booklist.

Hickman, Joseph

Murder at Camp Delta : a staff sergeant's pursuit of the truth about Guantanamo Bay / Joseph Hickman. Simon & Schuster, 2014. 256 p. **355.1**

1. Hickman, Joseph. 2. Guantanamo Bay Detention Camp. 3. United States. Marine Corps Officers. 4. War on Terrorism, 2001-2009. 5. Prisoner abuse 6. Military prisons. 7. Prisoners of war -- Abuse of

ISBN 9781451650792

LC 2014012099

A former team leader and Sergeant of the Guard at Guantanamo Naval Base offers a revelatory eyewitness account of the notorious prison, making claims of a secret CIA facility for torture, the murder of three detainees, and the subsequent U.S. government cover up.

"Some readers will see this book as a traitorous attack on patriots protecting the United States from fanatics by any means, while others will view it as confirmation from a veteran that an out-of-control government and individuals went way beyond the lawand gained nothing but trouble from it." Library Journal.

O'Donnell, Patrick K., 1969-

The **Unknowns** : the untold story of America's Unknown Soldier and WWI's most decorated heroes who brought him home / Patrick K. O'Donnell. Atlantic Monthly Press, 2018. 288 p. **355.1**

1. Arlington National Cemetery (Arlington, Va.) 2. Tomb of the Unknowns (Va.) 3. Veterans 4. Military cemeteries 5. National cemeteries. 6. Virginia
ISBN 9780802128331

LC bl2018085731

A critically acclaimed medical historian describes the history of the Tomb of the Unknown Soldier in Arlington National Cemetery and tells the stories of those laid to rest there as well as those veterans serving as Body Bearers.

355.120973 Military living conditions--United States

Lawhorne Scott, Cheryl, 1968-
Raising children in the military / Cheryl Lawhorne-Scott, Don Philpott, and Jeff Scott. Rowman & Littlefield, 2014 xii, 336 p. ; **355.120973**

1. Children of military personnel -- United States -- Handbooks, manuals, etc. 2. Families of military personnel -- United States -- Handbooks, manuals, etc. 3. Child rearing -- United States -- Handbooks, manuals, etc. 4. United States -- Armed Forces -- Military life Handbooks, manuals, etc..
ISBN 9781442227484

LC 2013046688

Includes index.

Military families with children face many of the everyday challenges that those families not in the military face, but they also face other challenges that the rest of us don't. This book looks at the special issues and concerns of military families raising children and provides support and resources for those families. --Provided by publisher

355.20973 Military resources--United States

Klare, Michael T., 1942-
All hell breaking loose : the Pentagon's perspective on climate change / Michael T. Klare. Metropolitan Books, 2019. 304 p. **355.20973**

1. Pentagon (Va.) 2. Climate change 3. Global environmental change 4. National security -- United States. 5. Military policy 6. United states -- Politics and government 7. United States -- Armed Forces 8. United States -- Military policy.
ISBN 9781627792486

LC bl2019033834

The author of Resource Wars reveals how the American military regards climate change as a top threat to national security and is developing new strategies for responding to catastrophic weather, droughts and food shortages.

355.3 Organization and personnel of military forces

Geraghty, Tony
Soldiers of fortune : a history of the mercenary in modern warfare / Tony Geraghty. Pegasus Books, 2009. xvii, 392 p., 12 p. of plates : **355.3**

1. Mercenaries 2. Military history 3. Armed Forces -- History 4. Expatriate soldiers.
ISBN 9781605980485

LC bl2009014369

A history of mercenaries explores the ways in which soldiers for hire have been an essential component of modern and privatized warfare in Iraq and Afghanistan, describing the myriad ways in which they are viewed in different parts of the world while offering insight into their lesser-known military activities.

"Covering the 1960s to the present, with revealing interviews, Geraghty looks at the virtues and failings of the world's second-oldest profession. This serious study should find its way to most readers of military history." Library Journal.

Harris, Shane
@WAR : the rise of the military-Internet complex / Shane Harris. Houghton Mifflin Harcourt, [2014] 256 p. **355.3**

1. United States. Strategic Command (2002-). Cyber Command. 2. United States. National Security Agency. 3. Information warfare 4. Cyberspace -- Security measures -- Government policy. 5. Cyberterrorism -- Prevention -- Government policy. 6. Computer crimes -- Prevention -- Government policy.
ISBN 9780544251793

LC 2014016741

"An Eamon Dolan Book."

Investigates how the Pentagon, NSA and other government agencies are working with corporations in anticipation of cyberspace warfare against enemy targets.

Lawhorne Scott, Cheryl, 1968-
★**Military** mental health care : a guide for service members, veterans, families, and community / Cheryl Lawhorne and Don Philpott. Rowman & Littlefield Publishers, c2013. x, 229 p. ; **355.3**

1. Psychology, Military 2. Soldiers -- Mental health -- United States 3. Veterans' families -- United States 4. Veterans -- Mental health -- United States
ISBN 9781442220935

LC 2012034879

"This guide makes it clear that every veteran deserves to get better, and highlights the various kinds of help available to military personnel." Booklist.

Paglen, Trevor
Blank spots on the map : the dark geography of the Pentagon's secret world / Trevor Paglen. Dutton, 2010, c2009. 324 p. **355.3**

1. Military bases, American. 2. Intelligence service -- United States. 3. Military secrets 4. Military bases -- United States.
ISBN 9780451229168

A geography scholar and artist recounts his research into ungoverned regions of the world where the military conducts some of its most clandestine operations, in an account that includes coverage of his investigation into a covert site in Nevada near where a construction worker was poisoned by toxic chemicals.

"The author explores the clandestine activities of the U.S. military and the CIA, giving readers a thorough and provocative tour of places that officially do not exist. Paglen has a brisk reporting style and is an engaging storyteller. His journey into what he calls the black world of classified locations from research facilities to secret prisons this time takes him across the country and around the world." Library Journal.

Stengel, Richard

Information wars : how we lost the global battle against disinformation and what we can do about it / Richard Stengel. Atlantic Monthly Press, 2019. 357 p. **355.3**

1. ISIS (Islamic State of Iraq and Syria) 2. United States. Department of State Officials and employees 3. Fake news 4. Information warfare 5. Terrorism in mass media 6. Propaganda 7. Russia -- Foreign relations United States 8. United States -- Foreign relations Russia

ISBN 9780802147981

LC 2019033532

The former Under Secretary of State for Public Diplomacy and Public Affairs presents an insider's account of how the U.S. tried, and failed, to combat the disinformation that directly influenced the 2016 election and continues to impact global society.

355.4 Military operations

Gaddis, John Lewis

On grand strategy / John Lewis Gaddis. Penguin Group USA, 2018 304 p. **355.4**

1. Strategy. 2. Leadership. 3. Military art and science. 4. Civilization, Western.

ISBN 9781594203510

LC 2018285468

Distilled from the Yale University seminar, "Studies in Grand Strategy," a master class in strategic thinking surveys statecraft from the ancient Greeks through FDR and beyond as vital historical lessons for future world leaders.

Kilcullen, David

The **accidental** guerrilla : fighting small wars in the midst of a big one / David Kilcullen. Oxford University Press, 2009. 304 p. **355.4**

1. Guerrilla warfare. 2. Unconventional warfare. 3. Military history -- 20th century. 4. Military history -- 21st century. 5. United States -- Military policy.

ISBN 9780195368345

LC 2008054870

"This excellent book has an anthropologist's sense of social dynamics and a reporter's eye for telling detail. [The author's] account of how the Americans use soft and hard power to pacify parts of eastern Afghanistan . . . should be compulsory reading in military academies on both sides of the Atlantic." The Economist.

Marx, Karl, 1818-1883

★The **communist** manifesto / Karl Marx and Friedrich Engels. Penguin Books, 2006, c1848. 119 p. ; **355.4**

1. Communism. 2. Political science. 3. World politics. 4. Social contract.

ISBN 014303751X

LC 2006043993

First published in 1848.

Translation of: Manifest der Kommunistischen Partei

Examines the theory and goals expounded by Marx in the Communist Manifesto and the influence on Marx of Hegel, Feuerbach, and other philosophers. Second presentation explores Rousseau's concept of social order and its implications for individual freedom and the good of society.

Springer, Paul J.,

Encyclopedia of cyber warfare / Paul J. Springer, editor. ABC-CLIO, 2017 xx, 379 p. **355.4**

1. Cyberspace operations (Military science) -- United States 2. Cyberterrorism

ISBN 9781440844249

LC oc2018143865

"This current volume seeks to provide some clarity regarding the history and current capabilities of the cyber domain. Its authors have largely, though not exclusively, focused upon the Western experience, particularly the United States. In part, this is due to the availability of open source, unclassified data. Not only are the sources more readily available, but they tend to be more applicable to the target audience for this work. The authors come from a wide variety of backgrounds, with a substantial number of them serving in the military or other governmental institutions. As such, it needs to be stated that the ideas and arguments presented in this volume are the opinions of the individual authors, based upon their expertise, and do not represent the position of any government, military entity, or institution."--Provided by publisher.

"Most of us are familiar with the concepts of identity theft, cybercrime, and related computer-security issues, but we do not know much about cyberwarfare, in which hacking techniques are used to support a state, organization, or ideology. This new reference work serves to document and inform readers about those activities. Written by both academics and members of the military and edited by a professor at a military college, this encyclopedia provides an excellent review of this sensitive topic." Booklist.

355.409 Military operations -- History

Nolan, Cathal J.

The **allure** of battle : a history of how wars have been won and lost / Cathal J. Nolan. Oxford University Press, 2017 viii, 709 p. **355.409**

1. Battles. 2. Military history. 3. War.

ISBN 9780195383782

LC 2016016391

Cathal Nolan's The Allure of Battle shows that while wars have shaped the history of the modern world, their outcomes are decided by many other factors. The book argues that major battles are not decisive to the outcome of wars; rather, wars depend on longer-term attrition in which the side that wins gradually and remorselessly overwhelms the other with larger arsenals and greater reserves of manpower.

"Nonetheless, this is one of the most valuable military histories in years. A must - read for students of military history." Kirkus.

355.5 Military training

Ambinder, Marc

The **brink** : President Reagan and the nuclear war scare of 1983 / Marc Ambinder. Simon & Schuster, 2018 320 p. **355.5**

1. Reagan, Ronald 2. Cold War 3. Nuclear warfare 4. Political leadership 5. World politics 6. United States -- Military relations Soviet Union 7. Soviet Union -- Military relations United States

ISBN 9781476760377

LC bl2018080040

Documents the story of the 1983 war game that intensified nuclear brinkmanship between the U.S. and the former Soviet Union, recounting a series of close calls that tested period leadership over the course of an anxious two-year nuclear stalemate. Illustrations.

Man, John, 1941-

Ninja : 1,000 years of the shadow warrior / John Man. William Morrow, c2013. vi, 288 p. : **355.5**

1. Ninjutsu. 2. Ninja -- History. 3. Martial artists -- Japan. 4. Assassination -- History. 5. Japan -- History -- 15th century.
ISBN 9780062222022

LC 2012031912

Blends mythology and anthropology to trace the history of the warriors with extraordinary skills in combat, climbing, deception, disguise, and camouflage from their first appearance in feudal Japan to the present.

355.6 Military administration

Cotton, Tom

Sacred duty : a soldier's tour at Arlington National Cemetery / Tom Cotton. William Morrow & Co, 2019. 352 p. **355.6**

1. Cotton, Tom 2. Arlington National Cemetery (Arlington, Va.) 3. United States. Army. Infantry Division, 3rd 4. Military history. 5. Cemeteries. 6. Memorials. 7. Funerals 8. Arlington, Virginia 9. United States -- History, Military
ISBN 9780062863157

LC 2019006676

The conservative Arkansas senator presents an intimate and uplifting portrait of Arlington National Cemetery's Old Guard, in a historical memoir that draws on his tradition-inspired service as a unit platoon leader in wartime.

"An Arkansas senator and Bronze Star recipient delivers a first book full of information, history, and remarkable facts about true heroes. A must-read for military members and their families that is sure to appeal to patriotic Americans of all stripes." Kirkus.

355.60973 Military administration--United States

Vogel, Steve, 1960-

The **Pentagon** : a history : the untold story of the wartime race to build the Pentagon--and to restore it sixty years later / Steve Vogel. Random House, c2007. xxv, 626 p. : **355.60973**

1. United States. Department of Defense Procurement 2. Pentagon (Va.) -- History 3. Public buildings -- Designs and plans 4. Architecture -- Washington, D.C. 5. Military architecture -- History 6. September 11 Terrorist Attacks, 2001 7. United States -- History, Military -- 20th century 8. United States -- History, Military -- 21st century 9. Washington, D.C. -- History
ISBN 1400063035

LC 2006050873

Describes the design and construction of the Pentagon during World War II, the subsequent history of the building and its role during key historical events, the September 11th attack and its aftermath, and the massive efforts to rebuild the structure.

"Vogel's work recounts the construction of one of the world's most iconic buildingsthe Pentagon. But more compelling by far, he relates the human stories underlying this huge construction effort. All this would of itself be enough to warrant a book but Vogel plunges on to an appropriate second story: the terrorist assault of 9/11 and the Pentagon's subsequent resurrection. This section of the book, due perhaps to the proximity of the event, is all the more compelling." New York Post

355.8 Military equipment and supplies

Baggott, J. E.

The **first** war of physics : the secret history of the Atomic Bomb, 1939-1949 / Jim Baggott. W. W. Norton & Co. Inc., 2010. xiv, 576 p. : **355.8**

1. Nuclear physics 2. Atomic bomb -- History. 3. Nuclear weapons. 4. Physics
ISBN 9781605980843

Originally published under title: Atomic. London : Icon, 2009.

Relates the politics and the physics of the ten-year race to build the world's most destructive weapon, from the discovery of nuclear fission to the aftermath of the first Soviet atomic bomb test.

Kaplan, Fred M.

The **bomb** : presidents, generals, and the secret history of nuclear war / Fred Kaplan. Simon & Schuster, 2020. 372 pages, 8 unnumbered pages of plates : **355.8**

1. Nuclear weapons 2. Weapons of mass destruction 3. Nuclear warfare 4. Military policy 5. United States
ISBN 9781982107291

LC bl2020002407

The national-security columnist for Slate and Pulitzer Prize finalist, combining deep reporting with historical research, and discussing theories that have dominated nightmare scenarios, presents a history of American policy on nuclear war.

"A well-written, exhaustively researched history of American leaders' efforts to manage their nuclear arsenal." Kirkus

Kean, Sam

The **bastard** brigade : the true story of the renegade scientists and spies who sabotaged the Nazi atomic bomb / Sam Kean. Little, Brown and Company, 2019. xii, 447 pages, 24 unnumbered pages of plates : **355.8**

1. Sabotage 2. Espionage 3. Atomic bomb -- Germany -- History 4. Nazis
ISBN 9780316381680

LC 2019939370

Traces the remarkable story of how a renegade group of soldiers, scientists and spies prevented Hitler from obtaining a nuclear bomb.

"Vivid derring-do moves swiftly through a carefully constructed espionage thriller." Kirkus.

Levy, Joel, 1971-

Fifty weapons that changed the course of history / written by Joel Levy. Firefly Books, 2014. 224 p. : **355.8**

1. Military weapons -- History. 2. Weapons -- History.
ISBN 1770854266

LC 2015300332

Looks at fifty weapons that have helped shape the last 3,500 years, from the very first hand-ax to the AK-47 and beyond.

"The format, layout, and liveliness of the text enhance its readability. A list of further reading, useful websites, and an accurate index further the volumes usefulness. With its modest price, this book is recommended for a wide range of public, school, and academic libraries." Booklist.

356 Specific kinds of military forces and warfare

Carney, John T.

No room for error : the covert operations of America's special tactics units from Iran to Afghanistan / John T. Carney Jr. and Benjamin F. Schemmer. Ballantine Books, 2002. xii, 334 p., 16 p. of plates : **356**

1. Special forces 2. United States -- History, Military -- 20th century. 3. United States -- History, Military -- 21st century.
ISBN 9780345453334

LC 2002028158

The creator and first commanding officer of the USAF's Special Tactics Units reveals the inside workings of the U.S. military's special forces and provides information on the war against terrorism on the front lines in Afghanistan.

"The author's dramatic tales place special operations history in perspective, particularly as the war in Afghanistan has been led by special forces units." Publishers Weekly.

Couch, Dick, 1943-

Sua sponte : the forging of a modern American Ranger / Dick Couch. Berkley Books, 2012. xviii, 364 p. : **356**

1. United States. Army. Ranger Regiment, 75th 2. United States. Army Commando troops 3. Special forces. 4. Commando troops. 5. Special operations (Military science) 6. Military education.
ISBN 9780425247587

LC 2011038693

Describes the ranger training and direct-action missions undertaken by the young warriors deployed in Afghanistan to fight the Taliban as part of the 75th Ranger Regiment.

Klein Halevi, Yossi, 1953-

Like dreamers : the story of the Israeli paratroopers who reunited Jerusalem and divided a nation / Yossi Klein Halevi. HarperCollins Publishers, 2013. 608 p. **356**

1. Haganah (Organization) 2. Arab-Israeli conflict. 3. Israel-Arab War, 1967. 4. Parachute troops. 5. Israel
ISBN 9780060545765

LC 2013018850

Sophie Brody Medal, 2014.

In Like Dreamers, acclaimed journalist Yossi Klein Halevi interweaves the stories of a group of 1967 paratroopers who reunited Jerusalem, tracing the history of Israel and the divergent ideologies shaping it from the Six-Day War to the present.

Mazzetti, Mark

The **way** of the knife : the CIA, a secret army, and a war at the ends of the Earth / Mark Mazzetti. The Penguin Press, 2013. 400 p. **356**

1. CIA 2. United States. Department of Defense 3. National security -- United States -- Decision-making 4. Assassination -- United States -- History -- 21st century 5. Military policy -- Decision-making 6. Spies 7. United States -- History, Military -- 21st century 8. United States -- Military policy
ISBN 9781594204807

LC 2013006820

Includes bibliographical references and index.

Presents a revelatory account of the transformation of the CIA and America's special forces into competing covert paramilitary agencies responsible for the defeat of Osama bin Laden and other strategic war efforts, offering insight into the new ways thatthe nation is fighting wars.

357 Mounted forces and warfare

Cotterell, Arthur

Chariot : the astounding rise and fall of the world's first war machine / Arthur Cotterell. Overlook Press, 2005. 352 p. **357**

1. Chariot -- History. 2. Military art and science -- History -- To 500. 3. Ancient military history. 4. Vehicles.
ISBN 1585676675

LC 2004065980

Traces the rise and fall of chariot use in civilizations throughout the ancient world, recounting key military confrontations in which the chariot played a significant role in the outcome of battles and directly impacted the fates of nations, in an account that also reveals the chariot's role in sports, as a religious symbol, and as an element in literature and film.

"This work is a welcome addition to a collection specializing in military history or ancient history but will appeal to general readers as well because the writing is accessible despite the plethora of detail." Library Journal.

358 Air and other specialized forces and warfare; engineering and related services

Baker, Nicholson, 1957-

Baseless : my search for secrets in the ruins of the Freedom of Information Act / Nicholson Baker. Penguin Press, 2020. xiv, 450 p. **358**

1. Baker, Nicholson, 1957- 2. United States. Freedom of Information Act 3. Biological weapons 4. Biological warfare research 5. Intelligence service -- United States -- History 6. Authors, American
ISBN 9780735215757

LC 2019043384

The National Book Critics Circle Award-winning author presents a deeply researched assessment of the Freedom of Information Act that reveals how deliberate obstructions, from extensive wait times to copious redactions, conceal government corruption and human-rights violations.

"This flowing account reveals the dark side of wartime strategies clouded by denials of FOIA requests. It will fascinate Cold War-era historians and readers concerned about access to government information." Library Journal

Emery, Theo

Hellfire boys : the birth of the U.S. Chemical Warfare Service and the race for the world's deadliest weapons / Theo Emery. Little Brown & Co 2017 368 p. **358**

1. United States. Army. Gas Regiment, 1st 2. United States. Army. Engineer Regiment, 30th (Gas and Flame) 3. United States. Army. Chemical Warfare Service 4. World War I 5. Chemical warfare 6. Chemical weapons 7. Military engineering
ISBN 9780316264105

LC bl2017037105

Traces the actions of the "Hellfire Battalion," a group of American engineers who were trained in gas warfare and were sent to the front lines in France to launch multiple assaults against the Germans.

Guillemin, Jeanne

★**Biological** weapons : from the invention of state-sponsored programs to contemporary bioterrorism / Jeanne Guillemin.

Columbia University Press, c2005. xii, 258 p. ; **358**

1. Biological warfare -- History. 2. Biological terrorism 3. International security. 4. Terrorism.
ISBN 0231129424

LC 2004051911

A timely account of how resources for biological weapons programs were mobilized and why such weapons have never been deployed in major conflicts offers an understanding of the relevance of the historical restraints placed on the use of biological weapons and looks at what can to done to prevent their proliferation in the post-September 11th world.

"This is a history of biological weaponry, beginning with the British, American and Japanese programs that predate WWII. Admirably free of finger-pointing, shrillness and Luddite tendencies, the book ranks high as a historical introduction to the subject and a handbook on contemporary remedies." Publishers Weekly.

Miller, Judith, 1948-

Germs : biological weapons and America's secret war / Judith Miller, Stephen Engelberg, William Broad. Simon & Schuster, 2001. 382 p. **358**

1. Biological weapons -- Control. 2. Biological warfare -- United States. 3. Biological warfare research.
ISBN 0684871580

LC 2001042690

Presents an account of germ weaponry around the globe, including the Soviet Union's biological weapons program that contains an abundance of anthrax germs, and the United States' attempt to put an end to these efforts.

Tucker, Jonathan B.

★**War** of nerves : chemical warfare from World War I to al-Qaeda / Jonathan B. Tucker. Pantheon Books, 2006. xi, 479 p. : **358**

1. Chemical warfare -- History. 2. Chemical weapons -- History. 3. Biological warfare -- History. 4. Biological weapons -- History.
ISBN 9780375422294

LC 2005050053

Traces the military applications of toxic weaponry from World War I to the present day, the development of potent nerve agents during the Cold War, and the efforts of such terrorist groups as Al-Qaeda to acquire deadly nerve agents.

"This book makes a sobering case for a less poisonous world." New York Times Book Review.

358.4 Air forces and warfare

Jacobsen, Annie

Area 51 : an uncensored history of America's top secret military base / Annie Jacobsen. Little, Brown and Co., 2011. xv, 523 p. : **358.4**

1. Military bases, American -- Nevada 2. Secrecy in government 3. Military history 4. Government information 5. Area 51 region, Nevada 6. Nevada
ISBN 9780316132947

LC 2011925205

Presents a history of the most famous secret military installation in the world, assembled from interviews with the people who served there and formerly classified information.

358.400941 Air forces--Great Britain

Hamilton-Paterson, James

Marked for death : the first war in the air / James Hamilton-Paterson. Pegasus Books, [2016] 356 p., 16 unnumbered p. of plates : **358.400941**

1. Fighter planes. 2. Military jet planes. 3. Military aviation. 4. World War I -- Aerial operations
ISBN 9781681771588

LC 2017304411

A dramatic and fascinating account of aerial combat during World War I, revealing the terrible risks taken by the men who fought and died in the world's first war in the air.

"Best of all, the authorwho has a solid body of fiction to his creditis a consummate storyteller; not only does the book tell a fascinating story, it is nearly impossible to put down." Kirkus.

359 Sea forces and warfare

Stavridis, James

Sea power : the history and geopolitics of the world's oceans / James Stavridis. Penguin Group USA, 2017 368 p. **359**

1. Sea-power -- History. 2. Naval history. 3. Geopolitics -- History. 4. International security.
ISBN 9780735220591

LC 2016056758

A general and former commander of NATO describes the history and geography of the world's oceans and the battles that have spanned them during the whole of human existence, from the Athenians to the nuclear submarines of the 20th century Cold War.

"A highly readable, instructive look at the role of the oceans in our civilization, past and present." Kirkus.

Tucker, Spencer, 1937-

★**Naval** warfare : an international encyclopedia / edited by Spencer C. Tucker ; associate editors, John Fredriksen ... [et al.] ; introduction by James C. Bradford. ABC-CLIO, c2002. 3 v. (1231 p.) : **359**

1. Naval art and science -- Encyclopedias. 2. Naval history -- Encyclopedias. 3. Naval biography -- Encyclopedias.
ISBN 9781576072196

LC 2002004401

"This new resource is international in scope, covering the subject of naval warfare from ancient times to the present. Some 157 contributors are responsible for more than 1,500 signed entries. Most entries include see also references and a short bibliography with one to four citations." Booklist

359.00973 Naval forces--United States

Toll, Ian W.

★**Six** frigates : the epic history of the founding of the U.S. Navy / Ian W. Toll. W.W. Norton & Co., c2006. xii, 560 p., 16 p. of plates : **359.00973**

1. United States. Navy -- History 2. Sea-power. 3. Military power. 4. Frigates -- United States -- History. 5. Pirates. 6. United States -- History, Naval.
ISBN 0393058476

LC 2006020769

Describes the origins and early history of the American Navy, discussing the debates by the founding fathers over the need for a permanent military, the decision to construct six heavy frigates, the campaign against Tripoli, and the War of 1812.

"This is a must-read for fans of naval history and the early American Republic." Publishers Weekly.

359.9 Specialized combat forces engineering and related services

Couch, Dick, 1943-

The **warrior** elite : the forging of Seal Class 228 / Dick Couch ; photographs by Cliff Hollenbeck. Three Rivers Press, 2003, c2001. x, 330 p. : **359.9**

1. United States. Navy. SEALs 2. United States. Navy Commando troops 3. Commando troops -- United States. 4. Special forces 5. Armed Forces 6. Navy SEALs

ISBN 1400046955

LC bl2004107971

Sequel: The finishing school.

Originally published: New York : Crown Publishers, 2001. With a new postscript.

A former Navy SEAL and Vietnam War hero chronicles the grueling physical training and psychological conditioning that every SEAL must successfully endure in order to graduate.

"This book is unique. Couch, a Vietnam-era SEAL and retired naval reserve captain was given the most complete access possible. On view is much serious thought by serious thinkers on the making of warriors at the dawn of the twenty-first century." Booklist.

Denver, Rorke

Worth dying for : a Navy SEAL's call to a nation / Rorke Denver and Ellis Henican. Howard Books, 2016. 224 p. **359.9**

1. Denver, Rorke. 2. United States. Navy Commando troops. 3. United States. Navy. SEALs 4. War on Terrorism, 2001-2009. 5. Terrorism -- Prevention. 6. Soldiers 7. Special forces.

ISBN 9781501124112

LC 2015034024

A Navy SEAL commander explores the practical and philosophical questions of heroic service that have emerged about America's past decade at war, from the qualities of heroes and the reasons we fight to how war impacts families and whether or not soldiers can be held accountable for wartime actions.

Parrish, Thomas D.

★The **submarine** : a history / Thomas Parrish. Viking, 2004. x, 576 p. : **359.9**

1. Submarines -- History. 2. Warships.

ISBN 0670033138

LC 2003070515

Chronicles the history and evolution of submarines and of the inventors and engineers who developed them, from eighteenth-century conception to twentieth-century reality, and discusses the military deployment, strategic implications, and future of the submarine.

"This brilliant, dramatic account of submarines and the men who sailed in them is a required acquisition for every military history collection." Choice.

361.3 Social work

Blumenfeld, Jeff

Travel with purpose : a field guide to voluntourism / Jeff Blumenfeld. Rowman & Littlefield, 2019 x, 198 p. ; **361.3**

1. Volunteer tourism

ISBN 9781538115329

LC 2018041035

"Blumenfeld leaves almost nothing to the imagination, with appendixes on volunteerism resources, best travel applications, favorite travel books, and volunteerism videos, along with notes and a bibliography." Booklist

362.1 People with physical illnesses

Coste, Joanne Koenig

Learning to speak Alzheimer's : a groundbreaking approach for everyone dealing with the disease / Joanne Koenig Coste. Houghton Mifflin, 2004, c2003. xv, 240 p. : **362.1**

1. Alzheimer's disease -- Patients -- Care 2. Alzheimer's disease -- Patients -- Rehabilitation 3. Caregivers

ISBN 9780618485178

LC bl2009016680

"A Mariner book."

Reprint. Originally published: 2003.

A new approach to dealing with Alzheimer's disease offers a five step method for caring for people with progressive dementia, while offering hundreds of practical tips to ease life for patients and caregivers.

Dorris, Michael

The **broken** cord : a family's ongoing struggle with fetal alcohol syndrome / Michael Dorris ; with a foreword by Louise Erdrich. Harper & Row, 1989. xix, 300 p. **362.1**

1. Adopted boys. 2. People with fetal alcohol spectrum disorders -- Family relationships 3. Fathers and sons. 4. Native American children. 5. United States -- Social life and customs -- 20th century.

ISBN 9780060160715

LC 88045893

ALA Notable Book, 1990.

National Book Critics Circle Award for Non-Fiction, 1989.

Considers the problems of Fetal Alcohol Syndrome on both a personal and national level, documenting the author's struggle to understand his adopted son's health and learning problems within a larger context.

"The alarming statistics and consequences of fetal alcohol syndrome are skillfully interwoven with the human story of one of its victims in The Broken Cord. Mr. Dorris's prose is clear and affecting." New York Times Book Review.

Kelly, Christopher R.

Am I dying?! : a complete guide to your symptoms--and what to do next / Christopher Kelly, M.D., M.S. ; Marc Eisenberg, M.D., F.A.C.C.. William Morrow, 2019 xii, 337 p. ; **362.1**

1. Health risk assessment 2. Symptoms -- Handbooks, manuals, etc. 3. Diagnosis -- Handbooks, manuals, etc. 4. Self-care, Health

ISBN 9780062847607

LC bl2018197570

Includes index.

Presents the most common symptoms--from bloating and chest pain to fatigue, rashes, and weakness--and provides guidance on seeking medical care, including whether to make a doctor's appointment or go to the hospital.

Offit, Paul A

Bad advice : or why celebrities, politicians, and activists aren't your best source of health information / Paul A. Offit, M.D. Columbia University Press, [2018] 224 p. **362.101**

1. Public health. 2. Medicine. 3. Mass media. 4. Science. 5. Social medicine.
ISBN 9780231186988

LC 2017056425

A psychologist, pediatrician and champion of sound science and public health humorously describes how he has taken on celebrities, advocates and lobbyists who flood the media with misleading health claims and conspiracy theories.

Khan, Ali, MD

The **next** pandemic : on the front lines against humankind's gravest dangers / Ali S. Khan with William Patrick. PublicAffairs, 2016 288 p. ; **362.1**

1. Public health 2. Epidemics 3. Disasters. 4. Diseases
ISBN 9781610395915

LC 2016001718

A former director of the Office of Public Health Preparedness and Response (PHPR) at the Centers for Disease Control and Prevention lays out his theories on when, where and how the next major disease outbreak will arrive.

"The details are sometimes disturbing, but Khan writes with verve, clarity, and a touch of humor." Kirkus.

Shah, Sonia

Pandemic : tracking contagions, from cholera to ebola and beyond / Sonia Shah. Sarah Crichton Books/Farrar, Straus and Giroux , 2016. 320 p. **362.1**

1. Communicable diseases -- Epidemiology -- History. 2. Epidemics 3. Public health 4. Cholera
ISBN 9780374122881

LC 2015010246

Includes index.

By tracking the story of cholera, a science journalist and award-winning author explores the origins of epidemics and discusses modern pathogens that have the potential to follow in the disease's pandemic footsteps.

362.108 Groups of people

Glezerman, Marek

Gender medicine : the groundbreaking new science of gender- and sex-based diagnosis and treatment / Marek Glezerman. Overlook Press, 2016 320 p. **362.108**

1. Medical care. 2. Sex differences. 3. Medical research
ISBN 9781468313185

LC bl2016028905

Over millions of years, male and female bodies developed crucial physiological differences to improve the chances for human survival. These differences have become culturally obsolete with the overturning of traditional gender roles. But they are nevertheless very real, and they go well beyond the obvious sexual and reproductive variances: men and women differ in terms of digestion, which affects the way medications are absorbed. Sensitivity to pain is dependent on gender. Even the symptoms of a heart attack manifest differently in a man than in a woman.And yet the medical establishment largely treats male and female patients as though their needs are identical.

"This fascinating work will teach readers a great deal about sex, gender, and the human body." Library Journal.

362.10973 Health services--United States

Brawley, Otis Webb

How we do harm : a doctor breaks ranks about being sick in America / Otis Webb Brawley with Paul Goldberg. St. Martin's Press, c2012. 256 p. **362.10973**

1. Medical care -- United States. 2. Health policy -- United States. 3. Medical care reform. 4. Medicine -- Corrupt practices.
ISBN 9780312672973

LC 2011035843

An American Cancer Society chief medical and scientific officer presents a call for the rational and skeptical practice of medicine that does not under-serve or favor patients based on wealth or insurance coverage and follows scientifically based protocols that do not kowtow to trendy drugs.

Reid, T. R.

★The **healing** of America : a global quest for better, cheaper, and fairer health care / T.R. Reid. Penguin Press, 2009. 288 p. **362.10973**

1. Health policy -- United States 2. Medical care reform 3. Medical care -- United States. 4. Health services regulation. 5. United States -- Politics and government.
ISBN 9781594202346

LC 2009009555

A best-selling author guides a whirlwind tour of successful healthcare systems worldwide, disproving American myths of "socialized medicine" to find possible paths toward reform.

Rosenthal, Elisabeth, 1956-

An **American** sickness : how healthcare became big business and how you can take it back / Elisabeth Rosenthal. Penguin Press, 2017. 384 p. **362.10973**

1. Medical care -- Costs 2. Medical care services 3. Health insurance 4. Health policy
ISBN 9781594206757

LC 2016042934

An award-winning New York Times reporter reveals expensive dysfunctions in America's healthcare system, outlining practical guidelines for recognizing misleading information and obtaining the care and pharmaceuticals needed to safeguard family health interests.

"After laying out the problem, Rosenthal presents solutions both personal and societal in this commanding and necessary call to arms." Booklist.

362.1109747 Hospitals--New York

Manheimer, Eric

Twelve patients : life and death at Bellevue Hospital / Eric Manheimer. Grand Central Pub., 2012. 272 p. **362.1109747**

1. Bellevue Hospital, New York 2. Hospital patients. 3. Hospital care. 4. Public hospitals. 5. Hospitals.
ISBN 9781455503889

LC 2012005513

Includes index.

"Manheimer offers a window onto a unique hospital and the wisdom of a healer who tends with equal skill to patients and the world." Publishers Weekly.

Oshinsky, David M., 1944-

Bellevue : three centuries of medicine and mayhem at America's most storied hospital / David Oshinsky. Doubleday, 2016 384 p. ; **362.1109747**

1. Bellevue Hospital, New York 2. Hospital care. 3. Hospitals. 4. Medicine -- History 5. Hospital patients. 6. New York City.

ISBN 9780385523363

LC 2016027568

ALA Notable Book, 2018.

A history of the iconic public hospital on New York City's East Side describes the changes in American medicine from 1730 to modern times as it traces building's origins as an almshouse and pesthouse to its current status as a revered place of first-class care.

362.1109763 Hospitals--Louisiana

Fink, Sheri

★**Five** days at Memorial : life and death in a storm-ravaged hospital / Sheri Fink. Crown Publishers, 2013. 432 p. **362.1109763**

1. Hospitals 2. Medical malpractice 3. Survival (after hurricanes) 4. Death 5. New Orleans, Louisiana

ISBN 9780307718969

LC 2013019693

ALA Notable Book, 2014

J. Anthony Lukas Book Prize, 2014.

National Book Critics Circle Award for Non-Fiction, 2013.

Andrew Carnegie Medal for Excellence in Non-Fiction finalist, 2014.

"Fink draws those few days in the hospital's life with a fine, lively pen, providing stunningly framed vignettes of activities in the hospital and sharp pocket profiles of many of the characters. She gives measured consideration to such explosive issues as class and race discrimination in medicine, end-of-life care, medical rationing and euthanasia, and she presents the injection of some patients with a cocktail of drugs to reduce their breathing in such a manner that readers will be able to fully fashion their own opinions." Kirkus.

362.17 Specific services

Gawande, Atul

★**Being** mortal : medicine and what matters in the end / Atul Gawande. Metropolitan Books : 2014. 304 p. ; **362.17**

1. Terminal Care. 2. Quality of Life. 3. Aging. 4. Prognosis.

ISBN 9780805095159

LC 2014017442

A prominent surgeon argues against modern medical practices that extend life at the expense of quality of life while isolating the dying, outlining suggestions for freer, more fulfilling approaches to death that enable more dignified and comfortable choices.

"A sensitive, intelligent and heartfelt examination of the processes of aging and dying." Kirkus.

Kaufman, Sharon R.

--And a time to die : how American hospitals shape the end of life / Sharon R. Kaufman. Scribner, 2005. x, 400 p. ; **362.17**

1. Terminal care. 2. Hospital care. 3. Death -- Social aspects -- United States.

ISBN 0743264762

LC 2004052530

"A Lisa Drew book."

"The author reveals the dilemmas of hospital death in America today: the shift to patients' control of decision making despite the doctors' greater knowledge; the ethics and practical effects of resuscitation versus pain relief; the complexities of assessing quality of life while guessing at the desires of an unconscious patient. This deeply probing study lays bare the cultural and institutional assumptions and rhetoric that frame our search for a good death." Publishers Weekly.

362.196 Specific conditions

France, David, 1959-

★**How** to survive a plague : the inside story of how citizens and science tamed AIDS / David France. Alfred A. Knopf, 2016. 640 p. **362.196**

1. ACT UP. 2. LGBTQIA rights -- History. 3. AIDS activists. 4. People with HIV 5. Gay and Lesbian Movement -- History. 6. New York (State)

ISBN 9780307700636

LC 2016010685

Baillie Gifford Prize for Non-Fiction, 2017.

Lambda Literary Award for LGBT Nonfiction, 2017

Stonewall Book Awards: Israel Fishman Non-fiction Award, 2017.

A definitive history of the successful battle to halt the AIDS epidemic, written by the creator of and inspired by the seminal documentary of the same name, also shares the poignant stories of gay activists who resolved to make their life battles purposeful.

Shilts, Randy, 1951-1994

★**And** the band played on : politics, people, and the AIDS epidemic / Randy Shilts. St. Martin's Griffin, 2007, c1987. xxiii, 630 p. ; **362.196**

1. AIDS (Disease) -- History. 2. AIDS (Disease) -- Political aspects. 3. AIDS (Disease) -- Social aspects.

ISBN 0312009941

LC 87016528

National Book Critics Circle Award for Nonfiction finalist, 1987.

An examination of the AIDS crisis exposes the federal government for its inaction, health authorities for their greed, and scientists for their desire for prestige in the face of the AIDS pandemic.

"Shilts successfully weaves comprehensive investigative reporting and commercial page-turner pacing, political intrigue and personal tragedy into a landmark work." Publishers Weekly.

362.19699 Patients with tumors and miscellaneous communicable diseases

Fessler, Pam

Carville's cure : leprosy, stigma, and the fight for justice / Pam Fessler. Liveright Publishing Corporation, 2020 352 p. **362.19699**

1. Louisiana Leper Home. 2. United States Marine Hospital No. 66 (Carville, La.) 3. Public Health Service Hospital at Carville, La. 4. People with leprosy 5. Leprosy 6. Stigma (Social psychology). 7. Skin -- Diseases -- Treatment 8. Louisiana

ISBN 9781631495038

LC 2020008057

Explores the hidden history of Carville, the only leprosy colony in the continental United States which lasted from 1894 to 1999, and the shameful treatment of the thousands of Americans who were needlessly exiled there.

"NPR correspondent Fessler's polished and compassionate debut examines the history of Hansen's disease (the modern name for leprosy) in America through the story of the Louisiana Leper Home in Carville, LA. . . . Readers will be enlightened and encouraged." Publishers Weekly

Hutton, Andrea

Bald is better with earrings : a survivor's guide to getting through breast cancer / Andrea Hutton. HarperWave, 2015 xiv, 205 p. ; **362.19699**

1. Breast -- Cancer 2. Breast -- Cancer -- Patients 3. Cancer -- Psychological aspects

ISBN 9780062375650

LC bl2015026747

A guide for women with breast cancer shares step-by-step coverage of how to navigate the emotional and physical challenges of every stage of treatment.

"Readers will be equally overwhelmed and overjoyed by Hutton's prescriptions. This book could be a lifesaver for breast cancer club members." Library Journal.

362.1988 Obstetrical surgery and abortion

Foster, Diana Greene, 1971-

The **turnaway** study : ten years, a thousand women, and the consequences of having--or being denied--an abortion / Diana Greene Foster. Scribner, [2020] 360 p. **362.1988**

1. Reproductive rights 2. Abortion -- Psychological aspects 3. Women's rights 4. Late-term abortion

ISBN 9781982141561

LC 2020004923

The principal investigator of the Turnaway Study and internationally renowned expert on contraception presents an illuminating report on the long-term consequences of receiving versus being denied an abortion in accordance with the access of today's America.

"Policy makers and abortion rights activists should consider it a must-read." Publishers Weekly

Peters, Rebecca Todd

Trust women : a progressive Christian argument for reproductive justice / Rebecca Todd Peters. Beacon Press, 2018. 240 p. **362.1988**

1. Abortion -- Religious aspects -- Christianity 2. Religion 3. Motherhood 4. Faith (Christianity)

ISBN 9780807069981

LC 2017042045

Rebecca Todd Peters, a Presbyterian minister and social ethicist, argues that the shaming and judging associated with abortion reflects deep, often unspoken patriarchal and racist assumptions about women and women's sexual activity. These assumptions are at the heart of what she calls the justification framework, which governs our public debate about abortion, and disrupts our ability to have authentic public discussions about the health and well-being of women and their families.

362.19888 Abortion services

Shah, Meera

You're the only one I've told : the stories behind abortion / Dr. Meera Shah. Chicago Review Press, 2020. 298 p. ; **362.19888**

1. Shah, Meera 2. Abortion 3. Abortion providers 4. Unplanned pregnancy 5. Abortion -- Law and legislation

ISBN 9781641603638

LC 2020939551

"Chief medical officer of Planned Parenthood Hudson Peconic tells the myriad stories of diverse individuals whose abortion experiences bring vital and threatened reproductive rights to life".-- Provided by publisher.

"A strong contribution to discussions of reproductive rights." Kirkus

362.19892 Pediatric care

Klass, Perri, 1958-

A **good** time to be born : how science and public health gave children a future / Perri Klass. W. W. Norton & Company, 2020. viii, 376 p. : **362.19892**

1. Child health 2. Children -- Mortality 3. Women physicians 4. Medical research

ISBN 9780393609998

LC 2020022472

A history of the world-transforming fight against child mortality interweaves the author's experiences as a medical student and doctor while paying tribute to the barrier-breaking women who introduced new approaches and scientific ideas about sanitation and vaccination.

"Klass masterfully introduces readers to the people coming up with solutions for many of the dangers of childhood and shows how the pediatric specialty over time has worked to improve children's lives. Essential reading for parents." Library Journal

362.2 People with mental illness and disabilities

Bering, Jesse

★**Suicidal** : why we kill ourselves / Jesse Bering. The University of Chicago Press, 2018. 272 p. **362.2**

1. Suicide 2. Social psychology 3. Depression 4. Mental illness

ISBN 9780226463322

LC 2018021904

"Bering illuminates a murky, misunderstood human quandary with compassion, confessional honesty, and academic perception." Kirkus.

Horn, Stacy

Damnation Island : poor, sick, mad & criminal in 19th-century New York / Stacy Horn. Algonquin Books of Chapel Hill, 2018. 304 p. **362.2**

1. French, William Glenney, 1814-1895. 2. Psychiatric hospitals 3. Mental illness 4. Psychiatry -- History 5. Prisoners 6. Roosevelt Island, New York City -- 19th century -- History 7. New York City -- 19th century -- History

ISBN 9781616205768

LC 2017052414

"It's now known as New York City's Roosevelt Island. Originally called Blackwell's Island, it housed a lunatic asylum, prison, hospital, workhouse and almshouse in the 19th century. This book re-creates what daily life was like on the island, what politics shaped it, and what constituted therapy and charity in the nineteenth century".-- Provided by publisher.

Marcus, Eric

Why suicide? : questions and answers about suicide, suicide prevention, and coping with the suicide of someone you know / Eric Marcus. HarperOne, 2010, c1996. xv, 240 p. ; **362.2**

1. Assisted suicide. 2. Suicide -- Prevention. 3. Suicide.
ISBN 9780062003911

LC 95033431

Originally published: San Francisco, Calif. : HarperSanFrancisco, 1996.

A nonjudgemental guide for people whose lives have been touched by suicide offers practical answers to such related concerns as what to tell others, insurance coverage, preventability, and what to do with suicidal feelings.

"The author's questions range from 'Does everyone have thoughts of suicide?' to 'What are the arguments against legalizing doctor-assisted suicide?' His responses reflect not only a knowledgeable and well-informed consideration of suicidology but also empathetic treatment. The typical response aims to educate by giving factual information and/or practical advice as well as to console by providing personal stories from suicide survivors." Library Journal.

Morton, Kati

Are u ok? : a guide to caring for your mental health / Kati Morton, LMFT. Da Capo Lifelong, 2018. xiii, 236 p. ; **362.2**

1. Mental health 2. Mental health.
ISBN 0738234990

LC bl2018188809

"How to know if you need help & where to find it"--Cover.

A licensed family therapist and YouTube personality clarifies the difference between mental health and mental illness, answering common questions to reduce stigmas while offering advice on how to pursue beneficial therapy.

362.28 Suicide

Case, Anne, 1958-

Deaths of despair and the future of capitalism / Anne Case, Angus Deaton. Princeton University Press, [2020] 312 p. : **362.28**

1. Capitalism and inequality 2. Depression 3. Working class -- United States. 4. Suicide -- Economic aspects. 5. United States -- Economic conditions -- 1945- 6. United States -- Social conditions -- 1945-
ISBN 9780691190785

LC 2019040360

This book documents the decline of white-working class lives over the last half-century and examines the social and economic forces that have slowly made these lives more difficult. Case and Deaton argue that market and political power in the United States have moved away from labor towards capital-as unions have weakened and politics have become more favorable to business, corporations have become more powerful. Consolidation in some American industries, healthcare especially, has brought an increase in monopoly power in some product markets so that it is possible for firms to raise prices above what they would be in a freely competitive market. This, the authors argue, is a major cause of wage stagnation among working-class Americans and has played a substantial role in the increase in deaths of despair. Case and Deaton offer a way forward, including ideas that, even in our current political situation, may be feasible and improve lives".-- Provided by publisher.

"Complementing their candid prose with enlightening charts and graphs, Case and Deaton make the scale and immediacy of the problem crystal clear. This is an essential portrait of America in crisis." Publishers Weekly

Humphry, Derek, 1930-

★**Final** exit : the practicalities of self-deliverance and assisted suicide for the dying / Derek Humphry. Delta Trade Paperback, c2002. xxviii, 220 p. ; **362.28**

1. Assisted suicide. 2. Euthanasia. 3. Suicide.
ISBN 0385336535

LC 2002019403

An updated edition of a controversial best-seller shows people looking to end their suffering from unbearable pain due to terminal or incurable illness how to prepare for and commit suicide and offers other relevant information on such issues as euthanasia, living wills, hospice care, legal implications, and more.

362.29 Substance abuse

Berenson, Alex

Tell your children : the truth about marijuana, mental illness, and violence / Alex Berenson. Simon & Schuster, 2019 256 p. **362.29**

1. Marijuana 2. Mental health 3. Marijuana abuse 4. Violence and drugs
ISBN 9781982103668

LC bl2018192602

A report from an award-winning author and former New York Times reporter reveals the link between teenage marijuana use and mental illness, and a hidden epidemic of violence caused by the drug?facts that the author believes have been ignored as the U.S. rushes to legalize cannabis.

"Those who favor legalization are likely to remain unmoved, but Berenson is certainly meticulous and coherent about making his case, and his well-written treatise never descends into Reefer Madnesslike hysteria." Publishers Weekly.

Dahl, Linda, 1949-

Loving our addicted daughters back to life : a guidebook for parents / Linda Dahl. Central Recovery Press, 2015. xix, 154 p. ; **362.29**

1. Parents of drug addicts 2. Parents of alcoholics 3. Teenage girls -- Substance use 4. Substance abuse
ISBN 9781937612856

LC bl2015035050

Provides parents with resources for getting their addicted daughters on the path to recovery, offering coverage of communication tools, when to intervene, treatment options, and how to deal with relapse and long-term recovery.

Dufton, Emily

Grass roots : the rise and fall and rise of marijuana in America / Emiliy Dufton. Basic Books, 2017. 336 p. **362.29**

1. Medical marijuana 2. Decriminalization of marijuana. 3. Drug control. 4. Marijuana -- Law and legislation. 5. United States -- Laws, statutes, etc.
ISBN 9780465096169

LC 2017956164

A chronicle of marijuana's journey toward and away from legalization examines how grassroots activists from the 1970s nearly secured its decriminalization before conservative parents and the Reagan administration transformed cannabis into a focus for the War on Drugs.

"Dufton's balanced and thoroughly researched book traces the long and still unwinding history of marijuana policy and activism in the U.S." Booklist.

Eyre, Eric

Death in Mud Lick : a coal country fight against the drug companies that delivered the opioid epidemic / Eric Eyre. Scribner, 2020. 320 p. **362.29**

1. Opioid epidemic 2. Addiction 3. Corruption 4. Drug industry and trade 5. West Virginia 6. United States -- Social conditions
ISBN 9781982105310

LC bl2020004776

A Pulitzer Prize-winning reporter presents an urgent investigation into the role of corporate and government greed on the opioid epidemic as it devastatingly unfolded throughout small and vulnerable Appalachian communities.

"This is an infuriating story, compellingly told, and adds another layer to the reporting of the opioid crisis laid out in Beth Macy's Dopesick (2018). It is also a tale of compassionate people deeply wronged and a dogged journalist who won't stand for it." Booklist

Feiling, Thomas

Cocaine nation : how the white trade took over the world / Thomas Feiling. W W Norton & Co Inc, 2010. 368 p. **362.29**

1. Cocaine. 2. Cocaine economy. 3. Cocaine smuggling. 4. Cocaine traffic.
ISBN 9781605981017

LC bl2010017632

The author investigates the global cocaine trade--meeting and talking to Medillin hitmen, U.S. kingpins and Brazilian traffickers, as well as the soldiers and narcotics officers who fight the gangs and cartels--explores how the cocaine business got so big and argues that the U.S.'s anti-drugs crusade is actually increasing demand.

"Studying the cultivation, distribution, and use of cocaine he probes the drug's meteoric rise in sales and traces traffic from Colombian coca fields to Miami, Kingston, Tijuana, London, and New York. He follows consumers, traders, producers, police officers, doctors, and custom officials. Packed with facts and figures, this is a well-researched survey of the subject." Publishers Weekly.

Fletcher, Anne M.

Inside rehab : the surprising truth about addiction treatment : and how to get help that works / Anne M. Fletcher. Viking, [2013] 432 p. **362.29**

1. Addicts -- Rehabilitation 2. Drug abuse -- Treatment 3. Drug addicts -- Rehabilitation 4. Alcoholics -- Rehabilitation
ISBN 9780670025220

LC 2012037030

A bracingly honest insider's view of America's drug and alcohol rehab industry explores its strengths and weaknesses while revealing a disturbing gap between best practice and reality, tracing the author's investigations of programs ranging from indigent and famous facilities to 12-step and unconventional therapies.

Inglis, Lucy

Milk of paradise : a history of opium / Lucy Inglis. Pegasus Books, 2019. 448 p. **362.29**

1. Opium industry and trade 2. Opium use -- History 3. Opium 4. Opioids
ISBN 9781643130552

LC bl2018196003

The creator of the award-winning Georgian London blog presents an authoritative history of opium that explores its many uses and controversies, covering subjects ranging from the heroin underworld to the development of synthetic opiates.

"The narrative offers breadth rather than depth, but Inglis builds interest by emphasizing the places where intersections among historical strands yielded unexpected results and new trajectories in our relationship with opium; heroin, for example, was originally marketed as relief for tuberculosis symptoms, while the medical crisis of WWI encouraged Mexican opium production." Booklist.

Kuhn, Cynthia

Buzzed : the straight facts about the most used and abused drugs from alcohol to ecstasy / Cynthia Kuhn, PhD, Scott Swartzwelder, PhD, Wilkie Wilson, PhD, Duke University and Duke University School of Medicine, with Leigh Heather Wilson and Jeremy Foster. W. W. Norton & Company, 2019. 398 p., 8 unnumbered p. of plates ; **362.29**

1. Drug abuse 2. Drugs
ISBN 9780393356465

LC 2019015003

The essential source for understanding how drugs affect the body and behavior. --Provided by publisher

Larsen, Laura

Drug abuse sourcebook : basic consumer health information about the abuse of cocaine, club drugs, marijuana, inhalants, heroin, hallucinogens, and other illicit substances and the misuse of prescription and over-the-counter medications; along with facts and statistics about drug use and addiction, treatment and recovery, drug testing, drug abuse prevention and intervention, glossaries of related terms, and directories of resources for additional help and information / edited by Laura Larsen. Omnigraphics, Inc., 2014 xx, 636 p. ; **362.29**

1. Drug abuse -- Prevention -- Handbooks, manuals, etc. 2. Drug abuse -- Treatment -- Handbooks, manuals, etc. 3. Drug addiction -- Treatment -- Handbooks, manuals, etc.
ISBN 9780780813076

LC 2013037324

"Provides basic consumer health information about the abuse of illegal drugs and misuse of prescription and over-the-counter medications, along with facts about prevention, treatment, and recovery. Includes index, glossary of related terms and directory of resources".-- Provided by publisher.

Lupick, Travis, 1985-

Fighting for space : how a group of drug users transformed one city's struggle with addiction / Travis Lupick. Arsenal Pulp Press, 2017 407 p. : **362.29**

1. Drug addicts. 2. Civil rights. 3. Drug addiction -- Treatment. 4. Political participation 5. Vancouver, British Columbia
ISBN 9781551527123

Tells the story of a grassroots group of addicts in downtown Vancouver who throughout the 1990s and 2000s demanded that they be given the same rights as other citizens.

Macy, Beth

★**Dopesick** : dealers, doctors, and the drug company that addicted America / Beth Macy. Little Brown & Co 2018 336 p. **362.29**

1. Opioid abuse 2. Drug addiction 3. Drug industry and trade 4. Heroin 5. United States -- Social conditions

ISBN 9780316551243

LC 2017961068

ALA Notable Book, 2019.

Andrew Carnegie Medal for Excellence in Non-Fiction Finalist, 2019

Kirkus Prize for Nonfiction finalist, 2018.

In a book that includes deeply human and unforgettable portraits of the families and first responders affected, the author takes readers into the epicenter of America's more than 20-year struggle with opioid addiction.

"Award-winning Virginia-based journalist Macy, author of bestsellers Factory Man (2014) and Truevine (2016), carefully constructs the through line from the midnineties introduction of the prescription painkiller OxyContin to the current U.S. opioid crisis: 300,000 deaths over the last 15 years, with that number predicted to double in the next 5." Booklist.

McGreal, Chris

American overdose : the opioid tragedy in three acts / Chris McGreal. PublicAffairs, 2018. 320 p. **362.29**

1. United States. Food and Drug Administration. 2. Opioid abuse. 3. Chronic pain -- Treatment. 4. Prescription drugs. 5. Prescription drug abuse.

ISBN 9781610398619

LC 2018025909

Describes how the current opioid crisis was driven by greed, incompetence and indifference and exposes Big Pharma's control of the healthcare system and the how the FDA was duped into pushing painkillers.

"This urgent, readable chronicle, which names names and pulls no punches, clearly and compassionately illuminates the evolution of Americas mass addiction problem." Publishers Weekly.

Mohammad, Akikur

The **anatomy** of addiction : what science and research tell us about the true causes, best preventive techniques, and most successful treatments / Akikur Mohammad, MD. Perigee, 2016. xiv, 256 p. ; **362.29**

1. Substance abuse -- Etiology. 2. Compulsive behavior -- Etiology. 3. Drug abuse -- Treatment

ISBN 9781101981832

LC 2015041635

"As compelling as it is informative and authoritative, The Anatomy of Addiction will lead you to a better understanding about the causes, prevention, and treatment of addiction. It explains in layman's terms what constitutes effective, evidence-based addiction medicine and how to find it. This book provides actionable, scientific information for addicts and their families and details how to avoid so-called rehab clinics that are at best useless and at worst dangerous and even life threatening".-- Provided by publisher.

"A useful and educative primer introducing but not elaborating on a new clinical perspective on addiction." Kirkus.

Quinones, Sam, 1958-

Dreamland : the true tale of America's opiate epidemic / Sam Quinones. Bloomsbury Press, [2014] 320 p. **362.29**

1. Drug traffic -- Mexico. 2. Drug addiction -- United States. 3. Heroin addiction 4. Narcotics.

ISBN 9781620402504

LC 2014025398

National Book Critics Circle Award for Non-Fiction, 2015.

An explosive true account of addiction, marketing and the making of an epidemic weaves together the story of Purdue Pharma's campaign to market OxyContin, while, at the same time, a massive influx of black tar heroin took the county by storm through an almost unbreakable marking and distribution system.

"Journalist Quinones weaves an extraordinary story, including the personal journeys of the addicted, the drug traffickers, law enforcement, and scores of families affected by the scourge, as he details the social, economic, and political forces that eventually destroyed communities in the American heartland and continues to have a resounding impact." Booklist.

Reding, Nick

Methland : the death and life of an American small town / Nick Reding. Bloomsbury, 2009. 272 p. **362.29**

1. Drug abuse. 2. Methamphetamine. 3. Small towns. 4. Small town life. 5. Iowa. 6. Oelwein, Iowa.

ISBN 9781596916500

LC 2008045398

Traces the efforts of a small Iowa community to counter the pervasiveness of crystal methamphetamine, in an account that offers insight into the drug's appeal while chronicling the author's visits with the town's doctor, the local prosecutor, and a long-time addict.

"The author traces rise of meth use across the Midwest, focusing on Oelwein, an Iowa railroad town (pop. 6,772) that by 2005 had been destroyed by the drug. An important report on an extremely dangerous drug and the consequences of addiction." Kirkus.

Sederer, Lloyd I.

The **addiction** solution : treating our dependence on opioids and other drugs / Lloyd I. Sederer, MD. Scribner, 2018. xii, 226 p. : **362.29**

1. Drug abuse -- Treatment 2. Health policy 3. Opioid abuse 4. Mental health

ISBN 9781501179440

LC 2017061754

A groundbreaking examination of addiction from the Chief Medical Officer for the New York State Office of Mental Health, offering practical, proven solutions for individuals, families, and communities dealing with substance use and abuse.

"Enriched with patient case studies that illustrate the complex nature of this disease, Sederer's balanced and compassionate approach makes this a valuable addition to the conversation on this timely topic." Library Journal.

Streatfeild, Dominic

Cocaine : an unauthorized biography / Dominic Streatfeild. Thomas Dunne Books, 2002, c2001. xii, 510 p. **362.29**

1. Cocaine -- History. 2. Cocaine traffic 3. Crack (Drug) 4. Crack traffic

ISBN 9780312286248

LC 2002725642

Originally published: London : Virgin, c2001.

Examines the history of cocaine from its first medical uses to the worldwide issues it presents today, taking readers into such locations as the isolation cells of America's prisons, crack houses in New York, and the jungles of Bolivia and Colombia, tracing its manufacture and chronicling the accounts of its cultivators, traffickers, and fighters.

"Thorough, engrossing, balanced, and entertaining, it is important social history in palatable form." Booklist.

Weil, Andrew

Mind over meds : know when drugs are necessary, when alternatives are better-- and when to let your body heal on its own / Andrew Weil, MD.. Little, Brown and Company, 2017. xiv, 289 p. **362.29**

1. Alternative medicine 2. Medication abuse
ISBN 9780316269704

LC OC2018158460

The Harvard graduate, public health professor and best-selling author of Spontaneous Happiness explores the dangers of overmedication while outlining lifestyle changes and alternative treatments for common ailments.

"Weil's (Univ. of Arizona; Spontaneous Happiness, Healthy Aging) revolutionary book casts a critical eye on modern medicine, examining the very serious risks that medicine can carry." Library Journal.

Westhoff, Ben

Fentanyl, Inc. : how rogue chemists are creating the deadliest wave of the opioid epidemic / Ben Westhoff. Atlantic Monthly Press, 2019. 288 p. **362.29**

1. Opioid epidemic 2. Drug control 3. Drug industry and trade 4. Chemical industry and trade
ISBN 9780802127433

LC 2019033267

An in-depth investigation into the dangerous world of synthetic drugs predicts a next wave in the opioid epidemic while examining the roles of black-market Chinese drug factories, European harm reduction activists and American dealers and users.

362.3 People with intellectual disabilities

Barry, Dan, 1958-

The **boys** in the bunkhouse : servitude and salvation in the heartland / Dan Barry. HarperCollins, 2016 224 p. **362.3**

1. People with developmental disabilities 2. Exploitation 3. Forced labor. 4. People with disabilities. 5. Iowa
ISBN 9780062372130

LC bl2016013131

ALA Notable Book, 2017.

A full-length account of the author's prize-winning New York Times story chronicles the exploitation and abuse case of a group of developmentally disabled workers, who for 25 years, were forced to work under harrowing conditions for virtually no wages until tenacious advocates helped them achieve their freedom.

"Gently, empathetically, and indelibly, Barry conveys a tale of unthinkable brutality." Kirkus.

362.4 People with physical disabilities

Kisor, Henry

Traveling with service animals : by air, road, rail, and ship across North America / Henry Kisor and Christine Goodier. University of Illinois Press, 2019 xii, 249 p. : **362.4**

1. Animals as aids for people with disabilities -- United States. 2. Working animals -- United States. 3. Animals -- Transportation -- United States. 4. Animals as aids for people with disabilities -- Canada.
ISBN 9780252084508

LC 2019014752

Includes index.

"Chicago Sun-Times columnist Kisor and freelance travel writer Goodier, both seasoned travelers with service dogs, offer a guide for those wishing to do the same. Only dogs and miniature horses are recognized by the U.S. government as service animals. Coverage is for North America only, and includes chapters on air travel (getting through TSA, negotiating airports), train travel (finding elusive potty stops), cruise ships (dining and onshore excursions), and on the road, including buses." Library Journal

362.4083 Children with disabilities--Social welfare

Solomon, Andrew, 1963-

Far from the tree : parents, children and the search for identity / Andrew Solomon. Scribner, c2012. 672 p. **362.4083**

1. Children with disabilities -- Psychology. 2. Parents of children with disabilities 3. Identity (Psychology) 4. Parent and child -- Psychological aspects. 5. United States
ISBN 9780743236713

LC 2012020878

J. Anthony Lukas Book Prize, 2013.

National Book Critics Circle Award for Non-Fiction, 2012.

The National Book Award-winning author explores the consequences of extreme personal differences between parents and children, describing his own experiences as a gay child of straight parents while evaluating the circumstances of people affected by physical, developmental or cultural factors that divide families.

362.40973 Children with disabilities--United States

Nielsen, Kim E.

A **disability** history of the United States / Kim E. Nielsen. Beacon Press, c2012. 272 p. **362.40973**

1. People with disabilities -- United States -- History. 2. Disabilities -- Social aspects 3. Sociology. 4. Social history.
ISBN 9780807022023

LC 2012014236

"American history examined sensitively and skillfully from the bottom up, grounded in the often shabby and sometimes exemplary treatment of disabled individuals. . . . A lively historical record that fills a gap in the literature." Kirkus

362.5 Poor people

Edelman, Peter B.

Not a crime to be poor : the criminalization of poverty in America / Peter Edelman. New Press, 2017. 224 p. **362.5**

1. Poverty. 2. Criminal justice system 3. Discrimination 4. Racism in the criminal justice system.
ISBN 9781620971635

LC 2017025523

A nationally known expert on poverty shows how not having money has been criminalized and shines a light on lawyers, activists, and policy makers working for a more humane approach.

Kozol, Jonathan

Rachel and her children : homeless families in America / Jonathan Kozol. Crown Publishers, 1988. ix, 261 p. ; **362.5**

1. Homeless persons 2. Poor people. 3. Poverty.
ISBN 9780517567302

LC 87022273

Robert F. Kennedy Book Award, 1989.

Argues that homelessness is caused by the lack of low-cost housing, describes the experiences of the homeless, and explains why the current welfare system is inadequate and misdirected.

"While the individual stories that Kozol tells so affectingly point out the vivid realities of urban poverty, the book also supplies statistics that detail the more abstract-and inhuman-attitudes that contemporary society assumes when attempting to deal with its victims." Booklist.

Vollmann, William T.

★**Poor** people / William T. Vollmann. Ecco, c2007. xx, 314, 120 p. : **362.5**

1. Poor families. 2. Poor people. 3. Poverty. 4. Social classes.
ISBN 0060878827

LC 2006048547

Examines and analyzes the diversity of poverty, using a series of interviews with impoverished people from around the world, who draw on their belief systems to account for their financial disadvantages.

"The author brings to bear his keen powers of observation on the world around him and, not incidentally, on himself; he is unabashed about allowing his emotional reactions to inform his thoughts about what it means to be poor. This remarkable book is sui generis and should be in all collections." Library Journal.

362.60973 Older people--Social welfare--United States

Aronson, Louise

Elderhood : redefining aging, transforming medicine, reimagining life / Louise Aronson. Bloomsbury Publishing, 2019. 446 p. **362.60973**

1. Seniors 2. Aging 3. Medical care 4. Geriatrics
ISBN 9781620405468

LC 2018040491

ALA Notable Book, 2020.

Pulitzer Prize for General Nonfiction finalist, 2020.

Reminiscent of Oliver Sacks, noted Harvard-trained geriatrician Louise Aronson uses stories from her quarter century of caring for patients, and draws from history, science, literature, popular culture, and her own life to weave a vision of old age that's neither nightmare nor utopian fantasy--a vision full of joy, wonder, frustration, outrage, and hope about aging, medicine, and humanity itself.

"Aronson's deep empathy, hard-won knowledge, and vivid reportage makes for one of the best accounts around of the medical mistreatment of the old." Publishers Weekly.

362.7 Young people

Whittington, Hillary

Raising Ryland : our story of parenting a transgender child with no strings attached / Hillary Whittington. William Morrow, 2016. 304 p. **362.7**

1. Whittington family 2. Whittington, Hillary Family 3. Transgender persons 4. Parent and child. 5. Child rearing. 6. Transgenderism 7. Autobiographies and memoirs
ISBN 9780062388889

LC bl2016007221

The author describes her and her husband's journey of support and unconditional love for their child Ryland, who identified as a boy from a very young age, as they decided to embrace his transgender transition.

"An uplifting testimonial to the power of unconditional familial love and acceptance." Kirkus.

362.7086 Young people by miscellaneous social attributes

Madrick, Jeffrey G.

Invisible Americans : the tragic cost of child poverty / Jeff Madrick. Alfred A. Knopf, 2020. 240 p. **362.7086**

1. Poor children 2. Poverty -- United States. 3. Child welfare -- United States. 4. Poor people -- United States. 5. United States -- Social conditions
ISBN 9780451494184

LC 2019022606

Includes index.

Citing the alarming percentage of children who live in poverty in today's America, an urgent report examines contributing factors, including government indifference, a failing social welfare system and entrenched racism, while outlining a politically feasible option for next steps.

"With passionate advocacy, Madrick addresses a systemic problem with a simple solution. His argument will appeal to those who champion economic policy change that centers the child." Library Journal

362.73 Institutional and related services

Beam, Cris

To the end of June : the intimate life of American foster care / Cris Beam. Houghton Mifflin Harcourt, 2013. 288 p. **362.73**

1. Foster home care 2. Foster children 3. Children -- Institutional care 4. Child welfare
ISBN 9780151014125

LC 2013001331

ALA Notable Book, 2014

An intimate, authoritative look at the foster care system that examines why it is failing the kids it is supposed to protect and what can be done to change it.

Bernstein, Nina, 1949-

The **lost** children of Wilder : the epic struggle to change foster care / Nina Bernstein. Pantheon Books 2001. xiv, 482 p. ; **362.73**

1. Wilder, Shirley Trials, litigation, etc. 2. Foster children -- New York City. 3. Foster children -- Legal status, laws, etc. 4. Foster care -- New York City. 5. Child welfare -- New York City.
ISBN 067943979X

LC 00057456

National Book Award for Nonfiction finalist, 2001

National Book Critics Circle Award for Nonfiction finalist, 2001.

"Bernstein explores the genesis and aftermath of the landmark 1973 legal case filed by young ACLU attorney Marcia Lowry against the New York State foster-care system. Known as Wilder for its 14-year-old African-American plaintiff, Shirley Pinky Wilder, the suit claimed Jewish and Catholic child welfare services had a lock on foster care funding and placements. This viscerally powerful history of institutionalized child abuse and the criminalization of poverty, of civil rights and social change, is compelling and essential reading." Publishers Weekly.

Moody, Anne

The **children** money can buy : stories from the frontlines of foster care and adoption / Anne Moody. Rowman & Littlefield, [2018] 266 p. **362.73**

1. Moody, Anne Family 2. Foster home care 3. Adoption 4. Foster children 5. Adoptive families
ISBN 9781538108024

LC 2017034191

Includes index.

Foster care and adoption can be rewarding ways to become parents. But the system itself seems almost rigged for failure, confusion, fraud, and disappointment. This book takes readers on an insider's tour of the system, its successes and failures, and the joys adoption can bring through the real stories of those involved on all sides.

362.734 Adoption

Aronson, Jane, 1951-

Carried in our hearts : the gift of adoption inspiring stories of families created across continents / Dr. Jane Aronson. Jeremy P. Tarcher/Penguin, Inc., 2013 xiv, 314 p. : **362.734**

1. Adoption 2. Adoptive parents 3. Families
ISBN 9780399161056

LC 2013001138

Shares first-person accounts of children and parents whose lives have been positively touched by international adoption.

"There is a wealth of information--and hope--here for people looking at possibilities for international adoption, and there is certainly no better advocate on the long journey than the upbeat, passionate Aronson." Publishers Weekly.

Caughman, Susan

You can adopt : an adoptive families guide / Susan Caughman and Isolde Motley ; with the editors and readers of Adoptive Families magazine. Ballantine Books, c2009. xi, 296 p. : **362.734**

1. Adoption -- Handbooks, manuals, etc. 2. Adoptive parents -- Handbooks, manuals, etc.
ISBN 9780345504012

LC 2009020252

Provides answers to common questions on adoption, including advice and honest stories from lawyers, social workers, parents, and childen.

"This thorough and honest resource stands out among other books on the topic in both its comprehensiveness and the authors' candor in discussing potentially controversial adoption-related issues. Domestic or international adoption? An infant or an older child? A sibling group? What about adopting transracially? These questions and many more are addressed here via a straightforward text interspersed with firsthand, sometimes wrenching accounts by adoptive parents, birth parents, and adoptees themselves." Booklist.

Joyce, Kathryn, 1979-

★The **child** catchers : rescue, trafficking, and the new gospel of adoption / Kathryn Joyce. PublicAffairs, 2013. 352 p. **362.734**

1. Fundamentalism 2. Christianity 3. International adoption 4. Adoption -- Religious aspects -- Christianity
ISBN 9781586489427

LC 2012044316

Reveals how adoption has become entangled in the conservative Christian agenda as a reflection of pro-life initiatives, explaining how child and family well-being has become a lesser priority in a market increasingly driven by profit and religious ideology.

"This intricate investigation of adoption ethics and religion is an incisive, evenhanded corrective to the view of child adoption as benign and salvific. ... Joyce details cases involving children from Haiti, Ethiopia, Liberia, Rwanda, South Korea, and the United States, shares the voices of a huge array of interviewees, and allows the facts to reveal how removing children from poverty has come to be seen as a virtue. Grim but not downbeat, Joyce's reporting also indicates signs of hope for reform." Library Journal.

362.74 Specific kinds of young people

Tough, Paul

Whatever it takes : one man's plan to change Harlem and America / Paul Tough. Houghton Mifflin, 2008. 304 p. **362.74**

1. Canada, Geoffrey. 2. Poverty -- New York City -- Prevention. 3. African American children -- Education -- New York City. 4. Inner city. 5. Poor people -- New York City -- Social conditions. 6. Harlem, New York City -- Economic conditions.
ISBN 9780618569892

LC 2008013303

A portrait of African-American activist Geoffrey Canada describes his radical approach to eliminating inner-city poverty, one that proposes to transform the lives of poor children by changing their schools, their families, and their neighborhoods at the same time.

DeRogatis, Jim

Soulless : the case against R. Kelly/ Jim DeRogatis Abrams Press, 2019. 306 p. **362.76**

1. Kelly, R. 2. Sexually abused teenagers 3. Child pornography 4. Trials (Sex crimes) 5. Musicians
ISBN 9781419740077

LC 2019930879

In November 2000, Chicago journalist and music critic Jim DeRogatis received an anonymous fax that alleged R. Kelly had a problem with "young girls." Weeks later, DeRogatis broke the shocking story, publishing allegations that the R&B superstar and local hero had groomed girls, sexually abused them, and paid them off. DeRogatis thought his work would have an impact. Instead, Kelly's career flourished. DeRogatis's work tells the story of Kelly's career, DeRogatis's investigations, and the world in which the two crossed paths, and brings the story up to the moment when things finally seem to have changed. Decades in the making, this is an outrageous, darkly riveting account of the life and actions of R. Kelly, and their horrible impact on dozens of girls, by the only person to tell it.

"Individuals who have experienced abuse may want to avoid this book entirely. For readers interested in the cult of celebrity, the life of R. Kelly, true crime, journalism, and the #MeToo movement." Library Journal.

362.76092 Abused children--Social welfare--Biography

Glatt, John

The **family** next door : the heartbreaking imprisonment of the 13 Turpin siblings and their extraordinary rescue / John Glatt. St. Martin's Press, [2019] 320 p. **362.76092**

1. Turpin, David Allen, 1961- 2. Turpin, Louise Ann, 1968- 3. Child

abuse 4. Child abuse victims 5. Captives 6. Family violence 7. California
ISBN 9781250202130

LC 2019006614

An investigative journalist details the disturbing case of Louise and David Turpin who outwardly displayed the perfect picture of domestic bliss, but in reality perpetrated shocking abuse, including isolation, torture and near starvation on their thirteen children.

"This chilling portrayal of abuse and secrecy may leave readers looking differently at their neighbors." Publishers Weekly.

362.77 Social problems of and services to young people

Kozol, Jonathan

Fire in the ashes : twenty-five years among the poorest children in America / Jonathan Kozol. Random House, 2012. 368 p. **362.77**

1. Inequality. 2. Urban schools. 3. Poor children -- Education -- Case studies. 4. Poverty. 5. United States -- Social conditions -- 21st century.
ISBN 9781400052462

LC 2012005183

Continuing the stories of inner-city children he has known for many years, the author shares the personal journeys of youths who have struggled to work through formidable racial and economic inequalities while approaching adulthood.

362.82 Families

Shannon, Joyce Brennfleck

Domestic violence sourcebook : basic consumer health information about warning signs, risk factors, and health consequences of intimate partner violence, sexual violence and rape, stalking, human trafficking, child maltreatment, teen dating violence, and elder abuse : along with factsabout victims and perpetrators, strategies for violence prevention, and emergency interventions, safety plans, and financial and legal tips for victims, a glossary of related terms, and directories of resources for additional information and support / edited by Joyce Brennfleck Shannon. Omnigraphics, c2009. xviii, 665 p. : **362.82**

1. Family violence -- United States. 2. Victims of family violence -- Services for -- United States. 3. Sexual abuse victims -- Services for -- United States.
ISBN 9780780810389

LC 2009004386

"Provides basic consumer health information about the physical, mental, and social effects of violence against intimate partners, children, teens, parents, and the elderly, along with prevention and intervention strategies. Includes index, glossary of related terms and directory of resources".--Provided by publisher.

Dalpiaz, Christina

Breaking free, starting over : parenting in the aftermath of family violence / Christina Dalpiaz. Praeger, 2004. xviii, 232 p. ; **362.82**

1. Children of abused wives 2. Family violence 3. Parenting 4. Victims of family violence
ISBN 9780275981679

LC 2003062436

Aids parents raising children in families that have suffered through abuse, providing an understanding of the impact of the violence and how to address the damage by rebuilding trust.

"This guide provides techniques for reparenting children who've been exposed to domestic violence. Lacking a safe haven, many of these children exhibit significant behavior, communication, and self-management problems." Library Journal.

Denham, Wes

Arrested : what to do when your loved one's in jail / Wes Denham. Chicago, Ill. :Review Press, c2010. 263 p. : **362.82**

1. Prisoners' families -- United States 2. Prisoners -- Family relationships -- United States 3. Prisoners -- United States
ISBN 9781556528347

LC 2009042270

A guide to supporting family members who are facing criminal charges, including how to make decisions with the whole family in mind, not just the defendant.

"This book is an extended checklist for those coping with the incarceration of a family member or significant friend, from the time the phone rings with news of the arrest onward. Denham shares the jargon, procedures, tricks, and traps in his coverage of jail visits, bail, public defenders, jail medical care, and legal and jail costs, and he outlines a decision-making process that considers the well-being of the entire family. Hard-hitting, blunt, and practical, this book is packed with inside knowledge of the jail experience. It's a necessary purchase for criminal justice collections in public libraries." Library Journal.

Fessler, Ann

The **girls** who went away : the hidden history of women who surrendered children for adoption in the decades before Roe v. Wade / Ann Fessler. Penguin Press, 2006. 354 p. **362.82**

1. Birthmothers -- United States. 2. Adoption -- Psychological aspects. 3. Unplanned pregnancy 4. Single mothers.
ISBN 9781594200946

LC 2005058179

National Book Critics Circle Award for Nonfiction finalist, 2006.

This book brings to light the lives of 1.5 million single American women in the years following World War II who, under enormous social and family pressure, were coerced to give up their newborn children. It tells not of wild and carefree sexual liberation, but rather of a devastating double standard that has had punishing long-term effects on these women and on the children they gave up. Single pregnant women were shunned by family and friends, evicted from schools, sent away to maternity homes to have their children alone, and often treated with cold contempt by doctors, nurses, and clergy. The majority of the women interviewed by Fessler, herself an adoptee, have never spoken of their experiences, and most have been haunted by grief and shame their entire adult lives.--From publisher description.

"These knowing oral histories are an emotional boon for birth mothers and adoptees struggling to make sense of troubled pasts." Publishers Weekly.

Lambert, Carol A.

Women with controlling partners : taking back your life from a manipulative or abusive partner / Carol A. Lambert, MSW. New Harbinger Publications, Inc., 2016 226 p. **362.82**

1. Abused women 2. Intimate partner violence -- Prevention 3. Family violence -- Prevention 4. Psychological abuse -- Prevention
ISBN 9781626254718

LC 2018136359

Cites the negative impact of controlling or abusive partners on women, identifying behaviors women should be aware of while sharing strategies for recognizing a problem, standing up for oneself, and making informed choices.

Snyder, Rachel Louise

No visible bruises : what we don't know about domestic violence can kill us / Rachel Louise Snyder. Bloomsbury Publishing, 2019. viii, 307 p. ; **362.82**

1. Family violence 2. Family violence victims 3. Violence against women 4. Abused women

ISBN 9781635570977

National Book Critics Circle Award for Nonfiction finalist, 2019

Kirkus Prize for Nonfiction finalist, 2019.

A journalist explores America's epidemic of domestic violence and how it has been misunderstood, sharing insights into what domestic violence portends about other types of violence and what countermeasures are needed today.

"Although domestic violence is a difficult subject, this sympathetic look at victims, perpetrators, and intervention efforts by law enforcement and social agencies makes for compelling reading. Journalist Snyder takes readers beyond headlines and mind-numbing statistics, sharing specific cases brought to life through her thorough research.'" Booklist.

Weiss, Elaine

Surviving domestic violence : voices of women who broke free / Elaine Weiss. Volcano Press, c2004. 214 p. ; **362.82**

1. Abused wives -- United States -- Case studies. 2. Abused wives -- United States -- Psychology. 3. Wife abuse -- United States. 4. Marital violence -- United States.

ISBN 9781884244278

LC 2003027829

Originally published: [Sandy, UT] : Agreka Books, 2000.

"Weiss eloquently tells the tragic yet inspiring stories of 12 survivors, ranging in age and socioeconomic circumstances." Library Journal

362.83 Women

Goudeau, Jessica

★**After** the last border : two families and the story of refuge in America / Jessica Goudeau. Viking, 2020. 336 p. **362.83**

1. Women refugees 2. American Dream. 3. Immigration policy 4. Refugee policy 5. United States -- History -- 21st century 6. Austin, Texas

ISBN 9780525559139

LC 2019033736

Documents the intimate stories of two refugees in present-day Texas, describing how a Christian from Myanmar and a Muslim from Syria narrowly escaped their home countries only to be introduced to the worst and best of the American dream.

"An excellent choice for readers seeking to understand the human effects of government immigration and refugee policy. Goudeau's sometimes heartbreaking narratives personalize the refugee crisis in ways cold news accounts cannot." Library Journal

Kristof, Nicholas D., 1959-

★**Half** the sky : turning oppression into opportunity for women worldwide / Nicholas D. Kristof and Sheryl WuDunn. Alfred A. Knopf, 2009. xxii, 294 p. : **362.83**

1. Women's rights. 2. Crimes against women. 3. Women -- Social conditions. 4. Human rights. 5. Developing countries.

ISBN 9780307267146

Two Pulitzer Prize winners issue a call to action against our era's most pervasive human rights violation: the oppression of women in the developing world. They show that a little help can transform the lives of women and girls abroad and that the key to economic progress lies in unleashing women's potential.

362.86 Veterans of military service

Bannerman, Stacy

Homefront 911 : how families of veterans are wounded by our wars / Stacy Bannerman. Arcade Publishing, 2015. 272 p. **362.86**

1. Families of military personnel. 2. Civil-military relations. 3. Veterans -- Mental health. 4. Post-traumatic stress disorder.

ISBN 9781628725698

LC 2015019123

The hallmarks of America's War on Terror have been repeated long deployments and a high percentage of troops returning with psychological problems. Family members of combat veterans are at a higher risk of potentially lethal domestic violence than almost any other demographic; it's estimated that one in four children of active-duty service members have symptoms of depression; and nearly one million veterans of Iraq and Afghanistan require increased care due to physical or psychological trauma. But, despite these staggering trends, civilian America has not been mobilized to take care of the families left behind; the American homefront, which traditionally has been rallied to support the nation's war efforts, has disappeared. In Homefront 911 Stacy Bannerman, a nationally-recognized advocate for military families, provides an insider's view of how more than a decade of war has contributed to the emerging crisis we are experiencing in today's military and veteran families as they battle with overwhelmed VA offices, a public they feel doesn't understand their sacrifices, and a nation that still isn't fully prepared to help those who have given so much.

"An activist, Bannerman has set up programs for women, drafted legislation, and testified before congressional committees. Here, she takes her message to a broader public in a disturbing cry for help." Kirkus.

362.88 Victims of crime

Crompton, Vicki

Saving beauty from the beast : how to protect your daughter from an unhealthy relationship / Vicki Crompton and Ellen Zelda Kessner. Little, Brown, c2003. xii, 259 p. : **362.88**

1. Dating violence -- Prevention 2. Teenage girls -- Abuse of -- Prevention 3. Interpersonal relations in adolescence 4. Parent and teenager

ISBN 9780316090582

LC 2002019153

Offers advice for dealing with teen dating abuse, from stalking to physical assault, discussing the warning signs of an unhealthy relationship, steps that friends and parents can take, and ways to intervene effectively.

"This book illuminates the problems of dangerous relationships by describing their characteristics, mapping out warning signs of abuse and offering sound advice for parents seeking to empower their daughters. The authors interviewed psychologists, counselors and girls who have had violent boyfriends; the girls' stories, as well as first-person accounts from parents and abusive boyfriends, are woven throughout the text. This book serves as both fervent friend and practical coach to parents whose daughters may be facing abuse." Publishers Weekly.

Krakauer, Jon
Missoula : rape and the justice system in a college town / Jon Krakauer. Doubleday, 2015. 384 p. **362.88309786**

1. University of Montana 2. Rape 3. Universities and colleges 4. Rape victims 5. Victims of crimes -- Rights.
ISBN 9780385538732
LC 2015002686

In Missoula, Krakauer chronicles the searing experiences of several women in Missoula ? the nights when they were raped; their fear and self-doubt in the aftermath; the way they were treated by the police, prosecutors, defense attorneys; the public vilification and private anguish; their bravery in pushing forward and what it cost them.

"Krakauer has done considerable research into acquaintance rape, and his recounting of trials, both legal and university proceedings, is riveting. His focus on quoting from testimony means that it is harder for readers to understand the motivations of someone like Kirsten Pabst, a former prosecutor who became a lawyer for an accused football player; an interview with her could have been useful. A raw and difficult but necessary read." Kirkus.

Nelson, Maggie, 1973-
The **red** parts : a memoir / Maggie Nelson. Free Press, c2007. xiv, 201 p. ; **362.88**

1. Nelson, Maggie, 1973 Family. 2. Mixer, Jane Louise, d. 1969. 3. Families of murder victims 4. Murder -- Psychological aspects 5. Loss (Psychology) 6. Cold cases (Criminal investigation) 7. Michigan
ISBN 9781416532033
LC 2006049664

Documents how the murder case of the author's aunt was reopened more than three decades later upon the discovery of new DNA findings, describing how the subsequent investigation and trial reopened long-standing wounds for the author and her family.

362.88086 Victims of crimes--People by miscellaneous social attributes

Yeung, Bernice
In a day's work : the fight to end sexual violence against America's most vulnerable workers / Bernice Yeung. New Press, 2018 272 p. **362.88086**

1. Sexual harassment. 2. Women foreign workers -- Crimes against. 3. Women immigrants -- Crimes against. 4. Sexual violence victims
ISBN 9781620973158
LC 2017053297

Pulitzer Prize for General Nonfiction finalist, 2019.

Yeung takes readers on a journey across the country, introducing us to women who came to America to escape grinding poverty only to encounter sexual violence in the United States. In a Day's Work exposes the underbelly of economies filled with employers who take advantage of immigrant women's need to earn a basic living. When these women find the courage to speak up, Yeung reveals, they are too often met by apathetic bosses and underresourced government agencies.

362.88092 Crime victims--Biography

Weinman, Sarah
The **real** Lolita : the kidnapping of Sally Horner and the novel that scandalized the world / Sarah Weinman. Ecco, 2018 xii, 306 p. : **362.88092**

1. Nabokov, Vladimir Vladimirovich, 1899-1977. Lolita 2. Horner, Sally 3. Kidnapping victims 4. Authors 5. Writing 6. Inspiration
ISBN 9780062661920

Arthur Ellis Award for Best Nonfiction, 2019.
Macavity Award for Best Non-Fiction, 2019.

A gripping true-crime investigation of the 1948 abduction of Sally Horner details the crime itself and how it inspired Vladimir Nabokov's classic novel, Lolita.

"This intricate balance of journalism and cultural critique is perfect for historical crime readers, feminist scholars, victims' rights advocates, and literature lovers. Recommended as a squirm-inducing read-along with Nabokov's novel." Library Journal.

362.883 Rape

Bryant-Davis, Thema
Surviving sexual violence : a guide to recovery and empowerment / edited by Thema Bryant-Davis. Rowman & Littlefield Publishers, c2011. ix, 372 p. ; **362.883**

1. Sexual abuse victims -- Psychology. 2. Sexual abuse victims -- Rehabilitation.
ISBN 144220639X
LC 2011013937

This book helps to empower survivors of sexual violation to navigate through the healing process. Sexual violation affects survivors but does not have to dictate their future, and this book shows readers how various paths to healing can help them, not only overcome the trauma of sexual assault, but also thrive as they move on with their lives. -- From publisher description.

"This book is useful for survivors, significant others, and counselors seeking a broad array of positive and supportive interventions. Resources and suggested activities are helpful." Choice.

Fowles, Stacey May,
Whatever gets you through : twelve survivors on life after sexual assault / edited by Stacey May Fowles & Jen Sookfong Lee ; foreword by Jessica Valenti. Greystone Books, 2019 xii, 219 p. **362.883**

1. Coping 2. Rape victims 3. Sexual violence victims 4. Feminism 5. Essays 6. Anthologies
ISBN 9781771643733

A collection of writers discuss how they have been sexually assaulted and survived.

"The authors present difficult truths often overlooked by popular narratives of survivordom, such as feeling abandoned by parents who didn't protect them or responsible for the friends they themselves couldn't protect...These writers' prose and generosity are nothing short of profound." Booklist.

363.11 Occupational and industrial hazards

Hamby, Chris
Soul full of coal dust : a fight for breath and justice in Appalachia

/ Chris Hamby. Little Brown & Co 2019 384 p. **363.11**

1. Black lung disease 2. Corporate cover-ups 3. Coal miners -- Health and safety 4. Miners -- Health and safety
ISBN 9780316299473
LC bl2018192156

An urgent report by a Pulitzer Prize-winning journalist uncovers the sobering resurgence of black lung disease in Appalachia, the cover-up activities of Big Coal and the awareness activities of regional mining communities.

"Pulitzer Prize-winning investigative reporter Hamby has compiled years of research into his story of coal miners in Appalachia who have endured black lung disease, and of their struggles to secure benefits from coal companies whose purposely hijacked safety procedures had led to their disability. . . . An engrossing read for those interested in social justice." Library Journal

363.12 Transportation hazards

Kluger, Jeffrey

Disaster strikes! : the most dangerous space missions of all time / Jeffrey Kluger. Philomel Books, 2019. 224 p. **363.12**

1. United States. National Aeronautics and Space Administration. NASA. 2. Project Apollo (U.S.) 3. Project Gemini (U.S.) 4. International Space Station 5. Space vehicle accidents 6. Space flight 7. Space exploration -- History 8. Accidents 9. Space
ISBN 9781984812759
LC 2018038095

Collects accounts of space missions gone awry at the height of the space race, from a botched space walk during the Gemini program to the famed Apollo 13 disaster.

"This well-researched book offers a series of compelling, real-life stories for kids intrigued by the history, the dangers, and the thrill of space exploration." Booklist.

Leinbach, Michael D.

Bringing Columbia home : the final mission of a lost space shuttle and her crew / Michael D. Leinbach, and Jonathan H. Ward Arcade Publishing, 2018 352 p. **363.12**

1. Columbia (Spacecraft) Accidents 2. Space Shuttle Program (U.S.) 3. Space shuttles 4. Space shuttle accidents 5. Explosions 6. Space exploration -- History
ISBN 9781628728514
LC 2017046190

Mike Leinbach was the launch director of the space shuttle program when Columbia disintegrated on reentry before a nation's eyes on February 1, 2003. And it would be Mike Leinbach who would be a key leader in the search and recovery effort as NASA, FEMA, the FBI, the US Forest Service, and dozens more federal, state, and local agencies combed an area of rural east Texas the size of Rhode Island for every piece of the shuttle and her crew they could find.

"A gripping account of a fatal tragedy and the impressive and deeply emotional human response that ensued." Kirkus.

363.17 Hazardous materials

Brown, Kate (Kathryn L.)

Plutopia : nuclear families, atomic cities, and the great Soviet and American plutonium disasters / Kate Brown. Oxford University Press, 2013. 384 p. **363.17**

1. Plutonium industry and trade 2. Occupational health and safety 3. Negligence 4. Working class families 5. Soviet Union 6. Washington (State)
ISBN 9780199855766
LC 2012041758

While many transnational histories of the nuclear arms race have been written, Kate Brown provides the first definitive account of the great plutonium disasters of the United States and the Soviet Union. --Provided by publisher

Higginbotham, Adam

Midnight in Chernobyl : the untold story of the world's greatest nuclear disaster / Adam Higginbotham. Simon & Schuster, 2019. 320 p. **363.17**

1. Chernobyl Nuclear Accident, 1986. 2. Nuclear accidents. 3. Political corruption. 4. Government cover-ups. 5. Ukraine -- History -- 1917-1991. 6. Soviet Union -- History -- 1985-1991.
ISBN 9781501134616
LC bl2018196001

ALA Notable Book, 2020.

Andrew Carnegie Medal for Excellence in Non-Fiction, 2020.

Draws on 20 years of research, recently declassified files and interviews with first-person survivors in an account of the 1986 Chernobyl nuclear power plant disaster that also reveals how propaganda and secrets have created additional dangers.

"Written with authority, this superb book reads like a classic disaster story and reveals a Soviet empire on the brink." Kirkus.

Moore, Kate (Writer and editor)

The **radium** girls : the dark story of America's shining women / Kate Moore. Sourcebooks, Inc., [2017] 480 p. **363.17**

1. Radioactive pollution 2. Womens rights 3. Occupational health and safety -- United States -- History -- 20th century. 4. Watch dial painters -- Diseases.
ISBN 9781492649359
LC 2016040681

"Originally published as: The Radium Girls : they paid with their lives, their final fight was for justice, in 2016 in the United Kingdom by Simon & Schuster UK."

ALA Notable Book, 2018.

"Moore's well-researched narrative is written with clarity and a sympathetic voice that brings these figures and their struggles to life." Library Journal.

Schlosser, Eric

Command and control : nuclear weapons, the Damascus Accident, and the illusion of safety / Eric Schlosser. The Penguin Press, 2013. xxiii, 632 p. ; **363.17**

1. Cold War 2. Weapons of mass destruction. 3. Nuclear weapons -- United States. 4. Nuclear accidents. 5. United States -- History, Military.
ISBN 9781594202278
ALA Notable Book, 2014
Pulitzer Prize for History finalist, 2014.

Presents a minute-by-minute account of an H-bomb accident that nearly caused a nuclear disaster, examining other near misses and America's growing susceptibility to a catastrophic event.

363.19 Product hazards

Nestle, Marion

Pet food politics : the Chihuahua in the coal mine / Marion Nestle. University of California Press, c2008. 232 p. **363.19**

1. Pet food -- Contamination. 2. Pet food industry and trade 3. Business -- Corrupt practices 4. Product recall.

ISBN 9780520257818

LC 2008003995

Marion Nestle, acclaimed author of Food Politics, now tells the gripping story of how, in early 2007, a few telephone calls about sick cats set off the largest recall of consumer products in U.S. history and an international crisis over the safety of imported goods ranging from food to toothpaste, tires, and toys. Nestle follows the trail of tainted pet food ingredients back to their source in China and along the supply chain to their introduction into feed for pigs, chickens, and fish in the United States, Canada, and other countries throughout the world. What begins as a problem "merely" for cats and dogs soon becomes an issue of tremendous concern to everyone. Nestle uncovers unexpected connections among the food supplies for pets, farm animals, and people and identifies glaring gaps in the global oversight of food safety.

"This book provides a vivid and detailed account of the [contaminated pet food] affair and its aftermath. The book ... deserves a wider readership." The Economist.

363.2 Police services

Butler, Paul, 1961-

Chokehold : policing black men / Paul Butler. New Press, The, 2017. 256 p. **363.2**

1. Discrimination in law enforcement 2. African American men -- Social conditions. 3. Criminal justice system -- Corrupt practices 4. Racism 5. United States -- Social conditions -- 21st century

ISBN 9781595589057

LC 2017000239

An African American former federal prosecutor and author of Let's Get Free uses new data to argue that white men commit the majority of violent crime in the United States and discusses the problem of black-on-black violence and how to keep communities safer without relying so much on the police.

"Smart, filled rightfully with righteous indignation, and demanding broad discussion and the widest audience." Kirkus.

Taibbi, Matt

★**I** can't breathe : a killing on Bay Street / Matt Taibbi. Spiegel & Grau, 2017. 256 p. **363.2**

1. Garner, Eric, -2014 2. New York City. Police Department 3. African American men 4. Black Lives Matter movement 5. Police brutality 6. Injustice 7. New York City -- Social conditions -- 21st century 8. New York City -- Politics and government

ISBN 9780812988840

LC bl2017035731

On July 17, 2014, a forty-three-year-old black man named Eric Garner died on a Staten Island sidewalk after a police officer put him in what has been described as an illegal chokehold during an arrest for selling bootleg cigarettes. The final moments of Garner's life were captured on video and seen by millions. His agonized last words, "I can't breathe," became a rallying cry for the nascent Black Lives Matter protest movement.

"This is a necessary and riveting work." Booklist.

Zimring, Franklin E.

When police kill / Franklin E. Zimring. Harvard University Press, 2017. xii, 305 p. ; **363.2**

1. Police shootings -- United States 2. Police -- Violence against -- United States 3. Police administration -- United States 4. Police-community relations -- United States

ISBN 9780674972186

LC 2016036666

When Police Kill is the first comprehensive analysis of police use of lethal force in the United States. The first seven chapters of this volume provide a summary and analysis of the known facts about killings by police. The final five chapters of the book provide an account of how federal, state and local governments can reduce killings by police without risking the lives of police officers. There are many strategies that federal and state government can use to motivate changes by police chiefs and sheriffs, but local law enforcement agencies are the main arena for reducing the carnage from police violence in the United States.-- Provided by publisher

"[A] valuable and important book. . . . It needs to be read." Huffington Post

363.20973 Police services--United States

Vitale, Alex S.

The **end** of policing / Alex Vitale. Verso, 2017. 288 p. **363.20973**

1. Police. 2. Police misconduct. 3. Police brutality.

ISBN 9781784782894

LC 2017020713

This book attempts to spark public discussion by revealing the tainted origins of modern policing as a tool of social control. It shows how the expansion of police authority is inconsistent with community empowerment, social justice--even public safety.

"A clearly argued, sure-to-be-controversial book." Kirkus.

363.25 Detection of crime (Criminal investigation)

Barnes-Svarney, Patricia L

The **handy** forensic science answer book : Reading Clues at the Crime Scene, Crime Lab and in Court / Patricia Barnes-Svarney and Thomas E. Svarney. Visible Ink Press, 2019 xii, 372 p. : **363.25**

1. Forensic sciences -- Miscellanea

ISBN 9781578596218

LC 2018019729

"Well-phrased questions are followed by succinct answers covering topics as diverse as the history of forensic science (1800 BCE through present day): crime scene investigations, lab work, controversies, and more." Library Journal

Bowden, Mark, 1951-

The **last** stone : a masterpiece of criminal interrogation / Mark Bowden. Atlantic Monthly Press, 2019. 304 p. **363.25**

1. Journalists 2. Detectives 3. Cold cases (Criminal investigation) 4. Missing girls

ISBN 9780802147301

LC 2018058489

The author of Black Hawk Down documents the story of how five skilled detectives navigated the deceptions of a prisoner who hid his role in the 1975 disappearance of two young sisters.

"An intriguing firsthand look at the nebulous justice meted out by necessities of time and the desire for closure, as seen through the focused lens of a seasoned journalist." Library Journal.

363.28 Services of special kinds of security and law enforcement agencies

Crooks, Pete

The **setup** : a true story of dirty cops, soccer moms, and reality TV / Pete Crooks. BenBella Books, Inc., [2014] 400 p. **363.28**

1. Butler, Chris (Private investigator) 2. Police corruption. 3. Private investigators. 4. Women private investigators. 5. Reality television programs. 6. California -- History.
ISBN 9781940363318

LC 2014027929

Documents how while writing a magazine piece about a private investigator firm that exclusively employed soccer moms, the author learned that the business was heavily engaged in fabricated sting operations and police corruption.

363.32 Social conflict

Gillon, Steven M

Separate and unequal : the Kerner Commission and the unraveling of American liberalism / Steven M. Gillon. Basic Books, 2018. 368 p. **363.32**

1. Johnson, Lyndon B., 1908-1973 2. United States. National Advisory Commission on Civil Disorders 3. Riots -- United States -- History 4. Urban poor people -- United States 5. African Americans -- Social conditions 6. Liberalism -- United States 7. United States -- Race relations -- Political aspects. 8. United States -- Politics and government -- 1963-1969. 9. United States -- Social conditions
ISBN 9780465096084

LC 2017035839

The definitive history of the Kerner Commission, whose report on urban unrest reshaped American debates about race and inequality.

Moore, Wes, 1978-

★**Five** days : the fiery reckoning of an American city / Wes Moore with Erica L. Green. One World, 2020 256 p. **363.32**

1. Gray, Freddie, 1989-2015. 2. Baltimore Riots, Baltimore, Md., 2015. 3. Police brutality 4. Police misconduct 5. Civil rights 6. Baltimore, Maryland -- Race relations. 7. Oral histories
ISBN 9780525512363

LC 2019048820

Includes index.

An account of the 2015 police-brutality killing of Freddie Gray retraces key events from the perspectives of seven insiders, including a conflicted Baltimore Police Department captain, the victim's sister and the owner of the Baltimore Orioles.

"Moore provides important context in the history of Baltimore's racial and income inequality and the emergence of the Black Lives Matter movement. Readers will be enthralled by this propulsive account." Publishers Weekly

363.3215 Social action

Okeowo, Alexis

A **moonless,** starless sky : ordinary women and men fighting extremism in Africa / Alexis Okeowo. Hachette Books, 2017. 256 p. **363.3215**

1. Extremists -- Africa, Sub-Saharan. 2. Islamic fundamentalism 3. Abduction -- Uganda. 4. Forced marriage -- Uganda. 5. Sub-Saharan Africa 6. Nigeria. 7. Mauritania. 8. Uganda. 9. Africa.
ISBN 9780316382939

LC 2017020071

A staff writer for the New Yorker describes the true stories of Africans who are bravely resisting the fundamentalism sweeping their country, including a women's basketball team in Somalia, a vigilante against Boko Haram, and kidnapping victims of Joseph Kony's LRA.

"In this memorable debut, Okeowo's in-depth, perceptive reporting gives a voice to the extraordinarily courageous--and resilient--women and men fighting malevolent ideologies and organizations in their native countries." Publishers Weekly.

363.325 Terrorism

Bergen, Peter L., 1962-

Manhunt : the ten-year search for Bin Laden--from 9/11 to Abbottabad / Peter L. Bergen. Crown Publishers, c2012. 288 p. **363.325**

1. Bin Laden, Osama, 1957-2011. 2. Qaida (Organization) 3. Terrorists -- Saudi Arabia. 4. Fugitives from justice -- United States. 5. Terrorism -- United States -- Prevention. 6. Special operations (Military science) -- United States.
ISBN 9780307955579

LC 2012004258

The author of the best-selling Holy War, Inc. presents a definitive account of the decade-long search for Osama bin Laden, sharing coverage of such topics as the CIA analyst team that gathered critical intelligence and what bin Laden's demise means for al Qaeda.

Katz, Samuel M., 1963-

No shadows in the desert : murder, vengeance, and espionage in the war against ISIS / Samuel M. Katz. Hanover Square Press, 2020. 352 p. **363.325**

1. ISIS (Islamic State of Iraq and Syria) 2. Jordan. General Intelligence Department. 3. CIA 4. Terrorism -- Prevention. 5. Strategic alliances (Military) 6. Fundamentalism 7. Murder victims
ISBN 9781335013835

LC bl2020010338

Offers the inside story of the destruction of ISIS, showing how the operations were carried out on the ground, drawing on sources throughout the anti-ISIS coalition.

"Though Katz's staccato prose can be clunky, he packs a wealth of information into the book and skillfully draws on an extensive network of sources in the U.S. and the Middle East. Espionage fans will savor this detailed and immersive account." Publishers Weekly

Pandith, Farah

How we win : how cutting-edge entrepreneurs, political visionaries, enlightened business leaders, and social media mavens can defeat the extremist threat / Farah Pandith. Custom House, 2019. 511 p. **363.325**

1. Terrorism 2. Extremism 3. Antiterrorist policy. 4. Radicalism
ISBN 9780062471154

An expert on countering violent extremism who served under the Secretary of State for two presidential administrations describes how to disrupt the dynamic that veers Muslim millennials toward extremism.

Sesay, Isha, 1976-

Beneath the tamarind tree : a story of courage, family, and the lost schoolgirls of Boko Haram / Isha Sesay. Dey Street Books,

2019. 382 p., 8 unnumbered p. of plates : **363.32509669**

1. Boko Haram 2. Terrorism 3. Fundamentalism 4. Girl kidnapping victims 5. Kidnapping 6. Nigeria 7. West Africa

ISBN 9780062686671

Presents a definitive account of Boko Haram's 2014 abduction of 276 Chibok schoolgirls, sharing first-person insights based on the author's escape with 21 survivors.

Soufan, Ali H.

★**Anatomy** of terror : from the death of Bin Laden to the rise of the Islamic State / Ali Soufan. W. W. Norton & Company, 2017. 336 p. **363.325**

1. Bin Laden, Osama, 1957-2011. 2. Qaida (Organization). 3. ISIS (Islamic State of Iraq and Syria) 4. Terrorism -- Religious aspects -- Islam. 5. Radicalism -- Religious aspects -- Islam.

ISBN 9780393241174

LC 2016055805

When Osama bin Laden was killed by a U.S. Navy SEAL, many prophesied al-Qaeda's imminent demise. In reality the opposite has occurred. Why? Watching the Arab Spring from his Pakistani safe house, bin Laden had seen an historic opportunity: "The next stage will be the return of the caliphate." In the six years since bin Laden's death, al-Qaeda's affiliates metastasized, and the Islamic State, its most brutal spinoff, proclaimed itself the reborn caliphate bin Laden had foreseen.

"Former FBI agent Soufan ... composes a concise, accessible, enormously readable account of the trajectory of al-Qaida, especially through the actions of its murderous main protagonists." Kirkus.

The **black** banners declassified : how torture derailed the war on terror after 9/11 / Ali Soufan, with Daniel Freedman. W. W. Norton & Co., 2020, c2011 xxx, 594 p. : **363.325**

1. Qaida (Organization) 2. Military intelligence. 3. Antiterrorist policy. 4. Terrorism. 5. Terrorists. 6. United States -- Politics and government -- 2001-2009

ISBN 9780393540727

LC 2020023446

The definitive account of an FBI special agent's al-Qaeda story, unredacted for the first time. In the fight against al-Qaeda, former FBI special agent Ali H. Soufan became a legend on the basis of his deft questioning of prisoners, which often short-circuited al-Qaeda plots in the pipeline. Physical or mental violence played no part in this success. He never laid a hand on the suspected terrorists. Other U.S. intelligence agencies took orders directly from the Oval Office, using other methods. The CIA's decision to employ "enhanced interrogation techniques" backfired, says Soufan. It made the job of defending the United States more difficult and dangerous.

"The best and most original book published in the West on al-Qaeda, this is highly recommended." Library Journal.

Wood, Graeme

The **way** of the strangers : encounters with the Islamic State / Graeme Wood. Random House Inc 2017. 224 p. **363.325**

1. ISIS (Islamic State of Iraq and Syria) 2. Terrorism -- Religious aspects -- Islam. 3. Fundamentalism -- Middle East. 4. Violence 5. Terrorists -- Iraq. 6. Middle East -- History -- 21st century.

ISBN 9780812988758

LC 2017302379

Governor General's Literary Award for English-Language Nonfiction, 2017

The writer of The Atlantic's cover story, "What ISIS Really Wants," presents an intimate and unsettling examination of the motivations that drive the men and women of the Islamic State, sharing the stories of individual followers against a backdrop of the violent events of today.

363.325082 Terrorism--Women

Rosenau, William

Tonight we bombed the U.S. Capitol : the explosive story of M19, America's first female terrorist group / William Rosenau. Atria Books, [2019] 320 p. **363.325082**

1. May 19th Communist Organization. 2. Women terrorists 3. Domestic terrorism 4. Women radicals 5. Women revolutionaries 6. United States -- History -- 20th century 7. United States -- Politics and government -- 20th century

ISBN 9781501170126

LC 2019014374

Describes how six veteran women extremists joined together in the late 1970s to create M19, a terrorist organization that carried out acts of domestic terrorism, including prison breaks, armed robberies and a bombing campaign on the nation's capital.

"Journalist Rosenau makes his debut with a gripping, meticulously researched account of the May 19 Communist Organization, a female-led violent revolutionary group active in America from 1978 to 1985." Publishers Weekly.

363.3250956 Terrorism--Middle East

Gerges, Fawaz A., 1958-

ISIS : a history / Fawaz A. Gerges. Princeton University Press, 2016 368 p. **363.3250956**

1. ISIS (Islamic State of Iraq and Syria) 2. Terrorism -- Religious aspects -- Islam. 3. Terrorists -- Iraq. 4. Fundamentalism 5. Violence 6. Middle East -- History -- 21st century.

ISBN 9780691170008

LC 2015956950

The Islamic State has stunned the world with its savagery, destructiveness, and military and recruiting successes. What explains the rise of ISIS and what does it portend for the future of the Middle East? In this book, one of the world's leading authorities on political Islam and jihadism sheds new light on these questions as he provides a unique history of the rise and growth of ISIS.

"A specific, timely, well-rendered exegesis of the unfolding global threat." Kirkus.

Wright, Lawrence, 1947-

The **terror** years : from al-Qaeda to the Islamic State / Lawrence Wright. Knopf, 2016. 336 p. **363.3250956**

1. Qaida (Organization). 2. ISIS (Islamic State of Iraq and Syria) 3. Terrorism. 4. Extremism. 5. Fundamentalism. 6. War on Terrorism, 2001-2009 7. Middle East -- Politics and government -- 1945- 8. Islamic countries -- Foreign relations 9. Essays

ISBN 9780385352055

LC 2015046064

Ten powerful pieces first published in "The New Yorker" recall the path terror in the Middle East has taken from the rise of al-Qaeda in the 1990s to the recent beheadings of reporters and aid workers by ISIS.

"The research that Wright did for the 10 essays contained in his latest work, all of which first appeared in the magazine, also contributed to Wright's deeper insight into the jihadist mindset, including its latest embodiment in ISIS. In The Man behind Bin Laden Wright recounts his return to Egypt, where he taught English decades earlier, to investigate the background of Bin Laden's sidekick Ayman al-Zawahiri, describing a country embroiled in post-9/11 political turmoil. Other pieces on Saudi Arabia, ISIS violence, and Israel round out a brilliant volume that is a must-read for anyone looking for greater illumination of the baffling world of religious extremism." Booklist.

363.3250973 Terrorism--United States

Bergen, Peter L., 1962-

United States of Jihad : investigating America's homegrown terrorists / Peter Bergen. Crown, 2016 384 p. **363.3250973**

1. Terrorists -- Recruiting. 2. Terrorism -- United States. 3. Jihad. 4. National security 5. Books to TV
ISBN 9780804139540

LC 2015034447

The television documentary Homegrown is based on this book.

Lucid, rigorously researched, and packed with fascinating new details, United States of Jihad is the definitive account of the Americans who have embraced militant Islam both here and abroad.

"Both balanced and galvanizing, Bergen's meticulous portrait of violent extremism is required reading for anyone who truly wants to understand the nature of the evolving threats from within and without." Booklist.

363.33 Control of firearms

Melville House (Brooklyn, New York),

Too many times : how to end gun violence in a divided America / Melville House. Melville House, 2020 198 p. **363.33**

1. Guns 2. Crime and guns 3. Violence and guns 4. Gun control 5. United States -- Social conditions 6. Essays 7. Anthologies
ISBN 9781612198798

LC 2020942670

Gun violence is a problem with many faces, but seemingly no solution. From mass shootings to deadly domestic abuse to police officers opening fire, it permeates American life. And yet it feels impossible to address. The lines are firmly drawn and the federal government has not passed any legislation to reduce gun ownership in over twenty-five years. That's why it's time to look at the issue differently. In this revelatory collection, gun violence in America is addressed from three angles: how gun violence affects us today, how we have gotten to this juncture legally and socially, and finally, what we can do to reduce and end gun violence in America.

"Readers will walk away well informed and inspired to act." Booklist

Overton, Iain

The **way** of the gun : a bloody journey into the world of firearms / Iain Overton. HarperCollins 2016. 320 p. **363.33**

1. Guns 2. Violence and guns 3. Gun ownership 4. Gun control
ISBN 9780062346063

LC 2016498146

An investigation into the life cycle of the gun draws on interviews with U.S. gun makers, lobbyists, doctors, hunters, shooting victims and others to illuminate harsh realities about gun crimes and how guns have become an integral part of 21st-century life.

"A passionate mix of rhetoric and travelogue, Overton's book takes the gun debate into impressive new territory." Kirkus.

363.330973 Gun control--United States

Giffords, Gabrielle D. (Gabrielle Dee), 1970-

Enough : our fight to keep America safe from gun violence / Gabrielle Giffords, and Mark Kelly. Scribner, 2014. 256 p. **363.330973**

1. United States. Constitution. 2nd Amendment 2. Gun control 3. Violence and guns 4. Gun ownership -- Law and legislation 5. Political rights. 6. United States -- Politics and government -- 21st century
ISBN 9781476750071

LC bl2014032786

Former Congresswoman Gabrielle Giffords--disabled from an assassination attempt in Tucson, Arizona--and her husband, astronaut Mark Kelly, share their impassioned argument for responsible gun ownership and more responsible gun control laws, despite being gun owners and staunch supporters of the Second Amendment themselves.

"Lay readers and political science students who want to understand the emotional debate surrounding gun ownership and current efforts to limit access to lethal weapons will appreciate the balanced discussion of the issues facing those who intend to change current firearms legislation." Library Journal.

Hogg, David

#NeverAgain : a new generation draws the line / David Hogg (Class of 2018), Lauren Hogg (Class of 2021), Marjory Stoneman Douglas High School, Parkland, Florida. Random House, [2018] 165 p. ; **363.330973**

1. Gun control 2. School shootings 3. Mass shootings 4. Social movements
ISBN 9781984801838

LC bl2018108177

Two survivors of the mass shooting at Marjory Stoneman Douglas High School in Parkland, Florida, offer an in-depth look at the creation of the #NeverAgain movement, which advocates for tighter gun regulations to prevent gun violence.

363.34 Disasters

Dolin, Eric Jay

A **furious** sky : the five-hundred-year history of America's hurricanes / Eric Jay Dolin. Liveright Publishing, 2020. xxvii, 392 p. **363.34**

1. Hurricanes 2. Storms 3. Natural disasters -- History 4. Humans -- Effect of environment on 5. United States -- History 6. Atlantic Ocean 7. Gulf of Mexico
ISBN 9781631495274

LC 2019059367

Presents the five-hundred-year story of American hurricanes, from the nameless storms that threatened Columbus' New World voyages, to the devastation wrought by Hurricane Maria in Puerto Rico and the escalation of hurricane season as a result of global warming.

Mooallem, Jon

This is Chance! : the shaking of an all-American city, a voice that held it together / Jon Mooallem. Random House, 2020 304 p. **363.34**

1. Chance, Genie, 1927-1998. 2. Alaska Earthquake, Alaska, 1964. 3. Women journalists 4. Radio programs 5. Earthquakes -- Alaska 6.

Anchorage, Alaska 7. Alaska
ISBN 9780525509912

LC 2019015815

"This is a work of nonfiction. Some names and identifying details have been changed"--T.p. verso.

The Good Friday, 1964, Anchorage, Alaska earthquake, and newscaster Genie Chance remaining on-air to broadcast events.

"A great crossover read for teens as well as adults about community, tenacity, and the power of one person to make a difference." Library Journal

363.350973 Civil defense--United States

Graff, Garrett M., 1981-

Raven Rock : the story of the U.S. Government's secret plan to save itself -- while the rest of us die / Garrett M. Graff. Simon & Schuster, 2017. 560 p. **363.350973**

1. National security 2. Crisis management 3. Secrecy in government 4. Emergency planning 5. United States -- Politics and government 6. United States -- Armed Forces
ISBN 9781476735405

LC 2017004895

Describes the secret Doomsday plans, developed for over 60 years, that would evacuate high-ranking government officials in the event of a massive terrorist or nuclear attack on Washington, DC, while leaving ordinary citizens to fend for themselves.

"A chilling portrait of how the government planned to continue to function during and after a nuclear holocaust is brilliantly told in this new valuable addition to Cold War literature that goes beyond policy and delves into logistical plans." Library Journal.

363.37 Fire hazards

Gee, Alastair

Fire in paradise : an American tragedy / Alastair Gee and Dani Anguiano W.W. Norton & Company, [2020] 244 pages : **363.37**

1. Wildfires 2. Climate change 3. Business -- Corrupt practices 4. Disasters 5. California
ISBN 9781324005148

LC bl2020011201

An account of the 2018 Camp Fire that razed the town of Paradise, California draws on hundreds of interviews with residents, firefighters, police and scientific experts to document its horrific impact, including the establishment of an unfolding refugee crisis.

"A vividly descriptive, compelling, well-researched, page-turning work of narrative nonfiction, both heartbreaking and uplifting." Library Journal

363.3709745 Fire hazards--Rhode Island

James, Scott, 1962-

Trial by fire : a devastating tragedy, a hundred lives lost, and a fifteen-year search for truth / Scott James. Thomas Dunne Books, 2020. 384 p. **363.3709745**

1. Station (Nightclub : West Warwick, R.I.) Fire, 2003. 2. Great White (Musical group) 3. Nightclubs. 4. Fires. 5. Rock concerts. 6. Fireworks 7. Rhode Island.
ISBN 9781250131263

LC 2020019383

In only 90 seconds, a fire in the Station nightclub killed 100 people and injured hundreds more. It would take nearly 20 years to find out why--and who was really at fault. All it took for a hundred people to die during a show by the hair metal band Great White was a sudden burst from two giant sparklers that ignited the acoustical foam lining the Station nightclub. But who was at fault? Trial By Fire is the heartwrenching story of the fire's aftermath because while the fire, one of America's deadliest, lasted fewer than two minutes, the search for the truth would take twenty years.

"This is not an easy book, but it is well worth reading for true crime fans who are tired of serial killers." Booklist

363.4 Controversies related to public morals and customs

McGirr, Lisa, 1962-

The **war** on alcohol : prohibition and the rise of the American state / Lisa McGirr. W. W. NORTON & COMPANY, 2016. 384 p. **363.4**

1. Prohibition 2. Temperance movements 3. Social history 4. Alcohol 5. United States -- History -- 20th century.
ISBN 9780393066951

LC 2015028038

Argues that Prohibition was not simply a curious interlude that left no trace on American history, but was the seed bed for a huge expansion of the federal government, especially in its law-enforcement capacities.

"McGirr's new perspective on Prohibition is recommended for all readers interested in American history." Library Journal.

Okrent, Daniel, 1948-

Last call : the rise and fall of Prohibition, 1920-1933 / Daniel Okrent. Scribner, 2010. 480 p. **363.4**

1. Prohibition 2. Drinking -- United States -- History -- 20th century. 3. Alcohol. 4. Bootleggers. 5. United States -- History -- 20th century.
ISBN 9780743277020

LC 2009051127

ALA Notable Book, 2011.

Okrent explores the origins, implementation, and failure of that great American delusion known as Prohibition. "Last Call" explains how Prohibition happened, what life under it was like, and what it did to the country.

363.4509861 Illegal drugs--Colombia

Muse, Toby

Kilo : inside the deadliest cocaine cartels--from the jungles to the streets / Toby Muse. William Morrow & Company, 2020. 303 p. **363.4509861**

1. Muse, Toby 2. War correspondents 3. Cocaine traffic 4. Cocaine smuggling 5. Drug cartels 6. Colombia
ISBN 9780062905291

LC bl2020004943

Seasoned war correspondent Toby Muse has witnessed each level of the cocaine business, fueled by the appetite for the drug in America and Europe. In this riveting chronicle, he takes the reader inside Colombia's notorious cartels to offer a never before look at the drug trade. Piercing this veiled world, Kilo is a gripping portrait of a country struggling to end this deadly trade even as the riches flow. A human portrait of criminals and the shocking details of their lives, Kilo is a chilling, unforgettable story that takes you deep into the belly of the beast.

"Cocaine darkens the souls of all it touches in a foreign correspondent's chilling eyewitness account of the barbarous world of Colombian drug trafficking. . . . An unrelentingly tragic yet indispensable expose." Kirkus

363.5 Housing

Satter, Beryl, 1959-

Family properties : race, real estate, and the exploitation of Black urban America / Beryl Satter. Metropolitan Books, 2009. 512 p. **363.5**

1. Satter, Mark J., 1916-1965. 2. African Americans -- Housing -- Chicago, Illinois 3. Discrimination in housing -- Chicago, Illinois -- History -- 20th century. 4. Housing policy -- Chicago, Illinois -- History -- 20th century. 5. African Americans -- Chicago, Illinois -- Social conditions 6. Chicago, Illinois -- Social conditions -- 20th century. 7. Chicago, Illinois -- Race relations -- History -- 20th century.

ISBN 9780805076769

LC 2008033005

National Jewish Book Award, 2009.

An investigation into practices of segregation and urban decay in post-war Chicago and other major American cities reveals how legal and financial exploitation, more than race pathology and poverty, are responsible for creating slums, in an account that cites the reform efforts of the author's father.

"The author leaps from the particulars of one man's story to become a panoramic retelling of the Chicago real-estate wars during a period when, after the postwar migration of Southern blacks, that city was the most segregated in the North." New York Times.

363.509794 Housing--California

Dougherty, Conor

Golden gates : the fight for housing--and democracy--in America's most prosperous city / Conor Dougherty. Penguin Press, 2020. 384 p. **363.509794**

1. Housing 2. Working class 3. Zoning 4. Urban planning 5. San Francisco, California 6. California

ISBN 9780525560210

LC 2019039425

An economics reporter at The New York Times, through ground-level reporting, chronicles America's housing crisis from its West Coast epicenter, revealing the decades of history and economic forces that have brought us here.

"Readers who assume there's no solution to sky-high rents in America's big cities should consult this detailed and optimistic counter-narrative." Publishers Weekly

363.6 Public utilities and related services

Clark, Anna (Anna Leigh)

The **poisoned** city : Flint's water and the American urban tragedy / Anna Clark. Henry Holt & Co., 2018 336 p. **363.6**

1. Public health 2. Water-supply 3. Lead contamination 4. Lead in drinking water -- Health hazards 5. Flint, Michigan 6. Michigan -- Politics and government

ISBN 9781250125149

LC 2018021437

Documents the 2014 poisoning of the residents of Flint, Michigan, by contaminated water, and the ensuing 18-month activism case that only got the state to admit its complicity after 12 people died and many others suffered permanent injuries.

"A compelling must-read about issues of environmental activism, urban issues, systemic racism, and the accountability of the government to the people whom it serves." Library Journal.

Heacox, Kim

National Geographic the national parks : an illustrated history / Kim Heacox. National Geographic, 2016 367 p. : **363.6**

1. National parks and reserves -- United States -- History.

ISBN 1426215592

LC 2015014107

Includes index.

A lavishly photographed celebration of the National Park Service's 100th anniversary combines top-selected National Geographic photography with expert historical coverage of topics ranging from the Grand Canyon to the Statue of Liberty.

"Gorgeous in every way, and essential for travel and history shelves." Library Journal.

363.7 Environmental problems

Shulman, Seth

Cooler smarter : practical steps for low-carbon living : expert advice from the Union of Concerned Scientists / Seth Shulman ... [et al.]. Island Press, c2012. xii, 321 p. : **363.7**

1. Sustainable living -- United States. 2. Environmental protection -- United States -- Citizen participation.

ISBN 9781610911924

LC 2012008656

"How can each of us live Cooler Smarter? While the routine decisions that shape our days--what to have for dinner, where to shop, how to get to work--may seem small, collectively they have a big effect on global warming. But which changes in our lifestyles might make the biggest difference to the climate? This science-based guide shows you the most effective ways to cut your own global warming emissions by twenty percent or more, and explains why your individual contribution is so vital to addressing this global problem. Cooler Smarter is based on an in-depth, two-year study by the experts at The Union of Concerned Scientists. While other green guides suggest an array of tips, Cooler Smarter offers proven strategies to cut carbon, with chapters on transportation, home energy use, diet, personal consumption, as well as how best to influence your workplace, your community, and elected officials. The book explains how to make the biggest impact and when not to sweat the small stuff. It also turns many eco-myths on their head, like the importance of locally produced food or the superiority of all hybrid cars. The advice in Cooler Smarter can help save you money and live healthier. But its central purpose is to empower you, through low carbon-living, to confront one of society's greatest threats".-- Provided by publisher.

Nesbit, Jeffrey Asher

This is the way the world ends : how droughts and die-offs, heat waves and hurricanes are converging on America / Jeff Nesbit. Thomas Dunne Books/St. Martin's Press, 2018. 320 p. **363.7**

1. Global environmental change. 2. Environmental policy 3. Global

warming 4. Climate change
ISBN 9781250160461

LC 2018011503

Telling real stories of substantial impacts to Earth's systems across each continent, an environmental expert presents a unique view of climate change as seen through the world's resources that are disappearing and describes what we can do to stop it.

"This vital summary of dire facts offers no-nonsense proposals for a way forward." Publishers Weekly.

Robinson, Mary, 1944-

Climate justice : hope, resilience, and the fight for a sustainable future / Mary Robinson. Bloomsbury Publishing, 2018. 176 p. **363.7**

1. Environmental justice. 2. Climate change -- Social aspects. 3. Global environmental change. 4. Communities
ISBN 9781632869289

LC 2018027314

A former president of Ireland and U.S. special envoy on climate change describes the impact of climate change and offers uplifting stories of ordinary people who have stepped up to help save our planet, including a Mississippi hair dresser and a Ugandan farmer.

"This brief but cogent account reminds readers that climate change is not academic or abstract; it is real and it has consequences." Publishers Weekly.

363.70092 Environmentalists

Thunberg, Greta, 2003-

No one is too small to make a difference / Greta Thunberg. Penguin Books, 2019 112 p. ; **363.70092**

1. Nature -- Effect of humans on 2. Teenage girl social advocates. 3. Environmentalism. 4. Sustainable living. 5. Speeches, addresses, etc.
ISBN 9780143133568

"With clarity and unbridled passion, Thunberg presents her message that climate change is an emergency that must be addressed immediately." Publishers Weekly.

363.7209749 Sanitation--New Jersey

Fagin, Dan

Toms River : a small town, a cancer cluster, and the epic quest to expose pollution's hidden consequences / Dan Fagin. Bantam Books, 2013. xv, 538 p. : **363.7209749**

1. Corporate cover-ups. 2. Pollution -- Health hazards. 3. Illegal hazardous waste disposal. 4. Cancer. 5. New Jersey. 6. Toms River, New Jersey -- Environmental conditions.
ISBN 9780553806533
National Academies Communication Award, 2014.
Pulitzer Prize for General Nonfiction, 2014.

Recounts the decades-long saga of the New Jersey seaside town plagued by childhood cancers caused by air and water pollution due to the indiscriminate dumping of toxic chemicals.

363.73 Pollution

Blackwell, Andrew, 1972-

Visit sunny Chernobyl : and other adventures in the world's most polluted places / Andrew Blackwell. Rodale, c2012. 320 p. **363.73**

1. Ecotourism. 2. Pollution. 3. Environmental degradation. 4. Nature -- Effect of humans on 5. Satire.
ISBN 9781605294452

LC 2011053229

Includes index.

A tour of the world's most environmentally compromised regions provides satirical analysis of "destinations" ranging from hidden bars and convenience stores to radioactive wildernesses and the waters of India, providing measured consideration of the relevance of degraded ecosystems.

363.730973 Pollution--United States

Vallianatos, E. G.

Poison spring : the secret history of pollution and the EPA / E.G. Vallianatos with McKay Jenkins. Bloomsbury Press, 2013. 320 p. **363.730973**

1. United States. Environmental Protection Agency. 2. Environmental responsibility -- United States. 3. Environmental policy -- United States. 4. Pollution 5. Corporate power 6. United States -- Politics and government -- 21st century.
ISBN 9781608199143

LC 2013041923

An insider's account discusses how political pressure and corporate co-optation have undermined the Environmental Protection Agency, with devastating effects on public safety and the natural world.

"The authors tout healthier living through small, nontoxic family farms while delivering an alarming, comprehensive account of a 'fatally compromised' EPA mission crippled by bad enforcement practices and numerous corrupting influences." Publishers Weekly.

363.7309748 Pollution--Pennsylvania

Griswold, Eliza, 1973-

Amity and Prosperity : one family and the fracturing of America / Eliza Griswold. Farrar, Straus and Giroux, 2018. 320 p. **363.7309748**

1. Hydraulic fracturing 2. Rural development 3. Oil industry and trade 4. Nature -- Effect of humans on 5. Pennsylvania 6. Amity (Washington County, Pennsylvania. : Township) -- Social conditions. 7. Prosperity, Pennsylvania -- Social conditions.
ISBN 9780374103118

LC 2017057605

Pulitzer Prize for General Nonfiction, 2019.

The award-winning author of The Tenth Parallel explores the costs of fracking as demonstrated by the volatile personalities and politics of a rural Allegheny town where an unlikely whistle-blower tried to investigate the sources of mysterious local illnesses.

"Griswold's (The Tenth Parallel, 2010) empathetic yet analytical account of Haney's indefatigable role as advocate for justice is a thorough and thoroughly blood-pressure-raising account of the greed and fraud embedded in the environmentally ruinous natural-gas industry. As honest and unvarnished an account of the human cost of corporate corruption as one will find." Booklist.

363.738 Pollutants

Berners-Lee, Mike

How bad are bananas? : the carbon footprint of everything / Mike Berners-Lee. Greystone Books, c2011. 232 p. : **363.738**

1. Global warming -- Prevention. 2. Carbon dioxide mitigation. 3. Sustainable living.
ISBN 9781553658313

LC bl2011006958

"First published in Great Britain in 2010 by Profile Books Ltd."-- T.p. verso.

Discusses the carbon footprint--the carbon emissions used to manufacture and transport--everyday items, including paper bags and imported produce, and provides information to help build carbon considerations into everyday purchases.

Carson, Rachel, 1907-1964

★**Silent** spring / Rachel Carson ; introduction by Linda Lear ; afterword by Edward O. Wilson ; drawings by Lois and Louis Darling. Houghton Mifflin, 2002, c1962. xix, 378 p. : **363.738**

1. Pesticides -- Environmental aspects. 2. Insect pests -- Biological control. 3. Insecticides. 4. Poisons.
ISBN 9780618253050

LC BL2002012485

Originally published in 1962.

Discusses the reckless annihilation of fish and birds by the use of pesticides and warns of the possible genetic effects on humans.

"Understand, yes, and shudder, for she has drawn a living portrait of what is happening to this balance nature has decreed in the science of life -- and what man is doing (and has done) to destroy it and create a science of death." Kirkus.

Flannery, Tim F. (Tim Fridtjof), 1956-

The **weather** makers : how man is changing the climate and what it means for life on Earth / Tim Flannery. Atlantic Monthly Press, 2005. xv, 357 p., 4 p. of plates : **363.738**

1. Global warming. 2. Climate change 3. Greenhouse effect, Atmospheric. 4. Natural disasters.
ISBN 0871139359

LC 2005052350

Australian Book Industry Awards, General Non Fiction Book of the Year, 2006.

ALA Notable Book, 2007.

Originally skeptical of global warming, Flannery spent years compiling his own research. What he learned is sobering. Human beings are weather makers whose production of carbon dioxide is polluting the planet at a devastating rate. Species are disappearing, the natural world is changing, and weather events, like Hurricane Katrina, are becoming increasingly disastrous. But as Flannery shows, there are cleaner ways to live--and doing so is the only wat to avoid global catastrophe.

"This work is distinctive in its marriage of science to an act-now attitude and should energize environmentally minded readers." Booklist.

Gore, Albert, 1948-

An **inconvenient** truth : the planetary emergency of global warming and what we can do about it / Al Gore. Rodale Press, 2006. 325 p. : **363.738**

1. Global warming. 2. Greenhouse effect, Atmospheric -- Government policy 3. Atmosphere. 4. Environmental policy.
ISBN 1594865671

Green Prize for Sustainable Literature: Adult Nonfiction, 2007.

The former vice-president details the factors contributing to the growing climate crisis, describes changes to the environment caused by global warming, and discusses the shift in environmental policy that is needed to avert disaster.

"Gore has put together a coherent account of a complex topic that Americans desperately need to understand. . . . By telling the story of climate change with striking clarity . . . Al Gore may have done for global warming what [Rachel Carson's] Silent Spring [1962] did for pesticides." New York Review of Books.

Hauter, Wenonah

Frackopoly : the battle for the future of energy and the environment / Wenonah Hauter. The New Press, 2016. 336 p. **363.738**

1. Energy development -- Environmental aspects. 2. Hydraulic fracturing -- Environmental aspects. 3. Energy industry and trade -- Environmental aspects 4. Environmental policy. 5. United States -- Environmental conditions.
ISBN 9781620970072

LC 2015050032

One of the nation's leading public interest advocates, describing the onset of the fracking industry, argues that the rush to fracking is dangerous to the environment and human health, examines the powerful interests that have supported it and offers a thorough debunking of its supposed economic benefits.

Holthaus, Eric, 1981-

The **future** earth : a radical vision for what's possible in the age of warming / Eric Holthaus. HarperOne, 2020. 247 p. ; **363.738**

1. Climate change 2. Climatology. 3. Global environmental change
ISBN 9780062883162

A hopeful book about climate change shows readers how to reverse the short- and long-term effects of climate change over the next three decades.

"Climate journalist Holthaus imagines a different world in his cautionary but guardedly optimistic debut about how humanity might meet the climate change challenge. . . . Serious and substantial, this will give readers plenty to consider." Publishers Weekly

Klein, Naomi, 1970-

This changes everything : capitalism vs. the climate / Naomi Klein. Simon & Schuster, 2014. 576 p. **363.738**

1. Economic policy. 2. Green economics. 3. Environmentalism. 4. Environmental policy.
ISBN 9781451697384

LC 2014013864

Green Prize for Sustainable Literature: Adult Nonfiction, 2015.

Hilary Weston Writers' Trust Prize, 2014.

Award-winning journalist Naomi Klein offers an explanation of why the climate crisis challenges us to abandon the core "free market" ideology of our time, restructure the global economy, and remake our political systems.

"In part, Klein's narrative is a personal story about her own awakening to and increasing engagement with the climate issue. But this always-interesting polemic is built mostly on her interviews with experts, environmentalists and activists and her colorful on-site reporting from various international meetings and conferences." Kirkus.

Kolbert, Elizabeth

Field notes from a catastrophe : man, nature, and climate change / Elizabeth Kolbert. Bloomsbury Pub., 2006. 210 p.

: 363.738

1. Global warming. 2. Climate change 3. Global temperature changes. 4. Global environmental change.

ISBN 9781596911253

ALA Notable Book, 2007.

A New Yorker writer tackles the controversial issue of global warming from every angle, incorporating interviews with researchers and environmentalists, explaining the science and the studies, unpacking the politics, drawing parallels to lost ancient civilizations, and presenting the personal tales of those who are being affected most.

"On the burgeoning shelf of cautionary but occasionally alarmist books warning about the consequences of dramatic climate change, Kolbert's calmly persuasive reporting stands out for its sobering clarity." Publishers Weekly.

Lappe, Anna, 1973-

Diet for a hot planet : the climate crisis at the end of your fork and what you can do about it / Anna Lappe ; foreward by Bill McKibben. Bloomsbury USA, 2010. 304 p. **363.738**

1. Food industry and trade. 2. Global warming. 3. Sustainable agriculture. 4. Climate change

ISBN 9781596916593

LC 2010017363

Predicts that, if nothing is done, food-system-related greenhouse gas emissions will continue to rise, exposes that food industry as a key opponent to system-wide reform, offers six principles for a climate-friendly diet and provides examples of farmers who are demonstrating the potential of sustainable farming.

McGraw, Seamus

Betting the farm on a drought : stories from the front lines of climate change / Seamus McGraw. University of Texas Press, 2015. 192 p. **363.738**

1. Climate change 2. Environmentalism 3. Environmental movement 4. Environmental protection 5. Essays

ISBN 9780292756618

LC 2014027613

This book takes a survey of climate change today: it lays out for the everyman what is happening, why it's happening, and what some people are doing about it. But rather than get mired in polemics or scientific jargon, as so many other books have done, Tempest tackles the issue through the people who are dealing with it -- scientists, yes, but also fishermen and farmers who, even if they're not ready to concede global warming is a manmade problem, are adapting to a world of stronger storms and more intense droughts in creative ways. By telling such human stories, McGraw hopes to move readers beyond partisan divisions and into the much-needed common ground. Otherwise, as he says, "if the melting ice caps and rising oceans don't get us, we're all going to drown in the viscera of each other's gored oxen."

"Effectively blending story, science, and context, this engaging, readable book will be invaluable for those studying or working on issues associated with climate change, especially those with a social science or policy focus." Choice.

Rich, Nathaniel, 1980-

Losing Earth : a recent history / Nathaniel Rich. MCD/Farrar, Straus and Giroux, 2019 x, 206 p. : **363.738**

1. Global warming -- History. 2. Global environmental change -- History. 3. Carbon dioxide -- Environmental aspects. 4. Greenhouse effect, Atmospheric

ISBN 9780374191337

LC 2018056269

An account of the failures that prevented the world from committing to taking measures against climate change documents key negotiations against the backdrop of 1980s history while explaining what the choices of the past mean for today's world.

Remnick, David,

The **fragile** Earth : writing from the New Yorker on climate change / edited by David Remnick and Henry Finder ; with an afterword by Elizabeth Kolbert. Ecco Press, 2020 xvi, 541 p. ; **363.738**

1. Climate change 2. Nature -- Effect of humans on 3. Humans -- Effect of climate on 4. Environmental movement 5. Essays 6. Anthologies

ISBN 9780063017542

LC 2020039157

The Fragile Earth tells the story of climate change - its past, present, and future--taking readers from Greenland to the Great Plains, and into both laboratories and rain forests. It features some of the best writing for the New Yorker on global warming from the last three decades, including Bill McKibben's seminal essay "The End of Nature," the first piece to popularize both the science and politics of climate change for a general audience, and the Pulitzer Prize-winning work of Elizabeth Kolbert, as well as Kathryn Schulz, Dexter Filkins, Jonathan Franzen, Ian Frazier, Eric Klinenberg, and others.

"This illuminating and powerful collection is filled with pieces on climate change originally published in the New Yorker." Publishers Weekly

363.739 Pollution of specific environments

Brockovich, Erin

★**Superman's** not coming : our national water crisis and what we the people can do about it / Erin Brockovich. Pantheon Books, 2020. 400 p. **363.739**

1. Brockovich, Erin 2. Women political activists 3. Women environmentalists 4. Drinking water -- Contamination 5. Water-supply 6. United States

ISBN 9781524746964

LC 2019041751

The environmental activist and consumer advocate, whose case against Pacific Gas and Electric was dramatized in an Oscar-winning film, looks at our present situation with water and reveals the imminent threats and shows us how we can each take action.

"A convincing call to arms about the global water crisis from a sharp, plainspoken activist." Kirkus

363.8 Food supply

Caparrós, Martín, 1957-

Hunger : the oldest problem / Martín Caparrós ; translated by Katherine Silver. Melville House, 2019, 2014. 544 p. **363.8**

1. Hunger 2. Food supply 3. Families 4. Survival

ISBN 9781612198040

LC 2019020095

Translation of: El hambre.

Originally published: Barcelona : Editorial Planeta , 2014.

There are now over 800 million starving people in the world. An average of 25,000 men and women, and in particular children, perish from hunger every day. Yet we produce enough food to feed the entire human population one-and-a-half times over. So why is it that world hunger remains such a deadly problem? Martín Caparrós travels the globe in search of an answer.

"A chronicle of righteous testimony and rage that must be read." Booklist.

Puleo, Stephen

Voyage of mercy : the USS Jamestown, the Irish famine, and the remarkable story of America's first humanitarian mission / Stephen Puleo. St. Martin's Press, [2020] xviii, 313 p. : **363.8**

1. Forbes, R. B. (Robert Bennet), 1804-1889. 2. Mathew, Theobald, 1790-1856. 3. Jamestown (Ship) 4. Famines -- Ireland -- History -- 19th century. 5. Food relief -- Ireland -- History -- 19th century. 6. Humanitarianism 7. Economic assistance, American 8. Ireland -- Great Famine, 1845-1849 9. United States -- Foreign economic relations Ireland. 10. Ireland -- Foreign economic relations United States.

ISBN 9781250200471

LC 2019043128

A historian tells the extraordinary story of Ireland's great potato famine in the late 1840s, the Jamestown voyage and the commitment of thousands of ordinary Americans to offer relief to Ireland, establishing the US as the leader in international aid.

"An uplifting historical account of humanitarianism with lessons in this increasingly isolationist time." Kirkus

Stuart, Tristram

Waste : uncovering the global food scandal / Tristram Stuart. W.W. Norton & Co., 2009. 352 p. **363.8**

1. Food industry and trade -- Waste minimization. 2. Recycling (Waste, etc.) 3. Waste products 4. Solid waste disposal

ISBN 9780393068368

LC 2009030964

IACP Cookbook Awards, Literary Food Writing, 2010.

Challenges popular beliefs about dire food shortages, outlining possible solutions based on actual western-world consumption, in a report that tours the world's food industry to reveal how hunger issues could be amply addressed by strategically adjusting production and distribution practices.

"The author shows how we could have much more food overnight simply by not tossing away so much of it. This simple concept ingeniously unites many food scandals that often do not get the attention they deserve: the mould that destroys a third or more of Third World harvests, … [and] the millions of tonnes of edible food wasted by modern food processing and sell-by dates. Usefully, Stuart offers examples of what we could be doing better, from processing technologies to offal sausages." The New Scientist.

364 Criminology

Flynn, Kevin,

The **New** York Times book of crime : more than 166 years of covering the beat / edited by Kevin Flynn, foreword Richard Price. Sterling, 2017 400 p. **364**

1. New York Times. 2. Crime 3. Criminals 4. Crime and the press.

ISBN 9781402793233

LC 2018275289

Includes index.

For 164 years, the Times has been a rich source of information about crime. This compilation--edited by seasoned Times crime-beat veteran Kevin Flynn--captures the full sweep of the newspaper's coverage of the subject, from vice, serial killers, and white-collar crimes to kidnapping, assassinations, and the Mob. Chronologically organized by type of crime and drawn from the Times's archives.

364.1 Criminal offenses

Bernstein, Carl, 1944-

★**All** the President's men / Carl Bernstein, Bob Woodward. Simon & Schuster, 1999, c1974. 349 p. : **364.1**

1. Bernstein, Carl, 1944- 2. Woodward, Bob, 1943- 3. Washington Post. 4. Watergate Scandal. 5. Presidents -- United States. 6. Political corruption. 7. Politicians -- United States.

ISBN 0684863553

LC 98054773

Includes index.

Originally published: New York : Simon & Schuster, 1974.

The two Washington Post reporters present the inside story of their inquiry into the persons involved in the Watergate scandal.

"Bernstein and Woodward, the two Washington Post journalists who broke the Big Story, tell how they did it by old fashioned seat-of-the-pants reporting -- in other words, lots of intuition and a thick stack of phone numbers." Kirkus.

Bradley, Mark A. (Mark Andrew), 1956-

Blood runs coal : the Yablonski murders and the battle for the United Mine Workers of America / Mark A. Bradley. W.W. Norton & Company, 2020 334 p. **364.1**

1. Boyle, William Anthony, 1904-1985. 2. Yablonski, Joseph A., 1910-1969. 3. United Mine Workers of America. 4. Labor unions -- Corrupt practices 5. Corruption 6. Labor leaders 7. Family-killing. 8. Pennsylvania

ISBN 9780393652536

LC 2020016358

Documents the 1969 assassination of the Yablonski family amid a campaign to oust the corrupt president of the UMWA, in a timely account that reflects the violent labor movements, industrial transformations and socioeconomic realities of fossil-fuel dependency.

"An absorbing narrative of pride, greed, arrogance, and retribution that will find a place in history and true crime collections." Library Journal

Bugliosi, Vincent, 1934-

★**Helter** skelter : the true story of the Manson murders / Vincent Bugliosi with Curt Gentry. W. W. Norton, 1994, c1974. 687 p. : **364.1**

1. Manson, Charles, 1934-2017 2. Murder -- California -- Case studies. 3. Murderers. 4. Trials (Murder) 5. Mind control.

ISBN 0393322238

LC bl2005022570

Includes index.

Originally published: New York : Norton, 1974.

Edgar Allan Poe Award for Best Fact Crime, 1975.

The prosecutor of the Tate-LaBianca trials presents the inside story behind the Manson killings, explaining how Charles Manson was able to make his "family" murder for him, chronicling the investigation, and describing the court trial that brought him and his accomplices to justice.

Bullough, Oliver, 1977-

Moneyland : the inside story of the crooks and kleptocrats who rule the world / Oliver Bullough. St. Martin's Press, 2019, c2018. 320 p. **364.1**

1. Money laundering investigation 2. Money laundering -- Prevention. 3. Organized crime. 4. Political corruption.

ISBN 9781250208705

An investigative journalist's deep dive into the corrupt workings of the world's kleptocrats takes him from ruined towns on the edge of Siberia, to Bond-villain lairs in London and Manhattan.

"An indefatigable investigative journalist, Bullough has traveled the world, from Siberia to the Seychelles, to untangle this web of deceit, avarice, and amorality. The result is an eye-opening and stomach-churning expos of financial transgressions on a global scale that threatens democracy and the institutions charged with its protection." Booklist.

Cacho, Lydia, 1963-

The **sorrows** of Mexico : an indictment of their country's failings by seven exceptional writers / Lydia Cacho, Anabel Hernandez, Sergio Rodriguez Gonzalez, Diego Enrique Orsono, Emiliano Ruiz Parra, Marcela Turati, Juan Villoro. MacLehose Press, 2017, c2016. 352 p. : **364.1**

1. Political corruption -- Mexico. 2. Violence -- Mexico. 3. Journalism -- Mexico. 4. Mexico -- Politics and government.

ISBN 9780857056221

LC bl2020046491

A crucial testament--bringing together work from seven of Mexico's finest journalists--that lays bare the outrageous circumstances of more than a hundred journalists who have been murdered while investigating corruption and criminality.

Capote, Truman, 1924-1984

★**In** cold blood : a true account of a multiple murder and its consequences / Truman Capote. Vintage Books, 1994, c1965. 343 p. ; **364.1**

1. Smith, Perry Edward, 1928-1965. 2. Clutter family. 3. Hickok, Richard Eugene, 1931-1965. 4. Murder -- Holcomb, Kansas. 5. Crime scenes. 6. Murder victims. 7. Murder investigation. 8. Kansas -- History -- 20th century. 9. Holcomb, Kansas -- History -- 20th century.

ISBN 0679745580

LC 93006282

"Appeared originally in the New Yorker in slightly different form."

Originally published: New York : Random House, 1965.

Edgar Allan Poe Award for Best Fact Crime, 1966.

Presents Capote's masterful account of the senseless 1959 murders of four members of a farm family in Holcomb, Kansas, and the search for the killers, Richard Eugene Hickock and Perry Edward Smith.

Dray, Philip

At the hands of persons unknown : the lynching of black America / Philip Dray. Random House, 2002. xii, 528 p., 8 p. of plates : **364.1**

1. Lynching -- Southern States -- History. 2. Crimes against African Americans 3. Southern States -- Race relations.

ISBN 9780375503245

LC 2001040366

Robert F. Kennedy Book Award, 2003.

Pulitzer Prize for History finalist, 2003.

A history of lynching in America describes its common use, especially in the southern United States, and discusses the crusade by a handful of black and white citizens to eliminate the shameful practice.

"Dray balances moral indignation with a sound understanding of history and politics. The result is vital, hard-hitting cultural history." Publishers Weekly.

Giroux, Robert, 1914-2008

A **deed** of death : the story behind the unsolved murder of Hollywood director William Desmond Taylor / Robert Giroux. Knopf, 1990. xix, 275 p. : **364.1**

1. Taylor, William Desmond, 1877-1922. 2. Murder investigation -- Los Angeles, California -- Case studies. 3. Film producers and directors -- Hollywood, California -- Case studies. 4. Cold cases (Criminal investigation)

ISBN 0394580753

LC 89030451

An analysis of the 1922 unsolved murder of film director William Desmond Taylor focuses on the two actresses in Taylor's life--ingenue Mary Miles Minter and Mabel Normand, a star and a drug addict.

Posner, Gerald L.

Case closed : Lee Harvey Oswald and the assassination of JFK / Gerald L. Posner. Random House, c1993. xv, 607 p. : **364.1**

1. Kennedy, John F. (John Fitzgerald), 1917-1963 Assassination. 2. Oswald, Lee Harvey, 1939-1963. 3. Assassination. 4. Conspiracies -- United States. 5. Presidents -- Assassination. 6. United States -- History -- 1961-1969.

ISBN 9780679418252

LC 93012821

Pulitzer Prize for History finalist, 1994.

"Posner, a lawyer and investigative reporter (Mengele), has set himself a major task here and brought it off with considerable panache. In the face of a multitude of assassination books propounding dozens of theories, all of them critical of the lone-assassin/no-conspiracy case, he has come out square for Oswald as the sole culprit." Publishers Weekly.

Trillin, Calvin

Killings / Calvin Trillin. Penguin Books, 1985. xxi, 231 p. ; **364.1**

1. Murder -- United States. 2. Murder victims -- United States. 3. Death. 4. Accidental death. 5. United States -- Social life and customs -- 20th century. 6. Essays

ISBN 0140079777

LC 84026633

Reprint. Originally published: New York : Ticknor & Fields, 1984.

Reprinted by Random House in 2017

"Violent deaths illuminate complex lives and desperate circumstances in this expanded reissue of the classic collection of the authors true-crime reporting for the New Yorker." Publishers Weekly.

Tyson, Timothy B.

The **blood** of Emmett Till / Timothy B. Tyson. Simon & Schuster, 2017 304 p. **364.1**

1. Till, Emmett, 1941-1955. 2. Lynching. 3. Crimes against African Americans 4. Racism. 5. Trials (Murder). 6. Southern States -- Race relations. 7. United States -- Race relations -- History -- 20th century. 8. Mississippi -- Race relations.

ISBN 9781476714844

LC 2016021595

ALA Notable Book, 2018.

Robert F. Kennedy Book Award, 2018.

Longlisted for the National Book Award for Nonfiction, 2017.

Though several books have covered the 60-year-old case of Emmett Till's lynching in Mississippi, historian Timothy Tyson's new history freshly illuminates the trial of Till's murderers. He analyzes the trial transcript, which had been missing since 1955, interviews the key witness (now 80 years old) to Till's allegedly inappropriate behavior, and provides details from a recent FBI investigation. This riveting account immerses readers in the case and offers the definitive summary of its impact on subsequent history.

"Cinematically engaging, harrowing, and poignant, Tyson's monumental work illuminates Emmett Till's murder and serves as a powerful reminder that certain stories in history merit frequent retelling." Publishers Weekly.

Vorobyov, Niko

Dopeworld : adventures in the global drug trade / Niko Vorobyov. St. Martin's Press, 2020, c2019. 432 p. **364.1**

1. Vorobyov, Niko Travel 2. Drug traffic 3. Drug dealers 4. Drug abuse 5. Drug control

ISBN 9781250270016

LC 2020010724

Originally published: London : Hodder & Stoughton, 2019.

Just as Anthony Bourdain's No Reservations did for the world of food, Dopeworld is an intoxicating journey into the world of drugs. From the cocaine farms in South America to the streets of Manila, Dopeworld traces the emergence of psychoactive substances and our intimate relationship with them. As a former drug dealer turned subversive scholar, with unparalleled access to drug lords, cartel leaders, street dealers and government officials, journalist Niko Vorobyov attempts to shine a light on the dark underbelly of the drug world.

"Vorobyov makes a persuasive case for the legalization of drugs in what he aptly calls 'a true crime, gonzo, social, historical-memoir meets fucked-up travel book.' It could well become a classic." Publishers Weekly

Weinman, Sarah

★**Unspeakable** acts : true tales of crime, murder, deceit, and obsession / Sarah Weinman ; introduction by Patrick Radden Keefe. Ecco Press, 2020. 288 p. **364.1**

1. True-crime television programs 2. Popular culture 3. Victims of crimes 4. Podcasts 5. Essays

ISBN 9780062839886

LC bl2020016866

An anthology of modern true-crime writing illustrating the appeal of this powerful and popular genre; as a collection, they, showcase writing about true crime across the broadest possible spectrum, while also reflecting what makes crime stories so transfixing and irresistible to the modern reader.

"This anthology is essential reading for all true crime fans." Booklist

364.106 Organized crime

Dudley, Steven S.

MS-13 : the making of America's most notorious gang / Steven Dudley. Hanover Square Press, 2020. 352 p. **364.106**

1. MS-13 (Gang) 2. Gangs 3. Organized crime 4. Gang members 5. Immigrants 6. Los Angeles, California 7. United States 8. El Salvador

ISBN 9781335005540

LC bl2020013289

Looks at the most dangerous street gang in America--the MS13--as seen through the lives of one family caught in its malicious web.

"An outstanding book for true crime readers." Library Journal

364.106089 Organized crime--Ethnic and national groups

English, T. J., 1957-

The **Corporation** : an epic story of the Cuban American underworld / T.J. English. William Morrow, 2018 400 p. **364.106089**

1. Gangsters 2. Organized crime 3. Cubans in the United States 4. Cuban Americans

ISBN 9780062568960

LC 2017039510

A multigenerational history of the Cuban mob in the U.S., written by the best-selling author of Havana Nocturne, examines the role of South Florida's exile community in building a criminal empire as part of a plot to reclaim Cuba from the Castro regime.

"English capably covers half a century of criminal enterprise, avoiding the clichs of the true-crime genre while stocking his narrative with familiar players: the capos and goons, the cops and informants, a mistress or two, and John F. Kennedy." Kirkus.

364.1060973 Organized crime--United States

Maier, Thomas, 1956-

Mafia spies : the inside story of the CIA, gangsters, JFK, and Castro / Thomas Maier. Simon & Schuster, 2019. xii, 388 p. **364.1060973**

1. Giancana, Sam, 1908-1975. 2. Rosselli, Johnny, 1905-1976. 3. Kennedy, John F. (John Fitzgerald), 1917-1963. 4. Castro, Fidel, 1926-2016 Attempted assassination. 5. CIA. 6. Espionage. 7. Organized crime. 8. Assassins. 9. Mafia. 10. United States -- Foreign relations Cuba. 11. Cuba -- Foreign relations United States.

ISBN 9781510741713

LC bl2019010606

The definitive account of America's most remarkable espionage plots ever?with CIA agents, mob hitmen, and James Bond-like killing devices together in a top-secret mystery full of surprise twists and deadly intrigue. In the early 1960s, two top gangsters, Johnny Roselli and Sam Giancana, were hired by the CIA to kill Cuba's Communist leader, Fidel Castro, only to wind up murdered themselves amidst Congressional hearings and a national debate about the JFK assassination.

"As he has done before, Maier offers another deft translation of murky American history, focused on dynamic, improbable protagonists." Kirkus.

364.10973 Criminal offenses--United States

Bowden, Mark, 1951-

The **case** of the vanishing blonde : and other true crime stories / Mark Bowden. Atlantic Monthly Press, 2020. 232 p. **364.10973**

1. Crime 2. Criminal investigation 3. Murder 4. Murder investigation 5. Essays

ISBN 9780802128447

LC 2020025999

These captivating true-crime stories, spanning Mark Bowden's long and illustrious career, cover a variety of crimes complicated by extraordinary circumstances. The Case of the Vanishing Blonde collects six of his most riveting pieces--accounts spanning four decades of searing characters and unsettling tales to illustrate all manner of crimes and the ways technology has progressively altered criminal investigation.

"This true crime master expands the limits of the genre, digging to find answers and revealing that even the most horrific crimes are often linked to a larger story about America." Library Journal

364.15 Offenses against the person

Abdulali, Sohaila

What we talk about when we talk about rape / Sohaila Abdulali. New Press, [2018] 224 p. **364.15**

1. Rape 2. Rape victims 3. Violence against women 4. Sexual violence.

ISBN 9781620974735

LC 2018034364

The acclaimed viral Mumbai journalist draws on personal experiences, inspiring survivor testimonies and meticulous research in an urgent call to action that illuminates the socio-economics and cultural realities of rape from the perspectives of survivors, counselors and activists.

" She writes in a conversational style and injects a levity that, rather than betraying the seriousness of her subject, makes it more possible to handle the necessary yet horrifying details of rape of all kinds." Booklist.

Barr, John (Sportswriter)

★**Start** by believing : Larry Nassar's crimes, the institutions that enabled him, and the brave women who stopped a monster / John Barr and Dan Murphy. Hachette Books, 2020. 320 p. **364.15**

1. Nassar, Larry 2. Women athletes 3. Child sexual abuse 4. Physicians 5. Child sexual abusers

ISBN 9780316532150

LC 2019031505

Includes index.

For decades, osteopathic physician Larry Nassar built a sterling reputation as the go-to doctor for America's Olympians while treating countless others at his office on Michigan State University's campus. It was largely within the high-pressure world of competitive gymnastics that Nassar exploited young girls, who were otherwise motivated by fear and intimidation, sexually assaulting hundreds of them under the guise of medical treatment. Following the paths traveled by courageous women--featuring a once-shy Christian attorney and a brash, outspoken Olympic medalist--Barr and Murphy detail the stories of those who fought back against the dysfunction within their sport to claim a far-from-inevitable victory.

"The authors' exhaustive research and relentless pursuit of the truth create an unsettling and stark record of the abuse scandal that sent shockwaves across America and which continues to resonate deeply." Library Journal.

Bolkovac, Kathryn

The **whistleblower** : private contractors, sex trafficking, and one woman's fight for justice / Kathryn Bolkovac with Cari Lynn. Palgrave Macmillan, 2010. 256 p. **364.15**

1. Bolkovac, Kathryn. 2. Whistle blowing -- Bosnia and Hercegovina. 3. Human trafficking -- Bosnia and Hercegovina. 4. Contractors. 5. Crimes against women. 6. Bosnia and Hercegovina

ISBN 9780230108028

LC 2010023196

"When Nebraska police officer and divorced mother of three Kathryn Bolkovac saw a recruiting announcement for private military contractor DynCorp International, she applied and was hired. Good money, world travel, and the chance to help rebuild a war-torn country sounded like the perfect job. Bolkovac was shipped out to Bosnia, where DynCorp had been contracted to support the UN peacekeeping mission. She was assigned as a human rights investigator, heading the gender affairs unit. The lack of proper training sounded the first alarm bell, but once she arrived in Sarajevo, she found out that things were a lot worse. At great risk to her personal safety, she began to unravel the ugly truth about officers involved in human trafficking and forced prostitution and their connections to private mercenary contractors, the UN, and the U.S. State Department. After bringing this evidence to light, Bolkovac was demoted, threatened with bodily harm, fired, and ultimately forced to flee the country under cover of darkness--bringing the incriminating documents with her. Thanks to the evidence she collected, she won a lawsuit against DynCorp, finally exposing them for what they were. This is her story and the story of the women left behind."-- Provided by publisher.

"This story bristles with disturbing details and heartfelt compassion." Publishers Weekly.

Cohan, William D.

The **price** of silence : the Duke lacrosse scandal, the power of the elite, and the corruption of our great universities / William D. Cohan. Scribner, 2014. 672 p. **364.15**

1. Duke University. 2. Rape. 3. Malicious accusation. 4. Trials (Rape). 5. Lacrosse players. 6. Durham, North Carolina.

ISBN 9781451681796

LC 2013043923

Based on in-depth reporting, this authoritative account of the Duke lacrosse team rape case illuminates the ever-widening gap between America's rich and poor, and shows just how far the powerful will go to protect themselves.

"Cohan explores the usual disconnects that occur in high-profile crime cases between what is reported by the press, chronicled in official records, and perceived as public opinion and what really happened. A gripping account of a sensational case." Booklist.

Gourevitch, Philip, 1961-

We wish to inform you that tomorrow we will be killed with our families : stories from Rwanda / Philip Gourevitch. Farrar, Straus, and Giroux, 1998. 355 p. : **364.15**

1. Hutu (African people) -- Rwanda. 2. Tutsi (African people) -- Rwanda. 3. Genocide -- Rwanda. 4. Rwanda -- Politics and government. 5. Rwanda -- Interethnic relations.

ISBN 0374286973

LC 98022132

National Book Critics Circle Award for Non-Fiction, 1998.

Guardian First Book Award, 1999.

In 1994, when the Rwanda government called on everyone in the Hutu majority to kill everyone in the Tutsi minority, 800,000 Tutsis were murdered. This haunting work is an anatomy of the killings and a vivid history of the genocide's background and aftermath.

"In 1994, the world was informed of the inexplicable mass killings in Rwanda, in which over 800,000 were killed in 100 days. Gourevitch . . . spent over three years putting together an oral history of the mass killing that occurred in this small country." Library Journal.

Kantor, Jodi, 1975-

★**She** said : breaking the sexual harassment story that ignited a movement / Jodi Kantor & Megan Twohey Penguin Press, 2019 310 p. ; **364.15**

1. Me Too Movement 2. Sex crimes 3. Sexual harassment 4. Investigative journalism 5. United States -- Social conditions

ISBN 9780525560340

LC 2019300465

The Pulitzer Prize-winning reporters who broke the story of Harvey Weinstein's sexual abuses discuss the suspenseful untold story of their investigation, the way it changed their careers and whether or not the #MeToo movement changed things for the better.

"Both admirable and suspenseful, the narrative is a fitting testament to the power of persistence and dedication in exposing critical crimes. Keenly executed, exemplary spadework dedicated to justice for all women caught in the crosshairs of privileged power." Kirkus.

King, David, 1970-

Six days in August : the story of Stockholm syndrome / David King. W.W. Norton & Company, 2020. 282 p. **364.15**

1. Bank robberies 2. Stockholm syndrome. 3. Hostages 4. Bank robbers 5. Stockholm, Sweden. 6. Sweden
ISBN 9780393635089

LC 2019058100

The definitive account of the bizarre hostage drama that gave rise to the term "Stockholm syndrome."

"Engrossing, well researched, and tailor-made for true crime enthusiasts." Library Journal

Miller, T. Christian

A **false** report : a true story of rape in America / T. Christian Miller and Ken Armstrong. Crown Publishers, 2018. 320 p. **364.15**

1. Rape 2. Rape victims 3. Police charges 4. Rape investigation 5. Books to TV.
ISBN 9781524759933

LC 2017037935

Adapted into the television series Unbelievable, Fall 2019.

Two Pulitzer Prize-winning journalists present the true story of two detectives who teamed up to discern the truth about a case involving a teen who was charged with falsely reporting a rape, an investigation that revealed the work of a serial rapist in multiple states.

"This timely, well-researched, highly readable account will appeal to readers interested in true crime and social justice issues." Booklist.

Murakami, Haruki, 1949-

Underground / Haruki Murakami ; translated from the Japanese by Alfred Birnbaum and Philip Gabriel. Vintage International, 2001. x, 366 p. ; **364.15**

1. Aum Supreme Truth cult 2. Religious terrorism. 3. Terrorism -- Religious aspects. 4. Violence -- Religious aspects. 5. Survival 6. Japan
ISBN 0375725806

LC 00069310

Covers the 1995 Tokyo Gas Attack, during which agents of a Japanese cult released sarin gas into the subway system, as documented in interviews with its survivors, perpetrators, and victims's family members.

"On March 20, 1995, followers of the religious cult Aum Shinrikyo unleashed lethal sarin gas into cars of the Tokyo subway system. Many died, many more were injured. This is [Murakami's] ... account of this episode." Publishers Weekly.

Standiford, Les

Bringing Adam home : the abduction that changed America / Les Standiford with Detective Sergeant Joe Matthews. Ecco, [2011], c2011. 304 p. **364.15**

1. Walsh, Adam. 2. Kidnapping -- Florida -- Case studies. 3. Murder investigation -- Florida -- Case studies 4. Crimes against boys 5. Kidnapping victims 6. Florida -- History -- 20th century
ISBN 9780061983900

LC 2010043572

Relates the full, twenty-seven-year story behind the abduction and murder of Adam Walsh, the six-year-old son of "America's Most Wanted" host John Walsh, as well as the decades-long search for the boy's elusive killer.

Stout, David, 1942-

The **kidnap** years : the astonishing true history of the forgotten kidnapping epidemic that shook Depression-era America / David Stout. Sourcebooks, 2020 xxix, 430 p. **364.15**

1. Kidnapping. 2. Crime -- United States -- History -- 20th century. 3. Gangsters. 4. Missing persons. 5. United States -- History
ISBN 9781492694793

LC 2019032997

Chronicles the less-remembered outbreak in kidnappings in Great Depression America, sharing insight into how the crime's low legal risks led to a sweep of abductions throughout the country.

"Stout presents a deeply researched, perfectly paced history of kidnappings that affected everyone from bank presidents and lumber barons to beer brewers and the children of wealthy families. Interspersed with the nail-biting tales of the kidnappings are details about the trials, the criminals, and the formation of the FBI and J. Edgar Hoover's rise to power." Library Journal

Talty, Stephan

The **good** assassin : how a Mossad agent and a band of survivors hunted down the Butcher of Latvia / Stephan Talty. New York : 2020. xiv, 304 p. **364.15**

1. Cukurs, Herbert, 1900-1965 Assassination. 2. Medad, Jacob, 1919-2012. 3. Mossad. 4. Fugitives -- Uruguay. 5. Holocaust (1933-1945) -- Riga, Latvia. 6. War criminals -- Riga, Latvia. 7. Jews -- Persecutions -- Latvia. 8. Riga, Latvia. 9. Brazil. 10. Uruguay.
ISBN 9781328613080

LC 2019027262

Provides the untold story of an Israeli spy's epic journey to bring the notorious Butcher of Latvia to justice--a case that altered the fates of all ex-Nazis.

"A fast-paced, recommended work that enthralls, edifies, and reveals the disturbing extent to which Latvians and others participated in genocide." Library Journal

Worrall, Simon

The **poet** and the murderer : a true story of literary crime and the art of forgery / Simon Worrall. Dutton, 2002. xv, 270 p. : **364.15**

1. Hofmann, Mark. 2. Dickinson, Emily, 1830-1886 Forgeries. 3. Forgery 4. Manuscripts -- Forgeries. 5. Murder -- Salt Lake City, Utah -- Case studies.
ISBN 0525945962

LC 2001053878

A renowned journalist delves into the deeply disturbed mind of Mark Hofmann, one of the most daring literary forgers and merciless killers of the late twentieth century, whose greatest deception was a forged Emily Dickinson poem, which led to fame and fortune, forcing him to commit atrocious crimes in order to keep his forgery a secret.

364.152 Homicide

Anastasia, George

Doctor dealer : a doctor high on greed, a biker gang high on opioids, and the woman who paid the ultimate price / George Anastasia and Ralph Cipriano. Berkley, 2020. 304 p. **364.152**

1. Kauffman, James, -2018 2. Kauffman, April, -2012 3. Married women -- Death 4. Physicians 5. Murder for hire 6. Drug traffic 7. New Jersey
ISBN 9780593097762

LC 2019059055

Includes index.

In May 2012, April Kauffman, a well-known local radio personality and staunch advocate of military veterans rights, was found shot to death in the bedroom of the home she shared with her husband, Dr. James Kauffman. Six years later, in the fall of 2018, Freddy Augello, a leader of the notorious motorcycle gang the Pagans, went on trial for drug dealing and murder. He was charged with arranging the death of April Kauffman in exchange for $50,000 from her husband, who, in addition to practicing medicine, was one of the area's most prolific drug traffickers. Told by two accomplished reporters and authors with exclusive insights and details provided by two principal players, this is the story about one man's descent into evil and the people he took with him.

"An entertaining story with broad appeal for true crime fans." Library Journal

Brown, Vanessa, 1980-

The **Forest** City Killer : a serial murderer, a cold-case sleuth, and a search for justice / Vanessa Brown. ECW Press, 2019. 328 p. **364.152**

1. Serial murder investigation -- Ontario 2. Serial murders -- Ontario 3. Cold cases (Criminal investigation) 4. London, Ontario 5. Ontario 6. Canada

ISBN 9781770415034

Investigates a cold-case serial killer case from London, Ontario in the 1960s.

Callahan, Maureen

American predator : the hunt for the most meticulous serial killer of the 21st century / Maureen Callahan. Viking, 2019. 304 p. **364.152**

1. Keyes, Israel. 2. Serial murderers. 3. Serial murder investigation. 4. Serial murderers -- United States 5. Murderers.

ISBN 9780525428640

LC 2018058203

An investigative journalist documents the story of enigmatic serial killer Israel Keyes and the efforts of the Anchorage PD and the FBI to capture him, discussing what his case reveals about twenty-first-century law enforcement.

Cep, Casey N.

★**Furious** hours : murder, fraud, and the last trial of Harper Lee / Casey Cep. Knopf, 2019. 304 p. **364.152**

1. Lee, Harper 2. Maxwell, Willie. 3. Serial murderers 4. Women true crime writers 5. Creativity in women 6. Rural life 7. Alabama -- History -- 20th century

ISBN 9781101947869

LC 2018043337

Documents the remarkable story of 1970s Alabama serial killer Willie Maxwell and the true-crime book on the Deep South's racial politics and justice system that consumed Harper Lee in the years after To Kill a Mockingbird.

"Cep has vividly and insightfully retrieved a grimly fascinating true-crime story and done Lee justice in a fresh and compelling portrait of this essential American writer." Booklist.

Cornwell, Patricia Daniels

Ripper : the secret life of Walter Sickert / Patricia Daniels Cornwell. Thomas & Mercer, 2017. 553 pages : **364.152**

1. Sickert, Walter Richard, 1860-1942 2. Jack, the Ripper. 3. Whitechapel murders, 1888. 4. Serial murderers. 5. Murder. 6. Serial murders. 7. London, England -- History -- 19th century. 8. Whitechapel (London, England)

ISBN 9781503936874

LC 2017276829

A comprehensive and intriguing expose of one of the world's most chilling cases of serial murder--and the police force that failed to solve it.

Eisenberg, Emma Copley

★The **third** rainbow girl : the long life of a double murder in Appalachia / Emma Copley Eisenberg. Hachette Books, 2020. 318 pages : **364.152**

1. Murder 2. Murder investigation 3. Communities 4. Rural life 5. West Virginia 6. Appalachian Region.

ISBN 9780316449236

LC bl2020004072

A stunningly written investigation of the murder of two young women--showing how a violent crime casts a shadow over an entire community.

"The book is more than just another true crime memoir; Eisenberg has crafted a beautiful and complicated ode to West Virginia. Exquisitely written, this is a powerful commentary on society's notions of gender, violence, and rural America. Readers of literary nonfiction will devour this title in one sitting." Booklist.

Epstein, Edward Jay, 1935-

The **annals** of unsolved crime / Edward Jay Epstein. Melville House, 2013. 347 p. ; **364.152**

1. Criminal investigation. 2. Cold cases (Criminal investigation) 3. Investigative journalism

ISBN 9781612190488

LC 2012049984

An insider's guide to the art of reporting draws on more than four decades of investigative work to provide revisionary insights into some of the most controversial and mysterious crimes from the past two centuries.

Fieseler, Robert W.

Tinderbox : the untold story of the Up Stairs Lounge fire and the rise of gay liberation / Robert W. Fieseler. Liveright Publishing, [2018] 320 p. **364.152**

1. Violence against gay men and lesbians 2. Mass murder 3. Arson 4. Gay bars and restaurants 5. New Orleans, Louisiana

ISBN 9781631491641

LC 2018004765

Edgar Allan Poe Award for Best Fact Crime, 2019.

A reconstruction of the 1973 fire that devastated New Orleans' subterranean gay community describes how the Up Stairs Lounge and dozens of innocent patrons were targeted in what became a catalyzing event in the gay liberation movement.

"Though Fieseler's prose leans toward overreach --Humidity, so thick with vapor that breathing air could feel like crying tears, would almost routinely reach 100 percent--his attention to detail and intricate exploration of the material is spot-on. Fieseler shines a bright light on a dark and largely forgotten moment in the history of the gay rights movement." Publishers Weekly.

Glatt, John

★The **perfect** father : the true story of Chris Watts, his all-American family, and a shocking murder / John Glatt. St. Martin's Press, 2020. x, 288 p. **364.152**

1. Watts, Chris (Christopher Lee), 1985- 2. Murder 3. Family violence 4. Husband and wife 5. Pregnant women 6. Denver, Colorado

ISBN 9781250231611

LC 2020009570

Documents the August 2018 murders of Shanann Watts and her young daughters, describing how viewers watched her husband's televised plea for help less than 24 hours before he confessed to killing his family.

"Fans of the Investigation Discovery show Nightmare Next Door are sure to appreciate this gripping read." Library Journal

Goldman, Francisco

The **art** of political murder : who killed the bishop? / Francisco Goldman. Grove Press, 2007. 208 p. **364.152**

1. Gerardi, Juan Jose, d. 1998 2. Assassination 3. Genocide -- Guatemala 4. Bishops -- Death. 5. Political crimes and offenses 6. Guatemala -- History -- 1985- 7. United States -- Foreign relations Guatemala 8. Guatemala -- Foreign relations United States

ISBN 0802118283

LC 2008298720

Details the story of a remarkable group of engaging, courageous young people known as Los Intocables and their fight for justice in an in-depth account of the murder of Guatemalan Bishop Juan Gerardi, the country's leading human rights activist, as well as the killing or forced exiles of multiple witnesses, prosecutors, and judges.

Harman, Claire

Murder by the book : the crime that shocked Dickens's London / Claire Harman. Alfred A. Knopf, 2019. 256 p. **364.152**

1. Courvoisier, Francois Benjamin, d. 1840 Trials, litigation, etc. 2. Russell, William, Lord, 1767-1840. 3. Ainsworth, William Harrison, 1805-1882. Jack Sheppard. 4. Murder. 5. Murder in literature. 6. Books and reading. 7. Trials (Murder) 8. London, England -- History -- 19th century.

ISBN 9780525520399

LC 2018029773

"This is a Borzoi Book."

Traces the lesser-known story of a Victorian-era murder that rocked literary London, revealing how the killer organized his defense by blaming his behavior on a popular crime novel.

Hawes, Jennifer (Jennifer Berry)

Grace will lead us home : the Charleston Church Massacre and the hard, inspiring journey to forgiveness / Jennifer Berry Hawes. St. Martin's Press, 2019. 352 p. **364.152**

1. Emanuel AME Church (Charleston, S.C.) 2. African Methodist Episcopal Church 3. Hate crimes 4. Mass shootings 5. Emanuel AME Church shooting, Charleston, South Carolina, 2015 6. Crimes against African Americans 7. South Carolina -- Race relations 8. United States -- Race relations 9. Southern States -- Race relations

ISBN 9781250117762

LC bl2018053071

Follows the experiences of the survivors and victims' families following the 2015 shootings at Charleston's Mother Emanuel AME Church, chronicling the events and emotions that came in the aftermath of the shooting.

"A groundbreaking, accessible work of investigative reporting that spans a variety of topics, including gun violence and the historic role of the Emanuel AME Church. It will appeal to general readers interested in these topics, as well as historians and political scientists." Library Journal.

Herman, Eleanor, 1960-

The **royal** art of poison : fatal cosmetics, deadly medicine, filthy palaces, and murder most foul / Eleanor Herman. St. Martin's Press, [2018] 288 p. **364.152**

1. Courts and courtiers. 2. Poisons. 3. Poisoning. 4. Power (Social sciences)

ISBN 9781250140869

LC 2017060759

This history of the role that poison has played in centuries of royal courts discusses both the intentional poisoning of royals by their underlings as well as the unintentional health effects of the makeup and medications they commonly used.

"Murder and scandal always sell, and Herman applies this philosophy to her examination--and frequent exhumation--of history's dubiously dispatched royalty." Booklist.

Jimenez, Stephen

The **book** of Matt : hidden truths about the murder of Matthew Shepard / Stephen Jimenez. Steerforth Press, 2013. 368 p. **364.152**

1. Shepard, Matthew, 1976-1998 2. Young gay men. 3. Violence against gay men and lesbians 4. Drug use. 5. Drug industry and trade

ISBN 9781586422141

LC 2013431178

A controversial account of the 1998 murder of Matthew Shepard describes the evening of the assault that ended his life and the ways in which the victim became a symbol of anti-hate crime activism, sharing additional details that suggest that Shepard was killed for more complicated and daunting reasons.

"In claiming that Shepard was killed because of drugs, and the 'gay panic' story was offered as a cover and heavily pushed by media and politicians as part of a larger agenda, Jimenez completely changes the meaning and impact of Shepard's death." Publishers Weekly.

Keefe, Patrick Radden, 1976-

★**Say** nothing : a true story of murder and memory in Northern Ireland / Patrick Radden Keefe. Doubleday, 2019. 304 p. **364.152**

1. McConville, Jean 2. Irish Republican Army 3. The Troubles, 1968-1998 4. Murder 5. Kidnapping 6. Domestic terrorism 7. Belfast, Northern Ireland 8. Northern Ireland -- History -- 1969-1994

ISBN 9780385521314

LC 2018031745

ALA Notable Book, 2020.

Orwell Prize, 2019.

National Book Critics Circle Award for Non-Fiction, 2019

Kirkus Prize for Nonfiction finalist, 2019.

Longlisted for the National Book Award for Nonfiction, 2019.

Documents the notorious abduction and murder of I.R.A. Troubles victim Jean McConville in 1972 Belfast, exploring how the case reflected the brutal conflicts of Northern Ireland and their ongoing repercussions.

"Tinged with immense sadness, this work never loses sight of the humanity of even those who committed horrible acts in support of what they believed in." Publishers Weekly.

King, David, 1970-

★**Death** in the city of light : the serial killer of occupied Paris / David King. Crown, c2011. 432 p. **364.152**

1. Petiot, Marcel. 2. Serial murderers. 3. Physicians 4. Serial murders 5. World War II -- France. 6. France -- History -- German occupation, 1940-1945.

ISBN 9780307452894

LC 2011014412

"This fascinating, often painful account combines a police procedural with a vivid historical portrait of culture and law enforcement in Nazi-occupied France." Publishers Weekly.

Leovy, Jill

Ghettoside : a true story of murder in America / Jill Leovy. Spiegel & Grau, [2014] 336 p. **364.152**

1. Murder 2. African American men 3. Inner city violence 4. Detectives 5. Los Angeles, California.
ISBN 9780385529983

LC 2013046367

National Book Critics Circle Award for Nonfiction finalist

"Readers may come for Leovy's detective story; they will stay for her lucid social critique." Publishers Weekly.

McDiarmid, Jessica

Highway of tears : a true story of racism, indifference, and the pursuit of justice for missing and murdered indigenous women and girls / Jessica McDiarmid. Atria Books, 2019. 320 p. **364.152**

1. First Nations (Canada) 2. Native American women 3. Violence against women 4. Missing women 5. British Columbia
ISBN 9781501160288

LC bl2019033987

Along northern Canada's Highway 16, a yellow billboard reads GIRLS, DON'T HITCHHIKE. KILLER ON THE LOOSE. The highway is a 450-mile stretch of dirt and asphalt, surrounded by rugged wilderness and snowy mountain peaks. It is known as the Highway of Tears. It is here that countless women and girls--most of them Indigenous--have vanished since 1969. Highway of Tears explores the true story of what has happened along this troubled road. Journalist Jessica McDiarmid reassembles the lives of the victims--who they were, where they came from, who loved them, and what led them to the highway--and takes us into their families--determined fight for the truth.

McGough, Matthew

The **Lazarus** files : a cold case investigation / Matthew McGough. Henry Holt, [2019] 595 p. **364.152**

1. Rasmussen, Sherri Death and burial. 2. Lazarus, Stephanie. 3. Women murder victims. 4. Cold cases (Criminal investigation) 5. Police corruption. 6. Murder. 7. Los Angeles, California.
ISBN 9780805095593

LC 2018037256

Traces the investigation surrounding a deeply reported cold case from 1986 Los Angeles that remained unsolved until DNA evidence shockingly implicated a woman LAPD detective.

McNamara, Michelle, 1970-2016

I'll be gone in the dark : one woman's obsessive search for the Golden State Killer / Michelle McNamara, introduction by Gillian Flynn, afterword by Patton Oswalt. HarperCollins, 2018 368 p. **364.152**

1. McNamara, Michelle, 1970-2016 2. Cold cases (Criminal investigation) 3. Home invasions 4. Criminal investigation 5. Crimes against women.
ISBN 9780062319784

LC 2017301180

Anthony Award for Best Critical/Nonfiction, 2019.

An account of the unsolved Golden State Killer case, written by the late author of the TrueCrimeDiary.com website traces the rapes and murders of dozens of victims and the author's determined efforts to help identify the killer and bring him to justice.

"McNamaras posthumously published book tells both the nightmarish story of the Golden State Killer (GSK) and the neighborhoods he terrorized and her own story of true-crime addiction." Booklist.

O'Neill, Tom

★**Chaos** : Charles Manson, the CIA, and the secret history of the Sixties / Tom O'Neill, with Dan Piepenbring. Little, Brown & Company, 2019. 528 p. **364.152**

1. O'Neill, Tom 2. Manson, Charles, 1934-2017 3. CIA 4. Investigative journalists 5. Murder investigation 6. Murder suspects 7. Police misconduct
ISBN 9780316477550

LC bl2019011669

A journalist's 20-year obsession with the 1969 Manson murders brings shocking revelations about one of the most infamous crimes in American history: carelessness from police, misconduct by prosecutors and even potential surveillance by intelligence agents.

Sanders, Eli

While the city slept : a love lost to violence and a young man's descent into madness / Eli Sanders. Viking, 2016. 336 p. **364.152**

1. Kalebu, Isaiah. 2. Murder -- Seattle, Washington -- Case studies. 3. Rape -- Seattle, Washington -- Case studies. 4. Men with mental illnesses 5. People with mental illnesses and crime 6. Seattle, Washington
ISBN 9780670015719

LC 2015041289

A Pulitzer Prize-winning reporter describes our failing mental-health system through the story of Isaiah Kalebu, who invaded the home of an engaged Seattle lesbian couple, raped and cut them both and murdered one of them.

Sides, Hampton

Hellhound on his trail : the stalking of Martin Luther King, Jr. and the international hunt for his assassin / Hampton Sides. Doubleday, 2010. 320 p. **364.152**

1. King, Martin Luther, Jr., 1929-1968 2. Ray, James Earl, 1928-1998 3. African American civil rights workers 4. Murderers -- United States 5. Assassination -- United States 6. Social history -- 20th century. 7. United States -- History -- 20th century
ISBN 9780385523929

LC 2009043659

From the acclaimed bestselling author of "Ghost Soldiers" and "Blood and Thunder," a taut, intense narrative about the assassination of Martin Luther King, Jr., and the largest manhunt in American history--a sixty-five-day search that led investigators to Canada, Portugal, and England.

"Sides begins with Ray's escape from a maximum security prison in Missouri the prior April. In short, crisp chapters, Sides then cuts back and forth between Ray's movements during the ensuing year and King's increasing challenges during the same period, as a fraying civil rights movement struggled to transform hard-won legal equality into economic justice. Along the way, we're treated to vignettes featuring J. Edgar Hoover's vicious anti-King smear tactics; George Wallace's race-driven politics of hate during the 1968 presidential campaign; and an embittered Lyndon Johnson's estrangement from King over the ongoing war in Vietnam. None of this is new, but Sides ensures that it's still compulsively readable." Milwaukee Journal Sentinel.

Singular, Stephen

The **spiral** notebook : the Aurora Theater shooter and the epidemic of mass violence committed by American youth / Stephen and Joyce Singular. Counterpoint Press, 2015 304 p. **364.152**

1. Mass murder 2. Mass shootings 3. Guns 4. Violence in teenagers

5. United States -- Social conditions
ISBN 9781619025349

LC bl2015021057

"Tragic, gripping, and authentic, this book deserves a wide audience." Kirkus.

Thompson, Jamie (Journalist)

★**Standoff** : race, policing, and a deadly assault that gripped a nation / Jamie Thompson. Henry Holt & Company, 2020 xix, 294 p. **364.152**

1. Police murders 2. Police -- Violence against 3. Mass shootings 4. Mass murder 5. Dallas, Texas
ISBN 9781250204219

LC 2019055941

On the evening of July 7, 2016, protesters gathered in cities across the nation after police shot two black men, Philando Castile and Alton Sterling. As officers patrolled a march in Dallas, a young man stepped out of an SUV wearing a bulletproof vest and carrying a high-powered rifle. He killed five officers and wounded eleven others. An award-winning journalist documents the shooting, offering character portraits of its first responders, negotiator, doctors and victims while examining how the tragedy reflects ongoing challenges in racial injustice and law enforcement.

"This standout account is both a riveting page-turner and a nuanced portrait of one of contemporary America's most divisive social issues." Publishers Weekly

Wiehl, Lis W.

Hunting Charles Manson : the quest for justice in the days of helter skelter / Lis Wiehl. Nelson Books, 2018. 319 p. **364.152**

1. Manson, Charles, 1934-2017. 2. Cults -- California 3. Trials (Murder) 4. Murderers -- California -- Case studies. 5. Mass murder investigation -- California -- Case studies.
ISBN 9780718092085

LC 2017059418

Recounts the life of Charles Manson, describing his troubled past, his formation of a group of dedicated followers, the murder spree that resulted from his orders, intense investigation by law enforcement, final capture, homicide trial, and imprisonment.

"Mystery writer, lawyer, and legal analyst Wiehl presents an accessible reboot of prosecutor Vincent Bugliosi's classic Helter Skelter that for the most part doesn't add new information to the highly publicized case." Library Journal.

Wiehl, Lis W.

Hunting the Unabomber : the FBI, Ted Kaczynski, and the capture of America's most notorious domestic terrorist / Lis Wiehl, with Lisa Pulitzer. Nelson Books, [2020] xiv, 317 p. **364.152**

1. Kaczynski, Theodore John, 1942- 2. FBI 3. Terrorists 4. Domestic terrorism 5. Bombing investigation 6. Serial murder investigation
ISBN 9780718092122

LC 2019031034

On April 3, 1996, a team of FBI agents closed in on an isolated cabin in remote Montana, marking the end of the longest and most expensive investigation in FBI history. The cabin's lone inhabitant was a former mathematics prodigy and professor who had abandoned society decades earlier. Few people knew his name, Theodore Kaczynski, but everyone knew the mayhem and death associated with his nickname: the Unabomber.

"The action progresses with drama and nail-biting intensity, the conclusion foregone yet nonetheless compelling. A true-crime masterpiece." Booklist

Zacharias, Karen Spears

A **silence** of mockingbirds : the memoir of a murder / Karen Spears Zacharias. MacAdam/Cage, c2012. 322 p. **364.152**

1. Murder. 2. Girl murder victims. 3. Child abuse. 4. Divorced women.
ISBN 9781596923751

LC 2012000748

An examination of the abuse that led to the murder of a three-year-old girl reveals the tendency of people to disregard or keep silent about predatory behavior, and brings to light many instances in which the abuse could have been stopped.

"Journalist Zacharias presents a searing account of child abuse and murder, bringing to life a tragedy with which she is intimately familiar...A harrowing cautionary tale that will touch fans of Ann Rule's chilling works." Library Journal.

Collins, Paul, 1969-

Duel with the devil : the true story of how Alexander Hamilton and Aaron Burr teamed up to take on America's first sensational murder mystery / Paul Collins. Crown, 2013 288 p. **364.1523**

1. Hamilton, Alexander, 1757-1804 2. Burr, Aaron, 1756-1836 3. Weeks, Levi 4. Murder investigation 5. Trials (Murder) 6. Sensationalism in journalism 7. Cooperation 8. New York City -- History -- 19th century
ISBN 9780307956453

LC 2013371593

Documents the sensational 1799 murder mystery that inspired rivals Alexander Hamilton and Aaron Burr to join forces, revealing the links between the accused killer and both men and the public outcry that nearly prevented the suspect's fair trial.

364.16 Offenses against property

Bilefsky, Dan

The **last** job : the "bad grandpas" and the Hatton Garden heist / Dan Bilefsky. W.W. Norton & Company, [2019] 304 p. **364.16**

1. Hatton Garden Safe Deposit Company. 2. Burglary 3. Jewelry theft 4. Seniors 5. Thieves 6. London, England
ISBN 9780393609516

LC 2018046576

The definitive account of one of the most brazen jewel heists in history. Over Easter weekend 2015, a motley crew of six English thieves, several in their sixties and seventies, couldn't resist coming out of retirement for one last career-topping heist. Their target: the Hatton Garden Safe Deposit, in the heart of London's medieval diamond district.

"Former New York Times London correspondent Bilefsky makes good use of his access to the Scotland Yarders investigating the biggest burglary in English history to recreate a daring theft carried out by five thieves, who ended their retirement from a life of crime in 2015 by breaking into safety-deposit boxes." Publishers Weekly.

Crosby, Molly Caldwell

The **great** pearl heist : London's greatest jewel thief and Scotland Yard's hunt for the world's most valuable necklace / Molly Caldwell Crosby. Berkely Books, c2012. 304 p. **364.16**

1. Jewelry theft 2. Robbery investigation 3. Burglary 4. Receiving stolen goods. 5. London, England 6. England
ISBN 9780425252802

LC 2012008261

Describes the true story of a 1913 collaboration between a notorious jewel thief and the Chief Inspector of Scotland Yard as they hunted for a precious pearl necklace, worth more than the Hope diamond.

Dolnick, Edward, 1952-

The **rescue** artist : a true story of art, thieves, and the hunt for a missing masterpiece / Edward Dolnick. Harper Collins Publishers, c2005. 270 p. : **364.16**

1. Munch, Edvard, 1863-1944. Scream (Nasjonalgalleriet (Norway)) 2. Art thefts. 3. Robbery investigation. 4. Museum thefts -- Norway. 5. Norway.

ISBN 0060531177

LC 2004062060

Edgar Allan Poe Award for Best Fact Crime, 2006.

Traces the theft of Edvard Munch's "The Scream" from Oslo's National Gallery in 1994, recounting the efforts of art detective Charley Hill to recover the painting in an investigation ranging from the estates of aristocrats to the art underworld.

"[A] tightly woven, fast-paced story." School Library Journal.

Goodman, Marc

Future crimes : everything is connected, everyone is vulnerable and what we can do about it / Marc Goodman. Doubleday, 2015 viii, 392, lx p. ; **364.16**

1. Computer crimes. 2. Technological forecasting. 3. Technology -- Social aspects. 4. Hackers.

ISBN 9780385539005

LC 2014038053

An FBI futurist and senior advisor to Interpol analyzes the digital underground to reveal the alarming ways criminals, corporations and countries are using emerging technologies to target individuals and wage war

Greenberg, Andy

Sandworm : a new era of cyberwar and the hunt for the Kremlin's most dangerous hackers / Andy Greenberg. Doubleday, [2019] 368 p. **364.16**

1. Cyberterrorism 2. Computer crimes 3. Spies -- Russia 4. Hackers

ISBN 9780385544405

LC 2019006755

The award-winning Wired senior writer and author of This Machine Kills Secrets documents the story of the hunt to identify and track an elite team of Russian agents behind the world's most dangerous digital attacks.

Hammer, Joshua, 1957-

★The **falcon** thief : a true tale of adventure, treachery, and the hunt for the perfect bird / Joshua Hammer. Simon & Schuster, 2020. 288 p. **364.16**

1. Wildlife crimes. 2. Wild bird industry and trade 3. Falcons 4. Rare and endangered birds

ISBN 9781501191886

LC 2019031607

Documents the true story of Irish national Jeffrey Lendrum and his globetrotting adventures as a smuggler of rare birds, detailing the efforts of British wildlife detective Andy McWilliam to protect the world's endangered birds of prey.

"A sleek, winning nonfiction thriller." Kirkus

Hvistendahl, Mara

★The **scientist** and the spy : a true story of China, the FBI, and industrial espionage / Mara Hvistendahl. Riverhead Books, 2020. 320 p. **364.16**

1. FBI 2. Business intelligence 3. Trade secrets 4. Spies 5. Governmental investigations 6. United States 7. China

ISBN 9780735214286

LC 2019037842

In September 2011, sheriff's deputies in Iowa encountered three ethnic Chinese men near a field where a farmer was growing corn seed under contract with Monsanto. What began as a simple trespassing inquiry mushroomed into a two-year FBI operation in which investigators bugged the men's rental cars, used a warrant intended for foreign terrorists and spies, and flew surveillance planes over corn country--all in the name of protecting trade secrets of corporate giants Monsanto and DuPont Pioneer. Hvistendahl gives a gripping account of this unusually far-reaching investigation, which pitted a veteran FBI special agent against Florida resident Robert Mo, who after his academic career foundered took a questionable job with the Chinese agricultural company DBG--and became a pawn in a global rivalry.

"This engaging book has something for everyone; it can be read as a spy thriller, an examination of U.S.-China relations, or a case study of agricultural espionage." Library Journal

Johnson, Kirk W.

The **feather** thief : beauty, obsession, and the natural history heist of the century / Kirk Wallace Johnson. Viking, 2018. x, 308 p., 16 unnumbered p. of plates : **364.16**

1. Johnson, Kirk W. 2. Rist, Edwin 3. Investigative journalism 4. Thieves 5. Natural history 6. Feathers

ISBN 9781101981610

ALA Notable Book, 2019.

Documents the astonishing 2009 theft of an invaluable collection of ornithological displays from the British Museum of Natural History by a talented American musician, tracing the author's years-long investigation to track down the culprit and understand his motives, which were possibly linked to an obsession with the Victorian art of salmon fly-tying.

"This is a remarkably compelling story of obsession and history and a man who so loved his art that he would break the law for it." Booklist.

Kolhatkar, Sheelah

Black edge : inside information, dirty money, and the quest to bring down the most wanted man on wall street / Sheelah Kolhatkar. Random House, 2017 368 p. **364.16**

1. Cohen, Steven A., 1956- 2. White collar crime 3. Hedge funds 4. Investments 5. Business -- Corrupt practices

ISBN 9780812995800

LC 2016031776

Longlisted for the Andrew Carnegie Medal for Excellence in Non-Fiction, 2018.

Traces the rise and fall of stock trader Steven Cohen and his hedge fund, SAC Capital, to offer insight into personalities behind the largest insider-trading investigation in Wall Street history while revealing how Cohen continues to make billions as a free man.

"Well-written, with pointed characterizations of the ambitious players and their motives, this book is highly recommended for readers interested in finance, crime, and politics." Library Journal.

Mueller, Tom, 1963-

Crisis of conscience : whistleblowing in an age of fraud / Tom Mueller. Riverhead Books, 2019. 596 p. ; **364.16**

1. Whistle blowing 2. Whistle blowers 3. Business -- Corrupt practices 4. Political corruption

ISBN 9781594634437

A riveting account of the heroes who are combating corporate, medical and government fraud traces the rise of whistleblowing through a series of important cases that reflect fundamental questions about the balance between free speech and state power.

Posner, Gerald L.

God's bankers : a history of money and power at the Vatican / Gerald Posner. Simon & Schuster, 2015. 496 p. **364.16**

1. Catholic Church Finance. 2. Catholic Church Corrupt practices. 3. Catholic Church -- History 20th century. 4. Catholic Church -- History 21st century. 5. Catholic Church Controversial literature. 6. Corruption 7. Banks and banking -- Vatican City. 8. Religious corruption

ISBN 9781416576570

LC 2014021061

From a master chronicler of legal and financial misconduct, a magnificent investigation nine years in the making, this book traces the political intrigue and inner workings of the Catholic Church. Decidedly not about faith, belief in God, or religious doctrine, this book is about the church's accumulation of wealth and its byzantine entanglements with financial markets across the world. Told through 200 years of prelates, bishops, cardinals, and the Popes who oversee it all, Gerald Posner uncovers an eyebrow-raising account of money and power in perhaps the most influential organization in the history of the world.

"The destruction of documents, stonewalling by prelates, and closed Vatican archives made Posner's work harder, necessitating conjectures. This sad tale is known in its outlines, but Posner provides much more detail." Choice.

Taub, Jennifer

Big dirty money : the shocking injustice and unseen cost of white collar crime / Jennifer Taub. Viking, 2020 xxxvi, 298 p. **364.16**

1. White collar crime 2. Corruption 3. Social classes 4. Income distribution. 5. United States -- Economic conditions -- 21st century. 6. United States -- Social conditions -- 21st century.

ISBN 9781984879974

LC 2020024366

A Harvard Law School visiting scholar and banking law advocate reveals how unchecked white-collar crimes, from fraud and embezzlement to obstruction of justice and bribery, continue to benefit the wealthy at the expense of everyday Americans.

"A significant manifesto for judicial reform that aims at cracking the cabal of big-money grifters at the top." Kirkus

364.2 Causes of crime and delinquency

Muhammad, Khalil Gibran

The **condemnation** of blackness : race, crime, and the making of modern urban America / Khalil Gibran Muhammad. Harvard University Press, 2010. 380 p. **364.2**

1. African Americans 2. Racism -- United States 3. Racism in the criminal justice system 4. Racism in the judicial system 5. United States -- Race relations

ISBN 9780674035973

Lynch mobs, chain gangs, and popular views of black southern criminals that defined the Jim Crow South are well known. We know less about the role of the urban North in shaping views of race and crime in American society.

"A brilliant work that tells us how directly the past has formed us." New York Review of Books

364.3 Offenders

Hayes, Christopher, 1979-

A **colony** in a nation / Chris Hayes. W W Norton & Co Inc, 2017. 256 p. **364.3**

1. Racism 2. Race relations 3. Racism in the criminal justice system 4. Criminal justice system 5. United States -- Social life and customs -- 21st century

ISBN 9780393254228

LC 2016053392

An Emmy Award-winning news anchor and New York Times best-selling author argues that there are really two Americas--a Colony and a Nation.

"A timely and impassioned argument for social justice." Kirkus.

364.40973 Prevention of crime and delinquency--United States

Stuntz, William J.

The **collapse** of American criminal justice / William J. Stuntz. Belknap Press of Harvard University Press, c2011. viii, 413 p. ; **364.40973**

1. Crime prevention. 2. Criminal justice system. 3. Racism in the criminal justice system. 4. Race relations. 5. United States -- Race relations.

ISBN 9780674051751

LC 2011006905

"This is a fascinating, passionate, compassionate, often brilliant book. Flawless? No. But it's a work that deserves to have a significant influence on American criminal-justice thinkers from across the political spectrum." National Review.

364.6 Penology

Sered, Danielle

Until we reckon : violence, mass incarceration, and a road to repair / Danielle Sered. New Press, [2019] 336 p. **364.6**

1. Restorative justice. 2. Imprisonment. 3. Prison reform. 4. Prisons.

ISBN 9781620974797

LC 2018047561

Asking us to reconsider the purposes of incarceration, an award-winning leader in the movement to end mass incarceration shows how her organization, which offers alternatives to people who commit serious violent crime, has produced immensely promising results.

364.60973 Penology--United States

Law, Vikki

Prison by any other name : the harmful consequences of popular reforms / Victoria Law and Maya Schenwar ; with a foreword by Michelle Alexander. The New Press, 2020. 240 p. **364.60973**

1. Correctional institutions 2. Imprisonment 3. Prison-industrial complex

ISBN 9781620973103

LC 2019055151

Situating this book in the context of criminal justice, two activist journalists reveal the way the kinder, gentler narrative of reform can obscure agendas of social control and challenge us to question the ways we replicate the status quo when pursuing change.

"Necessary reading for any critic of mass incarceration seeking to understand the myriad policy alternatives and the path to lasting liberation." Library Journal

364.66 Capital punishment

Prejean, Helen

★The **death** of innocents : an eyewitness account of wrongful executions / Helen Prejean. Random House, c2005. xvi, 310 p. ; **364.66**

1. Capital punishment -- United States -- Case studies. 2. Death row prisoners. 3. Judicial system 4. Capital punishment -- Law and legislation. 5. United States -- Politics and government.

ISBN 9780679440567

LC 2004054154

Raises constitutional questions about the legality of the death penalty and reveals how race, poverty, publicity, and prosecutorial ambition can determine who lives and dies after a murder conviction.

"The author reexamines the cases of two men she fervently believes were executed for crimes they did not commit. In addition to providing a searing indictment of capital punishment, Prejean also exposes the fundamental inadequacies of the American court system. Expect demand for this extremely thought-provoking book." Booklist.

364.973 Crime -- United States

Alexander, Michelle

★The **new** Jim Crow : mass incarceration in the age of colorblindness / Michelle Alexander. New Press, 2010. 352 p. **364.973**

1. Criminal justice system. 2. African American prisoners 3. Racism. 4. Interethnic relations. 5. United States -- Race relations.

ISBN 9781595581037

LC 2009022519

Street Lit Book Award Medal: Adult Non-Fiction, 2013

Argues that the War on Drugs and policies that deny convicted felons equal access to employment, housing, education, and public benefits create a permanent under caste based largely on race.

"Most provocatively, she reveals how both the move toward colorblindness and affirmative action may blur our vision of injustice: "most Americans know and don't know the truth about mass incarceration"-- but her carefully researched, deeply engaging, and thoroughly readable book should change that." Publishers Weekly

Caldwell, Laura,

Anatomy of innocence : testimonies of the wrongfully convicted / edited by Laura Caldwell and Leslie S. Klinger, introduction by Scott Turow and Barry Scheck. Liveright Publishing Corporation, 2017. 320 p. **364.973**

1. Judicial error 2. Innocence (Law) 3. Criminal justice system 4. Injustice 5. Anthologies

ISBN 9781631490880

LC 2016052528

A collective literary protest against wrongful convictions tells the stories of more than a dozen innocent men and women who were convicted of serious crimes and forced to endure a flawed criminal justice system before their exonerations, in an anthology that includes contributions by Lee Child, Sara Paretsky, Michael Harvey, Laurie King, Phillip M. Margolin and Jan Burke.

"A searing, unforgettable anthology, with valuable insights provided at the end of each chapter by the editors." Kirkus.

Forman, James, 1967-

★**Locking** up our own : crime and punishment in Black America / James Forman, Jr. Farrar, Straus and Giroux, 2017. 352 p. **364.973**

1. Criminal justice system 2. African American police 3. African American judges 4. Racism in the criminal justice system 5. United States -- Race relations. 6. Essays

ISBN 9780374189976

LC 2016041345

Includes index.

Pulitzer Prize for General Nonfiction, 2018.

Longlisted for the Andrew Carnegie Medal for Excellence in Non-Fiction, 2018.

Longlisted for the National Book Award for Nonfiction, 2017.

In Locking Up Our Own, author James Forman Jr. offers historical background to the U.S. War on Crime's aggressive policing and long criminal sentences. African American leaders welcomed these approaches, which began in the 1970s, but the measures now seem to be disproportionately targeting poor black men. Forman, a Yale law professor and former public defender, offers a thought-provoking perspective on combating drugs and violent crime.

"Possibly controversial, undoubtedly argumentative, Forman's survey offers a refreshing breath of fresh air on the crisis in American policing." Publishers Weekly.

King, Shaun, 1979-

★**Make** change : how to fight injustice, dismantle systemic oppression, and own our future / Shaun King ; foreword by Bernie Sanders. Houghton Mifflin Harcourt, 2020. 320 p. **364.973**

1. King, Shaun, 1979- 2. Social advocates 3. Black Lives Matter movement 4. Criminal justice system 5. Police brutality. 6. United States

ISBN 9780358048008

LC 2019049814

An activist and journalist reflects on the events that led to him becoming a prominent social justice leader and lays out a clear action plan for you to join the fight.

"A blend of memoir and manifesto by Black Lives Matter leader King. . . . A vigorous complement to other primers in political activism and social justice." Kirkus

Platt, Tony, 1942-

Beyond these walls : rethinking crime and punishment in the United States / Tony Platt. St. Martin's Press, [2019] 304 p. **364.973**

1. Criminal justice system -- History 2. Punishment -- United States 3. Racism in the criminal justice system 4. Crime -- United States -- History.

ISBN 9781250085115

LC 2018029156

The author of Grave Matters presents a groundbreaking investigation into the roots of the American criminal justice system to link the broken practices of the Trump administration to failures in past racial, gender and class reforms.

365 Penal and related institutions

Applebaum, Anne, 1964-

★**Gulag** : a history / Anne Applebaum. Doubleday, 2003. 677 p. : **365**

1. Concentration camps -- Soviet Union. 2. Forced labor -- Soviet Union. 3. Prisons -- Soviet Union. 4. Convict labor. 5. Soviet Union -- Politics and government. 6. Soviet Union -- History -- 1917-1953. 7. Soviet Union -- History -- 1953-1991.

ISBN 0767900561

LC 2002041344

Pulitzer Prize for General Nonfiction, 2004.

National Book Award for Nonfiction finalist, 2003.

National Book Critics Circle Award for Nonfiction finalist, 2003.

"This describes how, largely under Stalin's watch, a regulated, centralized system of prison labor--unprecedented in scope--gradually arose out of the chaos of the Russian Revolution. Applebaum details camp life, including strategies for survival; the experiences of women and children in the camps; sexual relationships and marriages between prisoners; and rebellions, strikes and escapes. Applebaum's lucid prose and painstaking consideration of the competing theories about aspects of camp life and policy are always compelling." Publishers Weekly.

Bauer, Shane

American prison : a reporter's undercover journey into the business of punishment / Shane Bauer. Penguin Press, 2018. 368 p. **365**

1. Prison industry and trade -- Corrupt practices -- United States. 2. Criminal justice system. 3. Corruption. 4. Prisons -- United States. 5. United States -- Social life and customs -- 21st century. 6. Louisiana -- Social life and customs -- 21st century.

ISBN 9780735223585

LC 2018018293

ALA Notable Book, 2019.

J. Anthony Lukas Book Prize, 2019.

Robert F. Kennedy Book Award, 2019.

Kirkus Prize for Nonfiction finalist, 2018.

The investigative journalist draws on his experiences working in a Louisiana private prison to connect today's brutal for-profit prison system to the Civil War-era mass incarcerations of African-American workers.

"Bauer's amazing book examines one of slaverys toxic legacies, using convicted people to make profit, through a dual approach." Booklist.

Gessen, Masha

Never remember : the gulags in Putin's Russia / Masha Gessen, Michael Friedman. Columbia Global Reports, 2018. 176 p. **365**

1. Stalin, Joseph, 1879-1953. 2. Putin, Vladimir Vladimirovich, 1952- 3. GULag. 4. Concentration camps -- Soviet Union. 5. Political prisoners -- Soviet Union. 6. Political persecution. 7. Totalitarianism. 8. Russia -- Politics and government -- 21st century. 9. Soviet Union -- History -- 1925-1953.

ISBN 9780997722963

LC 2016962829

" Friedman's moody, panoramic black-and-white photos of the memorial sites convey a narrative that's fragmented, blurry, and ultimately incomplete, perfectly underscoring Gessen's text. The combination is a powerful meditation on contemporary Russia as seen through its relationship to the past." Publishers Weekly.

Oshinsky, David M., 1944-

Worse than slavery : Parchman Farm and the ordeal of Jim Crow justice / David M. Oshinsky. Free Press, 1996. xiv, 306 p., [16] p. of plates : **365**

1. Mississippi State Penitentiary -- History. 2. Criminal justice system -- Mississippi -- History. 3. Prisoners -- Mississippi -- History.

ISBN 0684822989

LC 95052880

Robert F. Kennedy Book Award, 1997.

Draws on police records, prison documents, and oral history to examine Mississippi's state penitentiary and Jim Crow justice, from the era of the cottonfield chain gangs to the 1960s.

Solzhenitsyn, Aleksandr Isaevich, 1918-2008

★The **Gulag** Archipelago 1918-1956 : an experiment in literary investigation / Aleksandr I. Solzhenitsyn ; translated from the Russian by Thomas P. Whitney and Harry Willetts ; abridged by Edward E. Ericson. Perennial, 2002, c1985. xxiv, 472 p. : **365**

1. Prisons -- Soviet Union. 2. Political prisoners -- Soviet Union. 3. Concentration camps -- Soviet Union.

ISBN 9780060007768

LC 2001046504

Previously published: New York : Harper & Row, 1985.

An account of four decades of oppression describes individual escapes and attempted escapes from Stalin's camps, a disciplined, sustained resistance put down with tanks after forty days, and the forced removal and extermination of millions of peasants, in a special abridged edition of the classic by the Russian Nobel laureate.

★The **Gulag** Archipelago, 1918-1956 : an experiment in literary investigation / Aleksandr I. Solzhenitsyn ; translated from the Russian by Harry Willetts ; foreword by Anne Applebaum. Harper Perennial Modern Classics, 2007. xviii, 558, 24 p. : **365**

1. Concentration camps -- Soviet Union. 2. Political prisoners -- Soviet Union. 3. Prisons -- Soviet Union.

ISBN 9780061253737

LC bl2017038566

Describes individual escapes and attempted escapes from Stalin's camps.

Thompson, Heather Ann, 1963-

Blood in the water : the Attica prison uprising of 1971 and its legacy / Heather Ann Thompson. Pantheon, 2016. 720 p. **365**

1. Attica Prison. 2. Prison riots -- New York (State) 3. Violence in prisons 4. Prisoner abuse 5. Police brutality

ISBN 9780375423222

LC 2016000477

Includes index.

Pulitzer Prize for History, 2017.

An account of the infamous 1971 Attica prison uprising, the state's violent response, and the victims' decades-long quest for justice draws on previously unreleased information while detailing how the event has influenced civil rights practices in the criminal justice system.

"Thompson's superb and thorough study serves as a powerful tale of the search for justice in the face of the abuses of institutional power." Publishers Weekly.

368.38 Health insurance, accident insurance, disability income insurance

Brill, Steven

America's bitter pill : money, politics, backroom deals, and the fight to fix our broken healthcare system

/ Steven Brill. Random House., 2015 384 p. **368.38**

1. United States. Patient Protection and Affordable Care Act 2. Medical care -- United States -- Government policy 3. Medical care reform 4. Health policy 5. Health insurance
ISBN 9780812996951

LC 2014037908

Tells the story of the fight to pass and implement the Affordable Care Act, more popularly known as Obamacare.

"Brill breaks down insider language, asks fundamental and surprising questions, and leaves the reader … full of more questions yet with a much clearer map of the lines of debate." New York Times.

369.463 Girl's scouting organizations

Stewart, Nikita

Troop 6000 : the Girl Scout troop that began in a shelter and inspired the world / Nikita Stewart. Ballantine Books, 2020. 304 p. **369.46309747**

1. Girl Scouts of Greater New York. Troop 6000. 2. Girl Scouts 3. Homeless girls 4. Homelessness 5. Shelters for the homeless. 6. New York City
ISBN 9781984820754

LC 2019038599

Describes how hardworking mother of five Giselle Burgess rose from poverty and homelessness to establish Girl Scout troops in 15 New York City shelters to bring pride, life-skill training and community to disadvantaged urban girls.

"A tale of how grassroots spirit and gritty determination can bloom into hope." Kirkus

370 Education

Braun, Adam

The **promise** of a pencil : how an ordinary person can create extraordinary change / Adam Braun. Scribner, [2014] 272 p. **370**

1. Braun, Adam. 2. Pencils of Promise (Organization) 3. Schools 4. Education -- Developing countries. 5. Nonprofit organizations. 6. Social action. 7. Developing countries.
ISBN 9781476730622

LC 2014000425

One of Wired Magazine's "50 People Who Are Changing the World" recounts how he left a lucrative career to found the award-winning Pencils of Promise nonprofit, describing his travels through dozens of countries and the evolution of his "for-purpose" combination of nonprofit idealism with for-profit business principles.

Carroll, Rebecca,

Uncle Tom or new Negro? : African Americans reflect on Booker T. Washington and Up from slavery one hundred years later / edited by Rebecca Carroll. Broadway Books/Harlem Moon, 2006. viii, 320 p. ; **370**

1. Washington, Booker T., 1856-1915 2. Washington, Booker T., 1859?-1915. Up from slavery. 3. African Americans 4. Educators -- United States
ISBN 0767919556

LC 2005050161

A study of the complex legacy of Booker T. Washington draws on his classic autobiography, "Up from Slavery," to examine his role as one of the most influential voices in post-slavery America and to assess his controversial impact on African-American life.

Postman, Neil

The **end** of education : redefining the value of school / Neil Postman. Knopf, 1995. xi, 209 p. **370**

1. Education -- United States. 2. Educational reform. 3. Educational innovations. 4. Education -- Philosophy.
ISBN 9780679430063

LC 94046605

ALA Notable Book, 1996.

A critical analysis of American education states that poor motivational techniques and a lack of focus are at the core of most problems and offers four methods that can be implemented to promote education reform.

"Beautifully written, breathtakingly high-minded, this is Postman's best book on American education." Booklist.

370.1130973 Vocational education--United States

Newman, Katherine S., 1953-

Reskilling America : learning to labor in the twenty-first century / Katherine S. Newman, Hella Winston. Metropolitan Books, 2016. 288 p. **370.1130973**

1. Vocational education -- United States. 2. Blue collar workers 3. Occupational training -- United States. 4. Technical education
ISBN 9781627793285

LC 2015048810

Includes index.

From the award-winning author of No Shame in My Game, and a respected sociologist, comes a sharp and irrefutable call to reenergize the United States' long-neglected system of vocational training.

"A top-notch, highly accessible contribution to the business and popular economics literature." Kirkus.

370.15 Educational psychology

Heffron, Claire

Playful learning lab for kids : whole-body sensory adventures to enhance focus, engagement, and curiosity / Claire Heffron and Lauren Drobnjak. Quarry, 2019. 144 p. : **370.15**

1. Perceptual learning 2. Sensory stimulation 3. Teaching -- Aids and devices
ISBN 9781631595561

LC 2018027955

Outlines activities using the senses and the whole body for teaching language arts, mathematics, science, social studies, art, music, and geography.

LaGarde, Jennifer

Fact vs. fiction : teaching critical thinking skills in the age of fake news / Jennifer LaGarde and Darren Hudgins. International Society for Technology in Education, 2018 xi, 147 p. ; **370.15**

1. Critical thinking -- Study and teaching 2. Fake news -- Study and teaching 3. Information literacy -- Study and teaching 4. Mass media -- Study and teaching
ISBN 9781564847041

LC 2018051063

"A thought-provoking resource for teachers and librarians seeking to foster their students' critical thinking." School Library Journal

Levine, Melvin D.

A **mind** at a time : America's Top Learning Expert Shows How

Every Child Can Succeed / Mel Levine. Simon & Schuster, 2002. 352 p. : **370.15**

1. Child development 2. Cognition in children 3. Individual differences in children 4. Learning disabilities
ISBN 9780743202237

LC BL2002014592

Reprint. Originally published: 2002.

A professor of pediatrics reveals the many modes of learning and arms parents and teachers with the knowledge they need to help children prosper in a school environment.

"The author discusses eight areas of learning (the memory system, the language system, the spatial ordering system, the motor system, etc.). He provides chapters describing how each type of learning works and advises parents and teachers on how to help kids struggling in these areas. This is a must-read for parents and educators who want to understand and improve the school lives of children." Publishers Weekly.

Sarma, Sanjay E., 1948-

Grasp : the science transforming how we learn / Sanjay Sarma, with Luke Yoquinto. Doubleday, [2020] 304 p. **370.15**

1. Learning 2. Cognition 3. Research institutes 4. Brain
ISBN 9780385541824

LC 2019054620

As the head of Open Learning at MIT, Sanjay Sarma has a daunting job description: to fling open the doors of the MIT experience for the benefit of the wider world. But if you're going to undertake such an ambitious project, it behooves you to ask: How exactly does learning work? What conditions are most conducive? Are our traditional classroom methods actually effective? Grasp takes readers across multiple frontiers, from fundamental neuroscience to cognitive psychology and beyond, as it explores the future of learning. Along the way, Sarma debunks long-held views, while equipping readers with a set of practical tools for absorbing and retaining information across a lifetime. He presents a vision for learning that's more inclusive and democratic - revealing a world bursting with powerful learners, just waiting for the chance they deserve.

"Compelling advice on how to improve education. . . . Delightful as well as convincing in its plea that educators place learning over winnowing and access over exclusivity." Kirkus

370.19 Psychological principles

Lukas, J. Anthony, 1933-1997

Common ground : a turbulent decade in the lives of three American families / J. Anthony Lukas. Knopf, 1985. x, 659 p. **370.19**

1. Diver family. 2. Twyman family. 3. Goff family. 4. Busing (School integration) -- Boston, Massachusetts. 5. School integration -- Boston, Massachusetts. 6. Riots -- Boston, Massachusetts -- History. 7. Race riots 8. Boston, Massachusetts -- Race relations.
ISBN 9780394411507

LC 85000127

National Book Award for Nonfiction, 1985.
National Book Critics Circle Award for Non-Fiction, 1985.
Pulitzer Prize for General Nonfiction, 1986.
Robert F. Kennedy Book Award, 1986.

Probes the school integration crisis that shattered Boston during the decade 1968-1978 through portraits of three families--black, Irish and Yankee.

370.89 Ethnic groups in education

Ewing, Eve L.

Ghosts in the schoolyard : racism and school closings on Chicago's South side / Eve L. Ewing. The University of Chicago Press, 2018. xiii, 222 p. : **370.89**

1. Walter H. Dyett High School (Chicago, Ill.). 2. African Americans -- Education 3. Racism in education 4. Public schools 5. High schools 6. South Side, Chicago, Illinois 7. Chicago, Illinois
ISBN 9780226526027

LC 2018010065

"Failing schools. Underprivileged schools. Just plain bad schools." That's how Eve L. Ewing opens Ghosts in the Schoolyard: describing Chicago Public Schools from the outside. But Ewing knows Chicago Public Schools from the inside: as a student, then a teacher, and now a scholar who studies them. And that perspective has shown her that public schools are not buildings full of failures--they're an integral part of their neighborhoods, at the heart of their communities, storehouses of history and memory that bring people together.

370.9 History, geographic treatment, biography

Ripley, Amanda

The **smartest** kids in the world : and how they got that way / Amanda Ripley. Simon & Schuster, 2013. 320 p. **370.9**

1. Comparative education. 2. Exchange students 3. Education -- Finland. 4. Teenagers
ISBN 9781451654424

LC 2013002021

Following three teenagers who chose to spend one school year living and learning in Finland, South Korea and Poland, a literary journalist, through their adventures, discovers startling truths about how attitudes, parenting and rigorous teaching have revolutionized these countries' education results.

370.9173 Urban and rural education

Falk, Beverly

Teaching matters : stories from inside city schools / Beverly Falk and Megan Blumenreich with Adesina Abani ... [et al.]. New Press, 2012. 432 p. **370.9173**

1. Urban education. 2. Teachers. 3. Public schools. 4. Education.
ISBN 9781595584908

LC 2012004564

Drawing upon teachers' first-hand experiences, provides an account of what inner-city students need in order to learn and what is being done to satisfy those needs.

370.92 Educators -- Biography

Walker, Vanessa Siddle

The **lost** education of Horace Tate : uncovering the hidden heroes who fought for justice in schools / Vanessa Siddle Walker. The New Press, 2018. viii, 468 pages : **370.92**

1. Tate, Horace, 1922-2002 2. Georgia Teachers and Education Association 3. Racism in education 4. Segregation in education 5. African American teachers 6. Social justice 7. Georgia -- Race

relations 8. United States -- Race relations
ISBN 9781620971055

LC 2018007468

Draws on hidden archives to reveal the achievements of a devoted network of African-American educators who battled Southern school segregation and inequality on either side of Brown v. Board of Education.

"Walker's extensively documented work is a much-needed corrective contextualizing the landscape of school desegregation; required reading for those interested in the past, present, and future of education of African American children." Library Journal.

370.973 Education--United States

Robinson, Ken
Creative schools : the grassroots revolution that's transforming education / Ken Robinson, Lou Aronica. Viking Press, 2015 272 p. **370.973**

1. Educational reform 2. Education 3. Educational policy. 4. Educational innovations
ISBN 9780670016716

LC 2015001098

In a book filled with anecdotes, observations and recommendations from professionals on the front line of transformative education, case histories and groundbreaking research, the author of The Element argues for an end to our outmoded industrial educational system and proposes a highly personalized, organic approach that draws on today's unprecedented technological and professional resources to engage all students, develop their love of learning and enable them to face the real challenges of the 21st century.

"For readers who are ardent about changing education for the better, believing that they can be part of the forces that will revolutionize the future." Library Journal.

371.010973 Public schools--United States

Brill, Steven, 1950-
Class warfare : inside the fight to fix America's schools / Steven Brill. Simon & Schuster, c2011. 352 p. **371.010973**

1. Public schools 2. School improvement programs. 3. Educational policy 4. Education -- United States 5. United States -- Politics and government -- 21st century
ISBN 9781451611991

LC 2011016196

Looks at why many of America's schools are failing and offers ways to improve grades K-12 and offer children a better future.

Ravitch, Diane
★**Slaying** Goliath : the passionate resistance to privatization and the fight to save America's public schools / Diane Ravitch. Alfred A. Knopf, [2020] 352 p. **371.010973**

1. Education -- Privatization. 2. Public schools 3. Educational policy 4. Public education 5. United States
ISBN 9780525655374

LC 2019022776

An in-depth look at the failed efforts to privatize public schools and the victories of those who have fought to save America's public school system.

"This extensive analysis is required reading for anyone concerned about American education." Library Journal.

Rhee, Michelle
Radical : fighting to put students first / Michelle Rhee. HarperCollins, 2013. 352 p. **371.010973**

1. Women teachers 2. Women social advocates 3. Inner city -- Baltimore, Maryland 4. Educational reform 5. Baltimore, Maryland
ISBN 9780062203984

LC 2012038474

A teacher in inner-city Baltimore, chancellor of the Washington, D.C. schools, and the founder of the advocacy organization StudentsFirst shares her 18-year mission to prioritize the interests of children through education reform, offering inspiration and a sense of possibility for a brighter future.

371.1 Schools and their activities

Kozol, Jonathan
Letters to a young teacher / Jonathan Kozol. Crown Publishers, c2007. x, 288 p. ; **371.1**

1. Kozol, Jonathan Correspondence. 2. First-year teachers. 3. Teachers -- United States -- Anecdotes. 4. Teaching -- United States -- Anecdotes. 5. Education -- United States 6. United States -- Social life and customs -- 20th century
ISBN 0307393712

LC 2007002689

The author shares a series of personal reflections, anecdotes, wisdom, and guidance in his letters to Francesca, a first-year teacher in a Boston elementary school, as he attempts to help her deal with the challenges she encounters.

"The book will delight and encourage first-year (or for that matter, 40th-year) teachers who need Kozol's reminders of the ways that their beautiful profession can bring joy and beauty, mystery and mischievous delight into the hearts of little people in their years of greatest curiosity." Publishers Weekly.

371.1020973 Teaching--United States

Goldstein, Dana
The **teacher** wars : a history of America's most embattled profession / Dana Goldstein. Doubleday, 2014. 368 p.. **371.1020973**

1. Teaching -- United States. 2. Teachers -- United States. 3. Public schools -- History. 4. Education -- Social aspects. 5. United States -- Social conditions.
ISBN 9780385536950

LC 2014007024

Traces 175 years of teaching in America to demonstrate how educators have characteristically endured shifting and often impossible expectations, comparing the practices and test scores of other nations while revealing the cultural and political factors compromising education today.

371.19 Community-school relations

Bauer, Susan Wise
Rethinking school : how to take charge of your child's education / Susan Wise Bauer. W. W. Norton & Company, 2018 xiv, 264 p. ; **371.19**

1. Academic achievement 2. Education -- Parent participation
ISBN 9780393285963

LC 2017051513

"A best-selling expert on education shows how to make the school system work for your child. Our K-12 school system is an artificial product of market forces. It isn't a good fit for all--or even most--students. It prioritizes a single way of understanding the world over all others, pushes children into a rigid set of grades with little regard for individual maturity, and slaps "disability" labels over differences in learning style. Caught in this system, far too many young learners end up discouraged, disconnected, and unhappy. And when they struggle, school pressures parents, with overwhelming force, into "fixing" their children rather than questioning the system. With boldness, experience, and humor, Susan Wise Bauer turns conventional wisdom on its head: When a serious problem arises at school, the fault is more likely to lie with the school, or the educational system itself, than with the child. In five illuminating sections, Bauer teaches parents how to flex the K-12 system, rather than the child. She closely analyzes the traditional school structure, gives trenchant criticisms of its weaknesses, and offers a wealth of advice for parents of children whose difficulties may stem from struggling with learning differences, maturity differences, toxic classroom environments, and even from giftedness (not as much of a "gift" as you might think!). Rethinking School is a guide to one aspect of sane, humane parenting: negotiating the twelve-grade school system in a way that nurtures and protects your child's mind, emotions, and spirit"-- Provided by publisher.

"Bauer's guide to the various options available to struggling kids, inside and outside the educational system, will be both comforting and instructive to their parents." Publishers Weekly.

371.2 School administration administration of student academic activities

Russakoff, Dale

The **prize** : who's in charge of America's schools? / Dale Russakoff. Houghton Mifflin Harcourt, 2015 304 p. **371.2**

1. Education, Elementary -- United States 2. Educational reform 3. Newark, New Jersey.

ISBN 9780547840055

LC 2015017454

As serialized in the New Yorker, a roiling, behind-the-scenes look at the high-pressure race to turn around Newark's failing schools, with Facebook's Mark Zuckerberg, Governor Chris Christie, and Senator Cory Booker in eyebrow-raising leading roles

"An absorbing entry into the burgeoning genre about necessary education reforms." Kirkus.

Reese, William J., 1951-

Testing wars in the public schools : a forgotten history / William J. Reese. Harvard University Press, 2013. 298 p. ;

1. Educational tests and measurements -- United States -- History -- 19th century 2. Public schools -- United States -- History -- 19th century

ISBN 9780674073043

LC 2012033665

Despite claims that written exams narrowed the curriculum, ruined children's health, and turned teachers into automatons, once tests took root in American schools their legitimacy was never seriously challenged. William Reese puts today's battles over standards and benchmarks into perspective by showcasing the history of the pencil-and-paper exam. --Provided by publisher

371.2620973 Standardized tests--United States

Hagopian, Jesse,

More than a score : the new uprising against high stakes testing / edited by Jesse Hagopian ; forword by Diane Ravitch ; introduction by Alfie Kohn. Haymarket Books, 2014 180 p. **371.2620973**

1. Public schools. 2. Standardized tests. 3. Educational tests and measurements. 4. Program evaluation in education. 5. Essays 6. Interviews

ISBN 9781608463923

LC bl2014052985

Voices from the growing movement of teachers, students, and parents organizing against high-stakes testing.

"An array of outraged, insightful, and inspiring selections, this necessary collection should be required reading for educators, parents, and students affected by unremitting corporate education strategies." Booklist.

371.30281 Techniques of study

Donaldson-Pressman, Stephanie

The **learning** habit : a groundbreaking approach to homework and parenting that helps our children succeed in school and life / Stephanie Donaldson-Pressman, Rebecca Jackson, Dr. Robert M. Pressman. A Perigee Book, 2014. xiii, 306 p. : **371.30281**

1. Homework 2. Study skills 3. Parenting 4. Families

ISBN 9780399167119

LC 2014011124

"A groundbreaking approach to building learning habits for life, based on a major new study revealing what works--and what doesn't Life is different for kids today. Between standardized testing, the Common Core Curriculum, copious homework assignments, and seemingly endless amounts of "screen time," it's hard for kids-and parents-to know what's most essential. How can parents help their kids succeed - not just do well "on the test"--but develop the learning habits they'll need to thrive throughout their lives? This important and parent-friendly book presents new solutions based on the largest study of family routines ever conducted. The Learning Habit offers a blueprint for navigating the maze of homework, media use, and the everyday stress that families with school-age children face; turning those "stress times" into opportunities to develop the eight critical skills kids will need to succeed in college and in the highly competitive job market of tomorrow--skills including concentration andfocus, time management, decision-making, goal-setting, and self-reliance. Along with hands-on advice and compelling real-life case studies, the book includes 21 fun family challenges for parents and kids, bringing together the latest research with simple, everyday solutions to help kids thrive, academically and beyond".-- Provided by publisher.

371.33 Teaching aids, equipment, materials

Vander Ark, Tom, 1959-

Getting smart : how digital learning is changing the world / Tom Vander Ark ; foreword by Bob Wise. Jossey-Bass, c2012. xxi, 213 p. ; **371.33**

1. Blended learning -- United States 2. Computer-assisted instruction -- United States 3. Internet in education -- United States

ISBN 9781118007235

LC 2011024028

"A comprehensive look at the promise and potential of online learning. In our digital age, students have dramatically new learning needs and must be prepared for the idea economy of the future. In Getting Smart, well-known global education expert Tom Vander Ark examines the facets of educational innovation in the United States and abroad. Vander Ark makes a convincing case for a blend of online and onsite learning, shares inspiring stories of schools and programs that effectively offer "personal digital learning" opportunities, and discusses what we need to do to remake our schools into "smart schools." Examines the innovation-driven world, discusses how to combine online and onsite learning, and reviews "smart tools" for learning. Investigates the lives of learning professionals, outlines the new employment bargain, examines online universities and "smart schools". Makes the case for smart capital, advocates for policies that create better learning, studies smart cultures".-- Provided by publisher.

371.39 Other methods of instruction

Davies, Simone

The **Montessori** toddler : a parent's guide to raising a curious and responsible human being / Simone Davies ; illustrated by Hiyoko Imai. Workman Publishing, 2019 248 p. : **371.39**

1. Parenting 2. Montessori method of education 3. Education, Preschool

ISBN 9781523506897

LC 2019007032

Examines how to incorporate the Montessori education principles into daily routines at home, offering tips on setting up the home, discussing how to cultivate cooperation and set limits, and providing useful skills toddlers can learn.

371.58 Specific discipline problems

Hirsch, Lee

Bully : an action plan for teachers and parents to combat the bullying crisis / edited by Lee Hirsch and Cynthia Lowen ; with Dina Santorelli. Weinstein Books, c2012. viii, 295 p. : **371.58**

1. Bullying. 2. Bullying -- Prevention. 3. Bullying in schools -- Prevention. 4. Cyberbullying -- Prevention.

ISBN 9781602861848

LC 2012289039

A companion to the controversial documentary film that is raising awareness about the millions of child victims of bullying shares expert essays outlining recommendations for concerned caregivers and educators, offers celebrity contributions and includes an account of how young Katy Butler successfully campaigned to change the movie's rating to make it available to teen viewers..

371.7 Student welfare

Cullen, David, 1961-

★**Parkland** : birth of a movement / Dave Cullen. HarperCollins 2019 385 p. **371.7**

1. National Rifle Association of America 2. High school students 3. School shootings 4. Gun control 5. Mass shootings 6. Florida

ISBN 9780062882943

LC bl2018196564

The author of Columbine offers a deeply moving account of the extraordinary teenage survivors of Parkland who became activists and pushed back against the NRA and Congressional leaders--inspiring millions of Americans to join their grassroots #neveragain movement.

"Cullen, the author of the groundbreaking Columbine (2009), brings his eloquence, expertise, combination of deep research and concision, and unbiased perspective to yet another mass school shooting, revealing its deepest layers and resonance." Booklist.

Grigoriadis, Vanessa

Blurred lines : rethinking sex, power, and consent on campus / Vanessa Grigoriadis. Houghton Mifflin Harcourt 2017 320 p. **371.7**

1. Rape 2. Universities and colleges 3. Rape victims 4. Violence in universities and colleges

ISBN 9780544702554

LC 2017297003

A National Magazine Award winner draws on extensive on-campus research to examine the sexual revolution of today's America, exploring such subjects as how young women are both protecting and expressing themselves, how young men are becoming more sensitive and aggressive and how schools can make college a safer experience.

"Grigoriadis adds context to the often-polarizing topics with numerous first-person accounts. Her view that 'we, as a society, are terrified to look at boys as boys rather than men and give them a break as such' seems to make excuses for criminal behavior. However, the breadth of her research, including her discussion of how university administrators deal with rape allegations and her exploration of toxic gender roles and stereotypes, are reason enough to pick up this book." Publishers Weekly.

Hirsch, Jennifer S.

Sexual citizens : a landmark study of sex, power, and assault on campus / Jennifer S. Hirsch and Shamus Khan. W.W. Norton & Company, 2020. 384 p. **371.7**

1. Rape 2. Universities and colleges 3. College students -- Sexuality 4. Power (Social sciences)

ISBN 9781324001706

LC bl2019037477

The fear of campus sexual assault has become an inextricable part of the college experience. Research has shown that by the time they graduate, as many as one in three women and almost one in six men will have been sexually assaulted. But why is sexual assault such a common feature of college life? And what can be done to prevent it? Drawing on the Sexual Health Initiative to Foster Transformation (SHIFT) at Columbia University, the most comprehensive study of sexual assault on a campus to date, Jennifer S. Hirsch and Shamus Khan present an entirely new framework that emphasizes sexual assault's social roots.

"Taking into account gender, sexuality, and race, Hirsch and Khan do an excellent job of exploring the complexities of sexual assault and how to make campuses safer for all students." Booklist.

Lysiak, Matthew

Newtown : an American tragedy / Matthew Lysiak. Gallery Books, 2013. 352 p. **371.7**

1. Sandy Hook Elementary School (Newtown, Conn.) 2. Sandy Hook Elementary School Shooting, Newtown, Conn., 2012 3. School shootings. 4. Mass shootings 5. Crimes against children. 6. Connecticut.

ISBN 9781476753744

LC 2013034956

Chronicling the horrific events of December 14, 2012, this first comprehensive account of the Sandy Hook shootings sheds new light on the unstable killer, Adam Lanza, and shows how this American tragedy became a lighting rod for political agendas, much like Columbine 10 years earlier.

371.8 Students

Robbins, Alexandra, 1976-

Fraternity : an inside look at a year of college boys becoming men / Alexandra Robbins. Dutton, [2019] 368 p. **371.8**

1. Fraternities 2. Campus life. 3. College students 4. Personal conduct

ISBN 9781101986721

LC 2018027905

An exploration of fraternity life in the twenty-first century examines the state of masculinity today and explores how fraternities provide support to boys at a vulnerable age as they make the complicated transition to manhood.

"This engaging behind-the-scenes account of fraternities, their traditions, and how they influence (a certain strain of) American men will interest college-bound students, their parents, and readers contemplating American culture." Publishers Weekly.

371.826 Students by miscellaneous social attributes

Cianciotto, Jason

LGBT youth in America's schools / Jason Cianciotto and Sean Cahill. The University of Michigan Press, 2012. 236 p. ; **371.826**

1. Bisexual students -- United States. 2. Gay students -- United States. 3. Homosexuality and education -- United States. 4. Lesbian students -- United States.

ISBN 0472031406

LC 2011045478

Jason Cianciotto and Sean Cahill, experts on lesbian, gay, bisexual, and transgender public policy advocacy, combine an accessible review of social science research with analyses of school practices and local, state, and federal laws that affect LGBT students. In addition, portraits of LGBT youth and their experiences with discrimination at school bring human faces to the issues the authors discuss. -- From publisher description.

"Organized into three sections (research, current policies, and an agenda for looking forward), Cianciotto and Cahill's treatise is an informative and compelling basis for continuing the discussion (especially as regards LGBT students of color) of how best to protect the rights of a vulnerable and largely disenfranchised group. While their approach is accessible enough for the concerned lay reader, policymakers and educational professionals will likely get the most out of this study." Publishers Weekly.

371.85 Greek-letter societies

Hechinger, John (John Edward)

★**True** gentlemen : the broken pledge of America's fraternities / John Hechinger. PublicAffairs, 2017. 306 p. **371.85**

1. Fraternities 2. College students 3. Personal conduct 4. Universities and colleges.

ISBN 9781610396820

LC 2017008179

A journalist investigates modern fraternity culture, particularly the embattled Sigma Alpha Epsilon, who have been involved in hazing rituals that resulted in deaths, racism and sexual assaults on campus and discusses whether or not an institution so broken can be saved.

"A highly disquieting but important investigation of one of the most influential subcultures in American higher education." Kirkus.

371.9 Special education

Flink, David

Thinking differently : an inspiring guide for parents of children with learning disabilities / David Flink. William Morrow, 2014 x, 308 p. : **371.9**

1. Attention-deficit hyperactivity disorder 2. Attention-deficit-disordered children -- Education 3. Learning disabilities 4. Learning disabled children -- Education

ISBN 9780062225931

LC 2015300888

"When parents are told their child has a learning disability, they need more information. Thinking Differently is just the resource to meet that need. David Flink, leader of Eye to Eye, a national mentoring program for children with learning differences,explains each learning disability in layman's terms to prepare parents to speak knowledgeably with teachers about their child's specific challenges..." Provided by publisher.

Kravets, Marybeth

The **K** & W guide to colleges for students with learning differences : 338 schools with programs or services for students with ADHD, Asd, or learning differences / Marybeth Kravets, MA and Imy F. Wax, MS. Penguin Random House, 2019 xi, 739 p. ; **371.9**

1. Learning disabilities 2. College choice 3. Universities and colleges -- United States

ISBN 9780525567899

LC bl2019004811

"338 schools with programs or services for students with ADHD, ASD, or learning differences"--Cover.

At head of title: The Princeton Review.

Includes index.

Hundreds of thousands of students with ADHD, Autism Spectrum Disorder, or other learning differences head to college every year. This comprehensive guide makes it easy for those students and their families and guidance counselors to tackle the daunting process of finding the school that fits their needs best. -- From publisher description

371.91 Students with physical disabilities

Marschark, Marc

★**How** deaf children learn : what parents and teachers need to know / Marc Marschark and Peter C. Hauser. Oxford University Press, 2012. ix, 156 p. : **371.91**

1. Deaf children -- Language 2. Deaf children -- Means of communication 3. Deaf -- Education 4. Parents of deaf children

ISBN 9780195389753

LC 2011012553

"The authors believe the best way to lead deaf children to academic success is by understanding who they are, what they know, and how they think. After reading this book, parents who may be feeling inadequate about their parenting skills or fearful about providing a good education for their deaf or hard-of-hearing child should be more at ease, and teachers will gain insight into the complexities involved in deaf education and be better equipped to teach these children." Library Journal.

371.93 Delinquent and problem students

Shalaby, Carla

Troublemakers : lessons in freedom from young children at school / Carla Shalaby. The New Press, 2017. 192 p. **371.93**

1. School children 2. Misbehavior 3. Punishment 4. Personal conduct
ISBN 9781620972366

LC 2016048199

"Teachers and noneducators alike will appreciate Shalaby's sensitive reorientation of the idea of troublemakers." Booklist.

371.950973 Gifted students--United States

Hulbert, Ann

Off the charts : the hidden lives and lessons of American child prodigies / Ann Hulbert. Alfred A. Knopf, 2018. 400 p. **371.950973**

1. Gifted children. 2. Child prodigies. 3. Success (Concept) 4. Children and success
ISBN 9781101947296

LC 2017003438

Presents an exploration of child genius through the stories of fifteen exceptionally gifted young people, from cybernetics founder Norbert Wiener and chess master Bobby Fischer to movie icon Shirley Temple and African-American musician Philippa Schuyler.

"In this beautifully written, thoroughly reported look at young 'geniuses,' Hulbert … poses fascinating questions about the roles of both genetics and pushy parents." Booklist.

371.96 Special education -- Students by socioeconomic status

Kozol, Jonathan

Savage inequalities : children in America's schools / Jonathan Kozol. Crown Pub., 1991. ix, 262 p. **371.96**

1. Children with social disabilities -- Education -- United States. 2. Minority children -- Education. 3. Segregation in education -- United States. 4. Urban education -- Social aspects.
ISBN 9780517582213

LC 91017574

ALA Notable Book, 1992.

National Book Critics Circle Award for Nonfiction finalist, 1991.

A look at the systematic denial of a good education to lower-class children in the United States and the built-in inequality of the public school system examines urban schools in Camden, Chicago, San Antonio, and other cities.

"Jonathan Kozol has written an impassioned book, laced with anger and indignation, about how our public education system scorns so many of our children. Savage Inequalities is also an important book, and warrants widespread attention." New York Times Book Review.

372 Primary education

Montessori, Maria, 1870-1952

★The **Montessori** method / Maria Montessori ; [translated from the Italian by Anne E. George] ; introduction by J. McV. Hunt. Schocken Books c1964. xxxix, 376 p. : **372**

1. Montessori method of education
ISBN 9780805209228

LC 64024014

Translation of Il metodo della pedagogia scientifica.

Reprint. Edition first published by Schocken Books in 1964 ; text unaltered from original edition.

This book is Montessori's own exposition of the theory behind her innovative educational techniques. She shows parents, teachers and administrators how to 'free a child to learn through his own efforts'. --Provided by publisher

372.21 Preschool education

Alvarez, Celine

The **natural** laws of children : why children thrive when we understand how their brains are wired / Celine Alvarez ; translated by Sherab Chodzin Kohn. Shambhala, 2019. viii, 354 p. : **372.21**

1. Education -- Experimental methods 2. Early childhood education -- Activity programs 3. Montessori method of education
ISBN 9781611806731

LC 2018050411

"Shambhala Publications is distributed worldwide by Penguin Random House, Inc., and its subsidiaries"--T.p. verso.

Originally published: Paris, France : Les Arnes, [2016], under title Les lois naturelles de l'enfant.

A powerful, neuroscience-based approach to revolutionize early childhood learning through natural creativity, strong human connections, spontaneous free play, and more. --From publisher description.

"An indispensable resource for teachers and parents alike, this highly readable book offers strategies, anecdotes, and evidence without downplaying the complexity of the cognitive science that informs it." Library Journal.

Christakis, Erika

The **importance** of being little : what preschoolers really need from grownups / Erika Christakis. Viking Press, 2016 384 p. **372.21**

1. Early childhood education 2. Preschool children 3. Learning 4. Children -- Personal conduct
ISBN 9780525429074

LC 2015044529

Drawing on her strong foundation in the study of child development and early education, as well as her classroom experience, the author challenges the conventional wisdom about early childhood, encouraging parents to rethink how and where young children learn best.

"A deep, provocative analysis of the current modes of teaching preschoolers and what should be changed to create a more effective learning environment for everyone." Kirkus.

372.210973 Day care--preschool education--United States

Tough, Paul

★**How** children succeed : grit, curiosity, and the hidden power of character / Paul Tough. Houghton Mifflin Harcourt, 2012. 256 p. **372.210973**

1. Early childhood education 2. Cognitive styles in children 3. Success (Concept) 4. Characters and characteristics
ISBN 9780547564654

LC 2012019000

"Well-written and bursting with ideas." Kirkus.

372.4 Reading

Cleaver, Samantha, 1981-
Raising an active reader : the case for reading aloud to engage elementary school youngsters / Samantha Cleaver. Rowman & Littlefield, 2020. xviii, 181 p.; **372.4**

1. Reading (Preschool) 2. Reading comprehension. 3. Literacy. 4. Active learning.
ISBN 9781475849288

LC 2019051662

"Raising an Active Reader explains research on reading aloud with children who are in early elementary school (grades K-3). Upon completion, adults will know how read aloud works for children who are learning to read, and how the ABCs of Active Reading (Ask questions, Build vocabulary, and make Connections) build important reading skills".--Provided by publisher.

"This book will prove a valuable resource for parents, teachers, and librarians on the vital topic of reading aloud. With many titles geared toward reading aloud to babies, toddlers, and preschoolers, this helpful work will be ideal for school libraries." Library Journal

Gurdon, Meghan Cox
The **enchanted** hour : the miraculous power of reading aloud in the age of distraction / Meghan Cox Gurdon. HarperCollins, 2019. 304 p. **372.4**

1. Books and reading 2. Reading aloud 3. Intellectual life 4. Cognitive neuroscience
ISBN 9780062562814

LC bl2018192389

A Wall Street Journal writer looks at how reading aloud makes adults and children smarter, happier, healthier, more successful and more closely attached, even as technology pulls in the other direction.

"Gurdon combines a consciously old-fashioned, anti-technology perspective with modern, data-driven cognitive arguments to advocate for face-to-face reading with children early and often. Gurdon focuses especially on the value of the picture book to build connection, regulate attention and emotional awareness, transmit cultural values, and give children feelings of mastery through repetition." Publishers Weekly.

Trelease, Jim
Jim Trelease's read-aloud handbook / [Jim Trelease] ; edited and revised by Cyndi Giorgis. PENGUIN BOOKS, 2019. 358 p. : **372.4**

1. Reading aloud
ISBN 9780143133797

LC 2019014911

"Portions of this book were originally published in pamphlet form"--T.p. verso.

"The Read-Aloud Handbook first published in Penguin Books 1982. First revised edition published 1985. Second revised edition (with the title The New Read-Aloud Handbook) published 1989"--T.p. verso.

The classic million-copy bestselling handbook on reading aloud to children -- revised and updated for a new generation of readers. --From publisher description.

"Like its predecessors, this is an excellent choice to recommend to parents and also useful for beginning teachers and librarians." School Library Journal.

372.42 Remedial reading

Fertig, Beth, 1966-
Why cant u teach me 2 read? : three students and a mayor put a city's schools to the test / Beth Fertig. Farrar, Straus and Giroux, 2009. 368 p. **372.42**

1. Reading -- Remedial teaching. 2. Reading disability. 3. Children with disabilities -- Education. 4. Learning disabilities. 5. New York City -- Social conditions.
ISBN 9780374299057

LC 2009011520

Evaluates current debates about the most effective methods by which children are being taught how to read, sharing the stories of three teenagers with learning disabilities who legally challenged their city schools to reevaluate their educational methods and purposes.

"This is an overall excellent, thoroughly grounding survey of the state of literacy and education." Publishers Weekly.

372.63 Spelling and handwriting

Maguire, James, 1959-
American bee : the National Spelling Bee and the culture of word nerds : the lives of five top spellers as they compete for glory and fame / James Maguire. Rodale, 2006. x, 371 p. ; **372.63**

1. National Spelling Bee. 2. Spelling ability. 3. Spelling bees.
ISBN 9781594862144

LC 2005037443

A narrative portrait of the America's national spelling bee competition offers insight into its subculture of young wordsmiths, competitive parents, and spectator tension, sharing the stories of five top contestants to offer insight into their ambitions and winning strategies.

372.67 Other oral presentations

Ford, Lyn, 1951-
★**Supporting** diversity and inclusion with story : authentic folktales and discussion guides / Lyn Ford and Sherry Norfolk, editors Libraries Unlimited, 2020. 126 p. **372.67**

1. Storytelling. 2. Multicultural education.
ISBN 9781440867071

LC 2019036532

Professional storytellers including editors Sherry Norfolk and Lyn Ford are deeply committed to bringing people together through story. In this book, they have identified a group of culturally diverse storytellers whose carefully researched tales authentically reflect the cultures from which they come. The book includes well-crafted, culturally authentic folktales contributed by storytellers of varying cultures and ethnicities. Commentaries from the contributors follow each tale, reflecting on the story and its significance to the culture it represents. Sets of questions for teachers and librarians also accompany each story to facilitate discussion.

373 Secondary education

Cullen, David, 1961-
Columbine / Dave Cullen. Twelve, 2009. x, 417 p. ; **373**

1. Columbine High School (Littleton, Colo.) 2. Columbine High

School Shooting, Littleton, Colo., 1999 3. Teenage murderers -- Psychology. 4. School shootings -- Littleton, Colorado. 5. News media. 6. Colorado.
ISBN 9780446546935

LC 2008031441

ALA Notable Book, 2010.

Edgar Allan Poe Award for Best Fact Crime, 2010.

Ten years in the making and a masterpiece of reportage, "Columbine" is an award-winning journalist's definitive account of one of the most shocking massacres in American history.

Hobbs, Jeff, 1980-

★**Show** them you're good : a portrait of boys in the City of Angels the year before college / Jeff Hobbs. Scribner, 2020. 336 p. **373**

1. High school seniors 2. Boys 3. Student achievement 4. College applicants 5. High school students 6. Los Angeles, California
ISBN 9781982116330

LC bl2020013211

Four teenage boys are high school seniors at two very different schools within the city of Los Angeles, the second largest school district in the nation with nearly 700,000 students. Author Jeff Hobbs, writing with heart, sensitivity, and insight, stunningly captures the challenges and triumphs of being a young person confronting the future--both their own and the cultures in which they live--in contemporary America.

"It's sure to cheer school librarians looking for true stories of male high school students known for something besides their athletic talents or troubles with the law. A unique slice of male high school life with strong crossover appeal for YA readers." Kirkus

373.18 Students--secondary education

Thorpe, Helen, 1965-

The **newcomers** : finding refuge, friendship, and hope in an American classroom / Helen Thorpe. Scribner, 2017. 416 p. **373.18**

1. Teenage immigrants 2. Teenage refugees 3. Education, Secondary 4. High school students
ISBN 9781501159091

LC bl2017036773

Traces the lives of twenty-two immigrant teens throughout the course of a year at Denver's South High School who attended a specially created English Language Acquisition class and who were helped to adapt through strategic introductions to American culture.

373.22 Private and public secondary schools

Brick, Michael, 1974-

Saving the school : the true story of a principal, a teacher, a coach, a bunch of kids, and a year in the crosshairs of education reform / Michael Brick. Penguin Press, 2012. 320 p. **373.22**

1. Garza, Anabel. 2. John H. Reagan High School (Austin, Tex.) 3. School improvement programs. 4. Educational reform. 5. High school principals. 6. High schools.
ISBN 9781594203442

LC 2011050569

Documents the efforts of a dedicated principal's year-long race to save a Texas high school from closure in the face of failing standards, teen dropout rates and jaded officials who sought to replace the public school with a charter company system.

373.236 Secondary education -- Lower level

Fagell, Phyllis L.

★**Middle** school matters : the 10 key skills kids need to thrive in middle school and beyond--and how parents can help / Phyllis L. Fagell, LCPC. Lifelong, 2019. xix, 298 p. ; **373.236**

1. Adolescence 2. Home and school 3. Middle school education -- Parent participation 4. Middle school students -- Social conditions
ISBN 9780738235080

LC 2019022000

"Middle school is its own important, distinct territory, and yet it's either written off as an uncomfortable rite of passage or lumped in with other developmental phases. Based on her many years working in schools, professional counselor Phyllis Fagell sees these years instead as a critical stage that parents can't afford to ignore (and though "middle school" includes different grades in various regions, Fagell maintains that the ages make more of a difference than the setting). Though the transition from childhood to adolescence can be tough for kids, this time of rapid physical, intellectual, moral, social, and emotional change is a unique opportunity to proactively build character and confidence. Fagell helps parents use the middle school years as a low-stakes training ground to teach kids the key skills they'll need to thrive now and in the future, including making good friend choices, negotiating conflict, regulating their own emotions, be their own advocates, and more. To answer parents' most common questions and struggles with middle school-aged children, Fagell combines her professional and personal expertise with stories and advice from prominent psychologists, doctors, parents, educators, school professionals, and middle schoolers themselves".-- Provided by publisher.

"Readers will appreciate Fagell's straightforward advice on the wide array of challenges that can appear during the influential years between elementary and high school. This is a must-read for all parents and educators of kids in this unique and often misunderstood age group." Booklist.

374 Adult education

Klein-Collins, Rebecca

Never too late : the adult student's guide to college / Rebecca Klein-Collins, with the Washington Monthly. The New Press, 2018. vi, 376 p. : **374**

1. Adult college students 2. Adult education
ISBN 9781620973219

LC 2018017798

"Distributed by Perseus Distribution"--T.p. verso.

This authoritative resource for adults who are applying to college or hoping to finish earning a degree is filled with a wealth of practical advice for those seeking a richer life and a meaningful place in our rapidly changing economy and world.

Rose, Mike (Michael Anthony)

Back to school : why everyone deserves a second chance at education / Mike Rose. New Press, The, 2012. 256 p. **374**

1. Adult learners. 2. Adult education. 3. Higher education. 4. Education.
ISBN 9781595587862

LC 2012021135

"It's a statistic that's sure to surprise: close to 45 percent of postsecondary students in the United States today do not enroll in college directly out of high school and many attend part-time. Following a tradition of self-improvement as old as the Republic, the 'nontraditional' college student is becoming the norm. Back to School is the first book to look at the schools that serve a growing population of 'second-chancers,' exploring what higher education--in the fullest sense of the term--can offer our rapidly changing society and why it is so critical to support the institutions that make it possible for millions of Americans to better their lot in life. In the anecdotal style of his bestselling Possible Lives, Rose crafts rich and moving vignettes of people in tough circumstances who find their way; who get a second . . . or third . . . or even fourth chance; and who, in a surprising number of cases, reinvent themselves as educated, engaged citizens. Rose reminds us that our nation's economic and civic future rests heavily on the health of the institutions that serve millions of everyday people-not simply the top twenty universities in U.S. News and World Report--and paints a vivid picture of the community colleges and adult education programs that give so many a shot at reaching their aspirations".-- Provided by publisher.

378 Higher education (Tertiary education)

Perkins, Anne Gardiner

Yale needs women : how the first group of girls rewrote the rules of an Ivy League giant / Anne Gardiner Perkins. Sourcebooks, [2019] xv, 367 p. **378**

1. Yale University -- History 2. Women college students 3. Sexism in education 4. Feminism 5. Sexism in universities and colleges 6. New Haven, Connecticut
ISBN 9781492687740

LC 2019024227

"Yale University, along with the rest of the Ivy League, kept its gates closed to women until the class of 1969. The reason for letting them in? As an incentive for men to attend. Yale Needs Women is the story of why the most elite schools in the nation refused women for so long, and what the first women to enter those halls faced when they stepped onto campus".-- Provided by publisher.

Selingo, Jeffrey J.

College (un)bound : the future of higher education and what it means for students / Jeffrey J. Selingo. Houghton Mifflin Harcourt, 2013. 224 p. **378**

1. Higher education -- Aims and objectives. 2. Universities and colleges -- United States. 3. College students -- United States. 4. Educational policy 5. United States -- Social conditions.
ISBN 9780544027077

LC 2013001941

Discusses the problems facing four-year colleges in the wake of the 2008 recession that left graduates with enormous debts and slim job prospects in a tough economy and describes institutions that are innovating to better prepare students in the future.

378.1 Organization and activities in higher education

Bain, Ken

What the best college students do / Ken Bain. The Belknap Press of Harvard University Press, 2012 289 p. ; **378.1**

1. Academic achievement -- United States 2. College students -- United States
ISBN 9780674066649

LC 2012015548

"A soundly encouraging guide for college students to think deeply and for as long as it takes." Kirkus.

Belasco, Andrew

The **enlightened** college applicant : a new approach to the search and admissions process / Andrew Belasco and Dave Bergman. Rowman & Littlefield, 2016 xi, 240 p. ; **378.1**

1. College choice -- United States 2. Universities and colleges -- United States -- Admission
ISBN 9781475826906

LC 2016032477

The Enlightened College Applicant presents a no-nonsense account of how students should approach the college search and admissions process. Instead of providing recycled entrance statistics or anecdotal generalizations about campus life, authors Belasco and Bergman incorporate cutting-edge data and research to pull back the curtain on critical topics. --From publisher description.

"Families seeking enlightenment about how to rationally and reasonably advise their teens in the higher-education arms race would do well to seek out this title." Booklist.

Brenner, Andrea (Andrea Malkin)

How to college : what to know before you go (and when you're there) / Andrea Malkin Brenner and Lara Hope Schwartz. St. Martin's Griffin, 2019. viii, 294 p. : **378.1**

1. College student orientation -- United States -- Handbooks, manuals, etc. 2. College freshmen -- United States -- Life skills guides. 3. College students -- United States -- Personal conduct 4. Higher education -- United States.
ISBN 9781250225184

LC 2019000551

A practical guide to help first-year students and their families transition smoothly from high school to college prepares students to succeed and thrive as they adapt to college.

"Some of the best advice comes from other college students and professors. Anyone planning to attend college will find this practical guide useful." Booklist.

Bruni, Frank

Where you go is not who you'll be : an antidote to the college admissions mania / Frank Bruni. Grand Central Pub., 2015 176 p. **378.1**

1. Universities and colleges -- Admission 2. College choice 3. Competition 4. Higher education
ISBN 9781455532704

LC 2014049043

"Written in a lively style but carrying a wallop, this is a book that family and educators cannot afford to overlook as they try to navigate the treacherous waters of college admissions." Kirkus.

Fiske, Edward B

Fiske guide to getting into the right college / Edward B. Fiske & Bruce G. Hammond. Sourcebooks, 2016 385 p. ; **378.1**

1. College choice -- United States 2. Universities and colleges -- United States -- Admission
ISBN 9781492633303

LC bl2016029392

Includes index.

Provides information on each step of the college admissions process, including selecting a college, writing application essays, handling college interviews, and obtaining financial aid.

Rosenfeld, Seth, 1956-

Subversives : the FBI's war on student radicals, and Reagan's rise to power / Seth Rosenfeld. Farrar, Straus and Giroux,

2012. 528 p. **378.1**

1. Reagan, Ronald. 2. Hoover, J. Edgar, 1895-1972 3. University of California, Berkeley Students -- History. 4. United States. Federal Bureau of Investigation. 5. Student movements -- Berkeley, California -- History. 6. College students -- Political activity -- Berkeley, California -- History. 7. Subversive activities -- Berkeley, California -- History. 8. California -- Politics and government -- 1951-

ISBN 9780374257002

LC 2011041204

A narrative report on the FBI's covert involvement with future President Ronald Reagan, radical Mario Savio and liberal university president Clark Kerr to suppress the 1960s student movement at Berkeley reveals J. Edgar Hoover's campaign of planted news stories, illegal break-ins and other acts designed to undermine the Democratic party.

Selingo, Jeffrey J.

There is life after college : what parents and students should know about navigating school to prepare for the jobs of tomorrow / Jeffrey J. Selingo. William Morrow, 2016 xix, 297 p. ; **378.1**

1. College students -- Vocational guidance -- United States 2. College student orientation -- United States 3. College graduates -- Employment -- United States

ISBN 9780062388865

LC 2015046199

"From the bestselling author of College Unbound comes a hopeful, inspiring blueprint to help alleviate parents' anxiety and prepare their college-educated child to successfully land a good job after graduation. Saddled with thousands of dollars of debt, today's college students are graduating into an uncertain job market that is leaving them financially dependent on their parents for years to come--a reality that has left moms and dads wondering: What did I pay all that money for? There Is Life After College offers students, parents, and even recent graduates the practical advice and insight they need to jumpstart their careers. Education expert Jeffrey Selingo answers key questions--Why is the transition to post-college life so difficult for many recent graduates? How can graduates market themselves to employers that are reluctant to provide on-the-job training? What can institutions and individuals do to end the current educational and economic stalemate?--and offers a practical step-by-step plan every young professional can follow. From the end of high school through college graduation, he lays out exactly what students need to do to acquire the skills companies want. Full of tips, advice, and insight, this wise, practical guide will help every student,no matter their major or degree, find real employment--and give their parents some peace of mind".-- Provided by publisher.

Who gets in and why : a year inside college admissions / Jeffrey J. Selingo. Scribner, 2020 xiv, 306 p. **378.1**

1. Universities and colleges -- Admission 2. Discrimination in universities and colleges 3. Inequality in education 4. Educational reform 5. United States

ISBN 9781982116293

LC bl2020018371

A higher-education journalist draws on insider access to explain the nuts and bolts of college admissions today, outlining the unexpected agendas that reflect which and why prospective students receive admission into better schools.

"This well-researched work is an invaluable tool for college-bound students and their families, guidance counselors, and college admissions personnel." Library Journal

Shachtman, Tom, 1942-

Airlift to America : how Barack Obama, Sr., John F. Kennedy, Tom Mboya, and 800 East African students changed their world and ours / Tom Shachtman. St. Martin's Press, 2009. 288 p. **378.1**

1. African-American Students Federation. 2. College students -- Africa, East -- History -- 20th century. 3. Africans in the United States. 4. Foreign students. 5. Universities and colleges. 6. United States -- Foreign relations East Africa. 7. East Africa -- Foreign relations United States.

ISBN 9780312570750

LC 2009013186

Describes how a brave group of individuals helped fly East African men and women, including the forty-fourth president's father and a future Nobel Prize winner, to schools in North America, an international transport effort that influenced presidential politics.

"In the late 1950s, before Kenya's independence from Britain, Kenyan leader Tom Mboya and American philanthropist William Scheinman joined to develop a cadre of educated young people to staff the government and schools. Between 1959 and 1963, nearly 800 African students were flown to the U.S. to be educated and to return to become the founding brothers and sisters of their East African nations. Among them were Wangari Maathai, who went on to become an environmentalist and 2004 Nobel Peace Prize winner, and Barack Obama Sr., father of the future president of the U.S. Shachtman provides historical perspective of cold war politics in African nations, countervailing loyalties to European colonial powers, and the appeal of U.S. ideals of independence." Booklist.

Steinberg, Jacques

The **gatekeepers** : inside the admissions process of a premier college / Jacques Steinberg. Viking, 2002. xxiii, 292 p. **378.1**

1. Wesleyan University (Middletown, Connecticutt) 2. Universities and colleges -- Admission -- Case studies.

ISBN 0670031356

LC 2002016884

A revealing study of the college admissions process sheds light on the inside workings of America's "meritocracy," focusing on SAT scores, student essays, transcripts, and other factors vital in the process.

"This insightful and readable book should be purchased by all academic and large public libraries." Library Journal.

Tough, Paul

The **years** that matter most : how college makes or breaks us / Paul Tough. Houghton Mifflin Harcourt, [2019] viii, 390 p. ; **378.1**

1. Universities and colleges -- Admission 2. College students -- Social conditions 3. Equal education policy 4. Social mobility

ISBN 9780544944480

LC 2019013123

Drawing on new research, the book reveals how the landscape of higher education has shifted in recent decades and exposes the hidden truths of how the system works and for whom it works. And it introduces us to the people who really make higher education go: admissions directors trying to balance the class and balance the budget, College Board officials scrambling to defend the SAT in the face of mounting evidence that it favors the wealthy, researchers working to unlock the mysteries of the college-student brain, and educators trying to transform potential dropouts into successful graduates.

"Drawing on broad reading and visits to campuses across the country, Tough's work offers an indictment of American society and political structures and persuasively argues that universities must fulfill the American commitment to equality of opportunity." Library Journal.

Ventrone, Jillian, 1973-

From the Marine Corps to college : transitioning from the service to higher education / Jillian Ventrone. Rowan & Littlefield, 2014 vii, 215 p. ; **378.1**

1. United States. Marine Corps. 2. Marines -- Education -- United States 3. Veterans -- Education -- United States
ISBN 9781442237209

LC 2014013314

"Despite its limitations, this title will appeal to marines and do well in libraries serving this population; otherwise, it is a supplemental purchase." Library Journal.

Shotton, Heather, 1976-

Beyond the asterisk : understanding Native students in higher education / edited by Heather Shotton, Shelly Lowe, and Stephanie J. Waterman. Stylus, 2013. xvi, 189 p. : **378.1**

1. Indian students -- United States 2. Indians of North America -- Education (Higher) -- United States
ISBN 9781579226237

LC 2012040238

As the editors note in their introduction, a critical element of higher education is understanding the students it serves. But there is little general understanding of Native American students in higher education, possibly because of their "invisibility" within the confines of academia. The contributors, some of them Native Americans, offer insights and a framework for understanding and providing for the needs of those students. Subjects discussed include: first-year experience for Native American freshmen, the historically Native American fraternity and sorority movement, incorporating native culture into student affairs, tribal college collaborations, how institutions can support native professional and graduate students, and best practices. --From publisher description.

378.19 Guidance, discipline, physical plant, welfare, students, curricula

Valverde, Leonard A.

The **Latino** student's guide to college success / Leonard A. Valverde, editor. Greenwood, c2012. xiv, 270 p. ; **378.19**

1. Hispanic Americans -- Education (Higher) 2. Universities and colleges -- United States
ISBN 9780313397974

LC 2012010827

Includes index.

"This book provides Latino students with a step-by-step roadmap for navigating the college process--from overcoming cultural barriers to attending college, to selecting the right school, to considering advanced degrees".--Provided by publisher.

378.3 Student aid and related topics

Collinge, Alan, 1970-

The **student** loan scam : the most oppressive debt in U.S. history, and how we can fight back / Alan Collinge. Beacon Press, c2009. 256 p. **378.3**

1. Student loans -- Corrupt practices 2. College graduates -- Personal finance 3. Debt -- United States. 4. Consumer protection -- Law and legislation 5. United States -- Politics and government -- 21st century
ISBN 9780807042298

LC 2008012230

"Comprehensive and stirring, this extraordinary book is whistle-blowing at its finest." Publishers Weekly.

Goldrick-Rab, Sara

Paying the price : college costs, financial aid, and the betrayal of the American dream / Sara Goldrick-Rab. The University of Chicago Press, 2016. 368 p. **378.3**

1. College costs 2. Student aid 3. Higher Education -- Economic aspects 4. Federal aid to higher education 5. Wisconsin
ISBN 9780226404349

LC 2016007474

For the last decade, sociologist Sara Goldrick-Rab has been studying what happens when economically vulnerable people try to make their way through public higher education.

"This cogent and persuasive argument for a more humane and efficient program to make higher education accessible to all capable students draws upon thorough research and an array of personal portraits. Highly recommended for parents and taxpayers." Library Journal.

378.73 Colleges--United States

Bok, Derek Curtis

The **struggle** to reform our colleges / Derek Bok. Princeton University Press, [2017] 228 p. **378.73**

1. Universities and colleges 2. Higher education 3. Student achievement 4. Educational reform 5. United States -- Social conditions
ISBN 9780691177472

LC 2017012202

Why efforts to improve American higher educational attainment haven't worked, and where to go from here.

Cottom, Tressie McMillan

★**Lower** ed : how for-profit colleges deepen inequality in America / Tressie Mcmillan Cottom. The New Press, 2016 256 p. **378.73**

1. Universities and colleges 2. Higher education 3. For-profit universities and colleges 4. Education 5. United States -- Social life and customs
ISBN 9781620970607

LC 2016048195

Drawing on her personal experience as a former counselor at two for-profit colleges and interviews with students, senior executives and activists, a renowned sociologist reveals how for-profit schools have become so successful and deciphers the benefits, credentials pitfalls and real costs of a for-profit education.

"The best book yet on the complex lives and choices of for-profit students." New York Times Book Review.

Delbanco, Andrew, 1952-

College : what it was, is, and should be / Andrew Delbanco. Princeton University Press, c2012. 229 p. **378.73**

1. Higher education. 2. Universities and colleges. 3. Education.
ISBN 9780691130736

LC 2011039399

"Recommended for academic and general audiences as a thoughtful, literate, and gracefully written reminder of what higher education needs to be." Library Journal.

Hacker, Andrew

Higher education? : how colleges are wasting our money and failing our kids, and what we can do about it / Andrew Hacker and Claudia Dreifus. Times Books, 2010. 288 p. **378.73**

1. Higher education. 2. Educational reform. 3. College costs -- United States. 4. College teachers -- United States.
ISBN 9780805087345
LC 2010007219
Includes index.

"Hacker and Dreifus draw up a powerful, if rambling, indictment of academic careerism. The authors are not shy about making biting judgments along the way. [They conclude] with capsule summaries of, as they put it, Schools We Like, that is, schools that offer superior undergraduate educations at relatively low cost." Wall Street Journal.

Mettler, Suzanne

Degrees of inequality : how the politics of higher education sabotaged the American dream / Suzanne Mettler. Basic Books, 2014. 320 p. **378.73**

1. Higher education -- Political aspects. 2. For-profit universities and colleges 3. Higher education policy 4. Universities and colleges -- Political aspects.
ISBN 9780465044962
LC 2013043678

An acclaimed political scientist describes how political partisanship, corporate interests and for-profit colleges have negatively impacted America's higher education system, which has been skewed to benefit only those in the highest income brackets.

"Though the book orbits the central theme of the for-profits and their outsized political influence, [Mettler] frames this with a history of higher education and its attendant laws, as well as an excellent introduction to political science that explains--in approachable language--the myriad impacts of law and the ways in which the intentions of legislators are often deformed." Publishers Weekly.

Williams, Juan

I'll find a way or make one : a tribute to historically Black colleges and universities / Juan Williams and Dwayne Ashley with Shawn Rhea. Amistad, c2004. xxiv, 453 p. : **378.73**

1. African American universities and colleges -- History. 2. African Americans -- Education -- History.
ISBN 0060094532
LC 2004046450

A commemorative exploration of the history and cultural significance of 108 American Historically Black Colleges and Universities discusses how post-Civil War abolitionists worked to formally educate newly freed slaves; provides a wealth of historical narrative, personal memoir, and archival material; and identifies prominent African-Americans who have graduated to become societal leaders.

"The authors explore America's 107 historically black colleges and universities, in existence for 172 years, showing how the schools were created and how black and white abolitionists united to educate newly freed slaves." Library Journal.

378.77137 Higher education--Portage County (Ohio)

Derf

Kent State : four dead in Ohio / Derf Backderf. Abrams ComicArts, 2020 288 p. **378.77137**

1. Kent State University. 2. Kent State shootings, May 4, 1970. 3. College students -- Political activity -- United States -- History -- 20th century 4. Vietnam War, 1961-1975 -- Protest movements. 5. Student movements -- United States -- History -- 20th century 6. Ohio -- History. 7. Comics and Graphic novels
ISBN 9781419734847
LC bl2020033759
Illustrated by the author.

A commemorative 50th anniversary graphic-novel account of the May 4, 1970 shootings of Vietnam War college student protesters by the Ohio National Guard draws on in-depth interviews to profile the tragedy's four victims.

"Backderf's tightly drawn, muscular figures and busy layouts anchored by choice period details are consistent with his established style, with flourishes (from hairstyles to smirks) that individualize the ensemble cast. His expertly crafted chronicle of this defining moment in U.S. history serves as a deeply moving elegy for the victims." Publishers Weekly

379 Public policy issues in education

Duncan, Arne

How schools work : an inside account of failure and success from one of the nation's longest-serving secretaries of education / Arne Duncan. Simon & Schuster 2018 352 p. **379**

1. Schools 2. Public schools 3. Educational policy 4. Education -- United States 5. United States -- Social conditions
ISBN 9781501173059
LC 2018016716

"Duncan's experienced perspective will interest anyone invested in American public education." Publishers Weekly.

379.1

Ravitch, Diane

The **death** and life of the great American school system : how testing and choice are undermining education / Diane Ravitch. Basic Books, 2009. 296 p. **379.1**

1. Public schools. 2. Educational reform. 3. School choice. 4. Educational planning.
ISBN 9780465014910
LC 2009050406

"The author provides an important and highly readable examination of the educational system, how it fails to prepare students for life after graduation, and how we can put it back on track. Anyone interested in education should definitely read this accessible, riveting book." Library Journal.

379.2 Specific policy issues in public education

Kozol, Jonathan

★The **shame** of the nation : the restoration of apartheid schooling in America / Jonathan Kozol. Three Rivers Press, 2006, c2005. 423 p. ; **379.2**

1. Segregation in education -- United States 2. Educational reform 3. Education -- United States -- Evaluation 4. Urban children -- Education 5. United States -- Politics and government -- 21st century 6. United States -- Social life and customs -- 20th century 7. United States -- Social life and customs -- 21st century
ISBN 9781400052455
LC bl2006022039
Originally published: New York : Crown Publishers, 2005.

An analysis of urban education argues that conditions have worsened for inner-city children, looking at how liberal education is being replaced by high-stakes testing procedures, culturally barren and robotic methods of instruction, and harsh discipline.

Margolick, David

Elizabeth and Hazel : two women of Little Rock / David Margolick. Yale University Press, 2011. 320 p. **379.2**

1. Eckford, Elizabeth, 1941- 2. Massery, Hazel Bryan, 1942- 3. Central High School, Little Rock, Arkanas -- History. 4. School integration -- Little Rock, Arkansas -- History. 5. African American students -- Little Rock, Arkansas -- History 6. Racism. 7. Interracial friendship 8. Little Rock, Arkansas -- Race relations

ISBN 9780300141931

LC 2011014101

Looks at the lives of the two women at the center of a famous historic photograph taken during the Little Rock school desegregation crisis in 1957, in a book that discusses how each dealt with the fallout from that day.

"Margolick draws on interviews and press reports of the time to present a very nuanced analysis of how Elizabeth and Hazel were affected by the scene that made them famous. . . . A complex look at two women at the center of a historic moment." Booklist.

Wilder, Craig Steven

★**Ebony** and ivy : race, slavery, and the troubled history of America's universities / Craig Wilder. Bloomsbury, 2013 352 p. **379.2**

1. Universities and colleges. 2. Race relations. 3. Slavery 4. Higher education. 5. United States -- History

ISBN 9781596916814

LC 2013011971

BCALA Literary Award for Nonfiction, 2014.

Hurston/Wright Legacy Award: Nonfiction, 2014.

A leading African-American historian of race in America exposes the uncomfortable truths about race, slavery and the American academy, revealing that our leading universities, dependent on human bondage, became breeding grounds for the racist ideas that sustained it.

"A groundbreaking history that will no doubt contribute to a reappraisal of some deep-rooted founding myths." Kirkus.

379.28 Place of religion in public schools

Greenawalt, Kent, 1936-

Does God belong in public schools? / Kent Greenawalt. Princeton University Press, c2005. x, 261 p. ; **379.28**

1. Religion in the public schools 2. Educational policy 3. Religion in the public schools -- Law and legislation 4. Educational reform 5. United States -- Politics and government -- 20th century 6. United States -- Politics and government -- 21st century

ISBN 0691121117

LC 2004045779

"The author considers issues ranging from the teaching of evolution to parents' rights that their children not be exposed to offensive curriculum. He grounds his analyses in a review of the history and purposes of schooling. His legal and philosophical lines of scholarship come together to produce a nonpartisan consideration of the crucial issues facing US courts and the country." Choice.

381 Commerce (Trade)

Fili, Louise

The **cognoscenti's** guide to Florence : shop and eat like a Florentine / Louise Fili & Lise Apatoff. Princeton Architectural Press, 2017. 224 p. **381**

1. Shopping -- Florence, Italy 2. Restaurants -- Florence, Italy 3. Walking -- Florence, Italy 4. Florence, Italy

ISBN 9781616896362

Shop and eat like a Florentine with this pocket-sized guide to the best of the magnificent Tuscan city known for its art, culture, and cuisine. Celebrated graphic designer and self-described Italophile Louise Fili, with connoisseur of all things Lisa Apatoff, takes you on eight walks through Florence, discussing more than seventy of the city's most alluring shop -- some run by the same families for generations, others offering young entrepreneurs' fresh interpretations of traditional techniques. --From publisher description.

Jacobs, Ryan McMahon, 1989-

The **truffle** underground : a tale of mystery, mayhem, and manipulation in the shadowy market of the world's most expensive fungus / Ryan Jacobs. Clarkson Potter, 2019. vi, 279 p. **381**

1. Truffles 2. Mushrooms 3. Black market 4. Cooking (Truffles) 5. France 6. Italy

ISBN 9780451495693

LC 2018053998

"This deeply researched and eye-opening account of the lengths people will go for wealth, gratification, and a taste of the prized fungus will captivate readers." Publishers Weekly.

Minter, Adam, 1970-

Secondhand : travels in the new global garage sale / Adam Minter. Bloomsbury, 2019. 304 p. **381**

1. Consumerism 2. Secondhand industry and trade 3. Consumer behavior 4. Used clothing

ISBN 9781635570106

LC bl2019027524

From the author of Junkyard Planet comes a global exploration of the hidden market for used stuff and a travelogue that follows unwanted, obsolescent objects? journeys into a reusable future.

381.4 Commerce (Trade)--Specific products and services

Lorr, Benjamin

The **secret** life of groceries : the dark miracle of the American supermarket / Benjamin Lorr. Avery, 2020 328 p. ; **381.4**

1. Supermarkets -- United States -- Management. 2. Food industry and trade. 3. Grocery industry and trade 4. Grocery industry and trade employees

ISBN 9780553459395

LC 2020004949

"An extraordinary investigation into the human lives at the heart of the American grocery store. What does it take to run the American supermarket? How do products get to shelves? Who sets the price? And who suffers the consequences of increased convenience end efficiency? In this alarming exposé, author Benjamin Lorr pulls back the curtain on this highly secretive industry. Combining deep sourcing, immersive reporting, and compulsively readable prose, Lorr leads a wild investigation in which we learn: The secrets of Trader Joe's success from Trader Joe himself, Why truckers call their job 'sharecropping on wheels,'

What it takes for a product to earn certification labels like 'organic' and 'fair trade.'

"Lorr's exploration of the systems and individuals that create the modern grocery store will move readers to ask far more probing questions about what they're putting on the table. For fans of Michael Pollan's work and Michael Ruhlman's Grocery (2017)." Booklist

384 Communications

Basinger, Jeanine

The **star** machine / Jeanine Basinger. A. A. Knopf, 2007. xiv, 586 p. : **384**

1. Film industry and trade -- Los Angeles, California -- History 2. Film actors and actresses -- United States 3. Films -- History 4. United States -- Social life and customs -- 20th century

ISBN 9781400041305

LC 2007005268

In an entertaining compilation of Hollywood lore, trivia, and analysis, a leading film historian provides a close-up look at the golden era of filmmaking and the creation of stars at the height of the studio system, from the 1930s to the 1950s, explaining how the star machine worked, the grooming of actors, and the careers of such actors as Tyrone Power, Errol Flynn, Lana Turner, and others.

Goldman, William, 1931-2018

Adventures in the screen trade : a personal view of Hollywood and screenwriting / William Goldman. Warner Books, 1984, c1983. xiii, 594 p. ; **384**

1. Goldman, William, 1931-2018 Motion picture plays. 2. Screenplay writing 3. Film industry and trade 4. Screenwriters. 5. Film production services.

ISBN 9780446391177

LC BL 99758446

Includes index.

The Academy Award-winning screenwriter and bestselling author combines observations on Hollywood stars, studios, power plays, filming, directors, and producers with a point-by-point review of script writing

Which lie did I tell? : more adventures in the screen trade / William Goldman. Vintage Books, 2001, c2000. x, 485 p. ; **384**

1. Goldman, William, 1931-2018 2. Film industry and trade -- United States. 3. Screenplay writing. 4. Screenwriters -- United States 5. Hollywood, California -- History.

ISBN 9780375703195

LC BL2001000876

Includes index.

Originally published: New York : Pantheon Books, c2000.

An insider's take on Hollywood shares behind-the-scenes views of celebrities.

"An engaging expose that is not mean-spirited; recommended for public and academic libraries and film collections." Library Journal.

384.55 Television

Hastings, Reed, 1960-

No rules rules : Netflix and the culture of reinvention / Reed Hastings and Erin Meyer. Penguin Press, 2020. 288 p. **384.55**

1. Hastings, Reed, 1960- 2. Netflix (Firm) Management 3. Netflix (Firm) Employees Interviews 4. Chief executive officers 5. Corporate culture 6. Adaptability (Psychology) 7. Communication in organizations

ISBN 9781984877864

LC 2019058039

Includes index.

Netflix cofounder Reed Hastings reveals for the first time the unorthodox culture behind one of the world's most innovative, imaginative, and successful companies. There has never before been a company like Netflix. It has led nothing short of a revolution in the entertainment industries, generating billions of dollars in annual revenue while capturing the imaginations of hundreds of millions of people in over 190 countries. But to reach these great heights, Netflix has had to reinvent itself over and over again. This type of unprecedented flexibility would have been impossible without the counterintuitive and radical management principles that cofounder Reed Hastings established from the very beginning. Hastings rejected the conventional wisdom under which other companies operate and defied tradition to instead build a culture focused on freedom and responsibility, one that has allowed Netflix to adapt and innovate as the needs of its members and the world have simultaneously transformed.

"Aspiring tech moguls should flock to Hastings and Meyer's energetic and fascinating account." Publishers Weekly

Napoli, Lisa, 1963-

Up all night : Ted Turner, CNN, and the birth of 24-hour news / Lisa Napoli. Harry N. Abrams, 2020. 304 p. **384.55**

1. Turner, Ted 2. CNN 3. Current events. 4. Broadcast journalism 5. Mass media

ISBN 9781419743061

LC bl2020013378

Blends media and history in an account of the founding of CNN by Ted Turner and a motley assortment of cable-television visionaries, big-league rejects and non-union newcomers, whose collective successes exceeded their wildest ambitions.

"A page-turning hybrid of biography, media analysis, and business history." Kirkus

385 Railroad transportation

Ambrose, Stephen E.

Nothing like it in the world : the men who built the transcontinental railroad, 1863-1869 / Stephen E. Ambrose. Simon & Schuster, 2000. 471 p. : **385**

1. Central Pacific Railroad -- History 19th century. 2. Union Pacific Railroad -- History 19th century. 3. Transcontinental railroad (United States) 4. Railroads -- United States -- History -- 19th century. 5. Railroad construction workers. 6. Railroad workers -- United States -- History -- 19th century. 7. The West (United States) -- History -- 19th century. 8. United States -- History -- 19th century.

ISBN 0684846098

LC 00041005

Chronicles the race to finish the transcontinental railroad in the 1860s and the exploits, sacrifices, triumphs, and tragedies of the individuals who made it happen.

"Ambrose's scholarship seems impeccable. . . . He writes a brisk, colloquial, straightforward prose that not only is easy to read but also bears the reader on shoulders of wonder and excitement. " New York Times Book Review.

McCommons, James, 1957-

Waiting on a train : the embattled future of passenger rail service / James McCommons ; foreword by James Howard Kunstler. Chelsea Green Pub. Company, 2009. 304 p. **385**

1. Amtrak. 2. Railroads -- United States. 3. Train passengers. 4. Train rides. 5. Transportation -- United States. 6. United States -- Description and travel.

ISBN 9781603580649

LC 2009030142

Includes index.

McCommons spent much of 2008 on Amtrak researching this book. Here he celebrates the joy of train-riding and, gracefully preaches its efficiency together with a sketch of passenger train history, its current progress, the oil- and votes-loving opponents, and the proponents--even among the freight roads' executives. One UP executive spoke the company line about its obligation to move Amtrak over the road expeditiously: "...we don't care." A fine primer on economics, politics, engineering. --From publisher description.

"Essential reading for rail fans, policymakers, and anyone curious about the future of transportation." Library Journal.

Parks, Tim

Italian ways : on and off the rails from Milan to Palermo / Tim Parks. W.W. Norton & Company, 2013. 320 p. **385**

1. Parks, Tim Travel Italy. 2. Railroad travel -- Italy. 3. Transportation -- Italy 4. Train passengers. 5. Train rides. 6. Italy -- Description and travel. 7. Italy -- Social life and customs.

ISBN 9780393239324

LC 2013011386

English ex-pat Tim Parks (a resident in Italy since 1981) explores the wonderful, awful experience of traveling Italy with wry, insightful humor. Riding the rails from Italy top to bottom presents an up-close experiences of Italian life, past and present. With memorable vignettes of those he meets along the way (many of whom hate the train system) interspersed with railway history (he boards cars from pre-World War II, to modern high-speed ones), this entertaining travelogue delivers a slice of Italian culture at large.

385.09 Railroad atlases--specific areas

Zoellner, Tom

Train : riding the rails that created the modern world - from the Trans-Siberian to the Southwest Chief / Tom Zoellner. Viking Adult, 2014. 384 p. **385.09**

1. Trans-Siberian Railway 2. Trains 3. Railroads -- History. 4. Railroad travel 5. Public transportation.

ISBN 9780670025282

LC 2013036816

Do you love trains or wonder what the world would be like without them? Then climb on board the Train express! Combining fascinating social history and a sparkling travelogue, author (and train buff) Tom Zoellner engagingly chronicles the innovation and sociological impact of railway technologies that have changed and continue to change the world. Lucky him, he also travels to such far-flung locales as India, Britain, Russia, China, Peru, Spain, and the United States, soaking up local culture and riding an assortment of trains, from old stalwarts to modern bullet trains.

"An absorbing and lively reflection on an enduring marvel of modern industrial technology." Booklist.

385.0973 Railroad transportation--United States

Hiltzik, Michael A.

Iron empires : robber barons, railroads, and the making of modern America / Michael Hiltzik. Houghton Mifflin Harcourt, 2020. 416 p. **385.0973**

1. Big business 2. Capitalists and financiers 3. Industrialists 4. Railroads 5. United States -- Economic conditions -- 1865-1918. 6. United States -- History -- 1865-1921.

ISBN 9780544770317

LC 2019033911

"From Pulitzer Prize-winner Michael Hiltzik, the epic tale of the clash for supremacy between America's railroad titans".-- Provided by publisher.

"Pulitzer Prize-winning Los Angeles Times journalist Hiltzik chronicles the men who controlled the colossal railroad organizations that transformed the United States during the 19th century. . . . Lively storytelling and accessible writing makes Hiltzik's work suitable for all types of readers interested in railroad history." Library Journal

387.1 Ports

Dolin, Eric Jay

Brilliant beacons : a history of the American lighthouse / Eric Jay Dolin. Liveright Publishing Corporation, 2016 448 p. **387.1**

1. United States. Bureau of Light-Houses -- History. 2. United States. Lighthouse Service -- History. 3. Lighthouses.

ISBN 9780871406682

LC 2015044089

A history of America as reflected by the nation's lighthouses combines rich maritime lore with original details to trace coastal political, military and technological expansions, citing the roles of key contributors and incorporating more than 100 photos and illustrations.

"A delightful journey with excellent sketches, renderings, and resources for museums and organizations." Kirkus.

387.2 Ships

Graham, Ian, 1953-

Fifty ships that changed the course of history : a nautical history of the world / Ian Graham. Firefly Books, 2016. 224 p. : **387.2**

1. Ships -- History. 2. Navigation -- History.

ISBN 9781770857193

LC bl2018012054

Looks at fifty ships that have influenced human civilization and world history from ancient times to the present, covering such famous vessels as the Amistad, the Mayflower, the Bismarck, and the HMS Beagle.

"Well researched and illustrated, this 'reference-y' title will be a good addition to any collection covering seafaring and transport." Booklist.

Henry, John, 1939-

Great White Fleet : celebrating Canada Steamship Lines passenger ships / John Henry ; foreword by Paul Martin. Dundurn Press, c2013. 142 p. : **387.24309710904**

1. Canada Steamship Lines -- History. 2. Passenger ships -- History -- 20th century. 3. Steamboats 4. Voyages and travels 5. North

Atlantic Region 6. North Atlantic Ocean
ISBN 1459710460
The history of the passenger steamers of Canada Steamship Lines. Known as the Great White Fleet, Canada Steamship Lines operated 51 passenger steamers from 1913-1965 that plied the waterways from the Great Lakes to the St. Lawrence Seaway.

387.5 Ocean transportation (Marine transportation)

Ujifusa, Steven
Barons of the sea : and their race to build the world's fastest clipper ship / Steven Ujifusa. Simon & Schuster, 2018. xiv, 427 pages : **387.5**
1. Clipper-ships. 2. Shipping industry and trade. 3. Shipping -- United States -- History. 4. Import export business -- China.
ISBN 9781476745978
LC 2017037340
Describes the competition between merchants who imported luxury goods from China during the 1800s and their cutthroat race to build the best, fastest and most profitable clipper ships to promote their genteel, but sordid business.
"A vivid account of larger-than-life if not always attractive characters and a technological marvel that briefly captivated the Victorian world." Kirkus.

387.7 Air transportation

Holmes, Richard, 1945-
Falling upwards : how we took to the air / Richard Holmes. Pantheon Books, c2013. 400 p. **387.7**
1. Balloonists -- History. 2. Ballooning -- History. 3. Balloons (Aeronautics) 4. Aviation -- History
ISBN 9780307379665
LC 2013011128
Documents the experiences of the enigmatic pioneers of human flight including Sophie Blanchard, John Wise and Felix Nadar to offer insight into the character qualities that inspired their ambitions and the ways in which their achievements have shaped culture, technology and meteorology. By the award-winning author of The Age of Wonder.

388 Transportation

McPhee, John, 1931-
Uncommon carriers / John McPhee. Farrar, Straus, and Giroux, 2006. 248 p. ; **388**
1. Freight and freightage. 2. Transportation. 3. Trucking industry and trade 4. Trains.
ISBN 9780374280390
LC 2006007953
A staff writer for The New Yorker recounts his experiences with the freight transportation workers he has encountered during rides between Atlanta and Tacoma, from an eighteen-wheel hazmat tank operator to the skipper of a twenty-foot scale model of an ocean liner.
"The author sums up eight years of riding around with people who haul freight in vehicles ranging from 18-wheelers to towboats." Library Journal.

388.09 Transportation -- History, geographic treatment, biography

Humes, Edward
Door to door : the magnificent, maddening, mysterious world of transportation / Edward Humes. Harper, 2016 384 p. **388.09**
1. Transportation -- History. 2. Communication and traffic 3. Infrastructure 4. Transportation planning
ISBN 9780062372079
LC 2015037315
A Pulitzer Prize-winning journalist discusses the truths and challenges behind our modern world of transportation, describes the car culture that built modern America and predicts a coming revolution that stands to change every aspect of our lives.
"This timely book will inspire many readers to change their habits and their views of the future." Booklist.

388.1 Roads

Conover, Ted
The **routes** of man : how roads are changing the world, and the way we live today / Ted Conover. Alfred A. Knopf, 2010. 352 p. **388.1**
1. Conover, Ted Travel 2. Roads -- Social aspects. 3. Voyages and travels. 4. Travelers.
ISBN 9781400042449
LC 2009024007
Explores how roads literally and metaphorically bind the world and change its landscape, citing examples in such regions as China, the Andes, and the West Bank.
"A readable, fact-filled, well-written exploration of how roads work, for good and ill, and what their future likely holds." Kirkus.

Mask, Deirdre
The **address** book : what street addresses reveal about identity, race, wealth, and power / Deirdre Mask. St. Martin's Press, 2020. 320 p. **388.1**
1. Urban planning 2. Street names 3. Social classes 4. Inequality 5. United States -- Social conditions
ISBN 9781250134769
LC 2019048694
Tells the story of how streets got their names and houses their numbers, and why something as seemingly mundane as an address can save lives or enforce power.
"An impressive book-length answer to a question few of us consider: 'Why do street addresses matter? . . . combines deep research with skillfully written, memorable anecdotes to illuminate the vast influence of street addresses as well as the negative consequences of not having a fixed address . . . A standout book of sociological history and current affairs." Kirkus

388.4 Local transportation

Lashinsky, Adam
Wild ride : inside Uber's quest for world domination / Adam Lashinsky. Portfolio, 2017. 288 p. **388.4**
1. Uber (Firm). 2. Ridesharing. 3. Entrepreneurship 4. Computer

industry and trade 5. High technology
ISBN 9780735211391

LC 2017006832

Describes the history of Uber and the startup's rapid growth, including its contributions to on-demand economy and the mobile revolution while also fighting politicians and tax companies all around the world and the company's expansion into vastly different industries.

390 Customs, etiquette, folklore

Jenkins, Jessica Kerwin

All the time in the world : a book of hours / Jessica Kerwin Jenkins. Nan A. Talese/Doubleday, 2013 303 p. : **390**

1. Manners and customs 2. Time 3. Literary curiosities 4. Life
ISBN 9780385535410

LC 2013000795

A follow-up to Encyclopedia of the Exquisite presents a miscellany of engaging stories about intriguing customs, traditions and guilty pleasures pursued throughout history, from the day-long ceremony of laying a royal Elizabethan tablecloth to Nostradamus's beliefs about the aphrodisiac power of jam.

390.09 Customs, etiquette & folklore--History, geographic treatment, biography

Sagan, Sasha (Alexandra Rachel Druyan)

For small creatures such as we : rituals for finding meaning in our unlikely world / Sasha Sagan. G. P. Putnam's Sons, 2019. 304 p. **390.09**

1. Sagan, Sasha (Alexandra Rachel Druyan). 2. Sagan, Sasha (Alexandra Rachel Druyan) Family. 3. Rites and ceremonies 4. Spirituality 5. Nature 6. Secularism
ISBN 9780735218772

LC 2019021246

The daughter of astronomer Carl Sagan and writer Ann Druyan describes how motherhood inspired her investigations into the phenomena behind treasured human milestones to provide her daughter with a secular appreciation of the natural world.

391 Customs

Bari, Shahidha K.

Dressed : a philosophy of clothes / Shahidha Bari. Basic Books, 2020. 330 p. **391**

1. Fashion 2. Costume -- History 3. Identity (Philosophical concept) 4. Philosophy
ISBN 9781541645981

LC 2019033789

We all get dressed. But how often do we pause to think about the place of our clothes in our world? What unconscious thoughts do we express when we dress every day? Dressed ranges freely from suits to suitcases, from Marx's coat to Madame X's gown. Through art and literature, film and philosophy, philosopher Shahidha Bari unveils the surprising personal implications of what we choose to wear. The impeccable cut of Cary Grant's suit projects masculine confidence, just as Madonna's oversized denim jacket and her armful of orange bangles loudly announces big ambition. How others dress tells us something fundamental about them -- we can better understand how people live and what they think through their garments. Clothes tell our stories.

"Devoted fashion students will eagerly eat up every word of Bari's well-researched and passionate work." Publishers Weekly

DeJean, Joan E.

The **essence** of style : how the French invented high fashion, fine food, chic cafes, style, sophistication, and glamour / Joan DeJean. Free Press, 2005. 303 p. : **391**

1. Louis XIV, King of France, 1638-1715 Influence. 2. Fashion -- France -- History -- 17th century. 3. Cooking, French -- History -- 17th century. 4. Haute cuisine 5. France -- Social life and customs -- 17th century
ISBN 0743264134

LC 2005040019

An exploration of how French culture during the reign of Louis XIV has had an enduring influence on modern traditions and style cites the French origins of haute cuisine, interior design, and the consumption of celebratory champagne.

"An unusual and delightfully educational perspective on snob appeal." Booklist.

Edwards, Lydia (Lydia Jenny)

How to read a dress : a guide to changing fashion from the 16th to the 20th century / Lydia Edwards. Bloomsbury Academic, 2017. 211 p. : **391**

1. Women's clothing -- History. 2. Fashion -- History.
ISBN 9781472533272

LC 2016029748

Fashion is ever-changing, and while some styles mark a dramatic departure from the past, many exhibit subtle differences from year to year that are not always easily identifiable. With overviews of each key period and detailed illustrations for each new style, How to Read a Dress is an authoritative visual guide to women's fashion across five centuries. --From publisher description.

"Although the intended audience is fashion students, anyone interested in history or women's fashion will enjoy this volume." Booklist.

Esquire, inc,

Esquire dress code : a man's guide to personal style / Esquire Hearst Books, 2019 191 p. : **391**

1. Men's clothing 2. Clothing and dress 3. Fashion
ISBN 9781618372826

LC bl2019029401

Includes index.

Clothes make the man, and Esquire Dress Code helps you put together a great wardrobe. Visually bold, and told with Esquire's signature wit and humor, this sophisticated guide explains how to dress for any occasion, no matter your age, shape, or size. It covers closet must-haves, investment pieces (like a watch or winter coat), choosing the perfect suit, selecting office attire, outerwear, and accessories, and much more. Inspiring photos of style icons range from Mick Jagger and Steve McQueen to Lenny Kravitz and Robert Redford. Fashion might change from season to season, but once a man learns to adapt these fashion fundamentals for his personal look, he'll be set for life. --From publisher description.

"Given the wayward nature of fashion trends, this guide will help the discerning consumer work a foundation for tried-and-true looks." Booklist.

Kelly, Clinton

Dress your best : the complete guide to finding the style that's right for your body / Clinton Kelly and Stacy London. Three

Rivers Press, c2005. 255 p. : **391**

1. Clothing and dress -- Psychological aspects. 2. Fashion -- Psychological aspects.

ISBN 9780307236715

LC 2005013681

Presents a guide to fashion for the modern man or woman, offering tips on different male and female body types, how to select the right outfit for every occasion, great fashion for every budget, and other suggestions.

Moses, Susan

The **art** of dressing curves : the best-kept secrets of a fashion stylist / Susan Moses, with Jelani Bandele ; foreword by Emme. Harper Design, 2016. 254 p. : **391**

1. Fashion. 2. Women's clothing. 3. Overweight women -- Clothing. 4. Beauty

ISBN 9780062362032

LC bl2016016326

Presents a style guide for plus-size women who want to dress fashionably, covering such topics as foundation garments, hair styles, and makeup tips.

391.009 History, geographic treatment, biography

Cox, Caroline

The **world** atlas of street fashion / Caroline Cox. Yale University Press, 2017 399 p. : **391.009**

1. Fashion -- History -- 21st century. 2. Fashion -- History -- 20th century. 3. Clothing and dress -- History -- 21st century. 4. Clothing and dress -- History -- 20th century.

ISBN 9780300224030

LC bl2018004000

Includes index.

A global tour of street fashion, organized by continent, shows the history of each look and how it has developed over time.

Leventon, Melissa

What people wore when : a complete illustrated history of costume from ancient times to the nineteenth century for every level of society / Melissa Leventon. St. Martin's Griffin, 2008. 352 p. : **391.009**

1. Clothing -- History

ISBN 9780312383213

LC 2008012938

A history of costume and fashion spanning the civilizations of ancient Greece and Egypt through nineteenth-century Europe, including the clothing, footwear, accessories, and hairstyles of individuals from all levels of society.

"This attractive book will appeal to teens looking for quick answers for a last-minute assignment, and it will also be of interest to budding fashionistas and social historians. Leventon has combined current research on costume and dress through the ages with the detailed beauty of the work of two 19th-century illustrators, Auguste Racinet and Friedrich Hottenroth, to provide a historical and thematic examination of fashion and dress that is both comprehensive and readable." School Library Journal.

Stevenson, N. J.

Fashion : a visual history from regency & romance to retro & revolution : a complete illustrated chronology of fashion from the 1800s to the present day / NJ Stevenson. St. Martin's Griffin, 2012, c2011. 288 p. : **391.009**

1. Clothing and dress -- History. 2. Fashion -- History -- 19th century. 3. Fashion -- History -- 20th century. 4. Fashion -- History -- 21st century.

ISBN 031262445X

LC 2011278257

A chronological look at fashion trends from the Regency period to the current day discusses the evolution of the designer, key styles that defined each fashion movement, and the connection between fashion and society.

391.5 Hairstyles

Dabiri, Emma

Twisted : the tangled history of Black hair culture / Emma Dabiri. Harper Perennial, 2020, c2019. 259 p. : **391.5**

1. Identity (Psychology) 2. Feminism 3. Racism 4. Discrimination

ISBN 9780062966728

Originally published in Great Britain with the title Don't touch my hair : Penguin Books, 2019.

Describes the stigmatism of black hair and its encoded racism through history, from pre-colonial Africa through the Harlem Renaissance, to the modern Natural Hair Movement.

"Part memoir, part social history, and sure to become the definitive book on the politics, culture, and economics of black hair." Kirkus

Tarlo, Emma

Entanglement : the secret lives of hair / Emma Tarlo. Oneworld Publications, 2016. 320 p. **391.5**

1. Hair 2. Wigs 3. Haircutting 4. Culture

ISBN 9781780749921

LC bl2016051771

"From eccentric wig makers in China to hair hunters in India and customers in Europe, Tarlo takes us on an eye-opening journey that will make us wonder if our own hair doesnt have a secret life of its own." Booklist.

391.6 Personal appearance

Aitken-Smith, Trent

The **tattoo** dictionary : an A-Z guide to choosing your tattoo / Trent Aitken-Smith ; illustrated by Ashley Tyson. Mitchell Beazley, 2016. 255 p. : **391.6**

1. Tattooing 2. Tattooing -- Pictorial works

ISBN 9781784721770

LC bl2017046237

Includes index.

A book that includes over one hundred tattoo designs explains the true meanings behind them, from sailors' swallows and Mexican skulls to prisoners' barbed wire and intricate Maori patterns.

Eldridge, Lisa, 1974-

Face paint : the story of makeup / Lisa Eldridge. Abrams Image, 2015. 240 p. : **391.6**

1. Cosmetics -- History

ISBN 9781419717963

LC 2014959338

Reveals the entire history of the art form of makeup, from Egyptian and Classical times through the Victorian age and Golden Era of Hollywood, and also examines the cutting-edge makeup science of today and tomorrow.

392 Customs of life cycle and domestic life

Feiler, Bruce, 1964-

Life is the story you tell yourself : mastering transitions in a nonlinear age / Bruce Feiler. Penguin Press, 2020. 352 p. **392**

1. Personal conduct 2. Life change events 3. Change (Psychology) 4. Human life cycle
ISBN 9781594206825

LC 2019044488

The best-selling author of Council of Dads presents a pioneering study of the disruptions that are upending contemporary life, outlining bold recommendations for how to manage today's incremental transitions with more meaning, balance and satisfaction.

"All this advice is laid out in logical, sequential chapters, and occasional graphs and checklists bolster Feiler's reasoning. His relaxed, informal style is reassuring, and the numerous anecdotes gleaned from his wide variety of interview subjects keep the narrative fresh. His encouraging counsel will appeal to many." Booklist

392.5 Wedding and marriage customs

Jellison, Katherine, 1960-

It's our day : America's love affair with the white wedding, 1945-2005 / Katherine Jellison. University Press of Kansas, c2008. xi, 297 p. : **392.5**

1. Marriage customs and rites -- United States. 2. United States -- Social life and customs -- 1945-1970. 3. United States -- Social life and customs -- 1971-
ISBN 0700615598

LC 2007035444

A comprehensive cultural history of American weddings since World War II examines the development of the precise and expensive standards for celebrating weddings and the staying power of this phenomenon despite social, political, and economic upheaval.

"The author takes an in-depth look at the history and popularity of the American white wedding and in doing so provides a unique exploration of late 20th- and early 21st-century American culture. She starts right after World War II and progresses through celebrity, royal, and movie weddings to the reality weddings of today and how the ritual of a white wedding has been adapted in many same-sex marriages. An enlightening and fascinating read, her book is sure to be of interest in most libraries." Library Journal.

Monger, George

Marriage customs of the world : an encyclopedia of dating customs and wedding traditions / George P. Monger. ABC-CLIO, c2013. 2 v. (xxxiii, 743 p.) : **392.5**

1. Marriage customs and rites 2. Dating (Social customs) 3. Mate selection 4. Encyclopedias.
ISBN 9781598846638

LC 2012031375

This book presents a comprehensive overview of global courtship and marriage customs, from ancient history to contemporary society, demonstrating the vast differences as well as the similarities across all of human culture. --From publisher description.

"As little is published on this subject, this set would be a good addition to public and academic libraries." Booklist.

393 Death customs

Doughty, Caitlin

From here to eternity : traveling the world to find the good death / Caitlin Doughty. W. W. Norton & Company, 2017. 224 p. **393**

1. Doughty, Caitlin. 2. Death -- Social aspects 3. Mourning customs 4. Burial. 5. Funerals
ISBN 9780393249897

LC 2017025059

"These observances demonstrate how to diminish the stigma associated with death, burial, and eternal remembrance. Death gets the last word in this affably written, meticulously researched study of funerary customs." Kirkus.

Herring, Lucinda

Reimagining death : stories and practical wisdom for home funerals and green burials / Lucinda Herring ; foreword by David Spangler. North Atlantic Books, 2019. xix, 272 p. ; **393**

1. Burial -- Environmental aspects -- United States 2. Funeral rites and ceremonies -- Environmental aspects -- United States 3. Environmental responsibility -- United States
ISBN 9781623172923

LC 2018031617

"For all those seeking to reclaim their innate and legal right to care for their own dead, create home funeral vigils, and choose greener after-death care options that are less toxic and more sustainable for the earth More natural after-death care options are transforming the paradigm of the existing funeral industry, helping families and communities recover their instinctive capacity to care for a loved one after death and do so in creative, nourishing, and healing ways. In reclaiming these practices and creating new, innovative options, we are greening the gateway of death and returning home to ourselves, our bodies, and the earth. Lucinda Herring reminds us of the sacredness of death itself; her compelling stories, poetry, and guidance come from years of experience as a home funeral/ green burial consultant and licensed funeral director dedicated to more natural and healing death practices. In Reimagining Death she shares with readers her experience caring for her own mother after death. Through storytelling and resources Herring also reveals to families the gifts of partnering with nature, home funeral vigils, sacred care at death, conscious dying (through the story of a Death with Dignity with accompanying photos of one man's planned death and after-death care), bringing laughter and a greater lightness of being to death, natural burials, and emerging eco-conscious dispositions. A valuable resource in planning for all deaths in all circumstances (with a chapter on what to do when a death occurs outside of the home), this book also guides readers on how to create an advance after-death care directive".-- Provided by publisher.

Kammen, Michael G.

Digging up the dead : a history of notable American reburials / Michael Kammen. University of Chicago Press, 2010. xi, 260 p. : **393**

1. Exhumation -- Political aspects 2. Burial -- History. 3. Funerals -- History. 4. United States -- History
ISBN 9780226423296

LC 2009023515

Profiles the reburials of famous Americans throughout history, describing the reasons for the exhumation, the role of politics and geography on the final resting place, and how rivalries and greed can hinder the process.

"Kammen has a good sense of the details that make historical stories memorable. His occasional flashes of humor add a winsome, professionally geeky element to the telling." Dallas Morning News.

Pringle, Heather Anne, 1952-
The **mummy** congress : science, obsession, and the everlasting dead / Heather Pringle. Hyperion, 2001. 368 p. **393**
1. Mummies. 2. Human remains (Archaeology) 3. Forensic anthropology. 4. Physical anthropology.
ISBN 0786865512
LC 00054487

A study of the mysteries of mummies explores the world of the scientists who devote their own lives to the study of them and examines how mummies have been used, venerated, worshiped, collected, and studied over the course of nearly seven thousand years of history.

"More astounding than all the fright flicks about shambling, gauze-wrapped menaces wound together." Booklist.

394 General customs

Schutt, Bill
Cannibalism : a perfectly natural history / Bill Schutt. Algonquin Books, 2017. 329 p. **394**
1. Cannibalism 2. Animal behavior 3. Human behavior 4. Taboo
ISBN 9781616204624
LC 2016023112

"Published simultaneously in Canada by Thomas Allen & Son Limited."

Eating one's own kind is completely natural behavior in thousands of species, including humans. Throughout history we have engaged in cannibalism for reasons of famine, burial rites, and medicinal remedies. With unexpected wit and a wealth of knowledge, biologist Bill Schutt takes us on a tour of the field, dissecting exciting new research on the topic.

"With plenty of examples of cannibalism in humans past and present, Schutt's well researched and suspenseful work is a must read for anyone who's interested in the topic--and can stomach the gore. " Publishers Weekly.

Visser, Margaret
The **gift** of thanks : the roots, persistence, and paradoxical meanings of a social ritual / Margaret Visser. Houghton Mifflin Harcourt, 2009, c2008. 458 p. ; **394**
1. Gratitude. 2. Thank-you notes. 3. Generosity. 4. Attitude (Psychology)
ISBN 9780151013319
LC 2009014018

Originally published: Toronto : HarperCollins, 2008.

This inquiry into all aspects of gratitude ranges from the unusual determination with which parents teach their children to thank, to the difference between speaking the words and feeling them, to the ways different cultures handle the complex matters of giving, receiving, and returning favors and presents. It also illuminates the modern battle of social scientists to pin down the notion of thankfulness and discover its biological and evolutionary roots.

394.1 Eating, drinking; using drugs

Anthony, Jason C.
Hoosh : roast penguin, scurvy day, and other stories of Antarctic cuisine / Jason C. Anthony. University of Nebraska Press, c2012. 286 p. **394.1**
1. Food habits -- Antarctica 2. Outdoor cooking -- Antarctica 3. Antarctica -- Social life and customs. 4. Antarctica -- History
ISBN 9780803226661
LC 2012011994

"A singular, engrossing take on a region that until now has been mostly documented from a scientific angle or romanticized by adventurers." Kirkus.

Cheever, Susan
Drinking in America : our secret history / Susan Cheever. Twelve, 2015 240 p. **394.1**
1. Drinking customs -- United States -- History. 2. National characteristics, American. 3. Alcoholic beverages -- Social aspects. 4. Social drinking -- History 5. United States -- History.
ISBN 9781455513871
LC 2015025648

Presents an exploration of the history of drinking in the United States and its effects on the American character.

Collingham, E. M. (Elizabeth M.)
Curry : a tale of cooks and conquerors / Lizzie Collingham. Oxford University Press, 2006. 352 p. **394.1**
1. Curry powder. 2. Cooking, Indic. 3. Cooking (Curry) 4. Food habits -- India -- History. 5. India -- Civilization.
ISBN 0195172418
LC 2005016641

An authoritative history of the foods of India, complete with delicious recipes, ranges from the imperial kitchen of the Mughal invader Babur to the smoky cookhouse of the British Raj and includes information on the influence of various food traditions on the evolution of Indian specialties.

Cowen, Tyler
An **economist** gets lunch : new rules for everyday foodies / Tyler Cowen. Dutton, 2012. 304 p. **394.1**
1. Food habits. 2. Food industry and trade. 3. Economics.
ISBN 9780525952664
LC 2011035174

An influential economist challenges popular opinions about the superiority of locally grown and expensive foods, demonstrating how to eat responsibly without submitting to fashion-driven trends.

Downie, David
A **taste** of Paris : a history of the Parisian love affair with food / David Downie. St. Martin's Press, [2017] 320 p. **394.1**
1. Food 2. Gastronomy 3. Cooking, French 4. Food habits 5. Paris, France -- Description and travel. 6. France -- Description and travel. 7. Essays
ISBN 9781250082930
LC 2017018869

A critically acclaimed author, using his trademark wit and informative style, embarks on a quest to discover "What is it about the history of Paris that has made it a food lover's paradise?" by following the contours of history and geography of the city.

"Downie relishes in debunking myths about French culinary exceptionalism ... while unabashedly proclaiming his adoration for French culture and history in and out of the kitchen. Readers don't have to be foodies to get the flavor of the French character in this delightful, thoroughly researched culinary history." Publishers Weekly.

Goulding, Matt
Grape, olive, pig : deep travels through Spain's food culture / Matt Goulding ; edited by Nathan Thornburgh ; designed by Doul-

gas Hughmanick. Harper Wave, [2016] xiii, 347 p. : **394.1**

1. Food habits 2. Manners and customs 3. Cooking 4. Food 5. Spain -- Description and travel. 6. Spain -- Social life and customs

ISBN 9780062394132

LC 2016018185

"An Anthony Bourdain book."

IACP Cookbook Awards, Literary Food Writing, 2017.

A celebration of the culture and cuisine of Spain contextualizes meals with the stories behind them, offering a tour of everything from Barcelona's tapas bars to the coastal Cadiz bluefin tuna hunts to the small-plate flavors of Madrid.

Goulding, Matt

Rice, noodle, fish : deep travels through Japan's food culture / Matt Goulding ; edited by Nathan Thornburgh. HarperWave, 2015 352 p. : **394.1**

1. Goulding, Matt 2. Food habits -- Japan. 3. Food tourism 4. Cooking, Japanese. 5. Ramen. 6. Japan -- Description and travel.

ISBN 9780062394033

LC 2015005013

A gastronomic tour of Japan by the founders of the political and culinary "Roads & Kingdoms" website combines detailed narrative, insider advice and practical information with lavish full-color photography celebrating the traditions of seven key regions.

Henaut, Stephane

A **bite-sized** history of France : gastronomic tales of revolution, war, and enlightenment / Stephane Henaut and Jeni Mitchell. New Press, 2018. 256 p. **394.1**

1. Gastronomy -- France -- History. 2. Food -- France -- History. 3. Food habits -- France -- History. 4. Dinners and dining -- France -- History. 5. France -- Social life and customs.

ISBN 9781620972519

LC 2018001242

Describes the history of France through a gastronomic lens, discussing the country's legendary cuisine and wine, from Roquefort cheese to cognac and croissants along with the social and political trends that influenced its innovations and traditions.

"Henault and Mitchell are often witty (perhaps most amusingly illustrated by a chapter called War and Peas) even as they present their exceptionally well-researched material. This culinary history is a treat for Francophiles." Publishers Weekly.

Kauffman, Jonathan

Hippie food : how back-to-the-landers, longhairs, and revolutionaries changed the way we eat / Jonathan Kauffman. William Morrow & Company, 2018. 352 p. **394.1**

1. Food habits. 2. Counterculture 3. Diet 4. Natural foods.

ISBN 9780062437303

LC 2017278622

A narrative history of the alternative-foods movement of the past half century explores the diverse fringe trends, charismatic personalities and counterculture elements that have rendered quotidian wholefoods, from whole grain bread and tofu to yogurt and brown rice, part of the mainstream American diet.

"An astute, highly informative food expos that educates without bias, leaving the culinary decision-making to readers." Kirkus.

Kurlansky, Mark,

The **food** of a younger land : a portrait of American food : before the national highway system, before chain restaurants, and before frozen food, when the nation's food was seasonal, regional, and traditional : from the lost WPA files / edited and illustrated by Mark Kurlansky. Riverhead Books, 2009. 416 p. **394.1**

1. Cooking, American -- History. 2. Food habits -- United States -- History. 3. Food industry and trade. 4. Cooking, American. 5. United States -- History.

ISBN 9781594488658

LC 2009008100

FDR's little-known Depression-era program, "America Eats," sent writers to diverse regional niches gathering stories, photos, anecdotes, and authentic recipes reflecting local peoples? struggle for food. From New York automats to Arkansas possum-eating clubs, from Puget Sound salmon feasts to Choctaw funerals, discover a history of pre-WWII food cultures and curiosities recovered from Library of Congress records.

"In the late 1930s the WPA farmed out a writing project with the ambition of other New Deal programs: an encyclopedia of American food and food traditions from coast-to-coast similar to the federal travel guides. After Pearl Harbor, the war effort halted the project for good; the book was never published, and the files were archived in the Library of Congress. [The editor] brought the unassembled materials to light and created this version of the guide that never was. This extraordinary collectionat once history, anthropology, cookbook, almanac and family albumprovides a vivid and revitalizing sense of the rural and regional characteristics and distinctions that we've lost and can find again here." Publishers Weekly.

McWilliams, James E.

Just food : where locavores get it wrong and how we can truly eat responsibly / James E. McWilliams. Little, Brown, 2009. viii, 258 p. ; **394.1**

1. Food habits -- Moral and ethical aspects. 2. Food industry and trade. 3. Natural foods. 4. Organic farming.

ISBN 9780316033749

LC 2009015514

A provocative response to mixed messages surrounding the "locally grown" movement challenges popular opinions about the nutritional and environmental realities of food, revealing such information as the superior energy efficiency of imported tomatoes and the greater sustainability of farm-raised freshwater fish.

"The author argues for moderation and compromise in today's raging food fights. Until recently, the author was a locavore--one who eats locally produced food. Though he still believes that it is a dietary commitment with many virtues, he argues that it's also a feeble, ineffective way to feed the world's hungry billions. McWilliams presents some appealing alternatives to the views of both the agrarian romantics on the left and the agribusiness capitalists on the right. Rich in research, provocative in conception and nettlesome to both the right and the left." Kirkus.

Pollan, Michael

★The **omnivore's** dilemma : a natural history of four meals / Michael Pollan. Penguin Press, 2006. 450 p. **394.1**

1. Food habits. 2. Corn. 3. Natural foods. 4. Food consumption.

ISBN 1594200823

LC 2005056557

James Beard Foundation Book Awards, Writing and Literature, 2007.

National Book Critics Circle Award for Nonfiction finalist, 2006.

Offers insight into food consumption in the twenty-first century, explaining how an abundance of unlimited food varieties reveals the responsibilities of consumers to protect their health and the environment.

"The author defines the Omnivore's Dilemma as the confusing maze of choices facing Americans trying to eat healthfully in a society that he calls notably unhealthy. He seeks answers to this dilemma by taking readers through the industrial, organic, and hunter-gatherer stages of the food chain. This folksy narrative provides a wealth of information about agriculture, the natural world, and human desires." Library Journal.

Schlosser, Eric

★**Fast** food nation : the dark side of the all-American meal / Eric Schlosser. Houghton Mifflin, 2001. 356 p. : **394.1**

1. Fast food restaurants, chains, etc. 2. Food industry and trade. 3. Convenience foods. 4. Fast foods -- Nutritional aspects.
ISBN 0395977894

LC 00053886

ALA Notable Book, 2002.

A journalist explores the homogenization of American culture and the impact of the fast food industry on modern-day health, economy, politics, popular culture, entertainment, and food production.

Standage, Tom

A **history** of the world in 6 glasses / Tom Standage. Walker & Co., 2005. 240 p. **394.1**

1. Beverages -- History. 2. Drinking -- History 3. Tea -- History. 4. Coffee -- History.
ISBN 0802714471

LC 2004061209

An offbeat history of the world traces the story of humankind from the Stone Age to the twenty-first century from the perspective of six different drinks--beer, wine, spirits, coffee, tea, and cola--describing their pervasive influence during pivotal eras of world history, from humankind's adoption of agriculture to the advent of globalization.

"Standage has the ability to connect the smallest detail to the big picture and a knack for summarizing vast concepts in a few sentences." Publishers Weekly.

Standage, Tom

An **edible** history of humanity / Tom Standage. Walker & Company, c2009. 288 p. **394.1**

1. Food habits -- History. 2. Food industry and trade -- History. 3. Agriculture -- History. 4. Food -- Symbolic aspects.
ISBN 9780802715883

LC 2009005610

A lighthearted chronicle of how foods have transformed human culture throughout the ages traces the barley- and wheat-driven early civilizations of the near East through the corn and potato industries in America, comparing the progress of farming cultures to those of hunter-gatherers while citing the pivotal contributions of global trade.

Wrangham, Richard W., 1948-

Catching fire : how cooking made us human / Richard Wrangham. Basic Books, c2009. 320 p. **394.1**

1. Prehistoric humans -- Food 2. Cooking -- History. 3. Human evolution. 4. Fire -- History.
ISBN 9780465013623

LC 2009001742

Presents the theory that it was the introduction of cooking in the prehistoric past that led to physiological changes in the human brain and such advancements in human behavior as the development of social skills, bonding, and the division of labor in family groups.

"This is a plainspoken and thoroughly gripping scientific essay that presents nothing less than a new theory of human evolution. . . . [This book] contains serious science yet is related in direct, no-nonsense prose. It is toothsome, skillfully prepared brain food." New York Times.

Ying, Chris,

★**You** and I eat the same : on the countless ways food and cooking connect us to one another / edited by Chris Ying ; foreword by Rene Redzepi. MAD/Artisan, 2018 214 p. : **394.1**

1. Food habits. 2. Cultural relations -- United States. 3. Emigration and immigration -- United States.
ISBN 9781579658403

LC 2018024652

Proposing that immigration is fundamental to cuisine, and that good food is the common ground between cultures, the chef and owner of noma in Copenhagen and the founder of international nonprofit organization MAD takes our ideas about food to the next level.

394.26 Holidays

Abbey, Cherie D.

Holidays, festivals, and celebrations of the world dictionary : detailing more than 3,000 observances from all 50 states and more than 100 nations : a compendious reference guide to popular, ethnic, religious, national, and ancient holidays.... / edited by Cherie D. Abbey. Omnigraphics, c2010. xviii, 1323 p. ; **394.26**

1. Holidays -- Dictionaries. 2. Festivals -- Dictionaries.
ISBN 9780780809949

LC 2009041138

"A comprehensive dictionary that describes more than 3,000 holidays and festivals celebrated around the world. Features both secular and religious events from many different cultures, countries, and ethnic groups. Includes contact information for events;multiple appendices with background information on world holidays; extensive bibliography; multiple indexes".--Provided by publisher.

Henderson, Helene, 1963-

Holiday symbols and customs : a guide to the legend and lore behind the traditions, rituals, foods, games, animals, and other symbols and activities associated with holidays and holy days, feasts and fasts, and other celebrations, covering ancient, calendar, religious, historic, folkloric, national, promotional, and sporting events, as observed in the united states and around the world. / Helene (EDT) Henderson, Cherie D. (EDT) Abbey, Peggy Daniels, Tanya Gulevich, Sue Ellen Thompson. Omnigraphics, c2009. xix, 1321 p. ; **394.26**

1. Holidays. 2. Festivals. 3. Fasts and feasts.
ISBN 9780780809901

LC 2008028403

Rev. ed. of: Holiday symbols and customs / by Sue Ellen Thompson. 3rd ed.

"Describes the origins of 323 holidays around the world. Explains where, when, and how each event is celebrated, with detailed information on the symbols and customs associated with the holiday. Includes contact information and web sites for related organizations".--Provided by publisher.

394.2646 Halloween

Morton, Lisa, 1958-

Trick or treat : a history of Halloween / Lisa Morton. Reaktion Books, 2012. 229 p. : **394.2646**

1. Halloween -- History. 2. Holidays -- History. 3. Trick or treat. 4.

Halloween candy.
ISBN 9781780230474

LC bl2013007309

Bram Stoker Award for Best Nonfiction, 2012.

Every year, children and adults alike take to the streets dressed as witches, demons, animals, celebrities, and more. They carve pumpkins and play pranks, and the braver ones watch scary movies and go on ghost tours. There are parades, fireworks displays, cornfield mazes, and haunted houses and, most important, copious amounts of bite-sized candy. The popularity of Halloween has spread around the globe to places as diverse as Russia, China, and Japan, but its association with death and the supernatural and its inevitable commercialization has made it one of our most misunderstood holidays. How did it become what it is today?

394.2649 Thanksgiving

Baker, James W., 1926-

Thanksgiving : the biography of an American holiday / James W. Baker ; foreword by Peter J. Gomes. University of New Hampshire Press ; 2009. xii, 273 p. : **394.2649**

1. Thanksgiving Day -- History. 2. Holidays.
ISBN 9781584658016

LC 2009012348

In this, the first in-depth study of the most American of holidays, James Baker sweeps away lingering myths and misconceptions to show how this celebration day was born and grew to be an essential part of our national spirit. Thanksgiving: The Biography of an American Holiday opens with an overview of the popular mythos of the holiday before discussing its possible religious and cultural precedents. This classic Yankee holiday is examined in historical and contemporary detail that embraces everything from proclamations, sermons, and local and regional traditions to family reunions, turkey dinners, and recipes. Thanksgiving's evolving face is illustrated with charming and often revealing period prints that chart our changing attitudes: the influence of Victorian sentiment in Thanksgiving's development, Progressive utilitarianism, intellectual "debunking," patriotic wartime reclamation, and 1960s-era protest. Thanksgiving remains controversial up to the present day, as Mayflower descendants, Native Americans, and commercial exploiters compete for the American public's opinion of the holiday's contemporary significance and its future status. This is an intelligent and illuminating introduction to a beloved holiday and a fascinating cultural history of America and Americana. --From publisher description.

"This is destined to become the accepted text for research on the history and myth of this most American holiday, and it will be an enjoyable, fascinating read both for students and for anyone looking for a good story." Library Journal.

Hillstrom, Laurie Collier, 1965-

The **Thanksgiving** book : a companion to the holiday covering its history, lore, traditions, foods, and symbols, including primary sources, poems, prayers, songs, hymns, and recipes : supplemented by a chronology, bibliography with web sites, and index / Laurie C. Hillstrom. Omnigraphics, c2008. xi, 328 p. : **394.2649**

1. Thanksgiving Day.
ISBN 9780780804036

LC 2007025708

"Provides information about the history, lore, traditions, foods, and symbols of the Thanksgiving celebration. Features include narrative overviews and primary source documents, chronology, and resources for further information".--Provided by publisher.

394.2663 Christmas

Flanders, Judith

Christmas : a biography / Judith Flanders. St Martin's Press, 2017 304 p. **394.2663**

1. Christmas -- History. 2. Holidays -- History.
ISBN 9781250118349

LC 2017027330

The best-selling author of The Making of Home presents a tour of Christmas holiday traditions from the original festival through today, touching on subjects ranging from gift wrap and the holiday parade to the first gag holiday gift book and the first official appearance of Santa Claus.

"Christmas evokes both memories of the past and expectations for future celebrations, but Flanders posits that the holiday never was the quiet, thoughtful, religious observance we think it was. Separating fact from myth and traditional practice, Flanders provides a well-researched 'biography' of how Christmas came to be observed through the ages and in various cultures." Booklist.

Forbes, Bruce David

Christmas : a candid history / Bruce David Forbes. University of California Press, 2007. xiv, 179 p. : **394.2663**

1. Christmas -- History. 2. Holidays -- History.
ISBN 0520251040

LC 2007000366

Written for everyone who loves and is simultaneously driven crazy by the holiday season, Christmas: A Candid History provides an enlightening, entertaining perspective on how the annual Yuletide celebration got to be what it is today. In a fascinating, concise tour through history, the book tells the story of Christmas--from its pre-Christian roots, through the birth of Jesus, to the holiday's spread across Europe into the Americas and beyond, and to its mind-boggling transformation through modern consumerism. Packed with intriguing stories, based on research into myriad sources, full of insights, the book explores the historical origins of traditions including Santa, the reindeer, gift giving, the Christmas tree, Christmas songs and movies, and more. The book also offers some provocative ideas for reclaiming the joy and meaning of this beloved, yet often frustrating, season amid the pressures of our fast-paced consumer culture. --From publisher description.

Stibbe, Nina

An **almost** perfect Christmas / Nina Stibbe. Little, Brown and Co., 2018. 240 p. **394.2663**

1. Christmas cooking. 2. Holidays. 3. Family traditions. 4. Family recipes.
ISBN 9780316415811

LC 2018944946

From perennially dry turkeys to Christmas pudding fires, from the round robin code of conduct to the risks and rewards of re-gifting, An Almost Perfect Christmas is an ode to the joy and insanity of the most wonderful time of the year.

"Funny, smart, sweet, and tender, this is greater than a gift book and readable any time of year." Booklist.

394.8 Dueling and suicide

Durkheim, Emile, 1858-1917

★**Suicide,** a study in sociology: / translated by John A. Spaulding and George Simpson. Edited, with an introd., by

George Simpson. Free Press 1951 405 p. **394.8**

1. Suicide -- Sociological aspects
ISBN 9780684836324

LC 51009585

Emile Durkheim's Suicide addresses the phenomenon of suicide and its social causes. Written by one of the world's most influential sociologists, this classic argues that suicide primarily results from a lack of integration of the individual into society. Suicide provides readers with an understanding of the impetus for suicide and its psychological impact on the victim, family, and society. --From publisher description.

395 Etiquette (Manners)

Alkon, Amy

Good manners for nice people : who sometimes say f*ck / Amy Alkon. St. Martin's Griffin, 2014. x, 289 p. ; **395**

1. Courtesy -- United States. 2. Etiquette -- United States. 3. Manners and customs. 4. United States -- Social life and customs -- 21st century.
ISBN 9781250030719

LC 2014008115

Combining science with humor, this in-your-face modern guide to manners for regular people provides a new set of rules for our 21st century lives that show us how to avoid being rude and stand up to those who are.

Berman, Lea

Treating people well : the extraordinary power of civility at work and in life / Lea Berman and Jeremy Bernard. Simon & Schuster, 2018. 256 p. **395**

1. Courtesy 2. Cooperation 3. Success in business 4. Social skills
ISBN 9781501157981

LC 2017061756

"Berman and Bernard winningly call on their experiences as White House social secretaries under, respectively, George W. Bush and Barack Obama to make a case that manners and civility can be the basis for success in work and life." Publishers Weekly.

Dresser, Norine

Multicultural manners : essential rules of etiquette for the 21st century / Norine Dresser. John Wiley & Sons, c2005. xviii, 285 p. : **395**

1. Etiquette -- United States. 2. Multiculturalism -- United States.
ISBN 9780471684282

LC 2004027079

Reveals the dos and don'ts of international etiquette, covering body language, food, child rearing, clothing, colors, entertaining, weddings, funerals, and gift giving.

Forni, Pier Massimo

The **civility** solution : what to do when people are rude / P.M. Forni. St. Martin's Press, c2008. xxi, 166 p. ; **395**

1. Courtesy. 2. Etiquette.
ISBN 9780312368494

LC 2008009448

A founder of the Johns Hopkins Civility Project presents dozens of real-world examples and strategic advice on how to conduct oneself when confronted with the rude behavior of others, in a guide that makes recommendations for breaking rude cycles by being both polite and assertive.

Martin, Judith, 1938-

Miss Manners' guide to excruciatingly correct behavior / Judith Martin ; illustrated by Gloria Kamen. W.W. Norton & Co. ; c2005. 858 p. : **395**

1. Etiquette.
ISBN 9780393058741

LC 2005000264

An updated edition of the best-selling classic by the popular author of the "Miss Manners" columns and etiquette guides is a new volume of letters, essays, illustrations, and humorous advice on how to navigate the world of civilized behavior.

Post, Lizzie

Emily Post's etiquette : manners for today / Lizzie Post, Daniel Post Senning ; illustrations by Janice Richter. William Morrow & Company, 2017. xi, 722 p. : **395**

1. Etiquette 2. Personal conduct 3. Manners and customs 4. Courtesy
ISBN 9780062439253

A revised and updated edition addresses such contemporary issues as social-media etiquette, email and texting and covering tattoos and piercings before interviews, as well as such classic conundrums as names and titles, official forms of address and dress codes.

395.2 Etiquette for stages in life cycle

Abby, Laura Leigh

2brides 2be : a same-sex guide for the modern bride / Laura Leigh Abby. Archer/Rare Bird, 2017 296 p. : **395.2**

1. Weddings -- Planning 2. Same-sex marriage 3. Lesbian couples
ISBN 9781941729175

LC bl2017035961

Offers advice for planning a same-sex wedding, from the proposal and the logistics of walking down the aisle to wording on the invitation and booking vendors.

Harrison, Kate L.

The **green** bride guide : how to create an earth-friendly wedding on any budget / Kate L. Harrison. Sourcebooks, c2008. xix, 284 p. ; **395.2**

1. Weddings -- Planning
ISBN 9781402213458

LC 2008021154

A comprehensive guide to an eco-friendly wedding celebration covers all aspects of wedding planning, including engagements, location, invitation, fashion, flowers, the ceremony, the reception, gifts, and the honeymoon, with hundreds of beautiful, sustainable, and earth-friendly ideas for any budget.

Mead, Rebecca

One perfect day : the selling of the American wedding / Rebecca Mead. Penguin Press, 2007. 245 p. ; **395.2**

1. Weddings -- United States -- Planning. 2. Shopping -- United States. 3. Wedding consultants. 4. Consumer education. 5. United States -- Social life and customs.
ISBN 1594200882

LC 2006052461

Includes index.

A critique of the American wedding industry and the psychology behind the expense, stress, and pressure associated with typical weddings features a tour of the inner workings of wedding planners, commercial registries, and wedding management programs.

"Part investigative journalism, part social commentary, Mead's wry, insightful work offers an illuminating glimpse at the ugly underbelly of our Bridezilla culture." Publishers Weekly.

Outcalt, Todd

Your beautiful wedding on any budget / Todd Outcalt. Sourcebooks Casablanca, c2009. 227 p. ; **395.2**

1. Wedding planning 2. Weddings -- Costs. 3. Budget -- Personal finance

ISBN 9781402217883

LC 2008046864

"How to get what you want while paying less. Go on your honeymoon without a care in the world. Pay for your wedding with no hassles and no debt. Financial worksheets, checklists, and more."

With costs rising, the economy faltering, and the future uncertain, Outcalt provides an overall plan for cost-saving and dream-building. Unlike other books, Your Beautiful Wedding on Any Budget creates a plan tailored to your financial reality, not a specific dollar amount. --from publisher description

"A terrific resource for couples trying to start their marriage on a financially sound footing. The Methodist pastor offers suggestions for building a wedding fund and creative cost-cutting measures based on his debt-free wedding seminars and blog." Library Journal.

Post, Anna

Emily Post's wedding etiquette / Anna Post and Lizzie Post ; with illustrations by Happy Menocal. William Morrow, 2014 xx, 380 p. : **395.2**

1. Wedding etiquette.

ISBN 9780062326102

LC 2013498453

"Now completely updated and expanded in a new edition."

Includes index.

This trusted guide to planning the perfect wedding helps brides and their friends and family have a memorable, yet stress-free affair by covering such topics as handling awkward family situations, blending family traditions, using technology and creating a timeline of events.

Vivaldo, Denise

Do it for le$$! weddings : how to create your dream wedding without breaking the bank / Denise Vivaldo. Sellers Pub., c2008. 272 p. : **395.2**

1. Weddings -- Economic aspects. 2. Weddings -- Planning.

ISBN 9781416205197

LC 2008923779

Explains how to plan an affordable wedding that covers timelines, themes, budgets, necessary items, the reception, and menu plans.

Weiss, Mindy

The **wedding** book : the big book for your big day / Mindy Weiss with Lisbeth Levine. Workman Pub., c2007. 485 p. : **395.2**

1. Weddings -- Planning.

ISBN 9780761150947

LC bl2008009191

Includes index.

Provides a comprehensive guide to planning a wedding, including contract negotiations, creating a budget, planning guest lists, and obtaining a marriage license.

395.4 Social correspondence

Allert, Tilman

Heil Hitler : on the meaning of a gesture / Tilman Allert. Henry Holt and Company, 2008. 128 p. **395.4**

1. Salutations -- Germany. 2. Nazism -- Social aspects -- Germany. 3. Rites and ceremonies -- Germany. 4. Germany -- History -- 1933-1945.

ISBN 9780312428303

LC 2007035667

Translation of: Der deutsche Gruss.

Published in paperback as The Hitler salute, 2009.

Provides a critical look at the origins, history, and dissemination of the infamous Heil Hitler salute in Nazi Germany from its compulsory adoption in 1933, assessing its meaning in terms of a symbol of loyalty to the Nazi regime, as a means of vesting Hitler with a divine aura, and as a ritual of consent that paved the way for the erosion of social morality.

Scott, Andy

One kiss or two? : the art and science of saying hello / Andy Scott. Overlook Press, 2018. 304 p. **395.4**

1. Manners and customs. 2. Communication. 3. Social psychology. 4. Salutations.

ISBN 9781468316018

LC bl2018037444

In an increasingly global and connected world, our ways of saying hello have become more confusing than ever. This book is essential reading for anyone traveling and working in the cross-cultural, modern age and global citizens determined to avoid social gaffes in important situations.

"Emphasizing the virtue of human connection throughout, Scott's buoyant study is reminiscent of the work of A.J. Jacobs in its breezy mix of pop sociology, personal anecdote, and self-help." Publishers Weekly.

395.5 Etiquette by situations

Blyth, Catherine

The **art** of conversation : a guided tour of a neglected pleasure / Catherine Blyth. Gotham Books, 2009. 289 p. **395.5**

1. Conversation. 2. Oral communication. 3. Interpersonal communication. 4. Personal conduct.

ISBN 9781592404193

LC 2008024276

Draws on examples from history, literature, and other disciplines to offer advice on how to rebuild conversational tools in order to make more qualitative connections with other people.

Morrison, Terri

★**Kiss,** bow, or shake hands : the bestselling guide to doing business in more than 60 countries / Terri Morrison and Wayne A. Conaway. Adams Media, c2006. xiii, 593 p. : **395.5**

1. Business etiquette 2. Corporate culture 3. Business communication 4. Negotiation in business

ISBN 9781593373689

LC 2006013587

Includes index.

Presents information on the practices needed to do business in over sixty countries, covering such topics as historical background, cultural orientation, protocol, negotiations, entertainment, dress, and forms of address.

Oliver, Vicky

301 smart answers to tough business etiquette questions / Vicky Oliver. Skyhorse Pub., c2010. xii, 370 p. ; **395.5**

1. Business etiquette
ISBN 9781616081416

LC 2010021474

Presents a guide to professional etiquette in business situations, covering such topics as meetings, email, social networking, travel, dress, and restaurants in a question and answer format.

Schweitzer, Sharon, 1961-

Access to Asia : your multicultural guide to building trust, inspiring respect, and creating long-lasting business relationships / Sharon Schweitzer, J.D. , Liz Alexander, Ph.D. John Wiley & Sons, Inc., 2015 xxiv, 374 p.: **395.5**

1. Business etiquette -- Asia 2. Corporate culture -- Asia 3. Intercultural communication 4. Management
ISBN 9781118919019

LC 2014039933

"Beautifully constructed and expertly written in straightforward language; will make it far easier for anyone to navigate the cultural differences of doing business in Asia." Kirkus.

Tower, Jeremiah

Table manners : how to behave in the modern world and why bother / Jeremiah Tower ; illustrations by Libby VanderPloeg. Farrar, Straus and Giroux, 2016. 148 p. : **395.5**

1. Table etiquette.
ISBN 9780374272340

LC 2016007141

Funny and practical, a modern guide to table manners for all occasions by one of the world's most acclaimed chefs and restaurateurs tells readers how to behave, what to talk about, what to wear and how to eat, and serves up advice on everything from RSVPs, iPhones and running late to food allergies and what to do when you are served something disgusting.

398 Folklore

Guiley, Rosemary

The **encyclopedia** of vampires & werewolves / Rosemary Ellen Guiley ; foreword by Jeanne Keyes Youngson. Facts On File, c2011. xiv, 430 p. : **398**

1. Monsters 2. Vampires 3. Werewolves
ISBN 9780816081790

LC 2010034839

Rev. ed. of The encyclopedia of vampires, werewolves, and other monsters.

From ancient customs to famous cases of beasts and vampires and their reflections in popular culture, five hundred entries provide definitions, explanations, and lists of suggested further reading on the macabre.

Melton, J. Gordon

The **vampire** book : the encyclopedia of the undead / J. Gordon Melton. Visible Ink Press, c2011. xxxiii, 909 p. : **398**

1. Vampires -- Encyclopedias.
ISBN 9781578592814

LC 2010024263

Explores the myth, lore, and representation in popular culture of vampires and vampire legends from around the globe.

Prahlad, Anand

The **Greenwood** encyclopedia of African American folklore / edited by Anand Prahlad. Greenwood Press, 2006. 3 v. (xl, 1557 p.) : **398**

1. African Americans -- Folklore 2. African Americans -- Social life and customs 3. Folklore -- United States
ISBN 0313330352

LC 2005019214

Covering a wealth of topics -- in areas that include conversational genres, language, dance, festivals, events, folklore scholars and collectors, foods, material culture, music, quilting, and religion -- the over 700 entries of this reference demonstrate the wide impact of African American folklore throughout American culture. Many entries are devoted to countries and regions, particularly in Africa and parts of Central and South America, describing genres found there and their areas of influence. Characters in Black folklore are well represented in separate entries, and many entries are biographies. Cross references are incorporated in bold type within the text. Each entry is signed and includes a list of further reading. Many inset boxes are included, containing quotes gathered from oral history and literature. This fascinating and thought-provoking resource is suitable for high school and undergraduate students as well as the general reader. --From publisher description.

"This 'first comprehensive general reference work' on African American folklore is highly recommended for academic and public libraries." Booklist.

398.09 History, geographic treatment, biography of folklore

Bronner, Simon J.

Encyclopedia of American folklife / Simon J. Bronner, editor. M.E. Sharpe, c2006. 4 volumes : **398.09**

1. Folklore -- United States 2. United States -- Social life and customs 3. Encyclopedias
ISBN 9780765680525

LC 2005032119

Offers approximately 270 essays on topics in American folklife as diverse as chain letters, the Internet, Little Havana, fans of heavy metal music, Wiccans, and zydeco.

Sherman, Josepha

World folklore for storytellers : tales of wonder, wisdom, fools, and heroes / Josepha Sherman. Sharpe Reference, c2009. xvi, 368 p. : **398.09**

1. Folklore -- Classification 2. Folk literature -- History and criticism 3. Storytelling 4. Oral tradition
ISBN 9780765681744

LC 2009010525

Sherman, who is not otherwise identified, retells stories from folktale collections and literature around the world, removing any element that adults might think unsuitable for children of any age, and providing role models and cautionary tales for both boys and girls. The arrangement is first by the themes enumerated in the title. Subsections include Beauty and the Beast and other transformed males and females, dragon-slayers and monster-slayer, undersea kingdoms, legendary heroes, the master thief, kindness repaid, hope and redemption, fools, and wise people. In addition to story titles, the index includes topics that cut across the themes, and countries and cultures. --From publisher description.

"Sherman (Young Warriors) puts together a wonderfully wide-ranging collection of nearly 200 ethnically diverse folktales." Library Journal.

398.2 Folk literature

Bly, Robert
More than true : the wisdom of fairy tales / Robert Bly. Henry Holt and Company, 2018. 192 p. **398.2**
1. Fairy tales -- History and criticism 2. Wisdom 3. Archetype (Psychology) 4. Personal conduct 5. Essays
ISBN 9781250158192
LC 2017024789

Bly looks at six tales that have stood the test of time and have captivated the poet for decades, from "The Six Swans" to "The Frog Prince." Drawing on his own creative genius, and the work of a range of thinkers from Kirkegaard and Yeats to Freud and Jung, Bly turns these stories over in his mind to bring new meaning and illumination to these timeless tales.

Brunvand, Jan Harold
The **vanishing** hitchhiker : American urban legends and their meanings / Jan Harold Brunvand. Norton, c1981. xiv, 208 p. ; **398.2**
1. Urban folklore -- United States 2. Legends -- United States 3. Legends -- United States -- History and criticism
ISBN 9780393951691
LC 81004744

Presents a collection of examples of major American urban legends, one of the most common forms of contemporary American folklore, and explains their popular appeal

Haase, Donald
The **Greenwood** encyclopedia of folktales and fairy tales / edited by Donald Haase. Greenwood Press, 2008. 3 vols. : **398.2**
1. Folklore -- Encyclopedias. 2. Tales -- Encyclopedias. 3. Fairy tales -- Encyclopedias. 4. Encyclopedias.
ISBN 9780313334412
LC 2007031698

Provides alphabetically arranged entries on folk and fairy tales from around the world, including information on authors, subjects, themes, characters, and national traditions.

Orenstein, Catherine, 1968-
Little Red Riding Hood uncloaked : sex, morality, and the evolution of a fairy tale / Catherine Orenstein. Basic Books, c2002. xiii, 289 p. : **398.2**
1. Little Red Riding Hood (Tale).
ISBN 0465041256
LC 2002004240

Reveals the intricate sexual politics, moral ambiguities, and philosophical underpinnings of the folktale, tracing its history from the court of Louis XIV to its applications in modern marketing, and showing how it has served as a measure of social and sexual mores for women.

"Once upon a time, Red Riding Hood was a good little girl. When she foolishly strayed from the path in the forest and spoke to strangers, she fell prey to the wicked wolf, but fortunately, the heroic woodcutter rescued her just in time. With wit and insight, Orenstein makes us look again at the old childhood story, how it has changed and what that says about us. From Perrault and the Brothers Grimm to Bruno Bettelheim and Andrea Dworkin, the lively informal narrative surveys the stories and the scholarship in terms of folklore, psychology, feminism, and pornography." Booklist.

Seale, Yasmine
Aladdin : a new translation / translated by Yasmine Seale ; edited by Paulo Lemos Horta. Liveright Publishing, 2018 144 p. **398.2**
1. Genies 2. Magic lamps 3. Aladdin (Legendary character) 4. Middle East 5. Arab countries
ISBN 9781631495168
LC 2018036789

A new translation of the beloved folktale highlights the whimsy and also the darker themes often lost in previous English translations of the story of a rebellious 15-year old who is double-crossed by a sorcerer and saved by a princess.

"This exhilarating translation will thrill fans of darker, more complex fairy tales and upend readers preconceived image of Aladdin." Publishers Weekly.

Yolen, Jane,
Favorite folktales from around the world / edited by Jane Yolen. Pantheon Books, c1986. 498 p. ; **398.2**
ISBN 9780394543826
LC 86042644

"Selections include tales from the American Indians, the brother's Grimm, Italo Calvino's Italian folk-tales, as well as stories from Iceland, Afghanistan, Scotland, and many other countries. Yolen provides each section with a relevant introduction, often including historical and literary factors, thus alerting readers as to what to look for." School Library Journal.

398.2089 Ethnic and national groups

Patai, Raphael, 1910-1996
Encyclopedia of Jewish folklore and traditions / Raphael Patai, founding editor ; Haya Bar-Itzhak, editor. M.E. Sharpe, c2013. 2 v. (xvi, 593, I-44 p.) : **398.2089**
1. Jews -- Folklore -- Encyclopedias. 2. Jews -- Social life and customs -- Encyclopedias.
ISBN 9780765620255
LC 2012042203

"An outstanding ready-reference source presenting hard-to-find information, this work will interest students, academics, and general readers. Highly recommended." Library Journal.

398.209 History, geographic treatment, biography

Zipes, Jack, 1937-
The **irresistible** fairy tale : the cultural and social history of a genre / Jack Zipes. Princeton University Press, c2012. xvii, 235 p. : **398.209**
1. Fairy tales -- History and criticism. 2. Fairy tales -- Social aspects.
ISBN 0691153388
LC 2011040188

"A rich, persuasive, magical brew, graced by seven illustrations." Choice.

398.2093802 Persons (Individuals)--folklore--Greece--ancient

Wroe, Ann
Orpheus : the song of life / Ann Wroe. Overlook Press, 2012,

c2011. 262 p. : 398.2093802
1. Orpheus (Greek mythology)
ISBN 9781590207789
Originally published: London : Jonathan Cape, 2011.
A history of the legend of Orpheus traces his mythical achievements and enduring influence, covering topics ranging from his passion for Eurydice to his role in inspiring Plato and Monteverdi and his treatment by the early Church.

398.20943 Folk literature--Germany

Pullman, Philip, 1946-
★**Fairy** tales from the Brothers Grimm : a new English version / [edited by] Philip Pullman. Viking, c2012. 400 p. 398.20943
1. Parent and child. 2. Stepmothers.
ISBN 9780670024971
LC 2012027181
Presents mature and scholarly retellings of fifty favorite and lesser-known fairy tales on the two hundredth anniversary of the Grimm brothers' Children's and Household Tales, in a volume that includes such stories as Cinderella, Rapunzel, and Briar-Rose.
"Pullman's collection is noteworthy for the energetic pace of the stories and the subtle adaptations that make it accessible to modern readers. This is a collection for librarians and teachers to read aloud and to encourage listeners to imagine and retell in their own words." School Library Journal.

Schönwerth, Franz Xaver von, 1809-1886
The **turnip** princess : and other newly discovered fairy tales / Franz Xaver von Schönwerth ; compiled and edited with a foreword by Erika Eichenseer ; translated with an introduction and commentary by Maria Tatar ; illustrations by Engelbert Suss. Penguin Books, 2015. 264 p. 398.20943
1. Anthologies.
ISBN 9780143107422
LC bl2015033117
"These eminently enjoyable tales offer a rich new take on the material of the Grimms and Andersen." Library Journal.

Grimm, Jacob, 1785-1863,
The **original** folk and fairy tales of the Brothers Grimm : the complete first edition / Jacob and Wilhelm Grimm ; translated and edited by Jack Zipes ; illustrated by Andrea Dezso. Princeton University Press, [2014] xliii, 519 p. : 398.20943
1. Consequences. 2. Good and evil. 3. Magic.
ISBN 9780691160597
LC 2014004127
Collects the Grimm brothers' "Children's and Household Tales," a group of stories that include such famous tales as "Rapunzel," "Hansel and Gretel," and "Cinderella."

398.21 Tales and lore of paranatural beings of human and semihuman form

Bane, Theresa, 1969-
Encyclopedia of vampire mythology / Theresa Bane. McFarland & Co., Pub., c2010. vii, 199 p. ; 398.21
1. Vampires -- Encyclopedias 2. Encyclopedias
ISBN 9780786444526
LC 2010015576
"From the earliest days of oral history to brightly illuminated modern times, the vampire myth persists among mankind's deeply rooted fears. This encyclopedia, with entries ranging from "Abchanchu" to "Zmeus," catalogs nearly 600 different species of historical and mythological vampires, fully described and detailed. This is a cultural resource tool as well as literary entertainment".--Provided by publisher.

398.23 Tales and lore of places and times

Adams, Mark, 1967-
Meet me in Atlantis : my quest to find the 2,500-year-old sunken city / Mark Adams. Penguin Group USA, 2015. 336 p. 398.23
1. Adams, Mark, 1967- Travel 2. Plato, 428-347 B.C. Influence. 3. Atlantis (Legendary place) 4. Explorers 5. Quests. 6. Obsession.
ISBN 9780525953708
LC 2014025735
The best-selling author of Turn Right at Machu Picchu documents his investigation into the legend of Atlantis, surveying the efforts of amateur explorers and the clues left by the Greek philosopher Plato to consider its possible existence.
"Adams's excellent examination frames much of Atlantis research on an intimate level. In its own right, this work serves as an important contribution to the search for Atlantis. Readers of history, adventure, travel, scientific inquiry, or the history of science will find this book provocative and entertaining." Library Journal.

398.24 Tales and lore of plants and animals

Asma, Stephen T.
On monsters : an unnatural history of our worst fears / Stephen T. Asma. Oxford University Press, 2009. 368 p. 398.24
1. Monsters. 2. Fear. 3. Social psychology.
ISBN 9780195336160
LC 2009007219
Follows the evolution of monsters throughout time from Behemoth and Leviathan to the post-human cyborgs of tomorrow, in order to understand the mysterious territory outside of rational thought.
"The author is insightful and entertaining in his discussion of monsters of the deep, supernatural doppelgangers, zombies, and vampires, and intense in his discussion of Freud and the science of monstrous feelings. Asma's far-reaching book of monsterology is original, captivating, and profoundly elucidating." Booklist.

398.8 Rhymes and rhyming games

Brown, Marc Tolon
Marc Brown's playtime rhymes : a treasury for families to learn and play together. / Marc Tolon Brown. Little, Brown and Company, 2013. 47 p. : 398.8
1. Finger play. 2. Nursery rhymes.
ISBN 9780316207355
LC 2012048542
A collection of the artist's twenty favorite read-and-play-along finger rhymes complements such entries as "The Itsy-Bitsy Spider"

and "I'm a Little Teapot" with pictorial instructions for correlating finger movements.

Opie, Iona, 1923-2017
The **Oxford** dictionary of nursery rhymes / edited by Iona and Peter Opie. Oxford University Press, 1997. xxix, 559 p. : **398.8**

1. Nursery rhymes. 2. Children's poetry.
ISBN 9780198600886

LC 98140995

Includes indexes.

A reference source for scholars, book collectors, and parents and their children, a new edition of the standard anthology of more than five hundred nursery rhymes, songs, nonsense jingles, and lullabies is complemented by nearly a hundred period illustrations. UP.

400 Language

Everett, Daniel Leonard
Language : the cultural tool / Daniel L. Everett. Pantheon Books, 2011. 320 p. **400**

1. Language and culture. 2. Communication. 3. Sociolinguistics. 4. Language and languages.
ISBN 9780307378538

LC 2011034829

Includes index.

Building on a controversial premise that refutes the opinions of most linguists to argue that language is a unique and essential cultural tool, an anthropological and psychological report contends that language is a human, societally driven invention that can be reinvented and lost.

"Everett unfolds a compelling analysis of how language informs all the activities we recognize as distinctively human. A linguistic study certain to attract many general readers." Booklist.

Kenneally, Christine
The **first** word : the search for the origins of language / Christine Kenneally. Viking, 2007. viii, 357 p. ; **400**

1. Language and languages. 2. Evolution.
ISBN 9780670034901

LC 2007003182

A history of the quest for human language origins is comprised of two intertwined narratives that respectively trace the development of language and the process through which scientists have explored the subject, in an account that also documents the contributions of such figures as Noam Chomsky and Steven Pinker.

Pinker, Steven, 1954-
The **language** instinct / Steven Pinker. W. Morrow and Co., c1994. 494 p. : **400**

1. Language and languages. 2. Biolinguistics. 3. Speech.
ISBN 9780688121419

LC 93031842

The codirector of the MIT Center for Cognitive Science explains how language works, how it differs from thought, why adults have difficulty learning foreign languages, and why computers cannot learn human language.

"The author argues that an innate grammatical machinery of the brain exists, which allows children to reinvent language on their own. Basing his ideas on Noam Chomsky's Universal Grammar theory, Pinker describes language as a discrete combinatorial system that might easily have evolved via natural selection. Pinker steps on a few toes . but his work, while controversial, is well argued, challenging, often humorous, and always fascinating." Library Journal.

401 Philosophy and theory

Everett, Daniel Leonard
How language began : the story of humanity's greatest invention / Daniel Everett. Liveright Publishing Corporation, a division of W. W. Norton & Company, [2017] 384 p. **401**

1. Language and languages -- Origin 2. Oral communication 3. Semiotics 4. Psycholinguistics
ISBN 9780871407955

LC 2017025673

A pioneering linguist upends widely held beliefs about the acquisition and use of language by debunking theories on a wide range of disciplines and through citing examples from his four decades of field work with Amazonian hunter-gatherers.

"In this provocative and ambitious book, linguist Everett . demonstrates the complex and expansive nature of human language and its many communicative forms." Library Journal.

Pinker, Steven, 1954-
The **stuff** of thought : language as a window into human nature / Steven Pinker. Viking, 2007. ix, 499 p. : **401**

1. Language and languages -- Philosophy. 2. Thought and thinking. 3. Language and culture. 4. Language acquisition.
ISBN 9780670063277

LC 2007026601

The Pulitzer Prize finalist author presents an accessible study of the relationship between language and human nature, explaining how everything from swearing and innuendo to prepositions and baby names reveal facts about key human concepts, emotions, and relationships.

"The author's vivid prose and down-to-earth attitude will once again attract an enthusiastic audience outside academia." Publishers Weekly.

Wolfe, Tom
The **kingdom** of speech / Tom Wolfe. Little Brown & Co., 2016. 160 p. **401**

1. Speech. 2. Human evolution. 3. Language and culture. 4. Oral communication.
ISBN 9780316404624

LC 2016942707

Taking readers on a rollicking ride through history, a master storyteller and reporter, whose legend began in journalism, presents a paradigm-shifting argument that speech, not evolution, is responsible for humanity's complex societies and achievements.

"Wolfe is at his best when portraying the lives of the scientists and their respective eras, and his vibrant study manages to be clever, funny, serious, satirical, and instructive." Publishers Weekly.

Yang, Charles D.
★The **infinite** gift : how children learn and unlearn the languages of the world / Charles Yang. Scribner, c2006. vii, 273 p. : **401**

1. Language acquisition. 2. Cognitive styles in children. 3. Linguistics. 4. Child development.
ISBN 9780743237567

LC 2006044307

Draws on cutting-edge scientific findings to address key issues about language development, demonstrating how human beings are born with an innate ability to speak any language but customize their communication abilities to accommodate the language that they hear.

"Anyone with the slightest interest in the English language should read his book." Library Journal.

402 Miscellany

Tammet, Daniel, 1979-

Every word is a bird we teach to sing : encounters with the mysteries and meanings of language / Daniel Tammet. Little, Brown & Company, 2017. 288 p. **402**

1. Communication 2. Language and languages 3. Words 4. Semantics (Philosophy) 5. Essays

ISBN 9780316353052

LC 2017935940

An awareness-raising, deeply humane tour of language by the best-selling author of Born on a Blue Day is presented through a series of essays that explore such questions as whether vocabulary is destiny, why clocks "talk" to the Nahua of Mexico and whether or not A.I. researchers will ever produce true human-machine dialogue.

409 Geographic treatment and biography

Dorren, Gaston

Lingo : around Europe in sixty languages / Gaston Dorren. Atlantic Monthly, 2015. 320 p. **409**

1. Language and languages 2. Language and culture 3. Europe

ISBN 9780802124074

LC bl2015051930

Spanning six millenia and sixty languages in bite-size chapters, Lingo is a hilarious and highly edifying exploration of how Europe speaks.

"This intriguing, thoughtful book will delight those who love words; it is also a round, solid education in the vastness of the worlds citizens ability and desire to express themselves, intended, Dorren states, 'as an amuse-bouche.' Amusing, too! " Booklist.

410 Linguistics

Crystal, David, 1941-

★A **dictionary** of language / David Crystal. University of Chicago, Ill. :Press, 2001. vii, 390 p. : **410**

1. Language and languages 2. Linguistics

ISBN 0226122034

LC 00069076

Includes index.

Rev. ed. of: An encyclopedic dictionary of language and languages. 1992.

Originally published: The Penguin dictionary of language. 2nd ed. London : Penguin, 1999.

No ordinary dictionary, David Crystal's Dictionary of Language includes not only descriptions of hundreds of languages literally from A to Z (Abkhaz to Zyryan) and definitions of literary and grammatical concepts, but also explanations of terms used in linguistics, language teaching, and speech pathology. If you are wondering how many people speak Macedonian, Malay, or Makua, or if you're curious about various theories of the origins of language, or if you were always unsure of the difference between structuralism, semiotics, and sociolinguistics, this superbly authoritative dictionary will answer all of your questions and hundred of others. --From publisher description.

★**How** language works : how babies babble, words change meaning, and languages live or die / David Crystal. Overlook Press, 2006, c2005. xii, 500 p. : **410**

1. Linguistics. 2. Language and languages. 3. Words 4. Speech.

ISBN 1585678481

LC bl2006030001

Originally published: London : Penguin Books, 2005.

A lighthearted exploration of the origin, function and purpose of language addresses a wide range of topics to offer insight into what can be learned through verbal and body language, from the role of gestures and the evolution of grammar to the intricacies of different languages and the layout of the human throat.

"Crystal offers an impeccably organized guide to language and communication that brings clarity to a scholarly subject, and is sure to become a standard reference." Publishers Weekly.

411 Writing systems of standard forms of languages

Houston, Keith, 1977-

Shady characters : the secret life of punctuation, symbols, & other typographical marks / Keith Houston. W.W. Norton & Company, 2013 320 p. **411**

1. Punctuation -- History. 2. Signs and symbols -- History. 3. Type and type-founding -- History. 4. Writing -- History.

ISBN 9780393064421

LC 2013017324

Revealing the secret history of punctuation, this delightful tour of 2,000 years of the written word, from ancient Greece to the Internet, explores the parallel histories of language and typography throughout the world and across time.

Trubek, Anne, 1966-

The **history** and uncertain future of handwriting / Anne Trubek. Bloomsbury, 2016 272 p. **411**

1. Communication. 2. Writing methods and systems. 3. Handwriting 4. Paleography.

ISBN 9781620402153

LC 2016005079

In the digital age of instant communication, handwriting is less necessary than ever before, and indeed fewer and fewer schoolchildren are being taught how to write in cursive. Signatures--far from John Hancock's elegant model--have become scrawls. In her recent and widely discussed and debated essays, Anne Trubek argues that the decline and even elimination of handwriting from daily life does not signal a decline in civilization, but rather the next stage in the evolution of communication.

413 Dictionaries of standard forms of languages

Corbeil, Jean Claude

The **Firefly** five language visual dictionary / Jean-Claude Corbeil, Ariane Archambault. Firefly Books, 2009, c2004. viii, 1092 p. : **413**

1. Picture dictionaries, Polyglot 2. Dictionaries, Polyglot

ISBN 9781554074921

LC 2010290437

Includes indexes.

"English, Spanish, French, German, Italian"--Cover.

Presents an illustrated general reference dictionary that covers subjects and themes ranging from astronomy to sports.

413.028 Auxiliary techniques and procedures apparatus, equipment, materials

Stamper, Kory

Word by word : the secret life of dictionaries / Kory Stamper. Pantheon Books, 2017. 320 p. **413.028**

1. English language 2. Words 3. Vocabulary 4. Lexicography
ISBN 9781101870945

LC 2016024253

While most of us might take dictionaries for granted, the process of writing them is in fact as lively and dynamic as language itself. Stamper cracks open the complex, obsessive world of lexicography, from the agonizing decisions about what and how to define, to the knotty questions of usage in an ever-changing language.

"Word by Word offers marvelous insight into the messy world behind the tidy definitions on the page." Booklist.

415 Grammar of standard forms of languages

Pinker, Steven, 1954-

Words and rules : the ingredients of language / Steven Pinker. Basic Books, c1999. xi, 348 p. : **415**

1. Language and languages. 2. Grammar, Comparative and general -- Verb. 3. Words 4. Terms and phrases.
ISBN 0465072690

LC 99043013

An examination of the human ability to use language by an MIT professor traces the history and evolution of the English language, the theories of Noam Chomsky, the way children learn to use language, and much more.

"This book with its crisp prose and neat analogies, makes required reading for anyone interested in cognition and language." Publishers Weekly.

418 Standard usage (Prescriptive linguistics)

Dehaene, Stanislas

Reading in the brain : the science and evolution of a cultural invention / Stanislas Dehaene. Viking, c2009. 400 p. **418**

1. Reading -- Psychological aspects 2. Books and reading. 3. Brain. 4. Comprehension.
ISBN 9780670021109

LC 2009009389

An accessible introduction to the process through which the brain reads considers a paradox through which the human brain adapted to create and recognize words, in an account that draws on pioneering research to offer insight into language, spelling logic, dyslexia, and more.

Grossman, Edith, 1936-

Why translation matters / Edith Grossman. Yale University Press, c2010. xi, 135 p. ; **418**

1. Literature -- Translations. 2. Translating and interpreting.
ISBN 9780300126563

LC 2009026510

"Based on lectures Grossman gave at Yale, this book provides a succinct argument for the importance of those who 'bring a text over' from another language and make it accessible to a wider audience." Publishers Weekly.

Wolf, Maryanne

Reader, come home : the reading brain in a digital world / Maryanne Wolf. HarperCollins, 2018. 160 p. **418**

1. Books and reading 2. Thought and thinking 3. Technology and civilization 4. Brain -- Physiology
ISBN 9780062388780

LC bl2018117004

Draws on the author's extensive research from *Proust and the Squid* to consider the future of the reading brain and its capacity for critical thinking, empathy and reflection in today's highly digitized world.

"Overall, a hopeful look at the future of reading that will resonate with those who worry that we are losing our ability to think in the digital age." Library Journal.

419 Sign languages

Costello, Elaine

Random House Webster's American Sign Language dictionary : unabridged, / Elaine Costello. Random House Reference, c2008. xxxii, 1200 p. : **419**

1. American Sign Language -- Dictionaries.
ISBN 9780375426162

LC 2009286045

Previously published as: Random House American Sign Language dictionary. 1994.

An updated new edition, written by a former educator at the world's only liberal arts college for the deaf, illustrates that different meanings of the same word might require different signs and includes complete descriptions of each sign and full-torso illustrations for more than 5,600 signs.

Tennant, Richard A.

The **American** Sign Language handshape dictionary / Richard A. Tennant, Marianne Gluszak Brown ; illustrated by Valerie Nelson-Metlay. Clerc Books, Gallaudet University Press, c1998. 407 p. : **419**

1. American Sign Language -- Dictionaries 2. Dictionaries
ISBN 9781563680434

LC 97048389

Includes index.

"The unique feature of this dictionary is that it is organized by handshape rather than by alphabetical order. An American Sign Language learner can look up an unfamiliar sign by looking for the handshape rather than by looking up the word in an alphabetical English glossary. At the same time, an English speaker can look up a sign for a specific word by looking at the Index of English Glossaries located at the end of the dictionary. The introduction includes a history of sign language in the United States. Detailed instructions explain the organization of the handshape sections and the ordering of signs. The illustrations are clear and are described in terms of configuration, location, movement, orientation, and nonmanual markers" -- "Outstanding Reference Sources : the 1999 Selection of New Titles", American Libraries, May 1999. Comp. by the Reference Sources Committee, RUSA, ALA.

420 Specific languages

Bragg, Melvyn, 1939-

The **adventure** of English : the biography of a language / Melvyn Bragg. Arcade Pub., 2004. xii, 322 p. : **420**

1. English language -- History. 2. Etymology 3. Words
ISBN 1559707100

LC 2003019583

"The author offers a biography of the English language, highlighting key individuals, places, and literature that advanced it, as well as the political and social trends that influenced it. Bragg discusses its evolution in the English colonies, devoting four chapters to the United States and one each to India, the West Indies, and Australia. Well researched yet more accessible to a wide audience than scholarly treatments by linguists or historians." Library Journal.

Bryson, Bill

Made in America : an informal history of the English language in the United States / Bill Bryson. W. Morrow, c1994. xii, 417 p. ; **420**

1. English language -- United States -- History. 2. Americanisms -- History. 3. Language and culture. 4. National characteristics, American. 5. United States -- Civilization.
ISBN 9780688103125

LC 94046451

Traces America's history through the language of the time and discusses words culled from everyday activities in a discussion of American English.

McCrum, Robert

★The **story** of English / Robert McCrum, William Cran, Robert MacNeil. Penguin Books, 2003. xxi, 468 p. : **420**

1. English language -- History. 2. Language and languages -- Grammars. 3. Language arts
ISBN 0142002313

LC 2002029818

Sequel: Do you speak American?.

Thoroughly revised and updated, the new edition of the international bestseller tells the anecdotal history of the English language from its obscure Anglo-Saxon origins to its present status as the world's most prominent, expressive, and fast-growing international language.

Metcalf, Allan A.

Predicting new words : the secrets of their success / Allan Metcalf. Houghton Mifflin, c2002. xvi, 206 p. : **420**

1. New words. 2. Lexicology. 3. English language
ISBN 0618130063

LC 2002068593

Includes index.

Examines the phenomenon of new word creation, offering criteria for predicting the success of new words and including the American Dialect Society's listing of words of the year from 1991 to 2001.

"This book traces the origins of an array of words and phrases: Marlboro Man, Frankenfood, blurb, skycap, quark, scofflaw. It also introduces us to a fascinating array of would-be words, coinages that never quite caught on. The book is jam-packed with treats for word lovers." Booklist.

420.9 English language--history

Hitchings, Henry, 1974-

The **language** wars : a history of proper English / Henry Hitchings. Farrar, Straus and Giroux, 2011. 416 p. **420.9**

1. English language -- History. 2. Language and languages. 3. Grammar, Comparative and general.
ISBN 9780374183295

LC 2011010701

Examines modern debates about correct language use while exploring the roles of morality, politics and class on historical style arguments, evaluating the input of key contributors while covering topics ranging from regional accents and slang to political correctness and e-communications.

"As the author points out, there is probably not a person alive who does not have some bee in his bonnet about the way other people speak and write. Maybe it is the errant apostrophe, the splitting of the poor old infinitive, or the use of like as a comma. Or perhaps it is the exclamation mark, once known as the shriek mark. Mr Hitchings's book is a corrective to some of these linguistic prejudices. It is bracing to learn, for example, that the prohibition on splitting the infinitive is fairly recent. Pre-Victorians did not object. Chaucer was a splitter, and even Shakespeare had a go. Same story with the apostrophe: in the 18th-century authors were sprinkling apostrophes over everything. Mr Hitchings reviews such matters with cool erudition. He is resolutely relaxed about usage, understanding that correctitude and intelligibility are not the same." The Economist.

421 Writing system, phonology, phonetics of standard English

Crystal, David, 1941-

Spell it out : the curious, enthralling and extraordinary story of English spelling / David Crystal. St Martins Press, 2013 336 p. **421**

1. Spelling 2. Language and languages. 3. Words 4. English language.
ISBN 9781250003478

LC 2013010521

A lesser-known history of English spelling by the award-winning author of The Story of English in 100 Words is presented through engaging, pithy chapters that cover such topics as the introduction of the Roman alphabet, each letter's origins and the development of long and short vowels.

Rosen, Michael, 1946-

Alphabetical : how every letter tells a story / Michael Rosen. Counterpoint Press, 2015. 448 p. **421**

1. Writing. 2. Alphabet -- History. 3. Writing methods and systems -- History. 4. Alphabet in literature.
ISBN 9781619024830

LC 2014035051

"How on Earth did we fix upon our twenty-six letters, what do they really mean, and how did we come to write them down in the first place? Michael Rosen takes you on an unforgettable adventure through the history of the alphabet in twenty-six vivid chapters, fizzing with personal anecdotes and fascinating facts. Starting with the mysterious Phoenicians and how sounds first came to be written down, he races on to show how nonsense poems work, pins down the strange story of OK, traces our five lost letters and tackles the tyranny of spelling, among many many other things. His heroes of the alphabet range from Edward Lear to Phyllis Pearsall (the inventor of the A-Z), and from the two scribes of

Beowulf to rappers. Each chapter takes on a different subject - whether it's codes, umlauts or the writing of dictionaries. Rosen's enthusiasm for letters positively leaps off the page, whether it's the story of his life told through the typewriters he's owned or a chapter on jokes written in a string of gags and word games. This is the book for anyone who's ever wondered why Hawaiian only has a thirteen-letter alphabet or how exactly to write down the sound of a wild raspberry".-- Provided by publisher.

"Rosen also is mellow about correctness in usage and punctuation (Our personal histories and feelings are wrapped up in what the letters and their means of transmission mean to each of us) and shows little sorrow for the disappearance of handwriting in schools; in fact, he thinks our current emphasis on it doesn't make much sense. A delightfully informative book about letters, their meanings, and the words and meanings we derive from them." Kirkus.

422 Etymology of standard English

Crystal, David, 1941-

The **story** of English in 100 words / David Crystal. St. Martin's Press, 2012, c2011. xxi, 260 p. : **422**

1. Etymology 2. Language and languages. 3. Words 4. Native language.

ISBN 9781250003461

LC 2012003038

Includes index.

Originally published: Profile Books, LTD : Great Britain, 2011.

Demonstrates how the history of English vernacular is reflected in one hundred words with sources in key influences and events, from "roe" and "loaf" to "fopdoodle" and "twittersphere."

Dignen, Sheila

Adonis to Zorro : Oxford dictionary of reference and allusion / edited by Andrew Delahunty and Sheila Dignen. Oxford University Press, 2010. ix, 406 p. ; **422**

1. Allusions -- Dictionaries.

ISBN 9780199567454

LC 2010549367

"First and second editions edited by Andrew Delahunty, Sheila Dignen, and Penny Stock."

Previous ed.: Delahunty, Andrew. The Oxford dictionary of allusions. 2nd ed. c2005.

"It will be a valuable addition to any literature reference collection. Highly recommended." Library Journal.

Forsyth, Mark

The **etymologicon** : a circular stroll through the hidden connections of the English language / Mark Forsyth. Berkley Books, 2012. xvii, 279 p. ; **422**

1. English language -- Etymology

ISBN 9780425260791

LC 2012533123

Unauthorized guide to the underpinnings of the English language.

Hitchings, Henry, 1974-

The **secret** life of words : how English became English / Henry Hitchings. John Murray, 2008. 448 p. **422**

1. Lexicography -- History 2. Etymology 3. Language and culture. 4. Communication.

ISBN 9780374254100

LC 2008026055

Somerset Maugham Award, 2009.

A wide-ranging history of English language and vocabulary reveals hidden etymologies to reveal how English has absorbed words from hundreds of other languages and reflects key social changes.

Houghton Mifflin Company

Word histories and mysteries : from abracadabra to Zeus / from the editors of the American Heritage dictionaries. Houghton Mifflin Co., c2004. xvi, 348 p. : **422**

1. English language -- Etymology -- Dictionaries.

ISBN 9780618454501

LC 2004014798

Conveniently organized in alphabetical order, an entertaining and informative look at the rich diversity of the English language traces the origins and histories of five hundred everyday words.

Manser, Martin H.

★The **Facts** on File dictionary of foreign words and phrases / Martin H. Manser ; associate editors: David H. Pickering, Alice Grandison. Facts on File, c2008. xvii, 469 p. ; **422**

1. English language -- Foreign words and phrases

ISBN 0816070350

LC 2007029711

Provides pronunciations in American English, etymologies, definitions, and sample usage for words, expressions, and phrases from foreign sources, with more than 4,500 entries that include frequently used terms, prefixes and suffixes, words in the news, and the specialized languages of cooking, religion, and other fields. Simultaneous.

"This is a captivating title to browse." School Library Journal.

Rosten, Leo, 1908-1997

The **new** Joys of Yiddish / Leo Rosten ; revisions and commentary by Lawrence Bush ; illustrations by R.O. Blechman. Crown Publishers, c2001. xxxii, 458 p. : **422**

1. Yiddish language -- Influence on English -- Humor 2. English language -- Foreign words and phrases -- Yiddish -- Humor 3. Jewish wit and humor

ISBN 9780609607855

LC 2001028366

An updated version of the informal dictionary which offers the history and folklore behind Yiddish and Hebrew words as well as literal translations adds information on linguistic and cultural changes since Rosten's day.

422.03 English language--etymology--dictionaries

Houghton Mifflin Company

More word histories and mysteries : from aardvark to zombie / from the editors of the American Heritage dictionaries. Houghton Mifflin, c2006. xvi, 288 p. : **422.03**

1. English language -- Etymology -- Dictionaries.

ISBN 9780618716814

LC 2006020835

Sequel to: Word histories and mysteries : from abracadabra to Zeus.

Includes index.

Arranged in alphabetical order, a companion volume to Word Histories and Mysteries offers an entertaining and informative look at the rich diversity of the English language as it traces the origins and histories of additional everyday words.

423 Dictionaries of standard English

Adelson-Goldstein, Jayme

Oxford picture dictionary. Monolingual / Jayme Adelson-Goldstein, Norma Shapiro. Oxford University Press, c2008. xi, 285 p. : **423**

1. English language -- Dictionaries 2. Picture dictionaries
ISBN 9780194369763

LC 2007041017

A picture dictionary of 4,000 words arranged by such topics as everyday language, people, housing, food, clothing, health, community, work, and recreation designed to help English learners.

Ammer, Christine

The **American** Heritage dictionary of idioms / Christine Ammer. Houghton Mifflin Harcourt, 2013 v, 506 p. ; **423**

1. Americanisms 2. English language -- United States 3. English language -- United States -- Idioms
ISBN 0547676581

LC 2012026443

Covering almost ten thousand phrases, including bite the bullet, take the cake, buy the farm, and says who, a unique reference on common American vocabulary and idiomatic expressions defines each entry and provides a contextual sentence.

"This book makes for fun browsing and could be very helpful to foreign speakers." Choice.

Brewer, Ebenezer Cobham, 1810-1897

★**Brewer's** dictionary of phrase & fable / edited by Susie Dent. Brewer's, c2012. xxii, 1480 p. : **423**

1. Allusions. 2. English language 3. Literature 4. Mythology 5. Terms and phrases Dictionaries.
ISBN 0550107649

LC 2012464049

Provides definitions of typical phrases and words and explains their historical origins.

Corbeil, Jean-Claude

★**Merriam-Webster's** visual dictionary / under the direction of Jean-Claude Corbeil. Merriam-Webster, Incorporated, 2012. 1112 p. : **423**

1. Picture dictionaries, English.
ISBN 0877791511

LC 2013498156

Includes index.

25,000 terms and their definitions with 8,000 full-color illustrations of a wide variety of objects from all aspects of life.

Espy, Willard R.

Words to rhyme with : a rhyming dictionary : including a primer of prosody, a list of more than 80,000 words that rhyme, a glossary defining 9,000 of the more eccentric rhyming words, and a variety of exemplary verses, one of which does not rhyme at all / Willard R. Espy. Facts On File, c2006. xix, 683 p. ; **423**

1. English language -- Rhyme -- Dictionaries 2. English language -- Versification 3. Dictionaries
ISBN 9780816063031

LC 2005051122

Includes index.

Lists more than 80,000 rhyming words, including single, double, and triple rhymes, and offers information on rhyme schemes, meter, and poetic forms.

Houghton Mifflin Harcourt Publishing Company,

★The **American** Heritage dictionary of the English language Houghton Mifflin Harcourt, 2016 xxvii, 2084 p. : **423**

1. English language -- Dictionaries.
ISBN 9780544454453

LC bl2016012256

Bound in eco-friendly linen cloth, a latest edition of the top-selling reference incorporates more than 10,000 new words and terms as well as the latest research on word origins and meanings, providing guidelines on accurate usage and more than 4,000 new full-color images.

Lindberg, Christine A., 1954-

★**Oxford** American Writer's Thesaurus / Compiled by Christine A. Lindberg. Oxford University Press, 2012. xxv, 1050 p. ; **423**

1. English language -- Synonyms and antonyms
ISBN 9780199829927

LC 2012454696

Features more than three hundred thousand synonyms and ten thousand antonyms, as well as nearly two hundred collections of nouns to add detail to writing and quick guides to easily confused words.

Merriam-Webster, Inc

★**Merriam-Webster's** collegiate dictionary Merriam-Webster, Inc., 2003. 1623 p. : **423**

1. English language -- Dictionaries.
ISBN 9780877798088

LC 2003003674

Includes index.

Presents concise definitions, pronunciations, abbreviations, some illustrations, usage examples, and synonyms with ten thousand new words and meanings.

Mugglestone, Lynda

Lost for words : the hidden history of the Oxford English dictionary / Lynda Mugglestone. Yale University Press, 2005. xxi, 273 p. : **423**

1. Oxford English dictionary. 2. Encyclopedias -- History and criticism 3. Lexicography. 4. Dictionaries -- History and criticism 5. Etymology
ISBN 0300106998

LC 2004029344

"This is a history of the making of the OED." Am Sch.

"Serious word lovers will appreciate … [this book's] fascinating revelations." Booklist.

Simpson, J. A., 1953-

The **Oxford** English dictionary / John A. Simpson, Edmund (EDT) Weiner. Oxford University Press, 1989. 20 v. ; **423**

1. English language -- Dictionaries 2. Dictionaries
ISBN 9780198611868

LC 88005330

A dictionary like no other in the world, the OED has been described as "among the wonders of the world of scholarship." --From publisher description.

Stevenson, Angus

★**Concise** Oxford English dictionary / edited by Angus Stevenson, Maurice Waite. Oxford University Press, c2011. xxix, 1682 p. ; **423**

1. English language -- Dictionaries.
ISBN 9780199601080

LC 2011389902

Features more than 240,000 words, phrases and definitions, covering technical and scientific vocabulary as well as English from around the world.

425.55 English language -- Pronouns

Baron, Dennis E.

What's your pronoun? : beyond he and she / Dennis Baron. Liveright Publishing, 2020. 272 p. **425.55**

1. Grammar, Comparative and general 2. Pronouns 3. Gender identity 4. Gender equity
ISBN 9781631496042

LC 2019021998

The University of Illinois linguistics professor and national commentator on language issues explores evolving debates regarding modern pronoun usage, tracing the history of pronouns, the creations of new gender pronouns and the role of pronouns in establishing identity and rights.

"Based on decades of research, Baron's masterly work documents the historical and continued importance of personal pronouns. Those interested in gender politics or English grammar, or who feel that 'he' and 'she' are inadequate, would benefit greatly from perusing this book." Library Journal.

427 Historical and geographic variations, modern nongeographic variations of English

Axelrod, Alan, 1952-

Whiskey tango foxtrot : the real language of the modern American military / Alan Axelrod. Skyhorse Publishing, 2013 212 p. ; **427**

1. English language -- United States -- Slang 2. Military art and science -- United States 3. Sailors -- United States -- Language 4. Soldiers -- United States -- Language
ISBN 9781620876473

LC 2013011431

Explores military slang, explaining acronyms, words, and phrases in a text arranged by topic.

Bailey, Richard W.

Speaking American : a history of English in the United States / Richard W. Bailey. Oxford University Press, 2011. 240 p. **427**

1. English language -- United States -- History. 2. Americanisms. 3. Language and languages.
ISBN 9780195179347

LC 2011011042

Investigates the history and continuing evolution of American English, from the 16th century to the present, to celebrate the endless variety and remarkable inventiveness that have always been at the heart of our language. By the author of Images of English: A Cultural History of the Language.

Crystal, David, 1941-

★**English** as a global language / David Crystal. Cambridge University Press, 2012, c2003. xv, 212 p. : **427**

1. English language -- Foreign countries. 2. English language -- Social aspects -- Foreign countries. 3. English language -- Social aspects -- English-speaking countries. 4. Communication, International.
ISBN 9781107611801

LC 2013498883

Written in a detailed and fascinating manner, this book is ideal for general readers interested in the English language.

The **stories** of English / David Crystal. Overlook Press, 2004. [viii], 584 p. : **427**

1. Language and languages. 2. Linguistics. 3. English language -- Variation -- English-speaking countries.
ISBN 1585676012

LC 2004054727

"The author traces the diverse and unpredictable influences that have shaped English into an unruly family of dialects, creoles, and patois. Crystal acknowledges the emergence during the fourteenth and fifteenth centuries of a prestigious standard version of English. Yet he shows in instance after instance that the tempests of linguistic change have often overwhelmed the custodians of the King's English, compelling them to accommodate forces they could not control. And though he never loses his focus on language, Crystal allows some of its more colorful users--including Chaucer, Shakespeare, Samuel Johnson, and Thomas Jefferson--to bring their personalities and voices into the chronicle." Booklist.

Dalzell, Tom, 1951-

The **Routledge** dictionary of Modern American slang and unconventional English / edited by Tom Dalzell. Routledge, 2018. viii, 892 p. ; **427**

1. English language -- Slang -- Dictionaries.
ISBN 9781138779655

LC 2017001815

The Routledge Dictionary of Modern American Slang offers the ultimate record of modern, post WW2 American Slang. The 25,000 entries are accompanied by citations that authenticate the words as well as offer examples of usage from popular literature, newspapers, magazines, movies, television shows, musical lyrics, and Internet user groups. Etymology, cultural context, country of origin and the date the word was first used are also provided. In terms of content, the cultural transformations since 1945 are astounding. Television, computers, drugs, music, unpopular wars, youth movements, changing racial sensitivities and attitudes towards sex and sexuality are all substantial factors that have shaped culture and language. --From publisher description.

Holder, R. W.

★**How** not to say what you mean : a dictionary of euphemisms / R.W. Holder. Oxford University Press, 2007. xvi, 410 p. ; **427**

1. English language -- Euphemism 2. English language -- Synonyms and antonyms. 3. Vocabulary.
ISBN 0199208395

LC 2007037558

This thoroughly updated new edition of How Not to Say What You Mean celebrates 20 years of R. W. Holder's popular and successful dictionary of euphemisms, offering a delightful collection of jocular and evasive expressions for sex, death, murder, crime, prison, and much more. --From publisher description.

"Holder's collection, first published in 1987, has become the standard reference in the UK." Booklist.

MacNeil, Robert, 1931-

Do you speak American? : a companion to the PBS television series / Robert MacNeil and William Cran. Nan A. Talese/ Doubleday, 2005. 228 p. ; **427**

1. Americanisms. 2. English language -- History. 3. Language and languages -- Grammars. 4. Language arts

ISBN 9780385511988

LC 2004053735

Sequel to: The story of English.

Offers a look at the origins, history, and current state of American spoken and written language, looking at the linguistic traditions in diverse regions of the country and assessing the influence of e-mail, ethnic boundaries, and other factors on the language.

"Whether talking to crab fishermen in Maryland or country-and-western singers in Tennessee, the authors discover that regional dialects are thriving despite the uniformity of our national tastes in clothing, fast-food chains, and movies. The authors show how mobility, immigration, and racial and ethnic mixing are rapidly and profoundly changing the language. This is colorful, witty, and insightful commentary on American speech patterns." Booklist.

McMahon, Sean

Brewer's dictionary of Irish phrase & fable / Sean McMahon and Jo O'Donoghue. Brewer's, 2009. xiii, 867 p. ; **427**

1. Irish philology -- Encyclopedias 2. Mythology, Celtic -- Ireland -- Encyclopedias 3. Ireland Encyclopedias. 4. Ireland -- Languages Encyclopedias. 5. Ireland -- Civilization Encyclopedias. 6. Ireland -- In literature Encyclopedias. 7. Encyclopedias 8. Dictionaries

ISBN 9780550105653

LC bl2010032190

Originally published: London : Weidenfeld & Nicholson, 2004.

Provides definitions of Irish phrases and words and explains their historical origins.

McWhorter, John H.

Talking back, talking black : truths about America's lingua franca / John McWhorter. Bellevue Literary Press, 2017. 190 p. **427**

1. African Americans -- Language 2. English language -- Social aspects 3. Language and languages 4. Language and education -- United States. 5. Essays

ISBN 9781942658207

LC 2017276522

A linguistic expert explains the fundamentals and rich history of Black English while carefully examining the cultural, educational and political issues that have undermined recognition of the transformative, empowering dialect.

"This is an engaging look at the English language as spoken by many black Americans as well as the long history of stereotyping that has prevented an objective analysis of a rich language tradition." Booklist.

Nunberg, Geoffrey, 1945-

The **ascent** of the A-word : assholism, the first sixty years / Geoffrey Nunberg. PublicAffairs, 2012. 256 p. **427**

1. Obscene words 2. Swearing. 3. Vocabulary. 4. Words

ISBN 9781610391757

LC 2012017027

Includes index.

A renowned linguist looks at the surprisingly short history of the word "asshole"--from its use by World War II servicemen to express their frustration at arrogant superiors to its first use in print by Norman Mailer to George W. Bush's use of the word to describe a journalist and beyond.

428 Standard English usage (Prescriptive linguistics)

Dunn, Patricia A., 1952-

Grammar rants : how a backstage tour of writing complaints can help students make informed, savvy choices about their writing / Patricia A. Dunn and Ken Lindblom. Heinemann/ Boynton/Cook Publishers, c2011. xvi, 134 p. : **428**

1. English language -- Grammar -- Study and teaching 2. English language -- Rhetoric -- Study and teaching 3. English language -- Usage

ISBN 9780867096057

LC 2011005689

Grammar Rants provides the background teachers need to speak with authority about punctuation, correctness, and other hot-button issues. Its practical activities, handouts, and lessons will promote savvy writing by empowering teachers and students to see for themselves how best to raise the quality of their written and spoken language without resorting to ranting. --From publisher description.

Jetton, Tamara L.

Adolescent literacy in the academic disciplines : general principles and practical strategies / edited by Tamara L. Jetton, Cynthia Shanahan. The Guilford Press, 2012. xiv, 274 p. : **428**

1. Language arts (Secondary) 2. Language arts -- Correlation with content subjects.

ISBN 9781462502806

LC 2011035689

"From leading authorities in both adolescent literacy and content-area teaching, this book addresses the particular challenges of literacy learning in each of the major academic disciplines. Chapters focus on how to help students successfully engage with texts and ideas in English/literature, science, math, history, and arts classrooms. The book shows that while general strategies for reading informational texts are essential, they are not enough--students also need to learn processing strategies that are quite specific to each subject and its typical tasks or problems. Vignettes from exemplary classrooms illustrate research-based ways to build content-area knowledge while targeting essential reading and writing skills".-- Provided by publisher.

428.1 Vocabulary--English language--usage (Applied linguistics)

Elster, Charles Harrington

How to tell fate from destiny : and other skillful word distinctions / Charles Harrington Elster ; [illustrations by Chi Birmingham]. Houghton Mifflin Harcourt, 2018. viii, 312 p. : **428.1**

1. English language -- Usage. 2. English language -- Errors of usage.

ISBN 9781328884077

LC 2018028262

"If you have trouble distinguishing the verbs imitate and emulate, the relative pronouns that and which, or the adjectives pliant, pliable, and supple, never fear--How to Tell Fate from Destiny is here to help! With more than 500 headwords, the book is replete with advice on how to differentiate commonly confused words and steer clear of verbal trouble".-- Provided by publisher.

428.2 English language grammar

Florey, Kitty Burns

Sister Bernadette's barking dog : the quirky history and lost art of diagramming sentences / Kitty Burns Florey. Melville House, c2006. 154 p. : **428.2**

1. English language -- Grammar 2. English language -- Sentences 3. English language -- Syntax 4. Essays
ISBN 9781933633107

LC 2006024703

"The author writes with verve about the nuns who taught her to render the English language as a mess of slanted lines, explains how diagrams work, and traces the bizarre history of the men who invented this odd pedagogical tool. And unlike so many of today's microhistorians, who seek to demonstrate how zippers, azaleas, or hopscotch explain the world, Florey is refreshingly content to recount her tale without any suggestion that the diagramming of sentences somehow illuminates the American character. It's a great read." Slate.

Garner, Bryan A

The **Chicago** guide to grammar, usage, and punctuation / Bryan A. Garner. The University of Chicago Press, 2016. xxvii, 583 p. ; **428.2**

1. English language -- Grammar -- Handbooks, manuals, etc. 2. English language -- Grammar -- Study and teaching (Higher).
ISBN 9780226188850

LC 2015047425

Discusses standard literary English with sections about usage, grammar, punctuation, and word formation.

Hult, Christine A

The **handy** English grammar answer book / Christine A. Hult, Ph.D.. Visible Ink Press, 2016 xii, 419 p. : **428.2**

1. English language -- Grammar -- Handbooks, manuals, etc.
ISBN 9781578595204

LC 2015015787

Includes index.

Explains the rules of English grammar, explores common mistakes, and offers situational examples of correct usage.

O'Conner, Patricia T.

★**Woe** is I : the grammarphobe's guide to better English in plain English / Patricia T. O'Conner, Riverhead Books, 2003. xvi, 240 p. ; **428.2**

1. Grammar 2. English language -- Usage.
ISBN 1573222526

LC 2003041416

A guide to English grammar and style reveals the underlying logic of the language with the help of examples organized according to specific problems.

"The author doesn't take herself or the subject matter too seriously, offering a delightful romp through the intricacies of our language. . . . She knows her subject, can convey her message with wit and ease, and does it all in a compact, easy-to-read format. In short, this is an entertaining and useful grammar reference." Library Journal.

Strumpf, Michael

The **grammar** bible : everything you always wanted to know about grammar but didn't know whom to ask / Michael Strumpf and Auriel Douglas. H. Holt, 2004, c1999. xvi, 489 p. ; **428.2**

1. Grammar 2. Grammar, Comparative and general.
ISBN 0805075607

LC 2003057129

"First published by Knowledgeopolis in 1999"--T.p. verso.

"An Owl book."

A quick and easy reference guide to the English language, grammar, and usage answers a host of queries on verb tenses and moods, punctuation, capitalization, phrases, clauses, common and proper nouns, and other problematic language issues.

"The authors move from the parts of speech to the parts of the sentence and then to spelling, vocabulary, and punctuation, even encompassing thorny issues (e.g., sexist language, split infinitives) and complex grammatical terms (e.g., objective complements, gerund phrases). The authors also include a useful list of collocations and intersperse informative and often amusing Hot Line queries throughout. This book is thorough, combining practical information not easily found in trade books, and is lively without trying to be too witty, cute, or humorous." Library Journal.

Truss, Lynne

Eats, shoots & leaves : the zero tolerance approach to punctuation / Lynne Truss; Pat Byrnes, illustrator. Gotham Books, 2009, c2004. 176 p. : **428.2**

1. Language and languages -- Grammars. 2. English language -- Usage -- Humor 3. Language arts 4. Writing -- Philosophy
ISBN 9781592404889

LC 2009291769

Looks at the history of punctuation and the rules governing the use of apostrophes, commas, dashes, hyphens, colons, and semicolons.

"The author dissects common errors that grammar mavens have long deplored (often, as she readily points out, in isolation) and makes . . . arguments for increased attention to punctuation correctness. . . . Truss serves up delightful, unabashedly strict and sometimes snobby little book, with cheery Britishisms (Lawks-a-mussy!) dotting pages that express a more international righteous indignation." Publishers Weekly.

440 French and related Romance languages

Nadeau, Jean-Benoit

★The **story** of French / Jean-Benoit Nadeau and Julie Barlow. St. Martin's Press, 2006. 483 p. **440**

1. French language -- History. 2. Linguistics. 3. Language and languages.
ISBN 0312341830

Explores the origins and evolution of the French language, from the first extant document written in French in the mid-ninth century and the purging of Latin from the French courts to the obsession of French speakers to protect the purity of the language.

"This is a well-told, highly accessible history of the French language that leads to a spirited discussion of the prospects for French in an increasingly English-dominated world." New York Times.

443 Dictionaries of standard French

Correard, Marie-Helene

★**Larousse** French-English, English-French dictionary : advanced / [managing editor, Janice McNeillie ; editors, Marie-Helene Correard ... et al.]. Larousse ; c2007. 2331 p. ; **443**

1. English language -- French. 2. French language -- English.
ISBN 2035421322

LC bl2007023873

Previous ed. published with title: Grand dictionnaire francais-anglais, anglais-francais.

Features more than 250,000 entries and 400,000 translations; a bilingual atlas; coverage of Canadian, Belgian, and Swiss French; sidebars on French life and culture; and models for letters, faxes, and e-mails.

460 Spanish, Portuguese, Galician

Nadeau, Jean-Benoit

The **story** of Spanish / Jean-Benoit Nadeau and Julie Barlow. St. Martin's Press, 2013. 496 p. **460**

1. Spanish language -- History. 2. Linguistics. 3. Language and languages.
ISBN 9780312656027

LC 2013002633

Jean-Benoit Nadeau and Julie Barlow chronicle the history of the Spanish language.

463 Dictionaries of standard Spanish

Oxford Dictionaries (COR)

The **Oxford** Spanish dictionary : Spanish-English, English-Spanish / chief editors Beatriz Galimberti Jarman, Roy Russell. Oxford University Press Inc., 2008. xlviii, 1943 p. ; **463**

1. English language -- Spanish 2. Spanish language -- English
ISBN 9780199208975

LC 2008026099

"4th ed. edited by Nicholas Rollin, Carol Styles Carvajal" - - Cover.

A bilingual dictionary containing more than 300,000 words covers basic vocabulary as well as slang, American English, and Latin American Spanish.

"No serious Hispanist in the English-speaking world can do without the magnificent Oxford Spanish dictionaries." Times Literary Supplement.

470 Latin and related Italic languages

Ostler, Nicholas

Ad infinitum : a biography of Latin / Nicholas Ostler. Walker & Co., 2007. 400 p. **470**

1. Latin language -- History. 2. Language and languages -- Origin. 3. Lingua francas. 4. Language and culture.
ISBN 080271515X

LC bl2007012214

A study of the Latin language examines its role in the evolution of Western culture and civilization; its relationship with ancient Greek language, science, and philosophy; its place in the Catholic Church; and its function as an ancestor of modern-day languages.

"In four parts, Ostler covers the origins and development of Latin in the Roman world, Latin's taking over the church, its medieval continuation and fracturing into vernaculars, and a nuanced rebirth in the Renaissance and its legacy in the contemporary world. Incredibly well documented, with examples from antiquity to the modern era." Library Journal.

473 Dictionaries of classical Latin

Stone, Jon R., 1959-

★**Latin** for the illiterati : a modern phrase book for an ancient language / Jon R. Stone. Routledge, 2009. xxii, 338 p. ; **473**

1. Latin language 2. Latin language -- English
ISBN 9780415777674

LC 2010481624

Previous ed.: 1996.

This revised and updated edition includes a brand new foreword by Richard LaFleur and more than fifteen hundred new entries and abbreviations. Organized alphabetically within the categories of verba (common words and expressions), dicta (common phrases and familiar sayings), and abbreviations, this practical and helpful reference guide is a comprehensive compendium of more than 7,000 Latin words, expressions, phrases, and sayings taken from the world of art, music, law, philosophy, theology, medicine and the theatre, as well as witty remarks and sage advice from ancient writers such as Virgil, Ovid, Cicero, and more. --From publisher description.

483 Dictionaries of classical Greek

Liddell, Henry George, 1811-1898

A **Greek-English** lexicon / compiled by Henry George Liddell and Robert Scott. Oxford University Press, 1996. xlv, 2042, xxxi, 320 p. ; **483**

1. Greek language -- English
ISBN 9780198642268

LC 95032369

"With a revised supplement, 1996."

Liddell & Scott's Greek-English Lexicon is the most comprehensive and up-to-date ancient Greek dictionary in the world. Used by every student of ancient Greek in the English-speaking world, the dictionary covers every surviving ancient Greek author and text discovered up to 1940, from the Pre-Classical Greek of Homer and Hesiod to Classical Greek to the Hellenistic Period, including the Greek Old and New Testaments. This monumental work is now available with a brand new Revised Supplement. Representing the culmination of thirteen years' work, the new Supplement is a complete replacement of the 1968 Supplement. Nearly twice the size of the 1968 edition, with over 20,000 entries, it adds to the dictionary words and forms from papyri and inscriptions discovered between 1940 and the 1990s as well as a host of other revisions, updatings, and corrections to the main dictionary. Linear B forms are shown within entries for the first time, and the Revised Supplement gives the dictionary a date-range from 1200 BC to 600 AD. It is fully cross-referenced to the main text, but additions have been designed to be easily used without constant reference to the main text. --From publisher description.

492.4 Hebrew

Glinert, Lewis

The **story** of Hebrew / Lewis Glinert. Princeton University Press, 2016. 296 p. **492.4**

1. Hebrew language 2. Linguistics 3. Hebrew language -- Revival 4. Hebrew language -- Usage 5. Israel
ISBN 9780691153292

LC 2016022084

An examination of the Hebrew language, and its transition from the language of the Judaic scriptures, through its decline and abandonment, and eventually to its re-adoption in the 20th century in a largely unchanged form.

"This is a must-read for students of language and Jewish history." Publishers Weekly.

495.6 Japanese

Waley, Arthur

The **no** plays of Japan : an anthology / Arthur Waley. Dover Publications, 1998. 270 p. ; **495.6**

1. No plays -- Translations into English
ISBN 9780486401560

LC 97046053

Originally published: New York : Alfred A. Knopf, 1922.

Part prose, part verse, the visually stunning No plays of Japan deal with such subjects as insanity, obsession and historical characters, and frequently have as their focal points demons, gods, and beautiful women. Among the 19 works and 15 summaries included here are Ukai (The Cormorant-Fisher), Hatsuyuki (Early Snow), as well as a farcical interlude, or kyogen, titled The Bird-Catcher in Hell. A unique introduction for Western theater-goers to classic Japanese drama. --From publisher description.

498 South American native languages

Kierkegaard, Soren, 1813-1855

Fear and trembling / Soren Kierkegaard ; translated from the Danish by Alastair Hannay. Penguin Books, 2006. 151 p. **498**

1. Christianity -- Philosophy
ISBN 9780143037576

LC OC2012121048

This ed. originally published: London : Penguin Books (UK), 2005.

Uses the story of Abraham and Isaac to discuss the "theological suspension of ethics," a philosophical concept that claims when one acts out of direction from God, one is not necessarily subject to the ethical laws of the universe.

499 Non-Austronesian languages of Oceania, Austronesian languages, miscellaneous languages

Okrent, Arika

In the land of invented languages : Esperanto rock stars, Klingon poets, Loglan lovers, and the mad dreamers who tried to build a perfect language / Arika Okrent. Spiegel & Grau, 2009. 352 p. **499**

1. Language and languages. 2. Linguistics 3. Artificial languages
ISBN 9780385527880

LC 2008038732

Explores the fascinating and highly entertaining history of man's enduring quest to build a better language, including Babm, Blissymbolics, and the nearly nine hundred other languages that represent the hard work, high hopes, and full-blown delusions of so many misguided souls.

"The author explores some of the themes and shortcomings of 900 years worth of artificial languages. . . . [Her] prose is a model of clarity and grace; through it, she conveys fascinating insights into why natural language, with its corruptions, ambiguities and arbitrary conventions, trips so fluently off our tongues." Publishers Weekly.

Pukui, Mary Kawena, 1895-1986

Hawaiian dictionary : Hawaiian-English, English-Hawaiian / Mary Kawena Pukui, Samuel H. Elbert. University of Hawaii Press, c1986. xxvi, 572 p. ; **499**

1. Hawaiian language -- Dictionaries -- English 2. English language -- Dictionaries -- Hawaiian 3. Dictionaries
ISBN 9780824807030

LC 85024583

Includes definitions, a grammar, and a pronunciation key

Schor, Esther H.

Bridge of words : Esperanto and the dream of a universal language / Esther Schor. Metropolitan Books, 2016 384 p. **499**

1. Esperanto -- History. 2. Language and languages
ISBN 9780805090796

LC 2015018907

In 1887, Ludwig Lazarus Zamenhof, a Polish Jew, had the idea of putting an end to tribalism by creating a universal language, one that would be equally accessible to everyone in the world. The result was Esperanto, a utopian scheme full of the brilliance, craziness, and grandiosity that characterize all such messianic visions. In this first full history of a constructed language, poet and scholar Esther Schor traces the life of Esperanto.

"Must reading for those fascinated by linguistics and utopian endeavors and an essential volume for every library's language collection." Booklist.

500 Natural sciences and mathematics

Balaban, Naomi E.

The **handy** science answer book / compiled by the Carnegie Library of Pittsburgh ; [edited by Naomi E. Balaban and James E. Bobick]. Visible Ink Press, 2011. viii, 679 p. : **500**

1. Science -- Miscellanea.
ISBN 9781578593217

LC 2011000429

"Presenting a fun and educational way to explore the wonders of the world of science, this newly updated edition poses and answers 2,200 questions, providing an abundance of original and interesting science facts. Children and adults will uncover some of the most interesting, unusual, and quirky science curiosities such as: Are cell phones dangerous to your health? Is the same strain of yeast used to make different types of beer? What is the cleanest fossil fuel? What is the largest invertebrate? Readers will find this informative and enjoyable resource is chock full of hundreds of intriguing science and technology topics, from the inner workings of the human body and outer space to math, computers, planes, trains, and automobiles".-- Provided by publisher.

Bais, Sander

In praise of science : curiosity, understanding, and progress / Sander Bais. MIT Press, c2010. 192 p. : **500**

1. Science.
ISBN 0262014351

LC 2009035675

In this book, author and physicist Sander Bais shows how science can liberate us from our cultural straitjacket of prejudice and intolerance. We're living in a time in which technology is taken for granted, yet belief in such standard scientific facts as evolution is actually decreasing. How is it possible for cell phones and Creationism to coexist? Science--fundamental, fact-based knowledge, not the latest technological gadget--can give us the global and local perspectives we need to make the world a better place. The author argues that turning points in the history of science have been accompanied by similar milestones in social change, deeply affecting our view of nature, our perception of the human condition, and our understanding of the universe andour place in it.

"The polemical nature of Bais' arguments might spark debate for some readers, but he never comes across as ranting. He employs many (at times lengthy) quotes from a variety of sources, and near the end of the book there's a tendency to let the quotes make the case for him. But for the vast majority of the book, Bais seems like the quirky professor everyone loves and/or wishes they had, one who inspires lifelong interests." PopMatters.

Benamran, Bruce, 1977-

How to speak science : gravity, relativity, and other ideas that were crazy until proven brilliant / Bruce Benamran ; translated by Stephanie Delozier Strobel. The Experiment, 2018, c2015. 320 p. **500**

1. Science 2. Scientists -- History 3. Scientific discoveries

ISBN 9781615194032

LC 2018018275

Originally published in France: Prenez le temps d'e-penser (Paris : Editions Marabout, 2015).

A scientist and popular YouTube personality, reminding us that we've lost touch with many of the most basic science concepts that launched our information age, presents simple, math-free explanations and to-the-point historical recaps of landmark science and history's greatest scientists.

Bloom, Howard K., 1943-

The **God** problem : how a godless cosmos creates / Howard Bloom. Prometheus Books, 2012. 575 p. **500**

1. Science -- Social aspects. 2. Religion and science. 3. Cosmology -- Miscellanea. 4. Atheism

ISBN 9781616145514

LC 2012013460

Argues that there is no God and explains how the universe can pull off all the complexities that come with creation.

Brockman, John, 1941-

This explains everything : deep, beautiful, and elegant theories of how the world works / edited by John Brockman. Harper Perennial, c2013. 416 p. **500**

1. Science -- Miscellanea 2. Essays

ISBN 9780062230171

LC 2012032107

Presents responses from 150 of the world's brightest and most influential minds when asked to reveal their favorite deep, elegant, or beautiful explanation of how the human mind, society, and the universe work.

This idea is brilliant : lost, overlooked, and underappreciated scientific concepts everyone should know / John Brockman. HarperPerennial, 2018 864 p. **500**

1. Science -- Popular works. 2. Essays

ISBN 9780062698216

LC bl2018001260

As science informs public policy, decision making, and so many aspects of our everyday lives, a scientifically literate society is crucial. In that spirit, Edge.org publisher and author of Know This, John Brockman, asks 206 of the world's most brilliant minds the 2017 Edge Question: What scientific term or concept ought to be more widely known?

Bronowski, Jacob, 1908-1974

Science and human values / J. Bronowski. Perennial Library, 1990, c1965. xiv, 199 p. : **500**

1. Science. 2. Philosophy and science. 3. Essays.

ISBN 0060972815

LC 89045631

"The three essays which make up Science and human values were first given as lectures at the Massachusetts Institute of Technology on 26 February, 5 March, and 19 March 1953." The dialogue was originally broadcast by the BBC Third Programme in 1962.

Reprint. Originally published 1965.

Professor Bronowski explains the need to recognize science as an integral part of modern culture.

"The dialogue discusses the theme that science is as integral a part of the culture of our age as the arts are." Scientific American.

Bryson, Bill

★A **short** history of nearly everything / Bill Bryson. Broadway Books, 2003. ix, 544 p. **500**

1. Science -- History.

ISBN 0767908171

LC 2003046006

Royal Society General Prizes for Science Books, 2004.

"Neither oversimplified nor overstuffed, this exceptionally skillful tour of the physical world covers the basic principles and still has room for profiles of some of the more engaging scientists. " New York Times Book Review.

Dawkins, Richard, 1941-

A **devil's** chaplain : reflections on hope, lies, science, and love / Richard Dawkins. Houghton Mifflin Co., 2003. vi, 263 p. : **500**

1. Evolution. 2. Mysticism. 3. Science -- Philosophy. 4. Religion and science. 5. Africa -- History 6. Essays.

ISBN 0618335404

LC 2003050859

Presents a collection of essays that explore such topics as religion, mysticism, modern educational methods, pseudoscience, Africa, and late colleagues Douglas Adams and Stephen Jay Gould.

"This is a collection of essays that span 25 years of writing on evolution, education and science versus nonsense. Dawkins is creative, articulate and, above all, emotional." New York Times Book Review.

Science in the soul : selected writings of a passionate rationalist / Richard Dawkins. Random House, 2017. 320 p. **500**

1. Evolution 2. Reason 3. Truth 4. Science 5. Essays

ISBN 9780399592249

LC 2017025118

An evolutionary biologist and provocateur, in a collection of 42 essays, focuses on what science is and how it is done, the inexhaustible wonders of nature, the importance of critical thinking and the great minds who have changed his life

"These 41 short pieces suitably capture evolutionary biologist Dawkins's . reputation as a fierce proponent of rationalism, who possesses an exacting and questioning scientific mind and an acerbic wit." Library Journal.

Dean, Cornelia

Making sense of science : separating substance from spin / Cornelia Dean. The Belknap Press of Harvard University Press, 2017. 280 p. **500**

1. Science news 2. Science in mass media 3. Science in popular culture 4. Science journalism

ISBN 9780674059696

LC 2016037738

Cornelia Dean draws on her 30 years as a science journalist with the New York Times to expose the flawed reasoning and knowledge gaps that handicap readers when they try to make sense of science. She calls attention to conflicts of interest in research and the price society pays when science journalism declines and funding dries up.--Provided by publisher

"Deans excellent primer will be welcomed by those who find themselves lost in the fog of rival claims about scientific issues that affect us all." Publishers Weekly.

Du Sautoy, Marcus

The **great** unknown : seven journeys to the frontiers of science / Marcus du Sautoy. Viking, 2017. 464 p. **500**

1. Scientific discoveries. 2. Knowledge theory. 3. Science -- History.
ISBN 9780735221802

LC 2016056835

The award-winning author of The Music of the Primes and popular presenter of Netflix's The Story of Math explores the once-ridiculed theories of history's greatest innovators and the outer reaches of human knowledge to consider what discoveries may lie beyond the predictive powers of science.

"This brilliant, well-written exploration of our universes biggest mysteries will captivate the curious and leave them pondering 'natural phenomena that will never be tamed and known.' " Publishers Weekly.

Dyson, Freeman J.

Dreams of earth and sky / Freeman Dyson. New York Review Books, [2015] 300 p. **500**

1. Serendipity in science. 2. Scientific discoveries 3. Science 4. Essays
ISBN 9781590178546

LC 2014038482

Freeman Dyson's new collection of pieces from The New York Review of Books investigates and celebrates what he calls openness to unconventional ideas in science. His subjects range from the seventeenth-century scientific revolution, to the scientific inquiries of the Romantic generation, to important recent works by Daniel Kahneman and Malcolm Gladwell. He discusses twentieth-century giants of physics such as Richard Feynman, J. Robert Oppenheimer, and Paul Dirac, many of whom he knew personally, and explores some of today's most pressing scientific issues, from global warming, to the future of biotechnology, to the flood of information in the digital age.

"Readers who enjoyed the first volume of reviews will be pleased with this follow-up, and new readers will be delighted by the fascinating insider's view of the scientific community and its intersection with the political establishment." Kirkus.

Feynman, Richard P., (Richard Phillips), 1918-1988

★The **meaning** of it all : thoughts of a citizen scientist / Richard P. Feynman. Addison Wesley, 1998. 133 p. ; **500**

1. Feynman, Richard P., (Richard Phillips), 1918-1988 2. Science -- Social aspects -- Miscellanea 3. Physicists -- United States 4. Religion and science. 5. Science -- Political aspects 6. United States -- History -- 20th century
ISBN 0201360802

LC 97048250

Includes index.

In a series of previously unpublished lectures given at the University of Washington in 1963, one of the century's leading physicists reveals his thoughts on religion, life, politics, and science

Gardner, Martin, 1914-2010

★**Did** Adam and Eve have navels? : discourses on reflexology, numerology, urine therapy, and other dubious subjects / Martin Gardner. W.W. Norton, 2000. xi, 333 p. ; **500**

1. Science -- Miscellanea. 2. Numerology -- History. 3. Pseudoscience. 4. Urine therapy. 5. Essays.
ISBN 9780393049633

LC 00034870

A master debunker of scientific fraud and psuedo-science takes on numerology, Freud's dream theory, reflexology, and the Heaven's Gate cult, among other assaults on reason and rational thought.

"This is a collection of the author's pieces culled from the Skeptical Inquirer. Gardner gives succinct and amusing critiques of a number of the fallacies that abound in alternative medicine (including the very peculiar urine-therapy treatment) and many other dubious subjects." Library Journal.

Goldacre, Ben

Bad science : quacks, hacks, and big pharma flacks / Ben Goldacre. Faber and Faber, 2010, c2008. xii, 288 p. : **500**

1. Pseudoscience. 2. Scientific errors. 3. Science in mass media. 4. Experiments.
ISBN 9780865479180

Originally published, in different form: London : Fourth Estate, 2008.

While exposing quack doctors and nutritionists, bogus credentialing programs, and biased scientific studies, the author takes the media to task for its willingness to throw facts and proof out the window in its quest to sell more copies. He also teaches you how to evaluate placebo effects, double-blind studies, and sample size, so that you can recognize bad science when you see it.

"The author has written a very funny and biting book critiquing what he calls Bad Science. Under this heading he includes homeopathy, cosmetics manufacturers whose claims about their products defy plausibility, proponents of miracle vitamins, and drug companies and physicians who design faulty studies and manipulate the results. While it is a very entertaining book, it also provides important insight into the horrifying outcomes that can result when willful anti-intellectualism is allowed equal footing with scientific methodology." Boston Globe.

Green, Bill, 1942-

Boltzmann's tomb : travels in search of science / Bill Green. Bellevue Literary Press, 2011 288 p. **500**

1. Green, Bill, 1942- Travel 2. Scientists 3. Scientific discoveries 4. Voyages and travels.
ISBN 9781934137352

LC 2011026404

From Cambridge to Ohio, Vienna to Antarctica, Bill Green takes us on a globe-spanning pilgrimage to important sites of scientific discovery and along the way relates the captivating stories of the scientists who lived and worked there. Green interweaves the story of his own lifelong evolution as a scientist with a travelogue that is a personal and universal history of science. -- From the publisher.

"This book is very readable and should be especially appealing to young people contemplating a life in science." Science Books & Films.

Gribbin, John, 1946-

Almost everyone's guide to science : the universe, life, and everything / John Gribbin with Mary Gribbin. Yale University Press, 1999, c1998. 232 p. ; **500**

1. Physics. 2. Evolution. 3. Atoms. 4. Big Bang Theory (Astronomy)
ISBN 0300081014

LC 99026755

Originally published: London : Weidenfeld & Nicolson, 1998.

Discusses the major issues in science, including the structure of particles within the atom, origins of species, and the birth of the universe.

"In this general guide to science for the layperson . Gribbin combines biographies and history, on the one hand, with the major theories in science, on the other. The text is clear, is based on solid research, and clearly reflects a lifetime love for science." Science Books & Films.

Harvey, Derek

★**How** science works / contributors, Derek Harvey, Tom Jackson, Ginny Smith, Alison Sturgeon, John Woodward. DK Publishing, 2018. 255 p. : **500**

1. Science -- Miscellanea.

ISBN 9781465464194

LC bl2018028856

At head of title: DK.

Includes index.

Using clear, easy-to-understand graphics, an ultimate science book explores answers to questions on 70 topics in the areas of matter, physics, energy, chemistry, life science, earth science, technology and the universe.

Hawking, Stephen, 1942-2018

Brief answers to the big questions / Stephen W. Hawking. Bantam Dell Pub Group, 2018. 144 p. **500**

1. Questions and answers 2. Science 3. Cosmogony

ISBN 9781984819192

LC bl2018179891

The world-famous cosmologist and #1 best-selling author of A Brief History of Time leaves us with his final thoughts on the universe's biggest questions in a posthumous work.

Henderson, Mark

100 most important science ideas : key concepts in genetics, physics, and mathematics / Mark Henderson, Joanne Baker, Tony Crilly. Firefly Books, 2009. 431 p. : **500**

1. Science 2. Genetics 3. Physics 4. Mathematics

ISBN 9781554075270

LC bl2009025819

Includes index.

Explains the fundamental concepts in genetics, physics, and mathematics.

Munroe, Randall

How to : absurd scientific advice for common real-world problems / Randall Munroe. Riverhead Books, 2019. 307 p. : **500**

1. Science 2. Essays

ISBN 9780525537090

LC bl2019023579

The creator of the web comic xkcd and best-selling author of What If? and Thing Explainer shares inadvisable advice for responding to today's problems, from using social-media for weather forecasts to powering a home by destroying the fabric of space-time. Illustrations.

"With illustrated formulas that humorously explain the science behind Munroe's conjectures, this book is sure to entertain and educate thinkers from high school on up." Library Journal.

Munroe, Randall

Thing explainer: complicated stuff in simple words / Randall Munroe. Houghton Mifflin Harcourt, 2015. 61 p. : **500**

1. Science 2. Technology

ISBN 9780544668256

LC bl2015042919

The creator of the popular webcomic "xkcd" uses line drawings and common words to provide simple explanations for how things work, including microwaves, bridges, tectonic plates, the solar system, the periodic table, helicopters, and other essential concepts.

What if? : serious scientific answers to absurd hypothetical questions / Randall Munroe. Houghton Mifflin Harcourt, 2014. xii, 303 p. : **500**

1. Science -- Miscellanea. 2. Questions and answers.

ISBN 9780544272996

LC 2014016311

The creator of the webcomic xkcd.com provides hilarious and scientifically informative answers to questions that can never be physically solved, but are fun to think about.

"Those who enjoyed the irreverent style of Allie Brosh's best-selling memoir, Hyperbole and a Half, will enjoy Munroe's serious and silly musings on everything from science to romance. One question submitted to his blog: 'If all digital data were stored on punch cards, how big would Google's data warehouse be?' was even answered by the search-engine behemoth. The response, 'No comment.' " Library Journal.

Novella, Steven

The **skeptics'** guide to the universe : how to know what's really real in a world increasingly full of fake / Dr. Steven Novella with Bob Novella, Cara Santa Maria, Jay Novella, and Evan Bernstein. Grand Central Publishing, 2018. xviii, 494 p. **500**

1. Science -- Popular works 2. Scientific errors 3. Pseudoscience 4. Conspiracy theories

ISBN 9781538760536

LC 2018013089

Based on a podcast.

Based on the podcast known for battling sloppy reasoning, bad arguments and superstitions with logical thinking, the "Skeptical Rogues" help readers try to make sense of an increasingly crazy world using critical thinking skills, science and philosophy.

"This important addition to the literature of skepticism deserves shelf space beside the works of such notables as Michael Shermer, James Randi, Robert A. Baker, and Martin Gardner." Booklist.

Orzel, Chad

Eureka : discovering your inner scientist / Chad Orzel. Basic Books, 2014 240 p. **500**

1. Science 2. Scientists 3. Science -- History

ISBN 9780465074969

LC 2014034615

Even in the twenty-first century the popular image of a scientist is a reclusive genius in a lab coat, mixing formulas or working out equations inaccessible to all but the initiated few. The idea that scientists are somehow smarter than the rest of us is a common, yet dangerous, misconception, getting us off the hook for not knowing -- or caring -- how the world works. How did science become so divorced from our everyday experience? Is scientific understanding so far out of reach for the non-scientists among us?

Randall, Lisa

Knocking on heaven's door : how physics and scientific thinking illuminate the universe and the modern world / Lisa Randall. Ecco, 2011. 400 p. **500**

1. Science -- Social aspects. 2. Physics. 3. Particles (Nuclear physics)

ISBN 9780061723728

LC 2011010521

"From the one of Time magazine's "100 Most Influential People in the World"-- and bestselling author of Warped Passages--an exhilarating and readable overview of the latest ideas in physics and a rousing defense of the role of science in our lives".-- Provided by publisher.

"To explain how science works, Randall analyzes the way two researchers at Bell Labs turned the annoying static coming through their radio telescope into a cosmic breakthrough. For in this piquant episode--and others that Randall examines--science advances by testing theoretical ingenuity against technologically acquired data. Randall offers an insider's perspective into this cutting-edge science. Yet she illuminates that science with lucid language, laced with references to popular culture, political controversy, and even comic-strip art. The general reader's indispensable passport to the frontiers of science." Booklist.

Rees, Martin J., 1942-

From here to infinity : a vision for the future of science / Martin Rees. W.W. Norton, c2012. 160 p. **500**

1. Science -- Philosophy. 2. Research. 3. Science policy. 4. Science -- Social aspects. 5. Essays.

ISBN 9780393063073

LC 2012003421

A leading cosmologist and astrophysicist discusses the effect that science has on important issues from health care and energy policies to space travel and advocates for better communication between scientists and ordinary people in an effort to solve today's challenges.

Ritchie, Stuart (Stuart J.)

Science fictions : how fraud, bias, negligence, and hype undermine the search for truth / Stuart Ritchie. 2020 320 p. **500**

1. Science -- Methodology 2. Scientific errors 3. Research 4. Fraud

ISBN 9781250222695

LC 2020011654

Science is how we understand the world. Yet failures in peer review and mistakes in statistics have rendered a shocking number of scientific studies useless--or, worse, badly misleading. As Science Fictions makes clear, the current system of research funding and publication not only fails to safeguard us from blunders but actively encourages bad science. By illustrating the many ways that scientists go wrong, Ritchie gives us the knowledge we need to spot dubious research and points the way to reforms that could make science trustworthy once again.

"Thorough and detailed, this is a sobering and convincing treatise for anyone invested in the intellectual credibility of science." Publishers Weekly

Sagan, Carl, 1934-1996

Billions and billions : thoughts on life and death at the brink of the millennium / Carl Sagan. Random House, c1997. xii, 241 p. : **500**

1. Science -- Miscellanea 2. Essays.

ISBN 0679411607

LC 96052730

The author draws on the most recent research into science, mathematics, and space in a study of the mysteries of life, addressing such topics as global warming, the abortion debate, life on Mars, and his own battle with myelodysplasia.

"This collection of essays covers such topics as: the invention of chess, life on Mars, global warming, abortion, international affairs, the nature of government, and the meaning of morality. Writing with clarity and an understanding of human nature, Sagan offers hope for humanity's future." Library Journal.

Scientific American's ask the experts : answers to the most puzzling and mind-blowing science questions / the editors of Scientific American. HarperResource, c2003. 267 p. : **500**

1. Science -- Miscellanea.

ISBN 9780060523367

LC 2004555579

Includes index.

Provides thought-provoking answers to a variety of baffling questions about the world of science, providing an intriguing glimpse into everything from astronomy and biology to human anatomy and physiology, chemistry, physics, zooloogy, and more.

Strevens, Michael

The **knowledge** machine : how irrationality created modern science / Michael Strevens. Liveright Publishing Corporation, 2020 x, 350 p. **500**

1. Irrationalism (Philosophy) 2. Knowledge theory 3. Science -- History. 4. Science -- Methodology.

ISBN 9781631491375

LC 2020018496

Citing historical events from Newton's alchemy to Hurricane Sandy's storm surge, a paradigm-shifting investigation into the origins and structure of science urges scientists to intentionally disregard religion, theoretical beauty and philosophy to channel focus into tangible experimentation and observation.

"A thought-provoking and likely-to-be-controversial explanation of how scientists finally got it right. One of the better examinations of the origins of the scientific revolution." Kirkus

Wilkinson, Karen

The **art** of tinkering : meet 150+ makers working at the intersection of art, science & technology / Karen Wilkinson & Mike Petrich. Weldon Owen, 2013 223 p. : **500**

1. Creative ability in technology. 2. Technology. 3. Inventions.

ISBN 9781616286095

LC bl2014003406

"Exploratorium"--Cover.

Includes index.

Displays the best exhibits, artwork, and projects in the Exploratorium museum, including a city built out of one hundred thousand toothpicks and a musical instrument that is powered by the ocean.

Woodford, Chris

Atoms under the floorboards : the surprising science hidden in your home / Chris Woodford. Bloomsbury Sigma, 2015. 336 p. : **500**

1. Home furnishings 2. Scientific discoveries. 3. Science -- Miscellanea. 4. Science -- Popular works.

ISBN 9781472912220

LC bl2015018531

Explains scientific concepts by using household examples, including what kitchen knives and golf clubs have in common, how much heat energy a typical home holds in the winter, and why sunlight makes clothes look brighter.

500.201 Physical sciences--philosophy

Ball, Philip, 1962-

Nature's patterns : a tapestry in three parts / Philip Ball. Branches. Oxford University Press, 2008. 308 p. **500.201**

1. Chaos theory 2. Pattern formation (Biology) 3. Pattern formation

(Physical sciences) 4. Essays
ISBN 9780199237968

LC oc2007206161

"From the curl of a ram's horn to patterns of spider webs and the development of an embryo, Mr Ball examines the possible causes of the shapes and forms we observe. His book contains a lot of fascinating detail about the different physical, chemical and evolutionary processes at work." The Economist.

Patterns in nature : why the natural world looks the way it does / Philip Ball. The University of Chicago, Ill. :Press, 2016. 288 p. : **500.201**

1. Geometry in nature 2. Nature 3. Pattern formation (Biology) 4. Pattern formation (Physical sciences)
ISBN 9780226332420

LC 2015034568

The natural world is replete with patterned order underpinned by scientific and mathematical principles. Take, for example, the veins of a leaf to the fingerprint-like blotches of the leopard and the labyrinthine structure of a termite's nest to the majestic profile of a mountain range. These patterns have inspired artists, writers, designers, and musicians for thousands of years. Patterns in Nature: Why the Natural World Looks the Way It Does explores the science behind the amazing diversity of patterns in the natural world and takes readers on a visual tour of some of the world's most incredible natural wonders. Featuring awe-inspiring galleries of nature's most ingenious designs, Patterns in Nature is a synergy of art and science that will fascinate artists and nature lovers alike. --From publisher description.

"This is formidable eye candy for the I-love-science crowd, sure to spark a sense of impressed wonder at the beauty of our universe and our ability to photograph it." Publishers Weekly.

501 Philosophy and theory

Arbesman, Samuel

★The **half-life** of facts : why everything we know has an expiration date / Samuel Arbesman. Current, 2012. 256 p. **501**

1. Evolution. 2. Science -- Philosophy 3. Probabilities.
ISBN 9781591844723

LC 2012019142

A new approach to uderstanding the ever-changing information that bombards us. Arbesman is an expert in scientometrics, literally the science of science--how we know what we know. It turns out that knowledge in most fields evolves in systematic and predictable ways, and understanding that evolution can enormously powerful.

Dawkins, Richard, 1941-

The **magic** of reality : how we know what's really true / Richard Dawkins ; illustrated by Dave McKean. Free Press, 2011. 288 p. **501**

1. Science 2. Nature 3. Reality 4. Atheism
ISBN 9781439192818

LC 2011025607

Dawkins examines how people use science to make sense of the world and to answer the basic questions of existence. He also chronicles the time before the scientific method was developed, when society had only myth to explain the unknown.

"In this outstanding graphic science book, evolutionary biologist Dawkins . . . teams up with illustrator Dave McKean . . . to examine questions in everyday science, such as: why seasons occur; what things are made of; and whether there's life on other planets. They explain the answers from mythological and cultural points of view before diving into the chemistry, biology, and physics--all in language that advanced middle school, or most high school, students can absorb." Publishers Weekly.

Deutsch, David, 1953-

The **beginning** of infinity : explanations that transform the world / David Deutsch. Viking Adult, 2011. 496 p. **501**

1. Infinity. 2. Science -- Philosophy. 3. Cosmology 4. Quantum theory
ISBN 9780670022755

LC 2011004120

"A bold and all-embracing exploration of the nature and progress of knowledge from one of today's great thinkers. Throughout history, mankind has struggled to understand life's mysteries, from the mundane to the seemingly miraculous. In this important new book, David Deutsch, an award-winning pioneer in the field of quantum computation, argues that explanations have a fundamental place in the universe. They have unlimited scope and power to cause change, and the quest to improve them is the basic regulating principle not only of science but of all successful human endeavor. This stream of ever improving explanations has infinite reach, according to Deutsch: we are subject only to the laws of physics, and they impose no upper boundary to what we can eventually understand, control, and achieve. In his previous book, The Fabric of Reality, Deutsch describe the four deepest strands of existing knowledge--the theories of evolution, quantum physics, knowledge, and computation--arguing jointly they reveal a unified fabric of reality. In this new book, he applies that worldview to a wide range of issues and unsolved problems, from creativity and free will to the origin and future of the human species. Filled with startling new conclusions about human choice, optimism, scientific explanation, and the evolution of culture, The Beginning of Infinity is a groundbreaking book that will become a classic of its kind".-- Provided by publisher.

"Anyone who loves to grapple with profound ideas should love reading this very ambitious and challenging look at the history and (possibly unlimited) future of human understanding." Science Books & Films.

Firestein, Stuart

Ignorance : how it drives science / Stuart Firestein. Oxford University Press, 2012. 208 p. **501**

1. Science -- Philosophy. 2. Ignorance. 3. Scientific discoveries. 4. Science -- Experiments
ISBN 9780199828074

LC 2011051395

Knowledge is a big subject, says Stuart Firestein, but ignorance is a bigger one. And it is ignorance--not knowledge--that is the true engine of science.

Mitchell, Melanie (Melanie S.)

Complexity : a guided tour / Melanie Mitchell. Oxford University Press, 2009. xvi, 349 p. : **501**

1. Chaos theory. 2. Hypothesis. 3. Systems theory. 4. Science.
ISBN 9780195124415

Leading complex systems scientist Melanie Mitchell provides an intimate tour of the sciences of complexity, a broad set of efforts that seek to explain how large-scale complex, organized, and adaptive behavior can emerge from simple interactions among myriad individuals.

"The author offers a snapshot of the growing field of complex-systems science. Mitchell explores the historical roots of this area in the work of visionaries such as Henri Poincar and Edward Lorenz in dynamical-systems theory, and of John von Neumann, Alan Turing and others in computation. The book hits its stride in its latter half, with an insightful survey of recent developments in complex-network theory and scaling in biology." Nature.

Shtulman, Andrew
Scienceblind : why our intuitive theories about the world are so often wrong / Andrew Shtulman. Basic Books, 2017 viii, 311 p. **501**

1. Fallacies (Logic). 2. Intuition. 3. Reasoning. 4. Science -- Methodology.
ISBN 9780465053940

LC 2016050643

A cognitive and developmental psychologist describes how our misconceptions about the world around us, often stemming from childhood, have a negative impact on our ability to learn science and advocates for dismantling our intuitive theories and rebuilding from the ground up.

"Although this book is thoroughly researched with a wealth of scholarly sources cited, Shtulman reaches a broad audience by investigating topics that everyone can understand." Library Journal.

Stannard, Russell
The **end** of discovery / Russell Stannard. Oxford University Press, 2010. viii, 228 p. : **501**

1. Science -- Philosophy. 2. Physics -- History. 3. Knowledge theory
ISBN 9780199585243

LC 2010930293

Includes index.

Proposes that science will eventually reach the limits of what can be discovered, explained, or imagined, using unanswered questions about such topics as free will, consciousness, and the existence of extraterrestrial life as examples.

Webb, Jeremy, 1958-
Nothing : surprising insights everywhere from zero to oblivion / edited by Jeremy Webb. The Experiment, 2014, c2013 266 p. **501**

1. Nothingness. 2. Science -- Philosophy. 3. Big Bang Theory (Astronomy) 4. Essays
ISBN 9781615192052

LC 2014002254

First published in Great Britain in 2013 by Profile Books Ltd.

It turns out that almost nothing is as curious--or as enlightening--as, well, nothing. What is nothingness? Where can it be found? The writers of the world's top-selling science magazine investigate--from the big bang, dark energy, and the void to superconductors, vestigial organs, hypnosis, and the placebo effect--and discover that understanding nothing may be the key to understanding everything.

501.4 Science--terminology

Olson, Randy, 1955-
★**Don't** be such a scientist : talking substance in an age of style / Randy Olson. Island Press, c2009. vii, 206 p. : **501.4**

1. Communication in science. 2. Science in motion pictures.
ISBN 1597265632

LC 2009007081

"After nearly a decade on the defensive, the world of science is about to be restored to its rightful place. But is the American public really ready for science? And is the world of science ready for the American public? Scientists wear ragged clothes, forget to comb their hair, and speak in a language that even they don't understand. Or so people think. Most scientists don't care how they are perceived, but in our media-dominated age, style points count. Enter Randy Olson. Fifteen years ago, Olson bid farewell to the science world and shipped off to Hollywood ready to change the world. With films like Flock of Dodos: The Evolution-Intelligent Design Circus (Tribeca '06, Showtime) and Sizzle: A Global Warming Comedy (Outfest '08), he has tried to bridge the cultural divide that has too often left science on the outside looking in. Now, in his first book, Olson, with a Harvard Ph.D. and formerly a tenured professor of marine biology at the University of New Hampshire, recounts the lessons from his own hilarious-and at times humiliating-evolution from science professor to Hollywood filmmaker. In Don't Be Such a Scientist, he shares the secrets of talking substance in an age of style. The key, he argues, is to stay true to the facts while tapping into something more primordial, more irrational, and ultimately more human. In a book enlivened by a profane acting teacher who made Olson realize that "nobody wants to watch you think," he offers up serious insights and poignant stories. You'll laugh, you may cry,and as a communicator you'll certainly learn the importance of not only knowing how to fulfill, but also how to arouse."--Publisher's description.

"Olson packs this highly entertaining book with more good stories than good advice, spurring readers to rethink their personal communication styles rather than ape Olson's example." Publishers Weekly.

506.041 Organizations and management

Bryson, Bill,
Seeing further : the story of science, discovery & the genius of the Royal Society / edited & introduced by Bill Bryson. William Morrow, 2010. 512 p. **506.041**

1. Royal Society (Great Britain) -- History. 2. Scientific discoveries 3. Science -- History 4. Essays.
ISBN 9780061999765

LC 2011381700

Originally published: London : HarperPress, 2010.

"Bryson presents a remarkable collection of essays celebrating the 350th anniversary of the founding of the Royal Society of London and its many contributions to science. Society members have included such illustrious names as Darwin, Newton, Leibniz, and Francis Bacon, to name a few. The volume's 23 contributors are both uniformly excellent and remarkable for their diversity." Publishers Weekly.

507.1 Science education

Tesoriero, Heather Won
The **class** : a life-changing teacher and his world-changing kids / Heather Won Tesoriero. Ballantine Books, 2018. 288 p. **507.1**

1. Bramante, Andy. 2. Teacher/student relationships. 3. High school students. 4. Science projects. 5. Science fairs. 6. Greenwich, Connecticut.
ISBN 9780399181849

Traces a year in the life of a visionary high school science teacher, describing how he left a successful corporate career to guide a diverse range of students through prestigious science competitions, personal challenges and college applications.

507.8 Use of apparatus and equipment in study and teaching

Johnson, George, 1952 January 20-
The **ten** most beautiful experiments / George Johnson. Alfred A. Knopf, 2008. xiv, 192 p. : **507.8**

1. Galilei, Galileo, 1564-1642 2. Newton, Isaac, 1642-1727

3. Harvey, William, 1578-1657 4. Scientists -- 16th century 5. Scientists -- 17th century 6. Color theory 7. Gravity -- Measurement -- Experiments 8. England -- History 9. Italy -- History
ISBN 1400041015
LC 2007027839

Analyzes ten key experiments in the history of science and their implications for human knowledge, ranging from Galileo's measurement of the pull of gravity to Isaac Newton's examination of how light causes vibrations in the retina.

508 Science -- Natural history

Barnes, Simon

Rewild yourself : making nature more visible in our lives / Simon Barnes. Pegasus Books, 2019. 198 p. **508**

1. Nature 2. Nature study 3. Observing things 4. Beauty in nature
ISBN 9781643132167

We're not just losing the wild world. We're forgetting it. We're no longer noticing it. We've lost the habit of looking and seeing and listening and hearing. For those readers who want to get closer to the nature all around them and bring it back into focus within their lives, this book is the ideal companion.

Carroll, Sean B.

Remarkable creatures : epic adventures in the search for the origin of species / Sean B. Carroll. Houghton Mifflin Harcourt, 2009. 352 p. **508**

1. Evolution -- History 2. Naturalists -- History. 3. Life -- Origin 4. Natural history
ISBN 9780151014859
LC 2008025438

National Book Award for Nonfiction finalist, 2009

An award-winning biologist traces the contributions of pioneering scientists to the modern understanding of how Earth and the planet's life evolved, recounting such important discoveries as Darwin's trip around the world, Charles Walcott's discovery of pre-Cambrian life, the Leakeys' probe into humankind's remote past, and the mysteries of DNA.

Darwin, Charles, 1809-1882

★The **voyage** of the Beagle : journal of researches into the natural history and geology of the countries visited during the voyage of H.M.S. Beagle round the world / Charles Darwin ; introduction by Steve Jones. Modern Library, 2001. xix, 468 p. : **508**

1. Beagle Expedition, 1831-1836 2. Geology 3. Natural history 4. Trips around the world -- 19th century 5. South America -- Exploration
ISBN 9780375756801
LC 00046294

Originally published: New York : P.F. Collier & Son, 1909.

A youthful Charles Darwin records his impressions of the flora, fauna, and geology of the South American coasts.

De Villiers, Marq

Sahara : a natural history / Marq de Villiers and Sheila Hirtle. Walker & Co., 2002. 326 p. : **508**

1. Sand-dunes. 2. Ecology -- Sahara. 3. Natural history -- Sahara. 4. Sahara -- Description and travel. 5. Sahara -- Civilization.
ISBN 0802713726
LC 2002071391

Map on lining papers.

Offers a glimpse of the extraordinary Sarhara Desert, describing the people who live there, the forces of nature that shaped it, and the impact of the desert upon global weather.

"Insightful and intelligent, this fascinating book will appeal to anyone with a curiosity about the world's largest desert and the people who inhabit it." Booklist.

DK Publishing, Inc

Natural history : the ultimate visual guide to everything on Earth DK Pub., 2010. 648 p. : **508**

1. Natural history
ISBN 9780756667528
LC bl2010026981

At head of title: Smithsonian.

Includes index.

Produced in association with the Smithsonian Institution.

With oversight from the Smithsonian Institution's National Museum of Natural History, this detailed visual guide examines thousands of species and specimens of animals, plants and minerals that make Earth unique.

"This is an international encyclopedia of life-forms e.g., fossils, fungi, plants, animals, mammals that includes vital facts and two to three sentences about each as well as more than 5000 color illustrations in all. Each grouping is introduced by an essay that puts it in biological and evolutionary perspective." Library Journal.

Dillard, Annie

Pilgrim at Tinker Creek / Annie Dillard. Harper Perennial, 1998, c1974. 288 p. **508**

1. Nature. 2. Women and nature. 3. Seasons. 4. Virginia. 5. Blue Ridge Mountains. 6. Essays
ISBN 0061233323
LC 98029765

Originally published: New York : Harper's Magazine Press, 1974.

Pulitzer Prize for General Nonfiction, 1975.

Pulitzer Prize-winning writer Annie Dillard presents a series of connected essays that chronicle a year at Tinker Creek in Virginia's Blue Ridge valley. Observant, deeply contemplative, and beautifully written, Pilgrim at Tinker Creek challenges listeners to study their surroundings beyond their familiar surfaces and uncover new and refreshing milieus.

Teaching a stone to talk : expeditions and encounters / Annie Dillard. Harper & Row, c1982. 177 p. ; **508**

1. Nature. 2. Life. 3. Spirituality
ISBN 0060150300
LC 82047520

"In the fourteen penses that make up this book {the author} bears witness, reflects on her observations of the order and disorder, the splendor and horror of the natural world." The New Yorker.

Flannery, Tim F. (Tim Fridtjof), 1956-

The **eternal** frontier : an ecological history of North America and its peoples / Tim Flannery. Atlantic Monthly Press, 2001. 404 p. : **508**

1. Natural history -- North America. 2. Ecology -- North America. 3. North America -- Historical geography. 4. North America -- Climate.
ISBN 0871137895
LC 2001018841

Simultaneously published: Melbourne : Text Publishing, 2001.

"This book weaves ecological, cultural, and social history together in a marvelous way." Science Books & Films.

Fothergill, Alastair

Planet Earth as you've never seen it before / Alastair Fothergill ... [et al.] ; foreword by David Attenborough. University of California Press, c2006. 309 p. : **508**

1. Habitat (Ecology) 2. Earth (Planet)
ISBN 9780520250543

LC 2006050073

Includes index.

Presents a tour of the Earth, depicting an assortment of animals and plants, and such natural wonders as mountains, forests, rivers, deserts, oceans, and rainforests.

Gould, Stephen Jay, 1941-

The **flamingo's** smile : reflections in natural history / Stephen Jay Gould. Norton, c1985. 476 p. : **508**

1. Natural history. 2. Evolution. 3. Academic freedom. 4. Probabilities.
ISBN 0393022285

LC 85004916

Includes index.

Evolutionary theory is the theme that binds together these essays on such seemingly disparate topics as the feeding habits of flamingos, flowers and snails that change from male to female and sometimes back again, and the extinction from baseball of the .400 hitter.

"In this collection the theme is history, both natural and human. The essays are marked by Gould's usual careful scholarship and erudition and clear and nontechnical language." Science Books & Films.

★The **richness** of life : the essential Stephen Jay Gould / Stephen Jay Gould ; edited by Paul McGarr and Steven Rose ; with an introduction by Steven Rose ; and a foreword by Oliver Sacks. Norton, 2007. xiv, 654 p. : **508**

1. Gould, Stephen Jay. 2. Evolution (Biology) 3. Natural history.
ISBN 0393064980

LC 2006029208

Collects forty-four key segments from the late renowned paleontologist and evolutionary biologist's best-selling and award-winning books, papers, and essays, in a collection that includes an assortment of previously unpublished articles and speeches.

Higgins, Lila M.

Wild LA : explore the amazing nature in and around Los Angeles / The Natural History Museum of Los Angeles County ; Lila M. Higgins and Gregory B. Pauly ; with Jason G. Goldman and Charles Hood. Natural History Museum of Los Angeles County, 2019. 332 p. **508**

1. Natural history -- California -- Los Angeles.
ISBN 1604697105

LC 2018038899

Includes index.

"A dynamic, fact-filled guide to the natural world of Los Angeles from the experts at the Natural History Museum".-- Provided by publisher.

"No matter how much one thinks one knows about L.A., this travel companion will shed new light on all that flourishes and flowers, or creeps and crawls in the vast urban-yet-still-wild sprawl of the city and surrounding area." Publishers Weekly.

Keffer, Ken (Naturalist)

Earth almanac : nature's calendar for year-round discovery / Ken Keffer ; illustrations by Jeremy Collins. Skipstone, 2020 251 p.: **508**

1. Natural history -- North America. 2. Phenology -- North America. 3. Almanacs.
ISBN 9781680512823

LC 2019036902

"Earth Almanac presents the greatest hits of North American nature. Structured around phenology, the study of seasonal patterns in nature, these day-by-day descriptions offer insight into activities and connections throughout the natural world. Beginning with the Winter Solstice in December, Earth Almanac highlights a wide range of natural history, including mammals, birds, fish, reptiles, insects, intertidal and marine life, trees, plants, fungi, environmental activists, and more, all the while revealing the ebb and flow of nature across the planet. Each season features more than 90 entries, and sidebars throughout provide calls to environmental action, citizen science opportunities, and details on special dates or holidays. It makes an excellent gift to celebrate the fiftieth anniversary of Earth Day (April 22, 2020)".-- Provided by publisher.

Leach, Amy,

Things that are / Amy Leach. Milkweed Editions, c2012. 185 p. **508**

1. Life. 2. Essays.
ISBN 9781571313348

LC 2011040887

This collection of essays from an award-winning writer describes the similarities between love and vines and how exploding stars are related to exploding sea cucumbers, as well as tackling subjects like jellyfish, fainting goats and placid caterpillars.

Macdonald, Helen, 1970-

★**Vesper** flights / Helen MacDonald. Grove Press, 2020 288 p. **508**

1. Macdonald, Helen, 1970- 2. Humans -- Effect of environment on 3. Memory 4. Wildlife 5. Nature and culture. 6. Essays
ISBN 9780802128812

LC bl2020016185

The award-winning author of H Is for Hawk presents a collection of essays about humanity's relationship with nature, exploring subjects ranging from captivity and immigration to ostrich farming and the migrations of songbirds from the Empire State Building.

"English naturalist Macdonald (H Is for Hawk) offers meditations on the natural world and its inhabitants in an inviting collection of 41 new and previously published essays that are infused with wonder, nostalgia, and melancholy. . . . The message throughout is clear: the world humans enjoy today may not be around tomorrow, so it should not be taken for granted." Publishers Weekly

Matthiessen, Peter

End of the Earth : voyages to Antarctica / Peter Matthiessen. National Geographic, 2003. 242 p. : **508**

1. Matthiessen, Peter Travel Antarctica 2. South Pole expeditions. 3. Biotic communities. 4. Travelers. 5. Voyages and travels. 6. Antarctica -- Exploration 7. South Pole.
ISBN 0792250591

LC 2003051254

The author recounts his voyage through the islands around Antarctica, describing the region's wildlife as well as the region itself while sharing historical information about the pioneers and adventurers who preceded him.

"Vivid and empathic accounts of the high drama and petty rivalries of Antarctic exploration alternate with Matthiessen's own adventures as he shares his indelible impressions of this cold, white wonderland in the hope that they will inspire readers to appreciate the beauty and bounty of the earth's shimmering web of biodiversity enough to defend and preserve it." Booklist.

Nicholls, Steve

Paradise found : nature in America at the time of discovery / Steve Nicholls. University of Chicago Press, 2009. x, 524 p. ; **508**

1. Natural history -- North America 2. Nature -- Effect of humans on 3. Human ecology 4. Nature 5. North American -- Exploration 6. North America -- Environmental conditions -- History.
ISBN 9780226583402

LC 2008036076

Here Steve Nicholls demonstrates with both historical narrative and scientific inquiry just what an amazing place North America was and how it looked when the explorers first found it. --from publisher description

"The author turns to the writings of forgotten early naturalists to gain understanding both of the natural abundance of the New World when the first Europeans arrived and of how so much of this living bounty was destroyed so quickly. Not only does Nicholls present arresting material, he also offers fresh interpretations and connections in this grandly spanning and affecting look to the past for guidance in facing a future of further diminishment." Booklist.

Peck, Robert McCracken, 1952-

A **glorious** enterprise : the Academy of Natural Sciences of Philadelphia and the making of American science / Robert McCracken Peck and Patricia Tyson Stroud ; photographs by Rosamond Purcell. University of Pennsylvania Press, c2012. xvii, 437 p. : **508**

1. Academy of Natural Sciences of Philadelphia -- History. 2. Natural history -- Research -- Philadelphia, Pennsylvania
ISBN 9780812243802

LC 2011034991

A history of the renowned museum recounts key moments in its evolution as a research and education center, as well as the role of such individuals as Thomas Jefferson and John James Audubon in championing its purpose.

"Highly recommended for all academic libraries and larger public library systems. Readers of all levels will find this book useful." Library Journal.

Pyle, Robert Michael

Nature matrix : new and selected essays / Robert Michael Pyle. Counterpoint, 2020. 288 p. **508**

1. Pyle, Robert Michael 2. Nabokov, Vladimir Vladimirovich, 1899-1977 3. Astor, John Jacob, 1763-1848. 4. Natural history 5. Nature study 6. Wilderness areas 7. Naturalists 8. Essays
ISBN 9781640092761

LC 2019017872

A selection of nature-themed essays by the biologist author of Magdalena Mountain explores such subjects as his early years as a national park ranger, the "wilderness" of modern times and the life of Vladimir Nabokov.

"Pyle proves yet again that he is one of the most nourishing nature writers at work today." Kirkus

Rothman, Julia

Nature anatomy : the curious parts & pieces of the natural world / Julia Rothman, with help from John Niekrasz. Storey Publishing, 2015 224 p. : **508**

1. Natural history
ISBN 9781612122311

LC 2014033664

Drawings and diagrams depict the curosities and wonders of the natural world, illustrating everything from the rock cycle, the phases of the moon, and the harvesting of seaweed to the anatomy of flowers, tree trunks, mushrooms, and jellyfish.

"With its wide range of topics, from landforms to leaf identification, bird beaks, and water bugs, Nature Anatomy is designed as the ultimate book for browsers with an insatiable curiosity about the great outdoors. Rothman has clearly found a structure and design in which she excels; this title is an informative charmer from start to finish. More, please." Booklist.

Safina, Carl, 1955-

The **view** from lazy point : a natural year in an unnatural world / Carl Safina. Henry Holt and Co., 2010. 416 p. **508**

1. Coastal ecology. 2. Marine ecology. 3. Environmental degradation 4. Human ecology -- Philosophy. 5. Essays
ISBN 9780805090406

LC 2009040108

"A John Macrae Book."

The award-winning conservationist and author of Song for the Blue Ocean takes readers throughout various global regions to investigate examples of environmental degradation and renewal while identifying a link between environmental dangers and human rights issues.

"A superb work of environmental reportage and reflection." Kirkus.

Sampson, Scott D.

How to raise a wild child : the art and science of falling in love with nature / Scott D. Sampson. Houghton Mifflin Harcourt, 2015. xix, 327 p. ; **508**

1. Child development. 2. Natural history -- Study and teaching. 3. Nature study. 4. Outdoor education.
ISBN 0544279328

LC 2014048565

"From the beloved host of PBS Kids' Dinosaur Train, an easy-to-use guide for parents, teachers, and others looking to foster a strong connection between children and nature, complete with engaging activities, troubleshooting advice, and much more American children spend four to seven minutes a day playing outdoors--90 percent less time than their parents did. Yet recent research indicates that experiences in nature are essential for healthy growth. Regular exposure to nature can help relieve stress, depression, and attention deficits. It can reduce bullying, combat illness, and boost academic scores. Most critical of all, abundant time in nature seems to yield long-term benefits in kids' cognitive, emotional, and social development. Yet teachers, parents, and other caregivers lack a basic understanding of how to engender a meaningful, lasting connection between children and the natural world. How to Raise a Wild Child offers a timely and engaging antidote, showing how kids' connection to nature changes as they mature. Distilling the latest research in multiple disciplines, Sampson reveals how adults can help kids fall in love with nature--enlisting technology as an ally, taking advantage of urban nature, and instilling a sense of place along the way".-- Provided by publisher.

Shetterly, Susan Hand, 1942-

Settled in the wild : notes from the edge of town / Susan Hand Shetterly. Algonquin Books of Chapel Hill, 2010. 256 p. **508**

1. Natural history -- Maine. 2. Wildlife watching. 3. Women and

nature. 4. Rural life 5. Maine. 6. Essays.
ISBN 9781565126183

LC 2009030802

Through observations within her own neighborhood in rural Maine, a naturalist looks at how animals, humans and plants share the land, issuing warnings to the reader even as she celebrates the resilience that abounds.

Steelquist, Robert

The **Northwest** coastal explorer : your guide to the places, plants, and animals of the Pacific Coast / Robert Steelquist. Timber Press, 2016. 283 p. : **508**

1. Coastal ecology -- Northwest, Pacific 2. Coastal ecology -- Pacific Coast (North America) 3. Natural areas -- Northwest, Pacific 4. Natural areas -- Pacific Coast (North America) 5. Northwest, Pacific Guidebooks. 6. Guidebooks.
ISBN 1604696311

LC 2015047572

"A fun, engaging, and full-color field guide to the marine life in Oregon, Washington, and British Columbia".--Provided by publisher.

Steinberg, Theodore, 1961-

★**Gotham** unbound : the ecological history of greater New York / Ted Steinberg. Simon & Schuster, 2014. xxii, 517 p. : **508**

1. Urban planning. 2. Cities and towns. 3. City life 4. New York City
ISBN 9781476741246

This book is a powerful account of the relentless development that New Yorkers wrought as they plunged headfirst into the floodplain and transformed untold amounts of salt marsh and shellfish beds into a land jam-packed with people, asphalt and steel, and the reeds and gulls that thrive among them.

"A fascinating and cautionary unnatural history, a staggering epic of human will, might, and folly that affirms a crucial truth, 'the control of nature is an illusion.' " Booklist.

Wohlleben, Peter, 1964-

The **secret** wisdom of nature : trees, animals, and the extraordinary balance of all living things - stories from science and observation / Peter Wohlleben and translated by Jane Billinghurst. Greystone Books, 2019 272 p. Mysteries of nature trilogy ; **508**

1. Biotic communities 2. Biodiversity 3. Habitat (Ecology) 4. Ecology
ISBN 9781771643887

LC bl2019004698

In The Secret Wisdom of Nature, master storyteller and international sensation Peter Wohlleben takes readers on a thought-provoking exploration of the vast natural systems that make life on Earth possible. In this tour of an almost unfathomable world, Wohlleben describes the fascinating interplay between animals and plants and answers such questions as: How do they influence each other? Do lifeforms communicate across species boundaries? And what happens when this finely tuned system gets out of sync? By introducing us to the latest scientific discoveries and recounting his own insights from decades of observing nature, one of the world's most famous foresters shows us how to recapture our sense of awe so we can see the world around us with completely new eyes.

"This deep appreciation for ecology includes a passionate look at many animals, including wolves, salmon, and bears, and reflections on how their presence affects everything around them, from what they eat to plants and trees, bodies of water, rivers, and the very air they pass through." Booklist.

508.4 Natural history--Europe

Flannery, Tim F. (Tim Fridtjof), 1956-

Europe : a natural history / Tim Flannery with Luigi Boitani. Atlantic Monthly Press, 2019, c2018. 288 p. **508.4**

1. Natural history -- Europe 2. Paleontology 3. Zoology 4. Geology 5. Europe -- History
ISBN 9780802129161

LC 2018047048

First published in Australia in 2018 by The Text Publishing Company.

An ecological account of Europe and the forces shaping life on it.

"Throughout, the author employs crisp, lively language suitable for readers without a background in natural history; the level of research and detail, however, means that it can also be used as an uncommonly approachable natural history textbook." Library Journal.

Goulson, Dave

A **buzz** in the meadow : the natural history of a French farm / Dave Goulson. Picador, 2015 288 p. **508.4**

1. Honeybee. 2. Nature 3. Conservation of natural resources 4. Wildlife. 5. France
ISBN 9781250065889

LC bl2015017040

"Unexpectedly, Goulson also moves beyond his home to reflect on the work of biologists of the past and present, particularly when considering the critical state of the world's pollinators, for whom he issues a gentle call to arms. The book is, therefore, less a meditative reflection of wildlife in the country and more an artful blend of E. O. Wilson and Barry Lopez, with a continental flair. Backyard naturalists, regardless of their locale, will delight in the amiable company of this witty and thoughtful guide." Booklist.

509 History, geographic treatment, biography

Al-Khalili, Jim, 1962-

The **house** of wisdom : how Arabic science saved ancient knowledge and gave us the Renaissance / Jim Al-Khalili. Penguin Group, 2011. 352 p. **509.17**

1. Islam and science 2. Religion and science. 3. Science -- History 4. Philosophy, Islamic -- Greek influences 5. Middle East -- History
ISBN 9781594202797

LC 2010053136

Challenges popular misconceptions to reveal the unrecognized scientific accomplishments of medieval Islam, profiling innovations that played significant roles in bridging the ancient and modern worlds while promoting the European Renaissance.

Bauer, Susan Wise

The **story** of science : from the writings of Aristotle to the big bang theory / S. Wise Bauer. W W Norton & Co Inc 2015. 320 p. **509**

1. Science -- History 2. Scientists
ISBN 9780393243260

LC 2015000136

An anthology of top-selected science writings includes pieces by thinkers ranging from Hippocrates and Aristotle to Einstein and Schrödinger while sharing insights into how their achievements have changed the way people think about the world, the universe and themselves.

"What is especially enriching in the text is the focus on the science writing of these inquiring pioneers, and each chapter contains names of websites and e-book versions and recommendations for books written by individual scientists. A remarkable resource for a wide audience." Choice.

Close, F. E.

Nothing : a very short introduction / Frank Close. Oxford University Press, 2009. ix, 166 p. : **509**

1. Beginning 2. Science -- History 3. Space and time
ISBN 9780199225866

LC bl2013001020

Originally published: The void. 2007.

An exploration of the concept of "nothing" journeys from ancient ideas and cultural traditions to the latest scientific research, discussing the history of the vacuum, theories on the nature of time and space, and other discoveries.

Crease, Robert P.

The **great** equations : breakthroughs in science from Pythagoras to Heisenberg / Robert P. Crease. W.W. Norton, c2009. 315 p. **509**

1. Science -- Philosophy. 2. Mathematical physics -- History 3. Scientific discoveries -- History 4. Science -- Influence
ISBN 9780393062045

LC 2008042494

Shares behind-the-scenes stories for ten of the most significant equations in human history, covering a range of topics, from Feynman's statement about Maxwell's pivotal electromagnetic equations and the influence of Newton's law of gravitation to the reason Euler's formula has been called "God's equation" and Heisenberg's uncertainty principle.

"Any reader who aspires to be scientifically literate will find this a good starting place." Publishers Weekly.

Fara, Patricia

★**Science** : a four thousand year history / Patricia Fara. Oxford University Press, 2009. xv, 408 p. : **509**

1. Science -- History. 2. Scientists -- History. 3. Experiments. 4. Theories.
ISBN 019922689X

"This survey of 4,000 years of scientific discovery from Babylon to the present confirms that historians of science often have quite different perspectives from those of the actual practitioners. Readers learn about the contributions of famous scientists as though they were almost puppets responding to religious, social, and practical influences in both their choices of research topics and their methods of investigation--in contrast to their possessing an inherent desire to better understand the behavior of nature. In this highly readable book that tells a magnificent story, Fara weaves together the bits and pieces in a unique way." Choice.

Freely, John

The **flame** of Miletus : the birth of science in ancient Greece (and how it changed the world) / John Freely. I.B. Tauris, 2012. ix, 238 p., 8 p. of plates : **509.38**

1. Science -- Greece -- History 2. Science, Ancient 3. Greece -- Intellectual life -- To 146 B.C. 4. Byzantium. 5. Europe. 6. Greece. 7. Grekland -- kultur- och samhallsliv -- historia -- antiken. sao 8. Griechenland. gnd (DE-601)10481408X
ISBN 9781780760513

LC oc2017030566

Miletus: one of the wealthiest and most important towns in ancient Greece. It was here, in the 6th century BC, that the great traditions of Greek science and philosophy sparked into life, setting in motion a chain of knowledge that would change the world, forever. This title tells the story of Greek science from its earliest beginnings onwards.

Goddard, Jolyon

Concise history of science & invention : an illustrated time line / edited by Jolyon Goddard. National Geographic, c2010. 352 p. : **509**

1. Science -- History -- Chronology. 2. Inventions -- History -- Chronology.
ISBN 9781426205446

LC 2009018460

An accessible reference offers a panoramic perspective on scientific inventions that reflect the human race's efforts to understand and master the universe, sharing chronological and geocultural coverage of ten distinct eras.

Holmes, Richard, 1945-

★The **age** of wonder : how the romantic generation discovered the beauty and terror of science / Richard Holmes. Pantheon Books, c2009. 576 p.

1. Herschel, William, 1738-1822. 2. Herschel, Caroline Lucretia, 1750-1848. 3. Davy, Humphry, Sir, 1778-1829. 4. Science -- Social aspects -- History. 5. Scientists -- Great Britain -- 18th century. 6. Science -- History -- 18th century. 7. Romanticism -- Great Britain.
ISBN 9780375422225

LC 2008049587

ALA Notable Book, 2010.
National Book Critics Circle Award for Non-Fiction, 2009.
National Academies Communication Award, 2010.
Royal Society General Prizes for Science Books, 2009.

"The Age of Wonder" explores the earliest ideas of deep time and space, and the explorers of "dynamic science": an infinite, mysterious Nature waiting to be discovered. Three lives dominate the book: William Herschel, his sister Caroline, and Humphry Davy.

Ings, Simon

Stalin and the scientists : a history of triumph and tragedy, 1905-1953 / Simon Ings. Atlantic Monthly Press, 2017. 528 p. **509.47**

1. Stalin, Joseph, 1879-1953. 2. Scientists 3. Scientific discoveries 4. Science -- Political aspects 5. Science -- Social aspects 6. Russia -- History -- 20th century. 7. Soviet Union
ISBN 9780802125989

LC 2017300043

Stalin and the Scientists tells the story of the many gifted scientists who worked in Russia from the years leading up to the Revolution through the death of the "Great Scientist" himself, Joseph Stalin. It weaves together the stories of scientists, politicians, and ideologues into an intimate and sometimes horrifying portrait of a state determined to remake the world.

"A provocative and increasingly chilling work that shows how scientists in the nascent Soviet Union were sacrificed to the Soviet dream of building the ideal state." Kirkus.

Lightman, Alan P., 1948-

★The **discoveries** / Alan Lightman. Pantheon Books, 2005. xviii, 553 p. : **509**

1. Scientific discoveries -- History. 2. Research. 3. Technology -- Social aspects. 4. Science -- Historiography. 5. Essays..
ISBN 0375421688

LC 2005040854

"This book chronicles 25 landmark findings in astronomy, physics, chemistry, and biology in the 20th century. Beginning with Max Planck's quantum theory and ending with Paul Berg's recombinant DNA, these breakthroughs are academically and playfully explored via the nature of the unknown, the circumstances and influences of discovery, and, most originally, the actual words of the scientists." Library Journal.

McCray, Patrick (W. Patrick)

The **visioneers** : how a group of elite scientists pursued space colonies, nanotechnologies, and a limitless future / W. Patrick McCray. Princeton University Press, 2012. 328 p. **509**

1. Science -- History. 2. Visionaries. 3. Technological innovations. 4. Nanotechnology
ISBN 9780691139838

LC 2012017061

"In 1969, Princeton physicist Gerard O'Neill began looking outward to space colonies as the new frontier for humanity's expansion. A decade later, Eric Drexler, an MIT-trained engineer, turned his attention to the molecular world as the place where society's future needs could be met using self-replicating nanoscale machines. These modern utopians predicted that their technologies could transform society as humans mastered the ability to create new worlds, undertook atomic-scale engineering, and, if truly successful, overcame their own biological limits. The Visioneers tells the story of how these scientists and the communities they fostered imagined, designed, and popularized speculative technologies such as space colonies and nanotechnologies. Patrick McCray traces how these visioneers blended countercultural ideals with hard science, entrepreneurship, libertarianism, and unbridled optimism about the future. He shows how they built networks that communicated their ideas to writers, politicians, and corporate leaders. But the visioneers were not immune to failure--or to the lures of profit, celebrity, and hype. O'Neill and Drexler faced difficulty funding their work and overcoming colleagues' skepticism, and saw their ideas co-opted and transformed by Timothy Leary, the scriptwriters of Star Trek, and many others. Ultimately, both men struggled to overcome stigma and ostracism as they tried to unshackle their visioneering from pejorative labels like "fringe" and "pseudoscience." The Visioneers provides a balanced look at the successes and pitfalls they encountered. The book exposes the dangers of promotion--oversimplification, misuse, and misunderstanding--that can plague exploratory science. But above all, it highlights the importance of radical new ideas that inspire us to support cutting-edge research into tomorrow's technologies".-- Provided by publisher.

Mlodinow, Leonard, 1954-

The **upright** thinkers : the human journey from living in trees to understanding the cosmos / Leonard Mlodinow. Pantheon Books, 2015. 304 p. **509**

1. Knowledge 2. Intelligence 3. Science -- History. 4. Humans
ISBN 9780307908230

LC 2014040067

Includes index.

The best-selling co-author of The Grand Design chronicles the history of scientific discovery, from the invention of stone tools through modern-world understandings of quantum physics, tracing key moments in human progress to bravely asked, simple questions.

"Attending to the real people involved in the story he tells, and gifted with a knack for inserting a personal anecdote, a biographical tidbit, or a laugh line just when one is needed, Mlodinow never bores or exhausts. His structuring of the book is also exemplary. It's in three sections, the first ranging from H. habilis to Aristotle and the formalization of reason, the second from Renaissance cosmology to Darwin, and the third from Planck's and Einstein's invention of the quantum onward. Amateur science mavens couldn't ask for a better brief, introductory text." Booklist.

Park, Robert L.

Voodoo science : the road from foolishness to fraud / Robert L. Park. Oxford University Press, 2000. x, 230 p. ; **509**

1. Science -- Social aspects -- United States. 2. Fraud in science -- United States.
ISBN 9780195135152

LC 99040911

Includes index.

"The author aims to expose various beliefs and schemes put forth in the popular press and other places as scientifically real and factual. {He} turns a critical eye on cold fusion, magnet therapy, homeopathy, perpetual motion, and other recent examples of fringe science. Park's book should be required reading for all science writers, journalists, and politicians." Library Journal.

Teresi, Dick

Lost discoveries : the ancient roots of modern science-- from the Babylonians to the Maya / Dick Teresi. Simon & Schuster, 2002. ix, 453 p. : **509.3**

1. Ancient science. 2. Mathematics -- History. 3. Science -- History.
ISBN 0684837188

LC 2002075457

Documents scientific investigations and discoveries that were made by ancient civilizations, including the lowest common denominator, negative numbers, eclipses, the awareness of a round planet, and geocentric cosmology.

"Teresi offers a great deal of fascinating material largely ignored by many histories of science." Publishers Weekly.

Watson, Peter, 1943-

Convergence : the idea at the heart of science / Peter Watson. Simon & Schuster, 2017 512 p. **509**

1. Science -- History. 2. Convergence (Biology)
ISBN 9781476754345

LC 2016059213

Convergence is a history of modern science with an original and significant twist. Various scientific disciplines, despite their very different beginnings, have been coming together over the past 150 years, converging and coalescing. Intimate connections have been discovered between physics and chemistry, psychology and biology, genetics and linguistics.

"Bringing in ideas from geology, mythology, psychology, economics, and more to investigate the origins of civilization, Watson persuasively presents a deep and challenging idea." Publishers Weekly.

Weinberg, Steven, 1933-

To explain the world : the discovery of modern science / Steven Weinberg. Harper, 2015 368 p. **509**

1. Ancient science. 2. Science -- Greece -- History. 3. Medieval science 4. Science -- History.
ISBN 9780062346650

LC 2014030253

A Nobel Prize-winning physicist presents a masterful commentary on the history of science that examines historic clashes and collaborations between science and the competing realms of religion, technology, poetry, mathematics and philosophy, from the Ancient Greece to the world of today,.

"The author provides an almost 100-page appendix of technical notes, mathematical explanations of many of the theories and ideas discussed in the book. Overall, the book is interesting because it shows a scientist's perspective on the history of science; however, it does not measure up to the strict requirements of historiography expected by professional historian." Choice.

Wootton, David, 1952-
The **invention** of science : a new history of the Scientific Revolution / David Wootton. HarperCollins, 2015 xiv,769 p. **509**
1. Science -- History. 2. Scientific discoveries -- History
ISBN 9780061759529
LC bl2015054399

Cundill Prize in Historical Literature finalist, 2016

A groundbreaking examination of the Scientific Revolution by the author of Bad Medicine chronicles the essential transformations that were made possible by science throughout the past five centuries, profiles forefront iconoclasts and identifies links between key discoveries and the rise of industrialization.

"Although academics, who will catch the foreshadowing, will have no trouble following Wootton's argument, casual readers are likely to quit before they reach the payoff." Library Journal.

509.2 Scientists

Arianrhod, Robyn
Thomas Harriot : a life in science / Robyn Arianrhod. Oxford University Press, 2019. viii, 361 p. **509.2**
1. Harriot, Thomas, 1560-1621 2. Scientists 3. Scientific discoveries 4. Research 5. Physics 6. Great Britain -- History -- 16th century
ISBN 9780190271855
LC 2018024943

As Robyn Arianrhod shows in this new biography, the most complete to date, Thomas Harriot was a pioneer in both the figurative and literal sense. Indeed many have argued that Harriot was the best mathematician of his age, and one of the finest experimental scientists of all time. Yet he has remained an elusive figure. He had no close family to pass down records, and few of his letters survive. Most importantly, he never published his scientific discoveries, and not long after his death in 1621 had all but been forgotten. Using Harriot's re-discovered manuscripts, Arianrhod illuminates the full extent of his scientific and cultural achievements, expertly guiding us through what makes them original and important, and the story behind them.

"Filling in the gaps of a transitional era with deep background, the author alternates between straight histories and a close examination of Harriot's calculations, experiments, and theories. Although designed for a general audience, readers must be prepared to wade through tables and formulae better grasped by fellow mathematicians. theless, the richness of biographical and historical detail more than compensates for the effort." Kirkus.

Feldman, Burton
112 Mercer Street : Einstein, Russell, Godel, Pauli, and the end of innocence in science / Burton Feldman ; edited and completed by Katherine Williams. Arcade Pub., c2007. xx, 243 p. ; **509.2**
1. Einstein, Albert, 1879-1955. 2. Russell, Bertrand, 1872-1970. 3. Godel, Kurt, 1906-1978 4. Pauli, Wolfgang, 1869-1955. 5. Scientists -- History. 6. Scientists -- Philosophy. 7. Science -- History.
ISBN 1559707046
LC 2007001194

Portrays four of science's top minds as reflected during the historic 1944 meetings between Albert Einstein, Bertrand Russell, Wolfgang Pauli, and Kurt Godel at Einstein's Princeton home, offering insight into their remarkable personalities as friends, colleagues, and rivals.

"During the winter of 19431944, Albert Einstein met weekly with three other aging geniuses--philosopher Bertrand Russell, mathematician Kurt Godel and physicist Wolfgang Pauli--in the study of his home at 112 Mercer Street in Princeton, N.J. What the authors present are illuminating biographical sketches of these men and their earlier, groundbreaking work." Publishers Weekly.

Millar, David (Geophysicist)
★The **Cambridge** dictionary of scientists / David Millar ... [et al.]. Cambridge University Press, 2002. xii, 428 p. : **509.2**
1. Science -- History 2. Scientists
ISBN 9780521000628
LC 2002512240

From Ernst Abbe, a 19th-century German physicist, to Vladimir Zworykin, the 20th-century Russian inventor, this dictionary contains some 1,500 entries detailing the achievements of scientists in a variety of fields.

509.4 Science -- History, geographic treatment, biography -- Europe

Dolnick, Edward, 1952-
The **clockwork** universe : Isaac Newton, the Royal Society, and the birth of the modern world / Edward Dolnick. HarperCollins, 2011. 320 p. **509.4**
1. Newton, Isaac, 1642-1727. 2. Royal Society (Great Britain) 3. Science -- Europe -- History -- 17th century. 4. Religion and science -- History. 5. Intellectual life.
ISBN 9780061719516
LC 2010024321

A 350th anniversary tribute to the Royal Society documents the work of late 17th-century scientific geniuses who in spite of period ignorance forged lasting understandings about the organization of the universe.

"The author focuses on the 17th century and the giants of early science--Galileo, Kepler, Descartes, and particularly Newton and Leibniz, whose independent invention of calculus made it possible to describe the moving, changing world and opened up a literal universe of possibilities." Publishers Weekly.

Hofstadter, Dan
The **Earth** moves : Galileo and the Roman Inquisition / Dan Hofstadter. Atlas & Co. : c2009. 240 p. **509.4**
1. Galilei, Galileo, 1564-1642 Trials, litigation, etc. 2. Catholic Church Italy -- History 17th century. 3. Catholic theology -- History 4. Inquisition -- Italy 5. Astronomy -- Religious aspects -- Christianity 6. Renaissance science 7. Italy -- History -- 17th century.
ISBN 9780393066500
LC 2009004325

An analysis of Galileo Galilei's historic 1633 trial evaluates the period as a turning point in the history of science covers such topics as the execution of Giordano Bruno in 1600, Galileo's Catholic faith, and Rome's Holy Office of the Inquisition.

"This is a political, scientific and psychological examination of the first great clash of religion and science, between Galileo and Pope Urban VIII, two seminal figures who were, incredibly, once friends." Publishers Weekly.

510 Mathematics

Adam, John A.
★A **mathematical** nature walk / John A. Adam. Princeton University Press, c2009. xx, 248 p., 8 p. of plates : **510**
1. Mathematics in nature 2. Mathematical analysis. 3. Nature 4.

Mathematics
ISBN 9780691128955

LC 2008044828

"The general reader will find here a remarkably lucid explanation of how mathematicians create a formulaic model that mimics the key features of some natural phenomenon. . . . Ordinary math becomes adventure." Booklist.

Barrow, John D., 1952-

100 essential things you didn't know you didn't know : math explains your world / John D. Barrow. W. W. Norton & Co., 2009. 298 p. **510**

1. Mathematics -- Miscellanea 2. Essays.
ISBN 9780393070071

LC 2008055910

Originally published in London, England (Bodley Head, 2008).

"Barrow successfully conveys the idea that mathematics provides a key to understanding both ordinary and extraordinary phenomena." Publishers Weekly.

Benjamin, Arthur

The **magic** of math : solving for x and figuring out why / Arthur Benjamin. Basic Books, 2015 321 p. : **510**

1. Mathematics 2. Mathematical recreations. 3. Mathematics -- Study and teaching.
ISBN 9780465054725

LC bl2015034757

Includes index.

An engaging introduction to the beauty, simplicity and fun of mathematical formulas explains its essentials and disciplines through everyday examples, mnemonics and brain-teasing tricks. By the author of The Secrets of Mental Math.

Beveridge, Colin (Maths coach)

The **math** behind... : discover the mathematics of everyday things / Colin Beveridge. Firefly Books, 2017. 192 p. : **510**

1. Mathematics 2. Probabilities
ISBN 1770859985

LC bl2017047651

Includes index.

Examines the mathematical principles behind everyday things, including the odds of winning the lottery, the reason for "causeless" traffic jams, and how predictive text works.

"Whether readers are math geeks looking for new ways of applying mathematics principles or just curious to see how math might actually be applicable in everyday life, this fun, enlightening book will not disappoint." Publishers Weekly.

Cheng, Eugenia

How to bake pi : an edible exploration of the mathematics of mathematics / Eugenia Cheng. Basic Books, 2015. 320 p. **510**

1. Mathematics 2. Food. 3. Cooking. 4. Mathematicians
ISBN 9780465051717

LC bl2015018104

A math expert uses cooking to shed light on the heart of mathematics.

"Despite her zeal for mathematical logic, Cheng recognizes that such logic begins in faith--irrational faith--and ultimately requires poetry and art to complement its findings. A singular humanization of the mathematical project." Booklist.

Clegg, Brian

Are numbers real? : the uncanny relationship of mathematics and the physical world. / Brian Clegg. St. Martin's Press, 2016 320 p. **510**

1. Mathematics. 2. Number concept. 3. Arithmetic. 4. Number theory
ISBN 9781250081049

LC 2016027287

The critically acclaimed author of Ten Billion Tomorrows and The Final Frontier presents an accessible, in-depth look at the history of numbers and their applications in life and science, from math's surreal presence in the virtual world to the debates about the role of math in science.

"Clegg is an outstanding science writer, and this book lives up to his usual standard. Highly recommended for those interested in math or science." Library Journal.

Darling, David J.

The **universal** book of mathematics : from Abracadabra to Zeno's paradoxes / David Darling. Wiley, c2004. ix, 383 p. : **510**

1. Mathematics
ISBN 9780471270478

LC 2003024670

"The book's entries include numerous mathematical terms, brief biographies of mathematicians from ancient times to the present, and famous mathematical problems (both solved and unsolved), as well as problems and puzzles of a more recreational nature. It is a spirit of whimsy, the fanciful, and the outrageous that makes this book much more than a dry encyclopedia of mathematical terms, however. Darling's writing style and choice of entries make this an easy book to pick up and page through." Choice.

Dunham, William, 1947-

The **mathematical** universe : an alphabetical journey through the great proofs, problems, and personalities / William Dunham. Wiley & Sons, c1994. vi, 314 p. : **510**

1. Mathematics -- History. 2. Mathematicians.
ISBN 0471536563

LC 93046702

"In this history of mathematics, Dunham sheds light not only on the personalities--eccentric, vain, brilliant--of major mathematicians, but also on contemporary social issues, such as multiculturalism and gender equity. Readers who want to understand the cultural significance of mathematics would do well to begin with this book." Booklist.

Ellenberg, Jordan, 1971-

★ **How** not to be wrong : the power of mathematical thinking / Jordan Ellenberg. The Penguin Press, 2014. 480 p. **510**

1. Mathematics -- Miscellanea. 2. Mathematical analysis. 3. Everyday life
ISBN 9781594205224

LC 2014005394

In How Not to Be Wrong, Jordan Ellenberg shows us that math isn't confined to abstract incidents that never occur in real life, but rather touches everything we do -- the whole world is shot through with it. Math allows us to see the hidden structures underneath the messy and chaotic surface of our world. It's a science of not being wrong, hammered out by centuries of hard work and argument. Armed with the tools of mathematics, we can see through to the true meaning of information we take for granted: How early should you get to the airport? What does "public opinion" really represent? Why do tall parents have shorter children? Who really won Florida in 2000? And how likely are you, really, to develop cancer? How Not to Be Wrong presents the surprising revelations behind all of these questions and many more, using the mathematician's method of analyzing life and exposing the hard-won insights of the academic community to the layman--minus the jargon. Ellenberg pulls from history as well as from the latest theoretical developments to provide those not trained in math with the knowledge they need.

"Ellenberg finds the common-sense math at work in the everyday world, and his vivid examples and clear descriptions show how 'math is woven into the way we reason.' " Publishers Weekly.

Huber, Michael R., 1960-

Mythematics : solving the Twelve Labors of Hercules / Michael Huber. Princeton University Press, c2009. xix, 183 p. : **510**

1. Heracles (Greek mythological character). 2. Problem solving
ISBN 9780691135755

LC 2009008535

How might Hercules, the most famous of the Greek heroes, have used mathematics to complete his astonishing Twelve Labors? From conquering the Nemean Lion and cleaning out the Augean Stables, to capturing the Erymanthean Boar and entering the Underworld to defeat the three-headed dog Cerberus, Hercules and his legend are the inspiration for this book of fun and original math puzzles. --From publisher description.

"Though Mythematics is probably best viewed as a recreational mathematics book, the methods used should provide insight into how one applies mathematics to a physical, real-world problem." Choice.

Mahajan, Sanjoy, 1969-

Street-fighting mathematics : the art of educated guessing and opportunistic problem solving / Sanjoy Mahajan ; foreword by Carver A. Mead. MIT Press, c2010. xv, 134 p. : **510**

1. Estimation theory. 2. Hypothesis. 3. Problem solving.
ISBN 026251429X

LC 2009028867

In Street-Fighting Mathematics, Sanjoy Mahajan builds, sharpens, and demonstrates tools for educated guessing and down-and-dirty, opportunistic problem solving across diverse fields of knowledge--from mathematics to management. Mahajan describes six tools: dimensional analysis, easy cases, lumping, picture proofs, successive approximation, and reasoning by analogy. Illustrating each tool with numerous examples, he carefully separates the tool--the general principle--from the particular application so that the reader can most easily grasp the tool itself to use on problems of particular interest. --From publisher description.

Parker, Matt (Mathematician)

Humble pi : when math goes wrong in the real world / Matt Parker. Riverhead Books, 2020, c2019. 336 p. **510**

1. Mathematics 2. Errors 3. Mathematics -- Miscellanea 4. Mathematics -- Humor
ISBN 9780593084687

LC 2019029057

Includes index.

Originally published: London : Allen Lane, 2019.

This tour of real-world mathematical disasters reveals the importance of math in everyday life. All sorts of seemingly innocuous mathematical mistakes can have significant consequences. Exploring and explaining a litany of glitches, near misses, and mathematical mishaps involving the internet, big data, elections, street signs, lotteries, the Roman Empire, and an Olympic team, Matt Parker uncovers the ways math trips us up.

"Nonsense, blunders, and delusions make for good reading, so Parker's relentless litany will have a wide appeal. Fun reading for nonmathematicians." Kirkus.

★**Things** to make and do in the fourth dimension : a mathematician's journey through narcissistic numbers, optimal dating algorithms, at least two kinds of infinity, and more / Matt Parker. Farrar Straus & Giroux, 2014. 320 p. **510**

1. Mathematics 2. Fourth dimension 3. Numbers 4. Number theory
ISBN 9780374275655

LC bl2014050395

A stand-up comedian and mathematician offers games, puzzles and hands-on activities to help those with a fear of math understand and enjoy the logical tools and abstract concepts of the subject normally only accessible at college-level study.

"Parker makes it sound easy, even when it is not, and some of the material can be pretty heavy going. However, most important, he reveals the social aspects of the field, describing his interactions with other mathematicians as they bounce problems around, challenging one another's imaginations." Library Journal.

Posamentier, Alfred S.

Magnificent mistakes in mathematics / Alfred S. Posamentier, Ingmar Lehmann. Prometheus Books, 2013. 296 p. : **510**

1. Mathematics -- Miscellanea 2. Errors, Scientific 3. Discoveries in science
ISBN 9781616147471

LC 2013012126

Demonstrates how historical mistakes have had profound consequences, providing coverage of such events as the 1946 discovery of Shank's infamous pi miscalculation, the concept-violating method used to prove that every triangle is isosceles.

Seife, Charles

★**Proofiness** : the dark arts of mathematical deception / Charles Seife. Viking, 2010. 320 p. **510**

1. Mathematics. 2. Pseudoscience. 3. Statistics.
ISBN 9780670022168

LC 2010012127

"The author examines the many ways that people fudge with numbers, sometimes just to sell more moisturizer but also to ruin our economy, rig our elections, convict the innocent and undercount the needy. . . . [This book] reveals the truly corrosive effects on a society awash in numerical mendacity. This is more than a math book; it's an eye-opening civics lesson. " New York Times Book Review.

Singh, Simon

The **Simpsons** and their mathematical secrets / Simon Singh. Bloomsbury USA, 2013. 272 p. **510**

1. Simpsons (Television program). 2. Mathematics. 3. Number theory. 4. Mathematics fun.
ISBN 9781620402771

LC 2013020884

Based on interviews with the writers of The Simpsons and accompanied by images from the show, facsimiles of scripts, paintings and drawings and other imagery, this fascinating book reveals the meaningful mathematical concepts behind the most successful show in TV history.

"Perhaps Simpsons nerds have known this all along, but for the rest of us who think of the TV show as primarily a sharp piece of comic writing, it may come as a surprise to learn that it is riddled with sophisticated mathematics." Kirkus.

Stewart, Ian, 1945-

Visions of infinity : the great mathematical problems / Ian

Stewart. Basic Books, 2013. 320 p. **510**

1. Mathematics 2. Mathematicians 3. Mathematics -- Problems, exercises, etc.
ISBN 9780465022403
LC bl2013003267

A celebrated mathematician, explaining why mathematical problems exist, what drives mathematicians to solve them, and why their efforts matter in the context of science as a whole, presents a fascinating history of mathematics as told through 14 of its greatest problems.

Szpiro, George, 1950-
Numbers rule : the vexing mathematics of democracy, from Plato to the present / George G. Szpiro. Princeton University Press, c2010. xi, 226 p. ; **510**

1. Mathematics -- Anecdotes
ISBN 9780691139944
LC 2009028615

Traces the epic quest of philosophers, statesmen and mathematicians throughout history to create a more perfect democracy and adapt to the ever-changing demands of each new generation by analyzing the mathematical anomalies in voting results.

Tammet, Daniel, 1979-
★**Thinking** in numbers : on life, love, meaning, and math / Daniel Tammet. Little Brown & Co 2013. 288 p. **510**

1. Mathematics 2. Numbers. 3. Mathematical ability 4. Numeration -- History. 5. Essays
ISBN 9780316187374
LC bl2013030566

The mathematical savant and best-selling author of Born on a Blue Day uses personal stories and everyday examples to describe the way numbers and equations form the basis of our lives, from snowflakes to Anne Boleyn's extra finger.

Tymony, Cy
Sneaky math : a graphic primer with projects : ace the basics of algebra, geometry, trigonometry, and calculus with everyday things / Cy Tymony. Andrews McMeel Publishing, 2014 viii, 179 p. : **510**

1. Mathematics 2. Mathematics 3. Problems, exercises, etc.
ISBN 9781449445201
LC bl2015001740

Offers projects designed to improve readers' understanding of arithmetic, algebra, geometry, trigonometry, and calculus.

"Math lessons in school have a reputation for being rote and forgettable, but the content has a way of sneaking into everyday life, and by capitalizing on these real-world applications, Tymony helps conquer much of the fear and dread associated with traditional math lessons." Booklist.

Yates, Kit
The **math** of life and death : 7 mathematical principles that shape our lives / Kit Yates. Scribner, 2020. 256 p. **510**

1. Mathematics -- Popular works. 2. Statistics 3. Misinformation 4. Errors
ISBN 9781982111878
LC 2019024831

A first book by an Oxford-trained mathematician illuminates seven mathematical principles that shape our lives, from the controversies of DNA testing to the probabilities that shaped the Chernobyl disaster.

"A welcome addition to the math-for-people-who-hate-math genre." Kirkus.

Kolata, Gina Bari, 1948-
The **New** York Times book of mathematics : more than 100 years of writing by the numbers / edited by Gina Kolata ; foreword by Paul Hoffman. Sterling, [2013], ©2013. xiv, 480 p. : **510**

1. Mathematics. 2. Essays
ISBN 9781402793226
LC 2012045019

Includes index.

Presents a selection from the archives of the New York newspaper of its writings on mathematics from 1892 to 2010, covering such topics as chaos theory, statistics, cryptography, and computers.

510.76 Mathematics--examinations

Szpiro, George, 1950-
Poincare's prize : the hundred-year quest to solve one of math's greatest puzzles / George G. Szpiro. Dutton, c2007. ix, 309 p. ; **510.76**

1. Perelman, Grigory. 2. Mathematics -- Problems, exercises, etc. 3. Mathematics.
ISBN 0525950249
LC 2007012792

Traces the hundred-year effort to solve the Poincare Conjecture and its successful solution by Grigory Perelman, an impoverished Russian recluse who refused all prizes and academic appointments while solving an array of mathematical conundrums.

"Never has mathematics provided more fascinating human drama!" Booklist.

510.9 Mathematics--history

Merzbach, Uta C., 1933-
A **history** of mathematics / Uta C. Merzbach and Carl B. Boyer. John Wiley, c2011. xx, 668 p. : **510.9**

1. Mathematics -- History
ISBN 9780470525487
LC 2010003424

For more than forty years, A History of Mathematics has been the reference of choice for those looking to learn about the fascinating history of humankind's relationship with numbers, shapes, and patterns. This revised edition features up-to-date coverage of topics such as Fermat's Last Theorem and the Poincare Conjecture, in addition to recent advances in areas such as finite group theory and computer-aided proofs. --From publisher description.

Pickover, Clifford A.
The **math** book : From Pythagoras to the 57th Dimension, 250 Milestones in the History of Mathematics / Clifford A. Pickover. Sterling Pub., c2009. 527, 1 p. : **510.9**

1. Mathematics -- History.
ISBN 1402788290
LC 2008043214

"Pickover's love of mathematics shines through the text and images, and it is likely that the reader will catch at least some of his enthusiasm." Choice.

Rudman, Peter Strom
The **Babylonian** theorem : the mathematical journey to Pythagoras and Euclid / Peter S. Rudman. Prometheus Books,

2010. 248 p. : **510.9**

1. Pythagoras. 2. Euclides. 3. Mathematics -- History 4. Ancient mathematics 5. Mathematics, Babylonian. 6. Mathematics -- Egypt -- History.

ISBN 9781591027737

LC 2009039196

Sequel to: How mathematics happened: the first 50,000 years.

In this book on ancient Near Eastern and Egyptian mathematics, Rudman (physics, Technion Institute, Haifa, emeritus) explores the ways in which ancient mathematicians worked out mathematical solutions to practical problems, like building pyramids and ziggurats, or tracing the square root of two apparently just for fun. He begins by explaining the numbering systems of Egyptians, Babylonians and Greeks, including explaining the use of agricultural measurements and parts of the body as standards. Along the way, we learn that the Babylonians worked in base 60 and the Egyptians wrote fractions using the hieroglyph for the eye of Horus. Much of the book, though, consists of formulae that demonstrate the mathematical skill of these societies and how much Greeks like Pythagoras and Euclid were building on earlier work. The text is sprinkled with "fun questions" that can be used to enliven the teaching of geometry and algebra even at a high school level. --From publisher description.

510.92 Mathematicians

Lee Shetterly, Margot

Hidden figures : the American dream and the untold story of the Black women mathematicians who helped win the space race / Margot Lee Shetterly. William Morrow, 2016. xviii, 346 p. ; **510.92**

1. United States. National Aeronautics and Space Administration Officials and employees 2. Women mathematicians 3. African American women 4. Space programs -- International competition 5. Racism in politics and government. 6. United States -- History -- 20th century

ISBN 9780062363596

ALA Notable Book, 2017.

BCALA Literary Award for Nonfiction, 2017.

National Academies Communication Award, 2017.

An account of the previously unheralded but pivotal contributions of NASA's African-American women mathematicians to America's space program describes how they were segregated from their white counterparts by Jim Crow laws in spite of their groundbreaking successes.

"Shetterly's highly recommended work offers up a crucial history that had previously and unforgivably been lost. We'd do well to put this book into the hands of young women who have long since been told that there's no room for them at the scientific table." Library Journal.

Pasles, Paul C., 1968-

Benjamin Franklin's numbers : an unsung mathematical odyssey / Paul C. Pasles. Princeton University Press, c2008. 254 p., 8 p. of plates : **510.92**

1. Franklin, Benjamin, 1706-1790. 2. Politicians -- United States -- History -- 18th century 3. Inventors -- United States -- 18th century 4. Diplomats -- United States -- History -- 18th century 5. Scientists -- United States -- History -- 18th century 6. United States -- History -- 18th century

ISBN 0691129568

LC 2006102508

Paul Pasles reveals a side of the iconic statesman, scientist, and writer that few Americans know -- his mathematical side. In fact, Franklin indulged in many areas of mathematics, including number theory, geometry, statistics, and economics. Franklin's genius for numbers includes the math behind his hugely popular Poor Richard's Almanac and much more! Optional math problems challenge readers to match wits with the bespectacled Founding Father himself. Written for a general audience, this book assumes no technical skills beyond basic arithmetic. -- Description by the publisher.

"The author documents the famous scientist-statesman's lively interest in numerical enigmas, most particularly those known as Magic Squares. An unexpected but welcome perspective on the genial genius of Philadelphia." Booklist.

511 General principles of mathematics

Alexander, Amir R.

Infinitesimal : how a dangerous mathematical theory shaped the modern world / Amir Alexander. Scientific American/Farrar, Straus and Giroux, 2014. 368 p. **511**

1. Calculus -- History. 2. Infinitesimal geometry. 3. Mathematics -- History 4. Renaissance science. 5. Europe -- History -- 17th century.

ISBN 9780374176815

LC 2013033923

"The epic battle over a mathematical concept that shook the old order and shaped the world as we know it".-- Provided by publisher.

"The author navigates even the most abstract mathematical concepts as deftly as he does the layered social history, and the result is a book about math that is actually fun to read. A fast-paced history of the singular idea that shaped a multitude of modern achievements." Kirkus.

Michael, T. S., 1960-

How to guard an art gallery and other discrete mathematical adventures : And Other Discrete Mathematical Adventures / T.S. Michael. Johns Hopkins University Press, 2009. xi, 257 p. : **511**

1. Algorithms. 2. Combinatorial analysis. 3. Computer science -- Mathematics.

ISBN 0801892988

LC 2009000435

The time-honored story problem, central to mathematics and an expression of its fascination or frustration (depending on the student's success), is the protagonist of this delightful work on discrete mathematics. Written for advanced high school and undergraduate students who have learned algebra and geometry, the text contains 7 chapters, each one devoted to a different story problem and its variations. Pick's formula, art gallery problems, quadratic residues of primes and squares, and stamps and coins and Sylvester's formula are some of the problems presented, with each chapter consisting of a group of problems of increasing difficulty. Each chapter concludes with an annotated list of references. The author teaches at the United States Naval Academy. --From publisher description.

511.3 Mathematical logic (Symbolic logic)

Fortnow, Lance, 1963-

The **golden** ticket : P, NP, and the search for the impossible / Lance Fortnow. Princeton University Press, [2013] 200 p. **511.3**

1. Mathematics -- Problems, exercises, etc. 2. Computer science 3. Algorithms 4. NP-complete problems.

ISBN 9780691156491

LC 2012039523

Provides a nontechnical introduction to the P-NP problem in computing - which asks whether every problem than can be verified quickly by a computer can also be solved quickly by a computer - its rich history, and its algorithmic implications for everything we do with computers and beyond.

Stillwell, John
Roads to infinity : the mathematics of truth and proof / John Stillwell. A K Peters, c2010. xi, 203 p. : **511.3**
1. Infinite. 2. Logic, Symbolic and mathematical. 3. Set theory.
ISBN 1568814666
LC 2010014077

This book offers an introduction to modern ideas about infinity and their implications for mathematics. It unifies ideas from set theory and mathematical logic, and traces their effects on mainstream mathematical topics of today, such as number theory and combinatorics. The treatment is historical and partly informal, but with due attention to the subtleties of the subject. --From publisher description.

"This is a book that anyone with an interest in mathematics should have in their library." Choice.

512 Algebra

Conway, John Horton
The **book** of numbers / John H. Conway, Richard K. Guy. Copernicus c1996. ix, 310 p. : **512**
1. Number theory -- Popular works
ISBN 9780387979939
LC 95032588

Explores number theory and patterns that emerge in arithmetic, algebra, and geometry

Livio, Mario, 1945-
The **equation** that couldn't be solved : how mathematical genius discovered the language of symmetry / Mario Livio. Simon & Schuster, c2005. x, 353 p. : **512**
1. Abel, Niels Henrik, 1802-1829. 2. Galois, Evariste, 1811-1832. 3. Group theory -- History. 4. Number theory -- History. 5. Symmetry (Physics) 6. Diophantine analysis -- History.
ISBN 9780743258203
LC 2005044123

Traces the four-thousand-year-old mathematical effort to discover and define the laws of symmetry, citing the achievements of doomed geniuses Niels Henrick Abel and Evariste Galois to solve the quintic equation and give birth to group theory.

"Even the mathematically fainthearted can learn a great deal about symmetry from this book." Science Books & Films.

Singh, Simon
Fermat's enigma : the epic quest to solve the world's greatest mathematical problem / Simon Singh ; foreword by John Lynch. Walker, 1997. xviii, 315 p. : **512**
1. Wiles, Andrew, 1953- 2. Mathematicians -- Princeton, New Jersey. 3. Fermat's last theorem. 4. Mathematics -- Problems, exercises, etc. 5. Mathematics -- History.
ISBN 0802713319
LC 97020748

Also published as Fermat's last theorem.

The story of Fermat's Last Theorem, devised by the seventeenth-century French mathematician Pierre de Fermat, recounts the struggles of three and a half centuries of scientists to devise a proof for it.

"This vivid account is fascinating reading for anyone interested in mathematics, its history, and the passionate quest for solutions to unsolved riddles." School Library Journal.

512.7 Number theory

Derbyshire, John
Prime obsession : Bernhard Riemann and the greatest unsolved problem in mathematics / John Derbyshire. Joseph Henry Press, 2003. xv, 422 p. : **512.7**
1. Riemann, Bernhard, 1826-1866. 2. Prime numbers. 3. Series.
ISBN 0309085497
LC 2002156310

Includes index.

An intriguing look inside one of the great mathematical mysteries explains the fundamental elements of the nineteenth-century German mathematician's discovery and its implications, and features a profile of Bernhard Reimann and a history of mathematics in relation to his hypothesis.

"The author first takes readers through . mathematical fundamentals in order to give them a good understanding of Riemann's discovery and its consequences. Interspersed with the hardcore math, other chapters profile Riemann the man and trace the history of mathematics in relation to his still-unproven hypothesis. Derbyshire shows how after 150 years, the world's greatest minds still haven't found a solution." Library Journal.

Havil, Julian
The **irrationals** : a story of the numbers you can't count on / Julian Havil. Princeton University Press, 2012. 298 p. **512.7**
1. Irrational numbers. 2. Numbers 3. Mathematics
ISBN 9780691143422
LC 2012931844

Discusses the history of irrational numbers, surveys the work of mathematicians who have worked with them, and explores the questions and difficulties that still exist about them.

512.9 Foundations of algebra

Mackenzie, Dana
The **universe** in zero words : the story of mathematics as told through equations / Dana Mackenzie. Princeton University Press, 2012. 224 p. : **512.9**
1. Equations 2. Mathematics -- History
ISBN 0691152829
LC 2011936364

Looks at the history of twenty-four equations that have shaped the history of mathematics, science, and civilization.

513 Arithmetic

Bellos, Alex, 1969-
Here's looking at Euclid : a surprising excursion through the astonishing world of math / Alex Bellos. Free Press, 2010. xi, 319 p. : **513**
1. Mathematics 2. Numbers -- Social aspects 3. Mathematical ability

4. Number concept
ISBN 9781416588252

LC 2009036815

Also published as Alex's adventures in numberland: London : Bloomsbury, 2010.

A layperson's introduction to the mathematical world describes his travels to regions of lesser-known mathematical quality, from the lair of Japan's Sudoku to the Manhattan apartment of the creators of the world's fastest computer.

513.5 Numeration systems

Aczel, Amir D.

Finding zero : a mathematician's odyssey to uncover the origins of numbers / Amir D. Aczel. Palgrave Macmillan, [2015] 256 p. **513.5**

1. Numerals 2. Numbers 3. Mathematics -- History 4. Science -- History
ISBN 9781137279842

LC 2014024462

"The invention of numerals is perhaps the greatest abstraction the human mind has ever created. Virtually everything in our lives is digital, numerical, or quantified. The story of how and where we got these numerals, which we so depend on, has for thousands of years been shrouded in mystery. Finding Zero is an adventure filled saga of Amir Aczel's lifelong obsession: to find the original sources of our numerals. Aczel has doggedly crisscrossed the ancient world, scouring dusty, moldy texts, cross examining so-called scholars who offered wildly differing sets of facts, and ultimately penetrating deep into a Cambodian jungle to find a definitive proof. Here, he takes the reader along for the ride. The history begins with the early Babylonian cuneiform numbers, followed by the later Greek and Roman letter numerals. Then Aczel asks the key question: where do the numbers we use today, the so-called Hindu-Arabic numerals, come from? It is this search that leads him to explore uncharted territory, to go on a grand quest into India, Thailand, Laos, Vietnam, and ultimately into the wilds of Cambodia. There he is blown away to find the earliest zero--the keystone of our entire system of numbers--on a crumbling, vine-covered wall of a seventh-century temple adorned with eaten-away erotic sculptures. While on this odyssey, Aczel meets a host of fascinating characters: academics in search of truth, jungle trekkers looking for adventure, surprisingly honest politicians, shameless smugglers, and treacherous archaeological thieves--who finally reveal where our numbers come from. "-- Provided by publisher.

"The story brims with local color, as well as insights into the history of mathematics and philosophy." Publishers Weekly.

Posamentier, Alfred S.

Numbers : their tales, types, and treasures / Alfred S. Posamentier & Bernd Thaller. Prometheus Books, 2015. 300 p. **513.5**

1. Number concept. 2. Numbers. 3. Counting. 4. Arithmetic -- Foundations.
ISBN 9781633880306

LC 2015011662

Two experienced math educators aim to make math appealing and understandable to everyone through a discussion of the history of numbers, why we need them and what is so special about pi and the Fibonacci sequence.

"Overall the book is extremely well written and entertaining. Its rich, satisfying variety encompasses Piaget, multicultural references, Bertrand Russell, number patterns, and historical surprises. Summing Up: Highly recommended. All readers." Choice.

515 Analysis

Ash, Avner, 1949-

Elliptic tales : curves, counting, and number theory / Avner Ash, Robert Gross. Princeton University Press, c2012. xvii, 253 p. : **515**

1. Curves, Elliptic. 2. Elliptic functions. 3. Number theory.
ISBN 0691151199

LC 2011044712

Elliptic Tales describes the latest developments in number theory by looking at one of the most exciting unsolved problems in contemporary mathematics: the Birch and Swinnerton-Dyer Conjecture. In this book, Avner Ash and Robert Gross guide readers through the mathematics they need to understand this captivating problem. --From publisher description.

"This book will captivate math enthusiasts as well as readers curious about an intriguing and still unanswered question." Library Journal.

Ouellette, Jennifer

The **calculus** diaries : how math can help you lose weight, win in Vegas, and survive a zombie apocalypse / Jennifer Ouellette. Penguin Books, 2010. xv, 318 p. : **515**

1. Calculus -- Miscellanea. 2. Mathematics -- Miscellanea.
ISBN 9780143117377

LC 2010025843

Explains calculus in an effort to combat math phobia, and how it can make daily life, from gas mileage to gambling in Vegas, more understandable.

516 Geometry

Posamentier, Alfred S.

The **secrets** of triangles : a mathematical journey / Alfred S. Posamentier and Ingmar Lehmann. Prometheus Books, 2012. 387 p. **516**

1. Trigonometry. 2. Triangles 3. Geometry 4. Mathematics
ISBN 9781616145873

LC 2012013635

Reveals interesting geometrical properties designed to present the discipline as fun, and improve the reader's problem-solving skills.

"While some constructions are technically involved, others are refreshingly straightforward yet still disclose secrets hidden within this simple geometric shape. Moreover, the illustrations are excellent, clearly illustrating the points under consideration, even in the most complicated of settings." Choice.

516.2 Euclidean geometry

Berlinski, David, 1942-

★The **king** of infinite space : Euclid and his elements / David Berlinski. Basic Books, 2013. 176 p. **516.2**

1. Euclides. 2. Geometry. 3. Logic. 4. Mathematics -- History.
ISBN 9780465014811

LC 2012042492

"An impressively concise distillation of the wizardry that transforms points, lines, and planes into sheer genius." Booklist.

Livio, Mario, 1945-

The **golden** ratio : the story of phi, the world's most astonishing number / Mario Livio. Broadway Books, 2003, c2002. viii, 294 p. : **516.2**

1. Golden section. 2. Mathematics. 3. Ratios. 4. Numbers.
ISBN 0767908163

LC bl2004111069

Reprint. Originally published: 2002.

Offers a look at phi, or "the golden ratio," discovered by Euclid more than two thousand years ago, examining the meaning of this remarkable mathematical proportion in terms of science, biology, philosophy, and other fields.

"Overall, an enjoyable work, amply supported by index, extensive references, and ten appendixes presenting mathematical elaborations of text material." Choice.

516.22 Plane geometry

Kaplan, Robert, 1933-

Hidden harmonies : the lives and times of the Pythagorean theorem / Robert and Ellen Kaplan. Bloomsbury Press, 2010. 204 p. **516.22**

1. Pythagoras 2. Pythagorean theorem 3. Mathematics -- History. 4. Plane geometry. 5. Geometry
ISBN 9781596915220

LC 2010019959

The Harvard mathematician authors of The Art of the Infinite present a history of the famous relation "A squared plus B squared equals C squared" that assesses its contributors from da Vinci to the Freemasons while analyzing its numerous proofs and applications.

516.3 Analytic geometries

O'Rourke, Joseph

How to fold it : the mathematics of linkages, origami, and polyhedra / Joseph O'Rourke. Cambridge University Press, 2011. xii, 177 p. : **516.3**

1. Liaison theory (Mathematics). 2. Origami -- Mathematics. 3. Polyhedra. 4. Protein folding.
ISBN 0521145473

LC 2011001236

Includes index.

"What do proteins and pop-up cards have in common? How is opening a grocery bag different from opening a gift box? How can you cut out the letters for a whole word all at once with one straight scissors cut? How many ways are there to flatten a cube? With the help of 200 colour figures, author Joseph O'Rourke explains these fascinating folding problems starting from high school algebra and geometry and introducing more advanced concepts in tangible contexts as they arise. He shows how variations on these basic problems lead directly to the frontiers of current mathematical research and offers ten accessible unsolved problems for the enterprising reader. Before tackling these, you can test your skills on fifty exercises with complete solutions. The book's website, http://www.howtofoldit.org, has dynamic animations of many of the foldings and downloadable templates for readers to fold or cut out".--Provided by publisher.

519.2 Probabilities

Devlin, Keith J.

The **unfinished** game : Pascal, Fermat, and the seventeenth-century letter that made the world modern / Keith Devlin. Basic Books, c2008. x, 191 p. : **519.2**

1. Pascal, Blaise, 1623-1662 Correspondence. 2. Fermat, Pierre de, 1601-1665 Correspondence. 3. Probabilities. 4. Mathematicians -- France -- Correspondence. 5. Statistics. 6. Science -- History 7. France -- History -- 17th century
ISBN 9780465009107

LC 2008012222

Examines a letter written by Blaise Pascal to Pierre de Fermat in 1654 that speaks of probability and numerical values that have had an impact on the modern world with regard to calculating insurance rates, the housing markets, and car safety.

Mazur, Joseph

Fluke : the math and myth of coincidences / Joseph Mazur. Basic Books, 2016 272 p. **519.2**

1. Coincidence. 2. Chance. 3. Mathematics 4. Coincidence theory (Mathematics).
ISBN 9780465060955

LC 2015043288

Presents a mathematical guide to understanding why life can seem to be one big coincidence--and why the odds of just about everything are better than we think.

"The author draws examples and illustrations from a variety of fields--law enforcement, economics, the sciences--and, when he unavoidably gets into some fairly complicated mathematical discussions, he explains his terms and remembers that, for the most part, his readers aren't mathematicians. An ideal book, then, for the lay reader who is curious about the nature of coincidence." Booklist.

Mlodinow, Leonard, 1954-

The **drunkard's** walk : how randomness rules our lives / Leonard Mlodinow. Pantheon Books, 2008. xi, 252 p. : **519.2**

1. Random data (Statistics) 2. Probabilities. 3. Chance. 4. Statistics.
ISBN 9780375424045

LC 2007042507

Includes index.

Critically analyzes the role of chance and random events, forces, and factors in shaping human existence, in a readable study of how the mathematical laws of randomness control the world around us.

Smith, Gary, 1945-

What the luck? : the surprising role of chance in our everyday lives / Gary Smith. The Overlook Press, 2016. 304 p. **519.2**

1. Chance. 2. Options, alternatives, choices. 3. Statistics. 4. Probabilities.
ISBN 9781468313758

LC bl2016036451

The economics professor author of Standard Deviations explores the role of luck, specifically the "Regression to the Mean" concept, in everyday life, exploring how failures to understand chance and random variations influence choices and perceptions of truth.

"For anyone interested in statistics, fantasy sports players, and those curious about the role of chance." Library Journal.

519.3 Game theory

Nowak, M. A. (Martin A.)

★**Supercooperators** : altruism, evolution, and why we need each other to succeed / Martin A. Nowak, Roger Highfield.

Free Press, c2011. 352 p. **519.3**

1. Game theory. 2. Evolution -- Mathematical models. 3. Natural selection. 4. Human evolution.

ISBN 9781439100189

LC 2010035517

Looks at the importance of cooperation in human beings and in nature, arguing that this social tool is as an important aspect of evolution as mutation and natural selection.

"Nowak aims to tackle the mysteries of nature with paper, pencil and computer. ... In Nowak's view, figuring out how cooperation comes about and breaks down, as well as actively pursuing the snuggle for existence, is the key to our survival as a species." New York Times Book Review.

519.5 Statistical mathematics

Reinhart, Alex, 1991-

Statistics done wrong : the woefully complete guide / Alex Reinhart. No Starch Press, 2015 xviii, 152 p. : **519.5**

1. Missing observations (Statistics) 2. Statistics -- Methodology

ISBN 9781593276201

LC 2015002128

"Discusses how to avoid the most common statistical errors in modern research, and perform more accurate statistical analyses".-- Provided by publisher.

"Overall, this concise guide aims at helping the scientific community better understand the strengths and weaknesses of the research process. A comprehensive bibliography is included, as are numerous references for the statistical misconceptions that are addressed." Choice.

Santos, Aaron

Ballparking : practical math for impractical sports questions / Aaron Santos. Running Press, c2012. 220 p. : **519.5**

1. Estimation theory -- Miscellanea. 2. Mathematics -- Miscellanea. 3. Sports -- Mathematics.

ISBN 9780762443451

LC bl2012015506

Includes index.

A collection of sports trivia and athletic estimations shares such entries as how big a person needs to be to completely block a hockey goal and how hard a baseball would need to be hit to make contact with the Goodyear blimp.

Silver, Nate, 1978-

The **signal** and the noise : why most predictions fail--but some don't / Nate Silver. Penguin Group USA 2012 352 p. **519.5**

1. Forecasting -- Statistical methods. 2. Bayesian statistical decision theory. 3. Knowledge theory 4. Logic.

ISBN 9781594204111

LC 2012027308

The founder of FiveThirtyEight.com challenges myths about predictions in subjects ranging from the financial market and weather to sports and politics, profiling the world of prediction to explain how readers can distinguish true signals from hype, in a report that also reveals the sources and societal costs of wrongful predictions.

Smith, Gary, 1945-

Standard deviations : flawed assumptions, tortured data, and other ways to lie with statistics / Gary Smith. Overlook Duckworth, 2014. 304 p.. **519.5**

1. Manipulation (Social sciences) 2. Research -- Moral and ethical aspects. 3. Statistics -- Moral and ethical aspects. 4. Analysis of variance.

ISBN 9781468309201

LC 2014017052

An economics professor reveals the tricks and traps that researchers often use to reinforce, defend and backup their ridiculous theories and explains how data can so easily be manipulated to deliberately mislead and fool readers.

"We believe these stories if they seem reasonable and love them if they're provocativesee Freakonomics, whose authors have admitted some mistakes.We are too easily seduced by explanations for the inexplicable, writes the author in this amusing, informative account of how many arguments are backed by meaningless statistics." Kirkus.

Wheelan, Charles J.

Naked statistics : stripping the dread from the data / Charles Wheelan. W. W. Norton & Co., 2013. xviii, 282 p. : **519.5**

1. Statistics 2. Mathematics. 3. Probabilities. 4. Statistical services.

ISBN 9780393071955

LC 2012034411

The author takes on the stuffy study of statistics to describe and demystify another essential discipline by explaining how Netflix knows which movies you'll like and how to catch schools that cheat on standardized tests.

"Wheelan has provided an intuitive presentation of statistical concepts without getting bogged down by extensive data lists or computation. The author begins by generally introducing each idea with an idealized situation to illustrate that statistical setting and its impact on effective interpretation, and then moves on to current real-world settings to legitimize his discussion. He also clearly discusses subtleties that can be encountered, showing how data users must be careful to avoid oversimplifying the implications of a given result. The presentation is nonthreatening, yet readers will find it a suitably thoughtful consideration of statistical ideas." Choice.

520 Science -- Astronomy

Bely, Pierre-Yves

A **question** and answer guide to astronomy / Carol Christian,Space Telscope Science Institute, Baltimore, USA, Jean-Rene Roy, Laval University, Quebec, Canada. Cambridge University Press, 2017. xiv, 344 p. : **520**

1. Astronomy -- Miscellanea 2. Astronomy

ISBN 9781316615263

LC 2016040127

"English translation published 2010, revised 2016"--T.p. verso.

"First published 2008 as 250 reponses vos questions sur l'astronomie"--T.p. verso.

Contains 250 questions and answers about astronomy, particular for the amateur astronomer.

Consolmagno, Guy, 1952-

Turn left at Orion : hundreds of night sky objects to see in a home telescope-- and how to find them / Guy Consolmagno, Dan M. Davis ; illustrated by the authors ; cover and title page, Mary Lynn Skirvin ; additional illustrations by Karen Kotash Sepp, Todd Johnson, and Anne Drogin. Cambridge University Press, 2011. 255 p. : **520**

1. Astronomy

ISBN 9780521153973

LC 2011027048

"With over 100,000 copies sold since first publication, this is one of the most popular astronomy books of all time. It is a unique guidebook to the night sky, providing all the information you need to observe a whole host of celestial objects. With a new spiral binding, this edition is even easier to use outdoors at the telescope and is the ideal beginner's book. Keeping its distinct one-object-per-spread format, this edition is also designed for Dobsonian telescopes, as well as for smaller reflectors and refractors, and covers Southern hemisphere objects in more detail. Large-format eyepiece views, positioned side-by-side, show objects exactly as they are seen through a telescope, and with improved directions, updated tables of astronomical informationand an expanded night-by-night Moon section, it has never been easier to explore the night sky on your own".-- Provided by publisher.

Couper, Heather

The **history** of astronomy / Heather Couper and Nigel Henbest. Firefly Books, 2007. 288 p. **520**

1. Astronomy -- History.
ISBN 1554073251

LC oc2007164156

Includes index.

Traces the stories of humans interacting with the endless wonders of the night sky, beginning with the earliest superstitions and continuing through to the birth and development of the science of astronomy.

Dickinson, Terence,

Astronomy photographer of the year : prize-winning images by top astrophotographers / the Royal Observatory, Greenwich ; foreword by Terence Dickinson. Firefly Books, 2015. 287 p. **520**

1. Astronomy -- Pictorial works. 2. Astronomical photography. 3. Astronomical photography -- Competitions.
ISBN 9781770854734

LC oc2015048727

Includes index.

"The Royal Observatory, Greenwich, has compiled a collection of stunning images from the Astronomy Photographer of the Year competition. Capturing an amazing variety of astronomical phenomena within our solar system and far into deep space, the photos represent the best amateur astrophotography from around the world. The book includes the first six years of the competition (2009-2014) and features overall winners from each year along with a carefully curated selection of short-listed entries."-- Provided by publisher.

Ferris, Timothy

Seeing in the dark : how backyard stargazers are probing deep space and guarding Earth from interplanetary peril / Timothy Ferris. Simon & Schuster, 2002. xvii, 379 p. : **520**

1. Astronomers. 2. Cosmology. 3. Stars -- Observers' manuals. 4. Astronomy -- Amateurs' manuals.
ISBN 0684865793

LC 2002020693

"This book should turn many novices on to astronomy and captivate those already fascinated by the heavens." Publishers Weekly.

Miller, Arthur I.

Empire of the stars : obsession, friendship, and betrayal in the quest for black holes / Arthur I. Miller. Houghton Mifflin, 2005. xx, 364 p. : **520**

1. Chandrasekhar, Subrahmanyan, 1910-1995 2. Eddington, Arthur Stanley, Sir, 1882-1944. 3. Astrophysicists -- India 4. Astrophysicists -- Great Britain 5. Astrophysics -- History -- 20th century. 6. Black holes (Astronomy) 7. Great Britain -- Social life and customs -- 20th century
ISBN 061834151X

LC 2004060909

A history of the idea of "black holes" explores the tumultuous debate over the existence of this now well-accepted phenomenon, focusing particular attention on Indian scientist Subrahmanyan Chandrasekhar.

"Astronomy buffs and readers fascinated by the history of science will find this a compelling read." Publishers Weekly.

Plait, Philip C.

Death from the skies! : these are the ways the world will end / Philip Plait. Viking, 2008. 304 p. **520**

1. End of the world (Astronomy) 2. Astronomy. 3. Physics. 4. Science. 5. Earth. 6. Space.
ISBN 9780670019977

LC 2008022943

Includes index.

A lively astronomy primer uses cataclysmic scenarios to explain some of the universe's most interest-piquing phenomena, in a comprehensive guide that also explains how life on Earth would be affected should depicted events occur.

Ridpath, Ian

★**Stars** & planets : the complete guide to the stars, constellations, and the solar system / Ian Ridpath & Wil Tirion. Princeton University Press, 2017. 400 p. : **520**

1. Astronomy 2. Planets 3. Stars 4. Observers' manuals.
ISBN 0691177880

LC bl2018003900

Includes index.

Offers information about all eighty-eight constellations of the Northern and Southern skies and provides simple star charts for easy identification.

Sagan, Carl, 1934-1996

Cosmos / Carl Sagan. Random House, 2002, c1980. xvi, 365 p. : **520**

1. Astronomy. 2. Science -- Social aspects.
ISBN 0375508325

LC 2002069744

Originally published: New York : Random House, 1980.

Hugo Award for Best Related Non-Fiction Book, 1981.

"Based on the author's television series of the same name, this volume covers the 10- to 20-billion-year history of the universe, from the big bang and subsequent evolution of molecular material through the evolution of human culture." Library Journal. {review of 1980 edition}

Sanders, Ella Frances

Eating the sun : small musings on a vast universe / Ella Frances Sanders. Penguin Books, an imprint of Penguin Random House LLC, [2019] 160 p. **520**

1. Astronomy. 2. Astrophysics. 3. Everyday life. 4. Natural history. 5. Solar system. 6. Earth.
ISBN 9780143133162

Explores the principles, laws, and wonders of the universe, the solar system, the world, and daily life alongside these phenomena.

Schaaf, Fred

The **50** best sights in astronomy and how to see them : observing eclipses, bright comets, meteor showers, and other celestial wonders / Fred Schaaf. John Wiley, c2007. vii, 280 p. : **520**

1. Astronomy 2. Amateurs' manuals. 3. Observers' manuals.
ISBN 0471696579

LC 2006036221

Arranged in order of decreasing field of view and increasing technology, offers fifty night sky sights from comets and meteor showers that can be seen with the naked eye to distant galaxies requiring instruments.

"The author begins with some basic information and terminology (altazimuth system, for example, or right ascension) and then plunges right in with the most easily accessible astronomical sight, the starry sky above our heads. For each sight, he not only explains what it is and the best conditions under which to observe it, he also tells us about its historical, mythological, or scientific importance and explores how these far-off wonders can have a very real effect on our humble home world. This could so easily have been a dry-as-dust tome, but Schaaf's enthusiasm overflows every page." Booklist.

Schilling, Govert

Deep space : beyond the solar system to the end of the universe and the beginning of time / Govert Schilling. Black Dog and Leventhal Publishers, 2014. 224 p. **520**

1. Astronomy. 2. Cosmology. 3. Science 4. Solar system.
ISBN 9781579129781

LC bl2015006954

Filled with hundreds of photographs and custom illustrations, along with a star atlas that shows the full celestial sky, a mind-bending exploration of the mysteries of space that lie beyond our solar system takes readers on an exhilarating journey to the far reaches of the cosmos.

"A well-conceived, absorbing survey of the wonders of the cosmos that truly reinforces the author's point that space is big. Unimaginably big. Recommended for space enthusiasts and astronomy aficionados." Library Journal.

Trefil, James, 1938-

Space atlas : mapping the universe and beyond / James Trefil ; with a foreword by Buzz Aldrin. National Geographic, 2019 351 p. : **520**

1. Astronomy 2. Planets 3. Planets 4. Solar system. 5. Sun. 6. Solar system. 7. Sun.
ISBN 9781426219696

LC 2018410255

In this guided tour of our planetary neighborhood, the Milky Way and other galaxies, and beyond, detailed maps and fascinating imagery from recent space missions partner with clear, authoritative scientific information. Starting with the sun and moving outward into space, acclaimed science writer and physicist James Trefil illuminates each planet, the most important moons, significant asteroids, and other objects in our solar system. Looking beyond, he explains what we know about the Milky Way and other galaxies--and how we know it, with clear explanations of the basics of astrophysics, including dark matter and gravitational waves. For this new edition, and to celebrate the 50th anniversary of his moonwalk, astronaut and American hero Buzz Aldrin offers a new special section on Earth's moon and its essential role in space exploration past and future.

Trotta, Roberto

The **edge** of the sky : all you need to know about the all-there-is : (using only the ten hundred most-used words in our tongue) / Roberto Trotta. Basic Books, [2014] 144 p. **520**

1. Cosmology 2. Astronomy 3. Cosmogony
ISBN 9780465044719

LC 2014020067

"The book barely qualifies as a book at all, just squeaking past booklet status. An entertaining exercise, in the end, for those student-people who like to ponder the All-There-Is while testing the always-inadequate limits of language." Kirkus.

520.9 Astronomy--history

Bartusiak, Marcia, 1950-

The **day** we found the universe / Marcia Bartusiak. Pantheon Books, c2009. 368 p. **520.9**

1. Hubble, Edwin Powell, 1899-1953. 2. Einstein, Albert, 1879-1955. 3. Shapley, Harlow, 1885- 4. Astronomy -- History. 5. Astronomers. 6. Galaxies. 7. Expanding universe.
ISBN 9780375424298

LC 2008034377

Looks at the discovery of the true nature and immense size of the universe, tracing the decades of work done by a select group of scientists to make it possible.

"This is a superb book that interweaves the fascinating story of a major scientific quest with a cast of characters, situations, painstaking observations, and imaginative thinking that reminds us all of the human side of scientific endeavors and the ways in which the universe itself continuously surprises us." Science Books & Films.

Hirshfeld, Alan

Starlight detectives : how astronomers, inventors, and eccentrics discovered the modern universe / Alan Hirshfeld. Bellevue Literary Press, 2014. 400 p. **520.9**

1. Hubble, Edwin Powell, 1889-1953 2. Astronomers. 3. Astronomical discoveries. 4. Galaxies 5. Expanding universe
ISBN 9781934137789

LC bl2014027886

In 1929, Edwin Hubble announced the greatest discovery in the history of astronomy since Galileo first turned a telescope to the heavens. The galaxies, previously believed to float serenely in the void, are in fact hurtling apart at an incredible speed: the universe is expanding. This stunning discovery was the culmination of a decades-long arc of scientific and technical advancement. The path to a broader mode of cosmic observation was blazed by a cadre of nineteenth-century amateur astronomers and inventors, galvanized by the advent of photography, spectral analysis, and innovative technology to create the entirely new field of astrophysics. Hirshfeld reveals the incredible stories--and the ambitious dreamers--behind the birth of modern astronomy.

"Although the story fizzles toward the end, this is a well-written and enjoyable title for astronomers--professional and amateur alike--as well as science history fans." Library Journal.

Hughes, David W. (David Wolstenholme), 1941-

The **astronomy** book / contributors, David W. Hughes, Robert Dinwiddie, Penny Johnson, Tom Jackson. DK Publishing, 2017. 352 p. : **520.9**

1. Astronomy 2. Astronomy -- History.
ISBN 1465464182

LC bl2017030325

Includes index.

A guide to milestone developments in astronomical history explores topics ranging from planets and black holes to space telescopes and dark matter.

520.92 Astronomers

Fauber, L. S.

Heaven on Earth : how Copernicus, Brahe, Kepler, and Galileo discovered the modern world / L. S. Fauber. Pegasus Books, 2019. 336 p. **520.92**

1. Copernicus, Nicolaus, 1473-1543. 2. Brahe, Tycho, 1546-1601. 3. Kepler, Johannes, 1571-1630. 4. Galilei, Galileo, 1564-1642. 5. Renaissance science 6. Astronomy. 7. Astronomers. 8. Mathematicians. 9. Solar system. 10. Europe -- History -- 16th century

ISBN 9781643132044

LC bl2019033971

A vivid narrative that connects the lives of four great astronomers as they discovered, refined, and popularized the first major scientific discovery of the modern era: that the Earth moves around the Sun.

McCray, W. Patrick

Keep watching the skies! : the story of operation moonwatch and the dawn of the space age / W. Patrick McCray. Princeton University Press, 2008. 308 p. **520.92**

1. Astronomers -- United States -- History -- 20th century. 2. Amateur astronomy -- United States -- History -- 20th century. 3. Space programs -- International competition -- History

ISBN 9780691128542

LC 2007941755

After the launch of Sputnik, thousands of ordinary Americans became "Moonwatchers," a network of citizen-scientists who helped professional astronomers by providing critical and otherwise unavailable information about the first satellites.

521 Astronomy

Goodstein, David L., 1939-

Feynman's lost lecture : the motion of planets around the sun / David L. Goodstein and Judith R. Goodstein. Norton, c1996. 191 p. : **521**

1. Feynman, Richard Phillips. 2. Planets -- Orbits 3. Celestial mechanics 4. Conic sections

ISBN 9780393039184

LC 95038719

The text and a sound recording of one of Feynman's lectures, is accompanied by a discussion of the lecture and a brief remembrance of the influential physicist

522 Techniques, procedures, apparatus, equipment, materials

Bowen, Mark (Mark Stander)

The **telescope** in the ice : inventing a new astronomy at the South Pole / Mark Bowen. St. Martins Press, [2017] 320 p. **522**

1. IceCube South Pole Neutrino Observatory. 2. Neutrino astrophysics 3. Astrophysics 4. Particles (Nuclear physics) 5. Scientific apparatus and instruments 6. South pole 7. Antarctica

ISBN 9781137280084

LC 2017026874

Traces the story of the IceCube Observatory and its landmark studies observing high-energy neutrinos at the South Pole, celebrating its role in establishing a new field of astronomy while sharing insights into what the research station hopes to achieve in the near future.

Dickinson, Terence

The **backyard** astronomer's guide / Terence Dickinson & Alan Dyer. Firefly Books, 2008. 368 p. : **522**

1. Astronomy

ISBN 9781554073443

LC 2008279173

Discusses the practical aspects of stargazing, including how to choose appropriate equipment, contending with light pollution, taking successful photographs of galaxies and nebulas, and selecting an observing site.

Hubble's universe : greatest discoveries and latest images / Terrence Dickinson. Firefly Books, 2017. 332 p. **522**

1. Hubble Space Telescope (Spacecraft) 2. Galaxies -- Pictorial works 3. Astronomy -- Pictorial works 4. Deep space Pictorial works.

ISBN 9781770859975

The first edition of Hubble's Universe displayed 300 pages of high-resolution celestial portraits selected by bestselling astronomy writer Terence Dickinson from the initial 22 years of the Hubble Space Telescope's exploration of distant galaxies. With the telescope now at the apex of its imaging capabilities, this second edition adds another chapter with more than 36 completely new images, including the first publication of a four-page fold-out of the Andromeda Galaxy, the nearest spiral galaxy to Earth, revealing more than one million individual stars. --From publisher description.

"Part gorgeous coffee-table book, part accessible and mesmerizing astronomy book, Dickinson's latest is a treasure map to the majesty of our universe." Publishers Weekly.

Kerrod, Robin

Hubble : the mirror on the universe / Robin Kerrod & Carole Stott. Firefly Books, 2011 224 p. : **522**

1. Hubble Space Telescope (Spacecraft) 2. Space astronomy

ISBN 9781554079728

LC 2011292195

Includes index.

The latest images from the Hubble Space Telescope's recent discoveries and fascinating updates. --From publisher description.

Zimmerman, Robert, 1953-

The **universe** in a mirror : the saga of the Hubble Telescope and the visionaries who built it / Robert Zimmerman. Princeton University Press, c2008. xv, 287 p., 16 p. of plates : **522**

1. Hubble Space Telescope. 2. Orbiting astronomical observatories. 3. Space astronomy -- History -- 20th century. 4. Space exploration. 5. Space.

ISBN 9780691132976

LC 2007943159

A study of the Hubble Space Telescope and the visionary scientists responsible for its extraordinary accomplishments describes the heated battle between scientists and bureaucrats and the perseverance of astronauts to repair and maintain the telescope, in a volume highlighted by striking color images from the Hubble telescope.

"Must reading for armchair astrophysicists." Booklist.

523 Specific celestial bodies and phenomena

North, Chris (Chris E.)

How to read the solar system : a guide to the stars and planets / Chris North and Paul Abel. Pegasus Books, 2015. 320 p. : **523**

1. Stars 2. Astronomy 3. Solar system.
ISBN 9781605986715

LC bl2014054979

Includes index.

Introduces the development and techniques of astronomy; surveys the Sun and each of the planets and their moons; describes asteroids, comets, and other phenomena; and discusses the search for planets beyond the solar system.

Raymo, Chet

An **intimate** look at the night sky / Chet Raymo. Walker & Co., 2003, c2001. xii, 242 p. : **523**

1. Astronomy 2. Observers' manuals.
ISBN 0802776701

LC BL2003009375

Reprint. Originally published: 2001.

A star guide features twenty-four star maps that cycle through the seasons and across the heavens, revealing what one can see with the naked eye throughout the year on a clear night in the Northern Hemisphere.

"A delightful, inspiring introduction to astronomy." Booklist.

Scagell, Robin

Firefly complete guide to stargazing / Robin Scagell. Firefly Books, 2015. 320 p. : **523**

1. Astronomy 2. Constellations 3. Stars 4. Observers' manuals.
ISBN 1770854746

LC bl2016025178

Includes indexes.

A handbook for observing the stars describes how the wonders of the night sky change throughout the year and offers star charts, a dictionary of astronomy terms, and a guide to viewing constellations.

Shore, Linda

The **total** skywatcher's manual : 275+ skills and tricks for exploring stars, planets & beyond / Linda Shore, David Prosper & Vivian White of the Astronomical Society of the Pacific. Weldon Owen, 2015 1 volume (unpaged) : **523**

1. Stars -- Observers' manuals 2. Constellations -- Observers' manuals 3. Astronomy -- Observers' manuals 4. Handbooks and manuals.
ISBN 9781616288716

LC bl2015041893

Includes index.

Shares useful information for beginning and advanced stargazers, including sky charts and diagrams, advice on choosing equipment, and suggestions for DIY projects.

523.01 Astrophysics

Tyson, Neil deGrasse

★**Astrophysics** for people in a hurry / Neil deGrasse Tyson. W.W. Norton & Company, [2017] 144 p. **523.01**

1. Astrophysics. 2. Cosmology. 3. Space and time. 4. Cosmogony
ISBN 9780393609394

LC 2017005442

Includes index.

The notable host of StarTalk reveals just what people need to be fluent and ready for the next cosmic headlines: from the Big Bang to black holes, from quarks to quantum mechanics, and from the search for planets to the search for life in the universe.

"Substituting down-to-earth wit for unnecessary jargon, Tyson presents ideas in clean, straightforward language and allows for the awesome nature of the universe to impress itself on readers unadorned." Kirkus.

523.1 The universe, galaxies, quasars

Aczel, Amir D.

God's equation : Einstein, relativity, and the expanding universe / Amir D. Aczel. Four Walls Eight Windows, 1999. xvii, 236 p. : **523.1**

1. Einstein, Albert, 1879-1955. 2. Einstein, Albert, 1879-1955 Correspondence 3. Physicists -- Germany 4. Cosmology. 5. Relativity (Physics) -- History 6. Physics.
ISBN 1568581394

LC 99036319

Celebrates the great physicist through his research and personal correspondence, arguing that his work stands at the center of the search for the origins of the universe.

"Though Aczel's analysis of Einstein's work requires familiarity with advanced mathematics, that analysis makes up only a minor portion of his book, and most readers will appreciate the author's inclusion of the great physicist's letters to astronomer Erwin Freundlich." Publishers Weekly.

Bell, Jim, 1965-

The **space** book : from the beginning to the end of time, 250 milestones in the history of space & astronomy / Jim Bell. Sterling, c2013. 527 p. : **523.1**

1. Astronomy -- History. 2. Cosmology -- History. 3. Cosmology.
ISBN 9781402780714

LC bl2013016052

Presents a series of 250 significant events in the history of astronomy and space exploration, from the original formation of the galaxies, to the space mission to the planet Mars, to speculation about the end of the universe.

"This is a fine coffee-table book, suitable for either deep study or a few moments' perusal. Recommended for readers with a casual interest in the history of astronomy and the universe, or for sparking such an interest in others." Library Journal.

Berman, Bob

Earth-shattering : violent supernovas, galactic explosions, biological mayhem, nuclear meltdowns, and other hazards to life in our universe / Bob Berman. Little, Brown & Company, 2019. 336 p. **523.1**

1. Big Bang Theory (Astronomy) 2. Cosmology 3. Explosions 4. Catastrophism
ISBN 9780316511353

LC 2018026997

Includes index.

A heart-pumping exploration of the biggest explosions in history, from the Big Bang to mysterious activity on Earth and everything in between. In Earth-Shattering, astronomy writer Bob Berman guides us through an epic, all-inclusive investigation into these instances of violence both mammoth and microscopic.

"This lively menagerie of astrophysical oddities will entertain any reader whos ever wondered what the biggest, most dangerous bangs in the universe might be." Publishers Weekly.

Brockman, John, 1941-

The **universe** : leading scientists explore the origin, mysteries, and future of the cosmos / edited by John Brockman. Harper Perennial, 2014. 400 p. **523.1**

1. Cosmology. 2. Astronomy. 3. Physicists. 4. Science. 5. Essays.
ISBN 9780062296085

LC bl2014028475

"Edge.org presents Brian Greene, Alan Guth, Andrei Linde, Frank Wilczek, Benoit Mandelbrot, Lisa Randall, and more"--Cover.

"Fourth volume in the Best of Edge series"--Page ix.

"Original works from the online pages of Edge.org"--Page ix.

Collects writings from several leading theoretical physicists and cosmologists that offer an overview of our scientific understanding of the universe as it stands today.

Cham, Jorge

We have no idea : a guide to the unknown universe / Jorge Cham and Daniel Whiteson. Riverhead Books, 2017. 336 p. **523.1**

1. Cosmology 2. Physics 3. Science 4. Quarks
ISBN 9780735211513

LC 2016049070

The creator of PHD Comics and a University of California particle physicist blend infographics, cartoons and lighthearted scientific explanations to fill in gaps in layperson cosmological knowledge, offering coverage of topics ranging from quarks and neutrinos to gravitational wave and exploding black holes.

"Cham and Whiteson mesh comics, lighthearted infographics, and lively explanations to painlessly introduce curious readers to complex concepts in easily digestible chapters. This fun guide is just the ticket for science fans of any age." Publishers Weekly.

Chown, Marcus

Infinity in the palm of your hand : fifty wonders that reveal an extraordinary universe / Marcus Chown. Diversion Books, 2019, c2018 214 p. ; **523.1**

1. Science -- Miscellanea 2. Theories 3. Information
ISBN 9781635765946

Originally published: London : Michael O'Mara Books, 2018.

Explores some of the most profound and important science about us, our world, and beyond by examining some astonishing facts that reveal the vast complexities of the universe.

"A genial tour of the universe and its mysteries...Heavy stuff lightly spunjust the thing for the science buff in the house." Kirkus.

Clark, Stuart (Stuart G.)

The **unknown** universe : a new exploration of time, space, and modern cosmology / Stuart Clark. Pegasus Books, 2016. 288 p. **523.1**

1. Cosmology 2. Quantum theory. 3. String theory (Nuclear physics) 4. Time. 5. Space
ISBN 9781681771533

LC bl2016027526

A groundbreaking guide to the universe and how our latest deep-space discoveries are forcing us to revisit what we know--and what we don't.

"Since satisfying results have yet to turn up, Clark's book ends on a cliffhanger, but readers will be entirely pleased with the experience." Kirkus.

Cox, Brian, 1968-

Universal : a guide to the cosmos / Brian Cox and Jeff Forshaw. Da Capo Press, 2017. 320 p. **523.1**

1. Astrophysics 2. Space sciences 3. Astronomy 4. Cosmology
ISBN 9780306822704

LC 2017930821

Providing explanations, diagrams and photos, two physicists reveal how we can all understand some of the most fundamental questions about our Earth, Sun, solar system and the galaxies beyond, presenting a world of simple questions with sublime answers.

Dauber, Philip M.

The **three** big bangs : comet crashes, exploding stars, and the creation of the universe / Philip M. Dauber, Richard A. Muller. Addison-Wesley Pub. Co., 1996. viii, 207 p., 16 unnumbered p. of plates : **523.1**

1. Big bang theory 2. Catastrophes (Geology) 3. Supernovae
ISBN 9780201407525

LC 95024451

Examines the original "Big Bang," the explosion of a supernova that scattered heavy elements, and the crash of the comet that killed the dinosaurs.

Frank, Adam, 1962-

About time : cosmology, time and culture at the twilight of the big bang / Adam Frank. Free Press, 2011. 320 p. **523.1**

1. Cosmology 2. Big Bang Theory (Astronomy) 3. Space and time 4. Beginning
ISBN 9781439169599

LC 2011011345

"The Big Bang is dead! It is no longer the beginning of time. Allowing us a peek into the cutting edge of cosmology, astrophysicist Adam Frank explains how this change in our origins will affect every aspect of our lives".-- Provided by publisher.

Lightofthestars:alienworldsandthefateoftheEarth/AdamFrank. W.W. Norton & Company, Inc., [2018] 288 p. **523.1**

1. Cosmology 2. Human ecology 3. Exobiology 4. Civilization 5. Earth
ISBN 9780393609011

LC 2017061640

The astrophysicist traces beliefs about alien intelligence from the ancient Greeks to the theories of today's leading minds, drawing on the latest research to consider how other worlds may have addressed civilization-driven climate change.

Galfard, Christophe

The **universe** in your hand : a journey through space, time, and beyond / Christophe Galfard. Flatiron Books, 2016. 386 pages ; **523.1**

1. Astronomy 2. Cosmology 3. Space exploration 4. Space and time 5. Space
ISBN 9781250069528

LC 2016005257

A theoretical physicist who has worked closely with Stephen Hawking uses direct and simple language to demonstrate the theories behind the functioning of the universe, including what happens when a star dies and the basics of the quantum world.

"Readers looking to expand their knowledge of physics and cosmology will find everything they need here." Publishers Weekly.

Geach, James

Galaxy : mapping the cosmos / James Geach. Reaktion Books, 2014. 270 p. : **523.1**

1. Galaxies. 2. Universe.
ISBN 1780233639

LC bl2015016571

Presents stories of the evolution of galaxies and astronomers' quest to map them.

"Advanced researchers may be frustrated by the purposeful lack of higher-level mathematics, but the casual reader will appreciate how well Geach presents a clear narrative of the science." Choice.

Greene, B. (Brian), 1963-

The **fabric** of the cosmos : space, time, and the texture of reality / Brian Greene. A.A. Knopf, 2004. xii, 569 p. : **523.1**

1. Cosmology. 2. String theory (Nuclear physics) 3. Heisenberg uncertainty principle. 4. Inflationary universe.
ISBN 0375412883

LC 2003058918

"Frogs in bowls, falling eggs, loaves of bread, pennies on balloons, ping pong balls in molasses, and babushka dolls are just some of the analogies used to explain complex concepts cleverly. After reading this book, you will never look at a starry night sky the same way again." Library Journal.

Until the end of time : mind, matter, and our search for meaning in an evolving universe / Brian Greene. Alfred A. Knopf, 2020. 320 p. **523.1**

1. Cosmology. 2. Big Bang Theory (Astronomy) 3. Physics -- Philosophy. 4. Quantum theory
ISBN 9781524731670

LC 2019022442

The Columbia University theoretical physicist and best-selling author of The Elegant Universe explores subjects ranging from quantum mechanics to black holes, sharing insights into how human life and consciousness emerged from chaos.

"Curious readers interested in some of the most fundamental questions of existence, and willing to invest some time and thought, will be richly rewarded by his fascinating exploration." Publishers Weekly

Gribbin, John, 1946-

13.8 : the quest to find the true age of the universe and the theory of everything / John Gribbin. Yale University Press, 2016 256 p. **523.1**

1. General relativity (Physics) 2. Cosmology -- History. 3. Quantum theory.
ISBN 9780300218275

LC 2015951744

The twentieth century gave us two great theories of physics. The general theory of relativity describes the behavior of very large things, and quantum theory the behavior of very small things. In this landmark book, John Gribbin--one of the best-known science writers of the past thirty years--presents his own version of the Holy Grail of physics, the search that has been going on for decades to find a unified "Theory of Everything" that combines these ideas into one mathematical package.

"In order to bring lay readers up to speed, Gribbin first reprises the crucial developments, beginning in the 19th century, that have led scientists to their current understanding. An exciting chronicle of a monumental scientific accomplishment by a scientist who participated in the measur i ng of the age of the universe." Kirkus.

Halpern, Paul, 1961-

Edge of the universe : a voyage to the cosmic horizon and beyond / Paul Halpern. Wiley, c2012. iv, 236 p. ; **523.1**

1. Cosmology. 2. Astronomy. 3. Space.
ISBN 9780470636244

LC 2012002028

Explaining what we know about the Big Bang, the accelerating universe, dark energy, dark flow and dark matter, a physicist and popular science writer examines some of the theories about the nature of the universe.

Hawking, Stephen, 1942-2018

A **brief** history of time / Stephen W. Hawking. Bantam Books, 1998, c1988. ix, 212 p. : **523.1**

1. Cosmology. 2. Astronomy. 3. Time. 4. Big Bang Theory (Astronomy)
ISBN 9780553380163
Includes index.

Stephen W. Hawking, widely regarded as the most brilliant physicist since Einstein, discusses in a friendly and self-deprecating manner age-old questions about the origin and fate of the universe. Difficult concepts are made simple by Hawking's familiar, accessible prose.

★A **briefer** history of time / Stephen Hawking and Leonard Mlodinow. Bantam Books, c2005. 162 p. : **523.1**

1. Cosmology. 2. Astronomy. 3. Time. 4. Grand unified theories (Nuclear physics)
ISBN 0553804367

LC 2005042949

A shorter, more accessible edition of a now-classic survey of the origin and nature of the universe features new full-color illustrations and an expanded, easier to understand treatment of the volume's more important theoretical concepts.

"Hawking and Mlodinow provide one of the most lucid discussions of this complex topic ever written for a general audience. Readers will come away with an excellent understanding of the apparent contradictions and conundrums at the forefront of contemporary physics." Publishers Weekly.

Kaku, Michio

Parallel worlds : a journey through creation, higher dimensions, and the future of the cosmos / Michio Kaku. Doubleday, 2005. xvii, 428 p. : **523.1**

1. Cosmology. 2. Big Bang Theory (Astronomy) 3. Superstring theories. 4. Supergravity.
ISBN 9780385509862

LC 2004056039

A distinguished physicist sheds new light on the groundbreaking discoveries that have revolutionized the field of cosmology and transformed understanding of the universe, offering an incisive explanation of the multiverse M-theory and its implications in terms of the fate of our own universe.

"This is a riveting popular treatment of the string revolution in physics written by a pioneering theorist in the field. Kaku expounds comprehensibly on why astrophysicists love strings and branes and the way they resolve various vexatious cosmological paradoxes." Booklist.

Krauss, Lawrence Maxwell

A **universe** from nothing : why there is something rather than nothing / Lawrence M. Krauss ; with a foreword by Christopher Hitchens and an afterword by Richard Dawkins. Free Press,

2012. 256 p. **523.1**

1. Cosmology. 2. Beginning. 3. Physics. 4. Religion and science.
ISBN 9781451624458

LC 2011032519

Includes index.

One of the few prominent scientists today to have actively crossed the chasm between science and popular culture, Krauss reveals that modern science is addressing the question of why there is something rather than nothing, with surprising and fascinating results. He takes listeners back to the beginning of the beginning, presenting the most recent evidence for how the universe evolved, and the implications for how it's going to end.

Lightman, Alan P., 1948-

Searching for stars on an island in Maine / Alan Lightman. Pantheon Books, 2018 240 p. **523.1**

1. Cosmology -- Miscellanea. 2. Philosophy 3. Religion and science.
ISBN 9781101871867

LC 2017014750

The acclaimed author of Einstein's Dreams presents a lyrical meditation on religion and science as they relate to the human yearning for permanence and certainty in spite of discoveries that prove the world's impermanent and uncertain nature.

"Lightman's illuminating language and crisp imagery aim to ignite a sense of wonder in any reader whos ever pondered the universe, our world, and the nature of human consciousness." Publishers Weekly.

Mack, Katie

The **end** of everything : (astrophysically speaking) / Katie Mack. Scribner, 2020 240 p. **523.1**

1. Quantum theory 2. Astrophysics 3. End of the universe 4. Cosmology
ISBN 9781982103545

LC bl2020016348

Includes index.

An eye-opening look at five ways the universe could end, and the mind-blowing lessons each scenario reveals about the most important concepts in cosmology.

"Readers with some background in physical sciences, philosophers of science, and anyone wondering what to read after Brian Greene's Until the End of Time will relish this blend of wit and deep thought." Library Journal

Marchant, Jo, 1973-

The **human** cosmos : a secret history of the stars / Jo Marchant. Dutton, 2020. xii, 386 p. **523.1**

1. Cosmology -- History. 2. Civilization 3. Culture -- History 4. Humans -- Effect of environment on
ISBN 9780593183014

LC 2020004943

Revealing how early cultures celebrated the mysteries of a night sky now hidden by today's pollution and tech, the best-selling author of Cure invites readers to reconnect the human experience to the remarkable cosmic cycles that shaped it.

Merali, Zeeya

A **big** bang in a little room : the quest to create new universes / Zeeya Merali. Basic Books, [2017] 320 p. **523.1**

1. Cosmology 2. Cosmogony 3. Physics 4. Research
ISBN 9780465065912

LC 2016036546

An award-winning science writer provides a guided tour through the history of cosmology and uncovers why modern physicists believe that they will soon have the ability to create a brand new baby universe with its own physical laws, star systems and lifeforms.

"A rich and wonderful cosmological history that illuminates the scientific possibility of the nearly unthinkable." Kirkus.

Ostriker, J. P.

Heart of darkness : unraveling the mysteries of the invisible universe / Jeremiah P. Ostriker, Simon Mitton. Princeton University Press, 2013 288 p. **523.1**

1. Cosmology. 2. Astronomy. 3. Astrophysics -- History.
ISBN 9780691134307

LC bl2013003059

Describes humankind's quest to unravel the deepest secrets of the universe.

Randall, Lisa

Dark matter and the dinosaurs : the astounding interconnectedness of the universe / Lisa Randall. Ecco Press, 2015. 256 p. **523.1**

1. Dark matter (Astronomy) 2. Astrophysics. 3. Life -- Origin. 4. Life sciences -- History 5. Earth -- History
ISBN 9780062328472

LC bl2015035307

The renowned particle physicist and New York Times best-selling author of Warped Passages draws on original research into dark matter to illuminate the surprising connections between deep space and life on Earth.

"Writing in a deceptively chatty narrative style, Randall provides a fascinating window into the excitement of discovery and the rigor required to test and elaborate new hypotheses. A top-notch science book from a leading researcher." Kirkus.

Rees, Martin J., 1942-

Universe / general editor, Martin Rees. DK, 2012, c2005. 512 p. : **523.1**

1. Cosmology
ISBN 9780756698416

LC bl2012033291

At head of title: Smithsonian.

Includes index.

Full-color photographs representing the latest captures from space telescopes and detailed digital artwork enhance a comprehensive study of the world of outer space, from Earth's closest neighbors in the solar system to the farthest galaxies.

Scharf, Caleb A., 1968-

The **Copernicus** complex : our cosmic significance in a universe of planets and probabilities / Caleb Scharf. Scientific American/Farrar, Straus and Giroux, 2014. 288 p. **523.1**

1. Cosmology. 2. Space and time. 3. Astrophysics 4. Life.
ISBN 9780374129217

LC 2014008035

A groundbreaking revision of the Copernican principle Though the concept of "the universe" suggests the containment of everything, the latest ideas in cosmology hint that our universe may be just one of a multitude of others--a single slice of an infinity of parallel realities. In The Copernicus Complex, the renowned astrophysicist and author Caleb Scharf takes us on a cosmic adventure like no other, from tiny microbes within the Earth to distant exoplanets and beyond, asserting that the age-old Copernican principle is in need of updating. As Scharf argues, when Copernicus proposed that the Earth was not the fixed point at the center of the known universe (and therefore we are not unique), he set in motion a colossal scientific juggernaut, forever changing our vision of nature. But the principle has never been entirely true--we do live at a particular time, in a particular location, under particular circumstances. To solve this conundrum we must put aside our Copernican worldview and embrace the possibility that we are in a delicate balance between mediocrity and significance, order and chaos. Weaving together cutting-edge science and classic storytelling, historical accounts and speculations on what the future holds, The Copernicus Complex presents a compelling argument for what our true cosmic status is, and proposes a way forward for the ultimate quest: to determine life's abundance not just across this universe but across all realities.

"Scharf covers a lot of ground, and his entertaining, accessible approach offers valuable insight not just into science, but also into the way our assumptions can make a difficult task, like finding life in the universe, even harder." Publishers Weekly.

The **zoomable** universe : an epic tour through cosmic scale, from almost everything to nearly nothing / Caleb Scharf ; illustrations by Ron Miller ; and 5W Infographics. Scientific American/Farrar, Straus, and Giroux, 2017. xi, 206 p. : **523.1**

1. Astrophysics 2. Cosmology 3. Inflationary universe 4. Large scale structure (Astronomy)

ISBN 9780374279745

LC 2017001222

Inspired by the classic "Powers of Ten," an award-winning astrobiologist and an acclaimed artist take readers, in a full-color celebration of scientific discovery, on an extraordinary, cutting-edge journey through all known scales of reality, from the largest possible magnitude to the smallest.

"A beautifully illustrated survey of the universe and its constituent parts, from quarks to galaxies and beyond. .A superb composite of scientific knowledge that will no doubt inspire readers of all ages to learn more about our enigmatic universe." Kirkus.

Singh, Simon

Big bang : the origin of the universe / Simon Singh. Fourth Estate, c2004. 532 p. : **523.1**

1. Big Bang Theory (Astronomy) 2. General relativity (Physics) 3. Cosmology. 4. Astronomy.

ISBN 0007162200

LC 2004056306

Shares the stories of Big Bang theorists who fought against establishment beliefs about an eternal and unchanging universe to investigate the universe's origins, and continues with an explanation of the Big Bang theory.

"The author presents a brief history of the origins of the universe. He begins with a historical overview of how scientific thought changed from mythology to cosmology, then moves to the debate between the steady state model of an eternal universe and the Big Bang theory, which saw the universe as beginning at a unique moment that was followed by rapid extension. This readable book provides an accessible overview of this complex scientific theory." Library Journal.

Smoot, George

Wrinkles in time : witness to the birth of the universe / George Smoot and Keay Davidson. Harper Perennial, 2007. vi, 331 p. , 8 p. of plates : **523.1**

1. Cosmology

ISBN 9780061344442

LC oc2008078309

Provides a provocative and personal saga of two adventure-laden decades of discovery in which the author, an astrophysicist, and his colleagues searched for the universe's "seeds" and the nature of existence itself.

Tucker, Wallace H.

Chandra's cosmos : dark matter, black holes, and other wonders revealed by NASA's premier X-ray observatory / Wallace H. Tucker. Smithsonian Books, [2017] 304 p. **523.1**

1. Chandra X-ray Observatory (U.S.) 2. Astronomy 3. X-ray astronomy 4. Space telescopes 5. Extrasolar planets

ISBN 9781588345875

LC 2016016560

"Its one astonishment after another in this invaluable, imagination-stirring overview of cutting-edge astrophysics." Booklist.

Tyson, Neil deGrasse

Origins : fourteen billion years of cosmic evolution / Neil deGrasse Tyson and Donald Goldsmith. W.W. Norton & Co., c2004. 345 p., 32 p. of plates : **523.1**

1. Cosmology. 2. Evolution. 3. Life -- Origin. 4. Earth -- History 5. Mars (Planet) -- Exploration

ISBN 9780393059922

LC 2004012201

An exploration of new theories about the formation and evolution of the universe traces from the big bang, through the first three billion years on Earth, to today's search for life on other planets.

"Amateur astronomers--in fact, any reader who enjoys popular science--will find fascinating information presented in clear but never patronizing language." Library Journal.

Startalk : everything you ever need to know about space travel, sci-fi, the human race, the universe, and beyond / with Neil deGrasse Tyson. National Geographic, 2016. 302 p. : **523.1**

1. Cosmology -- Popular works. 2. Earth sciences -- Popular works. 3. Human beings -- Popular works. 4. Science fiction -- Social aspects. 5. Outer space -- Exploration Popular works.

ISBN 9781426217272

LC 2016019357

Contributing editors, Charles Liu, astrophysics professor at the City University of New York's College of Staten Island, and Jeffrey Lee Simons, social media director of StarTalk Radio.

A sumptuously photographed companion to the celebrated scientist's popular podcast and National Geographic Channel series combines the subjects of his most favorite Emmy-nominated talks with comprehensive fun facts, thought-provoking sidebars and vivid imagery.

Welcome to the universe : an astrophysical tour / Neil deGrasse Tyson, Michael A. Strauss, and J. Richard Gott. Princeton University Press, 2016. 432 p. **523.1**

1. Cosmology. 2. Astronomy. 3. Astrophysics. 4. Relativity (Physics)

ISBN 9780691157245

LC 2016013487

Three of today's leading astrophysicists offer a guided tour of the cosmos, discussing the latest discoveries in the field, explaining why Pluto lost its planet status, and covering everything you need to know about planets, stars, galaxies, black holes, wormholes and time travel.

"An accessible and comprehensive overview of our universe by three eminent astrophysicists, based on an introductory course they have taught at Princeton University." Kirkus.

Weintraub, David A. (David Andrew), 1958-

How old is the universe? / David A. Weintraub. Princeton

University Press, c2011. 370 **523.1**

1. Cosmology. 2. Astronomy. 3. Solar system -- Age. 4. Earth -- Age.
ISBN 9780691147314

LC 2010009117

Includes index.

"This is no-nonsense science writing that will be enjoyed for years: David Weintraub is an expert guide, laying out the evidence in just the right amount of detail." The New Scientist.

523.2 Science -- Astronomy and allied sciences -- Specific celestial bodies and phenomena -- Planetary systems

Benson, Michael, 1962-

Otherworlds : visions of our solar system / Michael Benson. Abrams, 2017. 160 p. : **523.2**

1. Space photography. 2. Solar system Photographs from space. 3. Solar system Pictorial works.
ISBN 1419724452

LC bl2017004928

Presents a visual journey through the planets of the solar system.

Chown, Marcus

Solar system : a visual exploration of the planets, moons, and other heavenly bodies that orbit our Sun / written by Marcus Chown. Black Dog & Leventhal Publishers, c2011. 224 p. : **523.2**

1. Astronomy 2. Cosmology. 3. Solar system. 4. Space
ISBN 9781579128852

LC bl2011034919

"Published in partnership with Touch Press, creators of 'The elements and solar system for iPad'; Faber and Faber; and Planetary Visions."

Includes index.

A guide to the solar system provides a photographic tour of its eight planets, as well as asteroids and comets, and presents its history from its birth to the present.

Daniels, Patricia, 1955-

The **new** solar system : ice worlds, moons, and planets redefined / Patricia Daniels ; foreword by Robert Burnham. National Geographic Society, 2009. 224 p. : **523.2**

1. Astronomy 2. Space sciences. 3. Astrophysics 4. Planets 5. Solar system. 6. Solar system Pictorial works. 7. Essays
ISBN 9781426204623

LC 2009010117

Explores the new technologies and discoveries that are showing us an ever more detailed vision of the solar system, in a resource that also includes diagrams, maps, essays, sidebars, and fact boxes.

Lang, Kenneth R.

The **Cambridge** guide to the solar system / Kenneth R. Lang. Cambridge University Press, 2011. xxv, 475 p. : **523.2**

1. Solar system.
ISBN 0521198577

LC 2011411432

Includes indexes.

"Anyone with a need for information on the solar system should find fulfillment in the pages of this handsome work, and it is a beautiful browsing book." Booklist.

Summers, Michael E.

Exoplanets : diamonds worlds, super-Earths, pulsar planets, and the new search for life beyond our solar system / Michael Summers, and James Trefil. Smithsonian Books, 2017 240 p. **523.2**

1. Extrasolar planets. 2. Space environment 3. Life on other planets. 4. Habitable planets
ISBN 9781588345943

LC 2016018596

Includes index.

The past few years have seen an incredible explosion in our knowledge of the universe. Since its 2009 launch, the Kepler satellite has discovered more than two thousand exoplanets, or planets outside our solar system. More exoplanets are being discovered all the time, and even more remarkable than the sheer number of exoplanets is their variety. In Exoplanets, astronomer Michael Summers and physicist James Trefil explore these remarkable recent discoveries: planets revolving around pulsars, planets made of diamond, planets that are mostly water, and numerous rogue planets wandering through the emptiness of space.

"These revelations, how they were made, imaginative voyages to five un-Earthly types of planets, and their implications for life and intelligence elsewhere than on Earth are concisely illuminated by astrophysicists Summers and Trefil in this marvelously fascinating and wonderfully accessible illustrated book." Booklist.

523.3 Moon

Morton, Oliver

The **Moon** : a history for the future / Oliver Morton. Public Affairs, 2019. 333 p. **523.3**

1. Project Apollo (U.S.) 2. Astronomy. 3. Space flight to the moon 4. Lunar geology 5. Space exploration 6. Moon 7. Moon -- Exploration. 8. Moon -- Orbit. 9. Moon -- Phases. 10. Moon -- Surface. 11. Moon -- Observations.
ISBN 9781541774322

LC 2019004627

Explores different perceptions of the relationship between the Earth and the Moon, including what early astronomers thought, the Cold War space race, and the potential future use of the Moon as a stepping stone to more space exploration.

"Accessible, informative, and entertainingfirst-rate popular science reporting." Kirkus.

523.4 Science -- Astronomy and allied sciences -- Specific celestial bodies and phenomena -- Planets, asteroids, trans-Neptunian objects of solar system

Hubbard, Scott, 1948-

Exploring Mars : chronicles from a decade of discovery / Scott Hubbard ; foreword by Bill Nye. University of Arizona Press, c2011. xix, 194 p. : **523.4**

1. United States. National Aeronautics and Space Administration. 2. Space flight. 3. Space exploration. 4. Space programs. 5. Mars (Planet) -- Exploration.
ISBN 9780816528967

LC 2011036184

Includes index.

Hubbard (aeronautics and astronautics, Stanford University) became known as the Czar of Mars when he was named the first director of NASA's Mars Exploration Program after the Mars Polar Lander fiasco in 1999. In this book, he recounts the program's comeback under his direction and offers a behind-the-scenes look at the program and specific Mars missions. The science is explained in plain language for general readers, with many b&w diagrams explaining scientific concepts and images from Mars cameras. The book also includes b&w photos of key figures.

"At once a fascinating scientific artifact and political thriller, Hubbard writes with wit and a passion for his work to uncover the secrets of our sister planet." Publishers Weekly.

Levenson, Thomas

The **hunt** for Vulcan : ...and how Albert Einstein destroyed a planet, discovered relativity, and deciphered the universe / Thomas Levenson. Random House, 2015 xv, 229 p. **523.4**

1. Einstein, Albert, 1879-1955. 2. Vulcan (Hypothetical planet). 3. General relativity (Physics) 4. Astronomical discoveries. 5. Solar system 6. Mercury (Planet).

ISBN 9780812998986

LC 2015018989

The story of the fifty-year search by the world's top scientists for a "missing" planet, and Albert Einstein's remarkable proof of the theory of relativity, which showed once and for all that the planet never existed in the first place.

"Though brief, Levenson's narrative is a well-structured, fast-paced example of exemplary science writing. A scintillating popular account of the interplay between mathematical physics and astronomical observations." Kirkus.

Murdin, Paul

The **secret** lives of planets : order, chaos, and uniqueness in the solar system / Paul Murdin. Pegasus Books, 2020. 272 p. ; **523.4**

1. Astronomy 2. Planets 3. Solar system

ISBN 9781643133362

LC bl2020052488

"An insider's guide to astronomy reveals everything you need to know about the planets, their satellites, and our place in the solar system. We have the impression that the solar system is perfectly regular like a clock or a planetarium instrument. On a short timescale it is. But, seen in a longer perspective, the planets, and their satellites, have exciting lives, full of events." Provided by publisher.

"Murdin's fondness for his subject is evident throughout this elegant, imaginative survey and should be contagious to all who encounter it." Publishers Weekly

Weintraub, David A. (David Andrew), 1958-

Is Pluto a planet? : a historical journey through the solar system / David A. Weintraub. Princeton University Press, c2007. ix, 254 p. : **523.4**

1. Planets. 2. Astronomy -- History 3. Physics. 4. Science -- History 5. Solar system. 6. Pluto (Dwarf planet)

ISBN 0691123489

LC 2006929630

Introduces the historical, philosophical, and physical aspects of the definition of "planet," and applies them to Pluto.

"The author places the Pluto controversy in context in his . . . account of the development of our solar system and the evolution of the meaning of the word planet, from Aristotle's theories to recent decrees by the International Astronomical Union." Publishers Weekly.

523.43 Mars

Aldrin, Buzz

Mission to Mars : my vision for space exploration / Buzz Aldrin ; with Leonard David. National Geographic, 2013 258 p. **523.43**

1. Space colonies 2. Space flight to Mars 3. Space exploration. 4. Mars probes 5. Mars (Planet) -- Exploration.

ISBN 9781426210174

LC bl2013020786

The history-making astronaut, aerospace engineer and respected advocate for space colonization outlines a plan for taking humans to Mars within the next quarter century, posing business-specific arguments while outlining practical strategies for travel and planetary homesteading.

"Aldrin makes a daring proposal for further space exploration in this exciting glimpse of the new new frontier." Publishers Weekly.

Jenner, Nicky

4th rock from the sun : the story of Mars / Nicky Jenner. St Martins Pr., 2017. 288 p. **523.43**

1. Space flight to Mars 2. Martians in mass media 3. Space exploration 4. Life on other planets 5. Mars (Planet) 6. Solar system -- Exploration

ISBN 9781472922496

LC bl2017032687

"Everything you ever wanted to know about the Red Planet, revealed in an up-close and personal tour of Mars."--Provided by the publisher.

"Science writer Jenner illuminates the significance of Mars to humankind, covering geology, pop culture, history, and more." Publishers Weekly.

Kessler, Andrew

Martian summer : robot arms, cowboy spacemen, and my 90 days with the Phoenix Mars Mission / Andrew Kessler. Pegasus Books, 2011 352 p. **523.43**

1. Phoenix Mars Mission (U.S.) 2. Space flight to Mars 3. Space exploration. 4. Space vehicles 5. Space flight 6. Mars (Planet) -- Exploration

ISBN 9781605981765

LC bl2011010099

The author chronicles the three fascinating months he spent in Mission Control for NASA's Phoenix Mars Mission, a project that lead to the discovery of liquid water on Mars, as well as a giant frozen ocean trapped beneath the planet's north pole.

Morton, Oliver

Mapping Mars : science, imagination, and the birth of a world / Oliver Morton. Picador, 2002. viii, 357 p., [16] p. of plates : **523.43**

1. Mars (Planet) -- Exploration. 2. Mars (Planet) Maps.

ISBN 9780312245511

LC 2002491494

Sheds light on the geologists, scientists, astrophysicists, and other visionaries who are mapping the surface of Mars in anticipation of future visits to the planet by the human race.

"The author traces scientists' efforts to map and understand the surface of Mars. Morton writes eloquently and displays a breadth of knowledge not often found in science writing." Publishers Weekly.

523.49 Trans-Neptunian objects

Brown, Mike, 1965-
How I killed Pluto and why it had it coming / Mike Brown. Spiegel & Grau, 2010. 288 p. **523.49**

1. Planets. 2. Scientific discoveries. 3. Dwarf planets. 4. Astronomy. 5. Pluto (Dwarf planet) 6. Solar system.
ISBN 9780385531085

LC 2010015074

The astronomer who inadvertently triggered the "demotion" of Pluto in his effort to officially recognize the solar system's tenth planet describes the ensuing debates and public outcry while revealing the behind-the-scenes story of his discovery.

"Deftly pulling readers along on his journey of discovery and destruction, Brown sets the record straight and strongly defends his science with a conversational, rational, and calm voice that may change the public's opinion of scientists as poor communicators." Publishers Weekly.

523.5 Meteors, solar wind, zodiacal light

Bevan, Alex
Meteorites : a journey through space and time / Alex Bevan and John de Laeter. Smithsonian Institution Press in association with the University of New South Wales Press, 2002. 215 p. : **523.5**

1. Meteorites. 2. Astronomy 3. Meteors. 4. Geochemistry 5. Solar system -- Questions and answers. 6. Earth -- Questions and answers
ISBN 158834021X

LC 2001049551

Describes the formation of meteorites, their recovery, and the information they hold.

"Informative and visually appealing, this title meets any library's need for a basic source on meteorites." Booklist.

Cokinos, Christopher
The **fallen** sky : an intimate history of shooting stars / Christopher Cokinos. Jeremy P. Tarcher/Penguin, c2009. 528 p. **523.5**

1. Meteorites -- Antarctica 2. Astronomy 3. Meteors 4. Cosmology. 5. Antarctica -- Exploration 6. Greenland -- Exploration 7. Solar system
ISBN 9781585427208

LC 2009017493

Chronicles how the study of meteorites became a modern science, in a natural history that documents the contributions of key individuals and traces landmark discoveries in Antarctica, Greenland, and other world regions.

"In 1894, fifteen years before his storied expedition to the North Pole, Robert Peary crossed a treacherous expanse of ice in Greenland in search of another prize: a massive meteorite laden with rare metals from outer space. In this hefty, industrious book, Cokinos retraces Peary's steps, and those of other meteor obsessives, in an idiosyncratic hunt of his own." The New Yorker.

523.6 Comets

Sagan, Carl, 1934-1996
Comet / Carl Sagan and Ann Druyan. Random House, c1985. xiv, 398 p. : **523.6**

1. Comets. 2. Halley's Comet 3. Astronomy.
ISBN 0394549082

LC 85008308

Documents the history of Halley's Comet and describes, in two hundred photographs and an informative text, the path of the comet and the astronomical details of its existence.

"The authors explore the myth and science of comets in a lavishly illustrated, slightly oversize volume that is both fascinating and authoritative." Booklist.

523.7 Sun

Baron, David, 1964-
American eclipse : a nation's epic race to catch the shadow of the moon and win the glory of the world / David Baron. Liveright Publishing Corporation, 2017 xiii, 330 p. **523.7**

1. Watson, James C. (James Craig), 1838-1880 2. Mitchell, Maria, 1818-1889 3. Edison, Thomas A. (Thomas Alva), 1847-1931. 4. Science. 5. Eclipses -- History. 6. Astronomy. 7. Astronomers 8. United States -- Civilization -- 1865-1918.
ISBN 9781631490163

LC 2017009679

Documents the efforts of three late-19th-century scientists to observe the rare total solar eclipse of 1878, citing how the respective ambitions of James Craig Watson, Maria Mitchell and Thomas Edison, juxtaposed against the challenges of the Wild West, helped America's early pursuits as a scientific superpower.

"With a wealth of choice details about their lives, Baron brilliantly presents these three pioneers, their ambitions, and their struggles." Booklist.

Dvorak, John
Mask of the sun : the science, history and forgotten lore of eclipses / John Dvorak. Pegasus Books, 2017. 336 p. **523.7**

1. Solar eclipses 2. Astronomy 3. Humans -- Effect of environment on 4. Eclipses
ISBN 9781681773308

LC 2017449069

An astronomer explores the ways eclipses have shaped the course of human history, from the ancient Chinese who recorded their occurrences on turtle shells and the Mayan "Dresden Codex," to appearances in literature and historic events, up through modern times.

"This book provides an excellent overview of how eclipses work and how people have interpreted them through time." Library Journal.

Golub, Leon
Nearest star : the surprising science of our sun / Leon Golub & Jay M. Pasachoff. Harvard University Press, 2001. xii, 267 p. : **523.7**

1. Sun. 2. Solar system. 3. Space.
ISBN 0674004671

LC 00063213

Offers an illustrated survey of the current state of solar knowledge, covering a range of topics from the birth of the sun and its composition to the various tools used to understand its history and makeup.

"This is a brilliant, richly illustrated survey." Booklist.

Nordgren, Tyler E. (Tyler Eugene), 1969-
Sun, moon, Earth : the history of solar eclipses, from omens of doom to Einstein and exoplanets / Tyler Nordgren. Basic

Books, [2016] 256 p. **523.7**

1. Eclipses 2. Astronomy -- History. 3. Archaeoastronomy. 4. Lunar eclipses 5. Solar system 6. Sun 7. Moon

ISBN 9780465060924

LC 2016013888

Ahead of the first total eclipse of the sun in 40 years, which will take place on August 21, 2017, an astronomer describes how solar eclipses were treated and interpreted by past civilizations, philosophers and Victorian scientists.

"A charming natural history of eclipses and a guide to witnessing the awe-inspiring event yourself." Kirkus.

523.8 Stars

Bartusiak, Marcia, 1950-

Black hole : how an idea abandoned by Newtonians, hated by Einstein, and gambled on by Hawking became loved / Marcia Bartusiak. Yale University Press, 2015 224 p. **523.8**

1. Black holes (Astronomy) 2. Scientific discoveries 3. Science -- Social aspects. 4. Astrophysics

ISBN 9780300210859

LC 2014038950

Chronicles the contentious history of the idea of the black hole--one of the most fascinating and bizarre celestial objects in the heavens.

"Superior science writing that eschews the usual fulsome biographies of eccentric geniuses, droll anecdotes and breathless prognostication to deliver a persistently fascinating portrait of an odd but routine feature of the cosmos." Kirkus.

Dickinson, Terence

Nightwatch : a practical guide to viewing the universe / Terence Dickinson ; foreword by Timothy Ferris ; illustrations by Adolf Schaller ... [et al.] ; principal photography by Terence Dickinson. Firefly Books, c2006. 192 p. : **523.8**

1. Astronomy 2. Stars 3. Observers' manuals.

ISBN 155407147X

LC bl2006021073

A reference guide for stargazers offers star charts and information on equipment, planets, and stellar photography.

"This handbook for amateur astronomers combines a text both meaty and hard to put down with a great array of charts, boxes, tables, and dazzling full-color photos of the sky." School Library Journal. [review of 1998 edition]

Dinwiddie, Robert, 1953-

The **stars** / authors, Robert Dinwiddie, David W. Hughes, Geraint Jones, Ian Ridpath, Carole Stott, Giles Sparrow. DK, 2016. 256 p. : **523.8**

1. Constellations. 2. Stars.

ISBN 1465453407

LC bl2016042507

At head of title: DK.

Includes index.

A guide filled with 3D artworks of each constellation and incredible new imagery from the Hubble Space Telescope and more combines astrology and cosmology, exploring the wonders of the universe, from the Big Bang to the search for extraterrestrial life.

Fletcher, Seth, 1979-

Einstein's shadow : a black hole, a band of astronomers, and the quest to see the unseeable / Seth Fletcher. Ecco Press, 2018. 288 p. **523.8**

1. Astrophysics 2. Astronomers 3. Black holes (Astronomy) 4. Relativity (Physics)

ISBN 9780062312020

LC 2018276358

Traces the efforts of an elite scientific team that put Einstein's theory to an ultimate test during a historic mission to photograph a black hole, addressing key questions about time, space and the nature of the universe.

Gubser, Steven Scott, 1972-

The **little** book of black holes / Steven S. Gubser and Frans Pretorius. Princeton University Press, 2017 240 p. **523.8**

1. Black holes (Astronomy).

ISBN 9780691163727

LC 2017024783

Black holes, predicted by Albert Einstein's general theory of relativity more than a century ago, have long intrigued scientists and the public with their bizarre and fantastical properties. Although Einstein understood that black holes were mathematical solutions to his equations, he never accepted their physical reality--a viewpoint many shared. This all changed in the 1960s and 1970s, when a deeper conceptual understanding of black holes developed just as new observations revealed the existence of quasars and X-ray binary star systems, whose mysterious properties could be explained by the presence of black holes. Black holes have since been the subject of intense research--and the physics governing how they behave and affect their surroundings is stranger and more mind-bending than any fiction.

"A comprehensive overview of the science of black holes, among the most mysterious, powerful, and mesmerizing entities in the universe." Kirkus. Reviews

Impey, Chris

Einstein's monsters : the life and times of black holes / Chris Impey. W.W. Norton & Company, [2019] 304 p. **523.8**

1. Black holes (Astronomy) 2. Gravity 3. Physics 4. String theory (Nuclear physics)

ISBN 9781324000938

LC 2018019192

An astronomer and critically-acclaimed author answers questions on the cutting edge of astrophysics to explores the fascinating science of black holes and their role in theoretical physics from Einstein's equations of general relativity to testing string theory.

Kaler, James B.

Extreme stars : at the edge of creation / James B. Kaler. Cambridge University Press, 2001. xi, 236 p. : **523.8**

1. Stars.

ISBN 052140262X

LC 00058522

Includes index.

"Each chapter covers extreme stars of a different kind, including the faintest, the coolest, the brightest, the largest, the smallest, the youngest, the oldest, and the strangest. {Kaler} piques the curiosity of the novice, while encouraging knowledgeable readers to think about stars from a different perspective. There is a wealth of information, much of it not available elsewhere at this semipopular level." Choice.

Scharf, Charles A.

Gravity's engines : how bubble-blowing black holes rule galaxies, stars, and life in the cosmos / Caleb Scharf. Scientific

American/Farrar, Straus and Giroux, 2012. 256 p. **523.8**

1. Black holes (Astronomy) 2. Gravity. 3. Cosmology.

ISBN 9780374114121

LC 2011047089

Includes index.

An astrobiologist describes the powerful, mysterious holes in the space-time continuum called black holes, explains how they not only suck in everything around them, but also spit back out clouds of matter and discusses their role in the universe.

Schneider, Howard

Backyard guide to the night sky / Howard Schneider ; foreword by Sandy Wood. National Geographic, c2009. 286 p. : **523.8**

1. Stars -- Observers' manuals. 2. Astronomy -- Observers' manuals.

ISBN 9781426202810

LC bl2010005616

At head of title: National Geographic.

An extensively illustrated reference for beginner-level stargazing enthusiasts covers basic principles without using complicated scientific language, providing star charts and tables that list key facts in an easy-to-understand format.

Tirion, Wil

The **Cambridge** star atlas / Wil Tirion. Cambridge University Press, 2011. 1 atlas (vi, 90 p.) : **523.8**

1. Stars -- Charts, diagrams, etc. 2. Astronomy -- Charts, diagrams, etc. 3. Stars -- Atlases. 4. Southern Hemisphere -- Charts, diagrams, etc. 5. Northern Hemisphere -- Charts, diagrams, etc. 6. Atlases.

ISBN 9780521173636

LC 2012589778

Provides information about the moon, star charts and monthly sky maps covering that which is visible each month in different hemispheres.

Tyson, Neil deGrasse

Death by black hole : and other cosmic quandaries / Neil deGrasse Tyson. W. W. Norton, c2007. 384 p. ; **523.8**

1. Cosmology. 2. Space biology. 3. Life on other planets. 4. Religion and science. 5. Solar system. 6. Essays

ISBN 0393062244

LC 2006022058

This is a vibrant collection of essays on the cosmos from the nation's best-known astrophysicist, Neil deGrasse Tyson, renowned for his ability to blend content, accessibility, and humor. Here he covers astral life at the frontiers of astrobiology to the movie industry's feeble efforts to get its night skies right.

"A wonderfully informed viewpoint on the slowly expanding boundaries of human knowledge." Boston Globe.

523.9 Satellites and rings eclipses, transits, occultations

Wulf, Andrea

Chasing Venus : the race to measure the heavens / Andrea Wulf. Knopf, 2012. 336 p. **523.9**

1. Geodetic astronomy -- History -- 18th century. 2. Astronomy -- History -- 18th century. 3. Scientific discoveries 4. Venus (Planet) -- Transit.

ISBN 9780307700179

LC 2011049136

The award-winning author chronicles the 18th-century quest to observe the transit of Venus and measure the solar system, explaining the political strife and weather challenges that were overcome to enable an international team of astronomers to work together.

526 Mathematical geography

Alder, Ken

The **measure** of all things : the seven-year odyssey and hidden error that transformed the world / Ken Alder. Free Press, 2002. x, 422 p. : **526**

1. Delambre, J. B. J. (Jean Baptiste Joseph), 1749-1822. 2. Mechain, Pierre, 1744-1804. 3. Arc measures -- History. 4. Metric system. 5. Measurement -- Standards.

ISBN 074321675X

LC 2002070267

"In 1792, two astronomers set out from Paris in opposite directions to measure the meridian and thereby define the length of the meter. Alder's marvelous account of their quest is a dramatic tale of revolution, science, and human error." Library Journal.

Danson, Edwin, 1948-

Weighing the world : the quest to measure the Earth / Edwin Danson. Oxford University Press, 2006. x, 289 p. : **526**

1. Science -- Europe -- History -- 18th century. 2. Geodesy. 3. Earth -- Figure -- Measurement.

ISBN 9780195181692

LC 2004066284

British surveyor and civil engineer Danson looks at the earliest efforts in what is now called geodesy during the age of rationality and enlightenment between 1688 and 1789 -- the English and French revolutions. The information became increasingly critical, he points out, as Europeans explored and conquered what had been the far corners of the round planet, and needed to know, for example, where exactly they were.

"With biographical sketches of the French and British organizers, Danson enlivens data about geodetic surveying, transforming them into greatly interesting dramas of science." Booklist.

Ferreiro, Larrie D.

The **measure** of the Earth : the Enlightenment expedition that reshaped our world / Larrie D. Ferreiro. Basic Books, 2011. 400 p. **526**

1. Bouguer, M. (Pierre), 1698-1758 2. La Condamine, Charles-Marie de, 1701-1774 3. Godin, Louis, 1704-1760 4. Scientific expeditions 5. Equator 6. Latitude 7. Peru -- Exploration

ISBN 9780465017232

LC 2011007173

Describes the early 18th-century expedition of scientists sent by France and Spain to colonial Peru to measure the degree of equatorial latitude, which could resolve the debate between whether the earth was spherical or flattened at the poles.

"This book reads like a script from an Indiana Jones adventure film. [It is] very well written and will interest any reader as it gives insight into the 18th Century and introduces some fascinating and unforgettable characters." Science Books & Films.

Nicastro, Nicholas

Circumference : Eratosthenes and the ancient quest to measure the globe / Nicholas Nicastro. St. Martin's Press, c2008. xi, 223 p. : **526**

1. Eratosthenes. 2. Ancient geography. 3. Mathematics, Greek. 4. Arc measures. 5. Weights and measures, Ancient. 6. Earth -- Figure

-- Measurement.
ISBN 9780312372477

LC 2008025773

Profiles the pioneering ancient Alexandria librarian and the experiment during which he accurately calculated the distance around the earth using elementary tools, in a narrative account that reveals his awareness of such principles as the earth's round shape and the nature of the sun's rays.

Raymo, Chet

Walking zero : discovering cosmic space and time along the Prime Meridian / Chet Raymo. Walker & Company : c2006. xiii, 194 p. : **526**

1. Raymo, Chet Travel England. 2. Walking -- England. 3. Prime Meridian 4. England -- Description and travel.
ISBN 0802714943

"This is the author's expression of his personal exploration of space, time, and scientific history, inspired partly by his walking the footpaths of southeast England in close proximity to the 0 degrees longitude line. . . . . This work is a thought-provoking, highly enlightening discussion of some of the most fascinating concepts in physics, astronomy, and geology, among other subjects." Science Books & Films.

Sobel, Dava

★**Longitude** : the true story of a lone genius who solved the greatest scientific problem of his time / Dava Sobel. Walker, 1995. viii, 184 p. **526**

1. Harrison, John, 1693-1776. 2. Longitude -- Measurement -- History. 3. Clock and watch makers -- Great Britain. 4. Orientation. 5. Chronometers -- History. 6. Great Britain -- History -- 18th century.
ISBN 9780802713124

LC 95017402

ALA Notable Book, 1997.

Traces the forty-year endeavor of John Harrison to safeguard financial interests and the lives of countless sailors by building the first chronometer, a mechanical device that would enable effective timekeeping on the sea.

"Sobel tells his story (and the larger history of the search for longitude) clearly, entertainingly, and with a fine sense of the era in which it took place. Breezily written and full of fascinating characters and facts, here's a science book as enjoyable as any novel." Kirkus.

526.09 Cartography--history

Garfield, Simon

On the map : a mind-expanding exploration of the way the world looks / Simon Garfield. Gotham Books, 2012. 368 p. **526.09**

1. Cartography -- History 2. Maps -- History 3. Surveying
ISBN 9781592407798

LC 2013375048

ALA Notable Book, 2014

Examines the pivotal relationship between mapping and civilization, demonstrating the unique ways that maps relate and realign history in an account that also shares engaging cartography stories and map lore.

529 Chronology

Burdick, Alan

Why time flies : a mostly scientific investigation / Alan Burdick. Simon & Schuster, [2017] 352 p. **529**

1. Time measurements 2. Time -- History.
ISBN 9781416540274

LC 2016025791

The award-winning author of Out of Eden presents an intimate exploration of how life is organized around time and its conflicting perceptions, drawing on international travels and research lab visits where he witnessed fascinating time-altering phenomena.

"A highly illuminating intellectual investigation." Kirkus.

Falk, Dan

In search of time : the science of a curious dimension / Dan Falk. Thomas Dunne Books, St. Martin's Press, c2008. 352 p. **529**

1. Time -- History. 2. Space and time. 3. Time measurements 4. Science -- Social aspects.
ISBN 9780312374785

LC 2008024875

"The book's scope is audaciously broad. Relying on reportage and humour to offset writing that is occasionally prolix, Falk deftly weaves together elements of religion, anthropology, philosophy, and physics into an engaging narrative." Quill & Quire

Galison, Peter Louis

Einstein's clocks and Poincare's maps : empires of time / Peter Galison. W.W. Norton, 2003. 389 p. : **529**

1. Einstein, Albert, 1879-1955. 2. Poincare, Henri, 1854-1912 3. Time. 4. Relativity (Physics)
ISBN 0393020010

LC 2002155114

"Gallison shows how Einstein's work was influenced by French cartographer Henri Poincar and by the physicist's own experience working in a Bern patent office, where the numerous patent requests for devices designed to coordinate distant clocks may have prompted further inquiry into the problem of simultaneity, which lies at the heart of relativity. Few books have ever made Einstein's theories more accessible--or more engrossing--for general readers." Booklist.

Garfield, Simon

Timekeepers : how the world became obsessed with time / Simon Garfield. Canongate Books, 2017. 368 p. **529**

1. Time 2. Perception 3. Measurement 4. Time management
ISBN 9781782113195

LC bl2017042091

An authoritative, upbeat exploration of how and why time has become a dominating force in a world that not long ago was measured by the movement of the sun shares stories that reflect humanity's growing obsession with time and its management throughout the past 250 years.

"Exhibiting dry wit and fizzing with insatiable curiosity, Garfield collects enough eccentric characters, places, and ideas to entertain every reader." Publishers Weekly.

Sims, Michael, 1958-

Apollo's fire : a day on Earth in nature and imagination / Michael Sims. Viking, 2007. xxiv, 296 p. ; **529**

1. Time -- History. 2. Days. 3. Astronomy -- Miscellanea. 4.

Mythology and astrology
ISBN 9780670063284

LC 2007006024

A lighthearted tour of the developmental synergies of life throughout the course of a single day touches on a broad variety of cultural and natural topics, from the color of the sky and the course of the sun to the iconography of prehistoric Egyptian sculpture.

"The author takes a single day and guides readers through the history of what we know, and what we've imagined, about sunrises, clouds and other natural phenomena. . . . His delightful tour of day and night skies will inspire many readers to look up with a marveling new perspective." Publishers Weekly.

530 Science -- Physics

Ananthaswamy, Anil

The **edge** of physics : a journey to Earth's extremes to unlock the secrets of the universe / Anil Ananthaswamy. Houghton Mifflin Harcourt, 2010. 336 p. **530**

1. Physics. 2. Experiments. 3. Science -- Experiments. 4. Cosmology.
ISBN 9780618884681

LC 2009020225

"A meticulous, accessible update of the latest ideas and instruments that contribute to the clarification of an increasingly puzzling universe." Kirkus.

Baggott, Jim

Mass : the quest to understand matter from greek atoms to quantum fields / Dr Jim Baggott. Oxford University Press, 2017. 320 p. **530**

1. Matter 2. Atoms 3. Quantum theory 4. Science -- History
ISBN 9780198759713

LC 2016960645

"Jim Baggott explains how we come to find ourselves here, confronted by a very different understanding of the nature of matter, the origin of mass, and its implications for our understanding of the material world. Ranging from the Greek philosophers Leucippus and Democritus, and their theories of atoms and void, to the development of quantum field theory and the discovery of a Higgs boson-like particle, he explores our changing understanding of the nature of matter, and the fundamental related concept of mass."--Provided by the publisher.

"Baggott smartly renders particle physics, typically a dense and opaque topic for the nonexpert, clear and captivating. Not only will readers grasp the building blocks of the standard model, they will forever look at mass differently." Publishers Weekly.

The **quantum** story : a history in 40 moments / Jim Baggott. Oxford University Press, 2011. 320 p. **530**

1. Quantum theory -- History. 2. Atomic research. 3. Physics. 4. Science.
ISBN 9780199566846

LC oc2010073057

Includes index.

Presents forty turning points in the history of the development of quantum theory and describes the personalities of the physicists involved in the discoveries.

"Quantum theorychallenging, disconcerting and heavy on mathis not going to be pinned down and dissected for lay readers without a lot of kicking and screaming. Baggott succeeds, however, imbuing the narrative with important context, his own communicable enthusiasm and the instances of dense theoretical exposition mediated by historical and biographical storytelling. His survey runs roughly chronologically, starting with Max Planck's contention that energy is composed of a definite number of equal finite packages, through Einstein, Bohr, Heisenberg, Dirac, Feynman, Hawking et al. the author then looks at the Standard Model and the more amorphous superstring theory." Kirkus.

Balibar, Sebastien

The **atom** and the apple : twelve tales from contemporary physics / Sebastien Balibar ; translated by Nathanael Stein. Princeton University Press, c2008. 200 p. **530**

1. Physics 2. Essays.
ISBN 9780691131085

LC 2008018027

Includes index.

Balibar examines twelve problems spanning the frontiers of physics, and he devotes a chapter to each issue. -- from publisher description

Cole, K. C.

The **hole** in the universe : how scientists peered over the edge of emptiness and found everything / K.C. Cole. Harcourt, 2001. xiv, 274 p. : **530**

1. Physics -- Philosophy. 2. Nothingness. 3. Black holes (Astronomy) 4. Cosmology.
ISBN 0156013177

LC BL2001010698

"A Harvest book."

A look at cutting-edge science shows how physicists have been able to pierce previous voids and limitations to discover black holes, repulsive anti-gravity, the undulating string, and other phenomena.

Czerski, Helen, 1978-

Storm in a teacup : the physics of everyday life / Helen Czerski. W.W. Norton & Company, 2017, c2016. 336 p. **530**

1. Science 2. Physics -- Miscellanea.
ISBN 9780393248968

LC 2016046555

Explanations of scientific principles as they can be observed in everyday examples, from the billowing cloud appearance of milk in hot drinks to how ducks keep their feet warm while walking on ice, reveal how they are linked to major challenges, including climate change and the energy crisis.

Einstein, Albert, 1879-1955

★The **evolution** of physics : the growth of ideas from early concepts to relativity and quanta / Albert Einstein and Leopold Infeld. Simon and Schuster, 1938. x, 319, 1 p. **530**

1. Physics -- History. 2. Relativity (Physics) 3. Quantum theory.
ISBN 0671201565

LC 38027272

Clear and concise explanations of the development of theories explaining physical phenomena.

"An exposition for the layman of the growth of ideas in physical science." Publishers Weekly.

Feynman, Richard P., (Richard Phillips), 1918-1988

★**Six** easy pieces : essentials of physics, explained by its most brilliant teacher / Richard P. Feynman ; originally prepared for publication by Robert B. Leighton and Matthew Sands; new introduction by Paul Davies. Addison Wesley, 1995. xxix, 145 p. : **530**

1. Physics. 2. Atoms. 3. Science.
ISBN 0201409550

LC 94030894

Includes index.

The six easiest chapters from Feynman's celebrated lectures on physics, which the Nobel Prize-winning scientist delivered from 1961 to 1963 at the California Institute of Technology, have been reprinted in this volume.

Goldberg, Dave, 1974-

A **user's** guide to the universe : surviving the perils of black holes, time paradoxes, and quantum uncertainty / Dave Goldberg and Jeff Blomquist. Wiley, c2010. vii, 296 p. : **530**

1. Physics

ISBN 9780470496510

LC 2009028773

Explains string theory, quantum mechanics, parallel universes and the beginning of time in a conversational, easy-to-understand way and answers enduring questions about life on other planets and breaking the light-speed barrier.

Gray, Theodore W

Reactions : an illustrated exploration of elements, molecules, and change in the universe / Theodore Gray ; photographs by Nick Mann. Black Dog & Leventhal Publishers, 2017. vii, 216 p. : **530**

1. Chemical elements. 2. Chemistry. 3. Molecular structure. 4. Molecules.

ISBN 0316391220

LC 2017020093

Includes index.

In a follow-up to The Elements and Molecules, a internationally best-selling author and app creator demonstrates how the focus of his first two books combine to create chemical reactions including combustion, photosynthesis, respiration and oxidation.

Kakalios, James, 1958-

The **physics** of everyday things : the extraordinary science of an ordinary day / James Kakalios. Crown Publishers, 2017 256 p. **530**

1. Physics. 2. Everyday life. 3. Science in popular culture.

ISBN 9780770437732

LC 2016046355

A physics professor reveals the invisible science behind the functioning of everyday things and activities that we often take for granted, including how electricity is transported from a power station to our toasters and what really makes digital "clouds" and electric cars function.

"Kakalios makes physics relatable, this time demonstrating how profoundly its principles enable our way of life." Kirkus.

Krauss, Lawrence Maxwell

★**Fear** of physics : a guide for the perplexed / Lawrence M. Krauss. Basic Books, c2007. xvii, 257 p. : **530**

1. Physics.

ISBN 9780465002184

LC 2007004700

"Revised with a new preface."--P. [1] cover.

"The writing style genuinely keeps the reader interested. This book is a great resource if you want insight into what physics really is and what physicists do." Science Books & Films.

Levi, Mark, 1951-

Why cats land on their feet : and 76 other physical paradoxes and puzzles / Mark Levi. Princeton University Press, c2012. x, 190 p. : **530**

1. Science

ISBN 0691148546

LC 2011045728

Ever wonder why cats land on their feet? Or what holds a spinning top upright? Or whether it is possible to feel the Earth's rotation in an airplane? Why Cats Land on Their Feet is a compendium of paradoxes and puzzles that readers can solve using their own physical intuition. And the surprising answers to virtually all of these astonishing paradoxes can be arrived at with no formal knowledge of physics. --From publisher description.

"Readers will find themselves coaxed into learning because they want to satisfy their curiosity as they examine each puzzle." Library Journal.

Randall, Lisa

Warped passages : unraveling the mysteries of the Universe's hidden dimensions / Lisa Randall. Ecco, 2005. xii, 499 p. : **530**

1. Physics -- Philosophy. 2. Particles (Nuclear physics) 3. Cosmology. 4. String theory (Nuclear physics)

ISBN 0060531088

LC 2004056376

Discusses dimensions of space, early twentieth-century advances, the physics of elementary particles, string theory and branes, and proposals for extra-dimension universes.

Robinson, Andrew, 1957-

The **story** of measurement / Andrew Robinson. Thames & Hudson, 2007. 224 p. : **530**

1. Measurement -- History 2. Weights and measures -- History 3. Scientific apparatus and instruments -- History 4. Science -- History

ISBN 9780500513675

LC 2007921450

An upbeat survey of humanity's fascination with measurement covers a wide range of topics, from currency and the birth of the meter to natural disasters and body mass index, in a volume that explains each measuring method within a historical context.

"Robinson has the knack to explain any number of complex concepts lucidly and with simplicity, without being condescending. He has produced a highly readable book." Times Literary Supplement.

Rovelli, Carlo, 1956-

★**Seven** brief lessons on physics / Carlo Rovelli. Riverhead Books, 2016 96 p. **530**

1. Physics 2. Science 3. Relativity (Physics) 4. Gravity

ISBN 9780399184413

LC bl2016001513

A introduction to modern physics by a founder of the loop quantum gravity theory shares seven succinct lessons on topics ranging from general relativity and quantum mechanics to elementary particles and black holes. An international best-seller.

Stanley, Matthew, 1975-

Einstein's war : how relativity triumphed amid the vicious nationalism of World War I / Matthew Stanley. Dutton, an imprint of Penguin Random House LLC, [2019] 384 p. **530**

1. Einstein, Albert, 1879-1955 2. Eddington, Arthur Stanley, Sir, 1882-1944 3. Scientists 4. Relativity (Physics) 5. Science -- Social aspects 6. World War I

ISBN 9781524745417

LC 2019001286

The history of science podcaster behind What the If?!? reveals how the life of Einstein and the acceptance of his theory of relativity were challenged by the harsh realities of World War I and nationalist bigotry that criminalized his ideas.

"Fans of popular science, Einstein, physics, and World War I will find this to be entertaining and informative." Library Journal.

Susskind, Leonard

The **theoretical** minimum : what you need to know to start doing physics / Leonard Susskind and George Hrabovsky. Basic Books, c2013. xi, 238 p. : **530**

1. Physics
ISBN 046502811X

LC bl2013002787

Includes index.

A string theorist and a citizen scientist instruct lay readers on elementary principles of physics and associated math that amateur enthusiasts should know in order to study more advanced topics, in a reference that covers such topics as classical mechanics, electromagnetic fields and chaos theory.

"Excellent as an introduction to theoretical physics for the educated layperson, the book will also be useful to students and physicists for its elegant summary of the complete structure of classical mechanics." Choice.

Wertheim, Margaret

Physics on the fringe : smoke rings, circlons, and alternative theories of everything / Margaret Wertheim. St Martins Press, 2011. 304 p. **530**

1. Physics. 2. Physicists.
ISBN 9780802715135

LC 2012045577

"The author offers a look into the hearts and minds of the outsider physicists: solitary figures who, usually with little or no formal training, strive to explain our world. Wertheim builds the book around the affable Jim Carter, explorer, self-taught physicist, trailer park owner, and proponent of circlon synchronicity, with atoms shaped like tiny circles of coiled spring. This sympathetic portrayal of one outsider's work offers an entry point into a fascinating corner of pseudoscience." Publishers Weekly.

530.01 Philosophy and theory

Krauss, Lawrence Maxwell

The **greatest** story ever told--so far : why are we here? / Lawrence M. Krauss. Pocket Books, 2017. 320 p. **530.01**

1. Physics 2. Cosmogony 3. Cosmology 4. Gravity 5. Solar system -- Origin
ISBN 9781476777610

LC bl2017004042

An award-winning theoretical physicist and best-selling author of A Universe from Nothing traces the dramatic discovery of the counterintuitive world of reality, explaining how readers can shift their perspectives to gain greater understandings of our individual roles in the universe.

"An admirable complement to the author's previous book and equally satisfying for those willing to read carefully." Kirkus.

530.09 Physics--history--serials

Ohanian, Hans C.

Einstein's mistakes : the human failings of genius / Hans C. Ohanian. W.W. Norton & Company, 2008. 256 p. **530.09**

1. Einstein, Albert, 1879-1955. 2. Physics -- History. 3. Science -- History. 4. Errors. 5. Physicists.
ISBN 9780393062939

LC 2008013155

Evaluates the contributions and achievements of Einstein from an alternative perspective of his mistakes and reliance on his predecessors, offering insight into how the discoveries of such figures as Galileo, Newton, and Copernicus shaped Einstein's career and how failures in his personal and professional arenas influenced his iconic character.

Pickover, Clifford A.

The **physics** book : from the big bang to quantum resurrection, 250 milestones in the history of physics / Clifford A. Pickover. Sterling Pub., c2011. 527 p. : **530.09**

1. Physics -- History.
ISBN 1402778619

LC 2010051365

"This attractive reference by biophysicist, biochemist, and science writer Pickover is composed of lucid one-page explanations of physics concepts, alternating with full-page color illustrations." Library Journal.

Simonyi, Karoly

A **cultural** history of physics / Karoly Simonyi ; translated by David Kramer. CRC Press, c2012. xiv, 622 p. : **530.09**

1. Physics -- History.
ISBN 1568813295

LC 2010009407

"An A K Peters book."

Translated from the German and Hungarian.

Offers a comprehensive history of physics, offering the cultural contexts in which many discoveries were made.

530.092 Physicists

Einstein, Albert, 1879-1955

★A **stubbornly** persistent illusion : the essential scientific writings of Albert Einstein / edited, with commentary, by Stephen Hawking. Running Press, c2007. xi, 468 p. : **530.092**

1. Einstein, Albert, 1879-1955. 2. Physicists -- Germany 3. Physics -- History 4. Science -- Experiments -- History 5. Quantum theory -- History 6. Germany -- History -- 20th century 7. Essays
ISBN 0762430036

LC bl2007020342

Brings together a compilation of the most important works by Albert Einstein, presenting his papers on the Theory of Relativity, quantum theory, statistical mechanics, the photoelectric effect, and other studies that transformed modern physics.

"Hawking adds a brief but effective introduction to each section, making this gem of a collection really shine." Publishers Weekly.

The **ultimate** quotable Einstein / collected and edited by Alice Calaprice ; with a foreword by Freeman Dyson. Princeton University Press, c2011. xxviii, 578 p. : **530.092**

1. Einstein, Albert, 1879-1955 Quotations.
ISBN 0691138176

LC 2010002855

Here is the definitive new edition of the hugely popular collection of Einstein quotations that has sold tens of thousands of copies worldwide and been translated into twenty-five languages. --From publisher description.

Kaiser, David

How the hippies saved physics : science, counterculture, and the quantum revival / David Kaiser. W.W. Norton, c2011. 400 p. **530.092**

1. Physicists -- Berkeley, California 2. Quantum theory. 3. Counterculture. 4. Physics -- History -- 20th century 5. Berkeley, California -- History
ISBN 9780393076363

LC 2010053415

Describes how a quirky band of misfit science students at Berkeley in the 1970s altered the course of modern physics while studying quantum theory alongside Eastern mysticism and psychic mind reading while lounging in hot tubs and dabbling with LSD.

"This entertaining, worthwhile read is as much about the nature of society at the dawn of the New Age as it is about quantum physics." Choice.

530.1 Theories and mathematical physics

Gribbin, John, 1946-

In search of Schrodinger's cat : quantum physics and reality / John Gribbin. Bantam Books, 1984. xvi, 302 p. : **530.1**

1. Schrodinger, Erwin, 1887-1961. 2. Quantum theory -- History. 3. Reality. 4. Heisenberg uncertainty principle 5. Physics.
ISBN 0553341030

LC 84002975

"This book contains many vignettes from the history of science and many insights into the researchers and the work that has led to our current understanding of the quantum theory. Excellent analogies and graphic illustrations are used to present difficult ideas." Science Books & Films.

Hawking, Stephen, 1942-2018

Black holes and baby universes and other essays / Stephen Hawking. Bantam Books, c1993. ix, 182 p. ; **530.1**

1. Hawking, Stephen, 1942-2018 2. Cosmology. 3. Physics. 4. Astronomy. 5. Unified field theories. 6. Essays.
ISBN 0553095234

LC 93008269

Includes index.

A collection of essays from the noted scientist includes personal reminiscences, a call for better science education, and explorations of the origins of the universe

"The author sprinkles his explanations with a wry sense of humor and a keen awareness that the sciences today delve not only into the far reaches of the cosmos, but into the inner philosophical world as well." New York Times Book Review.

The **nature** of space and time / Stephen Hawking and Roger Penrose. Princeton University Press, c1996. viii, 141 p. : **530.1**

1. Space and time. 2. Theories. 3. Quantum theory. 4. Astrophysics. 5. Speeches, addresses, etc.
ISBN 9780691037912

LC 95035582

"This volume takes the form of a debate between Hawking and Penrose at Cambridge in 1994. At the center of the discussion is a pair of powerful theories: the quantum theory of fields and the general theory of relativity. The issue is how--it at all--one can merge the two into a quantum theory of gravity. A substantial background in theoretical physics is needed for full comprehension." Library Journal.

Kaku, Michio

Hyperspace : a scientific odyssey through parallel universes, time warps, and the tenth dimension / Michio Kaku. Oxford University Press, 1994. xvi, 359 p. : **530.1**

1. Kaluza-Klein theories. 2. Superstring theories. 3. Hyperspace. 4. Physics -- Research -- United States -- History 5. United States -- Social life and customs -- 20th century
ISBN 9780195085143

LC 93007910

Offers insights into research on the tenth dimension, time warps, black holes, and multiple universes.

"This is an overview of the major scientists, discoveries, and ideas involved in an ongoing quest for synthesizing quantum mechanics and relativity physics into a superstring theory of our entire universe." Library Journal.

Thorne, Kip S.

Black holes and time warps : Einstein's outrageous legacy / Kip S. Thorne. W.W. Norton, 1994. 619 p. : **530.1**

1. Physics -- Philosophy. 2. Relativity (Physics) 3. General relativity (Physics) 4. Astrophysics.
ISBN 0393035050

LC 93002014

"This book is about black holes, white holes, wormholes, parallel universes, time travel, 10-dimensional space-time, the origin and fate of the universe and a lot of other subjects dear to science fiction fans." New York Times Book Review.

Yau, Shing-Tung, 1949-

The **shape** of inner space : string theory and the geometry of the universe's hidden dimensions / Shing-tung Yau and Steve Nadis ; illustrations by Xianfeng (David) Gu and Xiaotian (Tim) Yin. Basic Books, 2010. 400 p. **530.1**

1. Hyperspace. 2. String theory (Nuclear physics) 3. Fourth dimension. 4. Physics.
ISBN 9780465020232

LC 2010009956

"It is a testimony to [Yau's] careful prose (and no doubt to the skills of co-author Steve Nadis) that this book so compellingly captures the essence of what pushes string theorists forward in the face of formidable obstacles. It gives us a rare glimpse into a world as alien as the moons of Jupiter, and just as fascinating. Yau and Nadis have produced a strangely mesmerizing account of geometry's role in the universe." The New Scientist.

530.11 Relativity theory

Bodanis, David

E=mc2 : a biography of the world's most famous equation / David Bodanis. Walker, 2000. ix, 337 p. : **530.11**

1. Einstein, Albert, 1879-1955. 2. Force. 3. Energy. 4. Mass (Physics) 5. Physicists -- Germany
ISBN 9780802713520

LC 00040857

Examines the science and scientists who provided the backdrop to Einstein's seminal 1905 discovery, and offers a definitive explanation of the equation from a mathematical, historical, and scientific perspective.

"Bodanis rescues the masses from ignorance in an entertaining story about Einstein's formulation of the equation in 1905 and its association ever after with relativity and nuclear energy. Parallel with the science, Bodanis populates his tale with dramatic lives...With anecdotes and illustrations, Bodanis effectively opens up E = 2 to the widest audience." Booklist.

Carroll, Sean M., 1966-

★**From** eternity to here : the quest for the ultimate theory of time / Sean Carroll. Dutton, c2009. 448 p. **530.11**

1. Space and time. 2. Physics. 3. Time. 4. Physical sciences

ISBN 9780525951339

LC 2009023828

A cofounder of the blog Cosmic Variance outlines a comprehensive vision of the universe that attempts to explain why time moves forward, building on a premise that time owes its existence to conditions before the Big Bang and may be explained by theoretical space-time properties.

"Understanding time requires an acquaintance with entropy, relativity, cosmology, thermodynamics and statistical mechanics, which Carroll enthusiastically delivers at great length. Not for the scientifically disinclined, but determined readers will come away with a rewarding grasp of a complex subject." Kirkus.

Einstein, Albert, 1879-1955

The **meaning** of relativity / Albert Einstein. Princeton University Press, c2005. xxiv, 166 p. : The Stafford Little lectures ; **530.11**

1. Relativity (Physics)

ISBN 9780691120270

LC 2004111082

"Including the Relativistic theory of the non-symmetric field."

Includes index.

Simplified version of Einstein's theories that explain that the measurements of motion or rest are relative to the motion or rest of the observer.

Ferreira, Pedro G.

The **perfect** theory : a century of geniuses and the battle over general relativity / Pedro G. Ferreira. Houghton Mifflin Harcourt, 2014. 304 p. **530.11**

1. General relativity (Physics) -- History -- 20th century. 2. Physicists 3. Physics -- History -- 20th century. 4. Science -- Social aspects -- History -- 20th century.

ISBN 9780547554891

LC 2013021741

"At the core of Einstein's general theory of relativity are a set of equations that explain the relationship among gravity, space, and time--possibly the most perfect intellectual achievement of modern physics. For over a century, physicists have been exploring, debating, and at times neglecting Einstein's theory in their quest to uncover the history of the universe, the origin of time, and the evolution of solar systems, stars, and galaxies. In this sweeping narrative of science and culture, Pedro Ferreira explains the theory through the human drama surrounding it: the personal feuds and intellectual battles of the biggest names in twentieth-century physics, from Einstein and Eddington to Hawking and Penrose. We are in the midst of a momentous transformation in modern physics. As scientists look farther and more clearly into space than ever before, The Perfect Theory engagingly reveals the greater relevance of general relativity, showing us where it started, where it has led, and where it can still takeus"-- Provided by publisher.

"Ferreira does not downplay relativity's complexity and avoids the easy route of oversimplifying it into a cosmic magic show. The result is one of the best popular accounts of how Einstein and his followers have been trying to explain the universe for decades." Kirkus.

Gleick, James

Time travel : a history / James Gleick. Pantheon Books, 2016 256 p. **530.11**

1. Space and time. 2. Time travel.

ISBN 9780307908797

LC 2016002323

Presents an exploration of time travel that details its subversive origins, evolution in literature and science, and enduring influence on the understanding of time itself.

Muller, R. (Richard)

Now : the physics of time / Richard A. Muller. W.W. Norton & Company, 2016 352 p. **530.11**

1. Space and time. 2. Entropy. 3. Physics -- Philosophy.

ISBN 9780393285239

LC 2016012496

Includes index.

"Now" is a simple concept--you're reading this sentence now. Yet a real definition of "now" has eluded even the great Einstein. We know that time stretches and is affected by gravity and velocity. Yet, as eminent physicist Richard A. Muller points out, it is only today that we have all the physics at hand--relativity, entropy, entanglement, antimatter, and the Big Bang--to explain the flow of time. With these building blocks in place, Muller reaches a startling conclusion: our expanding universe is continuously creating not only new space but also new time. The front edge of this new time is what we call "now," and this moment is truly unique--it is the only moment in which we can exercise our free will.

"Not for the faint of heart or mathematically averse, but Muller is a masterful guide within this survey of cosmology." Kirkus.

Musser, George

Spooky action at a distance : the phenomenon that reimagines space and time : and what it means for black holes, the big bang, and theories of everything / George Musser. Scientific American/Farrar, Straus and Giroux, 2015. 288 p. **530.11**

1. Space and time -- Philosophy. 2. Relativity (Physics). 3. Physics

ISBN 9780374298517

LC 2015010155

"Clarity and humor illuminate Musser's writing, and he adroitly captures the excitement and frustration involved in investigating the mysteries of our universe." Publishers Weekly.

Rigden, John S.

★**Einstein** 1905 : the standard of greatness / John S. Rigden. Harvard University Press, 2005. ix, 173 p. : **530.11**

1. Einstein, Albert, 1879-1955 Influence. 2. Physicists. 3. Quantum theory.

ISBN 0674015444

Analyzes several of Albert Einstein's theories, including his particle theory of light, theory of Brownian motion, and theory of special relativity, and explores the context of these ideas and their continued impact on society.

"The book is a delight to read, with a lot of interesting, useful information." Choice.

Rovelli, Carlo, 1956-

The **order** of time / Carlo Rovelli ; translated by Erica Segre and Simon Carnell. Riverhead Books, 2018, c2017. 224 p. **530.11**

1. Space and time. 2. Time. 3. Presentism (Philosophy). 4. Cosmology.
ISBN 9780735216105

LC 2017060293

Originally published in Italian: L'ordine del tempo (Milan : Adelphi Edizioni, 2017).

The best-selling author of Seven Brief Lessons on Physics presents an accessible exploration of the nature of time that illuminates the questions debated by physicists and philosophers, challenging assumptions that time is linear or even measurable while explaining the critical role of perception.

Toomey, David

The **new** time travelers : a journey to the frontiers of physics / David Toomey. W. W. Norton, c2007. 391 p., 4 p. of plates : **530.11**

1. Space and time. 2. Time travel. 3. Physics.
ISBN 0393060136

LC 2007011307

In the 1990s, a group of theoretical physicists at Caltech undertook a serious investigation of the possibility of pastward time travel and concluded that it might be possible, inspiring a serious and sustained study that engaged more than thirty physicists around the world.

"This book on the physics of time travel illustrates dimension-bending concepts with space-time diagrams, M. C. Escher drawings, and the plot of H.G. Wells' Time Machine. Toomey gets a grip on bending the fourth dimension by historically chronicling physicists who have theorized about time travel . . . . If you dream of getting outside your personal light cone, Toomey shows how it might be imagined." Booklist.

Wolfson, Richard

Simply Einstein : relativity demystified / Richard Wolfson. W.W. Norton, c2003. x, 261 p. : **530.11**

1. Relativity (Physics) 2. Time travel. 3. Black holes (Astronomy) 4. Big Bang Theory (Astronomy)
ISBN 0393051544

LC 2002002984

A layperson's introduction to the theory of relativity and its significance discusses such topics as time travel, curved space, black holes, the big bang, gravity, and twenty-first-century physics.

"Wolfson's economical and vivid tutorial should open doors for lay readers encountering Einstein's principles for the first time. His popular style, with a minimum of math, should make this a must-have book for Einstein buffs as well." Publishers Weekly.

530.12 Quantum mechanics (Quantum theory)

Ananthaswamy, Anil

Through two doors at once : the elegant experiment that captures the enigma of our quantum reality / Anil Ananthaswamy. Penguin Group USA 2018 304 p. **530.12**

1. Quantum theory 2. Experiments 3. Light 4. Physics
ISBN 9781101986097

LC 2018008272

The award-winning author of *The Man Who Wasn't There* traces the story of the "double-slit" experiment that demonstrated how a sunbeam split into two paths, which challenged 19th-century understandings about light and the nature of reality, triggering debates that continue today.

"An engaging and accessible history of a fascinating and baffling experiment that remains inconclusive to this day. Recommended for those interested in the subject or anyone wishing to delve further into the double-slit experiment." Library Journal.

Bolles, Edmund Blair, 1942-

Einstein defiant : genius versus genius in the quantum revolution / Edmund Blair Bolles. Joseph Henry Press, 2004. viii, 348 p. : **530.12**

1. Einstein, Albert, 1879-1955. 2. Bohr, Niels Henrik David, 1885-1962. 3. Quantum theory -- History. 4. Physics -- History -- 20th century.
ISBN 0309089980

LC 2003023735

"This carefully researched book achieves a nice balance between science and history. The author provides enough scientific information to illuminate the unfolding drama for nonscientists and constructs a marvelously choreographed tale of how just about every physicist of note in the last century contributed to the debate." Science Books & Films.

Carroll, Sean M., 1966-

Something deeply hidden : quantum worlds and the emergence of spacetime / Sean Carroll. E.P. Dutton, 2019. 345 p. **530.12**

1. Quantum theory 2. Reality 3. Space and time 4. Physics
ISBN 9781524743017

LC bl2019021305

A Caltech physicist and author of The Big Picture argues in favor of the Many Worlds theory of quantum behavior that argues that there are innumerable multiple worlds with copies of everything and everyone in them.

Cox, Brian, 1968-

The **quantum** universe : and why anything that can happen, does / Brian Cox and Jeff Forshaw. Da Capo Press, 2012. 256 p. **530.12**

1. Quantum theory 2. Physics 3. Mechanics
ISBN 9780306819643

LC 2011942393

The authors of the best-selling Why Does E=MC2? render fundamental scientific principles in the areas of quantum mechanics comprehensive and engaging to lay readers, working through obscure and vague aspects to explain related natural world observations, how the quantum world was constructed and why it is important.

Crease, Robert P.

The **quantum** moment : how Planck, Bohr, Einstein, and Heisenberg taught us to love uncertainty / Robert P. Crease and Alfred Scharff Goldhaber. W.W. Norton & Company, [2014] 352 p. **530.12**

1. Quantum theory -- Popular works. 2. Popular culture 3. Physics -- Popular works. 4. Creativity
ISBN 9780393067927

LC 2014011427

Describes how the early-20th-century discoveries in quantum physics found their way into today's modern language and collective culture, appearing in everything from television shows and movies to coffee mugs and T-shirts to art forms like sculpture and prose.

"Though the authors acknowledge that many of those appropriating the jargon of quantum physics have no clue as to its scientific meaning, readers will learn to appreciate the imaginative process that transforms quantum formulas into new metaphors for understanding the human condition. An exhilarating romp for the intellectually adventurous! " Booklist.

Ford, Kenneth William, 1926-

The **quantum** world : quantum physics for everyone / Kenneth W. Ford. Harvard University Press, 2004. ix, 270 p. : **530.12**

1. Quantum theory. 2. Physics.
ISBN 0674013425

LC 2003068565

Includes index.

Helps the serious reader make sense of the mysterious science of quantum physics, covering the key discoveries of the twentieth century, such as granularity, the uncertainty principle, and superposition and entanglement, among other important topics.

Gilder, Louisa

The **age** of entanglement : when quantum physics was reborn / Louisa Gilder. Alfred A. Knopf, 2008. 464 p. **530.12**

1. Quantum theory. 2. Physics -- History 3. Particles (Nuclear physics) 4. Bell's theorem
ISBN 9781400044177

LC 2008011796

A study of one of the fundamental concept of quantum physics examines the strange correlation between two separated particles, entitled "entanglement" by physicist John Bell, drawing on the work of leading physicists to explain the phenomenon.

"This is the story of quantum mechanics and its lively cast of supporters. Gilder's history is rife with curious characters and dramatizes how difficult it was for even these brilliant scientists to grasp the paradigm-changing concepts of quantum science." Publishers Weekly.

Greene, B. (Brian), 1963-

★The **hidden** reality : parallel universes and the deep laws of the cosmos / Brian Greene. Alfred A. Knopf, 2011. 384 p. **530.12**

1. Cosmology. 2. Relativity (Physics) 3. Physics. 4. String theory (Nuclear physics)
ISBN 9780307265630

LC 2010042710

"The author explores the possibility that there is not one big uncharted universe, but many. Those universes take the form of Swiss cheese, suds in a bubble bath, passageways right out of Star Trek, and realms right next to us. The danger of writing a mind-blower like The Hidden Reality is that, if the author isn't careful, it can become mind-numbing to read. A caution here upfront: There are points where Greene walks perilously close to that precipice. Black holes, parallel universes, the idea that we and our world may have doppelgngers in different dimensions are heady concepts. For some, such conjecture is religious heresy; for others, it aims to answer the ultimate questions as to how and why we are here, with science, not faith, forming a necessary and--so far--inadequate, bridge to explore the mystery. What Greene does exceedingly well is to lay out the prevailing theories, advanced by the brightest human minds, as to how the whole of everything may be ordered." Christian Science Monitor.

Hawking, Stephen, 1942-2018

★The **universe** in a nutshell / Stephen Hawking. Bantam Books, 2001. viii, 216 p. ; **530.12**

1. Quantum theory. 2. String theory (Nuclear physics) 3. Time. 4. Space and time -- History.
ISBN 9780553802023

LC 2001035757

Includes index.

Royal Society General Prizes for Science Books, 2002.

The author explores recent scientific breakthroughs in the fields of supergravity, supersymmetry, quantum theory, superstring theory, and p-branes as he searches for the Theory of Everything that lies at the heart of the cosmos.

"Admirers of Hawking's previous book will continue to appreciate his ability not only to air fresh, provocative ideas but also to say what he means clearly and without watering down his material or condescending to his audience--he even injects humor into his narrative. The profuse, beautifully rendered illustrations contribute greatly to the reader's understanding of his points." Booklist.

Kakalios, James, 1958-

The **amazing** story of quantum mechanics : a math-free exploration of the science that made our world / James Kakalios. Penguin Group USA, 2010. 336 p. : **530.12**

1. Quantum theory -- Miscellanea 2. Science in popular culture 3. Mechanics 4. Physics -- Miscellanea
ISBN 9781592404797

LC 2010029568

Explains how everyday products were made possible by quantum mechanics, covering the Schrödinger equation, the Heisenberg uncertainty principle, and nanoscience.

"Though the book does not quite live up to the subtitle's promise of a math-free text, readers need no more than basic algebra to accompany comic-book heroes into well-illustrated explanations of quantum packets of light energy, of the wave functions of particles, and even of the angular spin inherent in both energy and matter. These basic principles illuminate the solid-state physics of semiconductors, the atomic magnetism of MRIs, and the nanotechnology of high-capacity storage batteries. And all of this conceptual heavy lifting comes with entertaining episodes from DC Comics and H. G. Wells' fiction. Physics has never been more fun!" Booklist.

Kumar, Manjit

★**Quantum** : Einstein, Bohr, and the great debate about the nature of reality / Manjit Kumar. W.W. Norton, 2010, c2008. xvi, 448 p. : **530.12**

1. Einstein, Albert, 1879-1955. 2. Bohr, Niels Henrik David, 1885-1962. 3. Quantum theory. 4. Physics. 5. Particles (Nuclear physics) 6. Nuclear physics.
ISBN 9780393078299

Originally published: Thriplow, Cambridge, England : Icon Books, 2008.

A journey through science history closely examines the golden age of physics, focusing on the central conflict between Einstein and Bohr over the nature of reality and the soul of science.

"A staggering account of the scientific revolution that still challenges our notions of reality. Kumar evokes the passion and excitement of the period and writes with sparkling clarity and wit. Expertly delineates complex scientific issues in nontechnical language, using telling detail to weave together personal, political and scientific elements." Kirkus.

Lloyd, Seth, 1960-

★**Programming** the universe : a quantum computer scientist takes on the cosmos / Seth Lloyd. Knopf, 2006. xii, 221 p. : **530.12**

1. Quantum theory. 2. Mathematical models. 3. Microcomputers -- Programming. 4. Quantum computers.
ISBN 1400040922

LC 2005050408

Is the universe actually a giant quantum computer? According to Seth Lloyd--professor of quantum-mechanical engineering at MIT and originator of the first technologically feasible design for a working quantum computer--the answer is yes. This book illuminates the professional and personal paths that led him to this remarkable conclusion. All interactions between particles in the universe, Lloyd explains, convey not only energy but also information--in other words, particles not only collide, they compute. And what is the entire universe computing, ultimately? "Its own dynamical evolution," he says. "As the computation proceeds, reality unfolds." To elucidate his theory, Lloyd examines the history of the cosmos, posing questions that in other hands might seem unfathomably complex: How much information is there in the universe? What information existed at the moment of the Big Bang and what happened to it? How do quantum mechanics and chaos theory interact to create our world? Could we attempt to re-create it on a giant quantum computer?--From publisher description.

Parker, Barry R.

Quantum legacy : the discovery that changed our universe / Barry Parker. Prometheus Books, 2002. 282 p. : **530.12**

1. Quantum theory.
ISBN 157392993X

LC 2002067966

Looks at the scientific breakthroughs in the field of quantum physics, discussing the scientists who made important discoveries, its philosophial implications, and the practical applications of quantum theory.

Susskind, Leonard

The **black** hole war : my battle with Stephen Hawking to make the world safe for quantum mechanics / Leonard Susskind. Little, Brown, 2008. 480 p. **530.12**

1. Hawking, Stephen, 1942-2018 2. Physicists -- England 3. Quantum theory. 4. General relativity (Physics) 5. Black holes (Astronomy)
ISBN 9780316016407

LC 2007048355

Includes index.

A mind-bending book about modern physics, quantum mechanics, the fate of stars and the deep mysteries of black holes. What happens when something is sucked into a black hole? Does it disappear? Three decades ago, a young physicist named Stephen Hawking claimed it did--and in doing so put at risk everything we know about physics and the fundamental laws of the universe. Most scientists didn't recognize the import of Hawking's claims, but Leonard Susskind and Gerard t'Hooft realized the threat, and responded with a counterattack that changed the course of physics. This is the story of their united effort to reconcile Hawking's revolutionary theories with their own sense of reality--effort that would eventually result in Hawking admitting he was wrong, paying up, and Susskind and t'Hooft realizing that our world is a hologram projected from the outer boundaries of space.

"The author delves into the related and disturbingly dangerous subject of black holes. Here, he describes disagreements that he and his Dutch friend, Gerard d'Hooft, had with the famous British mathematician/physicist Stephen Hawking on his predictions regarding the interaction of objects with black holes. This book provides an anecdotal, highly readable discussion of the background to black holes and the consequences of their existence." Choice.

530.14 Field and wave theories

Close, F. E.

The **infinity** puzzle : quantum field theory and the hunt for an orderly universe / Frank Close. Basic Books, c2011. xii, 435 p. : **530.14**

1. Quantum theory. 2. Higgs bosons. 3. Infinity. 4. Particles (Nuclear physics)
ISBN 9780465021444

LC 2011022966

Many mysteries of the atom have came unraveled, but one remains intractable- what Frank Close calls the "Infinity puzzle'. The problem was simple to describe. Although clearly very powerful, quantum field theory was making one utterly ridiculous prediction: that certain events had an infinite probability of occurring. The Infinity Puzzle charts the birth and life of the idea, and the scientists, who realized it. Based on numerous firsthand interviews and extensive research, this book captures an era of great mystery and greater discovery. Even if the Higgs boson is never found, renormalization- the pursuit of an orderly universe- has led to one of the richest and most productive intellectual periods in human history.--[book jacket]

"Close offers a compelling history and sociology of modern particle theory. We discover the motivations and achievements of a rich cast of brilliant individuals, and get enough of the science to grasp what they were trying to do. Where Close really shines is in exposing the fraught process of recognition in science, focusing on key players such as Pakistani theoretical physicist Abdus Salam and the man after whom the famous boson is named, British physicist Peter Higgs." Nature.

Hawking, Stephen, 1942-2018

★The **grand** design / Stephen W. Hawking, Leonard Mlodinow. Random House Inc, 2010. 192 p. **530.14**

1. Physics. 2. Cosmology. 3. Quantum theory. 4. Evolution.
ISBN 9780553805376

LC 2010287390

The best-selling author of A Brief History of Time presents a new study of the cosmos that will blow peoples' minds, presented in clear, concise language this is easy to understand.

Rovelli, Carlo, 1956-

Reality is not what it seems : the elementary structure of things / Carlo Rovelli ; translated by Simon Carnell and Erica Segre. Riverhead Books, an imprint of Penguin Random House LLC, 2017. 256 p. **530.14**

1. Physics 2. Gravity 3. Space-time 4. Quantum gravity.
ISBN 9780735213920

LC 2016036293

Originally published in Italian under the title: La Realta non e come ci appare.

English translation published in Great Britain by Allen Lane, an imprint of Penguin Random House UK.

The theoretical physicist author of the best-selling Seven Brief Lessons on Physics traces how the human image of the world has changed throughout history, demonstrating the evolution of the idea of reality while touching on subjects ranging from the Higgs boson to quantum gravity.

"Rovelli's work is challenging, but his excitement is contagious and he delights in the possibilities of human understanding." Publishers Weekly.

Smolin, Lee, 1955-

The **trouble** with physics : the rise of string theory, the fall of a science, and what comes next / Lee Smolin. Houghton Mifflin, c2006. xxiii, 392 p. ; **530.14**

1. Physics -- Methodology -- History -- 20th century. 2. String theory

(Nuclear physics) 3. Cosmology 4. Quantum theory
ISBN 0618551050

LC 2006007235

A theoretical physicist describes the evolution of modern-day string theory, the flaws in the attempt to formulate a "theory of everything" to explain all the forces and particles of nature and the origins of the universe, and their repercussions for physics.

"This is a well-written, critical profile of the theoretical physics community, free of equations, from the perspective of a member." Library Journal.

530.4 States of matter

Miodownik, Mark

Liquid rules : the delightful and dangerous substances that flow through our lives / Mark Miodownik. Houghton Mifflin Harcourt, 2019. 288 p. **530.4**

1. Liquids -- Popular works. 2. Matter -- Properties -- Popular works. 3. Science -- Popular works. 4. Materials science.
ISBN 9780544850194

LC 2018024866

Originally published in Great Britain by Penguin Books, 2018.

Sometimes explosive, often delicious, occasionally poisonous, but always interesting: the New York Times-bestselling author of Stuff Matters shows us the secret lives of liquids: the shadow counterpart of our solid "stuff."

"n this informative, casual narrative, Miodownik (Stuff Matters), a science professor at University College London, gives a guided tour of the strange, wondrous liquids that flow through everyday life." Publishers Weekly.

530.8 Measurement

Barrow, John D., 1952-

The **constants** of nature : from Alpha to Omega--the numbers that encode the deepest secrets of the universe / John D. Barrow. Pantheon Books, c2002. xv, 352 p. : **530.8**

1. Physical constants
ISBN 0375422218

LC 2002075975

A leading physicist and author of Theories of Everything describes what the constants of nature--the numbers that define the universe--tell us about the inner workings of the world around us and reveals how, despite our expertise at measuring the values of such constants, we cannot explain or predict them.

"Barrow traces scientists' evolving understanding of natural constants, like the speed of light, in this erudite and enthralling work of popular science." Publishers Weekly.

531 Classical mechanics

Chown, Marcus

The **ascent** of gravity : the quest to understand the force that explains everything / Marcus Chown. Pegasus Books, 2017. 256 p. **531**

1. Gravity 2. Cosmogony. 3. Physics 4. Space-time
ISBN 9781681775371

LC bl2017037487

Explains why gravity holds the key to understanding the nature of time and the origin of the universe.

"Adults and teens interested in science history and exciting new physics and astronomy discoveries will thoroughly enjoy." Library Journal.

Panek, Richard

The **trouble** with gravity : solving the mystery beneath our feet / Richard Panek. Houghton Mifflin Harcourt, 2019. 320 p. **531**

1. Gravity. 2. Mass (Physics) 3. Physics. 4. Gravitational waves
ISBN 9780544526747

LC 2018057178

An award-winning science writer traces our millennia-long effort to understand the phenomenon of gravity--the greatest mystery in physics, and a force that has shaped our universe and our minds in ways we have never fully understood until now.

"Teen and adult readers interested in better understanding the force of gravity and gaining insight into humanity's expanding knowledge of the universe will find this highly recommended book to be both accessible and enjoyable." Library Journal.

535 Light and related radiation

Ball, Philip, 1962-

Invisible : the dangerous allure of the unseen / Philip Ball. The University of Chicago Press, 2015. 256 p. ; **535**

1. Invisibility. 2. Human nature. 3. Science -- Moral and ethical aspects. 4. Ethics.
ISBN 9780226238890

LC 2014035709

"If offered the chance--by cloak, spell, or superpower--to be invisible, who wouldn't want to give it a try? We are drawn to the idea of stealthy voyeurism and the ability to conceal our own acts, but as desirable as it may seem, invisibility is also dangerous. It is not just an optical phenomenon, but a condition full of ethical questions. As esteemed science writer Philip Ball reveals in this book, the story of invisibility is not so much a matter of how it might be achieved but of why we want it and what we would do with it."--Publisher's description

Pendergrast, Mark

Mirror mirror : a history of the human love affair with reflection / Mark Pendergrast. Basic Books, 2004. xii, 404 p. : **535**

1. Mirrors -- History. 2. Reflection (Optics) 3. Reflecting telescopes.
ISBN 0465054714

LC 2003002544

"Those with a historical and scientific bent may profitably read this book for insight into the manufacture of mirrors--along with descendents the telescope and microscope--down through the ages. Whether for pleasure or profit, this well-written, entertaining book, packed with historical information, should be read!" Choice.

535.6 Color

Eckstut, Arielle

The **secret** language of color : science, nature, history, culture, beauty and joy of red, orange, yellow, green, blue, and violet / Arielle Eckstut and Joann Eckstut. Black Dog & Leventhal Pub,

2013. 240 p. : **535.6**
1. Color 2. Color in nature 3. Brain 4. Light
ISBN 9781579129491
LC bl2013047954

"The book's dynamic design and short entries make it easy to skim, but it's likely that those intending just a casual perusal will find themselves engrossed by this terrifically entertaining and informative volume." Publishers Weekly.

536 Heat

Shachtman, Tom, 1942-
Absolute zero and the conquest of cold / Tom Shachtman. Houghton Mifflin Co., 1999. 261 p. ; **536**
1. Low temperatures -- Research. 2. Thermometers -- History. 3. Air conditioning -- History. 4. Physics -- Experiments. 5. London, England -- History -- 16th century 6. Europe -- History 7. United States -- History
ISBN 0395938880
LC 99033305

The history of "cold" covers the wide gamut of scientific inquiry into the subject, from the invention of the thermometer to the "air conditioning" of Westminster Abbey in the sixteenth century, to the latest revelations from the field of physics.

"The author analyzes the social impact of the chill factor, explains the science of cold and tells the curious tales behind inventions like the thermometer, the fridge and the thermos flask." New York Times Book Review.

537 Electricity and electronics

Bodanis, David
Electric universe : the shocking true story of electricity / David Bodanis. Crown Publishers, 2005. 308 p. **537**
1. Electricity. 2. Force. 3. Energy. 4. Electrons.
ISBN 1400045509
LC 2004011275

Royal Society General Prizes for Science Books, 2006.

"As a storyteller, author David Bodanis is wonderful. This book is directed at a general audience, but it should be required reading for all scientific professionals." Science Books & Films.

538 Magnetism

Mitchell, Alanna
The **spinning** magnet : the force that created the modern world--and could destroy it / Alanna Mitchell. Dutton, 2018. 304 p. **538**
1. Electromagnetism. 2. Magnetism 3. Geomagnetism. 4. Solar radiation -- Health aspects. 5. Earth -- Mantle
ISBN 9781101985168
LC 2017034554

A prize-winning science journalist narrates the history of electromagnetism and discusses how the earth's magnetic force field is eroding 10 times faster than previously believed, which will result in pole reversal and seriously dire consequences for modern technology.

"This immersion in magnetism is an invaluable contribution to the popular science shelf." Booklist.

539.2 Radiation (Radiant energy)

Blatner, David
Spectrums : our mindboggling universe from infinitesimal to infinity / David Blatner. Walker & Co., c2012. 192 p. **539.2**
1. Spectrum analysis. 2. Science.
ISBN 9780802717702
LC 2012010727

"In Spectrums, David Blatner blends narrative and illustration to illuminate the variety of spectrums that affect our lives every day: numbers, size, light, sound, heat, and time. There is actually very little in this universe that we can feel, touch, see, hear, or possibly even comprehend. It's not an easy task to stretch the mind to encompass both billions of years and billionths of seconds; the distance to Jupiter and the size of a proton; the tiny waves of visible light and gargantuan but invisible gamma rays; or the freezing point of Helium and the heat generated by the blast of an atom bomb. Exploring these far-reaching spectrums gives us fascinating perspective on our small but not insignificant place in the universe. With easy-to-read, engaging, and insightful observations, illustrated by a wealth of photographs and diagrams, Blatner helps us "grok"--understand intuitively--six spectrums we encounter constantly, making our daily lives richer and more meaningful through greater appreciation of thebizarre and beautiful world in which we live".-- Provided by publisher.

Jorgensen, Timothy J.
Strange glow : the story of radiation / Timothy J. Jorgensen. Princeton University Press, 2016. 496 p. **539.2**
1. Radiation 2. Radiation victims 3. Health
ISBN 9780691165035
LC bl2016006701

Blends narrative history and current science to explore humanity's challenging relationship with radiation, tracing how it helps and harms health and how lessons from the past century can help people make more informed decisions about today's exposures.

"Jorgensen's easy-to-follow and enthusiastic style will appeal to readers who are interested in the study of radiation yet have plenty of time on their hands to get to the information they seek." Library Journal.

539.7 Atomic and nuclear physics

Aczel, Amir D.
Present at the creation : the story of CERN and the large hadron collider / Amir Aczel. Crown Publishers/Harmony Books, c2010. xvi, 271 p., 8 p. of plates : **539.7**
1. European Organization for Nuclear Research. 2. Colliders (Nuclear physics) 3. Large Hadron Collider (France and Switzerland)
ISBN 0307591670
LC 2010014835

Documents the large-scale 2008 experiment to determine the origins of the universe using the world's most powerful particle accelerator, an effort designed to help the scientific community to test the validity of key theories in physics and cosmology.

"Aczel has produced an excellent review of past, current, and possible future theories of particle physics and how they relate to the field of cosmology. He uses the Large Hadron Collider (LHC), the most energetic particle accelerator ever built, as a focal point for a discussion of these theories." Choice.

Butterworth, Jon
Atom land : a guided tour through the strange and impossibly

small world of particle physics / Jon Butterworth. The Experiment, 2018. xvi, 284 pages : **539.7**

1. Particles (Nuclear physics) 2. Nuclear physics 3. Physics 4. Dark matter (Astronomy)
ISBN 9781615193738

LC 2017052472

From a top physicist at CERN, the first guide to the fundamental units of matter and the forces that act on them--particle physics--since the discovery of the Higgs boson, the missing piece of the Standard Model, leading the reader from basic concepts to the cutting edge.

Carroll, Sean B.

The **particle** at the end of the universe : how the hunt for the Higgs Boson leads us to the edge of a new world / Sean Carroll. Dutton, c2012. x, 341 p., [16] p. of plates : **539.7**

1. Higgs bosons. 2. Particles (Nuclear physics) 3. Mass (Physics) 4. Dark matter (Astronomy)
ISBN 9780525953593
Royal Society General Prizes for Science Books, 2013.

Examines the effort to discover the Higgs boson particle by tracing the development and use of the Large Hadron Collider and how its findings are dramatically shaping scientific understandings while enabling world-changing innovations.

Challoner, Jack

The **atom** : a visual tour / Jack Challoner. The MIT Press, 2018. 192 p. **539.7**

1. Atoms 2. Matter -- Constitution 3. Nuclear physics 4. Physical chemistry
ISBN 9780262037365

LC bl2019032384

Illustrated in full-color, an accessible and engaging guide investigates the quest to identify the smallest, most fundamental constituents of matter--and how that quest helps us to understand what everything is made of and how it all works.

Goldberg, Dave, 1974-

The **universe** in the rearview mirror : how hidden symmetries shape reality / Dave Goldberg. Dutton, 2013. 336 p. **539.7**

1. Symmetry (Physics) 2. Reality. 3. Physics. 4. Physics -- Philosophy.
ISBN 9780525953661

LC 2013016178

The "Ask a Physicist" columnist for io9.com explains how space, time, and everything in between are shaped by hidden symmetries that have driven recent discoveries about the universe.

"An informative, math-free, and completely entertaining look at the concept of symmetry in physics." Publishers Weekly.

Greene, B. (Brian), 1963-

★The **elegant** universe : superstrings, hidden dimensions, and the quest for the ultimate theory / Brian Greene. W. W. Norton, 1999. xiii, 448 p. : **539.7**

1. Superstring theories. 2. Cosmology. 3. Relativity (Physics) 4. Quantum theory.
ISBN 9780393046885

LC 98025695

ALA Notable Book, 2000.
Royal Society General Prizes for Science Books, 2000.
Pulitzer Prize for General Nonfiction finalist

"[Greene] develops one fresh new insight after another ... In the great tradition of physicists writing for the masses, The elegant universe sets a standard that will be hard to beat."

"The author makes the terribly complex theory of strings accessible to all. He possesses a remarkable gift for using the everyday to illustrate what may be going on in dimensions beyond our feeble human perception." Publishers Weekly.

Lederman, Leon M.

Beyond the god particle / Leon M. Lederman, Christopher T. Hill. Prometheus Books, 2013, c1993. 340 p. **539.7**

1. Higgs bosons. 2. Particles (Nuclear physics). 3. Matter -- Constitution. 4. Nuclear physics
ISBN 9781616148010

LC 2013022346

Originally published in 1993

Two leading physicists discuss the importance of the Higgs Boson, the future of particle physics, and the mysteries of the universe yet to be unraveled.

Levin, Janna

Black hole blues : and other songs from outer space / Janna Levin. Alfred A. Knopf, 2016. 241 p. ; **539.7**

1. Gravitational waves 2. Black holes (Astronomy) 3. Astronomy
ISBN 9780307958198

LC 2015046692

Recounts the fifty-year search for gravitational waves, explaining how the waves are created in the collision of black holes and why they can never be detected by telescope, and profiles four scientists currently engaged in the quest.

"A superb alignment of author and subject: Levin is among the best contemporary science writers, and LIGO is arguably the most compelling experiment on the planet." Kirkus.

Lincoln, Don

The **Large** Hadron Collider : the extraordinary story of the Higgs boson and other stuff that will blow your mind / Don Lincoln. Johns Hopkins University Press, 2014. 240 p. **539.7**

1. Higgs bosons. 2. Large Hadron Collider (France and Switzerland) 3. Mass (Physics) 4. Quantum theory.
ISBN 9781421413518

LC 2013040921

Sequel to: The quantum frontier : the Large Hadron Collider

The Large Hadron Collider (or what scientists call "the LHC") is one of the wonders of the modern world - a highly sophisticated scientific instrument designed to recreate in miniature the conditions of the universe as they existed in the microseconds following the big bang. Among many notable LHC discoveries, one led to the 2013 Nobel Prize in Physics for revealing evidence of the existence of the Higgs boson, the so-called God particle. Picking up where he left off in The Quantum Frontier, physicist Don Lincoln shares an insider's account of the LHC's operational history and gives readers everything they need to become well informed on this marvel of technology.

"Readers will be fascinated by the projects sheer mechanical challenges and the failure that caused it to be shut down and rebuilt before being operated at its design power. This engaging story will be appreciated by readers interested in the frontiers of science. Summing Up: Highly recommended. All levels/libraries." Choice.

Malley, Marjorie Caroline, 1941-

Radioactivity : a history of a mysterious science / Marjorie

C. Malley. Oxford University Press, 2011. 288 p. **539.7**

1. Radioactivity. 2. Nuclear physics. 3. Physics.
ISBN 9780199766413

LC 2010038979

This is the story of a new science. Beginning with an obscure discovery in 1896, radioactivity led researchers on a quest for understanding that ultimately confronted the intersection of knowledge and mystery. --From publisher description.

"Malley does a wonderful job of demonstrating how scientific discovery functions, as opposed to the usual approach in which facts and figures are given as tidbits along a chronology." Library Journal.

Nelson, Craig, 1955-

The **age** of radiance : the epic rise and dramatic fall of the atomic era / Craig Nelson. Scribner, 2014. 416 p. **539.7**

1. Radioactivity -- History. 2. Nuclear weapons development. 3. Nuclear power -- History. 4. Nuclear weapons -- History.
ISBN 9781451660432

LC 2013042192

A narrative of the Atomic Age by the award-winning author of Rocket Man explores the complexities of nuclear energy, citing the contributions of such individuals as Marie Curie, Albert Einstein and Robert Oppenheimer while sharing lesser-known historical details.

"An engaging history that raises provocative questions about the future of nuclear science." Kirkus.

Randall, Lisa

Higgs discovery : the power of empty space / Lisa Randall. Ecco Solo, 2013 99 p. : **539.7**

1. Higgs bosons.
ISBN 0062300474

LC 2015300802

"On July 4, 2012, physicists at the Large Hadron Collider in Geneva made history when they discovered an entirely new type of subatomic particle that many scientists believe is the Higgs boson. For forty years, physicists searched for this capstone to the Standard Model of particle physics--the theory that describes both the most elementary components that are known in matter and the forces through which they interact. This particle points to the Higgs field, which provides the key to understanding why elementary particles have mass."-- Page 4 of cover.

Seife, Charles

Sun in a bottle : the strange history of fusion and the science of wishful thinking / Charles Seife. Viking, 2008. vi, 294 p. : **539.7**

1. Nuclear fusion -- History. 2. Fusion reactors. 3. Nuclear reactors -- History 4. Physics -- Research -- United States -- History 5. United States -- History -- 20th century
ISBN 9780670020331

LC 2008013135

Chronicles the last half century's haphazard attempt to harness fusion energy, describing how governments and research teams throughout the world have employed measures ranging from the controversial to the humorous.

Stewart, Ian, 1945-

Why beauty is truth : a history of symmetry / Ian Stewart. Basic Books, 2007. xiii, 290 p. **539.7**

1. Symmetry (Art) -- History. 2. Symmetry (Biology) -- History. 3. Mathematics.
ISBN 9780465082360

LC 2006038274

The renowned mathematician traces the history of the concept of symmetry, from the early Babylonians' efforts to solve quadratics to today's theoretical physics, citing the achievements of the mathematicians behind key discoveries.

"Beginning with the early struggles of the Babylonians to solve quadratics, Stewart guides his readers through the often-tangled history of symmetry, illuminating for nonspecialists how a concept easily recognized in geometry acquired new meanings in algebra. . . . An exciting foray for any armchair physicist!" Booklist.

Still, Ben

Particle physics brick by brick : atomic and subatomic physics explained... in Lego / Dr. Ben Still. Firefly Books, 2018. 176 p. **539.7**

1. Physics 2. Particles (Nuclear physics) 3. LEGO toys 4. Quantum theory
ISBN 9780228100126

LC bl2018197504

Includes index.

Particle Physics Brick by Brick is a succinct introduction for anyone that wants to gain a basic understanding of the atomic world, its elements and how they interact. By using tangible substitutes -- bricks -- it brings the unseen atomic world into the realm of the visual.

540 Science -- Chemistry -- Chemistry and allied sciences

Bruno, Thomas J,

CRC handbook of chemistry and physics : a ready-reference book of chemical and physical data / editor-in-chief, W.M. Haynes, Ph.D. Scientist Emeritus, National Institute of Standards and Technology ; associate editors, David R. Lide, Ph.D. Former Director, standard reference data, National Institute of Standards and Technology, Thomas J. Bruno, Ph.D. Former Director, National Institute of Standards and Technology. CRC Press, 2014 1 volume (various pagings) : **540**

1. Chemistry 2. Physics
ISBN 9781482208672

LC bl2014027850

Proudly serving the scientific community for over a century, this 95th edition of the CRC Handbook of Chemistry and Physics is an update of a classic reference, mirroring the growth and direction of science. This venerable work continues to be the most accessed and respected scientific reference in the world. An authoritative resource consisting of tables of data and current international recommendations on nomenclature, symbols, and units, its usefulness spans not only the physical sciences but also related areas of biology, geology, and environmental science. --From publisher description.

Cobb, Cathy

The **joy** of chemistry : the amazing science of familiar things / Cathy Cobb & Monty L. Fetterolf. Prometheus Books, 2005. 393 p. : **540**

1. Chemistry -- Experiments 2. Organic chemistry. 3. Inorganic chemistry. 4. Analytical chemistry.
ISBN 1591022312

LC 2004020144

"The authors cover the material of a general chemistry course along with organic, inorganic and analytical chemistry and biochemistry; there's even a chapter on forensic chemistry. . . . They explain everything from flatulence (the chemical composition of intestinal gas) to pizza cheese (why mozzarella rather than, say, parmesan?)." Publishers Weekly.

Coffey, Patrick
Cathedrals of science : the personalities and rivalries that made modern chemistry / Patrick Coffey. Oxford University Press, 2008. xix, 379 p. : **540**

1. Langmuir, Irving, 1881-1957. 2. Lewis, Gilbert Newton, 1875-1946. 3. Chemistry -- History -- 20th century. 4. Scientific discoveries 5. Chemical weapons. 6. Chemists -- Psychology.
ISBN 9780195321340

A history of modern chemistry discusses the development of the field, the battles for credit, the arguments over results, personal likes and antipathies and, the quest for the Nobel Prize.

540.9 Chemistry--history

Cobb, Cathy
Creations of fire : chemistry's lively history from alchemy to the atomic age / Cathy Cobb and Harold Goldwhite. Perseus Pub., 2001 xvi, 475 p. : **540.9**

1. Chemistry -- History
ISBN 9780738205946

LC 2001099001

Originally published: New York : Plenum Press, c1995.

In this fascinating history, Cathy Cobb and Harold Goldwhite celebrate not only chemistry's theories and breakthroughs but also the provocative times and personalities that shaped this amazing science and brought it to life. Throughout the book, the reader will meet the hedonists and swindlers, monks and heretics, and men and women laboring in garages and over kitchen sinks who expanded our understanding of the elements and discovered such new substances as plastic, rubber, and aspirin. Creations of Fire expands our vision of the meaning of chemistry and reveals the oddballs and academics who have helped shape our world. --From publisher description.

Greenberg, Arthur
From alchemy to chemistry in picture and story / Arthur Greenberg. Wiley-Interscience, c2007. xxiii, 637 p., 24 p. of plates : **540.9**

1. Chemistry 2. Chemistry -- History.
ISBN 9780471751540

LC 2006033564

"According to the author, this is a combination of his two previous books, A Chemical History Tour and The Art of Chemistry, with some additions and revisions. One could open the book at almost any page to learn something about the remarkable history of the chemical sciences." Science Books & Films.

541 Physical chemistry

Atkins, P.W. (Peter William), 1940-
Reactions : the private life of atoms / Peter Atkins. Oxford University Press, 2011. viii, 191 p. : **541**

1. Chemical reactions. 2. Atoms. 3. Molecules. 4. Matter.
ISBN 9780199695126
Includes index.

Explains how different kinds of chemical reactions ranging from precipitation and combustion to polymerization and catalysis are formed, including examples, color illustrations, and real-life applications for each reaction.

Gray, Theodore W.
Molecules : the elements and the architecture of everything / Theodore Gray. Black Dog & Leventhal Publishers, 2014 240 p. **541**

1. Molecules. 2. Organic compounds. 3. Inorganic compounds.
ISBN 9781579129712

LC bl2014050626

"Readers who wish to learn more about chemistry would be better served with another work that isn't so strongly focused on photography. Those already familiar with the topic are sure to enjoy the images." Library Journal.

546 Inorganic chemistry

Aldersey-Williams, Hugh
Periodic tales : a cultural history of the elements, from arsenic to zinc / Hugh Aldersey-Williams. Ecco, 2011. 428 p. **546**

1. Periodic law -- History. 2. Chemical elements -- History. 3. Scientific discoveries 4. Science
ISBN 9780061824722

LC 2011009864

"In the spirit of A SHORT HISTORY OF NEARLY EVERYTHING, an energetic and wide-ranging book of discovery and discoverers, of exploitation and celebration, and of superstition and science, all in search of the ways the chemical elements are woven into our culture, history, and language".-- Provided by publisher.

"Because Aldersey-Williams's ultimate subject is human civilization rather than simply the elements, he gives himself room to expound on just about everything, treating the components of the table as though they were sorted by an anthropologist. So his book is organized (loosely) into five sections: power (elements hoarded as riches or used to exert control); fire (elements that can best be understood by what happens when they are burned); craft (elements used to create and the cultural meaning we ascribe to them); beauty (elements used to colour our world); and earth (elements that have marked the place where they were discovered in a notable way). It's an ambitious project. [The book] is swollen with names, places, and long-forgotten (or simply unknown to most of us) figures, with zigzagging detours into almost every subject imaginable. It is almost more of a question of what the book does not touch upon than what it does." Boston Globe.

Bernstein, Jeremy, 1929-
Plutonium : a history of the world's most dangerous element / Jeremy Bernstein. Joseph Henry Press, c2007. x, 194 p., 8 p. of plates : **546**

1. Plutonium -- History. 2. Chemical elements. 3. Chemistry. 4. Chemicals.
ISBN 9780309102964

LC 2006038466

"This historical record of the growth of chemistry and its effect on history is suitable for public and academic libraries." Library Journal.

Challoner, Jack
The **elements** : the new guide to the building blocks of our universe / Jack Challoner. Carlton Books, 2012. 160 p. : **546**

1. Chemical elements 2. Chemical elements. 3. Periodic law.
ISBN 1780971257

LC bl2013000870

Includes index.

Presents photographic representations of the one hundred and eighteen elements in the period table, along with facts, figures and stories about each one.

Chapman, Kit, (Science journalist)

Superheavy : making and breaking the periodic table / Kit Chapman. Bloomsbury Sigma, 2019. 304 p. **546**

1. Chemical elements 2. Atoms 3. Atomic theory 4. Physical chemistry

ISBN 9781472953896

LC bl2019024639

The science of element discovery is a truly fascinating field, and is constantly rewriting the laws of chemistry and physics as we know them. Superheavy is the first book to take an in-depth look at how synthetic elements are discovered, why they matter and where they will take us. From the Cold War nuclear race to the present day, scientists have stretched the periodic table to 118 elements. They have broken the rules of the periodic table, rewriting the science we're taught in school, and have the potential to revolutionize our lives.

"This is a must-read for anyone interested in how humans have expanded, and continue to expand, the boundaries of scientific knowledge." Publishers Weekly.

Gray, Theodore W.

★The **elements** : a visual exploration of every known atom in the universe / Theodore Gray ; photographs by Theodore Gray and Nick Mann. Black Dog & Leventhal Publishers, c2009. 240 p. **546**

1. Chemical elements 2. Atoms 3. Periodic law 4. Chemistry.

ISBN 9781579128142

LC 2009034931

"This gorgeously photographed guide to the elements can be used as a visual reference, but its brief entries are packed with intriguing tidbits that also make it a fascinating read." Library Journal.

Kean, Sam

★The **disappearing** spoon : and other true tales of madness, love, and the history of the world from the periodic table of the elements / Sam Kean. Little, Brown and Co., 2010. vi, 391 p.: **546**

1. Periodic law. 2. Chemical elements. 3. Chemistry. 4. Carbon.

ISBN 9780316051644

LC 2009040754

The periodic table of the elements is a crowning scientific achievement, but it's also a treasure trove of passion, adventure, obsession, and betrayal. These tales follow carbon, neon, silicon, gold, and all the elements in the table as they play out their parts in human history.

"With the anecdotal flourishes of Oliver Sacks and the populist accessibility of Malcolm Gladwell, but without the latter's occasional facileness, he makes even the most abstract concepts graspable for armchair scientists. His keen sense of humor is a particular pleasure." Entertainment Weekly.

Rigden, John S.

Hydrogen : the essential element / John S. Rigden. Harvard University Press, 2002. 280 p. : **546**

1. Hydrogen. 2. Science -- Methodology.

ISBN 0674007387

LC 2001051708

"The author chronicles how one enduring conundrum--that of explaining the element hydrogen--has challenged two centuries of brilliant scientists. In the process, he clarifies for general readers the nature of the scientific enterprise, in which elegant theories must meet the test of empirical verification." Booklist.

Zoellner, Tom

Uranium : war, energy, and the rock that shaped the world / Tom Zoellner. Viking, 2009. 352 p. **546**

1. Uranium. 2. Radioactive materials. 3. Nuclear weapons -- History. 4. Nuclear warfare.

ISBN 9780670020645

LC 2008029023

A history of the powerful mineral element explores its role as a virtually limitless energy source, its controversial applications as a healing tool and weapon, and the ways in which its reputation has been used to promote war agendas in the Middle East.

547 Organic chemistry

Gorman, Hugh S. (Hugh Scott), 1957-

The **story** of N : a social history of the nitrogen cycle and the challenge of sustainability / Hugh S. Gorman. Rutgers University Press, c2013. xiii, 241 p. ; **547**

1. Nitrogen -- Environmental aspects 2. Nitrogen cycle 3. Sustainable development 4. Nature -- Effect of human beings on

ISBN 9780813554389

LC 2012009901

In The Story of N, Hugh S. Gorman analyzes the notion of sustainability from a fresh perspective--the integration of human activities with the biogeochemical cycling of nitrogen--and provides a supportive alternative to studying sustainability through the lens of climate change and the cycling of carbon. It is the first book to examine the social processes by which industrial societies learned to bypass a fundamental ecological limit and, later, began addressing the resulting concerns by establishing limits of their own. --From publisher description.

"A well-written, well-documented, and fascinating work, accessible to laypersons and useful to students and professionals." Choice.

549 Mineralogy

Johnsen, Ole

Minerals of the world / Ole Johnsen. Princeton University Press, c2002. 439 p. : **549**

1. Crystallography. 2. Mineralogy. 3. Minerals.

ISBN 069109537X

LC 2001097695

Includes index.

Originally published as: Mineralernes verden. København : Gads Forlag, 2000.

Describes more than five hundred minerals, providing such information as the mineral's crystallography, chemical properties, occurence, and names and varieties.

"The author provides descriptive information for the identification of more than 500 minerals. This book follows the standard mineralogy textbook approach in which the mineral sections are arranged according to mineral composition and structure. The book's suitability as a field guide is completed by the addition of hundreds of excellent color photographs and drawings. The content material is solid, and superb illustrations on high-quality paper make for an attractive volume." Choice.

Klein, Cornelis, 1937-

The **23rd** edition of the manual of mineral science : (after

James D. Dana) / Cornelis Klein, Barbara Dutrow. J. Wiley, c2008. xxi, 675 p. : **549**

1. Mineralogy
ISBN 9780471721574

LC 2007273750

Rev. ed. of: Manual of mineralogy. 21st ed., rev. c1999.

The classic in the field since 1848, this extraordinary reference offers readers unsurpassed coverage of mineralogy and crystallography. The book is known for integrating complete coverage of concepts and principles with a more systematic and descriptive treatment of mineralogy. The revised edition now includes a CD-ROM to let readers see the minerals and crystals, while also viewing chemical composition, symmetry, and morphological crystallography. --From publisher description.

Pellant, Chris

Rocks and minerals : a photographic field guide / Chris and Helen Pellant. Bloomsbury, 2014. 192 p. : **549**

1. Minerals 2. Rocks
ISBN 1472909933

LC bl2015024195

A field guide to identifying rocks and minerals provides information on their formation, classification, main characteristics, and economic uses and includes photographs showcasing examples from around the world.

"Students, nature photographers, and budding geologists will find this book both easy to use and highly informative." Library Journal.

Pough, Frederick H.

★A **field** guide to rocks and minerals / Frederick H. Pough, photographs by Jeffrey Scovil. Houghton Mifflin, 1996. xv, 396 p. : The Peterson field guide series ; **549**

1. Mineralogy, Determinative 2. Rocks
ISBN 9780395910962

LC 94049005

"Sponsored by the National Audubon Society, the National Wildlife Federation, and the Roger Tory Peterson Institute."

Describes hundreds of minerals and lists their geographic distribution, physical properties, chemical composition, and crystalline structure

Sofianides, Anna S.

Gems & crystals from one of the world's great collections / George E. Harlow, curator of gems and minerals, American Museum of Natural History, and Anna S Sofianides ; photographs by Erica and Harold Van Pelt. Sterling Signature, 2015 xiii, 215 p. : **549**

1. American Museum of Natural -- History Catalogs. 2. Minerals 3. Precious stones
ISBN 9781454917113

LC bl2015046321

At head of title: American Museum of Natural History.

Discusses the properties, history, lore, and sources of gems and crystals in the collection of the American Museum of Natural History.

549.09 Minerals -- History, geographic treatment, biography

Chaline, Eric

Fifty minerals that changed the course of history / written by Eric Chaline. Firefly Books, 2012. 223 p. : **549.09**

1. Civilization -- History. 2. Minerals -- History. 3. Minerals -- Social aspects.
ISBN 1554079845

LC bl2012029533

A guide to fifty metals, alloys, rocks, and organic minerals that have impacted history discusses the use of plutonium to power the Voyager space probes and the possiblity that Napoleon was poisoned by wallpaper containing arsenic.

550 Science -- Earth sciences & geology -- Earth sciences

Alvarez, Walter, 1940-

A **most** improbable journey : a big history of our planet and ourselves / Walter Alvarez. W W Norton & Company, 2016 288 p. **550**

1. Science -- History. 2. Human evolution.
ISBN 9780393292695

LC 2016022704

Famed geologist Walter Alvarez expands our view of human history by revealing the cosmic, geologic, and evolutionary forces that have shaped us.

Childs, Craig

Apocalyptic planet : field guide to the everending Earth / Craig Childs. Pantheon Books, c2012. 352 p. **550**

1. Regeneration (Biology) 2. Geology. 3. Earth -- History.
ISBN 9780307379092

LC 2012006012

An award-winning commentator for NPR's Morning Edition discusses the planet's inherent instability and susceptibility toward violent natural disasters and climate extremes, challenging beliefs about apocalyptic inevitabilities while revealing how to change humanity's place within the planet's cycles.

Hazen, Robert M., 1948-

★The **story** of Earth : the first 4.5 billion years, from stardust to living planet / Robert M. Hazen. Viking, 2012. 320 p. **550**

1. Planets. 2. Geology. 3. Evolution. 4. Earth.
ISBN 9780670023554

LC 2011043713

Includes index.

The author of the best-selling Science Matters outlines a radical new approach to geologic history that advances controversial theories that the Earth evolved and that life evolved from minerals, assessing supportive findings while explaining the impact of human actions.

"This is a thoroughly accessible book, deftly mixing a variety of scientific disciplines to tell an unforgettable story." Publishers Weekly.

Lambert, David, 1932-

The **field** guide to geology / David Lambert and the Diagram Group. Facts on File, c2007. 304 p. : **550**

1. Geology.
ISBN 0816065101

LC 2006048533

Rev. ed. of: The field guide to geology. Updated ed. c1998.

An updated title provides information on earth's origin, the shaping of the continents, the forming of rocks, erosion, earth's geological history, and the impact of the oceans and rivers.

Luhr, James F,

★**Earth** : the definitive visual guide / editors-in-chief, James F. Luhr and Jeffrey E. Post. DK Publishing, 2013. 528 p.

: 550

1. Earth.
ISBN 9781465414373

LC bl2013035792

At head of title: Smithsonian.
Includes index.

Featuring specially commissioned 3-D digital artwork, this ultimate guide to our planet describes more than 400 of the Earth's most fascinating features, explains the scientific processes that govern our world, and examines the complex relationship between humans and the natural environment.

Scigliano, Eric, 1953-

The **big** thaw : ancient carbon, modern science, and a race to save the world / Eric Scigliano with Dr. Robert Max Holmes, Dr. Susan Natali, and Dr. John Schade ; photography by Chris Linder ; epilogue by Theodore Roosevelt IV. Braided River, 2019. 163 p. : **550**

1. Climate change -- Arctic regions 2. Global warming 3. Carbon 4. Ice 5. Arctic regions
ISBN 9781680512472

LC 2019015089

"The book demonstrates the demanding activity of collecting data that is an antidote to the depression and helplessness many feel in the face of climate change. In its splendid design, well-written text, and revealing photos of the Arctic world and those who probe the impact of thawing permafrost on the climate, this book perfectly captures this critical issue and those who are meeting the challenge. This wondrous and timely work--featuring stunning photos--explores a crucial environmental problem that endangers the planet." Kirkus.

551 Geology, hydrology, meteorology

Flannery, Tim F. (Tim Fridtjof), 1956-

Here on Earth : a natural history of the planet / Tim Flannery. Atlantic Monthly Press, 2011, c2010. xviii, 316 p., 8 p. of plates (some col.) : **551**

1. Climate and civilization. 2. Sustainable societies. 3. Social evolution. 4. Evolution -- History. 5. Earth -- History.
ISBN 9780802119766

LC bl2011005925

Originally published: Melbourne : Text Publishing, 2010.

"The author expands on the proposition that humans inherently exhaust their resources, triggering all manner of ecological and societal trauma. To evaluate the idea, he ranges over the entirety of human existence, remarking within each subtopic he raises--for example, the Aborigines' relation to Australian ecosystems--the ramifications of human use of available natural resources." Booklist.

551.1 Gross structure and properties of the earth

Whitehouse, David

Into the heart of our world : a journey to the center of the Earth: a remarkable voyage of scientific discovery / David Whitehouse. Pegasus Books, 2016 288 p. **551.1**

1. Geology. 2. Geological expeditions. 3. Physical sciences. 4. Earth sciences. 5. Earth.
ISBN 9781605989594

A vivid exploration of the mysteries of the deep Earth profiles the latest discoveries and what they reveal about the planet's history, sharing engaging coverage of such topics as the disciplines of seismology, the planet's vast subterranean subcontinents and the connection between surface conditions and core phenomena.

551.2 Volcanoes, earthquakes, thermal waters and gases

Dvorak, John (John J.)

Earthquake storms : the fascinating history and volatile future of the San Andreas Fault / John Dvorak. Pegasus Books, 2014. xviii, 254 p. : **551.2**

1. Earthquakes -- California -- History. 2. Earthquakes -- California. 3. San Andreas Fault (Calif.) 4. San Andreas Fault (Calif.) -- History.
ISBN 1605984957

LC bl2014002537

Includes index.

A prominent geologist explains why the San Andreas Fault is ready for a colossal earthquake and how the network of subsidiaries it has created can wreak havoc on the highways, interstates and housing developments not directly on the Fault.

"Although almost entirely focused on California, this is a fine popular primer on the subject, lucidly written and no more technical than necessary." Kirkus.

Gates, Alexander E., 1957-

★**Encyclopedia** of earthquakes and volcanoes / Alexander E. Gates and David Ritchie. Checkmark Books, c2007. xvi, 346 p. : **551.2**

1. Earthquakes 2. Volcanoes 3. Encyclopedias.
ISBN 9780816071203

LC bl2007011320

Authors' names in reverse order on 2nd ed.

Provides information on earthquakes and volcanic eruptions in various regions of the world, major quakes and eruptions throughout history, and geologic and scientific terms.

Scarth, Alwyn

Vesuvius : a biography / Alwyn Scarth. Princeton University Press, 2009. ix, 342 p. : **551.2**

1. Volcanoes -- Italy 2. Seismology 3. Volcanology 4. Vesuvius -- History
ISBN 9780691143903

LC bl2009034613

Describes the complex relationship between the volcano Vesuvius and the people who live in the area, chronicles the causes behind each eruption, and discusses concerns about the severity of the next eruption.

551.21 Volcanoes

Thompson, Dick

Volcano cowboys : the rocky evolution of a dangerous science / Dick Thompson. St. Martin's Press, 2000. viii, 326 p. : **551.21**

1. Volcanological research -- History -- 20th century
ISBN 9780312208813

LC 00026158

An absorbing exploration of the sometimes deadly science of volcanology shows how this steadily developing discipline has evolved since the Mt. St. Helens eruption and describes the dangerous conditions under which its researchers work.

551.31 Glaciology

Gosnell, Mariana
Ice : the nature, the history, and the uses of an astonishing substance / Mariana Gosnell. The University of Chicago Press, 2007, c2005. 560 p. **551.31**

1. Ice -- Popular works.
ISBN 9780226304960
LC 2007003804

Originally published: New York : Knopf, 2005.

"The author opens with a description of the sound and sight of a small lake freezing, expanding from there to discuss the seasonal advance and retreat of ice, as on the Great Lakes or Lake Baikal. Taking the next natural step, the persistence of ice through the summer, brings Gosnell to the 1800s origin of glaciology in Louis Agassiz's study of Mont Blanc's Mer de Glace, and subsequently into the contemporary specialty of ice cores in ice-age research. En route through the science, which Gosnell condenses from the technical literature, the author imparts eclectic information through excerpts from poems, adventure and disaster stories, and discussions of ice sports and diversions." Booklist.

Pollack, H. N.
A **world** without ice / Henry Pollack. Avery, c2009. xv, 287 p. : **551.31**

1. Glaciers. 2. Ice 3. Global warming. 4. Climate change
ISBN 9781583333570
LC 2009030326

A cowinner of the 2007 Nobel Peace Prize shares a comprehensive survey of ice as a force of nature while describing potential catastrophic consequences of ice shortages, in a reference that outlines recommended steps for avoiding environmental threats.

"Seldom has a scientist written so well and so clearly for the lay reader. Pollack's explanations of how researchers can tell that the climate is warming faster than normal are free of the usual scientific jargon and understandable. All readers concerned about global warming and students writing papers on the topic will want this excellent and important volume." Library Journal.

551.43 Elevations

Dech, Stefan Werner
Mountains : mapping the earth's extremes / Stefan Dech, Reinhold Messner, Nils Sparwasser. Thames & Hudson, 2016. 241 p. : **551.43**

1. Mountains -- Discovery and exploration. 2. Mountain mapping. 3. Image processing -- Digital techniques.
ISBN 9780500518892
LC 2016931310

This thrilling combination of science, history, geography and adventure brings together more than 170 breathtaking virtual images of mountains, created using modern satellite technology with unprecedented precision and detail, allowing viewpoints that have never before been possible; the history of mountaineering, retold by world-class adventurer Reinhold Messner; first-hand accounts of expeditions by great climbers: Sandy Allan, Hansjorg Auer, Herve Barmasse, Yannick Graziani, Tomaž Humar, Gerlinde Kaltenbrunner, Pierre Mazeaud, Robert Paragot, John Roskelley, Adolf Schulze, Stephen Venables, and Barbara Washburn.

551.45 Plane and coastal regions

Goodell, Jeff
The **water** will come : rising seas, sinking cities, and the remaking of the civilized world / Jeff Goodell. Little Brown & Co., 2017. 336 p. **551.45**

1. Sea level 2. Climate change 3. Coast changes 4. Floods
ISBN 9780316260244
LC bl2017042941

An acclaimed journalist uses fact, science and on-the-ground reporting to provide an account of the coming new age of great flooding, due to rapidly rising sea levels that promise to inundate our coasts and transform existing landscapes.

"A frightening, scientifically grounded, and starkly relevant look at how climate change will affect coastal cities." Kirkus.

Rush, Elizabeth A.
Rising : dispatches from the new American shore / Elizabeth Rush. Milkweed Editions, 2018. 256 p. **551.45**

1. Rush, Elizabeth A. Travel. 2. Climate change 3. Coasts. 4. Sea level. 5. Hurricanes.
ISBN 9781571313676
LC 2017059870

ALA Notable Book, 2019.
Pulitzer Prize for General Nonfiction finalist, 2019.

A journalist, weaving firsthand accounts from the people and places imperiled by climate change in the United States today, takes readers to the places hardest hit by the rising seas, which are transforming the coastline of the U.S. in irrevocable ways.

551.46 Oceanography and submarine geology

Aldersey-Williams, Hugh
The **tide** : the science and stories behind the greatest force on earth / Hugh Aldersey-Williams. W. W. Norton & Co., 2016 368 p. **551.46**

1. Tides. 2. Beaches 3. Coasts 4. Earth -- Rotation.
ISBN 9780393241631
LC 2016018456

A sweeping exploration into the science and history of the earth's tides draws on centuries of intellectual thought, literature and folklore to chronicle humanity's efforts to understand its cycles as reflected by the strong tides of Nova Scotia's Bay of Fundy, Norway's Maelstrom tidal whirlpool, the Homeric tale of Scylla and other examples.

Kandel, Robert S.
★**Water** from heaven : the story of water from the big bang to the rise of civilization, and beyond / Robert Kandel. Columbia University Press, c2003. xiii, 311 p. : **551.46**

1. Water -- Origin. 2. Hydrology. 3. Hydrologic cycle. 4. Oceanography.
ISBN 9780231122443
LC 2002031229

Offers a scientific history of water molecules, explaining the importance of water to the origin of life and the role water plays in the world today.

Prager, Ellen J.
Chasing science at sea : racing hurricanes, stalking sharks, and living undersea with ocean experts / Ellen Prager. Univer-

sity of Chicago Press, 2008. 200 p. **551.46**

1. Oceanography. 2. Oceans. 3. Marine biology. 4. Marine animals.
ISBN 9780226678702

LC 2007049486

Using the first-hand accounts of her colleagues, a marine scientists offers a look into the lives and experiences of people who regularly go to sea--tall-ship captains, marine biologists, and aquanauts.

Roberts, Callum

The **ocean** of life : the fate of man and the sea / Callum Roberts. Viking, c2012. 416 p. **551.46**

1. Oceans -- History. 2. Marine ecology. 3. Oceanography. 4. Men and nature.
ISBN 9780670023547

LC 2012000252

ALA Notable Book, 2013

Traces the human race's relationship to the ocean, identifying the consequences of modern fishing, pollution, and climate change on marine life while making urgent recommendations for reversing damage.

Streever, Bill

In oceans deep : courage, innovation, and adventure beneath the waves / Bill Streever. Little Brown & Co, 2019. 320 p. **551.46**

1. Oceans 2. Deep diving 3. Oceanographic submersibles 4. Underwater exploration
ISBN 9780316551311

LC 2018965114

The award-winning author of Cold presents a dramatic exploration of the science and history of the deep sea that touches on such subjects as the Challenger Deep lowest oceanic point, submarine technology and competitive diving.

"A buoyant, at times thrilling, account of the deep sea experience, perfect for divers and other lovers of life beneath the waves." Kirkus.

Winchester, Simon

Atlantic : great sea battles, heroic discoveries, titanic storms, and a vast ocean of a million stories / Simon Winchester. William Morrow, 2010. 492 p. **551.46**

1. Ocean and civilization. 2. Atlantic Ocean -- Geography. 3. Atlantic Ocean -- History.
ISBN 9780061702587

LC 2010015229

Blends history and anecdote, geography and reminiscence, and science and exposition, to relate the saga of the Atlantic Ocean, setting it against the backdrop of mankind's intellectual evolution.

"Writing the history of the Atlantic Ocean from tectonic labor pains to its lead role in modern European and American history might be one of the more difficult tasks Simon Winchester has set for himself. Luckily, the author comes armed with a knowledge almost as vast and deep as his subject, as well as a clever yet functional organizational scheme that divides his oceanic biography Atlantic into the seven ages of a man's life as proposed by Shakespeare. A formidable writer and storyteller, Winchester still gets distracted by the occasional unworthy anecdote or superfluous specificity, but for all the densely packed information in this work, the one thing it never becomes, quite appropriately, is dry." Entertainment Weekly.

551.48 Hydrology

Montgomery, David R., 1961-

The **rocks** don't lie : a geologist investigates Noah's flood / David R. Montgomery. W. W. Norton, c2012. 288 p. **551.48**

1. Floods. 2. Creationism. 3. Religion and science. 4. Limnology.
ISBN 9780393082395

LC 2012015146

Using rocks as proof, a geologist examines the great flood stories found in many cultures and religions and travels across countries and landscapes to discover a place where theology and science converge.

Postel, Sandra

Replenish : the virtuous cycle of water and prosperity / Sandra Postel. Island Press, 2017. 323 p. **551.48**

1. Natural resources 2. Water-supply 3. Droughts 4. Water use
ISBN 9781610917902

LC 2017936498

Postel, who lectures, writes, and consults on global water issues, illustrates the evolving mindset in water management and how farmers, businesses, and conservationists are rejuvenating watersheds and floodplains and replenishing rivers, groundwater, and soils, to mitigate flood damages, prepare for droughts, restore habitats, grow food, augment water supplies, and strengthen water security.

551.5 Meteorology

Buckley, Bruce

★**Weather** : a visual guide / Bruce Buckley, Edward J. Hopkins, Richard Whitaker. Firefly Books, 2004. 303 p. : **551.5**

1. Weather. 2. Meteorology.
ISBN 9781552979570

LC bl2004112873

Includes index.

Explores how weather works and its effects and includes diagrams providing explanations for interpreting weather signs, as well as up-to-the-minute information on extreme weather and natural events that predict the weather.

Dewdney, Christopher, 1951-

18 miles : the epic drama of our atmosphere and its weather / Christopher Dewdney. ECW Press, 2018. 320 p. **551.5**

1. Atmosphere 2. Air 3. Meteorology 4. Weather
ISBN 9781770413467

LC bl2018188875

Also published in Great Britain by Bloomsbury, 2019.

We live at the bottom of an ocean of air--5,200 million million tons, to be exact. It sounds like a lot, but Earth's atmosphere is smeared onto its surface in an alarmingly thin layer--99 percent contained within 18 miles. Yet, within this fragile margin lies a magnificent realm--at once gorgeous, terrifying, capricious, and elusive. With his keen eye for identifying and uniting seemingly unrelated events, Chris Dewdney reveals to us the invisible rivers in the sky that affect how our weather works and the structure of clouds and storms and seasons, the rollercoaster of climate.

"Equal parts science, historical journey, and whimsical reflection that traces to Dewdney's childhood fascination with meteorology, this book marks an accessible and enjoyable entry into a field more often characterized by dry, uninspired texts." Publishers Weekly.

Logan, William Bryant

Air : the restless shaper of the world / William Bryant Logan. W.W. Norton & Co., 2012. 256 p. **551.5**

1. Air 2. Atmosphere 3. Meteorology 4. Earth sciences
ISBN 9780393067989

LC 2012013823

The award-winning writer and documentarian behind Oak and Dirt tackles the life-sustaining element all around us by discussing the science around the air we breathe and how the smallest molecular changes in composition can make the difference between life and death.

"For everyone who has wondered just how a 747 manages to get off the ground, luxuriated in the intoxicating aroma of a bed of roses, or marveled at a tropical sunset, Logan's meticulously researched and engagingly presented treatise is a breath of, well, fresh air." Booklist.

Williams, Jack, 1936-

★The **AMS** weather book : the ultimate guide to America's weather / Jack Williams. University of Chicago, Ill. :Press, 2009. xi, 316 p. : **551.5**

1. Climatology 2. Meteorology 3. Weather
ISBN 9780226898988

LC 2008035916

"Copublished with the American Meteorological Society."

Includes index.

Discusses the variety of weather patterns found in America, introduces the science behind meteorology, and answers common weather questions.

"This work, with its attractive, easy-to-understand graphics, offers a useful, engaging basic introduction to a wide variety of weather-related topics." Choice.

551.51 Composition, regions, dynamics of atmosphere

Kean, Sam

Caesar's last breath : decoding the secrets of the air around us / Sam Kean. Little, Brown & Co., 2017. 384 p. **551.51**

1. Air 2. Atmosphere 3. Chemistry 4. Atmospheric chemistry
ISBN 9780316381642

LC bl2017021331

An engaging round-the-globe journey through the periodic table explains how the air we breathe reflects the world's history, tracing the origins and ingredients of the atmosphere to explain air's role in reshaping continents, steering human progress and powering revolutions.

"A witty book that turns the science of the stuff we breathe into a delightful romp through history." Kirkus.

Marder, Michael, 1980-

Dust / Michael Marder. Bloomsbury Academic, 2016. xii, 129 p. : **551.51**

1. Dust 2. Cosmic dust 3. Allergens 4. Sweeping and dusting
ISBN 9781628925586

LC 2015024508

No matter how much you fight against it, dust pervades everything. It gathers in even layers, adapting to the contours of things and marking the passage of time. In itself, it is also a gathering place, a random community of what has been and what is yet to be, a catalog of traces and a set of promises: dead skin cells and plant pollen, hair and paper fibers, not to mention dust mites who make it their home. And so, dust blurs the boundaries between the living and the dead, plant and animal matter, the inside and the outside, you and the world ("or dust thou art, and unto dust shalt thou return"). This book treats one of the most mundane and familiar phenomena, showing how it can provide a key to thinking about existence, community, and justice today. --From publisher description.

551.55 Atmospheric disturbances and formations

Miles, Kathryn, 1974-

Superstorm : nine days inside Hurricane Sandy / Kathryn Miles. Dutton, 2014. 368 p. **551.55**

1. Bounty (Ship : 1960) 2. Hurricane Sandy, 2012. 3. Hurricanes -- United States -- History -- 21st century. 4. Weather broadcasting -- United States. 5. Hurricanes
ISBN 9780525954408

LC 2014031087

A moment-by-moment account of the largest Atlantic storm system ever recorded examines Hurricane Sandy's exponentially growing threat and devastating aftermath, in a book that follows the actions of the National Hurricane Center, National Weather Service, the crew of the ill-fated ship Bounty, New York Mayor Michael Bloomberg, New Jersey Governor Chris Christie and the countless residents who were affected.

"Miles spends a lot of time talking not just about the storms severity and significance (there hadn't been anything quite like it before) but also about the people who saw the early warning signs but didn't understand what they meant (one weather-forecasting center was warned the storm was coming, but the forecasted storm seemed so impossible that they dismissed the warnings as a computer anomaly). A fascinating and often moving account of a widely talked about disaster." Booklist.

Sandlin, Lee

★**Storm** kings : the untold history of America's first tornado chasers / Lee Sandlin. Pantheon Books, c2013. 304 p. **551.55**

1. Tornadoes 2. Storm chasers 3. Weather -- History. 4. Weather forecasting.
ISBN 9780307378521

LC 2012027314

Traces the historical efforts to study and understand super cell tornadoes and the role of storm chasers in shaping meteorology, citing the early experiments of Ben Franklin, the "great storm debates" of the 19th century and the development of the National Weather Service.

Sobel, Adam H., 1967-

Storm surge : Hurricane Sandy, our changing climate, and extreme weather of the past and future / Adam Sobel. HarperWave, 2014. xxii, 314 p., 8 unnumbered p. of plates : **551.55**

1. Hurricane Sandy, 2012. 2. Climatic extremes. 3. Hurricanes. 4. Cyclones.
ISBN 9780062304766

LC bl2014037302

A renowned scientist takes us through the devastating and unprecedented events of Hurricane Sandy, using it to explain our planet's changing climate, and what we need to do to protect ourselves and our cities for the future. Was Hurricane Sandy a freak event - or a harbinger of things to come? Was climate change responsible? What connects the spiraling clouds our satellites saw from space, the brackish water that rose up over the city's seawalls, and the slow simmer of greenhouse gases? Why weren't we better prepared?

"In 28 absorbing and instructive chapters, Sobel recounts the full history of the hurricane, including its warning signs and an explanation of the weather anomalies that forced Sandy to make a sudden left turn into the New Jersey coastline. He also explores the debate about how much climate change played a role in Sandy's devastating impact and examines how we can better respond to other extreme weather events. Must reading for earth-science and weather buffs and anyone living along the vulnerable passageways of potential future hurricanes." Booklist.

551.56 Atmospheric electricity and optics

Bogard, Paul, 1966-

The **end** of night : searching for natural darkness in an age of artificial light / Paul Bogard. Little, Brown, and Company, July 2013. 304 p. **551.56**

1. Light. 2. Light and darkness 3. Night -- Psychological aspects. 4. Lighting -- Physiological aspects.
ISBN 9780316182904

LC 2012027287

Describes how ever-present, modern artificial lights have changed the way humans experience darkness and bemoans the fact that the primal dark sky can no longer influence science and art.

"In this artful blend of environmental and cultural history, Bogard manages to make a book about light pollution pure reading pleasure." Booklist.

551.57 Hydrometeorology

Barnett, Cynthia, 1966-

★**Rain** : a natural and cultural history / Cynthia Barnett. Crown Publishers, 2014 320 p. **551.57**

1. Rain and rainfall. 2. Weather. 3. Rainfall anomalies. 4. Droughts.
ISBN 9780804137096

LC 2014034180

A natural history of rain draws on myriad disciplines to trace the ocean-filling torrents from 4 billion years ago through the storms of the present world's climate change while sharing stories about humanity's efforts to control rain through science and magic.

"Barnett explores every facet of the substance. A seamless blending of personal narrative with scientific and cultural explanations makes the book both informative and entertaining." Library Journal.

551.6 Climatology and weather

Dow, Kirstin, 1963-

The **atlas** of climate change : mapping the world's greatest challenge / Kirstin Dow and Thomas E. Downing. University of California Press, c2011. 128 p. : **551.6**

1. Climatic changes 2. Climatic changes -- Maps 3. Climatic changes -- Charts, diagrams, etc
ISBN 9780520268234

LC 2011922284

A resource with more than 50 full-color maps and graphics illustrates the causes and consequences of climate change on populations around the world, the progress made on fulfilling commitments regarding the issue and local efforts needed to reverse some of the long-term effects.

Dumanoski, Dianne

★The **end** of the long summer : why we must remake our civilization to survive on a volatile Earth / Dianne Dumanoski. Crown Publishing, 2009. 256 p. **551.6**

1. Climate and civilization 2. Global environmental change 3. Climate change 4. Climatology
ISBN 9780307396075

LC bl2009012670

A noted environmental journalist discusses the possible ecological consequences beyond global warming resulting from modern human activity, and describes the possibility of massive instability and climate swings, including a possible return to ice ages of the past.

"A passionate, precise account of climate change and a persuasive strategy for dealing with Nature's return to center stage as a critical player in human history." Kirkus.

Fagan, Brian M.

The **long** summer : how climate changed civilization / Brian Fagan. Basic Books, c2004. xvii, 284 p. : **551.6**

1. Climate change -- Environmental aspects. 2. Civilization -- History. 3. Humans -- Effect of climate on 4. Global warming.
ISBN 9780465022816

LC 2003013917

The anthropologist-author of "The Little Ice Age" analyzes the seminal impact of climatic change on the evolution of all of human history.

Fry, Juliane L. (Juliane Loraine)

The **encyclopedia** of weather and climate change : a complete visual guide / [authors, Juliane L. Fry ... [et al.]. University of California Press, 2010. 512 p. : **551.6**

1. Weather -- Encyclopedias. 2. Climatic changes -- Encyclopedias. 3. Climatology -- Encyclopedias. 4. Meteorology -- Encyclopedias.
ISBN 9780520261013

LC 2009943908

Includes index.

Offers a guide on weather around the world, describing how it forms, specific phenomena, how humans face extreme climates, and the possible long-term consequences and solutions to climate change on Earth.

Goodell, Jeff

How to cool the planet : geoengineering and the audacious quest to fix earth's climate / Jeff Goodell. Houghton Mifflin Harcourt, 2010. 262 p. ; **551.6**

1. Climate change -- Environmental aspects. 2. Global warming. 3. Engineering geology. 4. Environmental engineering.
ISBN 9780618990610

LC 2009046565

Documents the controversial efforts of a team of geo-engineers who are working to counter global warming through the development of technologies that may lower the planet's temperatures, assessing the arguments in favor of and against the effort.

"There is no trace of climate alarmism or political advocacy here. Goodell takes a detailed look at the range of hard choices humanity faces and explores how complicated moral and ethical considerations will dictate our response. Goodell is also a skilled writer. He splices complicated ideas into pithy turns of phrase". Business Week

Lynas, Mark, 1973-

Six degrees : our future on a hotter planet / Mark Lynas. National Geographic, 2008, c2007. 336 p. **551.6**

1. Global warming -- Environmental aspects 2. Humans -- Effect of climate on 3. Climate change -- Social aspects.
ISBN 9781426202131

LC 2007030864

Originally published: London : Fourth Estate, 2007.

Royal Society General Prizes for Science Books, 2008.

Features a degree-by-degree account of how the effects of global climate change will impact people, the environment, and natural species in every region of the world, and offers recommendations on what can be done to manage the problem.

Redniss, Lauren
Thunder & lightning : weather past, present, future / Lauren Redniss. Random House Inc., 2015. 272 p. : **551.6**
1. Weather. 2. Meteorology. 3. Climatology. 4. Fog. 5. Comics and Graphic novels
ISBN 9780812993172
LC bl2015042809

Focusing on the intricate nature of the world around us, as well as the personal relationship we all have to the weather, a National Book Award finalist--combining personal stories with history, interviews, scientific research and full-color photos--explores the transformative power of weather.

551.68 Artificial modification and control of weather

Fleming, James Rodger
Fixing the sky : the checkered history of weather and climate control / James Rodger Fleming. Columbia University Press, c2010. xiv, 325 p. : **551.68**
1. Weather control -- History. 2. Nature -- Effect of humans on
ISBN 9780231144124
LC 2010015482

"This book should be read by all who want a better understanding of global climate change and the debate over geoengineering our environment." Science Books & Films.

551.7 Historical geology

Bjornerud, Marcia
Reading the rocks : the autobiography of the earth / Marcia Bjornerud. Westview Press, a member of the Perseus Books Group, 2005. x, 237 p. ; **551.7**
1. Geology.
ISBN 081334249X
LC 2004022738

"This wonderful book should be examined by anyone with a curiosity about the natural history of our planet and how one science in particular has done such an impressive job of deciphering key mysteries of its origin and evolution." Science Books & Films.

Childs, Craig
Atlas of a lost world : travels in ice age America / Craig Childs. Pantheon, 2018. 288 p. **551.7**
1. Prehistoric humans -- North America 2. Stone age 3. Ice Age (Geology) 4. Paleo-Indians 5. North America -- Antiquities
ISBN 9780307908650
LC 2017033037

In a blend of science and personal narrative that takes readers on a fascinating journey through prehistory, the author of Apocalyptic Planet, chronicling the last millennia of the Ice Age and tracing the First People in North America, shows how much has changed since the time of mammoth hunters, and also what hasn't changed.

Macdougall, J. D., 1944-
Frozen Earth : the once and future story of ice ages / Doug Macdougall. University of California Press, c2004. xi, 256 p. : **551.7**
1. Ice age (Geology) 2. Paleoclimatology. 3. Global environmental change.
ISBN 0520239229
LC 2004008502

Explores the causes and effects of ice ages, explains how the Pleistocene Ice Age shaped the earth's landscape and influenced human evolution, and offers speculation and explanations of future climate changes.

"The author presents the scientific history behind ice ages, emphasizing the roles of four great scientists in the field . . . . Macdougall's account promotes a welcome reasoning attitude toward ice-age research and its relevance to global warming." Booklist.

Richet, Pascal
A **natural** history of time / Pascal Richet ; translated by John Venerella. University of Chicago Press, 2007. xiv, 471 p. : **551.7**
1. Geological time. 2. Earth -- Age.
ISBN 0226712877

The quest to pinpoint the age of the Earth is nearly as old as humanity itself. For most of history, people trusted mythology or religion to provide the answer, even though nature abounds with clues to the past of the Earth and the stars. Geophysicist Pascal Richet tells the fascinating story of how scientists and philosophers examined those clues and from them built a chronological scale that has made it possible to reconstruct the history of nature itself. --From publisher description.

"Geology and natural science buffs will discover a rich, baroquely embellished birthday cake to dig into and enjoy." Publishers Weekly.

552 Petrology

Coenraads, Robert Raymond, 1956-
Rocks & fossils : a visual guide / Robert R. Coenraads. Firefly Books, 2005. 304 p. : **552**
1. Fossils. 2. Minerals. 3. Rocks.
ISBN 1554070686
LC bl2006029600

Includes index.

Describes how the Earth's interior has shaped oceans and continents and explains the formation of rocks and fossils, as well as their importance to understanding life on Earth.

"In this introduction to geology and paleontology . [the author presents the] facts of how fossils are formed, how rocks are formed, and how plate tectonics work. A science work perfectly suited for general use." Booklist.

553.5 Structural and sculptural stone

Williams, David B., 1965-
Stories in stone : travels through urban geology / David B. Williams. Walker & Co., c2009. x, 260 p. : **553.5**
1. Urban geology. 2. Rocks. 3. Stone building. 4. Building materials -- History
ISBN 9780802716224
LC 2008051667

Documents the author's discoveries of geologically relevant materials that have been used as construction and artistic elements in major cities, revealing what can be learned about ancient and recent history through such structures as the Bunker Hill Monument, a 1935 gas station, and a St. Augustine fort.

553.6 Other economic materials

Kurlansky, Mark

★**Salt** : a world history / Mark Kurlansky. Walker and Co., c2002. xii, 484 p. : **553.6**

1. Salt. 2. Commodity exchanges. 3. Salt mines and mining. 4. Salt -- History.

ISBN 9780802713735

LC 2002391600

Explores the role of salt in shaping history, discussing how one of the world's most sought-after commodities has influenced economics, science, politics, religion, and eating customs.

"Throughout his engaging, well-researched history, Kurlansky sprinkles witty asides and amusing anecdotes. A piquant blend of the historic, political, commercial, scientific and culinary, the book is sure to entertain as well as educate." Publishers Weekly.

Welland, Michael, 1946-

Sand : the never-ending story / Michael Welland. University of California Press, c2009. xiv, 343 p., 15 p. of plates : **553.6**

1. Sand -- Miscellanea. 2. Sandstone -- Miscellanea. 3. Geology

ISBN 9780520254374

LC 2008009084

Describes the geological history of sand, examining the science behind the material as well as the human context of sand and how it has played important roles in history, commerce, and imagination.

553.7 Water

Solomon, Steven

Water : the epic struggle for wealth, power, and civilization / Steven Solomon. Harper, 2010. 608 p. **553.7**

1. Water -- Social aspects. 2. Natural resources. 3. Water-supply. 4. Droughts.

ISBN 9780060548308

LC 2009027500

"A narrative account of how water has shaped human society from the ancient past to the present".--Provided by publisher.

"Solomon's unprecedented inquiry into the history, science, and politics of water use provides fascinating and ample testimony to the need to place a higher value on water and its preservation." Booklist.

553.8 Gems

Bergstein, Rachelle

Brilliance and fire : a biography of diamonds / Rachelle Bergstein. Harper, 2016 xvii, 375 pages, 16 unnumbered pages of plates : **553.8**

1. Diamonds 2. Diamond industry and trade. 3. Gems.

ISBN 9780062323774

LC 2017304186

Sheds new light on the enticing, often surprising, story of our society's enduring obsession with the hardest gemstone, offering a fascinating history of its origins and revealing its greatest champions and most colorful enthusiasts.

"Bergstein's book is an informative, well-written, and entertaining window onto another way of life." Kirkus.

Hart, Matthew, 1945-

Diamond : a journey to the heart of an obsession / Matthew Hart. Walker & Company, 2001. 276 p. : **553.8**

1. Diamonds. 2. Diamond industry and trade. 3. Diamond mines and mining. 4. Diamond smuggling.

ISBN 0802713688

LC 2001026348

"Hart's account of the glittering business of mining and marketing diamonds is also a story of avarice, theft, aesthetics, monopoly, and war. A thoroughly entrancing book." Booklist.

Oldershaw, Cally

★**Firefly** guide to gems / Cally Oldershaw. Firefly Books, 2003. 224 p. : **553.8**

1. Gems. 2. Precious stones.

ISBN 1552978141

LC bl2005011968

Includes index.

A guide to gems and precious stones covers such topics as gem formation, structural properties, fashioning and cutting, and gem classification.

Raden, Aja,

Gem : the definitive visual guide / foreword by Aja Raden. DK Publishing, 2016. 440 p. : **553.8**

1. Precious stones. 2. Precious metals. 3. Gems. 4. Jewelry.

ISBN 9781465453563

LC 2016427871

Includes index.

Offers an illustrated guide to precious and semiprecious stones, metals, organic gems, and famous pieces, looking at the science, history, and mythology surrounding all the major gem types.

559 Science -- Earth sciences & geology -- Earth sciences of Australasia, Pacific Ocean islands, Atlantic Ocean islands, Arctic islands, Antarctica, extraterrestrial worlds

Sykes, Bryan

DNA USA : a genetic portrait of America / Bryan Sykes. Liveright Pub. Corp., c2012. 320 p. **559**

1. Human population genetics 2. Human genetics 3. DNA 4. Genetics

ISBN 9780871404121

LC 2011053182

"The geneticist and best-selling author of The Seven Daughters of Eve conducts a historical genetic tour of the United States and reveals interesting facts about who our ancestors really are and how Americans perceive race."

559.9 Earth sciences of extraterrestrial worlds

Baker, David, 1967-

The **50** most extreme places in our solar system / David Baker and Todd Ratcliff. Belknap Press of Harvard University Press, 2010. xiv, 290 p. : **559.9**

1. Extreme environments. 2. Solar system

ISBN 9780674049987

LC 2010006126

Explains the solar system in terms of storms, natural disasters, volcanoes, hail, tornadoes, and the possibility of life on other planets.

560 Paleontology

Eldredge, Niles

Extinction and evolution : what fossils reveal about the history of life / Niles Eldredge ; introduction by Carl Zimmer. Firefly Books, 2014. 256 p. : **560**

1. Evolution (Biology). 2. Extinction (Biology). 3. Fossils. 4. Paleontology.

ISBN 1770853596

LC bl2015015517

"A Peter N. Nevraumont book."

Chronicles the work and discoveries of paleontologist Niles Eldredge, tracing the history of life through the lense of paleontology, geology, ecology, anthropology, biology, zoology, mammalogy, herpetology, entomology, and botany.

"Though the text and photo captions are plagued by an assortment of typographical errors, the fossils and theories could not be presented in a more attractive, readable format. This handsome book should appeal to anyone with even the slightest curiosity about how life evolved on this planet. Highly recommended for all science collections." Library Journal.

Martin, Anthony J., 1960-

The **evolution** underground : burrows, bunkers, and the marvelous subterranean world beneath our feet / Anthony J. Martin. Pegasus Books, 2017. 400 p. **560**

1. Burrowing animals 2. Animal burrowing 3. Animal behavior 4. Animals

ISBN 9781681773124

LC 2017275625

The author of Dinosaurs Without Bones explores the subterranean secrets of survival, revealing how most of the planet's animal life survived the cataclysmic meteor strike 65 million years ago by hiding underground and continuing to take refuge in burrows today.

"A spry exercise in popular science." Kirkus.

Prothero, Donald R.

The **story** of life in 25 fossils : tales of intrepid fossil hunters and the wonders of evolution / Donald R. Prothero. Columbia University Press, 2015 viii, 389 p. : **560**

1. Fossils. 2. Paleontology. 3. Life -- Origin. 4. Evolution

ISBN 9780231171908

LC 2015003667

"Of particular appeal to those who enjoy the writings of Stephen Jay Gould but ideal for anyone interested in the origins of life on earth." Library Journal.

Taylor, Paul D

A **history** of life in 100 fossils / Paul D. Taylor & Aaron O'Dea. Smithsonian Books, 2014 224 p. : **560**

1. Evolution (Biology) 2. Fossils. 3. Historical geology. 4. Paleontology.

ISBN 1588344827

LC bl2014044030

Includes index.

Examines one hundred fossils of animals and plants that helped shape the Earth, with stories of how they were discovered and why they are important.

"From single-celled foraminifera to gigantic steppe mammoths, this volume presents a sweeping panorama of ancient life and is recommended for nonspecialists interested in paleontology or evolutionary biology." Library Journal.

Thompson, Ida

★The **Audubon** Society field guide to North American fossils / Ida Thompson ; with photographs by Townsend P. Dickinson ; visual key by Carol Nehring. Knopf : 1982 846 p. : The Audubon Society field guide series **560**

1. Fossils -- Collection and preservation -- North America

ISBN 9780394524122

LC 81084772

"A Chanticleer Press edition."

Includes index.

Aids in identifying eight hundred species of common North American fossils with color photographs and line drawings

567.9 Reptiles

Brusatte, Stephen

The **rise** and fall of the dinosaurs : a new history of a lost world / Stephen Brusatte. HarperCollins 2018 400 p. **567.9**

1. Dinosaurs 2. Evolution 3. Paleontology

ISBN 9780062490421

LC 2017038066

The "resident paleontologist" for BBC's Walking with Dinosaurs presents a narrative scientific history of the dinosaur eras that examines their origins, habitats, extinction and living legacy, chronicling nearly 200 million years of their evolution from small shadow dwellers through the emergences of prehistoric ancestors that became more than 10,000 modern bird species.

"His explanations of how sauropods became so large, the reasons for the dominance of Tyrannosaurus rex, the evolution of flying ability in some dinosaurs, and the factors leading to the demise of most of these creatures are carefully crafted and presented. Brusatte is not shy about saying what is not yet known, while making it clear that this is a truly exciting period, in which new fossils are being uncovered at a dizzying pace." Publishers Weekly.

Kainen, Dan,

Dinosaur : a photicular book / created by Dan Kainen ; written by Kathy Wollard. Workman Publishing, 2018 1 volume (unpaged) : **567.9**

1. Dinosaurs. 2. Photicular books.

ISBN 9781523504725

LC bl2018135305

Presents a dinosaur-themed series entry that features animated images of species ranging from the T. Rex to the triceratops.

Lacovara, Kenneth

Why dinosaurs matter / Kenneth Lacovara. Simon & Schuster, 2017. 120 p. **567.9**

1. Dinosaurs -- Extinction. 2. Climate change -- Environmental aspects. 3. Extinction (Biology) 4. Paleontology.

ISBN 9781501120107

LC bl2017038106

A paleontologist examines the importance of the way dinosaurs lived and may have died, the meaning of fossils, the nature of deep time, and humans' place in the world as the earth moves into an uncertain environmental future.

"As paleontologist Lacovara has dug up the bones of some mighty dinosaurs, … he's just the man to tell us what dinosaurs can tell us about ourselves." Library Journal.

Meier, John J.

Dinosaurs / edited by John J. Meier. H.W. Wilson Company, 2011. viii, 221 p. : **567.9**

1. Dinosaurs. 2. Paleontologists. 3. Dinosaurs -- Evolution. 4. Dinosaurs -- Extinction.

ISBN 9780824211073

LC 2011007540

"The articles collected in this volume ... are meant to give an overview of what we've come to learn about dinosaurs. Because our understanding grows and changes with each new discovery, the selections were culled exclusively from the past decade. Most are examples of what some would call "popular" science writing: pieces intended for anyone interested in the topic, not just experts." -- Preface

Naish, Darren

Dinosaurs : how they lived and evolved / Darren Naish and Paul Barrett. Smithsonian Books, [2016] 224 pages : **567.9**

1. Dinosaurs 2. Prehistoric animals 3. Paleontology. 4. Fossil dinosaurs.

ISBN 9781588345820

LC 2016937682

Dinosaurs are one of the most spectacular groups of animals that have ever existed. Many were fantastic, bizarre creatures that still capture our imagination: the super-predator Tyrannosaurus, the plate-backed Stegosaurus, and the long-necked, long-tailed Diplodocus. Dinosaurs: The Ultimate Guide to How They Lived taps into our enduring interest in dinosaurs, shedding new light on different dinosaur groups.

Paul, Gregory S.

The **Princeton** field guide to dinosaurs / Gregory S. Paul. Princeton University Press, 2016 360 p. : **567.9**

1. Dinosaurs.

ISBN 9780691167664

LC 2016933929

World-renowned dinosaur illustrator and researcher Gregory Paul provides comprehensive visual and textual coverage of the great Mesozoic animals that gave rise to the living dinosaurs, the birds. Paul presents thorough descriptions of more than 735 dinosaur species and features more than 600 color and black-and-white images, including unique skeletal drawings, "life" studies, and scenic views.

Pim, Keiron

Dinosaurs the grand tour : everything worth knowing about dinosaurs from Aardonyx to Zuniceratops / Keiron Pim with field notes by Jack Horner ; illustrated by Fabio Pastori. The Experiment, 2014 352 p. : **567.9**

1. Dinosaurs 2. Dinosaurs.

ISBN 1615192123

LC 2014018581

First published in Great Britain as The Bumper book of dinosaurs by Square Peg, 2013.

Collects information on paleontological expeditions, highlights from recent research, and profiles over three hundred dinosaurs, providing information on anatomy and evolution.

"This book provides detailed analyses of more than 300 different dinosaurs, grouped by the period (Triassic, Jurassic, or Cretaceous) in which they lived. Information is provided for each dinosaur on name pronunciation, the creatures diet and weight, where bones have been found, and when it lived. . . . This is a good, inexpensive choice for those who want the most up-to-date, comprehensive information on dinosaurs, and it is suitable for school and public libraries." Booklist.

569 Fossil mammals

Johanson, Donald C., 1943-

Lucy : the beginnings of humankind / Donald C. Johanson and Maitland A. Edey. Simon and Schuster, 1981. 409 p., [4] leaves of plates : **569**

1. Australopithecus afarensis. 2. Lucy (Prehistoric hominid) 3. Prehistoric humans -- Africa. 4. Prehistoric humans -- Ethiopia.

ISBN 0671250361

LC 80021759

Johanson, the discoverer, in 1974, of "Lucy"--the oldest skelton of an erect-walking human yet found--reports the story of his internationally acclaimed find and speculates on its meaning for the understanding of our origin.

Lister, Adrian

Mammoths : giants of the ice age / Adrian Lister and Paul Bahn ; foreword by Jean M. Auel. University of California Press, c2007. 192 p. : **569**

1. Mammoths

ISBN 9780520253193

LC 2007026369

A dazzling visual record of one of Earth's most extraordinary species, this updated and revised edition of Mammoths: Giants of the Ice Age integrates exciting new research to piece together the story of mammoths, mastodons, and their relatives, icons of the Ice Age. Incorporating recent genetic work, new fossil finds, new extinction theories, and more, Mammoths is a captivating exploration of how these mighty creatures evolved, lived, and mysteriously disappeared. The book features a wealth of color illustrations that depict mammoths in their dramatic Ice Age habitats, scores of photographs of mammoth remains, and images of the art of prehistoric people who saw these animals in the flesh. Full of intriguing facts, boxed features, and clear graphics, Mammoths examines the findings--including intact frozen carcasses from Siberia and fossilized remains from South Dakota, California, England, France, and elsewhere--that have provided clues to the mammoths' geographic range, body structure, way of life, and interactions with early humans. It is an enthralling story of paleontological, archaeological, and geological exploration and of the fascinating investigations of biologists, anthropologists, and art historians worldwide. --From publisher description.

"Valuable for all science libraries." Choice.

569.67 Mammoths

McKay, John J.

Discovering the mammoth : a tale of giants, unicorns, ivory, and the birth of a new science / John J. McKay. Pegasus Books, 2017. xiii, 241 p., 8 unnumbered p. of plates : **569.67**

1. Fossils 2. Paleontology 3. Scientific discoveries 4. Mammoths

ISBN 9781681774244

LC 2017471037

Describes how the discovery of mammoth fossils was handled throughout human history, from the Greeks, who believed they were Titans vanquished by the Gods, to the Chinese who believed they were dragon's teeth and through the Age of Reason and modern science.

"McKay masterfully weaves an intricate story of the events, politics, people, and scientific development associated with the 'rediscovery' of mammoths." Booklist.

569.9 Humans and related genera

Bahrami, Beebe

Cafe Neandertal : excavating our past in one of Europe's most ancient places / Beebe Bahrami. Counterpoint, 2017. 300 p. **569.9**

1. Neanderthals 2. Archaeologists 3. Archaeological sites 4. Prehistoric anthropology 5. Dordogne River Valley -- Description and travel 6. France -- Description and travel

ISBN 9781619027770

LC 2017004034

Describes the research, exploration and recovery of modern humans' ancient relatives, the Neanderthals, based on the work of archaeologists who are doing comprehensive work in the Dordogne region of France as well as elsewhere around the globe.

"Written with all the flair and enthusiasm of an experienced writer eager to share her love of her subject." Kirkus.

Pyne, Lydia V.

Seven skeletons : the evolution of the world's most famous human fossils / Lydia Pyne. Viking, 2016. 336 p. **569.9**

1. Prehistoric humans 2. Human evolution.

ISBN 9780525429852

LC 2016008398

A science historian describes seven famous ancestral fossils that have become known around the world, including the three-foot tall "hobbit" from Flores, the Neanderthal of La Chapelle, the Taung Child, the Piltdown Man hoax, Peking Man, Australopithecus sediba and Lucy.

"Pyne's tales complement and flesh out the well-known narratives already associated with these fossils; her work impressively blends the humanities and science to greatly enrich both." Publishers Weekly.

Sawyer, G. J.

★The **last** human : a guide to twenty species of extinct humans / created by G. J. Sawyer and Viktor Deak. Yale University Press, 2006. 256 p. **569.9**

1. Humans. 2. Human behavior. 3. Human evolution. 4. Evolution.

ISBN 0300100477

LC 2006928034

Creates three-dimensional scientific reconstructions for twenty-two species of extinct humans, providing information for each one on its emergence, chronology, geographic range, classification, physiology, environment, habitat, cultural achievements, coexisting species, and possible reasons for extinction.

"This is fascinating stuff, not least because it drives home just how much of our knowledge about the past is based on inference." The New Scientist.

Walker, Alan, 1938-

The **wisdom** of the bones : in search of human origins / Alan Walker and Pat Shipman. Knopf, 1996. x, 338 p., 8 p. of plates : **569.9**

1. Homo erectus 2. Evolution. 3. Prehistoric humans. 4. Skeleton. 5. Kenya. 6. Nariokotome Boy (Homo erectus)

ISBN 0679426248

LC 95037525

Royal Society General Prizes for Science Books, 1997.

Describes the discovery in Africa of a nearly complete skeleton of a teenage male that may represent the "missing link" between apes and modern humans and provides a step-by-step analysis of the find and its significance

"In 1984 Walker, along with colleague Richard Leakey and their 'hominidgang' of experienced Kenyan excavators, discovered a near-intact fossil of Homo erectus. The find was a veritable trove of theory-busting information, which the authors take up after recounting the scientists who preceded Walker in investigating the species. A fluidly presented portrait of the people and process of paleoanthropology." Booklist.

Walter, Chip

Last ape standing : the seven-million-year story of how and why we survived / Chip Walter. St Martins Press, 2013. 304 p. **569.9**

1. Evolution. 2. Humans -- Origin. 3. Apes. 4. Life -- Origin.

ISBN 9780802717566

LC 2012037484

Draws on new scientific discoveries to explain why homo sapiens were the only human species to survive among more than two dozen others, profiling such extinct species as the Neanderthals and the Red Deer Cave people while identifying such survival factors as premature births, long childhoods and a highly social nature.

Wragg Sykes, Rebecca

Kindred : Neanderthal life, love, death and art / Rebecca Wragg Sykes. Bloomsbury Sigma, 2020 400 p., 8 unnumbered p. of plates : **569.9**

1. Prehistoric humans. 2. Neanderthals. 3. Evolution 4. Manners and customs

ISBN 9781472937490

This book sheds new light on where Neanderthals lived, what they ate, and the increasingly complex Neanderthal culture that researchers have discovered.

"Accumulated from the approximately 200 known Neanderthal sites, the information that Sykes evocatively and enthusiastically presents enables readers to appreciate Neanderthals as sentient creatures, and possibly imagine themselves sharing, Jean Auel-like, a Pleistocene encounter with them." Booklist

570 Biology

Carroll, Sean B.

The **Serengeti** rules : the quest to discover how life works and why it matters / Sean B. Carroll. Princeton University Press, 2016. 272 p. **570**

1. Life (Biology) 2. Biofeedback 3. Ecology. 4. Nature -- Effect of humans on

ISBN 9780691167428

LC 2015038116

"Carroll superbly animates biological principles while providing important insights." Publishers Weekly.

De Queiroz, Alan

The **monkey's** voyage : how improbable journeys shaped the history of life / Alan de Queiroz. Basic Books, '2013. 304 p. **570**

1. Evolution 2. Zoogeography 3. Biogeography. 4. Animals

ISBN 9780465020515

LC 2013036248

An evolutionary biologist describes how diverse species of life--including monkeys, frogs and baobab trees--made long-distance trips across the ocean and made their homes around the world, opposing the long-held theory of continental drift.

Sinclair, David A., 1969-
Lifespan : the revolutionary science of why we age - and why we don't have to / David A. Sinclair, Ph.D., A.O. with Matthew D. LaPlante ; illustrations by Catherine L. Delphia. Atria Books, 2019. 416 p. ; **570**

1. Longevity. 2. Cytology. 3. Life expectancy 4. Aging
ISBN 9781501191978

LC 2019007196

From an acclaimed Harvard professor and one of Time's most influential people, this paradigm-shifting book shows how almost everything we think we know about aging is wrong, offers a front-row seat to the amazing global effort to slow, stop, and reverseaging, and calls readers to consider a future where aging can be treated.

570.1 Philosophy and theory

Lovelock, James, 1919-
The **ages** of Gaia : a biography of our living earth / James Lovelock. W. W. Norton & Company, 1995. xxi, 255 p.: **570.1**

1. Biology -- Philosophy 2. Gaia hypothesis 3. Biosphere 4. Life (Biology)
ISBN 9780393312393

LC 2017302885

Proposes that all living species are components of a single organism and theorizes that the biological processes of the Earth naturally change environmental conditions to enable survival.

Thomas, Lewis, 1913-1993
The **lives** of a cell : notes of a biology watcher / Lewis Thomas. Viking Press, 1974. 153 p. ; **570.1**

1. Biology -- Philosophy. 2. Cells. 3. Essays.
ISBN 9780670434428

LC 73018888

Essays which appeared in the New England journal of medicine, 1971-73.

A physician and cancer researcher shares his personal observations on the uniformity, diversity, interdependence, and strange powers of the earth's life forms.

"In this collection of twenty-nine short essays the author does not confine his scientist's eye to a microscope. He takes a much wider view of the world, looking at insect behavior and the possibility of intelligent life in outer space or bird songs and the evolution of language. He also offers a modest proposal for saving ourselves from nuclear self-destruction." Time.

Turner, J. Scott, 1951-
Purpose & desire : what makes something "alive" why modern darwinism has failed to explain it / J. Scott Turner. HarperOne, 2017. xvi, 332 pages : **570.1**

1. Evolution 2. Life (Biology) 3. Biology -- Philosophy 4. Evolutionary genetics.
ISBN 9780062651563

LC 2017019588

Helping us bridge the ideological divide, a professor, biologist and physiologist, drawing on the work of Claude Bernard, argues that modern Darwinism's materialist and mechanistic biases have led to a scientific dead end and only an openness to the qualities of "purpose and desire" will move the field forward.

"An unsettling but highly thought-provoking book." Kirkus.

570.3 Biology--dictionaries

Hine, Robert,
A **dictionary** of biology / edited by Robert Hine. Oxford University Press, 2015. vii, 662 p. : **570.3**

1. Biology -- Dictionaries.
ISBN 9780198714378

LC 2015934059

Previous edition: 2008.

Fully revised and updated for the seventh edition, this market-leading dictionary is the perfect guide for anyone studying biology, either at school or university. --From publisher description.

570.9 History, geographic treatment, biography

Jackson, Tom, 1972-
Biology : an illustrated history of life science / edited by Tom Jackson ; contributors, Richard Beatty [and five others]. Shelter Harbor Press, 2017 144 p. : **570.9**

1. Biology -- History. 2. Biology
ISBN 9781627950930

LC bl2018000988

Presents a history of biology, discussing notable biologists and their discoveries.

570.92 Biologists

Wilson, Edward O.
★**Letters** to a young scientist / Edward O. Wilson. Liveright Publishing Corporation, 2013. 256 p. **570.92**

1. Wilson, Edward O. Correspondence. 2. Advice 3. Scientists 4. Science 5. Biologists -- United States -- Correspondence.
ISBN 9780871403773

LC 2012051412

Includes index.

Green Prize for Sustainable Literature: Adult Nonfiction, 2014.

Weaves together more than twenty letters that illuminate the author's career and his motivations for becoming a biologist, explaining how success in the sciences depends on a passion for finding a problem and solving it.

"Critically aware of his--and his successors'--moments in time, and what kinds of problems the next generation of scientists will be dealing with (e.g., environmental issues), Wilson ultimately offers an encouraging call to arms: 'Time is growing short...you are needed.'" Publishers Weekly.

571 Internal biological processes and structures

Toomey, David
Weird life : the search for life that is very, very different from our own / David Toomey. W.W. Norton & Co., Inc., 2013. 288 p. **571**

1. Microbiology. 2. Life (Biology) 3. Extreme environments --

Microbiology. 4. Biology.
ISBN 9780393071580

LC 2012042391

An introduction to some of the universe's more unusual life-forms and the maverick scientists who search for them includes organisms that consume acid and organisms that reproduce without DNA, tracing the discoveries of unfamiliar life forms in extreme areas of the solar system.

571.0919 Space

Roach, Mary

★**Packing** for Mars : the curious science of life in the void / Mary Roach. W. W. Norton, 2010. 336 p. : **571.0919**

1. Space biology 2. Space exploration 3. Astronautics 4. Space sciences
ISBN 9780393068474

LC 2010017113

Describes the weirdness of space travel, answers questions about the long-term effects of living in zero gravity on the human body, and explains how space simulations on Earth can provide a preview to life in space.

"The author explores the organic aspects of the space program, such as the dangerous bane of space motion sickness and the challenges of space hygiene. . . . She devotes one chapter to space food and another to zero-gravity elimination, which is a serious matter, even with a term like fecal popcorning. An impish and adventurous writer with a gleefully inquisitive mind and a standup comic's timing, Roach celebrates human ingenuity (the odder the better), and calls for us to marshal our resources, unchain our imaginations, and start packing for Mars." Booklist.

571.2 Plants and microorganisms

Tetro, Jason

The **germ** files : the surprising ways microbes can improve your health and life (and how to protect yourself from the bad ones) / Jason Tetro. Doubleday Canada, 2016 273 p. **571.2**

1. Bacteria 2. Germ theory of disease 3. Microorganisms 4. Colds 5. Essays
ISBN 9780385685771

LC bl2016003556

Includes index.

Jason Tetro, author of The Germ Code, is back with a very different book but the same message: microbes are amazing, they deserve our respect and we should learn to live with them in harmony.

"Written in an engaging, fluid style that is nonacademic, this book also imparts a plethora of in-depth information." Library Journal.

572 Biochemistry

McFadden, Johnjoe

Life on the edge : the coming of age of quantum biology / Johnjoe McFadden and Jim Al-Khalili. Crown 2015, c2014. xi, 355 p. : **572**

1. Quantum biochemistry. 2. Quantum theory. 3. Molecular biology 4. Biology.
ISBN 9780307986818

LC 2015018948

Originally published: London : Bantam Press, 2014.

"Of interest to readers curious about the inner workings of life; suitable for public and undergraduate academic libraries." Library Journal.

Morton, Oliver

Eating the sun : how plants power the planet / Oliver Morton. HarperCollins, 2008. 480 p. **572**

1. Photosynthesis. 2. Plants. 3. Energy production. 4. Energy.
ISBN 9780007163649

LC bl2008023433

Traces the science of photosysthesis and its relevance in both history and the modern world, exploring the phenomenon's key role in confronting today's environmental challenges.

"This book is a work of flowing prose that makes vivid why our leafy nub of cosmic dust, swirling around an average star, is an extraordinarily beautiful and rare place to reside in the universe." Christian Science Monitor.

572.8 Biochemical genetics

Cobb, Matthew

Life's greatest secret : the race to crack the genetic code / Matthew Cobb. Basic Books, 2015. xiv, 434 p. : **572.8**

1. Genetic code 2. DNA 3. Genes. 4. Genetics.
ISBN 9780465062676

LC 2015937254

"First published in Great Britain in 2015 by Profile Books Ltd"--Title-page verso.

Looks at the story behind the discovery and cracking of the genetic code as it played out across the globe, following the diverse and eccentric characters who contributed to its discovery.

"Like Cobb's other titles, this scholarly work reflects extensive research and draws upon primary documents. Upper-level students and researchers in biology or the history of science are best equipped to appreciate this detailed book. Other readers should consider Michel Morange's A History of Molecular Biology." Library Journal.

Francis, Richard C., 1953-

Epigenetics : the ultimate mystery of inheritance / Richard C. Francis. W.W. Norton, c2011. 256 p. **572.8**

1. Genetic regulation. 2. Epigenesis. 3. Adaptation (Biology) 4. Physiology
ISBN 9780393070057

LC 2011000696

Discusses how scientific evidence is increasingly showing a link between the stress of the environment on an individual and the seemingly inherited traits of his or her subsequent generations. By the author of Why Men Won't Ask for Directions.

"The author sets out to dethrone the notion that genes are the directors of the plays that are our lives, orchestrating our development and determining our risk for disease and sundry physical and behavioral traits. Yes, genes are important, writes the author, but they are subject to regulation by forces that can turn them on or off, sometimes for a lifetime, sometimes across generations...To illustrate, Francis provides a dizzying array of examples." Kirkus.

Heine, Steven J.

DNA is not destiny : the remarkable, completely misunderstood relationship between you and your genes / Steven

J. Heine. W W Norton & Co Inc., 2017. 336 p. **572.8**

1. DNA 2. Social psychology 3. Genetics -- Influence 4. Genes
ISBN 9780393244083

LC 2017000693

A leading cultural psychologist challenges current understandings about the role of DNA in health, drawing on his own genome sequencing results to explain what genes can actually tell us and why psychological biases can render people vulnerable to media hype.

"An accessible contribution to what the author calls 'genetic literacy' and a satisfyingly hard-edged work of popular science." Kirkus.

Lewontin, Richard C., 1929-

The **triple** helix : gene, organism, and environment / Richard Lewontin. Harvard University Press, 2000. 136 p. : **572.8**

1. Developmental biology -- Philosophy. 2. Ecology -- Philosophy. 3. Evolution (Biology) 4. Molecular biology -- Philosophy.
ISBN 0674001591

LC 99053879

Portions previously published as: Gene, organismo e ambiente. Roma : Laterza, 1998.

Explores the themes, controversies, and debates in biology over the last quarter century and warns against reducing evolution to a sequence of events predetermined by genetic programming.

Wagner, Andreas, 1967 January 26-

Arrival of the fittest : the hidden mechanism of evolution / Andreas Wagner. Current, 2014. 304 p. **572.8**

1. Natural selection. 2. Biodiversity. 3. Evolutionary genetics. 4. Evolution
ISBN 9781591846468

LC 2014009774

"A book of startling congruencies, insightful flashes and an artful enthusiasm that delivers knowledge from the inorganic page to our organic brains." Kirkus.

573.6 Reproductive system

Long, John A., 1957-

The **dawn** of the deed : the prehistoric origins of sex / John A. Long. The University of Chicago Press, 2012. 278 p. : **573.6**

1. Sex (Biology) 2. Evolution (Biology) 3. Sexual behavior in animals 4. Sexual instinct
ISBN 9780226492544

LC 2012007439

Originally published under the title: Hung like an Argentine Duck: a journey back in time to the origins of sexual intimacy.

Discusses the evolution of sex and reproduction, from the first embryonic organism found to live over 380 million years ago to modern humans, and explains how discoveries in reproductive theory have helped inform our own sexual anatomy.

573.7 Musculoskeletal system

Winchester, Simon

Skulls : an exploration of Alan Dudley's curious collection / Simon Winchester ; photography by Nick Mann. Black Dog & Leventhal, c2012. 253 p. : **573.7**

1. Dudley, Alan, 1957- Natural history collections. 2. Naturalists 3. Skull -- Catalogs and collections. 4. Collectors and collecting
ISBN 9781579129125

LC bl2012042252

Includes index.

Shares photographs of a variety of skulls, including those of mammals, birds, and fish.

575 Specific parts of and physiological systems in plants

Darwin, Charles, 1809-1882

★The **origin** of species by means of natural selection, or, The preservation of favored races in the struggle for life : By Means of Natural Selection or the Preservation of Favored Races in the Struggle for Life / Charles Darwin. Modern Library, 1993. xvi, 689 p. ; **575**

1. Evolution (Biology) 2. Natural selection. 3. Essays
ISBN 0679600701

LC 93003598

Includes index.

States the evidence for a theory of evolution, explains how evolution takes place, and discusses instinct, hybrids, fossils, distribution, and classification.

Thomas, Chris D.

Inheritors of the Earth : how nature is thriving in an age of extinction / Chris D. Thomas. PublicAffairs, 2017. 304 p. **575**

1. Nature -- Effect of humans on 2. Biodiversity 3. Extinction (Biology) 4. Ecology
ISBN 9781610397278

LC bl2017035907

Combining a naturalist's eye for wildlife with an ecologist's wide lens, Inheritors of the Earth offers an authoritative account of the Anthropocene present and future, a challenge to conventional views of almost everything we do that relates to our interaction with the environment, and an illuminating reexamination of the relationship between humanity and the natural world.

575.5 Roots and leaves

Vogel, Steven, 1940-

The **life** of a leaf / Steven Vogel. The University of Chicago Press, 2012. 312 p. **575.5**

1. Leaves -- Growth. 2. Nature 3. Plants 4. Leaves -- Physiology.
ISBN 9780226859392

LC 2011037295

In its essence, science is a way of looking at and thinking about the world. In The Life of a Leaf, Steven Vogel illuminates this approach, using the humble leaf as a model. Whether plant or person, every organism must contend with its immediate physical environment, a world that both limits what organisms can do and offers innumerable opportunities for evolving fascinating ways of challenging those limits. Here, Vogel explains these interactions, examining through the example of the leaf the extraordinary designs that enable life to adapt to its physical world. --From publisher description.

"Vogel's obvious enthusiasm for the subject and his skill at writing shine through with clarity and joy." Library Journal.

576.5 Genetics

Arney, Kat

Herding Hemingway's cats : understanding how our genes work / Kat Arney. Bloomsbury, 2016 288 p. **576.5**

1. DNA 2. Genetics 3. Human genome 4. Genes

ISBN 9781472910042

LC bl2016008091

How DNA is packed, unpacked, and read--a companion reader to the book of life itself.

"A robust, bouncy, pellucid introduction to DNA and genetics." Kirkus.

Keller, Evelyn Fox, 1936-

The **century** of the gene / Evelyn Fox Keller. Harvard University Press, c2000. 186 p. : **576.5**

1. Genetics -- History -- 20th century

ISBN 9780674003729

LC 00038319

Arguing for a new vocabulary of genetics, the author shows why the past century of gene research and molecular biology was so revolutionary and assesses the potential implications of the Human Genome Project and other biological and genetic advances.

Zimmer, Carl, 1966-

She has her mother's laugh : the powers, perversions, and potential of heredity / Carl Zimmer. Dutton, an imprint of Penguin Random House LLC, 2018 544 p. ; **576.5**

1. Heredity. 2. Genetics 3. Genetic research 4. Human evolution.

ISBN 9781101984598

LC 2017046101

The award-winning columnist and author of Parasite Rex presents a history of our understanding of heredity and how it has shaped human society, chronicling the transitions brought about by genetic research and sharing anecdotal insights into his own family's experiences while making predictions about how evolving understandings are likely to impact the future.

576.8 Evolution

Ayala, Francisco J., 1934-

Darwin's gift to science and religion / Francisco J. Ayala. Joseph Henry Press, 2007. xi, 237 p. : **576.8**

1. Darwin, Charles, 1809-1882 2. Natural selection. 3. Evolution. 4. Intelligent design (Teleology) 5. Religion and science.

ISBN 9780309102315

LC 2007005821

"This elegant book provides the single best introduction to Darwin and the development of evolutionary biology now available." Publishers Weekly.

Barnosky, Anthony D.

Dodging extinction : power, food, money and the future of life on Earth / Anthony D. Barnosky. University of California Press, 2014 256 p. **576.8**

1. Mass extinctions. 2. Extinction (Biology) 3. Conservation of natural resources.

ISBN 9780520274372

LC 2013048773

"The author is an optimist who suggests a way through the present crisis: implement reasonable and responsible resource management and sustainable agricultural and energy practices along with habitat restoration and conservation biology. It can be done. This is a must read for college students and a well-informed citizenry. Summing Up: Essential. All levels/libraries." Choice..

Brannen, Peter

The **ends** of the world : volcanic apocalypses, lethal oceans, and our quest to understand Earth's past mass extinctions / Peter Brannen. Ecco Press, 2017. 256 p. **576.8**

1. Mass extinctions. 2. Extinction (Biology) 3. Environmental disasters. 4. Disaster forecasting

ISBN 9780062364807

LC bl2017017905

A vivid tour of Earth's five mass extinctions profiles the vibrant worlds that were destroyed and rebuilt during each cycle, explaining what today's scientists are learning from ancient fossils about 21st-century climate change.

"If readers have time for only one book on the subject, this wonderfully written, well-balanced, and intricately researched (though not too dense) selection is the one to choose." Library Journal.

Browne, E. J. (E. Janet), 1950-

Darwin's Origin of species : a biography / Janet Browne. Atlantic Monthly Press, 2007, c2006. x, 174 p. ; **576.8**

1. Darwin, Charles, 1809-1882 2. Darwin, Charles, 1809-1882. On the origin of species. 3. Naturalists -- England. 4. Evolution.

ISBN 0871139537

LC 2006043623

"First published in Great Britain in hardback in 2006 by Atlantic Books"--T.p. verso.

Describes the genesis of Darwin's theories, from his university studies and five-year voyage on the Beagle to his debates with contemporaries and his garden experiments, in a history that also illuminates controversies surrounding the work's publication.

"This excellent introduction is highly recommended for all readers who want to better understand the heated debates that this book still causes today." Publishers Weekly.

Catania, Kenneth, 1965-

Great adaptations : star-nosed moles, electric eels & and other tales of evolution's mysteries solved / Kenneth Catania. Princeton University Press, 2020. 240 p. **576.8**

1. Adaptation (Biology) 2. Animals -- Adaptation 3. Animal anatomy 4. Animal behavior

ISBN 9780691195254

LC bl2020052401

From star-nosed moles that have super-sensing snouts to electric eels that paralyze their prey, animals possess unique and extraordinary abilities. In Great Adaptations, Kenneth Catania presents an entertaining and engaging look at some of nature's most remarkable creatures. Telling the story of his biological detective work, Catania sheds light on the mysteries behind the behaviors of tentacled snakes, tiny shrews, zombie-making wasps, and more. He shows not only how studying these animals can provide deep insights into how life evolved, but also how scientific discovery can be filled with adventure and fun.

"The joy Catania takes in the process of exploring the natural world will delight readers." Publishers Weekly

Costa, James T., 1963-

Darwin's backyard : how small experiments led to a big theory / James T. Costa. W. W. Norton & Company, 2017 416

p. **576.8**

1. Darwin, Charles, 1809-1882 2. Naturalists -- England. 3. Natural selection. 4. Experiments 5. Evolution
ISBN 9780393239898

LC 2017017865

Goes beyond the portrait of Charles Darwin as a brilliant thinker to concentrate on him as a nimble experimenter delving into some of evolution's great mysteries.

"An instructive and entertaining look at Darwin's 'experimentising' and how it can be readily duplicated using mostly simple household tools." Kirkus.

Darwin, Charles, 1809-1882

Charles Darwin : the Beagle letters / edited by Frederick Burkhardt ; introduction by Janet Browne. Cambridge University Press, 2008. 500 p. **576.8**

1. Darwin, Charles, 1809-1882 2. Beagle Expedition, 1831-1836 3. Naturalists -- England -- Correspondence. 4. Expeditions. 5. Biological discoveries 6. Natural selection
ISBN 9780521898386

LC bl2009001752

"The complete correspondence both to and from Charles Darwin during his five years circumnavigating the globe on the HMS Beagle, beginning in 1831, documents his growth as a naturalist and offers a picture of life in the England he left behind. It is fascinating to watch Darwin attempt to come to grips with the huge amount of data he collected and make sense of the patterns he observed. We get an intimate look at an adventurous young Darwin, so unlike his more familiar, sedentary older self who would write On the Origin of Species." Publishers Weekly.

Davies, P. C. W.

The **eerie** silence : renewing our search for alien intelligence / Paul Davies. Houghton Mifflin Harcourt, 2010. 288 p. **576.8**

1. SETI. 2. Aliens (Non-humanoid) 3. Artificial intelligence. 4. Life on other planets. 5. Interstellar communication. 6. Space.
ISBN 9780547133249

LC 2010003088

Argues that erroneous searching is the cause of the lack of success of the Search for Extraterrestrial Intelligence project over the last fifty years and recommends broader parameters that include searches for non-human-like life.

Dawkins, Richard, 1941-

★The **ancestor's** tale : a pilgrimage to the dawn of evolution / Richard Dawkins. Houghton Mifflin, 2004. xii, 673 p. : **576.8**

1. Humans. 2. Life (Biology) 3. Evolution -- History. 4. Evolution -- Philosophy.
ISBN 0618005838

LC 2004059864

"The author sets out on a pilgrimage tracing the history of the human species back to the very origins of life, marking along the way 39 rendezvous points where the human genealogical path crosses that of other terrestrial species. Lively and daring, a book certain to draw even casual readers deep into the adventureand controversyof science." Booklist.

The **greatest** show on Earth : the evidence for evolution / Richard Dawkins. Free Press, 2009. 480 p. **576.8**

1. Evolution 2. Biology. 3. Humans. 4. Science.
ISBN 9781416594789

LC 2009025330

The acclaimed author of The God Delusion and Selfish Gene lays out evidence in defense of the theory of evolution in a thrilling tour into our distant past and into the the interstices of life on Earth that will be released in time for the 150th anniversary of Charles Darwin's On the Origin of Species.

Goldman, Lee (Physician)

Too much of a good thing : how four key survival traits are now killing us / Lee Goldman. Little, Brown, & Co., 2015 viii, 344 p. ; **576.8**

1. Human body 2. Survival 3. Adaptation (Biology) 4. Prehistoric humans
ISBN 9780316236812

LC 2015937505

The dean of Columbia University's medical school explains how rising rates of obesity, heart disease and other life-threatening conditions are reflecting how the human body is out of sync with today's environment, making recommendations for changing causative lifestyle habits.

Gould, Stephen Jay, 1941-

The **structure** of evolutionary theory / Stephen Jay Gould. Belknap Press of Harvard University Press, 2002. xxii, 1433 p. : **576.8**

1. Evolution. 2. Punctuated equilibria (Evolution) 3. Human evolution
ISBN 0674006135

LC 2001043556

"This is a history and analysis of classical and twentieth-century evolutionary theory." Booklist.

Johnson, Sarah Stewart

The **sirens** of Mars : searching for life on another world / Sarah Stewart Johnson. Crown, [2020] xiii, 266 p. **576.8**

1. Johnson, Sarah Stewart 2. Women scientists 3. Planets 4. Life on other planets 5. Extreme environments 6. Mars (Planet)
ISBN 9781101904817

LC 2020007280

Mars was once similar to Earth, but today there are no rivers, no lakes, no oceans. Coated in red dust, the terrain is bewilderingly empty. And yet multiple spacecraft are circling Mars, sweeping over Terra Sabaea, Syrtis Major, the dunes of Elysium, and Mare Sirenum--on the brink, perhaps, of a staggering find, one that would inspire humankind as much as any discovery in the history of modern science. In this beautifully observed, deeply personal book, Georgetown scientist Sarah Stewart Johnson tells the story of how she and other researchers have scoured Mars for signs of life, transforming the planet from a distant point of light into a world of its own.

"A vivid, poetic account that leaves readers eager to see what's next in the quest to find extraterrestrial life." Kirkus

Kaufman, Marc

First contact : scientific breakthroughs in the hunt for life beyond Earth / Marc Kaufman. Simon & Schuster, 2011. 213 p., [8] p. of plates : **576.8**

1. Life on other planets 2. Habitable planets 3. Cosmobiology. 4. Aliens
ISBN 9781439109007

LC 2010044630

Includes bibliographical references and index.

Documents the scientific community's search for the beginnings of life on Earth and other planets, drawing on recent discoveries that support the existence of extraterrestrial life while exploring how the search for life on other planets is changing what humans think about their own history.

Keller, Michael, 1976-

Charles Darwin's on the origin of species : a graphic adaptation / story by Michael Keller ; art by Nicolle Rager Fuller. Rodale, c2009. 192 p. **576.8**

1. Darwin, Charles, 1809-1882. Origin of species Illustrations. 2. Evolution. 3. Natural selection. 4. Biology. 5. Comics and Graphic novels

ISBN 9781605296975

LC 2009011387

"The graphic novel follows Origin's original chapters, combining snippets of Darwin's text with quotes from letters, illustrative examples from his time and from the present, and occasional invented dialog. Fuller's images of people seem clumsy, but her full-color plants, animals, charts, maps, and scientific accoutrements are attractive and effective. . . . [This] version well conveys both the science and the wonder of Origin." Library Journal.

Larson, Edward J. (Edward John)

Evolution : the remarkable history of a scientific theory / Edward J. Larson. Modern Library, 2006. 347 p. : **576.8**

1. Evolution -- Philosophy -- History. 2. Paleontology -- Philosophy. 3. Sociobiology. 4. Genetics -- History

ISBN 0812968492

LC oc2007047137

Traces the history of evolutionary theory, from the eighteenth-century emergence of paleontology, through the breakthroughs of Darwin, to the backlash against evolutionism, to its resurrection through the science of genetics.

"This is an overview of evolutionary thought from ancient speculations to the emergence of a neo-Darwinian synthesis. It focuses on those essential facts, events, and ideas that have contributed to the successes of scientific evolutionism. Larson is to be commended for stressing the value of both scientific inquiry and the evolutionary framework. This outstanding book is highly recommended for all academic and public libraries." Library Journal.

Lister, Adrian

★**Darwin's** fossils : the collection that shaped the theory of evolution / Adrian Lister. Smithsonian Books, c2018. 160 p. **576.8**

1. Darwin, Charles, 1809-1882. 2. Beagle Expedition, 1831-1836 3. Evolution 4. Fossils

ISBN 9781588346179

LC 2017046415

"Copyrighted by the Trustees of the Natural History Museum, London."

Reveals how Darwin's study of fossils shaped his scientific thinking and led to his development of the theory of evolution. -- Provided by publisher.

"Richly illustrated with photos from the fossil collection and line drawings produced when Darwin was alive, Lister's work is an essential acquisition for every library prizing quality books on evolution." Booklist.

Lloyd, Christopher, 1968-

The **story** of the world in 100 species / Christopher Lloyd. Bloomsbury, 2016. 416 p. **576.8**

1. History. 2. Civilization -- History. 3. Humans.

ISBN 9781408876381

"The author of What on Earth Happened? offers a radical new look at the story of Earth, seen through the prism of the living things that have had the greatest impacts on the planet."--From publisher's description.

"Lloyd shares the history of each of his entrants with casual enthusiasm and a sense of wonder, in articles that stand alone well for readers interested in browsing and which together give a sense of biodiversity as a source of joy." Publishers Weekly.

Losos, Jonathan B.

Improbable destinies : fate, chance, and the future of evolution / Jonathan B. Losos. Riverhead Books, 2017. 384 p. **576.8**

1. Evolution. 2. Adaptation (Biology) 3. Natural selection.

ISBN 9780399184925

LC 2016054594

A Harvard museum curator draws on the latest breakthroughs in evolutionary biology to challenge popular assumptions about how evolution works, examining how tiny, random convergences, from mutations to butterfly sneezes, have triggered remarkable evolutionary changes.

"A cheerful, delightfully lucid primer on evolution and the predictive possibilities within the field." Kirkus.

Margulis, Lynn, 1938-

Symbiotic planet : a new look at evolution / Lynn Margulis. Basic Books, c1998. vi, 147 p. : **576.8**

1. Symbiosis. 2. Evolution 3. Symbiogenesis.

ISBN 0465072712

LC 98038921

"From the origin of life to the classification and phylogeny of living organisms, from a discussion of Gaia--belief that Earth operates like a living being--to a discussion of the underlying reasons for sex, iconoclastic biologist Margulis ... takes on many of the big questions in biology. In a book that is part autobiography and part biological primer, Margulis . advances the idea that a large part of organic evolution can be explained by symbiosis." Publishers Weekly.

McCalman, Iain

Darwin's armada : four voyages and the battle for the theory of evolution / Iain McCalman. Norton, 2009. 432 p. **576.8**

1. Darwin, Charles, 1809-1882 2. Hooker, Joseph Dalton, Sir, 1817-1911. 3. Huxley, Thomas Henry, 1825-1895. 4. Wallace, Alfred Russel, 1823-1913. 5. Naturalists -- Great Britain. 6. Evolution -- History -- 19th century 7. Scientific discoveries -- History 8. Voyages and travels -- 19th century. 9. Great Britain -- History -- 19th century

ISBN 9780393068146

LC 2009016055

Profiles three British voyagers who became fierce defenders of Darwin's theory of evolution, tracing the lives and scientific discoveries of Joseph Hooker, Thomas Huxley, and Alfred Wallace during respective voyages to the southern hemisphere.

National Academy of Sciences (U.S.)

Science, evolution, and creationism / National Academy of Sciences, Institute of Medicine. National Academies Press, c2008. xv, 70 p. : **576.8**

1. Evolution (Biology) 2. Creationism. 3. Science.

ISBN 9780309105866

LC 2007015904

This beautifully illustrated and well-organized volume comes down firmly on the necessity of teaching evolution as the cornerstone for any science curriculum, articulating in gentle but clear language why the religious belief behind creationism invalidates its usefulness or even its appropriateness in science classrooms in America. The history of the theory of evolution, the basis of modern scientific method and study, and the history and religious background of the theories of creationism and intelligent design are described in separate chapters. The book is written to be accessible to public school teachers and parents by a committee of educators in the U.S. --From publisher description.

"This book will be important to educators at all levels, and gives valuable assistance to those who are fighting against willful ignorance." Choice.

Newitz, Annalee, 1969-
Scatter, adapt, and remember : how humans will survive a mass extinction / Annalee Newitz. Doubleday, [2013] 320 p. **576.8**

1. Survival. 2. Extinction (Biology) 3. End of the world 4. Humans. 5. Apocalyptic literature
ISBN 9780385535915
LC 2012042409

A speculative, optimistic work of popular science suggests practical ways to promote the human race's survival of a mass extinction induced by climate change, pandemics and catastrophic natural disasters, citing innovations ranging from the bacteria labs of St. Louis to the underground cities of central Turkey.

"Humans may be experts at destroying the planet, but we are no slouches at preserving it, either, and Newitz's shrewd speculations are heartening." Kirkus.

Nye, Bill
Undeniable : evolution and the science of creation / Bill Nye with Corey Powell. St. Martin's Press, 2014. 320 p. **576.8**

1. Natural history -- Philosophy -- Popular works. 2. Evolution (Biology) -- Popular works. 3. Creationism 4. Creationism in the public schools.
ISBN 9781250007131
LC 2014027163

Revealing the mechanics of evolutionary theory, the scientist, engineer and inventor presents a compelling argument for the scientific unviability of creationism and insists that creationism's place in the science classroom is harmful not only to our children, but to the future of the greater world as well.

"The straightforward, accessible language and clear explanations make this ideal reading to understand lifes origins, especially for those new to the evidence of evolution." Library Journal.

Preston, Louisa
Goldilocks and the water bears : the search for life in the universe / Louisa Preston. Bloomsbury Sigma, 2016 288 p. **576.8**

1. Cosmogony. 2. Cosmology. 3. Life on other planets.
ISBN 9781472920096
LC bl2016048937

Includes index.

Across billions of planets, life cannot be restricted solely to Earth--or can it? Scientist Louisa Preston chronicles what astrobiology tells us about the likelihood of extraterrestrial life.

"Preston's accessible writing style, enthusiasm, and optimism succeed at informing as well as tickling readers imaginations." Publishers Weekly.

Stott, Rebecca
★**Darwin's** ghosts : the secret history of evolution / Rebecca Stott. Spiegel & Grau, 2012. 320 p. **576.8**

1. Darwin, Charles, 1809-1882. On the origin of species. 2. Evolution -- History 3. Science -- History 4. Scientists 5. Naturalists
ISBN 9781400069378
LC 2011041951

Evolution was not discovered single-handedly, Rebecca Stott argues, contrary to what has become standard lore, but is an idea that emerged over many centuries, advanced by daring individuals across the globe who had the imagination to speculate on nature's extraordinary ways, and who had the courage to articulate such speculations at a time when to do so was often considered heresy.

Ward, Peter D. (Peter Douglas), 1949-
A **new** history of life : the radical new discoveries about the origins and evolution of life on earth / Peter Ward & Joe Kirschvink. Bloomsbury Press, 2015. 352 p. **576.8**

1. Evolution 2. Life -- Origin. 3. Biology
ISBN 9781608199075
LC 2014029828

Draws on cutting-edge research in a variety of scientific disciplines to outline provocative new theories about the evolution of life on Earth that challenge mainstream Darwinian beliefs and make predictions about future evolutions.

576.801 Philosophy and theory

Wilson, David Sloan
★**Evolution** for everyone : how Darwin's theory can change the way we think about our lives / David Sloan Wilson. Delacorte Press, 2007. viii, 390 p. ; **576.801**

1. Evolution. 2. Evolution -- History. 3. Life sciences
ISBN 0385340214
LC 2006023685

Wilson outlines the basic principles of evolution with stories that entertain as much as they inform, and shows how, properly understood, these principles can illuminate the length and breadth of creation, from the origin of life to the nature of religion. Now everyone can move beyond the sterile debates about creationism and intelligent design to share Darwin's panoramic view of animal and human life, seamlessly connected to each other. Evolution, as Wilson explains, is not just about dinosaurs and human origins, but about why all species behave as they do--from beetles that devour their own young, to bees that function as a collective brain, to dogs that are smarter in some respects than our closest ape relatives. And basic evolutionary principles are also the foundation for humanity's capacity for symbolic thought, culture, and morality.--From publisher description.

"Rather than catalog its successes, denounce its detractors or in any way present evolutionary theory as the province of expert tacticians like himself, Wilson invites readers inside and shows them how Darwinism is done, and at lesson's end urges us to go ahead, feel free to try it at home. The result is a sprightly, absorbing and charmingly earnest book that manages a minor miracle, the near-complete emulsifying of science and the real world, ingredients too often kept stubbornly, senselessly apart." New York Times Book Review.

576.839 Extraterrestrial life

Ward, Peter Douglas, 1949-
Life as we do not know it : the NASA search for (and synthesis of) alien life / Peter Ward. Penguin, 2007, c2005. xxi, 298 p. ; **576.839**

1. United States. National Aeronautics and Space Administration 2. Life on other planets. 3. Civilization -- Extraterrestrial influences. 4.

Astronomy -- Research. 5. Space biology
ISBN 0143038494

LC oc2007070096

Originally published: New York: Viking, 2005.

A revealing exploration of the latest NASA research into the possibility of extraterrestrial life also poses a hypothesis about the origins of life on Earth, examining the controversial idea of creating non-DNA life in a laboratory as well as the scientific possibilities of the range of life throughout the universe.

"The author believes researchers might be taking the wrong approach by looking only for earthly DNA-based life forms. Truly alien life, he argues, might have completely different origins. . . . The science is neatly laid out, and readers willing to follow his daring, scientifically based speculations will find their imaginations spurred." Publishers Weekly.

577 Ecology

Carroll, Sean M., 1966-

The **big** picture : on the origins of life, meaning, and the universe itself / Sean Carroll. Dutton est. 1852, an imprint of Penguin Random House LLC, 2016 352 p. **577**

1. Cosmology. 2. Scientific discoveries. 3. Life -- Origin. 4. Semantics (Philosophy)
ISBN 9780525954828

LC 2015050590

The award-winning Caltech physicist and author of The Particle at the End of the Universe shares sweeping perspectives into how human purpose and meaning naturally fit into a scientific worldview.

"Carroll is the perfect guide on this wondrous journey of discovery. A brilliantly lucid exposition of profound philosophical and scientific issues in a language accessible to lay readers." Kirkus.

Roston, Eric

The **carbon** age : how life's core element has become civilization's greatest threat / Eric Roston. Walker, 2008. 320 p. **577**

1. Carbon cycle (Biogeochemistry) 2. Carbon. 3. Carbon compounds.
ISBN 9780802715579

LC 2008002754

A historical and scientific assessment of carbon evaluates its ironic dual role as both a key building block of life on Earth and a component of such threats as carbon dioxide emissions, chlorofluorocarbons, and simple carbohydrates.

577.27 Effects of humans on ecology

Nuccitelli, Dana

Climatology versus pseudoscience : exposing the failed predictions of global warming skeptics / Dana Nuccitelli. Praeger, an imprint of ABC-CLIO, LLC, 2015 xiii, 212 p. : **577.27**

1. Climatic changes. 2. Global warming.
ISBN 1440832013

LC 2014046795

"The book includes the best available short account of the history of climate science and describes climate change models and controversies in brief but incisive and well-illustrated detail." Choice..

Wills, Christopher

Green equilibrium : the vital balance of humans & nature / / Christopher Wills. Oxford University Press 2013 320 p. **577.27**

1. Biotic communities. 2. Evolution 3. Nature -- Effect of humans on 4. Biology.
ISBN 9780199645701

LC bl2013024396

Explores the rules that govern such diverse ecosystems as the coral reefs in the Philippines and California's grasslands and looks at the role of human populations in maintaining a healthy balance in the world's ecosystems.

577.3 Forest ecology

Fortey, Richard A.

The **wood** for the trees : one man's long view of nature / Richard Fortey. Alfred A. Knopf, 2016. 320 p. **577.3**

1. Forest ecology. 2. Biotic communities 3. Natural history. 4. Phenology. 5. England 6. Chiltern Hills, England 7. Oxfordshire, England
ISBN 9781101875759

LC 2015048791

The author traces a year in his four-acre woodland property in the Chiltern Hills of Oxfordshire, England, where he discovered a new species and explored the myriad connections in the natural world and how they reflect history and our role in the universe.

"An eloquent, eccentric, and precise nature memoir." Kirkus.

577.4 Grassland ecology

Cowen, Rob

Common ground : encounters with nature at the edges of life / Rob Cowen ; with a new preface. The University of Chicago Press, 2016. 352 p. **577.4**

1. Cowen, Rob Homes and haunts 2. Nature 3. Natural history 4. Humans -- Effect of environment on 5. Nature conservation 6. Yorkshire, England 7. Northern England 8. England
ISBN 9780226424262

LC 2016014736

"Common Ground is a fascinating tour of the edges of ecosystem--surban and natural. It is in these heterogeneous landscapes that human animals encounter those of the non human variety."--Provided by the publisher.

577.5 Ecology of miscellaneous environments

Lawson, Nancy, 1970-

The **humane** gardener : nurturing a backyard habitat for wildlife / Nancy Lawson. Princeton Architectural Press, 2017 223 p. : **577.5**

1. Gardening to attract wildlife 2. Garden ecology
ISBN 9781616895549

LC 2016029007

A philosophical and practical guide for the gardener who wants to create a backyard garden in harmony with nature. --From publisher description.

"This gorgeously written, well-argued title will help backyard gardeners see all creatures, from insects to elk, as visitors to be welcomed rather than pests to be removed." Library Journal.

Schilthuizen, Menno

Darwin comes to town : how the urban jungle drives evolution / Menno Schilthuizen. Picador USA, 2018. 304 p. **577.5**

1. Cities and towns 2. Nature 3. Urban ecology 4. Urbanization
ISBN 9781250127822

LC 2017059153

An evolutionary biologist explains how scientists are discovering that evolution can actually happen very quickly in the most unlikely of places--the heart of the city.

Wolfe, David W.

Tales from the underground : a natural history of subterranean life / David W. Wolfe. Perseus Pub., 2002, c2001. x, 221 p. : **577.5**

1. Soil animals. 2. Soil biology. 3. Soil ecology. 4. Underground ecology.
ISBN 9780738206790

LC BL2002004640

Reprint. Originally published: 2001.

"Wolfe explains in a straightforward, readable style that there is probably as much biodiversity and even as much biomass below ground as above." New Scientist.

577.6 Aquatic ecology

Egan, Dan

★The **death** and life of the Great Lakes / Dan Egan. W.W. Norton & Company, 2017. 384 p. **577.6**

1. Lake ecology. 2. Water quality. 3. Lakes 4. Organism introduction 5. Great Lakes. 6. Great Lakes region
ISBN 9780393246438

LC 2016039546

Traces the scientific, historical, and ecological factors endangering the Great Lakes, discussing late-nineteenth century efforts to connect the lakes to the Atlantic, which unexpectedly introduced invasive species from the natural world.

"Egan...effectively calls attention to the inherent fragility of the Great Lakes in this thought-provoking investigation, providing a modern history of the lakes...and the problems that have plagued them." Publishers Weekly.

577.7 Marine ecology

Ellis, Richard, 1938-

★The **empty** ocean : plundering the world's marine life / written and illustrated by Richard Ellis. Island Press ; Shearwater Books, 2003. xiv, 367 p. : **577.7**

1. Marine animals. 2. Rare and endangered animals. 3. Rare and endangered plants. 4. Marine biology.
ISBN 1559639741

LC 2003002077

Explains the detrimental affects that commercial fishing and other depeletions of marine wildlife have on ocean ecology, and suggests remedies for the growing problem.

"Rather than writing the Silent Spring of the oceans, [Ellis] has produced a book that is likely to provide the inspiration and source materials for such a badly needed work. It is also a splendid example of history illuminating ecology, with well-chosen facts that enable us to picture a largely invisible catastrophe." New York Times Book Review.

578 Natural history of organisms and related subjects

Weidensaul, Scott

Return to wild America : a yearlong search for the continent's natural soul / Scott Weidensaul. North Point Press, 2005. xx, 394 p. : **578**

1. Weidensaul, Scott Travel North America. 2. Peterson, Roger Tory, 1908-1996 Travel North America. 3. Fisher, James, 1912- Travel North America. 4. Natural history -- North America. 5. Wildlife -- United States.
ISBN 9780865476882

LC 2005047720

"Fifty years after the publishing of Roger Tory Peterson's and James Fisher's Wild America, the author retraces Peterson and Fisher's steps from Newfoundland's craggy coastline, down the East Coast, into Mexico and up the West Coast to Alaska. This engrossing state-of-nature memoir, making a vibrant case for preserving America's wild past for future Americans, promises to become a classic in its own right." Publishers Weekly.

578.4 Adaptation

Forbes, Peter, 1947-

Dazzled and deceived : mimicry and camouflage / Peter Forbes. Yale University Press, c2009. xv, 283 p., 16 p. of plates : **578.4**

1. Mimicry (Biology) 2. Camouflage (Biology)
ISBN 9780300125399

LC 2009023577

Dazzled and Deceived tells the unique and fascinating story of mimicry and camouflage in science, art, warfare, and the natural world. Discovered in the 1850s by the young English naturalists Henry Walter Bates and Alfred Russel Wallace in the Amazonian rainforest, the phenomenon of mimicry was seized upon as the first independent validation of Darwin's theory of natural selection. But mimicry and camouflage also created a huge impact outside the laboratory walls. Peter Forbes's cultural history links mimicry and camouflage to art, literature, military tactics, and medical cures across the twentieth century, and charts its intricate involvement with the perennial dispute between evolution and creationism.

"Forbes has produced a colorful look at camouflage in nature and battle, with a focus on the two world wars. [The book] straddles the worlds of evolutionary biology, art, and military strategy with a world-class cast of characters..." Boston Globe.

Simon, Matt

The **wasp** that brainwashed the caterpillar : evolution's most unbelievable solutions to life's biggest problems / Matt Simon ; illustrated by Vladimir Stankovic. Penguin Books, 2016. xii, 260 p. : **578.4**

1. Animals -- Adaptation 2. Predation (Biology) 3. Parasitism 4. Natural selection 5. Essays
ISBN 9780143128687

LC 2016001823

Profiles animals that have adapted to solve some of nature's more perplexing problems of everyday life, from the pangolin's keratinized armor and the anglerfish's mating habits to the axolotl's regenerative limbs.

578.6 Miscellaneous nontaxonomic kinds of organisms

Anthony, Leslie, 1957-

The **aliens** among us : how invasive species are transforming the planet - and ourselves / Leslie Anthony. Yale University Press, 2017. 367 p. **578.6**

1. Biotic communities 2. Biological invasions 3. Adaptation (Biology) 4. Competition (Biology)
ISBN 9780300208900
LC 2017937194

A thoughtful, accessible look at the rapidly growing issue of invasive plants, animals, and microbes around the globe with a focus on the scientific issues and ecological, health, and other challenges.

Hamilton, Garry, 1962-

Super species : the creatures that will dominate the planet / Garry Hamilton. Firefly Books, 2010. 271 p. : **578.6**

1. Organism introduction. 2. Biological invasions. 3. Invasive species. 4. Invasive plants.
ISBN 9781554076307
LC oc2010078285

A gripping examination of invasive species' impact. --From publisher description.

"Well researched and written, with an abundance of excellent photos, this work provides an outstanding, balanced look at this group of species." Choice.

578.68 Rare and endangered species

Ackerman, Diane, 1948-

The **rarest** of the rare : vanishing animals, timeless worlds / Diane Ackerman. Random House, c1995. xxi, 184 p. ; **578.68**

1. Rare and endangered insects. 2. Wildlife conservation. 3. Rare and endangered animals 4. Rare and endangered plants.
ISBN 0679403469
LC 95008499

Includes index.

"Every species that is endangered or becomes extinct deserves so poetic a chronicler as Ackerman." Library Journal.

578.769 Saltwater wetlands--biology

Carson, Rachel, 1907-1964

The **edge** of the sea / Rachel Carson ; with illustrations by Bob Hines. Houghton Mifflin, 1955. 276 p. : **578.769**

1. Seashore biology. 2. Seashore animals. 3. Seashore. 4. Seashore ecology.
ISBN 0395924960
LC 54010759

The Edge of the Sea introduces a world of teeming life where the sea meets the land.

578.77 Oceans--biology

Carson, Rachel, 1907-1964

Under the sea wind / Rachel Carson. Penguin Books, 2007, c1941. 184 p. **578.77**

1. Marine biology -- Atlantic Ocean. 2. Marine ecology. 3. Sea birds. 4. Marine animals.
ISBN 0143104969

Originally published: United States : Simon and Schuster, 1941.

Uses the life and migrations of Scomber the mackerel and Anguilla the eel to depict marine ecology along the Atlantic shore.

Crist, Darlene Trew

World ocean census : a global survey of marine life / Darlene Trew Crist, Gail Scowcroft, James M. Harding, Jr. Firefly Books, c2009. 256 p. : **578.77**

1. Census of Marine Life (Program) 2. Marine biology -- Research -- Methodology 3. Marine animals -- Counting -- Methodology 4. Zoological surveys -- Methodology 5. Marine ecology
ISBN 9781554074341
LC 2009675176

An insider's description of the comprehensive Census of Marine Life and what it reveals about a seriously threatened ecosystem.

Kirby, Richard R.

Ocean drifters : a secret world beneath the waves / Richard R. Kirby. Firefly Books, 2011, c2010. 192 p. : **578.77**

1. Marine plankton
ISBN 9781554079827
LC 2011284690

"Kirby (Marine Inst. Research Fellow, Plymouth Univ., UK), who has published widely in scientific journals, combines in this book his area of expertise--plankton--with magnificent color photography of each species. He details the importance of the ocean's plankton layer to the health of the globe and its effects on sea and human life in the photos' descriptions...Recommended for readers interested in the smaller denizens of the natural world, the ocean, or microphotography." Library Journal.

Koslow, J. Anthony (Julian Anthony), 1947-

The **silent** deep : the discovery, ecology and conservation of the deep sea / Tony Koslow. University of Chicago, Ill. :Press, 2007. 270 p. : **578.77**

1. Deep-sea ecology. 2. Marine resources conservation.
ISBN 0226451259
LC 2006022282

Discusses the ecology of the deep sea, the impact being made by humans, and advocates for protection of this ecosystem.

Sardet, Christian

Plankton : wonders of the drifting world / Christian Sardet ; edited by Rafael D. Rosengarten and Theodore Rosengarten ; translated from the French by Christian Sardet and Dana Sardet ; prologue by Mark Ohman. University of Chicago Press, 2015 222 p. : **578.77**

1. Plankton -- Pictorial works.
ISBN 9780226188713
LC 2014034445

"Originally published in France as Plancton, aux origines du vivant. © 2013 Les Editions Eugen Ulmer, Paris"--Title page verso.

"A fascinating book that will cause readers to think deeply about plankton and its importance to human and animal life. A biology or general science background is not necessary to read this book; the reader needs only a desire to learn more about these intriguing organisms." Library Journal.

579 Natural history of microorganisms, fungi, algae

Ben-Barak, Idan

The **invisible** kingdom : from the tips of our fingers to the tops of our trash, inside the curious world of microbes / Idan Ben-Barak. Basic Books, 2009, c2008. x, 204 p. ; **579**

1. Microbiology. 2. Microorganisms. 3. Proteins. 4. Bacteria.
ISBN 9780465018871

LC 2009019655

Originally published as: Small wonders : how microbes rule our world: Carlton North, Vic. : Scribe Publications, 2008.

Introduces the lives of genes, proteins, bacteria, and viruses and explains the numerous ways in which they influence and benefit life on Earth, from creating antibiotics, to manufacturing food, to eliminating radioactive waste.

579.5 Fungi

Sheldrake, Merlin

Entangled life : how fungi make our worlds, change our minds and shape our futures / Merlin Sheldrake. Random House, 2020. 352 p. ; **579.5**

1. Fungi. 2. Mycology. 3. Botany. 4. Biotic communities
ISBN 9780525510314

Citing the ubiquitous role of fungi in the environment, a scientific tour of examples ranging from yeast to psychedelics reveals the complex fungi networks that link plants together and make most biological life processes possible.

"From bread to booze to the very fiber of life, the world turns on fungi, and Sheldrake provides a top-notch portrait." Kirkus

579.6 Mushrooms

McKnight, Kent H.

A **field** guide to mushrooms, North America / Kent H. McKnight and Vera B. McKnight ; illustrations by Vera B. McKnight. Houghton Mifflin, 1998, c1987. xii, 429 p. : The Peterson field guide series ; **579.6**

1. Mushrooms -- North America -- Identification 2. Mushrooms -- North America -- Pictorial works
ISBN 9780395910900

LC bl2006021494

"Sponsored by the National Audubon Society and the National Wildlife Federation."

Reprint. Originally published: 1987.

More than 1,000 species of mushrooms described in detail. Over 700 paintings and drawings reveal subtle field marks that cannot be captured into photographs. --From publisher description.

580 Science -- Natural history of plants and animals -- Plants (Botany)

Darcey, Cheralyn

Flowerpaedia : 1000 flowers and their meanings / Cheralyn Darcey. Rockpool Publishing, 2017. 258 p. : **580**

1. Flowers -- Australia -- Dictionaries 2. Dictionaries
ISBN 9781925429466

LC bl2018193106

An A-Z reference guide of over one thousand flowers explains what each flower means emotionally, spiritually, and symbolically.

Mabey, Richard, 1941-

The **cabaret** of plants : forty thousand years of plant life and the human imagination / Richard Mabey. W. W. Norton & Company, 2016, c2015 400 p. **580**

1. Botany -- History. 2. Plants 3. Nature 4. Natural history
ISBN 9780393239973

LC 2015033568

First published in Great Britain in 2015 under the title: The cabaret of plants: botany and the imagination.

Taking readers from the Himalayas to Madagascar to the Amazon to our backyards, a renowned naturalist presents a sweeping botanical history in which he explores dozens of plant species that have challenged our imaginations, awoken our wonder and upturned our ideas about history, science, beauty and belief.

"What Mabey does best is invite readers to think about plants in a radical new way, even posing the question as to whether a plant's sensory abilities--electrostatic charges, chemical communication through pheromones and bioacoustic sound waves--actually constitute intelligence. An unusual and vastly entertaining journey into the world of mysterious plant life as experienced by a gifted nature writer." Kirkus

580.92 Botanists

Kassinger, Ruth, 1954-

★A **garden** of marvels : how we discovered that flowers have sex, leaves eat air, and other secrets of plants / Ruth Kassinger. William Morrow & Co., 2014. 256 p. **580.92**

1. Botany 2. Plants 3. Horticulture 4. Gardeners
ISBN 9780062048998

LC 2014002824

"[A]n informal, entertaining account of how early researchers discovered how plants work and what scientists are still learning about plants today." Kirkus.

581.4 Adaptation

Dunn Chace, Teri

Seeing seeds : a journey into the world of seedheads, pods, and fruit / photography by Robert Llewellyn ; written by Teri Dunn Chace. Timber Press, 2015 284 p. : **581.4**

1. Seeds 2. Seeds.
ISBN 1604694920

LC 2015006910

Provides an overview of how seeds are formed and dispersed, and profiles common seeds from garden flowers, herbs, fruits and vegetables, and shrubs and trees.

581.6 Miscellaneous nontaxonomic kinds of plants

Angier, Bradford

Field guide to edible wild plants / Bradford Angier ; revisions by David K. Foster ; illustrations by Arthur J. Anderson ; additional illustrations by Jacqueline Mahannah, Michelle L. Meneghini, and Kristen E. Workman. Stackpole Books, c2008.

vi, 282 p. : **581.6**

1. Wild plants, Edible -- Identification
ISBN 9780811734479

LC 2007040125

Includes index.

First-ever revision of a classic guidebook. Essential information on each plant's characteristics, distribution, and edibility as well as updated taxonomy and 18 new species. How to find, prepare, and eat plants growing in the wild. --From publisher description.

Davis, Wade

One river : explorations and discoveries in the Amazon rain forest / Wade Davis. Simon & Schuster, 1996. 537 p. : **581.6**

1. Schultes, Richard Evans, 1915-2001. 2. Plowman, Timothy. 3. Ethnobotanists 4. Botanists 5. Ethnobotany -- Amazon Valley. 6. Hallucinogenic plants -- Amazon Valley -- Collection and preservation. 7. Amazon Valley.
ISBN 0684808862

LC 96021516

Governor General's Literary Awards, English-language Nonfiction finalist

An account of two generations of ethnobotanists who explored the Amazon--Richard Evans Schultes in the 1940s, and his students Timothy Plowman and Wade Davis in the 1970s--and their research into hallucinogenic and medicinal plants.

"Davis writes magnificently, with verve when describing his many adventurous field trips, accurately and efficiently when telling science or history, and with vivid fantasy when portraying hallucinogenic trances." New York Times Book Review.

Gibbons, Euell

Stalking the wild asparagus / Euell Gibbons ; with illustrations by Margaret F. Schroeder ; including a remembrance of the author by John McPhee. A.C. Hood, 1987, c1962. xiii, 303 p. : **581.6**

1. Wild plants, Edible -- United States. 2. Wild plants, Edible -- Canada. 3. Cooking (Wild foods) 4. Recipes 5. Cookbooks
ISBN 9780911469035

LC 87016933

Includes index.

Originally published: New York : D. McKay, 1962.

An imaginative approach to cooking, offering numerous recipes for main dishes and accompaniments made from wild berries, roots, nuts, and leaves

Stewart, Amy

Wicked plants : the weed that killed Lincoln's mother & other botanical atrocities / Amy Stewart ; etchings by Briony Morrow-Cribbs ; illustrations by Jonathon Rosen. Algonquin Books of Chapel Hill, 2009. xvii, 235 p. : **581.6**

1. Poisonous plants. 2. Dangerous plants. 3. Plants. 4. Botany
ISBN 9781565126831

LC 2009006192

Reveals the truth behind the harmful--even deadly--effects that many plants can have. From exploding shrubs to the weed that killed Abraham Lincoln's mother, not all plants are good for the garden.

"Stewart's book has two components: in-depth discussions of uniquely wicked plants like angel's trumpet, ergot and the water hyacinth and then guides to certain types of plants that share one common characteristic. These categories include common, garden-variety plants that have the potential to be killers (azalea, black locust, daphne, foxglove, lantana, etc.); blindness-inducing plants (poison sumac, tansy mustard, milky mangrove, etc.); and poison-producing plants that have been used to kill (curare, strychnine vine, kombe, upas tree, etc.). What makes Stewart's book even more fascinating is that it deftly blends botany, politics, and history into a very appealing format." PopMatters.

Turner, Nancy J., 1947-

★**Plants** of Haida Gwaii / Nancy J. Turner ; with Florence Davidson ... [et al.] ; illustrations by _Giits_xaa (Ron Wilson) ; prayer for Haida medicine by Gwaaganad (Diane Brown) ; epilologue by _K'iilljuus (Barbara Wilson) ; current Haida names checked and revised by John Enrico ; many originally recorded by Robert D. Levine ; writing system from Golie Hans' developed for use in school curriculum, Queen Charlotte City, B.C. Sono Nis Press, 2004. 264 p. : **581.6**

1. First Nations (Canada) 2. Haida Indians -- Ethnobotany. 3. Ethnobotany -- Queen Charlotte Islands (B.C.) 4. Economic botany -- Queen Charlotte Islands (B.C.) 5. Queen Charlotte Islands (B.C.) 6. British Columbia. 7. Canada.
ISBN 9781550391442

Haida Gwaii is the traditional name for that beautiful group of islands, sometimes called the Queen Charlottes, off the northern mainland coast of British Columbia. For thousands of years these islands have been the home of the Haida. Plants of Haida Gwaii, written with the cooperation and collaboration of the Haida, is a detailed and insightful record of the uses and importance to the Haida of over 150 species of native plants. --Provided by publisher.

581.7 Plant ecology, plants characteristic of specific environments

Speichert, C. Greg

Encyclopedia of water garden plants / Greg Speichert & Sue Speichert ; foreword by Ann Lovejoy. Timber Press, 2004. 386 p. : **581.7**

1. Aquatic plants 2. Water gardens
ISBN 9780881926255

LC 2003016619

The choice water garden plants are all here in gorgeous color. Waterlilies and lotuses, marginal plants, floating plants, bog plants, and submerged plants are discussed, with complete information on hardiness, culture, propagation, and pests and diseases. --From publisher description.

"The Speicherts have spent years working on this comprehensive resource, offering gardeners beautifully written entries that take in all the characteristics and cultivation requirements of hundreds of plants." Booklist.

582.16 Trees

Brockman, Christian Frank, 1902-

Trees of North America : a field guide to the major native and introduced species north of Mexico / C. Frank Brockman ; illustrated by Rebecca Merrilees ; revised by Jonathan P. Latimer and Karen Stray Nolting with David Challinor. St. Martin's Press, c2001. 280 p. : A golden guide **582.16**

1. Trees -- United States -- Identification 2. Trees -- Canada -- Identification 3. Trees -- North America -- Pictorial works
ISBN 9781582380926

LC 2001272405

Presents a handbook for the identification of over five hundred species of trees by illustration and text.

Drori, Jonathan

Around the world in 80 trees / Jonathan Drori ; illustrations by Lucille Clerc. Laurence King Publishing, 2018. 240 p. : **582.16**

1. Human-plant relationships. 2. Trees -- Ecology. 3. Trees.
ISBN 1786271613

LC bl2018146060

"This exploration is both educational and visually exceptional." Publishers Weekly.

Hugo, Nancy R.

★**Seeing** trees : discover the extraordinary secrets of everyday trees / Nancy Ross Hugo ; photography by Robert J. Llewellyn. Timber Press, 2011. 242 p. : **582.16**

1. Trees -- Identification.
ISBN 9781604692198

LC 2010052455

National Outdoor Book Award for Nature and the Environment, 2011.

Introduces trees, describing such topics as leaves, flowers, fruit, cones, and bark and profiling the uniques features of ten common North American trees.

"This fascinating celebration of trees will delight gardeners, botanists, students of natural history, and nature photographers." Library Journal.

Logan, William Bryant

Sprout lands : tending the endless gift of trees / William Bryant Logan. W.W. Norton & Company, 2019 384 p. **582.16**

1. Trees 2. Sustainable living 3. Humans and plants 4. Sustainable societies
ISBN 9780393609417

LC 2018055376

A practicing arborist discusses how people once used trees as an endless and self-renewing source of food and building materials, and presents practical knowledge about how we can again learn to tend to them in this way.

"Bryant knows trees, and much more. Tree lovers--even those who consider pollarded trees ghastly and strange--will be drawn in by Bryant's vast cultural and scientific references, and charmed by passages that read like prose poems." Library Journal.

Petrides, George A.

A **field** guide to western trees : eastern [i.e. western] United States and Canada / George A. Petrides ; illustrated by Olivia Petrides. Houghton Mifflin, 1998. xiv, 428 p. : The Peterson field guide series **582.16**

1. Trees -- West (US) -- Identification 2. Trees -- Canada, Western -- Identification 3. Trees -- West (US) -- Pictorial works 4. Trees -- Canada, Western -- Pictorial works
ISBN 9780395904541

LC 98013624

"Sponsored by the National Audubon Society, the National Wildlife Federation, and the Roger Tory Peterson Institute."

This newly designed field guide features detailed descriptions of 387 species, arranged in six major groups by visual similarity. The 47 color plates and 5 text drawings show distinctive details needed for identification. Color photographs and 295 color range maps accompany the species descriptions. --From publisher description.

Rodd, Tony

Trees : a visual guide / Tony Rodd and Jennifer Stackhouse. University of California Press, c2008. 304 p. : **582.16**

1. Trees 2. Trees -- Ecology
ISBN 9780520256507

LC 2007043797

Beautifully illustrated and designed, this gorgeous reference book explores the world of trees from every perspective--from the world's great forests to the lifespan of a single leaf. Arresting color photographs of a wide variety of trees and close-ups of many of their remarkable features provide an enormous amount of information in a highly accessible format. The volume illustrates how trees grow and function, looks at their astounding diversity and adaptations, documents the key role they play in ecosystems, and explores the multitude of uses to which we put trees--from timber and pharmaceuticals to shade and shelter. A highly absorbing read cover to cover or dipped into at random, Trees: A Visual Guide delves into many specific topics: the details of flowers, bark, and roots; profiles of favorite trees; how animals and insects interact with trees; trees in urban landscapes; the role trees play in our changing climate; deforestation and reforestation; and much more. With clear diagrams, illustrations, and intriguing sidebars on many featured topics, this unique volume is a complete visual guide to the magnificence of the arboreal world. --From publisher description.

"This is a beautifully photographed visual guide to one of the most important resources of the natural world." Booklist.

Wohlleben, Peter, 1964-

The **hidden** life of trees : what they feel, how they communicate: discoveries from a secret world / Peter Wohlleben, foreword by Tim Flannery. Greystone Books, 2016, c2015. 240 p. Mysteries of nature trilogy ; **582.16**

1. Wohlleben, Peter, 1964- 2. Men and nature 3. Trees 4. Forests. 5. Nature
ISBN 9781771642484

LC bl2016036121

Translated from the German Das geheime Leben der Baume by Jane Billinghurst.

Originally published by Ludwig Buchverlag, 2015.

Draws on research and engaging forester stories to reveal how trees nurture each other and communicate, outlining the life cycles of "tree families" that support mutual growth, share nutrients, and contribute to a resilient ecosystem.

"In this spirited exploration, he guarantees that readers will never look at these life forms in quite the same way again." Library Journal.

582.16097 Trees--North America

Little, Elbert L. (Elbert Luther), 1907-2004

★The **Audubon** Society field guide to North American trees : Eastern region / Elbert L. Little ; photos. by Sonja Bullaty and Angelo Lomeo, and others ; visual key by Susan Rayfield and Olivia Buehl. Knopf, c1980. 714 pages : **582.16097**

1. Trees -- United States -- Identification 2. Trees -- Canada -- Identification
ISBN 9780394507606

LC 79003474

Includes indexes.

Identifies and illustrates 360 species in the area ranging from the eastern seaboard to the Rocky Mountains

Sibley, David, 1961-

★The **Sibley** guide to trees / written and illustrated by David Allen Sibley. Alfred A. Knopf, 2009. xxxviii, 426 p. : **582.16097**

1. Trees -- North America -- Identification

ISBN 9780375415197

LC bl2009026363

Featuring more than 4,100 detailed paintings and five hundred maps, highlights the similarities and distinctions between approximately six hundred North American tree species.

583 Dicotyledons

Anderson, Edward F., 1932-

The **cactus** family / Edward F. Anderson ; with a foreword by Wilhelm Barthlott ; and a chapter on cactus cultivation by Roger Brown. Timber Press, c2001. 776 p. : **583**

1. Cactus 2. Cactus.

ISBN 0881924989

LC 00060700

"While more than 1,000 photographs overall illustrate the extraordinary diversity and beautiful flowers of cacti, the main section--an alphabetically arranged reference--will arguably rank as the definitive work readers will use to examine and identify cactus genera, species, and subspecies." Booklist.

Pappalardo, Joe

Sunflowers : a secret history / Joe Pappalardo. Overlook, 2008. 256 p. **583**

1. Sunflowers. 2. Flowers -- History 3. Annuals (Plants) 4. Economic botany

ISBN 1585679917

LC bl2008010104

"A look at a flower so ubiquitous that its critical role in cultural development since the dawn of time often goes overlooked. A glib, upbeat writer and fiercely determined researcher, Pappalardo intrepidly investigates everything from the sunflower's genetic history and recent bioengineering discoveries to its influence on global economies from the U.S. to Uganda." Booklist.

585 Pinophyta

Preston, Richard, 1954-

The **wild** trees : a story of passion and daring / Richard Preston. Random House, 2007. 294 p. : **585**

1. Redwood -- Ecology -- Northern California. 2. Forest canopies -- Northern California. 3. Forest conservation -- Northern California. 4. Tree climbing -- Northern California. -- Anecdotes. 5. Northern California.

ISBN 1400064899

LC 2006048646

The best-selling author of The Hot Zone takes a close-up look at the world's tallest trees, the coast redwoods that grow only in the coastal regions of California, and at the previously unknown ecosystem that the trees form high in the air in the forest canopy, profiling the scientists and researchers that study this unique, labyrinthine ecological niche.

"There is something so elementally boyish in searching out the biggest and tallest, poring over maps and measurements, dubbing these trees with names lifted from J.R.R. Tolkein's Middle Earth. . . . Preston knows how to fold the science into the seams of his narrative, and his dry humor crops up, pleasurably, at the edges of his observations." Cleveland Plain Dealer.

590 Animals

Chaline, Eric

Fifty animals that changed the course of history / written by Eric Chaline. Firefly Books, 2015. 223 p. : **590**

1. Animals and civilization. 2. Animals and history. 3. Human/animal relationships -- History 4. Natural history

ISBN 9781770856349

LC 2015490640

A guide to the animals that have had the greatest impact on human civilization and the evolution of humankind include the horse, dog, rat, beaver, leech, and shark.

"Each two- to six-page essay recounts an animals relationship with humans and highlights...contributions to human history." Booklist.

Stewart, Tracey

Do unto animals : a friendly guide to how animals live, and how we can make their lives better / Tracey Stewart ; illustrations by Lisel Ashlock. Artisan, 2015 199 p. : **590**

1. Human-animal relationships. 2. Animal habitations 3. Animal communication. 4. Pets.

ISBN 9781579656232

LC 2015010995

Includes index.

A former veterinary technician and animal advocate through hundreds of wonderful illustrations, homemade projects and expert advice provides insight into the secret lives of animals and the kindest ways to live with and alongside them.

590.2 Animals -- Miscellany

Cooke, Lucy, 1970-

The **truth** about animals : stoned sloths, lovelorn hippos, and other tales from the wild side of wildlife / Lucy Cooke. Perseus Books Group 2018, c2017. 304 p. **590.2**

1. Animals 2. Misconceptions 3. Animal behavior 4. Sloths

ISBN 9780465094646

LC 2019301387

Originally published under the title The unexpected truth about animals : a menagerie of the misunderstood by Doubleday, 2017.

An uproarious tour of some of the basest instincts and vice-related mysteries of the animal world includes profiles of drunken moose, cheating penguins, lazy worker ants, castrating hippos and porn-peddling Chinese pandas.

590.73 Collections and exhibits of living mammals

Baratay, Eric

★**Zoo** : a history of zoological gardens in the west / Eric Baratay, Elisabeth Hardouin-Fugier ; translated by Oliver Welsh. University of Chicago Press, 2002. 356 p. **590.73**

1. Zoos -- History. 2. Zoological societies.

ISBN 1861891113

LC bl2008017447

"In this history of zoos the authors take a social history focus, examining how people view wild animals and how that has changed over time. One can read the text or spend hours simply enjoying the images. Libraries that have other titles on zoos will still want to purchase this." Library Journal.

Charman, Isobel

The zoo : the wild and wonderful tale of the founding of London Zoo: 1826-1851 / Isobel Charman. Pegasus Books, 2017. 349 p. **590.73**

1. London Zoo (London, England) 2. Zoo animals. 3. Zoos. 4. Captive wild animals.
ISBN 9781681773568

Relates the creation of the London Zoo, the first zoo in history, describing the role of the diplomats, traders, scientists, and amateur naturalists who were charged with collecting animals from around the world, and the characters--both animal and human--who became part of it.

"A deeply researched, terrifically entertaining exploration of the London Zoo 'through the eyes of some of the people who made it happen.'" Kirkus.

590.75 Museum activities and services

Milgrom, Melissa

Still life : adventures in taxidermy / Melissa Milgrom. Houghton Mifflin Harcourt, 2010. 304 p. **590.75**

1. Taxidermy. 2. Taxidermists. 3. Zoological specimens -- Collection and preservation. 4. Animal specialists.
ISBN 9780618405473
LC 2009013511

Transformed from a curious onlooker to an empathetic participant, journalist Milgrom delves deeply into the world of taxidermy, encountering a world of intrepid hunter-explorers, eccentric naturalists, and gifted museum artisans, all devoted to the paradoxical pursuit of creating the illusion of life.

590.9 History, geographic treatment, biography

Roberts, Alice M.

Tamed : ten species that changed our world / Alice Roberts. Hutchinson, 2017. 360 p. ; **590.9**

1. Agriculture 2. Domestication 3. Civilization -- History 4. Food habits
ISBN 9781786330611
LC 2017479893

Dogs, apples and wheat; cattle, potatoes and chickens; rice, maize and horses--and, finally, humans. She reveals how becoming part of our world changed these animals and plants, and shows how they became our allies, essential to the survival and success of our own species.

"Anthropologist Roberts, who has written of humans (Evolution: The Human Story, 2017), now turns her attention to our most important domesticated plants and animals." Booklist.

591.4 Physical adaptation

MacPhee, R. D. E.

End of the megafauna : the fate of the world's hugest, fiercest, and strangest animals / Ross D. E. MacPhee ; with Illustrations by Peter Schouten. W.W. Norton & Company, [2018] 144 p. **591.4**

1. Extinct animals 2. Body size 3. Extinction (Biology) 4. Causation
ISBN 9780393249293
LC 2018029730

Investigates the yet-unsolved disappearances of the planet's giant prehistoric animals, exploring leading extinction theories to reveal the implausibility of human overhunting and catastrophic climate change and how new technologies may be able to reintroduce extinct species.

591.47 Protective and locomotor adaptations, color

Cheshire, James

Where the animals go : tracking wildlife with technology in 50 maps and graphics / James Cheshire, Oliver Uberti. W. W. Norton & Company, 2017. 174 p. : **591.47**

1. Animals 2. Animal behavior 3. Tracking and trailing 4. Maps
ISBN 9780393634020

Incorporating sophisticated infographics, a comprehensive, data-driven portrait of the behaviors of the planet's wildlife draws on pioneering research made possible by current advances in satellite, camera and other digital technologies to reveal nature's unique talents and survival skills.

Emlen, Douglas John, 1967-

Animal weapons : the evolution of battle / Douglas J. Emlen ; illustrated by David J. Tuss. Henry Holt and Company, 2014. 304 p. **591.47**

1. Animal weapons. 2. Animal defenses. 3. Defensive (Military science) 4. Animals.
ISBN 9780805094503
LC 2014004772

An exploration of the extreme weapons seen in the animal world--teeth, horns, and claws--draws parallels to the way humans develop and employ their own weapons.

"Emlen's excellent writing will draw in readers intrigued by astonishingly powerful weapons, both in the wild and in the military, and how they have evolved owing to selective pressures. Though Philip Street's Animal Weapons describes a greater variety of animal defenses, Emlen's book is a more compelling read because it focuses on the parallels between animal and humans in this regard." Library Journal.

591.5 Behavior

Bekoff, Marc

Wild justice : the moral lives of animals / Marc Bekoff and Jessica Pierce. University of Chicago Press, 2009. 192 p. **591.5**

1. Social behavior in animals 2. Animal behavior 3. Zoology 4. Ethics
ISBN 9780226041612
LC 2008040173

"The authors discuss recent scientific studies documenting that great apes, monkeys, wolves, coyotes, hyenas, dolphins, whales, elephants, rats, and mice are capable of a wide range of moral behavior. They strongly urge the scientific and philosophical communities to recognize that these animals can act as moral agents within the context of their own social groups. This provocative and well-argued view of animal morality may surprise some readers as it challenges outdated assumptions about animals." Library Journal.

Berger, Joel

The **better** to eat you with : fear in the animal world / Joel Berger. University of Chicago Press, 2008. xii, 305 p., 40 p. of plates : **591.5**

1. Fear in animals. 2. Animal behavior. 3. Animals. 4. Nature.
ISBN 9780226043630

LC 2008000418

"The author ostensibly attempts to answer whether the fear of predation in animals is innate or learned. In reality, his book is a memoir of a research career spent in some of the most inhospitable places on Earth, including Alaska, Greenland, Siberia, and Mongolia. [He] recounts his research as a series of adventure stories that portray the rewards and pitfalls of conducting biological field investigations." Choice.

Braitman, Laurel

Animal madness : how anxious dogs, compulsive parrots, and elephants in recovery help us understand ourselves / Laurel Braitman. Simon & Schuster, 2014. 384 p. **591.5**

1. Animal behavior. 2. Mental illness. 3. Convalescence
ISBN 9781451627008

LC 2014000791

For the first time, a historian of science draws evidence from across the world to show how humans and other animals are astonishingly similar when it comes to their feelings and the ways in which they lose their minds.

"Braitman's gradual accretion of reasons to believe in animal emotional states that we can relate to, including the loopy ones, gives pause and sparks curiosity." Kirkus.

Durrani, Matin

Furry logic : the physics of animal life / Matin Durrani, Liz Kalaugher. Bloomsbury Sigma, 2016. 304 pages : **591.5**

1. Biomechanics 2. Animal behavior 3. Biophysics 4. Zoology
ISBN 9781472914095

LC 2016497302

The properties of physics are behind many of the ways animals go about their daily lives. Scientists researching the field of biomechanics have discovered that the way cats and dogs lap up milk can be explained by the laws of surface tension, the way ants navigate is due to magnetic fields, and why pistol shrimps are able to generate enough force to destroy aquarium glass using their claws!

"Another offbeat factoid--in a book full of them--is the way that elephants raise one foot from the ground in order to use their other three to triangulate vibrations. Light science reading that informs while it entertainsgood for dipping into and out of." Kirkus.

Fagan, Brian M.

The **intimate** bond : how animals shaped human history / Brian Fagan. Bloomsbury Press, [2014] 288 p. **591.5**

1. Human-animal relationships -- History. 2. Working animals -- History. 3. Animals and civilization. 4. Animals and history.
ISBN 9781620405727

LC 2014027152

"History, anthropology, and cultural studies enthusiasts will enjoy this excellent, intelligent book, as will animal lovers of all stripes." Library Journal.

Grandin, Temple

★**Animals** in translation : using the mysteries of autism to decode animal behavior / Temple Grandin and Catherine Johnson. Scribner, 2005. 356 p. ; **591.5**

1. Animal behavior. 2. Senses and sensation. 3. People with autism 4. Autism.
ISBN 0743247698

LC 2004058498

An animal scientist draws on her experience as an autistic to identify commonalities between animals and autistics, offering insight into how animals process sensory information and how they often possess unrecognized savant-level talents.

"This fascinating book will teach readers to see as animals see, to be a little more visual and a little less verbal, and, as a unique analysis of animal behavior, it belongs in all libraries." Booklist.

McCarthy, Susan

★**Becoming** a tiger : how baby animals learn to live in the wild / Susan McCarthy. Harper Collins, 2004. xi, 418 p. ; **591.5**

1. Animal intelligence. 2. Animal behavior. 3. Animal babies.
ISBN 0066209242

LC 2003067553

The author shares natural wildlife stories to offer insight into the biological survival and learning processes of young animals, from a bear's efforts to preserve territory for her cubs to a bat's endeavor to win group acceptance.

"McCarthy writes clearly and her penchant for humor . . . makes the book an easy read, both for students of learning and those who can't get enough of television's Animal Planet." Publishers Weekly.

Wilson, Edward O.

Genesis : the deep origin of societies / Edward O. Wilson. Liveright Publishing Corporation, 2019. 224 p. **591.5**

1. Animal behavior. 2. Behavior evolution. 3. Evolution 4. Behavior genetics.
ISBN 9781631495540

LC 2018050101

Forming a 21st-century statement on Darwinian evolution, one shorn of "religious and political dogma," the author offers a bold work of scientific thought and synthesis.

"A challenging read best suited for specialists in the fields of evolutionary biology and sociobiology." Library Journal.

591.56 Behavior relating to life cycle

Bondar, Carin

Wild moms : motherhood in the animal kingdom / Dr. Carin Bondar. Pegasus Books, 2018. 400 p. **591.56**

1. Wildlife 2. Animal behavior 3. Motherhood 4. Mother and child
ISBN 9781681776651

LC bl2018052906

An expert in population ecology and the host of online and television programs discusses the ins and outs of what it means to be a mother in the animal kingdom, including gestation, pregnancy and child-rearing and caring for disabled offspring.

"Well-researched and with a large bibliography, Bondars study celebrates the idea that motherhood may be the most important job ever created by evolution." Booklist.

Wild sex : the science behind mating in the animal kingdom / Carin Bondar. Pegasus Books, 2016. 320 p. **591.56**

1. Biodiversity 2. Courtship of animals. 3. Animal behavior. 4. Sexual selection in animals.
ISBN 9781681771663

LC bl2016027931

An ecologist who has worked with Scientific American, PBS Digital Studios and Discovery World describes the difficult, varied, often violent and utterly fascinating mating and reproductive habits of the animal kingdom in their natural habitats.

"A fascinating peek into the intimate behavior of our animal cousins that provides new insight into the benefits of being human." Kirkus.

Gould, James L., 1945-

Nature's compass : the mystery of animal navigation / James L. Gould, Carol Grant Gould. Princeton University Press, c2012. xiii, 294 p. : **591.56**

1. Animal navigation. 2. Animal behavior. 3. Animal migration. 4. Senses and sensation.

ISBN 9780691140452

LC 2011035086

Explores the methods by which animals navigate throughout the world, examining such examples as the monarch butterfly's use of an internal clock and the honey bee's reliance on the sun and mental maps.

Safina, Carl, 1955-

Beyond words : what animals think and feel / Carl Safina. Henry Holt and Company, 2015. 320 p. **591.56**

1. Animal behavior. 2. Elephants. 3. Wolves. 4. Whales.

ISBN 9780805098884

LC 2014045385

"A John Macrae Book."

Weaving decades of field observations with exciting new discoveries about the brain, Carl Safina's landmark book offers an intimate view of animal behavior to challenge the fixed boundary between humans and nonhuman animals.

"With forays into neurology and diverse animal-behavior studies, Safina reveals that ours is just one of many powerful minds at work on Earth and that we share many profound traits with our fellow animals. By turns mesmerizing, thrilling, and tragic, Safinas enlightening inquiry into animal intelligence calls for a new, compassionate perspective before we unwittingly drive our precious animal kin into extinction." Booklist.

Zernicka-Goetz, Magdalena

The **dance** of life : the new science of how a single cell becomes a human being / Magdalena Zernicka-Goetz and Roger Highfield. Basic Books, 2020. vii, 289 p. ; **591.56**

1. Pregnancy 2. Embryology 3. Fetus -- Growth 4. Fertilization (Biology)

ISBN 9781541699069

LC 2019020177

Scientists have long struggled to make pregnancy easier, safer, and more successful. In The Dance of Life, developmental and stem-cell biologist Magdalena Zernicka-Goetz takes us to the front lines of efforts to understand the creation of a human life. She has spent two decades unraveling the mysteries of development, as a simple fertilized egg becomes a complex human being of forty trillion cells. Zernicka-Goetz's work is both incredibly practical and astonishingly vast: her groundbreaking experiments with mouse, human, and artificial embryo models give hope to how more women can sustain viable pregnancies.

"Meaty and entertaining, with the effort extended well worth the energy." Kirkus

591.59 Communication

Friend, Tim

Animal talk : breaking the codes of animal language / Tim Friend. Free Press, c2004. ix, 274 p. : **591.59**

1. Animal communication. 2. Animal behavior. 3. Animals.

ISBN 0743201574

LC 2003063107

A study of the mysteries of animal communication draws on the latest scientific research and real-life animal stories to explain the diverse ways in which wild animals of various species communicate with one another.

"The author describes the methods of, and reasons behind, animal communication and demonstrates that human and animal communication are not so widely disparate as once believed. Friend also gives background details on the basics of communication theory, genetics, evolution, and the progression of scientific thought regarding animal communication. . . . His humorous and engaging prose style makes this a captivating read." Library Journal.

Slobodchikoff, C. N.

Chasing Doctor Dolittle : learning the language of animals / Con Slobodchikoff. St. Martin's Press, 2012. 320 p. **591.59**

1. Animal communication. 2. Language and languages. 3. Human/animal communication

ISBN 9780312611798

LC 2012033696

Discusses how animals are capable of interacting intelligently through vocal and physical methods, drawing on work with prairie dogs to present evidence of animal communication methods and how they can be imitated by human researchers.

591.6 Miscellaneous nontaxonomic kinds of animals

Simon, Matt

Plight of the living dead : what the animal kingdom's real-life zombies reveal about nature -- and ourselves / Matt Simon. Penguin Group USA 2018 272 p. **591.6**

1. Parasites 2. Mind control 3. Predation (Biology) 4. Evolution

ISBN 9780143131410

LC 2018004526

"Simon's work is easily the most fun one could ever expect to have reading about the mind-controlling insects, insidious fungi, and parasites living alongside humanity." Publishers Weekly.

591.68 Rare and endangered animals

Girling, Richard

The **hunt** for the golden mole : all creatures great and small and why they matter / Richard Girling. Counterpoint Press, 2014. 312 p. **591.68**

1. Extinct animals. 2. Hunting -- Moral and ethical aspects. 3. Nature conservation. 4. Golden moles -- Somalia.

ISBN 9781619024502

LC 2014022506

Taking as its narrative engine the hunt for an animal that is legendarily rare, Richard Girling writes an engaging and highly informative history of humankind's interest in hunting and collecting -- what prompts us to do this? What good might come of our need to catalog all the living things of the natural world?

"Though Girling presents a sobering assessment of the state of the world's fauna, he does so with the dramatic flair of a novelist and eye for detail of a travel journalist. The result is a page-turning, thought-provoking treatise on a desperate environmental crisis." Booklist.

O'Connor, Maura R.
Resurrection science : conservation, de-extinction and the precarious future of wild things / Maura R. O'connor. St. Martin's Press, 2015 288 p. **591.68**
1. Evolution 2. Rare and endangered animals 3. Wildlife conservation
ISBN 9781137279293
LC 2015004485

A tour of current advances in biology and ethics demonstrates how humans are increasingly in control of evolution, exploring how as the scientific community endeavors to save near-extinct species, the creatures being saved become less wild and more dependent.

591.7 Animal ecology, animals characteristic of specific

Heinrich, Bernd, 1940-
Life everlasting : the animal way of death / Bernd Heinrich. Houghton Mifflin Harcourt, 2012. 256 p. **591.7**
1. Animal ecology. 2. Animal life cycles. 3. Animal behavior. 4. Animals -- Psychological aspects.
ISBN 9780547752662
LC 2012010583

"Bernd Heinrich receives a letter from a severely ill friend asking if he might have a 'green burial' at Heinrich's hunting camp, and the acclaimed biologist/author sets out to explore exactly how the animal world deals with the death-to-life cycle and what we can learn from the process, both ecologically and spiritually".-- Provided by publisher.

591.9 Animals by specific continents, countries, localities

Bambaradeniya, Channa N. B.,
The **illustrated** atlas of wildlife / Channa Bambaradeniya... et al. University of California Press, 2009 288 p. **591.9**
1. Zoogeography. 2. Wildlife. 3. Animals.
ISBN 9780520257856

Details the ecology and wildlife of the continents, oceans, and poles, and includes up-to-date conservation and preservation data and the human impact on the world's ecosystems.

"Stunning wildlife photography appears on every page, along with vibrant photographs, illustrations, and maps, accompanied by detailed annotations that complement the text." School Library Journal.

592 Specific taxonomic groups of animals

Attenborough, David, 1926-
Life in the undergrowth / David Attenborough. Princeton University Press, 2005. 288 p. **592**
1. Invertebrates. 2. Insects. 3. Adaptation (Biology) 4. Natural history.
ISBN 9780691127033
LC 2005934727

National Outdoor Book Award for Nature and the Environment, 2006.

A richly illustrated companion to the Animal Planet television program offers a rare, close-up study of the secret life of invertebrates, focusing on a broad spectrum of tiny, diverse creatures that have had a profound impact on not only the evolutionary cycle but also the environmental health of the planet.

"This wonderful exploration of invertebrates exceeds the requirements for a great nature book through the strength of its photographs and the quality of its prose." Publishers Weekly.

Meinkoth, Norman August, 1913-
The **Audubon** Society field guide to North American seashore creatures / Norman A. Meinkoth. A.A. Knopf, c1981. 799 p. : The Audubon Society field guide series **592**
1. Marine invertebrates -- North America -- Identification
ISBN 9780394519937
LC 81080828

Includes index.

Presents a comprehensive guide to more than six hundred species of sea creatures living along the coasts of North America, with full-color photographs, anecdotes, identification key, and other information

594 Mollusks and molluscoids

Harasewych, M. G.
The **book** of shells : a life-size guide to identifying and classifying six hundred seashells / M.G. Harasewych and Fabio Moretzsohn. University of Chicago Press, 2010. 655 p. : **594**
1. Shells 2. Mollusks
ISBN 9780226315775
LC 2009034321

The Book of Shells offers a visually stunning and scientifically engaging guide to six hundred of the most intriguing mollusk shells, each chosen to convey the range of shapes and sizes that occur across a range of species. Each shell is reproduced here at its actual size, in full color, and is accompanied by an explanation of the shell's range, distribution, abundance, habitat, and operculum; the piece that protects the mollusk when it's in the shell. Brief scientific and historical accounts of each shell and related species include fun-filled facts and anecdotes that broaden its portrait. --From publisher description.

"Distinguished by outstanding color visuals, The Book of Shells is highly recommended for libraries in need of an overview of seashells worldwide." Booklist.

Rehder, Harald Alfred, 1907-
The **Audubon** Society field guide to North American seashells / Harald A. Rehder, with photographs by James H. Carmichael, Jr. ; visual key by Carol Nehring and Mary Beth Brewer. Knopf, c1981. 894 p. : The Audubon Society field guide series **594**
1. Shells -- North America -- Identification
ISBN 9780394519135
LC 80084239

Includes index.

Surveys the habitat, range, behavior, biology, and reproductive habits of marine mullusks

"The more than 700 color plates are arranged according to shape and color rather than family or genus, making identification very simple for even the rankest amateur. . . . The text gives the common name, scientific name, description, habitat, range, and comments for each species. This is the most comprehensive field guide to North American seashells." Library Journal.

Williams, Wendy, 1950-
Kraken : the curious, exciting, and slightly disturbing, science of squid / Wendy Williams. Abrams Image, 2010. 222 p.

: 594

1. Squids 2. Giant squids 3. Marine biology. 4. Marine animals.
ISBN 9780810984653

LC 2010032489

Includes bibliographical references (p. 204-211), filmography (p. 212), and index.

Presents a study on squids and other cephalopods that describe their resilience throughout history, the truth behind the misconceptions about them, and the research being done on them that could help scientists understand the human brain.

"This serves as a good introduction to the subject for general readers and an inspiration to young people interested in marine biology." Library Journal.

595.4 Chelicerates

Hillyard, P. D.

The **private** life of spiders / Paul Hillyard. Princeton University Press, 2008. 160 p. : **595.4**

1. Spiders
ISBN 9780691135526

LC 2007929921

Presents an illustrated guide to the anatomy, behavior, social organization, reproduction, hunting techniques, and web construction of a variety of spiders from around the world.

"The author explains the two major spider lifestyles (those that actively hunt and those that spin webs), discusses silk production and all the uses spiders make of silk, mating and the resulting young, venom, sociality, and spiders and humans. Full of fascinating facts, the absorbing text teaches the reader all about the lives of spiders." Booklist.

595.7 Insects

Brock, James P.

Kaufman field guide to butterflies of North America / Jim P. Brock and Kenn Kaufman ; with the collaboration of Rick and Nora Bowers and Lynn Hassler. Houghton Mifflin, c2003. 391 p. : **595.7**

1. Butterflies -- North America -- Identification 2. Butterflies -- North America -- Pictorial works
ISBN 9780618768264

LC 2006287515

"Previously published as the Kaufman focus guide to Butterflies of North America"--P. [6].

The most user-friendly butterfly guide ever published, still handy and compact. --From publisher description.

Holldobler, Bert, 1936-

The **superorganism** : the beauty, elegance, and strangeness of insect societies / Bert Holldobler and Edward O. Wilson ; line drawings by Margaret C. Nelson. W.W. Norton & Company, 2008. 576 p. **595.7**

1. Insect societies. 2. Sociobiology 3. Social behavior in insects 4. Animal behavior.
ISBN 9780393067040

The Pulitzer Prize-winning authors present a lavishly detailed account of the extraordinary lives of social insects that draws on more than two decades of research and offers insight into how bees, termites, and other insect societies thrive in systems of altruistic cooperation, complex communication, and labor division.

MacNeal, David, 1985-

Bugged : the insects who rule the world and the people obsessed with them / David MacNeal ; with illustrations by Michael Kennedy. St. Martin's Press, 2017. 288 p. **595.7**

1. Insects. 2. Entomology. 3. Entomologists 4. Humans and insects
ISBN 9781250095503

LC 2017006880

Weaving together history, travel and culture, an off-beat scientific journey into the insects, which have been shaping our ecological world and plant life for over 400 million years, introduces a cast of mini-monsters that are as necessary to life as water and the people who love them.

"MacNeal delivers a joy-filled dose of science, reminding readers that the strange and alien creatures in our midst are not to be feared, but celebrated." Publishers Weekly.

Paulson, Dennis, 1937-

Dragonflies & damselflies : a natural history / Dennis Paulson. Princeton University Press, 2019. 224 p. : **595.7**

1. Damselflies 2. Damselflies. 3. Dragonflies 4. Dragonflies.
ISBN 0691180369

LC 2018961573

First published in the UK in 2019 by Ivy Press.

Dragonflies and damselflies are often called birdwatchers' insects. Large, brightly colored, active in the daytime, and displaying complex and interesting behaviors, they have existed since the days of the dinosaurs, and they continue to flourish. Their ancestors were the biggest insects ever, and they still impress us with their size, the largest bigger than a small hummingbird. There are more than 6,000 odonate species known at present, and you need only visit any wetland on a warm summer day to be enthralled by their stunning colors and fascinating behavior. In this lavishly illustrated natural history, leading dragonfly expert Dennis Paulson offers a comprehensive, accessible, and appealing introduction to the world's dragonflies and damselflies. --From publisher description.

"The appreciation of this group will be enhanced for everyone reading this work." Choice.

Raffles, Hugh, 1958-

Insectopedia / Hugh Raffles. Pantheon Books, c2010. x, 465 p. : **595.7**

1. Insects. 2. Entomology 3. Human/animal relationships 4. Zoology
ISBN 9780375423864

LC 2009024302

An alphabetical tour of the world of insects features short vignettes, meditations, and extended essays from a range of disciplines, covering such topics as Chinese cricket fighting and the use of Chernobyl-deformed insects in art.

"In addition to the fine writing, Raffles includes many intriguing drawings and illustrations, as well as a fascinating Notes section. Because of his manner of organization, there is little reason to read the book in order; you can simply open it anywhere and discover a new way to reflect on not only insects but people." Seattle Times.

Schmidt, Justin O., 1947-

The **sting** of the wild / Justin O. Schmidt. Johns Hopkins University Press, 2016. 280 p. **595.7**

1. Poisonous insects. 2. Insect pests. 3. Insects
ISBN 9781421419282

LC 2015026989

In The Sting of the Wild, the colorful Dr. Schmidt takes us on a journey inside the lives of stinging insects, seeing the world through their eyes as well as his own. He explains how and why they attack and reveals the powerful punch they can deliver with a small venom gland

and a "sting," the name for the apparatus that delivers the venom. We learn which insects are the worst to encounter and why some are barely worth considering.

"Schmidts tales will prove infectiously engaging even to entomophobes." Publishers Weekly.

Sverdrup-Thygeson, Anne

Buzz, sting, bite : why we need insects / Anne Sverdrup-Thygeson ; translated by Lucy Moffatt. Simon & Schuster, 2019, c2018. 256 p. **595.7**

1. Insects 2. Humans and insects 3. Entomology
ISBN 9781982112875

LC 2018059668

"Originally published in 2018 in Norway by J.M. Stenersens Forlag as Insektenes Planet."

Published in the UK by Mudlark as Extraordinary insects, 2019.

An enthusiastic, witty and informative introduction to the world of insects explains why we?and the planet we inhabit?could not survive without them.

"A classy and brightly informative appreciation of insectsall you could ask for in a popular natural history." Kirkus.

595.7097 Insects--North America

Milne, Lorus Johnson, 1910-1987

★The **Audubon** Society field guide to North American insects and spiders / Lorus and Margery Milne ; visual key by Susan Rayfield. Knopf, c1980. 989 p. : **595.7097**

1. Insects -- North America -- Identification 2. Spiders -- North America -- Identification 3. Arachnida -- North America -- Identification
ISBN 9780394507637

LC 80007620

"A Chanticleer Press edition."

Includes index.

Identifies, discusses, and illustrates every important family and species in North America, providing information on the habits and characteristics of each insect and spider covered.

595.717 Ecology--insects

Waldbauer, Gilbert

★**What** good are bugs? : insects in the web of life / Gilbert Waldbauer. Harvard University Press, 2003. 366 p. ; **595.717**

1. Insects -- Ecology. 2. Entomology. 3. Animal behavior.
ISBN 9780674010277

LC 2002027335

Looks at the behavior of insects and their importance to life on Earth.

595.76 Beetles

Lewis, Sara, 1953-

Silent sparks : the wondrous world of fireflies / Sara Lewis. Princeton University Press, 2016. 240 p. **595.76**

1. Fireflies. 2. Insects.
ISBN 9780691162683

LC 2015037057

For centuries, the beauty of fireflies has evoked wonder and delight. Yet for most of us, fireflies remain shrouded in mystery: How do fireflies make their light? What are they saying with their flashing? And what do fireflies look for in a mate? In Silent Sparks, noted biologist and firefly expert Sara Lewis dives into the fascinating world of fireflies and reveals the most up-to-date discoveries about these beloved insects.

595.77 Flies (Diptera) and fleas

Spielman, Andrew

Mosquito : the story of man's deadliest foe / Andrew Spielman, Michael D'Antonio. Hyperion Books, 2001. 256 p. **595.77**

1. Mosquitoes. 2. Mosquitoes as carriers of disease.
ISBN 0786886676

LC bl2016010898

An expert on this vexing insect traces the mosquito's origins, its role in history, and its ongoing threat to humankind as the bearer of diseases such as malaria, yellow fever, and encephalitis.

"This is truly an unexpected delight, an informative, entertaining, and sometimes skin-crawly book that should appeal to anyone with a taste for popular science." Booklist.

595.78 Moths and butterflies

Marren, Peter

Rainbow dust : three centuries of butterfly delight, with a New Preface / Peter Marren. The University of Chicago Press, 2017. 320 p. ; **595.78**

1. Butterflies 2. Philosophy of nature 3. Nature conservation 4. Men and nature
ISBN 9780226395883

LC 2016014269

Like fluttering shards of stained glass, butterflies possess a unique power to pierce and stir the human soul. Indeed, the ancient Greeks explicitly equated the two in a single word, psyche, so that from early times butterflies were not only a form of life, but also an idea. Profound and deeply personal, written with both wisdom and wit, Peter Marren's Rainbow Dust explores this idea of butterflies--the why behind the mysterious power of these insects we do not flee, but rather chase.

"An erudite, engaging book that will find the broadest readership among nature lovers on the other side of the Atlantic." Kirkus.

Stokes, Donald W.

The **butterfly** book : an easy guide to butterfly gardening, identification, and behavior / Donald and Lillian Stokes and Ernest Williams. Little, Brown, c1991. 96 p. : **595.78**

1. Butterflies -- North America -- Identification. 2. Butterfly gardening. 3. Butterflies -- Behavior.
ISBN 9780316817806

LC 91015323

Tells how to plan a garden that will attract butterflies, identifies the most common species, and describes the lifecyle and behavior of butterflies

Oberhauser, Karen Suzanne

Monarch butterfly biology & conservation : Biology and Conservation / edited by Karen S. Oberhauser and Michelle J. Solensky. Cornell University Press, 2004. viii, 248 p. : **595.78**

1. Monarch butterfly. 2. Wildlife conservation.
ISBN 9780801441882

LC 2004000884

Presents twenty-seven studies on the monarch butterfly's life cycle including papers presented at the 2001 Monarch Population Dynamics Conference and data compiled by both Journey North and the Monarch Larva Monitoring Project.

595.79 Hymenoptera

Frey, Kate, 1960-

The **bee-friendly** garden : design an abundant, flower-filled yard that nurtures bees and supports biodiversity / Kate Frey and Gretchen LeBuhn. Ten Speed Press, 2016 ix, 213 p. : **595.79**

1. Bees 2. Gardening to attract wildlife 3. Honey plants
ISBN 9781607747635

LC 2015025815

Includes index.

A guide to gardening shows readers how to create an organic, pesticide-free, and ecologically sustainable bee garden that can provide an impressive increase in yields and better-tasting produce.

"Frey and LeBuhn's accessible and inspiring advice, if correctly followed by growers around the world, could profoundly help restore diminishing bee populations to thriving good health, which is essential to our crops and our well-being." Booklist.

Wilson, Edward O.

Tales from the ant world / Edward O. Wilson. Liveright Publishing, 2020. 240 p. **595.79**

1. Wilson, Edward O. 2. Ants 3. Ants -- Behavior 4. Insects 5. Habitat (Ecology)
ISBN 9781631495564

LC 2020017595

Edward O. Wilson recalls his lifetime with ants--from his first boyhood encounters in the woods of Alabama to perilous journeys into the Brazilian rainforest. "Ants are the most warlike of all animals, with colony pitted against colony. . . . Their clashes dwarf Waterloo and Gettysburg," writes Edward O. Wilson in his most finely observed work in decades. In a myrmecological tour to such far-flung destinations as Mozambique and New Guinea, the Gulf of Mexico's Dauphin Island and even his parents' overgrown yard back in Alabama, Wilson thrillingly evokes his nine-decade-long scientific obsession with more than 15,000 ant species.

"Wilson's passion for his subject, for the scientific method, and for the natural world comes through clearly in this enjoyable survey." Publishers Weekly

Wilson, Joseph S., 1980-

The **bees** in your backyard : a guide to North America's bees / Joseph S. Wilson & Olivia Messinger Carril. Princeton University Press, 2016 288 p. : **595.79**

1. Bees -- North America. 2. Bees -- North America -- Identification. 3. Bee culture -- North America. 4. Honeybee -- North America.
ISBN 9780691160771

LC 2015007075

Includes index.

The Bees in Your Backyard provides an engaging introduction to the roughly 4,000 different bee species found in the United States and Canada, dispelling common myths about bees while offering essential tips for telling them apart in the field. --From publisher description.

"This is the best general guide to bees this reviewer has seen." Choice.

596 Chordata

Dinerstein, Eric, 1952-

The **kingdom** of rarities / Eric Dinerstein. Island Press, c2013. xiii, 295 p. : **596**

1. Rare and endangered animals 2. Biodiversity conservation. 3. Animals
ISBN 9781610911955

LC 2012025535

An eye-opening tour of the rare and exotic, The Kingdom of Rarities offers us a new understanding of the natural world, one that places rarity at the center of conservation biology. Looking at real-time threats to biodiversity, from climate change to habitat fragmentation, and drawing on his long and distinguished scientific career, Dinerstein offers readers fresh insights into fascinating questions about the science of rarity and unforgettable experiences from the field. --From publisher description.

"Though the author wrote the book primarily for those with an understanding of natural history/biology, he expertly weaves in examples to provide a solid context for laypersons." Choice.

597 Cold-blooded vertebrates

Gilbert, Carter Rowell, 1930-

★**National** Audubon Society field guide to fishes. Carter R. Gilbert, James D. Williams. Alfred A. Knopf, 2002. 607 p. : **597**

1. Fishes -- North America -- Identification.
ISBN 9780375412240

LC 2002020773

Rev. ed. of: National Audubon Society field guide to fishes, whales & dolphins / by the National Audubon Society staff. 1983.

"A Chanticleer Press edition."

Covering both freshwater and saltwater species of fish, this fully revised edition brings a new level of accuracy and usefulness to the National Audubon Society's acclaimed field guides.

Schweid, Richard, 1946-

Consider the eel / Richard Schweid. University of North Carolina Press, c2002. xiv, 181 p. : **597**

1. Anguillidae. 2. Eels. 3. Cooking (Seafood) 4. Recipes. 5. Sargasso Sea -- Natural history 6. Europe -- Natural history 7. United States -- Natural history
ISBN 0807826936

LC 2001048067

A culinary and natural history of the eel follows its life cycle from the Sargasso Sea to the rivers of North America and Europe, touring the eel's economic and gastronomic role throughout the world.

"The author tries to fill in the gaps in the eel's astonishing natural history and tie that to sketches of fishery traditions, folklore, literary excerpts and reportage. . . . Anyone with a curiosity about the sea will find Schweid's taste of the eel strangely appealing." Publishers Weekly.

Svensson, Patrik, 1972-

The **book** of eels : our enduring fascination with the most mysterious creature in the natural world / Patrik Svensson. Ecco, 2020, c2019 320 p. **597**

1. Eels 2. Marine animals 3. Nature -- Effect of humans on 4.

Humans 5. Europe
ISBN 9780062968814

LC 2019054460

A first book by the Sydsvenskan arts and culture journalist draws on research in literature, history and marine biology in a portrait of the enigmatic European eel that share insights into the species' complicated origins and nature.

"An account of the mysterious life of eels that also serves as a meditation on consciousness, faith, time, light and darkness, and life and death. . . . a highly readable place to begin learning. Unsentimental nature writing that sheds as much light on humans as on eels." Kirkus

597.15 Behavior--fishes

Balcombe, Jonathan P.

What a fish knows : the inner lives of our underwater cousins / Jonathan Balcombe. Scientific American/Farrar, Straus, and Giroux, 2016. 224 p. **597.15**

1. Fishes -- Behavior. 2. Animal communication. 3. Animal intelligence. 4. Fishes -- Physiology.
ISBN 9780374288211

LC 2015048629

The author of Second Nature challenges popular misconceptions to explore the complex lives of the planet's diverse fish species, drawing on the latest understandings in animal behavior and biology to reveal their self-awareness, elaborate courtship rituals and cooperative intelligence.

"This is a lively and surprising work that makes a strong argument for sport and food fishing reform." Library Journal.

597.17 Fishes

Page, Lawrence M.

★Peterson field guide to freshwater fishes of North America north of Mexico / Lawrence M. Page, Brooks M. Burr ; illustrations by Eugene C. Beckham III ... [et al.] ; maps by Griffin E. Sheehy. Houghton Mifflin Harcourt, c2011. xix, 663 p.: **597.17**

1. Freshwater fishes -- United States -- Identification 2. Freshwater fishes -- Canada -- Identification
ISBN 9780547242064

LC 2010049219

Rev. ed. of: A field guide to freshwater fishes : North America north of Mexico. 1991.

This second edition incorporates almost 150 more freshwater fish species, plus all-new maps and a collection of new and revised plates.

597.176 Freshwater fishes

Voigt, Emily

The **dragon** behind the glass : a true story of power, obsession, and the world's most coveted fish / Emily Voigt. Scribner, 2016 320 p. **597.176**

1. Fishes 2. Fish as pets 3. Rare and endangered fishes. 4. Aquariums
ISBN 9781451678949

LC 2015040075

A tour of the surprising world of the endangered Asian arowana, otherwise known as the dragon fish, describes the violence, expense, cultural beliefs and sophisticated smuggling operations surrounding its illegal possession, tracing the author's years-long quest in search of surviving populations.

"A fresh, lively look at an obsessive desire to own a piece of the wild." Kirkus.

597.177 Marine fishes

Schultz, Ken, 1950-

Ken Schultz's field guide to saltwater fish / Ken Schultz. John Wiley & Sons, c2004. viii, 274 p. : **597.177**

1. Marine fishes -- North America. 2. Marine fishes -- North America -- Identification.
ISBN 9780471449959

LC 2003015773

Includes index.

Based on the reference book Ken Schultz's Fishing Encyclopedia, this handy field guide compresses the essence of its bestselling predecessor into a more manageable, compact size. Arranged alphabetically by species, each entry covers the identification, size/age, distribution, habitat, life history/behavior, and feeding habits of each fish. This fully illustrated, full-color guide makes it easy to identify what's at the end of your line.

597.3 Sharks

Ebert, David A

A **pocket** guide to sharks of the world / illustrated by Marc Dando ; text by David A. Ebert and Sarah Fowler. Princeton University Press, 2015 256 p. : **597.3**

1. Sharks -- Identification. 2. Sharks.
ISBN 0691165998

LC bl2016054734

Includes index.

A guide to sharks profiles each of the five hundred and one different species, with full color illustrations and an identification guide for teeth and fins.

Eilperin, Juliet

Demon fish : travels through the hidden world of sharks / Juliet Eilperin. Pantheon Books, 2011. 320 p. **597.3**

1. Sharks. 2. Marine biology 3. Fishes 4. Marine fishes
ISBN 9780375425127

LC 2010030264

A global investigation into the surprising ways in which people and cultures relate to and engage with sharks includes coverage of Papua New Guinea's creation myths, the finning practices of mainland China and the counsel of a Miami shark-fishing guide to his celebrity clients.

597.5 Protacanthopterygii

Behnke, Robert J.

Trout and salmon of North America / Robert J. Behnke ; illustrated by Joseph R. Tomelleri ; foreword by Thomas McGuane ; introduction by Donald S. Proebstel ; edited by George Scott. Free Press, 2002. viii, 359 p. : **597.5**

1. Salmon -- North America. 2. Trout -- North America.
ISBN 0743222202

LC 2002069256

A fly fisher's guide to trout and salmon considers their evolution, relationship, and conservation efforts, complementing more than one hundred illustrations with the author's field notes, observations, and specimen photographs.

"Along with full and clearly written scientific explanations, statistics and analysis, the author provides anecdotal and historical details that make this not just a field guide, but a fascinating read for those interested in the natural world." Publishers Weekly.

597.8 Amphibians

Moore, Robin, 1975-

In search of lost frogs : The Campaign to Discover the World's Rarest Amphibians / Robin Moore ; Lisa Thomas, editor. Firefly Books, 2014. 256 p. **597.8**

1. Frogs 2. Frogs -- Conservation.
ISBN 1770854649

LC oc2014012016

"This is a superb resource for general readers and for specialists with advanced training in herpetology. It not only makes fascinating reading but also provides numerous, excellent color photos of rare frogs and salamanders. Summing Up: Highly recommended. All readership levels and libraries." Choice.

597.9 Reptilia

Ernst, Carl H.

Venomous reptiles of the United States, Canada, and northern Mexico : Crotalus / Carl H. Ernst and Evelyn M. Ernst. Johns Hopkins University Press, c2011-c2012. 391 p. ; **597.9**

1. Heloderma -- North America. 2. Poisonous snakes -- North America.
ISBN 0801898765

LC 2010036966

Presenting the latest research on venomous reptiles in the United States, Canada, and northern Mexico and featuring an extensive bibliography of literature on the subject, this volume contains a wealth of information for anyone with an interest in venom, snakes, or herpetology in general. --From publisher description.

"A current, vital addition to herpetology collections." Library Journal.

McGinnis, Samuel M

★**Peterson** field guide to western reptiles and amphibians / Samuel M. McGinnis and Robert C. Stebbins ; illustrations by Robert C. Stebbins ; sponsored by the National Audubon Society, the National Wildlife Federation and the Roger Tory Peterson Institute. Houghton Mifflin Harcourt Company, 2018. xi, 560 p. : **597.9**

1. Reptiles -- North America -- Identification 2. Amphibians -- North America -- Identification 3. Reptiles -- West (US) -- Identification 4. Amphibians -- West (US) -- Identification
ISBN 9781328715500

LC 2017059616

Revised edition of: A field guide to western reptiles and amphibians / text and illustrations by Robert C. Stebbins. 3rd ed. 2003.

This is the most comprehensive and trusted guide to reptiles and amphibians of western North America. The new edition retains the realistic and accurate paintings by Robert Stebbins and includes 160 color photographs for additional detail. All range maps are up to date and placed within their species accounts. Family, genus, species, and subspecies names have been updated to the currently accepted usage. Illustrations of eggs and larvae, which can aid in identifying salamanders and frogs, are a particularly helpful feature. --From publisher description.

597.96 Snakes

Campbell, Jonathan A.

The **venomous** reptiles of the Western Hemisphere / Jonathan A. Campbell and William W. Lamar, with contributions by Edmund D. Brodie III ... [et al.]. Comstock Pub. Associates, 2004. 2 v. (xviii, 870 p., 28 p.) : **597.96**

1. Poisonous snakes -- Western Hemisphere. 2. Reptiles -- Western Hemisphere.
ISBN 9780801441417

LC 2003007834

"The authors describe two species of lizards (the Gila monster and the beaded lizard) and 190 species of dangerously venomous snakes of North, Central and South America. Provided are . . . accounts of each species--from the smallest to the largest--complete with descriptions, habitats, and geographic distribution." Library Journal.

O'Shea, Mark

Venomous snakes of the world / Mark O'Shea. Princeton University Press, c2005. 160 p. : **597.96**

1. Poisonous snakes -- Pictorial works. 2. Encyclopedias.
ISBN 9780691124360

LC 2005920576

"First published in 2005 by New Holland Publishers (UK) Ltd."--T.p. verso.

Contains illustrated guide to the venomous snakes of the world, arranged by geographic region, and includes general information on snake anatomy, diversity and distribution, types of venoms, and conservation, as well as a look at venomous lizards.

"The author has produced a compendium of more than 170 venomous snakes, along with their markings, geographical distribution, maximum length, venom, prey, and similar species. But instead of opting for the traditional taxonomic arrangement, he lists these snakes geographically by continent (a final chapter on sea snakes is also included)." Library Journal.

598 Birds

Alderfer, Jonathan K.

National Geographic birding essentials : all the tools, techniques, and tips you need to begin and become a better birder / Jonathan Alderfer and Jon L. Dunn. National Geographic, c2007. 224 p. : **598**

1. Bird watching 2. Birds -- Identification
ISBN 9781426201356

LC 2007030960

Offers tips and advice for how to improve bird watching skills, from choosing equipment and guides to where to watch and what features to look for when trying to identify a bird.

Barnes, Simon

The **meaning** of birds / Simon Barnes. W.W. Norton & Company, 2018, c2016. 208 p. **598**

1. Birds. 2. Human/animal relationships 3. Humans and birds.
ISBN 9781681776262

LC bl2017046417

Includes index.

An illustrated examination of the lives of birds looks at how they achieve the miracle of flight, why they sing, what they tell us about the seasons of the year, the uses of feathers, and what the migration of birds can tell us about climate change.

"This is an entertaining peek into the world of birds and birding that is sure to delight nature lovers." Booklist.

Birkhead, T. R.

Bird sense : what it's like to be a bird / Tim Birkhead. Walker & Company, 2012. 288 p. **598**

1. Birds. 2. Animal behavior. 3. Senses and sensation.
ISBN 9780802779663

LC 2011043684

Describes the senses of birds that enable them to interpret their environments and interact with one another, drawing on cutting-edge science to explain how bird senses compare with those of humans and how they are able to detect distant and extraordinary elements from an upcoming storm to the Earth's magnetic field.

The **most** perfect thing : inside (and outside) a bird's egg / Tim Birkhead. St. Martin's Press, 2016 288 p. **598**

1. Birds 2. Eggs 3. Reproduction 4. Biology
ISBN 9781632863690

LC bl2016015249

A bird's egg is a nearly perfect survival capsule--an external womb--and one of natural selection's most wonderful creations.

"Birkhead manages to contain what could have become an unwieldy topic, and readers with little familiarity in guillemot eggs specifically will still find the material fascinating." Publishers Weekly.

Cocker, Mark, 1959-

Birds and people / Mark Cocker and [photography by] David Tipling ; with specialist research by and the support of Jonathan Elphick and John Fanshawe. Jonathan Cape, 2013 592 pa. : **598**

1. Birds. 2. Human/animal relationships 3. Art. 4. Literature.
ISBN 9780224081740

Describes and maps the spectrum of human engagements with birds, drawing in themes of history, literature, art, cuisine, language, lore, politics, and the environment.

Floyd, Ted, 1968-

How to know the birds : the art & adventure of birding / Ted Floyd ; illustrations by N. John Schmitt. National Geographic Kids, 2019 303 p. : **598**

1. Bird watching -- United States 2. Birds -- United States -- Nomenclature
ISBN 9781426220036

LC 2018037630

Includes index.

Offers a holistic approach to bird-watching by noting how behaviors, settings, and seasonal cycles connect with shape, song, color, gender, and other characteristics traditionally used to identify species.

"Highly recommended for those interested in the natural world. This is a book to be read; there is nothing else quite like it." Library Journal.

Gentile, Olivia

★**Life** list : a woman's quest for the world's most amazing birds/ Olivia Gentile. Bloomsbury, 2009. 353 p. **598**

1. Snetsinger, Phoebe, 1931-1999 2. Women bird watchers -- United States 3. Bird watching 4. Cancer -- Diagnosis 5. Self-fulfillment 6. United States -- Social life and customs -- 20th century
ISBN 9781596911697

LC 2008027036

"Compassionate and comprehensive." Kirkus.

Jones, Darryl N.

The **birds** at my table : why we feed wild birds and why it matters / Darryl Jones. Comstock Publishing Associates, an imprint of Cornell University Press, 2018. 352 p. **598**

1. Birds -- Effect of human on 2. Human-animal relationships 3. Wildlife 4. Animal behavior
ISBN 9781501710780

LC 2017046553

Darryl Jones is fascinated by bird feeders. Not the containers supplying food to our winged friends, but the people who fill the containers. Why do people do this? Jones asks in The Birds at My Table. Does the food even benefit the birds? What are the unintended consequences of providing additional food to our winged friends? Jones takes us on a wild flight through the history of bird feeding. --From publisher description.

Knapp, Eli J.

The **delightful** horror of family birding : sharing nature with the next generation / Eli Knapp. Torrey House Press, 2018. 267 p. : **598**

1. Bird watching 2. Nature study 3. Families 4. Father and child 5. Essays
ISBN 9781937226916

Exuberant and insightful essays soar to Tanzania, Ecuador, and beyond in search of truth, adventure, and birds of all feathers. --Provided by publisher.

Lederer, Roger J.

Beaks, bones, and bird songs : how the struggle for survival has shaped birds and their behavior / Roger J. Lederer. Timber Press, 2016. 288 p. **598**

1. Birds -- Evolution. 2. Birds -- Behavior.
ISBN 9781604696486

LC 2015045261

"This is an exceptional overview of the life, adaptations, and impressive skill sets of wild birds." Library Journal.

Montgomery, Sy

Birdology : lessons learned from a pack of hens, a peck of pigeons, cantankerous crows, fierce falcons, hip hop parrots, baby hummingbirds, and one murderously big cassowary / Sy Montgomery. Free Press, 2010. vii, 260 p. **598**

1. Birds. 2. Birds as pets. 3. Bird watching. 4. Women and birds.
ISBN 9781416569848

LC 2009031303

"Montgomery assists a hummingbird rehabilitator in the delicate raising of two tiny orphans, and meets the most dangerous bird on earth, the enormous, razor-clawed cassowary in Australia, one bird whose dinosaur ancestry is blazingly apparent. She also writes from unexpected perspectives about falcons, crows, pigeons, chickens, and parrots. Inspired equally by all that we share with birds--similarities in intelligence, emotion, language, and music--and all that is mysterious (birds remain fundamentally wild), Montgomery expresses profound appreciation for the living web of life in a book that both bird lovers and readers new to bird lore will find evocative, enlightening, and uplifting." Booklist.

Östling, Brutus

Between the wingtips : the secret life of birds / Photographs,

Brutus Östling ; text, Magnus Ullman. Collins, c2006. 203 p. : 598

1. Birds 2. Pictorial works.
ISBN 9780061136856

LC bl2006024187

Includes index.

Organized by theme, presents one hundred forty photographs of common and rare bird species shown in their natural habitats, and offers musings on, and descriptions of, their most distinctive features and behaviors.

Perrins, Christopher M.

The **Princeton** encyclopedia of birds / edited by Christopher Perrins. Princeton University Press, 2009. 656 p. : 598

1. Birds -- Encyclopedias.
ISBN 9780691140704

LC bl2013035731

Presents a comprehensive and illustrated reference to the world's birds and provides accounts of every bird family, covering form and function, distribution, diet, social behavior, breeding biology, and conservation and status.

Robbins, Jim

The **wonder** of birds : what they tell us about ourselves, the world, and a better future / Jim Robbins. Spiegel & Grau, 2017. 256 p. 598

1. Birds. 2. Humans and birds 3. Human/animal relationships
ISBN 9780812993530

LC 2016049366

From New York Times science writer Jim Robbins comes a powerful examination of the fascinating and surprising world of birds: how they enrich our lives, help sustain the planet, and have a lot to teach us about being human.

Sibley, David, 1961-

Sibley birds East : field guide to birds of eastern North America / written and illustrated by David Allen Sibley. Alfred A. Knopf, 2016, c2003. xxv, 438 p. : 598

1. Birds -- North America
ISBN 9780307957917

LC BL2003007994

Includes indexes.

A new edition of the eastern North American guide for bird enthusiasts profiles 550 species, and features new illustrations and maps, in a guide specifically designed for use in the field.

"All the qualities to be expected in a field guide are here. Image reproduction is crisp, colors are distinct, shading shows well, and despite the very small size, range map colors are clear. Sibley has accomplished the difficult task of condensing [The Sibley guide to birds] to practical field size." Library Journal

★**Sibley** birds west : field guide to birds of western North America / written and illustrated by David Allen Sibley. Alfred A. Knopf, 2016. xxv, 471 p. : 598

1. Birds -- North America -- Identification.
ISBN 9780307957924

LC bl2016012774

"A Scott & Nix edition."

Includes indexes.

Features clear and detailed descriptions of 650 species of birds from the western regions of North America and several new maps and illustrations that feature depicted species from at least six different views.

★**Sibley's** birding basics / written and illustrated by David Allen Sibley. Alfred A. Knopf, 2002. 154 : 598

1. Bird watching. 2. Birds -- Identification.
ISBN 9780375709661

LC 2002020768

A noted bird painter and author of the Sibley Guide to Bird Life and Behavior offers an easy-to-follow introduction to birding, explaining how to identify various species of birds from their habitats, behaviors, characteristic feathers, and sounds and providing tips on where to look for birds.

The **Sibley** guide to birds / written and illustrated by David Sibley. Alfred A. Knopf, c2000. 544 p. : 598

1. Birds -- North America -- Identification. 2. Birds -- North America -- Behavior.
ISBN 0679451226

LC 00041239

A new edition of the North American guide for bird enthusiasts profiles hundreds of species, and features new full-color illustrations and migration-range maps, in a guide specifically designed for use in the field.

"Published to universal acclaim in 2000, Sibley expands the first edition of his guide by over 50 pages, with more than 100 species added... More than 600 paintings are new, the range maps revised, and information on habitat, behavior, and food preferences--largely lacking previously--enhance this superb guide." Library Journal.

Stokes, Donald W.

The **new** Stokes field guide to birds. Donald & Lillian Stokes. Little, Brown, 2013. xv, 574 p. : 598

1. Birds -- The West (United States) -- Identification 2. Birds -- The West (Canada) -- Identification 3. Bird watching -- North America -- Guidebooks 4. Reference books
ISBN 9780316213929

LC bl2013010778

Includes indexes.

Presents a resource that covers all species of birds including all subspecies in the western regions of North America, with detailed information on range maps, migration routes, bird shape, significant plumages, habitat, and scientific and common names.

Strycker, Noah K.

The **thing** with feathers : the surprising lives of birds and what they reveal about being human / Noah Strycker. Riverhead Books, 2014. 256 p. 598

1. Birds -- Behavior. 2. Bird watching -- Anecdotes. 3. Human/animal relationships 4. Natural history
ISBN 9781594486357

LC 2013030320

"The Thing with Feathers by Noah Strycker is a fun and profound look at the lives of birds, illuminating their surprising world--and deep connection with humanity".-- Provided by publisher.

"Strycker...here combines the latest in ornithological science with snippets of history and his own vast experience in the field to hatch a thoroughly entertaining examination of bird behavior." Booklist.

Tougias, Robert

Birder on Berry Lane : three acres, twelve months, thousands of birds / Robert Tougias ; with illustrations by Mark Szantyr. Charlesbridge, 2020 256 p. 598

1. Bird watching -- Connecticut. 2. Bird watchers -- Connecticut. 3.

Birds -- Migration. 4. Backyards.
ISBN 9781623545413

LC 2019019734

A writer, birder and naturalist presents a month-by-month guide to the birds that flock to his New England backyard, revealing the miracles of the ordinary in the subtle changes, season to season and the ecosystem of the land surrounding him.

"Bird-loving readers will adore Tougias's celebratory account of how wild animals can become an intrinsic part of one's daily life." Publishers Weekly

598.072 Descriptive research

Zickefoose, Julie

The **bluebird** effect : uncommon bonds with common birds / Julie Zickefoose. Houghton Mifflin Harcourt Co., 2012. 352 p. **598.072**

1. Zickefoose, Julie Anecdotes. 2. Birds -- Behavior 3. Wildlife rescue. 4. Bird watching. 5. Birds -- Wounds and injuries -- Treatment
ISBN 9780547003092

LC 2011036692

A wild bird rehabilitator and natural history artist describes her painstaking efforts to rescue sick and injured wild birds and the experience of rereleasing a bird that subsequently visits, dedicating 25 chapters to a sequence of individual birds to offer insight into species personality, habits and quirks. By the author of Letters from Eden.

598.097 Birds--North America

Bull, John L.

★The **National** Audubon Society field guide to North American birds. John Bull and John Farrand, Jr. ; revised by John Farrand ; visual Key by Amanda Wilson and Lori Hogan. Knopf, 1994. 796 p. : **598.097**

1. Birds -- North America -- Identification.
ISBN 9780679428527

LC 94007768

Rev. ed. of: The Audubon Society field guide to North American birds. 1977.

Includes index.

A revised edition of the popular field guide includes hundreds of all new, full-color photographs, along with information on diverse species of eastern birds, their characteristics, habitats and ranges, identification tips, and more.

Floyd, Ted, 1968-

Smithsonian field guide to the birds of North America / Ted Floyd ; edited by Paul Hess and George Scott ; designed by Charles Nix ; maps by Paul Lehman ; photographs by Brian E. Small ... [et al.]. Collins, c2008. vii, 512 p. : **598.097**

1. Birds -- North America.
ISBN 9780061120404

LC 2008001395

A reference guide to North American wild birds features descriptive entries on 730 species, essays on bird behavior and identification, and maps based on the latest range information.

"Ideal for beginners, but also has formidable resources for experienced birders. Perfect for field use. Birders of any experience level will be happy with this volume on their bookshelf." Publishers Weekly.

598.147 Feathers

Hanson, Thor

★**Feathers** : the evolution of a natural miracle / Thor Hanson. Basic Books, 2011. 256 p. **598.147**

1. Feathers. 2. Body covering (Anatomy)
ISBN 9780465020133

A biologist presents the natural history of feathers, applying the findings of paleontologists, ornithologists, biologists, engineers, and art historians to answer questions about the origin of feathers, their evolution, and their uses throughout the ages.

"Readers from science buffs to those interested in cultural history will find this a worthwhile afternoon's read." Publishers Weekly.

598.15 Behavior--birds

Ackerman, Jennifer, 1959-

The **bird** way : a new look at how birds talk, work, play, parent, and think / Jennifer Ackerman. Penguin Press, 2020. 352 p. **598.15**

1. Birds -- Behavior. 2. Animal intelligence. 3. Birds. 4. Animal behavior.
ISBN 9780735223011

LC 2020002317

"'There is the mammal way and there is the bird way.' This is one scientist's pithy distinction between mammal brains and bird brains: two ways to make a highly intelligent mind. But the bird way is much more than a unique pattern of brain wiring, and lately, scientists have taken a new look at bird behaviors they have, for years, dismissed as anomalies or mysteries. What they are finding is upending the traditional view of how birds conduct their lives, how they communicate, forage, court, breed, survive. They're also revealing the remarkable intelligence underlying these activities, abilities we once considered uniquely our own--deception, manipulation, cheating, kidnapping, infanticide, but also, ingenious communication between species, cooperation, collaboration, altruism, culture, and play. Some of these extraordinary behaviors are biological conundrums that seem to push the edges of--well--birdness: A mother bird that kills her own infant sons, and another that selflessly tends to the young of other birds as if they were her own. Young birds that devote themselves to feeding their siblings and others so competitive they'll stab their nestmates to death. Birds that give gifts and birds that steal, birds that dance or drum, that paint their creationsor paint themselves, birds that build walls of sound to keep out intruders and birds that summon playmates with a special call--and may hold the secret to our own penchant for playfulness and the evolution of laughter. Drawing on personal observations, the latest science, and her bird-related travel around the world, from the tropical rainforests of eastern Australia and the remote woodlands of northern Japan, to the rolling hills of lower Austria and the islands of Alaska's Kachemak Bay, Ackerman shows there is clearly no single bird way of being. In every respect, in plumage, form, song, flight, lifestyle, niche, and behavior, birds vary. It's what we love about them. As E.O Wilson once said, when you have seen one bird, you have not seen them all".-- Provided by publisher.

"A brightly original book sure to please any nature lover." Kirkus

Attenborough, David, 1926-

The **life** of birds / David Attenborough. Princeton University Press, 1998. 320 p. : **598.15**

1. Birds -- Behavior. 2. Ornithology. 3. Bird watching. 4. Bird

ecology.
ISBN 069101633X

LC 98030705

"Well illustrated with color photographs, Attenborough's latest goes a long way to converting all readers into bird lovers." Booklist.

Erickson, Laura, 1951-

The **love** lives of birds : courting and mating rituals / Laura Erickson. Storey Publishing, 2020 152 p. **598.15**

1. Birds -- Behavior 2. Birds -- Sexual behavior 3. Courtship of animals 4. Parental behavior in animals

ISBN 9781635862751

LC 2020029587

Ornithologist Laura Erickson combines her bird expertise with a touch of romance writing in this exploration of the courtship and mating rituals of 35 bird species. From the lifelong devotion of the American crow to the dalliances of the eastern bluebird, from the bald eagle's dazzling aerial display to the male ruby-throated hummingbird's reputation as a "deadbeat dad"--courtship, mating, and parenting differ dramatically among birds.

"Terrific color illustrations by Veronica Lilja add to the fun. Bird enthusiasts and nature lovers in general shouldn't miss this." Publishers Weekly

Kroodsma, Donald E.

The **singing** life of birds : the art and science of listening to birdsong / Donald E. Kroodsma ; drawings by Nancy Haver. Houghton Mifflin, 2005. xii, 482 p. : **598.15**

1. Birdsongs. 2. Bird watching 3. Birds -- Behavior

ISBN 0618405682

LC 2004065130

A recognized authority on birdsong discusses the reasons why birds sing, covering a wide range of birds that might be found warbling or chirping in any backyard, including whippoorwills, wrens, woodcocks, thrushes, flycatchers, sparrows, and thrashers.

"Kroodsma's is a warm, encouraging guide to the world of birdsong, and his enthusiasm is contagious." Publishers Weekly.

598.177 Sea birds

Nicolson, Adam, 1957-

★The **seabird's** cry : the lives and loves of the planet's great ocean voyagers / Adam Nicolson. Henry Holt and Company, 2018, c2017. 400 p. : **598.177**

1. Sea birds 2. Marine ecology 3. Birds -- Behavior 4. Puffins 5. Hebrides

ISBN 9781250134189

LC 2017031320

Originally published: London : William Collins, 2017.

"Marveling at lives lived in some of the harshest places on the planet, Nicolson writes lyrically of birds most of us only briefly notice when visiting a rocky shoreline, beings possessing extraordinary forms of understanding we have never shared." Booklist.

598.7 Miscellaneous orders of land birds

Davies, N. B. (Nicholas B.), 1952-

Cuckoo : cheating by nature / Nick Davies. Bloomsbury USA, 2015. 289 p. **598.7**

1. Cuckoos. 2. Birds. 3. Ornithology.

ISBN 9781620409527

LC bl2015012933

A gifted biologist's careful and beguiling study of why cuckoos have got away with tricking other birds into hatching and raising their young for thousands of years.

"He describes experiments involving recorded bird calls, radio transmitters, and egg substitutions, and he reports findings that suggest how predators and prey continue to adapt. Readers may gain some respect, if not affection, for a hard-to-understand bird." Booklist.

Orenstein, Ronald I. (Ronald Isaac), 1946-

Hummingbirds / text by Ronald Orenstein ; photography by Michael and Patricia Fogden. Firefly Books, 2014 256 p. : **598.7**

1. Hummingbirds.

ISBN 1770854002

Hummingbirds reveals the various adaptations of this avian species.

"Of optional interest to naturalists, nature buffs, and birders." Library Journal.

Shunk, Stephen A.

Peterson reference guide to woodpeckers of North America / Stephen A. Shunk. Houghton Mifflin Harcourt, 2016. xi, 298 p. : **598.7**

1. Woodpeckers -- North America. 2. Woodpeckers -- North America -- Identification.

ISBN 9780618739950

LC bl2016018082

"Sponsored by the Roger Tory Peterson Institute and the National Wildlife Federation."

Presents a comprehensive guide to twenty-three species of woodpeckers, describing their anatomy, physical features, distribution, habitat, behavior, diet, and conservation status.

West, George C.

Do hummingbirds hum? : fascinating answers to questions about hummingbirds / George C. West and Carol A. Butler. Rutgers University Press, c2010. xvi, 185 p. : **598.7**

1. Hummingbirds -- Miscellanea.

ISBN 9780813547381

LC 2009049511

In Do Hummingbirds Hum? George C. West, who has studied and banded over 13,500 hummingbirds in Arizona, and Carol A. Butler provide an overview of hummingbird biology for the general reader, and more detailed discussions of their morphology and behavior for those who want to fly beyond the basics. Enriched with beautiful and rare photography, including a section in vivid color, this engaging question and answer guide offers readers a wide range of information about these glorious pollinators as well as tips for attracting, photographing, and observing hummingbirds in the wild or in captivity. --From publisher description.

598.8 Perching birds (Passeriformes)

Heinrich, Bernd, 1940-

White feathers : the nesting lives of tree swallows / Bernd Heinrich. Houghton Mifflin Harcourt, 2020. 352 p. **598.8**

1. Birds -- Behavior 2. Tree swallow. 3. Swallows. 4. Tree swallow

-- Nests.
ISBN 9781328604415

LC 2019024927

An acclaimed scientist, naturalist and best-selling author offers an engaging, detailed look at the lives of wild birds, after becoming fascinated by a pair of swallows who have a preference for white feathers as nest lining.

"This inviting work will draw in naturalists and birders, along with anyone wishing to learn more about animal behavior from a trusted guide." Library Journal

598.9 Falconiformes, Strigiformes, Caprimulgiformes

Clark, William S., 1937-

A **field** guide to hawks of North America / William S. Clark and Brian K. Wheeler ; illustrations by Brian K. Wheeler. Houghton Mifflin, 2001. x, 316 p., 81 p. of plates : **598.9**

1. Birds of prey -- North America -- Identification
ISBN 9780395670682

LC 2001024477

Identifies all species of North American hawks, eagles, falcons, vultures, kites, and ospreys, describing their characteristics and markings.

Duncan, James R.

Owls of the world / James Duncan. Johns Hopkins University Press, 2018. 192 p. : **598.9**

1. Owls
ISBN 9781421427188

LC bl2018191746

"There is no shortage of books devoted to the world's owls, and for good reason. Owls fascinate. This coffee-table-sized book is most noteworthy for its splendid photos of owls, which make the book a visual treat." Choice.

599 Mammals

Drew, Liam

I, mammal : the story of what makes us mammals / Liam Drew. Bloomsbury Sigma, 2018. 288 p. **599**

1. Humans 2. Mammals 3. Human evolution 4. Human anatomy
ISBN 9781472922892

LC bl2018000456

A freelance writer and former neurobiologist examines the biology, evolution and traits of humans and explores the anatomical and physiological attributes that make us mammals and that ultimately separate us from other members of the same scientific class designation.

"With wit and passion, Drew, a freelance writer and former neurobiologist, explores what it means to be a mammal by taking an evolutionary look at how and where mammals arose." Publishers Weekly.

Elbroch, Mark

Mammal tracks & sign : a guide to North American species / Mark Elbroch. Stackpole Books, c2003. vii, 779 p. : **599**

1. Animal tracks -- North America. 2. Mammals -- North America
ISBN 9780811726269

LC 2002010549

"The author brings an ideal combination of practical experience and careful research to this work. . . . A definitive treatment, Elbroch's book will set the standard for years to come and is essential to anyone interested in tracking this continent's mammals." Library Journal.

Hoyt, Erich

Encyclopedia of whales, dolphins and porpoises / Erich Hoyt ; principal photography by Brandon Cole ; illustrations by Uko Gorter. Firefly Books, 2017 300 p. : **599**

1. Marine mammals -- Encyclopedias 2. Cetacea 3. Whales 4. Dolphins 5. Encyclopedias
ISBN 9781770859418

LC 2017300268

"In [this book], award-winning author and whale researcher Erich Hoyt takes readers into the field for an intimate encounter with some 90 species of cetaceans that make their homes in the world's oceans. Drawing on decades of firsthand experience and a comprehensive familiarity with the current revolution in cetacean studies, Hoyt provides unique insights into the life histories of these compelling marine mammals. Here are discoveries about cetacean biology and behavior, from the physical differences and adaptations among the baleen and toothed whales to their highly intelligent hunting and feeding methods. The courtship and mating practices, family relationships and the lifelong bonds among some family members are fascinating. The symphonic composerof the whale world is the humpback whale, whose complex 30-minute songs reverberate across the liquid universe of the ocean . Some cetaceans survive deep diving and negotiate lengthy migrations across oceans. This book is a fascinating compilation of the latest data on cetaceans and an impassioned argument for the ongoing need for international protection of at-risk populations and their increasingly damaged habitat."-- provided by the Publisher.

Kelsey, Elin

Watching giants : the secret lives of whales / Elin Kelsey ; with photographs by Doc White ; additional photographs by Francois Gohier. University of California Press, c2008. xiii, 201 p., 16 p. of plates : **599**

1. Whale watching -- Sea of Cortez 2. Marine biology 3. Oceanography 4. Marine mammals 5. Sea of Cortez.
ISBN 9780520249769

LC 2008007782

"An appealing, agitating foray into the world of whales that ignites both protective instincts and a hungry curiosity to know more." Kirkus.

Murie, Olaus J. (Olaus Johan), 1889-1963

★A **field** guide to animal tracks / Olaus J. Murie and Mark Elbroch ; illustrated by Olaus J. Murie and Mark Elbroch. Houghton Mifflin Company, 2005. xxvi, 391 p. : The Peterson field guide series **599**

1. Animal tracks -- North America -- Identification 2. Animals -- North America
ISBN 9780618517435

LC 2005013108

A new edition of the classic guide to animal tracking includes descriptions of habitats, habits, signs, and much more, providing thousands of line drawings of bird, reptiles, amphibians, and insects that leave tracks.

Nowak, Ronald M.

Walker's mammals of the world. / Ronald M. Nowak. Johns Hopkins University Press, 1999. 2 v. (li, 1936 p.) : **599**

1. Mammals -- Classification. 2. Mammals.
ISBN 0801857899

LC 98023686

Gives an historical account of the world's mammals since 3,000 B.C., and then provides detailed information about every mammal on earth, divided by genus.

Vaillant, John

The **tiger** : a true story of vengeance and survival / John Vaillant. Alfred A. Knopf, 2010. 352 p. **599**

1. Tiger hunting. 2. Poaching. 3. Wildlife conservation. 4. Tiger attacks. 5. Russia. 6. Russian Far East.

ISBN 9780307268938

LC 2010004068

"A Borzoi Book."

ALA Notable Book, 2011.

Documents the efforts of a tiger conservation leader who was forced to hunt a man-eating tiger through the brutal Siberian winter, an effort that familiarized him with the creature's history, motives, and unique method of attack.

"What makes The Tiger a grand addition to the animal-pursuit subgenre is the sensitive way in which Vaillant . evokes his cat. Few writers have taken such pains to understand their monsters, and few depict them in such arresting prose." New York Times Book Review.

599.03 Mammals--dictionaries

Macdonald, David W. (David Whyte)

The **Princeton** encyclopedia of mammals / edited by David W. Macdonald. Princeton University Press, 2009, c2006. xii, 936 p. : **599.03**

1. Mammals.

ISBN 9780691140698

LC bl2010032703

Originally published: The encyclopedia of mammals. New York : Oxford University Press, 2006.

Presents a guide to the world's mammals, with information on anatomy, behavior, conservation, and distribution.

599.097 Mammals--North America

Kays, Roland, 1971-

★**Mammals** of North America / Roland W. Kays and Don E. Wilson. Princeton University Press, 2009. 248 p. : **599.097**

1. Mammals -- North America -- Identification

ISBN 9780691142784

LC 2009001417

The best-selling field guide that "sets new standards" (New Scientist) and "makes all other field guides for mammals of the United States. . . and Canada obsolete" (Journal of Mammalogy) is now even better. Covering 20 species recognized since 2002 and including 13 new color plates, this fully revised edition of Mammals of North America illustrates all 462 known mammal species in the United States and Canada -- each in beautiful color and accurate detail. With a more up-to-date species list than any other guide, improved facing-page descriptions, easier-to-read distribution maps, updated common and scientific names, and track and scat illustrations, this slim, light, and easy-to-use volume is the must-have source for identifying North American mammals. --From publisher description.

Whitaker, John O.

★**National** Audubon Society field guide to North American mammals / John O. Whitaker, Jr. Knopf , c1996. 937 p. : **599.097**

1. Mammals -- North America -- Identification.

ISBN 9780679446316

LC 95081456

"A Chanticleer Press edition"--P. opposite t.p.

Includes index.

Presents information on 390 species of North American mammals, along with keys for identification, range maps, and information on tracks and anatomy

599.4 Bats

Taylor, Marianne, 1972-

Bats : an illustrated guide to all species / Marianne Taylor, Merlin D. Tuttle, science editor & photographer. Smithsonian Books, 2018 400 p. : **599.4**

1. Bats. 2. Bats -- Ecology.

ISBN 9781588346476

LC 2018043061

Includes indexes.

Bats: An Illustrated Guide to All Species explores bats and their fundamental role in our ecosystems through lavish full-color photographs and lively narrative. From the Giant Golden Crowned Flying Fox, a megabat with a wingspan of more than five feet, to the aptly named Bumblebee Bat, the world's smallest mammal, the number and diversity of bat species have proven to be both rich and underestimated. Nocturnal, fast-flying, and secretive, bats are difficult to observe and catalog. This richly illustrated handbook presents bats' evolution, biology, behavior, and ecology. It offers in-depth profiles of four hundred megabats and microbats and detailed summaries of all the species identified to date. Complete with an introduction exploring bats' natural history and their unique adaptations to life on the wing, Bats includes close-up images of these animals' delicate and intricate forms and faces, each shaped by evolution to meet the demands of an extraordinarily specialized life. --From publisher description.

"This comprehensive, clear, and concise guide is sure to appeal to any armchair enthusiast or researcher with an interest in the topic." Booklist.

599.5 Cetaceans and sea cows

Hoare, Philip

The **whale** : in search of the giants of the sea / Philip Hoare. HarperCollins, 2010, c2008 448 p. **599.5**

1. Whales. 2. Whales in art. 3. Whales in literature. 4. Whaling.

ISBN 9780061976216

LC bl2009036210

Originally published: London : Fourth Estate, 2008.

Samuel Johnson Prize for Nonfiction, 2009.

An extraordinary journey into the underwater world of the whale.

Pyenson, Nick

Spying on whales : the past, present, and future of Earth's most awesome creatures / Nick Pyenson. Viking, 2018 xii, 322 p. : **599.5**

1. Whales 2. Marine biology 3. Marine mammals 4. Evolution

ISBN 9780735224568

Tracing the evolution of whales from small land-roamers to the intelligent, massive creatures of today, an award-winning Smithsonian researcher shares scientific and archaeological insights into their mysteries and survival challenges.

599.53 Dolphins and porpoises

Neiwert, David A., 1956-

Of orcas and men : what killer whales can teach us / David Neiwert. Overlook Pr., 2015. 368 p. **599.53**

1. Killer whale. 2. Humans and whales. 3. Human/animal relationships. 4. Natural history. 5. Puget Sound. 6. Pacific Northwest literature.

ISBN 9781468308655

LC 2015010796

A revelatory history of orcas evaluates them as one of the planet's most intelligent animals, challenging beliefs about their "killer" natures while citing the threats to their populations. By the author of Strawberry Days.

"This narrative is perhaps a bit long but accessible and persuasive. The author authoritatively presents his facts and will likely inspire readers to share what they've learned from his call to action to ensure the orcas' survival. His tone isn't alarmist or strident, but his message is urgent. A wide-ranging, interesting book that should be required reading for school-aged environmentalists." Kirkus.

599.638 Giraffe and okapi

Peterson, Dale

Giraffe reflections / text by Dale Peterson ; photographs by Karl Ammann. University of Calif. Press, 2013 221 p. : **599.638**

1. Giraffe 2. Giraffe.

ISBN 0520266854

LC 2012038611

Presents a cultural, historical, and pictorial history of giraffes, describing their biology and behavior and demonstrating their grace and elegance through over one hundred photographs.

599.64 Bovids

Castello, Jose R.

Bovids of the world : antelopes, gazelles, cattle, goats, sheep, and relatives / Jose R. Castello ; foreword by Brent Huffman and Colin Groves. Princeton University Press, 2016 664 p. : **599.64**

1. Bovidae

ISBN 0691167176

LC 2015035946

Bovids are a diverse group of ruminant mammals that have hooves and unbranched hollow horns. Bovids of the World is the first comprehensive field guide to cover all 279 bovid species, including antelopes, gazelles, cattle, buffaloes, sheep, and goats. From the hartebeest of Africa and the takin of Asia to the muskox of North America, bovids are among the world's most spectacular animals and this stunningly illustrated and easy-to-use field guide is an ideal way to learn more about them. --From publisher description.

Rinella, Steven

American buffalo : in search of a lost icon / Steven Rinella. Spiegel & Grau, 2008. 288 p. **599.64**

1. Rinella, Steven. 2. Buffaloes. 3. American bison hunting 4. Hunting. 5. Symbolism. 6. Alaska.

ISBN 9780385521680

LC 2008013624

A correspondent for "Outside" magazine details his participation in a hunt for American bison in the Alaskan wilderness while reflecting on the history of the buffalo and the future of an animal that has haunted the American imagination.

"In 2005, [Rinella] won an Alaska state lottery permit making him one of 24 hunters allowed to kill one wild buffalo each to thin out the Copper River herd in the Wrangell-Saint Elias National Park. The book's core is Rinella's entertaining and often harrowing account of that hunting trip into Alaska's frozen south-central wilderness, where he bagged his first buffalo. But entwined throughout that story line is an engaging back story a stampede of facts and factoids, legends and lore, hard-core science and staggering history of North America's largest land animal. Everything you ever wanted to know about the buffalo or didn't going back to Pleistocene days." USA Today.

599.67 Elephants

Ammann, Karl

Elephant reflections / photographs by Karl Ammann ; text by Dale Peterson. University of California Press, c2009. xv, 272 p. : **599.67**

1. Elephants 2. Elephants -- Pictorial works

ISBN 9780520253773

LC 2008042391

Presents a pictorial celebration of the elephant, moving from the informative to the purely aesthetic, and introduces the natural history and conservation of the animal as well as the politics of the ivory trade.

Wood, Levison, 1982-

The **last** giants : the rise and fall of the African elephant / Levison Wood. Black Cat, 2020 272 p. **599.67**

1. Wood, Levison, 1982- 2. African elephant 3. Rare and endangered animals. 4. Social behavior in animals 5. Mammals 6. Botswana -- Description and travel

ISBN 9780802158475

LC 2020038634

The Last Giants is a comprehensive exploration of the fascinating past, difficult present, and imperiled future of the African elephant.

"Comprehensively yet accessibly conveying Wood's lifelong fascination with African elephants, his discussion will appeal to anyone keen on learning more about them." Publishers Weekly

599.75 Cat family

Hunter, Luke

Wild cats of the world / Luke Hunter ; illustrated by Priscilla Barrett. Bloomsbury, 2015. 240 p. : **599.75**

1. Felidae.

ISBN 1472912195

LC bl2015040226

Looks at the wild members of the cat family throughout the world, with illustrated profiles of each species containing detailed factual material about their behavior, habitats, ecological presence, and demographic status.

Pittman, Craig

Cat tale : the wild, weird battle to save the Florida panther / Craig Pittman. Hanover Square Press, 2020. 336 pages, 16 unnumbered pages of plates : **599.75**

1. Florida panther 2. Panthers 3. Wildlife conservation 4. Rare and

endangered animals 5. Florida
ISBN 9781335938800
LC bl2020002934

Traces the story of the unlikely rescue of the Florida panther from extinction while revealing the political factors and colorful personalities that are impacting the species today.

"A bright, intriguing story of people and panthers with strong appeal for readers interested in endangered species." Kirkus.

Sunquist, Fiona

The **wild** cat book / Fiona Sunquist and Mel Sunquist ; with photos by Terry Whittaker and others. University of Chicago, Ill. :Press, 2014 v, 268 p. : **599.75**

1. Felidae.
ISBN 0226780260
LC 2013048755

Presents information about the physical features, behavior, habitats, and geographical distribution of wild and feral cats throughout the world, and the dangers they face from humans and changes to their environment.

"An extensive bibliography for each species provides sources of additional information for interested readers. The clearly written text and attractive layout of photographs make this book a valuable resource for both academic and public libraries." Choice.

Williams, Jim

Path of the puma : the remarkable resilience of the mountain lion / Jim Williams, with Joe Glickman and a foreword by Douglas Chadwick. Patagonia, Inc., 2018. 288 p. **599.75**

1. Puma 2. Wild cats 3. Wildlife 4. Wildlife conservation
ISBN 9781938340727
LC bl2019003695

During a time when most wild animals are experiencing decline in the face of development and climate change, the intrepid mountain lion--also known as a puma, a cougar, and by many other names--has experienced reinvigoration as well as expansion of territory. What makes this cat, the fourth carnivore in the food chain--just ahead of humans ? so resilient and resourceful?

"The many spectacular landscape photographs are a treasure on their own and worth the cover price. A handsome book that is well-balanced, instructive, and authoritative." Kirkus.

599.773 Canis lupus and Canis rufus

Busch, Robert (Robert H.)

The **wolf** almanac : a celebration of wolves and their world / Robert H. Busch ; foreword by Rick Bass. The Lyons Press, 2018 xiv, 303 p. : **599.773**

1. Wolves.
ISBN 9781493033751
LC 2017057201

The Wolf Almanac is the most widely respected compendium on wolves. With hundreds of full-color photos, graphs, charts, maps, and more, The Wolf Almanac covers every aspect of the wolf kingdom, from the animal's evolution, to its anatomy, physiology, behavior, social dynamics, and interactions with other species. Important updates about wolf conservation and reintroductions are included, making The Wolf Almanac an indispensable addition to any naturalist's library. --From publisher description.

Lopez, Barry Holstun, 1945-

★**Of** wolves and men / Barry Lopez ; with photographs by John Bauguess ; including a new afterword by the author and expanded bibliography. Scribner Classics, 2004, c1978. ix, 323 p. : **599.773**

1. Wolves. 2. Humans and wolves 3. Rare and endangered animals. 4. Nature. 5. Essays
ISBN 0743249364
LC 2004045429

Originally published: New York : Scribner, 1978.

A National Book Award finalist, originally published twenty-five years ago, examines the relationship between wolves and humans throughout history, drawing on a range of historical, mythological, and literary sources to discuss what wolves represent to people and present a case for their protection.

"The author infuses his natural history of the long relationship between wolves and humankind with both myth and science." Booklist.

599.773097 Wolves--North America

Blakeslee, Nate, 1970-

★**American** wolf : a true story of survival and obsession in the West / Nate Blakeslee. Crown Publishers, 2017 336 p.

1. Wolves. 2. Rare and endangered animals 3. Wildlife management. 4. Animal conservation. 5. Yellowstone National Park. 6. The West (United States)
ISBN 9781101902783
LC 2017008953

The story of O-Six, a female wolf in Yellowstone National Park who became something of a social media star, and the challenges she, her pups, and her pack faced from hunters, cattle ranchers, and other Yellowstone wolves. It is also a larger story of the clash in the American West between those who want to restore the wolf population of Yellowstone, and those who oppose it.

"The fight between federal and state control of Yellowstones wolves is embodied in O-Six's story, told with great immediacy and empathy in a tale that reads like fiction. This one will grab readers and impel them into the heart of the conflict." Booklist.

McAllister, Ian, 1969-

The **last** wild wolves : ghosts of the rain forest / Ian McAllister ; with contributions by Chris Darimont ; introduction by Paul Paquet. University of California Press, 2007. 191 p. **599.773097**

1. Wolves -- British Columbia. 2. Wolves -- Canada. 3. Wolves -- Behavior. 4. British Columbia. 5. Canada.
ISBN 9780520254732

"The text is particularly well written and engaging. . . . However, it is the dozens of unique photos sprinkled liberally throughout the book that provide the greatest appeal." Science Books & Films.

599.775 Vulpes

Brand, Adele

The **hidden** world of the fox / Adele Brand. William Morrow & Company, 2019. 224 p. **599.775**

1. Foxes 2. Predatory animals 3. Human/animal relationships 4. Animals -- Adaptation
ISBN 9780062966100
LC bl2019023587

A mammal ecologist's intimate portrait of the fox draws on scientific research in multiple countries to share insights into the species' evolution, its highly adaptable nature and the cultural history it has inspired. Adele Brand's observations have convinced her that the fox is arguably the most modern of all wildlife, uniquely suited to survival in the rapidly expanding urban/wild interface.

599.786 Polar bear

Derocher, Andrew E.

Polar bears : a complete guide to their biology and behavior / text by Andrew E. Derocher ; photographs by Wayne Lynch. Johns Hopkins University Press ; 2012. ix, 249 p. : **599.786**

1. Polar bear -- Behavior. 2. Polar bear.

ISBN 1421403056

LC 2011021303

Presents an introduction to the polar bear, discussing its evolution, physical characteristics, life cycle, predatory behavior, habitat, and the threats to its existence from global warming.

599.789 Ailuropoda

Nicholls, Henry, 1973-

The **way** of the panda : the curious history of China's political animal / Henry Nicholls. W W Norton & Co Inc, 2011. 304 p. **599.789**

1. Pandas. 2. Bears. 3. Animal conservation. 4. Wildlife conservation. 5. China.

ISBN 9781605981888

LC bl2011015768

Chronicles the formal scientific discovery, conservation and current understandings of giant pandas to trace their dramatic story and reveal how the species reflects changing attitudes toward the natural world and contributes to China's rise to a 21st-century super-power.

"When the Chinese government brings Giant Pandas to the negotiating table, the stakes change. Whole populations and their leaders clamor for access to these animals, as if they were toddlers reaching for toys. Washington, London and Moscow have all succumbed to this awesome (a chorus of Awwwwwww! accompanies every panda appearance) force. That is only one reason that Henry Nicholls refers to the Giant Panda as a political animal in his charmingly written The Way of the Panda. At times everything concerning the creatures seems to have a political angle: not only their value as state gifts (with heavy strings attached) but also their precise scientific classification; their mating habits and offspring; and the efforts to ensure their preservation. The author compares the history of the panda in the modern world to that of China itself, complete with a great leap forward in the 1960s, when the captive breeding of pandas first became possible." Wall Street Journal.

599.8 Primates

Goodall, Jane, 1934-

★**In** the shadow of man / Jane Goodall ; photos. by Hugo van Lawick. Houghton Mifflin, 1971. xx, 297 p. : **599.8**

1. Chimpanzees -- Behavior. 2. Social behavior in animals. 3. Social behavior in chimpanzees. 4. Primatology

ISBN 0395127262

LC 71162007

A personal account of the author's life among wild chimpanzees in Africa offers insight into animal behavior and draws parallels between chimpanzee and human relationships.

599.88 Great apes and gibbons

Stanford, Craig B. (Craig Britton), 1956-

Planet without apes / Craig B. Stanford. Belknap Press of Harvard University Press, 2012. 248 p. **599.88**

1. Apes 2. Rare and endangered animals 3. Extinct animals 4. Primates

ISBN 9780674067042

LC 2012023985

Predicting the imminent extinction of the world's great apes, a leading primatologist explains the loss of evolutionary knowledge that would result from losing the world's animal species that most closely resemble humans.

Waal, F. B. M. de (Frans B. M.), 1948-

Bonobo : the forgotten ape / Frans de Waal ; photographs, Frans Lanting. University of California Press, 1997. xv, 210 p. : **599.88**

1. Primatologists. 2. Bonobos. 3. Bonobos -- Behavior. 4. Photographs.

ISBN 0520205359

LC 96041095

"The subject of this monograph is the bonobo, a species of ape. In six chapters, de Waal describes the history of the discovery of bonobos as a separate species; he compares them with common chimps; he describes their natural habitat and their . use of sex as social currency, particularly in moderating aggression; he examines bonobo social structure in relation to that of common chimps and humans; and he finishes with an exploration of bonobos' highly developed sense of empathy." The New Scientist.

599.884 Gorilla

Fossey, Dian, 1932-1985

★**Gorillas** in the mist / Dian Fossey. Houghton Mifflin, 2000, c1983. xviii, 326 p. ; **599.884**

1. Fossey, Dian, 1932-1985. 2. Gorillas -- Behavior 3. Animal behavior. 4. Women and gorillas. 5. Humans and gorillas.

ISBN 061808360X

LC 2001265471

"Whatever the mountain gorillas' future, their immediate past is here in Fossey's vibrant and invaluable study." Kirkus.

599.885 Chimpanzees

Halloran, Andrew R.

The **song** of the ape : understanding the languages of chimpanzees / Andrew R. Halloran. St. Martin's Press, 2012. 288 p. **599.885**

1. Halloran, Andrew R. 2. Chimpanzees -- Behavior. 3. Animal communication. 4. Primates. 5. Chimpanzees -- Psychology.

ISBN 9780312563110

LC 2011041344

An investigation into chimpanzee communication documents the astonishing experiences that inspired the author's zoology work, the individual histories of five captive chimpanzees and the attempts of the scientific community to teach human language to chimps.

"Halloran has written a fascinating book that easily spans the gap between scientific research and popular reading tastes." Booklist.

Waal, F. B. M. de (Frans B. M.), 1948-

★**Mama's** last hug : animal emotions and what they tell us about ourselves / Frans de Waal ; with photographs and drawings by the author. W.W. Norton & Company, 2019. 336 p. **599.885**

1. Emotions in animals. 2. Empathy 3. Emotions 4. Animal behavior

ISBN 9780393635065

LC 2018047218

ALA Notable Book, 2020.

The influential primatologist draws on renowned primate studies in an exploration of animal emotions that touches on such subjects as expressions, animal sentience, and free will.

"Most of the author's observations involve the spontaneous behavior of chimpanzees, bonobos, and other primates, but readers will also be rewarded with tales of birds, dogs, horses, elephants, and rats. As he has shown in nearly all of his books, de Waal is a skilled storyteller, and his love for animals always shines through." Kirkus.

599.9 Humans

Meals, Roy A.

Bones : inside and out / Roy A. Meals, MD. W. W. Norton & Company, 2020 x, 294 p. **599.9**

1. Bones. 2. Human anatomy 3. Culture -- History 4. Skeleton

ISBN 9781324005322

LC 2020013491

A 500-million-year history of bone as a focus for understanding vertebrate life and human culture examines the biological makeup of bones, how medical innovations have enhanced human knowledge and what can be learned from bones even millions of years later.

"This appealing and kaleidoscopic narrative on bone topics, ranging from x-ray technology to the Paris catacombs, will appeal to readers interested in medicine and medical history, anthropology, archaeology, and material culture. Enjoyable and recommended." Library Journal

599.93 Genetics, sex and age characteristics, evolution

Finkel, Elizabeth

The **genome** generation / Elizabeth Finkel. Melbourne University Press, 2012. xiv, 274 p. : **599.93**

1. Gene mapping 2. Human genetics. 3. DNA research 4. Genetic engineering

ISBN 9780522856477

"With consummate skill and a flair for storytelling, Finkel, an award-winning journalist and molecular biologist, uncoils the mystery of the genome and its ramifications." Choice.

Leakey, Richard E.

★The **origin** of humankind / Richard Leakey. BasicBooks, 1994. xvi, 171 p. : **599.93**

1. Human evolution. 2. Prehistoric humans. 3. Evolution.

ISBN 0465031358

LC 94003617

Discusses the evolution of the human species, relates the distinctions that set humans apart from apes, and explains how and why we developed social and cultural organizations

"This is a worthwhile addition to many kinds of libraries: public, general, science, biological, and psychological." Science Books & Films.

Rutherford, Adam

Humanimal : how homo sapiens became nature's most paradoxical creature--a new evolutionary history / Adam Rutherford. The Experiment, LLC, 2019. 256 p. **599.93**

1. Human evolution 2. Humans 3. Evolution 4. Animals

ISBN 9781615195312

LC bl2019001361

Originally published in 2018 as "The Book of Humans".

The author of A Brief History of Everyone Who Ever Lived draws on current genetic research to explore the paradox of the human identity as a member of the animal kingdom that is distinct from all others.

"A smooth, expert, and often startling history that emphasizes that no behavior separates us from other animals, but we remain an utterly unique species." Kirkus.

Tattersall, Ian

The **fossil** trail : how we know what we think we know about human evolution / Ian Tattersall. Oxford University Press, 2009. xxiii, 327 p. : **599.93**

1. Human evolution. 2. Prehistoric humans. 3. Fossils. 4. Evolution.

ISBN 9780195367669

"The task of organising such complex material into a narrative account would have defeated most writers, but Tattersall has mastered it with remarkable skill." The New Scientist. [review of 1995 edition]

Masters of the planet : seeking the origins of human singularity / Ian Tattersall. Palgrave Macmillan, 2012. 272 p. **599.93**

1. Prehistoric humans. 2. Human evolution. 3. Genetic psychology. 4. Humans -- Origin.

ISBN 9780230108752

LC 2011034415

An award-winning Museum of Natural History curator and author traces the evolution of homo sapiens to demonstrate how they prevailed among other early humans because of their unique cognitive ability, in an account that also explains how their superior mental abilities were acquired.

Vince, Gaia

Transcendence : how humans evolved through fire, language, beauty, and time / Gaia Vince. Basic Books, 2020, c2019. 320 p. **599.93**

1. Human evolution 2. Technology 3. Communication 4. Culture

ISBN 9780465094905

LC bl2020004892

Originally published: London : Allen Lane, 2019.

The author of Adventures in the Anthropocene traces the dramatic evolutionary changes that enabled intelligence in humans, explaining how our species established dominion through our growing understandings of four key elements.

Wilson, Edward O.

★The **social** conquest of Earth / Edward O. Wilson. Liveright Pub. Corporation, c2012. 352 p. **599.93**

1. Social evolution 2. Human evolution -- Philosophy. 3. Evolution

-- Philosophy.
ISBN 9780871404138

LC 2011052680

"An acclaimed biologist and author of the Pulitzer Prize-winning The Ants discusses how morality, religion and the creative arts are biological in nature and defends his theory that the origin of the human condition is due to group, not family, selection."

"Wilson is a prolific and popular biological theorist, and this significant addition to his legacy of thought will be controversial, provocative, and influential." Library Journal.

Yi, Sang-hui (Professor of anthropology)

Close encounters with humankind : a paleoanthropologist investigates our evolving species / Sang-hee Lee With Shin-young Yoon. W. W. Norton & Company, 2018. 304 p. **599.93**

1. Forensic anthropology 2. Prehistoric humans 3. Human evolution 4. Paleontology
ISBN 9780393634822

"Originally published in Korea by ScienceBooks Publishing Co., Ltd, Seoul, a division of Minumsa Publishing Group."

Explores how the field enables new insights into some of the world's leading evolutionary questions, drawing on cutting-edge findings to explore such topics as the life cycles of ancient people, the origins of social nature and the common traits between today's humans and Neanderthals.

"Lee, professor of anthropology at the University of California, Riverside, approaches an array of topics in the field of human evolution with candor, clarity, and brevity." Publishers Weekly.

600 Technology (Applied sciences)

Doorley, Rachelle

Tinkerlab : a hands-on guide for little inventors / Rachelle Doorley. Roost Books, 2014. xv, 219 p. : **600**

1. Creative activities and seat work 2. Inventions 3. Playrooms
ISBN 9781611800654

LC 2013027910

Features creative experiments designed to encourage young children to use their natural curiosity to explore, test, play, and tinker.

"Young children will relish the projects provided here. From paper houses to marble runs to marker explosions, Doorley's designs have more of an engineering essence than those found in the standard arts and crafts book, and they will also take more preparation, but early educators, in particular, will delight in the volume's possibilities. For all budding inventors." Library Journal.

Harman, Jay

The **shark's** paintbrush : biomimicry and how nature is inspiring innovation / Jay Harman. White Cloud Press, 2013. 339 p. : **600**

1. Technological innovations
ISBN 9780385535717

An introduction to the scientific practice through which natural models are inspiring innovative, environmentally friendly solutions to pressing industrial challenges profiles such remarkable examples as energy-efficient wind turbines based on whale fins and cockroach-emulating prosthetic limbs.

"A useful update on recent developments in biomimicry and an intriguing case for innovative green technology that goes beyond sustainability." Kirkus.

Macaulay, David

The **way** things work now : from levers to lasers, windmills to wi-fi, a visual guide to the world of machines / David Macaulay, with Neil Ardley. Houghton Mifflin Harcourt, 2016, 1988. 400 p. **600**

1. Technology. 2. Machinery. 3. Mechanics. 4. Science. 5. Toy and movable books.
ISBN 9780544824386

LC bl2016040252

"Revised and updated" -- Cover.

Originally published as The new way things work: Boston, MA : Houghton Mifflin, 1988.

The sweeping new update to the worldwide bestseller, The New Way Things Work includes all new sections on the technology that most impacts our everyday lives.

"Macaulay's brilliantly designed, engagingly informal diagrams and cutaways bring within the grasp of even casual viewers a greater understanding of the technological wonders of both past and present." Kirkus.

601 Technology -- Philosophy and theory

Weinersmith, Kelly

Soonish : emerging technologies that'll improve and/or ruin everything / Kelly and Zach Weinersmith. Penguin Press, 2017. 368 p. **601**

1. Technological forecasting 2. Technological innovations 3. Science 4. Comics and Graphic novels
ISBN 9780399563829

LC 2017008654

Presents an illustrated investigation into the technologies of the near future, from deep-space travel to 3D organ printing, to offer insight into how they will work and what is needed to advance their readiness.

"With infectious enthusiasm, the Weinersmiths serve up the perfect combination for curious, critical minds. Popular-science writing has rarely been so whip-smart, captivating, or hilarious (albeit occasionally terrifying)." Booklist.

602 Technology -- Miscellany

Lupi, Giorgia

Dear data / Giorgia Lupi, Stefanie Posavec. Princeton Architectural Press, 2016. 289 p. : **602**

1. Posavec, Stefanie Correspondence Pictorial works. 2. Communication of technical information -- Pictorial works.
ISBN 9781616895327

LC bl2016038435

"A friendship in 52 weeks of postcards"--Cover.

Chiefly illustrations.

Collects the data filled post cards the authors exchanged over the course of a year, covering topics that range from time and music to travel and touch.

607 Education, research, related topics

Creighton, Margaret S., 1949-

The **electrifying** fall of Rainbow City : spectacle and assassination at the 1901 World's Fair / Margaret Creighton. W.W.

Norton & Company, 2016 320 p. **607**

1. McKinley, William, 1843-1901 Assassination. 2. Pan-American Exposition (1901 : Buffalo, N.Y.). 3. Exhibitions. 4. Scandals. 5. Social values 6. Buffalo, New York.
ISBN 9780393247503

LC 2016018256

Traces the events surrounding the 1901 Pan American Exposition in Buffalo, New York, describing how it was organized to bring millions into the region before the assassination of President William McKinley and a host of controversies reshaped the dawn of the century.

"An excellent and entertaining history for all readers." Library Journal.

Tirella, Joseph

Tomorrow-land : the 1964-65 World's Fair and the transformation of America / Joseph Tirella. Lyons Press, 2014. 360 p. **607**

1. Moses, Robert, 1888-1981. 2. New York World's Fair (1964-1965) 3. Technological innovations. 4. Social change -- United States -- History -- 20th century. 5. Political culture -- United States -- History -- 20th century. 6. United States.
ISBN 9780762780358

LC 2013015055

Though considered a financial failure, the 1964-65 World's Fair was a Sixties flashpoint in areas from politics to pop culture, technology to urban planning, and civil rights to violent crime. In an epic narrative, Tomorrow-Land shows the astonishing pivots taken by New York City, America, and the world during the Fair.

"A model of accessible narrative, showing the author's immersion in archival research, this book will be appreciated most by those who love reading about Sixties or New York City history or, of course, world's fairs." Library Journal.

609 Technology -- History, geographic treatment, biography

Ashton, Kevin

How to fly a horse : the secret history of creation, invention, and discovery / Kevin Ashton. Doubleday, 2015. xviii, 314 p. ; **609**

1. Scientific discoveries. 2. Inventions -- History. 3. Creativity. 4. Technological innovations.
ISBN 9780385538596

LC 2014030841

Celebrating the acts of seemingly unremarkable individuals that led to humanity's most astounding breakthroughs, an eye-opening exploration of the world's greatest creations reveals the true process of discovery, shedding new light on how the "new" comes to be.

Benford, Gregory, 1941-

The **wonderful** future that never was : Flying Cars, Mail Delivery by Parachute, and Other Predictions from the Past / Gregory Benford and the editors of Popular mechanics. Hearst Books, c2010. 207 p. : **609**

1. Technological forecasting. 2. Inventions -- History.
ISBN 9781588168221

LC 2010003998

Includes indexes.

Dust jacket folds out into wall poster.

"The illustrations, text, and photographs in this volume previously appeared in Popular mechanics issues between 1903 and 1970"--Colophon.

"Flying cars, mail delivery by parachute, and other predictions from the past"--Dust jacket.

Reveals predictions made in "Popular Mechanics" magazine between 1903 and 1969 about what the future would hold! "Surrounded by wonders and a fast-evolving culture of innovation, it's just as chalenging today for us to imagine the next century as it must have been for our early 20th century colleagues to envision the fabled year 2000."-- P. 6.

"Profusely illustrated (there's something on nearly every page), the book is endlessly fascinating, a collage of snapshots of the present the way people saw it when it was still the distant future." Booklist.

Harford, Tim, 1973-

50 inventions that shaped the modern economy / Tim Harford. Riverhead Books, 2017. 321 p. ; **609**

1. Inventions. 2. Technological innovations. 3. Economic history. 4. Essays
ISBN 9780735216136
Includes index.

Describes the history of economic change through the 50 inventions that had the most impact and explores the hidden connections they share, from paper money and the horse collar, to bar codes and spreadsheets.

"And while the essays stand on their own, he has a broader point to make. 'Inventions shape our lives in unpredictable ways,' he writes, 'and while they're solving a problem for someone, they're often creating a problem for someone else.' Harford's contagious delight in his subject reminds readers not to take for granted the impact of objects and ideas so familiar they're easy to overlook." Kirkus.

North, Ryan, 1980-

How to invent everything : a survival guide for the stranded time traveler / Ryan North. Penguin Group USA 2018 464 p. **609**

1. Time travel (Past) 2. Civilization 3. Technology and civilization 4. Illustrated books
ISBN 9780735220140

LC 2018003730

A best-selling author and time-travel enthusiast details the science, engineering, mathematics, art, music, philosophy, facts and figures required for even the most clueless time traveler to build a civilization from the ground up.

"North's survival guide is a fun, thoughtful, and thoroughly accessible reference for curious readers, students, and world-builders, as well as wayward time travelers." Publishers Weekly.

609.2 Biography

Carey, Charles W.

American inventors, entrepreneurs, and business visionaries / Charles W. Carey, Jr. Facts On File, 2011. xxi, 455 p. : **609.2**

1. Inventors -- United States 2. Businesspeople -- United States 3. United States
ISBN 9780816081462

LC 2009054269

American Inventors, Entrepreneurs, and Business Visionaries, Revised Edition profiles more than 300 important Americans from colonial times to the present. Featuring such inventors and entrepreneurs as Thomas Edison, this revised resource provides in-depth information on robber barons and their counterparts as well as current visionaries such as Steve Jobs. This A-to-Z biographical dictionary has been fully updated to include an array of new and fascinating biographies, from financier Warren Buffet to music mogul Jay-Z. --From publisher description.

"With its eclectic list of visionaries, this work will not only educate, but it will also inspire and entertain." School Library Journal.

Evans, Harold, 1928-

They made America : from the steam engine to the search engine : two centuries of innovators / Harold Evans, with Gail Buckland and David Lefer. Little, Brown, c2004. 496 p. : **609.2**

1. Inventors -- United States -- History. 2. Inventions -- History. 3. Technological innovations. 4. Technology. 5. United States -- History.

ISBN 0316277665

LC 2003065954

A history of the United States's major inventors and innovators includes coverage of such figures as Henry and Edsel Ford, cosmetics entrepreneur C. J. Walker, and Google founders Sergey Brin and Larry Page, in a tie-in to a PBS four-part series that shares lesser-known background information and features lavish duotone and full-color photography.

610 Medicine and health

Groopman, Jerome E.

How doctors think / Jerome Groopman. Houghton Mifflin, 2007. 307 p. : **610**

1. Medicine -- Decision making. 2. Medical logic. 3. Physicians -- Psychology. 4. Judgment.

ISBN 0618610030

ALA Notable Book, 2008.

A physician discusses the thought patterns and actions that lead to misdiagnosis on the part of healthcare providers, and suggests methods that patients can use to help doctors assess conditions more accurately.

"By turns inspired and dismaying, it explains how even the best doctor can draw the wrong conclusion, and why that same doctor might also come up with a brilliant diagnosis that has eluded [their] peers. Uncertainty hovers over the practice of medicine, which Dr. Groopman, a clear writer and a humane thinker, presents as an art as well as a science, despite the spectacular advances in medical technology." New York Times.

Pogrebin, Letty Cottin

How to be a friend to a friend who's sick / Letty Cottin Pogrebin. PublicAffairs, [2013] 288 p. **610**

1. Communication. 2. Sick persons -- Care. 3. Visiting sick persons. 4. People with breast cancer

ISBN 9781610392839

LC 2012049749

Draws on the experiences of sick people to counsel family, friends, and caregivers on how to cope with managing another's illness, sharing advice, stories, and tips on the challenges involved.

"A useful refresher course on navigating the complicated territory of compassionate companionship." Kirkus.

Porter, Roy, 1946-2002

The **greatest** benefit to mankind : a medical history of humanity / Roy Porter. W. W. Norton, 1998. xvi, 831 p. : **610**

1. Medicine -- History. 2. Medicine -- Practice -- History. 3. Diseases -- Treatment. 4. Social medicine -- History.

ISBN 0393046346

LC 98010219

British ed. published with subtitle: A medical history of humanity from antiquity to the present.

National Book Critics Circle Award for Nonfiction finalist, 1998.

"Porter's study traces Western medical thought and practices from their origins in classical Greece to today's biomedical developments. Although scholarly, the text is elegantly written, accessible to the general reader, and filled with fascinating details." Library Journal.

Shapiro, Nina, 1947-

Hype : a doctor's guide to medical myths, exaggerated claims and bad advice - how to tell what's real and what's not / Nina Shapiro, M.D., with Kristin Loberg. St. Martin's Press, [2018] 288 p. **610**

1. Medical misconceptions. 2. Popular medicine 3. Medical care 4. Physicians

ISBN 9781250149305

LC 2017055072

An award-winning Otolaryngologist examines the actual science behind our collective health beliefs, dispelling misinformation and myths including the idea that sugar is toxic and the importance of drinking 8 glasses of water a day.

610.1 Medicine and health -- Medicine--philosophy

Mukherjee, Siddhartha

The **laws** of medicine : field notes from an uncertain science / Siddhartha Mukherjee. Simon & Schuster 2015 120 p. **610.1**

1. Medical care 2. Physicians 3. Medicine -- Philosophy 4. Science

ISBN 9781476784847

LC bl2015034883

The Pulitzer Prize-winning author of The Emperor of All Maladies and one of the world's premiere cancer researchers reveals an urgent philosophy on the little-known principles that govern medicine--and how understanding these principles can empower us all.

Rakel, David

The **compassionate** connection : the healing power of empathy and mindful listening / David Rakel, MD, with Susan K. Golant, MA. W.W. Norton & Company, 2018 xiv, 280 p. : **610.1**

1. Healing -- Psychological aspects 2. Compassion 3. Interpersonal relations -- Health aspects 4. Interpersonal communication -- Health aspects

ISBN 9780393247749

LC 2017056375

Draws on a range of disciplines to outline the concept of bio-psycho-spiritual authentic awareness and how to strengthen empathy bonds with others to promote healing and overall wellness.

610.28 Auxiliary techniques and procedures; apparatus, equipment, materials

Gawande, Atul

★The **checklist** manifesto : how to get things right / Atul Gawande. Metropolitan Books, 2010. x, 209 p. ; **610.28**

1. Medical care -- Quality control. 2. Lists. 3. Clinical competence -- Personal Narratives. 4. Decision-making

ISBN 9780805091748

LC 2009046888

Reveals the surprising power of the ordinary checklist now being used in medicine, aviation, the armed services, homeland security, investment banking, skyscraper construction, and businesses of all kinds.

"Few medical writers working today can transmit the gore-drenched terror of an operation that suddenly goes wrong--a terror that has a special resonance when it is Dr. Gawande himself who makes the initial horrifying mistake. And few can make it as clear as he can what exactly is at stake in the effort to minimize calamities." New York Times.

610.285 Medicine and health -- Medicine -- Computer applications

Topol, Eric J., 1954-

The **creative** destruction of medicine : how the digital revolution will create better health care / Eric Topol. Basic Books, c2012. xi, 303 p. : **610.285**

1. Information resources management 2. Medical informatics

ISBN 9780465025503

LC 2011041162

A leading professor of innovative medicine who conducted one of the first trials of a genetically engineered protein for treating heart attacks reveals how technologies in the areas of wireless internet, individual data and personal genomics are revolutionizing medicine in life-saving ways.

610.3 Medicine and health -- Medicine -- Dictionaries

★**Dorland's** illustrated medical dictionary Elsevier Science Health Science, 2020. xxiii, 2116 p. : **610.3**

1. Medicine -- Dictionaries. 2. Dictionaries

ISBN 9781455756438

Illustrates and defines terms used in different branches of medicine and health science.

O'Toole, Marie T,

Mosby's medical dictionary / editor, Marie T. O'Toole, EdD, RN, FAAN, senior associate dean & professor, School of Nursing--Camden, Rutgers Unviersity, Camden, New Jersey. Elsevier, 2016 xiv, A1-A43, 1942 p. : **610.3**

1. Medicine -- Dictionaries.

ISBN 9780323414258

LC bl2016027352

Provides detailed definitions for medical terms, updated to reflect the latest advancements in health care, nursing, and pharmacology.

610.69 Medical personnel and relationships

Epstein, Ronald

Attending : medicine, mindfulness, and humanity / Ronald Epstein, MD. Scribner, 2018. xii, 292 p. ; **610.69**

1. Mindfulness (Psychology) 2. Physicians -- Psychology. 3. Physician and patient

ISBN 9781501121715

LC 2017470848

"While focusing primarily on health-care professionals, Epstein presents for general readers a concise guide to his view of what mindfulness is, its value, and how it is a skill that anyone can work to acquire." Library Journal.

Goldberg, Sana

How to be a patient : the essential guide to navigating the world of modern medicine / Sana Goldberg, RN. Harper Wave, 2019 xxvi, 432 p. ; **610.69**

1. Communication in medicine 2. Physician and patient

ISBN 9780062797186

LC 2018041369

A registered nurse and public health advocate provides a quick-reference guide for confronting the challenges of trying to navigate common medical situations, from making the most of routine appointments to understanding hospital culture.

"This essential resource, which can also double as ready reference, complements Karen A. Friedman and Sara L. Merwins The Informed Patient but can, and should, stand on its own." Library Journal.

Michelson, Leslie D.

★The **patient's** playbook : how to save your life and the lives of those you love / Leslie D. Michelson. Alfred A. Knopf, 2015 xi, 320 p. ; **610.69**

1. Patient advocacy 2. Patient education 3. Medical errors -- Prevention 4. Medicine -- Decision making

ISBN 9780385352284

LC 2015014325

"The Patient's Playbook is a compelling narrative of personal stories that imparts lessons and illuminates strategies for better, and even life-saving, medical decision-making. With clarity and as a call to action, the book presents the most effective approach to getting the best from a broken system: sourcing excellent doctors, choosing the right treatment protocols in the "no mistake zone," researching with precision, and structuring the ideal support team. Leslie D. Michelson has devoted his life's work to helping people access the best quality medical care--serving as an expert navigator for hundreds of clients. As the former head of the Prostate Cancer Foundation and the CEO of Private Health Management he has dedicated his life's work to helping individuals find the courage and confidence to get what they need in a challenging health system"-- Provided by publisher.

Ofri, Danielle

What doctors feel : how emotions affect the practice of medicine / Danielle Ofri. Beacon Press, 2013. 208 p. **610.69**

1. Physicians -- Attitudes. 2. Empathy. 3. Physician and patient 4. Emotions

ISBN 9780807073322

LC 2012049349

An assessment of the role of doctor emotions in health care draws on scientific studies and real-life stories to explore how fear, empathy and other strong feelings affect the decision making practices of medical professionals, discussing how experiences ranging from mistakes and tragedies to legal disputes and personal mortality are distinctly influencing medical care.

610.92 Medicine -- Biography

Deer, Brian

The **doctor** who fooled the world : science, deception, and the war on vaccines / Brian Deer. Johns Hopkins University Press, 2020. 320 p. ; **610.92**

1. Wakefield, Andrew J. 2. Anti-vaccination movement -- History. 3. Deception. 4. Propaganda 5. Former physicians.

ISBN 9781421438009

LC 2019033966

Includes index.

Also published in Australia in 2020 by Scribe Publications.

Andrew Wakefield, a former British doctor, has been a leading proponent of the discredited view that vaccines cause autism. The discrediting of Wakefield and the anti-vax position he propelled is due largely to the work of Brian Deer, an investigative reporter from the United Kingdom. In this book Deer tells the story of how Wakefield fabricated research results for his Lancet paper, failed to disclose financial conflicts of interest, manipulated researchers and parents, and lied to the public. Provided by publisher.

"This riveting history of Andrew Wakefield's career as an advocate for the discredited link between the measles vaccine and autism serves as a stirring demonstration of the process and power of investigative journalism. . . . Readers who love a good debunking will find Deer's narrative logical, exciting, and enraging." Publishers Weekly

611 Human anatomy, cytology, histology

Balaban, Naomi E.

The **handy** anatomy answer book / Naomi E. Balaban and James E. Bobick. Visible Ink Press, c2008. xiii, 362 p. ; **611**

1. Human anatomy -- Miscellanea. 2. Physiology -- Miscellanea. 3. Human body. 4. Human physiology.

ISBN 9781578591909

LC 2008001595

"This book can provide an excellent way to read and self-test for health and human biology classes. Adults wanting to know more about the subjects covered will also find a wealth of useful and accessible information." Voice of Youth Advocates.

Roach, Mary

★**Stiff** : the curious lives of human cadavers / Mary Roach. W.W. Norton & Co., 2003. 303 p. : **611**

1. Human experimentation in medicine. 2. Dead. 3. Human dissection. 4. Medical research.

ISBN 0393050939

LC 2002152908

A look inside the world of forensics examines the use of human cadavers in a wide range of endeavors, including research into new surgical procedures, space exploration, and a Tennessee human decay research facility.

"Roach writes in an insouciant style and displays her metier in tangents about bizarre incidents in pathological history. Death may have the last laugh, but, in the meantime, Roach finds merriment in the macabre." Booklist.

Rutherford, Adam

★A **brief** history of everyone who ever lived : the stories in our genes / Adam Rutherford. The Experiment, 2017, c2016. 400 p. **611**

1. Genetics 2. Human genetics 3. Evolution. 4. DNA.

ISBN 9781615194049

LC 2017022566

Originally published: London : Weidenfeld & Nicolson, 2016.

National Book Critics Circle Award for Nonfiction finalist, 2017

A science writer and broadcaster with a background in genetics reveals what our genes can tell us about history and how unraveling the human genome has shattered deeply held beliefs about our heritage and identities.

"An enthusiastic history of mankind in which DNA plays a far greater role than the traditional bones and stones approach, followed by a hopeful if cautionary account of what the recent revolution in genomics foretells." Kirkus.

Shubin, Neil

Your inner fish : a journey into the 3.5-billion-year history of the human body / Neil Shubin. Pantheon Books, 2008. 229 p. : **611**

1. Human anatomy. 2. Human evolution. 3. Humans. 4. Anatomy.

ISBN 9780375424472

National Academies Communication Award, 2009.

A fascinating chronicle of the evolution of humankind traces the genetic history of the organs of the human body, offering a revealing correlation between the distant past and present-day human anatomy and physiology, behavior, illness, and DNA.

"This is a look at how the human body evolved into its present state. . . . Shubin excels at explaining the science, making each discovery an adventure, whether it's a Pennsylvania roadcut or a stony outcrop beset by polar bears and howling Arctic winds." Publishers Weekly.

Standring, Susan,

Gray's anatomy : the anatomical basis of clinical practice / editor-in-chief, Susan Standring ; section editors, Neel Anand [and 11 others]. Elsevier Limited, 2016. 1562 p. ; **611**

ISBN 9780702052309

LC 2015027527

In 1858, Drs. Henry Gray and Henry Vandyke Carter created a book for their surgical colleagues that established an enduring standard among anatomical texts. After more than 150 years of continuous publication, Gray's Anatomy remains the definitive, comprehensive reference on the subject, offering ready access to the information you need to ensure safe, effective practice. --From publisher description.

Sulston, John

The **common** thread : a story of science, politics, ethics, and the human genome / John Sulston, Georgina Ferry. Joseph Henry Press, c2002. x, 310 p. : **611**

1. Human Genome Project.

ISBN 9780309084093

LC 2002014007

Previously published: London ; New York : Bantam, 2002.

"Overall, a fascinating account of science conducted in an atmosphere of big money, politics, and personalities." Choice.

Switek, Brian

Skeleton keys : the secret life of bone / Brian Switek. Riverhead Books, 2019. 288 p. **611**

1. Skeleton 2. Human anatomy 3. Bones 4. Human remains (Archaeology)

ISBN 9780399184901

LC 2018037813

Presents a natural and cultural history of bone that explains how human skeletons evolved over 500 million years, what they do inside the body and how they record a person's history.

612 Human physiology

Ashcroft, Frances M.

The **spark** of life : electricity in the human body / Frances Ashcroft ; line drawings by Ronan Mahon. Norton, 2012. 352 p. **612**

1. Electrophysiology 2. Human physiology. 3. Human body 4.

Nervous system
ISBN 9780393078039
LC 2012021264

Presents the history of the discovery of electricity in the human body as well as present-day research and real-life stories that aim to explain death, consciousness and how these physiological electrical signals drive human thoughts, movements and lives.

Bryson, Bill

The **body** : a guide for occupants / Bill Bryson. Doubleday, 2019. 400 p. **612**

1. Human anatomy. 2. Human physiology. 3. Human body
ISBN 9780385539302
LC 2019012407

The award-winning author presents an engaging head-to-toe tour of the human body that shares anecdotal insights into its functions, ability to heal and vulnerability to disease.

Cassidy, Cody

And then you're dead : what really happens if you get swallowed by a whale, are shot from a cannon, or go barreling over Niagara / Cody Cassidy and Paul Doherty, PhD. Penguin Books, 2017. xiii, 235 p. ; **612**

1. Human anatomy 2. Human physiology 3. Accidents
ISBN 9780143108443
LC 2016040949

In a delightfully gruesome look at the actual science behind the most outlandish, cartoonish and impossible deaths imaginable, the senior staff scientist at the San Francisco Exploratorium Museum and a writer examine a vast array of fantastic scenarios, teaching readers about physics, astronomy, anatomy and more along the way.

"With bite-size morsels of astonishing science and the perfect combination of smart-alecky writing and black humor, this page-turner will surely debunk any misapprehension that science is dull." Booklist.

Clayman, Charles B.

The **human** body : an illustrated guide to its structure, function, and disorders / editor-in-chief, Charles Clayman. Dorling Kindersley Pub., 1995. 240 p. : **612**

1. Human physiology 2. Human anatomy 3. Medicine, Popular.
ISBN 9781564589927
LC 94037165

Filled with facts about every system and component and valuable information about problems, diagnostic techniques, treatments, and surgical procedures, a unique visual approach to understanding the human body emphasizes the ways individual parts of the body work together.

Damasio, Antonio R.

The **strange** order of things : life, feeling, and the making of the cultures / Antonio Damasio. Pantheon Books, 2017. 320 p. **612**

1. Homeostasis 2. Neuroscience 3. Culture 4. Emotions
ISBN 9780307908759
LC 2017019925

A neuroscientist reflects on the origins of life, culture and emotions describing the biological and psychological processes that modern man inherited from single living cells and the development of genes that regulate the maintenance of life.

"Damasio's sophisticated and complex theory on the role of feelings in the emergence of culture incorporates hard science, neuroscience, and even philosophy." Library Journal.

Hutchinson, Alex

★**Endure** : mind, body, and the curiously elastic limits of human performance / Alex Hutchinson ; with a foreword by Malcolm Gladwell. William Morrow, 2018. 320 p. **612**

1. Athletes 2. Runners. 3. Competition. 4. Distance running.
ISBN 9780062499868
LC 2017035195

An elite distance runner explores the science of human endurance and performance and discusses the cutting-edge studies that show it is the brain--and not heart size, lung capacity or muscle strength--that dictates how far a person can go.

"The science shines (though, occasionally, its a hefty lift), and it can be fun: the human body at rest produces about 100 watts of heat, but bicycling boosts that figure to 1,000 watts, and running a six-minute mile generates 1,500 watts. 'When it comes to pushing our limits, we're just getting started,' Hutchinson writes. Persuasive and motivating." Booklist.

Lieberman, Daniel, 1964-

The **story** of the human body : evolution, health, and disease / Daniel Lieberman. Pantheon Books, 2013. 464 p. **612**

1. Human body. 2. Human evolution. 3. Adaptation (Biology) 4. Biology.
ISBN 9780307379412
LC 2013011811

The Story of the Human Body brilliantly illuminates as never before the major transformations that contributed key adaptations to the body: the rise of bipedalism; the shift to a non-fruit-based diet; the advent of hunting and gathering, leading to our superlative endurance athleticism; the development of a very large brain; and the incipience of cultural proficiencies.

"Lieberman's discussion of type 2 diabetes, heart disease, and breast cancer are as clear as any yet published, and he offers a well-articulated case for why an evolutionary perspective can greatly enrich the practice of medicine." Publishers Weekly.

612.1 Specific functions, systems, organs

Amidon, Stephen

The **sublime** engine : a biography of the human heart / Stephen Amidon and Thomas Amidon. Rodale, c2011. 242 p. **612.1**

1. Heart in art. 2. Heart in literature. 3. Heart -- Religious aspects.
ISBN 9781605295848
LC 2010030227

A lyrical history of the human heart draws on scientific, religious and literary sources to reveal the heart's role in human imagination and culture from the ancient world to today. Co-written by the author of Human Capital.

"This book presents a multifaceted picture of the heart's influences on mythology, science, and popular culture through the ages. In six lyrically written chapters, they trace humanity's perennial fascination with the heart through the eyes of history's greatest artists and medical explorers, beginning with the Greeks and fancifully ending with a peek into the future of cardiological innovation." Booklist.

George, Rose, 1969-

★**Nine** pints : a journey through the money, medicine, and mysteries of blood / Rose George. Metropolitan Books/ Henry

Holt and Company, 2018. 304 p. **612.1**

1. Blood 2. Blood plasma 3. Phlebotomy 4. Blood donors
ISBN 9781627796378

LC 2018013647

A freelance journalist explores the science, traditions and myths surrounding blood, from ancient bloodletting practices to the development of mass blood donations during the Blitz and from researchers working on synthetic blood to the lucrative business of plasma transfusions.

"The author packs her book with the kinds of provocative, witty, and rigorously reported facts and stories sure to make readers view the integral fluid coursing through our veins in a whole new way. An intensive, humanistic examination of blood in all its dazzling forms and functions." Kirkus.

612.3 Digestive system

Collen, Alanna

10% human : how your body's microbes hold the key to health and happiness / Alanna Collen. HarperCollins, 2015 320 p. **612.3**

1. Health. 2. Microorganisms 3. Bacteria. 4. Microbiology
ISBN 9780062345981

LC 2015004721

An argument for the importance of gut bacteria in the human body and how this affects our health and well-being

"Collen never claims that she has uncovered the answers to modern health woes, but she points out the markers that may one day lead to such answers. Everything you wanted to know about microbes but were afraid to ask." Kirkus.

Price, Catherine, 1978-

Vitamania : our obsessive quest for nutritional perfection / Catherine Price. Penguin Press, 2015. xv, 318 p. ; **612.3**

1. Vitamins -- History. 2. Vitamins in human nutrition. 3. Food supplements. 4. Nutritionally induced diseases
ISBN 9781594205040

LC 2014036657

Delves into the big business of synthetic vitamins and dietary supplements and uncovers the truths about the long-held nutritional myths the industry has been championing for the past century.

"Prices sharp wit, skillful and vivid translation of science into story, and valiant inquisitiveness (she insists on tasting synthetic vitamins and gets buzzed on the military's caffeinated meat sticks) make for an electrifying dissection of our vitamin habit in contrast to our irrevocable need for naturally nutrient-rich food." Booklist.

Roach, Mary

★**Gulp** : adventures on the alimentary canal / Mary Roach. W.W. Norton & Company, [2013] 336 p. **612.3**

1. Digestion 2. Food habits 3. Gastrointestinal system 4. Digestive organs
ISBN 9780393081572

LC 2012050391

The humor scientist behind Stiff: The Curious Lives of Human Cadavers and Spook: Science Tackles the Afterlife takes a tour of the human digestive system, explaining why the stomach doesn't digest itself and whether constipation can kill you.

612.4 Hematopoietic, lymphatic, glandular, urinary systems

Epstein, Randi Hutter

Aroused : the history of hormones and how they control just about everything / Randi Hutter Epstein. W. W. Norton & Company, 2018 272 p. ; **612.4**

1. Hormones 2. Human body. 3. Human physiology. 4. Genetic psychology
ISBN 9780393239607

LC 2017061090

A guided tour through the strange science of hormones and the age-old quest to control them.

612.6 Reproduction, development, maturation

Angier, Natalie

Woman : an intimate geography / Natalie Angier. Houghton Mifflin Co., 1999. xvi, 398 p. **612.6**

1. Women -- Anatomy. 2. Sex differences. 3. Physiology. 4. Anatomy.
ISBN 0395691303

LC 98047634

"A Peter Davison book."

National Book Award for Nonfiction finalist, 1999

"Angier proves a knowledgeable, witty guide on our illustrative journey through hordes of cultures and species." Ms.

Dolnick, Edward, 1952-

Seeds of life : from Aristotle to Da Vinci, from shark's teeth to frog's pants, the long and strange quest to discover where babies come from / Edward Dolnick. Basic Books, 2017. 272 p. **612.6**

1. Human reproduction 2. Conception 3. Scientific discoveries 4. Scientists
ISBN 9780465082957

LC 2016054195

Kirkus Prize for Nonfiction finalist, 2017.

An upbeat history of the early scientists who engaged in genius or quack experiments in their effort to explain human conception profiles the remarkable theories that reflected period innovation, religious beliefs and personal biases.

"The best sort of science history, explaining not only how great men made great discoveries, but why equally great men, trapped by prejudices and what seemed to be plain common sense, missed what was in front of their noses." Kirkus.

Eliot, Lise

Pink brain, blue brain : how small differences grow into troublesome gaps--and what we can do about it / Lise Eliot. Houghton Mifflin Harcourt, 2009. 432 p. **612.6**

1. Sex differences (Psychology) 2. Gender gap. 3. Developmental neurobiology. 4. Sex differences.
ISBN 9780618393114

LC 2009014746

A neuroscientist shatters the myths about gender differences, arguing that the brains of boys and girls are largely shaped by how they spend their time, in a book where she offers parents and teachers concrete ways to avoid reinforcing harmful stereotypes.

"This is an important book and highly recommended for parents, teachers, and anyone who works with children." Library Journal.

Enright, Lynn

Vagina : a re-education / Lynn Enright. Allen & Unwin, 2019.

229 p. : **612.6**

1. Vagina 2. Women -- Health 3. Human anatomy 4. Human physiology

ISBN 9781911630012

This indispensable book sifts through myths and misinformation with the aim of empowering women with vital knowledge about their own bodies.

"A necessary resource on an often-stigmatized subject, this book will appeal to anyone looking to learn more about the vagina and women's health." Library Journal

Esty, Katharaine C.

Eightysomethings : a practical guide to letting go, aging well, and finding unexpected happiness / Katharine Esty, PhD. Skyhorse Publishing, 2019. viii, 231 p. : **612.6**

1. Aging. 2. Aging -- Psychological aspects. 3. Quality of life 4. Seniors

ISBN 9781510743120

LC bl2019027387

This invaluable guide will help the historical number of eightysomethings live fulfilled, happy lives long into their twilight years. Personal stories illustrate how real people in their eighties are living and how they make sense of their lives.

Gunter, Jennifer

★The **vagina** bible : the vulva and the vagina - separating the myth from the medicine. / Jen Gunter. Citadel Press, 2019. 432 p. **612.6**

1. Vagina 2. Women -- Health 3. Women -- Anatomy 4. Female reproductive system

ISBN 9780806539317

LC bl2019026835

Dr. Jen Gunter now delivers the definitive book on vaginal health, answering the questions you've always had but were afraid to ask--or couldn't find the right answers to. She has been called Twitter's resident gynecologist, the Internet's OB/GYN, and one of the fiercest advocates for women's health--and she's here to give you the straight talk on the topics she knows best.

Jensen, Frances E

The **teenage** brain : a neuroscientist's survival guide to raising adolescents and young adults / Frances E. Jensen, MD ; with Amy Ellis Nutt. Harper, 2015 xvii, 358 p. : **612.6**

1. Adolescent psychology. 2. Brain -- Growth. 3. Developmental neurobiology. 4. Developmental psychobiology.

ISBN 9780062067845

LC bl2015003741

An internationally renowned neurologist, parent and speaker demystifies the teen brain by presenting new findings, dispelling widespread myths and providing practical advice for negotiating this difficult and dynamic life stage for both adults and teens.

"Recommended for readers who enjoyed Laurence Steinberg's Age of Opportunity, this title applies new science to the frustrating dilemma of how to live with teenage kids." Library Journal.

Katz, Rebecca

The **longevity** kitchen : satisfying, big-flavor recipes featuring the top 16 age-busting power foods / Rebecca Katz with Mat Edelson ; photography by Leo Gong. Ten Speed Press, 2013 xi, 243 p. : **612.6**

1. Longevity -- Nutritional aspects 2. Natural foods 3. Older people -- Health and hygiene 4. Recipes 5. Cookbooks

ISBN 9781607742944

LC 2012035097

"A collection of 120 whole-foods, big-flavor recipes that combat and prevent chronic diseases and other conditions that plague American adults, enabling readers to live longer, healthier lives".-- Provided by publisher.

Mansberg, Ginni

The **M** word : how to thrive in menopause / Ginni Mansberg. Murdoch Books, 2020. 314 p. ; **612.6**

1. Menopause 2. Perimenopause 3. Women -- Health

ISBN 9781911632382

"Perimenopausal and menopausal women, as well as health-care professionals, will appreciate the wealth of evidence, advice, and topics covered in Mansberg's candid guide." Publishers Weekly.

Mitteldorf, Josh

Cracking the aging code : the new science of growing old--and what it means for staying young / Josh Mitteldorf and Dorion Sagan. Flatiron Books, 2016 320 p. **612.6**

1. Aging -- Physiological aspects 2. Human evolution 3. Evolution 4. Population genetics

ISBN 9781250061706

LC 2016001602

Argues that aging is not something that "just happens," nor is it the result of wear and tear or a genetic inevitability, rather, it has the evolutionary purpose of stabilizing populations and ecosystems.

"A thoughtful examination of the role of aging and death in supporting life." Kirkus.

Nilsson, Lennart, 1922-2017

A **child** is born / [photography], Lennart Nilsson ; text, Lars Hamberger ; translated from the Swedish by Linda Schenck. Delacorte Press, 2020 219 p. : **612.6**

1. Pregnancy 2. Childbirth

ISBN 9780593157961

LC 2003043854

"Merloyd Lawrence book.

Includes index.

A new edition of the classic work on the miracle of human reproduction contains historic new photos of life before birth, accompanied by a detailed account of every stage of development and advice for expectant parents.

Roach, Mary

Bonk : the curious coupling of science and sex / Mary Roach. Norton, c2008. 288 p. **612.6**

1. Sex (Biology) -- Popular works. 2. Sexuality 3. Sex customs 4. Sexual excitement

ISBN 9780393064643

LC 2007051990

Roach shows how and why sexual arousal and orgasm can be so hard to achieve and what science is doing to make the bedroom a more satisfying place

"Tucked between the jokes and anecdotes, you will find lessons on impotence, orgasm, unusual and unusually brave scientists, and the sexual behaviour of other species, including a hilarious description of porcupine sex." The New Scientist.

Stein, Elissa

Flow : the cultural story of menstruation / Elissa Stein and

Susan Kim. St. Martin's Griffin, c2009. 288 p. **612.6**

1. Menstruation -- Social aspects. 2. Women -- Sexuality 3. Menstruation -- Humor. 4. Women -- Physiology

ISBN 9780312379964

LC 2009017046

An irreverent history of the cultural experience of menstruation shares the misconceptions and outright superstitions that have complicated its natural process, from the ancient Roman belief in the evil supernatural qualities of menstrual blood to 20th-century edicts about menstrual hygiene.

Walters, Jacqueline

The **Queen** V : everything you need to know about intimacy, sex, and down there healthcare / Dr. Jackie Walters. Henry Holt and Company, 2020. xxxiv, 265 p. : **612.6**

1. Sexual health 2. Vagina -- Care and hygiene 3. Women -- Health and hygiene

ISBN 9781250209177

LC 2019038046

The celebrity OB-GYN and star of Married to Medicine outlines 12 principles for caring for the female reproductive system, sharing straightforward advice on taboo subjects ranging from libido and contraception to fertility and labiaplasty.

Weil, Andrew

Healthy aging : a lifelong guide to your physical and spiritual well-being / Andrew Weil. Alfred A. Knopf, 2005. 293 p. ; **612.6**

1. Aging 2. Older people -- Health and hygiene

ISBN 9780375407550

LC 2005045183

Simultaneously published in Large Print by Random House.

Draws on the latest medical research, as well as a combination of conventional and alternative approaches, to present a guide to healthy living that offers strategies to deal with physical, mental, and emotional problems that come with aging.

"The author explores common Western beliefs and attitudes about aging and urges readers to develop healthier perspectives. The 60-year-old author assesses the growing and lucrative field of anti-aging medicine, takes the position that aging is not reversible, and offers many ways for readers to prevent conditions and illnesses that limit mortality and ensure well-being into the later years. The real value is Weil's courageous stand, one likely to meet resistance in a culture devoted to external indicators of eternal youth." Publishers Weekly.

Williams, Florence, 1967-

Breasts : a natural and unnatural history / Florence Williams. W. W. Norton & Co. Inc., 2012. 336 p. **612.6**

1. Breast -- History 2. Human body 3. Women -- Body -- Psychological aspects

ISBN 9780393063189

LC 2011053153

"A science journalist draws from the fields of anthropology, biology and medicine to describe the life cycle of the human female breast, from puberty to pregnancy to menopause and discusses the organ's modern susceptibility to toxins and disease."

612.7 Musculoskeletal system, integument

Lyman, Monty

★The **remarkable** life of the skin : an intimate journey across our surface / Monty Lyman Atlantic Monthly Press, 2020, c2019. xvii, 283 p. : **612.7**

1. Skin 2. Human body 3. Body covering (Anatomy) 4. Human skin color.

ISBN 9780802129406

LC 2020026004

Originally published: London : Bantam Press, 2019.

An engaging exploration of the human body's skin and its multifaceted physical, psychological and social relevance explains how our skin provides a habitat to a complex world of microorganisms and physical functions that are vital to health and survival.

"At first blush dermatology may not seem the most enticing subject, but this brilliant synthesis will be an engrossing read for anyone interested in human health and biology." Library Journal

612.8 Nervous system

Adam, David, 1972-

The **genius** within : unlocking your brain's potential / David Adam. Pegasus Books, 2018. 326 p. : **612.8**

1. Cognition 2. Intelligence 3. Neuroscience 4. Research

ISBN 9781681776743

Draws on the latest research in cognitive enhancement to explore how new revelations in neuroscience are changing the way the mind works to render it more focused and more intelligent, sharing case studies and stories from the author's own personal experimentations with "smart pills" and electrical brain stimulation.

"Adam provides readers with a lucidly written and enticing look at cutting-edge neuroscience discoveries that may eventually benefit us all." Booklist.

Aftel, Mandy

Fragrant : the secret life of scent / Mandy Aftel. Riverhead Books, 2014. 288 p. **612.8**

1. Smell. 2. Odors. 3. Cinnamon. 4. Mints (Plants) 5. Essays

ISBN 9781594631412

LC 2014018554

From a trailblazer in natural perfumery comes a celebration of our most potent sense: scent. Through five major players in the epic of aroma (cinnamon, mint, frankincense, ambergris, and jasmine) Mandy Aftel explores the profound connection between our sense of smell and the appetites that move us, give us pleasure, and make us fully alive. Includes recipes for easy-to-make fragrances and edible, drinkable, and useful concoctions that reveal the imaginative possibilities of creating with--and reveling in--aroma.

"Targeted toward those new to the perfume world, this book is strongly recommended for casual readers interested in the basics of scent and perfumery." Library Journal.

Biever, John A., 1947-

The **wandering** mind : understanding dissociation, from daydreams to disorders / John A. Biever and Maryann Karinch. Rowman & Littlefield Publishers, c2012. xv, 167 p. ; **612.8**

1. Consciousness. 2. Dissociation (Psychology) 3. Mental health.

ISBN 9781442216150

LC 2012013303

Introduces readers to dissociative states and helps them understand the nature of serious dissociative disorders, such as those involving multiple personalities. The authors pinpoint the differences between normal dissociation and disordered thinking that requires evaluation and treatment.

Buonomano, Dean

Brain bugs : how the brain's flaws shape our lives / Dean Buonomano. W. W. Norton & Co. Inc., 2011. 336 p. : **612.8**

1. Memory -- Physiological aspects. 2. Neuroscience 3. Brain -- Research 4. Human biology.
ISBN 9780393076028

LC 2011014934

A neuroscientist examines the imperfections in the human brain and highlights the causes, consequences, and evolutionary purpose of these "bugs" and discusses how they function and malfunction in the modern world.

Your brain is a time machine : the neuroscience and physics of time / Dean Buonomano. W. W. Norton & Company, 2017 304 p. **612.8**

1. Brain -- Physiology. 2. Time measurements 3. Time perception. 4. Memory.
ISBN 9780393247947

LC 2016046898

A leading neuroscientist presents a groundbreaking exploration of how time works inside the mind, arguing that the human brain's complex system constructs our sense of chronological flow in ways that are essential to evolution and everyday survival.

"Fascinating throughout and a pleasing vehicle by which to think about thinking--and the passing hours." Kirkus.

Burnett, Dean

Idiot brain : what your head is really up to / Dean Burnett. W.W. Norton & Company, 2016. 336 p. **612.8**

1. Consciousness. 2. Brain. 3. Neuroscience 4. Memory.
ISBN 9780393253788

LC 2016009451

A delightful tour of our mysterious, mischievous gray matter from neuroscientist and massively popular Guardian blogger Dean Burnett.

"Burnett manages to both entertain and inform in engaging ways that would benefit the performance of the most humorless pedant." Kirkus.

Carr, Nicholas G., 1959-

The **shallows** : what the Internet is doing to our brains / Nicholas Carr. W.W. Norton, 2010. 288 p. **612.8**

1. Neuropsychology. 2. Cognitive science. 3. Internet -- Physiological effect. 4. Brain.
ISBN 9780393072228

LC 2010007639

Pulitzer Prize for General Nonfiction finalist

Describes how human thought has been shaped through the centuries by "tools of the mind", from the alphabet to maps, to the printing press, the clock, and the computer. The technologies we use to find, store, and share information can literally reroute our neural pathways. Building on the insights of thinkers from Plato to McLuhan, the author makes a convincing case that every information technology carries an intellectual ethic, a set of assumptions about the nature of knowledge and intelligence.

"Drawing from neuroscience, history and social-science research, Carr reviews evidence that learning how to solve a problem, how to play a piece of music or how to speak a language physically changes the brain. It's a mistake, he argues, to think of the brain as a hard drive that stores information; it's far more than that and changes dynamically as it processes information, altering itself as it confronts challenges for better or worse. Reading a book, he notes, is vastly different from reading hyperlinked Internet text. Reading a book is solitary, requiring deep thought, analysis of the text and sustaining a narrative thread for the duration. By contrast, Internet reading invites shallow skimming for relevant passages, incessant clicking to hyperlinked articles and reliance on Google's search algorithms to determine relevance. Carr argues that the result is an emerging nation of shallow and impatient readers." Seattle Times.

Carter, Rita, 1949-

The **human** brain book / Rita Carter ... [et al.]. DK Pub., 2014 264 p. : **612.8**

1. Brain. 2. Neurology. 3. Neuroscience. 4. Neurophysiology.
ISBN 9781465416025

LC bl2009025937

Includes index.

Combines the latest findings from the field of neuroscience with expert text and state-of-the-art illustrations and imaging techniques to provide insight into every facet of the brain.

"Using computer-generated three-dimensional images, graphics, and clear explanatory text presented in brief sections, the follow-up to The Human Body Book (2007) examines each aspect of the brains structure and functions...This is a valuable resource for any high-school, college, and public library collection. Libraries should be aware that it comes with a DVD." Booklist.

DeSalle, Rob

The **brain** : big bangs, behaviors, and beliefs / Rob DeSalle & Ian Tattersall ; illustrated by Patricia J. Wynne. Yale University Press, c2012. xiv, 354 p. : **612.8**

1. Cognition. 2. Neurophysiology. 3. Brain -- Evolution. 4. Evolution.
ISBN 9780300175226

LC 2011044329

Based the latest findings in evolutionary biology, neuroscience and molecular biology, this first full, step-by-step account of the evolution of the brain and nervous system explains the how the cognitive gulf that separates us from all other living creatures could have occurred.

Doidge, Norman

The **brain** that changes itself : stories of personal triumph from the frontiers of brain science / Norman Doidge. Viking, 2007. xvi, 427 p. ; **612.8**

1. Neuroplasticity. 2. People with brain injuries -- Rehabilitation. 3. Molecular evolution.
ISBN 067003830X

LC 2006049224

A new science called neuroplasticity is overthrowing the old notion that the human brain is immutable. Psychoanalyst Doidge traveled the country to meet both the brilliant scientists championing neuroplasticity and the people whose lives they've transformed--people whose mental limitations or brain damage were seen as unalterable. We see a woman born with half a brain that rewired itself to work as a whole, blind people who learn to see, learning disorders cured, IQs raised, aging brains rejuvenated, stroke patients learning to speak, children with cerebral palsy learning to move with more grace, depression and anxiety disorders successfully treated, and lifelong character traits changed. Using these stories to probe mysteries of the body, emotion, love,sex, culture, and education, Dr. Doidge has written an inspiring book that will permanently alter the way we look at our brains, human nature, and human potential.--From publisher description.

The **brain's** way of healing : remarkable discoveries and recoveries from the frontiers of neuroplasticity / Norman Doidge, M.D. Viking, 2015. 432 p. **612.8**

1. Neuroplasticity. 2. Brain. 3. Healing. 4. Pain.
ISBN 9780670025503

LC 2014038471

"A James H. Silberman Book."

"Norman Doidge's revolutionary new book shows, for the first time, how the amazing process of neuroplastic healing really works. It describes natural, non-invasive avenues into the brain provided by the forms of energy around us--light, sound, vibration, movement--which pass through our senses and our bodies to awaken the brain's own healing capacities without producing unpleasant side effects. Doidge explores cases where patients alleviated years of chronic pain or recovered from debilitating strokes or accidents; children on the autistic spectrum or with learning disorders normalizing; symptoms of multiple sclerosis, Parkinson's disease, and cerebral palsy radically improved, and other near-miracle recoveries. And we learn how to vastly reduce the risk of dementia with simple approaches anyone can use. For centuries it was believed that the brain's complexity prevented recovery from damage or disease. The Brain's Way of Healing shows that this very sophistication is the source of a unique kind of healing".-- Provided by publisher.

"A fascinating study on brain science that shows the way to major therapeutic discoveries." Library Journal.

Eagleman, David

The **brain** : the story of you / David Eagleman. Pantheon Books, 2015. 256 p. **612.8**

1. Brain. 2. Neuroscience. 3. Medical research. 4. Humans.
ISBN 9781101870532

LC 2015023281

The best-selling author of Incognito examines how the human brain creates the multisensory experiences that culminate in human reality, examining the brain's role in everything from developmental disorders to extreme sports while speculating on the provocative potential of scanning a brain into a computer, in a companion to the PBS series.

"This is a straightforward, stimulating companion book to the PBS series on the subject." Publishers Weekly.

Livewired : the inside story of the ever-changing brain / David Eagleman. Pantheon Books, [2020] 320 p. **612.8**

1. Brain 2. Neuroplasticity 3. Adaptation (Biology) 4. Brain stimulation
ISBN 9780307907493

LC 2020000081

The magic of the brain is not found in the parts it's made of but in the way those parts unceasingly reweave themselves in an electric living fabric. With his hallmark clarity and enthusiasm, David Eagleman reveals the myriad ways that the brain absorbs experience: developing, redeploying, organizing, and arranging the data it receives from the body's own absorption of external stimuli, which enables us to gain the skills, the facilities, and the practices that make us who we are.

"Neuroscientist Eagleman (The Brain) delivers an intellectually exhilarating look at neuroplasticity. . . . Eagleman's skill as teacher, bold vision, and command of current research will make this superb work a curious reader's delight." Publishers Weekly

Eliot, Lise

What's going on in there? : how the brain and mind develop in the first five years of life / Lise Eliot. Bantam Books, c1999. viii, 533 p. : **612.8**

1. Developmental neurophysiology 2. Developmental psychobiology
ISBN 9780553102741

A study of how the human brain forms in the first five years of life describes the critical period of development a child goes through and what parents can do to help their children's brains develop.

Emmons, Henry

Staying sharp : 9 keys for a youthful brain through modern science and ageless wisdom / Henry Emmons, MD, David Alter, PhD. Touchstone, 2015. viii, 280 p. ; **612.8**

1. Brain -- Care and hygiene
ISBN 9781476758947

LC 2015000723

A practical guidebook for maintaining a sharp and healthy mind combines the latest neuroscience research with Eastern holistic mindfulness practices to outline a drug-free program for resilient mental aging.

"The authors, who have worked together for over 25 years, dub their approach an intersection of Eastern tradition and Western science. Some readers may be skeptical, but for those open to new ways of thinking and acting, this book will provide a valuable start." Publishers Weekly.

Gazzaniga, Michael S

The **consciousness** instinct : unraveling the mystery of how the brain makes the mind / Michael S. Gazzaniga. Farrar, Straus and Giroux, 2018. 288 p. **612.8**

1. Brain. 2. Mind and body. 3. Consciousness. 4. Cognitive neuroscience.
ISBN 9780374715502

LC 2017038333

How do neurons turn into minds? How does physical "stuff"--atoms, molecules, chemicals, and cells--create the vivid and various worlds inside our heads? The problem of consciousness has gnawed at us for millennia. In the last century there have been massive breakthroughs that have rewritten the science of the brain, and yet the puzzles faced by the ancient Greeks are still present. In The Consciousness Instinct, the neuroscience pioneer Michael S. Gazzaniga puts the latest research in conversation with the history of human thinking about the mind, giving a big-picture view of what science has revealed about consciousness.

"Gazzaniga's accessible, well-organized arguments are bound to provoke deep metathoughts, and readers should find his treatise delightful." Publishers Weekly.

Human : the science behind what makes us unique / Michael S. Gazzaniga. Ecco Press, 2008. 352 p. **612.8**

1. Brain. 2. Neuroscience. 3. Medical research. 4. Humans.
ISBN 9780060892883

LC 2008297703

A leading neuroscientist presents an accessible discussion of the psychological brain, drawing on the last fifty years of findings in such areas as language, memory, and biology to offer insight into the unique qualities of the human mind and the relevance of language and art in defining the human condition.

Godfrey-Smith, Peter

Other minds : the octopus, the sea, and the deep origins of consciousness / Peter Godfrey-Smith. Farrar, Straus and Giroux, 2016. 288 p. **612.8**

1. Nervous system -- Evolution. 2. Consciousness. 3. Octopuses 4. Developmental neurobiology.
ISBN 9780374227760

LC 2016016696

The leading philosopher of science and award-winning author of Darwinian Populations and Natural Selection provides photos taken during his advanced scuba dives to share stories of cephalopod encounters and insights into how nature became self-aware.

"He makes the case that cephalopods demonstrate a type of intelligence that is largely alien to our understanding of the concept but is no less worthy of wonder. He also ponders how and why such intelligence developed in such short-lived creatures (they generally live only a few years). Godfrey-Smith doesn't provide definitive answers to his questions, but the journey he leads is both thoroughly enjoyable and informative." Publishers Weekly.

Holmes, Bob (Evolutionary biologist)

Flavor : the science of our most neglected sense / Bob Holmes. W.W. Norton & Company, [2017] 320 p. **612.8**

1. Taste 2. Taste buds 3. Flavor 4. Senses and sensation
ISBN 9780393244427

LC 2016046897

"Independent Publishers Since 1923."

A journey into the surprising science of the sense of flavor by a veteran New Scientist correspondent outlines narrative principles in neurobiology and modern food production to reveal the broad range of factors that can affect one's appreciation of what we consume.

Kaku, Michio

The **future** of the mind : the scientific quest to understand, enhance, and empower the mind / Michio Kaku. Doubleday, 2014. 352 p. **612.8**

1. Physics -- Miscellanea. 2. Neuroscience 3. Forecasting. 4. Scientific forecasting.
ISBN 9780385530828

LC 2013017338

An authoritative survey of current groundbreaking research into the human mind reveals how top international laboratories have innovated unique technologies for recording profound mental capabilities and enabling controversial opportunities in the field of cognition enhancement.

"Kaku delivers ingenious predictions extrapolated from good research already in progress." Kirkus.

Kounios, John

The **Eureka** factor : aha moments, creative insight, and the brain / John Kounios and Mark Jung-Beeman. Random House, 2015 304 p. **612.8**

1. Insight. 2. Epiphanies. 3. Intuition. 4. Cognition.
ISBN 9781400068548

LC 2014022220

Includes index.

Eureka or aha moments are sudden realizations that expand our understanding of the world and ourselves, conferring both personal growth and practical advantage. Such creative insights, as psychological scientists call them, were what conveyed an important discovery in the science of genetics to Nobel laureate Barbara McClintock, the melody of a Beatles ballad to Paul McCartney, and an understanding of the cause of human suffering to the Buddha. But these moments of clarity are not given only to the famous. Anyone can have them. In The Eureka Factor, John Kounios and Mark Beeman explain how insights arise and what the scientific research says about stimulating more of them.

"An excellent title for those interested in neuroscience or creativity, or those who enjoy reading about brain research." Library Journal.

Kurzweil, Ray

How to create a mind : the secret of human thought revealed / Ray Kurzweil. Viking Adult, 2012. 384 p. **612.8**

1. Brain 2. Thought and thinking 3. Neuroscience -- Research. 4. Consciousness
ISBN 9780670025299

LC 2012027185

Explores the limitless potential of reverse-engineering the human brain, outlining the controversial implications of increasing intelligence in order to address global problems while comparing emotional and moral intelligence and considering the origins of consciousness.

Linden, David J., 1961-

Touch : the science of hand, heart, and mind / David J. Linden. Viking, 2015. 256 p. **612.8**

1. Touch -- Physiological aspects. 2. Emotions -- Physiological aspects. 3. Neuroscience 4. Human body
ISBN 9780670014873

LC 2014038475

The New York Times best-selling author of The Compass of Pleasure explores scientific advances in the understanding of interpersonal touch to offer insight into its role in shaping one's experiences and sense of self.

"An exciting book for those interested in learning more about the sense of touch and how the brain performs." Library Journal.

Masley, Steven

The **better** brain solution : how to start now--at any age--to reverse and prevent insulin resistance of the brain, sharpen cognitive function, and avoid memory loss / Steven Masley, M.D. Alfred A. Knopf, 2018. xiv, 367 p. ; **612.8**

1. Brain 2. Mental health 3. Nutrition 4. Self-care, Health
ISBN 9781524732387

LC 2017016326

"This is a Borzoi Book" -- title page verso.

Explains how diet and lifestyle can render the brain insulin resistant, leading to cognitive declines and memory loss, and identifies brain-bolstering foods and supplements while providing fifty easy-to-prepare recipes.

"Masleys book will appeal to anyone interested in a well-substantiated guide to mental health." Publishers Weekly.

McAuliffe, Kathleen

This is your brain on parasites : how tiny creatures manipulate our behavior and shape society / Kathleen McAuliffe. Houghton Mifflin Harcourt, 2016. 272 p. **612.8**

1. Parasitology. 2. Microorganisms 3. Nervous system -- Diseases. 4. Human evolution.
ISBN 9780544192225

LC 2016002949

"An Eamon Dolan book."

An expansion of a popular "Atlantic" article investigates the world of microbes and the myriad ways they control how other creatures--including humans--act, feel, and think.

"McAuliffe presents her collected research--often from small, nearly anecdotal studies--less as fact than in a spirit of exploration." Publishers Weekly.

McGee, Harold

★**Nose** dive : a field guide to the world's smells / Harold McGee. Penguin Press, 2020. 654 p. **612.8**

1. Odors. 2. Smell.
ISBN 9781594203954

LC 2020003220

The James Beard Award-winning author presents a sensory tour of the universe's smells from the ambrosial to the malodorous that reveals the science behind scent and how humans perceive it in nature, products and food.

"Perfect for foodies, those interested in science, and the innately curious. Engagingly written, this would be a wonderful ready reference to have on hand." Library Journal

Mlodinow, Leonard, 1954-

Elastic : flexible thinking in a time of change / Leonard Mlodinow. Pantheon Books, 2018 352 p. **612.8**

1. Neuroscience. 2. Neurology -- Technological innovations. 3.

Decision making.
ISBN 9781101870921

LC 2017015377

An award-winning theoretical physicist and author of Subliminal draws on cutting-edge research in neuroscience and psychology to introduce the theory of "elastic thinking" as it can advance the mind's cognitive abilities to adapt to today's rapidly evolving technologies.

"With elements of self-help and business writing and including entertaining anecdotes and turns of phrase, this fantastically accessible science writing about the brain can be enjoyed by anyone. Of particular interest to those wishing to understand how to cope with the pace of change in the modern world." Library Journal.

Nakazawa, Donna Jackson

The **angel** and the assassin : the tiny brain cell that changed the course of medicine / Donna Jackson Nakazawa. Ballantine Books, [2020] xii, 300 pages ; **612.8**

1. Microglia. 2. Cells 3. Healing 4. Brain.
ISBN 9781524799175

LC 2019034927

The award-winning journalist, Guillain-Barre Syndrome patient and author reveals the role of microglia on brain health and disease, describing emerging treatments for brain diseases ranging from depression to Alzheimer's.

"Indispensable for psychology professionals and students and fans of Susannah Cahalan's Brain on Fire: My Month of Madness." Library Journal

Palca, Joe

Annoying : the science of what bugs us / Joe Palca and Flora Lichtman. Wiley, 2011. 272 p. **612.8**

1. Neuropsychology. 2. Discontent. 3. Annoyance. 4. Human physiology.
ISBN 9780470638699

LC 2010054046

"A scientific look at something that affects us all--annoying spouses, car alarms, fingernails on a chalkboard, coworkers, missed planes, bad dreams, dropped calls, bed bugs, even the sounds coming out of everyone else's iPod--while still being humorous, surprising, and helpful".--Provided by publisher.

"Palca and Lichtman skitter all over the map in pursuit of their subject, and at first their progress seems peculiarly random, like one of those robotic vacuums. But in the end they do indeed cover every part of the terrain: from physics and psychology to aesthetics, genetics and even treatment for the miserably, terminally annoyed." New York Times.

Randall, David K.

Dreamland : adventures in the strange science of sleep / David K. Randall. W.W. Norton, c2012. 336 p. **612.8**

1. Dreams. 2. Sleep disorders. 3. Sleep -- Health aspects. 4. Insomnia.
ISBN 9780393080209

LC 2012014932

A reporter for the Associated Press examines the complex world of sleep and discusses interesting questions as to whether or not women sleep differently than men and if you killed someone while sleepwalking, whether it would count as murder.

Sacks, Oliver, 1933-2015

★The **river** of consciousness / Oliver Sacks. Alfred A. Knopf, 2017. 320 p. **612.8**

1. Consciousness. 2. Neuropsychology. 3. Creativity. 4. Essays
ISBN 9780385352567

LC 2017000815

"A Borzoi book."

Presents a collection of essays reflecting the author's passionate engagement with compelling and seminal ideas of human endeavor, from evolution and creativity to memory and consciousness.

"The essays are all enlightening, entertaining, and a pleasure to read and are of value to scholars and lay readers alike." Choice.

Sapolsky, Robert M.

★**Behave** : the biology of humans at our best and worst / Robert M. Sapolsky. Penguin Press, 2017. 496 p. **612.8**

1. Neurophysiology. 2. Neurobiology. 3. Human behavior 4. Human nature
ISBN 9781594205071

LC 2016056755

A professor of biology and neurology at Stanford reveals what makes humans do the things they do, delving into environmental stimuli, things that trigger the nervous system, hormonal responses and how they work in conjunction with evolutionary and cultural factors.

"An exemplary work of popular science, challenging but accessible." Kirkus.

Suskind, Dana

Thirty million words : building a child's brain / Dana Suskind. Dutton, 2015 320 p. **612.8**

1. Cognitive learning. 2. Children -- Intelligence levels. 3. Cognition in children. 4. Child rearing.
ISBN 9780525954873

LC 2015016306

A doctor encourages parents to help improve their child's neural development and their vocabularies through tuning in to what they are doing, speaking to them using many descriptive words and engaging them in conversations

Thomson, Helen

Unthinkable : an extraordinary journey through the world's strangest brains / Helen Thomson. HarperCollins 2018 256 p. **612.8**

1. Brain -- Diseases 2. Thought and thinking 3. Consciousness 4. Neuroscience
ISBN 9780062391162

LC 2018303642

An award-winning science writer draws on years investigating some of the world's rarest brain disorders and the cases of nine extraordinary people to share insights into how the brain shapes life in unexpected, alarming and vibrant ways.

"Thomson has a gift for making the complex and strange understandable and relatable." Library Journal.

Walker, Matthew

★**Why** we sleep : unlocking the power of sleep and dreams / Matthew Walker. Scribner, 2017. 352 p. **612.8**

1. Sleep -- Health aspects 2. Neuroscience 3. Dreams 4. Sleep disorders
ISBN 9781501144318

LC 2017033123

A first book by the director of UC Berkeley's Sleep and Neuroimaging Lab outlines a groundbreaking exploration of sleep that explains how to harness its transformative power to improve overall health and life quality, covering subjects ranging from caffeine and REM sleep to sleep patterns and the role of sleep in illness.

613 Personal health and safety

Block, Jennifer

Everything below the waist : why health care needs a feminist revolution / Jennifer Block. St. Martin's Press, [2019] 304 p. **613**

1. Women -- Health 2. Women -- Medical care 3. Feminism. 4. Women's Health Movement. 5. United States

ISBN 9781250110053

LC 2019007959

The award-winning journalist and author of Pushed presents a critical assessment of women's healthcare in present-day America, citing declining life expectancies and common examples of how today's healthcare routinely compromises women's sexual lives.

"Thought-provoking, empowering information that all women should have; essential for public and consumer health libraries." Library Journal.

Chopra, Deepak

Super genes : unlock the astonishing power of your DNA for optimum health and well-being / Deepak Chopra, MD and Rudoph E. Tanzi, PhD. Harmony Books, 2015. 320 p. **613**

1. Health 2. Self-care 3. Genetics 4. Genes

ISBN 9780804140133

LC 2015028562

The New York Times best-selling authors of Super Brain blend cutting-edge science and spiritual advice to outline new understandings about human genes and how lifestyle changes may enable better health and happiness. Includes four graphs.

"Chopra's name, along with his trademark blend of concrete suggestions with spiritual principles, will guarantee popularity." Booklist.

Crowley, Chris

Younger next year : live strong, fit, sexy, and smart - until you're 80 and beyond / Chris Crowley and Henry S. Lodge, MD; with Allan J. Hamilton, MD. Workman Publishing Company 2019 xiii, 321 p. ; **613**

1. Longevity 2. Older men -- Health and hygiene

ISBN 9781523507924

Previously published as: Younger next year : a guide to living like 50 until you're 80 and beyond, 2004.

Draws on the research into the science of aging to explain how men over the age of fifty can turn back their biological clocks to live stronger, healthier, injury-free, and more alert lives.

Dietert, Rodney R.

The **human** superorganism : how the microbiome is revolutionizing the pursuit of a healthy life / Rodney Dietert. Dutton, 2016 368 p. **613**

1. Microorganisms. 2. Health. 3. Human biology

ISBN 9781101983904

LC 2015041110

The award-winning immunogenetics researcher and co-author of Immunotoxicity outlines a new biological paradigm about the origins of such non-communicable diseases as asthma, autism and cancer, arguing in favor of ancient-world dietary practices and protective measures against unsafe chemicals.

"Dietert makes a fascinating case for an exciting, emerging field that offers a new way of thinking about the human body and health." Publishers Weekly.

Dusenbery, Maya

Doing harm : the truth about how bad medicine and lazy science leave women dismissed, misdiagnosed, and sick / Maya Dusenbery. HarperOne, 2018 320 p. **613**

1. Women -- Health and hygiene. 2. Sexism in medicine. 3. Health education. 4. Medical care.

ISBN 9780062470805

LC 2017019560

The editorial director of the award-winning site Feministing.com explains how gender biases are negatively impacting every level of medicine and health care today, arguing that incorrect diagnoses and treatments are threatening women's lives

"For readers interested in a feminist critique of health care, especially in the treatment of women." Library Journal.

Falter, Suzanne

The **extremely** busy woman's guide to self-care : do less, achieve more, and live the life you want / Suzanne Falter. Sourcebooks Inc., 2019. 288 p. **613**

1. Self-care, Health

ISBN 9781492698531

LC bl2019029090

A dedicated self-care guide for today's over-scheduled women draws on the author's experiences as a highly stressed workaholic who, in the face of a tragedy, discovered simple strategies for promoting wholeness and balance.

Garcia, Hector, 1981-

Ikigai : the Japanese secret to a long and happy life / Hector Garcia and Francesc Miralles ; translated by Heather Cleary. Penguin Books, 2017 194 p. : **613**

1. Longevity -- Japan 2. Longevity 3. Happiness 4. Quality of life

ISBN 9780143130727

LC 2017005811

"Originally published in Spanish as Ikigai: Los secretos de Japon para una vida larga y feliz by Ediciones Urano in 2016."

Interviews with the residents of a Japanese village that has the world's highest percentage of centenarians reveals the secrets to happiness and longevity through "ikigai," the intersection of passion, purpose, and mission.

Guiliano, Mireille, 1946-

French women don't get facelifts : the secret of aging with style & attitude / Mireille Guiliano. Grand Central Life & Style, 2013. 258 p. ; **613**

1. Older women -- Health and hygiene -- France. 2. Older women -- France -- Attitudes. 3. Aging -- Psychological aspects.

ISBN 9781455524112

LC 2013017824

Includes index.

Discusses how to grow old gracefully while looking and feeling great without having to resort to plastic surgery.

Hamblin, James

Clean : / the new science of skin and the beauty of doing less. James Hamblin. Riverhead Books 2020. 288 p. ; **613**

1. Hygiene 2. Beauty care 3. Skin care

ISBN 9780525538318

Clean reveals the harm that excessive soap, washing and skin-care products are doing to our health and environment--and introduces a new way to think about cleanliness. Every time you wash, you are harming your skin's natural ecology and defences. Hygiene prevents the spread of disease and saves countless lives. But in recent decades, rather than safeguarding us from illness, an obsession with 'cleanliness' seems to have been having the opposite effect. As we are now starting to realise, our overuse of soap, sanitizers and untested, misleading skin-care products is doing untold damage to our skin's vital microbial layer, which influences everything from acne, eczema and dry skin to how we smell. Not only might our obsession with soap-based cleanliness be exacerbating or even causing many of the skin conditions we seek to remedy or avoid, it may even be weaking our immune defences and increasing our vulnerability to allergies. Lucid, accessible, and deeply researched, Clean explains how we got here--thanks to the concerted efforts of the multi-billion-dollar cosmetics industry--and introduces us to the emerging science that will be at the forefront of health and wellness conversations in coming years. It shows that the new goal of skin care will be to cultivate a healthy biome and to embrace a natural approach to being clean--one that is cheaper, simpler and better both for our health and the environment.

"A quick, engaging read for everyone concerned with caring for their skin, and the science behind it." Library Journal

If our bodies could talk : a guide to operating and maintaining a human body / James Hamblin. Doubleday, 2016 352 p. **613**

1. Human body. 2. Health 3. Medical care. 4. Wellness lifestyle.
ISBN 9780385540971

LC 2016046694

Explores the stories behind persistent health questions that are subject to mischaracterization and oversimplification by marketing and the media, covering health topics ranging from sleep and aging to diet and the immune system.

"He does a stellar job with nutrition, covering supplements, multivitamins, energy drinks, and gluten. He calls out medical misinformation and marketing myths. He is troubled... by how money, politics, and industry distort scientific data and muddle health policy. Educational, entertaining, and a bit eccentric." Booklist.

Mcgregor, Alyson J.

Sex matters : how male-centric medicine endangers women's health and what we can do about it / Alyson J. Mcgregor. Hachette Go, 2020 254 p. **613**

1. Women -- Health 2. Medical care 3. Sex discrimination in medicine 4. Medical research
ISBN 073824676X

LC bl2020013069

Sex Matters tackles one of the most urgent, yet unspoken issues facing women's health care today: all models of medical research and practice are based on male-centric models that ignore the unique biological and emotional differences between men and women--an omission that can endanger women's lives. Sex Matters is an empowering roadmap for reinventing modern medicine--and for self-care.

"The author is to be commended for showing how medicine has long skewed male and harmed women. . . . Good ammunition for mandating sex- and gender-based differences in health professional education, research, and practice." Kirkus

Northrup, Christiane

Goddesses never age : the secret prescription for radiance, vitality, and well-being / Christiane Northrup, M.D.. Hay House, Inc., 2015. xvi, 386 p. : **613**

1. Aging 2. Physical fitness 3. Women -- Health and hygiene
ISBN 9781401945169

LC 2014029338

"Includes the 14-day ageless goddess program"--Jacket.

"Though we talk about wanting to "age gracefully," the truth is that when it comes to getting older, we're programmed to dread an inevitable decline: in our health, our looks, our sexual relationships, even the pleasure we take in living life. But as Christiane Northrup, M.D., shows us in this profoundly empowering book, we have it in us to make growing older an entirely different experience, for both our bodies and our souls. In chapters that blend personal stories and practical exercises with the latest research on health and aging, Dr. Northrup lays out the principles of ageless living, from rejecting processed foods to releasing stuck emotions, from embracing our sensuality to connecting deeply with our Divine Source. Explaining that the state of our health is dictated far more by our beliefs than by our biology, she works to shift our perceptions about getting older and show us what we are entitled to expect from our later years--no matter what our culture tries to teach us to the contrary--including: Vibrant good health, A fulfilling sex life, The capacity to love without losing ourselves, The ability to move our bodies with ease and joy, Clarity and authenticity in all our relationships--especially the one we have with ourselves And she brings it all together in a 14-day Ageless Goddess Program, offering tools and inspiration for creating a healthful and soulful new way of being at any stage of life"-- Provided by publisher.

Pollan, Michael

In defense of food : an eater's manifesto / Michael Pollan. Penguin Press, 2008. 176 p. **613**

1. Diet. 2. Food habits. 3. Natural foods. 4. Nutrition.
ISBN 9781594201455

LC 2007037552

ALA Notable Book, 2009.

James Beard Foundation Book Awards, Writing and Literature, 2009.

Cites the reasons why people have become so confused about their dietary choices and discusses the importance of enjoyable moderate eating of mostly traditional plant foods.

"Pollan will succeed in making you think twice about what you are piling up in your grocery cart or on your plate." Christian Science Monitor.

Roizen, Michael F.

This is your do-over : the 7 secrets to losing weight, living longer, and getting a second chance at the life you want / Michael F. Roizen, M.D. ; with Ted Spiker ; foreword by Mehmet C. Oz, M.D. Scribner, 2015 xxiv, 358 p. : **613**

1. Health 2. Rejuvenation 3. Self-care, Health 4. Vitality
ISBN 9781501103339

LC 2014049798

Includes index.

"From one of America's most trusted physicians and the bestselling coauthor of the YOU series with Dr. Mehmet Oz--this practical and empowering guide shares the seven secrets to losing weight, restoring peak vitality, and regaining optimal health at any age. No matter whether you're a stressed-out workaholic, a couch potato, or a marshmallow addict, it's never too late to get a second chance. You do not have to let genetics or bad choices of the past dictate your health outcomes. In fact, you have the power to change your body--as well as which of your genes are switched on--no matter how you've lived in the past. In This Is Your Do-Over, Dr.Michael Roizen, four-time New York Times #1 bestselling author and renowned Chief Wellness Officer of the Cleveland Clinic, provides the tools you need to slam the brakes on bad health and press the gas pedal to good health. In the book, he addresses all the areas that contribute to total-body wellness, including nutrition, exercise, sex, stress, sleep, and the brain. Using concrete strategies that anyone of any age can use, Dr. Roizen shows you how to change your heath destiny with his seven simple secrets to earning a Do-Over. He even shares the key step missing in most other programs: how to select and partner with the proper buddy or coach to get you to your goals. Grounded in cutting-edge scientific research and culled from Dr. Roizen's experience coaching thousands, This Is Your Do-Over is the ultimate guide to reversing damage, optimizing health, and living a life filled with energy and happiness. It is not too late; your Do-Over starts now".-- Provided by publisher.

613.2 Dietetics

Barrett, Pearl

★**Trim** healthy mama trim healthy table : more than 300 all-new healthy and delicious recipes from our homes to yours / Pearl Barrett & Serene Allison. Harmony Books, 2017 559 p. : **613.2**

1. Dieting 2. Weight loss. 3. Nutrition. 4. Recipes 5. Cookbooks
ISBN 9780804189989

LC 2017030325

Includes indexes.

"Gather the family, eat up, and trim down"--Cover.

The best-selling authors share tips and more than 250 recipes for promoting health in entire families through better eating, offering time-saving advice and culinary options that focus on quick-and-easy one-pot meals that minimize sugar and processed foods.

Bauer, Juli

The **paleo** kitchen : finding primal joy in modern cooking / Juli Bauer & George Bryant. Victory Belt Publishing, Inc., 2014. 327 p. : **613.2**

1. Cooking (Natural foods) 2. High-protein diet 3. Prehistoric peoples -- Nutrition. 4. Recipes 5. Cookbooks
ISBN 1628600101

LC bl2014023107

Includes index.

Presents a collection of one hundred gluten- and grain-free Paleo recipes, including such options as blackberry lavender muffins, creamy seafood risotto, and blueberry cheesecake.

Brown, Harriet

Body of truth : how science, history, and culture drive our obsession with weight--and what we can do about it / Harriet Brown. Da Capo Lifelong Books, 2015. 304 p. **613.2**

1. Weight loss -- Psychological aspects. 2. Dieting -- Evaluation. 3. Body image. 4. Weight loss -- Social aspects.
ISBN 9780738217697

LC 2014043431

"Over the last 25 years, our longing for thinness has morphed into a relentless cultural obsession with weight and body image. You can't be a woman or girl (or, increasingly, a man or boy) in America today and not grapple with the size and shape of your body, your daughter's body, other women's bodies. Even the most confident people have to find a way through a daily gauntlet of voices and images talking, admonishing, warning us about what size we should be, how much we should weigh, what we should eat and what we shouldn't. Obsessing about weight has become a ritual and a refrain, punctuating our every relationship, including the ones with ourselves. It's time to change the conversation around weight. Harriet Brown has explored the conundrums of weight and body image for more than a decade, as a science journalist, as a woman who has struggled with weight, as a mother, wife, and professor. In this book, she describes how biology, psychology, metabolism, media, and culture come together to shape our ongoing obsession with our bodies, and what we can learn from them to help us shift the way we think. Brown exposes some of the myths behind the rhetoric of obesity, gives historical and contemporary context for what it means to be "fat," and offers readers ways to set aside the hysteria and think about weight and health in more nuanced and accurate ways".-- Provided by publisher.

"A solid general overview of the scientific and cultural issues surrounding fatness and weight loss with an excellent starter bibliography." Library Journal.

Campbell, T. Colin, 1934-

The **China** study : the most comprehensive study of nutrition ever conducted and the startling implications for diet, weight loss and long-term health / T. Colin Campbell, PhD, Thomas M. Campbell II, MD. BenBella Books, 2017. xxx, 451 p. : **613.2**

1. Nutrition 2. Nutritionally induced diseases 3. Diet in disease
ISBN 9781942952831

LC bl2017051571

The updated and expanded edition of a groundbreaking book describes the findings of a comprehensive nutritional study that shows the relationship between a diet high in animal protein and an increased risk of developing disease.

Carroll, Aaron E.

The **bad** food bible : why you can (and maybe should) eat everything you thought you couldn't / Aaron Carroll, MD. Houghton Mifflin Harcourt, 2017. xxxiv, 234 p. : **613.2**

1. Nutrition 2. Diet
ISBN 9780544952560

LC 2017044244

Revealing how foods we are trained to avoid can actually improve health, a science-based cookbook reveals the positive benefits of enjoying moderate portions of vilified ingredients ranging from red meat and alcohol to gluten and salt.

Cruikshank, Tiffany

Meditate your weight : the 21-day retreat to optimize your metabolism and feel great / Tiffany Cruikshank, LAc, MAOM ; with Mariska Van Aalst. Harmony Books, 2016 321 p. ; **613.2**

1. Weight loss -- Psychological aspects. 2. Metabolism -- Regulation.
ISBN 9780804187961

LC 2015033619

An international yoga teacher and meditation, health and wellness expert presents a 21-day weight-loss plan that employs daily journaling and meditation practice to coach readers through the various mental blocks, thoughts, habits and behaviors and help them achieve and sustain a healthy weight and body image.

Davis, Brenda, 1959-

Becoming vegan : the complete reference to plant-based nutrition / Brenda Davis, RD, Vesanto Melina, MS, RD. Book Publishing Company, 2014 ix, 611 p. : **613.2**

1. Nutrition 2. Veganism -- Health aspects 3. Veganism
ISBN 9781570672972

LC 2014018034

"The book also carefully considers specific issues surrounding veganism during pregnancy and lactation, infancy, childhood, the teen years, and adulthood and provides practical advice for athletes and for those seeking to maintain a healthy weight. The science behind the recommendations is well documented with extensive chapter references. Summing Up: Highly recommended. All nutrition collections." Choice.

Davis, Garth

Proteinaholic : how our obsession with meat is killing us and what we can do about it / Garth Davis, M.D. ; with Howard Jacobson, Ph.D.. HarperOne, 2015 377 p. ; **613.2**

1. Diet in disease 2. Meat 3. Proteins in human nutrition
ISBN 9780062279309

LC 2015020233

"An acclaimed surgeon specializing in weight loss delivers a paradigm-shifting examination of the diet and health industry's focus on protein, explaining why it is detrimental to our health, and can prevent us from losing weight. Whether you are seeing a doctor, nutritionist, or a trainer, all of them advise to eat more protein. Foods, drinks, and supplements are loaded with extra protein. Many people use protein for weight control, to gain or lose pounds, while others believe it gives them more energy and is essential for a longer, healthier life. Now, Dr. Garth Davis, an expert in weight loss asks, "Is all this protein making us healthier?" The answer, he emphatically argues, is NO. Too much protein is actually making us sick, fat, and tired, according to Dr. Davis. If you are getting adequate calories in your diet, there is no such thing as protein deficiency. The healthiest countries in the world eat far less protein than we do and yet we have an entire nation on a protein binge getting sicker by the day. As a surgeon treating obese patients, Dr. Davis was frustrated by the ever-increasing number of sick and overweight patients, but it wasn't until his own health scare that he realized he could do something about it. Combining cutting-edge research, with his hands-on patient experience and his years dedicated to analyzing studies of the world's longest-lived populations, this explosive, groundbreaking book reveals the truth about the dangers of protein and shares a proven approach to weight loss, health, and longevity".-- Provided by publisher.

Dickerman, Sara, 1971-

The **food** lover's cleanse : 140 delicious, nourishing recipes that will tempt you back into healthful eating / Sara Dickerman ; nutritional adviser, Marissa Lippert, MA, RD ; foreword by Adam Rapoport ; photographs by Michael Graydon and Nikole Herriott. William Morrow, 2015 341 p. : **613.2**

1. Cooking (Natural foods) 2. Detoxification (Health) 3. Recipes 4. Cookbooks
ISBN 9780062390233

LC bl2015056475

At head of title: Bon appetit.
Includes index.

Collects recipes to use on four different two-week plans for rebooting eating habits, which emphasize whole foods like fruits, vegetables, and whole grains; controlling portion sizes; and eliminating refined flour, dairy, alcohol, and caffeine.

"Dickerman's approachable guide to whole foods-centric, occasionally meatless healthy eating can help readers curb their postholiday guilt and adopt sustainable life changes. For vegetarians and vegans, Mark Bittman's The VB6 Cookbook is a better choice." Library Journal.

Ehrenreich, Barbara

★**Natural** causes : an epidemic of wellness, the certainty of dying, and killing ourselves to live longer / Barbara Ehrenreich. Twelve, 2018 288 p. **613.2**

1. Death education. 2. Aging. 3. Life expectancy 4. Longevity
ISBN 9781455535910

LC 2017041893

The respected cellular immunologist and author of the best-selling Nickel and Dimed shares cautionary insights into today's healthcare practices to identify the cellular sources of aging and illness while revealing how most treatments are aggressive and offer only the illusion of control and better survivability at the cost of life quality.

"In assessing our quest for a longer, healthier life, Ehrenreich provides a contemplative vision of an active, engaged health care that goes far beyond the physical restraints of the body and into the realm of metaphysical possibilities." Booklist.

Fuhrman, Joel

Eat to live : the amazing nutrient-rich program for fast and sustained weight loss / Joel Fuhrman. Little, Brown, 2011. xx, 380 p. : **613.2**

1. Dieting 2. Weight loss.
ISBN 9780316120913

LC 2010038834

Fuhrman offers a highly effective and scientifically proven way to lose weight quickly, with the simple formula of health = nutrients/calories.

Hartwig, Melissa

Food freedom forever : letting go of bad habits, guilt, and anxiety around food / Melissa Hartwig. Houghton Mifflin Harcourt, 2016. xx, 249 p. ; **613.2**

1. Diet therapy 2. Food habits 3. Nutrition 4. Recipes
ISBN 9780544838291

LC bl2016035910

Includes index.

Shares advice on how to improve energy and health while letting go of negative food habits, outlining a three-part plan for long-term control and recovery from restriction breaks taken during the holidays, vacations, and times of stress.

Heller, Marla

The **everyday** DASH diet cookbook : over 150 fresh and delicious recipes to speed weight loss, lower blood pressure, and prevent diabetes / Marla Heller, MS, RD ; with Rick Rodgers. Grand Central Life & Style, 2013 xxiii, 214 p. : **613.2**

1. Dieting 2. Salt-free diet 3. Hypertension -- Diet therapy 4. Diabetes -- Diet therapy 5. Cookbooks.
ISBN 9781455528066

LC 2012045485

Includes index.

Features healthy recipes for those following the DASH diet (Dietary Approaches to Stop Hypertension).

Hyman, Mark, 1959-

Food : what the heck should I eat? / Mark Hyman, MD. Little, Brown and Company, 2018. xiv, 386 p. ; **613.2**

1. Cooking (Natural foods) 2. Diet therapy 3. Food habits 4. High-protein diet
ISBN 9780316338868

LC 2017958899

Demystifies conflicting dietary advice to explain the crucial role of food in health, examining each food group to reveal what popular opinions have gotten right and wrong so that dieters can make informed choices to lose weight and promote wellness.

Joulwan, Melissa

Well fed : paleo recipes for people who love to eat / Melissa Joulwan ; foreword by Melissa and Dallas Hartwig ; photos by David Humphreys ; design by Kathleen Shannon. Smudge Publishing, LLC, 2011 160 p. : **613.2**

1. High-protein diet 2. Prehistoric people -- Nutrition. 3. Recipes 4. Cookbooks
ISBN 061557226X

LC bl2013040308

"Grain, sugar, legume, dairy free"--Cover.

Includes index.

Offers information on following the paleo diet along with a collection of recipes, and variations, for sauces and seasonings, proteins, vegetables, salads, and fruits.

Ludwig, David, 1957-

Always hungry? : conquer cravings, retrain your fat cells, and lose weight permanently / David Ludwig, MD, PhD. Grand Central Life & Style, 2016. xxiii, 357 p. : **613.2**

1. Metabolism -- Regulation 2. Recipes 3. Reducing diets 4. Self-care, Health

ISBN 9781455533862

LC 2015032645

"Inspired by the New York Times op-ed "Always Hungry," ALWAYS HUNGRY? will change everything readers ever thought about weight loss, diet, and health. Groundbreaking new research shows that calorie counting does not work for weight loss: one diet causes weight gain whereas another diet with the same calorie count doesn't. It's your fat cells that are to blame for causing excessive hunger and increased weight. By eating the wrong foods, our fat cells are triggered to take in too many calories for themselves, setting off a dangerous chain reaction of increased appetite and a slower metabolism. Now, Harvard Medical School's David Ludwig, MD, PhD, offers an impeccably researched diet that will turn dieting on its head, teaching readers to reprogram their fat cells, tame hunger, boost metabolism, and lose weight--for good".-- Provided by publisher.

"Ludwig's meal plans and recipes are excellent. This quality book on the basics of losing weight will appeal to all types of readers." Library Journal.

Mann, Traci

Secrets from the eating lab : the science of weight loss, the myth of willpower, and why you should never diet again / Traci Mann, Ph.D.. HarperWave, 2015 xii, 254 p. : **613.2**

1. Reducing diets -- Psychological aspects 2. Reducing diets -- Social aspects 3. Weight loss -- Psychological aspects 4. Weight loss -- Social aspects

ISBN 9780062329233

LC 2014049872

"A provocative exposé of the dieting industry from one of the nation's leading researchers in self-control and the psychology of weight loss that offers proven strategies for sustainable weight loss. From her office in the University of Minnesota's Healthand Eating Lab, professor Traci Mann researches self-control and dieting. And what she has discovered is groundbreaking. Not only do diets not work; they often result in weight gain. Americans are losing the battle of the bulge because our bodies and brains are not hardwired to resist food--the very idea of it works against our biological imperative to survive. In Secrets From the Eating Lab, Mann challenges assumptions--including those that make up the very foundation of the weight loss industry--about how diets work and why they fail. The result of more than two decades of research, it offers cutting-edge science and exciting new insights into the American obesity epidemic and our relationship with eating and food. Secrets From the Eating Lab also gives readers the practical tools they need to actually lose weight and get healthy. Mann argues that the idea of willpower is a myth--we shouldn't waste time and money trying to combat our natural tendencies. Instead, she offers 12 simple, effective strategies that take advantage of human nature instead of fighting it--from changing the size of your plates to socializing with people with healthy habits, removing 'healthy' labels that send negative messages to redefining comfort food".-- Provided by publisher.

"Mann cites study after study to make her case; titles her last chapter, 'Final Words: Diet Schmiet'; and declares that no single eating plan will ever make the pounds melt away forever. 'The fragility of willpower' and 'a culture of ubiquitous temptations' conspire against the best-laid plans. Her bottom-line recommendation: 'reach your leanest livable weight.' Sold." Booklist.

Moss, Michael, 1955-

★**Salt,** sugar, fat : how the food giants hooked us / Michael Moss. Random House, c2013. 352 p. **613.2**

1. Nutrition -- Economic aspects -- United States 2. Food habits -- Economic aspects -- United States 3. Food industry and trade -- United States 4. Salt

ISBN 9781400069804

LC 2012033034

Published in Canada as Sugar, salt, fat: Toronto : Signal, 2013.

James Beard Foundation Book Awards, Writing and Literature, 2014.

Traces the rise of the processed food industry and how addictive salt, sugar, and fat have enabled its dominance in the past half century, revealing deliberate corporate practices behind current trends in obesity, diabetes, and other health challenges.

Moyad, Mark A., 1965-

The **supplement** handbook : a trusted expert's guide to what works & what's worthless for more than 100 conditions / Mark Moyad, MD, MPH, Jenkins/Pokempner Director of Complementary and Alternative Medicine at the University of Michigan Medical Center ; with Janet Lee, LAc. Rodale, 2014 ix, 502 p. ; **613.2**

1. Dietary supplements

ISBN 9781623360351

LC 2014035702

Includes index.

"Nearly half of Americans use supplements and many more are curious about them, but there's a lot of misinformation out there. Mark Moyad is the only physician in the United States who has an endowed position to study vitamins, minerals, herbs, and other supplements. For the past 25 years, he's been researching supplements and using them in his practice. He's the doctor that other doctors go to when they want research-backed information on natural remedies. In The Supplement Handbook, he takes the guesswork out of what to use and when by providing clear, authoritative advice on more than 200 ailments and 200 supplements. In this discerning guide, readers will learn how to treat or alleviate common conditions such as arthritis, heartburn, high cholesterol, high blood pressure, migraines, and hot flashes. Dr. Moyad is also up front about when prescription or over-the-counter drugs are the better choice. And he reveals the truth about popular supplements that are touted for their effectiveness, but actually do nothing, or are harmful. More than an overview, The Supplement Handbook delivers prescriptive, reliable advice. Both the alternative medicine convert and the novice interested in supplements but confused about what to take, will learn surprising and useful information from Dr. Moyad's expertise and put themselves on the road to better health, naturally."-- Provided by publisher.

"This book explains what supplements are, what they can and can't do, and when to use them. It also tells readers how to evaluate the information that is available about supplements.The bulk of the book discusses specific medical conditions, with recommendations for supplements based on evidence from research." Booklist.

Nestle, Marion

Why calories count : from science to politics / Marion Nestle and Malden Nesheim. University of California Press, c2012.

288 p. : **613.2**

1. Food -- Caloric content. 2. Diet. 3. Obesity -- Prevention
ISBN 9780520262881

LC 2011044785

Explores food issues in America including understanding how calories work in the body and understanding how the food industry presents calories on labels.

Oates, Carla

The **beauty** chef gut guide / Carla Oates. Hardie Grant Books, 2019. 255 p. : **613.2**

1. Gastrointestinal system -- Diseases -- Diet therapy 2. Health. 3. Nutrition. 4. Well-being.
ISBN 9781743795002

The Beauty Chef Gut Guide is the practical companion to Carla Oates' acclaimed book, The Beauty Chef. It is a compelling resource for people who want to better understand the science underpinning the link between gut and skin health. The 8-week program includes information on the importance of gut functionality, weekly meal plans for repairing and reprogramming your gut, and more than 90 recipes. In addition to recipes and information about repairing your gut, it covers broader advice for wellbeing, from the importance of cleaning products to mindfulness and yoga.

Oxmoor House,

Cooking that counts : 1,200- to 1,500-calorie meal plans to lose weight deliciously / the editors of Cooking light. Oxmoor House, 2017. 288 p. : **613.2**

1. Low-calorie diet -- Recipes. 2. Weight loss. 3. Cookbooks
ISBN 9780848749507

LC bl2016054494

Includes index.

Easy-to-use, sustainable meal plans and more than 150 calorie-controlled recipes place an emphasis on whole, natural foods, portion sizes and flexibility while offering suggestions for busy schedules and strategic shopping.

Prescott, Matthew

Food is the solution : what to eat to save the world : 80+ recipes for a greener planet and a healthier you / Matthew Prescott ; foreword by Academy Award-winning director James Cameron. Flatiron Books, 2018. 272 p. : **613.2**

1. Cooking (Vegetables) 2. Recipes 3. Vegan cooking 4. Veganism 5. Cookbooks
ISBN 9781250144454

LC bl2018001272

A senior food policy director for the Humane Society presents a guide to supporting key agendas in ecological responsibility and sustainability that includes environmentally friendly, healthy, plant-based recipes.

Sanfilippo, Diane

Practical paleo : a customized approach to health and a whole-foods lifestyle / Diane Sanfilippo. Victory Belt Pub., 2016, c2012 480 p. : **613.2**

1. Cooking (Natural foods) 2. High-protein diet 3. Prehistoric peoples -- Nutrition
ISBN 9781628600025

LC bl2012027906

Includes index.

Jam-packed with more than 100 easy recipes, all with notes about common food allergens, a collection of meal plans targets the right way to eat to improve blood sugar regulation and athletic performance, as well as brain, joint, skin, heart, digestive and immune system health.

Tam, Michelle

Nom nom paleo : food for humans / Michelle Tam + Henry Fong. Andrews McMeel Publishing, 2013 277 p. : **613.2**

1. Cooking (Natural foods) 2. High-protein diet 3. Prehistoric peoples -- Nutrition. 4. Recipes 5. Cookbooks
ISBN 1449450334

LC bl2013053904

Offers a variety of family-friendly paleo recipes as well as strategies for stocking the pantry, feeding kids, maximizing flavor, and saving time in the kitchen.

Tara, Sylvia

The **secret** life of fat : the science behind the body's least understood organ and what it means for you / Sylvia Tara, PhD. W.W. Norton & Company, 2017 xiv, 235 p. : **613.2**

1. Fat -- Health aspects 2. Fat
ISBN 9780393244830

LC bl2017012214

Blends historical perspectives with cutting-edge research to examine body fat as a critical endocrine organ that can be better understood and managed when recognized as a necessary component of human health.

Taubes, Gary

The **case** against sugar / Gary Taubes. Alfred A. Knopf, 2016. 272 p. **613.2**

1. Sugar-free diet. 2. Cooking, Sugar-free. 3. Sugar -- Health hazards. 4. Food habits -- United States.
ISBN 9780307701640

LC 2016018147

From the best-selling author of Why We Get Fat, a groundbreaking, eye-opening exposé that makes the convincing case that sugar is the tobacco of the new millennium: backed by powerful lobbies, entrenched in our lives, and making us very sick. Among Americans, diabetes is more prevalent today than ever; obesity is at epidemic proportions; nearly 10% of children are thought to have nonalcoholic fatty liver disease. And sugar is at the root of these, and other, critical society-wide, health-related problems.

Urban, Melissa

★The **whole30** : the 30-day guide to total health and food freedom / Melissa Hartwig and Dallas Hartwig ; with Chef Richard Bradford ; photography by Alexandra Grablewski. Houghton Mifflin Harcourt, 2015. ix, 421 p. : **613.2**

1. Diet therapy 2. Food habits 3. Nutrition 4. Self-care, Health
ISBN 9780544609716

LC 2015007139

Includes index.

"Millions of people visit Whole30.com every month and share their stories of weight loss and lifestyle makeovers. Hundreds of thousands of them have read It Starts With Food, which explains the science behind the program. At last, The Whole30 provides the step-by-step, recipe-by-recipe guidebook that will allow millions of people to experience the transformation of their entire life in just one month. Melissa and Dallas Hartwig's critically-acclaimed Whole30 program has helped hundreds of thousands of people transform how they think about their food, bodies, and lives. Their approach leads to effortless weight loss and better health--along with stunning improvements in sleep quality, energy levels, mood, and self-esteem. Their first book, the New York Times best-selling It Starts With Food, explained the science behind their life-changing program. Now they bring you The Whole30, a stand-alone, step-by-step plan to break unhealthy habits, reduce cravings, improve digestion, and strengthen your immune system. The Whole30 features more than 100 chef-developed recipes, like Chimichurri Beef Kabobs and Halibut with Citrus Ginger Glaze, designed to build your confidence in the kitchen and inspire your taste buds. The book also includes real-life success stories, community resources, and an extensive FAQ to give you the support you need on your journey to 'food freedom.'-- Provided by publisher.

613.2083 Personal health and safety -- Dietetics -- Young people

Avena, Nicole M., 1978-

What to feed your baby & toddler : a month-by-month guide to support your child's health & development / Nicole M. Avena, PhD with recipes by Charity Ferreira. Ten Speed Press, 2018 ix, 214 p. : **613.2083**

1. Baby foods 2. Child development 3. Infants -- Nutrition 4. Toddlers -- Nutrition

ISBN 9780399580239

LC 2018010055

A science-based manual for feeding babies schedules out meal plans designed to provide the optimal nutrition for respective physical and intellectual milestones from 6 to 24 months, providing dozens of recipes as well as advice for common concerns about fussiness, allergies, dining out and food safety.

"Specific nutritional information and straightforward, fun-to-eat recipes make this a great primer for new parents." Library Journal.

613.25 Weight-losing diet

Wansink, Brian

Slim by design : mindless eating solutions for everyday life / Brian Wansink, Ph.D. William Morrow, 2014. 312 p. : **613.25**

1. Health behavior. 2. Eating disorders -- Alternative treatment. 3. Food habits -- Psychological aspects. 4. Weight loss -- Psychological aspects.

ISBN 9780062136527

LC 2015304142

Using research from his Food and Brand Lab at Cornell University, an expert in eating behavior reveals how innovative, inexpensive design changes can make it mindlessly easy and profitable for people to eat healthier.

613.6 Personal safety and special topics of health

Canterbury, Dave

Advanced bushcraft : an expert field guide to the art of wilderness survival / Dave Canterbury. Adams Media, 2015 256 p. ; **613.6**

1. Camping 2. Camping -- Equipment and supplies 3. Outdoor life 4. Outdoor recreation

ISBN 9781440587962

LC 2015008301

Includes index.

"Meant to follow "Bushcraft 101" by providing more advanced techniques for making tools, traps, shelters, and more, in the wilderness".-- Provided by publisher.

Bushcraft 101 : a field guide to the art of wilderness survival / Dave Canterbury. Adams Media, 2014 256 p. ; **613.6**

1. Camping 2. Camping -- Equipment and supplies 3. Outdoor life 4. Outdoor recreation

ISBN 9781440579776

LC 2014012976

Includes index.

Offers survival skills on using the surrounding wilderness as a useful resource, including how to manufacture needed tools, how to collect and cook food, and how to guard against the elements.

Dorn, Michael Stephen, 1961-

Staying alive : how to act fast and survive deadly encounters / Michael Dorn, Stephen Satterly, Dr. Sonayia Shepherd, Chris Dorn. Barron's Educational Series, 2014 xi, 292 p. : **613.6**

1. Survival. 2. Survival skills

ISBN 9781438004082

LC 2013031901

Mass shootings, home invasions, attacks on the general public ... these are no longer the rare exception they once were. What can the average person do to stay safe? This book takes an honest look at the myths and truths surrounding mass casualty events, provides proven strategies for surviving violent incidents, and gives you safety concepts that can be applied to any emergency, man-made or natural.

"A chilling and comprehensive crisis-preparedness guide." Library Journal.

Gervasi, Lori Hartman

Fight like a girl-- and win : defense decisions for women / Lori Hartman Gervasi. St. Martin's Griffin, 2007. xvi, 285 p. ; **613.6**

1. Self-defense for women. 2. Safety education.

ISBN 9780312357726

LC 2007017216

A television journalist explains why women need to learn how to consider their options and train their reflexes to react before they find themselves in a dangerous situation, walking readers through thirty-five key decisions they need to make in order to save their lives.

"Although the author has a black belt in karate, she maintains that 90 percent of self-defense is awareness and common sense. She helps readers set up absolute rules and boundaries, sharpen their observation skills, and trust in their intuition. Physical fitness is stressed, and resources are provided for further training." Library Journal.

Kostigen, Thomas

National Geographic extreme weather survival guide : understand, prepare, survive, recover / Thomas M. Kostigen. National Geographic, 2014. 382 p. : **613.6**

1. Severe storms. 2. Natural disasters. 3. Weather. 4. Emergency management -- Handbooks, manuals, etc.

ISBN 9781426213762

LC 2014005362

Accompanied by first-hand accounts from survivors, this must-have resource helps readers plan ahead and prepare, respond to emergencies and survive the worst-case scenarios during extreme weather events such as hurricanes, floods, wildfires and tornadoes.

Marquis, Sarah, 1972-

Wild by nature : from Siberia to Australia, three years alone in the wilderness on foot / Sarah Marquis. Thomas Dunne Books/ St. Martin's Press , 2016, c2015 320 p. **613.6**

1. Marquis, Sarah, 1972- Travel. 2. Wilderness survival. 3. Hiking. 4. Women travelers 5. Voyages and travels. 6. Asia 7. Australia
ISBN 9781250081971

LC 2015039458

Using her wits and skills as a hunter to get by, a woman describes her solo 10,000-mile trek across the Gobi desert where she encountered mafiosos, drug dealers, thieves on horseback, temperature extremes, dehydration, ringworm and dengue fever.

"Her tales of whom she meets and what she sees are as bracing as she is. Straightforward and forthright, this is adventure writing as it was meant to be." Booklist.

Moore, Alexis, 1951-

Cyber self-defense : expert advice to avoid online predators, identity theft, and cyberbullying / Alexis Moore and Laurie J. Edwards. Lyons Press, 2014. 259 p. : **613.6**

1. Internet -- Safety measures. 2. Computer security. 3. Cyberbullying. 4. Online identity theft -- Prevention.
ISBN 9781493005697

LC 2014027221

"Explains how to identify potential cyberattackers and how to recover from a cybercrime if you've been attacked".-- Provided by publisher.

Rawles, James Wesley

Tools for survival : what you need to survive when you're on your own / James Wesley, Rawles. Plume, 2015. xxxii, 315 p. ; **613.6**

1. Survival. 2. Self-reliant living. 3. Alternative lifestyles.
ISBN 9780452298125

LC 2014032904

Includes index.

A preparedness expert describes how to survive any disaster event--from a minor disruption to the end of the world--including preserving food and cooking; welding and blacksmithing; the basics of timber, firewood and lumber; firefighting; and more. By the author of How to Survive the End of the World as We Know It.

Sprinkle, Timothy

Lost and stranded : expert advice on how to survive being alone in the wilderness / Timothy Sprinkle. Skyhorse Publishing, 2017. 275 p. **613.6**

1. Outdoor recreation. 2. Outdoor life. 3. Wilderness survival. 4. Wilderness areas.
ISBN 9781510727700

Breaking down the perils that can befall hikers, hunters, and other outdoor enthusiasts, information from expert sources fills in the details around exactly how each scenario plays out on the ground, followed by suggestions on how to avoid or survive each risk factor--making this book a vital resource for outdoor travelers.

Wiseman, John, 1940-

SAS survival handbook : the ultimate guide to surviving anywhere / John "Lofty" Wiseman. William Morrow, 2014. 672 p. : **613.6**

1. Survival -- Handbooks, manuals, etc.
ISBN 9780062378071

LC 2014956877

"Featuring 100 pages of additional material, including a new chapter on urban survival"--Cover.

Includes index.

A survival guide from the Special Air Service offers a complete course on how to be prepared for any type of emergency--from natural disasters to terrorist attacks to wilderness adventures--explaining how to adapt successfully to various climates, how toidentify edible plants, and how to build a fire, with tips on first aid, campcraft, emergency preparation, and more. The SAS Survival Handbook is the Special Air Service's complete course in being prepared for any type of emergency. John Wiseman presentsreal strategies for surviving in any type of situation, from accidents and escape procedures, including chemical and nuclear to successfully adapting to various climates (polar, tropical, desert), to identifying edible plants and creating fire. The book is extremely practical and is illustrated throughout with easy-to-understand line art and diagrams.

613.7 Physical fitness

Baleka, Siphiwe

4-minute fit : the metabolism accelerator for the time-crunched, deskbound, and stressed-out / Siphiwe Baleka, "America's Fittest Trucker", with L. Jon Wertheim. Touchstone, 2017. xiii, 224 p. : **613.7**

1. Weight loss -- Popular works. 2. Exercise -- Popular works. 3. Physical fitness 4. Metabolism
ISBN 9781501129773

LC 2016038003

The founder of Fitness Trucking, LLC and full-time fitness coach for one of the nation's largest trucking companies presents a revolutionary metabolism-spiking program for anyone who feels they don't have enough time, equipment or money to get in shape and lose those extra pounds.

Bercovici, Jeff

Play on : the new science of elite performance at any age / Jeff Bercovici. Houghton Mifflin Harcourt, 2018. 288 p. **613.7**

1. Aging -- Physiological aspects. 2. Physical fitness for seniors 3. Sports for seniors 4. Exercise for seniors
ISBN 9780544809987

LC 2017050323

"A lively, thoroughly researched tour of the latest in fitness science and technology, and the strategies of elite and amateur athletes who are performing at peak levels for decades longer than before".-- Provided by publisher.

"Bercovici smartly separates science from quackery--avoiding GMO foods won't help, he argues, but taking creatine will--while offering colorful reportage on sports trainers, physiologists, and gurus, and using his own achy frame to road test their wares, from -286 F cryotherapy chamber to an exercise/torture device called the Versaclimber." Publishers Weekly.

Broad, William J.

The **science** of yoga : the myths and the rewards / William J. Broad. Simon & Schuster, 2012. 320 p. **613.7**

1. Hatha yoga. 2. Yoga. 3. Stretching exercises 4. Physical fitness
ISBN 9781451641424

LC 2011020408

A two-time Pulitzer Prize-winning New York Times senior writer challenges popular misconceptions to separate out modern yoga's true discipline from the inauthentic activities of charlatans and trend-hoppers, drawing on scientific and cultural research to counsel readers on how to recognize an authentic practice and gain actual benefits. By the author of the best-selling Germs.

Brooks, Amanda (Runner)

Run to the finish : the everyday runner's guide to avoiding injury, ignoring the clock, and loving the run / Amanda Brooks. Lifelong Books, 2020. 288 p. **613.7**

1. Running -- Training. 2. Running -- Physiological aspects. 3. Marathons 4. Runners

ISBN 9780738285993

LC 2019043017

In her first book, popular runner blogger Amanda Brooks lays out the path to finding greater fulfillment in running for those who consider themselves "middle of the pack runners"--they're not trying to win Boston (or even qualify for Boston); they just want to get strong and stay injury-free so they can continue to enjoy running.

"While there are plenty of books about running, few are as approachable and helpful as this one. Highly recommended for anyone looking to improve their running ability." Library Journal

Brown, Jeff, 1969-

The **runner's** brain : how to think smarter to run better / Dr. Jeff Brown with Liz Neporent ; foreword by Meb Keflezighi. Rodale, 2015 x, 228 p. ; **613.7**

1. Running -- Psychological aspects 2. Running -- Training

ISBN 9781623363475

LC bl2015037966

At head of title: Runner's world.

Offers runners psychological techniques designed to rewire the mind for athletic success.

Budig, Kathryn

Aim true : love your body, eat without fear, nourish your spirit, discover true balance! / Kathryn Budig. William Morrow, 2016 322 p. : **613.7**

1. Hatha yoga. 2. Exercise. 3. Physical fitness. 4. Women -- Health and hygiene.

ISBN 9780062419712

LC 2015034599

"Yoga teacher and inspirational speaker Kathryn Budig extends her empowering message beyond the mat, in this ultimate girl's guide to yoga, diet, and mindfulness".-- Provided by publisher.

"In an age that increasingly commercializes the ancient practice of yoga, Budig's wholesome, down-to-earth outlook is welcome, sure to aid readers of all shapes and sizes in establishing healthy food and exercise patterns while practicing self-love and acceptance." Publishers Weekly.

Contreras, Bret, 1976-

Strong curves : a woman's guide to building a better butt and body / Bret Contreras & Kellie Davis. Victory Belt Publishing, 2013. 320 p. : **613.7**

1. Bodybuilding for women 2. Buttocks exercises 3. Buttocks -- Muscles 4. Exercise

ISBN 9781936608645

LC 2018300807

Based on years of research and field-testing the best methods for building shapelier bodies, the world's leading expert in gluteal muscle functioning and development offers an extensive fitness and nutrition guide for women seeking to improve their physique, function, strength and mobility.

Cucuzzella, Mark

Run for your life : how to run, walk, and move without pain or injury and achieve a sense of well-being and joy / Mark Cucuzzella, M.D., with Broughton Coburn. Alfred A. Knopf, 2018. xviii, 364 p. : **613.7**

1. Running injuries -- Prevention 2. Running -- Physiological aspects 3. Running -- Training

ISBN 9781101946305

LC 2017056684

"The first running book by a world's leading pioneering running doctor and athlete, creator of the Air Force's Efficient Running program--the result of more than three decades of study, practice, and science that shows us in clearly illustrated and accessible text how easy it is to run efficiently and injury-free, whether you're in your 20s, 60s or 70s; for beginning runners and experienced marathoners. In Run for Your Life, Dr. Mark Cucuzzella explains the simple mechanics of how our bodies have evolved and adapted to run. Despite our natural ability and our human need to run, each year more than half of all runners suffer injuries. Pain and discouragement inevitably follow. Cucuzzella's book outlines the proven, practical techniques to avoid injury and reach the goal of personal fitness and overall health. His book--the first running book to be written by a Professor of Medicine with the credibility of the Air Force behind him--gives us a straightforward, easy-to-follow look at the anatomy, bio-mechanics, nutrition, and/or clinical medicine with clear drawings and black-and-white photographs. The book provides illustrated exercises designed to teach healthy running, along with simple progressions, a weekly/monthly schedule detailing common mistakes and cautions that allow the reader to tailor the training regime to individual needs and abilities. With corresponding online videos and other innovative, book-Internet links".-- Provided by publisher.

De Sena, Joe, 1969-

Spartan fit! : 30 days. Transform your mind. Transform your body. Commit to grit. / Joe De Sena with John Durant. Houghton Mifflin Harcourt, 2016 xvi, 239 p. : **613.7**

1. Endurance sports -- Training 2. Exercise 3. Health 4. Physical fitness

ISBN 9780544439603

LC 2016440092

Offers a thirty-one-day fitness and diet plan to help achieve peak physical and mental fitness through full-body workouts that don't require gym access or weights.

"This book is ideal for workout enthusiasts who want to push themselves to the limit." Publishers Weekly.

Epstein, David J., 1983-

The **sports** gene : inside the science of extraordinary athletic performance / David Epstein. Current, 2013. xiv, 338 p. **613.7**

1. Sports -- Physiological aspects. 2. Human genetics. 3. Sports sciences 4. Athletic ability.

ISBN 9781591845119

LC 2013013443

"[T]his book is essential reading for sports fans interested in the science of sports, and for readers (not scholars) interested in the science of human differences." Library Journal.

Esmonde-White, Miranda

Aging backwards : reverse the aging process and look 10 years younger in 30 minutes a day / Miranda Esmonde-White. Harper Wave, 2018 vi, 278 p. : **613.7**

1. Rejuvenation. 2. Longevity. 3. Aging -- Prevention. 4. Physical fitness.

ISBN 9780062859327

LC 2014028452

Originally published: New York : Harper Wave, 2014

"PBS fitness personality and creator of the fitness phenomenon The Esmonde Technique, Miranda Esmonde-White offers an eye-opening guide to anti-aging that provides essential tools to help anyone turn back the clock and look and feel younger. Miranda Esmonde-White trains everyone from prima ballerinas to professional hockey players to MS patients: what do they all have in common? All of these people are hoping to heal their bodies, prevent further injury, and move optimally and without pain. In fact, they have the same goals as any of us who are trying to stay young, fit, and reverse the hands of time. Because the aging of our bodies occurs in our cells, it must be repaired there too--that's where Miranda's highly effective and sought-after techniques come in. The body isn't programmed to self-destruct as we age. Bones don't have to become brittle; muscles don't have to atrophy; bellies don't have to be soft. In Aging Backwards, Miranda offers a revolutionary program that shows readers how to keep fit and healthy through lifestyle changes and gentle exercises that don't require you to spend hours in the gym. From losing weight to improving skin tone to getting stronger and fitter, Miranda offers readers of all ages the tools they need to look and feel younger. Complete with tips, tools, and her Eight Basic Age-Reversing Workouts accompanied by instructional photos, Aging Backwards will help you turn back the clock form the inside out".-- Provided by publisher.

Fitzgerald, Matt

How bad do you want it? : mastering the psychology of mind over muscle / Matt Fitzgerald ; foreword by Samuele Marcora, PhD. VeloPress, 2015 xiii, 282 p. ; **613.7**

1. Running -- Psychological aspects 2. Running -- Training
ISBN 9781937715410

LC bl2015047425

Examines the way elite athletes strengthen their mental toughness and approach their true physical limits, offering a psychobiological model of endurance performance to help readers master the psychology of mind over muscle.

Green, Louise

Big fit girl : embrace the body you have / Louise Green. Greystone Books, 2017 xi, 236 p. : **613.7**

1. Physical fitness for women 2. Overweight women -- Health and hygiene
ISBN 9781771642125

LC bl2017009337

Offers a guide for plus-sized women to overcome cultural stereotypes and achieve high levels of fitness, from motivation, gear, and goals to appropriate nutrition for athletes and overcoming performance plateaus.

Gregory, Alice

Nodding off : the science of sleep from cradle to grave / Alice Gregory. St Martins Pr 2018 288 p. **613.7**

1. Sleep 2. Sleepiness 3. Human biology 4. Sleep deprivation
ISBN 9781472946188

LC bl2018179681

A well-respected sleep expert takes readers on a scientific journey through slumber, exploring every aspect of sleep, from the different stages of sleep all the way to what happens when getting some shut-eye becomes more of a trial than a pleasure.

"Of particular interest to parents and educators who deal with issues surrounding children's and teen's sleep (or lack thereof), but also useful to those of any age who suffer from problems that prevent proper rest." Library Journal.

Grossman, Gail Boorstein

Restorative yoga for life : a relaxing way to de-stress, re-energize, and find balance / Gail Boorstein Grossman. Adams Media, 2015 254 p. : **613.7**

1. Hatha yoga. 2. Relaxation.
ISBN 9781440575204

LC 2014026432

Includes index.

A certified YogaKids trainer demonstrates how to practice a restorative form of yoga that focuses on prop-aided physical and mental relaxation while treating a range of ailments, from headaches and digestive imbalances to weight gain and back pain.

Hanoch, Doron, 1971-

The **yoga** lifestyle : using the flexitarian method to ease stress, find balance & create a healthy life / Doron Hanoch. Llewellyn Publications, 2016. xviii, 365 p. : **613.7**

1. Hatha yoga. 2. Medicine, Ayurvedic. 3. Vegetarians. 4. Health.
ISBN 9780738748665

LC 2016002999

Introduces and explains what the flexitarian lifestyle is, an integration of yoga, Ayurveda, breathing practices, meditation, and nutrition.

Huffington, Arianna Stassinopoulos, 1950-

The **sleep** revolution : transforming your life, one night at a time / Arianna Huffington. Harmony Books, 2016 viii, 392 p. ; **613.7**

1. Sleep deprivation 2. Sleep -- Health aspects
ISBN 9781101904008

LC 2015039918

Evaluates the role of sleep as a cultural and historical unifier, the impact of sleep deprivation on health, and the science community's recommendations for how to achieve more restorative sleep.

Isacowitz, Rael, 1955-

Pilates / Rael Isacowitz. Human Kinetics, 2014 xvii, 373 p. : **613.7**

1. Pilates
ISBN 9781450434164

LC 2013019507

Offers an in-depth explanation of mat work and breathing, features exercises and variations that can be applied to the full range of pilates apparatus, and includes tools for creating customized routines.

Krasno, Jeff

Wanderlust : a modern yogi's guide to discovering your best self / Jeff Krasno, with Sarah Herrington & Nicole Lindstrom. Rodale, 2015. 289 p. : **613.7**

1. Hatha yoga 2. Yoga 3. Self-actualization (Psychology)
ISBN 9781623363505

LC 2015023375

Includes index.

A road map to pursuing a spiritual life of yoga practices, mindfulness techniques, and healthy eating outlines adaptable principles for living while providing uplifting messages and recommended music playlists.

Kunitz, Daniel

Lift : fitness culture, from naked Greeks and dumbbells to jazzercise and ninja warriors / Daniel Kunitz. Harper Wave,

2016. 272 p. **613.7**

1. Physical fitness. 2. Physical education and training. 3. Exercise.
ISBN 9780062336187

LC 2016004087

A cultural history of fitness explores the ways in which human exercise has changed over time and what can be learned from our athletic ancestors, evaluating whether today's high-tech exercise machines are actually productive while making recommendations based on early health practices.

"Kunitz includes his own challenges with fitness along the way, making this a book not just for those interested in the roots of fitness, but for anyone who struggles to live healthily." Publishers Weekly.

Lacerda, Daniel (Yoga teacher)

2,100 Asanas : the complete yoga poses / Daniel Lacerda, Founder of Mr. Yoga, Inc. Black Dog & Leventhal Publishers, 2015. 736 p. : **613.7**

1. Hatha yoga 2. Yoga 3. Exercise
ISBN 9781631910104

LC 2015026283

Includes index.

An extensive catalog of yoga asanas for practitioners of any experience level showcases the form's beauty and athleticism and is organized under eight major types, from standing and seated poses to inversion and quadruped poses.

Lasater, Judith

Yoga myths : what you need to learn and unlearn for a safe and healthy yoga practice / Judith Hanson Lasater. Shambhala, 2020 xiv, 255 p. : **613.7**

1. Hatha yoga.
ISBN 9781611807967

LC 2019042112

"Because yoga has become more and more popular and integrated into Western culture, millions of people outside of India study and practice yoga. Along with this has been a proliferation in the numbers of yoga teachers. In this book, Judith Hanson Lasater introduces 'yoga myths' in each chapter. These are the beliefs commonly held about how movements should be practiced which in fact do not represent the actual physical anatomical reality of the body's structure and how it moves. These yoga myths are very common among virtually all systems of yoga asana practice. This book creates the opportunity to choose something different in our practice and teaching of yoga. This difference is that we now have the power to stop injuring ourselves, and to begin to move with more joy and ease."-- Provided by publisher.

"This wise and detailed guidebook (accompanied by black-and-white photos) will help students and teachers alike to remember to listen to their bodies and practice yoga with awareness." Publishers Weekly

Liebman, Hollis Lance

Encyclopedia of exercise anatomy / Hollis Lance Liebman. Firefly Books U.S., 2014. 392 p. : **613.7**

1. Exercise -- Encyclopedias. 2. Muscles -- Anatomy -- Encyclopedias.
ISBN 9781770854437

LC 2015301045

"This useful title, which will also work well as a circulating item, presents that something extra for fitness enthusiasts who want to become serious about their conditioning." Library Journal.

Marcum, Andrea

Close to om : stretching yoga from your mat to your life / Andrea Marcum. St. Martin's Griffin, 2018. x, 214 p. : **613.7**

1. Hatha yoga. 2. Meditation. 3. Mindfulness (Psychology). 4. Self-care, Health.
ISBN 9781250127594

LC bl2017052802

Includes index.

A veteran celebrity yoga instructor offers a program that combines yoga poses, an exploration of yoga philosophy, and tips and techniques for practicing meditation and mindfulness to improve your physical health and mental well-being.

McClusky, Mark

Faster, higher, stronger : how sports science is creating a new generation of superathletes, and what we can learn from them / Mark McClusky. Hudson Street Press, 2014. 288 p. **613.7**

1. Sports sciences. 2. Sports -- Physiological aspects. 3. Athletes -- Training.
ISBN 9781594631535

LC 2014021223

In Faster, Higher, Stronger, veteran journalist Mark McClusky brings readers behind the scenes with a new generation of athletes, coaches, and scientists whose accomplishments are changing our understanding of human physical achievement and completely redefining the limits of the human body.

"All of this trickles down to amateur athletics as well, and McClusky does a good job of relating cutting-edge science to people wanting to run their 5K a little faster or shave a few strokes off their golf handicap." Booklist.

Pohlman, Dean

Yoga fitness for men : build strength, improve performance, increase flexibility / Dean Pohlman. DK Publishing, 2018. 191 p. : **613.7**

1. Hatha yoga. 2. Exercise for men. 3. Physical fitness for men.
ISBN 9781465473486

LC bl2018085674

Includes index.

Perfect for beginners! With straightforward language and easy-to-follow steps, Yoga Fitness for Men will teach you how to execute the yoga postures you need for greater endurance, flexibility, balance, and strength. Prop the book in front of your mat and let the full-color, step-by-step photography guide you through everything you need to know for an effective yoga practice. --From publisher description.

"A solid introduction or supplemental guide for men wishing to try yoga." Library Journal.

Reynolds, Gretchen

The **first** 20 minutes : surprising science reveals how we can exercise better, train smarter, live longer / Gretchen Reynolds. Hudson Street Press, c2012. xvii, 266 p. ; **613.7**

1. Exercise -- Physiological aspects 2. Physical education and training -- Physiological aspects 3. Physical fitness
ISBN 9781594630934

LC 2012000321

Includes index.

The New York Times 'Phys Ed' columnist counsels casual and serious exercisers on the latest understandings about the mental and physical aspects of a fitness program, sharing recommendations for current 'best practices' for a range of goals. BT.

Rountree, Sage Hamilton

The **professional** yoga teacher's handbook : the ultimate guide for current and aspiring instructors / Sage Rountree. The Experiment, 2020 x, 240 p. ; **613.7**

1. Yoga -- Study and teaching.
ISBN 9781615196975

LC 2020024420

Includes index.

"For yoga teachers at every stage of their careers, this is a how-to-teach guide from navigating client relationships and publicizing classes to avoiding burnout and financial planning. It's complete with journal prompts and thoughtful workbook exercisesto help aspiring yoga teachers learn their path and to help current teachers continue their education." Provided by publisher.

"This clear-cut guide will help readers approach yoga teaching with professionalism and passion." Publishers Weekly

Schuler, Lou

Strong : nine workout programs for women to burn fat, boost metabolism, and build strength for life / Lou Schuler and Alwyn Cosgrove. Avery, 2015. xviii, 285 p. : **613.7**

1. Exercise for women. 2. Weight training for women.
ISBN 9781583335758

LC 2015015248

"A groundbreaking strength and conditioning plan for women, from the authors of The New Rules of Lifting for Women".-- Provided by publisher.

"This book is thoughtful, precise, and well-geared to providing women of all ages and fitness backgrounds with the knowledge and tools necessary for building strength." Publishers Weekly.

Stanley, Jessamyn

Every body yoga : let go of fear, get on the mat, love your body / Jessamyn Stanley. Workman Publishing, 2017. ix, 222 p. : **613.7**

1. Hatha yoga. 2. Yoga. 3. Exercise. 4. Physical fitness.
ISBN 9780761193111

LC 2017009009

An internationally recognized, stereotype-shattering yogi welcomes people of all shapes and sizes to start practicing yoga with simple instructions for 50 basic yoga poses and 10 sequences and reinforces the idea that yoga is about how someone feels, not looks.

Starrett, Kelly

Becoming a supple leopard : the ultimate guide to resolving pain, preventing injury, and optimizing athletic performance / Kelly Starrett with Glen Cordoza. Victory Belt Pub., 2015. 400 p. : **613.7**

1. Exercise 2. Physical education and training 3. Sports injuries -- Prevention 4. Sports -- Physiological aspects
ISBN 9781628600834

LC bl2013015369

Offers more than two hundred techniques for improving athletic performance, treating body stiffness and achy joints, and rehabilitating injuries.

Ready to run : unlocking your potential to run naturally / Dr. Kelly Starrett with T.J. Murphy. Victory Belt Publishing, 2014. 288 p. : **613.7**

1. Running -- Training
ISBN 9781628600094

LC 2018420181

Includes index.

Are you ready to run? Is there a bridge from the injury-ridden world of the modern runner to the promised land that barefoot running and Born to Run have led us to believe exists? Can we run faster, longer, and more efficiently? Dr. Kelly Starrett has focused his movement and mobility philosophy on the injury-plagued world of running. Despite the promises of the growing minimalist-shoe industry and a rush of new ideas on how to transform running technique, more than three out of four runners suffer at least one injury per year. The harsh effects of too much sitting and too much time wearing the wrong shoes has left us shackled to lower back problems, chronic knee injuries, and debilitating foot pain. In this guide, you will learn the 12 standards that will prepare your body for a lifetime of top-performance running.

Taubes, Gary

Why we get fat and what to do about it / Gary Taubes. Alfred A. Knopf, 2011. xii, 257 p. : **613.7**

1. Low-carbohydrate diet 2. Obesity -- Etiology 3. Weight loss
ISBN 9780307272706

LC 2010034248

An award-winning science journalist reveals the role of certain carbohydrates in today's obesity epidemic while denouncing calorie-based nutritional practices, in a report that includes coverage of such topics as genetics, the politics behind nutritional guidelines and foods to eat and avoid.

"The author assures readers that overweight and obesity are not character flaws but a disorder of fat accumulation; most of the book deals with this issue in detail. This brave, paradigm-shifting man uses logic and the primary literature to unhinge the nutritional mantra of the last 80 years that an imbalance of calories in versus calories out leads to weight change." Choice.

Vonn, Lindsey

Strong is the new beautiful : embrace your natural beauty, eat clean, and harness your power / Lindsey Vonn and Sarah Toland. Dey St., an imprint of William Morrow, 2016 242 p. : **613.7**

1. Exercise for women 2. Nutrition 3. Physical fitness for women
ISBN 9780062400581

LC bl2016035911

A popular world champion, Olympic gold medalist skier and beauty icon provides lessons in strength, fitness, food and more.

"Vonn has created an inspiring narrative, along with a seductive means of getting healthy and fit." Publishers Weekly.

Wayne, Peter

The **Harvard** medical school guide to tai chi : 12 weeks to a healthy body, strong heart, and sharp mind / Peter M. Wayne, with Mark Fuerst. Shambhala, 2013. xiii, 336 p. : **613.7**

1. Health. 2. Tai chi -- Therapeutic use.
ISBN 9781590309421

LC 2012025187

Presents the basic principles of tai chi and provides instructions for integrating tai chi into everyday activities to improve health and well-being.

613.835 Cannabis

Dolce, Joe

Brave new weed : adventures into the uncharted world of cannabis / Joe Dolce. Harperwave, 2016 256 p. **613.835**

1. Cannabis. 2. Marijuana -- History. 3. Drug use -- Social aspects. 4. Recreational drugs.
ISBN 9780062499912

LC 2016288356

The former editor-in-chief of Details and Star adventures into the fascinating "brave new world" of cannabis, tracing its history and possible future as he investigates the social, medical, legal, and cultural ramifications of this surprisingly versatile plant.

613.85 Personal health and safety -- Substance abuse -- Tobacco

Fisher, Edwin B., 1946-

American Lung Association 7 steps to a smoke-free life / Edwin B. Fisher, Jr. with Toni L. Goldfarb. John Wiley, c1998. xi, 226 p. ; **613.85**

1. Smoking cessation.
ISBN 9780471247005

LC 97038826

Includes index.

Offers a seven-step program for kicking the smoking habit, with advice on coping with cravings, managing stress, and avoiding setbacks.

"Based on the American Lung Association's smoking cessation program, this book coaches smokers through discovering their own personal motivations and obstacles to quitting, planning effective strategies to meet and conquer the temptation to pick up a cigarette, and tailoring a cessation program to individual lifestyles." Library Journal.

613.9 Birth control, reproductive technology, sex hygiene, sexual techniques

Comfort, Alex, 1920-2000

The **joy** of sex / Alex Comfort, Susan Quilliam. Crown Publishers, c2008. 288 p. : **613.9**

1. Sex instruction 2. Sex customs
ISBN 9780307452030

LC 2008017531

Originally published: New York : Crown, 1972; 1st American ed. of revision originally published in Great Britain in 2008 by Mitchell Beazley.

An updated version of the guide first published in 1972 features updated text and illustrations and covers such topics as sexually transmitted diseases and achieving healthy intimacy.

Graham, Jessica, 1980-

Good sex : getting off without checking out / Jessica Graham. North Atlantic Books, 2017. 285 p. **613.9**

1. Sexuality 2. Self-discovery 3. Mindfulness (Psychology) 4. Meditation
ISBN 9781623172343

LC 2017036252

Jessica Graham demonstrates that a deep spiritual life and an extraordinary sex life are not mutually exclusive in this keenly personal and unflinchingly frank guide to finding mindfulness in sex without losing the fun and adventure. Not only a tool kit for creating a rich and deeply satisfying sex life, this playful, explicit, and transformative book conveys the deeper message of how combining meditation with sex can bring about profound spiritual awakenings.

Kerner, Ian

She comes first : the thinking man's guide to pleasuring a woman / Ian Kerner. ReganBooks, c2004. xii, 228 p. ; **613.9**

1. Female orgasm. 2. Oral sex. 3. Sex instruction for men.
ISBN 0060538252

LC 2004041787

A man's guide on how to enhance a woman's sexual experience through oral sex explains how to make cunnilingus a key part of an overall romantic relationship, outlining a system of intimate techniques designed to maximize female gratification.

"Dispelling the widely held myth of genital penetration as the apogee of sexual pleasure, Kerner, who holds a doctorate in clinical sexology, offers this witty, well-researched manual for 'consistently leading women to orgasm' through cunnilingus." Publishers Weekly.

Nagoski, Emily

Come as you are : the surprising new science that will transform your sex life / Emily Nagoski, Ph.D. Simon & Schuster Paperbacks, 2015 xi, 400 p. ; **613.9**

1. Sex instruction for women. 2. Sexual health. 3. Women -- Sexual behavior. 4. Women -- Health and hygiene.
ISBN 9781476762098

LC 2014017773

Drawing upon multiple research disciplines, a counselor at the Kinsey Institute describes the factors that affect a woman's sexual wellbeing, including stress, mood, trust and body image and explains how the complications of daily life can affect arousal and desire.

Weschler, Toni, 1955-

Taking charge of your fertility : the definitive guide to natural birth control, pregnancy achievement, and reproductive health / Toni Weschler, MPH. William Morrow, 2015 xxi, 536 p. : **613.9**

1. Natural family planning
ISBN 9780062326034

LC bl2015026782

"20th anniversary edition."

Offers a natural alternative to ineffective procedures and a biologically proven method of fertility control for avoiding or achieving pregnancy.

613.9071 Personal health and safety -- Birth control, reproductive technology, sex hygiene, sexual techniques -- Sex education--secondary level

Roffman, Deborah M.

Talk to me first : everything you need to know to become your kids' go-to person about sex / Deborah Roffman. Da Capo Lifelong, c2012. xii, 281 p. ; **613.9071**

1. Sex instruction for children. 2. Sex instruction for teenagers. 3. Sexual ethics for teenagers. 4. Parent and child.
ISBN 9780738215082

LC 2012006068

Informs parents on how to become a knowledgable and accessible authority for their children on sex, detailing education tips, talking-point suggestions for each age, and guidance on giving teenagers sexual freedom.

Smiler, Andrew P., 1965-

Dating and sex : a guide for the 21st century teen boy / Andrew P. Smiler, PhD. Magination Press, American Psychological Association, [2016] 288 p. : **613.9071**

1. Sex education for teenagers 2. Dating (Social customs) 3.

Sexuality 4. Interpersonal attraction
ISBN 9781433820458

LC 2015019582

Presents information about dating and sex for teenage boys, including such topics as puberty, asking someone out on a date, and sexual orientation.

Vernacchio, Al

For goodness sex : changing the way we talk to teens about sexuality, values, and health / Al Vernacchio, with Brooke Lea Foster. Harper, 2014 xiii, 254 p. ; **613.9071**

1. Sex instruction. 2. Sex instruction for teenagers. 3. Sexual ethics. 4. Teenagers -- Sexual behavior.
ISBN 9780062269515

LC 2014019134

A high school sexuality educator presents a new approach to sex education for parents and teens that challenges traditional teaching models and instead embraces 21st-century realities by promoting healthy sexuality, values and body image in young people, in a book that includes real-life examples from the classroom, exercises and quizzes.

614 Forensic medicine; incidence of injuries, wounds, disease; public preventive medicine

Balko, Radley

★The **cadaver** king and the country dentist : a true story of injustice in the American South / Radley Balko and Tucker Carrington. PublicAffairs, 2018 336 p. **614**

1. Hayne, Steven (Forensic pathologist). 2. West, Michael (Dentist). 3. Brooks, Levon, 1959- Trials, litigation, etc. 4. Brewer, Kennedy Trials, litigation, etc. 5. Criminal justice system. 6. Racism in the criminal justice system. 7. Judicial error. 8. Trials (Rape). 9. Mississippi
ISBN 9781610396912

LC 2017009508

Relates the stories of two innocent men who were wrongly accused and convicted of crimes due largely to the legally condoned failures perpetrated by invalid forensic science and institutional racism.

"Through the intensive scrutiny of how the men were speedily tried, convicted, and then released after years in prison, the authors uncover an unholy alliance of racist cops and prosecutors with questionable death investigations and misapplied forensics. This work should spark both admiration and outrageand, one hopes, reform." Booklist.

Bass, William M., 1928-

Death's acre : inside the legendary forensic lab the Body Farm where the dead do tell tales / Bill Bass and Jon Jefferson ; foreword by Patricia Cornwell. G. P. Putnam's Sons, 2003. xii, 304 p., 16 p. of plates : **614**

1. Forensic anthropology. 2. Crime laboratories 3. Dead -- Identification 4. Skeleton -- Identification 5. Tennessee.
ISBN 0399151346

LC 2003046908

Includes index.

Nowhere is there another lab like Dr. Bill Bass's: On a hillside in Tennessee, human bodies decompose in the open air, aided by insects, bacteria and birds, unhindered by coffins or mausoleums. At the "Body Farm," nature takes its course, with corpses buried in shallow graves, submerged in water, concealed beneath slabs of concrete, locked in trunks of cars. As stand-ins for murder victims, they serve the needs of science -- and the cause of justice.

"The author explains the process of decomposition and how bones give clues to identify: approximate age, sex, height, and race, all of which are needed to bring the forensic scientist one step closer to putting a name to a corpse. He describes some of the cases he has been involved with and laughs at himself when he shares stories of mistakes and assumptions. Young adults will gain insight into the forensic process and appreciate Bass's dedication to the truth and his work." School Library Journal.

Blum, Deborah, 1954-

The **poisoner's** handbook : murder and the birth of forensic medicine in jazz age New York / Deborah Blum. Penguin Press, 2010. 336 p. **614**

1. Poisoning. 2. Forensic sciences. 3. Forensic medicine. 4. Forensic toxicology. 5. New York (State) -- History -- 20th century
ISBN 9781594202438

LC 2009026461

Chronicles the story of New York City's first forensic scientists to describe Jazz Age poisoning cases, including a family's inexplicable balding, Barnum and Bailey's Blue Man, and the crumbling bones of factory workers.

"Blum effectively balances the fast-moving detective story with a clear view of the scientific advances that her protagonists brought to the field. Caviar for true-crime fans and science buffs alike." Kirkus.

Maples, William R., died 1997

Dead men do tell tales / William R. Maples and Michael Browning. Doubleday, 1994. 292 p., [32] p. of plates : **614**

1. Maples, William R., died 1997 2. Physical anthropologists. 3. Physical anthropology. 4. Forensic anthropology -- United States.
ISBN 0385474903

LC 94012290

Includes index.

While explaining the behavior of maggots and the biology of putrefaction a forensic anthropologist recounts his strangest and most horrifying criminal cases, from puzzles of dismemberment to the revelation of the identity of long-buried skeletons.

614.4 Incidence of and public measures to prevent disease

Biss, Eula

★**On** immunity : an inoculation / Eula Biss. Graywolf Press, 2014. 192 p. **614.4**

1. Immunization 2. Vaccination 3. Communities 4. Diseases
ISBN 9781555976897

LC bl2014041482

"Artfully mixing motherhood, myth, maladies, and metaphors into her presentation, Biss transcends medical science and trepidation." Booklist.

Honigsbaum, Mark

The **pandemic** century : one hundred years of panic, hysteria, and hubris / Mark Honigsbaum. W. W. Norton & Company, [2019] 448 p. ; **614.4**

1. Epidemics. 2. Diseases. 3. Epidemiology. 4. Communicable diseases.
ISBN 9780393254754

LC 2018048424

Chronicles the last century of scientific struggle against deadly contagious disease--from the 1918 Spanish influenza pandemic to the recent

SARS, Ebola and Zika epidemics--examining related epidemiological mysteries and the role of disease in exacerbating world conflicts.

Kohn, George C.

Encyclopedia of plague and pestilence : from ancient times to the present / George Childs Kohn, editor. Facts On File, c2008. xiv, 529 p. : **614.4**

1. Epidemics -- History -- Encyclopedias.

ISBN 9780816069354

LC 2006041296

Articles document major, outstanding, and unusual epidemics throughout the world from the dawn of history to the present, describing how the epidemics started and spread, who was affected, and the eventual outcome.

Kinch, Michael S.

Between hope and fear : a history of vaccines and human immunity / Michael Kinch. Pegasus Books, 2018. 360 p. **614.4**

1. Vaccines 2. Communicable diseases 3. Epidemics 4. Vaccination -- History

ISBN 9781681777511

LC bl2018080363

The author of A Prescription for Change presents an informed examination of the science of immunity, the public policy implications of vaccine denial and the real-world outcomes of failing to vaccinate.

"Kinch (radiation oncology, Washington Univ.; director, Ctr. for Research Innovation in Business; Prescription for Change), ostensibly writing to refute the dangerous rise of antivaccinators, provides readers with an interdisciplinary cornucopia of meticulously researched information on the intersection of history, disease, and vaccine invention." Library Journal.

McNeill, William Hardy, 1917-2016

Plagues and peoples / William H. McNeill. Anchor Press, 1976. viii, 369 p. : **614.4**

1. Plague -- History. 2. Epidemics -- History. 3. Diseases -- Social aspects. 4. Smallpox -- History.

ISBN 9780385112567

Includes index.

New edition released in 2008 by Paw Prints Media.

"Upon its original publication, Plagues and Peoples was an immediate critical and popular success, offering a radically new interpretation of world history as seen through the extraordinary impact--political, demographic, ecological, and psychological--of disease on cultures. From the conquest of Mexico by smallpox as much as by the Spanish, to the bubonic plague in China, to the typhoid epidemic in Europe, the history of disease is the history of humankind. With the identification of AIDS in the early 1980s, another chapter has been added to this chronicle of events, which William McNeill explores in his new introduction to this updated editon." --Provided by publisher.

Quammen, David, 1948-

★**Spillover** : animal infections and the next human pandemic / David Quammen. W.W. Norton & Co., c2012. 587 p. ; **614.4**

1. Epidemics 2. Communicable diseases 3. Public health 4. Ebola virus disease

ISBN 9780393066807

Andrew Carnegie Medal for Excellence in Non-Fiction finalist, 2013.

National Book Critics Circle Award for Nonfiction finalist, 2012.

"A wonderful, eye-opening account of humans versus disease that deserves to share the shelf with such classics as Microbe Hunters and Rats, Lice and History." Kirkus.

Quick, Jonathan D.

The **end** of epidemics : the looming threat to humanity and how to stop it / Jonathan D. Quick, with Bronwyn Fryer. St. Martin's Press, 2018. 304 p. ; **614.4**

1. Epidemics 2. Communicable diseases 3. Public health 4. Emergency planning

ISBN 9781250117779

LC 2017037542

A Harvard Medical School instructor and chair of the Global Health Council outlines recommendations for preventing the next global pandemic, drawing on the examples of epidemics ranging from smallpox and AIDS to SARS and Ebola to outline specific measures for appropriate spending, communication and innovation.

Senthilingam, Meera

Outbreaks and epidemics : battling infection from measles to coronavirus / Meera Senthilingam. Icon Books, 2020 176 p. **614.4**

1. Epidemics -- History. 2. Plague -- History. 3. Diseases. 4. Communicable diseases.

ISBN 9781785785634

A journey through the history and science of epidemics and pandemics--from measles to coronavirus.

"Of considerable interest to anyone who wishes to learn about infections, how they spread, and how they are managed. Required reading for anyone new to learning about issues of public health." Library Journal

614.5 Incidence of and public measures to prevent specific diseases and kinds of diseases

Allen, Arthur, 1959-

★The **fantastic** laboratory of Dr. Weigl : how two brave scientists battled typhus and sabotaged the Nazis / Arthur Allen. W.W. Norton & Company, 2014 352 p. **614.5**

1. Weigl, Rudolf, 1883-1957. 2. Fleck, Ludwik, 1896-1961. 3. World War II 4. Resistance to military occupation 5. Anti-Nazi movement -- Poland. 6. Scientists -- Poland. 7. Poland

ISBN 9780393081015

LC 2014003246

Describes the true story of how the eccentric Polish scientist tasked by the Nazis to create a typhus vaccine hid the intelligentsia from the Gestapo by hiring them to work in his laboratory.

"Allen is unflinching in his retelling of this monstrous era, but he manages to avoid writing a depressing narrative. Instead, Weigl, Fleck and their vaccines illuminate the inherent social complexities of science and truth and reinforce the overriding good of man." Kirkus.

Barry, John M., 1947-

★The **great** influenza : the epic story of the deadliest plague in history / John M. Barry. Viking, 2004. 546 p. : **614.5**

1. Influenza Epidemic, 1918-1919 2. Plague -- History. 3. Influenza -- Prevention. 4. Vaccines.

ISBN 0670894737

LC 2003057646

National Academies Communication Award, 2005.

An in-depth account of the deadly influenza epidemic of 1918, a plague that took the lives of millions of people around the world, examines the causes of the pandemic, its devastating impact on early twentieth-century society, the researchers who risked their lives to confront the disease, and the lasting implications of the crisis and the scientific discoveries that resulted.

Cantor, Norman F.

In the wake of the plague : the Black death and the world it made / Norman F. Cantor. Harper Collins Perennial, 2002, c2001. 245 p. : **614.5**

1. Black Death -- History. 2. Plague -- History. 3. Civilization, Medieval.

ISBN 9780060014346

LC 2001051819

Originally published: New York : Free Press, 2001.

Through profiles of merchants, peasants, priests, and kings, argues that despite devastation, the Black Death resulted in a scientific revoltuion, a new wave of art, and the emergence of independent farmers.

"By animating history and demonstrating our times' connections to even as remote an event as the Black Death, Cantor's erudite excursion proves most engrossing." Booklist.

Crosby, Molly Caldwell

The **American** plague : the untold story of yellow fever, the epidemic that shaped our history / Molly Caldwell Crosby. Berkley Books, 2006. viii, 308 p., 16 p. of plates : **614.5**

1. Yellow fever -- History. 2. Epidemics. 3. Medicine. 4. Yellow fever -- Memphis, Tennessee -- History. 5. Memphis, Tennessee -- History. 6. United States -- History.

ISBN 0425212025

LC 2006050497

Map on lining papers.

Traces the impact on American history of yellow fever from the mid-seventeenth century onward, examining in particular the near-destruction of Memphis from the disease and the efforts of four men to combat the deadly scourge.

"The author offers a forceful narrative of a disease's ravages and the quest to find its cause and cure." Publishers Weekly.

Farmer, Paul, 1959-

★ **Fevers,** feuds, and diamonds : Ebola and the ravages of history / Paul Farmer. Farrar, Straus and Giroux, 2020. 688 p. **614.5**

1. Ebola virus disease 2. Epidemics. 3. Humanitarian assistance 4. Injustice 5. Africa -- Social conditions

ISBN 9780374234324

LC 2020027255

The Harvard University global-health authority documents the 2014 Ebola crisis and the stories of victims and first responders while revealing the centuries of exploitation, injustice and state failures that rendered it history's worst outbreak.

Holt, Nathalia, 1980-

Cured : how the Berlin patients defeated HIV and forever changed medical science / Nathalia Holt. Dutton, published by the Penguin Group, 2014. 368 p. **614.5**

1. World health. 2. People with HIV 3. Gene therapy. 4. HIV (Viruses)

ISBN 9780525953920

LC 2013037181

An award-winning research scientist and HIV fellow at the Ragon Institute reveals the science behind the discovery of a potential cure for HIV, tracing the groundbreaking contributions of the two Berlin patients and how their cases have influenced HIV researchers throughout the world.

"[I]n this accessible and fascinating account, Holt...juggles genetic mysteries, research perils, the agonies of these two reserved and sensitive men diagnosed with what was considered a death sentence, and the dogged doctors who successfully treated them during the later stages of AIDS epidemic." Publishers Weekly.

Johnson, Steven, 1968-

The **ghost** map : the story of London's deadliest epidemic--and how it changed the way we think about disease, cities, science, and the modern world / Steven Johnson. Riverhead Books, 2006. 299 p. : **614.5**

1. Cholera -- London, England -- History -- 19th century. 2. Epidemics -- History. 3. Communicable diseases. 4. Diseases -- Causes. 5. London, England -- History -- 19th century.

ISBN 9781594489259

LC 2006023114

A thrilling historical account of the worst cholera outbreak in Victorian London--and a brilliant exploration of how Dr. John Snow's solution revolutionized the way we think about disease, cities, science, and the modern world. The ghost map is an endlessly compelling and utterly gripping account of that London summer of 1854, from the microbial level to the macro-urban-theory level--including, most important, the human level.

"From Snow's discovery of patient zero to Johnson's compelling argument for and celebration of cities, this makes for an illuminating and satisfying read." Publishers Weekly.

Kelly, John, 1945-

The **great** mortality : an intimate history of the Black Death, the most devastating plague of all time / John Kelly. HarperCollins Publishers, 2005. xvii, 304 p. : **614.5**

1. Black Death -- History. 2. Plague -- Europe. 3. Epidemics 4. Floods 5. Europe -- History -- 14th century 6. Asia -- History -- 14th century

ISBN 9780060006921

LC 2004054213

Chronicles the Great Plague that devastated Asia and Europe in the fourteenth century, documenting the experiences of people who lived during its height while describing the decline of moral boundaries that also marked the period.

"Western Europe is the primary focus of Kelly's compact history, which is intimate in that it highlights many particular persons' passages through the crucible years, 1348-49. Kelly proceeds chronologically, beginning with the plague's prehistory in north central Asia and its spread through China before empire-building Mongols brought it west. This sweeping, viscerally exciting book contributes to a literature of perpetual fascination: the chronicles of pestilence." Booklist.

Kolata, Gina Bari, 1948-

★ **Flu** : the story of the great influenza pandemic of 1918 and the search for the virus that caused it / Gina Kolata. Farrar, Straus and Giroux, 1999. xi, 330 p. : **614.5**

1. Influenza Epidemic, 1918-1919. 2. Influenza -- History -- 20th century. 3. Epidemics -- History. 4. Virus diseases -- History.

ISBN 9780374157067

LC 99039665

Describes the great flu epidemic of 1918, an outbreak that killed some forty million people worldwide, and discusses the efforts of scientists and public health officials to understand and prevent another lethal pandemic.

"Clearly explaining both the science and the social toll of the pandemic, Kolata writes an admirable history and soberly spells out how the U.S. government is preparedor unpreparedfor a similar public health threat today." Publishers Weekly.

Oshinsky, David M., 1944-

★**Polio** : an American story / David M. Oshinsky. Oxford University Press, 2005. 342, 16 p. of plates : **614.5**

1. Salk, Jonas, 1914-1995. 2. March of Dimes. 3. Vaccines. 4. Viruses -- History. 5. Poliomyelitis -- United States -- History.

ISBN 0195152948

LC 2004025249

Pulitzer Prize for History, 2006.

This comprehensive and gripping narrative covers all the challenges, characters, and controversies in America's relentless struggle against polio. Funded by philanthropy and grassroots contributions, Salk's killed-virus vaccine (1954) and Sabin's live-virus vaccine (1961) began to eradicate this dreaded disease.

"This book is a rich and illuminating analysis that convincingly grounds the ways and means of modern American research in the response to polio." New York Times Book Review.

Preston, Richard, 1954-

Crisis in the red zone : the story of the deadliest Ebola outbreak in history, and of the outbreaks to come / Richard Preston. Random House, [2019] 384 p. ; **614.5**

1. Ebola virus disease 2. Epidemics 3. Epidemics 4. Public health 5. West Africa 6. Africa -- Social conditions

ISBN 9780812998832

LC 2019010492

Chronicles the 2013-2014 Ebola outbreak in West Africa and the global efforts of health professionals to contain the virus, and provides an urgent wake-up call about the future of emerging viruses.

"Medical thriller, cautionary tale, and a public health call-to-arms are all bundled together in this powerful read." Booklist.

The **hot** zone / Richard Preston. Random House, 1994. xiii, 300 p. : Dark biology ; **614.5**

1. Ebola virus disease -- Reston, Virginia. 2. Diseases. 3. Epidemics. 4. Viruses.

ISBN 0679430946

LC 94013415

Volumes 1 and 3 of this series are nonfiction titles, while volume 2 is a fictional novel.

A highly infectious, deadly virus from the central African rain forest suddenly appears in the suburbs of Washington, D.C. There is no cure. In a few days 90 percent of its victims are dead. A secret military SWAT team of soldiers and scientists is mobilized to stop the outbreak of this exotic "hot" virus. The Hot Zone tells this dramatic story, giving a hair-raising account of the appearance of rare and lethal viruses and their "crashes" into the human race...

"Ebola, a lethal virus that slumbers in an unknown host somewhere in the rain forest, sneaked into the United States in 1989 in a shipment of primates that ended up in a monkey house in Reston, Virginia. This virus jumps between species easily, and takes only weeks to kill its victim, with gory hemorrhaging from various orifices. Preston tells the suspenseful tale of its detection, and gives vivid life to the members of the SWAT team that, for eighteen bio-hazardous days, combatted the strain now known as Ebola Reston." The New Yorker.

Quammen, David, 1948-

Ebola : the natural and human history of a deadly virus / David Quammen. W.W. Norton & Company, [2014] 128 p. **614.5**

1. Ebola virus disease 2. Epidemics 3. Communicable diseases 4. Public health

ISBN 9780393351552

LC 2014038144

Extracted, but with updated and additional material from: Spillover : animal infections and the next human pandemic / David Quammen. c2012.

"This book will appeal to a wide range of readers. Those who have not previously read Spillover but want to learn more about Ebola will find much to interest them here. Summing Up: Recommended. All levels/libraries." Choice.

Spinney, Laura

★**Pale** rider : the Spanish Flu of 1918 and how it changed the world / Laura Spinney. PublicAffairs, 2017. viii, 332 p. : **614.5**

1. Influenza Epidemic, 1918-1919 2. Influenza 3. Epidemics 4. Sick persons

ISBN 9781610397674

LC 2017933356

Describes the enormous-scale human disaster caused by the 1918 Spanish Flu and uses the latest findings in history, virology, epidemiology, psychology and economics to show how the pandemic permanently changed global politics, race relations, medicine, religion and the arts.

"A compelling, expert account of a half-forgotten historical catastrophe." Kirkus.

Tayman, John

The **colony** : the harrowing true story of the exiles of Molokai / John Tayman. Scribner, c2006. vi, 421 p. : **614.5**

1. Kalaupapa Leper Settlement, Molokai. 2. Segregation. 3. People with leprosy 4. Leprosy -- Hawaii 5. Human experimentation in medicine. 6. Molokai, Hawaii -- History -- 19th century 7. United States -- Social conditions -- 19th century.

ISBN 9780743233002

LC 2005047767

"A Lisa Drew book."

Reveals the untold history of the infamous American leprosy colony on Molokai and the extraordinary people who struggled to survive under the most horrific circumstances. Tracked by bounty hunters and torn screaming from their families, the luckless were loaded into shipboard cattle stalls and abandoned in a lawless place where brutality held sway. Many did not have leprosy, and most of those who did were not contagoius, yet all were caught in a shared nightmare. The colony had little food, little medicine, and very little hope. Exile continued for more than a century, the longest and deadliest instance of medical segregation in American history. Nearly 9,000 people were banished to the colony, trapped by pounding surf and armed guards and the highest sea cliffs in the world. Twenty-eight live there still.

"This is a history of the leper colony at the Hawaiian island Molokai. Tayman's crisp, flowing writing and inclusion of personal stories and details make this an utterly engrossing look at a heartbreaking chapter in Hawaiian history." Booklist.

Wadman, Meredith

The **vaccine** race : science, politics, and the human costs of defeating disease / Meredith Wadman. Viking, 2017 400 p. ; **614.5**

1. Vaccination -- History. 2. Communicable diseases -- Prevention -- History. 3. Vaccines. 4. Human experimentation in medicine.

ISBN 9780525427537

LC 2016044189

Longlisted for the Andrew Carnegie Medal for Excellence in Non-Fiction, 2018.

Documents the controversial story of the development of the first widely used normal human cell line, paving the way for some of the world's most important vaccines, against a backdrop of the devastating rubella epidemic of the mid-1960s.

Wasik, Bill

Rabid : a cultural history of the world's most diabolical virus / Bill Wasik and Monica Murphy. Viking, 2012. 240 p. **614.5**

1. Rabies -- Epidemiology -- History. 2. Diseases. 3. Animals as carriers of disease. 4. Rabies -- Treatment -- History.
ISBN 9780670023738

LC 2011043903

Includes index.

Charts the history, science and cultural mythology of rabies, documenting how before its vaccine the disease caused fatal brain infections and sparked the creations of famous monsters including werewolves, vampires and zombies.

615.1 Pharmacology and therapeutics -- Drugs

Goldacre, Ben

Bad pharma : how drug companies mislead doctors and harm patients / Ben Goldacre. Faber and Faber, Inc., an affiliate of Farrar, Straus and Giroux, 2013, c2012. 240 p. **615.1**

1. Drugs -- Testing. 2. Science -- Moral and ethical aspects. 3. Drug industry and trade -- Corrupt practices. 4. Pharmaceutical research -- Corrupt practices.
ISBN 9780865478008

LC 2012038902

Originally published: London : Fourth Estate, 2012.

Argues that doctors are deliberately misinformed by profit-seeking pharmaceutical companies that casually withhold information about drug efficacy and side effects, explaining the process of pharmaceutical data manipulation and its global consequences. By the best-selling author of Bad Science.

PDR Network, LLC,

PDR for nonprescription drugs PDR Network, LLC, 2013. 360 p., 74 p., 31 p. ; **615.1**

1. Drugs, Nonprescription -- Handbooks, manuals, etc.
ISBN 9781563638275

LC bl2014002023

Includes indexes.

The 35th edition of PDR for Nonprescription Drugs is the most comprehensive and valuable to date. The 2014 book offers an updated guide to hundreds of the most commonly used OTC medications, including analgesics, cough and cold preparations, fever reducers, allergy medications, and more. Organized for easy use, PDR for Nonprescription Drugs offers comprehensive drug information such as usage, dosage, warnings and precautions, side effects, ingredients, and more. --From publisher description.

615.3 Pharmacology and therapeutics -- Organic drugs

Chevallier, Andrew

Encyclopedia of herbal medicine : 550 Herbs and Remedies for Common Ailments / Andrew Chevallier, FNIMH. DK, 2016. 336 p. : **615.3**

1. Materia medica, Vegetable 2. Medicinal plants
ISBN 9781465449818

LC bl2016021377

Provides an herb directory with photographic index, guidelines for growing medicinal plants and making home remedies, and historical and cultural perspectives for herbal medicine around the world.

"Though this selection should not be used as a medical reference on its own, it goes into enough depth for average readers looking for home remedies." Library Journal.

Davidson, Tish

The **vaccine** debate / Tish Davidson. Greenwood, 2019 xii, 236 p. : **615.3**

ISBN 9781440843532

LC 2018030122

Providing accurate, accessible information on vaccines and the controversies that surround them, this book outlines the history of vaccine regulation and interactions between vaccines and the immune system, and thoughtfully considers each vaccine debate. --From publisher description.

"This is an excellent resource for public, consumer-health, and school libraries." Booklist.

Pursell, J. J., 1973-

The **herbal** apothecary : 100 medicinal herbs and how to use them / JJ Pursell ; with photos by Shawn Linehan. Timber Press, 2015. 292 p. : **615.3**

1. Herbs -- Therapeutic use 2. Materia medica, Vegetable
ISBN 9781604696622

LC 2015009786

A guide to more than one hundred healing plants, with information on medicinal uses, identification and cultivation, benefits, and side effects, includes instructions for formulating a variety of herbal blends and remedies.

"It is not a quick read, but will quickly become indispensable for understanding a neglected field that is ripe with great benefits." Publishers Weekly.

615.5 Therapeutics

Bland, Jeffrey, 1946-

The **disease** delusion : conquering the causes of chronic illness for a healthier, longer, and happier life / Dr. Jeffrey S. Bland. HarperWave, 2014 xiii, 409 p. : **615.5**

1. Functional medicine 2. Holistic medicine
ISBN 9780062290731

LC bl2014013853

A biochemist and pioneer in naturopathic medicine introduces the concept of functional medicine, discussing the reasons for a host of ailments and offering achievable, science-based solutions that can alleviate chronic illness.

Borins, Mel

A **doctor's** guide to alternative medicine : what works, what doesn't, and why / Mel Borins, MD, FCFP ; foreword by Dr. Bernie Siegel ; with contributions by Heather Boon, BScPhm, Phd, Carol Chan, BScPhm, ACPR, RPh, Jennifer Fink, MD, Scott Forman, MD, Jason Mackie, BSc, Linda Rapson, MD, Cherry Tanega, BSc, Cheryl Tyler, BScPhm. Lyons Press,,

2014 xx, 314 p. ; **615.5**

1. Alternative medicine
ISBN 9781493005956

LC 2014015122

"In the United States alone, more than 38 percent of people use Alternative Medicine to treat and prevent medical issues and more than 50 percent of people have tried Alternative Medicine at some point in their life. But because some people don't feel their doctors see those methods as legitimate, patients often turn to unreliable sources such as the internet, celebrities, etc. for guidance. With so much misinformation out there, how does anyone know which advice to follow and what actually works? In this book, Dr. Mel Borins answers these questions using the latest scientific research and double-blind studies to educate patients and physicians alike on which alternative treatments work, which don't, and why. And more importantly, it teaches them how to safely use these alternative treatments, as a reputable source of information to supplement their conventional medicine treatments. Written in clear, accessible language for the layperson while providing citations to full studies for the medical professional, the book covers traditional healing and herbal remedies, physical therapies, psychological therapies, and natural health products--making it perfect for alternative medicine skeptics looking for hard evidence, doctors of conventional medicine seeking to understand why alternative therapies work, and for those open to alternative medicine but who want to understand the benefits and dangers; these include America's 78 million Baby Boomers who purchase 77 percent of all prescriptions drugs and are seeking ways to treat their health issues without causing more of them. "-- Provided by publisher.

Low Dog, Tieraona

Healthy at home : get well and stay well without prescriptions / Tieraona Low Dog, M.D. National Geographic, 2014 335 p. ; **615.5**

1. Naturopathy. 2. Nutritional therapy 3. Self-care, Health.
ISBN 9781426212581

LC 2013034581

Includes index.

An internationally respected doctor and expert in herbal medicine and dietary supplements outlines recommendations for identifying, responding to and caring for common ailments using herbal remedies, offering complementary advice on when it is better to consult a health-care professional instead.

"Accessible and reliable, this title will appeal to readers interested in alternative medicine and those who enjoyed the authors other books (Life Is Your Best Medicine: A Womans Guide to Health, Healing, and Wholeness at Every Age; National Geographic Guide to Medicinal Herbs: The Worlds Most Effective Healing Plants). Recommended." Library Journal.

Murray, Michael T.

The **encyclopedia** of natural medicine / Michael T. Murray, Joseph E. Pizzorno. Atria Books, c2012. x, 1219 p. : **615.5**

1. Naturopathy -- Encyclopedias.
ISBN 9781451687347

LC 2012023268

Features up-to-date coverage of holistic remedies for more than eighty common ailments, drawing on research in naturopathy to provide recommendations for topics ranging from prevention and safety to herbs and supplements.

Offit, Paul A.

★**Do** you believe in magic? : the sense and nonsense of alternative medicine / Paul A. Offit. Harper, 2013 x, 322 p. **615.5**

1. Alternative medicine. 2. Natural healing 3. Drug industry and trade 4. Medicine
ISBN 9780062222961

LC bl2013029279

Using dramatic real-life stories, the Chief of the Division of Infectious Diseases at Children's Hospital of Philadelphia presents a scathing exposé of the alternative medicine industry that debunks the treatments that don't work and takes on the media celebrities who promote alternative medicine.

"This excellent, easy-to-read look at the alternative-medicine industry is highly recommended." Library Journal.

The **Gale** encyclopedia of alternative medicine Gale, a Cengage Company, 2019 3,217 p. **615.5**

1. Alternative medicine
ISBN 9781410394279

LC 2019028693

"Provides alternative medical information about complementary therapies, herbs and remedies, and common medical disease and conditions. Minimizes medical jargon, using language that any reader can understand while still providing thorough coverage of each topic".--Provided by publisher.

615.7 Pharmacokinetics

Backes, Michael

Cannabis pharmacy : a practical guide to medical marijuana / Michael Backes. Black Dog & Leventhal Publishers, 2014 272 p. : **615.7**

1. Medical marijuana
ISBN 9781579129514

LC bl2014040100

Introduces the use of medical marijuana, offering information on the effects of the drug on the body, practical ways of using it medicinally, notes on distinct marijuana varieties and their properties, and an overview of conditions treated by marijuana.

"Suitable as an at-home reader for patients (and their families) considering medicinal marijuana as a treatment option." Library Journal.

Blaser, Martin J.

★**Missing** microbes : how the overuse of antibiotics is fueling our modern plagues / Dr. Martin Blaser. Henry Holt and Company, 2014 288 p. **615.7**

1. Antibiotics. 2. Drug resistance in microorganisms. 3. Diseases.
ISBN 9780805098105

LC 2013042578

Includes index.

A critically important and startling look at the harmful effects of overusing antibiotics, from the field's leading expert. Tracing one scientist's journey toward understanding the crucial importance of the microbiome, this revolutionary book will take readers to the forefront of trail-blazing research while revealing the damage that overuse of antibiotics is doing to our health: contributing to the rise of obesity, asthma, diabetes, and certain forms of cancer. In Missing Microbes, Dr. Martin Blaser invites us into the wilds of the human microbiome where for hundreds of thousands of years bacterial and human cells have existed in a peaceful symbiosis that is responsible for the health and equilibrium of our body. Now, this invisible eden is being irrevocably damaged by some of our most revered medical advances--antibiotics--threatening the extinction of our irreplaceable microbes with terrible health consequences.

"A masterful work of preventive health and superb science writing." Booklist.

Kramer, Peter D.

★**Ordinarily** well : the case for antidepressants / Peter D. Kramer. Farrar, Straus and Giroux, 2016. 336 p. **615.7**

1. Antidepressants -- History. 2. Psychotropic drugs. 3. Depression 4. Mental health

ISBN 9780374280673

LC 2015036472

Includes index.

"An eminent psychologist and writer discusses the value of antidepressant drugs".-- Provided by publisher.

"Kramer (Listening to Prozac), a psychiatrist and professor at Brown Medical School, makes an energetic and personal case for the role of antidepressants in easing crippling depression. Starting with the history of psychotherapy, when infinite patience was the norm in treatment for depression, Kramer delves into the breakthrough use of imipramine for treatment in the mid-1950s that helped redefine the disorder and invigorate psychopharmacology. Kramer shows that the tools may be imperfect, but people battling severe depression are lucky to have them." Publishers Weekly.

Pollan, Michael

★**How** to change your mind : what the new science of psychedelics teaches us about consciousness, dying, addiction, depression, and transcendence / Michael Pollan. Penguin, 2018. 496 p. **615.7**

1. Drug use 2. Altered states of consciousness 3. Medical research 4. Psychedelic experience

ISBN 9781594204227

LC 2018006190

The best-selling author of The Omnivore's Dilemma presents a groundbreaking investigation into the medical and scientific revolution currently taking place in the field of psychedelic drugs, drawing on a range of experiences to trace the criminalization of such substances as LSD and psychedelic mushrooms and how they may offer treatment options for difficult health challenges.

"This nuanced and sophisticated exploration, which asks big questions about meaning-making and spiritual experience, is thought-provoking and eminently readable." Publishers Weekly.

Rosen, William, 1955-

Miracle cure : the creation of antibiotics and the birth of modern medicine / William Rosen. Viking Press, 2017. 368 p. **615.7**

1. Antibiotics 2. Communicable diseases 3. Inventions 4. Bacteria

ISBN 9780525428107

LC 2016029488

Describes the history of the discovery of antibiotics, including the eccentric characters whose false starts and lucky accidents led to humans having much greater control over the microbes that resulted in previously deadly infections.

"An encyclopedic reference for researchers and practitioners but also accessible for general readers due to Rosen's lively depiction of the people, places, and politics that color the history of the fight against infectious disease." Kirkus.

Slater, Lauren

Blue dreams : the science and the story of the drugs that changed our minds / Lauren Slater. Little Brown & Co 2018 368 p. **615.7**

1. Psychotropic drugs 2. Drug industry and trade 3. Pharmaceutical research 4. Science

ISBN 9780316370646

LC bl2018004078

Explores the discovery, invention, science and people behind today's major psychotropic drugs, from the earliest, Thorazine and Lithium, to Prozac, Ecstasy, "magic mushrooms" and through today's most cutting-edge memory drugs and neural implants.

615.8 Specific therapies and kinds of therapies

Brock, Pope

Charlatan : America's most dangerous huckster, the man who pursued him, and the age of flimflam / Pope Brock. Crown Publishers, 2008. 336 p. **615.8**

1. Brinkley, John Richard, 1885-1942. 2. Fishbein, Morris, 1889-1976. 3. Quacks and quackery -- History. 4. Deception in men. 5. Impostors 6. Swindlers and swindling. 7. Kansas

ISBN 0307339882

LC 2007010074

Tells the story of the little-known Dr. John Brinkley and his unquenchable thirst for fame and fortune and Morris Fishbein, a quackbuster extraordinaire who relentlessly pursued the greatest charlatan of the 1920s and 1930s.

"Presentation is everything in telling this elaborate, many-faceted story. And Mr. Brock's has three outstanding virtues. First of all, he has a terrific ear for singling out quotations. Second, he is selective. This fast-moving, light-stepping book takes care not to throw in extraneous detail. Third, his own voice is wry enough to compete with the actual Brinkley material, which is saying a great deal." New York Times.

Chopra, Deepak

The **healing** self : a revolutionary new plan to supercharge your immunity and stay well for life / Deepak Chopra, M.D. and Rudolph E. Tanzi, Ph.D.. Harmony Books, 2018 290 p. ; **615.8**

1. Integrative medicine 2. Mind and body therapies

ISBN 9780451495525

LC 2017030783

"Combining the best current medical knowledge with a new approach grounded in integrative medicine, Chopra and Tanzi offer a groundbreaking new model of healing and the healing system, one of the main mysteries in the mind-body connection".-- Provided by publisher.

Louv, Richard

Our wild calling : how connecting with animals can transform our lives; and save theirs / Richard Louv. Algonquin Books of Chapel Hill, 2019. 288 p. **615.8**

1. Human-animal relationships. 2. Animals -- Therapeutic use. 3. Human-animal communication. 4. Nature -- Psychological aspects.

ISBN 9781616205607

LC 2019019787

The bestselling author of the landmark work Last Child in the Woods now shows how cultivating the powerful, mysterious, and fragile bond between humans and other animals can improve our mental, physical, and spiritual health, protect our planet, and serve as an antidote to the loneliness of our species.

Quest, Penelope

Reiki for life : the complete guide to reiki practice for levels 1, 2 & 3 / Penelope Quest. Jeremy P. Tarcher/Penguin, 2010. x,

310 p. ; **615.8**
1. Reiki (Healing system)
ISBN 9781585427901
LC 2009051213
Originally published: London : Piatkus, 2002.
Provides information about the healing art of Reiki, covering such subjects as basic routines, special techniques, and Reiki's use in spiritual growth.
"A definitive manual on the use and possibilities of the healing energies of reiki. An instant classic." Library Journal.

Taylor, Madisyn
Unmedicated : the four pillars of natural wellness / Madisyn Taylor. Beyond Words, 2018. xxxviii, 165 p. **615.8**
1. Mind and body therapies -- Methodology 2. Depression, Mental -- Alternative treatment 3. Anxiety disorders -- Alternative treatment
ISBN 9781582706573
LC 2018170141
"The cofounder of the holistic lifestyle website DailyOM presents a gentle and accessible step-by-step guide to moving from excessive reliance on medications to fundamentally healing yourself through four pillars of natural wellness. Madisyn Taylor was plagued by depression and anxiety, suffering from chronic physical problems that left her desperate for solutions. Spending decades searching for answers, she first turned to the medical community, which put her on a rollercoaster course of numerous doctors, tests, and an unhealthy reliance on medications that left her numb and lifeless. With her happiness and future on the line, she then made the decision to become unmedicated, reaching out to the natural, holistic health realm. And after years of practice and research, Madisyn developed an integrative wellness program that put her back in the driver's seat of her health, and ultimately, her life. Unmedicated is her thoughtful account of how she broke free from binding mental chains and physical ailments to be happy, healthy, and productive; it is also a guide for you to apply her practical techniques to your own healing journey. Madisyn offers a daily program of easy-to-follow actions based on four pillars that will build a lifelong foundation for health: clear your mind; strengthen your body; nurture your spirit; and find your tribe. Whether you want to be happy and stay happy, find relief from depression and anxiety, or heal and create a healthy change, Unmedicated is a gentle, compassionate, and achievable path that empowers you to take back your life and live fully".-- Provided by publisher.
"Taylor . shares her story of her own overreliance on medications that numbed her to her full potential in this instructive take on holistic medicine." Publishers Weekly.

616 Diseases

Biddle, Wayne
A **field** guide to germs / Wayne Biddle. Anchor Books, c2002. xiv, 209 p. : **616**
1. Medical microbiology
ISBN 9781400030514
LC 2002511927
Previously published: New York : Henry Holt and Co., 1995.
Discusses nearly one-hundred notorious pathogens, describing their physical characteristics, the afflictions they cause, and their impact on folklore, philosophy, and history.
"Relaying essential information about the 100 most prevalent, powerful, or literarily famous microbiological malefactors in dictionary-encyclopedia style, Biddle injects social and political history into the exposition to provide fuller understanding of germs, their roles in society, their histories, and their current statuses. Eminently entertaining, the book yet has the serious purpose of showing how concerns other than science and the relief of human suffering have affected the course of medical history." Booklist. {review of 1995 edition}

Brody, Jane E.
Jane Brody's Guide to the great beyond : a practical primer to help you and your loved ones prepare medically, legally, and emotionally for the end of life / Jane Brody. Random House, c2009. xxiv, 287 p. : **616**
1. Advance directives (Medical care) 2. Palliative treatment 3. Terminal care
ISBN 9781400066544
LC 2008016583
A guide to proactively prepare for the end of life covers topics ranging from financial planning and medical issues to emotional considerations, with advice on health care proxies, wills, funeral preparations, and palliative care.
"An instructive, inspiring and reassuring work full of compassion and humor (along with several cartoons from various New Yorker illustrators), this volume belongs on every family's bookshelf." Publishers Weekly.

Collins, Francis S.
The **language** of life : DNA and the revolution in personalized medicine / Francis S. Collins. Harper, 2009. 368 p. **616**
1. Medical genetics. 2. DNA. 3. Genetics. 4. Genetic screening.
ISBN 9780061733178
LC 2009025832
The best-selling author of The Language of God and leader of the Human Genome Project explains how ongoing improvements in DNA testing will usher in a new era of customized medicine.
"This readable book...can help anyone understand more about how genetics and our DNA contribute to our health." Library Journal.

Gawande, Atul
Better : a surgeon's notes on performance / Atul Gawande. Metropolitan, 2007. x, 273 p. ; **616**
1. Gawande, Atul. 2. Internal medicine -- Case studies. 3. Medicine -- Miscellanea. 4. Surgery.
ISBN 0805082115
LC 2006046962
Explores the efforts of physicians to close the gap between best intentions and best performance in the face of insurmountable obstacles, discussing such topics as the ethical considerations of lethal injections, malpractice, and surgical errors.
"Mostly, and repeatedly, the question Gawande pose at the heart of each of his essays is deceptively straightforward and can-do: How do we get it right, or barring that, just an iota better? ... Gawande is unassuming in every way, and yet his prose is infused with steadfast determination and hope." Boston Globe.

Kaplan, Gary, 1953-
Total recovery : solving the mystery of chronic pain and depression : how we get sick, why we stay sick, how we can recover / Dr. Gary Kaplan, D.O., with Donna Beech. Rodale, 2014 xxii, 250 p. ; **616**
1. Chronic pain -- Complications 2. Chronic pain 3. Depression, Mental
ISBN 9781623362751
LC 2013046868
A leading integrative doctor outlines new theories about illness and recovery based on the experiences of patients with chronic pain whose

medical exams reveal no clear sources, exploring the theory that disease can be a cumulative effect of inflammation-triggering traumas.

Kenneally, Christine

The **invisible** history of the human race : how DNA and history shape our identities and our futures / Christine Kenneally. Viking, 2014. 320 p. **616**

1. Genetics -- History 2. DNA 3. Heredity
ISBN 9780670025558

LC 2014021679

Shortlisted for the Stella Prize, 2015.

Draws on cutting-edge research to reveal how both historical artifacts and DNA tell us where we come from and where we may be going, showing everything from DNA to emotions to names and stories are all part of our human legacy and explaining how the history of nations is written in our DNA.

"Those interested in learning basic human genetics or seeking a more accurate story of eugenics might prefer Ricki Lewis's Human Genetics: The Basics or Paul A. Lombardo's A Century of Eugenics in America. For appreciating genealogy and family history in a new light, Kenneally's work shines." Library Journal.

Kolata, Gina Bari, 1948-

Mercies in disguise : a story of hope, a family's genetic destiny, and the science that rescued them / Gina Kolata. St. Martin's Press, 2017. 272 p. **616**

1. Baxley family 2. Baxley, Amanda 3. Medical genetics 4. Families 5. Medical ethics 6. Kuru
ISBN 9781250064349

LC 2016044044

Includes index.

A New York Times science reporter follows a family through genetic illness and one courageous daughter who decides her fate shall no longer be decided by a genetic flaw.

"Kolata's book reads like a medical thriller and readers will be caught up in the lives of the protagonists." Publishers Weekly.

Mangalik, Aroop, 1935-

Dealing with doctors, denial, and death : a guide to living well with serious illness / Aroop Mangalik, MD. Rowman & Littlefield, 2017 xiv, 260 p. ; **616**

1. Chronically ill -- Care 2. Chronically ill -- Family relationships 3. Chronically ill -- Treatment 4. Medical ethics
ISBN 9781442272804

LC 2016025054

A guide for patients facing chronic, serious illnesses details hospice and palliative care, explains what to ask doctors, and describes the importance of obtaining clear information about all treatment options.

"Mangalik provides invaluable information everyone can use to be prepared to face the inevitability of death and celebrate each life." Booklist.

Mukherjee, Siddhartha

★The **gene** : an intimate history / Siddhartha Mukherjee. Scribner, 2016. 592 p. ; **616**

1. Genetics -- History. 2. Heredity. 3. Genes.
ISBN 9781476733500

LC 2015039962

ALA Notable Book, 2017.

From the Pulitzer Prize-winning, best-selling author of The Emperor of All Maladies comes a magnificent history of the gene and a response to the defining question of the future: What becomes of being human when we learn to "read" and "write" our own genetic information?

"Sobering, humbling, and extraordinarily rich reading from a wise and gifted writer who sees how far we have comebut how much farther we have to go to understand our human nature and destiny." Kirkus.

Murphree, Rodger H

Treating and beating fibromyalgia and chronic fatigue syndrome : a step-by-step program proven to help you feel good again / Dr. Rodger H. Murphree. Harrison Hampton, 2013 544 p. : **616**

1. Chronic fatigue syndrome 2. Fibromyalgia
ISBN 9780972893879

LC bl2014008864

Dr. Murphree exposes the medical myths, pharmaceutical propaganda and doctor ignorance that sabotages those with chronic illness. The only way to beat these illnesses is to get healthy. Dr. Murphree explains in easy to understand terms how and why using scientifically researched and clinically proven natural vitamins, minerals, amino acids, and other over the counter supplements, corrects the problems associated with these illnesses. --From publisher description.

Rochman, Bonnie, 1972-

The **gene** machine : how genetic technologies are changing the way we have kids--and the kids we have / Bonnie Rochman. Scientific American / Farrar, Straus and Giroux, 2017. 288 p. ; **616**

1. Genetic engineering 2. Genetic screening 3. Medical genetics 4. Human chromosome abnormalities -- Diagnosis
ISBN 9780374160784

LC 2016035006

A researched exploration of the promises and vulnerabilities of having children in an age of genetic tests and interventions considers key scientific, technological and political factors while sharing the stories of men and women struggling to understand the range of the tests and their revelations.

Knight, Jeffrey A., 1948-

Genetics & inherited conditions / editor, Jeffrey A. Knight. Salem Press, c2010. 3 v. (xxxii, 1366, l p.) : **616**

1. Genetic disorders. 2. Genetics.
ISBN 9781587656507

LC 2010005289

"The latest edition to the Salem Health family, Salem Health: Genetics and Inherited Conditions alphabetically arranges 459 essays on diseases, biology, techniques, methodologies, genetic engineering, biotechnology, ethics, and social issues. Written for nonspecialists by professors and professional medical writers, this comprehensive reference publication will interest health-care consumers, premedical students, public library patrons, and librarians building scientific collections. Designed for the general reader, Salem Health: Genetics and Inherited Conditions is a revised and expanded version of Salem's award-winning Encyclopedia of Genetics, published in 2004. It adds 237 topics new to the encyclopedia, many of them diseases and conditions that are known to be genetic in origin to some degree. In addition, two entries from the last edition were replaced and 79 were heavily revised by experts to bring them up to date. All other previously published entries were reedited and their bibliographies updated with the latest sources. All appendixes were updated by science experts."--Publisher's description.

Hach, Shannon,

Medical symptoms : a visual guide / consulting medical

editor, Shannon Hach, MD; STAT editing ; contributors: Dina Kaufman, MBBS, MRCGP, DCH, DRCGP, Michael Dawson, MMedSc, FRCGP, Mike Wyndham, MBBS, MRCGP, Martyn Page. DK, 2018. 256 p. : **616**

1. Symptoms -- Encyclopedias. 2. Diagnosis -- Encyclopedias. 3. Medicine, Popular.
ISBN 9781465459145

LC bl2018001565

"The easy way to identify medical problems.
Includes index.

A resource with head-to-toe visual diagnostics helps readers identify suspected conditions or injuries based on symptoms and then a cross-reference takes them to easy-to-follow descriptions of the condition at the back of the book.

Gutkind, Lee,

Twelve breaths a minute : end-of-life essays / edited by Lee Gutkind ; foreword by Karen Wolk Feinstein ; introduction by Francine Prose. Southern Methodist University Press, 2011. 240 p. **616**

1. Terminal care. 2. Death. 3. Caregivers. 4. People with terminal illnesses -- Family relationships. 5. Essays.
ISBN 9780870745713

LC 2010045874

"A collection of creative nonfiction essays about end-of-life issues. How depressing, a friend said. I thought the same thing until I read one and then another and then another. Sad, yes. But depressing? No. Twelve Breaths a Minute, a book commissioned by the Jewish Healthcare Foundation as part of its ongoing end-of-life initiative, is uplifting. The 23 essays, chosen from among more than 400 submissions, also are beautifully written. The writers are the sons, daughters and parents who have had to deal with the deaths of family, as well as members of the medical profession who have had to balance the oath to save lives with the desires of a patient to die without extraordinary medical measures. Sometimes they are both." Pittsburgh Post-Gazette.

616.02 Special topics of diseases

Anthes, Emily

Frankenstein's cat : cuddling up to biotech's brave new beasts / Emily Anthes. Scientific American / Farrar, Straus and Giroux, 2013. 272 p. **616.02**

1. Animal experimentation 2. Clones and cloning 3. Bioethics 4. Biotechnology
ISBN 9780374158590

LC 2012029045

This thought-provoking examination of the most current advances in cloning technology, which can reproduce a cherished pet, protect endangered species, create disease-resistant livestock and more, takes readers on a wild ride through a world where science fiction is fast becoming reality.

Butler, Katy, 1949-

The **art** of dying well : a practical guide to a good end of life / Katy Butler. Scribner, 2019. xi, 274 p. : **616.02**

1. Terminal care -- Decision making. 2. Death -- Psychological aspects 3. Human comfort
ISBN 9781501135316

LC 2018037020

Draws on patient insights to counsel readers on how to navigate the health-care system for best-possible life quality and how to achieve an optimal end-of-life experience.

"Journalist Butler offers a straightforward, well-organized, non-depressing guide to managing the run-up to one's inevitable demise." Publishers Weekly.

Knocking on heaven's door : the path to a better way of death / Katy Butler. Scribner, 2013. 288 p. **616.02**

1. Terminal care -- Decision making. 2. Euthanasia -- Moral and ethical aspects. 3. Children of aging parents -- Family relationships. 4. Aging parents
ISBN 9781451641974

LC 2013017659

A blend of memoir and investigation of the choices we face when our terror of death collides with the technological imperatives of modern medicine.

"With candidness and reverence, Butler examines one of the most challenging questions a child may face: how to let a parent die with dignity and integrity when the body has stopped functioning." Kirkus.

Fersko-Weiss, Henry

★**Caring** for the dying : the doula approach to a meaningful death / Henry Fersko-Weiss. Conari Press, an imprint of Red Wheel/Weiser, LLC, 2017. xiv, 222 p. ; **616.02**

1. Doulas 2. Terminal care 3. Terminally ill -- Care
ISBN 9781573246965

LC 2016041229

"An Open Center Book"--Title page.

Provides a way to care for the dying based on the model of care birth doulas provide.

Harrington, Samuel (Physician)

At peace : choosing a good death after a long life / Samuel Harrington, MD. Grand Central Life & Style, 2018. xix, 282 p. **616.02**

1. Geriatrics 2. Terminal care 3. Terminally ill
ISBN 9781478917410

LC OC2018170062

A practical follow-up to Being Mortal cites current practices in aggressive medical intervention that are compromising end-of-life quality, counseling older patients and their health-care proxies on the patterns of six chronic diseases while sharing compassionate advice on recognizing a terminal diagnosis, dementia, and hospice care.

Lamas, Daniela J.

You can stop humming now : a doctor's stories of life, death, and in between / Daniela J. Lamas. Little, Brown and Company, 2018. vii, 245 pages ; **616.02**

1. Critical care 2. Physicians 3. Medicine 4. Patients
ISBN 9780316393171

LC 2017947289

A critical care doctor examines the lives of people who were given a second chance through treatments and technologies including a man whose heart was replaced by a battery-operated pump and a man who found a kidney donor on social media.

"This thoughtful, reflective, and beautifully rendered book examines the costs of modern medicine. Readers who enjoy books by Oliver Sacks and Atul Gawande, or Paul Kalanithi's When Breath Becomes Air will find this volume moving and provocative." Library Journal.

Monte, Tom

Unexpected recoveries : seven steps to healing body, mind

& soul when serious illness strikes / Tom Monte. Square One Publishers, 2017 ix, 242 p. ; **616.02**

1. People with terminal illnesses 2. People with chronic illnesses. 3. Healing.

ISBN 9780757004001

LC 2016043898

Readers are introduced to twelve people who have recovered from incurable illness. Also included are a helpful resource section, a twenty-one-day menu planner, and over sixty kitchen-tested recipes.

"The easy-to-follow format, combined with compelling and dramatic patient recovery stories, makes for an appealing read." Publishers Weekly.

Piazza, Gina M,

First aid manual : the step-by-step guide for everyone / American College of Emergency Physicians ; medical editor-in-chief, Gina M. Piazza, DO, FACEP. DK, 2014. 288 p. : **616.02**

1. First aid in illness and injury

ISBN 9781465419507

LC 2014430333

Includes index

A manual for diagnosing illnesses and injuries and acting in emergency situations provides techniques on treating burns, wounds, muscle injuries, shock, bites, concussions, and poisoning.

Volandes, Angelo, 1971-

The **conversation** : a revolutionary plan for end-of-life care / Angelo Volandes. Bloomsbury, 2015. 256 p. ; **616.02**

1. Terminal care. 2. Last days. 3. Palliative treatment 4. Quality of life.

ISBN 9781620408544

LC 2014028386

Harvard Medical School physician Angelo Volandes offers a solution to traumatic end-of-life care: talking, medicine's oldest and least technological tool in the proverbial black bag.

"Written with passion and clarity, this book moves beyond others on the topic by including empirical evidence of how to make such conversations about end-of-life care most effective." Library Journal.

Zitter, Jessica Nutik

Extreme measures : finding a better path to the end of life / Jessica Nutik Zitter. Avery, 2017 352 p. **616.02**

1. Zitter, Jessica Nutik 2. Terminal Care. 3. Quality of Life. 4. Aging. 5. Medical students

ISBN 9781101982556

LC 2016056303

An ICU and Palliative Care specialist reveals medical school training gaps in caring for dying patients, describing the professional experiences that compelled her to become a caregiver for the dying and counselor to patients and caregivers about enabling a positive end of life.

616.07 Pathology

Carver, Catherine

Immune : how your body defends and protects you / Catherine Carver. Bloomsbury USA, 2017. 304 p. **616.07**

1. Immune system 2. Human body 3. Immunology 4. Human anatomy

ISBN 9781472915115

LC bl2017045451

Includes index.

Immune explores the incredible arsenal that lives within us--how it knows what to attack and what to defend, and how it kills everything from the common cold to the plague bacterium. We see what happens when the immune system turns on us, and conversely how impossible life is without its protection.

"This book is jam-packed with hard-core science, and Carver engages readers with her cheeky, playful style and the inclusion of fascinating human-interest anecdotes." Library Journal.

Nuland, Sherwin B.

How we die : reflections on life's final chapter / Sherwin B. Nuland. Alfred A. Knopf, 1994. xviii, 278 p. : **616.07**

1. Death. 2. Last days.

ISBN 0679414614

LC 93024590

Includes index.

ALA Notable Book, 1995.

National Book Award for Nonfiction, 1994.

National Book Critics Circle Award for Nonfiction finalist, 1994.

Pulitzer Prize for General Nonfiction finalist, 1995.

"The author provides information on the clinical, biological and emotional details of deaths resulting from heart disease, stroke, cancer, AIDS, Alzheimer's disease, old age, accidents, suicide, euthanasia and murder or violent physical assault." Publishers Weekly.,Nuland is one of those rare physicians who know a great deal about a great deal, not only medicine but also its history and, beyond that, literature and the humanities. Commentary

Richtel, Matt

★An **elegant** defense : the extraordinary new science of the immune system : a tale in four lives / Matt Richtel. William Morrow, 2019. 416 p. **616.07**

1. Immune system 2. Immunology 3. Sick persons 4. Autoimmune diseases

ISBN 9780062698537

LC 2018038019

Includes index.

A terminal cancer patient rises from the grave. A medical marvel defies HIV. Two women with autoimmunity discover their own bodies have turned against them. An Elegant Defense uniquely entwines these intimate stories with science's centuries-long quest to unlock the mysteries of sickness and health, and illuminates the immune system as never before.

"Pulitzer Prize-winning reporter, nonfiction writer, and crime novelist Richtel adroitly mingles cellular biology, scientific history, medical research, and patients experiences as he explains how the immune system primarily protects our health but is also implicated in cancer, AIDS, and autoimmune disorders." Booklist.

Sanders, Lisa, 1956-

Every patient tells a story : medical mysteries and the art of diagnosis / Lisa Sanders. Broadway Books, c2009. 256 p. **616.07**

1. Diagnosis -- Popular works. 2. Medicine. 3. Physician and patient. 4. Physicians.

ISBN 9780767922463

LC 2008041478

"The author discusses how doctors deal with diagnostic dilemmas. Sanders not only collects difficult cases, she reflects on what each means for both patient and struggling physician. Readers who enjoy dramatic stories of doctors fighting disease will get their fill, and they will also encounter thoughtful essays on how doctors think and go about their work, and how they might do it better." Publishers Weekly.

616.1 Specific diseases

Fuhrman, Joel

The **end** of heart disease : the eat to live plan to prevent and reverse heart disease / Joel Fuhrman, M.D. HarperOne, 2016 430 p. : **616.1**

1. Heart -- Diseases -- Diet therapy 2. Heart -- Diseases -- Nutritional aspects 3. Heart -- Diseases -- Prevention

ISBN 9780062249357

LC 2015033616

"The New York Times bestselling author of Eat to Live, Super Immunity, The End of Diabetes, and The End of Dieting presents a scientifically proven, practical program to prevent and reverse heart disease, the leading cause of death in America--coinciding with the author's new medical study revealing headline-making findings. Dr. Joel Fuhrman, one of the country's leading experts on preventative medicine, offers his science-backed nutritional plan that addresses the leading cause of death in America: heartdisease. An expert in the science of food, Dr. Fuhrman speaks directly to readers who want to take control of their health and avoid taking medication or undergoing complicated, expensive surgery, the two standard treatments prescribed today. Following the model of his previous programs that have successfully tackled conditions from diabetes to dieting, Dr. Fuhrman's plan begins with the food we eat. He focuses on a high nutrient per calorie ratio, with a range of options for different needs and conditions. He shows us what to remove and what to add to our diets for optimum heart health, provides menu plans and recipes for heart-healthy meals and snacks, and includes helpful questions for doctors and patients.By understanding heart disease and its triggers, Dr. Fuhrman gives us the knowledge to counter-attack this widespread epidemic and lead longer, healthier lives".-- Provided by publisher.

"It's obvious Furhman's zeal is genuine as he passionately tries to convince the general public to make smarter choices." Booklist.

Parnia, Sam

Erasing death : the science that is rewriting the boundaries between life and death / Dr. Sam Parnia with Josh Young. HarperOne, 2013. 256 p. **616.1**

1. Near-death experience 2. Heart attack 3. Sudden death 4. C P R.

ISBN 9780062080608

LC 2012041098

Drawn from meticulous research, one of the world's leading experts on the scientific study of death, the human mind-brain relationship and near-death experiences demystifies what happens to human consciousness during and after death.

616.2 Diseases of respiratory system

Mackenzie, Debora

★Covid-19 : the pandemic that never should have happened and how to stop the next one / Debora Mackenzie. Hachette Books, 2020. 279 p. **616.2**

1. COVID-19 (Disease) 2. Viruses 3. Epidemics 4. Diseases

ISBN 9780306924248

LC bl2020016355

Over the last 30 years of epidemics and pandemics, we learned nearly every lesson needed to stop this coronavirus outbreak in its tracks. We heeded almost none of them. The result is a pandemic on a scale never before seen in our lifetimes. In this captivating, authoritative, and eye-opening book, science journalist Debora MacKenzie lays out the full story of how and why it happened: the previous viruses that should have prepared us, the shocking public health failures that paved the way, the failure to contain the outbreak, and most importantly, what we must do to prevent future pandemics.

"MacKenzie delivers a wise and accurate account of the COVID-19 pandemic, supplying readers with an objective assessment of where we are, how we got here, and how to prepare for future emerging infections. . . . Surely one of the best books available about the virus that has altered how we live and work, worry and interact with others." Booklist

616.3 Diseases of digestive system

Ali, Naheed, 1981-

Understanding celiac disease : an introduction for patients and caregivers / Naheed Ali. Rowman & Littlefield, 2014 xiii, 317 p. ; **616.3**

1. Celiac disease

ISBN 9781442226555

LC 2014016086

Presents an introduction to celiac disease, discussing the causes, symptoms, and treatment options for sufferers.

"Those who want a more technical description of celiac disease will find this book useful; readers looking for a basic overview and understanding of the condition and how to live with it may want to consider David L. Burns's 100 Questions & Answers About Celiac Disease and Sprue or Celiac Disease by Sylvia Llewelyn Bower, et al." Library Journal.

Understanding hepatitis : an introduction for patients and caregivers / Naheed Ali. Rowman & Littlefield, 2018 xiv, 175 p. ; **616.3**

1. Hepatitis 2. Liver -- Diseases

ISBN 9781538117248

LC 2018019972

Hepatitis afflicts many people and is a growing cause for concern. Naheed Ali, MD, breaks down the history, causes, symptoms, and treatment of hepatitis so readers, both patients and those who love them, can better understand the disease and address the needs of the sufferer from a whole person perspective. --From publisher description.

"Ali's guide may help improve or save lives." Booklist.

Freuman, Tamara Duker

The **bloated** belly whisperer : see results within a week, and tame digestive distress once and for all / Tamara Duker Freuman, MS, RD, CDN ; recipes by Kristine Kidd. St. Martin's Press, 2018. x, 324 p. : **616.3**

1. Gastrointestinal system -- Diseases -- Diet therapy. 2. Digestive system 3. Diet therapy -- Popular works

ISBN 9781250195234

LC 2018026747

A leading digestive diagnostician shares consultation methods to outline a program for eliminating uncomfortable bloat, helping to identify specific needs from an informed perspective based on the latest research and patient stories.

616.4 Diseases of endocrine, hematopoietic, lymphatic, glandular systems; diseases of male breast

American Diabetes Association

American Diabetes Association complete guide to diabetes / American Diabetes Association. American Diabetes Association, c2011. vii, 499 p. : **616.4**

1. Diabetes

ISBN 9781580403306

LC 2010041272

The latest edition of this comprehensive, easy-to-use home reference from the most trusted organization on diabetes offers expert advice to diabetics on living an active, healthy life.

American Diabetes Association

Ask the experts : expert answers about your diabetes American Diabetes Association, 2014 viii, 159 p. ; **616.4**

1. Diabetes -- Miscellanea.

ISBN 9781580405393

LC 2013046542

"This book is a compilation of questions sent in to the editors of Diabetes Forecast. They were from diabetes patients and were chosen to provide information on general issues that diabetics face".-- Provided by publisher.

Mayo Clinic,

The **essential** diabetes book Time Home Entertainment Inc., 2014 vii, 223 p. : **616.4**

1. Diabetes

ISBN 9780848743390

LC bl2014017224

At head of title: Mayo Clinic

Includes index.

A resource for the millions of people who have or are at risk of developing diabetes provides practical advice to help successfully manage diabetes and reduce the risk of serious complications, and includes delicious recipes created especially for diabetics.

Saudek, Christopher D.

The **Johns** Hopkins guide to diabetes : for patients and families / Christopher D. Saudek, M.D., Richard R. Rubin, Ph.D., CDE, Thomas W. Donner, M.D. The Johns Hopkins University Press, 2014 xi, 488 p. : **616.4**

1. Diabetes -- Treatment

ISBN 9781421411798

LC 2013015256

Includes index.

A comprehensive guide to the disease includes up-to-date information and answers questions for sufferers and their families.

Wright, Hillary

The **prediabetes** diet plan : how to reverse prediabetes and prevent diabetes through healthy eating and exercise / Hillary Wright, MEd, RD. Ten Speed Press, 2013 ix, 245 p. : **616.4**

1. Diabetes -- Diet therapy 2. Diabetes -- Prevention 3. Physical fitness 4. Prediabetic state -- Patients -- Diet therapy

ISBN 9781607744627

LC 2013018751

An empowering guide to managing and reversing prediabetes through diet and exercise shares comprehensive, jargon-free coverage of topics ranging from meal planning and grocery shopping to dining out and using supplements.

"This excellent introduction for readers recently diagnosed with (or at risk for) prediabetes will also interest readers with other forms of insulin resistance." Library Journal.

616.6 Diseases of urogenital system

Kang, Mandip S.

The **doctor's** kidney diet : a nutritional guide to managing and slowing the progression of chronic kidney disease / Mandip S. Kang, MD, FASN. Square One Publishers, 2015 x, 208 p. : **616.6**

1. Kidneys -- Diseases -- Diet therapy 2. Kidneys -- Diseases -- Nutritional aspects 3. Kidneys -- Diseases 4. Self-care, Health

ISBN 9780757003738

LC 2015018370

"Smart nutrition is essential to the treatment of kidney disease. With The Doctor's Kidney Diets, you can become an active, effective participant in your own treatment plan". --From publisher description.

"This well-written manual is essential for anyone diagnosed with kidney disease, or their caregivers, and is a needed addition for all consumer health collections." Library Journal.

616.7 Diseases of musculoskeletal system

Fishman, Loren

Yoga for arthritis : the complete guide / Loren M. Fishman, Ellen Saltonstall. W.W. Norton, c2008. 335 p. : **616.7**

1. Arthritis -- Exercise therapy 2. Yoga -- Therapeutic use

ISBN 9780393330588

LC 2007044693

Pizzorno, Lara

Your bones : how you can prevent osteoporosis & have strong bones for life-naturally / Lara Pizzorno, MA, LMT ; with Jonathan V. Wright, MD. Praktikos Books, 2013 xiii, 496 p. : **616.7**

1. Osteoporosis -- Prevention. 2. Bones. 3. Nutritional therapy. 4. Nutrition.

ISBN 9781607660132

LC 2012047340

"Consumer health collections looking for another book about the natural ways to prevent osteoporosis would do well to choose this title. Those looking for recipes or photos of recommended exercises need to look elsewhere." Library Journal.

616.8 Diseases of nervous system and mental disorders

Jebelli, Joseph

★**In** pursuit of memory / Joseph Jebelli. Little, Brown and Co., 2017. 304 p. **616.8**

1. Dementia. 2. Alzheimer's disease -- Research. 3. Medical research. 4. Memory disorders.

ISBN 9780316360791

LC bl2017042236

In a very human history of Alzheimer's disease that doubles as a scientific detective story, a neuroscientist takes readers on a journey around the world where we meet hero scientists who are working against the clock to find a cure.

"Jebelli analyzes every facet of Alzheimer's with personal empathy and scientific rigor, a combination that makes for enthralling reading." Kirkus.

Kosik, K. S. (Kenneth S.), 1950-

Outsmarting Alzheimer's : what you can do to reduce your risk / Kenneth S. Kosik, MD, with Alisa Bowman. The Reader's Digest Association, 2015 xviii, 301 p. : **616.8**

1. Alzheimer's disease -- Prevention 2. Self-care, Health

ISBN 9781621452447

LC 2015025509

"An easy-to-follow, research-based guide to the simple, low-cost lifestyle choices you can make to reduce the risk or slow the progression of Alzheimer's disease and dementia. Develop a personalized plan, including recipes, brain-training games, exercises. Includes advice for caregivers".-- Provided by publisher.

Leschziner, Guy

The **nocturnal** brain : nightmares, neuroscience, and the secret world of sleep / Guy Leschziner. St. Martin's Press, 2019. 288 p. **616.8**

1. Sleep disorders 2. Sleep deprivation. 3. Sleep -- Health aspects. 4. Sleep deprivation -- Health aspects.

ISBN 9781250202703

LC 2019005309

A clinical neurologist and global authority on narcolepsy presents a tour of the sleeping human brain, sharing remarkable patient stories that demonstrate the neuroscience behind what happens in different mind states.

"Readers will find Leschziners stories fascinating, and might even pick up a few tips for getting a more restorative nights sleep in the process." Publishers Weekly.

Mace, Nancy L.

★The **36-hour** day : a family guide to caring for people who have Alzheimer disease, other dementias, and memory loss / Nancy L. Mace and Peter V. Rabins. Johns Hopkins University Press, c2017. xx, 393 p. ; Johns Hopkins Press Health Book **616.8**

1. Alzheimer's disease -- Patients -- Home care. 2. Senile dementia -- Patients -- Home care.

ISBN 9781421422220

LC 2016033545

Includes index.

Originally published in 1981, The 36-Hour Day was the first book of its kind. Thirty years later, with dozens of other books on the market, it remains the definitive guide for people caring for someone with dementia. Now in a new and updated edition, this best-selling book features thoroughly revised chapters on the causes of dementia, managing the early stages of dementia, the prevention of dementia, and finding appropriate living arrangements for the person who has dementia when home care is no longer an option. --From publisher description.

Nicholls, Henry, 1973-

Sleepyhead : The neuroscience of a good night's rest / Henry Nicholls. Perseus Books Group, 2018 288 p. **616.8**

1. Sleep 2. Narcolepsy 3. Sleep disorders 4. Neuroscience

ISBN 9781541672574

LC bl2018142107

A science writer recounts his life dealing with chronic narcolepsy and explores the world of sleeping disorders and its victims--including insomniacs, fellow narcoleptics and sleep-apnea sufferers--and uncovers the secrets of a good night's rest.

Owen, Adrian M.

Into the gray zone : a neuroscientist explores the border between life and death / Adrian Owen. Simon & Schuster, 2017. 320 p. **616.8**

1. Brain death 2. Neuroscience 3. Consciousness 4. Death

ISBN 9781501135200

LC bl2017024227

A world-renowned neuroscientist reveals his controversial, groundbreaking work with patients believed to be brain dead to explain how up to 20 percent of them were still vibrantly alive, sharing his team's insights into what life may be like for such patients and the moral implications for religious organizations, politicians and families.

"An exploration of the current medical research on brain health and the consciousness of patients who suffer catastrophic head trauma." Kirkus.

Palfreman, Jon

Brain storms : the race to unlock the mysteries of Parkinson's disease / Jon Palfreman. Scientific American/Farrar, Straus and Giroux, 2015. 272 p. ; **616.8**

1. Parkinson's disease 2. People with Parkinson's disease 3. Diseases 4. Medical research

ISBN 9780374116170

LC 2015003861

Includes index.

Jon Palfreman writes about the history of Parkinson's from his perspective as a journalist and as a patient.

"In this illuminating book, Palfreman reminds patients that exercise and a positive attitude help, and he urges them to participate in clinical trials and take to task drug companies reluctant to initiate huge trials for what they dismiss as a non-life-threatening disease." Kirkus.

Powell, Tia (Psychiatrist)

Dementia reimagined : building a life of joy and dignity from beginning to end / Tia Powell, MD. Avery, 2019 310 p. ; **616.8**

1. Alzheimer's disease 2. Alzheimer's disease -- Patients -- Care 3. Dementia 4. Dementia -- Patients -- Care

ISBN 9780735210905

LC 2018049886

"The cultural and medical history of dementia and Alzheimer's disease by a leading psychiatrist and bioethicist who urges us to turn our focus from cure to care".-- Provided by publisher.

Radin, Gary, 1969-

What if it's not Alzheimer's? : a caregiver's guide to dementia / edited by Gary Radin and Lisa Radin ; foreword by Murray Grossman, MD EdD. Prometheus Books, 2014. 444 p. : **616.8**

1. Dementia -- Nursing -- Handbooks, manuals, etc. 2. Dementia -- Patients -- Care -- Handbooks, manuals, etc. 3. Caregivers -- Handbooks, manuals, etc.

ISBN 9781616149680

LC 2014015843

A guide to dealing with non-Alzheimer's dementias defines frontotemporal degeneration and provides information on diagnosis, managing care, finding the right doctors and managing care for a loved one.

Ramachandran, V. S.

The **tell-tale** brain : a neuroscientist's quest for what makes us human / V. S. Ramachandran. W W Norton, 2011. 384 p. **616.8**

1. Neuroscience 2. Neurology. 3. Brain. 4. Anatomy.

ISBN 9780393077827

LC 2010044913

Traces the links between neurology and behavior, discusses the evolution of normal brain function through the examination of several baffling and extreme case studies, and describes a new direction for the treatment of autism.

"Ramachandran produces an exhilarating and at times funny text that invites discussion and experimentation." Kirkus.

Reiss, Benjamin

Wild nights : how taming sleep created our restless world / Benjamin Reiss. Basic Books, [2017] 288 p. **616.8**

1. Sleep. 2. Lifestyle change. 3. Social change. 4. Industrialization -- Social aspects.

ISBN 9780465061952

LC 2016043568

Based on centuries of literary, medical and scientific writings, an English professor explains how the modern rules of sleeping, which have been ingrained in our culture for two centuries, have had a detrimental impact on our overall well-being.

"This is a captivating examination and Reiss gives readers much to ponder long into the night." Publishers Weekly.

Sacks, Oliver, 1933-2015

An **anthropologist** on Mars : seven paradoxical tales / Oliver Sacks. Knopf, 1995. xix, 327 p. : **616.8**

1. Neurology. 2. Human behavior. 3. Brain -- Diseases. 4. Essays.

ISBN 0679437851

LC 94026733

"In this collection of previously published essays, the noted neurologist describes his meetings with seven people whose abnormalities in brain function generate new perspectives on the workings of that organ, the nature of experience and concepts of personality and consciousness. Writing with eloquent particularity and compassionate respect, Sacks enlarges our view of the nature of human experience." Publishers Weekly.

★The **man** who mistook his wife for a hat and other clinical tales / Oliver Sacks. Summit Books, c1985. xvi, 233 p. : **616.8**

1. Neurologists 2. Neurology -- Anecdotes 3. Physician and patient. 4. Medical care.

ISBN 9780671554712

LC 85017220

Spine title: The man who mistook his wife for a hat.

Presents a series of stories about men and women who, representing both medical and literary oddities, raise fundamental questions about the nature of reality.

"Sacks introduces the reader to real people who suffer from a variety of neurological syndromes which includes symptoms such as amnesia, uncontrolled movements, and musical hallucinations. Sacks recounts their stories in a riveting, compassionate, and thoughtful manner." Library Journal.

Small, Gary, 1951

2 weeks to a younger brain / Gary Small, MD and Gigi Vorgan. Humanix Books, 2015 x, 297 p. : **616.8**

1. Intellect -- Deterioration -- Prevention. 2. Brain -- Degeneration -- Prevention. 3. Brain -- Aging -- Prevention.

ISBN 9781630060305

LC bl2015017247

Offers science-based, practical strategies for preventing mental decline and improving brain function, covering such topics as cognitive exercises, stress reduction, nutrition, exercise, and social stimulation.

Winter, W. Chris

The **sleep** solution : why your sleep is broken and how to fix it / W. Chris Winter, MD. New American Library, 2017. viii, 262 p. : **616.8**

1. Sleep 2. Sleep disorders

ISBN 9780399583605

LC 2016034735

A guide to sleep problems, including insomnia, sleep apnea, and circadian sleep disorders, discusses how to minimize medication dependency and offers time-tested techniques.

"This highly recommended title will appeal to those who have trouble sleeping--and who hasn't?" Library Journal.

616.85 Miscellaneous diseases of nervous system and mental disorders

Bass, Ellen

★The **courage** to heal : a guide for women survivors of child sexual abuse / Ellen Bass & Laura Davis. Collins Living, c2008. xxxiv, 606 p. ; **616.85**

1. Child sexual abuse -- United States 2. Women -- United States -- Psychology 3. Adult child abuse victims -- United States

ISBN 9780061284335

LC 2008011616

Offers inspiration and encouragement to women who have been sexually abused as children, providing self-help guidelines, a timely Resource Guide, healing tools, and new stories, insights, and wisdom.

Begley, Sharon, 1956-

Can't just stop : an investigation of compulsions / Sharon Begley. Simon & Schuster, 2017. 304 p. **616.85**

1. Obsessive-compulsive disorder. 2. Compulsive behavior. 3. Obsession 4. Anxiety

ISBN 9781476725826

LC 2016016745

Examines the science behind both mild and extreme compulsive behavior?using fascinating case studies to understand its deeper meaning and reveal the truth about human compulsion.

"Due to Begley's dense explanations of brain science, the book requires close attention at times, but her captivating, accessible anecdotes of individual cases lead to unforgettable scenarios." Kirkus.

Boyes, Alice

The **anxiety** toolkit : strategies for fine-tuning your mind and moving past your stuck points / Alice Boyes, PhD. Perigee, 2015 232 p. ; **616.85**

1. Anxiety 2. Anxiety -- Treatment

ISBN 9780399169250

LC 2014040065

"Drawing on extensive social psychology research, and the author's training and clinical experience in Cognitive-Behavioral therapy, The Anxiety Toolkit offers actionable strategies that anyone can use to manage their anxiety--both personal and professional".-- Provided by publisher.

"Boyes's tone is friendly but never saccharine, and endlessly practical. Her tips and exercises, drawn from cognitive behavioral therapies that she herself has administered, should make a valuable reference for anxiety sufferers, and an ideal companion to readers undergoing psychotherapy themselves." Publishers Weekly.

Bullmore, Edward T.

The **inflamed** mind : a radical new approach to depression

/ Edward Bullmore. Picador, 2019. xv, 240 p. : **616.85**

1. Neuroscience 2. Depression 3. Mental health 4. Psychiatry
ISBN 9781250318145

Worldwide, depression will be the single biggest cause of disability in the next 20 years. But treatment for it has not changed much in the last three decades. In the world of psychiatry, time has apparently stood still... until now.

"Readers looking for current treatments for depression or self-help advice will not find it here, but those concerned with the science behind depression or autoimmune disorders will discover the current state of research very compelling." Library Journal.

Dittrich, Luke

★**Patient** H.M. : a story of memory, madness and family secrets / Luke Dittrich. Random House, 2016. 320 p. ; **616.85**

1. H. M., 1926-2008 2. Scoville, William Beecher, 1906-1984. 3. Neurosurgeons. 4. Neuroscience. 5. Amnesia. 6. Experimental medicine -- Moral and ethical aspects.
ISBN 9780812992731

LC 2015048638

Explores the scientific, ethical, and human dimensions of the 1953 brain operation by William Beecher Scoville on an epileptic patient that transformed understandings of memory science and triggered profound legal and medical debates.

"Though long, there's not a wasted word in the book, which should make readers glad we live in the age of Prozac and not the scalpel. A mesmerizing, maddening story and a model of journalistic investigation." Kirkus.

Donvan, John (John Joseph) 1955-

★**In** a different key : the story of autism / John Donvan and Caren Zucker. Crown Publishers, 2016 448 p. **616.85**

1. Autism spectrum disorders. 2. People with disabilities. 3. Autism 4. People with autism
ISBN 9780307985675

LC 2015024706

Pulitzer Prize for General Nonfiction finalist, 2017.

The story of the discovery of autism and the first child diagnosed with the disorder draws on extensive research to trace how understandings about the condition have evolved through eight decades and how it has affected families in different historical periods.

"This book will not educate researchers with new information on autism. It will, however, introduce a human aspect to the chronology. Parents of autistic children will recognize themselves in many of these stories but also learn more about the truth behind them. Autistic individuals will take away lessons to forgive the past and to recognize the vast spectrum of differencenot just among those on the autism spectrum but among all people, who are always learning and growing." Library Journal.

Frost, Randy O.

Stuff : compulsive hoarding and the meaning of things / Randy O. Frost and Gail Steketee. Houghton Mifflin Harcourt, 2010. 300 p. **616.85**

1. Obsessive-compulsive disorder. 2. Compulsive hoarding 3. Mental health. 4. Psychology.
ISBN 9780151014231

LC 2009028273

Two respected psychologists analyze the sources of compulsive hoarding behaviors, presenting case studies of sufferers who have rendered their homes virtually unlivable, in a report that also outlines typical ineffective treatments and the impact of the disorder on families.

"Writing with authority and compassion, the authors tell the stories of diverse men and women who acquire and accumulate possessions to the point where their apartments or homes are dangerously cluttered with mounds of newspapers, clothing and other objects. An absorbing, gripping, important report." Kirkus.

Gillard, Arthur,

Asperger syndrome / Arthur Gillard, book editor. Greenhaven Press, 2011. 144 p. Perspectives on diseases and disorders **616.85**

1. Asperger's syndrome. 2. People with Asperger's syndrome 3. Syndromes
ISBN 9780737757712

LC 2011006229

"Asperger Syndrome: Understanding Asperger Syndrome; Controversies About Asperger Syndrome; Personal Experiences with Asperger Syndrome".-- Provided by publisher.

Grandin, Temple

★The **autistic** brain : thinking across the spectrum / Temple Grandin and Richard Panek. Houghton Mifflin Harcourt 2013 304 p. **616.85**

1. Grandin, Temple. 2. Autism. 3. Children with autism 4. Asperger's syndrome. 5. Syndromes.
ISBN 9780547636450

LC 2013000662

Offers the latest research and science on autism, including new neuroimaging and genetic research that provide new theories on what causes autism spectrum disorders as well as new ways to treat and diagnose them.

Grinker, Roy Richard, 1961-

Unstrange minds : remapping the world of autism / Roy Richard Grinker. Basic Books, c2007. vii, 340 p. ; **616.85**

1. Autism. 2. People with autism 3. Medicine.
ISBN 0465027636

LC 2006023003

A father's attempt to understand his daughter's autism leads him on a journey around the world to learn how societies view the widely diagnosed disorder.

"The first part of the book is an expanded essay on the history of the classification of psychiatric disorders and how these definitions continue to evolve. The second part of the book explores the cultural issues related to autism in societies as diverse as those of India, South Korea, and South Africa and how the place of the autistic child is changing in those countries. Grinker's experiences as a father of an autistic child are woven throughout the volume. The text is scholarly, but easily read, and is useful not only for providing an understanding of autism, but also for understanding the issues associated with changing diagnoses of psychiatric disorders." Science Books & Films.

Guyenet, Stephan

The **hungry** brain : outsmarting the instincts that make us overeat / Stephan, M.D. Guyenet. Flatiron Books, 2017. 288 p. **616.85**

1. Overeating 2. Brain chemistry. 3. Obesity 4. Diet.
ISBN 9781250081193

LC 2016057553

Explores how the brain's dual thinking processes regulate when, what and how much we eat.

"This fun, insightful, and important text will appeal to both science lovers and fitness fanatics." Publishers Weekly.

Hallowell, Edward M.

Driven to distraction : recognizing and coping with attention deficit disorder from childhood through adulthood / Edward M. Hallowell and John J. Ratey. Anchor Books, 2011. xviii, 382 p. : **616.85**

1. Attention-deficit disorder in adults 2. Attention-deficit hyperactivity disorder

ISBN 0307743152

LC bl2012020871

A revised and updated edition of a best-selling reference for adults and children with ADHD draws on vivid patient stories and case histories while incorporating current medical information on everything from ADHD myths and current diagnostic methods to family management options and the positive aspects of the disorder.

Kluger, Jeffrey

The **narcissist** next door : understanding the monster in your family, in your office, in your bed--in your world / Jeffrey Kluger. Riverhead Books, 2014. 277 p. ; **616.85**

1. Narcissism.

ISBN 1594486360

LC 2014006297

Includes index.

"A lively and perceptive exploration of narcissism that examines its causes, the science and psychology at its core, and the opportunities and challenges it presents to those who suffer from it (and those who contend with it in others)".-- Provided by publisher.

"In addition to being informative and engaging, Kluger's account provides some effective tools for dealing with potential narcissists." Publishers Weekly.

LeDoux, Joseph E

Anxious : using the brain to understand and treat fear and anxiety / Joseph LeDoux. Penguin Books, 2016. xii, 468 p. : **616.85**

1. Anxiety disorders -- Treatment 2. Anxiety -- Treatment

ISBN 9780143109044

LC bl2016034817

Profiles a range of anxiety disorders to challenge common misconceptions while identifying breakthroughs that are enabling effective new approaches in psychotherapy.

"Life is dangerous, and professor of neuroscience LeDoux is an expert on the way the brain gathers, stores, and processes data about danger." Booklist.

Lock, James

Help your teenager beat an eating disorder / James Lock, MD, PhD, Daniel Le Grange, PhD. The Guilford Press, 2015 viii, 310 p. ; **616.85**

1. Eating disorders in adolescence 2. Parent and teanager

ISBN 9781462517480

LC 2014034977

"Tens of thousands of parents have turned to this compassionate resource for support and practical advice grounded in cutting edge scientific knowledge. Numerous vivid stories show how to recognize and address anorexia nervosa, bulimia nervosa, and otherdevastating eating disorders that wreak havoc on teens and their families. James Lock and Daniel Le Grange present strong evidence that parents--who have often been told to take a back seat in eating disorder treatment--can and must play a key role in recovery. Whether pursuing family based treatment or other options, parents learn specific, doable steps for monitoring their teen's eating and exercise habits, managing mealtimes, ending weight related power struggles, and collaborating successfully with health care providers. Featuring the latest research and resources, the second-edition now addresses additional disorders recognized in DSM 5 (including binge eating disorder)".-- Provided by publisher.

McBride, Karyl

Will I ever be good enough? : healing the daughters of narcissistic mothers / Karyl McBride. Free Press, 2008. xvi, 243 p. ; **616.85**

1. Mothers and daughters -- Psychological aspects 2. Narcissism. 3. Self-acceptance. 4. Interpersonal relations

ISBN 9781416551324

A resource for daughters of mothers with narcissistic personality disorder explains how to manage feelings of inadequacy and abandonment in the face of inappropriate maternal expectations and conditional love.

"In this book aimed at women whose mothers have narcissistic personality disorder, McBride presents specific steps toward recovery that daughters of any age can use as they grieve for the love and support they didn't receive, set healthy boundaries with their mothers and access an internal mother as a source of self-comforting. The author provides parenting tips as well as advice on maintaining healthy love relationships and friendshipsall of which tend to be weak points of the daughters of narcissistic mothers." Publishers Weekly.

Milliken, Kirsten

PlayDHD : permission to play... a prescription for adults with ADHD / Kirsten Milliken, Ph.D., PCC, psychologist and ADHD coach ; design and illustration by Morgan Pickard, Howler Monkey Design Studio. Bookbaby, 2016 144 p. : **616.85**

1. Attention-deficit disorder in adults. 2. Attention-deficit hyperactivity disorder. 3. Play therapy.

ISBN 0997004509

LC bl2017005825

"This book is a must for those with ADHD and their loved ones." Publishers Weekly.

Power, Thomas J.

If your adolescent has ADHD : an essential resource for parents / Thomas J. Power, PhD, Linda Wasmer Andrews. Oxford University Press, 2018 xi, 218 p. ; **616.85**

1. Attention-deficit hyperactivity disorder in adolescence 2. Attention-deficit disordered youth 3. Parents of attention-deficit disordered children

ISBN 9780190873103

LC 2017037994

Provides evidence-based treatments and behavioral strategies for parents of adolescents coping with attention-deficit hyperactivity disorder as they transition through high school into college, work, and moving away from home.

Ronson, Jon, 1967-

★The **psychopath** test : a journey through the madness industry / Jon Ronson. Riverhead Books, 2011. 288 p. ; **616.85**

1. Antisocial personality disorders 2. Mental illness 3. Psychopathology. 4. Mental health

ISBN 9781594488016

LC 2011003133

"In this madcap journey, a bestselling journalist investigates psychopaths and the industry of doctors, scientists, and journalists who study them".-- Provided by publisher.

Sacks, Oliver, 1933-2015

The **mind's** eye / Oliver Sacks. Knopf, 2010. 256

p. **616.85**

1. Vision. 2. Vision disorders. 3. Perception. 4. People with communicative disorders

ISBN 9780307272089

LC 2010012791

"This is a Borzoi book."

Traces the stories of six individuals whose lives have been profoundly altered by unusual changes to essential senses and abilities, including a renowned pianist who lost the ability to read scores and a novelist whose ability to read was destroyed by a stroke.

"[A] riveting exploration of how we use our vision to perceive and understand the world and our place in it and how our brains teach us to see those things we need to lead a complete, fulfilled life." Booklist.

Smith, R. Garth

ASD, the complete autism spectrum disorder health & diet guide : The complete Autism Spectrum Disorder health & diet guide / R. Garth Smith, MBBS, FRCPC, Susan Hannah, BA, BScH, and Elke Sengmueller, BASc, RD. Robert Rose, 2014 408 p. ; **616.85**

1. Autism -- Diet therapy 2. Autism -- Nutritional aspects 3. Casein-free diet 4. Gluten-free diet 5. Cookbooks

ISBN 9780778804734

LC oc2014020110

Includes index.

"With sections for all parts of the day, there are plenty of recipes to work through for even the pickiest/limited eater. This should be required reading for anyone wanting to best address healthy options for Autistic people." Publishers Weekly.

Stewart, Alison, 1966-

Junk : digging through America's love affair with stuff / Alison Stewart. Chicago Review Press, 2016. 304 p. **616.85**

1. Consumer society 2. Compulsive hoarding 3. Housekeeping.

ISBN 9781613730553

LC 2015050224

When journalist and author Alison Stewart was confronted with emptying her late parents' overloaded basement, a job that dragged on for months, it got her thinking: How did it come to this? Why do smart, successful people hold on to old Christmas bows, chipped knick-knacks, and books they would likely never reread? Junk details Stewart's three-year investigation into America's stuff, lots and lots and lots of stuff.

"Absorbing and enjoyably compelling research on the packrat conundrum in our society." Kirkus.

Van der Kolk, Bessel A., 1943-

The **body** keeps the score : brain, mind, and body in the healing of trauma / Bessel A. van der Kolk, M.D. Viking, 2014 xvi, 443 p. : **616.85**

1. Stress Disorders, Post-Traumatic -- physiopathology. 2. Stress Disorders, Post-Traumatic -- therapy.

ISBN 9780670785933

LC 2014021365

A forefront expert on traumatic stress outlines his own take on healing, explaining how traumatic stress affects brain processes and how to use innovative treatments to reactivate the mind's abilities to trust, engage others and experience pleasure.

Wilson, Sarah, 1974-

First, we make the beast beautiful : a new journey through anxiety / Sarah Wilson. Dey Street, 2018, c2017. 312 p. ; **616.85**

1. Wilson, Sarah, 1974- Mental health. 2. Anxiety 3. Mental health 4. Coping 5. Spirituality 6. Australian

ISBN 9780062836786

"Originally published in Australia in 2017 by Pan Macmillan Australia Pty Ltd."--Title page verso.

Challenges cultural beliefs about anxiety from the perspectives of medical and spiritual leaders to explore how the condition needs to be viewed less as a burdensome affliction and more as a source of divine growth.

"Amusing, practical, and filled with delightful asides, this book will appeal to anxiety-prone readers, who will find much to calm them in these pages." Publishers Weekly.

Wood, David

★**What** have we done : the moral injury of our longest wars / David Wood. Little Brown & Co, 2016 320 p. **616.85**

1. Political ethics. 2. War -- Moral and ethical aspects. 3. Killing (Ethics)

ISBN 9780316264150

LC 2016932416

Featuring portraits of combat veterans and leading mental health researchers, a Pulitzer Prize-winning journalist presents a meticulously researched and deeply personal look at war and those who volunteer for it, and, too often, receive the scars of moral injury.

616.86 Substance abuse (Drug abuse)

Beattie, Melody

★**Codependent** no more : Stop Controlling Others And Start Caring for Yourself / Melody Beattie. Hazelden, 1987. 231 p. ; **616.86**

1. Codependency. 2. Self-care, Health. 3. Substance abuse -- Patients -- Family relationships.

ISBN 0894864025

LC 86082660

The healing touchstone of millions, this modern classic by one of America's best-loved and most inspirational authors holds the key to understanding codependency and to unlocking its stultifying hold on your life. --From publisher description.

616.89 Mental disorders

Cahalan, Susannah

The **great** pretender : the undercover mission that changed our understanding of madness / Susannah Cahalan. Grand Central Publishing, 2019. 336 p. ; **616.89**

1. Rosenhan, David L. 2. Mental illness -- diagnosis 3. Mental Health Services 4. Human experimentation in psychology 5. Psychiatric hospitals 6. United States

ISBN 9781538715284

LC 2019017569

The award-winning, bestselling author investigates the 50-year-old mystery behind a dramatic experiment that broke open the field of psychology, closing down institutions and changing mental health diagnosis forever.

Frances, Allen, 1942-

★**Saving** normal : an insider's revolt against out-of-control psychiatric diagnosis, DSM-5, big pharma, and the medicalization of ordinary life / Allen Frances. William Morrow, 2013

304 p. **616.89**

1. Diagnostic and statistical manual of mental disorders. 2. Medical ethics. 3. Psychiatry. 4. Psychopathology -- Classification. 5. Mental health.
ISBN 9780062229250
LC bl2013015157

Published to coincide with the new edition of the Diagnostic and Statistical Manual of Mental Disorders (DSM 5), the author argues that the DSM 5 threatens to destroy what is considered normal and that grief, sorrow, stress, disappointment and other feelings are part of life, not a psychiatric disease.

"A valuable assessment for clinicians and potential patients." Kirkus.

Greenberger, Dennis

★**Mind** over mood : change how you feel by changing the way you think / Dennis Greenberger, PhD, Christine A. Padesky, PhD ; foreword by Aaron T. Beck, MD. The Guilford Press, 2016 xx, 341 p. : **616.89**

1. Affective disorders -- Treatment. 2. Cognitive therapy
ISBN 1462520421
LC 2015025241

"Discover simple yet powerful steps you can take to overcome emotional distress--and feel happier, calmer, and more confident. This life-changing book has already helped more than 1,000,000 readers use cognitive-behavioral therapy--one of today's most effective forms of psychotherapy--to conquer depression, anxiety, panic attacks, anger, guilt, shame, low self-esteem, eating disorders, substance abuse, and relationship problems. Revised and expanded to reflect significant scientific developments of the past 20 years, the second edition contains numerous new features: expanded content on anxiety; chapters on setting personal goals and maintaining progress; happiness rating scales; gratitude journals; innovative exercises focused on mindfulness, acceptance, and forgiveness; new worksheets; and much more." -- Amazon.com.

"Recommended for dedicated readers willing to spend an hour a day working on new skills." Library Journal.

Harrington, Anne, 1960-

Mind fixers : psychiatry's troubled search for the biology of mental illness / Anne Harrington. W.W. Norton & Company, [2019] 384 p. **616.89**

1. Mental illness -- Physiological aspects. 2. Psychotropic drugs -- History. 3. Neuropsychiatry. 4. Psychiatry.
ISBN 9780393071221

Documents the unfulfilled 1980s quest to identify the biological basis of mental illness, documenting the cultural upheavals, activism, public policy change, rivalries and profit-mongering that shaped efforts to address mental illness with biochemical treatments.

"In this erudite work, Harrington explores the history of psychiatry from the French neurologist Jean-Martin Charcot to the Swiss American neurologist Adolf Meyer to Sigmund Freud and up to the present day." Booklist.

Hibbs, B. Janet

The **stressed** years of their lives : helping your kid survive and thrive during their college years / B. Janet Hibbs, Ph.D., M.F.T. & Anthony Rostain, M.D., M.A.. St. Martin's Press, 2019. xiii, 322 p. : **616.89**

1. College students -- Mental health 2. College students -- Psychology 3. Education, Higher -- Parent participation
ISBN 9781250113139
LC 2018041166

A guide for parents of college-bound students cites the emergence of mood disorders and other mental-health challenges in mid to late adolescence, sharing counsel on typical versus atypical mental health and what behaviors necessitate intervention.

"Packing in just the right amount of statistics and real-world scenarios, two doctors offer sound advice on how parents can better prepare their children for the challenging college years that lie ahead of them." Kirkus.

Kandel, Eric R

The **disordered** mind : what unusual brains tell us about ourselves / Eric R. Kandel. Farrar, Straus and Giroux, 2018. 352 p. ; **616.89**

1. Self 2. Neuroscience 3. Brain -- Diseases 4. Mental health
ISBN 9780374287863
LC 2017049274

A Nobel Prize-winning neuroscientist draws on his extensive research to explore how the mind and one's individual sense of self arise from the physical matter of the brain, explaining what brain disorders can teach us about human nature.

"Emphasizing advances in the fields of genetics, brain imaging, and animal research, Kandel writes about decision-making, sense of self, emotion, mood, addiction, and gender identity." Booklist.

Lieberman, Jeffrey A., 1948-

Shrinks : the untold story of psychiatry / Jeffrey A. Lieberman with Ogi Ogas. Little Brown & Co 2015. 304 p. **616.89**

1. Psychiatry -- History 2. Mental illness -- History. 3. People with mental illnesses -- Care and treatment -- History.
ISBN 9780316278867
LC bl2015006112

A former president of the American Psychiatric Association presents the fascinating story of psychiatry's origins, downfall and redemption.

"A lively defense of psychiatry that extols brain science and pharmaceutical treatment. A contrasting approach is found in Philip Thomas's Psychiatry in Context; critical of routine overuse of pharmaceuticals, Thomas makes a case for understanding the unique experience of each patient, even in schizophrenia." Library Journal.

Marchant, Jo

Cure : a journey into the science of mind over body / Jo Marchant. Crown Publishers, 2016 288 p. **616.89**

1. Mind and body therapies. 2. Mind and body 3. Alternative medicine. 4. Healing
ISBN 9780385348157
LC 2015024707

Drawing on the latest research and traveling the world to interview physicians, patients and researchers on the cutting edge of a new world of medicine, an award-winning science writer presents a rigorous, skeptical, deeply reported examination into the science behind the vast potential of the mind's ability to heal the body.

Nerenberg, Jenara

Divergent mind : thriving in a world that wasn't designed for you / Jenara Nerenberg. HarperOne, 2019 256 p. **616.89**

1. Nerenberg, Jenara 2. Women -- Mental health 3. Neuropsychology 4. Women with autism 5. Brain -- Sex differences
ISBN 9780062876799
LC 2019033534

A journalist who suffered into adulthood with autism and ADHD reveals why these conditions are often overlooked and misdiagnosed in women and shares real stories from fellow females to dispel widely-held misconceptions while offering a path forward.

"An extraordinary, jaw-dropping take on a topic with which many women will identify. Of special interest to those in the human resources, counseling, and education fields." Library Journal

Nesse, Randolph M.

Good reasons for bad feelings : insights from the frontier of evolutionary psychiatry / Randolph M. Nesse, MD. Dutton, [2019] 384 p. **616.89**

1. Mental illness 2. Genetics 3. Human evolution 4. Psychiatry -- History

ISBN 9781101985663

LC 2018045094

A founder of the field of evolutionary medicine uses his decades of experience as a psychiatrist to provide a much-needed new framework for making sense of mental illness.

"Nesse fully meets his modest but laudable goal of providing a conversation-starter on why mental illness should be viewed from an evolutionary perspective." Publishers Weekly.

Porter, Roy, 1946-2002

Madness : a brief history / Roy Porter. Oxford University Press, 2002. xii, 241 p. : **616.89**

1. Mental illness -- History. 2. People with mental illnesses -- Care and treatment -- History. 3. Psychiatry -- History.

ISBN 0192802666

LC 2001052329

A history of "madness" offers readers a sweeping history of mental illness and its treatment, from holes drilled in five-thousand-year-old skulls to the latest in modern psychotropic drugs.

"This book combines the appeal of history as narrative with the intellectual stimulation derived from cogent analysis." Library Journal.

Sederer, Lloyd I.

The **family** guide to mental health care / Lloyd I. Sederer, MD ; foreword by Glenn Close. W.W. Norton & Company, 2013 xxii, 312 p. ; **616.89**

1. Families of the mentally ill -- Counseling of 2. Mental health services -- United States 3. Mental illness -- United States

ISBN 9780393707946

LC 2013007244

Counsels those dealing with a family member's mental illness on medications, medical privacy laws, depression, anxiety, bipolar illness, and eating disorders, and includes a checklist of questions to ask at a doctor's visit.

Shatkin, Jess P.

Born to be wild : why teens take risks, and how we can help keep them safe / Jess P. Shatkin, MD, MPH. TarcherPerigee, [2017] 304 p. **616.89**

1. Risk-taking (Psychology) 2. Adolescence 3. Adolescent psychology 4. Risk

ISBN 9780143129790

LC 2017016376

"Decoding the adolescent brain, ages 12-26" -- cover.

A research-backed guide that illuminates the psychological sources of such high-risk teen behaviors as texting while driving, binge drinking, bullying and unprotected sex draws on decades of clinical experience and cutting-edge scientific findings to share anecdotal insights into how to engage in specific teachable activities to promote safe behavior.

"An accessible and compelling look at a frequently misunderstood developmental stage that will provoke talk around the family dinner table." Booklist.

Torrey, E. Fuller (Edwin Fuller), 1937-

Surviving schizophrenia : a family manual / E. Fuller Torrey, M.D.. Harper Perennial, 2019. xxii, 496 p. : **616.89**

1. Schizophrenia

ISBN 9780062880802

LC bl2013053517

First published 1983

Describes the symptoms, causes, and treatment of schizophrenia, tells those concerned how to take care of a schizophrenic, and discusses legal and ethical problems related to the mental illness.

Washington, Harriet A.

Infectious madness : the surprising science of how we "catch" mental illness / Harriet A. Washington. Little, Brown, & Company, 2015 304 p. **616.89**

1. Mental illness 2. Infection 3. Medical care 4. Psychology

ISBN 9780316277808

LC 2015935999

The National Book Critics Circle Award-winning author of Medical Apartheid presents a groundbreaking look at the connection between germs and mental illness, and how we can protect ourselves.

"Recommended for fans of science journalism and readers interested in the next 'hot topic' in biological psychiatry." Library Journal.

Young, Joel L.

When your adult child breaks your heart : coping with mental illness, substance abuse, and the problems that tear families apart / Joel L. Young, MD and Christine Adamec. Lyons Press, 2013 xii, 251 p. ; **616.89**

1. Parents of mentally ill children -- Psychology 2. Parent and adult child 3. Self-care, Health

ISBN 9780762792979

LC 2013023047

"Urgently needed practical advice for parents of adult children whose mental health disorders, addictions, and/or violent tendencies continue to traumatize their family's lives".-- Provided by publisher.

616.9 Other diseases

Broudy, Oliver

The **sensitives** : The rise of environmental illness and the search for America's last pure place / Oliver Broudy. Simon & Schuster, 2020. 288 p. **616.9**

1. Environmentally induced diseases 2. Environmental health 3. Sick persons 4. Journalists 5. United States

ISBN 9781982128500

LC 2019050181

A dramatic exploration of the mysteries of Environmental Illness visits an eastern Arizona community where people who have been marginalized for their hypersensitivities are learning how to respond to and avoid common symptom-triggering toxins.

"Throughout this balanced account, Broudy weaves a history of the mind-body connection, the chemical industry, and the specialty of allergy-immunology, providing a solid introduction to a widespread but often invisible problem." Library Journal

Fallon, Brian, M.D

Conquering Lyme disease : science bridges the great divide / Brian A. Fallon, MD, and Jennifer Sotsky, MD ; with Carl Brenner, Carolyn Britton, MD, Marina Makous, MD, Jenifer

Nields, MD, and Barbara Strobino, PhD. Columbia University Press, 2018 xxviii, 421 p. : **616.9**

1. Lyme disease

ISBN 9780231183840

LC 2017031085

In this authoritative book, the Columbia University Medical Center physicians Brian A. Fallon and Jennifer Sotsky explain that, despite the vexing "Lyme Wars," there is cause for both doctors and patients to be optimistic. The past decade's advances in precision medicine and biotechnology are reshaping our understanding of Lyme disease and accelerating the discovery of new tools to diagnose and treat it, such that the great divide previously separating medical communities is now being bridged. Drawing on both extensive clinical experience and cutting-edge research, Fallon, Sotsky, and their colleagues present these paradigm-shifting breakthroughs in language accessible to both sides. They clearly explain the immunologic, infectious, and neurologic basis of chronic symptoms, the cognitive and psychological impact of the disease, as well as current and emerging diagnostic tests, treatments, and prevention strategies. Written for the educated patient and health care provider seeking to learn more, Conquering Lyme Disease gives an up-to-the-minute overview of the science that is transforming the way we address this complex illness. It argues forcefully that the expanding plague of Lyme and other tick-borne diseases can be confronted successfully and may soon even be reversed. --From publisher description.

"Aimed at specialists, Fallon and Sotsky's heady volume presents the multidisciplinary cadre aiming to restore Lyme patients 'to their former well-being and good grace.'" Publishers Weekly.

Finlay, B. Brett, 1959-

Let them eat dirt : saving your child from an oversanitized world / B. Brett Finlay, PhD, Marie-Claire Arrieta, PhD. Algonquin Books of Chapel Hill, 2016. xiii, 288 p. ; **616.9**

1. Bacteria -- Health aspects 2. Medical microbiology 3. Pathogenic microorganisms

ISBN 9781616206499

LC 2016018794

Drawing on recent scientific findings that suggest that exposure to infectious microbes can actually promote long-term health in children links microbe imbalances to a range of health problems while sharing insights into the pros and cons of such parenting choices as natural childbirth, breastfeeding, antibiotics and having pets.

Horowitz, Richard I.

Why can't I get better? : solving the mystery of Lyme and chronic disease : pain, fatigue, memory and concentration problems, and much more / Richard I. Horowitz, MD. St. Martin's Press, 2013. xii, 532 p. ; **616.9**

1. Diagnosis 2. Lyme disease 3. Symptoms

ISBN 9781250019400

LC 2013013336

A groundbreaking reference about diagnosing Lyme disease and chronic illness traces the heated debate that has prevented patients from obtaining adequate care, outlining the author's plan for identifying and treating chronic illness using methods for promoting best-possible outcomes.

"Less self-help and more educational, this work is recommended for health sciences professionals and medically literate audiences, not necessarily for introductory or casual readers." Library Journal.

Ingels, Darin

The **Lyme** solution : a 5-part plan to fight the inflammatory auto-immune response and beat Lyme disease / Darin Ingels, ND, FAAEM. Avery, 2018. xi, 372 p. : **616.9**

1. Lyme disease 2. Lyme disease -- Alternative treatment 3. Naturopathy

ISBN 9780735216303

LC bl2018000933

Shares comprehensive, whole-body approaches to treating acute and chronic Lyme disease, outlining a five-step plan that involves prevention, early detection, bolstering the immune system, strategic uses of medication and overall lifestyle quality improvement.

Masterson, Karen, 1964-

The **malaria** project : the U.S. government's secret mission to find a miracle cure / Karen Masterson. New American Library, 2014. 320 p. ; **616.9**

1. Malaria -- History. 2. Human experimentation in medicine. 3. Vaccines 4. Malaria -- Prevention -- History.

ISBN 9780451467324

LC 2014018351

Describes the secret, American World War II initiative to develop a Malaria vaccine, spearheaded by Dr. Lowell T. Coggeshall and the nation's top chemists and researchers, who tested their drugs on birds, mental-health patients and criminals

Newby, Kris

Bitten : the secret history of lyme disease and biological weapons / Kris Newby. Harper Wave, [2019] 352 p. **616.9**

1. Burgdorfer, Willy, 1925-2014 2. Lyme disease -- History. 3. Lyme disease -- Diagnosis. 4. Tick-borne diseases 5. Lyme disease -- Treatment.

ISBN 9780062896278

LC 2019006357

Examines the mystery surrounding Lyme disease, the difficulty in diagnosing it, the different treatments that are available, and addresses the questions of possible biological warfare surrounding the disease.

Oldstone, Michael B. A.

Viruses, plagues, and history : past, present, and future / Michael B.A. Oldstone. Oxford University Press, 2020 495 p. : **616.9**

1. Virus diseases -- History

ISBN 9780190056780

LC 2009003550

First published 1998.

Documents the major viral outbreaks throughout history, the devastating toll they have taken on human life, and the heroic scientists and health workers who fight a continuing battle to eradicate current and future plagues. UP.

Peterson, Phillip K.

Microbes : the life-changing story of germs / Phillip K. Peterson. Prometheus, 2020 294 p. **616.9**

1. Microorganisms 2. Viruses 3. Medical microbiology 4. Epidemics

ISBN 9781633886346

LC 2019057113

With straight-forward and engaging writing, infectious diseases physician Phillip Peterson surveys how our understanding of viruses has changed throughout history, from early plagues and pandemics to more recent outbreaks like HIV/AIDS, Ebola, and the Zika virus. Microbes also takes on contemporary issues like the importance of vaccinations in the face of the growing anti-vaxxer movement, as well as the rise of cutting-edge health treatments like fecal transplants. Microbes explains for general readers where these germs came from, what they do to and for us, and what can be done to stop the bad actors and foster the benefactors.

"Lay readers should find this an eye-opening and illuminating look at the pressing issue of infectious disease." Publishers Weekly

Pfeiffer, Mary Beth

Lyme : the first epidemic of climate change / Mary Beth Pfeiffer. Island Press, [2018] xiii, 288 pages ; **616.9**

1. Lyme disease 2. Ticks 3. Tick-borne diseases 4. Global environmental change

ISBN 9781610918442

LC 2017958888

Lyme disease is spreading rapidly around the globe as ticks move into places they could not survive before. Mary Beth Pfeiffer argues it is the first epidemic to emerge in the era of climate change, infecting millions around the globe.

Preston, Richard, 1954-

The **demon** in the freezer / Richard Preston. Random House, 2002. 240 p. Dark biology ; **616.9**

1. Smallpox -- Prevention. 2. Biological terrorism. 3. Biological weapons. 4. Viruses.

ISBN 0375508562

LC 2004271019

Volumes 1 and 3 of this series are nonfiction titles, while volume 2 is a fictional novel.

The author explores the return of smallpox, eradicated in 1979 but now returning on the black market as a weapon of bioterrorism, and the crusade of three doctors to uncover the mastermind of the 2001 anthrax attacks.

"Preston humanizes his science reportage by focusing on individuals-scientists, patients, physicians, government figures. That, and a flair for teasing out without overstatement the drama in his inherently compelling topics, plus a prose style that's simple and forceful, make this book as exciting as the best thrillers, yet scarier by far, for Preston's pages deal with clear, present and very real dangers." Publishers Weekly.

Randall, David K.

Black Death at the Golden Gate : the race to save America from the bubonic plague / David K. Randall. W. W. Norton & Co., 2019. 273 p. **616.9**

1. Plague 2. Black Death 3. Quarantine 4. Immigrants 5. San Francisco, California

ISBN 9780393609455

LC 2018055377

Traces the massive effort to contain an outbreak of bubonic plague in 1900 San Francisco, detailing how the process was complicated by virulent racism, pseudoscience, and political cover-ups.

Weintraub, Pamela

Cure unknown : inside the Lyme disease epidemic / Pamela Weintraub. St. Martin's Griffin, 2013. xxii, 456 p. ; **616.9**

1. Lyme disease. 2. Communicable diseases. 3. Medical care. 4. Lyme disease -- Treatment.

ISBN 9781250044563

LC 2008007816

An investigation into the science, history, and politics of Lyme disease as observed by a journalist whose entire family contracted the illness traces its significant rise and the atypical presentations that have made its diagnosis and treatment difficult.

"The author deftly weaves top-notch research and reporting on this malevolent infection ... with the personal narrative of a family's encounters with ignorance and bias while fighting a tenacious, disabling illness. The result is a compelling read that is also important journalism." Discover.

Zaman, Muhammad H. (Muhammad Hamid)

Biography of resistance : the epic battle between people and pathogens / Muhammad H. Zaman, Ph.D. Harper Wave, 2020. 304 p. **616.9**

1. Antibiotics 2. Drug resistance in microorganisms 3. Pathogenic microorganisms 4. Virus diseases

ISBN 9780062862976

LC 2020002198

An award-winning Boston University educator and researcher provides a chilling look at the rise of antibiotic-resistant superbugs, explaining how we got here and what we must do to address this growing global health crisis.

"Recommended for readers interested in the history of science and medicine, and how human response to global issues informs and impacts pathogen research and antibacterial use." Library Journal

616.95 Sexually transmitted diseases, zoonoses

Grimes, Jill

Sexually transmitted disease : an encyclopedia of diseases, prevention, treatment, and issues / Jill Grimes, MD, editor ; Kristyn Fagerberg, MD and Lori Smith, MD, coeditors. Greenwood, 2014 2 volumes (xxxiii, 784 p.) : **616.95**

1. Sexually transmitted diseases -- Encyclopedias.

ISBN 9781440801341

LC 2013016319

This up-to-date, two-volume work provides A-Z coverage of all topics related to sexually transmitted disease, ranging from anatomy to modern legal and social implications to past and present methods of prevention, diagnosis, and treatment. --From publisher description.

"Simply written, this title will be of interest to both the general public and undergraduate students studying health care, sociology, and social work." Library Journal.

616.97 Diseases of immune system

Blum, Susan S.

The **immune** system recovery plan : a doctor's 4-step plan to : achieve optimal health and feel your best, strengthen your immune system, treat autoimmune disease, see immediate results / Susan S. Blum, M.D., M.P.H. ; with Michele Bender. Scribner, 2013. xiv, 378 p. : **616.97**

1. Autoimmune diseases -- Treatment 2. Immune system 3. Self-care, Health

ISBN 9781451694994

LC 2012031929

Outlines a four-step program for treating, reversing, and preventing autoimmune conditions and repairing the immune system, arguing that autoimmune disease occurs as a result of environmental toxins.

"By cycling back to the nonnegotiable role of food (for example, Blum expresses frustration with people who think low-calorie packaged snacks are healthy and states that most people are guilty of food amnesia) and examining the effects of infections on specific conditions, Blum encourages readers to play detective, find the root causes of their problem, and take control of recovery." Publishers Weekly.

Myers, Amy (Physician)
The **autoimmune** solution : prevent and reverse the full spectrum of inflammatory symptoms and diseases / Amy Myers, M.D. HarperOne, an imprint of HarperCollinsPublsihers, 2015 viii, 390 p. : **616.97**

1. Autoimmune diseases
ISBN 9780062347473

LC 2014017620

A leader in the paleo and functional medicine worlds introduces an accessible, easy-to-follow, and scientifically proven plan for preventing and reversing the full spectrum of autoimmune diseases.

"Americans who suffer from psoriasis, type 1 diabetes, and other autoimmune diseases and want to treat them without conventional medicine will find many alternative ideas in this guide from medical doctor Myers." Booklist.

Sicherer, Scott H.
Food allergies : a complete guide for eating when your life depends on it / Scott H. Sicherer ; foreword by Maria Laura Acebal ; introduction by Hugh A. Sampson. Johns Hopkins University Press, c2013. xvii, 279 p. : **616.97**

1. Food allergy -- Diet therapy
ISBN 1421408988

LC 2012025274

"A Johns Hopkins Press health book"

Offers readers guidance on living with food allergies, discussing how the allergies develop, symptoms of a reaction, and recommendations for tests for diagnosing the allergies and the chronic health problems they can cause.

"This book is practical and informative without being overwhelming." Library Journal.

616.99 Tumors and miscellaneous communicable diseases

Aaronson, Naomi
Pilates for breast cancer survivors : a guide to recovery, healing, and wellness / Naomi Aaronson, MA, OTR/L CHT, CPI, CET, Ann Marie Turo, OTR/L. Demos Health, 2014 xvii, 227 p. : **616.99**

ISBN 9781936303571

LC 2014020932

Uses Pilates to guide women recovering from breast cancer through a series of exercises designed to strengthen arms and regain range of motion, reduce pain and swelling in tight areas affected by scars, and relieve stress.

Alschuler, Lise
The **definitive** guide to thriving after cancer : a five-step integrative plan to reduce the risk of recurrence and build lifelong health / Lise N. Alschuler, ND, FABNO and Karolyn A. Gazella. Ten Speed Press, 2013 viii, 216 p. ; **616.99**

1. Cancer -- Diet therapy 2. Cancer -- Prevention
ISBN 9781607745648

LC 2013014557

Revision of: Five to thrive. -- El Segundo, California : Active Interest, 2011.

"A companion to The Definitive Guide to Cancer, outlining a 5-step integrative plan to living well after cancer, reducing the risk of a recurrence, and building a foundation for lifelong health".-- Provided by publisher.

"For cancer survivors and caregivers who need a well-organized, comprehensible manual for healthy living after cancer and who don't already have the previous titles by these authors." Library Journal.

Funk, Kristi
Breasts : the owner's manual : every woman's guide to reducing cancer risk, making treatment choices, and optimizing outcomes / Dr. Kristi Funk. Thomas Nelson, 2018 xxiii, 392 p. : **616.99**

1. Breast care 2. Breast cancer -- Prevention. 3. Breast cancer -- Risk factors. 4. Breast cancer -- Treatment.
ISBN 9780785218722

LC 2018000692

A holistic guide to total breast health arms women with the most up-to-date tools for prevention and includes compassionate and complete explanations of treatment options.

Graeber, Charles
The **breakthrough** : immunotherapy and the race to cure cancer / Charles Graeber. Grand Central Pub 2018 352 p. **616.99**

1. Immunotherapy 2. Cancer research 3. Cancer -- Treatment
ISBN 9781455568505

LC bl2018183865

The New York Times best-selling author of The Good Nurse, details the astonishing scientific discovery of the code to unleashing the human immune system to fight--and possibly even cure--cancer.

Mukherjee, Siddhartha
★The **emperor** of all maladies : a biography of cancer / Siddhartha Mukherjee. Scribner, 2010. xiv, 571 p., 8 p. of plates : **616.99**

1. Cancer. 2. Oncology. 3. Chemotherapy. 4. Leukemia
ISBN 9781439107959

LC 2010024114

ALA Notable Book, 2012.
Guardian First Book Award, 2011.
Pulitzer Prize for General Nonfiction, 2011.
National Book Critics Circle Award for Nonfiction finalist, 2010.

A historical assessment of cancer addresses both the courageous battles against the complex disease and the misperceptions and hubris that have compromised modern understandings, covering such topics as ancient-world surgeries and the developments of present-day treatments.

"Mukherjee's formidable intelligence and compassion produce a stunning account of the effort to disrobe the emperor of maladies." Publishers Weekly.

Port, Elisa
★The **new** generation breast cancer book : how to navigate your diagnosis and treatment options--and remain optimistic--in an age of information overload / Elisa Port, MD, FACS, Chief of Breast Surgery at The Mount Sinai Hospital and Co-director of the Dubin Breast Center. Ballantine Books, 2015 xix, 298 p. ; **616.99**

1. Breast -- Cancer -- Treatment 2. Breast -- Cancer 3. Women -- Health and hygiene
ISBN 9781101883143

LC 2015022841

Includes index.

Offers a comprehensive resource for diagnosis, prognosis and treatment of breast cancer, and includes information on mammograms, chemotherapy, where to get care and how to support someone with breast cancer.

Raza, Azra
The **first** cell : and the human costs of pursuing cancer to the last / Azra Raza. Basic Books, 2019 336 p. ; **616.99**
1. Raza, Azra 2. Cancer -- Prevention 3. Oncologists 4. People with cancer 5. Physician and patient
ISBN 9781541699526
LC 2019016257

A world-class oncologist and coeditor of the 3QuarksDaily website explores the medical, scientific, cultural and personal impact of cancer while outlining more beneficial alternatives to today's high-cost, largely ineffective treatments.

Ross, Theodora
A **cancer** in the family : take control of your genetic inheritance / Theodora Ross, M.D., PH.D. Avery, 2016 xv, 286 p. : **616.99**
1. Cancer -- Genetic aspects 2. Families -- History
ISBN 9781101982839
LC 2015026294

An authoritative reference for people facing a genetic predisposition to cancer draws on the author's experiences as both an oncologist and genetic melanoma survivor to explain how to identify risk patterns, obtain testing and make informed decisions without fear.

"Recommended for readers seeking appropriate information on hereditary cancers, including their causes, and risk management as well as those beyond the target audience who are interested in sound writing on medical topics." Library Journal.

Roth, Andrew J.
Managing prostate cancer : a guide for living better / Andrew J. Roth, MD. Oxford University Press, 2015 xi, 354 p. : **616.99**
1. Men -- Health and hygiene -- United States 2. Physician and patient 3. Prostate -- Cancer -- Psychological aspects 4. Prostate -- Cancer -- United States
ISBN 9780199336920
LC 2015016699

A psychiatrist who specializes in support for cancer patients provides the emotional skills and strategies needed to healthfully deal with the challenges that a prostate cancer diagnosis brings to daily life. These tools, which he terms "Emotional Judo," will also help healthcare givers to provide improved support for their patients and families.

"Roth offers a first-rate overview of how best to respond to a diagnosis of prostate cancer." Booklist.

Servan-Schreiber, David
Anticancer : a new way of life / David Servan-Schreiber. Viking, 2008. 304 p. **616.99**
1. Cancer -- Prevention. 2. Medicine. 3. People with cancer 4. Research.
ISBN 9780670020348
LC 2008015721

The author describes his treatment for brain cancer, challenges beliefs about the body's ability to heal, identifies the environmental and lifestyle factors that promote cancer growth, and outlines conventional and alternative therapies.

"Servan-Schreiber underscores that his advice should be an adjunct to, not a replacement for, conventional treatments like surgery and chemotherapy, in this spirited mixture of good medical information, helpful suggestions and alternative medicine." Publishers Weekly.

Silver, Marc, 1951-
Breast cancer husband : how to help your wife (and yourself) through diagnosis, treatment, and beyond / Marc Silver ; foreword by Frederick P. Smith. Rodale, 2004. xv, 319 p. ; **616.99**
1. Breast -- Cancer 2. Breast -- Cancer -- Patients -- Family relationships 3. Breast -- Cancer -- Psychological aspects 4. Caregivers
ISBN 9781579548339
LC 2004007914

Includes index.

A guide for men whose wives contract breast cancer offers emotional support and advice every husband needs, including guidance from breast cancer doctors and the shared experiences of those who have gone through the same ordeal.

"Silver's prose is funny, tender, and filled with rock-solid advice." Library Journal.

Walsh, Patrick C., 1938-
★**Dr.** Patrick Walsh's guide to surviving prostate cancer / Patrick C. Walsh, M.D., and Janet Farrar Worthington. Grand Central Life & Style, 2018. xvi, 524 p. : **616.99**
1. Prostate -- Cancer
ISBN 9781538727478
LC bl2018072795

Includes index.

This guide covers every aspect of prostate cancer, from potential causes including diet to tests for diagnosis, curative treatment, and innovative means of controlling advanced stages of cancer. --From publisher description.

Wapner, Jessica
The **Philadelphia** chromosome : a mutant gene and the quest to cure cancer at the genetic level / Jessica Wapner ; foreword by Robert A. Weinberg. The Experiment, LLC, 2013. 272 p. **616.99**
1. Drug industry and trade. 2. Leukemia 3. Chromosomes 4. Mutation (Biology)
ISBN 9781615190676
LC 2012047686

Discusses the history of a single genetic mutation, discovered in 1959, that causes chronic myeloid leukemia and traces the important scientific research and breakthroughs over decades that led to the development of a drug that makes this once-fatal illness now treatable.

"Wapner weaves together the basic and applied science with the stories of the dedicated researchers, the broader supporting superstructure of modern medicine and the process of bringing pharmaceuticals to market. An absorbing, complex medical detective story." Kirkus.

617 Surgery, regional medicine, dentistry, ophthalmology, otology, audiology

Anshel, Jeffrey
What you must know about dry eye : how to prevent, stop, or reverse dry eye disease / Jeffrey Anshel, OD. Square One Publishers, 2019 135 p. **617**
1. Dry eye syndromes
ISBN 9780757004797
LC 2019018125

If you are one of the millions of people who suffer from dry eye, you know that this disorder can affect both your feeling of well-being and your ability to function in the world. What You Must Know About Dry Eye tells you how to relieve this common condition while improving and safeguarding your vision. --From publisher description.

"It's an eye-opening look at a condition that affects quality of life, especially for people over 40." Booklist.

Clements, Carol (Personal trainer)

Better balance for life : banish the fear of falling with simple activities added to your everyday routine a 10-week plan / Carol Clements. The Experiment, 2018 182 p. **617**

1. Falls (Accidents) in old age -- Prevention 2. Exercise for older people

ISBN 9781615194155

LC 2017026289

As you age, stumbling blocks are everywhere: the bottom step, the roadside curb, and even the living room carpet. But you don't have to live in fear of falling. With Better Balance for Life, you will learn all-new, simple activities to help you build strength and increase flexibility to improve your balance! In this ten-week program, personal trainer Carol Clements shows you effortless moves to slide into your everyday routine. --From publisher description.

"These excellent illustrated instructions that can easily be performed will help seniors increase their strength and avoid injury." Library Journal.

Laar, Arnold van de

Under the knife : a history of surgery in 28 remarkable operations / Arnold van de Laar. St. Martin's Press, 2018 320 p. **617**

1. Surgery -- History 2. Medicine -- History 3. Surgeons

ISBN 9781250200105

LC 2018019684

Translation of: Onder het mes : de beroemdste patiënten en operaties uit de geschiedenis van de chirurgie.

Originally published: Amsterdam : Thomas Rap, 2014.

From the story of the desperate man from seventeenth-century Amsterdam who grimly cut a stone out of his own bladder to Bob Marley's deadly toe, Under the Knife offers a wealth of fascinating and unforgettable insights into medicine and history via the operating room.

"Beyond his interesting review of surgical history, van de Laar also offers insight into the thought process and philosophy of those who cut to heal." Booklist.

Otto, Mary

Teeth : the story of beauty, inequality, and the struggle for oral health in America / Mary Otto. The New Press, 2016. 288 p. ; **617**

1. Dental care 2. Medical care 3. Inequality 4. Health policy 5. United States

ISBN 9781620971444

LC 2016041484

Takes readers on a disturbing journey into the role teeth play in our health and our social mobility. Muckraking and paradigm-shifting, Teeth exposes for the first time the extent and meaning of our oral health crisis.

"A focused, well-researched depiction of the dental industry's social and cultural relevance and its dire need for reform." Kirkus.

Sacks, Oliver, 1933-2015

The **island** of the colorblind and, Cycad island / Oliver Sacks. A.A. Knopf, 1997. xv, 298 p. : **617**

1. Color-blindness -- Micronesia -- Case studies. 2. Medical anthropology. 3. Neuroscience -- Research. 4. Parkinson's disease -- Case studies. 5. Micronesia -- Description and travel. 6. Caroline Islands. 7. Guam.

ISBN 0679451145

LC 96034252

Colored maps on endpapers.

The best-selling author of The Man Who Mistook His Wife for a Hat describes his journey to the remote islands of the Pacific--one that is inhabited by an isolated colorblind community and another that is the site of a baffling neurodegenerative paralysis.

"As a travel writer, Sacks ranks with Paul Theroux and Bruce Chatwin. As an investigator of the mind's mysteries, he is in a class by himself." Publishers Weekly.

617.1 Injuries and wounds

Fainaru-Wada, Mark.

League of denial : the NFL, concussions, and the battle for truth / Mark Fainaru-Wada; and Steve Fainaru. Crown Archetype, 2013. 399 p. **617.1**

1. NFL 2. Football injuries 3. Brain -- Concussion 4. Corporate cover-ups. 5. Head -- Wounds and injuries

ISBN 9780770437541

LC bl2013043145

Award-winning ESPN investigative reporters Mark Fainaru-Wada and Steve Fainaru reveal how the NFL, over a period of nearly two decades, sought to cover up and deny mounting evidence of the connection between football and brain damage.

John, Tommy

Minimize injury, maximize performance : a sport parent's survival guide / Dr. Tommy John, with Myatt Murphy. DeCapo, Lifelong, 2018. xvii, 285 p. : **617.1**

1. Athletes -- Nutrition 2. Sports injuries -- Prevention 3. Sports medicine

ISBN 9780738233802

LC bl2018181787

Outlines a diet, lifestyle, and movement plan to minimize sports injuries in young athletes.

Krabak, Brian,

The **long** distance runner's guide to injury prevention and treatment : how to avoid common problems and deal with them when they happen / edited by Brian J. Krabak, MD, MBA, FACSM, Grant S. Lipman, MD, FACEP, and Brandee L. Waite, MD, FAAPMR. Skyhorse Publishing, 2017 424 p. : **617.1**

1. Running -- Physiological aspects. 2. Running injuries -- Prevention. 3. Running injuries -- Treatment.

ISBN 9781510717909

LC 2017021922

Medical professsionals explain the most common causes of injuries to long distance runners and offers advice on how best to avoid and treat athletic ailments.

617.4 Surgery by systems and regions

Jones, Chip

The **organ** thieves : the shocking story of the first heart transplant in the segregated South / Chip Jones. Jeter Publishing, 2020 399 p. **617.4**

1. Human experimentation in medicine 2. Heart -- Transplantation 3. African Americans -- Medical care -- History. 4. Racism in medical care 5. Southern States

ISBN 9781982107529

LC bl2020015982

An investigation into how racial inequality has shaped the heart transplant race describes how in 1968 an injured black man checked into a hospital before his heart was removed and donated without his family's knowledge or consent.

"A dramatic and fine-grained expose of the mistreatment of black Americans by the country's white medical establishment." Publishers Weekly

Kean, Sam

The **tale** of the dueling neurosurgeons : the history of the human brain as revealed by true stories of trauma, madness, and recovery / Sam Kean. Little, Brown and Company, 2014. 400 p. **617.4**

1. Brain -- Physiology. 2. Neuroscience -- History. 3. Brain -- Diseases 4. Neurology.

ISBN 9780316182348

LC 2014004910

The author of the best-seller The Disappearing Spoon offers fascinating tales of the brain and the history of neuroscience

"Entertaining and quotable, Kean's writing is sharp, and each individual story brings the history of neuroscience to life. Compulsively readable, wicked scientific fun." Kirkus.

Snyder, Rich

What you must know about dialysis : the secrets to surviving and thriving on dialysis / Rich Snyder. Square One Publishers, c2013. vii, 197 p. ; **617.4**

1. Hemodialysis 2. Hemodialysis -- Patients

ISBN 9780757003493

LC 2012028692

"Dialysis can be a life-saving technique for the individual whose kidneys are unable to remove toxic waste and excess water from the blood. But over time, the process can become both physically debilitating and psychologically difficult. To address these issues, kidney specialist Dr. Rich Snyder has written a complete guide to dialysis. This book not only provides answers to common questions about the process, but also offers practical advice and strategies, as well as complementary options that can help you deal successfully with the many aspects of your treatment plan. --From publisher description."

"A great consumer health resource, especially for those just beginning dialysis, this is also recommended as a support tool for family, friends, and caregivers of dialysis patients." Library Journal.

Stoler, Diane Roberts

Coping with concussion and mild traumatic brain injury : a guide to living with the challenges associated with post concussion syndrome and brain trauma / Diane Roberts Stoler, Ed.D., and Barbara Albers Hill. Avery, 2013 xi, 378 : p. : **617.4**

1. Brain damage -- Patients -- Rehabilitation 2. Brain damage -- Psychological aspects 3. Brain damage 4. Brain -- Wounds and injuries -- Complications

ISBN 9781583334768

LC 2013016860

A comprehensive guide to improving mental clarity and quality of life in the aftermath of a concussion draws on the expertise of a neuropsychologist and concussion survivor to counsel patients and caregivers on how to manage symptoms.

"Filled with practical advice on understanding and living with concussion and TBI, this well-written and well-organized volume is an excellent resource for patients who have suffered from this condition and for their family members." Library Journal.

Swartz, Mimi

Ticker : the quest to create an artificial heart / Mimi Swartz. Crown, [2018] 304 p. ; **617.4**

1. Frazier, O. Howard 2. Cohn, Billy 3. Artificial heart 4. Surgeons 5. Heart 6. Cardiology 7. Houston, Texas

ISBN 9780804138000

LC 2017058910

A two-time National Magazine Award winner traces the medical and technological quest to develop a successful artificial heart implant, chronicling the evolution of cardiac medicine while exploring the pioneering work of two Texas Heart Institute innovators.

"Told in an appropriately over-the-top style, this is a quintessentially Texas story: sprawling, unpredictable, and teeming with risk and opportunity." Publishers Weekly.

617.5 Regional medicine

Deyo, Richard A.

Watch your back! : how the back pain industry is costing us more and giving us less, and what you can do to inform and empower yourself in seeking treatment / Richard A. Deyo MD. 212 p. **617.5**

1. Backache -- Treatment. 2. Back -- Diseases -- Treatment. 3. Medical care 4. Health

ISBN 9780801453243

LC 2014006972

"Concise, clearly written, and evidence based, Deyo's work would be invaluable to those facing the onset of back pain and the dizzying range of treatment choices, as well as to practitioners and policy makers." Library Journal.

Laskas, Jeanne Marie, 1958-

Concussion / Jeanne Marie Laskas. Random House, 2015 269 p., 8 unnumbered p. of plates : **617.5**

1. Omalu, Bennet I. (Bennet Ifeakandu) 2. NFL 3. Sports -- Moral and ethical aspects 4. Football injuries 5. Sports injuries 6. Sports medicine

ISBN 9780812989267

Tells the true story of how forensic neuropathologist Bennet Omalu discovered a dangerous secret that the National Football League desperately tried to keep silent.

"Effectively sobering. Suffice it to say that Pop Warner parents will want to armor their kids from head to toe upon reading it." Kirkus.

617.6 Dentistry

Artemis, Nadine, 1971-

Holistic dental care : the complete guide to healthy teeth and gums / Nadine Artemis ; foreword by Victor Zeines. North Atlantic Books, c2013. xvii, 130 p. : **617.6**

ISBN 9781583947203

LC 2013014011

A full-color comprehensive guide to natural, do-it-yourself oral care introduces simple, at-home dental procedures that anyone can do.

Sterling, Evelina Weidman, 1970-

Your child's teeth : a complete guide for parents / Evelina Weidman Sterling and Angie Best-Boss. The Johns Hopkins

University Press, 2013 x, 284 p. : **617.6**

1. Children -- Dental care 2. Pedodontics
ISBN 9781421410623
LC 2012047776

"Untypical, too, but much appreciated are Days admissions of difficult times and how to overcome them. A super (and superquirky) memoir." Booklist.

Wynbrandt, James
The **excruciating** history of dentistry : toothsome tales & oral oddities from Babylon to braces / James Wynbrandt. St. Martin's Griffin, 2000, c1998. viii, 248 p. : **617.6**

1. Dentistry -- History.
ISBN 9780312263195
LC BL2001005603

An informative and often humorous look at how people have been caring for their teeth since biblical times explores how the painful, sometimes fatal procedures of the past have developed into the high-tech protocols of today.

"The author discusses the development of dentistry as a profession, the use of different anesthetics, and the evolution of dentures and dental prosthetics, among other topics. Much of the book is devoted to anecdotes illustrating discontinued dental practices." Library Journal.

617.8 Otology and audiology

Owen, David, 1955-
Volume control : hearing in a deafening world / David Owen. Riverhead Books, 2019. 288 p. **617.8**

1. Medical innovations 2. Deafness 3. Hearing 4. Cochlear implants
ISBN 9780525534228

Citing the millions of Americans suffering from hearing loss and the stigmas and costs that challenge treatment, a New Yorker staff writer outlines the science of hearing while profiling the remarkable new technologies of today's medical community.

617.9 Operative surgery and special fields of surgery

Cole-Adams, Kate
Anesthesia : the gift of oblivion and the mystery of consciousness / Kate Cole-Adams. Counterpoint Press, 2017. 408 p. **617.9**

1. Surgery 2. Consciousness 3. Medical research 4. Anesthesia 5. Australian
ISBN 9781619029507
LC 2017034798

Originally published: Melbourne: Text Publishing, 2017.

The author examines what happens to the unconscious mind while under the effects of anesthesia, tracing her own experiences with surgery and the accounts of people who have reported trauma, waking mid-surgery, dreams, hallucinations and submerged memories while under anesthesia.

" While the author raises more questions than she answers, and some readers may be put off by her less-that-straightforward style, these are thought-provoking questions, and Cole-Adams presents a lyrical journey through the vital question of what it means to be human." Kirkus.

618.1 Gynecology and obstetrics

Allmen, Tara
Menopause confidential : a doctor reveals the secrets to thriving through midlife / Tara Allmen, MD. HarperOne, 2016 248 p. ; **618.1**

1. Menopause 2. Middle-aged women -- Health and hygiene
ISBN 9780062447265
LC 2016028325

"An authoritative guide to understanding and navigating the hormonal changes and health issues women experience in midlife and beyond, from one of the leading medical experts in the field. The physical changes that occur after women turn forty are unavoidable--and can be unnerving. Menopause affects every aspect of life--from sex and sleep to mood and mental clarity to weight and body temperature. While there are a number of resources available, many are confusing and contradictory. Now, Manhattan gynecologist Dr. Tara Allmen, an experienced, nationally board-certified menopause practitioner and the recipient of the 2015 Doctor's Choice National Award for Obstetrics & Gynecology, shares her knowledge to help women be their happiest and healthiest, and turn this challenging time into an exciting one. Written in her effervescent yet assured voice, Menopause Confidential provides simple strategies and cutting-edge information on: hormonal changes and the symptoms of perimenopause and menopause; the health risks associated with midlife--from cutting through the conflicting opinions and advice about health screenings (Do I really need a colonoscopy? How often should I get a mammogram?) to common medical conditions, such as osteoporosis; various remedies, both allopathic and natural, to combat symptoms and empower women to make the best choices for their individual needs; practical tips and resources for mitigating the effects of menopause. Fifty-one-year-old Dr. Allmen knows firsthand what women are going through, and shares stories of her own personal travails and solutions. Women can't turn back the clock, but they can take control of their health and flourish in midlife. Menopause Confidential encourages them to be informed, be proactive, and be their greatest selves".-- Provided by publisher.

"Board-certified gynecologist and nationally certified menopause practitioner Allmen offers a comprehensive health guide for women over 40." Library Journal.

Anstett, Patricia, 1947-
Breast cancer surgery and reconstruction : what's right for you / Patricia Anstett ; with photography by Kathleen Galligan. Rowman & Littlefield, 2016 ix, 229 p. : **618.1**

1. Breast -- Surgery 2. Surgery, Plastic
ISBN 9781442242623
LC 2016003294

"This important, well-reported guide should empower women with breast cancer to figure out their own best treatment." Booklist.

Greer, Germaine, 1939-
The **change** : women, aging, and the menopause / Germaine Greer. Fawcett Columbine, 1993, c1991. 422 p. ; **618.1**

1. Menopause -- Psychological aspects 2. Menopause 3. Middle aged women -- Psychology 4. Self-actualization (Psychology)
ISBN 9780449908532
LC BL 99740521

Originally published: London : Hamish Hamilton, 1991.

Challenges accepted notions about the physical and emotional effects of menopause and aging.

"In a wise, witty and inspiring book, Greer rebukes doctors, psychiatrists--and women themselves--who blame the aging female for her menopausal distress. Greer dispels all manner of myths and misconceptions about menopause." Publishers Weekly.

Love, Susan M.

Dr. Susan Love's breast book / Susan M. Love, M.D. ; with Elizabeth Love and Karen Lindsey ; illustrations by Marcia Williams. Da Capo Lifelong, 2015 xiii, 690 p. : **618.1**

1. Breast -- Diseases 2. Breast cancer 3. Cancer -- Diagnosis 4. Breast care

ISBN 9780738218212

LC 2015458675

"A Merloyd Lawrence Book."

Offers the most cutting-edge information for those at risk of getting breast cancer or those who already have it, including the latest in genetic research, advances in imaging, recognition of breast density as a risk factor, a section focused on personalized medicine and much more.

Potter, Daniel A. (Physician)

What to do when you can't get pregnant : the complete guide to all the options for couples facing fertility issues / Daniel A. Potter, MD, and Jennifer S. Hanin, MA ; foreword by Pamela Madsen. Da Capo Press, a member of the Perseus Books Group, 2013. xxii, 329 p. : **618.1**

1. Human reproductive technology 2. Infertility -- Treatment

ISBN 9780738216911

LC 2013372225

An internationally renowned fertility expert offers an up-to-date guide on the latest technology, procedures, and drugs available to women who are having difficulty conceiving, offering useful advice on how to make the right fertility choices.

"This solid, up-to-date resource supplants Debra Fulghum Bruce and Samuel Thatcher's Making a Baby: Everything You Need To Know To Get Pregnant. Recommended for most consumer health collections." Library Journal.

Sheehy, Gail, 1937-2020

The **silent** passage : menopause / Gail Sheehy. Pocket Books, 1998. xxvi, 293 p. ; **618.1**

1. Menopause -- Psychological aspects. 2. Menopause -- Social aspects. 3. Women -- Health. 4. Middle age.

ISBN 0671017748

LC 98065873

Includes index.

Looks at menopause, discussing the disquieting approach the medical community takes to it and offering commentary by some of today's most notable post-menopausal women.

Streicher, Lauren F.

The **essential** guide to hysterectomy : advice from a gynecologist on your choices before, during, and after surgery / Lauren F. Streicher, M.D. M. Evans, 2013 xiv, 466 p. : **618.1**

1. Hysterectomy 2. Patient education

ISBN 9781590772119

LC 2012043565

Includes index.

An updated guide to a delicate medical subject discusses all the options, technological advances, and new procedures involved in having a hysterectomy.

618.2 Obstetrics

Amato, Paula,

The **pregnancy** encyclopedia : all your questions answered / consultant editor Paula Amato ; editor-in-chief Dr. Chandrima Biswas, consultant obstetrician. DK Publishing, 2016. 351 p. : **618.2**

1. Pregnancy 2. Childbirth

ISBN 9781465443786

LC bl2015057786

Includes index.

Overflowing with full-color photos and illustrations, an ultimate pregnancy guide is filled with advice from top experts in the field who cover more than 300 topics of interest, including fertility, birth, nutrition, exercise and lifestyle changes, to expecting mothers and their partners.

Curtis, Glade B.

★**Your** pregnancy week by week / Glade B. Curtis, M.D., M.P.H., OB/GYN and Judith Schuler, M.S. DaCapo Lifelong, 2016. xii, 463 p. : **618.2**

1. Fetus -- Growth 2. Pregnancy

ISBN 9780738218939

LC 2016303069

Includes index.

A completely revised edition of the detailed pregnancy handbook that has been helping expectant parents for the last quarter century provides up-to-date information on the latest medical tests and procedures, safe exercises for moms and helpful hints for fathers.

Harshe, January

Birth without fear : The Judgment-Free Guide to Taking Charge of Your Pregnancy, Birth, and Postpartum / January Harshe. Hachette Books, 2019. xix, 267 p. ; **618.2**

1. Childbirth 2. Pregnancy 3. Pregnant women -- Health and hygiene 4. Puerperium

ISBN 9780316515597

LC 2018020001

The founder of the global online community Birth Without Fear presents an all-encompassing, nonjudgmental and empowering guide to pregnancy, childbirth and postpartum life that puts mothers first.

"Practical, positive, and empowering." Booklist.

Murkoff, Heidi Eisenberg

★**What** to expect when you're expecting / Heidi Murkoff and Sharon Mazel ; foreword by Charles J. Lockwood, MD, Professor of obstetrics and gynecology and public health, Dean, Morsani College of Medicine, University of South Florida. Workman Publishing, 2016 xii, 644 p. : **618.2**

1. Pregnancy 2. Childbirth 3. Postnatal care

ISBN 9780761189244

LC 2015044527

Includes index.

Offers advice, insight, and tips for moms and dads, discussing pregnancy and birthing practices, prenatal screenings, postpartum birth control, and nutrition.

Oster, Emily

Cribsheet : a data-driven guide to better, more relaxed parenting, from birth to preschool / Emily Oster. Penguin Press, 2019. xxv, 322 p. : **618.2**

1. Pregnancy -- Decision making. 2. Pregnant women -- Health and

hygiene. 3. Pregnancy -- Economic aspects. 4. Parenthood.
ISBN 9780525559252

LC 2018041564

"From the author of EXPECTING BETTER, an economist's guide to the early years of parenting With Expecting Better, award-winning economist Emily Oster spotted a need in the pregnancy market for advice that gave women the information they needed to make the best decision for their own pregnancies. By digging into the data, Oster found that much of the conventional pregnancy wisdom was wrong. In Cribsheet, she now tackles an even great challenge: decision making in the early years of parenting. As any new parent knows, there is an abundance of often-conflicting advice hurled at you from doctors, family, friends, and the internet. From the earliest days, parents get the message that they must make certain choices around feeding, sleep, and schedule or all will be lost. There's a rule--or three--for everything. But the benefits of these choices can be overstated, and the tradeoffs can be profound. How do you make your own best decision? Armed with the data, Oster finds that the conventional wisdom doesn't always hold up. She debunks myths around breastfeeding (not a panacea), sleep training (not so bad!), potty training (wait until they're ready or possibly bribe with M&Ms), language acquisition (early talkers aren't necessarily geniuses), and many other topics. She also shows parents how to think through freighted questions like if and how to go back to work, how to think about toddler discipline, and how to have a relationship and parent at the same time. Economics is the science of decision-making, and CRIBSHEET is a thinking parent's guide to the chaos and frequent misinformation of the early years. Emily Oster is a trained expert--and mom of two--who can empower us to make better, less fraught decisions--and stay sane in the years before preschool".-- Provided by publisher.

Romm, Aviva Jill

The **natural** pregnancy book : your complete guide to a safe, organic pregnancy and childbirth with herbs, nutrition, and other holistic choices / Aviva Jill Romm ; foreword by Ina May Gaskin. Ten Speed Press, 2014 304 p. **618.2**

1. Alternative medicine 2. Holistic medicine 3. Pregnancy
ISBN 9781607744481

LC OC2014102207

"A revised and updated edition of the classic handbook for women seeking a safe, organic, eco-friendly, and natural pregnancy, featuring an integrative-based approach with new medical, herbal, and nutritional information. Over the last two decades, The Natural Pregnancy Book has ushered thousands of women through happy and healthy pregnancies. Addressing women's health from conception to birth, Dr. Romm describes herbs that can promote and maintain a healthy pregnancy, and allays such familiar concerns as anxiety, fatigue, morning sickness, and stretch marks. She also discusses the components of a healthy diet, with an emphasis on natural foods. New to this edition is integrative health advice based on Dr. Romm's new credentials as a Yale-trained physician, combined with her twenty years of experience as a midwife and herbalist".-- Provided by publisher.

Rope, Kate

Strong as a mother : how to stay healthy, happy, and (most importantly) sane from pregnancy to parenthood : the only guide to taking care of you! / Kate Rope. St. Martin's Griffin, 2018 xii, 388 p. ; **618.2**

1. Pregnancy -- Health aspects. 2. Pregnant women -- Health and hygiene.
ISBN 9781250105585

LC 2017059644

Includes index.

Kate Rope's Strong as a Mother is a practical and compassionate guide to preparing for a smooth start to motherhood. Everyone knows the secret to having "the Happiest Baby on the Block." This is your guide to being the Sanest Mommy on the Block. It will prepare you with humor and grace for what lies ahead, give you the tools you need to take care of yourself, permission to struggle at times, and professional advice on how to move through it when you do. This book will become a dog-eared resource on your nightstand, offering you the same care and support that you are working so hard to provide to your child. It will help you prioritize your emotional health, set boundaries and ask for help, make choices about feeding and childcare that feel good to you, get good sleep, create a strong relationship with your partner, make self care an everyday priority, trust your instincts, and actually enjoy the hardest job you will ever love. --From publisher description.

"Rope's book offers women commonsense guidance and vigorous reassurances on coping with the tumultuous changes of pregnancy and parenthood." Publishers Weekly.

Rowland, Kelly, 1981-

Whoa, baby! : a guide for new moms who feel overwhelmed and freaked out (and wonder what the #*$& just happened) / Kelly Rowland and Tristan Emily Bickman, MD with Laura Moser. Da Capo Lifelong, 2017. xv, 176 p. : **618.2**

1. Childbirth 2. Parenting 3. Pregnancy 4. Women -- Health and hygiene
ISBN 9780738219424

LC 2016043406

"When vocalist and actress Kelly Rowland, whose albums have sold millions of copies worldwide, gave birth to her son, it was love at first sight. But she was also a little freaked out about what had happened to her body and the overwhelming new thoughts and emotions. In Whoa Baby!, Rowland and her OB-GYN Dr. Tristan Emily Bickman team up to cover everything a first-time mom needs to know: the gross physical stuff, the hormonal and emotional stuff, and the just plain weird stuff. Whoa, Baby! is often hilarious and always honest and down-to-earth. Readers will empathize with the candid unglamorous experiences of parenting. From falling asleep with the pump on to swollen legs and lack of sleep, Rowland and Dr. Bickman cover every surprising challenge that new moms face".-- Provided by publisher.

Simkin, Penny, 1938-

The **birth** partner : a complete guide to childbirth for dads, doulas, and all other labor companions / Penny Simkin. The Harvard Common Press, 2013 xx, 396 p. : **618.2**

1. Childbirth 2. Labor (Obstetrics) -- Complications 3. Natural childbirth -- Coaching 4. Pregnancy
ISBN 9781558328198

LC 2013007371

"Since the original publication of The Birth Partner in 1989, new mothers' mates, friends, and relatives and doulas (professional birth assistants) have relied on Penny Simkin's guidance in caring for the new mother from the last few weeks of pregnancy through the early postpartum period. Fully revised in its third edition, The Birth Partner remains the definitive guide for preparing to help a woman through childbirth and the essential manual to have at hand during the event. This completely updated edition includes thorough information on: Preparing for labor and knowing when it has begun; Normal labor and how to help the woman every step of the way; Epidurals and other medications for labor; Non-drug techniques for easing labor pain; Cesarean birth and complications that may require it; Breastfeeding and newborn care; And much more. For the partner who wishes to be truly helpful in the birthing room, this book is indispensable".-- Provided by publisher.

Vincent, Peggy, 1942-

Baby catcher : chronicles of a modern midwife / Peggy Vincent. Scribner, 2002. 336 p. ; **618.2**

1. Midwives. 2. Childbirth.
ISBN 0743219333

LC 2001054988

"This is an account of a midwife specializing in home births who over the course of 40 years, brought some 2,000 babies into the world. A solid writer, Vincent doesn't preach the virtues of unmedicated birthing; she just lays consistent stories of women doing itChristian Science moms, Muslim moms, spiritualist moms, lesbian moms, teen moms and just plain ordinary moms." Publishers Weekly.

Wick, Myra

Mayo Clinic guide to a healthy pregnancy / Myra J. Wick Mayo Clinic c2018. 518 p. : **618.2**

1. Pregnancy 2. Prenatal care
ISBN 9781893005600

LC bl2011008457

Includes index.

Fully revised and updated.

In this fully reviewed and revised second edition, you'll find updated guidance and practical tips.

618.3 Diseases, disorders, management of pregnancy, childbirth, puerperium

Azri, Stephanie, 1977-

The **prenatal** bombshell : help and hope when continuing or ending a precious pregnancy after an abnormal diagnosis / Stephanie Azri and Sherokee Ilse. Rowman & Littlefield, 2015 xl88 p. ; **618.3**

ISBN 9781442239425

LC 2014040890

The Prenatal Bombshell is for women who have received a poor or fatal prenatal diagnosis for their unborn child and have made the decision to either carry to term or terminate their pregnancies. The authors share emotional and practical information, as well as real accounts from women who have made these decisions and how they moved forward. --From publisher description.

"This book is an excellent vehicle for coming to grips with a very difficult situation." Publishers Weekly.

Guthrie, Julian

Good blood : a doctor, a donor, and the incredible breakthrough that saved millions of babies / Julian Guthrie. Abrams Press, 2020 246 p. **618.3**

1. Physicians 2. Blood donors 3. Blood -- Diseases 4. Anemia
ISBN 9781419743313

LC bl2020033611

In 1951 in Sydney, Australia, a fourteen-year-old boy named James Harrison was near death when he received a transfusion of blood that saved his life. A few years later, and half a world away, a shy young doctor at Columbia University realized he was more comfortable in the lab than in the examination room. Neither could have imagined how their paths would cross, or how they would change the world.

"Guthrie narrates her account like a novel, as her characters chat, think, brood, agonize, and ultimately triumph just as in a Hollywood movie. A readable pop-history account of medical research that turned out spectacularly." Kirkus

618.4 Childbirth

Silbernagel, Shantel

The **many** faces of home birth : 25 honest, firsthand accounts from parents around the world / Shantel Silbernagel. Skyhorse Publishing, 2017 xv, 169 p. ; **618.4**

1. Childbirth at home 2. Childbirth at home 3. Natural childbirth
ISBN 9781510724976

LC bl2017041965

Shares the personal narratives of twenty-five families who had a home birth.

618.6 Normal puerperium

Serrallach, Oscar

The **postnatal** depletion cure : a complete guide to rebuilding your health and reclaiming your energy for mothers of newborns, toddlers, and young children / Dr. Oscar Serrallach. Grand Central Life & Style, 2018. xv, 287 p. ; **618.6**

1. Postnatal care 2. Postnatal care -- Treatment
ISBN 9781478970293

LC 2017046606

A guide to navigating postpartum depression by treating the nutrient depletion, sleep loss and emotional shifts that affect women for years after childbirth also shares insights into how pregnancy affects the body and how to find support.

"A practical volume that will be of use to mothers everywhere." Library Journal.

618.7 Puerperal diseases

Fox Starr, Rebecca, 1985-

Beyond the baby blues : anxiety and depression during and after pregnancy / Rebecca Fox Starr. Rowman & Littlefield, 2018 xi, 141 p. ; **618.7**

1. Postpartum depression -- Treatment 2. Postpartum depression
ISBN 9781442273900

LC 2017023086

"This work promises to be a valuable refuge for expectant mothers and their families confronting the specter of prenatal and postpartum depression." Publishers Weekly.

618.92 Pediatrics

Barkley, Russell A., 1949-

Taking charge of ADHD : the complete, authoritative guide for parents / Russell A. Barkley, PhD. The Guilford Press, 2013 xvi, 363 p. ; **618.92**

1. Attention-deficit hyperactivity disorder 2. Child rearing
ISBN 9781462508518

LC 2012050510

Provides a step-by-step plan for ADHD diagnosis and treatment, behavior management, strategies for helping children succeed at school and in social situations, and information on advances in research.

"The author reports on his own theory, recent research, and strategies for parents in the challenge of raising children with attention problems. His view is that attention-deficit hyperactivity disorder (ADHD) is a 'disorder of self-regulation' and that the problems of inattention, overactivity, and lack of inhibition become a developmental disability when extreme. ADHD is described as a neurologically based disorder with a probable genetic base." Science Books & Films.

Bryson, Tina Payne

The **bottom** line for baby : from sleep training to screens, thumb sucking to tummy time--what the science says / Tina Payne Bryson, Ph.D.. Ballantine Books, 2020 xxvii, 297 p. ; **618.92**

1. Infant care 2. Parent and infant. 3. Infant psychology.

ISBN 9780593129968

LC 2019053246

"What the Science Says About Your Biggest Questions and Concerns"-- Provided by publisher.

"Psychotherapist Bryson (No-Drama Discipline) offers a splendid guide to help parents and caregivers 'wade through the cacophony' of sometimes conflicting information and opinions about baby care. . . . Parents, grandparents, and caretakers would do well to pick up this comprehensive work." Publishers Weekly

Chansky, Tamar E. (Tamar Ellsas), 1962-

Freeing your child from anxiety : practical strategies to overcome fears, worries, and phobias and be prepared for life--from toddlers to teens / Tamar E. Chansky, Ph.D. ; illustrations by Phillip Stern. Harmony Books, 2014. viii, 468 p. : **618.92**

1. Anxiety in children.

ISBN 0804139806

LC 2013050665

An authoritative resource written by a prominent childhood-anxiety expert guides parents through a proven program that will help their children overcome their fears, worries and anxieties to lead happier, healthier lives.

Chicoine, Brian

The **guide** to good health for teens & adults with Down syndrome / Brian Chicoine and Dennis McGuire. Woodbine House, c2010. xvi, 391 p. : **618.92**

1. Down syndrome -- Patients -- Health and hygiene 2. Down syndrome -- Complications

ISBN 9781890627898

LC 2010018783

Provides invaluable insight into what health problems are more common in their patients, and how medical issues can present differently in people with Down syndrome.

Cohen, Scott W.

Eat, sleep, poop : a common sense guide to your baby's first year--essential information from an award-winning pediatrician and new dad / Scott W. Cohen. Scribner, 2010. xi, 291 p. : **618.92**

1. Infants -- Care.

ISBN 1439117063

LC 2009037966

Includes index.

Cohen, a Beverly Hills pediatrician on the Cedars Sinai Medical Center teaching staff, penned this guide during his daughter's first year of life. Neither starchy reference tome nor sentimental diary, the book weaves useful facts and information with Cohen's often comical, personal accounts of being a regular dad who is also a pediatrician (sidebars called "Daddy vs. Doctor" probe such topics as sleeping through the night, Apgar scores, and birthmarks). In keeping with the book's title, Cohen maintains that three mundane activities--eating, sleeping, and defecating--make up "most of baby's agenda." He devotes a good portion of his text to these three subjects, but also delves into a flurry of other concerns, such as vaccinations, why babies cry, and whatto do about colic (presenting a viable theory relating to stress). For each issue, Cohen concludes with "common sense bottom line" summaries, advising parents to stick to the essentials, whether planning a nursery or choosing a pediatrician. Doing what works for one's individual family is what counts--for instance, he counsels moms that breast is best but not to feel guilty if they choose to bottle-feed. Cohen's practical approach is sure to pacify and entertain first-time parents who can easily become overwhelmed by both the joys and challenges of baby's first year.

"Cohen is great at identifying parental concerns, and he responds with reassuring answers, providing just enough information to assuage worries. Of the multitude of baby guides out there, this is, hands down, one of the best in years." Library Journal.

Delmolino, Lara

Essential first steps for parents of children with autism : helping the littlest learners / Lara Delmolino, PhD., BCBA-D & Sandra L. Harris, PhD. Woodbine House, 2013. xiv, 152 p. : **618.92**

1. Autistic children 2. Autistic children -- Education 3. Parents of autistic children

ISBN 9781606131893

LC 2013038047

When autism is diagnosed or suspected in young children, overwhelmed parents wonder where to turn and how to begin helping their child. Drs. Delmolino and Harris, experienced clinicians and ABA therapists, eliminate the confusion and guesswork by outlining the pivotal steps parents can take now to optimize learning and functioning for children age 5 and younger. The book covers: -- early indicators of ASD in children younger than 3 years -- behaviors of 3 to 5 year olds with a confirmed diagnosis -- research about effective treatments & teaching methods -- social, play, communication & self-help skills -- support for the rest of the family Case studies and a review of evidence-based interventions and proven practices help parents prepare a strong foundation for their child's future development. --From publisher description.

"Highly recommended for those with newly diagnosed children, this helpful work is essential for all public library collections." Library Journal.

DiGregorio, Sarah

Early : an intimate history of premature birth and what it teaches us about being human / Sarah DiGregorio. HarperCollins, 2020. 320 p. **618.92**

1. DiGregorio, Sarah 2. Premature infants 3. Neonatal intensive care 4. Premature labor 5. Mothers

ISBN 9780062820303

LC bl2020002787

Inspired by the author's harrowing experience giving birth to her premature daughter, a compelling and empathetic work that combines memoir with rigorous reporting to tell the story of neonatology--and to meditate on the questions raised by premature birth.

"A well-written, carefully researched book that should be of vital interest to potential parents and their friends and families." Library Journal.

Foss, Ben

The **dyslexia** empowerment plan : a blueprint for renewing your child's confidence and love of learning / Ben Foss. Ballantine Books, 2013 xxviii, 304 p. : **618.92**

1. Dyslexia. 2. Children with dyslexia -- Education 3. Parents of children with disabilities.

ISBN 9780345541239

LC 2013023931

The inventor of the Intel Reader shares inspirational ideas for accessing the tools and learning accommodations needed by dyslexic students in school and life, outlining a three-step strategy for skill building and advocacy while sharing advice on how to harness personal strengths to advance long-term goals.

Gnaulati, Enrico

Back to normal : why ordinary childhood behavior is mistaken for ADHD, bipolar disorder, and Autism Spectrum Disorder / Enrico Gnaulati, PHD. Beacon Press, c2013. xv, 239 p. ; **618.92**

ISBN 0807073342

LC 2013009182

A veteran clinical psychologist argues that today's children are routinely misdiagnosed with serious psychiatric conditions, explaining how the misdiagnoses are occurring while sharing tools for parents on how to differentiate serious conditions from behavior disturbances stemming from developmental, familial and social issues.

"Gnaulati makes a strong case that an incorrect diagnosis of behavioral problems can be stigmatizing and that prescription drugs frequently have overlooked, negative side effects. A valuable guide for parents and educators that includes tips on choosing a therapist and parenting strategies." Kirkus.

Greenspan, Stanley I.

Engaging autism : using the floortime approach to help children relate, communicate, and think / Stanley I. Greenspan, Serena Wieder. Da Capo Lifelong Books, 2009. xiv, 434 p. ; **618.92**

1. Children with autism -- Behavior modification 2. Behavior therapy 3. Social control 4. Parents of children with autism

ISBN 9780738210940

LC bl2014003387

In [this book, the authors] describe the DIR/Floortime approach and show how to enter a child's world and bring her or him into a shared world of relating, communicating, and thinking. Part I presents a new, more accurate way of defining autism and ASD and observing a child's earliest signs, and describes goals for working with children with ASD and other special needs within the DIR framework. Part II shows how families can take the lead in working with their children toward these goals. In Part III [the authors] describe the DIR model's Floortime technique and illustrate it in various contexts. Part IV looks at how to create a comprehensive treatment plan and how school environments can be modified to support treatment plans. In Part V, [they] address working with specific problems in greater depth. Appendices A-C present research that supports the DIR model. -Introd.

Jassey, Lewis

The **newborn** sleep book : a simple, proven method for training your new baby to sleep through the night / Dr. Lewis Jassey and Dr. Jonathan Jassey. Penguin Group, 2014. xxxiii, 190 p. ; **618.92**

1. Infants -- Sleep

ISBN 9780399167980

LC 2014011339

"A Perigee Book"--Title page.

"The first and only proven, safe plan for a sound night's sleep for newborns--and parents. Here is the first and only guide to lay out a detailed sleep program for newborns--as early as the first few weeks of life. Developed and refined by two successful pediatricians, the "Jassey Way" boasts a more than 90% success rate of getting children to sleep through the night prior to their one month birthday. A safe and proven technique, the Jassey Way uses a feeding schedule that allows newborns (and their parents) a full night's sleep at a younger age than other sleep training techniques".-- Provided by publisher.

Karp, Harvey

The **happiest** baby guide to great sleep : simple solutions for kids from birth to 5 years / Harvey Karp. William Morrow, 2012. xiii, 367 p. : **618.92**

1. Children -- Sleep 2. Infants -- Sleep 3. Sleep disorders in children

ISBN 0062113313

LC bl2012014329

A parenting expert debunks common myths about sleep, explains a child's sleep needs, and presents advice for parents that will help them get their child to sleep soundly through the night.

"While the advice is sound, the book is embarrassingly long while the author belabors the obvious, and the pace is insufferable. Despite the critique, patrons may likely request." Library Journal.

Keene, Nancy

★**Childhood** leukemia : a guide for families, friends & caregivers / Nancy Keene. Childhood Cancer Guides, 2018 xvi, 476 p. : **618.92**

1. Childhood leukemia

ISBN 9781941089040

LC 2017031837

The go-to guide for families of children with leukemia. Reviewed by renowned experts, it contains up-to-date medical information along with practical advice and poignant stories from more than 150 families of children with leukemia. Definitive, comprehensive and easy to read.

Latson, Jennifer

The **boy** who loved too much : a true story of pathological friendliness / Jennifer Latson. Simon & Schuster, 2017. 304 p. **618.92**

1. Williams syndrome 2. Children -- Friendship 3. Social interaction in children 4. Developmental disabilities

ISBN 9781476774046

LC 2016043207

A journalist describes the story of a twelve-year-old boy suffering from Williams syndrome, a genetic, developmental disorder that makes him impervious to social inhibitions and incapable of distrust, putting him at an extreme disadvantage for life in modern times.

"A well-researched, perceptive exploration of a rare genetic disorder seen through the eyes of a mother and son." Kirkus.

Leach, Penelope

Your baby & child : from birth to age five / Penelope Leach ; photography by Jenny Matthews. Alfred A. Knopf, 2010. 559 p. : **618.92**

1. Child care. 2. Child development. 3. Infants -- Care.

ISBN 0375712038

LC 2010022848

"New version for today."

Includes index.

Previous ed.: 2003.

A latest edition of a classic reference shares authoritative early child-care guidelines for today's parents, describing each stage of development from birth through the preschool years while defining child behaviors and addressing common concerns.

"In addition to physical growth and progress, Leach addresses the psychosocial needs of children. She also includes parent concerns and responses similar to those found in Workman's 'What To Expect' series. Public and academic libraries would do well to stock the new version of this primer on children and their development for circulation as well as for the reference shelf." Library Journal.

Linden, Dana Wechsler

Preemies : the essential guide for parents of premature babies / Dana Wechsler Linden, Emma Trenti Paroli, and Mia Wechsler Doron. Gallery Books, c2010. xxii, 633 p. : **618.92**

1. Premature infants 2. Premature infants -- Care 3. Birth weight, Low -- Complications 4. Pregnancy -- Complications
ISBN 9781416572329

LC 2011289347

Includes index.

Updated to incorporate the latest neonatology advances, a comprehensive guide shares advice on everything from risk factors and progress monitoring to homecoming preparations and development prospects.

Moon, Rachel,

Sleep : what every parent needs to know / Rachel Y. Moon, MD, FAAP, editor in chief. American Academy of Pediatrics, 2013 xxvi, 219 p. ; **618.92**

1. Sleep disorders in children. 2. Sleep disorders in adolescents. 3. Sleep -- Stages.
ISBN 9781581107814

LC bl2013043238

Includes index.

Identifies a variety of sleep problems in children from infancy through adolescence, and provides practical strategies for establishing good sleep habits and solving common sleep problems such as difficulties falling asleep and night fears.

Nigg, Joel T.

Getting ahead of ADHD : what next-generation science says about treatments that work -- and how you can make them work for your child / Joel T. Nigg. Guilford Press, 2017. 272 p. **618.92**

1. Attention-deficit hyperactivity disorder -- Alternative treatment. 2. Neuroscience. 3. Children with ADHD. 4. Genes.
ISBN 9781462524938

Presents exciting treatment advances to maximize the positive effects of healthy nutrition, exercise, and sleep, and minimize the damage from stress and other known risk factors.

"Parents will find reassurance, hope, and step-by-step action plans in this coherent guide to the current and evolving science on ADHD." Publishers Weekly.

Ozonoff, Sally

A **parent's** guide to high-functioning autism spectrum disorder : how to meet the challenges and help your child thrive / Sally Ozonoff, Geraldine Dawson, James C. McPartland. The Guilford Press, 2015 xi, 308 p. ; **618.92**

1. Asperger's syndrome 2. Autism spectrum disorders 3. Parents of autistic children
ISBN 9781462517473

LC 2014026326

"Packed with real-life stories and everyday problem-solving ideas, this book has given many tens of thousands of parents the facts they need about high-functioning autism spectrum disorder (ASD), including Asperger syndrome. The authors are leading experts who describe ways to work with these kids' unique impairments and capabilities so they can grow into happy, self-sufficient adults. Parents learn practical strategies for helping their son or daughter relate more comfortably to peers, learn the rules of appropriate behavior, and succeed in school. The book also discusses what scientists currently know about ASD and how it is diagnosed, as well as what treatments and educational supports have been shown to work. Updated with the latest research, resources, and clinical strategies, the second edition clearly explains the diagnostic changes in DSM-5".-- Provided by publisher.

Porto, Anthony

The **pediatrician's** guide to feeding babies & toddlers : practical answers to your questions on nutrition, starting solids, allergies, picky eating, and more / Anthony Porto, MD, MPH, Dina DiMaggio, MD. Ten Speed Press, 2016 viii, 247 p. : **618.92**

1. Children -- Nutrition 2. Food habits 3. Infants -- Nutrition
ISBN 9781607749011

LC 2015031409

An authoritative guide written by a team of medical and culinary experts--including a pediatrician, pediatric gastroenterologist, pediatric allergist and a personal chef--helps parents give their children the optimum nutrition they need to thrive during the crucial first years of life.

Prizant, Barry M.

Uniquely human : a different way of seeing autism / Barry M. Prizant, PhD ; with Tom Fields-Meyer. Simon & Schuster, 2015. x, 256 p. ; **618.92**

1. Autism in children. 2. Autism.
ISBN 1476776237

LC 2014035241

"Simon & Schuster nonfiction original hardcover."

In a book that aims to be essential reading for any parent, teacher, therapist or caregiver of a person with autism, one of the world's leading authorities on autism suggests a major shift in understanding autism and offers inspiring stories and practical advice drawn from his more than four-decade career.

"This positive volume should reassure parents and caregivers of kids with autism and any other disability that their kids are not broken, but, indeed, special." Booklist.

Saline, Sharon

What your ADHD child wishes you knew : working together to empower kids for success in school and life / Dr. Sharon Saline ; foreword by Laura Markham. A TarcherPerigee Book, 2018 xviii, 254 p. ; **618.92**

1. Attention-deficit hyperactivity disorder 2. Attention-deficit-disordered children 3. Attention-deficit hyperactivity disorder -- Social aspects 4. Parent and child
ISBN 9780143132394

LC 2018017661

"A veteran psychologist presents a proven roadmap to help ADHD kids succeed in school and life. You've read all the expert advice, but despite countless efforts to help your child cope better and stay on track, you're still struggling with everyday issues like homework, chores, getting to soccer practice on time, and simply getting along without push-back and power struggles. What if you could work with your child, motivating and engaging them in the process, to create positive change once and for all? In this insightful and practical book, veteran psychologist Sharon Saline shares the words and inner struggles of children and teens living with ADHD--and a blueprint for achieving lasting success by working together. Based on more than 25 years of experience counseling young people and their families, Dr. Saline's advice and real-world examples reveal how parents can shift the dynamic and truly help kids succeed. Topics include: * Setting mutual goals that foster cooperation * Easing academic struggles * Tackling everyday challenges, from tantrums and backtalk to staying organized, building friendships, and more. With useful exercises and easy-to-remember techniques, you'll discover a variety of practical strategies that really work, creating positive change that will last a lifetime"-- Provided by publisher.

Saul, Richard

ADHD does not exist : the truth about attention deficit and hyperactivity disorder / Richard Saul. HarperWave, 2014 336 p. **618.92**

1. Attention-deficit hyperactivity disorder. 2. Diagnosis. 3. Mental health

ISBN 9780062266736

LC 2013030794

Over the course of half a century, physician Richard Saul has worked with thousands of patients demonstrating symptoms of ADHD. Based on his experience, he offers a shocking conclusion: ADHD is not a condition on its own, but rather a symptom complex caused by over twenty separate conditions - from poor eyesight and giftedness to bipolar disorder and depression - each requiring its own specific treatment.

Schwarz, Alan, 1968-

ADHD nation : children, doctors, big pharma, and the making of an American epidemic / Alan Schwarz. Scribner, 2016. 352 p. **618.92**

1. Attention-deficit hyperactivity disorder. 2. Diagnostic errors. 3. Drug industry and trade 4. Adults with ADHD

ISBN 9781501105913

LC 2016018493

A cautionary assessment of what the author believes to be widespread misdiagnoses of ADHD argues that doctors and pharmaceutical companies are improperly targeting adults and children for commercial gain, sharing the dramatic stories of two patients while denouncing the work of ADHD expert Keith Conners.

"In this powerful, necessary book, Schwarz exposes the dirty secrets of the growing ADHD epidemic." Kirkus.

Sears, Robert W.

The **allergy** book : solving your family's nasal allergies, asthma, food sensitivities, and related health and behavioral problems / Robert W. Sears, MD, FAAP, and William Sears, MD, FRCP. Little, Brown and Company, 2015. xviii, 332 p. ; **618.92**

1. Allergy in children -- Prevention 2. Allergy in children -- Treatment

ISBN 9780316324809

LC bl2015014077

Includes index.

America's most trusted name in pediatrics presents an authoritative guide to treating and preventing nasal allergies, asthmas, food allergies and intolerances and more, which uses a proven science-based approach for both treatment and prevention.

"The authors warn readers about hidden sources of allergens (eggs can turn up in canned soups and in salad dressings), and discuss healthy eating, favoring fruits and vegetables over gluten-filled foods. Even allergy-free people will benefit from checking out the Searses easy-to-read, clearly laid-out guidebook." Booklist.

Sears, William, 1939-

The **baby** book : everything you need to know about your baby from birth to age two / William Sears ... [et al.]. Little, Brown, 2013. xiv, 769 p. : **618.92**

1. Newborn infants -- Care 2. Infants -- Care 3. Infants -- Development

ISBN 9780316198264

LC bl2013000990

A comprehensive baby care book features information on every aspect of infant care, including the treatment of illnesses and infant nutritional requirements, and focuses on a baby's five needs: eating, sleeping, development, health, and comfort.

"The authors teach new parents how to bond with their babies through seven fundamental behaviors, including breastfeeding, 'baby-wearing' and setting proper boundaries. From tips for a healthy birth, getting your baby to sleep and feeding him the 'right fats,' to information about early health concerns, the major steps in infant development and troublesome but typical toddler behavior, the authors of this comprehensive volume . are assured and reassuring experts." Publishers Weekly.

Sheffer, Edith

Asperger's children : the origins of autism in Nazi Vienna / Edith Sheffer. W.W. Norton & Company, 2018 288 p. **618.92**

1. Asperger, Hans. 2. Asperger's syndrome 3. Children with Asperger's syndrome 4. Autism. 5. Nazism 6. Vienna, Austria

ISBN 9780393609646

LC 2018003422

The prizewinning author of Burned Bridge: How East and West Germans Made the Iron Curtain presents an exploration of the sobering history behind Asperger's Syndrome that reveals child psychiatrist Hans Asperger's influence by Nazi psychiatry and his use of one of the Reich's deadliest killing centers to experiment on disabled children.

Shetreat-Klein, Maya

The **dirt** cure : growing healthy kids with food straight from soil / Maya Shetreat-Klein, MD ; with Rachel Holtzman. Atria Books, 2016. viii, 374 p. ; **618.92**

1. Children -- Health and hygiene 2. Children -- Nutrition 3. Diet therapy for children

ISBN 9781476796970

LC bl2015054163

An integrative pediatric neurologist reveals harmful ingredients in children's food and their potential for injuring developing brains and bodies, outlining a nutritional plan for promoting health through informed, child-friendly food choices.

"The text is full of scientific information presented in a fun and informative way, giving concrete evidence that good food can transform ones life." Publishers Weekly.

Thurow, Roger

The **first** 1,000 days : a crucial time for mothers and children-and the world / Roger Thurow. PublicAffairs, 2016. 336 p. **618.92**

1. Infants -- Nutrition -- Case studies. 2. Nutrition 3. Malnutrition 4. Parenting

ISBN 9781610395854

LC 2015050285

Proper nutrition during the 1,000 days can profoundly influence an entire life, particularly an individual's ability to grow, learn and work. It can also determine a society's long-term health and prosperity. The 1,000 days is where everyone starts out equal, and where the world's inequalities begin.

"You may find yourself cheering and crying with the families you meet. 1,000 Days is a valuable addition to larger public and academic libraries, and for any library where mothers and healthcare providers can share the information." Booklist.

Trainor, Kathleen, 1955-

Calming your anxious child : words to say and things to do / Kathleen Trainor, PsyD. Johns Hopkins University Press, 2016. 249 p. ; **618.92**

1. Anxiety disorders -- Treatment 2. Anxiety in children 3. Parent

and child
ISBN 9781421420097

LC 2015034014

Provides parents with practical steps and a seven-step method for helping children manage anxiety and worry and cope with such problems as phobias, tics, and selective mutism.

"Anxiety can be a tough condition to beat, but parents with the organizational skills to stick to the Trainor approach will in all likelihood achieve improvement. A solid offering." Library Journal.

Trubo, Richard

★**Caring** for your baby and young child : birth to age 5 / Steven P. Shelov, MD, MS, FAAP, editor-in-chief, Associate Dean, Undergraduate Medical Education Winthrop University Hospital, Mineola, New York, Professor of Pediatrics, Stony Brook School of Medicine Stony Brook, New York ; Tanya Remer Altmann, MD, FAAP, associate medical editor, Community Pediatrics Medical Group, Westlake Village, California, Clinical Instructor, Mattel Children's Hospital at UCLA ; Robert E. Hannemann, MD, FAAP, associate medical editor, Emeritus Visiting Professor, Child Psychology, Biomedical and Chemical Engineering Purdue University ; Richard Trubo, writer. Bantam Books, 2014. xxxix, 917 p. : **618.92**

1. Infants -- Care. 2. Child care. 3. Child development.
ISBN 9780553393828

LC 2014013096

Includes index.

Provides a comprehensive guide to early child care from birth to preschool, covering topics ranging from food allergies, sleeping habits, autism and breastfeeding.

Vlock, Deborah

Parenting children with mental health challenges : a guide to life with emotionally complex kids / Deborah Vlock. Rowman & Littlefield, 2018 xx, 177 p. ; **618.92**

1. Mentally ill children. 2. Parent and child. 3. Parents of mentally ill children.
ISBN 1538105241

LC 2018009447

Written by a mother, expressly for other parents, this work supports parents as they help their kids manage life with mental illness. It offers insight into the various life "hurdles" every mom or dad must guide their children over--but which loom higher and more frightening when a child's emotional disorder is thrown into the mix. --From publisher description.

"Readers who feel overwhelmed by the numerous and ever-present challenges of parenting a child with mental health issues will find opportunities to feel connected, supported, and hopeful in this book." Booklist.

Zaichkin, Jeanette, 1956-

Understanding the NICU : what parents of preemies and other hospitalized newborns need to know / Jeanette Zaichkin, RN, MN, NNP-BC, editor in chief, Gary Weiner, MD, FAAP, contributing editor, David Loren, MD, FAAP, contributing editor. American Academy of Pediatrics, 2017 xix, 304 p. : **618.92**

1. Neonatal intensive care. 2. Parent and infant. 3. Hospitals -- Nurseries.
ISBN 9781610020480

LC bl2016049722

Includes index.

Understanding the NICU will guide you through your NICU journey, help you communicate with members of the NICU team, and learn about your baby's condition so that you can ask questions and participate as a valuable partner in your baby's care. It will also provide important information about how to care for your baby after you leave the hospital and head home with your little one. --From publisher description.

"It's hard to imagine a better guide for parents of premature babies than this title from the American Academy of Pediatrics." Booklist.

618.97 Geriatrics

Serani, Deborah, 1961-

Depression in later life : an essential guide / Deborah Serani. Rowman & Littlefield, 2016 xi, 273 p. : **618.97**

1. Depression in old age
ISBN 144225582X

LC 2015045280

"Though the author uses a lot of technical jargon, overall this is a valuable resource that can help improve the quality of life for a highly at-risk group." Booklist.

620 Engineering and allied operations

Khan, Amina

Adapt : how humans are tapping into nature's secrets to design and build a better future / Amina Khan. St. Martin's Press, 2017. 352 p. **620**

1. Nature 2. Biotechnology 3. Technological innovations 4. Engineering design
ISBN 9781250060402

LC 2016049027

In a meticulously researched volume, the author, a renowned science writer, presents fascinating examples of how nature effortlessly solves the problems that humans attempt to solve with decades worth of the latest and greatest technologies, time and money.

"These well-crafted tales of bio-inspired innovation will entrance general readers and warrant the close attention of scientists and technologists." Kirkus.

Petroski, Henry

The **essential** engineer : why science alone will not solve our global problems / Henry Petroski. Alfred A. Knopf, 2010. 288 p. **620**

1. Technological innovations. 2. Engineering. 3. Technology and civilization. 4. Research.
ISBN 9780307272454

LC 2009021216

"A Borzoi book."

"Petroski presents a book-length argument for the place of engineering in humanity's future, especially when it comes to ensuring that future in the face of climate change, natural disasters, dwindling oil supplies and other global problems. Scientists get the credit for everything from the moon landing to the construction of the Large Hadron Collider, he complains, when in reality those and myriad other projects large and small couldn't have been achieved without the creative, intelligent and rigorous input of engineers." Washington Post Book World.

★**To** forgive design : understanding failure / Henry Petroski. Belknap Press of Harvard University Press, 2012. xii, 410 p.

: **620**

1. Structural failures. 2. Engineering. 3. Engineering design.
ISBN 9780674065840

LC 2011044194

Argues that failures in structural engineering are not necessarily due to the physical design of the structures, but instead a misunderstanding of how cultural and socioeconomic constraints would affect the structures.

Success through failure : the paradox of design / Henry Petroski. Princeton University Press, 2006. 256 p. **620**

1. Engineering design -- Case studies. 2. Structural failures -- Case studies. 3. Building failures. 4. Engineering.
ISBN 9780691122250

LC 2005034126

Contends that modeling engineering designs solely on past successes and ignoring past missteps is a path toward eventual failure.

"The author explores the relationship between success and failure in engineering design. Ingenuity is explored as a pendulum that swings between success and failure, driven by design philosophy and practices in a given place and time. Case studies and examples include bridges, spacecrafts, airports, buildings with architectural celebrity, New Coke, U-Locks, and notable structures that have suffered from performance issues." Library Journal.,An engaging and readable book. Petroski uses countless interesting case histories to show how failure motivates technological advancement. IEEE Spectrum

620.009 History, geographic treatment, biography

Winchester, Simon

★The **perfectionists** : how precision engineers created the modern world / Simon Winchester. HarperCollins, 2018 384 p. **620.009**

1. Inventions -- History. 2. Technology -- History. 3. Modern history.
ISBN 9780062652553

LC bl2018052538

Published in Great Britain under the title: Exactly: How Precision Engineers Created the Modern World.

Traces the development of technology from the Industrial Age to the Digital Age to explore the crucial role of precision in advancement, in a chronicle that stands as both an homage and cautionary assessment for the future.

"Winchester smoothly mixes history, science, and biographical sketches to pay homage to the work of precision engineers [A] rollicking work of pop science that entertains and informs." Publishers Weekly.

620.1 Engineering mechanics and materials

Beiser, Vince, 1965-

The **world** in a grain : the story of sand and how it shaped civilization / Vince Beiser. Riverhead Books, 2018. 304 p. **620.1**

1. Sand 2. Natural resources 3. Sand and gravel industry and trade 4. Black market
ISBN 9780399576423

LC 2017053122

Reveals the world's absolute dependence on sand as a resource material used in virtually every structure and consumer product, describing how the planet's dwindling sand levels and related human practices are incurring significant environmental consequences.

"Beiser is a diligent researcher, and his sources and interviews build a strong case in this entirely absorbing, if troubling, read to argue that the many grains of sand, often associated with abundance, are in fact, finite." Library Journal.

Freinkel, Susan, 1957-

Plastic : a toxic love story / Susan Freinkel. Houghton Mifflin Harcourt, c2011. 320 p. **620.1**

1. Plastics. 2. Synthetic products. 3. Materials
ISBN 9780547152400

LC 2010043019

Green Prize for Sustainable Literature: Adult Nonfiction, 2012.

Relates the near-crisis status of the world's usage of plastic and the environmentally harmful disposal of it through the story of eight familiar plastic objects--a comb, a chair, a Frisbee, an IV bag, a disposable lighter, a grocery bag, a soda bottle, and a credit card.

Johnson, Les (Charles Les)

Graphene : the superstrong, superthin, and superversatile material that will revolutionize the world / Les Johnson and Joseph E. Meany, PhD. Prometheus Books, 2018. 269 p. **620.1**

1. Graphene. 2. Materials science 3. Materials 4. Carbon
ISBN 9781633883253

LC 2017032965

Two scientists give an enthusiastic, layperson's overview of a new supermaterial now in development that could transform many features of daily life, from creating new conveniences to improving health and safety.

Miodownik, Mark

Stuff matters : exploring the marvelous materials that shape our manmade world / Mark Miodownik. Houghton Mifflin Harcourt, 2014. 256 p. **620.1**

1. Materials science 2. Manufacturing processes 3. Chemistry 4. Scientific discoveries
ISBN 9780544236042

LC 2013047575

Reprint of: London : Penguin, 2013.

National Academies Communication Award, 2015.

Royal Society General Prizes for Science Books, 2014.

A world-leading materials scientist presents an engrossing collection of stories that explain the science and history of materials, from the plastic in our appliances to the elastic in our underpants, revealing the miracles of engineering that seep into our everyday lives.

"At a time when science is maligned, first-rate storyteller Miodownik entertains and educates with pop-culture references, scholarly asides, and nods to everyone from the Six Million Dollar Man to the Lumière brothers. A delight for the curious reader." Booklist.

Waldman, Jonathan

Rust : the longest war / Jonathan Waldman. Simon & Schuster, 2015. 304 p. **620.1**

1. Corrosion and anti-corrosives -- History. 2. Corrosion and anti-corrosives -- Anecdotes.
ISBN 9781451691597

LC 2014043291

An environmental journalist traces the historical war against rust, revealing how rust-related damage costs more than all other natural disasters combined and how it is combated by industrial workers, the government, universities and everyday people. Map(s).

"A brilliantly written and fascinating close-up look at one of natures most neglected threats to man-made structures and machines." Booklist.

621 Applied physics

Alley, Richard B.
Earth : the operators' manual / Richard B. Alley. W.W. Norton, c2011. 496 p. **621**
1. Energy development -- Environmental aspects -- History. 2. Renewable energy sources. 3. Global warming. 4. Greenhouse effect, Atmospheric
ISBN 9780393081091
LC 2010054016

The book companion to the PBS series combines accessible scientific facts with engaging stories to explore the history of energy use by humans over the centuries, and how this use is profoundly and negatively changing the environment.

Davy, Phil
The **tool** book : a tool lover's guide to more than 200 hand tools / writers, Phil Davy, Luke Edwardes-Evans, Jo Behari, Matthew Jackson ; foreword by Nick Offerman. DK Publishing, 2018. 256 p. : **621**
1. Tools.
ISBN 1465468544
LC 2017276784

Includes index.
A visual guide to hand tools. The writers show you each tool from every angle, and help you visualize how it works. They also provide information on choosing a tool, and how to keep it in the best condition. Own the best, treat them well, and use them effectively.

Hearst Books (Firm),
The **ultimate** tool book. / Popular Mechanics Hearst Books, 2019 239 p. : **621**
1. Tools
ISBN 9781618372925
LC bl2019011605

At head of title: Popular Mechanics.
Includes index.
Offers information on hand tools, including how to use them effectively, how to choose the right one for a project, and how to keep them in great shape.

Horne, Richard
3D printing for dummies / Richard Horne and Kalani Kirk Hausman. John Wiley & Sons, Inc., 2017 xii, 392 p. : **621**
1. Three-dimensional printing.
ISBN 1119386314
LC bl2017026664

Includes index.
Each book covers all the necessary information a beginner needs to know about a particular topic, providing an index for easy reference and using the series' signature set of symbols to clue the reader in to key topics, categorized under such titles as Tip, Remember, Warning!, Technical Stuff and True Story.

Jackson, Tom, 1972-
Chilled : how refrigeration changed the world and might do so again / Tom Jackson. Bloomsbury USA, 2015. 288 p. **621**
1. Cooling. 2. Refrigeration and refrigerating machinery. 3. Refrigerators.
ISBN 9781472911438
LC bl2015038695

The refrigerator may seem mundane nowadays, but it is one of the wonders of twentieth-century science--lifesaver, food preserver, social liberator. Part historical narrative, part scientific decoder, Chilled looks at early efforts to harness the cold at the ice pits of Persia (Iranians still call their fridges the "ice pit") and ice harvests on the Regents Canal. As people learned more about what cold actually was, scientists invented machines for producing it on demand. The discovery of refrigeration and its applications features a cast of characters that includes the Ice King of Boston, Galileo, Francis Bacon, an expert on gnomes, a magician who chilled a cathedral, a Renaissance duke addicted to iced eggnog, and a Bavarian nobleman from New England.

Rigsby, Mike, 1950-
A **beginner's** guide to 3D printing : 14 simple toy designs to get you started / Mike Rigsby. Chicago, Ill. :Review Press, 2014 291 p. : **621**
1. SketchUp. 2. CAD/CAM systems 3. Computer-aided design 4. Rapid prototyping 5. Three-dimensional printing
ISBN 9781569761977
LC 2014026069

"A Beginner's Guide to 3D Printing is the perfect resource for those who would like to experiment with 3D design and manufacturing, but have little or no technical experience with the standard software. Author Mike Rigsby leads readers step-by-step through 15 simple toy projects, each illustrated with screen caps of Autodesk 123D Design, the most common free 3D software available. The projects are later described using Sketchup, another free popular software package. Beginning with basic projects that will take longer to print than design, readers are then given instruction on more advanced toys, including a baking-powder submarine, a train with expandable track, a multipiece airplane, a rubber band-powered car, and a noise-making push toy with froggy eyes. Once trained in the basics of computer-aided design, readers will be able to embark on even more elaborate projects of their own creation".-- Provided by publisher.

621.3 Electrical, magnetic, optical, communications, computer engineering; electronics, lighting

Abramson, Albert
The **history** of television, 1880 to 1941 / Albert Abramson. McFarland, 2009, c1987. xiv, 354 p. : **621.3**
1. Television -- History.
ISBN 0786440864
LC bl2010029572

Reprint. Originally published: c1987.
Uses interviews with scientists, archival research, and rare photographs to present a history of television, discussing the interactions of the several hundred scientists that made it possible and examining the first devices, early camera tubes, the kinescope, and the iconoscope.

The **history** of television, 1942 to 2000 / Albert Abramson ; foreword by Christopher H. Sterling. McFarland & Co., Publishers, 2008, c2003. x, 309 p. : **621.3**
1. Television -- History.
ISBN 9780786432431
LC bl2010033279

Reprint. Originally published: 2003.
A technical history of television covers significany developments from 1942 to 2000, including television during World War II, the change from helical to high band technology, and the rise of electronic journalism.

"No reference work available in print right now matches the attention to detail that is obvious here. A significant work on how the machinery of television has evolved, this . . . should stand as the authority for years to come." Library Journal.

Black & Decker Corporation (Towson, Md.),

The **complete** guide to wiring : current with 2017-2020 electrical codes Cool Springs Press, 2018. 335 p. : **621.3**

1. Electric wiring, Interior -- Amateurs' manuals. 2. Dwellings -- Maintenance and repair -- Amateurs' manuals. 3. Dwellings -- Electric equipment -- Amateurs' manuals.

ISBN 9780760353578

LC bl2017052689

At head of title: Black & Decker.

Presents a full range of wiring repair and upgrade projects, along with detailed circuit diagrams, instructions on how to connect and network home electronics, and the latest requirements of the National Electrical Code.

Brox, Jane, 1956-

Brilliant : the evolution of artificial light / Jane Brox. Houghton Mifflin Harcourt, 2010. 320 p. **621.3**

1. Lighting -- History. 2. Light bulbs. 3. Electric lighting. 4. Light.

ISBN 9780547055275

LC 2009035441

Documents the role of light in history, tracing how the development of specific innovations had a pivotal influence on social and cultural evolution. By the National Book Critics Circle Award-winning author of Five Thousand Days Like This One.

"The author examines our relationship with light, our attempts to harness it to brighten places we cannot see, and its impact on American psychology and culture. This well-written, well-researched, and thought-provoking book has much to offer. The general reader with an interest in the (social) history of technology will find it...a source of inspiration for considering technology's impact on our lives." Library Journal.

Croft, Terrell, 1880-1967

American electricians' handbook / Terrell Croft (deceased), Frederick P. Hartwell, Wilford I. Summers. McGraw-Hill Education, 2013 1712 p. : **621.3**

1. Electricians 2. Electric industry and trade

ISBN 9780071798808

LC bl2013043391

Includes index.

A comprehensive guide to electrical equipment and techniques, with useful diagrams, photographs, and tables.

Fletcher, Seth, 1979-

Bottled lightning : superbatteries, electric cars, and the new lithium economy / Seth Fletcher. Hill and Wang, 2011. 304 p. **621.3**

1. Lithium industry and trade 2. Electronics industry and trade 3. Electric batteries. 4. Electric vehicles.

ISBN 9780809030538

LC 2010047695

Shares strategies for meeting the near-future world's energy needs, citing the prevalence of lithium in everyday technologies while explaining the metal's potential role in reducing oil dependency, shifting geopolitical power, and enabling sustainability.

"Provides an entertaining, surprisingly eventful history of human efforts to harness energy in the form of battery power . A fine, readable work of popular science." Kirkus.

Hartwell, Frederic P

Wiring simplified : based on the 2014 National Electrical Code / Frederic P. Hartwell, W. Creighton Schwan, H. P. Richter. Park Publishing, Inc., 2014 xii, 256 p. : **621.3**

1. Electric wiring, Interior.

ISBN 9780979294556

LC bl2014028854

Includes index.

Provides information on standards, codes, and safety practices of interior electric wiring along with instructions for a variety of wiring projects.

McAlister, Michael

Taunton's wiring complete : includes the latest in Wi-Fi, smart-house technology / Michael McAlister & Michael Litchfield. The Taunton Press, 2017 284 p. : **621.3**

1. Electric wiring, Interior 2. Dwellings -- Electric equipment

ISBN 9781631868382

LC 2017014083

At head of title: Taunton's.

Shares information and instructions with homeowners for different wiring projects, including installing recessed lighting, stripping cable, and running power to an outbuilding.

Roach, Craig

Simply electrifying : the technology that transformed the world, from Benjamin Franklin to Elon Musk / Craig R. Roach. BenBella Books, Inc., [2017] 400 p. **621.3**

1. Electricity -- History. 2. Electrical engineering -- History. 3. Inventors 4. Science

ISBN 9781944648268

LC 2017004508

Looks at the stories of the researchers, innovators, businesspeople, and regulators who shaped how electricity was understood and used, from early researchers like Benjamin Franklin to contemporary innovators like Elon Musk.

"Simply Electrifying provides a comprehensive history of this life-changing discovery and is a fascinating and deeply engaging look at how we live today and where we may be headed in the future." Booklist.

Shulman, Seth

★The **telephone** gambit : chasing Alexander Graham Bell's secret / Seth Shulman. W. W. Norton & Co., c2008. 256 p. : **621.3**

1. Bell, Alexander Graham, 1847-1922. 2. Gray, Elisha, 1835-1901. 3. Telephones -- History. 4. Patents. 5. Inventors -- United States

ISBN 0393062066

LC 2007030904

Documents the illicit beginnings of the lucrative telephone monopoly, revealing how Bell's journals acknowledged his illegal copying of Elisha Gray's invention in order to secure what would become the nation's most valuable patent.

"This book does a neat job of painting, in rapid brush strokes, a portrait of the thrilling era of innovation in which Bell lived and also of the interesting circumstances of his life. [He] also manages to lace his work with just enough technology to tell his story without losing the interest of any low-tech readers." Christian Science Monitor.

Silver, H. Ward

Ham radio for dummies / H. Ward Silver. John Wiley & Sons,

Inc., 2013 xvi, 358 p. : **621.3**

1. Amateur radio stations 2. Radio 3. Amateurs' manuals.
ISBN 9781118592113

LC bl2013039581

An introduction to amateur radio offers information and advice on getting a license, communicating with other hams, and setting up radio equipment.

621.381 Electronics

Horowitz, Paul, 1942-

The **art** of electronics / Paul Horowitz, Harvard University, Winfield Hill, Rowland Institute. Cambridge University Press, 2015 xxxi, 1192 p. : **621.381**

1. Electronics. 2. Electronic circuit design.
ISBN 9780521809269

LC 2015002303

At long last, here is the thoroughly revised and updated third edition of the hugely successful The Art of Electronics. It is widely accepted as the best single authoritative book on electronic circuit design. In addition to new or enhanced coverage of many topics, the third edition includes 90 oscilloscope screenshots illustrating the behavior of working circuits, dozens of graphs giving highly useful measured data of the sort that is often buried or omitted in datasheets but which you need when designing circuits, and 80 tables (listing some 1650 active components), enabling intelligent choice of circuit components by listing essential characteristics (both specified and measured) of available parts. The new Art of Electronics retains the feeling of informality and easy access that helped make the earlier editions so successful and popular. It is an indispensable reference and the gold standard for anyone, student or researcher, professional or amateur, who works with electronic circuits.

Platt, Charles

Make: more electronics / Charles Platt. Maker Media, 2014. xxxii, 357 p. : **621.381**

1. Electronic apparatus and appliances -- Design and construction
ISBN 9781449344047

LC bl2014023844

"36 illustrated experiments that explain logic chips, amplifiers, sensors, and more"--Cover.

Includes index.

Shares step-by-step experiments that teach how to add computational power to projects, including light bars, timers, decoders, phototransistors, op-amps, and various sensors.

Schultz, Mitchel E.

Grob's basic electronics / Mitchel E. Schultz, Western Technical College. McGraw-Hill Education, 2016 xxvii, 1232 p. ; **621.381**

1. Electronics 2. Textbooks.
ISBN 9780073373874

LC 2014042490

Includes index.

Grob's Basic Electronics is written for the beginning student pursuing a technical degree in Electronics Technology.ſrThis longtime best-selling text has been refined, updated and made more student friendly. The focus on absolutely essential knowledge for technicians, and focus on real-world applications of these basic concepts makes it ideal for today's technology students. In covering the fundamentals of electricity and electronics, this text focuses on essential topics for the technician, and the all-important development of testing and troubleshooting skills. This highly practical approach combines clear, carefully-laid-out explanations of key topics with good, worked-out examples and problems to solve. Review problems that follow each section reinforce the material just completed, making this a very student-friendly text. It is a thoroughly accessible introduction to basic DC and AC circuits and electronic devices. --From publisher description.

621.389 Security, sound recording, related systems

Mixerman

Zen and the art of recording / Mixerman. Hal Leonard Books, 2014 xii, 291 p. : **621.389**

1. Sound recordings -- Production and direction -- Vocational guidance. 2. Popular music -- Production and direction. 3. Sound recording industry -- Vocational guidance.
ISBN 9781480387430

LC 2014035146

In this book, the third in the Zen and the Art Of series, Mixerman distills the inescapable technical realities of recording down to understandable and practical terms. Whether musician or self-taught recordist, whether at home or in a full-blown studio complex, you'll discover a definitive blueprint for recording within the current realities of the business, without ever losing focus on the core consideration the music itself. As Mixerman writes: "The moment you start to think in musical terms, your recordings will improve a hundredfold." This book is an absolute must-have for anyone who enjoys recording music and wants to get better doing it. --From publisher description.

621.48 Nuclear engineering

Smith, Gar

Nuclear roulette : the truth about the most dangerous energy source on earth / Gar Smith ; foreword by Jerry Mander and Ernest Callenbach. Chelsea Green Pub., 2012. 248 p. **621.48**

1. Nuclear power 2. Nuclear power plants -- Risk assessment. 3. Energy policy. 4. Antinuclear movement
ISBN 9781603584777

LC 2012027407

Argues against the "nuclear renaissance" that U.S. corporations claim is underway, exposing the critiques of nuclear power and near daily system failures that plague the industry, and proposes potential energy solutions.

623 Military and nautical engineering

Powell, John, 1954-

Weapons & warfare / editor, John Powell. Salem Press, c2010. 3 v. (xxix, 1260 p.) : **623**

1. Military weapons -- History. 2. Military art and science -- History.
ISBN 9781587655944

LC 2009050491

Presents information about weaponry, tactics, and modes of warfare worldwide, from ancient times to the present, and discusses the cultural, sociopolitical, and ethical aspects of weaponry and warfare.

623.4 Ordnance

Sheinkin, Steve

Bomb : the race to build--and steal--the world's most dangerous weapon / Steve Sheinkin. Henry Holt & Co., 2012. 192 p. **623.4**

1. Manhattan Project (U.S.) -- History 2. Atomic bomb -- History -- 20th century. 3. Nuclear power research. 4. Spies 5. World War II 6. United States -- History -- 1939-1945 7. United States -- History, Military -- 20th century.

ISBN 9781596434875

National Book Award for Young People's Literature finalist, 2012
Newbery Honor Book, 2013.

Recounts the scientific discoveries that enabled atom splitting, the military intelligence operations that occurred in rival countries, and the work of brilliant scientists hidden at Los Alamos.

623.74 Vehicles

Cockburn, Andrew, 1947-

Kill chain : the rise of the high-tech assassins / Andrew Cockburn. Henry Holt & Co 2015. 320 p. : **623.74**

1. Drone aircraft. 2. Military engineering. 3. High technology weapons. 4. Assassination.

ISBN 9780805099263

LC 2014029340

A narrative history of drone warfare explores its innovations and key contributors while revealing the less-understood, real-world military and economic consequences of targeted killing as a means of waging war.

"Despite some problems, this is an informative and easy-to-read book for those interested in this hot topic. Perhaps a drone will drop it off at your front door." Library Journal.

623.88 Seamanship

Maloney, Elbert S,

Chapman piloting & seamanship / editorial team, Elbert S. Maloney, Peter A. Janssen, and Jonathan Eaton. Hearst Books, 2013 919 p. : **623.88**

1. Navigation. 2. Pilots and pilotage. 3. Motorboats.

ISBN 9781588169617

LC bl2013056060

"Completely updated & revised"--Cover.

Includes index.

Surveys the latest developments in safety systems, marine electronics, radar, and communications, and includes information on tides and currents, weather, and navigation.

Bigon, Mario

The **Morrow** guide to knots : for sailing, fishing, camping, climbing / Mario Bigon and Guido Regazzoni ; translated from the Italian by Maria Piotrowska. W. Morrow, 1982. 255 p. : **623.88**

1. Knots and splices.

ISBN 9780688012267

LC 82006308

Translation of: Guida ai nodi.

Includes index.

Demonstrates how to tie a variety of practical and ornamental knots and offers advice on selecting rope.

Naranjo, Ralph J.

The **art** of seamanship manual : evolving skills, exploring oceans, and handling wind, waves, and weather / Ralph Naranjo. International Marine/McGraw-Hill Education, 2015 xi, 496 p. : **623.88**

1. Sailing. 2. Seamanship.

ISBN 0071493425

LC 2015300840

Around-the-world sailor Ralph Naranjo--technical expert, ocean racer, former Vanderstar Chair at the U.S. Naval Academy--delivers a priceless reference for anything that comes up while on the water, sharing all the knowledge today's sailors need to "hand, reef, and steer" -- an enduring reference to the collective skills of the bluewater sailor. Naranjo's vast knowledge is supported by real-life examples of sailing mishaps, sample itineraries, vibrant photos, as well as first-hand accounts and sidebars from top sailors and marine experts, including Shelia McCurdy, Chuck Hawley, Lee Chesneau, and Paul Miller, N.A.Seamanship is a dynamic art, demanding full attention from the sailor amidst a constant flow of information and knowledge. --From publisher description.

Pawson, Des

The **handbook** of knots / Des Pawson. DK, 2004. 176 p. : **623.88**

1. Knots and splices.

ISBN 0756603749

LC 2004274491

Includes index.

Explains how to use rope and provides annotated step-by-step photographs and detailed instructions for tying more than one hundred stopper knots, binding knots, bends, hitches, loops, braids, and splices.

Rousmaniere, John

The **Annapolis** book of seamanship / John Rousmaniere ; illustrated by Mark Smith. Simon & Schuster, 2014. xi, 403 p. : **623.88**

1. Seamanship

ISBN 9781451650198

LC 2014412287

"The art of sailing, maneuvering, and preserving a ship or a boat in all positions and under all reasonable circumstances." With the addition of the words, "and some unreasonable circumstances, too," this definition of "seamanship" is as valid today as when the first edition of this book was published in 1983. This edition has been extensively updated with new or updated text, and many new photographs.

623.89 Navigation

Grant, R. G.

Lighthouse : an illuminating history of the world's coastal sentinels / R.G. Grant. Black Dog & Leventhal Publishers, 2018. 155 p. : **623.89**

1. Lighthouses -- History. 2. Lighthouses -- Design and construction -- History.

ISBN 9780316414470

LC bl2018185164

Presents a visual exploration of lighthouses from around the world, featuring towers built during seafaring's golden age, from 1700-1900.

624 Civil engineering

Parkyn, Neil, 1943-

The **seventy** wonders of the modern world : 1500 years of extraordinary feats of engineering and construction / edited by Neil Parkyn. Thames & Hudson, 2002. 304 p. : **624**

1. Civil engineering -- History. 2. Building -- History. 3. Architecture.
ISBN 0500510474

LC 2002100549

Describes the history, usage, and architectural uniqueness of seventy structures from around the world, including places of worship, castles, skyscrapers, bridges, dams, and statues.

"Most of the featured wonders date from the second half of the 20th century. The selections are divided into seven categories: churches, palaces, public buildings, towers and skyscrapers, bridges and railways, canals and dams, and statues. Each entry includes basic information on history, structural and engineering details, innovations, aesthetics, and a sidebar fact-file." Library Journal.

624.1 Structural engineering and underground construction

Agrawal, Roma

Built : the hidden stories behind our structures / Roma Agrawal. Bloomsbury, 2018. 352 p. **624.1**

1. Architecture 2. Buildings 3. Structural engineering 4. Engineering
ISBN 9781635570229

LC 2018000409

A structural engineer specializing in large construction projects discusses the fascinating science behind her field, describing how they keep modern buildings from falling down, how a bridge can span distances and comparing modern solutions with those from ancient cultures.

"A unique addition to public library collections on technology and engineering." Library Journal.

Hunt, Will (Urban adventurer)

Underground : a human history of the worlds beneath our feet / Will Hunt. Spiegel & Grau, 2019. 288 p. **624.1**

1. Underground areas 2. Underground construction 3. Exploration 4. Subways
ISBN 9780812996746

LC 2018005540

The first book by an urban adventurer, spelunker and photographer explores the history, science, architecture and mythology of the subterranean landscape to evaluate humanity's relationship with the underground, from sacred caves and hidden catacombs to abandoned mines and subway systems.

"This unique book is a real-life Journey to the Center of the Earth, a maze of dark corners and subterranean denizens that encompass unknown or forgotten worlds." Library Journal.

625.1 Railroads

Smithsonian Institution,

Train : the definitive visual history DK Publishing, 2014 320 p. : **625.1**

1. Railroads -- History. 2. Railroads -- History -- Pictorial works. 3. Locomotives -- History. 4. Locomotives -- History -- Pictorial works.
ISBN 9781465422293

LC 2012287667

Includes index.

Featuring amazing images of trains, virtual tours of engines, and profiles of key innovators, designers, and engineers, Train: The Definitive Visual History traces the history of the railroad and the role of trains, from the first steam engines to today's high speed bullet trains. Comprehensive catalogs feature the most important trains from each period, exploring in detail iconic trains such as the Fairy Queen, Orient Express, and Javelin, and follows the development of trains from early steam to diesel engines and modern electronic locomotives. Beautiful photographs and detailed maps explore some of the world's most impressive rail routes from South Africa to Siberia, including the Darjeeling Himalayan Railway, the trans-Siberian Railway, and the high-speed Japanese Tokaido Shinkansen line. Includes 2 exclusive prints.

625.2 Railroad rolling stock

Solomon, Brian, 1966-

The **field** guide to trains : locomotives and rolling stock / Brian Solomon. Voyageur Press, 2016. 208 p. : **625.2**

1. Diesel locomotives. 2. Locomotives -- History. 3. Locomotives. 4. Railroad cars -- History.
ISBN 0760349975

LC 2015047962

"This book is an indispensable illustrated resource for railfans and families on road trips, filled with easy-to-find information on locomotives and rolling stock, such as railroad cars, coaches, and wagons".--Provided by publisher.

627 Hydraulic engineering

Hiltzik, Michael A.

Colossus : Hoover Dam and the making of the American century / Michael Hiltzik. Free Press, 2010. 512 p. **627**

1. Dams. 2. Depressions -- 1929-1941. 3. Public works. 4. Building. 5. Hoover Dam -- History. 6. Colorado River.
ISBN 9781416532163

LC 2009033833

"Drawing on extensive research, a Pulitzer Prize winner details the construction and lasting impact of the Hoover Dam., highlighting such historical figures as Teddy and Franklin D. Roosevelt and the dam's colorful architect, Frank Crowe."

"In this account of the Hoover Dam story, Hiltzik explains the technological and physical difficulties posed by the dam project, but he also fixes the endeavor in its time and captures the personalities of the people involved. The author is at his best in a masterly portrayal of Frank Crowe, the central figure in the dam's construction. A born engineer who demanded much from his workmen, Crowe had to solve a myriad of problems on the fly as he confronted the unexpected difficulties of an unprecedented project in an unprecedented location. One of the nice things about nonfiction such as Colossus is that the stories don't need to be believable; they just need to be true." Wall Street Journal.

Matson, Tim, 1943-

Earth ponds : the country pond maker's guide to building, maintenance and restoration / Tim Matson. Countryman Press

; 2012. 150 p. : **627**

1. Ponds 2. Water-supply, Rural 3. Amateurs' manuals.
ISBN 158157147X

LC bl2012029309

A fully redesigned, third edition of a guide to pond making cites its aesthetic and environmental benefits while providing step-by-step coverage of everything from site planning and soil sampling to drainage and wildlife management.

628 Sanitary engineering

Pernick, Ron

Clean tech nation : how the U.S. can lead in the new global economy / Ron Pernick, Clint Wilder. HarperCollins, 2012. 320 p. **628**

1. Technology -- Environmental aspects 2. Business -- Environmental aspects 3. Eco-entrepreneurship 4. Renewable energy sources
ISBN 9780062088444

LC 2012474099

Combining expert analysis with lively storytelling, this follow-up to The Clean Tech Revolution explores the latest clean technology being implemented around the world and outlines the tools the U.S. needs to compete and win on this fast-changing, competitive global battlefield.

Winkless, Laurie

Science and the city : the mechanics behind the metropolis / Laurie Winkless. Bloomsbury Sigma, 2016. 288 p. **628**

1. Cities and towns 2. Urban planning 3. Architecture 4. City life
ISBN 9781472913210

Uncovering the science and engineering that shapes our cities, a physicist reveals how technology will help us meet the challenges of a soaring world population, from an ever-increasing demand for power, water and Internet access, to simply how to get about in a megacity of tens of millions of people.

628.4 Waste technology, public toilets, street cleaning

Humes, Edward

Garbology : our dirty love affair with trash / Edward Humes. Avery, c2012. 288 p. **628.4**

1. Solid waste. 2. Solid waste disposal. 3. Garbage collection. 4. Environmental engineering.
ISBN 9781583334348

LC 2012001701

The author identifies trash as America's largest export, discussing how the nation reached current garbage levels while explaining what families, communities, and countries are doing to reverse waste trends.

629 Other branches of engineering

Dorling Kindersley Publishing, Inc,

Tractor : the definitive visual history DK Publishing, 2015. 256 p. : **629**

1. Tractors -- History. 2. Tractors -- Pictorial works.
ISBN 9781465435996

LC 2015288087

Includes index.

This is the definitive visual history of the tractor. The complete history of farm machinery, from steam and vintage tractors to the latest combine harvesters is showcased in this lavishly illustrated volume. Packed with images and tractor data on more than 200 iconic machines, The Tractor Book explores the entire range of tractors and farming machines from around the world, such as Fordson Model F and Massey-Harris GP. Histories of famous models, such as John Deere and Massey Ferguson, sit alongside immersive visual tours of celebrated machines. The Tractor Book covers how tractors work, their history, major models and catalogues tractors from every era making this a must-have for anyone fascinated by these extraordinary machines.

629.1 Aerospace engineering

Branson, Richard

Reach for the skies : ballooning, birdmen, and blasting into space / Richard Branson. Current, 2011. 352 p. **629.1**

1. Aviation -- History 2. Air travel 3. Technological innovations
ISBN 9781617230035

LC 2010052340

The billionaire entrepreneur and pioneer of the first commercial spaceliner examines the history of aviation, citing the achievements of such leading contributors as Tony Jannus, Leon Valentin and Steve Fossett.

629.13 Aeronautics

Alexander, David E., 1955-

Why don't jumbo jets flap their wings? : flying animals, flying machines, and how they are different / David E. Alexander. Rutgers University Press, c2009. 288 p. **629.13**

1. Aviation 2. Animal flight 3. Flying-machines 4. Aerodynamics
ISBN 9780813544793

LC 2008035425

"Anyone interested in the flight of birds or insects or the flight of various types of aircraft will find this volume fascinating. . . . [This book] is very well written and approaches complex topics in a manner that readers at any level of expertise will find understandable and interesting." Science Books & Films.

Bell, Dana

Smithsonian atlas of world aviation : charting the history of flight from the first balloons to today's most advanced aircraft / [compiled by] Dana Bell. HarperCollins, 2008? 230 p. : **629.13**

1. Aviation -- History 2. Historical geography -- Maps. 3. Atlases 4. Reference books
ISBN 9780061251443

LC 2007047574

A world history of flight provides a lavishly illustrated tour of everything from wartime air campaigns to the latest experimental planes, in an oversized volume that is complemented by descriptive charts and flight-pattern layouts.

"Bell's writing ... adds immeasurably to the value of this atlas: it is articulate, clear, informative, and, above all, accurate." School Library Journal.

Grant, R. G.

Flight : the complete history of aviation / R. G. Grant. DK

Pub., 2017. 452 p. : **629.13**
1. Aviation -- History.
ISBN 9781465463272

LC 2016461395

Includes index.

A visual history of the past one hundred years of aviation utilizes thousands of images, accompanied by text and captions, to capture humankind's efforts to fly, from the earliest medieval experiments to the dramatic accomplishments of the Space Shuttle.

"The impressive illustrations include over 300 gorgeous, full-color profiles of the world's major military and civilian aircraft and space vehicles." Library Journal.

Hampton, Dan

The **flight** : Charles Lindbergh's 1927 transatlantic crossing / Dan Hampton. William Morrow & Co, 2017. 400 p. **629.13**
1. Lindbergh, Charles A. (Charles Augustus), 1902-1974 2. Transatlantic flights 3. Pilots 4. Flight 5. Aviation -- United States -- History
ISBN 9780062464392

LC bl2017019791

"A celebration of a heroic feat sure to interest fans of aviation history." Kirkus.

Jackson, Joe, 1955-

Atlantic fever : Lindbergh, his competitors, and the race to cross the Atlantic / Joe Jackson. Farrar, Straus and Giroux, 2012. 592 p. **629.13**
1. Lindbergh, Charles A. (Charles Augustus), 1902-1974. 2. Transatlantic flights. 3. Aviation -- History. 4. Pilots. 5. Competition. 6. Atlantic Ocean.
ISBN 9780374106751

LC 2011046068

"A fast-paced, dynamic account of the race to cross the Atlantic, and the larger-than-life personalities of the aviators who captured the world's attention. In 1919, a prize of $25,000 was offered to the first aviator to cross the Atlantic in either direction between France and America. Although it was one of the most coveted prizes in the world, it sat unclaimed (not without efforts) for eight long years, until the spring of 1927. It was then, during five incredibly tense weeks, that one of those magical windows in history opened, when there occurred a nexus of technology, innovation, character, and spirit that led so many contenders (from different parts of the world) to all suddenly be on the cusp of the exact same achievement at the exact same time. Atlantic Fever is about the race; it is a milestone in American history whose story has never been fully told. Richard Byrd, Noel Davis, Stanton Wooster, Clarence Chamberlin, Charles Levine, Rene; Fonck, Charles Nungesser, and François Coli--all had equal weight in the race with Charles Lindbergh. Although the story starts in September 1926 with the crash of the first competitor, or even further back with the 1919 establishment of the prize, its heart is found in a short period, those five weeks from April 14 to May 21, 1927, when the world held its breath and the aviators met their separate fates in the air".-- Provided by publisher.

Mortimer, Gavin

The **chasing** Icarus : the seventeen days in 1910 that forever changed American aviation / Gavin Mortimer. St Martins Press, 2009. 320 p. **629.13**
1. Flight. 2. Aviation. 3. Airships. 4. Ballooning.
ISBN 9780802717115

LC bl2009017350

A dramatic chronicle of a pivotal moment in the history of aviation sets events against a backdrop of heated debates about which flight technology was the most viable, in an account that covers such topics as Walter Wellman's attempt to cross the Atlantic by dirigible, the Gordon Bennett International Balloon Cup competition, and record-setting demonstrations by airplane pilots at Belmont Park.

"Mortimer effectively places the reader at the vital center.... A singular contribution to early aviation history." Library Journal.

Ryan, Jason (Journalist)

Race to Hawaii : the 1927 Dole Air Derby and the thrilling first flights that opened the Pacific / Jason Ryan. Chicago Review Press Incorporated, [2018] 304 p. **629.13**
1. Dole Air Race (1927). 2. Transpacific flights 3. Airplane racing. 4. Aviation 5. Hawaii
ISBN 9780912777252

LC 2017057554

Race to Hawaii chronicles the thrilling first flights during the Golden Age of Aviation, a time when new airplanes traveled farther and faster but were also unreliable, fragile, and hampered by primitive air navigation equipment.

"Ryan builds suspense skillfully and makes heroes out of the men and one woman who vied in the derby." Booklist.

629.132 Mechanics of flight flying and related topics

Hampton, Dan

Chasing the demon : a secret history of the quest for the sound barrier, and the band of American aces who conquered it / Dan Hampton. William Morrow & Company, 2018. 400 p. **629.132**
1. United States. Air Force 2. Military aviation 3. Test pilots 4. Supersonic planes 5. High-speed aviation
ISBN 9780062688729

LC 2018024770

The New York Times best-selling author of Viper Pilot and The Flight chronicles another thrilling chapter in American aviation history: the race to break the sound barrier.

"Author of the New York Times best-selling Viper Pilot and a decorated military pilot well acquainted with flying supersonic fighter jets, Hampton chronicles the U.S. effort to break the sound barrier, starting with the founding of the U.S. Air Force in 1947 and ending with Capt. Chuck Yeager's triumph on October 14, 1947." Library Journal.

629.133 Aircraft types

Chiles, James R.

The **god** machine : from boomerangs to black hawks, the story of the helicopter / James R. Chiles. Bantam Dell, 2007. 368 p. **629.133**
1. Helicopters -- History. 2. Aviation -- History 3. Aeronautics -- History. 4. Black Hawk (Military transport helicopter)
ISBN 0553804472

LC 2007028575

Traces the development of the helicopter from its earliest origins to the high-tech craft of today, looking at the many ways in which the helicopter has revolutionized rescue techniques, the art of modern warfare, and the transportation industry.

"The author chronicles helicopter development from ancient observations of birds and boomerangs in flight to Leonardo da Vinci's aerodynamic ideas to modern police, fire, and medical response helicopters." Library Journal.

629.2 Motor land vehicles, cycles

Hadland, Tony

Bicycle design : an illustrated history / Tony Hadland and Hans-Erhard Lessing ; with contributions from Nick Clayton and Gary W. Sanderson. The MIT Press, 2014 xiii, 564 p. : **629.2**

1. Bicycles -- Design and construction -- History 2. Bicycles -- Parts -- History

ISBN 9780262026758

LC 2013023698

Written by two leading bicycle historians and generously illustrated with historic drawings, designs, and photographs, Bicycle Design describes the key stages in the evolution of the bicycle, beginning with the counterintuitive idea of balancing on two wheels in line, through the development of tension-spoked wheels, indirect drives (employing levers, pulleys, chains, and chainwheels), and pneumatic tires. The authors examine the further development of the bicycle for such specific purposes as racing, portability, and all-terrain use; and they describe the evolution of bicycle components including seats, transmission, brakes, lights (at first candle-based), and carriers (racks, panniers, saddlebags, child seats, and sidecars). They consider not only commercially successful designs but also commercial failures that pointed the way to future technological developments. And they debunk some myths about bicycles--for example, the mistaken but often-cited idea that Leonardo sketched a chain-drive bike in his notebooks. Despite the bicycle's long history and mass appeal, its technological history has been neglected. This volume, with its engaging and wide-ranging coverage, fills that gap. It will be the starting point for all future histories of the bicycle. --From publisher description.

629.222 Vehicles powered by fossil fuels and human-powered vehicles

Cagle, Gregory A

Scenes from an automotive wonderland : remarkable cars spotted in postwar Europe / Gregory A. Cagle ; foreword by Jeff Lane. McFarland & Company,, 2018 viii, 231 p. ; **629.222**

1. Automobiles -- Europe 2. Automobiles -- Europe -- History -- 20th century. 3. Photography of automobiles.

ISBN 1476671788

LC 2017055037

"Gregory Cagle was a 10 year-old car fanatic when his family moved from New Jersey to Germany in 1956. For the next five years he photographed unusual, rare and sometimes bizarre automobiles throughout Europe. This book features 105 specimens of auto exotica, captured with Cagle's Iloca Rapid-B 35mm camera".-- Provided by publisher.

"Cagle makes it easy to feel the excitement and enthusiasm he felt as a young boy. Any car spotter will enjoy this book, and may find a 26 horsepower favorite. The book is presented in a pleasant, easily readable format and contains a useful index and excellent bibliography." Choice. Reviews

DK Publishing, Inc

Car : the definitive visual history of the automobile DK Pub., 2011. 360 p. : **629.222**

1. Automobiles -- Pictorial works. 2. Automobiles -- History.

ISBN 9780756671679

LC bl2011014019

Includes index.

Traces the history of the automobile, from technological developments and manufacturers to the changing cultural backdrop of various models, and features photographs of the most noted cars of each decade.

Gurdon, Martin

Classic car : the definitive visual history / writers, Martin Gurdon, David Long, Andrew Noakes, Chris Quiller-Rees. DK Publishing, 2016. 320 p. : **629.222**

1. Antique and classic cars 2. Antique and classic cars. 3. Automobiles -- History.

ISBN 1465453393

LC bl2017002230

Includes index.

Features over 250 classic car models from the 1940s to the 1980s, highlighting their specificiations and key features.

"Obviously, this is a book to savor, to be pored over time and again." Booklist.

Ingrassia, Paul

Engines of change : a history of the American dream in fifteen cars / Paul Ingrassia. Simon & Schuster, 2012. xx, 395 p., [32] p. of plates : **629.222**

1. Automobiles -- Social aspects -- History 2. Transportation -- United States -- History 3. Transportation, Automotive 4. Social change. 5. United States -- History -- 20th century

ISBN 9781451640632

LC 2012002303

ALA Notable Book, 2013.

Chronicles the history reflected by 15 iconic car models including the VW Beetle, the Mustang and Honda Accord to discuss how automobiles reflect key cultural shifts as well as developments in such areas as manufacturing, women's rights and environmental awareness.

Klara, Robert

The devil's Mercedes : the bizarre and disturbing adventures of Hitler's limousine in America / Robert Klara. Thomas Dunne Books, 2017. 336 p. **629.222**

1. Hitler, Adolf 1889-1945 2. Automobiles 3. Antique and classic cars 4. Publicity stunts 5. World War II -- Post-war aspects

ISBN 9781250069726

LC 2016058801

The author chases down the improbable story of the national drama that erupted when Hitler's armored limousine surfaced in the U.S.

"An entertaining story of the irresistible cult of a creepy car." Kirkus.

Noakes, Andrew

Drive : the definitive history of driving / editor-in chief, Giles Chapman ; contributors, Andrew Noakes, Chris Rees, Martin Gurdon, Richard Truett, Sam Skelton, Richard Bremner, Peter Nunn, Simon Heptinstall, Alexandra Black. DK Publishing, 2018. 360 p. : **629.222**

1. Automobiles -- History 2. Automobile driving -- History 3. Transportation, Automotive -- History

ISBN 9781465469243

LC bl2019001993

At head of title: DK Smithsonian.

Includes index.

A history of the automobile, from the arrival of horseless carriages to the advent of driverless vehicles, explores the early glamour of driving, motor sport, and car design, and looks at how the automobile has shaped the modern world.

Parissien, Steven

The **life** of the automobile : the complete history of the motor car / Steven Parissien. Thomas Dunne Books, 2014. 432 p. **629.222**

1. Automobiles -- History. 2. Transportation -- History. 3. Mass production. 4. Automobile industry and trade.
ISBN 9781250040633

LC 2013045750

This all-encompassing world history of the most important transport innovation of the modern age explores the impact, development and significance of the automobile through its tumultuous and colorful 130-year history.

"This elegant and authoritative work demonstrates the historical links among people, machines, and cultures on a global scale." Library Journal.

Schleuning, Sarah

Dream cars : innovative design, visionary ideas / Sarah Schleunung, Ken Gross. Skira Rizzoli, 2014 134 p. : **629.222**

1. High Museum of Art Catalogs. 2. Experimental automobiles -- Exhibitions. 3. Antique and classic cars -- Exhibitions. 4. Automobiles -- Drawings -- Exhibitions. 5. Product design -- Exhibitions.
ISBN 9780847842636

LC 2014000794

"A sensuously designed showcase of covetable concept or limited-edition cars by the best American and European manufacturers. Dream Cars presents some of the world's most breathtaking concept cars built between 1934 and 2001, a series of visionary designs that influenced the automotive industry and challenged notions of what is possible both aesthetically and technologically. Stunning all-new photography of design pioneers such as the 1935 Bugatti Type 57 Aerolithe, the 1951 LeSabre concept car, and the 1954 Alfa Romeo B.A.T. 7 accompany lush images of dream sports cars, including the 1970 Ferrari Modulo and the 1955 Ghia Streamline X "Gilda." Meticulously restored and brought to life by all-new photography, these images trace a lineage of innovation in automobile design. Comprehensive descriptions by celebrated automotive writer Ken Gross as well as drawings and scaled models further illustrate the imaginative force of individual designers and famed manufacturers. Surprising insights into familiar models like the minivan, based on the streamlined silhouette of the Stout Scarab concept car developed in 1936, are juxtaposed with startling new technologies such as the 2001 BMW GINA Light Visionary Model's ingenious use of fabric as a retractable skin. An extended essay by Sarah Schleuning explores the effects of aerodynamics and aeronautics on car design and considers how groundbreaking events-such as General Motors's Motorama-fueled the creativity of automobile styles".-- Provided by publisher.

629.227 Cycles

Hallett, Richard, 1960-

The **bike** deconstructed : a grand tour of the modern bicycle / Richard Hallett. Princeton Architectural Press, 2014. 192 p. : **629.227**

1. Bicycles -- Design and construction -- History. 2. Bicycles -- Parts. 3. Road bicycles -- Parts.
ISBN 1616892285

LC 2013029264

Includes index.

Looks at the parts that make up a modern road bike, examining the history of each component, their uses, and how they work.

"The author includes historical background for many topics, as well as the advantages and disadvantages of different materials used in terms of weight, strength, and flexibility. A fascinating work of interest to a wide audience." Choice.

Holmstrom, Darwin,

Harley-Davidson : the complete history / Darwin Holmstrom, editor ; text, Darwin Holmstrom, Herbert Wagner, Jerry Hatfield, Greg Fields, Allan Girdler, Steve Anderson. Motorbooks, 2016. 240 p. : **629.227**

1. Harley-Davidson motorcycle 2. Harley-Davidson motorcycle -- History.
ISBN 9780760350003

LC bl2017029677

Includes index.

Issued in slipcase.

Traces the history of the Harley-Davidson motorcycle, highlighting the company's most iconic bikes while featuring never-before-seen archival images from celebrated motorcycle photographers.

629.28 Tests, driving, maintenance, repair

Downs, Todd

Essential road bike maintenance handbook / Todd Downs with Brian Fiske. Rodale, 2014 ix, 166 p. : **629.28**

1. Bicycles -- Maintenance and repair
ISBN 9781623361662

LC bl2014005451

Includes index.

A guide to repairing and maintaining bicycles includes instructions with step-by-step photographs, troubleshooting tips, links to videos, and sidebar material.

Henderson, Bob, 1962-

The **Haynes** bicycle book : the Haynes repair manual for maintaining and repairing your bike / Bob Henderson. Haynes North America, 2013 224 p. : **629.28**

1. Bicycles -- Maintenance and repair -- Handbooks, manuals, etc.
ISBN 9781620920404

LC 2013930927

Includes index.

This revised and updated third edition of The Haynes Bicycle Book contains everything you need to know to help you enjoy and maintain your bicycle. --From publisher description.

Little, Jamie, 1978-

Essential car care for women / Jamie Little & Danielle McCormick. Seal Press, c2013. xiii, 171 p. : **629.28**

1. Automobiles -- Maintenance and repair 2. Amateurs' manuals.
ISBN 9781580054362

LC 2011045604

Includes index.

"Despite the many advances women have made since the internal combustion engine was invented, there is still one widely held belief that won't seem to go away: that when it comes to cars, women should just leave it to the men. In Essential Car Care for Women, ESPN NASCAR pit reporter Jamie Little and Discovery Channel "Turbo Expert" Danielle McCormick team up to dispel this myth once and for all--and to offer the indispensable, hard-won advice women need to buy, sell, and care for their cars with confidence. With this handy guide, women will learn how to save themselves money by performing basic--but essential-

-maintenance tasks on their own. Little and McCormick explain what an alternator, regulator, distributor, and timing belt are; how to change a tire, recharge a flat battery, check the oil, and assess tire pressure; what to do when a car breaks down or when an accident occurs; how to buy a car without being taken advantage of; and more. Straightforward and easy to follow--and including simple step-by-step diagrams and pictures to help along the way--Essential Car Care for Women is the ultimate handbook to everything a woman should know about her set of wheels. "-- Provided by publisher.

"This is a good update for Julie Sussman & Stephanie Glakas-Tenet's Dare To Repair Your Car. As it lacks an overwhelming amount of mechanical instruction, this book proves useful and approachable. It will appeal to high school to adult audiences, male or female, though guys may be leery of the pink cover. Very strongly recommended." Library Journal.

Ramsey, Dan, 1945-

Teach yourself visually car care & maintenance / Dan Ramsey and Judy Ramsey. Wiley Pub., c2009. 210 p. : **629.28**

1. Automobiles -- Maintenance and repair

ISBN 9780470377277

LC bl2009012449

Includes index.

Describes how to repair and maintain automobiles, including information on how each part of the engine functions, performing basic maintenance checks, repairing and cleaning automobiles, and handling road emergencies.

Vanderbilt, Tom

Traffic : why we drive the way we do (and what it says about us) / Tom Vanderbilt. Alfred A. Knopf, 2008. viii, 402 p. ; **629.28**

1. Automobile driving -- Psychological aspects. 2. Traffic congestion. 3. Human behavior 4. Sociology

ISBN 9780307264787

LC 2008011507

ALA Notable Book, 2009.

Analyzes the complex social, physical, psychological, and technical factors that dictate how traffic works, why we drive the way we do, and what our driving reveals about us, discussing the unintended consequences of attempts to engineer safety.

"This may be the most insightful and comprehensive study ever done of driving behavior and how it reveals truths about the types of people we are." Booklist.

Zinn, Lennard

Zinn & the art of road bike maintenance : the world's best-selling bicycle repair and maintenance guide / / Lennard Zinn ; illustrated by Todd Telander and Mike Reisel. VeloPress, 2016 xvii, 465 p. : **629.28**

1. Bicycles -- Maintenance and repair 2. Road bicycles -- Maintenance and repair

ISBN 9781937715373

LC 2015039577

Offers advice and instructions on how to maintain and repair a bicycle, including freeing a jammed chain, cleaning rear cogs, and overhauling pedals.

629.4 Astronautics

Brinkley, Douglas

American Moonshot : John F. Kennedy and the great space race / Douglas Brinkley. HarperCollins, 2019. 448 p. **629.4**

1. Kennedy, John F. (John Fitzgerald), 1917-1963 2. National Aeronautics and Space Aministration 3. Space programs -- International competition 4. Space exploration 5. Cold War 6. Presidents -- United States 7. Moon -- Exploration 8. Space

ISBN 9780062655066

LC 2019300429

The historian author of Cronkite draws on new primary source material and firsthand interviews in a reassessment of the space program that examines the political, cultural and scientific factors that launched NASA and the space race.

Clegg, Brian

Final frontier : the pioneering science and technology of exploring the universe / Brian Clegg. St. Martin's Press, 2014. 296 p. **629.4**

1. Astronautics. 2. Space flight 3. Space exploration

ISBN 9781250039439

LC 2014010056

The best-selling author of How to Build a Time Machine outlines the massive challenges to space exploration while surveying current and near-future technologies that may enable greater advances in space travel.

"This fine work belongs in all college libraries. Summing Up: Highly recommended." Choice.

Holt, Nathalia, 1980-

Rise of the rocket girls : the women who propelled us, from missiles to the moon to Mars / Nathalia Holt. Little Brown & Co., 2016 304 p. **629.4**

1. Space exploration 2. Women scientists 3. Women engineers 4. Space flight

ISBN 9780316338929

LC 2015954384

Traces the pivotal achievements of the elite female science recruits at the Jet Propulsion Laboratory, where in the mid-20th century they transformed rocket design and enabled the creations of the first American satellites.

"This is an excellent contribution to American history, valuable not only for what it reveals about the space program and gender equality but even more as great reading. Book clubs will be lining up." Booklist.

Launius, Roger D

The **Smithsonian** history of space exploration : from the ancient world to the extraterrestrial future / Roger D. Launius. Smithsonian Books, 2018 400 p. **629.4**

1. Astronautics 2. Space flight 3. Space flight to Mars 4. Space exploration 5. Illustrated books

ISBN 9781588346377

LC 2018017014

Offers an illustrated history of space exploration, from the pioneering work of ancient astronomers to the latest technological and mechanical marvels that allow extraterrestrial exploration, as well as what the future may hold.

Neufeld, Michael J., 1951-

Milestones of space : eleven iconic objects from the Smithsonian National Air and Space Museum / Michael J. Neufeld, [editor]. Smithsonian National Air and Space Museum in association with Zenith Press, 2014 176 p. : **629.4**

1. National Air and Space Museum Catalogs. 2. Astronautics --

United States -- Equipment and supplies -- Pictorial works.
ISBN 9780760344446

LC 2013045152

"A beautifully illustrated history of the exploration of space through the most iconic objects from the Smithsonian National Air and Space Museum. Throughout the whole of human history, across all of Earth's cultures and landscapes, countless individuals have gazed with wonder in the same direction: upwards. Getting to space was no easy task, and our curiosity with the surrounding universe has long been a source of earthly pride and competition. At the bottom of this international technological rivalry, though, lies one unifying purpose, which is to understand the impossibly vast heavens. In Milestones of Space, Michael Neufeld and select curators of the Smithsonian National Air and Space Museum present a gorgeous photographic celebration of some of the most groundbreaking artifacts that played key parts in giving humanity its first steps into the cosmos. Focusing on the most iconic objects and technology--such as Friendship 7,the Lunar Module 2, Neil Armstrong's Lunar Suit, the Hubble Space Telescope, and Space Shuttle Discovery--this book extensively profiles eleven of the NASM's most important breakthroughs in space technology. The NASM curators feature each object in incredible detail with compelling timelines, sidebars and captions, and over 150 archival images that provide new and little-known insights into their development and historical context. We are still a long way from grasping our universe. But for now, Milestones of Space magnificently commemorates the individuals and inventions that havetaken us this far".-- Provided by publisher.

Piantadosi, Claude A.

Mankind beyond Earth : the history, science, and future of human space exploration / Claude A. Piantadosi. Columbia University Press, c2012. 336 p. **629.4**

1. Astronautics. 2. Space flight. 3. Space exploration. 4. Space programs. 5. Space.
ISBN 9780231162425

LC 2012017631

Seeking to reenergize Americans' passion for the space program, the value of further exploration of the Moon, and the importance of human beings on the final frontier, Claude A. Piantadosi presents a rich history of American space exploration and its major achievements. He emphasizes the importance of reclaiming national command of our manned program and continuing our unmanned space missions, and he stresses the many adventures that still await us in the unfolding universe. Acknowledging space exploration's practical and financial obstacles, Piantadosi challenges us to revitalize American leadership in space exploration in order to reap its scientific bounty. --From publisher description.

"This nicely written volume will appeal to the general public and space enthusiasts who want to learn about the hazards of human space exploration." Choice.

Scott, Jonathan (Freelance writer)

★The **vinyl** frontier : the story of the Voyager Golden Record / Jonathan Scott. Bloomsbury Sigma, 2019. 288 p. ; **629.4**

1. Sagan, Carl, 1934-1996. 2. Voyager Project. 3. Outer space -- Exploration.
ISBN 1472956133

LC bl2019012682

Shares the story of the Voyager Golden Record, a multi-media LP of music, spoken greetings in multiple languages, and over one hundred photographs and diagrams sent up with Voyagers 1 and 2 on their grand tour of the outer planets.

"The most intriguing stories are often found in the details, and this is the case for music writer Scott's engaging and conversational look at the creation of the gold-plated records that are still traveling throughout the universe on the two Voyager probes launched in 1977...This is also a very relatable and human way to approach deep space exploration." Library Journal.

Sparrow, Giles, 1970-

★**Spaceflight** : the complete story from Sputnik to Curiosity / Giles Sparrow. DK Publishing, 2019. 320 p. : **629.4**

1. Space exploration 2. Space flight 3. Astronautics. 4. Space probes 5. Space 6. Solar system -- Exploration.
ISBN 9781465479655

LC bl2019005785

At head of title: DK Smithsonian.
Includes index.

A comprehensive history of space exploration chronicles the development of space technology, including rockets, vehicles, and equipment; the role of the "space race;" tragedies; key accomplishments; and past and future missions.

"This volume serves as an inspiring ode to scientific progress and a humble reminder of how much more of the galaxy there is to explore." Publishers Weekly.

Stern, Alan, 1957-

Chasing New Horizons : inside the epic first mission to Pluto / Alan Stern and David Grinspoon. Picador, 2018 320 p. **629.4**

1. New Horizons (Spacecraft). 2. Space flight to Pluto. 3. Pluto probes. 4. Pluto (Dwarf planet) -- Exploration.
ISBN 9781250098962

LC 2017060114

Includes index.

A New Horizons Principal Investigator and an award-winning NASA advisor share a behind-the-scenes account of the science, politics, egos and public expectations that shaped the New Horizons' mission to Pluto and beyond, citing the endeavor's boundary-breaking achievements and how they reflect the collective power of shared human goals.

"Armchair space explorers and budding scientists will relish this inspiring aerospace adventure." Library Journal.

Teitel, Amy Shira

Breaking the chains of gravity : the story of spaceflight before NASA / Amy Shira Teitel. Bloomsbury Sigma, 2016 288 p. **629.4**

1. United States. National Advisory Committee for Aeronautics 2. Rocketry. 3. Rockets (Aviation) 4. Space flight
ISBN 9781472911179

LC 2015046643

A history of pre-NASA spaceflight describes how America's space agency drew some of the world's leading minds, discussing such subjects as Wernher von Braun's Jupiter rocket, the cutting-edge aircraft flown by NACA test pilot Neil Armstrong and the rivalries between the various arms of the U.S. military.

"Aircraft and rocketry geeks will find the most to love in this jet-powered history, but it's a great primer for anyone interested in the origins of space travel." Library Journal.

Tyson, Neil deGrasse

Space chronicles : facing the ultimate frontier / Neil deGrasse Tyson ; edited by Avis Lang. W. W. Norton, c2012. 240 p. **629.4**

1. United States. National Aeronautics and Space Administration. 2. Space flight. 3. Space exploration. 4. Space policy. 5. Astronautics.
ISBN 9780393082104

LC 2011032481

Includes index.

Presents the astrophysicist's views on the future of space travel and America's role in that future, giving his readers an eye-opening manifesto on the importance of space exploration for America's economy, security, and morale.

Wolfe, Tom

★The **right** stuff / Tom Wolfe. Farrar, Straus, Giroux, c1983. 436 p. ; **629.4**

1. United States. National Aeronautics and Space Administration -- History 2. Astronautics -- United States. 3. Astronauts -- United States 4. Space flight. 5. Space accidents. 6. United States -- History -- 20th century.

ISBN 0374250332

LC 84162805

National Book Award for Nonfiction, 1980.

National Book Critics Circle Award for Nonfiction finalist, 1979.

"This volume chronicles the handful of adrenaline-junkie military test pilots who became the Mercury astronauts. Their story is juxtaposed against that of Chuck Yeager, the ace of aces pilot who broke the sound barrier but couldn't apply to the space program because he lacked a college degree. . . . A terrific read from beginning to end." Library Journal.

629.44 Auxiliary spacecraft

Kitmacher, Gary

Space stations : the art, science, and reality of working in space / Dr. Gary Kitmacher, Ron Miller, Robert Pearlman ; foreword, Nicole Stott. Smithsonian Books, 2018. 240 p. : **629.44**

1. Space stations 2. Space stations -- History 3. Outer space -- Exploration

ISBN 9781588346322

LC 2018004838

Copyrighted by Elephant Book Company Limited.

"A rich visual history of real and fictional space stations, illustrating pop culture's influence on the development of actual space stations and vice versa."-- Provided by publisher.

"Covering technical breakthroughs as well as Star Trek and comic book references, their work will win high marks from space buffs and sf fans alike." Booklist.

629.45 Manned space flight

Donovan, Jim, 1954-

★**Shoot** for the moon : the space race and the extraordinary voyage of Apollo 11 / James Donovan. Little, Brown, 2019. 448 p. **629.45**

1. United States. National Aeronautics and Space Administration 2. Project Apollo (U.S.) -- History. 3. Space programs -- International competition -- History. 4. Cold War. 5. Apollo 11 (Spacecraft) 6. Space flight to the moon. 7. Moon -- Exploration.

ISBN 9780316341783

LC 2018947611

Published to coincide with the mission's 50th anniversary, a meticulously researched account of the Apollo 11 program also examines its astronauts, flight controllers and engineers, as well as its role in shaping the Mercury and Gemini missions.

"Drawing on dozens of interviews with the era's engineers and scientists, Donovan's history is a powerfully written and irresistible celebration of the Apollo missions." Booklist.

Fishman, Charles, 1961-

One giant leap : the impossible mission that flew us to the moon / Charles Fishman. Simon & Schuster 2019 416 p. **629.45**

1. Project Apollo (U.S.) 2. Space programs -- United States 3. Technological innovations 4. Space flight to the moon 5. Scientists 6. Moon -- Exploration 7. United States -- Politics and government -- 20th century

ISBN 9781501106293

LC bl2019011666

The award-winning author of The Wal-Mart Effect shares the story of the remarkable NASA scientists and engineers who created America's space program and fulfilled President Kennedy's mandate to put a man on the Moon before 1970.

"With the upcoming 50th anniversary of the Apollo 11 landing, this compelling read is highly recommended for all public libraries." Library Journal.

Kaku, Michio

The **future** of humanity : terraforming Mars, interstellar travel, immortality, and our destiny beyond Earth / Michio Kaku. Doubleday, 2018. 416 p. **629.45**

1. Scientific forecasting 2. Technological forecasting 3. Space colonies 4. Space flight

ISBN 9780385542760

LC 2017046597

The co-founder of string field theory and best-selling author of The Future of the Mind traverses the frontiers of astrophysics, artificial intelligence and technology to outline a remarkable vision of humanity's future in space, from colonizing Mars to traveling to distant galaxies.

"Kaku's writings have garnered a reputation for combining hard science with clever speculation, and his latest book continues that winning trend. A breathtaking voyage through what is almost certainly the next major period in the history of humanity." Booklist.

Kluger, Jeffrey

★**Apollo** 8 : the thrilling story of the first mission to the Moon / Jeffrey Kluger. Henry Holt and Co., 2017. 336 p. **629.45**

1. Project Apollo (U.S.). 2. Apollo 8 (Spacecraft). 3. Space flight to the moon. 4. Astronauts. 5. Cold War.

ISBN 9781627798327

LC 2016046157

In Apollo 8, acclaimed science writer Jeffrey Kluger provides a you-were-there reading experience as he recounts the preparations that culminated in the first manned flight to the moon. Drawing on his interviews with crew members Frank Borman, Jim Lovell, and Bill Anders, as well as the NASA Oral History Project and other records, Kluger enriches the personal and technical details of the mission with facets of the Cold War-era politics that spurred the race to the moon.

"Readers will relish Kluger's multisensory prose, and the whole gamut of space flight comes alive in the details. Moreover, extensive interviews lend authenticity to the dialogue and character sketches." Publishers Weekly.

Kurson, Robert

★**Rocket** men : the daring odyssey of Apollo 8 and the astronauts who made man's first journey to the Moon / Robert Kurson. Random House, [2018] 352 p. **629.45**

1. Project Apollo (U.S.) 2. Apollo 8 (Spacecraft) 3. Space flight to the moon 4. Astronauts 5. Space exploration

ISBN 9780812988703

LC 2017009386

Shares the lesser-known inside story of the dangerous Apollo 8 mission, focusing in particular on the lives and families of astronaut heroes Frank Borman, Jim Lovell and Bill Anders, while illuminating the political factors that prompted America to risk lives to save the Apollo program and define the space race.

"An exuberant history of a major turning point in early American spaceflight, possibly 'the riskiest and most thrilling of all the Apollo missions.'" Kirkus.

Mailer, Norman

Of a fire on the moon / Norman Mailer. Random House Trade Paperbacks, 2004. 463 p. ; **629.45**

1. Project Apollo (U.S.) 2. Space flight to the moon. 3. Astronauts -- United States. 4. United States -- Civilization -- 1945-

ISBN 9780553390612

LC 2014415502

For many, the moon landing was the defining event of the twentieth century. So it seems only fitting that Norman Mailer--the literary provocateur who altered the landscape of American nonfiction--wrote the most wide-ranging, far-seeing chronicle of the Apollo 11 mission. A classic chronicle of America's reach for greatness in the midst of the Cold War, Of a Fire on the Moon compiles the reportage Mailer published between 1969 and 1970 in Life magazine: gripping firsthand dispatches from inside NASA's clandestine operations in Houston and Cape Kennedy; technical insights into the magnitude of their awe-inspiring feat; and prescient meditations that place the event in human context as only Mailer could. --From publisher description.

Nelson, Craig, 1955-

Rocket men : the triumph and tragedy of the first Americans on the moon / Craig Nelson. Viking, 2009. 416 p. **629.45**

1. Project Apollo (U.S.) 2. United States. National Aeronautics and Space Administration 3. Space flight to the moon. 4. Astronauts -- United States 5. Space programs -- United States. 6. Astronautics -- United States -- History.

ISBN 9780670021031

LC 2008051175

Recreates the story of the Apollo 11 moon mission through interviews, NASA oral histories, and declassified CIA documents.

"A thorough recountingas full in human terms as in scientific and technical detail of NASA's first manned Moon landing. The definitive account of a watershed in American history." Kirkus.

Potter, Christopher, 1959-

The **Earth** gazers : on seeing ourselves / Christopher Potter. Pegasus Books, 2018 400 p. **629.45**

1. Project Apollo (U.S.) 2. Space flight to the moon 3. Astronauts -- United States 4. Moon -- Exploration

ISBN 9781681776361

LC bl2018004393

To commemorate the 50th anniversary of the moon landing, a full-color book examines the beautiful images of the whole earth taken by the mission's astronauts and the long road that led to that point by showcasing the visionaries that came before.

"Potter (You Are Here: A Portable History of the Universe) pens this excellent account of the people and events that brought about the first photographs of the earth taken from outer space." Library Journal.

Pyle, Rod

Destination moon : the Apollo missions in the astronauts' own words / Rod Pyle. First Person Productions in association with Collins, 2005. 192 p. : **629.45**

1. Project Apollo (U.S.) 2. Space flight to the moon -- History. 3. Astronauts -- United States

ISBN 0060873493

LC 2005051350

Encompassing the firsthand accounts of the astronauts and other participants, a complete history of NASA's Apollo program includes coverage of the Apollo 11 moon landing and the near-catastrophic Apollo 13 mission.

"Space collections of all sizes should welcome Pyle's book, and smaller ones will find it invaluable." Booklist.

Stone, Robert, 1958-

Chasing the moon : the people, the politics, and the promise that launched America into the space age / Robert Stone and Alan Andres. Ballantine Books, [2019] 240 p. **629.45**

1. Space policy 2. Space exploration 3. Space programs -- International competition 4. Space flight to the moon 5. United States -- History -- 20th century

ISBN 9781524798123

LC 2018059390

A companion to PBS's American Experience draws on eyewitness accounts and newly discovered archival material to chronicle the stories of the visionaries who helped America win the space race with the first lunar landing.

"In an informative companion book to the PBS miniseries of the same name, documentary filmmaker Stone, the program's writer, producer, and director, and Andres, a consulting producer and researcher on the series, chronicle the quest for space travel that culminated in Neil Armstrong's first step on the lunar surface." Kirkus.

Stuart, Colin (Science writer)

How to live in space : everything you need to know for the not-so-distant future / Colin Stuart. Smithsonian Books, 2018. 192 p. **629.45**

1. Space flight 2. Space stations 3. Life on other planets 4. Terraforming

ISBN 9781588346384

LC 2018011524

Includes index.

"Suitable for space-happy tweens as well as nonscientist adults, Stuart's captivating handbook has something to amaze and entertain every reader." Publishers Weekly.

Virts, Terry, 1967-

How to astronaut : an insider's guide to leaving planet earth / Terry Virts. Workman Publishing Company, 2020 ix, 310 p. **629.45**

1. Virts, Terry, 1967- 2. International Space Station. 3. Astronauts 4. Astronautics. 5. Space flight 6. Space exploration 7. Essays

ISBN 9781523509614

LC bl2020018719

Includes index.

A behind-the-scenes look at the training, basic rules, lessons and procedures of space travel by the former astronaut, space-shuttle pilot and International Space Station commander includes coverage of the realities of living long-term in space.

"This is an eye-opening insider's view on what it's really like to be an astronaut: the joys, the dangers, the fear, and the day-to-day reality of it. Virts' writing is humorous, playful, down to earth, and often wise." Booklist

Wohlforth, Charles P.

Beyond Earth : our path to a new home in the planets / Charles

Wohlforth and Amanda R. Hendrix. Pantheon Books, 2016. 288 p. **629.45**

1. Space flight. 2. Astronautics. 3. Space exploration. 4. Space colonies

ISBN 9780804197977

LC 2016009498

Includes index.

A leading planetary scientist and an award-winning science writer present a chronicle of the developments and initiatives that have transformed the idea of space colonization into an achievable goal, sharing arguments in favor of targeting Saturn's moon, Titan.

"On the whole, the fictional chapters are entertaining, chilling, and put the science in a more human context. The two halves work together to create a striking, reality-based possible future thats seen through the lens of current knowledge." Publishers Weekly.

629.47 Astronautical engineering

Guthrie, Julian

How to make a spaceship : a band of renegades, an epic race, and the birth of private spaceflight / Julian Guthrie, foreword by Richard Branson, afterword by Stephen Hawking. Penguin Group USA, 2016 400 p. **629.47**

1. Diamandis, Peter H. 2. SpaceShipOne (Spacecraft) 3. Aeronautical engineers 4. Space flight

ISBN 9781594206726

LC bl2016030308

Traces the efforts of science prodigy Peter Diamandis and other pioneering space hopefuls to create the private spaceflight industry, launching a historic race to win the $10 million XPrize and inspiring the triumphant 2004 launch of SpaceShipOne.

"Guthrie well captures the high-risk, buccaneering spirit of privately financed spaceflight." Booklist.

629.8 Automatic control engineering

Bascomb, Neal

The **new** cool : a visionary teacher, his first robotics team, and the ultimate battle of smarts / Neal Bascomb. Crown Publishers, 2011. xiii, 337 p. **629.8**

1. FIRST (Organization) 2. Science teachers. 3. High school teachers. 4. Robotics. 5. High school students.

ISBN 9780307588890

LC 2010021646

A report on genius inventor Dean Kaman's FIRST program follows a team of brilliant, misfit high school students through the program's 2009 robotics competition, during which the teens under the guidance of a dedicated teacher confronted other hopefuls in stadiums throughout the country.

"Aside from a mind-numbing plethora of physics terminology, Bascomb skillfully translates the exhilarating challenge to the page via intricately descriptive, expertly paced sketches of the group and their combined handiwork. A nail-biting thrill ride for techies and armchair engineers." Kirkus.

Davis, Joshua, 1974-

Spare parts : four Mexican teenagers, one ugly robot, and the battle for the American dream / Joshua Davis. Farrar, Straus, and Giroux, 2014. 240 p. **629.8**

1. Robotics 2. Mexican American boys 3. Undocumented immigrants. 4. Robots 5. Phoenix, Arizona.

ISBN 9780374183370

LC 2014018569

Tells the story of four Mexican American high school students who built a submersible robot and entered it in a national competition.

"Davis pulls no punches as he describes the grim sociopolitical atmosphere that allows the oppression of talented people for no morally acceptable reason. The four young inventors and their struggles helped spur the DREAMers movement, and their story will also be told in a forthcoming Hollywood movie. This is important reading." Booklist.

Dufty, David F.

How to build an android : the true story of Philip K. Dick's robotic resurrection / David F. Dufty. H. Holt, 2012, c2011. 272 p. : **629.8**

1. PKD Android Project 2. Androids. 3. Robots. 4. Artificial intelligence. 5. Robotics.

ISBN 9780805095517

LC 2011043674

Originally published: Lost in transit. Carlton, Vic. : Melbourne University Pub., 2011.

The stranger-than-fiction story of the creation and loss of an artificially intelligent android of science-fiction writer Philip K. Dick.

Long, John, 1964 January 12-

Darwin's devices : what evolving robots can teach us about the history of life and,the future of technology / John Long. Basic Books, 2012. 320 p. **629.8**

1. Robotics. 2. Evolution -- Simulation methods. 3. Technology -- Forecasting. 4. Evolutionary robotics.

ISBN 9780465021413

LC 2011051804

"What happens when we let robots play the game of life? The challenge of studying evolution is that the history of life is buried in the past--we can't witness the dramatic events that shaped the adaptations we see today. But biorobotics expert John Longhas found an ingenious way to overcome this problem: he creates robots that look and behave like extinct animals, subjects them to evolutionary pressures, lets them compete for mates and resources, and mutates their 'genes'. In short, he lets robots play the game of life. In Darwin's Devices, Long tells the story of these evolving biorobots--how they came to be, and what they can teach us about the biology of living and extinct species. Evolving biorobots can replicate creatures that disappeared from the Earth long ago, showing us in real time what happens in the face of unexpected environmental challenges. Biomechanically correct models of backbones functioning as part of an autonomous robot, for example, can help us understand why the first vertebrates evolved them. But the most impressive feature of these robots, as Long shows, is their ability to illustrate the power of evolution to solve difficult technological challenges autonomously--without human input regarding what a workable solution might be. Even a simple robot can create complex behavior, often learning or evolving greater intelligence than humans could possibly program. This remarkable idea could forever alter the face of engineering, design, and even warfare. An amazing tour through the workings of a fertile mind, Darwin's Devices will make you rethink everything you thought you knew about evolution, robot intelligence, and life itself".-- Provided by publisher.

Mindell, David A.

Our robots, ourselves : robotics and the myths of autonomy / David A. Mindell. Penguin Publishing Group, 2015 272 p. **629.8**

1. Robotics 2. Automation 3. Technological innovations 4. Artificial intelligence
ISBN 9780525426974

LC bl2015034077

An MIT professor outlines provocative arguments for the crucial role of people in a changing technological landscape, discussing cutting-edge advances and the unintended consequences of a robotics-driven future.

"An expansively researched and enjoyably accessible treatment of robotic automation, recommended for readers of popular science and those with an interest in artificial intelligence and automation." Library Journal.

Waldman, Jonathan

Sam : one robot, a dozen engineers, and the race to revolutionize the way we build / Jonathan Waldman. Avid Reader Press, 2020. 288 p. **629.8**

1. Engineers 2. Construction industry and trade 3. Technological innovations 4. Robots
ISBN 9781501140594

LC bl2019037483

A true story of innovation centers on a scrappy team of engineers--far from the Silicon Valley limelight--and their quest to achieve a surprisingly difficult technological feat: building a robot that can lay bricks.

"As one learns a great deal about geology from John McPhee and computers from Tracy Kidder, Waldman offers a lively, accessible overview of the bricklayer's art, which is much more complex than one might think." Kirkus.

630 Agriculture and related technologies

English, Ashley, 1976-

The **essential** book of homesteading : the ultimate guide to sustainable living / Ashley English. LARK, 2017 vii, 360 p. : **630**

1. Agriculture 2. Bee culture. 3. Canning and preserving. 4. Dairying.
ISBN 1454710209

LC bl2017012049

Includes index.

A homesteading expert shares her time-honored tips for successfully overseeing food production in one's own home, covering everything from preserving jams and jellies to whipping butter and keeping a hive of honeybees.

Levatino, Audrey

Woman-powered farm : manual for a self-sufficient lifestyle from homestead to field / Audrey Levatino. The Countryman Press, 2015 343 p. : **630**

1. Farm management 2. Women farmers
ISBN 9781581572414

LC 2015006642

Presents advice for women on how to manage a farm, discussing internships, buying or leasing a farm, tools, animals, planting techniques, sources of funding, and best business practices.

"A comprehensive volume on farming for women beginning to contemplate the industry, whether as a hobby or for a living. Personal anecdotes and a friendly tone don't overshadow the wealth of information in this book." Library Journal.

630.68 Agriculture management

Lanier, Karen, 1975-

The **woman** hobby farmer : female guidance for growing food, raising livestock, and building a farm-based business / Karen Lanier. CompanionHouse Books, 2017 238 p. **630.68**

1. Women farmers
ISBN 9781620082607

LC 2017013667

Hobby farming is alive and thriving in semi-rural, suburban, and rural areas across the country, and female farmers have been cited as the fastest growing sector within the farming community in recent years. With more than 1 million women in the United States and Canada describing farming as their primary source of income, and many more for whom hobby farming is just that--a hobby--the time is right for a publication dedicated to hobby farming from a female perspective. Written for women, by a woman, this insightful volume is packed with stories and advice from women hobby farmers and looks at female-specific farming challenges as well as issues that all farmers face. --From publisher description.

"An uplifting, can-do book that is sure to present encouragement and inspiration to women interested in small-scale farming." Library Journal.

630.9 Agriculture -- History

Genoways, Ted

This blessed earth : a year in the life of an American family farm / Ted Genoways. W.W. Norton & Company, [2017] 288 p. **630.9**

1. Hammond family 2. Farm life. 3. Family farms. 4. Farmers 5. Ranchers 6. Nebraska
ISBN 9780393292572

LC 2017025062

"By following a single family through time, the book captures the complex reality of farmers in America today both in terms of the future of the industry and of their everyday lives. It is an unvarnished portrait striking for both its depth and humanity." Publishers Weekly.

Hanson, David, 1978-

Breaking through concrete : building an urban farm revival / David Hanson and Edwin Marty ; photographs by Michael Hanson ; foreword by Mark Winne. University of California Press, c2012. xv, 181 p. : **630.9**

1. Gardening -- Environmental aspects 2. Urban agriculture -- United States. 3. Community gardens -- United States. 4. Community gardening -- United States.
ISBN 9780520270541

LC 2011024485

People have always grown food in urban spaces--on windowsills and sidewalks, and in backyards and neighborhood parks--but today, urban farmers are leading an environmental and social movement that transforms our national food system. To explore this agricultural renaissance, brothers David and Michael Hanson and urban farmer Edwin Marty document twelve successful urban farm programs, from an alternative school for girls in Detroit, to a backyard food swap in New Orleans, to a restaurant supply garden on a rooftop in Brooklyn. Each beautifully illustrated essay offers practical advice for budding farmers, such as composting and keeping livestock in the city, decontaminating toxic soil, even changing zoning laws. --From publisher description.

"Gardeners and foodies may be inspired by this book to hit the road themselves and visit some of the urban oases described." Library Journal.

630.973 Agriculture -- History -- United States

Berry, Wendell, 1934-

Bringing it to the table : on farming and food / Wendell Berry ; introduction by Michael Pollan. Counterpoint, c2009. xvi, 234 p. ; **630.973**

1. Agriculture -- United States 2. Family farms -- United States 3. Farmers -- United States 4. Local foods -- United States 5. Essays
ISBN 9781582435435

LC 2009024437

A collection of essays that address the origins of the food you eat, including how organically-grown food measures up against locally-grown produce, and how the differences between large and small farms can affect the food on your table.

Hodgkins, Martha,

Letters to a young farmer : on food, farming, and our future / edited by Martha Hodgkins, Illustrations by Chris Wormell. Princeton Architectural Press, 2017 176 p. **630.973**

1. Farmers 2. Farm life 3. Sustainable agriculture 4. Farms
ISBN 9781616895303

LC 2016013820

"Three dozen esteemed writers, farmers, chefs, activists, and visionaries address the highs and lows of farming life--as well as larger questions of how our food is produced and consumed--in vivid and personal detail."-- provided by the publisher.

"Longtime advocates of sustainable agriculture join with new voices for a comradely take on the challenging future of farming." Kirkus.

631.4 Soil science

Pavlis, Robert

Soil science for gardeners : working with nature to build soil health / Robert Pavlis. New Society Publishers, 2020 xi, 209 p. : **631.4**

1. Garden soils. 2. Soil science. 3. Soil management. 4. Gardening.
ISBN 9780865719309

LC bl2020046377

Includes index.

"Soil Science for Gardeners is an easy-to-read, practical guide to the science behind a healthy soil ecosystem and thriving plants. The book debunks common myths, explains soil science basics, and provides the reader with the knowledge to create a personalized soil fertility improvement program for better plants."-- Provided by publisher.

631.5 Cultivation and harvesting

Bradley, Steve, 1949-

★**Pruning** simplified : a visual guide to 50 trees and shrubs / Steven Bradley. Timber Press, 2019. 192 p. : **631.5**

1. Pruning. 2. Shrubs -- Pruning. 3. Trees -- Pruning.
ISBN 1604698888

LC bl2019012456

Includes index.

Filled with expert advice, a plant-by-plant guide profiles 50 of the most popular trees and shrubs and provides easy-to-follow instructions for pruning and shaping each one.

"British horticulturist Bradley, known for his long career providing gardening advice, focuses his latest book on the evergreen subject of pruning. He outlines the many reasons for pruning, basic pruning techniques, and necessary equipment in brief, using general terms to start with, before moving on to the specific details for pruning 50 plants commonly grown in residential gardens." Booklist.

Jenkins, McKay, 1963-

Food fight : GMOs and the future of the American diet / McKay Jenkins. Avery, 2017. 322 p. **631.5**

1. Biotechnology in agriculture. 2. Genetically engineered food 3. Food crops -- Genetics. 4. Food -- Biotechnology.
ISBN 9781594634604

LC 2016054194

The noted environmental journalist and author examines the rise of GMOs and offers a fresh, nuanced, and informative look at how they're shaping our food system--for better and for worse.

"Highlighting the pros and cons of this contentious topic, Jenkins gives conscientious readers plenty to chew on." Publishers Weekly.

631.6 Clearing, drainage, revegetation

Fukuoka, Masanobu

Sowing seeds in the desert : natural farming, global restoration, and ultimate food security / Masanobu Fukuoka ; edited by Larry Korn. Chelsea Green Pub., c2012. xxxv, 168 p. : **631.6**

1. Desert reclamation 2. Desertification -- Control 3. Revegetation
ISBN 9781603584180

LC 2012007330

"Translated into English and adapted from the book originally published in Japanese in 1996 by Shou Shin Sha, Japan, as The Ultimatum of God, Nature"--T.p. verso.

Argues that the Earth's deteriorating condition is man-made and outlines a way for the process to be reversed by rehabilitating the deserts using natural farming.

631.8 Fertilizers, soil conditioners, growth regulators

Pleasant, Barbara

★The **complete** compost gardening guide : banner batches, grow heaps, comforter compost, and other amazing techniques for saving time and money, and producing the most flavorful, nutritious vegetables ever / Barbara Pleasant & Deborah L. Martin. Storey Pub., c2008. 319 p. : **631.8**

1. Compost
ISBN 9781580177030

LC 2007049729

Explains how to transform one's garden into a nourishing, organic environment with the use of compost customized to the special needs and soil of each garden.

632 Plant injuries, diseases, pests

Dickinson, Richard, 1960-

Weeds of North America / Richard Dickinson and France Royer. The University of Chicago Press, 2014. xxxii, 797 p. : **632**

1. Weeds -- North America -- Identification. 2. Weeds -- North America -- Handbooks, manuals, etc.
ISBN 9780226076447

LC 2013038953

Organized by plant family and featuring more than 500 species, a visually stunning and informative guide to North American weeds at every stage of growth provides much-needed background on these intrusive organisms, arming readers with the knowledge they need to win the battle with weeds.

Mabey, Richard, 1941-
Weeds : in defense of nature's most unloved plants / Richard Mabey. HarperCollins, c2011. 320 p. **632**

1. Weeds -- History. 2. Plants. 3. Horticulture -- Sociological aspects. 4. Nature.
ISBN 9780062065452

LC 2011010483

First printed in Great Britain in 2010 by Profile Books Ltd. as Weeds: how vagabond plants gatecrashed civilisation and changed the way we think about nature.

Weaving together natural history, botanical science and insight from his own travels, a prominent nature writer reveals the many hidden truths behind these scourges of lawns and gardens, and explores how weeds have been portrayed from the Bible all the way to Invasion of the Body Snatchers.

"This lively, erudite work invites readers to take a new look at the lowly and unloved weed. Mabey explains how weeds have cunningly evolved to survive natural disasters, human devastation, climate change, and almost every attempt to eradicate them. He weaves together a complex, fascinating tale of history and botany that travels from the first farm fields of Mesopotamia to the bomb craters of the London Blitz and the lowly industrial outfields of our modern cities." Publishers Weekly.

Orlando, Richard, 1942-
Weeds in the urban landscape : where they come from, why they're here, and how to live with them / Richard Orlando. North Atlantic Books, [2018] 392 p. **632**

1. Weeds -- Identification 2. Weed control 3. Urban gardening 4. The West (United States)
ISBN 9781623172114

LC 2017043940

This engaging field guide for the urban explorer, gardener, or armchair enthusiast traces the history of weeds as they migrated out of the Middle East with human tribes and spread across Europe and the Americas, details the folklore surrounding them, and explains their role in the evolution of agriculture and human civilizations as well as their many uses for medicine, food, animal fodder, and soil enhancement. Richard Orlando provides detailed descriptions of 189 common weeds found across the U.S., describing their families and characteristics, and suggesting strategies for managing their presence in the garden and field. Abundant illustrations enhance the text and facilitate plant identification. An annotated bibliography and index of botanical names, in addition to a detailed explanation of Integrated Pest Management, make this an essential reference for anyone with an interest in the world outside our doors. --From publisher description.

"While the book is primarily a reference guide for controlling weeds, the historical context and cultural references add a holistic dimension that will appeal to general readers with an interest in botany." Publishers Weekly.

Stewart, Amy
Wicked bugs : the louse that conquered Napoleon's army & other diabolical insects / Amy Stewart ; etchings and drawings by Briony Morrow-Cribbs. Algonquin Books of Chapel Hill, 2011. xiii, 271 p. ; **632**

1. Insect pests. 2. Entomology 3. Insects. 4. Arachnids
ISBN 9781565129603

LC 2011003629

Chronicles the insects, worms, and spiders that have tormented humankind for centuries.

633 Field and plantation crops

Cervantes, Jorge, 1953-
The **cannabis** encyclopedia : the definitive guide to cultivation & consumption of medical marijuana / Jorge Cervantes. Van Patten Publishing, 2015 594 p. : **633**

1. Cannabis -- Encyclopedias 2. Marijuana -- Encyclopedias 3. Cannabis 4. Cannabis -- Utilization 5. Encyclopedias
ISBN 9781878823397

LC bl2017007045

Includes index.

Examines aspects of cannabis cultivation, discussing the plant life cycle, detailing how to create the ideal growing environment, and offering diagnostic information on diseases and pests.

"Essential where patrons grow, or are interested in growing, their own cannabis." Library Journal.

Dewitt, Dave
Chile peppers : a global history / Dave Dewitt. University of New Mexico Press, 2020. 368 p. : **633**

1. Chile peppers 2. Cooking (Peppers) 3. Chile pepper industry and trade 4. Peppers. 5. Illustrated books
ISBN 9780826361806

LC 2020008831

In Chile Peppers: A Global History, Dave DeWitt, a world expert on chiles, travels from New Mexico across the Americas, Europe, Africa, and Asia chronicling the history, mystery, and mythology of chiles around the world and their abundant uses in seventy mouth-tingling recipes.

"A richly illustrated guided tour of chile peppers and their uses in cuisines around the world. . . . If you're a fan of the hot stuff, you'll definitely want this deep-diving work of natural and food history." Kirkus

Graf, Nicole
Grow your own : understanding, cultivating, and enjoying cannabis / Nicole Graf, Micah Sherman, David Stein, and Liz Crain. Tin House Books, 2017. 193 p. : **633**

1. Cannabis 2. Marijuana
ISBN 9781941040584

LC bl2017039229

Presents a guide for cannabis home-growers of all abilities, discussing such topics as how to set up a grow space and harvest buds, as well as providing recipes that feature the drug.

633.1 Cereals

Yafa, Stephen H., 1941-
Grain of truth : the real case for and against wheat and gluten / Stephen Yafa. Avery, 2015. 272 p. **633.1**

1. Gluten-free diet. 2. Wheat-free diet. 3. Wheat. 4. Gluten.
ISBN 9781594632495

LC 2015005944

The author of Cotton analyzes the current trend against wheat consumption, tracing its role in history and science to share facts about how wheat has been wrongly demonized and holds an important and nutritious role in dietary health.

"Well researched and accessible, this title is recommended for libraries where people look for Michael Pollan's titles (Cooked; Food Rules; The Omnivore's Dilemma). Worth considering for any collection with copies of William Davis's Wheat Belly or David Perlmutter's Grain Brain." Library Journal.

633.5 Fiber crops

Fine, Doug

Hemp bound : dispatches from the front lines of the next agricultural revolution / Doug Fine. Chelsea Green Publishing Company, 2014. 144 p. **633.5**

1. Hemp. 2. Hemp industry and trade. 3. Agriculture

ISBN 9781603585439

LC 2013048926

"A short, sweet, logical and funny argument for the potential of one of the world's most dynamic cash crops." Kirkus.

634 Orchards, fruits, forestry

Attlee, Helena

The **land** where lemons grow : the story of Italy and its citrus fruit / Helena Attlee. The Countryman Press, 2015. ix, 247 p. : **634**

1. Citrus fruits 2. Recipes 3. Italy

ISBN 9781581572902

Transporting readers back in time, a fascinating foray into Italian cultural history is told through the history of its citrus crops, from the early migration of citrus from the foothills of the Himalayas to Italy's shores to the persistent role of the unique crops in the perfume and cosmetics industries of today.

Begos, Kevin (Kevin Paul)

Tasting the past : the science of flavor and the search for the original wine grapes / Kevin Begos. Algonquin Books of Chapel Hill, 2018. 224 p. **634**

1. Grapes -- Varieties 2. Viticulture. 3. Wine and wine making -- History. 4. Travelers

ISBN 9781616205775

LC 2017046783

Blending together journalism, history, science and adventure travel, a journalist, after a chance encounter with an obscure vintage made near Jerusalem, embarks on a journey around the world to discover the multicultural roots of wine and encounters a colorful cast of characters along the way.

Bowling, Barbara L.

Homegrown berries : successfully grow your own strawberries, raspberries, blueberries, blackberries, and more Timber Press, 2014 208 p. : **634**

1. Berries. 2. Ornamental berries.

ISBN 9781604693171

LC 2014009483

"This work incorporates portions of The Berry Grower's Companion copyright 2000 by Barbara L. Bowling."

Includes index.

A primer on the basics of growing berries at home provides details on site selection, cultivation needs, pest control and more for an array of climates and varieties.

"From Berry Basics to the listings of recommended cultivars by region, suggested reading, and resources, this comprehensive guide will inspire and instruct everyone interested in homegrown berries." Booklist.

Deardorff, David C.

What's wrong with my fruit garden? : 100% organic solutions for berries, trees, nuts, vines, and tropicals / David Deardorff and Kathryn Wadsworth. Timber Press, 2013. 312 p. : **634**

1. Fruit-culture 2. Fruit -- Diseases and pests -- Control 3. Fruit trees -- Wounds and injuries -- Diagnosis 4. Organic gardening

ISBN 9781604694888

LC 2013009257

Counsels fruit gardeners on how to diagnose a range of plant problems, providing growth portraits and organic solutions for treating thirty-seven popular berry, nut, and fruit-producing plants.

Pilbeam, John,

Happy cactus : cacti, succulents, and more / consulting editor: John Pilbeam. DK Publishing, 2018. 144 p. : **634**

1. Cactus. 2. Succulent plants.

ISBN 9781465474537

LC bl2018080087

Includes index.

From potting to propagating, this one-of-a-kind, practical guide to cacti and succulents provides in-depth profiles of more than 50 popular varieties, including the pincushion cactus and the prickly pear, care tips and display inspiration, and much more.

Ralph, Ann (Horticulturist)

Grow a little fruit tree : simple pruning techniques for small-space, easy-harvest fruit trees / Ann Ralph. Storey Publishing, 2014. 168 p. : **634**

1. Fruit trees -- Pruning.

ISBN 1612120547

LC 2014025665

Includes index.

Outlines simple but effective techniques for growing apples, plums, cherries and peaches on smaller trees that take up less space and require minimal care in smaller home gardens.

634.8 Grapes

Cox, Jeff, 1940-

From vines to wines : the complete guide to growing grapes & making your own wine / Jeff Cox ; foreword by Tim Mondavi. Storey Publishing, 2015 x, 253 p. : **634.8**

1. Viticulture. 2. Wine and wine making. 3. Viticulture -- United States.

ISBN 9781612124384

LC 2014033708

Includes index.

Tells how to select, plant, cultivate, train, prune, protect, and harvest grapes, and explains each step in making wine.

"A must-have for anyone interested in making their own wine." Library Journal.

634.9 Forestry

Maclean, Norman, 1902-1990

Young men & fire / Norman Maclean. University of Chicago Press 1992. viii, 301 p., 16 p. of plates : **634.9**

1. United States. Forest Service Officials and employees. 2. Forest fires -- Mann Gulch, Montana -- Prevention and control. 3. Forest fire fighters. 4. Smokejumpers. 5. Rocky Mountains 6. Montana.
ISBN 9780226500614

LC 92011890

ALA Notable Book, 1993.

National Book Critics Circle Award for Non-Fiction, 1992.

A witness to the Montana Mann Gulch fire of 1949 explores the mysteries of the tragedy, with eyewitness accounts, new evidence, and research from fire scientists.

"On Aug. 5, 1949, 16 Forest Service smoke jumpers landed at a fire in remote Mann Gulch, Mont. Within an hour, 13 were dead or irrevocably burned, caught in a 'blowup'--a rare explosion of wind and flame. . . . [A]n engrossing account of human fallibility and natural violence." Publishers Weekly.

635 Garden crops (Horticulture)

Allaby, Michael

The **gardener's** guide to weather & climate / Michael Allaby. Timber Press, 2015. 333 p. : **635**

1. Crops and climate. 2. Gardening.
ISBN 9781604695540

LC 2014040762

Includes index.

"This book provides a clear and accessible explanation of how the weather works and how it affects the garden. It takes readers from the macro to the micro, from the effects of global warming on our planet to finding the micro-climates in their own backyards".-- Provided by publisher.

"Color illustrations enhance the value of this book for the reference shelf; its probably best read in winter by those seeking the really big picture for their gardens." Publishers Weekly.

Balick, Michael J., 1952-

Rodale's 21st-century herbal : a practical guide for healthy living using nature's most powerful plants / Michael J. Balick ; foreword by Andrew Weil ; edited by Vicki Mattern and featuring top healing herbs from Tieraona Low Dog. Rodale, 2014 xiii, 498 p. : **635**

1. Herb gardening 2. Herbals 3. Herbs -- Utilization 4. Herbs
ISBN 9781609618049

LC 2013022312

Includes index.

Exploring the evolution of the relationship between people and herbal plants over time, this must-have holistic resource introduces 180 of the most useful herbs from around the world that can be used to improve our health and well-being.

Bellamy, Andrea

Small-space vegetable gardens : growing great edibles in containers, raised beds, and small plots / Andrea Bellamy. Timber Press, 2014 213 p. : **635**

1. Farms, Small. 2. Vegetable gardening.
ISBN 1604695471

LC 2014009485

Offers advice, tips, and techniques on choosing a space to garden, how to care for the plants, and preparing the soil.

"Recommended for readers interested in gardening on a smaller scale or growing food where lack of physical space is challenging." Library Journal.

Bonine, Paul

Gardening in the Pacific Northwest : the complete homeowner's guide / Paul Bonine and Amy Campion. Timber Press, 2017. 319 p. : **635**

1. Gardening -- Northwest, Pacific 2. Landscape gardening -- Northwest, Pacific
ISBN 9781604693331

LC bl2018086886

A gardener's plant choices and garden style are inextricably linked to the place they call home. In order to grow a flourishing garden, every gardener must know the specifics of their region's climate, soil, and geography. Gardening in the Pacific Northwest, by regional gardening experts Paul Bonine and Amy Campion, is comprehensive, enthusiastic, and accessible to gardeners of all levels. It features information on site and plant selection, soil preparation and maintenance, and basic design principles. Plant profiles highlight the region's best perennials, shrubs, trees, and vines. Color photographs throughout show wonderful examples of Northwest garden style. --From publisher description.

"Useful for libraries in the massive region of the U.S. that extends from the Pacific Northwest coast all the way east to the Rockies." Booklist.

Bradley, Fern Marshall,

★**Rodale's** ultimate encyclopedia of organic gardening : the indispensable green resource for every gardener / edited by Fern Marshall Bradley, Barbara W. Ellis, and Ellen Phillips, with Deborah L. Martin. Rodale, 2017 xiii, 706 p. : **635**

1. Organic gardening -- Encyclopedias 2. Encyclopedias
ISBN 9781635650983

LC bl2018002434

Features over four hundred entries covering all aspects of organic gardening and includes step-by-step gardening techniques.

Bradley, Fern Marshall

Saving vegetable seeds : harvest, clean, store, and plant seeds from your garden / Fern Marshall Bradley. Storey Publishing, 2014. 91 p. : **635**

1. Vegetables -- Seeds -- Harvesting. 2. Vegetables -- Seeds.
ISBN 9781612123639

LC bl2014028389

Includes index.

"Five stages--plant maintenance for producing top-quality seeds, harvesting, cleaning and drying, packaging and storing, and testing for viability--are thoroughly explored for each crop, including lettuce, radishes, cucumbers, and more. Wonderfully user-friendly, this will be in demand." Booklist.

Buckingham, Alan

The **kitchen** garden : a month by month guide to growing your own fruits and vegetables / Alan Buckingham. DK, 2019. 352 p. : **635**

1. Fruit growing 2. Gardening. 3. Kitchen gardens. 4. Vegetable gardening.
ISBN 9781465479792

LC bl2018197787

Includes index.

Presents a gardening guide that provides month-to-month advice on increasing the amount and variety of produce that can be grown in a kitchen garden and reducing the money spent on buying fruits and vegetables in the supermarket.

Campbell, Stu

How to mulch : save water, feed the soil, and suppress weeds / Stu Campbell and Jennifer Kujawski. Storey Publishing, 2015 91 p. : **635**

1. Mulching.
ISBN 9781612124445

LC 2014029013

Includes index.

Presents a guide to mulching, discussing its advantages and disadvantages, its different types, and the best methods to use for vegetables, fruits, and flowers.

"Campbell's sound, experienced advice, supported by excellent illustrations, makes this handbook an indispensable one for both veteran and novice gardeners." Booklist.

Coleman, Eliot, 1938-

The **new** organic grower : a master's manual of tools and techniques for the home and market gardener / Eliot Coleman ; photographs by Barbara Damrosch. Chelsea Green Publishing, 2018. xi, 288 p. : **635**

1. Vegetable gardening 2. Organic gardening 3. Truck farming 4. Organic farming
ISBN 9781603588171

LC 2018015247

Shares information on soil, farm economics and labor, crop planning, equipment, green manures, tillage, organic fertilizers, pests, and livestock.

"This thirtieth-anniversary edition of a foundational book on small-scale organic growing has been revised and updated to reflect the changes that have happened in the intervening years." Booklist.

Cranshaw, Whitney

Garden insects of North America : the ultimate guide to backyard bugs / Whitney Cranshaw and David Shetlar. Princeton University Press, 2017. 704 p. **635**

1. Garden pests -- North America -- Identification.
ISBN 9780691167442

LC 2017013286

This second edition of Garden Insects of North America solidifies its place as the most comprehensive guide to the common insects, mites, and other "bugs" found in the backyards and gardens of the United States and Canada. Featuring 3,300 full-color photos and concise, detailed text, this fully revised book covers the hundreds of species of insects and mites associated with fruits and vegetables, shade trees and shrubs, flowers and ornamental plants, and turfgrass--from aphids and bumble bees to leafhoppers and mealybugs to woollybears and yellowjacket wasps--and much more. This new edition also provides a greatly expanded treatment of common pollinators and flower visitors, the natural enemies of garden pests, and the earthworms, insects, and other arthropods that help with decomposing plant matter in the garden. --From publisher description.

Damrosch, Barbara

The **garden** primer / Barbara Damrosch ; illustrations by Linda Heppes Funk, Ray Maher, and carol Bolt. Workman Pub., c2008. x, 820 p. : **635**

1. Gardening. 2. Organic gardening 3. Reference books
ISBN 9780761122753

LC 2007051425

"A Regina Ryan book."

Offers advice on buying and growing different kinds of plants with an emphasis on the use of native plant species and the techniques of organic gardening.

"This is a book for the new gardener that clearly explains the basics of garden planning, plant care, and equipment. Detailed chapters on the different categories of plantsannuals, perennials, vegetables, fruits, lawns, shrubs, roses, vines, trees, wildflowers, and even house plantsgive general advice on how to use and care for these varieties. A valuable book for public libraries." Library Journal.

Deardorff, David C.

What's wrong with my plant (and how do I fix it?) : a visual guide to easy diagnosis and organic remedies / David Deardorff and Kathryn Wadsworth. Timber Press, 2009. 451 p. : **635**

1. Plants, Ornamental -- Wounds and injuries -- Diagnosis 2. Plant diseases -- Diagnosis 3. Garden pests -- Control 4. Natural pesticides
ISBN 9780881929614

LC 2009019447

Provides visual treatments for diagnosing and curing sick plants, sharing illustrations of stressed or diseased examples, flow charts organized by the parts of a plant where symptoms appear, and comprehensive organic fixes.

What's wrong with my vegetable garden? : 100% organic solutions for all your vegetables, from artichokes to zucchini / David Deardorff and Kathryn Wadsworth. Timber Press, 2011. 249 p. : **635**

1. Organic gardening 2. Vegetable gardening 3. Vegetables -- Diseases and pests -- Control
ISBN 9781604692839

LC 2011018443

Provides information about the most common home-grown vegetables, describing techniques for growing healthy plants and for treating diseases and pests with effective organic solutions.

DK Publishing, Inc,

The **gardener's** year DK, Penguin Random House, 2015. 317 p. : **635**

1. Gardening. 2. Gardens.
ISBN 9781465424570

LC bl2015039504

Includes index.

Provides a year's worth of timely gardening tips and techniques as well as easy to follow, season-by-season projects suitable for any level gardener, all accompanied by gorgeous photos of each project's flowers, plants, fruits, vegetables and herbs.

Elliott, Shaye

Welcome to the farm : how-to wisdom from the Elliott homestead / Shaye Elliott. Lyons Press, 2017 313 p. **635**

1. Agriculture 2. Country life
ISBN 1493026011

LC 2016057686

Includes index.

Whether you want to dabble or immerse yourself completely in the back-to-basics lifestyle, Welcome to the Farm is a fully illustrated guide to growing the very best food right in your own backyard. Shaye Elliott shows you how to harvest baskets full of organic produce, milk a dairy cow (and make butter), plant a homestead orchard, can jams and jellies, and even raise chickens and bees. --From publisher description.

"This is a book for the armchair wannabe farmer and for those seriously considering homesteading." Publishers Weekly.

Etty, Thomas

Heirloom plants : a complete compendium of heritage vegetables, fruits, herbs & flowers / Thomas Etty & Lorraine Harrison. Ball Publishing, 2016. 224 p. : **635**

1. Gardening 2. Heirloom varieties (Plants)
ISBN 9781613735756

LC bl2016011344

Based on the extensive seed catalogs of Thomas Etty, the popular heirloom seedsman, Heirloom Plants includes information on almost 500 exciting cultivars to be grown and harvested, along with detailed profiles and cultivation tips for each plant. Responsible gardening, certainly, but with more than a hint of romance. In addition to edibles, the book also has chapters on antique herbs and flowers, from Cup and Saucer vines and Sweet William carnations to hollyhocks and Empress of India nasturtiums. Trowel and book in hand, let your motto be, "Growing the past, saving the future." Do not allow Forget-Me-Nots to be forgotten! --From publisher description.

"This encyclopedic delineation of "directories" of vegetable, fruit, herbs, and flowers offers practical help to the gardener who's interested in preserving heirloom cultivars and turning a green-thumb hobby into an all-out mission." Publishers Weekly.

Gardiner, Mary M.

Good garden bugs : everything you need to know about beneficial predatory insects / Mary M. Gardiner, Ph.D. Quarry Books, 2015. 176 p. : **635**

1. Beneficial insects. 2. Garden pests -- Biological control. 3. Predatory insects.
ISBN 1592539092

LC 2014049089

Provides information on using "good" insects as natural pesticide alternatives, including how to identify the beneficial bugs, how to enhance their garden habitat, and how to use them to grow garden plants.

Hildebrand, Caz

Herbarium / Caz Hildebrand. Thames & Hudson, 2016. 224 p. : **635**

1. Herbs 2. Recipes
ISBN 0500518939

LC bl2016034693

A modern approach to the traditional herbarium explores the histories, associations and uses of 100 herbs, providing ideas for how each herb can be used to improve both food and well-being and helping readers expand their knowledge, improve their culinary skills and enhance their appreciation of the incredible world of tastes offered by herbs.

"The point of the book is that the earth is filled with these horticultural gifts, which are plentiful, useful, beneficial, beautiful, and, most importantly, right there in front of you." Publishers Weekly.

Jabbour, Niki

Groundbreaking food gardens : 73 plans that will change the way you grow your garden / Niki Jabbour. Storey Pub., 2014 263 p. : **635**

1. Edible landscaping. 2. Food crops. 3. Fruit. 4. Vegetable gardening.
ISBN 161212061X

LC 2013030517

Featuring contributions from such gardening superstars as Amy Stewart, Jessi Bloom and Joe Lampl, this must-have gardening resource presents 73 plans for unique and inspiring food gardens along with photographs, plant lists, the story behind the design and more.

"Every plan is accompanied by full-color illustrations, growing tips, and tweakable lists of crop possibilities. The abundance of creative advice here will help perk up the gardens of both novice and professional growers." Booklist.

Niki Jabbour's veggie garden remix : 224 new plants to shake up your garden and add variety, flavor, and fun / Niki Jabbour. Storey Publishing, 2018 231 p. : **635**

1. Vegetables. 2. Vegetable gardening.
ISBN 9781612126708

LC 2017034219

Includes index.

Presents planting and growing advice for 224 varieties of unusual vegetable and herbs from around the world, including the Cape gooseberry, Middle Eastern molokhia, Asian celtuce, Japanese winter squash, and Thai basil.

"Loaded with lush photos throughout, this attractive book will appeal to gardeners and gourmands alike." Publishers Weekly.

Jason, Dan

The **power** of pulses : saving the world with peas, beans, chickpeas, favas, & lentils / Dan Jason, Hilary Malone, and Alison Malone Eathorne. Doublas & McIntyre, 2016 xiv, 192 p. : **635**

1. Legumes. 2. Cooking (Legumes). 3. Gardening. 4. Recipes 5. Cookbooks
ISBN 9781771621021

LC bl2016026118

"Includes 50 vegetarian recipes"--Cover.

"This is a perfect book for gardeners, vegetarians, and others looking to expand beyond their tried-and-true pulses." Booklist.

Joffe, Daron

Citizen farmers : the biodynamic way to grow healthy food, build thriving communities, and give back to the Earth / Daron "Farmer D" Joffe with Susan Puckett ; photography by Rinne Allen. Stewart, Tabori & Chang, 2014. 224 p. : **635**

1. Gardens -- Design. 2. Organic gardening. 3. Sustainable agriculture. 4. Sustainable living.
ISBN 1617691011

LC bl2014012023

Includes index.

Teaches readers how to create biodynamic gardens and encourages the development of a holistic approach to growing food, offering advice on such topics as composting, soil replenishment, pest control, and cooperative gardening practices.

Johnsen, Kate,

Grow all you can eat in 3 square feet / US editor, Kate Johnsen. DK Publishing, 2015. 255 p. : **635**

1. Small gardens. 2. Square foot gardening. 3. Container gardening.
ISBN 9781465429803

LC bl2015002954

Includes index.

Describes how to grow your own organic produce in small spaces, detailing how to make a raised bed or a hanging basket to maximize every square foot of valuable space and how to manage seed collecting, successional gardening and companion planting methods.

Karsten, Joel, 1969-

Straw bale gardens complete : breakthrough vegetable gardening method / Joel Karsten. Cool Springs Press, 2015. 176 p. : **635**

1. Compost. 2. Container gardening. 3. Raised bed gardening. 4. Vegetable gardening.

ISBN 1591869072

LC bl2015007891

"All-new information on urban & small spaces, organics, saving water"--Cover.

Includes index.

A follow-up to Straw Bale Gardens, which introduced a revolutionary new way to grow vegetables anywhere with no weeding, contains all-new advice and photos on such subjects as growing in a tight urban setting and making your straw bale garden completely organic.

LeHoullier, Craig

Epic tomatoes : how to select & grow the best varieties of all time / Craig LeHoullier. Storey Publishing, 2015. 255 p. : **635**

1. Tomatoes

ISBN 9781612124643

LC 2014029010

Offers advice on growing and harvesting tomatoes and takes a look at the author's thirty-three favorite varieties, including the Green Giant, Red Zebra, and Yellow Oxheart.

Leendertz, Lia

My tiny veg plot : grow your own in surprisingly small spaces / Lia Leendertz ; photography by Mark Diacono. Pavilion, 2017 159 p. : **635**

1. Vegetable gardening 2. Container gardening 3. Small gardens 4. Urban gardening

ISBN 9781910904015

LC OC2018158428

Food can be grown just about anywhere, and lack of space should not put you off growing and enjoying the taste of your own fresh vegetables. This book offers solutions and inspirations for these tricky spots that we frequently overlook or neglect, and highlights some unusual growing spaces such as a minuscule balcony in Bristol, an innovative installation of hexagonal polytunnels full of salad leaves in Amiens, France, and an ingenious self-sufficient growing system that provides a wealth of vegetables in an old swimming pool in Phoenix, Arizona. Filled with practical advice, inspiration and planting and design ideas, My Tiny Veg Plot tells you how to prepare your beds whatever the size and situation; there is advice on filling containers, creating ingenious planters, using planting mediums, soil and water and which fruit and vegetables will thrive in which spot. My Tiny Veg Plot contains straightforward information on what to grow and how to grow it, from seed to ready to eat. --From publisher description.

Lehmkuhl, Greg,

Terrain : ideas and inspiration for decorating the home and garden / edited by Greg Lehmkuhl and the gardeners of Terrain ; words by Caroline Lees ; principal photography by Isa Salazar. Artisan, 2018 367 p. : **635**

1. Gardening. 2. Interior decoration.

ISBN 9781579658076

LC 2018023578

Includes index.

Provides suggestions for container gardening, wreaths from natural materials, flower arrangements using wild items, and holiday decorations, and considers possibilities for each of the seasons as well as for Christmastime.

Loades, Greg

The **modern** cottage garden : a fresh approach to a classic style / Greg Loades ; with photography by Neil Hepworth. Timber Press, 2020. 227 p. : **635**

1. Cottage gardening. 2. Cottage gardens. 3. Gardening 4. Plants.

ISBN 9781604699081

LC bl2020052338

The editor of The Alpine Gardener presents a new style of planting, in this design-forward guide that teaches gardeners how to blend together big, colorful blooms and a striking mix of grasses and native plants into one space.

"Loades, editor of The Alpine Gardener, inspires with this delightful exploration of the process of creating a 'modern cottage garden'. . . . Gorgeous, full-page color photos of gardens designed using Loades's approach will propel readers to the nearest plant nursery." Publishers Weekly

Markham, Brett L.

Mini farming : self sufficiency on a 1/4 acre / Brett L. Markham. Skyhorse Pub., c2010. 227 p. : **635**

1. Agriculture 2. Farms, Small 3. Self-reliant living

ISBN 1602399840

LC 2009041561

Mini Farming describes a holistic approach to small-area farming that will show you how to produce 85 percent of an average family's food on just a quarter acre -- and earn $10,000 in cash annually while spending less than half the time that an ordinary job would require. Even if you have never been a farmer or a gardener, this book covers everything you need to know to get started: buying and saving seeds, starting seedlings, establishing raised beds, soil fertility practices, composting, pest and disease problems, crop rotation, farm planning, and much more. Because self-sufficiency is the objective, subjects such as raising backyard chickens and home canning are also covered. Materials, tools, and techniques are detailed with photographs, tables, diagrams, and illustrations. - Publisher.

"An excellent guide for gardeners wanting to eliminate most of their grocery bills. Markham's approach combines his own experience with the best practices from several raised-bed methods. Advice includes how to select vegetables that are calorie-dense and budget friendly, how to raise poultry, how to build both a plucker and a thresher, and how to preserve food." Library Journal.

McCrate, Colin

High-yield vegetable gardening : grow more of what you want in the space you have / Colin McCrate and Brad Halm. Storey Publishing, 2015 319 p. : **635**

1. Vegetable gardening.

ISBN 9781612123967

LC bl2015057624

Offers tips and techniques for making a home garden of any size much more productive, offering planning guidelines and advice on all aspects of planting and growing in order to bring a garden to its fullest potential.

"With worksheets, charts, and tables galore, the volume also includes an extensive collection of links for people who prefer to do their record keeping, an essential tool of the high-yield garden arsenal, on a computer. Appendixes and a list of suppliers round out this rich, thoughtful resource." Library Journal.

Pleasant, Barbara

Homegrown pantry : a gardener's guide to selecting the best varieties & planting the perfect amounts for what you want to eat year-round / Barbara Pleasant. Storey Publishing, 2017 319 p. : **635**

1. Food crops 2. Food -- Preservation 3. Vegetables 4. Herbs
ISBN 9781612125787

LC 2016055527

Includes index.

Presents guidance on how to stock a pantry for year-round use, discussing fifty-five crops and how best to harvest and preserve them, including canning, pickling, and fermenting, and at what amounts.

Starter vegetable gardens : 24 no-fail plans for small organic gardens : 24 No-Fail Plans for Small Organic Gardens / Barbara Pleasant ; photography by John Gruen. Storey Pub., c2010. 179 p. : **635**

1. Vegetable gardening.
ISBN 1603425292

LC 2009049114

Includes index.

Presents a guide to cultivating an efficient and beautiful vegetable garden, from growing seedlings to preventing diseases, and provides twenty-four different plans for optimum crop yield.

"From simple bag gardens to bountiful food cornucopias, each garden plan is...laid out with precise lists of materials and plants based on detailed landscape plans suitable for small city gardens as well as larger suburban backyards. Along with year-by-year overviews that allow gardeners to anticipate growth and adapt to changes, Pleasant provides essential cultivation and maintenance techniques." Booklist.

Russell, Stephen (Stephen D.), 1984-

The **essential** guide to cultivating mushrooms : simple and advanced techniques for growing shiitake, oyster, lion's mane, and maitake mushrooms at home / Stephen Russell. Storey Publishing, 2014 232 p. : **635**

1. Edible mushrooms. 2. Mushrooms. 3. Mushroom growing. 4. Gardening
ISBN 9781612121468

LC 2014015198

Offers guidance and instructions for creating ideal environments for growing oyster, shiitake, lion's mane, and maitake mushrooms.

"Thorough and clearly written with helpful photos on nearly every page, this guide is a must for anyone who wants to move beyond premade growing kits. With Russell's emphasis on building basic skills, advice for avoiding common mistakes, and sections on troubleshooting, the book will be a valuable resource for those interested in growing a variety of gourmet mushrooms." Library Journal.

Schwartz, Bobbie

Garden renovation : transform your yard into the garden of your dreams / Bobbie Schwartz. Timber Press, 2017. 259 p. : **635**

1. Gardens -- Design. 2. Landscape gardening 3. Gardening.
ISBN 9781604696127

LC 2016055618

A guide to garden makeovers provides information on tackling problem areas, deciding where to start, and how to choose the right plants and design plans.

Slatalla, Michelle

Gardenista : the definitive guide to stylish outdoor spaces / Michelle Slatalla, with the editors of Gardenista ; edited by Julie Carlson ; photographs by Matthew Williams. Artisan, 2016 ix, 397 p. : **635**

1. Gardens -- Design. 2. Outdoor living spaces.
ISBN 9781579656522

LC 2016012874

Includes index.

"The end result is a display of outdoor living space that integrates plants, color, balance, design, and also functionality." Publishers Weekly.

Smith, Edward C. (Edward Clarke), 1941-

★The **vegetable** gardener's bible : discover Ed's high-yield W-O-R-D system for all North American gardening regions / Edward C. Smith. Storey Pub., c2009. 351 p. : **635**

1. Organic gardening. 2. Vegetable gardening.
ISBN 160342475X

LC 2009023862

First ed. published in 2000.

A fully updated 10th-anniversary edition covers more vegetables, fruits and herbs than the first edition and includes full-color photos, extended-season growing advice, sections on organic gardening and solutions for small-space gardening.

Stross, Amy

The **suburban** micro-farm : modern solutions for busy people / Amy Stross. Twisted Creek Press, 2018. 347 p. : **635**

1. Edible landscaping 2. Farms, Small 3. Organic gardening 4. Permaculture
ISBN 9780997520835

LC bl2018045302

Outlines the ways to run a suburban homesteading garden, covering such topics as developing and nurturing healthy soil, using permaculture techniques, and making money with crops.

Swift, Vivian, 1956-

Gardens of awe and folly : a traveler's journal of the meaning of life and gardening / Vivian Swift. Bloomsbury, 2016. 166 p. : **635**

1. Swift, Vivian, 1956- Travel. 2. Gardens.
ISBN 1632860279

LC 2015019652

A round-the-world tour of 10 idiosyncratic gardens by the author of "Le Road Trip" combines her signature watercolors with reflections on such subjects as a green fescue on a Scottish rainy day, a Tahitian Dawn Bougainvillea garden that survived Hurricane Katrina and a Rambling Rose that has overtaken a FEMA trailer.

Waldin, Monty

Biodynamic gardening / Monty Waldin. DK, Penguin Random House, 2015. 253 p. : **635**

1. Organic gardening.
ISBN 1465429867

LC bl2015008324

Offers guidance for entirely organic gardening, making use of natural methods of avoiding pests and disease, while enhancing the flavor of produce, the appearance of the plants, and the garden's environmental impact.

"For people with an interest in environmentally aware gardening and a willingness to experiment with nontraditional methods." Library Journal.

Walliser, Jessica
Attracting beneficial bugs to your garden : a natural approach to pest control / Jessica Walliser. Timber Press, 2014. 240 p. : **628.9**

1. Beneficial insects. 2. Garden pests -- Biological control.
ISBN 1604693886

LC 2013015303

Profiles nineteen bugs which are helpful to gardeners, with descriptions, illustrations, and a list of their benefits, along with planting and zone details about thirty-nine plants which can be used to attract them.

"While the subject matter and close-up photographs of insects eating insects may make some readers squirm, dedicated gardeners will discover enough solid information and genuine motivation to finally put down their bug spray." Booklist.

Ziegler, Lisa Mason
Vegetables love flowers : companion planting for beauty and bounty / Lisa Mason Ziegler. Cool Springs Press, 2018. 176 p. : **635**

1. Companion planting. 2. Flowers. 3. Vegetables.
ISBN 0760357587

LC 2017043293

A guide to pairing vegetables and flowers to create a bountiful garden includes tips, timetables, and planting schedules for companion planting.

635.022 Gardening -- Photographs

Woods, Christopher, 1953-
Gardenlust : a botanical tour of the world's best new gardens / Christopher Woods. Timber Press, 2018. 414 p. : **635.022**

1. Gardens
ISBN 9781604697971

LC 2018019654

A renowned gardening authority explores the world's most beautiful gardens in an illustrated guide to over 50 locations in the Americas, Europe, Africa, Australia and Asia including the Geelong Botanic Gardens, Sunnylands Center and Garden's and the Golden Rock Inn.

" A recommended purchase for public libraries that have patrons interested in gardening as well as those who combine gardening and travel." Booklist.

Yglesias, Caren
Desert gardens of Steve Martino / Caren Yglesias ; photographs by Steve Gunther ; foreword by Obie G. Bowman. The Monacelli Press, 2018 235 p. : **635.022**

1. Desert gardening
ISBN 1580934919

LC 2017962354

"A beautifully made book that will appeal to gardeners and designers interested in the Southwest." Library Journal.

635.09 Gardening -- History

Culp, David L.
The **layered** garden : design lessons for year-round beauty from Brandywine Cottage / David L. Culp ; with Adam Levine ; photographs by Rob Cardillo. Timber Press, 2012. 312 p. : **635.09**

1. Gardening -- Pennsylvania 2. Gardens -- Pennsylvania -- Design.
ISBN 1604692367

LC 2012007640

A book based on the garden at Brandywine Cottage offers inspiration and expert tips on how to create a beautiful, layered garden in every season, describing how to combine heirloom daffodils and hellebores in spring that give way to Asian wildflowers in winter.

"In the tradition of classics like Beverly Nichols's Merry Hall, this is a marvelous account of how one gardener created his garden and a sense of place. It's an essential title in the 'how I did it' genre of garden writing." Library Journal.

McDowell, Marta
All the presidents' gardens : Madison's cabbages to Kennedy's roses : how the White House grounds have grown with America / Marta McDowell. Timber Press, Inc., 2016. 328 p. **635.09**

1. Gardens -- United States -- History. 2. Historic gardens. 3. Presidents' spouses -- United States -- History. 4. Presidents -- United States -- History. 5. White House Gardens, Washington, D.C. 6. Washington, D.C. -- History.
ISBN 9781604695892

LC 2015029811

"Photographs, line drawings, paintings, maps, and other documents add to the interesting stories. Short biographies of the 14 head gardeners, a lengthy chart of the plants in the gardens, and two bibliographies add to this delightful and elucidating work." Booklist.

635.9 Flowers and ornamental plants

Armitage, A. M. (Allan M.)
Armitage's garden perennials / Allan M. Armitage. Timber Press, 2011. 347 p. : **635.9**

1. Perennials
ISBN 1604690380

LC 2011293867

"More than 1250 plants"--Cover.

Includes indexes.

Profiles one hundred and thirty-six genera of perennials, providing desctiptions and color illustrations for each.

"This is an illustrated compilation of Booklist.

Armitage's vines and climbers: a gardener's guide to the best vertical plants / Allan M. Armitage. Timber Press, 2010. 212 p. : **635.9**

1. Climbing plants -- Canada 2. Climbing plants -- United States 3. Ornamental climbing plants -- Canada 4. Ornamental climbing plants -- United States
ISBN 1604690399

LC 2009032437

Includes indexes.

Presents descriptions of 115 ornamental climbing plants, with information on each plant's size, habit, hardiness, flowers, propagation methods, and cultural needs.

Bainbridge, David A
Gardening with less water : low-tech, low-cost techniques : use up to 90% less water in your garden / David A. Bainbridge. Storey Publishing, 2015 127 p. : **635.9**

1. Xeriscaping. 2. Gardening 3. Horticulture 4. Landscape gardening

-- Water conservation
ISBN 9781612125824

LC 2015036487

Includes index.

Presents inexpensive methods of irrigating plants with efficient water systems, discussing such techniques as clay pots, wicks, porous hoses, vertical pipes, and grow tubes.

"Beyond soaker hoses, the title offers a varied range of scalable options for growers of all types committed to the exploration and use of optimal water-sparing techniques." Library Journal.

Baldwin, Debra Lee

Succulents simplified : growing, designing, and crafting with 100 easy-care varieties / Debra Lee Baldwin. Timber Press, 2013. 272 p. : **635.9**

1. Drought-tolerant plants 2. Landscape gardening 3. Succulent plants 4. Succulent plants -- Varieties
ISBN 9781604693935

LC 2012038829

A complete primer on choosing, growing and designing with succulents. Along with gorgeous photos packed with design ideas, Debra offers her top 100 plant picks and explains how to grow and care for succulents no matter where you live. Step-by-step projects, including a cake-stand centerpiece, special-occasion bouquets, a vertical garden, and a succulent topiary sphere, will inspire you to express your individual style -- Publishers Description.

"This fresh and entertaining volume certainly deserves a green thumbs up." Library Journal.

Bender, Richard W.

Bountiful bonsai : create instant indoor container gardens with edible fruits, herbs and flowers / Richard W. Bender. Tuttle Pub., c2014. 128 p. : **635.9**

1. Bonsai 2. Indoor gardening
ISBN 9784805312704

LC 2013040431

Includes index.

An expert in the Japanese art of training plants to grow into beautiful sculptures provides instructions for making instant bonsai using common houseplants, herbs and fruit, to create artistic and beautifully-scented mini works of art.

Bender, Steve,

The **new** Southern living garden book : the ultimate guide to gardening / edited by Steve Bender. Oxmoor House, 2015 767 p. : **635.9**

1. Gardening -- Southern States. 2. Landscape plants -- Southern States. 3. Landscape gardening -- Southern States.
ISBN 9780848742980

LC bl2015001198

"2,000 full-color photos, 500 garden ideas, 8,000 flowers, vegetables, trees and more."

Includes indexes.

Presents a guide to selecting trees, berries, perennials, and vines for the Southern garden, and offers more than eight thousand plant listings with information on varieties, cultivation, and maintenance.

Benzakein, Erin

Floret Farm's Cut Flower Garden : grow, harvest & arrange stunning seasonal blooms / Erin Benzakein with Julie Chai ; photographs by Michaele M. Waite. Chronicle Books, 2017 308 p. : **635.9**

1. Cut flowers 2. Flower arrangement
ISBN 9781452145761

LC 2016011482

A guide to arranging fresh cut flowers year-round features advice for planting, cultivating, and harvesting over one hundred and seventy-five flower varieties, along with step-by-step instructions for floral decor for every season.

Branhagen, Alan

Native plants of the Midwest : a comprehensive guide to the best 500 species for the garden / Alan Branhagen. Timber Press, 2016. 440 p. : **635.9**

1. Endemic plants -- Middle West. 2. Native plants for cultivation -- Middle West.
ISBN 9781604695939

LC oc2018091642

"As more people are incorporating more natives in their landscapes for their own pleasure, pollinators, and birds, this book will be used by novice and experienced gardeners alike." Booklist.

Brickell, Christopher

American Horticultural Society encyclopedia of plants & flowers / editor-in-chief, Christopher Brickell. DK Pub., 2011. 744 p. : **635.9**

1. Plants, Ornamental -- Encyclopedias. 2. Plants, Ornamental -- Pictorial works.
ISBN 9780756668570

LC 2011290703

Includes indexes.

Revised and updated, this guide provides gardeners with information and photos of 8,000 different plants, from shrubs and trees to perennials, annuals, biennials and bulbs and cacti, cataloged and organized by color, growing season and size.

Pruning & training / Christopher Brickell, David Joyce. DK, 2011. 336 p. : **635.9**

1. Plants -- Training 2. Pruning
ISBN 0756671892

LC 2011290797

Includes index.

Rev. ed. of: Pruning & training / Lin Hawthorne. 1st American ed. 2003.

Offers the information gardeners need to maintain attractive, well-pruned, and trained trees, shrubs, climbers, roses, and fruit.

Brown, George E. (George Ernest), 1917-1980

Essential pruning techniques : trees, shrubs, and conifers / George E. Brown ; revised and enlarged by Tony Kirkham ; with photography from Andrea Jones and a new foreword by Hugh Johnson. Timber Press, 2017. 404 p. **635.9**

1. Trees -- Pruning. 2. Shrubs -- Pruning. 3. Conifers -- Pruning. 4. Pruning.
ISBN 9781604692884

LC 2016017684

"This work incorporates portions of The Pruning of Trees, Shrubs and Conifers, first published in 1972 by Faber and Faber Limited ... by the estate of George E. Brown."

Pruning is an indispensable part of garden maintenance, but it is also one of the most difficult. Successful pruning requires a thorough knowledge of a plant's growth and flowering habits. In Essential Pruning Techniques, Tony Kirkham, the head of the arboretum and gardens at the Royal Botanic Gardens, Kew shares his decades of knowledge and expertise and expands on the groundbreaking work done by George E. Brown. Step-by-step photographs clearly show the general principles of pruning, and profiles of 379 woody plants include advice on habit, attributes, reasons for pruning, and the best time to prune. Essential Pruning Techniques is a must-have reference for home gardeners and professionals. --From publisher description.

"All in all, an even more excellent text for shaping trees, shrubs, and conifers." Booklist.

Calvo, Janit

The **gardening** in miniature prop shop : handmade accessories for your tiny living world / Janit Calvo ; with photographs by Kate Baldwin. Timber Press, 2017. 248 p. **635.9**

1. Gardens, Miniature. 2. Garden ornaments and furniture. 3. Garden structures.

ISBN 9781604698091

LC 2017005197

A fun-filled guide to creating unique miniature gardens and accessories, which features 37 projects that are accompanied by fully illustrated, step-by-step instructions, is perfect for anyone enchanted by the whimsy of creating a tiny world. By the author of Gardening in Miniature.

"Fairy gardens and miniature gardens are extremely popular right now, and this book offers a guide to creating one (or many) of your own." Booklist.

Carey, Jenny Rose

Glorious shade : dazzling plants, design ideas, and proven techniques for your shady garden / Jenny Rose Carey. Timber Press, 2017. 323 p. : **635.9**

1. Gardening in the shade. 2. Shade-tolerant plants.

ISBN 1604696818

LC 2016036949

Explains how to maintain a shade garden and offers a calendar of seasonal tasks, a plant directory of choices, and techniques for garden design.

"As much as Glorious Shade strives to help the amateur gardener, the text is also a professional botanist's primer on how to talk about plants to a lay audience and have them listen." Choice.

Chapman, Baylor

Decorating with plants : what to choose, ways to style, and how to make them thrive / Baylor Chapman ; photographs by Aubrie Pick. Artisan, 2019 272 p. : **635.9**

1. House plants in interior decoration 2. House plants

ISBN 9781579657765

LC 2018030427

Includes index.

Focusing on houseplants, which are more popular than ever before, the founder of a San Francisco-based plant design studio presents this complete guide to "greening" any space along with ideas and inspiration for adding plants to every room in the home.

"Chapmans inviting tone mixed with the gorgeous photography makes for an ideal volume for the brown- and green-thumbed alike." Publishers Weekly.

Chezar, Ariella

Seasonal flower arranging : fill your home with blooms, branches, and foraged materials all year round / Ariella Chezar with Julie Michaels ; photography by Erin Kunkel. Ten Speed Press, 2019 xvi, 204 p. : **635.9**

1. Flower gardening -- Seasonal variations. 2. Flower arrangement.

ISBN 9780399580765

LC 2018023747

Includes index.

Provides step-by-step instructions for thirty-nine themed floral arrangements and projects that reflect the changing seasons and the wild beauty of nature.

"The combination of instructions, photographs, and elegant prose makes for a delightful companion for gardeners, florists, or armchair naturalists." Publishers Weekly.

Claffey, Bree

Indoor green : living with plants / Mr Kitly's Bree Claffey ; photography by Lauren Bamford. Thames & Hudson Australia, 2015. 206 p. : **635.9**

1. House plants in interior decoration. 2. House plants. 3. Indoor gardening. 4. Interior landscaping.

ISBN 0500500533

LC bl2017006774

Showing how plants can transform any home, a visual ode to indoor green provides readers with practical information for introducing living, growing, joyful things rooted in community and creativity to their living space.

"This enlivening exploration will inspire even the most timid of indoor plant lovers, providing a fresh look at an affordable type of gardening that both beautifies a home and expands the soul." Publishers Weekly.

Cullina, William

Native trees, shrubs, & vines : a guide to using, growing, and propagating North American woody plants / William Cullina. Houghton Mifflin, 2002. xi, 354 p. : **635.9**

1. Native plants for cultivation -- Canada. 2. Native plants for cultivation -- United States. 3. Ornamental woody plants -- Canada. 4. Ornamental woody plants -- United States.

ISBN 0618098585

LC 2002022586

"A Frances Tenenbaum book."

"New England Wildflower Society."

A comprehensive, illustrated reference covering nearly one thousand native woody plants discusses the benefits of using such trees, shrubs, and vines in ecological gardening to provide food and shelter to attract birds and butterflies and offers helpful instructions on how to select, cultivate, and propagate a variety of native species.

"Cullina's writing is a pleasure to read beautifully descriptive, informative, and personal. His useful, authoritative work is highly recommended for North American libraries." Library Journal.

Dash, Mike

Tulipomania : the story of the world's most coveted flower and the extraordinary passions it aroused / Mike Dash. Crown Publishers, 1999. x, 273 p. : **635.9**

1. Tulips -- History. 2. Tulip mania, 17th century. 3. Netherlands -- History -- 17th century. 4. Netherlands -- Economic conditions -- 17th century.

ISBN 0609604392

LC 99039186

Follows the plant from the steppes of Central Asia as it headed west into Europe, becoming even more prized by the time it reached the Netherlands.

"Stripped to its basics, this would be a dry case study in an economics textbook. But Dash adds depth to the tale by including relevant bits of botany, sociology and history, as well as glimpses of the personalities involved in the creation of the tulip market." Publishers Weekly.;

Deardorff, David C

What's wrong with my houseplant? : save your indoor plants with 100% organic solutions / David Deardoff and Kathryn Wadsworth. Timber Press, 2016. 292 p. : **635.9**

1. House plants 2. Organic gardening
ISBN 9781604696332

LC 2015013389

Provides advice on caring for over one hundred thirty different houseplants, including watering, sunlight exposure, potting space, and organic solutions to common plant problems.

Dirr, Michael

Dirr's trees and shrubs for warm climates : an illustrated encyclopedia / Michael A. Dirr. Timber Press, 2002. 446 p. : **635.9**

1. Landscape plants -- Sunbelt States 2. Ornamental shrubs -- Sunbelt States 3. Ornamental trees -- Sunbelt States
ISBN 088192525X

LC 2001035810

Includes indexes.

"This volume, in conjunction with Dirr's Hardy Trees and Shrubs, completes [the author's] coverage of the woody ornamentals cultivated in North America. In a witty and informative style, Dirr presents botanic, cultural, and landscaping details on over 400 species. Entries are accompanied by magnificent color photos." Library Journal.

Manual of woody landscape plants : their identification, ornamental characteristics, culture, propagation, and uses / Michael A. Dirr ; illustrations by Bonnie Dirr ... [et al.]. Stipes Pub., 2009. xxxix, 1325 p. : **635.9**

1. Landscape plants -- Handbooks, manuals, etc. 2. Landscape plants -- United States -- Handbooks, manuals, etc. 3. Ornamental woody plants -- Handbooks, manuals, etc. 4. Ornamental woody plants -- United States -- Handbooks, manuals, etc.
ISBN 1588748685

LC 2009905492

A reference guide to the identification and culture of over 1,600 species and over 7,800 cultivars of woody landscape plants. Includes bibliography, common name and scientific index.

The **reference** manual of woody plant propagation : from seed to tissue culture : a practical working guide to the propagation of over 1100 species, varieties, and cultivars / Michael A. Dirr and Charles W. Heuser, Jr. Varsity Press, c2006. ix, 410 p. : **635.9**

1. Woody plants -- Propagation -- Handbooks, manuals, etc.
ISBN 1604690046

LC 2009497202

Includes indexes.

Compiled by two distinguished professors of horticulture, The Reference Manual of Woody Plant Propagation is a must for professionals and students of horticulture. Over 1,100 species and their propagation requirements by seeds, cuttings, grafting and budding, and tissue culture are discussed in exhaustive detail. Essentially a recipe book for making more trees and shrubs, this reference is a high-level how-to. --From publisher description.

The **tree** book : superior selections for landscapes, streetscapes, and gardens / Michael A. Dirr and Keith S. Warren. Timber Press, 2019. 939 p. : **635.9**

1. Ornamental trees
ISBN 9781604697148

LC 2018038897

Includes index.

"An enormous undertaking passionately and expertly performed, and an invaluable resource." Booklist.

Druse, Kenneth

The **new** shade garden / Ken Druse. Stewart, Tabori & Chang, 2015. 255 p. : **635.9**

1. Gardening in the shade. 2. Natural gardens.
ISBN 1617691046

LC bl2015015164

Includes index.

Presents a comprehensive guide to creating a shade garden with emphasis on the adjustments necessary for a changing climate, offering advice on such subjects as sustainable watering, container gardening, and dealing with foraging animals.

"Even in cutlines, his delight in gardening percolates: for example, he notes attentively that prairie dropseed smells like popcorn. Druse sells shade masterfully." Publishers Weekly.

Duffield, Mary Rose

Plants for dry climates : how to select, grow, and enjoy / Mary Rose Duffield and Warren D. Jones. Perseus Pub., c2001. 216 p. : **635.9**

1. Arid regions plants 2. Arid regions plants -- Pictorial works 3. Desert gardening 4. Desert gardening -- Southwest, New
ISBN 9781555612511

LC 2001280011

The classic color reference for choosing and tending plants that thrive in hot climates, now revised and expanded-almost 450 plants in all, with 200 new to this edition. --From publisher description.

Ellis, Barbara W.

Covering ground : unexpected ideas for landscaping with colorful, low-maintenance ground covers / Barbara W. Ellis. Storey Pub., c2007. 224 p. : **635.9**

1. Ground cover plants. 2. Landscape gardening.
ISBN 1580176658

LC 2007000335

Includes index.

The author of Shady Retreats offers a fresh approach to using a variety of beautiful ground covers throughout the home landscape, explaining how to incorporate flowering plants, herbs, mosses, ground-hugging shrubs, heathers, and other species into a low-maintenance, creative yard and including how-to guidelines on site preparation, plant selection, weed control, and more. Simultaneous.

"Divided into three main sections, the book addresses why one should consider using ground covers, types of plants for different areas, and planting, growing, and propagating. Suitable for all gardening collections, this easy and fun read is essential for the home gardener looking for low-maintenance or problem-area ground covers." Library Journal.

Fourwords,

Miniature terrariums / Fourwords ; translated from Japanese by Leeyong Soo. Tuttle Publishing, 2018 96 p. : **635.9**

1. Gardens, Miniature. 2. Plant terrariums 3. Terrariums.
ISBN 9784805314777

LC bl2018085984

A guide to creating terrariums offers tips and techniques on using repurposed glass, as well as choosing and arranging soils, stone, and plants.

Gardiner, James M. (James Milton), 1946-

The **Timber** Press encyclopedia of flowering shrubs : More Than 1700 Outstanding Garden Plants / Jim Gardiner. Timber Press, 2011. 436 p. : **635.9**

1. Flowering shrubs -- Encyclopedias 2. Flowering shrubs -- Pictorial works 3. Encyclopedias

ISBN 9780881928235

LC 2011020264

Gardiner has distilled the knowledge of several decades to come up with an incomparable pictorial reference of hardy flowering shrubs that excel in temperate-zone gardens.

Greenlee, John

The **American** meadow garden : creating a natural alternative to the traditional lawn / John Greenlee ; photography by Saxon Holt. Timber Press, 2009. 278 p. : **635.9**

1. Meadow gardening -- United States 2. Grasses -- United States 3. Natural landscaping -- United States

ISBN 9780881928716

LC 2009019438

Offers guidance for designing, planting, and taking care of a meadow with information on plants, styles, and examples from all over the country.

Gutierrez, Annette Goliti

Potted : make your own stylish garden containers / Annette Goliti Gutierrez & Mary Gray. Timber Press, 2017. 227 p. : **635.9**

1. Plant containers

ISBN 9781604696974

LC 2016036945

Outdoor style often comes at a high price, but it doesn't have to! This lushly designed guide empowers you to create your own show-stopping containers made from everyday materials such as concrete, plastic, metal, terracotta, rope, driftwood, and fabric. The 23 step-by-step projects are affordable, and most importantly, gorgeous. They include new spins on old favorites, like the cinderblock garden and hanging planters made from enamelware bowls, along with never-before-seen ideas like a chimney flue planter and wall planters made from paint cans. Packed with color photographs and simple instruction, Potted will help you turn your outdoor space into a stylish oasis. --From publisher description.

"Gutierrez and Gray combine design prowess and essential plant knowledge for a winning how-to." Booklist.

Heibel, Tara

Rooted in design : Sprout Home's guide to creative indoor planting / Tara Heibel & Tassy de Give ; photos by Ramsay de Give & Maria Lawson. Ten Speed Press, 2015 217 p. : **635.9**

1. House plants. 2. Indoor gardening.

ISBN 1607746972

LC 2014036284

Includes index.

A guide to modern interior design using indoor gardening techniques such as succulents, air plants, terrariums, and moss walls.

"While the authors concentrate more on design than the practicalities of indoor gardening, they do address many common issues, such as watering and lighting. Buried in the last few pages is a plant directory that answers questions of what plants work best in low light and with varying levels of water and soil." Publishers Weekly.

Helm, Ben

The **water** gardener's bible : A Step-by-step Guide to Building, Planting, Stocking, and Maintaining a Backyard Water Garden / Ben Helm, Kelly Billing. Rodale, c2008. 192 p. : **635.9**

1. Water gardens.

ISBN 1594866589

LC 2007045129

An accessible reference to water gardening provides guidelines for creating and managing gardens of any size, counseling readers on such details as water-garden kits, selecting aquatic plants and fish, and electrical and child safety.

Hitchmough, James

Sowing beauty : designing flowering meadows from seed / James Hitchmough. Timber Press, 2017. 364 p. : **635.9**

1. Meadow gardening. 2. Meadows.

ISBN 160469632X

LC 2016036943

Filled with gorgeous photographs, a new approach to creating meadow gardens from an expert in the design, ecology and management of herbaceous vegetation shows readers how to design and sow seed mixes that include a range of plants, both native and exotic, and how to maintain the sown spaces over time.

"This is a hopeful and expansive book for the gardener who can see a field as a canvas." Publishers Weekly.

Iwai, Terutoshi

Miniature bonsai : the complete guide to super-mini bonsai / Terutoshi Iwai. Tuttle Publishing, 2017 80 p. : **635.9**

1. Bonsai.

ISBN 4805314389

LC bl2017031467

A guide to the Japanese practice of miniature bonsai provides step-by-step instructions and basic techniques for growing such tiny plants as flowering trees, pines, maples, oaks, and junipers.

"An excellent introduction to the practice and deserves a spot on a shelf with conventional bonsai-gardening books." Booklist.

Keville, Kathi

The **aromatherapy** garden : growing fragrant plants for happiness and well-being / Kathi Keville. Timber Press, 2016 276 p. : **635.9**

1. Aromatherapy 2. Aromatic plants -- Therapeutic use 3. Fragrant gardens

ISBN 9781604695496

LC 2015029697

Includes index.

Presents a guide to creating a garden of fragrant plants, with descriptions and therapeutic uses for each plant and advice for making herbal blends and vinegars, teas, scents, and body oils.

"With such rich descriptions, readers will long for the actual aroma." Publishers Weekly.

Kukielski, Peter

Roses without chemicals : 150 disease-free varieties that will change the way you grow roses / Peter E. Kukielski. Timber Press, 2015. 265 p. : **635.9**

1. Roses -- Disease and pest resistance -- North America. 2. Roses

-- Varieties -- North America.
ISBN 1604693541

LC 2014020741

Includes index.

A former curator at the New York Botanical Garden describes 150 different varieties of roses that can be grown without the use of pesticides, fungicides or fertilizers and provides information on planting, pruning and caring for these gorgeous blooms.

"This valuable guide for gardeners wanting to try roses that are less disease-prone is recommended for public libraries and horticultural collections." Library Journal.

Luu, Amanda

Ikebana unbound : A Modern Approach to the Ancient Japanese Art of Flower Arranging / Amanda Luu and Ivanka Matsuba of Studio Mondine ; photographs by M. K. Sadler. Artisan, 2020. 176 p. **635.9**

1. Flower arrangement, Japanese
ISBN 9781579659134

LC 2019050289

Includes index.

"Ikebana is a Japanese art form that began in the fifteenth century, but a new generation of florists around the world have begun embracing its natural, minimalist ethos and reimagining it for the modern age. Studio Mondine is at the forefront of this movement; with their restrained approach, a few foraged branches and a single flower stem can feel as dramatic and elevated as a whole bouquet of pricey blooms. The book is organized around four central tenets of ikebana: naturalness, movement, balance, and simplicity. Every chapter includes an essay explaining the key tenet followed by a series of representative seasonal arrangements. For each one, Luu and Matsuba discuss the design's connection to ikebana philosophy and then offer readers step-by-step instructions for re-creating the arrangement, with photos showing the mechanics of building the piece (foliage manipulation, working with floral frogs, etc.). In the Simplicity chapter, two bittersweet vines and single stem of amaryllis make for a dramatic fall statement. In Naturalness, a springtime "pondscape" takes shape, brought to life with a collection of muscari blooms, butterfly ranunculus, and leggy alliums. And in the chapter on Movement, palm bark is bent to resemble a strong current of wind, blowing through a valley of coreopsis. With hundreds of beautiful photographs and the authors' expert intel, Ikebana Unbound is at once a primer on contemporary ikebana design and an inspiration for readers to create their own exceptional arrangements".-- Provided by publisher.

"This graceful book will enable even the amateur arranger to appreciate and participate in a beautiful tradition." Publishers Weekly

Martin, Tovah

The **indestructible** houseplant : 200 beautiful plants that everyone can grow / Tovah Martin ; photographs by Kindra Clineff. Timber Press, 2015. 288 p. : **635.9**

1. House plants.
ISBN 1604695013

LC 2014042918

Includes index.

An expert gardener and best-selling author offers plant profiles with information on light, water care and blooming times for an array of hardy, pretty, resilient and easy-to-find indoor plants that even the most neglectful gardener can grow.

"The green-thumb-challenged will give Martin a standing ovation for this much-needed book created for windowsill-gardener wannabees desiring plants to survive tough love and transform lives. New England-based Martin appreciates interest in an indoor gardening approach requiring minimal time investment." Booklist.

Martin, Tovah

The **new** terrarium : creating beautiful displays for plants and nature / Tovah Martin ; photographs by Kindra Clineff. Clarkson Potter/Publishers, c2009. 176 p. : **635.9**

1. Glass gardens 2. Terrariums
ISBN 9780307407313

LC 2008027713

Includes index.

One of America's favorite gardeners introduces the whimsical yet practical world of gardens under glass--the perfect way to spark creativity while incorporating favorite plants in a home.

The **unexpected** houseplant : 220 extraordinary choices for every spot in your home / Tovah Martin ; photography by Kindra Clineff. Timber Press, 2012. 328 p. **635.9**

1. House plants. 2. Indoor gardening.
ISBN 1604694262

LC oc2012633870

The Unexpected Houseplant, by renowned plant authority Tovah Martin, offers a revolutionary approach to houseplants. Instead of the typical varieties, Martin suggests hundreds of creative choices--brilliant spring bulbs, lush perennials brought in from the garden, quirky succulents, and flowering vines and small trees. Along with loads of visual inspiration, you will learn how to make unusual selections, where to best position plants in the home, and valuable tips on watering, feeding, and pruning. --From publisher description.

"All indoor plant hobbyists in every geographic area will enjoy and learn from this book. Its fresh approach deserves a thumbs-up." Library Journal.

McGowan, Alice

Bulbs in the basement, geraniums on the windowsill : how to grow and overwinter 165 tender plants / Alice and Brian McGowan. Storey Pub., c2008. 208 p. : **635.9**

1. Perennials -- Massachusetts 2. Plants, Ornamental -- Massachusetts 3. Greenhouse gardening -- Massachusetts
ISBN 9781603420426

LC 2008022440

Explains that many plants grown in cool climates as annuals can thrive for many years through overwintering in containers.

McIndoe, Andrew, 1956-

The **creative** shrub garden : eye-catching combinations for year-round interest / Andy McIndoe. Timber Press, 2014. 247 p. : **635.9**

1. Ornamental shrubs. 2. Shrubs.
ISBN 1604694343

LC 2013040985

A professional garden designer describes the benefits of planting low-maintenance, hardy shrubs to beautify a home and garden and offers tips for choosing the best types based on climate, soil type and pruning requirements.

"A plant directory; alphabetical guide for planting and maintaining various shrubs, including container planting; suggested readings; and an index round out this comprehensive text sure to please gardeners who love perennials." Booklist.

O'Sullivan, Penelope

The **homeowner's** complete tree & shrub handbook : the essential guide to choosing, planting, and maintaining perfect landscape plants / Penelope O'Sullivan ; photography by Karen Bussolini. Storey Pub., c2007. 408 p. : **635.9**

1. Ornamental shrubs. 2. Ornamental trees.
ISBN 1580175708

LC 2007010718

A definitive resource on selecting woody plants for the home landscape covers every aspect of choosing trees and shrubs, with an encyclopedia of hundreds of trees and shrubs that features profiles of each plant's hardiness, cultivation requirements, history, size, growth rate, availability, and special characteristics, as well as complete maintenance and care guidelines.

"The real jewel of this volume is the extensive A-Z directory of nearly 350 trees and shrubs, many offering more than one season of interest. There is even a handy pronounciation guide for every plant name." Library Journal.

Penick, Pam

The **water-saving** garden : how to grow a gorgeous garden with a lot less water / Pam Penick. Ten Speed Press, 2016 233 p. : **635.9**

1. Xeriscaping. 2. Water conservation. 3. Drought-tolerant plants.
ISBN 9781607747932

LC 2015025964

A guide to growing gardens in drought-prone areas teaches home gardeners how to use minimal water to achieve maximum results, from using permeable paving and irrigation to limiting grass and timing the planting season.

"With the growing popularity of permaculture and sustainable cultivation techniques, Penicks how-to offers gardeners at all levels of experience much timely advice on working with one of the Earths most precious natural resources." Booklist.

Pleasant, Barbara

The **complete** houseplant survival manual : essential know-how for keeping (not killing) more than 160 indoor plants / Barbara Pleasant ; photography by Rosemary Kautzky. Storey Pub., c2005. xvii, 365 p. : **635.9**

1. House plants.
ISBN 1580175694

LC 2005014205

Includes index.

A definitive home gardening handbook provides comprehensive, hands-on advice on how to care for 160 common houseplants, with helpful information on how to identify different plants, how to select the right container and soil mixture, lighting needs, feeding and watering, propagation, and how to identify causes, symptoms, and remedies for common problems on a plant by plant basis.

"Following an enlightening introduction that discusses the history, uses, and benefits that houseplants bestow, the manual is divided into three main sections. The first two are plant directories offering in-depth plant profiles of first flowering, then foliage, houseplants. The third is an extensive compilation of houseplant-care topics, from acclimatization to watering. With vivid color photographs, precise illustrations, appendixes listing helpful resources, definitions, and a cross-reference chart of botanical and common names, this is a must-have manual for anyone who shares home or office space with potted plants." Booklist.

Seaton, Philip

★The **Kew** gardener's guide to growing orchids : the art and science to grow your own orchids / Philip Seaton. Frances Lincoln, 2020. 144 p. : **635.9**

1. Orchid culture. 2. Orchids.
ISBN 0711242801

LC bl2020002079

Includes index.

"Educating both the novice and expert orchid-fancier (without overwhelming the first or boring the latter), Seaton's infectiously enthusiastic handbook does a wonderful job of illuminating these captivating horticultural beauties." Publishers Weekly.

Sengo, Zenaida

Air plants : the curious world of Tillandsias / Zenaida Sengo ; foreword by Flora Grubb ; photos by Caitlin Atkinson. Timber Press, 2014. 224 p. : **635.9**

1. Epiphytes 2. Tillandsia
ISBN 9781604694895

LC 2014009480

A passionate horticulturist and designer describes how to grow air plants and use them in craft projects and decor, including as living bows on presents, additions to jewelry, mounted on walls and suspended from the ceiling.

"The coverage of air-plant display, design, and decor is dazzling as Sengo offers guidance in using these virtually weightless plants in ceiling suspensions and wall displays and even as wearable, living art. This comprehensive guide is an invaluable resource that delights the eye with the dizzying variety and beauty of air plants and the possibilities for inventive installments." Booklist.

Silver, Johanna

The **bold** dry garden : lessons from the Ruth Bancroft Garden / Johanna Silver ; photographs by Marion Brenner. Timber Press, 2016. 235 p. : **635.9**

1. Landscape gardening -- Water conservation. 2. Xeriscaping. 3. Ruth Bancroft Garden (Walnut Creek, Calif.). 4. Essays
ISBN 1604696702

LC 2016001680

"Replete with brilliant color photography, this hopeful book will win over anyone who doubts that a desolate landscape can support thriving life." Publishers Weekly.

Stearns, Jen

The **inspired** houseplant : transform your home with indoor plants from kokedama to terrariums and water gardens to edibles / Jen Stearns. Sasquatch Books, 2019 xi, 192 p. : **635.9**

1. House plants
ISBN 9781632171771

LC 2018014482

Includes index.

Presents the basic principles of potting, watering, and pruning house plants, a guide for favorite plants, and instructions for such plant projects as a hanging air globe, succulent bowl, and an underwater landscape.

Sterman, Nan

Hot color in the dry garden : inspiring designs and vibrant plants for the waterwise gardener / Nan Sterman. Timber Press, 2018. 319 p. : **635.9**

1. Drought-tolerant plants. 2. Xeriscaping.
ISBN 1604694572

LC 2017046300

Dry weather defines the southwest, and it's getting dryer. As water becomes more precious, our gardens suffer. If we want to keep gardening, we must revolutionize our plant choices and garden practices. Hot

Color, Dry Garden provides a joyful, color-filled way to exuberantly garden in low-water conditions. Garden expert Nan Sterman highlights inspiring examples of brilliant gardens filled with water-smart plants. You'll find information about designing for color using plants, architecture, and accessories, along with a plant directory that features drought-tolerant plants that dazzle. --From publisher description.

"Gardeners in water-challenged areas will find here expert guidance in plant selection for optimum color impact." Library Journal.

Stewart, Martha, 1941-
Martha's flowers : a practical guide to growing, gathering, and enjoying / Martha Stewart with Kevin Sharkey. Clarkson Potter Publishers, 2018 287 p. : **635.9**

1. Flower arrangement. 2. Flower gardening. 3. Flowers.
ISBN 9781984822345

LC bl2019002404

Includes index.

The well-known author and decorator discusses her love of flowers from a young age, describes the different flower gardens she has had, and provides gardening advice on planting, growing, troubleshooting, and arranging specific flowers.

Tallamy, Douglas W.
★**Nature's** best hope : a new approach to conservation that starts in your yard / Douglas W. Tallamy. Timber Press, 2019. 254 p. : **635.9**

1. Human ecology. 2. Native plants for cultivation. 3. Natural landscaping.
ISBN 1604699000

LC bl2020005246

The best-selling author of Bringing Nature Home outlines practical next-step approaches to conservation, instructing homeowners on how to turn yards into supportive wildlife habitats that do not require government regulation. Illustrations.

"Recent reports of massive declines in bird populations across North America make this book both timely and apposite. An essential addition to most gardening collections." Library Journal.

Tychonievich, Joseph
Rock gardening : reimagining a classic style / Joseph Tychonievich. Timber Press, 2016. 295 p. : **635.9**

1. Rock gardens 2. Rock plants
ISBN 9781604695878

LC OC2018139553

"This useful work targets a wide range of garden enthusiasts and/or horticulturalists. While comparable to the North American Rock Garden Society's Rock Garden Design and Construction, this stands on its own merits." Library Journal.

Weathington, Mark
Gardening in the South : the complete homeowner's guide / Mark Weathington. Timber Press, 2017. 319 p. : **635.9**

1. Gardening -- Southern States. 2. Plants, Ornamental -- Southern States.
ISBN 1604695919

LC 2016036944

"Plant picks - growing advice - style tips."

A gardener's plant choice and garden style are inextricably linked to the place they call home. In order to grow a flourishing garden, every gardener must know the specifics of their region's climate, soil, and geography. Gardening in the South is comprehensive, enthusiastic, and accessible to gardeners of all levels. It features information on site and plant selection, soil preparation and maintenance, and basic design principles. Plant profiles highlight the region's best perennials, annuals, trees, shrubs, and bulbs. Color photographs throughout show wonderful examples of southern garden style. Gardening in the South is for home gardeners in Virginia, Kentucky, North Carolina, South Carolina, Georgia, Alabama, Mississippi, Arkansas, and Louisiana. --From publisher description.

"Should find an eager audience." Booklist.

Whitman, John, 1944-
Fresh from the garden : an organic guide to growing vegetables, berries, and herbs in cold climates / John Whitman. University of Minnesota Press, 2017. 514 p. **635.9**

1. Organic gardening -- Snowbelt States 2. Organic gardening -- Canada 3. Vegetable gardening -- Snowbelt States 4. Vegetable gardening -- Canada
ISBN 9780816698394

LC 2016027971

Includes index.

Emphasizing organic gardening, Whitman, a professional gardener and author, offers a guide to growing vegetables, berries, and herbs in cold climates, in areas where temperatures can get to 20 degrees below zero during the winter. He explains where to plant, planting seed, starting vegetables from seed indoors, caring for plants, propagation, solving growing problems, harvesting and culinary uses, and tools, materials, and gardening aids, then offers a guide to about 150 plants and how they grow, where and how to plant them, how to care for them, problems, propagation, harvesting, storing, culinary uses, and varieties, along with nutrition facts. --From publisher description.

"An excellent handbook deserving a larger audience than it may receive." Booklist.

Wiley, Keith
Designing and planting a woodland garden : plants and combinations that thrive in the shade / Keith Wiley. Timber Press, 2014. 227 p. : **635.9**

1. Shade-tolerant plants. 2. Woodland garden plants. 3. Woodland gardening.
ISBN 1604693851

LC 2014011045

Provides a guide to creating a garden in the shade of the woods, detailing plants that thrive in dark conditions, design tips, and how to create shade in a home garden.

"The helpful garden designs and diagrams (such as how to plant a tree), along with hundreds of color photographs, facilitate choosing perennials, shrubs, trees, bulbs, tubers, and ferns. Gardeners, who are dreamers, writes Wiley, can dream that, once established, this magical garden will in fact grow itself." Publishers Weekly.

636 Animal husbandry

Brown, Sarah L.
The **cat** : a natural and cultural history / Sarah Brown. Princeton University Press, 2020. 224 p. : **636**

1. Cats 2. Cats as pets 3. Domestic animals 4. Humans and cats
ISBN 9780691183732

A comprehensive, richly illustrated exploration of the natural and cultural history of this much-loved pet. Filled with surprising facts, The Cat will enchant anyone with an interest in, or a love for, these animals.

"Chapters flow easily, with paragraph entries under headings and subheadings. Adding diverting interest, many blue-boxed pop-outs appear throughout the book on topics like cats' third eyelid and their ability to (almost) always land on their feet; and every page features a photo, graphic, or both, with informational captions." Booklist

Ehringer, Gavin

Leaving the wild : the unnatural history of dogs, cats, cows, and horses / Gavin Ehringer. Pegasus Books, 2017. xii, 356 p. ; **636**

1. Human/animal relationships. 2. Animals and civilization. 3. Domestic animals. 4. Animal breeding.
ISBN 9781681775562
Includes index.

Presents a thought-provoking and surprising exploration of the ever-evolving relationship between humans and domesticated animals.

"Solid, well-reported popular science for animal lovers." Kirkus.

Foer, Jonathan Safran, 1977-

★**We** are the weather : saving the planet begins at breakfast / Jonathan Safran Foer. Farrar, Straus and Giroux, 2019. 192 p. **636**

1. Climate change 2. Global warming 3. Livestock -- Climatic factors 4. Animal culture
ISBN 9780374280000
LC 2019020218

Green Prize for Sustainable Literature: Adult Nonfiction, 2020.

An urgent call to action on climate change by the author of Eating Animals shares insight into the climate denial mindset while identifying meat farms as a primary source of environmental pollutants.

"In his desire to convince others to take action, Foer raises the philosophical bar, which is, perhaps, the most effective way of fomenting sincere and long-lasting commitment to this life-threatening crisis." Booklist.

DK publishing, Inc

The **cat** encyclopedia DK, 2014. 320 p. : **636**

1. Cats -- Encyclopedias. 2. Cat breeds -- Encyclopedias.
ISBN 9781465419590
LC bl2014016861
Includes index.

Purr-fect for cat lovers of all ages, this visual resource profiles cat breeds from around the world, provides expert advice on kitten and cat care and celebrates cats in both art and culture.

Francis, Richard C., 1953-

Domesticated : evolution in a man-made world / Richard C. Francis. W. W. Norton & Co. Inc., 2015 400 p. **636**

1. Domestic animals -- History 2. Animals and civilization 3. Animals 4. Human/animal relationships
ISBN 9780393064605
LC 2014046934

Explains how certain ancient animals chose to live near humans, thus sealing their evolutionary fate.

"The cited literature is extensive and an excellent source for those wishing to pursue specific topics further. This treatise will be valuable to a wide readership, from animal lovers to a large array of professionals." Choice.

Grandin, Temple

★**Animals** make us human : creating the best life for animals / Temple Grandin & Catherine Johnson. Houghton Mifflin Harcourt, 2009. 352 p. **636**

1. Emotions in animals. 2. Animal welfare 3. Human/animal relationships -- Psychological aspects 4. Consciousness in animals
ISBN 9780151014897
LC 2008034892

Drawing on the latest research and her own work, Grandin identifies the core emotional needs of animals and explains how to fulfill them for dogs and cats, horses, farm animals, and zoo animals.

"Packed with fascinating insights, unexpected observations and a wealth of how-to tips, Grandin's peppy work ably challenges assumptions about what makes animals happy." Publishers Weekly.

★**Temple** Grandin's guide to working with farm animals : safe, humane, livestock handling practices for the small farm / Temple Grandin. Storey Publishing, 2017 181 p. : **636**

1. Domestic animals
ISBN 9781612127446
LC 2016055528

The animal behavior expert provides insight into the minds of livestock and presents practical advice on how to handle these animals humanely.

Kavin, Kim

The **dog** merchants : inside the big business of breeders, pet stores, and rescuers / Kim Kavin. Lyons Press, 2016. 336 p. **636**

1. Pet industry and trade 2. Dogs as pets 3. Dog breeding 4. Dogs
ISBN 9781681771403
LC 2015014827

Reveals the complex network behind the $11 billion-a-year business of selling dogs; discusses how all dogs are treated, from puppy mills to high-kill shelters; and shows how all dog lovers can come together, with one voice as consumers, on behalf of canines everywhere.

"A scathing indictment of an industry run amok; belongs on every pet lover's bookshelf." Kirkus.

Kerasote, Ted

Merle's door : lessons from a freethinking dog / Ted Kerasote. Harcourt, Inc., c2007. 398 p. ; **636**

1. Kerasote, Ted. 2. Humans and dogs. 3. Abandoned animals. 4. Human/animal relationships 5. Dogs. 6. Wyoming.
ISBN 0151012709
LC 2006038041

Describes how the author adopted a dog living on its own in the wild and his decision to install a dog door in his house so that the dog could live both inside and outside, in a study of the human-dog partnership and animal consciousness and behavior.

"A In telling Merle's story, Kerasote also explores the science behind canine behavior and evolution, weaving in research on the human-canine bond and musing on the way dogs see the world. Merle is a true character, yet Merle is also Everydog. An absolute treasure of a book." Booklist.

Lawler, Andrew

Why did the chicken cross the world? : the epic saga of the bird that powers civilization / Andrew Lawler. Atria Books, 2014. 320 p. **636**

1. Chickens -- History. 2. Civilization -- History. 3. Animals and civilization -- History. 4. Human/animal relationships -- History.
ISBN 9781476729893
LC 2014031979

In a combination of historical sleuthing and journalistic exploration on four continents, a renowned science writer takes readers on an adventure from prehistory to the modern era that follows the animal most crucial to the spread of civilization across the globe?the chicken.

"Recommended for readers of popular nonfiction as well as those with a specific interest in accessible scientific and anthropological studies." Library Journal.

Myron, Vicki

Dewey : the small-town library cat who touched the world / Vicki Myron, with Bret Witter. Grand Central Pub., 2008. 288 p. **636**

1. Dewey (Marmalade cat) 2. Cats -- Iowa 3. Libraries. 4. Mascots. 5. Pets. 6. Iowa -- Social life and customs.

ISBN 9780446407410

LC 2008004498

Traces the author's discovery of a half-frozen kitten in the drop-box of her small-community Iowa library and the feline's development into an affable library mascot whose intuitive nature prompted hundreds of abiding friendships.

"Myron's beguiling, poignant, and tender tale of survival, loyalty, and love is an unforgettable study in the mysterious and wondrous ways animals, and libraries, enrich humanity." Booklist.

Pierce, Jessica, 1965-

Run, Spot, run : the ethics of keeping pets / Jessica Pierce. The University of Chicago Press, 2016. 256 p. **636**

1. Pets -- Moral and ethical aspects. 2. Animal welfare -- Moral and ethical aspects. 3. Human/animal relationships -- Moral and ethical aspects.

ISBN 9780226209890

LC 2015038627

Through a mix of personal stories, philosophical reflections and scientifically informed analyses of animal behavior and natural history, a bioethicist takes readers on a mindful exploration of the ethics and experiences of pet ownership, and asks if we are doing the right thing, keeping these independent beings locked up, subject to our control.

"A thoughtful book that should spark debate, with the author stressing that bringing a companion animal into one's life is an ethical commitment that should not to be taken lightly." Kirkus.

Rousseau, Elise, 1977-

★**Horses** of the world / Elise Rousseau ; illustrated by Yann Le Bris ; translated by Teresa Lavender Fagan. Princeton University Press, 2017 536 p. : **636**

1. Horses -- Encyclopedias.

ISBN 9780691167206

LC 2016042566

Title of the original edition: Tous les chevaux du monde : pres de 570 races et types decrits et illustres (Paris : Delachaux et Niestle, 2014).

An encyclopedia of horses covers five hundred seventy breeds from around the world, including hybrids between domestic breeds and other such other equids as zebras.

Toutonghi, Pauls

Dog gone : a lost pet's extraordinary journey and the family who brought him home / Pauls Toutonghi. Alfred A. Knopf, 2016 240 p. **636**

1. Lost dogs 2. Dogs as pets. 3. Families 4. Addison's disease

ISBN 9781101947012

LC 2015034739

After its dog, Gonker, disappears along the Appalachian Trail, a family begins a frantic search, one that is spurred on by the fact that Gonker will die from Addison's disease if he is not found within 23 days.

"This book offers a poignant reminder of the important role dogs often fill as they help their human companions traverse difficult life passages." Library Journal.

Westoll, Andrew

The **chimps** of Fauna Sanctuary : a true story of resilience and recovery / Andrew Westoll. Houghton Mifflin Harcourt, 2011. 256 p. **636**

1. Grow, Gloria 2. Laboratory animals. 3. Chimpanzees -- Conservation. 4. Animal rescue. 5. Animal welfare.

ISBN 9780547327808

LC 2010049783

Charles Taylor Prize for Literary Non-Fiction (Canada), 2012.

Journalist Andrew Westoll recounts his time spent at the Fauna Sanctuary in rural Quebec as a volunteer caregiver for a family of chimpanzees rescued from a research lab.

636.088 Animals for specific purposes

Link, Tim, 1964-

Talking with dogs and cats : joining the conversation to improve behavior and bond with your animals / Tim Link ; foreword by Victoria Stilwell. New World Library, 2015 xv, 220 p. ; **636.088**

1. Human-animal communication 2. Pets -- Behavior 3. Pets -- Psychology

ISBN 9781608683222

LC 2015004274

"For readers who enjoyed Amelia Kinkade's Straight from the Horse's Mouth, Link's easygoing attitude and sincerity will be a welcome addition to those interested in alternative forms of animal communication." Library Journal.

Masson, J. Moussaieff (Jeffrey Moussaieff), 1941-

★**Lost** companions : reflections on the death of pets / Jeffrey Moussaieff Masson. St. Martin's Press, 2020. 272 p. **636.088**

1. Pets -- Death 2. Pet owners -- Psychology 3. Grief 4. Loss (Psychology)

ISBN 9781250202239

LC 2019058388

A heartfelt exploration of human grief after the loss of a pet by the New York Times bestselling author of Dogs Never Lie About Love.

"Highly recommended for all animal lovers who inevitably must deal with the death of their pets." Library Journal

Sheldrake, Rupert

Dogs that know when their owners are coming home : and other unexplained powers of animals / Rupert Sheldrake. Three Rivers Press, c2011. xiv, 385 p. : **636.088**

1. Pets -- Psychological aspects 2. Psychic animals 3. Human/animal relationships -- Psychological aspects

ISBN 9780307885968

LC 2011004065

A study of the psychic powers of animals provides anecdotal evidence of animals' telepathic communication, along with analyses of the unique relationships that exist between pet owners and their companions.

"The author reports the results of five years of extensive research as he followed up on anecdotal accounts from pet owners on the homing abilities of lost pets, animals that show premonitions of earthquakes or epileptic seizures, and the fact that animals anticipate the arrival home of their owners." Booklist.

Weitzman, Gary
National Geographic complete guide to pet health, behavior, and happiness : the veterinarian's approach to at-home animal care / Gary Weitzman, DVM, MPH, CAWA. National Geographic, 2019 399 p. : **636.088**

1. Pets -- Health. 2. Pets -- Behavior. 3. Pets -- Psychology.
ISBN 9781426219658

LC 2018027275

"Combining first aid, medical reference, and tips and tricks of the trade, here is your go-to-guide for at-home animal care, focusing on dogs, cats, rabbits, birds, and more! Building on more than two decades of veterinary experience, Dr. Gary Weitzman covers topics including upset stomachs, house training, physical ailments and behavior tips. The president and CEO of the San Diego Humane Society and former co-host of the weekly NPR show The Animal House, 'Dr. Gary' brings a wealth of experience to essential veterinary questions, revealing basic first-aid techniques, when a trip to the vet is necessary, dietary recommendations, simple training techniques, necessary supplies, essential behavior cues, and much more."-- Publisher's website.

636.089 Veterinary medicine

Goldstein, Martin, 1947-
The **nature** of animal healing : the path to your pet's health, happiness, and longevity / Martin Goldstein. Ballantine Books, 2000, c1999. 361 p. ; **636.089**

1. Pets -- Diseases -- Alternative treatment. 2. Pets -- Feeding and feeds. 3. Pets -- Health. 4. Holistic veterinary medicine.
ISBN 9780345439192

LC BL 00014880

Originally published: New York : Knopf, 1999.

A guide to pet health by a holistic veterinarian whose clinic is renowned for its pioneering alternative therapies sheds new light on the various causes of disease in animals and the most effective methods for treatment.

636.1 Horses

Forrest, Susanna
The **age** of the horse : an equine journey through human history / Susanna Forrest. Atlantic Monthly Press, 2017. 432 p. **636.1**

1. Horses -- History. 2. Human/animal relationships 3. Horses -- Evolution.
ISBN 9780802126511

LC 2017003334

An evolutionary chronicle of the horse from its origins 56 million years ago to the present examines its prominent role in diverse societies throughout history, sharing anthropological details, personal anecdotes and archival materials to illustrate the parallel development of humans and horses.

"In clear, introspective prose that underscores the astonishing depth of her research, Forrest tracks human history through the eyes of our equine companions." Booklist.

Hill, Cherry, 1947-
How to think like a horse : the essential handbook for understanding why horses do what they do / Cherry Hill. Storey Pub., c2006. ix, 181 p. : **636.1**

1. Horsemanship. 2. Horses -- Behavior. 3. Human-animal communication.
ISBN 1580178359

LC 2005027792

In this fascinating best seller, Cherry Hill explores the way horses think and how it affects their behavior. Explaining why certain smells and sounds appeal to your horse's sensibility and what sets off his sudden movements, Hill stresses how recognizing the thought processes behind your horse's actions can help you communicate effectively and develop a trusting relationship based on mutual respect. --From publisher description.

Philipps, David
Wild horse country : the history, myth, and future of the mustang / David Philips. W. W. Norton & Company, 2017. 336 p. **636.1**

1. Mustangs 2. Horses 3. Wild horses 4. Humans and horses 5. The West (United States)
ISBN 9780393247138

LC 2017018261

A Pulitzer Prize--winning reporter's history of wild horses in America--and an eye-opening story of their treatment in our own time.

"A fine, readable work of advocacy journalism . that deserves to inform discussion about the mustang issue as it plays out in courts and in Congress." Kirkus.

Raulff, Ulrich, 1950-
Farewell to the horse : a cultural history / Ulrich Raulff. Liveright Publishing Corporation, a Division of W.W. Norton & Company, 2018, c2015. 480 p. **636.1**

1. Horses -- History 2. Humans and horses 3. Human/animal relationships 4. Animals and civilization
ISBN 9781631494321

LC 2017047848

Translated from the German by Ruth Ahmedzai Kemp.

First published in German by Verlag C. H. Beck oHG Munchen in 2015 under the title Das letzte Jahrhundert der Pferde.

A scholarly history of the relationship between horses and humans traces their essential roles in early civilization through the transformations of an increasingly mechanized modern world, exploring how horses have been sources of artistic, military and athletic inspiration. Illustrations.

"A top-notch addition to the library of any cultured equestrian; highly readable from start to finish." Kirkus.

Williams, Wendy, 1950-
The **horse** : the epic history of our noble companion / Wendy Williams. Scientific American/Farrar, Straus and Giroux, 2015. 320 p. **636.1**

1. Horses -- History. 2. Human/animal relationships 3. Animals 4. Horses -- Evolution.
ISBN 9780374224400

LC 2015003860

Journalist Wendy Williams chronicles the 56-million-year journey of horses, from protohorse to the Thoroughbred and cow ponies of the twenty-first century.

"Williams's book educates, entertains, and enthralls; its part scientific discovery, part social commentary, and part history lesson, while always focusing on the relationship between horses and humans. This accessible profile of equines through the ages pays homage to an animal that had a crucial role in the modernization of the world." Publishers Weekly.

636.2 Cattle and related animals

Lewis, Celia, 1948-

The **illustrated** guide to cows : how to choose them - how to keep them / Celia Lewis. Bloomsbury, 2014. 160 p. : **636.2**

1. Cattle 2. Cattle breeds. 3. Cattle.
ISBN 1408181355

LC bl2014040488

Includes index.

Profiles the various cattle breeds, guides readers in choosing the best breed for their land, and offers an overview of feeding, caring, and handling cattle.

"Lewis concludes with instructions on milking, dairy production, tanning, and more. This guide, with its abundance of friendly illustrations, is an informative and fun homage to an animal of great importance." Publishers Weekly.

Young, Rosamund

The **secret** life of cows / Rosamund Young. Penguin Group USA 2018, c2003. 208 p. **636.2**

1. Cows 2. Animal behavior 3. Animal intelligence 4. Cognition in animals 5. England 6. Worcestershire, England
ISBN 9780525557319

LC 2018025176

Previously published: London : Faber & Faber, 2017. Originally published by Good Life Press, 2003.

The author distills a lifetime of organic-farming wisdom, describing the surprising personalities of her cows and other animals.

636.4 Swine

Estabrook, Barry

Pig tales : an omnivore's quest for sustainable meat / Barry Estabrook. W W Norton & Co Inc 2015. 320 p. **636.4**

1. Pig farming 2. Sustainable agriculture 3. Organic farming 4. Factory farming.
ISBN 9780393240245

LC 2014048321

The author of Tomatoland offers an eye-opening investigation of the commercial pork industry and an inspiring alternative to the way pigs are raised and consumed in America.

"An enjoyable and erudite read, the book will appeal to a broad audience. It includes detailed notes; photos and illustrations would have been welcome." Choice.

636.5 Chickens and other kinds of domestic birds

Hyman, Frank

Hentopia : create a hassle-free habitat for happy chickens : 21 innovative projects / Frank Hyman. Storey Publishing, 2018 206 p. : **636.5**

1. Chickens -- Housing.
ISBN 9781612129945

LC 2018012736

Includes index.

A sequence of innovative building projects for backyard chicken owners assumes no previous carpentry experience and offers such practical options as a predator-proof pen, nest boxes, a self-filling waterer and automatic coop doors.

"This lively read is a handy resource for chicken keepers, like having a happy, helpful neighbor to call on any time you need advice about the flock." Library Journal.

Johnson, Samantha

How to build chicken coops : everything you need to know / Samantha Johnson and Daniel Johnson. Voyageur Press, 2015. 176 p. : **636.5**

1. Chickens -- Housing.
ISBN 9780760347331

LC 2014039439

"This book is ideal for high school students or adults who need an introduction on raising chickens and coop building." Library Journal.

Litt, Robert

The **new** rules of the roost : organic care & feeding for the family flock / Robert and Hannah Litt. Timber Press, 2018. 207 p. : **636.5**

1. Chickens 2. Organic farming 3. Poultry farms
ISBN 9781604698459

LC 2018001915

The owners of the Urban Farm Store and authors of the bestselling <I>A Chicken in Every Yard<I> present an essential guide to backyard chicken keeping that goes beyond the basics, covering such topics as organic health remedies and disease prevention and pest management.

McKenna, Maryn

Big chicken : the incredible story of how antibiotics created modern agriculture and changed the way the world eats / Maryn McKenna. National Geographic, [2017] 288 p. **636.5**

1. Antibiotics in animal feed 2. Drug resistance in microorganisms. 3. Chickens -- Microbiology. 4. Poultry -- Marketing.
ISBN 9781426217661

LC 2017011586

The acclaimed, award-winning health journalist behind Superbug exposes the shocking role of antibiotics in industrial farming and the profound impact these mass food-processing practices are having on our lives and our health.

"In this well-written expose, McKenna (Superbug) dissects the controversy of the routine use of antibiotics to fatten chicken, which has lead to the rise of drug-resistant bacteria... Throughout, McKenna offers spot-on commentary on the dangerous additives in chickens and concludes on a relatively hopeful note." Publishers Weekly.

636.7 Dogs

American Kennel Club

Meet the breeds / American Kennel Club. I-5 Press, 2016 238 p. : **636.7**

1. Dog breeds 2. Dogs
ISBN 9781621871170

LC 2017303181

"A Guide to 198 AKC Breeds"--Cover.

Revised edition of: The American Kennel Club's meet the breeds : dog breeds from A to Z / an official publication of the American Kennel Club. 4th edition. 2013.

Includes index.

Presents information on dog breeds, including size, color, life expectancy, grooming, activity level, and temperament.

American Kennel Club

★The **new** complete dog book / American Kennel Club. Fox Chapel Publishing, 2017 919 p. : **636.7**

1. Dog breeds 2. Dogs 3. Dogs -- Standards -- United States
ISBN 9781621871736

LC 2017020403

Includes index.

Describes the official breed standards for the American Kennel Club recognized dog breeds, offering a history and photographs of each breed, and covering such topics as advice on selecting a puppy and living with and caring for each breed.

Anderson, Teoti

The **ultimate** guide to dog training : puppy training to advance techniques plus 25 problem behaviors solved! / Teoti Anderson, CPDT-KA, KPA-CTP. I-5 Press, 2014 239 p. : **636.7**

1. Dogs -- Behavior. 2. Dogs -- Training.
ISBN 1621870901

LC 2014015365

"A dogster book."

A dog trainer and behavior expert presents an essential training manual for dog owners that is filled with practical advice, easy-to-follow instructions and her trademark success-oriented positive-training methods.

Bendersky, Jorge

From puppy cuts to best in show, DIY dog grooming : everything you need to know, step by step / Jorge Bendersky ; foreword by Cesar Millan. Quarry Books, 2014. 160 p. : **636.7**

1. Dogs -- Grooming.
ISBN 1592538886

LC 2013038975

Includes index.

A dog groomer offers the tricks of his trade, including instructions on bathing and brushing, practical solutions to problems such as fleas and ticks, and creative suggestions for grooming a picture-perfect dog.

Blackwell, Lewis, 1958-

The **life** & love of dogs / Lewis Blackwell. Abrams, in association with PQ Blackwell, 2014. 214 p. : **636.7**

1. Dogs 2. Dogs. 3. Human-animal relationships.
ISBN 1419713930

LC bl2014041866

Combines facts and full-page photographs in a book that discusses the history of dogs and their relationship to humans.

"Readers who have enjoyed Blackwell's other books will delight in this beautiful, contemplative analysis of dogs as a species and as human companions." Library Journal.

Bradshaw, John, 1950-

★**Dog** sense : how the new science of dog behavior can make you a better friend to your pet / John Bradshaw. Basic Books, 2011. 320 p. **636.7**

1. Dogs -- Behavior 2. Animal intelligence. 3. Human/animal relationships 4. Dogs -- Psychology.
ISBN 9780465019441

LC 2010054337

A renowned anthrozoologist shows how humans can live in harmony with their canine friends, explaining why positive reinforcement is a more effective way to control behavior and how to weigh a dog's unique personality against stereotypes about its breed.

"Pet owners and those interested in the animal mind will learn from this balanced, well-referenced guide to the science of canine behavior." Library Journal.

Burch, Mary R.

Citizen canine : ten essential skills every well-mannered dog should know / Mary R. Burch. Kennel Club Books, c2010. 256 p. : **636.7**

1. Dogs -- Training 2. Dogs -- Behavior -- Standards
ISBN 9781593786441

LC 2009028847

Includes index.

"An official training publication of the American Kennel Club"--Cover.

Inside Citizen Canine, you'll learn about: The ten test items of the CGC [Canine good citizen] test and how to teach your dog the skills needed to pass them; [accepting a friendly stranger; sitting politely for petting; appearance and grooming; walking on a loose leash; walking through a crowd; sit and down on command and staying in place; coming when called; reaction to another dog or distractions; supervised separation). The book reviews aspects of the AKC CGC Responsible Dog Owner's Pledge suggests training resources. The author describes opportunities that might follow the program for CGC graduates, including competition, therapy dog work, and American Kennel Club possibilities. An apendix lists CGC evaluators by State.

Charleson, Susannah

Where the lost dogs go : a story of love, search, and the power of reunion / Susannah Charleson. Houghton Mifflin Harcourt, 2019. 320 p. **636.7**

1. Charleson, Susannah 2. Lost dogs 3. Search dogs. 4. Search and rescue operations. 5. Humans and dogs.
ISBN 9781328995056

LC 2018046441

Draws on expert studies in animal behavior, lost-pet search tactics, and the psychology of loss in an analysis of the world of lost dogs and the power of reunion.

"Charleston [sic] suffuses her tale with insight and well-earned sentiment, skillfully weaving in anecdotes of searches for lost dogs with those of her blossoming relationship with a new addition to her household, rescued Maltese-poodle mix Ace...This inspiring and informative work will resonate with pet lovers everywhere." Publishers Weekly.

Coile, D. Caroline

Encyclopedia of dog breeds / D. Caroline Coile, Ph.D. ; illustrations by Michele Earle-Bridges. Barron's, 2015 vii, 392 p. : **636.7**

1. Dog breeds -- Encyclopedias. 2. Dog breeds -- Pictorial works.
ISBN 9780764167294

LC 2015935573

Includes index.

Profiles each AKC breed, covering breed history, physical traits, health, longevity, behavior, and exercise needs.

Coren, Stanley

Why we love the dogs we do : how to find the dog that matches your personality / Stanley Coren. Fireside, 2000, c1998. xii, 308 p. : **636.7**

1. Dog breeds. 2. Dog owners 3. Dogs -- Selection. 4. Dogs. 5. Psychology.
ISBN 068485502X

LC BL 00009338

Originally published: New York : Free Press, 1998.

Illuminates the relationships of people and their dogs throughout history, showing what types of dog--and owner--make for harmony or disharmony and helping readers choose a dog.

"Coren offers insight into dog-and-owner personality conflicts and shows prospective owners how to choose the dog that is right for them. His book shows why some breeds of dogs turn out to be disasters for certain people, provides personality tests for readers to determine their own distinctive personality types, and includes amusing 'famous pet' anecdotes. Humanitarian, witty, and full of common sense, this is a perfect primer for novice dog owners." Booklist.

Dibenedetto, David

The **good** dog : true stories of love, loss, and loyalty / [edited by] David DiBenedetto & the editors of Garden & Gun. HarperWave, 2014. 336 p. **636.7**

1. Dogs -- Anecdotes 2. Dog owners 3. Human/animal relationships -- Anecdotes.

ISBN 9780062242358

LC 2014015874

Good Dog offers memorable, beautifully written stories of dog ownership, companionship, friendship, and kinship. From the troublemakers who can't be fenced in to the lifelong companions who won't leave our sides, this poignant anthology showcases man's best friend through all of his most endearing - and sometimes maddening - attributes. By turns inspirational and humorous (just like the dogs we love), Good Dog is a must-have collection for dog lovers everywhere.

"Bird lovers may blanch at feather-in-the-mouth hunting tales, but this selection of vignettes is varied, entertaining and frequently heartwarming." Kirkus.

Eldredge, Debra

Dog owner's home veterinary handbook. / Debra M. Eldredge, Delbert G. Carlson, Liisa D. Carlson, James M. Giffin. Wiley, c2007. xxviii, 628 p. : **636.7**

1. Dogs -- Diseases -- Handbooks, manuals, etc.

ISBN 9780470067857

LC 2007016275

Includes index.

Rev. ed. of: Dog owner's home veterinary handbook / James M. Giffin and Liisa Carlson. 3rd ed. 2000.

Presents a comprehensive guide to dog diseases and medical conditions, organized into such categories as emergencies, infectious diseases, the eyes, pregnancy, pediatrics, and medications.

Franklin, Jon

★The **wolf** in the parlor : the eternal connection between humans and dogs / Jon Franklin. Henry Holt, 2009. 304 p. **636.7**

1. Dogs -- Behavior. 2. Human/animal relationships 3. Bonding (Human/animal) 4. Humans and dogs

ISBN 9780805090772

LC 2009002227

Building on evolutionary science, archaeology, behavioral science, and the firsthand experience of watching his own dog evolve from puppy to family member, Franklin posits that man and dog are more than just inseparable; they are part and parcel of the same creature.

"Among a plethora of books on breeding, disciplining, loving and lamenting the loss of man's best friend, this thoughtful discourse is a best of breed." Publishers Weekly.

Goldberg, Marc

Let dogs be dogs : understanding canine nature and mastering the art of living with your dog / the monks of New Skete and Marc Goldberg. Little, Brown and Company, 2017. xiii, 272 p. : **636.7**

1. Dogs -- Training 2. Dogs -- Philosophy 3. Human-animal relationships

ISBN 9780316387934

LC bl2017035779

Includes index.

Presents a foundational guide for dog owners on dog care and training that shows them how to lead, provide for, and be a friend to their canine companions.

Horowitz, Alexandra

★**Being** a dog : following the dog into a world of smell / Alexandra Horowitz. Scribner, 2016 368 p. **636.7**

1. Dogs -- Behavior 2. Smell. 3. Cognition in animals. 4. Animal behavior

ISBN 9781476795997

LC 2016006968

The author of the New York Times best-selling Inside of a Dog explains how dogs perceive the world through their acute sense of smell and how humans can reconnect with their own underused senses to further human-canine bonds and gain insights into dog cognition.

"Both dog lovers and pop science readers will want to stick their noses in this book, and they may find themselves using their noses, like Horowitz and dogs everywhere, to experience the world more vividly." Publishers Weekly.

Inside of a dog : what dogs see, smell, and know / Alexandra Horowitz. Scribner, c2009. x, 353 p. ; **636.7**

1. Dogs -- Psychology. 2. Animal behavior 3. Dog owners -- Anecdotes 4. Dogs -- Behavior

ISBN 9781416583400

A psychologist offers insight into the canine mind, drawing on current cognitive research to illuminate a dog's perceptual abilities and the experiences that shape dog behavior, with stories about the author and her canine friend.

Our dogs, ourselves : the story of a singular bond / Alexandra Horowitz. Scribner, 2019. 352 p. **636.7**

1. Dogs 2. Human/animal relationships 3. Humans and dogs 4. Dog owners

ISBN 9781501175008

LC 2019017043

We keep dogs and are kept by them. We love dogs and (we assume) we are loved by them. We buy them sweaters, toys, shoes; we are concerned with their social lives, their food, and their health. The story of humans and dogs is thousands of years old but is far from understood. In Our Dogs, Ourselves, Alexandra Horowitz explores all aspects of this unique and complex interspecies pairing.

Katz, Jon

★**Katz** on dogs : a commonsense guide to training and living with dogs / Jon Katz. Villard, c2005. xxviii, 240 p. : **636.7**

1. Dogs -- Training. 2. Dogs.

ISBN 1400064031

LC 2005046209

Provides a detailed plan for living with a canine, covering everything from selecting the right dog and the importance of effective training to how to live with multiple dogs and the art of housebreaking.

"Katz's commonsense approach and skill as a storyteller make this an appealing, informative book." Library Journal.

Kress, Rory

The **doggie** in the window : how one dog led me from the pet store to the factory farm to uncover the truth of where puppies really come from / Rory Kress. Sourcebooks, [2018] 346 p. **636.7**

1. Pets 2. Dog breeding 3. Pet shops 4. Pet industry and trade
ISBN 9781492651826

LC 2017046006

The Doggie in the Window is a story of hope and redemption. It upends the notion that purchased dogs are a safer bet than rescues, examines how internet puppy sales allow customers to get even farther from the truth of dog breeding, and offers fresh insights into one of the oldest bonds known to humanity. With Izzie's help, we learn the real story behind the dog in the window--and how she got there in the first place.

McConnell, Patricia B.

For the love of a dog : understanding emotion in you and your best friend / Patricia B. McConnell. Ballantine Books, c2006. xxxi, 332 p., 16 p. of plates : **636.7**

1. Dogs -- Behavior. 2. Dogs -- Psychology. 3. Dog owners -- Psychology. 4. Emotions in animals.
ISBN 0345477146

LC 2006045200

An animal behaviorist draws on case studies and the latest scientific research to discuss the truth about a dog's emotional life, its implications for the human-canine bond, and its impact on dog training.

"This is not a book on how to train dogs, but McConnell's examination of cases from her veterinary practice, backed up by her scientific study of animal behavior, will help readers better understand their closest companions." Booklist.

Monks of New Skete

The **art** of raising a puppy / the Monks of New Skete ; [photographs by the Monks of New Skete]. Little, Brown and Co., 2011, 1991. x, 341 p. : **636.7**

1. Puppies -- Training. 2. Puppies.
ISBN 0316083275

LC 2011002744

"Completely revised and updated."

"For more than thirty years the Monks of New Skete have been among America's most trusted authorities on dog training, canine behavior, and the animal/human bond. In their two now-classic bestsellers, How to be Your Dog's Best Friend and THE ART OF RAISING A PUPPY, the Monks draw on their experience as long-time breeders of German shepherds and as trainers of dogs of all breeds to provide--brilliantly distilled--the indispensable information and advice that every dog owner needs. This new edition of THE ART OF RAISING A PUPPY features new photographs throughout, along with updated chapters on play, crating, adopting dogs from shelters and rescue organizations, raising dogs in an urban environment, and the latest developments in canine health and canine behavioral theory".-- Provided by publisher.

Monks of New Skete

How to be your dog's best friend : the classic training manual for dog owners / the Monks of New Skete. Little, Brown, c2002. xvi, 336 p. : **636.7**

1. Dogs -- Training.
ISBN 9780316610001

LC BL2002011737

Thoroughly revised to incorporate the latest trends in training and reflections on the canine-human relationship, a new edition of the classic illustrated guide to dog training helps the dog owner understand his dog's nature, know when and how to discipline, and to select a dog breed that is appropriate to the owner's lifestyle.

Ogden, Paul W.

★**Chelsea,** the story of a signal dog / Paul Ogden. Little, Brown, c1992. viii, 169 p. : **636.7**

1. Ogden, Paul W. 2. Canine Companions for Independence (Firm) 3. Hearing ear dogs -- California -- Case studies 4. People who are deaf 5. Service dogs. 6. Chelsea (Dog)
ISBN 0316633755

LC 91020928

"In this third edition of this esteemed text, coauthors Ogden . and Smith...deliver a foundational approach to raising deaf and hard-of-hearing children, emphasizing that 'being deaf is not about hearing but about communication.'" Library Journal.

Pierson, Melissa Holbrook

The **secret** history of kindness : learning from how dogs learn / Melissa Holbrook Pierson. W. W. Norton & Company, Inc., 2015. 256 p. **636.7**

1. Dogs -- Training -- Philosophy. 2. Animal behavior 3. Humans and dogs 4. Dog trainers -- Psychology.
ISBN 9780393066197

LC 2014045932

An intimate, surprising look at man's best friend and what the leading philosophies of dog training teach us about ourselves.

"A well-researched and thorough examination of current methods of dog training based on psychology; useful to those who want a deeper, beyond-the-basics understanding of the techniques." Library Journal.

Rutherford, Clarice

How to raise a puppy you can live with / Clarice Rutherford, David H. Neil. Alpine Blue Ribbon Books, c2005. x, 153 p. : **636.7**

1. Puppies -- Training 2. Puppies -- Behavior 3. Puppies 4. Dogs -- Training
ISBN 9781577790761

LC 2005041038

This substantially revised and expanded edition benefits from an additional decade of observation of puppy behavior by its authors and includes effective, up-to-date methods for educating puppies to become good canine citizens. Covers planning for the new puppy, selecting a breeder, house training, where to sleep at night, bonding with your new puppy, socialization, discipline, simple commands and leash training. Learn the stages of development and what to expect as the puppy grows. Breeders, this is a good book to give to your buyers when you collect that deposit on the new puppy! Help them plan ahead and be prepared.

Schlimm, John, 1971-

Extraordinary dogs : stories from search and rescue dogs, comfort dogs, and other canine heroes / essays by John Schlimm ; photographs by Liz Stavrinides. St. Martin's Press, 2019. 256 p. **636.7**

1. Dogs 2. Search dogs 3. Rescue dogs 4. Working dogs
ISBN 9781250201409

LC 2019025386

Beautiful stories accompany portraits of over 50 heroic working dogs in their uniforms, alongside the police officers, firefighters, veterans, and other trained handlers who serve side-by-side with them, including search and rescue dogs, bomb-sniffing dogs and comfort dogs.

Stilwell, Victoria

Train your dog positively : understand your dog and solve common behavior problems including separation anxiety, excessive barking, aggression, housetraining, leash pulling, and more! / Victoria Stilwell. Ten Speed Press, 2013 viii 248 p. : **636.7**

1. Dogs -- Training. 2. Dogs -- Behavior.
ISBN 9781607744146

LC 2012045637

The positive reinforcement canine trainer and host of It's Me or the Dog counsels owners on how to strategically improve problem behaviors in dogs, offering insight into how canines think, feel and learn.

Sykes, Bryan

Once a wolf : the science behind our dogs' astonishing genetic evolution / Bryan Sykes. Liveright Publishing Corporation, 2019, c2018. 304 p. **636.7**

1. Dogs -- History 2. Evolution 3. Human/animal relationships 4. Wolves
ISBN 9781631493799

LC 2018055788

Originally published: The wolf within : the astonishing evolution of the wolf into man's best friend. London : William Collins, 2018.

How did wolves evolve into dogs? When did this happen, and what role did humans play? Oxford geneticist Bryan Sykes used the full array of modern technology to explore the canine genetic journey that likely began when a human child decided to adopt a wolf cub thousands of years ago. In the process, he discovered that only a handful of genes have created the huge range of shapes, sizes, and colors in modern dogs.

Wynne, Clive D. L.

Dog is love : why and how your dog loves you / Clive Wynne. Houghton Mifflin Harcourt, 2019. 272 p. **636.7**

1. Dogs. 2. Dogs -- Psychology. 3. Humans and dogs 4. Dogs -- Behavior
ISBN 9781328543967

LC 2019002729

A pioneering canine behaviorist draws on cutting-edge research to show that a single, simple trait?the capacity to love?is what makes dogs such perfect companions for humans, and to explain how we can better reciprocate their affection.

636.737 Herding dogs

Dohner, Janet Vorwald, 1951-

★**Farm** dogs : a comprehensive breed guide to 93 guardians, herders, terriers, and other canine working partners / Janet Vorwald Dohner. Storey Publishing, 2016 351 p. : **636.737**

1. Herding dogs 2. Livestock protection dogs 3. Terriers 4. Working dogs
ISBN 9781612126005

LC 2016014115

A guide to ninety-three breeds of livestock guardian dogs, herding dogs, terriers, and traditional multipurpose farm dogs highlights the tasks each dog is best suited for and describes its physical characteristics and temperament.

636.755 Terriers

Dickey, Bronwen

Pit bull : the battle over an American icon / Bronwen Dickey. Alfred A. Knopf, 2016 288 p. **636.755**

1. Dogs as pets 2. Dog owners. 3. Pit bull terriers
ISBN 9780307961761

LC 2015033292

Describes how the loyal and affectionate dog breed that once earned presidential recognition for their roles on the battlefields of Gettysburg and the Marne and appeared in films and TV, became demonized and stigmatized through urban dog-fighting rings.

"This exceptional, thoroughly researched, and expertly written work is a must for all libraries." Library Journal.

636.8 Cats

Bradshaw, John, 1950-

★**Cat** sense : how the new feline science can make you a better friend to your pet / John Bradshaw. Basic Books, 2013. 320 p. **636.8**

1. Cats -- Behavior. 2. Animal intelligence. 3. Human/animal relationships 4. Cats -- Psychology.
ISBN 9780465031016

LC 2013020749

The best-selling anthrozoologist author draws on the latest scientific and behavioral research to explain the origins, evolution and modern-day needs of domestic cats, revealing how an understanding of a cat's ancient instincts is an essential part of a healthy cat-human relationship.

"Bradshaw teases out a better understanding of what our cats want (and need) from their owners. . . . This fascinating book will be a bible for cat owners." Booklist.

Dennis-Bryan, Kim

The **complete** cat breed book / consultant editor, Kim Dennis-Bryan. DK, 2013. 256 p. ; **636.8**

1. Cat breeds.
ISBN 9781465408518

LC bl2013016208

Includes index.

Profiles one hundred cat breeds, including size, looks, and history, also features information on choosing and owning a cat.

DK Publishing, Inc,

Complete cat care. / Dorling Kindersley. DK Publishing, 2014. 96 p. : **636.8**

1. Cats. 2. Cats as pets. 3. Pet care.
ISBN 9781465416049

LC bl2014001601

"How to keep your cat healthy and happy"--Cover.

Includes index.

A visual and practical guide to cat care covers everything from selecting a kitten to providing for day-to-day needs for a feline companion at every stage of life, discussing such topics as behavior, nutrition, and disease.

Ewing, Susan M.

77 things to know before getting a cat : the essential guide to preparing your family and home for a feline companion / Susan M. Ewing. CompanionHouse Books, an imprint of Fox

Chapel Publishers International Ltd, 2018 223 p. : **636.8**

1. Cats 2. Cat adoption

ISBN 9781620082911

LC 2018032320

Includes index.

This book starts with the process of selecting a suitable cat for your home and lifestyle and goes on to discuss the present and future requirements of feeding, grooming, training, healthcare, and much more to fully educate prospective new cat owners. --From publisher description.

"Even if owning a pet might not fit existing lifestyles, Ewing provides a well-written narrative that educates as well as entertains -- and just might encourage adoption." Booklist.

Galaxy, Jackson

Catification : designing a happy and stylish home for your cat (and you!) / Jackson Galaxy, Kate Benjamin. Jeremy P. Tarcher, 2014. 291 p. : **636.8**

1. Cats -- Equipment and supplies. 2. Cats -- Housing. 3. Interior decoration.

ISBN 9780399166013

LC 2014019022

Includes index.

The host of Animal Planet's My Cat from Hell and the designer behind the cat design website hauspanther.com offer DIY projects to make one's home both stylish and functionally hospitable for felines.

"If you have cats, you need this book." Library Journal.

★**Total** cat mojo : the ultimate guide to life with your cat / Jackson Galaxy with Mikel Delgado and Bobby Rock. TarcherPerigee Book, 2017 xviii, 365 p. : **636.8**

1. Cats. 2. Cats -- Health.

ISBN 9780143131618

LC 2017026753

"A TarcherPerigee book."

The star of Animal Planet's My Cat from Hell describes how to keep your feline pets happy and healthy by harnessing their |cat mojo| which allows them to safely stay in touch with their natural instincts in your home.

Hart, Benjamin L.

Your ideal cat : insights into breed and gender differences in cat behavior / Benjamin L. Hart, DVM, PhD, and Lynette A. Hart, PhD. Purdue University Press, 2013 x, 147 p. : **636.8**

1. Cat breeds. 2. Cats -- Behavior.

ISBN 1557536481

LC 2012034713

For a happy relationship with your cat, go beyond the looks and make your pick based on demonstrated breed behavior. This is the advice of the Harts, two experts in animal communication and behavior, whose new book takes the process of selecting a cat to the next level by offering data-based behavioral profiles of a wide range of cat breeds. Developed over a lifetime of research and through extensive interviews with eighty veterinary experts, the profiles are presented in easy-to-use graphical form. A history of the development of different breeds is presented, and then breed-specific differences across a range of variables are discussed. These include twelve behavioral traits, in areas such as affection, sociality, activity level, and litter box use. After giving guidance about choosing a cat, the authors present some strategies for avoiding problem behaviors and resolving those that emerge. They also share fascinating theories about the origins of various common cat behaviors, including purring, yawning, eating grass, flipping out on catnip, and staking out territory. While the focus is on purebred cats, there is also lots of good information for owners of blends. The book ends with helpful guidance on further reading. Based on the latest science, this is a great book for anyone interested in the fundamental building blocks of feline behavior, and an invaluable handbook for cat owners. --From publisher description.

Johnson-Bennett, Pam, 1954-

CatWise : America's favorite cat expert answers your cat behavior questions / Pam Johnson-Bennett. Penguin Books, 2016 xxiii, 325 p. : **636.8**

1. Cats -- Behavior.

ISBN 9780143129561

LC 2016000873

Includes index.

Presents answers to a variety of questions about cats, covering such topics as feeding, communication, litter boxes, interactive play, scratching, and cat training.

"The book is an excellent choice for someone planning to adopt a kitten as well as for experienced cat owners with senior cats." Publishers Weekly.

Schotz, Susanne, 1958-

The **secret** language of cats : how to understand your cat for a better, happier relationship / Susanne Schotz ; translated by Peter Kuras. Hanover Square Press, 2018 265 p. : **636.8**

1. Cats -- Behavior. 2. Animal communication. 3. Human-animal communication. 4. Animal sounds.

ISBN 9781335013897

LC bl2018184204

A Swedish professor of phonetics and leading authority on cat communication provides a crash course in speaking cat, describing what feline vocalizations mean in different situations and provides practical advice to help better understand your pets.

Tucker, Abigail

The **lion** in the living room : how house cats tamed us and took over the world / Abigail Tucker. Simon & Schuster, 2016. 256 p. **636.8**

1. Cats as pets 2. Cats -- History. 3. Human-animal relationships. 4. Humans and cats.

ISBN 9781476738239

LC 2016000722

"Tucker's informative interviews with werewolf cat breeders, cat lobbyists, and Internet star Little Bub's owner round out a thoughtful look at the illogical human love of felines." Publishers Weekly.

637 Processing dairy and related products

Caldwell, Gianaclis, 1961-

Mastering artisan cheesemaking : the ultimate guide for home-scale and market producer / Gianaclis Caldwell ; foreword by Ricki Carroll. Chelsea Green Publishing, 2012 vi, 345 p. : **637**

1. Cheesemaking. 2. Recipes 3. Cookbooks

ISBN 9781603583329

LC 2012023148

"Every serious home-scale artisan cheesemaker--even those just beginning to experiment--will want this book as their bible to take them from their first quick mozzarella, to a French mimolette, and ultimately to designing their own unique cheeses. This comprehensive and user-friendly guide thoroughly explains the art and science that allow milk to be transformed into epicurean masterpieces. Caldwell offers a deep look at the history, science, culture, and art of making artisan cheese on a small scale, and includes detailed information on equipment and setting up a home-scale operation. A large part of the book includes extensive process-based recipes dictating not only the hard numbers, but also the concepts behind each style of cheese and everything youwant to know about affinage (aging), and using oils, brushes, waxes, infusions, and other creative aging and flavoring techniques. Mastering Artisan Cheesemaking will also prove an invaluable resource for those with, or thinking of starting, a small-scale creamery. Let Gianaclis Caldwell be your mentor, guide, and cheering section as you follow the pathway to a mastery of cheesemaking".-- Provided by publisher.

"Recipes are offered and explained in very easy terms. A complete package." Booklist.

Carroll, Ricki

Home cheese making : from fresh and soft to firm, blue, goat's milk, and more / Ricki Carroll ; additional recipe development by Jim Wallace. Storey Publishing, 2018. xv, 366 p. : **637**

1. Cheesemaking. 2. Cooking (Cheese). 3. Cookbooks.
ISBN 9781612128672

LC 2018030470

Includes index.

Revised and updated, the fourth edition of a guide to making artisanal cheese at home includes 35 new recipes including burrata, stracchino, Brillat-Savarin, Cambrales and Drunk Gouda, as well as recipes for cheese plate condiments and classic cheese recipes.

"The introductory chapters outline the ingredients, equipment, and techniques used in a way designed to help the reader build a foundational understanding of the chemistry that creates cheese " Booklist.

Donnelly, Catherine W,

The **Oxford** companion to cheese / edited by Catherine Donnelly. Oxford University Press, 2016 xx, 849 p. : **637**

1. Cheese -- Encyclopedias.
ISBN 9780199330881

LC 2016034026

A reference on cheese for experts and novices alike includes over eight hundred entries on cheese history, culture, science, and production from around the world.

English, Ashley, 1976-

Home dairy with Ashley English : all you need to know to make cheese, yogurt, butter & more / Ashley English. Lark Crafts, c2011. 135 p. : **637**

1. Cooking (Dairy products) 2. Dairy processing.
ISBN 9781600596278

LC 2010020669

"Includes 40 dairy recipes + plans for DIY cheese press"--Cover.

Instructs readers on how to make their own butter, cheese, cultured dairy products, and ice cream from scratch, while also providing such recipes as macaroni and cheese and chilled cucumber yogurt soup.

"English is no slouch at demystifying the intricacies of home dairy; from the simplicities of churning out your own delectable butter to pressing your very first gouda, the author covers it all in clean, unpretentious, step-by-step instruction. Excellent for those looking to take a slight step off the grid." Kirkus.

Kurlansky, Mark

★**Milk!** : a 10,000-year food fracas / Mark Kurlansky. Bloomsbury, 2018. 352 p. **637**

1. Dairy products -- History. 2. Milk -- History. 3. Dairying 4. Beverages
ISBN 9781632863829

LC 2017039795

Profoundly intertwined with human civilization, milk has a compelling and a surprisingly global story to tell. Tracing the liquid's diverse history from antiquity to the present, Mark Kurlansky details its curious and crucial role in cultural evolution, religion, nutrition, politics, and economics.

"A fascinating and comprehensive book that will keep readers engaged and entertained. The recipes, especially those on the historical side, are a unique and complimentary addition. Will appeal to both foodies and readers of world history. Highly recommended." Library Journal.

Lucero, Claudia

One-hour cheese : ricotta, mozzarella, chevre, paneer--even burrata, fresh and simple cheeses you can make in an hour or less! / Claudia Lucero, founder of Urban Cheesecraft and Creator of DIY Cheese Kits. Workman Publishing, 2014 xi, 260 p. : **637**

1. Cheesemaking. 2. Quick and easy cooking 3. Recipes 4. Cookbooks
ISBN 9780761177487

LC 2014001166

Presents step-by-step instructions for crafting sixteen different cheeses at home in an hour or less, and provides recipes in which to include these cheeses.

"A fantastic introduction for novices who want simple, delicious, DIY cheese." Library Journal.

638 Insect culture

Black, Scott Hoffman

Gardening for butterflies : how you can attract and protect beautiful, beneficial insects / The Xerces Society (Scott Hoffman Black, Brianna Borders, Candace Fallon, Eric Lee-Mader, Matthew Shepherd) ; foreword by Robert Michael Pyle. Timber Press, 2016. 287 p. : **638**

1. Butterflies. 2. Butterfly gardening.
ISBN 1604695986

LC 2015029810

Discusses the life cycle of butterflies and the current threats to their existence and describes how to design and maintain a butterfly garden and select appropriate plants.

"This book will help even those without green thumbs support the much-needed effort to assist and protect pollinators." Booklist.

Flottum, Kim

★The **backyard** beekeeper : an absolute beginner's guide to keeping bees in your yard and garden / Kim Flottum. Quarry Books, 2018. 240 p. : **638**

1. Bee culture 2. Honeybee
ISBN 9781631593321

LC 2019302955

Includes index.

Features information about bees, beeswax, and the modern rules of beekeeping with do-it-yourself tips for safe and fun beekeeping.

Jones, Richard, 1958 July 14-

★The **beekeeper's** bible : bees, honey, recipes & other home uses / Richard A. Jones and Sharon Sweeney-Lynch. Stewart,

Tabori & Chang, 2011. 413 p. : **638**

1. Bee culture 2. Bee products 3. Cooking (Honey)
ISBN 9781584799184

LC 2010041458

Includes index.

Originally published: London : HarperCollins, 2010.

Provides a history of beekeeping, discussing bee culture, managing hives, and harvesting, with recipes featuring honey and instructions for craft projects using beeswax.

Nordhaus, Hannah

The **beekeeper's** lament : how one man and half a billion honey bees help feed America / Hannah Nordhaus. Harpercollins 2011 256 p. **638**

1. Bees. 2. Beekeeping. 3. Pollination. 4. Bee products.
ISBN 9780061873256

LC 2011283445

An awarding-winning journalist tells the extraordinary story of John Miller, one of America's foremost migratory beekeepers, who, despite mysterious epidemics that threaten American honey populations--and the nation's agribusiness--forges on and moves ahead in a new natural world.

Sammataro, Diana

The **beekeeper's** handbook / Diana Sammataro and Alphonse Avitabile ; foreword by Dewey M. Caron. Comstock Pub. Associates, 2011. x, 308 p. : **638**

1. Bee culture
ISBN 0801476941

LC 2010050047

The fourth edition of this comprehensive beekeeper's handbook provides new and updated information throughout including new information on important contemporary issues such as Colony Collapse Disorder, Africanized honey bees and bee mite control. Packed with detailed illustrations and step-by-step instructions, this guide provides beginner and experienced beekeepers with the fundamentals of bee theory as well as practical information on hive construction, obtaining bees, feeding, seasonal management and honey and pollen harvesting procedures. The work includes useful sidebars throughout as well as a large section of web and print resource recommendations on a wide variety of beekeeping and related topics. --From publisher description.

639 Hunting, fishing, conservation, related technologies

Dray, Philip

The **fair** chase : the epic story of hunting in America / Philip Dray. Basic Books, 2018. 368 p. **639**

1. Hunting -- United States -- History. 2. Hunters 3. Environmental ethics 4. Guns 5. United States -- Social life and customs
ISBN 9780465061723

LC 2018005078

"While steering clear of taking sides in the matter of recreational hunting, Dray provides a lively history that can be enjoyed by hunters and conservationists alike." Kirkus.

Greenlaw, Linda, 1960-

The **lobster** chronicles : life on a very small island / Linda Greenlaw. Hyperion, 2003, c2002. xii, 238 p. : **639**

1. Greenlaw, Linda, 1960- 2. Lobster fisheries. 3. Fishing. 4. Small town life. 5. Fishers. 6. Maine. 7. Isle au Haut, Maine -- Social life and customs.
ISBN 0786885912

LC BL2003009755

Reprint. Originally published: 2002.

The author details her return to Isle au Haut, a tiny Maine island with a population of seventy year-round residents, many of whom are her relatives, to describe small-town life in a lobster-fishing village.

"In this companion to The Hungry Ocean, the author gives up swordfishing to return to her parents' home on Isle Au Haut off the coast of Maine and fish for lobster. She intersperses her narrative with plenty of eccentrics who live on her tiny island. Self-speculation and uncertainties . nicely balance her delightfully cocky essays of island life." Publishers Weekly.

Jacobsen, Rowan

The **essential** oyster : a salty appreciation of taste and temptation / Rowan Jacobsen ; photography, David Malosh ; styling, Adrienne Anderson. Bloomsbury, 2016. 293 p. : **639**

1. Oyster culture. 2. Cooking (Oysters). 3. Recipes 4. Cookbooks
ISBN 9781632862563

LC bl2016044544

Includes indexes.

Describes the oysters that can be found globally, discussing their habitats and how they are harvested, as well as provides such recipes as oyster pan roast and fiddlehead mignonette.

"A handful of recipes from top chefs round out the book, chased down with a dirty oyster-brine martini." Publishers Weekly.

Swift, Earl, 1958-

Chesapeake requiem : a year with the watermen of vanishing Tangier Island / Earl Swift. Dey Street, 2018. 434 p. : **639**

1. Crabs 2. Fishers 3. Island life 4. Islands 5. Chesapeake Bay 6. Tangier Island (Va.) 7. Virginia
ISBN 9780062661395

LC 2018024659

Presents a 200-year history of Chesapeake Bay's Tangier Island crabbing community while explaining how rapidly rising sea levels will render the island uninhabitable within 20 years.

639.2 Commercial fishing, whaling, sealing

Clark, Doug Bock

The **last** whalers : three years in the far Pacific with a courageous tribe and a vanishing way of life / Doug Bock Clark. Little Brown & Co, 2019. 384 p. **639.2**

1. Whalers 2. Hunting and gathering societies 3. Indigenous peoples 4. Rites and ceremonies 5. Indonesia 6. Islands of the Pacific
ISBN 9780316390620

LC bl2018192737

Deeply empathetic and richly reported, The Last Whalers is a riveting, powerful chronicle of the collision between one of the planet's dwindling indigenous peoples and the irresistible enticements and upheavals of a rapidly transforming world.

"Over several years, Clark lived among the Lamalerans in an attempt to tell their story and, in a larger context, the human story. The result is a wonderful ethnography that comes alive through a novelistic approach in which Clark explains whale hunting culture and keys in on a few individuals and their families in his effort to inform readers about their lives, ultimately exemplifying how the juggernaut nature of the modern world impacts all of its inhabitants." Library Journal.

Cook, Langdon, 1966-

Upstream : searching for wild salmon, from river to table / Langdon Cook. Ballantine Books, 2017 320 p. **639.2**

1. Pacific salmon. 2. Salmon fisheries 3. Salmon fishing 4. Salmon 5. Pacific Northwest.
ISBN 9781101882887

LC 2017012853

Combining information about nature and animal behavior, cuisine, environmental issues and outdoor adventures, the author of The Mushroom Hunters examines the life and culture of wild salmon, from Alaskan spawning grounds to restaurant menus.

"The Pacific salmon is a great American fish, and by writing about it with such care and curiosity, Cook establishes its ecological importance and tells a great American story." Booklist.

Dolin, Eric Jay

Leviathan : the history of whaling in America / Eric Jay Dolin. W.W. Norton, c2007. 479 p. : **639.2**

1. Whaling -- United States -- History. 2. Seafaring life. 3. Whalers. 4. United States -- History.
ISBN 0393060578

LC 2007006113

The epic history of the "iron men in wooden boats" who built an industrial empire through the pursuit of whales. Few things can capture the sheer danger and desperation of men on the deep sea as dramatically as whaling. Environmental writer Dolin chronicles the rise of a burgeoning industry, from its brutal struggles during the Revolutionary period to its golden age in the mid-1800s when a fleet of more than 700 ships hunted the seas and American whale oil lit the world, to its decline as the twentieth century dawned. This sweeping social and economic history provides rich and often fantastic accounts of the men themselves, who mutinied, murdered, rioted, deserted, drank, scrimshawed, and recorded their experiences in journals and memoirs. The book also contains a wealth of naturalistic detail on whales.--From publisher description.

"The author chronicles the long history of whaling in North America, from the voyages of Capt. John Smith, who, like many after him, found this Whale-fishing a costly conclusion, to the last voyage of the Wanderer, a whaler that set sail from the once-teeming port of New Bedford, Mass., in 1924 and promptly wrecked in the shallows before a crowd of curious onlookers. Anyone whose knowledge of whaling begins and ends with Moby Dick will get a solid education from Mr. Dolin, who fills in the historical record and sets the stage for the glory years when men like Melville set out from Nantucket, New Bedford, Sag Harbor and dozens of other ports on voyages lasting as long as four years." New York Times.

Kurlansky, Mark

★The **last** fish tale : the fate of the Atlantic and survival in Gloucester, America's oldest fishing port and most original town / Mark Kurlansky. Ballantine Books, 2008. 304 p. **639.2**

1. Fisheries -- Gloucester, Massachusetts -- History -- Anecdotes. 2. Fishing -- Gloucester, Massachusetts -- History -- Anecdotes. 3. Small town life. 4. Tourism 5. Gloucester, Massachusetts -- History Anecdotes.
ISBN 9780345487278

LC 2007051116

Provides a close-up look at the history of Gloucester, Massachusetts, America's oldest fishing port, how fishing and the culture of fishing have defined the coastal region, and how the disappearance of this way of life has transformed Gloucester.

"The author provides a delightful, intimate history and contemporary portrait of the quintessential northeastern coastal fishing town: Gloucester, Mass., on Cape Anne. Illustrated with his own beautifully executed drawings, Kurlansky's book vividly depicts the contemporary tension between the traditional fishing trade and modern commerce, which in Gloucester means beach-going tourists." Publishers Weekly.

Urbina, Ian

The **outlaw** ocean : journeys across the last untamed frontier / Ian Urbina. Alfred A. Knopf, 2019. 448 p. **639.2**

1. Urbina, Ian Travel. 2. Fisheries -- Corrupt practices. 3. Corruption 4. Piracy 5. Maritime law. 6. Oceania
ISBN 9780451492944

LC 2019001735

A Pulitzer Prize-winning investigative reporter profiles the rampant criminal and exploitative activities of the world's unmonitored ocean regions, uncovering a vast global network of industry corruption, piracy and trafficking.

639.34 Fish culture in aquariums

Bailey, Mary (Writer on aquarium fish)

The **ultimate** encyclopedia of aquarium fish & fish care : a definitive guide to identifying and keeping freshwater and marine fishes / Mary Bailey & Gina Sandford. Southwater, 2015 256 p. : **639.34**

1. Aquarium fishes 2. Aquariums
ISBN 1780193416

LC bl2016019931

Presents a comprehensive guide to setting up and maintaining an aquarium, and provides information on identifying and caring for fish.

Paletta, Michael S.

The **new** marine aquarium : step-by-step setup & stocking guide / Michael S. Paletta ; illustrations by Edward Kadunc ; principle photographers, Scott W. Michael & John Goodman. Microcosm, c1999. 144 p. : **639.34**

1. Marine aquariums.
ISBN 1890087521

LC 98034407

Creating a beautiful, thriving first saltwater aquarium has never been easier, using the natural, simplified methods learned and practiced by the world's leading reef hobbyists. By helping newcomers avoid the pitfalls of outdated, high-maintenance filtration techniques, the author offers an easy-to-follow route to long-term success with live rock, appropriate equipment, aquascaping, disease prevention, and essential husbandry techniques. Includes a photographic guide to selecting fishes, with dozens of hardy choices that are highly recommended for beginning hobbyists or others wanting beautiful, interesting, and long-lived marine species. --From publisher description.

639.9 Conservation of biological resources

Jacobsen, Rowan

The **living** shore : rediscovering a lost world / Rowan Jacobsen. Bloomsbury, 2009. 176 p. **639.9**

1. Oyster fisheries. 2. Oysters. 3. Endangered ecosystems. 4. Habitat (Ecology) 5. Puget Sound area. 6. Pacific Coast (North America)
ISBN 9781596916845

LC 2009008903

The James Beard-winning author of A Geography of Oysters models a modern environmental story on Steinbeck's The Sea of Cortez and traces the efforts of a team of scientists to study the Olympias oysters to see if their habitat could provide a blueprint for ocean restoration efforts.

639.97 Specific kinds of animals

Bradley, Carol, 1957-
Last chain on Billie : how one extraordinary elephant escaped the big top / Carol Bradley. St. Martin's Press, [2014] 288 p. **639.97**

1. Animal welfare. 2. Elephants -- United States. 3. Circus animals. 4. Cruelty
ISBN 9781250025692

LC 2014008568

The award-winning author of Saving Gracie chronicles the story of a psychologically traumatized zoo and circus elephant who was removed and rehabilitated as part of the largest government elephant rescue in U.S. history.

"Graphic details of animal abuse may offend some readers, but the overall story is worth enduring those passages. A moving and informative account of the plight of trained elephants in the U.S. and the efforts of those who have created an asylum for them." Kirkus.

640 Home and family management

Alink, Merissa
Little house living : the make-your-own guide to a frugal, simple, and self-sufficient life / Merissa A. Alink. Gallery Books, 2015 xi, 306 p. : **640**

1. Home economics. 2. Housekeeping. 3. Quick and easy cooking
ISBN 9781501104268

LC 2015024538

Encourages readers to live an entirely made-from-scratch life through recipes and DIY projects to help save money and simplify the everyday.

"With chapters on Body and Beauty, Household, Children and Pets, and Make-Ahead Mixes, plus additional stories, Alink brings a bit of Wilder's life into the present." Library Journal.

Bried, Erin
How to sew a button : and other nifty things your grandmother knew / Erin Bried. Ballantine Books, c2009. xxii, 278 p. : **640**

1. Homemaking 2. Handicraft 3. Life skills
ISBN 9780345518750

LC 2009036046

Presents step-by-step instructions for more than one hundred basic domestic life skills from building a fire and hemming pants to rolling a pie crust and planting a vegetable garden, in a guide that includes tips for saving money.

"These anecdotes and tutorials gleaned from subject experts and grandmothers who were children during the Great Depression cover a broad swath of homemaking skills. Instead of systematic how-tos, Bried presents these lessons as a means to improve the quality of the reader's life." Library Journal

Carroll, Ryder
The **bullet** journal method : track the past, order the present, design the future / Ryder Carroll. Portfolio/Penguin, 2018 310 p. ; **640**

1. Appointment books 2. Diaries -- Authorship 3. Time management
ISBN 9780525533337

LC 2018041565

A digital product designer and inventor of the Bullet Journal organizational system shows us how to track the past, order the present and design the future, providing the structure needed to go from passenger and pilot of your own life.

Mendelson, Cheryl, 1946-
Home comforts : the art and science of keeping house / Cheryl Mendelson ; illustrations by Harry Bates. Scribner, c1999. x, 884 p. : **640**

1. Home economics.
ISBN 068481465X

LC 99037555

Ranging from suggestions for the care of musical instruments to maintaining home safety, a celebration of and guide to the finer points of home-keeping offers a contemporary, creative, and positive take on a traditional subject

"Mendelson includes sections on food, clothing, cleanliness, daily life, and safety, with information on negligence, domestic employment laws, insurance, and even the impact of clothing label laws on our laundry. Preferred methods are explained in detail, and some alternatives are offered for those who need to compromise. This is a valuable tool." Library Journal.

Stewart, Martha, 1941-
★The **Martha** manual : how to do (almost) everything / Martha Stewart. Houghton Mifflin Harcourt, 2019. 400 p. : **640**

1. Dwellings -- Maintenance and repair 2. Entertaining 3. Gardening 4. Homemaking
ISBN 9781328927323

LC 2018051333

Includes index.

An authoritative handbook by the domestic-lifestyle expert shares hundreds of ideas and instructions for homemaker skills, from transporting a decorated cake and folding an American flag to playing a classic lawn game and bathing a cat.

"This wide-ranging guide is designed as a household reference that sums up the breadth of Stewarts expertise. " Booklist.

Sundeen, Mark, 1970-
The **unsettlers** : in search of the good life in today's America / Mark Sundeen. Riverhead Books, 2017. 336 p. **640**

1. Sustainable living 2. Sustainable development 3. Sustainable communities 4. Simple life 5. United States -- Civilization -- 21st century.
ISBN 9781594631580

LC 2016026360

In a world of immersive journalism steeped in a distinctively American social history and sparked by a personal quest, the author chronicles the quest for the simple life through both the stories of three very different couples and the visionaries, ascetics and artists that inspired each of them to create a sustainable, ethical and authentic existence.

"An engaging read for those with an interest in sustainable living, urban farming, and homesteading." Library Journal.

Tracy, Brian
Eat that frog! : 21 great ways to stop procrastinating and get more done in less time / Brian Tracy. Berrett-Koehler Publish-

ers, c2007. xiv, 128 p. ; **640**

1. Procrastination

ISBN 9781576754221

LC 2006021172

An expert in personal development shows readers how to overcome the urge to procrastinate in both one's personal and professional lives and offers twenty-one practical steps designed to end procrastination, get important tasks done, and utilize the principles and techniques of time management.

Watkins, Julia

Simply living well : a guide to creating a natural, low-waste home / Julia Watkins. Houghton Mifflin Harcourt, 2020. xiv, 271 p. : **640**

1. Home economics 2. House cleaning 3. Formulas, recipes, etc 4. Waste minimization

ISBN 9780358202189

LC 2019045719

"Easy recipes, DIY projects, and other ideas for living a beautiful and low-waste life, from the expert behind @simply.living.well on Instagram".-- Provided by publisher.

640.73 Evaluation and purchasing guides

Pogue, David, 1963-

Pogue's basics: money : essential tips and shortcuts (that no one bothers to tell you) about beating the system / David Pogue. Flatiron Books, 2016 287 p. : **640.73**

1. Consumer education. 2. Personal finance 3. Shopping.

ISBN 1250081416

LC 2016033301

A follow-up to Pogue's Basics: Tech and Pogue's Basics: Life shares 200 simple tips and tricks for making financial management easier, offering insights into top-recommended ways to make and save money while avoiding costly scams.

641 Food and drink

Barr, Luke

Provence, 1970 : M.F.K. Fisher, Julia Child, James Beard, and the reinvention of American taste/ Luke Barr. Clarkson Potter, 2013 320 p. **641**

1. Fisher, M. F. K. (Mary Frances Kennedy), 1908-1992. 2. Child, Julia. 3. Jones, Judith. 4. Beard, James, 1903-1985. 5. Olney, Richard, 1927-1999 6. Cooking, American -- History -- 20th century. 7. Cooking, American -- Philosophy. 8. Americans in France. 9. Provence, France.

ISBN 9780307718341

LC 2013007782

The grand-nephew of M. F. K. Fisher presents a dramatic account of the 1970 gathering in Provence where such culinary luminaries as James Beard and Julia Child debated and inadvertently launched the modern food movement in America, sharing engaging details about the strong personalities, friendships and rivalries behind current traditions.

Bourdain, Anthony

A **cook's** tour : in search of the perfect meal / Anthony Bourdain. Bloomsbury, 2001. x, 274 p. **641**

1. Gastronomy 2. Dinners and dining 3. Food habits. 4. Cooking.

ISBN 1582341400

LC 2001052428

From Japan where he eats traditional fugu, a poisonous blowfish that can only be prepared by specially licensed chefs, to a delectable snack in the Mecong Delta, follows the author as he embarks on a quest around the world to find the ultimate meal.

Davies, Katie Quinn

What Katie ate on the weekend... / photography by Katie Quinn Davies. Viking Studio, 2015. 310 p. : **641**

1. Cooking 2. Entertaining 3. Seasonal cooking 4. Recipes 5. Cookbooks.

ISBN 9780525428954

LC bl2015017105

Includes index.

Shares food photography and recipes for over one hundred easy recipes for weekend entertaining, as well as stories from the author's dinner parties and Sunday brunches.

Fisher, M. F. K. (Mary Frances Kennedy), 1908-1992

The **art** of eating / M.F.K. Fisher ; with an introduction by Clifton Fadiman ; an appreciation by James A. Beard ; and a retrospective essay by Joan Reardon. Wiley Pub., 2004, c1954. xxxiv, 749 p. ; **641**

1. Gastronomy. 2. Food. 3. Food habits.

ISBN 0764542613

LC 2003026124

Originally published under title: Collected gastronomical works of M.F.K. Fisher. 1954.

Includes index.

A commemorative keepsake edition of the food writing classic is a compilation of many of the author's best writings and features an introductory tribute by Fisher's leading biographer and quotes from some of today's top culinary names.

Kamp, David

The **United** States of Arugula: how we became a gourmet nation/ David Kamp. Broadway Books, 2006. xxi, 392 p. : **641**

1. Gastronomy. 2. Cooking, American. 3. Local foods 4. Food habits -- United States -- History -- 20th century

ISBN 0767915798

LC 2006042599

"The author details the development of fine dining in the U.S. and proves healthy, even exotic food movements are having an effect on our diet. This cultural history makes for an engrossing read, documenting the dramas and rivalries of the food industry." Publishers Weekly.

Madigan, Carleen

The **backyard** homestead / edited by Carleen Madigan. Storey Pub., c2009. 367 p. : **641**

1. Kitchen gardens. 2. Food -- Preservation. 3. Meat animals.

ISBN 9781603421386

LC 2009001338

Suggests organic methods for growing plants and raising animals on a small plot of land, explains how to determine the proper times for planting, and provides tips for using and preserving food.

Mayle, Peter

French lessons : adventures with knife, fork, and corkscrew

/ Peter Mayle. Alfred A. Knopf, 2001. ix, 227 p. : **641**

1. Mayle, Peter Travel France. 2. Cooking, French. 3. Food habits -- France. 4. Americans in France. 5. Gastronomy. 6. France -- Social life and customs.

ISBN 0375405909

LC 2001087658

In French Lessons, Mayle broadens his horizons and sets out on a gastronomic voyage to every region of France, ready to eat and drink his way into blissful oblivion. Along the way, Mayle unearths rare local delicacies, irresistible recipes, and eccentric characters, while ingesting plenty of red wine, piquant cheese, and escargots.

"Mayle relives some of his most precious moments reveling in the cuisine of his adopted homeland. {He tells} savory, sensual, positively transporting stories about his encounters with Gallic gustatory delights and about his growing appreciation of the central place food occupies in French life." Booklist.

Raeburn, Paul

The **game** theorist's guide to parenting : how the science of strategic thinking can help you deal with the toughest negotiators you know--your kids / Paul Raeburn and Kevin Zollman. Scientific American/Farrar, Straus and Giroux, 2016. 222 p. ; **641**

1. Parenting. 2. Game theory -- Social aspects. 3. Negotiation.

ISBN 9780374160012

LC 2015036381

Uses tactics from the world of business and economics to help parents more effectively negotiate with their children, offering advice and case studies of game theory in action.

"Tantalizing perspectives on cultivating sharing, honesty, and cooperation via game theory." Kirkus.

Westmoreland, Susan

★The **Good** Housekeeping cookbook : 1,275 recipes from America's favorite test kitchen / edited by Susan Westmoreland. Hearst Books, c2010. 752 p. : **641**

1. Cooking, American. 2. Recipes 3. Cookbooks.

ISBN 9781588168139

LC 2010018437

Includes index.

Filled with 1,275 delicious recipes and plenty of full-color photos, this handy kitchen reference also offers dependable information on cooking techniques, tools, ingredients, food handling, nutrition, canning, freezing, holiday celebrations and much more.

"Quick recipes and simple dessert preparations, like Fire-Roasted Nectarines and Coffee Granita, will please anyone pressed for time, but the encyclopedic inclusion of recipes for everything from Egg Salad, Lobster Bisque, and Chocolate Souffle to Pad Thai, Salmon with Mustard-Dill Sauce, and Muffuletta is its true benefit, making it a cookbook readers will grow with." Publishers Weekly.

641.01 Philosophy and theory

Frank, Dana

Wine food : new adventures in drinking and cooking / Dana Frank and Andrea Slonecker ; photographs by Eva Kolenko. Lorena Jones Books, 2018 255 p. : **641.01**

1. Food and wine pairing 2. Cooking 3. Cookbooks.

ISBN 9780399579592

LC 2017058757

Offers over seventy-five recipes with suggestions on wine pairings for each dish, including shrimp aguachile, tomato chaat, falafel waffles, ratatouille gratin, deviled ham hand pies, butternut lamb chili, and porcini mushroom stroganoff.

Harrison, Jim, 1937-2016

A **really** big lunch : the roving gourmand on food and life / Jim Harrison with an introduction by Mario Batali. Grove Press, an imprint of Grove Atlantic, [2017] 272 p. **641.01**

1. Harrison, Jim, 1937-2016. 2. Cooking 3. Gastronomy 4. Dinners and dining 5. Essays

ISBN 9780802126467

LC 2016056292

"The pieces collected in this volume have originally appeared in Smoke Signals, The Kermit Lynch Wine Newsletter, Brick, The New Yorker, Martha Stewart Living, Playboy, Edible Baja Arizona, Big Sky Cooking by Meredith Brokaw and Ellen Wright, The Montana Writers"

An array to be published on the one-year anniversary of the author's death collects many of his food essays for the first time--from the titular New Yorker piece about a French lunch that went to 37 courses to pieces on the relationship between hunter and prey and the obscure language of wine reviews.

"With an introduction from Harrison's longtime friend Mario Batali, this makes a great addition to popular food and wine collections and will be a savory treat for Harrison fans." Booklist.

Mohammadi, Kamin

Bella figura : how to live, love, and eat the Italian way / Kamin Mohammadi. Alfred A. Knopf, 2018. 284 p. ; **641.01**

1. Mohammadi, Kamin Friends and associates. 2. Mohammadi, Kamin Travel Italy. 3. Cooking, Italian. 4. Gastronomy -- Italy. 5. Travel writers -- England 6. Italy -- Description and travel.

ISBN 0385354010

LC 2017055692

An Iranian exile and British journalist describes how in spite of her successful career she began to experience stress-related health setbacks and accepted a friend's invitation to Florence, where she discovered the Italian approach to slowing down and enjoying everyday life.

Wilson, Bee

First bite : how we learn to eat / Bee Wilson ; with illustrations by Annabel Lee. Basic Books, 2015 336 p. **641.01**

1. Gastronomy. 2. Food habits 3. Nutrition

ISBN 9780465064984

LC 2015027683

The award-winning food writer and author draws on current research to trace the origins of food habits in culture, memory and appetite to explain how to alter one's palate to promote better health and fulfillment.

"This work will appeal to food scientists, parents wishing to know the roots of their children's meal choices, and curious readers in general." Library Journal.

Wilson, Bee

The **way** we eat now / Bee Wilson. Basic Books, 2019. 384 p. **641.01**

1. Food habits 2. Food supply 3. Food 4. Nutrition

ISBN 9780465093977

An award-winning food writer takes us on a global tour of what the world eats--and shows us how we can change it for the better.

"This compelling overview of global eating habits by acclaimed food writer and Wall Street Journal columnist Wilson...seesaws back and forth between alarming paradoxes...Wilsons many fans and new converts alike will find her arguments convincing. This diet advice goes down easy." Booklist.

641.2 Food and drink -- Beverages (Drinks)

Acitelli, Tom

The **audacity** of hops : the history of America's craft beer revolution / Tom Acitelli. Chicago Review Press, 2013. 384 p. **641.2**

1. Beer -- United States. 2. Brewing 3. Brewing industry and trade 4. Breweries.
ISBN 9781613743881

LC 2013002264

"Charting the birth and growth of craft beer across the United States, Tom Acitelli offers an epic, story-driven account of one of the most inspiring and surprising American grassroots movements. In 1975, there was a single craft brewery in the United States; today there are more than 2,000. Now this once-fledgling movement has become ubiquitous nationwide--there's even a honey ale brewed at the White House. This book not only tells the stories of the major figures and businesses within the movement, but it also ties in the movement with larger American culinary developments. It also charts the explosion of the mass-market craft beer culture, including magazines, festivals, home brewing, and more. This entertaining and informative history brims with charming, remarkable stories, which together weave a very American business tale of formidable odds and refreshing success".-- Provided by publisher.

Alworth, Jeff

The **beer** bible / Jeff Alworth. Workman Publishing, 2015 xi, 644 p. : **641.2**

1. Beer. 2. Recipes
ISBN 0761168117

LC 2015024777

Shares extensive information about beer, including the different ways it's made, the different styles of beer, and beer suggestions based on taste preferences.

"Beer enthusiasts will welcome this guide that feels like one is spending time with a well-versed drinking pal." Library Journal.

Basset, Gerard,

Know-it-all wine : the 50 essential topics, each explained in under a minute / editor, Gerard Basset, OBE ; foreword, Annette Alvarez-Peters ; contributors, Gerard Basset, OBE, David Bird, MW, Martin Campion, Jeremy Dixon, Paul Lukacs, Debra Meiburg, MW, Jane Parkinson, Stephen Skelton, MW. Wellfleet Press, 2018. 160 p. : **641.2**

1. Recipes 2. Wine and wine making.
ISBN 1577151763

LC bl2018184440

Provides information about wine and wine making through short entries that each thoroughly explain a single topic.

"Basset, the 2010 Worlds Best Sommelier, instructs budding oenophiles on what differentiates, say, a sauvignon blanc from a cabernet sauvingon (besides color), the importance of terroir, wines religious connections, and emerging regions of wine production." Booklist.

Bauer, Bryce T

The **new** rum : a modern guide to the spirit of the Americas / Bryce T. Bauer. The Countryman Press, 2018 333 p. : **641.2**

1. Alcoholic beverages. 2. Cocktails. 3. Recipes 4. Rum -- Brazil.
ISBN 1682680002

LC 2018009537

Rum, traditionally relegated to cloying cocktails or tropical- themed novelty drinks, is undergoing a global renaissance. In bars and distilleries across the world, rum is being defined as a dynamic, complex, and versatile drink. New to the scene of connoisseurship, rum is a spirit of possibilities, inviting imaginative bartenders and mixologists to leave their marks on this burgeoning movement. In The New Rum, award-winning drinks author Bryce T. Bauer charts the historical and cultural journey of the spirit of the Americas from its origins in the Caribbean, to its long- held status as a cheap vacation drink, to today's inspiring craft revival. This rum-spiked travelogue also includes a producer- focused drinks guide, covering dozens of the world's most innovative and iconic producers, making everything from Martinique rhum agricole to long-aged sippers from Barbados and the Dominican Republic. --From publisher description.

"Fast and funny, this offering is like a craft cocktail -- delightfully conceived and executed." Publishers Weekly.

Broom, Dave

The **world** atlas of whisky : more than 200 distilleries explored and 750 expressions tasted / Dave Broom, Glenfiddich Award-winning author. Mitchell Beazley, 2014. 336 p. : **641.2**

1. Recipes 2. Whiskey industry. 3. Whiskey.
ISBN 1845339428

LC bl2014047760

Provides a guide to over two hundred distilleries around the world, covering the offerings of each and the five different flavor camps of whiskey.

"A perfect complement to Dominic Roskrow's expansive The World's Best Whiskies, which includes distiller interviews." Library Journal.

Centamore, Adam

Tasting wine & cheese : an insider's guide to mastering the principles of pairing / Adam Centamore. Quarry Books, 2015. 160 p. : **641.2**

1. Wine and wine making 2. Cheese -- Varieties 3. Food and wine pairing
ISBN 9781631590672

LC bl2015042956

Includes index.

A guide to pairing wine and cheese explains how to properly taste the two, pair condiments, and broaden the appreciation of gourmet combinations.

Huckelbridge, Dane

The **United** States of beer : a freewheeling history of the all-American drink / Dane Huckelbridge. William Morrow & Co., 2016. 288 p. **641.2**

1. Beer. 2. Alcoholic beverages. 3. Beverages.
ISBN 9780062389756

LC bl2016024833

A history of beer in America by the author of Bourbon chronicles how beer has evolved in every nation from a regional product to a global mega-brand, sharing anecdotes about such subjects as Washington's failed attempt to brew molasses at Mount Vernon and the manufacturing technologies that introduced beer to the Wild West.

"The author's breezy style is a perfect match for his subject." Library Journal.

Johnson, Hugh, 1939

Hugh Johnson on wine : good bits from 55 years of scribbling. / Hugh Johnson. Mitchell Beazley, 2016. 288 p. : **641.2**

1. Wine and wine making. 2. Vineyards. 3. Wineries.
ISBN 9781784722623

LC bl2017021295

Includes index.

Collects the best of the author's writings on wine, from the 1960s to the present day.

"Every page presents careful thought and nuanced presentation. This work is highly recommended to beginners learning about wine and for established professionals. Johnson's writing is a joy to read." Choice.

Larousse (Firm),

Larousse wine : the definitive reference for wine lovers : how to understand & enjoy the world's best wines Hamlyn, 2017. 654 p. : **641.2**

1. Wine and wine making.
ISBN 9780600635093

LC bl2019019779

"Completely revised & updated with additional content."
Includes index.

Profiles winemaking regions around the globe, from Europe and the Americas to Africa and the Far East, offering information on grapes, vineyards, and vintages, and explaining how to buy, choose, store, serve, and taste wine.

Liem, Peter

★**Champagne** : the essential guide to the wines, producers, and terroirs of the iconic region / Peter Liem, with Kate Leahy Ten Speed Press, 2017 321 p. : **641.2**

1. Champagne (Wine) 2. Wine and wine making -- Champagne-Ardenne, France 3. Champagne-Ardenne, France 4. Essays.
ISBN 9781607748427

LC 2017022013

"From Peter Liem, the lauded expert behind the top-rated online resource ChampagneGuide.net, comes this groundbreaking guide to the modern wines of Champagne--a region that in recent years has undergone one of the most dramatic transformations in the wine-growing world. This luxurious box set includes a pullout tray with a complete set of seven vintage vineyard maps by Louis Larmat, a rare and indispensable resource that beautifully documents the region's terroirs. With extensive grower and vintner profiles, as well as a fascinating look at Champagne's history and lore, Champagne explores this legendary wine as never before".-- Provided by publisher.

"In writing that pairs authoritative knowledge with an inviting tone, the author guides readers through the history of champagne, the process of producing the wine, the geography of the Champagne region, and the major manufacturers." Library Journal.

Neiman, Ophelie

Wine isn't rocket science : a quick and easy guide to understanding, buying, tasting, and pairing every type of wine / Ophelie Neiman ; illustrations by Yannis Varoutsikos ; translated by Nysa Kline. Black Dog & Leventhal Publishers, 2017. 272 p. : **641.2**

1. Recipes 2. Wine and wine making.
ISBN 9780316431309

LC OC2018017219

Includes index.

"This book is a terrific introduction to an often intimidating subject." Publishers Weekly.

Old, Marnie

Wine : a tasting course / Marnie Old. DK Publishing, 2014. 256 p. : **641.2**

1. Wine tasting.
ISBN 1465405887

LC bl2013056284

Includes index.

This visual guide helps readers understand the concepts and subtleties surrounding the taste of wine, how to detect and discuss its various qualities and how to describe what is being processed on the tongue and in the nose.

Proulx, Annie

Cider : making, using & enjoying sweet & hard cider / Annie Proulx & Lew Nichols. Storey Pub., c2003. iv, 219 p. : **641.2**

1. Apples. 2. Cider.
ISBN 1580175201

LC 2003272271

Includes index.

Discover the pleasures of making and drinking cider. From choosing the right apples through reaping the liquid rewards of a successful pressing, this classic guide has you covered. With detailed drawings of cider-making equipment, methods, and set-up, even a novice juicer will enjoy sweet and spicy gallons in no time. Annie Proulx and Lew Nichols provide insightful, time-tested advice enlivened by a smattering of historical anecdotes. Whether you like your cider sweet or hard, you're sure to find a recipe that satisfies. --From publisher description.

Puckette, Madeline

Wine folly : the master guide / Madeline Puckette and Justin Hammack. Avery, 2018 317 p. : **641.2**

1. Recipes 2. Wine and wine making.
ISBN 0525533893

LC bl2018186804

An expanded edition of a popular guide for budding oenophiles provides illustrated, accessibly organized profiles of leading vintages, detailed maps of major and up-and-coming regions, expanded food-and-wine pairing listings and essential tasting tips.

Risen, Clay

American whiskey, bourbon, & rye : a guide to the nation's favorite spirit / Clay Risen. Sterling Epicure, 2013 297 p. : **641.2**

1. Recipes 2. Whiskey -- United States.
ISBN 1402798407

LC bl2013049547

Offers brief histories, ratings, and tasting notes for 206 types of American whiskey, including Eagle Rare, Jim Beam, and Whistlepig.

"Risen...deftly combines history and assessment in this informative volume that covers more than 200 of the titular spirits." Library Journal.

Robinson, Jancis,

The **Oxford** companion to wine / edited by Jancis Robinson ; assistant editor: Julia Harding ; advisory editor, viticulture: Richard E. Smart ; advisory editors, oenology: Valerie Lavigne & Denis Dubourdieu. Oxford University Press, 2015. xlvii, 859 p. : **641.2**

1. Recipes 2. Wine and wine making.
ISBN 0198705387

LC bl2015036448

A comprehensive, illustrated reference for wine presents almost four thousand entries on every wine-related topic imaginable, including viticulture, grape varieties, and wine consumption.

"This hefty volume is certain not just to answer both broad and obscure questions on viniculture, but also to pique the interest of the reader who dips into its pages." Library Journal.

Tardi, Alan, 1956-

Champagne, uncorked : the house of Krug and the timeless allure of the world's most celebrated drink / Alan Tardi. PublicAffairs, [2016] 296 p. **641.2**

1. Champagne (Wine). 2. Wine and wine making 3. Wineries
ISBN 9781610396882

LC 2016007400

"Tardi deftly melds the process of creating champagne with the story of the winery from its earliest days. The result is fascinating, all the more so for the rich side stories captured in endnotes." Library Journal.

Theise, Terry, 1953-
What makes a wine worth drinking : in praise of the sublime / Terry Theise. Houghton Mifflin Harcourt, 2018. 176 p. ; **641.2**

1. Recipes 2. Wine and wine making. 3. Essays
ISBN 1328762211

LC 2018012317

A James Beard Award-winning wine writer celebrates the role of authenticity in quality wines, describing how crafted, artisanal and regional family wines have the power to improve and enrich the world.

"This intoxicating book illuminates a path to savoring good wine, body, and spirit." Publishers Weekly.

Wallace, Benjamin, 1968-
The **billionaire's** vinegar : the mystery of the world's most expensive bottle of wine / Benjamin Wallace. Crown Publishers, c2008. 336 p. **641.2**

1. Wine and wine making -- Miscellanea. 2. Collectors and collecting. 3. Wine industry and trade 4. Wine bottles.
ISBN 9780307338778

LC 2007031645

Describes the 1985 purchase of a bottle of 1787 Chateau Lafite Bordeaux for $156,000, the mysterious background of the wine, and the enigmatic wine collector who discoverd the bottle, once supposedly owned by Thomas Jefferson, in a bricked-up Paris cellar.

"This is a gripping story, expertly handled by Benjamin Wallace who writes with wit and verve, drawing the reader into a subculture strewn with eccentrics and monomaniacs. Full of detail that will delight wine lovers. It will also appeal to anyone who merely savours a great tale, well told." The Economist.

Webb, Tim, 1955-
The **world** atlas of beer : The Essential Guide to the Beers of the World / Tim Webb & Stephen Beaumont. Sterling Epicure, c2012. 256 p. : **641.2**

1. Beer. 2. Recipes
ISBN 1402789610

LC bl2013000448

Originally published: London : Mitchell Beazley, 2012.

Surveys noteworthy beers around the world, along with information on the production process, different styles, purchasing and storage tips, pouring techniques, food pairings, emerging trends, and popular festivals.

Wilson, Tonia
Beer at my table : recipes, beer styles and food pairings / Tonia Wilson. Whitecap Books, 2019. 208 p. : **641.2**

1. Food and beer pairing 2. Beer tasting. 3. Beer -- Flavor and odor. 4. Recipes 5. Cookbooks
ISBN 9781770503182

Includes index.

"Cookbook of recipes and culinary food pairings for beers from across the globe including information needed to know and understand beer and its interactions with food and the palate."-- Provided by publisher.

Zraly, Kevin
Windows on the World complete wine course / Kevin Zraly. Sterling Epicure, 2014 xxi, 346 p. : **641.2**

1. Windows on the World (New York, N.Y.) 2. Vineyards. 3. Wine and wine making.
ISBN 1454913649

LC bl2014041180

Includes index.

Looks at how and where wine is made and how this affects its quality and pricing, including information on how the professionals taste and rate wine and a country-by-country tour of the latest vintages.

"The casual browser will find fascinating trivia and facts about wine in numerous sidebars, but may not be able to resist becoming involved in the main text, making this difficult to put down. Highly recommended for all wine connoisseurs." Library Journal.

641.3 Food

Adarme, Adrianna
The **year** of cozy : 125 recipes, crafts, and other homemade adventures / Adrianna Adarme. Rodale, 2015 x, 259 p. : **641.3**

1. Comfort food. 2. Handicraft. 3. Do-it-yourself work. 4. Recipes 5. Cookbooks.
ISBN 9781623365103

LC 2015034972

Includes index.

"From blogger, recipe developer, and photographer Adrianna Adarme comes a beautiful book of advice for simplifying, beautifying, and living a more thoughtful life. Organized by the months of the year, and by categories such as "Live," "Do," and "Make," Adarme shares ideas for activities, recipes, and projects that make the little moments in life just as exciting as the big. Like her blog, A Cozy Kitchen, The Year of Cozy features warm and comforting photos and cozy inspiration. Adarme gives us special (but totally doable) things we can do for others and ourselves. From recipes to DIY crafts, Adarme focuses on easy, inexpensive undertakings that have a big reward: happiness. The best moments in life don't require stuff, they just require intention. Adarme's clear and easy-to-follow instructions and recipes will excite and motivate you to march into your kitchen and craft closet to make something you can be proud of".-- Provided by publisher.

America's Test Kitchen (Firm)
★**Nutritious** delicious : turbocharge your favorite recipes with 50 everyday superfoods / the editors at America's Test Kitchen. America's Test Kitchen, 2018 x, 318 p. : **641.3**

1. Natural foods 2. Cooking (Natural foods) 3. Cookbooks.
ISBN 9781945256110

LC 2017030625

Includes index.

Presents a collection of 125 recipes for dishes made up of superfood combinations, with a discussion on the health benefits of using fresh fruits and vegetables and advice on stocking a pantry with nutrient dense foods.

Bacon, Josephine, 1942-
The **story** of food : an illustrated history of everything we eat / contributors, Josephine Bacon, Alexandra Black, Liz Calvert

Smith, Jane Garton, Jeremy Harwood, Patsy Westcott. DK Publishing, 2018. 360 p. : **641.3**

1. Food -- History. 2. Diet -- History. 3. Food habits. 4. Food preferences.

ISBN 9781465473363

LC bl2019020233

Includes index.

A montage of food reveals the cultural impact of the foods we eat, explores the early efforts of humans in their quest for sustenance and tells the stories behind individual foods.

Barber, Dan, 1969-

★The **third** plate : field notes on a new cuisine / Dan Barber. The Penguin Press, 2014. 496 p. **641.3**

1. Cooking, American 2. Natural foods. 3. Cooking (Natural foods) 4. Seasonal cooking.

ISBN 9781594204074

LC 2013039966

Green Prize for Sustainable Literature: Adult Nonfiction, 2015.

James Beard Foundation Book Awards, Writing and Literature, 2015.

Renowned chef Dan Barber introduces a new kind of cuisine that represents the future of American dining in THE THIRD PLATE. Barber explores the evolution of American food from the "first plate," or industrially-produced, meat-heavy dishes, to the "second plate" of grass-fed meat and organic greens, and says that both of these approaches are ultimately neither sustainable nor healthy. Instead, Barber proposes Americans should move to the "third plate," a cuisine rooted in seasonal productivity, natural livestock rhythms, whole-grains, and small portions of free-range meat. Barber's book charts a bright path for eaters and chefs alike towards a healthy and sustainable future for American cuisine.

"In this bold and impassioned analysis, Barber insists that chefs have the power to transform American cuisine to achieve a sustainable and nutritious future." Kirkus.

Bittman, Mark

The **food** matters cookbook : 500 revolutionary recipes for better living / Mark Bittman. Simon & Schuster, c2010. x, 645 p. ; **641.3**

1. Food. 2. Nutrition. 3. Health. 4. Cooking. 5. Cookbooks.

ISBN 9781439120231

LC 2010028623

This follow up to Mark Bittman's 'NY Times' bestseller, 'Food Matters: The Cookbook' offers around 450 recipes that will save your health and the planet.

"The author provides a rational approach to eating that not only improves health but also helps the environment. Extolling the benefits of a plant-heavy diet, Bittman offers more than 500 healthful recipes that feature unprocessed fruits, vegetables, legumes, nuts, and whole grains and reduce all types of meat to backup players. In addition, he shares five basic principles for sane eating that are easy to implement and understand as well as an unusually helpful pantry section and handy charts for substituting produce and seafood by season. Practical and balanced, this collection will shape the way we cook at home for years to come." Publishers Weekly.

Blount, Roy

Save room for pie : food songs and chewy ruminations / Roy Blount, Jr. Sarah Crichton Books/Farrar, Straus and Giroux, 2016 304 p. **641.3**

1. Blount, Roy 2. Food -- Anecdotes. 3. Food in literature.

ISBN 9780374175207

LC 2015036049

"Eminently quotable, informative, and entertaining, Blount makes for a genial host, regaling the reader with story after story." Publishers Weekly.

Britton, Sarah

My new roots : inspired plant-based recipes for every season / Sarah Britton. Clarkson Potter/Publishers, 2015. 256 p. : **641.3**

1. Cooking (Natural foods) 2. Recipes 3. Vegetarian cooking 4. Cookbooks.

ISBN 9780804185387

LC 2014018135

Includes index.

The holistic nutritionist and writer behind the popular food blog MyNewRoots.org offers 100 healthy, whole food, vegetarian recipes that don't use processed ingredients, refined flours or sugar, including Butternut Squash Lasagna, Savory Sprint Hand Pies and Carrot Rhubarb Muffins.

"Britton's approachable guide to healthy eating will appeal to many readers." Library Journal.

Chaplin, Amy

★**At** home in the whole food kitchen : celebrating the art of eating well / Amy Chaplin. Roost Books, 2014 xi, 386 p. : **641.3**

1. Cooking (Natural foods). 2. Natural foods. 3. Cookbooks.

ISBN 9781611800852

LC 2013043411

Includes index.

Presents an introduction to cooking with natural foods, discussing ingredients, equipment, and pantry essentials, and providing recipes for vegetarian and vegan dishes for breakfast foods, soups, salads, main meals, and desserts.

"After introducing whole food pantry essentials ranging from ancient grains to superfoods, [Chaplin] presents mostly vegan and gluten-free recipes. [She] also offers lifestyle advice, weighing in on the benefits of cleansing and eating organic." Library Journal.

Whole food cooking every day : transform the way you eat with 250 vegetarian recipes free of gluten, dairy, and refined sugar / Amy Chaplin ; photographs by Anson Smart. Artisan, 2019 400 p. : **641.3**

1. Cooking (Natural foods). 2. Natural foods. 3. Recipes 4. Cookbooks

ISBN 9781579658021

LC 2018039183

Includes index.

The James Beard Award-winning author of a healthy eating cookbook shares her brilliant recipes incorporating whole foods that can transform a diet including Butternut Squash Soup with Toasted Hazelnut Milk and Sautěd Root Vegetables with Parsley, Poppy Seeds and Lemon. Illustrations.

Crosby, Guy

The **science** of good cooking : master 50 simple concepts to enjoy a lifetime of success in the kitchen / the editors at America's Test Kitchen and Guy Crosby ; illustrations by Michael Newhouse and John Burgoyne. America's Test Kitchen, 2012 xvii, 486 p. : **641.3**

1. Cooking. 2. Food. 3. Cookbooks.
ISBN 9781933615981

LC 2012012807

Collects tips and advice on cooking and provides answers to common culinary questions, including how to melt cheese well and how to create flaky pastry.

David, Laurie

The **family** cooks : 100+ recipes to get your family craving food that's simple, tasty, and incredibly good for you / Laurie David ; foreword by Katie Couric ; photographs by Quentin Bacon. Rodale Books, 2014. ix, 277 p. : **641.3**

1. Cooking (Natural foods) 2. Families -- Nutrition. 3. Recipes 4. Cookbooks.
ISBN 9781623362508

LC 2014003505

Includes index.

Citing high-priced marketing campaigns designed to promote processed foods, a guide to promoting long-term healthy eating habits shares more than 100 recipes that emphasize minimal preparation times, healthy ingredients and low-stress cooking practices.

"Written primarily for busy families with children, David's attractive guide to reclaiming the family dinner will also appeal to young couples and professionals trying to shop smarter and eat less-processed meals at home." Library Journal.

Dinki, Nikki

Meat on the side : delicious vegetable-focused recipes for every day / Nikki Dinki ; photographs by Ellen Silverman. St. Martin's Griffin, 2016 xviii, 270 p. : **641.3**

1. Cooking (Vegetables). 2. Cookbooks.
ISBN 9781250067166

LC 2015043188

Shares plant-based recipes that feature some meat.

"For those who like flexible recipes that can be both meaty and meatless, this cookbook provides excellent choices." Library Journal.

DiSpirito, Rocco

Rocco's healthy+delicious : more than 200 (mostly) plant-based recipes for everyday life / Rocco Dispirito. Harper Wave, 2017 xiii, 383 p. : **641.3**

1. Cooking (Natural foods). 2. Nutrition. 3. Vegan cooking. 4. Recipes 5. Cookbooks
ISBN 9780062378125

LC 2017012595

Includes index.

Presents the health benefits of eating a plant-based diet, with information about natural ingredients and a collection of recipes for snacks, smoothies, main dishes, sides, and desserts.

Fernandez-Armesto, Felipe

Near a thousand tables : a history of food / Felipe Fernandez-Armesto. The Free Press, 2002. xiii, 258 p. **641.3**

1. Food -- History. 2. Food habits. 3. Cooking -- History. 4. Agriculture -- History.
ISBN 0743226445

LC 2002023318

Originally published as: Food: A History.

IACP Cookbook Awards, Literary Food Writing, 2003.

"This is a well-written, thought-provoking overview of food history." Library Journal.

Foer, Jonathan Safran, 1977-

Eating animals / Jonathan Safran Foer. Little Brown & Co., 2009. 256 p. **641.3**

1. Vegetarianism. 2. Food -- Philosophy. 3. Animal welfare. 4. Meat industry and trade.
ISBN 9780316069908

LC 2009034434

Foer dissects our dietary choices in an intriguing look at why we eat the things we do.

Forte, Sara

The **sprouted** kitchen : a tastier take on whole foods / Sara Forte ; photography by Hugh Forte. Ten Speed Press, c2012. 241 p. : **641.3**

1. Cooking (Cereals) 2. Cooking (Natural foods) 3. Cooking, Sugar-free. 4. Recipes 5. Cookbooks.
ISBN 9781607741145

LC 2012008143

Includes index.

"Sara Forte showcases her tasty take on whole foods with 100 easy, produce-rich recipes that take advantage of whole grains, unsaturated fats, natural sugar alternatives, and bright, seasonal flavors".--Provided by publisher.

The **sprouted** kitchen bowl and spoon : simple and inspired whole foods recipes to savor and share / Sara Forte ; photography by Hugh Forte. Ten Speed Press, 2015. xxix, p. : **641.3**

1. Cooking (Natural foods) 2. Recipes 3. Salads. 4. Cookbooks.
ISBN 9781607746553

LC 2014036843

"Vegetarians and flexitarians will find plenty to love here, as will vegans, though they'll have fewer choices. Readers interested in healthy bowl foods may also like Ruth Tal and Jennifer Houston's Fresh: New Vegetarian and Vegan Recipes from Fresh Restaurants." Library Journal.

Ganeshram, Ramin

Future Chefs : recipes by tomorrow's cooks across the nation and the world / Ramin Ganeshram ; photography by Jean Paul Vellotti. Rodale, 2014 xi, 276 p. : **641.3**

1. Cooking -- United States. 2. Recipes 3. Teenage cooks -- United States. 4. Cookbooks
ISBN 1623362067

LC 2014025322

Includes index.

"A curated collection of 150 recipes drawn from the experience and kitchens of young cooks all over America and the world, FutureChefs brings exciting and unique recipes to your kitchen for you or your kids to make at home! Here you'll find the real, cooking-obsessed tweens and teens from diverse social and cultural backgrounds--the face of America's culinary future. Veteran journalist and trained chef Ramin Ganeshram has crafted profiles of serious young chefs whose experience varies from culinary contest winners and prolific food bloggers to brand new cooks in the kitchen. Whether these kids have taken to cooking out of necessity, inspiration, or sheer passion, their stories all share common threads of creativity, hard work, and a look at what's ahead in America's culinary scene. This generation is more interested in hands-on cooking than ever, but they're lacking the platform to showcase their talents. FutureChefs is the perfect vehicle for these kids to share their passion, their stories, and, of course, their recipes. "-- Provided by publisher.

Gascoyne, Kevin, 1966-

Tea : history, terroirs, varieties / Kevin Gascoyne, François Marchand, Jasmin Desharnais, and Hugo Americi. Firefly

Books, 2014. 271 p. : **641.3**

1. Cooking (Tea) 2. Recipes 3. Tea -- History. 4. Tea -- Varieties.
ISBN 1770853197

LC bl2014000503

"The Camellia Sinensis Tea House."

Offers a survey of tea through profiles of the areas around the world where the leaves of the Camellia sinensis plant are cultivated and harvested, along with information about its history, varieties, preparation, and health benefits.

"While there is no shortage of tea-related tomes, this definitive guide will appeal to die-hard tea enthusiasts interested in learning about the modern, global industry as well as the history and enjoyment of this ubiquitous beverage." Library Journal.

Garrett, Natalie Eve,

Eat joy : stories & comfort food from 31 celebrated writers / edited by Natalie Eve Garrett ; with illustrations by Meryl Rowin. Black Balloon Publishing, 2019. ix, 194 p. : **641.3**

1. Authors, American -- Miscellanea. 2. Comfort food. 3. Cooking. 4. Food habits. 5. Essays
ISBN 9781936787791

LC bl2019035371

Each essay is accompanied by a recipe.

Essays and recipes.

A collection of illustrated, personal essays about comfort foods from a number of celebrated literary writers, including Lev Grossman and Carmen Maria Machado, reveal the way these dishes helped them cope with dark times and pain.

"Garrett has selected the best kind of culinary writingunfussy recipes and heartfelt stories that use food as an avenue for reflection. Foodies and fiction readers alike will devour this excellent collection." Publishers Weekly.

Gaylard, Linda

The **tea** book / Linda Gaylard. DK, 2015 224 p. : **641.3**

1. Recipes 2. Tea. 3. Cookbooks
ISBN 1465436065

LC bl2015022434

Includes index.

A guide to tea explores the blends, tastings, and ceremonies from around the world, presents the health benefits of the beverage, and provides recipes for different types of tea and foods and other drinks incorporating it.

Hamilton, Gabrielle

★Prune / Gabrielle Hamilton. Random House, 2014 567 p. : **641.3**

1. Prune (Restaurant). 2. Cooking, French. 3. Cooking, American. 4. Recipes 5. Cookbooks.
ISBN 9780812994094

LC 2014003617

"A full repertoire of the many recipes served at the beloved Lower East Side restaurant Prune over the last thirteen years from one of America's most recognized chefs and established literary talents. The recipes are written from the unique perspective of cook to cook, as if Gabrielle were addressing her own line cooks, some seasoned, some green, with all of the essential elements provided to getting a dish just right--all presented in a way that will make total sense to home cooks, too".-- Provided by publisher.

"Recipes range from a complex cold pork with tuna sauce to a simple butter-and-sugar sandwich. Despite the books address to fellow restaurateurs, skilled home chefs can find a number of ways to profit from a fair number of Hamilton's creations." Booklist.

Hamshaw, Gena

Choosing raw : making raw foods part of the way you eat / Gena Hamshaw. Da Capo Lifelong, a member of the Perseus Books Group, 2014. x, 276 p. : **641.3**

1. Cooking (Natural foods) 2. Raw food diet. 3. Raw foods 4. Recipes 5. Cookbooks.
ISBN 9780738216874

LC 2014017394

A certified clinical nutritionist and author of the popular blog Choosing Raw, sharing the health journey that led her to a plant-based diet, presents 100 recipes for innovative and wholesome meals that are perfect for both newcomers and plant-based pros.

"Among vegan cookbooks, this volume will appeal most to those who are interested in better understanding a vegan diet and curious about raw foods. Cooks looking for vegan recipes without the raw focus have lots of other great recent titles to choose from, such as The Oh She Glows Cookbook by and Isa Does It by Isa Chandra Moskowitz." Library Journal.

Harbutt, Juliet,

World cheese book / editor-in-chief, Juliet Harbutt ; contributors, Androuet [and twenty others]. DK, 2015. 352 p. : **641.3**

1. Cheese. 2. Cooking (Cheese).
ISBN 9781465436054

LC 2015413323

Includes index.

Features over 750 of the world's most significant cheeses, and offers guidance on how to choose a cheese in accordance with occasion and personal taste.

"A must for cheese connoisseurs, this title will delight with its extensive detail and full-color, up-close pictures. The tasting and enjoyment notes for each entry will guide the new cheese enthusiast." Library Journal.

Helwig, Jenna

Baby-led feeding : a natural way to raise happy, independent eaters / Jenna Helwig with Natalia Stasenko, MS, RD. Houghton Mifflin Harcourt, 2018. 205 p. : **641.3**

1. Baby foods 2. Infants -- Weaning
ISBN 0544963407

LC 2017051889

Includes index.

What if you could skip the tiny jars and pouches of bland baby food in favor of a more natural, flavor-filled, and family-friendly transition to solid foods? Baby-led feeding (also known as baby-led weaning) is just that. Feeding your baby a variety of healthy, wholesome solid foods, rather than relying solely on purees, is thought to promote motor skills and establish lifelong healthy eating habits. Here, author and food editor at Parents magazine Jenna Helwig gives an easy-to-follow introduction to this popular new method. With more than 100 ideas and recipes, this bright, photo-driven book includes chapters on the benefits of this approach, when and how to get started, essential safety and nutrition guidelines, frequently asked questions, basic fruit and vegetable prep, more complex finger foods, and family meals. All recipes have been reviewed by a registered dietitian and include nutrition information to ensure a healthy mealtime. --From publisher description.

"The baby gets to choose (and have more variety) in this easy-to-use guide." Library Journal.

Hemphill, Ian, 1949-
The **spice** & herb bible / Ian Hemphill with recipes by Kate Hemphill. Robert Rose, 2014 800 p. : **641.3**
1. Spices. 2. Herbs. 3. Cooking (Spices). 4. Cooking (Herbs). 5. Cookbooks.
ISBN 9780778804963
LC 2014472224
Includes index.
"This truly beautiful and quite comprehensive volume will appeal to lovers of food, amateur and professional chefs, and everyone in between. While other works may address similar information, the author gives a personal touch to this one, which creates an uncommon warmth." Library Journal.

Hill, McKel
Nutrition stripped : whole-food recipes made deliciously simple / McKel Hill, MS, RDN. William Morrow, 2016 295 p. : **641.3**
1. Cooking (Natural foods). 2. Natural foods. 3. Recipes 4. Cookbooks.
ISBN 9780062419927
LC bl2016036178
Includes index.
Collects recipes from the Nutrition Stripped website, showing readers how to make simple, healthy meals, snacks, and beverages using whole foods.
"Best known for the anti-inflammatory turmeric milk recipe on her healthy living site, Nutrition Stripped, Hill offers elixirs and more in her first cookbook. But this is more than a cookbook; its a healthy living guide." Booklist.

Hoffman, James
The **world** atlas of coffee : from beans to brewing--coffees explored, explained, and enjoyed / James Hoffman. Firefly Books, 2014. 256 p. : **641.3**
1. Coffee.
ISBN 1770854703
LC bl2014051146
Includes index.
Provides an all-encompassing guide to coffee, presenting its origins and cultural impact, detailing where it is grown around the world, and chronicling the modern fascination with it.
"An unusual offering that will be of value in collections serving agriculture, business, and nutrition students." Library Journal.

Kass, Sam, 1980-
Eat a little better : great flavor, good health, better world / Sam Kass. Clarkson Potter/Publishers, 2018 287 p. : **641.3**
1. Cooking. 2. Health. 3. Nutrition. 4. Seasonal cooking 5. Cookbooks.
ISBN 9780451494948
LC 2017019841
Includes index.
Collects recipes from the former chef to the Obamas and White House food policy advisor features such dishes as slow roasted salmon and grilled rib eye, and shares recommendations for ecologically responsible grocery shopping, cooking, and eating.

Katzinger, Jennifer
Gluten-free & vegan pie : more than 50 sweet and savory pies to make at home / Jennifer Katzinger ; photographs by Charity Burggraaf. Sasquatch Books, 2013 xvii, 140 p. : **641.3**
1. Pies. 2. Vegan cooking. 3. Gluten-free diet 4. Baking 5. Cookbooks.
ISBN 9781570618680
LC 2012050141
Includes index.
Presents more than fifty-five gluten-free and vegan recipes, with tips and techniques for mixing and working with dough that doesn't contain butter or lard and for pie fillings that do not contain cream or eggs.
"Katzinger presents a breadth of pastry doughs, press-in crusts, and sweet and savory fillings that can be used to make pies, turnovers, cobblers, crisps, galettes, tarts, and more." Library Journal.

La Cerva, Gina Rae
Feasting wild : in search of the last untamed food / Gina Rae La Cerva. Greystone Books, [2020] xvi, 317 p. ; **641.3**
1. La Cerva, Gina Rae, 1983- Travel. 2. Wild foods. 3. Manners and customs 4. Natural foods. 5. Food habits.
ISBN 9781771645331
LC 2019458957
Challenging us to take a closer look at what we eat today, a geographer and anthropologist traces our relationship to wild foods and shows what we sacrifice when we domesticate them, including biodiversity, indigenous knowledge and a vital connection to nature.
"La Cerva's beautifully written narrative is as tantalizing as it is edifying." Publishers Weekly

Lakshmi, Padma
The **encyclopedia** of spices and herbs : an essential guide to the flavors of the world / Padma Lakshmi ; with Judith Sutton and Kalustyan's Spice Shop ; photographs by Evan Sung. Ecco, 2016 xii, 335 p. : **641.3**
1. Cooking (Herbs). 2. Cooking (Spices). 3. Herbs 4. Spices
ISBN 9780062375230
LC bl2016042330
The Emmy-nominated host of Top Chef presents an A-to-Z compendium of spices, herbs, salts, peppers and blends that combines sumptuous photography with culinary lore and advice.
"Cooks will appreciate Lakshmi's explanations of what goes into spice blends such as Chinese five spice powder, curries, dukkah, and garam masala. Full-color photographs appear every few pages, showing spices and herbs in various states, from just-harvested to finely ground." Library Journal.

Le, Stephen
One hundred million years of food : what our ancestors ate and why it matters today / Stephen Le. Picador, 2015. 384 p. **641.3**
1. Food -- History. 2. Nutrition. 3. Prehistoric humans -- Food 4. Human evolution.
ISBN 9781250050410
LC 2015029501
"An intriguing viewpoint on how dietary practices have changed over time, but further research is needed to support some of Le's healthy living recommendations." Library Journal.

Leonti, Adam
Flour lab : an at-home guide to baking, with freshly milled grains / Adam Leonti with Katie Parla ; foreword by Marc Vewtri ; .photographs by Andrew Thomas Lee. Clarkson Potter/ Publishers, 2019. 255 p. : **641.3**
1. Baking. 2. Flour. 3. Recipes 4. Cookbooks
ISBN 152476096X
LC 2018004040

Includes index.

A guide to sourcing and milling your own wheat to make flour at home, which is better-tasting and more nutritious than store-bought flours, contains 20 recipes for breads, pasta, pizza, cakes and pastries. Illustrations.

Lillien, Lisa

Hungry girl clean & hungry ; easy all-natural recipes for healthy eating in the real world / Lisa Lillien. St. Martin's Griffin, 2016 xix, 348 p. : **641.3**

1. Cooking (Natural foods). 2. Low-fat diet -- Recipes. 3. Cookbooks.
ISBN 9780312676773

LC 2015048585

Focuses on recipes that use natural ingredients and features such low-calorie dishes as Tex-Mex egg bakes, fork 'n' knife skillet pizza, blackened shrimp tacos, flourless chocolate cake, and clean and hungry blondies.

"Most readers will simply rejoice at the fact that pumpkin spice waffles, barbecue meatloaf, and fudgy flourless chocolate cake are now legit diet foods." Publishers Weekly.

McLagan, Jennifer

Odd bits : how to cook the rest of the animal / Jennifer McLagan ; photography by Leigh Beisch. Ten Speed Press, c2011. 248 p. : **641.3**

1. Cooking (Variety meats) 2. Cookbooks.
ISBN 9781580083348

LC 2011011575

A follow-up to the award-winning Bones and Fat provides accessible coverage of less-consumed, low-priced cuts and organ meats to counsel home cooks on how to prepare appetizing meals from such ingredients as oxtail, pork belly and marrow bones.

"A unique, informative, and readable cookbook. The ingredients used for the 100 recipes include lungs, necks, spleens, tongues, cheeks, testicles, and feet, as well as a few more common cuts (ribs, brisket, and shanks). In her introduction, McLagan traces the history of eating meat and why in earlier times the odd bits were considered the prime parts. In the last 75 to 100 years, most of these parts have been discarded or used for cat and dog food in the United States. McLagan encourages readers with a detailed and clear discussion of how to choose, prepare, and cook them. She draws the line at eyeballs and notes that lungs are not sold in the United States." Library Journal.

Medrich, Alice

★**Flavor** flours : a new way to bake with teff, buckwheat, sorghum, other whole & ancient grains, nuts & non-wheat flowers / Alice Medrich with Maya Klein. Artisan Books, 2014 368 p. : **641.3**

1. Baking. 2. Desserts 3. Flour. 4. Recipes 5. Cookbooks
ISBN 1579655130

LC 2014004631

Includes index.

Demonstrates how to bake with flour alternatives, presenting such recipes as silky butterscotch pudding, buckwheat cake with rose apples, bittersweet teff brownies,and sorghum cinnamon sticks.

Mitchell, Andie

Eating in the middle : a mostly wholesome cookbook / Andie Mitchell ; photographs by Aran Goyoaga. Clarkson Potter, 2016 240 p. : **641.3**

1. Cooking, American. 2. Diet. 3. Food. 4. Health. 5. Cookbooks
ISBN 0770433278

LC 2015034879

Includes index.

From the author of the New York times bestselling It was me all along, a cookbook for eating in balance, featuring mostly healthy recipes to help anyone stay fit, and a few "special occasion" sweets and entrees, with the author's moving story of weight loss and thoughts on managing cravings throughout. -- Publisher.

Montagne, Prosper, 1864-1948

★**Larousse** gastronomique : the world's greatest culinary encyclopedia / with the assistance of the Gastronomic Committee, President Joel Robuchon. Clarkson Potter/Publishers, c2009. 1206 p. : **641.3**

1. Cooking -- Encyclopedias. 2. Food -- Encyclopedias.
ISBN 9780307464910

LC 2009075160

Based on the work of Prosper Montagne.

Includes indexes.

This resource offers an index of classic and modern cooking techniques, tools of the trade, and recipes; four-color ingredient glossaries; culinary histories/biographies of the greatest chefs; full-color photos, including over four hundred behind-the-scenes images of upscale restaurants; and more.

"The alphabetical entries range in length from a few sentences to several pages. They cover types of food (Apples, Locusts); cooking techniques (Braising, Grilling); famous chefs (Auguste Escoffier, Alice Waters); culinary jobs (Matre d'htel, Sommelier); countries (China, Greece); and tools of the trade (Knife, Saucepan). This is an essential resource for most library reference collections as well as a wonderful book to browse." Booklist.

Olmsted, Larry

Real food/fake food : why you don't know what you're eating & what you can do about it / Larry Olmsted. Algonquin Books of Chapel Hill, 2016. 320 p. **641.3**

1. Food -- Quality. 2. Fraud. 3. Consumer education. 4. Artificial foods.
ISBN 9781616204211

LC 2016018797

"Published simultaneously in Canada by Thomas Allen & Son Limited."

"You've seen the headlines: Parmesan cheese made from sawdust. Lobster rolls containing no lobster at all. Extra virgin olive oil that isn't. Fake foods are in our supermarkets, our restaurants, and our kitchen cabinets. Award-winning food journalist and travel writer Larry Olmsted exposes the pervasive and dangerous fraud perpetrated on unsuspecting Americans. Real Food/Fake Food brings readers into the unregulated food industry, revealing the alarming truth: What we think we're eating is not what we're really eating.

"A provocative yet grounded look at the U.S. food industry. Though the prospect of finding quality food products may prove increasingly challenging for most consumers, Olmsted provides encouraging tips to help navigate the many obstacles." Kirkus.

Paltrow, Gwyneth, 1972-

The **clean** plate : eat, reset, heal / Gwyneth Paltrow ; photographs by Ditte Isager. Goop Press, Grand Central Life & Style, 2019. xvi, 268 p. : **641.3**

1. Cooking (Natural foods) 2. Detoxification (Health) 3. Recipes 4.

Cookbooks.
ISBN 9781538730461

LC 2018953666

Includes index.

Shares more than one hundred recipes that focus on clean ingredients, delicious flavors, and targeted health benefits, and includes meal plans, detoxes, and cleanses to address specific health needs in accordance with specialist recommendations.

Rathbone, Olivia

The **Occidental** Arts and Ecology Center cookbook : fresh-from-the-garden recipes for gatherings large and small / The OAEC Collective with Olivia Rathbone ; foreword by Alice Waters. Chelsea Green Publishing, 2015 ix, 404 p. ; **641.3**

1. Cooking (Natural foods). 2. Kitchen gardens. 3. Seasonal cooking 4. Recipes 5. Cookbooks.
ISBN 9781603585132

LC 2014043698

Collects two hundred recipes from the California-based farm, educational retreat, and ecology center, including such dishes as roasted fennel soup, crispy garlic scapes, curries mashua and potatoes, wild mushroom barley risotto, and blood peach torta.

" Vegetarians--and even omnivores who appreciate the diversity of veg-focused cuisine--will find much to love in this book from the Mother Garden." Booklist.

Robinson, Jo, 1947-

Eating on the wild side : the missing link to optimum health / Jo Robinson ; illustrations by Andie Styner. Little, Brown and Company, 2013. viii, 407 p. : **641.3**

1. Natural foods.
ISBN 9780316227940

LC 2013934815

Describes how to replace modern fruits and vegetables, which are high in starch and sugar and lower in nutrients than earlier generations of the plants, with different varieties, easily located in grocery stores and farmers markets, that have better nutritional value.

Rodale, Maria

Scratch : home cooking for everyone made simple, fun, and totally delicious / Maria Rodale, with Melanie Hansche ; photographs by Con Poulos and Stacey Cramp. Rodale, 2016 xxx, 352 p. : **641.3**

1. Comfort food. 2. Cooking. 3. Seasonal cooking 4. Cookbooks.
ISBN 9781623366438

LC 2016033950

Includes index.

"Maria Rodale was raised on real food. She doesn't think of eating homemade, from scratch meals as part of a trend or movement; it has always been her life. Raised in a family of farmers, bakers, chefs, gardeners, and publishers, Maria is used to growing, cooking, reading and writing about, and eating organic, delicious food. And now, for the first time ever, she's sharing her tried-and-true family recipes. Scratch is full of comfort food recipes that aren't focused on any one healthy trend, but are instead innately healthy, because Maria inspires you to return to your kitchen and cook with real, organic food. Recipes like Pasta Fagiole, Maria's Fried Chicken, and Lamb & Barley Soup will be crowd pleasers for sure, but Maria throws in some unique-to-the-family recipes that are going to delight as well, such as her Pennsylvania Dutch Dandelion Salad with Bacon Dressing, Ardie's Pasties, and Homemade Hoppin' John (a black-eyed pea stew made with smoked turkey or ham). Besides sharing her family's favorite recipes, Maria's book also gives you a peek into her life as a Rodale, with personal family portraits and stories. With this cookbook, you can eat like the Rodale family every night of the week with delicious food to make at home, from scratch. Naturally healthy, bacon included.".-- Provided by publisher.

"This down-to-earth, totally accessible cookbook will take any cook from breakfast to dessert." Publishers Weekly.

Rosenblum, Mort

Chocolate : a bittersweet saga of dark and light / Mort Rosenblum. North Point Press, 2005. 290 p. : **641.3**

1. Cacao -- History. 2. Chocolate -- History. 3. Cocoa industry and trade -- History.
ISBN 0865476357

LC 2004054734

IACP Cookbook Awards, Literary Food Writing, 2006.

A food journalist tackles one of the world's most popular narcotics--chocolate--in search of the biological, historical, and social reasons why this substance has so tantilized humans the world over.

"The author unveils chocolate's history and its various incarnations, including in his fresh and insightful discussions the origins of mole; the differences between, say, Hershey's kisses and Valrhona's products; the invention of Nutella; and the small boutique chocolate artisans found nearly everywhere. . . . A compelling and tasty read." Booklist.

Sacasa, Maria del Mar

The **quinoa** [keen-wah] cookbook / Maria del Mar Sacasa. HarperWave, 2015 xi, 193 p. : **641.3**

1. Cooking (Quinoa) 2. Cookbooks
ISBN 9780062411211

LC 2015009849

Includes index.

"Inspired by the success of health-minded, irreverent cookbooks such as Fifty Shades of Kale and Thug Kitchen, The Quinoa [KEEN-WAH] Cookbook offers a sendup of the latest hipster grain, along with 75 seriously delicious recipes. In the increasingly trend-driven and health-conscious food world, there are a handful of foods that inspire both admiration and irritation. Quinoa is one of them. Not only has it become as ubiquitous as kale salads or açai bowls on hipster café menus, it is also frustratingly difficult to pronounce and can be even more challenging to prepare. Enter The Quinoa [KEEN-WAH] Cookbook. With more than seventy-five fresh and fun takes on this ancient grain, foolproof cooking instructions for getting perfect results every time, and a nutritional overview that explains why everyone has gone quinoa-crazy, this cookbook will appeal to both quinoa converts and novices alike. Accompanied by gorgeous four-color photography, the cookbook features recipes for breakfast, lunch, dinner, snacks, and desserts, and will show readers inventive and often offbeat methods for utilizing the protein-rich grain in ways they'd never expect--such as quinoa tacos, a '50s-inspired quinoa casserole, and even quinoa cupcakes. Move over kale: it's quinoa's time to shine".-- Provided by publisher.

Sacks, Stefanie

What the fork are you eating? : an action plan for your pantry and plate / Stefanie Sacks, MS, CNS, CDN. Jeremy P. Tarcher/ Penguin, a member of Penguin Group, (USA), 2014 xviii, 380 p. ; **641.3**

1. Food additives 2. Grocery shopping 3. Natural foods 4. Nutrition
ISBN 9780399167966

LC 2014027015

"When your grocery list is full of items labeled "low-fat," "sugar-free," and even "natural," it's easy to assume that you're making healthy choices. Yet even some of those seemingly wholesome offerings contain chemical preservatives, pesticides, and artificial flavors and coloring that negatively affect your health. In WHAT THE FORK ARE YOU EATING?, a practical guide written by certified chef and nutritionist Stefanie Sacks, we learn exactly what the most offensive ingredients in our food are and how we can remove (or at least minimize) them in our diets. Sacks gives us an aisle-by-aisle rundown of how to shop for healthier items and create simple, nutritious, and delicious meals, including more than forty of her own recipes".-- Provided by publisher.

"While Sacks writes in a similar style to Marion Nestle and Michael Pollan, her book is more accessible and practical for people seeking the motivation and tools to follow a healthier lifestyle, emphasizing that even very small changes in diet can make a big difference in health. Although some readers may object to the mildly offensive language she deploys as part of her no-nonsense shtick, this is a valuable guide to evaluating, choosing, and preparing food for wellness." Library Journal.

Schatzker, Mark

The **Dorito** effect : the surprising new truth about food and flavor / Mark Schatzker. Simon & Schuster, 2015. 288 p. **641.3**

1. Junk food. 2. Nutrition. 3. Taste 4. Dieting
ISBN 9781476724218

LC 2014044543

The award-winning author of Steak argues that the key to reversing America's health crisis lies in the overlooked link between nutrition and flavor, explaining how technologically advanced but plentiful foods have been rendered less nutritious and taste-appealing.

"This is a provocative new take on American eating." Booklist.

Seo, Danny

Naturally, delicious : 100 recipes for healthy eats that make you happy / Danny Seo ; photographs by Armando Rafael. Pam Krauss Books / Avery, 2016 237 p. : **641.3**

1. Cooking (Natural foods). 2. Recipes 3. Quick and easy cooking 4. Quick and easy cooking 5. Cookbooks
ISBN 9781101905302

LC 2015038829

Includes index.

A collection of recipes from the sustainable lifestyle expert for preparing healthy, easy, organic meals, including such options as buckwheat pancakes with sauteed cinnamon apple, wilted spinach salad with coconut bacon, and Mexican shrimp skewers.

"Overall, this is an interesting approach to good-for-you food without sacrificing flavor and appeal." Publishers Weekly.

Thompson, Jennifer Trainer

Fresh fish : a fearless guide to grilling, shucking, searing, poaching and roasting seafood / Jennifer Trainer Thompson ; photographs by Keller + Keller. Storey Publishing, 2016 351 p. : **641.3**

1. Cooking (Fish). 2. Cookbooks.
ISBN 9781612128085

LC 2015041612

Includes index.

Collects recipes that showcase the versatility of seafood, including such options as curried lobster roll and New-Haven style white clam pizza, and offers tips on everything from shucking oysters and roasting whole fish to organizing a clambake.

Venezia, Ray

The **everyday** meat guide : a neighborhood butcher's advice book / Ray Venezia with Chris Peterson. Chronicle Books, 2016 184 p. : **641.3**

1. Meat. 2. Meat cuts. 3. Grocery shopping.
ISBN 9781452142883

LC 2015008240

Includes index.

Presents advice on choosing meat from a market, explaining grades, best values, and common cuts for poultry, pork, lamb, veal, and beef.

"Venezia clearly and succinctly leads consumers through the butcher shop, from poultry--including ducks, geese, turkey, and, of course, chicken--right up to beef." Library Journal.

Walker, Danielle (Chef)

Danielle Walker's Eat what you love : everyday comfort food you crave : gluten-free, dairy-free and paleo recipes / photographs by Aubrie Pick. Ten Speed Press, 2018 329 p. : **641.3**

1. Comfort food 2. Comfort food. 3. Cooking (Natural foods). 4. Cooking, American. 5. Cookbooks.
ISBN 9781607749448

LC 2017053030

Includes indexes.

The best-selling author of the Against All Grain series shares 125 recipes for gluten-free and paleo comfort foods for weeknight meals, featuring allergen-safe and healthful adaptations of such classics as fried chicken, sloppy Joes and chicken pot pie.

Ward, Tess, 1990-

The **naked** cookbook / Tess Ward ; photography by Columbus Leth. Ten Speed Press, 2015 128 p. : **641.3**

1. Cooking (Natural foods). 2. Health. 3. Cookbooks.
ISBN 9781607749943

LC 2015039084

Includes index.

Collects recipes composed of nutrient-rich and simple foods from the London-based food blogger and Le Cordon Bleu-trained chef, including such options as lamb meatballs with rhubarb sauce, Hainanese chicken, and chilled avocado and yogurt soup.

Weil, Andrew

Fast food, good food : more than 150 quick and easy ways to put healthy, delicious food on the table / Andrew Weil, MD ; photographs by Ditte Isager. Little, Brown and company, 2015. 293 p. : **641.3**

1. Cooking (Natural foods). 2. Quick and easy cooking 3. Recipes 4. Cookbooks
ISBN 9780316329422

LC 2015931944

Includes index.

These days, fewer people than ever are cooking meals at home. Convincing ourselves that we don't have time to cook, we've forgotten how fast, simple, and wonderfully satisfying it can be to prepare delicious meals in our own kitchens for the people we love. With guidance on following an anti-inflammatory diet and mouth-wateringly gorgeous photographs, FAST FOOD, GOOD FOOD will inspire the inner nutritionist and chef in every reader.

"Weil's accessible recipes will attract flexitarians, especially those with a penchant for seafood, vegetables, whole grains, and olive oil." Library Journal.

White, Dana Angelo

First bites : superfoods for babies and toddlers / Dana Angelo White, MS, RD, ATC. Perigree, 2015 xii, 180 p. ; **641.3**

1. Infants -- Nutrition. 2. Toddlers -- Nutrition. 3. Baby foods. 4.

Recipes 5. Cookbooks.
ISBN 9780399172465

LC 2014040028

A handy reference guide for parents of babies and toddlers offers more than 75 recipes using 50 superfoods that can be incorporated into nutritious meals masquerading as kid favorites--such as macaroni and cheese, pizza and chicken fingers--with minimal processing.

"Most parents eventually conclude that little ones can eat whatever healthy dish you are enjoying (just smash up or blend), but White's focus on the known 50 superfoods will get everyone off to a great start. Bon Appetit!" Library Journal.

Ying, Chris

The **wurst** of Lucky peach : a treasury of encased meat / Chris Ying and the editors of Lucky peach ; illustrations by Tim Lahan. Clarkson Potter/Publishers, 2016 240 p. : **641.3**

1. Cooking (Meat) 2. Recipes 3. Sausages. 4. Cookbooks
ISBN 0804187770

LC 2015038559

Includes index.

A cookbook culled from the quarterly journal of food and writing includes inspiration, advice, and support for cooks seeking to make sausage at home.

641.4 Food preservation and storage

America's Test Kitchen (Firm)

Foolproof preserving : a guide to small batch jams, jellies, pickles, condiments, and more / The editors at America's Test Kitchen. America's Test Kitchen, 2016 viii, 310 p. : **641.4**

1. Canning and preserving. 2. Jams and jellies 3. Condiments. 4. Cookbooks.
ISBN 9781940352510

LC 2015045561

Includes index.

A detailed guide to home preserving offers more than one hundred recipes, from sweet jams to whole fruits, along with detailed tutorials, troubleshooting tips, equipment information, and insight into the science behind canning.

"An exceptional resource for novice canners, though preserving veterans will find plenty here to love as well." Library Journal.

Atwood, Lisa

The **art** of preserving / authors, Lisa Atwood, Rebecca Courchesne, Rick Field ; photographer, France Ruffenach. Weldon Owen, c2010. 239 p. : **641.4**

1. Canning and preserving. 2. Food -- Preservation. 3. Recipes 4. Cookbooks
ISBN 9781740899789

LC bl2010017707

Includes index.

Provides instructions on how to preserve seasonal fruits and vegetables for year-round dishes, creating such items as jams, relishes, condiments, salsas, marmalades, pickled foods, sweet butters, and sauces.

Butcher, Meredith L.,

The **all** new Ball book of canning and preserving : over 350 of the best canned, jammed, pickled, and preserved recipes / editor: Meredith L. Butcher. Oxmoor House, 2016. 368 p. : **641.4**

1. Canning and preserving. 2. Recipes 3. Cookbooks.
ISBN 9780848746780

LC bl2016021312

Includes index.

A guide to preserving offers a wide assortment of recipes for classic jams, smoked favorites, and fermented foods organized by techniques ranging from water bath and pressure canning to freezing and dehydrating.

"These 200-plus recipes prove that jellies and chutneys, salsas and syrups contain enough seasoning magic to flavor any meal. The book also shows how thoroughly the experts at Ball approach the subject." Booklist.

Barrow, Cathy

Mrs. Wheelbarrow's practical pantry : recipes and techniques for year-round preserving / Cathy Barrow ; photographs by Christopher Hirsheimer and Melissa Hamilton. W.W. Norton, 2014 428 p. : **641.4**

1. Canning and preserving. 2. Recipes 3. Cookbooks
ISBN 9780393240733

LC 2014017291

A guide to preserving foods demonstrates how to make the most out of seasonal ingredients throughout the year, covering such preserving techniques as canning, salt-curing, smoking, and air-curing.

"Barrow offers a well-rounded look at home preserving and this book will appeal to those looking to expand their pantry." Library Journal.

Boetticher, Taylor

★**Jerky** : the Fatted Calf's guide to preserving & cooking dried meaty goods / Taylor Boetticher & Toponia Miller ; photography by Ed Anderson. Ten Speed Press, 2018 121 p. : **641.4**

1. Dried beef. 2. Dried meat 3. Meat -- Preservation. 4. Cooking (Meat). 5. Cookbooks
ISBN 9781524759025

LC 2017040523

Includes index.

"A cookbook dedicated to homemade jerky from the founders of San Francisco's Fatted Calf Charcuterie, with 40 easy-to-follow recipes perfect for home canners and preservers; hunters; followers of a Paleo, Keto, or high-protein diet; fans of dehydrators; or anyone looking to explore the centuries-old craft of drying meat".-- Provided by publisher.

Costenbader, Carol W.

The **big** book of preserving the harvest : 150 recipes for freezing, canning, drying and pickling fruits and vegetables / Carol W. Costenbader ; [foreword by Joanne Lamb Hayes]. Storey Books, c2002. iv, 347 p. : **641.4**

1. Canning and preserving. 2. Recipes 3. Cookbooks
ISBN 9781580174589

LC 2002021172

Includes index.

Learn how to preserve a summer day -- in batches -- from this classic primer on drying, freezing, canning, and pickling techniques. Did you know that a cluttered garage works just as well as a root cellar for cool-drying? That even the experts use store-bought frozen juice concentrate from time to time? With more than 150 easy-to-follow recipes for jams, sauces, vinegars, chutneys, and more, you'll enjoy a pantry stocked with the tastes of summer year-round. --From publisher description.

Day, Alex

★**Cocktail** codex : fundamentals, formulas, and evolutions /

Alex Day, Nick Fauchald, and David Kaplan. Ten Speed Press, 2018 ix, 309 p. : **641.4**

1. Bartending 2. Cocktails. 3. Flavor.
ISBN 9781607749707

LC 2018011137

From the authors of the best-selling and genre-defining cocktail book Death & Co, Coctail Codex is a comprehensive primer on the craft of mixing drinks that employs the authors' unique "cocktail families" approach to give drink-makers of every level the tools to understand, execute, and improvise both classic and original cocktails-- Provided by publisher.

"Experienced cocktail makers looking to take a deeper dive into mixology will find this to be a wonderfully detailed volume." Publishers Weekly.

Krissoff, Liana

Canning for a new generation : bold, fresh, flavors for the modern pantry / Liana Krissoff ; photographs by Rinne Allen. Abrams, 2016. 399 p. : **641.4**

1. Canning and preserving. 2. Fruit -- Preservation. 3. Vegetables -- Preservation. 4. Recipes 5. Cookbooks
ISBN 9781617691850

LC 2015949289

The revised and expanded edition of the bestselling resource for canning and preserving, with 50 new recipes plus all-new sidebars and tips. --From publisher description.

MacKenzie, Jennifer

The **complete** book of pickling : 250 recipes from pickles & relishes to chutneys & salsas / Jennifer MacKenzie. Robert Rose, c2009. 335 p. : **641.4**

1. Canning and preservation. 2. Pickles. 3. Cooking (Relishes) 4. Chutney. 5. Cookbooks
ISBN 9780778802167

LC bl2011004724

Includes index.

Offers an overview on canning food at home, instructions on the process, and over two hundred recipes for pickles, relishes, chutneys, and salsas.

"This is a terrific collection of 250 pickles, sauces, chutneys and relishes. Even readers without an appreciation for the tang of a good pickle will appreciate MacKenzie's 50 chutneys, including variations such as Sangria Citrus, classic cranberry and peach, pineapple ginger and spiced tomato; six chili sauces; 18 salsas; and homemade ketchup." Publishers Weekly.

Macdonald, Emma (Chef)

Artisan preserving : a complete collection of classic and contemporary ideas / Emma Macdonald ; with Susanna Tee. Nourish, 2014. 223 p. : **641.4**

1. Canning and preserving. 2. Recipes 3. Cookbooks.
ISBN 9781848991958

LC bl2014049114

Includes index.

Shares over two hundred recipes for preserving everything from fruits and vegetables to meat, flowers, and nuts, featuring such options as pink grapefruit and elderflower marmalade, lemon curd, and pickled black grapes.

"This chic, thoughtful overview of many types of food preservation has the potential to become a staple for novice and veteran cooks alike." Library Journal.

West, Kevin, 1970-

Saving the season : a cook's guide to home canning, pickling, and preserving / Kevin West. Alfred A. Knopf, 2013. 532 p. : **641.4**

1. Canning and preserving. 2. Seasonal cooking 3. Recipes 4. Cookbooks
ISBN 9780307599483

LC 2012037844

"A stylish, richly illustrated, practical guide for home cooks and preserving enthusiasts, the first cookbook from journalist Kevin West, author of the popular blog Savingtheseason.com. Incorporating classic favorites and new flavors, West gives us more than one hundred recipes, organized by season, for sweet preserves and savory pickles; easy-to-can vegetables and fruits; condiments such as relishes, chutneys, and salsas; and cordials, candies, and cocktails. Interspersed with the recipes are chroniclesof West's travels and the history of American preserving traditions from California to New Mexico to Long Island. A witty and erudite culinary companion, West makes a rich and entertaining story of the introductions to the recipes. Also included is a primer on preserving techniques that addresses issues of food safety and nutrition".-- Provided by publisher.

Kingry, Judi

Complete book of home preserving : 400 delicious and creative recipes for today / edited by Judi Kingry and Lauren Devine. R. Rose, 2006. 448 p., 32 p. of plates : **641.4**

1. Canning and preserving. 2. Cooking (Fruit) 3. Cooking (Vegetables) 4. Recipes 5. Cookbooks
ISBN 9780778801399

LC 2007701974

Includes index.

Encompassing four hundred delicious recipes, a comprehensive guide to home preserves features a wide array of salsas, savory sauces, chutneys, pickles, relishes, jams, jellies, fruit spreads, and more, along with complete instructions for safe canning and preserving methods, lists of essential equipment and kitchen utensils, and handy cooking tips.

641.5 Cooking

Acheson, Hugh

The **chef** and the slow cooker : a cookbook / Hugh Acheson ; photographs by Andy Lee. Clarkson Potter/Publishers, 2017 256 p. **641.5**

1. Electric cooking 2. Quick and easy cooking 3. Cookbooks.
ISBN 9780451498540

LC 2017011173

Presents a collection of recipes for the slow cooker, including options for broths, soups, beans, meats, fish, vegetables, butters, chutneys, and desserts.

Ahern, Shauna James

Gluten-free girl every day / Shauna James Ahern, with Daniel Ahern ; photography by Penny De Los Santos. Houghton Mifflin Harcourt, c2013. 319 p. : **641.5**

1. Gluten-free diet 2. Recipes 3. Cookbooks
ISBN 111811521X

LC 2012030520

Includes index.

Presents a cookbook for busy people that focuses on gluten-free lifestyles and seasonal vegetables, sharing practical tips for stocking a pantry and baking without gluten while providing a variety of options.

Alford, Jeffrey

★**Hot,** sour, salty, sweet : a culinary journey through Southeast Asia / Jeffrey Alford and Naomi Duguid ; studio photographs by Richard Jung ; location photographs by Jeffrey Alford and Naomi Duguid. Artisan, c2000. 346 p. : **641.5**

1. Gastronomy 2. Voyages and travels 3. Cooking, Southeast Asian. 4. Food -- Southeast Asia. 5. Southeast Asia.
ISBN 1579651143

LC 00022092

"Part travel essay and part culinary exploration, this is a perfect choice for both adventurous cooks and armchair travelers." Library Journal.

Ali, Laila

Food for life : delicious & healthy comfort food from my table to yours! / Laila Ali ; with Leida Scheintaub. St. Martin's Press, 2017 312 p. : **641.5**

1. Comfort food. 2. Cooking. 3. Cookbooks.
ISBN 9781250131096

LC 2017045756

Collects one hundred hearty and flavor-focused recipes that can fit into any busy schedule, including oven "fried" chicken, cheesy cauliflower pizza, and heavenly lemon yogurt cake.

The **New** York Times passover cookbook : more than 200 holiday recipes from top chefs and writers / edited by Linda Amster. Morrow, c1999. xxii, 328 p. : **641.5**

1. Holiday cooking 2. Kosher food 3. Passover cooking. 4. Recipes 5. Cookbooks
ISBN 0688155901

LC 98041282

A compendium of recipes for Passover covers all the favorites and taps the wisdom of Wolfgang Puck, Barbara Kafka, Joyce Goldstein, and other renowned food critics

"This book's recipes range from the traditional to the innovative and are drawn from European, Mediterranean and Middle Eastern traditions. Amster has produced what may be the definitive word in Passover cookbooks, from recipes to the feelings evoked by sitting at a beautifully set, bountifully laden table." Publishers Weekly.

America's Test Kitchen (Firm),

Easy everyday keto : healthy kitchen-perfected recipes / America's Test Kitchen. America's Test Kitchen, 2020 ix, 246 p. : **641.5**

1. Ketogenic diet. 2. Low-carbohydrate diet 3. Dieting 4. Quick and easy cooking 5. Cookbooks.
ISBN 9781948703123

LC 2019053814

Includes index.

Keeping mealtime easy but interesting, this meticulously tested, must-have collection of foolproof recipes for naturally keto dishes delivers inspiration, variety and great taste to help make your keto goals achievable.

"This information-packed volume rises above the rest of the keto cookbooks." Publishers Weekly

America's Test Kitchen (Firm)

The **America's** Test Kitchen healthy family cookbook : a new, healthier way to cook everything from America's most trusted test kitchen / the editors at America's Test Kitchen ; photography, Daniel J. Van Ackere, Carl Tremblay. America's Test Kitchen, 2010. viii, 520 p. : **641.5**

1. Cooking, American. 2. Recipes 3. Cookbooks.
ISBN 9781933615561

LC bl2010029410

Includes index.

Spiral binding.

Presents advice on cooking techniques, equipment, food preparation, and selection of ingredients, along with more than 750 recipes for healthy dishes, including appetizers, soups, meats, fish, vegetables, sauces, breads, and desserts.

"[A] well-tested collection of more than 750 recipes that employ vetted techniques and abundant flavor to create dishes that are as healthy as they can be, given what they are, without sacrificing a pleasurable eating experience." Publishers Weekly.

America's Test Kitchen (Firm)

The **make-ahead** cook : 8 smart strategies for dinner tonight / the editors at America's Test Kitchen. America's Test Kitchen, 2014 328 p. : **641.5**

1. Dinners and dining. 2. Make-ahead cooking. 3. Recipes 4. Cookbooks.
ISBN 9781936493845

LC 2014014386

Includes index.

Perfect for cooks who are pressed for time, a revolutionary resource for make-ahead cooking, going way beyond the freezer, presents eight smart new strategies and more than 150 recipes, including oven-ready casseroles, slow-cooker favorites, make-ahead braises and more.

"Indispensable for busy families and anyone who has limited time to cook during the week." Library Journal.

Anderson, Pam, 1957-

How to cook without a book : recipes and techniques every cook should know by heart / Pam Anderson. Broadway Books, 2000. 290 p. ; **641.5**

1. Quick and easy cooking. 2. Recipes 3. Cookbooks.
ISBN 9780767902793

LC 99043776

Recalling an earlier era when cooks relied on sight, touch, and taste rather than cookbooks, the author encourages readers to rediscover the lost art of preparing food and use their imagination in the kitchen.

"Former executive editor of Cook's magazine and author of The Perfect Recipe, Anderson wants to teach Americans a new way to cook without relying on recipes. It's somewhat surprising, then, to discover that this book is full of recipes. However, readers may cotton to Anderson's method: each chapter consists of a simple technique, basic recipe, variations, key points and a little mnemonic device used to recall the technique. The techniques are, for the most part, terrific time-savers." Publishers Weekly.

Andres, Jose, 1969-

Vegetables unleashed : a cookbook / Jose Andres and Matt Goulding ; photography by Peter Frank Edwards. Ecco, 2019 357 p.. : **641.5**

1. Cooking (Vegetables) 2. Vegetarian cooking. 3. Recipes 4. Cookbooks
ISBN 9780062668387

LC bl2019014702

"An Anthony Bourdain book."

Includes index.

A world-renowned Spanish chef and an award-winning food author present a collection of tricks and tips that focus on the vibrancy and diversity of vegetable-based dishes such as lentil stew, vegetable paella and the classic Spanish gazpacho.

"Recommendations for composting, in-season and farmer's-market shopping, and using seeds and scraps all underscore their waste-reducing ethos and their goal to get people excited about things that sprout from the ground." Booklist.

Aron, Jules

★**Vegan** cheese : simple, delicious, plant-based recipes / Jules Aron. The Countryman Press, 2017 190 p. : **641.5**

1. Cheese -- Varieties. 2. Dairy substitutes. 3. Recipes 4. Vegan cooking. 5. Cookbooks

ISBN 9781581574036

LC oc2018007570

Includes index.

"Aron's book is a useful, fun, and necessary addition to both the beginner and advanced vegan cooks repertoire." Publishers Weekly.

Batali, Mario

Italian grill / Mario Batali with Judith Sutton ; photography by Beatriz Da Costa. Ecco, c2008. 246 p. : **641.5**

1. Barbecuing 2. Cooking, Italian

ISBN 9780061450976

LC bl2008010757

Includes index.

A collection of eighty recipes for grilled Italian food is divided into categories for antipasti, pizza, meat, fish, and vegetables, and includes information on grilling basics, different heat-source options, and differences in grilling equipment.

"This is an essential collection for any serious backyard cook." Publishers Weekly.

Beard, James, 1903-1985

★**James** Beard's American cookery / James Beard ; with illus. by Earl Thollander. Little, Brown 1972 877 p. **641.5**

1. Cooking, American. 2. Recipes 3. Cookbooks.

ISBN 9780316085663

LC 70165755

An illustrated, nostalgic excursion into America's culinary past presents more than fifteen hundred of Beard's favorite--and most popular--recipes, suitable for all levels of cooking skills and all types of entertainment.

"Comprehensive in scope the cookbook gives eighteenth-and nineteenth-century recipes as well as modern directions for preparation of a full range of U.S. cookery. The format is attractive and the historical data add to the value of an authoritative guide." Booklist.

Berry, Mary, 1935-

Cooking with Mary Berry. / Mary Berry. DK Publishing, 2016. 256 p. : **641.5**

1. Cooking. 2. Recipes 3. Cookbooks.

ISBN 9781465459510

LC bl2016040254

Includes index.

In her first cookbook for Americans, a British food writer and television host offers 150 of her favorite recipes, including Butternut Squash Soup, Chicken With Sage and Orange, Chelsea Buns and Lemon Cheesecake.

"This is a basic, go-to volume, with the flair that Berry's growing U.S. fan base will expect." Booklist.

The **best** international recipe : a best recipe classic / the editors of Cook's illustrated ; photography, Daniel J. Van Ackere and Carl Tremblay ; illustrations, John Burgoyne. America's Test Kitchen, c2007. xii, 579 p. : A Best Recipe Classic **641.5**

1. International cooking. 2. Recipes 3. Cookbooks

ISBN 9781933615172

LC 2010281412

Includes index.

Collects three hundred fifty favorite recipes from around the world, arranged by country of origin and providing step-by-step instructions, advice, and tips for preparation.

Better Homes & Gardens fast or slow : delicious meals for slow cookers, pressure cookers, or multicookers. / Better Homes and Gardens Books (COR). Houghton Mifflin Harcourt, 2018. 304 p. : **641.5**

1. Electric cooking, Slow. 2. Pressure cooking. 3. Cookbooks

ISBN 9781328918499

LC 2018006349

Includes index.

The iconic cooking brand provides delicious recipes that can be made in either the Crock-Pot, pressure cooker or the Instant Pot, with instructions for both slow-cooking and quick-prep meals.

Better Homes and Gardens new cook book J. Wiley, c2010. 660 p. (loose-leaf) : **641.5**

1. Cooking. 2. Recipes 3. Cookbooks

ISBN 9780470556863

LC 2010025417

Includes index.

"The updated and revised 15th edition of America's favorite cookbook The Better Homes and Gardens New Cook Book has been an American favorite since 1930, selling 40 million copies through fourteen editions. This new 15th Edition is the best yet, with hundreds of all-new recipes and a fresh, contemporary style. Plenty of new chapters have been added to meet the needs of today's everyday cooks, including new chapters on breakfast and brunch, casseroles, and convenience cooking. 1,000 photos accompany this wide selection of recipes, which cover everything from Pad Thai to a Thanksgiving turkey. NEW FEATURES: icons that call out fast, healthy, or classic dishes; an expanded and revised chapter on canning and freezing foods; and new chapters on pizza, sandwiches, wraps, and more. Presents more than 1,200 recipes, including 750 brand new to this edition. More than 800 helpful step-by-step, how-to images and photos. New suggestions for personalizing family dinners, new twists on favorite dishes, and plenty of recipes that yield leftovers you can use again in other recipes. Better Homes and Gardens New Cook Book, 15th Edition covers it all! Completely revised, revamped and updated, this is a must for every kitchen."--Provided by publisher.

Better Homes and Gardens new cook book Houghton Mifflin Harcourt, 2018. 708 p. : **641.5**

1. Cooking. 2. Recipes 3. Cookbooks.

ISBN 9781328498854

LC 2018028246

Includes index.

Presents hundreds of new recipes along with traditional favorites; includes chapters on breakfast, casseroles, and convenience cooking; and features a bonus chapter of food gifts and packaging ideas.

Bianco, Chris

Bianco : pizza, pasta, and other food I like / Chris Bianco. Ecco, 2016 xi, 212 p. : **641.5**

1. Cooking, Italian 2. Cooking. 3. Pizza. 4. Recipes 5. Cookbooks

ISBN 9780062224378

LC bl2017039570

Includes index.

An award-winning chef presents the basic techniques of pizza making, with a discussion on dough, tomato sauce, and ingredients and options for pizza, sandwiches, pasta, and vegetable sides.

"Thanks to Bianco's focus on simple recipes and outstanding ingredients, home cooks get appealing, classic dishes great for any day of the week." Publishers Weekly.

Bittman, Mark

Dinner for everyone : 100 iconic dishes made 3 ways--easy, vegan, or perfect for company / Mark Bittman ; photographs by Ava Brackett. Clarkson Potter/Publishers, 2019 432 p. : **641.5**

1. Cooking. 2. Quick and easy cooking. 3. Recipes 4. Cookbooks
ISBN 9780385344760

LC 2018003810

Includes index.

Provides instructions for one hundred dishes with three variations, easy, complex, and vegan.

"The all-out, or perfect-for-company recipes are for those who wish to take their time and cook for pleasure, not survival." Library Journal.

How to cook everything fast : a better way to cook great food / Mark Bittman ; illustrations by Olivia de Salve Villedieu. Houghton Mifflin Harcourt, 2014. 1056 p. : **641.5**

1. Quick and easy cooking. 2. Quick and easy cooking 3. Quick and easy cooking 4. Cookbooks.
ISBN 9780470936306

LC bl2014041639

Includes index.

Demonstrates how to minimize cooking times while becoming more intuitive in the kitchen, sharing hundreds of simple, flavorful dishes that can be prepared in fifteen to forty-five minutes.

"Bittman's latest is fantastic for busy, novice, and noncooks. It's also a practical tool for anyone who aspires but struggles to cook more often." Library Journal.

★**How** to cook everything : simple recipes for great food / Mark Bittman ; illustrations by Alan Witschonke. J. Wiley, c2019. viii, 951 p. **641.5**

1. Cooking. 2. Recipes 3. Quick and easy cooking 4. Cookbooks
ISBN 9781328545435

LC 2008018984

A full-color 20th-annivesary edition includes hundreds of brand new features, recipes and variations plus old favorites from the previous editions, in many cases reimagined with new methods or flavors.

"The author presents more than 1000 basic recipes and simple and inventive variations. The enormous breadth of recipes along with Bittman's engaging, straightforward prose will appeal to cooks looking for reliable help with kitchen fundamentals." Publishers Weekly.

★**How** to cook everything : the basics / Mark Bittman ; photography by Romulo Yanes. Wiley, c2012. ix, 486 p. : **641.5**

1. Cooking. 2. Recipes 3. Cookbooks
ISBN 9780470528068

LC 2011048881

Includes index.

The New York Times columnist and author demonstrates fundamental cooking techniques while providing 171 recipes using basic staples and methods, covering everything from equipping a kitchen and stocking a pantry to making food selections and performing essential cooking tasks.

★**How** to cook everything vegetarian : simple meatless recipes for great food / Mark Bittman ; photography by Burcu Avsar & Zach DeSart ; illustrations by Alan Witschonke. Houghton Mifflin Harcourt, 2017. 830 p. : **641.5**

1. Cooking (Vegetables) 2. Recipes 3. Vegetarian cooking. 4. Cookbooks
ISBN 1118455649

LC 2017051874

Includes index.

Provides more than one thousand recipes and variations for simple meatless meals, including salads, soups, dairy, vegan, vegetables, fruit, pasta, grains, legumes, and meat substitutes.

"Bittman's evenhanded tone and his ability to cover a gamut of recipes . . . render this book as relevant today as it was when it first appeared, and confirm its status as an indispensable resource." Publishers Weekly.

Mark Bittman's kitchen express : 404 inspired seasonal dishes you can make in 20 minutes or less / Mark Bittman. Simon & Schuster, 2009. 233 p. ; **641.5**

1. Quick and easy cooking. 2. Seasonal cooking 3. Recipes 4. Cookbooks
ISBN 9781416575665

LC 2008054823

Presents over four hundred recipes that require short preparation times, organized by the season in which the meal's ingredients are fresh and enjoyed best.

"Bittman here offers a sampling of 404 inspiring recipes. The no-sweat recipes are divided into four sections: summer, fall, winter and spring, capitalizing on the freshest ingredients of each season while whittling down the prep time of ordinarily elaborate dishes like coq au vin and ricotta cheesecake to 10 minutes or less. The book includes a drill-down of how best to stock your kitchen, and given the impromptu nature of the book, the substitution grid proves indispensable." Publishers Weekly.

Mark Bittman's kitchen matrix : more than 700 simple recipes and techniques to mix and match for endless possibilities / Mark Bittman. Pam Krauss Books, 2015 304 p. : **641.5**

1. Cooking. 2. Recipes 3. Cookbooks.
ISBN 9780804188012

LC 2015020733

An anthology of the best-selling food writer's popular Matrix writings is presented in the form of a boldly graphic cookbook that features single ingredients served up a dozen ways to demonstrate the versatility of recipe alterations.

"This unconventional cookbook can help proficient cooks develop ideas for creating their own recipe variations." Library Journal.

The **VB6** cookbook : more than 350 recipes for healthy vegan meals all day and delicious flexitarian dinners at night / Mark Bittman ; photographs by Quentin Bacon. Clarkson Potter/Publishers, 2014 272 p. : **641.5**

1. Recipes 2. Reducing diets 3. Vegan cooking 4. Cookbooks
ISBN 9780385344821

LC 2013050637

Includes index.

A companion to the Minimalist host's best-selling VB6 provides a broad selection of everyday vegan and vegetable-forward meals while outlining the potential health benefits of a diet that focuses on fruits and vegetables while minimizing meats and dairy.

"Rather than overload readers with prescriptive rules, unfamiliar ingredients, and complicated preparations, Bittman gives them a memorable charge (eat more plants, less meat and processed foods) and tools to help them follow it." Library Journal.

VB6 : eat vegan before 6:00 to lose weight and restore your health... for good : the flexible diet you can really stick to, with more than 60 easy, delicious recipes / Mark Bittman ; foreword by Dean Ornish, M.D. Clarkson Potter/Publishers, 2013. xi,

276 p. ; **641.5**
1. Vegan cooking. 2. Dieting 3. Cookbooks.
ISBN 9780385344746
LC 2012046866

The popular New York Times columnist builds on the theories of his hit book, Food Matters, to outline a menu plan that eliminates meat and animal products throughout the day to promote weight loss and overall better health.

Blais, Richard, 1972-

So good : 100 recipes from my kitchen to yours / Richard Blais with Mary Goodbody ; photography by Evan Sung. Houghton Mifflin Harcourt, 2017. 255 p. ; **641.5**
1. Cooking. 2. Cookbooks.
ISBN 9780544663312
LC 2017017426

Includes index.

The television personality and restaurateur presents recipes that he cooks in his own kitchen, including rabbit au vin, triple-cooked fries, and marshmallow ice cream.

"Home cooks interested in upping their game will want to give this one a look." Publishers Weekly.

Blue Apron Culinary Team,

The **Blue** Apron cookbook : 165 essential recipes and lessons for a lifetime of home cooking / from the Blue Apron Culinary Team. Harper Wave, 2017 ix, 389 p. : **641.5**
1. Cooking. 2. Cooking (Natural foods). 3. Recipes 4. Quick and easy cooking 5. Cookbooks
ISBN 9780062562760
LC 2017018933

Includes index.

Combining simple, delicious and original recipes with culinary education, the trusted national brand and beloved meal-delivery service presents 165 step-by-step, technique-driven dishes that will transform novice cooks into confident home chefs.

Bourdain, Anthony

Appetites : a cookbook / Anthony Bourdain, with Laurie Woolever. HarperCollins 2016. 320 p. **641.5**
1. Cooking 2. Dinners and dining 3. Cooking for families 4. Cooks
ISBN 9780062409959
LC 2017394114

Draws on more than four decades of professional cooking and world traveling, as well as the author's more recent experiences as a father, to present a collection of personal home-cooking favorites that deconstructs the structural aspects of satisfying meals.

"In what might be his most accessible book yet, Bourdain reveals his 'Ina Gartenlike need to feed the people around me' with a terrific collection of recipes for family and friends." Publishers Weekly.

Bracken, Peg

The **I** hate to cook book / Peg Bracken ; with a new foreword by Jo Bracken ; drawings by Hilary Knight. Grand Central Pub., 2010. xiv, 207 p. ; **641.5**
1. Cooking. 2. Recipes
ISBN 0446545929
LC 2009001249

"50th Anniversary Edition."

Includes index.

A commemorative edition of a classic, humorous cookbook includes more than 180 easy recipes for those who fear the kitchen, from Philosopher's Chowder and Skinny Meatloaf to Fat Man's Shrimp and Immediate Fudge Cake.

Britton, Sarah

Naturally nourished : healthy, delicious meals made with everyday ingredients / Sarah Britton. Clarkson Potter/Publishers, 2017 240 p. : **641.5**
1. Vegetarian cooking 2. Cooking (Natural foods) 3. Nutrition 4. Cookbooks.
ISBN 9780804185400
LC 2018139474

Includes index.

An acclaimed holistic nutritionist and blogger simplifies whole food, vegetarian cooking for any budget and any night of the week with 100 recipes including Grilled Caesar Salad, Cauliflower Steaks, Baked Feta and Stone Fruit Ginger Salad.

Brown, Leanne

★**Good** and cheap : eat well on $4/day / Leanne Brown. Workman Publishing, 2015 xviii, 190 p. : **641.5**
1. Low budget cooking. 2. Recipes 3. Cookbooks
ISBN 0761184996
LC 2015011072

"A special edition of Good and Cheap."

Includes index.

A call-to-arms guide to ending hunger shares 120 recipes for satisfying, healthful meals on a daily budget equivalent to the amount of government food-stamp allowances, offering complementary information about economical cooking methods.

"Brown estimates the cost per serving for all dishes, including potato leek pizzas, dark and spicy chili, and peanut chicken and broccoli with coconut rice." Library Journal.

Byres, Tim

Smoke : new firewood cooking : how to build flavor with fire, on the grill and in the kitchen / Tim Byres ; photography by Jody Horton. Rizzoli, 2013. 255 p. : **641.5**
1. Barbecuing. 2. Cooking (Smoked foods). 3. Outdoor cooking. 4. Cookbooks.
ISBN 9780847839797
LC 2012950104

Shares recipes for imbuing foods with smoky flavors, including vegetables, seafood, poultry, meats, and sweets, and discusses techniques for stovetop smoking, grilling with wood planks, and building firepits and spit roasts.

Calderone, Athena

Cook beautiful / Athena Calderone ; photography by Johnny Miller. Abrams, 2017. 288 p. : **641.5**
1. Cooking. 2. Party decorations. 3. Recipes 4. Seasonal cooking. 5. Cookbooks
ISBN 1419726528
LC 2016960601

"Creator of Eyeswoon."

Includes index.

A collection of recipes by the creator of EyeSwoon includes such offerings as cherry and apricot polenta crisp, delicata squash agrodolce, and blood orange bundt cake with orange bitters glaze.

Carruthers, John

Eat street : the ManBQue guide to making street food at home / John Carruthers, John Scholl and Jesse Valenciana ; photography by Clayton Hauck. Running Press, 2016 328 p. : **641.5**

1. Street food. 2. Barbecuing. 3. Recipes 4. Cookbooks
ISBN 9780762458691

LC bl2016016903

Includes index.

The creators of ManBQue share recipes for two hundred street foods from around the world, including bacon s'mores, jalapeno popper pizza, and triple-peach fried pies.

Cavallari, Kristin, 1987-

True roots : a mindful kitchen with more than 100 recipes free of gluten, dairy, and refined sugar / Kristin Cavallari, with Mike Kubiesa. Rodale, 2018 xviii, 252 p. : **641.5**

1. Cooking (Natural foods) 2. Gluten-free diet 3. Milk-free diet 4. Recipes 5. Cookbooks.
ISBN 9781623369163

LC bl2018055271

Includes index.

A collection of healthy, clean-eating recipes from the actress and New York times bestselling author features such dishes as butternut squash pancakes, leek and zucchini quiche, raw honey planked salmon, and zesty quinoa salad.

Cayne, Alison

The **Haven's** Kitchen cooking school : recipes and inspiration to build a lifetime of confidence in the kitchen / Alison Cayne. Artisan, 2017 374 p. : **641.5**

1. Haven's Kitchen (Firm). 2. Cooking. 3. Seasonal cooking 4. Recipes 5. Quick and easy cooking 6. Cookbooks.
ISBN 9781579656737

LC 2016038079

Includes index.

Presents cooking basics for beginners, discussing how to season vegetables and which knives to use for particular tasks, and includes such recipes as apple beignets, poached eggs, and beef bourguignon.

"This book will remain a staple in kitchens long after readers have mastered the basics of boiling an egg and searing a steak." Publishers Weekly.

Chang, Joanne

Baking with less sugar : recipes for desserts using natural sweeteners and little-to-no white sugar / Joanne Chang of Flour Bakery + Cafe. Chronicle Books, 2015 200 p. ; **641.5**

1. Baking. 2. Recipes 3. Sugar-free diet 4. Cookbooks
ISBN 145213300X

LC 2014023855

Includes index.

Shares over sixty recipes for desserts that use very little or no refined white sugar and instead rely on chocolate, honey, maple syrup, molasses, and fruit as sweeteners.

Chapple, Justin

Just cook it! : 145 built-to-be-easy recipes that are totally delicious / Justin Chapple ; photography by David Malosh. Houghton Mifflin Harcourt, 2018. 288 p. : **641.5**

1. Quick and easy cooking. 2. Recipes 3. Cookbooks.
ISBN 9780544968837

LC 2017051913

Includes index.

Presents quick and easy recipes from the Test Kitchen Editor of Food & Wine, including such dishes as avocado pizza, cassoulet, oven-fried cornflake chicken, and butter-basted scallops, along with time-saving tips and hacks.

"Folksy introductions to each recipe, good tips (go ahead and wash mushrooms quickly), and favorite dishes--red-curry peanut soup, classic meat-loaf sandwiches and tomato jam, chocolate-peanut pie, Reuben toast with poached eggs--done simply and well make this a must-have." Booklist.

Child, Julia

★The **way** to cook / Julia Child ; photographs by Brian Leatart and Jim Scherer. Knopf, 1989. xi, 511 p. : **641.5**

1. Cooking.
ISBN 9780394532646

LC 88045838

Includes index.

Blending classic techniques with free-style American cooking and emphasizing freshness, lightness, and simpler preparations, this treasury of cooking from the "French Chef" features eight hundred master recipes and variations.

Chitnis, Christine

Little bites : 100 healthy, kid-friendly snacks / Christine Chitnis and Sarah Waldman ; photographs by Christine Chitnis. Roost Books, 2015. x, 277 p. : **641.5**

1. Children -- Nutrition. 2. Recipes 3. Snack foods. 4. Cookbooks
ISBN 161180177X

LC 2014022055

Offers recipes for one hundred healthy, kid-friendly snacks that use seasonal ingredients, including raspberry French toast sticks, cherry tomato cheddar bites, and carrot-apple cinnamon sticks.

Clair, Jennifer

Six basic cooking techniques : culinary essentials for the home cook / Jennifer Clair ; photographs by Meredith Heuer. HCNY Press, 2018 112 p. : **641.5**

1. Cooking -- Technique. 2. Quick and easy cooking 3. Quick and easy cooking 4. Cookbooks
ISBN 9780998979205

LC bl2018045284

Includes index.

A culinary instructor details the six basic techniques needed to successfully cook at home, form learning how to handle a chef's knife to properly cooking leafy greens.

"This quick course in how-tos can also serve as a refresher course." Booklist.

Clark, Melissa

Comfort in an instant : 75 comfort food recipes for your pressure cooker, multicooker + Instant Pot / Melissa Clark. Clarkson Potter/Publishers, 2018 159 p. : **641.5**

1. Comfort food. 2. Pressure cooking. 3. Recipes 4. Quick and easy cooking 5. Cookbooks
ISBN 9780525576150

LC 2018019955

Includes index.

Collects classic comfort food recipes adapted for slow and pressure cookers, including such dishes as cheddar-spinach strata, matzo ball soup, chicken cacciatore, chili, and ginger-lemon cheesecake.

Dinner : changing the game / Melissa Clark ; photographs by Eric Wolfinger. Clarkson Potter, 2017 399 p. : **641.5**

1. Cooking. 2. Quick and easy cooking 3. Quick and easy cooking

4. Cookbooks.
ISBN 9780553448238
LC 2016013021

Includes index.

A collection of recipes for home cooks from the New York Times food columnist that are easy and quick enough to prepare on weeknights, includng such dishes as herb-marinated steak, maple-roasted tofu, and coconut curry chicken.

Dinner in an instant : 75 modern recipes for your pressure cooker, slow cooker, and instant pot / Melissa Clark. Clarkson Potter/Publishers, 2017 159 p. : **641.5**

1. Quick and easy cooking. 2. Recipes 3. Cookbooks
ISBN 9781524762964
LC 2017021737

Trademark sign appears after Pot in title.

Includes index.

"With 75 all-new recipes, Melissa Clark,New York Times food columnist, web star, and our generation's authority on upping your cooking game without fuss, brings her signature flavor-forward dishes and dinner brand to everyone's favorite countertop appliance, the Instant Pot®. With 75 recipes for slow cooker, pressure cooker, and other Instant Pot settings, Dinner in an Instant proves that home cooks do not have to sacrifice flavor and quality for the convenience of countertop appliance cooking. With Melissa's signature arsenal of flavors (garlic, ginger, preserved lemons, gochujang, harissa, and more!) and chock-full of tips--each of the recipes will be annotated with dietary information and notes on which setting is best for each dish. Recipes will also include instructions for cooking on multiple settings--busy home cooks can decide whether they want to have their dinner cook throughout the day while they tend to other tasks, or in a quick twenty minutes before the family sits down to eat. As in her previous book,Dinner,all of Melissa's recipes are never before published, fresh, approachable, and practical for weeknight cooking, without ever sacrificing quality and taste"-- Provided by publisher.

Colwin, Laurie 1944-1992

Home cooking : a writer in the kitchen / Laurie Colwin ; illustrated by Anna Shapiro. Vintage Books, 2010, c1988. x, 193 p. : **641.5**

1. Cooking. 2. Essays.
ISBN 9780307474414
LC 2010455796

"Portions of this text were originally published in Gourmet magazine, Inside magazine, and 7 Days magazine"--Verso t.p.

Includes index.

Originally published: New York : Knopf, 1988.

From the humble hotplate of her one-room apartment to the crowded kitchens of bustling parties, Colwin regales us with tales of meals gone both magnificently well and disastrously wrong. Hilarious, personal, and full of Colwin's hard-won expertise, Home Cooking will speak to the heart of any amateur cook, professional chef, or food lover. --From publisher description.

"Friendly, warm, and inviting, Colwin's essay collection is a charming and funny mix of recipes, memories, and ruminations on building a life." Library Journal.

Comerford, Hope

Fix-it and forget-it healthy 5-ingredient cookbook : 150 easy and nutritious slow cooker recipes / Hope Comerford. Good Books, 2019 336 p. : **641.5**

1. Electric cooking, slow 2. Quick and easy cooking 3. Cookbooks.
ISBN 9781680994124
LC bl2019005951

Includes index.

A collection of recipes featuring five ingredients or less, including Southwestern chili, butternut squash soup, and spinach frittata, with tips on purchasing and using a slow cooker.

Comerford, Hope

Fix-it and forget-it slow cooker freezer meals : 150 make-ahead meals to save you time and money / Hope Comerford ; photos by Bonnie Matthews. Good Books, 2018. 343 p. : **641.5**

1. Cooking (Frozen foods) 2. Crockpot cooking 3. Make-ahead cooking. 4. Recipes 5. Cookbooks.
ISBN 9781680993905

Includes index.

A collection of make-ahead, family-friendly recipes offers shopping strategies, freezer cooking basics, and tips on purchasing a slow cooker.

Coscarelli, Chloe

Chloe flavor : saucy, spicy, crunchy, vegan / Chloe Coscarelli ; photographs by Christina Holmes ; foreword by Michael Symon. Clarkson Potter/Publishers, 2018 271 p. : **641.5**

1. Vegan cooking. 2. Quick and easy cooking 3. Recipes 4. Cookbooks.
ISBN 9780451499622
LC 2017021732

Includes index.

Shares vegan recipes for over a hundred dishes that focus on simplicity and flavor, including fiesta taco bowl, oatmeal cake with coconut caramel glaze, and butternut bisque.

"For those who want to try vegan cooking, this is the perfect cookbook." Publishers Weekly.

The **little** book of lunch : 100 recipes & ideas to reclaim the lunch hour / Caroline Craig and Sophie Missing. Regan Arts, 2015. 207 p. : **641.5**

1. Lunchbox cooking. 2. Recipes 3. Quick and easy cooking 4. Quick and easy cooking 5. Cookbooks.
ISBN 9781941393222
LC bl2015017347

Includes index.

Presents a collection of easy lunch recipes for busy employees, including chickpea salad with cumin, balt sourdough sandwich, and simple guacamole & tomato salsa on rye.

Crandall, Russ

Paleo takeout : restaurant favorites without the junk / Russ Crandall ; photography by Russ Crandall and Giang Cao. Victory Belt Publishing, Inc., 2015. 320 p. : **641.5**

1. Cooking (Natural foods). 2. High-protein diet 3. Prehistoric peoples -- Nutrition. 4. Cookbooks.
ISBN 9781628600872
LC bl2015024183

Includes indexes.

A guide to recreating popular takeout meals with wholesome ingredients includes recipes for such dishes as Vietnamese spring rolls, Hawaiian pizza, chicken nuggets, gyros, lamb vindaloo, and guacamole.

Cristofano, Jana

Eat well, be well : 100+ healthy re-creations of the food you crave : plant based, gluten-free, refined sugar-free / Jana Cristofano. Sterling Epicure, 2020 250 p. : **641.5**

1. Cooking (Natural foods) 2. Gluten-free diet 3. Sugar-free diet 4. Vegan cooking
ISBN 9781454933779

LC 2019019084

"Satisfy your cravings and boost your vitality with good food that tastes great and is vegan." Provided by publisher.

"Not only fans of Cristofano's blog, but also everyday cooks looking to explore gluten-free and vegan recipes will find plenty to enjoy." Library Journal

Crocker, Betty

★**Betty** Crocker cookbook : 1500 recipes for the way you cook today / Betty Crocker. John Wiley & Sons, c2011. 684 p. : **641.5**

1. Cooking. 2. Recipes 3. Cookbooks.
ISBN 9780470906026

LC 2011009744

In ringbinder.
Includes index.

This 11th edition of the Betty Crocker Cookbook is the most thorough update in the book's 60-year history, with 1,100 all-new photos, 1,500 recipes, a fully contemporized design and features that highlight the heritage and expertise of this trusted classic. An exclusive bonus area on BettyCrocker.com features 80 videos demonstrating recipes and techniques from the book, plus 400 additional recipes just for Big Red consumers.

Culinary Institute of America

The **professional** chef / the Culinary Institute of America. John Wiley & Sons, 2006. xvi, 1215 p. : **641.5**

1. Quantity cooking. 2. Recipes 3. Cookbooks
ISBN 9780764557347

LC 2004027110

Includes bibliographical references (p. 1190-1196) index.

Filled with stunning photography and instructional text, the ultimate guide to culinary excellence is filled with an abundance of tips and techniques and contains more than six hundred recipes, both classic and contemporary, identifies key tools and ingredients, and discusses food science, cooking techniques, and food and kitchen safety.

"The nation's most prestigious training school for food careerists concentrates the essence of its course work within a comprehensive volume that competent students must master. Every aspect of the restaurant business is addressed, from nutrition and portion sizing to fiscal and human resource management. ... Although beyond the need of most home cooks, this massive tome is a necessary reference-collection purchase for any library whose community includes food-service-training programs." Booklist.

Curry, Kevin (Health and fitness writer)

Fit men cook : 100+ meal prep recipes for men and women - always #HealthyAF, never boring / Kevin Curry. Touchstone, 2018. 319 p. : **641.5**

1. Cooking 2. Health 3. Nutrition 4. Recipes 5. Cookbooks
ISBN 9781501178726

LC 2018041649

Includes index.

The fitness influencer and creator of the best-selling Food & Drink app, FitMenCook, shares 100 satisfying, quick-prep recipes designed to support personal health goals on a budget.

David, Elizabeth, 1913-1992

Summer cooking / Elizabeth David ; illustrated by Adrian Daintrey. New York Review Books, 2002, c1955. 234 p. : **641.5**

1. Cooking, English. 2. Summer. 3. Cooking. 4. Food.
ISBN 1590170040

LC 2002000744

Includes index.

For the great English food writer Elizabeth David, summer fare means neither tepid nor timid. Her stress is always on fresh, seasonal food--recipes that can be quickly prepared and slowly savored, from Gnocchi alla Genovese ("simply an excuse for eating pesto") to La Poule au Pot to Gooseberry Fool. Divided into such sections as Soup, Poultry and Game, Vegetables, and Dessert, her 1955 classic includes an overview of herbs as well as chapters on impromptu cooking for holidays and picnics. Chockablock with both invaluable instructions and tart rejoinders to the pallid and the overblown, Summer Cooking is a witty, precise companion for feasting in the warmer months. --From publisher description.

Davies, Katie Quinn

What Katie ate : recipes and other bits & pieces / photography by Katie Quinn Davies. Viking, 2012. 297 p. : **641.5**

1. Cooking. 2. Cookbooks.
ISBN 9780670026180

LC bl2012037029

Includes index.

The creator of the renowned What Katie Ate blog combines her acclaimed photography with favorite simple recipes, providing diary-style culinary tips and personal stories.

"This gorgeous title begs to be displayed. Readers who value excellent food photography and styling won't be able to resist." Library Journal.

De Laurentiis, Giada

Happy cooking : make every meal count-- without stressing out / Giada De Laurentiis. Pam Krauss Books, 2015 311 p. : **641.5**

1. Cooking. 2. Cookbooks.
ISBN 9780804187923

LC 2015022028

Outlines the author's year-round approach to enjoying a happy and healthy lifestyle based on strategic wellness practices, nutritious foods, and occasional indulgences.

DeBenedetti, Christian

Beer bites : tasty recipes and perfect pairings for brew lovers / Christian DeBenedetti & Andrea Slonecker ; foreword by Eric Asimov ; photographs by John Lee. Chronicle Books, 2015 168 p. : **641.5**

1. Cooking. 2. Food and beer pairing 3. Recipes 4. Cookbooks.
ISBN 9781452135243

LC 2014032763

Includes index.

" This superb collection features of recipes that are sure to be hits at any gathering. Highly recommended for all cooking collections." Library Journal.

DiGregorio, Sarah

Adventures in slow cooking : 120 slow-cooker recipes for people who love food / Sarah DiGregorio ; photography by Andrew

Purcell. William Morrow, 2017 xxvii, 228 p. : **641.5**

1. Electric cooking 2. Recipes 3. Crockpot cooking. 4. Cookbooks.
ISBN 9780062661371

LC bl2017041532

Includes index.

Collects recipes for slow cooker meals, including such offerings as gingery cranberry chutney, farro puttanesca, and oxtail and short rib pho.

"Essential for most collections, this is an exciting and refreshingly unbiased guide to slow cooking." Library Journal.

DiSpirito, Rocco

Now eat this! : 150 of America's favorite comfort foods, all under 350 calories / Rocco DiSpirito. Ballantine Books, c2010. xxiii, 246 p. : **641.5**

1. Cooking, American. 2. Low-calorie diet 3. Recipes 4. Cookbooks
ISBN 9780345520906

LC 2009052470

"A Ballantine Books trade paperback original"--Verso, t.p.

Includes index.

A popular chef takes 150 familiar recipes and puts a healthy spin on them, all without sacrificing the well-loved flavors of these classic American dishes.

"The author retools diet cookery in the hope of convincing even the most stubborn gourmand to cut calories without giving up delicious, satisfying foods." Booklist.

Diamond, Kerry

The **Cherry** bombe : the cookbook : recipes and stories from 100 of the most creative and inspiring women in food today / Kerry Diamond and Claudia Wu ; photographs by Alpha Smoot ; food styling by Claudia Ficca. Clarkson Potter/Publishers, 2017 242 p. ; **641.5**

1. Cooking. 2. Recipes 3. Seasonal cooking 4. Cookbooks.
ISBN 9780553459524

LC 2016044131

Selection of recipes from noted food writers from the editors of the quarterly Cherry bombe.

Includes index.

Collects recipes from some of the most interesting female chefs, bakers, food stylists, and pastry chefs on the food scene today, including such options as crab rolls with avocado, watermelon gazpacho, latkes with pear sauce, and ginger cookies.

Disbrowe, Paula

Thank you for smoking : fun and fearless recipes cooked with a whiff of wood fire on your grill or smoker / Paula Disbrowe ; photographs by Johnny Autry. Ten Speed Press, 2019 233 p. : **641.5**

1. Smoking (Cooking) 2. Recipes 3. Cookbooks.
ISBN 9780399582134

LC 2018038937

"Featuring an impressive array of smoke-infused recipes that extend well beyond the realm of rib joints, Thank You for Smoking shows home cooks how easy it is to rig a gas or charcoal grill or use a backyard smoker to infuse everything you love to eat--from veggies and greens to meat and fish--with a smoky nuance".-- Provided by publisher.

"Readers who enjoy trying new cooking techniques, and those looking for creative ways to incorporate smoky flavor into their foods will find this a treasure." Library Journal.

Donofrio, Jeanine

The **love** & lemons cookbook : an apple-to-zucchini celebration of impromptu cooking / Jeanine Donofrio, Jack Mathews. Avery, 2016 xv, 291 p. : **641.5**

1. Cooking. 2. Recipes 3. Cookbooks.
ISBN 9781583335864

LC 2016006543

Includes index.

Collects recipes for vegetable-centric dishes, including apple, brie and thyme crostini, broccoli rabe and sunchoke orecchiette, and crispy shiitake BLTs.

"Celebrating spontaneity in cooking with plant-based inspiration, this imaginative recipe collection will please cooks who take their cue from ingredients as much as from recipes." Publishers Weekly.

Drummond, Ree

The **pioneer** woman cooks : come and get it! : simple, scrumptious recipes for crazy busy lives / Ree Drummond. William Morrow, 2017 xvii, 381 p. : **641.5**

1. Quick and easy cooking 2. Recipes 3. Cookbooks
ISBN 9780062225269

LC bl2017037717

Includes index.

The Food Network star and best-selling author shares a collection of recipes that provide for the needs of today's busy families, outlining a wide range of quick-prepare, nutritious and satisfying options for every meal of the day.

Duclos, Andrea

The **plantiful** table : easy, from-the-earth recipes for the whole family / Andrea Duclos. The Experiment, 2015 311 p. ; **641.5**

1. Vegetarian cooking. 2. Recipes 3. Cookbooks.
ISBN 9781615192472

LC 2015003784

Shares family-friendly vegan recipes, including garam masala pancakes, chickpea pot pie, and chocolate chip coffee brownies.

Duyff, Roberta Larson

American Dietetic Association complete food and nutrition guide / Roberta Larson Duyff. John Wiley & Sons, c2012. xii, 708 p. : **641.5**

1. Nutrition -- Popular works.
ISBN 9780470912072

LC 2012382537

Includes index.

Offers tips and guidelines for following a healthy diet, from choosing the right food at the supermarket to eating well at every stage in life.

"The author's goal is 'to answer the whats, hows, and whys about food and nutrition' for wellness. This new edition . is divided into six sections covering food choices for wellness; the basics of nutrition; food selection and safety; special needs for various life stages; food choices for some selected health problems; and a selected list of resources." Choice.

Elliot, Jeffrey

Zwilling J.A. Henckels complete book of knife skills : the essential guide to use, techniques & care / Jeffrey Elliot & James P. DeWan. R. Rose, 2010. 400 p. **641.5**

1. Knives
ISBN 9780778802563

LC oc2010024939

Includes index.

The definitive book on knife skills from the knife manufacturer recognized worldwide as the symbol of the best quality and function. --From publisher description.

"This step-by-step manual of age-old culinary tradition will have readers who are looking to sharpen their kitchen skills preparing frenched lamb rack with tourne potatoes and fluted mushrooms in no time." Booklist.

Esposito, Jennifer, 1972-

Jennifer's Way kitchen : easy allergen-free, anti-inflammatory recipes for a delicious life / Jennifer Esposito with Eve Adamson. Grand Central Life & Style, 2017. 304 p. : **641.5**

1. Cooking (Natural foods). 2. Gluten-free diet 3. Dairy-free diet 4. Sugar-free diet 5. Cookbooks

ISBN 9781455596713

LC bl2017038332

"Gluten-free, grain-free, dairy-free, egg-free, soy-free, corn-free, refined sugar-free recipes from the owner of the beloved Jennifer's Way bakery."

Includes index.

A collection of anti-inflammatory, allergen-free recipes from the actress and owner of New York City-based Jennifer's Way bakery features such offerings as spaghetti squash with garlic and oil, one-dish chicken with asparagus, and spring risotto.

"This solid foray into allergen-free cooking is packed with information that can help those with dietary problems." Publishers Weekly.

Esselstyn, Rip

The **Engine** 2 cookbook : more than 130 lip-smacking, rib-sticking, body-slimming recipes to live plant-strong / Rip Esselstyn & Jane Esselstyn. Grand Central Life & Style, 2017 278 p. : **641.5**

1. Community cookbooks. 2. Health. 3. Recipes 4. Vegetarian cooking.

ISBN 1455591203

LC 2017029721

Includes index.

A cookbook companion to the popularly endorsed The Engine 2 Diet shares more than 130 satisfying recipes designed to help readers lose weight, lower cholesterol and improve overall health.

Fairchild, Barbara, 1951-

The **Bon** appétit cookbook / Barbara Fairchild. Wiley, c2006. xxiv, 792 p., 32 p. of plates : **641.5**

1. Cooking.

ISBN 9780764596865

LC 2005005181

Includes index.

A comprehensive cooking compendium from America's leading food and entertaining magazine, Bon Appétit, selects more than 1,200 of the periodical's best-loved recipes for every meal, taste, budget, and occasion, including a variety of easy-to-make dishes that range from family favorites and classics to regional and international specialties.

"Mirroring the magazine on which it is based, this collection of 1,200 recipes is accessible, applicable to most home cooks' lives and a pleasure to cook from." Publishers Weekly.

The **bon** appétit fast easy fresh cookbook / Barbara Fairchild. John Wiley & Sons, Inc., c2008. xxiv, 770 p., 32 p. of plates : **641.5**

1. Cooking. 2. Recipes 3. Quick and easy cooking 4. Cookbooks

ISBN 9780470226308

LC 2007044562

Includes index.

A comprehensive cooking compendium from Bon Appetit, selects more than 1,100 quick and easy recipes for special weeknight meals for every taste and budget.

"This cookbook presents hundreds of quick and simple recipes from the magazine's popular Fast Easy Fresh feature. An introductory Shopping Guide covers buying and storing produce, meat, and fish, and dozens of sidebars and boxes provide more information on ingredients and techniques. Sure to appeal to any busy cook as well as the magazine's numerous fans, this is highly recommended." Library Journal.

Fearnley-Whittingstall, Hugh

River Cottage every day / Hugh Fearnley-Whittingstall ; photography by Simon Wheeler. Ten Speed Press, 2011 415 p. : **641.5**

1. River Cottage (Television program). 2. Cooking (Natural foods). 3. Cooking, English. 4. Recipes 5. Cookbooks

ISBN 9781607740988

LC 2010046949

"Originally published in slightly different form in Great Britain by Bloomsbury Publishing Plc, London, in 2009"--T.p. verso.

Includes index.

"A collection of more than 180 appealing everyday recipes from the bestselling author of the River Cottage series".--Provided by publisher.

"An advocate of a back-to-basics approach to cooking and sustainable agriculture...[the author] delivers thoughtful insight and colorful narratives that celebrate the joy of good family food, which will inspire and compel readers into the kitchen, book in hand. Simple ingredients become brilliant when combined in fresh and easy recipes like Baked Breakfast Cheesecake, Curried Fish Pie, breads, boxed lunches, and frittatas." Library Journal.

River Cottage veg : 200 inspired vegetable recipes / Hugh Fearnley-Whittingstall ; photography by Simon Wheeler ; illustrations by Mariko Jesse. Ten Speed Press, 2013, c2011. 415 p. : **641.5**

1. River Cottage (Television program) 2. Vegetarian cooking. 3. Recipes 4. Cookbooks.

ISBN 9781607744726

LC bl2013021941

"Originally published in slightly different form in hardcover in Great Britain as River Cottage Veg Everyday by Bloomsbury Publishing Plc, London, in 2011"--T.p. verso.

Includes index.

Collects vegetarian recipes, including kale and mushroom lasagna, winter stir-fry with Chinese five-spice, and herby, peanutty, noodly salad.

Fernald, Anya

Home cooked : essential recipes for a new way to cook / Anya Fernald, Belcampo founder and CEO ; with Jessica Battilana ; photography by Brown W. Cannon III. Ten Speed Press, 2016 295 p. : **641.5**

1. Cooking. 2. Quick and easy cooking 3. Recipes 4. Cookbooks

ISBN 9781607748403

LC 2015033515

Includes index.

"A recipe collection and how-to guide for preparing base ingredients that can be used to make simple, weeknight meals, while also teaching skills like building and cooking over a fire, and preserving meat and produce, written by a sustainable food expert--and founder of Belcampo Meat Co. Anya Fernald's style of cooking is rustic and simple, shaped by her years working on farms, living in Italy, and running Slow Food Nation--but it's also sophisticated and brilliant. Her secret is that by taking the time to create beautiful, super-flavorful base ingredients ahead of time--such as homemade sauces, preserves, pickles, and cured meats--you can easily create fast but luscious meals later using these components. In Home Cooked, Fernald teaches readers her methods and heritage skills to help them become more intuitive, natural home cooks who don't need to rely on recipes. Along the way, she shares kitchen tips and tricks for transforming food into something truly special, as well as her food philosophy and inspired approach to home cooking"-- Provided by publisher.

"Fernald's approach advances the importance of celebration, traditional ways of food and farm, and viable food production techniques." Publishers Weekly.

Firth, Henry

Bosh! : simple recipes, amazing food, all plants / Henry Firth & Ian Theasby. William Morrow, 2018 288 p. : **641.5**

1. Vegetarian cooking 2. Cooking (Vegetables) 3. Cookbooks.
ISBN 9780062820686

LC bl2018071448

Includes index.

Shares over one hundred and forty plant-based recipes that span from daily meals to special-occasion fare, including sweet and sour crispy tofu, satay maki rolls, and creamy garlic mushroom toast.

Flanagan, Shalane

Run fast, cook fast, eat slow : quick-fix recipes for hangry athletes / Shalane Flanagan & Elyse Kopecky ; photography by Alan Weiner. Rodale, 2018 253 p. : **641.5**

1. Cooking (Natural foods). 2. Natural foods. 3. Recipes 4. Runners (Sports) -- Nutrition. 5. Cookbooks.
ISBN 9781635651911

LC bl2018179666

Includes index.

A follow-up to the *New York Times* best-seller *Run Fast. Eat Slow* is aimed at busy young athletes looking for nutritious recipes to fuel their lives, in a book that includes recipes for such dishes as Superhero Muffins, Pizza Bolognese, Baked Avocado and more.

Run fast, eat slow : nourishing recipes for athletes / Shalane Flanagan and Elyse Kopecky ; photography by Alan Weiner. Rodale, 2016 xiii, 242 p. : **641.5**

1. Cooking (Natural foods). 2. Natural foods. 3. Recipes 4. Runners (Sports) -- Nutrition. 5. Cookbooks.
ISBN 9781623366810

LC bl2016032457

A leading distance runner and a culinary nutritionist offer this indulgent and nourishing cookbook of more than 100 recipes to help fuel athletes, including Can't Beet Me Smoothie, Arugula CashewPesto, High-Altitude Bison Meatballs, Superhero Muffins and Double ChocolateTeff Cookies.

Flay, Bobby

Bobby at home : fearless flavors from my kitchen / Bobby Flay with Stephanie Banyas and Sally Jackson. Clarkson Potter/ Publishers, 2019 255 p. : **641.5**

1. Cooking. 2. Recipes 3. Cookbooks.
ISBN 9780385345910

LC 2018052578

Includes index.

The James Beard Award-winning celebrity chef shares 165 advice-laden recipes, from pumpkin pancakes with apple-cider syrup to Korean BBQ chicken, that he prepares at home for friends and family members.

Bobby Flay fit : 200 recipes for a healthy lifestyle / Bobby Flay with Stephanie Banyas and Sally Jackson. Clarkson Potter/ Publishers, 2017. 256 p. : **641.5**

1. Cooking. 2. Health. 3. Recipes 4. Cookbooks.
ISBN 9780385345934

LC 2016044398

"The book does an excellent job of addressing different dining styles--it's easy to pick full breakfasts, lunches, and dinners from dedicated chapters, or to assemble a meal-sized assortment of snacks, sides, and small plates." Library Journal.

Bobby Flay's grill it! / Bobby Flay, with Stephanie Banyas and Sally Jackson ; photographs by Ben Fink. Clarkson Potter/ Publishers, c2008. vii, 280 p. : **641.5**

1. Barbecuing. 2. Recipes 3. Cookbooks
ISBN 9780307351425

LC 2007032662

Includes index.

Presents a guide to grilling that features more than 150 simple recipes, organized by ingredients, for a wide variety of meat, poultry, seafood, vegetable, fruit, and dessert dishes.

Bobby Flay's grilling for life : 75 healthier ideas for big flavor from the fire / Bobby Flay with Stephanie Banyas and Sally Jackson ; foreword by Joy Bauer ; color photographs by Gentl & Hyers ; black-and-white photographs by John Dolan. Scribner, 2005. xiv, 210 p. : **641.5**

1. Barbecuing. 2. Recipes 3. Cookbooks
ISBN 9780743272728

LC 2005045053

A collection of recipes instructs readers on the importance of discerning good carbs from bad carbs, sharing a wealth of barbecue tips and recommendations.

"The author's trademark use of bold flavors in dishes like Grilled Red Snapper with Grapefruit-Thyme Mojo, and (skinless) Grilled Duck Breast with Black Pepper-Sweet Mustard Sauce bring out appealing contrasts and result in food that's satisfying even if it's reduced in calories, carbs or fat." Publishers Weekly.

Brunch @ Bobby's : 140 recipes for the best part of the weekend / Bobby Flay with Stephanie Banyas & Sally Jackson ; photographs by Ben Fink. Clarkson Potter/Publishers, 2015 256 p. : **641.5**

1. Brunch @ Bobby's (Television program). 2. Brunches. 3. Cooking, American. 4. Recipes 5. Cookbooks
ISBN 0385345895

LC 2014012752

Includes index.

A treasury of favorite, simple and most-sought recipes centering on the celebrity's chef's brunches includes a variety of beverages, main dishes and sides, from Sangria Sunrise and Carrot Cake Pancakes to Sautěd Bitter Green Omelets and Wild Mushroom-Yukon Gold Hash.

"These bold, flavorful moves from Flay's breakfast playbook will leave readers salivating." Publishers Weekly.

Friedman, Andrew, 1967-

Knives at dawn : the American quest for culinary glory at the legendary Bocuse d'Or competition / Andrew Friedman. Free Press, 2009. 320 p. **641.5**

1. Bocuse d'Or, USA (Competition) (2008 : Orlando, Fla.) 2. Bocuse d'Or (Competition) (2009 : Lyon, France) 3. Cooking contests. 4. Cooking. 5. Cooks -- United States. 6. Competition in men.
ISBN 9781439153079

LC 2009035271

Just when you thought you've read enough culinary memoirs and single subject studies on every esoteric food topic imaginable comes

Knives at Dawn, Andrew Friedman's sharp, insider account of America's quest to win the Bocuse d'Or--the epicurean equivalent of the World Cup, held biannually in Lyon, France. For over two decades, international teams have entered the arena, cooking for five-and-a-half hours from a glass-walled pod in full view of the intimidating judges and howling spectators (who add to the frenzy with chants and clanging cowbells). In 2009, Paul Bocuse himself enlisted legendary chefs Daniel Boulud and Thomas Keller (well-known for his obsession with perfection) to field the U.S. team. French Laundry chef Timothy Hollingsworth and his commis, Adina Guest, continued to work their grueling day jobs over three-and-a-half months of intense training, and set the bar for future U.S. brigades.

"A vibrant portrait of the world's most significant cooking competition, the Bocuse d'Or, in Lyon, France. [The author] dynamically illustrates the colorful personalities, ego-battering conflicts, career-defining aspirations, politicking, precision planning, naked missteps and the final judges' decisions regarding the 2009 U.S. team's shot for the culinary gold medal. The book is infused with the muscular, meticulous gusto of a sportswriter covering the Olympics. Edge-of-your-seat food writing of the highest caliber." Kirkus.

Fuentes, Laura (Chef)

The **best** homemade kids' lunches on the planet : make lunches your kids will love with over 200 deliciously nutritious meal ideas / Laura Fuentes. Fair Winds Press, 2014. 240 p. : **641.5**

1. Lunchbox cooking 2. Recipes 3. Cookbooks
ISBN 9781592336081

LC 2013049151

Includes index.

Collects over two hundred ideas and recipes for creating nutricious and delicious lunches, including ninja turtle grilled cheese, olive strips, chicken taco soup, and white chocolate peanut butter strawberry crostinis.

"Stocked with good ideas, these recipes will give families (not just the kids!) nutritional snacking options." Library Journal.

The **best** homemade kids' snacks on the planet : more than 200 healthy homemade snacks you and your kids will love / Laura Fuentes, founder of MOMables.com. Fair Winds Press, 2015. 240 p. : **641.5**

1. Cooking (Natural foods) 2. Quick and easy cooking. 3. Recipes 4. Snack foods. 5. Cookbooks
ISBN 1592336612

LC 2014047820

Includes index.

Overflowing with quick and healthy ideas for the whole family, this cookbook features delicious recipes for more than 200 homemade snacks that solve the snack conundrum and can be made in minutes without fuss in the kitchen.

Fuhrman, Joel

Eat to live quick & easy cookbook : 131 delicious, nutrient-rich recipes for fast and sustained weight loss, reversing disease, and lifelong health / Joel Fuhrman, M.D. HarperOne, 2017 vii, 294 p. : **641.5**

1. Weight loss. 2. Dieting 3. Nutrition. 4. Recipes 5. Cookbooks.
ISBN 9780062684950

LC 2017013630

Includes index.

A full-color companion cookbook to the author's popular Eat to Live shares dozens of easy-to-prepare, plant-based recipes designed to promote health and weight loss.

"Most recipes take only minutes to assemble; vegans, nonvegans, and raw foodies also will find suitable options." Publishers Weekly.

Gand, Gale

Gale Gand's brunch! : 100 fantastic recipes for the weekend's best meal / Gale Gand with Christie Matheson ; photographs by Ben Fink. Clarkson Potter/Publishers, c2009. 208 p. : **641.5**

1. Brunches. 2. Recipes
ISBN 0307406989

LC 2008036988

Includes index.

Every weekend is worth celebrating when you can relax over a good brunch.

"Accessible instructions, basic preparation tips and make-ahead hints ensure that both beginners and those who think cooking brunch is too bothersome will find this volume to be inspiring." Publishers Weekly.

Garten, Ina

Cook like a pro : recipes & tips for home cooks / Ina Garten ; photographs by Quentin Bacon. Clarkson Potter/Publishers, 2018 272 p. : **641.5**

1. Barefoot Contessa (Store) 2. Cooking. 3. Recipes 4. Cookbooks
ISBN 9780804187046

LC 2018006753

Includes index.

Presents simple, streamlined recipes with tips and techniques for cooking like a chef.

Cooking for Jeffrey : a barefoot contessa cookbook / Ina Garten ; photographs by Quentin Bacon ; garden photographs by John M. Hall. Clarkson Potter/Publishers, 2016 256 p. : **641.5**

1. Barefoot Contessa (Store). 2. Cooking. 3. Cooking for two. 4. Cookbooks
ISBN 9780307464897

LC 2016025974

Includes index.

Collects recipes for the author's most requested dishes, including brisket with onions and leeks, maple-roasted carrot salad, and vanilla rum panna cotta with salted caramel.

"True to form, this culinary love letter is as warm and comforting as Gartens dishes." Publishers Weekly.

Modern comfort food : A Barefoot Contessa cookbook / Ina Garten ; photographs by Quentin Bacon ; party photographs by Jean-Pierre Uys. Clarkson Potter/Publishers, [2020] 256 p. : **641.5**

1. Comfort food.
ISBN 9780804187060

LC bl2020046541

Includes indexes.

A collection of eighty-five all-new recipes by the James Beard Award-winning host of the Emmy Award-winning Food Network series features comforting twists on childhood favorites, including cheesy chicken enchiladas, tomato and goat cheese crostata, and banana rum trifle.

"Garten's cookbooks are perennial best sellers. Anyone in search of nostalgic American comfort food with a twist will enjoy her latest offering." Library Journal

Barefoot Contessa at home : everyday recipes you'll make over and over again / Ina Garten ; photographs by Quentin Bacon. Clarkson Potter, c2006. 256 p. : **641.5**

1. Cooking. 2. Menus. 3. Recipes 4. Cookbooks.
ISBN 9781400054343

LC 2006014257

Includes indexes.

Collects recipes featuring elegant but easy-to-prepare dishes for breakfast, lunch, dinner, and dessert for both everyday meals or special occasions, accompanied by tips on the art of entertaining with style.

Barefoot Contessa family style : easy ideas and recipes that make everyone feel like family / Ina Garten ; photographs by Maura McEvoy ; food styling by Rori Trovato. Clarkson Potter, 2002. 240 p. : **641.5**

1. Cooking. 2. Recipes
ISBN 060961066X

LC 2002074979

Includes index.

Offers a collection of recipes for everday cooking, including clam chowder, penne with five cheeses, and linguine with shrimp scampi.

"This is simple, elegant home cooking with good ingredients and a minimum of fuss. It takes a certain amount of chutzpah to include ordinary chicken noodle soup and mashed potatoes and gravy in a cookbook, but Garten pulls it off with heart and style." Publishers Weekly.

Barefoot Contessa, how easy is that? : fabulous recipes & easy tips / Ina Garten ; photographs by Quentin Bacon. Clarkson Potter/Publishers, c2010. 256 p. : **641.5**

1. Barefoot Contessa (Store) 2. Cooking. 3. Recipes 4. Cookbooks
ISBN 9780307238764

LC 2010002025

Includes index.

Food Network guru Ina Garten offers simple yet appetizing dishes that save time and minimize stress in the kitchen. Featuring over 200 recipes, including everything from easy parmesan risotto and French toast bread pudding to spicy turkey meatballs.

Make it ahead / Ina Garten ; photographs by Quentin Bacon ; garden photographs by John M. Hall. Clarkson Potter/Publishers, 2014 272 p. : **641.5**

1. Barefoot Contessa (Store). 2. Make-ahead cooking. 3. Quick and easy cooking 4. Cookbooks.
ISBN 9780307464880

LC 2014004486

Includes index.

The Emmy Award-winning celebrity chef shares favorite make-ahead recipes and meal-planning tips for a variety of occasions, suggesting preparation options for low-stress dishes that improve if prepared in advance.

"A quieter, simpler, more accessible version of Martha Stewart in the kitchen. Make-ahead meals appended." Booklist.

Garutti, Randy

Shake Shack : recipes and stories / Randy Garutti and Mark Rosati ; introduction by Danny Meyer ; photographs by Christopher Hirsheimer and Melissa Hamilton. Clarkson Potter/Publishers, 2017. 240 p. **641.5**

1. Frankfurters 2. French fries 3. Milkshakes 4. Hamburger
ISBN 9780553459814

LC 2016055794

Includes index.

With each chapter focusing on a main menu item, this cookbook for fans of the burger restaurant chain includes photos, infographics and 70 recipes for how to make your own ShackBurgers, crinkle fries, Chick?'n Shack and limited edition burgers.

Gellar, Sarah Michelle, 1977-

Stirring up fun with food : over 115 simple delicious ways to be creative in the kitchen / Sarah Michelle Gellar and Gia Russo ; photographs by Amy Neunsinger. Grand Central Life & Style, 2017. xvi, 269 p. : **641.5**

1. Cooking. 2. Recipes 3. Cookbooks.
ISBN 9781455538744

LC 2016054252

Includes index.

The Emmy Award-winning actress and an editor and owner of a successful lifestyle brand offer over 100 fun and delicious food-crafting ideas and recipes to help kids become more adventurous, confident and creative in the kitchen.

"With carefully curated recipes for every month of the year...parents and kids alike will enjoy seeing what kind of fun they can cook up in the kitchen all year long." Booklist.

Gentry, Ann, 1954-

The **Real** Food Daily cookbook : really fresh, really good, really vegetarian / Ann Gentry with Anthony Head. Ten Speed Press, c2005. vii, 232 p. : **641.5**

1. Real Food Daily (Restaurant). 2. Vegetarian cooking. 3. Cookbooks.
ISBN 9781580086189

LC 2005016245

Includes index.

The founder-chef of Real Food Daily showcases a collection of 150 trademark recipes that exemplify the best in healthful, vegetarian cooking, with such creative dishes as Lentil-Walnut Pt,̌ Country-Style Miso Soup, Tuscan Bean Salad with Herb Vinaigrette, Southern-Style Skillet Cornbread, and Coconut Cream Pie with Chocolate Sauce.

"The author presents what she has learned about seasonal, organic, macrobiotic and vegan cooking. Gentry doesn't break new ground--sandwiches made with tempeh instead of meat, and nut cheeses like cashew cheddar will be familiar to most vegans--but she provides clear and comprehensive directions on how to make them more interesting and flavorful. Gentry explains the basics without preaching or condescending to readers, and discusses nutritional benefits without unnecessary jargon." Publishers Weekly.

Ghayour, Sabrina

Bazaar : vibrant vegetarian recipes / Sabrina Ghayour. Mitchell Beazley, 2019. 239 p. : **641.5**

1. Vegetarian cooking 2. Cooking, Middle Eastern. 3. Recipes 4. Cookbooks.
ISBN 9781784725754

LC bl2019018402

Includes index.

Presents vegetarian recipes with a Middle Eastern flavor profile, including such dishes as date-stuffed naan, cabbage and sesame salad, roasted eggplant and carrot couscous, and kaffir lime and spice-roasted chickpeas.

"An ancient cuisine expanded with a world of distinct flavors; readers will find dishes to savor again and again." Library Journal.

Gill, Sasha

East meets vegan : the best of Asian home cooking, plant-based and delicious / Sasha Gill. The Experiment, 2019 223 p. : **641.5**

1. Vegetarian cooking -- Asia 2. Cooking, Asian 3. Cookbooks.
ISBN 9781615195633

LC 2018043596

"Published as Jackfruit and Blue Ginger in the UK, Australia, and New Zealand by Murdoch Books in 2019."

"Ninety affordable, delicious vegan recipes that capture the color, spice and flavor of dishes from six Asian countries: India, Thailand, Singapore, Malaysia, China, and Japan."--Publisher.

Gillingham-Ryan, Sara Kate

The **kitchn** cookbook : recipes, kitchens & tips in inspire your cooking / Sara Kate Gillingham & Faith Durand ; photographs by Leela Cyd. Clarkson Potter/Publishers, 2014 304 p. : **641.5**

1. Cooking. 2. Kitchens. 3. Recipes 4. Cookbooks.
ISBN 9780770434434

LC 2014029477

Includes index.

A book from Apartment Therapy's cooking site provides fifty essential techniques as well as over one hundred recipes, including such offerings as breakfast pizza, three-cheese tomato tart, green papaya pad thai, and Vietnamese beef pho.

Goldman, Jessica, 1982-

Sodium girls limitless low-salt cookbook / Jessica Goldman ; photography by Matt Armendariz. Wiley, c2012. 256 p. : **641.5**

1. Low-salt diet 2. Cooking, Low-salt. 3. Cookbooks.
ISBN 9781118123775

LC 2011040042

Includes index.

Packed with creative and delicious low-sodium recipes, this healthful cookbook can help lower your daily recommended intake of salt to promote and sustain good health while still enjoying tasty meals and foods that you love.

Goldstein, Joyce Esersky

The **new** Mediterranean Jewish table : Old World recipes for the modern home / Joyce Goldstein ; illustrations by Hugh D'Andrade. University of California Press, 2016 458 p. ; **641.5**

1. Jewish cooking. 2. Cooking, Mediterranean. 3. Recipes 4. Cookbooks.
ISBN 9780520284999

LC 2015043306

"For thousands of years, Jewish people have lived in a global diaspora, carrying culinary traditions bound by kosher law. For many, Ashkenazi and Sephardic cooking define Jewish cuisine today, but in The New Mediterranean Jewish Table, Joyce Goldstein expands the repertoire with a comprehensive collection of over 400 recipes from the greater Mediterranean, including North Africa, Italy, Greece, Turkey, Spain, Portugal, and the Middle East. This vibrant treasury is filled with vibrant and seasonal recipesthat embrace fresh fruits and vegetables, whole grains, small portions of meat, poultry, and fish, enhanced by herbs and spices that create distinct regional flavors. By bringing Old World Mediterranean recipes into the modern home, Joyce Goldstein will inspire a new generation of home cooks as they prepare everyday meals and build their Shabbat and holiday menus".--Provided by publisher.

"Thorough research and excellent recipes make Goldstein's latest an instant classic, worthy of shelf space alongside complementary works by Claudia Roden and Joan Nathan." Library Journal.

Good, Phyllis Pellman, 1948-

Fix-it and forget-it new cookbook : 250 new delicious slow-cooker recipes! / New York Times bestselling author Phyllis Good. Good Books, 2013 384 p. : Fix-it and Forget-it **641.5**

1. Electric slow cookers 2. Quick and easy cooking. 3. Cooking. 4. Recipes 5. Cookbooks.
ISBN 9781561488001

LC bl2013041707

Includes index.

Presents over two hundred recipes designed for the slow cooker, from such easy-to-prepare dishes as wild rice with chicken and lentil soup to more advanced recipes including oatmeal tandy cake, beef carbonnade, and braised beef short ribs.

Goodall, Tiffany

The **ultimate** student cookbook : from chicken to chili / Tiffany Goodall ; photography by Claire Peters. Firefly Books, 2010, c2009. 160 p. : **641.5**

1. Quick and easy cooking. 2. Low budget cooking. 3. Cooking, American. 4. Quick and easy cooking 5. Cookbooks.
ISBN 9781554076024

LC bl2011005792

Originally published under title: From pasta to pancakes. London : Quadrille Pub., 2009.

Includes index.

Presents instructions and color photographs for simple meals that suit a collegiate budget and lifestyle.

"The author outlines basic kitchen equipment, pantry ingredients, and food hygiene. Writing for the student with no cooking experience, she offers step-by-step photos that will make cooking a breeze. Goodall discusses basics like how to cook noodles, rice, and potatoes and presents dishes like wraps, salads, soups, chili, pizza, kebabs, and cakes. Two alcoholic drinks are included. Highly recommended for the numerous photographs and the variety of recipes." Library Journal.

Goyoaga, Aran

Cannelle et Vanille : nourishing, gluten-free recipes for every meal and mood / written and photograhed by Aran Goyoaga. Sasquatch Books, 2019. 337 p. : **641.5**

1. Gluten-free diet 2. Gluten-free foods 3. Cooking (Natural foods) 4. Recipes 5. Cookbooks.
ISBN 9781632172006

LC 2019003267

From the James Beard-recognized creator of Cannelle et Vanille--lauded by everyone from Bon Appetit to Heidi Swanson--comes 100 gluten-free recipes that show us how to bring more joy and mindfulness to the kitchen, and connection around the table, through family-friendly meals that are satisfying, yet decidedly unfussy. Filled with Aran's gorgeous photographs, you will also find suggestions sprinkled throughout the book for creating a welcoming space with lighting, linens, flowers and flatware.

"Goyoaga relies on a whole-food philosophy that shines through each recipe; however, these are not quick weekday meals (most start with preheating or boiling). . . . Recommended for home cooks with experience in the kitchen and those looking to expand their gluten-free options. These are flexible meals to impress." Library Journal

Greenspan, Dorie

★**Everyday** Dorie : the way I cook / Dorie Greenspan ; photographs by Ellen Silverman. Houghton Mifflin Harcourt, 2018. 357 p. : **641.5**

1. Cooking. 2. Cookbooks.
ISBN 9780544826984

LC 2017061484

"A Rux Martin book."
Includes index.

The James Beard Award-winning and New York Times magazine columnist shares the irresistibly informal food she makes for her husband and friends.-- Provided by publisher.

"Greenspan (Around My French Table), five-time James Beard Award winner, shares her favorite day-to-day recipes in this standout cookbook." Publishers Weekly.

Griffin, Brooke

Skinny suppers : 125 lightened up, healthier meals for your family / Brooke Griffin. William Morrow, an Imprint of HarperCollins Publishers, 2016 xi, 307 p. : **641.5**

1. Low-calorie diet 2. Quick and easy cooking 3. Recipes 4. Cookbooks

ISBN 9780062419156

LC 2015034595

Includes index.

Collects light recipes for quick-and-easy suppers from the Skinny Mom website founder, including such options as supreme pizza pasta casserole, loaded nacho soup, and un-sloppy Janes, with meal-planning techniques and time-saving grocery lists.

"Having this cookbook on hand will be like having your own personal cheerleader in the kitchen." Booklist.

Guggiana, Marissa

Off the menu : staff meals from America's top restaurants / Marissa Guggiana. Welcome Books, 2011. 287 p. : **641.5**

1. Cooking. 2. Restaurants -- United States. 3. Recipes.

ISBN 9781599621029

LC oc2011041877

Includes index.

Inside Off the Menu you will find 100 recipes from more than 50 of the nation's top restaurants. Each entry includes profiles of the restaurants, Q&As with the chefs, behind-the-scenes trips to the kitchens, and dining out tips, restaurant tricks, and cooking techniques from the cream of the culinary crop. Pull back the curtain on the staff meal, and find new, exciting ways to feed your family from the best in the business. --From publisher description.

"A wonderfully original resource to inspire inventive family or group dinners." Booklist.

Hamilton, Melissa

Canal House cooks every day / Hamilton & Hirsheimer. Andrews McMeel Pub., c2012. xxiii, 359 p. : **641.5**

1. Seasonal cooking 2. Seasonal cooking 3. Cookbooks.

ISBN 9781449421472

LC bl2012039792

Includes index.

From the award-winning authors of the Canal House Cooking series, their first comprehensive collection of recipes by home cooks for home cooks. This magnificent compilation celebrates the everyday practice of simple cooking and the enjoyment of eating -- two of the greatest pleasures in life. --From publisher description.

"this transporting title successfully captures a year in a beautiful setting." Library Journal.

Hamshaw, Gena

Food 52 vegan : 60 vegetable-driven recipes for any kitchen / Gena Hamshaw ; photography by James Ransom. Ten Speed Press, 2015. xii, 145 p. ; **641.5**

1. Vegan cooking. 2. Veganism. 3. Cooking (Vegetables). 4. Recipes 5. Cookbooks.

ISBN 9781607747994

LC 2015002837

Includes index.

Presents a collection of hassle-free vegan recipes, including such offerings as baked kale chips, butternut squash mac and cheese, and blackberry coconut ice cream.

Hart, Alice

Good veg : ebullient vegetables, global flavors : a modern vegetarian cookbook / Alice Hart. Experiment, 2017 xiii, 321 p. : **641.5**

1. Vegetarian cooking. 2. Cookbooks.

ISBN 9781615192861

LC 2016045768

Includes index.

Shares recipes for vegetarian dishes, including Greek coddled eggs, tomato-lentil rasam with spelt, Vietnamese coconut and pomelo salad, and toasted marzipan ice cream.

"The 200 colorful creations presented here represent a veritable master class in meat-free cooking and would be a worthy addition to any cook's shelf, no matter vegetarian or omnivore." Booklist.

Hartwig, Melissa

The **whole30** fast & easy : 150 simply delicious everday recipes for your Whole30 / Melissa Hartwig, co-author of the New York Times best-selling The Whole30 ; photography by Ghazalle Badiozamani. Houghton Mifflin Harcourt, 2017 xix, 300 p. : **641.5**

1. Diet therapy 2. Nutrition 3. Food habits 4. Self-care, Health 5. Cookbooks

ISBN 9781328839206

LC 2017302891

Includes index.

Presents Whole30 diet compliant meals in thirty minutes or less, including roasted salmon with tomatoes and fennel, shrimp stir-fry over cauliflower grits, and Moroccan chicken and sweet potatoes.

"Readers interested in preparing and serving healthier meals that come together quickly (even if theyre not participating in the Whole30 program) are sure to appreciate this thoughtful collection." Publishers Weekly.

Hartwig, Melissa

The **Whole30** friends & family : 150 recipes for every social occasion / Melissa Hartwig Urban ; photography by Ghazalle Badiozaman. Houghton Mifflin Harcourt, 2019. xxi, 265 p. : **641.5**

1. Cooking (Natural foods). 2. Diet therapy -- Popular works. 3. Dieting 4. Low-carbohydrate diet 5. Cookbooks.

ISBN 9780358112136

LC 2019024061

Includes index.

"Whole30 menus and recipes for everyday social occasions from birthday parties and baby showers, to movie night, date night, and more".-- Provided by publisher.

Hartwig, Melissa

The **Whole30** slow cooker : 150 totally compliant prep-and-go recipes for your Whole30 / Melissa Hartwig ; photography by Ghazalle Badiozamani. Houghton Mifflin Harcourt, 2018. xxi,

313 p. : **641.5**

1. Nutritional therapy 2. Nutrition 3. Food habits 4. Self-care, Health 5. Cookbooks.
ISBN 9781328531049

LC 2018032711

Includes index.

Presents slow cooker recipes, including ribs, soups, and noodle bowls that comply with the Whole30 lifestyle.

"Each of the books recipes includes modifications for the Instant Pot, as well as an additional chapter of more than 30 dishes best suited for the device, such as smoky beef and bacon chili, and Chinese sesame chicken." Publishers Weekly.

Hasselbrink, Kimberley

Vibrant food : celebrating the ingredients, recipes, and colors of each season / written and photographed by Kimberley Hasselbrink. Ten Speed Press, 2014 215 p. : **641.5**

1. Seasonal cooking. 2. Color of food 3. Food 4. Recipes 5. Cookbooks.
ISBN 9781607745419

LC 2013040310

Includes index.

An artistic collection of whole-foods recipes by the creator of the acclaimed Year in Food blog reflects the role of color in the author's produce choices, providing such aesthetic options as Pasta with Nettle Pesto and Broiled Figs with Za'atar and Pecans.

"This enjoyable title would be a nice addition to the shelves of voracious seasonal cookbook readers, but it does not do enough to distinguish itself for most cooks, other than readers of the author's blog, to seek it out specifically." Library Journal.

Hay, Donna

Life in balance : a fresher approach to eating / Donna Hay. Fourth Estate, 2015. 237 p. : **641.5**

1. Cooking (Natural foods). 2. Nutrition. 3. Cookbooks.
ISBN 9781460750322

LC bl2016039686

Includes index.

A cookbook focusing on fresher eating includes such recipes as roasted zucchini lasagna, beef pho, kingfish ceviche, and caramel sticky date cookies.

"Recommended for readers who dislike the idea of dieting but want to explore popular health foods." Library Journal.

Headley, Brooks

Superiority Burger cookbook : the vegetarian hamburger is now delicious / Brooks Headley ; with Julia Goldberg, Gabe Rosner, Matthew Silverstein, and Matt Sweeney ; photographs by Sunny Shokrae. W. W. Norton & Company, 2018 223 p. : **641.5**

1. Superiority Burger (Restaurant). 2. Meat substitutes. 3. Hamburger 4. Vegetarian cooking. 5. Recipes 6. Cookbooks.
ISBN 9780393253986

LC 2018015069

Includes index.

The chef-owner of America's most talked-about vegetarian restaurant located in New York City's East Village presents 90 delicious recipes, some of which are the restaurant's favorites, that are innovative, irresistible and incredibly simple to make.

Hearst Books (Firm),

Christmas cookies : 75 irresistible holiday treats / Good Housekeeping Institute Hearst Books, 2016 128 p. : **641.5**

1. Christmas cooking. 2. Cookies. 3. Holiday cooking 4. Baking 5. Cookbooks.
ISBN 9781618371454

LC bl2016043060

At head of title: Good housekeeping.

Includes index.

Serving up the best from Good Housekeeping, a delightful holiday collection of 75 triple-tested cookie recipes--including Gingerbread Cutouts, Chocolate-Peanut Butter Thumbprints, Mint Peppermint Sticks and more--along with do-ahead tips and easy decorating and gift-wrapping ideas, is perfect for both expert bakers and enthusiastic home cooks.

Henry, Diana

A **change** of appetite : where healthy meets delicious / Diana Henry. Mitchell Beazley, 2014. 336 p. : **641.5**

1. Cooking. 2. International cooking 3. Seasonal cooking 4. Recipes 5. Cookbooks.
ISBN 9781845338923

LC oc2014022250

"Broken down by season, the book offers a nice mix of food from around the world that will not take a toll on the digestive system." Publishers Weekly.

How to eat a peach : menus, stories and places / Diana Henry. Mitchell Beazley, 2018. 224 p. **641.5**

1. Menus 2. Cooking 3. Food writers 4. Food writing 5. Essays
ISBN 9781784724115

LC bl2018064231

Personal essays about places, journeys, and particular times introduce twenty-four menus and explain the choice of dishes for each.

Plenty : good, uncomplicated food for the sustainable kitchen / Diana Henry. Mitchell Beazley, 2017. 320 p. : **641.5**

1. Seasonal cooking 2. Sustainable living. 3. Recipes 4. Cookbooks.
ISBN 9781784723002

Includes index.

"A very timely book--sure to appeal to many cooks." Library Journal.

Simple : effortless food, big flavors / Diana Henry. Mitchell Beazley, 2016. 335 p. : **641.5**

1. Cooking. 2. Quick and easy cooking 3. Recipes 4. Cookbooks.
ISBN 9781784722043

LC bl2016037984

Includes index.

Presents simple recipes that use common ingredients found in most kitchens, including such dishes as lamb chops with walnut, chiles, and honey salsa verde, cod with a crab and herb crust, Turkish pasta with feta, yogurt, and dill, and melon granita.

"Those looking to enliven their daily toast, eggs, pastas, and salads will find particularly fabulous choices here, along with other delicious mains and desserts." Library Journal.

Hesser, Amanda

The **essential** New York Times cook book : classic recipes for a new century / Amanda Hesser. W.W. Norton, c2010. xxiv, 932 p. : **641.5**

1. Cooking -- United States. 2. Recipes 3. Cookbooks.
ISBN 9780393061031

LC 2010033311

Text on lining papers.

The newspaper|s food columnist presents a compendium of more than 1,000 of the best recipes from the past 150 years of food journalism, including classics like Plum Torte, David Eyre|s Pancake and Pamela Sherrid|s Summer Pasta to modern-day fava bean salad.

"The author spent six years combing the Times's vast recipe archive, cooking her way through more than 1000 recipes to assemble this indispensible tome culled from 150 years of the paper's food columns. This daunting compendium features both noteworthy classics (Osso Buco) and modern recipes (Smoked Mashed Potatoes) that have been tested and, in some cases, updated for the contemporary cook. Chapters begin with a time line and are arranged by type of food (e.g., soups, vegetables, cakes) then chronologically within the chapter, making for a fascinating historic overview of the interests of American cooks." Library Journal.

Homolka, Gina

Skinnytaste fast and slow : knockout quick-fix and slow cooker recipes / Gina Homolka with Heather K. Jones, R.D.. Clarkson Potter/Publishers, 2016. 304 p. : **641.5**

1. Quick and easy cooking. 2. Electric cooking 3. Low-calorie diet 4. Dieting 5. Cookbooks.
ISBN 9780553459609

LC bl2016054008

Includes index.

Shares over one hundred recipes for dishes that are easy to prep, whether for cooking in the oven, on the stovetop or in a slow cooker, including such options as Korean-style beef tacos, pizza-stuffed chicken roll-ups, and peach-strawberry crumble.

"With its attractive design and easy everyday dishes, Homolka's latest may strike advanced cooks as too basic, but these recipes are excellent for novices. Expect demand." Library Journal.

Skinnytaste one & done : 140 no-fuss dinners for your Instant Pot, slow cooker, sheet pan, air fryer, dutch oven, & more / Gina Homolka with Heather K. Jones, R.D. Clarkson Potter/Publishers, 2018 303 p. : **641.5**

1. Quick and easy cooking. 2. Electric slow cookers 3. Dutch oven cooking. 4. One-dish meals. 5. Cookbooks
ISBN 9781524762155

LC 2018015876

Includes index.

Presents quick and easy, family-friendly recipes, with tips and nutritional information, for one-pot cooker convenience.

Hunt, Lindsay Maitland

Healthyish : a cookbook with seriously satisfying, truly simple, good-for-you (but not too good-for-you) recipes for real life / Lindsay Maitland Hunt ; photography by Linda Pugliese. Abrams, 2017. 255 p. : **641.5**

1. Cooking. 2. Recipes 3. Cookbooks.
ISBN 9781419726569

LC bl2018000448

Includes indexes.

A collection of simple, healthy recipes features such dishes as toasted coconut muesli, hummus and veggie pita, summer corn soup, pork and mushroom stroganoff, and salmon and quinoa bowl.

"Whether you like to leave cooking till the last minute or enjoy whipping up a big batch of something to eat throughout the week, this book will serve you well." Library Journal.

Help yourself : a guide to gut health for people who love delicious food / Lindsay Maitland Hunt ; photography by Linda Pugliese. Houghton Mifflin Harcourt, 2020. 352 p. **641.5**

1. Cooking. 2. Health. 3. Low-calorie diet 4. Nutrition. 5. Cookbooks.
ISBN 9780358008385

LC 2019045851

Emphasizing plant-based and whole ingredients this cookbook offers more than 125 recipes, including Brussels Sprouts and Peanut Butter Curry Bowl and Seeded Almond Flour Waffles with Raspberry-Flax Smash, that will help restore microbial balance in the gut.

"This is a lightning bolt of lucidity in a crowded and jargon-laden field of often impractical and unsustainable dietary approaches." Publishers Weekly

Hyland, Emily

Emily : the cookbook / Emily & Matthew Hyland with Rick Rodgers ; with photographs by Evan Sung. Ballantine Books, 2018 xvi, 221 p. : **641.5**

1. Cooking. 2. Pizza. 3. Cookbooks.
ISBN 9781524796839

LC 2018018964

Includes index.

The husband and wife team responsible for restaurants Emily and Emmy Squared share some of their pizza and burger recipes, as well as recipes for sandwiches, pasta, desserts, and cocktails.

"The husband-and-wife culinary team behind the New York City restaurants Emily and Emmy Squared serve up more than 100 recipes in their excellent debut collection." Publishers Weekly.

Jaffrey, Madhur

Madhur Jaffrey's world vegetarian. / Madhur Jaffrey. Clarkson Potter, 2002, c1999. ix, 758 p. : **641.5**

1. Vegetarian cooking. 2. Cooking, International. 3. Recipes 4. Cookbooks
ISBN 9780609809235

LC BL2002005317

Reprint. Originally published: 1999.
Includes index.

An international assortment of more than 650 meatless recipes representing a host of ethnic culinary traditions includes soups and salads, vegetable dishes, beans and grains, and chutneys and sauces.

"A compendium of vegetarian recipes from all over the world. Grouped mostly into broad categories by main ingredient (beans, grain, vegetables, etc.), they are as likely to come from a Palestinian restaurant in Toronto, the nuns at the Ormylia Monastery in Macedonia, or a home cook in Mexico as from Jaffrey's own Indian background or her experience as a cooking teacher." Library Journal.

Johnson, Elaine,

The **great** outdoors cookbook : adventures in cooking under the open sky / edited by Elaine Johnson and Margo True. Oxmoor House, 2014 254 p. : **641.5**

1. Outdoor cooking. 2. Recipes 3. Cookbooks.
ISBN 9780376028075

LC bl2014015505

At head of title: Sunset.

Offers recipes that can be prepared in an outdoor setting, utilizing such techniques as grilling, smoking, and Dutch and solar oven cooking, and provides the most up-to-date expert advice on cooking equipment.

Jones, Anna (Food writer)

A **modern** way to eat : 200+ satisfying vegetarian recipes (that will make you feel amazing) / Anna Jones. Ten Speed Press, 2014 352 p. : **641.5**

1. Vegetarian cooking. 2. Cookbooks.
ISBN 9781607748038

LC 2014035561

Includes index.

Collects quick, healthy recipes that explore the full breadth of vegetarian ingredients--grains, nuts, seeds, and seasonal vegetables.

Jones, Judith, 1924-2017

The **pleasures** of cooking for one / Judith Jones. Alfred A. Knopf, 2009. x, 273 p. : **641.5**

1. Cooking for one. 2. Quick and easy cooking 3. Recipes 4. Cookbooks
ISBN 9780307270726

LC 2009012307

Counsels readers on how to enjoy a solitary culinary life by preparing meals in accordance with one's own preferences, outlining a range of basic through sophisticated recipes that work in weekly menus and make use of leftovers.

"This is a civilized, unfussy guide to cooking--and cooking well--for solitary diners. [The author] doesn't skip desserts, entertaining or self-indulgence, and best of all, her whole book benefits from the diverse and cumulative gleanings of work with many of the great cooks and cookbook writers (including Julia Child, of course) of the latter half of the 20th century." Publishers Weekly.

Kaminsky, Peter

The **essential** New York times grilling cookbook : more than 100 years of sizzling food writing and recipes / edited by Peter Kaminsky ; foreword by Mark Bittman. Sterling Epicure, 2014 xvi, A-P, 384 p. : **641.5**

1. Barbecuing. 2. Recipes 3. Cookbooks.
ISBN 9781402793240

LC 2013026602

Includes index.

Collects notable recipes and stories, chosen from the past century of New York times articles on barbecuing and grilling, including Texas-style brisket, grilled plums with star fruit, and barbecued pork tenderloin.

"A fascinating look at how various innovators, personalities, and cultural trends have shaped the evolution of grilling and barbecue." Library Journal.

Kamozawa, Aki

Ideas in food : great recipes and why they work / Aki Kamozawa and H. Alexander Talbot. Clarkson Potter, c2010. 9-320 p. ; **641.5**

1. Chemistry. 2. Cooking. 3. Recipes
ISBN 9780307717405

LC 2010017633

The writers of Popular Science's "Kitchen Alchemy" online column share informative essays that explain both food-preparation methods and underlying science, building on today's popular "geek-chic" trends with more than 75 recipes.

"The authors break down the science behind correctly and deliciously preparing everything from bread, pasta, and eggs (including soft scrambled eggs; hardboiled eggs, and brown butter hollandaise sauce) to homemade butter and yogurt. Most recipes fall into the Ideas for Everyone category, which composes about the first three-quarters of the book; the final section is Ideas for Professionals, which explores trendy molecular gastronomy topics like liquid nitrogen--used to make popcorn gelato--and carbon dioxide, a necessary tool for making coffee onion rings. Straightforward prose and anecdotes with personality keep this from being a dry food science tome. And accessible recipes for such dishes as a simple roast chicken, green beans almondine, and root beer-braised short ribs mean it never gets too lofty." Publishers Weekly.

Kasper, Lynne Rossetto, 1943-

The **Splendid** table's, how to eat supper : recipes, stories, and opinions from public radio's award-winning food show / Lynne Rossetto Kasper and Sally Swift. Clarkson Potter/Publishers, 2008. xii, 338 p. : **641.5**

1. Suppers. 2. Cooking, American. 3. Recipes
ISBN 9780307346711

LC 2007024749

Includes index.

"This superb book should grace the shelves of even the most infrequent of cooks." Publishers Weekly.

Kassoff, Anya

Simply vibrant : all-day vegetarian recipes for colorful plant-based cooking / Anya Kassoff ; photography by Masha Davydova. Roost, 2018. 328 p. ; **641.5**

1. Vegetarian cooking 2. Seasonal cooking 3. Cookbooks.
ISBN 9781611803846

LC 2016057919

Includes index.

The author of The Vibrant Table, through everyday recipes inspired by the seasons and practical preparations, shows home cooks how to create colorful foods using flavors from around the world, including Superfood Summer Porridge, Grilled Pineapple and Avocado Salsa, Roasted Portobello & Eggplant Gyros, Daikon Radish Pad Thai and many more.

Katz, Rebecca

The **cancer-fighting** kitchen : nourishing big-flavor recipes for cancer treatment and recovery / Rebecca Katz with Mat Edelson. Celestial Arts, c2009. x, 222 p. : **641.5**

1. Cancer -- Diet therapy 2. Recipes
ISBN 9781587613449

LC 2009014359

A cookbook for cancer patients with more than 100 specially formulated recipes for their specific nutritional and appetite needs, featuring a step-by-step guide to nutritionally preparing for chemotherapy and radiation, and using powerhouse ingredients to create a cancer-fighting culinary toolkit.--Provided by publisher.

Katzen, Mollie, 1950-

The **heart** of the plate : vegetarian recipes for a new generation / recipes, photographs, and illustrations by Mollie Katzen. Houghton Mifflin Harcourt 2013. 456 p. : **641.5**

1. Vegetarian cooking. 2. International cooking. 3. Cooking (Natural foods) 4. Recipes 5. Cookbooks
ISBN 9780547571591

LC 2013010180

"A Rux Martin book."

Includes index.

Reinventing the traditional vegetarian repertoire, offers 250 recipes for simple and healthful dishes that celebrate vegetables in all their glory and juxtapose colors and textures to make weeknight dinners fresh and exciting.

Katzen, Mollie, 1950-

The **Moosewood** cookbook / Mollie Katzen. Ten Speed Press, 2014 xvi, 231 p. : **641.5**

1. Moosewood Restaurant. 2. Vegetarian cooking. 3. Cooking (Natural foods) 4. Cookbooks.
ISBN 9781607747390

LC 2014015685

Includes index.

Traditional cooking styles and eclectic cuisines are reflected in a collection of vegetarian recipes served at the Moosewood Restaurant.

Kimball, Christopher

Christopher Kimball's Milk Street : the new home cooking / with Matthew Card, J.M. Hirsch, Michelle Locke and Jennifer Baldino Cox. Little, Brown and Company, 2017. xxv, 310 p. : **641.5**

1. International cooking 2. Recipes 3. Cookbooks.
ISBN 9780316437288

LC bl2017037212

Includes index.

A collection of recipes for the home cook, inspired by Christopher Kimballs Milk Street Television show and arranged by type of dish features such offerings as curry braised eggs, Vietnamese caramel fish, multigrain soda bread, and pumpkin tart.

"Overall, with its testing notes, short ingredient lists, and firm directions (each recipe has a dont section), this volume is a trustworthy and easy-to-use collection of international flavors from one of the nations best cooking teachers." Booklist.

Kimball, Christopher

★**Christopher** Kimball's Milk Street : Tuesday nights / Christopher Kimball, J.M. Hirsch, Matthew Card, Michelle Locke, Jennifer Baldino Cox, and the editors and cooks of Milk Street ; photography by Connie Miller. Little, Brown and Company, 2018. ix, 405 p. : **641.5**

1. Quick and easy cooking 2. Cookbooks.
ISBN 9780316437318

LC bl2018186299

Includes index.

A collection of quick recipes for weeknight dining, inspired by Christopher Kimball's Milk Street Television show, include such dishes as yakiudon with pickled ginger, pork schnitzel, kale and white bean soup, Indonesian fried tofu salad, and three-cheese pizza.

"Milk Street's globally inspired approach to fast cooking is anything but bland. Turn to their latest for flavorful weeknight winners." Library Journal.

Milk Street : the new rules : recipes that will change the way you cook / Christopher Kimball ; with writing and editing by J.M. Hirsch and Michelle Locke ; recipes by Matthew Card, Diane Unger and the Cooks at Milk Street ; art direction by Jennifer Baldino Cox and Brianna Coleman ; photography by Connie Miller of CB Creatives. Voracious, Little, Brown and Company, 2019. xv, 302 p. : **641.5**

1. Christopher Kimball's Milk Street (Firm) 2. Cooking. 3. Recipes 4. Cookbooks.
ISBN 9780316423052

LC bl2019032149

Includes index.

The Milk Street chef and his team offer such recipes as Vietnamese Chicken Salad and Malaysian-Style Noodles while demonstrating adaptable tips, tricks and ideas for dramatically improving preparation times and overall results.

"Highly recommended for fans of Kimball and Cook's Illustrated, with delicious recipes and sound techniques to improve and spice up everyday cooking routines." Library Journal

Kish, Kristen, 1983-

Kristen Kish cooking : recipes and techniques / Kristen Kish ; with Meredith Erickson. Clarkson Potter/Publishers, 2017 287 p. : **641.5**

1. Cooking -- Technique. 2. Creative ability in cooking. 3. Gourmet cooking 4. Recipes 5. Cookbooks.
ISBN 9780553459760

LC 2016055343

Includes index.

The winner of the tenth season of "Top Chef" shares her personal history as an adopted child from Korea and offers insights into cooking technqiues and flavor combinations, with a collection of recipes that showcase her unique pairing of ingredients to create signature dishes.

Knauer, Ian

The **farm** cooking school : techniques and recipes that celebrate the seasons / Ian Knauer and Shelley Wiseman ; photography by Guy Ambrosino. BLP, 2017. 250 p. : **641.5**

1. Cooking (Vegetables) 2. Cooking, American. 3. Recipes 4. Seasonal cooking. 5. Cookbooks
ISBN 0997211342

LC bl2017050465

Includes index.

A cookbook that celebrates the seasons includes such recipes as rhubarb chutney, pistachio baklava, cheddar and caramelized onion pizza, honey panna cotta with candied orange zest, and lemon chiffon mousse.

Koenig, Leah

Modern Jewish cooking : recipes & customs for today's kitchen / Leah Koenig ; photographs by Sang An. Chronicle Books, 2015 352 p. : **641.5**

1. Jewish cooking. 2. Kosher food 3. Recipes 4. Cookbooks
ISBN 1452127484

LC 2014012075

Presents a collection of 175 recipes which represent updated versions of traditional Jewish dishes, including potato-leek kugel, fattoush, beet latkes with chive goat cheese, and chicken schnitzel with caper vinaigrette.

"The beautiful photography, pleasing layout on heavy paper, and excellent recipes make this a fine gift book as well as a suitable purchase for cookbook collections, especially in communities with large Jewish populations." Library Journal.

Krieger, Ellie

The **food** you crave : luscious recipes for a healthy life / Ellie Krieger. Taunton Press, c2008. 316 p. : **641.5**

1. Cooking. 2. Nutrition. 3. Recipes
ISBN 9781600850219

LC 2007037528

Presents a selection of two hundred recipes for every type of meal that emphasizes such healthy ingredients as herbs, spices, vegetables, grains, fruits, meats, and fish, and provides a nutritional breakdown for each dish.

Krieger, Ellie

You have it made! : delicious, healthy do-ahead meals / Ellie Krieger ; with photography by Quentin Bacon. Houghton Mifflin Harcourt, 2016. 352 p. : **641.5**

1. Make-ahead cooking. 2. Recipes 3. Cookbooks
ISBN 0544579305

LC 2015028798

A longtime Food Network star and best-selling author offers make-ahead recipes for breakfast, salads, soups, entrees, vegetarian dishes and much more.

Lagasse, Emeril

Emeril at the grill : a cookbook for all seasons / Emeril Lagasse ; with photography by Steven Freeman. HarperStudio, c2009. xxii, 248 p. : **641.5**

1. Barbecuing. 2. Cookouts 3. Recipes 4. Cookbooks
ISBN 9780061742743

LC 2010275712

Includes index.

Presents techniques for both indoor and outdoor cooking, so you can keep the party going all year round. From drinks (watermelon margaritas) to meats (grilled marinated flank steak with chimichurri sauce, from salads (watercress, avocado, and mango Salad) to desserts (ever grill a banana split?), this is a grilling book like no other. Features 158 recipes.

Lagasse, Emeril

Essential Emeril : favorite recipes and hard-won wisdom from a life in the kitchen / Emeril Lagasse with Pam Hoenig. Oxmoor House, 2015 304 p. : **641.5**

1. Cooking. 2. Recipes 3. Cookbooks
ISBN 9780848744786

LC bl2015038121

Includes indexes.

The celebrity chef shares anecdotes, cooking instructions, and recipes for iconic dishes that have shaped his career from easy barbecue shrimp and duck confit with killer bacon waffles to lobster and saffron risotto and grilled calamari salad.

"More advanced than some of his other titles, Lagasse's latest showcases his skill. Emeril fans will savor these delicious and iconic dishes." Library Journal.

Lancaster, Bridget

★**Cooking** at home with Bridget & Julia : the TV hosts of America's Test Kitchen share their favorite recipes for feeding family and friends / Bridget Lancaster, Julia Collin Davison, and the editors at America's Test Kitchen. America's Test Kitchen, 2017 xv, 304 p. : **641.5**

1. Cooking. 2. Recipes 3. Cookbooks.
ISBN 9781945256165

LC 2017018306

Includes index.

The television hosts share their favorite recipes, including muffin tin doughnuts, corned beef hash, hearty beef and vegetable stew, tomato and mozzarella tart, and florentine lace cookies.

Larsen, Jeffrey, 1962-

Gluten-free baking at home : 102 foolproof recipes for delicious breads, cakes, cookies, and more / Jeffrey Larsen ; photographs by Kelly Puleio. Ten Speed Press, 2019. 277 p. : **641.5**

1. Baking. 2. Gluten-free diet 3. Pies. 4. Bread. 5. Cookbooks
ISBN 9780399582790

LC 2018060697

A comprehensive, fully illustrated collection of more than 80 master recipes and variations for gluten- and allergen-free baked goods includes options ranging from chocolate chip cookies and banana bread to brioche and biscuits. Illustrations.

"A lovingly precise collection of gluten-free baking classics, stunning yet never showy. Highly recommended for bakers of all skill levels." Library Journal.

Larson, Elsie

A **beautiful** mess : weekday weekend : how to live a healthy veggie life ... and still eat treats / text and photographs by Elsie Larson and Emma Chapman. Chronicle Books, 2017 208 p. : **641.5**

1. Vegetarian cooking. 2. Recipes 3. Cookbooks.
ISBN 9781452154718

LC 2016053237

A collection of vegetarian recipes from the popular style bloggers that help readers embrace their philosophy of eating responsibly during the week--avoiding refined flours, sugars, alcohol, and dairy--and indulging on weekends.

Lawson, Nigella, 1960-

How to eat : the pleasures and principles of good food / Nigella Lawson. John Wiley, 2002, c2000. xx, 474 p. ; **641.5**

1. Cooking. 2. Food.
ISBN 0471257508

LC 2003265369

Originally published: New York : John Wiley, 2000.

Earthy, witty, and totally passionate about eating, British food phenomenon Nigella Lawson has taken North American kitchens by storm with the huge success of her television show, Nigella Bites. How to Eat is the book that started it all -- her signature, all-purpose cookbook that became a blockbuster bestseller on its publication in England and has now sold hundreds of thousands of copies on both sides of the Atlantic.

Lawson, Nigella, 1960-

Nigella express : good food, fast / Nigella Lawson ; photography by Lis Parsons. Hyperion, c2007. 390 p. : **641.5**

1. Quick and easy cooking. 2. Recipes 3. Cookbooks
ISBN 9781401322434

LC bl2007024380

Includes index.

Presents a collection of over a hundred fast recipes, including Asian-flavored chowder and no-worries chocolate mousse, accompanied by time-saving tips, recommendations for stocking a kitchen, and culinary strategies.

Lawson, Nigella, 1960-

Simply Nigella / Nigella Lawson ; photographs by Keiko Oikawa. Flatiron Books, 2015. xiii, 402 p. : **641.5**

1. Cooking. 2. Comfort food. 3. Cookbooks.
ISBN 9781250073754

LC 2015036267

Includes index.

" Whatever the occasion, food--in the making and the eating--should always be pleasurable. Simply Nigella taps into the rhythms of our cooking lives with recipes that are uncomplicated and relaxed yet always satisfying. From quick and calm workday dinners (Miso Salmon; Cauliflower & Cashew Nut Curry) to stress-free ideas when feeding a crowd (Chicken Traybake with Bitter Orange & Fennel) to the instant joy of bowlfood for cozy nights on the sofa (Thai Noodles with Cinnamon and Shrimp), here is food guaranteed to make everyone feel good. Whether you need to create some breathing space at the end of a long week (Asian-Flavored Short Ribs), indulge in a sweet treat (Lemon Pavlova; Chocolate Chip Cookie Dough Pots), or wake up to a strength-giving breakfast (Toasty Olive Oil Granola), Nigella's new cookbook is filled with recipes destined to become firm favorites. Simply Nigella is the perfect antidote to our busy lives: a calm and glad celebration of food to soothe and uplift".-- Provided by publisher.

"Home cooks who love planning relaxed meals by whim will be well served by Lawson's latest, which offers a winning selection of recipes for all occasions." Library Journal.

Le, Stephanie

Easy gourmet : awesome recipes anyone can cook / from

the creator of "I am a Food Blog" named top cooking blog by Saveur magazine, Stephanie Le. Page Street Publishing Co., 2014. 240 p. : **641.5**

1. Cooking. 2. Recipes 3. Quick and easy cooking 4. Gourmet cooking 5. Cookbooks.
ISBN 9781624140624

LC bl2014037483

Includes index.

Collects simple recipes with gourmet flavor from the creator of the popular website, "I am a Food Blog," including chicken and waffles, glazed duck, miso cod and quinoa, braised beef brisket, and raspberry pistachio pavlova.

"Simple recipes, attractive photographs, an easy-to-read layout, and a functional lie-flat binding make this a great choice for young and aspiring cooks, small families, and anyone looking for easy meal ideas." Library Journal.

Leake, Lisa

100 days of real food : how we did it, what we learned, and 100 easy, wholesome recipes your family will love / Lisa Leake. William Morrow, 2014 360 p. : **641.5**

1. Cooking (Natural foods) 2. Recipes 3. Cookbooks.
ISBN 9780062252555

LC bl2014036664

Presents a hands-on cookbook and guide that provides family-friendly recipes and practical advice for eating wholesome natural food that is not highly processed or refined.

100 days of real food on a budget : simple tips and tasty recipes to help you cut out processed food without breaking the bank / Lisa Leake. William Morrow, 2018 295 p. : **641.5**

1. Cooking (Natural foods). 2. Low-cost cooking 3. Recipes 4. Quick and easy cooking 5. Cookbooks
ISBN 9780062668554

LC bl2018156978

Shares shopping lists and meal plans designed to eliminate processed foods while on a tight budget.

Lee, Cecilia Hae-Jin

Quick & easy Korean cooking : more than 70 everyday recipes / bcby Cecilia Hae-Jin Lee ; photographs by Julie Toy and Cecilia Hae-Jin Lee. Chronicle Books, c2009. 168 p. : **641.5**

1. Cooking, Korean. 2. Quick and easy cooking. 3. Recipes 4. Cookbooks
ISBN 9780811861465

LC 2008033629

"Gourmet cook book club selection"--Cover.

Imagine sitting down to a sumptuous and fragrant dinner of Dumpling Soup with Rice Cakes after a long day of work. And a hot summer afternoon just begs for a picnic basket stocked with Chilled Cucumber Soup, delicate Chicken Skewers with Green Onions, and Seaweed Rice Rolls. Using ingredients that are readily available and techniques already familiar to home cooks, these Korean specialties can easily be dinner any night of the week. With appetizers and snacks, soups and hot pots, side dishes, entrees, rice, noodles, and a whole chapter devoted to kimchi, Quick & Easy Korean Cooking will bring new flavors to the dinner table. --From publisher description.

Lee, Matt

★The **Lee** Bros. Southern cookbook : stories and recipes for Southerners and would-be Southerners / Matt Lee and Ted Lee. W. W. Norton, c2006. 589 p. : **641.5**

1. Lee, Matt. 2. Lee, Ted. 3. Cooking, American -- Southern style 4. Food writers -- United States 5. Brothers -- South Carolina 6. Recipes 7. South Carolina -- Social life and customs -- 20th century 8. South Carolina -- Social life and customs -- 21st century
ISBN 9780393057812

LC 2006022745

Includes index.

Two brothers describe their culinary coming-of-age in Charleston, South Carolina, in a cookbook that features recipes for such dishes as fried chicken, crab cakes, pecan pie, and buttermilk-sweet potato pie, accompanied by helpful hints and substitution tips.

"Every recipe has a story attached, and the large format makes for easy reading." Booklist.

Leidich, Shari Koolik

Two Moms in the Raw : simple, clean, irresistible recipes for your family's health / Shari Koolik Leidich ; photography by Iain Bagwell. Houghton Mifflin Harcourt, 2015 288 p. : **641.5**

1. Two Moms in the Raw (Firm). 2. Quick and easy cooking. 3. Raw foods. 4. Cooking (Natural foods). 5. Raw food diet 6. Cookbooks.
ISBN 9780544253254

LC 2014036934

The founder of the national award-winning healthy snack company Two Moms in the Raw presents a raw, cooked and gluten-free guide to eating well that includes more than 130 recipes that will help anyone get back on track, enjoy greater vitality, reduce stress and achieve their best health.

"Home cooks may be daunted by her inclusive list of basic exotics--including gomaiso, ashwagandha, coconut aminos, and psyllium husks--but her kid-friendly 'coconutty' chicken breasts and raw key lime pie bring a fun nutritional boost to the family table." Publishers Weekly.

Levine, Sarabeth

Sarabeth's good morning cookbook : breakfast, brunch, and baking / Sarabeth Levine with Genevieve Ko ; photographs by Quentin Bacon. Rizzoli, 2015 282 p. : **641.5**

1. Breakfasts. 2. Brunches. 3. Baking. 4. Recipes 5. Cookbooks
ISBN 9780847846382

LC 2015938571

Includes index.

Legendary New York City baker and restaurateur Sarabeth Levine shares her most beloved breakfast and brunch recipes.

Liddon, Angela

Oh she glows every day cookbook : quick and simple satisfying plant-based recipes / Angela Liddon. Avery, 2016 xvi, 333 p. : **641.5**

1. Cooking (Vegetables) 2. Recipes 3. Seasonal cooking 4. Vegan cooking. 5. Cookbooks
ISBN 1583335749

LC 2016009038

A follow-up to the best-selling The Oh She Glows Cookbook shares more than 100 quick-and-easy whole-food, plant-based recipes designed for today's busy lifestyles, from Fusilli Lentil-Mushroom Bolognese to Ultimate Flourless Brownies.

Lightner, Jill

Cooking from scratch : 120 recipes for colorful, seasonal food from PCC Community Markets / with Jill Lightner ; photographs by Charity Burggraff. Sasquatch Books, 2018 xxi, 279 p. : **641.5**

1. PCC Community Markets. 2. Cooking (Natural foods) 3. Recipes

4. Seasonal cooking 5. Seattle, Washington 6. Cookbooks.
ISBN 9781632171887

LC 2018000128

Includes index.

120 simple and delicious recipes in a cookbook that's chock-full of nutritional information and expert advice from Seattle's popular grocer, PCC Community Markets. --From publisher description.

"This diverse collection of easy-to-follow and flavorful recipes is a delicious, memorable addition to any home kitchen." Library Journal.

Lillien, Lisa

Hungry girl 1-2-3 : the easiest, most delicious, guilt-free recipes on the planet / Lisa Lillien. St. Martin's Griffin, c2010. xv, 333 p., [16] p. of plates : **641.5**

1. Quick and easy cooking 2. Low-calorie diet -- Recipes. 3. Low-fat diet -- Recipes. 4. Recipes 5. Cookbooks.
ISBN 9780312556181

LC 2009046743

Includes index.

With a focus on quick-to-prepare meals, offers recipes that require four ingredients or less and make use of the microwave, crockpot, and foil-pack baking, as well as some dishes that require no cooking.

Hungry girl simply 6 : all-natural recipes with 6 ingredients or less / Lisa Lillien. St. Martin's Griffin, 2019. 384 p. : **641.5**

1. Quick and easy cooking 2. Low-calorie diet -- Recipes. 3. Low-fat diet -- Recipes. 4. Cookbooks.
ISBN 9781250154521

LC 2018050709

Includes index.

A collection of recipes with six ingredients or less for meals, snacks, and desserts includes vegetarian and gluten-free recipes.

Ly, Linda, 1980-

The **new** camp cookbook / Linda Ly ; photography by Will Taylor. Voyager Press, 2017 224 p. ; **641.5**

1. Outdoor cooking. 2. Seasonal cooking 3. Cookbooks.
ISBN 9780760352014

LC 2016054283

Shares campfire recipes for anyone who enjoys cooking outdoors, including chai-spiced oatmeal with cinnamon apples, egg-in-a-hole grilled cheese, tin foil seafood boil, and homemade hot chocolate mix.

Madison, Deborah

★**In** my kitchen : a collection of new and favorite vegetarian recipes / Deborah Madison ; photography by Erin Scott. Ten Speed Press, 2017 285 p. : **641.5**

1. Vegetarian cooking. 2. Cooking. 3. Recipes 4. Cookbooks.
ISBN 9780399578885

LC 2016038957

Presents an updated collection of recipes from the country's leading authority on vegetarian cooking, including such dishes as cheese souffle, braised summer vegetables, and zucchini cake, with menu suggestions and tips for modifications.

"One glance will quickly show why the dishes here are Madison's go-to meals, and they will soon become reader's favorites as well." Publishers Weekly.

Madison, Deborah

The **new** vegetarian cooking for everyone / Deborah Madison. Ten Speed Press, 2014 vi, 665 p. ; **641.5**

1. Vegetarian cooking. 2. Recipes 3. Cookbooks.
ISBN 9781607745532

LC 2013046540

Includes index.

Originally published: New York : Broadway Books, 1997.

Presents a vegetarian primer cookbook with basic, stylish cooking techniques, including more than 1,600 classic recipes, with comprehensive information on vegetarian and vegan ingredients.

Madison, Deborah

★**Vegetarian** cooking for everyone / Deborah Madison. Broadway Books, c2007. x, 742 p., 24 p. of plates : **641.5**

1. Recipes 2. Vegetarian cooking.
ISBN 0767927478

LC 2007010075

Includes index.

Originally published: New York : Broadway Books, 1997.

The founding chef of San Francisco's Greens restaurant and award-winning author of The Greens Cookbook presents a lavishly illustrated cookbook of more than 1,400 innovative vegetarian and vegan recipes and comprehensive information on a myriad of vegetables dishes, in a tenth anniversary edition of the James Beard Award-winning cookbook.

"Following information on ingredients and techniques, the recipes focus mainly on vegetables and grains, aiming at flavor and variety, both often arrived at via assorted ethnic approaches." Publishers Weekly.

Marks, Gil

The **world** of Jewish cooking / Gil Marks. Simon & Schuster, 1999, c1996. 406 p. : **641.5**

1. Cooking, Kosher 2. Jewish cooking 3. Kosher food
ISBN 9780684835594

LC BL 99012334

A Fireside book."

Includes index.

Reprint. Originally published: c1996.

A collection of kosher recipes from two dozen communities around the world also includes holiday dishes and lore about the history of Jewish food throughout the ages.

"This cookbook is loosely arranged by food category, with chapters on appetizers, soups, and main dishes, as well as side items, breads, and desserts. You'll find recipes from India, Africa, even China, here, alongside many dishes that originated in one of the two major Jewish cultural communities, Ashkenazic and Sephardic." Booklist.

McFadden, Joshua

★**Six** seasons : a new way with vegetables / Joshua McFadden with Martha Holmberg ; foreword by Barbara Damrosch and Eliot Coleman. Artisan, 2017 397 p. ; **641.5**

1. Cooking (Vegetables) 2. Recipes 3. Seasonal cooking. 4. Cookbooks.
ISBN 9781579656317

LC OC2018135929

Includes index.

A chef and "vegetable whisperer" offers 225 vegetable-centric recipes that provide a new way to view and utilize their attributes throughout their growing seasons including Farro and Tomato Salad, Carrot and Beet Slaw and Fried Farro with Pickled Carrots and Runny Eggs.

"McFadden's debut cookbook is an invaluable resource for all things veggie." Booklist.

McGee, Harold

Keys to good cooking : a guide to making the best of foods and recipes / Harold McGee. Penguin Books, 2012, c2010. xvii, 552 p. ; **641.5**

1. Cooking. 2. Food. 3. Cookbooks
ISBN 9780143122319

LC bl2012043471

Originally published: New York : Penguin Press, 2010.

A one-stop reference answers common kitchen conundrums the home cook may have, from equipment and cooking methods to how to handle nearly every ingredient.

Miglore, Kristen

Food52 genius recipes : 100 recipes that will change the way you cook / Kristen Miglore ; photography by James Ransom. Ten Speed Press, 2015 xvii, 251 p. : **641.5**

1. Cooking. 2. Recipes 3. Cookbooks.
ISBN 9781607747970

LC 2014034413

Includes index.

"An essential collection of more than 100 foolproof recipes from food luminaries such as Julia Child, Alice Waters, and David Chang--curated, introduced, and photographed by the team behind the leading food website Food52. This debut title from Food52 Works, a new imprint from Ten Speed Press, draws from Food52's James Beard Award-nominated Genius Recipes column, which features inventive recipes that rethink cooking tropes and, simply put, are nothing short of genius. In this inspired book for the modern cook, Food52's executive editor Kristen Miglore combines new genius recipes, greatest hits from the column, and her own kitchen wisdom in a sleek, lushly illustrated package. Whether it's fail-safe Fried Chicken from Michael Ruhlman or the imaginative Black Pepper Tofu from Yotam Ottolenghi, once you try these recipes, you'll never need to go back to other versions. Plus with abundant how-to and finished dish photographs throughout, Genius Recipes is destined to become every home cook's go-to reference for smart, enjoyable cooking. "-- Provided by publisher.

"Miglore's addition to Food52's growing list of cookbooks is a treat for readers who enjoy casual gourmet food." Library Journal.

Miller, Klancy

★**Cooking** solo : the joy of cooking for yourself / Klancy Miller ; photographs by Tara Donne. Houghton Mifflin Harcourt, 2016 xiii, 225 p.: **641.5**

1. Cooking for one. 2. Quick and easy cooking. 3. Recipes 4. Cookbooks.
ISBN 9780544176485

LC 2015015219

Collects one hundred simple, quick recipes designed for single-diner meals, eliminating the need for scaling down ingredients, including such options as Tahitian noodle sandwich, smoked duck breast salad, and mackerel with lemon and capers.

"This cookbook reframes cooking, which can seem like a chore, as a form of self-care. Solo diners looking to revive the pleasure of cooking for one will enjoy this." Library Journal

Miller, Laura (Cook)

Raw, vegan, not gross : all vegan and mostly raw recipes for people who love to eat / Laura Miller ; photography by David Loftus. Flatiron Books, 2016. 215 p. : **641.5**

1. Raw foods. 2. Vegan cooking. 3. Cookbooks.
ISBN 9781250066909

LC 2016014385

Includes index.

The creator and star of YouTube's Tastemade show by the same name shares more than 100 vegan and mostly raw recipes for people who want to enjoy a vibrant and satisfying diet, providing options for a range of occasions while sharing her perspectives on food and body image in her signature frank and self-deprecating style.

Mills, Ella

Natural feasts : 100+ healthy, plant-based recipes to share and enjoy with friends and family / Ella Mills. Scribner, 2017. 286 p. : **641.5**

1. Cooking (Natural foods). 2. Recipes 3. Vegetarian cooking. 4. Cookbooks
ISBN 1501174274

LC bl2017042156

Includes index.

In this follow-up to her best-selling, debut cookbook, Deliciously Ella, the popular blogger and healthy living advocate offers over 100 plant-based, gluten-free, clean-eating recipes for easy weeknight dinners, large feasts, birthday parties, picnics and cocktails.

"For a plant-based entertainer who wants to serve the most delicious, natural, and healthy food, this cookbook is a must purchase." Publishers Weekly.

Moody, Liz

Healthier together : recipes for two--nourish your body, nourish your relationships / Liz Moody ; photographs by Lauren Volo. Clarkson Potter/Publishers, 2019 239 p. : **641.5**

1. Cooking. 2. Dinners and dining. 3. Nutrition. 4. Recipes 5. Cookbooks.
ISBN 9780525573272

LC 2018027627

Includes index.

Presents a collection of gluten-free, dairy-free, and plant-centered recipes designed to serve two, along with a twenty-one-day cleanup and information on recommended equipment and ingredients.

"Moody, the food editor of the Mindbodygreen website, focuses on a largely vegetable diet with no refined sugars or grains, and gut-healthy anti-inflammatory foods (in considering breads, for example, she suggests sourdough or sprouted)." Publishers Weekly.

Moosewood Collective

Moosewood Restaurant cooks at home : fast and easy recipes for any day / the Moosewood Collective. Simon and Schuster, c1994. 416 p. : **641.5**

1. Moosewood Restaurant. 2. Vegetarian cooking. 3. Cooking (Natural foods). 4. Recipes 5. Cookbooks
ISBN 9780671679927

LC 93039126

"A Fireside book."

Includes index.

Offers more than 150 time-efficient and easy-to-follow recipes for healthy dishes, many of them vegetarian, along with tips on cooking techniques, menu planning, and more.

Moosewood Collective

Moosewood restaurant favorites : the 250 most-requested naturally delicious recipes from one of America's best-loved restaurants / The Moosewood Collective ; food photography by Jim Scherer. St. Martin's Griffin, 2013. xiv, 402 p. : **641.5**

1. Moosewood Restaurant. 2. Vegetarian cooking. 3. Cooking

(Natural foods) 4. Recipes 5. Cookbooks.
ISBN 9781250006257

LC 2013013841

Includes index.

A collection of classic vegetarian recipes from the first four decades of the Moosewood Restaurant features 250 most-requested favorites updated to reflect today's practices and includes such options as Red Lentil Soup with Ginger and Cilantro, Caramelized Onion Pie and Vegan Chocolate Cake.

"Throughout, recipes are concise and confident, accompanied by helpful preparation tips and serving ideas. Whether vegetarian or not, home cooks looking for fresh inspiration will appreciate this book built on years of experience." Booklist.

Moosewood Collective

The **Moosewood** Restaurant table : 250 brand-new recipes from the natural foods restaurant that revolutionized eating in America / The Moosewood Collective ; food photography by Al Karevy ; food styling by Patti Harville. St. Martin's Griffin, 2017 xii, 400 p. : **641.5**

1. Moosewood Restaurant. 2. Vegetarian cooking 3. Pescatarian cooking 4. Cooking (Natural foods) 5. Cookbooks.
ISBN 9781250074331

LC 2018173546

A collection of new recipes from the New York natural foods restaurant consistent with its farm-to-table philosophy features such dishes as Asian filo rolls, spring risotto, and sweet potato gnocchi, along with vegan and gluten-free options.

The **best** recipe / the editors of Cook's illustrated Boston Common Press, 1999. 575 p. : **641.5**

1. Cooking, American 2. Recipes 3. Cookbooks.
ISBN 9780936184388

LC 2002512594

Morgan, Jeff (Winemaker)

The **covenant** kitchen : food and wine for the new Jewish table / Jeff and Jodie Morgan. Schocken Books, 2015. xi, 262 p. : **641.5**

1. Jewish cooking 2. Food and wine pairing. 3. Kosher food 4. Recipes 5. Cookbooks.
ISBN 9780805243253

LC 2014025769

Includes index.

Features over 100 delicious, kosher recipes incorporating flavors from around the world.

"This hip, fresh cookbook is just the thing for foodies desiring to keep kosher while elevating their repertoire of dishes for the benefit of themselves or their dinner guests--and there's plenty to interest cooks who lack a kosher kitchen as well." Library Journal.

Morris, Julie

Superfood kitchen : cooking with nature's most amazing foods / Julie Morris. Sterling Epicure, 2012. xv, 238 p. : **641.5**

1. Cooking (Natural foods) 2. Natural foods. 3. Cookbooks.
ISBN 9781454903529

LC bl2012043346

Originally published: Superfood cuisine. Novato, CA : Navitas Naturals, c2011.

Collects recipes composed of plant-based whole foods and superfoods; describes the history, benefits, use, and taste of each superfood; and provides a list of foods that should be in the pantry and where to find them.

Moskowitz, Isa Chandra

Vegan pie in the sky : 75 out-of-this-world recipes for pies, tarts, cobblers, and more / Isa Chandra Moskowitz & Terry Hope Romero. Lifelong Books, c2011. ix, 223 p. : **641.5**

1. Vegan cooking. 2. Pies. 3. Cookbooks.
ISBN 9780738212746

LC bl2011030830

Includes index.

Presents recipes for pies, tarts, and cobblers made without dairy, eggs, or animal products.

"The authors focus on dessert in this collection of 75 egg, dairy and animal-free pies, cheesecakes, cobblers and tarts. The duo deserves plaudits for their user-friendly approach as well as their ability to keep scarcer ingredients to a minimum. Bakers who fear they won't be able to recreate these will be happy to discover that once they've mastered a crust or two they'll be able to whip together a Strawberry Field Hand Pie, Chocolate Mousse Tart, or even a Coconut Cream with confidence." Publishers Weekly.

Mullen, Seamus

Real food heals : eat to feel younger + stronger every day / Seamus Mullen with Genevieve Ko. Avery, 2017 319 p. : **641.5**

1. Low-carbohydrate diet 2. Nutritional therapy 3. High-protein diet 4. Recipes
ISBN 9780735213852

LC 2017012317

Includes index.

"Healthy cooking reinvented by top chef Seamus Mullen, with over 125 Paleo-inspired recipes designed to revitalize your health every day".-- Provided by publisher.

"Readers interested in transitioning to a healthier diet--particularly those new to the kitchen--are sure to appreciate this terrifically accessible approach." Publishers Weekly.

Music, Carla Lalli

Where cooking begins : uncomplicated recipes to make you a great cook / Carla Lalli Music. Clarkson Potter/Publishers, 2019 271 p. : **641.5**

1. Cooking. 2. Recipes 3. Cookbooks.
ISBN 9780525573340

LC 2018024658

"Home cooks looking to expand their repertoire with vibrant and easy meals need look no further than this remarkable, flavorsome new collection." Publishers Weekly

Myers, Amy (Physician)

The **autoimmune** solution cookbook : over 150 delicious recipes to prevent and reverse the full spectrum of inflammatory symptoms and diseases / Amy Myers, MD. HarperOne, 2018. x, 325 p. : **641.5**

1. Autoimmune diseases -- Diet therapy 2. Recipes 3. Cookbooks
ISBN 9780062853547

LC 2018010173

A companion cookbook to the best-selling <I>The Autoimmune Solution<I> provides dozens of recipes for foods that can help reduce inflammation and reverse other debilitating symptoms related to autoimmune disorders.

Nathan, Joan

Jewish cooking in America / Joan Nathan. Alfred A. Knopf,

1998. xvi, 518 p. : Knopf cooks American **641.5**

1. Jewish cooking. 2. Kosher food 3. Recipes 4. Cookbooks.
ISBN 9780375402760

LC 98027952

Traces three centuries of Jewish-American culinary history, with more than three hundred kosher recipes, a historical overview, and an explanation of dietary laws.

"This companion volume to the PBS television series contains nearly 300 recipes. It is also a history of the Jewish people through their food. Nathan introduces both people and food in a preface that discusses dietary laws, Jewish holidays, Jewish immigration to the U.S., and the impact of Jews--and their food--on American culture. With every recipe comes an original story or a reprint of an article or a personal vignette that intrigues and/or edifies." Booklist.

Nathan, Joan

★**King** Solomon's table ; a culinary exploration of Jewish cooking from around the world / Joan Nathan ; photographs by Gabriela Herman. Alfred A. Knopf, 2017 xxviii, 382 p. **641.5**

1. Jewish cooking 2. Jewish way of life 3. Food habits. 4. Food.
ISBN 9780385351140

LC 2016047294

Filled with historical details and personal histories, an around-the-world collection of recipes from a James Beard Award-winning cookbook author, with King Solomon's appetites and explorations in mind, showcases the diversity of Jewish cuisine.

Nathan, Joan

Quiches, kugels, and couscous : my search for Jewish cooking in France / Joan Nathan. Alfred A. Knopf, 2010. x, 387 p. : **641.5**

1. Jewish cooking 2. Cooking, French. 3. Jews, French -- Social life and customs. 4. Food habits. 5. France -- Social life and customs.
ISBN 9780307267597

LC 2010020280

A celebration of Jewish cuisine in Paris, Alsace and the Loire Valley describes the author's visits to regional marketplaces and home kitchens, where she discovered thriving Jewish-French culinary traditions shaped by centuries of international influence. By the James Beard Award-winning author of Jewish Cooking in America.

The **new** best recipe / the editors of Cook's illustrated ; photography, Carl Tremblay, Daniel J. Van Ackere ; illustrations, John Burgoyne. America's Test Kitchen, c2004. xi, 1028 p. : **641.5**

1. Cooking. 2. Recipes 3. Cookbooks.
ISBN 9780936184746

LC bl2005002631

Includes index.

Rev. ed. of: The best recipe. Brookline, Mass. : Boston Common Press, 1999.

Presents a collection of more than one thousand recipes along with cooking tutorials and opinons on equipment and ingredients.

"A compendium of more than 1,000 recipes. Twenty-two chapters cover appetizers to desserts. Even the simplest tasks, such as blanching vegetables or peeling an egg, are explained and illustrated in detail. More involved techniques include brining poultry and roasting a turkey. Well organized and extremely clear." Publishers Weekly.

The **new** classics cookbook / the editors of Saveur. Weldon Owen Inc., 2014 624 p. : **641.5**

1. Cooking. 2. Gourmet cooking 3. Recipes 4. Cookbooks.
ISBN 9781616287351

LC bl2014049529

At head of title: Saveur.

Includes indexes.

Features more than one thousand recipes from around the world, including such offerings as deviled eggs with smoked trout, oyster po'boy, crispy Chinese roast pork, spicy Tunisian fish stew, and cardamom-buttermilk pie.

"Highly recommended for most collections and home cooks who'd like a contemporary, all-purpose kitchen reference." Library Journal.

Nathan, Zoe

Huckleberry : stories, secrets, and recipes from our kitchen / Zoe Nathan, with Josh Loeb and Laurel Almerinda ; photographs by Matt Armendariz. Chronicle Books, 2014 288 p. : **641.5**

1. Huckleberry (Restaurant). 2. Baking. 3. Cookbooks.
ISBN 9781452123523

LC 2013037996

Includes index.

The authors offer recipes from their Santa Monica bakery, including herb biscuits, mixed berry cobbler, and powdered sugar beignets.

"Filled with entertaining behind-the-scenes stories and technical tips relayed in plain English, this cookbook will thrill meticulous bakers and Huckleberry's devotees." Library Journal.

Nosrat, Samin

★**Salt,** fat, acid, heat / Samin Nosrat. Simon & Schuster, 2017. 469 p. **641.5**

1. Cooking 2. Cooks 3. Food habits 4. Food science 5. Books to TV
ISBN 9781476753836

LC 2016040649

Salt, Fat, Acid, Heat inspired the 2018 Netflix series of the same name.

A first book by the acclaimed chef from New York's Chez Panisse distills decades of professional experience into four simple elements that if properly applied can lead to better results in the kitchen, in a reference complemented by 100 essential remedies and dozens of variations.

"This exceptional debut is sure to inspire greater confidence in readers and enable them to create better meals on their own." Publishers Weekly.

Oliver, Jamie, 1975-

Jamie Oliver's Christmas cookbook / Jamie Oliver. Flatiron Books, 2017 405 p. ' **641.5**

1. Christmas 2. Holiday cooking. 3. Recipes 4. Cookbooks.
ISBN 9781250146267

LC 2017032269

Includes index.

A collection of tried-and-tested Christmas recipes by the celebrity chef and best-selling author of Jamie's Food Revolution shares a wealth of ideas for edible gifts, entertaining for the holidays and using leftovers.

Oliver, Jamie, 1975-

Jamie Oliver's comfort food : the ultimate weekend cookbook / Jamie Oliver ; photography by David Loftus. Ecco, 2014 406 p. : **641.5**

1. Comfort food. 2. Cooking. 3. Recipes 4. Cookbooks.
ISBN 9780062305619

LC bl2014040929

Includes index.

From moussaka, gyoza with crispy wings and ramen, to sticky toffee pudding and eggs Benedict, one of the world's best-loved television personalities brings together 100 recipes from around the world that celebrate the beauty of good food and the joy of cooking.

Oliver, Jamie, 1975-

Jamie's dinners / Jamie Oliver ; with photographs by David Loftus and Chris Terry and illustrations by Marion Deuchars. Hyperion, c2004. 321 p. : **641.5**

1. Cooking 2. Recipes 3. Cookbooks
ISBN 9781401301941

LC bl2004115582

Includes index.

Offers recipes using common ingredients to create soups, salads, sandwiches, vegetable dishes, pasta, meat dishes, and desserts that draw on new ideas to add a twist to old favorites.

Olivier, Michele (Food blogger)

Little bento : 32 irresistible bento box lunches for kids / Michele Olivier, author of Little foodie. Sonoma Press, 2016 177 p. : **641.5**

1. Bento cooking 2. Lunchbox cooking 3. Cookbooks.
ISBN 9781943451289

LC bl2017030679

Includes indexes.

Shares over one hundred healthy bento box recipes for children's lunches.

Ottolenghi, Yotam

★**Jerusalem** : a cookbook / Yotam Ottolenghi, Sami Tamimi. Ten Speed Press, c2012. 318 p. : **641.5**

1. Cooking, Middle Eastern. 2. Recipes 3. Jerusalem -- Description and travel. 4. Cookbooks
ISBN 9781607743941

LC 2012017560

Includes index.

The London restaurateur and best-selling author of Plenty offers a tribute to the vibrant cuisine of Jerusalem that explores its cross-cultural influences and includes such options as Charred Baby Okra With Tomato and Preserved Lemon, Clementine and Almond Cake and Braised Lamb Meatballs With Sour Cherries.

Ottolenghi Simple : a cookbook / Yotam Ottolenghi, with Tara Wigley and Esme Howarth ; photographs by Jonathan Lovekin. Ten Speed Press, 2018 xiii, 307 p. : **641.5**

1. Cooking, Middle Eastern 2. Quick and easy cooking. 3. Make-ahead cooking. 4. Quick and easy cooking 5. Cookbooks.
ISBN 9781607749165

LC 2018020229

An author, chef, and restaurateur presents 130 Middle Eastern recipes that can be made easily in one or more ways: in 30 minutes or less, with 10 or fewer ingredients, in a single pot, using pantry staples, or prepared ahead of time for easy weeknight meals.

"Ottolenghi's many fans will want this book, but it will also appeal to home cooks looking for exciting, approachable recipes." Library Journal.

Oz, Daphne

The **happy** cook : 125 recipes for eating every day like it's the weekend / Daphne Oz ; photographs by Amy Neunsinger. William Morrow, 2016. 328 p. : **641.5**

1. Cooking. 2. Quick and easy cooking 3. Recipes 4. Cookbooks.
ISBN 9780062426901

LC 2016037715

Includes index.

"Tips, variations, and sidebars will guide inexperienced cooks to consider shortcuts and alternatives (try refrigerated piecrust, or include horseradish for its healing properties)." Booklist.

Page, Karen

The **flavor** bible : the essential guide to culinary creativity, based on the wisdom of America's most Imaginative chefs / Karen Page and Andrew Dornenburg ; photographs by Barry Salzman. Little, Brown and Company, 2008. xi, 380 p. : **641.5**

1. Cooking. 2. Flavor. 3. Gastronomy.
ISBN 9780316118408

LC 2007033064

"The authors first discuss the four basic tastes and the roles played by weather, the season of the year, and other environmental factors in cooking. The rest of the book is an extensive alphabetic guide to different culinary ingredients. Rather than just another collection of recipes, this is a unique resource that both beginning cooks and serious chefs will find wonderfully inspiring and immensely useful." Library Journal.

Paltrow, Gwyneth, 1972-

It's all easy : delicious weekday recipes for the super-busy home cook / Gwyneth Paltrow with Thea Baumann ; photographs by Ditte Isager. goop press, Grand Central Life & Style, 2016 xiv, 267 p. ; **641.5**

1. Quick and easy cooking. 2. Recipes 3. Quick and easy cooking 4. Quick and easy cooking 5. Cookbooks.
ISBN 9781455584215

LC 2015044440

Includes index.

Collects more than one hundred healthy quick and easy recipes, including chopped salad with grilled shrimp, chocolate cinnamon overnight oats, and chicken enchiladas.

Pascal, Cybele

The **whole** foods allergy cookbook : two hundred gourmet and homestyle recipes for the food allergic family / Cybele Pascal. Square One Publishers, c2009. xviii, 215 p. : **641.5**

1. Food allergy -- Diet therapy 2. Recipes
ISBN 1890612456

LC 2009012565

Provides recipes free of milk, eggs, wheat, soy, peanuts, tree nuts, fish, and shellfish, and includes such dishes as cherry dijon pork chops, Greek salad, lemon quinoa, soft pretzels, and orange zucchini bread.

Patalsky, Kathy

Healthy happy vegan kitchen / Kathy Patalsky. Houghton Mifflin Harcourt, 2015 352 p. : **641.5**

1. Vegan cooking. 2. Cooking (Natural foods). 3. Cookbooks.
ISBN 9780544379800

LC 2014014408

Includes index.

A collection of plant-based recipes from the creator of the blog HealthyHappyLife.com, including breakfasts, sandwiches, soups, salads, main dishes, desserts, and smoothies.

"Headnotes and information on the author's own vegan journey offer encouragement and background for anyone interested in embracing the meatless life or simply incorporating meatless meals into their diet." Publishers Weekly.

Pépin, Jacques, 1935-

Jacques Pépin celebrates / Jacques Pépin with Claudine Pepin ; photographs by Christopher Hirsheimer ; illustrations by Jacques Pépin. Alfred A. Knopf, 2001. xvi, 458 p. : **641.5**

1. Cooking. 2. Entertaining.
ISBN 9780375412097

LC 2001029929

Includes index.

Shares two hundred recipes for dishes, organized from soup to dessert, that range from simple meals to elaborate menus for holiday celebrations, accompanied by special sections on the techniques of working with bread and pastry doughs.

"In this companion to a new PBS series, Pépin builds on a broad definition of celebrations--encompassing holidays, special occasions, and simply nice weather--to present a collection of typically solid French recipes and numerous useful tips and techniques. More valuable than the recipes...are the many notes on chopping, garnishing, carving and so forth." Publishers Weekly.

Perelman, Deb

★The **smitten** kitchen cookbook / Deb Perelman. Alfred A. Knopf, 2012. xiv, 321 p. : **641.5**

1. Cooking. 2. Recipes 3. Cookbooks.
ISBN 9780307595652

LC 2012007711

Includes index.

The award-winning blogger for Smitten Kitchen presents a long-awaited first cookbook of 100 new and favorite recipes, from Mushroom Bourguignon and Pancetta to Buttered Popcorn Cookies and Chocolate Hazelnut Layer Cake, in a volume that features adapted options for busy home cooks.

★**Smitten** kitchen every day : triumphant and unfussy new favorites / Deb Perelman. Alfred A. Knopf, 2017. xvii, 330 p. ; **641.5**

1. Cooking, American 2. Recipes 3. Cookbooks.
ISBN 9781101874813

LC 2017010179

Includes index.

Shares unfussy, foolproof recipes that yield indulgent, flavorful dishes, including such options as sticky toffee waffles, bacony baked pintos, beefsteak skirt steak salad, and chocolate peanut butter icebox cake.

"Blogger and cookbook author Perelman (The Smitten Kitchen Cookbook) found she had to modify her approach to mealtime to accommodate a young, hungry family. This cookbook is her attempt to inspire herself and others to take a relaxed yet celebratory approach to feeding our families. The result is a joyous cookbook filled with delectable, creative possibilities for every meal." Publishers Weekly.

Perry Lang, Adam

Serious barbecue : smoke, char, baste, and brush your way to great outdoor cooking / Adam Perry Lang, with J.J. Goode and Amy Vogler ; photographs by David Loftus. Hyperion, c2009. 390 p. : **641.5**

1. Barbecuing. 2. Recipes 3. Cookbooks
ISBN 9781401323066

LC 2009001765

Includes index.

An introductory guide to barbecue cooking that covers everything from equipment fundamentals to preparing a diverse range of fare, including honey-glazed baby back ribs, quick cook Texas-style brisket, and rack of lamb crusted with grain mustard and chile powder.

Peternell, Cal

A **recipe** for cooking / Cal Peternell. William Morrow, 2016 xiii, 336 p. : **641.5**

1. Cooking, American 2. Recipes 3. Seasonal cooking 4. Cookbooks.
ISBN 9780062427861

LC bl2016046678

Includes index.

In a follow-up to the New York Times best-selling cookbook, Twelve Recipes, a celebrated chef and restaurateur provides delicious and easily mastered recipes for family gatherings of any size, including Savory Tart With Onions, Olive, and Anchovies; Lasagna Bolognese; and Fish and Shellfish Soup.

"Cookbooks for relaxed entertaining are making a comeback." Library Journal.

★**Twelve** recipes / Cal Peternell. William Morrow, 2014 xv, 288 p. : **641.5**

1. Cooking. 2. Cookbooks.
ISBN 9780062270306

LC bl2014045081

Includes index.

A cookbook and kitchen manual filled with photos and drawings offers basic techniques and essential recipes that transform standard ingredients--including eggs, beans, and pasta--into simple, elegant dishes.

"Marked by Peternell's zeal for good, simple food, this title takes a very different approach from cooking handbooks that emphasize science or technical precision." Library Journal.

Peterson, James

Cooking / James Peterson. Ten Speed Press, c2007. xviii, 534 p. : **641.5**

1. Cooking. 2. Recipes 3. Cookbooks
ISBN 9781580087896

LC 2007021065

Includes index.

"600 recipes, 1500 photographs, one kitchen education".--Provided by publisher.

"This book opens with a fairly brief description of ten basic cooking techniques and then moves on to Recipes To Learn By, organized by course or main ingredient. Many of the recipes are traditional French standbys, from Celeriac Remoulade to Beef la Mode, although there are dishes inspired by Thai, Mexican, and other cuisines as well. Essentially an intensive course for home cooks in the classic techniques that underlie good cooking, this is recommended for all cooking collections." Library Journal.

Pierson, Joy

Vegan holiday cooking from Candle Cafe : celebratory menus and recipes from New York's premier plant-based restaurants / Joy Pierson, Angel Ramos, & Jorge Pineda ; photography by Jim Franco ; forewords by Alicia Silverstone and Laura and Woody Harrelson. Ten Speed Press, 2014 viii, 168 p. : **641.5**

1. Candle Cafe. 2. Candle 79 (Restaurant). 3. Vegan cooking. 4. Holiday cooking. 5. Recipes 6. Cookbooks.
ISBN 9781607746478

LC 2014005259

A first-of-its-kind vegan holiday cookbook from professional chefs takes plant-based fare to a fresh, inventive new level through special-occasion menus and recipes for main dishes and sides, along with wine and cocktail pairings, which will impress vegans and omnivores alike.

"You'll be proud to serve and eat these vegan foods, and party hosts won't be tempted to hide them at the end of their holiday buffet." Library Journal.

Pollan, Corky

The **Pollan** family table : the best recipes and kitchen wisdom for delicious, healthy family meals / Corky, Lori, Dana, and Tracy Pollan ; foreword by Michael Pollan ; photographs by John Kernick. Scribner, 2014. xvii, 334 p. : **641.5**

1. Cooking (Natural foods) 2. Cooking. 3. Recipes 4. Cookbooks.
ISBN 9781476746371

Includes index.

A family known for their commitment to fresh, local and healthy food presents a book of more than 100 of their best recipes.

Pollan, Michael

★**Cooked** : a natural history of transformation / Michael Pollan. The Penguin Press, 2013. 464 p. **641.5**

1. Cooking 2. Cooks 3. Four elements 4. Food habits
ISBN 9781594204210

LC 2012039705

A New York Times contributor and best-selling author of The Omnivore's Dilemma recounts the story of his culinary education and the roles of the four classical elements of fire, water, air and earth in transforming natural ingredients into delicious meals and drinks, in an account that traces his efforts to master classic recipes using one of the four elements.

"The author mixes journalistic encounters with tales of skilled, often relentlessly obsessive cooks who demonstrated the art of transforming the products of nature into tasty food and then tried, with spotty success, to teach him to do the same. Four sections describe this transformation with the four classical elements: fire, water, air and earth." Kirkus.

Pomeroy, Naomi

Taste & technique : recipes to elevate your home cooking / Naomi Pomeroy with Jamie Feldmar. Ten Speed Press, 2016 400 p. **641.5**

1. Cooking. 2. Recipes 3. Cookbooks.
ISBN 9781607748991

LC 2016031265

The James Beard Award-winning chef shares 140 recipes that focus on cooking fundamentals, with sections on ingredients, techniques and equipment and recipes such as Orange-Caraway Glazed Carrots and Herbed Leg of Lamb.

"Her debut cookbook offers home cooks a superb arsenal of methods and elegant, do-able dishes designed to increase competence, confidence, and cooking pleasure." Publishers Weekly.

Pulde, Alona

★The **forks** over knives plan : how to transition to the life-saving, whole-food, plant-based diet / Alona Pulde, MD, and Matthew Lederman, MD ; with Marah Stets and Brian Wendel, recipes by Darshana Thacker and Del Sroufe. Simon & Schuster, 2014. x, 322 p. : **641.5**

1. Cooking (Natural foods) 2. Menus 3. Natural foods -- Health aspects 4. Recipes 5. Cookbooks
ISBN 9781476753294

LC 2014009582

"A Touchstone book."

The physician creators of the documentary by the same name present a four-week, celebrity-recommended plan for transitioning to a whole-food, plant-based diet to bolster the body's resistance to disease.

Purviance, Jamie

Weber's greatest hits : 125 classic recipes for every grill / Jamie Purviance ; photography by Ray Kachatorian. Houghton Mifflin Harcourt, 2017. 318 p. : **641.5**

1. Barbecuing. 2. Outdoor cooking 3. Recipes 4. Cookbooks.
ISBN 9780544952379

LC bl2017013608

Includes index.

Collects over one hundred barbecue recipes from the grilling company, including such offerings as grilled oysters, Korean beef barbecue, jerk-spiced ribs, and Greek seafood salad.

"Accompanied by all-new photographs and practical tips, these easy dishes will interest just about everyone." Library Journal.

Purviance, Jamie

★**Weber's** ultimate grilling / Jamie Purviance ; photography by Ray Kachatorian. Houghton Mifflin Harcourt, 2019. 351 p. : **641.5**

1. Barbecuing. 2. Outdoor cooking 3. Recipes 4. Cookbooks.
ISBN 9781328589934

LC 2019010097

Includes index.

Shares advice and instruction on grilling, as well as over one hundred grilling recipes, including charred rib-eye steak with mushrooms, Tuscan rotisserie pork roast, spatchcocked chicken with chimichurri, and planked salon with gremolata.

"Purviance offers a banquet for visual learners in this easy-to-use guide for the grill." Publishers Weekly.

Raichlen, Steven

★The **barbecue!** bible / Steven Raichlen ; photography by Ben Fink. Workman, c2008. xvii, 556 p. : **641.5**

1. Barbecue cooking 2. Outdoor cooking.
ISBN 0761149449

LC bl2008018079

Includes index.

Redesigned inside and out for its 10th anniversary, The Barbecue! Bible now includes full-color photographs illustrating food preparation, grilling techniques, ingredients, and of course those irresistible finished dishes. A new section has been added with answers to the most frequently asked grilling questions, plus Steven's proven tips, quick solutions to common mistakes, and more. --From publisher description.

Man made meals : the essential cookbook for guys / Steven Raichlen. Workman Publishing, 2014 631 p. : **641.5**

1. Cooking. 2. Recipes 3. Cookbooks
ISBN 9780761166443

LC 2014004022

Offers recipes for cooking a variety of different foods including breakfasts, appetizers, beef, porks, breads, rubs, sauces, and desserts.

Steven Raichlen's BBQ USA : 425 fiery recipes from all across America. / Steven Raichlen. Workman Pub., c2003. x, 774 p. : **641.5**

1. Barbecuing. 2. Recipes 3. Cookbooks
ISBN 9780761131335

LC 2003042287

Collects over four hundred barbecue recipes from across the United States, Puerto Rico, and Canada, including appetizers, soups, and entrees, accompanied by numerous tips and techniques.

Ramsay, Gordon

Quick and delicious : 100 recipes to cook in 30 minutes or less / Gordon Ramsay. Grand Central Publishing, 2020. 250 p. : **641.5**

1. Quick and easy cooking.
ISBN 9781538719336

LC bl2020033663

Includes index.

The celebrity chef star of Kitchen Nightmares shares 100 tried-and-tested recipes for straightforward, expert-quality meals from his 3

Michelin-star restaurant and Las Vegas burger joint that can be made in 30 minutes or less.

"Chef, restaurateur, and TV personality Ramsay (Gordon Ramsay's Healthy, Lean & Fit) extends a guiding hand to those who need to quickly get dinner on the table in his excellent latest." Publishers Weekly

Rea, Andrew

Eat what you watch : a cookbook for movie lovers / Andrew Rea ; photography by Scott Gordon Bleicher. Dovetail, 2017 131 p. : **641.5**

1. Cooking. 2. Food in motion pictures. 3. Motion pictures -- Themes, motives. 4. Recipes 5. Cookbooks.

ISBN 9780998739953

LC bl2017042600

Includes index.

Collects recipes for food featured in forty classic and cult films, including courtesan au chocolat from "The Grand Budapest Hotel" and hazelnut gelato from "Roman Holiday."

Real Simple (Firm),

Dinner made simple : 35 everyday ingredients, 250 easy recipes / the editors of Real Simple. Independent Pub Group 2016 349 p. : **641.5**

1. Quick and easy cooking. 2. Recipes 3. Quick and easy cooking 4. Quick and easy cooking 5. Cookbooks.

ISBN 9780848746896

LC bl2016014444

Includes index.

Collects three hundred and fifty recipes that use thirty-five everyday ingredients to create easy and inventive dishes, including coconut bass over rice noodles, whipped ricotta with pomegranate and mint, and margherita tortilla pizzas.

"With plenty of ideas for meals that can be prepared in less than 30 minutes, this cookbook will satisfy busy home cooks and eaters who enjoy browsing by photo." Library Journal.

Riggs, Taylor

Real food, real simple : 80 delicious paleo-friendly, gluten-free recipes in 5 steps or less / Taylor Riggs, founder of Simply Taylor. Page Street Publishing Co, 2017. 192 p. : **641.5**

1. Gluten-free diet 2. High-protein diet 3. Quick and easy cooking. 4. Cooking (Natural foods). 5. Cookbooks

ISBN 9781624143373

LC 2016940924

Includes index.

"Real food, real simple makes preparing whole, nutrient-dense foods as easy as one, two, three, four, five with delicious recipes that are gluten-free, Paleo-friendly and exceptionally healthy. Taylor Riggs, Registered Dietician Nutritionist and founder of Simply Taylor, shares 80 incredible recipes that encompass her healthy lifestyle manifesto in five steps or less."--Back cover.

"It's a terrific introduction to paleo and gluten-free cooking for novices and experts interested in expanding their repertoires with new dishes that come together quickly and easily." Publishers Weekly.

Robertson, Robin (Robin G.)

Robin Robertson's vegan without borders : easy everyday meals from around the world / Robin Robertson ; photography by Sara Remington. Andrews McMeel Publishing, 2014 xxiii, 280 p. : **641.5**

1. Vegan cooking. 2. International cooking. 3. Recipes 4. Quick and easy cooking 5. Cookbooks

ISBN 9781449447083

LC bl2014042982

Includes indexes.

Collects recipes for plant-based dishes from the great cuisines of the world, including Europe, the Americas, Africa, the Middle East, India, and Asia, with such recipes as Tuscan white bean soup, vegan feta, cottage pie, and vegetable tagine.

"Robertson's existing fans will be joined by many new ones on this tasty whirlwind tour of the globe." Library Journal.

Robertson, Robin (Robin G.)

Vegan planet : more than 425 irresistible recipes with fantastic flavors from home and around the world / Robin Robertson. The Harvard Common Press, 2014 xii, 532 p. ; **641.5**

1. International cooking. 2. Vegan cooking. 3. Recipes 4. Cookbooks

ISBN 9781558328310

LC 2013022919

Newly revised and updated, this classic collection of vegan recipes offers diverse ethnic dishes and popular street foods from all over the world reworked into healthy, meatless meals and covers such topics as whole grains, super greens, sauces and global flavoring ideas.

"The author offers dozens of imaginative vegan recipes inspired by a wide range of cuisines." Library Journal.

Roden, Claudia

The **book** of Jewish food : an odyssey from Samarkand to New York / Claudia Roden. Knopf : 1996. xiv, 668 p. : **641.5**

1. Jewish cooking. 2. Kosher food 3. Recipes

ISBN 0394532589

LC 96028758

Eight hundred delicious recipes from around the world represent the finest in traditional and contemporary Jewish cookery, featuring dishes from such diverse places as Russia, Syria, India, North and South America, Africa, the Mediterranean, and Israel.

Roll, Rich

The **plantpower** way : whole food plant-based recipes and guidance for the whole family / Rich Roll and Julie Piatt. Avery, 2015 xv, 319 p. : **641.5**

1. Vegetarian cooking. 2. Vegan cooking. 3. Cooking (Natural foods). 4. Recipes 5. Cookbooks.

ISBN 9781583335871

LC bl2015017042

Presents more than one hundred and twenty whole food recipes for every meal of the day, plus recipes for smoothies, juices, and desserts, along with advice on maintaining a plant-based lifestyle.

Rondinelli-Hamilton, Lara, 1974-

The **diabetes** cookbook : 300 recipes for healthy living Powered by the Diabetes Food Hub / Lara Rondinelli-Hamilton, RD, LDN, CDE & Chef Jennifer Bucko Lamplough. American Diabetes Association, 2019 x, 398 p. : **641.5**

1. Diabetes -- Diet therapy 2. Recipes 3. Cookbooks.

ISBN 9781580406802

LC 2018009603

Backed by decades of evidence-based research, a cookbook from the American Diabetes Association shares low-carb, diabetes-friendly adaptations of classic favorites, including Slow Cooker Pulled Pork, Jalapeno Mac and Cheese and Paleo 10-Minute Taco Salad.

"The authors include standards like roasted turkey and vegetables, and salmon burgers (both are categorized as budget-friendly), but also surprise with mole pork tenderloin with zucchini and refried beans (in the chapter on low-glycemic index recipes); reduced-carb sangria; and, to satisfy snack cravings, sweet and spicy nuts. Directions are clear and succinct, and virtually all the ingredients can be sourced at the local grocery store." Publishers Weekly.

Rose, Evelyn

100 best Jewish recipes : traditional and contemporary Kosher cuisine from around the world / Evelyn Rose ; with Judi Rose. Interlink Books, 2016. 192 p. : **641.5**

1. Jewish cooking 2. Kosher food 3. Cookbooks.
ISBN 9781566560733

LC bl2016049394

Includes index.

Collects one hundred of the late author's best-loved recipes, including traditional Jewish dishes, international and regional favorites, festival foods, and originally non-Jewish dishes adapted for the Jewish kitchen.

"Condensing the world's vast tradition of Jewish cookery to just 100 dishes presents a formidable challenge. The late Evelyn Rose spent a lifetime scouring Europe, Africa, and Asia and documenting the foods consumed in those continents Jewish communities. Duck breast glazed with ginger, honey, and soy recalls the seasonings of Chinese food. Sephardi-style pizza evokes Armenian or Turkish lahmacun, and further topping it with kosher salami transforms it almost into American pepperoni pizza. Because Jewish holidays have so many food traditions supplementing religious ones, Rose gives advice on dishes to celebrate the eight major festivals that Jews observe. An excellent addition to most library collections." Booklist.

Rosenstrach, Jenny

How to celebrate everything : recipes and rituals for birthdays, holidays, family dinners, and every day in between / Jenny Rosenstrach ; photography by Chelsea Cavanaugh. Ballantine Books, 2016 xxix, 288 p. : **641.5**

1. Dinners and dining. 2. Entertaining. 3. Families. 4. Holiday cooking. 5. Cookbooks
ISBN 0804176302

LC 2016001416

Includes index.

"From the creator of the popular blog and book Dinner: A Love Story and author of theNew York Times bestseller Dinner: The Playbook comes a warm and inviting guide with more than one hundred time-tested recipes and a host of inspiring ideas for turning birthdays, holidays, and everyday occasions into cherished traditions. "Families crave rituals," says Jenny Rosenstrach, and by rituals she means not just the big celebrations--Valentine's Day dinners, Mother's Day brunches, Thanksgiving feasts--but the littleones we may not even realize are rituals: A platter of deluxe nachos on Super Bowl Sunday or a bowl of creamy mashed potatoes after every braces-tightening session. Whether simple or elaborate, daily or annually, these rituals all serve the same purpose for Rosenstrach: to bring comfort, connection, and meaning to everyday family life. Recipes here are organized into groupings unique to Rosenstrach but familiar to everyone: Our Family Rituals (think tomato sandwiches for lunch after a family walk to the market, or homemade popovers on sleepover mornings); Holidays We Didn't Invent, including Friday Challah and Easter Ham (yes, both, more on that inside); a Halloween Launch Party for trick-or-treaters, featuring a self-serve simmering pot of Chicken Chorizo Chili. A section on Birthdays includes Rosenstrach's legendary chocolate frosted "mud" cake as well as a one-size-fits-all party planner with menus that do not rely on pizza. Lastly, in Family Dinners you'll find celebratory Sunday meals (Soy-Glazed Grilled Pork Chops, HarissaRoasted Chicken, Summer Cobbler) alongside Rosenstrach's signature easy weeknight fare (Crispy Chickpeas and Yogurt, Shrimp Tacos with Avocado "Butter," and vegetable-packed Burrito Bowls)--all of which translate to prime quality time with the family. In this digital, overscheduled age, How to Celebrate Everything helps families slow down, capture the moments that matter--and eat well while doing it".-- Provided by publisher.

Rosso, Julee

The **Silver** Palate cookbook / Julee Rosso & Sheila Lukins with Michael McLaughlin ; photographs by Patrick Tregenza and Susan Goldman ; illustrations by Sheila Lukins. Workman, c2007. xi, 452 p. : **641.5**

1. Cooking. 2. Gourmet cooking 3. Cookbooks.
ISBN 9780761145974

LC 2007276244

Includes index.

Provides recipes for appetizers, soups, pasta, main dishes, vegetables, salads, breads, and desserts, and includes tips on planning menus and entertaining.

Ruhlman, Michael, 1963-

Ratio : the simple codes behind the craft of everyday cooking / Michael Ruhlman. Scribner, c2009. xxv, 224 p. : **641.5**

1. Cooking. 2. Ratio and proportion. 3. Recipes 4. Cookbooks
ISBN 9781416566113

LC 2008032679

Demonstrates how to master western cooking fundamentals through an understanding of ingredient ratios, in a guide that introduces twenty-six basic recipes broken down into ratio-style measurements as well as a variety of accessible variations that enable more flavorful or creative taste combinations.

"While Ruhlman was attending the Culinary Institute of America for a book project, a chef showed him a copy of the golden rules, which boiled down the elements of (French) cooking into ratios. [In this volume] Ruhlman guides readers through the ratios for a variety of doughs, batters, stocks, sauces, custards and sausages, explaining their chemical and culinary basis in clear, earnest prose and providing tasteful recipes that lay out the technique for each formula." New York Times Book Review.

Ruhlman's twenty : the ideas and techniques that will make you a better cook / Michael Ruhlman ; photographs by Donna Turner Ruhlman. Chronicle Books, c2011. 367 p. : **641.5**

1. Cooking. 2. Cookbooks.
ISBN 9780811876438

LC 2011036735

Includes index.

Presents twenty basic elements of cooking and explains their importance in order to become a better cook, from proper salting techniques to mastering such basic ingredients as eggs and butter.

"Thorough, clearly explained, and stunningly beautiful, this collection will appeal to cooks of all levels." Publishers Weekly.

Saltz, Joanna

Delish : eat like every day's the weekend / Joanna Saltz & the editors of Delish. Houghton Mifflin Harcourt, 2018 415 p. : **641.5**

1. Cooking. 2. Entertaining. 3. Recipes. 4. Quick and easy cooking 5. Cookbooks
ISBN 9781328498861

LC 2018012229

Includes index.

"Amazingly delicious recipes from the team behind Hearst's wildly popular Delish.com website."

Shares recipes for the home cook from the popular Internet food site, including such options as Boston cream pancakes, chicken fried steak fingers, pizza pinwheels, quesadilla burgers, avocado pesto linguine, and snickerdoodle blondies.

Samuelsson, Marcus

Marcus off duty : the recipes I cook at home / Marcus Samuelsson with Roy Finamore ; photographs by Paul Brissman. Houghton Mifflin Harcourt, 2014 352 p. : **641.5**

1. Samuelsson, Marcus. 2. Cooking. 3. Recipes 4. Cookbooks.
ISBN 9780470940587

LC 2014018169

"A Rux Martin Book."

Includes index.

The award-winning chef presents over one hundred twenty recipes he likes to prepare at home, incorporating Ethiopian, Swedish, Caribbean, Italian, and Southern soul food cuisines.

"Highly recommended for adventurous and well-traveled home cooks, as well as fans of Susan Feniger's Street Food." Library Journal.

Sauvage, Jeanne

Gluten-free wish list : sweet & savory treats you've missed the most / Jeanne Sauvage ; photographs by Eva Kolenko. Chronicle Books, 2015 255 p. : **641.5**

1. Baking. 2. Gluten-free diet 3. Recipes 4. Cookbooks
ISBN 1452138338

LC 2015000533

Offers gluten-free recipes for popular treats, including soft pretzels, crêpes, deep-dish pizza, and churros.

"For those looking to expand their specialty cooking section or who are thinking of going gluten-free themselves, this book would seem to be the ticket. For all cookbook collections." Library Journal.

Scala Quinn, Lucinda

Mad hungry family : 120 essential recipes to feed the whole crew / Lucinda Scala Quinn ; photographs by Jonathan Lovekin. Artisan 2016 xi, 260 p. : **641.5**

1. Cooking. 2. Recipes 3. Quick and easy cooking 4. Quick and easy cooking 5. Cookbooks.
ISBN 9781579656645

LC 2015037712

Includes index.

A cookbook that focuses on high-flavor, easy-to-prepare options that provide for time-limited families, shares such recipes as second-day spaghetti pancakes, flat roast chicken, and double-melt pork tacos.

"Quinn's Mad Hungry books are fantastic for novice cooks who like simple, everyday recipes without heavy-handed diet and lifestyle advice. Her latest doesn't disappoint." Library Journal.

Shepherd, Sue

The **2-step** low-FODMAP eating plan : how to build a custom diet that relieves the symptoms of IBS, lactose intolerance and gluten sensitivity / Dr. Sue Shepherd. The Experiment, 2016 279 p. : **641.5**

1. Malabsorption syndromes -- Diet therapy 2. Recipes 3. Irritable colon -- Diet therapy
ISBN 9781615193158

LC 2015042268

Includes index.

"First published in Australia in 2015 as The two-step low-FODMAP diet and recipe book by Pan Macmillan Australia."

Offers a diet plan, complete with eighty recipes designed to help those suffering from IBS and other digestive issues, including menu plans, a guide to food labels, and lists of restricted ingredients.

Shulman, Martha Rose

Mediterranean harvest : vegetarian recipes from the world's healthiest cuisine / Martha Rose Shulman. Rodale, c2007. 398 p. : **641.5**

1. Vegetarian cooking. 2. Cooking, Mediterranean. 3. Recipes 4. Cookbooks
ISBN 9781594862342

LC 2007031561

Presents more than five hundred vegetarian recipes for Mediterranean dishes, from tabbouleh and gnocchi to stuffed artichokes and honey-roasted figs, and includes information about common spices and ingredients of Mediterranean cuisine.

The **simple** art of vegetarian cooking : templates and lessons for making delicious meatless meals every day / Martha Rose Shulman. Rodale, 2014 xvii, 270 p. : **641.5**

1. Vegetarian cooking. 2. Vegan cooking 3. Quick and easy cooking 4. Cookbooks.
ISBN 9781623361297

LC 2013049184

Includes index.

"Martha Rose Shulman's The Simple Art of Vegetarian Cooking is an accessible, delicious-recipe-packed teaching book designed to give home cooks a plan ("templates") and a language for cooking mouth-watering plant-based meals every day. What is a template?It's a generic recipe for a basic dish--a risotto, a frittata, a rice bowl, a pasta bowl, a soup base--into which you put any suitable combination of vegetables and herbs based on seasonality and availability. By having these basic templates in hand, readers--wherever they live and whatever the season--will be able to prepare meatless dishes simply and easily, making this plan ideal for busy families, working moms, and anyone who wants to be able to put a mouthwatering vegetarian dish on the table, angst-free.Template cooking--providing a reliable, sensible framework for dishes that can change fluidly with seasonal availability--is enjoying rising popularity in the food world, and Shulman is a Rodale house author and legend. Whether the reader is a working parent trying to decipher the overflowing CSA box or a new vegetarian trying to navigate a world where meals can't be summed up as "steak," "chicken," or "pork chops," The Simple Art of Vegetarian Cooking, with 125 recipes, is the perfect tool"-- Provided by publisher.

The **very** best of recipes for health : 250 recipes and more from the popular feature on NYTimes.com / Martha Rose Shulman. Rodale, c2010. xvi, 352 p. : **641.5**

1. Cooking (Natural foods) 2. Health. 3. Nutrition. 4. Recipes
ISBN 9781605295732

LC 2010021608

Includes index.

Drawing on her newspaper column, the author explains how to stock up on healthy, seasonal ingredients and use them to create easy-to-prepare meals, with recipes in such categories as soups, salads, pizza, vegetables, rice, fish, and poultry.

Shumski, Daniel

How to Instant Pot : mastering all the functions of the one pot that will change the way you cook / Daniel Shumski. Workman Publishing, 2017 viii, 279 p. : **641.5**

1. One-dish meals. 2. Pressure cooking. 3. Quick and easy cooking.

4. Recipes 5. Cookbooks
ISBN 9781523502066

LC bl2017051578

Includes index.

Presents over one hundred recipes specifically designed for use in the Instant Pot, including such dishes as beef barbacoa tacos, gorzonzola polenta, beet and blue cheese salad, chipotle tomato soup, and saffron rice pudding.

Sifton, Sam

See you on Sunday : a cookbook for family and friends / Sam Sifton ; photographs by David Malosh ; food stylist: Simon Andrews. Random House, 2019. 368 p. : **641.5**

1. Cooking. 2. Entertaining. 3. Recipes 4. Cookbooks
ISBN 9781400069927

LC 2018032051

Includes index.

The award-winning New York Times food editor celebrates the art of Sunday suppers and the joys of gathering with friends and family, complementing simple, traditional recipes for small and larger groups with tips about rendering classics distinctive.

"[D]elivers a lush and fun guide to creating memorable Sunday dinners for large groups of friends and family . . . This is an excellent resource for family meals that readers will turn to time and again." Publishers Weekly

Thanksgiving : how to cook it well / Sam Sifton. Random House, 2012. 133 p. : **641.5**

1. Holiday cooking 2. Thanksgiving Day 3. Cooking, American. 4. Recipes 5. Cookbooks
ISBN 9781400069910

LC 2012013919

Includes index.

A former New York Times restaurant critic and Thanksgiving Help Line contact presents an accessible and authoritative guide to cooking and surviving a stylish Thanksgiving dinner, drawing on his extensive experiences to counsel home cooks on everything from different ways to prepare a turkey and selecting accompanying wines to managing difficult relatives and timing side dishes.

Simmons, Gail

Bringing it home : favorite recipes from a life of adventurous eating / Gail Simmons with Mindy Fox ; foreword by Tom Colicchio ; photographs by Johnny Miller. Life & Style, 2017. xxxvii, 249 p. : **641.5**

1. Cooking. 2. Recipes 3. Cookbooks.
ISBN 9781455542208

LC 2017020073

"Top Chef judge and food-media powerhouse Simmons serves up 100 recipes drawn from her journeys in the culinary world. The recipes, which consist of Simmons's personal favorites inspired by food memories and famous mentors, aim to elevate the home cooks 'everyday cooking game.'" Publishers Weekly.

Smith, Michelle, 1980-

The **Whole** Smiths good food cookbook : delicious real food recipes to cook all year long / Michelle Smith. Houghton Mifflin Harcourt, 2018. xxi, 261 p. : **641.5**

1. Nutritional therapy 2. Cooking (Natural foods) 3. Nutrition 4. Self-care, Health 5. Cookbooks.
ISBN 9781328915092

LC 2017051915

Includes index.

Fully endorsed by Whole30, a collection of 150 recipes for the other 335 days of the year includes both gluten-free and low-grain options as well as meals that can be customized for dietary restraints.

Snodgrass, Alex

The **defined** dish : healthy and wholesome weeknight recipes / Alex Snodgrass ; photography by Kristen Kilpatrick ; foreword by Melissa Urban, co-creator of the Whole30. Houghton Mifflin Harcourt, 2020. xi, 291 p. : **641.5**

1. Cooking (Natural foods). 2. Gluten-free diet 3. Wheat-free diet 4. Low-carbohydrate diet 5. Cookbooks
ISBN 9780358004417

LC 2019032812

"Whole30 endorsed"--Cover.

Includes index.

With gluten-free, dairy-free and grain-free recipes that sound and look way too delicious to be healthy, this is a cookbook people can turn to after completing a Whole30, when they're looking to reintroduce healthful ingredients like tortillas, yogurt, beans and legumes.

Sobel, Adam

Street vegan : recipes and dispatches from the Cinnamon Snail food truck / Adam Sobel ; photographs by Kate Lewis. Clarkson Potter/Publishers, 2015 272 p. : **641.5**

1. Vegan cooking. 2. Street food -- New York City 3. Recipes 4. Cookbooks.
ISBN 9780385346191

LC 2014047446

Includes index.

Presents vegan recipes from the owner of the Cinnamon Snails food truck, including fresh fig pancakes, vanilla sesame milk, gochujang burger deluxe, and lavender pear fritters.

Sobon, Jackie

Vegan yack attack on the go! : plant-based recipes for your fast-paced vegan lifestyle / Jackie Sobon. Fair Winds, 2018. 208 p. : **641.5**

1. Vegan cooking. 2. Recipes 3. Quick and easy cooking 4. Cookbooks
ISBN 9781631594229

LC 2017059560

Includes index.

A collection of vegan recipes that can be prepared quickly or made in advance features such dishes as tropical trail mix, no-bake apricot almond bars, whole wheat empanadas, portobello fajita salad, and white bean marinara penne.

"This cookbook is proof that vegan food can be portable, healthy, and tasty." Publishers Weekly.

Solfrini, Valentina

Naturally vegetarian : recipes & stories form my Italian family farm / Valentina Solfrini. Avery, 2017 255 p. : **641.5**

1. Vegetarian cooking. 2. Cooking, Italian. 3. Recipes 4. Seasonal cooking 5. Cookbooks.
ISBN 9781101983591

LC bl2017045054

Includes index.

Drawing upon the traditions of her Italian farming family, the author and blogger shares vegetarian recipes that use fresh, local, seasonal ingredients.

"In this thoroughly enjoyable book, Solfrini, a graphic designer and blogger (Hortus Cuisine) who lives on her family's farm in central Italy, takes the reader through seasonal chapters on vegetarian Italian cooking." Publishers Weekly.

Stevens, Molly

All about dinner : simple meals, expert advice / Molly Stevens ; photography by Jennifer May. W. W. Norton & Company, 2019 335 p. : **641.5**

1. Dinners and dining. 2. Recipes 3. Cookbooks.
ISBN 9780393246278

LC 2019020817

Includes index.

The James Beard Award-winning cooking instructor and author of All About Braising demonstrates how to add flair to everyday staples, sharing such family-favorite recipes as Arugula Salad, Creamy Parsnip-Leek Soup and Butter-Poached Shrimp.

"A solid and attractive addition for any home cook." Library Journal

Stewart, Martha, 1941-

Martha Stewart's cooking school : lessons and recipes for the home cook / Martha Stewart with Sarah Carey. Clarkson Potter/Publishers, c2008. vii, 504 p. : **641.5**

1. Cooking 2. Recipes 3. Cookbooks
ISBN 9780307396440

LC bl2008027017

Introduces common cooking methods, including techniques for making stocks and soups, eggs, pasta, vegetables, beans, and desserts, and broiling, braising, and sautéing meats and fish, along with recipes and descriptions of basic kitchen equipment, seasonings, and herbs.

Stewart, Martha

Martha Stewart's pressure cooker : 100+ fabulous new recipes for the pressure cooker, multicooker, and instant pot / from the editors of Martha Stewart Living ; photographs by Marcus Nilsso. Clarkson Potter/Publishers, 2018. 255 p. : **641.5**

1. Pressure cooking. 2. Recipes 3. Quick and easy cooking 4. Quick and easy cooking 5. Cookbooks
ISBN 9781524763350

LC 2017050562

Includes index.

Offers over one hundred recipes using a pressure cooker, including such dishes as spicy shrimp and polenta, pork shoulder stew, lamb and potato curry, Mexican tortilla soup, coq au vin, and cinnamon-caramel flan.

Sussman, Adeena

Sababa : fresh, sunny flavors from my Israeli kitchen / Adeena Sussman. Avery, 2019 368 p. : **641.5**

1. Cooking, Jewish 2. Seasonal cooking 3. Cookbooks.
ISBN 9780525533450

LC 2019004726

Includes index.

An American food writer and expatriate living in Tel Aviv presents 125 recipes from Israel, including Freekeh and Roasted Grape Salad, Crudo with Cherries and Squeezed Tomatoes, Schug Marinated Lamb Chops and Tahini Caramel Tart. Illustrations.

"Sababa, which translates as everything is awesome, makes for an appropriate title for this outstanding collection of fresh variations on an old-world cuisine." Publishers Weekly.

Swanson, Heidi, 1973-

Super natural every day : well-loved recipes from my natural foods kitchen / Heidi Swanson. Ten Speed Press, c2011. 247 p. : **641.5**

1. Cooking (Natural foods). 2. Recipes 3. Cookbooks.
ISBN 9781580082778

LC 2010043749

Includes index.

"The eagerly anticipated follow-up to Heidi Swanson's James Beard-nominated Super Natural Cooking features 100 vegetarian recipes for nutritious, gratifying, weekday-friendly dishes from the popular blogger behind 101 Cookbooks. In Super Natural Cooking, Heidi taught us how to navigate a healthier, less-processed world of cooking by restocking our pantries and getting acquainted with organic, nutrient-rich whole foods. Now, in Super Natural Every Day, Heidi presents a sumptuous collection of seductively flavored dishes that are simple enough to prepare for breakfast on the fly, a hearty brown bag lunch, or a weeknight dinner with friends. Nearly 100 vegetarian recipes, including Pomegranate-Glazed Eggplant, Black Sesame Otsu, Mostly Not Potato Salad, Chickpea Saffron Stew, Salted Buttermilk Cake, and a new version of the ever-popular Pan-Fried Beans and Greens, are presented in Heidi's signature nonpreachy style. Gorgeously photographed, this stylish cookbook reveals the beauty of uncomplicated food prepared well and reflects a realistic yet gourmet approach to a healthy and sophisticated urban lifestyle".--Provided by publisher.

Symon, Michael, 1969-

Fix it with food : more than 125 recipes to address autoimmune issues and inflammation / Michael Symon and Douglas Trattner ; [photographs by Ed Anderson]. Clarkson Potter/Publishers, 2019. 255 p. : **641.5**

1. Cooking. 2. Health. 3. Recipes 4. Cookbooks
ISBN 9781984825537

LC 2019008836

Includes index.

A health-focused cookbook by the celebrity cohost of Iron Chef America draws on his experiences with chronic illness and food-triggering pain to offer satisfying recipes that do not include red meat, white flour, sugar, dairy or alcohol.

Tam, Michelle

Ready or not! : 150+ make-ahead, make-over, and make-now recipes by Nom Nom Paleo / Michelle Tam + Henry Fong. Andrews McMeel Publishing, 2017 344 p. : **641.5**

1. Cooking (Natural foods). 2. Quick and easy cooking. 3. High-protein diet 4. Recipes 5. Cookbooks.
ISBN 9781449478292

LC bl2017030627

"No gluten, grains, dairy, refined sugar, or excuses!"--Cover.

Includes indexes.

Presents paleo diet recipes that are intended to be prepared quickly and with simple ingredients, including rustic chocolate cake, hangry soup, flank steak super salad, and sunnyside salad.

Tanis, David

David Tanis market cooking : recipes and revelations ingredient by ingredient / David Tanis ; photographs by Evan Sung. Artisan, 2017. 478 p. : **641.5**

1. Cooking. 2. Farm produce. 3. Recipes 4. Cookbooks.
ISBN 9781579656287

LC 2017000348

Includes index.

"With this elegant collection of vegetable-based dishes, chef and New York Times columnist Tanis (One Good Dish) makes the task of meal planning a little easier." Library Journal.

Tarlow, Andrew

Dinner at the long table / Andrew Tarlow & Anna Dunn ; with Scarlett Lindeman : introduction by Kate Huling : photographs by Michael Graydon & Nichole Herriott. Ten Speed Press, 2016 xxii, 312 p. : **641.5**

1. Cooking. 2. Entertaining 3. Cookbooks
ISBN 9781607748465

LC 2016012177

Includes index.

A collection of menus from the restaurateur for creating celebrations with food and friends, from intimate gatherings to large-scale parties, including such options as a cold night cassoulet, an afternoon around the fire, and a New Year's eve party.

"With nine outer-borough eateries and shops in his portfolio, Tarlow, more than anyone, has been responsible for defining Brooklyn's artisinal food scene." Publishers Weekly.

Tasty (Website)

Tasty ultimate : how to cook basically everything / Tasty. Clarkson Potter/Publishers, 2018. 303 p. : **641.5**

1. Cooking. 2. Recipes 3. Quick and easy cooking 4. Cookbooks
ISBN 9780525575863

LC 2018012828

Includes index.

Presents 150 recipes from the popular Buzzfeed video series, with detailed instructions for favorite dishes, including fried cod tacos with cabbage slaw, potato-crusted quiche, baked avocado eggs, and pumpkin spice latte bars.

Taylor, Kathryne

Love real food : more than 100 feel-good vegetarian favorites to delight the senses and nourish the body / Kathryne Taylor. Rodale, 2017 xxvii, 243 p. : **641.5**

1. Vegetarian cooking. 2. Recipes 3. Cookbooks
ISBN 9781623367411

LC 2017007675

Includes index.

The author presents vegetarian recipes that are popular on her blog, including heirloom tomato pesto pizza, peanut butter chocolate chip cookies, and olive oil and black pepper popcorn.

"Taylor, creator of the vegetarian food blog Cookie and Kate (cookieandkate.com), debuts an approachable collection that will coax even reluctant cooks toward healthy eating." Library Journal.

Taylor, Marvin J.

101 classic cookbooks ; 501 classic recipes / The Fales Library, New York University ; Marvin J. Taylor and Clark Wolf, editors ; text by Marvin J. Taylor. Rizzoli, 2012. 688 p. : **641.5**

1. Cookbooks -- History -- 20th century. 2. Cooking -- History -- 20th century. 3. Cooks -- History -- 20th century. 4. Recipes 5. Cookbooks.
ISBN 9780847837939

LC bl2013028567

Respected figures in the food world choose the most important cookbooks of the twentieth century and select recipes that reflect the author's unique viewpoint, codify a new technique, or invoke a particular time and place.

Better Homes & Gardens fast or slow : delicious meals for slow cookers, pressure cookers, or multicookers. / Better Homes and Gardens Books (COR). Houghton Mifflin Harcourt, 2018. 304 p. : **641.5**

1. Electric cooking, Slow. 2. Pressure cooking. 3. Cookbooks
ISBN 9781328918499

LC 2018006349

Includes index.

The iconic cooking brand provides delicious recipes that can be made in either the Crock-Pot, pressure cooker or the Instant Pot, with instructions for both slow-cooking and quick-prep meals.

Better Homes and Gardens new cook book J. Wiley, c2010. 660 p. (loose-leaf) : **641.5**

1. Cooking. 2. Recipes 3. Cookbooks
ISBN 9780470556863

LC 2010025417

Includes index.

"The updated and revised 15th edition of America's favorite cookbook The Better Homes and Gardens New Cook Book has been an American favorite since 1930, selling 40 million copies through fourteen editions. This new 15th Edition is the best yet, with hundreds of all-new recipes and a fresh, contemporary style. Plenty of new chapters have been added to meet the needs of today's everyday cooks, including new chapters on breakfast and brunch, casseroles, and convenience cooking. 1,000 photos accompany this wide selection of recipes, which cover everything from Pad Thai to a Thanksgiving turkey. NEW FEATURES: icons that call out fast, healthy, or classic dishes; an expanded and revised chapter on canning and freezing foods; and new chapters on pizza, sandwiches, wraps, and more. Presents more than 1,200 recipes, including 750 brand new to this edition. More than 800 helpful step-by-step, how-to images and photos. New suggestions for personalizing family dinners, new twists on favorite dishes, and plenty of recipes that yield leftovers you can use again in other recipes. Better Homes and Gardens New Cook Book, 15th Edition covers it all! Completely revised, revamped and updated, this is a must for every kitchen."--Provided by publisher.

Better Homes and Gardens new cook book Houghton Mifflin Harcourt, 2018. 708 p. : **641.5**

1. Cooking. 2. Recipes 3. Cookbooks.
ISBN 9781328498854

LC 2018028246

Includes index.

Presents hundreds of new recipes along with traditional favorites; includes chapters on breakfast, casseroles, and convenience cooking; and features a bonus chapter of food gifts and packaging ideas.

Terry, Bryant, 1974-

Vegan Soul kitchen : fresh, healthy, and creative African American cuisine / Bryant Terry. Da Capo Press, 2009. xxviii, 223 p., 8 p. of plates : **641.5**

1. Vegan cooking. 2. Cooking, African American 3. Cooking, American -- Southern style. 4. Cooking, Low-salt. 5. Cookbooks.
ISBN 9780738212289

LC 2008046945

Offers recipes for low-fat African American dishes made with fresh ingredients and minimal amounts of salt and refined sugar, along with tips on using healthy cooking techniques and buying local, seasonal products.

★**Vegetable** kingdom : the abundant world of vegan recipes / Bryant Terry ; photographs by Ed Anderson. Ten Speed Press, 2020 249 p.: **641.5**

1. Vegan cooking. 2. Cooking (Natural foods). 3. Recipes 4. Cookbooks.
ISBN 9780399581045

LC 2019038413

Includes index.

A guide to the fundamentals of plant-based cooking features over 100 recipes for such dishes as Dirty Cauliflower, Barbecued Carrots With Slow-Cooked White Beans and Millet Roux Mushroom Gumbo, as well as tips on vegan cooking.

"Terry's approach to food and its preparation is complex, even when recipes are simple. His previous book, Afro-Vegan, explored dishes of the African diaspora. This newest work broadens the global reach with international influences that blend traditional methods with the culinary techniques and training of the James Beard Award-winning chef and writer." Library Journal

Thiessen, Tiffani, 1974-

Pull up a chair : recipes from my family to yours / Tiffani Thiessen with Rachel Holtzman ; photography by Rebecca Sanabria. Houghton Mifflin Harcourt, 2018. xi, 323 p. : **641.5**

1. Cooking. 2. Recipes 3. Cookbooks.
ISBN 9781328710307

LC 2017059617

Includes index.

Presents a collection of family recipes from the television star with her take on classic American dishes, including roasted chicken potpie, whole grilled trout, arugula, grape, & ricotta pizza, and vanilla bean bread pudding with bourbon-caramel sauce.

"Thiessen's simple recipes and presentation truly inspire meals to reconnect and celebrate with friends and family." Publishers Weekly.

Thomas, Anna

Love soup : 160 all-new vegetarian recipes from the author of The Vegetarian Epicure / Anna Thomas ; illustrations by Annika Huett. W. W. Norton & Co., c2009. 528 p. : **641.5**

1. Soups. 2. Vegetarian cooking. 3. Recipes
ISBN 9780393064797

LC 2009019632

Includes index.

A volume of vegetarian soup recipes by the author of the Vegetarian Epicure series places an emphasis on fresh seasonal produce and is complemented by accompanying bread, salad, and dessert options

"The author presents 160 enticing recipes that may just charm even a die-hard carnivore. Soups are organized by season and range from hearty selections like rustic leek and potato, and minestrone for a crowd, to lighter summer options including tomato and fennel soup with blood orange and sweet corn. Recipes for breads, dips and spreads, salads and a collection of desserts, as well as sample menus at the start of each chapter, make it easy to plan a full meal." Publishers Weekly.

Thomas, Anna

Vegan vegetarian omnivore : dinner for everyone at the table / Anna Thomas ; photography by Victoria Pearson. W.W. Norton & Company, 2016 414 p. : **641.5**

1. Cooking. 2. Recipes 3. Cookbooks.
ISBN 9780393083019

LC 2015043951

Includes index.

Presents a collection of 150 recipes to accommodate every type of eater, including vegans, vegetarians, and meat eaters, with options for appetizers, dips, sauces, salads, soups, pasta, sides, main courses, and desserts.

"Armed with nearly 200 of Thomas's versatile recipes, hosts can feel confident cooking one menu for all their guests." Library Journal.

Thomas, Biju

Feed zone portables : a cookbook of on-the-go food for athletes / Biju Thomas & Allen Lim. Velo Press, 2013 xv, 271 p. : **641.5**

1. Athletes -- Nutrition 2. Snack foods 3. Cookbooks
ISBN 9781937715007

LC 2013003073

Includes index.

"When Dr. Allen Lim left the lab to work with pro cyclists, he found athletes weary of food. For decades the sport's elite athletes had been underperforming on bland fare and processed bars and gels. So Lim and professional chef Biju Thomas set out to make eating delicious and practical. Chef Biju and Dr. Lim vetted countless meals with the world's best endurance athletes during the world's most demanding races. Their groundbreaking Feed Zone Cookbook brought the favorite recipes of the pros to everyday athletes. In Feed Zone Portables, Lim and Biju expand on the success of The Feed Zone Cookbook to offer athletes 50 new portable snacks that will nourish better performance. Feed Zone Portables maintains all the most popular features of The Feed Zone Cookbook including simple recipes that are easy to prepare, beautiful full-color photographs of every dish, complete nutrition information, tips on how each snack can benefit athletic performance, and time-saving ways to make real food the basis of an athletic diet. New in Portables are: Two-Bite Portables: Tasty treats for a breakaway from the norm; Aha! Portables: Clever twists on favorite snacks; Portable Bars: Sweet and savory flavors featuring whole foods; Take & Make: Plan-ahead meals and snacks for traveling athletes. With simple recipes requiring just a handful of ingredients, Feed Zone Portables from chef Biju and Allen Lim shows how easy it is for athletes to prepare their own food, whether at home or on the go".-- Provided by publisher.

Thomas, Haile

Living lively : 80 plant-based recipes to activate your power and feed your potential / Haile Thomas. William Morrow, 2020. 256 p.: **641.5**

1. Vegetarian cooking. 2. Cooking (Natural foods) 3. Recipes 4. Cookbooks
ISBN 9780062943415

LC 2019054725

"By a superstar eighteen-year-old activist and motivational speaker, and the youngest Certified Integrative Health Coach in America, an inspiring plant-based cookbook featuring 80 delicious, wholesome recipes to boost confidence, happiness, energy, and positivity along with '7 points of power' to motivate the next generation of leaders".-- Provided by publisher.

"Plant-based foodstuffs are the backbone of her 80 recipes, including comfort foods in new guises and variations, like chickpea flour pancakes, overnight oats, cauliflower steaks, and spicy Southwestern falafel." Booklist

Thompson, Antony Worrall

The **essential** diabetes cookbook : good healthy eating from around the world / Antony Worrall Thompson ; with Louise Blair. Kyle Books, 2010. 287 p. : **641.5**

1. Diabetes -- Diet therapy 2. Recipes 3. International cooking 4. Cookbooks.
ISBN 9781906868154

LC bl2011009565

Includes index.

Features two hundred recipes inspired by international cuisine that have been modified to meet the requirements of a diabetic diet.

Thug Kitchen LLC.

Thug Kitchen : eat like you give a f*ck. / Thug Kitchen. Rodale, 2014 xxvii, 212 p. : **641.5**

1. Vegetarian cooking. 2. Cooking (Vegetables). 3. Recipes 4. Cookbooks.

ISBN 9781623363581

LC 2014036430

Includes index.

The creators of the popular healthy food blog share recipes for 100 of their most popular dishes, offering comprehensive, accessible recommendations for such options as Roasted Beer and Lime Cauliflower Tacos, Pumpkin Chili and Grilled Peach Salsa.

Tila, Jet

101 epic dishes : recipes that teach you how to make the classics even more delicious / Jet Tila, Ali Tila. Page Street Pub., 2019. 208 p. **641.5**

1. Recipes 2. Cookbooks

ISBN 9781624145735

LC 2018961523

"This is an excellent and accessible guide for home cooks who are interested in developing their kitchen skills." Publishers Weekly.

Tourles, Stephanie L., 1962-

Raw energy : 124 raw food recipes for energy bars, smoothies, and other snacks to supercharge your body / Stephanie Tourles. Storey Pub., c2009. 271 p. : **641.5**

1. Cooking (Natural foods). 2. Raw food diet. 3. Vegetarian cooking. 4. Raw foods. 5. Cookbooks.

ISBN 9781603424677

LC 2009028675

Presents recipes made with raw foods for trail mixes, parfaits, energy bars, juice blends, smoothies, soups, veggie chips, dips, candies, and cookies that contain less than 250 calories per serving.

"This delightful addition is easily accessible even to readers looking to make small changes in their diets. [The author] shares a list of ingredients with pictures of each item. A list of kitchen equipment is also provided to accompany these recipes for shakes, bars, and soups, some of which require the use of a juicer or dehydrator. For libraries that don't have any books on the topic, this is an excellent introduction." Library Journal.

Turner, Kristy

But I could never go : -vegan!- 125 recipes that prove you can live without cheese, it's not all rabbit food, and your friends will still come over for dinner / Kristy Turner, photographs by Chris Miller. The Experiment, 2014 xi, 308 p. : **641.5**

1. Cooking (Vegetables) 2. Recipes 3. Vegan cooking. 4. Cookbooks

ISBN 1615192107

LC 2014020051

Includes index.

Collects easy-to-follow vegan recipes for every meal of the day, including pizza, nachos, entree salads, and brownies.

"Vegan foodies and foodies considering becoming vegan will be eager to break out their farro, sriracha, and liquid smoke, and have fun in the kitchen." Library Journal.

Turshen, Julia

Feed the resistance : recipes + ideas for getting involved / Julia Turshen with contributions from Maya-Camille Broussard, Anthony Thosh Collins and Chelsea Luger, Erika Council, Devita Davison, Cheryl Day, Jocelyn Delk Adams, Von Diaz, Yana Gilbuena, Mikki Halpin, Hawa Hassan, Jocelyn Jackson, Callie Jayne, Jordyn Lexton, Preeti Mistry, People's Kitchen Collective, Stephen Satterfield, Nik Sharma, Shakirah Simley, Bill Smith and Antonio Lopez, Bryant Terry, Tunde Wey, and Caleb Zigas. Chronicle Books, 2017 143 p. ; **641.5**

1. Cooking. 2. Recipes 3. Cookbooks.

ISBN 9781452168388

LC 2017024414

Includes index.

A popular cookbook author offers a collection of recipes aimed at fostering community and providing sustenance for those actively fighting to |resist| social injustice and express support for civil rights along with political activism resources, lists and essays from other activists. Proceeds will be donated to the ACLU.

Now & again : go-to recipes, inspired menus + endless ideas for reinventing leftovers / Julia Turshen ; photographs by David Loftus. Chronicle Books, 2018 303 p. : **641.5**

1. Cooking (Leftovers) 2. Cookbooks.

ISBN 9781452164922

LC 2017040842

Includes Index.

Offers over one hundred recipes and menu ideas for reinventing leftovers, including such dishes as kale salad with pepita dressing, baked saffron rice, chicken and black-eyed pea chili, and black forest cake.

Small victories : recipes, advice + hundreds of ideas for home-cooking triumphs / Julia Turshen ; foreword by Ina Garten ; photographs by Gentl + Hyers. Chronicle Books, 2016 303 p. **641.5**

1. Cooking. 2. Recipes 3. Cookbooks.

ISBN 9781452143095

LC OC2018153478

Includes index.

Overflowing with instruction and inspiration, a writer and go-to recipe developer shares a lifetime of lessons learned through cooking thousands of meals along with more than 400 bold, flavorful recipes, that are simple and achievable, for breakfast, lunch, dinner and dessert.

"Home cooks aiming to produce delicious, unpretentious fare or those who enjoyed such cookbooks as Deb Perelman's The Smitten Kitchen Cookbook or Kristen Miglore's Food52 Genius Recipes would do well to add this to their shelves." Library Journal.

Unell, Barbara C., 1951-

The **back** in the swing cookbook : recipes for eating and living well every day after breast cancer / Barbara C. Unell and Judith Fertig ; foreword by Rachel S. Beller ; photography by Sara Remington. Andrews McMeel Pub., c2012. xxiv, 261 p. : **641.5**

1. Breast -- Cancer -- Diet therapy 2. Cooking (Natural foods) 3. Recipes 4. Cookbooks.

ISBN 9781449418328

LC bl2012027801

Includes index.

Collects over one hundred fifty recipes for breast cancer survivors that feature natural ingredients, and offers suggestions on adopting a positive attitude and lifestyle and focusing on long-term wellness.

Vinton, Sherri Brooks, 1968-

Eat it up! : 150 recipes to use every bit and enjoy every bite of the food you buy / Sherri Brooks Vinton. Da Capo, Lifelong, a member of the Perseus Books Group, 2016 xiv, 241 p. ; **641.5**

1. Food conservation. 2. Food waste -- Prevention. 3. Cooking. 4.

Recipes 5. Cookbooks.
ISBN 9780738218182

LC 2015045183

Offers one hundred fifty recipes that use elements of food products normally thrown away, from stale bread and carrot tops to citrus peels, chicken fat, olive juice, and parsley stems.

"A sterling resource for the ecologically minded cook." Booklist.

Vongerichten, Jean-Georges

Home cooking with Jean-Georges : my favorite simple recipes / Jean-Georges Vongerichten ; with Genevieve Ko. Clarkson Potter/Publishers, 2011. 256 p. : **641.5**

1. Cooking. 2. Cookbooks.
ISBN 9780307717955

LC 2010053808

Includes index.

The celebrated French-born chef of New York's Jean George presents his most personal book to date in a collection of favorite casual recipes inspired by his family's dedication to two-day weekends, providing instructions for preparing such options as Crab Toasts with Sriacha Mayonnaise, Parmesan-Crusted Chicken and Buttermilk Pancakes with Warm Berry Syrup.

"After working 18-hour days six days a week, Vongerichten buys a weekend country home and rediscovers the joys of unfussy cooking. He shares recipes for the meals he and his family enjoy in this pleasingly accessible volume. ... Dotted with culinary reminiscences both personal and professional, this book shows Vongerichten at his simple best and offers his many fans the opportunity to cook and enjoy his favorite meals without being chained to the kitchen for hours." Publishers Weekly.

Walker, Danielle (Chef)

Danielle Walker's against all grain : meals made simple : gluten-free, dairy-free, and paleo recipes to make anytime / written and photographed by Danielle Walker ; cover photography by Jennifer Skog. Victory Belt Publishing, 2014. 319 p. : **641.5**

1. Cooking (Natural foods) 2. Gluten-free diet 3. High-protein diet 4. Milk-free diet 5. Cookbooks
ISBN 162860042X

LC bl2014037018

Includes index.

In a follow-up to her New York Times best-selling Against All Grain the popular blogger offers 100 new, enjoyable, gluten-free, dairy-free and Paleo-friendly recipes, including a month of dinner ideas and complete shopping lists.

Waters, Alice

The **art** of simple food / Alice Waters ; with Patricia Curtan, Kelsie Kerr & Fritz Streiff ; illustrations by Patricia Curtan. Clarkson Potter, c2007. ix, 405 p. : **641.5**

1. Cooking. 2. Seasonal cooking
ISBN 9780307336798

LC bl2007022117

Includes index.

Reveals how to select seasonal, local, fresh, and sustainable foods; provides a series of lessons on everyday principles and practices of good eating; and presents more than two hundred recipes that range from appetizers to desserts.

"After a useful discussion of ingredients and equipment come chapters on techniques, such as making broth and soup. Each of these includes three or four recipes that rely on the technique described. The final third of the book divides many more recipes traditionally into salads, pasta and so forth. Waters taps an almost endless supply of ideas for appealing and fresh yet low-stress dishes." Publishers Weekly.

Waters, Alice

In the green kitchen : techniques to learn by heart / Alice Waters ; photographs by Hirsheimer & Hamilton. Clarkson Potter Publishers, 2010. 151 p. : **641.5**

1. Cooking (Natural foods) 2. Sustainable living. 3. Slow food movement. 4. Recipes 5. Cookbooks
ISBN 9780307336804

LC bl2010008705

Includes index.

A sustainable-food advocate and author of The Art of Simple Food features 30 basic cooking techniques and 50 corresponding recipes, each demonstrated by chefs and friends of the author, including Lidia Bastianich, Thomas Keller and Deborah Madison..

"The author showcases basic cooking techniques every cook can and should master along with recipes using each method in this slim and attractive book. Derived from a Slow Food Nation event she helped organize, where notable chefs and foodies provided demonstrations on foundational procedures, Waters highlights a set of techniques that are universal to all cuisines. She covers the most basic of the basics, from stocking the pantry and washing lettuce to boiling pasta and wilting greens. Ideal for the cooking novice, this gem of a book captures the expertise of world-class chefs in an accessible, straightforward manner." Publishers Weekly.

Weight Watchers International

Weight Watchers 50th anniversary cookbook : 280 delicious recipes for every meal St. Martin's Griffin, 2013. xv, 335 p. : **641.5**

1. Reducing diets -- Recipes. 2. Cookbooks
ISBN 9781250036407

LC bl2013018084

Includes index.

Features 250 recipes that conform to the WeightWatchers360 PointsPlus system.

Weil, Andrew

The **healthy** kitchen : recipes for a better body, life, and spirit / Andrew Weil and Rosie Daley ; photographs by Sang An, Amy Haskell, and Eric Studer. Alfred A. Knopf, 2002. xxxviii, 325 p. : **641.5**

1. Cooking (Natural foods) 2. Recipes 3. Cookbooks
ISBN 9780375413063

LC 2001050391

Includes index.

Presents 135 recipes for a range of healthful dishes, in a cookbook that features information on the art of healthy eating.

"This is a stimulating invitation to healthy, pleasurable eating." Publishers Weekly.

Weinstein, Bruce, 1960-

The **great** big pressure cooker book : 500 easy recipes for every machine, both stovetop and electric / Bruce Weinstein and Mark Scarbrough ; photographs by Tina Rupp. Clarkson Potter/Publishers, 2015 512 p. : **641.5**

1. Pressure cooking. 2. Quick and easy cooking 3. Cookbooks.
ISBN 9780804185325

LC 2014022862

Includes index.

Provides over five hundred recipes for stovetop and electric pressure cookers, including French toast bread pudding, osso bucco, tamarind beef stew, chicken fricassee, spicy steamed clams, and chocolate pudding.

Weir, Joanne

Kitchen gypsy : recipes and stories from a lifelong romance with food / Joanne Weir ; foreword by Alice Waters. Oxmore House, 2015. 288 p. **641.5**

1. Cooks. 2. Recipes. 3. Cooking -- Anecdotes. 4. Cooking, Mediterranean.
ISBN 9780848746032

LC bl2015034577

"A compelling read with worldly recipes and evocative writing. If you like this title, try following it with Alex Guarnaschelli's Old-School Comfort Food or Hubert Keller's Souvenirs." Library Journal.

Wells, Patricia

★**My** master recipes : 165 recipes to inspire confidence in the kitchen, with dozens of variations / Patricia Wells ; in collaboration with Emily Buchanan. William Morrow, 2017 xxix, 466 p. : **641.5**

1. Cooking -- Recipes. 2. Gourmet cooking. 3. Recipes 4. Cookbooks
ISBN 0062424823

LC bl2017009407

Includes index.

A best-selling cookbook author, drawing on the lessons taught at her cooking schools in France, presents an instructional cookbook that provides a vast array of recipes that teach particular techniques--including blanching, searching, braising and steaming--and gives home cooks the knowledge and assurance to expand their cooking even further.

"Simple, seasonal dishes...will send gourmands to the kitchen for leisurely cooking. Wells's recipes are fiercely precise and personal." Library Journal.

Wex, Michael, 1954-

Rhapsody in schmaltz : Yiddish food and why we can't stop eating it / Michael Wex. St. Martin's Press, 2016. 320 p. **641.5**

1. Jewish cooking 2. Jews -- Food. 3. Ashkenazim -- Social life and customs. 4. Food habits
ISBN 9781250071514

LC 2015044974

Rhapsody in Schmaltz is a journey into the sociology, humor, history, and traditions of food and Judaism.

"Informative, merrily entertaining culinary and cultural history." Kirkus.

Wilson, Maya

The **Alaska** from scratch cookbook : seasonal, scenic, homemade / written & photographed by Maya Wilson. Rodale, 2018 xxxiii, 237 p. : **641.5**

1. Cooking, American -- Alaska. 2. Seasonal cooking 3. Recipes 4. Cookbooks.
ISBN 9781635650631

LC 2017279589

Includes index.

Presents a collection of tasty, family-friendly recipes that use fresh Alaskan seasonal ingredients, including breakfasts, soups, seafood dishes, main dishes, beverages, and desserts.

Winfrey, Oprah, 1954-

Food, health, and happiness : 115 on-point recipes for great meals and a better life / Oprah Winfrey ; with Lisa Kogan. Flatiron Books, 2017. 231 p. : **641.5**

1. Winfrey, Oprah, 1954- 2. Cooking (Natural foods). 3. Cooking. 4. Cookbooks.
ISBN 9781250126535

LC 2016963619

"An Oprah book."

Includes index.

A four-color cookbook collecting 100 top-selected recipes by the iconic host of The Oprah Winfrey Show draws on the expertise of such fan-favorite chefs as Rosie Daley and Taryn Huebner and shares insights into how Winfrey learned to enjoy favorite meals while controlling her weight.

Wolf, Robb

Wired to eat : turn off cravings, rewire your appetite for weight loss, and determine the foods that work for you / Robb Wolf. Harmony Books, 2017 xii, 388 p. : **641.5**

1. Low-carbohydrate diet 2. Recipes 3. Reducing diets
ISBN 9780451498564

LC BL2017031726

A recipe-complemented guide by the best-selling author of The Paleo Solution outlines a 30-day program based on the latest research to help readers rewire their appetites, regulate blood sugar, and lose weight more easily by consuming paleo-based, whole foods.

Wolfert, Paula

Couscous and other good food from Morocco / Paula Wolfert ; introd. by Gael Green ; color photos. by Bill Bayer ; drawings by Sidonie Coryn. Harper & Row, 1973. xv, 351 p. : **641.5**

1. Cooking, Moroccan. 2. Recipes. 3. Morocco -- Social life and customs. 4. Cookbooks
ISBN 0060147210

LC 72009165

Woodward, Ella

Deliciously Ella : 100+ easy, healthy, and delicious plant-based, gluten-free recipes / Ella Woodward. Scribner, 2015. 255 p. : **641.5**

1. Cooking (Natural foods) 2. Gluten-free diet 3. Recipes 4. Vegan cooking 5. Cookbooks
ISBN 9781476793283

LC bl2015006672

Includes index.

The author of a popular food blog shares plant-based recipes designed to combat chronic illness and improve life quality without refined foods or deprivation.

Workman, Katie

Dinner solved! : 100 ingenious recipes that make the whole family happy, including you / Katie Workman ; photographs by Todd Coleman. Workman Publishing, 2015 xii, 372 p. ; **641.5**

1. Cooking, American. 2. Cooking. 3. Recipes 4. Cookbooks
ISBN 0761181873

LC 2015011304

Collects family-friendly recipes with "Fork-in-the-Road" variations that make it easy to adapt dishes to appeal to both adults and children, including appetizers, burgers, one-dish meals, vegetarian meals, and desserts.

Workman, Katie

The **mom** 100 cookbook : 100 recipes every mom needs in her back pocket / Katie Workman ; photographs by Todd Coleman. Workman Pub., c2012. xxix, 366 p. : **641.5**

1. Cooking. 2. Recipes 3. Quick and easy cooking 4. Cookbooks.
ISBN 9780761166030

LC 2012001330

Includes index.

Contains several recipes designed to make life easier for mothers and choosy children.

"Families can use this practical, mix-and-match recipe collection to lessen the stress of meal planning." Library Journal.

Zakarian, Geoffrey

My perfect pantry : 150 Easy Recipes from 50 Essential Ingredients / Geoffrey Zakarian ; with Amy Stevenson and Margaret Zakarian ; photographs by Sara Remington. Clarkson Potter/ Publishers, 2014 304 p. : **641.5**

1. Cooking. 2. Recipes 3. Cookbooks.
ISBN 9780385345668

LC 2013050636

Includes index.

Details fifty essential ingredients that every cook should have in the pantry, including barley, chocolate, maple syrup, pasta, pecans, vegetable stock, and yeast, and provides recipes incorporating each.

"Zakarian's list of 50 pantry necessities includes beans, oils, pastas, sauces, and nuts. For each of these staples he proffers a trio of recipes. Color photographs enhance the text and encourage readers to pursue Zakarians culinary vision." Booklist.

641.502 Miscellaneous

Warner, Justin, 1984-

The **laws** of cooking* : and how to break them / Justin Warner, photography by Daniel Krieger. Flatiron Books, 2015 332 p. : **641.502**

1. Cooking -- Technique. 2. Recipes 3. Cookbooks.
ISBN 9781250065131

LC 2015034388

Includes index.

"The Laws of Cooking . . . and How to Break Them encourages improvisation and play, while explaining Justin Warner's unique ideas about "flavor theory"--like color theory, but for your tongue. By introducing eleven laws based on familiar foods (e.g., "The Law of Peanut Butter and Jelly"; "The Law of Coffee, Cream, and Sugar"), the book will teach you why certain flavors combine brilliantly, and then show how these combinations work in 110 more complex and inventive recipes (Tomato Soup with "Grilled Cheese" Ravioli; Scallops with Black Sesame and Cherry). At the end of every recipe, Justin "breaks the law" by adding a seemingly discordant flavor that takes the combination to a new level".-- Provided by publisher.

"Warner's focus is on the food, and encouraging readers to stretch their palates and skills to create something truly unique. This is a refreshingly new take from an author to watch." Publishers Weekly.

641.509 History, geographic treatment, biography

Sitwell, William (William Ronald Sacheverell)

A **history** of food in 100 recipes / William Sitwell. Little, Brown, 2013, c2012. 360 p. : **641.509**

1. Cooking -- History. 2. Food -- History. 3. Food habits
ISBN 9780316229975

Originally published: London : Collins, 2012.

A British food writer and culinary expert traces the history of many people's favorite edibles, from the creation of the first cupcake to the invention of the sandwich, describing the origins of and methods used to make 100 different dishes.

Willan, Anne

The **cookbook** library : four centuries of the cooks, writers, and recipes that made the modern cookbook / Anne Willan ; with Mark Cherniavsky and Kyri Claflin. University of California Press, c2012. xii, 328 p. : **641.509**

1. Cooks -- History. 2. Cooking -- History. 3. Cookbooks -- History and criticism. 4. Food habits -- History.
ISBN 9780520244009

LC 2011024489

This gorgeously illustrated volume began as notes on the collection of cookbooks and culinary images gathered by renowned cookbook author Anne Willan and her husband Mark Cherniavsky. From the spiced sauces of medieval times to the massive roasts and ragouts of Louis XIV's court to elegant eighteenth-century chilled desserts, The Cookbook Library draws from renowned cookbook author Anne Willan's and her husband Mark Cherniavsky's antiquarian cookbook library to guide readers through four centuries of European and early American cuisine. As the authors taste their way through the centuries, describing how each cookbook reflects its time, Willan illuminates culinary cross-currents among the cuisines of England, France, Italy, Germany, and Spain. A deeply personal labor of love, The Cookbook Library traces the history of the recipe and includes some of their favorites. --From publisher description.

"A valuable acquisition for libraries with strong food collections." Choice.

641.5092 Cooks

Bourdain, Anthony

The **nasty** bits : collected varietal cuts, usable trim, scraps, and bones / Anthony Bourdain. Bloomsbury Pub., 2006. xii, 288 p. ; **641.5092**

1. Cooking. 2. Food. 3. Restaurants. 4. Food industry and trade.
ISBN 1582344515

LC 2005033245

Presents a candid collection of culinary misadventures, from scrounging for eel in backstreet Hanoi, to quarreling with raw-food activist Woody Harrelson and revealing the less than glamorous aspects of making television.

"The author is a vivid and witty writer, but his greatest gift is his ability to convey his passion for professional cooking." New York Times Book Review.

Galarza, Daniela

Beyond the plate : includes 60 recipes / foreword by Adam Sachs ; text by Daniela Galarza. Prestel, 2017 200 p. : **641.5092**

1. Cooks. 2. Cooking -- Blogs. 3. Food -- Blogs. 4. Recipes 5. Cookbooks.
ISBN 9783791382777

LC 2016037475

Includes index.

"Beautiful, full-page food photos tantalize throughout, while recipes cover a vast range of trends and techniques." Booklist.

Reardon, Joan, 1930-
As always, Julia : letters of Julia Child and Avis DeVoto : food, friendship, and the making of a masterpiece / selected and edited by Joan Reardon. Houghton Mifflin Harcourt, 2010. 320 p. **641.5092**

1. Child, Julia Correspondence. 2. De Voto, Avis Correspondence. 3. Cooks -- United States -- Correspondence. 4. Literary agents. 5. Women cooks. 6. Female friendship.
ISBN 9780547417714

LC 2010025840

Includes index.
IACP Cookbook Awards, Literary Food Writing, 2011.
Shares the previously unpublished correspondence between the iconic celebrity chef and her unofficial literary agent from 1952 to 1965, offering insight Julia's early experiences as a new bride in Paris, her support of her diplomat husband, and her views on period politics.
"Their letters span a wide range of topics, from cookbooks, menus, recipes, and restaurants to Balzac, sex, goose stuffing, gardening, learning languages, the political climate, Sunday afternoon cocktail parties, and proofreading. Witty, enlightening and entertaining." Publishers Weekly.

641.555 Timesaving cooking

Weinstein, Bruce, 1960-
The **kitchen** shortcut bible : more than 200 recipes to make real food real fast / Bruce Weinstein and Mark Scarbrough ; photographs by Eric medsker. Little, Brown and Company, 2018. 352 p. : **641.555**

1. Quick and easy cooking 2. Recipes 3. Cookbooks.
ISBN 9780316509718

LC 2017964191

Includes index.
A collection of quick and easy recipes features such dishes as blender salsa verde, microwave pasta carbonara, one-skillet loaded mac and cheese, and no-churn butter pecan ice cream.
"Basic directions and easy-to-find ingredients guarantee this book will be embraced by everyday cooks, who will welcome a respite from complicated, time-consuming, and multi-ingredient recipes." Library Journal.

641.59 Cooking characteristic of specific geographic

Acquista, Angelo
The **Mediterranean** family table : 125 simple, everyday recipes made with the most delicious and healthiest food on Earth / Angelo Acquista, M.D. with Laurie Anne Vandermolen ; photography by Liz Clayman ; styling by Rebekah Peppler. William Morrow, 2015 xi, 324 p. : **641.59**

1. Cooking, Mediterranean. 2. Recipes 3. Cookbooks.
ISBN 9780062407184

LC bl2015048900

Including index.
Collects family-friendly recipes based on the Mediterranean diet, including salads, soups, vegetables, pastas, seafood and meat dishes, and desserts, along with nostalgic family anecdotes and advice for making healthy eating choices.
"For those interested in changing their life through diet, Acquista is an infectiously positive coach, and his recipes make a fine playbook." Publishers Weekly.

Bishara, Rawia
Levant : new Middle Eastern cooking from Tanoreen / Rawia Bishara, with Sarah Zorn ; photographs by Con Poulos. Kyle Books, 2018. 223 p. : **641.59**

1. Cooking, Middle Eastern. 2. Recipes 3. Cookbooks.
ISBN 9781909487727

LC bl2018117650

Includes index.
The owner of the Brooklyn restaurant Tanoreen presents a collection of recipes inspired by her Palestinian-Arab heritage, including stuffed eggplant over toasted pita, bahraini chicken, walnut-crusted fish fillets, and triple almond cake.

Olives, lemons & za'atar : the best Middle Eastern home cooking / Rawia Bishara ; photography by Peter Cassidy. Kyle Books, 2014. 224 p. : **641.59**

1. Cooking, Middle Eastern. 2. Cookbooks.
ISBN 9781906868840

LC bl2014006120

Includes index.
Draws on the author's Palestinian-Arab family life and her experiences as the owner of Brooklyn's Tanoreen restaurant to present a collection of Middle-Eastern recipes, including red snapper in grape leaves and cheese knafeh.
"Themes of food, family, and personal growth flow throughout this gorgeous cookbook, which balances both simple and challenging recipes." Library Journal.

Clark, Melissa
In the kitchen with a good appetite : 150 recipes and stories about the food you love / Melissa Clark. Hyperion, c2010. xix, 444 p. : **641.59**

1. International cooking. 2. Recipes 3. Essays
ISBN 1401323766

LC 2010005760

A James Beard Award winner and New York Times food columnist offers an inviting collection of stories and recipes organized into such quirky chapters as Things With Cheese, It Tastes Like Chicken and more, in a book that includes such dishes as Roasted Spiced Cauliflower and Almonds and Baked Camembert With Walnut Crumble and Ginger Marmalade.

David, Elizabeth, 1913-1992
A **book** of Mediterranean food / Elizabeth David ; decorated by John Minton. New York Review Books, 2002, c1950. xvi, 203 p. : **641.59**

1. Cooking, Mediterranean.
ISBN 1590170032

LC 2002000749

Includes index.
Originally published: London : Lehmann, 1950.
Long acknowledged as the inspiration for such modern masters as Julia Child and Claudia Roden, A Book of Mediterranean Food is Elizabeth David's passionate mixture of recipes, culinary lore, and frank talk. In bleak postwar Great Britain, when basics were rationed and fresh food a fantasy, David set about to cheer herself --and her audience -- up with dishes from the south of France, Italy, Spain, Portugal, Greece, and

the Middle East. Some are sumptuous, many are simple, most are sublime. --From publisher description.

Deetz, Kelley Fanto

Bound to the fire : how Virginia's enslaved cooks helped invent American cuisine / Kelley Fanto Deetz. The University Press of Kentucky, 2017. 162 p. **641.59**

1. Slaves. 2. Cooking, African American 3. Cooking, American. 4. African Americans -- Food. 5. Virginia -- Race relations -- History.

ISBN 9780813174730

LC 2017029779

In grocery store aisles and kitchens across the country, smiling images of 'Aunt Jemima' and other historical and fictional black cooks can be found on various food products and in advertising. Although these images are sanitized and romanticized in American popular culture, they represent the untold stories of enslaved men and women who had a significant impact on the nation's culinary and hospitality traditions even as they were forced to prepare food for their oppressors.

"Scholarly yet readable, Deetz's book honors these American ancestors by reclaiming their rightful places and stories." Booklist.

Feniger, Susan

Susan Feniger's street food : irresistibly crispy, creamy, crunchy, spicy, sticky, sweet recipes / Susan Feniger, with Kajsa Alger, and Liz Lachman ; photographs by Jennifer May. Clarkson Potter/Publishers, 2012, 224 p. : **641.59**

1. International cooking. 2. Street food. 3. Recipes 4. Cookbooks.

ISBN 9780307952585

LC 2011041175

Includes index.

A popular television chef shares eighty-three of her favorite recipes culled during visits to eateries throughout the world, offering insights into spice and ingredient combinations.

Galimberti, Gabriele

In her kitchen : stories and recipes from grandmas around the World / Gabriele Galimberti. Clarkson Potter/Publishers, 2014 248 p. : **641.59**

1. International cooking. 2. Galimberti, Gabriele -- Travel. 3. Grandmothers. 4. Recipes 5. Cookbooks.

ISBN 9780804185554

LC 2013050635

Includes index.

The author provides recipes from grandmothers from sixty different countries he has visited, from a Swedish housewife and her homemade lox and vegetables to a Zambian villager and her roasted spiced chicken.

"While drawing on some academic sources, this book is written in lively narrative prose that is more appropriate for general readers than scholars." Library Journal.

Gibney, Michael

Sous chef : 24 hours on the line / Michael Gibney. Ballantine Books, 2014 240 p. **641.59**

1. Cooks 2. Restaurants. 3. Cooking. 4. Food preparation. 5. Second person narratives

ISBN 9780804177870

LC 2014002153

An executive sous chef who has worked alongside cooks from some of the nation's leading restaurants documents an intense 24-hour period that illuminates the allures and adversities of a professional culinary life.

Guy, Jerrelle, 1990-

Black girl baking : wholesome recipes inspired by a soulful upbringing / Jerrelle Guy, founder of Chocolate for Basil. Page Street Publishing Co., 2018. 207 p. : **641.59**

1. Guy, Jerrelle, 1990- 2. Baking. 3. African American cooking. 4. Cooking (Natural foods). 5. Recipes 6. Cookbooks.

ISBN 9781624145124

LC 2017943529

Includes index.

Growing up sensitive and slightly awkward in a race-conscious space, Guy decided early on that good food is the most powerful way to connect, understand, and heal. She leads readers on a sensual baking journey, using the fives senses, as she retells food memories with ingredients that involve whole flours, less refined sugar, and vegan alternatives.

Hall, Carla

Carla's comfort foods : favorite dishes from around the world / Carla Hall with Genevieve Ko ; photography by Frances Janisch ; design by Jennifer Barry. Atria Books, 2014. xvii, 221 p. : **641.59**

1. International cooking 2. Comfort food. 3. Recipes 4. Cookbooks.

ISBN 9781451662221

LC 2013035094

Includes index.

"Featuring 130 recipes with new variations on soulful favorites, this cookbook covers the globe to capture the international flavors of comfort".-- Provided by publisher.

"The executive chef and co-host of The Chew presents 130 recipes that offer new variations on international and American South favorites, from Southern Chicken with Milk Gravy and West African Spicy-Sweet Stew to Irish Shepherd's Pie and Mexican Enchiladas.

Harris, Jessica B.

High on the hog : a culinary journey from Africa to America / Jessica B. Harris. Bloomsbury USA, 2011. 288 p. **641.59**

1. Cooking, African American. 2. Food habits. 3. African diaspora 4. Identity (Psychology)

ISBN 9781596913950

LC 2010024899

Includes index.

"A narrative history--and travel memoir--of African American cuisine by the author of numerous popular cookbooks. Harris explains the rich provenance of African America's foodways and meals." Library Journal

Harris, Jessica B.

My soul looks back : a memoir / Jessica B. Harris. Scribner, 2017. 288 p. **641.59**

1. Harris, Jessica B. 2. Baldwin, James, 1924-1987 3. Angelou, Maya 4. Morrison, Toni 1931-2019 5. Identity (Psychology) 6. Food habits 7. Friendship 8. Interpersonal relations 9. New York City 10. Manhattan, New York City

ISBN 9781501125904

LC 2017012143

The award-winning writer describes what it was like growing up and hanging out with other members of the Black Intelligentsia in 1970s New York City, including Maya Angelou, James Baldwin, and Toni Morrison and their ongoing friendships.

"This is a lively, entertaining, and informative recounting of a time and place that shaped and greatly enriched American culture." Publishers Weekly.

Helou, Anissa, 1952-

Mediterranean street food : stories, soups, snacks, sandwiches, barbecues, sweets, and more, from Europe, North Africa, and the Middle East / Anissa Helou ; photographs by the author. William Morrow, 2006, c2002. xxvi, 277 p. : **641.59**

1. Cooking, Mediterranean. 2. Cookbooks.
ISBN 9780060891510

LC bl2006024674

Originally published: New York : HarperCollins, c2002.

Celebrates the foods of Mediterranean street vendors and simple shopkeepers, offering a host of recipes for soups, salads, snacks, sandwiches, breads, one-pot meals, desserts and sweets, barbecues, and drinks.

Jenkins, Nancy Harmon

The **new** Mediterranean diet cookbook : a delicious alternative for lifelong health / Nancy Harmon Jenkins ; with a foreword by Marion Nestle. Bantam Books, c2009. xiii, 496 p. ; **641.59182**

1. Cooking, Mediterranean. 2. Low-fat diet 3. Recipes 4. Cookbooks.
ISBN 9780553385090

LC 2008040982

Prev. ed. published under title: The Mediterranean diet cookbook.

Discusses the nutritional and health benefits of Mediterranean culinary practices and presents two hundred recipes adapted for the modern American kitchen.

"Jenkins' knowledge of these cuisines is both personal and informed. An essential purchase." Library Journal.

Joachim, David

Cooking light global kitchen : the world's most delicious food made easy / David Joachim. Oxmoor House/Time Home Entertainment, 2014. 319 p. : **641.59**

1. International cooking. 2. Recipes
ISBN 0848739981

LC 2013956992

Includes index.

Presents over 150 recipes from around the world to help cooks of any level easily prepare a variety of international and ethnic meals including Mexican chile rellenos, homemade Italian pasta, Thai sticky rice and Egyptian koshari.

Johnson, J. J., 1984-

Between Harlem and Heaven : Afro-Asian-American cooking for big nights, weeknights, & every day / JJ Johnson and Alexander Smalls ; with Veronica Chambers ; photography by Beatriz da Costa ; food styling by Roscoe Betsill. Flatiron Books, 2018. 269 p. : **641.59**

1. Cooking, African American 2. Cooking, Asian American 3. Cookbooks.
ISBN 9781250108715

LC 2018000426

Includes index.

Describes how the authors created the Afro-Asian-American flavor profile in their Harlem restaurant, and provides recipes for such dishes as pineapple black fried rice, grilled octopus salad, tamarind glazed oxtails, and West African peanut punch.

Kassis, Reem

The **Palestinian** table / Reem Kassis. Phaidon Press, 2017. 255 p. : **641.59**

1. Cooking, Palestinian Arab. 2. Recipes 3. Cookbooks.
ISBN 9780714874968

LC 2017446720

Includes index.

Collects 150 authentic Palestinian food recipes ranging from breakfasts and breads to dinners and desserts.

Khanna, Vikas, 1971-

Return to the rivers : recipes and memories of the Himalayan river valleys / Vikas Khanna with Andrew Blackmore-Dobbyn. Lake Isle Press, 2013. 443 p. **641.59**

1. Cooking, Nepali. 2. Cooking, Bhutanese. 3. Cooking, Indic. 4. Cooking, Indic -- Northern style. 5. Cookbooks
ISBN 9781891105531

Return to the Rivers is an incredible collection of recipes, photos, and memories as a means to preserve and share the sacred foodways, values, and simple gifts of friendship that the Himalayan people bestowed Khanna. Exploring the regions the great Himalayas directly touch upon ſτ Bhutan, Nepal, Tibet, Northern India, Myanmar, Western China, Pakistan ſτ Khanna was met with immeasurable kindness and hospitality. The dishes are beautifully simple and appealing, such as Eggplant Fritters with Ginger, Spinach and Cheese Momos, Chile-Scallion Buckwheat Noodles, Nepalese Black Lentils and Rice, Burmese Fish Noodle Soup, Pressed Rice with Yogurt and Almonds, and Tibetan Scallion Pancakes. --From publisher description.

Koehler, Jeff

Spain : recipes and traditions from the Verdant Hills of the Basque Country to the costal waters of Andalucia / Jeff Koehler ; location photographs by Jeff Koehler , food photographs by Kevin Miyazaki. Chronicle Books, 2013 352 p. **641.59**

1. Cooking, Spanish. 2. Recipes 3. Cookbooks.
ISBN 9780811875011

LC 2013026594

From the craggy Catalan coastline to the undulating, red-soiled hills of Andalucſτa, the diversity of the Spanish countryside is without rival. Its cuisine directly reflects this landscape, with each region celebrating its own ingredients and culinary traditions. In Spain, long-time Barcelona resident Jeff Koehler gathers the country's many time-honored dishes and age-old culinary customs, and distills the Spanish table down to its essence -- food that is prepared simply but full of homemade flavors, and always meant to be shared. --From publisher description.

Lawson, Nigella, 1960-

At my table : a celebration of home cooking / Nigella Lawson. Flatiron Books, 2018 288 p. : **641.59**

1. Cooking. 2. Quick and easy cooking 3. Cooking, Mediterranean. 4. Cooking, English. 5. Cookbooks
ISBN 9781250154286

LC 2018000297

Includes index.

A recipe collection that celebrates home cooking offers recipes that are simple to prepare and feature new ingredients to enrich classic flavors and tastes, including such dishes as parmesan French toast, meatballs with orzo, and apple pork chops.

Lee, Edward, 1972-

Buttermilk graffiti : a chef's journey to discover America's new melting-pot cuisine / Edward Lee. Artisan, [2018] 272 p. **641.59**

1. Lee, Edward, 1972- Friends and associates. 2. Voyages and travels

3. Restaurateurs. 4. Automobile travel 5. Cooks 6. United States -- Description and travel
ISBN 9781579657383
LC 2017051428

James Beard Foundation Book Awards, Writing and Literature, 2019.

A chef, restaurateur and author describes the two years he spent traveling the United States learning about the different cultures, traditions, memories and innovations that keep adding to, reshaping and helping to evolve what makes up American cuisine.

Lukas, Albert, 1968-

Sweet Home Cafe cookbook : a celebration of African American cooking / Albert Lukas and Jessica B. Harris, with contributions by Jerome Grant ; foreword by Lonnie G. Bunch III ; introduction by Jacquelyn Serwer ; in association with the National Museum of African American History and Culture and Restaurant Associates. Smithsonian Books, 2018 216 p. : **641.59**

1. Sweet Home Cafe. 2. African American cooking. 3. Cooking, American -- Southern style. 4. Recipes 5. Cookbooks
ISBN 9781588346407
LC 2018016725

A celebration of African-American cooking focuses on locally sourced ingredients and includes modern adaptations of such traditional recipes as fried green tomatoes, grits, hush puppies, fried chicken, and gumbo.

"Named for the cafe at the National Museum of African American History and Culture in Washington, DC, this cookbook collects classic and contemporary dishes inspired by historically African American foods." Library Journal.

McTernan, Cynthia Chen

A **common** table : 80 recipes and stories from my shared cultures / Cynthia Chen McTernan, creator of Two red bowls. Rodale, 2018 285 p. : **641.59**

1. McTernan, Cynthia Chen. 2. International cooking 3. Cookbooks.
ISBN 9781635650020
LC bl2018190042

Includes index.

In A Common Table, Two Red Bowls blogger Cynthia Chen McTernan shares more than 80 Asian-inspired, modern recipes that marry food from her Chinese roots, Southern upbringing, and Korean mother-in-law's table. --From publisher description.

"This beautiful book is a pleasure to read and cook from." Library Journal.

Miller, Adrian

Soul food : the surprising story of an American cuisine, one plate at a time / Adrian Miller. The University of North Carolina Press, 2013. 344 P. **641.59**

1. Cooking, African American -- History 2. Cooking, American -- Southern style. 3. Food 4. Recipes
ISBN 9781469607627
LC 2013002823

"An engaging, tradition-rich look at an often overlooked American cuisine--certainly to be of interest to foodies from all walks of life." Kirkus.

Morin, Frederic, 1975-

Joe Beef : surviving the apocalypse : another cookbook of sorts / Frederic Morin, David McMillan, and Meredith Erickson ; photographs by Jennifer May. Alfred A. Knopf, 2018. xiii, 333 p. : **641.59**

1. Joe Beef (Restaurant) 2. Cooking, French-Canadian. 3. Recipes 4. Montreal, Quebec -- Social life and customs 5. Cookbooks.
ISBN 9781524732301
LC 2018004088

"This is a Borzoi Book."

A new cookbook/survival guide/love letter to Montreal for these apocalyptic times, from the James Beard Award–nominated culinary adventurists and proprietors of the beloved restaurant, Joe Beef. --From publisher description.

"Quirky, comprehensive and cutting, this is the ideal tome to have on any bomb shelter bookshelf." Publishers Weekly.

Moushabeck, Leyla,

The **immigrant** cookbook : recipes that make America great / collected and edited by Leyla Moushabeck. Interlink Books, 2018. 224 p. : **641.59**

1. International cooking 2. Cooking, American. 3. Recipes 4. Cookbooks.
ISBN 9781566560382
LC bl2018100177

Includes index.

A culinary celebration of the many ethnic groups that have contributed to America's vibrant food culture collects recipes by renowned chefs from Africa, Asia, Latin America, the Middle East, and Europe.

Nguyen, Luke

The **food** of Vietnam / Luke Nguyen. Hardie Grant Books, 2013. 367 p. : **641.59**

1. Cooking, Vietnamese. 2. Vietnam -- Description and travel. 3. Cookbooks.
ISBN 9781742706207
LC bl2013045719

Includes index.

Presents brief descriptions of different regions of Vietnam along with recipes that are commonly prepared there.

Ottolenghi, Yotam

Ottolenghi : the cookbook / Yotam Ottolenghi and Sami Tamimi ; photography by Richard Learoyd. Ten Speed Press, 2013 xv, 287 p. : **641.59**

1. Ottolenghi (Restaurant) 2. Cooking, Mediterranean. 3. Cooking, Middle Eastern. 4. Cookbooks.
ISBN 9781607744184
LC bl2013037719

Includes index.

Shares 140 recipes from the Mediterranean-inspired chain restaurant, including options for such dishes as stuffed grape leaves, harissa-marinated chicken with red grapefruit salad, and sour cherry amaretti.

"Although Ottolenghi's latest will challenge readers in ways its predecessors did not, it reliably delivers unique recipes with flavor combinations unmatched in their inventiveness." Library Journal.

Parla, Katie

Tasting Rome : fresh flavors & forgotten recipes from an ancient city / Katie Parla and Kristina Gill ; foreword by Mario Batali. Clarkson Potter/Publishers, 2016 255 p. : **641.5937**

1. Cooking, Italian. 2. Recipes 3. Cookbooks.
ISBN 9780804187183
LC 2015023715

Presents recipes for modern dishes influenced by Roman regional traditions and culture, demonstrating how classic favorites, street-food innovations, and forgotten recipes reveal Italy's unique culinary evolution.

Phan, Charles

Vietnamese home cooking / Charles Phan with Jessica Battilana ; photography by Eric Wolfinger. Ten Speed Press, c2012. xxix, 222 p. : **641.59**

1. Cooking, Vietnamese. 2. Recipes 3. Cookbooks
ISBN 9781607740537

LC 2012014119

"Charles Phan -- chef-owner, The Slanted Door".

Includes index.

Introduces traditional Vietnamese cooking techniques and ingredients used in the author's restaurant "The Slanted Door," providing one hundred twenty-five recipes for such dishes as pork and shrimp spring rolls, banh mi, and sweet and sour fish.

Psilakis, Michael

How to roast a lamb : new Greek classic cooking / Michael Psilakis ; with Brigit Binns, Ellen Shapiro ; foreword by Barbara Kafka ; photography Christopher Hirsheimer & Melissa Hamilton. Little, Brown and Co., c2009. xiv, 288 p. : **641.59182**

1. Cooking, Greek. 2. Cooking, Mediterranean. 3. Cookbooks.
ISBN 9780316041218

LC 2008054932

Includes index.

Celebrates contemporary Greek cuisine through a restaurant owner's stories about his life, and recipes that use familiar techniques and readily available ingredients.

Psilakis, Michael

Live to eat : cooking the Mediterranean way / Michael Psilakis with Kathleen Hackett ; photography and design, Hirsheimer & Hamilton. Little, Brown and Company, 2017. xvii, 219 p. : **641.59**

1. Cooking, Mediterranean. 2. Quick and easy cooking 3. Cookbooks.
ISBN 9780316380133

LC bl2017002337

Includes indexes.

Offers recipes for quick, healthy Mediterranean dishes, including Greek turkey burgers, haricot verts with tomatoes and feta, whole wheat spaghetti with roasted tomato sauce, and Greek paella.

Randall, Alice

Soul food love : 100 years of cooking and eating in one Black family, with recipes / Alice Randall and Caroline Randall Williams ; photographs by Penny De Los Santos. Clarkson Potter/Publishers, [2015] 224 p. : **641.59**

1. Cooking, African American 2. African American families 3. Food habits 4. Recipes 5. United States
ISBN 9780804137935

LC 2014014423

Includes index.

"The Wind Done Gone author Randall and daughter, poet Randall Williams, write about the history of black cooking in America and offer recipes that are both traditional and nutritious." Library Journal.

Randall, Joe

A **taste** of heritage : the new African-American cuisine / Chef Joe Randall & Toni Tipton-Martin. Macmillan, 1998. xvii, 334 p. ; **641.59**

1. Cooking, African American 2. Recipes 3. Cookbooks
ISBN 9780028603827

LC 97043736

Includes index.

A collection of more than three hundred recipes provides an array of African American meals and treats, such as corn fritters, beef tenderloin soup, catfish stew, and chit'lin pizza on a cornmeal crust

"Honoring a legacy and its elaborations simultaneously, Randall and Tipton-Martin deliver a lively and valuable cultural portrait." Publishers Weekly

Reichl, Ruth

The **gourmet** cookbook : more than 1000 recipes / edited by Ruth Reichl. Houghton Mifflin, c2004. xvi, 1040 p. ; **641.59**

1. Cooking. 2. International cooking. 3. Recipes 4. Cookbooks.
ISBN 9780618374083

LC 2004047873

Gathers recipes published in Gourmet magazine over the last six decades, including beef Wellington, seared salmon with balsamic glaze, and other entrees, hors d'oeuvres, side dishes, ethnic specialties, and desserts.

"Recipes culled from issues of Gourmet magazine include concoctions like Coq au Vin, Beef Wellington, Coulibiac, Chop Suey, Bananas Foster, and Black Forest Cake. Every chapter begins with an overview of its subject; each recipe has an introduction; and many dishes feature helpful cook's notes, which give tips for food preparation, technique and storage." Publishers Weekly.

Reichl, Ruth

Gourmet today : more than 1000 all-new recipes for the contemporary kitchen / edited by Ruth Reichl. Hougton Mifflin Harcourt, 2009. xv, 1008 p. : **641.59**

1. International cooking.
ISBN 9780618610181

LC 2009019781

Includes index.

Edited by Gourmet magazine's editor-in-chief, this cookbook designed for today's modern palette offers over 650 recipes that can be prepared in 30 minutes or less, hundreds of vegetarian dishes, nearly 100 drinks, dozens of grilled dishes, nearly 100 seafood recipes, and over 300 deserts.

Roden, Claudia

Arabesque : a taste of Morocco, Turkey, and Lebanon / Claudia Roden. Knopf, 2006, c2005. 341 p. : **641.59**

1. Cooking, Arabic. 2. Cooking, Moroccan. 3. Cooking, Turkish. 4. Cooking, Lebanese.
ISBN 9780307264985

LC 2006045258

Includes index.

"Originally published in Great Britain by Michael Joseph, Penguin Books, Ltd., London, in 2005"--T.p. verso.

An authority on Middle Eastern and North African cuisine explores the culinary heritage of Morocco, Turkey, and Lebanon in a colorful cookbook that features more than 150 tempting recipes that transform the unique flavors, foods, cooking techniques, and traditions for the modern home cook.

Rodriguez, Jessamyn Waldman

The **Hot** Bread Kitchen cookbook : artisanal baking from around the world / Jessamyn Waldman Rodriguez and the Bakers of Hot Bread Kitchen with Julia Turshen. Clarkson Potter/Publishers, 2015 301 p. ; **641.59**

1. Hot Bread Kitchen. 2. Bread. 3. International cooking. 4. Recipes 5. Cookbooks.

ISBN 9780804186179

LC 2014048697

A cookbook from the New York-based bakery that supplies ethnic breads to dozens of retail outlets while employing and empowering immigrant women shares the baker's regional breads from the international locales these women called home.

"Hot Bread Kitchen's first cookbook foray is essential reading for serious foodies, bakers and anyone inspired by the bakery's philanthropic mission." Library Journal.

Ronnen, Tal

Crossroads / Tal Ronnen, Scot Jones and Serafina Magnussen with JoAnn Cianciulli ; photographs by Lisa Romerein. Artisan, 2015 xviii, 283 p. ; **641.59**

1. Cooking, Mediterranean. 2. Vegan cooking. 3. Recipes 4. Cookbooks.

ISBN 9781579656362

LC 2015010988

Includes index.

A collection of vegan recipes by the chef of Los Angeles' Crossroads restaurant turns seasonal vegetables, legumes, and grains into Mediterranean fare that readily offers favorite flavors without animal products.

"Vegan cooking taken to a new level of refinement. Epicures and professionals should take note." Library Journal.

Shepherd, Chris, 1972-

Cook like a local : flavors that can change how you cook and see the world / Chris Shepherd ; with Kaitlyn Goalen ; photographs by Julie Goalen. Clarkson Potter/Publishers, 2019. 288 p. : **641.59**

1. International cooking. 2. Cooking -- Houston, Texas 3. Recipes 4. Cookbooks.

ISBN 9781524761264

LC 2019013832

Includes index.

The James Beard Award-winning chef of Underbelly Hospitality in Houston champions, not appropriates, the city's diverse immigrant communities and their cuisines in this collection of recipes including Fried Chicken Tamales and Korean Braised Goat and Dumplings.

"Flavors from around the world redefine the concept of home cooking in this rich and satisfying collection." Publishers Weekly.

Sherman, Sean, 1974-

★The **Sioux** chef's indigenous kitchen / Sean Sherman ; with Beth Dooley. University of Minnesota Press, 2017 225 p. : **641.59**

1. Indians of North America -- Food. 2. Indian cooking. 3. Recipes 4. Cookbooks

ISBN 9780816699797

LC 2017020954

"Here is real food--our indigenous American fruits and vegetables, the wild and foraged ingredients, game and fish. Locally sourced, seasonal, "clean" ingredients and nose-to-tail cooking are nothing new to Sean Sherman, the Oglala Lakota chef and founder of The Sioux Chef. In his breakout book, The Sioux Chef's Indigenous Kitchen, Sherman shares his approach to creating boldly seasoned foods that are vibrant, healthful, at once elegant and easy. Sherman dispels outdated notions of Native American fare--no fry bread or Indian tacos here--and no European staples such as wheat flour, dairy products, sugar, and domestic pork and beef. The Sioux Chef's healthful plates embrace venison and rabbit, river and lake trout, duck and quail, wild turkey, blueberries, sage, sumac, timpsula or wild turnip, plums, purslane, and abundant wildflowers. Contemporary and authentic, his dishes feature cedar braised bison, griddled wild rice cakes, amaranth crackers with smoked white bean paste, three sisters salad, deviled duck eggs, smoked turkey soup, dried meats, roasted corn sorbet, and hazelnut-maple bites. The Sioux Chef's Indigenous Kitchen is a rich education and a delectable introduction to modern indigenous cuisine of the Dakota and Minnesota territories, with a vision and approach to food that travels well beyond those borders".--Provided by publisher.

"Oglala Lakota chef Sherman has set out to educate the U.S. about its indigenous fruits and vegetables. Starting from his base in the northern Midwest and Great Plains and extending into Navajo lands, he ably demonstrates just how tasty and sophisticated the produce of the nation's heartland can be." Booklist.

Smalls, Alexander, 1952-

Meals, music, and muses : recipes from my African American kitchen / Alexander Smalls with Veronica Chambers ; food and author photography by Beatriz da Costa ; food styling by Roscoe Betsill. Flatiron Books, 2020. xiii, 224 p.: **641.59**

1. Cooking, African American 2. Cooking, American -- Southern style. 3. Recipes 4. Cookbooks.

ISBN 9781250098092

LC 2019054745

Includes index.

The acclaimed James Beard award-winning restaurateur, while sharing anecdotes from his childhood in the Low Country, and examinations of Southern musical tradition, presents classic African American dishes that originated in the South,

"Home cooks are sure to give this excellent recipe collection a standing ovation." Publishers Weekly

Sterling, David, 1951-

★**Yucatan** : recipes from a culinary expedition / David Sterling. University of Texas Press, 2014. xiv, 560 p. : **641.59**

1. Cooking -- Yucatan Peninsula. 2. Maya cooking. 3. Mayas -- Social life and customs. 4. Recipes 5. Yucatan Peninsula -- Description and travel. 6. Yucatan Peninsula -- Social life and customs. 7. Cookbooks.

ISBN 9780292735811

LC 2013021911

"Some recipes are multiday affairs, but they're clearly written and intended for home cooks. An introductory index provides an invaluable reference to unique Mesoamerican ingredients." Library Journal.

Swanson, Heidi, 1973-

Near & far : recipes inspired by home and travels / Heidi Swanson. Ten Speed Press, 2015 329 p. : **641.59**

1. Cooking (Natural foods) 2. International cooking. 3. Recipes 4. Cookbooks 5. Essays

ISBN 1607745496

LC 2014047586

Includes index.

The New York Times best-selling author of Super Natural Every Day combines a cookbook, a journal and a photo album as she chronicles her travels around the world and the delicious things she tasted.

"Highly recommended for anyone who loves unassuming and easy gourmet cooking. Fans of David Tanis (One Good Dish) and Alice Waters (The Art of Simple Food) will love this." Library Journal.

Tanis, David

Heart of the artichoke and other kitchen journeys / David Tanis ; photographs by Christopher Hirsheimer. Artisan, c2010. vii, 344 p. : **641.59**

1. Entertaining. 2. International cooking. 3. Menus. 4. Recipes 5. Cookbooks
ISBN 157965407X

LC 2010004538

Includes index.

A chef of the well-known California restaurant Chez Panisse offers recipes and menus that center around ingredients that are seasonal and locally available, covering main courses, side dishes, and desserts.

A **platter** of figs and other recipes / David Tanis. Artisan, c008. x, 294 p. : **641.59**

1. Entertaining. 2. International cooking. 3. Menus. 4. Recipes 5. Essays
ISBN 1579653464

LC 2007049384

Offers a natural approach to sustainable American cuisine in a beautifully illustrated cookbook that introduces twenty-four seasonal, market-driven menus that anyone can re-create, ranging from spring's Supper of the Lamb to winter's North African Comfort Food.

"This volums is both a meditation on the powerful rites of cooking and serving a meal and a gentle but serious education in doing both. With 24 menus distributed over the course of a year, Tanis emphasizes seasonality with ingredients (blueberry-blackberry crumble in summer; celery root mashed potatoes in winter) and with the types of dishes provided for each menu (as with a divine, warming lobster risotto as part of a menu for a cold spring day). Anecdotes from his peripatetic life of enjoying good food around the world, from Venice to Morocco to New Mexico, add another intimate dimension and help the book appear written just for the reader by a kind, patient friend." Publishers Weekly.

Terry, Bryant, 1974-

★**Afro-vegan** : farm-fresh African, Caribbean & Southern flavors remixed / Bryant Terry ; photography by Paige Green. Ten Speed Press, 2014 viii, 215 p. color illustrations ; **641.59**

1. Cooking, African American 2. Cooking, African. 3. Cooking, Caribbean. 4. Cooking, American -- Southern style. 5. Cookbooks
ISBN 9781607745310

LC 2013048560

Includes index.

The rising star chef, food activist and author of The Inspired Vegan remixes foods of the African diaspora to outline creative but comprehensive vegan recipes.

"Chef-author Terry . . . introduces the concept of food justice, a philosophy that he defines as good food being an everyday right, and not just a privilege. His book is also an introduction to the various ways (more than 100, in short) that African cuisine can go mainstream." Booklist

Tipton-Martin, Toni

★The **Jemima** code : two centuries of African American cookbooks / Toni Tipton-Martin ; forewords by John Egerton and Barbara Haber. University of Texas Press, 2015. xv, 246 p. : **641.59**

1. Cooking, African American 2. Cookbook writing -- History 3. African American women cooks. 4. Recipes.
ISBN 9780292745483

LC 2014033779

Includes index.

"Women of African descent have contributed to America's food culture for centuries, but their rich and varied involvement is still overshadowed by the demeaning stereotype of an illiterate "Aunt Jemima" who cooked mostly by natural instinct. To discover the true role of black women in the creation of American, and especially southern, cuisine, Toni Tipton-Martin has spent years amassing one of the world's largest private collections of cookbooks published by African American authors, looking for evidence of their impact on American food, families, and communities and for ways we might use that knowledge to inspire community wellness of every kind."--Provided by the publisher.

"In this collection of two centuries worth of black cookbooks, from an 1827 manual to contemporary titles, Tipton-Martin . . . uncovers the central role of black women in American food." Library Journal

★**Jubilee** : recipes from two centuries of African-American cooking / Toni Tipton-Martin. Clarkson Potter, 2019. 319 p. : **641.59**

1. Cooking, African American 2. African American cooks 3. Slaves. 4. African Americans -- Food.
ISBN 9781524761738

LC 2019006495

Drawing from historical texts and rare African-American cookbooks, a collection of 125 recipes takes readers into the world of African-American cuisine made by enslaved master chefs, free caterers and black entrepreneurs and culinary stars that goes far beyond soul food.

"More than a cookbook, this collections of recipes offers an excellent starting point for anyone interested in African American culinary history." Library Journal

Twitty, Michael, 1977-

★The **cooking** gene : a journey through African-American culinary history in the Old South / Michael W. Twitty. HarperCollins Publishers, 2017. 336 p. **641.59**

1. Cooking, African American 2. Cooking, American -- Southern States 3. Food habits -- Southern States 4. Southern States -- Social life and customs -- 20th century
ISBN 9780062379290

LC 2017003374

James Beard Foundation Book Awards, Writing and Literature, 2018.

Finalist for the Hurston/Wright Legacy Awards for Nonfiction, 2018
Kirkus Prize for Nonfiction finalist, 2017.

Food blogger (Afroculinaria), Judaic studies scholar, and Southerner Michael Twitty connects family history with food and culture in this wide-ranging -- and often mouth-watering -- study. Primarily a narrative cultural history that examines slavery, race relations, soul food, and even kosher cooking, The Cooking Gene includes recipes that Twitty extensively researched and personally tested.

Wadi, Sameh

The **new** Mediterranean table : modern and rustic recipes inspired by cooking traditions spanning three continents / Sameh Wadi, chef/owner of the critically acclaimed and award-winning Saffron Restaurant and Lounge in Minneapolis. Page Street Publishing Co., 2015. 224 p. : **641.59**

1. Cooking, Mediterranean. 2. Recipes 3. Cookbooks.
ISBN 9781624140952

LC BL2015021723

Includes index.

Provides easy-to-make recipes that represent the flavors and cooking techniques that define the Mediterranean, including such dishes as duck kefta tagine, fresh chickpeas with cumin butter, and hibiscus tea with dark spices.

Wolfert, Paula

Mediterranean clay pot cooking : traditional and modern recipes to savor and share / Paula Wolfert. John Wiley & Sons, c2009. xviii, 334 p., 16 p. of plates : **641.59182**

1. Clay pot cooking. 2. Cooking, Mediterranean. 3. Recipes 4. Cookbooks

ISBN 9780764576331

LC 2008055912

Showcases recipes for soups, poultry, meats, vegetables, pastas, grains, legumes, and desserts, accompanied by stories and personal insights on the people, places, foods, and traditions related to each recipe.

"Wolfert is a true cook's author, and . this book is not for the casual home cook. But for those willing to tackle them, Wolfert's clay pot dishes do indeed merit the hype." Publishers Weekly.

The **slow** Mediterranean kitchen : recipes for the passionate cook / Paula Wolfert. Wiley, c2003. xviii, 350 p. : **641.59**

1. Cooking, Mediterranean. 2. Cookbooks.

ISBN 9780471262886

LC 2002153265

A treasury of more than 150 recipes with a Mediterranean flair, featuring traditional dishes from North Africa, the Eastern Mediterranean, Italy, Spain, and the South of France that use a slow-cooked, flavorful approach to great food.

"The author offers dishes from all the countries of the region: brodetto Pasquale (Italian Easter Lamb Soup), Expatriate Roast Chicken with Lemon and Olives from Morocco, and Catalonian Fall-Apart Lamb Shanks. Although many recipes call for braising, stewing, and other techniques of long cooking, others are not limited to those techniques, for Wolfert's definition of slow cooking also encompasses marinating and similar techniques." Library Journal.

Woods, Sylvia (Sylvia Pressley)

Sylvia's family soul food cookbook : from Hemingway, South Carolina to Harlem / Sylvia Woods and family with Melissa Clark. Morrow, c1999. xi, 275 p. : **641.59**

1. Cooking, African American 2. Cooking, American -- Southern style. 3. Cookbooks.

ISBN 9780688162191

LC 98049126

Includes index.

The inspiring story of the "Queen of Soul Food," from her youth in the Deep South to her rise to culinary fame, is combined with 125 recipes, as well as a collection of family photographs

641.591822 Cooking--Mediterranean region

Eden, Caroline

Black sea : dispatches and recipes-through darkness and light / Caroline Eden. Quadrille Publishing. 2018 279 p. : **641.5918229**

1. Cooking. 2. Recipes 3. Black Sea region 4. Cookbooks.

ISBN 9781787131316

This is the tale of a journey between three great cities - Odessa, built on a dream by Catherine the Great, through Istanbul, the fulcrum balancing Europe and Asia and on to tough, stoic, lyrical Trabzon. With a nose for a good recipe and an ear for an extraordinary story, Caroline Eden travels from Odessa to Bessarabia, Romania, Bulgaria and Turkey's Black Sea region, exploring interconnecting culinary cultures. From the Jewish table of Odessa, to meeting the last fisherwoman of Bulgaria and charting the legacies of the White Russian emigres in Istanbul, Caroline gives readers a unique insight into a part of the world that is both shaded by darkness and illuminated by light. Meticulously researched and documenting unprecedented meetings with remarkable individuals, Black Sea is like no other piece of travel writing. Packed with rich photography and sumptuous food, this biography of a region, its people and its recipes truly breaks new ground.

"Enticing to home cooks and armchair travelers alike, Eden's spectacular cookbook transports readers." Publishers Weekly

641.5926872073 Mexican American cooking

Casares, Sylvia

The **enchilada** queen cookbook : enchiladas, fajitas, tamales, and more classic recipes from Texas-Mexico border kitchens / Sylvia Casares with Dotty Griffith. St. Martin's Griffin, 2016 xii, 224 p. : **641.5926872073**

1. Cooking, Mexican American 2. Cookbooks.

ISBN 9781250082916

LC 2016033309

Includes index.

Presents a recipe collection representing the best in Texas-Mexico border town cooking from the founder and chef of Texas' Sylvia's Enchilada Kitchen, including such dishes as salsa verde, corn and crab soup, Gulf coast fish tacos, and braised pork.

"A satisfying combination of autobiography and popular Mexican foods." Library Journal.

641.59296073 African American cooking

Richards, Todd (Chef)

★**Soul** : a chef's culinary evolution in 150 recipes / Todd Richards ; foreword by Sean Brock. Oxmoor House, 2018. 366 p. : **641.59296073**

1. Cooking, African American 2. Cooking, American -- Southern style. 3. Recipes 4. Cookbooks.

ISBN 9780848754419

Includes index.

"Lovers of Southern cuisine will find grits, corn, shrimp, and peaches showcased, but in unexpected, delightful ways (grilled peach toast with pimiento cheese; and peach salsa, chicken liver pate on zucchini bread)." Publishers Weekly.

Strobel, Pamela

Princess Pamela's soul food cookbook : a mouth-watering treasury of Afro-American recipes / Pamela Strobel ; introduction by Matt Lee and Ted Lee. Rizzoli International Publications, 2017. 239 p. : **641.59296073**

1. African American cooking. 2. Cooking, American -- Southern style. 3. Recipes 4. Cookbooks.

ISBN 9780847858422

LC 2016952695

"Lee brothers library classic."

"The beloved classic now back in print after 45 years."

"A Bible for those looking to learn about soul food--Marcus Samuelsson"--Cover.

Includes index.

Presents recipes for traditional African American dishes, including fried chicken, okra fritters, Southern fries, and coconut pie.

641.5929992 Basque cooking

Raij, Alex

The **Basque** book : a love letter in recipes from the kitchen of Txikito / Alexandra Raij with Eder Montero and Rebecca Flint Marx ; photography by Penny De Los Santos. Ten Speed Press, 2016. 295 p. ; **641.5929992**

1. Cooking, Basque. 2. Recipes 3. Cookbooks.
ISBN 9781607747611

LC 2015041924

Collects one hundred traditional recipes for Basque dishes and Basque-inspired dishes from the author's New York restauraunts.

"Part cookbook, part travelog, this richly descriptive title is a pleasure to read and recalls evocative, landscape photography-rich works such as Giorgio Locatelli's Made in Sicily." Library Journal.

641.594 Cooking -- Europe

Allibhoy, Omar

Spanish made simple : foolproof Spanish recipes for every day / Omar Allibhoy ; photography by Martin Poole. Quadrille, 2016. 207 p. : **641.594**

1. Cooking, Spanish. 2. Recipes 3. Cookbooks.
ISBN 9781849497602

LC bl2017032188

Includes index.

Presents recipes for one hundred classic Spanish dishes, including tuna-stuffed eggs, squid in black ink sauce, pea soup with Serrano ham, seafood paella, and roasted almond nougat.

Andrews, Colman

The **country** cooking of Ireland / Colman Andrews ; photographs by Christopher Hirsheimer ; foreword by Darina Allen. Chronicle Books, c2009. 383 p. : **641.594**

1. Cooking, Irish.
ISBN 9780811866705

LC bl2009032505

Portraits of the Irish countryside and its people accompany recipes and cooking instructions for traditional Irish fare.

"The author provides new perspectives on the often maligned Irish cuisine. The breathtakingly beautiful photographs are alone enough to convince, but Andrews, calling Irish cuisine one of the most exciting food stories in the world today, lets the dishes make his case. ... Andrews has done the near impossible in elevating a cuisine thought to be humble and drab into tantalizing fare that will have worldwide appeal." Publishers Weekly.

Barrenechea, Teresa, 1956-

The **Basque** table : passionate home cooking from one of Europe's great regional cuisines / Teresa Barrenechea, with Mary Goodbody. The Harvard Common Press, c1998. viii, 232 p. : **641.594**

1. Cooking, Basque. 2. Food habits -- Spain 3. Recipes 4. Cookbooks
ISBN 9781558321403

LC 98029295

Includes index.

Offers more than 130 recipes for soups, salads, vegetable dishes, meat, poultry, fish and seafood, and desserts.

"The author's Basque dishes are characterized by fresh, lively flavors; garlic, hot chilis, and roasted sweet peppers, fish of all types, and beef and lamb are favorite ingredients. While home-style dishes are her emphasis here, there are some entries from nueva cocina as well. A chapter on pinchos, the Basque version of tapas, is a highlight, and there are sidebars on Basque ingredients and traditions throughout." Library Journal.

Bastianich, Lidia

Felidia : recipes from my flagship restaurant / Lidia Matticchio Bastianich with Chef Fortunato Nicotra and Tanya Bastianich Manuali ; photographs by Jennifer May. Alfred A. Knopf, 2019. xxxiii, 240 p. : **641.594**

1. Felidia (Restaurant) 2. Cooking, Italian. 3. Recipes 4. Cookbooks.
ISBN 9781524733087

LC 2018060923

The best-selling author and award-winning chef and her culinary partners share 115 recipes from their popular New York restaurant including Pasta Primavera; Linguine with Mussels, Clams and Broccoli; Pear and Pecorino Ravioli; Chicken Piazzaiola; Chocolate Hazelnut Flan and Open Cannoli

Lidia's : celebrate like an Italian / Lidia Matticchio Bastianich and Tanya Bastianich Manuali ; photographs by Steve Giralt. Alfred A. Knopf, 2017. xxvii, 383 p. ; **641.594**

1. Cooking, Italian. 2. Recipes 3. Cookbooks.
ISBN 9780385349482

LC 2017010180

Includes index.

In a guide for entertaining with that distinctly Bastianich flare, the beloved TV chef and her daughter present 220 easy-to-follow recipes with a welcoming Italian flavor that are perfect for any occasion, including Fragoli Daiquiri, Mussels With Zucchini Salsaverde, Peach Almond Cake, Roasted Olives With Orange and Rosemary, Campanelle With Fennel and much more.

Lidia's commonsense Italian cooking : 150 delicious and simple recipes anyone can master / Lidia Matticchio Bastianich and Tanya Bastianich Manuali ; photographs by Marcus Nilsson. Alfred A. Knopf, 2013. xxi, 277 p. : **641.594**

1. Cooking, Italian. 2. Recipes 3. Cookbooks.
ISBN 9780385349444

LC 2013005067

"This is a Borzoi book"--Title page verso.

Includes index.

Collects recipes outlining accessible culinary tips that channel instructive elements from the author's television show while sharing preparation guidelines for such fare as citrus roasted veal, rustic ricotta tart, and raw garden salad.

Lidia cooks from the heart of Italy / Lidia Matticchio Bastianich and Tanya Bastianich Manuali, with David Nussbaum ; photographs by Hirsheimer & Hamilton and Lidia Matticchio Bastianich. Alfred A. Knopf, 2009. xv, 411 p. : **641.594**

1. Cooking, Italian. 2. Cooking -- Italy. 3. Recipes 4. Cookbooks
ISBN 9780307267511

LC 2009022021

"A feast of 175 regional recipes"--jacket.

Includes index.

Shares recipes from lesser-known regions of Italy and secret dishes from famous areas, in a treasury that includes such options as risotto milan-style with marrow and saffron and roast lobster with bread crumb topping.

"Bastianich and daughter Tanya take readers on a culinary tour of Italy's 12 regions. Grouped by those areas, the recipes are simple enough for novice cooks. Included are appetizers, soups, salads and side dishes, condiments, pastas and risottos/rice, vegetarian main courses (aside from pasta), fish and seafood, meat and poultry, and desserts. In addition, there are stories about the history of the dishes." Library Journal.

★**Lidia's** family table / Lidia Matticchio Bastianich, with David Nussbaum ; photographs by Christopher Hirsheimer. Alfred A. Knopf, 2004. xxiv, 419 p. : **641.594**

1. Cooking, Italian. 2. Recipes 3. Cookbooks
ISBN 9781400040353

LC 2004022411

Includes index.

A guide to family cookery features more than two hundred master recipes for everyday dining and special family occasions, along with imaginative ideas for variations and improvisations, including seasonal salads, vegetables, soups, pastas, sauces, main courses, and desserts.

"Step-by-step photographs illustrate kitchen techniques, and charming photos of the author's grandchildren and other family scenes add to the appeal of this engaging, immensely practical book." Library Journal.

Lidia's favorite recipes : 100 foolproof Italian dishes, from basic sauces to irresistible entrees / Lidia Matticchio Bastianich and Tanya Bastianich Manuali ; photographs by Marcus Nilsson. Alfred A. Knopf, 2012. xv, 220 p. : **641.594**

1. Cooking, Italian. 2. Recipes 3. Cookbooks.
ISBN 9780307595669

LC 2012023455

Includes index.

The proprietor of New York City's Felidia restaurant and her daughter present a collection of favorite Italian recipes, with nutritional information for ingredients and suggestions for recipe variations.

"More compact than Bastianich's other titles, this practical collection is perfect for families as well as readers who enjoyed Viana La Place and Evan Kleimans Cucina Rustica." Library Journal.

Lidia's Italian-American kitchen / Lidia Matticchio Bastianich ; photographs by Christopher Hirsheimer. Alfred A. Knopf, c2001. xxvi, 432 p.: **641.594**

1. Cooking, Italian. 2. Cooking, American. 3. Recipes 4. Cookbooks
ISBN 9780375411502

LC 2001045009

Includes index.

Explores the secrets of Italian-American cuisine with recipes for such dishes as veal parmigiana, baked cannelloni, lasagna, and pizza, as well as a variety of dishes that use authentic Italian ingredients and cooking techniques.

"Bastianich has a warm, engaging style, and she's a teacher as well as a chef: throughout, she provides thoughtful head-notes and sidebars along with useful boxes on cooking with wine, resting soup, and other such practicalities." Library Journal.

Lidia's mastering the art of Italian cuisine : everything you need to know to be a great Italian cook / Lidia Mattichio Bastianich, with Tanya Bastianich Manuali. Alfred A. Knopf, 2015. xiii, 461 p. ; **641.594**

1. Cooking, Italian. 2. Recipes 3. Cookbooks.
ISBN 9780385349468

LC 2015001871

The Emmy-winning host of "Lidia's Kitchen," along with her daughter, provides an authoritative guide to Italian cooking that features 400 recipes along with the techniques needed to master Italian cuisine and a comprehensive guide to the tools every kitchen should have to produce the best results.

"The book completes its course with a charming chapter on Italian culture and language, as well as an extensive glossary of food terms. With this passionate treatise on Italian food and culture, readers dreaming of la dolce vita may find armchair travels enough to satisfy their hunger." Publishers Weekly.

Baxter, John, 1939-

The **perfect** meal : in search of the lost tastes of France / John Baxter. Harper Perennial, c2013. 336 p. **641.594**

1. Baxter, John, 1939- Travel 2. Cooking (Game) 3. Cooking, French. 4. Food habits -- France -- History. 5. Scarcity -- Social aspects. 6. France -- Social life and customs.
ISBN 9780062088062

LC 2012019240

"Baxter skillfully blends what could be considered merely entertaining food trivia into a satisfying full-course meal." Publishers Weekly.

Behr, Edward, 1951-

The **food** and wine of France : eating and drinking from Champagne to Provence / Edward Behr. Penguin Group USA, 2016 352 p. **641.594**

1. Cooking, French. 2. Food habits -- France. 3. France
ISBN 9781594204524

LC bl2016024274

An investigation into French cuisine by the founding editor of The Art of Eating and author of 50 Foods traces the stories of leading French artisans and chefs while drawing on their expertise in traditional methods and optimal ingredient pairings.

"What resonates is that whether a cuisine is defined by its ingredients, techniques, or even the logistical structure of its menu, it is perhaps the story and the telling that remain most important." Library Journal.

Bennison, Vicky

Pasta Grannies : the secrets of Italy's best home cooks / Vicky Bennison ; photography by Emma Lee. Hardie Grant Books, 2019. 255 p. : **641.594**

1. Cooking (Pasta). 2. Cooking, Italian. 3. Cookbooks.
ISBN 9781784882884

LC bl2019035961

Includes index.

"Bennison's inviting cookbook of homey recipes celebrates pasta-making traditions. . . . The recipes are easy to follow and include callouts to the YouTube channel for a visual guide." Publishers Weekly

Bishop, Jack, 1963-

Tasting Italy : a culinary journey / foreword by Jack Bishop ; Essays by Eugenia Bone and Julia della Croce ; recipes by America's Test Kitchen. National Geographic, 2018 382 p. : **641.594**

1. Cooking, Italian. 2. Food habits -- Italy 3. Recipes 4. Cookbooks.
ISBN 9781426219740

LC 2018003169

The experts at America's Test Kitchen team up with National Geographic to take readers on a culinary journey through the rich history of

Italian cuisine, region by region, that is accompanied by 100 innovative, kitchen-tested recipes that bring it all home.

"This beautifully illustrated book takes readers on a vivid culinary journey of Italys 20 provinces, from the Italian Alps of Valle dAosta to the juniper-scented coastlines of Sardinia." Publishers Weekly.

Björk, Katrín

From the north : a simple and modern approach to authentic Nordic cooking / Katrin Bjork founder of Modern Wifestyle. Page Street Publishing Co., 2018. 192 p. : **641.594**

1. Cooking, Scandinavian. 2. Entertaining -- Scandinavia. 3. Recipes 4. Cookbooks.

ISBN 9781624145308

LC 2017952212

Includes index.

In From the North, Katrín Björk celebrates the flavors of her childhood with fresh ingredients and unique twists. Her modern techniques make traditional Nordic cooking simple and approachable, no matter how far south your kitchen. --From publisher description.

"This cookbook -- with its solid, simple recipes -- serves as an excellent introduction to Nordic cuisine." Publishers Weekly.

Bottura, Massimo, 1962

Never trust a skinny Italian chef / Massimo Bottura, Osteria Francescana ; photography by Carlo Benvenuto and Stefan Graziani. Phaidon Press Limited, 2014 301 p. : **641.594**

1. Bottura, Massimo, 1962- 2. Osteria Francescana. 3. Restaurants -- Italy 4. Cooking, Italian. 5. Recipes 6. Cookbooks.

ISBN 9780714867144

LC bl2014049357

Includes index.

A tribute to Bottura's career and the evolution of his restaurant in Modena deals with four distinct periods in his life and shares fifty recipes along with stories that explain his inspirations, ingredients, and techniques.

"Quirky dishes such as a deconstructed mortadella sandwich made with mortadella foam; bread, butter, and anchovies; and a compression of pasta and beans make this a fun collection to peruse, but one unlikely to inspire home cooks. Professionals, however, will relish the opportunity for guided experimentation with Italian classics." Publishers Weekly.

Boulud, Daniel

Daniel : my French cuisine / Daniel Boulud and Sylvie Bigar ; essays by Bill Buford ; photography by Thomas Schauer. Grand Central Life & Style, 2013. xix, 395 p. : **641.594**

1. Cooking, French. 2. Cookbooks.

ISBN 9781455513925

LC bl2013044423

Includes index.

A chef and restaurateur best known for his eponymous restaurant in Manhattan presents seventy-five signature French recipes along with essays on bread and cheese as well as a humorous take on the preparation of several famous French dishes.

Carmellini, Andrew

Urban Italian : simple recipes and true stories from a life in food / Andrew Carmellini and Gwen Hyman ; photographs by Quentin Bacon. Bloomsbury USA, 2008. 311 p. : **641.594**

1. Carmellini, Andrew. 2. Cooking, Italian. 3. Cooking, Italian American 4. Recipes 5. Cookbooks

ISBN 9781596914704

LC bl2009000702

Includes index.

Offers one hundred recipes that blend sophisticated ingredients with instructions for such dishes as lamb meatballs stuffed with goat cheese, roast pork with Italian plums and grappa, and honey-flavored pine nut cake.

"The author presents spectacular recipes while opening a window onto his life with food, from his Italian-American boyhood and cooking school to revelations while traveling in Italy and being a top New York chef. The recipes, which come from all over Italy and mix regional Italian and American influences, are arranged classically, from antipasti to dolci." Publishers Weekly.

Child, Julia

From Julia Child's kitchen / Julia Child ; photographs and drawings by Paul Child ; additional technical photographs by Albie Walton. Gramercy Books, 1999. xvi, 677, xxvi p. : **641.594**

1. Cooking, French.

ISBN 9780517207123

LC 99020209

Includes index.

A new edition of one of the beloved chef's earliest cookbooks presents an American approach to classic French cookery, along with a host of delectable recipes and cooking techniqes for both novice and experienced cooks.

"The author has taken many of the recipes she demonstrated in her 72 'French Chef' TV shows; grouped them by subject {soups, appetizers, egg dishes, fish, poultry, meat, vegetables, salads, bread} added variations and additional recipes; and introduced each section and most recipes with commentaries." Library Journal.

Child, Julia

Julia and Jacques cooking at home / Julia Child and Jacques Pepin, with David Nussbaum. Alfred A. Knopf, 1999. xii, 430 p. : **641.594**

1. Child, Julia. 2. Pepin, Jacques, 1935- 3. Cooking, French. 4. Recipes 5. Cookbooks.

ISBN 9780375404313

LC 98032418

Two culinary masters join their talents in a cookbook that demonstrates the best in traditional French home cooking, with an assortment of recipes that ranges from soups to desserts

"A companion volume to the PBS series. For each show, the two chefs started out with ideas and ingredients but no set recipes, so they improvised as they went along, cooking a lot of their favorite traditional dishes and coming up with new ones as well. Dozens of boxes throughout the text provide information on a wide variety of topics." Library Journal.

★**Mastering** the art of French cooking / Julia Child, Louisette Bertholle, Simone Beck ; illustrations by Sidonie Coryn. Alfred A. Knopf, 2018. xxxi, 684, xxxii p. : **641.594**

1. Cooking, French. 2. Recipes 3. Cookbooks.

ISBN 0375413405

LC 2009288212

"This is a Borzoi Book"--Title page verso.

Includes index.

Revised edition of: Mastering the art of French cooking / by Simone Beck, Louisette Bertholle, Julia Child. [1st ed]. 1961-1970.

Explains for the novice American cook the special ingredients and cooking techniques involved in preparing the wide variety of French dishes featured.

Clark, Melissa

Dinner in French : my recipes by way of France / Melissa Clark. Clarkson Potter/Publishers, 2020. 335 p. : **641.594**

1. Cooking, French. 2. Recipes 3. Seasonal cooking 4. Cookbooks.
ISBN 9780553448252

LC 2019013485

Includes index.

An authoritative but comprehensive French cookbook by the James Beard Award-winning New York Times food writer and author of Dinner shares 150 wide-ranging recipes and modern updates of classic favorites, from Ratatouille Sheet-pan Chicken to Scalloped Potato Gratin.

"This remarkable volume will entice avid home cooks to return to it time and again." Publishers Weekly

Coscarelli, Chloe

Chloe's vegan Italian kitchen : 150 pizzas, pastas, pestos, risottos, & lots of creamy Italian classics / Chloe Coscarelli. Atria Books, 2014 xv, 271 p. : **641.594**

1. Cooking, Italian. 2. Vegan cooking. 3. Recipes 4. Cookbooks.
ISBN 9781476736075

LC 2013045234

Includes index.

"Vegan chef Chloe Coscarelli creates more than 150 recipes inspired by Italian cuisine".-- Provided by publisher.

Costantini, Elisa, 1938-

Italian moms : something old, something new : 150 family recipes / Elisa Costantini with Frank Costanitini. Sterling Epicure, 2018 viii, 246 p. : **641.594**

1. Cooking, Italian. 2. Recipes 3. Cookbooks.
ISBN 9781454927983

LC bl2018048924

Includes index.

A collection of homestyle Italian recipes features such dishes as fried mozzarella, pancetta corn cakes, penne with lobsters, stuffed eggplant, veal marsala, seafood paella, panna cotta, and Italian rum truffle.

"Color photographs accompany most recipes, and, helping time-starved cooks, most preparations are contained in one page or less...The best reason of all to say Mamma mia!" Booklist.

Crapanzano, Aleksandra

The **London** cookbook : recipes from the restaurants, cafes, and hole-in-the-wall gems of a modern city / Aleksandra Crapanzano ; photography by Sang An. Ten Speed Press, 2016 xxvii, 289 p. : **641.594**

1. Cooking, English. 2. Cooking -- England -- London. 3. Restaurants -- England -- London. 4. Recipes 5. Cookbooks.
ISBN 9781607748137

LC 2016012459

Collects more than one hundred eclectic recipes from some of London's best restaurants, dessert shops, coffee houses, cocktail lounges, and hole-in-the-wall gems--all adapted for the home kitchen.

"Crapanzano perfectly captures all that's exciting about the people, places, and foods that make up London's modern culinary scene. After reading this cookbook, home cooks may find themselves planning a London vacation." Library Journal.

Danford, Natalie

How to Eataly : a guide to buying, cooking, and eating Italian food / written by Natalie Danford ; photographs by Francesco Sapienza ; introduction by Oscar Farinetti, founder ; forewords by Joe Bastianich, Lidia Bastianich, Mario Batali, and Adam & Alex Saper. Rizzoli, 2014. 304 p. : **641.594**

1. Eataly alti cibi (Italian marketplace) 2. Cooking, Italian. 3. Recipes 4. Cookbooks.
ISBN 9780847843350

LC bl2014044028

Includes index.

Collects recipes from the Eataly food emporium experts for contemporary Italian classics, with information about Italian food and cooking, including how to source the best-quality ingredients, drink coffee Italian style, and cook pasta al dente.

David, Elizabeth, 1913-1992

French provincial cooking / Elizabeth David ; illustrations by Juliet Renny. Grub Street, 2008 519 p. **641.594**

1. Cooking, French 2. Recipes 3. Cookbooks.
ISBN 9781904943716

LC 2008411778

Contains a long essay on French cuisine and offers background stories and sketches of recipes. This book starts with a short essay on each of the major culinary regions of France. It consists of chapters on cuisine by type of dish such as: Sauces, Hors-D'oeuvres and Salads, Soups, Eggs and Cheese, Pates and Terrines, Vegetables, Fish, and others. --From publisher description.

Italian food / Elizabeth David. Penguin Books, 1999, c1958. xxxiii, 376 p. ; **641.594**

1. Cooking, Italian. 2. Food. 3. Cooking.
ISBN 0141181559

LC 99200031

Originally published: New York : Knopf, 1958.

"David studies and analyzes cooking the way a scholar analyzes literature, and, as a result, her titles are far more than just cookbooks. Along with the recipes, of which there are many, she explains at length the histories of the dishes and offers splendid advice on serving wine with the meals." Library Journal.

De Laurentiis, Giada

Giada's Italy : my recipes for La Dolce Vita / Giada De Laurentiis. Clarkson Potter, 2018 288 p. : **641.594**

1. Cooking, Italian. 2. Recipes 3. Cookbooks.
ISBN 9780307987228

LC 2017049489

Includes index.

A lavish exploration of the author's food heritage in her native Rome also celebrates the lifestyle traditions that define la bella vita, sharing authentic Italian recipes enhanced with a contemporary California twist, including Grilled Swordfish with Candied Lemon Salad, Spaghetti with Chianti and Fava Beans and Fennel Upside Down Cake.

Giada's kitchen : new Italian favorites / Giada De Laurentiis ; photographs by Tina Rupp. Clarkson Potter/Publishers, c2008. 240 p. : **641.594**

1. Cooking, Italian. 2. Cooking, Italian-American 3. Recipes 4. Cookbooks
ISBN 9780307346599

LC 2008005004

Includes index.

The host of Food Network's Everyday Italian presents a new collection of nearly one hundred tempting recipes for classic Italian dishes with a California-inspired twist, including lighter versions of such traditional dishes as Osso Bucco, as well as regional specialties, pasta, salads, meats, desserts, and special meals for kids.

Dusoulier, Clotilde, 1979-

The **French** market cookbook : vegetarian recipes from my Parisian kitchen / Clotilde Dusoulier of chocolateandzucchini.com. Clarkson Potter Publishers, 2013 224 p. : **641.594**

1. Vegetarian cooking. 2. Cooking, French. 3. Recipes 4. Cookbooks.
ISBN 9780307984821

LC 2012554926

Includes indexes.

Presents a collection of vegetarian recipes inspired by French cooking, using basic, readily available ingredients and including several options that are dairy- and gluten-free.

"Organized by season and peppered with tips on how to select and store vegetables, this cookbook will excite readers looking for substantial vegetarian meals they can feel good about eating." Library Journal.

Tasting Paris : 100 recipes to eat like a local / Clotilde Dusoulier. Clarkson Potter/Publishers, [2018] 256 p. **641.594**

1. Cooking, French 2. Cultural fusion 3. Food habits 4. City life 5. Paris, France
ISBN 9780451499141

LC 2017025780

A culinary tour of the French capital and food destination includes iconic bistro and brasserie fare, as well as such newer dishes as carrot chickpea crepes and ratatouille tahini sandwiches.

"Chapters are organized by time of day, so that one for afternoon treats, for instance, proffers light sweets, which are differentiated from dinner desserts. The setup can be a bit confusing at first, but it does ultimately lend reading this volume the same feel as of discovering something new while strolling down a city street." Publishers Weekly.

Feinberg, Andrew, 1974-

Franny's: simple seasonal Italian / Andrew Feinberg, Francine Stephens, Melissa Clark. Artisan, 2013 ix, 366 p. : **641.594**

1. Cooking, Italian. 2. Cooking -- New York (State) -- Brooklyn. 3. Seasonal cooking 4. Cookbooks.
ISBN 9781579654641

LC 2012028954

Offers modern Southern Italian recipes including roasted romano beans with calabrese olives, linguine with meyer lemon, marinated artichokes, baked sausage and polenta, and bucatini alla puttanesca.

Fourmont, Camille

★**La** Buvette : recipes & wine notes from Paris / Camille Fourmont and Kate Leahy ; photographs by Marcus Nilsson. Ten Speed Press, 2020 xi, 211 p.: **641.594**

1. Buvette (Restaurant : Paris, France). 2. Cooking, French. 3. Wine and wine making -- France. 4. Recipes 5. Cookbooks.
ISBN 9781984856692

LC 2019040994

Includes index.

The owner of a beloved Paris wine shop, bar and café, while introducing some of Paris's best wine and food makers in intimate portraits, presents 50 recipes for simple, grazing-style food along with her wine notes.

"Fourmont transports readers to Paris in this pleasant volume of simple recipes." Publishers Weekly

Garten, Ina

Barefoot in Paris : easy French food you can make at home/ Ina Garten ; photographs by Quentin Bacon ; food styling by Rori Trovato ; styling by Miguel Flores-Vianna. Clarkson Potter/Publishers, c2004. 238 p. : **641.594**

1. Cooking, French. 2. Cookbooks
ISBN 9781400049356

LC 2004003280

Includes indexes.

Provides recipes for simple dishes from France, using fresh, quality ingredients to concoct new twists on traditional French favorites, including steak au poivre, and creme brulé.

Gislason, Gunnar Karl

North : the new Nordic cuisine of Iceland / Gunnar Karl Gislason and Jody Eddy ; foreword by Rene Redzepi ; photography by Evan Sung. Ten Speed Press, 2014 ix, 341 p. : **641.594**

1. Cooking, Icelandic. 2. Recipes 3. Cookbooks.
ISBN 9781607744986

LC 2014003525

A collection of recipes celebrating the cuisine of Iceland, including main dishes, sides, and desserts, with stories about the people and traditions of the island nation.

"Many of the recipes reflect the natural resources of Iceland, for example, the sea-salt employed is Icelandic and the fact that so many recipes involve pickled items is a direct product of the necessity of storing food items in a harsh climate. There are many recipes, though, for which the chef does not need to have access to Iceland." Publishers Weekly.

Goin, Suzanne, 1966-

★**Sunday** suppers at Lucques : seasonal recipes from market to table / Suzanne Goin with Teri Gelber ; photographs by Shimon and Tammar. Alfred A. Knopf, 2005. xviii, 398 p. : **641.594**

1. Lucques (Restaurant) 2. Cooking, French. 3. Seasonal cooking 4. Recipes 5. Cookbooks
ISBN 9781400042159

LC 2004058604

Includes index.

Introduces Sunday supper recipes served at the Los Angeles restaurant, Lucques, organized according to season, demonstrating the importance of fresh ingredients combined in unexpected ways to create appetizers, main courses, and desserts.

"The author writes with passion and humor, and while her recipes are sophisticated and sometimes complicated, they are written with the home cook in mind." Library Journal.

Greenspan, Dorie

Around my French table : more than 300 recipes from my home to yours / Dorie Greenspan ; photographs by Alan Richardson. Houghton Mifflin Harcourt, c2010. xiii, 530 p. : **641.594**

1. Cooking, French. 2. Recipes
ISBN 9780618875535

LC 2010014232

Includes product source list and index.

A James Beard Award winner offers personable recipes for French home cooking, presenting more than 300 recipes for hors d'oeuvres, salads, soups, meat dishes, fish, vegetables, and desserts, with a separate section on making dough, vinaigrettes, and sauces.

"A part-time Paris resident for more than a decade, Greenspan focuses on what French people really eat at home: easy-to-prepare yet flavorful dishes that are suitable for just about any time of day. From Bacon and Eggs and Asparagus Salad to Chicken in a Pot to Veal Chops with Rosemary Butter, her offerings are hardy, mostly uncomplicated, and superbly appetizing. She also provides sidebars on a wide range of topics, including whether or not to wash raw chicken, several ways of cooking beets, mussels, and more." Publishers Weekly.

Hazan, Marcella

★**Essentials** of classic Italian cooking / Marcella Hazan ; illustrated by Karin Kretschmann. A. A. Knopf, 1992. xi, 688 p. : **641.594**

1. Cooking, Italian. 2. Recipes 3. Cookbooks
ISBN 9780394584041

LC 92052954

Includes index.

"This could readily assume the mantle of the definitive resource for Italian cuisine." Booklist.

Hazan, Marcella

Ingredienti : Marcella's guide to the market / Marcella Hazan and Victor Hazan ; illustrated by Karin Kretschmann Lubart. Scribner, 2016. xiii, 238 p. : **641.594**

1. Cooking, Italian. 2. Grocery shopping. 3. Recipes 4. Cookbooks
ISBN 9781451627367

LC bl2016028117

The husband of the late "Godmother of Italian cooking" shares Marcella's vignettes on how to buy and use fresh produce for authentic Italian cuisine, sharing tips for using ingredients from supermarkets, farmers' markets, and online sources.

"This little volume offers a treasury of lifetime observations to serious, inquisitive cooks." Booklist.

Hazan, Marcella

Marcella cucina / Marcella Hazan ; photography by Alison Harris, design by Joel Avirom. HarperCollins Publishers, c1997. 471 p. : **641.594**

1. Cooking, Italian. 2. Recipes 3. Cookbooks.
ISBN 9780060171032

LC 97001253

Includes index.

A culinary tour of Italy offers regional specialties and includes a guide to shopping for ingredients

"This book includes both the author's old favorites and recent creations, along with her versions of regional dishes from chefs and home cooks throughout Italy. She offers an intimate, at times nostalgic glimpse at her life with cooking." Library Journal.

Hazan, Marcella

Marcella says ... : Italian cooking wisdom from the legendary teacher's master classes, with 120 of her irresistible new recipes / Marcella Hazan. HarperCollins, c2004. 390 p. : **641.594**

1. Cooking, Italian. 2. Recipes 3. Cookbooks
ISBN 9780066209678

LC 2004042892

Includes index.

The master chef and cooking instructor presents a follow-up to Marcella Cucina, explaining traditional cooking techniques, outlining detailed Italian menus, and providing 100 new recipes complemented by preparation essays, narratives, and historical information.

Hercules, Olia

Mamushka : a cookbook / Olia Hercules. Weldon Owen, 2015 240 p. : **641.594**

1. Cooking -- Europe, Eastern. 2. Cooking, Ukrainian. 3. Cookbooks.
ISBN 9781616289614

LC bl2016009808

Includes index.

Shares a collection of traditional Ukrainian and Eastern European recipes, featuring such fare as curd cheese, stuffed cabbage leages, chickpea and mutton soup, apricot jam, and honey cake.

"Hercules's unexpected Ukranian, Azerbaijani, Russian, and Armenian comfort foods can help home cooks transition to colder months." Library Journal.

Hoffman, Susanna

The **olive** and the caper : adventures in Greek cooking / Susanna Hofman ; in collaboration with Victoria Wise. Workman Pub., 2004. xvii, 589 p. : **641.594**

1. Cooking, Greek. 2. Food habits -- Greece. 3. Greece -- Social life and customs.
ISBN 1563058480

LC 2004040862

"With its fascinating trove of information, this work will please armchair cooks and traveling foodies. For those willing to surrender to its searingly bright palate of flavors, it's a boon to the kitchen, too. Publishers Weekly.

Jones, Catherine Cheremeteff

A **year** of Russian feasts / Catherine Cheremeteff Jones ; illustrations by Barbara Stott McCoy. Jellyroll Press, c2002. 192 p. : **641.594**

1. Cooking, Russian. 2. Food habits -- Russia. 3. Russia -- Social life and customs.
ISBN 0971601305

LC BL2002014081

Equal parts travel memoir and cookbook, Catherine Jones's critically acclaimed and award-winning book, A Year of Russian Feasts, combines her warm, insightful writing style with her sensitive approach to discovering her family's Russian cultural heritage and its cuisine. --From publisher description.

"Rich and hearty, the recipes evoke a strong sense of the Russian landscape." Booklist.

Kahan, Paul, 1962-

Cheers to the Publican, repast and present : recipes and ramblings from an American beer hall / Paul Kahan and Cosmo Goss with Rachel Holtzman ; photographs, Peden + Munk ; poems, Jason Pickleman. Lorena Jones Books, an imprint of Ten Speed Press, 2017 xi, 324 p. : **641.594**

1. Publican (Restaurant : Chicago, Ill.) 2. Cooking, European. 3. Recipes 4. Cookbooks.
ISBN 9780399578564

LC 2017013468

The chef behind an incredibly popular restaurant in Chicago, known for its beer-friendly cooking and massive communal tables, offers 125 recipes for meat, seafood and vegetable dishes along with entertaining stories from the kitchen and dining room.

Keller, Thomas, 1955-

★**Bouchon** Bakery / Thomas Keller and Sebastien Rouxel with Susie Heller, Matthew McDonald, Michael Ruhlman, and Amy Vogler ; photographs by Deborah Jones. Artisan, c2012. 399 p. : **641.594**

1. Bouchon Bakery. 2. Baking. 3. Cookbooks.
ISBN 9781579654351

LC 2012000695

Collects recipes from the famed Bouchon Bakery, including chocolate eclairs, cherry-whipped cream doughnuts, poached pears, and sourdough boule.

"[T]his lovely volume is a must-have for cooks who want to take baking to the next level." Publishers Weekly.

Khoo, Rachel

The **little** Swedish kitchen : over 100 recipes to celebrate every season / Rachel Khoo. Michael Joseph, 2018. 302 p. : **641.594**

1. Cooking, Swedish. 2. Cookbooks.
ISBN 9780718188917

LC bl2019037519

Includes index.

Complete with stunning location and food photography, and over 100 beautiful, fuss-free recipes, this cookbook lets you in on what the Swedish call lagom...the art of not too little, not too much, but just the right amount. --from publisher description

"This excellent offering is stylish, tempting, and just plain fun." Publishers Weekly.

Kiros, Tessa

Food from many Greek kitchens / Tessa Kiros. Andrews McMeel Pub., 2011. 333 p. : **641.594**

1. Cooking, Greek. 2. Cookbooks.
ISBN 9781449406523

LC bl2011034130

Includes index.

Originally published: Millers Point, N.S.W. : Murdoch Books, 2010.

Features recipes of traditional Greek cuisine for each meal of the day and special holidays, with color photographs, synonymous title names, cooking tips, and background information for each recipe.

"For each recipe, [the author] gives the title in English and Greek and offers an introduction to the dish and thorough instruction. From Baklava to Keftedes Fried Meatballs to Pita Bread, the accessible dishes are accompanied by beautiful photography. Greek cookbooks written for the beginner are rare, so this book is a gem. It provides a good foundation and is sure to be a gateway to more advanced Greek cooking." Library Journal.

Kochilas, Diane

The **glorious** foods of Greece : traditional recipes from the islands, cities, and villages / Diane Kochilas. William Morrow, c2001. xv, 496 p. : **641.594**

1. Cooking, Greek. 2. Food habits -- Greece. 3. Recipes 4. Cookbooks
ISBN 9780688154578

LC 00028158

A region-by-region cookbook introduces the diverse cuisine of Greece, offering a collection of 400 authentic traditional and contemporary recipes representing three thousand years of history, culture, and culinary lore.

"This cookbook includes over 400 recipes from various regions, starting with the Peloponnesus and the Ionian Islands, moving on to Macedonia, the islands of the Aegean, and Crete, and finishing up in the city of Athens. Kochilas also provides extensive historical background, cultural as well as culinary, along with detailed descriptions and explanations of ingredients." Library Journal.

Ikaria : lessons on food, life, and longevity from the Greek island where people forget to die / Diane Kochilas ; photography by Vassilis Stenos. Rodale, 2014 xii, 306 p. : **641.594**

1. Cooking -- Greece 2. Cooking, Greek. 3. Food -- Greece 4. Recipes 5. Ikaria (Greece : Municipality) 6. Cookbooks.
ISBN 9781623362959

LC 2014032164

"Ikaria is mythical, beautiful, enigmatic--and, as we learned after reading the New York Times article about it, a place where residents live unaccountably long lives. Part cookbook, part travelogue, filled with gorgeous photography, stunning recipes, and interviews with locals, and packed with the often quirky secrets to a long life that Ikarians are spoon-fed at birth, Ikaria is award-winning author Diane Kochilas's ethno-culinary paean to this magical island. Here, Kochilas will marry lore to lesson and recipe to interview: we'll meet a 101-year-old weaver--the best on the island--and taste the combinations of herbs that he cooks with and that he believes give him life. We'll learn about the life-giving benefits of delicious salads both raw and cooked, the gorgeous breads and savory pies that are a part of every meal, the bean dishes that are passed down through generations, and the seafood that is at the root of the Ikarian culinary culture. Filled with mouthwatering recipes and remarkable stories, this book will introduce many Americans to food as life, as only the Ikarians know it"-- Provided by publisher.

Korkosz, Michal

Fresh from Poland : new vegetarian cooking from the old country / Michal Korkosz The Experiment, 2020 245 p. : **641.594**

1. Cooking, Polish. 2. Vegetarian cooking. 3. Recipes 4. Cookbooks.
ISBN 9781615196555

LC 2019054739

Includes index.

"The first Polish vegetarian cookbook, with new Polish recipes and meat-free versions of traditional dishes"-- Provided by publisher.

"This charming collection offers both traditional vegetable dishes of Poland, such as creamy cucumber salad and chilled beet soup, and vegetarian versions of the Polish canon. . . . A light and delicious take on a cuisine often underrepresented in cooking collections. Vegetarian or not, most cooks will find something to savor." Library Journal

Ladner, Mark

The **Del** Posto cookbook / Mark Ladner with Michael R. Wilson ; forewords by Mario Batali and Joe Bastianich ; food photography by Paulette Tavormina. Grand Central Life & Style, 2016. xxxi, 239 p. : **641.594**

1. Del Posto (Restaurant). 2. Cooking, Italian. 3. Restaurants -- New York (State) -- New York. 4. Cookbooks.
ISBN 9781455561544

LC OC2018159199

Includes index.

The celebrated chef at Mario Batali's and Lidia Bastianich's award-winning destination restaurant in New York City redefines excellence in Italian cooking in America, focusing on regional Italian ingredients and traditions to present a collection of sophisticated old-country recipes.

"In addition to a thorough index, Ladner provides a welcome rarity: an allergen guide, three pages of charts listing all the recipes and the common allergens they include." Publishers Weekly.

Le Goff, Audrey

Rustic French cooking made easy : authentic, regional flavors from Provence, Brittany, Alsace and beyond / Audrey Le Goff, creator of Pardon your French. Page Street Publishing Co., 2019. 175 p. : **641.594**

1. Cooking, French. 2. Recipes 3. Cookbooks.
ISBN 9781624148637

LC bl2019029908

Includes index.

Real French home cooking is easier than you think! Leave haute cuisine to fussy restaurants, and dive into these uncomplicated classics from Audrey Le Goff, founder of the blog Pardon Your French. Drawing inspiration from her childhood in the north of France, Audrey shares simple fare, full of the rich, complex flavors French cuisine is known for. From quiche to cr]urpes, these homey dishes are anything but humble. --From publisher description.

"This is a superb collection of lesser-known regional French dishes." Publishers Weekly.

Lebovitz, David

★**My** Paris kitchen : recipes and stories / David Lebovitz. Ten Speed Press, 2014. 352 p. **641.594**

1. Lebovitz, David Anecdotes. 2. Cooking, French. 3. Cooking -- Anecdotes. 4. Bloggers 5. Food habits -- France 6. Paris, France -- Social life and customs Anecdotes.

ISBN 9781607742678

LC 2013032561

"A collection of stories and 100 sweet and savory French-inspired recipes from Chez Panisse pastry chef turned popular food blogger David Lebovitz, reflecting the way modern Parisians eat today and featuring lush photography taken around Paris and in David's Parisian kitchen. French cooking has come a long way since the days of Escoffier. The culinary culture of France has changed and the current generation of French cooks, most notably in Paris, are incorporating ingredients and techniques from around the world. In My Paris Kitchen, David Lebovitz remasters the French classics, introduces lesser known French fare, and presents 100 recipes using ingredients foraged in the ethnic neighborhoods of Paris. Stories told in David's trademark style describe thequirks, trials, and joys of cooking, shopping, and eating in France, while food and location photographs reveal modern life in Paris".-- Provided by publisher.

"French food personalized and demystified for the home cook in the best way." Publishers Weekly.

Leite, David

The **new** Portuguese table : exciting flavors from Europe's western coast / David Leite ; photographs by Nuno Correia. Clarkson Potter/Publishers, c2009. 256 p. : **641.594**

1. Cooking, Portuguese. 2. Recipes 3. Cookbooks

ISBN 9780307394415

LC 2008051283

Includes index.

A culinary journey of Portugal spanning thirteen different historical regions covers the nation's food and culture, and includes recipes for such dishes as slowly simmered white beans and sausage and olive oil-poached fresh cod with roasted tomato sauce.

"The author begins by outlining Portugal's diverse regional cuisines and then describes traditional ingredients. From there it is a straightforward listing of appetizers, soups, fish, meat, poultry, vegetable/egg/ rice dishes, breads, sweets, liqueurs, and condiments, with approximately 150 recipes overall. Full of delicious-sounding recipes, this title is sure to appeal to adventurous cooks wanting to try a new ethnic cuisine and will also be popular with Portuguese American communities." Library Journal.

Loomis, Susan Herrmann

In a French kitchen : tales and traditions of everyday home cooking in France / Susan Herrmann Loomis. Gotham Books, 2015 352 p. **641.594**

1. Loomis, Susan Herrmann. 2. Cooking, French. 3. Food habits -- France. 4. Food writers 5. Americans in France 6. Normandy -- Social life and customs. 7. Louviers, France -- Social life and customs.

ISBN 9781592408863

LC 2014035856

Includes index.

With In a French Kitchen, Loomis an expat who long ago traded her American grocery store for a bustling French farmer's market demystifies in lively prose the seemingly effortless je ne sais quoi behind a simple French meal. One by one, readers are invited to meet the busy people of Louviers and surrounding villages and towns of Loomis's adopted home, from runway-chic Edith, who has zero passion for cooking but a love of food that inspires her to whip up an array of mouthwatering dishes to Nathalie, who becomes misty-eyed as she talks about her mother's Breton cooking, then goes on to reproduce it.

"Loomis also shares scores of recipes from her own repertoire and those of her friends, including a 12-month meal plan based on fresh, seasonal ingredients. A tempting and helpful guide to delectable food." Kirkus.

McDonnell, Imen

The **Farmette** cookbook : recipes and adventures from my life on an Irish farm / Imen McDonnell. Roost Books, 2016. xx, 361 p. : **641.594**

1. Cooking, Irish. 2. Country life -- Ireland. 3. Recipes 4. Cookbooks.

ISBN 9781611802047

LC 2015026646

Includes indexes.

The author documents her move to Ireland and marriage to an Irish dairy farmer through over one hundred recipes, including such offerings as Irish dulse miso soup, tater tot shepherd's pie, and coffee-walnut cake.

"An outstanding debut, with just the right amount of sentimentality." Library Journal.

Mendes, Nuno

My Lisbon : a cookbook from Portugal's city of light / Nuno Mendes, photography by Andrew Montgomery. Ten Speed Press, 2018 315 p. : **641.594**

1. Cooking, Portuguese. 2. Cooking -- Lisbon, Portugal 3. Recipes 4. Cookbooks.

ISBN 9780399581717

LC 2017049818

"Sharing recipes inspired by the dishes that he grew up eating, Mendes takes you to his beloved Lisbon, revealing the secrets for recreating the city's most vibrant dishes"-- Provided by publisher.

"Pitch-perfect and mouthwatering, this book is a joy from start to finish." Publishers Weekly.

Morales, Bonnie Frumkin

Kachka : a return to Russian cooking / Bonnie Frumkin Morales ; with Deena Prichep ; photography by Leela Cyd. Flatiron Books, 2017 389 p. ; **641.594**

1. Kachka (Restaurant) 2. Cooking, Russian. 3. Recipes 4. Cookbooks.

ISBN 9781250087607

LC 2017022390

Includes index.

"This fantastic cookbook from the chef at Kachka in Portland, Ore., is by turns funny, moving, informative, and appetite-whetting." Publishers Weekly.

Moulle, Jean-Pierre

French roots : two cooks, two countries, and the beautiful food along the way / Jean-Pierre Moulle and Denise Lurton Moulle. Ten Speed Press, 2014 272 p. **641.594**

1. Moulle, Jean-Pierre. 2. Moulle, Denise Lurton. 3. Cooking, French. 4. Cooks -- United States 5. Cooking 6. Autobiographies and memoirs

ISBN 9781607745471

LC 2014023823

Includes index.

"Readers who have an active imaginary life in France will relish poring over this cookbook's extensive narrative. Fans of Chez Panisse will enjoy pairing it with titles from other chef alums, such as David Tanis and David Lebovitz." Library Journal.

Necchio, Valeria

Veneto : recipes from an Italian country kitchen / Valeria Necchio. Guardian Books, 2017. 288 p. : **641.594**

1. Cooking, Italian -- Northern style. 2. Cooking, Italian -- Venetian style. 3. Recipes 4. Cookbooks.

ISBN 9781783351084

Includes index.

"Necchio writes in lovely elegiac prose about her small hometown... and the recipes themselves are clear and appealing, no matter from which time in the author's life they originate." Publishers Weekly.

Nilsson, Magnus, 1983-

The **Nordic** cookbook / Magnus Nilsson. Phaidon Press Limited, 2015. 767 p. : **641.594**

1. Cooking, Scandinavian. 2. Cookbooks.

ISBN 9780714868721

LC bl2018045351

Includes index.

Collects more than seven hundred authentic Scandinavian recipes that showcase the region's unique culinary culture, including such offerings as fresh eel cooked on straw, Icelandic grouse soup, and Finnish mutton and herring casserole.

Nolen, Jeremy

New German cooking : recipes for classics revisited / Jeremy and Jessica Nolen with Drew Lazor ; photographs by Jason Varney. Chronicle Books, 2014 235 p. : **641.594**

1. Cooking, German. 2. Recipes 3. Cookbooks.

ISBN 9781452128061

LC 2014000717

Shares recipes for familiar German classics that have been updated to reflect contemporary dining preferences, including such options as smoked pork and bacon sausage, mushroom and sauerkraut goulash, and apple strudel.

Ojakangas, Beatrice A.

Scandinavian feasts : celebrating traditions throughout the year / Beatrice Ojakangas ; photography by Michael Grimaldi. University of Minnesota Press, 2001, c1992. xiv, 281 p. ; **641.594**

1. Cooking, Scandinavian.

ISBN 9780816637454

Includes index.

Originally published: New York : Stewart, Tabori & Chang, 1992.

Drawing upon her rich knowledge of Scandinavian cuisine and culture, expert chef and veteran writer Beatrice Ojakangas presents a multitude of delicious yet remarkably simple recipes in this cookbook classic, available in paperback for the first time. Scandinavian Feasts features the cuisine of Denmark, Norway, Sweden, and Finland, and it includes menus made up of a bounty of appetizers, drinks, smorgasbord, meats, fish, soups, vegetables, desserts, and baked goods. Easily as engaging as the dishes themselves, each recipe comes with an introduction that explains the cultural importance of the feast and details its seasonal significance. --From publisher description.

Olivella, Daniel

Catalan food : culture & flavors from the Mediterranean / Daniel Olivella with Caroline Wright ; photographs by Johnny Autry. Clarkson Potter/Publishers, 2018 271 p. : **641.594**

1. Cooking, Spanish -- Catalonian style. 2. Recipes 3. Cookbooks.

ISBN 9780451495884

LC 2017048094

Includes index.

A collection of recipes from Catalan cuisine for the home cook features such dishes as paella, fried squid with fennel, clams in white sauce, brisket canelones, and churros with hot chocolate.

Oliver, Jamie, 1975-

Jamie's Italy / Jamie Oliver ; photographs by David Loftus and Chris Terry. Hyperion, c2006. xv, 319 p. : **641.594**

1. Cooking, Italian. 2. Recipes 3. Cookbooks

ISBN 9781401301958

LC bl2006024728

Includes index.

The author presents recipes and cooking tips he received from real Italians during a tour of Italy along with anecdotes from his trip.

Olney, Richard

Lulu's Provencal table / Richard Olney. Grub Street, 2013. 224 p. : **641.594**

1. Cooking, French -- Provencal style. 2. Recipes 3. Cookbooks

ISBN 9781909166189

LC oc2014007655

Includes index.

Richard Olney, responsible for the legendary Time-Life cooking series as well as other cooking classics such as his wonderful Simple French Food (also published by Grub Street), moved to Provence in 1961 and had the good fortune to befriend Lulu and Lucien Peyraud, the owners of the noted Domaine Tempier vineyard in Provence, not far from Marseilles.

Simple French food / Richard Olney ; new foreword by Mark Bittman ; foreword by James Beard ; introduction by Patricia Wells ; drawings by Richard Olney. Houghton Mifflin Harcourt, 2014. xvii, 455 p. : **641.594**

1. Cooking, French. 2. Cooking, French -- Provencal style. 3. Quick and easy cooking 4. Cookbooks.

ISBN 9780544242203

LC 2014012324

Includes index.

Presents recipes for a wide variety of dishes, sauces, and desserts representing the full range of French regional cooking.

Ortega, Simone

1080 recipes / Simon and Ines Ortega ; illustrations, Javier Mariscal. Phaidon Press, 2007. 975 p. : **641.594**

1. Cooking, Spanish. 2. Recipes 3. Cookbooks

ISBN 9780714848365

LC bl2008019796

Includes index.

Presents a collection of recipes from every region in Spain for appetizers, sauces, stews, soups, main dishes, flans, vegetable dishes, and desserts.

"Something like the Joy of Cooking for the Spanish home cook... [this book] includes recipes for both traditional regional fare and dishes inspired by a variety of other cuisines. An essential purchase." Library Journal.

Parla, Katie

Food of the Italian south : recipes for classic, disappearing, and lost dishes / Katie Parla ; photographs by Ed Anderson. Clarkson Potter/Publishers, 2019 255 p. : **641.594**

1. Cooking, Southern Italian 2. Cookbooks.
ISBN 9781524760465

LC 2018020557

Offers eighty-five recipes from southern Italy, including stuffed eggplant, fried marinated sardines with saffron, and jam tart with lard crust.

"This excellent volume proves that no matter how well-trodden the Italian cookbook path is, an expert with genuine curiosity and a well-developed voice can still find new material." Publishers Weekly.

Peltre, Beatrice

My French family table : recipes for a life filled with food, love & joie de vivre / Beatrice Peltre. Roost Books, 2016. 392 p. : **641.594**

1. Cooking, French. 2. Recipes 3. Cookbooks.
ISBN 9781611801361

LC 2015026649

Includes index.

Presents a collection of 120 recipes for healthy dishes inspired by classic French cooking, made with ingedients that are gluten free and include whole grains, seasonal produce, and distinct spices.

"Peltre's latest shows how cooking for gluten-free eaters doesn't have to be stressful. Highly recommended for foodies, flexitarians, and confident home cooks who are new to gluten-free cooking." Library Journal.

Pepin, Claudine

Let's cook French : a family cookbook / Claudine Pepin with illustrations by Jacques Pepin ; translation, Christel Mazquiaran = Cuisinons français : un livre pour toute la famille Claudine Pepin with illustrations by Jacques Pepin. Quarry Books, 2016. 96 p. **641.594**

1. Cooking, French 2. Cooking and children
ISBN 9781631591471

Published earlier as "Kids cook French = Les enfants cuisinent a la francaise".

With an emphasis on fresh ingredients and hands-on preparation, Let's Cook French offers a total immersion in French culinary culture. Each left-hand page in English is mirrored in French on the right and food terms are called out bilingually throughout, creating the perfect format for language learning. Featured are authentic French recipes that are easy for young chefs to follow, including starters, main courses, sides, and desserts. Sweet illustrations by Claudine's father, legendary chef Jacques Pepin, and daughter Shorey, add charm to the pages throughout. --From publisher description.

Pepin, Jacques, 1935-

Essential Pepin : more than 700 all-time favorites from my life in food / Jacques Pepin. Houghton Mifflin Harcourt, 2011. xv, 685 p. : **641.594**

1. Cooking, French. 2. Cooking. 3. Recipes 4. Cookbooks.
ISBN 9780547232799

LC 2011016057

Includes index.

Collects updated versions of the James Beard Award-winning celebrity chef's favorite recipes from his six-decade career, discussing the international flavors that inspired his cuisine while providing on an accompanying DVD demonstrations of a complete range of cooking techniques. First serial, Food & Wine. TV tie-in.

"Pepin offers more than 700 of his best French and French-accented dishes from decades of cooking and teaching. They're simple without being dumbed down; approachable yet still adventurous. Whether he's explaining how to make Escoffier quenelles with mushroom sauce; black sea bass gravlax; chicken livers sauted with vinegar; duck cassoulet; artichoke hearts with tarragon and mushrooms; or tarte tatin, he makes it seem doable and shares tidbits of wisdom to boost confidence and kitchen knowledge. His head notes are brief but informative, warm but not cloying. Pepin's own line drawings accompany the recipes, and they are, appropriately, at once homey and sophisticated. A DVD teaching a variety of cooking techniques accompanies the book, promising to make even the more challenging recipes less intimidating. For serious cooks and beginners alike, this is an instant classic." Publishers Weekly.

Pepin, Jacques, 1935-

Jacques Pepin : heart & soul in the kitchen / photography by Tom Hopkins Studio. Houghton Mifflin Harcourt, 2015. ix, 435 p. : **641.594**

1. Cooking. 2. Recipes 3. Cookbooks.
ISBN 9780544301986

LC bl2015038122

"A Rux Martin Book."

Includes index.

Shares 200 recipes from the chef's final PBS series that emphasize his close relationship to the land and sea, including herbed omelet with shrimp, baked rabbit with mustard crust, and caramelized pear custard.

"Readers can expect effortless, entertaining-worthy fare...along with humorous and informative anecdotes from Pepin's storied career... Highly recommended for fans of the chef and most public libraries." Library Journal.

Peterson, James

Glorious French food : a fresh approach to the classics / James Peterson. J. Wiley, c2002. xxv, 742 p. : **641.594**

1. Cooking, French.
ISBN 9780471442769

LC 2001046972

Explores ingredients, techniques, and recipes for making such dishes as asparagus with Maltaise sauce, chicken liver flans with tomato-marjoram sauce, roast turkey with giblet gravy, and orange-flavored crème caramel.

"The author presents 50 classic recipes as the starting point for his wide-ranging exploration of French food and techniques; each recipe serves both to demonstrate a variety of techniques and as the inspiration for a diverse collection of other recipes related to it in one way or another. Each chapter includes boxes and charts on improvising with different ingredients and flavors. The suggested variations for individual recipes, often mini-essays in themselves, open up dozens of other possibilities. Peterson is both passionate and knowledgeable about his subject, and his...book is an essential purchase." Library Journal.

Recipes from an Italian summer / translation, Mary Consonni ; photographs of Italy by Joel Meyerowitz ; photographs of recipes and ingredients by Andy Sewell ; illustrations by Jeffrey Fisher. Phaidon Press Limited, 2010. 431 p. : **641.594**

1. Cooking, Italian. 2. Seasonal cooking. 3. Cookbooks.
ISBN 9780714857732

LC bl2013054552

"Originates from Il cucchiaio d'argento estate, first published in 2005, and Il cucchiaio d'argento, first published in 1950, eighth edition (revised, expanded and updated in 1997)"--Colophon.

Includes indexes.

Presents seasonal Italian recipes for all occasions using summer produce such as tomatoes, fresh herbs, peas, beans, fresh fruit, and berries.

★The **silver** spoon / Phaidon Press Phaidon Press, 2011. 1504 p. : **641.594**

1. Cooking, Italian. 2. Food habits -- Italy 3. Recipes 4. Cookbooks
ISBN 9780714862569

LC bl2011036139

Includes index.

Presents more than 2000 recipes for traditional Italian dishes.

"Globe-trotting gourmands will appreciate the menu and 'signature dish' contributions by famous Italian chefs that round out the book. The most exhaustive Italian cookbook in recent memory, this volume offers something for every cook, regardless of their skill level, and deserves to be a fixture in American kitchens." Publishers Weekly.

Plum, Camilla

The **Scandinavian** kitchen / Camilla Plum ; photography by Anne-Li Engstrom. Kyle, 2011 272 p. **641.594**

1. Cooking, Scandinavian 2. Recipes 3. Cookbooks
ISBN 9781906868475

"Plum, a leading Danish food writer, broadcaster, and cookbook author, extols the virtues of Scandinavian cuisine in this beautiful and fascinating collection. More of a guide to Scandinavian agriculture and its bounty than a full-fledged cookbook, this work showcases the diverse ingredients that make up the Scandinavian diet, including the wide array of both fresh and preserved fish, meat, and vegetables. Recipes are numerous but feel almost secondary." Publishers Weekly.

Ray, Rachael

Everyone is Italian on Sunday / Rachael Ray. Atria Books, 2015 ix, 396 p. : **641.594**

1. Cooking, Italian. 2. Recipes 3. Cookbooks
ISBN 9781476766072

LC 2014043645

Includes index.

Presents a comprehensive collection of Italian recipes from the celebrated television chef, with traditional and original versions of options for appetizers, soups, risotto, pasta, meats, vegetables, cocktails, and desserts.

"For those who are looking for a new angle , this cookbook satisfies in spades." Publishers Weekly.

Redzepi, Rene

Noma : time and place in Nordic cuisine / Rene Redzepi. Phaidon Press Limited, 2010. 354 p. : **641.594**

1. Redzepi, Rene. 2. Noma (Restaurant : Copenhagen, Denmark). 3. Cooking, Scandinavian. 4. Recipes 5. Cookbooks
ISBN 9780714859033

LC 2012515490

Includes index.

Noma: Time and Place in Nordic Cuisine offers an exclusive insight into the food, philosophy and creativity of Rene Redzepi. It reveals the first behind the scenes look at the restaurant, Noma, and features over 90 recipes as well as excerpts from Redzepi's diary from the period leading up to the opening of the restaurant and texts on some the most enigmatic of Noma's suppliers. The book includes 200 new specially commissioned color photographs of the dishes, unique local ingredients and landscapes from across the Nordic region. It also includes a foreword by the artist Olafur Eliasson. --From publisher description.

"This is an envelope-pushing exercise that deserves respect." Publishers Weekly.

Roden, Claudia

The **food** of Spain / Claudia Roden ; photography by Jason Lowe. Ecco, c2011. 609 p. : **641.594**

1. Cooking, Spanish. 2. Recipes 3. Cookbooks.
ISBN 9780061969621

LC bl2011015492

Includes index.

Presents hundreds of recipes from the different regions of Spain, from Andalusia to Galicia, and provides a guide to the peoples and cultures that develop the different cuisines.

Rogers, Ruth, 1948-

River Cafe London : thirty years of recipes and the story of a much-loved restaurant / Ruth Rogers, Rose Gray, Sian Wyn Owen, Joseph Trivelli, Matthew Donaldson, Jean Pigozzi, Stephanie Nash, Anthony Michael; with a foreword by April Bloomfield. Alfred A. Knopf, 2018. 311 p. : **641.594**

1. River Cafe (London, England). 2. Cooking, Italian -- Tuscan style. 3. Quick and easy cooking 4. Recipes 5. Cookbooks
ISBN 9780525521303

LC 2017044066

Published in Great Britain under the title: River Cafe 30.

Includes index.

Presents a look at the historic Italian restaurant and provides 120 recipes for its signature dishes, including langoustines with borlotti beans, penne with zucchini and lemon zest, ravioli with ricotta, and scallops with sage and capers.

Rosin, Frank

Modern German cookbook / Frank Rosin ; photography: Klaus Arras. DK Publishing, 2015. 223 p. : **641.594**

1. Cooking, German. 2. Cooking -- Germany. 3. Cookbooks.
ISBN 9781465443946

LC bl2015046061

Includes index.

100 recipes of modern German favorites from Michelin-starred chef Frank Rosin. --From publisher description.

"An innovative collection from an impassioned chef." Booklist.

Roux, Michel, Jr

The **French** kitchen : recipes from the master of French cooking / Michel Roux, Jr.. Weldon Owen, 2016 352 p. : **641.594**

1. Cooking, French. 2. Recipes 3. Cookbooks.
ISBN 9781681880600

LC bl2015057875

Includes index.

A comprehensive guide to French cooking contains two hundred classic recipes for mastering French cooking, including soups, terrines and pates, meat dishes, vegetables, salads, desserts, breads, stocks, and sauces.

"Today, chefs of all statures are adored, revered for their kitchen talent, devotion to the cause, and painstaking meticulousness in this art and craft of food. Yet not all can translate those competencies into a collection of recipes for the home cook to follow. Roux, of London's Michelin-starred La Gavroche, can..." Booklist.

Sachs, Adam,

Saveur Italian comfort foods / the editors of Saveur ; editor-in-chief, Adam Sachs. Weldon Owens Inc., 2015 221 p.

: 641.594

1. Cooking, Italian. 2. Cookbooks.
ISBN 9781616289645

LC bl2015052468

Includes index.

Presents over one hundred recipes for simple, authentic Italian food, including salads, soups, pasta dishes, pizza, main dishes, side dishes, and desserts.

Samuelsson, Marcus

Aquavit and the new Scandinavian cuisine / Marcus Samuelsson ; with a preface by Hakan Swahn ; photographs by Shimon & Tammar. Houghton Mifflin, 2003. x, 302 p. : **641.594**

1. Aquavit (Restaurant) 2. Cooking, Scandinavian. 3. Recipes 4. Cookbooks
ISBN 9780618109418

LC 2003042018

An award-winning chef offers an innovative collection of recipes that emphasize the best in Scandinavian cuisine, including such unique dishes as Gravlax with Mustard Sauce, Swedish Roast Chicken with Spiced Apples, and Fois Gras Ganache, all tested for the home kitchen and accompanied by full-color photographs.

Silverton, Nancy

Mozza at home : more than 150 crowd-pleasing recipes for relaxed, family-style entertaining / Nancy Silverton with Carolynn Carreño ; photographs by Christopher Hirsheimer. Alfred A. Knopf, 2016. xiii, 411 p. : **641.594**

1. Pizzeria Mozza. 2. Cooking, Italian. 3. Quick and easy cooking 4. Entertaining. 5. Recipes 6. Cookbooks
ISBN 9780385354325

LC 2015029125

Includes index.

Collects menus with easy-to-follow recipes for simple foods to serve family style, including such options as eggplant lasagne, braised oxtails, grilled lamb shoulder chops with mint yogurt sauce, cheese pie, and chai chocolate chip cookies.

"The exceptional foods of Nancy Silverton's wildly popular Los Angeles restaurants now come to delight home kitchens. Silverton's recipes reflect her attention to detail, her sophistication, and her creative imagination." Booklist.

Sivrioglu, Somer

Anatolia : adventures in Turkish cooking / Somer Sivrioglu, David Dale. Murdoch Books, 2015. 359 p. **641.594**

1. Cooking, Turkish 2. Food habits -- Istanbul, Turkey 3. Recipes 4. Cookbooks
ISBN 9781743360491

Anatolia is a richly illustrated, entertaining and informative exploration of the regional cooking culture of Turkey. Turkish-born chef Somer Sivrioglu and co-author David Dale re-imagine the traditions of Turkish cooking, presenting recipes ranging from the grand banquets of the Ottoman empire to the spicy snacks of Istanbul's street stalls. In doing so they explain their take on the classics and reveal the surrounding rituals, myths, jokes and folk wisdom of both the old and new Turkey. --From publisher description.

Theroux, Jessica

Cooking with Italian grandmothers : recipes and stories from Tuscany to Sicily / Jessica Theroux ; introduction by Alice Waters ; illustrations by Zach Hewitt ; edited by Katherina Fried. Welcome Books, 2010. 295 p. : **641.594**

1. Theroux, Jessica Travel Italy 2. Cooking, Italian. 3. Grandmothers 4. Families 5. Women cooks 6. Italy -- Description and travel
ISBN 9781599620893

LC 2010021657

Includes index.

Presents a collection of recipes, techniques, anecdotes, and photographs that celebrate the culinary traditions of Italy.

Thorisson, Mimi

French country cooking : meals and moments from a village in the vineyards / Mimi Thorisson ; photographs by Oddur Thorisson. Clarkson Potter / Publishers, 2016 335 p. : **641.594**

1. Thorisson, Mimi Homes and haunts France Medoc. 2. Cooking, French 3. Cooking -- France -- Medoc 4. Wineries -- France 5. Seasonal cooking 6. Cookbooks.
ISBN 9780553459586

LC 2016004585

Features 100 simple artisan recipes and stories inspired by life in a small village in French wine-country, including such options as fig and pistachio cake, simple vegetable potage, country terrine, cassoulet, and strawberry tart.

A **kitchen** in France : a year of cooking in my farmhouse / Mimi Thorisson ; photographs by Oddur Thorisson. Clarkson Potter/Publishers 2014 304 p. : **641.594**

1. Thorisson, Mimi Homes and haunts France Medoc. 2. Cooking, French. 3. Cooking -- France 4. Seasonal cooking 5. Recipes 6. Medoc, France -- Social life and customs. 7. Medoc, France -- Description and travel. 8. Cookbooks
ISBN 9780804185592

LC 2013049107

Includes index.

A French-cooking blogger describes and photographs her family's meals--made using local ingredients--at their farmhouse in Medoc, including almond gazpacho, quail grilled over grapevines, and apple tart with orange flower water.

"Francophiles and armchair travelers who loved Dorie Greenspan's Around My French Table and David Lebovitz's My Paris Kitchen will gladly add this classic title to their collections." Library Journal.

Vetri, Marc

Il viaggio di Vetri : a culinary journey / Marc Vetri with David Joachim ; wine notes by Jeff Benjamin ; photography by Douglas Takeshi Wolfe. Ten Speed Press, c2008. xiii, 289 p. : **641.594**

1. Vetri, Marc. 2. Cooking, Italian. 3. Recipes 4. Cookbooks
ISBN 9781580088886

LC 2008021667

Includes index.

A debut cookbook from the chef of Philadelphia's Vetri Ristorante showcases the best in classic and innovative rustic Italian cuisine, accompanied by extensive wine notes that match each dish with an appropriate vintage.

"More than a cookbook, this...is a guide through the particular Italian cuisine and culture on which...[the author] has based his career. Amateur chefs may have only dreamed of having a culinary journey like Vetri's, but with this book he has given them a reliable key to turning dream into reality." Publishers Weekly.

Rustic Italian food / Marc Vetri with David Joachim ; beverage notes by Jeff Benjamin ; photography by Kelly Campbell ; foreword by Mario Batali. Ten Speed Press, c2011. xi, 291 p.

: **641.594**

1. Cooking, Italian. 2. Recipes 3. Cookbooks.
ISBN 9781580085892

LC 2011015301

Includes index.

A follow-up to Il Viaggio di Vetri celebrates the rustic, handcrafted cuisine of Italian home cooking while advocating a hands-on, back-to-basics approach in a volume that provides 120 recipes for a variety of slow-cooked meats, homemade breads and flavorful pastas.

"Advanced cooks looking to master bread and pasta will value Vetri's patient, masterful explanation of underlying techniques." Library Journal.

Waters, Alice

My pantry / Alice Waters with Fanny Singer ; illustrations by Fanny Singer. Pam Krauss Books, 2015 143 p. : **641.594**

1. Cooking, French. 2. Seasonal cooking 3. Spices 4. Recipes 5. Cookbooks.
ISBN 9780804185288

LC 2014042977

Collects recipes showcasing simple building-block ingredients for creating quick, satisfying meals all year long, sharing how to shop, store, and prepare the pantry staples and preserves that form the core of a meal.

"The truly ambitious may make their own simple, unaged cheeses. Not everyone has access to the sorts of ingredients available in Waters Mediterranean climate, but creative cooks can adapt local produce in season to Water's techniques." Booklist.

Weiss, Jeffrey, 1977-

Charcuteria : the soul of Spain / Jeffrey Weiss. Surrey Books, 2014 460 p. : **641.594**

1. Cooking (Meat). 2. Cooking, Spanish. 3. Cookbooks.
ISBN 9781572841529

LC 2013018755

Includes index.

"A guide to Spanish charcuteria, with recipes"-- Provided by publisher.

Weiss, Luisa

Classic German baking : the very best recipes for traditional favorites, from pfeffernusse to streuselkuchen / Luisa Weiss ; photographs by Aubrie Pick. Ten Speed Press, 2016 xi, 275 p. ; **641.594**

1. Cooking, German. 2. Baking. 3. Recipes 4. Cookbooks.
ISBN 9781607748250

LC 2016015734

Presents a collection of recipes for classic German desserts, including glazed apple cake, chocolate-hazelnut cookie bars, lemon cream roll, braided almond-cream wreath and carrot-nut torte.

"Collected from various places and people--whether it's a cookbook or from her German assistant--this cookbook presents a beautiful piece of German tradition." Publishers Weekly.

Wells, Patricia

The **French** kitchen cookbook : recipes and lessons from Paris and Provence / Patricia Wells ; photographs by Jeff Kauck. William Morrow, 2013 312 p. : **641.594**

1. Cooking, French. 2. Cooking -- Paris, France 3. Cooking, French -- Provencal style 4. Food habits -- France 5. Cookbooks
ISBN 9780062088918

LC 2013013311

Includes index.

The culinary legend reflects on what she and her students have learned throughout the years and presents some of her best recipes--all of which are inspired by the colorful Provençal countryside and the bustle of Parisian life.

Patricia Wells at home in Provence : recipes inspired by her farmhouse in France / Patricia Wells ; photographs by Robert Freson. Fireside, 1999. 355 p. : **641.594**

1. Cooking, French -- Provencal style. 2. Cooking, Provencal. 3. Recipes
ISBN 0684863286

LC 00266924

Includes index.

A culinary tour of the author's farmhouse in Provence offers 175 recipes, including olive oil brioche, grape harvest cake, and duck with lime and honey.

Wells, Patricia

The **Provence** cookbook : 175 recipes and a select guide to the markets, shops, & restaurants of France's sunny south / Patricia Wells. Harper Collins Publishers, 2004. 338 p. : **641.594**

1. Cooking, French -- Provencal style. 2. Recipes
ISBN 0060507829

LC 2003056977

Includes index.

"Wells offers her own recipes, along with some from her butcher, fishmonger, other merchants, neighborhood restaurants, and other sources slightly farther afield. Most of the dishes are simple, allowing the flavors of Provence's wonderfully fresh produce and other ingredients to come through. Wine suggestions are included throughout--sometimes for Wells's own label, since her vineyard is now productive--and she provides addresses and other relevant details about her favorite restaurants and purveyors." Library Journal.

White, Michael, 1971-

Classico e moderno : essential Italian cooking / Michael White and Andrew Friedman ; foreword by Thomas Keller. Ballantine Books, 2013 xxxiii, 405 p. : **641.594**

1. Cooking, Italian. 2. Recipes 3. Gourmet cooking 4. Cookbooks
ISBN 9780345530523

LC 2013009625

Includes index.

Collects over 200 recipes for traditional and contemporary Italian dishes, including warm radicchio and prosciutto salad, ricotta tortelli with butter and sage, and filet mignon with balsamic vinegar pan sauce.

Willan, Anne

The **country** cooking of France / Anne Willan ; photographs by France Ruffenach. Chronicle Books, c2007. 390 p. : **641.594**

1. Cooking, French. 2. Recipes 3. Cookbooks
ISBN 9780811846462

LC 2007004773

Includes index.

Celebrates the cooking traditions of France's country kitchens in a tempting cookbook containing more than 250 recipes that include La Truffade, Cassoulet de Toulouse, Crêpes au Caramel et Beurre Sal,̌ and Galette Landaise, among others, along with historical tidbits and culinary lore.

641.595 Cooking -- Asia

Abood, Maureen

Rose water & orange blossoms : fresh and classic recipes from my Lebanese kitchen / Maureen Abood ; photography by Jason Varney. Running Press, 2015 256 p. : **641.595**

1. Cooking, Lebanese. 2. Recipes 3. Cookbooks.
ISBN 9780762454860

LC bl2015030723

Includes index.

Shares over 100 Lebanese recipes that emphasize spices and herbs, lean meats, grains, and fruits and vegetables, including such options as yogurt-cucumber salad, green bean and lamb stew, and spinach pies.

Admony, Einat

Shuk : from market to table, the heart of Israeli home cooking / Einat Admony & Janna Gur ; photographs by Quentin Bacon. Artisan, 2019 367 p. : **641.595**

1. Cooking, Israeli. 2. Cookbooks.
ISBN 9781579656720

LC 2019018638

Includes index.

Taking readers on a culinary journey through Israel where they are introduced to the fragrances and flavors of the mishmash of foods represented in its shuks or markets, this book presents 140 home-cook-friendly recipes for creating a multicultural table.

Alford, Jeffrey

Beyond the Great Wall : recipes and travels in the other China / Jeffrey Alford and Naomi Duguid ; studio photographs by Richard Jung ; location photographs by Jeffrey Alford and Naomi Duguid. Artisan, c2008. 376 p. : **641.595**

1. Cooking, Tibetan. 2. Cooking, Chinese -- Yunnan style. 3. Recipes 4. Tibet Autonomous Region (China) -- Description and travel. 5. Yunnan Sheng (China) -- Description and travel. 6. Silk Road -- Description and travel. 7. Cookbooks
ISBN 9781579653019

LC 2007028556

Collects recipes from in and around China including Hani chile-garlic paste, ham sesame coils, Lhasa beef and potato stew, and tomato bell pepper salad.

"The authors explore the food and peoples of the outlaying regions of present-day China, historically home to those not ethnically Chinese. Part travel guide and part cookbook, this collection looks at the cultural survival and preservation of food in smaller societies including that of the Tibetan, Mongol, Tuvan and Kirghiz peoples, among others. A handsome and engaging collection suitable for travelers and cooks alike, this book will delight anyone with an interest in this part of the world." Publishers Weekly.

Algar, Ayla Esen

Classical Turkish cooking : traditional Turkish food for the American kitchen / Ayla Algar. HarperPerennial, 1999, c1991. xii, 306 p. ; **641.595**

1. Cooking, Turkish. 2. Recipes 3. Cookbooks.
ISBN 9780060931636

LC BL 99004033

Originally published: New York : HarperCollins, 1991.

Offers recipes from all types of Turkish cuisine, including fava bean soup, Circassian chicken, lamb morsels, and poached sea bass

"A cuisine that melds the fragrances and flavors of the Far East, Central Asia, Iran, Anatolia, and the Mediterranean is enriched by Algar as she goes well beyond the standard recipes (160 of them) to explain Turkey's historical, cultural, and culinary traditionsand, along the way, to include a glimpse of her personal family heritage." Booklist.

Anjari, Mayada

The **bread** and salt between us : recipes and stories from a Syrian refugee's kitchen / Mayada Anjari with Jennifer Sit ; foreword by Jose Andres ; photography by Liz Clayman. Lake Isle Press, 2018 176 p. : **641.595**

1. Cooking, Syrian. 2. Recipes 3. Cookbooks.
ISBN 9781891105630

LC 2018931230

Includes index.

Delicious family recipes from the kitchen of a Syrian refugee mother. --From publisher description.

"A thoughtful and attractive work." Library Journal.

Arokiasamy, Christina

The **Malaysian** kitchen : 150 recipes for simple home cooking / Christina Arokiasamy. Houghton Mifflin Harcourt, 2017. xi, 340 p. : **641.595**

1. Cooking, Malaysian. 2. Recipes 3. Cookbooks.
ISBN 9780544809994

LC bl2017007022

Collects recipes that use classic Malaysian flavors to create such dishes as chili prawns, beef rendang, and Hainanese chicken rice.

"A mouthwatering introduction to Malaysian cooking, this book offers home cooks a wealth of delicious everyday meals sure to delight." Publishers Weekly.

Bajaj, Ashok

Rasika : flavors of India / stories by Ashok Bajaj ; recipes by Vikram Sunderam ; coauthored by David Hagedorn. Ecco, 2017 xxv, 310 p. : **641.595**

1. Cooking, Indic. 2. Recipes 3. Cookbooks.
ISBN 9780062435552

LC bl2017041559

A cookbook that showcases the cuisine of a popular Indian restaurant in Washington, DC includes such recipes as okra with mango powder, tandoori-style mango shrimp, and garlic naan with cilantro.

"Innovative yet familiar, this collection offers many excellent, appetizing recipes home cooks are sure to embrace." Publishers Weekly.

Bharadwaj, Monisha

The **Indian** cooking course : techniques, masterclasses, ingredients, 300 recipes / Monisha Bharadwaj ; photography by Gareth Morgans. Kyle Books, 2016. 496 p. : **641.595**

1. Cooking, Indic. 2. Recipes 3. Cookbooks.
ISBN 9781909487468

LC bl2018185195

A comprehensive guide to Indian cooking explores regional varieties and includes such recipes as North Indian chicken biryani, saoji mutton, palak murgh, sweet khoya, and karela masala.

"This is a must-have for almost any public-library cookbook collection." Booklist.

Bowien, Danny

The **Mission** Chinese Food cookbook / Danny Bowien and Chris Ying. ECCO, 2015 xv, 318 p. : **641.595**

1. Cooking, Chinese. 2. Recipes 3. Cookbooks.
ISBN 9780062243416

LC bl2015045980

"An Anthony Bourdain book."

Includes index.

Shares the story of Mission Chinese Food along with forty-nine recipes for dishes that include braised pork belly, beggar's duck, and mapo tofu.

"To hear Bowien in his own words is a treat, and his debut cookbook is not to be missed. Like Gabrielle Hamilton's Prune, this will thrill foodies and aspiring chefs." Library Journal.

Bush, Austin

The **food** of Northern Thailand / written and photographed by Austin Bush ; illustrated by Kathy MacLeod. Clarkson Potter/ Publishers, 2018. 336 p. : **641.595**

1. Cooking, Thai -- Northeastern style. 2. Cooking, Thai. 3. Cookbooks.
ISBN 9780451497499

LC 2017061193

A culinary tour of northern Thailand explores the distinctive cuisines and flavors of individual provinces, drawing on insights from cooks, academics and restaurateurs to include coverage of staple ingredients, cooking methods and regional practices.

Cailan, Alvin

Amboy : recipes from the Filipino-American dream / Alivin Cailan with Alexandra Cuerdo and Susan Choung ; photography by Wyatt Conlon. Houghton Mifflin Harcourt, 2020. 352 p. **641.595**

1. Cailan, Alvin 2. Cooks 3. Filipino Americans 4. Cooking, Philippine 5. Food preparation
ISBN 9781328931733

LC 2019045713

Includes index.

Alvin Cailan has risen to become arguably the most high-profile chef in America's Filipino food movement. He took the food scene by storm when he opened the now-legendary Eggslut in Los Angeles, as well as hosting the popular The Burger Show on First We Feast's YouTube channel. Alvin's story of success, however, is an unlikely one. He emerged from his youth spent as part of an immigrant family in East LA feeling like he wasn't Filipino enough to be Filipino and not American enough to be an American, thus amboy, the term for a Filipino raised in America. He had to first overcome cultural traditions and family expectations to find his own path to success, and this unique cookbook tells that story through his recipes.

"It's impossible not to engage with Cailan's energy and commentary: his persona virtually leaps off the page. Readers who enjoy personality-driven memoirs will discover something inimitable and poignant here, in both Cailan's story and his delicious food." Library Journal

Chang, David, 1977-

Momofuku / David Change and Peter Meehan ; photographs by Gabriele Stabile. Clarkson Potter, c2009. 303 p. : **641.595**

1. Momofuko (Restaurant) 2. Cooking, Asian. 3. Recipes 4. Cookbooks
ISBN 9780307451958

LC bl2009030920

Includes index.

Offers recipes for a variety of dishes from the author's Momofuku restaurant, including quick pickled dishes, one-pan vegetable sautes, flavorful soups, and a myriad pork dishes, all accompanied by 150 full-color photographs.

"Chang's Virginia upbringing, upscale restaurant experience and love of certain Korean and Japanese flavors result in the kind of dishes that will jam your eyeballs into the back of your head, like brussels sprouts with bacon and kimchi puree. This fawningly produced book is fueled by Chang's hard-core attitude and punctuated with a Hell's Kitchen season's worth of unprintable words. The dude's intense, and he wants you to know it. The food is intense, too, especially as the recipes increase in difficulty as the chapters move up the Momofuku restaurant scale, from Noodle Bar to Ssam Bar to Ko." New York Times Book Review.

Chang, Joanne

Myers+Chang at home : yum me yum you : recipes from the beloved Boston eatery / Joanne Chang with Karen Akunowicz ; preface by Christopher Myers ; photography by Kristin Teig. Houghton Mifflin Harcourt, 2017. 320 p. ; **641.595**

1. Myers+Chang. 2. Cooking, Chinese -- Taiwan style. 3. Recipes 4. Cookbooks.
ISBN 9780544836471

LC 2017018562

Includes index.

"The first cookbook from Boston's acclaimed and beloved Myers+Chang restaurant".-- Provided by publisher.

"Readers will feel confident re-creating these flavorful foods, even the ones that aren't ultrasimple." Library Journal.

Chio-Lauri, Jacqueline,

The **new** Filipino kitchen : stories and recipes from around the globe / edited by Jacqueline Chio-Lauri ; photography by Rowena Dumlao-Giardina ; foreword by John Birdsall. Surrey Books, 2018 ix, 238 p. : **641.595**

1. Cooking, Philippine. 2. Recipes 3. Philippines -- Social life and customs. 4. Cookbooks
ISBN 9781572842588

LC 2018007796

Includes index.

Thirty chefs and home cooks present personal anecdotes and a collection of recipes for updated versions of Philippine dishes, including rice noodles with seafood and shrimp sauce, crab torta, meat and shrimp dumplings soup, and purple yam ice cream.

"Standouts include White House executive chef Cristeta Comerfords Ani Pambihirang Lutoni Nanay and escabeche-inspired fried snapper (an homage to her mother Nana Pate) and in-flight chef Novel Omamalins sylvana dessert. A gentle, inspiring, and exciting introduction to a savory world still new to many U.S. readers." Booklist.

Choi, Roy, 1970-

★**L.A.** son : my life, my city, my food / Roy Choi with Tien Nguyen and Natasha Phan. Ecco, 2013. 340 p. : **641.595**

1. Choi, Roy, 1970- 2. Cooks 3. Korean Americans 4. City life 5. Recipes 6. Los Angeles, California
ISBN 9780062202635

The co-founder of the wildly popular Kogi BBQ taco trucks pays tribute to the city he loves with this cookbook that combines his appreciation of food and his evolution as a chef with 60 recipes for everything from kalbi and kimchi to chorizo and carno asada.

Chou, Hsiao-Ching, 1972-

Chinese soul food : a friendly guide for homemade dumplings, stir-fries, soups, and more / Hsiao-Ching Chou ; photography by Clare Barboza. Sasquatch Books, 2018 256 p. : **641.595**

1. Cooking, Chinese. 2. Cookbooks.
ISBN 9781632171238

LC 2017041434

Presents eighty recipes for Chinese soul food that any home cook can make, including such dishes as pork and Chinese cabbage dumplings, vegetable fried rice with curry, wonton soup, red-braised beef shank, and pork spare ribs.

"This is a fun guide to creating favorite restaurant recipes at home." Publishers Weekly.

Cole, Tyson

Uchi : the cookbook / Tyson Cole, Jessica Dupuy University of Texas Press, 2011 268 p. **641.595**

1. Cooking, Japanese 2. Cooking (Seafood) 3. Cooking (Fish) 4. Sushi 5. Cookbooks
ISBN 9780292771291

Invites sushi lovers and novices alike to explore their gastronomic boundaries with some of the restaurant's most celebrated recipes.

Conlon, Abraham

The **adventures** of Fat Rice : recipes from the Chicago restaurant inspired by Macau / Abraham Conlon, Adrienne Lo, Hugh Amano ; photography by Dan Goldberg ; illustrations by Sarah Becan. Ten Speed Press, 2016 311 p. : **641.595**

1. Fat Rice (Restaurant) 2. Cooking, Chinese -- Macanese style 3. Cultural fusion 4. Restaurants -- Chicago, Illinois 5. Recipes 6. Macau (China : Special Administrative Region) -- Social life and customs
ISBN 9781607748953

LC 2016014121

Includes index.

Shares recipes from the Chicago restaurant that serves food from Macau, including crazy squid rice, Macau roast pigeon, and almond gelee.

Dagdeviren, Musa

The **Turkish** cookbook : the culinary traditions & recipes from Turkey / Musa Dagdeviren. Phaidon Press, 2019 511 p. **641.595**

1. Cooking, Turkish 2. Food habits -- Turkey 3. Recipes 4. Cookbooks.
ISBN 9780714878157

LC 2018459863

"Dagdeviren, a Turkish restaurateur and chronicler of the countrys foodways, draws clear lines between culture and cuisine in this impressive, comprehensive work." Publishers Weekly.

Deravian, Naz

★**Bottom** of the pot : Persian recipes and stories / Naz Deravian ; photography by Eric Wolfinger. Flatiron Books, 2018. 373 p. **641.595**

1. Cooking, Iranian. 2. Recipes 3. Cookbooks.
ISBN 9781250134417

LC 2018028300

Includes index.

An award-winning, Iranian-born food blogger offers over 100 Persian recipes, adapted for American kitchens, as well as the story of her family, who immigrated to Rome and then Vancouver during the height of Iran's revolution and hostage crisis in 1979.

"A delicious introduction to Iranian life and food. Recommended for all cookbook collections." Library Journal

Duguid, Naomi

★**Burma** : rivers of flavor / Naomi Duguid. Artisan, c2012. xii, 372 p. : **641.595**

1. Cooking (Spices) 2. Cooking, Burmese. 3. Food habits -- Southeast Asia. 4. Cooking, Southeast Asian. 5. Burma -- Description and travel.
ISBN 9781579654139

LC 2011052121

"A colorful immersion into the daily market and table of the Burmese people, this volume is an invitation to celebrate the Burmese people and their transformation." Publishers Weekly.

Taste of Persia : a cook's travels through Armenia, Azerbaijan, Georgia, Iran, and Kurdistan / Naomi Duguid. Artisan, [2016] 384 p. **641.595**

1. Cooking, Iranian. 2. Food habits. 3. Dinners and dining. 4. Taste. 5. Central Asia -- Description and travel.
ISBN 9781579655488

LC 2016012875

Overflowing with exotic flavors, fascinating stories and ancient history, a collection of recipes from the heart of the Persian Empire introduces readers to the food traditions from this culinary paradise where diverse religions, cultures, languages and politics are linked by a love for the fresh and the tart.

"This gorgeous and compelling title will transport home cooks and armchair travelers to another time and place." Library Journal.

Dunlop, Fuchsia

Every grain of rice : simple Chinese home cooking / Fuchsia Dunlop ; photography by Chris Terry. W.W. Norton, 2013. 351 p. : **641.595**

1. Cooking, Chinese. 2. Cookbooks.
ISBN 9780393089042

LC 2012004741

Includes index.

A culinary reference features southern Chinese recipes, shares a comprehensive introduction to key seasonings and techniques, and offers such options as smoky eggplant with garlic, twice-cooked pork, and emergency midnight noodles.

The **food** of Sichuan / Fuchsia Dunlop ; photography by Yuki Sugiura with additional location photography by Ian Cumming. W. W. Norton & Company, 2019. 495 p. **641.595**

1. Cooking, Chinese -- Sichuan style 2. Cookbooks
ISBN 9781324004837

LC 2019020111

This revised and updated edition first published in 2019 by Bloomsbury Publishing.

First published in the UK in 2001 by Michael Joseph as Sichuan Cookery and in the US in 2003 by W. W. Norton & Company as Land of Plenty.

Twenty years after the publication of her groundbreaking cookbook, Land of Plenty, the author returns to Sichuan and adds over 70 new, regional recipes for home cooks, including Mapo Tofu, Twice- Cooked Pork and Gong Bao Chicken.

Land of fish and rice : recipes from the culinary heart of China / Fuchsia Dunlop ; photography by Yuki Sugiura. W. W. Norton & Company, Inc., 2016. 367 p. : **641.595**

1. Cooking, Chinese. 2. Recipes 3. Cookbooks.
ISBN 9780393254389

LC 2016013124

An exploration of techniques and ingredients key to the Jiangnan kitchen collects recipes for dishes that celebrate the culinary delights of the Yangtze region, featuring such dishes as clear-steamed sea bass, fresh soybeans with pickled greens, and dingpo pork.

"The Jiangnan is an exquisite 'crucible of Chinese gastronomy,' and Dunlop's scholarly homage to the region will captivate the culinary imagination." Publishers Weekly.

Eckhardt, Robyn

Istanbul & beyond : exploring the diverse cuisines of Turkey / Robyn Eckhardt ; photographs by David Hagerman. Houghton Mifflin Harcourt, 2017. 352 p. : **641.595**

1. Cooking, Turkish. 2. Cookbooks.
ISBN 9780544444317

LC 2017016108

"A Rux Martin book."

"The most extensive and lushly photographed Turkish cookbook to date, by two internationally acclaimed experts. Standing at the crossroads between the Mediterranean, the Middle East, and Asia, Turkey boasts astonishingly rich and diverse culinary traditions. Journalist Robyn Eckhardt and her husband, photographer David Hagerman, have spent almost twenty years discovering the country's very best dishes. Now they take readers on an unforgettable epicurean adventure, beginning in Istanbul, home to one of the world's great fusion cuisines. From there, they journey to the lesser-known provinces, opening a vivid world of flavors influenced by neighboring Syria, Iran, Iraq, Armenia, and Georgia. From village home cooks, community bakers, cafe chefs, farmers, and fishermen, they have assembled a broad, one-of-a-kind collection of authentic, easy-to-follow recipes: 'The Imam Fainted' Stuffed Eggplant; Pillowy Fingerprint Flatbread; Pot-Roasted Chicken with Caramelized Onions; Stovetop Lamb Meatballs with Spice Butter; Artichoke Ragout with Peas and Favas; Green Olive Salad with Pomegranate Molasses; Apple and Raisin Hand Pies. Many of these have never before been published in English".-- Provided by publisher.

"This collection will delight and inspire home cooks who are unfamiliar with the regions food but are looking to broaden their culinary horizons." Publishers Weekly.

Ghayour, Sabrina

Persiana : recipes from the Middle East & beyond / Sabrina Ghayour. Interlink Books, an imprint of Interlink Publishing Group, Inc., 2015. 240 p. : **641.595**

1. Cooking, Middle Eastern. 2. International cooking. 3. Recipes 4. Cookbooks.
ISBN 9781566569958

LC 2014021227

Includes index.

"Though the decidedly 70's font and presentation wears a little thin, this is an outstanding collection that will surely win readers over and inspire many a meal." Publishers Weekly.

Gomez, Asha

My two souths : blending the flavors of India into a Southern kitchen / Asha Gomez, with Martha Hall Foose. Running Press, 2016 288 p. : **641.595**

1. Cooking, Indic -- Southern style. 2. Cooking, American -- Southern style. 3. Cookbooks.
ISBN 9780762457830

LC bl2016045088

Includes index.

Collects recipes that meld the culinary stylings of southern India and the American South, including such offerings as green cardamom shrimp etouffee, banana leaf grilled catfish, and clove baked sweet potatoes.

"Guaranteed to spice up your dinner routine, Gomez's debut enlivens Indian and Southern foods." Library Journal.

Goodwin, Jason, 1964-

Yashim cooks Istanbul / Jason Goodwin. Argonaut Books, 2016. 221 p. **641.595**

1. Cooking, Turkish 2. Food habits -- Istanbul, Turkey 3. Recipes 4. Cookbooks
ISBN 9780957254015

Inspired by recipes in Jason Goodwin's bestselling historical Investigator Yashim series, Yashim Cooks Istanbul evokes the colors and flavors of the Ottoman world, combining Turkish recipes, illustrations and tempting descriptions from the novels. --From publisher description.

Gur, Janna

The **book** of New Israeli food : a culinary journey / Janna Gur ; photography, Eilon Paz ; contributing writers Rami Hann... [et al.]. Schocken Books, c2007. 303 p. : **641.595**

1. Cooking, Israeli. 2. Kosher food. 3. Israel -- Social life and customs.
ISBN 9780805212242

LC 2008300413

"Originally published in English in Israel in slightly different form by Al Hashulchan Gastronomic Meida Ltd., Tel Aviv, in 2007."

Includes indexes.

"All recipes are kosher".

Brings together a collection of kosher recipes and culinary history in a volume that captures the broad diversity of modern-day Israeli cuisine, with dishes ranging from new interpretations of traditional classics to innovative exotic specialities.

"Beautiful and comprehensive, this book will become an immediate favorite with anyone with even a passing interest in Israeli cuisine." Publishers Weekly.

Ha, Robin,

Cook Korean! : a comic book with recipes / Robin Ha. Ten Speed Press, 2016. 176 p. : **641.595**

1. Cooking, Korean. 2. Cooking -- Anecdotes. 3. Cooking, Asian. 4. Recipes. 5. Korea -- Social life and customs. 6. Comics and Graphic novels
ISBN 9781607748878

LC 2015047866

An introduction to the basics of Korean cooking in graphic novel form, with 64 recipes, ingredient profiles, and more, presented through light-hearted comics.

Hair, Jaden

The **steamy** kitchen cookbook : 101 Asian recipes simple enough for tonight's dinner / Jaden Hair. Tuttle Pub., c2009. 160 p. : **641.595**

1. Cooking, Asian. 2. Dinners and dining. 3. Recipes 4. Cookbooks.
ISBN 9780804840286

LC 2009017461

Includes index.

Collects authentic, easy-to-prepare recipes focusing on Chinese, Japanese, Korean, and Thai cuisine.

"For home cooks of all levels of experience seeking to expand their repertoire of Asian recipes, Hair has written an extremely accessible cookbook that blends great recipes with mouthwatering photographs she took." Library Journal.

Helou, Anissa, 1952-

★**Feast** : food of the Islamic world / Anissa Helou. ECCO, 2018 529 p. : **641.595**

1. Cooking -- Islamic countries. 2. Islamic cooking. 3. Cooking, Middle Eastern. 4. Cooking, North African. 5. Cookbooks.
ISBN 9780062363039
LC bl2018190099

Includes index.

A collection of recipes from North Africa, the Mediterranean, and the Middle East.

"Renowned chef Helou takes readers on a culinary tour of the Muslim world, showcasing more than 300 recipes from the Middle East, Africa, and Indonesia, while exploring the history and tradition of Islamic cuisine." Library Journal.

Hong, Deuki

Koreatown : a cookbook / Deuki Hong & Matt Rodbard ; photographs by Sam Horine. Clarkson Potter/Publishers, 2016 272 p. : **641.595**

1. Cooking, Korean. 2. Recipes 3. Cookbooks.
ISBN 9780804186131
LC 2015009587

Collects recipes, stories, interviews, and photographs from Korean American neighborhoods across the country, to create a portrait of a culture and community through dishes that range from mixed rice bowls, spicy seafood noodle soup, and sweet soy-braised chicken.

Iyer, Raghavan, 1961-

660 curries / Raghavan Iyer ; food photography by Ben Fink. Workman Pub., 2008. vi, 809 p. : **641.595**

1. Cooking, Indic. 2. Cooking (Curry) 3. Recipes 4. Cookbooks
ISBN 9780761137870
LC 2008001288

"The gateway to the world of Indian cooking"--Cover.

Presented by an award-winning cooking instructor and author of "Betty Crocker's Indian Home Cooking," this collection is the gateway to the world of Indian curries.

"A wide-ranging guide to the curries of the Indian subcontinent, including Pakistan, Nepal, and Sri Lanka. Iyer explains that Indian curries are not based on a can of curry powder and that the term curry refers to any dish simmered in or covered with a fragrant, spicy (though not necessarily hot) sauce or gravy. The hundreds of recipes include appetizer curries such as Skewered Chicken with Creamy Fenugreek Sauce, main-course curries like Yogurt-Marinated Lamb with Ginger and Garlic, and contemporary curries such as Wild Salmon with Chiles, Scallions, and Tomato; there are also recipes for curry cohorts--rice, bread, and other accompaniments." Library Journal.

Indian cooking unfolded : a master class in Indian cooking, with 100 easy recipes using 10 ingredients or less / Raghavan Iyer ; photography by TK. Workman Publishing, 2013 330 p. : **641.595**

1. Cooking, Indic. 2. Recipes 3. Cookbooks.
ISBN 9780761165217
LC 2013004247

Reveals how to create one hundred of Indian cuisine's most popular dishes and is complemented by step-by-step photo gatefolds.

Jaffrey, Madhur, 1933-

At home with Madhur Jaffrey : simple, delectable dishes from India, Pakistan, Bangladesh, & Sri Lanka / Madhur Jaffrey ; photographs by Christopher Hirsheimer ; decorative drawings by Madhur Jaffrey. Alfred A. Knopf, 2010. xi, 301 p. : **641.595**

1. Cooking, Asian. 2. Quick and easy cooking 3. Cooking -- South Asia. 4. Cookbooks.
ISBN 9780307268242
LC 2010019678

Includes index.

"Originally published in different form in Great Britain as Curry Easy by Ebury Press, ... London." --T.p. verso.

A James Beard Award-winning author outlines a revisionist approach to classic Indian cooking, instructing home cooks on the potentially health-bolstering properties of correctly applied seasonings and spices.

"This is a cookbook of easily prepared, thoughtful, and unusual dishes from India, Pakistan, Bangladesh, and Sri Lanka. Anyone looking to explore Indian cooking for the first time will find this volume uniquely helpful." Booklist.

An **invitation** to Indian cooking / Madhur Jaffrey ; with a new preface by the author. Ecco Press, 1999. 285, 15 p. ; **641.595**

1. Cooking, Indic. 2. Recipes 3. Cookbooks
ISBN 9780880016643
LC 98030321

Includes index.

Carefully worked out for American cooks in American kitchens, Madhur Jaffrey's classic An Invitation to Indian Cooking demonstrates how varied, irresistible, and inexpensive Indian cooking can be and how easily you can prepare authentic dishes at home. --From publisher description.

Madhur Jaffrey's instantly Indian cookbook / Madhur Jaffrey ; photographs by Dana Gallagher Alfred A. Knopf, 2019. xiii, 170 p. : **641.595**

1. Cooking, Indic. 2. Pressure cooking. 3. Recipes 4. Cookbooks.
ISBN 9780525655794
LC 2018040124

"This is a Borzoi Book published by Alfred A. Knopf."

Includes index.

The James Beard Award-winning cookbook author presents new and classic Indian recipes that can be made using an Instant Pot, including South Indian mixed-vegetable korma, simple mung dal, butter chicken, Kerala lamb stew, and pork kabobs.

★**Vegetarian** India : a journey through the best of Indian home cooking / Madhur Jaffrey. Alfred A. Knopf, 2015. xxii, 416 p. : **641.595**

1. Cooking, Indic. 2. Vegetarian cooking. 3. Recipes 4. Cookbooks.
ISBN 9781101874868
LC 2014048953

Includes index.

Presents a collection of Indian vegetarian recipes from the award-winning chef, with options for soups, dals, grains, eggs and dairy, chutneys, and desserts, and a separate section on ingredients.

"Jaffrey's fresh compilation features extraordinary variety and achieves approachability without oversimplification. Highly recommended for vegetarians and Indian food enthusiasts." Library Journal.

Joo, Judy

Korean food made simple / Judy Joo ; With Vivian Jao ; Photography by Jean Cazals. Houghton Mifflin Harcourt, 2016. 286 p. ; **641.595**

1. Cooking, Korean. 2. Cookbooks.
ISBN 9780544663305
LC 2015049784

"125 simple Korean recipes from the host of the Cooking Channel television show of the same name In Korean Food Made Simple, Judy Joo, host of the Cooking Channel's show of the same name and Food Network regular, brings Korean food to the masses, proving that it's fun and easy to prepare at home. As a Korean-American, Judy understands how to make dishes that may seem exotic and difficult accessible to the everyday cook. The book has over 100 recipes including well-loved dishes like kimchi, sweet potato noodles (japchae), beef and vegetable rice bowl (bibimbap), and Korean fried chicken, along with creative, less-traditional recipes like Spicy Pork Belly Cheese Steak, Krazy Korean Burgers, and Fried Fish with Kimchi Mayo and Sesame Mushy Peas. In addition, there are chapters devoted to sauces, desserts, and drinks as well as a detailed list for stocking a Korean pantry, making this book a comprehensive guide on Korean food and flavors. Enjoying the spotlight as the hot Asian cuisine, Korean food is on the rise, and Judy's bold and exciting recipes are go-tos for making it at home. "-- Provided by publisher.

"Cooks looking to make a first foray into Korean cooking or those wishing to enhance their knowledge will delight in Joo's uncommon approach and her tasty creations." Publishers Weekly.

Khan, Yasmin (Cook)

Zaitoun : recipes from the Palestinian kitchen / Yasmin Khan ; recipe photography by Matt Russell ; travel photography by Raya Manaa'and Hosam Salem. W. W. Norton & Co., 2018. 256 p. : **641.595**

1. Cooking, Middle Eastern 2. Recipes 3. Culture 4. Food habits -- Middle East 5. Palestine -- Social life and customs 6. Cookbooks
ISBN 9781324002628

LC 2018050132

Includes index.

"A dazzling celebration of Palestinian cuisine, featuring more than 80 modern recipes, captivating stories, and stunning travel photography."--Publisher's description.

Kho, Kian Lam

Phoenix claws and jade trees : essential techniques of authentic Chinese cooking / Kian Lam Kho ; photographs by Jody Horton. Clarkson Potter/Publishers, 2015 368 p. : **641.595**

1. Cooking, Chinese. 2. Cookbooks.
ISBN 9780385344685

LC 2014046694

Includes index.

"Kho rounds out his excellent book with recipes and lessons on smoking as well as cold and sweet dishes. This extraordinary collection is a must-have for anyone interested in Chinese cuisine." Publishers Weekly.

Kim, Bill

Korean BBQ : master your grill in seven sauces / Bill Kim with Chandra Ram ; photograps by Johnny Autry. Ten Speed Press, 2017 232 p. : **641.595**

1. Cooking, Korean. 2. Barbecuing. 3. Outdoor cooking. 4. Cookbooks.
ISBN 9780399580789

LC 2017040334

Includes index.

Offers recipes from the chef that combine flavors and sauces from Korea and grilling, along with suitable substitutions for hard-to-find ingredients, including such dishes as spicy grilled crabs, lemongrass chicken, and kimchi potato salad.

"Although some of the recipes may seem daunting, Kim provides even the most basic cook with a guide to understanding their way around a grill." Library Journal.

Kim, Hooni

My Korea : traditional flavors, modern recipes / Hooni Kim with Aki Kamozawa, photography by Kristin Teig. W. W. Norton & Company, 2020. 272 p. **641.595**

1. Cooking, Korean. 2. Cooking, American. 3. Recipes 4. Cookbooks
ISBN 9780393239720

LC 2019057930

Includes index.

"The long-awaited debut cookbook from the Michelin-star chef known for defining Korean food in America. Hooni Kim is a chef who cooks with jung sung, heart and devotion. My Korea embraces his gastronomic heritage. From simple rice cakes drenched in a spicy sauce to a 12-Hour Korean Ramyeon (ramen), Hooni uses his background in world-class French and Japanese kitchens to fine-tune techniques in classic Korean cuisine, which often originated in home kitchens. Readers will discover the Korean culinary trinity: gochujang, doenjang, and ganjang (Korean chili pepper paste, fermented soybean paste, and soy sauce). These key ingredients add a savory depth and flavor to the entire spectrum of Korean cuisine, from banchan to robust stews. Enhanced with gorgeous photography that highlights food creation and enjoyment across Korea today, My Korea brings a powerful culinary legacy into your kitchen".-- Provided by publisher.

"This thoughtful, comprehensive, and inventive volume sets a high bar for Korean cookbooks." Publishers Weekly

Krishna, Priya

★**Indian-ish** : recipes and antics from a modern American family / Priya Krishna with Ritu Krishna ; photography by Mackenzie Kelly ; illustrations by Maria Qamar ; foreword by Padma Lakshmi. Houghton Mifflin Harcourt, 2019. ix, 241 p. : **641.595**

1. Cooking, Indic. 2. Cooking, American 3. Recipes 4. Cookbooks.
ISBN 9781328482471

LC 2018043605

Includes index.

Collects recipes for the home cook that merge Indian and American cuisine, including such dishes as tomato-cheese masala toast, roti noodle stir-fry, herby avocado sandwich, and garlic-ginger chicken with cilantro and mint.

"Krishna's newest offering will delight cooks seeking to expand their palate and knowledge of Indian cuisine. With easy-to-follow recipes, the 'Indian-ish' additions to many American homestyle favorites will appeal to even the pickiest eaters." Library Journal.

Lo, Eileen Yin-Fei

Mastering the art of Chinese cooking / Eileen Yin-Fei Lo ; photographs by Susie Cushner ; brush calligraphy by San Yan Wong. Chronicle Books, c2009. 384 p. : **641.595**

1. Cooking, Chinese. 2. Cookbooks.
ISBN 9780811859332

LC 2010027670

Includes index.

Presents more than 150 recipes along with step-by-step instructions on the techniques of Chinese cooking.

"[V]isually stunning with brush calligraphy, decorative borders, and full-page color photographs as well as a comprehensive and educational guide that fulfills the promise of how to master Chinese cooking." Publishers Weekly.

Maangchi

Maangchi's big book of Korean cooking : from everyday meals to celebration cuisine / Maangchi ; with Martha Rose Shulman ; photographs by Maangchi. Houghton Mifflin Harcourt, 2019. 447 p. : **641.595**

1. Cooking, Korean. 2. Cookbooks.
ISBN 9781328988126

LC 2019013139

"A Rux Martin book."
Includes index.

The creator of maangchi.com presents a comprehensive collection of favorite Maangchi recipes, from Korean barbecue to bulgogi, while sharing advice for Buddhist vegan options, hosting parties and Korean-cooking techniques.

Maangchi's real Korean cooking : authentic dishes for the home cook / Maangchi with Lauren Chattman ; photographs by Maangchi. Houghton Mifflin Harcourt, 2015 310 p. ; **641.595**

1. Cooking, Korean. 2. Cookbooks.
ISBN 9780544129894

LC 2015004571

Offers a complete Korean cuisine cooking course for home chefs, with step-by-step, illustrated recipes for a variety of the country's best dishes, including bulgogi, Korean fried chicken, spicy beef and vegetable soup, and seafood-scallion pancake.

"Like Robert Danhi's Easy Thai Cooking and Bee Yin Low's Easy Chinese Recipes, this encouraging and instructional cookbook demystifies Asian home cooking. First-timers to Korean restaurants and grocery stores will be grateful for Maangchi's introductory chapters." Library Journal.

Maffei, Yvonne M.

My halal kitchen : global recipes, cooking tips, lifestyle inspiration / Yvonne Maffei. Surrey Books, an Agate imprint, 2016 xvii, 214 p. : **641.595**

1. Halal food 2. Cooking, Middle Eastern. 3. Food -- Religious aspects -- Islam. 4. Cookbooks.
ISBN 9781572841741

LC 2016001808

The founder of the cooking blog MyHalalKitchen.com serves up more than 100 recipes from a variety of culinary traditions, including such offerings as Hawaiian pizza, berry hot sipping chocolate, and shredded goat tacos.

"An approachable introduction to halal home cooking for Muslim and non-Muslim families alike." Library Journal.

Makan, Chetna

The **cardamom** trail : Chetna bakes with flavours of the East / Chetna Makan. Mitchell Beazley, 2016. 240 p. : **641.595**

1. Cooking, Indic 2. Cookbooks.
ISBN 9781784721299

LC bl2016019000

Includes index.

Presents recipes featuring Indian spices, describing the flavor, uses, and author's personal experience with each spice, including saffron, star anise, coriander, and tamarind.

"Infuse the vibrant flavors of India into your baked goods with this beautiful volume of recipes redolent with herbs, spices, and surprising ingredients." Booklist.

Massaad, Barbara Abdeni

Man'oushe : inside the Lebanese street corner bakery / Barbara Abdeni Massaad ; photography by Barbara Abdeni Massaad and Raymond Yazbeck. Interlink Books, 2014. 199 p. : **641.595**

1. Cooking, Lebanese. 2. Recipes 3. Cookbooks.
ISBN 9781566569286

LC 2013032109

Includes index.

Offers recipes for creating different varieties of the Lebanese national pie for anytime of day.

"A reasonably adept home baker will find Massaad's recipes easy to follow. The book's full-color photographs bring into focus not just the foods but also the lively characters who constitute a remarkably diverse nation." Booklist.

Matar, Marlene

The **Aleppo** cookbook : celebrating the legendary cuisine of Syria = Kitb al-abkh al-alab / Marlene Matar. Interlink Books, 2017. 352 p. : **641.595**

1. Cooking, Syrian. 2. Cooking -- Syria -- Aleppo. 3. Cookbooks.
ISBN 9781566569866

LC 2014032555

"This introduction to Middle Eastern cooking techniques will equally satisfy beginners or experienced fans of the regional fare." Publishers Weekly.

Meehan, Peter, 1977-

Lucky peach presents 101 easy Asian recipes / Peter Meehan and the editors of Lucky peach ; photographs by Gabriele Stabile. Clarkson Potter/Publishers, 2015 271 p. : **641.595**

1. Cooking, Asian. 2. Quick and easy cooking 3. Recipes 4. Cookbooks.
ISBN 9780804187794

LC 2015015729

Includes index.

A collection of simple recipes for favorite Asian dishes from the popular indie food magazine, including dumplings, rice, soups, noodles, meat dishes, sauces, and desserts.

"Readers will also appreciate the surprising lack of prep for many dishes; few require chopping and dicing multitudes of vegetables or sourcing ingredients that are difficult to find in the U.S. This is an outstanding, practical guide sure to inspire even the most discouraged home cook." Publishers Weekly.

Mistry, Preeti

The **Juhu** Beach Club cookbook : Indian spice, Oakland soul / Preeti Mistry with Sarah Henry ; photographs by Alanna Hale. Running Press, 2017. 288 p. : **641.595**

1. Juhu Beach Club (Restaurant) 2. Cooking, Indic. 3. Recipes 4. Restaurants -- Oakland, California 5. Cookbooks.
ISBN 9780762462452

LC 2017945078

Includes indexes.

"Vibrant and unexpected, The Juhu Beach Club Cookbook brings the outsized opinions and culinary daring of Preeti Mistry, chef/owner of Oakland's Juhu Beach Club, to the page. Influenced by her background as a second-generation Indian -- born in London, raised across the US, now based in the Bay Area -- Preeti's irreverent style informs her personality and her food. This collection of street food, comfort classics, and restaurant favorites blends cuisines from across India with American influences to create irresistible combinations. Organized by feeling rather than course or season, with sections like Mom Meals, Masala Mashups, and JBC Classics, The Juhu Beach Club Cookbook weaves Preeti's culinary journey together with bold, flavor-forward recipes to excite and inspire home cooks. Illustrated throughout with full-color photography and playful line art, this book captures the eclectic energy and wide-ranging influences of one of the West Coast's most up-and-coming chefs."-- Provided by publisher.

Moorman, Tom

Elizabeth Street Cafe : breakfast lunch dinner sweets / Tom Moorman, Larry McGuire, with Julia Turshen. Phaidon Press Limited, 2017. 239 p. : **641.595**

1. Cooking, Vietnamese. 2. Cooking, French. 3. Restaurants -- Texas -- Austin. 4. Recipes 5. Cookbooks

ISBN 9780714873954

LC bl2017044321

Includes index.

Presents 100 French-inspired Vietnamese cooking recipes that are served at the critically acclaimed restaurant located in Austin, Texas, including bun bo hue, Nutella and banana crêpes with candied hazelnuts, and Manila clam and ginger fried rice.

Morimoto, Masaharu, 1955-

Mastering the art of Japanese home cooking / Masahuru Morimoto. Ecco, 2016 vii, 275 p. : **641.595**

1. Coooking, Japanese. 2. Cookbooks.

ISBN 9780062344380

LC bl2016048973

Includes index.

A collection of traditional Japanese recipes for the home cook from the legendary chef and restaurateur features such dishes as miso soup, pork and cabbage dumplings, salt-grilled salmon, and chicken teriyaki.

"Soups, stir-fry, and noodles each have their own chapter and a section on the underappreciated art of simmering features fish simmered with sake, soy sauce, and sugar, as well as slow-cooked pork belly with beer-teriyaki glaze. The 177 color photos range from utilitarian instruction on flipping a Japanese omelet to an artistic interpretation of rice grains clustered in the hand of the chef." Publishers Weekly.

Nguyen, Andrea Quynhgiao

Asian dumplings : mastering gyza, spring rolls, samosas, and more / Andrea Quynhgiao Nguyen. Ten Speed Press, c2009. 234 p. : **641.595**

1. Cooking, Asian. 2. Dumplings. 3. Recipes 4. Gourmet cooking 5. Cookbooks

ISBN 9781580089753

LC 2010286323

A guide to making authentic versions of the most popular regional dumplings also includes instructions for preparing dim sum favorites, in an illustrated reference that outlines such options as spicy potato samosas and Shanghai wonton soup.

The **banh** mi handbook : recipes for crazy-delicious Vietnamese sandwiches / Andrea Quynhgiao Nguyen ; photography by Paige Green. Ten Speed Press, 2014 125 p. : **641.595**

1. Cooking, Vietnamese. 2. Sandwiches -- Vietnam. 3. Recipes 4. Cookbooks.

ISBN 9781607745334

LC 2014002924

Includes index.

An introduction to the popular Vietnamese sandwich shares dozens of recipes for classic through innovative modern varieties, including peppery grilled chicken, lemongrass pork and coconut curry tofu.

★The **pho** cookbook : easy to adventurous recipes for Vietnam's favorite soup and noodles / Andrea Quynhgiao Nguyen. Ten Speed Press, 2017 160 p. : **641.595**

1. Cooking, Vietnamese. 2. Noodle soups 3. Cookbooks.

ISBN 9781607749585

LC 2016022687

Looks at the Vietnamese dish's roots with information on ingredients and techniques and offers instructions for making different versions of the noodle soup and recipes for snacks, salads, companion dishes, and vegetarian and gluten-free options.

Vietnamese food any day : simple recipes for true, fresh flavors / Andrea Nguyen ; photographs by Aubrie Pick. Ten Speed Press, 2019 233 p. : **641.595**

1. Cooking, Vietnamese. 2. Recipes 3. Quick and easy cooking 4. Cookbooks.

ISBN 9780399580352

LC 2018017922

Includes index.

Collects accessible, easy recipes for Vietnamese food, including such options as honey-glazed pork riblets, curry-scented grilled beef lettuce wraps, turmeric coconut rice, crispy lemongrass salmon, and orange-rum flan.

"The first chapter is extremely useful in its offering of several sauces essential to Vietnamese dishes, such as Caramel sauce and Nuoc Cham. In many of the recipes, Nguyen gives notes on substitutions to make them vegetarian friendly. Beautiful photographs are a bonus." Library Journal.

Nongkran Daks

Nong's Thai kitchen : 84 classic recipes that are quick healthy and delicious / Nongkran Daks and Alexandra Greeley. Tuttle Publishing, 2015 160 p. ; **641.595**

1. Cooking, Thai. 2. Recipes 3. Cookbooks.

ISBN 9780804843317

LC 2014030057

Collects recipes for quick-prepare Thai dishes from the master chef, offering such options as grilled pork skewers, rice soup with shrimp, eggplant salad, steamed seafood curry, spicy beef with mint leaves, and sweet black rice pudding.

"Chef in suburban Washington, D.C., Daks offers recipes for all manner of Thai dishes to re-create at home. Ever-popular satay can be grilled indoors or out, and the spicy peanut-coconut sauce that makes satay almost universally appreciated turns out to be easy to reproduce from ingredients available in most well-stocked supermarkets." Booklist.

Orkin, Ivan

The **gaijin** cookbook : Japanese recipes from a chef, father, eater, and lifelong outsider / Ivan Orkin and Chris Ying ; photographs by Aubrie Pick. Houghton Mifflin Harcourt, 2019. 256 p. : **641.595**

1. Cooking, Japanese. 2. Recipes 3. Cookbooks

ISBN 9781328954350

LC 2019002730

Includes index.

"This passionate, welcoming volume serves as an excellent guide to Japanese home cooking." Publishers Weekly.

Orkin, Ivan

Ivan Ramen : love, obsession, and recipes from Tokyo's most unlikely noodle joint / Ivan Orkin with Chris Ying. Ten Speed Press, 2013 xi, 211 p. : **641.595**

1. Orkin, Ivan. 2. Ivan Ramen (Restaurant) 3. Cooking, Japanese. 4.

Ramen. 5. Noodles 6. Recipes 7. Cookbooks
ISBN 9781607744467

LC 2013025984

"The end-all-be-all guide to ramen from Ivan Orkin, the iconoclastic New York-born owner of Tokyo's top ramen shop. While scores of people line up outside American ramen powerhouses like Momofuku Noodle Bar, chefs and food writers in the know revere Ivan Orkin's traditional Japanese take on ramen. Ivan Ramen chronicles Orkin's journey from dyed-in-the-wool New Yorker to the chef and owner of one of Japan's most-loved ramen restaurants, Ivan Ramen. His passion for ramen is contagious, his story fascinating, and his recipes to-die-for, including master recipes for the fundamental types of ramen, and variations on each. Likely the only chef in the world with the knowledge and access to convey such a candid look at Japanese cuisine to a Western audience, Orkin is perfectly positioned to author what will be the ultimate English-language overview on ramen and all of its components".-- Provided by publisher.

Ottolenghi, Yotam

Nopi : the cookbook / Yotam Ottolenghi, Ramael Scully ; with Tara Wigley. Ten Speed Press, 2015 xv, 331 p. : **641.595**

1. Nopi (Restaurant). 2. Cooking, Mediterranean 3. Cooking, Middle Eastern 4. Recipes 5. Cookbooks
ISBN 9781607746232

LC OC2018154188

Includes index.

"Yotam Ottolenghi is beloved in the food world for his beautiful, inspirational cookbooks, as well as his Ottolenghi delis and his fine-dining restaurant, Nopi. In The NOPI Cookbook, head chef Ramael Scully's Asian-inspired pantry meets Ottolenghi's Middle Eastern influences and brings the restaurant's favorite dishes within reach of the home cook".-- Provided by publisher.

Packer, Sarit

Honey & Co. : the cookbook / Sarit Packer & Itamar Srulovich ; photography by Patricia Niven. Little, Brown and Company, 2015. xiii, 289 p. : **641.595**

1. Honey & Co. (London, England). 2. Cooking, Middle Eastern. 3. Recipes 4. Cookbooks.
ISBN 9780316284301

LC 2014953286

Includes index.

Offers a selection of accessible Middle Eastern recipes from the restaurateurs, including spreads and dips, salads, one-pan dishes, soups, Persian entrees, tagines of North Africa, sofritos of Jerusalem, and stews of Iran.

"This restaurant cookbook is representative of the hottest trends and has enough variety to be suitable for everyday use." Library Journal.

Paskin, Layo, 1970-

The **Palomar** cookbook : modern Israeli cuisine / Layo Paskin and Tomer Amedi ; photography by Helen Cathcart. Clarkson Potter/Publishers, 2016 256 p. ; **641.595**

1. Palomar (Restaurant). 2. Cooking, Israeli. 3. Recipes 4. Cookbooks.
ISBN 9780451496614

LC 2016031350

Includes index.

Over 100 modern Israeli recipes include such dishes as watercress pesto, fattoush salad, Jerusalem polenta, mussels hamusta, labneh kreplach tortellini, and tahini ice cream.

Phan, Charles

★The **Slanted** Door : modern Vietnamese food / Charles Phan, with Janny Hu ; photography by Ed Anderson. Ten Speed Press, 2014 xxiii, 261 p. : **641.595**

1. Cooking, Vietnamese. 2. Recipes 3. Cookbooks.
ISBN 9781607740544

LC 2014015943

Includes index.

Collects recipes from San Francisco's Vietnamese eatery, including vegetarian imperial rolls, papaya salad, spicy squid stir-fry, roasted lobster with butter-herb dressing, and mussels in red curry.

"Phan's cuisine illustrates the synthesis that is Vietnam's culinary heritage: Chinese ingredients and traditions blended with French techniques. The Slanted Door's bar also mixes extensive lists of innovative cocktails, and these, along with Phan's cooking, are here documented." Booklist.

Phillips, Carolyn J.

All under heaven : recipes from the 35 cuisines of China / written and illustrated by Carolyn Phillips ; foreward by Ken Hom. McSweeney's, Ten Speed Press, 2016 xiii, 514 p. ; **641.595**

1. Cooking, Chinese. 2. Recipes 3. Cookbooks.
ISBN 9781607749820

LC 2015029244

Includes index.

A comprehensive portrait of China's culinary landscape, and the history and geography that shaped it, examines all thirty-five cuisines of China, with more than 300 recipes for everything from fried green onion soup to camphor tea duck.

"Those who enjoy the thoroughly researched cookbooks of experts such as Claudia Roden (The New Book of Middle Eastern Food) will appreciate Phillips's comprehensive treatment, which includes historical information, an extensive ingredient glossary, suggested menus, and useful advice." Library Journal.

The **dim** sum field guide : a taxonomy of dumplings, buns, meats, sweets, and other specialties of the Chinese teahouse / written and illustrated by Carolyn Phillips. Ten Speed Press, 2016 169 p. : **641.595**

1. Cooking, Chinese -- Cantonese style. 2. Dim sum.
ISBN 9781607749561

LC 2015036911

Includes index.

A guide to the dishes served during Chinese dim sum meals includes information on the dish's origins, variations, and accompanying sauces, profiling such foods as siu mai, char siu, roast duck, and black sesame rolls.

Ponseca, Nicole

I am a Filipino and this is how we cook / Nicole Ponseca & Miguel Trinidad with Rachel Wharton ; foreword by Jose Antonio Vargas ; photographs by Justin Walker. Artisan, 2018 352 p. : **641.595**

1. Cooking, Philippine. 2. Recipes 3. Cookbooks
ISBN 9781579657673

LC 2018014210

Includes index.

Two trailblazing restaurateurs present a modern cookbook filled with a vast array of Filipino recipes that capture the unexpected and addictive flavors of this vibrant and diverse cuisine.

Punyaratabandhu, Leela

★**Bangkok** : recipes and stories from the heart of Thailand / Leela Punyaratabandhu ; photography by David Loftus. Ten Speed Press, 2017 359 p. : **641.595**

1. Cooking, Thai 2. Recipes 3. Bangkok (Thailand) -- Description and travel. 4. Cookbooks

ISBN 9780399578311

LC 2016051340

Includes index.

A native of Thailand with an award-winning cooking blog writes a love letter to her hometown with 120 recipes that capture the vibrant spirit of the city, including Steamed Dumplings with Chicken-peanut Filling, Beef Green Curry and Kudi Chin Sponge Cakes.

Raines, Abigail Sotto

Rice. Noodles. Yum. : everyone's favorite Southeast Asian dishes / Abigail Sotto Raines. Page Street Publishing Co., 2019. 191 p. : **641.595**

1. Cooking, Asian. 2. Cooking, Southeast Asian. 3. Recipes 4. Cookbooks.

ISBN 9781624147715

LC 2018957262

Includes index.

"This is an outstanding assembly of dishes, and a book sure to get plenty of use." Publishers Weekly.

Ramineni, Shubhra

Entice with spice : easy Indian recipes for busy people / Shubhra Ramineni ; photography by Masano Kawana ; styling by Christina Ong and Magdalene Ong. Tuttle Pub., c2010. 160 p. : **641.595**

1. Cooking, Indic. 2. Quick and easy cooking 3. Recipes 4. Cookbooks.

ISBN 9780804840293

LC 2009049092

Includes index.

"In this easy-to-follow cookbook, author Shubhra Ramineni shows Indian food enthusiasts how to prepare delicious meals at home without spending hours in the kitchen. A first generation Indian-American, Shubhra has developed a no-fuss cooking style that recreates authentic Indian flavors using easy techniques and fresh and easily available ingredients. The Indian food lover will find nearly 100 recipes--from samosa to naan and mouth watering curries--for easy-to-make versions of popular dishes from all over India"--Cover, p. 2.

"This is a cookbook full of traditional Indian recipes adapted for busy American kitchens. Beginning with thorough explanations, from terminology to spice mixtures, she provides time-saving suggestions and tips for preparing ingredients. This may be the Indian cookbook that American foodies have been waiting for." Publishers Weekly.

Ricker, Andy

★**Pok** Pok : Food and stories from the streets, homes, and roadside restaurants of Thailand / Andy Ricker with JJ Goode ; photography by Austin Bush. Ten Speed Press, 2013 viii, 295 p. : **641.595**

1. Pok Pok (Restaurant). 2. Cooking, Thai. 3. Recipes 4. Cookbooks.

ISBN 9781607742883

LC 2013012451

Includes index.

A guide to bold and authentic Thai cooking by the chef and owner of the popular Pok Pok chain draws on the traditional preparations he learned in his decades in Thailand and shares 50 accessible recipes for options ranging from Grilled Pork Collar with Spicy Dipping Sauce to Vietnamese Fish Sauce Wings.

★**Pok** Pok noodles : recipes from Thailand and beyond / Andy Ricker with JJ Goode ; photographs by Austin Bush. Ten Speed Press, 2019 263 p. : **641.595**

1. Pok Pok (Restaurant) 2. Cooking, Thai. 3. Recipes 4. Cookbooks.

ISBN 9781607747758

LC 2018046259

Includes index.

"Ricker's expertise with and affinity for Thai fare make for dishes well worth slurping up." Publishers Weekly.

Pok Pok : the drinking food of Thailand / Andy Ricker with JJ Goode ; photography by Austin Bush. Ten Speed Press, 2017 265 p. : **641.595**

1. Pok Pok (Restaurant). 2. Cooking, Thai. 3. Food and beer pairing. 4. Cookbooks.

ISBN 9781607747734

LC 2017025853

Includes index.

A guide to the food and drink of Thailand from the owner of Portland's Whiskey Soda Lounge features such exotic recipes as fried sour pork ribs, frog soup, squid salad, and fried peanuts with makrut lime leaves, garlic, and chilies.

Roden, Claudia

The **new** book of Middle Eastern food / Claudia Roden. Knopf, c2000. x, 513 p., 24 p. of plates : **641.595**

1. Cooking, Middle Eastern. 2. Recipes 3. Cookbooks

ISBN 9780375405068

LC 00708864

Contains an assortment of more than 800 recipes for traditional and modern dishes from Morocco, Tunisia, Turkey, Greece, Lebanon, Iran, and other Middle Eastern countries.

"This volume includes 800 recipes and variations, as well as historical background, an introduction to essential ingredients and regional dietary practices, folktales, and a vast amount of other information." Library Journal.

Rushdie, Sameen

Sameen Rushdie's Indian cookery / Sameen Rushdie ; foreword by Salman Rushdie. Picador Cookstr Classics, 2018, c1988. xvi, 256 p. : **641.595**

1. Cooking, Indic -- Northern style. 2. Cooking, Indic 3. Vegetarian cooking 4. Recipes 5. Cookbooks

ISBN 9781250102812

Originally published: London, England : Century Hutchinson Ltd, 1988.

Drawing together the traditional recipes from different Indian cuisines, Sameen Rushdie's invitation to share in the pleasures of Indian cookery is irresistible. --From publisher description.

Sageer, Julie Ann

Julie Taboulie's Lebanese kitchen : authentic recipes for fresh and flavorful Mediterranean home cooking / Julie Ann Sageer with Leah Bhabha ; photographs by Alexandra Grablewski. St. Martin's Griffin, 2017. 295 p. : **641.595**

1. Cooking, Lebanese. 2. Cooking, Mediterranean 3. Cookbooks.
ISBN 9781250094933

LC bl2017023073

Includes index.

Presents a collection of 125 authentic Lebanese recipes, including such dishes as roasted eggplant dip, yogurt mint soup, stuffed kousa squash, salmon and saffron rice stew, and lamb, potato, and tomato casserole.

"Sageer documents dozens of recipes from broadcasts in this new volume." Booklist.

Sakai, Sonoko, 1955-

Japanese home cooking : simple meals, authentic flavors / Sonoko Sakai ; photographs by Rick Poon ; illustrations by Juliette Bellocq. Roost Books, 2019. 304 p. **641.595**

1. Cooking, Japanese. 2. Quick and easy cooking 3. Cookbooks.
ISBN 9781611806168

LC 2018041562

Includes index.

The essential guide to Japanese home cooking--the ingredients, techniques and over 100 recipes--for seasoned cooks and beginners who are craving authentic Japanese flavors. Using high-quality, seasonal ingredients in simple preparations, Sakai offers recipes with a gentle voice and a passion for authentic Japanese cooking. Beginning with the pantry, the flavors of this cuisine are explored alongside fundamental recipes, such as dashi and pickles, and traditional techniques, like making noodles and properly cooking rice.

Shimbo, Hiroko

Hiroko's American kitchen : cooking with Japanese flavors / Hiroko Shimbo ; photography by Frances Janisch. Andrews McMeel Pub., c2012. 215 p. : **641.595**

1. Cooking, Japanese. 2. Recipes 3. Cookbooks
ISBN 9781449409784

LC bl2012042628

Includes index.

Introduces six core items--two stocks and four sauces--that can be used to prepare Japanese dishes designed for American tastes, including gingered pork burger, curried miso peanuts, and chunky potato and leek soup with miso.

Sodha, Meera

Fresh India : 130 quick, easy, and delicious vegetarian recipes for every day / Meera Sodha ; photography by David Loftus. Flatiron Books, 2016. 302 p. : **641.595**

1. Cooking, Indic. 2. Recipes 3. Vegetarian cooking. 4. Cookbooks.
ISBN 9781250123831

LC 2018000170

Includes index.

In a follow-up to her best-selling Made in India, the author, through more than 100 vegetable-based recipes, incorporates exotic flavors with simple ingredients to reveal a new side of Indian food that is fresh, delicious and quick to make.

Made in India : recipes from an Indian family kitchen / Meera Sodha ; photography by David Loftus. Flatiron Books, 2015. 319 p. : **641.595**

1. Cooking, Indic. 2. Cooking (Spices). 3. Recipes 4. Cookbooks
ISBN 9781250071019

LC 2015950828

Includes index.

Presents a collection of over 130 family recipes for Indian dishes, with advice on ingredients, equipment, weights, and measurement and options for starters, meat entrees, vegetables, sides, breads, chutneys, and desserts.

"Sodha offers helpful sections explaining how each Indian ingredient tastes and the best ways to use it, and how to fix a dish thats too spicy or salty. The power of this book lies in its simplicityboth in terms of ingredients and technique." Publishers Weekly.

Solomonov, Michael

★**Israeli** soul : easy, essential, delicious / Michael Solomonov, Steven Cook. Houghton Mifflin Harcourt, [2018] 384 p. **641.595**

1. Cooking, Israeli 2. Kosher food 3. Recipes 4. Cooking, Middle Eastern 5. Israel -- Social life and customs 6. Philadelphia, Pennsylvania -- Social life and customs
ISBN 9780544970373

LC 2018017712

"A Rux Martin book."

focuses on the great dishes that are the soul of Israeli cuisine, including varieties of shawarma, hummus, falafel, mountain bread, schnitzel, Ashkenazi and much more. Each chapter weaves history with contemporary portrayals of the food.

"Whether they're seeking an entertaining travelogue, an engrossing gourmet history, or an amazing collection of admirably imitable Israeli cuisine, readers won't be disappointed by Philadelphia chef Solomonov and his business partner Cook's (Federal Donuts, 2017; Zahav, 2015) third collection." Booklist.

Syhabout, James

Hawker Fare : stories & recipes from a refugee chef's Isan Thai & Lao roots / James Syhabout with John Birdsall ; foreword by Roy Choi ; introduction by Anthony Bourdain. Ecco, an Imprint of HarperCollins Publishers, 2018. 368 p. **641.595**

1. Syhabout, James 2. Hawker Fare (Restaurant) 3. Cooks 4. Cooking, Asian 5. Immigrant families 6. Cooking, Thai
ISBN 9780062656094

LC 2017038047

The chef and restaurateur who initially ignored his Asian heritage to become classically trained in Europe describes his eventual travels into his parent's respective homelands of Thailand and Laos and offers recipes inspired by his childhood.

"Syhabout's outstanding debut is a combination immersive deep dive into authentic Thai and Lao cuisine and personal memoir of Syhabout's journey to chefdom and owner of the restaurants Commis and Hawker Fare in the San Francisco Bay Area." Publishers Weekly.

Tamimi, Sami

Falastin : a cookbook / Sami Tamimi, Tara Wigley ; foreword by Yotam Ottolenghi ; photographs by Jenny Zarins. Ten Speed Press, 2020. 352 p. **641.595**

1. Cooking, Palestinian Arab. 2. Food -- Palestine. 3. Recipes 4. Cookbooks.
ISBN 9780399581731

LC 2019050435

"A soulful tour of Palestinian cooking today from the Ottolenghi restaurants' executive chef and partner--120 recipes shaped by his personal story as well as the history of Palestine".-- Provided by publisher.

"Ottolenghi alums Tamimi (coauthor, Jerusalem and Ottolenghi) and Wigley (coauthor, Ottolenghi Simple) set out on their own with this expert dive into the food of Palestine. The dishes overflow with bold flavors . . . Like the best cookbooks, this one opens a window to expand both palates and minds." Publishers Weekly

Tan, Desmond, 1966-

Burma Superstar : addictive recipes from the crossroads of Southeast Asia / Desmond Tan and Kate Leahy ; photography by John Lee. Ten Speed Press, 2017 xi, 256 p. : **641.595**

1. Burma Superstar (Restaurant). 2. Cooking, Burmese. 3. Recipes 4. Cookbooks.
ISBN 9781607749509

LC 2016025785

Presents an eclectic collection of recipes that feature the vivid flavors of Burmese cooking from the famed San Francisco Bay Area Burmese restaurant, including such dishes as coconut curry chicken, chili lamb, samusa salad, and chin corn soup.

Thomas, Deepa

★**Deepa's** secrets : slow carb, new Indian cuisine / foreword by Curt Ellis ; Deepa Thomas. Skyhorse Publishing, 2017 227 p. : **641.595**

1. Cooking, Indic. 2. Low-carbohydrate diet 3. Recipes 4. Convenience cooking 5. Cookbooks.
ISBN 9781510718982

LC bl2017051528

Includes index.

Presents a collection of 70 low-carbohydrate Indian recipes that incorporate time-saving cooking techniques.

"Engaging personal stories combined with artfully scattered notes and hints make this book reminiscent of the earliest Moosewood Cookbook in its tone and inviting narrative." Publishers Weekly.

Thompson, David, 1960-

Thai food=: Arharn Thai / David Thompson ; with photography by Earl Carter. Ten Speed Press, c2002. xiii, 673 p. : **641.595**

1. Cooking, Thai. 2. Cookbooks
ISBN 9781580084628

LC 2002018117

"A Kirsty Melville book."

"The first section of the book provides detailed cultural and social history and a guide to the regions and regional cuisines of Thailand. Then a detailed glossary of ingredients and a guide to techniques introduce the hundreds of recipes. These are grouped into chapters on relishes, soups, curries, salads, and sides, followed by one of menus with recipes. [This] culinary history/cookbook is unique and will be an important purchase for any Asian cookery collection." Library Journal.

Tila, Jet

101 Asian dishes you need to cook before you die : discover a new world of flavors in authentic recipes / Jet Tila, award-winning chef and TV personality. Page Street Publishing Co., 2017. 192 p. : **641.595**

1. Cooking, Asian. 2. Recipes 3. Cookbooks.
ISBN 9781624143823

LC bl2017025759

Includes index.

A collection of authentic Asian recipes for the home cook from the celebrity chef and television personality features such dishes as kung pao shrimp, Korean spicy grilled chicken, spicy tuna roll, and Vietnamese crispy imperial rolls.

"Readers of all skill levels and heat tolerances will appreciate Tila's instructions, which emphasize flavor without calling for hours of prep or multiple trips to specialty stores." Publishers Weekly.

Tsai, Ming, 1964-

Blue Ginger : East meets West cooking with Ming Tsai / Ming Tsai and Arthur Boehm ; photographs by Alan Richardson ; foreword by Ken Hom. Clarkson Potter, 1999. 275 p. : **641.595**

1. Cooking, Asian. 2. Recipes 3. Cookbooks
ISBN 9780609605301

LC 99036393

Includes index.

Presents a collecttion of more than 125 innovative recipes for dishes that blend the best in Western and Eastern ingredients and cooking techniques.

"Chapters divide the 125-plus recipes into soups, dim sum, rice and noodles, poultry, meat, seafood, elaborate side dishes and desserts, with mail-order sources. Instructions are clearly written and often include tips for wine and food pairings and advice on ingredient substitutions and techniques." Publishers Weekly.

West, Da-Hae

K food : Korean home cooking and street food / Da-Hae and Gareth West. Mitchell Beazley, 2016. 240 p. : **641.595**

1. Cooking, Korean. 2. Street food -- Korea. 3. Cookbooks.
ISBN 9781784721596

LC bl2016023211

Includes index.

Collects recipes for modern Korean food, with classic Korean recipes and recipes combining Korean and Western flavors and ingredients, including such options as bulgogi burgers, corn on the cob with kimchi butter, and pomegranate-glazed lamb kebobs.

"Korean cookbooks are very popular right now--this one will satisfy adventurous cooks looking for contemporary recipes." Library Journal.

Wong, Lee Anne

Dumplings all day Wong : a cookbook of Asian delights from a top chef / Lee Anne Wong, celebrity chef and TV personality ; foreword by Marcus Samuelsson. Page Street Publishing Co., 2014. 256 p. : **641.595**

1. Dumplings. 2. Cooking, Asian. 3. Cookbooks.
ISBN 9781624140594

LC bl2014035539

Includes index.

Collects dumpling recipes using a variety of folds, including potstickers, wontons, gyozas, shumai, and har gow, along with countless fillings and such cooking methods as steaming, pan-frying, baking, and deep-frying.

"This excellent dumpling cookbook highlights a wealth of flavors and techniques and advocates a from-scratch approach. The simpler dumplings in Bee Yin Low's Easy Chinese Recipes would make a great starting point for novices." Library Journal.

Young, Grace, 1956-

The **breath** of a wok : unlocking the spirit of Chinese wok cooking through recipes and lore / Grace Young and Alan Richardson ; with text and recipes by Grace Young. Simon & Schuster, c2004. xv, 240 p. : **641.595**

1. Cooking, Chinese. 2. Food habits -- China. 3. Recipes 4. Wok cooking. 5. Cookbooks.
ISBN 9780743238274

LC 2003070403

A collection of wok recipes includes such dishes as Kung Pao Chicken, Sizzling Pepper and Salt Shrimp, and Scallion and Ginger Lo Mein, in a Chinese cooking primer that also features food preparation tips and anecdotes about the author's culinary experiences in the international kitchens of famous chefs, teachers, and celebrities.

641.596 Cooking -- Africa

Adjonyoh, Zoe

Zoe's Ghana kitchen : traditional Ghanaian recipes remixed for the modern kitchen / Zoe Adjonyoh. Mitchell Beazley, 2017. 256 p. : **641.596**

1. Cooking, Ghanaian. 2. Recipes 3. Cookbooks.
ISBN 9781784721633

LC bl2018002329

Includes index.

The author, whose pop-up restaurant was very successful in the United Kingdom, presents a new take on traditional Ghanaian recipes, including such dishes as Jamestown grilled prawns, smoked fish stew, baked cassava fries, and a mango and lime smoothie.

Aki, Evi

Flavors of Africa : discover authentic family recipes from all over the continent / Evi Aki. Page Street Publishing Co., 2018. 176 p. : **641.596**

1. Cooking, African. 2. Recipes 3. Cookbooks.
ISBN 9781624146749

LC 2018943550

Includes index.

Showcasing the tried and true--and incredibly flavorful--recipes that have survived generations, the founder of EV's Eats introduces home cooks to a wide range of trendy culinary traditions from all over Africa.

Gebreysus, Yohanis

Ethiopia : recipes and traditions from the horn of Africa / Yohanis Gebreysus with Jeff Koehler. Interlink Book, 2019. 224 p. **641.596**

1. Cooking, Ethiopian. 2. Recipes 3. Cookbooks.
ISBN 9781623719630

LC 2019002531

Includes index.

Chef Yohanis takes the reader on a journey through all the essential dishes of his native country, including the traditional Injera synonymous with an Ethiopia feast, along the way telling wondrous stories of the local communities and customs. Complete with photography of the country's stunning landscapes and vibrant artisans, this book demonstrates why Ethiopian food should be considered as one of the world's greatest, most enchanting cuisines.

Gregory-Smith, John

Orange blossom & honey : magical Moroccan recipes from the Souks to the Sahara / John Gregory-Smith ; food photography by Martin Poole ; location photography by Alen Kechane Kyle Books, 2018. 192 p. **641.596**

1. Cooking, Moroccan 2. Cooking, North African 3. Recipes
ISBN 9781909487901

LC bl2019003691

"Food and travel writer Gregory-Smith has been collecting recipes in Morocco since 2007 and this stellar collection proves to be a great entry point...Colorful photos round out this excellent and inviting primer on Moroccan cuisine." Publishers Weekly.

Harris, Jessica B.

The **Africa** cookbook : tastes of a continent / Jessica B. Harris. Simon & Schuster, 1998. xi, 382 p. : **641.596**

1. Cooking, African. 2. Africa -- Description and travel.
ISBN 0684802759

LC 98038882

"[The author] begins with a a wide-ranging introductory section that provides history...background on the four general divisions of the continent, and a very good glossary of ingredients and equipment. Recipes are organized by course, with country of origin listed for each, and headnotes offer context as well as useful tips. Harris writes well, and her accounts of various visits and encounters are particularly readable. With few other cookbooks available even on specific African cuisines, her ambitious new book is unique." Library Journal.

Hassan, Hawa, 1982-

In Bibi's kitchen : the recipes and stories of grandmothers from the eight African countries that touch the Indian Ocean / Hawa Hassan with Julia Turshen ; photographs by Khadija M. Farah & Jennifer May ; illustrations by Araki Koman. Ten Speed Press, 2020. 281 p. : **641.596**

1. Cooking, African. 2. Cooking -- East Africa 3. Cooking -- Indian Ocean Region. 4. Recipes 5. East Africa -- Description and travel. 6. Indian Ocean Region -- Description and travel. 7. Cookbooks
ISBN 9781984856739

LC 2020003798

The best-selling cookbook author of Feed the Resistance teams up with the founder and CEO of a company that makes condiments inspired by Somalia to present 75 recipes and stories gathered from grandmothers of eight African nations.

Samuelsson, Marcus

The **soul** of a new cuisine : a discovery of the foods and flavors of Africa / Marcus Samuelsson with Heidi Sacko Walters ; photographs by Gediyon Kifle ; foreword by Desmond Tutu. John Wiley & Sons, c2006. xxii, 344 p. : **641.596**

1. Cooking, African. 2. Recipes 3. Cookbooks
ISBN 9780764569111

LC 2005028312

An award-winning chef introduces readers to the eating traditions of Africa in a collection of more than two hundred recipes representing diverse cultures and cuisines, accompanied by a commentary on his journey of culinary exploration across the continent.

"For this African cookbook, the author traveled to Africa and even took cooking lessons in Ethiopia, the country of his birth. Samuelsson emphasizes that this is not the definitive cookbook of an area with over 800 languages and dialects, but an overview of what he saw and ate in his travels. This is a unique cookbook about a little-known cuisine, including travel essays and enhanced by beautiful color photographs that depict the food and the people of Africa. A necessary acquisition for international cooking collections." Library Journal.

Thiam, Pierre

Senegal : modern Senegalese recipes from the source to the bowl / Pierre Thiam with Jennifer Sit. Lake Isle Press 2015 320 p. : **641.596**

1. Cooking, Senegalese.
ISBN 9781891105555

LC 2015930449

"This is not merely a beautiful cookbook, full of lavish full-color photographs and numerous recipes; it also serves to profile today's Senegal, adding a welcome layer of meaning and context, and providing a glimpse into the culture as a whole." Library Journal

Wolfert, Paula

The **food** of Morocco / Paula Wolfert ; photographs by Quentin Bacon ; drawings by Mark Marthaler. Ecco, c2011. 517 p. : **641.596**

1. Cooking, Moroccan. 2. Cookbooks.
ISBN 9780061957550

LC bl2011027656

Presents almost 200 recipes for Moroccan dishes, including salads, breads, main dishes, soups, desserts, and beverages.

"Deftly balancing authenticity with ease of preparation...Wolfert is an eager and encouraging host, walking readers through the various regions and their signature dishes as well as the handful of ingredients that make the cuisine so distinctive." Publishers Weekly.

641.5971 Cooking -- Canada

Matheson, Matty

Matty Matheson : a cookbook / Matty Matheson ; photographs by Quentin Bacon and Pat O'Rourke. Abrams, 2018 299 p. : **641.5971**

1. Matheson, Matty. 2. Cooking, Canadian. 3. Cooking -- Prince Edward Island. 4. Recipes. 5. Cookbooks
ISBN 9781419732454

LC 2017956845

Includes index.

The Canadian chef recounts his memories through the recipes from his boyhood and from his work in restaurants that shaped his personality as well as his cooking style.

O'Brady, Tara

Seven spoons : my favorite recipes for any and every day / Tara O'Brady. Ten Speed Press, 2015 285 p. : **641.5971**

1. Cooking. 2. Cooking, Canadian. 3. Recipes 4. Cookbooks.
ISBN 9781607746379

LC 2014036366

Includes index.

"The much-anticipated debut from the author behind the popular food blog Seven Spoons, featuring distinctive, crowd-pleasing recipes; engaging, writerly essays; and the same stunning photography that has earned her website a devoted following. Tara O'Brady was one of the earliest food bloggers to enter the scene, and now, nearly ten years after she first started Seven Spoons, she has become one of the most highly regarded and unique voices in the culinary arena. In her debut cookbook, Seven Spoons, O'Brady shares stories and recipes from her Canadian home--fresh, ingredient-driven food that is easy to make yet refined. Recipes like Roasted Carrots with Dukkah and Harissa Mayonnaise, Braised Beef Short Ribs with Gremolata, and Plum Macaroon Cake are wholesome, hearty, and showcase the myriad culinary influences at work in O'Brady's kitchen. Her evocative writing and gorgeously simple, elegant photography has earned her accolades from Saveur magazine, the Daily Mail, and more. Impeccable food photography and a lavish package round out this beautiful, personal collection. "-- Provided by publisher.

"Recommended for fans of O'Brady's blog (sevenspoons.net) and readers who'd like a globally influenced home cooking collection." Library Journal.

641.5972 Cooking -- Mexico

Bayless, Rick

Authentic Mexican : regional cooking from the heart of Mexico / Rick Bayless with Deann Groen Bayless ; illustrations by John Sandford ; photographs by Christopher Hirsheimer. William Morrow, 2007 384 p., 16 unnumbered p. of plates : **641.5972**

1. Cooking, Mexican. 2. Recipes 3. Cookbooks.
ISBN 9780061373268

Collects recipes that show readers how to recreate the textures and flavors of Mexico's regional specialties in North American kitchens.

Fiesta at Rick's : fabulous food for great times with friends / Rick Bayless with Deann Groen Bayless ; photographs by Paul Elledge. W. W. Norton, c2010. 348 p. : **641.5972**

1. Cooking, Mexican. 2. Entertaining. 3. Menus. 4. Recipes 5. Cookbooks.
ISBN 9780393058994

LC 2010013128

Includes indexes.

"The book loosely packages recipes around fiestas, from a luxury guacamole and cocktail party for 12 to classic mole for 24, complete with game-plan checklists. The hardest thing about using this book isn't finding the ingredients (today, practically every small town has a great Mexican grocery), it's keeping yourself from eating everything before the guests arrive." New York Times Book Review.

Mexican everyday / Rick Bayless, with Deann Groen Bayless ; color photographs by Christopher Hirsheimer. Norton, c2005. 336 p. : **641.5972**

1. Cooking, Mexican. 2. Recipes 3. Cookbooks.
ISBN 9780393061543

LC 2005023129

Includes index.

Presents easy-to-prepare recipes for nutritious Mexican dishes including salads, soups, soft tacos, enchiladas, tostadas, tortas, entrees, grilled fare, marinades, salsas, and desserts.

"Befitting the Mexican origins of these dishes, Bayless uses a wide variety of chiles, especially the deeply flavorful poblano. With virtually every recipe in the book, Bayless adds riffs that offer imaginative variations on the main recipe's techniques." Booklist.

More Mexican everyday : simple, seasonal, celebratory / Rick Bayless, with Deann Groen Bayless and David Tamarkin ; photographs by Hirsheimer and Hamilton. W.W. Norton & Company, 2015 384 p. : **641.5972**

1. Cooking, Mexican. 2. Recipes 3. Seasonal cooking. 4. Cookbooks.
ISBN 9780393081145

LC 2015005985

Includes index.

Presents easy-to-prepare recipes for Mexican dishes using seasonal ingredients, including salads, soups, tacos, enchiladas, tostadas, tortas, entrees, salsas, and desserts.

"Recipes conclude with quick summaries of ingredients to ease shopping. An effective starting point for the would-be home Mexican cook." Booklist.

Rick Bayless Mexico one plate at a time / Rick Bayless, with Jeanmarie Brownson and Deann Groen Bayless ; color photographs by Gentl & Hayers ; Mexican location photographs by James Baigrie ; glossary photographs by James Isberner. Scribner, c2000. x, 374 p. : **641.5972**

1. Cooking, Mexican. 2. Recipes 3. Cookbooks

ISBN 9780684841861

LC 00058327

An authority on Mexican cuisine shares his wisdom and experience on cooking south of the border in this collection of 120 recipes that includes classics as well as some of his own creations.

"There are helpful questions and answers at the end of each section, based on questions generated by recipe testers, an addition that may be unique to the cookbook genre. There is much here for both neophytes and experienced cooks. Highly recommended for all public libraries." Library Journal.

Rick Bayless's Mexican kitchen : capturing the vibrant flavors of a world-class cuisine / with Deann Groen Bayless and JeanMarie Brownson ; photographs by Maria Robledo ; illustrations by John Sandford. Scribner, c1996. 448 p. : **641.5972**

1. Cooking, Mexican. 2. Recipes 3. Cookbooks

ISBN 9780684800066

LC 96218444

Presents recipes for more than 200 authentic Mexican dishes, as well as introducing the major components of Mexican food

Camara, Gabriela, 1975-

My Mexico City kitchen : recipes and convictions / Gabriela Camara with Malena Watrous ; photographs by Marcus Nilsson. Lorena Jones Books, 2019 367 p. : **641.5972**

1. Cooking, Mexican. 2. Recipes 3. Food habits -- Mexico City, Mexico 4. Mexico City, Mexico -- Social life and customs. 5. Cookbooks

ISBN 9780399580574

LC 2018042689

Includes index.

"Inspired by the flavors, ingredients, and flair of culinary and cultural hotspot Mexico City, Gabriela Camara's style of fresh-first, vegetable-forward, legume-loving, and seafood-centric Mexican cooking is a siren call to home cooks who crave authentic, on-trend recipes they can make with confidence and regularity. With 150 recipes for Basicos (basics), Desayunos (breakfasts), Primeros (starters), Platos Fuertos (mains), and Postres (sweets), Mexican food-lovers will find all the dishes they want to cook--from Chilaquiles Verdes to Chiles Rellenos and Flan de Cajeta--and will discover many sure-to-be favorites, such as her signature tuna tostadas".-- Provided by publisher.

"This simple yet authentic and extensive collection could easily replace every other Mexican cookbook in your library's collection." Library Journal.

Carrillo Arronte, Margarita

★**Mexico** : the cookbook / Margarita Carrillo Arronte. Phaidon Press Limited, 2014. 704 p. : **641.5972**

1. Cooking, Mexican. 2. Recipes 3. Cookbooks.

ISBN 9780714867526

LC bl2014050104

Features seven hundred recipes from across Mexico, from snacks and street food to meats and desserts, including such offerings as Sonora-style cheesy broth, stuffed supreme chiles, pickled chipotles, and stuffed candied limes.

"Full-color photos of food, landscapes, and people round out this hefty and appealing collection. For those interested in learning how to make authentic Mexican cuisine, Arronte has provided the definitive guide." Publishers Weekly.

Cramby, Jonas

Tex-mex from scratch / Jonas Cramby ; photography by: Roland Persson. Sterling Epicure, 2015. 141 p. : **641.5972**

1. Cooking, American -- Southwestern style. 2. Cooking, Mexican American 3. Cooking, Tex-Mex 4. Recipes 5. Cookbooks.

ISBN 9781454916291

LC bl2015017178

Includes index.

Collects recipes for traditional tex-mex dishes and drinks created from scratch, including shrimp taquitos, poblano potato salad, and green scallop tostado.

"Texas BBQ is a treat for armchair cooks and can broaden regional collections. Cramby, whose daughters are named Dixie Margarita and Lone Star, has an infectious passion for Tex-Mex food and a talent for food photography. Of his available and forthcoming titles, Tex-Mex from Scratch offers the best value." Library Journal.

Gerson, Fany

My sweet Mexico : recipes for authentic pastries, breads, candies, beverages, and frozen treats / Fany Gerson ; photography by Ed Anderson. Ten Speed Press, c2010. vii, 215 p. : **641.5972**

1. Cooking, Mexican. 2. Desserts -- Mexico. 3. Recipes 4. Cookbooks.

ISBN 9781580089944

LC 2010014469

"The first cookbook to present authentic versions of beloved Mexican sweets plus a creative selection of new recipes rooted in traditional flavors and ingredients".--Provided by publisher.

"The author has dutifully catalogued the confections of her native Mexico. American readers who have only encountered the occasional tres leches cake in a Mexican restaurant will be stunned by the breadth and depth of recipes here, ranging from coffee-flavored corn cookies to guava caramel pecan rolls and hibiscus ice pops, all culled from Gerson's family, friends, and generous strangers. Gerson's vivid descriptions, exacting instruction, and obvious passion for her subject matter make this volume a substantial read about the most tempting indulgences." Publishers Weekly.

Goldberg, Dan

¡Cuba! : recipes and stories from the Cuban kitchen / Dan Goldberg, Andrea Kuhn, and Jody Eddy. Ten Speed Press, 2016 249 p. : **641.5972**

1. Cooking, Cuban. 2. Cookbooks.

ISBN 9781607749868

LC 2016011291

Explores Cuban cuisine and culture through meticulously tested recipes, complemented by stories about life on the island, including such options as Cuban-style fried chicken, tostones stuffed with lobster and conch, and squid-ink empanadas.

"Photographer Goldberg, art director Kuhn, and food writer Eddy made three visits to Havana and its environs over a five-year period, feasting on the local cuisine and meeting the proud cooks and farmers of the area. They now report back on their sightseeing, with scores of photos and 75 recipes in tow." Publishers Weekly.

Guzman, Gonzalo Gonzalez

★**Nopalito** : a Mexican kitchen / Gonzalo Gonzalez Guzman, with Stacy Adimando ; photography by Eva Kolenko. Ten Speed Press, 2017. xiii, 241 p. : **641.5972**

1. Nopalito (Restaurant). 2. Cooking, Mexican. 3. Cooking,

American -- California 4. Recipes 5. Cookbooks.
ISBN 9780399578281

LC 2016030890

"More challenging than low-effort or quick-and-easy offerings, Guzman's compelling debut will appeal to foodies and Mexican food lovers who enjoy leisurely cooking." Library Journal.

Hernandez, Eddie

Turnip greens & tortillas : a Mexican chef spices up the southern kitchen / Eddie Hernandez and Susan Puckett ; photographs by Angie Mosier. Houghton Mifflin Harcourt, 2018. vii, 310 p. : **641.5972**

1. Cooking, Mexican. 2. Cookbooks.
ISBN 9780544618824

LC 2017051352

Includes index.

"A Rux Martin Book."

A collection of recipes for Southern fare with a Mexican flair from the chef and restaurateur features such dishes as Cajun hash, cheeseburger tacos, chicken enchilada casserole, and Creole red beans and rice burritos.

"A stellar debut imbued with Hernandez's infectious excitement for cooking." Library Journal.

Hoyer, Daniel

Mayan cuisine : recipes from the Yucatan region / Daniel Hoyer ; photographs by Marty Snortum. Gibbs Smith, Publisher, c2008. 224 p. : **641.5972**

1. Maya cooking. 2. Cooking -- Mexico 3. Recipes 4. Cookbooks
ISBN 9781423601319

LC 2007033541

Includes index.

"Hoyer is encouraging and enthusiastic, offering salient tips for key techniques like working with tamale wrappers and charring tomatoes, as well as sources for hard-to-locate ingredients." Publishers Weekly.

Jinich, Pati

Mexican today : new and rediscovered recipes for contemporary kitchens / Pati Jinich ; photography by Ellen Silverman. Houghton Mifflin Harcourt, 2016 320 p. : **641.5972**

1. Cooking, Mexican. 2. Recipes 3. Cookbooks.
ISBN 9780544557246

LC 2015042717

"A Rux Martin Book."

A collection of recipes from the host of PBS series Pati's Mexican Table for traditional Mexican dishes and modified recipes that show the evolution of Mexican food, including such options as guacamoles, salsa, tacos, enchiladas, and guisados.

"Many of her recipes can be made in advance or in less than 30 minutes and rely on easy-to-find ingredients. A highlight of this cookbook is its playful variations such as baked huevos rancheros casserole." Library Journal.

Kennedy, Diana

The **essential** cuisines of Mexico / Diana Kennedy. Clarkson Potter, c2000. xviii, 526 p. ; **641.5972**

1. Cooking, Mexican. 2. Food habits -- Mexico 3. Recipes 4. Cookbooks
ISBN 9780609603550

LC 00023156

Includes index.

A recognized authority on authentic Mexican cuisine has revised, updated, and expanded several of her classic cookbooks to present hundreds of traditional recipes, as well as new instructions for ingredient use, new cooking techniques, and additional recipes.

"Every aspect of the Mexican kitchen is covered; you can be quite sure that if it isn't here, it isn't worth cooking." BookPage.

From my Mexican kitchen : techniques and ingredients / Diana Kennedy ; photographs by Michael Calderwood ; and styled by the author. Clarkson Potter/Publishers, c2003. 320 p. : **641.5972**

1. Cooking, Mexican. 2. Recipes 3. Cookbooks
ISBN 9780609607008

LC 2002070405

Includes index.

"This is an indispensable addition to any library cookbook collection." Booklist.

Mason, Taymer

Caribbean vegan : meat-free, egg-free, dairy-free authentic island cuisine for every occasion. / Taymer Mason. The Experiment, 2016 311 p. ; **641.5972**

1. Cooking, Caribbean. 2. Vegan cooking. 3. Cookbooks.
ISBN 9781615193608

LC 2016020831

Presents vegan versions of classic Caribbean dishes, including creole spaghetti, citrus tofu jerk kebabs, christophenes farcies, and vegan fish pie.

"Mason invites home cooks to sample a rich array of dishes, from callaloo fritters to...guava bread pudding with coconut rum sauce." Library Journal.

Pelaez, Ana Sofia

The **Cuban** table : a celebration of food, flavors, and history / Ana Sofia Pelaez ; photographs by Ellen Silverman. St. Martin's Press, 2014. xi, 323 p. : **641.5972**

1. Cooking, Cuban. 2. Recipes 3. Cookbooks.
ISBN 9781250036087

LC 2014026974

A Cuban-American food writer and blogger offers an illustrated, comprehensive overview of Cuban cuisine, providing historical context for dishes that include Spanish and African ingredients as well as 110 delicious, authentic recipes.

"Let's hope Pelaez and Silverman undertake more collaborations. Their thorough and respectful treatment of their subject results in a compelling cookbook that conveys a strong sense of place." Library Journal.

Presilla, Maricel E.

★**Gran** cocina latina : the food of Latin America / Maricel E. Presilla ; photographs by Gentl & Hyers/Edge ; drawings by Julio Figueroa. Norton & Company, c2012. vii, 901 p., 32 p. of plates : **641.5972**

1. Cooking, Latin American. 2. Cooking, Caribbean. 3. Cooking, Mexican. 4. Recipes 5. Cookbooks.
ISBN 9780393050691

LC 2012017701

Includes index.

Presents 500 recipes from the Latin world ranging from Mexico to Argentina and all the Spanish-speaking countries of the Caribbean including adobos, sofritos, empanadas, tamales, ceviches, moles, and flan.

Rousseau, Michelle

Provisions : the roots of Caribbean cooking : 150 vegetarian recipes / Michelle Rousseau & Suzanne Rousseau. Da Capo Press, 2018. xv, 301 p. : **641.5972**

1. Cooking, Caribbean. 2. Vegetarian cooking 3. Cookbooks.
ISBN 9780738234670

LC 2018014939

Putting a modern twist on traditional island ingredients and flavors, this sumptuous vegetarian cookbook combines the region|s culinary past with creative recipes that represent the best of Caribbean food today.

Santibanez, Roberto

Truly Mexican / Roberto Santibanez with J.J. Goode and Shelley Wiseman. John Wiley, c2011. vii, 264 p. : **641.5972**

1. Cooking, Mexican 2. Sauces 3. Cookbooks.
ISBN 9780470499559

LC 2010013151

Includes index.

Introduces traditional Mexican sauces with recipes for authentic favorites, from tacos and tamales to braised short ribs adobo and red snapper papillotes in green mole and includes instructions on essential ingredients and techniques.

Tellez, Lesley

Eat Mexico : recipes from Mexico City's streets, markets & fondas / Lesley Tellez ; photographs by Penny De Los Santos. Kyle Books, 2015. 192 p. : **641.5972**

1. Cooking, Mexican. 2. Recipes 3. Cookbooks.
ISBN 9781909487277

LC bl2015025408

Includes index.

Showcases recipes from Mexico City's streets, neighborhood markets, casual fondas, the more rustic dishes from the rural outskirts, and the Mexican-inspired dishes that Lesley cooks at home in New York.

Von Bremzen, Anya

Paladares : recipes inspired by the private restaurants of Cuba / Anya Von Bremzen ; recipe development and photography by Megan Fawn Schlow. Abrams, 2017. 351 p.: **641.5972**

1. Cooking, Cuban. 2. Food habits -- Cuba. 3. Recipes 4. Cookbooks.
ISBN 9781419727030

LC 2016961368

Includes index.

A full-color cookbook describes the history of Cuban cuisine by focusing on the country's private restaurants, called paladares, and featuring 150 authentic, but easily prepared at home, recipes, including Ham and Cheese Empanadas, Pumpkin Flan and Salmorejo.

Werner, Eric

Hartwood : bright, wild flavors from the edge of the Yucatan / Eric Werner, Mya Henry, with Christine Muhlke and Oliver Strand ; photographs by Gentl & Hyers ; foreword by Rene Redzepi. Artisan, 2015. 301 p. ; **641.5972**

1. Hartwood (Restaurant : Tulum, Mexico). 2. Cooking, Mexican. 3. Maya cooking. 4. Recipes 5. Cookbooks.
ISBN 9781579656201

LC 2015013061

Includes index.

Collects recipes from the Tulum restaurant, including such offerings as ceviche de robalo, chicken legs recado rojo, lime tart with lime caramel, and chilled avocado soup with erazote.

"Vibrant flavors dominate this warm and welcoming collection, bringing the local tastes of the Yucatn region into the home kitchen." Publishers Weekly.

641.5973 United States

America's Test Kitchen (Firm)

The **America's** test kitchen do-it-yourself cookbook : 100+ foolproof kitchen projects for the adventurous home cook / the editors at America's test kitchen ; photography by Anthony Tieuli. America's Test Kitchen, 2012 viii, 360 p. : **641.5973**

1. Cooking, American. 2. Recipes 3. Cookbooks.
ISBN 9781936493081

LC 2012022144

Includes index.

From smoked bacon and dill pickles to your own home-brewed ale, trust the test kitchen experts to guide you through more than 100 foolproof kitchen projects. --From publisher description.

America's Test Kitchen twentieth anniversary TV show cookbook : best-ever recipes from the most successful cook show on TV / America's Test Kitchen. America's Test Kitchen, 2019 vii, 581 p. : **641.5973**

1. Cooking, American. 2. Recipes 3. Cookbooks.
ISBN 9781945256882

LC bl2019038344

Includes index.

A collection of over 500 recipes from the long-running PBS series features such dishes as Chicken Enchiladas With Red Chili Sauce, Chinese-style Oven-Steamed Fish and Maple-glazed Pork Tenderloin, as well as a behind-the-scenes look at cast members.

Cook's Country eats local : 150 regional recipes you should be making no matter where you live / the editors at America's Test Kitchen. America's Test Kitchen, 2015 ix, 310 p. ; **641.5973**

1. Cooking, American. 2. Recipes 3. Cookbooks.
ISBN 9781936493999

LC 2015005574

Includes index.

Collects one hundred fifty local recipes from around the United States, from Philadelphia cheesesteaks and Utica greens to Carolina red slaw and Texas chicken-fried steak.

"For families and home cooks seeking foolproof classic fare for potlucks, picnics, tailgates, and other occasions." Library Journal.

★**Cook's** illustrated revolutionary recipes : groundbreaking techniques, compelling voices, one-of-a-kind recipes. / America's Test Kitchen. America's Test Kitchen, 2018 564 p. : **641.5973**

1. Cooking, American. 2. Recipes 3. Cookbooks.
ISBN 9781945256479

LC 2018017995

Includes index.

Published to coincide with its 25th anniversary, this special collection of groundbreaking recipes and extraordinary innovations shows how *Cook's Illustrated* has changed the way America cooks.

The **new** family cookbook : all-new edition of the best-selling classic with 1,100 new recipes / the editors at America's Test Kitchen. America's Test Kitchen, 2014 ix, 878 p. : **641.5973**

1. Cooking, American. 2. Recipes 3. Gourmet cooking 4. Cookbooks.
ISBN 9781936493852

LC 2014009517

Includes index.

A comprehensive A to Z cookbook for anyone looking for an approachable timeless collection of foolproof recipes, cooking techniques, and product ratings from America's Test Kitchen. The America's Test

Kitchen Family Cookbook, published in 2005, has sold more than 800,000 copies. We've completely updated and redesigned this edition, adding more than 1,100 new recipes to 200 best-loved classics from the original book. --From publisher description.

Ahern, Shauna James

Gluten-Free Girl American classics reinvented / Shauna James Ahern with Daniel Ahern ; photography by Lauren Volo. Houghton Mifflin Harcourt, 2015 320 p. : **641.5973**

1. Cooking, American. 2. Cooking, Gluten-free 3. Recipes 4. Cookbooks.

ISBN 9780544219885

LC 2015007133

Includes index.

Shares a collection of gluten-free recipes for classic comfort food from cinnamon rolls with cream cheese frosting and chicken-fried steak to New England clam chowder and baked artichoke dip.

"Those who feel limited on a gluten-free diet will rejoice in this extensive and appetizing collection of family favorites that can once again be on the menu." Publishers Weekly.

Angelou, Maya

Hallelujah! the welcome table / Maya Angelou. Random House, 2004. xiii, 218 p. : **641.5973**

1. Angelou, Maya Anecdotes. 2. Cooking, American. 3. Cooking.

ISBN 1400062896

LC 2004044902

"The author couples brief anecdotes from her life with more than 60 recipes for food enjoyed at that time. Readers will be torn between losing themselves in the evocative text and rushing to the kitchen to whip up such delights as her grandmother's caramel cake or the white bean cassoulet that Angelou prepared for food writer M.F.K. Fisher." Library Journal.

Anthony, Michael, 1968-

The **Gramercy** Tavern cookbook / Michael Anthony ; with a history by Danny Meyer ; produced by Dorothy Kalins ; photographs by Maura McEvoy. Clarkson Potter, 2013. 351 p. : **641.5973**

1. Gramercy Tavern. 2. Cooking, American. 3. Gourmet cooking 4. Seasonal cooking 5. Recipes 6. Cookbooks.

ISBN 9780307888334

LC 2012047367

Includes index.

"One of the best New York restaurants, a culinary landmark that has been changing the face of American dining for decades, now shares its beloved recipes, stories, and pioneering philosophy. Opened in 1994, Gramercy Tavern is more than just a restaurant. It has become a New York institution earning dozens of accolades, including six James Beard awards. Its impeccable, fiercely seasonal cooking, welcoming and convivial atmosphere, and steadfast commitment to hospitality are unparalleled. The restaurant has its own magic--a sense of community and generosity--that's captured in these pages for everyone to bring home and savor through 125 recipes. Restaurateur Danny Meyer's intimate story of how Gramercy was born sets the stage for executive chef-partner Michael Anthony's appealing approach to American cooking and recipes that highlight the bounty of the farmer's market. With 200 sumptuous photographs and personal stories, The Gramercy Tavern Cookbook also gives an insider look into the things that make this establishment unique, from the artists who have shaped its decor and ambience, to the staff members who share what it is like to be a part of this close-knit restaurant family. Above all, food lovers will be inspired to make memorable meals and bring the warmth of Gramercy into their homes".-- Provided by publisher.

"[T]he authors encourage cooks to approach their restaurant recipes as inspirational points of departure to produce dishes that 'look great by virtue of the beauty of the ingredients.' Signature tavern cocktails are followed by recipes organized by season, from appetizers through main dishes to desserts." Publishers Weekly.

Batali, Mario

America farm to table : simple, delicious recipes celebrating local farmers / Mario Batali and Jim Webster ; art direction by Douglas Riccardi ; recipe photography by Quentin Bacon ; farm photography by Christine Birch Ferrelli and Lara Cerri. Grand Central Life & Style, 2014. 351 p. : **641.5973**

1. Cooking, American. 2. Local foods -- United States. 3. Farms, Small -- United States. 4. Seasonal cooking 5. Cookbooks.

ISBN 9781455584680

LC 2014011984

Includes index.

The renowned celebrity chef presents a tribute to the American farmer through stories and photos that evince their way of life, sharing regional recipes for such fare as Lamb Shank Sloppy Joes and Grilled Salmon With Strawberry Salsa.

"No particular ingredient is sacred; all ingredients are celebrated in the unique farmer-chef-home-cook collaboration." Booklist.

Mario Batali big American cookbook : 250 favorite recipes from across the USA / Mario Batali ; with Jim Webster ; art direction by Douglas Riccardi ; photography by Quentin Bacon, Grand Central Life & Style, 2016 xv, 495 p. ; **641.5973**

1. Cooking, American. 2. Local foods -- United States. 3. Recipes 4. Cookbooks.

ISBN 9781455584710

LC 2016022712

Includes index.

Presents two hundred fifty recipes using regional ingredients from around the United States, sharing such dishes as lobster pot pie, oyster fritters, shrimp and grits, key lime pie, stuffed cabbages, fried pickles, huevos rancheros, and Kahlua pork.

"Boosting recipes with color photographs, Batali makes every dish look like great fun, and its impossible not to share his enthusiasm." Booklist.

Beard, James, 1903-1985

The **essential** James Beard cookbook : 450 recipes that shaped the tradition of American cooking / James Beard ; edited by Rick Rodgers ; with John Ferrone, editorial consultant. St. Martin's Press, 2012. xx, 380 p. ; **641.5973**

1. Cooking, American. 2. Cookbooks.

ISBN 9780312642181

LC 2012028372

Includes index.

A treasury of updated recipes culled from 12 of the influential cooking personality's classic books provides basic and favorite options in categories ranging from appetizers and soups to meats and desserts.

"Home cooking has evolved considerably since Beard's cookbooks were first published, so it's wonderful to see his recipes reprinted in this functional collection." Library Journal.

Besh, John

Cooking from the heart : my favorite lessons learned along the way / John Besh ; produced by Dorothy Kalins ; photographs by Maura McEvoy. Andrews McMeel Publishing, 2013 xi, 308 p.

: **641.5973**

1. Cooking, American. 2. Cookbooks.
ISBN 9781449430566

LC bl2013049022

Includes index.

Traces the culinary journey of chef John Besh by visting his mentors around the world, including heartfelt stories and recipes from each.

Brennan, Kathy

Keepers : two home cooks share their tried-and-true weeknight recipes and the secrets to happiness in the kitchen / Kathy Brennan and Caroline Campion. Rodale, 2013. xiv, 240 p. : **641.5973**

1. Cooking -- Philosophy. 2. Cooking, American. 3. Kitchens -- Management. 4. Low budget cooking. 5. Cookbooks.
ISBN 9781609613549

LC 2013005481

Includes index.

A collection of 120 accessible, affordable recipes for families, written by two award-winning food journalists, draws on the expertise of professional chefs and the authors' own home-kitchen experiences to provide adaptations of classic dishes, old favorites and one-pot convenience meals that can be readily prepared on busy weeknights.

Clark, Melissa

Cook this now : 120 easy and delectable dishes you can't wait to make / Melissa Clark. Hyperion, c2011. xviii, 396 p. : **641.5973**

1. Cooking, American. 2. COOKING / General. 3. Quick and easy cooking 4. Quick and easy cooking 5. Cookbooks.
ISBN 9781401323981

LC 2011010420

Includes index.

"A journal-style narrative about the author's first year of feeding her family seasonally, sustainably, and sumptuously -- eating real, fresh, whole, non-processed foods, choosing local and seasonal and sustainable whenever possible, and eschewing factory meats and overfished seafood. But also about eating well and not making herself crazy. This will be a look at her choices, how she succeeds and fails, and most importantly, what she's choosing to cook. Including approx. 135 recipes".--Provided by publisher.

"Clark presents readers with 120 recipes organized by season and month. With a candid opening essay on weekly trips to her local NYC farmers' market in the dead of winter--think frosty fingers, and ice-topped milk--Clark sets the course for this down-to-earth, realistic guide to cooking throughout the year, finding and highlighting seasonal gems in mains, side dishes, and desserts. Even with a multitude of cooking-by-season titles in the marketplace, the author's inspiring use of fresh ingredients and flexible attitude toward cooking make this a solid addition to any kitchen cookbook shelf." Publishers Weekly.

Cunningham, Marion

The **Fannie** Farmer cookbook / Marion Cunningham ; illustrated by Lauren Jarrett. Knopf , 1996. xi, 874 p. : **641.5973**

1. Cooking, American. 2. Recipes
ISBN 9780679450818

LC 97162330

Rev. ed. of: The Fannie Farmer cookbook / [Fannie Merritt Farmer]. 12th ed.

Includes index.

Features nearly 2000 recipes and includes chapters dealing with microwave, outdoor, and vegetarian cooking.

Dufresne, Wylie

wd~50 : the cookbook / Wylie Dufresne with Peter Meehan ; photography by Eric Medsker. Ecco, 2017 343 p. : **641.5973**

1. Cooking, American. 2. Restaurants -- New York City 3. Recipes 4. Gourmet cooking 5. Cookbooks.
ISBN 9780062318534

LC bl2018012049

"An Anthony Bourdain book."

Issued in slipcase.

Includes index.

Collects the recipes from the now-closed New York restaurant, wd~50, that featured New American cooking.

"Dufresne himself is a rock star of the kitchen, and his recipes here are clever and inspirational." Publishers Weekly.

Dupree, Nathalie

Mastering the art of Southern cooking / Nathalie Dupree & Cynthia Graubart ; photographs by Rick McKee ; with a foreword by Pat Conroy. Gibbs Smith, 2012. 720 p. : **641.5973**

1. Cooking, American -- Southern style. 2. Cookbooks.
ISBN 9781423602750

LC 2012017365

Offers recipes for both old-fashioned and new Southern cuisine, including oven-fried chicken breasts with pecan crust, cheese grits souffle, and Nana's banana cream pie.

Estrine, Darryl

Harvest to heat : cooking with America's best chefs, farmers, and artisans / Darryl Estrine and Kelly Kochendorfer. Taunton Press, 2010. 295 p. : **641.5973**

1. Cooking, American. 2. Recipes 3. Seasonal cooking 4. Cookbooks.
ISBN 9781600852541

LC 2010011943

Includes index.

"The authors match farmers and artisans with chefs and restaurants across the country to present 100 original recipes from, e.g., Eric Ripert (Le Bernardin, New York), Paul Kahan (Blackbird, Chicago), and Vitaly Paley (Paley's Place, Portland, OR), for the home cook, for starters and salads, main courses, sides, and desserts. Each recipe is accompanied by a description of the farmer or artisan who provided the main ingredients. Sustainable food is in, and this book will encourage home cooks to follow the tenets of the movement." Library Journal.

Falk, Daina

The **hungry** fan's game day cookbook : 165 recipes for eating, drinking & watching sports / Daina Falk. Oxmoor House, 2016. 256 p. : **641.5973**

1. Cooking, American. 2. Recipes 3. Cookbooks.
ISBN 9780848745837

LC bl2016032888

Includes index.

Offers game-day recipes from a nationally recognized sports expert and fan, including such options as Cajun shrimp skewers, empanadas, buffalo chicken salad, and Italian hero sandwich, along with signature recipes from professional athletes.

"Regardless of culinary preferences or skill level, every hungry sports fan can find something appealing in this go-to guide for game days all year long." Publishers Weekly.

Freedman, Paul, 1949-

American cuisine : and how it got this way / Paul Freedman. Liveright Publishing Corporation, A division of W.W.

Norton & Company, 2019. 528 p. **641.5973**

1. Food habits -- United States -- History 2. Cooking, American 3. Processed foods 4. Advertising 5. United States -- Social life and customs

ISBN 9781631494628

LC 2019029642

A leading food historian details the culinary habits of Americans from the days of the colonies to the present, exploring how regional dishes like New England clam Chowder and Louisiana gumbo moved aside for processed and packaged food. With an ambitious sweep over two hundred years, Paul Freedman's lavishly illustrated history shows that there actually is an American cuisine.

Goin, Suzanne, 1966-

The **A.O.C.** cookbook / Suzanne Goin with wine notes by Caroline Styne ; photographs by Shimon and Tammar Rothstein. Alfred A. Knopf, 2013. xvi, 429 p. : **641.5973**

1. A.O.C. (Restaurant) 2. Appetizers. 3. Cooking, American. 4. Food and wine pairing. 5. Recipes 6. Cookbooks.

ISBN 9780307958235

LC 2013005068

Recipes from the author's "sophomore restaurant, A.O.C., turning the small-plate, shared-style dishes that she made so famous into main courses for the home chef".--Dust jacket flap.

Guarnaschelli, Alex, 1969-

The **home** cook : recipes to know by heart / Alex Guarnaschelli. Clarkson Potter/Publishers, 2017 368 p. ; **641.5973**

1. Cooking, American. 2. Recipes 3. Cookbooks.

ISBN 9780307956583

LC 2016045628

Includes index.

A collection of modern recipes from the accomplished chef that features vibrant international flavors, including such dishes as whole pork loin roast with Cajun rub, lamb tagine, and roasted eggplant dip with garlic butter naan.

Holland, Tanya

Brown sugar kitchen : new-style, down-home recipes from sweet West Oakland / Tanya Holland with Jan Newberry ; foreword by Michael Chabon ; photographs by Jody Horton. Chronicle Books, 2014 223 p. : **641.5973**

1. Cooking, American. 2. Cooking, African American 3. Restaurants -- Oakland, California 4. Restaurateurs -- Oakland, California 5. Oakland, California 6. Cookbooks

ISBN 9781452122342

LC bl2014041061

Includes index.

The author offers recipes from her West Oakland restaurants, including spiced winter squash soup, Creole meatloaf, and buttermilk cornbread pudding.

"Bold and soulful Southern foods, gorgeously photographed by Horton, will have readers' stomachs rumbling." Library Journal

Keller, Thomas, 1955-

★**Ad** Hoc at home / Thomas Keller with Dave Cruz ; along with Susie Heller, Michael Ruhlman, and Amy Vogler ; photographs by Deborah Jones. Artisan Books, 2009. 359 p. : **641.5973**

1. Ad Hoc (Restaurant). 2. Cooking, American. 3. Recipes 4. Cookbooks

ISBN 9781579653774

LC 2009013258

Includes index.

Offers recipes inspired by the author's restaurant, Ad Hoc, with emphasis on casual, family-style dining, and including recipes for such dishes as "Buttermilk Fried Chicken" and "Pineapple Upside-Down Cake."

"For this cookbook, the author focuses on family-style meals for the home cook in this accessible and dazzlingly beautiful book based on the fare served at his Ad Hoc restaurant, in Napa, Calif. [He provides] a thorough primer on the foundations of cooking, offering clear and easy-to-follow instructions on techniques such as butchering and trussing chickens and tying a pork loin. Dishes such as braised beef short ribs, buttermilk fried chicken, and fig-stuffed roast pork loin highlight a vast array of offerings that range from crab cakes to shortbread cookies." Publishers Weekly.

Langholtz, Gabrielle

America : the cookbook / Gabrielle Langholtz. Phaidon Press, 2017. 767 p. : **641.5973**

1. Cooking, American. 2. Recipes 3. Cookbooks.

ISBN 9780714873961

LC 2017446984

"1 country, 50 states, 800 recipes, 50 chefs, 50 essays, 50 states menus"--Page 4 of cover.

"A culinary road trip through the 50 states"--Cover.

Includes index.

With 800 home-cooking recipes, America: The Cookbook is a celebration of the remarkable diversity of American food and food culture state by state. Features 50 essays and menus from a 'who's who' of 100 foremost food experts and chefs.

"Rather than simply offering a rote recitation of well-worn classics, Langholtz artfully includes recipes that show America's kaleidoscopic culinary landscape. (" Publishers Weekly.)

Lewis, Edna

★The **gift** of Southern cooking : recipes and revelations from two great Southern cooks / Edna Lewis and Scott Peacock. Alfred A. Knopf, 2003. xiv, 332 p. : **641.5973**

1. Cooking, American -- Southern style. 2. Recipes 3. Cookbooks.

ISBN 9780375400353

LC 2002073153

Includes index.

Virginian Edna Lewis and Alabama-born chef Scott Peacock provide 225 of their favorite Southern recipes, including pole beans simmered in pork stock, asparagus and scallion pie, and cornmeal crisps.

"If you care--and I mean really care--about coleslaw, pan-fried chicken, trout, greens simmered in pork stock and Southern-style ketchups, relishes and vinegars, this is a book you shouldn't be without." New York Times Book Review.

Lohman, Sarah

Eight flavors : the untold story of American cuisine / Sarah Lohman. Simon & Schuster, [2016] 280 p. **641.5973**

1. Food habits -- United States 2. Cooking, American 3. Flavor 4. Cooking 5. United States -- Social life and customs

ISBN 9781476753959

LC 2016040059

The young gastronomist formerly behind New York magazine's Grub Street food blog presents a culinary history of America that chronicles the diverse cultures that shaped the nation's cuisine, using long-forgotten recipes to explain how eight distinct flavors changed how we eat.

"A tantalizing look at flavors of the American table that foodies will absolutely devour." Kirkus.

McBride, Martina

Martina's kitchen mix : my recipe playlist for real life / Martina McBride. Oxmoor House, 2018. 271 p. : **641.5973**

1. Cooking, American. 2. Cookbooks.
ISBN 9780848757632

LC bl2018190482

Includes index.

The country music star shares recipes from her kitchen for meals, beverages, appetizers, and desserts, that feature fresh seasonal ingredients.

Moulton, Sara, 1952-

Sara Moulton's home cooking 101 : how to make everything taste better / Sara Moulton. Oxmoor House, 2016. 367 p. : **641.5973**

1. Cooking, American. 2. Recipes 3. Cookbooks.
ISBN 9780848744410

LC bl2016007835

Includes indexes.

Collects more than one hundred fifty recipes that exhibit the essentials of flavor and taste, including such offerings as tomato paella soup, grilled jerk pork, and spicy greens ravioli.

"Busy home cooks will find much to savor in this approachable, elegant collection of recipes." Publishers Weekly.

Rich, Sarah K.

Rich table / Sarah & Evan Rich ; with Carolyn Alburger ; recipe development by Kate Williams ; photographs by Alanna Hale. Chronicle Books, 2018 287 p. : **641.5973**

1. Rich Table (Restaurant). 2. Cooking, American. 3. Gourmet cooking 4. Cookbooks
ISBN 9781452156378

LC 2017036518

Includes index.

The owners of a well-known San Francisco restaurant present a collection of 86 recipes for some of their signature dishes, including porcini doughnuts with raclette dipping sauce, rabbit cannelloni with mustard, and lemon icebox pie.

Rombauer, Irma S., 1877-1962

★**Joy** of cooking / Irma S. Rombauer, Marion Rombauer Becker, Ethan Becker, John Becker, Megan Scott ; illustrations by John Norton ; papercuts by Anna Brones. Scribner, 2019. xliv, 1156 p. : **641.5973**

1. Cooking, American. 2. Cookbooks.
ISBN 9781501169717

LC bl2019032676

Revised and updated with more than 600 new recipes, a new edition of the classic cookbook, which has become a kitchen bible, combines classic recipes, new dishes and indispensable reference information for today's home cooks.

"In an era when thousands of recipes are at our fingertips online, this classic collection proves its worth as a source of dependable culinary guidance and reliable recipes; a first purchase." Library Journal.

★**Joy** of cooking / Irma S. Rombauer, Marion Rombauer Becker, Ethan Becker ; illustrated by John Norton. Scribner, c2006. xiii, 1132 p. : **641.5973**

1. Cooking, American 2. Cookbooks.
ISBN 9780743246262

LC 2006051231

75th anniversary ed.

Includes index.

A classic guide to American cooking features thousands of traditional recipes and five hundred new dishes, in a volume that includes an array of favorite casserole, dessert, and soup options.

Rosen, Ali

Bring it! : tried and true recipes for potlucks and casual entertaining / Ali Rosen ; photography by Noah Fecks. / Ali Rosen, Noah (PHT) Fecks. Running Press, 2018. 239 p. ; **641.5973**

1. Cooking, American. 2. Recipes 3. Quick and easy cooking 4. Seasonal cooking 5. Cookbooks.
ISBN 9780762462728

LC 2017955766

Presents advice about preparing foods for entertainment, discussing ingredients and serving sizes and providing a collection of recipes for appetizers, dips, salads, casseroles, main dishes, and desserts.

Sappington, Adam

Heartlandia : heritage recipes from the Country Cat / Adam and Jackie Sappington with Ashley Gartland ; photography by John Valls. Houghton Mifflin Harcourt, 2015 304 p. ; **641.5973**

1. Country Cat Dinner House & Bar (Portland, Ore.). 2. Cooking, American. 3. Recipes 4. Cookbooks.
ISBN 9780544363779

LC 2014036933

Includes index.

The owners of The Country Cat Dinner House & Bar shares recipes that reflect the flavor of Portland, including skillet-fried chicken, red-wine braised beef with wild mushroom steak sauce, and crispy fried oysters with smoky bacon and green apple ragout.

Selengut, Becky

How to taste : the curious cook's handbook to seasoning and balance, from umami to acid and beyond--with recipes / Becky Selengut. Sasquatch Books, 2018 xv, 223 p. ; **641.5973**

1. Cooking, American. 2. Flavor. 3. Cooking (Spices). 4. Recipes 5. Cookbooks.
ISBN 9781632171054

LC 2017041100

How to Taste outlines the underlying principles of taste, and then takes a deep dive into salt, acid, bitter, sweet, fat, umami, bite (heat), aromatics, and texture. You'll find out how temperature impacts your enjoyment of the dishes you make as does color, alcohol, and more. The handbook goes beyond telling home cooks what ingredients go well together or explaining cooking ratios. You'll learn how to adjust a dish that's too salty or too acidic and how to determine when something might be lacking. It also includes recipes and simple kitchen experiments that illustrate the importance of salt in a dish, or identifies whether you're a "supertaster" or not. Each recipe and experiment highlights the chapter's main lesson. How to Taste will ultimately help you feel confident about why and how various components of a dish are used to create balance, harmony, and deliciousness. --From publisher description.

"A wealth of accessible, practical information marks this as a singular achievement." Booklist.

Voltaggio, Bryan, 1976-

Home : recipes to cook with family and friends / Bryan Voltaggio, with Aki Kamozawa ; photography by Ed Anderson. Little, Brown and Company, 2015. ix, 257 p. : **641.5973**

1. Cooking, American. 2. Comfort food. 3. Recipes 4. Cookbooks.
ISBN 9780316323888

LC bl2015013413

Includes index.

A cookbook featuring distinctive adaptations of classic American comfort foods includes such offerings as lobster rolls, cheese grits, meat loaf, crab and artichoke dip, and maple-pecan tart.

"This is a celebrity chef cookbook that readers will want to use, not relegate to the coffee table." Library Journal.

Yeh, Molly

Molly on the range : recipes and stories from an unlikely life on a farm / Molly Yeh, creator of My name is Yeh. Rodale, 2016 xix, 283 p. : **641.5973**

1. Yeh, Molly Anecdotes. 2. Cooking, American. 3. Cooking, American -- Middle West 4. Seasonal cooking 5. Recipes 6. Cookbooks.

ISBN 9781623366957

Includes index.

The author and mega-blogger behind My Name is Yeh, shares recipes, stories and photos from her unlikely life on a Midwestern farm on the North Dakota/Minnesota border, where she learned intricate family recipes, threw picnics in the snow and created countless whimsical cakes in her farm kitchen.

Ziegelman, Jane

A **square** meal : a culinary history of the Great Depression / Jane Ziegelman and Andrew Coe. Harper, [2016] 336 p. **641.5973**

1. Cooking, American -- History -- 20th century. 2. Depressions -- 1929-1941 3. Crises -- United States -- History -- 20th century. 4. Social change -- United States -- History -- 20th century. 5. United States -- Social conditions -- 1933-1945. 6. United States -- Environmental conditions -- History -- 20th century.

ISBN 9780062216410

LC 2016016051

"Jane Ziegelman, author of the acclaimed 97 Orchard, and her husband, Andrew Coe, team up for an in-depth exploration of America's greatest food crisis".-- Provided by publisher.

641.5974 United States -- New England

Altiero, Kerry

The **best** comfort food on the planet / Kerry Altiero, chef/owner of Cafe Miranda in Rockland, Maine, with Katherine Gaudet ; photographs by Stacey Cramp. Page Street Publishing Co., 2018 240 p. : **641.5974**

1. Cafe Miranda (Rockland, Me.). 2. Comfort food 3. Comfort food. 4. Cooking, American. 5. Cookbooks.

ISBN 9781624146848

LC 2018945563

Includes index.

Originally published in 2014 as Adventures in comfort food.

Shares a collection of comfort food recipes with a twist that are served up at Rockland, Maine's Cafe Miranda, including such options as black bean soup, lobster mac 'n cheese, pot roast bleu, haddock enchilada, and oven-roasted fish tacos.

"Altieros instructions are clear, and his ingredient list for any recipe is kept simple. While the book is not for the health-minded cook (heavy cream is incorporated into 20 dishes), this is an exciting and inventive collection." Publishers Weekly.

Dojny, Brooke

The **New** England cookbook : 350 recipes from town and country, land and sea, hearth and home / Brooke Dojny ; illustrations by John MacDonald. Harvard Common Press, c1999. xvi, 652 p. ; **641.5974**

1. Cooking, American -- New England style. 2. Recipes 3. Cookbooks

ISBN 9781558321397

LC 99014393

Collects recipes that encompass a wide range of dishes, from oysters-on-the-half-shell to blackberry patch cobbled cobbler, with stories about the entire area included in sidebars.

"This volume includes traditional dishes as well as dozens of ethnic specialties from the various immigrant groups who have helped populate New England: Oregano-Scented Greek Lamb Shanks, Portuguese Tuna Escabeche, and Garlicky Mussels, Italian-style, to name a few." Library Journal.

Jennings, Matthew (Chef)

Homegrown : cooking from my New England roots / Matthew Jennings with Jessica Battilana. Artisan, 2017. 304 p. **641.5974**

1. Cooking, American -- New England style 2. Recipes 3. Cookbooks.

ISBN 9781579656744

LC 2016058708

A James Beard Award-nominated chef and culinary innovator, honoring the iconic New England foods of his heritage and celebrating fresh ingredients, presents a collection of 100 recipes that include modern spins on favorite recipes, including Classic Lobster Rolls, Clam and Corn Chowder, Boston Cream Whoopie Pies and more.

"His debut cookbook is a treasury of ingenious takes on New England and American classics, with some challenging but most well within reach." Library Journal.

Lundy, Ronni

Victuals : an Appalachian journey, with recipes / Ronni Lundy ; photographs by Johnny Autry. Clarkson Potter/Publishers, 2016. 256 p. **641.5974**

1. Cooking, American. 2. Cooking 3. Food -- History 4. Recipes 5. Appalachian Region -- Social life and customs.

ISBN 9780804186742

LC 2016013454

Victuals is an exploration of the foodways, people, and places of Appalachia. Written by Ronni Lundy, regarded as the most engaging authority on the region, the book guides us through the surprisingly diverse history--and vibrant present--of food in the Mountain South. Victuals explores the diverse and complex food scene of the Mountain South through recipes, stories, traditions, and innovations.

"Fans of locally sourced foods and Southern cooking will find a lot to like here, as Lundy does a terrific job of showcasing Appalachia's breadth and depth." Publishers Weekly.

Sewall, Jeremy

The **New** England kitchen : fresh takes on seasonal recipes / Jeremy Sewall & Erin Byers Murray ; photography by Michael Harlan Turkell. Rizzoli International Publications, 2014 255 p. : **641.5974**

1. Cooking, American -- New England style. 2. Recipes 3. Seasonal cooking 4. Cookbooks.

ISBN 9780789327475

LC 2014942046

Award-winning Boston chef Jeremy Sewall presents contemporary versions of New England classics that capture the flavors of this time-honored cuisine. In this first cookbook to explore contemporary New England fare, Jeremy Sewall adapts the region's fresh, simple flavors into refined dishes for the home cook. More than 100 delectable recipes highlight the area's celebrated farms and fisheries to incorporate distinct flavors throughout the year. For fall and winter, there are hearty dishes such as Maple-Brined Pork Rack with Apple and Leeks and Creamy Oyster Stew with Fennel. Dayboat Cod with Green Garlic Puree perfectly captures springtime, while summer brings the arrival of Sweet Corn, Bacon, and Crab Chowder and Hand-Dug Steamers with Bay Leaf and Thyme. Artful photographs illustrate thoughtful presentations for serving this satisfying food. There is a prep section demonstrating how to cook and eat a lobster, shuck oysters, and cure bacon. The book also includes profiles of a New England farmer, fishermen, and an artisanal beer brewer to capture the new revolutionary spirit. --From publisher description.

641.59747 Cooking--New York

Humm, Daniel

I [heart] New York : ingredients and recipes : a moment in New York cuisine / Daniel Humm and Will Guidara ; phtography by Francesco Tonelli. Ten Speed Press, 2013 511 p. : **641.59747**

1. Cooking, American. 2. Cooking -- New York (State) -- New York. 3. Local foods -- New York (State) -- New York. 4. Recipes 5. Cookbooks.

ISBN 9781607744405

LC 2012026491

Includes index.

Celebrates the food, ingredients, and culinary history of New York City while sharing innovative adaptations of classic New York recipes.

"Superb in both substance and scope, this collection offers a feast for the senses that will be savored at length." Publishers Weekly.

Humm, Daniel

The **NoMad** cookbook / Daniel Humm & Will Guidara ; photography by Francesco Tonelli ; desserts by Mark Welker. Ten Speed Press, 2015 317 p. : **641.59747**

1. NoMad Hotel (New York, N.Y.). 2. Cooking. 3. Recipes 4. Cookbooks

ISBN 1607748223

LC 2015007694

Includes index.

Includes map and book "The Nomad coctail book," Leo Robitscheck in pocket.

The chefs of The NoMad Hotel present a collection of recipes from their restaurant and bar, focusing on unique combinations of ingredients for snacks, appetizers, main dishes, desserts, and cocktails.

Phillips, Michael, 1969-

Chelsea Market cookbook : 100 recipes from New York's premier indoor food hall / Michael Phillips with Rick Rodgers ; photography by Jennifer May. Stewart, Tabori & Chang, 2013. 223 p. : **641.59747**

1. Chelsea Market (New York, N.Y.) 2. Cooking, American. 3. International cooking. 4. Recipes 5. Cookbooks

ISBN 9781617690372

LC 2013009924

Includes index.

Presents one hundred recipes from the fifteen-year-old New York City market compiled by vendors, local chefs, and food celebrities, along with anecdotes and tips on entertaining.

Ridge, Brent

The **Beekman** 1802 heirloom dessert cookbook : 100 delicious heritage recipes from the farm and garden / Brent Ridge and Josh Kilmer-Purcell and Sandy Gluck ; photography by Paulette Tavormina. Rodale, 2013 260 p. : **641.59747**

1. Cooking, American. 2. Desserts. 3. Recipes 4. Cookbooks.

ISBN 9781609615734

LC 2013010502

Includes index.

The founders of the upstate New York-based farm company share favorite eco-conscious, vintage-modern recipes collected from generations of their family, complementing such entries as Fourth of July Fruitcake and Hot Chocolate Dumplings with nostalgic personal stories.

Samuelsson, Marcus

★The **Red** Rooster Cookbook : the story of food and hustle in Harlem / Marcus Samuelsson ; photographs by Bobby Fisher ; foreword by Hilton Als ; text with April Reynolds ; recipes and text with Roy Finamore ; illustrations by Rebekah Maysles and Leon Johnson. Houghton Mifflin Harcourt, 2016 384 p. ; **641.59747**

1. Red Rooster (Restaurant). 2. International cooking. 3. Cooking -- New York (State) -- New York. 4. Food -- New York (State) -- New York. 5. Harlem (New York, N.Y.). 6. Cookbooks.

ISBN 9780544639775

LC 2016037226

"A Rux Martin Book."

Includes index.

A cookbook by the chef and owner of Red Rooster Harlem offers Southern comfort food and other multicultural recipes, including brown butter biscuits, killer collards, donuts with sweet potato cream, and Chinese steamed bass.

"Fisher's food and street photography colorfully captures the character of Samuelsson's dishes as well as the characters that inhabit his neighborhood." Publishers Weekly.

Taylor, Nicole A.

The **up** South cookbook : chasing Dixie in a Brooklyn kitchen / Nicole A. Taylor. The Countryman Press, 2015 235 p.; **641.59747**

1. Cooking, American -- Southern style. 2. Cooking -- New York City 3. Cookbooks.

ISBN 9781581573015

LC 2015018282

The podcast host of "Hot Grease" shares recipes for favorite Southern foods from her childhood adapted in the Brooklyn kitchen of her professional world, demonstrating how to achieve classic comfort with healthier ingredients.

641.5975 United States -- Southern

Acheson, Hugh

The **broad** fork : recipes for the wide world of vegetables and fruits / Hugh Acheson ; photographs by Rinne Allen. Clarkson Potter/Publishers, 2015 336 p. : **641.5975**

1. Cooking, American -- Southern style. 2. Seasonal cooking. 3. Farm produce. 4. Recipes 5. Cookbooks.

ISBN 9780385345026

LC 2014023531

Includes index.

Demystifies fifty fruits and vegetables by providing over two hundred seasonal recipes for such dishes as sweet potato gratin, salmon with ramps and peas, chanterelle and goat cheese tarts, and spaghetti squash caponata.

A **new** turn in the South : Southern flavors reinvented for your kitchen / Hugh Acheson. Clarkson Potter, c2011. 299 p. : **641.5975**

1. Cooking, American -- Southern style. 2. Cookbooks.
ISBN 9780307719553

LC 2010052632

Includes index.

Presents numerous recipes for modern dishes based on elements of traditional southern cooking.

Brock, Sean

★**Heritage** / Sean Brock ; with contributions by Marion Sullivan and Jeff Allen ; photgraphs by Peter Frank Edwards. Artisan, 2014 335 p. : **641.5975**

1. Cooking, American -- Southern style. 2. Recipes 3. Cookbooks.
ISBN 9781579654634

LC 2014005022

Includes index.

The chef of Husk collects recipes that showcase Southern food and culture with dishes that include lobster with parsnip puree, leeks braised with orange and vadouvan jus, brown oyster stew with benne, and slow-cooked pork shoulder with tomato gravy, creamed corn, and roasted baby vidalias.

"The recipes (e.g., butter-bean chowchow; pork belly with herbed farro, pickled elderberries, chanterelles, and sumac; buttermilk pie with cornmeal crust) range from simple to sophisticated, and some call for unusual preparations. Within chapters, Brock profiles producers who supply his restaurants, explains various ingredient categories, and touches on topics from industrial agriculture to the origins of bourbon to 19th-century books on food and drink." Library Journal.

South : essential recipes and new explorations / Sean Brock, with Lucas Weir and Marion Sullivan ; photographs by Peter Frank Edwards. Artisan, 2019 374 p. : **641.5975**

1. Cooking, American -- Southern States 2. Seasonal cooking 3. Recipes 4. Cookbooks.
ISBN 9781579657161

LC 2019016960

Includes index.

An award-winning chef, cookbook author, Nashville restauranteur and Southern cuisine promoter shares his mix-and-match component recipes for grits, fried chicken, collard greens, corn bread, tomato okra stew and buttermilk biscuits.

"Brimming with exquisite interpretations of Southern cooking, this is a great collection for intermediate to advanced cooks looking to broaden their culinary repertoire." Library Journal

Brule, Jennifer

Learn to cook 25 Southern classics 3 ways : traditional, contemporary, international / Jennifer Brule. The University of North Carolina Press, 2016 xvi, 228 p. : **641.5975**

1. Cooking, American -- Southern style. 2. Cookbooks.
ISBN 9781469629124

LC 2016012031

Includes index.

Offers variations on traditional American Southern recipes and step-by-step instructions for basic cooking techniques.

"An ingenious cookbook that will appeal to cooks of all stripes." Booklist.

Buffett, Lucy Anne

Gumbo love : recipes for Gulf Coast cooking, entertaining, and savoring the good life / Lucy Buffett ; foreword by Thomas McGuane. Grand Central Life & Style, 2017. xxxi, 303 p. : **641.5975**

1. Cooking, American -- Southern style. 2. Cooking -- Gulf States. 3. Recipes 4. Cookbooks.
ISBN 9781455566440

LC 2016056560

Includes index.

Presents recipes that draw upon such cooking styles as Cajun, Old Florida, Caribbean, and Mexican, including shrimp fritters, muffuletta salad, and Key West tuna burger.

"Restaurateur Buffett (Lulus Kitchen) packs Gumbo Love with stories and recipes reflecting her love of the Gulf Coast." Publishers Weekly.

Castle, Sheri

The **Southern** Living community cookbook : celebrating food & fellowship in the American South / Sheri Castle. Oxmoor House, 2014 319 p. : **641.5975**

1. Cooking, American -- Southern style. 2. Cookbooks.
ISBN 9780848743543

LC bl2014043254

Includes index.

Brings together the best recipes from Southern hometown cooks, including Mom's signature pot roast, cream of peanut soup, and hummingbird cake.

Christensen, Ashley

Poole's : recipes and stories from a modern diner / Ashley Christensen with Kaitlyn Goalen ; photography by Johnny Autry. Ten Speed Press, 2016 vii, 295 p. : **641.5975**

1. Poole's (Restaurant). 2. Cooking, American -- Southern style. 3. Recipes 4. Cookbooks.
ISBN 9781607746874

LC 2016018885

Includes index.

Teaches home cooks how to make the best foundational recipes and then turn them into exceptional sides, mains, and desserts, with recipes from the celebrated Southern restaurant, Poole's Downtown Diner.

"Mouthwatering Southern foods beckon to readers from the pages of this attractive restaurant cookbook, which recalls other excellent titles such as Frank Stitt's Southern Table. Highly recommended." Library Journal.

Cobbs, Katherine,

Southern Living 2018 annual recipes : an entire year of recipes! / executive editor: Katherine Cobbs ; project editor: Lacie Pinyan. Oxmoor House, 2018. 368 p. : **641.5975**

1. Cooking, American -- Southern style. 2. Recipes 3. Cookbooks.
ISBN 9780848757601

LC bl2018196421

Includes indexes.

Collects every recipe published in 2018, sharing easy-to-follow instructions for an array of everyday and special-occasion meals complemented by cooking and preparation times.

Currence, John

Pickles, pigs & whiskey : recipes from my three favorite food groups (and then some) / John Currence ; foreplay by John T. Edge ; photography by Angie Mosier. Andrew McMeel Publishing, 2013 259 p. : **641.5975**

1. Cooking, American -- Southern style. 2. Cooks -- Anecdotes. 3. Recipes 4. Cookbooks.
ISBN 9781449428808

LC 2013940033

Includes index.

Presents 130 Southern-style recipes, divided by ten different cooking techniques, and includes recipes for such dishes as pickled sweet potatoes, rabbit cacciatore, bourbon-braised pork cheeks, and cayenne-praline ice cream.

"Recipes for mint julep redux, deep South ramen with fried poached eggs, hill country cioppino, and bourbon-pecan pie with tonka bean ice cream, showcase some of the most exciting trends in Southern food and drink." Library Journal.

Edge, John T.

The **potlikker** papers : a food history of the modern South 1955-2015 / John T. Edge. Penguin Press, 2017. 384 p. **641.5975**

1. Food 2. Food habits 3. Cooking, American -- Southern style 4. Cooking, American -- Southern States 5. Southern States -- Politics and government -- 1951- 6. Southern States -- Social conditions
ISBN 9781594206559

LC 2016029615

Describes how the culinary traditions of the poor, rural South played a large part in the region's revitalization and renaissance, eventually becoming incorporated into the gentrification and artesian renaissance that gave rise to popular figures in Southern food, from Paul Prudhomme to Craig Claiborne.

"Edge's research and command of prose make this a necessary history." Booklist.

Foose, Martha Hall

★**Screen** doors and sweet tea : recipes and tales from a Southern cook / Martha Hall Foose. Clarkson Potter/Publishers, 2008. vii, 248 p. : **641.5975**

1. Cooking, American -- Southern style 2. Recipes 3. Cooking -- Anecdotes 4. Southern States -- Social life and customs
ISBN 9780307351401

LC 2007031646

Includes index.

A noted chef and raconteur celebrates the people, landscape, and traditions of America's South in a cookbook that presents Southern food with a contemporary twist in more than 150 original recipes for creative dishes that range from Sweet Potato Soup to Sweet Tea Pie, accompanied by personal anecdotes, cooking shortcuts and variations, and tips on ingredients, preparation techniques, storage, and more.

"As much fun to read as it will be to cook from, this is highly recommended." Library Journal.

A **Southerly** course : recipes & stories from close to home / Martha Hall Foose. Clarkson Potter, c2011. 256 p. : **641.5975**

1. Cooking, American -- Southern style. 2. Recipes 3. Cookbooks
ISBN 9780307464286

LC 2010022969

Includes index.

The author reflects on the role of food in her life while observing the dynamic nature of Southern foodways, in a volume that includes personal anecdotes and recipes that incorporate locally grown ingredients.

"Offering meditations on subjects like congealed salads and family china, Foose has all the savvy of a local tour guide, leading the way through her native state with poetry and wit." Publishers Weekly.

Franklin, Sara B.,

Edna Lewis : at the table with an American original / edited by Sara B. Franklin. The University of North Carolina Press, 2018 xi, 259 p. : **641.5975**

1. Lewis, Edna. 2. African American cooks. 3. Cookbooks -- History and criticism. 4. Cooking, American -- Southern style.
ISBN 9781469638553

LC 2017036473

"Edna Lewis (1916-2006) wrote some of America's most resonant, evocative, and significant cookbooks ever, including the now classic The Taste of Country Cooking. Lewis cooked and wrote first as a means to explore her memories of childhood on a farm in Freetown, Virginia, a community originally founded by freed black families. Later, she wrote to commemorate and document the seasonal richness of southern foodways ... She moved from the rural South to New York City, where she became a chef and a political activist, and eventually returned to the South. Her reputation as a trailblazer in the revival of regional cooking and as a progenitor of the farm-to-table movement only continues to burgeon."-- Provided by publisher.

Gaines, Joanna, 1978-

★**Magnolia** Table : a collection of recipes for gathering / Joanna Gaines with Marah Stets ; photography by Amy Neunsinger. William Morrow, 2018 328 p. : **641.5975**

1. Cooking, American -- Southern style. 2. Cooking, American -- Southwestern style. 3. Recipes 4. Seasonal cooking 5. Cookbooks.
ISBN 9780062820150

LC 2018438643

Includes index.

Jo Gaines believes there's no better way to celebrate family and friendship than through the art of togetherness, celebrating tradition, and sharing a great meal. She provides 125 classic recipes -- from breakfast, lunch, and dinner to small plates, snacks, and desserts -- presenting a modern selection of American classics, personal family favorites, and comfort food from the couple's new restaurant, Magnolia Table. Complemented by her love for her garden, these dishes also incorporate homegrown, seasonal produce at the peak of its flavor. Dishes include fried chicken with sticky poppy seed jam, white Cheddar bisque, peach caprese, and lemon pie.

Hall, Carla

★**Carla** Hall's soul food : everyday and celebration / Carla Hall with Genevieve Ko. Harper Wave, 2018 x, 322 p. : **641.5975**

1. African American cooking. 2. Cooking, American -- Southern style. 3. Recipes 4. Cookbooks
ISBN 9780062669834

LC 2018020071

Includes index.

Presents a collection of recipes inspired by traditional African American cooking, including flaky buttermilk biscuits, grilled okra with spiced sprinkle, black-eyed pea salad with hot sauce vinaigrette, and oxtail stew with brown sauce.

Hesser, Amanda

Food52 : a new way to dinner : a playbook of recipes and strategies for the week ahead / Amanda Hesser & Merrill Stubbs ; photography by James Ransom. Ten Speed Press, 2016 279 p. : **641.5975**

1. Cooking, American. 2. Seasonal cooking. 3. Dinners and dining.

4. Recipes 5. Cookbooks.
ISBN 9780399578007

LC 2016022690

Includes index.

Presents meal plans, shopping lists, and recipes for weekly meals using fresh ingredients for each season of the year.

Howard, Vivian (Vivian S.), 1978-

Deep Run roots : stories and recipes from my corner of the South / Vivian Howard. Little, Brown, 2016. 576 p. **641.5975**

1. Howard, Vivian (Vivian S.), 1978- 2. Cooking 3. Local foods 4. Cooking, American -- North Carolina 5. Recipes 6. North Carolina -- Social life and customs 7. Southern States -- Social life and customs
ISBN 9780316381109

LC 2016931447

As much a storybook as it is a cookbook, Deep Run roots imparts the true tale of Southern food: rooted in family and tradition, yet calling out to the rest of the world.

Jordan, Christy

Sweetness : Southern recipes to celebrate the warmth, the love, and the blessings of a full life / Christy Jordan. Workman Publishing, 2016. ix, 294 p. : **641.5975**

1. Cooking, American -- Southern style. 2. Desserts. 3. Recipes 4. Cookbooks.
ISBN 9780761189428

LC 2016040308

"Published simultaneously in Canada by Thomas Allen & Son Limited".

"What is sweetness? It's life: Memories made in our parents' and grandparents' kitchens. Welcoming guests with an open heart. And it's food: Passing slices of old-fashioned Peach Buttermilk Pie around the table. Greeting kids after school with Chocolate Chip Dream Bars. Laughing together over glasses of cold Sweet Tea on the front porch. Christy Jordan is the doyenne of Southern cooking for a new generation. Talk about soul-satisfying: Love at First Bite Brown Sugar Bars. Icebox Oatmeal Cookies. Gooey Cherry Bars. Mama Reed's Jam Cake. Chocolate Chess Pie. Plus decadent ice cream toppings, refreshing fruit salads, candies (including three kinds of fudge!), spiced nuts, floats, punches, and more. Life is sweet--cultivate it, savor it, share it, celebrate it.

"Filled with family stories and cheerful advice, this cookbook is a reasonably priced volume of easy-to-make sweets." Library Journal.

Lee, Edward, 1972-

Smoke & pickles : recipes and stories from a new Southern kitchen / Edward Lee. Artisan, 2013 xi, 292 p. : **641.5975**

1. Cooking, American -- Southern style. 2. Recipes 3. Cookbooks.
ISBN 9781579654924

LC 2012039653

Includes index.

A Korean-American chef offers his take on Southern cooking, including chicken-fried pork steak with ramen crust and buttermilk pepper gravy, collards and kimchi, and miso-smothered chicken.

"An irresistible collection for any adventurous home cook." Publishers Weekly.

Lee, Matt

The **Lee** Bros. Charleston kitchen / Matt Lee and Ted Lee. Clarkson Potter, c2012. 256 p. **641.5975**

1. Cooking, American -- Southern style. 2. Cities and towns -- Southern States. 3. Brothers 4. Family businesses. 5. Charleston, South Carolina. 6. Southern States -- Social life and customs
ISBN 9780307889737

LC 2012013331

Includes index.

A celebration of the storied cuisines of Charleston, South Carolina, provides 100 regionally inspired recipes by the James Beard Award-winning authors of The Lee Bros. Southern Cookbook, including Flounder in Parchment With Shaved Vegetables, Hugenot Torte and Shrimp and Grits.

"The brothers also provide two excellent addendums: a comprehensive bibliography of Charleston cookbooks dating back to 1756 and directions for a walking or driving tour featuring eateries from which many of their recipes were derived." Publishers Weekly.

Lewis, Edna

In pursuit of flavor / Edna Lewis, with Mary Goodbody ; foreword by Mashama Bailey ; illustrated by Louisa Jones Waller. Alfred A. Knopf, 2019. 354 p. **641.5975**

1. Cooking, American -- Southern States 2. Food habits 3. Food preparation
ISBN 9780525655510

LC 2018035278

Includes index.

Originally published: New York : Knopf, 1988.

Decades before cornbread, shrimp and grits, and peach cobbler were mainstays on menus everywhere, Edna Lewis was pioneering the celebration of seasonal food as a distinctly American cuisine. In this James Beard Foundation Cookbook Hall of Fame-inducted cookbook, Miss Lewis (as she was almost universally known) shares the recipes of her childhood, spent in a Virginia farming community founded by her grandfather and his friends after emancipation, as well as those that made her one of the most revered American chefs of all time.

Lewis, Edna

★The **taste** of country cooking / Edna Lewis. Knopf, 2006, c1976. xxi, 268 p. : **641.5975**

1. Cooking, American -- Virginia. 2. Recipes 3. Freetown, Virginia -- History. 4. Cookbooks.
ISBN 9780307265609

LC bl2006018974

Includes index.

A special thirtieth anniversary edition of the classic guide to Southern cookery features recipes for specific dishes and entire meals based on the culinary traditions of the author's Virginia Piedmont farming village, originally settled by freed slaves, interspersed with reminiscences of the author's childhood.

Link, Donald

Down south : bourbon, pork, gulf shrimp & second helpings of everything / Donald Link with Paula Disbrowe ; photographs by Chris Granger. Clarkson Potter, 2014 256 p. : **641.5975**

1. Cooking, American -- Southern style. 2. Cooking, Cajun. 3. Recipes 4. Cookbooks
ISBN 9780770433185

LC 2013020280

A celebrated New Orleans chef presents a culturally evocative collection of Southern and Cajun recipes that reflect classic regional flavors, from slow-cooked pork barbecue from Memphis to single-barrel bourbon from Kentucky.

Lynch, Lazarus

★**Son** of a Southern chef: cook with soul / Lazarus Lynch photography ; by Anisha Sisodia. Avery, 2019 288 p.: **641.5975**

1. Cooking, American -- Southern style. 2. Recipes 3. Cookbooks.
ISBN 9780525534174

LC 2018059322

Includes index.

Presents a collection of recipes which include new versions of favorite classic Southern dishes, including hot catfish sandwich with ranch sauce, jerk-spiced grilled corn with coconut confetti, brown stew chicken, and curried shrimp and okra.

"With a personality and presence as bold as his food, Lynch, a two-time winner of Food Network's Chopped, here offers a bevy of dishes with Southern roots." Publishers Weekly

Neely, Patrick

Down home with the Neelys : a Southern family cookbook / Patrick Neely and Gina Neely ; with Paula Disbrowe. Alfred A. Knopf, 2009. ix, 278 p. : **641.5975**

1. Cooking, American -- Southern style. 2. Barbecuing. 3. Recipes 4. Cookbooks.
ISBN 9780307269942

LC 2008054393

Includes index.

"This is a Borzoi book"--T.p. verso.

Collects over 120 southern style recipes and cooking secrets, from adding barbeque sauce to spaghetti and nachos to molasses-baked beans and a kitchen sink omelet.

"This cookbook written by husband-and-wife television personalities with their own Tennessee chain of barbecue joints...[is] full of 120 recipes that pull back the curtain on their award-winning seasonings, sauce, and fixings. Emphasizing their personal story and family recipes, this cookbook is brimming with down-home personality...and dishes that are simple, stylish, and not too fussy." Publishers Weekly.

Roahen, Sara

The **Southern** Foodways Alliance community cookbook / edited by Sara Roahen and John T. Edge. University of Georgia Press, c2010. xv, 285 p. : **641.5975**

1. Cooking, American -- Southern style. 2. Recipes 3. Cookbooks
ISBN 9780820332758

LC 2010011415

"Published in association with The Southern Foodways Alliance at the Center for the Study of Southern Culture at the University of Mississippi."

Includes indexes.

Including more than 170 tested recipes, this cookbook is a true reflection of southern foodways and the people, regardless of residence or birthplace, who claim this food as their own. Traditional and adapted, fancy and unapologetically plain, these recipes are powerful expressions of collective identity. There is something from -- and something for --everyone. The recipes and the stories that accompany them came from academics, writers, catfish farmers, ham curers, attorneys, toqued chefs, and people who just like to cook -- spiritual Southerners of myriad ethnicities, origins, and culinary skill levels. --From publisher description.

"Recommended for readers interested in the South." Library Journal.

Stone, Robyn, 1972-

Add a Pinch cookbook : easier, faster, fresher southern classics / Robyn Stone ; foreword by Ree Drummond. Clarkson Potter/ Publishers, 2017 240 p. : **641.5975**

1. Cooking, American -- Southern style. 2. Cooking, American -- Southern States 3. Quick and easy cooking 4. Cookbooks.
ISBN 9780553496413

LC 2016044983

Includes index.

A blogger who was featured in Southern Living magazine offers 100 traditional Southern recipes that have been reworked to be faster and healthier including Southern Buttermilk Fried Chicken, Pepper Jelly Pork Medallions, Weeknight Chicken Pot Pie and Buttermilk Praline Cheesecake.

Van Beuren, Alexe

The **B.T.C.** Old-Fashioned Grocery cookbook : recipes and stories from a Southern revival / Alexe van Beuren ; with recipes by Dixie Grimes. Clarkson Potter/Publishers, 2014 239 p. : **641.5975**

1. B.T.C. Old-Fashioned Grocery. 2. Cooking, American -- Southern style. 3. Recipes 4. Water Valley, Miss. -- Social life and customs. 5. Cookbooks
ISBN 9780385345002

LC 2013019690

Includes index.

Documents how a simple grocery and prepared foods store empowered community life in a crumbling Mississippi town, and shares 120 of the establishment's best recipes that range from shrimp and sweet corn chowder to peach pound cake.

"Water Valley, Miss., is a small, rural village saved from obscurity by being just 25 minutes from the campus town of Oxford, and by being fortunate enough to be the home of chef Grimes and self-made business woman van Beuren. Van Beuren's unadorned prose keeps the character studies pure, with a refreshingly minimal amount of folksiness, while Grimes's 120 recipes alternate between classic and surprising." Publishers Weekly.

Willis, Virginia, 1966-

Bon appetit, y'all : recipes and stories from three generations of Southern cooking / Virginia Willis ; photography by Ellen Silverman. Ten Speed Press, c2008. vii, 312 p. : **641.5975**

1. Cooking, American -- Southern style. 2. Recipes 3. Cookbooks
ISBN 9781580088534

LC 2008009233

Includes index.

Two divergent influences--Southern cooking and French cuisine--come together in Bon Appetit, Y'all, a modern Southern chef's passionate and utterly appealing homage to her culinary roots. --From publisher description.

"Magnificent color photos; detailed, helpful tips; and Willis's cheerful, trustworthy guidance make this an original and welcome newcomer to a classic cookbook library." Publishers Weekly.

641.5976 United States -- South Central

Besh, John

My New Orleans : the cookbook : 200 of my favorite recipes & stories from my hometown / John Besh. Andrews McMeel Universal, c2009. 374 p. : **641.5976**

1. Cooking, American -- New Orleans, Louisiana 2. Cooking, American -- Louisiana 3. Cooking, Creole. 4. Cooking, Cajun. 5. New Orleans, Louisiana -- Social life and customs. 6. Cookbooks.
ISBN 9780740784132

LC 2009920846

Includes index.

A Southern chef offers an introduction to the cooking of New Orleans, with over two hundred recipes, descriptions of traditional ingredients, as well as a discussion of the social customs of the city and his own family history.

Chase, Leah

The **Dooky** Chase cookbook / Leah Chase. Pelican Pub. Co., 1990. 224 p. : **641.5976**

1. Dooky Chase (Restaurant) 2. Cooking, American -- Louisiana style. 3. Cooking, Creole. 4. Recipes 5. Cookbooks

ISBN 9780882896618

LC 89048272

Includes index.

"The Dooky Chase Restaurant is a New Orleans landmark, famous for Chase's down-home Creole cooking. She offers her favorite recipes here, from Crab Soup and Crawfish Etouffee to Squirrel Pie and Stewed Snapper Turtle, and includes lively reminiscences of her childhood and restaurant experiences." Library Journal

Link, Donald

Real Cajun : rustic home cooking from Donald Link's Louisiana / Donald Link ; with Paula Disbrowe ; photographs by Chris Granger. Clarkson Potter /Publishers, c2009. 255 p. : **641.5976**

1. Cochon Restaurant (New Orleans, La.) 2. Cooking, American -- Louisiana style. 3. Cooking, Cajun. 4. Recipes 5. Cookbooks

ISBN 9780307395818

LC 2008036989

Includes index.

A well-known New Orleans chef presents an introduction to traditional Cajun cooking, along with a collection of recipes for seafood, meat, poultry, side, and vegetable dishes, and desserts.

"Link shares the fare he ate growing up on the bayou, as well as what he cooks for family, friends and funerals. Some recipes are aspirationally insanefried chicken and andouille gumbo, or game day choucroute with sausage, tasso and duck confitwhile others I simply aspire to make, like a fried oyster and bacon sandwich (bacon recipe included), and Link's outstanding boudin, which he also uses as a heart-stopping beignet filling. The tone is easygoing, the explanations clear." New York Times Book Review.

Thompson-Anderson, Terry, 1946-

Texas on the table : people, places, and recipes celebrating the flavors of the Lone Star State / Terry Thompson-Anderson ; photos by Sandy Wilson. University of Texas Press, 2014. xi, 452 p. : **641.5976**

1. Cooking -- Texas. 2. Cooking, American -- Southwestern style. 3. Recipes 4. Cookbooks

ISBN 9780292744097

LC 2013048386

Includes indexes.

Shares a collection of new and classic Texan recipes, ranging from soups and first courses to meat and vegetarian dinners, complemented by stories of the farmers, cheesemakers, and others who are changing the face of Texas cuisine.

Toups, Isaac

Chasing the gator : Isaac Toups and the new Cajun cooking / Isaac Toups and Jennifer V. Cole ; photography by Denny Culbert. Little, Brown and Company, 2018. 237 p. : **641.5976**

1. Cooking, American -- Louisiana style. 2. Cooking, Cajun. 3. Cooking, Creole -- Louisiana style. 4. Cookbooks.

ISBN 9780316465779

LC bl2018190282

Includes index.

Collects recipes that showcase the foods of the Louisiana bayou, including such dishes as hog backbone stew, boiled crawfish, pickled quail eggs, French bread-fried oysters, and smoked duck gumbo.

641.5977 United States -- Midwest

Brownson, JeanMarie

Dinner at home : 140 recipes to enjoy with family and friends / JeanMarie Brownson. Surrey Books, 2015. 282 p. : **641.5977**

1. Cooking, American -- Midwestern style. 2. Recipes 3. Cookbooks.

ISBN 9781572841789

LC 2015031410

Includes index.

"Recipes for home cooking from Chicago Tribune food columnist".-- Provided by publisher.

Sever, Shauna

Midwest made : big, bold baking from the heartland / Shauna Sever ; photographs by Paul Strabbing. Running Press, 2019. 318 p. : **641.5977**

1. Baking. 2. Cooking, American -- Midwestern style. 3. Recipes 4. Cookbooks.

ISBN 9780762464500

LC bl2019034670

Includes index.

When it comes to defining what we know as all-American baking, everything from Bundt cakes to brownies have roots that can be traced to the great Midwest. German, Scandinavian, Polish, French, and Italian immigrant families baked their way to the American Midwest, instilling in it pies, breads, cookies, and pastries that manage to feel distinctly home-grown.

Thielen, Amy

The **New** Midwestern table : 200 heartland recipes / Amy Thielen. Clarkson Potter Publisher, 2013 399 p. : **641.5977**

1. Cooking, American. 2. Cooking, American -- Middle West 3. Food habits -- Middle West 4. Seasonal cooking 5. Cookbooks.

ISBN 9780307954879

LC 2012047058

Includes index.

Applies the author's professional expertise as gleaned from work under such chefs as David Bouley and Shea Gallante to classic Midwestern dishes from her childhood, demonstrating how to best enjoy simple heritage fare that is plentiful, affordable and seasonal.

641.5978 United States -- Western

Rollins, Kent

A **taste** of cowboy : ranch recipes and tales from the trail / Kent Rollins with Shannon Keller Rollins ; photographs by Shannon Keller Rollins. Houghton Mifflin Harcourt, 2015 248 p. : **641.5978**

1. Cooking, American -- Western style. 2. Recipes 3. Cookbooks.

ISBN 9780544275003

LC 2014036936

"A Rux Martin book."
Includes index.

Accompanied by entertaining stories and poetry, an authentic cowboy and TV veteran presents a guide to comfort food that gets creative with pantry ingredients to create such dishes as Sweet Heat Chopped Barbecue Sandwiches and Bread Pudding With Whisky Cream Sauce.

"Though Rollins offers sage advice on choosing and caring for cast-iron cookware, readers won't need to worry about building a fire, since these recipes have been adjusted to allow followers to recreate cowboy fare in the comfort of their own kitchens. However, Rollins remains true to his methods by incorporating a wide variety of boxed, canned, and prepared ingredients such as creamed soups and processed cheese. Rollins's campfire stories and DIY cures for ailments such as arthritis (honey in your coffee) and spider bites (tape a penny on it) give warmth and personality to a book that even city slickers will enjoy spending time with." Publishers Weekly.

641.5979 United States -- Pacific Slope

Balla, Nicolaus, 1977-

★**Bar** Tartine : techniques & recipes / Nicolaus Balla and Cortney Burns ; with Jan Newberry ; photographs by Chad Robertson. Chronicle Books, 2014 366 p. : **641.5979**

1. Bar Tartine (San Francisco, Calif.). 2. Cooking, American -- California style. 3. Recipes 4. Cookbooks.

ISBN 9781452126463

LC 2014011157

Collects recipes from the California restaurant reflecting the cuisines of Central Europe, Japan, and Scandinavia for a range of dishes from soups to salads, to shared plates and sweets, with a section on cooking techniques.

"Many of these techniques are doable for home cooks, though it's hard to imagine amateurs making their own bottarga (which involves drying cured sacs of fish roe for five to seven weeks)." Library Journal.

Brioza, Stuart

State Bird Provisions : a cookbook / Stuart Brioza + Nicole Krasinski ; with JJ Goode. Ten Speed Press, 2017. 375 p. ; **641.5979**

1. State Bird Provisions (Restaurant). 2. Cooking, American -- California style. 3. Cookbooks.

ISBN 9781607748441

LC 2017026602

Includes index.

"The debut cookbook from one of the country's most celebrated and pioneering restaurants, Michelin-starred State Bird Provisions in San Francisco. Few restaurants have taken the nation by storm in the way that State Bird Provisions has. Inspired by their years catering parties, chefs Stuart Brioza and Nicole Krasinski use dim sum style carts to offer guests small but finely crafted dishes ranging from Potato Chips with Cre||me Fraiche and Cured Trout Roe, to Black Butter-Balsamic Figs with Wagon Wheel Cheese Fondue, to their famous savory pancakes (such as Chanterelle Pancakes with Lardo and Maple Vinegar), along with a menu of more substantial dishes such as their signature fried quail with stewed onions. Their singular and original approach to cooking, which expertly blends seemingly disparate influences, flavors, and textures, is a style that has influenced other restaurants throughout the country and is beloved by diners, chefs, and critics alike. In the debut cookbook from this acclaimed restaurant, Brioza and Krasinski share recipes for their most popular dishes along with stunning photography, and inspire readers to craft an unforgettable meal of textures, temperatures, aromas, and colors that excite all of the senses".-- Provided by publisher.

"This earnest debut book... has all the elements of a great restaurant cookbook: artful photographs, enlightening recipes, and a compelling story of triumph in the face of hardship." Library Journal.

Centeno, Josef

Ama : a modern Tex-Mex kitchen / Josef Centeno & Betty Hallock ; photographs by Ren Fuller. Chronicle Books, 2019 272 p. : **641.5979**

1. Cooking, Mexican American 2. Cooking, American -- Southwestern style. 3. Recipes 4. Cookbooks

ISBN 9781452155869

LC 2018052019

Includes index.

A San Antonio native and Los Angeles chef and restauranteur introduces Tex-Mex, a cuisine that combines the deep traditions of Texan and Mexican cooking, in this collection of more than 100 recipes that celebrate down-home cooking and grilling at its most inspiring. Illustrations.

Dixon, Kirsten

The **Tutka** Bay Lodge cookbook : coastal cuisine from the wilds of Alaska / with Kirsten Dixon and Mandy Dixon ; food photography by Tyrone Potgieter. Alaska Northwest Books, 2014 224 p. : **641.5979**

1. Tutka Bay Lodge (Alaska). 2. Cooking, American -- Pacific Northwest style. 3. Cooking -- Alaska. 4. Cookbooks.

ISBN 9781941821152

LC 2014017785

Includes index.

In personal stories, evocative photographs, and recipes that are purposefully simple and designed for the home cook, Chef Kirsten Dixon and her family share fresh, rustic cuisine offering friendship, communicating passion, and bringing comfort and delight to the table.This recipe collection represents the cuisine at Tutka Bay Lodge, the Dixons' seaside lodge nestled within the curve of a quiet cove at the entrance to Tutka Bay, a deep seven-mile fjord in Kachemak Bay, Alaska. In old-world tradition, Kirsten Dixon's family works together to craft a lifestyle that centers around three themes: the natural world, their culinary lives, and living a life of adventure. The cookbook is organized by sections for breakfast, lunch, appetizers, dinner, and the Cooking School at Tutka Bay. Among the one hundred recipes are Brioche Doughnuts with Cider Black Currant Marmalade, Hot-Smoked Salmon Croquettes, Grilled Oysters with Salmon Bacon and Pernod, Braised Short Rib Ravioli, and Wild Berry Chocolate Shortcake. --From publisher description.

Erickson, Renee

A **boat,** a whale, and a walrus : a year of menus / Renee Erickson with Jess Thomson. Sasquatch Books, [2014] 304 p. **641.5979**

1. Cooking 2. Seafood 3. Cooking (Seafood) 4. Women cooks

ISBN 9781570619267

LC 2014021808

The chef and owner of such popular Seattle restaurants as the Narwhal Oyster Truck and the Boat Street Café shares seasonal menus for entertaining, combining culinary traditions from the Puget Sound region and France with reminiscences about her youth and restaurant experiences.

"If a trip to Seattle isn't possible, this book provides the next best way to enjoy Erickson's beautiful seafood." Library Journal.

Jamison, Cheryl Alters

The **border** cookbook : authentic home cooking of the American Southwest and Northern Mexico / Cheryl Alters Jamison and Bill Jamison. Harvard Common Press, c1995. xii, 500 p. : **641.5979**

1. Cooking, American -- Southwestern style. 2. Cooking, Mexican. 3. Recipes 4. Cookbooks.
ISBN 9781558321038

LC 95010799

Includes indexes.

Gathers recipes for salsas, tacos, tortillas, rice, beans, soups, stews, seafood, game, and desserts.

Kinch, David, 1961-

Manresa : an edible reflection / David Kinch with Christine Muhlke ; photography by Eric Wolfinger. Ten Speed Press, 2013. 327 p. : **641.5979**

1. Manresa (Restaurant). 2. Cooking, American -- California style. 3. Recipes 4. Cookbooks.
ISBN 9781607743972

LC 2013016098

Includes index.

Collects recipes made famous by the restaurant Manresa, including pork belly with green tomato verjus, garden veloute with mustard cream, rooster in zinfandel, and local milk panna cotta with abalone.

Moore, Russell (Chef)

This is Camino / Russell Moore + Alison Hopelain with Chris Colin and Maria Zizka ; photographs by Yoko Takahashi. Ten Speed Press, 2015 258 p. : **641.5979**

1. Camino (Restaurant). 2. Cooking, American -- California style. 3. Cooking -- California 4. Recipes 5. Cookbooks.
ISBN 9781607747284

LC 2015013757

Includes index.

An introduction to the fire-based cooking approach and ingredient-centric philosophy of San Francisco's Camino restaurant features such recipes as grilled king salmon, grilled duck wing confit, and slow-cooked lamb shoulder.

"A compelling look at an innovative restaurant. Aspiring chefs and advanced cooks may also enjoy Suzanne Goin's The A.O.C. Cookbook and Nancy Silverton's The Mozza Cookbook (also from California restaurants)." Library Journal.

Prueitt, Elisabeth M

Tartine all day : modern recipes for the home cook / Elisabeth Prueitt ; with Jessica Washburn and Maria Zizka , Photographs by Paige Green. Lorena Jones Books, 2017 373 p. : **641.5979**

1. Tartine (Bakery). 2. Cooking, American -- California style. 3. Recipes 4. Cookbooks
ISBN 9780399578823

LC 2016049912

"Lorena Jones books."

"An all-purpose, comprehensive cookbook with 225 recipes for the whole-foods way people want to eat and bake at home today, from James Beard Award-winning and best-selling author Elisabeth Prueitt, cofounder of San Francisco's acclaimed Tartine Bakery. In 1993, Elisabeth Prueitt and Chad Robertson opened Tartine Bakery in a modest storefront in the heart of San Francisco's Mission District and immediately changed the city's--and nation's--culinary landscape by popularizing rustic, wild yeast-leavened bread and wholesome and delicious cooking. In Tartine All Day, Tartine's first all-purpose (non-baking) cookbook, Prueitt shares 125 master recipes and 75 variations plus 25 DIY from-scratch techniques from her incredible repertoire of breakfasts, soups, salads, packable lunches, suppers, holiday staples, breads, and desserts, all guaranteed to transform daily home cooking. With 150 compelling photographs and recipes for instant classics (such as White Cheddar Macaroni and Cheese with Toasted Grain Gratin, Brined Pork Chops with Roasted Apples and Corn Spoon Bread, and Chicory Salad with Farro and Lemon-Buttermilk Dressing), plus Prueitt's gluten-free stand-bys, this hardworking resource will inspire and instruct home cooks in new and enduring ways".-- Provided by publisher.

Rosenthal, Mitchell, 1960-

Cooking my way back home : recipes from San Francisco's Town Hall, Anchor & Hope, and Salt House / Mitchell Rosenthal with Jon Pult, foreword by wolfgang Puck ; photography by Paige Green. Ten Speed Press, c2011. vii, 263 p. : **641.5979**

1. Town Hall (Restaurant : San Francisco, Calif.) 2. Anchor & Hope (Restaurant) 3. Salt House (Restaurant) 4. Cooking, American -- California style. 5. Cooking, American -- Southern style. 6. Recipes 7. Cookbooks.
ISBN 9781580085922

LC 2011011631

The owner of three San Francisco restaurants showcases more than one hundred recipes, including fried oysters with spinach salad and herbsaint dressing, smoked chicken-hock gumbo with andouille sausage and green onion, and hot beignets with powdered sugar.

Saltsman, Amelia

The **Santa** Monica farmers' market cookbook : seasonal foods, simple recipes, and stories from the market and farm / Amelia Saltsman ; foreword by Deborah Madison. Blenheim Press, c2007. 216 p. : **641.5979**

1. Santa Monica Farmers' Market (Santa Monica, Calif.) 2. Seasonal cooking 3. Recipes 4. Cookbooks
ISBN 9780979042904

LC oc2008082986

Includes index.

"In her first book, Saltsman proves that minimal effort, coupled with high-quality food, can produce extraordinary results." Publishers Weekly.

Trejo, Danny

Trejo's tacos : recipes and stories from L.A. / Danny Trejo with Hugh Garvey ; photography by Ed Anderson. Clarkson Potter, 2020 223 p. **641.5979**

1. Cooking, Mexican American 2. Tacos 3. Recipes 4. Cookbooks.
ISBN 9781984826855

LC bl2020046500

The legendary actor and L.A. restauranteur shares his favorite--and badass--recipes for bold, fun and versatile Mexican dishes along with stories about his lifelong love of food, in this cookbook that is symbolic of L.A.'s vibrant Latino culture.

"This fiendishly creative collection is a must-have for taco lovers." Publishers Weekly

Valladolid, Marcela

Casa Marcela : recipes and food stories of my life in the Californias / Marcela Valladolid ; foreword by Geoffrey Zakarian ; photography by Coral Von Zumwalt. Houghton Mifflin Harcourt, 2017. xix, 265 p. ; **641.5979**

1. Cooking, American -- California style. 2. Cooking, Mexican. 3. Recipes 4. Cookbooks.
ISBN 9780544808553

LC bl2017016347

Includes index.

The author presents personal recipes that she has collected over her years of traveling between San Diego, California and Tijuana, Mexico, including sweet potato enchiladas, spicy turkey breast, poblano rings, and salsa verde.

"In Valladolid's latest cookbook, the Food Network host warmly welcomes readers into her new southern California home." Publishers Weekly.

Wangler, Justin

★**Season** : a year of wine country food, farming, family & friends / Justin Wangler & Tracey Shepos Cenami ; with culinary gardener Tucker Taylor, Jackson Family Wines ; photographer, Alan Campbell ; writer, Steve Siegelman ; designers, Iain R. Morris & Suzi Hutsell. Cameron + Company, 2018 302 p. : **641.5979**

1. Cooking, American -- California style. 2. Food and wine pairing. 3. Recipes 4. Seasonal cooking. 5. Cookbooks.

ISBN 9781944903374

LC 2018042526

"A cookbook put together by the chefs and gardeners at Jackson Family Wines, offering season-specific recipes for every occasion".-- Provided by publisher.

"This high-end farmers almanac pairs seasonal food with Jackson Family wines... the entire package is an appealing advertisement for not just wines and food, but for the California wine country lifestyle." Publishers Weekly.

641.598 Cooking -- South America

Acurio, Gaston

Peru : the cookbook / Gaston Acurio ; translation by Lingoleaf. Phaidon Press Limited, 2015. 432 p. : **641.598**

1. Cooking, Peruvian. 2. Recipes 3. Cookbooks.

ISBN 9780714869209

LC bl2015019459

Includes index.

Bursting with flavor, a definitive Peruvian cookbook features 500 traditional recipes from the country's most acclaimed chef who introduces home cooks to the full range of Peru's vibrant cuisine, from popular classics like quinoa and ceviche to lesser known dishes.

"In chef and restaurant owner Acurios first foray into English-language cookbooks, the cuisine of Peru shines. The color-coded sections book break down the usual Western groupings of dishes (appetizers, first course, etc.) with a more Peruvian sensibility in mind." Publishers Weekly.

Castanho, Thiago

Brazilian food / Thiago Castanho & Luciana Bianchi. Firefly Books, 2014. 255 p. : **641.598**

1. Cooking, Brazilian 2. Food habits -- Brazil 3. Recipes 4. Cookbooks.

ISBN 9781770854727

"With beautiful, splashy photos of the recipes, markets, food producers and even street artists at work, this book is elevated above a simple collection of recipes. It's an ode to the author's foodscape, and his passion for it is infectious. Readers who have never heard of manteiga de garrafa or tried pickled peppers will be excited about Castanho's recipes and may be inspired to visit Brazil." Publishers Weekly.

Kijac, Maria Baez

The **South** American table : the flavor and soul of authentic home cooking from Patagonia to Rio de Janeiro, with 450 recipes / Maria Baez Kijac ; foreword by Charlie Trotter. Harvard Common Press, c2003. xvii, 478 p. : **641.598**

1. Cooking, Latin American. 2. Cooking -- South America. 3. Recipes 4. South America -- Social life and customs. 5. Cookbooks

ISBN 9781558322486

LC 2003011100

Highlighting the culinary range of South America, the author introduces readers to Brazilian feijoada, Argentine barbecue, and Ecuadorian seafood specialties, with 450 recipes in all from ten countries.

Mallmann, Francis

Mallmann on fire / Francis Mallmann with Peter Kaminsky and Donna Gelb ; principal photography by Santiago Soto Monllor. Artisan, 2014 ix, 305 p. : **641.598**

1. Cooking, Argentine. 2. Barbecuing. 3. Frying. 4. Broiling. 5. Cookbooks.

ISBN 9781579655372

LC 2014004632

Includes index.

Shares the author's live fire recipes, as well as his experiences cooking in places all over the world, including New York, Garzon, and Trancosa.

Mallmann, Francis

Seven fires : grilling the Argentine way / Francis Mallmann, with Peter Kaminsky. Artisan, c2009. x, 278 p. : **641.598**

1. Cooking, Argentine. 2. Barbecuing. 3. Outdoor cooking. 4. Cookbooks

ISBN 9781579653545

LC 2008037367

Includes index.

"Mallmann cooks with the elegant purity achieved only after attaining a mastery of complicated food. He also reconnects us to the primal simplicity and visceral pleasure of cooking over a fire--though his recipes can be made over charcoal or in a grill pan, too." New York Times Book Review.

Speck, Maria

Ancient grains for modern meals : Mediterranean whole grain recipes for barley, farro, kamut, polenta, wheat berries & more / Maria Speck ; photography by Sara Remington. Ten Speed Press, 2011. ix, 230 p. : **641.598**

1. Cooking (Cereals). 2. Grain. 3. Cooking, Mediterranean. 4. Cookbooks.

ISBN 9781580083546

LC 2010045867

"A whole-grain cookbook featuring well-balanced and wholesome recipes inspired by the Mediterranean cuisines of Greece, southern France, Italy, and Turkey".-- Provided by publisher.

"Speck simplifies cooking with grains without sacrificing flavor. Her recipes--including minted barley and fennel stew with marinated feta, New England cider mussels with fresh cranberries and bulgur, and walnut spelt biscotti with olive oil--are deliciously nourishing and not to be missed." Library Journal.

Van Aken, Norman, 1951-

New World kitchen : Latin American and Caribbean cuisine / Norman Van Aken, with Janet Van Aken ; photographs by Tim Turner. Ecco, c2003 xiv, 322 p. : **641.598**

1. Cooking, Caribbean. 2. Cooking, Latin American. 3. Recipes 4.

Cookbooks.
ISBN 9780060185053

LC 2002027158

One of the stars of American cuisine turns his attention south to Latin America, collecting delicious recipes from across the continent and integrating the African-inspired Creole cuisines of Cuba, Jamaica, and Puerto Rico, to create a sumptuous array of inventive dishes.

"Combined with Van Aken's many thoughtful sidebars and notations, the sophistication of these recipes make this a treat for serious home cooks." Publishers Weekly.

641.59969 Cooking--Hawaii

Kysar, Alana, 1985-

Aloha kitchen : recipes from Hawai'i / Alana Kysar ; photography by Alana Kysar and Brooklyn Dombroski. Ten Speed Press, 2019 230 p. : **641.59969**

1. Cooking, Hawaiian. 2. Recipes 3. Cookbooks.
ISBN 9780399581366

LC 2018034179

Includes index.

A native Hawaiian food blogger explores the multicultural influences behind the cuisine of the islands with recipes for such staples as saimin, loco moco, shave ice, and shoyu chicken, tracing their geographic origin and history on the islands.

"Kysar, a food blogger (Fix Feast Flair) born in Maui, presents an eye-opening portrait of the cultural diversity behind Hawaiis cuisine in 85 recipes celebrating the aloha spirit at the core of Hawaiian food." Publishers Weekly.

641.6 Cooking specific materials

Aidells, Bruce

The **complete** meat cookbook : a juicy and authoritative guide to selecting, seasoning, and cooking today's beef, pork, lamb, and veal / Bruce Aidells and Denis Kelly ; photographs by Beatriz Da Costa ; illustrations by Mary DePalma. Houghton Mifflin, 1998. 604 p. : **641.6**

1. Cooking (Meat) 2. Recipes 3. Cookbooks
ISBN 9780618135127

LC 98028216

Includes index.

Demystifies the meat-buying process, meat cuts, and seasoning techniques, and includes more than two hundred recipes.

"More than 230 recipes, many with several variations, are presented along with charts and illustrations to help the reader understand different types of meat." Library Journal.

America's Test Kitchen (Firm)

The **Cook's** Illustrated meat book : the game-changing guide that teaches you how to cook meat and poultry with 425 bulletproof recipes / the editors of America's Test Kitchen. America's Test Kitchen, 2014 xi, 492 p. : **641.6**

1. Cooking (Meat). 2. Recipes 3. Cookbooks.
ISBN 9781936493869

LC 2014016170

Includes index.

This ultimate meat and poultry guide from America's most-trusted food magazine is filled with 450 foolproof recipes and a wealth of information on selecting and cooking the best meat and poultry available.

"That said, carnivores with an obsession for perfection will likely have found their new bible in this comprehensive collection." Publishers Weekly.

America's Test Kitchen (Firm)

Foolproof fish : modern recipes for everyone, everywhere / America's Test Kitchen. America's Test Kitchen, 2020 ix, 374 p. : **641.6**

1. Cooking (Fish) 2. Cooking (Seafood) 3. Recipes 4. Cookbooks.
ISBN 9781948703109

LC 2020002583

Includes index.

A fact-filled seafood cookbook by the experts from America's Test Kitchen shares fish profiles, essential culinary techniques and recipes for such fare as Sizzling Garlic Shrimp, Roasted Salmon with Orange Beurre Blanc and grease-free Fish and Chips.

"The book's depth, breadth, and practicality makes it a must-have for seafood lovers. . . . Wildly useful." Publishers Weekly

Anthony, Michael, 1968-

V is for vegetables : inspired recipes and techniques for home cooks from artichokes to zucchini / Michael Anthony with Dorothy Kalins ; photographs by Maura McEvoy ; design by Don Morris Design. Little, Brown and Company, 2015. ix, 374 p. : **641.6**

1. Cooking (Vegetables). 2. Recipes 3. Cookbooks.
ISBN 9780316373357

LC bl2015042210

Includes index.

Collects simple recipes and techniques for cooking imaginative vegetable-based dishes, including salads, herb sauces, gratins, and stews.

"With its distinctive recipes, this title can augment and supplement collections that already include classics such as James Peterson's Vegetables, Revised and Deborah Madison's Vegetable Literacy." Library Journal.

Arokiasamy, Christina

The **spice** merchant's daughter : recipes and simple spice blends for the American kitchen / Christina Arokiasamy. Clarkson Potter/Publishers, c2008. 231 p. : **641.6**

1. Cooking (Spices) 2. Cooking, Southeast Asian. 3. Recipes 4. Cookbooks
ISBN 9780307396280

LC 2007050015

A guide to creatively blending and cooking with spices explains how to combine and use spices in both traditional and innovative ways and offers one hundred recipes inspired by Southeast Asian cuisine that includes such dishes as lemon pepper wings, spicy beef salad, and cardamom butter rice with sultanas.

Bevill, Amanda

World spice at home : new flavors for 75 favorite dishes / Amanda Bevill & Julie Kramis Hearne, photography by Charity Burggraaf. Sasquatch Books, 2014 xi, 226 p. : **641.6**

1. Cooking (Spices). 2. Cookbooks.
ISBN 9781570619076

LC 2014011114

Presents a collection of seventy-five recipes which incorporate spices from around the world, with information about each spice and options for soups, stews, meat and seafood dishes, bread, desserts, and condiments.

"Bevill and Kramis Hearnes's spice blends, which contain 714 spices (compared to 40-plus in some ethnic cookbooks), taste superior to many premade and shelf-weary equivalents. Their approachable recipes offer home cooks a gentle introduction to new flavorings." Library Journal.

Bir, Sara, 1976-

★The **fruit** forager's companion : ferments, desserts, main dishes, and more from your neighborhood and beyond / Sara Bir. Chelsea Green Publishing, 2018. xiv, 379 p. : **641.6**

1. Cooking (Fruit) 2. Forage plants
ISBN 9781603587167

LC 2017058242

Includes bibliographical references and index.

Presents a guide to the basics of fruit foraging, gathering techniques, and preservation methods, with a collection of recipes for sauces, butters, salsas, jellies, cakes, sherbets, and breads.

" Even if readers don't have a lemon or apple tree in the backyard, they're sure to find some useful advice, as Bir does an outstanding job of illustrating how to get the most out of simple, often neglected or discarded ingredients." Publishers Weekly.

Bitterman, Mark

Salted : a manifesto on the world's most essential mineral, with recipes / Mark Bitterman ; photography by Mark Bitterman and Jennifer Martine. Ten Speed Press, c2010. viii, 312 p. : **641.6**

1. Salt. 2. Cooking. 3. Recipes 4. Cookbooks
ISBN 9781580082624

LC 2010021043

Includes index.

"An authoritative field guide to an indispensable and increasingly fashionable ingredient--featuring 80 salt profiles, a reference guide with 160 salts, and more than 50 recipes--written by the country's top purveyor of artisanal salts".-- Provided by publisher.

Bloomfield, April

A **girl** and her greens : hearty meals from the garden / April Bloomfield with JJ Goode ; photographs by David Loftus ; illustrations by Sun Young Park. Ecco, 2015 261 p. : **641.6**

1. Cooking (Vegetables) 2. Seasonal cooking. 3. Recipes 4. Cookbooks
ISBN 9780062225887

LC bl2015016502

Includes index.

Presents a collection of seasonal vegetable recipes that offers such options as snap pea salad, asparagus quiches with mint, potato soup with garlic and parsley, Swiss chard cannelloni, and broccoli with bacon.

"Bloomfield's latest is an excellent companion to its popular predecessor, offering a second helping of narrative-rich recipes and Sun Young Park's charming illustrations." Library Journal.

Caldwell, Gianaclis, 1961-

Homemade yogurt & kefir : 71 recipes for making & using probiotic-rich ferments / Gianaclis Caldwell ; photography by Carmen Troesser. Storey Publishing, 2020. 223 p. **641.6**

1. Cooking (Yogurt). 2. Fermented milk. 3. Recipes 4. Cookbooks.
ISBN 9781635861099

LC 2019051400

"Step-by-step instructions cover the basics of making dairy ferments, from necessary equipment to the myriad options for thickening, sweetening, and flavoring".-- Provided by publisher.

"This is a practical addition to any cookery collection, especially with the growing trend toward self-sufficiency." Booklist

Cameron, Angus (Donald Angus)

The **L.L.** Bean game and fish cookbook / Angus Cameron and Judith Jones ; illustrations by Bill Elliott. Random House, c1983. xiii, 475 p. : **641.6**

1. Cooking (Game) 2. Cooking (Fish) 3. Recipes 4. Cookbooks.
ISBN 9780394511917

LC 82015089

Includes index.

Provides recipes for preparing venison, rabbit, squirrel, woodchuck, pheasant, quail, duck, geese, trout, salmon, shad, bass, sole and swordfish, and offers tips on cooking outdoors

"With handsome wildlife and botanical drawings by Bill Elliott, the book was written by two experts and is complete and comprehensive." Christian Science Monitor.

Canterbury, Dave

The **Bushcraft** field guide to trapping, gathering, & cooking in the wild / Dave Canterbury Adams Media, 2016 256 p., 8 unnumbered color plates : **641.6**

1. Camping -- Handbooks, manuals, etc. 2. Cooking (Game) -- Technique. 3. Cooking (Wild foods) -- Technique. 4. Hunting -- Handbooks, manuals, etc.
ISBN 9781440598524

LC 2016024921

Includes index.

Renowned outdoors expert and New York Times bestselling author Dave Canterbury provides you with all you need to know about packing, trapping, and preparing food for your treks and wilderness travels. Whether you're headed out for a day hike or a weeklong expedition, you'll find everything you need to survive--and eat well--out in the wild. --From publisher description.

Chernila, Alana

Eating from the ground up : recipes for simple, perfect vegetables / Alana Chernila ; photographs by Johnny Autry. Clarkson Potter/Publishers, 2018 271 p. : **641.6**

1. Cooking (Vegetables) 2. Cooking (Vegetables). 3. Recipes 4. Vegetables. 5. Cookbooks
ISBN 0451494997

LC 2017013871

Includes index.

A collection of 100 recipes teaches home cooks how to prepare dishes with vegetables in ways that help showcase the unique flavor and texture properties of each, including arugula, celeriac, kohlrabi, fennel, asparagus in recipes like Winter Borscht and Cucumber Yogurt Pops.

Coffey, Bennett

Chocolate every day : 85+ plant-based recipes for cacao treats that support your health snd well-being / not your sugar mamas Bennett Coffey + Kyleen Keenan, Martha's Vineyard's favorite chocolatiers, with Rebecca Miller Ffrench ; photography by Elizabeth Cecil. Avery, 2018 223 p. : **641.6**

1. Baking. 2. Chocolate desserts. 3. Cooking (Chocolate). 4. Recipes 5. Cookbooks.
ISBN 9780735216044

LC bl2018117461

The cofounders of Not Your Sugar Mamas, a holistic chocolate company based on Martha's Vineyard, show chocolate for what it really is through more than 75 recipes for a vast array of decadent delights that do away with refined sugar, dairy and gluten and only rely on raw cacao and high-quality, unprocessed ingredients.

"With fruit and nut ingredients, such as orange zest for chocolaty orange scones, pomegranate seeds for chocolate bark, and peanut butter and honey frosting for chocolate cupcakes, this book is filled with dozens of wonderful flavor combinations." Publishers Weekly.

Corbin, Pam

The **River** Cottage preserves handbook / Pam Corbin ; introduced by Hugh Fearnley-Whittingstall. Ten Speed Press, c2010. 216 p. : **641.6**

1. River Cottage (Television program) 2. Cooking (Jam) 3. Condiments. 4. Chutney. 5. Cookbooks.
ISBN 9781580081726

LC 2010010617

Includes index.

Includes "Notes to the U.S. edition" (p. 202).

Shares practical guidelines for preserving locally grown fruits, vegetables and herbs while offering seventy-five recipes for such preserves as raspberry jam and apple butter.

Darlington, Tenaya, 1971-

Di Bruno Bros. House of Cheese : a guide to wedges, recipes, and pairings / Tenaya Darlington ; photography by Jason Varney. Running Press, 2013. 256 p. : **641.6**

1. Di Bruno Bros. "The House of Cheese." 2. Cooking (Cheese) 3. Cheese. 4. Cheese -- Varieties. 5. Cheese shops -- Philadelphia, Pennsylvania 6. Cookbooks.
ISBN 9780762446049

LC 2012942524

The Philadelphia institution and self proclaimed "Culinary Pioneers Since 1939" offers this guide to cheese pairing with information on 170 different varieties of artisan cheeses and 30 recipes.

Flores, Eva Kosmas

Adventures in chicken : 150 amazing recipes form the creator of adventures in cooking.com / Eva Kosmas Flores. Houghton Mifflin Harcourt, 2016. 288 p. : **641.6**

1. Cooking (Chicken). 2. Recipes 3. Cookbooks.
ISBN 9780544558205

LC 2015038041

Includes index.

Presents chicken recipes, including such dishes as sausage-stuffed savory French toast and chicken and feta filo pockets.

"An aptly titled book that takes everyday chicken to the ends of the earth." Booklist.

Franklin, Aaron

Franklin steak : dry-aged, live-fired, pure beef / Aaron Franklin and Jordan Mackay ; photography by Wyatt McSpadden ; illustrations by Bryan B. Butler. Ten Speed Press, 2019 vii, 215 p. : **641.6**

1. Beef steaks. 2. Cooking (Beef) 3. Cookbooks.
ISBN 9780399580963

LC 2018045052

"The be-all, end-all guide to cooking the perfect steak--from buying top-notch beef, seasoning to perfection, and finding or building the ideal cooking vessel--from the team behind the acclaimed and best-selling book Franklin Barbecue. Aaron Franklin may be the reigning king of brisket, but in his off-time, what he really loves to cook and eat at home is steak. So, in this follow-up to his New York Times best-selling book Franklin Barbecue, the pitmaster extraordinaire teaches readers how to cook his favorite food to absolute perfection. With their trademark rigor and expertise, Franklin and coauthor Jordan Mackay go deeper into the art and science of cooking steak than anyone has gone before. They travel the world--beyond Franklin's native Texas to Spain, Scotland, California, and Japan--to uncover global steak preparations and traditions. They demystify cattle breeds, explore the technique of dry-aging, and even teach readers how to build custom, backyard grill setups inspired by the best steak chefs in the world. For any meat-lover, backyard grillmaster, or fan of Franklin's fun yet authoritative approach, this book is a must-have".-- Provided by publisher.

Giller, Megan

Bean to bar chocolate : America's craft chocolate revolution : the origins, the makers, the mind-blowing flavors / Megan Giller ; recipe photography by Jody Horton. Storey Publishing, 2017 vii, 231 p. ; **641.6**

1. Chocolate. 2. Cocoa. 3. Cooking (Chocolate). 4. Recipes 5. Cookbooks.
ISBN 9781612128214

LC 2017011628

A journey through Americas craft chocolate scene explains what to look for in a chocolate bar, explores food pairings, introduces more than a dozen artisanal chocolate makers, and presents recipes.

Good Housekeeping Institute (New York, N.Y.),

Burgers : 125 mouthwatering recipes & tips Hearst Books, 2016 127 p. : **641.6**

1. Hamburgers. 2. Cooking (Meat). 3. Recipes 4. Cookbooks.
ISBN 9781618372017

LC bl2016012764

At head of title: Good Housekeeping.

"Good food guaranteed."

Includes index.

Presents a collection of hamburger recipes, along with fresh fixings, sides, and spiced-up toppings, including such options as Texas chicken burgers, rosemary-cabernet sliders, Greek lamb burgers, and portobello pesto burgers.

Greenspan, Eric

The **great** grilled cheese book : grown-up recipes for a childhood classic / Eric Greenspan ; photography by Colin Price. Ten Speed Press, 2018 143 p. : **641.6**

1. Sandwiches. 2. Cooking (Cheese). 3. Recipes 4. Quick and easy cooking 5. Cookbooks
ISBN 9780399580741

LC 2017049573

Includes index.

Offers fifty recipes for grilled cheese sandwiches, from the simple to the sophisticated, and includes tips on the best cheeses and breads and notes on the best cooking techniques.

Grescoe, Taras

Bottomfeeder : a seafood lover's journey to the end of the food chain / Taras Grescoe. Bloomsbury USA, 2008. 327 p. ; **641.6**

1. Seafood. 2. Cooking (Seafood) 3. Seafood industry and trade 4. Marine resources conservation.
ISBN 9781596912250

LC 2007049843

IACP Cookbook Awards, Literary Food Writing, 2009.

Writers' Trust Non-Fiction Prize, 2008.

A tour of the lucrative seafood industry, which occurred as a result of the author's search for both satisfying and humane seafood, reports on his discoveries about the consequences of pollution, unregulated fishing, and climate change, in an account that also identifies which fish varieties are the healthiest for the body and the environment.

Grigson, Jane

Charcuterie and French pork cooking / Jane Grigson. Grub Street, 2001. 347 p. : **641.6**

1. Cooking (Pork) 2. Cooking, French. 3. Cookbooks.
ISBN 9781902304885

LC bl2011024508

"First published in Great Britain by Michael Joseph, 1967"--T.p. verso.

Includes index.

Introduces the techniques of charcuterie and offers recipes for sauces and relishes, terrines, pâtes, sausages, ham, and fresh pork.

Guittard, Amy

Guittard Chocolate cookbook : decadent recipes from San Francisco's premium bean-to-bar chocolate company / Amy Guittard ; foreword by Alice Medrich ; photographs by Antonis Achilleos. Chronicle Books, 2015 177 p. : **641.6**

1. Cooking, Chocolate. 2. Recipes 3. Cookbooks.
ISBN 9781452135335

LC 2014033173

Includes index.

A collection of recipes from the famous chocolate-maker presents a variety of ways to enjoy chocolate, including chocolate cherry scones, chocolate bread pudding, chocolate banana blondies, chocolate mousse pie, and dark chocolate raspberry bonbons.

Higgins, Katie

Chocolate-covered Katie : over 80 delicious recipes that are secretly good for you / Katie Higgins. Grand Central Life & Style, 2015 207 p. : **641.6**

1. Chocolate desserts. 2. Cooking (Chocolate). 3. Recipes 4. Cookbooks.
ISBN 9781455599707

LC 2014017846

Includes index.

The blogger behind ChocolateCoveredKatie.com shares 80 never-before-seen recipes--including Cookie Dough Cheesecake, Cake Batter Ice Cream and Peanut Butter Brownie Pie--for healthy desserts that only use real ingredients without any unnecessary fats, sugars or empty calories.

Hodgkin, Sophie,

Recipes from an Italian butcher : roasting, stewing, braising / Silver Spoon Kitchen ; Project editor: Sophie Hodgkin. Phaidon Press Limited, 2017. 303 p. : **641.6**

1. Cooking (Meat). 2. Cooking, Italian. 3. Cookbooks.
ISBN 9780714874975

LC bl2017044235

"A Silver Spoon book. Authentic recipes from Italy's most trusted kitchen"--Cover.

"Recipes from an Italian Butcher originates from Il cucchiano d'argento, first published in 1950, tenth edition (revised, expanded and updated in 2016), Il cucchiaio d'argento piccoli arrosti, first published in 2016, Il cucchiaio d'argento carni da i secondi piatti, first published in 2004, and Il cucchioaio d'argento scuola di cucina arrosti, brasati e polpettoni, first published in 2013"--Colophon.

At head of title: The Silver Spoon Kitchen.

Includes index.

Provides 150 authentic Italian recipes that feature meat, poultry, and game, including veal shank in cider, Milanese osso buco, roasted veal with egg yolk sauce, braised beef, and spiced guinea fowl with yogurt.

Iyer, Raghavan, 1961-

Smashed, mashed, boiled, and baked and fried, too! / Raghavan Iyer. Workman Publishing, 2016 250 p. : **641.6**

1. Cooking (Potatoes). 2. Potatoes. 3. Cookbooks.
ISBN 9780761185475

LC 2016023744

Includes index.

"Published simultaneously in Canada by Thomas Allen & Sons Limited."

"You say potato...? Not anymore. You'll say, Wow! Fantastic! Incredible! You'll say, Who knew you could make a potato taste so good? Raghavan knew. A master teacher and beloved and award-winning cookbook author, Raghavan Iyer celebrates his favorite ingredient in Smashed, Mashed, Boiled, and Baked--And Fried, Too!, a continent-by-continent celebration of the amazing potato. Its recipes, inspired by a diversity of cuisines, are accompanied by enticing full-color photographs and feature scrumptious starters, like Ecuadorean Llapingachos and Sweet Potato Samosas. Hearty mains: Canadian Lamb-Potato Tortiere, Moroccan Potato Stew with Saffron Biscuits, Potato Lasagne with Lemon Ricotta. Plus rich gratins, a boundary-defying Mojito Potato-Pomegrante Salad, luscious sauces and condiments, and even desserts, including a decadent Chocolate Sweet Potato Pound Cake and Thick-Cut Potato Crisps with Dark Chocolate--a match made in sweet-salty heaven. The book includes a guide to potato varieties, uses and storage, plus fascinating stories in potato history for the truly obsessed".-- Provided by publisher.

Kafka, Barbara

★**Vegetable** love / Barbara Kafka with Christopher Styler ; photographs by Christina Cornish. Artisan, c2005. 708 p. : **641.6**

1. Cooking (Vegetables) 2. Vegetables. 3. Recipes 4. Cookbooks.
ISBN 9781579651688

LC 2005047818

Provides instructions for seven hundred and fifty recipes that utilize vegetables, including tabbouleh with red and hot peppers, chard gratin, creamy carrot soup, and morels with rhubarb and asparagus.

"The author has triumphed with an outstanding, indispensable cookbook that not only summons the reader to get into the kitchen and cook but also constitutes a valuable and comprehensive reference tool." Booklist.

Khong, Rachel, 1985-

All about eggs : everything we know about the world's most important food / Rachel Khong and the editors of Lucky peach. Clarkson Potter/Publishers, 2017 256 p. : **641.6**

1. Cooking (Eggs). 2. Eggs as food. 3. Recipes 4. Cookbooks.
ISBN 9780804187756

LC 2016048977

Presents a collection of foolproof egg recipes, including such dishes as Taiwanese oyster omelet, eggs Benedict, egg curry, and soft-boiled egg, along with anecdotes and techniques.

"In usual Lucky Peach style, this well-rounded, informative cookbook has a hip vibe and quirky illustrations." Publishers Weekly.

La Place, Viana

Verdura : vegetables Italian style / Viana La Place. Grub Street, 2010. 320 p. ; **641.6**

1. Cooking (Vegetables) 2. Cooking, Italian. 3. Recipes 4. Cookbooks
ISBN 9781906502782

LC 2010537034

Originally published: New York: Morrow, 1991. London: Macmillan, 1994.

With a vegetable and herb guide and an ingredient glossary, Verdura provides comprehensive information while exciting the palate.

Kingsley, Lisa,

EatingWell vegetables : the essential reference / project editor: Lisa Kingsley. Houghton Mifflin Harcourt, 2016. 515 p. : **641.6**

1. Cooking (Vegetables). 2. Vegetables. 3. Recipes 4. Cookbooks.
ISBN 9780544715288

LC bl2016023847

Includes indexes.

A reference to purchasing, storing, preparing, and enjoying vegetables at their peak includes alphabetized coverage of one hundred common vegetables, sharing complementary recipes and nutritional information.

"Food trends such as the cauliflower pizza crust and raw kale salads also get their due. Throughout, bonus tips for growing cucumbers and stale-ing bread offer added value. This is a useful addition to a veg-centric cooks collection." Publishers Weekly.

LaFrieda, Pat

Meat : everything there is to know / Pat LaFrieda and Carolynn Carreno ; photographs by Evan Sung. Atria Books, 2014. xix, 234 p. : **641.6**

1. Cooking (Meat) 2. Recipes 3. Cookbooks.
ISBN 9781476725994

LC 2014000898

Includes index.

A third-generation butcher and owner of New York's premier meatpacking business introduces home cooks to a full range of cuts and butchering skills while sharing 75 recipes for beef, pork, lamb, veal and poultry.

"LaFreida's emphasis is in educating readers on the various animals, diagramming cuts, and showing how to best utilize them. Tips like how to break down a chicken or cut pockets in veal or pork chops for stuffing make this a valuable reference that will give readers a greater appreciation for not only their favorite cuts of meat, but their butcher as well." Publishers Weekly.

Landau, Rich, 1967-

Vedge : 100 plates large and small that redefine vegetable cooking / Rich Landau & Kate Jacoby ; foreword by Joe Yonan. The Experiment, 2013 xv, 240 p. ; **641.6**

1. Vedge (Restaurant : Philadelphia, Pa.). 2. Cooking (Vegetables). 3. Cooking (Fruit). 4. Vegan cooking. 5. Recipes 6. Cookbooks
ISBN 9781615190850

LC 2013012098

Includes index.

Presents one hundred recipes from the Philadelphia-based, vegetarian restaurant, including porcini and celery root shepherd's pie, charred shishito peppers, and chocolate stuffed beignets.

Lang, Rebecca D., 1976-

The **Southern** vegetable book : a root-to-stalk guide to the South's favorite produce / Rebecca Lang. Oxmoor House, 2016 256 p. : **641.6**

1. Cooking (Vegetables). 2. Cooking, American -- Southern style. 3. Recipes 4. Cookbooks.
ISBN 9780848746889

LC bl2016006151

Includes index.

Collects more than one hundred recipes that showcase thirty vegetables favored in Southern cuisine, organized by season, including such staples as tomatoes, okra, and corn, and such lesser-known gems as Jerusalem artichokes and ramps.

" Many recent cookbooks feature creative vegetable preparations... this one has a distinct Southern twist." Library Journal.

Lobel, Stanley

Lobel's meat bible : all you need to know about meat and poultry from America's master butchers / Stanley Lobel ... et al. ; with Mary Goodbody and David Whiteman ; photographs by Lucy Schaeffer. Chronicle Books, c2009. 319 p. : **641.6**

1. Cooking (Meat) 2. Cooking (Poultry) 3. Meat. 4. Poultry.
ISBN 9780811858267

LC 2008033441

Includes index.

For anyone who ever wanted to know the difference between Porterhouse and Chateaubriand, the Lobel family of master butchers has all the answers in the Meat Bible. Covering every imaginable meat--beef, veal, pork, lamb, poultry, rabbit, and more--the Lobels share their extensive knowledge of the differing tastes, textures, flavors, fat contents, and uses for each cut of meat. More than 150 recipes include such savory dishes as Thai Beef Salad, Braised Pork Tacos with Ancho Chile Sauce, Lamb Loin Chops with Eggplant Caponata and Andalusian-Style Quail with Dates and Almonds. How-to instructions take the mystery out of techniques such as butterflying a chicken. When it comes to meat, no one knows more than the Lobels. --From publisher description.

Louis, Jenn

The **book** of greens : a cook's compendium of 40 varieties, from arugula to watercress, with over 150 recipes / Jenn Louis with Kathleen Squires ; photographs by Ed Anderson. Ten Speed Press, 2017 328 p. **641.6**

1. Cooking (Greens). 2. Cooking (Natural foods) 3. Recipes 4. Cookbooks
ISBN 9781607749844

LC 2016048674

This reference guide to 50 different types of greens includes information on each one's origin, season, flavor, and nutrition, along with tips on how to shop for, store and clean them, as well as 150 delicious recipes that incorporate greens.

Madison, Deborah

Vegetable literacy : cooking and gardening with twelve families from the edible plant kingdom, with over 300 deliciously simple recipes / Deborah Madison ; photography by Christopher Hirsheimer and Melissa Hamilton. Ten Speed Press, 2013 405 p. : **641.6**

1. Cooking (Vegetables) 2. Food crops -- Identification. 3. Recipes 4. Cookbooks.
ISBN 9781607741916

LC 2012030968

Shows how vegetables from the same family can be interchanged to complement other flavors and includes over one hundred recipes, including grilled asparagus with tarragon butter, potato cakes with red chile molido, and chive and saffron crepes.

Mangini, Cara

The **vegetable** butcher : how to select, prep, slice, dice, and masterfully cook vegetables from artichokes to zucchini / Cara Mangini. Workman Publishing, 2016 iv, 346 p. ; **641.6**

1. Cooking (Vegetables). 2. Vegetables. 3. Recipes 4. Cookbooks.
ISBN 9780761180524

LC 2016004215

Includes index.

Marrying the art of butchery with the joy of seasonal produce, an essential guide demystifies the world of vegetables, providing a complete vegetable education through 100 vegetarian recipes that celebrate the soul-satisfying flavor of each vegetable.

Masonis, Todd

Making chocolate : from bean to bar to s'more / Todd Masonis, Greg D'Alesandre, Lisa Vega & Molly Gore ; photographs by Eric Wolfinger. Clarkson Potter/Publishers, 2017 366 p. : **641.6**

1. Cacao beans. 2. Chocolate. 3. Cooking (Cocoa). 4. Recipes 5. Cookbooks.
ISBN 9780451495358

LC 2017005182

A guide from the chocolate maker Dandelion Chocolate offers their approach to making chocolate with only cocoa beans and sugar and covers everything from bean-sourcing tips through their chocolate-making method, along with recipes from their kitchen.

Mast, Rick

Mast Brothers Chocolate : a family cookbook / Rick Mast & Michael Mast ; foreword by Thomas Keller ; photography by Tuukka Koski. Little, Brown and Company, 2013. 276 p. : **641.6**

1. Mast Brothers Chocolate. 2. Cooking (Chocolate) 3. Desserts. 4. Recipes 5. Cookbooks.
ISBN 9780316234849

LC bl2013046099

Includes index.

Craft chocolate pioneers who have a factory and specialty shop in Brooklyn share their story and their recipes for classic desserts including chocolate cookies and cakes, brownies, bars, milkshakes, and homemade whoopie pies.

Moonen, Rick

Fish without a doubt : the cook's essential companion / Rick Moonen and Roy Finamore ; photographs by Ben Fink. Houghton Mifflin Co., 2008. 496 p. : **641.6**

1. Cooking (Seafood) 2. Cooking (Fish) 3. Recipes 4. Cookbooks
ISBN 9780618531196

LC 2007052084

Includes index.

An guide to cooking with fish introduces more than 250 recipes that encompass all the techniques of fish and seafood cooking for appetizers, soups and salads, pastas, and main courses.

"In this cookbook that covers the preparing of sustainable fish, the authors show how to clean, bone, and portion both finfish and shellfish. Recipes are organized by cooking method: broiling, poaching, roasting, grilling, steaming, [and] frying. Succeeding chapters cover such fish basics as chowders, fish cakes, and salads. Both the book's organization and its comprehensive coverage make this a necessary addition to any cookbook collections." Booklist.

Mullen, Marissa

That cheese plate will change your life : creative gatherings and self-care with the cheese by numbers method / Marissa Mullen ; illustrated by Sara Gilanchi. The Dial Press, 2020. 285 p. : **641.6**

1. Cheese -- Varieties. 2. Appetizers. 3. Cooking (Cheese) 4. Cookbooks
ISBN 9780593157596

LC 2019036418

Includes index.

Celebrates the ways in which cheese brings people together, and how just crafting a cheese plate can be a meditative act that lets us tap into our creativity. With over 50 easy-to-make yet showstopping cheese plates, this book will teach you how to relax, enjoy, and indulge--and let cheese spark joy.

"This is a fun, attractive, and unique guide to a favorite party dish." Publishers Weekly

Music, Debra

Theo Chocolate : recipes & sweet secrets from Seattle's favorite chocolate maker / Debra Music and Joe Whinney with Leora Bloom ; photographs by Charity Burggraaf. Sasquatch Books, 2015 xxvii, 223 p. ; **641.6**

1. Theo Chocolate. 2. Chocolate desserts. 3. Chocolate candy. 4. Recipes 5. Cookbooks.
ISBN 9781570619977

LC 2015011364

Includes index.

Presents a collection of recipes from the owners of Theo Chocolate, a Seattle establishment which makes organic chocolate, with descriptions of the chocolate-making process and basic information on working and cooking with chocolate.

"Though light on technical instruction, this book contains a compelling range of sweet and savory recipes." Library Journal.

Ottolenghi, Yotam

★**Plenty** more : vibrant vegetable cooking from London's Ottolenghi / Yotam Ottolenghi. Ten Speed Press, 2014. x, 339 p. : **641.6**

1. Ottolenghi (Restaurant) 2. Cooking (Vegetables) 3. Recipes 4. Cookbooks.
ISBN 9781607746218

LC 2014017924

Includes index.

"While the recipes require time and finesse . they are often revelatory, introducing textures and flavor combinations that readers won't find elsewhere." Library Journal.

★**Plenty** : vibrant vegetable recipes from London's Ottolenghi / Yotam Ottolenghi. Chronicle Books, 2011. 287 p. : **641.6**

1. Ottolenghi (Restaurant) 2. Cooking (Vegetables) 3. Recipes 4. Cookbooks.
ISBN 9781452101248

LC 2011036741

A collection of vegetarian recipes based on freshness and seasonality, and drawn from the diverse food cultures represented in London.

Phipps, Catherine

Citrus : recipes that celebrate the sour and the sweet / Catherine Phipps. Quadrille, 2017. 255 p. : **641.6**

1. Cooking (Citrus fruits). 2. Recipes 3. Cookbooks.
ISBN 9781849499002

LC bl2017009126

Includes index.

Offers over one hundred recipes featuring citrus fruits, including lime and chicken tortilla soup, Szechuan peppercorn and orange beef, blood orange and rhubarb meringue pie, and orange and pistachio cake.

Pollinger, Ben

School of fish / Ben Pollinger and Stephanie Lyness. Gallery Books, 2014. 439 p. : **641.6**

1. Cooking (Seafood) 2. Recipes 3. Cookbooks

ISBN 9781451665130

LC 2014000760

Includes index.

"From the acclaimed executive chef of a Michelin-starred seafood restaurant comes a comprehensive, beautifully designed guide to cooking fish, for home cooks of all skill levels. School of Fish is an all-encompassing culinary education in one handy--not to mention gorgeously photographed--cookbook. Ben Pollinger, executive chef of upscale Manhattan restaurant Oceana, distills years of experience working in some of the world's best restaurants in this no-nonsense book that demystifies the art of cooking seafood. With more than 100 recipes organized by technique from the easiest to the most advanced, Pollinger takes you through the ins and outs of baking, roasting, braising, broiling, steaming, poaching, grilling, frying, saute;ing, and of course seasoning. In addition, he offers up terrific recipes for basics (like Homemade Hot Sauce and Fish Fumet); dressed fish (from ceviche to tartars); salads, pasta, rice, and sides (such as Salmon Salad with Spinach, Dill, and Mustard Vinaigrette); soups and chowders (including Gazpacho with Seared Scallops); and one-pot meals (like Caribbean Fish Stew and Thai-Style Bouillabaisse). And to round out your seafood education, School of Fish includes a Fish-ionary, a Guide to Unusual Ingredients, and detailed step-by-step photos to complement the 100 photographed recipes. As appealing in its presentation as it is useful, this guide outlines all the skills you need for perfecting your culinary craft. So whether you're a home cook trying something new or an experienced "afishionado," School of Fish will turn you into a better cook and an authority on all things seafood".-- Provided by publisher.

Presilla, Maricel E.

Peppers of the Americas : the remarkable capsicums that forever changed flavor / Maricel E. Presilla ; photographs by Romulo Yanes. Ten Speed Press, 201. 288 p. **641.6**

1. Peppers. 2. Chile pepper industry and trade. 3. Cooking (Chile peppers) 4. Cooking (Peppers)

ISBN 9780399578922

Presents a culinary and ethnobotanical survey of the pepper and its many varieties, providing an abundance of information on this essential ingredient central to our multicultural palate, and includes 40 recipes that celebrate its complex flavors and health benefits.

"Presilla is both 'botanical sleuth' and chef, presenting a scholarly and stunning visual guide to peppers in this definitive guide." Publishers Weekly.

Raichlen, Steven

The **brisket** chronicles : how to barbecue, braise, smoke, and cure the world's most epic cut of meat / Steven Raichlen ; food photography by Matthew Benson. Workman Publishing, 2019 ix, 278 p. : **641.6**

1. Cooking (Beef). 2. Meat cuts. 3. Cookbooks.

ISBN 9781523505487

LC bl2019012911

Includes index.

Collects more than sixty recipes that incorporate America's favorite cut of meat, including such offerings as bacon-smoked brisket flat, Korean grilled brisket, old school pastrami, brisket ramen, and smoky brisket cheese pockets.

"Barbecue guru Raichlen (Project Smoke) turns his expert attention to that collagen-laced chest cut of beef known, in 1450 England, as brukette, revealing it as the modern-day centerpiece for an international menu of delicacies. Over 60 recipes and numerous cooking techniques are interwoven with a look at the foods history, along with brief profiles of a few of who Raichlen considers America's best pit masters." Publishers Weekly.

Project smoke : seven steps to smoked food nirvana, plus 100 irresistible recipes from classic (slam-dunk brisket) to adventurous (smoked bacon-bourbon apple crisp) / Steven Raichlen. Workman Publishing, 2016. 293 p. ; **641.6**

1. Cooking (Smoked foods). 2. Smoked foods. 3. Smoking (Cooking). 4. Recipes 5. Cookbooks.

ISBN 9780761181866

LC 2015044528

"Project Smoke is the How to Grill of smoking, both a complete step-by-step guide to mastering the gear and techniques and a collection of 100 explosively flavorful recipes for smoking every kind of food, from starters to desserts. Project Smoke describes Raichlen's seven steps to smoked food nirvana, including: 1. Choose Your Smoker; 4. Source Your Fuel; 7. Know When Your Food Is Done. There's an in-depth rundown on various smokers; the essential brines, rubs, marinades, and barbecue sauces; and a complete exposition of woods: and ways to smoke--cold smoking, hot smoking, smoke-roasting and smoke-braising. Then the recipes, all big-flavored dishes. Bacon-Crab Poppers, Cherry-Glazed Baby Back Ribs. Slam-Dunk Brisket, Porkstrami, and Jamaican Jerk Chicken. Even desserts and cocktails--Smoked Chocolate Bread Pudding or a Mezcalini, anyone? Illustrated throughout with gorgeous full-color photographs, it's a book that inspires hunger at every glance, and satisfies with every recipe tried".-- Provided by publisher.

"An excellent how-to for those fired up about smoke." Booklist.

Rinella, Steven

The **MeatEater** game and fish cookbook : recipes and techniques for every hunter and angler / Steven Rinella. Spiegel & Grau, 2018 xii, 350 p. : **641.6**

1. MeatEater (Television program). 2. Cooking (Meat). 3. Cooking (Game) 4. Cookbooks.

ISBN 9780399590078

LC 2018002015

Includes index.

Offers wild game and fish recipes as well as techniques on the best way to butcher the animals for cooking.

"Rinella is at the top of his game in this must-read cookbook for those seeking a taste of the wild." Publishers Weekly.

Ruhlman, Michael, 1963-

★**Egg** : a culinary exploration of the world's most versatile ingredient / Michael Ruhlman ; photography by Donna Turner Ruhlman. Little, Brown, and Company, 2014. xix, 235 p. : **641.6**

1. Cooking (Eggs) 2. Recipes 3. Cookbooks.

ISBN 9780316254069

LC bl2014013408

Includes indexes.

An award-winning author dedicates his latest work to the common egg, taking a tour of all the wonders this ordinary but powerful ingredient can help create, from poached and scrambled breakfasts, to brioche, Italian meringue, mayonnaise, custards, quiches and cakes.

"Ruhlman's regard for this simple ingredient is evident as he describes the multiple functions it serves and then offers up recipes for a wide array of appetizing dishes." Publishers Weekly.

Rule, Cheryl Sternman

Yogurt culture : a global look at how to make, bake, sip, and chill the world's creamiest, healthiest food / Cheryl Sternman Rule ; photography by Ellen Silverman. Houghton Mifflin Harcourt, 2015 352 p. : **641.6**

1. Cooking (Yogurt). 2. Recipes 3. Cookbooks.
ISBN 9780544252325
LC 2014039690

"A Rux Martin Book."
Includes index.

Collects over one hundred flavorful recipes for each meal of the day using yogurt as an ingredient, including tomato, avocado, and cucumber salad, challah French toast, creamy beef curry, and goat cheese cheesecake.

"This excellent cookbook belongs in most collections, along with Arto de Hartounian's The Yogurt Cookbook." Library Journal.

Seaver, Barton

For cod & country / Barton Seaver. Sterling Epicure, c2011. ix, 294 p. : **641.6**

1. Cooking (Fish) 2. Cooking (Seafood) 3. Recipes 4. Cookbooks
ISBN 9781402777752
LC 2011283174

Includes index.

"Barton Seaver...became one of the most important voices in food today because of his take on seafood and sustainability. Combining freshness with tastes, textures, and flavors, Seaver has created an entirely new kind of fun, fabulous, and casual food featuring seafood that hasn't been overfished or caught in an environmentally destructive way...Is also an essential cook's guide, brimming with great advice on how to shop for affordable fish, wine pairings, basic cooking, and prep techniques plus spice mix recipes..."--Dust jacket flap.

"A user's manual for any seafood lover who wants to eat sustainably--and very well. Seaver's book vibrates with personality, practical advice, photographs (both evocative and how-to), and stovetop wisdom: never be shy about adding butter, but go easy on the black pepper. With the help of step-by-step photographs, he demonstrates seafood-savvy techniques, everything from how to fillet a bass to how to open an oyster without severing one of your arteries. He also provides a list of substitutions for overexploited species: Use Pacific cod in place of Atlantic cod; sablefish instead of Chilean sea bass; squid instead of octopus." The Atlantic.

Seaver, Barton

The **joy** of seafood : the all-purpose seafood cookbook with more than 900 recipes / Barton Seaver. Sterling Epicure, 2019 ix, 485 p. : **641.6**

1. Cooking (Fish) 2. Cooking (Seafood) 3. Cookbooks.
ISBN 9781454921981
LC bl2019027789

Includes index.

Inspired by American regional cuisine and classic preparations, and curated to give home cooks complete confidence, these thoroughly modern dishes include such crowd-pleasing fare as Citrus-Crusted Fried Halibut, New Orleans BBQ Shrimp, Clam Risotto, Cod Cakes, and Hot Smoked Salmon, along with flavored butters, marinades, vinaigrettes, sauces, spice mixes, chowders, stock, soups, and stews.

"Chef Seaver (For Cod and Country) distills his vast knowledge of seafood in this encyclopedic work... This superb collection conveys Seaver's experience, enthusiasm, and creativity." Publishers Weekly.

Seaver, Barton

Two if by sea : delicious sustainable seafood / Barton Seaver. Sterling Epicure, 2016 304 p. : **641.6**

1. Cooking (Fish). 2. Cooking (Seafood). 3. Cookbooks.
ISBN 9781454917878
LC bl2016017575

Includes index.

Offers more than 150 recipes for dishes featuring sustainable fish and seafood, including broiled scallop gratin, shrimp al ajillo, seafood pot pie, smoked trout puffs, green curry fish stew, and grilled sardine skewers.

"From a quick weeknight meal of canned shrimp and pasta to a show-stopping stew for guests, the ideas here will fit any bill. Essential for seafood lovers." Library Journal.

Selengut, Becky

Good fish : 100 sustainable seafood recipes from the Pacific Coast / Becky Selengut ; photography by Clare Barboza. Sasquatch Books, 2018 321 p. : **641.6**

1. Cooking, American -- Pacific Northwest style. 2. Cooking (Seafood). 3. Recipes 4. Cookbooks
ISBN 9781632171078
LC 2017041101

Learn to shop for -- and cook -- Pacific coast seafood that's good for your health and the planet, with 100 recipes, plus cooking techniques and practical tips for buying. --From publisher description.

"Despite its regional focus, this capable seafood cookbook will appeal to fish fans across the country." Library Journal.

Sharma, Nik

Season : big flavors, beautiful food / recipes & photographs by Nik Sharma. Chronicle Books, 2018 288 p. : **641.6**

1. Cooking (Spices). 2. Spices -- India. 3. Cooking, Indic. 4. Cookbooks.
ISBN 9781452163994
LC 2017051015

Includes index.

A collection of recipes in which the flavors of Indian cooking combine with familiar ingredients and recipes of the American South and California, including such dishes as spiced beef kebabs, ginger-garlic stir-fried crab, and roast leg of lamb.

Simonds, Nina

★**Spices** of life : simple and delicious recipes for great health / Nina Simonds ; photographs by Tina Rupp. Alfred A. Knopf, 2005. xi, 383 p. : **641.6**

1. Cooking (Herbs) 2. Spices. 3. Quick and easy cooking. 4. Recipes 5. Cookbooks
ISBN 9780375411601
LC 2004021089

With an emphasis on the tonic properties of foods, including herbs and spices, presents recipes for a variety of healthful dishes that reflect an array of ethnic cuisines and utilize health-restoring foods to make good eating a way of life.

"Simonds' book is full of straightforward but practical recipes, and peppered with loads of health information." Publishers Weekly.

Slater, Nigel
Ripe : a cook in the orchard / Nigel Slater ; photography by Jonathan Lovekin. Ten Speed Press, 2012. 591 p. : **641.6**
1. Cooking (Fruit) 2. Recipes 3. Cookbooks.
ISBN 9781607743323
LC 2011043551
Includes index.
Originally published: Tender, volume II : a cook's guide to the fruit garden. London : Fourth Estate, 2010.
"A comprehensive guide to growing and cooking with fruit, featuring more than 300 recipes for sweet and savory dishes".--Provided by publisher.

Speck, Maria
Simply ancient grains : fresh and flavorful whole grain recipes for living well / Maria Speck ; photography by Erin Kunkel. Ten Speed Press, 2015 viii, 261 p. : **641.6**
1. Cooking (Cereals) 2. Grain 3. Heirloom varieties (Plants) 4. Cookbooks.
ISBN 9781607745884
LC 2014036879
Shares family-friendly recipes for every meal of the day that feature bulgur, spelt, farro, teff, and other whole grains, as well as tips for cooking with these ingredients.

Stein, Rick
Rick Stein's complete seafood : a step-by-step reference / Rick Stein. Ten Speed Press, 2008. 264 p. **641.6**
1. Cooking (Seafood) 2. Cooking (Fish) 3. Recipes 4. Cookbooks
ISBN 9781580089142
LC 2006298920
Offers an almost limitless repertoire, with detailed instructions and extensive charts. Hundreds of photographs and illustrations show how to scale and gut fish for the grill, bake whole fish in a salt or pastry casing, hot-smoke fish, prepare live crabs, and clean and stuff squid, along with other essential techniques.-- from publisher description.

Vegetables from an Italian garden : season-by-season recipes Phaidon, 2011. 431 p. **641.6**
1. Seasonal cooking 2. Cooking (Vegetables) 3. Recipes 4. Cookbooks
ISBN 9780714861173
Vegetables from an Italian Garden features 400 delicious recipes showcasing over 40 different kinds of vegetables newly collected by the editors behind the classic Italian cooking bible, The Silver Spoon. Authentic and easy-to-use, the book will reveal how Italians use vegetables year-round to prepare simple yet crowd-pleasing dishes. --From publisher description.

Vegetables illustrated : an inspiring guide with 700+ kitchen-tested recipes / America's Test Kitchen. America's Test Kitchen, 2019 xvi, 528 p. : **641.6**
1. Cooking (Vegetables). 2. Recipes 3. Cookbooks.
ISBN 9781945256738
LC 2018048691
Includes index.
Filled with more than 700 recipes for enjoying vegetables to their fullest, a book from America's Test Kitchen reveals hundreds of ways to cook nearly every vegetable and showcases vegetables' versatility in everything from sides to mains.
"This sturdy must-have cookbook is a highly informative reference highlighting the versatility of vegetables." Publishers Weekly

Viljoen, Marie
Forage, harvest, feast : a wild-inspired cuisine / Marie Viljoen. Chelsea Green Publishing, 2018 469 p. : **641.6**
1. Cooking (Wild foods). 2. Wild foods. 3. Seasonal cooking 4. Cookbooks.
ISBN 9781603587501
LC 2018007866
Includes indexes.
A collection of recipes that incorporate wild ingredients into everyday and special occasion fare features such dishes as rhubarb and ground elder soup, rabbit with field garlic and morels, juniper black currant chutney, and pawpaw spice cake.
"As long as readers heed Viljoens explanations--typically related to sourcing, preparation or, in the case of ramps, sustainability--theyll be set. The book's imaginative yet practical recipes make it one of the best resources of its type. Its a terrific entry point for would-be foragers, as well as experts interested in making the most of their bounty." Publishers Weekly.

Vinton, Sherri Brooks, 1968-
Put 'em up! : a comprehensive home preserving guide for the creative cook, from drying and freezing to canning and pickling / Sherri Brooks Vinton. Storey Pub., 2010. 303 p. : **641.6**
1. Canning and preservation. 2. Vegetables -- Preservation 3. Fruit -- Preservation. 4. Cooking (Vegetables)
ISBN 9781603425469
LC 2010009609
Includes bibliographical references (p. 288) and index.
"Vinton provides an excellent introduction to multiple food preservation methods. Organized first by technique, then by fruit or vegetable, this volume contains many easy-to-follow options for prepared and preserved foods." Library Journal.

Wells, Patricia
Vegetable harvest / Patricia Wells. William Morrow, 2007. 336 p. **641.6**
1. Cooking (Vegetables)
ISBN 9780060752446
LC 2006043723
Includes index.
"After surveying the bounty of her backyard garden, Wells became inspired to build meals around vegetables rather than starting with meat, fish or poultry. She tripled the number she served at each meal and tried different cooking methods, looking for the best-tasting, most wholesome ways of cooking each type. She includes nutritional information and an equipment list for each recipe, and selectively offers wine suggestions, translations of French food idioms, and nuggets of folklore connected to the dish or main ingredient. This collection is highly recommended for cooks and gardeners alike." Publishers Weekly.

641.658 Mushrooms

Selengut, Becky
Shroom : mind-bendingly good recipes for cultivated and wild mushrooms / Becky Selengut ; foreword by Langdon Cook ; wine pairings by sommelier April Pogue ; photography by Clare Barboza. Andrews McMeel Publishing, 2014 xxxiv, 205 p. : **641.658**
1. Cooking (Mushrooms) 2. Recipes 3. Cookbooks
ISBN 9781449448264
LC 2014931303

Includes index.

Chef and cooking teacher Becky Selengut's Shroom feeds our enduring passion for foraged and wild foods by exploring 15 types of mushrooms, including detailed how-to's on everything home cooks need to know to create 75 inventive, internationally-flavored mushroom dishes.-- "From publisher description".

"A delight to read and cook from, this is one of the most welcoming and unintimidating mushroom books to hit shelves in ages." Library Journal.

641.665 Poultry

The **best** chicken recipes : a best recipe classic / the editors of Cook's illustrated America's Test Kitchen, c2008. 422 p. **641.665**

1. Cooking (Chicken) 2. Cooking, American 3. Recipes 4. Cookbooks.

ISBN 9781933615233

LC 2010282817

"This volume offers more than 300 recipes for chicken, along with a primer called Chicken 101, information on techniques (including step-by-step illustrations), and ratings of equipment and ingredients." Library Journal.

641.7 Specific cooking processes and techniques

America's Test Kitchen (Firm)

Cook it in cast iron : kitchen-tested recipes for the one pan that does it all / the editors at America's Test Kitchen. America's Test Kitchen, 2015 ix, 293 p. : **641.7**

1. Skillet cooking. 2. Recipes 3. Cookbooks.

ISBN 9781940352480

LC 2015037708

Includes index.

A culinary celebration of the versatile cast-iron skillet demonstrates the correct use and maintenance of cast-iron cookware and the wide range of dishes that it can prepare, from classic entrees and breakfasts to baked goods and surprising favorites.

"The editors of Cooks Country undertake a comprehensive exploration of the classic cast iron skillet, as well as the panoply of meals it can provide." Publishers Weekly.

The **America's** Test Kitchen family baking book : featuring more than 700 kitchen-tested recipes, 800 step-by-step photos, opinionated product ratings, and at-a-glance tutorials that guarantee success every time you bake / the editors at America's test kitchen ; photography, Daniel J. Van Ackere, Carl Tremblay. America's Test Kitchen, c2008. viii, 544, 24 p. : **641.7**

1. Baking. 2. Recipes 3. Cookbooks

ISBN 9781933615226

LC 2012371858

Includes index.

Presents over 700 recipes, organized into such categories as rustic breads, fancy cookies, and fruit desserts, along with step-by-step instructions for some dishes and tips on procedures, equipment, and ingredients.

"Expert bakers and novices scared of baking's requisite exactitude can all learn something from this hefty, all-purpose home baking volume." Publishers Weekly.

How to braise everything : classic, modern, and global dishes using a time-honored technique / America's Test Kitchen. America's Test Kitchen, 2019 ix, 398 p. : **641.7**

1. Braising (Cooking) 2. Recipes 3. Cookbooks.

ISBN 9781945256714

LC 2018033789

Includes index.

A cook's guide to braising from America's Test Kitchen includes more than two hundred recipes, including such offerings as coq au vin, cider-braised pork roast, shredded beef tacos, and drunken beans.

The **best** skillet recipes : a best recipe classic / the editors of Cook's illustrated ; photography, Keller + Keller, Carl Tremblay, and Daniel J. Van Ackere ; illustrations, John Burgoyne. America's Test Kitchen, c2009. x, 355 p. : **641.7**

1. Skillet cooking. 2. One-dish meals. 3. Quick and easy cooking. 4. Recipes 5. Cookbooks

ISBN 9781933615417

LC bl2009009444

Includes index.

Features recipes made from start to finish in a skillet and tips on how to cook specific foods such as vegetables, thick cuts of meat, and pasta in a skillet.

"This cookbook celebrates the versatility of that ordinary workhorse, the 12-inch skillet. An indispensable tool for eggs, pan-seared meats and sauted vegetables, the skillet can also be used for stovetop-to-oven dishes such as All-American Mini Meatloaves; layered dishes such as tamale pie and Tuscan bean casserole; and even desserts such as hot fudge pudding cake. Whether or not you properly appreciate your skillet, this book will at least teach you to wield it gracefully." Publishers Weekly.

Bittman, Mark

★**How** to grill everything : simple recipes for great flame-cooked food / Mark Bittman ; photography by Christina Holmes. Houghton Mifflin Harcourt, 2018. vii, 568 p. : **641.7**

1. Barbecuing. 2. Barbecue cooking 3. Recipes 4. Cookbooks.

ISBN 9780544790308

LC 2017051933

Includes index.

"Regardless of one's grilling experience, fans of outdoor cooking will find this volume to be essential." Publishers Weekly.

Carroll, Joe, 1970-

Feeding the fire : recipes & strategies for better barbecue & grilling / Joe Carroll and Nick Fauchald ; photographs by William Hereford. Artisan Books, 2015 264 p. ; **641.7**

1. Barbecuing. 2. Recipes 3. Cookbooks

ISBN 9781579655570

LC 2014035876

A guide to barbecue cooking features seventy-five recipes, including such offerings as smoked mackerel, Maryland pit beef, and dry rub-brined chicken.

Davis, Timothy Charles

The **Hot** Chicken cookbook : the fiery history & red-hot recipes of Nashville's beloved bird / Timothy Charles Davis ; photography by Danielle Atkins. Spring House Press, 2015 122 p. : **641.7**

1. Cooking (Chicken) 2. Cooking, American -- Southern style. 3. Deep frying 4. Recipes 5. Nashville, Tennessee 6. Cookbooks.

ISBN 9781940611198

LC 2015951464

"Reading Davis's cookbook, it's easy to understand why hot chicken has a cult following. A fascinating exploration of food culture and highly recommended." Library Journal.

Disbrowe, Paula

Food52 any night grilling : 60 ways to fire up dinner (& more) / Paula Disbrowe ; photography by James Ransom. Ten Speed Press, 2018. xi, 211 p. : **641.7**

1. Barbecuing. 2. Cooking (Smoked foods) 3. Recipes 4. Cookbooks.
ISBN 9781524758967

LC 2017028346

Includes index.

An innovative collection of recipes by creators of the Food52 culinary website coaches home cooks through the fundamentals of grilling for everyday occasions, sharing time-saving tips and flavor-enhancing techniques for such recipes as Porchetta-Style Pork Kebabs, Sweet & Smoky Drumsticks and Gulf Coast Shrimp Tacos.

Fine Cooking

Fine Cooking roasting / editors and contributors of Fine Cooking. The Taunton Press, Inc., 2014. 153 p. : **641.7**

1. Roasting (Cooking). 2. Cookbooks.
ISBN 9781627108072

LC 2014024594

Includes index.

This must-have collection serves up the best recipes and techniques so home cooks can successfully produce bold-flavored, juicy meat and vegetable dishes time and again.

Franklin, Aaron

Franklin barbecue : a meat-smoking manifesto / Aaron Franklin and Jordan Mackay ; photography by Wyatt McSpadden. Ten Speed Press, 2015 ix, 213 p. : **641.7**

1. Barbecuing -- Technique. 2. Cooking (Smoked foods) 3. Recipes 4. Cookbooks.
ISBN 9781607747208

LC 2014036177

Includes index.

A resource for home cooks from an award-winning pitmaster unlocks the secrets behind great barbecue, including building a smoker, curing the right wood, and tending fires, with recipes for brisket, spare ribs, beef ribs, and turkey breast.

Goldwyn, Meathead

Meathead : the science of great barbecue and grilling / text and photos by Meathead Goldwyn ; with Greg Blonder, Ph.D. Houghton Mifflin Harcourt, 2016 xv, 384 p. ; **641.7**

1. Barbecuing. 2. Cookbooks.
ISBN 9780544018464

LC 2015049143

Includes index.

The founder and editor behind AmazingRibs.com provides a definitive guide to understanding the science behind barbecuing and grilling, explaining how marinades work, the importance of digital thermometers, how to calibrate a grill or smoker, along with 118 delicious recipes.

"This highly recommended food-science focused guide to grilling and barbecue will satisfy amateurs and professionals alike." Library Journal.

Mills, Mike, 1941-

Praise the lard : recipes and revelations from a legendary life in barbecue / Mike Mills and Amy Mills ; photographs by Ken Goodman. Houghton Mifflin Harcourt, 2017. 336 p. : **641.7**

1. Barbecuing. 2. Barbecue cooking 3. Recipes 4. Cookbooks.
ISBN 9780544702493

LC 2016051671

"A Rux Martin Book."

Collects recipes from a legendary Illinois barbecue joint, including such offerings as pimento cheeseburgers, lone star beef ribs, brisket dumplings, and pork belly porchetta.

Noyes, Brian, (Baker)

Red Truck Bakery cookbook : gold-standard recipes from America's favorite rural bakery / Brian Noyes ; photographs by Andrew Thomas Lee. Clarkson Potter/Publishers, 2018 223 p. : **641.7**

1. Red Truck Bakery. 2. Baking. 3. Cupcakes. 4. Desserts 5. Desserts. 6. Cookbooks
ISBN 0804189617

LC 2018002249

Shares recipes from the rural Virginia bakery for such favorites as Southern shoofly pie, wild raspberry buckle, sweet potato pecan pie, persimmon cookies, and bourbon balls.

Perry Lang, Adam

Charred & scruffed : Bold New Techniques for Explosive Flavor On and Off the Grill / Adam Perry Lang with Peter Kaminsky. Artisan, c2012. xiv, 266 p. : **641.7**

1. Barbecuing. 2. Cookbooks.
ISBN 9781579654658

LC 2011031786

A collection of recipes for barbecuing different types of meat and fish emphasizes grilling techniques while presenting ideas for side dishes, sauces, bastes, and brines.

Raichlen, Steven

Project fire : cutting-edge techniques and sizzling recipes from the caveman porterhouse to salt slab brownie s'mores / Steven Raichlen ; food photography by Matthew Benson. Workman Publishing, 2018 325 p. : **641.7**

1. Barbecuing. 2. Cooking. 3. Recipes 4. Cookbooks.
ISBN 9781523502769

LC 2018011117

Includes index.

The author of the New York Times best-selling Barbecue Bible' cookbook series and winner of five James Beard awards and three IACP awards, drawing on a combination of classic and boldly contemporary techniques, presents 100 recipes that put the latest grilling methods' from spit-roasting to salt-grilling'to work.

Steven Raichlen's Planet Barbecue! : an electrifying journey around the world's barbecue trail / Steven Raichlen. Workman Pub., c2010. xviii, 638 p. : **641.7**

1. Barbecuing. 2. Barbecue cooking 3. Cookbooks.
ISBN 9780761148012

LC 2010008444

Includes index.

Contains barbecue recipes from sixty countries, including Argentina, South Africa, Greece, India, Malaysia, and Australia.

Rapoport, Adam

The **grilling** book : the definitive guide from bon appetit / edited by Adam Rapoport ; photography by Peden + Munk. Andrews McMeel Publishing, 2013 432 p. ; **641.7**

1. Barbecuing. 2. Cookbooks.
ISBN 9781449427528

LC 2012952341

Features over three hundred fifty recipes for the grill, including rosemary-basted chicken, Yucatan-style pork chops, and corn with hoisin-orange butter.

Ruhlman, Michael, 1963-

Ruhlman's how to braise : foolproof techniques and recipes for the home cook / Michael Ruhlman. Little, Brown and Company, 2015. xi, 147 p. : How-To **641.7**

1. Braising (Cooking). 2. Recipes 3. Cookbooks.
ISBN 9780316254137

LC 2014941487

Includes index.

A guide to braising includes such recipes as Moroccan lamb tagine, classic yankee pot roast, Mexican pork and posole stew, braised fennel, and corned beef and cabbage braise.

"... Ruhlman (How to Roast) notes, 'There is pleasure to be had in the aroma of floured meat sizzling in hot fat.' Anyone who shares that sentiment will want to dive into this handy guide, and anyone without a Dutch oven would be well advised to purchase one along with the book." Publishers Weekly.

Stevens, Molly

★**All** about braising : the art of uncomplicated cooking / Molly Stevens ; color photographs by Gentl & Hyers/Edge ; black-and-white illustrations by Yevgeniy Solovyev ; wine notes and selections by Tim Gaiser. W.W. Norton & Co., c2004. xiii, 481 p. : **641.7**

1. Braising (Cooking). 2. Recipes 3. Cookbooks
ISBN 9780393052305

LC 2004017907

A comprehensive guide to the braising method of cooking provides a detailed explanation of the principles of good braising, tips on how to select the best ingredients and cooking equipment, wine suggestions, and 125 easy-to-follow recipes for a range of dishes.

"[T]he book contains interesting tasting notes and cultural information, and Stevens's lengthy instructions will be particularly valuable to beginners." Publishers Weekly.

Stone, Tuffy

Cool smoke : the art of great barbecue / Tuffy Stone ; photographs by Ken St. Martin's Griffin, 2018 xv, 288 p. ; **641.7**

1. Barbecuing. 2. Outdoor cooking 3. Cookbooks.
ISBN 9781250137845

LC 2017055075

Includes index.

A former marine, classically-trained chef and World Record-breaking champion pitmaster offers 100 recipes and tips for making great barbecue including how to prepare your own brines, rubs and sauces and the best way to trim meat.

Symon, Michael, 1969-

Michael Symon's playing with fire : BBQ and more from the grill, smoker, and fireplace / Michael Symon and Douglas Trattner ; photographs by Ed Anderson. Clarkson Potter/Publishers, 2018 239 p. : **641.7**

1. Barbecuing. 2. Cooking (Meat) 3. Recipes 4. Cookbooks.
ISBN 9780804186582

LC 2017034644

"With just 42 main-dish recipes spread across the first 167 pages, the gaps are filled with an overabundance of 'pitmaster profiles,' in which barbecue chefs from across the country are briefly interviewed and their own eateries promoted. Meanwhile, Ed Andersons color photography of savory cuts encrusted with dry rub or slathered with sauce is nearly enough to make Cleveland synonymous with mouthwatering. This is an excellent guide to live-fire cooking." Publishers Weekly.

641.8 Cooking specific kinds of dishes and preparing beverages

Alexander, William, 1953-

52 loaves : one man's relentless pursuit of truth, meaning, and a perfect crust / William Alexander. Algonquin Books of Chapel Hill, 2010. x, 339 p. : **641.8**

1. Alexander, William, 1953- 2. Bread. 3. Baking. 4. Perfection.
ISBN 9781565125834

LC 2009049656

"Bakers will delight in his often humorous mission as he relates leaving out salt, growing his own wheat, discovering parchment paper, and splashing water into the oven in an effort to create steam. This humorous memoir is recommended for anyone who has ever tried to bake a loaf." Library Journal.

Alford, Jeffrey

Flatbreads and flavors : a baker's atlas / Jeffrey Alford and Naomi Duguid. Morrow, c1995. xvi, 441 p., 16 p. of plates : **641.8**

1. Bread. 2. Baking 3. International cooking. 4. Recipes 5. Cookbooks
ISBN 9780688114114

LC 94030892

A cookbook-travelogue of unusual flatbread recipes, including Afghan naan, Indian chapattis, Middle Eastern pita, and Mexican tortilla, with complimentary meat and vegetable dishes.

Anderson, Pam, 1957-

Perfect one-dish dinners : all you need for easy get-togethers / Pam Anderson ; photographs by Judd Pilossof. Houghton Mifflin Harcourt, 2010. xii, 266 p. : **641.8**

1. One-dish meals. 2. Entertaining. 3. Quick and easy cooking 4. Recipes 5. Cookbooks
ISBN 9780547195957

LC 2010021447

Includes index.

"Pam Anderson, the New York Times bestselling author beloved by millions, whose recipes are consistently lauded as 'foolproof,' 'infallible,' and 'the best they can be' by publications from Food & Wine to the New York Times, serves up dozens of one-dish wonders perfect for every occasion and any time of year. These dishes will wow your family and guests--and leave you calm and collected at the end of the evening".--Cover, p. 2.

"This is an accessible, engaging collection of meals based around a singular dish. Grouped into four sections--summer salads and grilled platters; casseroles; the roasting pan; and stews--Anderson smartly mixes classics like Osso Bucco, Paella, and Lasagna with riffs on standards like Coq Au Vin (here with white wine and spring vegetables) and a Spanish beef stew (with bell peppers, chickpeas, saffron, paprika, and orange). Whether readers are new to cooking or simply looking for new ideas for meals, Anderson's winning collection is sure to encourage and inspire." Publishers Weekly.

Andres, Jose, 1969-

Tapas : a taste of Spain in America / Jose Andres ; with Richard Wolffe. Clarkson Potter/Publishers, c2005. 256 p. : **641.8**

1. Tapas 2. Cooking, Spanish. 3. Recipes 4. Cookbooks

ISBN 9781400053599

LC 2004027466

Includes index.

Integrating the traditions of Spanish cuisine with a variety of American foods, a collection of tapa recipes and advice on obtaining the right ingredients from an award-winning chef.

"The author presents some of the small-plate dishes he serves at his tapas restaurants, including traditional favorites recreated with American ingredients. Recipes are organized by ingredient, from olives and olive oil to citrus to fish, shellfish, and meat, and they are mouth-watering: Oven-Roasted Potatoes and Oyster Mushrooms, for example, or Lobster with Pimento and Olive Oil." Library Journal.

Baking illustrated : a best recipe classic / the editors of Cook's illustrated ; illustrations, John Burgoyne ; photography, Carl Tremblay, Keller & Keller, Daniel Van Ackere. America's Test Kitchen, c2004. ix, 513 p. : **641.8**

1. Baking. 2. Desserts. 3. Recipes 4. Cookbooks

ISBN 9780936184753

LC BL2004001760

Includes index.

A comprehensive baking reference offers 350 recipes for baking pies, breads, cookies, cakes, pastry, crisps, cobblers, and tarts.

"Test kitchen cooks analyzed brand-name baking ingredients and equipment and . make best buy recommendations. The test summaries preceding each recipe include both successes and failures; the resulting recipes (more than 350) cover everything from the simplest quick breads to more complex yeast breads and cookies and pastries. This is the best instructional book on baking this reviewer has seen." Library Journal.

Bauer, Jeni Britton

Jeni's splendid ice creams at home / Jeni Britton Bauer. Artisan, c2011. 217 p. : **641.8**

1. Desserts 2. Ice cream, ices, etc. 3. Recipes

ISBN 1579654363

LC 2010039453

Includes index.

A debut cookbook by the founder of Jeni's Splendid Ice Creams in Ohio demonstrates how to prepare professional-quality ice creams, yogurts and sorbets using unique flavors and minimally processed milk, in a volume that includes recipes for such signature favorites as Salty Caramel and Bourbon with Toasted Buttered Pecans.

"This inspiring collection of seasonal ice cream recipes from Ohio-based ice cream whiz Bauer stands apart for its creative, unconventional flavors like Sweet Basil & Honeyed Pine Nut and Sweet Potato with Torched Marshmallows." Library Journal.

Beard, James, 1903-1985

Beard on bread / James Beard ; drawings by Karl Stuecklen ; with and introduction by Chuck Williams for the 1995 edition. Knopf, 1995. xiii, 228, viii p. : **641.8**

1. Bread.

ISBN 9780679755043

LC 95127290

Includes index.

A guide to mastering the art of making bread that contains both simple and complex recipes prepared by the renowned chef.

"An inclusive guide to the preparation of a variety of breads with recipes for coffee cakes, rolls, flat breads, fried cakes. The recipes included are those Beard considers the best from around the world which can be made in a U.S. kitchen." Booklist.

Beranbaum, Rose Levy

The **cake** bible / Rose Levy Beranbaum ; edited by Maria D. Guarnaschelli ; photographs by Vincent Lee ; foreword by Maida Heatter. W. Morrow, c1988. 555 p., 30 p. of plates : **641.8**

1. Cake

ISBN 9780688044022

LC 88001369

Includes index.

Providing countless solutions and tips for commonly encountered baking problems, this comprehensive cake cookbook provides precise instructions for baking and decorating spectacular special-occasion cakes of any size up to eighteen inches in diameter

The **best** one-dish suppers : a best recipe classic / the editors of Cook's illustrated ; photography, Keller + Keller, Carl Tremblay, and Daniel J. Van Ackere ; illustrations, John Burgoyne. America's Test Kitchen, c2011. 342 p. : **641.8**

1. One-dish meals. 2. Quick and easy cooking 3. Recipes 4. Cookbooks

ISBN 9781933615813

LC bl2011018548

Includes index.

A comprehensive guide to the quick and easy one-dish meal presents 175 recipes and tips to minimize preparation time and cleanup chores.

Boyle, Tish

The **cake** book / Tish Boyle ; photography by John Uher. Wiley, c2006. vii, 376 p., 16 p. of plates : **641.8**

1. Cake. 2. Recipes 3. Cookbooks.

ISBN 9780471469339

LC 2005021384

Includes index.

From simple pound cakes to elaborately decorated wedding cakes, an introduction to the art of cake making furnishes practical guidelines on kitchen equipment, ingredients, and baking techniques, as well as nearly two hundred recipes for such tempting sweets as Banana Walnut Chiffon Cake and Espresso Meringue Rounds.

Chang, Joanne

Flour : spectacular recipes from Boston's Flour Bakery + Cafe / Joanne Chang ; with Christie Matheson ; photographs by Keller + Keller. Chronicle Books, c2010. 319 p. : **641.8**

1. Flour Bakery + Cafe (Boston, Mass.) 2. Baked products. 3. Baking 4. Recipes 5. Cookbooks

ISBN 9780811869447

LC oc2010088463

Includes index.

Almost 150 Flour recipes such as Milky Way Tart and Dried Fruit Focaccia are included, plus Joanne's essential baking tips, making this mouthwatering collection an accessible, instant classic cookbook for the home baker.

Colicchio, Tom

'wichcraft : craft a sandwich into a meal--and a meal into a sandwich / Tom Colicchio ; with Sisha Ortuzar ; text by Rhona Silverbush ; photographs by Bill Bettencourt. Clarkson Potter/

Publishers, c2009. 208 p. : **641.8**

1. 'wichcraft (Restaurant). 2. Sandwiches. 3. Recipes 4. Cookbooks
ISBN 9780609610510

LC 2008027803

Includes index.

Shares the secrets behind the 'wichcraft restaurant group's spin on the sandwich, with recipes for their most popular offerings, essays on stocking the sandwich pantry, and an interview with the owners.

"The authors offer an entire cookbook featuring the sandwiches served at...[their] New York restaurant, 'wichcraft. This book's table of contents alone will have grab-and-go eaters and sophisticated gastronomes alike salivating." Booklist.

The **complete** book of pasta and noodles / the editors of Cook's illustrated. America's Test Kitchen, 2000. 496 p. **641.8**

1. Cooking (Pasta) 2. Cooking (Noodles) 3. Recipes 4. Cookbooks
ISBN 9780609600641

LC 99040076

Featuring more than five hundred recipes, this celebration of pasta and noodles includes instructions for preparing a wide range of fresh pastas and hundreds of tasty sauces, casseroles, and side dishes.

"This work brings together information and recipes covering pasta's worldwide range from North America's beloved macaroni and cheese through Italy's sophisticated sauces, across China's exotic rice noodles, and up to Japan's modest Zen noodles in broth. Content and organization combine to make this a superior cooking reference book for libraries." Booklist.

Corriher, Shirley O.

BakeWise : the hows and whys of successful baking with over 200 magnificent recipes / Shirley O. Corriher. Scribner, 2008. ix, 532 p., 16 p. of plates : **641.8**

1. Baking. 2. Cookies. 3. Cake. 4. Desserts. 5. Cookbooks
ISBN 9781416560784

LC 2008032681

A compendium of baking recipes combines food science with practical kitchen techniques to explain how to obtain ideal results, in a comprehensive volume that is complemented by 250 recipes.

"This collection of more than 200 recipes offers amateur and expert bakers alike clear, numbered steps and a plethora of information on ingredients, equipment and method. Invaluable troubleshooting sections solve pesky problems on everything from pale and crumbly cookies to fallen souffls. Astute references to a variety of chefs, cookbook authors and restaurants add a knowing punch to this solid collection that's sure to please bakers of all skill levels." Publishers Weekly.

DeGroff, Dale

★The **new** craft of the cocktail : everything you need to know to think like a master mixologist, with 500 recipes / Dale DeGroff ; photographs by Daniel Krieger. Clarkson Potter/Publishers, 2020. 255 p. : **641.8**

1. Cocktails. 2. Bartending.
ISBN 9781984823571

LC bl2020046399

Revision of the author's The craft of the cocktail.

Offers five hundred recipes for classic and original cocktails, includes advice on how to set up a bar and use the correct techniques and tools, and discusses the history and development of mixed drinks.

"In this excellent update of bartender DeGroff's seminal 2002 work, The Craft of the Cocktail, DeGroff serves up a whopping 500 recipes. . . . Home bartenders will be thrilled by this authoritative and satisfying reference." Publishers Weekly

DeMasco, Karen

The **craft** of baking : cakes, cookies & other sweets with ideas for inventing your own / Karen DeMasco & Mindy Fox ; photographs by Ellen Silverman. Clarkson Potter Publishers, c2009. 256 p. : **641.8**

1. Cake. 2. Cookies. 3. Candy. 4. Confectionery. 5. Cookbooks
ISBN 9780307408105

LC 2010278700

Includes index.

Features new ideas, different variations, and creative combinations of classic desserts and other baked goods.

"In the first sections, [DeMarco] covers ingredients and techniques accessible even to novice bakers. Then come her new modern-day treats, created with traditional recipes and familiar home baking techniques, e.g., Lemon Olive Cake (an interesting variation on the traditional lemon cake using butter and extra virgin olive oil). Sources are listed for hard-to-find items. Owing to DeMasco's well-respected culinary pedigree, home bakers will want this." Library Journal.

Desaulniers, Marcel

Death by chocolate cakes : an astonishing array of chocolate enchantment / Marcel Desaulniers ; recipes with Brett Bailey and Kelly Bailey ; photography by Duane Winfield. Morrow, 2000. 216 p. : **641.8**

1. Cake. 2. Cooking (Chocolate). 3. Recipes 4. Cookbooks.
ISBN 9780688162979

LC 00056247

Collects recipes and cooking techniques for such desserts as chocolate peanut root beer rumble, midnight truffle cake, and excessively expressive espresso ecstasy that feature chocolate as the main ingredient.

"This cookbook features indulgent showstoppers, from Happy All the Time Cakes to Excessively Expressive Espresso Ecstasy, each one shown in a full-page color photograph. Although many of the recipes are complicated, instructions are detailed and clear; there are no headnotes per se to introduce these creations, but 'The Chef's Touch' section at the end of each recipe provides tips and some background." Library Journal.

Fine cooking appetizers : 200 recipes for small bites with big flavor / from the editors and contributors of Fine cooking. Taunton Press, 2010. 252 p. : **641.8**

1. Appetizers. 2. Recipes 3. Quick and easy cooking 4. Cookbooks
ISBN 9781600853302

LC 2010028598

Includes index.

In these collections the editors of Fine Cooking have gathered a tempting and satisfying range of recipes on favorite topics. Each listing below tells you which recipes are included in each downloadable collection. As always, clear instructions, full-color photos, plus tips and techniques help you get delicious results.

The **Gourmet** cookie book : the single best recipe from each year 1941-2009. / Gourmet Magazine. Houghton Mifflin Harcourt, c2010. xiii, 161 p. : **641.8**

1. Cookies. 2. Baking 3. Recipes 4. Cookbooks.
ISBN 9780547328164

LC 2010018882

Includes index.

A treasury of top-selected cookie recipes draws on the archives of Gourmet magazine to represent several varieties, cultures, and special occasions.

"This cookbook features one recipe for every year Gourmet magazine was in business. The recipes are grouped by decade, from the ration-era pluck of the 1940s (honey refrigerator cookies and Scotch oat crunchies), when the magazine was published out of a penthouse in the Plaza Hotel, to the twisted classics of the oughts (cranberry turtle bars and glittering lemon sandwich cookies). The wistful headnotes offer historical insight into our past tastes and aspirations." New York Times Book Review.

Greenspan, Dorie

Baking : from my home to yours / Dorie Greenspan ; photographs by Alan Richardson. Houghton Mifflin, 2006. xiii, 514 p. : **641.8**

1. Baking. 2. Recipes 3. Cookbooks

ISBN 9780618443369

LC 2006003101

Includes index.

Offers more than three hundred of the author's favorite recipes, including split-level pudding, gingered carrot cookies, and fold-over pear torte, and provides baking tips and a glossary.

"This collection of recipes covers all the baking bases, from muffins, cookies and brownies to spoon desserts, pies and cobblers. Instructions are clear and easy to follow, and Greenspan uses everyday ingredients readily available to the home chef. This is baking at its best." Publishers Weekly.

Greenspan, Dorie

Baking with Julia : based on the PBS series hosted by Julia Child / written by Dorie Greenspan ; photographs by Gentl & Hyers. Morrow, c1996. xvii, 480 p. : **641.8**

1. Baking. 2. Recipes 3. Cookbooks

ISBN 9780688146573

LC 96023061

Includes index.

A companion volume to the PBS series hosted by Julia Child presents more than 250 recipes for baked goods including simple white breads, muffins, pastry, chocolate creations, and a wedding cake

"The 200 recipes are organized as a course in baking, with an early, energetic section on the basic batters and doughs for cakes and pastries. The book moves on to recipes of varying degrees of complexity. But the book's success is due to more than organization: the text never misses a chance to explain, expand and entertain." New York Times Book Review.

Haedrich, Ken, 1954-

★**Pie** : 300 tried-and-true recipes for delicious homemade pie / Ken Haedrich. Harvard Common Press, c2004. xiv, 639 p., 16 p. of plates : **641.8**

1. Pies. 2. Recipes

ISBN 1558322531

LC 2004003635

Includes index.

Presenting three hundred delicious recipes, the most comprehensive book ever written on American pie focuses on how to make this classic dessert at home, paying attention to ingredients, cooking utensils, oven temperatures, and of course, crust.

Heatter, Maida

Maida Heatter's cookies / illustrations by Melanie Marder Parks. Cader Books, c1997. xii, 308 p. : **641.8**

1. Cookies. 2. Recipes 3. Cookbooks.

ISBN 9780836237337

LC 97031043

Includes index.

Drawing on her previous, award-winning cookie book, the author presents more than two hundred recipes for bar cookies, drop cookies, rolling-pin cookies, icebox cookies, crackers, brownies, biscotti, and more, including her famous Palm Beach Brownies.

Hellmich, Mittie, 1960-

Ultimate bar book : the comprehensive guide to over 1,000 cocktails / Mittie Hellmich ; illustrations by Arthur Mount. Chronicle Books, c2006. 474, 1 p. : **641.8**

1. Bartending 2. Cocktails.

ISBN 9780811843515

LC 2005030720

The Ultimate Bar Book is an indispensable guide to classic cocktails and new drink recipes. Loaded with essential-to-know topics such as barware, tools, and mixing tips.

Hensperger, Beth

The **best** quick breads: 150 recipes for muffins, scones, shortcakes, gingerbreads, cornbreads, coffeecakes, and more / Beth Hensperger. Harvard Commomon Press, c2000. xi, 382 p. : **641.8**

1. Bread. 2. Recipes 3. Quick and easy cooking 4. Cookbooks

ISBN 9781558321717

LC 00036962

Includes index.

Originally published under title: The art of quick breads. San Francisco : Chronicle Books, 1994.

Mixing favorites from the author's collection with new recipes, this guide to great bread includes instructions for making brandy-glazed zucchini bread, raspberry corneal muffins, and much more.

"This book includes about 150 recipes. In addition to quick loaves, both sweet and savory, there are waffles, dumplings, biscuits, popovers, and a variety of other easy baked goods, along with some tasty accompaniments, such as the Fruit Salsa for her Hopi Blue Corn Hotcakes." Library Journal.

Hirigoyen, Gerald

Pintxos : small plates in the Basque tradition / Gerald Hirigoyen with Lisa Weiss ; photography by Maren Caruso. Ten Speed Press, c2009. 201 p. : **641.8**

1. Tapas 2. Cooking, Basque 3. Cooking, American -- California style

ISBN 9781580089227

LC 2008043518

Includes index.

This book features 75 distinctive California-inflected versions of Spanish tapas and French Basque dishes specially written for the home cook. It is organized by type of dish--grilled, soups, braises, skewers and toasts, sandwiches, bean dishes, and fried foods--and illustrated with the photography of James Beard award-winning photographer Maren Caruso.

"With 75 recipes and 50 full-color photographs, Hirigoyen showcases a tasty and broad array of small plates that will tantalize and satisfy." Publishers Weekly.

Holtz, Deborah

Tacopedia / Deborah Holtz ; Juan Carlos Mena. Phaidon Press Limited, 2015. 317 p. : **641.8**

1. Tacos -- Mexico. 2. Cooking, Mexican. 3. Recipes 4. Cookbooks.

ISBN 9780714870472

LC bl2015038089

Includes indexes.

A guide to the different taco traditions of Mexico includes interviews, maps, graphics, and recipes.

Lawson, Nigella, 1960-

How to be a domestic goddess : baking and the art of comfort cooking / Nigella Lawson ; photography by Petrina Tinslay. Hyperion, c2001. viii, 374 p. : **641.8**

1. Baking. 2. Recipes 3. Cookbooks

ISBN 9780786867974

LC 2001024170

A leading British chef shares her secrets of fine baking with a selection of more than 220 recipes for cakes, pies, pastries, preserves, puddings, breads, and cookies.

Lebovitz, David

Ready for dessert: my best recipes/David Lebovitz; photography by Maren Caruso. Ten Speed Press, c2010. 278 p. : **641.8**

1. Desserts. 2. Recipes

ISBN 9781580081382

LC 2009049281

Includes index.

"A compendium of recipes for desserts, including cakes, pies, tarts, fruit desserts, custards, souffles, puddings, frozen treats, cookies, candies, and accompaniments, from noted pastry chef, cookbook author, and food blogger David Lebovitz -- Provided by publisher.

Medrich, Alice

Chewy gooey crispy crunchy melt-in-your-mouth cookies / Alice Medrich ; photographs by Deborah Jones. Artisan Books, c2010. 384 p. : **641.8**

1. Cookies. 2. Cookbooks.

ISBN 9781579653972

LC 2010019491

Includes index.

Brand-new cookies and delicious new spins on the classics are here, with simple well-tested recipes and all the tips, techniques, and ideas that you need to please a crowd or satisfy the most sophisticated palate around.

"Medrich presents a compendium of exciting and enticing cookie recipes that reflects every aspect of our widening culinary landscape. The recipes are organized by texture, hence the title, but there's also a section grouping cookies into categories like those containing whole grains, those that keep at least two weeks, ridiculously quick and easy cookies, and cookies to make with kids. This book has redesigned and reframed the often-overlooked cookie and is a boon to the modern, conscious baker." Publishers Weekly.

Meyer, Danny

Mix shake stir : cocktails for the home bar : recipes from Danny Meyer's acclaimed New York City restaurants / foreword by Danny Meyer. Little, Brown, 2008. 223 p. : **641.8**

1. Cocktails. 2. Bartending. 3. Bartending -- New York City -- Quotations, maxims, etc. 4. Bartenders -- New York City -- Quotations.

ISBN 9780316045124

LC 2008934947

Includes index.

A volume of stylish and creatively mixed cocktail recipes from Danny Meyer's popular New York City restaurants draws on expert tips from his chefs and bartenders while suggesting an array of accompanying snacks.

"Restauranteur Meyer delivers a terrific collection of 140 tempting recipes for cocktails created by bartenders in his award-winning dining establishments. Included are old favorites like the Ritz as well as new classics like the Winter Mojito, and the book's clear instructions and luscious photographs will inspire even nondrinkers to pick up a cocktail shaker. As a bonus, basic tips on mixing drinks, recipes for simple syrups and garnishes, and a concise collection of recipes for bar snacks are offered." Library Journal.

Nevins, Jerry

Sloshies : 102 boozy cocktails straight from the freezer / Jerry Nevins of Snow & Co. Workman Publishing, 2017 152 p. ; **641.8**

1. Alcoholic beverages. 2. Blenders (Cooking). 3. Cocktails. 4. Seasonal cooking 5. Cookbooks.

ISBN 9780761189466

LC 2017024296

"It's not your mother's Pina Colada! Sophisticated, flavorful, with fresh ingredients and the perfect hit of booze, a sloshie is a high-octane slushie--the ideal summer drink that's a far cry from the cloyingly sweet blender cocktails of yore. Written by Jerry Nevins, cofounder of Kansas City's Snow & Co.--named the #1 frozen cocktail bar in the United States--Sloshies features more than 100 innovative refreshers guaranteed to jazz up (and cool down) backyard parties, barbecues, or any gathering with family and friends. And they are so easy to make: Based on a simple granita technique, sloshies require little to no special equipment. Just mix the ingredients, stick them in the freezer, and wait until they're slushy. There's the tart: the Whisky Smashed,a frozen mint julep; the cucumber-kissed Limey Bastard; and the Sunshine Boulevard, a stone-cold shandy starring beer, vodka, and citrus juice. The sweet: the alluringly exotic Blue Roses (featuring a bouquet of curacao, vodka, and rose hip liqueur). The spiced and herbal: including a Manhattan with rye-infused cherries, and the Proud Mary--yes, that's a frozen Bloody Mary. Plus drinks with floral notes, like the Midnight Orchard, a beguiling combination of whiskey, elderflower, bitters, and maraschino,and a few nonalcoholic granitas to refresh the palate. The book includes recipes for the syrups and infused liquors that many of the drinks are built upon, plus information on garnishes, serving suggestions, and other finishing touches".-- Provided by publisher.

Parsons, Brad Thomas

Bitters : a spirited history of a classic cure-all, with cocktails, recipes, and formulas / Brad Thomas Parsons. Ten Speed Press, 2011. 231 p. : **641.8**

1. Bitters. 2. Cocktails. 3. Mineral waters. 4. Drinking behavior.

ISBN 9781580083591

LC 2011017774

Presents a history of bitters, cocktail recipes, and how to make bitters at home.

Peterson, James

Baking / James Peterson. Ten Speed Press, c2009. xv, 378 p. : **641.8**

1. Baking. 2. Recipes 3. Cookbooks

ISBN 9781580089913

LC bl2009027157

Includes index.

Offers a step-by-step instructional for baking the best-loved basics as well as new and fresh versions of pies, tarts, cakes, cookies, pastries, and breads.

"This workhorse of a guidebook...is a worthy baking school between covers. The work features over 300 recipes, mostly classics based in the French tradition. The five chapters--Cakes; Pies, Tarts and Pastries; Cookies; Breads, Quick Breads, and Bread-based Desserts; and Custards, Soufflés, Fruit Curds and Mousses--include a comprehensive overview, sidebars on techniques and recipes designed to teach techniques that can be used in more than the recipe listed." Publishers Weekly.

Prueitt, Elisabeth M.

Tartine / Elisabeth M. Prueitt and Chad Robertson ; foreword by Alice Waters ; photographs by France Ruffenach. Chronicle Books, c2006. 223 p. : **641.8**

1. Tartine (Bakery). 2. Desserts. 3. Pastry. 4. Cookbooks.
ISBN 9780811851503

LC 2006004651

Includes index.

The owner-chefs of the acclaimed Tartine Bakery share the secrets of the baker's art with a collection of easy-to-follow recipes for the home kitchen, featuring such luscious treats as Banana Cream Pie, Apple Crisp, Brioche Bread Pudding, Devil's Food Cake, Lemon Pound Cake, and other tarts, crackers, cookies, breads, cakes, and dishes for every meal of the day.

Sax, Richard

★**Classic** home desserts : a treasury of heirloom and contemporary recipes from around the world / Richard Sax ; photography by Alan Richardson. Houghton Mifflin Harcourt, 2010. 648 p., [48] p. of plates : **641.8**

1. Desserts. 2. International cooking 3. Recipes 4. Cookbooks
ISBN 9780618057085

LC 2010025552

Originally published: Shelburne, Vt. : Chapters Pub., c1994.

Presents a collection of classic, old-fashioned desserts, updated for today's tastes, with advice on kitchen equipment, ingredients, and cooking techniques.

Schreiber, Cory, 1961-

Rustic fruit desserts : crumbles, buckles, cobblers, pandowdies, and more / Cory Schreiber and Julie Richardson ; photography by Sara Remington. Ten Speed Press, c2009. 164 p. : **641.8**

1. Cooking (Fruit) 2. Desserts. 3. Recipes 4. Cookbooks.
ISBN 9781580089760

LC 2008049349

Includes index.

"A collection of simple and satisfying recipes for crisps, slumps, buckles, grunts, and other old-timey desserts by a beloved Portland bakery owner in collaboration with one of the region's top chefs".--Provided by publisher.

"A seasonal mini-bible that goes beyond basics." New York Times Book Review.

Stevens, Daniel (Dan)

The **River** Cottage bread handbook / Daniel Stevens ; introduced by Hugh Fearnley-Whittingstall. Ten Speed Press, c2010. 223 p. : **641.8**

1. River Cottage (Television program). 2. Bread.
ISBN 9781580081863

LC 2010010618

Includes index.

A newest addition to an award-winning series inspired by the locally grown and sustainable food movement combines informative recipes with step-by-step photos covering such options as ciabatta, pizza dough and bagels, in a volume complemented by instructions for building a backyard wood-fired oven.

Stewart, Martha, 1941-

Martha Stewart's baking handbook / Martha Stewart. Clarkson Potter/Publishers, c2005. 415 p. : **641.8**

1. Baking. 2. Recipes 3. Cookbooks
ISBN 9780307236722

LC 2005053532

Includes index.

Combines instructions for a variety of baking techniques, a visual glossary of equipment, tips on storage and make-ahead preparation, and more than 250 recipes for cakes, pies, biscuits, muffins, scones, breads, and pastries.

"This volume may add to global warming as cooks all over the country start up their ovens to produce the extraordinary baked goods that Stewart proposes." Booklist.

Tosi, Christina

Momofuku Milk Bar / Christina Tosi with Courtney McBroom ; photographs by Gabriele Stabile and Mark Ibold. Clarkson Potter, c2011. 255 p. : **641.8**

1. Momofuku Milk Bar 2. Desserts. 3. Recipes 4. Cookbooks.
ISBN 9780307720498

LC 2011007720

Includes index.

The pastry chef from the Momofuku restaurant group reveals the recipes behind her delicious cookies, pies, cakes, ice creams and more.

Walter, Carole

Great cookies : secrets to sensational sweets / Carole Walter ; photographs by Duane Winfield. Clarkson Potter/Publishers, c2003. 418 p. : **641.8**

1. Cookies.
ISBN 9780609609699

LC 2003007633

A master baker shares her secrets for baking the perfect cookie every time, introducing two hundred taste-tempting recipes for drop cookies, chocolate chip variations, macaroons, brownies, meringues, and other delectable treats from around the world, along with advice on essential equipment, ingredients, foolproof techniques, storage, and more.

Wells, Patricia

Salad as a meal : healthy main-dish salads for every season / Patricia Wells ; photography by Jeff Kauck. William Morrow, c2011. 360 p. : **641.8**

1. Cooking (Vegetables) 2. Recipes 3. Salads.
ISBN 006123883X

LC 2010027043

Includes index.

A collection of recipes for more than one hundred salads that can be served as a main dish, featuring salads for each season as well as recipes for soup sides and breads.

"Given Wells's high profile and the book's useful focus, this can't miss wherever cookbooks are popular." Library Journal.

641.81 Side dishes, sauces, garnishes

Allison, Courtney

The **soup** club cookbook : feed your friends, feed your family, feed yourself / Courtney Allison [and 3 others], photographs by Annie Schlechter ; illustrations by Kate Neckel. Clarkson Potter

Publishers, 2015 240 p. : **641.81**

1. Cooking, American. 2. One-dish meals. 3. Recipes 4. Soups. 5. Cookbooks

ISBN 0770434622

LC 2014009496

"Who doesn't want a delicious, home-cooked meal to appear magically at their doorstep on a chilly evening? But work, kids, and life get in the way, even in the most well-intentioned homes. In The Soup Club Cookbook four moms show how to make this fantasy a reality with 150 recipes for soups from favorites (Jewish Chicken Noodle, Italian Wedding) to fancy (Sunchoke Bisque, Sengalese Peanut), and dozens of filling and delish sides, such as Soy Simmered Chicken Wings and Pickled Brussels Spouts. The authors, who are neighbors on New York's Lower East Side, make this soup book extra delicious--and inspring--by explaining how to start the same kind of soup club that they did: each person makes soup once a month and delivers it to the other women with garnishes and instructions for serving. That's at least three meals a month you don't have to cook or order. And you have a good excuse to see your friends".-- Provided by publisher.

Beranbaum, Rose Levy

★The **baking** bible / Rose Levy Beranbaum ; photography by Ben Fink. Houghton Mifflin Harcourt, 2014 xv, 560 p. : **641.81**

1. Baking. 2. Cookbooks.

ISBN 9781118338612

LC 2014016319

Offers baking tips and techniques, with recipes for cakes, tarts, pies, cookies, and breads.

"Berenbaum successfully bridges the gap between popular home baking collections and professional texts." Library Journal.

★**Rose's** baking basics : 100 essential recipes, with more than 600 step-by-step photos / Rose Levy Beranbaum ; photography by Matthew Septimus. Houghton Mifflin Harcourt, 2018. xxvi, 372 p. : **641.81**

1. Baking. 2. Cookies. 3. Pies. 4. Pastry. 5. Cookbooks.

ISBN 9780544816220

LC 2017058732

Includes index.

Provides illustrated no-fuss recipes for cookies, pies, pastries, cakes, and breads, including such options as marzipan cookies, chocolate butterscotch toffee, blueberry muffins, lemon meringue pie, cream puffs, and whole wheat sandwich bread.

"Instructions for creating related toppings and fillings such as classic ganache, along with solutions for problems during the baking process, will help guide new bakers to create treats such as basic chocolate cupcakes, apple cinnamon coffee cake, and butter biscuits. Lavish step-by-step photographs and storing information accompany each recipe." Library Journal.

Berry, Mary, 1935-

Baking with Mary Berry / Mary Berry. DK Publishing, 2015. 192 p. : **641.81**

1. Baking. 2. Cakes 3. Cookies 4. Desserts 5. Cookbooks

ISBN 1465453237

LC bl2015052930

Includes index.

Collects more than one hundred recipes for cakes, cupcakes, pies, tarts, crumbles, brownies, cookies, and special occasion desserts.

"The recipes themselves are clear and concise and the offerings wide ranging, everything from the usual, brownies and lemon meringue pie, to the unusual, almond and apricot tartlets to the exotic, figgy-seeded bites. A solid guide, not just for fans of the show but its those fans (and their numbers are growing in the U.S.) who will be clamoring for copies." Booklist.

Bertinet, Richard

Crumb : show the dough who's boss / Richard Bertinet ; photography by Jean Cazals. Kyle Books, 2019. 224 p. : **641.81**

1. Bread. 2. Cooking (Bread). 3. Cookbooks.

ISBN 9780857835543

LC bl2019024230

Includes index.

"Armed with that confidence and knowledge (the book?s early chapters include vital information on the role of the rise, timing, moisture, and heat), home bakers are well on their way ... . With Bertinet as an expert guide, this volume proves to be an outstanding bread making primer for those new to baking." Publishers Weekly.

Bittman, Mark

★**How** to bake everything : simple recipes for best baking / Mark Bittman ; illustrated by Alan Witschinke. Houghton Mifflin Harcourt, 2016. 703 p. : **641.81**

1. Baking. 2. Recipes 3. Cookbooks.

ISBN 9780470526880

LC bl2016040259

Includes index.

A comprehensive baker's resource collects more than 2000 recipes for a wide variety of baked products, sharing illustrated how-to instructions as well as advice for adapting recipes for vegan and other customizable needs.

Black, Sarah

One dough, ten breads : making great bread by hand / Sarah Black ; photography by Lauren Volo. Houghton Mifflin Harcourt,, 2016 xiv, 209 p. : **641.81**

1. Bread. 2. Recipes 3. Cookbooks.

ISBN 9780470260951

LC 2015004574

Teaches how to make artisan-style breads by hand, starting with simple, white dough, and then making small changes to ingredients, proportions, and shapes to craft ten foundation breads, and includes additional recipes that build on these basics.

"Black, who believes getting your hands in the dough is the best way to learn about bread, provides easy-to-follow directions for 10 types of bread, each created from one dough and with less than 30 minutes of active time." Publishers Weekly.

Conners, Rachel

Bakerita : 100+ no-fuss gluten-free, dairy-free, and refined sugar-free recipes for the modern baker / Rachel Conners with Mary Goodbody. Houghton Mifflin Harcourt, 2020. 288 p. : **641.81**

1. Baking. 2. Desserts. 3. Gluten-free diet. 4. Dairy-free diet 5. Cookbooks

ISBN 9780358116677

LC 2019033897

Includes index.

"Amazingly delicious and beautiful gluten-free, grain-free, dairy-free, and refined sugar-free desserts from the popular Bakerita blog".-- Provided by publisher.

"A great choice for health-conscious bakers interested in exploring flavors beyond the nut-and-chocolate staples prevalent in gluten-free and vegan baking." Library Journal

Day, Cheryl

Back in the Day Bakery, made with love : more than 100 recipes and make-it-yourself projects to create and share / Cheryl Day & Griffith Day. Artisan, 2015 302 p. ; **641.81**

1. Back in the Day Bakery (Savannah, Ga.). 2. Baking. 3. Cake. 4. Pies. 5. Recipes 6. Cookbooks.
ISBN 9781579655563

LC 2014035874

Offers more than 100 recipes for treats, breakfast pastries, breads, pizza, and condiments, including jam muffins, breakfast bread pudding, rustic plum pie, tomato pie, spoon bread, salted caramel popcorn, and rosemary focaccia.

"Though the Days are wordy at times, the narrative is instructive and warming. The inclusion of crafts like a marshmallow chandelier and a keepsake cake topper seems jarring rather than jovial, the only off note. This is a terrific sequel, and fans of Southern baking (not to mention baking in general) will want to add it to their collection." Publishers Weekly.

Daykin, Rosie

Butter baked goods : nostalgic recipes from a little neighborhood bakery / Rosie Daykin ; photography by Janis Nicolay. Alfred A. Knopf, 2015. 263 p. : **641.81**

1. Butter Baked Goods (Vancouver, B.C.). 2. Pastry. 3. Cake. 4. Recipes 5. Cookbooks.
ISBN 9781101875087

LC 2014039534

"Originally published in Canada by Appetite by Random House, Toronto, in 2013."

Includes index.

Collects more than one hundred recipes using readily available ingredients for delectable desserts from the owner of Vancouver's Butter Baked Goods, including Butter's famous marshmallows, red velvet cupcakes, coconut cake, and lemon walnut bar.

Dodge, Abigail Johnson

The **everyday** baker : recipes & techniques for foolproof baking breads, pastries, cakes, pies, cookies, and more / Abigail Johnson Dodge. Taunton Press, Inc., 2015 615 p. : **641.81**

1. Baking 2. Desserts 3. Bread 4. Cookbooks.
ISBN 9781621138105

LC 2015032688

Collects over 150 recipes, with step-by-step photographs, for the home baker, including donuts, scones, cookies, turnovers, pies, cakes, baguettes, croissants, and tarts, complemented by must-know tips and techniques.

Emberling, Amy

Zingerman's Bakehouse / Amy Emberling & Frank Carollo ; photographs by Antonis Achilleos. Chronicle Books, 2017 255 p. : **641.81**

1. Zingerman's Bakehouse. 2. Baking 3. Recipes 4. Cookbooks.
ISBN 9781452156583

LC 2016057669

Includes indexes.

A collection of recipes from Michigan's renowned artisanal bakery in celebration of its twenty-fifth anniversary features such options as sour cream coffee cake, Jewish rye, challah, Boston cream pie, French crullers, and pecan sandies with bacon.

"All home bakers will recognize its merit, made visible in precise recipes...stunning photographs, and deeply reflective storytelling." Library Journal.

Ford, Bryan

New world sourdough : artisan techniques for creative homemade fermented breads; with recipes for birote, bagels, Pan de coco, beignets and more / Bryan Ford. Quarry, 2020. 159 p.: **641.81**

1. Cooking (Sourdough) 2. Sourdough bread. 3. Fermentation. 4. Recipes 5. Cookbooks.
ISBN 9781631598708

LC 2020000169

Includes index.

"New World Sourdough teaches handmade artisan bread baking for beginner to intermediate home bakers who want to learn how to bake fermented breads at home with New World twists".-- Provided by publisher.

"Instructions for the 35 recipes are direct, and the accompanying photographs of finished breads, mouthwatering. Really, a whole-world approach to bread baking." Booklist

Forkish, Ken

Flour water salt yeast : the fundamentals of artisan bread and pizza / Ken Forkish ; photographs by alan Weiner. Ten Speed Press, c2012. 265 p. : **641.81**

1. Bread. 2. Pizza. 3. Recipes 4. Cookbooks.
ISBN 9781607742739

LC 2012012080

Includes index.

A treasury of recipes for world-class breads and pizzas is complemented by schedules that can be adapted for busy home bakers, sharing instructions for preparing high-quality artisan recipes using basic straight dough, pre-ferment dough and complex levain.

"Committed bakers will find plenty here to keep ovens hot and families' plates filled with honest versions of one of the nations most beloved foods." Booklist.

Francois, Zoe

Holiday and celebration bread in five minutes a day : sweet and decadent baking for every occasion / Zoe Francois and Jeff Hertzberg, M.D. ; photographs by Sarah Kieffer and Zoe Francois. St. Martin's Press, 2018 xix, 378 p. : **641.81**

1. Bread. 2. Holiday cooking. 3. Recipes 4. Cookbooks
ISBN 9781250077561

LC 2018017182

Includes index.

This new cookbook from the authors of the <I>*Artisan Bread in Five Minutes a Day*</I> series contains 100 recipes for every occasion, using stored doughs that can be used as the basis for celebration breads from all over the globe.

Garbacz, Angela

★Perfectly golden : adaptable recipes for sweet and simple treats / Angela Garbacz, Owner, Goldenrod Pastries ; photographs by Daniel Muller. The Countryman Press, 2020. 256 p. : **641.81**

1. Baking. 2. Desserts. 3. Gluten-free foods
ISBN 9781682684764

LC 2020002620

Includes index.

"A cookbook of treats from the Great Plains to satisfy every sweet tooth Based in Lincoln, Nebraska, Goldenrod Pastries is a community bakery with an ambitious and talented baker at the helm. Angela Garbacz learned at her mother's and grandmothers' elbows, mixing up cookies and rolling sweet buns. Her training continued in New York City before she returned home and opened her dream shop. From her grandma's famous peach coffee cake to caramel-covered pecan rolls, lemon meringue pie and frosted brownies to fluffernutter buns and confetti cookies, Garbacz's pastries come out of the oven perfectly golden and regularly sell out. At her bakery, she creates delicious treats without dairy or gluten, but every recipe in this book can be made with butter and all-purpose flour just as easily as any alternative. With her positive attitude and confident voice, Garbacz makes it easy and fun to bake a perfect dessert that everyone can eat. This beautiful cookbook--the photography, the philosophy, and the desserts!--is an instant classic."-- Provided by publisher.

"An essential purchase for regional libraries and a top recommendation for all baking collections." Library Journal

Goldman, Duff

Duff bakes : think and bake like a pro at home / Duff Goldman and Sara Gonzales ; photography by Caren Alpert. William Morrow, 2015 343 p. : **641.81**

1. Baking. 2. Desserts. 3. Recipes 4. Cookbooks.
ISBN 9780062349804

LC bl2015046059

The graffiti artist-turned-Ace of Cakes star presents a collection of down-to-earth baking recipes that outlines the essentials that home cooks need to create satisfying favorites, from cookies and brownies to muffins and pizza dough.

"Rounded out with plenty of salient tips on everything from selecting the right blowtorch (hit the hardware store) to getting cheesecake out of a cake pan (briefly warm the bottom over the stove top), Goldman and Gonzalez's thoughtful instructions are sure to inspire and embolden readers." Publishers Weekly.

Golper, Zachary

Bien cuit : the art of bread / Zachary Golper and Peter Kaminsky ; photographs by Thomas Schauer. Regan Arts, 2015. ix, 324 p. : **641.81**

1. Bread. 2. Recipes 3. Cookbooks.
ISBN 9781941393413

LC bl2015048825

Includes index.

Two bread experts offer recipes, techniques, and tales of their work and travel experiences to help home bakers craft their own from-scratch rolls, loaves and quick breads, including Whole Wheat With Pumpkin Seeds, Bourbon Bread and Ciabatta.

Haedrich, Ken, 1954-

The **harvest** baker : 150 sweet & savory recipes celebrating the fresh-picked flavors of fruits, herbs & vegetables / Ken Haedrich ; photography by Johnny Autry. Storey Publishing, 2017 303 p. : **641.81**

1. Bread. 2. Pastry. 3. Baking. 4. Cookbooks.
ISBN 9781612127675

LC 2016059746

Includes index.

A collection of sweet and savory recipes that incorporate a wide variety of vegetables, fruits, and herbs into all types of baking features such options as muffins, scones, flatbreads, calzones, cookies, cakes, and pies.

"Renowned author and teacher Haedrich (Dinner Pies) returns with a new collection of hearty baked goods featuring garden and farm fresh produce." Library Journal.

Helding, Patricia

Fat witch bake sale : 67 recipes from the beloved Fat Witch Bakery for your next bake sale or party / Patricia Helding with Lucy Baker ; photography by Alexandra Grablewski. Rodale Books, 2014 184 p. : **641.81**

1. Fat Witch Bakery. 2. Baked products. 3. Baking. 4. Desserts 5. Recipes 6. Cookbooks
ISBN 1623362261

LC 2014038513

Includes index.

"Fat Witch brownies are a chocolate obsession, not just for the locals from New York City, but also for the many tourists who visit Chelsea Market. Patricia Helding and staff bake tender, moist, classic, and decadent morsels that people are willing to wait in line to buy. And following on the heels of Helding's very successful Fat Witch Brownies, which revealed the author's secret recipe (at long last), comes her new personal collection of yummy brownies, blondies, barks, bars, and more. along with tips and tricks for packaging and selling them at your next bake sale. Here are mouthwatering recipes for Pecan Caramel Brownies; Red Velvet Brownies; Five Layer Chocolate Bars; Jelly Blondies; Cinnamon Bars; Pumpkin Oatmeal Bars; Coconut Macadamia Cookies; uniquely grownup flavors like Fruitcake Brownies and Rum Raisin Spice Bars; and even gluten-free treats like Meringue Drops and Almond Flour White Chocolate Cookies. Packed with astonishingly good, easy-to-bake recipes that will leave your family and friends agog, Fat Witch Bake Sale will be the go-to recipe source for bake sale season--or anytime".-- Provided by publisher.

Hesser, Amanda

Food52 baking : 60 sensational treats you can pull off in a snap / editors of Food52 ; foreword by Amanda Hesser & Merrill Stubbs ; photography by James Ransom. Ten Speed Press, 2015 xiii, 157 p. ; **641.81**

1. Baking. 2. Quick and easy cooking 3. Recipes 4. Cookbooks.
ISBN 9781607748014

LC 2015027663

Includes index.

The editors of the popular culinary website Food52 offer 60 recipes for baking simple and delicious treats, including Brown Butter Cupcake Brownies, Peach Tart, Buttermilk Dutch Baby with Caramelized Pears and Black Pepper Popovers.

"A troubleshooting guide collects tips scattered through the book, explaining how to stale fresh bread in a hurry, how to pit cherries without a cherry pitter, and how to package cookies for the mail. This title may just become that one baking book kept out on the counter for use time and time again." Publishers Weekly.

Hoffman, Brian Hart

Bake from scratch. Brian Hart Hoffman. 83 Press, 2018 400 p. : **641.81**

1. Baking. 2. Bread. 3. Desserts. 4. Cookbooks.
ISBN 9781940772486

LC bl2018052577

Includes index.

Collects recipes for artisan breads, cakes, cookies, and confections for the home cook, including such dishes as spiced persimmon coconut cake, carrot coffee cake, honey pear swirl bread, apricot-almond hand pies, salted chocolate chip cookies, and pecan-toffee bites.

Kulaga, Agatha

Ovenly : sweet & salty recipes from New York's most creative bakery / Agatha Kulaga & Erin Patinkin ; photography by Winona Barton-Ballentine. Harlequin, 2014 xxi, 217 p. : **641.81**

1. Ovenly (Bakery) 2. Bread. 3. Baked products. 4. Recipes 5. Cookbooks.

ISBN 9780373892952

LC 2014005173

Includes index.

Presents a collection of recipes from the award-winning Brooklyn bakery, with a discussion on baking tools and ingredients and options for breads, muffins, cookies, pies, brownies, and cakes.

"Complemented by an attractive design and step-by-step photographs of important techniques, this is a satisfying everyday baking collection, perfect for readers who like substantial baked goods with a salty streak." Library Journal.

Lahey, Jim

The **Sullivan** Street Bakery cookbook / Jim Lahey with Maya Joseph ; photography by Squire Fox. W. W. Norton & Company, 2017 240 p. : **641.81**

1. Sullivan Street Bakery. 2. Baking. 3. Recipes 4. Cookbooks

ISBN 0393247287

LC 2017029427

Collects recipes for the Italian-inspired cafe dishes and breads from the popular Manhattan bakery, including such options as asparagus pizza, ciabatta, bran and blackberry muffins, oven-baked pasta, and brisket braised in black tea.

"A terrific addition to the bread-making canon." Publishers Weekly.

Leader, Daniel

Living bread : tradition and innovation in artisan bread making / Daniel Leader with Lauren Chattman. Avery, 2019 367 p. **641.81**

1. Bread. 2. Recipes 3. Cookbooks

ISBN 9780735213838

LC 2019015854

"This vital addition to the dough canon will resonate with serious home bakers as well as professionals." Publishers Weekly

Lenzer, Suzanne

Graze : inspiration for small plates and meandering meals / Suzanne Lenzer ; photography by Nicole Franzen. Rodale, 2017 xxxiii, 205 p. : **641.81**

1. Appetizers 2. Cookbooks.

ISBN 9781623367534

LC bl2017027909

Includes index.

Collects recipes for dishes and snacks for creating small plates that work together as a meal, including such options as Spanish-style shrimp with chile, duck rillettes on toast, and crab, avocado, and black bean tostadas.

Lin, Irvin F.

Marbled, swirled and layered : 150 recipes and variations for artful bars, cookies, pies, cakes, and more / Irvin Lin ; photography by Linda Xiao. Houghton Mifflin Harcourt, 2016 346 p. : **641.81**

1. Baking. 2. Desserts 3. Recipes 4. Cookbooks

ISBN 0544453735

LC 2015038040

Includes index.

An award-winning photographer and the founder of the nationally recognized blog, Eat the Love, offers 150 recipes, along with baking and decorating tips, to help readers make gorgeous, tasty desserts including cinnamon spiral icebox cookies, pistachio-swirl brownies and triple-chocolate pie.

Manning, Ivy

Easy soups from scratch with quick breads to match : 70 recipes to pair and share / Ivy Manning ; photographs by Dina Avila. Chronicle Books, 2017 175 p. : **641.81**

1. Bread. 2. Recipes 3. Soups. 4. Cookbooks

ISBN 145215502X

LC 2016032627

Includes index.

Presents a collection of seventy soup recipes, including Korean kimchi and tofu soup, roasted cauliflower and paprika soup, black bean soup with roasted red pepper cream, and coconut chicken soup.

McDowell, Erin Jeanne

The **fearless** baker : simple secrets for baking like a pro / Erin Jeanne McDowell ; photographs by Jennifer May. Houghton Mifflin Harcourt, 2017 383 p. : **641.81**

1. Baking. 2. Cookbooks.

ISBN 9780544791435

LC bl2017043684

"A Rux Martin book."

Includes index.

Shares tips and techniques for baking to make professional-quality cakes, pies, and other desserts, and provides recipes for such confections as flourless cocoa cookies, apple cider pie, and strawberry popovers.

"Comprehensive tips on baking and decorating cakes and pies accompany tempting recipes, including for pound cupcakes made with honey-caramel glaze, mocha cake with a coffee and white chocolate ganache, and a simple cider caramel apple pie. Her clearly written recipes and tips, explained in a friendly, encouraging voice, will inspire confidence in experienced and novice bakers alike." Publishers Weekly.

Moore, Christine, 1963-

Little Flower baking / Christine Moore with Cecilia Leung ; photographs by Staci Valentine. Prospect Park Books, 2016 260 p. : **641.81**

1. Little Flower (Restaurant). 2. Baking. 3. Cooking, American. 4. Cookbooks.

ISBN 9781938849602

LC 2015042873

Includes index.

"Recipes are written clearly enough, even for kitchen novices, and she includes a helpful prologue of baking and ingredient tips. This ones a must-read for serious bakers." Booklist.

Nelson, Candace, 1974-

The **Sprinkles** baking book : 100 secret recipes from Candace's kitchen / Candace Nelson with Adeena Sussman ; photographs by Amy Neunsinger. Grand Central Life & Style, 2016. xiii, 321 p. : **641.81**

1. Desserts. 2. Cake. 3. Cupcakes. 4. Baking. 5. Cookbooks.

ISBN 9781455592579

LC OC2018140580

The founder and pastry chef of Sprinkles Bakery and judge of Cupcake Wars shares the stories and recipes that have been a part of her life and her customers' lives, including 50 Sprinkles cupcake recipes in all their variations along with 50 of her favorite dessert recipes for cakes, pies, cookies, bars and more.

A **new** way to bake : classic recipes updated with better-for-you ingredients from the modern pantry / from the kitchens of Martha Stewart. Clarkson Potter/Publishers, 2017 319 p. ; **641.81**

1. Baking. 2. Recipes 3. Cookbooks.
ISBN 9780307954718

LC 2016008583

Includes index.

Shares classic recipes for baked goods using whole-grain flours, natural sweeteners, and other healthy ingredients.

"This is a healthier, yet no less tasty collection to rely on." Publishers Weekly.

Norman, David, 1963-

Bread on the table : recipes for making and enjoying Europe's most beloved breads / David Norman, owner of Austin's easy tiger bake shop & beer garden ; photographs by Johnny Autry. Ten Speed Press, 2019 vii, 244 p. : **641.81**

1. Bread 2. Recipes 3. Cookbooks.
ISBN 9781607749257

LC 2019008705

Includes index.

Culinary instructor and baker David Norman explores the European breadmaking traditions that inspire him most. Norman also offers recipes for traditional foods to accompany these regional specialties, so home bakers can showcase their freshly made breads alongside traditional meals.

"This terrific work is sure to appeal to veterans and novices alike." Publishers Weekly.

Peterson, James

★**Sauces** : classical and contemporary sauce making / James Peterson. Houghton Mifflin Harcourt, 2017. xxi, 666 p. : **641.81**

1. Recipes 2. Sauces. 3. Cookbooks
ISBN 0544819829

LC bl2017051518

Offers practical tips for making sauces, as well as hundreds of recipes for stocks, glaces, and purees using easy-to-follow charts, healthier ingredients, and standardized terminology.

Poilane, Apollonia

Poilane : the secrets of the world-famous bread bakery / Apollonia Poilane ; foreword by Alice Waters ; photographs by Philippe Vaurès Santamaria. Houghton Mifflin Harcourt, 2019. 288 p. **641.81**

1. Poilane, Apollonia 2. Poilâne (Bakery). 3. Baking. 4. Bread. 5. Sourdough baking 6. Pastry.
ISBN 9781328810786

LC 2019024020

Includes index.

"For the first time, Poilâne provides detailed instructions so bakers can reproduce its unique "hug-sized" sourdough loaves at home, as well as the bakery's other much-loved breads and pastries. It tells the story of how Apollonia Poilâne, the third-generation baker and owner, took over the global business at eighteen and steered it into the future as a Harvard University freshman after her parents were killed in a helicopter crash".-- Provided by publisher.

Robertson, Chad

Tartine. modern, ancient, classic, whole. Chad Robertson. Chronicle Books, 2013 336 p. : **641.81**

1. Tartine (Bakery) 2. Cooking (Bread) 3. Recipes 4. Cookbooks.
ISBN 9781452114309

LC bl2014000228

Includes index.

Shares techniques and master recipes for different styles of bread and recipes for pastry, fruit galettes, and cookies.

"Acclaimed baker and Tartine Bakery cofounder Robertson's third cookbook is as visually impressive as its predecessors. Its recipes, however, are far more challenging, providing spare instructions and assuming considerable technical knowledge. Robertson breaks up chapters of intriguing and innovative breads, crispbreads, and pastries (e.g., sprouted quinoa kamut bread, lemon-poppy-kefir pound cake) with accounts of baking-related travels in Denmark, Sweden, Germany, Austria, France, and Mexico." Library Journal.

Tartine bread / Chad Robertson ; photographs by Eric Wolfinger. Chronicle Books, c2010. 303 p. : **641.81**

1. Tartine (Bakery) 2. Cooking (Bread) 3. Cookbooks.
ISBN 9780811870412

LC 2011029736

Includes index.

"This baker's guidebook is divided into four parts: Basic Country Bread; Semolina and Whole-Wheat Breads; Baguettes and Enriched Breads; and Day-Old Bread. Robertson's basic recipe is explained in depth with numbered steps, and consists of making a natural leaven and baking in a cast-iron cooker. The author's passionate tone and tales of baking apprenticeships, along with top-notch step-by-step photos, elevate the title from mere manual to enjoyable read." Publishers Weekly.

Saltz, Joanna

Delish insane sweets : bake yourself a little crazy / Joanna Saltz & the Editors of Delish. Houghton Mifflin Harcourt, 2019. 238 p. : **641.81**

1. Baking. 2. Cookies. 3. Cake. 4. Cupcakes. 5. Cookbooks.
ISBN 9780358193340

LC 2019025607

"100+ cookies bars & bites inside!"

Includes index.

"The first dessert recipe collection from the editors of the wildly popular site and magazine, Delish"-- Provided by publisher.

Scheft, Uri

Breaking breads / Uri Scheft with Raquel Pelzel. Artisan Books, 2016 351 p. : **641.81**

1. Bread. 2. Cookbooks.
ISBN 9781579656829

LC 2016027530

Includes index.

Presents a collection of sweet and savory baking recipes that combine flavors from both Europe and the Middle East, including such options as challah rolls, rum raisin and cheese babka, ciabatta, chocolate rugelach, and tahini cookies.

"An essential modern Middle Eastern baking collection featuring delights such as shakshuka focaccia and chocolate rugelach." Library Journal.

Smith, Ed (Food writer)

On the side : a sourcebook of inspiring side dishes / Ed Smith ; photography by Joe Woodhouse. Bloomsbury, 2017. xv, 335

p. : **641.81**

1. Side dishes (Cooking). 2. Quick and easy cooking 3. Quick and easy cooking 4. Cookbooks.
ISBN 9781408873151

LC bl2018071843

Includes index.

A revolutionary cookbook that moves the humble side dish to centre stage.

"They're incredibly easy to browse and select thanks to abundant cross-references and "recipe directories" addressing key questions... This is a UK title, so be ready for metric measurements and some potentially unfamiliar terms." Library Journal.

Symon, Michael, 1969-

Michael Symon's 5 in 5 for every season : 165 quick dinners, sides, holiday dishes and more / Michael Symon, with Douglas Trattner ; photographs by Jennifer May. Clarkson Potter, 2015 255 p. : **641.81**

1. Dinners and dining. 2. Side dishes (Cooking). 3. Seasonal cooking. 4. Quick and easy cooking. 5. Cookbooks.
ISBN 9780804186568

LC 2015006128

Includes index.

A collection of simple, from-scratch recipes by the television personality organizes entries according to the season, including such offerings as sweet corn fritters, vegetable stir-fry, and pork tenderloin with fresh cranberries.

Volger, Lukas

Bowl : vegetarian recipes for ramen, pho, bibimbap, dumplings, and other one-dish meals / Lukas Volger ; photography by Michael Harlan Turkell. Houghton Mifflin Harcourt, 2016 255 p. : **641.81**

1. Soups. 2. Stews. 3. One-dish meals. 4. Vegetarian cooking. 5. Cookbooks.
ISBN 9780544325289

LC 2015037777

Putting a vegetarian twist on ramen, pho, bibimbap, dumplings and burrito bowls, this unique cookbook, capturing the full flavor of the popular one-bowl meals, shows readers how to make improvisational meals full of seasonal produce and herbs that can be made quickly and inexpensively.

"A go-to cookbook for Asian-inspired vegetarian soups, noodle bowls, and dumplings." Library Journal.

Volland, Susan

Mastering sauces : the home cook's guide to new techniques for fresh flavors / Susan Volland ; photography by Angie Norwood Browne. W.W. Norton & Company, 2015 495 p. ; **641.81**

1. Recipes 2. Sauces. 3. Cookbooks
ISBN 0393241858

LC 2015017677

Includes index.

Based on three fundamental principles for making great sauces--Maximizing Flavor, Manipulating Texture and Seasoning Confidently--an ultimate resource, filled with more than 150 recipes that reflect today's tastes, teaches home cooks the "whys" and "hows" of sauce-making.

"This is an excellent culinary reference with a thoroughness that recalls titles such as Shirley Corriher's Cookwise and Karen Page and Andrew Dornenburg's The Flavor Bible. Highly recommended, along with Martha Holmberg's Modern Sauces." Library Journal.

Weber, Kathleen (Baker)

Della Fattoria bread : 63 foolproof recipes for yeasted, enriched & naturally leavened breads / Kathleen Weber ; with Amy Albert & Amy Vogler ; photographs by Ed Anderson ; foreword by Thomas Keller. Artisan, 2014 xix, 284 p. : **641.81**

1. Della Fattoria (Bakery). 2. Bread. 3. Recipes 4. Cookbooks.
ISBN 9781579655310

LC 2014004630

Collects tips and techniques for baking bread along with recipes from the author's award winning bakery, including brioche braid, olive oil wreath, and olive campagne boule.

"Highly recommended for serious home bakers, especially those looking to move on from easier titles such as Jeff Hertzberg and Zoe Francois's Artisan Bread in Five Minutes a Day." Library Journal.

641.815 Bread and bread-like foods

Meyer, Claus (Cook)

Meyer's Bakery : bread and baking in the Nordic kitchen / Claus Meyer. Mitchell Beazley, 2017. 296 p. : **641.815**

1. Meyers Bageri. 2. Baking. 3. Bread. 4. Cooking (Natural foods) 5. Cooking, Scandinavian. 6. Cookbooks.
ISBN 9781784722715
Includes index.
Translation of: Meyers bageskole.

"Originally published in Danish in 2014 by Lindhardt og Ringof"--Colophon.

Meyer shares his knowledge of bread and baking. He begins with the simple idea that bread made with lots whole grain and slow fermentation is one of the healthiest things we can eat-- and everyone can learn to make it. Building around four types of dough, he provides recipes that will expand your range with Nordic baking in its many forms.

Nilsson, Magnus, 1983-

The **Nordic** baking book / Magnus Nilsson. Phaidon Press Limited, 2018. 575 p. : **641.815**

1. Baking -- Faroe Islands. 2. Baking -- Finland. 3. Baking -- Iceland. 4. Baking -- Scandinavia. 5. Cookbooks
ISBN 0714876844

LC 2018420391

Includes index.

The acclaimed chef featured in the Emmy-Award winning US PBS series The Mind of a Chef and the Netflix docuseries Chef's Table explores the rich baking tradition of the Nordic region, with 450 tempting recipes for home bakers

641.82 Main dishes

Bastianich, Joseph

Healthy pasta : the sexy, skinny, and smart way to eat your favorite food / Joseph Bastianich and Tanya Bastianich Manuali, PhD. Alfred A. Knopf, 2015. x, 185 p. : **641.82**

1. Cooking (Pasta). 2. Cooking, Italian. 3. Recipes 4. Cookbooks.
ISBN 9780385352246

LC 2014025460

Includes index.

A guide to making pasta an integral part of a healthy and well-balanced lifestyle offers one hundred recipes under 500 calories per serving, including spaghetti primavera, rigatoni with chicken and zucchini, and vegetable lasagna.

"Though their sexiness is debatable, these recipes are tasty, practical, and in line with current dietary trends. Recommended for pasta lovers in search of healthier everyday recipes." Library Journal.

Beddia, Joe

Pizza camp : recipes from Pizzeria Beddia / Joe Beddia ; photography by Randy Morris. Adams, 2017 223 p. : **641.82**

1. Pizzeria Beddia. 2. Pizza 3. Cookbooks.
ISBN 9781419724091

LC bl2017020047

Includes index.

Presents over fifty recipes for pizza from the famous Philadelphia pizzeria, including pistachio pesto, roasted fennel and sausage, and stromboli.

Bruni, Frank

A **meatloaf** in every oven : two chatty cooks, one iconic comfort dish and dozens of recipes-from Mom's to Mario Batali's / Frank Bruni and Jennifer Steinhauer ; illustrations by Marilyn Pollack Naron. GCP Life & Style, [2017] 208 p. **641.82**

1. Meat loaf 2. Cooking, American 3. Journalists 4. Cooking
ISBN 9781455563050

LC 2016025917

Includes index.

A guide to American meatloaf as traced through the culinary friendship of two New York Times journalists shares 50 recipes that incorporate an international range of flavors.

"Liberally peppered with Bruni and Steinhauer's snappy dialogue, this is a terrific collection that deserves a look from meatloaf lovers of all ages." Publishers Weekly.

Carluccio, Antonio

Pasta : the essential new collection from the master of Italian cookery / Antonio Carluccio ; photography by Laura Edwards. Quadrille, 2014. 224 p. : **641.82**

1. Cooking (Pasta). 2. Cooking, Italian. 3. Recipes 4. Cookbooks.
ISBN 9781849496643

LC bl2015043187

Includes index.

"This is a superb addition to shelves already groaning with Italian cookbooks. Pasta lovers will want to give this one some serious consideration." Publishers Weekly.

Forkish, Ken

The **elements** of pizza : unlocking the secrets to world-class pies at home / Ken Forkish ; photography by Alan Weiner. Ten Speed Press, 2016 249 p. : **641.82**

1. Cooking, Italian 2. Pizza. 3. Recipes 4. Cookbooks
ISBN 160774838X

LC 2015032247

A follow-up to the James Beard and IACP award-winning Flour Water Salt Yeast shares in-depth explanations of the complicated mechanics of preparing excellent pizza dough, sharing dozens of recipes for a wide range of pizza styles, from Neapolitan and American Pan to gluten free and New York.

Green, Aliza

Making artisan pasta : how to make a world of handmade noodles, stuffed pasta, dumplings, and more / [Aliza Green ; with photography by Steve Legato]. Quarry Books, 2012. 176 p. : **641.82**

1. Cooking (Pasta) 2. Noodles. 3. Gourmet cooking 4. Recipes 5. Cookbooks
ISBN 9781592537327

LC 2011031326

"Homemade rules in the kitchen, and everyone from artisan bakers to canners and picklers know it. Culinary enthusiasts and hungry home cooks are exploring classic skills again, and making homemade, hand-shaped pasta is on the rise. With the simplest ingredients and easier-than-you-think instructions, Making Artisan Pasta teaches you how make your own linguine, ravioli, lasagna, and dozens of other styles of pasta and noodles by hand. The fully illustrated, step-by-step tutorials will walk you through the entire tasty process, from mixing dough, rolling, and shaping pasta through cooking, serving, and storing pasta for later. Going way beyond noodles, though, this book includes tutorials on gnocchi, Chinese pot stickers, pierogi, and dozens of other world pastas. Through author and chef Aliza Green's expertise and encyclopedia knowledge of all things culinary, plus hundreds of gorgeous photos by acclaimed food photographer Steve Legato, you will learn everything there is to know about making fresh, delicious pasta in your home kitchen....and you'll never look at the supermarket pasta aisle the same way again".-- Provided by publisher.

"The book contains many useful extras such as nutrition information, resources, and a glossary, but those who want to serve a homemade sauce along with their pasta fresca may need to consult another resource." Library Journal.

Henry, Colu

Back pocket pasta : inspired dinners to cook on the fly / Colu Henry ; photographs by Peden + Munk. Clarkson Potter/Publishers, 2017 239 p. : **641.82**

1. Cooking (Pasta). 2. Quick and easy cooking. 3. Recipes 4. Cookbooks.
ISBN 9780553459746

LC 2016010616

Includes index.

Includes 100 recipes for making delicious pasta dishes on the fly, including Linguine With Chili Oil, Capers and Lemon, Roasted Fennel and Garlic With White Beans and Spinach and Penne With Red Cabbage, Caraway and Pancetta.

Henry, Diana

From the oven to the table : simple dishes that look after themselves / Diana Henry. Mitchell Beazley, 2019. 240 p. : **641.82**

1. Cooking. 2. Quick and easy cooking 3. One-dish meals. 4. Cookbooks.
ISBN 9781784726096

LC bl2019029485

Includes index.

"An appealing resource for home cooks, curious dabblers, serious chefs." Library Journal

Louis, Jenn

Pasta by hand : a collection of Italy's regional hand-shaped pasta / Jenn Louis ; foreword by Mario Batali ; photographs by Ed Anderson. Chronicle Books, 2015 200 p. : **641.82**

1. Cooking (Pasta) 2. Cooking, Italian 3. Pasta 4. Dumplings. 5. Cookbooks.
ISBN 9781452121888

LC 2014032602

Collects over sixty-five recipes for hand-shaped pastas and dumplings, including ricotta gnocchetti, spinach spatzli, and semolina cavatelli.

"The luxurious sauce recipes in the last chapter are worth the price of admission alone and feature traditional rags of lamb, rabbit, porcini, tomato, beef, and wild boar. This single-focus cookbook is written with both authority and a passion for 'some of the most soulful Italian food we can eat.'" Publishers Weekly.

Marchetti, Domenica

The **glorious** pasta of Italy / Domenica Marchetti. Chronicle Books, 2011. 280 p. : **641.82**

1. Cooking (Pasta) 2. Cooking, Italian. 3. Cookbooks.
ISBN 9780811872591

LC 2011030010

Celebrating pasta in all its glorious forms, author Domenica Marchetti draws from her Italian heritage to share 100 classic and modern recipes. Step-by-step instructions for making fresh pasta offer plenty of variations on the classic egg pasta, while a glossary of pasta shapes, a source list for unusual ingredients, and a handy guide for stocking the pantry with pasta essentials encourage the home cook to look beyond simple spaghetti.

Martha Stewart Living Omnimedia

One pot : 120+ easy meals from your skillet, slow cooker, stockpot, and more / from the kitchens of Martha Stewart Living, photographs by Christine Holmes and others. Clarkson Potter/Publishers, 2014 256 p. : **641.82**

1. Stews. 2. One-dish meals. 3. Electric slow cookers 4. Quick and easy cooking 5. Cookbooks.
ISBN 9780307954411

LC 2013050638

Includes index.

Collects recipes for comfort foods that can be make using a single pot or pan, offering such options as Cajun stew made in a Dutch oven, slow cooker lamb shanks and potatoes, and kale and white bean soup made in a pressure cooker.

"Useful for weeknight home cooking, this survey of one-pot preparations features consistent, classic recipes and vibrant photographs. Readers interested in the slow-cooking chapters will also enjoy Andrew Schloss's Cooking Slow." Library Journal.

Mirarchi, Carlo

Roberta's / Carlo Mirarchi, Brandon Hoy, Chris Parachini and Katherine Wheelock, art direction by Ryan Rice. Clarkson Potter/Publishers, 2013 287 p. : **641.82**

1. Roberta's (Restaurant) 2. Pizza. 3. Gourmet cooking 4. Cookbooks.
ISBN 9780770433710

LC 2013004300

Includes index.

Presents a collection of recipes from the owners of Roberta's pizzeria in Bushwick, Brooklyn, along with the story of how the owners transformed a concrete bunker into an highly acclaimed and innovative restaurant and rooftop garden.

Reinhart, Peter

Perfect pan pizza : square pies to make at home, from Roman, Sicilian, and Detroit, to grandma pies and focaccia / Peter Reinhart. Ten Speed Press, 2019 185 p. : **641.82**

1. Pizza 2. Cooking, Italian 3. Cookbooks.
ISBN 9780399581953

LC 2018054093

A guide to pan pizza illustrates how to make several styles in a home oven, including Detroit-style deep-pan, focaccia, Sicilian, and Roman, and features recipes for such options as pepperoni deluxe, kundalini cauliflower, and bacon and egg.

Segan, Francine

Pasta modern : new & inspired recipes from Italy / Francine Segan ; photographs by Lucy Schaeffer. Stewart, Tabori & Chang, 2013. 208 p. : **641.82**

1. Cooking (Pasta) 2. Cooking, Italian. 3. Recipes 4. Cookbooks.
ISBN 9781617690624

LC bl2013040230

Includes index.

Offers 100 illustrated recipes for unusual and innovative Italian pasta dishes, covering appetizers, soups, main dishes, and desserts.

"Meticulously researched, thoughtfully curated, and artfully designed, this unique collection will inspire readers to try new preparations and flavors." Library Journal.

Tanis, David

One good dish / David Tanis ; photographs by Gentl & Hyers. Artisan, 2013 256 p. : **641.82**

1. One-dish meals. 2. Recipes
ISBN 1579654673

LC 2013006289

Includes index.

Offers 100 recipes for simple, casual meals appropriate for any time of the day, including breaded eggplant cutlets, scallion kimchee, and peppery duck steaks with parsley salad.

Vetri, Marc

Mastering pasta : the art and practice of handmade pasta, gnocchi, and risotto / Marc Vetri with David Joachim ; photography by Ed Anderson. Ten Speed Press, 2015 ix, 261 p. : **641.82**

1. Cooking (Pasta). 2. Recipes 3. Cookbooks.
ISBN 9781607746072

LC 2014020868

Collects directions for making fresh pastas along with recipes for dishes, including asparagus and egg yolk rotolo, doppio ravioli with lamb and polenta, and saffron fusilli with lobster and leeks.

"This lavish pasta cookbook has lots of science-based information and an overview of 15 types of wheat flours. Perfect for dedicated pasta lovers looking to hone their skills." Library Journal.

Vetri, Marc

Mastering pizza : the art and practice of handmade pizza, focaccia and calzone / Marc Vetri and David Joachim ; photography by Ed Anderson. Ten Speed Press, 2018 261 p. : **641.82**

1. Pizza. 2. Cooking, Italian. 3. Cookbooks
ISBN 9780399579226

LC 2017049095

A noted, award-winning chef and restauranteur offers a step-by-step guide for making the perfect pizza by selecting from a variety of base doughs with different hydration levels that can work perfectly in a regular home kitchen oven.

641.83 Salads

Caldesi, Katie

Around the world in 120 salads : fresh, healthy, delicious / Katie & Giancarlo Caldesi ; photography by Helen Cathcart. Kyle

Books, 2017. 208 p. : **641.83**

1. Salads 2. International cooking 3. Recipes 4. Cookbooks.
ISBN 9781909487611

LC bl2017017639

Includes index.

Presents a collection of healthful salad recipes from around the world, including spiced green beans with tomatoes from Kuwait, hot spicy shrimp meet cool cucumber salad from Spain, and fish tacos with shredded cabbage from Mexico.

Romero, Terry Hope

Salad samurai : 100 cutting-edge, ultra-hearty, easy-to-make salads you don't have to be vegan to love / Terry Hope Romero. Da Capo Lifelong,, 2014 180 p. : **641.83**

1. Recipes 2. Salads. 3. Cookbooks
ISBN 0738214876

LC 2014002618

Includes index.

Introduces a versatile world of meatless, dairy-free dishes built on whole-food ingredients and includes recipes for dressings.

Rosen, Ilene

Saladish : a crunchier, grainier, herbier, heartier, tastier way with vegetables / Ilene Rosen with Donna Gelb ; photographs by Joseph De Leo ; illustrations by Emma Dibben. Artisan, 2018 207 p. : **641.83**

1. Salads. 2. Salad greens. 3. Salad vegetables. 4. Cookbooks
ISBN 9781579656959

LC 2017036051

A collection of seasonally organized recipes for creative salads and vegetable dishes that blend a wide range of ingredients, flavors, and textures, features such options as Vietnamese-style tofu salad, roasted grapes, and Bosc pear and fennel slaw.

"Highly recommended for fans of grain bowls, meal-sized salads, and meatless meals." Library Journal.

641.84 Sandwiches and related dishes

Avila, Wesley

Guerrilla Tacos : recipes from the streets of L.A. / Wesley Avila ; with Richard Parks III ; photographs by Dylan James .Ho, Jeni Afuso ; illustrations by Michael Hirshon. Ten Speed Press, 2017 269 p. : **641.84**

1. Guerilla Tacos. 2. Tacos. 3. Cooking, American -- California style. 4. Recipes 5. Cookbooks
ISBN 9780399578632

LC 2017024762

Includes index.

"The definitive word on tacos from native Angeleno Wes Avila of Guerrilla Tacos, who draws on his Mexican heritage as well as his time in the kitchens of some of the world's best restaurants to create taco perfection. In a town overrun with taco trucks, Wes Avila's Guerrilla Tacos has managed to win almost every accolade there is, from being crowned Best Taco Truck by LA Weekly to being called one of the best things to eat in Los Angeles by living legend Jonathan Gold. Avila's approach stands out in a crowded field because it's unique; the 50 base recipes in this book are grounded in authenticity but never tied down to tradition. Wes uses ingredients like kurobata sausage and sea urchin, but his best-selling taco is made from the humble sweet potato. From basic building blocks to how to balance flavor and texture, with comic-inspired illustrations and stories throughout, Guerrilla Tacos is the final word on tacos from the streets of L.A".-- Provided by publisher.

Fuentes, Laura (Chef)

The **taco** Tuesday cookbook : 52 tasty taco recipes to make every week the best ever / Laura Fuentes, founder of MOMables.com. Fair Winds, 2018. 175 p. : **641.84**

1. Tacos. 2. Mexican American cooking. 3. Recipes 4. Quick and easy cooking 5. Cookbooks
ISBN 9781592338191

LC 2018012263

Includes index.

Presents family-friendly taco recipes--one for every week of the year--that are all made with real-food ingredients, including such options as chickpea and butternut squash, Mexican short rib, and baja fish tacos.

Garcia, Lorena (Chef)

Lorena Garcia's new taco classics / Lorena Garcia with Liz Balmaseda. Celebra, 2015 xiv, 352 p. : **641.84**

1. Tacos. 2. Recipes 3. Cookbooks.
ISBN 9780451476913

LC 2015008294

Collects quick and easy-to-follow recipes for the street foods of Latin America, breaking down each new-style taco into its elements, from the shell to the fillings to the toppings, including slaws, salads, and sauces.

"Traditionalists will appreciate the inclusion of tamales with green tomatillo and pulled chicken and tostadas al pastor, as well as tips on making the best chile de arbol sauce. This book is approachable enough for the novice, and packed with must-try dishes for everyday dining as well as special occasions. Readers might want to buy two copies, since the first ones going to be stained and tattered in no time." Publishers Weekly.

Kord, Tyler

A **super** upsetting cookbook about sandwiches / Tyler Kord ; photography by Noah Fecks ; artwork by William Wegman. Clarkson Potter/Publishers, 2016 191 p. ; **641.84**

1. Sandwiches. 2. Recipes 3. Cookbooks.
ISBN 9780804186414

LC 2015028505

Includes index.

The chef of a popular New York sandwich shop presents a collection of recipes for unique sandwich combinations, using meat, fish, veggie burgers, condiments, sauces, purees, and sides.

Stupak, Alex

Tacos : recipes and provocations / Alex Stupak and Jordana Rothman ; photographs by Evan Sung. Clarkson Potter, 2015 239 p. : **641.84**

1. Tacos. 2. Tortillas. 3. Cooking, Mexican. 4. Gourmet cooking 5. Cookbooks.
ISBN 9780553447293

LC 2015006214

In a full-color, highly visual book, the owner of Empellón Taqueria and a food journalist teach readers how to make a variety of gourmet tacos from scratch.

641.85 Preserves and candy

Curl, Jami

Candy is magic : real ingredients, modern recipes / Jami Curl ; photography by Maggie Kirkland ; illustrations by Michelle Ott. Ten Speed Press, 2017 vii, 303 p. ; **641.85**

1. Candy. 2. Confectionery. 3. Recipes 4. Cookbooks.
ISBN 9780399578397

LC 2016047716

Shares recipes for two hundred confectionaries made from real, natural ingredients, including donut magic dust, vanilla bean and roasted fruit caramels, and toasted coconut marshmallows.

"Curls enthusiasm for her craft makes this cookbook a pleasure to read; she is the ideal coach for would-be candy makers." Publishers Weekly. Annex

Goldstein, Joyce Esersky, author

Jam session : a fruit-preserving handbook / Joyce Goldstein ; photographs by Ed Anderson. Lorena Jones Books, an imprint of the Crown Publishing Group, 2018 263 p. : **641.85**

1. Jam 2. Jelly 3. Seasonal cooking 4. Cookbooks.
ISBN 9780399579615

LC 2018001021

Includes index.

Offers instructions for all-natural fruit preserving and includes ideas on how to use fruit preserves to elevate common foods.

641.86 Desserts

Adams, Jocelyn Delk

Grandbaby cakes : modern recipes, vintage charm, soulful memories / Jocelyn Delk Adams. Surrey Books, An Agate Imprint, 2015 224 p. ; **641.86**

1. Cake. 2. Baking 3. Recipes 4. Cookbooks.
ISBN 9781572841734

LC 2015013216

Includes index.

"Cookbook featuring 50 vintage cakes with modern twists and memoir tracing the roots of the author's family recipes".--Provided by publisher.

"Adams's cake recipes are familiar yet unlike any you'll find in similar cookbooks. An instant classic, this title belongs in most baking collections." Library Journal.

America's Test Kitchen (Firm)

Naturally sweet : bake all your favorites with 30% to 50% less sugar / the editors at America's Test Kitchen. America's Test Kitchen, 2016 x, 309 p. : **641.86**

1. Desserts. 2. Baking. 3. Sugar-free diet. 4. Recipes 5. Cookbooks.
ISBN 9781940352589

LC 2016009055

Includes index.

Collects recipes for baked goods and desserts that rely on natural alternatives to white sugar, including such options as peach pie, honey buns, blueberry scones, chocolate chip cookies, chocolate layer cake, and red velvet cupcakes.

"Cooks with a powerful sweet tooth should scoop up this well-researched recipe book for healthier takes on classic sweet treats." Booklist.

America's Test Kitchen (Firm)

The **perfect** cake : your ultimate guide to classic, modern, and whimsical cakes / the editors at America's Test Kitchen. America's Test Kitchen, 2018 422 p. : **641.86**

1. Cake. 2. Recipes 3. Cookbooks.
ISBN 9781945256264

LC 2017049045

Includes index.

"Gathering together years of baking knowledge in their first-ever cake book, America's Test Kitchen offers a comprehensive collection of recipes for any cake you can imagine--from better-than-the-rest yellow cake layers for birthday parties to fanciful creations and elegant holiday desserts. Cakes are the ultimate all-occasion dessert. Whether you are looking for a party-worthy cake that's sure to bring smiles or a rustic treat for any time, America's Test Kitchen has the perfect recipe in this definitive guide to cake baking. The Perfect Cake opens with a valuable chapter of mix-and-match layer cakes, frostings, and fillings, allowing anyone to find just the combination they're looking for. The following chapters traverse a range of styles, touching on easy crowd-pleasers, sky-high stunners, American classics, holiday cakes, charming minature cakes, and more. Rigorously tested to ensure the perfect outcome, these never-fail recipes will improve any baker's game, from White Cake Layers with an ultradowny crumb to a perfectly domed Pound Cake, a New York Cheesecake with a browned surface (and no cracks), and superlatively chocolaty Ultimate Chocolate Cupcakes. Discover new techniques and flavors with a Blueberry Jam Cake frosted in a stunning ombre pattern, a sweet-salty Chocolate-Caramel Layer Cake, and a naked-sided Blackberry-Lemon Mascarpone Cake. And as only the test kitchen can, we fill the book with insight on everything from batter mixing methods to slicing cakes into multiple even layers.The Table of Contents:IntroductionChapter 1: Build-a-Cake: Mix-and-Match Layers and FrostingsChapter 2: Cupcakes, Cake Pops, Mug Cakes, and MoreChapter 3: Crowd-Pleasing Sheet CakesChapter 4: Sky-High CakesChapter 5: Elegant Cakes and TortesChapter 6: Great American CakesChapter 7: Celebrate! Holiday CakesChapter 8: Snack Cakes and Rustic Fruit CakesChapter 9: Pound Cakes, Bundt Cakes and Tube CakesChapter 10: Cool Down: Cheesecakes, Ice Cream, and Icebox"--Provided by publisher.

America's Test Kitchen (Firm)

The **perfect** cookie : your ultimate guide to foolproof cookies, brownies & bars / the editors at America's Test Kitchen. America's Test Kitchen, 2017 ix, 438 p. : **641.86**

1. Cookies. 2. Brownies (Cookies) 3. Recipes 4. Cookbooks.
ISBN 9781940352954

LC 2017008692

Includes index.

Presents cookie recipes, from brownies and chocolate turtle cookies to classic chewy oatmeal cookies and spumoni bars, breaking down key steps and techniques.

"The editors at America's Test Kitchen pack decades of baking experience into this impressive volume of 250 recipes for cookies, brownies, bars, and no-bake confections." Library Journal.

America's Test Kitchen (Firm)

The **perfect** pie : your ultimate guide to classic and modern pies, tarts, galettes, and more / America's Test Kitchen. America's Test Kitchen, 2019 ix, 366 p. : **641.86**

1. Pies. 2. Cookbooks.
ISBN 9781945256912

LC 2019019130

Includes index.

Covers corner-bakery classics and French-patisserie favorites|plus a host of whimsical, modern pies and tarts of all kinds such as Crab Apple Rose Pie, Chocolate-Hazelnut Raspberry Mousse Tart, and Holiday Eggnog Custard Pie. Index.

Ansel, Dominique (Chef)

Dominique Ansel : the secret recipes / foreword by Daniel Boulud ; photographs by Thomas Schauer. Simon & Schuster, 2014. xi, 259 p. : **641.86**

1. Pastry. 2. Recipes 3. Cookbooks.
ISBN 9781476764191

LC 2014024377

Includes index.

The gourmet-baker creator of the Cronut', the croissant-doughnut hybrid that has taken the world by storm, shares the secret to transforming the most humble ingredients into the most extraordinary, tempting, and satisfying pastries imaginable, revealing the stories and recipes behind his most sought-after creations.

"Ansel's essays will delight his fans, as well as foodies who enjoy learning about the creative processes of famous chefs. Those new to French pastry will prefer collections with more recipes and instruction." Library Journal.

Austin, Maggie

Maggie Austin cake : artistry and technique / Maggie Austin ; photography by Kate Headley. Houghton Mifflin Harcourt, 2017. 303 p. : **641.86**

1. Cake decorating. 2. Recipes 3. Cookbooks.
ISBN 9780544765351

LC bl2017012970

Includes indexes.

The cake artist shares a collection of her cake designs along with illustrated, step-by-step instructions for each technique used to create them, covering such topics as shaping fondant ribbons, sculpting textured surfaces, and painting by hand.

"Filled with technical know-how and sumptuous photographs, this book will tempt all cake lovers." Library Journal.

Barrow, Cathy

Pie squared : irresistibly easy sweet & savory slab pies / Cathy Barrow ; Photographs by Christopher Hirsheimer. Grand Central Life & Style, 2018 xiv, 321 p. : **641.86**

1. Desserts. 2. Pastry. 3. Pies. 4. Recipes 5. Cookbooks.
ISBN 9781538729144

LC 2018003656

Shares recipes for the new food trend of slab pies, including such options as blueberry streusel, lemon cream, mushroom and kale, and Hawaiian pizza, along with such crust recipes as cracker, cornbread, cookie, and cheddar cheese crusts.

Barrow, Cathy

When pies fly : handmade pastries from strudels to stromboli, empanadas to knishes / Cathy Barrow ; photographs by Christopher Hirsheimer. Grand Central Publishing, 2019. xvi, 286 p. : **641.86**

1. Desserts. 2. Pastry. 3. Pies. 4. Recipes 5. Cookbooks.
ISBN 9781538731901

LC bl2019026811

Finds more ways to use pastry dough deliciously with crowd-pleasing (and easy to make) galettes and small tarts, as well as empanadas, strudels, and knishes. Barrow digs into a world of doughs for turnovers, fried pies, poppers, and Texas-by-way-of-Krakow kolaches, all offered in sweet and savory iterations.

"Barrow (Pie Squared) encourages readers to be fearless and creative in their pie-making endeavors in this accessible and fun baking guide. A primer on equipment called "Check Your Equipment" and nine steps to "Earn Your Pie Wings" (which explains, anong other things, how to avoid soggy pie bottoms and the uses of egg wash) set up home bakers for recipes categorized in chapters including 'Galettes,' 'Empanadas,' and 'Knishes.'" Publishers Weekly.

Beddall, Catherine

The **magic** of gingerbread : 16 beautiful projects to make and eat / written and photographed by Catherine Beddall. Peter Pauper Press, Inc., 2016. 184 p. : **641.86**

1. Gingerbread. 2. Holiday cooking
ISBN 1441319808

LC 2016003632

"All projects are elegantly crafted and simple in design yet impactful when completed: holiday place cards, two-inch-tall tree ornaments, a toy box any child would delight in receiving, and a haunted house that's not too frightening. Proof indeed that gingerbread is for more than Christmas." Booklist

Ben-Ishay, Melissa

Cakes by Melissa : life is what you bake it : 120+ recipes for cakes, icings, fillings, and toppings for endless flavor combinations from the creative force behind Baked by Melissa / Melissa Ben-Ishay ; photography by Ashley Sears. William Morrow, 2017 291 p. : **641.86**

1. Baking. 2. Cake. 3. Recipes 4. Cookbooks.
ISBN 9780062681270

LC bl2017040797

Includes index.

Offers tips and techniques for baking cakes, with recipes for more than 120 cakes, including tie-dye cupcakes, peanut butter banana, and traditional flavors.

Beranbaum, Rose Levy

Rose's ice cream bliss / Rose Levy Beranbaum ; photography by Matthew Septimus. Houghton Mifflin Harcourt, 2020. 336 p. **641.86**

1. Ice cream, ices, etc. 2. Recipes 3. Cookbooks.
ISBN 9781328506627

LC 2019033902

Includes index.

An award-winning cookbook author offers foolproof recipes for making ice cream at home including classic flavors like Peanut Butter and Chocolate Fudge as well as the more exotic like Brown Sugar and Black Pepper, Roasted Corn and Red Wine.

"Serious ice cream makers will want to add this to the shelf." Publishers Weekly

Bilderback, Leslie

No-churn ice cream : over 100 simply delicious no-machine frozen treats / Leslie Bilderback ; photographs by Teri Lyn Fisher. St. Martin's Griffin, 2015 168 p. **641.86**

1. Ice cream, ices, etc. 2. Quick and easy cooking 3. Quick and easy cooking 4. Cookbooks.
ISBN 9781250054388

LC 2015007286

Offers techniques, easy recipes, and instructions for creating a variety of ice creams and other frozen desserts without the machine churning of traditional recipes.

"Supplemented by Bilderback's professional pastry knowledge, this easy yet informative ice cream cookbook will appeal to a wide audience. Highly recommended for college students, apartment dwellers, and anyone lacking kitchen equipment or space." Library Journal.

Boyle, Tish

Flavorful : 150 irresistible desserts in all-time favorite flavors / Tish Boyle ; photography by Andrew Meade. Houghton Mifflin Harcourt, 2015 374 p. : **641.86**

1. Desserts 2. Cookbooks.
ISBN 9781118523551

LC 2015004678

Includes index.

Collects more than one hundred fifty recipes for desserts made with nine popular flavors, including chocolate, vanilla, apple, citrus, caramel, nuts, and coffee, organized into chapters by flavor.

Byrn, Anne

American cake : from colonial gingerbread to classic layer, the stories and recipes behind more than 125 of our best-loved cakes from past to present / Anne Byrn. Rodale Inc., 2016 344 p. : **641.86**

1. Cake -- United States -- History. 2. Cake. 3. Recipes 4. Cookbooks.
ISBN 9781623365431

LC 2016029092

Describes the rich history of American cake baking, from colonial times to the present, and includes such cake recipes as New Orleans king, chocolate stout, angel food, red velvet, and pineapple upside-down.

"These well researched and written pages go far beyond the average baking guide." Publishers Weekly.

Byrn, Anne

★**American** cookie : the snaps, drops, jumbles, tea cakes, bars & brownies that we have loved for generations / Anne Byrn ; photography by Tina Rupp. Rodale, 2018 312 p. : **641.86**

1. Cookies -- United States -- History. 2. Cookies. 3. Recipes 4. Cookbooks.
ISBN 9781623365455

LC bl2018180646

Describes the rich history of American cookie baking, from colonial times to the present, and includes such cookie recipes as macaroons, snickerdoodles, American gingersnaps, lavender tea cookies, and black and white cookies.

"The introduction sets the stage, outlining the basic ingredients and supplies required for the recipes. Sidebars offer baking suggestions and historical notes, and each recipe is introduced with a brief anecdote about its origins." Library Journal.

Chang, Joanne

Pastry love : a baker's journal of favorite recipes / Joanne Chang ; photography by Kristin Teig. Houghton Mifflin Harcourt, 2019. 463 p. : **641.86**

1. Baking. 2. Desserts 3. Pastry. 4. Recipes 5. Cookbooks
ISBN 9780544836488

LC 2019004919

Includes index.

An award-winning baker presents 125 of her favorite recipes--such as Strawberry Slab Pie, Mocha Chip Cookies and Malted Chocolate Cake--as well as lessons and techniques for both experienced bakers and beginners. Illustrations.

"An excellent volume of recipes that will work for bakers at any level." Library Journal

Cordon bleu (School : Paris, France),

Pastry school : 100 step-by-step recipes / Le Cordon Bleu ; photographs by Olivier Ploton. Grub Street, 2018. 511 p. : **641.86**

1. Pastry 2. Desserts 3. Cookbooks.
ISBN 9781911621201

LC bl2019015445

Includes indexes.

Presents one hundred pastry recipes from the world renowned cooking school, with step-by-step instructions.

Chicago Tribune (Firm)

Holiday cookies : prize-winning family recipes from the Chicago Tribune for cookies, bars, brownies and more. / Chicago Tribune Surrey Books, an Agate imprint, 2014 222 p. : **641.86**

1. Cookies. 2. Holiday cooking 3. Recipes 4. Cookbooks.
ISBN 9781572841642

LC 2014026785

"A collection of recipes from the Chicago Tribune's annual holiday cookie contest".-- Provided by publisher.

"A timely cookie collection that's big on variety and nostalgia." Library Journal.

Ebuehi, Benjamina

★The **new** way to cake : simple recipes with exceptional flavor / Benjamina Ebuehi Page Street Publishing Co., 2019. 159 p.: **641.86**

1. Cake 2. Recipes 3. Cookbooks.
ISBN 9781624148675

LC bl2019034041

Includes index.

Unlock a whole new world of flavor with Benjamina Ebuehi's signature cakes. Inspired by her journey to The Great British Bake Off and beyond, Benjamina's groundbreaking recipes put flavor at the forefront by letting the star ingredients--toasted nuts, fragrant spices, bold herbs and ripe fruit--do all the work.

Elsen, Emily

The **Four** & Twenty Blackbirds pie book : uncommon recipes from the celebrated Brooklyn pie shop / Emily Elsen & Melissa Elsen ; photography by Gentl & Hyers. Grand Central Life & Style, 2013. 224 p. : **641.86**

1. Four & Twenty Blackbirds (Firm). 2. Baking. 3. Pies. 4. Recipes 5. Cookbooks
ISBN 1455520519

LC 2013939669

Includes index.

"From the proprietors of the renowned Brooklyn shop and cafe comes the ultimate pie-baking book for a new generation of bakers. Melissa and Emily Elsen, the twenty-something sisters who are proprietors of the wildly popular Brooklyn pie shop and cafe Four & Twenty Blackbirds, have put together a pie-baking book that's anything but humble. This stunning collection features more than 60 delectable pie recipes organized by season, with unique and mouthwatering creations such as Salted Caramel Apple, Green Chili Chocolate, Black Currant Lemon Chiffon, and Salty Honey. There is also a detailed and informative techniques section."-- From publisher's description.

Ferroni, Lara

Doughnuts : 90 simple and delicious recipes to make at home / Lara Ferroni. Sasquatch Books, 2018 xvi, 188 p. : **641.86**

1. Doughnuts
ISBN 9781632171252

LC 2017041913

Collects ninety recipes for doughnuts to make at home, including such offerings as carrot cake doughnuts, red velvet doughnuts, and chocolate coconut macaroon doughnut holes.

Gallucci, Laurel

Sweet Laurel : recipes for whole food, grain-free desserts / Laurel Gallucci and Claire Thomas ; foreword by Lauren Conrad ; photography by Claire Thomas. Clarkson Potter/Publishers, 2018 255 p. : **641.86**

1. Sweet Laurel Bakery. 2. Desserts. 3. Low-fat diet 4. Recipes 5. Cookbooks.
ISBN 9781524761455

LC 2017031551

Includes index.

After being diagnosed with an aggressive autoimmune disease, the co-founder of Sweet Laurel Bakery, to avoid giving up dessert, learned how to bake with whole food ingredients and shares that knowledge in a cookbook that features 85 simple, yet decadent, dessert recipes that are grain-free, gluten-free, refined sugar-free and dairy free.

Gerson, Fany

Mexican ice cream : beloved recipes and stories / Fany Gerson ; photography by Justin Walker and Fernando Gomez Carbajal. Ten Speed Press, 2017 173 p. : **641.86**

1. Cooking, Mexican 2. Cooking, Mexican. 3. Desserts -- Mexico. 4. Frozen desserts. 5. Cookbooks 6. Essays
ISBN 1607747774

LC 2016051341

Presents recipes for Mexican ice cream that showcase its diverse flavors, including such options as goat's milk caramel, avocado, rice pudding, and chocolate-chile, while exploring the cultural aspects of preparing and consuming ice cream in Mexico.

"[Gerson's] extensive expertise underpins this inspiring cookbook, which collects classic and modern recipes for sorbets, ice creams, and accompaniments." Library Journal.

Greenspan, Dorie

★**Baking** chez moi : recipes from my Paris home to your home anywhere / Dorie Greenspan ; photographs by Alan Richardson. Houghton Mifflin Harcourt, 2014. ix, 477 p. : **641.86**

1. Desserts. 2. Cooking, French. 3. Baking. 4. Recipes 5. Cookbooks.
ISBN 9780547724249

LC 2014016312

"A Rux Martin book."

Includes index.

The author of the award-winning Around My French Table presents a collection of 180 radically simple desserts from French home cooks and pastry chefs.

"Combining everyday desserts with doable versions of extremely popular treats (think macarons, eclairs, and crackle-top cream puffs), Greenspan's new collection is an instant classic." Library Journal.

Greenspan, Dorie

★**Dorie's** cookies / Dorie Greenspan. Houghton Mifflin Harcourt, 2016 517 p. : **641.86**

1. Cookies. 2. Baking 3. Recipes 4. Cookbooks.
ISBN 9780547614847

LC 2015042719

A James Beard Foundation Who's Who inductee presents an all-occasions collection of top-selected cookie recipes, including Blueberry Buttermilk Pie Bars, Snowy-Topped Brownie Drops and Pink-Peppercorn Thumbprints.

Greenstein, George

A **Jewish** baker's pastry secrets : recipes from a New York baking legend for strudel, stollen, danishes, puff pastry, and more / George Greenstein with Elaine Greenstein, Julia Greenstein, and Isaac Bleicher. Ten Speed Press, 2015 202 p. ; **641.86**

1. Baking. 2. Cooking, European. 3. Kosher food 4. Pastry. 5. Cookbooks
ISBN 1607746735

LC 2015025814

Presents a collection of pastry recipes from an award-winning New York baker, covering basic technques, equipment, tools, and ingredients and offering variations on coffee cake, strudel, babka, and breads.

Heatter, Maida

Cookies are magic : classic cookies, brownies, bars, and more / Maida Heatter ; illustrations by Alice Oehr ; foreword by Deb Perelman. Voracious, Little Brown and Company, 2020. 266 p. : **641.86**

1. Cookies. 2. Cookbooks
ISBN 9780316460187

LC bl2020045691

Includes index.

Collects nearly one hundred cookie recipes, including classic sugar cookies, tart lemon bars, cookie kisses, and chocolate and peanut butter ripples, this is the only cookie book you will ever need.

Heatter, Maida

Happiness is baking : cakes, pies, tarts, muffins, brownies, cookies : favorite desserts from the Queen of Cake / Maida Heatter ; foreword by Dorie Greenspan ; illustrations by Alice Oehr. Little, Brown and Company, 2019. 287 p. : **641.86**

1. Desserts. 2. Baking. 3. Cookbooks.
ISBN 9780316420570

LC bl2019009880

Includes index.

A collection of the cookbook author's classic, foolproof recipes features such options as blueberry crumb cake, chocolate cupcakes, oatmeal molasses cookies, chocolate chip and almond biscotti, devil's food cake, and apricot tart.

"This is an excellent one-stop shop for Heatter's greatest hits, and a perfect introduction for any rising baker unfamiliar with her work." Booklist.

Hesser, Amanda

Food52 ice cream and friends : 60 recipes & riffs for sorbets, sandwiches, no-churn ice creams and more / editors of Food52 ; photography by James Ransom ; foreword, Amanda Hesser & Merrill Stubbs [editors of Food52]. Ten Speed Press, 2017 xii, 161 p. : **641.86**

1. Desserts 2. Frozen desserts. 3. Ice cream, ices, etc. 4. Recipes 5.

Cookbooks
ISBN 9780399578021
LC OC2018158442

Includes index.

"Impressive in its variety, the book blends all-new and reader-contributed recipes ." Library Journal.

Jaronsky, Shelly

The **cookies** & cups cookbook : 125+ sweet & savory recipes reminding you to always eat dessert first / Shelly Jaronsky. Gallery Books, 2016 xxi, 293 p. ; **641.86**

1. Desserts. 2. Cookies. 3. Recipes 4. Quick and easy cooking 5. Cookbooks.
ISBN 9781501102516
LC 2015027541

A collection of recipes for both sweet and savory treats from the popular blogger, including such options as tuxedo brownies, s'mores cookies, snickerdoodles, pretzel bark, salted caramel cupcakes, hot fudge sundae cake, and coconut cream pie.

"Jaronsky, the creator of the website Cookies & Cups, presents over 125 selections with sweets in the front. Her casual tone and concise recipes with numbered steps are inviting for those new to the kitchen." Publishers Weekly.

Johnstone, Christi Farr

Smart cookie : transform store-bought cookies into amazing treats / Christi Farr Johnstone. Running Press, 2014 192 p. : **641.86**

1. Cookies. 2. Cookbooks.
ISBN 9780762452521
LC bl2014037500

Includes index.

Explains how to forgo the baking and decorate store-bought cookies, including such designs as adorable acorns, mock macarons, halloween pops, and football cookies.

"Johnstone's charming decorated cookies require minimal time and equipment and no baking. This is her debut title and a great resource for kid-friendly decorating projects and last-minute party favors." Library Journal.

Kalman, Maira

Cake / Maira Kalman, with recipes by Barbara Scott-Goodman. Penguin Press, 2018 93 p. : **641.86**

1. Baking 2. Cake. 3. Recipes 4. Cookbooks.
ISBN 9781101981542
LC 2017025262

"With great style, wit, and joy, Maira Kalman and Barbara Scott-Goodman celebrate their favorite dessert. In Cake, renowned artist and author Maira Kalman and food writer Barbara Scott-Goodman bring us a beautifully illustrated book dedicated to their mutual love of cakes. Kalman's enchanting illustrations, in her inimitable style, and Scott-Goodman's mouthwatering recipes complement each other perfectly, making Cake a joyful whimsical celebration of a timeless dessert"-- Provided by publisher.

"Illustrator and author Kalman (And the Pursuit of Happiness) and Scott-Goodman (The Beach House Cookbook) charmingly write about the importance of cake in daily life." Publishers Weekly.

Kave, Allison

First prize pies : shoo-fly, candy apple & other deliciously inventive pies for every week of the year (and more) / Allison Kave ; photographs by Tina Rupp. Stewart, Tabori & Chang, 2014. 224 p. : **641.86**

1. Baking. 2. Pies. 3. Recipes
ISBN 161769102X
LC bl2014012089

Includes index.

Collects inventive recipes for a variety of pies such as root beer float pie, bourbon-ginger pecan pie, and chocolate lavender pie, with instructions for different crusts, including classic, vegan, gluten-free, and chocolate cookie crust.

Kieffer, Sarah

The **Vanilla** Bean baking book : recipes for irresistible everyday favorites and reinvented classics / Sarah Kieffer. Avery, 2016 336 p. ; **641.86**

1. Desserts. 2. Cake. 3. Recipes 4. Cookbooks.
ISBN 9781583335840
LC 2016016459

Recipes from the Vanilla Bean Blog.

Collects recipes for desserts and sweet treats from the founder of the popular Vanilla Bean baking blog, including such options as peanut butter cookies, coffee blondies, banana bread, apple-blackberry turnovers, and raspberry cream cake.

"Familiar and timeless without being superfluous, this highly recommended, well-executed baking book will thrill home bakers who like to keep things simple." Library Journal.

Lane, Christina

Dessert for two : small batch cookies, brownies, pies, and cakes / Christina Lane. The Countryman Press, 2015 231 p. : **641.86**

1. Desserts. 2. Recipes 3. Cookbooks.
ISBN 9781581572841
LC bl2015010260

Includes index.

A collection of small-batch dessert recipes takes favorite sweet treats and scales down the recipes to make only two servings using small pans, ramekins and muffin cups, including Br|lěd Lemon Bars, Banana Puddin', brownies, blondies and assorted cookies.

Lebo, Kate

Pie school : lessons in fruit, flour and butter / Kate Lebo, photography by Rina Jordan. Sasquatch Books, 2014 227 p. : **641.86**

1. Baking. 2. Pies. 3. Recipes 4. Cookbooks
ISBN 1570619107
LC 2014021810

"Unlock the secret to baking the perfect crust, and everything else is easy as pie. Seattle literary and culinary darling Kate Lebo shares her recipes for fifty perfect pies. Included are apple (of course), five ways with rhubarb, lemon chiffon, several blueberry pie variations, galettes, and more. Learn the tricks to making enviable baked goods and gluten-free crust while enjoying Kate Lebo's wonderfully humorous, thoughtful, and encouraging voice. In addition to recipes, Lebo invites readers to ruminate on the social history, the meaning, and the place of pie in the pantheon of favorite foods. When you have mastered the art, science and magic of creating the perfect pie in Pie School, everyone will want to be your friend".-- Provided by publisher.

"An informed and rather romantic take on the art of the handmade pie." Library Journal.

Lebovitz, David

The **perfect** scoop : 200 recipes for ice creams, sorbets, gelatos, granitas, and sweet accompaniments / David Lebovitz ; photography by Ed Anderson. Ten Speed Press, 2018 265 p. : **641.86**

1. Ice cream, ices, etc. 2. Frozen desserts 3. Recipes 4. Cookbooks.
ISBN 9780399580314

LC 2017030281

"The author's 25 years of experience as a frozen-dessert maker are put to excellent use in this wittily written, detailed volume. Step-by-step photos and advice on selecting an ice cream machine will reassure ice cream amateurs." Publishers Weekly.

Ludwinski, Lisa

★**Sister** Pie : the recipes & stories of a big-hearted bakery in Detroit / Lisa Ludwinski ; photographs by E.E. Berger. Lorena Jones Books, an imprint of Ten Speed Press, 2018 ix, 245 p. : **641.86**

1. Sister Pie Bakery. 2. Pies 3. Pastry 4. Cookbooks.
ISBN 9780399579769

LC 2018003428

Includes index.

A collection of favorite recipes for sweet and savory pies from the owner of Detroit's Sister Pie bakery features such options as ginger peach biscuit, toasted marshmallow butterscotch, and sour cherry bourbon pie.

McDermott, Kate, 1953-

Art of the pie : a practical guide to homemade crusts, fillings, and life / Kate McDermott ; photographs by Andrew Scrivani. The Countryman Press, a division of W. W. Norton & Company, 2016 352 p. : **641.86**

1. Baking. 2. Desserts 3. Pies. 4. Recipes 5. Cookbooks
ISBN 1581573278

LC 2016017593

An award-winning, self-taught home baker who hosts instructional Pie Camps around the country provides detailed recipes and instructions for making, rolling and baking perfect pie crusts and fillings every time, including Blackberry, Peach and Rhubarb.

"Its really all about the standards... McDermott excels, giving readers an informative guide theyll be referring to for years to come." Publishers Weekly.

McKenney, Sally

★**Sally's** cookie addiction : irresistible cookies, bars, shortbread, and more from the creator of Sally's baking addiction / Sally McKenney. Race Point Publishing, 2017. 199 p. : **641.86**

1. Cookies. 2. Recipes 3. Cookbooks.
ISBN 9781631063077

LC 2017018781

Includes index.

A collection of recipes for cookies, cookie bars, cookie dough dips, slice-and-bakes, and no-bakes includes such options as brown butter snickerdoodles, pinwheel cookies, fairy meringues, jam shortbread bars, and chocolate hazelnut thumbprints.

Medrich, Alice

Holiday cookies : the ultimate chewy, gooey, crispy, crunchy treats / Alice Medrich. Artisan, 2017 110 p. : **641.86**

1. Cookies. 2. Holiday cooking. 3. Recipes 4. Cookbooks.
ISBN 9781579658045

LC 2017005079

A collection of holiday cookie recipes includes such confections as currant and nib rugelach, coffee walnut cookies, Mexican wedding cakes, and caramel cheesecake bars.

Miglore, Kristen

★**Food52** genius desserts : 100 recipes that will change the way you bake / Kristen Miglore ; photography by James Ransom. Ten Speed Press, 2018 xi, 273 p. : Food52 Works **641.86**

1. Desserts. 2. Recipes 3. Cookbooks.
ISBN 9781524758981

LC 2017053167

Includes index.

A collection of game-changing dessert recipes includes the unconventional ingredients and methods used to make East 62nd Street Lemon Cake, Flourless Chocolate-Walnut Cookies, Butterscotch Budino, Peach Cobbler With Hot Sugar Crust, and Parsnip Cake With Blood Orange Buttercream.

Nederlanden, Elisabet der

Holiday cookies : showstopping recipes to sweeten the season / Elisabet der Nederlanden ; photography by Erin Scott. Ten Speed Press, 2017 161 p. : **641.86**

1. Baking. 2. Confectionery. 3. Cookies. 4. Holiday cooking. 5. Cookbooks
ISBN 0399580255

LC 2017015950

A collection of holiday cookie recipes from a veteran baker and recipe developer features such sweets as gingerbread cookies, black and whites, molasses spice cookies, fig and cardamom rugelach, and candy cane cookies.

Nelson, Kim (Kim Adams)

Daisy Cakes bakes : keepsake recipes for Southern layer cakes, pies, cookies, and more / Kim Nelson. Clarkson Potter/Publishers, [2017] 222 p. : **641.86**

1. Daisy Cakes (Bakery) 2. Cake. 3. Desserts. 4. Quick and easy cooking. 5. Recipes 6. Cookbooks.
ISBN 9780451499417

LC 2017044208

Includes index.

A collection of recipes from the founder of the Daisy Cakes mail-order bakery features such options as pumpkin whoopee pies, chocolate peanut butter bark, pecan pie, apple fritters, Mississippi mud cake, and buttermilk ice cream.

O'Neill, Laura, 1981-

Van Leeuwen artisan ice cream / Laura O'Neill, Ben Van Leeuwen, and Pete Van Leeuwen with Olga Massov ; photographs by Sidney Bensimon. Ecco, 2015. xxi, 228 p. : **641.86**

1. Ice cream, ices, etc. 2. Frozen desserts. 3. Recipes 4. Ice cream trucks. 5. Cookbooks.
ISBN 9780062329585

LC 2015487824

Collects frozen treat recipes made with natural ingredients from the owners of the popular Brooklyn homemade ice cream brand, including vegan ice cream, sorbet, frozen yogurt, and granita, with techniques and tips for making ice cream at home.

"This engagingly written cookbook is a recommended purchase for all libraries." Library Journal.

Ottolenghi, Yotam

Sweet : desserts from London's Ottolenghi / Yotam Ottolenghi, Helen Goh with Tara Wigley. Ten Speed Press, 2017 363 p.

: **641.86**

1. Confectionery. 2. Pastry. 3. Desserts. 4. Cookbooks.
ISBN 9781607749141

LC bl2017045258

Includes index.

A collection of recipes for sweets, baked goods, and confections from the superstar chef, including such dishes as banana cakes with rum caramel, pineapple and star anise chiffon cake, pecan snowballs, and lemon and poppy seed cake.

"Modern, creative, appealing, and, most importantly, fun--this is Ottolenghi at the top of his game." Publishers Weekly.

Pansino, Rosanna

Baking all year round / Rosanna Pansino. Atria Books, 2018. 255 p. : **641.86**

1. Baking. 2. Desserts. 3. Holiday cooking. 4. Recipes 5. Cookbooks.
ISBN 9781501179822

LC 2018015942

Includes index.

An award-winning YouTube star returns with a follow-up to her *New York Times* best-seller *The Nerdy Nummies Cookbook* that includes dishes for a variety of holidays and special occasions, including Heart-shaped Ravioli, Baseball Pizza and Confetti Pancakes.

Parks, Stella

★**Bravetart** : iconic American desserts / Stella Parks ; foreword by J. Kenji Lopez-Alt ; photography by Penny De Los Santos. W.W. Norton & Company, 2017 395 p. : **641.86**

1. Baking 2. Cooking, American 3. Desserts 4. Recipes 5. Cookbooks
ISBN 9780393239867

LC 2017007009

"Parks, a senior editor at Serious Eats and the creator of the Bravetart blog, has written a cookbook that is as interesting to read as it is to cook from." Publishers Weekly.

Payard, Francois

Payard cookies / Francois Payard with Anne E. McBride ; photography by Rogerio Voltan. Houghton Mifflin Harcourt, 2015 272 p. : **641.86**

1. Cookies. 2. Cooking, French. 3. Recipes 4. Cookbooks.
ISBN 9780544512986

LC 2014044010

Includes index.

A collection of 100 favorite cookie recipes by the James Beard Foundation Pastry Chef of the Year includes varieties learned from his father and baked at home, from simple butter cookies and picture-perfect macaroons to jam-filled linzers and iced cutout holiday cookies.

"Experienced bakers will have no trouble with Payard's pleasing and precise cookie recipes." Library Journal.

Pfeiffer, Jacquy

★The **art** of French pastry / Jacquy Pfeiffer ; with Martha Rose Shulman ; photographs by Paul Strabbing. Alfred A. Knopf, 2013. xxxi, 395 p. : **641.86**

1. Pastry. 2. Cooking, French. 3. Cookbooks
ISBN 9780307959355

LC 2013017643

"A Borzoi book."

"Anyone studying to be a professional baker will profit from Pfeiffer's guidance, and the amateur cook can vastly improve family desserts." Booklist.

Ptak, Claire

The **Violet** Bakery cookbook / Claire Ptak ; foreword by Alice Waters ; photography, Kristin Perers. Ten Speed Press, 2015 269 p. : **641.86**

1. Violet Bakery (London, England). 2. Desserts. 3. Baking. 4. Cookbooks.
ISBN 9781607746713

LC 2014036768

Includes index.

Presents recipes from the cake shop and cafe in east London using simple ingredients and seasonal fruits, including cinnamon buns, chocolate oat agave cookies, gingersnaps, hazelnut toffee cake, candied citrus peel, and coconut macaroons.

"Highly recommended for fans of baking books such as Elisabeth Prueitt and Chad Robertson's Tartine and Zoe Nathan's Huckleberry. Aspiring pastry chefs will find inspiration in Ptak's impressive career highlights." Library Journal.

Purchese, Darren

Lamingtons & lemon tarts : best-ever cakes, desserts & treats from a modern sweets maestro / Darren Purchese. Hardie Grant Books, 2016. 262 p. : **641.86**

1. Baking 2. Cake. 3. Desserts. 4. Recipes 5. Cookbooks.
ISBN 9781743791868
Includes index.

Hailed as Australia's Willy Wonka, Darren Purchese is renowned for his stunning high-end dessert creations.

"A treat for intermediate-level bakers and aspiring pastry chefs." Library Journal

Reynaud, Stephane

Pies and tarts for dinner and dessert / Stephane Reynaud ; photographs by Marie-Pierre Morel. Melville House, 2013 191 p. : **641.86**

1. Pies. 2. Cooking, French. 3. Baking. 4. Desserts. 5. Cookbooks.
ISBN 9781612194172

LC bl2014050005

Includes indexes.

Shares a collection of sweet and savory French pie and tart recipes, including options featuring vegetables, mushrooms, poultry and rabbit, meat, fish and seafood, and cheese, as well as a selection of dessert pies.

"Topped off with eminently useful indexes that allow bakers to select recipes based on key ingredients, recipe name or pastry dough, this is a terrific addition to the canon." Publishers Weekly.

Ricciardi, Holly

Magpie : sweets and savories from Philadelphia's favorite pie boutique / Holly Ricciardi with Miriam Harris. Running Press, 2015 256 p. : **641.86**

1. Pies. 2. Recipes 3. Cookbooks.
ISBN 9780762454532

LC 2015937006

Includes index.

"Magpie Artisan Pie Boutique is a jewel in Philadelphia's food-town crown. Since 2012, the pocket-size shop has been turning out flaky crusts and luscious fillings. Now this book serves up Magpie's seasonal menu for home bakers everywhere: the fruity, creamy, and nutty pies; hand pies, pot pies, and quiches; and even pie shakes and pie "fries," all fine-tuned to exacting standards and with lots of step-by-step instruction for that all-important crust. Baker-owner Holly Ricciardi's upbringing deep in the Central Pennsylvania countryside provided the basis for Magpie's perfect synthesis of classic favorites and new twists - alongside down-home favorites like Sweet Crumb Pie and Shoofly Pie you'll find Holly's bourbon-infused update of her great-grandmother's special butterscotch pie as well as the ingenious (and instant-sellout) Cookie Dough Hand Pies. Ninety-plus recipes also include sweets like Cranberry Curd Mini Meringue Pies, Blueberry Rhuby Rose Pie, and Chocolate Blackout Pie, and savories like Summer Squash Pie, Ham-Leek-Dijon Potpies, and Quiche Lorraine. From crusts to crumbles and sumptuous savories to sweet confections, there's a Magpie pie for every occasion."--provided from Amazon.com.

Richardson, Julie, 1970-

Vintage cakes : timeless cupcakes, flips, rolls, layer, angel, snack, chiffon, and icebox cakes for today's sweet tooth / Julie Richardson ; photography by Erin Kunke. Ten Speed Press, 2012. 166 p. : **641.86**

1. Cake. 2. Desserts 3. Baking 4. Cookbooks
ISBN 9781607741022

LC 2011041262

A collection of updated recipes for classic and forgotten cakes features such options as jam cake with caramel chocolate ganache, lemon icebox cake with white chocolate cream, and eggnog bundt cake with brandy butter glaze.

Robicelli, Allison

Robicelli's : a love story, with cupcakes : with 50 decidedly grown-up recipes / Allison & Matt Robicelli ; photographs by Eric Isaac. Viking Studio, 2013. viii, 306 p. : **641.86**

1. Robicelli's (Bakery) 2. Cupcakes. 3. Baking 4. Gourmet cooking 5. Recipes 6. Cookbooks.
ISBN 9780670785872

LC bl2013046044

Includes index.

A gourmet cupcake guide by the owners of New York's Robicelli's bakery provides a range of sophisticated recipes for cupcakes flavored by such exotic ingredients as figs, goat cheese, and prosciutto.

"Photos are lick-the-page enticing and proof that home bakers are going to enjoy the best bleeping cupcakes their side of the Brooklyn Bridge." Publishers Weekly.

Roden, Cesar

Ice pops! : 50 delicious, fresh and fabulous icy treats / Cesar and Nadia Roden ; photography by Adam Slama ; illustrations by Peter Roden & Divya Scialo. Sterling Epicure, 2015. 128 p. : **641.86**

1. Ice pops. 2. Frozen desserts. 3. Cookbooks.
ISBN 9781454916260

LC bl2015017986

Includes index.

Provides tips and techniques for making and putting ice pops together with recipes for fifty unique flavors, including three milks lemon dessert, drenched watermelon, and French twist.

"Fruit-focused ice pop books are commonplace. Recommend this superb collection to readers seeking a wide range of recipes." Library Journal.

Rucker, Nicole

Dappled : baking recipes for fruit lovers / Nicole Rucker. Avery, 2019 255 p. : **641.86**

1. Baking. 2. Cooking (Fruit). 3. Desserts. 4. Recipes 5. Cookbooks.
ISBN 9780735218017

LC 2018058468

Includes index.

The founder and owner of a popular Los Angeles pastry shop offers a fruit-based dessert cookbook using seasonal ingredients in new takes on classic dishes like Peach and Ricotta Biscuit Cobbler, Tomato Pudding, Spiced Tangerine Semolina Cake and Huckleberry Blondies.

"Festive recipes and enticing photos make this a top pick for home bakers eager to indulge in fruit." Publishers Weekly

Seneviratne, Samantha

The **new** sugar and spice : a recipe for bolder baking / Samantha Seneviratne ; photography by Erin Kunkel. Ten Speed Press, 2015 234 p. ; **641.86**

1. Baking. 2. Cookies. 3. Cooking (Spices). 4. Desserts 5. Cookbooks
ISBN 1607747464

LC 2015005473

Includes index.

Collects more than eighty unique dessert recipes using exotic spices, including chile-chocolate truffles, cinnamon toast bread pudding, Indonesian spiced layer cake, crêpe cake with pistachio cream, and fig and fennel seed biscotti.

"Marked by a sense of the exotic, Seneviratne's recipes will lure many home cooks, including fans of Alice Medrich's Pure Dessert and Claudia Fleming's The Last Course." Library Journal.

Smith, Brian

Ample Hills Creamery : secrets & stories from Brooklyn's favorite ice cream shop / Brian Smith, Jackie Cuscuna with Lauren Kaelin ; illustrated by Lauren Kaelin ; photography by Lucy Schaeffer. Stewart, Tabori & Chang, 2014. 222 p. : **641.86**

1. Desserts 2. Ice cream, ices, etc. 3. Recipes 4. Cookbooks
ISBN 1617690767

LC bl2014015596

Includes index.

Provides ice cream recipes from Brooklyn's Ample Hills Creamery, including ooey gooey butter cake, lemon sky, vanilla malted, and toffee bar crunch.

Solomonov, Michael

Federal Donuts / Mike Solomonov, Steven Cook, Tom Henneman, Bob Logue, Felicia D'Ambrosio ; produced by Dorothy Kalins INK ; photographs by Michael Persico ; design by Don Morris Design. Houghton Mifflin Harcourt, A Rux Martin Book, 2017 224 p. ; **641.86**

1. Federal Doughnuts (Restaurant). 2. Desserts 3. Doughnuts. 4. Recipes 5. Cookbooks
ISBN 0544969049

LC 2017015571

Presents the history of the famous doughnut restaurant founded by two James Beard Award winners and provides recipes for some of their popular flavors, including strawberry shortcake, grapefruit brulee, and pomegranate nutella.

Tosi, Christina

All about cake / Christina Tosi with Courtney McBroom ; photographs by Gabriele Stabile and Mark Ibold. Clarkson Potter/ Publishers, 2018. 287 p. : **641.86**

1. Cake. 2. Desserts. 3. Quick and easy cooking. 4. Recipes 5. Cookbooks.
ISBN 9780451499523

LC 2017050431

In this sugar-fueled cookbook, the chef, owner and founder of Milk Bar helps bakers of all levels to indulge in both classic flavors and true originals, revealing the method behind her team's creativity to help invent any cake flavor imaginable.

Tosi, Christina

Milk bar life : recipes & stories / Christina Tosi , with Courtney McBroom and spiritual Chaperone Peter Meehan ; photographs by Gabriele Stabile and Mark Ibold. Clarkson Potter/ Publishers, [2015] 256 p. : **641.86**

1. Momofuku Milk Bar. 2. Cooking, American. 3. Junk food. 4. Snack foods. 5. Convenience foods.
ISBN 9780770435103

LC 2014041740

Includes index.

"Go off the clock with Christina Tosi of Momofuku Milk Bar as she bakes one-bowl treats, grills with skills, and embraces simple, nostalgic--and often savory--recipes made from supermarket ingredients. For anyone addicted to crack pie, compost cookies, and cake truffles, here are their savory counterparts--such as Kimcheezits with Blue Cheese Dip, Burnt Honey-Butter Kale with Sesame Seeds, and Choose Your Own Adventure Chorizo Burgers--along with enough make-at-home sweets to satisfy a cookie-a-day habit. Join Christina and friends as they cook their way through "weaknights," sleepovers, and late-night snack attacks to make mind-blowingly delicious meals with whatever is in the pantry."--Provided by publisher.

Weinstein, Bruce, 1960-

A **la** mode : 120 recipes in 60 pairings : pies, tarts, cakes, crisps, and more topped with ice cream, gelato, frozen custard, and more / Bruce Weinstein & Mark Scarbrough ; photographs by Eric Medsker. St. Martin's Griffin, 2016. 224 p. : **641.86**

1. Pies. 2. Cake. 3. Ice cream, ices, etc. 4. Cookbooks.
ISBN 9781250072139

LC 2016000033

A pairing guide presents recipes for desserts and complementary ice cream to serve with each, including such options as bourbon peach pie and vanilla bean gelato, cinnamon roll cake and maple frozen custard, and blueberry pie and marzipan gelato.

"This isn't your average ice cream cookbook. Rather than providing just a few suggested accompaniments, Weinstein and Scarbrough ... pair each of the 60 ice cream recipes with a complementary dessert. They also forego a master ice cream base in favor of multiple ice cream types and techniques. ... [T]his cookbook is a playful collection of unusual ice cream pairings." Library Journal.

Weinstein, Bruce, 1960-

All-time favorite sheet cakes & slab pies : easy to make, easy to serve / Bruce Weinstein and Mark Scarbrough ; photographs by Eric Medsker. St. Martin's Griffin, 2017 ix, 211 p. ; **641.86**

1. Baking 2. Cake. 3. Quick and easy cooking 4. Cookbooks.
ISBN 9781250117588

LC 2017018871

Includes index.

"This laid-back approach to baking is sure to entice home bakers of all levels to get out that sheet pan and invite a hungry crowd." Publishers Weekly.

Wright, Caroline

Cake magic! : mix & match your way to 100 amazing combinations / Caroline Wright. Workman Publishing, 2016 186 p. ; **641.86**

1. Baking. 2. Cake. 3. Desserts. 4. Recipes 5. Cookbooks.
ISBN 9780761182030

LC 2016000666

Includes index.

"It's a simple formula for dessert bliss: batter + syrup + frosting = 100 different cakes! An innovative and remarkable easy way to bake luscious, flavorful cakes, Cake Magic! is a full-color visual cookbook--photos in the front, recipes in the back--for every cake lover, for fans of the genius of The Cake Mix Doctor series, and for home bakers who obsess over colorful cakes on Pinterest and Instagram (where cakes are consistently in the "most popular" feed). The key to the cakes' ease is the homemade Mix + Match Baking Mix -- the foundation of every cake in the book. From there it's just a matter of mixing and matching batters, flavoring syrups (the secret step that makes these cake recipes so versatile), frostings, and, sometimes, topping to create uniquecakes. Want something decadent and fudgy? Darkest Chocolate Cake + Milky Caramel Syrup + Malted Milk Chocolate Frosting + crushed candy bars = Candy Bar Cake. Swap in Bourbon Syrup + Cream Cheese Frosting, and you have the grown-up Drunken Tuxedo Cake. There's nothing vanilla about these vanilla cakes (Cookies + Cream Cake, Caramel-Pineapple Upside-Down Layer Cake); ethereal coconut cakes; and nutty cakes like Elvis-Peanut Butter Cake + Bacon Syrup + Nutella Frosting, topped with candied bacon. Fit for the Kind, indeed. Includes valuable baking tips, vegan and gluten-free variations, plus how to tweak the recipes to make sheet cakes, Bundt cakes, and cupcakes".-- Provided by publisher.

Wyss, Roxanne

Delicious dump cakes : 50 super simple desserts to make in 15 minutes or less / Roxanne Wyss and Kathy Moore ; photographs by Staci Valentine. St. Martin's Griffin, 2016 ix, 118 p. : **641.86**

1. Baking 2. Cobblers (Food) 3. Desserts 4. Quick and easy cooking 5. Cookbooks.
ISBN 9781250082633

LC 2015049003

Includes index.

A collection of recipes for quick desserts includes such offerings as triple berry cobbler, chocolate pudding dump cake, tropical mango dump cake, and cinnamon roll dump cake.

"Whatever readers' level of experience or inexperience in the kitchen, this cookbook will have them serving up delicious desserts in a flash." Library Journal.

Yosses, Bill

The **sweet** spot : dialing back sugar and amping up flavor / Bill Yosses & Peter Kaminsky with Kathleen Hackett ; photographs by Evan Sung. Pam Krauss Books, Avery, 2017 263 p. : **641.86**

1. Cooking (Sugar). 2. Desserts. 3. Recipes 4. Cookbooks.
ISBN 9780804189019

LC bl2017044672

Includes index.

The former White House pastry chef and the author of Pig Perfect presents a collection of healthy and satisfying dessert recipes, from Kabocha Persimmon Pie and Alfonso Mango Cake to Lemon Kaffir Semifreddo and Coconut Chocolate Apricot Cookies.

"Notes throughout the collection--with information such as how to work with dried fruit and what to do with leftover yolks--add value to any bakers arsenal. Yoses, with Kaminsky, has produced a thoughtful, inspiring title to bake through the seasons." Publishers Weekly.

Zabar, Tracey

One sweet cookie : celebrated chefs share favorite recipes / Tracey Zabar ; photography by Ellen Silverman. Rizzoli, 2011. 191 p. : **641.86**

1. Cookies. 2. Recipes 3. Cookbooks.
ISBN 9780847836666

LC bl2014005525

Includes index.

Offers a collection of cookie recipes from a variety of New York chefs for such treats as brownies, petits fours, meringues, macaroons, biscotti, and sugar cookies.

"When cookie-obsessed baker Zabar couldn't convince friends to participate in a cookie swap, she orchestrated a virtual exchange, the result of which is this outstanding collection of recipes from more than 50 well-known New York City chefs." Library Journal.

641.87 Preparing beverages

Arnold, Dave, 1971

★**Liquid** intelligence : the art and science of the perfect cocktail / Dave Arnold ; photography by Travis Huggett. W.W. Norton & Company, 2014 416 p. : **641.87**

1. Cocktails. 2. Measuring instruments.
ISBN 9780393089035

LC 2014022332

Outlines scientific approaches to making aesthetically appealing, better-tasting drinks through an awareness of ingredient properties, sharing illustrated recipes and instructions for using specific equipment and techniques.

"Professional bartenders will drink up this remarkable manual, and amateurs will find Arnold's step-by-step guide to gathering requisite hardware both achievable and fun." Booklist.

Boudreau, Jamie

The **canon** cocktail book : recipes from the award-winning bar / Jamie Boudreau & James O. Fraioli. Houghton Mifflin Harcourt, 2016. x, 338 p. : **641.87**

1. Cocktails -- Handbooks, manuals. 2. Bartending.
ISBN 9780544631038

LC bl2016043893

Includes index.

Shares classic cocktail recipes as well as recipes for more unusual and unique drinks, including the Tom Collins, French 75, Milk Punch, and Zim Zala Bim.

"This terrific resource is sure to send armchair bartenders scurrying to their shakers." Publishers Weekly.

Carducci, Tad

The **Tippling** bros. : a lime and a shaker / Tad Carducci & Paul Tanguay with Alia Akkam ; foreword by Doug Frost ; photography by Lauren Volo. Houghton Mifflin Harcourt, 2015. 256 p. : **641.87**

1. Bartending 2. Cocktails. 3. Cookbooks.
ISBN 9780544302327

LC 2014023051

Includes index.

Shares recipes for Mexican-inspired cocktails featuring tequila and mezcal, as well as information on techniques, ingredients, and preparing syrups and salts.

"A title that is sure to have readers looking for opportunities to try the recipes contained within. Highly recommended for any collection in which books on cocktails are prevalent." Library Journal.

Conigliaro, Tony, 1971-

The **cocktail** lab / Tony Conigliaro. Ten Speed Press, 2013 224 p. : **641.87**

1. Bartending 2. Cocktails.
ISBN 9781607745679

LC 2013004969

"Originally published in slightly different form in Great Britain as Drinks : unravelling the mysteries of flavour and aroma in drink, by Random House Group Company, London, in 2012"--Title page verso.

"Unraveling the mysteries of flavor and aroma in drink, with recipes."

"From the U.K.'s preeminent bartender and one of the leading authorities on "modernist mixology" comes this collection of 60 revolutionary cocktails, all grounded in the classics but utilizing technologies and techniques from the molecular gastronomy movement. The right cocktail is more than just a drink. It's the perfect combination of scent, color, sound, and taste. In the hands of Tony Conigliaro, drinks like the Vintage Manhattan, Dirty Martini by the Sea, and Cosmo Popcorn will redefine your understanding of what a cocktail can be. With this revolutionary new approach to drink-making, Conigliaro has established himself as a modern master of the form".-- Provided by publisher.

DeBary, John

Drink what you want : the subjective guide to making objectively delicious cocktails / John deBary ; illustrations by Sarah Tanat-Jones. Clarkson Potter/Publishers, 2020 224 p.: **641.87**

1. Cocktails. 2. Alcoholic beverages.
ISBN 9780525575771

LC 2019037791

"A non-judgmental, back-to-basics approach to cocktails that's as fun as it is definitive--from a renowned New York City bartender who's worked everywhere from Please Don't Tell to Momofuku"-- Provided by publisher.

"This is a terrific entry point that even veteran bartenders can appreciate." Publishers Weekly

Helwig, Jenna

Smoothie-licious : power-packed smoothies and juices the whole family will love / Jenna Helwig. Houghton Mifflin Harcourt, 2015 159 p. : **641.87**

1. Smoothies (Beverages). 2. Blenders (Cooking). 3. Recipes 4. Cookbooks
ISBN 9780544370081

LC bl2015020581

Includes index.

Collects recipes for seventy-five smoothies, juices, and treats made from superfoods, including kiwi-kale cooler, apple-walnut spinach, and cantaloupe-blackberry breeze juice.

Hoffman, Maggie (Food and drink writer)

Batch cocktails : make-ahead pitcher drinks for every occasion / Maggie Hoffman ; photographs by Kelly Puleio. Ten Speed Press, 2019 153 p. : **641.87**

1. Cocktails -- Handbooks, manuals. 2. Reference books
ISBN 9780399582530

LC 2018046944

Includes index.

Provides recipes for sixty-five pitcher cocktails for advance preparation to serve eight to twelve guests.

Huerta, Alba

★**Julep** : Southern cocktails refashioned / Alba Huerta & Marah Stets ; photography by Julie Soefer. Lorena Jones Books, 2018 ix, 212 p. : **641.87**

1. Cocktails -- Southern States. 2. Drinking customs -- Southern States.
ISBN 9780399579417

LC 2017040259

"A tribute to the spirits and drinking traditions of the South through a leading barwoman's glass, with 80 recipes and photos. Craft cocktail maven Alba Huerta succinctly tells the story of drinking in the South through themes such as "Trading with the Enemy," "the Rural South," "the Drinking Society," "the Saltwater South," and others that anchor the menu at her destination bar, Julep. With historical overviews, 15 bar snack recipes, and 65 bespoke cocktail recipes, ranging from the iconic Mint Julep (and variations such as Rye Julep and Sparkling Julep) to modern inventions like the Snakebit Sprout, Liquid Currency, and Hot July, Huerta recounts the tales and traditions that define drinking culture in the American South today. Approximately 80 evocative cocktail and location photographs convey the romance and style that distinguish Julep and serve to inspire beverage enthusiasts to relive Southern history via the bar cart".-- Provided by publisher.

Jones, Carey (Personal chef)

Brooklyn bartender : a modern guide to cocktails and spirits / Carey Jones ; photographs by Lucy Schaeffer ; illustrations by Rebecca Matt. Black Dog & Leventhal Publishers, 2016 304 p. ; **641.87**

1. Cocktails. 2. Liqueurs. 3. Recipes
ISBN 9780316390255

LC 2015050472

Includes index.

Shares three hundred modern cocktail recipes, including variations on old classics as well as the signature drinks of a few trendy Brooklyn bars.

"Even the staunchest teetotaler will work up quite a thirst while perusing what is easily one of the best cocktail books this year." Publishers Weekly.

Kaplan, David (Bartender)

★**Death** & Co : modern classic cocktails / David Kaplan, Nick Fauchald, Alex Day ; photographs by William Hereford ; illustrations by Tim Tomkinson. Ten Speed Press, 2014 xix, 299 p. illustrations (some color) ; **641.87**

1. Death & Co. (Bar : New York, N.Y.). 2. Bartending 3. Cocktails.
ISBN 9781607745259

LC 2014004245

A guide to creating cocktails collects recipes from the famous New York drinking establishment, including such offerings as a gin rickey, a mai tai, a "velvet Warhol," a "Dale Cooper," and an "East River underground."

"There's a clear, unpretentious spirits primer for those who have been bluffing their way through in-vogue varieties of rum, tequila, and whiskey; other sections tackle bitters, ice, glassware, and additional details without dictating. More than half the book is devoted to 450-plus recipes for classics, variations, and riffs." Library Journal.

Lebovitz, David

Drinking French : the iconic cocktails, aperitifs, and cafe traditions of France, with 160 recipes / David Lebovitz ; photographs by Ed Anderson. Ten Speed Press, 2020. viii, 293 p. : **641.87**

1. Cocktails. 2. Aperitifs -- France. 3. Drinking -- France 4. France -- Social life and customs
ISBN 9781607749295

LC 2019019161

Includes index.

"A recommended collection that makes accessible the sophistication of French cafe drinking to cocktail-crazed American audiences." Library Journal

McDonnell, Duggan

Drinking the devil's acre : a love letter to San Francisco and her cocktails / Duggan McDonnell ; photographs by Luke Abiol. Chronicle Books, 2015 256 p. : **641.87**

1. Cocktails. 2. Bars (Drinking establishments) 3. Drinking -- San Francisco, California 4. San Francisco, California
ISBN 9781452135250

LC 2014044040

Provides a history-packed, twenty-five cocktail drinking tour through the "City by the Bay," including such offerings as a mai tai, a Manhattan, and a mojito.

"Not just another cocktail recipe book but a great read peppered with drinks to be made. Highly recommended where books on cocktails are popular." Library Journal.

Meehan, Jim, 1976-

★**Meehan's** bartender manual / Jim Meehan ; photography by Doron Gild.; illustrations by Gianmarco Magnani Ten Speed Press, 2017 ix, 477 p. ; **641.87**

1. Bartending. 2. Cocktails. 3. Cocktails -- Handbooks, manuals. 4. Reference books
ISBN 9781607748625

LC 2017024758

"Meehan's Bartender Manual is acclaimed mixologist Jim Meehan's magnum opus--and the first book to explain the ins and outs of the modern bar industry. This work chronicles Meehan's storied career in the bar business through practical, enlightening chapters that mix history with professional insight. Meehan's deep dive covers the essential topics, including the history of cocktails and bartending, service, hospitality, menu development, bar design, spirits production, drink mixing technique, and the tools you'll need to create a well-stocked bar--all brought to life in over 150 black- and-white illustrations by artist Gianmarco Magnani".-- Provided by publisher.

"[D]ivulges the recipes for 100 classic and fanciful cocktails and gives away intel that is vital not only for would-be bartenders but for anyone who dreams of owning and operating their own establishment." Publishers Weekly.

Morgenthaler, Jeffrey

The **bar** book : elements of cocktail technique / Jeffrey Morgenthaler with Martha Holmberg ; photographs by Alanna Hale. Chronicle Books, 2014 288 p. : **641.87**

1. Cocktails. 2. Bartending -- Handbooks, manuals, etc. 3. Reference books
ISBN 9781452113845

LC bl2014025252

Includes index.

Teaches techniques for preparing a variety of cocktails, including juicing, garnishing, carbonating, and stirring, and includes over sixty recipes that illustrate each concept.

"Straightforward directions are matched with beautifully clear photographs that make homemade grenadine, limoncello, and ginger beer look enticingly simple. The author also demystifies shaking, muddling, and presentation." Library Journal.

Muldoon, Sean

The **Dead** Rabbit : grocery and grog : drinks manual : secret recipes and barroom tales from two Belfast boys who conquered the cocktail world / Sean Muldoon, Jack McGarry and Ben Schaffer ; photography by Brent Herrig. Houghton Mifflin Harcourt, 2015. 288 p. : **641.87**

1. Dead Rabbit Grocery and Grog (New York, N.Y.). 2. Cocktails. 3. Recipes

ISBN 9780544373204

LC 2014043215

The owners of The Dead Rabbit Grocery and Grog share recipes for their signature cocktails and drinks, including peach blow fizz, hot whiskey toddy, and scotch daisy.

"Like the best Irish bartender, this book is warm, welcoming, full of great stories, and dedicated to excellent drinks." Library Journal.

Munro, Lizzie,

Winter drinks : 70 essential cold-weather cocktails / the editors of PUNCH ; photography by Lizzie Munro. Ten Speed Press, 2018 ix, 149 p. : **641.87**

1. Bartending 2. Cocktails.

ISBN 9780399581663

LC 2018006298

Includes index.

Shares recipes for cold weather cocktails, including hot buttered rum, mulled punch, and spiked horchata.

"For those looking for ways to celebrate during the dead of winter, this is a smart and handy go-to guide." Publishers Weekly.

Peppler, Rebekah

Aperitif : cocktail hour the French way / Rebekah Peppler ; photographs by Joann Pai. Clarkson Potter/Publishers, 2018 223 p. : **641.87**

1. Cocktails -- France -- History. 2. Cocktails.

ISBN 9781524761752

LC 2018024058

Includes index.

Keeping true to the aperitif tradition, you'll find cocktail recipes that use lighter, low-alcohol spirits, fortified wines, and bitter liqueurs. The impressive drinks have influences from both Old World and New, but are always low fuss and served barely embellished--an easy feat to pull off for the relaxed host at home.

Reiner, Julie

The **craft** cocktail party : delicious drinks for every occasion / Julie Reiner with Kaitlyn Goalen ; photographs by Daniel Krieger. Grand Central Life & Style, 2015 xiii, 226 p. : **641.87**

1. Cocktails.

ISBN 9781455581597

LC 2014049853

Julie Reiner, the co-owner of The Clover Club in Brooklyn and The Flatiron Lounge in Manhattan, has written a book that provides inspiration for the rest of us, not only the cocktail geeks. She wants to balance the needs of the everyday drinker with those of the passionate mixologist.

Rollich, Christiaan

Bar chef : handcrafted cocktails / Christiaan Rollich and Carolynn Carreno. W. W. Norton & Company. 2019 304 p. ; **641.87**

1. Bartending 2. Cocktails.

ISBN 9780393651560

LC 2018053634

Celebrated Los Angeles bartender Christiaan Roellich approaches a drink the way a master chef approaches a dish: he draws on high-quality seasonal ingredients to create cocktails for every occasion. In Bar Chef, Rollich shares 100 original recipes for drinks that that are as beautiful as they are delicious, including the Quixote (gin with grapefruit); a Kentucky Sour (bourbon with homemade cola syrup); Eggnog for the holidays; and Rollich's signature drink, the Green Goddess (green tea vodka with cucumber, arugula, jalapeno, and absinthe), which has become a part of the language of LA. Including easy-to-follow recipes for syrups, tinctures, liqueurs, and bitters with herbs, spices, and seasonal fruit, Rollich guides you through his creative process, demystifying the craft of cocktail-making. With stunning color photography and the suave storytelling of your favorite bartender, Bar Chef will become a go-to bar book for home cooks and cocktail enthusiasts, inspiring and pleasing readers with every drink.

"This refreshing collection is a must-have for those seeking a no-nonsense approach to making high-end drinks." Publishers Weekly.

Sacasa, Maria del Mar

Summer cocktails : margaritas, mint juleps, punches, party snacks, and more / Maria del Mar Sacasa ; photographs by Tara Striano. Quirk Books, 2015 158 p. : **641.87**

1. Cocktails.

ISBN 9781594747854

LC bl2015020371

Includes index.

Presents one hundred summer cocktail recipes, including bourbon-peach punch, watermelon refresher, and martinis, with recipes for snacks and party meals.

"With clear instructions and bright color photographs it's easy to make a Pulparindo or a Pimm's your new summer staple, while handy guides to tools and prep techniques round out this essential primer." Library Journal.

Simonson, Robert

★**3-ingredient** cocktails : an opinionated guide to the most enduring drinks in the cocktail canon / Robert Simonson ; photographs by Colin Price. Ten Speed Press, 2017. 166 p. : **641.87**

1. Cocktails.

ISBN 9780399578540

LC 2017016197

Includes index.

Collects seventy-five recipes for both classic and contemporary cocktails which feature only three ingredients, including such options as the Harvey Wallbanger, Rob Roy, Manhattan, and Moscow Mule.

Simonson, Robert

The **martini** cocktail : a meditation on the world's greatest drink, with recipes / Robert Simonson ; photographs by Lizzie Munro. Ten Speed Press, 2019 165 p. : **641.87**

1. Martinis 2. Martinis -- History

ISBN 9780399581212

LC 2018060706

"This is a no-brainer for martini enthusiasts." Publishers Weekly

Simonson, Robert

A **proper** drink : the untold story of how a band of bartenders saved the civilized drinking world / Robert Simonson. Ten Speed Press, [2016] 352 p. **641.87**

1. Bartenders. 2. Bars (Drinking establishments) 3. Cocktails -- History. 4. Alcoholic beverages
ISBN 9781607747543

LC 2016014120

A Proper Drink is the first-ever book to tell the full, unflinching story of the contemporary craft cocktail revival. Award-winning writer Robert Simonson interviewed more than 200 key players from around the world, and the result is a rollicking (if slightly tipsy) story of the characters--bars, bartenders, patrons, and visionaries--who in the last 25 years have changed the course of modern drink-making. The book also features a curated list of about 40 cocktails--25 modern classics, plus an additional 15 to 20 rediscovered classics and classic contenders--to emerge from the movement.

"No matter which side of the bar readers are on, theyre sure to work up a powerful thirst." Publishers Weekly.

642 Meals and table service

Battista, Maggie

Food gift love : more than 100 recipes to make, wrap, and share / Maggie Battista, founder of Eat Boutique ; photography Heidi Murphy. Houghton Mifflin Harcourt, 2015 255 p. ; **642**

1. Canning and preserving. 2. Gift baskets. 3. Holiday cooking 4. Recipes 5. Cookbooks
ISBN 0544387678

LC 2015004480

Includes index.

Features one hundred simple-to-make edible gifts from flavored butters and pickles to infused salts and desserts.

English, Ashley, 1976-

A **year** of picnics : recipes for dining well in the great outdoors / Ashley English ; photographs by Jen Altman. Roost Books, 2017. 238 p. : **642**

1. Outdoor cooking. 2. Picnics. 3. Recipes 4. Cookbooks
ISBN 1611802156

LC 2015003041

Includes index.

Presents menus and over seventy recipes for various types of outdoor picnics, including such picnic themes as table-to-farm, afternoon tea, movie night, sacred tree, and rooftop.

"English (A Year of Pies) offers menus for 20 seasonal picnics, including a bird-watching picnic, a movie night picnic, and an afternoon tea picnic." Library Journal.

Hanel, Marnie

The **picnic** : recipes and inspiration from basket to blanket / Marnie Hanel, Andrea Slonecker & Jen Stevenson ; illustrations by Emily Isabella. Artisan, 2015 191 p. ; **642**

1. Picnics. 2. Recipes 3. Cookbooks.
ISBN 9781579656089

LC 2014036496

Includes an index.

Provides tips for planning and arranging picnics along with recipes for no-fail foods that include rainbow carrots with smoky paprika vinaigrette, Vietnamese noodle bowls with shrimp and vegetables, and spicy salted olive oil brownies.

"A fresh look at outdoor entertaining that's just in time for spring and summer. Highly recommended." Library Journal.

Hudson, Kate, 1979-

Pretty fun : creating and celebrating a lifetime of tradition / Kate Hudson with Rachel Holtzman ; photographs by Amy Neunsinger. Dey St., an imprint of William Morrow, 2017 258 p. : **642**

1. Cooking. 2. Entertaining. 3. Parties. 4. Recipes 5. Cookbooks
ISBN 0062685767

LC bl2017044234

Outlines tips for celebrating special events, offers advice on organizing more meaningful gatherings, and provides recipes for healthy snacks and beverages.

Reed, Julia

Julia Reed's South : spirited entertaining and high-style fun all year long / Julia Reed ; photography by Paul Costello. Rizzoli, 2016. 224 p. : **642**

1. Cooking, American -- Southern style 2. Cooking, American -- Southern style. 3. Entertaining -- Southern States. 4. Holiday cooking -- Southern States. 5. Cookbooks
ISBN 0847848280

LC bl2017020296

Includes index.

Presents a guide to throwing a Southern-style party, featuring ideas for invitations, table settings, and flower arrangements, as well as cocktails, lunches, and formal dinners.

Roman, Alison

Nothing fancy : unfussy food for having people over / Alison Roman ; photographs by Michael Graydon and Nikole Herriott. Clarkson Potter/Publishers, 2019 319 p. : **642**

1. Cooking. 2. Entertaining. 3. Quick and easy cooking 4. Seasonal cooking 5. Cookbooks
ISBN 9780451497017

LC 2019001089

Includes index.

Bringing her signature laid-back, approachable style to the table, a social media superstar and newly minted New York Times columnist presents 150 recipes that are high on 'wow' factors and low on effort. Illustrations.

Rosenstrach, Jenny

Dinner : the playbook : a 30-day plan for mastering the art of the family meal / Jenny Rosenstrach. Ballantine Books Trade Paperbacks, 2014 xx, 219 p. : **642**

1. Cooking. 2. Dinners and dining. 3. Families. 4. Quick and easy cooking 5. Cookbooks.
ISBN 9780345549808

LC 2013033023

Includes index.

Presents a primer on how to establish dinner as the family meal and a time for reconnection, collecting recipes for such offerings as shrimp rolls, hoisin turkey burgers, zucchini fritters, and stromboli.

"Families and novice cooks who accept Rosenstrach's challenge will definitely find a few keepers here to add to their repertoire." Library Journal.

Sims, Molly, 1973-

Everyday chic : my secrets for entertaining, organizing, and decorating at home / Molly Sims, with Tracy O'Connor. Dey

St./HarperCollins Publishers, 2017 296 p. : **642**

1. Entertaining. 2. Housekeeping. 3. Recipes 4. Cookbooks
ISBN 0062439634

LC 2017038316

A supermodel shares her secrets for keeping house, covering such topics as cooking family-friendly meals, party planning, decluttering a home, and staying positive.

643 Housing and household equipment

Black & Decker Corporation (Towson, Md.)

The **book** of home how-to : complete photo guide to home repair & improvement Cool Springs Press, 2014. 600 p. : **643**

1. Dwellings -- Maintenance and repair -- Amateurs' manuals.
ISBN 9781591865988

LC 2013047686

Includes index.

"Clear, step-by-step instructions with full-color photography show how to accomplish the most common home repair, maintenance and improvement tasks. A complete homeowners manual for jobs that cover every part of the home, including electrical, plumbing, flooring, walls, windows and doors, kitchens, bathrooms, cabinetry, garages, basements, and exteriors"-- Provided by publisher.

Black & Decker Corporation (Towson, Md.)

The **complete** guide to finishing basements : projects and practical solutions for converting basements into livable space Cool Springs Press, 2013. 239 p. : **643**

1. Basements -- Remodeling -- Amateurs' manuals.
ISBN 9781591865889

LC 2013009481

At head of title: Black & Decker.
Includes index.

An updated second edition of the most comprehensive guidebook for DIYers that provides the inspiration and information you'll need to conduct every phase of your basement remodeling project.

Black & Decker Corporation (Towson, Md.)

The **complete** photo guide to home improvement Creative Pub. International, c2009. 560 p. : **643**

1. Dwellings -- Maintenance and repair -- Amateurs' manuals. 2. Dwellings -- Remodeling -- Amateurs' manuals.
ISBN 9781589234529

LC 2008045755

At head of title: Black & Decker.
Includes index.

"Features more than 200 value-adding modeling projects"--Provided by publisher.

Black & Decker Corporation (Towson, Md.)

The **complete** photo guide to home repair Creative Pub. International, c2008. 559 p. : **643**

1. Dwellings -- Maintenance and repair -- Amateurs' manuals.
ISBN 9781589234178

LC 2008016520

At head of title: Black & Decker.
"With 350 projects and over 2,000 photos"--Cover.
Includes index.

"Features more than 200 essential home repair projects, including common wiring, plumbing, interior and exterior repairs".--Provided by publisher.

Bray, Ilona M., 1962-

Nolo's essential guide to buying your first home / Ilona Bray, J.D., Attorney Alayna Schroeder & Marcia Stewart. Nolo, Law for All 2017. 430 p. : **643**

1. House buying
ISBN 9781413323450

LC 2016026455

Includes index.

Presents a guide to buying a home, emphasizing that careful research is necessary before deciding what price and terms to include in an offer and discussing the changing requirements that affect financing.

Bryson, Bill

At home : an informal history of private life / Bill Bryson. Doubleday, 2010. 497 p. : **643**

1. Houses -- History. 2. Architecture, Domestic -- History. 3. Home (Social sciences) -- History. 4. Rooms -- History.
ISBN 9780767919388

LC 2010004008

Bryson, author of A Short History of Nearly Everything, takes readers on a tour of his house, a rural English parsonage, showing how each room has figured in the evolution of private life.

"It takes a very particular kind of thoughtfulness, as well as a bold temperament, to stuff all this research into a mattress that's supportive enough to loll about on while pondering the real subject of this book--the development of the modern world. Bryson is fascinated by everything, and his curiosity is infectious." New York Times Book Review.

Byers, Charles T.

★**Ultimate** guide home repair and improvement : Proven Money-Saving Projects: 3,400 Photos & Illustrations / Technical editor for updated edition: Charles T. Byers, assistant professor, residential remodeling technology, B.Sc., Thaddeus Stevens College of Technology. Creative Homeowner, 2017 599 p. : **643**

1. Dwellings -- Maintenance and repair 2. Dwellings -- Remodeling
ISBN 158011783X

LC bl2016042011

Includes index.

Presents information on home maintenance and remodeling with more than three hundred step-by-step projects that cover such topics as masonry, plumbing, insulation, flooring, trimwork, siding, roofing, and windows.

Crook, David, 1953-

The **Wall** Street journal complete home owner's guidebook : make the most of your biggest asset in any market / David Crook. Three Rivers Press, c2008. vi, 260 p. : **643**

1. Home ownership -- Costs 2. House buying -- Costs 3. Real estate investment
ISBN 9780307405920

LC 2008025355

A comprehensive guide to home ownership, even in a troubled real-estate market, covers everything readers need to know about buying, owning, and selling a home, with practical advice on how to make a profit on a home in any market, overcome potential problems if looking to trade up or cash out on a home for retirement, and more.

"This is a look at the pros and cons of owning a home--rather than renting one from a bank via a mortgage--along with its ultimate costs. For those aspiring to own a home and those trying to manage the affordability of their biggest asset, this is a must read." Publishers Weekly.

German, Roger
Remodeling a basement / Roger German. Taunton Press, c2010. 170 p. : **643**
1. Basements -- Remodeling
ISBN 9781600852923
LC 2009033545

Includes index.

In a new edition updated to meet the latest building codes, the author takes the reader through the entire remodeling process, showing how to construct new family rooms, bathrooms, laundry rooms, workshops and hobby rooms and covering wiring, plumbing, windows, doors and more, with 420 photos to support the text.

"Beginning with solving moisture problems, then renovating space, this book walks the reader through a logical process for repair and remodeling, with easy-to-follow instruction and illustrations. Design ideas and the latest building code data are also included." Library Journal.

Hearst Books (Firm),
★**How** to fix anything : essential home repairs anyone can do. / Popular Mechanics Hearst Books, 2018 190 p. : **643**
1. Dwellings -- Maintenance and repair
ISBN 9781618372604
LC bl2018070826

At head of title: Popular mechanics.
Includes index.

A guide to fixing household problems, big or small, is organized room by room, making it simple to find the solution necessary.

Litchfield, Michael W.
Renovation / Michael W. Litchfield ; Chip Harley, technical editor. The Taunton Press, 2012 615 p. : **643**
1. Dwellings -- Conservation and restoration 2. Dwellings -- Maintenance and repair 3. Dwellings -- Remodeling
ISBN 9781600854927
LC 2012028561

Includes index.

Following the complete sequence of a home remodeling project, an updated handbook demonstrates how to assess renovation needs and select the repair method, discusses what problems might arise during each step of renovation, and offers specific advice on renovating all types of homes.

"This guide covers all aspects of home renovation, including how to assess a house's structure, tools, materials, wiring, plumbing, painting, flooring, etc. Instructions are to the pointthere is less hand-holding here than in other titles because some remodeling experience is assumed. A classic." Library Journal.

O'Connor, Kevin (Kevin Douglas)
The **best** homes from This old house / Kevin O'Connor ; photographs by Michael Casey. Stewart, Tabori & Chang, 2011. 225 p. : **643**
1. Architecture, Domestic -- United States 2. Dwellings -- Remodeling -- United States 3. Dwellings -- United States -- Maintenance and repair
ISBN 9781584799351
LC 2011018212

Includes index.

This Old House is America's longest-running home improvement show, airing on PBS since 1979. In this book, host Kevin O'Connor will chronicle 10 of the finest transformations rendered by the craftsmen and artists from the past decade of filming the show.

Reader's Digest Association
101 Saturday morning projects : organize, decorate, rejuvenate Reader's Digest Association, 2010. 144 p. : **643**
1. Do-it-yourself work. 2. Dwellings -- Maintenance and repair 3. Dwellings -- Remodeling 4. Storage in the home 5. Amateurs' manuals.
ISBN 1606520180
LC 2009038049

Is your weekend to-do list filled with basic home repairs, projects, and wishful improvements? Let this book show you how easy it is to remove some of these projects from your list. No project takes more than 4 hours--some items will disappear in 15 minutes or less! You'll even save money with energy-saving ideas and repair and maintenance fixes.

Reader's Digest Association,
Complete do-it-yourself manual / the editors at the Family handyman. Reader's Digest, 2014 528 p. : **643**
1. Dwellings -- Maintenance and repair -- Amateurs' manuals.
ISBN 9781621452010
LC bl2014041462

Includes index.

A comprehensive quick reference guide to do-it-yourself home-improvement projects includes more than 3,000 photos and illustrations, teaches readers how to cope with emergencies and repairs and features information on financing home improvements, working with contractors, obtaining permits and more.

Scott, Jonathan, 1978 April 28-
Dream home : the Property Brothers' ultimate guide to finding & fixing your perfect house / Jonathan Scott & Drew Scott ; photography by David Tsay. Houghton Mifflin Harcourt, 2016. 304 p. : **643**
1. Dwellings -- Inspection 2. Dwellings -- Remodeling 3. House buying
ISBN 9780544715677
LC 2015037674

Includes index.

The celebrity designers from "Property Brothers" and other hit HGTV series share comprehensive guidelines to buying, selling, and renovating a house in a reference that includes strategic tips on hidden costs and finding good deals on home products.

"Dream Home is full of ideas and is a good source for anyone looking to buy, sell, or renovate a property." Booklist.

Soles, Clyde, 1959-
The **fire** smart home handbook : preparing for and surviving the threat of wildfire / Clyde Soles ; foreword by Molly Mowery. Lyons Press, 2014. xvii, 268 p. : **643**
1. Dwellings -- Fires and fire prevention -- United States. 2. Wildfires -- United States -- Prevention and control. 3. Wildfires -- United States -- Management.
ISBN 9780762796908
LC 2013050242

Includes index.

"Learn how wildfires begin and behave, how to evaluate your property, what essential tools you'll need and what they will cost, how to prepare your land and home--including tips on how to avoid insurance nightmares--when to stay and fight, when it's time to evacuate, how to clean up after a fire event, and more".-- Provided by publisher.

Susanka, Sarah
Not so big remodeling : tailoring your home for the way you

really live / Sarah Susanka and Marc Vassallo. Taunton Press, c2009. 329 p. : **643**

1. Dwellings -- Remodeling 2. Small houses
ISBN 9781600858246
LC 2008046632

Includes index.

Discusses how to evaluate, plan, and execute minor alterations to different rooms in the home which can maximize living space and improve its overall appearance.

Sussman, Julie (Julie Ellen)

Dare to repair : a do-it-herself guide to fixing (almost) anything in the home / Julie Sussman and Stephanie Glakas-Tenet ; illustrations by Yeorgos Lampathakis. HarperCollins Publishers, 2002. xiv, 253 p. : **643**

1. Do-it-yourself work. 2. Dwellings -- Maintenance and repair 3. Women. 4. Amateurs' manuals.
ISBN 0060959843
LC 2002027625

Includes index.

Detailed step-by-step instructions and more than three hundred illustrations take busy women through seventy-five simple, do-it-yourself home repairs, from unclogging a toilet to installing a window guard, providing essential background information, safety tips, lists of necessary tools and materials, and how-to advice.

"The authors show women how to perform a number of the most common repairs, including unclogging drains and toilets, replacing electrical switches and outlets, leveling appliances, lighting pilot lights, unsticking windows, and installing a door peephole. This is a wonderful book that should be purchased by every public library." Library Journal.

Taunton Press

Bathroom upgrades / editors of Fine Homebuilding. The Taunton Press, 2016 220 p. ; **643**

1. Bathrooms -- Remodeling
ISBN 9781631866548
LC 2016027698

Includes index.

"Bathroom remodels add value to any home, and this book covers everything from layout to fixtures to how-to projects. Considerations of design and accessibility are illustrated, along with bathroom storage, fixtures, surface options, and more. The helpful pros and cons comparisons aide with planning decisions." Library Journal.

Wilson, Bee

Consider the fork : a history of how we cook and eat / Bee Wilson ; with illustrations by Annabel Lee. Basic Books, 2012. xxiii, 327 p. **643**

1. Kitchen utensils -- History. 2. Cooking -- History. 3. Dinners and dining -- History. 4. Implements, utensils, etc.
ISBN 9780465021765
LC 2012016283

Traces the history of cooking through a series of engaging cultural anecdotes while demonstrating how technological innovations ranging from the mortar and pestle to the microwave have shaped how and what humans eat.

Wing, Charles, 1939-

★**How** your house works : a visual guide to understanding and maintaining your home / Charlie Wing. Wiley, 2018 xvi, 216 p. : **643**

1. Buildings -- Mechanical equipment. 2. Dwellings -- Maintenance and repair.
ISBN 1119467616
LC 2018008701

Includes index.

An illustrated guide to understanding how everything in a house works, including appliances, electrical, plumbing, heating, and air conditioning.

645 Household furnishings

Cone, Steve, 1948-

Singer upholstery basics plus : complete step-by-step photo guide / Steve Cone. Creative Pub. International, c2007. 155 p. : **645**

1. Upholstery.
ISBN 9781589233294
LC 2007007252

Includes index.

"Projects include all styles of chairs or couches, stools, different styles of ottomans, a bench, and a headboard. Includes stripping, repairing, and reupholstering old furniture pieces to like-new condition. Step-by-step instructions. Index".--Provided by publisher.

"If there ever was an upholstery bible, this is it." Library Journal.

Dobson, Cherry

The **complete** guide to upholstery : stuffed with step-by-step techniques for professional results / Cherry Dobson. St. Martin's Griffin, 2009. 143 p. : **645**

1. Furniture finishing 2. Furniture -- Repairing 3. Upholstery 4. Amateurs' manuals.
ISBN 0312383274
LC bl2009013431

Includes index.

From stripping and reupholstering to fixing a simple tear, this guide provides practical instructions, photos, and diagrams to complete a diverse collection of jobs with professional-looking results.

"Want to recycle your old furniture with reupholstery? This lovely manual...contains fine step-by-step photos and tips on technique. Master upholsterer Dobson easily walks the confident beginner through the basics." Library Journal.

Montano, Mark

The **big-ass** book of home decor / Mark Montano ; photographs by Auxy Espinoza. Stewart, Tabori & Chang, 2010. 271 p. : **645**

1. Home furnishings 2. Interior decoration
ISBN 9781584798255
LC 2009036376

Includes index.

A do-it-yourself guru and TV host presents 105 practical decorating projects--which utilize thrift store finds, hardware store materials and things around the house--for every space in the home, in a book with 400 color photos.

"The author presents over 100 projects for decorating, creating, and repurposing furniture and decorative accessories. He offers clearly written instructions illustrated with color photographs of the steps. The wealth of inspiring projects that require only basic skills e.g., decoupage, spray paint, glue gunwill make this a popular choice for both experienced and inexperienced crafters." Library Journal.

Petersik, Sherry
Lovable livable home : how to add beauty, get organized, and make your house work for you / Sherry & John Petersik of Young House Love. Artisan, 2015. 336 p. ; **645**
1. Dwellings -- Remodeling. 2. Interior decoration.
ISBN 1579656226
LC 2015010991

Offers illustrated guidance for creating beautiful, functional, and practical living spaces, including advice, DIY projects, and inspirational examples of interior decoration from real homes.

646 Sewing, clothing, management of personal and family life

Karen, Dawnn
Dress your best life : how to use fashion psychology to take your look -- and your life -- to the next level / Dawnn Karen. Little, Brown Spark, 2020. 280 p. ; **646**
1. Clothing and dress -- Psychological aspects 2. Women's clothing -- Psychological aspects 3. Fashion -- Psychological aspects
ISBN 9780316530996
LC bl2020009829

Packed with practical tips and cutting-edge advice, Dress Your Best Life will teach you to harness the power of fashion for the life you want to live.

"This is a thoughtful and fashion-forward approach to figuring out what to wear and understanding how clothes reflect lives well lived... Karen's very apt conclusion: Don't be eye candy. Be soul food. Engaging, well-written, and (gulp) rather piercing commentary on getting dressed." Booklist.

Montenegro, Sonya
Mending life : a handbook for repairing clothes and hearts / Sonya and Nina Montenegro. Sasquatch Books, 2020 191 p. : **646**
1. Clothing -- Repairing 2. Needlework.
ISBN 9781632172525
LC 2019015016

Teaching basic techniques along with more advanced stitches, this visually stunning, practical tool kit for repairing the clothes and belongings reveals how mending can strengthen not only the object we are repairing, but ourselves as well.

"With a guiding mantra that 'There's nothing broken that can't be fixed', this very accessible guide will encourage readers to look with hopeful possibility at their well-worn, well-loved clothes." Booklist

646.2 Sewing and related operations

Bednar, Nancy
Encyclopedia of sewing machine techniques / Nancy Bednar, JoAnn Pugh-Gannon. Sterling Pub., 2007, c1999. 336 p. : **646.2**
1. Machine sewing.
ISBN 9781402742934
LC bl2011004695

Reprint. Originally published: 2000.
"A Sterling/Sewing Information Resources book."
Includes index.

Demonstrates over seventy sewing machine techniques, including applique, embroidery, hemstitching, monogramming, quilting, tucks, bias binding, buttonholes, and zippers.

Bull, Jane, 1957
Get set, sew : the beginner's sewing machine book / Jane Bull. DK, 2015. 125 p. : **646.2**
1. Machine sewing. 2. Sewing.
ISBN 9781465435873
LC bl2015025944

"20 simple step-by-step projects"--Cover.
Includes index.
Provides advice for beginners on how to set up and use a sewing machine, sewing equipment and supplies, and related techniques, and outlines twenty simple projects, including bags, accessories, cushions, and toys.

Conahan, Gillian
The **hero's** closet : sewing for cosplay and costuming / Gillian Conahan ; photographs by Karen Pearson. Abrams, 2017. 207 p. : **646.2**
1. Sewing. 2. Costume. 3. Cosplay.
ISBN 9781419723964
LC bl2017015805

Includes index.
Offers step-by-step instructions and patterns that covers the basics of sewing costumes.

Creative Publishing International,
First time sewing : the absolute beginners guide / the editors of Creative Publishing international. Creative Publishing international, 2014 127 p. : **646.2**
1. Sewing.
ISBN 9781589238046
LC bl2014023797

"Learn by doing step-by-step + 8 projects"--Cover.
Includes index.
Teaches beginners how to sew, with detailed descriptions of materials and tools, step-by-step instructions for basic sewing techniques, and simple projects to practice such sewing skills as hems, seams, and how to use a pattern.

DK Publishing, Inc,
Handmade interiors DK Publishing, 2015. 304 p. : **646.2**
1. Home furnishings 2. Interior decoration. 3. Interior decoration accessories. 4. Sewing.
ISBN 9781465427083
LC bl2015028974

Includes index.
Provides step-by-step, illustrated instructions for creating soft furnishings ranging from cushion covers, curtains, and blinds to bedding and simple upholstery, with advice on fabrics and suggested variations to fit different budgets and styles.
"This book will soon become a well-worn reference." Library Journal.

Ellis, Cassandra
Home sewn : projects and inspiration for every room / Cassandra Ellis ; photography by Catherine Gratwicke. Clarkson

Potter/Publishers, 2016 160 p. : **646.2**
1. Sewing. 2. Home furnishings 3. Interior decoration.
ISBN 9781101906958
LC bl2016024454
Includes index.
Provides sewing projects for around the home, including leather and linen patchwork pillows, organic linen tea towels, and antique silk-scrap bed bolsters.

Gardiner, Wendy
The **sewing** machine accessory bible / Wendy Gardiner & Lorna Knight. St. Martin's Griffin, 2011. 128 p. : **646.2**
1. Machine sewing. 2. Sewing machines.
ISBN 9780312676582
LC bl2011019357
Includes index.
Explains which sewing-machine accessories to use when, with the aim of saving time, creating beautiful embellishments, and working effortlessly with difficult-to-handle fabrics.
"Beginners will find this book especially handy." Library Journal.

Gunn, Sarah, 1956-
The **tunic** bible : one pattern, interchangeable pieces, ready-to-wear results! / Sarah Gunn and Julie Starr. C&T Publishing, 2016 111 p. : **646.2**
1. Tunics. 2. Sewing.
ISBN 9781617453564
LC 2016014302
Offers instructions for ready-to-wear tunics using one pattern and interchangeable pieces.

Ishida, Sanae
Sewing happiness : a year of simple projects for living well / Sanae Ishida. Sasquatch Books, 2016 225 : **646.2**
1. Ishida, Sanae Health. 2. Machine sewing.
ISBN 9781570619953
LC 2015040697
"The instructions are thorough, the tips and advice are generous, and the overall presentation is thoughtful." Library Journal.

James, Chris
The **complete** serger handbook / Chris James. Sterling Pub. Co., 1998, c1997. 159 p. : **646.2**
1. Serging. 2. Sewing machines.
ISBN 9780806998077
LC BL 99002286
Reprint. Originally published: 1997.
"A Sterling/Sewing Information Resources book."
Includes index.
"This is a concise guide to the serger and serger techniques. Major sections of the book include identifying the parts of a serger (with photos of each part), serger accessories, types of threads, threading and testing the threading, learning to regulate tension, and techniques." Library Journal.

Lee, Linda, 1948-
Sewing edges and corners : decorative techniques for your home and wardrobe / Linda Lee. Taunton Press, 2000. 134 p. : **646.2**
1. Sewing. 2. Borders, Ornamental (Decorative arts) 3. Seams (Sewing) 4. Cushions.
ISBN 9781561584185
LC 00029919
Includes index.
"Readers appreciate the clarity of Lee's instructions, since each step is numbered, photographs and other illustrations ease difficult tasks, and sidebars ensure the comfortableness of the sewing." Booklist.

Lubin, Clementine
A **beginner's** guide to overlockers, sergers & coverlockers : 50 lessons and 15 projects to get you started / Clementine Lubin. Search Press, 2018. 159 p. : **646.2**
1. Serging 2. Machine sewing -- Technique 3. Sewing machines
ISBN 9781782214908
LC 2018285368
Translation of: J'apprends ̀coudre ̀la surjeteuse et ̀la recouvreuse.
"Includes 12 full-size patterns"--Cover.
Full of practical advice to help you master all the features and applications of your overlocker (serger) and coverlocker, you will learn how to handle your machine using its more complex features and will soon be finishing hems like a professional sewer. Hem and finish all your garments and accessories like a professional! This practical and comprehensive book helps you master all the functions and applications of your overlocker and coverlocker, from the simplest to the most complex. There are 50 beautifully photographed step-by-step lessons and 15 lovely projects to apply your knowledge and help you realize your sewing goals. You can make a dress, a T-shirt, a shoulder bag, a playsuit and more. There are 15 gorgeous projects to make including cushions,shoulder bags, soft toys and quilts. Full-size, fold-out patterns accompany the designs in addition to the 50 illustrated step-by-step lessons will guide you through all the skills you need to get started. This book includes full-size, fold-out patterns and is the essential guide for all aspiring seamstresses.

Paganelli, Jennifer
Happy home : twenty-one sewing and craft projects to pretty up your home / Jennifer Paganelli ; with Dolin O'Shea ; photographs by Tim Geaney. Chronicle Books, c2012. 175 p. : **646.2**
1. Home furnishings 2. Machine sewing.
ISBN 9780811874458
LC 2011018891
Includes index.
Featuring simple step-by-step instructions, a comprehensive glossary of techniques, pattern sheets tucked into a handy front pocket, and lush color photos, this book makes it exceptionally easy to pretty up every room in the house.

Reader's Digest Association
New complete guide to sewing : step-by-step techniques for making clothes and home accessories / Reader's Digest. Reader's Digest, c2011. 384 p. : Reader's Digest **646.2**
1. Sewing. 2. Dressmaking. 3. Tailoring. 4. Linens
ISBN 9781606522080
LC 2010029616
Provides general instructions for fitting, constructing, tailoring, and finishing women's, men's, and children's clothing and for making curtains and bedcoverings.

Sandqvist, Anton
Heavy-duty sewing : making backpacks and other stuff /

Anton Sandqvist. Frances Lincoln, 2018. 119 p. : **646.2**

1. Machine sewing 2. Sewing 3. Backpacks 4. Bags
ISBN 9780711239258

LC bl2018183849

Discusses the materials, equipment, and techniques needed to make and repair products that require heavy-duty sewing, including a rucksack, knife holder, and aprons.

"With awe-inspiring photos of mountain ranges and other Nordic landscapes throughout, Sandqvist encourages adventuresome sewers with projects that are practical and a lifestyle thats aspirational." Publishers Weekly.

Schlosser, Erin, 1982-

Sew home : learn design basics, techniques, fabrics & supplies : 30+ modern projects to turn a house into your home / Erin Schlosser. StashBooks, 2016 143 p. : **646.2**

1. Home furnishings 2. Sewing.
ISBN 9781617451584

LC 2015049120

"Each project includes step-by-step instructions, as well as measuring and cutting guides, a supply list, and a summary of techniques used. Incorporated throughout are design tips and suggestions for further customization." Library Journal.

Shore, Debbie

Half yard gifts : easy sewing projects using left-over pieces of fabric / Debbie Shore. Search Press, 2016. 96 p. : **646.2**

1. Sewing. 2. Handicraft.
ISBN 9781782211501

LC bl2015034015

Includes index.

Provides step-by-step, illustrated instructions for handicraft projects sewn from left over fabric, including pillows, aprons, and a cosmetic bag.

Singer Company

The **new** sewing essentials. Creative Publishing, c2008. 144 p. : **646.2**

1. Sewing. 2. Machine sewing.
ISBN 9781589234321

LC bl2009020122

At head of title: Singer.

Previous ed. published under title: Sewing essentials.

Includes index.

Shows how to use a sewing machine, looks at marking, measuring, cutting, and pressing tools, and discusses patterns, fabrics, layout and cutting, stitches, seams, and closures.

Smith, Alison (Alison Victoria)

The **sewing** book / Alison Smith. DK Pub., 2009. 400 p. : **646.2**

1. Sewing.
ISBN 9780756642808

LC 2009284133

Provides comprehensive instruction on sewing, including stitch and finish techniques, mending, and sewing projects for both apparel and household goods.

Staples, Heidi, 1977

Sew organized for the busy girl : tips to make the most of your time & space : 23 quick & clever sewing projects you'll love / Heidi Staples. Stashbooks, 2015 111 p. : **646.2**

1. Sewing. 2. Home furnishings
ISBN 9781607059790

LC 2014031103

Provides instructions for creating twenty sewing projects, including a dotty hexagon pillow, chevron table set, and double zip clutch, along with tips and techniques for organizing work areas, fitting craft time into personal schedules, and arranging projects.

"Staples's suggestions range from useful (gathering items related to an ongoing project into a project bag) to a little silly (using a weekly family meeting to declare your need for some sewing time), but the chronically disorganized--and those seeking a better system--will appreciate her low-stress, creative approach." Library Journal.

Yaker, Rebecca

Little one-yard wonders : irresistible clothes, toys, and accessories you can make for babies and kids / Rebecca Yaker & Patricia Hoskins. Storey Publishing, 2014 359 p. : **646.2**

1. Machine sewing. 2. Children's paraphernalia. 3. Children's clothing.
ISBN 9781612121246

LC 2013045043

Six sheets of pattern pieces in pocket.

Includes index.

Shares one hundred one projects for accessories, toys, and wearables for babies and children, focusing on single yards of fabric and minimal completion times.

"This title is a treasure trove of handmade kid's stuff, and sewists of all skill levels will find ideas and inspiration in this lighthearted collection." Library Journal.

Yaker, Rebecca

One-yard wonders : look how much you can make with just one yard of fabric! / Rebecca Yaker and Patricia Hoskins ; photography by John Gruen ; photo styling by Raina Kattelson. Storey Pub., c2009. 303 p. : **646.2**

1. Machine sewing. 2. Clothing 3. Home furnishings
ISBN 9781603424493

LC 2009023721

Enclosed spiral binding.

Includes index.

"This is a fundamental crafts book appropriate for most crafts collections." Booklist.

646.4 Clothing and accessories construction

Alicia, Anna

Bags : sew 18 stylish bags for every occasion / Anna Alicia ; photography by Anna Batchelor. Hardie Grant, Quadrille, 2019. 141 p. : **646.4**

1. Handbags. 2. Sewing.
ISBN 1787133761

LC bl2019038743

Includes index.

"Each project has a skill-level rating, keeping fledgling crafters from getting in over their heads. Laden with gorgeous color photography and easy-to-follow templates, Alicia's book will tempt many crafters into replicating her designs--and adding their own twists." Publishers Weekly.

Atherley, Kate

The **beginner's** guide to writing knitting patterns : learn to write patterns others can knit / Kate Atherley. Interweave, 2015 127 p. : **646.4**

1. Knitting -- Patterns. 2. Knitwear -- Pattern design.
ISBN 9781632504340

LC bl2016015874

Teaches knitters how to write knitting patterns, including how to handle multiple sizes and how to establish a personal style sheet.

"There's an abundance of information here, and designers of all skill levels who are interested in improving the structure and presentation of their knitting patterns will gain much from Atherley's expertise." Library Journal.

Blakeney, Justina

99 ways to cut, sew, trim & tie your t-shirt into something special Crown, 2006. 112 p. **646.4**

1. Sewing. 2. Fashion. 3. T-shirts. 4. Clothing -- Remaking
ISBN 0307345564

LC bl2007011876

Introduces a collection of ninety-nine do-it-yourself patterns, along with easy-to-follow instructions, materials lists, and project difficulty ratings, for transforming a simple T-shirt into a stylish, one-of-a-kind garment.

Butler, Amy

Amy Butler's style stitches : 112 modern bag projects to fit your fashionable life. / Amy Butler, David (PHT) Butler. Chronicle Books, 2010. 182 p. : **646.4**

1. Fancy work. 2. Handbags. 3. Sewing.
ISBN 0811866696

LC 2009025698

Includes index.

Presents twelve basic patterns to create twenty-six unique looks for clutches, wristlets, purses, and totes.

Dayton, Hilarie Wakefield

Sew bags : the practical guide to making purses, totes, clutches & more : 13 skill-building projects / Hilarie Wakefield Dayton. StashBooks, 2019 111 p. : **646.4**

1. Tote bags 2. Handbags 3. Sewing
ISBN 9781617457913

LC 2018037405

"Applicable to a variety of projects despite the handbag focus, this spirited primer will leave readers feeling well-prepared and ready to start sewing." Publishers Weekly.

Gunn, Sarah, 1956-

A **stylish** guide to classic sewing : explore 30 timeless garments with history, styling & tips for ready-to-wear results / Sarah Gunn and Julie Starr. C&T Publishing, Inc., [2019] 176 p. : **646.4**

1. Tailoring 2. Sewing
ISBN 9781617458729

LC 2019020879

This guide walks you through thirty timeless garments to create, including a must-have button-up shirt, a flattering A-line dress, and a modern classic pencil skirt (pattern included).

"Including some nods to the sustainability of creating one's own garments that will appeal to eco-conscious sewers, this primer should prove truly inspiring for any crafters interested in creating classic women's apparel." Publishers Weekly.

Hewett, Jen

Print, pattern, sew : block-printing basics + simple sewing projects for an inspired wardrobe / Jen Hewett ; photographs by Jen Siska. Roost Books, 2018. 162 p. : **646.4**

1. Textile printing 2. Repetitive patterns (Decorative arts) 3. Dressmaking -- Patterns 4. Dress accessories -- Patterns
ISBN 9781611804621

LC 2017016294

Create bold block prints for a completely custom wardrobe--print fabrics, customize patterns, and sew garments that truly express your own style.

"This alluring how-to guide combines block printing with garment sewing to yield dreamy bohemian scarves, preppy printed aprons, elegant summer dresses, and more." Publishers Weekly.

Hirsch, Gretchen, 1979

Gertie sews vintage casual : a modern guide to sportswear styles of the 1940s and 1950s / Gretchen Hirsch ; photographs by Karen Pearson ; illustrations by Sun Young Park. STC Craft, Stewart, Tabori & Chang, 2014. 223 p. : **646.4**

1. Tailoring (Women's) 2. Dressmaking. 3. Dressmaking -- Patterns. 4. Vintage clothing.
ISBN 9781617690747

LC bl2014041256

"A Melanie Falick book."

Includes index.

Celebrates post-war fashions by offering patterns and techniques for creating more than thirty pieces of casual-vintage clothing inspired by icons Katharine Hepburn, Audrey Hepburn, and Rosie the Riveter.

"The audience for Hirsch's second book will likely be wider than that for her first, since casualwear is more accessible than retro-cocktail dresses. Though a few pieces veer toward the costumey, women will find that the garments in this collection fall well within contemporary workplace and casual styles but with a clever, retro flair." Library Journal.

Hirsch, Gretchen, 1979-

Gertie's ultimate dress book : a modern guide to sewing fabulous vintage styles / Gretchen Hirsch ; photographs by Karen Pearson ; illustrations by Sun Young Park. STC & Craft, 2016. 235 p. : **646.4**

1. Dressmaking -- Patterns 2. Sewing 3. Dresses 4. Sewing -- Handbooks, manuals, etc
ISBN 9781617690754

LC 2015948555

Shares information on constructing and customizing dress designs as well as finishing details, techniques for special fabrics, and fitting, and includes instructions for sewing twenty-three dresses.

Johnson, Liz

Bags and totes : 10 easy, fashionable projects anyone can sew / Liz Johnson and Anne Adams, founders & managing editors of Sew4Home. Fons & Porter, 2016 127 p. : Sew4home **646.4**

1. Handbags -- Design and construction. 2. Tote bags -- Design and construction. 3. Sewing.
ISBN 9781440245046

LC bl2017029359

Includes index.

Presents step-by-step instructions for creating bags and totes, from yoga bags and clutches to shoulder bags and kids' satchels.

Kim, Sue, 1969-
Boutique bags : classic style for modern living : 19 projects, 76 bags / Sue Kim. Stash Books, 2015. 127 p. ; **646.4**
1. Handbags
ISBN 9781607059851
LC 2014038488
"Sewists who enjoy bags designed by Lexie Barnes, Amy Butler, or Sara Lawson will enjoy Kim's stylish designs." Library Journal.

Mallalieu, Nicole Claire, 1968-
The **better** bag maker : an illustrated handbook of handbag design--techniques, tips, and tricks / Nicole Claire Mallalieu. Stash Books, an imprint of C&T Publishing, 2014 191 p. : **646.4**
1. Handbags. 2. Sewing.
ISBN 9781607058052
LC 2013034373
Teaches how to make homemade bags using high-end techniques, shortcuts, and secrets for professional design and finishes.
"While these plans are useful, the technique tutorials are the highlight herethey contain information that can be applied to many bag patterns, not just the ones in this collection. Sewists of every ability level will appreciate having a wealth of bag-making information in a single volume." Library Journal.

Mitnick, Sarai
The **Colette** sewing handbook : inspired styles and classic techniques for the new seamstress / Sarai Mitnick. Krause Publications, c2011. 176 p. : **646.4**
1. Sewing. 2. Dressmaking. 3. Dressmaking -- Patterns.
ISBN 9781440215452
LC bl2012024162
Enclosed spiral binding.
Includes index.
Provides information on the fundamentals of sewing and choosing fabrics along with instructions for creating five different garments using the supplied patterns.
"Though the book is intended for beginners, it is appropriate for sewers of all levels who appreciate a well-tailored garment." Library Journal.

Mood Designer Fabrics (Firm),
The **Mood** guide to fabric and fashion : the essential guide from the world's most famous fabric store / foreword by Tim Gunn ; photography by Johnny Miller. Stewart, Tabori & Chang, an imprint of Abrams, 2015. 184 p. : **646.4**
1. Mood Designer Fabrics (Firm) -- History. 2. Textile fabrics 3. Dressmaking materials
ISBN 9781617690884
LC bl2015025968
"A Melanie Falick book."
"A complete resource from Mood Designer Fabrics"--Cover.
The staff of the noted fabric supply business recounts its history and the history of textiles, discusses how to choose materials and how to use them in fashion design, and provides information on specific fabric types.

Mooncie, Vanessa
The **gentleman's** wardrobe : vintage-style projects for the modern man / Vanessa Mooncie. The Guild of Master Craftsman Publications, 2017. 174 p. : **646.4**
1. Tailoring. 2. Men's clothing. 3. Men's clothing -- Design. 4. Sewing.
ISBN 9781861087478
LC bl2017051551
Includes pattern sheets in pocket attached to page 3 of cover.
Includes index.
Provides step-by-step illustrated instructions for classic garments, including pajamas, pants, and accessories.

Powell, Pamela (Fashion designer)
Lingerie design : a complete course / Pamela Powell. Laurence King Publishing, 2016. 304 p. : **646.4**
1. Lingerie -- Design. 2. Lingerie -- Design and construction.
ISBN 9781780677910
In this book, Pamela Powell takes a very practical approach, showing how to design and construct lingerie, sleepwear and foundation garments. Step-by-step illustrations demonstrate the basic blocks and show how to manipulate them into different styles. Advice is given about how to work with the speciality fabrics used in the industry including woven, knit, power stretch and bias-cut fabrics. Specially commissioned photographs and diagrams are used to showcase construction techniques specific to lingerie including boning, elastic and lace insertion and how and where to use the myriad of closures available. A final chapter on embellishment shows how to add unique and personal touches to garments and apply that luxurious finish.
"Lingerie sewing is increasingly popular among experienced garment sewists, and this guide provides a wealth of information for both home sewists who want to make custom-fit lingerie and designers interested in costuming." Library Journal.

Quindt, Svetlana
The **costume** making guide : creating armor & props for cosplay / Svetlana Quindt, aka Kamui Cosplay. Impact, 2016 128 p. : **646.4**
1. Armor. 2. Cosplay. 3. Costume design.
ISBN 1440345163
LC bl2017027597
Includes index.
Introduces costume making, offering tips and techniques on making bracers, armor, and weapons.
"Cosplay armor and props are the focus of Quindt's guide, which takes crafters through the steps of designing, fitting, and creating custom pieces." Library Journal.

Tsukiori, Yoshiko
Stylish wraps sewing book : ponchos, capes, coats and more--fashionable warmers that are easy to sew / Yoshiko Tsukiori, author of Stylish dress book. Tuttle Publishing, 2017. 80 p. : **646.4**
1. Coats. 2. Sewing -- Patterns.
ISBN 9780804846950
LC bl2018125027
A guide to sewing warm wraps includes five full-sized patterns that can be used to create twenty-two ponchos, capes, coats, and more.

Veblen, Sarah
The **complete** photo guide to perfect fitting / [Sarah Veblen]. Creative Pub. International, c2012. 224 p. : Complete Photo Guide **646.4**
1. Dressmaking -- Pattern design. 2. Clothing measurements. 3. Clothing -- Alteration.
ISBN 9781589236080
LC 2011023810

Includes index.

"Reference for sewers with step-by-step instructions for fitting test garments on the body, then transferring adjustments to paper patterns before cutting out and sewing the final garment"--Provided by publisher.

646.7 Management of personal and family life

Becker-Phelps, Leslie

Love : the psychology of attraction / Leslie Becker-Phelps Ph.D. with Megan Kaye. DK, 2016. 224 p. : **646.7**

1. Mate selection 2. Dating (Social customs) 3. Courtship 4. Interpersonal relations

ISBN 9781465429896

LC bl2015048890

Includes index.

Uses psychological research to help readers find and maintain a loving relationship.

Blake, Jenny

Life after college : the complete guide to getting what you want / Jenny Blake. Running Press, c2011. 293 p. ; **646.7**

1. College graduates -- Life skills guides. 2. College graduates -- Employment.

ISBN 9780762441273

LC 2010940614

Presents advice and written exercises for college graduates, covering issues that deal with work, friends, family, dating, health, leisure, personal growth, and life goals.

Bowe, Whitney

The **beauty** of dirty skin : the surprising science to looking and feeling radiant from the inside out / Whitney Bowe, MD with Kristin Loberg. Little, Brown and Company, 2018. viii, 278 p. ; **646.7**

1. Skin -- Care and hygiene 2. Skin -- Diseases -- Diet therapy

ISBN 9780316509824

LC bl2018003629

A leading dermatologist and research scientist identifies a connection between a healthy gut and radiant, clear skin, outlining a twenty-one-day program for maximizing skin health and beauty through a strategic diet, appropriate sleep habits, and do-it-yourself practical skin-care strategies.

Cullinane, Jan

The **new** retirement : the ultimate guide to the rest of your life / Jan Cullinane and Cathy Fitzgerald. Rodale, c2007. xii, 484 p. ; **646.7**

1. Retirement -- United States -- Planning

ISBN 9781594864797

LC 2007015947

A practical handbook on planning for a secure, financially stable, and rewarding retirement covers such topics as tax considerations, learning opportunities, leisure and volunteer activities, and relocation.

Dunn, Jancee

How not to hate your husband after kids / Jancee Dunn. Little, Brown and Company, 2017. viii, 269 p. ; **646.7**

1. Dunn, Jancee. 2. Communication in marriage. 3. Marriage. 4. Parenting.

ISBN 0316267104

LC 2016946111

A candid account of the author's struggles to revitalize her post-baby marriage describes how she resented societal roles that made her the only caregiver to her new daughter and the counseling and research that were part of her effort to resolve unbalanced family dynamics.

Hinden, Stan

How to retire happy : the 12 most important decisions you must make before you retire / Stan Hinden. McGraw-Hill, 2013 xx, 261 p. : **646.7**

1. Retirement income -- United States. 2. Retirement -- Economic aspects -- United States. 3. Retirement -- United States -- Planning.

ISBN 0071800697

LC 2012039679

"Fully revised and updated."

Includes index.

Helps you make the right decisions to ensure a happy, healthful retirement. It delivers all the expert advice you need in an easy-to-understand step-by-step style. How to Retire Happy includes everything that has made previous editions the go-to guides for retirees and near-retirees, plus brand new material on health insurance and Social Security strategies.

Johansen, Signe

How to hygge : the Nordic secrets to a happy life / Signe Johansen. St. Martin's Griffin, 2017. 206 p. ; **646.7**

1. Life. 2. Happiness -- Scandinavia. 3. Well-being -- Scandinavia. 4. Scandinavia -- Civilization.

ISBN 9781250122032

LC 2016059131

A chef and writer who grew up in Norway--using the concept of 'hygge,' which values the idea of cherishing yourself, celebrating experiences over possessions and being kind to yourself and others--presents a how-to guide that combines recipes, helpful tips and more for cozy living at home the Danish way.

"Readers interested in simplifying their homes and lives are sure to find plenty of practical recipes and suggestions here that they can implement immediately." Publishers Weekly.

Lofas, Jeannette

Stepparenting / Jeannette Lofas. Citadel Press, c2004. xiv, 241 p. ; **646.7**

1. Stepparents -- Family relationships 2. Stepchildren -- Family relationships 3. Blended families 4. Parenting -- United States.

ISBN 9780806526522

LC 2004556219

In this newly revised and updated edition Lofas draws on her twenty-year track record of counseling and coaching stepfamilies and provides up to the minute advice for dealing with the many baffling and emotional issues that beset them today.

Massey, Lorraine

Curly girl : the handbook / Lorraine Massey with Michele Bender. Workman Pub. Co., 2010. xi, 188 p. : **646.7**

1. Hair -- Care and hygiene

ISBN 9780761156789

LC 2011004311

Provides tips for curly hair, including shampooing, conditioners, drying, combing, styling, getting the right cut, and how to heal hair after years of strong detergents and damaging blow dryers.

Michaels, Melissa, 1967-
Dwelling / Melissa Michaels. Harvest House Publishers, 2019 222 p. ; **646.7**
1. Dwellings -- Religious aspects. 2. Home -- Religious aspects. 3. Self-care, Health. 4. Simplicity.
ISBN 0736963197
LC 2018049636

Encourages readers to find peace by taking better care of their homes, simplifying their lives, investing in positive relationships, and leaning into their faith.

Soukup, Ruth, 1978-
Unstuffed : decluttering your home, mind, & soul / Ruth Soukup. Zondervan, 2016 219 p. ; **646.7**
1. Simplicity -- Religious aspects -- Christianity.
ISBN 0310337690
LC 2015031891

Offers advice for removing clutter from the home, as well as from busy schedules and burdened minds and souls.

"Commonsense suggestions, personal anecdotes, and Soukup's Christian perspective give the book a friendly, nonthreatening feel. Hopefully delving into the why as well as the how may allow some of us to break the 'stuff' cycle." Booklist.

Storey Publishing,
★**Storey's** curious compendium of practical and obscure skills : 214 things you can actually learn how to do. Storey Publishing, 2020. 344 p. : **646.7**
1. Life skills
ISBN 9781635861914
LC 2020017296

"From the how-to experts at Storey Publishing."

"With dozens of visual tutorials, this rich compendium will educate and inspire new hobbies and experiences." Provided by publisher.

"No matter how complex, each skill is broken down into simple steps and expertly explained alongside beautiful illustrations and photography." Booklist

Taillac, Victoire de
An **atlas** of natural beauty : botanical ingredients for retaining and enhancing beauty / Victoire de Taillac and Ramdane Touhami from Officine Universelle Buly. Simon & Schuster, 2018. 256 p. : **646.7**
1. Beauty, Personal
ISBN 9781501197352
LC 2018033089

Includes indexes.

"Originally published in Great Britain in 2017 by Ebury Press"--Title page verso.

The aesthetic and heritage of a French apothecary are on display in this encyclopedic illustrated guide to home beauty recipes that use seeds, flowers, oils, fruits and herbs to smooth skin, brighten hair and make readers feel beautiful.

Thomas, Mathilde
The **French** beauty solution : time-tested secrets to look and feel beautiful inside and out / Mathilde Thomas. Avery, 2015 viii, 263 p. : **646.7**
1. Beauty, Personal 2. Self-care, Health 3. Skin -- Care and hygiene 4. Women -- Health and hygiene
ISBN 9781592409518
LC 2015003934

Includes index.

"Cofounder of the international beauty company Caudalíe shares the simple, natural, time-tested beauty secrets she learned growing up in France that any woman can use to look younger, healthier, and more radiant without harsh products or drastic procedures. When Mathilde Thomas moved from her native France to the United States to expand her skin-care company, Caudalíe, she wanted to find out what American women wanted from their beauty routines. She interviewed thousands of women and was struck by how different the French and American approaches to beauty were. American women are all about the quick fix--the elusive product or procedure that will instantly solve a nagging beauty problem, even if it hurts, is wildly expensive, or is damaging in the longterm. The French, by contrast, approach beauty as an essential and pleasurable part of the day, a lifelong and active investment that makes you look and feel good. Mathilde used these insights to turn Caudalíe into one of America's top beauty brands. Drawing on her company's twenty years of scientific skin-care expertise backed by the research of doctors and dermatologists--as well as the beauty secrets she learned growing up on a vineyard in Bordeaux--The French Beauty Solution covers everything from how to use natural ingredients such as oil and honey to wash your face; what foods to eat for healthier hair, skin, and nails; and the amazing properties of grapes and grapeseed oil. She also introduces an easy three-day grape cleanse that European aristocrats have been using to detox for hundreds of years. Blending stories, science, DIY recipes, and tons of savoir faire, The French Beauty Solution is the last beauty regimen you'll ever need. "-- Provided by publisher.

Tourles, Stephanie L., 1962-
Pure skin care : nourishing recipes for vibrant skin & natural beauty / Stephanie L. Tourles. Storey Publishing, 2018 247 p. : **646.7**
1. Skin -- Care and hygiene 2. Herbal cosmetics 3. Beauty, Personal
ISBN 9781635860504
LC 2018012689

Shares recipes for facial cleansers and scrubs, masks, moisturizers, and steams, along with creams, balms, and exfoliants for the entire body, all formulated to meet the most up-to-date green beauty standards.

Wiking, Meik
The **little** book of lykke : secrets of the world's happiest people / Meik Wiking. William Morrow, 2017. 285 p. : **646.7**
1. Contentment 2. Happiness 3. Quality of life
ISBN 9780062820334
LC bl2017042108

Shares inspirational writings and suggestions for achieving happiness by practicing the art of seeking out the good that exists in the world, and discusses how small adjustments in behavior can deepen contentment and increase happiness.

"Wiking provides common-sense, real-life applications for his advice in a light-hearted, easy-to-read presentation laced with statistics and personal anecdotes in support of his findings. Whether its used as a how-to or as inspirational reading, this little book is sure to bring a dose of happiness to all its readers." Booklist.

Ziegler, Sheryl
Mommy burnout : how to reclaim your life and raise healthier children in the process / Dr. Sheryl Ziegler. Dey St., an imprint of William Morrow, 2018 xiii, 311 p. ; **646.7**
1. Motherhood 2. Mothers -- Psychology
ISBN 9780062683687
LC bl2017051387

A practical handbook for modern moms outlines positive, liberating recommendations for avoiding debilitating social messages that impose impossible standards of perfection, sharing relatable anecdotes and real-world suggestions for breaking burnout cycles and protecting children from the damage of overwhelmed-parenting dynamics.

"Although this book is well researched and broad in scope of topics, it's written for a singular audience: the heterosexual, middle-class mother. Beyond this limitation, the harrowing descriptions of how women are suffering are anxiety-inducing in their own right and may make the reader opt to put down the book and call her therapist." Booklist.

647.94 Lodging for temporary residents

Mazzeo, Tilar J.

The **hotel** on Place Vendome : life, death, and betrayal at the Hotel Ritz in Paris / Tilar J. Mazzeo. Harper, 2014. xxii, 292 p. : **647.94**

1. Goring, Hermann, 1893-1946. 2. Chanel, Coco, 1883-1971 3. Hemingway, Ernest, 1899-1961 4. Arletty 1898-1992 5. Gellhorn, Martha, 1908-1998 6. Miller, Lee, 1907-1977. 7. Ritz Hotel (Paris, France) 8. Double agents 9. Nazi collaborators 10. Anti-Nazi movement.. 11. French Resistance (World War II) 12. Paris, France -- History -- German occupation, 1940-1944 13. France -- History -- German occupation, 1940-1945

ISBN 9780061791086

Taking readers behind the doors of Paris's Hotel Ritz during the Nazi occupation of World War II, this extraordinary chronicle reveals a hotbed of illicit affairs, deadly intrigues, courageous acts of defiance and treachery and the people and events that made this opulent cultural landmark legendary.

647.95 Eating and drinking places

Cate, Martin

Smuggler's Cove : exotic cocktails, rum, and the cult of tiki / Martin Cate with Rebecca Cate ; photography by Dylan + Jeni. Ten Speed Press, 2016 352 p. ; **647.95**

1. Smuggler's Cove (San Francisco, Calif.). 2. Bars (Drinking establishments) -- San Francisco, California 3. Bartending 4. Cocktails 5. Rum.

ISBN 9781607747321

LC 2016012487

"Cast aside your cares and worries. Make yourself a Mai Tai, put your favorite exotica record on the hi-fi, and prepare to lose yourself in the fantastical world of tiki, one of the most alluring--and often misunderstood--movements in American cultural history. Martin and Rebecca Cate, founders and owners of Smuggler's Cove (the most acclaimed tiki bar of the modern era) take you on a colorful journey into the lore and legend of tiki: its birth as an escapist fantasy for Depression-era Americans; how exotic cocktails were invented, stolen, and re-invented; Hollywood starlets and scandals; and tiki's modern-day revival. Featuring more than 100 delicious recipes (original and historic), plus a groundbreaking new approach to understanding rum, Smuggler's Cove is the magnum opus of the contemporary tiki renaissance. Whether you're looking for a new favorite cocktail, tips on how to trick out your home tiki grotto, help stocking your bar with great rums, or inspiration for your next tiki party, Smuggler's Cove has everything you need to transform your world into a Polynesian Pop fantasia".-- Provided by publisher.

"Even the most serious single-malt sipper will be charmed by this richly illustrated ode to escapism." Library Journal.

Chandler, Adam

Drive-thru dreams : a journey through the heart of America's fast-food kingdom / Adam Chandler. Flatiron Books, [2019] 272 p. **647.95**

1. Fast food restaurants, chains, etc. 2. Fast foods 3. Food habits -- United States -- History 4. Multinational corporations 5. United States -- Social life and customs

ISBN 9781250090720

LC 2019002978

Most any honest person can own up to harboring at least one fast-food guilty pleasure. In Drive-Thru Dreams, Adam Chandler explores the inseparable link between fast food and American life for the past century. The dark underbelly of the industry's largest players has long been scrutinized and gutted, characterized as impersonal, greedy, corporate, and worse. But, in unexpected ways, fast food is also deeply personal and emblematic of a larger than life image of America.

"This fun, argumentative, and frequently surprising pop history of American fast food will thrill and educate food lovers of all speeds." Publishers Weekly.

Freedman, Paul, 1949-

Ten restaurants that changed America / Paul Freedman ; introduction by Danny Meyer. Liveright Publishing Corporation, a division of W.W. Norton & Company, [2016] 528 p. **647.95**

1. Food habits -- United States 2. Restaurants -- United States -- History. 3. Gastronomy -- History -- 20th century. 4. Dinners and dining -- United States -- History -- 20th century.

ISBN 9780871406804

LC 2016029340

"This will appeal widely, engaging readers with both a casual or scholarly interest in food history and its influence on American culture in the late 19th and 20th centuries." Library Journal.

Friedman, Andrew, 1967-

Chefs, drugs and rock & roll : how food lovers, free spirits, misfits and wanderers created a new American profession / Andrew Friedman. HarperCollins 2018 368 p. **647.95**

1. Cooks 2. Restaurateurs 3. Business competition 4. Cooking, American 5. New York City -- Social life and customs 6. San Francisco, California -- Social life and customs 7. Los Angeles, California -- Social life and customs

ISBN 9780062225856

LC bl2018020725

A history of the U.S. restaurant chef in the 70s and 80s chronicles the profession's politically charged transformation as it reflected the rivalry between French-established masters in New York City and game-changing newcomers from California, in a book that recounts the stories of such notables as Mario Batali, Tom Colicchio and Bobby Flay.

"An easy-going history that will be devoured by foodies and cooking fans as well as those interested in American cultural history." Library Journal.

Levy, Shawn

The **castle** on Sunset : life, death, love, art, and scandal at Hollywood's Chateau Marmont / Shawn Levy. Doubleday, 2019. 384 p. **647.95**

1. Chateau Marmont Hotel, Hollywood, California 2. Hotels 3. Celebrities 4. Entertainment industry and trade 5. Film actors and actresses 6. Hollywood, California

ISBN 9780385543163

LC 2018023441

For ninety years, Hollywood's brightest stars have favored the Chateau Marmont as a home away from home. An apartment house-turned-hotel, it has been the backdrop for generations of gossip and folklore. The author of Rat Pack Confidential presents a deeply researched history of the iconic Hollywood hotel that explores its storied role in wild celebrity revelries, scandalous liaisons and creative breakthroughs.

"Levy focuses on Chateau Marmont as a living entity, bringing it to life through its guests and the changes on the Sunset Strip. This will appeal most to Hollywood history buffs, but may also pique the interest of general readers with its yarns of various stars." Library Journal.

Ripert, Eric

On the line / Eric Ripert and Christine Muhlke. Artisan, 2008. 240 p. **647.95**

1. Le Bernardin (Restaurant) 2. Restaurants -- New York City 3. Gourmet cooking 4. Restaurant management. 5. Dinners and dining 6. New York City -- Social life and customs -- 21st century
ISBN 9781579653699

LC 2008005930

Includes index.

A behind-the-scenes look at the inner workings of a top New York restaurant goes into the kitchens to capture the everyday drama, crises, organization, and culinary expertise of Le Bernardin, in a volume that also includes some of the institution's signature modern French dishes.

"A behind-the-scenes look at the famed New York restaurant Le Bernardin. Chef Ripert and New York Times writer Muhlke recount the restaurant's history, from its founding in 1986 by Gilbert and Maguy Le Coze, through Ripert's joining the team in 1991, to the present day. This thorough guide to how the restaurant operates teaches about various kitchen stations, tools of the trade, key personnel and their duties, how new dishes are born and what it's like to spend a night on the line. [Some recipes are included.] A huge treat for industry insiders, fans of Le Bernardin and foodies everywhere." Publishers Weekly.

Schultz, Howard

Onward : how fighting for what we believe reignited Starbucks / Howard Schultz with Joanne Gordon. St. Martins Press, 2011. 368 p. **647.95**

1. Schultz, Howard. 2. Starbucks Coffee Company. 3. Restaurateurs 4. Leadership in business 5. Management 6. Businesspeople -- United States
ISBN 9781605292885

LC 2011003239

Describes how the CEO of Starbucks gained new insights into leadership upon resuming his position eight years after stepping down, a comeback he accepted to restore the company's performance and sustainability values.

648 Housekeeping

Aarssen, Cassandra

Real life organizing : clean and clutter-free in 15 minutes a day / Cassandra Aarssen. Mango, 2017 149 p. : **648**

1. Storage in the home 2. Orderliness
ISBN 9781633535190

LC bl2017015519

Offers easy, inexpensive tips, tricks, and solutions for creating a clean, organized, and functional home with minimal effort needed to maintain it.

Bow, Sara Lyle,

Simple household wisdom : 425 easy ways to clean & organize your home / edited by Sara Lyle Bow. Hearst Books, 2016 209 p. : **648**

1. House cleaning 2. Housekeeping 3. Home economics
ISBN 9781618371690

LC 2016298071

Offers smart and stylish ways to find storage space, make the most of your yard, tidy up around the house, enjoy carefree entertaining and more-- Source other than Library of Congress.

Boyd, Nikki

★**Beautifully** organized : a guide to function and style in your home / Nikki Boyd, creator of Athomewithnikki.com. Paige Tate & Co., 2019 224 p. : **648**

1. Storage in the home. 2. Interior decoration.
ISBN 9781944515683

LC bl2019009998

Includes index.

In a full-color guide, the creator of the firm At Home With Nikki shares her best advice for how to create an organized, beautiful and welcoming home, including the five steps every homeowner should go through: Assess, Declutter, Clean, Organize and Beautify.

Carlson, Julie, 1960-

Remodelista : the organized home : simple, stylish storage ideas for all over the house / Julie Carlson and Margot Guralnick ; with the editors of Remodelista ; photographs by Matthew Williams ; creative direction by Alexa Hotz. Artisan, 2017 224 p. ; **648**

1. Interior decoration -- Themes, motives 2. Orderliness 3. Storage in the home
ISBN 9781579656935

LC 2017013398

Includes index.

The team behind Remodelista.com shares over one hundred tips for creating an organized home using common everyday items, along with guidance on tackling problem zones and turning clutter into stylish design.

Cilley, Marla

The **CHAOS*** cure : clean your house and calm your soul in 15 minutes / Marla Cilley aka The Fly Lady. Seal Press, 2018. 191 p. : **648**

1. House cleaning 2. Housekeeping
ISBN 9781580058025

LC 2018959608

The "FlyLady" author of the best-selling <I>Sink Reflections</I> shares practical advice, quick fixes and helpful tricks for transforming a perpetually messy home by embracing housekeeping as an act of self-care.

Ewer, Cynthia Townley

Cut the clutter : a simple organization plan for a clean and tidy home / Cynthia Townley Ewer of OrganizedHome.com. DK Publishing, 2016. 240 p. : **648**

1. House cleaning. 2. Orderliness. 3. Storage in the home.
ISBN 1465453059

LC bl2016039921

Includes index.

Explains how to declutter, organize, and clean the home, with easy-to-remember tips for every job, from keeping the bathroom clean and doing the laundry to sorting out paperwork and organizing the family photo album.

" The book delves into the nitty-gritty of list-making, menu planning, and the cycles of cleaning. Its best used as a reference guide for specific chores... rather than as a method to follow strictly. This practical guide will be a solid resource for young adults and new parents." Publishers Weekly.

Friedman, Virginia M.

Field guide to stains : how to identify and remove virtually every stain known to man / Virginia M. Friedman, Melissa Wagner, and Nancy Armstrong. Quirk Books, c2002. viii, 280 p., [64] p. of plates : **648**

1. Spot and stain removal
ISBN 9781931686075

LC 2002104065

Includes index.

A step-by-step guide to stain removal is divided into such sections as Fruits and Vegetables, Sauces and Condiments, Garage and Yard, and Office and School Products, in a resource complemented by one hundred cross-referenced photographs for easy identification.

Jameson, Marni

Downsizing the family home : what to save, what to let go / Marni Jameson ; foreword by Mark Brunetz. Sterling, 2015 xviii, 237 p. : **648**

1. House cleaning 2. Moving, Household 3. Older people -- Family relationships 4. Simplicity
ISBN 9781454916338

LC bl2016000493

"AARP."

Includes index.

Counsels readers on how to downsize a family home filled with a lifetime of memories, sharing practical recommendations for strategies based on the expertise of antiques appraisers, garage-sale gurus, professional organizers, and psychologists.

"The common-sense advice and practical information here will be of interest to persons facing downsizing or needing to get rid of stuff they no longer use." Library Journal.

Jones, Richard, 1958 July 14-

House guests, house pests : a natural history of animals in the home / Richard Jones. Bloomsbury, 2015. 256 p. **648**

1. Insect pests 2. Insects 3. Domestic animals 4. Urban pests
ISBN 9781472906236

Shares information on a wide range of pests that invade human homes, including bloodsucking bedbugs, furniture-destroying woodworms, and clothes-eating moths.

Kerr, Jolie

My boyfriend barfed in my handbag ... and other things you can't ask Martha / Jolie Kerr. Penguin Group, 2014. xii, 238 p. ; **648**

1. House cleaning.
ISBN 0142196932

LC 2013022730

"A Plume book."

Includes index.

Based on her column "Ask a Clean Person," the author, using her signature sass and straight talk, takes on the tough questions in this guide to cleaning up life's little emergencies that is perfect for college students and anyone new to living on their own.

Kond, Marie

★The **life-changing** magic of tidying up : the Japanese art of decluttering and organizing / Marie Kondo ; translated from Japanese by Cathy Hirano. Ten Speed Press, 2014 213 p. ; **648**

1. Home economics 2. Housekeeping 3. Orderliness 4. Storage in the home
ISBN 9781607747307

LC 2014017930

Includes index.

"This English translation by Cathy Hirano first published in Great Britain by Ebury Publishing, an imprint of Random House UK, London"--Copyright page.

Presents a guide to cleaning and organizing a living space, discussing best methods for decluttering and the impact that an organized home can have on mood and physical and mental health.

Magnusson, Margareta (Artist),

★The **gentle** art of Swedish death cleaning : how to free yourself and your family from a lifetime of clutter / text and drawings by Margareta Magnusson. Scribner, 2018. ix, 117 p. : **648**

1. Estate planning. 2. Hoarders. 3. House cleaning. 4. Orderliness. 5. Sweden -- Social life and customs.
ISBN 1501173243

LC 2017061728

A Swedish artist provides humorous commentary and advice on how to tidy up and declutter your unnecessary possessions to make life easier and more pleasant while you live it, as well as for those who will be cleaning up after you pass.

"Striking a balance of gentle encouragement, philosophical musing, and pragmatism, her recommendations are wholly practical and warmly convey her hope for a positive outcome." Library Journal.

McCubbin, Tracy

Making space, clutter free : the last book on decluttering you'll ever need / Tracy McCubbin. Sourcebooks, Inc., 2019 282 p. **648**

1. House cleaning. 2. Orderliness. 3. Storage in the home.
ISBN 1492675199

LC 2019006715

A Los Angeles clutter guru shares her unique approach to conquering clutter and discovering emotional cleansing, providing empowering advice, tips and tricks for creating a beautiful home devoid of emotional baggage and clutter--one that sparks a newfound feeling of freedom.

"While many books concentrate on either the emotional aspects of clutter or tips for getting rid of it, McCubbin interweaves both, resulting in highly practical guidance." Library Journal.

Mendelson, Cheryl, 1946-

Laundry : the home comforts book of caring for clothes and linens / Cheryl Mendelson ; illustrated by Harry Bates. Scribner, 2005. xvi, 400 p. ; **648**

1. Laundry 2. Home economics
ISBN 9780743271455

LC 2005051602

Explains how to care for a wide range of items from bedding and hand-washables to baby clothes and vintage linens, sharing advice on such topics as removing stains, ironing, and storing.

Platt, Stacey

What's a disorganized person to do? / Stacey Platt. Artisan, 2010. x, 277 p. : **648**

1. House cleaning. 2. Orderliness. 3. Storage in the home.
ISBN 1579653723

LC 2009013493

In a book illustrated with full-color photos, a professional organizer offers hundreds of solutions for gaining control of clutter, from quick fixes to hour-long projects, from organizing one's e-mails to sorting through the area beneath the bathroom sink.

"The author offers quick tips (e.g., storing sterling silver with chalk to prevent tarnish), instructions (e.g., folding silk scarves correctly), and one-hour projects (e.g., taking back the junk drawer) that anyone can immediately put into practice. Guidelines for organizing office space are designed for those who like to file and those who prefer to pile, and detailed steps for vacation packing and cross-country moving are also included. The employment of one idea alone is worth the price of the book." Library Journal.

Shearer, Clea, 1982-

★The **Home** Edit life : the no-guilt guide to owning what you want and organizing everything / Clea Shearer & Joanna Teplin ; photographs by Clea Shearer. Clarkson Potter/Publishers, 2020 255 p. : **648**

1. Storage in the home. 2. Orderliness.
ISBN 9780593138304

LC 2019056167

Includes index.

The stars of Home Edit outline holistic, tech-friendly approaches to rendering everyday work more productive and fulfilling through organization, offering customizable, guilt-free recommendations for everything from office spaces and holiday storage to luggage and pet supplies.

"Big photos of gorgeously organized spaces provide plenty of eye candy. This irresistible primer will delight and inspire the neat and messy alike." Publishers Weekly

Wenzke, Ali

★The **art** of happy moving : how to declutter, pack, and start over while maintaining your sanity and finding happiness / Ali Wenzke. William Morrow, 2019 xiv, 271 p. : **648**

1. Moving, Household
ISBN 9780062869739

LC bl2019012822

Includes index.

A blogger who moved ten times in eleven years shares tips on managing the moving process, including how to successfully list your home, declutter and pack and transition to a new community.

"A less-onerous-than-Marie Kondo method guide to decluttering. Appended with a moving checklist, moving resolutions, questions to ask before hiring a mover or realtor, moving-day survival kit, donation value guide, and dream-home wish list." Booklist.

649 Child rearing; home care of people with disabilities and illnesses

Adichie, Chimamanda Ngozi, 1977-

Dear Ijeawele : or a feminist manifesto in fifteen suggestions / Chimamanda Ngozi Adichie. Random House Inc 2017 63 p. **649**

1. Feminist theory 2. Feminism 3. Feminists 4. Advice
ISBN 9781524733131

LC bl2017007979

"This excellent series of essays is award-winning author Adichie's (Americanah) response to a friend's question on how to raise her daughter as a feminist." Library Journal.

Agnew, Connie L., 1957-

Twins! : pregnancy, birth, and the first year of life / Connie L. Agnew, Alan H. Klein, and Jill Alison Ganon ; illustrations by Victor Robert. Collins, c2005. viii, 360 p. : **649**

1. Twins
ISBN 9780060742195

LC 2005045585

Includes index.

An updated guide for parents preparing for a multiple birth is filled with practical advice and addresses such topics as a woman's relationship with her doctors, fetal development, prenatal nutrition, pre-term delivery, breast and bottle feeding, and family support.

Bailey, Rebecca Anne, 1952-

Easy to love, difficult to discipline : the seven basic skills for turning conflict into cooperation / Becky A. Bailey. Quill, 2002, c2000. x, 285 p. ; **649**

1. Child rearing 2. Discipline of children 3. Parent and child 4. Parenting
ISBN 9780060007751

LC BL2002003282

Originally published: New York : William Morrow, 2000.

And easy-to-adopt seven-step prpgram is designed to transform willful children into willing ones by applying basic rules of discipline and consistency to a child's daily life.

"Bailey contends that the difficult but rewarding task of guiding children's behavior starts only when parents are able to discipline themselves and become models of self-control. Bailey's underlying message is positive and hopeful, supported with humorous anecdotes and helpful solutions." Publishers Weekly.

Borba, Michele

Unselfie : why empathetic kids succeed in our all-about-me world / Michele Borba, Ed.D.. Touchstone, 2016 xxi, 262 p. ; **649**

1. Child rearing. 2. Empathy. 3. Interpersonal relations.
ISBN 1501110039

LC 2015049137

"According to Michele Borba, the woman Dr. Drew calls "the most trusted parenting expert in America," there's an empthy crisis among today's youth, who she dubs the "selfie generation." But the good news is that empathy is a skill that can -- and must --be taught, and in UNSELFIE (her first book for a general trade audience) Borba offers a 9-step program to help parents cultivate empathy in children, from birth to young adulthood".-- Provided by publisher.

"Her thought- provoking and practical book may very well tip over the parenting priority applecartand rightly so." Publishers Weekly.

Bowers, Mark (Psychologist)

8 keys to raising the quirky child : [how to help a kid who doesn't (quite) fit in] / Mark Bowers ; foreword by Babette Rothschild. W.W. Norton & Company, 2015 xii, 306 p. ; **649**

1. Child rearing. 2. Parenting. 3. Parents of autistic children. 4.

Parents of exceptional children.
ISBN 0393709205
LC 2015004622

Tips and strategies for parents of children who have difficulties connecting with others through personality traits unrelated to developmental disorders counsel parents on how to understand specific behaviors and facilitate better social functioning.

"Frustrated parents who believe their child is well-described by the 'quirky' profile will find Bower's attitude supportive, his psychological explanations of their childs motivations satisfying, and his specific strategies for helping these kids accept breadth of experience and build social competency usable and encouraging." Publishers Weekly.

Boyce, W. Thomas

The **orchid** and the dandelion : why some children struggle and how all can thrive / W. Thomas Boyce MD. Knopf, 2019. 304 p. **649**

1. Developmental psychology 2. Child development 3. Heredity and environment (Psychology) 4. Parenting
ISBN 9781101946565
LC 2017060895

"Based on groundbreaking research, a book on the idea that there are children who have the capacity to survive and thrive under any circumstances and those who are highly sensitive to their environment but, if properly nurtured, can survive and flourish".--Provided by publisher.

"This fascinating study of nurture vs. nature and how parents can play a positive role in a childs life comes highly recommended." Library Journal.

Brown, Christia Spears

Parenting beyond pink & blue : how to raise your kids free of gender stereotypes / Christia Spears Brown, PhD. Ten Speed Press, 2014 xi, 225 p. ; **649**

1. Parenting. 2. Sex differences (Psychology). 3. Sex role. 4. Stereotypes (Social psychology).
ISBN 160774502X
LC 2014001259

Outlines psychology-based strategies for focusing on a child's unique strengths rather than on gender expectations, counseling parents of infants through middle schoolers on how to avoid cultural inclinations that limit a child's potential.

"Brown argues that children are 'free to flourish' when gender is deemphasized and covers both the neuroscience and cultural influences of sex in language that is accessible and at times even humorous." Library Journal.

Dawson, Peg

Smart but scattered : the revolutionary "executive skills" approach to helping kids reach their potential / Peg Dawson, Richard Guare. Guilford Press, c2009. vi, 314 p. : **649**

1. Parenting 2. Executive ability in children 3. Children -- Life skills guides 4. Child development
ISBN 9781593859879
LC 2008026078

Presents advice for parents of children who lack basic "executive skills," providing strategies to help children become organized, increase concentration, follow instructions, be persistent, and complete homework and chores on time.

Eanes, Rebecca

Positive parenting : an essential guide / Rebecca Eanes ; foreword by Dr. Laura Markham. A TarcherPerigee Book, 2016. xx, 183 p. ; **649**

1. Parent and child. 2. Parenting.
ISBN 0143109227
LC 2016009096

"Popular parenting blogger Rebecca Eanes believes that parenting advice should be about more than just getting kids to behave. Struggling to maintain a meaningful connection with her two little ones and frustrated by the lack of emotionally aware books for parents, she began to share her own insights with readers online. Her following has grown into a thriving community--hundreds of thousands strong. In this eagerly anticipated guide, Eanes shares her hard-won wisdom for overcoming limiting thought patterns and recognizing emotional triggers, as well as advice for connecting with kids at each stage, from infancy to adolescence. This heartfelt, insightful advice comes not from an "expert," but from a learning, evolving parent. Filled with practical, solution-oriented advice, this is an empowering guide for any parent who longs to end the yelling, power struggles, and downward spiral of acting out, punishment, resentment, and shame--and instead foster an emotional connection that helps kids learn self-discipline, feel confident, and create lasting, loving bonds".-- Provided by publisher.

Edelman, Marian Wright, 1939-

The **measure** of our success : a letter to my children and yours / Marian Wright Edelman. Beacon Press, c1992. 97 p. ; **649**

1. Edelman, Marian Wright, 1939- 2. Child rearing -- United States. 3. Children -- Personal conduct. 4. African American children -- Personal conduct. 5. United States -- Moral conditions.
ISBN 9780807031025
LC 91042743

In a letter to her three sons, the author offers words of inspiration to young people, discussing work, education, failure, confidence, self-esteem, and more.

"The author presents her beliefs on child rearing and moral values. She includes a personal letter to her three sons, who were born into a family with a shared African American and Jewish heritage, and offers 25 lessons, or road maps, for life." Library Journal.

Ezzo, Gary

★**On** becoming baby wise : giving your infant the gift of nighttime sleep / Gary Ezzo, M.A. and Robert Bucknam, M.D.. Parent-Wise Solutions, Inc., 2012. 279 p. : **649**

1. Child rearing. 2. Infants -- Sleep. 3. Infants. 4. Parent and infant.
ISBN 1932740139
LC bl2014007776

Teaches parents about synchronized feedings so their baby will establish cycles for wake time and nighttime, giving both parent and child the rest they need.

Faber, Adele

★**How** to talk so kids will listen & listen so kids will talk / Adele Faber & Elaine Mazlish ; illustrations by Kimberly Ann Coe. Scribner Classics, 2012, c1980. xiv, 345 p. : **649**

1. Parenting 2. Interpersonal communication
ISBN 9781451663877
LC bl2012004319

"With a new afterword, 'The Next Generation' by Joanna Faber."

Details a program for improving communication between parents and children, providing sample dialogues and role-playing exercises.

Fonseca, Christine, 1966-

Raising the shy child : a parent's guide to social anxiety : advice for helping kids make friends, speak up, and stop worrying / Christine Fonseca. Prufrock Press, Inc., 2015 xvi, 223 p. : **649**

1. Bashfulness in children 2. Social phobia in children 3. Child rearing 4. Parenting
ISBN 9781618213983

LC 2014048544

Combines real-world examples and stories from people with social anxiety disorder to demonstrate how to help children overcome their fear and express social competence, covering such topics as bullying and identity.

Forgan, James W.

The **impulsive,** disorganized child : solutions for parenting kids with executive functioning difficulties / James W. Forgan, Ph.D., & Mary Anne Richey. Prufrock Press Inc., 2015 xiv, 258 p. : **649**

1. Child psychology 2. Children with mental disabilities -- Care 3. Executive functions (Neuropsychology) 4. Self-control in children
ISBN 9781618214010

LC 2015001880

Offers parenting advice to parents of children who cannot select, plan, initiate, or sustain action toward their goals.

"The advice presented has practical context and gives specifics for action. Using the SMART model (goals should be: specific, measurable, attainable, realistic, and timely), kids can join their parents in improving impulse control and organization." Library Journal.

Ginott, Haim G.

Between parent and child : the bestselling classic that revolutionized parent-child communication / Haim G. Ginott. Three Rivers Press, c2003. xiv, 231 p. : **649**

1. Child rearing 2. Domestic education 3. Emotions in children 4. Empathy
ISBN 9780609809884

LC 2003000626

A revised edition of the child development classic offers advice to a current generation of parents on how to develop empathetic yet disciplined child rearing skills that place an emphasis on good communication and avoid negative reinforcements.

Glickman, Elaine Rose

Your kid's a brat and it's all your fault / Elaine Rose Glickman. A TarcherPerigee Book, 2016 xii, 301 p. ; **649**

1. Parenting. 2. Parent and child. 3. Spoiled children 4. Children -- Behavior modification.
ISBN 9780399173127

LC 2015045423

"In this wise and informative parenting guide, Elaine Rose Glickman shows readers how loving your kid enough to be the boss will result in happier, healthier, and much easier-to-be-around children! You've seen them--kids running wild through restaurants while the parents avert their gaze and order another cappuccino. You've heard them--kids telling their parents to 'shut up' and 'get me that.' You've met them--kids who dress inappropriately and roll their eyes and never say thank you. Maybe one of those kids belongs to you. Combining incisive commentary with grounded, practical advice, Your Kid's a Brat and It's All Your Fault will have you recognizing and laughing at yourself, your fellow parents, and a culture that seems determined to turn our precious angels into not-so-precious brats. Divided into three sections--"Your Budding Brat" for toddlers and preschoolers, "Your Bratty Child" for grade-schoolers, and "Your Bratty Tween"--this book is packed with wisdom and tips culled from the trenches of child-rearing. Your Kid's a Brat and It's All Your Fault will not only help you grow adept at responding to specific misbehaviors, but will encourage and empower you to become the confident, respected parent you yearn to be".-- Provided by publisher.

"Most parents will find this humorous guide refreshing and truly helpful." Booklist.

Gold, Tammy

Secrets of the nanny whisperer : a practical guide for finding and achieving the gold standard of care for your child / Tammy Gold LCSW, MSW, LSW, CEC. Perigee, 2015. viii, 279 p. ; **649**

1. Child care services -- United States 2. Nannies -- Employment -- United States 3. Nannies -- Selection and appointment -- United States
ISBN 9780399169885

LC 2014040010

"A top expert reveals the most common mistakes parents make with their nannies--and how to avoid them".-- Provided by publisher.

"While many families view their nanny as a part of the family, Gold reminds readers that this is ultimately an employment relationship. She dispenses exceptional advice that will help families avoid common pitfalls and is especially strong when illustrating scenarios from the nanny's point of view. From her needs assessment to interview questions to problem-solving language, Gold's examples and crisp narrative gives readers one-stop shopping for nanny know-how. A required purchase. Well done." Library Journal.

Grayson, Jennifer

Unlatched : the evolution of breastfeeding and the making of a controversy / Jennifer Grayson. HarperCollins 2016. 272 p. **649**

1. Breast feeding 2. Infant formulas 3. Bottle feeding 4. Infants.
ISBN 9780062423399

LC bl2016027825

"Persuasive arguments backed by scientific research that clearly demonstrate the benefits of breast-feeding for as long as possible." Kirkus.

Haddad, Douglas, 1976-

The **ultimate** guide to raising teens and tweens : strategies for unlocking your child's full potential / Douglas Haddad. Rowman & Littlefield, 2017 xxi, 263 p. **649**

1. Parenting 2. Child rearing 3. Education -- Parent participation 4. Home and school
ISBN 9781442256958

LC OC2018140762

The Ultimate Guide to Raising Teens and Tweens is for parents of adolescents (ages 10-19). Parents are provided with the ten "child unlimited tools" to help raise smart, successful, and self-disciplined children. This book also discusses "child limiting challenges" and offers parents effective strategies to prevent and solve these issues with their children.

"This is a crucial, thoughtful guide that will aid any adults with responsibility for mentoring children between 10 and 19." Publishers Weekly.

Haelle, Tara

The **informed** parent : a science-based resource for your child's first four years / Tara Haelle and Emily Willingham, Ph.D. A TarcherPerigee Book, 2016 xii, 321 p. ; **649**

1. Child development 2. Child rearing 3. Families -- Health and

hygiene 4. Infants -- Care
ISBN 9780399171062
LC 2015046759
Includes index.

Science writers and parents themselves, the authors, sifting through research studies on dozens of essential topics, present the latest scientific research on home birth, breastfeeding, sleep training, vaccines and other important topics so that parents-to-be can make their own best-information decisions.

"For anyone headed into parenthood, this is a must-read, as it answers so many questions new parents are bound to ask. Easy-to-read, up-to-date information on the latest research into pregnancy, childbirth, and early childhood." Kirkus.

Harvey, Jennifer, 1971-

Raising white kids: bringing up children in a racially unjust America / Jennifer Harvey. Abingdon Press, 2018. xiii, 306 p. ; **649**

1. Race awareness in children. 2. Parenting. 3. Parent and child.
ISBN 9781501856426
LC 2017042214

Discusses how parents of white children should navigate the topic of race in the United States.

Huggins, Kathleen

★The **nursing** mother's companion : the breastfeeding book mothers trust, from pregnancy through weaning / Kathleen Huggins, R.N., M.S., I.B.C.L.C. ; foreword by Jessica Martin-Weber ; preface by Kelly Bonyata ; appendix on drug safety by Philip O. Anderson. Harvard Common Press, 2017. xii, 436 p. : **649**

1. Breastfeeding
ISBN 9781558328822
LC bl2018125682

Breastfeeding is natural, but it is not always instinctive for either mothers or babies. The Nursing Mother's Companion has been among the best-selling books on breastfeeding for more than 30 years, with more than 1 million copies sold. It is respected and recommended by professionals, including The International Lactation Consultant Association, T. Berry Brazelton and The American Academy of Pediatrics, and is well loved by new parents for its encouraging and accessible style.

Hurley, Katie

The **happy** kid handbook : how to raise joyful children in a stressful world / Katie Hurley, LCSW. Jeremy P.Tarcher/Penguin Random House, 2015 xii, 303 p. ; **649**

1. Happiness in children 2. Child rearing 3. Parenting
ISBN 9780399171819
LC 2015022156

"With all the parenting information out there and the constant pressure to be the "perfect" parent, it seems as if many parents have lost track of one very important piece of the parenting puzzle: raising happy kids. Parenting today has gotten far too complicated. It's never been the easiest job in the world, but with all the "parenting advice" parents are met with at every corner, it's hard not to become bewildered. It seems that in the past it was a good deal simpler. You made sure there was dinner onthe table and the kids got to school on time and no one set anything on fire, and you called it a success. But today everybody has a different method for dealing with the madness--attachment parenting, free-range parenting, mindful parenting. And who is to say one is more right or better than another? How do you choose? The truth is that whatever drumbeat you march to, all parents would agree that we just want our kids to be happy. It seems like a no-brainer, right? But in the face of all the many parenting theories out there, happiness feels like it has become incidental. That's where The Happy Kid Handbook by child and adolescent psychotherapist and parenting expert Katie Hurley comes in. She shows parents how happiness is the key to raising confident, capable children. It's not about giving in every time your child wants something so they won't feel bad when you say no, or making sure that they're taking that art class, and the ballet class, and the soccer class (to help with their creativity and their coordination and all that excess energy). Happiness is about parenting the individual, because not every child is the same, and not every child will respond to parenting the same way. By exploring the differences among introverts, extroverts, and everything in between, this definitive guide to parenting offers parents the specific strategies they need to meet their child exactly where he or she needs to be met from a social-emotional perspective. A back-to-basics guide to parenting, The Happy Kid Handbook is a must-have for any parent hoping to be the best parent they can be".-- Provided by publisher.

Ingall, Marjorie

Mamaleh knows best : what Jewish mothers do to raise successful, creative, empathetic, independent children / Marjorie Ingall. Harmony Books, 2016. 245 p. ; **649**

1. Child rearing -- Religious aspects -- Judaism. 2. Parenting.
ISBN 080414141X
LC 2016010796
Includes index.

"In this funny, insightful look at the best practices of Jewish mothering, Marjorie identifies the 10 key tenets of Jewish parenting, then uses a blend of funny anecdotes, modern research, and ancient texts to show how anyone can teach those values at home".-- Provided by publisher.

Karp, Harvey

The **happiest** baby on the block : the new way to calm crying and help your baby sleep longer / Harvey Karp. Bantam Books, 2015. xvii, 319 p. : **649**

1. Child rearing. 2. Crying in infants. 3. Infants -- Care. 4. Infants -- Sleep.
ISBN 9780553393231
LC 201512546
First Bantam hardcover ed. published 2002.
Includes index.

A completely revised and updated second edition of one of the most popular and bestselling parenting books of all time: A pediatrician and child development specialist combines cutting-edge medical research with personal experience to create a sensible, easy-to-follow, four-step plan for soothing a cranky infant.

Kazdin, Alan E.

The **everyday** parenting toolkit : the Kazdin method for easy, step-by-step, lasting change for you and your child / Alan E. Kazdin, with Carlo Rotella. Houghton Mifflin Harcourt, 2013. xiv, 192 p. ; **649**

1. Child rearing. 2. Parenting.
ISBN 0547985541
LC bl2013025761

Outlines accessible strategies for handling everyday child rearing challenges, outlining comprehensive approaches to such topics as fussiness, video game overindulgence, and respecting others.

Kennedy, Janet Krone

The **good** sleeper : the essential guide to sleep for your baby--and you / Janet Krone Kennedy, PhD. Holt Paperbacks, 2015 xv, 286 p. ; **649**

1. Infants -- Sleep. 2. Naps (Sleep). 3. Parent and infant.
ISBN 0805099433

LC 2014019607

Includes index.

"Cry it out or co-sleep? Bassinet or swing? White noise machine or Bach? How many hours anyway? For something so important, there's too much conflicting information about how best to get your baby to sleep through the night and nap successfully during the day. This book is a straightforward, no-nonsense answer to one of the biggest challenges new parents face when they welcome a brand new baby home. This book is written for exhausted parents, giving them immediate access to the information they need. Reassuring and easy to understand, Dr. Kennedy addresses head-on the fears and misinformation about the long-term effects of crying and takes a bold stand on controversial issues such as co-sleeping and attachment parenting. With polarizing figures and techniques dominating the marketplace--and spawning misinformation across the internet--Dr. Kennedy's methods and practices create an extensively researched and parent-tested approach to sleep training that takes both babies' and parents' needs into account to deliver good nights and days of sleep, and no small dose of peace of mind. THE GOOD SLEEPER is a practical, empowering--and even entertaining--guide to help parents understand infant sleep. This research-based book will teach parents the basics of sleep science, determine how and when to intervene, and provide tools to solve even the most seemingly impossible sleep problems".-- Provided by publisher.

Kennedy-Moore, Eileen

Smart parenting for smart kids : nurturing your child's true potential / Eileen Kennedy-Moore, Mark S. Lowenthal. Jossey-Bass, c2011. xii, 306 p. : **649**

1. Gifted children. 2. Parents of gifted children.
ISBN 0470640057

LC 2010043005

"'My kid is smart, but...' It takes more than school smarts to build a fulfilling life. In fact, many bright children face special challenges: Some are driven by perfectionism. Some are afraid of effort, because they're used to instant success. Some routinely butt heads with authority figures. Some struggle to get along with their peers. Some are outwardly successful but just don't feel good about themselves. This warm and practical book explains why and offers parents do-able strategies for raising capable, confident, and caring children. With wisdom and compassion, psychologists Eileen Kennedy-Moore and Mark S. Lowenthal describe specific approaches parents can use to guide children toward developing inner strength and outward empathy. Drawing from research as well as the authors' clinical experience, this book provides strategies for helping children learn to cope with feelings, build relationships, and embrace learning. It focuses on the essential skills children need to make the most of their abilities and find personal satisfaction".--Provided by publisher.

Kowal-Connelly, Suanne

Parenting through puberty : mood swings, acne, and growing pains / Suanne Kowal-Connelly, MD, FAAP. American Academy of Pediatrics, 2019 xvii, 246 p. : **649**

1. Parent and teenager. 2. Puberty.
ISBN 9781610022125

LC bl2018186502

Details the physical and emotional changes parents can expect to see in their child during puberty and explains how to help teenagers navigate through this tough time in their lives.

Kriegsman, Kay Harris

Just one of the kids : raising a resilient family when one of your children has a physical disability / Kay Harris Kriegsman, Ph.D., and Sara Palmer, Ph.D. The Johns Hopkins University Press, 2013 xiv, 226 p. ; **649**

1. Children with disabilities -- Family relationships 2. Parents of children with disabilities
ISBN 9781421409313

LC 2012035771

Presents parents with stories, tips, and tools for ensuring that children with physical disabilities meet acceptable risks, face challenges, and feel like "one of the kids" while meeting the needs of the whole family.

"A valuable resource for families looking for encouragement as they try to create an inclusive environment for their child with a physical disability." Library Journal.

Lahey, Jessica

The **gift** of failure : how the best parents learn to let go so their children can succeed / Jessica Lahey. Harper, 2015. 304 p. **649**

1. Self-reliance in children. 2. Child rearing -- United States. 3. Parenting -- United States. 4. Overprotectiveness in parents
ISBN 9780062299239

LC 2014039146

A full-length guide based on the author's provocative essay on the website of The Atlantic counsels parents of school-aged children on how to overcome tendencies toward over-protectiveness to allow children to develop independence.

"Lahey's conversational tone, combined with research and narratives from both children and parents, delivers in-depth insight into the value of mistakes. With chapters on specific age groups (middle schoolers and high schoolers) and hot-button issues, such as household chores, homework, and friendships, any parent who needs assistance reining in the supermom tendencies will find sound advice here." Library Journal.

Leach, Penelope

The **essential** first year / Penelope Leach. DK Pub., 2010. 288 p. : **649**

1. Infants -- Care 2. Child rearing
ISBN 9780756657994

LC bl2010015518

Presents a guide for new parents on properly caring for an infant, from pregnancy to its first year, and includes tips on feeding, sleeping, and crying, as well as providing new insights to infants' neurological development.

Lev, Arlene Istar

The **complete** lesbian & gay parenting guide / Arlene Istar Lev. Berkley Books, 2004. xvi, 379 p. ; **649**

1. Families -- United States 2. Gay parents -- United States 3. Parenting -- United States
ISBN 9780425191972

LC 2004057080

A comprehensive and practical handbook for gay, lesbian, and alternative lifestyle parents shares sensible advice and personal real-life stories about the challenges of twenty-first century family life.

Levine, Madeline

★**Ready** or not : preparing our kids to thrive in an uncertain and rapidly changing world / Madeline Levine. Harper360, 2020. 352 p. **649**

1. Parenting 2. Child rearing 3. Skills 4. Success (Concept)
ISBN 9780062657756

LC bl2020000501

The best-selling author explores how today's parenting techniques and our myopic educational system are failing to prepare children for their certain-to-be-uncertain future -- and how we can reverse course to ensure their lasting adaptability, resilience, health and happiness.

"With thorough research backing her up, Levine delivers advice with intelligence and compassion, but also with realistic expectations of what it's like to parent as well as grow up in today's world. Best of all, she masterfully balances this realism with positivity. Another invaluable resource from Levine." Booklist

Lewis, Lisa E.

Feed the baby hummus : pediatrician-backed secrets from cultures around the world / Lisa Lewis, MD. Familius LLC, 2018 288 p. ; **649**

1. Newborn infants -- Care 2. Infants -- Care 3. Parent and infant

ISBN 9781945547799

LC bl2018086082

"With tips from 40+ countries!"--Cover.

Offers readers parenting advice on bonding, nutrition, stages of development, and separation anxiety, with stories, customs, and traditions from around the world.

Lickona, Thomas

How to raise kind kids : and get respect, gratitude, and a happier family in the bargain / Thomas Lickona. Penguin Books, 2018 xxvii, 308 p. ; **649**

1. Parenting 2. Kindness 3. Moral education 4. Education -- Parent participation

ISBN 9780143131946

LC 2017058211

"Can you teach a child to be kind? This vital question is taking on a new urgency as our culture grows ever more abrasive and divided. We all want our kids to be kind. But that is not the same as knowing what to do when you catch your son being unkind. A world-renowned developmental psychologist, Dr. Thomas Lickona has led the character education movement in schools for forty years. Now he shares with parents the vital tools they need to bring peace and foster cooperation at home. Kindness doesn't stand on its own. It needs a supporting cast of other essential virtues--like courage, self-control, respect, and gratitude. With concrete examples drawn from the many families Dr. Lickona has worked with over the years and clear tips you can act on tonight, How to Raise Kind Kids will help you give and get respect, hold family meetings to tackle persistent problems, discipline in a way that builds character, and improve the dynamic of your relationship with your children while putting them on the path to ahappier and more fulfilling life".--Provided by publisher.

Markham, Laura

Peaceful parent, happy kids : how to stop yelling and start connecting / Laura Markham. Perigee Book, 2012. xxvii, 274 p. ; **649**

1. Child rearing. 2. Parent and child.

ISBN 0399160280

LC 2012031273

A clinical psychologist offers practical, easy-to-apply ideas to help parents regulate themselves and their own emotions in order to foster a better connection with their children to help them grow, thrive and learn emotional intelligence, empathy, and responsibility.

"In this compassionate yet practical text, Markham deftly leads parents down a gentler, kinder path to raising emotionally intelligent and happier children." Publishers Weekly.

Matthews, Dona J., 1951-

Beyond intelligence : secrets for raising happily productive kids / Dona Matthews, Ph.D., Joanne Foster, Ed.D.. Anansi, 2014. 290 p. ; **649**

1. Child development 2. Child rearing 3. Parenting 4. Children -- Intelligence levels

ISBN 9781770894778

LC bl2014032165

Includes bibliographical references (pages 249-269) and index.

Offers guidance on identifying a child's ability with information on fostering their creativity, and persistance, while exploring different ways of learning.

"Parents who have read other child rearing books may recognize but still appreciate the information and advice provided here: listen to, understand, and nurture children in order to foster their growth." Library Journal.

Medina, John, 1956-

Brain rules for baby : how to raise a smart and happy child from zero to five / John Medina. Pear Press, 2014 323 p. : **649**

1. Brain -- Development. 2. Child development. 3. Child rearing. 4. Infants -- Development.

ISBN 0983263388

LC bl2014016838

Includes index.

The best-selling author of Brain Rules extends his popular plan to infants, sharing what the latest science says about raising smart and happy children, in a book that includes such advice as: TV is harmful for children under 2, the best predictor of academic performance is a child's level of self-control, praising effort is better than praising intelligence and much more.

Miller, Lisa (Clinical psychologist)

The **spiritual** child : the new science on parenting for health and lifelong thriving / Lisa Miller ; with Teresa Barker. St. Martin's Press, 2015 viii, 374 p. ; **649**

1. Parenting -- Religious aspects. 2. Christian parenting 3. Child development. 4. Children -- Religious life.

ISBN 9781250032928

LC 2015005940

Combining research with broad anecdotal evidence from her work as a clinical psychologist to illustrate just how invaluable spirituality is to a child's mental and physical health, Miller translates these findings into practical advice for parents, giving them concrete ways to develop and encourage their children's--as well as their own--well-being. Provided by publisher.

"If the plights of Marin and Kurt had been introduced earlier, Miller could have established more emotional connection with her readers, who would then be more engaged with the science she presents. New science or a leap of faith? Either way, nurturing spirituality in your children may save them a world of pain." Kirkus.

Mogel, Wendy, 1951-

Voice lessons for parents : what to say, how to say it, and when to listen / Wendy Mogel, PhD. Scribner, 2018. xvi, 302 p. ; **649**

1. Interpersonal communication. 2. Parent and child. 3. Parenting.

ISBN 1501142399

LC bl2018004483

Presents an essential guide to the art of talking with children that demonstrates how a change of voice can transform conversations and ease parent-child relationships, sharing strategies for communicating with kids at different age levels.

Morgenstern, Julie

Time to parent : organizing your life to bring out the best in your child and you / Julie Morgenstern. Henry Holt and Company, 2018 xvi, 335 p. : **649**

1. Parenting 2. Time management
ISBN 9781627797436

LC 2018001408

Intends to help parents and caregivers craft a life schedule that builds in quality time with children.

Morin, Amy

13 things mentally strong parents don't do : raising self-assured children and training their brains for a life of happiness, meaning, and success / Amy Morin. William Morrow, 2017. 342 p. ; **649**

1. Parenting. 2. Child rearing. 3. Self-confidence in children.
ISBN 9780062565730

LC 2017470363

In today's world, many parents over-react to events by trying to shield their children from pain and reality. But children need to learn skills that will help them become mentally strong adults. Morin offers advice for providing appropriate support, guidance, and encouragement to help children deal with challenges and flourish in their everyday lives.

"Her combination of common sense backed by research--amply cited--will help parents make a midcourse correction. While the title focuses on the negative, the book itself accentuates the positive." Publishers Weekly.

Murkoff, Heidi Eisenberg

★**What** to expect the second year : from 12 to 24 months / Heidi Murkoff and Sharon Mazel ; foreword by Mark D. Widome. Workman Pub., c2011. xvi, 512 p. : **649**

1. Child rearing 2. Toddlers
ISBN 9780761163640

LC 2011281832

Includes index.

From the first birthday to the second, everything you need to know about caring for, nurturing, understanding, and keeping up with your incredible 1 year old.--Provided by publisher.

Natterson, Cara Familian, 1970-

★**Decoding** boys : new science behind the subtle art of raising sons / Cara Natterson, MD. Ballantine Books, 2020. 288 p. **649**

1. Boys -- Psychology. 2. Teenage boys -- Psychology. 3. Child rearing. 4. Puberty
ISBN 9781984819031

LC 2019037589

Citing the less-recognized behavioral tendencies of male adolescence that complicate communications between parents and children, a guide to raising teen boys shares strategic guidelines on effective parenting, managing screen time and understanding the sources of negative behavior.

"An essential and approachable resource for parents of preteen and teenage boys." Library Journal

Neifert, Marianne R.

The **essential** guide to breastfeeding / Marianne Neifert. Sterling, c2009. 312 p. : **649**

1. Breastfeeding
ISBN 9781402758171

LC 2009005248

Includes index.

Describes how to prepare for breastfeeding a newborn, from preparations before birth to breastfeeding with a busy schedule, proper storage, maintaining a healthy diet, and breastfeeding high-risk infants.

"The author combines detailed, readable medical explanations with practical tips for success and addresses potential challenges honestly rather than glossing over them with bland reassurances. Each chapter seems designed to stand alone, making it easy for time-pressed mothers to find the information they need without reading the entire book." Library Journal.

Newman, Nancy, 1944-

Raising passionate readers : 5 easy steps to success in school and life / Nancy Newman. Tribeca View Press, 2014 221 p. ; **649**

1. Children -- Books and reading 2. Reading (Early childhood) 3. Reading -- Parent participation
ISBN 9780615847542

LC bl2015024551

Grounded in scientific research and personal experience, details five simple steps for instilling a love of reading in children.

"While the subject literature has not changed much over the years, it is still widely accepted that reading is the greatest indicator of future academic success. Recommended for collections needing an update on the topic." Library Journal.

Ockwell-Smith, Sarah

Gentle discipline : using emotional connection-not punishment-to raise confident, capable kids / Sarah Ockwell-Smith. A TarcherPerigee Book, 2017 xxiv, 246 p. : **649**

1. Child rearing. 2. Discipline of children. 3. Emotions -- Social aspects.
ISBN 0143131893

LC 2017015635

Simultaneously published in London, UK as Gentle discipline book, 2017.

Drawing from research in child development, psychology, and neuroscience, debunks common myths about punishments and rewards in discipline and provides connection-based techniques that bring parents and kids close together.

"Ockwell-Smith, a parenting blogger, presents a primer on placing empathy and respect for children at the center of parenting." Publishers Weekly.

Ockwell-Smith, Sarah

Ready, set, go! : a gentle parenting guide to calmer, quicker potty training / Sarah Ockwell-Smith. A TarcherPerigee Book, 2017 xiii, 191 p. ; **649**

1. Toilet training.
ISBN 0143131907

LC 2018011129

A popular parenting expert presents this authoritative guide to potty-training that helps parents understand when to start the process, and provides step-by-step information on the most effective, gentle and compassionate approach, as well as how to handle setbacks.

"There is little new here, but potty training is of perennial interest to parents, and newbies may find this a solid starter manual." Library Journal.

Paul, Pamela

★**How** to raise a reader / Pamela Paul, Maria Russo ; illustrated by Dan Yaccarino. Workman Publishing, 2019. 208

p. **649**

1. Books and reading 2. Children -- Books and reading 3. Reading aloud 4. Families -- Books and reading
ISBN 9781523505302
LC bl2019021047

Includes index.

A parent's guide to raising a lifelong reader, packed with practical ideas for engaging children of all ages in books, plus wonderful lists of books, arranged by age and subject matter, will keep the shelves stocked and young readers' interests high from birth through teens.

"With the bottom line that 'If you want to raise a reader, be a reader,' their primer is recommended for all worried parents and anyone looking for suggestions of what books to read or give to children." Publishers Weekly.

Perry, Philippa, 1957-

★The **book** you wish your parents had read : (and your children will be glad that you did) / Philippa Perry. Pamela Dorman Books Life/Viking , 2019 xv, 304 p. ; **649**

1. Parenting 2. Parent and child
ISBN 9781984879554
LC 2019025255

"In this absorbing, clever, and warm book, renowned psychotherapist Philippa Perry tells us what really matters and what behavior it is important to avoid--the vital dos and don'ts of parenting".-- Provided by publisher.

Phelan, Thomas W., 1943-

★**1-2-3** magic : effective discipline for children 2-12 / Thomas W. Phelan, PhD. Sourcebooks, 2016 xx, 265 p. : **649**

1. Discipline of children 2. Child rearing 3. Parenting
ISBN 9781492631828
LC 2015021612

Outlines a three step parenting guide, offering readers tools to use in a variety of situations and advice for common problems.

Remer Altmann, Tanya

What to feed your baby : a pediatrician's guide to the eleven essential foods to guarantee veggie-loving, no-fuss, healthy-eating kids / Tanya Altmann, M.D., F.A.A.P. with Beth Saltz M.P.H., R.D. HarperOne, 2016 vii, 326 p. ; **649**

1. Food habits 2. Infants -- Nutrition
ISBN 9780062404930
LC 2015033614

An American Academy of Pediatrics spokesperson and best-selling author of Mommy Calls shares strategies for raising children to love healthy foods, clarifying the contradictory information that challenges parenting choices while identifying 11 foundation foods critical to brain development and growth.

"This clear, thorough guide will take the angst and confusion out of feeding time for parents and youngsters alike." Publishers Weekly.

Rende, Richard

Raising can-do kids : giving children the tools to thrive in a fast-changing world / Richard Rende, PhD & Jen Prosek. A Perigee Book, 2015. xvii, 252 p. ; **649**

1. Child rearing. 2. Parenting. 3. Self-reliance in children.
ISBN 0399168966
LC bl2015030247

Provides a guide for raising resourceful, resilient, and responsible children that can succeed in the world without a roadmap, highlighting such qualities as curiosity, inventiveness, and optimism.

"The authors' suggestions and insights cover a wide spectrum of child-raising situations and should, when properly applied, deliver lasting results." Kirkus.

Seals-Allers, Kimberly

The **big** letdown : how medicine, big business, and feminism undermine breastfeeding / Kimberly Seals Allers. St. Martin's Press, 2017. 288 p. **649**

1. Breast feeding 2. Infants. 3. Parenting
ISBN 9781250026965
LC 2016044039

A socio-historical look at the controversies surrounding breastfeeding examines the role of celebrities in shaping both sides of the debate, calling for candid discussions about the cultural, sociological and economic forces that are shaping breastfeeding culture and how the author believes they undermine women.

"Easily digested research and personal stories in support of breastfeeding and its importance to mothers and their children." Kirkus.

Seldin, Tim, 1946-

How to raise an amazing child the Montessori way / Tim Seldin. DK Pub., 2017. 208 p. : **649**

1. Child rearing. 2. Child development. 3. Learning. 4. Early childhood education.
ISBN 9781465462305
LC 2017302243

The president of The Montessori Foundation offers an inspirational handbook designed to help parents enhance a child's physical and intellectual growth from birth to six years of age, furnishing insights into each development stage; proven strategies for helping youngsters develop discipline, respect, and kindness; and tips on coping with problem behavior.

"Child psychiatrist Seldin, president of the Montessori Foundation, here adapts key Montessori principles for the home environment, maintaining the core tenets of 'kindness, partnership, and respect.'" Library Jouranl.

Siegel, Daniel J., 1957-

No-drama discipline : the whole-brain way to calm the chaos and nurture your child's developing mind / Daniel J. Siegel, M.D., Tina Payne Bryson, Ph.D. Bantam, 2014 xxviii, 255 p. : **649**

1. Parenting 2. Child development 3. Child rearing
ISBN 9780345548047
LC 2014008270

"The authors of the Los Angeles Times bestselling The Whole-Brain Child team up again to offer parents of children aged 2-13 a practical roadmap to effective, productive, and more peaceful discipline, highlighting the fascinating and important connection between the way a parent reacts to misbehavior and a child's neurological development".-- Provided by publisher.

Siegel, Daniel J., 1957-

Parenting from the inside out : how a deeper self-understanding can help you raise children who thrive / Daniel J. Siegel, M.D., and Mary Hartzell, M.Ed ; with a new preface by the authors. Jeremy P. Tarcher/Penguin, 2014 xxiv, 311 p. : **649**

1. Parent and child. 2. Parenting. 3. Self-perception.
ISBN 039916510X
LC 2013037883

Explores the extent to which our childhood experiences shape the way we parent, drawing on new findings in neurobiology and attachment research and explaining how interpersonal relationships directly impact the development of the brain. Offers parents a step-by-step approach to forming a deeper understanding of their own life stories.

Siegel, Daniel J., 1957-

The **power** of showing up : how parental presence shapes who our kids become and how their brains get wired / Daniel J. Siegel, M.D., Tina Payne Bryson, Ph.D. ; illustrations by Tuesday Mourning. Ballantine Books, 2020. xiv, 238 p. : **649**

1. Parenting -- Psychological aspects. 2. Parent and child -- Psychological aspects. 3. Self-help psychology for parents

ISBN 9781524797713

LC 2019034765

Drawa on the latest understandings in attachment research to explain the importance of a parent's involved presence in helping children feel safe, secure and loved.

Siegel, Daniel J., 1957-

The **whole-brain** child : 12 revolutionary strategies to nurture your child's developing mind / Daniel J. Siegel, Tina Payne Bryson. Delacorte Press, c2011. xiii, 176 p. : **649**

1. Parenting. 2. Child development. 3. Child rearing.

ISBN 9780553807912

LC 2010052988

Includes index.

Outlines twelve key strategies for fostering healthy brain development in children to promote a calm and happy outlook, explaining how challenging child behaviors are rooted in immature left and right brain coordination and how parents can make informed adjustments to enable positive learning experiences.

"Siegel and Bryson reveal that an integrated brain with parts that cooperate in a coordinated and balanced manner creates a better understanding of self, stronger relationships, and success in school, among other benefits. With illustrations, charts, and even a handy 'Refrigerator Sheet,' the authors have made every effort to make brain science parent-friendly." Publishers Weekly.

Small, Meredith F.

Our babies, ourselves : how biology and culture shape the way we parent / Meredith F. Small. Anchor Books, 1999, c1998. xxii, 292 p. : **649**

1. Infants -- Care -- Cross-cultural studies. 2. Infants -- Development -- Cross-cultural studies. 3. Parent and infant -- Cross-cultural studies.

ISBN 9780385483629

LC bl2007010441

An exploration into the new field of ethnopediatrics--the study of how and why parents raise their children the way they do--examines the effects of cultural traditions, which may actually sometimes run contrary to a baby's biological needs.

Spock, Benjamin, 1903-1998

Dr. Spock on parenting : sensible, reassuring advice for contemporary parents / Benjamin Spock ; edited by Martin T. Stein. Pocket Books, 2001, c1988. xi, 386 p. ; **649**

1. Parenting -- United States 2. Parent and child -- United States

ISBN 9780743426831

LC BL2001012660

Includes index.

Originally published: New York : Simon & Schuster, 1988.

Discusses the concerns of contemporary parents, including teaching sexual equality, raising "superkids," and keeping children safe in a dangerous world.

Spock, Benjamin, 1903-1998

Dr. Spock's baby and child care / Benjamin Spock. Gallery Books, 2012. xx, 1130 p. : **649**

1. Child care. 2. Child rearing. 3. Infant care

ISBN 9781439189283

LC 2012382318

Includes index.

This anniversary edition of the guide to baby and child care includes new material on obesity and nutrition, nontraditional family structures, environmental health, and such common disorders as ADHD and autism.

Spock, Benjamin, 1903-1998

Dr. Spock's the first two years : the emotional and physical needs of children from birth to age two / Benjamin Spock ; edited by Martin T. Stein. Pocket Books, c2001. xvii, 153 p. ; **649**

1. Child rearing. 2. Infant care 3. Infants -- Development and guidance 4. Infants -- Health and hygiene.

ISBN 9780743411226

LC BL2001011640

"This book is comprised of a series of essays previously published individually in Redbook (1985-1992) and Parenting (1992-1998)"--T.p. verso.

Includes index.

In a collection of previously uncollected essays, America's foremost parenting authority shares insight into a child's first two years of physical, emotional, and intellectual development, offering helpful advice on how to distinguish a baby's different cries, communicate with a small child, teach youngsters about sharing, toilet training, and more.

"In these articles culled from Redbook and Parenting Spock's advice to parents is that they should trust themselves and expands on this idea in his reply to the question, 'What has eroded so many parents' self-asssurance in asking for reasonably good behavior?' " Library Journal.

Swong, Sarah,

How do I explain this to my kids? : parenting in the age of Trump / edited by Sarah Swong and Diane Wachtell ; introduction and Commentary by Dr. Ava Siegler. The New Press, 2017. xii, 170 p. ; **649**

1. Trump, Donald, 1946- 2. Child rearing -- United States 3. Political culture -- United States

ISBN 9781620973561

LC 2017018179

Writers, artists, and activists discuss having to explain the Trump phenomenon to their children, and offers advice from child psychologists on how parents can deal with the issue.

White, Burton L., 1929-

The **new** first three years of life / Burton L. White. Fireside Book, c1995. 384 p. : **649**

1. Infant psychology.

ISBN 0684804190

LC 95018297

"The completely revised and updated edition of the parenting classic."

Includes index.

A childhood development manual features a weekly guide to the mental, physical, and emotional development of the young child, including discipline, sibling rivalry, toilet training, and more

"White describes the seven developmental phases of the first three years of life. He provides parents with a comprehensive treasury of techniques for enhancing development and establishing discipline that are refreshingly straight-forward and based on real-world experience." Publishers Weekly.

Wiessinger, Diane

Sweet sleep : nighttime and naptime strategies for the breastfeeding family / Diane Wiessinger and [three others]. Ballantine Books, 2014. xxiii, 484 p. : **649**

1. Breastfeeding 2. Sleep 3. Breastfeeding -- Safety measures
ISBN 9780345518477

LC 2014019411

At head of title: La Leche League International.

"Sweet Sleep is the first and most complete book on nights and naps for breastfeeding families. It's mother-wisdom, reassurance, and a how-to guide for making sane and safe decisions on how and where your family sleeps, backed by the latest research. It's 4 A.M. You've nursed your baby five times throughout the night. You're beyond exhausted. But where can you breastfeed safely when you might fall asleep? You've heard that your bed is dangerous for babies. Or is it? Is there a way to reduce the risk? Does life really have to be this hard? No, it doesn't. Sweet Sleep is within reach. This invaluable resource will help you sleep better tonight in under ten minutes with the Quick Start guide--and sleep safer every night with the Safe Sleep Seven. Sort out the facts and fictions of bedsharing and SIDS, learn about normal sleep at every age and stage, from newborn to new parent, direct your baby toward longer sleep when he's ready tailor your approach to your baby's temperament, uncover the hidden costs of sleep training and 'cry it out' techniques, navigate naps at home and daycare handle criticism from family, friends, and physicians, enjoy stories and tips from mothers like you, and make the soundest sleep decisions for your family and your life".-- Provided by publisher.

Wiessinger, Diane

The **womanly** art of breastfeeding. / Diane Wiessinger, Diana West, Teresa Pitman. Ballantine Books, c2010. xxiv, 550 p. : **649**

1. Breastfeeding
ISBN 9780345518446

LC 2010014031

"From pregnancy to weaning, the one book every nursing mother needs by her side"--Cover.

At head of title: La Leche League International.

Completely revised and updated 8th ed."--Cover.

A guide for expectant and new mothers on breastfeeding thier baby.

Wojcicki, Esther

How to raise successful people : simple lessons to help your child become self-driven, respectful, and resilient / Esther Wojcicki. Houghton Mifflin Harcourt, 2019 xxxi, 293 pages ; **649**

1. Parenting 2. Education -- Parent participation. 3. Child psychology 4. Child development
ISBN 9781328974860

LC 2018046436

The Godmother of Silicon Valley, legendary teacher, and mother of a Super Family shares her tried-and-tested methods for raising happy, healthy, successful children using Trust, Respect, Independence, Collaboration, and Kindness: TRICK.

"Written with honesty, heart, and a great deal of experience, How to Raise Successful People is a must-read for all parents." Booklist.

649.1 Child rearing

Bhattacharya, Shaoni

The **baby** book : Pregnancy, Birth, Baby & Childcare from 0 to 3 / writers Shaoni Bhattacharya, Claire Cross, Carol Dyce, Kate Ling, Susannah Marriott, Karen Sullivan, and Jo Wiltshire. DK Publishing, 2016. 320 p. : **649.1**

1. Child care 2. Childbirth 3. Infants -- Care 4. Pregnancy
ISBN 9781465444783

LC bl2015056898

A comprehensive guide for modern parents covers pregnancy through the first three years with recommendations on everything from prenatal superfoods and labor tips to first checkups and breastfeeding practices.

"While books on this subject are abundant, readers will be naturally drawn to the warm style and sheer beauty of the DK titles. Libraries can't go wrong with this acquisition." Library Journal.

649.33 Breast feeding

Shortall, Jessica

Work. Pump. Repeat : the new mom's survival guide to breastfeeding and going back to work / Jessica Shortall. Abrams Image, 2015. 208 p. ; **649.33**

1. Breastfeeding 2. Working mothers
ISBN 9781419718700

LC bl2015039799

A guide for new mothers trying to find the balance between breastfeeding and work.

649.8 Home care of people with disabilities and illnesses

Bucher, Julia A.

American Cancer Society complete guide to family caregiving : the essential guide to cancer caregiving at home / edited by Julia A. Bucher, Peter S. Houts, Terri Ades. American Cancer Society/Health Promotions, 2011. xviii, 354 p. : **649.8**

1. Cancer -- Palliative treatment. 2. Cancer -- Patients -- Home care. 3. Caregivers.
ISBN 9780944235003

LC 2010015968

Rev. ed. of: Caregiving. Rev. ed. 2003.

A resource for caregivers who are tending cancer patients in the home environment provides step-by-step recommendations for such issues as maintaining one's own quality of life, helping patients to manage treatment side effects and obtaining help from available community agencies.

McFarlane, Rodger

The **complete** bedside companion : no-nonsense advice on caring for the seriously ill / Rodger McFarlane, Philip Bashe. Simon & Schuster, 1999, c1998. 544 p. ; **649.8**

1. Home nursing. 2. Caregivers. 3. Critically ill -- Home care. 4. Terminal care.
ISBN 9780684843193

LC BL 99010132

"A Fireside book."

Drawing on the experiences of ordinary people, this guide to caring for the seriously ill offers valuable advice on managing symptoms, dealing with the medical system, battling insurance companies, maintaining cash flow, prearranging funerals, and much more.

650.1 Personal success in business

Aarons-Mele, Morra

Hiding in the bathroom : an introvert's roadmap to getting out there when you'd rather stay home / Morra Aarons-Mele. Dey Street Books, 2017. 287 p. **650.1**

1. Anxiety 2. Success in business 3. Self-fulfillment 4. Stress management

ISBN 9780062666086

LC 2017470333

Based on a podcast.

The marketing guru and host of the Forbes.com podcast of the same name challenges popular theories about the secrets to professional success to outline practical tips for building strong relationships and enabling achievements on one's own terms.

Anders, George, 1957-

You can do anything : the surprising power of a "useless" liberal arts education / George Anders. Little, Brown and Company, 2017. 342 p. ; **650.1**

1. Degrees, Academic -- United States 2. General education -- United States 3. Job hunting -- United States 4. Success in business -- United States

ISBN 9780316548809

LC bl2017031631

Argues for the value of a liberal arts degree in today's tech-dominated world, showing that the well-roundedness of this education can open the door to thousands of cutting-edge jobs.

Bennett, Jessica, 1981-

Feminist fight club : an office survival manual (for a sexist workplace) / Jessica Bennett ; illustrations by Saskia Wariner, with Hilary Fitzgerald Campbell. HarperWave, 2016 xxxiii, 294 p. : **650.1**

1. Sex discrimination against women 2. Sex role in the workplace 3. Sexism 4. Women employees

ISBN 9780062439789

LC bl2016032117

A humorous, incisive guide to navigating subtle sexism at work draws on the experiences of a group of women who gather regularly to discuss gender-related frustrations at the workplace and how to handle them, profiling a range of predatory male archetypes and more.

"Bennett is on a mission to reform today's workplaces, and this manifesto just might be the weapon modern women are looking for." Booklist.

Burkus, David, 1983-

Friend of a friend... : understanding the hidden networks that can transform your life and your career / David Burkus. Houghton Mifflin Harcourt, 2018. 256 p. **650.1**

1. Business networks 2. Networking 3. Career development 4. Networks

ISBN 9780544971264

LC 2017045593

"Burkus shows that most of your best connections do not come from close friends but rather from distant, even long-forgotten contacts; that it's the colleagues and influential acquaintances of your best friends who will play a major role in developing your connections; and that your most valuable network in business has much more to do with how you develop these secondary sources in order to springboard your career".-- Provided by publisher.

"This work offers thought-provoking case studies and practical guidelines on a popular but generally misunderstood topic. Of interest to social scientists, business professionals, and job seekers alike." Library Journal.

Burnett, William (Consulting professor of design)

Designing your life : how to build a well-lived, joyful life / Bill Burnett and Dave Evans. Alfred A. Knopf, 2016. xxxi, 238 p. : **650.1**

1. Decision making 2. Design -- Social aspects 3. Self-realization 4. Vocational guidance

ISBN 9781101875322

LC 2016008862

Outlines strategies for enabling a thriving life by incorporating "design thinking" habits that promote fulfillment and meaning by emulating the examples of the engineers of today's most popular technologies.

Cast, Carter

The **right--and** wrong--stuff : how brilliant careers are made and unmade / Carter Cast. PublicAffairs, [2017] 288 p. **650.1**

1. Success in business 2. Career development 3. Executive ability 4. Skills

ISBN 9781610397094

LC 2017042061

Drawing on his own experiences, as well as meticulous research, the author, a former rising star at a Fortune 100 company whose career was derailed by his attitude, shows readers how, through five defining archetypes, they can recognize blind spots that can lead to downfall and provides new ways for readers to take charge of their careers.

"This relatable career manual should inspire plenty of white-collar professionals to work on serious self-accounting, take responsibility for their own mistakes, and form support teams of friends, managers, and mentors." Publishers Weekly.

Chideya, Farai

The **episodic** career : how to thrive at work in the age of disruption / Farai Chideya. Atria Books, 2016. x, 290 p. : **650.1**

1. Job hunting -- United States -- History -- 21st century 2. Vocational guidance -- United States -- History -- 21st century

ISBN 9781476751504

LC 2015029936

"A practical guide to the ways in which work in America is changing and how you can navigate today's volatile job market".-- Provided by publisher.

"A fun, useful, and informative book for any stage of the career path. Recommended for public libraries and career collections." Library Journal.

Davis, Todd (Chief people officer)

Get better : 15 proven practices to build effective relationships at work / Todd Davis. Simon & Schuster, 2017. xiv, 230 p. ; **650.1**

1. Corporate culture 2. Interpersonal relations 3. Organizational behavior

ISBN 9781501158308

LC 2017301150

The Chief People Officer at FranklinCovey outlines anecdotal and practical recommendations for how organizations of any size or type can create a competitive advantage by building effective relationships.

"Making the office a safe place to speak the truth, trusting oneself as well as others, and reflecting on the intentions that drive one's actions are all sage practices, but the foundation of Davis's fundamental points is observing and listening to business partners, colleagues, and supervisors." Library Journal.

Fineman, Meredith

Brag better : master the art of fearless self-promotion / Meredith Fineman. Portfolio, 2020 288 p. **650.1**

1. Business communication. 2. Success in business 3. Branding (Marketing) 4. Interpersonal communication.

ISBN 9780593086810

LC 2020004061

An entrepreneur, writer and podcast host advocates for the power of talking about your accomplishments and offers tools and tips for bragging, including eliminating words that undermine your work and focusing on your personal brand and voice.

"Though the focus is on self-promotion, Fineman's upbeat ideas have crossover potential for finding confidence in other aspects of life. Women entrepreneurs will love these shrewd promotion strategies." Publishers Weekly

Golden, Gail, 1952-

Curating your life : ending the struggle for work-life balance / Gail Golden. Rowman & Littlefield, 2020 ix, 193 p. : **650.1**

1. Work-life balance 2. Time management 3. Values 4. Decision making

ISBN 9781538132876

LC 2019038955

"Building a work-life balance continues to be a growing challenge, as technology breaks down the physical boundaries between home and the office. Curating Your Life offers a new approach for business leaders looking for success at work and satisfaction at home".-- Provided by publisher.

Goulston, Mark

Just listen : discover the secret to getting through to absolutely anyone / Mark Goulston ; foreword by Keith Ferrazzi. AMACOM, c2010. xix, 234 p. : **650.1**

1. Business communication 2. Interpersonal communication

ISBN 9780814414033

LC 2009014386

Includes index.

Offers listening tools and techniques to make employees, bosses, and clients more willing to agree with proposals.

"This is a primer on dealing with hard-to-reach people in virtually every scenario--defiant executives, angry employees, families in turmoil, warring couples--through use of well-honed psychological techniques. . . . Chapter summaries feature action steps preparing readers to encounter similar scenarios, yielding a guide that is as entertaining as it is useful." Publishers Weekly.

Green, Alison

Ask a manager : how to navigate clueless colleagues, lunch-stealing bosses, and the rest of your life at work / Alison Green. Ballantine Books, 2018. 287 p. ; **650.1**

1. Industrial psychology 2. Work -- Psychological aspects. 3. Work environment. 4. Conflict resolution

ISBN 9780399181818

LC 2018288338

From the creator of the popular website Ask a Manager and New York magazine's work-advice columnist comes a witty, practical guide to navigating 200 difficult professional conversations--featuring all-new advice! There's a reason Alison Green has been called "the Dear Abby of the work world." Ten years as a workplace-advice columnist have taught her that people avoid awkward conversations in the office because they simply don't know what to say. Thankfully, Green does--and in this incredibly helpful book, she tackles the tough discussions you may need to have during your career.

Hansen, Morten T

Great at work : how top performers do less, work better, and achieve more / Morten T. Hansen. Simon & Schuster, 2018. viii, 310 p. ; **650.1**

1. Ability 2. Motivation (Psychology) 3. Performance 4. Self-management (Psychology)

ISBN 9781476765624

LC bl2017045786

Shares authoritative, practical advice on how to bolster individual performance, drawing on a study involving thousands of managers and employees to outline seven work practices for improving focus, scheduling, and organization.

"Based on this work, Hansen identifies the seven key factors that make people work smarter, not harder: do less, then obsess; redesign your work; dont just learn, loop; have passion and purpose; be a forceful champion; fight over ideas but unite on decisions; and use disciplined collaboration." Booklist.

Harris, Carla A.

Strategize to win : the new way to start out, step up, or start over in your career / Carla A. Harris. Hudson Street Press, 2014. ix, 243 p. ; **650.1**

1. Career changes 2. Career development 3. Success in business 4. Vocational guidance

ISBN 9781594633058

LC 2014031571

" The Wall Street powerhouse and author of Expect to Win offers a new way to conceptualize career strategies and gives us proven tools for successful change Whether we're starting out, striving toward a promotion, or looking for a new opportunity, the working world isn't what it used to be. Wall Street veteran Carla Harris knows this, and in Strategize to Win she gives readers the tools they need to get started; get "unstuck" from bad situations; redirect momentum; and position themselves to manage their careers no matter the environment. With her trademark galvanizing advice, Harris identifies and clarifies issues that are often murky, offering lessons on: Identifying and making the most of your work profile (are you a Good Soldier? a Leader? an Arguer?); preparing for a career change without going back to school or taking a step down: honing three essential skills industry leaders possess (and how to get them); tuning into unspoken cues; and thriving through change. Introducing a new way of planning one's career in five-year units, Strategize to Win distills battle-tested and step-by-step tools that Carla has used to launch and sustain her own successful career and help others move forward, recover from setbacks, and position themselves for success".-- Provided by publisher.

"Advice to those in the 'Starting Over' phase covers knowing when it's time to jump ship and recognizing what factors motivate one, whether it's increased compensation, improved chances for advancement, or escaping current unfair treatment. She also provides an informative chapter on repositioning oneself, which many will find especially insightful. Most professionals should be able to find something of value, whether they're just starting out, ready to move on, or somewhere in between." Publishers Weekly.

Hill, Napoleon, 1883-1970

Think and grow rich : the landmark bestseller--now revised and updated for the 21st century / Napoleon Hill ; rev. and expanded by Arthur R. Pell. Jeremy P. Tarcher/Penguin, 2005. xv, 302 p. ; **650.1**

1. Carnegie, Andrew, 1835-1919. 2. Success in business
ISBN 9781585424337

LC 2005044133

Orginally published: Meriden, Conn. : Ralston Society, 1937.
Includes index.

An updated edition of the best-selling guide features anecdotes about such modern figures as Bill Gates, Dave Thomas, and Sir John Templeton, explaining how their examples can enable modern readers to pursue wealth and overcome personal stumbling blocks.

Hoffman, Reid

The **start-up** of you : adapt to the future, invest in yourself, and transform your career / Reid Hoffman and Ben Casnocha. Crown Business, c2012. 272 p. **650.1**

1. Career changes. 2. Career development. 3. Business networks.
ISBN 9780307888907

LC 2011033835

The founder of LinkedIn demonstrates how to apply effective entrepreneurial strategies to an individual career, explaining how to navigate modern challenges by becoming more innovative, self-reliant, and networked.

"With plenty of valuable guidance relevant to any career stage, this book will help readers not only survive professionally in times of uncertainty but stand out from the pack and flourish." Publishers Weekly.

Jacobs, Bert, 1964-

Life is good : the book / Bert and John Jacobs. National Geographic, 2015 271 p. : **650.1**

1. Jacobs, Bert, 1964- 2. Jacobs, John, 1968- 3. Life Is Good (Firm). 4. Businesspeople -- United States -- Conduct of life. 5. Clothing trade -- United States. 6. Optimism.
ISBN 1426215630

LC 2015020909

"From Life is Good founders and brothers Bert and John Jacobs, this inspiring book of wisdom outlines the ten key "superpowers" readers need to live their best lives. Based on the brothers' personal and professional journey, this whimsically illustrated guide captures the unique voice and profound optimism that is the foundation of their beloved T-shirt and apparel company, now worth more than $100 million. Life Is Good: The Owner's Manual will inspire readers of all ages and passions to discover--and embrace--the good in their lives. Entertaining yet profound, easygoing yet powerful, this engaging book reveals how to tap into the hidden power of optimism. Beginning with their upbringing in working class Boston and following the arc of their lives from postgrad wanderlust to the birth of a small business, Bert and John use their experiences to illuminate the ten superpowers on which optimism is founded--from humor and compassion to gratitude and authenticity. Capturing their buoyant, community-focused outlook and supplementing with top-ten lists and the company's iconic stick-figure illustrations, this book doesn't preach. Instead, it offers lighthearted, practical self-help that will inspire and empower readers to embrace their lives with delight and daring".-- Provided by publisher.

"An outstanding book for all ages. One cannot browse through it without smiling and feeling that, despite everything, life is good." Library Journal.

Johnson, Jaclyn

WorkParty : how to create & cultivate the career of your dreams / Jaclyn Johnson ; illustrations by Chloe White. Gallery Books, 2018. xii, 244 p. : **650.1**

1. Businesswomen -- United States 2. Job satisfaction 3. Sex discrimination against women -- United States 4. Success in business -- United States
ISBN 9781501190834

LC 2018014251

The CEO of a popular online platform for millennial woman building their dream careers describes how she turned her frustration into fuel and her setbacks into successes and uses the stories of today's leading female entrepreneurs to inspire others.

Kerr, Hillary

The **career** code : must-know rules for a strategic, stylish, and self-made career / Hillary Kerr & Katherine Power. Abrams Image, 2016 167 p. : **650.1**

1. Career development. 2. Success in business. 3. Women executives.
ISBN 1419718029

LC 2015949324

Navigating your dream career can be a difficult thing. Whether you're starting out or starting over, Kerr and Power provide advice to help you navigate the corporate ladder. Their tried and tested rules to live by will give you the tools you need for each step up to success in your career.

"This savvy, smart guide will benefit professionals at all career stages." Library Journal.

Knapp, Jake

Make time : how to focus on what matters every day / Jake Knapp and John Zeratsky. Currency, 2018 xiv, 287 p. : **650.1**

1. Self-realization 2. Time management 3. Work-life balance
ISBN 9780525572428

LC 2017059817

Provides advice on organizing life to provide the time to do what one really wants by making that the highlight of the day, minimizing distractions, learning from the day's experiences, and taking care of health, one small step at a time.

Kotter, John P., 1947-

Buy-in : saving your good idea from being shot down / John P. Kotter and Lorne A. Whitehead. Harvard Business Review Press, c2010. xi, 192 p. ; **650.1**

1. Sales promotion 2. Creative ability in business 3. Public relations
ISBN 9781422157299

LC 2010016497

Explains how to effectively present and carry through one's business idea, focusing on the key areas of contention that opponents will offer and detailing how to combat each of them.

Kramer, Andrea S.

Breaking through bias : communication techniques for women to succeed at work / Andrea S. Kramer, Alton B. Harris. Bibliomotion, Inc., 2016 xxx, 226 p. ; **650.1**

1. Communication in management -- Sex differences 2. Communication in organizations -- Sex differences 3. Women -- Interpersonal communication. 4. Sex discrimination
ISBN 9781629561042

LC 2015040059

Argues that stereotypes about men, women, work, leadership, and family are to blame for the gender gap in employment and includes communication techniques that women can use to avoid the discriminatory consequences of these stereotypes.

Kreamer, Anne

Risk/reward : why intelligent leaps and daring choices are the best career moves you can make / Anne Kreamer. Random House, 2015 xxvi, 188 p. ; **650.1**

1. Career changes 2. Career development 3. Risk management 4. Success in business

ISBN 9780812997712

LC 2014046074

"Anne Kreamer makes the compelling case that embracing risk is one of the best career choices a person can make. Timely and insightful, Risk/Reward is a unique blend of original research and practical wisdom that even the most risk-averse person can harness to realize success".--Provided by publisher.

"Well-written with intriguing findings, this quick and relevant read is recommended for public libraries and career collections." Library Journal.

Licht, Aliza

Leave Your Mark : Land Your Dream Job. Kill it in Your Career. Rock Social Media / Aliza Licht, foreword by Donna Karan. Grand Central Publishing, 2015 xxii, 259 p. ; **650.1**

1. Career development 2. Social media 3. Success 4. Vocational guidance

ISBN 9781455584147

LC 2014049281

"LEAVE YOUR MARK isn't an advice book--it's a mentorship in 288 pages. Aliza Licht -- global fashion communications executive, AKA fashion's favorite "PR girl" and Twitter phenom -- is here to tell her story, complete with The Devil Wears Prada- like moments and insider secrets. Drawing invaluable lessons from her experience, Licht shares advice, inspiration, and a healthy dose of real talk in LEAVE YOUR MARK. She delivers personal and professional guidance for people just starting their careers and for people who are well on their way. With a particular emphasis on communicating and building your personal brand, something she knows a thing or two about, Aliza is your sassy, knowledgeable guide to the contemporary working world, where personal and professional lines are blurred and the most important thing you can have is a strong sense of self. "-- Provided by publisher.

Lidsky, Isaac

Eyes wide open : overcoming obstacles and recognizing opportunities in a world that can't see clearly / Isaac Lidsky. TarcherPerigee, 2017. 272 p. **650.1**

1. Lidsky, Isaac 2. Men who are blind 3. Self-fulfillment 4. Blindness 5. Affirmations

ISBN 9780143129578

LC 2016048498

Sharing his hard-won insights, the author, who started to go blind at the age of 13, used losing his sight as the catalyst to achieving immense success, joy and fulfillment as he graduated from Harvard College at age 19, served as a Supreme Court law clerk, fathered four children and turned a failing construction subcontractor into a highly profitable business.

"This master class in counting one's blessings will stay with readers long after the final page is turned." Publishers Weekly.

Mohr, Tara, 1968-

Playing big : find your voice, your mission, your message / Tara Sophia Mohr. Gotham Books, 2014 256 p. **650.1**

1. Self-fulfillment 2. Success (Concept) 3. Success in business 4. Leadership in women

ISBN 9781594206078

LC 2014021945

While not all women aspire to end up in the corner office, every woman aspires to something. Playing Big fills a major gap among women's career books; it isn't just for corporate women. The book offers tools to help every woman play bigger - whether she's an executive, community volunteer, artist, or stay-at-home mom.

"Recommended for women who have good ideas but are unsure of themselves or how to implement their innovative concepts. A useful book for public libraries and those with strong feminist or career collections." Library Journal.

Mulcahy, Diane

The **gig** economy : the complete guide to getting better work, taking more time off, and financing the life you want / Diane Mulcahy. AMACOM, American Management Assoication 2017 227 p. ; **650.1**

1. Career development 2. Flexible work arrangements 3. Part-time employment 4. Quality of work life

ISBN 9780814437339

LC 2016023117

Presents advice for managing employment in an economy characterized by contract work and freelance assignments, describing strategies for creating multiple sources of income, developing new skills, financing time off, and retaining a personal safety net.

"The book is filled with helpful step-by-step instructions, sound examples of good and bad approaches, and financial reality checks." Booklist.

Newport, Cal

Deep work : rules for focused success in a distracted world / Cal Newport. Grand Central Publishing, 2016. 295 p. ; **650.1**

1. Distractions 2. Mental work. 3. Cognition. 4. Success (Concept)

ISBN 9781455586691

LC 2015032646

Argues that the ability to apply sustained attention to a valuable task is the new key to achieving success and true meaning in one's professional life.

"It's tempting to blow off the message as the complaints of an admitted non-technophile, but Newport's disarming self-awareness... and emphasis on a meaningful work practice that's 'rich with productivity and meaning' makes for an excellent lesson in focusing on quality rather than quantity at work." Publishers Weekly.

Porath, Christine Lynne

Mastering civility : a manifesto for the workplace / Christine Porath. Grand Central Publishing, 2016 viii, 230 p. ; **650.1**

1. Courtesy in the workplace 2. Employee morale 3. Interpersonal relations 4. Organizational behavior

ISBN 9781455568987

LC 2016028809

A full-length guide based on the author's New York Times article, "No Time to Be Nice at Work," demonstrates how to enhance workplace effectiveness by mastering the skills of professional civility.

"This book will arm readers with the tools they need to move from defeat to empowerment and prompt change in the workplace." Publishers Weekly.

RoAne, Susan, 1948-

How to work a room : the ultimate guide to making lasting connections in person and online / Susan RoAne. William Morrow,

2014. xxviii, 370 p. : **650.1**

1. Business entertaining 2. Business etiquette 3. Interpersonal relations 4. Public relations
ISBN 9780062295347

LC bl2014001193

Offers techniques and tips for making profitable social and professional acquaintances at meetings, parties, and online, from learning how to remember names to using humor to "break the ice."

Samit, Jay

Disrupt you! : master personal transformation, seize opportunity, and thrive in the era of endless innovation / Jay Samit. Flatiron Books, 2015. x, 291 p. ; **650.1**

1. Creative ability in business 2. Decision making 3. Success in business 4. Technological innovations -- Economic aspects
ISBN 9781250059376

LC 2015017121

A serial entrepreneur reveals how he made a career launching businesses, selling them, and then reinventing himself in order to do it again and shows readers how to do it too.

"Throughout, Samit incorporates elements of his own success story as well as those of prominent figures such as actor Jim Carrey, Benihana founder Hiroaki Aoki, and Zappos CEO Tony Hsieh. Samit closes with a motivational 'Self-Disruptors Manifesto.' For readers seeking to get more out of their lives and careers, Samit is a wise teacher with valuable lessons to impart." Publishers Weekly.

Shell, G. Richard, 1949-

Springboard : launching your personal search for success / G. Richard Shell. Portfolio/Penguin, 2013 302 p. : **650.1**

1. Job satisfaction 2. Satisfaction 3. Self-realization 4. Success
ISBN 9781591845478

LC 2013017451

A Wharton School professor and award-winning author helps readers discard their old definitions of success, particularly ones promoted by outside influences, and create new ones based on their own unique talents, values, personalities and motivations.

Smith, Larry, 1945-

No fears, no excuses : what you need to do to have a great career / Larry Smith. Houghton Mifflin Harcourt, 2016. xvi, 255 p. ; **650.1**

1. Career development 2. Vocational guidance
ISBN 9780544663282

LC 2015037676

Outlines a provocative approach to discovering one's life calling and achieving a satisfying career, challenging the perspectives of college graduates while sharing strategies based on the author's popular TED talk.

Stanley, Thomas J.

★The **millionaire** next door : the surprising secrets of America's wealthy / Thomas J. Stanley, William D. Danko. Taylor Trade Pub., 2010. xiv, 258 p. ; **650.1**

1. Rich people -- United States. 2. Millionaires -- United States.
ISBN 9781589795471

LC 2011381748

"With a new preface for the 21st century" -- Cover.

The bestselling?The Millionaire Next Door?identifies seven common traits that show up again and again among those who have accumulated wealth. Most of the truly wealthy in this country don't live in Beverly Hills or on Park Avenue--they live next door. This new edition, the first since 1998, includes a new foreword for the twenty-first century by Dr. Thomas J. Stanley.

Steib, Mike

The **career** manifesto : discover your calling and create an extraordinary life / Mike Steib. TarcherPerigee, 2018 xi, 274 p. : **650.1**

1. Career development 2. Vocational guidance
ISBN 9780143129349

LC OC2018170784

An award-winning business leader uses his own experiences in his career as well as those of other successful business leaders to offer advice and exercises aimed at helping young professionals, entrepreneurs and creative people to bring purpose to their work and lives.

"His book lays out a sound and logical approach, with easily applicable and customizable advice aplenty." Publishers Weekly.

Sull, Donald N. (Donald Norman)

Simple rules : how to thrive in a complex world / Donald Sull, Kathleen M. Eisenhardt. Houghton Mifflin Harcourt, 2015. 280 p. ; **650.1**

1. Conduct of life 2. Decision making 3. Simplicity
ISBN 9780544409590

LC 2014044513

"How simplicity trumps complexity in nature, business, and life. We struggle to manage complexity every day. We follow intricate diets to lose weight, juggle multiple remotes to operate our home entertainment systems, face proliferating data at the office, and hack through thickets of regulation at tax time. But complexity isn't destiny. Sull and Eisenhardt argue there's a better way: By developing a few simple yet effective rules, you can tackle even the most complex problems. Simple rules are a hands-on tool to achieve some of our most pressing personal and professional objectives, from overcoming insomnia to becoming a better manager or a smarter investor. Simple rules can help solve some of our most urgent social challenges from setting interest rates at the Federal Reserve to protecting endangered marine wildlife along California's coast. Drawing on more than a decade of rigorous research, the authors provide a clear framework for developing effective rules and making them better over time. They find insights in unexpected places, from the way Tina Fey codified her experience working at Saturday Night Live into rules for producing 30 Rock (rule five: never tell a crazy person he's crazy) to burglars' rules to choose a house to rob ("avoid houses with a car parked outside") to Japanese engineers using the foraging rules of slime molds to optimize Tokyo's rail system. Whether you're struggling with information overload, pursuing opportunities with limited resources, or just trying to change your bad habits, Simple Rules provides a powerful way to tame complexity. "-- Provided by publisher.

"Feeling info-ed out? Sull, a senior lecturer at the MIT Sloan School of Management and a global expert on market strategy and execution, and Eisenhardt, professor of strategy and organization at Stanford University, offer a framework for the creation of a few simple rules to manage it all." Library Journal.

Sutton, Robert I.

The **asshole** survival guide : how to deal with people who treat you like dirt / Robert I. Sutton. Houghton Mifflin Harcourt, [2017] 224 p. **650.1**

1. Organizational behavior. 2. Interpersonal conflict. 3. Bullying in the workplace. 4. Emotional abuse
ISBN 9781328695918

LC 2017012053

The author of The No Asshole Rule provides field-tested, evidence-based and sometimes surprising strategies for dealing with toxic people-

-avoiding them, outwitting them, disarming them, sending them packing and developing protective psychological armor--as well as advice for not becoming toxic yourself.

Tracy, Brian

Master your time, master your life : the breakthrough system to get more results, faster, in every area of your life / Brian Tracy. A TarcherPerigee Book, 2016. vi, 226 p. ; **650.1**

1. Time management. 2. Decision-making 3. Self-help techniques 4. Efficiency.

ISBN 9780399183812

LC 2016021429

Drawing on his 30 years of experience, the international speaker, business consultant, and productivity expert presents a book that, based on the most recent research into the field of productivity, provides simple steps for determining WHAT to do WHEN and managing all the many details of our lives.

"Angled mostly for those in the twenty- to thirtysomething crowd, this book will be valuable to those looking to be more productive." Library Journal.

Vaden, Rory

Procrastinate on purpose : 5 permissions to multiply your time / Rory Vaden. Perigee Book, 2015. xix, 236 p. : **650.1**

1. Labor productivity 2. Time management

ISBN 9780399170621

LC 2014040004

"New York Times bestselling author and sales-performance trainer Rory Vaden brings his high-energy approach and can-do spirit to the most nagging problem in our professional lives: stalled productivity. Millions are overworked, organizationally challenged, or have a motivation issue that's holding them back. Vaden presents a simple yet powerful paradigm that will set readers free to do their best work--on time and without stress and anxiety".-- Provided by publisher.

Varol, Ozan O., 1981-

Think like a rocket scientist : simple strategies you can use to make giant leaps in work and life / Ozan Varol. PublicAffairs, 2020. vii, 353 p. ; **650.1**

1. Creative ability in business 2. Creative ability 3. Scientific ability

ISBN 9781541762596

LC 2019041750

"We're experiencing a second age of spaceflight, and the renaissance of rocket science is captivating the world. Movies and television shows set in this sphere consistently top the charts, and millions tune in to watch SpaceX launches. Although we glamorize rocket science, we assume that it's beyond comprehension by mere mortals who don't have a special kind of genius baked into their DNA (hence the common saying, "It's not rocket science"). Yet while the complex math and scientific details of building rockets may be out of our reach, the principles that guide the discipline don't have to be. In this mind-expanding book, Ozan Varol, an actual rocket scientist, shows how the strategies that built the Apollo 11 can help you achieve your own moon shot. Think Like a Rocket Scientist teaches you how to attack previously unsolved problems, how to overcome everyday obstacles to grand ambitions, and much more. A deeply knowledgeable scholar with a breezy, contrarian voice, Varol inspires us not only to dream big--but to achieve those dreams too".-- Provided by publisher.

Vaynerchuk, Gary

Crushing it! : how great entrepreneurs build business and influence-- and how you can, too / Gary Vaynerchuk. Harper-Business, 2018 272 p. ; **650.1**

1. New business enterprises 2. Entrepreneurship 3. Internet marketing 4. Branding (Marketing)

ISBN 9780062674678

LC bl2017045699

Shares new lessons and inspiration drawn from dozens of entrepreneurs who rejected traditional corporate careers in favor of pursuing their dreams.

Verveer, Melanne

Fast forward : how women can achieve power and purpose / Melanne Verveer and Kim K. Azzarelli ; foreword by Hillary Rodham Clinton. Houghton Mifflin Harcourt, 2015. 192 p. **650.1**

1. Women professional employees 2. Business success for women. 3. Women executives. 4. Women in development.

ISBN 9780544527195

LC 2015019683

Two women leaders with wide-reaching access throughout corporate America draw on interviews with 50 trailblazing women to explain how women can tap their growing economic powers to advance purposeful and successful agendas.

Wasmund, Shaa, 1972-

Do less, get more : how to work smart and live life your way / Shaa Wasmund. Portfolio Penguin, 2015. 218 p. : **650.1**

1. Success in business 2. Time management

ISBN 9781591847168

LC 2015295904

Offers advice on using time more effectively, including stop putting things off, nurturing support networks, and scheduling for value.

"Wasmund ultimately brings her reader to a place where they believe, along with her, that the 'things that will create your best life are perfectly attainable if you are willing to stop doing what's not important and start prioritizing what is.' Sage and sane advice." Booklist.

Webb, Caroline, 1971-

How to have a good day : harness the power of behavioral science to transform your working life / Caroline Webb. Crown Business, 2016 360 p. : **650.1**

1. Job satisfaction -- Psychological aspects 2. Neuropsychology 3. Performance -- Psychological aspects 4. Psychology, Industrial

ISBN 9780553419634

LC 2015026815

An economist and executive coach offers seven different practices to use to ensure you have a good day at work, including setting the right priorities, making productive use of time, having effective conversations, doing your very best work and sustaining energy. 7 charts.

Williams, Joan, 1952-

What works for women at work : four patterns working women need to know / Joan C. Williams and Rachel Dempsey ; foreword by Anne-Marie Slaughter. New York University Press, 2018. xxxvii, 365 p. ; **650.1**

1. Office politics 2. Women -- Employment 3. Gender role in the work environment 4. Glass ceiling

ISBN 9781479814312

LC bl2018001611

Provides a guide for mastering office politics as a woman, describing four patterns that affect working women and presenting strategies for overcoming them.

"[F]illed with street-smart advice and plain old savvy about the way life works in corporate America." Booklist.

650.14 Success in obtaining jobs and promotions

Aujla, Dev

50 ways to get a job : an unconventional guide to finding work on your terms / Dev Aujla. TarcherPerigee, 2018 xxv, 224 p. ; **650.14**

1. Job hunting 2. Vocational guidance
ISBN 9780143131533

LC 2017033682

"Based on the popular website of the same name, a guide to finding the right job while maintaining your sanity in the process In today's endlessly fluctuating job market, it's becoming more and more difficult to get hired. 50 Ways to Get a Job aims to fix that. Job search expert Dev Aujla created 50WaysToGetAJob.com as a way to offer practical, tangible steps to finding (and getting) the right job for you. Within only a few months, over 400,000 people used the site, and Aujla was able to gather data from thousands of individual job searches. In this cleverly constructed guide, Aujla presents the tried-and-tested steps to not only getting hired, but also the secrets to staying motivated and energized throughout the job hunting process. Filled with practical quick-step exercises, this book is designed so you can pick your path through the process, starting where it feels the most natural:*Feeling stuck? Start by sending a "looking for a job" email to five close friends. *Not sure what sort of job you want? Write some creative nonfiction about yourself.*Feeling overwhelmed? Learn the benefits of forty-five minutes of unplugged bliss. *Going on an interview? Practice with a conversation guide. Whether you've just decided to start the hunt or you're gearing up for a big interview, 50 Ways to Get a Job will keep you poised, on-track, and motivated right up to landing your dream career".-- Provided by publisher.

Berger, Lauren (Lauren E.)

All work, no pay : finding an internship, building your resume, making connections, and gaining job experience / Lauren Berger. Ten Speed Press, c2012. xii, 194 p. : **650.14**

1. Internship programs. 2. Vocational guidance.
ISBN 1607741687

LC 2011034540

"This guide from Intern Queen Lauren Berger shows college students (and others) how to find and land impressive internships and get the most out of them, from work experience to networking to resume building".--Provided by publisher.

Citrin, James M

The **career** playbook : essential advice for today's aspiring young professional / James M. Citrin. Crown Business, 2015 x, 241 p. : **650.14**

1. Career development 2. Success in business 3. Vocational guidance
ISBN 9780553446968

LC 2015288094

An executive placement guru counsels graduates and young professionals on how to land a first job and establish a satisfying and successful career, covering topics ranging from job searches and interviews to salaries and advancement potential.

Kay, Andrea, 1954-

This is how to get your next job : an inside look at what employers really want / Andrea Kay ; foreword by Richard N. Bolles. AMACOM, American Management Association, 2013 ix, 245 p. ; **650.14**

1. Career development. 2. Employment interviewing. 3. Job hunting.
ISBN 0814432212

LC 2012051814

Includes index.

Offers advice on how job hunters should present themselves to potential employers.

Mackay, Harvey

Use your head to get your foot in the door : job search secrets no one else will tell you / Harvey Mackay. Portfolio, 2010. xix, 329 p. : **650.14**

1. Job hunting.
ISBN 1591843219

LC 2009039791

Drawing on real-life stories, the best-selling author of Swim With the Sharks Without Being Eaten Alive explains how to rebuild one's confidence, take advantage of the way bosses make hiring decisions and blend the latest online tools with old-fashioned face-to-face networking.

"This collection of job search tips by Mackay...[comes] complete with humorous examples and Quickie one-page stories that illustrate his main points. Don't let the cover or any worry about his sense of humor dissuade you: this is a very useful book. The short chapters with descriptive titles make it easy to navigate, and Mackay offers tips--from changing your attitude to getting hired--both for those currently employed but wishing to position themselves better in their current companies and for those who are out of work." Library Journal.

Raskin, Don

The **dirty** little secrets of getting your dream job : everything you need to know to land your first job and find career success / Don Raskin. Regan Arts, 2016. viii, 182 p. : **650.14**

1. Job hunting
ISBN 9781942872764

LC bl2016013491

Includes index.

Offers a guide to job hunting that provides straightforward advice on how to stand out from competing applicants, as well as how to make the most of the opportunity a job affords.

Yate, Martin John

Knock 'em dead cover letters : cover letters and strategies to get the job you want / Martin Yate, CPC, New York times bestseller. Adams Media, 2016 319 p. : **650.14**

1. Cover letters. 2. Job hunting. 3. Resumes (Employment).
ISBN 1440596182

LC 2016020841

Includes indexes.

Offers advice on writing a professional-looking cover letter that complements the accompanying resume and draws attention to the job applicant, with guidance on resumes, interviews, and job hunting.

Knock 'em dead resumes / Martin Yate, CPC. Adams Media, 2014 320 p. ; **650.14**

1. Job hunting. 2. Resumes (Employment).
ISBN 1440579075

LC 2014019106

"A killer resume gets MORE job interviews!"

Includes index.

Revised edition of the author's Resumes that knock 'em dead.

Presents detailed information on resume writing, including step-by-step instruction for creating effective resumes, advice for online job searching, and examples of successful resumes with their cover letters.

651.56 Cooking for special situations, reasons, ages

Meyer, Linda (Writer on vegan cooking)

Great vegan BBQ without a grill : amazing plant-based ribs, burgers, steaks, kabobs and more smokey favorites / Linda Meyer & Alex Meyer, the mother-daughter team behind veganosity. Page Street Publishing Co., 2018. 191 p. : **651.56**

1. Barbecuing. 2. Recipes 3. Vegan cooking. 4. Cookbooks
ISBN 1624144969

LC 2017946105

"Amazing plant-based ribs, burgers, steaks, kabobs and more smoky favorites"--Cover.

Includes index.

Collects vegan recipes that replicate the smoky flavors and textures of classic BBQ meats, made using only a grill pan or cast iron skillet, including such dishes as chickpea sliders, Texas BBQ vegan brisket, and savory veggie skewers.

Moskowitz, Isa Chandra

The **superfun** times vegan holiday cookbook : entertaining for absolutely every occasion / Isa Chandra Moskowitz ; photographs by Vanessa Rees and Joshua Foo. Little, Brown and Company, 2016. 439 p. : color illustrations ; **651.56**

1. Holiday cooking. 2. Recipes 3. Vegan cooking. 4. Cookbooks
ISBN 0316221899

LC 2016941207

Includes index.

A best-selling vegan cookbook author presents her first book on entertaining, in a guide the includes menus and tips for every Holiday and every big celebration in between, as well as recipes for vegan versions of such dishes as Cinnamon Apple Crepes, Cheeseburger Pizza, Churro Biscotti, Biscuits and Gravy and many more.

Perlmutter, David, 1954-

The **grain** brain cookbook : more than 150 life-changing, gluten-free recipes to transform your health / David Perlmutter, MD. Little Brown and Company, 2014. 337 p. : **651.56**

1. Brain -- Diseases -- Nutritional aspects 2. Carbohydrates -- Metabolism 3. Gluten-free diet 4. Recipes 5. Cookbooks
ISBN 0316334251

LC 2014940575

Includes index.

Provides more than 150 delicious, gluten-free recipes, including Eggs Benedict With Zucchini Pancakes and Cauliflower "Couscous," to help maintain a healthy body and mind and reduce the risk of chronic diseases, in a follow-up to the best-selling Grain Brain.

"Recommended only for libraries where Perlmutter's books are in high demand." Library Journal.

Sarno, Chad

The **wicked** healthy cookbook : free. from. animals. / Chad Sarno, Derek Sarno, and David Joachim ; foreword by Woody Harrelson ; photographs by Eva Kosmas Flores. Grand Central Life & Style, 2018. xii, 306 p. : **651.56**

1. Cooking (Natural foods). 2. Cooking (Vegetables) 3. Recipes 4. Vegan cooking. 5. Cookbooks
ISBN 1455570281

LC 2018288838

Includes index.

Two former Whole Foods Market culinary experts combine innovative cooking techniques with attitude in a collection of vegan recipes that includes options for everyday meals and special occasions as well as tips for gluten-free cooking.

"This varied assortment will appeal mostly to herbivores wishing to comfort their inner carnivore." Publishers Weekly.

651.57 Quantity, institutional, travel, outdoor cooking

Kostow, Christopher, 1976-

★A **new** Napa cuisine / Christopher Kostow ; photographs by Peden + Munk. Ten Speed Press, 2014 296 p. : **651.57**

1. Cooking, American -- California style. 2. Recipes 3. Seasonal cooking 4. Napa Valley (Calif.) -- Description and travel. 5. Cookbooks.
ISBN 9781607745945

LC 2014010462

Includes indexes.

"The debut cookbook from the head chef at the three-Michelin-starred Restaurant at Meadowood, featuring nearly 100 recipes and spotlighting the artisans, gardeners, and growers, as well as the hidden landscapes of Napa Valley, that have influenced and inspired Kostow's unparalleled cuisine. A philosophy major with no formal culinary training, Christopher Kostow is not your typical Napa Valley chef. While there are many popular restaurants in Napa and cookbooks about its chefs, restaurants, and cooking styles, there is no chef who is more deeply rooted in and affected by the place in which he works. Beyond the Vineyard will follow Kostow's evolution from a line cook in a seaside town to a three-Michelin-starred chef at Meadowood, a Napa Valley mainstay that the Wall Street Journal recently labeled a "world class culinary splurge" and "temple of modern American cuisine." Through artfully constructed recipes and stories--of discovering a bounty of wild ingredients in the woods near his St. Helena home, or spending afternoons firing pottery with local ceramists--Kostow introduces readers to a new Napa, one that's rich in local flavor and a strong sense of community".-- Provided by publisher.

"This sort of food lies beyond even the most ambitious amateur, but culinary students will appreciate the challenge of seeing where their art and craft are headed, and the restaurants patrons will love documentation of a once-in-a-lifetime dinner." Booklist.

652.3 Keyboarding

Casillo, Anthony

Typewriters : iconic machines from the golden age of mechanical writing / Anthony Casillo ; foreword by Tom Hanks ; photography by Bruce Curtis & Anthony Casillo. Chronicle Books, 2017 207 p. : **652.3**

1. Typewriters
ISBN 9781452154886

LC 2016044392

From the creation of the QWERTY keyboard to the world's first portable typing machine, this handsome collection is a visual homage to the golden age of the typewriter.

"This is sure to delight typewriter lovers and those interested in machine or design history." Library Journal.

657 Accounting

Siegel, Joel G.

Accounting handbook. / Jae K., Ph.D. Shim, Joel G., Ph.D. Siegel, Nick Dauber, Anique A., Ph.D. Qureshi. Barrons Educational Series, 2015 1062 p. ; **657**

1. Accounting
ISBN 9780764166570

LC 2014009657

Revised edition of: Accounting handbook / Joel G. Siegel, Jae K. Shim. 5th ed.

Presents an overview of financial accounting, with a focus on financial statements, reporting requirements, and taxation, and features a dictionary of accounting terms.

658 General management

Collins, James C. (James Charles), 1958-

Good to great: why some companies make the leap--and others don't / Jim Collins. HarperBusiness, c2001. xii, 300 p. : **658**

1. Leadership. 2. Strategic planning. 3. Organizational change. 4. Technological innovations -- Management.
ISBN 0066620996

LC 2001024818

The author uses his research on the Fortune 500 to create a blueprint for turning good companies into spectacular ones.

"Starting with every company that ever appeared in the Fortune 500, Collins identifies 11 great ones and looks for similarities among them, and what he finds will both surprise and fascinate anyone involved in management." Booklist.

Drucker, Peter F. (Peter Ferdinand), 1909-2005

The **Drucker** lectures: essential lessons on management, society, and economy / Peter F. Drucker ; edited and with an introduction by Rick Wartzman. McGraw-Hill, c2010. xii, 266 p. ; **658**

1. Management -- Social aspects 2. Management
ISBN 9780071700450

LC 2010484567

This book presents thirty-three of Peter F. Drucker's most important speeches and talks delivered at professional gatherings and in the classroom.

"From his concern with continuous and full employment in the 1950s to globalization, nonprofit management, and the future of the corporation in the early 2000s, these lectures reflect a Drucker that many scholars and practitioners knew, but they also reveal new insights into the currency...of his thinking." Choice.

Michelli, Joseph A., 1960-

Driven to delight : delivering world-class customer experience the Mercedes-Benz way / Joseph Michelli. McGraw-Hill, 2016 xvii, 282 p. : **658**

1. DaimlerChrysler. 2. Automobile industry and trade -- Customer services -- Germany 3. Automobile industry and trade -- Germany -- Management 4. Mercedes automobiles
ISBN 9780071806305

LC 2015029398

A New York Times best-selling author, who worked closely with leaders inside the organization to understand the customer experience transformation as a top operational and cultural priority, offers an exclusive, behind-the-scenes look at how Mercedes-Benz transformed themselves into a best-in-class, customer-obsessed organization.

Murray, Alan S., 1954-

The **Wall** Street journal essential guide to management : lasting lessons from the best leadership minds of our time / Alan Murray. Harper Business, c2010. xxvii, 207 p. ; **658**

1. Management
ISBN 9780061840333

LC 2010002879

"From the Wall Street Journal comes the definitive guide to how to be a successful manager".--Provided by publisher.

"The author lays out in helpful order and understandable prose what he considers the best practices for a good manager to follow; especially instructive are his discussions of six different styles that leaders use to motivate others. For serious consideration for any library business collection." Booklist.

Peter, Laurence J.

The **Peter** principle: why things always go wrong / Laurence J. Peter and Raymond Hull. Collins Business, 2009. 192 p **658**

1. Executive ability -- Humor. 2. Work -- Humor. 3. Management -- Humor
ISBN 9780061699061

LC 2008044122

A re-release of the popular treatise on the rise and fall of civilizations as reflected by their professional organizations is based on a premise that every employee in a hierarchy tends to rise to his or her level of incompetence, an unfortunate fact that is shaping education, government, and business.

Thompson, Mark

Now, build a great business! : 7 ways to maximize your profits in any market / Mark Thompson and Brian Tracy ; foreword by Frances Hesselbein. American Management Association, c2011. xxii, 228 p. ; **658**

1. Leadership. 2. Strategic planning. 3. Marketing. 4. Consumer satisfaction.
ISBN 9780814416976

LC 2010030612

Includes index.

Reveals seven principles that can change one's business for the better, including becoming a great leader, attracting and keeping great people, developing a great business plan, offering a great product or service, and delivering superior customer service.

"The authors offer easy, tried-and-true ways to think about and plan organizational growth, especially in tough economic times. In seven steps (with a chapter devoted to each), the authors identify sustainable strategies for attracting customers and recruiting better leaders. They share seven simple questions that leaders ask themselves and provide helpful checklist exercises on a variety of key topics including creating a great business plan, designing an effective marketing plan, and creating a good customer experience." Publishers Weekly.

Travis, Nigel

The **challenge** culture : why the most successful organizations run on pushback / Nigel Travis. PublicAffairs, [2018] 288 p. **658**

1. Travis, Nigel 2. Dunkin' Donuts (Firm) 3. Businesspeople 4. Corporate culture 5. Success in business
ISBN 9781541762145

LC 2018010002

The CEO of Dunkin' Brands demonstrates how the discipline of "questioning everything without trashing anyone" can provide a unique, results-oriented approach to leading an organization to prosperity.

Webb, Maynard, 1955-

Dear founder : letters of advice for anyone who leads, manages, or wants to start a business / Maynard Webb, with Carlye Adler. St. Martin's Press, [2018] 272 p. **658**

1. New businesses. 2. Leadership in business. 3. Corporate culture. 4. Entrepreneurs.
ISBN 9781250195647

LC 2018013472

Includes index.

"This recommended book provides honest guidance about the work that goes into a new company, delivered in digestible chunks for the entrepreneur on the go." Library Journal.

Wooldridge, Adrian

Masters of management : how the business gurus and their ideas have changed the world--for better and for worse / Adrian Wooldridge ; with a foreword by John Micklethwait. HarperBusiness, 2011. xviii, 446 p. ; **658**

1. Industrial management. 2. Comparative management. 3. Corporate accountability 4. Reengineering (Management)
ISBN 9780061771132

LC 2011015690

Rev. ed. of: Witch doctors / John Micklethwait. 1996.

"A complete update of the 1996 bestselling The witch doctors, a penetrating and engaging history of management theory that sorts the wisdom from the dross, and the wise men from the charlatans".-- Provided by publisher.

658.02 Management of enterprises of specific sizes and scope

Sarillo, Nick

A **slice** of the pie : how to build a big little business / Nick Sarillo. Portfolio/Penguin, c2012. xviii, 253 p. : **658.02**

1. Employees -- Training of 2. Industrial management 3. New business enterprises 4. Success in business
ISBN 9781591844587

LC 2012019321

Includes index.

The founder and CEO of Nick's Pizza & Pub draws on the examples of his considerable successes to demonstrate how any business can build a high-performance, purpose-driven company culture, explaining how every member of a team must be equipped with the tools to perform their jobs well and advance a shared company purpose.

Strauss, Steven D., 1958-

The **small** business bible ; everything you need to know to succeed in your small business / Steven D. Strauss. Wiley, c2012. xiii, 578 p. ; **658.02**

1. New business enterprises -- United States 2. Small business -- United States -- Finance 3. Small business -- United States -- Management
ISBN 9781118135945

LC 2011042848

Includes index.

A reference guide to managing a small business provides strategies and advice on such topics as developing business plans, understanding insurance and legal issues, and using social media to advertise and forge partnerships.

"Chapters cover green businesses, online advertising and marketing, emerging technologies, and cutting-edge business building strategies." Library Journal.

658.1 Organization and financial management

Buelow, Beth L

The **introvert** entrepreneur : amplify your strengths and create success on your own terms / Beth L. Buelow. Perigee, LLC, 2015. xi, 260 p. ; **658.1**

1. Entrepreneurship 2. Introversion 3. Introverts 4. Success in business
ISBN 9780399174834

LC bl2015057904

A corporate trainer, certified coach and professional speaker shows introverts how to use their innate talents and balance their weaknesses with strengths in a business setting to become adept in networking, marketing, leadership and community building.

Duffy, Scott (Business consultant)

Launch! : the critical 90 days from idea to market / Scott Duffy. Portfolio Hardcover, 2014 xvii, 218 p. ; **658.1**

1. Entrepreneurship 2. New business enterprises 3. New products
ISBN 9781591846062

LC 2013039077

"A serial entrepreneur offers a plan for launching successful ventures . About ninety-seven percent of a rocket's fuel is used in the first three feet of its launch. The same is true in launching a new business, product, or service. Those first few steps are absolutely critical. Scott Duffy has developed a practical approach for turning your big idea into a thriving venture by focusing on the crucial period immediately before, during, and after opening your doors (literally or online). His approach is based on his experiences working with top entrepreneurs like Tony Robbins and Richard Branson, who taught him how to balance the two key sides of entrepreneurship: The personal side, including personal finances, relationships, and health. The business side, including raising capital, building teams, establishing partnerships, and closing sales. Duffy also draws on the true stories of other big names, such as Howard Schultz, Lou Holtz, and MC Hammer, to offer guidance on turning your vision into a full-fledged enterprise".-- Provided by publisher.

"A breezy handbook for entrepreneurs on how to launch a new business, product or service. Solid advice for novice risk-takers." Kirkus.

Guillebeau, Chris

The **$100** startup : reinvent the way you make a living, do what you love, and create a new future / Chris Guillebeau. Crown Business, c2012. xviii, 285 p. : **658.1**

1. Entrepreneurship 2. New business enterprises -- Management
ISBN 9780307951526

LC 2012003093

Includes index.

Shares advice for transitioning away from unfulfilling jobs to embark on adventurous, meaningful careers, outlining recommendations for starting a personal business with a minimum of time and investment while turning ideas into higher income levels.

John, Daymond, 1969-

The **power** of broke : how empty pockets, a tight budget, and a hunger for success can become your greatest competitive advantage / Daymond John with Daniel Paisner. Crown Business,

2016 x, 269 p. ; **658.1**

1. Creative ability in business 2. Entrepreneurship 3. New business enterprises 4. Strategic planning
ISBN 9781101903599
LC 2015021158

The star of ABC's "Shark Tank" demonstrates how starting a business on a shoestring can provide significant competitive advantages for entrepreneurs by forcing them to think creatively, use resources efficiently, and connect more authentically with customers.

Karlgaard, Rich

Team genius : the new science of high-performing organizations / Rich Karlgaard and Michael S. Malone. HarperCollins, 2015 336 p. **658.1**

1. Teams in the workplace 2. Interpersonal communication 3. Cooperation. 4. Business
ISBN 9780062302540
LC 2015431339

"Gems of insight and wisdom are offered here, such as the need for balance between creative and analytical skills to maintain a team's forward momentum, but not all readers will persevere to find and employ them. For fans of business history and theory." Library Journal.

Kawasaki, Guy, 1954-

The **art** of the start 2.0 : the time-tested, battle-hardened guide for anyone starting anything / Guy Kawasaki. Portfolio/Penguin, 2015. x, 326 p. : **658.1**

1. Entrepreneurship 2. New business enterprises
ISBN 9781591847847
LC 2015295069

Newly revised and updated, a 10th-anniversary edition of an iconic, best-selling guide for start-ups provides expert advice on a wealth of topics--including writing a business plan, recruiting, raising capital and branding.

"An excellent guide packed with valuable information for students, would-be entrepreneurs, and practicing entrepreneurs." Library Journal.

Kidder, David S.

The **Startup** playbook : secrets of the fastest-growing startups from their founding entrepreneurs / David S. Kidder ; foreword by LinkedIn founder Reid Hoffman. / David S. Kidder, Hanny (CON) Hindi, Reid (FRW) Hoffman. Chronicle Books, 2012. 291 p. : **658.1**

1. Entrepreneurship 2. New business enterprises -- Management
ISBN 9781452105048
LC 2012019684

Includes index.

Outlines the managerial decisions and leadership goals that guide a startup business to success, and provides tips and advice from the founders of such companies as Spanx, Zipcar, Flickr, Honest Tea, and LinkedIn.

Ries, Eric, 1978-

The **lean** startup : how today's entrepreneurs use continuous innovation to create radically successful businesses / Eric Ries. Crown Business, c2011. 320 p. ; **658.1**

1. Consumers' preferences 2. New business enterprises 3. Organizational effectiveness
ISBN 9780307887894
LC 2011012100

"Most startups are built to fail. But those failures, according to entrepreneur Eric Ries, are preventable. Startups don't fail because of bad execution, or missed deadlines, or blown budgets. They fail because they are building something nobody wants. Whether they arise from someone's garage or are created within a mature Fortune 500 organization, new ventures, by definition, are designed to create new products or services under conditions of extreme uncertainly. Their primary mission is to find out what customers ultimately will buy. One of the central premises of The Lean Startup movement is what Ries calls "validated learning" about the customer. It is a way of getting continuous feedback from customers so that the company can shift directions or alter its plans inch by inch, minute by minute. Rather than creating an elaborate business plan and a product-centric approach, Lean Startup prizes testing your vision continuously with your customers and making constant adjustments".-- Provided by publisher.

Wasserman, Noam, 1969-

The **founder's** dilemmas : anticipating and avoiding the pitfalls that can sink a startup / Noam Wasserman. Princeton University Press, c2012. ix, 480 p. : **658.1**

1. Entrepreneurship 2. New business enterprises -- Management
ISBN 9780691149134
LC 2011037954

Looks at whether it is a good idea to cofound with friends or relatives, how and when to split the equity within the founding team, and how to recognize when a successful founder-CEO should exit or be fired.

658.15 Financial management

Goldfayn, Alex L.

The **revenue** growth habit : the simple art of growing your business by 15% in 15 minutes a day / Alex Goldfayn. Wiley, 2015 xiii, 242 p. : **658.15**

1. Revenue management 2. Strategic planning
ISBN 9781119084068
LC 2015013431

Includes index.

"Grow your business by 15% with these proven daily growth actions. Do you have trouble finding time during your hectic day to grow your business? Is your company stalled because you are too busy reacting to customer problems? Do you lack the funds to jumpstart an effective marketing plan? The Revenue Growth Habit gives business owners, leaders, and all customer-facing staff a hands-on resource for increasing revenue that is fast, easy, and requires no financial investment. Alex Goldfayn, CEO of the Evangelist Marketing Institute, shows how to grow your organization by 15% or more in 15 minutes or less per day--without spending a penny of your money. Forget about relying on social media. Posting on Twitter, Facebook, and LinkedIn doesn't grow revenue, especially for business-to-business companies. The Revenue Growth Habit shows how to request and collect testimonials and how to communicate these testimonials to grow your business. You will discover how to write powerful case studies, ask for (and get!) referrals, grow your lists, and send a revenue-growing newsletter. Goldfayn also includes information for teaching your customer service people how to inform your current clients about what else they can buy from you. This proven approach revolves around letting your customers tell your story. There is nothing you can say about your products and services that is more effective than what your paying customers say. How does it work? Each day, take one quick, proactive communication action that tells someone about how they'll be improved after buying from you. Choose from the 22 actions Goldfayn details in The Revenue Growth Habit. Each technique is fast, simple, and free. It only requires your personal effort to communicate the value of your product or service to someone who can buy from you. Personal communication--the key to the 22 action steps--will make your company stand head-and-shoulders above the competition".-- Provided by publisher.

Johnson, Victoria M.

Grant writing 101 : everything you need to start raising funds today / Victoria M. Johnson. McGraw-Hill, c2011. xiii, 269 p. ; **658.15**

1. Fund raising 2. Proposal writing for grants
ISBN 9780071750189

LC 2010039599

In a book endorsed by the Association of Fundraising Professionals, the author explains how inexperienced grant writers can learn to write fundraising proposals and provides plenty of tables, lists and sample letters.

McKeever, Mike P

How to write a business plan / Mike P. McKeever. Nolo, 2017 331 p. ; **658.15**

1. Business planning 2. New business enterprises -- Finance 3. New business enterprises -- Planning 4. Small business -- Finance
ISBN 9781413323191

LC 2016026296

Explains how to create the loan package necessary to finance a business and make it work, covering such topics as assessing the potential of a business idea, estimating operating expenses, and finding sources of financing.

Rice, Condoleezza, 1954-

Political risk : how businesses and organizations can anticipate global insecurity / Condoleezza Rice and Amy Zegart. Twelve, 2018. 336 p. **658.15**

1. World politics 2. Risk analysis 3. Business and politics 4. Management
ISBN 9781455542352

LC 2017054476

Examines the topic of political risk, the authors look at the essential lessons, corrective measures and counterintuitive insights for executives, entrepreneurs and investors to navigate an uncertain, volatile world.

658.3 Personnel management (Human resource management)

Gostick, Adrian

All in : how the best managers create a culture of belief and drive big results / Adrian Gostick, Chester Elton. Free Press, 2012. 256 p. **658.3**

1. Organizational behavior. 2. Corporate culture. 3. Employee motivation. 4. Leadership in business
ISBN 9781451659825

LC 2011045590

Offers insight into the corporate cultures of high-performance organizations to explain the importance of engaged employees in business success, outlining a seven-step plan for managers to facilitate high-achieving teams.

Hallowell, Edward M.

Shine : using brain science to get the best from your people / Edward M. Hallowell. Harvard Business Review Press, c2011. 224 p. **658.3**

1. Employee motivation. 2. Job satisfaction. 3. Performance. 4. Management.
ISBN 9781591399230

LC 2010024950

Hallowell outlines a five-step process any manager can use to get the best out of his or her employees. By utilizing principles discovered through intense brain research, managers will be able to assign jobs to the right people, strengthen team bonds, cultivate imaginations, relieve and overcome stress, and stimulate loyalty and a desire to excel through rewards. This is an indispensable volume for leaders in any professional field.

Hewlett, Sylvia Ann, 1946-

#metoo in the corporate world : power, privilege, and the path forward / Sylvia Ann Hewlett. Harper Business, 2020. xviii, 232 p. : **658.3**

1. Sexual harassment 2. Me Too movement 3. Business -- Corrupt practices 4. Sexual violence victims 5. United States -- Social conditions
ISBN 9780062899194

LC bl2020003094

Economist and award-winning author Sylvia Ann Hewlett blends vivid stories with powerful new data in assessing the impact of the #MeToo movement in corporate America and provides concrete action to help executives and companies create more inclusive and safe work environments for women, people of color, and LGBTQ employees.

"Hewlett admits that we are in the early stages of understanding #MeToo in business, but her clear and practical book should be required reading for corporate leaders." Booklist.

Kelly, Matthew

The **dream** manager / Matthew Kelly. Hyperion, c2007. xi, 158 p. ; **658.3**

1. Employee motivation 2. Organizational effectiveness 3. Personnel management
ISBN 9781401303709

LC 2007013597

A business parable about how companies can achieve remarkable results by helping their employees fulfill their dreams. The fictional company in this book is grappling with real problems of high turnover and low morale--so the managers begin to investigate what really drives the employees. What they discover is that the key to motivation isn't necessarily the promise of a bigger paycheck or title, but rather the fulfillment of crucial personal dreams. Beginning with the thought that a company can only become the-best-version-of-itself to the extent that its employees are becoming better-versions-of-themselves, Kelly explores the connection between the dreams we are chasing personally and the way we all engage at work.--From publisher description.

"This business fable extols the virtues of helping those working for and with you to achieve their dreams. In this way . managers can boost morale and control turnover. This one's sure to appeal to business readers." Library Journal.

Newkirk, Pamela

Diversity, Inc. : the failed promise of a billion-dollar business / Pamela Newkirk. Bold Type Books, 2019. 261 p. **658.3**

1. Minorities -- Employment. 2. Multiculturalism -- Workplace aspects 3. Strategic planning 4. Leadership
ISBN 9781568588223

LC 2019941714

An award-winning journalist describes how well-intentioned and often costly workplace diversity initiatives have given way to a misguided industry and reveals the large gap between the rhetoric of inclusivity and actual accomplishments

"A must-read. . . . A well-sourced and succinctly written report that addresses the overall lack of progress in three key sectors: academia, corporate America, and the Hollywood entertainment establishment. . . . The book is valuable for many reasons, not the least of which is the context Newkirk provides." Fortune

Richards, Shola

Making work work : the positivity solution for any work environment / Shola Richards. Sterling Ethos, 2016 xiv, 239 p. ; **658.3**

1. Self-actualization (Psychology) 2. Work environment
ISBN 9781454918721

LC 2016016626

"Most books about creating a better work climate center on the role of management... Richard's focus on leading change from across title ranks will be appreciated by people at any stage of their careers who are seeking a more spirit-enriching workplace." Library Journal.

Tracy, Brian

Full engagement! : inspire, motivate, and bring out the best in your people / Brian Tracy. American Management Association, 2011. viii, 226 p. ; **658.3**

1. Employee motivation 2. Organizational behavior 3. Organizational effectiveness 4. Performance
ISBN 9780814416891

LC 2010048293

Includes index.

Tracy (president, Brian Tracy International and Business Growth Strategy) presents this guide to motivating team members which focuses on high-trust work environment creation, identifying and eliminating the fears that hinder productivity, goals and objectives, unlocking potential, the "X Factor", and recognizing and rewarding efforts.

658.4 Executive management

Bahcall, Safi

Loonshots : how to nurture the crazy ideas that win wars, cure diseases, and transform industries / Safi Bahcall. St. Martin's Press, [2019] 352 p. **658.4**

1. Creativity in business 2. Entrepreneurship 3. Success in business 4. Ideas (Philosophy)
ISBN 9781250185969

LC 2018041158

What do James Bond and Lipitor have in common? What can we learn about human nature and world history from a glass of water? In Loonshots, physicist and entrepreneur Safi Bahcall reveals a surprising new way of thinking about the mysteries of group behavior that challenges everything we thought we knew about nurturing radical breakthroughs.

"This thorough, fascinating study will appeal to a broader audience than just business wonks." Booklist.

Barsh, Joanna

Grow wherever you work : straight talk to help with your toughest challenges / Joanna Barsh. McGraw-Hill Education, 2018 xiv, 254 p. ; **658.4**

1. Leadership in business 2. Leadership -- Psychological aspects 3. Problem solving in management. 4. Coaching (Personnel management)
ISBN 9781260026467

LC 2017039530

"The essential coach's handbook for anyone in a position of leadership: engaging, wise, and extremely practical. A must-read for students of business, organizational communication, and psychology." Library Journal.

Bock, Laszlo

Work rules! : insights from inside Google that will transform how you live and lead / Laszlo Bock. Twelve, 2015. viii, 406 p. : **658.4**

1. Google (Firm) Management. 2. Corporate culture 3. Leadership 4. Management
ISBN 9781455554799

LC 2014020843

"'We spend more time working than doing anything else in life. It's not right that the experience of work should be so demotivating and dehumanizing.' So says Laszlo Bock, head of People Operations at the company that transformed how the world interacts with knowledge. This insight is the heart of WORK RULES!, a compelling and surprisingly playful manifesto with the potential to change how we work and live. Drawing on the latest research in behavioral economics and with a profound grasp of human psychology, Bock also provides teaching examples from a range of industries -- including companies that are household names but hideous places to work, and little-known companies that achieve spectacular results by valuing and listening to their employees. Bock takes us inside one of history's most explosively successful businesses to reveal why Google is consistently rated one of the best places to work in the world, distilling 15 years of intensive worker R&D into delightfully counterintuitive principles that are easy to put into action, whether you're a team of one or a team of thousands. Cleaving the knot of conventional management, some lessons from WORK RULES! include: Take away managers' power over employees; Learn from your best employees - and your worst Only hire people who are smarter than you are, no matter how long it takes to find them; Pay unfairly (it's fairer!); Don't trust your gut: use data to predict and shape the future; Default to open: be transparent, and welcome feedback; If you're comfortable with the amount of freedom you've given your employees, you haven't gone far enough; WORK RULES! shows how to strike a balance between creativity and structure, leading to success you can measure in quality of life as well as market share. Read it to build a better company from within rather than from above; read it to reawaken your joy in what you do. "-- Provided by publisher.

"Bock makes a persuasive case for ceding power to individual employees and teams. For visionary managers." Library Journal.

Bolman, Lee G.

How great leaders think : the art of reframing / Lee G. Bolman, Terrence E. Deal. Jossey-Bass, A Wiley Brand, 2014 xi, 228 ; **658.4**

1. Leadership 2. Organizational change
ISBN 9781118140987

LC 2014013595

"Reframing Leadership translates Bolman & Deal's influential four-frame model of leadership and organizations developed in their bestselling Jossey-Bass Book, Reframing Organizations: Artistry, Choice and Leadership, (over 300,000 copies sold in 4 editions, $7M in net revenue) into a thought-provoking and practical guide for leaders in business and other organizations. This book will offer leaders a template and guide for understanding four major dimensions of organizational life: structure, people, politics, and symbols (or culture) that will enable them to decode the messy world in which they live, see a broader range of options, and find more powerful and elegant strategies for leading".-- Provided by publisher.

Botelho, Elena L.

The **CEO** next door : what it takes to get to the top, and succeed / Elena L. Botelho and Kim R. Powell with Tahl Raz. Currency, [2017] 304 p. **658.4**

1. Chief executive officers 2. Executive ability 3. Career development 4. Success in business

ISBN 9781101906491

LC 2017035471

Drawing on a database of more than 17,000 leaders, as well as interviews with CEO candidates, two business consultants, dispelling myths about what it takes to get to the top, reveal the common attributes and hidden insights to success that have helped more than 6 million CEOs land their jobs and how these can be applied to our own careers. Includes six charts.

"Botelho and Powell have created a thought-provoking look at successful leadership without the typical bluster." Publishers Weekly.

Brown, Brene

★**Dare** to lead : brave work, tough conversations, whole hearts / Brene Brown. Random House, 2018. xix, 298 p. ; **658.4**

1. Leadership 2. Management 3. Growth (Psychology) 4. Courage

ISBN 9780399592522

"It's an absorbingly actionable handbook on creating a space for better work and more fulfilled people." Washington Post.

Catmull, Edwin E.

Creativity, Inc. : overcoming the unseen forces that stand in the way of true inspiration / Ed Catmull ; with Amy Wallace. Random House, 2014 xvi, 340 p., 8 unnumbered p. of plates : **658.4**

1. Pixar (Firm) 2. Creativity in business 3. Corporate culture. 4. Organizational effectiveness.

ISBN 9780812993011

LC 2013036026

Includes index.

The co-founder and president of Pixar Animation Studios presents a distillation of the ideas and management principles he has used to develop a the company's successful creative culture, reflecting on how Pixar's commitment to specific values has involved a daily effort.

Cerulo, Erica

Work wife : the power of female friendship to drive successful businesses / Erica Cerulo and Claire Mazur. Ballantine Books, [2019] 288 p. **658.4**

1. Women executives 2. Women-owned businesses 3. Female friendship 4. Business partnership

ISBN 9781524796778

LC 2018051136

When Erica Cerulo and Claire Mazur met in college in 2002, they bonded instantly. Fast-forward to 2010, when they founded the popular fashion and design website Of a Kind. Now, in their first book, Cerulo and Mazur bring to light the unique power of female friendship to fuel successful businesses. Drawing on their own experiences, as well as the stories of other thriving "work wives," they highlight the ways in which vulnerability, openness, and compassion--qualities central to so many women's relationships--lend themselves to professional accomplishment and innovation.

"This insightful, engaging work is an essential guidebook for friends considering a business collaboration." Library Journal

Chan, Ronald W.

Behind the Berkshire Hathaway curtain : lessons from Warren Buffett's top business leaders / Ronald W. Chan. John Wiley & Sons ; 2010. xiii, 178 p. : **658.4**

1. Buffett, Warren. 2. Berkshire Hathaway Inc. Management. 3. Business -- Decision making 4. Chief executive officers -- United States 5. Executive ability -- United States 6. Holding companies -- United States

ISBN 9780470560624

LC oc2012178490

Includes index.

Drawing on exclusive interviews from Berkshire leaders, Chan vividly describes how an exceptional group of managers has built a culture of achievement. With a keen eye for detail, he shows how their lessons can be applied for career success and personal fulfillment. Brimming with practical advice, the book will appeal to both executives and employees wanting to improve their leadership skills and work performance. --From publisher description.

Chapman, Bob (CEO)

Everybody matters : the extraordinary power of caring for your people like family / Bob Chapman and Raj Sisodia. Portfolio/Penguin, 2015 xii, 260 p. : **658.4**

1. Leadership. 2. Management. 3. Organizational effectiveness.

ISBN 9781591847793

LC 2015303330

"Chapman and coauthor Raj Sisodia show how any organization can reject the traumatic consequences of rolling layoffs, dehumanizing rules, and hypercompetitive cultures. Once you stop treating people like functions or costs, disengaged workers begin to share their gifts and talents toward a shared future. Uninspired workers stop feeling that their jobs have no meaning. Frustrated workers stop taking their bad days out on their spouses and kids. And everyone stops counting the minutes until it's time to go home. This book chronicles Chapman's journey to find his true calling, going behind the scenes as his team tackles real-world challenges with caring, empathy, and inspiration. It also provides clear steps to transform your own workplace, whether you lead two people or two hundred thousand. While the Barry-Wehmiller way isn't easy, it is simple. As the authors put it: 'Everyone wants to do better. Trust them. Leaders are everywhere. Find them. People achieve good things, big and small, every day. Celebrate them. Some people wish things were different. Listen to them. Everybody matters. Show them.'"--P. [2] of cover.

"Chapman is convincing in his appeal for a more human approach to management in all kinds of organizations. This inspirational read is recommended for all types of business collections." Library Journal.

Conant, Douglas R., 1951-

Touchpoints : creating powerful leadership connections in the smallest of moments / Douglas R. Conant, Mette Norgaard. Jossey-Bass, c2011. xxxi, 173 p. : **658.4**

1. Leadership

ISBN 9781118004357

LC 2011008907

Includes index.

"A fresh, effective, and enduring way to lead starting with your next interaction. Most leaders feel the inevitable interruptions in their jam-packed days are troublesome. But in TouchPoints, Conant and Norgaard argue that these--and every point of contact with other people--are overlooked opportunities for leaders to increase their impact and promote their organization's strategy and values. Through previously untold stories from Conant's tenure as CEO of Campbell Soup Company and Norgaard's vast consulting experience, the authors show that a leader's impact and legacy are built through hundreds, even thousands, of interactive moments in time. The good news is that anyone can develop "TouchPoint" mastery by focusing on four essential components: head, heart, hands and touch. Promotes a new intuitive model of rational, active, and wise leadership practices. Shows how the authenticity of a leader is tested during every informal interaction, every day. Introduces four integrated commitments that are foundational to mastering the TouchPoints: the commitment to inquiry, reflection, practice, and continuous improvement. Compelling and transformative, this book shows how TouchPoint mastery can turn otherwise ordinary moments into powerful opportunities for influence with lasting impact--one TouchPoint at a time."--Provided by publisher.

Davidds, Yasmin

★**Your** own terms : a woman's guide to taking charge of any negotiation / Yasmin Davidds, PsyD with Ann Bidou. AMACOM, American Management Association, 2015 xii, 260 p. ; **658.4**

1. Businesswomen 2. Negotiation in business 3. Negotiation
ISBN 9780814436028

LC 2015009457

A negotiating guide for women provides information about such topics as creating a strong presence, leveraging natural style, and handling difficult people.

Doerr, John E.

Measure what matters : how Google, Bono, and the Gates Foundation rock the world with OKRs / John Doerr. Portfolio/Penguin, 2018 xii, 306 p. : **658.4**

1. Business -- Planning 2. Goal (Psychology) 3. Organizational effectiveness 4. Performance
ISBN 9780525536222

LC 2018002727

A noted venture capitalist reveals how the goal-setting system of Objectives and Key Results (OKRs) has helped tech giants from Intel to Google achieve explosive growth--and how it can help any organization thrive.

Dreeke, Robin

The **code** of trust : an American counterintelligence expert's five rules to lead and succeed / Robin Dreeke and Cameron Stauth ; foreword by Joe Navarro. St. Martin's Press, 2017. xi, 371 p. ; **658.4**

1. Dreeke, Robin. 2. United States. Federal Bureau of Investigation Officials and employees 3. Leadership 4. Trust 5. Interpersonal communication 6. Organizational behavior
ISBN 9781250093462

LC 2017006882

"Robin Dreeke is a 28-year veteran of federal service, including the United States Naval Academy, United States Marine Corps. He served most recently as a senior agent in the FBI, with 20 years of experience. He was, until recently, the head of the Counterintelligence Behavioral Analysis Program, where his primary mission was to thwart the efforts of foreign spies, and to recruit American spies. His core approach in this mission was to inspire reasonable, well-founded trust among people who could providevaluable information. The Code of Trust is based on the system Dreeke devised, tested, and implemented during years of field work at the highest levels of national security. Applying his system first to himself, he rose up through federal law enforcement, and then taught his system to law enforcement and military officials throughout the country, and later to private sector clients. The Code of Trust has since elevated executives to leadership, and changed the culture of entire companies, making them happier and more productive, as morale soared. Inspiring trust is not a trick, nor is it an arcane art. It's an important, character-building endeavor that requires only a sincere desire to be helpful and sensitive, and the ambition to be more successful at work and at home. The Code of Trust is based on 5 simple principles: 1) Suspend Your Ego 2) Be Nonjudgmental 3) Honor Reason 4) Validate Others 5) Be Generous. To be successful with this system, a reader needs only the willingness to spend eight to ten hours learning a method of trust-building that took Robin Dreeke almost a lifetime to create".--Provided by publisher.

Duke, Annie, 1965-

Thinking in bets : making smarter decisions when you don't have all the facts / Annie Duke. Portfolio/Penguin, 2018 276 p. : **658.4**

1. Decision making 2. Management games
ISBN 9780735216358

LC 2017042666

"Poker champion turned business consultant Annie Duke teaches you how to get comfortable with uncertainty and make better decisions as a result. In Super Bowl XLIX, Seahawks coach Pete Carroll made one of the most controversial calls in football history: With 26 seconds remaining, and trailing by four at the Patriots' one-yard line, he called for a pass instead of a hand off to his star running back. The pass was intercepted and the Seahawks lost. Critics called it the dumbest play in history. But was the call really that bad? Or did Carroll actually make a great move that was ruined by bad luck? Even the best decision doesn't yield the best outcome every time. There's always an element of luck that you can't control, and there is always information that is hidden from view. So the key to long-term success (and avoiding worrying yourself to death) is to think in bets: How sure am I? What are the possible ways things could turn out? What decision has the highest odds of success? Did I land in the unlucky 10% on the strategy that works 90% of the time? Or is my success attributable to dumb luck rather than great decision making? Annie Duke, a former World Series of Poker champion turned business consultant, draws on examples from business, sports, politics, and (of course) poker to share tools anyone can use to embrace uncertainty and make better decisions. For most people, it's difficult to say "I'm not sure" in a world that values and, even, rewards the appearance of certainty. But professional pokerplayers are comfortable with the fact that great decisions don't always lead to great outcomes and bad decisions don't always lead to bad outcomes. By shifting your thinking from a need for certainty to a goal of accurately assessing what you know and what you don't, you'll be less vulnerable to reactive emotions, knee-jerk biases, and destructive habits in your decision making. You'll become more confident, calm, compassionate and successful in the long run".-- Provided by publisher.

Ferrazzi, Keith

Never eat alone : and other secrets to success, one relationship at a time / Keith Ferrazzi and Tahl Raz. Crown Business, 2014 xvii, 379 p. ; **658.4**

1. Success in business 2. Business networks 3. Online social networks 4. Generosity
ISBN 9780385346658

LC 2014381541

Explaining how to turn one-time contacts into a lifelong circle of mentors, colleagues, and friends, a guide to the art of networking reveals the fundamental principles of what it takes to build lasting, mutually beneficial relationships.

Gallo, Carmine

Talk like TED : the 9 public-speaking secrets of the world's top minds / Carmine Gallo. St. Martin's Press, 2014 x, 278 p.

: 658.4

1. Business presentations. 2. Public speaking.
ISBN 9781250041128

LC 2013031049

Reveals the nine strategies of the gold-standard presentation method, drawing on interviews with TED conference speakers to outline methods for overcoming public speaking fears, motivating teams, and making a presentation dynamic.

"The author ... includes successful outlines and guides to using both audio-visual aides and effective body language. Dramatic composition and vigorous presentation make this a powerful tool to improve mastery of speaking skills." Kirkus.

Gilkey, Charlie

Start finishing : how to go from idea to done / Charlie Gilkey. Sounds True, 2019. ix, 257 p. : 658.4

1. Time management 2. Procrastination
ISBN 9781683642633

LC 2018059665

Presents a 9-step method for success -- including identifying your genius, building a success pack of supporters, navigating multiple projects, and overcoming the challenges that come with doing work that matters.

"For those interested in project management and entrepreneurship, this book offers creative solutions for developing habits and routines that will set them on a path to starting and finishing projects successfully." Booklist

Goleman, Daniel

Primal leadership : unleashing the power of emotional intelligence / Daniel Goleman, Richard Boyatzis, Annie McKee. Harvard Business Review Press, 2013 xxi, 306 p. ; 658.4

1. Leadership -- Psychological aspects 2. Management -- Psychological aspects 3. Executive ability 4. Emotional intelligence
ISBN 9781422168035

LC 2013018294

This refreshed edition of Primal Leadership illustrates why the book is all the more timely today as leaders face ever-increasing pressures from globalization and the economic roller coaster to the hyper-speed of evolving information technologies and the ratcheting up of competitive forces.

Granet, Keith, 1956-

The **business** of creativity : how to build the right team for success / Keith Granet. Princeton Architectural Press, 2017 190 p. : 658.4

1. Creative ability in business 2. Business planning
ISBN 9781616893941

LC 2016018288

"Long known as the go-to management consultant of the design world, Keith Granet reveals more of his clear-eyed insights about running a creative business in this follow-up to his book The Business of Design. While aimed at creative enterprises, Granet's advice, quickly summarized as "know what you do best and focus on that," applies to any organization, small or large, commercial or nonprofit. He delves into the skill sets and people needed to grow a business, as well as the things you don't need (bad clients, bad employees, negative energy), in an engaging and easy-to-implement manner. His shrewd understanding, gleaned from decades of consulting for brands like Harrods, Pantone, John Varvatos, and Urban Archeology, makes this essential reading for anyone managing a business or thinking of starting one".-- Provided by publisher.

Horstman, Mark,

The **effective** manager / Mark Horstman, cofounder, manager tools. Wiley, 2016 xiv, 194 p. ; 658.4

1. Executive ability 2. Management 3. Supervision of employees 4. Teams in the workplace -- Management
ISBN 9781119244608

LC 2016018227

Includes index.

"The Effective Manager is written for every manager, at every level. It focuses on what you can do now, today, with your team members, to improve their performance and get better results and retention. It even tells you how fast to roll out each of the 4tools -- One on Ones, Feedback, Coaching and Delegation, week by week".-- Provided by publisher.

Johnson, Whitney (Whitney W.)

Disrupt yourself : putting the power of disruptive innovation to work / Whitney Johnson. Bibliomotion, 2015. xxvii, 162 p. : 658.4

1. Success in business 2. Disruptive technologies 3. Career changes 4. Organizational change
ISBN 9781629560526

LC 2015019271

"Are you a high potential charting your course within your current organization, a leader trying to jumpstart innovative thinking in your company? Or are you ready to do something new? Consider this simple yet powerful idea: disruptive companies and ideas upend markets by doing something truly different -- they see a need, an empty space waiting to be filled, and they dare to create something for which a market may not yet exist. An expert in driving innovation via personal disruption, Whitney Johnson, will help you understand how the frameworks of disruptive innovation can apply to you: if you want to be successful in unexpected ways, follow your own disruptive path. Dare to innovate. Dream big dreams. Do something astonishing. Disrupt yourself. In this book, you will learn how to apply these frameworks to building a business, career -- and you. We are living in an era of accelerating disruption -- those who can manage the S-curve waves of learning and maxing out will have a competitive advantage. But this is a skill set that needs to be learned. Disrupt Yourself will help people cope with the unpredictability of disruption, and use it to their competitive advantage".-- Provided by publisher.

Kethledge, Raymond Michael, 1966-

Lead yourself first : inspiring leadership through solitude / Raymond M. Kethledge and Michael S. Erwin ; foreword by Jim Collins. Bloomsbury Publishing USA, 2017. 288 p. 658.4

1. Leadership 2. Solitude 3. Self-improvement 4. Politicians
ISBN 9781632866318

LC 2016044432

Citing examples from great leaders in politics, business, sports and the military, makes the case for leaders to unplug from daily life and spend time alone to improve clarity and creativity, balance their emotions and sustain certainty.

"This book is a rare gem, offering an optimistic message that there remain powerful leaders intent on being courageous and moral, and on finding 'transcendent meaning' in their vocation." Publishers Weekly.

Klubeck, Martin

Why organizations struggle so hard to improve so little : overcoming organizational immaturity / Martin Klubeck, Michael Langth-

orne, and Donald Padgett. Praeger, c2010. xvi, 222 p. : **658.4**
1. Organizational change
ISBN 9780313380228
LC 2009046410

The book's audience includes organization leaders and other stakeholders, managers at all levels, and staff members.

"The text also includes charts, graphs and encouraging words, but readers shouldn't expect motivational directives here; rather, the book's clear-eyed practicality is its strength. A viable tool for business leaders who accept change as part of growth." Kirkus

Knapp, Jake
Sprint : how to solve big problems and test new ideas in just five days / Jake Knapp ; with John Zeratsky and Braden Kowitz. Simon & Schuster, 2016. 274 p. : **658.4**
1. Problem solving 2. Management 3. Creative ability in business
ISBN 9781501121746
LC 2015303348

Includes index.

From three design partners at Google Ventures, a unique five-day process--called the sprint--for solving tough problems using design, prototyping, and testing ideas with customers.

Kouzes, James M., 1945-
The **truth** about leadership : the no-fads, heart-of-the-matter facts you need to know / James M. Kouzes, Barry Z. Posner. Jossey-Bass, c2010. xxv, 197 p. ; **658.4**
1. Leadership 2. Executive ability
ISBN 9780470633540
LC 2010018715

"A fresh look at what it means to lead from two of the biggest names in leadership In these turbulent times, when the very foundations of organizations and societies are shaken, leaders need to move beyond pessimistic predictions, trendy fads, and simplistic solutions. They need to turn to what's real and what's proven. In their engaging, personal, and bold new book, Kouzes and Posner reveal ten time-tested truths that show what every leader must know, the questions they must be prepared to answer, and the real-world issues they will likely face. Based on thirty years of research, more than one million responses to Kouzes and Posner's leadership assessment, and the questions people most want leaders to answer. Explores the fundamental, enduring truths of leadership that hold constant regardless of context or circumstance-leaders make a difference, credibility, values, trust, leading by example, heart, and more. Shows emerging leaders what they need to know to be effective; fans of The Leadership Challenge will find a dynamic new look at the real challenges leaders face today. Drawing from cases spanning three generations of leaders from around the world, this is a book leaders can use to do their real and necessary work-bringing about the essential changes that will renew organizations and communities."-- Provided by publisher.

Lanik, Martin
The **leader** habit : master the skills you need to lead in just minutes a day / Martin Lanik. AMACOM, American Management Association, 2018 xiv, 238 p. ; **658.4**
1. Leadership
ISBN 9780814439340
LC 2017051455

Develop the habits necessary to become the most effective leader possible.

"Ultimately, the book provides a refreshing counterpoint to the standard idea that some people are simply gifted with good leadership skills, instead shifting the emphasis to daily attention. An engaging program that demystifies leadership skills with bite-sized exercises." Kirkus

Maroney, Tyler
The **modern** detective : how corporate intelligence is reshaping the world / Tyler Maroney. Riverhead Books, 2020. 262 p. **658.4**
1. Maroney, Tyler 2. Business intelligence. 3. Private investigators. 4. Intelligence service. 5. Ethics
ISBN 9781594632594
LC 2020018425

Includes index.

An insider's tour of the world of 21st-century private investigators examines how today's detectives use unique creativity and resources to help catch corrupt politicians, international embezzlers and corporate purveyors of human-rights abuses.

"Readers do not need a background in private investigative work to appreciate this fascinating read. Hand this to readers interested in the work and life of a private investigator, the role of technology in investigative work, and political and white-collar crime." Booklist

McChesney, Chris
The **4** disciplines of execution : achieving your wildly important goals / Chris McChesney, Sean Covey, Jim Huling. Free Press, c2012. 256 p. **658.4**
1. Goals and objectives in personnel management 2. Management 3. Goals and objectives 4. Business.
ISBN 9781451627053
LC 2012001672

The 4 Disciplines of Execution (4DX) is a simple, repeatable, and proven formula for executing on your most important strategic priorities in the midst of the whirlwind.

McGowan, Bill
Pitch perfect : how to say it right the first time, every time / Bill McGowan and Alisa Bowman. Harper Business, 2014 xi, 266 p. ; **658.4**
1. Business communication 2. Persuasion (Rhetoric) 3. Success in business
ISBN 9780062273222
LC bl2014013253

Introducing his simple principles of persuasion, the media guru and correspondent shows business leaders how to craft the right message and deliver it both verbally and nonverbally to get what they want.

Mueller, Jennifer
Creative change : why we resist it... how we can embrace it / Jennifer Mueller. Houghton Mifflin Harcourt, 2017 288 p. **658.4**
1. Creativity 2. Change. 3. Success in business 4. Business innovations.
ISBN 9780544703094
LC 2016036403

A forefront psychologist analyzes the paradox of how today's corporate leaders both desire and reject creative solutions, offering insight into the biases that compromise innovation while suggesting options for recognizing creative opportunities and overcoming unproductive beliefs.

"This enlightening book not only shows why people reject creativity but provides solutions on how to switch ones thinking and truly welcome it." Publishers Weekly.

Peshawaria, Rajeev
Too many bosses, too few leaders : the art of being a true leader /

Rajeev Peshawaria. Free Press, 2011. xxii, 222 p. : **658.4**

1. Leadership

ISBN 9781439197745

LC 2010042147

A founding member of the renowned Goldman Sachs leadership development program outlines a program for achieving consistent leadership excellence, explaining his definition of true leadership while sharing stories about effective role models from such companies as Coca-Cola, American Express and Morgan Stanley.

"Peshawaria's book ought to become required reading for all business people--from students to executives." Publishers Weekly.

Peters, Thomas J

The **excellence** dividend : meeting the tech tide with work that wows and jobs that last / Tom Peters. Vintage Books, 2018 xxxiv, 460 p. : **658.4**

1. Organizational change 2. Organizational effectiveness 3. Strategic planning 4. Automation -- Economic aspects

ISBN 9780525434627

LC 2017031994

"This book offers a fresh perspective on sustaining business in the tech age and is sure to be a popular read for both employees and business leaders." Booklist

The **little** big things : 163 ways to pursue excellence / Tom Peters. HarperStudio, c2010. xxix, 538 p. **658.4**

1. Excellence -- United States 2. Industrial management -- United States

ISBN 9780061894084

LC oc2012190130

Includes index.

The coauthor of the business classic In Search of Excellence offers a collection of business-success tips--including "Love Your Competitors," "Leave Your Wallet at Home" and "Cut Red Tape"--that encourage readers to get back to basics and excel at the people side of business.

"The author combines observations he has gleaned from his travels, current news items, conversations, and followers of his blog in a compact guide that aims to help readers realize effective projects, customer contentment, employee engagement, and business profitability. No doubt, Peters is on target as he advises readers to appreciate the angry customer, work on their last impressions, make sure that the restroom is clean, and 160 other ways to guarantee success. Each suggestion contains a rationale, example, and method of implementation, all in two pages apiece." Library Journal.

Pimsleur Levine, Julia

Million dollar women : the essential guide for female entrepreneurs who want to go big / Julia Pimsleur. Simon & Schuster, 2015. 242 p. : **658.4**

1. Fund raising 2. New business enterprises 3. Women-owned business enterprises

ISBN 9781476790299

LC 2015011025

The CEO and founder of a second-language-learning system offers tips and advice to women entrepreneurs for making their businesses big, including how to network, when to delegate, and how to jump the emotional hurdles that will come their way.

Pinson, Linda

Anatomy of a business plan : the step-by-step guide to building your business and securing your company's future / Linda Pinson. Out of Your Mind...and Into the Marketplace, 2014 xii, 372 p. : **658.4**

1. Business planning 2. New business enterprises -- Planning

ISBN 9780944205556

LC bl2018052167

Includes index.

Used by more than 1.5 million business owners since its original publication, the new edition of this classic how-to guide provides any entrepreneur the tools to create a well-constructed business plan. All steps are included -- from initial considerations to envisioning the organizational structure to creating a growth-powering marketing plan and building for the future with airtight financial documents. --From publisher description.

Port, Michael, 1970-

Steal the show : from speeches to job interviews to deal-closing pitches : how to guarantee a standing ovation for all the performances in your life / Michael Port. Houghton Mifflin Harcourt, 2015. xxviii, 237 p. ; **658.4**

1. Business communication 2. Business presentations 3. Employment interviewing 4. Interpersonal communication

ISBN 9780544555181

LC 2015017313

"An inspiring program full of essential advice for spotlight lovers and wallflowers alike that will teach readers how to bring any crowd to its feet Every day there are moments when you must persuade, inform, and motivate others effectively. Each of those moments requires you, in some way, to play a role, to heighten the impact of your words, and to manage your emotions and nerves. Every interaction is a performance, whether you're speaking up in a meeting, pitching a client, or walking into a job interview. In Steal the Show, New York Times best-selling author Michael Port draws on his experience as an actor and as a highly successful corporate speaker and trainer to teach readers how to make the most of every presentation and interaction. He demonstrates how the methods of successful actors can help you connect with, inspire, and persuade any audience. His key strategies for commanding an audience's attention include developing a clear focus for every performance, making sure you engage with your listeners, and finding the best role for yourself in order to convey your message with maximum impact. Michael Port is one of the most in-demand corporate speakers working today. His presentations are always powerful, engaging, and inspirational. And yes, audiences always give him a standing ovation. "-- Provided by publisher.

Reynolds, Garr

Presentation zen : simple ideas on presentation design and delivery / Garr Reynolds. New Riders, c2012. xi, 296 p. : **658.4**

1. Microsoft PowerPoint (Computer file) 2. Business presentations -- Graphic methods -- Computer programs 3. Business presentations 4. Multimedia systems in business presentations

ISBN 9780321811981

LC 2012382532

Includes index.

Provides lessons to help users design and deliver creative presentations using Microsoft PowerPoint.

"As the author himself notes, the book is not about Zen, but about a Zen approach to presentation, rather than a set of rules. Reynolds especially focuses on the differences that should exist between well-written detailed handouts as documents to be read, and slides as visual presentations to be viewed. The before-and-after slide illustrations support the author's main points. Is this book unique? Only in its approach to the tenets of Zen simplicity driving presentation design. Summing Up: Recommended. General readers; upper-division undergraduates and graduate students." Choice.

Riel, Jennifer

Creating great choices : a leader's guide to integrative thinking / Jennifer Riel, Roger L. Martin. Harvard Business Review Press, 2017 xvii, 242 p. : **658.4**

1. Problem solving 2. Contradiction 3. Thought and thinking 4. Decision making
ISBN 9781633692961

LC 2017012026

"Conventional wisdom--and business school curricula--teaches us that making trade-offs is inevitable when it comes to hard choices. But sometimes, accepting the obvious trade-off just isn't good enough: the choices in front of us don't get us what we need. In those cases, rather than choosing the least worst option, we can use the models in front of us to create a new and better answer. This is integrative thinking. First introduced by Roger Martin in The Opposable Mind, integrative thinking is an approach to problem solving that uses opposing ideas as the basis for innovation. Now, in Creating Great Choices, Martin and fellow Rotman expert Jennifer Riel vividly show how they have refined and enhanced the understanding and practice of integrative thinking through their work teaching the concept and its principles to business and nonprofit executives, MBA students, even kids. Integrative thinking has been embraced by organizations such as Procter & Gamble, Deloitte, Verizon, and the Toronto District School Board--all seeking a replicable, thoughtful approach to creating a "third and better way" to make important choices in the face of unacceptable trade-offs. The book includes new stories of successful integrative thinkers that will demystify the process of creative problem solving. It lays out the authors' practical four-step methodology, which can be applied in virtually any context: Articulating opposing models; Examining the models; Generating possibilities; Assessing prototypes. Stimulating and practical, Creating Great Choices blends storytelling, theory, and hands-on advice to help any leader or manager facing a tough choice".-- Provided by publisher

Sally, David

One step ahead : mastering the art and science of negotiation / David Sally. St. Martin's Press, 2020. x, 372 p. : **658.4**

1. Negotiation in business. 2. Negotiation.
ISBN 9781250166395

LC 2019054416

An innovative strategist and behavioral economist, drawing on 20 years of experience--and the stories of often misunderstood historical characters, introduces a revolutionary way of approaching negotiation that applies in any situation.

"Entertaining and conversational, this is an important tool for getting to yes, as well as understanding exactly what will prompt an opponent to say it." Publishers Weekly

Sandberg, Sheryl

Lean in : for graduates / Sheryl Sandberg. Alfred A. Knopf, 2014. 432 p. **658.4**

1. Women college graduates 2. Job hunting 3. Job applications 4. Leadership in women
ISBN 9780385353670

LC 2014002390

Expanded and updated for graduates just entering the workforce, a guide to finding and getting the most out of a first job shares professional advice for resume writing, recommended interviewing practices, and salary negotiation.

"An expanded version of Facebook COO Sandberg's 2013 bestseller, this time with additional material aimed specifically at women just entering the workforce. Sandberg recruits a considerable number of women, and a couple of men, to add their voices to hers." Kirkus.

Lean in : women, work, and the will to lead / Sheryl Sandberg. Alfred A. Knopf, 2013. 208 p. **658.4**

1. Sandberg, Sheryl 2. Women executives 3. Leadership in women
ISBN 9780385349949

LC 2012043371

The Facebook chief operating officer and Fortune top-ranked businesswoman shares provocative, anecdotal advice for women that urges them to take risks and seek new challenges in order to find work that they can love and engage in passionately.

Scott, Kim Malone

Radical candor : be a kick-ass boss without losing your humanity / Kim Scott. St. Martin's Press, 2017. 272 p. **658.4**

1. Management 2. Executives 3. Leadership 4. Decision-making
ISBN 9781250103505

LC 2016044291

A high-profile business manager describes her development of an optimal management course designed to help business leaders become balanced and effective without resorting to insensitive aggression or overt permissiveness.

"Informational and clear, this is necessary reading for anyone whos having trouble coming to terms with an underperforming workforce." Publishers Weekly.

Snow, Shane

Dream teams : working together without falling apart / Shane Snow. Portfolio/Penguin, 2018. xiii, 286 p. : **658.4**

1. Cooperation 2. Success in business 3. Small groups -- Psychological aspects. 4. Teams in the workplace.
ISBN 9780735217799

LC 2018014633

Includes index.

Uses research from history, neuroscience, psychology, and business to explore and determine how and why some partnerships break down and others thrive.

"Entrepreneur, journalist, and author Snow (Smartcuts, 2014) explains how the composition of teams can make or break ideas, progress, and even the outcomes of battles. Using a combination of historical events (like the Battle of New Orleans, against the British, with General Andrew Jackson at the helm) and psychological research, Snows narrative and perspective are clear: to become stronger, work must be collective in certain ways." Booklist.

Solovic, Susan Wilson

The **one-percent** edge : small changes that guarantee relevance and build sustainable success / Susan Solovic with Ray Manley. AMACOM Books, 2018 xxi, 256 p. **658.4**

1. Organizational change. 2. Corporate culture. 3. Organizational behavior. 4. Success in business
ISBN 9780814438800

LC 2017027592

Includes index.

When business is good, most leaders focus on maintaining the status quo. After all, why fix what's not broken? But doing the same thing leaves you vulnerable to new competitors and technologies. (Consider what happened to Polaroid when digital cameras hit the market, or to Firestone when Michelin introduced its superior radial tires.) To gain an advantage over old rivals and upstarts alike, The One-Percent Edge offers a simple but powerful formula: make small, incremental improvements in seven areas of your business.

Spetzler, Carl S.

Decision quality : value creation from better business decisions / Carl Spetzler, Hannah Winter, Jennifer Meyer. WILEY, 2016 xviii, 237 p. : **658.4**

1. Decision making

ISBN 9781119144670

LC 2015043777

"Add value with every decision using a simple yet powerful framework. Few things are as valuable in business, and in life, as the ability to make good decisions. Can you imagine how much more rewarding your life and your business would be if every decision you made were the best it could be? Decision Quality empowers you to make the best possible choice and get more of what you truly want from every decision. Dr. Carl Spetzler is a leader in the field of decision science and has worked with organizations across industries to improve their decision-making capabilities. He and his co-authors, all experienced consultants and educators in this field, show you how to frame a problem or opportunity, create a set of attractive alternatives, identify relevant uncertain information, clarify the values that are important in the decision, apply tools of analysis, and develop buy-in among stakeholders. Their straightforward approach is elegantly simple, yet practical and powerful. It can be applied to all types of decisions. Our business and our personal lives are marked by a stream of decisions. Some are small. Some are large. Some are life-altering or strategic. How well we make those decisions truly matters. This book gives you a framework and thinking tools that will help you to improve the odds of getting more of what you value from every choice. You will learn: The six element of decisions quality, and how to apply them; The difference between a good decision and a good outcome; Why a decision can only be as good as the best of the available alternative; Methods for making both 'significant' and strategic decisions; The mental traps that undermine decision quality and how to avoid them; How to deal with uncertainty--a factor in every important choice; How to judge the quality of a decision at the time you're making it; How organizations have benefited from building quality into their decisions. Many people are satisfied with 'good enough' when making important decisions. This book provides a method that will take you and your co-workers beyond 'good enough' to true Decision Quality".-- Provided by publisher.

Taylor, William, 1959-

Practically radical : not-so-crazy ways to transform your company, shake up your industry, and challenge yourself / William C. Taylor. William Morrow, c2011. 320 p. **658.4**

1. Organizational change. 2. Leadership in business 3. Business competition 4. Organizational development.

ISBN 9780061734618

LC 2010028021

Drawing on inspiration from such companies as Lexus, Zappos, MGM Grand Las Vegas and more, the author explains how looking at things from an outsider's view, caring and empathizing, emotionally engaging customers and much more can lead to radical, positive changes in an organization. By the co-author of Mavericks at Work.

"The author takes us on an inside look at 25 companies that have grown ever more adaptive to not merely survive but thrive in today's challenging environment. An engaging and briskly written read, this will captivate and benefit business people interested in change and innovation." Publishers Weekly.

Webb, Amy, 1974-

The **signals** are talking : why today's fringe is tomorrow's mainstream / Amy Webb. PublicAffairs, [2016] 322 p. **658.4**

1. Strategic planning 2. Business forecasting 3. Technological innovations 4. Technological forecasting

ISBN 9781610396660

LC 2016028425

"Webb provides a logical way to sift through todays onslaught of events and information to spot coming changes in your corner of the world." Kirkus.

Wheeler, Michael, 1943-

The **art** of negotiation : how to improvise agreement in a chaotic world / Michael Wheeler, Harvard Business School. Simon & Schuster, 2013 viii, 304 p. ; **658.4**

1. Negotiation in business 2. Negotiation

ISBN 9781451690422

LC 2013005793

Shedding new light on the improvisational nature of negotiation, a member of the world renowned Program on Negotiation at Harvard Law School explains how diplomats, deal-makers, and Hollywood producers apply their best practices to everyday transactions.

658.5 Management of production

Kolko, Jon

Well-designed : how to use empathy to create products people love / Jon Kolko. Harvard Business Review Press, 2014 viii, 234 p. : **658.5**

1. Consumer behavior 2. Marketing research 3. New products 4. Product design

ISBN 9781625274793

LC 2014032507

"A new way to create-and then disrupt Industry disruption is no longer isolated to a unique product or service. Today's consumer needs engagement in order to be swayed to interact, connect, and buy your next offering. Achieve this and you'll achieve success. Sharp and refreshing, design insider and expert Jon Kolko offers a new view and usable process for conceiving and building powerful, emotionally resonant new products in this new book. In Well-Designed, Kolko--VP at MyEdu and Founder and Director of the Austin Center for Design--shows how deep, meaningful engagement happens when products and services are delivered in an authentic way, when consumers see them less like manufactured artifacts and more like good friends. The key is empathy-driven design thinking, using a process of storytelling and iteration, with results that provoke emotion, change behavior, and create deep engagement. Kolko, who has been engaged in this process of design for more than 15 years, now shares a concrete set of steps for identifying lucrative opportunities, designing for innovation, and producing products that have deep, meaningful emotional engagement. By following this process, readers will learn how to raise the role of design to a strategic competency".-- Provided by publisher.

Tenner, Edward

The **efficiency** paradox : what big data can't do / Edward Tenner. Alfred A. Knopf, 2018. xxxi, 282 p. **658.5**

1. Artificial intelligence. 2. Big data. 3. Industrial efficiency. 4. Serendipity.

ISBN 9781400041398

LC 2017032040

Presents a scholarly challenge to today's focus on efficiency, citing the inherent waste of current practices while explaining how artificial intelligence can be combined with intuition to enable random, unexpected outcomes for overall better results.

658.8 Management of marketing

Burcher, Nick

Paid, owned, earned : maximizing marketing returns in a socially connected world / Nick Burcher. Kogan Page, 2012. xiv, 279 p. : **658.8**

1. Digital media 2. Internet marketing 3. Marketing -- Management 4. Online social networks
ISBN 9780749465629

LC oc2014085162

A guide to marketing in an increasingly fragmented media environment provides advice on creating an advertising framework that addresses social media optimization, seeding and viral distribution, and broadcast mass media.

Godin, Seth

This is marketing : you can't be seen until you learn to see / Seth Godin. Penguin Group USA, 2018 208 p. **658.8**

1. Marketing -- Social aspects 2. Marketing management 3. Market segmentation
ISBN 9780525540830

LC 2018041567

The author offers the core of his marketing wisdom, discussing how great marketing is grounded in empathy, generosity, and making a connection.

"Theres a very good reason Godin (and his 18 previous best-selling books) is so popular: simplicity, period. He boils down the principles of marketing (and, by the way, gently chides those who think social media is the be-all, end-all) in ways that anyone will understand and--he fervently hopes--adopt." Booklist.

Lindstrom, Martin, 1970-

Small data : the tiny clues that uncover huge trends / Martin Lindstrom. St. Martin's Press, 2016 256 p. **658.8**

1. Consumerism. 2. Human behavior. 3. Economic indicators. 4. Consumer behavior.
ISBN 9781250080684

LC 2015030202

An expert on branding and consumer behavior explains how instead of using Big Data, he personally gathers small clues, from a teddy bear in a bedroom to a simple pearl bracelet in Dubai, and uses them to predict demand for consumer goods.

"Lindstrom's uncanny ability to detect and decipher seemingly unrelated clues will inspire reporters and detectives as well as companies looking for ways to develop new products and ideas." Kirkus.

Miles, Jason, 1970-

YouTube marketing power : how to use video to find more prospects, launch your products, and reach a massive audience / Jason G. Miles. McGraw-Hill, 2014 xvii, 231 p. : **658.8**

1. YouTube (Electronic resource). 2. Internet advertising 3. Internet marketing 4. Internet videos 5. Video tape advertising
ISBN 9780071830546

LC 2013030881

Explains how to use YouTube videos to drive traffic to websites to increase sales, describing how to increase brand loyalty and avoid common mistakes.

Schaefer, Mark

Return on influence : the revolutionary power of Klout, social scoring, and influence marketing / Mark W. Schaefer. McGraw-Hill, c2012. xviii, 215 p. : **658.8**

1. Online social networks. 2. Social media -- Marketing. 3. Social influence. 4. Marketing.
ISBN 9780071791090

LC 2011052315

Looks at how brands are using the world's most powerful online celebrities, like bloggers and tweeters, to market products and shows how this same system can be used by the reader to achieve goals.

Underhill, Paco

★**Why** we buy : the science of shopping / Paco Underhill. Simon & Schuster, 2000, c1999. 255 p. ; **658.8**

1. Marketing research. 2. Consumer behavior. 3. Shopping. 4. Consumers.
ISBN 0684849143

LC BL 00009176

"A Touchstone book."
Includes index.
Originally published: c1999.

An expert on shopping behavior and motivation offers an analysis of consumers' tastes and habits, discussing why point-of-sale purchases are still the most significant, and why Internet shopping will not replace the mall.

Watkins, Alexandra

Hello, my name is awesome : how to create brand names that stick / Alexandra Watkins. Berrett-Koehler Publishers, 2014 x, 98 p. : **658.8**

1. Brand name products 2. Branding (Marketing)
ISBN 9781626561861

LC 2014018994

Includes index.

"Naming a business or product has always been challenging--and sometimes costly--for entrepreneurs and inventors, but it's one of the most important decisions they have to make. Alexandra Watkins presents a foolproof model that anyone can use to create and evaluate brand names like a pro".-- Provided by publisher.

"Useful for readers who are naming anything more important than a household pet." Library Journal.

659.1 Advertising

Auletta, Ken

Frenemies : the epic disruption of the ad business (and everything else) / Ken Auletta. Penguin Press, [2018] 400 p. **659.1**

1. Advertising agencies -- History. 2. Advertising -- History. 3. Marketing -- History. 4. Consumer behavior
ISBN 9780735220867

LC 2018006195

The "Annals of Communication" columnist and author of Googled presents an intimate and awareness-raising assessment of the changes buffeting the $2 trillion global advertising and marketing business as viewed by the industry's most powerful players.

Marshall, Perry S

Ultimate guide to Google AdWords / Perry Marshall, Mike Rhodes, Bryan Todd. Entrepreneur Media, Inc., 2017 xvi, 341 p. ; **659.1**

1. Google AdWords. 2. Internet advertising 3. Web search engines
ISBN 9781599186122

LC 2017027582

Includes index.

"Uncle Claude, as this outstanding guide affectionately calls him, pioneered results-driven advertising, so celebrating Hopkins by relating his timeless wisdom to modern-day marketing is a nice touch. An exemplary Google AdWords manual that could easily prevent costly mistakes and help boost profits." Kirkus. Reviews

Turow, Joseph

The **daily** you : how the new advertising industry is defining your identity and your world / Joseph Turow. Yale University Press, 2011. xi, 234 p. ; **659.1**

1. Consumer profiling 2. Marketing -- Technological innovations 3. Advertising 4. Internet marketing

ISBN 9780300165012

LC 2011028202

Describes the rise of media agencies which collect information about individuals from their Internet behavior and provide that data to to marketing firms for use in targeted marketing campaigns and examines the impact of these strategies on consumer power.

Wu, Tim

The **attention** merchants : the epic scramble to get inside our heads / Tim Wu. Knopf, 2016. 304 p. **659.1**

1. Manipulation (Social sciences) 2. Advertising -- Psychological aspects 3. Mass media -- History. 4. Technology -- Social aspects

LC 2016010140

The award-winning author of The Master Switch, who coined the term "net neutrality," discusses the companies that want to attract and harvest human attention and their relentless attempts to influence our consumption and purchases.

659.2 Public relations

Gramm, Jeff

Dear chairman : boardroom battles and the rise of shareholder activism / Jeff Gramm. Harper Business, 2016 304 p. **659.2**

1. Corporate governance. 2. Corporations -- Investor relations. 3. Stockholders. 4. Investors.

ISBN 9780062369833

LC 2015038177

Drawing on lively case studies and original letters from some of our most legendary and controversial investors and activists, a hedge-fund manager and an adjunct professor at Columbia Business School traces the rise in shareholder activism from the 1920s to today, providing a first-of-its-kind perspective on what it means to be a public company.

"Entertaining as well as intriguing, Gramm's work is a great read for both students of business and interested general readers." Library Journal.

660.6 Biotechnology

Kurpinski, Kyle

How to defeat your own clone : and other tips for surviving the biotech revolution / Kyle Kurpinski and Terry D. Johnson. Bantam Books Trade Paperbacks, 2010. viii, 180 p. : **660.6**

1. Biotechnology. 2. Clones and cloning. 3. Genetics. 4. Genetic engineering.

ISBN 9780553385786

LC 2009045899

A satirical guide to enduring a near future that will be inundated with bio-enhancements draws on actual and theoretical technologies to counsel readers on such strategies as eliminating unwanted genes and using viruses to make life better.

Piore, Adam

The **body** builders : inside the science of the engineered human / Adam Piore. Ecco Press, 2017. 400 p. **660.6**

1. Biotechnology 2. Medical genetics. 3. Human engineering. 4. Genetic engineering

ISBN 9780062347145

LC bl2017004021

A tour of the current revolution in human augmentation explores how the world's most innovative engineers are helping people repair traumatic injuries while transcending physical and mental limitations.

"Piore writes gracefully, and with deep insight, about complex scientific endeavors that could ease human suffering but are fraught with myriad ethical perils." Publishers Weekly.

661 Chemical engineering -- Technology of industrial chemicals

DK Publishing, Inc,

Essential oils : all-natural remedies and recipes for your mind, body, and home DK Publishing, 2016. 256 p. : **661**

1. Essences and essential oils. 2. Naturopathy.

ISBN 9781465454379

LC bl2016038747

Includes index.

Featuring comprehensive overviews of more than 80 essential oils, such as ylang-ylang, cedarwood and cinnamon, this introductory guide provides detailed information on blending, storing and applying these oils for home and beauty uses as well as for relieving common ailments.

663 Beverage technology

The **Brew** Your Own big book of homebrewing : all-grain and extract brewing, kegging, 50+ craft beer recipes, tips and tricks from the pros / editors of Brew Your Own. Voyageur Press, 2017. 240 p. **663**

1. Brewing 2. Recipes 3. Amateurs' manuals.

ISBN 0760350469

LC 2016033863

"Homebrew guides, recipes, troubleshooting, and tips from Brew Your Own magazine are brought together in one book"-- Provided by publisher.

Bryson, Lew

Tasting whiskey : an insiders guide to the unique pleasures of the world's finest spirits / Lew Bryson. Storey Publishing, 2014 255 p. ; **663**

1. Whiskey.

ISBN 9781612123011

LC 2014023260

Includes index.

This full-color book on all things whiskey offers whiskey aficionados and fans detailed information on the history, flavors, and more of this celebrated spirit.

Cioletti, Jeff

Sakepedia : a non-traditional guide to Japan's traditional beverage / Jeff Cioletti. Turner Publishing, 2019 201 p. ; **663**

1. Rice wines

ISBN 9781683367741

LC 2018008896

Booze journalist, expert and International Kikisake-shi--that's a fancy term for "sake sommelier"--Jeff Cioletti is passionate about Japan's classic national beverage, but he's tired of it being so misunderstood. Sake has been called "exotic," "mysterious," and even, at times, "intimidating." But Jeff's here to tell you that it's actually none of those things and he wants you to join him on his flavorful, unpretentious and demystifying journey across thousands of miles, centuries of tradition and hundreds of glasses of sake. Anyone who's enjoyed a good beer, wine or spirit from time to time and is looking for a new adventure is invited to come along.-- Provided by publisher.

Hoalst-Pullen, Nancy

National Geographic atlas of beer : a globe-trotting journey through the world of beer / Nancy Hoalst-Pullen & Mark W. Patterson ; foreword & tasting tips by Garrett Oliver. National Geographic, 2017 303 p. : **663**

1. Beer -- Guidebooks. 2. Breweries -- Guidebooks.

ISBN 9781426218330

LC 2017011583

Featuring 200 photos, 100 maps, interesting beer destinations and fascinating historical perspectives, an ultimate beer lover's guide to the world explores beer history, geography, trends and tasting on six continents.

Kirk, Mimi, 1938-

The **ultimate** book of modern juicing : more than 200 fresh recipes to cleanse, cure, and keep you healthy / Mimi Kirk ; photographs by Mike Mendell. Countryman Press, 2015 312 p. : **663**

1. Fruit juices. 2. Vegetable juices. 3. Cookbooks

ISBN 9781581572605

LC bl2014054804

Includes index.

A guide to juicing offers 200 recipes for turning fruits and vegetables into delicious, satisfying drinks that will promote health and vitality, and provides advice on how to get the most from these nutritious concoctions.

Kolpan, Steven

WineWise : your complete guide to understanding, selecting, and enjoying wine / Steven Kolpan, Brian H. Smith, and Michael A. Weiss, The Culinary Institute of America. Houghton Mifflin Harcourt, 2014. 376 p. : **663**

1. Wine and wine making 2. Wine tasting

ISBN 9780544334625

LC 2014016316

A comprehensive guide to wine covers such topics as buying and storing wine, understanding labels, grape varieties, flavor profiles, and how to taste wine, with advice on pairing wine with food, a bargain wines list, and opinions on wine gadgets.

"Brevity is the soul of keeping a reader's attention, and a lot of ground is covered here by breaking out the material into hundreds of short entries grouped across 17 chapters. Back-of-book gems include best practices for at-home wine tastings, a list of value wines, and full permission to enjoy wine from a box." Publishers Weekly.

Mitenbuler, Reid

Bourbon empire : the past and future of America's whiskey / Reid Mitenbuler. Viking Adult, 2015. 336 p. **663**

1. Bourbon whiskey -- United States. 2. Alcohol 3. Whiskey 4. Whiskey industry and trade.

ISBN 9780670016839

LC 2015001100

Unraveling the many myths and misconceptions surrounding America's most iconic spirit, Mitenbuler traces a history that spans frontier rebellion, Gilded Age corruption, and the magic of Madison Avenue.

"An illuminating, well-paced narrative that will interest students and imbibers of the wee drap, American-style." Kirkus.

Risen, Clay

Single malt : a guide to the whiskies of Scotland / Clay Risen. Quercus, 2018. 316 p. : **663**

1. Whiskey. 2. Whiskey -- Scotland.

ISBN 9781681441078

LC 2018941147

"Includes profiles, ratings, & tasting notes for more than 330 expressions"--Cover.

"Similar in tone and approach to his 2013 American Whiskey, Bourbon & Rye, New York Times deputy op-ed editor Risen covers everything in this entertaining and immersive guide to one of the world's favorite liquors. The volume is organized alphabetically, with Risen offering brief but specific tasting notes for more than 330 single malt whiskies (blends aren't covered) , along with profiles of distilleries, price ranges, and ratings." Publishers Weekly.

Rogers, Adam, 1970-

★**Proof** : the science of booze / Adam Rogers. Houghton Mifflin Harcourt, 2014. 256 p. **663**

1. Liquors. 2. Alcoholic beverages. 3. Distillation. 4. Beverage industry and trade

ISBN 9780547897967

LC 2013045770

Presents a look at the science of alcohol production and consumption, from the principles behind the fermentation, distillation, and aging of alcoholic beverages, to the psychology and neurobiology of what happens after it is consumed.

"The science here can be intimidating to process, but when enjoyed in leisurely sips, Rogerss cheeky and accessible writing style goes down smoothly, capturing the essence of this enigmatic, ancient social lubricant." Publishers Weekly.

White, April

Apples to cider : how to make sweet and hard cider at home / April White with Stephen M. Wood of Farnum Hill Ciders. Quarry Books, 2015. 151 p. **663**

1. Cider.

ISBN 9781592539185

LC 2015000551

With these easy-to-follow instructions for first-time cidermakers and advanced techniques for the more experienced, you'll be on your way to making your own delicious cider at home.

"This book is a fine introduction to the basics of hard cider and will surely pique the interest of home brewers looking to stretch beyond beer and wine." Library Journal

664 Food technology

Danforth, Adam

★**Butchering** poultry, rabbit, lamb, goat, and pork : the comprehensive photographic guide to humane slaughtering and butchering / Adam Danforth, Photograpy by Keller + Keller. Storey Pub., 2014. ix, 446 p. : **664**

1. Animal welfare 2. Cooking (Meat) 3. Game and game-birds, Dressing of 4. Meat animals
ISBN 9781612121826

LC 2013030702

Depicts the entire process of slaughtering and butchering small livestock, including chickens, rabbits, sheep, pigs and goats through detailed, explicit step-by-step photographs and also features information on food safety, freezing, packaging and equipment.

Katz, Sandor Ellix, 1962-

The **art** of fermentation : an in-depth exploration of essential concepts and processes from around the world / Sandor Ellix Katz ; foreword by Michael Pollan. Chelsea Green Pub., c2012. xxiii, 498 p. : **664**

1. Fermentation. 2. Fermented foods.
ISBN 9781603582865

LC 2011052014

"'The Art of Fermentation' is the most comprehensive guide to do-it-yourself home fermentation ever published. Sandor Katz presents the concepts and processes behind fermentation in ways that are simple enough to guide a reader through their first experience making sauerkraut or yogurt, and in-depth enough to provide greater understanding and insight for experienced practitioners. While Katz expertly contextualizes fermentation in terms of biological and cultural evolution, health and nutrition, and even economics, this is primarily a compendium of practical information--how the processes work; parameters for safety; techniques for effective preservation; troubleshooting; and more. With full-color illustrations and extended resources, this book provides essential wisdom for cooks, homesteaders, farmers, gleaners, foragers, and food lovers of any kind who want to develop a deeper understanding and appreciation for arguably the oldest form of food preservation, and part of the roots of culture itself. Readers will find detailed information on fermenting vegetables; sugars into alcohol (meads, wines, and ciders); sour tonic beverages; milk; grains and starchy tubers; beers (and other grain-based alcoholic beverages); beans; seeds; nuts; fish; meat; and eggs, as well as growing mold cultures, using fermentation in agriculture, art, and energy production, and considerations for commercial enterprises. Sandor Katz has introduced what will undoubtedly remain a classic in food literature, and is the first--and only--of its kind".-- Provided by publisher.

"Katz takes fermentation down to the molecular level while keeping it conversational and accessible to the generalist." Library Journal.

Kivirist, Lisa

Homemade for sale : how to set up and market a food business from your home kitchen / Lisa Kivirist & John D. Ivanko. New Society Publishers, 2015 xvii, 220 p. : **664**

1. Food industry and trade -- Management 2. Food industry and trade -- Marketing 3. Home-based businesses -- Management 4. Home-based businesses -- Marketing
ISBN 9780865717862

LC bl2015009549

Includes index.

Provides entrepreneurs with advice on all aspects of launching a home-based food business, covering product development and testing, marketing, structuring a business, managing regulations, and planning for the future.

Lopez-Alt, J. Kenji

The **food** lab / J. Kenji Lopez-Alt. W W Norton & Co, 2015. 958 p. **664**

1. Food science 2. Cooking, American 3. Cooking 4. Cooks
ISBN 9780393081084

LC 2015016358

Collects easy-to-prepare, illustrated recipes for practicing simple, fool-proof techniques, based on the science of cooking, for creating great food, including blanching, defatting stock, emulsions, and knife skills.

"This indispensable kitchen manual, which suggests visualizing heat capacity as a coop full of Red Bull-energized chickens, makes food science accessible." Library Journal.

McLagan, Jennifer

★**Bitter** : a taste of the world's most dangerous flavor, with recipes / Jennifer McLagan ; photography by Aya Brackett. Ten Speed Press, 2014 263 p. : **664**

1. Bitterness (Taste). 2. Cooking. 3. Recipes 4. Cookbooks.
ISBN 9781607745167

LC 2014023824

Collects over one hundred recipes which feature ingredients with a bitter taste.

Mueller, Tom

Extra virginity : the sublime and scandalous world of olive oil / Tom Mueller. W W Norton & Co Inc, 2011. 256 p. **664**

1. Olive oil. 2. Deception. 3. Food industry and trade.
ISBN 9780393070217

LC 2011041459

Expanding on his article in The New Yorker an olive oil expert uncovers corruption in the food industry, from ancient times to the present, and describes the lax rules that permit fake and even toxic foods into the United States.

Redzepi, Rene

★The **Noma** guide to fermentation : foundations of flavor / Renae Redzepi & David Zilber ; photographs by Evan Sung ; illustrations by Paula Troxler. Artisan, 2018 455 p. : **664**

1. Noma (Restaurant : Copenhagen, Denmark). 2. Fermentation -- Biotechnology. 3. Flavor. 4. Fermented foods 5. Recipes
ISBN 9781579657185

LC 2018003633

Includes index.

Describes how the chefs at the Copenhagen restaurant Noma make the fermented flavorings, based on fermentation traditions from throughout the world, that are basic to the foods they serve, and suggests possible uses for fermented foods.

"Practical applications abound, such as DIY lemon verbena kombucha, whiskey vinegar, and shoyu-buttermilk fried chicken (add shoyu to buttermilk for the marinade). Recipes are clearly written and accompanied by more than 500 photos." Publishers Weekly.

Robinson, Jancis

Wine grapes : a complete guide to 1,368 vine varieties, including their origins and flavours / Jancis Robinson, Julia Harding, Jose Vouillamoz. Ecco, c2012. xxxvii, 1242 p., 81 p. of col. plates : **664**

1. Grapes -- Varieties. 2. Recipes 3. Viticulture. 4. Wine and wine

making.
ISBN 0062206362

LC 2012019224

"A complete guide--the first in over a century--to all grape varieties relevant to the wine lover, charting their relationships (with some astounding family trees), where and how they are grown, and, most importantly, what wines made from them taste like!"-- Provided by publisher.

Ronald, Pamela C.
Tomorrow's table : organic farming, genetics, and the future of food / Pamela C. Ronald, Raoul W. Adamchak. Oxford University Press, 2008. xviii, 208 p. : **664**

1. Food -- Biotechnology. 2. Genetically engineered food. 3. Organic farming. 4. Genetic engineering.
ISBN 9780195301755

LC 2007007071

"The format is easy to follow and effective at highlighting...[the authors'] seemingly adverse positions on the subject. By the book's conclusion, their argument is elegantly presented in a logical fashion." Choice.

Shetterly, Caitlin
Modified:GMOsandthethreattoourfood,ourland,ourfuture/Caitlin Shetterly. G.P. Putnam's Sons, 2016 336 p. **664**

1. Biotechnology in agriculture. 2. Genetically engineered food 3. Food crops -- Genetics. 4. Food -- Biotechnology.
ISBN 9780399170676

LC 2016011424

An assessment of the hot-button debate about GMOs by a journalist who became convinced that genetically modified corn was causing family illnesses traces the evolution of ubiquitous modified products and how they are threatening human health.

Winter, Ruth, 1930-
A **consumer's** dictionary of food additives : Descriptions in Plain English of More Than 12,000 Ingredients Both Harmful and Desirable Found in Foods / Ruth Winter. Three Rivers Press, c2009. 595 p. ; **664**

1. Food additives
ISBN 9780307408921

LC 2008040601

Supplies consumers with vital information needed to judge the safety of a wide variety of food additives, updating the reference to encompass the more than twelve thousand ingredients in new food products, and offers detailed explanations of food production technologies, safe storage procedures, and the new label regulations.

Zanini De Vita, Oretta, 1936-
Encyclopedia of pasta / Oretta Zanini De Vita ; translated by Maureen B. Fant ; with a foreword by Carol Field. University of Calif. Press, c2009. xxi, 374 p. : **664**

1. Cooking (Pasta) 2. Pasta products -- Italy 3. Pasta products -- Italy -- History. 4. Recipes
ISBN 0520255224

LC 2009010522

Translated from the Italian.

Provides a complete history of pasta in Italian cooking, including the origins of each pasta shape, preparation techniques, and common pasta myths and misconceptions.

"This book provides a complete history of pasta in Italy, showcasing more than 300 types of pasta: from bucatini and gnocchetti to tortellini and ziti. Each entry is nicely displayed in a box and includes an overview of each pasta type: the primary ingredients, preparation techniques, the different names for each kind of pasta, how it is served, the region where it is found, and the author's remarks. This wonderful resource is destined to become the definitive book on pasta. It succeeds both as a scholarly achievement and as an entertaining and authentic overview of Italian history and geography." Library Journal.

665.8 Chemical engineering -- Other industrial gases

Hoffmann, Peter, 1935-
Tomorrow's energy : hydrogen, fuel cells, and the prospects for a cleaner planet / Peter Hoffmann ; foreword by Senator Byron L. Dorgan. MIT Press, c2012. xii, 367 p. : **665.8**

1. Hydrogen as fuel
ISBN 9780262516952

LC 2011030564

How the use of nonpolluting, zero-emission hydrogen as fuel could be the cornerstone of a new energy economy. --Publisher description.

666 Ceramic and allied technologies

Garfield, Simon
Mauve : how one man invented a color that changed the world / Simon Garfield. W.W. Norton & Co., 2001, c2000. 222 p. : **666**

1. Perkin, William Henry, 1838-1907. 2. Mauve (Color) 3. Dye industry and trade -- Great Britain -- History 4. Synthetic products. 5. Organic chemistry.
ISBN 9780756750251

LC 00069533

Originally published: London : Faber and Faber, 2000.

Relates how English chemist William Perkin's accidental discovery of the color mauve--and a method to mass-produce it--created new interest in the industrial applications of chemistry research.

"The text is understandable by the average layman and is enjoyable reading for the scientist and non-scientist alike." Science Books & Films.

Macfarlane, Alan
Glass : a world history / Alan Macfarlane and Gerry Martin. University of Chicago Press, 2002. xi, 255 p. : **666**

1. Glass -- History.
ISBN 0226500284

LC 2002020493

"The authors make the case for the centrality of glass in the artistic renaissance and scientific revolution that took place in Western Europe from the 14th to 17th centuries. They discuss the origins of glass making and trace its development and usage across centuries and multiple cultures (Europe, the Middle East, China, India, and Japan). Their discussion combines cultural, artistic, and aesthetic viewpoints of glass within these cultures with history and developments in science. The result is a thoroughly readable, carefully argued work, filled with delightful surprises. An excellent example of microhistory...this is required for history of science collections and recommended for large public and academic collections." Library Journal.

667 Cleaning, color, coating, related technologies

Greenfield, Amy Butler, 1968-

A **perfect** red : empire, espionage, and the quest for the color of desire / Amy Butler Greenfield. HarperCollins, 2005. viii, 338 p. : **667**

1. Cochineal -- History. 2. Dyes and dyeing -- Textile fibers -- Europe -- History. 3. Dyes and dyeing -- Mexico -- History. 4. Cochineal insect.
ISBN 0060522755

LC 2004042376

A history of the red dye cochineal cites its role in building the empires of monopoly holders in ancient Mexico and sixteenth-century Spain, tracing the efforts of European pirates, explorers, alchemists, scientists, and spies to discover the dye's origins.

"The author combines the investigative prowess of a detective with the intellectual reasoning of an academician to create an eminently entertaining and educational read." Booklist.

668 Technology of other organic products

Turin, Luca

The **secret** of scent : adventures in perfume and the science of smell / Luca Turin. Harper Perennial, 2007, c2006. ix, 207 p. : **668**

1. Perfumes
ISBN 0061133841

LC bl2008024255

"An Ecco book."

Originally published: London : Faber and Faber, 2006.

A celebrated biophysicist draws on cutting-edge discoveries to document the science of olfaction and its relationship with fragrance, in an account that chronicles the history of organic chemistry from its origins in the nineteenth century through the modern world's perfume industry.

"This volume is a triumph of popular science writing. Readers to whom scents and odorants were not at the top of their reading list will find that this volume propels a narrative they will hardly want to put down." Science Books & Films.

Winter, Ruth, 1930-

A **consumer's** dictionary of cosmetic ingredients : Complete Information About the Harmful and Desirable Ingredients in Cosmetics and Cosmeceuticals / Ruth Winter. Three Rivers Press, c2009. 567 p. ; **668**

1. Cosmetics
ISBN 9780307451118

LC 2010292417

An updated edition of a consumer resource explains how potentially harmful hybrid products that combine pharmaceuticals and cosmetics are not currently regulated by the FDA, in a volume that includes more than 800 new entries.

674 Lumber processing, wood products, cork

Petroski, Henry

The **pencil** : a history of design and circumstance / Henry Petroski. Knopf, 1992, c1990. xi, 434 p. : **674**

1. Pencils -- History. 2. Inventions. 3. Writing materials and instruments -- History.
ISBN 0679734155

LC BL 99734111

Reprint. Originally published: 1990.

Analyzes the common pencil, citing it as an example of engineering excellence, looks at its origins and the history of its production, and provides reasons for its survival into the computer age.

"An incredibly rich and complex history of this entirely unremarkable instrument of communication." School Library Journal.

Walker, Aidan

The **encyclopedia** of wood : a tree-by-tree guide to the world's most versatile resource / general editor, Aidan Walker. Facts on File, c2005. 192 p. : **674**

1. Wood -- Encyclopedias.
ISBN 9780816061815

LC 2004060849

Includes index.

Intended for anyone who works with wood, this oversize reference features a full-page entry for each of some 150 popular woods.

"The Encyclopedia of Wood is a beautifully crafted identification guide for practicing woodworkers and others whose professions depend on wood." Booklist

676 Pulp and paper technology

Basbanes, Nicholas A., 1943-

★**On** paper : the everything of its two-thousand-year history / Nicholas A. Basbanes. Alfred A. Knopf, 2013. 448 p. **676**

1. Papermaking 2. Paper 3. Paper products. 4. Paper industry and trade.
ISBN 9780307266422

LC 2012050267

ALA Notable Book, 2014

Andrew Carnegie Medal for Excellence in Non-Fiction finalist, 2014.

An award-winning investigative journalist presents a sweeping history of paper that traces its invention in China 1,800 years ago through its myriad applications in business, trade and culture to illuminate paper's crucial role in the unfolding of political scandals, the making of laws and more.

"An unhurried book that will be enjoyed not only by bibliophiles, librarians, and archivists but by many readers engaged by the study of the past and present." Library Journal.

Grummer, Arnold E., 1923-

Trash-to-treasure papermaking : Make Your Own Recycled Paper from Newspapers & Magazines, Can & Bottle Labels, Disgarded Gift Wrap, Old Phone Books, Junk Mail, Comic Books, and More / Arnold E. Grummer. Storey Publishing, 2011, ©2011. 207 p. : **676**

1. Handmade paper 2. Papermaking.
ISBN 9781603425476

LC 2010043056

Includes index.

Provides instructions on making paper, offers tips on everything from proper technique to troubleshooting problems with finished paper, and includes directions for dozens of projects.

"Grummer begins with basic papermaking, then progresses to more advanced skills. Ample tips on everything from proper technique to troubleshooting problems with finished paper are included. A gallery of clever projects with directions rounds out this friendly, accessible guide to papermaking." Library Journal.

Hiebert, Helen, 1965-

The **papermaker's** companion : the ultimate guide to making and using handmade paper / Helen Hiebert. Storey Books, c2000. 219 p. : **676**

1. Paper, Handmade

ISBN 9781580172004

LC 99087351

With tips on building your own papermaking equipment, ideas for transforming junk mail into dazzlingly unique notecards, and much more, you'll be inspired to let your creativity shine as you explore the endless possibilities of handcrafted papers.

"Some projects are included, but the emphasis is on processes and techniques. This good, basic manual is suitable for all crafts collections." Library Journal

Kurlansky, Mark

Paper : paging through history / Mark Kurlansky. W W Norton & Co., 2016 416 p. **676**

1. Papermaking 2. Paper industry and trade. 3. Paper 4. Printing -- History.

ISBN 9780393239614

LC 2016007084

The best-selling author of Cod and Salt presents a history of paper and the unexpected ways it shaped a modern world transitioning toward digital technologies, tracing the role of paper and paper-making in education, media, religion, commerce and art.

"Kurlansky profiles key individuals, from inventors to master printers, writers, artists, and revolutionaries, while incisively parsing technological breakthroughs and social conundrums." Booklist.

Monro, Alexander

The **paper** trail : an unexpected history of a revolutionary invention / Alexander Monro. Knopf, 2016. 384 p. **676**

1. Papermaking -- History. 2. Paper -- History. 3. Writing 4. Inventions

ISBN 9780307271662

LC 2015036988

Tracing the cultural, political and religious revolutions set in motion by the invention of paper, a fascinating history of the now globally ubiquitous material?which is populated by holy men and scholars, warriors and poets, war-makers and peacekeepers?takes readers from second-century China to today.

"The result is an engaging, lively, informative examination of a ubiquitous resource and its multimillennia influence on the world." Publishers Weekly.

677 Textiles

Goldsmith, Becky, 1956-

The **ultimate** thread guide : everything you need to know to choose the perfect thread for every project / Becky Goldsmith. C&T Publishing 2019 64 p. : **677**

1. Thread 2. Sewing

ISBN 9781617458705

"In addition to explanations about weight and thickness, Goldsmith provides practical guidance on which needles to use with which thread, whether for sewing by hand or with a machine. Her section dedicated to introducing various manufacturers and their particular offerings, meanwhile, will make for a handy shopping tool." Publishers Weekly

Parkes, Clara

The **knitter's** book of yarn : the ultimate guide to choosing, using, and enjoying yarn / Clara Parkes. Potter Craft, c2007. 255 p. : **677**

1. Knitting. 2. Yarn.

ISBN 9780307352163

LC 2007009363

A definitive guide to yarn explains how to pair a knitting project with the right type of available yarn, discussing the special characteristics and qualities of each category of yarn, the unique effects it creates, and available substitutions, and includes dozens of creative projects by experienced knitting designers.

Robson, Deborah

The **field** guide to fleece : 100 sheep breeds and how to use their fibers / Deborah Robson & Carol Ekarius. Storey Publishing, 2013 231 p. : **677**

1. Wool.

ISBN 9781612121789

LC 2013003107

Provides different breeds of sheep and explains the best way to prepare their fleece for spinning, the natural colors of the fleece and how well it dyes, the best use for the wool, and fleece weights, staple lengths, and fiber diameters.

Schoeser, Mary

Silk / Mary Schoeser ; with a foreword by Julien Macdonald and contributions by Bruno Marcandalli. Yale University Press, 2007. 256 p. : **677**

1. Silk -- History. 2. Textile fabrics -- History.

ISBN 9780300117417

LC 2006937044

"Arranged roughly into chronological periods, the book . details technique, materials, and designs and puts them in historical and cultural context. This is truly a fantastic history of textile arts. The text itself is a delight to read and more comprehensive than in other comparable works." Library Journal.

681.1 Instruments for measuring time, counting and calculating machines and instruments

Marchant, Jo

Decoding the heavens : a 2,000-year-old computer--and the century-long search to discover its secrets / Jo Marchant. Da Capo Press, 2009. 288 p. **681.1**

1. Computers. 2. Technology. 3. Technological innovations. 4. Ancient history. 5. Ancient Greece.

ISBN 030681742X

LC bl2009006460

"The author relates the century-long struggle of competing amateurs and scientists to understand the secrets of a 2000-year-old clock-like mechanism found in 1901 by Greek divers off the coast of Antikythera, a small island near Tunisia. This globe-trotting, era-spanning mystery should absorb armchair scientists of all kinds." Publishers Weekly.

683 Hardware, weapons, household appliances

Baum, Dan

Gun guys : a road trip / Dan Baum. Alfred A. Knopf, 2013. 336 p. **683**

1. Baum, Dan. 2. Gun owners 3. Gun ownership 4. Guns -- Social aspects

ISBN 9780307595416

LC 2012028767

A lifelong NRA supporter presents a raucous tour of gun culture that celebrates its stores, festivals, and colorful enthusiasts while offering insight into the power and appeal of guns in America.

DK publishing, Inc

Firearms : an illustrated history DK Publishing, 2014 320 p. : **683**

1. Firearms -- History. 2. Weapons -- History. 3. Ammunition -- History.

ISBN 9781465416056

LC 2012286690

At head of title: DK Smithsonian.

Includes index.

Two prints inserted in pocket in back cover.

Spanning more than 700 years, this historical guide to the evolution of the gun features virtual tours of the earliest muskets to modern-day military weapons and includes special sections on iconic gun-makers Colt, Smith & Wesson, Maxim and Kalashnikov.

683.4 Small firearms

Gun digest 2020 / edited by Jerry Lee. Gun Digest Books, 2019. 558 p. : **683.4**

1. Guns 2. Guns -- Catalogs. 3. Guns -- Directories.

ISBN 9781946267825

Presents articles on different gun models and accessories, and provides descriptions and prices for the latest domestic and imported guns.

684 Furnishings and home workshops

Abram, Norm

Measure twice, cut once : lessons from a master carpenter / Norm Abram. Little, Brown & Co., c1996. x, 196 p. : **684**

1. Woodworking. 2. Carpentry. 3. Carpenters.

ISBN 0316004944

LC 96007584

The resident master carpenter on PBS's "This Old House" presents an illustrated handbook containing sixty simple lessons in the nuts and bolts of carpentry.

"In this book about woodwork and carpentry the author deals mainly with hand tools. Abram covers items such as levels, chalk lines, and plumb-bobs, detailing his experiences with them and his preferences. Even experienced woodworkers will pick up a tip or two from this book." Library Journal.

Barn the Spoon

Woodcraft : master the art of green woodworking with key techniques and inspiring projects / Barn the Spoon. DK Publishing, 2019. 256 p. : **684**

1. Woodwork. 2. Wood-carving -- Technique. 3. Wood-carving.

ISBN 9781465479785

LC 2019285189

Includes index.

Explores the craft of green woodworking and offers instructions on different green woodworking projects, including a bangle, frame stool, and shaving horse.

"Barn the Spoon--aka Barnaby Carder, a London-based woodworker known for his spoon-carving workshops--uses incredible mastery and a touch of humor to instruct readers in the art of green woodcraft, with smart, calculated lessons that lead up to the from-scratch creation of a captains chair." Booklist.

Christiana, Asa

Build stuff with wood : make awesome projects with basic tools / Asa Christiana ; foreword by Nick Offerman. Taunton Press, 2017 202 p. : **684**

1. Woodworking

ISBN 9781631867118

LC 2017007163

Provides instructions for creating useful items from wood using only a few portable power tools, including an outdoor bench, postmodern coffee table, floating shelves, and hanging lamp.

"This solid, basic primer wonderfully reflects straightforward instruction with some very desirable projects." Library Journal.

Hoadley, R. Bruce

Understanding wood : a craftsman's guide to wood technology / R. Bruce Hoadley. Taunton Press, c2000. 280 p. : **684**

1. Woodworking. 2. Wood.

ISBN 9781561583584

LC 00044322

Instructs readers in the art of cutting, seasoning, machining, joining, and bending wood.

Horwood, Roger

Woodworker's handbook : the beginner's reference to tools, materials, and skills, plus essential projects to make / Roger Horwood. Fox Chapel Publishing, 2019. 168 p. : **684**

1. Woodworking. 2. Handicraft 3. Woodworking -- Equipment and supplies 4. Do-it-yourself work

ISBN 9781497100657

"The complete reference handbook for DIY home woodworking, this is an absolute must-have guide for beginners and even experienced craftsmen. Every tool you'll need is laid out with guidance on safety measures, care instructions, and how and when to use it, from gauges and shaping tools to clamps, drills, and more. Every technique you'll use is described and detailed, from constructing to finishing. You'll know what type of woods to use for certain projects, how they cut, and their durability. After learning the crucial fundamentals of woodworking, you'll complete 5 step-by-step projects that are beautiful and useful items for everyday use, ranging from a dining room table to a bedside cabinet. Concise and practical, and useful even for experienced woodworkers, Woodworker's Handbook will help you practice and improve your skills -- and learn new ones!" -- Provided by publisher.

Kelsey, John, 1946-

Woodworking : techniques & projects for the first-time woodworker / John Kelsey. Fox Chapel Publishing, 2013 111 p.

: **684**

1. Woodworking. 2. Carpentry.
ISBN 9781565238015

LC 2013017981

"Aimed at nine-year-olds through adults, this beautifully arranged title starts logically with wood selection and tool overviews and contains simple skill-building tasks that will develop DIYers' confidence and help them to learn technique. The quality of instruction is high, with large color photos showing each step." Library Journal.

Warner, Pat, 1943-
The **router** book : a complete guide to the router and its accessories / Pat Warner. Taunton Press, c2001. 185 p. : **684**

1. Routers (Tools) 2. Woodwork.
ISBN 1561584231

LC 2001027149

"Warner shows readers how to get the most from their router, covering tools, accessories, and its use. Fixed-base, plunge routers, and laminate trimmers are introduced with excellent evaluations of specific models of each type." Library Journal.

White, Ana
The **handbuilt** home : 34 simple, stylish & budget-friendly woodworking projects for every room / Ana White. Potter Craft, c2012. 1 online resource (192 p.) : **684**

1. Woodworking. 2. Furniture making
ISBN 9780307587329

LC oc2012643252

Includes index.

Demonstrates how to build inexpensive, quality home furnishings from beginner-friendly home accessories and sturdy tables to kids' items and storage solutions, featuring projects that can be made mostly with off-the-shelf materials and basic equipment.

"Generally a nice collection, but beginners will need tool instruction. Pair this with Fox Chapel's Missing Shop Manual series (Table Saw: The Tool Information You Need at Your Fingertips & others). Recommended for public libraries with popular woodworking collections." Library Journal.

★**Woodworking** : the complete step-by-step manual. DK Publishing, 2020. 399 p. : **684**

1. Woodworking 2. Carpentry.
ISBN 9781465491114

"This invaluable reference for anyone looking to explore woodworking as a hobby or profession offers a thorough detailing of each tool's functions and nuances, a multitude of joint and finishing techniques, profiles on the different types of woods, and projects sorted by increasing levels of difficulty." Library Journal

684.1 Furniture

Blair, Barb
Furniture makeovers : simple techniques for transforming furniture with paint, stains, paper, stencils, and more / Barb Blair ; photographs by J. Aaron Greene ; foreword by Holly Becker. Chronicle Books, c2013. 190 p. : **684.1**

1. Furniture finishing. 2. Furniture painting.
ISBN 1452104158

LC bl2013015035

Includes index.

Offers simple techniques to transforming drab furniture into showpieces, including easy-to-follow instructions for spray painting, applying gold leaf, wall papering, stenciling, and dip dyeing.

Furniture makes the room : create special pieces to style a home you love / Barb Blair ; Photographs by Paige French. Chronicle Books, 2016 190 p. : **684.1**

1. Furniture finishing. 2. Furniture painting. 3. Interior decoration -- Themes, motives.
ISBN 1452139997

LC 2015015943

Offers advice and inspiration for creatively altering furniture to function as distinctive design elements, and how to incorporate the pieces into stylish rooms suited to the individual.

Bruno, Isabelle
Reinventing IKEA : 70 DIY projects to transform IKEA essentials / Isabelle Bruno and Christine Baillet. Abrams Image, 2016. 215 p. : **684.1**

1. Ikea (Firm) 2. Furniture making 3. Furniture finishing 4. Home furnishings
ISBN 9781419722677

LC bl2017008167

Cover title.

Includes index.

Provides seventy customization projects that begin with IKEA products, from a cake stand to constructing a kitchen island, each project has a list of materials needed and step-by-step instructions.

Hingley, Brian D.
Furniture repair & restoration / Brian D. Hingley. Creative Homeowner, c2010. 175 p. : **684.1**

1. Furniture -- Repairing 2. Furniture finishing
ISBN 9781580114783

LC bl2010012453

"Green ed."

Includes index.

Presents a guide to repairing antique wooden furniture, and information on the tools, supplies, and equipment needed for each situation.

"With special sections on evaluation and repair of structural issues, this volume features an array of valuable information on furniture repair and refinishing. Geared toward beginners in wood restoration, the book highlights the author's professional experience, which shows through in the advice and thorough directions." Library Journal.

Huey, Glen, 1959-
Shaker furniture projects / Glen D. Huey & the editors of Popular woodworking. Popular Woodworking Books, 2014 190 p. : **684.1**

1. Furniture making 2. Shaker furniture. 3. Woodworking.
ISBN 9781440335310

LC bl2014029225

"Step-by-step plans for 31 traditional projects"--Cover.

Provides instructions for completing thirty-one furniture projects inspired by Shaker designs, including tables, cabinets and chests, seats, clocks, hanging shelves, and a firewood box.

"Many Shaker-style furniture project books exist, but this title rises above with very fine designs and excellent instruction. These are beautiful pieces and will be desirable to aspiring woodworkers with some experience under their belt. A solid purchase and a great addition to any furniture building collection." Library Journal.

Jones, Stephanie

Upstyle your furniture : techniques and creative inspiration to style your home / Stephanie Jones. Barron's, 2015. 160 p. : **684.1**

1. Furniture painting. 2. Furniture finishing.
ISBN 9781438005560

LC bl2015007434

Includes index.

Provides instructions for updating, fixing, and re-finishing furniture.

"Overall, this is a great example of styles that will appeal to a wide range of tastes and abilities. Don't let this be the only furniture project book on the shelf, though--pair it with another that has better step-by-step illustrations, such as Christophe Pourny's The Furniture Bible." Library Journal.

Paolini, Gregory

Arts & crafts furniture projects / Gregory Paolini. The Taunton Press, 2015 170 p. ; **684.1**

1. Furniture making. 2. Woodworking
ISBN 9781600857812

LC 2014046454

Shares nine furniture making projects in the style of the late-nineteenth-century aesthetic movement, each of which builds on previous skills while introducing new ones.

"Highly recommended for strong intermediate to more expert woodworkers who are well equipped to take on these beautiful projects, as there are no basic instructions for tool use or general techniques, though special tips appear throughout." Library Journal.

Pourny, Christophe

★The **furniture** bible / Christophe Pourny with Jen Renzi ; foreword by Martha Stewart ; photographs by James Wade ; illustrations by Christophe Pourny. Artisan, 2014 304 p. : **684.1**

1. Furniture finishing 2. Amateurs' manuals.
ISBN 1579655351

LC 2014004628

A comprehensive guide to restoring, preserving and refinishing furniture draws on the author's experience as the son of a French atelier to outline such step-by-step techniques as ceruse, vernis anglais and water gilding.

"Pourny explains how to assess damage, make repairs, and complete a final finish. A strong section on furniture care and cleaning argues that using the right methods will prolong the life of furniture. This guide will find a wide audience among those who simply want to learn about and appreciate good furniture, as well as those who are more hands-on." Publishers Weekly.

685 Manufacture for specific uses -- Leather and fur goods, and related products

Corral, Rodrigo

Sneakers / Rodrigo Corral, Alex French, Howie Kahn. Razorbill, 2017. 311 p. : **685**

1. Sneakers 2. Sneakers -- Social aspects 3. Shoes in art
ISBN 9780448494333

LC 2017289364

An absolute necessity for design devotees and sneakerheads of all ages! Sneakers is a definitive exploration of the creative energy, innovation, collaboration, and visionary intelligence behind the cultural phenomenon of sneakers, now an 85-billion-dollar-a-year industry.

686 Printing and related activities

Lee, Marshall, 1921-

Bookmaking : editing, design, production / Marshall Lee ; technical consultant Joseph Gannon. Norton, c2004. 494 p. : **686**

1. Books. 2. Book design. 3. Book industries and trade. 4. Editing.
ISBN 9780393730180

LC 2003059672

"A Balance House book."

Updated to reflect changes in the bookmaking process and in publishing practices, covers all processes from preparation of a manuscript to both print and electronic distribution.

Rivers, Charlotte

Little book of book making : timeless techniques and fresh ideas for beautiful handmade books / Charlotte Rivers. Potter Craft, 2014 192 p. : **686**

1. Book design. 2. Book designers. 3. Bookbinding. 4. Artists' books.
ISBN 9780770435141

LC 2013044724

"Making books by hand has never been cooler, with this inspiring guide to 30 top bookmakers working today, plus 21 tutorials for essential techniques to make your own books. Crafters, artists, writers, and book lovers can't resist a beautifully handbound book. Packed with wonderfully eclectic examples, this book explores the intriguing creative possibilities of bookmaking as a modern art form, including a wide range of bindings, materials, and embellishments. Featured techniques include everything from Coptic to concertina binding, as well as experimental page treatments such as sumi-e ink marbling and wheat paste. In addition to page after page of inspiration from leading contemporary binderies, Little Book of Bookmaking includes a practical section of21 easy-to-follow illustrated tutorials".-- Provided by publisher.

686.2 Printing

Garfield, Simon

Just my type : a book about fonts / Simon Garfield. Gotham Books, 2011 356 p. : **686.2**

1. Type and type-founding 2. Printing. 3. Graphic design. 4. Newspaper layout and typography.
ISBN 9781592406524

"First published in Great Britain in 2010 by Profile Books"--Title page verso.

Documents the history of typefaces from the early days of Gutenberg to the modern applications of digital fonts, tracing the impact of font usage in business and pop culture while explaining what favorite fonts reveal about personality.

Lupton, Ellen

Thinking with type : a critical guide for designers, writers, editors, & students / Ellen Lupton. Princeton Architectural Press, c2010. 224 p. : **686.2**

1. Graphic design (Typography) 2. Type and type-founding
ISBN 9781568989693

LC 2010005389

This revised edition includes forty-eight pages of new content.

Spiekermann, Erik

★**Stop** stealing sheep & find out how type works / Erik

Spiekermann. AdobePress, 2014 213 p. : **686.2**
1. Type and type-founding
ISBN 9780321934284
LC 2014378096

Explains what type is, demonstrates how to select it, and examines its use in printed communication.

"This updated edition uses an easygoing style to get readers from a variety of backgrounds up to speed on good use of type and general typography. The examples, images, and guidance not only are helpful to illustrate concepts, but also are up-to-date with current web and mobile trends and technologies." Choice.

686.3 Bookbinding

Cambras, Josep
Bookbinding : techniques and projects / Josep Cambras ; [translated from the Spanish by Michael Brunelle and Beatriz Cortabarria]. Barron's, c2007. 143 p. : Decorative techniques **686.3**
1. Bookbinding.
ISBN 9780764160844
LC bl2008012639

Describes the history, techniques, and processes of bookbinding along with instructions for seventeen bookbinding projects.

"Beginning with a historical overview, continuing to an explanation of tools and materials, Cambras showcases his expertise in chapters devoted to half a dozen techniques and the same quantity of paper-painting methods." Booklist.

Diehn, Gwen, 1943-
Real life journals : designing & using handmade books : Designing & Using Handmade Books / Gwen Diehn. Lark Books, c2010. 180 p. : AARP: Live & Learn **686.3**
1. Bookbinding. 2. Book design. 3. Diary writing
ISBN 9781600594922
LC 2009032647

Includes indexes.

Envelope containing booklet attached to inside of front cover ; envelope containing 1 folded chart attached to inside of back cover.

Shows how to design and create custom-made journals, along with suggestions on how they can enhance personal experiences.

"Chapters on tools, covers, paper choices, and bindings are detailed and fully illustrated, but Diehn...goes well beyond that, making a point to include information on creating a purposeful design, enriching textual content, and binding the words to the visual elements to reflect a bookmaker's interests and personality. [This is] a lovely, helpful volume that will inspire and attract journalers and scrapbookers alike." Booklist.

Ekrem, Erica
Bound : over 20 artful handmade books / Erica Ekrem. Lark, 2015 144 p. : **686.3**
1. Bookbinding 2. Book design
ISBN 9781454708674
LC 2013049059

Includes index.

"Bound offers approximately 25-30 bookbinding projects showcasing beautiful exposed bindings. Classified in chapters entitled Vintage, Nature, and Leather, projects include a mason jar book, a seashell book, and a classic-looking leather-bound photo album, to name a few. Beginners will find plenty of entry-level projects to enjoy, while more experienced book artists will learn new ways to do old binding techniques. The Basics section and each project are illustrated with gorgeous, bright beauty shots and whimsical, but-clear, illustrations. Ms. Ekrem uses her way with words and her talented hand at book arts to take readers on a little stroll into their own imagination (or their memory) with each creation".-- Provided by publisher.

"This fresh look at an old art will be in demand and is highly recommended." Library Journal.

Golden, Alisa J.
Making handmade books : 100+ bindings, structures & forms / Alisa Golden. Lark Crafts, c2010. 256 p. : **686.3**
1. Bookbinding 2. Book design
ISBN 9781600595875
LC 2010001546

Offers instructions on folding, gluing, and sewing handmade books in a variety of shapes and styles.

"This volume updates and combines Golden's previous Creating Handmade Books and Unique Handmade Books to provide an introduction to the fascinating world of artists' books. The specimens highlighted are far from your traditional book--they are works of art that will challenge readers' ideas of what books can be. Though there are plenty of inspiring photographs, there is also ample direction to guide readers interested in creating their own books. Golden also intersperses tidbits of bookmaking history and lore throughout, making this guide not only pleasurable and inspiring to look at but fun to read." Library Journal.

LaPlantz, Shereen, 1947-
Cover to cover : creative techniques for making beautiful books, journals & albums / Shereen LaPlantz. Lark Books, 2015 144 p. : **686.3**
1. Bookbinding.
ISBN 9781454708483
LC bl2015012580

Introduces the basic techniques of bookbinding and provides step-by-step instructions for creating a variety of journals, albums, and books.

687 Manufacture for specific uses -- Clothing and accessories

Smith, Alison (Alison Victoria)
Dressmaking : step by step / Alison Smith. DK, 2015. 224 p. : **687**
1. Dressmaking. 2. Tailoring (Women's). 3. Sewing. 4. Clothing
ISBN 9781465429810
LC 2015300522

Includes index.

Discusses how to make, alter, and customize clothes, includes classic patterns for skirts, dresses, tops, pants, and jackets, with step-by-step instructions for each project and demonstrations of key techniques.

688.7 Recreational equipment

Gathercole, Peter
The **fly-tying** bible : 100 deadly trout and salmon flies in step-by-step photographs / Peter Gathercole. Barron's, 2003. 256 p. : **688.7**
1. Flies, Artificial. 2. Fly tying. 3. Salmon fishing. 4. Trout fishing.
ISBN 0764155504
LC 2002109917

"A Quarto book"--T.p. verso.

Examples vary in complexity, with patterns to fit every skill level from novice to expert fly-tier. Here are dry flies, nymphs and bugs, wet flies, streamers, and hairwings a virtually complete selection of traditional and up-to-date examples of the art. The book's hidden spiral binding keeps its pages opened flat, which makes it ideal for reference at the workbench. -- From publisher description

Gathercole, Peter

Fly tying for beginners : how to tie 50 failsafe flies / Peter Gathercole. Barron's, c2006. 256 p. (spiral binding) : **688.7**

1. Flies, Artificial. 2. Fly fishing. 3. Fly tying.
ISBN 0764158457

LC 2005921781

"A Quarto book."
Includes index.

This profusely illustrated instruction book shows beginners how to craft 50 professional-looking flies for trout and salmon fishing. --From publisher description.

Whitelaw, Ian

The **history** of fly-fishing in fifty flies / Ian Whitelaw ; illustrations by Julie Spyropoulos. Stewart, Tabori & Chang, 2015. 223 p. : **688.7**

1. Flies, Artificial 2. Fly fishing -- History
ISBN 9781617691461

LC bl2015015009

Focuses on fifty flies chosen to represent the evolution of fly fishing, including the green drake, prince nymph, and bionic bug.

690 Construction of buildings

Black & Decker Corporation (Towson, Md.)

The **complete** guide to patios & walkways : money-saving do-it-yourself projects for improving outdoor living space Creative Pub. International, c2010. 255 p. : **690**

1. Patios -- Design and construction -- Amateurs' manuals. 2. Garden walks -- Design and construction -- Amateurs' manuals.
ISBN 9781589234819

LC 2009038316

At heaf of title: Black & Decker.
Includes index.

Each book in the series provides easy-to-follow step-by-step instructions coupled with scores of illustrative color photos to help the reader complete all the relevant projects for a particular area of the home.

The **complete** outdoor builder : from arbors to walkways : 150 DIY projects Creative Pub. International, c2009. 528 p. : **690**

1. Garden structures -- Design and construction -- Amateurs' manuals. 2. Building, Wooden -- Amateurs' manuals. 3. Outbuildings -- Design and construction -- Amateurs' manuals. 4. Woodwork -- Amateurs' manuals.
ISBN 9781589234833

LC 2009028983

More than 150 projects and hundreds of instructional photographs combine with informative tips, tricks and inspiration for at comprehensive patio and walkway book.

Brain, Marshall

The **engineering** book ; from the catapult to the curiosity rover: 250 miletones in the history of engineering / Marshall Brain. Sterling, 2015 527 p. : **690**

1. Engineering -- History 2. Technological innovations -- History 3. Technology and civilization -- History
ISBN 9781454908098

LC bl2015018008

Provides a detailed look at two hundred and fifty milestones in aerospace, architecture, chemistry, computer engineering, and more, from ancient history to the present, including the cotton gin, radar, space satellite, and genetic engineering.

"Despite some problems, this book is a solid introduction to its topic and can serve to generate interest in the applied sciences and engineering. For report use, however, it lacks the depth that high-school students and older readers would expect, thus it's recommended for middle schoolers only." Library Journal.

Cory, Steve

Ultimate guide : porches : building techniques for adding a new porch to your home / Steve Cory. Creative Homeowner, c2011. 191 p. : Creative Homeowner Ultimate Guide to... **690**

1. Porches -- Design and construction -- Amateurs' manuals. 2. Sunspaces -- Design and construction -- Amateurs' manuals.
ISBN 9781580114912

LC bl2011035873

At head of title: Creative homeowner.
Includes index.

Describes the process of building a porch, covering such topics as design features, tools, materials, roofs, and elaborate porch styles.

"In this manual, the author shares numerous, clear illustrations and detailed construction information and techniques. His confident, expert instruction..is apparent in the projects presented here. A solid addition to any home improvement collection." Library Journal.

Diedricksen, Derek

Micro shelters : 59 creative cabins, tiny houses, tree houses, and other small structures / Derek "Deek" Diedricksen. Storey Publishing, 2015 255 p. : **690**

1. Outbuildings. 2. Small houses -- United States -- Designs and plans. 3. Architecture, Domestic -- United States -- Designs and plans.
ISBN 9781612123530

LC 2015009864

Profiles some of the most creative and clever microshelters in the country and includes tips on scavenging materials, ideas from microshelter designers, and building plans for cabins, treehouses, and other small structures.

"A handy source for tiny-house enthusiasts. Pair this with Ryan Mitchell's Tiny House Living or Jay Shafer's The Tumbleweed DIY Book of Backyard Sheds & Tiny Houses." Library Journal.

Johnston, Amy

What your contractor can't tell you : the essential guide to building and renovating / Amy Johnston. Shube Pub., c2008. xvi, 208 p. : **690**

1. Dwellings -- Remodeling
ISBN 9780979983801

LC bl2011022583

Originally published: What the "experts" may not tell you about building or renovating your home. New York : Warner Books, 2004.

A comprehensive guide to getting the best results while building or renovating a home operates on the belief that homeowners can't know what goes into a plan unless someone tells them, which is based on the premise ... if homeowners knew even 10% of what the professionals know, they could avoid 90% of the problems.

Levy, Matthys
Why buildings fall down : how structures fail / Matthys Levy and Mario Salvadori ; illustrations by Kevin Woest. W.W. Norton, 1994, c1992. 334 p. : **690**
1. Building failures. 2. Structural failures. 3. Architectural design.
ISBN 039331152X
LC BL 99761591
Reprint. Originally published: 1992.
Includes index.
Takes readers on a journey through the history of architectural and structural disasters, from the Parthenon to the Tower of Pisa to the Tacoma Narrows Bridge
"Two structural engineers examine puzzling structural failures and collapses and the destruction of ancient and modern buildings, bridges, dams, and other constructions. Plenty of illustrations accent the lively text." Booklist.

Stiles, Jeanie, 1944-
Backyard building : treehouses, sheds, arbors, gates and other garden projects / Jeanie & David Stiles. The Countryman Press, 2014 253 p. : **690**
1. Outbuildings -- Design and construction 2. Sheds -- Design and construction 3. Garden structrues -- Design and construction
ISBN 9781581572384
LC bl2014022893
Features instructions on how to build backyard building projects, including a deck with benches, three-legged tree house, and garden shed.

Thorstensen, Ole
Making things right : the simple philosophy of a working life / Ole Thorstensen ; translated from the Norwegian by Sean Kinsella. Penguinbooks, an imprint of Penguin Random House, 2018, c2015. 240 p. **690**
1. Thorstensen, Ole Philosophy 2. Houses -- Remodeling 3. Carpenters 4. Building 5. Work ethic
ISBN 9780143130949
LC 2017058279
Originally published in 2015 as En snekkers dagbok by Pelikanen Forlag.
A carpenter and contractor, in this ode to manual labor, reflects on the philosophical aspects of life and work while renovating a loft, writing passionately about his profession and of the joy of seeing a vision for a space take shape.

Toht, David
★**Stanley** decks : a homeowner's guide / David Toht. The Taunton Press, Inc., 2017. 234 p. ; **690**
1. Decks (Architecture, Domestic) -- Design and construction
ISBN 9781631864506
LC 2016037011
Includes index.
Offers step-by-step guidance on how to build a deck, including choosing materials, installing footings and ledgers, framing, and building stairs and railings.

694 Wood construction

Purdy, Strother
Doormaking : materials, techniques, and projects for building your first door / Strother Purdy. Linden Publishing, 2017 viii, 144 p. : **694**
1. Wooden doors. 2. Doors.
ISBN 9781610352918
LC 2017001604
Includes index.
"Readers should look elsewhere for tool instruction, however, and more attention to modifications for accessibility would have been useful. That said, this book has few competitors, with instruction that is sufficient for an intermediate woodworker." Library Journal

Thallon, Rob
★**Graphic** guide to frame construction / Rob Thallon. The Taunton Press, 2016 xi, 243 p. : **694**
1. Wooden-frame buildings -- Design and construction 2. Wooden-frame buildings -- Drawings 3. Framing (Building) 4. House framing
ISBN 9781631863721
LC 2016008479
"Rather than step-by-step instruction, this is instead a visual encyclopedia of how elements of proper framing should look. With simple line drawings depicting surface and exposed view, builders can easily check for proper technique." Library Journal

695 Roof covering

Creative Publishing International
The **complete** guide to roofing & siding Cool Springs Press, 2013 255 p. : **695**
1. Roofing -- Handbooks, manuals, etc. 2. Roofing -- Installation -- Handbooks, manuals, etc. 3. Roofs -- Maintenance and repair -- Handbooks, manuals, etc. 4. Siding (Building materials) -- Handbooks, manuals, etc.
ISBN 9781589237179
LC 2011052377
Rev. ed. of: Complete guide to roofing, siding & trim / created by: the editors of Creative Publishing International, Inc., in cooperation with Black & Decker. 2008.
Includes index.
"This updated 3rd edition of Black & Decker's Complete Guide to Roofing & Siding provides detailed and updated information on modern materials and techniques for evaluating, installing, and maintaining a wide variety of roofing and siding materials".--Provided by publisher.

Creative Publishing International
The **complete** guide to roofing, siding & trim / created by: the editors of Creative Publishing International, Inc., in cooperation with Black & Decker. Creative Pub. International, c2008. 271 p. : **695**
1. Roofing -- Handbooks, manuals, etc. 2. Roofing -- Installation -- Handbooks, manuals, etc. 3. Roofs -- Maintenance and repair -- Handbooks, manuals, etc. 4. Siding (Building materials) -- Handbooks, manuals, etc.
ISBN 9781589234185
LC 2008026823
At head of title: Black & Decker.
Rev. ed. of: The complete guide to roofing & siding. 2004

"Provides all the information homeowners need in order to maintain, repair, and install all types of roofing, siding and trim".--Provided by publisher.

696 Utilities

Black & Decker Corporation (Towson, Md.)
The **complete** guide to plumbing : faucets & fixtures, PEX, tubs & toilets, water heaters, troubleshooting & repair, much more. / Black & Decker Corporation (COR), Creative Publishing International (COR). Creative Pub. International, c2012. 335 p. : **696**

1. Plumbing -- Amateurs' manuals. 2. Dwellings -- Remodeling -- Amateurs' manuals.
ISBN 9781589237001

LC 2011052378

At head of title: Black & Decker.
Includes index.

A latest edition of a best-selling guide to plumbing home repair shares illustrated, comprehensive directions on a range of topics from fixing faucets to installing basement drain lines and incorporates into the latest volume instructions for winterizing a house and installing an on-demand water heater.

Black & Decker Corporation (Towson, Md.)
The **complete** guide to plumbing : modern materials and current codes all new guide to working with gas pipe Creative Pub. International, c2008. 334 p. : **696**

1. Plumbing -- Amateurs' manuals. 2. Dwellings -- Remodeling -- Amateurs' manuals.
ISBN 9781589233782

LC 2008008636

Includes index.
At head of title: Black & Decker.

Provides step-by-step instructions for planning and carrying out home plumbing projects, including installing new plumbing, replacing old equipment, and repairing leaks, clogs, and other problems in existing fixtures, with new sections on how to work safely with gas hookups, outdoor plumbing projects, and updated information on the most recent Universal Plumbing Code.

Henkenius, Merle, 1950-
Ultimate guide to plumbing : complete projects for the home / Merle Henkenius. Creative Homeowner, c2006. 287 p. : **696**

1. Dwellings -- Maintenance and repair 2. Plumbing 3. Amateurs' manuals.
ISBN 1580113117

LC bl2007012672

At head of title: Creative Homeowner.
Includes index.

Provides step-by-step instructions for planning and carrying out home plumbing projects, from replacing a washer in a leaky faucet to cutting and joining cast-iron vent pipes.

697 Heating, ventilating, air-conditioning engineering

Ewing, Rex A.
Got sun? go solar : harness nature's free energy to heat and power your grid-tied home / Rex A. Ewing and Doug Pratt. PixyJack Press, c2009. vi, 191 p. : **697**

1. Photovoltaic power systems 2. Solar energy 3. Wind power 4. Wind turbines
ISBN 9780977372461

LC 2009019053

Includes indexes.

Examines renewable energy options for grid-tied homeowners, including solar- and wind-generated electricity, solar water heating, passive solar, and geothermal heating / cooling. System configurations and equipment, average costs, financial incentives, and installation considerations are also covered.--Provided by publisher.

Thurkettle, Vincent, 1954 or 1955-
The **wood** fire handbook : the complete guide to a perfect fire / Vincent Thurkettle. Mitchell Beazley, 2012. 224 p. : **697**

1. Firemaking 2. Fuelwood
ISBN 9781845336707

LC bl2016003280

Includes index.

Presents a guide to preparing a wood fire, covering everything from woodcutting, buying firewood, and seasoning logs to tending the fire and cooking over an open flame.

698 Detail finishing

Jenkins, Alison
300 tips for painting & decorating : tips, techniques & trade secrets / Alison Jenkins. Firefly Books, 2014. 176 p. : **698**

1. Interior decoration. 2. Interior painting.
ISBN 1770854525

LC bl2014051241

Includes index.

Provides information on decorating house interiors with paint, wallpaper, and tile, including surface preparation, application of materials, estimating quantities, using tools, and cleaning up, with fix-it solutions for common problems.

"All of the tips are illustrated, if not with photographs and drawings, then with graphic design. What counts most are the author's know-how sections. Great advice made accessible." Booklist.

Santos, Brian
Painting and wallpapering secrets from Brian Santos, the Wall Wizard / Brian Santos. Wiley, c2011. 240 p. : **698**

1. House painting 2. Paperhanging 3. Amateurs' manuals.
ISBN 0470593601

LC 2010028548

Includes index.

Drawing on the best tips from The Wall Wizard's previous books on painting, faux finishes and wallcoverings, this guide provides tricks for changing the appearance of a room quickly and effectively and provides green alternatives to environmentally harmful products.

"This guide contains useful information for wall treatments. The practical and reassuring advice includes important directions on what not to do. This is nitty-gritty do-it-yourself, with outstanding prep instruction, tool selection, well-thought-out tips and tricks, and technique photos. While inspirational wall-treatment photo books abound...this is the guide you'll need to achieve those looks." Library Journal.

700 The arts

Cumming, Robert, 1945-

Art : a visual history / Robert Cumming. DK Publishing, 2015 416 p. : **700**

1. Art
ISBN 9781465436610

LC 2015473824

Includes index.

A chronological book features information on the history of more than 650 artists, as well as details on the major schools and movements of the art world, from Ancient Greece to Pop Art, as well as an extended, detailed focus on 22 masterpieces.

"With its solid, accessible information and hundreds of excellent, full-color reproductions, this is ideal for high school or college students as well as any art lover or museum goer." Library Journal.

Fox, Dan (Daniel Luke), 1976-

Pretentiousness : why it matters / Dan Fox. Coffee House Press, 2016. 140 p. **700**

1. Performance. 2. Authenticity (Philosophy). 3. Creation (Literary, artistic, etc.). 4. Creativity.
ISBN 9781566894289

LC 2015033491

"Pretentiousness is for anyone who has braved being different, whether that's making a stand against artistic consensus or running the gauntlet of the last bus home dressed differently from everyone else. It's an essential ingredient in pop music and high art. Why do we choose accusations of elitism over open-mindedness? What do our anxieties about "pretending" say about us? Co-editor of Frieze, Europe's foremost magazine of contemporary art and culture, Dan Fox has authored over two hundred essays, interviews, and reviews, contributed to numerous catalogues and publications produced by major international art galleries and institutions".-- Provided by publisher.

"His book stands as a convincing philosophical investigation into a wide-ranging concept that governs much of the way people behave." Publishers Weekly.

Impelluso, Lucia

Gods and heroes in art / Lucia Impelluso ; edited by Stefano Zuffi ; translated by Thomas Michael Hartmann. J. Paul Getty Museum, c2002. 383 p. : **700**

1. Mythology, Classical, in art -- Dictionaries -- Italian 2. Mythology, Classical -- Dictionaries -- Italian 3. Dictionaries
ISBN 9780892367023

LC 2002013422

"[T]he focus of Gods and Heroes in Art as a practical, well-illustrated handbook for the museum audience is successful and welcome." Library Journal

Lindquist, Sherry C. M., 1964-

Medieval monsters : terrors, aliens, wonders / Sherry C. M. Lindquist, Asa Simon Mittman ; with a preface by China Mieville. The Morgan Library & Museum in association with D Giles Limited, 2018. 175 p. : **700**

1. Monsters in art -- Exhibitions. 2. Curiosities and wonders in art -- Exhibitions. 3. Illumination of books and manuscripts, Medieval -- Themes, motives -- Exhibitions. 4. Illumination of books and manuscripts, Renaissance -- Themes, motives -- Exhibitions.
ISBN 9781911282181

LC 2017046081

"Published to accompany an exhibition at the Morgan Library & Museum, 8 June to 23 September 2018."

Taps into our abiding fascination with monsters and monstrosities since the Middle Ages.

Murray, Albert

The **blue** devils of Nada : a contemporary American approach to aesthetic statement / Albert Murray. Vintage Books, 1997, c1996 viii, 238 p. ; **700**

1. Afro-American artists -- Psychology 2. Afro-American arts 3. Blues (Music) -- Influence
ISBN 9780679758594

LC BL 99789505

Includes index.

Originally published: New York : Pantheon Books, c1996.

A collection of essays on the blues and its impact on American culture includes such titles as "The writer as artist," "Duke Ellington vamping till ready," and "Comping for Count Basie".

"In these essays Murray presents Louis Armstrong, Count Basie, Duke Ellington, painter Romare Bearden and Ernest Hemingway as embodying, in their work and their lives, a peculiarly American strain of existential improvisation and epic storytelling. His theme, variously elaborated, is the effort of the engaged artist to document and give shape to the rootlessness and chaos underlying contemporary life in general--and African American life, in particular--in a way that transcends 'agit-prop journalism'." Publishers Weekly.

Ross, Clifford, 1952-

The **world** of Edward Gorey / Clifford Ross and Karen Wilkin. H. N. Abrams, 2002, c1996. 190 p. : **700**

1. Gorey, Edward, 1925- Criticism and interpretation.
ISBN 9780810990838

LC BL2002012846

Explores Gorey's roles as artist, illustrator, writer, and theater designer using criticism of his work and an interview with the artist.

Updike, John

Always looking : essays on art / John Updike ; edited by Christopher Carduff. Alfred A. Knopf, 2012. xiii, 204 p. : **700**

1. Art, American. 2. Art criticism, American -- History -- 20th century. 3. Art appreciation 4. Artists -- Psychology. 5. United States -- Social life and customs -- 20th century. 6. Essays.
ISBN 9780307957306

LC 2012005986

Includes index.

A posthumous anthology of the author's art writings includes his 2008 lecture "The Clarity of Things" as well as fourteen essays on Western art and the characterization of American art.

700.1 Philosophy and theory of the arts

James, Jamie, 1951-

The **glamour** of strangeness : artists and the last age of the exotic / Jamie James. Farrar, Straus & Giroux, 2016 xii, 364 p. **700.1**

1. Artists 2. Expatriates 3. Immigrants 4. Art history
ISBN 9780374163358

"Abundant primary sources inform James' sharply drawn, sympathetic portraits." Kirkus.

700.71 Arts--education

Kohl, Herbert, 1937-
The **muses** go to school : inspiring stories about the importance of arts in education / edited by Herbert Kohl and Thomas Oppenheim. New Press, 2012. 200 p. **700.71**

1. Arts -- Study and teaching. 2. Education -- Aims and objectives. 3. Influence (Psychology) 4. Artists. 5. Essays.
ISBN 9781595585394

LC 2011042803

Autobiographical pieces by artists and performers are paired with illuminating essays by educators to produce a powerful case for putting the arts at the center of primary and secondary school curricula.

"This superbly articulate assemblage of intensely personal, interdisciplinary voices is critically important, as arts education remains under siege." Booklist.

700.74 Arts--museums

Shister, Neil
Radical ritual : how burning man changed the world / Neil Shister. Counterpoint, 2019. 336 p. **700.74**

1. Shister, Neil. 2. Harvey, Larry, 1948-2018 3. Burning Man (Festival). 4. Festivals 5. Performance art 6. Sociocultural anthropology 7. Avant-garde (Aesthetics) 8. Nevada
ISBN 9781640092198

LC 2018051326

Includes index.

A journalist and festival participant explains why Burning Man is a historically significant event and describes the gathering's contributions to avant-garde postmodernism and new social paradigms by its fusing together of 1960s humanism with the modern tech of Silicon Valley.

" In this fascinating, immersive exploration of the annual weeklong bohemian festival, journalist Shister begins with the event's grassroots genesis in 1986 as a bonfire in San Francisco first lit by Larry Harvey to assuage a broken heart." Kirkus.

700.89 Arts -- Ethnic and national groups

Otfinoski, Steven
Latinos in the arts / Steven Otfinoski. Facts on File, c2007. x, 277 p. : **700.89**

1. Hispanic American arts -- United States -- 21st century. 2. Hispanic Americans.
ISBN 081606394X

LC 2006016900

Each volume in this invaluable resource contains more than 150 biographical profiles of Latinos who have influenced and continue to impact the Latino community, the United States, and the world in a variety of fields and professions.

700.9 History, geographic treatment, biography of the arts

Gardner, James, 1960-
The **Louvre** : the many lives of the world's most famous museum / James Gardner. Atlantic Monthly Press, 2020. xxi, 394 p. : **700.9**

1. Musee du Louvre -- History. 2. Louvre (Paris, France) -- History. 3. Paris, France -- Buildings, structures, etc.
ISBN 9780802148773

LC 2020010112

Describes the history of the Louvre, which was a clay quarry in the first centuries AD, a fortress in 1191 and a royal residence in the 1300s until finally becoming a place to display national treasures after the French Revolution.

"Recommended for readers interested in the history of France, the history of architecture, and museology. . . . A detailed, clearly marked floor plan helps readers navigate the different wings of this enormous and complicated building from the Louvre's days as a palace under various rulers to those as a museum." Library Journal

Volkov, Solomon
Romanov riches : Russian writers and artists under the tsars / Solomon Volkov ; translated from the Russian by Antonina W. Bouis. Alfred A. Knopf, 2011. xi, 274 p. ; **700.9**

1. Romanov, House of History. 2. Intellectual life -- Russia. 3. Art patronage. 4. Creativity in art. 5. Authors, Russian 6. Russia -- Rulers 7. Russia -- History -- 1613-1917.
ISBN 9780307270634

LC 2010045132

"Translation is from an unpublished manuscript"--T.p. verso.

"Published in ... Canada by Random House of Canada Limited, Toronto"--T.p. verso.

"This is a Borzoi book"--T.p. verso.

Analyzes the Russian royal family's distorted relationship with art throughout three centuries, providing coverage of such topics as how the poet Pushkin shared a power struggle with Alexander I and how Dostoevsky transitioned from a monarchy supporter to the tsarist cause. By the award-winning author of The Magical Chorus.

"Volkov revitalizes our understanding of rebellious poet Pushkin and offers fresh insights into Tchaikovsky, Dostoevsky, and Turgenev. A thrillingly anecdotal and incisive look at the paradigmatic and paradoxical Romanov world of politics, patronage, and the quest for artistic freedom." Booklist.

700.92 Biography

Byatt, A. S. (Antonia Susan), 1936-
Peacock & vine : on William Morris and Mariano Fortuny / A.S. Byatt. Knopf, 2016. 181 p. ; **700.92**

1. Morris, William, 1834-1896 Criticism and interpretation. 2. Fortuny, Mariano, 1871-1949 Criticism and interpretation. 3. BIOGRAPHY & AUTOBIOGRAPHY / Artists, Architects, Photographers.
ISBN 9781101947470

LC 2016008946

A dual portrait of two 19th-century artists describes their respective cultures and inspirations and how, through their revolutionary inventions and textiles, they helped establish an influential art form. By the Booker Prize-winning author of Possession.

Tomkins, Calvin, 1925-
Lives of the artists / Calvin Tomkins. Henry Holt, 2008. 272 p. **700.92**

1. Artists -- History and criticism 2. Modern art -- 20th century. 3. Art. 4. Painters. 5. Essays.
ISBN 9780805088724

LC 2008013121

"A John Macrae book."

Includes index.

"Tomkins is a ruthless observer. Books that trade on content that originally appeared in the New Yorker have become a small industry, but not all are as intimate as this one." Publishers Weekly.

701 Philosophy and theory of fine and decorative arts

Shnayerson, Michael

Boom : mad money, mega dealers, and the rise of contemporary art / Michael Shnayerson. PublicAffairs, 2019. 272 p. **701**

1. Art -- Collectors and collecting 2. Modern art 3. Art -- Economic aspects 4. Art -- Marketing

ISBN 9781610398404

LC 2018044679

A Vanity Fair editor discusses the explosive growth of the market for modern art and how it has created the largest unregulated financial market in the world through interviews with renowned art dealers such as Larry Gagosian and David Zwirner.

"Focusing on personalities as much as business development, Shnayerson's writing is conversational and accessible, even for those without deep art knowledge. Fast-paced and eye-opening, this is a wildly entertaining business history." Publishers Weekly.

702 Miscellany of fine and decorative arts

Congdon, Lisa

Art Inc. : the essential guide for building your career as an artist / Lisa Congdon ; edited by Meg Mateo Ilasco ; foreword by Jonathan Fields. Chronicle Books, 2014 184 p. : **702**

1. Artists -- Vocational guidance. 2. Art -- Vocational guidance.

ISBN 9781452128269

LC bl2014034127

Includes index.

Presents advice for aspiring artists on the best ways to manage their career, discussing the use of social media for promotion, signing with a gallery, preparing for exhibitions, and pricing and selling artwork.

"A useful resource for young adults, emerging artists, and creative people of all ages who seek a career change." Library Journal.

702.8 Auxiliary techniques and procedures; apparatus, equipment, materials

Amore, Anthony M.

The **art** of the con : the most notorious fakes, frauds, and forgeries in the art world / Anthony M. Amore. Palgrave Macmillan Trade, 2015. 272 p. **702.8**

1. Art forgeries 2. Art thefts. 3. Swindlers and swindling

ISBN 9781137279873

LC 2014046676

Art scams are today so numerous that the specter of a lawsuit arising from a mistaken attribution has scared a number of experts away from the business of authentication, and with good reason. Art scams are increasingly convincing and involve incredible sums of money. The cons perpetrated by unscrupulous art dealers and their accomplices are proportionately elaborate. The Art of the Con tells the stories of some of history's most notorious yet untold cons. They involve stolen art hidden for decades; elaborate ruses that involve the Nazis and allegedly plundered art; the theft of a conceptual prototype from a well-known artist by his assistant to be used later to create copies; the use of online and television auction sites to scam buyers out of millions; and other confidence scams incredible not only for their boldness but more so because they actually worked. Using interviews and newly released court documents, The Art of the Con will also take the reader into the investigations that led to the capture of the con men, who oftentimes return back to the world of crime.

"Of significant interest to art world aficionados, brokers, collectors, dealers, lawyers, professionals, and general readers, this ambitious, well-presented and well-documented survey belongs in public as well as academic and special libraries." Library Journal.

704 Special topics in fine and decorative arts

Arnett, William

Gee's Bend : the architecture of the quilt / contributions by William Arnett ... [et al.] ; edited by Paul Arnett, Joanne Cubbs, Eugene W. Metcalf. Tinwood Books, 2006. 223 p. : **704**

1. Tinwood Alliance Exhibitions. 2. African American quilts -- Alabama -- Wilcox County -- Exhibitions. 3. African American quiltmakers -- Alabama -- Wilcox County -- Exhibitions. 4. Quilts -- Alabama -- Wilcox County -- History -- Exhibitions. 5. African American women -- Alabama -- Wilcox County -- Exhibitions.

ISBN 9780971910454

LC oc2007062706

Published on the occasion of the exhibition organized by the Museum of Fine Arts, Houston and Tinwood Alliance--T.p. verso.

Since taking the art world by storm in 2002, the formerly downtrodden community of Gee's Bend, Alabama, has revitalized its one-of-a-kind quilt tradition. With nearly 100 never-before-seen modern masterpieces, this book documents the renaissance of a national artistic treasure.

Beckett, Wendy, 1930-2018

Contemporary women artists / Wendy Beckett. Universe Books, 1988. 127 p. : **704**

1. Feminism and art. 2. Women artists 3. Modern art -- 20th century. 4. Women's studies.

ISBN 0876636911

LC 88004413

"This work covers 350 women artists, mostly US painters and sculptors. Entries are helpfully indexed by nationality and medium and include photographers, performance and video artists, ceramicists, filmmakers, textile artists, and weavers from countries in Latin America and western and eastern Europe." Choice.

Farrington, Lisa E.

Creating their own image : the history of African-American women artists / Lisa E. Farrington. Oxford University Press, 2005. 354 p. : **704**

1. African American art. 2. African American women artists

ISBN 019516721X

LC 2003066171

An expansive collection of artists, styles, and periods are woven together into a survey that demonstrates how African-American women artists have created an alternative vision of how women of color can, are, and might be presented in American culture.

"A richly detailed yet fluent work of trailblazing research, fresh interpretations, and cogent argument, Farrington's treatise discusses vital aesthetic as well as social and cultural issues and creates a vibrant context for such seminal artists as Augusta Savage, Faith Ringgold, Barbara Chase-Riboud, Kara Walker, and many more." Booklist.

Heller, Nancy

Women artists : an illustrated history / Nancy G. Heller. Abbeville Press, 2003. 312 p. : **704**

1. Women artists

ISBN 9780789207685

LC 2004269241

"Organized in six chapters by century, the survey provides brief biographical information, some critical analysis and context, and at least one color plate of the work of 125 women artists who lived and worked in Europe or North America. An excellent resource." School Library Journal.

Holladay, Wilhelmina Cole, 1922-

A **museum** of their own : National Museum of Women in the Arts / Wilhelmina Cole Holladay ; text contributions by Philip Kopper. Abbeville Press, c2008. 240 p. : **704**

1. Holladay, Wilhelmina Cole, 1922- 2. National Museum of Women in the Arts -- History. 3. Women artists -- Museums -- Washington (D.C.) 4. Museums. 5. Art history 6. Washington (D.C.)

ISBN 9780789210036

LC 2008021646

Includes index.

"The National Museum of Women in the Arts...opened in 1987. It changed the status of women artists and the life of its founder, who now tells the museum's fascinating success story in an entertainingly anecdotal, inspiring, and beautifully illustrated [book]. This invaluable work of art history is enlivened by Holladay's encounters with artists...and gorgeous reproductions, many of works that will be new to even the most art-expert readers." Booklist.

McWilliams, Mary, 1954-

In harmony : the Norma Jean Calderwood collection of Islamic art / edited by Mary McWilliams ; with essays by Jessica Chloros and Katherine Eremin, Walter B. Denny, Penley Knipe, Oya Pancarolu, David J. Roxburgh, Sunil Sharma, Anthony B. Sigel, Marianna Shreve Simpson. Harvard Art Museum, 2013 303 p. : **704**

1. Calderwood, Norma Jean Art collections Exhibitions 2. Arthur M. Sackler Museum Exhibitions. 3. Islamic art -- Exhibitions 4. Art, Iranian -- Exhibitions 5. Art -- Private collections -- Exhibitions

ISBN 9780300176414

LC 2012030304

In Harmony: The Norma Jean Calderwood Collection of Islamic Art accompanies an exhibition organized by the Harvard Art Museums and shown at the Arthur M. Sackler Museum January 31-June 1, 2013.

Issued in a slipcase.

"Enthusiastically recommended to students of Islamic art and history, art enthusiasts, and collectors. This stunning volume will make an excellent addition to art history collections." Library Journal

704.03 Ethnic and national groups

Berlo, Janet Catherine

★**Native** North American art / Janet Catherine Berlo, University of Rochester, Ruth B. Phillips, Carleton University. Oxford University Press, 2015 xxix, 410 p. : **704.03**

1. Art, Native American. 2. North America -- Antiquities.

ISBN 9780199947546

LC 2014004553

This lively introductory survey of indigenous North American arts from ancient times to the present explores both the shared themes and imagery found across the continent and the distinctive traditions of each region. Focusing on the richness of artwork created in the US and Canada, Native North American Art, Second Edition, discusses 3,000 years of architecture, wood and rock carvings, basketry, dance masks, clothing and more.

Oehler, Sarah Kelly,

★**Charles** White : a retrospective / edited by Sarah Kelly Oehler and Esther Adler ; with essays by Esther Adler, Ilene Susan Fort, Kellie Jones, Sarah Kelly Oehler, Mark Pascale, and Deborah Willis ; and a preface by Kerry James Marshall. The Art Institute of Chicago, 2018. 247 p. : **704.03**

1. White, Charles, 1918-1979 Exhibitions. 2. African Americans in art -- Exhibitions.

ISBN 9780300232981

LC 2017057656

Published in conjunction with an exhibition of the same title organized by the Art Institute of Chicago and the Museum of Modern Art.

"This is a revelatory reassessment of one of the most influential American artists of the 20th century: Charles White (1918-1979) is best known for bold, large-scale paintings and drawings of African Americans, meticulously executed works that depict human relationships and socioeconomic struggles with a remarkable sensitivity. This comprehensive study offers a much-needed reexamination of the artist's career and legacy. With handsome reproductions of White's finest paintings, drawings, and prints, the volume introduces his work to contemporary audiences, reclaims his place in the art-historical narrative, and stresses the continuing relevance of his insistent dedication to producing positive social change through art. Tracing White's career from his emergence in Chicago to his mature practice as an artist, activist, and educator in New York and Los Angeles, leading experts provide insights into White's creative process, his work as a photographer, his political activism and interest in history, the relationship between his art and his teaching, and the importance of feminism in his work. A preface by Kerry James Marshall addresses White's significance as a mentor to an entire generation of practitioners and underlines the importance of this largely overlooked artist".-- Provided by publisher.

Patton, Sharon F.

African-American art / Sharon F. Patton. Oxford University Press, c1998. 319 p. : **704.03**

1. African American art

ISBN 9780192842138

LC 98190459

Discusses African American folk art, decorative art, photography, and fine arts

Stanislaus, Grace C.

Instill & inspire : the John & Vivian Hewitt collection of African-American art / text by Grace C. Stanislaus. University of Pittsburgh Press, 2017 xiv, 152 p. : **704.03**

1. Hewitt, John H., 1924-2000 Art collections Catalogs. 2. Hewitt, Vivian D. Art collections Catalogs. 3. Harvey B. Gantt Center for African-American Arts + Culture Catalogs. 4. African American art

5. Art -- Private collections -- North Carolina -- Charlotte
ISBN 9780822945048

LC 2017014500

"The John and Vivian Hewitt Collection of African-American Art represents works that celebrate the expression and passion of twenty artists, including Romare Bearden, Margaret Burroughs, Jonathan Green, Jacob Lawrence, Elizabeth Catlett, Ann Tanksley, and Henry Ossawa Tanner. This book contains all fifty-eight works from the collection, exquisitely reproduced in full color. Grace C. Stanislaus provides a text on the significance of the collection that is supplemented by interviews with Vivian Hewitt, David Taylor of the Gantt Center, art collectors Harmon and Harriett Kelley, and Nancy Washington".-- Provided by publisher.

White, Mark Andrew

The **James** T. Bialac Native American Art Collection : selected works / Mark Andrew White, General Editor. University of Oklahoma Press in cooperation with the Fred Jones Jr. Museum of Art, 2012. xi, 223 p. : **704.03**

1. Bialac, James T. Art collections Catalogs. 2. Fred Jones Jr. Museum of Art Catalogs. 3. Indian art -- Catalogs. 4. Art -- Private collections -- Oklahoma -- Norman -- Catalogs.
ISBN 9780806143040

LC 2012003005

The Bialac Collection represents indigenous cultures across North America, especially the Pueblos of the Southwest, Navajos, Hopis, and many of the tribes of the Great Plains.

"This is a beautifully rendered book about one of the most important collections of modern Native American art ever assembled by one person--James T. Bialac." Choice.

704.9 Iconography

Beard, Mary, 1955-

★**How** do we look : the body, the divine, and the question of civilization / Mary Beard. W. W. Norton, 2018. 240 p. : **704.9**

1. Art and religion. 2. Civilization, Ancient. 3. Religious art and symbolism. 4. Sculpture. 5. Central America -- Antiquities. 6. Ancient Egypt. 7. Ancient Greece.
ISBN 9781631494406

LC 2018027575

From prehistoric Mexico to modern Istanbul, Mary Beard looks beyond the familiar canon of Western imagery to explore the history of art, religion, and humanity.

"Recommended for fans of this popular author, the Civilizations program, and those looking for brief foray into an alternative form of art appreciation." Library Journal.

Christiansen, Keith

★The **Renaissance** portrait : from Donatello to Bellini / edited by Keith Christiansen and Stefan Weppelmann ; essays by Patricia Rubin ... [et al.]. Metropolitan Museum of Art, 2011. xii, 420 p. : **704.9**

1. Art, Renaissance (Europe) 2. Portrait painting. 3. Art, Italian -- Exhibitions. 4. Exhibition catalogs
ISBN 9781588394255

LC 2011027471

Published in conjunction with an exhibition held at the Bode-Museum, Berlin, Aug. 25-Nov. 20, 2011, and at the Metropolitan Museum of Art, New York, Dec. 21, 2011-Mar. 18, 2012.

"This beautiful, significant, expertly presented, and scholarly publication will be of considerable interest to many museum visitors, students, scholars, professionals, and others. It belongs on shelves everywhere." Library Journal.

Hall, James, 1963-

The **self-portrait** : a cultural history : 120 illustrations, 109 in color / James Hall. Thames & Hudson, 2014 288 p. : **704.9**

1. Art appreciation 2. Artists 3. Self-portraits -- History
ISBN 9780500239100

LC bl2014017378

From the earliest myths of Narcissus to the prolific self-image-making of today, this all-encompassing cultural history of self-portraiture, filled with beautiful illustrations, offers insights into artists' personal, psychological and creative worlds.

Schama, Simon

The **face** of Britain : a history of the nation through its portraits / Simon Schama. Oxford University Press, [2016] xxiv, 602 p. : **704.9**

1. Portraits 2. Art and culture 3. National characteristics 4. Persons 5. Great Britain 6. Great Britain -- History 7. Great Britain -- Social life and customs 8. Great Britain -- Social conditions
ISBN 9780190621872

LC 2016005776

Written to accompany a five-part BBC series and a major exhibition at London's National Portrait Gallery, Schama's compelling analysis and story-telling genius bring a whole nation to life, building a collective picture that at once reflects and transforms Britain's image.

708.1 Arts--North America

Galitz, Kathryn Calley, 1964-

The **Metropolitan** Museum of Art : masterpiece paintings / Kathryn Calley Galitz. Skira Rizzoli Publications, Inc. : 2016. 544 p. : **708.1**

1. Metropolitan Museum of Art (New York, N.Y.) Catalogs. 2. Painting -- Catalogs.
ISBN 9780847846597

LC bl2016055669

Celebrates over five thousand years of painting through reproductions of five hundred masterpieces from the Metropolitan Museum of Art's collection.

Gross, Michael, 1952-

Rogues' gallery : the secret history of the moguls and the money that made the Metropolitan Museum / Michael Gross. Broadway Books, 2009. 560 p. **708.1**

1. Metropolitan Museum of Art (New York, N.Y.) 2. Art -- Collectors and collecting -- United States 3. Capitalists and financiers. 4. Collectors and collecting. 5. Art patronage.
ISBN 9780767924887

LC 2008041480

"A deft rendering of the down-and-dirty politics of the art world." Kirkus.

708.19 Arts--United States

J. Paul Getty Museum

The **J.** Paul Getty Museum and its collections : a museum for the new century / John Walsh, Deborah Gribbon. J. Paul

Getty Museum, c1997. 288 p. : **708.19**

1. Getty, J. Paul (Jean Paul), 1892-1976. 2. J. Paul Getty Museum. 3. Art -- Collectors and collecting. 4. Art museums 5. Museums 6. Malibu, California -- Buildings. 7. California -- Social life and customs.

ISBN 0892364769

LC 97012170

Includes index.

Provides a history of the buildings that have housed the Getty Museum collections, overviews the collections themselves, and offers a biography of J. Paul Getty.

"This is a lavish visual compendium of J. Paul Getty's amazing art collection; in addition, the text reveals important background details surrounding Getty's life and his passion for art. Walsh and Gribbon communicate just how the magnate's fortunes were put to the test as planned acquisitions of artwork flourished." Booklist.

708.4 Arts -- France

Pomarede, Vincent

The **Louvre** : all the paintings / preface by Henri Loyrette ; photography by Erich Lessing ; edited and introductions by Vincent Pomarede ; text by Anja Grebe. Black Dog & Leventhal, c2011. xvi, 766 : **708.4**

1. Louvre Museum, Paris, France 2. Painting, European

ISBN 9781579128869

LC bl2011029885

Issued in slipcase.

Includes index.

Collects photographs of all of the 3,022 paintings from the permanent collection of the Louvre currently on display, with introductions to each of the four main museum collections, as well as descriptive and analytical text for over four hundred of the paintings.

709 History, geographic treatment, biography

Bailey, Gauvin A.

Art in time : a world history of styles and movements / Gauvin Alexander Bailey [and twenty four others]. Phaidon Press, 2014. 367 p. : **709.0**

1. Art movements 2. Art -- History

ISBN 9780714867373

LC 2014466680

Includes index.

"Regardless, this is an ambitious attempt to rethink the survey in light of contemporary art's global turn and a valuable addition to any library." Library Journal.

Beckett, Wendy, 1930-2018

Sister Wendy's American collection / Sister Wendy Beckett. Harper Collins Publishers, c2000. 288 p. : **709**

1. Art appreciation. 2. Art history 3. Art criticism. 4. Art -- United States.

ISBN 0060195568

LC 00040953

Includes index.

"The author provides a discussion of works in six of America's renowned art museums. {She} includes a variety of media--paintings, sculpture, decorative arts, armor, and other art objects--and the individual works originate from a dizzying array of time periods and several countries." Library Journal.

Boardman, John

★**Greek** art / John Boardman. Thames & Hudson, 2016. 320 p. : **709**

1. Art, Greek

ISBN 9780500204337

LC 2016933412

"This is a classic in the field made even more readable and useful than before. Highly recommended for all collections." Library Journal.

Dasal, Jennifer, 1980-

Artcurious : stories of the unexpected, slightly odd, and strangely wonderful in art history / Jennifer Dasal. Penguin Books, 2020. 256 p. **709**

1. Art history 2. Art -- Anecdotes. 3. Artists -- Anecdotes. 4. Art and society

ISBN 9780143134596

LC 2020013857

Based on a podcast.

From the host of the ArtCurious podcast, this book looks at the world of art history, revealing some of the strangest, funniest, and most fascinating stories behind the world's great artists and masterpieces. It demonstrates why art history is, and continues to be, a riveting and relevant world to explore.

"Both art aficionados and novices will find something to appreciate in this offbeat and informative outing." Publishers Weekly

Dickerman, Leah, 1964-

★**Dada** : Zurich, Berlin, Hannover, Cologne, New York, Paris / Leah Dickerman ; with essays by Brigid Doherty ... [et al.]. National Gallery of Art in association with D.A.P., c2005. xv, 519 p. : **709**

1. Arts, Modern -- 20th century 2. Dadaism

ISBN 9781933045207

LC 2005017984

Catalog of an exhibition held at the Musee national d'art moderne, Centre Pompidou, Paris, Oct. 5, 2005-Jan. 9, 2006; at the National Gallery of Art, Washington, Feb. 19-May 14, 2006; and at the Museum of Modern Art, New York, June 18-Sept. 11, 2006.

"Seven scholars and curators contribute essays that examine each of the various Dada centers in turn. Each essay examines key locations (e.g., the Cabaret Voltaire), individuals, publications (including Merz magazine), and inventions (such as ready-mades and photomontage.) ... Its comprehensive scholarship and color illustrations of many rarely seen works make this book essential for all art collections." Choice.

Gombrich, E. H. (Ernst Hans), 1909-2001

★The **story** of art / E.H. Gombrich. Prentice-Hall, 1995. 688 p. : **709**

1. Art history 2. Art history -- Chronology.

ISBN 0134401999

LC 96140698

"North American educational ed."--Copr. p.

An illustrated introduction to art appreciation with a survey of the major art periods and styles and descriptions of the work and world of the masters.

Gompertz, Will

What are you looking at? : the surprising, shocking, and sometimes strange story of one hundred years of modern art / Will

Gompertz. E. P. Dutton, 2012. 416 p. **709**

1. Art history 2. Modern art
ISBN 9780525952671

LC 2012027995

A BBC arts editor and former director of London's Tate Gallery presents an irreverent narrative tour of Modern Art that explains its cultural relevance and why it is so compelling, tracing a century's worth of movements, achievements and masterpieces that have reshaped the art world.

Guo li gu gong bo wu yuan

Splendors of Imperial China : treasures from the National Palace Museum, Taipei / Maxwell K. Hearn. Metropolitan Museum of Art ; c1996. 144 p. : **709**

1. Guo li gu gong bo wu yuan Exhibitions. 2. Art, Chinese -- Exhibitions. 3. Art -- Taiwan -- Taipei -- Exhibitions. 4. Exhibition catalogs
ISBN 9780870997662

LC 95046590

"Hearn selected more than 100 works to present here, drawn from an extensive traveling exhibition featuring Neolithic and Bronze Age works, as well as Sung, Ming, and other dynasty masterpieces. This beautifully produced book contains fine quality reproductions that illuminate a splendid collection of rare artwork. The text describes in accessible terms important background information, including cultural climate, historical events, and artistic elements." Booklist.

Hoving, Thomas, 1931-2009

Art for dummies / Thomas Hoving ; foreword by Andrew Wyeth. IDG Books Worldwide, Inc., 1999. xxiv, 382 p., 32 p. of col. plates : **709**

1. Art appreciation
ISBN 9780764551048

LC 99065838

Explains to the average person how to understand, appreciate, and evaluate art, and discusses starting an art collection and where to go to see art.

"In this delightful book, Hoving...leads readers gently through thousands of years of art history. His breathless enthusiasm is avuncular, scholarly, and quite infectious--an attitude that happily precludes condescension. A terrific book for students, travelers, tyros, and old hands alike." Library Journal.

Hughes, Robert, 1938-2012

American visions : the epic history of art in America / Robert Hughes. Alfred A. Knopf, 1997. ix, 635 p. : **709**

1. Art -- Themes. 2. Art, American. 3. Art, American -- History.
ISBN 0679426272

LC 96045111

"Hughes has orchestrated a spectacular integration of facts, observations, and insights in this ambitious, lively, and gloriously illustrated volume." Booklist.

Janson, H. W. (Horst Woldemar), 1913-1982

★**Janson's** history of art: the western tradition / Penelope J.E. Davies ... [et. al]. Prentice Hall, c2011. xxxi, 1152 p. : **709**

1. Art -- History
ISBN 9780205685172

LC 2009022617

Rewritten and reorganized, this new edition weaves together the most recent scholarship, the most current thinking in art history, and the most innovative online supplements, including digital art library.

Johnson, Paul, 1928-

★**Art** : a new history / Paul Johnson. Harper Collins, c2003. x, 777 p. : **709**

1. Art history 2. Artists.
ISBN 9780060530754

LC BL2003015116

Includes index.

A personal view of the history of art follows every period from prehistoric times to today, examining both major movements and lesser-known contributors.

"While [Johnson's] narrative is for the most part a conventional journey through the canon, his headlong pace, quirky views and pungent prose make it anything but dull." Publishers Weekly.

Kampen-O'Riley, Michael

Art beyond the West : the arts of the Islamic world, India and Southeast Asia, China, Japan and Korea, the Pacific, Africa, and the Americas. / Michael Kampen O'Riley. Pearson, 2013. 367 p. : **709**

1. Art -- History 2. Textbooks.
ISBN 9780205887897

LC 2012026414

A major survey of the visual arts that lie outside the Western tradition -- Art Beyond the West, 3e presents the vast range of arts that lie outside of the Western tradition. -- From publisher description

Livingstone, Marco

Pop art : a continuing history / Marco Livingstone. Thames & Hudson, 2000, c1990. 272 p. : **709**

1. Art, Modern -- 20th century -- History 2. Pop art -- History
ISBN 9780500282403

LC bl2006000563

Originally published: New York : H.N. Abrams, 1990.

This comprehensive and critical history of pop art charts its international development, and describes and illustrates the work of over 130 artists, including Andy Warhol, Jasper Johns, Peter Blake, Claes Oldenburg, and Roy Lichtenstein.

"Recommended as the best single historical survey on Pop Art." Library Journal.

Massie, Suzanne

Land of the Firebird : the beauty of old Russia / Suzanne Massie. Simon and Schuster, c1980. 493 p., [32] leaves of plates : **709**

1. Art and culture. 2. Art, Russian. 3. Russia -- Civilization.
ISBN 0671230514

LC 80012860

"The author's intent is to give a sense of the whole, now-vanished culture of old Russia...to describe that beauty which the Russians once knew how to create, what they loved, and admired and how they once lived and rejoiced." New York Times Book Review.

McPhee, John, 1931-

The **ransom** of Russian art / John McPhee. Farrar, Straus and Giroux, 1994. 181 p. : **709**

1. Dodge, Norton Townshend, 1927- Art patronage 2. Samizdat art. 3. Americans in the Soviet Union. 4. Art, Soviet 5. Dissident art 6. Soviet Union.
ISBN 0374246823

LC 94014723

Reveals the clandestine activities of an American professor who retrieved eight thousand works of Soviet art by visiting dissident artists in the Soviet Union

"McPhee's engaging narrative sheds light on this suppressed creative milieu." Publishers Weekly.

Phaidon Press

The **art** book / Lee Beard, Adam Butler, Claire Van Cleave, Diane Fortenberry, Susan Stirling. Phaidon Press, 2012. 592 p. : **709**

1. Artists -- Dictionaries. 2. Art -- History -- Pictorial works. 3. Art -- Themes, motives.

ISBN 9780714864679

LC bl2012033092

Features paintings, sculptures, and other mediums of art from the Middle Ages to the present, each by a different artist, with a brief description of the work and its place in both art history and the creator's career.

Robins, Gay

The **art** of ancient Egypt : Revised Edition / Gay Robins. Harvard University Press, 2008. 271 p. : **709**

1. Art, Ancient -- Egypt 2. Art, Egyptian

ISBN 9780674030657

LC 2008004264

"The first chapter orients the reader in the cultural, technical, and iconographic contexts needed to explore the evolution of the Egyptian artistic tradition in subsequent chapters. Beginning with the predynastic origins (5000 BCE) and concluding in the Ptolemaic Period (304-30 BCE), Robins traces the development of sculpture, painting, funerary and religious art, and architecture with over 300 illustrations, many in color." Library Journal. [review of 1997 edition]

Schama, Simon

The **power** of art / Simon Schama. Ecco Press, 2006. 448 p. **709**

1. Art history 2. Artists. 3. Creativity.

ISBN 9780061176104

A companion to the author's PBS series documents the creation processes of eight master artists including Rembrandt, Van Gogh, and Picasso, in an account that discusses how each featured masterpiece was created under tremendous pressure in response to the artist's troubled time.

"The author presents eight remarkable artists who created their masterworks against a backdrop of personal and professional distress. From politically charged commentaries (David, Picasso, Turner and Rembrandt) to intensely personal visions of the world (van Gogh and Rothko) and the reinvention of the divine (Bernini and Caravaggio), Schama takes these masters' hallowed works off the museum wall and drags them through the mud and muck that went into their creation." Publishers Weekly.

Scott, John F. (John Fredrik), 1936-

Latin American art : ancient to modern / John F. Scott. University Press of Florida, c1999. xxiv, 240 p. : **709**

1. Art, Latin American

ISBN 9780813016450

LC 98046535

Traces the development of Latin American art from 20,000 BCE to modern times, from the southern tip of Argentina to the Rio Grande.

Strickland, Carol

The **annotated** Mona Lisa : a crash course in art history from prehistoric to post-modern / Carol Strickland and John Boswell. Andrews and McMeel, 2018, c1992. 222 p. : **709**

1. Art history 2. Art appreciation. 3. Art -- Study and teaching.

ISBN 9781449482138

LC 2017931253

Includes index.

Presents the history of art from prehistoric times to the present day, describing major artists and movements and detailing the influence of art on society through the ages.

Ward, Gerald W. R.

Chihuly : through the looking glass / Gerald W.R. Ward. MFA Publications ; c2011. 149 p. : **709**

1. Chihuly, Dale, 1941- Exhibitions 2. Glass art -- United States -- History -- 20th century -- Exhibitions 3. Glass art -- United States -- History -- 21st century -- Exhibitions 4. Glass sculpture -- United States -- History -- 20th century -- Exhibitions 5. Glass sculpture -- United States -- History -- 21st century -- Exhibitions

ISBN 9780878467648

LC 2010941797

Catalog of an exhibition held at the Museum of Fine Arts, Boston, Apr. 10-Aug. 7, 2011.

"The book covers a rich set of vibrant work inspired predominantly by natural forms and makes the most of its large format. The documentation is superb, the scope is expansive, and the text is expertly presented." Library Journal.

Visona, Monica Blackmun, 1953-

A **history** of art in Africa / Monica Blackmun Visona ... [et al.] ; introduction by Suzanne Preston Blier ; preface by Rowland Abiodun. Harry N. Abrams, 2001. 544 p. : **709**

1. Art, African -- History. 2. Africa -- History.

ISBN 0810934485

LC 00022796

"Treating the subject from an art historical rather than an anthropological perspective, this groundbreaking book is organized geographically to cover the entire continent. Each of the five regional sections focuses on selected major art traditions. Accompanying the text are over 700 photos and scores of maps, plans, drawings, etc." Library Journal. [review of 2000 edition]

709.04 20th century, 1900-1999

Arnason, H. Harvard

★**History** of modern art : painting, sculpture, architecture, photography / H.H. Arnason, Elizabeth C. Mansfield, National Humanities Centre. Pearson, 2013 xvi, 816 p. : **709.04**

1. Art, Modern

ISBN 9780205259472

LC 2012029474

A visual comprehensive overview of the modern art field. --From publisher description.

Barnes, Julian

Keeping an eye open : essays on art / Julian Barnes. Alfred A. Knopf, 2015. 288 p. **709.04**

1. Modern art -- 19th century 2. Art criticism 3. Art -- Technique 4. Modern art -- 20th century. 5. Essays.

ISBN 9781101874783

LC 2015014317

Originally published in Great Britain by Jonathan Cape.

"Barnes knows that one of the immeasurable pleasures of art is its capacity to approach us from unexpected angles and excite our senses of wonder. The same may be said of his scholarly and astute yet accessible and exciting essays." Kirkus.

Cooke, Lynne

Outliers and American Vanguard Art / Lynne Cooke ; with Douglas Crimp, Darby English, Suzanne Hudson, Thomas J. Lax, Jennifer Jane Marshall, Richard Meyer, Jenni Sorkin. The University of Chicago Press, 2018 xv, 396 p. : **709.04**

1. Outsider art -- United States -- Exhibitions. 2. Outsider art -- United States -- Influence -- Exhibitions. 3. Folk art -- United States -- Exhibitions. 4. Folk art -- United States -- Influence -- Exhibitions. 5. Exhibition catalogs

ISBN 9780226522272

LC 2017035749

"The exhibition is organized by the National Gallery of Art, Washington"--Colophon.

Some 250 works explore three distinct periods in American history when mainstream and outlier artists intersected, ushering in new paradigms based on inclusion, integration, and assimilation. The exhibition aligns work by such diverse artists as Charles Sheeler, Christina Ramberg, and Matt Mullican with both historic folk art and works by self-taught artists ranging from Horace Pippin to Janet Sobel and Joseph Yoakum. It also examines a recent influx of radically expressive work made on the margins that redefined the boundaries of the mainstream art world, while challenging the very categories of "outsider" and "self-taught." Historicizing the shifting identity and role of this distinctly American version of modernism's "other," the exhibition probes assumptions about creativity, artistic practice, and the role of the artist in contemporary culture. The exhibition is curated by Lynne Cooke, senior curator, special projects in modern art, National Gallery of Art.--Provided by publisher.

"Accessible for most readers without extensive art history backgrounds, and for those looking to expand their understanding of American art and artists creating from the margins." Library Journal.

Morris, Desmond

The **lives** of the surrealists / Desmond Morris. Thames & Hudson, 2018. 272 p. **709.04**

1. Surrealism (Art) 2. Modern arts -- 20th century. 3. Arts -- History -- 20th century. 4. Collective biographies

ISBN 9780500021361

LC bl2018080005

Looks at the lives of surrealist artists, exploring their life histories, idiosyncrasies, personalities, characters, and love lives, with photographs of the artists and reproductions of their work.

Salle, David, 1952-

How to see : looking, talking, and thinking about art / David Salle. W.W. Norton & Company, 2016. viii, 271 p. : **709.04**

1. Modern art -- 20th century. 2. Modern art -- 21st century. 3. Art appreciation. 4. Essays

ISBN 9780393248135

LC 2016025215

Includes index.

The renowned artist whose work is among the permanent collections at the Whitney Museum and the National Gallery describes contemporary art in simple language and explores how an artist gives form to an idea and the difference between inventing and perfecting ideas.

"As he states in his introduction, Salle wants to avoid what he describes as the generalizing language of professional art writing (with its frequent recourse to broad art historical styles and obscure critical theory) and instead analyze art in direct and intimate fashion as befits a practicing artist. Although many may take issue with Salle?s dismissal of art history and theory, his writing is refreshingly engaging and original: conversational in tone, replete with personal anecdotes, and grounded in keen observational analysis." Library Journal.

709.05 Arts--21st century, 2000-2099

Thornton, Sarah

Seven days in the art world / Sarah Thornton. W.W. Norton, 2008. 256 p. **709.05**

1. Art contests 2. Art criticism. 3. Art and culture. 4. Art and society

ISBN 9780393067224

LC 2008035056

"The book is cleverly divided into seven day-in-the-life chapters, each focusing on a different facet of the contemporary art world: an auction (at Christie's New York), an art school crit (at the California Institute of the Arts in Valencia), an art fair (Art Basel), an artist's studio (that of the Japanese star Takashi Murakami), a prize (Britain's prestigious Turner Prize), a magazine (Artforum) and a biennale (Venice). Thornton is a smart and savvy guide with a keen understanding of the subtle power dynamics that animate each of these interconnected milieus." New York Times Book Review.

709.1 Arts--Areas, regions, places in general

Khalili, Nasser D.

Islamic art and culture : a visual history / Nasser D. Khalili. Overlook Press, 2006. 186 p. : **709.1**

1. Art, Islamic -- History 2. Islamic Empire -- History.

ISBN 9781585678396

LC bl2006029795

An oversized visual history of Islamic civilization as reflected in its fine art spans 1,200 years and surveys a range of media, from architecture and painting to silk textiles and calligraphy, in a volume that also demonstrates the relationship between Islamic artists and their western peers.

O'Kane, Bernard

★**Treasures** of Islam : artistic glories of the Muslim world / [Bernard O'Kane]. Duncan Baird, 2007. 224 p. : **709.1**

1. Art, Islamic -- History. 2. Architecture, Islamic -- History. 3. Islamic Empire -- History 4. Middle East -- History

ISBN 1844834832

LC bl2007021891

Presents a portrait of the cultural heritage of Islam looking at its artistic influences and offering examples of paintings, jewelry, sculpture, metalwork, and architecture.

"The wealth of glorious full-color illustrations make this beautifully designed book an excellent introduction to the art of Islam." Publishers Weekly.

709.2 Biography

Aquino, Lucia

Leonardo da Vinci / preface by Mario Pomilio ; [editor (English edition), Julie Di Filippo ; translation, Miriam Hurley]. Rizzoli, 2005. 173 p. : **709.2**

1. Leonardo, da Vinci, 1452-1519 Criticism and interpretation.
ISBN 9780847826773

LC bl2007009384

A discussion of the work of the Italian master includes commentary by famous art historians, a critical essay on the artist's life and art, a timeline, and a list of museums where the featured paintings can be found.

Hook, Philip

Rogues' gallery : the rise (and occasional fall) of art dealers, the hidden players in the history of art / Philip Hook. Experiment, 2017. 298 p. : **709.2**

1. Art dealers. 2. Art -- Collectors and collecting -- History.
ISBN 9781615194162

LC 2017025490

"Originally published in the UK as Rogues' Gallery: A History of Art and Its Dealers by Profile Books Ltd in 2017."

Philip Hook takes the lid off the world of art dealing to reveal the brilliance, cunning, greed, and daring of its practitioners. In a richly anecdotal chronological narrative he describes the rise and occasional fall of the extraordinary men and women who over the centuries have made it their business to sell art to kings, merchants, nobles, entrepreneurs, and museums.

Matisse, Henri, 1869-1954

Henri Matisse : the cut-outs / edited by Karl Buchberg, Nicholas Cullinan, Jodi Hauptman, and Nicholas Serota ; with essays by Karl Buchberg, Nicholas Cullinan, Samantha Friedman, Flavia Frigeri, Markus Gross, Jodi Hauptman, Stephan Lohrengel, and Nicholas Serota. The Museum of Modern Art, 2014 298 p. : **709.2**

1. Matisse, Henri, 1869-1954 Exhibitions. 2. Collage -- France -- 20th century 3. Decoupage -- France -- 20th century 4. Paper art -- France -- 20th century
ISBN 9780870709159

LC bl2015013492

"Published in conjunction with the exhibition Henri Matisse: The Cut-Outs, at The Museum of Modern Art, New York. The exhibition is organized by The Museum of Modern Art, New York, in collaboration with Tate Modern, London"--Title page verso.

Showcases the gouache-painted cut-outs created during the period of Matisse's life when he suffered from restricted physical mobility, while sharing new research on such topics as his methods and environmental ambitions for the works.

"The beautifully produced catalog of this exhibition includes essays that explore Matisses innovative process, brought to life by photographs of the artist with his assistants at work in his studio as well as a generous and representative selection of high-quality color reproductions of significant milestones from a decade of cut-out projects. Essential for art studio, history, and conservation collections." Choice.

709.45 Fine arts -- Italy, San Marino, Vatican City, Malta

Adams, Laurie

★**Italian** Renaissance art / Laurie Schneider Adams. Westview Press, 2013. 436 p. : **709.45**

1. Art, Italian 2. Art, Renaissance -- Italy
ISBN 9780813349022

LC bl2014000066

Presents a survey of Italian Renaissance art, focusing on the principal works of the most important and innovative artists, along with information on women artists, Mannerism, and the late Renaissance period.

Testa, Judith Anne, 1943-

An **art** lover's guide to Florence / Judith Testa. NIU Press, 2012 viii, 269 p. : **709.45**

1. Art, Italian -- Italy -- Florence 2. Art, Renaissance -- Italy -- Florence 3. Florence (Italy) Guidebooks. 4. Guidebooks.
ISBN 9780875806808

LC 2012005427

"Testa achieves her purpose admirably. This unindexed book, with approximately 40 black-and-white images, features an extensive thematic bibliography of sources in English." Choice.

709.51 Fine arts--China

Tregear, Mary

Chinese art / Mary Tregear. Thames and Hudson, 1997. 216 p. : **709.51**

1. Art, Chinese
ISBN 9780500202999

LC 96061015

Traces the history of Chinese painting and sculpture, and describes important movements and themes

Weiwei, Ai

Ai Weiwei : according to what? / [editor, Deborah E. Horowitz]. DelMonico Books-Prestel, 2012 144 p. : **709.51**

1. Ai, Weiwei Exhibitions. 2. Ai, Weiwei Interviews. 3. Installations (Art)
ISBN 9783791352404

LC bl2013035266

"This catalogue is published in conjunction with the exhibition Ai Weiwei: According to What?, organized by the Mori Art Museum, Tokyo, in association with the Hirshhorn Museum and Sculpture Garden, Smithsonian Institution, Washington, D.C."--T.p. verso.

Exhibition held at the Hirshhorn Museum and Sculpture Garden, Washington, D.C., October 7, 2012-February 24, 2013; Indianapolis Museum of Art, Indianapolis, Indiana, April 5-July 28, 2013; Art Gallery of Ontario, Toronto, Ontario, August 31-October 27, 2013; Perez Art Museum Miami, Miami, Florida, November 28, 2013-March 16, 2014; Brooklyn Museum, Brooklyn, New York, April 18-August 10, 2014.

Offers an introduction to Weiwei's work--from photographs and sculpture to documentation of several of his most well-known projects, including his collaboration on the "bird's nest" stadium for the 2008 Beijing Olympics.

709.6 Fine arts--Africa

Giblin, John (Curator),

South Africa : the art of a nation / John Giblin, Chris Spring. The British Museum, 2016. 255 p. : **709.6**

1. Art, South African -- Exhibitions 2. Art, South African -- Antiquities -- Exhibitions 3. Art, Modern -- Exhibitions 4. Apartheid -- South Africa -- Exhibitions 5. South Africa -- History. 6. South Africa -- Antiquities Exhibitions.
ISBN 9780500519066

LC 2016931258

"This publication accompanies the exhibition "South Africa: the art of a nation," at the British Museum from 27 October 2016 - 26 February 2017"--Title page verso.

A unique insight into South Africa's history, from iconic pre-colonial artifacts to the country's vibrant contemporary art scene.

"While other books focus more comprehensively on the traditional indigenous art of the many peoples of the region, the scope of this volume makes it invaluable to readers interested in the subject." Library Journal

709.73 Fine arts--United States

FitzGerald, Michael C.

★**Picasso** and American art / Michael FitzGerald ; with a chronology by Julia May Boddewyn. Whitney Museum of American Art, c2006. 400 p. : **709.73**

1. Picasso, Pablo, 1881-1973 Influence Exhibitions. 2. Art, American -- 20th century 3. Avant-garde (Aesthetics) -- United States -- History -- 20th century

ISBN 9780300114522

LC 2006001402

"The exhibition was organized by Michael FitzGerald, guest curator, in association with Dana Miller, associate curator, Whitney Museum of American Art."

Published on the occasion of an exhibition organized by the Whitney Museum of American Art, New York and held also at the San Francisco Museum of Modern Art and Walker Art Center, Minneapolis.

"A study of Picasso's influence on some of the most significant American artists of the 20th century. Fitzgerald moves chronologically, from the earliest Americans who engaged cubism in the teens (Max Weber, Mardsen Hartley, Man Ray, Stuart Davis), through the modernist investigations of Arshile Gorky, Willem De Kooning and Jackson Pollack, and winds up with Roy Lichtenstien's pop-art and Jasper Johns' postmodern responses to Picasso. Fitzgerald takes great pains to triangulate exhibition specifics with the work and words of each artist to document the precise nature and extent of the influence in each case. There is a generous supply of images presented with the text, and they are as successful as Fitzgerald's prose in illuminating the complexities of Picasso's influence on these artists." Publishers Weekly.

Marter, Joan M.

The **Grove** encyclopedia of American art / editor in chief, Joan Marter. Oxford University Press, c2011. 5 volumes : **709.73**

1. Art, American 2. Encyclopedias

ISBN 9780195335798

LC 2010030274

Arranged in alphabetical order, these 5 volumes encompass the history of the cultural development of America with over 2300 entries.

709.8 Fine arts--South America

Barnitz, Jacqueline

Twentieth-century art of Latin America / Jacqueline Barnitz. University of Texas Press, 2015. 415 p. : **709.8**

1. Art, Latin American -- 20th century. 2. Art, Latin American -- History.

ISBN 9781477308042

LC 99050871

This new edition has been refreshed throughout to include new scholarship on several modern movements, such as abstraction in the River Plate region and the Cuban avant-garde. A new chapter covers art since 1990. In all, 30 percent of the images in this edition are new, and thirty-four additional artists are discussed and illustrated.

"Latin American art, the fruit of violent collisions among diverse indigenous, European, and African cultures, is revealed as provocative and vibrant in Barnitz's well-illustrated and groundbreaking overview of its dazzling twentieth-century flowering." Booklist.

711 Area planning (Civic art)

McGregor, James H. (James Harvey), 1946-

Rome from the ground up / James H.S. McGregor Belknap Press of Harvard University Press, 2005. 344 p. : **711**

1. Urban planning -- Rome. 2. Architecture -- History. 3. Rome, Italy -- Description and travel. 4. Rome, Italy -- History.

ISBN 9780674019119

LC 2005048213

In this multifaceted historical portrait of Rome, the practical world of each period is explored to reveal the complex urban forms and shifting realities of the many cities that constitute Rome.

"The author chronologically traces the successive periods of intense architecture and planning that helped Rome achieve strategic greatness, from the Etruscan management of the Tiber Island ford 3,000 years ago, to the city's unparalleled artistic stamp by Bramante and Michelangelo during the Renaissance, to Mussolini's monumental Fascist vision, to the precarious repairs heralding the Jubilee Year of 2000. Here is a walking tour in stately, inviting prose that renders wonderfully manageable a massive history lesson for the intellectually curious and adept." Publishers Weekly.

712 Landscape architecture (Landscape design)

Alexander, Rosemary

★The **essential** garden design workbook : 3rd edition / Rosemary Alexander. Timber Press, 2017. 391 p. : **712**

1. Gardens -- Design.

ISBN 9781604696615

LC 2009008564

Guides you through every stage of designing a garden. Hundreds of explanatory drawings and quick-reference diagrams make this workbook a vital addition to your garden-planning library.

"Now in its third edition, expand[s] on the distinguished and experienced author's goal of providing guidance for a professional garden designer's career [and] maintains the earlier editions' well-written, straightforward text, instructive line drawings, and beautiful, informative color photographs." Choice

Brody, Mark

Mosaic garden projects : add color to your garden with tables, fountains, birdbaths, and more / Mark Brody ; with Sheila Ashdown ; with photographs by Justin Myers. Timber Press, 2015. 304 p. : **712**

1. Gardens -- Design. 2. Mosaics. 3. Color in design. 4. Garden ornaments and furniture.

ISBN 9781604694871

LC 2014020734

"25 colorful step-by-step projects"--Cover.

Includes index.

Presents detailed, step-by-step instructions for making mosaic garden structures and ornaments, including planters, stepping stones, tabletops, and a pagoda.

Buchanan, Rita

Taylor's master guide to landscaping / Rita Buchanan. Houghton Mifflin Co., c2000. 372 p. : **712**

1. Landscape gardening.
ISBN 0618055908

LC 99054110

"A Frances Tenenbaum book."
Includes index.

Reveals the vital components of landscape design, offering advice on choosing a site, selecting plants, creating garden accessories, and maintaining a landscape.

"Buchanan offers a comprehensive treatment of landscape design, emphasizing designing with plants and including extensive information about choosing and caring for plants, trees, shrubs, vines, and ground covers. A landmark work destined to become a classic." Library Journal.

Darke, Rick

The **living** landscape : designing for beauty and biodiversity in the home garden / Rick Darke & Doug Tallamy ; principal photography by Rick Darke. Timber Press, 2014. 392 p. : **712**

1. Ecological landscape design -- United States. 2. Natural landscaping -- United States.
ISBN 1604694084

LC 2013040141

Describes how gardeners can support sustainability and biodiversity by including in their garden plants that provide food for birds and bugs and serve as a pollination source for bees, suggesting plants for every climate and region.

Greayer, Rochelle

Cultivating garden style : inspired ideas and practical advice to unleash your garden personality / Rochelle Greayer. Timber Press, Inc., 2014. 323 p. : **712**

1. Gardening. 2. Gardens -- Styles.
ISBN 1604694777

LC 2014009479

Includes index.

Features examples of twenty-three different garden styles, with advice on selecting plants, trees, containers, and garden accessories to make a garden inviting and a reflection of individual taste.

"The extravagant use of color photos on each page brings visual clarity to otherwise improbable schemes. Whether depicting retro rockery, topiary, trellising, Danish or Zen features, the book offers needed guidance for designing outdoor space in a way that helps gardeners bring unique personality to their living, growing outdoor decor." Publishers Weekly.

Holmes, Roger

Midwest home landscaping : including South-central Canada / Roger Holmes & Rita Buchanan. Creative Homeowner Press, 2010. 223 p. : **712**

1. Gardens -- Middle West -- Design. 2. Gardens -- Ontario -- Design. 3. Landscape gardening -- Middle West. 4. Landscape gardening -- Ontario.
ISBN 9781580112567

LC bl2007010605

Includes index.

Previous ed. published under title: Home landscaping : Midwest Region, including southern Canada. 1999.

Provides information and guidance on designing plantings for the home yard and includes do-it-yourself outdoor building projects.

"The authors offer 46 designs for 23 common landscaping situations. Illustrated installation instructions are followed by solid plant choices for zone 4. Zone 3 gardeners are advised on plant substitutions." Library Journal.

Howcroft, Heidi

Garden design : a book of ideas / Heidi Howcroft & Marianne Majerus. Firefly Books, 2015. 320 p. : **712**

1. Gardens -- Design 2. Gardens -- Design -- Pictorial works
ISBN 9781770855243

LC oc2016048116

Includes index.

"More than 600 inspirational photographs, 24 case studies, [and] a must-have sourcebook for garden owners, architects and designers".--Page 4 of cover.

Mansfield, Stephen

Japanese stone gardens : origins, meaning, form / Stephen Mansfield ; foreword by Donald Richie. Tuttle Pub., c2009, 2017. 160 p. : **712**

1. Rock gardens, Japanese.
ISBN 9784805310564

LC bl2009035758

Japanese Stone Gardens provides a comprehensive introduction to the powerful mystique and dynamism of the Japanese stone garden--from their earliest use as props in animistic rituals, to their appropriation by Zen monks and priests to create settings conducive to contemplation and finally to their contemporary uses and meaning.

"An in-depth tour of 15 masterpiece stone gardens ancient and contemporary throughout Japan further deepens our appreciation for these landscapes of aesthetic precision and meditative repose in a book as lovely and restorative as its subject." Booklist.

Oudolf, Piet,

Gardens of the High Line : elevating the nature of modern landscapes / Piet Oudolf, Rick Darke. Timber Press, 2017. 319 p. : **712**

1. Gardens -- New York City -- Pictorial works 2. Urban parks -- New York City -- Pictorial works 3. High Line (New York, N.Y. : Park) Pictorial works.
ISBN 9781604696998

LC bl2017030163

Offers an in-depth view into the planting designs, plant palette, and maintenance of New York Citys iconic High Line gardens.

Pember, Mat

DIY garden projects : step -by-step activities for edible gardening and backyard fun / Mat Pember and Dillon Seitchik-Reardon. Hardie Grant Books, 2016. 383 p. : **712**

1. Garden structures -- Design and construction. 2. Gardens -- Design.
ISBN 1743790996

LC bl2016029905

Includes index.

Provides step-by-step instructions for thirty-eight activities in the garden, including garden basics, using recycled materials, and vertical gardening.

"Charming and hip projects emphasize recycled materials and small space gardens that will be attractive in urban settings. Highly recommended, especially where variety is desired." Library Journal.

Phaidon Press,
The **gardener's** garden Phaidon Press Ltd., 2014. 471 p. : **712**

1. Gardens -- Design. 2. Gardens -- Design -- Pictorial works. 3. Gardens. 4. Gardens -- Pictorial works.
ISBN 9780714867472

LC bl2014051288

Combines images, overviews, and key information on gardens from around the world, including Alice Springs Desert Park in Australia, Jardin des Colombieres in France, and Casa Soplo in Chile.

Rainer, Thomas (Landscape architect)
Planting in a post-wild world : designing plant communities for resilient landscapes / Thomas Rainer and Claudia West. Timber Press, 2015. 271 p. : **712**

1. Gardens -- Design 2. Plant communities
ISBN 9781604695533

LC 2015019338

Two leaders in ecological landscape design offer tips, instructions, and practical advice for creating beautiful and diverse gardens and landscapes that function in the same way as naturally occurring plant communities.

Williams, Bunny, 1944-
On garden style / Bunny Williams ; written with Nancy Drew ; book design by Doug Turshen with David Huang. Stewart, Tabori & Change, 2015. 287 p. : **712**

1. Gardening 2. Plants, Ornamental 3. Gardens -- Styles 4. Garden structures
ISBN 9781617691539

LC bl2015012051

A leading interior designer and a gardening journalist combine their expertise to provide an authoritative volume on how to design gardens of all kinds, as well as how to appreciate their aesthetic appeal.

712.09 Landscape architecture--history

Brown, Kendall H.
Quiet beauty : the Japanese gardens of North America / Kendall H. Brown ; photographs by David M. Cobb. Tuttle Pub., c2013. 176 p. : **712.09**

1. Gardens, Japanese -- North America
ISBN 4805311959

LC 2012036548

Japanese gardens have been part of North American culture for almost 150 years. Quiet Beauty is a thought-provoking look at the history of their introduction to the world of North American gardening and how this aspect of Japanese culture has taken root and flourished.

"Yet, the 150-year history of Japanese gardens in American culture raises complicated questions about authenticity, design, style, and meaning. In this lavishly illustrated book, art historian Brown and photographer Cobb act as tour guides to 26 such gardens." Publishers Weekly

Graham, Wade
American Eden : from Monticello to Central Park to our backyards : what our gardens tell us about who we are / Wade Graham. HarperCollins Publishers, c2011. 480 p. **712.09**

1. Gardens -- United States -- History. 2. Landscape architecture -- United States -- History. 3. Gardening.
ISBN 9780061583421

LC 2010024940

"Graham unveils the aesthetic, political, psychological, and ethical dimensions of the American garden. Graham is able to gently mock the fashions of history while astutely observing that we are still as vulnerable to gardening fads today... Graham's history is a fascinating and illuminating tour of this American landscape." Publishers Weekly.

Wulf, Andrea
Founding gardeners : the revolutionary generation, nature, and the shaping of the American nation / Andrea Wulf. Knopf, 2011, c2008. x, 349 p. : **712.09**

1. Washington, George, 1732-1799 2. Jefferson, Thomas, 1743-1826 3. Madison, James, 1751-1836 4. Adams, John, 1735-1826. 5. Gardening -- United States -- History -- 18th century. 6. Founding Fathers of the United States. 7. Gardens -- History -- 18th century. 8. Gardening -- Political aspects.
ISBN 9780307269904

LC 2010052920

Originally published: London : William Heinemann, 2008.

Reviews the lives of the founding fathers from their perspectives as gardeners, farmers, and plantsmen, revealing how a shared passion for agriculture shaped their beliefs and decisions.

"...Founding Gardeners is an excellent portrait of the early years of the federal republic. It will delight the general reader, not just the garden buff. But for the garden enthusiast, this is a book of special interest, reminding us that a garden has a purpose, a character, a soul, that's it's an expression of our relationship not just to the soil, but to a vision of the world." Cleveland Plain Dealer.

715 Woody plants in landscape architecture

Foley, Caroline (Writer on gardens)
Topiary, knots and parterres / Caroline Foley. Pimpernel Press Ltd., in association with the European Boxwood and Topiary Society, 2017 288 p. : **715**

1. Formal gardens -- History. 2. Hedges -- History. 3. Knot gardens -- History. 4. Topiary work -- History.
ISBN 1910258180

LC 2017431398

"Topiary, knots, and parterres come in many guises, from the grand and imposing to the humble and folksy. In this book Caroline Foley -- with the aid of diarists, writers, wits, designers, gardeners, and garden owners -- traces their story through the centuries and across the world".--Jacket flap.

Hobson, Jake
The **art** of creative pruning : inventive ideas for training and shaping trees and shrubs / Jake Hobson. Timber Press, 2011. 200 p. : **715**

1. Pruning. 2. Topiary work.
ISBN 160469114X

LC 2011007954

Offers instructions for creating unique topiary lanscapes using a blend of techniques gathered from Eastern and Western topiary gardens.

"Libraries already well stocked with titles such as Christopher Brickell and David Joyce's The American Horticultural Society Pruning & Training or Lewis Hill and Penelope O'Sullivan's The Pruning Answer Book will find Hobson's gorgeously illustrated, more philosophical book a good counterpart to those more nuts-and-bolts guides. Written with passion, verve, and a dash of dry wit, this title will inspire any gardener who wants to understand the how and why of creative pruning before picking up the shears and hacking off branches." Library Journal.

717 Structures in landscape architecture

Hayward, Gordon

Stone in the garden : inspiring designs and practical projects / Gordon Hayward ; illustrations by Gordon Morrison. W.W. Norton, c2001. 224 p. : **717**

1. Stone in landscape gardening.
ISBN 0393047792

LC 00069945

A guide to using stones in the garden, walls, walkways, and terraces features more than one hundred drawings and photographs that give instructions on how to complete a wide range of projects.

"The book's first half focuses on the philosophical and design considerations of stone forms as varied as walls, paths, terraces, and even benches. The second half is more practical, covering topics such as estimating the amount of stone needed for a wall, the methods of cutting and laying stone, and building pools and fountains." Library Journal.

720 Architecture

Cornille, Didier, 1951-

Who built that? : skyscrapers : an introduction to skyscrapers and their architects / Didier Cornille. Princeton Architectural Press, 2014. 83 p. : Who built that? **720**

1. Skyscrapers 2. Architecture 3. Architects 4. Buildings
ISBN 9781616892708

LC 2014004388

Originally published as: Tous les gratte-ciel sont dans la nature, France, 2012.

Illustrated by the author

An introduction to skyscrapers spotlights eight built between 1889 and 2010 in Europe, the United States, and Asia, with information about the architects, the circumstances when they were designed, and the elements that make them distinctive.

"Though the information is a little slight, the spare illustrations easily make up for itall of Cornilles drawings unmistakably reveal architectural components not visible in photographs, such as interior structures or foundations, and although they're very minimalistic, it's impossible not to see the structures' grandeur in each illustration. Though this resembles a picture book, the sometimes elevated language makes this better suited to middle- or even high-school students who already have an interest in architecture or graphic design." Booklist.

Glancey, Jonathan

The **story** of architecture / Jonathan Glancey. Dorling Kindersley, 2000. 240 p. : **720**

1. Architecture -- History. 2. Architectural criticism 3. Architectural photography.
ISBN 0789459655

LC 00030434

Includes index.

An illustrated study of architecture spans some five thousand years as it captures the finest achievements of human construction; discusses a variety of architectural styles and movements; and profiles some of the world's great architects, past and present.

"Devoting nearly half the text to the modern period, Glancey condenses history's panorama into a series of colorful vignettes, each described as having some contemporary relevance. Driven by a contagious enthusiasm, the narrative is enlivened by chatty, sometimes offbeat commentary." Library Journal.

Lewis, Miles

Architectura : elements of architectural style / general editor, Miles Lewis. Barrons Educational Series, 2008. 399 p. : **720**

1. Architecture.
ISBN 9780764161704

LC 2008929852

Includes index.

Surveys global architecture styles, describing different features common to cathedrals, mosques, museums, offices, and mansions.

Mars, Roman

★The **99%** invisible city : a field guide to the hidden world of everyday design / Roman Mars and Kurt Kohlstedt. Houghton Mifflin Harcourt, 2020 384 p. **720**

1. Urban planning 2. Cities and towns 3. Design 4. Public works
ISBN 9780358126607

LC 2020023323

Based on a podcast.

The creators of the record-setting 99% Invisible podcast celebrate the achievements of modern urban design and architecture, sharing the origin stories behind fundamental innovations, from power grids and fire escapes to drinking fountains and street signs.

"A user-friendly guide to all the overlooked things that make urban civilization tick. If you're an infrastructure nerd, a reader of David Macauley, Kate Ascher, or Brian Hayes, then you know that under the sidewalks of your town or city lies an endlessly complex world of pipes, cables, wires, and tunnels. If you want to understand the language spoken in that world, then this book is for you." Kirkus

Palladio, Andrea, 1508-1580

The **four** books of architecture / With a new introd. by Adolf K. Placzek. Dover Publications, [1965] vii, 110 p. : **720**

1. Architecture -- Early works to 1800. 2. Rome -- Antiquities Early works to 1800.
ISBN 0486213080

LC 64018862

"Unabridged and unaltered republication of the work first published by Isaac Ware in 1738."

"Drawing on the monuments of ancient Rome as well as the author's own villas and public works, this philosophical treatise and practical guide served as the pattern book for countless Palladian buildings by other architects around the world. Elegantly translated (in the first new English translation since 1738) and illustrated with the lyrical, rarely seen woodcuts of Palladio's original." New York Times Book Review.

Rybczynski, Witold

Mysteries of the mall : and other essays / Witold Rybczynski. Farrar, Straus and Giroux, 2018, c2015. 320 p. **720**

1. Cities and towns -- United States -- History. 2. Urban planning 3. Architecture and society -- United States. 4. Essays
ISBN 9780374269937

LC 2014046633

Includes index.

A collection of essays about modern life in our cities.

"A superb book for those interested in architectural history, written in an easygoing style by a man with encyclopedic knowledge and an obvious great love for building." Kirkus.

Watkin, David, 1941-2018

A **history** of Western architecture / David Watkin. Laurence King Publishing, 2015. 736 p. : **720**

1. Architecture -- History. 2. Architecture and society -- History.
ISBN 9781780675978

Previous edition: 2011. First edition published in 1986.

Traces the history of western architecture from the earliest times in Mesopotamia and Egypt to the eclectic styles of the twenty-first century. The author emphasizes that "traditional architecture has re-established itself as a solution to the many problems presented by new needs and new materials ... the classical language of architecture is always modern. ... This new edition covers...[structures] in [other areas of the world] as products of globalization, the attention paid to sustainability, energy; recycling elements of buildings; the passion for astonishing height but also architecture on a human scale, and urban planning [issues].

Wolfe, Tom

From Bauhaus to our house / Tom Wolfe. Farrar Straus Giroux, c1981. 143 p. : **720**

1. Bauhaus Influence 2. Architecture, American 3. Popular culture -- History -- 20th century 4. Conformity 5. Architecture, Modern -- 20th century -- United States 6. Satire.
ISBN 0374158924

LC 81012589

A short history of architecture in the twentieth century debunks the stuffy European contributions to both modern and post-modern building design.

720.1 Architecture--Philosophy and theory

Goldhagen, Sarah Williams

Welcome to your world : how the built environment shapes our lives / Sarah Williams Goldhagen. Harper, 2017 xxxiv, 347 p. : **720.1**

1. Architecture -- Human factors. 2. Architectural design. 3. Urban beautification 4. Urban planning.
ISBN 9780061957802

One of the nation's chief architecture critics, drawing on new discoveries in cognitive psychology and neuroscience, takes readers on an eye-opening journey through some of the world's best and worst landscapes, buildings and cityscapes, revealing how the environments we build profoundly shape our feelings and memories.

"An eye-opening look at the ways in which carefully planned and executed design and architecture can expand cognitive faculties and improve daily life." Kirkus.

720.9 History, geographic treatment, biography

Ching, Francis D. K., 1943-

★A **global** history of architecture / Francis D.K. Ching, Mark Jarzombek, Vikramaditya Prakash. Wiley, 2017 xiii, 850 p. : **720.9**

1. Architecture -- History
ISBN 9781118981337

LC 2017004046

"A Global History of Architecture, Third Edition has been updated and revised throughout to reflect current scholarship, including an expanded section on contemporary global architecture. Spanning from 3,500 b.c.e. to the present, this unique guide is written by an all-star team of architectural experts in their fields who emphasize the connections, contrasts, and influences of architectural movements throughout history".-- Provided by publisher.

Hollis, Edward

The **secret** lives of buildings : from the ruins of the Parthenon to the Vegas Strip in thirteen stories / Edward Hollis. Metropolitan Books, Henry Holt and Co., 2009. 352 p. **720.9**

1. Architecture and history. 2. Architecture and society. 3. Buildings. 4. Architecture. 5. Essays.
ISBN 9780805087857

LC 2009018715

A narrative history of western architecture offers insight into its reflection of cultural influences and transformations, documenting some of the most dramatic examples of dynamic western architecture from Notre Dame's cathedral to the Berlin Wall.

720.92 Architects

Storrer, William Allin

The **Frank** Lloyd Wright companion / William Allin Storrer. University of Chicago, Ill. :Press, 2006. xvi, 492 p. : **720.92**

1. Wright, Frank Lloyd, 1867-1959 Criticism and interpretation. 2. Wright, Frank Lloyd, 1867-1959.
ISBN 0226776212

LC 2006044502

Includes index.

The comprehensive source for as-built plans of Wright's work.

"With this volume, Storrer surpasses his previous catalog of Wright's work, The Architecture of Frank Lloyd Wright (MIT Pr., 1978), by compiling detailed plans, photographs, and brief histories of every structure built by America's most widely known architect." Library Journal

721 Architectural materials

Rybczynski, Witold

The **look** of architecture / Witold Rybczynski. Oxford University Press, c2001. xiv, 130 p. : **721**

1. Architecture. 2. Architectural design.
ISBN 0195156331

LC 00053077

One of the nation's foremost experts on architecture discusses the role of style in the "language" of the discipline, and shows how Frank Gehry, Mies van der Rohe, Allan Greenberg, and others are influenced by it.

"The author's deeply informed enthusiasm is infectious, and his removal of architectural writing from an airily theoretical discourse to the realm of practical experience is empowering for the lay reader." Publishers Weekly.

Smith, Nathan, 1981-

Color concrete garden projects : make your own planters, furniture, and fire pits using creative techniques and vibrant finishes / Nathan Smith & Michael Snyder ; photographs by Charles Coleman. Timber Press, 2015 206 p. : **721**

1. Garden ornaments and furniture -- Design and construction. 2.

Concrete construction -- Formwork.
ISBN 9781604695397
LC 2014048495
Includes index.

Presents step-by-step instructions for twenty garden projects that use concrete as a medium, from a tabletop candleholder and a doorstop to a large oval planter and a modern birdhouse.

"This book has taken concrete projects to a new high; there's nothing else quite as focused on the subject. For a general concrete container book, see Malin Nilsson and Camilla Arvidsson's Concrete Garden Projects. A true standoutsuperior instructions and innovative design and use of pigment. A must for any DIY collection." Library Journal.

724 Architecture from 1400

Curtis, William J. R.

Modern architecture since 1900 / William J.R. Curtis. Phaidon, 1996 736 p. : **724**

1. Architecture, Modern -- 20th century.
ISBN 9780714835242
LC 97112837

"The volume's well-detailed text is buttressed with 650 color and black-and-white illustrations. This should be a standard volume in all architecture collections." Library Journal.

Huxtable, Ada Louise

On architecture : collected reflections on a century of change / Ada Louise Huxtable. Walker & Co., 2008. 288 p. **724**

1. Architecture -- History 2. Architectural criticism 3. Architecture and society 4. Essays
ISBN 9780802717078
LC bl2009005866

A forefront and passionate critic evaluates architecture as a pivotal and controversial component of twentieth-century culture, in a collection of articles that covers such topics as Le Corbusier's Carpenter Center at Harvard, the mid-century shifts in style, and her selections for best and worst architectural examples.

"The author presents her penetrating and tough-minded criticism spanning half a century. Centering largely on modernism, its masters and its discontents, the volume opens with an overview of the past four decades, including startlingly powerful pieces on the late '60s urban decay and the '90s reinvention of architecture." Publishers Weekly.

725 Architecture--Public structures

Blockley, David

Bridges : the science and art of the world's most inspiring structures / David Blockley. Oxford University Press, 2010. 288 p. **725**

1. Bridges. 2. Architecture. 3. Structural engineering. 4. Suspension bridges.
ISBN 9780199543595
LC bl2010016758

Explains the importance of bridges, the process of constructing the four main types, and the reasons behind bridge disasters around the world.

726.5 Buildings associated with Christianity

Van Hensbergen, Gijs

The **Sagrada** Familia : Gaudi's heaven on Earth / Gijs van Hensbergen. Bloomsbury, 2017, c2016. 204 p. ; **726.5**

1. Gaudi, Antoni, 1852-1926 2. Sagrada Familia (Church : Barcelona, Spain) 3. Churches 4. Architects 5. Religious architecture 6. Barcelona, Spain 7. spain
ISBN 9781408854778
Includes index.
Originally published : Barcelona : Rosa dels Vents, 2016.

Explores the history of the Sagrada Fam?ilia, the unfinished minor basilica designed by Antoni Gaudi.

"Van Hensbergen serves as an enthusiastic guide in this more than thorough account of one of the world's most eccentric and stunning buildings." Publishers Weekly.

726.6 Cathedrals

King, Ross, 1962-

Brunelleschi's dome : how a Renaissance genius reinvented architecture / Ross King. Walker & Co., 2000. 194 p. : **726.6**

1. Brunelleschi, Filippo, 1377-1446. 2. Ghiberti, Lorenzo, 1378-1455. 3. Santa Maria del Fiore Cathedral, Florence, Italy. 4. Architects -- Italy 5. Domes -- Florence, Italy -- Design and construction. 6. Architecture, Renaissance -- Italy. 7. Architecture and religion. 8. Florence, Italy -- Buildings. 9. Florence, Italy -- History -- To 1421.
ISBN 0802713661
LC 00043524
Simultaneously published: London : Chatto & Windus, 2000.

"King illuminates the mysterious sources of inspiration and the secretive methods of architectural genius Filippo Brunelleschi in a fascinating chronicle of the building of his masterwork, the dome of Santa Maria del Fiore in Florence. A remarkable saga of how one incandescent mind performed the one matchless feat that would forever transform architecture from a mechanical craft into a creative art." Booklist.

727 Buildings for educational and research purposes

Holway, Tatiana M.

The **flower** of empire : the Amazon's largest water lily, the quest to make it bloom, and the world it helped create / Tatiana Holway. Oxford University Press, [2013] 336 p. **727**

1. Lindley, John, 1799-1865. 2. Schomburgk, Robert H. (Robert Hermann), Sir, 1804-1865. 3. Great Exhibition of the Works of Industry of All Nations, London, England, 1851. 4. Royal Geographic Society. 5. Victoria amazonica. 6. Fads and crazes. 7. Water lilies. 8. Botany. 9. Great Britain -- History -- 19th century.
ISBN 9780195373899
LC 2012034518

Narrates the story of the discovery of an Amazon water lily and its impact on Victorian life and culture, as prominent botanists of the day became obssessed in their quest to make the flower bloom in England.

Meier, Richard, 1934-

Building the Getty / Richard Meier. Alfred A. Knopf, 1997. xii, 204 p. : **727**

1. Getty Center (Los Angeles, Calif.) 2. Richard Meier & Partners.

3. Art centers -- Los Angeles, California 4. Los Angeles, California -- Buildings, structures, etc.
ISBN 0375400435

LC 97029326

"Charting his involvement in the Getty's construction, Meier recounts in an intriguingly candid, eminently personal style the formidable bureaucratic process entailed upon undertaking to realize this grandiose endeavor. Beginning with the competition itself, Meier's detailed reminiscences offer fascinating insights into the design process and the extraordinarily intricate procedures and systems, as well as endless setbacks, associated with executing a modern-day megalithic structure." Booklist.

728 Residential and related buildings

Barker, Margaret A.

Audubon birdhouse book : building, placing, and maintaining great homes for great birds / Margaret A. Barker and Elissa Wolfson ; foreword by Stephen W. Kress ; carpentry by Chris Willett. Voyageur Press, 2013. 160 p. : **728**

1. Birdhouses -- Design and construction 2. Bird attracting -- United States
ISBN 9780760342206

LC 2013018947

Produced in association with the National Audubon Society, Audubon Birdhouse Book explains how to build and place functional DIY bird homes that are safe and appropriate for more than 20 classic North American species, from wrens to raptors.

"Like Birdhouses You Can Build in a Day, this informative volume tailors designs to specific species. However, what sets this work apart is the inclusion of research and scientific study results on what makes a home suitable for a particular type of bird." Library Journal.

Bradbury, Dominic

Mountain modern : contemporary homes in high places / Dominic Bradbury ; photographs by Richard Powers. Thames & Hudson, 2014. 255 p. : **728**

1. Architecture, Domestic 2. Hillside architecture 3. Interior decoration
ISBN 9780500517468

LC bl2015006420

Showcases contemporary houses designed specifically for mountain settings and high-altitude locations, looking at how architects incorporate natural settings into their plans while highlighting interior design features.

Hirsch, William J., Jr

Designing your perfect house : lessons from an architect / William J. Hirsch Jr. Dalsimer Press, c2008, 2017. 239 p. : **728**

1. Architecture, Domestic 2. Dwellings -- Planning
ISBN 9780979882005

LC 2007936951

This second edition of Designing Your Perfect House includes a bonus lesson, Building Green, Naturally.

"Drawing many examples from his own practice, he explains the process and philosophy of residential design as seen from a professional's view and discusses what to consider when creating one's dream home." Library Journal.

Jordan, Wendy Adler, 1946-

Universal design for the home : great looking, great living design for all ages, abilities, and circumstances / Wendy A. Jordan. Quarry Books, c2008. 207 p. : **728**

1. Dwellings -- Barrier-free design -- United States 2. Universal design -- United States
ISBN 9781592533817

LC 2007032663

Includes index.

Showcases newly built or renovated homes that are accommodating to all and discusses the inhabitants' lifestyles and physical challenges.

"This book shows how a home that is accommodating to all can also have a stylish decor. Color photographs and some before-and-after floor plans show how accessibility standards have been incorporated. A list of resources is provided." Library Journal.

Koones, Sheri, 1949-

Prefabulous small houses / Sheri Koones ; foreword by Robert Redford. The Taunton Press, Inc., 2016 233 p. ; **728**

1. Prefabricated houses 2. Ecological houses 3. Small houses 4. Dwellings -- Energy conservation
ISBN 9781631864049

LC 2016021033

In Prefabulous Small Houses, best-selling author Sheri Koones presents 32 stunning prefabricated homes from around North America. 250 beautiful photographs and floorplans show the amazing breadth of styles available to today's homeowners.

"Lack of an index might hamper the use of this volume, but a multitude of cost-effective, energy-efficient ideas can be found here." Library Journal

Kotite, Erika, 1962-

She sheds : a room of your own / Erika Kotite. Cool Springs Press, 2017. 176 p. : **728**

1. Interior decoration 2. Outdoor living spaces 3. Sheds 4. Women -- Homes and haunts
ISBN 9781591866770

LC 2016033753

"She Sheds provides inspiration, tips, and tricks to help create the hideaway of your dreams".-- Provided by publisher.

McAlester, Virginia, 1943-

A **field** guide to American houses : the definitive guide to identifying and understanding America's domestic architecture / Virginia Savage McAlester ; with drawings by Suzanne Patton Matty and photographs by Steve Clicque ; revised and expanded from the original edition written by Virginia and Lee McAlester ; with drawings by Lauren Jarrett and model house drawings by Juan Rodriguez-Arnaiz. Alfred A. Knopf, 2013. xxv, 848 p. : **728**

1. Architecture, Domestic -- United States 2. United States Guidebooks. 3. Guidebooks.
ISBN 9781400043590

LC 2013018432

"First edition published June 12, 1984."--Title page verso

A guide for architecture aficionados explains how to identify the various styles and periods of American domestic architecture, focusing on typical dwellings in everyday neighborhoods to place distinct styles and characteristics within historical frames.

Paradis, Thomas W. (Thomas Wayne), 1970-

The **Greenwood** encyclopedia of homes through American

history / Thomas W. Paradis, general editor. Greenwood Press, 2008. 4 v., 32 p. of plates : **728**

1. Architecture, Domestic -- United States -- Encyclopedias. 2. Decorative arts -- United States -- Encyclopedias. 3. Dwellings -- United States -- Encyclopedias.

ISBN 9780313334962

LC 2008002946

Provides a survey of house architecture and use in the United States from 1492 through the present.

Pierce, D. (Deborah), 1938-

The **accessible** home : designing for all ages and abilities / Deborah Pierce. The Taunton Press, 2012 234 p. : **728**

1. Dwellings -- Barrier-free design 2. Universal design

ISBN 9781600854910

LC 2012029176

Includes index.

"Millions of baby boomers are approaching the golden years. While it's a marker worth celebrating, it can also be a reminder of uncertain times ahead. How will I manage? Can I stay in my home? The Accessible Home goes beyond ramps and grab-bars to help aging boomers, or those faced with disabilities, accomplish home accessibility on a deeper level. With a focus on closing the gap between home and homeowner, architect Deborah Pierce leads readers through the steps of universal design--from hiring the right architect to creating a pleasing space with the final details. Plus, an insider's look at 25 case studies shows that the best design is built in, not tacked on, and that "accessible" can be both beautiful and functional. The Accessible Home empowers people of all ages and challenges them to create homes that restore independence and the grace of daily living".-- Provided by publisher.

Schapdick, Chris

Building your tiny house dream : design and build a camper-style tiny house with your own hands / Chris Schapdick. Fox Chapel Pub Co Inc 2020 176 p. **728**

1. Small houses 2. House construction

ISBN 9781580118477

"Combining the 'why' with the 'how to,' Building Your Tiny House Dream will show you each step to constructing your own custom camper! Part one provides detailed guidance on essential information, from the skills needed and planning to tools, safety, and helpful resources. Start building your tiny home in part two that's carefully laid out in order from start to finish, from laying the foundation and framing to plumbing, adding personality, and towing so you can take your tiny home on wheels on the road! Also included is access to an online how-to video series of the author building the featured tiny home project from beginning to end." Provided by publisher

"Those looking to go small will appreciate this solid how-to." Publishers Weekly

Susanka, Sarah

Creating the not so big house : insights and ideas for the new American home / Sarah Susanka ; photographs by Grey Crawford. Taunton Press ; c2000. 258 p. : **728**

1. Architecture -- United States -- History -- 20th century 2. Architecture, Domestic -- United States 3. Interior architecture -- United States 4. Space (Architecture)

ISBN 9781561583775

LC 00044323

Includes index.

Offers a look at twenty-five examples of small house designs to show readers what they need to know to plan the home that best fits their goals and lifestyles.

"Architect Susanka has big ideas about small design. {This book promotes} well-designed, efficient, interesting modest-size homes. {She} includes 25 delightful examples of houses designed by architects from around the country." Booklist.

★The **not** so big house : a blueprint for the way we really live / Sarah Susanka with Kira Obolensky. Taunton Press, c2001, c1998. 199 p. : **728**

1. Architecture, Domestic -- Psychological aspects. 2. Space (Architecture) 3. Small houses 4. Interior architecture -- Psychological aspects.

ISBN 9781561583768

LC BL2001000853

Reprint. Originally published: 1998.

Proposes guidelines for creating intimate homes that serve both spiritual needs and material requirements, covering such topics as specific lifestyles, budgeting, and energy-efficient construction.

Not so big solutions for your home / Sarah Susanka. Taunton Press ; c2002. 155 p. : **728**

1. Architecture, Domestic 2. House construction 3. Interior architecture

ISBN 9781561586134

LC 2002007101

"From the pages of Fine homebuilding magazine."

Contains articles originally written for "Fine homebuilding" magazine's "Drawing board" column.

Offers ideas to increase usable space in a home and add warmth and character, including tips on designing a window seat, planning a recyling area, and using tile to personalize a kitchen or bathroon.

"The author presents a compilation of 31 essays from her Drawing Board column in Fine Homebuilding magazine that offer a number of solutions to household design problems both big and small. Susanka offers an eclectic mix: tips on site selection, mud room design, planning to fit specific furniture, creating a family room that works, personalizing with tile, and planning window seats, pantries, TV placement, and floor plan changes." Library Journal.

Van Doren, Adam, 1962-

The **house** tells the story : homes of the American presidents / Adam Van Doren ; foreword by David McCullough. David R. Godine, Publisher, 2015. 189 p. : **728**

1. Van Doren, Adam, 1962- 2. Dwellings in art. 3. Presidents -- Dwellings -- United States -- Pictorial works.

ISBN 9781567925425

LC 2015000579

Includes index.

The author shares the illustrated letters he sent his friend, historian David McCullough, over the course of three years that depict the homes of former presidents, focusing on the small details of everyday life to provide a more intimate look at the presidents' lives.

"Warm, accessible, and harmonious, this book marries history with art for a uniquely American vision." Publishers Weekly.

Versaci, Russell

Creating a new old house : yesterday's character for today's home / Russell Versaci ; photographs by Erik Kvalsvik. Taunton

Press, c2003. 218 p. : **728**

1. Architecture, Domestic -- United States
ISBN 9781561586158

LC 2003004993

Featuring 18 homes, this guidebook by a Virginia-based architect offers ideas and techniques for instilling "core pillars of tradition" in new homes.

Wilhide, Elizabeth

Scandinavian home : a comprehensive guide to mid-century modern Scandinavian designers / Elizabeth Wilhide. Quadrille Publishing, 2016. 192 p. : **728**

1. Architecture, Domestic -- Scandinavia 2. Architecture, Modern 3. Interior decoration -- Scandinavia
ISBN 9781849497497

LC bl2016032221

Includes index.

Explores the Scandinavian design movement, an approach characterized by the use of natural materials and organic forms with clean lines and comfort.

728.37 Separate houses

Mitchell, Ryan

Tiny house living : ideas for building and living well in less than 400 square feet / Ryan Mitchell. Betterway Home, 2014 175 p. : **728.37**

1. Small houses.
ISBN 9781440333163

LC bl2014029615

Explores the philosophies behind the tiny house lifestyle, and provides guidance for the transition to a smaller space, including practical strategies for paring down possessions and design tricks to maximize function in available space.

728.81 Castles

Morris, Marc, 1973-

Castles : their history and evolution in Medieval Britain / Marc Morris. Pegasus, 2017. 288 p. **728.81**

1. Castles -- History. 2. Medieval architecture. 3. Architecture, British. 4. Great Britain -- Buildings. 5. England -- Buildings. 6. Ireland -- Buildings. 7. Wales -- Buildings.
ISBN 9781681773599

LC 2017446173

From the author of The Norman Conquest and A Great and Terrible King comes a sweeping and stunning history of the most magnificent castles in Britain.

731.4 Sculpture--Techniques and procedures

Heaser, Sue

The **polymer** clay techniques book / Sue Heaser. North Light Books, c1999. 128 p. : **731.4**

1. Polymer clay sculpture
ISBN 9781581800081

LC BL 00001414

A step-by-step guide to creating different crafts, such as buttons, beads, and mosaics, using polymer clay.

"The Polymer Clay Technique Book, in particular, has detailed step-by-step instructions for many techniques such as marbling, cutting, and making millefiori canes." Library Journal.

736 Carving and carvings

Brown, Nancy Marie

Ivory Vikings : the mystery of the most famous chessmen in the world and the woman who made them / Nancy Marie Brown. Palgrave Macmillan Trade, 2015. 256 p. **736**

1. Lewis chessmen. 2. Antiquities 3. Vikings -- Antiquities 4. Civilization, Medieval 5. Chess sets 6. Scotland 7. Lewis with Harris Island (Scotland) -- Antiquities.
ISBN 9781137279378

LC 2015002532

"This book is a delight for chess players, of course, but also for gamers of all sorts as well as anyone interested in the intricacies of the provenance of art and in endlessly fascinating minutiae--the strength and uses of walrus skin, how to carve walrus ivory, and so much more." Booklist.

Jones, Andrew, 1934-

Stickmaking handbook / Andrew Jones & Clive George. Guild of Master Craftsman Publications, 2016. 143 p. : **736**

1. Wood-carving. 2. Staffs (Sticks, canes, etc.).
ISBN 9781784940980

LC bl2017008659

Includes index.

Explains how to carve a variety of traditional walking sticks using wood and alternative materials.

"There are few books on this traditional craft, making this title unique. Recommended as a different focus for woodworkers." Library Journal.

736.98 Paper cutting and folding

Baard, Nellianna van den

Better living through origami : 20 creative paper projects for a beautiful home / Nellianna van den Baard and Kenneth Veenenbos. Sew and So, 2018. 127 p. : **736.98**

1. Origami 2. Interior decoration accessories
ISBN 9781446307120

LC bl2019001192

Includes index.

"Patterns for finished objects that are both contemporary and versatile feature instructions that can be readily executed, covering all of the elements more specifically and including graphics, patterns, and metric measurements " Booklist.

Bolitho, Mark

The **art** and craft of geometric origami / Mark Bolitho. Princeton Architectural Press, 2017 128 p. : **736.98**

1. Origami
ISBN 9781616896348

LC bl2018000780

Origami paper sheets inserted in flap on page 3 of cover.

Presents instructions for making twenty-seven different geometric origami projects that utilize such shapes as pyramids and starbursts, in a book that includes thirty sheets of origami paper.

"The combination of thorough, helpful instruction, geometry, and one-piece and modular models will appeal to crafters interested in trying something different with origami." Library Journal.

Hayakawa, Hiroshi, 1962-

Kirigami menagerie : 38 paper animals to copy, cut & fold / Hiroshi Hayakawa. Sterling Pub. Co, 2009. 128 p. : **736.98**

1. Paper animal making. 2. Origami. 3. Kirigami. 4. Animals in art.
ISBN 9781600593185

LC 2008050622

Includes index.

In origami, a flat piece of paper is folded to create a dimensional object. Similarly, in traditional Japanese kirigami, paper is folded, cut, and unfolded to reveal complex patterns, like a paper snowflake. Here, author Hiroshi Hayakawa has ingeniously combined these two techniques to create a charming menagerie of 38 animals, from flocks of sheep and swirling dragons to stampeding ostriches and pandas in a bamboo grove. -- From publisher description

"Hayakawa's delightful animals start out with cutout shapes that are folded and joined together with slits and tabs." Library Journal.

Morin, John

Inspired origami : projects to calm the mind and soothe the soul / John Morin and Camilla Sanderson. Running Press, 2016 120 p. : **736.98**

1. Origami. 2. Origami -- Psychological aspects. 3. Mindfulness (Psychology).
ISBN 9780762461752

LC bl2018002539

Includes index.

Presents fifteen origami projects and explains how the practice of paper folding can calm people through mindfulness.

738 Ceramic arts

Nelson, Glenn C.

Ceramics : a potter's handbook / Glenn C. Nelson, Richard Burkett. Wadsworth/Thomson Learning, 2002. 439 p. : **738**

1. Ceramics.
ISBN 9780030289378

LC 2001096329

"This text introduces students to the fundamentals of the ceramic arts, beginning with a history of ceramic materials and techniques up to the present day and then moving on to a detailed presentation of basic and complex ceramic techniques. Techniques and results are illustrated with b&w and color photos, with a portfolio of contemporary work of the last 50 years. This sixth edition incorporates new resources and materials available as well as current technical and safety information. Burkett is affiliated with San Diego State University." -- From Book News, Inc., Portland, OR

738.1 Techniques, procedures, apparatus, equipment, materials

Burnett, Jason Bige, 1984-

Graphic clay : ceramic surfaces & printed image transfer techniques / Jason Bige Burnett. Lark Crafts, 2014 160 p. : **738.1**

1. Glazing (Ceramics). 2. Transfer-printing. 3. Pottery
ISBN 9781454707752

LC 2014016141

Presents information about decorative imagery for ceramics, describing techniques for applying slip, prepping bisqueware, firing decals, creating silk-screen stencils, and transferring screen-print images.

"Intermediate and experienced artists with some existing ceramics skills can find much inspiration here." Library Journal.

Muller, Kristin

The **potter's** studio handbook : a start-to-finish guide to hand-built and wheel-thrown ceramics / Kristin Muller. Quarry Books, c2007. 192 p. : Backyard Series **738.1**

1. Pottery 2. Artists' studios -- Design and construction
ISBN 9781592533732

LC 2007016693

"The author guides beginners through advanced students in equipping a ceramic studio, handling the design, preparing the clay, constructing slab projects, throwing on a wheel, glazing, and firing. The 16 clay projects featured here include teapots, vases, and dinner plates. Readers can draw inspiration from the creative painting and underglazing examples, as well as the unusual firing techniques for color and texture." Library Journal.

Pavelka, Lisa, 1960-

The **complete** book of polymer clay ; step-by-step instructions, original projects, inspirational gallery / Lisa Pavelka. Taunton Press, c2010. 221 p. : **738.1**

1. Polymer clay sculpture
ISBN 9781600851285

LC 2009042430

The Complete Book of Polymer Clay is an encyclopedic book by renowned expert Lisa Pavelka includes the latest techniques, handy tips, and trade secrets.

Taylor, Brian J.

Glaze : the ultimate ceramic artist's guide to glaze and color / Brian Taylor and Kate Doody. Barron's, 2014. 320 p. : **738.1**

1. Glazing (Ceramics)
ISBN 9780764166426

LC oc2014087346

"A Quarto book"--Title page verso.

"Anyone who loves creating ceramics knows that glazing can be a labor of great love or the bane of the entire ceramic process. In the instructional and inspirational Glaze, potters will find a wealth of guidance on the glazing process as several of today's leading ceramicists share the recipes and techniques behind their most stunning works of art--each selected specifically for its unique glaze".--Back cover.

"Pottery was never so alluring. Appended are a glossary, a bibliography, an Orton cone chart, a directory of ceramic materials, and teachers and artists." Booklist.

738.209 History and geographic treatment of porcelain

De Waal, Edmund

The **white** road : journey into an obsession / Edmund de Waal. Farrar, Straus and Giroux, 2015. 432 p. **738.209**

1. De Waal, Edmund Travel. 2. Porcelain -- History. 3. Ceramics 4.

Artists 5. Porcelain, Chinese.
ISBN 9780374289263

LC 2015022207

"An intimate narrative history of porcelain, structured around five journeys through landscapes where porcelain was dreamed about, fired, refined, collected, and coveted".-- Provided by publisher.

"De Waals passionately and elegantly elucidated story of porcelain, laced with memoir and travelogue, serves as a portal into the madness and transcendence of our covetous obsession with beauty." Booklist.

739.2092 Art metalwork--biography

Faber, Toby, 1965-

Faberge's eggs : the extraordinary story of the masterpieces that outlived an empire / Toby Faber. Random House, 2008. 320 p. **739.2092**

1. Faberge, Peter Carl, 1846-1920. 2. Romanov, House of Art patronage. 3. Faberge (Firm) 4. Faberge eggs. 5. Art patronage -- Russia -- History. 6. Eggs. 7. Art objects, Russian. 8. Russia -- History -- 1801-1917.
ISBN 9781400065509

LC 2007049635

Chronicles the history of Faberge's imperial Easter eggs and of their maker, the Russian tsars who commissioned them, and the collectors who fell in love with them, looking at their meticulous craftsmanship, unimaginable wealth, and significance both as a symbol of imperial splendor and for the revolution that brought down the Romanovs.

739.27 Jewelry

Burns, Cherie

Diving for starfish : the jeweler, the actress, the heiress and one of the world's most alluring pieces of jewelry / Cherie Burns. St. Martin's Press, 2018. 256 p. **739.27**

1. Rene Boivin (Firm). 2. Brooches. 3. Jewelry. 4. Fashion. 5. Starfish pins
ISBN 9781250056207

LC 2017037546

The author describes her search for one of the most famous pieces of jewelry ever made, a gold, articulated starfish brooch encrusted with rubies and amethysts made by Juliette Moutard for Paris jeweler Boivin in the early 1930s.

"Quick, fun, easy reading for devotees of high fashion and mystery fans, complete with wrong turns and false friends." Kirkus.

Codina, Carles

The **complete** book of jewelry making : a full-color introduction to the jeweler's art / [Carles Codina ; translation from the Spanish, Laurie C. Jones]. Lark Books, 2006. 160 p. : **739.27**

1. Jewelry making.
ISBN 9781579903046

LC oc2007055494

"This book covers the basics, from the ABCs of metallurgy to such complicated techniques as enameling and lacquering. Most of the examples are contemporary, taken from European designers, and all blessed with great color photographs." Booklist.

DeCoster, Marcia

★**Marcia** DeCoster's beaded opulence : elegant jewelry projects with right angle weave / Marcia DeCoster. Lark Books, 2009. 128 p. : **739.27**

1. Beadwork 2. Jewelry making
ISBN 9781600592928

LC 2008050857

Includes index.

"Uniformly good design characterizes both books." Library Journal

Haab, Sherri

The **art** of metal clay : techniques for creating jewelry and decorative objects / Sherri Haab. Watson-Guptill Publications, 2010. 160 p. : **739.27**

1. Metal-work. 2. Jewelry making. 3. Precious metal clay.
ISBN 9780823099320

LC 2009043781

Includes index.

Developed in Japan in the 1990s, metal clay consists of microscopic particles of silver or gold suspended in a pliable organic binder that can be worked with the hands and simple household tools. This book offers a comprehensive introduction to the medium designed specifically for crafters and jewelrymakers.

"An essential project book for anyone interested in learning to work with metal clay. [The projects included involve] bronze and copper metal clays, etching, and enameling. An included DVD has additional projects." Library Journal.

Michaels, Chris Franchetti

Teach yourself visually jewelry making & beading / Chris Franchetti Michaels. Wiley Pub., c2007. 290 p. : Teach Yourself Visually **739.27**

1. Jewelry making. 2. Beadwork.
ISBN 9780470101506

LC bl2007029159

Presents illustrated step-by-step instructions for jewelry making and beading, with advice on techniques, supplies, and design, and diagrams for easy and intermediate projects.

Raden, Aja

Stoned : jewelry, obsession, and how desire shapes the world / Aja Raden. HarperCollins, 2015 368 p. **739.27**

1. Precious stones 2. Precious metals 3. Greed 4. Social history
ISBN 9780062334695

LC bl2015044700

An account of how eight jewels shaped the course of history shares insights into the role of precious gemstones in triggering cultural movements, political dynasties and wars while exploring how jewels reflect darker aspects of human nature.

"History enthusiasts will be entertained by Raden's knowledge of famous names as well as her narrative approach to the topic. Occasional injections of humor will keep readers interested." Library Journal.

Young, Anastasia

The **workbench** guide to jewelry techniques / Anastasia Young. Interweave Press LLC, 2009. 320 p. : **739.27**

1. Jewelry making
ISBN 9781596681699

LC 2009041385

"A Quarto Book" -- T.p. verso.

Presents a comprehensive workshop reference for jewelry making and includes tips on tool shapes, an introduction to the history of jewelry, and suggestions for photographing and promoting finished pieces.

"This is a reference guide for all jewelers, amateur or professional. Includes extensive photographic illustrations of virtually all techniques needed to create quality jewelry. Also has an excellent chapter on design, and additional sections on photographing, exhibiting, marketing, and selling work." Library Journal.

739.27028 Jewelry--Auxiliary techniques and procedures

McGrath, Jinks

The **complete** jewelry making course / Jinks McGrath. Barron's, 2007. 144 p. : **739.27028**

1. Jewelry making

ISBN 9780764136603

LC bl2007026247

This comprehensive and heavily illustrated manual teaches the craft of jewelry making to students looking to create professional quality items.

740 Graphic arts

Eskilson, Stephen, 1964-

Graphic design : a new history / Stephen J. Eskilson. Yale University Press, c2012. 464 p. : **740**

1. Graphic arts -- History. 2. Commercial art -- History.

ISBN 9780300172607

LC 2011025963

A classic and indispensable account of graphic design history from the Industrial Revolution to the present.

"Given the sheer number of topics and concepts encompassed by graphic design, Eskilson isn't able to dwell on any specific subject for too long, which may frustrate some readers. Originally published in 2007, this newly-updated edition adds over eighty new images and revised text, making this an even more essential reference for designers as well as art historians." Publishers Weekly

Ogura, Yoshiko

The **complete** guide to drawing for beginners : 21 step-by-step lessons: over 450 illustrations! / Yoshiko Ogura. Tuttle Publishing 2020 127 p. **740**

1. Drawing

ISBN 9784805315767

"It's difficult to see how an in-person class could teach much more." Booklist

740.9 History, geographic treatment, biography of graphic arts and of decorative arts

Harvey, Eleanor Jones

The **Civil** War and American art / Eleanor Jones Harvey. Smithsonian American Art Museum ; 2012 xvii, 316 p. : **740.9**

1. Art and society -- United States -- History -- 19th century 2. Art, American -- 19th century -- Themes, motives 3. United States -- History -- Civil War, 1861-1865 Art and the war Exhibitions.

ISBN 9780300187335

LC 2012029342

Published in conjunction with the exhibition of the same name, on view at the Smithsonian American Art Museum in Washington, D.C., from November 16, 2012 through April 28, 2013, and at the Metropolitan Museum of Art, New York City, from May 21-September 2, 2013.

"The American Civil War was arguably the first modern war. Its grim reality, captured through the new medium of photography, was laid bare. American artists could not approach the conflict with the conventions of European history painting, which glamorized the hero on the battlefield. Instead, many artists found ways to weave the war into works of art that considered the human narrative--the daily experiences of soldiers, slaves, and families left behind. Artists and writers wrestled with the ambiguity and anxiety of the Civil War and used landscape imagery to give voice to their misgivings as well as their hopes for themselves and the nation.This important book looks at the range of artwork created before, during, and following the war, in the years between 1859 and 1876. Author Eleanor Jones Harvey examines the implications of the war on landscape and genre painting, history painting, and photography, as represented in some of the greatest masterpieces of 19th-century American art. The book features extensive quotations from men and women alive during the war years, alongside text by literary figures including Emily Dickinson, Mark Twain, and Walt Whitman, among many others".--Provided by publisher.

741.09 History, geographic treatment, biography

Kline, Fred R.

Leonardo's holy child : the discovery of a Leonardo da Vinci masterpiece: a connoiseur's search for lost art in America / Fred R. Kline. Pegasus Books, 2016 384 p. **741.09**

1. Leonardo, da Vinci, 1452-1519 2. Drawing. 3. Art -- Collectors and collecting 4. Art -- Provenance.

ISBN 9781605989792

LC bl2016018832

Fred Kline is a well-known art historian, dealer, connoisseur, and explorer who has made a career of scouring antique stores, estate sales, and auctions looking for unusual--and often misidentified--works of art. Many of the gems he has found are now in major museum collections like the Frick, the Getty, and the Metropolitan Museum of Art. But this book is about the discovery of one piece in particular: About ten years ago, when Kline was routinely combing through a Christie's catalog, a beautiful little drawing caught his eye. Attributed to Carracci, it came with a very low estimate, but Kline's every instinct told him that the attribution was wrong. He placed a bid at the low asking price and bought the drawing outright. And that was the beginning of how Kline discovered Leonardo da Vinci's model drawing for the Infant Jesus and the Infant St. John. It is the first work by da Vinci to have surfaced in over a century.

"Even the most casual museum goer will find something to appreciate in this fascinating account." Booklist.

Whistler, Catherine

Venice and drawing, 1500-1800 : theory, practice and collecting / Catherine Whistler. Yale University Press, 2016 xxxv, 344 p. : **741.09**

1. Drawing, Italian -- Collectors and collecting 2. Drawing, Italian -- Italy -- Venice

ISBN 9780300187731

LC 2015045305

"With its wealth of new information and its highlighting of superb examples of the craft, this book will be the gold standard for the study of Venetian drawings for years to come." Choice.

741.092 Biography

Lester, Toby
Da Vinci's ghost : genius, obsession, and how Leonardo created the world in his own image / Toby Lester. Free Press, 2012. 304 p. **741.092**
1. Leonardo, da Vinci, 1452-1519. Vitruvian man. 2. Leonardo, da Vinci, 1452-1519 Criticism and interpretation 3. Leonardo, da Vinci, 1452-1519. 4. Intellectual life -- History 5. Drawing -- History 6. Anatomy 7. Philosophy, Italian
ISBN 9781439189238
LC 2011027966

Citing the ubiquitous presence of the Renaissance master's meticulous rendering of an outstretched human form in a circle and square, an account of the epic intellectual journeys that inspired the Vitruvian Man's creation shares lesser-known aspects of da Vinci's life and how he served to bridge the Middle Ages to a monumental period of art, science and philosophy.

741.2 Techniques, procedures, apparatus, equipment, materials

Birch, Helen (Artist)
Freehand : sketching tips and tricks drawn from art / Helen Birch. Chronicle Books, 2013 224 p. : **741.2**
1. Creation (Literary, artistic, etc) 2. Drawing -- Technique
ISBN 9781452119779
LC 2013036430

Provides commentary on a selection of different freehand drawings, identifying tips, techniques, and different tools to inspire readers.

"Employing the formula of examples + explanations = inspiration, journalist and artist Birch presents the work of dozens of practicing contemporary artists, highlighting prominent techniques so that the reader can emulate and build upon them. Illustrations can be found on nearly every page, including many close-up views that break down for the reader what is happening in the more elaborate drawings." Library Journal.

De Reyna, Rudy, 1914-
How to draw what you see / Rudy de Reyna. Watson-Guptill Publications, 1996, c1970. 175 p. : **741.2**
1. Drawing -- Study and teaching
ISBN 9780823023752
LC BL 99786913

Includes index.

Reprint. Originally published: c1970.

Provides lessons in dimensions, proportions, the recognition of basic structure, lighting, shading, and the selection and use of various drawing materials.

"This compact 35th anniversary edition touches on still life, landscapes, and figure drawing in pencil, charcoal, watercolor wash, acrylic, and ink. De Reyna's dedication and enthusiasm are evident on every page." Library Journal.

Eagle, Ellen
Pastel painting atelier : essential lessons in techniques, practices, and materials / Ellen Eagle ; foreword by Maxine Hong Kingston. Watson-Guptill Publications, 2013 192 p. : **741.2**
1. Pastel drawing -- Technique
ISBN 9780823008414
LC 2012018761

A complete primer for serious beginners through advanced artists traces the history, materials and techniques of pastel artwork, featuring the pieces of old masters as well as a selection of notable contemporaries to cover each stage, discussing formal techniques as well as steps for pursuing personal aesthetics.

Edwards, Betty, 1926-
Drawing on the right side of the brain / Betty Edwards. Tarcher/Penguin, 2012. xxxiii, 284 p. : **741.2**
1. Cerebral dominance 2. Drawing -- Technique 3. Visual perception
ISBN 9781585429202
LC 2012001232

Rev. and expanded ed. of: New drawing on the right side of the brain. 1999.

Helps the reader gain access to right-brain functions, which affect artistic and creative abilities, by teaching drawing through unusual exercises designed to increase visual skills.

"This new edition of the hugely popular and influential drawing manual first published over 30 years ago incorporates new findings from neuroscience, like the discovery of brain plasticity, together with the tried-and-true exercises included in past editions." Library Journal.

Kaupelis, Robert
Experimental drawing / Robert Kaupelis. Watson-Guptill, 1992, c1980. 192 p. : **741.2**
1. Drawing -- Study and teaching 2. Drawing -- Technique
ISBN 9780823016228
LC BL 99732647

Reprint. Originally published: 1980.

Suggests new ways to use contour, gesture, organization, light, and dark, and new techniques involving photographs, grids, and photocopiers, to produce innovative drawings.

McKinley, Richard, 1958-
Pastel pointers : top secrets for beautiful pastel paintings / Richard McKinley. North Light Books, c2010. 127 p. : **741.2**
1. Pastel drawing -- Technique
ISBN 9781440308390
LC 2010028709

This book covers everything from the fundamentals to get you going (how to lay out your palette, create an underpainting, evoke luminous effects) to inspirations that will keep you growing (plein air painting, working in a series, keeping a painting journal). Whether you're a beginner or an experienced painter anxious to explore the expressive possibilities of pastel, this is your guide to making the most of the medium. --From publisher description.

Micklewright, Keith, 1933-
Drawing : mastering the language of visual expression / Keith Mickelwright. Harry N. Abrams, 2005. 168 p. : **741.2**
1. Communication in art 2. Drawing -- Technique
ISBN 9780810992382
LC 2005005862

Gives a history of drawing and includes chapters on such subjects as proportion, light, dimension, visual relationships, materials, and movement, and discusses how drawing is like language because it brings thoughts to life.

Price, Maggie, 1947-
Painting with pastels : easy techniques to master the medium /

Maggie Price. North Light Books, c2007. 128 p. : **741.2**
1. Pastel drawing -- Technique
ISBN 9781581808193
LC 2006029048
Includes index.
From selecting the right materials to learning the fundamentals of composition, Maggie starts with the basics and progresses to 21 complete pastel demonstrations that detail specific painting techniques and effects.

Scheinberger, Felix
Dare to sketch : a guide to drawing on the go / Felix Scheinberger. Watson-Guptill, 2017 159 p. ; **741.2**
1. Drawing -- Technique
ISBN 9780399579554
LC 2017020347
"An inspirational, instructional, and visually stimulating guide to sketching and drawing. Dare to Sketch is filled with practical tips about which materials to use, a variety of subject matter ranging from easy to more challenging, and wisdom about overcoming creative blocks and fear of making mistakes".-- Provided by publisher.
"Lots of practical advice helps with everything from how to confront a blank sketchbook to the best way to catch a subject that won't sit still." Library Journal.

Willenbrink, Mark, 1962-
Drawing for the absolute beginner : a clear & easy guide to successful drawing / Mark and Mary Willenbrink. North Light Books, c2006. 128 p. : **741.2**
1. Drawing -- Technique
ISBN 9781581807899
LC 2006008900
Includes index.
A series of confidence-building exercises take the reader from the basic fundamentals of drawing to the complexities of creating landscapes, still lifes, people, and much more in this helpful guide for artists of all skill levels.

741.5 Cartoons, graphic novels, caricatures, comics

Abel, Jessica
Drawing words, writing pictures : making comics from manga to graphic novels / Jessica Abel, Matt Madden. First Second Books, 2008. 206 p. : **741.5**
1. Comic book writing. 2. Cartooning -- Technique. 3. Comic books, strips, etc. -- Technique. 4. Comic book illustration -- Technique. 5. Comics and Graphic novels
ISBN 9781596431317
"This book offers step-by-step entry into a complicated series of skills in a nonscary and approachable way." Library Journal.

Mastering comics : drawing words & writing pictures continued / Jessica Abel and Matt Madden First Second Books, 2012. 336 p. : **741.5**
1. Comic book writing. 2. Cartooning -- Technique. 3. Comic books, strips, etc. -- Technique. 4. Comic book illustration -- Technique. 5. Comics and Graphic novels
ISBN 9781596436176
Presents instructions for mastering the creation of comic books and graphic novels, providing guidelines for the intermediate cartoonist on technique, story generation, narrative tools, and business and industry insights.

Barry, Lynda, 1956-
What it is / Lynda Barry. Drawn & Quarterly, 2008. 209 p. **741.5**
1. Writing -- Self-instruction. 2. Creative writing -- Study and teaching. 3. Comics and Graphic novels
ISBN 9781897299357
Eisner Awards, Best Reality-Based Work, 2009.
Presented as a series of lined-notebook cartoon collages, a visual testament to the creator's life-long quest for creative excellence explores such questions as the capacity of material objects for summoning memories and the tangible qualities of images.
"Every so often a book comes along that surpasses expectations, taking readers on an inspirational voyage that they don't want to leave. This is one such book." School Library Journal.

Brunetti, Ivan
Cartooning : philosophy and practice / Ivan Brunetti. Yale University Press, 2011. 77 p. : **741.5**
1. Cartooning -- Philosophy 2. Cartooning -- Technique
ISBN 9780300170993
LC 2010940419
Provides lessons on the art of cartooning along with information on terminology, tools, techniques, and theory.

Chelsea, David
Perspective in action : creative exercises for depicting spatial representation from the Renaissance to the digital age / David Chelsea. Watson-Guptill Publications, 2017 171 p. : **741.5**
1. Graphic novels 2. Perspective 3. Comic books, strips, etc.
ISBN 9781607749462
LC 2016045493
Chiefly illustrations.
Includes index.
"Using the graphic novel format, Perspective in Action features 33 easy-to-follow demonstrations to teach the major discoveries in perspective".-- Provided by publisher.
"Cleverly packaged in a graphic novel format, artist Chelsea's (Perspective! For Comic Book Artists) book covers all aspects of simple perspective drawing and depicts its more complex applications." Library Journal.

Cowsill, Alan
★The **DC** comics encyclopedia : the definitive guide to the characters of the DC universe / text by Alan Cowsill, Alex Irvine, Steve Korte, Matt Manning, Stephen (Win) Wiacek, Sven Wilson ; additional text by Scott Beatty, Robert Greenberger, Phil Jiminez, Nick Jones, Dan Wallace. DK Publishing, 2016. 368 p. : **741.5**
1. DC Comics Encyclopedias 2. Comic strip characters -- Encyclopedias 3. Superheroes -- Encyclopedias 4. Comic books, strips, etc. -- Encyclopedias 5. Encyclopedias
ISBN 9781465453570
Provides a guide to all of the superheroes and archvillains of the DC universe, featuring more than one thousand different characters, including images from the original comic books, from the past seventy-five years of DC Comics.

Derf
My friend Dahmer / written and illustrated by Derf Backderf.

Abrams ComicArts, 2012. 224 p. : **741.5**

1. Dahmer, Jeffrey, 1960-1994. 2. High school students. 3. Murderers. 4. Teenagers -- Friendship. 5. Suburban life. 6. Middle West -- History -- 20th century. 7. Biographical comics 8. Comics and Graphic novels
ISBN 9781419702167

LC 2011285306

YALSA Great Graphic Novel for Teens, 2013.

In graphic novel format, the author offers an account of growing up in the same schools as Jeffrey Dahmer, who went on to become one of the most notorious serial killers and cannibals in United States history.

Eisner, Will

★**Comics** and sequential art : principles and practices from the legendary cartoonist / Will Eisner. W. W. Norton, 2008. xii, 175 p. : **741.5**

1. Comic books, strips, etc. -- Technique. 2. Drawing -- Technique. 3. Cartooning -- Technique.
ISBN 9780393331264

LC 2008020042

Rev. ed. of: Comics & sequential art. 1985.

Includes index.

"This guide by one of the veterans of the industry provides a solid framework in the principles of drawing comic art." Library Journal.

Gitlin, Marty

A **celebration** of animation : the 100 greatest cartoon characters in television history / Marty Gitlin and Joe Wos. Lyons Press, 2017. 256 p. **741.5**

1. Cartoon characters 2. Television cartoon shows 3. Popular culture 4. Cartoons (Animated films) -- History and criticism
ISBN 9781630762780

LC 2017025749

Explores the greatest cartoon characters in television history, providing such information about each character as its creator, debut, voice artist, and antagonists.

Hart, Christopher

Cartooning for the beginner / Christopher Hart. Watson-Guptill, 2000. 144 p. : **741.5**

1. Cartooning -- Technique
ISBN 9780823005864

LC BL 00014882

Includes index.

"This guide to cartooning techniques covers the world of cartoon animals, animation, and edgy 'toons." Library Journal.

Howe, Sean

Marvel Comics : the untold story / Sean Howe. Harper, 2012. 320 p. **741.5**

1. Marvel Comics Group. 2. Publishers and publishing -- United States -- History. 3. Comic books, strips, etc. -- Publishing. 4. Popular culture -- History -- 20th century. 5. Comic book characters. 6. United States -- Popular culture -- History -- 20th century.
ISBN 9780061992100

LC 2012015058

Pulp magazine publisher Marvin Goodman reluctantly expanded into the new field of comic books in 1939, but Marvel Comics didn't really make the scene until 1961. Author Sean Howe delivers the scoop on the notoriously contentious relationships among Marvel's artists, writers, and editors throughout its publishing history. Stan Lee and Jack Kirby take center stage, as do their famous creations -- like the golden-boy Captain America, and lovable (if nerdy) Spiderman, four-color comic book heroes who are now among Hollywood's hottest stars.

Jones, Gerard

Men of tomorrow : geeks, gangsters, and the birth of the comic book / Gerard Jones. Basic Books, c2004. xv, 384 p. : **741.5**

1. Cartoonists -- United States 2. Comic books, strips, etc. -- History and criticism 3. United States -- History -- 20th century 4. United States -- Social life and customs -- 20th century 5. United States -- Social life and customs -- 21st century
ISBN 9780465036561

LC 2004009031

Springing from the depths of the Depression, the birth of the comic book superhero spawned a new genre that still resonates seventy years later, a journey chronicled in an in-depth look at the people and personalities behind the creations.

Karp, Jesse

Graphic novels in your school library / Jesse Karp ; illustrated by Rush Kress. American Library Association, c2012. xi, 146 p. : **741.5**

1. Graphic novels in education -- United States. 2. Graphic novels. 3. Libraries -- Special collections -- Graphic novels. 4. School libraries -- Collection development -- United States.
ISBN 0838910890

LC 2011026353

Explains how and when to use graphic novels in the library or classroom, detailing the differences in format, the history of the medium, and annotated lists of core titles.

"A graphic-novel expert and a librarian, Karp partners with illustrator Kress on this latest offering, intended for school librarians working in preschool through high-school settings... Most school libraries will benefit from this accessible and practical manual." Booklist.

Kawa, Abraham

Democracy / Abraham Kawa, illustrated by Alekos Papadatos. Bloomsbury, 2015. 352 p. **741.5**

1. Democracy -- Philosophy. 2. Political science. 3. Democracy -- Ancient Greece -- History. 4. Ancient Greece. 5. Comics and Graphic novels
ISBN 9781608197194

LC 2020289649

From a team including the artists of the New York Times bestseller Logicomix, another entertaining and educational graphic delight focusing on the origins and rise of democracy.

Kitchen, Denis, 1946-

The **art** of Harvey Kurtzman : the mad genius of comics / Denis Kitchen and Paul Buhle ; introduction by Harry Shearer. Abrams ComicArts, 2009. xiii, 241 p. : **741.5**

1. Kurtzman, Harvey Criticism and interpretation. 2. Cartoonists -- United States -- Criticism and interpretation.
ISBN 9780810972964

LC 2008004809

Essential Harvey Kurtzman bibliography: p. 241.

Shares hundreds of illustrations, paintings, pencil sketches, illustrated correspondence, and vintage photos from this master of American comics.

Kneece, Mark

The **art** of comic book writing : the definitive guide to outlining, scripting, and pitching your sequential art stories / Mark Kneece. Watson-Guptill Publications, 2015 184 p. : **741.5**

1. Comic books, strips, etc. -- Authorship.

ISBN 9780770436971

LC 2015007716

Includes index.

A successful writer and instructor offers practical advice, essential tools and simple examples for aspiring comic book writers at any level to use to better navigate the mysteries and pitfalls of getting published in the industry.

Lee, Stan, 1922-2018

Stan Lee's How to draw comics : from the legendary co-creator of Spider-Man, the Incredible Hulk, Fantastic Four, X-Men, and Iron Man. Watson-Guptill Publications, c2010. 224 p. : **741.5**

1. Comic books, strips, etc. -- Technique. 2. Drawing -- Technique.

ISBN 9780823000838

LC 2010005781

"The author includes chapters on creating comics with computer programs and online resources and how to get work in the 21st century. The book begins with a brief history of comics, then focuses on action-adventure style, romance, humor, horror, and Japanese manga. This is the one book anyone interested in drawing comics should own." Library Journal.

Leong, Sonia

101 top tips from professional manga artists / Sonia Leong. Barron's, 2013. 176 p. : **741.5**

1. Comic books, strips, etc. -- Japan -- Technique. 2. Cartooning -- Technique 3. Comic strip characters -- Japan

ISBN 9781438002064

LC 2012948428

Includes index.

"Freelance comic artist and illustrator Leong and several contributing artists provide over 100 tips grouped and organized around basic topics, highlighting key aspects of manga such as character design, backgrounds, props, software and media, and even practices of successful professionals." Library Journal.

Lepore, Jill, 1966-

★The **secret** history of Wonder Woman / Jill Lepore. Alfred A. Knopf, 2014. 432 p. **741.5**

1. Marston, William Moulton, 1893-1947. 2. Wonder Woman (Fictitious character) 3. Comic book writers 4. Comic books, strips, etc. -- History and criticism. 5. Nontraditional families

ISBN 9780385354042

LC 2014011064

ALA Notable Book, 2015.

American History Book Prize, 2014.

A cultural history of Wonder Woman traces the character's creation and enduring popularity, drawing on interviews and archival research to reveal the pivotal role of feminism in shaping her seven-decade story.

McCloud, Scott, 1960-

Making comics : storytelling secrets of comics, manga and graphic novels / Scott McCloud. Harper, 2006. 264 p. : **741.5**

1. Comic book writing. 2. Cartooning. 3. Drawing. 4. Storytelling. 5. Comics and Graphic novels

ISBN 9780060780944

LC 2006287667

"The author explores practical matters, including comics devices such as panels, word balloons, and sound effects; facial expressions and body language; the creation of convincing and evocative settings; and the different tools artists can use for the job, from pencils to computers. He also delves into the framing of images in panels, the flow of panels on a page, and the relationships between words and pictures in comics. . . . This is thoughtful, fascinating, stimulating, potentially controversial, and inspiring." Library Journal.

Reinventing comics Harper Collins, 2000. 237 p. **741.5**

1. Cartoons. 2. Comic books, strips, etc. -- History and criticism 3. Comic books, strips, etc. -- Technological innovations. 4. Comics and Graphic novels

ISBN 0060953500

Explains how digital revolutions are affecting the comic strip business, from the artist's creation of the comic strips to the distribution of the finished product to the consumers.

"The author maps out 12 revolutions, which, he believes, need to take place for comics to survive and finally be recognized as a legitimate art form. The topics progress from the oldest of comic-related arguments (seeking respect) to the use of computer technology to renew and expand its audience. These brilliantly presented discussions concern comics as literature, comics as art, creators' rights, industry innovation, and public perception, among other topics." Library Journal.

★**Understanding** comics : the invisible art / Scott McCloud. Tundra Pub., 1993. 215 p. : **741.5**

1. Cartooning -- Technique. 2. Comic books, strips, etc. -- History and criticism 3. Comic books, strips, etc. -- Illustrations. 4. Comics and Graphic novels

ISBN 1568620195

LC 93184802

Harvey Awards, Best Graphic Album - Original, 1994.

"The author traces the 3,000-year history (from Egyptian paintings on) of telling stories through pictures; describes the language of comicsits grammar and vocabulary; explains the use of different types of images ranging from ironic to realistic; depicts how artists convey movement and the passage of time and use various symbols as shorthand; and [seeks to demonstrate] the expressive emotional qualities of different drawing styles." Booklist. [review of 1993 edition]

Satrapi, Marjane, 1969-

Embroideries / Marjane Satrapi. Pantheon Books, 2005. 144 p. : **741.5**

1. Satrapi, Marjane, 1969- 2. Sexuality. 3. Women's role -- Iran. 4. Female friendship. 5. Regret. 6. Iran -- Social life and customs -- 20th century. 7. Comics and Graphic novels

ISBN 0375423052

LC 2004058660

A collection of stories and anecdotes, told in the form of a graphic novel, reveals the love and sex lives of a group of women as revealed during an afternoon of conversation and tea-drinking.

"Discussions of sex are frank and explicit and laced with high humor. . . . Satrapi's simple black-and-white cartooning style is tremendously effective, expertly portraying emotional nuances with just a few lines" Library Journal.

Spiegelman, Art

In the shadow of no towers / Art Spiegelman. Pantheon Books, 2004. 42 p. : **741.5**

1. Spiegelman, Art 2. World Trade Center, New York City. 3. September 11 Terrorist Attacks, 2001. 4. Grief 5. Anger 6. New

York City Comic books, strips, etc. 7. Comics and Graphic novels 8. Biographical comics
ISBN 9780375423079

LC 2004043870

The creator of Maus conveys experience of the September 11th tragedy in a series of drawings and text that capture the horror of the event, its impact on his own life, and the dangerous erosion of American democracy that has occured in the aftermath of the attack.

"The author provides a hair-raising and wry account of his family's frantic efforts to locate one another on September 11 as well as a morbidly funny survey of his trademark sense of existential doom. . . . This is a powerful and quirky work of visual storytelling by a master comics artist." Publishers Weekly.

Voloj, Julian

Ghetto brother : warrior to peacemaker / Julian Voloj ; illustrated by Claudia Ahlering. NBM Comics Lit, 2015. 127 p. : **741.5**

1. Melendez, Benjy. 2. Gang leaders. 3. Nonviolence. 4. Mediation. 5. Gangs. 6. Bronx, New York City. 7. New York City. 8. Biographical comics. 9. Comics and Graphic novels
ISBN 9781561639489

LC 2015931382

Tells the true story of Benjy Melendez, a Bronx legend, son of Puerto-Rican immigrants, who founded, at the end of the 1960s, the notorious Ghetto Brothers gang.

"A fine documentary graphic novel of cultural and personal change for the better." Booklist.

Watterson, Bill

The **complete** Calvin and Hobbes / Bill Watterson. Andrews McMeel Pub., 2005. 1440 p. **741.5**

1. Calvin (Fictitious character : Watterson) 2. Boy adventurers 3. Six-year-old boys 4. Boys 5. Newspaper comic strips 6. Comics and Graphic novels 7. Humorous comics
ISBN 0740748475

LC 2004062709

In three volumes.

Illustrated by the author.

Includes an introduction by the author.

Brings together every "Calvin and Hobbes" cartoon that has ever appeared in syndication, along with stories and poems from classic collections.

Weldon, Glen

★The **caped** crusade : Batman and the rise of nerd culture / Glen Weldon. Simon & Schuster, 2016 viii, 324 p. **741.5**

1. Batman (Fictitious character) 2. Popular culture -- History -- 20th century. 3. Superhero comics -- History and criticism. 4. Social history.
ISBN 9781476756691

Explains Batman's rises and falls throughout the ages--and what his story tells us about ourselves.

"Ostensibly written with non-nerds in mind, this will, nevertheless, have huge appeal for members of the very group it attempts to dissect. Includes a truly spectacular, comprehensive bibliography." Booklist.

741.6 Graphic design, illustration, commercial art

Bang, Molly

★**Picture** this : how pictures work / Molly Bang. SeaStar Books, c2000. 96 p. : **741.6**

1. Illustration of books -- Psychological aspects. 2. Visual perception -- Psychological aspects. 3. Illustrated children's books -- Psychological aspects.
ISBN 1587170299

LC 00024402

Republished in 2016 by Chronicle Books.

"A must-have book for anyone wanting to learn or teach about art elements and principles and their connections to (picture book) art and visual perception." Kirkus.

Crumb, R.

R. Crumb : the complete record cover collection. / R. Crumb. W.W. Norton, c2011. [108] pages : **741.6**

1. Crumb, R. 2. Graphic arts 3. Sound recordings -- Album covers
ISBN 9780393082784

LC bl2011026934

In slipcase.

A collection of album cover artwork from a founder of the underground comix movement.

"This volume is filled with the artist's designs for such ephemera as 'Unknown Detroit Bluesmen' or Cliff Edwards's 'I'm a Bear in a Ladies' Boudoir.' Starting in the 1970s, Mr. Crumb produced covers for reissues from labels like Yazoo, Blue Goose and Barrelhouse Records, and his love for the music is evident--a stippled Robert Johnson stares out in stark black and white, Bessie Smith sings 'Put a Little Sugar in My Bowl' and Charlie Patton gets his own mini-graphic novel. (The biggest act here is Big Brother and the Holding Company, with Janis Joplin done over to fit Crumb's zaftig ideal.) In this journeyman work, however, the discipline of playing second fiddle to his favorite musicians keeps the artist's self-loathing in check without taming the ribald humor that is also a hallmark of the blues. Few Crumb projects seem like so much fun--to read about, to look at or to listen along to." Wall Street Journal.

Heller, Steven

Becoming a graphic and digital designer : a guide to careers in design / Steven Heller, Veronique Vienne. John Wiley & Sons, Inc., 2015 xiii, 335 p. ; **741.6**

1. Commercial art -- Vocational guidance 2. Graphic arts -- Vocational guidance 3. Computer graphics -- Vocational guidance
ISBN 9781118771983

LC 2015011294

Includes index.

Becoming a Graphic and Digital Designer is a single source guide to the myriad of options available to those pursuing a graphic design career. With an emphasis on portfolio requirements and job opportunities, this guide helps both students and individuals interested in entering the design field prepare for successful careers. --From publisher description.

Kahng, Eik, 1963-

David Wiesner & the art of wordless storytelling / Eik Kahng, Ellen Keiter, Katherine Roeder, David Wiesner. Santa Barbara Museum of Art, 2016 110 p. : **741.6**

1. Wiesner, David Exhibitions 2. Art and literature -- United States -- Exhibitions 3. Illustrated children's books -- United States -- Exhibitions
ISBN 9780300226010

LC 2016041100

"This book is published in conjunction with the exhibition David Wiesner & the Art of Wordless Storytelling presented at the Santa Barbara Museum of Art from January 29 through May 14, 2017."

This handsome volume is the first to examine his creative process and his many sources of inspiration. The book features dozens of lavish color plates, from early work to the exquisitely wrought watercolors that are the basis of his best-known books, along with pages excerpted from his forthcoming first graphic novel, Fish Girl. --From publisher description.

Kidd, Chip

Book one : work, 1986-2006 : album / Chip Kidd. Rizzoli, c2005. 400 p. : **741.6**

1. Kidd, Chip. 2. Book design -- United States 3. Book jackets -- United States

ISBN 9780847827480

LC bl2006026118

Includes index.

"Stylishly designed and richly produced, this witty volume works both as a retrospective of Kidd's renowned book covers and as a memoir of his career in publishing." Publishers Weekly.

Meder, Danielle

Draw fashion now : techniques, inspiration, and ideas for illustrating and imagining your designs / Danielle Meder. Rockport, 2016. 143 p. : **741.6**

1. Fashion drawing -- Technique.

ISBN 9781631591204

LC bl2016030336

"With fashion paper dolls and a customizable, designer-inspired wardrobe"--Cover.

Provides step-by-step instructions for drawing fashion designs from basic forms to finished products in environments such as red carpet events and live fashion runway shows.

"Fashion buffs and aspiring designers of any skill level will enjoy this fun guide." Library Journal.

Rees, Darrel

How to be an illustrator / Darrel Rees. Laurence King Publishing Ltd, 2014. 167 p. : **741.6**

1. Commerical artists -- Vocational guidance 2. Illustrators -- Vocational guidance

ISBN 9781780673288

LC bl2014008473

Offers practical guidance to aspiring illustrators, including effective ways to approach would-be clients, how to negotiate contracts, and how to set up a studio.

"This guide...shares the author's insights on everything except the artistic aspects of the occupation, i.e., business concerns such as education, job hunting, project management, billing, and promoting yourself." Library Journal.

Rendgen, Sandra

Understanding the world : the atlas of infographics / Sandra Rendgen ; ed. Julius Wiedemann. Taschen, 2014 456 p. : **741.6**

1. Graphic arts 2. Graphic methods

ISBN 9783836548830

LC bl2014055105

"The atlas of infographics"--Cover.

Includes index.

Collects over 280 information graphics that render data on the environment, technology, economics, society, and culture into visual formats.

Schiller, Justin G.

Maurice Sendak : a celebration of the artist and his work / curated by Justin G. Schiller and Dennis M.V. David ; edited by Leonard S. Marcus. Abrams, 2013. 223 p. : **741.6**

1. Sendak, Maurice Exhibitions.

ISBN 9781419708268

LC 2013007227

"Published in conjunction with the exhibition Maurice Sendak: A Celebration of His Life and Art at the Society of Illustrators, New York, June 11-August 17, 2013, curated by Justin G. Schiller and Dennis M. V. David."

A companion guide to an exhibition at the Society of Illustrators features over two hundred illustrations by the artist, including previously unpublished pieces, preliminary drawings, and variant art for his famous works.

742 Perspective in drawing

Brehm, Matthew T., 1966-

Drawing perspective : how to see it, how to apply it / Matthew Brehm. Barrons Educational Series, Inc., 2016. 144 p. : **742**

1. Drawing -- Technique 2. Perspective

ISBN 9781438006598

LC 2014945484

"Put your skills to the test! Includes a 32-page workbook with grids to fill in and artwork to complete"--Cover.

A hands-on guide to perspective provides exercises designed to make drawing perspective effortless and easy.

"Dynamic layouts and simple structure make this guide fun to read and easy to comprehend." Library Journal.

Norling, Ernest R. (Ernest Ralph), 1892-

Perspective made easy / Ernest R. Norling. Dover Publications, 1999. xii, 203 p. : **742**

1. Drawing -- Technique 2. Perspective

ISBN 9780486404738

LC 99010310

Originally published: New York : Macmillian, 1939.

Mastery of perspective is a basic skill every artist must have. This simple, nontechnical guide will enable you to master its essentials in a relatively short time. Clear and concise, this book is an essential addition to any artist's bookshelf. --From publisher description.

743 Drawing and drawings by subject

Vanderpoel, John Henry, 1857-1911

The **human** figure / John H. Vanderpoel. Dover Publications, 1958, c1935. 143 p. : **743**

1. Figure drawing.

ISBN 9780486204321

LC BL 99965426

Originally published: New York : Sterling Pub. Co., 1935.

The classic text on drawing human anatomy offers instructions on depicting such difficult areas as the lips, knee, ear, and nose.

743.4 Drawing human figures

Bradley, Barbara, 1927-

Drawing people : how to portray the clothed figure / Barbara Bradley. North Light Books, c2003. 175 p. : **743.4**

1. Drapery in art 2. Drawing -- Technique 3. Human figure in art
ISBN 9781581803594

LC 2003042043

Includes index.

Teaches the fundamentals of any drawing, then illustrates how to draw clothed human figures that are active or at rest.

"Watson's Life Drawing Class is a rich and dynamic volume on the human form, clothed and unclothed, flabby and buff, indoors and out. Using pencil, charcoal, ink, and watercolor, Watson (Artists Sketchbook) utilizes photographs to complement lessons in balance and proportion, lighting, mood, and composition." Library Journal.

Hale, Robert Beverly, 1901-

Anatomy lessons from the great masters / Robert Beverly Hale and Terence Coyle. Watson-Guptill Publications, c2000. 271 p. : **743.4**

1. Anatomy, Artistic 2. Drawing, European -- Themes, motives
ISBN 9780823002818

LC 2003265337

"Advanced students will find Hale and Coyle's Anatomy Lessons from the Great Masters a rich source of inspiration." Library Journal

Hart, Christopher, 1957-

Human anatomy made amazingly easy / Christopher Hart. Watson-Guptill Publications, 2000. 144 p. : **743.4**

1. Anatomy, Artistic 2. Drawing -- Technique 3. Human figure in art
ISBN 9780823024971

LC 00043514

Includes index.

Offers instructions for drawing seated, reclining, and standing figures, and features twelve projects from simple charcoal drawings to complex watercolors.

Huston, Steve

Figure drawing for artists : making every mark count / Steve Huston. Rockport Publishers, 2016. 192 p. : **743.4**

1. Figure drawing -- Technique 2. Human figure in art -- Technique
ISBN 9781631590658

LC 2018277532

Teaches human figure drawing techniques for both beginner and advanced students, offering specific instructions for areas such as the head, torso, arms, and feet.

Loomis, Andrew, 1892-1959

Figure drawing for all it's worth : For All It's Worth / Andrew Loomis. Titan Books, 2011. 204 p. : **743.4**

1. Anatomy, Artistic 2. Figure drawing -- Technique
ISBN 9780857680983

LC 2011381456

"A book of fundamentals for an artistic career"--Jkt.

Originally published: New York : Viking Press, 1943.

The illustrator Andrew Loomis (1892-1959) is revered among artists -- including comics superstar Alex Ross -- for his mastery of figure drawing and clean, Realist style. His hugely influential series of art instruction books have never been bettered, and Figure Drawing is the first in Titan's programme of facsimile editions, returning these classic titles to print for the first time in decades. --From publisher description.

Parks, Carrie

Secrets to drawing realistic faces / Carrie Stuart Parks. North Light Books, c2003. 140 p. : **743.4**

1. Drawing -- Technique 2. Face in art
ISBN 9781581802160

LC 2002023509

Includes index.

Provides examples and exercises to teach readers how to draw faces, covering shapes, shading, eyes, noses, lips, teeth, the head, and hair.

"Her useful and far-ranging discussion of materials includes an evaluation of pencils' graphite grades, kneaded and electric erasers, blending tools, and papers." Booklist.

Ryder, Anthony

The **artist's** complete guide to figure drawing : a contemporary perspective on the classical tradition / Anthony Ryder. Watson-Guptill Publications, 2000. 160 p. : **743.4**

1. Figure drawing -- Technique
ISBN 9780823003037

LC 99022843

Includes index.

Demonstrates a three-step drawing method exploring outline, contour, and the capture of light, volume, and mass

Winslow, Valerie L.

Classic human anatomy : the artist's guide to form, function, and movement / Valerie L. Winslow. Watson-Guptill, c2009. 303 p. : **743.4**

1. Anatomy, Artistic 2. Figure drawing -- Technique
ISBN 9780823024155

LC 2009280099

"The study of anatomy has long been essential training for painters and sculptures who want to accurately portray the human form. With hundreds of drawings and meticulously researched text, this book includes: an overview of the history of artistic anatomy; an introduction to the "language of anatomy" that makes the meaning of anatomical terms transparent, accessible, and memorable; entries on all major muscles and muscle groups, depicting each muscle's form, its interactions with the skeletal system, and its role in creating movement; instruction on capturing the human figure through quick "gesture" drawings as well as highly detailed renderings; a selection of finished life studies--some of the whole figure, others focusing on discrete regions of the body--that translate anatomical knowledge into expressive art; and quick-reference study aids, including a guide to anatomical terminology and a glossary."--BOOK JACKET.

"A significant contribution to the literature of art reference." Library Journal.

743.6 Drawing animals

Hand, Diana

Draw horses in 15 minutes : capture the beauty of the equine form / Diana Hand. ILEX, 2015. 112 p. : **743.6**

1. Horses in art 2. Drawing -- Technique
ISBN 9781781572498

LC bl2016054519

Teaches essential skills and techniques for sketching horses, with guidance specific to each element of the horse's anatomy.

745 Decorative arts

Fiell, Charlotte, 1965-

Design now! / Charlotte & Peter Fiell. Taschen, c2007. 560 p. : **745**

1. Design -- History -- 21st century 2. Industrial design -- History -- 21st century

ISBN 9783822852675

LC 2008384048

"Not only an in-depth exploration of contemporary design practice, this book is also a rallying call for a more sustainable approach to product design of every type, from lighting and furniture design to consumer electronic equipment, transportation, product architecture, and environmental design." -- Publisher website.

Larson, Elsie

A **beautiful** mess happy handmade home : a room-by-room guide to painting, crafting, and decorating a cheerful, more inspiring space / Elsie Larson and Emma Chapman. Potter Style, 2014 240 p. : **745**

1. Handicraft. 2. Home furnishings 3. Interior decoration

ISBN 9780770434052

LC 2014008902

"Give your home a "happiness makeover" with the more than 90 DIY projects, decorating tips, and inspiring ideas in this first-ever home decor book from the creators of the mega-popular style blog A Beautiful Mess".-- Provided by publisher.

"In the introduction, the authors instruct readers to identify what features stand out in favorite spaces of all kinds, to make lists of how rooms might be used unconventionally (playing cards in a dining room), and to do some soul searching (Make a list of 100 things about YOU.) The idea is to make home an expression of one's personality, a skill that the authors have clearly mastered." Publishers Weekly.

745.103 Antiques -- Encyclopedias

Miller, Judith, 1951-

Miller's antiques encyclopedia / general editor, Judith Miller. Miller's, 2017 592 p. : **745.103**

1. Antiques -- Encyclopedias 2. Encyclopedias

ISBN 9781784723651

LC bl2019020761

Offers information on traditional and specialist collecting areas, including furniture, glass, textiles, toys, silver, and clocks.

745.4 Pure and applied design and decoration

Albrecht, Donald

The **work** of Charles and Ray Eames : a legacy of invention / essays by Donald Albrecht ... [et al.]. Harry N. Abrams in association with the Library of Congress and the Vitra Design Museum, 2005, c1997. 205 p. : **745.4**

1. Eames, Charles Criticism and interpretation. 2. Eames, Ray Criticism and interpretation. 3. Design -- United States -- History -- 20th century

ISBN 9780810992320

LC oc2007026006

"This publication accompanies an international traveling exhibition organized by the Library of Congress in partnership with the Vitra Design Museum"--T.p. verso.

"This overview of the work of two prominent American postwar designers features pictures of famous furniture, toys, exhibitions, promotional material, informal snapshots, stills from films, comics, advertisements, exhibitions for the federal government, and much more. The work features six major essays, each with extensive notes, by scholars, designers, academics, and architecture/design writers." Choice.

Black, Alexandra

Design : the definitive visual history / writers, Alexandra Black, R.G. Grant, Ann Kay, Philip Wilkinson, Iain Zaczek. DK, 2015. 480 p. : **745.4**

1. Design. 2. Design -- History.

ISBN 9781465438010

LC bl2015040100

"DK Smithsonian"--Cover.

Includes index.

Traces the history of design from early cultures to contemporary design, profiling major movements, designers, and manufacturers.

745.409034 Decoration--19th century

Miller, Judith, 1951-

Miller's arts & crafts : living with the arts & crafts style / Judith Miller. Millers, a division of Mitchell Beazley, 2014. 239 p. : **745.409034**

1. Arts and crafts movement

ISBN 9781845339432

LC oc2014163957

Includes index.

"Noteworthy for its breadth and its superb color images, this is an up-to-date resource for any art collection." Library Journal.

745.5 Handicrafts

Akiyama, Lance

Duct tape engineer : the book of big, bigger, and epic duct tape projects / Lance Akiyama. Rockport Publishers, 2017 160 p. : **745.5**

1. Tape craft 2. Duct tape

ISBN 9781631591303

LC 2016032103

"This volume will have great appeal to young adults and teens. And while the durability of cardboard and duct tape furniture may be questionable, it certainly is unique." Library Journal

Chapin, Kari

★The **handmade** marketplace : featuring new online strategies and crafter profiles / Kari Chapin. Storey Publishing, 2014 247 p. ; **745.5**

1. Handicraft industries 2. Handicraft -- Marketing 3. Selling -- Handicraft

ISBN 9781612123356

LC 2014004540

Presents advice on turning a creative interest into a profitable craft business, covering basic business start-up practices, marketing, networking, advertising and publicity, blogging, participating in craft fairs, and online selling.

Corwin, Lena
Printing by hand : a modern guide to printing with handmade stamps, stencils, and silk screens / Lena Corwin ; photography by Thayer Allyson Gowdy. Stewart, Tabori & Chang, 2008. 144 p. : **745.5**

1. Handicraft. 2. Rubber stamping 3. Stenciling 4. Screen process printing.
ISBN 9781584796725
LC 2007044503

A talented designer explains how to create a wide variety of unusual and innovative hand-printed fabrics, furnishings, accessories, and paper crafts by using stencils, master stamps, and screen printing, using step-by-step instructions to teach crafters the fundamentals of hand printing and offering an array of ingenious projects, from screen-printed bed linens to stationery.

Falick, Melanie
Making a life : working by hand and discovering the life you are meant to live / Melanie Falick ; photographs by Rinne Allen. Artisan, 2019. 319 p. **745.5**

1. Artisans 2. Handicraft -- Philosophy 3. Creation (Literary, artistic, etc.) -- Philosophy 4. Semantics (Philosophy)
ISBN 9781579657444
LC 2019016973

A writer, crafter and maker describes her travels around the world to meet with 30 potters, weavers, painters, metalsmiths, woodworkers, and more to explore the personal, inspiring and resonating reasons that they create with their hands.

Gorges, Eric
A **craftsman's** legacy : why working with our hands gives us meaning / Eric Gorges, with Jon Sternfeld. Algonquin Books, [2019] 244 p. **745.5**

1. Gorges, Eric 2. Handicraft 3. Happiness 4. Purpose in life 5. Work-life balance
ISBN 9781616208363
LC 2018042246

"The host of PBS's A Craftsman's Legacy makes the case that the craftsman's way--the philosophy, the skills, and the mindset--can provide a blueprint for all of us in our increasingly hurried, disposable world. In this book he tells the stories and shares the collective wisdom of these modern-day makers while also celebrating the culture of all craftsmen".-- Provided by publisher.

"Metalworker Gorges, who has profiled artisans of all stripes as host of the PBS series A Craftsmans Legacy, revisits some of his favorite interviews in this invigorating survey." Publishers Weekly.

Minter, Laura
Mini makers : crafty makes to create with your kids / Laura Minter & Tia Williams. Guild of Master Craftsman Publications Ltd, 2016. 159 p. : **745.5**

1. Handicraft. 2. Handicraft for children.
ISBN 9781784941017
LC bl2017003624

Includes index.

Presents ideas for crafts designed for parents and children to complete together, including rainy-day games, musical instruments, dress up costumes, and a cardboard vessel.

"Parents and caregivers will find plenty of ideas for creative play in this imaginative collection." Library Journal.

Nicholas, Kristin
Crafting a patterned home : painting, printing, and stitching projects to enliven every room / Kristin Nicholas ; photographs by Rikki Snyder. Roost Books, 2018. x, 191 p. **745.5**

1. Handicraft 2. Home furnishings
ISBN 9781611803495
LC 2017008660

Presents design ideas for adding patterns to home decor, giving advice on paints, materials, tools, the use of color, and the mixing and layering of different patterns, with projects for creating such items as pillows, murals, curtains, napkins, and upholstered chairs.

Pester, Sophie
Supercraft : easy projects for every weekend / Sophie Pester, Catharina Bruns. DK, 2016. 175 p. : **745.5**

1. Handicraft.
ISBN 9781465449207
LC bl2016008207

Shares instructions for a year of crafts broken down by season, from knitting hats and cutomizing stationary to painting hangers and creating concrete letters.

"The aesthetic is fresh and contemporary, with lots of bright colors and modern art-inspired style. Numerous techniques are covered, including paper craft, painting, crochet, embroidery, weaving, origami, and sewing, making this a veritable buffet of ideas." Library Journal.

Pigza, Jessica
Bibliocraft : a modern crafter's guide to using library resources to jumpstart creative projects / Jessica Pigza ; photographs by Johnny Miller ; photostyling by Shana Faust ; ilustrations by Sun Young Park. STC Craft, 2014. 207 p. : **745.5**

1. Handicraft in art. 2. Altered books.
ISBN 9781617690969
LC bl2014014668

"A Melanie Falick book."
Includes index.

Encourages using the library as a source of both creative inspiration and materials for handicraft projects, showcasing the projects from celebrated designers, including watermark pillows, cyanotype throws, and cartouche embroidery.

"Though bibliophiles and fans of libraries will be drawn in by the theme of the book, crafters who haven't visited a library since childhood will be thrilled with the wealth of talented artists whose projects are featured. (Bibliophiles will also be pleased that no books are harmed in the making of these crafts." Library Journal.

Rodabaugh, Katrina
The **paper** playhouse : awesome art projects for kids : using paper, boxes, and books / Katrina Rodabaugh. Quarry Books, 2015. 144 p. : **745.5**

1. Handicraft.
ISBN 9781592539802
LC bl2014053710

Offers different arts and crafts projects parents and their children can create together, including sculpture, printmaking, bookbinding, and collage.

"Craft projects using recycled or upcycled materials are perennially popular, and the kid-friendly angle adds a fun dimension." Library Journal.

Samuell, Kristine

A **year** of gingerbread houses : making & decorating gingerbread houses for all seasons / Kristine Samuell. Lark, an imprint of Sterling Publishing, 2015 vii, 135 p. : **745.5**

1. Gingerbread houses. 2. Gingerbread.
ISBN 1454708913

LC bl2015032357

Provides step-by-step instructions for six gingerbread house projects, including a haunted hideaway, a winter wonderland, and a birthday picnic, with project templates; advice on planning, baking, and assembling houses; and decorating tips.

"One of the best gingerbread books available, Samuell's debut is essential for serious gingerbread architects and decorators." Library Journal.

Stewart, Martha

Martha Stewart's encyclopedia of crafts : an A-to-Z guide with detailed instructions and endless inspiration. / Martha Stewart Living. Potter Craft, c2009. 416 p. : **745.5**

1. Handicraft.
ISBN 9780307450579

LC 2008033415

Includes index.

"The brilliant crafts editors at Martha Stewart living ... conceived, created, and produced the craft projects in this book"--P. [7].

Alphabetically arranged entries present step-by-step instructions for craft projects ranging from albums and scrapbooks to soap making and wreaths, along with detailed descriptions of tools and materials.

"In alphabetical order, from albums to wreaths, with intermediate stops at beading, jewelry making, mosaics, quilling, soap making, and more, Stewart presents easily absorbed directions for 200 projects; in each project profile, sumptuous illustrations are partnered with rich, full, stimulating discussion of materials, techniques, and tips. Of primary importance to all crafts collections." Booklist.

745.5083 Handicrafts--arts--children

Neuburger, Emily K.

Show me a story : 40 craft projects and activities to spark children's storytelling / Emily K. Neuburger. Storey Pub., 2012. 144 p. : **745.5083**

1. Handicraft for children 2. Storytelling
ISBN 9781603429887

LC 2012004610

Features instructions for creating and leading forty activities that encourage children to tell stories by using their imaginations, drawing, developing characters, and learning vocabulary.

Van't Hul, Jean

The **artful** parent : simple ways to fill your family's life with art and creativity / Jean Van't Hul. Roost Books, c2013. xxi, 320 p. : **745.5083**

1. Child artists 2. Creative activities and seat work 3. Handicraft for children 4. Parent and child
ISBN 9781590309643

LC 2012021168

Includes bibliographical references (p. 298-309) and index.

Provides over sixty art projects for children designed to inspire creativity and imagination, including creating artful envelopes, tracing shadow shapes, and making collage frames.

"Parents, teachers, and child-care providers will all find useful ideas and inspiration here." Library Journal.

745.53 Handicrafts--Leathers and furs

Gethin, Rosanna Clare

Sew luxe leather : over 20 stylish leather craft accessories / Rosanna Clare Gethin. SewandSo, 2018. 127 p. : **745.53**

1. Leatherwork 2. Handicraft
ISBN 9781446306765

LC bl2018072028

Includes index.

"All are ordered by level of difficulty, easiest to most complex, and include tools, materials, and numbered directions, with accompanying color photographs." Booklist.

Guild of Master Craftsman Publications,

Leathercraft : inspirations projects for you and your home. / Gmc Guild of Master Craftsman Publications, 2016. 119 p. : **745.53**

1. Leatherwork
ISBN 9781784941727

LC bl2017003347

"All projects first published in Making magazine"--Title page verso.

Includes index.

Provides instructions for twenty-five beginner-level leather projects, including a silk scarf belt, hand-sewn bag, punched leather purse, pencil case, and iPad cover.

"These easy, attractive designs will appeal to crafters who are interested in exploring the possibilities of leatherwork." Library Journal.

745.54 Papers

Bartkowski, Alli

Quilled Christmas : 30 festive paper projects / Alli Bartkowski. Lark Books, 2018 143 p. : **745.54**

1. Paper quillwork 2. Christmas decorations
ISBN 9781454710387

LC bl2018196996

Includes index.

"Remember sitting in class, aimlessly rolling paper around a pen or pencil? Thats the foundation of quilling, a popular paper craft with origins in Renaissance-era Europe that has evolved into a wide breadth of fashionable projectsthanks, in part, to Bartkowskis cache of how-tos " Booklist.

Descamps, Ghylenn, 1968-

Beginner's guide to kirigami : 24 skill-building projects using origami & papercrafting skills / Ghylenn Descamps. Fox Chapel Publishing, 2019. 94 p. **745.54**

1. Paper work. 2. Kirigami
ISBN 9781497100169

LC 2019024143

"Gives instructions for making 24 kirigami projects. Also offers tips on using papercrafting tools, paper selection, and folding techniques".--Provided by publisher.

Martin, Ann, 1954 July 5-

The **art** of quilling paper jewelry : techniques & projects for metallic earrings & pendants / Ann Martin. Interweave, 2017 144 p. : **745.54**

1. Paper quillwork. 2. Jewelry making.
ISBN 9781632505774

LC bl2017035569

Includes index.

"This beautiful collection opens up numerous options for quilling beyond the standard surface decoration and may inspire crafters to give this ages-old craft a try." Library Journal

Thuss, Rebecca

Paper to petal : 75 whimsical paper flower ideas to craft by hand / Rebecca Thuss and Patrick Farrell ; Foreward by Martha Stewart. Potter Craft, 2013 256 p. : **745.54**

1. Paper flowers.
ISBN 9780385345057

LC 2012048675

Includes index.

Shares step-by-step instructions for making dozens of sophisticated paper flowers, outlining creative projects ranging from wristlets and bookmarks to wreaths and a Mary Poppins-inspired flower.

745.57 Rubber and plastics

Akiyama, Lance

Rubber band engineer : build slingshot-powered rockets, rubber band rifles, unconventional catapults, and more guerilla gadgets from household hardware / Lance Akiyama. Rockport, 2016. 144 p. : **745.57**

1. Rubber band craft. 2. Toy making. 3. Handicraft.
ISBN 9781631591044

LC bl2016018730

Includes index.

Offers instructions for twenty-five different gadgets, including a crossbow, pneumatic magic box, and slingshot rocket.

745.592 Toys, models, miniatures, related objects

Baker, Mark, 1966-

Turned toys / Mark Baker. The Taunton Press, Inc., 2016. 191 p. : **745.592**

1. Wooden toy making. 2. Turning (Lathe work).
ISBN 9781631866531

LC 2016021953

Includes index.

Pick up a copy of Turned Toys today to sharpen your skills while creating toys that will easily become treasured family heirlooms for generations to come. --From publisher description.

Davis, Todd, 1972-

Handy dad : 25 awesome projects for dads and kids / Todd Davis ; photographs by Juli Stewart and Todd Davis ; illustrations by Nik Schulz. Chronicle Books, c2010. 167 p. : **745.592**

1. Handicraft -- Design. 2. Toy making. 3. Family recreation.
ISBN 9780811869584

LC 2009026020

Includes index.

In this super fun book, Todd Davis, star of HGTV's "Design Star", offers up 25 awesome projects for dads to build with their kids. Skate ramps, zip lines, go-carts, and more!

Finnanger, Tone

Tilda's toy box / Tone Finnanger. David & Charles, an imprint of F&W Media International, Ltd, 2015. 135 p. : **745.592**

1. Sewing 2. Soft toy making 3. Soft toys 4. Textile crafts
ISBN 9781446306154

LC bl2015056416

Includes index.

Provides instructions for quilts, soft toys, and doll clothes, offering tips on making the toys sturdier.

Frisoni, Christine-Lea

The **big** book of a miniature house : create and decorate a house room by room / Christine-Lea Frisoni ; translated by Stephen Haynes ; photographs by Bertrand Runtz. Guild of Master Craftsman Publications Ltd, 2014. 191 p. : **745.592**

1. Dollhouses. 2. Miniature craft. 3. Interior decoration.
ISBN 9781861089540

LC bl2016021468

Provides instructions for building and decorating a miniature French country house and adding furniture, plants, and other adornments.

Smith, Sally J., 1954-

Fairy houses : how to create whimsical homes for fairy folk / Sally J. Smith. Cool Springs Press, 2017. 192 p. ; **745.592**

1. Dollhouses 2. Fairies in art 3. Fairies -- Miscellanea 4. Miniature objects
ISBN 9781591866725

LC 2016033755

"While charming and sweet, the fairy houses here are not hardy enough to hold up to inclement weather and temperature. Nevertheless, this recommended title is fun and unique." Library Journal

745.5928 Models and miniatures

Garfield, Simon

In miniature : how small things illuminate the world / Simon Garfield. Atria Books, 2019, c2018. 323 p. **745.5928**

1. Collectibles 2. Collectors and collecting 3. Toys 4. Control (Psychology)
ISBN 9781501199585

LC 2020302037

Originally published: Edingburgh : Canongate Books, 2018.

Encouraging us to find greatness in the smallest of things, the author, focusing on miniatures -- and bringing together history, psychology, art and obsession -- explores what fuels the strong appeal of miniature objects among collectors, modelers and fans.

745.593 Useful objects

Oppenheimer, Betty, 1957-

The **candlemaker's** companion : a complete guide to rolling, pouring, dipping, and decorating your own candles / Betty

Oppenheimer. Storey Books, c2001. vii, 199 p. : **745.593**

1. Candlemaking.

ISBN 9781580173667

LC 00053802

From wax to wick to wrapping, The Candlemaker's Companion is a definitive guide to modern candle making. Learn how to create rolled, poured, molded, and dipped candles; play with your favorite scents and colors; and use specialty techniques to design glowing luminaria, candle holders, and other gorgeous accessories.

745.594 Decorative objects

Bluhm, Lisa, 1969-

Creative soldered jewelry & accessories : 20+ Earrings, Necklaces, Bracelets & More / Lisa Bluhm. Lark, 2015 126 p. : **745.594**

1. Jewelry making 2. Solder and soldering

ISBN 9781454708162

LC 2013044513

Includes index.

Presents step-by-step instructions for twenty-eight projects using todays most popular soldering torch and iron techniques, from fashionable cuffs and necklaces to unique frames and decorative bottle toppers.

"This is a practical introduction and overview of both hard and soft soldering for hobbyists. Creating fun pieces as part of the learning process is an added bonus." Library Journal.

Brown, Carrie, 1955-

The **new** Christmas tree : 24 dazzling trees and over 100 handcrafted projects for an inspired holiday / Carrie Brown ; photographs by Paige Green. Artisan, 2015 295 p. ; **745.594**

1. Christmas decorations 2. Handicraft. 3. Christmas trees.

ISBN 9781579655914

LC 2015010993

Provides inspiration for turning everyday items into one-of-a-kind Christmas decor, with step-by-step instructions for creating ornaments, tree toppers, and information on picking the right tree.

"There's no shortage of clever ideas, especially for those who'd like to produce ornaments without much fuss. Brown is at her best in suggesting simple crafts that will make an impressive statement." Publishers Weekly.

Brown, Stephen

Glitterville's handmade Christmas : a glittered guide for whimsical crafting / Stephen Brown. Andrews McMeel Publishing, 2014 xxiii, 181 p. : **745.594**

1. Handicraft. 2. Christmas decorations.

ISBN 9781449414559

LC bl2014038441

Provides step-by-step, illustrated instructions for twenty holiday craft projects, including ginger cookie kids, wacky woods felt ornaments, and a pinecone gnome.

Glitterville's handmade Halloween : a glittered guide for whimsical crafting / Stephen Brown. Andrews McMeel Pub., c2012. xxiv, 178 p. : **745.594**

1. Handicraft. 2. Halloween decorations.

ISBN 9781449414528

LC bl2012027048

Provides instructions for making whimsical Halloween crafts, from the oh-so wicked party hat and wacky Willie Webber spider puppet to the glittered cat silhouette party hat and pumpkin tiara.

Cetti, Livia

The **exquisite** book of paper flowers : a guide to making unbelievably realistic paper blooms / Livia Cetti ; photographs by Addie Juell. STC Craft, 2014. 192 p. : **745.594**

1. Paper flowers.

ISBN 9781617691003

LC bl2014040851

"A Melanie Falick book."

Provides step-by-step instructions for creating twenty-five paper flowers from tissue and crepe paper, and explains how to combine the flowers to arrange garlands, wreaths, table decorations, and corsages.

Combs, Rebecca Ann

Kumihimo : basics & beyond : 24 braided and beaded jewelry projects on the kumihimo disk / Rebecca Ann Combs. Kalmbach Books, 2014. 95 p. : **745.594**

1. Braid. 2. Beadwork -- Patterns. 3. Jewelry making.

ISBN 9781627000437

LC oc2013124525

Kumihimo Basics and Beyond presents techniques for creating all-cord braids and beaded braids, then teaches beaders how to transform them into finished jewelry.

Crowther, Janet

Make a statement : 25 handcrafted jewelry & accessory projects / Janet Crowther & Katie Covington. Chronicle Books, 2015 143 p. : **745.594**

1. Jewelry making. 2. Costume jewelry. 3. Fashion.

ISBN 9781452133201

LC 2014004103

Presents twenty-five projects for handcrafting jewelry and other accessories, including earrings, bracelets, necklaces, hair combs, and shoe clips.

Geary, Theresa Flores

The **illustrated** bead bible : terms, tips & techniques / Theresa Flores Geary ; photographs by Debra Whalen. Sterling Pub., c2008. viii, 406 p. : **745.594**

1. Beadwork.

ISBN 9781402723537

LC 2007026120

Offers information on bead types, styles, materials, and tools with tips and techniques for purchasing beads and materials.

"This may be the ultimate bead reference book. The majority of the text is made up of an illustrated alphabetical encyclopedia of beads, broadly defined, and beading terms. Additional chapters include tips and techniques, charts illustrating bead characteristics, and stitch diagrams." Library Journal.

Gedeon, Jade

Beautiful bracelets by hand : seventy-five one-of-a-kind baubles, bangles, and other wrist adornments you can make at home / Jade Gedeon. Page Street Publishing Co., 2014. 1 online resource (223 p.) : **745.594**

1. Bracelets. 2. Jewelry making.

ISBN 9781624140907

LC BL2015009513

Includes index.

Offers instructions on creating different types of bracelets from different types of materials, including leather, metal, and wood.

"The majority of the bracelets in this book are so simple and easy to make that absolute beginners can duplicate them successfully. Much of the writing reads like corny catalog copy, but there's enough Gedeon to make this a worthwhile purchase, especially where beginners' jewelry-making titles are popular." Library Journal.

Kan, Lisa

Bead metamorphosis : exquisite jewelry from custom components / Lisa Kan. Interweave, 2014 159 p. ; **745.594**

1. Jewelry making. 2. Beadwork.
ISBN 9781596688254

LC 2014028517

Shares sixteen beadweaving projects, each of which features a basic jewelry component that can be transformed into a new piece of jewelry through embellishment, disassembly, reassembly, or interchanging elements.

Karon, Karen

Advanced chain maille jewelry workshop : weaving with rings & scales / Karen Karon. Interweave, 2014 159 p. ; **745.594**

1. Jewelry making. 2. Chains (Jewelry). 3. Metal-work.
ISBN 9781620336595

LC 2014011104

Includes index.

"For experienced jewelry makers, since basic chain maille techniques such as opening and closing jump rings properly are not covered. Those looking to go beyond the techniques addressed in most related books will find a wealth of information within these pages." Library Journal.

Katz, Amy

Seed bead chic : 25 elegant projects inspired by fine jewelry / Amy Katz. Lark Jewelry & Beading, 2014 128 p. : Lark Jewelry & Beading Bead Inspirations **745.594**

1. Beadwork -- Patterns. 2. Jewelry making.
ISBN 9781454708179

LC 2013047476

Includes index.

"Upscale, elegant, CHIC: these 25 handcrafted projects look like the fine jewelry you'd find in high-end boutiques. But why splurge when all it takes to make them are some seed beads and intermediate-to-advanced skills? Featuring a variety of stitches--including the author's newly created right-angle ladder stitch--these stunning pieces cover everything from earrings to brooches. Gorgeous photographs, diagrams, and helpful tips make the beading process simple and pleasurable!"-- Provided by publisher.

"Katz's projects are sophisticated in both style and technique. Jewelry makers looking for a challenge will find one here." Library Journal.

Legenhausen, Courtney

Fashion jewelry : a beginner's guide to jewelry making / Courtney Legenhausen of Lotus Jewelry Studio. Lark, 2017 175 p. : **745.594**

1. Jewelry making.
ISBN 9781454710325

LC bl2017029491

Includes index.

Provides instructions for creating sixteen stylish jewelry pieces using such techniques as bead stringing, wire wrapping, knotting, and hammering.

Oxmoor House,

Christmas with Southern Living 2017 : the complete guide to holiday cooking and decorating Oxmoor House, 2017. 192 p. : Christmas with Southern Living **745.594**

1. Christmas cooking. 2. Christmas decorations. 3. Handicraft. 4. Holiday cooking 5. Cookbooks.
ISBN 9780848752262

LC bl2017028840

Includes indexes.

Offers recipes for meals, treats, and baked goods for gift-giving and holiday entertaining, along with seasonal decorating ideas, including festive centerpieces, mantels, and wreaths.

Papp, Csilla

Sensational soutache jewelry making : braided jewelry techniques for 15 statement pieces / Csilla Papp. Interweave, 2016 128 p. : **745.594**

1. Beadwork. 2. Jewelry making.
ISBN 9781440243745

LC bl2016010155

Includes index.

Presents fifteen designs for beadwork jewelry using decorative fabric braids known as soutache, with detailed instructions on using open and closed wraps, making curves, creating shapes, and securing beads.

"Jewelrymakers interested in experimenting with soutache, as well as fans of statement jewelry, will be drawn to Papp's intricate designs." Library Journal.

Pester, Sophie

Homemade holiday : craft your way through more than 40 festive projects/ Sophie Pester, Catharina Bruns. DK Publishing, 2017. 143 p. : **745.594**

1. Christmas decorations 2. Handicraft
ISBN 9781465463265

LC bl2017037715

Presents step-by-step, illustrated instructions for festive craft projects for gifts, decorations, and homemade wrapping paper.

Sheldon, Kathy, 1959-

Felt-o-ween : 40 scary-cute projects to celebrate Halloween / Kathy Sheldon & Amanda Carestio. Lark, 2014 132 p. : **745.594**

1. Halloween decorations. 2. Felt work.
ISBN 9781454708513

LC 2013039868

Includes index.

Presents easy instructions for more than three dozen felt crafts for the Halloween season.

Shore, Debbie

Sew advent calendars : count down to Christmas with 20 stylish designs to fill with festive treats / Debbie Shore. Search Press, 2017. 96 p. : **745.594**

1. Christmas decorations. 2. Sewing.
ISBN 9781782214885

LC bl2017048945

Includes index.

Presents instructions for sewing twenty personalized advent calendars, from traditional flat-pocket calendars to hanging cones and festive pouches.

Van't Hul, Jean

The **artful** year : celebrating the seasons and holidays with family arts and crafts / Jean Van't Hul. Roost Books, 2015. xv, 351 p. : **745.594**

1. Family recreation 2. Handicraft 3. Holiday decorations 4. Recipes 5. Cookbooks

ISBN 9781611801491

LC 2013048889

Shares a collection of child-friendly holiday crafts and seasonal recipes to inspire and enrich family traditions.

Watanabe, Judi, 1963

The **complete** photo guide to cardmaking / Judi Watanabe. Creative Publishing International, 2016 256 p. : Complete Photo Guide **745.594**

1. Greeting cards. 2. Paper work.

ISBN 9781589238824

LC bl2016002838

Includes index.

Shows readers a range of paper crafting techniques, from washi tape, origami, and quilling to cut-outs, stamping, and die cutting, for designing cards for all occasions.

"Although this is a cardmaking book, scrapbookers, art journalers, and mixed-media artists will also appreciate the image-based tutorials and the abundance of inspiring photos." Library Journal.

Wiseman, Jill

Jill Wiseman's beautiful beaded ropes : 24 wearable jewelry projects in multiple stitches. / Jill Wiseman. Lark Crafts, 2012. 119 p. : Beadweaving Master Class **745.594**

1. Beadwork -- Patterns. 2. Jewelry making.

ISBN 9781454703563

LC 2012002269

Includes indexes.

Join popular teacher and designer Jill Wiseman as she presents 24 beaded rope designs in this wonderful entry in Lark Jewelry & Beading's popular Beadweaving Master Class series. From dainty to heavy, and from simple to outrageously textured, these beautiful and wearable necklace, lariat, bangle, and bracelet projects (plus a few earrings!) utilize such popular stitch techniques as spiral rope, peyote, netting, herringbone, right angle weave, chevron, polygon weave, and oglala.

"Wiseman's designs have a lot of appeal and are easily customizable to suit individual tastes, and the variety of stitches used in the projects will pique beaders' interest." Library Journal.

Yamazaki, Hiromi

Japanese paper flowers : elegant kirigami blossoms, bouquets, wreaths and more / Hiromi Yamazaki. Tuttle Publishing, 2019 96 p. : **745.594**

1. Paper flowers. 2. Handicraft.

ISBN 9784805314982

LC bl2019012564

Provides instructions on how to create thirty-one paper flower designs and includes projects that incorporate them, including wreaths, garlands, and jewelry.

"Whether or not they're already familiar with the Japanese art of origami, crafters can follow Yamazaki's instructions for fashioning exquisite and realistic-looking flowers from paper." Booklist.

745.5941646 Halloween--handicrafts

Cupp, Lundy

Realistic pumpkin carving : 24 scary, spooky, and spine-chilling designs / Lundy Cupp. Fox Chapel Publishing, 2016. 96 p. : **745.5941646**

1. Halloween decorations. 2. Jack-o-lanterns. 3. Vegetable carving. 4. Pumpkin.

ISBN 9781565238947

LC 2017279887

"Portions of this book were originally published in Woodcarving Illustrated magazine"--Title page verso.

Includes index.

Showcases realistic faces carved on pumpkins, discussing how to choose a pumpkin, describing the tools and equipment, and offering step-by-step instructions and twenty ready-to-use patterns.

"Create the perfect pumpkin for Halloween with this stunning book. Artist Cupp presents a collection of pumpkin carving patterns. The galleries of brilliantly carved pumpkins, squashes, and sweet potatoes are tantalizing, and the author's level of expertise is clearly on display." Library Journal.

745.6 Calligraphy, heraldic design, illumination

Doh, Jenny

Creative lettering : techniques & tips from top artists / Jenny Doh. Lark, 2013 143 p. : **745.6**

1. Lettering -- Technique.

ISBN 9781454704003

LC 2012021130

Includes index.

Provides step-by-step instructions for lettering from top artists, including advice on the best tools, techniques and tips, and font samples.

"Artists of all skill levels can enjoy this title." Library Journal.

More creative lettering : techniques & tips from top artists / Jenny Doh. Lark, 2015 144 p. : **745.6**

1. Lettering -- Technique 2. Calligraphy -- Technique

ISBN 9781454708926

LC bl2015026125

Includes index.

Presents additional information and more step-by-step instructions for lettering from top artists, with advice on the best tools, techniques and tips, and font samples.

"With lots of practical and creative applications, this book can be appreciated by a wide range of audiences." Library Journal.

Flor, Martina

The **golden** secrets of lettering : letter design from first sketch to final artwork / Martina Flor. Princeton Architectural Press, 2017 167 p. : **745.6**

1. Lettering -- Technique

ISBN 9781616895730

LC 2016037057

"Readers with at least some prior drawing experience are best poised to benefit from this highly educational art instruction book." Library Journal.

Glynn, Kathy

Hand lettering step by step : techniques and projects to express yourself creatively / Kathy Glynn. Get Creative 6, 2018 143

p. : **745.6**

1. Lettering -- Technique 2. Handicraft
ISBN 9781942021858

LC 2017028519

"Each chapter contains step-by-step projects with lots of practical applications, including designs for love letters, monogrammed jewelry, business cards, fabric patterns, all sorts of signs, gift wrap, rubber stamps, and temporary tattoos. Detailed, close-up photographs of various pen types, nibs from all angles, a great variety of inks, paints, and other supplies are featured throughout." Library Journal

Owen, Imogen

Modern calligraphy workshop : the creative art of pen, brush and chalk lettering / Imogen Owen ; photography by Kim Lightbody. Quadrille, 2017. 143 p. : **745.6**

1. Calligraphy
ISBN 9781849499071

LC bl2017044850

Includes index.

Instructs readers on how to write calligraphy to create hand-lettered stationery, art, and other decorations through the use of interactive sample alphabets, exercises, and step-by-step projects.

Rodriguez, Dina

The **big** awesome book of hand & chalk lettering / Dina Rodriguez. DK Publishing, 2017. 206 p. : **745.6**

1. Alphabets 2. Decorative arts 3. Lettering -- Technique
ISBN 9781465462725

LC bl2017027950

Includes index.

Uses step-by-step instructions and photographs to teach beginners how the master the art of hand lettering, how to compose phrases on the page, and how to make letters look dimensional.

Shepherd, Margaret

Learn calligraphy : the complete book of lettering and design / Margaret Shepherd. Broadway Books, 2001. 167 p. : **745.6**

1. Calligraphy -- Technique
ISBN 9780767907323

LC 00053016

Offers step-by-step lessons on the techniques of calligraphy, providing historical information while suggesting advice for choosing alphabets for different messages and selecting the best materials.

Thames and Hudson,

Calligraphy & lettering : a maker's guide Thames & Hudson, 2019. 176 p. : **745.6**

1. Lettering. 2. Calligraphy.
ISBN 9780500294307

LC bl2019017322

Includes index.

A practical guide to calligraphy and hand-lettering traditions from around the world offers fifteen step-by-step projects that each take their cue from a different lettering technique.

Thorpe, Molly Suber

Modern calligraphy : everything you need to know to get started in script calligraphy / Molly Suber Thorpe ; photography by Molly Suber Thorpe. St. Martin's Griffin, 2013. vi, 184 p. : **745.6**

1. Calligraphy 2. Writing materials and instruments
ISBN 9781250016324

LC 2013013847

Includes index.

"Calligraphy is about creating something uniquely beautiful, whether to celebrate a special occasion like marriage or to use every day in the form of stationery. Author Molly Suber Thorpe, an award-winning designer and calligrapher based in Los Angeles, works closely with her international clients to give them the distinctive products they're looking for. Now you can learn from this experienced expert how to master this fresh modern lettering style. The first book to teach this bold new style breaks the calligraphy process down into simple steps so anyone can learn to create their own stunning wedding invitations, thank you cards, gift tags, and more. Starting with an overview of the supplies--from paper to ink to pens--you will learn how to form letters, words, and then phrases by following Molly's clear step-by-step instructions, and by practicing with the provided templates. After mastering letter forms using a pointed pen and ink you can take it to the next level by learning how to use watercolor and gouache, or how to digitize your calligraphy. The twenty projects in the book provide lots of inspiration for making your own and are grouped into three sections: weddings, entertainment, and personal stationery. With loads of ideas, practice exercises, and helpful tips, soon you will be turning out gorgeous script calligraphy pieces like the ones featured in wedding magazines and popular websites like Pinterest!"-- Provided by publisher.

745.61 Calligraphy

Godfrey-Nicholls, Gaye

Mastering calligraphy : the complete guide to hand lettering / Gaye Godfrey-Nicholls. Chronicle Books, 2013. 288 p. : **745.61**

1. Calligraphy -- Technique.
ISBN 9781452101125

LC 2015300387

Provides step-by-step instructions on creating such calligraphy styles as hand-lettering techniques, digital typography, and illumination.

"Godfrey-Nicholls, an Australia-based artist, elucidates the art of hand-lettering in this comprehensive work. The majority of the book is devoted to calligraphic hands, or different styles of writing. Each hand includes a brief history, exercises for practicing the basic shapes and strokes, foundational groups of letters arranged by type, and variations on the alphabet. Appropriate supplies are suggested for each hand." Library Journal.

745.7 Decorative coloring

Joyce, Anna

Stamp stencil paint : making extraordinary patterned projects by hand / Anna Joyce ; photography by Lisa Waringer ; photostyling by Chelsea Fuss. STC Craft 2015. 144 p. : **745.7**

1. Stenciling 2. Painting. 3. Handicraft.
ISBN 9781617691775

LC bl2015032839

"A Melanie Falick book."

Shares instructions for creating projects by stamping, stenciling, and painting, including beach towels, table linens, storage baskets, and plates.

Sloan, Annie, 1949-

Color recipes for painted furniture and more : 40 step-by-step projects to transform your home / Annie Sloan. Cico Books, c2013. 160 p. : **745.7**

1. Furniture painting. 2. Finishes and finishing.
ISBN 9781908862778

LC bl2013013989

Includes index.

Presents instructions for using a variety of decorative and color mixing techniques to transform furniture, floors, lighting fixtures, and walls, describing such methods as painting, gilding, waxing, stenciling, marbling, and decoupage.

745.92 Floral arts

Chezar, Ariella

★The **flower** workshop : lessons in arranging blooms, branches, fruits, and foraged materials / Ariella Chezar with Julie Michaels ; photography by Erin Kunkel. Ten Speed Press, 2016 245 p. : **745.92**

1. Flower arrangement.
ISBN 9781607747659

LC 2015027664

Includes index.

Presents a guide to to creating flower arrangements, with information on color, texture, foliage, techniques, and essential tools, and detailed instructions for specific types of arrangements for branches, flowers, and fruits.

"Infused with overwhelming appreciation for nature and including quotes from others and Chezar's own poetic phrases, the book offers beauty and inspiration to flower arrangers at most levels of skill." Booklist.

Cylinder, Carly

The **flower** chef : a modern guide to do-it-yourself floral arrangements / Carly Cylinder ; edited by Amara Holstein. Grand Central Life & Style, 2016. 223 p. : **745.92**

1. Flower arrangement.
ISBN 9781455555499

LC 2015039431

Includes index.

Provides instructions for creating fresh and original floral designs, from buying and caring for flowers to using foam, vases, and other decorative elements to create arrangements.

"This book creates a needed foundation for aspiring designers." Library Journal.

Harampolis, Alethea

The **flower** recipe book / Alethea Harampolis and Jill Rizzo of Studio Choo, photographs by Paige Green. Artisan, 2013 268 p. : **745.92**

1. Flower arrangement.
ISBN 9781579655303

LC 2012046704

Offers step-by-step instructions with accompanying photographs to make over one hundred different floral arrangements in a variety of styles, from single blooms to overflowing and layered blossoms, using easily located flowers.

Turner, Tiffanie

The **fine** art of paper flowers : a guide to making beautiful and lifelike botanicals / Tiffanie Turner ; photographs by Tiffanie Turner and Aya Brackett. Watson-Guptill, 2017 1 online resource (vii, 254 p.) : **745.92**

1. Paper flowers. 2. Flower arrangement.
ISBN 9780399578373

LC oc2018143426

Features step-by-step instructions for crafting over thirty of the author's lifelike paper flowers and their foliage, from bougainvillea to zinnias, along with instructions for using paper flowers in garlands, bouquets, and fashion accessories.

Underwood, Kiana

Color me floral : stunning monochromatic arrangements for every season / Kiana Underwood ; photographs by Nathan Underwood. Chronicle Books, 2018 240 p. : **745.92**

1. Flower arrangement
ISBN 9781452161174

LC 2017020489

Includes index.

Organized by season, the book includes how-to's for 40 arrangements, including a lush green display for spring, an astonishing black bouquet for summer, a striking magenta design for fall, and an unexpected, oh-so-pretty pink arrangement for winter.

"She builds each arrangement in steps and includes photos -- taken by her husband -- at each stage. Using a pin frog (and eschewing floral foam), she indicates which specimen is inserted at what point, considering height, breadth, and mass." Publishers Weekly

746 Textile arts

Adams, Liza

Needle felting : from basics to bears with step-by-step photos and instructions for creating cute little bears and bunnies from natural wools / Liza Adams. Stackpole Books, 2016 128 p. : **746**

1. Felt work. 2. Textile crafts.
ISBN 9780811716628

LC 2015045254

Make the cutest little creatures from wool! Needle felting is all the rage, and this book shows you how to create tiny bears, rabbits, dogs, cats, fairies, dolls, cupcakes, and more.

Lindsay, Virginia Keleher, 1975-

Sewing to sell : the beginner's guide to starting a craft business : bonus, 16 starter projects : how to sell locally & online / Virginia Lindsay. StashBooks, C&T Publishing, 2014 151 p. : **746**

1. Handicraft industries -- Management 2. Home-based businesses -- Management 3. Small business -- Management 4. Selling
ISBN 9781607059035

LC 2014013070

Provides tips for setting up a craft business along with instructions for sixteen sewing projects.

"Most appropriate for crafters who need a very basic guide to selling their handmade goods. Those looking to take their business to the next level will benefit from Kari Chapin's Grow Your Handmade Business and The Handmade Marketplace, which provide a more comprehensive view of operating a craft-based enterprise." Library Journal.

Susa, Sachiko
Sweet & simple needle felted animals : a step-by-step visual guide / Sachiko Susa. Tuttle Publishing, 2017 96 p. : **746**
1. Felt work 2. Handicraft
ISBN 9784805314548
LC bl2017041724
Offers step-by-step illustrated instructions to create felt animals, including kittens, a dachshund puppy, and rabbits.
"Novices and experienced needle felters alike will enjoy making these irresistible miniatures." Booklist.

White, Christine, 1962-
Uniquely felt : dozens of techniques from fulling and shaping to nuno and cobweb : includes 46 creative projects / Christine White. Storey Pub., c2007. 311 p. : **746**
1. Felt work. 2. Felt work.
ISBN 9781580176736
LC 2007023531
Describes the concepts and theories of feltmaking, equipment needed, and the techniques of feltmaking, along with a variety of projects for such items as bags, shawls, curtains, and bath mats.
"The author covers basic feltmaking techniques as well as needle, nuno, cobweb, 3-D, and carved techniques and featuring 46 projects. What makes this a title of lasting value for libraries is the depth of solid information it offers on the craft and its history, on various artists, and on related topics like setting up a feltmaking studio, teaching felt making, and leading community feltmaking projects." Library Journal.

746.0463 Felt--textiles--arts

Lapierre, Corinne
Folk embroidered felt birds : 20 Modern Folk Art Designs to Make & Embellish / Corinne Lapierre. Search Press Limited, 2019. 96 p. : **746.0463**
1. Felt work -- Technique 2. Embroidery -- Technique 3. Embroidery -- Patterns 4. Birds in art
ISBN 9781782216988
LC 2018289826
"20 modern folk art designs to make & embellish"-- cover.
"Lapierre provides clear introductory instructions on suggested materials and basic embroidery stitches, but the small size of the finished projects (based on the provided templates, most are a little over six inches long) and the detailed stitching work required to finish them make this an ideal challenge for more-experienced crafters." Booklist.

746.1 Products and processes

Anderson, Sarah (Sarah B.)
The **spinner's** book of yarn designs : techniques for creating 80 yarns / Sarah Anderson ; foreword by Judith MacKenzie. Storey Publishing, 2012 255 p. : **746.1**
1. Hand spinning. 2. Spun yarns.
ISBN 9781603427388
LC 2012039869
Offers step-by-step instructions for spinning yarn, explaining the process of working with fleece and how to manipulate and combine the fibers for creating eighty different types of yarn, from mohair boucle to supercoils.
"Inventive, accessible, and fun, this book is an invitation to spinners of all skill levels to venture into uncharted territory and try out something new. This beautiful reference is an essential addition to any spinner's library." Publishers Weekly.

Boggs, Jacey
Spin art : mastering the craft of spinning textured yarn / Jacey Boggs. Interweave Press, c2011. 143 p. : **746.1**
1. Hand spinning. 2. Spun yarns.
ISBN 9781596683624
LC bl2013019898
Includes index.
Presents step-by-step coverage of thirty yarn spinning techniques, including autowrap, halos, and spiral plying.

Daly, Fiona
Weaving on a little loom : techniques, patterns, and projects for beginners / Fiona Daly. Princeton Architectural Press, 2018 144 p. : **746.1**
1. Handlooms. 2. Weaving.
ISBN 9781616897123
LC 2018006741
Includes index.
Previously published: Little loom weaving. Berkeley, CA : Ulysses Press, 2017.
"Weaving, Daly explains, is not a weekend project but a commitment; her alluring book convinces readers its worth the time and effort." Publishers Weekly.

Dixon, Anne, 1939-
The **handweaver's** pattern directory : over 600 weaves for four-shaft looms / Anne Dixon. Interweave Press, 2007. 256 p. : **746.1**
1. Hand weaving -- Patterns. 2. Weaving -- Patterns
ISBN 9781596680401
LC 2007026351
Includes index.
Provides instructions on the basics of weaving and finishing techniques along with six hundred different weaving patterns for four-shaft looms.
"This guide to more than 600 different weaving patterns for four-shaft looms divides weaves into basic groups by structure (e.g., basic threadings, block drafts). Each weave is accompanied by warp threading and weaving drafts (the latter, explained in a handy extended flap), a tieup grid, closeup photos of the weave, and color photos of the actual woven fabric. Beginning weavers will appreciate the sections on weaving basics and finishing techniques as well as the glossary of common weaving terms." Library Journal.

The **weaver's** inkle pattern directory / Anne Dixon. Interweave Press, 2012 175 p. : **746.1**
1. Inkle weaving
ISBN 9781596686472
LC 2012002086
"Over 400 patterns for inkle weaving".-- Provided by publisher.

Jarchow, Deborah
The **weaving** explorer : ingenious techniques, accessible tools & creative projects with yarn, paper, wire & more / Deborah Jarchow & Gwen W. Steege. Storey Publishing, 2019 310 p. : **746.1**
1. Hand weaving. 2. Hand weaving -- Patterns
ISBN 9781635860283
LC 2019033543

Includes index.

"The Weaving Explorer takes inspiration from the world of folk weaving traditions, adding a contemporary spin by introducing an unexpected range of materials and home dec projects".-- Provided by publisher.

Mitchell, Syne, 1970-

Inventive weaving on a little loom : discover the full potential of the Rigid-Heddle loom, for beginners and beyond / Syne Mitchell. Storey Publishing, 2015 295 p. : **746.1**

1. Hand weaving. 2. Handlooms.

ISBN 9781603429726

LC 2015019702

A handbook to the tabletop loom provides step-by-step photographs to outline techniques that can be applied to a range of contemporary projects, from pillows and curtains to bags and jewelry.

Murphy, Marilyn

Woven to wear : 17 thoughtful designs with simple shapes / Marilyn Murphy. Interweave Press, 2013 143 p. : **746.1**

1. Hand weaving. 2. Clothing

ISBN 9781596686519

LC 2012048056

"A collection of woven wraps, shawls, and outwear that will appeal to beginner and advanced weavers alike".-- Provided by publisher.

"Beginners (or experienced weavers who could use a refresher) will appreciate the thorough introduction to weaving tools and technique." Library Journal.

Patrick, Jane

The **weaver's** idea book : creative cloth on a rigid-heddle loom / Jane Patrick. Interweave Press, c2010. 239 p. : **746.1**

1. Hand weaving -- Patterns.

ISBN 9781596681750

LC 2009039518

Presents a wide variety of weave-structure patterns along with swatches illustrating the techniques, accompanied by step-by-step photos, as well as project ideas ranging from wearables to home decor.

"Patrick's collection of patterns and projects explores the possibilities of weaving on a rigid heddle loom. From basic plain weaves to finger-controlled and pick-up techniques, Patrick guides weavers of all skill levels. This is an excellent addition to any weaving collection." Library Journal.

746.3 Pictures, hangings, tapestries

Brosens, Koenraad

European tapestries in the Art Institute of Chicago / Koenraad Brosens ; with contributions by Pascal-Francois Bertrand ... [et al.] ; Christa C. Mayer Thurman, general editor. Art Institute of Chicago, c2008. viii, 407 p. : **746.3**

1. Art Institute of Chicago Catalogs. 2. Tapestry -- Europe -- Catalogs. 3. Tapestry, Medieval -- Europe -- Catalogs. 4. Tapestry, Renaissance -- Europe -- Catalogs. 5. Tapestry, Baroque -- Europe -- Catalogs. 6. Europa (geografie). gtt

ISBN 9780300119602

LC 2008930401

Presents a catalog of the tapestries in the Art Institute of Chicago, from the medieval age to Baroque, and explains designer and workshop attributions, design and source identifications, and provenance information.

746.4 Needlework and handwork

Zimmermann, Elizabeth, 1910-1999

★**Knitting** without tears : basic techniques and easy-to-follow directions for garments to fit all sizes / Elizabeth Zimmermann. Scribner, 1971 120 p. : **746.4**

1. Knitting.

ISBN 9780684135052

LC 70140776

The author guides the novice and the experienced knitters in shortcuts and construction tricks and offers twenty original designs

746.412 Basketry

Irish, Lora S.

Basket essentials : rib basket weaving; techniques and projects for DIY woven reed baskets / Lora S. Irish. Fox Chapel Publishing, 2020 200 p. : **746.412**

1. Baskets 2. Basket making

ISBN 9781497100145

Includes index.

Go beyond just following the steps and learn the methods to traditional basket weaving. With step-by-step instructions and photography for 3 rib basket projects, followed by 12 additional designs to accomplish independently, you'll acquire all the proper techniques you need to become a successful basket-weaver, from measuring and adding spokes to learning various weaving patterns. Provided by publisher

"Her attractive illustrations and skillful instructions should inspire many newcomers to try out this laid-back craft." Publishers Weekly

746.42 Nonloom weaving and related techniques

Hartmann, Kat

Hot knots : fresh macrame ideas for jewelry, home, and fashion / Kat Hartmann. Barron's, 2015. 128 p. : **746.42**

1. Macrame. 2. Macrame -- Patterns.

ISBN 9781438005652

LC bl2015009725

Presents instructions and patterns for a variety of macrame projects, including drop earrings, cord bracelet, market bag, and knotted tank top.

"Up-to-date titles about macrame are difficult to find, and while Hartmann includes nods to 1970s-era classics such as owls and plant hangers, contemporary crafters will find that macrame is both simple and versatile." Library Journal.

Katz, Emily

Modern macrame : 33 stylish projects for your handmade home / Emily Katz with Johanna Kunin ; photographs by Nicole Franzen and Shannon Wolf. Ten Speed Press, 2018 247 p. : **746.42**

1. Macrame 2. Interior decoration

ISBN 9780399579578

LC bl2018157085

Includes index.

A guide to the traditional art of decorative knotting includes thirty-three projects for the home, including wall hangings, bohemian light fixtures, macrame baskets, rugs, and chairs.

"The step-by-step guidance for plant hangers, rugs, wall hangings, and general knotted miscellany will help even novice crafters achieve results that are both lovely and useful. Readers looking for an updated take on macrame will want to pick up this stylish and practical book." Publishers Weekly.

Zedenius, Fanny

Macrame : the craft of creative knotting for your home / Fanny Zedenius ; photography by Kim Lightbody. Quadrille, 2017. 143 p. : **746.42**

1. Macrame -- Patterns. 2. Macrame. 3. Home furnishings
ISBN 9781849499408

LC bl2017028164

Includes index.

Shares information on starting macrame, the most popular knots, and tips on how to create different patterns through various knot combinations, as well as over twenty projects to make for the home.

746.43 Knitting, crocheting, tatting

Atherley, Kate

The **knitter's** dictionary : knitting know-how from A to Z / Kate Atherley. Interweave, 2018 126 p. : **746.43**

1. Knitting -- Dictionaries.
ISBN 9781632506382

LC bl2018191533

Provides an A-to-Z guide to knitting, offering entries on knitting language and abbreviations, extended information on such challenging topics as understanding gauge, and tips on making knitting patterns.

"Unlike many knitting books, the diagrams and drawings included here are clearly drawn and easy to decipher. The book is small but filled with enough useful information to make it a go-to reference in any knitting library." Publishers Weekly.

Bara, Brett

Crochet at home : 25 clever projects for colorful living / edited by Brett Bara. Interweave Press, 2013 143 p. : **746.43**

1. Crocheting -- Patterns. 2. Home furnishings 3. Linens
ISBN 9781596688377

LC 2012048922

"Get 25 small and quick crochet projects from top designers to add color and cheer to your home! In Crochet at Home, editor Brett Bara and a team of crochet experts bring 25 exciting home projects to life. Explore a collection of practical, pretty pieces for your kitchen, living room, and bedroom: from a riotously colorful blanket, to a delicate bunting of crocheted snowflakes, to flower-inspired trivets that are anything but dull-and even a full-sized ottoman! Techniques such as felting, lace, and crocheting with wire will appeal to beginner and advanced crocheters alike. Projects are made in affordable yarns, especially for large pieces and ones that take a beating, like kitchen accessories. Join Brett and her team of all-star crocheters in this cheerful, affordable, and occasionally humorous take on home decor in this new and approachable resource".-- Provided by publisher.

Bassetti, Amanda

Arm knitting / Amanda Bassetti. Barron's, 2015. 144 p. : **746.43**

1. Knitting -- Patterns 2. Hand weaving.
ISBN 9781438007304

LC bl2015036233

"30 home and fashion projects for all your no-needle needs"--Cover.
Includes index.

Offers step-by-step instructions to learn a range of arm knitting stitches and thirty projects they can be used to create.

"Hands down (or arms up), one of the best-ever beginner craft books." Booklist.

Bergstrom, Lauren

Mini crochet creatures : 30 amigurumi animals to make / Lauren Bergstrom. The Guild of Master Craftsman Publications, 2018. 159 p. : **746.43**

1. Amigurumi -- Patterns 2. Crocheting -- Patterns 3. Soft toy making -- Patterns 4. Stuffed animals (Toys)
ISBN 9781784943899

LC bl2018183427

Includes index.

Presents thirty designs for amigurumi animals, including a bunny, otter, butterfly, and elephant, providing detailed instructions and explanations of all the techniques used.

"Photos of the finished products in cleverly crafted settings (the sea creatures surf in ocean blue-green yarn) add whimsy to the books general appeal. While the projects are designed for novice crocheters, experts may want to craft this menagerie as well." Publishers Weekly.

Bernard, Juliet,

Knitting masterclass : with over 20 technical workshops and 15 beautiful patterns / edited by Juliet Bernard. Collins & Brown, 2013. 160 p. : **746.43**

1. Knitting. 2. Knitting -- Patterns.
ISBN 9781908449023

LC bl2014043995

At head of title: The Knitter.
Includes index.

Presents fourteen knitting projects, from hats and jumpers to socks and cardigans, discussing how to cast on and off, how to hold the needles, and how to choose yarn.

Bernard, Wendy (Wendy Jo)

Up, down, all-around stitch dictionary : more than 150 stitch patterns to knit top down, bottom up, back and forth, and in the round / Wendy Bernard ; photography by Thayer Allyson Gowdy ; prop and wardrobe styling by Karen Schaupeter. Stewart, Tabori & Chang, 2014. 288 p. : **746.43**

1. Knitting -- Patterns.
ISBN 9781617690990

LC bl2014021762

"A Melanie Falick Book."
Includes index.

Provides instructions for more than one hundred-fifty stitch patterns, ranging from lace and cables to colorwork and fancy edgings.

"As with any solid stitch dictionary, the swatches show multiple repeats of the pattern, and the color photos are clear and large enough to display detail. Charts are present as needed." Library Journal.

Bliss, Debbie

★The **knitter's** book of knowledge : a complete guide to essential knitting techniques / Debbie Bliss ; illustrations by Cathy Brear ; photography by Kim Lightbody. Lark, 2015. 318 p. : **746.43**

1. Knitting. 2. Knitting -- Techniques.
ISBN 9781454709268

LC bl2016032794

Includes index.

A guide to knitting techniques discusses equipment and materials, shows readers basic, embellishing, and finishing techniques, and provides time-saving tips.

"Years in the knitwear industry have made Bliss a leading expert, but her ability to share her knowledge in a cohesive manner is special indeed." Library Journal.

Bogert, Kerry,

CoffeeHouse knits : knitting patterns and essays with robust flavor / [editorial director] Kerry Bogert. Interweave, 2019 143 p. : **746.43**

1. Knitting -- Patterns 2. Knitting -- Miscellanea 3. Patterns

ISBN 9781632506597

LC 2018289941

"The jolt of inspiration every knitter needs! Inspired by the ritual of sipping and stitching, CoffeeHouse Knits is a stimulating collection of knitwear with an extra shot of something special. Whether you're joining friends at the coffee shop for community knitting or you're home enjoying the first cup of the day, perk up your knitting with: 20 patterns that range in skill level from advanced beginner to intermediate--macchiato to espresso; Simple touches evoke the idea of everyone's favorite drink, from steaming swirls around a sweater yoke to coffee bean inspired motifs; Stirring essays from knitters explore community, connection, and caffeine. Pour yourself another cup and settle in with Coffeehouse Knits."--provided by Amazon.com.

Budd, Ann, 1956-

The **knitter's** handy book of patterns : basic designs in multiple sizes & gauges / Ann Budd. Interweave Press, c2002. 111 p. : **746.43**

1. Knitting -- Patterns

ISBN 1931499047

LC 2001059208

Includes index.

"The patterns in this book allow the knitter to create garments in any size from toddler to extra-large adult in any weight of yarn, from fingering to bulky. The knitter has only to knit a generous swatch with yarn and needles of her/his choice and plug the resulting gauge information into the charted instructions and schematics provided. Highly recommended for all knitting collections." Library Journal.

The **knitter's** handy book of top-down sweaters : basic designs in multiple sizes and gauges / Ann Budd. Interweave Press LLC, 2012, ©2012. 263 p. : **746.43**

1. Knitting -- Patterns. 2. Sweaters.

ISBN 9781596684836

LC 2012001366

"Fiber and yarn enthusiasts nationwide will celebrate Ann Budd's latest addition to The Knitter's Handy Book series. Answering to a growing interest in knitting sweaters from the top down and knitting seamless sweaters that require little finishing, this handy book offers instructions for knitting five basic sweater types: circular yoke, raglan, modified-drop shoulder, set-in sleeve, and saddle shoulder. Patterns are offered in multiple sizes and yarn gauges and for a broad age group. Following the basics for each of the five sweater types are three diverse patterns from top designers that illustrate some of the many ways that instructions can be used as springboards for creative expression, including color, texture, and shaping variations. Also included for intermediate to advanced knitters are personal design touches, detailed charts, clear instruction, and quick tips to expand knitting possibilities and maintain creative originality. A key reference for knitters of all skill levels, this is the new essential knitting resource on your bookshelf."-- Provided by publisher.

"Knitters who want to design their own sweaters but don't want to figure out all the math will appreciate Budd's straightforward approach to sweater design, while knitters who are just looking for patterns will enjoy the variety of ready-to-knit patterns in this collection." Library Journal.

New directions in sock knitting : 18 innovative designs knitted from every which way / Ann Budd. Interweave, 2015 167 p. : **746.43**

1. Knitting -- Patterns. 2. Socks.

ISBN 9781620339435

LC bl2016001628

Includes index.

Presents a collection of sock patterns categorized by type of knitting construction, including top-down, toe-up, zigzag, boomerang, and u-turn.

Sock knitting master class : innovative techniques + patterns from top designers / Ann Budd. Interweave, c2011. 183 p. : **746.43**

1. Knitting -- Patterns 2. Socks

ISBN 9781596683129

LC 2010049008

"Learn sock design from the masters while knitting 15+ spectacular, brand-new patterns featuring the widest variety of techniques".-- Provided by publisher.

Chachula, Robyn, 1978-

Unexpected afghans : innovative crochet designs with traditional techniques / Robyn Chachula. Interweave Press, 2012 159 p. : **746.43**

1. Afghans (Blankets) 2. Crocheting -- Patterns.

ISBN 9781596682993

LC 2012001563

"Unexpected Afghans presents 29 innovative interpretations of a favorite at-home essential. From best-selling author Robyn Chachula comes an in-depth look into crocheting traditional afghans using contemporary techniques, colors and patterns. Expert designers including Kristin Omdahl, Kathy Merrick, Kimberly McAlindin, and many more, provide an abundance of fresh patterns and projects that are perfect for new and advanced crocheters as they start out beginner-friendly and become more complex, allowing a crocheter to build skills and confidence. Designers at any level will enjoy: A detailed technique's workshop in every chapter including cables, motifs, color, lace, and Tunisian crochet. Helpful tips from designers for working through each afghan project. Easy-to-follow charts and diagrams. Along with tons of beautiful afghan projects for all skill levels, you'll find many of your favorite designer's biographies--giving you an exploration into their inspiration."-- Provided by publisher.

"With almost 30 different projects encompassing a variety of styles and techniques, this is an excellent value." Library Journal.

Corkhill, Betsan

Crochet therapy : the soothing art of savoring each stitch / Betsan Corkhill. Abrams, 2016. 144 p. : **746.43**

1. Crocheting. 2. Crocheting -- Patterns.

ISBN 9781419721113

LC 2015955482

"20+ projects for finding your zen"--Cover.

Includes index.

"Crochet Therapy will inspire you to pick up a hook and take some time out of your hectic day to dive into colorful whorls of yarn. Focus, relax, and become more mindful by making more than 20 simple and colorful projects comprised of crocheted mandalas, soothing circles, and other beautiful motifs. Each repetitive pattern helps you engage with your materials, increase your well-being, and unlock your creativity. Mindfulness exercises accompany the patterns and complement the therapeutic effect of crocheting for achieving calm, stress relief, and becoming 'effortlessly present' in your craft. Clear instructions and a host of finishing techniques round out the pretty projects and crocheted bounty." -- Publisher's description

"Corkhill's meditative projects, combined with the exercises throughout, will help crocheters reap the health and wellness benefits of mindful crafting." Library Journal.

Crowfoot, Jane

Ultimate crochet bible : a complete reference with step-by-step techniques / Jane Crowfoot. Collins & Brown, 2010. 304 p. : C&b Crafts **746.43**

1. Crocheting.
ISBN 9781843405634

LC bl2011026453

Includes index.

Provides step-by-step instructions for all aspects of crocheting, with information on such topics as choosing a hook; texture and lace stitches; Tunisian and entrelac crochet; working with color, beads and sequins; embellishments; and finishing techniques.

"This guide begins with an overview of the craft's origins and its requirements and necessities (for instance, hooks, needles, and knowledge of how to read a chart). Each chapter truly exposes the how-to details, not only in words but also, most important, in oversize illustrations. Included are a well-explained section of basics (for instance, how to differentiate between front and reverse sides and how to work crochet for left-handed crafters) and specific stitch categories: texture and lace, thread, Tunisian entrelac, color, beads and sequins, edgings, and professional finishing techniques." Booklist.

Dassau, Jennifer

Knitting short rows : techniques for great shapes & angles / Jennifer Dassau. Interweave, 2016 143 p. : **746.43**

1. Knitting -- Patterns.
ISBN 9781632502582

LC bl2017029398

Includes index.

Provides instructions for essential techniques to create seamless curves, soft angles, and finishing touches.

Dosen, Stephanie

Woodland knits : over 20 enchanting patterns : a Tiny Owl Knits Collection / Stephanie Dosen ; photographer, Tiffany Mumford. The Taunton Press, 2013 128 p. : Tiny Owl Knits **746.43**

1. Knitting -- Patterns. 2. Dress accessories.
ISBN 9781627100243

LC 2013026929

Presents over twenty knitting patterns incorporating flowers, vines, or woodland creatures in the designs, including scarves, hats, and mittens.

Durant, Judith, 1955-

Cable left, cable right : 94 knitted cables / Judith Durant ; photography by Mars Vilaubi. Storey Publishing, 2016 216 p. : **746.43**

1. Cable knitting 2. Knitting -- Technique
ISBN 9781612125169

LC 2015044820

Includes index.

"Each of the cables includes a full-color, close-up swatch illustrating clearly how the cables are formed as well as charted instructions. Helpful tips for troubleshooting--including a clever approach to remedying loose stitches before and after cables--are supplied throughout." Library Journal.

Crochet one-skein wonders for babies / edited by Judith Durant & Edie Eckman ; photography by Geneve Hoffman. Storey Publishing, 2016 286 p. : **746.43**

1. Crocheting -- Patterns 2. Infants' clothing.
ISBN 9781612125763

LC 2015050175

Includes index.

A crochet-focused collection of projects features single-skein items for babies and toddlers and includes an array of wearables, accessories, and toys.

"Handy tips on topics such as sizing and safety are scattered throughout, featuring valuable information the crocheter will continue to use in future projects. Covering a lot of ground in one volume, this thorough collection would be a valuable addition to libraries where crochet books are in demand." Booklist.

Increase, decrease : 99 step-by-step methods / Judith Durant ; photography by John Polak. Storey Publishing, 2015 256 p. : **746.43**

1. Knitting -- Patterns 2. Knitting -- Technique. 3. Knitting -- Stitches.
ISBN 9781612123318

LC 2014042919

Includes index.

Presents detailed instructions for making increases and decreases in knitting patterns, with a variety of techniques for bringing shape and structure to the finished garment.

One-skein wonders for babies : 101 knitting projects for infants & toddlers / edited by Judith Durant. Storey Publishing, 2015 287 p. ; **746.43**

1. Knitting -- Patterns 2. Infants' clothing.
ISBN 9781612124803

LC 2015010744

Features patterns for more than one hundred one-skein projects for outfitting and accessorizing babies and toddlers including mittens, hats, tees, sweaters, and hoodies.

"This is a popular series, and the collection of projects will appeal to knitters with little ones in their lives." Library Journal.

Durham, Teva

Loop-d-loop crochet : more than 25 novel designs for crocheters (and knitters taking up the hook) / Teva Durham ; photographs by Adrian Buckmaster. Stewart, Tabori & Chang, 2007. 144 p. : **746.43**

1. Crocheting. 2. Crocheting -- Patterns.
ISBN 9781584795803

LC 2006025052

"A Melanie Falick book."

Eckman, Edie

Around the corner crochet borders : 150 colorful, creative crocheted edgings with charts & instructions for turning the corner perfectly every time / Edie Eckman. Storey Pub., c2010. 316 p. : **746.43**

1. Crocheting -- Patterns.
ISBN 9781603425384

LC 2010001461

Includes index.

A crochet border is the perfect finishing touch on the edges of any fiber project, but creating one often means shaping the edging around an unforgiving 90-degree angle. It's no easy task, but Edie Eckman guides you through it with style and poise. --From publisher description.

Beyond the square crochet motifs : 144 circles, hexagons, triangles, squares, and other unexpected shapes / Edie Eckman. Storey Pub., 2008. vi, 201 p. : **746.43**

1. Crocheting
ISBN 1603428143

LC oc2012548281

Includes index.

Move beyond granny squares and get ready for crocheted circles, triangles, hexagons, and stars. Edie Eckman opens up the door to crocheting creativity with more than 140 motifs of every shape and size.

Connect the shapes crochet motifs : creative techniques for joining motifs of all shapes / Edie Eckman. Storey Publishing, 2012 271 p. : **746.43**

1. Crocheting -- Patterns.
ISBN 9781603429733

LC 2012013934

Includes index.

Presents 101 crochet motifs along with techniques for arranging and joining them together in a variety of patterns.

"Eckman's eye for color and design make this an excellent addition to any crafter's crochet collection." Library Journal.

The **crochet** answer book : solutions to every problem you'll ever face ; answers to every question you'll ever ask / Edie Eckman. Storey Publishing, 2015 408 p. : **746.43**

1. Crocheting -- Miscellanea.
ISBN 9781612124063

LC 2014033696

Includes index.

Discusses a range of topics about crocheting, from foundation chains and yarn types to charts, gauges, granny squares, borders, and tunisian crochet, in a question-and-answer format.

"Eckman presents a definitively revised guide that reflects the latest trends. In her inimitable question-and-answer style, she features the most recently unearthed techniques (do remember: what's old is new again in this and other needlework books), like Tunisian crochet and Bruges and Clones laces. There are brief illustrations, now, for both left- and right-handed stitchers. And new yarns and new tools (or adaptive ones) are explored with helpful tips and caveats." Booklist.

Epstein, Nicky

Nicky Epstein, the essential edgings collection : 500 of her favorite original borders / Nicky Epstein. Nicky Epstein Books, an imprint of Sixth&Spring Books, 2012 256 p. : **746.43**

1. Knitting -- Patterns. 2. Borders, Ornamental (Decorative arts)
ISBN 9781936096473

LC bl2013039645

Includes index.

Provides instructions on creating over five hundred decorative borders, trims, ribs, fringe, cords, twists, and edgings.

Gardner, Sue

★A **to** Z of crochet : the ultimate guide for the beginner to advanced crocheter / [editor, Sue Gardner]. Martingale & Co., 2008, c2007. 160 p. : **746.43**

1. Crocheting. 2. Crocheting -- Technique.
ISBN 9781564779984

LC bl2012046478

Includes index.

Originally published: Malvern, S. Aust. : Country Bumpkin Publications, 2007.

Presents step-by-step instructions and photographs covering the techniques of crocheting.

Gaughan, Norah

Norah Gaughan's knitted cable sourcebook : a breakthrough guide to knitting with cables and designing your own / photographs by Jared Flood. Abrams, 2016. 275 p. : **746.43**

1. Knitting -- Patterns
ISBN 9781419722394

LC bl2016042339

Presents more than one hundred and fifty cable stitch patterns, ranging from basic to complex, and information on how to mix and match cables in projects, along with instructions for fifteen garment patterns for wraps, sweaters, and accessories.

Gullberg, Maria

Tapestry crochet and more : a handbook of crochet techniques and patterns : tapestry crochet, granny squares, lacy stars, and 3D patterns / Maria Gullberg ; translator, Carol Huebscher Rhoades. Trafalgar Square, 2016. 82 p. : **746.43**

1. Crocheting. 2. Crocheting -- Patterns.
ISBN 9781570767678

LC bl2016047675

Presents tapestry crocheting techniques with practical tips and patterns for totes, hats, wrist warmers, and lace.

"This concealed ring-bound book focuses on tapestry crochet but also offers several other types of projects, including granny squares and three-dimensional flowers. The look of tapestry crochet is very distinctive and is rarely represented in craft books published in the U.S." Booklist.

Herzog, Amy, 1975-

Knit to flatter : The Only Instructions You'll Ever Need to Knit Sweaters That Make You Look Good and Feel Great! / Amy Herzog ; photographs by Karen Pearson ; photostyling by Karen Schaupeter. Stewart, Tabori & Chang, 2013. 159 p. : **746.43**

1. Knitting -- Patterns. 2. Clothing measurements.
ISBN 9781617690174

LC 2012022908

"STC Craft/A Melanie Falick Book."

Presents a guide to knitting sweaters that can be designed for every body type, providing ten patterns with instructions for up to ten sizes and for creating customized details.

"Featuring a variety of models and a beauty-at-all-sizes attitude, Herzog's positive, inspiring book will help knitters create attractive garments that make them feel gorgeous." Library Journal.

Knit wear love : foolproof instructions for knitting your best-fitting sweaters ever in the styles you love to wear / Amy Herzog ; photography by Karen Pearson ; photography creative direction and styling by Karen Schaupeter. Stewart, Tabori & Chang, 2015. 192 p. : **746.43**

1. Knitting. 2. Knitting -- Patterns. 3. Sweaters. 4. Clothing measurements.
ISBN 9781617691393

LC bl2015012057

"STC Craft/A Melanie Falick Book."
"24 sweaters for all shapes and sizes!"--Cover.
"Mix-and-match patterns in 12 sizes and 3 gauges!"--Page 4 of cover.
A guide to knitting sweaters explains how to customize such basic sweater patterns as cardigans, wraps, and pullovers to suit different shapes and personal styles, with a variety of customization details and twelve sizes.
"This classic-in-the-making will inspire knitters to make sweaters that fit well and suit their personal style." Library Journal.

Hiatt, June
The **principles** of knitting : methods and techniques of hand knitting / June Hemmons Hiatt ; illustrations by Jesse Hiatt. Simon & Schuster, 2012. xx, 712 p. : **746.43**

1. Knitting.
ISBN 9781416535171

LC 2012418278

"A Touchstone Book."
"The comprehensive & timeless guide"--Cover.
A revised and updated edition of a popular classic primer shares comprehensive guidelines for beginning and experienced knitters that demonstrate how to approach a full range of techniques.

Hubert, Margaret
10 granny squares, 30 blankets : color schemes, layouts, and edge finishes for 30 unique looks / Margaret Hubert. Creative Publishing International, 2016. 128 p. : **746.43**

1. Crocheting -- Patterns. 2. Blankets.
ISBN 9781589238930

LC bl2016047704

Provides instructions for crocheting thirty blankets, including baby blankets and full-size throws, using combinations of ten different granny squares.
"Hubert is one of the crocheters responsible for rescuing granny squares from the 1970s nostalgia heap, and here she continues her quest to modernize this tried-and-true favorite." Library Journal.

Hubert, Margaret
The **complete** photo guide to crochet : 1200 Photos: Basics, Stitch Patterns, and Projects / Margaret Hubert. Creative Pub. International, c2010. 272 p. : **746.43**

1. Crocheting 2. Crocheting.
ISBN 1589234723

LC 2009031798

"Reference for crocheters; includes instructions and diagrams for 200 stitch patterns, basic information about how to crochet, plus 20 patterns".--Provided by publisher.

Hubert, Margaret
The **granny** square book : timeless techniques & fresh ideas for crocheting square by square / Margaret Hubert. Creative Pub. International, c2011. 176 p. : **746.43**

1. Crocheting -- Patterns
ISBN 9781589236387

LC 2011013365

"Granny squares are to crochet what pieced squares are to quilting. They originated with pioneer women using up precious scraps of yarn to make blankets for their families, and over the years, many recognized, named patterns have been handed down from one generation to the next. Beyond this treasury of 75 different granny square motifs, Margaret Hubert shows the evolution of the granny square, how it can be used and interpreted in different ways with different yarns, and how today's crocheter can designher own projects using the granny squares of her choice with the yarn choices of today. Just as Margaret learned from her grandmother and mother and then passed the skill down to her daughter and granddaughter, each generation finds new uses and artistic ways to interpret granny squares".-- Provided by publisher.
"Crocheters looking to move beyond basic granny squares, as well as new crocheters drawn to these traditional motifs, will enjoy this collection." Library Journal.

Huff, Mary Scott
★The **mitten** handbook : knitting recipes to make your own/ Mary Scott Huff ; photographs by Lesley Unruh. Abrams, 2017. 158 p. : **746.43**

1. Mittens. 2. Knitting -- Patterns 3. Knitting. 4. Recipes
ISBN 9781419726620

LC 2016961383

Shares twenty patterns for knitting mittens.

Impelen, Helgrid van
Big knits big needles / Helgrid van Impelen ; photography: Katja Schubert. DK Publishing, 2015. 143 p. : **746.43**

1. Knitting -- Patterns. 2. Sweaters.
ISBN 9781465453983

LC 2016591051

"20+ stylish patterns on giant needles for super-fast results"-- Cover.
"Sophisticated and more rustic styles are featured and should please a variety of tastes." Booklist.

Interweave Press,
Crochet to calm / the editors at Interweave ; foreword by Mandy O'Sullivan of @craftastherapy. Interweave, 2016 111 p. : Craft to Calm **746.43**

1. Crocheting. 2. Crocheting -- Patterns.
ISBN 9781632504951

LC bl2017005562

"Stitch and de-stress with 18 simple crochet patterns"--Cover.
Provides eighteen crocheting projects to calm the mind, including a tote, a pillow, and a scarf.
"Many crafters are drawn to the relaxing properties of handwork, and crocheters seeking simple-yet-attractive projects will enjoy this collection." Library Journal.

Karlsson, Maja
Traditional Swedish knitting patterns : 40 motifs and 20 projects / Maja Karlsson ; photography: Maria Rosenlöf ; translator: Carol Huebscher Rhoades. Trafalgar Square, 2017. 159 p. : **746.43**

1. Knitting -- Sweden -- Patterns
ISBN 9781570768217

LC bl2017030611

Includes index.

Provides forty Swedish knitting motifs and twenty related projects, including hats, mittens, and shawls.

Kartus, Lisa, 1953-

Knit fix : problem solving for knitters / Lisa Kartus, author. Interweave Press, 2006. 111 p. : **746.43**

1. Knitting.

ISBN 1596680113

LC 2006002416

Includes index.

"Knitting teacher Kartus believes that there isn't any knitting faux pas that can't be fixed, and in this illustrated problem-solving manual, she proves her point." Library Journal

Knight, Erika

500 crochet stitches : the ultimate crochet stitch bible / Pavilion. St. Martin's Griffin, 2015. 287 p. : **746.43**

1. Crocheting -- Technique. 2. Stitches (Sewing).

ISBN 9781250067302

LC 2015016931

Includes index.

Presents an introduction to crocheting, discussing tools, equipment, basic and advanced stitches, edgings, and trims, with illustrations and detailed instructions for five hundred stitches.

"There are a number of crochet stitch dictionaries on the market, but most are focused on a specific type of stitch (e.g., edgings) or on motifs. This comprehensive work makes an excellent reference for crocheters of all skill levels." Library Journal.

750 knitting stitches : the ultimate knit stitch bible / [Erika Knight]. St. Martin's Griffin, 2015 287 p. : **746.43**

1. Knitting -- Technique. 2. Stitches (Sewing).

ISBN 9781250067180

LC 2015017155

Includes index.

Presents an introduction to knitting, discussing tools, equipment, techniques for basic and advanced stitches, colorwork, edgings, and trims, with illustrations and detailed instructions for 750 stitches.

"A close-up, full-color swatch is also included for each design, giving the knitter an idea of what multiple pattern repeats look like in a knitted sample. A directory of basic knitting abbreviations and a guide to knitting elementals appear in the introduction." Library Journal.

Leapman, Melissa

Mastering color knitting : simple instructions for stranded, intarsia, and double knitting / Melissa Leapman. Potter Craft, 2010. 175 p. : **746.43**

1. Knitting.

ISBN 9780307586506

LC 2010006097

Includes index.

Reveals how to create advanced results through stranded knitting, intarsia, and two-color double knitting techniques, with twelve projects and more than fifty stitch patterns that use multiple yarn colors or include reversible knitting options.

"Knitters who like to design their own projects will appreciate the variety of motifs in all three techniques, which can be used to create a one-of-a-kind garment or accessory." Library Journal.

Marchant, Nancy, 1949-

Knitting brioche : the essential guide to the brioche stitch / Nancy Marchant. North Light Books, 2009. 256 p. : **746.43**

1. Knitting -- Patterns

ISBN 9781600613012

LC 2009038643

"Marchant is widely recognized as the expert on brioche stitch, and her continued explorations of such knitting will appeal to experienced knitters looking for the next big trend." Library Journal.

Knitting fresh brioche : creating two-color twists & turns / Nancy Marchant. Sixth&Spring Books, 2014 240 p. : **746.43**

1. Knitting 2. Knitting.

ISBN 1936096773

LC 2014017015

Introduces an original brioche technique for two-color brioche rib, providing step-by-step instructions for all aspects of the technique, from basic stitches to repairing mistakes, and includes twelve shawl and scarf projects for practice.

Melville, Sally

Knitting pattern essentials : adapting and drafting knitting patterns for great knitwear / Sally Melville. Potter Craft, 2013 224 p. : **746.43**

1. Knitting 2. Knitwear -- Pattern design.

ISBN 0307965570

LC 2012015715

Includes index.

An acclaimed instructor and author of the best-selling Knitting Experience series presents a comprehensive guide to sweater construction that reveals how to modify garment patterns so that finished products look and fit as desired, in a volume complemented by 10 customizable patterns.

Mullett-Bowlsby, Shannon

★Complete crochet course : the ultimate reference guide / Shannon & Jason Mullett-Bowlsby. Lark, 2018 335 p. : **746.43**

1. Crocheting 2. Crocheting -- Patterns 3. Crocheting -- Technique

ISBN 9781454710523

LC bl2018029092

"Featuring more than 190 stitches, 125 tutorials, 98 techniques"--Cover.

Includes index.

Presents a guide to every aspect of crocheting, describing tools, yarn, chart reading, basic and advanced stitches, colorwork and finishing techniques, with detailed instructions for five crochet projects.

"It's a well-organized reference, up-to-date with the different cable, ribbing, and pattern stitches that are now popular." Booklist.

Newton, Deborah

Finishing school : a master class for knitters / Deborah Newton. Sixth&Spring Books, 2011. 164 p. : **746.43**

1. Knitting -- Patterns.

ISBN 9781936096190

LC 2011013424

"The word "finishing" fills many knitters, beginners and more experienced alike, with dread. Some even abandon projects at this stage, rather than complete the necessary steps to achieve beautiful, wearable garments. In Finishing School, master knitter and designer Deborah Newton, shares her expertise and love of (yes, love of) finishing with knitters of all skill levels. She takes them step by step through the ins and outs of blocking, seaming, edging and embellishments, giving knitting the confidence and skills needed to create professional-looking knitwear. In addition to in-depth instruction, the book includes patterns for 12 sweaters, jackets and scarves, many with variations".-- Provided by publisher.

Nico, Brooke

More lovely knitted lace : contemporary patterns in geometric shapes / Brooke Nico. Lark, 2016 127 p. : **746.43**

1. Knitting -- Patterns. 2. Knitwear. 3. Shapes.
ISBN 9781454709183

LC bl2017016125

"4 basic shapes, 16 stunning projects"--Cover.
Includes index.
Presents sixteen new lace knitting projects that use four basic shapes as the base for shawls, gauntlets, vests, and other wearables.

Noldeke, Marisa

50 knitted wraps and shawls / Marisa Noldeke. Stackpole Books 2020 167 p. **746.43**

1. Knitting -- Patterns 2. Shawls.
ISBN 9780811738613

LC bl2020045589

"With 50 patterns for knitted shawls and wraps to choose from, in so many styles and textures, choosing your first project will be a welcome challenge. From simple knit-purl designs to more complex colorwork, cables, and lace, there are designs to interest every level of knitter".-- Provided by publisher.
"This will be an excellent addition to the knitting library for crafters who enjoy experimenting with design choices to fashion stylish, one-size-fits-all creations." Publishers Weekly

Ohrenstein, Dora

The **crocheter's** skill-building workshop / Dora Ohrenstein. Storey Publishing, 2014 255 p. : **746.43**

1. Crocheting.
ISBN 1612122469

LC 2014028045

Includes index.
Covers basic crochet techniques and beyond, providing dozens of stitch-along swatches that teach specific skills that can be applied to five projects for a hat, shawl, neck warmer, bag and scarf.

Omdahl, Kristin

The **finer** edge : crocheted trims, motifs & borders / Kristin Omdahl. Interweave Press, 2013. 143 p. : **746.43**

1. Crocheting -- Patterns
ISBN 9781596685543

LC 2012029110

"Refine your taste with this innovative collection of 40 stitch and 12 garment crochet patterns from best-selling author Kristin Omdahl".-- Provided by publisher.
"Several crocheted edging/motif books have been published in the last few years. Omdahl is a big name in the field, and crocheters will appreciate this nicely curated ensemble." Library Journal.

Phelps, Isela

Loom knitting primer : a beginner's guide to knitting on a loom with over 35 fun projects / Isela Phelps. St. Martin's Griffin, 2016 160 p. ; **746.43**

1. Handlooms. 2. Knitting 3. Machine knitting.
ISBN 1250084199

LC 2015041185

"Fully revised and updated edition of the bestselling book."
Cover title.
Presents an introduction to loom knitting, with detailed instructions on techniques for round and rectangular looms and thirty-five patterns for making hats, scarves, socks, cowls, and an afghan.

Radcliffe, Margaret (Margaret K. K.)

Circular knitting workshop : essential techniques to master knitting in the round / Margaret Radcliffe; photography by John Polak. Storey Pub., LLC, c2012. 319 p. : **746.43**

1. Knitting. 2. Knitting -- Patterns.
ISBN 9781603429993

LC 2011025033

Includes index.
Provides step-by-step instructions for stitching items using the circular knitting method, a technique used to create socks, bags, gloves and mittens, sweaters, and vests.
"All knitters, from novice to expert, will find something new and useful in this comprehensive guide. Essential for knitting collections." Library Journal.

The **knitting** answer book : solutions to every problem you'll ever face ; answers to every question you'll ever ask / Margaret Radcliffe. Storey Publishing, 2015 439 p. : **746.43**

1. Knitting -- Miscellanea.
ISBN 9781612124049

LC 2014033661

Discusses a range of topics about knitting, from needle sizes and yarn weights to curling edges, chart reading, tight ribbing, and dropped stitches, in a question-and-answer format.

The **knowledgeable** knitter : understand the inner workings of knitting and make every project a success / Margaret Radcliffe. Storey Publishing, 2014 295 p. : **746.43**

1. Knitting. 2. Knitting -- Patterns
ISBN 9781612124148

LC 2014016057

Helps knitters with the challenges they face while undertaking a new project by demystifying and explaining every knitting technique, including how to read a pattern chart, select the right yarn, modify a pattern, fix a mistake, and create edges and seams.

Righetti, Maggie

Crocheting in plain English / Maggie Righetti. Thomas Dunne Books, 2008. xviii, 268 p. : **746.43**

1. Crocheting.
ISBN 9780312353544

LC 2008043913

Comprehensive, common-sense advice on all aspects of crocheting ranges from the basics for beginners to perfecting techniques for the advanced crocheter, and from selecting threads and yarns to blocking, cleaning, and storing crocheted articles, in a revised and updated edition of the best-selling crochet reference.

Seifert, Jacob

Noro Kureyon : the 30th anniversary collection. / edited by Jacob Seifert. Sixth & Spring Books, 2018. 143 p. : **746.43**

1. Eisaku Noro, Ltd. 2. Knitting -- Patterns 3. Yarn
ISBN 9781942021889

LC 2017029200

Includes index.
"Unlike in some knitting books, which don't illustrate enough, patterns here often get four photographs. Throughout, it's the full-size color

photographs, along with smaller additions, that will make knitters drool. Fans of Noro will adore this one, and those new to the yarn will want to get started ASAP." Booklist.

Shida, Hitomi

Japanese knitting stitch bible : 260 exquisite patterns / Hitomi Shida ; translated from the Japanese with an introduction by Gayle Roehm. Tuttle Publishing, 2017 160 p. : **746.43**

1. Knitting -- Patterns 2. Knitting -- Japan.
ISBN 9781462919406

LC bl2017043744

Offers 260 original knitting patterns for experienced knitters, including variations on classic stitches, as well as unique new creations, with diagrams showing how to execute the basic stitches and instructions and diagrams for a sampling of projects.

"For intrepid knitters looking for a challenge, the pages of stunning stitches will prove well worth the effort." Publishers Weekly.

Spainhower, Courtney

Elemental knits : a perennial knitwear collection / Courtney Spainhower. Interweave, 2020. 159 p. **746.43**

1. Knitting -- Patterns
ISBN 9781632506535

LC bl2020000199

A collection of 20 customizable knitting patterns counsels do-it-yourself crafters on how to select practical patterns and fibers while creating wardrobe-enhancing fashions for different times of the year.

Starmore, Alice

Alice Starmore's book of Fair Isle knitting / Alice Starmore. Dover Publications, 2009. 199 p. : **746.43**

1. Fair Isle knitting -- Patterns 2. Knitting
ISBN 9780486472188

LC 2009026197

Scotland's Fair Isle is celebrated the world over for its distinctive, stranded-color knitting, and Alice Starmore is famous for her expertise in designing and instructing knitters in this appealing regional tradition. Starmore's richly illustrated guide offers both beginning and advanced knitters a complete workshop in the Fair Isle style. It not only explores the art's history, patterns, and traditional techniques but also encourages knitters to develop their own creativity. --From publisher description.

Tudor roses / Alice Starmore. Calla Editions, 2013. 175 p. : **746.43**

1. Decoration and ornament -- Tudor style. 2. Knitting
ISBN 1606600478

LC bl2013053123

Features hand-knitted designs inspired by members of the Tudor dynasty, includes charts and instructions, color photographs, and historical background.

Stoller, Debbie

★Stitch 'n bitch : the knitter's handbook / Debbie Stoller ; illustrations by Adrienne Yan ; fashion photography by John Dolan. Workman, c2003. 248 p. : **746.43**

1. Knitting
ISBN 9780761128182

LC 2003053543

Includes index.

A guide to knitting offers instructions for a variety of techniques and stitches, as well as information on the different types of needles and yarns, tips on shopping for yarns, finishing techniques, and forty patterns.

"An introduction chronicles the history of knitting from the female perspective, while subsequent chapters cover topics such as yarn type, instruments, stitches, and patterns. Perhaps the most exciting bit is Stoller's knit-as-you-learn technique: with every new stitch, she presents a new pattern, thereby allowing knitters to build on their knowledge. Essential for all crafts collections and perfect for a display." Library Journal.

Stoller, Debbie

Stitch 'n bitch superstar knitting : go beyond the basics / Debbie Stoller ; with photography by Gabrielle Revere. Workman Pub, c2010. xii, 356 p. : **746.43**

1. Knitting.
ISBN 9780761135975

LC 2010051402

Includes index.

Presents instructions for a full array of advanced knitting techniques and skills, such as double-knitting, knitting lace, complicated color work, and beading, along with forty-one patterns for such items as sweaters, hats, socks, and scarves.

"Essential for the well-rounded knitting collection owing to the sections on techniques and designing; a few of the patterns are destined to be popular. The Frilly Filly Scarf (see pattern, above) is simple and sophisticated." Library Journal.

Storey, Martin, 1958-

Easy fair isle knitting : 27 projects with a modern twist / Martin Storey ; photography by Steven Wooster. Trafalgar Square, 2016. 128 p. : **746.43**

1. Knitting -- Patterns. 2. Knitting.
ISBN 9781570767852

LC bl2016037437

Presents instructions for Fair Isle knitting projects for the novice that feature patterns with only two colors in each row of knitting, including scarves, cowls, hats, and pillows.

"Knitters who are drawn to Fair Isle colorwork but aren't taken with traditional geometric motifs will appreciate Storey's modern take on the technique." Library Journal.

Todhunter, Tracey

Crochet, learn it. love it. : techniques and projects to build a lifelong passion for beginners up / Tracey Todhunter. Barron's Educational Series, Inc., 2016. 160 p. : **746.43**

1. Crocheting. 2. Crocheting -- Patterns.
ISBN 9781438007595

LC 2015951472

"A Quarto book"--Title page verso.

Includes index.

"The tone is straightforward but friendly, and the written and photographed instructions are thorough, making this appropriate for crafters who learn best either visually or by following written instructions." Library Journal.

Turner, Sharon, 1962-

Teach yourself visually knitting / Sharon Turner. Wiley Pub., c2010. 339 p. : **746.43**

1. Knitting -- Patterns
ISBN 9780470528327

LC bl2010003831

Includes index.

Uses color photographs and step-by-step instructions to provide a visual guide for creating a knitted scarf, hat, or sweater, covering such topics as casting, purling, correcting mistakes, and deciphering cryptic knitting patterns.

Varnam, Emma

Crocheted succulents : cacti and other succulent plants to make / Emma Varnam. The Guild of Master Craftsman Publications, 2019. 143 p. : **746.43**

1. Crocheting -- Patterns 2. Succulent plants 3. Plants in art
ISBN 9781784945046

LC bl2019032453

"25 fun and easy projects"--Cover.

Includes index.

"An adorable book that is a must for all crafting collections." Booklist.

★**Vogue** knitting. The Ultimate Knitting Book / the editors of Vogue knitting Magazine. Sixth&Spring Books, 2018 351 p. : **746.43**

1. Knitting
ISBN 9781942021698

LC 2017033626

Includes index.

An updated knitting reference offers an expanded library of stitches; sections on new favorite techniques; dozens of projects for hats, mittens, gloves, socks, and shawls; and revised chapters on finishing and garment care.

★**Vogue** knitting : the ultimate quick reference / the editors of Vogue knitting magazine. Sixth&Spring Books, [2019] 184 p. **746.43**

1. Knitting
ISBN 9781640210516

LC 2019019706

"Knitting: The Ultimate Knitting Book (2018) on steroids." Booklist.

Weil, Anne (Anne B.)

Knitting without needles : a stylish introduction to finger and arm knitting / Anne Weil. Potter Craft, 2015 191 p. : **746.43**

1. Finger weaving. 2. Knitting -- Patterns. 3. Knitting -- Technique.
ISBN 9780804186520

LC 2014036650

Includes index.

A guide to finger weaving explains how to create such projects as headbands, hats, scarves, and blankets.

Werker, Kim P.

Teach yourself visually crochet / Kim P. Werker and Cecily Keim. Wiley, c2011. 280 p. : Teach Yourself Visually **746.43**

1. Crocheting.
ISBN 9780470879979

LC bl2011003712

Includes index.

Uses color photographs and step-by-step instructions to provide a visual guide to crocheting, covering such topics as basic crochet stiches, advanced variations, blocks, edgings, patterns, and finishing.

Wood, Jennifer, 1963

Refined knits : sophisticated lace, cable, and Aran lace knitting / Jennifer Wood. Interweave, 2016 156 p. : **746.43**

1. Knitted lace -- Patterns 2. Cable knitting -- Patterns. 3. Knitwear.
ISBN 9781632500687

LC bl2016011985

Knitwear designer Jennifer Wood combines lace, cable, and Aran lace knitting techniques into patterns for pullover sweaters, cardigans, cowls, and shrugs.

"The patterns are comprehensive, including written and charted instructions, schematics, and notes on construction as needed." Library Journal.

746.432 Knitting

Bestor, Leslie Ann

Cast on, bind off : 54 step-by-step methods / Leslie Ann Bestor ; photography by John Polak. Storey Publishing, 2012 215 p. : **746.432**

1. Knitting -- Technique.
ISBN 9781603427241

LC 2012002769

Collects contemporary and creative cast-on and bind-off knitting methods, including the invisible circular cast on, the mobius cast on, and the Icelandic bind off.

Drysdale, Rosemary

Entrelac : the essential guide to interlace knitting / Rosemary Drysdale. Sixth & Spring, c2010. 160 p. : **746.432**

1. Knitting. 2. Knitting -- Patterns.
ISBN 9781936096008

LC oc2010080121

Includes index.

Entrelac introduces both the history and how-to of this fun style, along with 20 patterns for a variety of garments, home decor items, and baby accessories. Comprehensive instructions and a wide array of swatches provide endless possibilities in lace, colorwork, and much more.

Eaton, Jan

350+ crochet tips, techniques, and trade secrets / Jan Eaton. St. Martins Griffin, 2017. 160 p. ; **746.432**

1. Crocheting 2. Crocheting.
ISBN 1250125103

LC 2017938523

Includes index.

A treasury of tips, techniques, and trade secrets for crocheters provides step-by-step, illustrated instructions that cover everything from choosing the right hook and yarn to setting up a dye studio and managing yard ends.

Herzog, Amy, 1975

You can knit that : foolproof instructions for fabulous sweaters / Amy Herzog ; photography by Karen Pearson. Abrams, 2016 175 p. : **746.432**

1. Knitting. 2. Knitting -- Patterns. 3. Sweaters -- Patterns
ISBN 9781419722479

LC 2015955480

Intends to provide knitters of all skill levels with the sweater-making confidence they need through instructions for six sweater styles--vests, all-in-one construction, drop shoulders, raglans, yokes, and set-in sleeves.

"Herzog's expertise, combined with her ability to explain clearly the hows and whys of sweater knitting, will build confidence even in the most reluctant knitters." Library Journal.

Jurgrau, Andrea

New heights in lace knitting : 17 lace knit accessory patterns / Andrea Jurgrau. Interweave, 2016 142 p. : **746.432**

1. Knitted lace -- Patterns
ISBN 9781632502315

LC 2018419726

Offers seventeen patterns for knitted lace projects inspired by mountain climbing and the world's tallest peaks.

"Adventurous knitters will be drawn to Jurgrau's exquisite lace designsbut novices will find that these peaks are not insurmountable, thanks to an excellent introductory tutorial on lace-knitting techniques." Library Journal.

Meldrum, Carol

Freeform crochet with confidence : unlock the secrets of free-form crochet techniques with 30 fun projects / Carol Meldrum. Barrons Educational Series, Inc., 2015. 144 p. : **746.432**

1. Crocheting. 2. Crocheting -- Patterns.
ISBN 9781438007007

LC 2014956702

Includes index.

Presents thirty crochet projects for such articles as hats, shawls, and bags that incorporate themes and feature step-by-step photography and simple instructions.

"Knowledge enough to begin a freeform project without a veteran by your side. Even more encouraging are the 30 patterns with directions, from fingerless gloves and an infinity scarf to a layered brooch and granny chic top." Booklist.

Square, Vicki, 1954-

The **knitter's** companion : expanded and updated! / Vicki Square. Interweave, c2010. 138 p. : **746.432**

1. Knitting. 2. Sweaters.
ISBN 9781596683143

LC oc2010090182

Includes index.

Now with an instructional DVD, an ideal knitting reference guide includes plenty of techniques, illustrations and definitions, covering everything from stitches, gauges, seams, borders and buttonholes to tassels, fringe, knitting with beads and more. By the author of Knit Kimono.

"This is an excellent ready reference for a variety of knitting techniques, including cast-ons, bind-offs, finishing, and other basics. The demonstrations on the DVDs show knitters exactly what they should be doing. Every knitting collection needs a reference; this one is affordable and accessible." Library Journal.

746.44 Embroidery

Barbe, Karen

Colour confident stitching : how to create beautiful colour palettes / Karen Barbe. Pimpernel Press Ltd, 2017. 128 p. : **746.44**

1. Embroidery -- Technique 2. Color in art.
ISBN 9781910258651

LC bl2017032391

Includes index.

Guides readers through understanding color theory and color sensitivity to create color palettes, offering five stitching projects for readers to practice and build confidence.

Blomkamp, Hazel

Crewel intentions : fresh ideas for Jacobean embroidery / Hazel Blomkamp. Search Press, 2014. 160 p. : **746.44**

1. Crewelwork -- Patterns. 2. Crewelwork.
ISBN 9781782211068

LC bl2015019033

Provides instructions for completing crewelwork projects as well as coverage of techniques, stitches, and weaving methods.

Chanin, Natalie

★The **geometry** of hand-sewing : a romance in stitches and embroidery from Alabama Chanin and The School of Making / Natalie Chanin ; photographs by Abraham Rowe and Rinne Allen ; illustrations by Sun Young Park. Abrams, 2017. 143 p. : **746.44**

1. Stitches (Sewing) 2. Sewing
ISBN 9781419726637

LC bl2017051001

Includes indexes.

Explains that all stitches are based on gridlines and provides instructions for more than one hundred stitches, from straight to herringbone, in a book that includes two plastic stitch cards that can be used for practice.

"Her tone throughout is as measured as her grids and as serene as the gray backgrounds appearing in the photos of each stitch." Publishers Weekly.

Christensen, Jo Ippolito

★The **needlepoint** book / Jo Ippolito Christensen. Simon & Schuster, 1999. xix, 428 p. : **746.44**

1. Canvas embroidery.
ISBN 1476754101

LC oc2014027833

"A Fireside book."

A revision of the profusely illustrated, so-called "Black Bible" of needlepoint, first published in 1976, includes new information on the latest stitches, materials, and techniques and hundreds of new photographs and informational charts.

"Even though the book is a reference, the text is enjoyable to read. Sage advice from Christensen and a variety of other needle artists can be found throughout." Library Journal.

Eaton, Jan

Mary Thomas's dictionary of embroidery stitches. Trafalgar Square Pub., 1998. 208 p. : **746.44**

1. Embroidery -- Dictionaries.
ISBN 1570761183

LC 97081406

"Revised, full-color edition of this classic book, wtih over 100 new stitches."

Includes index.

"A comprehensive dictionary offering more than 400 stitches, this edition includes 100 new stitches, all described and pictured in full-color diagrams. Essential for public libraries and embroidery collections." Library Journal.

Ganderton, Lucinda

★**Embroidery** / Lucinda Ganderton. DK, 2015 160 p. : **746.44**

1. Embroidery. 2. Needlework.
ISBN 9781465436030

LC 2015431417

Previously published as: Stitch Sampler. 1999.

Includes index.

Demonstrates over two hundred stitches for embroidery, needlepoint, and dressmaking and offers advice on thread, needles, and fabrics.

" It's straightforward, simple, and easy to access, thanks not only to an appended index but also to an upfront visual table of contents. The quintessentially perfect reference." Booklist.

Glass, Alison

Alison Glass applique. the essential guide to modern applique / Alison Glass. Lucky Spool Media, 2014. 143 p. : **746.44**

1. Applique -- Patterns. 2. Quilting -- Patterns.

ISBN 9781940655031

LC bl2020045642

"Former interior designer turned award-winning pattern and textile designer, Alison Glass, brings you fresh, creative projects guaranteed to add warmth and style to your home. You'll love making eye-catching quilts and home decor that rival boutique-style accessories but made by hand. Alison introduces readers to a variety of fabric types, threads and techniques suitable for creating wonderful textures in applique. She also includes a series of embroidery stitch instructions to get you started with hand-stitched embellishments. Who says applique has to be from a single fabric? Learn how to piece interesting improv components to cut large-scale applique shapes to add more layers to your quilts. From heirloom-quality needle-turn applique to modern jersey and big-stitch accents, this book includes step-by-step photographs covering each technique in detail (from raw-edge, to needle-turn to reverse applique). With two large pull-out pages packed with mix-and-match shapes to use, Alison gets you drawing, cutting, snipping, turning and stitching to express your own style through each fabulous layer. 14 unique projects for those new to applique and Alison Glass enthusiasts alike".-- Provided by publisher.

Henry, Charles

Mindful embroidery : stitch your way to relaxation with charming European street scenes / Charles Henry and Elin Petronella, creators of Charles and Elin Academy. Page Street Publishing Co., 2020. 157 p. : **746.44**

1. Embroidery -- Patterns. 2. Cities and towns in art.

ISBN 9781645670520

LC bl2020052486

Includes index.

"Escape the chaos of everyday life by embroidering yourself a romantic and tranquil getaway. Allow Charles Henry and Elin Petronella to whisk you away to the calming villas of the French countryside. Discover the hidden gems of Paris, stroll down the colorful tiled streets of Lisbon or float along the canals of Venice. Let go of your worries stitch by stitch through these 20 delightful European scenescapes inspired by Charles and Elin's favorite places throughout Europe. Beginners can confidently complete any design in this book using five common and simple embroidery stitches. As leaders in the modern hand embroidery movement, Charles and Elin invite you to let go of perfectionism and instead slow down, unwind and enjoy the meditative process of creating something gorgeous one stitch, and breath, at a time." Provided by publisher.

"Hand embroidery teachers Henry and Petronella combine traveling with crafting in their charming book of designs. . . . Beginning or advanced embroiderers will find much to enjoy and create here as they armchair-travel with thread." Publishers Weekly

Mornu, Nathalie

Embroider your life : techniques + motifs + inspiration : simple techniques & 150 stylish motifs to embellish your world / Nathalie Mornu. Alpha, 2017. 124 p. : **746.44**

1. Embroidery. 2. Embroidery -- Patterns. 3. Needlework.

ISBN 9781465464859

LC bl2017037586

"Embroidery is on the upswing among crafters, and Mornu's nicely organized collection is full of helpful tutorials and clever ideas." Library Journal.

Prain, Leanne

Hoopla : the art of unexpected embroidery / Leanne Prain ; photography by Jeff Christenson. Aresnal Pulp Press, c2011. 400 p. : **746.44**

1. Embroidery. 2. Embroidery in art.

ISBN 9781551524061

LC bl2013012743

Includes index.

Showcases intricate and extreme embroidery projects that elevate the handicraft to an art form, focusing on innovative stitch artists and providing twenty-eight embroidery projects, including nipple doilies and a ransom note pillow.

"In this combination overview of embroidery and exploration of its current trends, Prain takes a traditional approach, beginning with a cursory look at the craft's history and highlighting practicalities, such as tools and equipment, finishing techniques, and stitching resources. But it is between these lines that the author's true innovation and fun starts: specifically, with interviews with 28 working embroiderers and the same number of unusual projects to complete. Projects don't disappoint, with directions as clear as the designs are funky: handkerchiefs emblazoned with microbes, a modern cuckoo clock stitched on Aida cloth, and knuckle-tattoo church gloves." Booklist.

Reader's Digest Association

The **big** book of cross-stitch designs : over 900 simple-to-stitch decorative motifs. / Reader's Digest Association (EDT). Reader's Digest Association, c2007. 320 p. : **746.44**

1. Cross-stitch -- Patterns

ISBN 9780762106738

LC 2006044634

A treasury of cross-stitch patterns and motifs is complemented by dozens of project ideas, in a volume that provides instructional information for every step, tips on how to select the most compatible materials, and recommendations for a variety of finishing embellishments.

"When editors at Reader's Digest identify a subject to publish, they explore its history, plumb the most popular techniques, then apply those learnings pragmatically. Here, cross-stitching takes on a more artistic bent, starting with the book's layout-big type fonts, step-by-step illustrations with full-color photographs of the projectsand ending with more than 900 designs." Booklist.

Ringquist, Rebecca

★**Rebecca** Ringquist's embroidery workshops : a bend-the-rules primer / photography by Johnny Miller ; photostyling by Shana Faust. STC Craft, 2015. 156 p. : **746.44**

1. Embroidery -- Technique

ISBN 9781617691416

LC bl2015014297

"A Melanie Falick book."

Teaches a variety of embroidery techniques, including stitching, tracing, drawing, layering, and mixing machine- and hand-sewing, and features projects that test each skill.

"Ringquist is a skilled instructor with a great deal of experience. Crafters who are intimidated by embroidery will find her free-spirited approach refreshing." Library Journal.

Search Press,
A-Z of ribbon embroidery : a comprehensive manual with over 40 gorgeous designs to stitch / Search Press Limited. Search Press, 2016. 132 p. : A-Z **746.44**

1. Silk ribbon embroidery. 2. Embroidery. 3. Ribbon work.
ISBN 9781782211730
LC bl2015041120

Includes index.

Provides step-by-step instructions for every stitch and technique involved in ribbon embroidery, and also offers advice from experts on choosing ribbons, fabrics, and other materials.

"Search Press, as always in this British series, excels, giving its readers good instructions and traditional designs, including Victorian bouquet, roses, violets, baby bears, and other animals and flowers. Occasional tips (e.g., test ribbons first for color fastness by washing) ensure that beginners are on the same page as experienced embroiderers. A fresh, instructive approach to a wonderful tradition." Booklist.

Search Press,
A-Z of whitework. Search Press, 2015. 159 p. : A-Z **746.44**

1. Holbein embroidery
ISBN 9781782211792
LC bl2015042932

"The ultimate resource for beginners and experienced needleworkers"--Cover.

Includes index.

Step-by-step photographs illustrate a variety of whitework embroidery techniques, including Ayrshire embroidery, broderie anglaise, candlewicking, cutwork, and shadow work.

"Traditional whitework embroidery--especially Mountmellick and cutwork--is starting to get some attention on embroidery blogs, and these classic techniques will appeal to stitchers with sophisticated tastes." Library Journal.

Shimoda, Naoko, 1953-
Artfully embroidered : motifs and patterns for bags and more / Naoko Shimoda. Interweave, 2014. 119 p. : **746.44**

1. Embroidery -- Patterns.
ISBN 9781620337288
LC 2014036871

Includes two folded sheets of patterns inside pocket on page 3 of cover.

Artfully Embroidered reinvents vintage embroidery through a modern aesthetic. Traditional Japanese and western motifs are made new with color and embellishment, and 25 embroidered patterns demonstrate the beauty of the traditional designs while keeping the projects fresh and modern-looking for today's sewists.

"Sewists interested in exploring the world of embroidery will find a wealth of inspiration here, though beginners may need to consult a reference or an online tutorial to get themselves up to speed on the basics." Library Journal

Victoria and Albert Museum,
Embroidery : a maker's guide, over 230 photographs and illustrations. / Victoria & Albert Museum. Thames & Hudson in association with the Victoria and Albert Museum, 2017. 176 p. : **746.44**

1. Embroidery -- Patterns 2. Embroidery
ISBN 9780500293270
LC 2017944788

"From Japanese kogin to Irish whitework. 15 projects inspired by the V & A collections"--Cover.

Includes index.

"While the coverage isn't comprehensive, this collection provides an overview of a wide variety of techniques, and stitchers interested in global traditions of embroidery will find plenty to explore." Library Journal.

Watson, Sarah
Pen to thread : 750+ hand-drawn embroidery designs to inspire your stitches / Sarah Watson. Interweave, 2015 159 p. : **746.44**

1. Embroidery.
ISBN 9781620339527
LC bl2015054045

Includes index.

Shares over seven hundred and fifty motifs to embroider inspired by everyday items, nature, and food, along with tips for choosing fabric and stitching basics.

"Illustrator and fabric designer Watson brings her whimsical, hand-drawn designs to embroiderers in this collection of small and medium motifs." Library Journal.

746.46 Patchwork and quilting

Adams, Katherine Jean
Comfort & glory : two centuries of American quilts from the Briscoe Center / Katherine Jean Adams. University of Texas Press, Briscoe Center for American History, 2016. xiv, 320 p. ; **746.46**

1. University of Texas at Austin. Center for American -- History Catalogs. 2. Quilts -- Texas 3. Quilts -- Texas -- History
ISBN 9781477309186
LC 2015033631

Includes index.

"This eminently accessible and thorough title will make a wonderful addition to academic, museum, and public libraries of all sizes." Library Journal.

Alexander, Lissa
Oh, scrap! : fabulous quilts that make the most of your stash / Lissa Alexander. Martingale, 2018 96 p. : **746.46**

1. Patchwork 2. Quilting
ISBN 1604688947
LC 2017044124

Best of all, with a dozen patterns to choose from you'll discover how to (finally!) use your unique stash to make scrap quilts that sing. Includes a preface by renowned quilt historian Barbara Brackman. --From publisher description.

Belyea, Patricia
East-meets-West quilts : explore improv with Japanese-inspired designs / Patricia Belyea ; photography by Kate Baldwin. Abrams, 2017. 191 p. : **746.46**

1. Quilting 2. Patchwork
ISBN 9781419726590
LC bl2017052290

The author presents her Quilt Manifesto of five rules for improvising while creating quilts and offers detailed instructions for fourteen quilt patterns using yukata cottons and inspired by Japanese design.

"The quilts' backs prove as interesting as the fronts, and Belyea's stitching designs are innovative, too. With fresh designs and useful directions, Belyea's book is both practical and aspirational." Publishers Weekly.

Beyer, Jinny

A **quilter's** album of patchwork patterns : 4050 pieced blocks for quilters / Jinny Beyer. Breckling Press, 2009. vii, 488 p. : **746.46**

1. Patchwork -- Patterns. 2. Quilting -- Patterns.
ISBN 9781933308081

LC 2009021009

A visual encyclopedia of quilt block designs that provides quilters, designers, researchers, and patchwork enthusiasts with a comprehensive tool for finding, identifying and drafting more than 4050 unique patterns.

"The author pored through newspapers, catalogs, patterns, and magazines of the 1800s and 1900s to prepare illustrations--along with grids, dates, and multiple names--of more than 4,000 quilting blocks, the foundation of this genre of stitching. Yet providing that resource wasn't enough; Beyer enhances her encyclopedic reference by featuring mini catalogs of like-minded design styles, like bow ties, airplanes, the Red Cross, and kaleidoscope blocks. She also details her sources with commentary and explains how she categorized the blocks. Worthy of any quilting (and quilter's) library." Booklist.

Brackman, Barbara

The **Kansas** City star quilts sampler : 60+ blocks from 1928 to 1961 / compiled by the editors of C&T Publishing. C&T Publishing, 2018 263 p. : **746.46**

1. Quilting -- Patterns -- Middle West 2. Quilting -- Patterns -- History 3. Patchwork quilts -- United States
ISBN 9781617456909

LC 2018030451

"Historical profiles by Barbara Brackman."

For the first time ever, the best of the quilt block patterns printed in the Kansas City Star since 1928 are present in one volume that features more than 60 vintage blocks that culminate in an unforgettable sampler quilt.

"More than just a pattern book, this dive into the archives of the Kansas City Star newspaper also serves as a fascinating look at the history of American quilting." Publishers Weekly.

Brandvig, Jera, 1985-

Quilt as-you-go made vintage : 51 blocks, 9 projects, 3 joining methods / Jera Brandvig. StashBooks, 2017 143 p. : **746.46**

1. Patchwork quilts 2. Patchwork -- Patterns 3. Machine sewing -- Technique
ISBN 9781617454721

LC 2017003179

Presents an innovative quilt-as-you-go technique for reversible quilts that encourages improvisation, providing patterns for nine quilting projects.

Denegre, Vivika Hansen,

Modern patchwork home : dynamic quilts & projects for every room / edited by Vivika Hansen Denegre. The Quilting Company, 2018 143 p. : **746.46**

1. Patchwork -- Patterns 2. Quilting -- Patterns
ISBN 9781440248856

LC bl2019006688

Includes index.

Presents designs for such patchwork projects as a table runner, yoga mat, log cabin quilt, and apron.

"Denegre selects two dozen samples of quilting for the home, complete with instructions and elegant color photographs and charts." Booklist.

Doughty, Kathy

Adding layers : color, design & imagination : 15 original quilt projects from Kathy Doughty of Material obsession. / Kathy Doughty. C&T Publishing, 2014 127 p. : **746.46**

1. Patchwork 2. Quilting
ISBN 1607058472

LC 2013024143

1 folded sheet.

"Techniques range from both simple to curved piecing to Y-seams and are best suited to intermediate quilters, although an ambitious beginner could easily follow Doughty's instructions and attempt any of the projects. Handy tips for everything from efficient cutting to design and layout are included." Library Journal

Fassett, Kaffe

Kaffe Fassett's bold blooms : quilts and other works celebrating flowers / Kaffe Fassett with Liza Prior Lucy ; photography by Debbie Patterson. Abrams, 2016. 223 p. : **746.46**

1. Quilting -- Patterns. 2. Flowers in art. 3. Canvas embroidery. 4. Needlework.
ISBN 9781419722363

LC 2015955663

Includes index.

Invites crafters to explore the behind-the-scenes process and fascinating design methods used to create Kaffe's bold fabrics and modern color palettes--from "sketching" with fabric swatches to creating mood boards and renderings to sewing visually striking quilts.

Fassett, Kaffe

Kaffe Fassett's quilts in Italy : 20 designs from Rowan for patchwork and quilting The Taunton Press, 2016. 152 p. : **746.46**

1. Quilting. 2. Patchwork.
ISBN 9781631867088

LC 2016288271

Provides detailed information on how to make each featured quilt, along with general practical patchwork and quilting information and a visual summary of Kaffe's latest fabrics.

Gering, Jacquie

Quilting modern : techniques and projects for improvisational quilts / Jacquie Gering, Katie Pedersen. Interweave Press, 2012. 175 p. : **746.46**

1. Patchwork -- Patterns. 2. Machine quilting -- Patterns. 3. Quilting.
ISBN 9781596683877

LC 2011039245

"Quilting Modern teaches quilters to use improvisational techniques to make graphic, contemporary quilts and quilted projects".-- Provided by publisher.

Walk : master machine quilting with your walking foot / Jacquie Gering. Lucky Spool Media, LLC, 2016. 160 p.

: 746.46

1. Machine quilting.
ISBN 9781940655215

LC bl2017037006

Covers the basics of quilting with a walking foot, featuring over forty traditional and advanced designs as well as tips for quilting with decorative stitches and reverse quilting.

Gilleland, Diane

All points patchwork : English paper piecing beyond the hexagon, for quilts & small projects / Diane Gilleland. Storey Publishing, 2015 222 p. ; **746.46**

1. Quilting -- Patterns. 2. Patchwork -- Patterns. 3. Paper work.
ISBN 9781612124209

LC 2014048235

A patchwork guide instructs quilters on how to use the traditional English paper piecing technique to achieve well-matched points, with step-by-step illustrations showing how to connect a variety of shapes, including diamonds, jewels, and curves.

"An essential reference for quilters interested in EPP." Library Journal.

Goertzen, Vanessa, 1984-

★**Charm** school : 18 quilts from 5" squares : a beginner's guide / Vanessa Goertzen of Lella Boutique. StashBooks, 2017 127 p. : **746.46**

1. Patchwork quilts. 2. Patchwork -- Patterns. 3. Quilting.
ISBN 9781617452710

LC 2016025934

"These cheery quilts demonstrate the versatility of charm squares and will inspire quilters to make use of these popular precuts." Library Journal.

Goldsworthy, Lynne

Quick & easy quilts : 20 machine quilting projects / Lynne Goldsworthy ; photography by Jan Baldwin. The Taunton Press, 2017. 128 p. : **746.46**

1. Patchwork -- Patterns 2. Quilting -- Patterns 3. Machine quilting -- Patterns 4. Patchwork quilts
ISBN 9781631869143

LC 2017026662

"First published in Great Britain in 2016 by Kyle Books, an imprint of Kyle Cathie Ltd."

"These projects will appeal to quilters looking for attractive, modern projects featuring bold interpretations of traditional blocks." Library Journal.

Grisham, Candyce Copp, 1954-

Dresden quilt blocks reimagined : sew your own playful plates : 25 elements to mix & match / Candyce Copp Grisham. C&T Publishing, Inc., 2019 79 p. **746.46**

1. Dresden plate quilts 2. Quilting -- Patterns 3. Patchwork quilts
ISBN 9781617457937

LC 2018054532

"Mix and match the 4 edge treatments, 16 sizes, and endless fabric combinations to make Dresden Plate quilts".-- Provided by publisher.

Hartman, Elizabeth (Elizabeth Anne)

Modern patchwork : 12 quilts to take you beyond the basics / Elizabeth Hartman. StashBooks, c2012. 143 p. : **746.46**

1. Patchwork quilts 2. Quilting -- Patterns
ISBN 9781607055488

LC 2011040928

Presents detailed instructions for twelve quilts which demonstrate modern color design and utilize such intermediate techniques as curved seams and hexagon blocks, with a section on construction basics.

Hogan, Mary M.

Classic to contemporary string quilts : techniques, inspiration, and 16 projects for strip quilting / Mary M. Hogan. Landauer Publishing, 2019 127 p. : **746.46**

1. Quilting -- Patterns 2. Quilting -- Technique
ISBN 9781947163041

LC bl2019020201

A book that presents sixteen projects for string quilts that utilize strips, scraps, and selvages of fabric includes step-by-step illustrated instructions, tips and suggestions, and information on required and recommended tools.

"Hogan's enthusiastic, well-explained primer will leave experienced quilters feeling inspired to start their own string-based projects." Publishers Weekly.

Hunter, Bonnie K.

String frenzy : 12 more string quilt projects : strips, strings & scrappy things! / Bonnie K. Hunter. C&T Publishing, 2018 95 p. ; **746.46**

1. Patchwork -- Patterns 2. Quilting -- Patterns
ISBN 9781617457326

LC 2018009853

A latest collection of playful string-quilt projects demonstrates the author's foundation piecing basics and instructs crafters on how to transform leftover fabric scraps into one-of-a-kind quilts.

"Short on fluff and long on useful information, this slim volume offers abundant, well-stated advice for creating unique heirloom quilts." Publishers Weekly.

Maxwell, Sarah (Sarah J.)

Fearless with fabric : fresh quilts from traditional blocks : an inspiring guide to making 14 quilt projects / Sarah J. Maxwell. Landauer Publishing, 2020 150 p. : **746.46**

1. Quilting -- Patterns
ISBN 9781947163232

Inspiring readers to quilt outside of their comfort zone, a project book designed to build confidence shows how, through step-by-step instructions, to mix and match fabrics and colors.

"Maxwell's instruction stands out in its encouragements." Booklist

Nyberg, Amanda Jean, 1975-

No scrap left behind : 16 quilt projects that celebrate scraps of all sizes / Amanda Jean Nyberg. ShashBooks, an imprint of C&T Publishing, 2017 127 p. ; **746.46**

1. Patchwork -- Patterns 2. Quilting -- Patterns
ISBN 9781617453366

LC 2016030821

Presents sixteen quilt projects which are categorized by the use of fabric scraps to form squares, triangles, snippets, strips, and strings.

Sunday morning quilts : 16 modern scrap projects : sort, store, and use every last bit of your treasured fabrics / Amanda Jean Nyberg and Cheryl Arkison. Stash Books, c2012. 143 p.

: **746.46**
1. Patchwork -- Patterns. 2. Quilting -- Patterns.
ISBN 9781607054276
LC 2011034028

Presents sixteen quilting projects using leftover fabric scraps that feature piecing, applique, and improvisational work, in a book that also includes tips for cutting, storing, and organizing fabric scraps.

Pink, Tula
Quilts from the house of Tula Pink : 20 fabric projects to make, use, and love / Tula Pink. Krause Publications, c2012. 144 p. : **746.46**
1. Quilting -- Patterns. 2. Patchwork -- Patterns. 3. Textile crafts.
ISBN 9781440218187
LC bl2012011429

Includes index.

Features ten large quilt patterns, ten accessory sewing projects, and tips on choosing and combining fabrics.

Tula Pink's city sampler : 100 modern quilt blocks / Tula Pink. D&C, David and Charles, 2013 255 p. : **746.46**
1. Quilting -- Patterns. 2. Patchwork -- Patterns.
ISBN 9781440232145
LC 2015431077

Includes index.

Offers advice and techniques on creating quilt blocks and shares five city-themed sampler quilt patterns.

Redford, Catherine
Modern machine quilting : make a perfectly finished quilt on your home machine / Catherine Redford. Fons & Porter, 2017 127 p. : **746.46**
1. Machine quilting. 2. Machine quilting -- Patterns. 3. Quilting -- Patterns. 4. Patchwork -- Patterns.
ISBN 9781440246319
LC bl2018052901

Includes index.

A guide to creating quilts on a home sewing machine includes step-by-step instructions for planning, constructing, and finishing a quilt; presents a multitude of designs; and provides projects for quilting practice.

Rosenthal, Maxine, 1944-
One-block wonders of the world : new ideas, design advice, a stunning collection of quilts / Maxine Rosenthal and Linda Bardes. C&T Publishing, Inc., 2017. 79 p. : **746.46**
1. Patchwork -- Patterns 2. Quilting
ISBN 9781617455186
LC 2017013882

"Quilters familiar with making kaleidoscopic quilts will find plenty of inspiration; those new to this style will want to consult Rosenthal's earlier book One-Block Wonders for instructions." Library Journal.

Schmidt, Denyse
Denyse Schmidt : modern quilts, traditional inspiration : 20 new designs with historic roots / Denyse Schmidt ; photographs by John Gruen. Stewart, Tabori & Chang, 2012. 160 p. : **746.46**
1. Quilting -- Patterns.
ISBN 9781584799009
LC 2011021075

"STC Craft/A Melanie Falick Book."

Offers modern reinterpretations of twenty traditional quilt designs, including basket weave, wagon wheel, and a Hawaiian-style applique, along with information on each one's history, patterns, and an overview of technique.

Denyse Schmidt quilts : 30 colorful quilt and patchwork projects / text by Denyse Schmidt with Bethany Lyttle ; photographs by Susie Cushner. Chronicle Books, c2005. 175 p. : **746.46**
1. Patchwork -- Patterns 2. Quilting -- Patterns
ISBN 9780811844420
LC 2004023094

Includes index.

A richly illustrated resource for home quilters presents a collection of thirty quilt projects, ranging from the simple to challenging items for the experienced quilter--including patchwork slippers, aprons, tote bags, pillows, and more--with a review of the fundamental principles and techniques of quilting, step-by-step instructions, detailed patterns, sewing tips, and more.

"It's wonderful to see quilting traditions treated with reverence in a modern quilting book, and the variety of designs, combined with the wealth of information on both quilting and the traditions of each design, make this an essential addition to quilting collections." Library Journal.

Shaw, Robert, 1951-
American quilts : the democratic art / Robert Shaw. Sterling, 2014. 375 p. : **746.46**
1. Quilts -- United States -- History.
ISBN 9781454913979
LC bl2014042061

Presents a history of American quilt making over a four-hundred-year period, covering the evolution of the art and describing the cultural and social conditions under which the quilts were made, with 350 examples of works created by a diverse group of artists.

"The story of American quilting is eloquently told here, set within a broad geographic scope, putting Shaw's expansive curatorial background to full advantage." Library Journal.

Stocker, Blair
Wise craft quilts : a guide to turning beloved fabrics into meaningful patchwork / Blair Stocker ; foreword by Denyse Schmidt ; photographs by Stephanie Congdon Barnes. Roost Books, 2017. xv, 173 p. : **746.46**
1. Patchwork quilts. 2. Patchwork -- Patterns. 3. Textile fabrics. 4. Textile waste -- Recycling.
ISBN 9781611803488
LC 2016012230

"There are so many innovative projects in this impressive collection that it's difficult to pick a standout. Quilters interested in nontraditional textiles will be inspired." Library Journal

Tomasson, Dara, 1973-
Walk, jog, run : a free-motion quilting workout : muscle-memory-building exercises, projects & tips / Dara Tomasson. Stash Books, 2020 143 p. : **746.46**
1. Machine quilting -- Patterns
ISBN 9781617459153
LC 2019049047

"Free-motion quilting book how to get started and 10 projects"--Provided by publisher.

"Tomasson, who blogs about and teaches free-motion quilting, fills this auspicious debut with instructions on the craft of using sewing machines to stitch something other than straight lines onto a quilt." Publishers Weekly

Victoria and Albert Museum,
Patchwork & quilting : a maker's guide, 210+ photographs and illustrations / Victoria and Albert Museum. Thames & Hudson in association with the Victoria and Albert Museum, 2017 176 p. : **746.46**

1. Patchwork quilts 2. Patchwork -- Patterns 3. Quilting -- Patterns
ISBN 9780500293263

LC 2017944789

Includes index.

"From Italian trapunto to Korean jogakbo, 15 projects inspired by the V&A collections"--Cover.

"The combination of diverse techniques, as well as the international scope, makes this an excellent guide for crafters interested in the history and traditions of quilting." Library Journal.

Walters, Angela, 1979-
Free-motion meandering : a beginner's guide to machine quilting / Angela Walters. StashBooks, 2017 79 p. : **746.46**

1. Machine quilting
ISBN 9781617455209

LC 2017006148

Presents step-by-step, illustrated instructions for eight meandering stitches for beginners to practice, along with unique modifications for each, to improve free-motion quilting, disguise mistakes, and transition between designs with ease.

Wolfe, Victoria Findlay, 1970-
Modern quilt magic : 5 parlor tricks to expand your piecing skills - 17 captivating projects / Victoria Findlay Wolfe. Stash Books, an imprint of C & T Publishing, Inc., 2017 128 p. : **746.46**

1. Patchwork -- Patterns. 2. Quilting -- Patterns.
ISBN 9781617455087

LC 2016059348

Presents detailed instructions for such quilting skills as partial-seams, y-seams, and free-form curves and offers seventeen projects which incorporate these techniques into quilts and pillows.

Wood, Sherri
The **improv** handbook for modern quilters : a guide to creating, quilting & living courageously / Sherri Lynn Wood ; photography by Sara Remington. STC Craft, 2015. 174 p. : **746.46**

1. Quilting -- Patterns.
ISBN 9781617691386

LC bl2015014300

"A Melanie Falick book."

Shares a flexible approach to quilting that features improvisational sewing and patchwork techniques, and includes ten patterns with loose parameters as well as mind exercises for experimenting with color.

"Improv quilting may not be to everyone's taste--it can be visually jarring at times--but many who love this style are downright passionate about it, and Wood provides a comprehensive overview of improvisational techniques." Library Journal.

746.5 Bead embroidery

Cox, Shelley (Teacher)
Bead embroidery / Shelley Cox. Search Press, 2013. 95 p. : **746.5**

1. Bead embroidery.
ISBN 184448923X

LC bl2014038270

"RSN, Royal School of Needlework"--Cover.

Includes index.

Focuses on bead embroidery, presenting a brief history and discussing basic techniques, counted thread embroidery, bead embroidery, surface embroidery, and fringes.

746.6 Printing, painting, dyeing

Callahan, Gail
Hand dyeing yarn and fleece : dip-dyeing, hand-painting, tie-dyeing, and other creative techniques / Gail Callahan ; photography by John Polak. Storey Pub., c2010. 168 p. : **746.6**

1. Dyes and dyeing -- Textile fibers. 2. Yarn. 3. Wool.
ISBN 9781603424684

LC 2009028676

Provides instructions for dyeing yarn and fleece using various techniques, designs, and dyes, along with information on supplies and finding the right colors.

Corwin, Lena
Lena Corwin's made by hand / Lena Corwin ; photography by Maria Alexandra Vettese and Stephanie Congdon Barnes. STC Craft/A Melanie Falick Book, Stewart, Tabori & Chang, 2013. 176 p. ; **746.6**

1. Dyes and dyeing 2. Handicraft 3. Knitting 4. Sewing
ISBN 9781617690594

LC 2013010186

"STC Craft/A Melanie Falick book."

Curates a collection of twenty-six studio classes hosted at the author's Brooklyn studio, offering step-by-step instructions for projects that use classic craft techniques showcased in modern styles.

Duerr, Sasha
Natural color : vibrant plant dye projects for your home and wardrobe / Sasha Duerr ; photography by Aya Brackett Watson-Guptill Publications, 2016 vi, 263 p. **746.6**

1. Dyes and dyeing -- Textile fibers 2. Dyes and dyeing, Domestic 3. Dye plants
ISBN 9781607749363

LC 2016002216

An illustrated guide to making natural plant dyes for clothing and home decor features more than two dozen projects, organized by season, including using mint to dye table runners and using sourgrass to color children's clothing.

"Duerr is knowledgeable and thorough, and fiber artists with an interest in incorporating natural dyeing into their work will find the information they need to get started, as well as insight into the dyeing process." Library Journal.

Joyce, Anna (Textile designer)
Hand dyed : a modern guide to dyeing in brilliant color for you and your home / Anna Joyce ; photography by Dane Tashima.

Abrams, 2019. 159 p. : **746.6**

1. Dyes and dyeing.

ISBN 9781419734281

LC 2018936227

A guide to dyeing explains the classic techniques and materials needed to create colored and patterned pieces, including swaddling blankets, a tie-dye swimsuit, and festive cotton buntings.

"A wide range of crafters and textile artists should find this to be a useful resource." Library Journal.

Swearington, Jen

Printing on fabric : techniques with screens, stencils, inks, and dyes / Jen Swearington. Lark Crafts, 2013 160 p. : **746.6**

1. Textile printing.

ISBN 9781454703945

LC 2012006729

Provides an accessible guide to hand-printing fabric, and includes tips on translating design ideas into prints, the different modes of transfer, and how to use effective color combinations.

746.7 Rugs

Denny, Walter B.

How to read Islamic carpets / Walter B. Denny. The Metropolitan Museum of Art, 2014. 143 p. : **746.7**

1. Metropolitan Museum of Art (New York, N.Y.) 2. Islamic rugs -- History. 3. Islamic rugs -- Technique.

ISBN 9781588395405

LC 2014035553

"This book explores the history, design techniques, materials, craftsmanship, and socio-economic contexts of these works. Fifty-five examples of Islamic carpets are illustrated with new photographs and revealing details. Walter B. Denny situates these carpets within the cultural and social realm of their production, be it in a nomadic encampment, a rural village, or an urban workshop."

"This slim, affordable book is highly recommended to both public and academic libraries of all sizes with collections on art, art history, or textile arts." Library Journal.

Rott, Ira

Crochet animal rugs : over 20 crochet patterns for fun floor mats and matching accessories / Ira Rott. SewandSo, 2018. 143 p. : **746.7**

1. Rugs 2. Home furnishings 3. Animals in art 4. Crocheting -- Patterns

ISBN 9781446307007

LC bl2018168472

Includes index.

"Following the online success of her elephant-rug pattern, Rott, in her first book, expands her animal-themed designs beyond rugs to over 20 patterns that include matching pillows, bags, blankets, and other accessories and the original elephant rug." Booklist

746.9 Other textile products

Bowles, Hamish

Vogue & the Metropolitan Museum of Art Costume Institute : parties, exhibitions, people / Hamish Bowles ; foreword by Thomas P. Campbell ; introduction by Anna Wintour ; edited by Chloe Malle. Abrams, 2014. 271 p. : **746.9**

1. Costume Institute (New York, N.Y.) Exhibitions Pictorial works. 2. Costume Institute (New York, N.Y.) Exhibitions -- History. 3. Balls (Parties) -- New York (NY) 4. Costume -- Exhibitions 5. Fashion photography -- New York (NY)

ISBN 9781419714245

LC bl2014047080

Offers pictorial highlights of the Metropolitan Museum of Art's spring Costume Institute exhibitions of the twenty-first century, curated by Harold Koda and Andrew Bolton, as well as the Vogue fashion shoots they inspired and galas that opened them.

Faerm, Steven

Fashion design course : Principles, Practice, and Techniques: the Practical Guide for Aspiring Fashion Designers / Steven Faerm. Barron's, 2017 160 p. : **746.9**

1. Clothing and dress. 2. Fashion design -- Vocational guidance. 3. Fashion design.

ISBN 1438011075

LC bl2018004126

"Principles, practice, and techniques: the practical guide for aspiring fashion designers"--Cover.

Includes index.

An introduction to fashion design offers practical exercises and interviews with industry professionals to help readers create their own collections and discover their unique design vision.

"The author takes readers through a thorough exploration of the fashion industry, from history to inspiration to the design process to landing a job. There are also 14 practical assignments to help budding designers learn more about the industry. Teens exploring careers in fashion will enjoy the practical advice from industry insiders, and fashion-mad readers of all ages will appreciate the information about how fashion design works." Library Journal.

Givhan, Robin

The **Battle** of Versailles : the night American fashion stumbled into the spotlight and made history / Robin Givhan. Flatiron Books, 2015. 320 p. **746.9**

1. Chateau de Versailles (Versailles, France) 2. Fashion shows 3. Fashion design -- History -- 20th century 4. Fashion designers 5. Fashion merchandising -- History -- 20th century 6. Versailles, France

ISBN 9781250052902

LC 2014040369

"Readers need not be fashion mavens to enjoy this entertaining episode of history, enhanced by Givhan's effortless ability to illustrate the models and designers (particularly Lambert) who changed how we dress." Kirkus.

Grumbach, Didier

History of international fashion / Didier Grumbach ; photo editor Isabelle d'Hauteville. Interlink Books, 2014. 462 p. : **746.9**

1. Fashion design -- History. 2. Fashion -- History. 3. Fashion design -- France -- History -- 20th century. 4. Fashion -- France -- History -- 20th century.

ISBN 9781566569767

LC 2014004755

"Originally published in French as Histoires de la mode"--Page facing title page.

"Industry veteran Grumbach takes you through the history of fashion in this lavishly illustrated book, from its humble beginnings to today's superstar designers." Publishers Weekly

Linett, Andrea

The **cool** factor : a guide to achieving effortless style, with secrets from the women who have it / Andrea Linett. Artisan, 2016 223 p. ; **746.9**

1. Fashion 2. Women's clothing

ISBN 9781579656485

LC 2015034242

Includes index.

"There's at least one tip or rule-busting, potentially game-changing suggestion for any woman looking to cultivate a coherent wardrobe and unique style by using her eyes, judgment, and Linett's six principles." Publishers Weekly.

Lowit, Roxanne

Yves Saint Laurent / Roxanne Lowit, photographs ; foreword by Pierre Berge. Thames & Hudson, 2014. 1 volume (unpaged) : **746.9**

1. Saint Laurent, Yves, 1936-2008 2. Fashion designers -- Paris, France -- Pictorial works. 3. Fashion design -- France -- History -- 20th century -- Pictorial works.

ISBN 9780500517604

LC 2014930896

A dazzling portrait of Yves Saint Laurent and his world of fashion over the last twenty-five years of his career, by legendary pioneer of backstage fashion photography, Roxanne Lowit. Yves Saint Laurent is a name synonymous with style, elegance, and high fashion. When he came on the scene at Dior and then started his own line, he quickly changed the way people regarded haute couture and the world of fashion itself. He revolutionized women's eveningwear when he introduced le smoking, a woman's tuxedo, and made couture accessible to a younger generation. Yves Saint Laurent is Roxanne Lowit's personal photographic history of Saint Laurent, the man and the fashion, from 1978, the year she first met him, to the last show he gave in 2002. With contributions from YSL's muses and admirers, including Catherine Deneuve, Betty Catroux, Lucie de la Falaise, Pat Cleveland, and Valerie Steele, this book represents the backstage experience at YSL's shows as Lowit experienced them herself. Whether surrounded by beautiful models or peeking at the catwalk from the wings, every moment was a magnificent photo opportunity. Lowit shares magical moments of YSL with the world; intimate, social, absorbed in fashion; and creates a unique portrait of this towering figure of postwar couture.

Righetti, Maggie

Knitting in plain English / Maggie Righetti. St. Martin's Press, c1986. xiii, 241 p. : **746.9**

1. Knitting.

ISBN 9780312458539

LC 86001800

Includes index.

An introduction to knitting covers patterns, gauges, yarns, needles, types of construction, casting on and off, increases, decreases, buttonholes, hems, color, pattern stitching, blocking, and alterations

"This is one of the most comprehensive and accessible guides to crochet available. This isn't a quick-start guide: Righetti provides an overview of the necessary supplies, a brief history of crochet, and information about gauge before guiding beginners through their first stitch, an ideal approach for readers who wish to understand crochet in-depth." Library Journal.

Arnold, Rebecca,

Know-it-all fashion : the 50 key modes, garments & designers, each explained in under a minute / editor, Rebecca Arnold ; contributors, Emma McClendon, Katerina Pantelides, Julia Rea, Rebecca Straub, Alison Toplis, Olgs Vainshtein. Wellfleet Press, 2018. 159 p. : **746.9**

1. Fashion -- History -- 20th century. 2. Fashion -- History -- 21st century. 3. Fashion design -- History -- 20th century. 4. Fashion design -- History -- 21st century.

ISBN 9781577151746

LC bl2018195769

Profiles notable people in the industry, discusses recurring themes and inspirations, and explores aspects of the modern fashion industry, from haute couture to high street, from catwalk to street style, and from magazine to blog.

746.92 Costume

Dirix, Emmanuelle

Dressing the decades : twentieth-century vintage style / Emmanuelle Dirix. Yale University Press, 2016. 224 p. **746.92**

1. Fashion 2. Clothing 3. Fashion design

ISBN 9780300215526

LC 2015953579

A visually dazzling tour of 20th-century fashion, spotlighting the leading designers and dominant styles of the past 100 years

"Her well-informed narrative is often laced with socioeconomic observations, including discussion of Hollywood's impact on designers and vice versa, the class divisions of haute couture vs. ready-to-wear, and how various social and political movements transformed how we dress and consume fashion. The accompanying photos and illustrations ... are stunning and often drool-worthy." Library Journal.

Trubert-Tollu, Chantal, 1946-

★The **House** of Worth 1858-1954 : the birth of haute couture / Chantal Trubert-Tollu, Francoise Tetart-Vittu, Jean-Marie Martin-Hattemberg, Fabrice Olivieri ; foreword by Christian Lacroix. Thames & Hudson, 2017. 335 p. : **746.92**

1. Worth, Charles Frederic, 1825-1895 2. House of Worth (Firm) -- History 3. Couture clothing 4. Fashion design -- France -- 19th century. 5. Fashion design -- France -- 20th century. 6. Fashion design -- England -- 20th century.

ISBN 9780500519431

LC 2017944380

A history of the House of Worth, the world's pioneering haute couture label, covers its founder, Charles Frederick Worth, the company's successes and failures, and its lasting legacy and influence in the realm of fashion.

"With gorgeous color images of Worth designs, paintings, and archival fashion drawings and photographs, this sumptuous book is recommended for readers interested in the history of haute couture and French fashion." Library Journal.

746.92092 Fashion design--biography

Barker, Nigel, 1972-

Models of influence : 50 women who reset the course of fashion

/ Nigel Barker. Harper Design, 2015. 255 p. : **746.92092**
1. Models (Persons) 2. Models (Persons) -- Portraits 3. Fashion -- History -- 20th century 4. Fashion -- History -- 20th century -- Pictorial works
ISBN 9780062345844
LC 2014930210

"Interweaving ... photographs and ... anecdotes, [this book] profiles 50 women who have made an unforgettable impression on fashion, the modeling industry, and our notions of beauty. Eight chronological chapters, each of which spotlight an era, feature the stories and images of women who made their mark".--Amazon.com.

747 Interior decoration

Adams, Michael Henry
Style and grace : African Americans at home / Michael Henry Adams ; photographs by Mick Hales. Bulfinch Press, c2003. 160 p. : **747**
1. African Americans -- Homes and haunts -- New York City 2. Interior decoration -- New York City -- History -- 20th century. 3. Architecture, Domestic -- New York City
ISBN 9780821228470
LC 2003103036

Includes index.
Celebrating the African-American tradition of style and creativity in home design and decoration, this richly illustrated study looks at the unique homes of hip-hop entrepreneur Russell Simmons, photographer Gordon Parks, Congressman Charles Rangel, and other African-American artists and professionals.

Atwood, Rebecca
Living with pattern : color, texture, and print at home / Rebecca Atwood. Clarkson Potter Publishers, 2016 288 p. ; **747**
1. Repetitive patterns (Decorative arts) in interior decoration. 2. Color in interior decoration. 3. Texture in interior decoration.
ISBN 9780553459449
LC 2016008549

Traveling room by room throughout the house--the expected main rooms as well as smaller, not-to-be-forgotten spaces like reading nooks and foyers--a textile designer provides information on how to create different levels of pattern, how color works, how prints can mix and match, how to enliven elements already in the home and more.

Becker, Holly
Decorate : 1,000 professional design ideas for every room in your home / Holly Becker & Joanna Copestick ; photographs by Debi Treloar. Chronicle Books, c2011. 288 p. : **747**
1. Interior decoration
ISBN 9780811877893
LC 2010048053

Collects tips from such professional interior designers as Kelly Wearstler, Amy Butler, and Jonathan Adler for every room and every budget, along with photographs, line illustrations, checklists, shortcuts, and floor plans.

Blair, Gabrielle Stanley
Design mom : how to live with kids : a room-by-room guide / Gabrielle Stanley Blair. Artisan, 2015 288 p. : **747**
1. Interior decoration -- Human factors. 2. Families. 3. Interior decoration.
ISBN 9781579655716
LC 2014038734

A mother of six and a popular blogger offers an illustrated manual for making the rooms of your house organized, creative, functional and stylish despite the insanity and chaos that comes with having a family.

Blakeney, Justina
The **new** bohemians : cool & collected homes / Justina Blakeney ; photography by Dabito. Abrams, 2015. 304 p.: **747**
1. Interior decoration. 2. Bohemianism in art.
ISBN 9781617691515
LC bl2015015762

Profiles twenty homes from around the country that capture the bohemian spirit along with twelve DIY projects, "adopt an idea" section, and plant guide.
"The youthful exuberance shown in these interiors will encourage amateurs to discover their own bohemian style." Library Journal

The **new** bohemians handbook : come home to good vibes / Justina Blakeney ; photography by Dabito. Abrams, 2017. 287 p.: **747**
1. Interior decoration. 2. Bohemianism in art.
ISBN 9781419724824
LC bl2017045393

A guide to affordable bohemian interior design presents ways to enhance the environment of the room with plants, colors, and do-it-yourself projects.

Bonney, Grace
Design*Sponge at home / Grace Bonney. Artisan, c2011. ix, 390 p. : **747**
1. Interior decoration 2. Amateurs' manuals.
ISBN 9781579654313
LC 2010039458

Presents seventy design interiors provided by the readers of the DesignSponge website, along with fifty projects with before and after pictures showing transformed rooms, furniture, and accessories.
"A highly recommended compendium of ideas to inspire amateur decorators." Library Journal.

Bradbury, Dominic
The **iconic** interior : private spaces of leading artists, architects, and designers / Dominic Bradbury ; with photography by Richard Powers. Abrams, 2012. 351 p. : **747**
1. Interior decoration -- History -- 20th century -- Themes, motives 2. Interior decoration -- History -- 21st century -- Themes, motives
ISBN 9781617690051
LC 2012007221

"With such a detailed description of the best of the best in 20th-century interior design and the range of styles represented, this book is an outstanding reference and fulfills Bradbury's intention of encouraging both amateurs and professionals to take a bold approach to design." Library Journal

Bridges, Sheila
Furnishing forward : a practical guide to furnishing for a lifetime / Sheila Bridges ; with photographs by Anna Williams. Bulfinch Press, 2005, c2002. 184 p. : **747**
1. Interior decoration -- United States
ISBN 9780821261804
LC 2001016480

A distinguished designer shares professional and personal anecdotes in this full-color guide on how to make the transition to eclectic and classic furniture that will endure for years to achieve an individual and elegant home.

Brits, Louisa Thomsen

The **book** of hygge : the Danish art of comfort, coziness, and connection / Louisa Thomsen Brits. Plume, 2017. 192 p. **747**

1. Human comfort -- Denmark. 2. Interior decoration -- Human factors -- Denmark.
ISBN 0735214107

LC 2016033937

"The centuries-old Danish tradition of Hygge (pronounced "hue-gah") comes from a country voted to be the happiest on earth, and its special custom of emotional warmth, slowness, and appreciation, is becoming increasingly familiar to an international audience. To hygge means to enjoy the good things in life with good people".-- Provided by publisher.

Brown, Amanda, 1982-

★**Spruce** : a step-by-step guide to upholstery and design / Amanda Brown ; photography by Ryann Ford. Storey Publishing, 2013 392 p. ; **747**

1. Do-it-yourself work 2. Upholstery.
ISBN 9781612121376

LC 2013012590

Includes index.

Accompanied by photographs and step-by-step instructions, an introduction to the craft of upholstery provides all of the techniques and skills needed to reupholster any piece of furniture and become a master upholsterer.

"[P]erfectly matches complete, precisely written directions with correspondingly crisp, helpful photographs." Booklist.

Carlson, Julie, 1960-

Remodelista : a manual for the considered home / Julie Carlson, with the editors of Remodelista ; written and edited by Margot Guralnick ; photographs by Matthew Williams. Artisan, 2013 xi, 387 p. : **747**

1. Dwellings -- Remodeling. 2. Interior decoration -- Themes, motives.
ISBN 157965536X

LC 2013006278

Includes index.

Featuring in-depth tours and lessons from 12 gorgeous homes, the creative team behind Remodelista.com reveals how to achieve a classic and timeless aesthetic on any budget and takes the guesswork out of the remodeling process.

"An excellent source of inspiration for those interested in renovating their house or just revamping a room." Library Journal.

Carter, Darryl, 1961-

The **collected** home : rooms with style, grace, and history / Darryl Carter with Trish Donnally ; photographs by Gordon Beall. Clarkson Potter/Publishers, 2012. 208 p. : **747**

1. Interior decoration -- Psychological aspects.
ISBN 9780307953940

LC 2011043291

Includes index.

Explores the role of textures, multi-purpose furniture, and unexpected objects in rendering spaces both comfortable and eye-catching, outlining a range of short- and long-term steps for overall home design.

The **new** traditional : reinvent, balance, define your home / Darryl Carter. Clarkson Potter, 2008. 208 p. : **747**

1. Interior decoration -- Psychological aspects.
ISBN 9780307408655

LC 2007045663

Includes index.

Presents an accessible guide to creating a stylish, inviting, and comfortable design that is responsive to the individual requirements of the people who live in it, explaining how to integrate modern elements with the classical using furnishings accessories, textiles, lighting, and color to make one's home a place to be enjoyed.

Crochet, Treena

Bungalow style : creating classic interiors in your arts and crafts home / Treena Crochet. Taunton Press, c2005. 186 p. : **747**

1. Arts and crafts movement -- Influence 2. Bungalows -- Conservation and restoration -- United States 3. Dwellings -- Remodeling -- United States 4. Interior decoration -- United States -- History -- 21st century
ISBN 9781561586233

LC 2004009748

Includes index.

The author features the American bungalow, illuminating the various elements of this Victorian classic while also discussing restoration techniques, adding modern conveniences, and much, much more.

DeGeneres, Ellen

Home / Ellen DeGeneres. Grand Central Life & Style, 2015. 304 p. : **747**

1. DeGeneres, Ellen Homes and haunts. 2. Interior decoration -- United States
ISBN 9781455533565

LC bl2015034855

The comedian and talk show host shares her passion for home design, a look at her homes, and the secrets she has learned over twenty-five years of renovation and decoration.

DK Publishing, Inc,

Pillows, curtains, & shades step by step DK Publishing, 2017. 224 p. : **747**

1. Interior decoration accessories.
ISBN 9781465455758

LC bl2016050128

Includes index.

Presents step-by-step, illustrated instructions for twenty-five soft-furnishing projects for the home, including pillow covers, shades, curtains, and bedding.

Domino : your guide to a stylish home / editors of Domino, Jessica Romm Perez, Shani Silver. Simon & Schuster, 2016. 224 p. **747**

1. Interior decoration
ISBN 9781501151873

LC 2016032162

The editors of domino magazine present a guide to discovering a personal style and creating loved personal spaces, building on the brand's best-selling first style guide, domino: The Book of Decorating, to share friendly and authoritative tips on everything from textiles and art to lighting and accessories.

Gates, Erin T

★**Elements** of family style : elegant spaces for everyday life / Erin Gates. Atria Books, 2019 xi, 355 p. : **747**

1. Interior decoration
ISBN 9781501137303

LC bl2019008480

Organized by room, this decorating guide offers advice, inspiration, and ideas for designing a home with children, pets, and all the messes of life, but still reflects the owner's personality and style.

Elements of style : designing a home and a life / Erin T. Gates. Simon & Schuster, 2014. xv, 318 p. : **747**

1. Interior decoration.
ISBN 1476744874

LC 2014012101

"From the rising-star designer and author of the hit blog, Elements of Style, a full-color, fully illustrated book packed with honest advice, inspiration, ideas, and lessons learned about designing a home that reflects your personality and style. Elements of Style is a uniquely personal and practical decorating guide that shows how designing a home can be an outlet of personal expression and an exercise in self-discovery. Drawing on her ten years of experience in the interior design industry, Erin combines honest design advice and gorgeous professional photographs and illustrations with personal essays about the lessons she has learned while designing her own home and her own life--the first being: none of our homes or lives is perfect. Like a funny best friend, she reveals the disasters she confronted in her own kitchen renovation, her struggles with anorexia, her epic fight with her husband over a Lucite table, and her secrets for starting a successful blog. Organized by rooms in the house, Elements of Style invites readers into Erin's own home as well as homes she has designed for clients. Fresh, modern, and colorful, it is brimming glamour and style as well as advice on practical matters from choosing kitchen counter materials to dressing a bed with pillows, picking a sofa, and decorating a nursery without cartoon characters. You'll also find a charming foreword by Erin's husband, Andrew, and an extensive Resource and Shopping Guide that provides an indispensable a roadmap for anyone embarking on their first serious home decorating adventure. With Erin's help, you can finally make your house your home".-- Provided by publisher.

Giramonti, Lisa Borgnes

Novel interiors : Living in Enchanted Rooms Inspired by Literature / Lisa Borgnes Giramonti ; photographs by Ivan Terestchenko ; foreword by David Netto. Potter Style, 2014 287 p. : **747**

1. Interior decoration in literature 2. Interior decoration -- Themes, motives
ISBN 9780385345996

LC 2013036923

Includes index.

A book with more than 250 full-color photos outlines an approach to home decorating inspired by classic works of literature and inspiring movie sets, combining strategic advice with lavish photography to explain how to incorporate key design elements in a home.

Grove, Kirsten

Simply styling : fresh & easy ways to personalize your home / Kirsten Grove of Simply Grove. Sterling, 2016 xxii, 199 p. : **747**

1. Interior decoration
ISBN 9781454918226

LC bl2016042188

Includes index.

Presents interior decorating advice on how to personalize a home, offering instructions for styling such items as a couch, coffee table, and bathtub, and such areas as the walls, foyer, and bedroom.

"With her blog, Simply Grove, self-taught interior stylist Grove's ideas have become quite influential, which has led to her contributing to numerous interior design publications and websites. Here, Grove explains how to achieve this popular look that she espouses of neutral-colored interiors bathed in light." Library Journal.

Gura, Judith

The **guide** to period styles for interiors : from the 17th century to the present / Judith Gura. Bloomsbury, Fairchild Books, an imprint of Bloomsbury Publishing Inc., 2016. xvi, 479 p. ; **747**

1. Interior decoration -- History
ISBN 9781628924718

LC 2015005290

"This updated pictorial guide to interior design features fully revised sections and a new chapter on twenty-first-century styles. There are 350 photographs, a bibliography, a glossary, and a chronology. Every era is covered in a brief narrative, along with photos of prime examples (mostly individual furniture pieces) of the style." Booklist

Hays, Jeanine

Remix : decorating with culture, objects, and soul / Jeanine Hays and Bryan Mason ; photographs by Patrick Cline, foreword by Danielle Colding. Clarkson Potter/Publishers, 2013 256 p.: **747**

1. Interior decoration -- United States. 2. African Americans -- Homes and haunts.
ISBN 9780770433024

LC 2012038317

Includes index.

Aphro-who? -- Elements. The culture of color -- Telling your story through pattern -- Original art -- Going global at home -- Modern soulful homes. Maiysha Simpson: Brooklyn lullaby -- Angela and Leon Belt: artists in residence -- Tara Bethea and BOA: a soulful abode -- Malene Barnett: island in the city -- Jeanine Hays and Bryan Mason: our homecoming.

Profiling homes throughout Brooklyn, Manhattan, Philadelphia, Los Angeles, and Washington, D.C., this design resource, influenced by African-American culture, showcases authentically designed homes that celebrate diversity in design.

Henderson, Emily

Styled : secrets for arranging rooms, from tabletops to bookshelves / Emily Henderson, with Angelin Borsics ; photographs by David Tsay. Potter Style, 2015. 304 p. ; **747**

1. Interior decoration
ISBN 9780804186278

LC 2014045185

Includes index.

An HGTV Design Star winner offers a full-color guide to thinking like a stylist, with 1,000 design ideas for creating the most beautiful, personal and livable rooms.

Lauder, Aerin, 1970-

Beauty at home / Aerin Lauder ; written with Christine Pittel ; photographs by Simon Upton. Potter Style, 2013 239 p. : **747**

1. Lauder, Aerin, 1970- Homes and haunts New York (State) 2. Interior decoration -- New York (State) -- Themes, motives. 3.

Lauder, Estee -- Homes and haunts -- New York (State)
ISBN 0770433618
LC 2012050518

Offers a look at the design style of Aerin Lauder by compiling photographs of the interiors of her home that combines her grandmother's heritage with modern-day taste.

Linsley, Leslie
Salvage style : decorate with vintage finds / Leslie Linsley. Hearst Books, 2017 160 p. : **747**

1. Found objects in interior decoration 2. Home furnishings 3. Interior decoration.
ISBN 9781588169280
LC 2017287731

Includes index.

"Decorate with repurposed, refurbished, and vintage items to stunning effect. Try wire cubbies for pretty bathroom storage; a tree trunk as a rustic nightstand; a bedspring as an inventive memo board; a breadbox to hold silverware and so much more!" --Back cover.

"Crafts and design author Linsley (Nantucket: Island Living) turns her attention to using junkyard finds in home decor." Library Journal.

Merhi, Farah
★**Inspire** your home : easy, affordable ideas to make every room glamorous / Farah Merhi. Tiller Press, 2019. 289 p.: **747**

1. Interior decoration.
ISBN 9781982131241
LC bl2019032425

The Instagram star and founder of Inspire Me! Home Decor offers strategic interior design secrets for creating glamorous but cozy living spaces on a budget, sharing related advice for home cleaning, organizing and customizing.

Moss, Charlotte
Garden inspirations / Charlotte Moss. Rizzoli, 2015. 287 p. : **747**

1. Flower arrangement in interior decoration. 2. Gardens 3. Interior decoration.
ISBN 9780847844777
LC bl2016015787

Shares ideas for bringing the garden into the home, including decorating with flower arrangements and setting up garden seating, and showcases a selection of notable gardens.

Needleman, Deborah
The **book** of decorating : a room-by-room guide to creating a home that makes you happy / Deborah Needleman, Sara Ruffin Costello, & Dara Caponigro. Simon & Schuster, 2008. 271 p. : **747**

1. Interior decoration
ISBN 9781416575467
LC 2008015072

The editors of "Domino" magazine present a guide to furnishing and decorating every room of a home, in a reference that demonstrates strategic layouts and includes insider shopping tips.

The **perfectly** imperfect home : How to Decorate & Live Well / Deborah Needleman. Clarkson Potter/Publishers, 2011. 255 p. : **747**

1. Interior decoration.
ISBN 0307720136
LC 2011020194

Includes index.

Describes eighty items that are what the author identifies as all one needs to live comfortably, practically, and stylishly, from essential furnishings to aesthetic accents.

New decorating book John Wiley & Sons, c2011. 312 p. : **747**

1. Interior decoration -- Handbooks, manuals, etc.
ISBN 9780470887141
LC bl2011030734

At head of title: Better homes and gardens.

Includes index.

A revised and updated edition of a top-selling guide reflects the latest approaches to decorating, counseling readers on how to combine personal expression with budget-friendly measures while making room-by-room decisions about colors, window treatments, wall art and more.

Petersik, Sherry
Young house love : 243 ways to paint, craft, update, & show your home some love / Sherry & John Petersik. Artisan, c2012. 336 p. : **747**

1. Petersik, John Homes and haunts Miscellanea. 2. Petersik, Sherry Homes and haunts Miscellanea. 3. Dwellings -- Maintenance and repair 4. Dwellings -- Remodeling 5. Housekeeping 6. Interior decoration
ISBN 1579654789
LC 2012009849

Includes index.

Offers more than two hundred tips and ideas for do-it-yourself home makeovers and ways to spruce up humble abodes.

"The clever ideas developed by these amateurs that adapt to the needs of busy families will motivate others to tackle their own spaces." Library Journal.

Richardson, Sarah, 1971-
Sarah style / Sarah Richardson. Simon & Schuster Canada, 2017. 338 p. **747**

1. Interior decoration.
ISBN 9781476784380
LC oc2016044080

Previously published: New York: Gallery Books, 2014.

"From bestselling author, HGTV star, and Canadian design queen Sarah Richardson comes the interior design book of the decade. Ever wondered how to transform your laundry room from drab to fab? Your kitchen from prison to paradise? Your bedroom from boring to beautiful? Now you can, in this comprehensive interior design tome by design maven extraordinaire Sarah Richardson. Within these beautiful, full-colour pages and photographs, Sarah walks you through each room in your home, from the master bedroom to the kids' rooms, to the kitchen, the bathroom, and everywhere in between, showing you how to turn a house into a home--Sarah style. Featuring full-page design spreads with stunning attention to detail, Sarah Style is a cache of creative, unique ideas for transforming your living spaces. You can make your dream home a reality, and the inspiration--and complete know-how--is right here in this premier source for all things interior design!"-- Provided by publisher.

Roney, Carley
[The nest] home design handbook : simple ways to decorate, organize, and personalize your place / Carley Roney and the editors of TheNest.com ; photographs by Ellen Silverman. Clark-

son Potter, c2008. 192 p. : **747**
1. Interior decoration
ISBN 0307341917
LC 2008299144

Includes index.

Explaining how to create a fun, stylish, and comfortable living space, this no-hassle handbook simplifies home decorating with innovative tricks and affordable style for every room in the house, in a volume that features organization advice, personalization pointers, tips on merging styles, DIY projects, and overviews on color, wood, and the fundamentals of good design.

"Roney, editor in chief of TheNest.com and cofounder of TheKnot.com, has created a practical guide aimed at the amateur decorator... Recommended for public libraries." Library Journal.

Schuman, Emily

Cupcakes and cashmere at home / Emily Schuman. Abrams Image, 2015. 175 p. : **747**
1. Entertaining. 2. Interior decoration.
ISBN 1419715836
LC bl2015020611

Offers accessible interior-design inspiration, entertaining ideas and DIY projects to help turn your home into a chic and inviting space.

Spencer, Lara

Flea market fabulous : designing gorgeous rooms with vintage treasures / Lara Spencer with Amy Feezor ; foreword by Jonathan Adler ; photographys by ChiChi Ubiña. Stewart, Tabori & Chang, 2014. 182 p. : **747**
1. Flea markets 2. Interior decoration
ISBN 9781617690952
LC bl2014036775

Presents information on how to find flea market treasures and incorporate them into home interiors, with tips on making a decorating plan, overcoming the limitations of each room, and the best ways to restore and reinvent flea market items.

Studholme, Joa

Farrow & Ball how to decorate / Joa Studholme & Charlotte Cosby. Mitchell Beazley, 2016. 268 p. : **747**
1. Interior decoration.
ISBN 1784720879
LC bl2016016029

Includes index.

A comprehensive guide to interior decoration that demystifies every aspect of home design, including the creative potential of floor paint and how light affects color.

"The wealth of information on topics such as room accessories, color combinations, and even ceilings makes this book an invaluable tool for the novice who feels inspired to give a living space a makeover." Publishers Weekly.

Tanov, Erica

Design by nature : creating layered, lived-in spaces inspired by the natural world / Erica Tanov. ; photographs by Ngoc Minh Ngo. Ten Speed Press, 2018 229 p. ; **747**
1. Interior decoration -- Themes, motives.
ISBN 9780399579073
LC 2017036480

"The first design book that translates elements of nature--flora, water, and wood--into elements of decor for beautiful, lived-in, bohemian interiors, from acclaimed designer and tastemaker Erica Tanov".-- Provided by publisher.

Van der Meer, Antonia

Coastal living beach house happy : the joy of living by the water / Antonia van der Meer. Oxmoor House, 2015 223 p. : **747**
1. Cottages. 2. Interior decoration. 3. Seaside architecture. 4. Vacation homes.
ISBN 0848744292
LC 2014953432

Includes index.

Describes how to incorporate the happiness of beach houses into non-coastal homes, detailing the warmth and beauty found in the style of shore houses' architecture, decor, walls, windows, doors and floors.

747.7 Decoration of specific rooms of residential buildings

Gold, Jamie, 1960-

Taunton's new bathroom idea book / Jamie Gold. The Taunton Press, Inc., 2017 217 p. ; **747.7**
1. Bathrooms. 2. Interior decoration.
ISBN 9781631864056
LC 2016056526

Shares design ideas for different types of bathrooms, including half-baths, standard his-and-hers bathrooms, and luxury home spas.

Lee, Vinny

Kitchenalia : furnishing and equipping your kitchen with flea market finds and period pieces / Vinny Lee. Jacqui Small, 2014. 224 p. : **747.7**
1. Interior decoration. 2. Kitchens -- Design. 3. Kitchens -- Equipment and supplies.
ISBN 1909342491
LC bl2015009104

Includes index.

Shows how to use vintage finds and accessories to furnish the kitchen, describing the themes that characterize seven distinct design styles as well as how to enhance each by focusing on furniture, surfaces, and other elements of the room.

"The variety of styles makes this book an inspiring choice for those looking for ideas on decorating kitchens." Library Journal.

747.98 Decorating with houseplants

Carter, Hilton, 1979-

★**Wild** interiors : beautiful plants in beautiful spaces / Hilton Carter. CICO Books, 2020. 224 p. : **747.98**
1. Interior decoration 2. House plants
ISBN 9781782498759

"...Hilton Carter takes you on a magical plant journey that highlights 12 unique, green-filled, interiors. Full of plant care advice, including a room by room guide profiling the plants that are best suited to each one, Hilton brings his unique eye and love of plants to inspire you to create your own Wild Interiors."--Back cover.

748.20973 Glassware--decorative arts--United States

Charbonneau, Diane,

Chihuly / edited by Diane Charbonneau. Montreal Museum of Fine Arts/DelMonico Books, 2013 230 p. : **748.20973**

1. Chihuly, Dale, 1941- Exhibitions 2. Glass art -- History -- 20th century -- Exhibitions 3. Glass art -- History -- 21st century -- Exhibitions

ISBN 9783791353241

LC bl2014021937

Discusses the work and influences of glass artist Dale Chihuly, looking at Baskets, Cyllinders, Seaforms, and other collections that were on display at the Montreal Museum of Fine Arts.

748.5 Stained, painted, leaded, mosaic glass

Rich, Chris, 1949-

Stained glass basics : techniques & projects / Chris Rich with Martha Mitchell and Rachel Ward. Sterling Pub., c1996. 144 p. : **748.5**

1. Glass craft. 2. Glass painting

ISBN 9780806948768

LC 95054102

"A Sterling/Lark book."

Includes index.

Introduces tools, materials, and techniques for working with stained glass, offers tips on safety, and suggests projects.

"This book presents the fundamental techniques of working with stained glass and is intended for those getting started in the craft. Excellent color photographs and diagrams show materials and tools, as well as the cutting, assembling, and soldering of glass items. The projects include hanging glass panels, boxes, and lamps." Library Journal.

748.50282 Glass painting and staining

Stevenson, Christine Kellmann

Creative stained glass : modern designs & simple techniques / Christine Kellman Stevenson. Lark, 2007. 128 p. : **748.50282**

1. Glass painting and staining -- Technique.

ISBN 9781600591327

LC oc2007073614

Includes index.

Originally published: 2004.

From in-a-weekend pieces to intricate designs that take more time, these 27 stained-glass projects shine with light, color, and texture, thanks to the great new glasses on the market today. More than 70 color photos present the techniques, all worked with easy-to-acquire, modern, and efficient tools. --From publisher description.

749 Furniture and accessories

Aronson, Joseph, 1898-

The **encyclopedia** of furniture / Joseph Aronson. Crown Publishers 1965 ix, 484 p. : **749**

1. Furniture -- Dictionaries 2. Encyclopedias

ISBN 9780517037355

LC 65024334

An illustrated up-to-date reference work which describes every period and development in furniture styling and construction.

Kistler, Vivian Carli

The **complete** photo guide to framing and displaying artwork : 500 Full-color How-to Photos / Vivian Carli Kistler. Creative Pub. International, 2009. 192 p. : Complete Photo Guide **749**

1. Picture frames and framing -- Technique.

ISBN 9781589234222

LC 2008046612

Includes index.

"In this guide, the author teaches the do-it-yourselfer to frame like a pro. Hundreds of photos illustrate conservation matting, working with premade elements or frame-building from scratch, glazing, and hanging." Library Journal.

Logan, M. David

Mat, mount, and frame it yourself / M. David Logan. Watson-Guptill Publications, c2002. 160 p. : **749**

1. Picture frames and framing. 2. Decorative arts

ISBN 9780823030385

LC 2001093246

Includes index.

Explains how to use frames and mats to skillfully and economically present artwork.

"Logan does a great job of explaining everything and supplements the text with attractive photos. There is something here for framers of all skill levels." Library Journal.

Miller, Judith

Furniture / Judith Miller. DK Pub., 2005. 560 p. : **749**

1. Furniture -- History. 2. Furniture -- Styles.

ISBN 075661340X

LC bl2006009577

A comprehensive reference spanning some three thousand years of design provides more than 3,500 full-color photographs and descriptions of furniture representing every style and form, along with an overview of decorative motifs from key periods, profiles of important designers and craftsmen, a study of important movements in furniture design, and more.

Rybczynski, Witold

Now I sit me down : from klismos to plastic chair : a natural history / Witold Rybczynski. Farrar, Straus and Giroux, 2016. 192 p. **749**

1. Chairs -- History. 2. Sitting customs. 3. Furniture -- History. 4. Leisure.

ISBN 9780374223212

LC 2015041604

Includes index.

A history of chairs from the folding stools of pharaonic Egypt to the stackable monobloc chairs we have today.

"Rybczynski is totally engaging in this smoothly flowing, sharp, witty narrative; another winner from a top-notch writer on design." Kirkus.

750.1 Philosophy and theory

Ward, Ossian

Look again : how to experience the old masters / Ossian Ward.

Thames & Hudson, 2019. 175 p. : **750.1**

1. Painting -- Appreciation 2. Painting -- Themes, motives 3. Visual perception

ISBN 9780500239674

LC bl2019027947

"With over 100 illustrations."

"This book is a primer, preparing readers to stop reading and start looking." Booklist.

751.4 Painting--Techniques and procedures

Bridle, Bob,

Artist's painting techniques / senior editor, Bob Bridle. DK Publishing 2016. 304 p. : **751.4**

1. Painting -- Technique.

ISBN 9781465450951

LC bl2016034459

Includes index.

Perfect for all skill levels, a definitive master class to a variety of painting techniques and styles teaches aspiring artists the basic principles of painting, provides a vast array of inspiration for creating masterpieces and explains the tools, materials and methods to be used along the way.

Crilley, Mark

The **realism** challenge : drawing and painting secrets from a modern master of hyperrealism / Mark Crilley. Watson-Guptill Publications, 2015 152 p. : **751.4**

1. Drawing -- Technique 2. Painting -- Technique 3. Photo-realism

ISBN 9780385346290

LC 2014024085

Includes index.

Discusses methods, tips, and techniques for creating realistic drawings and paintings with step-by-step process photos for over twenty works.

"Those with modest artistic skills can greatly improve their ability to draw and paint realistic objects by following the tips and tricks detailed here." Library Journal.

Jung, Kwan, 1932-

Chinese brush painting : step by step / Kwan Jung. North Light Books, c2003. 128 p. : **751.4**

1. Ink painting, Chinese -- Technique 2. Watercolor painting, Chinese -- Technique

ISBN 9781581802078

LC 2002071858

Includes index.

A guide to Chinese brush painting provides twelve projects that use a range of Chinese inks, brushes, and papers.

Marine, Carol

Daily painting : paint small and often to become a more creative, productive, and successful artist / Carol Marine. Watson-Guptill Publications, 2014 x, 182 p. : **751.4**

1. Painting -- Technique

ISBN 9780770435332

LC BL2014050373

Includes index.

A blogger, teacher and painter describes how the practice of painting small projects daily can help artists at all levels grow, improve their technique and skill level and keep the creative ideas flowing.

Self, Caroline, 1919-

Chinese brush painting : a hands-on introduction to the traditional art / Caroline Self and Susan Self Tuttle Pub., 2007. 64 p. : **751.4**

1. Ink painting, Chinese -- Technique. 2. Art. 3. Painting.

ISBN 9780804838771

LC 2006037838

"This introduces readers to the art of Chinese calligraphy and brush painting. The text is fluid and graceful . . . and the authors wrap succinct accounts of Chinese history and lore around their clear, step-by-step, illustrated instructions." Booklist.

751.42 Use of water-soluble mediums

Kersey, Geoff

Painting successful watercolours from photographs / Geoff Kersey. Search Press, 2015. 128 p. : **751.42**

1. Landscape painting -- Technique 2. Painting from photographs 3. Watercolor painting -- Technique

ISBN 9781844489985

LC bl2014050761

Includes index.

A master watercolorist counsels developing artists on how to adapt and improve photographic source material to create successful paintings, displaying reference images, color charts and preparatory sketches beside finished works. Includes illustrated glossary.

"This guide has solid crossover potential among avid travelers, hobbyist watercolor painters, and amateur photographers." Library Journal.

Kloosterboer, Lorena

Painting in acrylics : The Indispensable Guide / Lorena Kloosterboer. Firefly Books, 2014. 320 p. : **751.42**

1. Acrylic painting -- Technique

ISBN 9781770854086

LC bl2014055914

Includes index.

Provides an introduction to acrylic painting, with information on different paints, brushes, tools, surfaces, color theories, and painting techniques and advice on competitions and exhibits.

O'Connor, Birgit

Watercolor essentials : hands-on techniques for exploring watercolor in motion / Birgit O'Connor. North Light Books, c2009. 127 p. : **751.42**

1. Watercolor painting -- Technique

ISBN 9781600610943

LC 2008036576

Includes index.

"This is an exciting, comprehensive package for the beginning watercolor artist. O'Connor...keys her lessons to a 70-minute DVD. Her wet and loose technique and the personal touch of the DVD make this a great choice at a good price." Library Journal.

Robinson, Mario Andres, 1970-

Lessons in realistic watercolor : a contemporary approach to painting people and places in the classical tradition / Mario Andres Robinson. Monacelli Studio, 2016 176 p. : **751.42**

1. Realism in art 2. Watercolor painting -- Technique

ISBN 9781580934459

LC 2015038871

Includes index.

"Artists of intermediate skill level are best poised to benefit from these lessons." Library Journal.

Zickefoose, Julie

Baby birds : an artist looks into the nest / Julie Zickefoose. Houghton Mifflin Harcourt, 2016. xxi, 333 p. : **751.42**

1. Birds in art

ISBN 9780544206700

LC bl2016011031

An artist and a wildlife rehabilitator presents a visually stunning book, combining art and natural history, that is filled with more than 400 watercolor paintings that capture the breathtakingly swift development of 17 different species of wild birds.

751.45 Oil painting

Griffel, Lois

Painting the impressionist landscape : lessons in interpreting light and color / Lois Griffel. Watson-Guptill Publications, 2008, c1994. 144 p. : **751.45**

1. Hawthorne, Charles Webster, 1872-1930 Influence. 2. Color in art 3. Impressionism (Art) 4. Landscape painting -- Technique 5. Light in art

ISBN 9780823095193

LC bl2011004762

Includes index.

Reprint. Originally published: 1994.

Offers a study of Hawthorne's theories about the use of color and light in impressionism, features examples with classic and local reproductions, and provides exercises for creating simple pieces using the theories.

751.7 Specific forms

Felisbret, Eric

Graffiti New York / Eric Felisbret DEAL CIA ; contributions by Luke Felisbret SPAR ONE ; foreword by James Prigoff. Abrams, 2009. 339 p. : **751.7**

1. Street art 2. Graffiti 3. Visual nonfiction

ISBN 9780810951464

LC 2009011736

Presents the history of graffiti art in New York City, detailing the concepts, aesthetics, ideals, and social structures that have served as a cultural blueprint for graffiti movements across the world.

Ganz, Nicholas

★**Graffiti** world : street art from five continents / Nicholas Ganz ; edited by Tristan Manco. Abrams, 2009. 391 p. (some folded) : **751.7**

1. Street art. 2. Graffiti. 3. Murals. 4. Public art.

ISBN 9780810980495

LC 2004004248

Includes 8 folded pages.

"Ganz's survey of graffiti art includes upward of 2,000 full-color photographs. . . . An ephemeral, often despised, yet irrefutably powerful mode of expression, graffiti has always been political, and although many of the street artists Ganz succinctly profiles have moved away from illegal spray painting, they have not compromised the inherent subversiveness of their work. . . . Ganz's global array captures the power and synergy of this vibrant alternative art world in which artists form crews and collectiveness to ensure that their art is seen." Booklist.

752 Color

Edwards, Betty, 1926-

Color : a course in mastering the art of mixing colors / Betty Edwards. Jeremy P. Tarcher/Penguin, c2004. xvii, 206 p. : **752**

1. Color in art

ISBN 9781585421992

LC 2003067215

The author of The New Drawing on the Right Side of the Brain distills the complex principles of color theory into a practical, easy-to-follow method of working with color to produce harmonious and pleasing combinations, explaining how to see and use color and how to mix and combine hues.

758 Nature, architectural subjects and cityscapes, other specific subjects

Wilton, Andrew

American sublime : landscape painting in the United States, 1820-1880 / Andrew Wilton & Tim Barringer. Princeton University Press, 2002. 282 p. : **758**

1. Landscape painting, American -- 19th century -- Exhibitions 2. Sublime, The, in art -- Exhibitions

ISBN 9780691096704

LC 2001098792

"Published ... on the occasion of the exhibition at Tate Britain, London 21 February-19 May 2002, and touring to Pennsylvania Academy of the Fine Arts, Philadelphia 17 June-25 August 2002, Minneapolis Institute of Arts, 22 September-17 November 2002"--T.p. verso.

Published to accompany a major transatlantic exhibition, a tribute to U.S. landscape painting features more than one hundred works by the Hudson River School artists, complemented by three gatefolds, artist biographies, and essays on American landscape painting in the context of international traditions and national identity. (Fine Arts)

758.5 Plants

Woodin, Carol

Botanical art techniques : a comprehensive guide to watercolor, graphite, colored pencil, vellum, pen and ink, egg tempera, oils, printmaking, and more / The American Society of Botanical Artists ; edited by Carol Woodin and Robin A. Jess. Timber Press, 2020. 414 p. : **758.5**

1. Plant drawing 2. Plants in art 3. Flower painting and illustration

ISBN 9781604697902

LC bl2020045570

Includes index.

The ultimate how-to guide to the essential botanical art techniques from the people who know it best, the American Society of Botanical Artists.

"The ASBA, a community of practitioners and appreciators of botanical art, has produced this spectacular how-to book for those who are not-quite-beginners in the arts of drawing, sketching, and painting fruits, flowers, tree parts, and, occasionally, vegetables." Booklist

759.13 United States

Cikovsky, Nicolai, Jr., 1933-

Winslow Homer / Nicolai Cikovsky, Jr., Franklin Kelly ; with contributions by Judith Walsh and Charles Brock. National Gallery of Art ; c1995. 420 p. : **759.13**

1. Homer, Winslow, 1836-1910 Exhibitions. 2. Nationalism in art -- Exhibitions
ISBN 9780300065558

LC 95019025

"Exhibition dates, National Gallery of Art, Washington, 15 October 1995-28 January 1996, Boston Museum of Fine Arts, 21 February-26 May 1996, Metropolitan Museum of Art, New York, 20 June -22 September 1996"--T.p. verso.

" In this catalog of the American artist's retrospective exhibition, the contributors present a contextually rich and vibrant analysis of Homer's life and groundbreaking work." Booklist.

Gerdts, William H.

American impressionism / William H. Gerdts. Abbeville Press, 2001. 368 p. : **759.13**

1. Impressionism (Art) -- United States 2. Painting, American -- 19th century
ISBN 9780789207371

LC 2001022419

More than four hundred illustrations along with photographs of the artists and excerpts from their letters and journals illustrate a new expanded edition of the definitive study of American Impressionism by the preeminent scholar in the field.

"The best general source available on American Impressionism. [The] book covers the major artists in the movement, including expatriates working in Europe and regional schools throughout the United States during the late 19th and early 20th centuries. .The well-chosen illustrations include many full-page color reproductions as well as photographs of many of the artists." Library Journal.

Livingston, Jane

The **paintings** of Joan Mitchell / Jane Livingston ; with essays by Linda Nochelin, Yvette Lee, and Jane Livingston. Whitney Museum ; c2002. 237 p. : **759.13**

1. Mitchell, Joan, 1926-1992 Exhibitions 2. Abstract expressionism -- United States -- Exhibitions
ISBN 0520235681

LC 2001058514

Catalog of an exhibition held at the Whitney Museum of American Art, New York, June-Oct. 2002.

"This is a vivid portrait of the artist. Mitchell's compositions {are} gorgeously reproduced here in vibrant color." Booklist.

Lynes, Barbara Buhler, 1942-

Georgia O'Keeffe Museum collections / Barbara Buhler Lynes. Abrams, 2007. 352 p. : **759.13**

1. O'Keeffe, Georgia, 1887-1986 Catalogs 2. Georgia O'Keeffe Museum Catalogs. 3. Art -- New Mexico -- Santa Fe
ISBN 9780810909571

LC 2006019894

"In association with Georgia O'Keeffe Museum."

Provides a comprehensive view of O'Keeffe's paintings, drawings, and sculptures, and documents the growth of the collection at the Georgia O'Keeffe Museum from its inception to its ten-year anniversary.

Rothko, Mark, 1903-1970

Rothko : the color field paintings / foreword by Christopher Rothko ; essay by Janet Bishop ; picture editor, Jenny Moussa Spring. Chronicle Books, 2017 120 p. : **759.13**

1. Rothko, Mark, 1903-1970 Themes, motives. 2. Color-field painting -- United States -- Themes, motives
ISBN 9781452156606

LC oc2018144648

This collection presents fifty large-scale artworks from the American master's color field period (1949-1970) alongside essays by Rothko's son, Christopher Rothko, and San Francisco Museum of Modern Art curator of painting and sculpture Janet Bishop.

Sewell, Darrel, 1939-

Thomas Eakins / organized by Darrel Sewell with essays by Kathleen A. Foster ... [et al.] ; chronology by Kathleen Brown. Philadelphia Museum of Art, c2001. xli, 446 p. : **759.13**

1. Eakins, Thomas, 1844-1916 Exhibitions.
ISBN 9780300091113

LC 2001053142

Exhibition held at Philadelphia Museum of Art, Oct. 4, 2001 to Jan. 6, 2002, Musee d'Orsay, Paris, Feb. 5 to May 12, 2002, the Metropolitan Museum of Art, New York, June 18 to Sept. 15, 2002.

"This is clearly the definitive monograph on one of the most significant artists America has produced." Library Journal

Marin, Cheech

Chicano visions : American painters on the verge / Cheech Marin ; essays by Max Benavidez, Constance Cortez, Tere Romo. Little, Brown and Co., 2002. 160 p. : **759.13**

1. Marin, Cheech Art collections Exhibitions 2. Marin, Patti Art collections Exhibitions 3. Painting, Mexican-American -- 20th century -- Exhibitions 4. Painting -- Private collections -- California -- Exhibitions
ISBN 0821228064

LC 2002104645

Published on the occasion of the exhibition.

"A Bulfinch Press book."

The popular actor and comedian highlights the work of more than thirty Chicano artists in a volume that showcases Marin's own personal art collection and includes essays by leading scholars on the history and development of Chicano art.

De Kooning, Elaine,

Elaine de Kooning : portraits / Brandon Brame Fortune, Ann Eden Gibson, Simona Cupic. Published for the National Portrait Gallery, 2015 144 p. : **759.13**

1. De Kooning, Elaine Exhibitions 2. De Kooning, Elaine, 1918-1989 Exhibitions -- 2015 Washington (D.C.). 3. Portraits, American -- Exhibitions
ISBN 9783791354385

LC 2014958601

Catalogue published in conjunction with the exhibition "Elaine de Kooning: Portraits," at the National Portrait Gallery, Smithsonian Institution, Washington, D.C., March 13, 2015-January 10, 2016.

"John F. Kennedy, Frank O'Hara, Allen Ginsberg, Merce Cunningham, and Fairfield Porter were just some of the figures who sat for portraits by Elaine de Kooning. Famous for her marriage to the Abstract Expressionist Willem de Kooning, Elaine was herself a groundbreaking artist and writer who challenged many conventions during her career. Although she portrayed women, she was most engaged with portraits of men, sometimes painting multiple portraits of her subjects in order to explore and capture their most compelling likenesses. She focused intently on her subjects--as she wrote in 1965, "Like falling in love painting a portrait is a concentration on one particular person and no one else will do." This insightful book explores de Kooning's portraits as well as her artistic process and her position in the rise of Postmodernism. Illustrated throughout with full-color reproductions of paintings, drawings, and archival photos, this book is an important contribution to the literature on Abstract Expressionism, women artists, and feminism during a transformative period, and will also appeal to lovers of painting of all kinds." -- Publisher's description.

759.36 Austrian painting

O'Connor, Anne Marie, 1959-

The **lady** in gold : the extraordinary tale of Gustav Klimt's masterpiece, Portrait of Adele Bloch-Bauer / Anne-Marie O'Connor. Knopf, 2012. xviii, 349 p. : **759.36**

1. Klimt, Gustav, 1862-1918. Adele Bloch-Bauer I. 2. Bloch-Bauer, Adele, 1881-1925 Portraits. 3. Portraits. 4. Painting. 5. Art thefts. 6. Painters. 7. Vienna, Austria -- History -- 19th century. 8. Europe -- History -- 1945-

ISBN 9780307265647

LC 2011033578

Shares the events that shaped the creation of Gustav Klimt's most famous portrait, covering such topics as the story of the salon hostess who was his model, contributing factors in turn-of-the-century Vienna, and the painting's fate.

759.4 French painting

Cogeval, Guy

Edouard Vuillard / Guy Cogeval with Kimberly Jones, Laurence des Cars, MaryAnne Stevens ; contributions by Dario Gamboni, Elizabeth Easton, Mathias Chivot. National Gallery of Art, 2003. xviii, 501 p. : **759.4**

1. Vuillard, Edouard, 1868-1940 Exhibitions.

ISBN 0300097379

LC 2002151120

"National Gallery of Art, Washington, 19 January-20 April 2003, Montreal Museum of Fine Arts, 15 May-24 August 2003, Galeries nationales du Grand Palais, Paris, 23 September 2003-4 January 2004, Royal Academy of Arts, London, 27 January-27 April 2004."

"This authoritative study on an artist whose career spanned two centuries is recommended for all libraries that collect art books." Library Journal

Kelder, Diane

The **great** book of French impressionism / Diane Kelder. Abbeville Press, 2001?, c1980. 400 p. : **759.4**

1. Impressionism (Art) -- France 2. Painting, French

ISBN 9780789206886

LC 2001266313

Traces the development of impressionism and draws on anecdotes and excerpts from contemporary essays and letters to explore the lives of the major Impressionists.

King, Ross, 1962-

The **judgment** of Paris : the revolutionary decade that gave the world Impressionism / Ross King. Walker & Co., 2006. xiii, 448 p., 8 p. of plates : **759.4**

1. Manet, Edouard, 1832-1883 Criticism and interpretation. 2. Meissonier, Jean Louis Ernest, 1815-1891 Criticism and interpretation. 3. Impressionism (Art) -- France. 4. Painters -- France -- 19th century. 5. Visual art and society -- Paris, France -- 19th century. 6. Painting, French -- 19th century. 7. Paris, France -- History -- 19th century.

ISBN 0802714668

LC 2005031089

Governor General's Literary Award for English-Language Nonfiction, 2006.

ALA Notable Book, 2007.

Discusses the development of Impressionism in Paris during the 19th century.

"The book serves as an entertaining if broad account of a revolutionary transformation in visionnot least of all through art." Library Journal.

Morton, Mary G

Gustave Caillebotte : the painter's eye / Mary Morton, George T.M. Shackelford ; Essays by Michael Marrinan, Alexandra K. Wettlaufer, Elizabeth Benjamin, Stephane Guegan, Sarah Kennel. National Gallery of Art , 2015 283 p. : **759.4**

1. Caillebotte, Gustave, 1848-1894 Exhibitions

ISBN 9780226263557

LC 2015004438

"More than fifty of Gustave Caillebotte's (1848-1894) strongest paintings illustrate the fertile period from 1875 to 1885 when he was most closely allied with the impressionists. Accompanying the National Gallery of Art's major new exhibition, coorganized with the Kimbell Art Museum, this volume explores the inquisitive, experimental, almost fearless vision that inspired his masterworks".-- Provided by publisher.

Shackelford, George T. M., 1955-

Monet : the early years / George T.M. Shackelford ; with essays by Anthea Callen, Mary Dailey Desmarais, Richard Shiff, Richard Thomson. Kimbell Art Museum, 2016 206 p. : **759.4**

1. Monet, Claude, 1840-1926 Exhibitions. 2. Monet, Claude 1840-1926. gnd 3. Exhibition catalogs

ISBN 9780300221855

LC 2016951792

Catalog of the exhibition at Kimbell Art Museum, Fort Worth, October 16, 2016 - January 29, 2017; Fine Arts Museums of San Francisco, February 25 - May 29, 2017.

Errata sheet tipped in.

This elegant volume is the first to be devoted to the young genius of Claude Monet (1840-1926). Bringing together the greatest paintings from his early career--including his first Salon-exhibited work, the Kimbell Art Museum's La Pointe de la Heve at Low Tide; Dejeuner sur l'Herbe (Luncheon on the Grass) and The Magpie from the Musee d'Orsay; and The Green Wave and La Grenouillere from the Metropolitan Museum of Art--it features essays by distinguished scholars, focusing on the evolution of Monet's own distinctive mode of painting. Through the 1860s, the young painter absorbed and transformed a variety of influences, from the lessons of the Barbizon school and his mentor Boudin to the challenges posed by his friends Manet, Pissarro, Renoir, and Sisley. Artistic innovation and personal ambition shaped the work of the celebrated impressionist painter from the very start of his long and illustrious career.

"It offers a fresh, coherent reassessment of Monet's early career (1858-1872) before he participated in impressionistic exhibitions." Choice.

759.5 Italian painting

Brewer, John, 1947-

The **American** Leonardo : a tale of obsession, art and money / John Brewer. Oxford University Press, 2009. ix, 310 p., 8 p. of plates : **759.5**

1. Leonardo, da Vinci, 1452-1519. Belle Ferronniere. 2. Hahn, Harry (Harry J.), b. 1897 Art collections. 3. Painting, Renaissance -- Authenticity. 4. Art forgeries 5. United States -- History -- 20th century

ISBN 9780195396904

LC 2009008681

"In 1919, a Midwestern auto salesman named Harry Hahn and his French war bride, Andre, got in touch with Joseph Duveen, the famous New York art dealer, with an offer to sell what they claimed was an original painting by Leonardo da Vinci. Duveen publicly dismissed the work as a fake, and the Hahns, taking him to court for slander, began a decades-long struggle for authentication that scrutinized not only the art world's elitism but the validity of connoisseurship itself. Brewer skillfully outlines the conditions that made America ripe for such an incident and explores how Old Master art became the currency with which the country's new millionaires established their cultural credibility." The New Yorker.

King, Ross, 1962-

Florence : the paintings & frescoes, 1250-1743 / Introductions and essays by Ross King ; painting descriptions by Anja Grebe. Black Dog & Leventhal, 2015. x, 697 p. : **759.5**

1. Painting, Italian 2. Art history 3. Art, European 4. Painting, Renaissance (Europe) -- Florence, Italy 5. Florence, Italy

ISBN 9781631910012

LC 2015026785

"A comprehensive book on the paintings and frescoes of Florence, with more than 2,000 artworks from the city's great museums and churches".-- Provided by publisher.

"Written in an easy-to-read style, this surprisingly affordable tome, given its size and lavish illustrations, will interest general readers through art historians." Library Journal.

★**Leonardo** and the Last supper / Ross King. Walker & Company, 2012. 352 p. **759.5**

1. Leonardo, da Vinci, 1452-1519. Last Supper. 2. Mural painting and decoration, Italian 3. Painting, Italian 4. Artists 5. Signs and symbols in art

ISBN 9780802717054

LC 2012005358

Governor General's Literary Award for English-Language Nonfiction, 2012.

ALA Notable Book, 2013

Shortlisted for The Charles Taylor Prize for Literary Non-Fiction

Chronicles how Leonardo da Vinci created the mural painting, the Last Supper.

Michelangelo & the Pope's ceiling / Ross King. Walker & Company, 2003. 373 p., 8 p. of plates : **759.5**

1. Michelangelo Buonarroti, 1475-1564 Contemporaries. 2. Julius II, Pope, 1443-1513. 3. Vatican. Sistine Chapel. 4. Bible Illustrations. 5. Artists -- Florence, Italy. 6. Mural painting and decoration, Italian -- Vatican City. 7. Frescoes -- Italy. 8. Artistic rivalry. 9. Italy -- History -- 1492-1559. 10. Vatican City

ISBN 9780802713957

LC 2002038074

ALA Notable Book, 2004.

Governor General's Literary Awards, English-language Nonfiction finalist

An account of Michelangelo's creation of his masterpiece, the ceiling of the Sistine Chapel, from his original commission from Pope Julius II, through the artist's four years of work, to the final acclaim at the paintings' 1512 unveiling.

"This engaging narrative sets the record straight on a few points and is highly recommended for most public library collections." Library Journal.

Scotti, R. A.

Vanished smile : the mysterious theft of Mona Lisa / R.A. Scotti. Knopf Books, 2009. 256 p. **759.5**

1. Leonardo, da Vinci, 1452-1519. Mona Lisa. 2. Art thefts -- Paris, France. 3. Painting. 4. Art. 5. Paris, France.

ISBN 9780307265807

LC 2008047851

Reopens the case of one of the most perplexing art thefts ever committed--the still unsolved mystery of the disappearance of Leonardo da Vinci's "Mona Lisa" from the Louvre on August 21, 1911.

"The author reports on the 1911 theft of Mona Lisa. The lovely woman with the enigmatic smile was simply lifted off the wall and spirited away. The scandal was immense, the investigation feverish, the headlines screaming, and Scotti revels in every turn. Her lively, expert coverage encompasses the fascinating, many-chaptered story of Mona Lisa and ironic revelations about the frenzy among America's robber barons for old masters and the corresponding renaissance in art fraud. Scotti's avid, exciting true-life mystery yields intriguing disclosures and reaffirms Mona Lisa's unique powers." Booklist.

759.81 Norwegian painting

Knausgaard, Karl Ove, 1968-

So much longing in so little space : the art of Edvard Munch / Karl Ove Knausgaard ; translated from the Norwegian by Ingvild Burkey. Penguin Books, 2019, c2017. 233 p. : **759.81**

1. Munch, Edvard, 1863-1944 Criticism and interpretation 2. Artists -- Norway 3. Art -- Psychological aspects 4. Creation (Literary, artistic, etc.) 5. Authors

ISBN 9780143133131

LC 2018057501

Originally published by Forlaget Oktober, 2017.

The award-winning Norwegian novelist tackles nonfiction with his personal assessment of the work of the famous expressionist painter and fellow countryman, providing artistic insight with historical, biographical and autobiographical discussions surrounding works including My Struggle and Four Seasons.

"Fans of the author's acclaimed autobiographical novels will find this book to be of Rosetta Stone-like importance as he delves into Munch's exploration of memory and how the artist rendered the past in a way that still feels both intimate and universally relatable." Kirkus.

759.9492 Dutch painting

Fischer, Stefan (Writer on art)

Jheronimus Bosch / Stefan Fischer ; English translation, Karen Williams. Taschen, 2016. 517 p. : **759.9492**

1. Bosch, Hieronymus, died 1516. Catalogues raisonnes. 2. Artists

-- Netherlands. 3. Painting, Dutch. 4. Art appreciation.
ISBN 9783836538350

"The complete works"--Jacket.

Presents the artist's twenty-eight known drawings and paintings and analyzes key themes and influences in his work.

"As keen as the book's historical and technical sections are, its most enthralling passages contain the authors' insights into Bosch's original and satiric worldview and cosmic iconography." Booklist.

Silva Maroto, María Pilar,

Bosch : the 5th centenary exhibition / edited by Pilar Silva Maroto. Thames & Hudson, 2017. 396 p. : **759.9492**

1. Bosch, Hieronymus, -1516 Exhibitions. 2. Exhibition catalogs
ISBN 9780500970799

Published in conjunction with the exhibition of the same name held at the Museo Nacional del Prado, Madrid, 31st May-11th September 2016.

"Primary sources enrich the historical narrative of Bosch and his art, and the complete catalogue entries provide the history of ownership and recent technological research on the physical state of each richly reproduced painting." Choice.

759.9493 Belgian painting

Gohr, Siegfried

★**Magritte** : attempting the impossible / Siegfried Gohr. D.A.P./Distributed Art Publishers, c2009. 323 p. : **759.9493**

1. Magritte, Rene, 1898-1967 Criticism and interpretation. 2. Surrealism -- Belgium
ISBN 9781933045931

LC 2009022403

"This extremely well-illustrated tour de force combines new research with unique organization. Obligatory chapters introduce Magritte's early development (during which his work revealed the heavy influence of De Chirico, Leger, and Le Corbusier) and his use of other media (graphic design, illustration, drawings, collages) in addition to oil paintings. This structure will engage the novice's imagination and will intrigue the Magritte connoisseur. Gohr's book reminds readers that excellent art never ceases to provide new avenues for investigation, through both research and careful visual examination of the art as primary document." Choice Reviews.

760 Printmaking and prints

Harmon, Katharine A., 1960-

The **map** as art : contemporary artists explore cartography / Katharine Harmon ; with essays by Gayle Clemans. Princeton Architectural Press, 2009. 255 p. : **760**

1. Maps in art -- Exhibitions 2. Cartography in art -- Exhibitions
ISBN 9781568989723

LC 2008030929

Arranged by themes including personal terrain, inner visions, and global reckoning, a catalog collects 350 works by an international range of artists creating map-related works of art.

769.569 Postage stamps and related devices--History, geographic treatment, biography

Barron, James, 1954-

The **one-cent** magenta : inside the quest to own the most valuable stamp in the world / James Barron. Algonquin Books of Chapel Hill, 2017. 224 p. **769.569**

1. Rare postage stamps. 2. Stamp collecting. 3. Collectors and collecting. 4. Postage stamps. 5. Guyana
ISBN 9781616205188

LC 2016038074

"Published simultaneously in Canada by Thomas Allen & Son Limited."

When it was issued in 1856, it cost a penny. In 2014, this tiny square of faded red paper sold at Sotheby's for nearly $9.5 million, the largest amount ever paid for a postage stamp at auction. Through the stories of the eccentric characters who have bought, owned, and sold the one-cent magenta in the years in between, James Barron delivers a fascinating tale of global history and immense wealth, and of the human desire to collect.

"Readers of history, microhistory, and narrative nonfiction, and those with an interest in stamps, will appreciate this absorbing tale of the rarefied world of high-stakes philately." Library Journal.

769.92 Prints--biography

Katsushika, Hokusai, 1760-1849

Hokusai : beyond the great wave / edited by Timothy Clark. Thames & Hudson, 2017. 352 p. : **769.92**

1. Katsushika, Hokusai, 1760-1849 Exhibitions. 2. Color prints, Japanese -- Edo period, 1600-1868 3. Painting, Japanese -- Edo period, 1600-1868
ISBN 9780500094068

LC bl2018029569

"This publication accompanies the exhibition 'Hokusai : beyond the great wave' at the British Museum from 25 May to 13 August 2017 and the exhibition 'Hokusai - Fuji o koete' at Abeno Harukas Art Museum, Osaka, from 6 October to 19 November 2017"--Title page verso.

Examines the brush paintings, drawings, woodblock prints, and illustrated books of Hokusai and arranges them thematically into groups that are related to the major spiritual and artistic quests of his life.

770 Photography, computer art, cinematography, videography

Ang, Tom

Digital photography masterclass / Tom Ang. DK, 2013. 360 p. : **770**

1. Image processing -- Digital techniques 2. Photography -- Digital techniques
ISBN 9781465408563

LC bl2013033728

Includes index.

Explains how to see the world with a photographer's eyes through tutorials, image analyses, assignments, and step-by-step image manipulation exercises.

Campany, David

The **open** road : photography & the American road trip / David Campany. Aperture Foundation, 2014 334 p. ; **770**

1. Photographic criticism 2. Photography, Artistic 3. United States Pictorial works. 4. United States -- Description and travel Pictorial works. 5. United States -- Social life and customs Pictorial works.
ISBN 9781597112406

LC 2014020321

The Open Road considers the photographic road trip as a genre in and of itself, and presents the story of photographers for whom the American road is muse. The book features David Campany's introduction to the genre and 18 chapters presented chronologically, each exploring one American road trip in depth through a portfolio of images and informative texts. --From publisher description.

Cole, Teju

Blind spot / Teju Cole. Random House, [2017] 352 p. **770**

1. Cole, Teju Travel. 2. Voyages and travels 3. Photography 4. Authors -- Travel. 5. Perception
ISBN 9780399591075

LC 2016032505

The New York Times photography critic and award-winning author pairs more than 150 images with lyrical text to explore his complex relationship to the visual world through his great passions--writing and photography--in a testament to the art of seeing.

Fagans, Michael

iPhone photography for everybody / Michael Fagans. Amherst Media, Inc., 2017 127 p. : **770**

1. Photography -- Digital techniques 2. iPhone (Smartphone) 3. Photography, Artistic
ISBN 9781682032909

LC bl2017050802

Includes index.

Offers advice on how to shoot exceptional images with an iPhone camera, covering such topics as context and composition, lighting, and portraits and selfies.

Freeman, Michael, 1945-

The **photographer's** mind : creative thinking for better digital photos / Michael Freeman. Focal Press, c2011. 192 p. : **770**

1. Digital cameras 2. Image processing -- Digital techniques 3. Photography -- Digital techniques 4. Photography -- Psychological aspects
ISBN 9780240815176

LC bl2011023168

Describes the components of a good photograph--purpose, style, and technique--and offers illustrative examples of the concepts within each section that were created using digital technology.

"The author shares experience he has gained as a professional photographer to improve the quality of the digital pictures nearly everyone is now creating. The content is streamlined into three chapters, on intent, style, and process, that tackle both the practical and the intangible aspects of photography more thoughtfully than many similar books. Freeman is as adept at explaining composition as he is at discussing the problem of cliché or the philosophy of the sublime." Library Journal.

Gatcum, Chris

★The **beginner's** photography guide / written by Chris Gatcum. DK Publishing, 2016. 192 p. : **770**

1. Photography -- Digital techniques
ISBN 9781465449665

LC bl2016009693

Includes index.

Provides practical advice on the techniques of digital photography, with information on such topics as equipment, exposure, focusing, lenses, light, flash, and image enhancement.

"Though perfect for novices, this manual will also be helpful to readers with prior knowledge of analog photography wishing to translate their skills to the digital realm." Library Journal.

Horenstein, Henry

Digital photography : a basic manual / Henry Horenstein with Allison Carroll. Little, Brown and Co., 2011. 240 p. : **770**

1. Photography -- Digital techniques.
ISBN 9780316020749

LC 2011018758

Includes index.

A professional photographer and author presents a step-by-step course for beginning digital photography enthusiasts, covering topics such as exposure controls, shutter speed and information on image editing, printing methods and file storage.

Matter, Jordan,

Dancers among us : a celebration of joy in the everyday / Jordan Matter. Workman Publishing, 2012 ix, 229 p. : **770**

1. Matter, Jordan. 2. Dance 3. Dance in art. 4. Dancers 5. Portrait photography.
ISBN 0761171703

LC 2012033655

Collects pictures of dancers striking poses in everyday places and while doing everyday things, including in libraries, on subway platforms, at restaurants, and on beaches.

Museum of Modern Art (New York, N.Y.)

Photography at MoMA. edited by Quentin Bajac, Lucy Gallun, Roxana Marcoci, Sarah Hermannson Meister ; foreword, Glenn D. Lowry. MoMA, 2016 415 p. : **770**

1. Museum of Modern Art (New York, N.Y.) Photograph collections. 2. Artistic photography 3. Photography -- History -- 20th century. 4. Photograph collections -- New York City
ISBN 9781633450134

LC 2016941489

As the second volume in a set of three books that together present a new and comprehensive history of photography through works from MoMA's collection, this publication charts the medium during the height of the modernist period, from 1920 to 1960.

National Gallery of Art (U.S.)

★**Alfred** Stieglitz : the key set : the Alfred Stieglitz collection of photographs / Sarah Greenough. National Gallery of Art ; 2002. 2 v. (lxiii, 1012 p.) : **770**

1. Stieglitz, Alfred, 1864-1946 Catalogs 2. National Gallery of Art (U.S.) Photograph collections Catalogs. 3. Artistic photography 4. Art museums -- Washington (DC) 5. Photograph collections -- Washington (DC)
ISBN 9780810935334

LC 2002005066

A lavish two-volume boxed set is a definitive catalogue of the artist's collection at the National Gallery of Art and is published to coincide with a major traveling exhibition.

Peterson, Bryan, 1952-
Learning to see creatively : design, color, and composition in photography / Bryan Peterson. Amphoto Books, 2015 144 p. : **770**

1. Composition (Photography). 2. Artistic photography 3. Picture perception.
ISBN 9781607748274

LC 2014049147

Includes index.

"Completely revised and updated throughout, Bryan Peterson's classic guide to creativity helps photographers visualize their work, and the world, in a whole new light by developing their photographic vision. Fully revised with 100 percent new photography, this best-selling guide takes a radical approach to creativity by explaining how it is not just an inherent ability but a skill that can be learned and applied. Using inventive photos from his own stunning portfolio, author and veteran photographer Bryan Peterson deconstructs creativity for photographers. He details the basic techniques that go into not only taking a particular photo, but also provides insights on how to improve upon it--helping readers avoid the visual pitfalls and technical dead ends that can lead to dull, uninventive photographs. This revised edition features a complete section on color as a design element and all new photographs to illustrate Peterson's points. Learning to See Creatively is the definitive reference for any photographer looking for a fresh perspective on their work".--Provided by publisher.

Taylor, David, 1969 April 13-
Digital photography complete course / written by David Taylor, Tracy Hallett, Paul Lowe, Paul Sanders. DK, 2015. 360 p. : **770**

1. Photography -- Digital techniques
ISBN 9781465436078

LC bl2015031893

Includes index.

Using a combination of tutorials, step-by-step demonstrations, practical assignments and Q&As, a guide to digital photography explores a wide range of genres to help aspiring photographers build their skills.

"An affordable, uncomplicated way to learn about digital photography." Library Journal.

Willis, Deborah, 1948-
Reflections in Black : a history of Black photographers, 1840 to the present / Deborah Willis. W. W. Norton, c2000. xviii, 348 p. : **770**

1. African American photographers 2. African Americans in art 3. Photography -- United States -- History -- 19th century. 4. Photography -- United States -- History -- 20th century.
ISBN 0393048802

LC 99055185

The companion volume to a major exhibition at The Smithsonian Institution contains a photographic celebration of the power of family, endurance, spirituality, and the diverse range of the African-American experience over the last two centuries.

"Willis sketches important figures and traces both developments in photographic techniques and the practice of photography by African Americans. . . . A beautiful and informative album." Booklist.

770.23 Photography as a profession, occupation, hobby

Fordham, Demetrius
★**If** you're bored with your camera read this book / Demetrius Fordham. Ilex, 2017. 128 p. : **770.23**

1. Photography -- Digital techniques 2. Photography -- Technique
ISBN 9781781574317

LC bl2017044359

Includes index.

Shares tricks, tips, hacks, and exercises to help readers find new ideas for images and different techniques, covering such topics as creating an inspiration board, playing with shadows and highlights, and experimenting with double exposure.

770.9 History, geographical treatment, biography

Ang, Tom
Photography : the definitive visual history / Tom Ang. DK Publishing, 2014. 480 p. : **770.9**

1. Photography -- History
ISBN 9781465422880

LC bl2014039324

Includes index.

Traces the history of photography from its origins in the 1820s to the digital photography of the twenty-first century, profiling key photographers, highlighting important techniques, and showcasing iconic photographic images.

"While too basic for a professional or serious student, this volume will appeal to photo enthusiasts and general readers. Those wanting an extensive single-volume overview should stick with Michael R. Peres's The Focal Encyclopedia of Photography." Library Journal.

Morris, Errol
Believing is seeing : observations on the mysteries of photography / Errol Morris. Penguin Press, 2011. 336 p. **770.9**

1. Documentary photography. 2. Photojournalism 3. Truth 4. Reliability
ISBN 9781594203015

LC 2011013101

Presents an investigation into the truth behind a variety of documentary photographs throughout history, discussing the relationship between the photograph and the world they supposedly represent.

770.92 Biography

Alinder, Mary Street, 1946-
Group f.64 : Edward Weston, Ansel Adams, Imogen Cunningham, and the community of artists who revolutionized American photography / Mary Street Alinder. Bloomsbury USA, 2014. 320 p. **770.92**

1. Group f.64 -- History. 2. Photographers 3. Photography 4. Artists 5. California
ISBN 9781620405550

LC 2014011040

"As she chronicles the photographers' friendships, tempestuous love lives, epic parties, scrambles to survive, passionate manifestos, heated public debates, social and environmental concerns, and hard-won exhibitions, Alinder achieves an f.64 degree of crisp and commanding detail in this landmark group portrait of the visionary photographers who succeeded in 'forever changing our way of seeing.' " Booklist.

Brandow, Todd
Edward Steichen : lives in photography / Todd Brandow and

William A. Ewing ; with contributions by A.D. Coleman ... [et al.]. Foundation for the Exhibition of Photography ; 2008. 335 p. : **770.92**

1. Steichen, Edward, 1879-1973. 2. Photography, Artistic -- Exhibitions.
ISBN 9780393066265

LC 2007020128

Published on the occasion of the exhibition organized by the Foundation for the Exhibition of Photography and Musee de l'Elysee, Lausanne; Exhibition itinerary, Jeu de Paume, Paris, October 9-December 30, 2007; Musee de l'Elysee, Lausanne, January 17-March 23, 2008; Palazzo Magnani, Reggio Emilia, April 12-June 8, 2008; Museo Nacional Centro de Arte Reina Sofia, June 24-September 22, 2008.

A visual portrait of the influential and prolific fine-art photographer also includes an analysis of his commercial achievements and the continuing legacy of his exhibition, The Family of Man, in an account that features scholarly essays that evaluate such topics as his work with Condé Nast and his Museum of Modern Art directorship.

Curtis, Edward S., 1868-1952

Edward S. Curtis : one hundred masterworks / Christopher Cardozo ; with contributions by A. D. Coleman, Louise Erdrich, Eric J. Jolly, and Michael Charles Tobias. Foundation for the Exhibition of Photography, 2015. 183 p. : **770.92**

1. Curtis, Edward S., 1868-1952. 2. Indians of North America -- History -- Pictorial works 3. Indians of North America -- Portraits 4. Photographers -- United States 5. Photography in ethnology
ISBN 9783791354217

LC 2014049053

Galassi, Peter

Ansel Adams in Yosemite Valley : celebrating the park at 150 / Peter Galassi. Little, Brown and Company, 2014. 203 p. : **770.92**

1. Adams, Ansel, 1902-1984. 2. Landscape photography -- California -- Yosemite Valley. 3. Landscape photography -- United States. 4. National parks and reserves -- United States 5. Photographers -- United States. 6. Yosemite National Park (Calif.) Pictorial works. 7. Yosemite Valley (Calif.) Pictorial works.
ISBN 0316323403

LC 2014940622

A luminous collection of photographs that Ansel Adams made in Yosemite National Park during his long and remarkably productive life, published to celebrate the 150th anniversary of President Abraham Lincoln's signing of the Yosemite Land Grant.

Pich, Tom

Folk masters : a portrait of America / photographs by Tom Pich ; text by Barry Bergey. Indiana University Press, 2018. 245 p. : **770.92**

1. National Endowment for the Arts. National Heritage Fellowship. 2. Ethnic arts -- United States 3. Folk artists -- United States
ISBN 9780253032324

LC 2017032043

"Bergey, former director of folk and traditional arts at the National Endowment for the Arts (NEA), highlights the expansive and compelling photographs of Tom Pich, who has spent the last 25 years capturing recipients of the NEA's National Heritage Fellowship." Library Journal.

771 Techniques, procedures, apparatus, equipment, materials

Ang, Tom

Digital photographer's handbook / Tom Ang. DK, c2012. 408 p. : **771**

1. Digital cameras 2. Photography -- Digital techniques
ISBN 9780756692421

LC 2012418315

A latest edition provides revised and updated coverage of expert techniques related to current trends and developments in digital photography to counsel novice through professional photographers on how to capture the best possible shots and enhance existing pictures.

Peterson, Bryan, 1952-

Understanding exposure : how to shoot great photographs with any camera / Bryan Peterson. AmPhoto Books, 2016 168 p. ; **771**

1. Photography -- Exposure.
ISBN 9781607748502

LC 2015025905

Provides detailed lessons on the elements of exposure and how each relates to depth of field, freezing and blurring action, and shooting in low light, demonstrating a diversity of creative choices in exposing a picture.

777 Cinematography and videography

Pincus, Edward

The **filmmaker's** handbook : a comprehensive guide for the digital age / Steven Ascher & Edward Pincus ; drawings by Carol Keller and Robert Brun ; original photographs by Ted Spagna and Stephen McCarthy completely revised and updated by Steven Ascher With contributions by David Leitner. Plume, 2012 832 p. **777**

1. Cinematography 2. Digital cinematography 3. Digital video 4. Motion pictures -- Production and direction
ISBN 9780452297289

LC OC2012621105

Originally published as: The filmmaker's handbook / Edward Pincus and Steven Ascher. 1984.

A fully revised, comprehensive guide offers an in-depth exploration of today's recent technological advances, such as digital age filmmaking, while reviewing a collection of new methods and techniques in relation to various film formats and offering suggestions on the business aspects of financing and producing films.

778 Specific fields and special kinds of photography

Prud'homme, Alex

France is a feast : the photographic journey of Paul and Julia Child / Alex Prud'Homme & Katie Pratt. Thames & Hudson, 2017. 207 p. : **778**

1. Child, Julia. 2. Child, Paul, 1902-1994. 3. Americans in France 4. Artistic photography 5. Cooking, French. 6. Husband and wife 7. France
ISBN 9780500519073

LC 2016932144

As Paul and Julia Child traveled around France during his years as cultural attaché for the US Information Service, Julia focused on cooking and writing-- and Paul, an accomplished photographer, focused on photography. Some of his work is in the collection of the Museum of Modern Art. Here Prud'homme, his great-nephew, captures this magical period in Paul and Julia's lives in introductory essays, in a collection of photos curated by Pratt.

"This thoroughly delicious book illustrates how two creative minds can impact public taste." Publishers Weekly.

Williams, Richard, 1933-

The **animator's** survival kit : a manual of methods, principles and formulas for classical, computer, games, stop motion and internet animators / Richard Williams. Faber and Faber, 2009. x, 382 p. : **778**

1. Animation (Cinematography) 2. Drawing -- Technique.
ISBN 9780571238330

LC 2010294449

Previous ed.: 2001.

Title on accompanying DVD: The animator's survival kit animated.

The Academy Award-winning artist draws on his master instruction classes to demonstrate essential techniques required of animators of any skill level or method, in an updated edition that provides expanded coverage of such topics as animal gaits and liveaction.

778.3 Special kinds of photography

Benson, Michael, 1962-

Far out : a space-time chronicle / Michael Benson. Abrams, 2009. 328 p. : **778.3**

1. Space photography. 2. Outer space Pictorial works.
ISBN 0810949482

LC bl2009026130

Includes index.

Presents a collection of photographs depicting various sections of our solar system as well as of distant galaxies beyond the Milky Way taken by observatories around the world.

"Here are stars packed like golden sand, gas combed in delicate blue threads, piled into burgundy thunderheads and carved into sinuous rilles and ribbons, and galaxies clotted with star clusters dancing like spiders on the ceiling. . . . You can sit and look through this book for hours and never be bored, . . . or you can actually read the accompanying learned essays. Mr. Benson's prose is up to its visual surroundings, no mean feat. New York Times.

778.7 Photography under specific conditions

Mustard, Alex,

Underwater photography masterclass / Alex Mustard. Ammonite Press, 2016. 191 p. : **778.7**

1. Underwater photography -- Techniques. 2. Marine animals -- Pictorial works.
ISBN 9781781452226

LC bl2017005588

There is an astonishing world just waiting to be photographed underwater. From information about diving equipment and cameras, to crucial advice on understanding and controlling light underwater, this book provides all the background you need before you take the plunge.

Rotman, Jeffrey L.

The **last** fisherman : witness to the endangered oceans / Jeffrey L. Rotman with Yair Harel ; introduction by Les Kaufman. Abbeville Press, 2014 276 p. : **778.7**

1. Rotman, Jeffrey L. Travel. 2. Marine photography. 3. Overfishing. 4. Saltwater fishing 5. Underwater photography.
ISBN 0789211912

LC 2014016848

"An excellent cautionary tale, this work offers much to celebrate, too. Highly recommended to all interested in nature, the oceans, and fishing." Library Journal.

778.9 Photography of specific subjects

Watkins, Carleton E., 1829-1916

Carleton Watkins : the complete mammoth photographs / Weston Naef and Christine Hult-Lewis ; with contributions by Michael Hargraves, Jack von Euw, and Jennifer A. Watts. J. Paul Getty Museum, c2011. xxv, 572 p. : **778.9**

1. Watkins, Carleton E., 1829-1916 Exhibitions 2. Landscape photography -- California -- Exhibitions 3. View cameras -- Exhibitions 4. California Pictorial works Exhibitions.
ISBN 9781606060056

LC 2011005241

Discusses the life and work of the nineteenth century landscape photographer, presenting a selection of photographs of the American West taken between 1858 and 1891.

779 Photographic images

Buckland, Gail

Who shot rock & roll : a photographic history, 1955 to the present / Gail Buckland. Knopf, 2009. 304 p. **779**

1. Rock music -- History and criticism 2. Rock musicians -- Portraits. 3. United States -- Social life and customs -- 20th century 4. United States -- Social life and customs -- 21st century
ISBN 9780307270160

LC 2009019122

A former curator of the Royal Photographic Society of Great Britain presents a chronicle of rare and previously unseen images marking more than half a century of rock-and-roll history, in a tribute to star performers and leading photographers that also includes album covers and live concert shots.

"Here are nearly 300 iconic photographs by those photographers who understood the power of the image in the formation and sustenance of rock-and-roll culture from 1955 onward. The care with which Buckland selects representative photographers and their most significant images is matched by her interpretive prowess. [She] carefully but deliberately argues that the art of rock photography has been sacrificed to the paparazzi and corporate art departments. In light of this inclusive, heady and visceral collection of the genre's best, it would be hard to argue otherwise." Publishers Weekly.

Who shot sports : a photographic history, 1843 to the present / Gail Buckland. Alfred A. Knopf, 2016. xii, 329 p. : **779**

1. Photography of sports -- History.
ISBN 0385352239

LC 2015038089

Presents more than 280 amazing action photographs of athletes, including Willie Mays, Carl Lewis, Ian Botham, Kobe Bryant and Magic Johnson by such photographers as Robert Capa, Danny Lyon, Annie Leibovitz, Neil Leifer, Walter Iooss Jr. and Bob Martin.

"Buckland writes with such authority that her thoughts on photography, as an art form, and her analysis of individual images in and out of the sports context make this a must-read for pop culture enthusiasts and anyone interested in photography." Publishers Weekly.

Evans, Walker, 1903-1975

American photographs / Walker Evans ; with an essay by Lincoln Kirstein. Museum of Modern Art, c2012. 208 p. : **779**

1. Evans, Walker, 1903-1975. 2. Artistic photography 3. United States Pictorial works. 4. United States -- Social conditions -- 1918-1932 Pictorial works. 5. United States -- Social conditions -- 1933-1945 Pictorial works.

ISBN 9780870708350

LC 2012940325

This seventy-fifth anniversary edition of American Photographs, made with new reproductions, recreates the original 1938 edition as closely as possible to make the landmark publication available for a new generation.

Friedman, Elias Weiss

The **Dogist** : photographic encounters with 1,000 dogs / Elias Weiss Friedman. Artisan, 2015 303 p. : **779**

1. Photography of dogs.

ISBN 1579656714

LC 2015036708

A treasury of expressive and heartwarming canine portraits is complemented by subject stories and characteristics and is thematically organized under sections ranging from Puppies and Cones of Shame to Working Dogs and Dogs in Fancy Outfits.

"This delightful collection of photographs is likely to catch the eye of readers who follow Friedman's blog, Facebook page, tweets, and/or Instagram account. Animal portraiture enthusiasts may be especially interested in this title as an exemplar of the genre." Library Journal.

Gardullo, Paul

The **Scurlock** Studio and Black Washington : picturing the promise / edited by Paul Gardullo ... [et al.]. National Museum of African American History and Culture, c2009. 224 p. : **779**

1. Scurlock Studio (Washington, D.C.) -- History Exhibitions. 2. Scurlock Studio (Washington, D.C.) Photograph collections Exhibitions. 3. National Museum of African American -- History and Culture (U.S.) Photograph collections Exhibitions. 4. National Museum of American -- History (U.S.) Photograph collections Exhibitions. 5. African Americans -- Washington (D.C.) -- History -- Pictorial works -- Exhibitions. 6. African Americans -- Washington (D.C.) -- Social life and customs -- Pictorial works -- Exhibitions. 7. African Americans -- Washington (D.C.) -- Portraits -- Exhibitions. 8. Washington (D.C.) -- History Pictorial works Exhibitions. 9. Washington (D.C.) -- Social life and customs Pictorial works Exhibitions. 10. Washington (D.C.) Portraits Exhibitions.

ISBN 9781588342621

LC 2008032847

"Companion volume to the exhibition opening at the National Museum of American History in January 2009"--Jacket flap.

This volume collects examples of the work produced by the Scurlock Studio, much of which focuses on the elites and luminaries of Black Washington, portrayed in formal portraits and photographs of events such as weddings and balls, but also includes many looks into the social lives of the African American middle classes and a small handful portraying the lives of the working class and poor.

"With more than 100 images, this book is a proud celebration of a vibrant community from the early to the late twentieth century." Booklist

Hitchcock, Susan Tyler,

National Geographic rarely seen : photographs of the extraordinary / [compiled by] Susan Tyler Hitchcock ; foreword by Stephen Alvarez. National Geographic, 2015 399 p. : **779**

1. Travel photography. 2. Documentary photography. 3. Nature photography. 4. Landscape photography.

ISBN 9781426215612

LC 2015014900

Collects the work of National Geographic's best photographers, featuring striking images of places, events, natural phenomena, and manmade heirlooms seldom seen by human eyes, including ancient cave art and volcanic lightning.

Leibovitz, Annie, 1949-

A **photographer's** life, 1990-2005 / Annie Leibovitz. Random House, c2006. 480 p. ; **779**

1. Leibovitz, Annie, 1949- 2. Portrait photography.

ISBN 9780375505096

LC 2006045765

A visual narrative of the past fifteen years brings together more than three hundred photographs, including both personal images and professional work, that document her relationship with her late companion Susan Sontag, the birth of her daughters, the death of her father, and the world of such public figures as Demi Moore, Nelson Mandela, Bill Clinton, and others.

★**Portraits** : 2005-2016 / Annie Leibovitz. Phaidon Press Limited, 2017 313 p. : **779**

1. Celebrities 2. Portrait photography.

ISBN 0714875139

LC bl2018012067

Chiefly illustrations.

An extensive treasury of 21st-century portraits by one of today's most influential photographers includes several previously unpublished images and stand as a collective symbol of modern culture.

Women / [photographs by] Annie Leibovitz ; [essay by] Susan Sontag. Random House, c1999. 239 p. : **779**

1. Leibovitz, Annie, 1949- 2. Photography of women

ISBN 9780375500206

LC 99024968

Cover title.

The photographer turns her lens to a favorite topic, women, sharing her portraits of Hillary Rodham Clinton, Eudora Welty, Martina Navratilova, and Jodie Foster, as well as women from other walks of life, including a Navajo weaver, an astronaut, and a rancher.

Light, Michael

100 suns : 1945-1962 / Michael Light. ALfred A. Knopf, 2003. 208 p. : **779**

1. Nuclear weapons -- Testing -- United States -- History. 2. Nuclear weapons -- Pictorial works.

ISBN 1400041139

LC 2003106275

"Images in this book were made by photographers in the U.S. Army Signal Corps ... [and] the 1352nd Photographic Group of the U.S. Air Force"--Note on the photographs.

Contains 100 photographs of nuclear tests.

"The suns Light presents to readers in this photography collection are manmade: aboveground atomic detonations captured on film both in the Nevada desert and at sea, terrifyingly beautiful images that remind readers of the apocalyptic might of nuclear weapons." Booklist.

Malin, Gray,

Beaches / Gray Malin. Abrams, 2016. 143 p. : **779**

1. Aerial photography. 2. Beaches. 3. Photography, Artistic.
ISBN 1419720899

LC 2015946912

Provides an aerial perspective of bathing beaches throughout the world, including Bondi Beach in Sydney, Australia; Oak Street Beach in Chicago, Illinois; and Muizenberg Beach in Cape Town, South Africa.

Sartore, Joel

★The **photo** ark : one man's quest to document the world's animals / Joel Sartore ; foreword by Harrison Ford ; introduction by Douglas H. Chadwick. National Geographic, 2017 399 p. : **779**

1. Rare and endangered animals 2. Photography of animals. 3. Wildlife photography.
ISBN 9781426217777

LC 2016038616

Includes index.

Representing National Geographic's Photo Ark--a major cross-platform initiative and lifelong project by a veteran photographer to make portraits of the world's animals, especially those that are endangered--this showcase of 600 photos presents a thought-provoking argument for saving all the species of our planet.

"Satore more than succeeds in his goal to provide people with an opportunity to become aware of these animals, many endangered, before they disappear." Publishers Weekly.

Shaughnessy, Jim

The **call** of trains : railroad photographs by Jim Shaughnessy / text by Jeff Brouws. W.W. Norton & Co., c2008. 224 p. : **779**

1. Photography of railroads. 2. Railroads -- United States
ISBN 0393065928

LC 2008001295

A celebration of the life and work of the renowned railroad photographer includes photographs taken between 1946 and 1988, and emphasizes the railroad culture of the fifties and sixties.

"Shaughnessy began shooting trains in downtown Troy, New York (his hometown), in the middle 1940s. He eventually took lengthy trips, first in New England and Canada, later across the Midwest to the Southwest, to photograph trains. He initially focused on the big engines but quickly extended his purview to include railway workers, railway buildings, and the countrysides through which the trains rolled. A civil engineer rather than a professional photographer, he became as skilled as any pro. Appearing on full pages of this oversize volume, his pictures are engrossing, stunning masterpieces of photodocumentation." Booklist.

Smith, Joel, 1964-

Edward Steichen : the early years / Joel Smith. Princeton University Press in association with the Metropolitan Museum of Art, c1999. 167 p., 61 leaves of col. plates : **779**

1. Steichen, Edward, 1879-1973. 2. Photography, Artistic.
ISBN 0691048738

LC 99026617

"Smith examines the photography of Edward Steichen. Alfred Stieglitz was a patron of Steichen's, and Smith discusses the interrelationship between Steichen's work and Stieglitz's shifting aesthetic interests, as well as the influence of Paris on Steichen's development." New York Times Book Review.

Wegman, William,

William Wegman : being human / William A. Ewing. Chronicle Books, 2017. 352 p. : **779**

1. Photography of dogs
ISBN 9781452164991

LC 2017021743

Includes index.

"William Wegman's whimsical photographs of his Weimaraner dogs have been celebrated in the art world and enjoyed by pet lovers for nearly four decades. In this entirely new volume, renowned photography curator William A. Ewing presents more than 300 images from the artist's personal archive, unearthing previously unseen gems alongside the iconic images that have made Wegman--along with dressed-up dogs Man Ray, Fay Ray, and others--beloved worldwide. Presented in sixteen thematic chapters, William Wegman:Being Human foregrounds the photographer's penchant for play and his evergreen ability to create images that are at once funny, striking, and surreal. Audiences of all ages will fall in love--for the first time, or all over again--with Wegman and his friends".-- Provided by publisher.

779.092 Photographers

Eggleston, William, 1939-

William Eggleston's guide / essay by John Szarkowski. Museum of Modern Art : c2002. 110 p. : **779.092**

1. Photography, Artistic
ISBN 9780870703782

LC bl2009003149

Presents a collection of forty-eight photographs taken between 1969 and 1971 depicting people and places around the photographer's hometown of Memphis.

McCurry, Steve

The **iconic** photographs : The Iconic Photographs / Steve McCurry. Phaidon, 2012. 270 p. : **779.092**

1. Photography, Artistic. 2. Portrait photography.
ISBN 0714865133

LC bl2012046509

Presents a retrospective collection of the photographer's work over the past thirty years.

779.2 Portraits--photographs

Bethencourt, Kahran

Glory : magical visions of Black beauty / Kahran and Regis Bethencourt. St. Martin's Press, 2020 256 p. **779.2**

1. African American children 2. African Americans -- Portraits 3. Africans 4. Photography of children 5. Visual nonfiction
ISBN 9781250204561

LC 2020021905

The husband-and-wife team behind CreativeSoul Photography and the acclaimed AfroArt series combine striking photography of natural Black hairstyles with visual storytelling in a celebration of Black culture, heritage and self-acceptance.

"An exquisite pictorial love letter to Black children around the world." Kirkus

780 Music

Burrows, John, 1939-

The **complete** classical music guide / general editor, John Burrows with Charles Wiffen and contributions from Robert Ainsley ... [et al.]. DK Pub., c2012. 352 p. : **780**

1. Music appreciation.
ISBN 9780756692568

LC 2012562384

"Based on content previously published in Eyewitness companions : Classical music"--T.p. verso.

A visual guide to one thousand years of classical music introduces composers, performers, instruments, and key works.

Crawford, Richard, 1935-

America's musical life : a history / Richard Crawford. Norton, 2001. xv, 976 p. : **780**

1. Music -- United States -- History and criticism 2. Music, American -- History and criticism
ISBN 0393048101

LC 99047565

"This survey of music in America covers blues, jazz, swing, pop, rock, hip hop . with economics and history as cultural backdrops. Well researched and sensitively constructed, this is highly recommended." Library Journal.

Day, Timothy

★A **century** of recorded music : listening to musical history / Timothy Day. Yale University Press, c2000. x, 306 p. : **780**

1. Music -- 20th century -- History and criticism. 2. Sound recording industry -- History. 3. Sound recordings -- History. 4. Sound -- Recording and reproducing -- History.
ISBN 0300084420

LC 00043490

"This work provides a narrative of the evolution of recording from cylinders (1887), shellac discs, and acoustic rerecording through the reproducing piano, electrical amplifications (1925), and magnetic tape to the long-playing record (1948) and compact disc of the 1980s. Day also discusses studio practices and the emergence of influential record producers, the role of radio and recordings in creating a mass audience, the expansion of recorded repertoire, and new ways to experience music. Recommended for all music collections." Choice.

Gilbert, Steven E.

The **music** of Gershwin / Steven E. Gilbert. Yale University Press, c1995. xi, 255 p. : **780**

1. Gershwin, George, 1898-1937 Criticism and interpretation. 2. Musical analysis
ISBN 9780300062335

LC 95012086

"With this book, Gershwin's music finally gets the attention it deserves. Gilbert's book is not for the casual reader, since it requires an understanding of music theory and notation." Library Journal.

Ross, Alex, 1968-

Listen to this / Alex Ross. Farrar, Straus and Giroux, 2010. 416 p. **780**

1. Popular music. 2. Music -- History and criticism. 3. Music and society. 4. Composers 5. Essays.
ISBN 9780374187743

LC 2010010283

"Though the bulk of the book examines classical work both historical and contemporary, Ross veers effortlessly from Mozart to Radiohead, from Kurt Cobain to Brahms, bringing a pop fan's enthusiasm to the composers and treating the rock stars seriously as musicians. The triumph of Listen to This is that Ross dusts off music that's centuries old to reval the passion and brilliance that's too often hidden from a contemporary audience. It's a joy for a pop fan or a classical aficionado." New York Times Book Review.

Terkel, Studs, 1912-2008

And they all sang : adventures of an eclectic disc jockey / Studs Terkel. New Press, 2005. xxii, 301 p. ; **780**

1. Musicians -- Interviews. 2. Singers -- Interviews. 3. Composers -- Interviews. 4. Disc jockeys. 5. Interviews 6. Oral histories
ISBN 9781595580030

LC 2005043866

A selection of forty previously unpublished interviews with top musicians from the past half-century includes the Pulitzer Prize-winning oral historian's discussions with such figures as Bob Dylan, Janis Joplin, and Louis Armstrong.

"In each priceless give-and-take, Terkel captures the distinct personality of each artist and the spirit of his or her world-altering music. Terkel is like no other in his eloquence, humor, empathy, and generosity." Booklist.

Walker-Hill, Helen

From spirituals to symphonies : African-American women composers and their music / Helen Walker-Hill. Greenwood Press, 2002. xvi, 401 p. : **780**

1. African American women composers 2. Composers -- United States 3. Music by African American women composers -- History and criticism.
ISBN 9780313299476

LC 2001040600

"This excellent and beautifully produced publication will immediately interest those working in music history and women's studies." Choice

780.26 Texts treatises on music scores and recordings

Calamar, Gary

Record store days : from vinyl to digital and back again / Gary Calamar, Phil Gallo ; edited by Scott Calamar ; foreword by Peter Buck. Sterling Pub Co Inc, 2010. 238 p. **780.26**

1. Music stores. 2. Music industry and trade 3. Records, Phonograph. 4. Vintage record stores.
ISBN 9781402772320

LC bl2010016536

Uses interviews, photographs, anecdotes, and memorabilia to provide a nostalgic history of the record store in the United States and includes profiles of major shops and quotations from musicians, shop oweners, and fans.

780.3 Music dictionaries

Hoffman, Miles

The **NPR** classical music companion : an essential guide for enlightened listening / Miles Hoffman. Houghton Mifflin, 2005. x, 306 p. **780.3**

1. Music -- Dictionaries. 2. Music -- Terminology.
ISBN 9780618619450

LC 2006273343

Includes index.

Originally published: The NPR classical music companion : terms and concepts from A to Z, c1997.

Recently revised for the latest wave of classical music fans, this popular introduction to the genre by NPR commentator Miles Hoffman teaches readers how to distinguish between good and bad performances, explains why opera was invented, and shares fascinating facts designed to heighten appreciation for the form.

780.71 Music--education

Tunstall, Tricia

Changing lives : Gustavo Dudamel, El Sistema, and the transformative power of music / Tricia Tunstall. W.W. Norton, c2012. 320 p. **780.71**

1. Dudamel, Gustavo Anecdotes. 2. Fundacion del Estado para el Sistema Nacional de las Orquestas Juveniles e Infantiles de Venezuela -- History. 3. Music -- Instruction and study. 4. Children and music. 5. Poor children. 6. Music in education.
ISBN 9780393078961

LC 2011026504

Includes index.

Reveals the effect that education can have on positive social change by examining the life of a conductor of the Los Angeles Philharmonic and the unique program that nurtured his talent back home in Venezuela and its current availability in the U.S.

780.866 LGBTQ musicians

Bullock, Darryl W.

David Bowie made me gay : 100 years of LGBT music / Darryl W. Bullock. Overlook Duckworth, 2017. 358 pages, 8 unnumbered pages of plates : **780.86**

1. Gay culture -- History 2. Musicians 3. Music -- History and criticism 4. Popular culture
ISBN 9781468315592

LC bl2017049523

The most comprehensive history of LGBT music ever compiled, encompassing a century of music by and for the LGBT community.

"Well-researched and brimming with intrigue, Bullock's comprehensive study not only makes the work of scores of musicians sing anew; it also demonstrates how the pendulum of acceptance can swing from era to era." Kirkus.

780.9 History, geographic treatment, biography

Burton-Hill, Clemency

★**Year** of wonder : classical music to enjoy day by day / Clemency Burton-Hill. Harper, 2018 442 p. ; **780.9**

1. Music 2. Music appreciation 3. Music calendars
ISBN 9780062856203

LC 2019564819

"First published in Great Britain in 2017 by Headline Home"--Title page verso.

Classical music has a reputation for being stuffy, boring, and largely inaccessible, but Burton-Hill is here to change that. An award-winning writer, broadcaster and musician, with a deep love of the art form she wants everyone to feel welcome at the classical party, and her desire to share her passion for its diverse wonders inspired this unique, enlightening, and expertly curated treasury. As she says, "The only requirements for enjoying classical music are open ears and an open mind." Year of Wonder introduces readers to one piece of music each day of the year, artfully selected from across genres, time periods, and composers. Burton-Hill offers short introductions to contextualize each piece, and makes the music come alive in modern and playful ways. From Bach, Beethoven, Mozart, and Puccini to George Gershwin, Clara Schumann, Philip Glass, Duke Ellington, and many remarkable yet often-overlooked voices, Burton-Hill takes us on a dazzling journey through our most treasured musical landscape. Thoughtfully curated and masterfully researched, Year of Wonder is a book of classical music for everyone. Whether you're a newcomer or an aficionado, Burton-Hill's celebration will inspire, nourish, and enrich your life in unexpected ways.-- [Publisher description]

"Burton-Hill's delightful and informative guide provides a daily dose of the beauty of classical music and also an enticing introduction to it." Publishers Weekly.

Gioia, Ted

Music : a subversive history / Ted Gioia. Basic Books, 2019. 528 p. **780.9**

1. Popular culture 2. Music -- Political aspects.
ISBN 9781541644366

LC 2019001627

A music historian recounts four-thousand-years of music history focusing on the social outcasts, riffraff, insurgents and provocateurs who became trailblazers of this artistic expression and have repeatedly reinvented it, from Sappho to the Sex Pistols.

Grout, Donald Jay

A **history** of western music / J. Peter Burkholder, Donald Jay Grout, Claude V. Palisca. W. W. Norton & Company, 2014 xlii, 1009, 143 p. : **780.9**

1. Music -- History and criticism
ISBN 9780393918298

LC 2013035016

This music history textbook surveys the key musical styles and ideas of Western music.

Moody, Rick

On celestial music : and other adventures in listening / Rick Moody. Little, Brown and Company, 2012. 384 p. **780.9**

1. Music -- History and criticism. 2. Popular music 3. Music and literature 4. Popular culture 5. Essays
ISBN 9780316105217

LC 2011030556

Includes index.

The author of The Ice Storm and Garden State discusses his love of music and how it inspires his writing, including his infatuation with the Velvet Underground as well as more modern bands including Magnetic Fields, Wilco and The Pogues.

Rosen, Charles, 1927-

The **classical** style : Haydn, Mozart, Beethoven / Charles Rosen. W. W. Norton, c1997. xxx, 533 p. ; **780.9**

1. Haydn, Franz Joseph, 1732-1809 Criticism and interpretation 2. Mozart, Wolfgang Amadeus, 1756-1791 Criticism and interpretation 3. Beethoven, Ludwig van, 1770-1827 Criticism and interpretation 4. Classicism in music. 5. Music -- 18th century -- History and criticism
ISBN 0393317129

LC BL 98000020

Presents a detailed analysis of the musical styles and forms developed by Mozart, Haydn, and Beethoven

"This remains simply the most important book on the classical style in music." Choice.

Hamilton, Jill,

Music : the definitive visual history / US editors, Jill Hamilton, Margaret Parrish, Rebecca Warren. DK Publishing, 2015. 480 p. : **780.9**

1. Music -- History and criticism.

ISBN 9781465442468

LC bl2015042575

At head of title: DK Smithsonian.

Includes index.

A guide to the history of music and instruments begins in prehistoric times and progresses through all eras throughout the world and includes background music theory and advances in technology.

780.92 Biography

Cramer, Alfred William

Musicians & composers of the 20th century / editor Alfred W. Cramer. Salem Press, c2009. 5 vols. : **780.92**

1. Music -- 20th century -- Bio-bibliography -- Dictionaries. 2. Musicians -- History -- 20th century 3. Composers -- 20th century -- Bio-bibliography

ISBN 9781587655128

LC 2009002980

"The work covers 614 composers, performers, and teachers, chosen for musical influence as well as fame. All major genres are covered, from classical to rap, along with many subgenres, such as rockabilly, atonal, and funk. . . . This work provides valuable, basic information on the topic as well as multiple, easy-access routes to it. Highly recommended." Library Journal.

Everitt, Matt

The **first** time : stories & songs from music icons / Matt Everitt. Laurence King Publishing, 2018. 336 p. : **780.92**

1. Musicians 2. Popular music -- HIstory and criticism. 3. Rock music -- HIstory and criticism. 4. Interviews.

ISBN 9781786272980

LC bl2019018982

"BBC Radio 6 music"--Cover.

Includes index.

A collection of forty interviews gleaned from the BBC Radio 6 Music show includes talks with such artists as Paul Simon, Alice Cooper, Yoko Ono, Florence Welch, and Pete Townshend.

"A delight for browsers; put this eye-catching title on display and watch it fly off the shelves." Library Journal.

Moynahan, Brian, 1941-

Leningrad : siege and symphony: the story of the great city terrorized by Stalin, starved by Hitler, immortalized by Shostakovich / Brian Moynahan. Atlantic Monthly Press, 2014 496 p. **780.92**

1. Shostakovich, Dmitrii Dmitrievich, 1906-1975. 2. Sieges. 3. World War II 4. Starvation 5. Musicians 6. St. Petersburg, Russia -- Siege, 1941-1944

ISBN 9780802123169

LC bl2014044322

Describes the concert played in August 1942 by a cobbled-together group of starving survivors -- who were cold, sick and weak from Stalin's purges and the Nazi invasion of Russia -- which offered a glimmer of hope during the darkest days of World War II.

"Moynahan's rapturous commentary on the music at times amounts to puffery...nonetheless an admirable tribute to the human spirit and artistic integrity. Highly recommended for all readers interested in the era and the wellsprings of artistic creation." Library Journal.

781 Principles, forms, ensembles, voices, instruments

Mannes, Elena

The **power** of music : pioneering discoveries in the new science of song / Elena Mannes ; foreword by Dr. Aniruddh Patel. Walker & Company, 2011. 288 p. **781**

1. Music -- Psychological aspects. 2. Music and science. 3. Sound -- Psychological aspects 4. Music -- History and criticism

ISBN 9780802719966

LC 2010048255

The award-winning creator of the documentary The Music Instinct traces the efforts of visionary researchers and musicians to understand the biological foundations of music and its relationship to the brain and the physical world.

"An investigation of how music affects people and other animals. Detailing a variety of scientific experiments, [the author] shows the effects of sound frequencies and vibrations on body organs and brain waves; her study culminates in documentation supporting music therapy. Mannes's intercontinental explorations range from songbird studies to infants' melodic preferences to the origins of the universe (one topic on which her discussions seem rather far-fetched if fascinating). Interviews with influential musicians such as Bobby McFerrin help lighten an otherwise rather dense text." Library Journal.

781.1 Basic principles of music

Gasser, Nolan

Why you like it : the science and culture of musical taste / Nolan Gasser. Flatiron Books, 2019. 576 p. **781.1**

1. Music appreciation. 2. Popular music 3. Musicology 4. Musical style

ISBN 9781250057198

LC 2018037896

The chief architect of the Pandora Radio song recommendation engine presents a groundbreaking examination of how the body and mind affect music tastes, discussing how the brain processes music and what qualities trigger such human responses as humming and dancing.

"The book is a sprawl, but serious music lovers will find much fascinating science and lore to browse." Publishers Weekly.

Mauceri, John

For the love of music : a conductor's guide to the art of listening / John Mauceri. Alfred A. Knopf, 2019. 224 p. **781.1**

1. Music appreciation. 2. Classical music 3. Music -- History and criticism 4. Music -- Philosophy and aesthetics.

ISBN 9780525520658

LC 2018051290

In this beautifully written guide, a protege of Leonard Bernstein, his colleague for 18 years, draws on his profound knowledge to answer the questions: Why should I listen to classical music? How can a get the most from the listening experience?

"Even those who know classical music well will learn something from this lively and enthusiastic primer." Kirkus.

781.4 Techniques of music

Piston, Walter, 1894-1976

Counterpoint / Walter Piston ; with musical illustrations drawn by Mario Carmosino. W. W. Norton & Co., 1947 235 p. ; **781.4**

1. Counterpoint 2. Music -- Study and teaching
ISBN 9780393097283

LC 47001928

Explores the contrapuntal element in significant works from the eighteenth and nineteenth centuries for the music student who fully understands the composition of harmony.

781.45 Conducting

Mauceri, John

Maestros and their music : the art and alchemy of conducting / John Mauceri. Alfred A. Knopf, 2017. 272 p. **781.45**

1. Conductors (Music) 2. Music -- Performance 3. Orchestras 4. Conducting.
ISBN 9780451494023

LC 2016055932

Includes index.

An accessible tour of the enigmatic craft of conducting by the celebrated international conductor explores how the art of his profession is itself a composition of legacy, tradition, and techniques that involve intricate communicative gestures.

"Symphony-lovers will be thrilled with the behind-the-scenes details, and aspiring conductors will enjoy the rich industry insight. Those simply curious about how classical music happens will feel drawn in by Mauceri's palpable passion." Booklist.

781.49 Recording of music

Milner, Greg

Perfecting sound forever : an aural history of recorded music / Greg Milner. Faber and Faber, 2009. x, 416 p. : **781.49**

1. Music -- Psychological aspects 2. Sound -- Recording and reproducing -- History. 3. Popular music -- History and criticism 4. Sound -- Recording and reproducing
ISBN 9780571211654

LC 2008055444

Includes index.

A history of recorded music reveals the behind-the-scenes processes through which recorded sound is captured and produced, in a chronicle that also covers major recording achievements, the innovators who influence the way music is experienced, and the current debate about faithful versus transcendent recording practices.

"The author begins in the late 19th century, tracing the evolution from Edison's invention of the phonograph to the contemporary use of digital music files. Broad in scope and steeped in detail, the book strikes a mostly well-maintained balance between the history of the technological development of recordings and the more approachable accounts of the people and events surrounding it." Kirkus.

781.6 Traditions of music

Horowitz, Joseph, 1948-

★**Classical** music in America : a history of its rise and fall / Joseph Horowitz. W.W. Norton, c2005. xix, 606 p. : **781.6**

1. Classical music -- United States -- History and criticism 2. Music -- United States -- History and criticism
ISBN 0393057178

LC 2004027754

"Whether or not his conclusions are accepted in their totality, this fascinating book is an important social history and is highly recommended for all libraries." Library Journal.

781.62 Folk music

Lomax, John A. (John Avery), 1867-1948

American ballads and folk songs / [compiled by] John A. Lomax and Alan Lomax ; with a foreword by George Lyman Kittredge. Dover Publications, 1994. xxxix, 625 p. : **781.62**

1. Ballads, English -- United States. 2. Folk songs, English -- United States. 3. African Americans -- Music. 4. Folk music -- United States.
ISBN 9780486282763

LC bl2013012283

Originally published: New York : Macmillan Co., 1934.

Presents a collection of music and lyrics for more than two hundred American ballads and folk songs.

Strom, Yale

The **book** of klezmer : the history, the music, the folklore / Yale Strom. Chicago Review Press, 2011. 381 p. **781.62**

1. Klezmer music -- History 2. Music, Jewish 3. Folk music
ISBN 9781613740637

"This history of Klezmer music is divided into four chapters: 'From King David to Duvid the Klezmer,' 'From the Enlightenment to the Holocaust,' 'Klezmer in the New World, 1880-1960,' and 'From Zev to Zorn: The Masters of the Culture.' The first appendix, 'Klezmer Memories in the Memorial Books,' is one of the most moving sections, featuring a collection of commentaries on klezmer music and musicians from hundreds of memorial books written by Holocaust survivors." Library Journal.

Wade, Stephen

The **beautiful** music all around us : field recordings and the American experience / Stephen Wade. University of Illinois Press, c2012. xvii, 477 p. : **781.62**

1. Archive of Folk Culture (U.S.) 2. Folk music, American -- History and criticism. 3. Music, American -- History and criticism. 4. Music and society. 5. Music -- United States -- 20th century -- History and criticism. 6. United States -- Social life and customs -- 20th century. 7. Southern States -- Social life and customs -- 20th century. 8. Middle West -- Social life and customs -- 20th century.
ISBN 9780252036880

LC 2011044092

Highlights the stories behind thirteen field recordings captured between 1934 and 1942, focusing on the experiences of the people--ranging from students to prisoners--who contributed to the recordings.

Young, Rob, 1968-

Electric Eden : unearthing Britain's visionary music

/ Rob Young. Faber and Faber, 2011. 672 p. **781.62**

1. Folk music, British. 2. Music -- 20th century -- History and criticism 3. Folk music -- History and criticism
ISBN 9780865478565

LC 2011001987

Traces the 1960s effort to revive music in England that underscored the achievements of such period artists as Pink Floyd, Nick Drake and Led Zeppelin, providing insight into how their work reflected historical precedents while establishing models for present-day musicians.

"Young's narrative slips fluidly forward, backward, and through the cracks of canonical music history. And he doesn't just stick to music; like Greil Marcus with a thirst for ancient paganism and postmodern urban theory, Young weaves a poetic, philosophical tapestry as rich and heady as the songs he champions." AV Club.

781.63 Popular music

Piston, Walter, 1894-1976

Orchestration / Walter Piston. Norton, 1955 477 p. : **781.63**

1. Instrumentation and orchestration 2. Music -- Study and teaching 3. Orchestral music
ISBN 9780393097405

LC 55014230

A college-level music text that develops the student's knowledge of musical instruments, and their function in the orchestra.

781.64 Western popular music

Bradley, Andy, 1951-

House of hits : the story of Houston's Gold Star/SugarHill Recording Studios / Andy Bradley and Roger Wood. University of Texas Press, 2010. xvi, 334 p. : **781.64**

1. SugarHill Recording Studios. 2. Gold Star Studios. 3. Sound recording industry -- Texas -- Houston -- History
ISBN 9780292719194

LC 2009044441

The authors offer behind-the-scenes accounts of numerous hit recordings, spiced with anecdotes from studio insiders and musicians who recorded at SugarHill.

Darms, Lisa,

The **riot** grrrl collection / edited, with an introduction by Lisa Darms. Feminist Press, 2013. 326 p. : **781.64**

1. Punk rock music 2. Feminism. 3. Young women -- Empowerment. 4. Women rock musicians -- History.
ISBN 9781558618220

LC 2013014331

"The writers' desperation, anger, and desire translate vividly into the 21st century and will resonate strongly with today's feminists, misfits, and punks." Publishers Weekly.

Doggett, Peter, 1957-

Electric shock : from the Gramophone to the iPhone - 125 Years of Pop Music / Peter Doggett. Random House UK, 2017. 728 p. **781.64**

1. Popular music 2. Music -- Influence 3. Music -- Psychological aspects 4. Popular culture
ISBN 9780099575191

LC bl2018020209

Tells the story of popular music, from the birth of recording in the 1890s to the digital age, from the first pop superstars of the twentieth century to the omnipresence of music in our lives, in hit singles, ringtones and on Spotify. The author takes us on a rollercoaster ride through the history of music.

"This exhaustive work will be indispensable and go well alongside such books as Ed Wards The History of Rock & Roll: Volume 1, 1920-1963 (2016) and Ann Powers Good Booty (2017)." Booklist.

Hermes, Will

Love goes to buildings on fire : five years in New York that changed music forever / Will Hermes. Faber and Faber, 2011. xi, 368 p. : **781.64**

1. Popular music -- New York City -- 1971-1980 -- History and criticism. 2. Popular culture 3. Music -- New York City 4. United States -- Social life and customs -- 1970-1979.
ISBN 9780865479807

LC 2011008445

This is the first book to tell the full story of the New York City punk rock, hip-hop, disco, salsa, loft jazz scene, the downtown composers known in the mid-1970s as Minimalists, and the phenomenal and surprising ways they intersected. From New Year's Day 1973 to New Year's Eve 1977, the book moves panoramically from post-Dylan Greenwich Village, to the arson-scarred South Bronx barrios where salsa and hip-hop were created, to the Lower Manhattan lofts where jazz and classical music were reimagined, to ramshackle clubs like CBGB and the Gallery, where rock and dance music were hot-wired for a new generation.

Houghton, Mick

Becoming Elektra : the true story of Jac Holzman's visionary record label / Mick Houghton. Jawbone, 2010. 304 p. : **781.64**

1. Holzman, Jac. 2. Elektra Records (Firm) -- History. 3. Music -- Recording and reproducing 4. Sound recording industry and trade -- United States. 5. Popular music -- United States -- History and criticism.
ISBN 9781906002299

LC 2011477408

"Includes full-color reproductions of virtually every title in Elektra's catalog, themselves a revealing portrait of changing tastes and evolving consumer sophistication. Houghton's research is meticulous but he avoids the minutia that clogs many music books." Seattle Post-Intelligencer

McNally, Dennis

On Highway 61 : music, race, and the evolution of cultural freedom / Dennis McNally. Counterpoint, 2014. 384 p. **781.64**

1. African Americans 2. Popular music -- History and criticism. 3. Music 4. Race relations. 5. United States -- History 6. United States -- History
ISBN 9781619024496

LC 2014014417

Traces the progression of music created by post-Civil War black Americans "from ragtime to blues and jazz" and the white followers who adopted and embraced diversity and the sound to create bop, swing and rock and roll.

"A concise, Dylan-heavy history of the American relationship between race and music." Kirkus.

Powers, Ann, 1964-

Good booty : love and sex, black and white, body and soul in American music / Ann Powers. Dey Street Books, 2017. 256

p. **781.64**

1. Popular music 2. Sound recording industry and trade 3. Sexuality 4. Race (Social sciences)

ISBN 9780062463692

LC bl2017032952

The critic and correspondent for NPR Music explores the history of American popular music as an erotic art form, from 19th-century New Orleans and the Jazz Age in New York, to the screaming teens that welcomed The Beatles and modern day performers.

"Powers reveals an extraordinary breadth of knowledge and insight and has produced an absolutely essential addition to any pop-culture collection." Booklist.

Seabrook, John

The **song** machine : inside the hit factory / John Seabrook. W. W. Norton & Company, [2015] 288 p. **781.64**

1. Music industry and trade 2. Sound recording industry and trade 3. Popular music

ISBN 9780393241921

LC 2015022305

"Seabrook goes deeper into the career developments of Rihanna and Katy Perry, but most of the artists hold insignificant power within the international behemoth that this industry has become and even less control over their own musical progression. A revelatory ear-opener, as the music business remains in a state of significant flux." Kirkus.

Smirnoff, Marc

The **Oxford** American book of great music writing / edited by Marc Smirnoff ; foreword by Van Dyke Parks. University of Arkansas Press, 2008. 466 p. **781.64**

1. Popular music -- Southern States -- History and criticism 2. Music -- History and criticism 3. Musicians. 4. Music and society. 5. Essays.

ISBN 9781557288875

LC 2008026298

Contains 55 essays.

"With contributions from Nick Tosches, Robert Palmer, Robert Gordon, and Peter Guralnick, some of the top music writers, Smirnoff reminds us what good music writing is. This compilation is full of little gems, including Susan Straight's tender reminiscence of the music of Al Green, Tom Piazza's harrowing account of his encounter with bluegrass legend Jimmy Martin, and John Fergus Ryan's report of his time backstage with Jerry Lee Lewis in 1970. Also included are Jerry Wexler on Dusty Springfield, Roy Blount Jr. on Ray Charles, and John Jeremiah Sullivan on Chris Bell (of Big Star)." Booklist.

Stanley, Bob,

Yeah! Yeah! Yeah! : the story of pop music from Bill Haley to Beyonce / Bob Stanley. W. W. Norton & Company, 2014. 640 p. **781.64**

1. Popular music -- History and criticism. 2. Music and society. 3. Pop musicians.

ISBN 9780393242690

LC 2014002223

Everything you ever wanted to know about pop music but never thought to ask, delivered with wit -- and plenty of opinions. From longtime success stories like Simon & Garfunkel (they "looked as much fun as their undertaker name suggested") to one-hit wonders, this encyclopedic history covers about 60 years and multiple musical genres, like R&B, doo-wop, glam, grunge, disco, new wave, techno, and country. Some pieces are short and pithy, while others are a little more in-depth, but overall this addictive book is a must-read for fans of popular music of all stripes.

"The assemblage of irresistible, bite-size histories of top-of-the-charts stars is joyful, smart, and addictive, just like the best pop songs, and a must for music fans everywhere." Booklist.

Wald, Elijah

American epic : when music gave America her voice / Elijah Wald, and Bernard McMahon. Touchstone Books, 2016. 288 p. **781.64**

1. Music -- History. 2. Blues (Music) 3. Gospel music. 4. Folk music.

ISBN 9781501135606

LC 2016001493

A companion book to the groundbreaking PBS and BBC documentary series celebrates the pioneers and artists of American roots music--blues, gospel, folk, Cajun, Appalachian, Hawaiian, Native American--without which there would be no jazz, rock, country R&B, or hip hop today.

Wald, Elijah

How the Beatles destroyed rock 'n' roll : an alternative history of American popular music / Elijah Wald. Oxford University Press, 2009. 336 p. **781.64**

1. Beatles (Musical group) Influence 2. Rock groups 3. Popular music -- History and criticism 4. Rock music -- History and criticism 5. Music -- Influence 6. United States -- Social life and customs -- 21st century

ISBN 9780195341546

LC 2008042265

Surveys the history of American popular music in terms of the changes in technology and their effect on ordinary listeners as they changed music from something to be listened to and danced to live to something to be bought in recorded form.

781.642 Country music

Duncan, Dayton

★**Country** music : an illustrated history / Dayton Duncan and Ken Burns. Alfred A. Knopf, 2019. 464 p. **781.642**

1. Country music 2. Country musicians 3. Music -- History and criticism 4. United States -- Social life and customs

ISBN 9780525520542

LC 2018047629

Spur Award for Contemporary Nonfiction, 2020.

The rich and colorful story of America's most popular music and the singers and songwriters who captivated, entertained, and consoled listeners throughout the twentieth century--based on the upcoming eight-part film series to air on PBS in September 2019.

"Country music is America's music--which is to say, music from every culture and ethnicity. An essential guide." Kirkus.

Jennings, Dana Andrew

Sing me back home : love, death, and country music / Dana Jennings. Faber and Faber, 2008. 272 p. **781.642**

1. Country music -- History and criticism 2. Country musicians 3. Popular music -- History and criticism

ISBN 0865479607

LC 2007047955

"This quirky, endearing combination memoir, family history, music criticism, and love-of-place offering, made up of short, punchy chapters and sharp observations about country's appeal and how country has expressed the inchoate emotions of its largely rural following, essentially-presents the music as the portrayal of a way of life and a way of being." Booklist.

Kingsbury, Paul

The **encyclopedia** of country music : the ultimate guide to the music / compiled by the staff of the Country Music Hall of Fame and Museum ; edited by Paul Kingsbury, Michael McCall, and John W. Rumble ; with the assistance of Michael Gray and Jay Orr. Oxford University Press, c2012. xi, 626 p., 16 p. of plates : **781.642**

1. Country music -- Encyclopedias.
ISBN 9780195395631

LC 2010045104

More than 1,200 entries cover the important figures, trends and forms of country music throughout its history--from the Carter Family of the 1920s to Taylor Swift and Keith Urban today--in a resource with a photo insert and foreword by Grammy-winning artist Vince Gill.

781.643 Blues

Cohn, Lawrence, 1932-

Nothing but the blues : the music and the musicians / edited by Lawrence Cohn. Abbeville Press, 1999. 432 p. : **781.643**

1. Blues (Music) -- History and criticism.
ISBN 9780789206077

LC bl2013054563

A lively history of this distinctly American music form rewards blues lovers with a vivid retelling of the story of their favorite music, enhanced with images from record labels, posters, and ads, as well as photographs of the musicians, promoters, and venues.

Lomax, Alan, 1915-2002

★The **land** where the blues began / Alan Lomax. Pantheon Books, 1993. xv, 539 p. : **781.643**

1. Blues (Music) -- Delta region, Mississippi -- History and criticism 2. Blues (Music) -- Social aspects 3. Blues (Music) -- History and criticism 4. Music, American. 5. Delta Region, Mississippi.
ISBN 9780679404248

LC 91052627

National Book Critics Circle Award for Non-Fiction, 1993.

A journey of discovery through the Mississippi Delta explores the rich African-American musical heritage of the region, as recorded in the words and music of Muddy Waters, Fred Macdowell, Sid Hemphill, and other great masters of the blues.

"If it were a novel, Alan Lomax's long-awaited account of his adventures in the Mississippi Delta would be called sprawling and a must read. It is as delightful and hard to put down as any fictional epic." Booklist.

781.64309 Blues--history

Ferris, William R.

Give my poor heart ease : voices of the Mississippi blues / [interviews by] William Ferris. University of North Carolina Press, c2009. xiv, 302 p. : **781.64309**

1. African Americans -- Mississippi -- Music -- History and criticism. 2. Blues (Music) -- 1961-1970. 3. Blues (Music) -- 1971-1980. 4. Blues (Music) -- Mississippi -- History and criticism. 5. Interviews.
ISBN 9780807833254

LC 2009016647

"This book was published with the assistance of the H. Eugene and Lillian Youngs Lehman Fund of the University of North Carolina Press"--T.p. verso.

Collects interviews and commentary on blues and gospel music from the Mississippi Delta area, and discusses how race relations, connections to the sacred, and Southern life helped mold this style of music.

"Ferris presents transcriptions of stories he captured via films and recording devices from the 1960s and 1970s of Mississippi blues practitioners, preachers, and Parchman Prison inmates. The enclosed CD and DVD bring the package together with stories, blues songs, and gospel recordings. B.B. King and Willie Dixon are the most famous artists included, but the stories of desperately poor sharecroppers and ex-inmates are just as engrossing. The comprehensive bibliography is a great resource." Library Journal.

Gioia, Ted

Delta blues : the life and times of the Mississippi Masters who revolutionized American music / Ted Gioia ; artwork by Neil Harpe. W. W. Norton, c2008. 448 p. **781.64309**

1. Blues (Music) -- Mississippi -- History and criticism 2. Blues musicians. 3. Music. 4. Blues (Music) -- Influence 5. Mississippi -- Social life and customs.
ISBN 9780393062588

LC 2008009412

"Gioia describes the beginnings of the Delta sound with Charley Patton and former Parchman inmates Son House and Bukka White. He relates the stories of such obscure Delta artists as Tommy Johnson and Big Joe Williams before delivering the bulk of the book, which describes the lives and influences of Delta blues icons Robert Johnson, Muddy Waters, Howlin' Wolf, B.B. King, and John Lee Hooker. Gioia ends with a chapter about the rediscovery of Delta legends by rabid blues collectors during the 1960s and then oddly leaps to 1990s performers such as Chris Thomas King and Junior Kimbrough in the last few pages. Though presenting little new information and not geared for the blues fanatic, this is an excellent introduction to Delta blues for the novice and the general reader." Library Journal.

781.648 Electronica

Matos, Michaelangelo

The **underground** is massive : how electronic dance music conquered America / Michaelangelo Matos. Dey Street Books, 2015 368 p. **781.648**

1. Music and society 2. Technopop music 3. Rave culture 4. Electronic music
ISBN 9780062271785

LC bl2015006082

A music journalist chronicles the birth and escalating popularity of electronic dance music, describing how the Millennial generation's use of technology and social media helped fuel the rise and expansion of the musical subculture.

781.65 Jazz

DeVeaux, Scott Knowles

Jazz / Scott DeVeaux, University of Virginia, Gary Giddins, The Graduate Center, City University of New York. W. W. Norton & Company, 2015 xix, 475 p., 66 vari-

ously numbered p., 16 unnumbered p. of plates : **781.65**
1. Jazz -- History and criticism
ISBN 9780393937060
LC 2014038121

This streamlined second edition exposes students to the expressive power of jazz and brings its greatest players to life.

"There are numerous histories of jazz on the market, but renowned critic Giddins and scholar DeVeaux's offering jumps immediately to the top of the list." Booklist

Giddins, Gary

Weather bird : jazz at the dawn of its second century / Gary Giddins. Oxford University Press, 2004. xxiv, 632 p. ; **781.65**
1. Jazz music -- History and criticism 2. Performing arts.
ISBN 9780195156072
LC 2004000654

Includes index.

A companion volume to the landmark Visions of Jazz collects more than 140 writings celebrating jazz, with commentary on everything from modern jazz events and the current top musicians, to studies on the leading jazz figures of the past.

"This book collects more than 140 essays, articles, and reviews that Giddins wrote from 1990 to November 2003. The breadth and depth of his knowledge is extremely impressive, his ear is astounding, and his masterly style routinely achieves the near impossible in writing engagingly about something that inherently eludes description." Library Journal.

Kahn, Ashley

The **house** that Trane built : the story of Impulse Records / Ashley Kahn. W.W. Norton & Co., c2006. viii, 338 p. : **781.65**
1. Coltrane, John, 1926-1967. 2. Impulse! Records -- History. 3. Sound recording industry and trade 4. Jazz music -- History and criticism 5. United States -- Social life and customs -- 20th century.
ISBN 0393058794
LC 2005037218

Traces the story of Impulse Records and the pivotal contributions of avant-garde jazz musician John Coltrane in the 1960s and 1970s, explaining how the label was shaped by thirty-eight of his politically charged recordings.

"The author offers a fascinating insider's view of the sessions that produced not only Coltrane's classics but also top-grade albums by both fiery radicals and such timeless stars as Duke Ellington, Coleman Hawkins and Benny Carter." The Economist.

Marsalis, Wynton, 1961-

Moving to higher ground : how jazz can change your life / Wynton Marsalis with Geoffrey C. Ward. Random House, 2008. 208 p. **781.65**
1. Jazz music appreciation. 2. Jazz music. 3. Music and society. 4. Music appreciation. 5. First person narratives
ISBN 9781400060788
LC 2008016560

The Pulitzer Prize-winning musician offers his own take on jazz music as he discusses the secrets of listening to jazz, the different styles of various jazz musicians, its improvisational principles, and its influence on modern life and on one's view of the world around.

Morgenstern, Dan

Living with jazz : A Reader / Dan Morgenstern ; a reader edited by Sheldon Meyer. Pantheon Books, c2004. xvii, 712 p. ; **781.65**
1. Jazz -- History and criticism.
ISBN 037542072X
LC 2004043432

Includes index.

A collection of essays, biographical profiles, and critical analyses by one of the twentieth century's leading jazz writers includes commentary on the work of jazz entertainers, including Duke Ellington, Ella Fitzgerald, John Coltrane, Dizzy Gillespie, and Louis Armstrong, as well as assessment of the role of jazz in contemporary culture and its influence on modern music.

"This is a compilation of nearly half a century of Morgenstern's profiles, liner notes, record and show reviews and other musings. Morgenstern reminisces about his introduction to jazz in a brief opening memoir, then segues into lengthy sections on his greatest heroes, Louis Armstrong and Duke Ellington. His exuberant characterizations make this monumental volume a stimulating guide to jazz in the second half of the 20th century." Publishers Weekly.

Myers, Marc, 1956-

Why jazz happened / Marc Myers. University of California Press, c2013. 248 p. **781.65**
1. Jazz music -- History and criticism. 2. Music industry and trade. 3. Jazz musicians.
ISBN 9780520268784
LC 2012022218

A comprehensive social history looks at the many forces that shaped this most American of art forms and the many influences that gave rise to jazz's post-war styles.

Torgoff, Martin

Bop apocalypse : jazz, race, the beats, and drugs / Martin Torgoff. Da Capo Press, 2017. 320 p. **781.65**
1. Beat culture 2. Music and race (Social sciences) 3. Drugs -- Social aspects. 4. Jazz -- History and criticism.
ISBN 9780306824753
LC 2016015902

Describes the history of drug culture in America, interweaving tales of the birth of jazz in New Orleans, the rise of swing and bebop and the start of the Beat Generation with the first drug laws and the development of the Federal Bureau of Narcotics.

"A textured story of human hope and hopelessness, of artistry that blossomed in the most daunting and, in some cases, demeaning circumstances." Kirkus.

Ward, Geoffrey C.

Jazz : a history of America's music / Geoffrey C. Ward ; based on a documentary film by Ken Burns written by Geoffrey C. Ward ; with a preface by Ken Burns. Alfred A. Knopf, 2000. x, 489 p. : **781.65**
1. Jazz music -- History and criticism 2. Jazz musicians 3. Music -- History and criticism 4. African American jazz musicians
ISBN 067944551X
LC 00022604

A companion book to the PBS series furnishes a lavish photographic essay that celebrates the contributions of such artists as Louis Armstrong, Duke Ellington, Ella Fitzgerald, and John Coltrane.

"The illustrations are copious, including about 500 pieces and running from cover to cover; the text, picture captions, and sidebars reflect the research that went into the six-year project. A very competent and lovingly rendered history." Booklist.

781.6509 Jazz--history

Chinen, Nate

Playing changes : jazz for the new century / Nate Chinen. Pantheon Books, [2018] 256 p. **781.6509**

1. Jazz music -- History and criticism 2. Jazz musicians 3. Music -- History and criticism 4. African American jazz musicians
ISBN 9781101870341

LC 2017058677

A leading jazz critic charts the origins of jazz history and the influence of commercialized jazz education on the true spirit of the genre and discusses the synergy between jazz and postmillennial hip-hop and R&B music.

"Chinen's virtuoso jazz history will drive readers to listen to the music anew, or for the first time. " Publishers Weekly.

Cooke, Mervyn

The **chronicle** of jazz Oxford University Press, 2013. 256 p. **781.6509**

1. Jazz musicians. 2. Jazz music composers. 3. Jazz music -- History and criticism
ISBN 9780199341009

LC 2013019617

Originally published in 1998 (New York :Abbeville Press,1998).

A year-by-year history of people and events, this lively multi-layered account tells the whole story of jazz music and its personalities.

"This handsome and attractive volume by music professor and writer Cooke covers the entire history of the jazz medium in one accessible and colorful resource." Booklist.

Gioia, Ted

The **history** of jazz / Ted Gioia. Oxford University Press, c2011. 444 p. : **781.6509**

1. Jazz music -- History and criticism
ISBN 9780195399707

LC 2010023182

A panoramic history of the genre brings to life the diverse places in which jazz evolved, traces the origins of its various styles, and offers commentary on the music itself.

"The author relates the story of African American music from its roots in Africa to the international respect it enjoys today. This well-researched, extensively annotated volume covers the major trends and personalities that have shaped jazz. The excellent bibliography and list of recommended listening make this a valuable purchase for libraries building a jazz collection." Library Journal.

Sandke, Randy

Where the dark and the light folks meet : race and the mythology, politics, and business of jazz / Randall Sandke. Scarecrow Press, 2010. x, 277 p. ; **781.6509**

1. Jazz -- History and criticism. 2. Jazz -- Political aspects -- United States. 3. Music and race -- United States.
ISBN 0810866528

LC 2009037977

Looks at the history and nature of jazz, challenging the theory that the music was solely created and driven by African Americans.

"This book is thoroughly researched and documented. This is an important addition to the literature of jazz." Choice.

Alexander, Charles (Guitarist)

Know-it-all jazz : the 50 crucial concepts, styles & performers, each explained in under a minute / editor, Dave Gelly ; contributors, Charles Alexander, Kevin LeGendre, Chris Parker, Brian Priestley, Tony Russell. Wellfleet Press, 2018. 160 p. : **781.6509**

1. Jazz -- History and criticism.
ISBN 1577151755

LC bl2018184444

Provides information about jazz through short entries that each thoroughly explain a single topic.

"Although brief, the contents are not elementary; instead, the Know-It-All books are sophisticated fun. Musician and scholar Gelly encourages readers to trust their ears while they learn to 'get' jazz, then covers different styles of jazz, the major instruments and vocalists, key albums, and what is happening in jazz today." Booklist.

781.65092 Jazz--Biography

Ratliff, Ben

The **jazz** ear : conversations over music / Ben Ratliff. Times Books, 2008. 256 p. **781.65092**

1. Jazz musicians -- Interviews. 2. Jazz music. 3. Music. 4. Musicians. 5. United States -- Social life and customs.
ISBN 9780805081466

LC 2008010122

An intimate exploration into the musical achievements of fifteen living jazz artists profiles jazz as one of the most ephemeral and improvisational performing art forms, in an account that offers insight into the conceptual nature of jazz while drawing on interviews with such figures as Sonny Rollins, Ornette Coleman, and Branford Marsalis.

"Originally published as a series in the New York Times, the 15 conversations presented here consist of Ratliff sitting down with such diverse and talented luminaries as Sonny Rollins, Pat Metheny, Paul Motian, and Dianne Reeves. The treasure of these conversations is not just their fluid and intimate manner but their focus on the recordings that had the greatest influence on the artists and their musical paths. An added bonus is the recommended-listening section, in which Ratliff shares his list of his subjects' seminal recordings. Highly recommended." Library Journal.

781.66 Rock (Rock 'n' roll)

McNeil, Legs

Please kill me : the uncensored oral history of punk / Legs McNeil and Gillian McCain, editors. Grove Press, 1996. xvi, 424 p. : **781.66**

1. Punk rock music -- History and criticism 2. Punk rock musicians -- Interviews. 3. Punk culture. 4. Oral histories
ISBN 0802115888

LC 95049841

"An essential accompaniment to the first, still-thrilling punk records, this preposterously entertaining document just reeks with all the brilliance and filth of the Blank Generation." Kirkus.

Waksman, Steve

This ain't the summer of love : conflict and crossover in heavy metal and punk / Steve Waksman. University of Calif. Press, c2009. xi, 391 p. : **781.66**

1. Heavy metal (Music) -- History and criticism. 2. Punk rock music -- History and criticism.
ISBN 0520257170

LC 2008025957

"Roth Family Foundation music in America imprint"--Prelim. p.

"The number of fanzines and interviews cited is evidence that this is a comprehensively and enthusiastically researched book. As a critical study it provides an original critique of both the genres involved, and of genre itself; the only flipside is that this ends up playing second fiddle to a damn good story." PopMatters.

Yarm, Mark

Everybody loves our town : an oral history of Grunge / Mark Yarm. Crown Archetype, 2011. 592 p. **781.66**

1. Grunge music -- History and criticism 2. Grunge groups -- Interviews. 3. Heavy metal music -- History and criticism 4. Punk rock music -- History and criticism 5. Oral histories
ISBN 9780307464439

LC 2011009192

A tribute to the Pacific Northwest's grunge genre draws on the observations of individuals at the forefront of the movement from Soundgarden and the Melvins to Nirvana and Pearl Jam, citing the influences of such factors as the rise of Seattle's Sub Pop record label and the death of Kurt Cobain.

781.66078 Rock music - festivals

Austerlitz, Saul

★**Just** a shot away : peace, love, and tragedy with the Rolling Stones at Altamont / Saul Austerlitz. Thomas Dunne Books, 2018. 304 p. **781.66078**

1. Rolling Stones (Musical group) 2. Hell's Angels 3. Grateful Dead (Musical group) 4. Altamont Festival (1969 : Tracy, Calif.) 5. Rock concerts 6. Murder 7. Racism 8. Rock music 9. California -- History -- 20th century
ISBN 9781250083197

LC 2018001404

Includes index.

Explores how the 1969 Altamont Festival and the murder of 18-year-old Meredith Hunter during a performance by the Rolling Stones came to symbolize the end of an era and persistent racial tensions.

"Austerlitz (Money for Nothing) offers a blistering exploration of the deadly confluence of racism, stoned naivete, biker belligerence, and rockstar obliviousness that resulted in the murder of 18-year-old Berkeley arts student Meredith Hunter at the Rolling Stones infamously disastrous concert in Altamont, Calif." Publishers Weekly.

781.6609 Rock music--history

Browne, David, 1960-

Fire and rain : the Beatles, Simon and Garfunkel, James Taylor, CSNY and the lost story of 1970 / David Browne. Da Capo Press, 2011. 392 p. **781.6609**

1. Taylor, James, 1948- 2. Beatles (Musical group) 3. Simon and Garfunkel. 4. Crosby, Stills, Nash & Young (Musical group) 5. Musicians -- Interviews 6. Sound recording industry and trade -- History 7. Rock music -- History and criticism 8. Popular culture -- History -- 20th century
ISBN 9780306818509

LC 2011564229

Depicts the interactions between four groups of famous musicians who each released an iconic album in the year 1970, told against the backdrop of the events of that year, including the Kent State killings and the rescue of Apollo 13.

"Browne skillfully interleaves the stories of these musicians during this tumultuous year, making room for substantial walk-ons by other significant industry figures like Bill Graham, Peter Yarrow, Phil Spector, Rita Coolidge, Carole King and Joni Mitchell. Intimately familiar with the music, fully comprehending the cross-pollination among the artists, thoroughly awake to the dynamics of the decade's last gasp, the author expertly captures a volatile and hugely interesting moment in rock history." Kirkus.

Heller, Jason

Strange stars : David Bowie, pop music, and the decade sci-fi exploded / Jason Heller. Melville House Publishing ; London : Blackstock Mews, 2018. 272 p. **781.6609**

1. Popular music -- 1971-1980 -- History and criticism. 2. Science fiction in music. 3. Popular culture
ISBN 9781612196978

LC 2018013060

A Hugo Award-winning author and music journalist revisits a time of unparalleled creativity as the sci-fi world collides with the rock 'n' roll world of the 1970s, presenting a whole generation of revered musicians as the sci-fi obsessed conjurers they really were.

"The accessible title will have readers scouring local bookstores for old sf classics and used record bins for long-forgotten LPs such as Colonel Elliott & The Lunatics' Interstellar Reggae Drive (1973) and Zed's Visions of Dune (1979)." Library Journal.

Hopper, Jessica

The **first** collection of criticism by a living female rock critic / Jessica Hopper. Featherproof Books, 2015. 250 p. **781.6609**

1. Rock music 2. Rock musicians 3. Music critics
ISBN 9780983186335

LC bl2015023805

"Rock music fans of all genders and stripes will find a lot to chew on in these pages." Library Journal.

Hyden, Steven, 1977-

Twilight of the gods : a journey to the end of classic rock / Steven Hyden. Dey Street Books, 2018. 320 p. **781.6609**

1. Rock music -- History and criticism 2. Rock musicians 3. Popular music -- History and criticism 4. Musicians 5. Essays
ISBN 9780062657121

LC bl2018072576

The author of the critically acclaimed Your Favorite Band Is Killing Me presents a frank and revelatory assessment of the current state of classic rock, assessing its past and future, its enduring impact and what its loss could mean in economic and cultural arenas.

McKeen, William, 1954-

Everybody had an ocean : music and mayhem in 1960s Los Angeles / William McKeen. Chicago Review Press, 2017. 422 p. **781.6609**

1. Beach Boys (Musical group) 2. Byrds (Musical group) 3. Popular culture -- Los Angeles, California 4. Popular music -- History and criticism 5. Rock music -- 1961-1970 -- History and criticism. 6. Rock music -- Los Angeles, California -- History and criticism. 7. Los Angeles, California 8. Southern California, 9. California
ISBN 9781613734919

LC 2016029172

"Using a synthesis of memoirs and biographies, McKeen creates a sprawling, entertaining, and sometime lurid, narrative about artists who, bursting with creative energy, converged in L.A." Booklist.

Reynolds, Simon, 1963-

Shock and awe : glam rock and its legacy, from the seventies to the twenty-first century / Simon Reynolds. Dey Street Books, 2016 304 p. **781.6609**

1. Bowie, David, 1947-2016 2. T. Rex (Musical group) 3. Roxy Music (Musical group) 4. Progressive rock music 5. Rock musicians -- England 6. Fame 7. Excess (Philosophy)

ISBN 9780062279804

LC bl2016045701

A definitive history of glam and glitter rock, celebrating its outlandish fashion and outrageous stars, shows how the original glam artists' obsession with fame, extreme fashion and theatrical excess are still prevalent today.

"For neo-glamsters, a blueprint for how to get things done; for oldsters, a nostalgic look into a shining, glittery era." Kirkus.

Robb, John, 1961-

Punk rock : an oral history / John Robb ; edited by Oliver Craske. PM Press, 2012, c2006. xv, 562 p. : **781.6609**

1. Punk rock music -- History and criticism. 2. Rock music -- History and criticism. 3. Punk rock musicians -- Interviews. 4. Rock musicians -- Interviews. 5. Great Britain -- Popular culture -- History -- 20th century. 6. Oral histories

ISBN 9781604860054

LC 2011939680

Originally published: London : Ebury Press, 2006.

Through more than 150 interviews with key players in the punk-rock scene, the author gives a thorough account of the rise of his important new genre, from its roots in the 1960s to the the influence of such acts as The Clash, The Sex Pistols, Henry Rollins and Black Flag, the Buzzcocks and many more.

Savage, Jon

★**1966** : the year the decade exploded / Jon Savage. Faber & Faber, 2016 620 p. **781.6609**

1. Social history. 2. Popular culture. 3. Popular music. 4. Counterculture.

ISBN 9780571277629

LC bl2016036637

Paying tribute to the year that shaped the pop future of the century, an exploration into the social and cultural heart of the decade, drawing on archival primary sources, reveals a unique chemistry of ideas, substances, freedom of expression and dialogue that exploded in unparalleled creativity.

Wiederhorn, Jon

Louder than hell : the definitive oral history of metal / Jon Wiederhorn & Katherine Turman ; introduction by Scott Ian of Anthrax ; afterword by Rob Halford of Judas Priest. it Books, 2013. xiii, 718 p., 48 unnumbered p. of plates : **781.6609**

1. Heavy metal music -- History and criticism. 2. Heavy metal musicians -- Interviews. 3. Heavy metal groups. 4. Counterculture -- History -- 20th century. 5. Great Britain -- Popular culture -- History -- 20th century. 6. United States -- Popular culture -- History -- 20th century. 7. Oral histories 8. Interviews.

ISBN 9780061958281

LC bl2013023546

Introduction and afterword responsibility statements from dust jacket.

Offers a chronological look at the history of heavy metal music through the words of the artists themselves culled from over four hundred interviews conducted over twenty-five years.

781.68 Western art music (Classical music)

Chilingirian, Levon,

The **classical** music book / contributors: Levon Chilingirian [and 11 others]. DK Publishing, 2018. 352 p. : **781.68**

1. Music appreciation.

ISBN 9781465473424

LC 2018560171

Includes index.

Combines accessible, authoritative text and quotes with bold explanatory graphics in an accessible guide to classical music that covers dozens of essential compositions from early through modern times to demystify key salient themes and ideas.

782.1 Operas and related dramatic vocal forms

Gay, John, 1685-1732

The **beggar's** opera / edited by Edgar V. Roberts; music edited by Edward Smith University of Nebraska Press, 1969 xxix, 238 p. **782.1**

1. Ballad operas -- Librettos. 2. Ballad operas -- Vocal scores with piano. 3. English drama -- Restoration, 1660-1700.

ISBN 9780803253612

LC 68021878

Appendices (p. 84-238): A. The music of The beggar's opera, with keyboard accompaniments realized from the basses of John Christopher Pepusch by Edward Smith.--B. Chronology.

The Beggar's Opera introduced to theater the ballad-opera and an immortal cast of characters.

Hischak, Thomas S.

The **Oxford** companion to the American musical : theatre, film, and television / Thomas Hischak. Oxford University Press, c2008. xxxiv, 923 p. : **782.1**

1. Musicals -- United States

ISBN 9780195335330

LC 2007052436

A reference that covers American stage, film, and television musicals from 1860 to 2007 offers information on the musical productions and the historical evolution of the musical, as well as on performers, composers, and producers.

"This is an overview of the American musical theater on the stage, silver screen, and small screen. The 2000-plus entries are brief but detailed accounts of plots; production histories; careers of actors, dancers, musicians, lyricists, composers, choreographers, and directors; organizations; and genres (animated musicals, frontier musicals). . . . This thorough work provides enjoyable reading for anyone interested in American theatrical history in general and musicals in particular." School Library Journal.

Maslon, Laurence

★**Broadway** : the American musical / Laurence Maslon ; based on the documentary film by Michael Kantor. Applause Theatre & Cinema Books, 2010, c2004. 497 p. : **782.1**

1. Musicals -- New York City -- History and criticism 2. Broadway, New York City. 3. New York City.

ISBN 9781423491033

LC bl2010016394

Presents a history of the Broadway musical theater, including summaries of the shows, photographs of the stars, posters, sheet music, production stills, and essays by theater luminaries.

Miranda, Lin-Manuel, 1980-
Hamilton : the revolution / Lin-Manuel Miranda, with Jeremy McCarter. Grand Central Pub., 2016. 288 p. **782.1**

1. Miranda, Lin-Manuel, 1980- Hamilton. 2. Hamilton, Alexander, 1757-1804 3. Hamilton (Musical) 4. Musicals -- Production and direction. 5. Theater -- Production and direction. 6. Popular culture -- History -- 21st century. 7. Founding Fathers of the United States. 8. Broadway, New York City Musicals.
ISBN 9781455539741
LC 2015957946

The Tony Award-winning composer-lyricist-star takes readers behind the scenes of his groundbreaking hit musical, which is filled with romance, drama, violence, patriotism and adventure and details the many dramatic episodes in Alexander Hamilton's life.

"A treasure trove of information, they highlight his writing process, musical influences (ranging from show tunes to pop to hip-hop), amusing anecdotes, and so much more." Library Journal.

Mordden, Ethan, 1947-
Anything goes : a history of American musical theatre / Ethan Mordden. Oxford University Press, 2013. 360 p. **782.1**

1. Musicals. 2. Theater. 3. Dancing. 4. Musical writing. 5. Broadway, New York City.
ISBN 9780199892839
LC 2013000208

Discography.

Anything Goes stages a grand revue of the musical from the 1920s through the 1970s, narrated in Mordden's famously witty, scholarly, and conversational style.

"Mordden brightly differentiates those forms, citing hundreds and analyzing dozens of examples of them in a sweeping narrative that, with plenty of sass and tang, wit and even a little snark, not to mention scholarly precision, is obviously the best-ever history of the musical and likely to remain so for a very long time." Booklist.

Porter, Cole, 1891-1964
Selected lyrics : Selected Lyrics / Cole Porter ; Robert Kimball, editor. Library of America, c2006. xxii, 178 p. ; **782.1**

1. Musicals 2. Songs -- Texts.
ISBN 1931082944
LC 2006040809

Includes index.

A collection of lyrics by the twentieth-century American songwriter and lyricist features pieces that reflect the writer's observations about the pain of emotional relationships and tongue-in-cheek beliefs about the unlikely nature of permanence.

"For those hankering after a happy medium between American poetry and American Idolatry, Kimball's reading edition affords a golden opportunity to brush up on your Porterjust be sure to listen up, too, if you really want to be wowed." New York Times Book Review.

Rose, Michael, 1934-
The **birth** of an opera : fifteen masterpieces from Poppea to Wozzeck / Michael Rose. W.W. Norton & Company, c2013. 480 p. **782.1**

1. Operas -- History and criticism. 2. Creation (literary, artistic, etc.) 3. Composition (Music) 4. Composers.
ISBN 9780393060430
LC 2012039470

Including Monteverdi, Mozart, Puccini, Wagner and Berg, this guide describes the stories behind the writing and creation of fifteen different operas, detailing the circumstances of each composer's life and times and the impact their environment had on their art.

Sondheim, Stephen, 1930-
Look, I made a hat : collected lyrics (1981-2011) with attendant comments, amplifications, dogmas, harangues, digressions, anecdotes and miscellany / Stephen Sondheim. Alfred A. Knopf, 2011. 480 p. **782.1**

1. Musicals -- Excerpts -- Librettos 2. Composition (Music) 3. Lyric writing 4. Songwriting
ISBN 9780307593412
LC 2011014604

A second volume of collected lyrics by the iconic music artist features accompanying discussions of his experiences in the theater, memories about some of his important collaborations and dissections of what he believes to be his most significant successes and failures, providing additional coverage of his creative process and non-sequitur pieces.

"With this chronological continuation of Finishing the Hat, musical theater lyricist and composer Sondheim has produced another delightful book that melds lyrics, anecdotes, opinions, and whimsy...As in the previous volume, Sondheim includes descriptions about each show, as well as running commentary. Sondheim's general essays (the harangues and dogmas of the subtitle) show him at his opinionated and literate best.... certainly all libraries owning the first volume will want the second." Library Journal.

Romano, Renee Christine
Historians on Hamilton : how a blockbuster musical is restaging America's past / edited by Renee C. Romano and Claire Bond Potter. Rutgers University Press, 2018. 396 p. **782.1**

1. Miranda, Lin-Manuel, 1980- Hamilton 2. Hamilton, Alexander, 1757-1804 3. Musicals 4. Founding Fathers of the United States 5. Politicians 6. Theater -- History 7. United States -- History -- 1783-1815 8. Biographies
ISBN 9780813590295
LC 2017033851

America has gone Hamilton crazy. Lin-Manuel Miranda's Tony-winning musical has spawned sold-out performances, a triple platinum cast album, and a score so catchy that it is being used to teach U.S. history in classrooms across the country. But just how historically accurate is Hamilton? And how is the show itself making history?

782.103 Operas--dictionaries

Sadie, Stanley
The **Grove** book of operas / edited by Stanley Sadie. Oxford University Press, c2006. xxiii, 740 p., 16 p. of plates : **782.103**

1. Opera -- Encyclopedias 2. Encyclopedias
ISBN 9780195309072
LC 2006015323

Rev. ed. of: New Grove book of operas.

Synopses and descriptions of more than 250 operas are covered in this collection of entries that are written by leading authorities on the opera and include information on musicians and performers, performance style, operatic history, literary and social background, and more.

782.25 Small-scale vocal forms

Perry, Imani, 1972-
May we forever stand : a history of the Black National Anthem

/ Imani Perry. The University of North Carolina Press, 2018. xiv, 280 p. ; **782.25**

1. Johnson, James Weldon, 1871-1938 Lift every voice and sing 2. Johnson, John Rosamond 1873-1954. Lift every voice and sing 3. Civil rights 4. Social change 5. Intellectual life -- African Americans 6. African Americans -- Songs and music. 7. United States -- Race relations.

ISBN 9781469638607

Hurston/Wright Legacy Award: Nonfiction, 2019.

In this rich, poignant, and readable work, Imani Perry tells the story of the Black National Anthem as it traveled from South to North, from civil rights to black power, and from countless family reunions to Carnegie Hall and the Oval Office. Drawing on a wide array of sources, Perry uses "Lift Every Voice and Sing" as a window on the powerful ways African Americans have used music and culture to organize, mourn, challenge, and celebrate for more than a century.

782.4 Secular forms

Bostridge, Ian

Schubert's winter journey : anatomy of an obsession / Ian Bostridge. Alfred A. Knopf, 2015. 336 p. **782.4**

1. Bostridge, Ian 2. Schubert, Franz, 1797-1828. Winterreise. 3. Songs -- History and criticism 4. Composers -- Austria.

ISBN 9780307961631

LC 2014020088

Drawing on his first-hand experience with Schubert's Winterreise, considered by many to be the single greatest piece of music ever written for the male solo voice; his musical knowledge; and his training as a scholar, the author explores the enigmas and subtle meanings of each of the 24 songs comprising this legendary masterpiece.

782.42 Songs

Gioia, Ted

Work songs / Ted Gioia. Duke University Press, 2006. xiii, 352 p. ; **782.42**

1. Work songs -- History and criticism. 2. Working class -- History and criticism.

ISBN 0822337266

LC 2005026241

"Gioia poignantly tells the story of work songs sung by everyone from prehistoric hunters to today's consumers. His task involved drawing on multilayered and diverse resources that include travel literature, slave narratives, historical accounts and personal journals, myths and legends, biographies, and labor union writings; the focus is on the rhythms, melodies, and lyrics of music that has accompanied such tasks as raising and lowering sails, felling trees, and weaving and sewing garments. This book provides an opportunity to re-experience the history and dignity of our human toils. Highly recommended for public and academic libraries." Library Journal.

Lynskey, Dorian

33 revolutions per minute : a history of protest songs, from Billie Holiday to Green Day / Dorian Lynskey. Ecco, c2011. 320 p. **782.42**

1. Music -- Political aspects. 2. Popular music -- Political aspects 3. Protest songs, American -- History and criticism 4. Popular culture -- Political aspects. 5. United States -- Popular culture -- History -- 20th century. 6. Great Britain -- Popular culture -- History -- 20th century.

ISBN 9780061670152

LC 2010024247

"The author delves into the protest song movement from 1939 to the present. Dividing the time into discrete sections, he focuses on particular examples but also provides information on related songs. The author traces the historical context, using valuable contemporary sources and quotations from the artists. Lynskey's flowing prose and well-turned phrases bring the times to life. He is especially adept at integrating the songs into the wider social milieu, which extends the appeal to cultural historians as well as music lovers." Library Journal.

McMurray, Jacob,

Taking punk to the masses : from Nowhere to Nevermind / [edited by] Jacob McMurray. Fantographics Books, 2011 xi, 233 p. : **782.42**

1. Nirvana (Musical group) 2. Punk rock music -- United States -- History and criticism. 3. Grunge music -- Washington (State) -- Seattle -- History and criticism. 4. Punk rock musicians -- United States.

ISBN 9781606994337

LC 2013560052

Includes index.

Using key artifacts from the Experience Music Project collection, illustrates the evolution of punk rock from underground subculture to the mainstream.

Meacham, Jon

Songs of America : patriotism, protest, and the music that made a nation / Jon Meacham and Tim McGraw. Random House, [2019] 320 p. **782.42**

1. Music -- Political aspects -- United States. 2. Music -- Social aspects -- United States. 3. Protest songs -- United States -- History and criticism. 4. Patriotic music -- United States -- History and criticism.

ISBN 9780593132951

LC 2019014364

A Pulitzer Prize-winning author and Grammy-winning music artist celebrate America and the music that inspired people and illuminated eras, from the Revolutionary War to the present.

"Not in the musicological class of Alan Lomax or at the historical heights of David Hackett Fischer's Liberty and Freedom, but worthy reading for the anthemically minded." Kirkus.

Polenberg, Richard

Hear my sad story : the true tales that inspired Stagolee, John Henry, and other traditional American folk songs / Richard Polenberg. Cornell University Press, 2015 280 p. **782.42**

1. Folk songs, American -- History and criticism 2. Folk songs -- History and criticism 3. Folk music -- History and criticism

ISBN 9781501700026

LC 2015016652

In Hear My Sad Story, Richard Polenberg describes the historical events that led to the writing of many famous American folk songs that served as touchstones for generations of American musicians, lyricists, and folklorists.

"A well-written primer of American folk culture that should be in any serious popular music collection." Library Journal.

Sandburg, Carl

The **American** songbag / Carl Sandburg. Harcourt Brace Jovanovich, 1990, c1927. xxix, 495 p. : **782.42**

1. Ballads, English -- United States 2. Folk music -- United States 3. Folk-songs, English -- United States 4. Songs, English -- United States

ISBN 9780156056502

LC BL 99712752

"A Harvest/HBJ book."

Originally published: New York : Harcourt, Brace & Co., 1927.

Two hundred and eighty songs and ballads trace the growth of America

782.42164 Western popular songs

Kapilow, Robert

Listening for America : inside the great American songbook from Gershwin to Sondheim / Rob Kapilow. Liveright Publishing Corporation, 2019. 448 p. **782.421640973**

1. Popular music -- History and criticism 2. Songs -- United States -- 20th century -- Analysis, appreciation. 3. Musicals -- History and criticism 4. Songs -- History and criticism 5. United States -- Popular culture

ISBN 9781631490293

LC 2019026121

A composer, conductor, and the host of the NPR's What Makes It Great? explores the songs and stories of eight of the twentieth century's most beloved American composers, including Porter, Gershwin and Sondheim and celebrates what makes their work unforgettable.

"A treat for music fans and a great addition to any performing arts or popular culture collection." Booklist

Lehman, David, 1948-

A **fine** romance : Jewish songwriters, American songs / David Lehman. Nextbook/Schocken, c2009. 249 p. ; **782.42164**

1. Jewish composers -- United States. 2. Jewish lyricists -- United States. 3. Popular music -- United States -- History and criticism. 4. Popular music -- United States -- Jewish influences.

ISBN 0805242503

LC 2009005942

A look at the formation of the American songbook-the timeless numbers that became jazz standards, iconic love songs, and sound tracks to famous movies-and explores the extraordinary fact that this songbook was written almost exclusively by Jews. -- Dust jacket.

"Lehman investigates the lasting impact of 20th-century Jewish popular songwriters in America, ranging from Irving Berlin's and Jerome Kern's early efforts in the 1910s through George Gershwin, Harold Arlen, Richard Rodgers, Lorenz Hart, and Oscar Hammerstein II to Leonard Bernstein and the early 1960s. In fluid prose and expert foreshadowing and summations, the author conveys the personality of each musician or writer and recommends selected versions of his favorite songs." Library Journal.

Mike D., 1965-

Beastie Boys book / Mike D. and Adam Horovitz. Spiegel & Grau, [2018] 576 p. **782.42164**

1. Mike D, 1965- 2. Horovitz, Adam 3. Yauch, Adam, 1964-2012 4. Beastie Boys. 5. Rap music 6. Rap musicians. 7. Music industry and trade 8. Popular culture

ISBN 9780812995541

LC 2018004935

With a style as distinctive and eclectic as a Beastie Boys album, Beastie Boys Book upends the typical music memoir. Alongside the band narrative you will find rare photos, original illustrations, a cookbook by chef Roy Choi, a graphic novel, a map of Beastie Boys' New York, mixtape playlists, pieces by guest contributors, and many more surprises.

Thomas, Richard F., 1950-

Why Bob Dylan matters / Richard F. Thomas. Dey Street Books, 2017 256 p. **782.42164**

1. Dylan, Bob, 1941- 2. Folk music, American. 3. Popular music -- History and criticism 4. Rock music -- History and criticism 5. Rock musicians

ISBN 9780062685735

LC 2017041732

A Harvard classics professor and expert on Bob Dylan expands on his popular seminar in a full-length, meditative examination of the Nobel Prize-winning lyricist's enduring influence, sharing insights into Dylan's formative experiences against a backdrop of western and classical literature.

"This new work doesn't simply examine Dylan's appeal or the deep meaning of his lyrics but tracks his cultural importance and ongoing relevance in today's tumbled-around world." Library Journal.

Wald, Elijah

Dylan goes electric! : Newport, Seeger, Dylan, and the night that split the sixties / Elijah Wald. Dey Street Books, 2015. 256 p. **782.42164**

1. Dylan, Bob, 1941- 2. Folk-rock music (Vocal), American 3. Popular music -- 1961-1970 -- History and criticism 4. Music -- Influence 5. Folk music, American -- History and criticism. 6. United States -- Social life and customs -- 20th century

ISBN 9780062366689

LC 2017561065

On the evening of July 25, 1965, Bob Dylan took the stage at Newport Folk Festival, backed by an electric band, and roared into his new rock hit, Like a Rolling Stone. The audience of committed folk purists and political activists who had hailed him as their acoustic prophet reacted with a mix of shock, booing, and scattered cheers. It was the shot heard round the world--Dylan's declaration of musical independence, the end of the folk revival, and the birth of rock as the voice of a generation--and one of the defining moments in twentieth-century music.

"Some of this material has been covered before, but rarely has it been done so knowingly, lovingly, and felicitously. All the players, too, are here (Joan Baez, Dave Van Ronk, Johnny Cash, et al.), and, though nostalgic, the book makes a major contribution to modern musical history." Booklist.

782.421642092 Country musicians--singers

Smarsh, Sarah

She come by it natural : Dolly Parton and the women who lived her songs / Sarah Smarsh. Scribner, 2020 208 p. **782.421642092**

1. Parton, Dolly, 1946- Influence 2. Smarsh, Sarah 3. Women country musicians 4. Blue collar women 5. Poor women 6. Women's role

ISBN 9781982157289

Growing up amid Kansas wheat fields and airplane factories, Sarah Smarsh witnessed firsthand the particular vulnerabilities--and strengths --of women in working poverty. Meanwhile, country songs by female artists played in the background, telling powerful stories about life, men, hard times, and surviving. In her family, she writes, "country music was foremost a language among women. It's how we talked to each other in a place where feelings aren't discussed." And no one provided that language better than Dolly Parton. In She Come By It Natural, Smarsh explores the overlooked contributions to social progress by such women--including those averse to the term "feminism"--as exemplified by Dolly Parton's life and art.

"Smarsh's luminescent prose and briskly tempered storytelling make for an illuminating take on a one-of-a-kind artist." Publishers Weekly

782.421643 Blues--songs

Young, Kevin, 1970-

Blues poems / selected and edited by Kevin Young. Knopf, 2003. 256 p. ; **782.421643**

1. Blues (Music) -- Texts. 2. African American poetry 3. American poetry.

ISBN 9780375414589

LC 2003053149

The rich emotional palette of the blues is fully represented here in verse that pays tribute to the heart and humor of the music, and in poems that swing with its history and hard-bitten hope. --From publisher description.

782.421649 Rap songs

Abdurraqib, Hanif, 1983-

Go ahead in the rain : notes to A Tribe Called Quest / Hanif Abdurraqib. University of Texas Press, 2019. 200 p. **782.421649**

1. Abdurraqib, Hanif, 1983- 2. Tribe Called Quest (Musical group) 3. Rap music 4. Rap musicians 5. Hip-hop culture 6. Bands (Music)

ISBN 9781477316481

LC 2018031799

Kirkus Prize for Nonfiction finalist, 2019.

Longlisted for the National Book Award for Nonfiction, 2019.

How does one pay homage to A Tribe Called Quest? The seminal rap group brought jazz into the genre, resurrecting timeless rhythms to create masterpieces such as The Low End Theory and Midnight Marauders. Poet and essayist Hanif Abdurraqib digs into the group's history and draws from his own experience to reflect on how its distinctive sound resonated among fans like himself. The result is as ambitious and genre-bending as the rap group itself.

"Abdurraqib frames himself as a participant in the story. His journey is integral as the music weaves into his existence, and he conveys the passion felt when art gives voice to our lives. This is his homage, written at times directly to readers and at others to the members of the group." Library Journal

Ashon, Will

★**Chamber** music : Wu-Tang and America, in 36 pieces / Will Ashon. Faber & Faber, 2019. 374 p. **782.421649**

1. Wu-Tang Clan (Musical group) 2. Rap music 3. Rap musicians 4. Music and society 5. African American musicians 6. New York City -- Social life and customs -- 20th century

ISBN 9780571350001

LC bl2019021748

"This is nothing less than a literary tour de force through hundreds of years of American history as seen through one hip-hop band and one landmark album." Booklist.

Chuck D., 1960-

Chuck D presents this day in rap and hip-hop history / with Duke Eatmon, Ron Maskell, Lorrie Boula, and Jonathan Bernstein ; foreword by Shepard Fairey. Black Dog & Leventhal, 2017. ix, 342 p. : **782.421649**

1. Rap music -- History and criticism. 2. Hip-hop culture 3. Rap music industry and trade 4. Rap music -- Lyrics

ISBN 9780316430975

LC 2017568883

Includes index.

A comprehensive, chronological survey of rap and hip-hop from 1973 to the present, written by one of the industry's most influential lyricists, is based on his long-running show on Rapstation.com and details the most iconic moments and relevant songs from the genre's recorded history.

Edwards, Paul, 1982-

The **concise** guide to hip-hop music : a fresh look at the art of hip-hop, from old-school beats to freestyle rap / Paul Edwards. St. Martin's Griffin, 2015. 232 p. ; **782.421649**

1. Rap (Music) -- History and criticism. 2. Rap (Music) -- Analysis, appreciation. 3. Rap musicians.

ISBN 9781250034816

LC 2014034012

"In 1973, the music scene was forever changed by the emergence of hip-hop. Masterfully blending the rhythmic grooves of funk and soul with layered beats and chanted rhymes, artists such as DJ Kool Herc and Grandmaster Flash paved the way for an entire new genre and generation of musicians. In this comprehensive, accessible guide, Paul Edwards breaks down the difference between old school and new school, recaps the biggest influencers of the genre, and sets straight the myths and misconceptions of the artists and their music. Fans old and new alike will all learn something new about the history and development of hip-hop, from its inception up through the current day."--Back cover.

Greenburg, Zack O'Malley

3 kings : Diddy, Dr. Dre, Jay-Z, and hip-hop's multibillion-dollar rise / Zack O'Malley Greenburg. Little, Brown, 2018. 320 p. **782.421649**

1. Jay-Z, 1969- 2. Dr. Dre, 1965- 3. Diddy, 1969- 4. Death Row Records -- History 5. N. W. A. (Musical group) 6. Rap musicians -- United States 7. Rap music. 8. Hip-hop culture 9. African Americans 10. United States -- Social life and customs

ISBN 9780316316538

LC 2017021046

Tracing the careers of hip-hop's three most dynamic stars, this deeply reported history brilliantly examines the entrepreneurial genius of the first musician tycoons: Diddy, Dr. Dre, and Jay-Z.

"Greenburg details the thinking of these three tastemakers throughout their musical careers and into their corporate identities as they focus on shaping the way people enjoy their lives. Each approached rap music through a different outlet. Each carved out a different lasting mark. And all slowly but intentionally made decisions that impacted the business world on a grand scale. Greenburg offers a refreshing perspective on three immensely talented and popular personalities." Booklist.

Iandoli, Kathy

God Save the queens : the essential history of women in hip-hop / Kathy Iandoli. Dey Street Books, 2019. 320 p. **782.421649**

1. Women rap musicians 2. Hip-hop culture 3. Rap music 4. Women musicians

ISBN 9780062878502

LC bl2019035953

Paying tribute to the women of hip-hop, and exploring issues of gender, money, sexuality, violence, objectification and more, this important and monumental work of music journalism finally gives these influential artists the respect they have long deserved.

Riggs, Thomas, 1963-

St. James encyclopedia of hip hop culture / Thomas J. Riggs, editor. St. James Press, 2018 xxiv, 579 p. ; **782.421649**

1. Rap (Music) -- Encyclopedias. 2. Hip-hop -- Encyclopedias.
ISBN 9781410380814

LC 2017049826

"Examines the history and contributions of hip hop to American and global culture".-- Provided by publisher.

Tobak, Vikki

Contact high : a visual history of hip-hop / Vikki Tobak. Chlarkson Potter, 2018. 320 p. **782.421649**

1. Hip-hop culture 2. Rap music 3. Rap musicians 4. Rap music industry and trade
ISBN 9780525573883

LC 2017057961

A collection of photographic essays on rap and hip-hop legends draws on details from their intimate contact sheets, combining industry legend interviews and essays with rare photo-shoot outtakes to share related insights into the artistry of genre memorabilia.

"Journalist Tobak (Detroit News; Paper) provides a valuable lens into the history of hip-hop, offering iconic photographs spanning 19792012, along with the contact sheets." Library Journal.

Watkins, S. Craig (Samuel Craig)

★**Hip** hop matters : politics, pop culture, and the struggle for the soul of a movement / S. Craig Watkins. Beacon Press, c2005. 295 p. ; **782.421649**

1. Rap music -- History and criticism 2. Hip-hop culture.
ISBN 0807009865

LC 2004024187

Explores the evolution of hip-hop and the backlash against it, from Detroit Mayer Kwame Killpatrick, the nation's first hip-hop mayor, to the reception of the music on college campuses, where debates over its misogyny thrive.

"The author presents a concise, clear history of the hip-hop movement in the US and uses it as a springboard for discussion of contemporary issues of politics, pop culture, and struggle." Choice.

Westhoff, Ben

Dirty South : Outkast, Lil Wayne, Soulja Boy, and the Southern rappers who reinvented hip-hop / Ben Westhoff. Chicago Review Press, 2011. 288 p. **782.421649**

1. Rap (Music) -- Southern States -- History and criticism. 2. Rap musicians -- Southern States 3. Popular music -- Southern States 4. Hip-hop culture 5. Southern States -- Social life and customs -- 21st century
ISBN 9781569766064

LC 2010053907

"An exploration of the musical and personal terrain of what has come to be known as the Southern sound of rap by such artists as Lil Wayne, Young Jeezy, and Ludacris. Westhoff convincingly details how Southern rap music--party music, full of hypnotic hooks and sing-along choruses--took over from dominant East Coast and West Coast rap styles by replacing normal rap structures and metaphor-heavy rhymes, in favor of chants, grunts and shouts. In fact, the beauty of Westhoff's descriptions of the genre as a whole and various songs in particular will make old fans as well as newbies want to search out and play classic CDs such as OutKast's Aquemini and Kings of Crunk by Lil Jon. And Westhoff's personal trips to the home bases of each artist he presents show how the personalities of the artists reinforce their music." Publishers Weekly.

Original gangstas : the untold story of Dr. Dre, Eazy-E, Ice Cube, Tupac Shakur, and the birth of West Coast rap / Ben Westhoff. Hachette Books, 2016. viii, 422 p. **782.421649**

1. Dr. Dre, 1965- 2. Wright, Eric, 1964-1995 3. Ice Cube 4. Shakur, Tupac, 1971-1996 5. Notorious B.I.G., 1972-1997 6. Rap musicians 7. Hip-hop culture -- History 8. Inner city 9. Gangsta rap 10. South Central Los Angeles, California 11. Los Angeles, California 12. Oral histories
ISBN 9780316383899

LC 2016941451

Includes index.

This wide-ranging history of West Coast rap offers in-depth biographies of its leading artists -- including Eazy-E, Dr. Dre, Ice Cube, Tupac Shakur, and others -- as well as accounts of the rivalries between them. It also offers insightful examinations of the glamorizing of thug life and the popularity of hip hop, the consequences of fame, and the still-unsolved murders of Tupac and Biggie Smalls.

"Westhoff's impressive research makes this an invaluable overview of the musical influences and legal nightmares of West Coast raps main players ." Publishers Weekly.

add subject heading Rock musicians--singers

Cohen, Rich

★The **sun** and the moon and the Rolling Stones / Rich Cohen. Spiegel & Grau, 2016. 381 p. **782.42166092**

1. Rolling Stones (Musical group) 2. Rolling Stone Magazine 3. Journalists. 4. Rock musicians. 5. Rock groups.
ISBN 9780804179232

LC 2015035782

Describes the history of the English rock group, documenting the formation of the band in the 1960s, their rise to world fame, skills as innovative songwriters, and continuing endurance into the present day.

"A compact and conversant history that makes the story new again, capturing the Rolling Stones in all their Faustian glory." Kirkus.

Cross, Charles R.

Here we are now : the lasting impact of Kurt Cobain / Charles R. Cross. It Books, 2014. 192 p. **782.42166092**

1. Cobain, Kurt, 1967-1994 Influence. 2. Nirvana (Musical group) 3. Rock music -- 1991-2000 -- History and criticism. 4. Music -- Influence. 5. Rock musicians 6. Addiction
ISBN 9780062308214

LC 2013045769

"This short but intriguing book explores the troubled musician as a kind of muse for seemingly unrelated fields (modern hip-hop, medical studies, high-end fashion) as well as a champion for gay and women's rights and racial equality." Library Journal.

Cutler, Sam

You can't always get what you want : my life with the Rolling Stones, the Grateful Dead and other wonderful reprobates / Sam Cutler. ECW Press, 2009. 326 p. **782.42166092**

1. Cutler, Sam. 2. Concert agents 3. Road managers. 4. Entertainers -- Managers, booking agents, etc. 5. Rock music.
ISBN 9781550229325

LC oc2009052481

"Effortlessly readable, packed with entertaining, sleazy, behind-the-scenes tales." Portland Mercury.

Gould, Jonathan, 1951-

Can't buy me love : the Beatles, Britain, and America / Jonathan Gould. Harmony Books, 2007. 661 p. : **782.42166092**

1. Beatles (Musical group) 2. Rock music -- United States -- History and criticism 3. Rock music -- Great Britain -- History and criticism 4. Popular culture -- History -- 1960-1969.
ISBN 0307353370

LC 2007013240

A cultural and musical history of the 1960s in Britain and America captures the pulse of the era through the music of the Beatles, critically analyzing why the group became a trans-Atlantic phenomenon while discussing the evolution of the group's music.

"Gould's combination group biography, cultural history, and musical criticism artfully places the Beatles in their time and social context while examining with great skill how they became an international phenomenon comparable only to themselves." Booklist.

Gruen, Bob

New York Dolls : photographs / Bob Gruen ; [introduction by Lenny Kaye ; interviews by Lenny Kaye, David Johansen and Sylvain Sylvain ; afterword by Morrissey]. Abrams Image, 2008. 158 p. : **782.42166092**

1. New York Dolls (Musical group) Pictorial works. 2. Glam rock musicians -- United States 3. Rock musicians -- United States
ISBN 0810972719

LC 2008013074

Photographer Bob Gruen offers the first photography collection devoted to the New York Dolls, featuring over two hundred images celebrating their unprecedented style.

Guesdon, Jean-Michel

All the songs : the story behind every Beatles release / preface by Patti Smith ; Jean-Michel Guesdon & Philippe Margotin ; Scott Freiman, consulting editor. Black Dog & Leventhal Publishers, 2013 671 p. : **782.42166092**

1. Beatles (Musical group) 2. Songs -- Lyrics 3. Songwriting 4. Lyric writing 5. Composition (Music)
ISBN 9781579129521

LC bl2013048728

Presents the stories behind the writing and recording of all 213 songs released by The Beatles, in a work arranged chronologically and illustrated with hundreds of photographs.

"Arranged chronologically by album, the book includes for each song basic information (songwriter, track length, number of takes, etc.), a brief discussion of how it was written and recorded, and an overall assessment. [N]umerous anecdotes and quotations from the group keep the book entertaining and accessible even to more casual music fans." Library Journal.

Harrison, George, 1943-2001

George Harrison on George Harrison : interviews and encounters / edited by Ashley Kahn. Chicago Review Press, 2020. 432 p. **782.42166092**

1. Harrison, George, 1943-2001 2. Beatles (Musical group) 3. Rock musicians 4. Guitarists 5. Fame 6. Rock music 7. Interviews 8. Letters 9. Essays
ISBN 9781641600514

LC bl2020046154

George Harrison on George Harrison is an authoritative, chronologically arranged anthology of Harrison's most revealing and illuminating interviews, personal correspondence, and writings, spanning the years 1962 to 2001. Though known as the "Quiet Beatle," Harrison was arguably the most thoughtful and certainly the most outspoken of the famous four. This compendium of his words and ideas proves that point repeatedly, revealing his passion for music, his focus on spirituality, and his responsibility as a celebrity, as well as a sense of deep commitment and humor.

"A fascinating addition to the voluminous catalog of Beatle-related literature." Library Journal

Southall, Brian

Sgt. Pepper's Lonely Hearts Club Band : the album, the Beatles, and the world in 1967 / Brian Southall. Charlesbridge, 2017. 192 p. : **782.42166092**

1. Beatles. Sgt. Pepper's Lonely Hearts Club Band. 2. Rock music -- 1961-1970 -- Pictorial works
ISBN 9781623545260

LC 2017010577

"An Imagine Book."

First published: London : Carlton Books, 2017.

Sgt. Pepper's Lonely Heart Club Band is considered one of the most popular and influential albums of all time. Southall offers an insider's account of the album's creation, reception, and influence. He then discusses the music, the Beatles, and global events between 1966 and 1968 to paint a portrait of the social, cultural, and political changes that shaped the legacy of the album.

Blauner, Andrew,

In their lives : great writers on great Beatles songs / edited by Andrew Blauner ; a note from Paul McCartney. Blue Rider Press, 2017 320 p. **782.42166092**

1. Beatles (Musical group) 2. Rock musicians 3. Rock music -- History and criticism.
ISBN 9780735210691

LC 2016053859

This collection of essays from 30 authors, actors and musicians has each list their favorite Beatles song and explore and reflect on why they selected their song and discuss the enduring impact of the most popular band of all time.

"A charming, delightful collection for Beatles fans and music fans in general." Kirkus.

782.42166 Rock (Rock 'n' roll) songs

Margotin, Philippe

The **Rolling** Stones : all the songs : the story behind every track / Philippe Margotin and Jean-Michel Guesdon ; translation by Richard George Elliott. Black Dog & Leventhal Publishers, 2016. 703 p. : **782.42166**

1. Rolling Stones. 2. Rolling Stones Discography. 3. Rock music -- England -- History and criticism
ISBN 9780316317740

LC 2016564656

A visual, song-by-song history of The Rolling Stones covers their studio albums, compilation albums, and more than one hundred singles, providing photographs, musician lists, and recording and song development information.

782.8 Men's voices

Leigh, Mitch, 1928-2014

Man of La Mancha; a musical play, / Dale Wasserman. Lyrics by Joe Darion. Music by Mitch Leigh. Random House, 1966 xiv, 82 p. **782.8**

1. Musicals -- Librettos

ISBN 9780394406190

LC 66021454

Contains the script of the musical play which is based on Cervantes' classic, Don Quixote

783.9 Other types of voice

Hughes, Charles William, 1900-

American hymns old and new : notes on the hymns and biographies of the authors and composers / Albert Christ-Janer, Charles W. Hughes, Carleton Sprague Smith. Columbia University Press, 1980. xv, 838 p. : **783.9**

1. Hymns, English.

ISBN 9780231034586

LC 79004630

Includes index.

Presents over six hundred hymns from the American tradition of religious song, including folk hymns, patriotic songs, and spirituals, with explanatory notes and biographies of their composers

784.18 Musical forms

Hamilton-Paterson, James

Beethoven's Eroica : the first great romantic symphony / James Hamilton-Paterson. Basic Books, 2017. 176 p. **784.18**

1. Beethoven, Ludwig van, 1770-1827. Symphonies, no. 3-5 2. Classical music. 3. Symphonies.

ISBN 9781541697362

LC bl2017049925

A tribute to Beethoven's revolutionary Third Symphony explores how it was originally inscribed to Napoleon, broke the mold of the Viennese Classical style and revealed powerful new forms of musical expressiveness. By the award-winning author of Empire of the Clouds.

"Casual concertgoers and serious music aficionados alike will find much to savor in this elegant and insightful book." Booklist.

784.19 Instruments

Wilkinson, Philip, 1955-

The **history** of music in fifty instruments / written by Philip Wilkinson. Firefly Books, 2014. 224 p. : **784.19**

1. Musical instruments -- History

ISBN 9781770854284

LC 2014900697

Wilkinson charts the evolution of musical instruments, profiling the instruments that have joined the orchestra from the Baroque era of the 1600s up to the modern age. The origin and development of each instrument is described. Includes brief informationon the instrument makers, composers, and musicians who have made them famous.

"Wilkinson's history unfolds like a symphonic work with instrument makers, composers and virtuosic performers picking up these incredible creations and exposing their beauty and capability. To open it up is to be instantly hooked." Publishers Weekly.

784.2 Full orchestra (Symphony orchestra)

Sachs, Harvey, 1946-

The **Ninth** : Beethoven and the year 1824 / Harvey Sachs. Random House, 2010. 224 p. **784.2**

1. Beethoven, Ludwig van, 1770-1827. Symphony No. 9 in D minor, Op. 125, "Choral." 2. Music and society. 3. Music -- Political aspects. 4. Music -- 19th century -- History and criticism. 5. Romanticism in music. 6. Europe -- History -- 19th century

ISBN 9781400060771

LC 2009019716

An analysis of Beethoven's seminal Ninth Symphony identifies it as a key cultural event that reflected major social upheavals, from the emergence of a dynamic Western world and changes in philosophical perspectives on individuality.

"This discussion of the cornerstone of Romantic music, whose influence extended deep into the twentieth century, is concise, thorough, and written from the heart of a great biographer, musicologist, and lover of fine music." Booklist.

Steinberg, Michael, 1928-

The **symphony** : a listener's guide / Michael Steinberg. Oxford University Press, 1998, c1995. xvii, 678 p. ; **784.2**

1. Symphonies -- Analysis, appreciation

ISBN 0195126653

LC BL 98013621

Reprint. Originally published: 1995.

Presents an exhaustive listener's guide to the symphony, replete with musical examples, biographical details, historical background, and commentaries on more than one hundred major works.

"Steinberg describes 36 composers and, movement by movement, 118 symphonies, including all the standard repertory...as well as a few by less well known composers such as Gorecki, Harbison, Martinu, and Sessions. The writing varies from formal and factual to chatty, with candid asides and stories relevant to the composer, the composition, or an important performance." Library Journal.

786.2 Pianos

Isacoff, Stuart

A **natural** history of the piano : from Mozart to modern jazz, and everything in between / Stuart Isacoff. Alfred A. Knopf, 2011. 416 p. **786.2**

1. Piano -- History. 2. Piano music -- History and criticism. 3. Pianists.

ISBN 9780307266378

LC 2011011557

The award-winning founder of Piano Today magazine presents a historical tribute to the piano that evaluates the roles of forefront composers and pianists while exploring the artistic development of various genres and the influence of the piano on Western musical traditions.

786.2092 Pianists

Hafner, Katie

A **romance** on three legs : Glenn Gould's obsessive quest for the perfect piano / Katie Hafner. Bloomsburg USA, 2008. 272 p. **786.2092**

1. Gould, Glenn 2. Steinway & Sons History 3. Pianists -- Canada 4. People with Asperger's syndrome 5. Steinway piano -- History. 6. Piano -- Construction -- United states. 7. United States -- History -- 20th century

ISBN 9781596915244

LC 2007048808

Traces the complex and eccentric musician's psychologically charged relationship with a Steinway concert grand, from his discovery of the instrument and the seemingly endless coddling that went into its maintenance to his acquaintance with a long-suffering piano tuner.

"When Gould was paired with the right composer, Bach especially, he could make you wonder if he was altogether human. And reading Hafner on Gould is sometimes as much fun as listening to him play. And that's saying a lot." Newsweek.

Hough, Stephen, 1961-

Rough ideas : reflections on music and more / Stephen Hough. Farrar Straus & Giroux 2020, c2019. 304 p. **786.2092**

1. Hough, Stephen, 1961- 2. Classical music 3. Classical musicians 4. Pianists 5. Art 6. Essays

ISBN 9780374252540

LC bl2020005922

Originally published: London : Faber & Faber, 2019.

A world-renowned classical pianist, composer and polymath candidly and engagingly discusses music and the life of a musician as well as people, places, books, paintings, the existence of God and the challenges of being a gay Catholic.

"Hough writes with wit, grace, and a singular point of view. His book offers rare insight into the mind of one of the leading performers of classical music." Library Journal

786.5 Organs

Whitney, Craig R., 1943-

All the stops : the glorious pipe organ and its American masters / Craig R. Whitney. Public Affairs, 2003. xxv, 321 p. : **786.5**

1. Organ music -- History and criticism 2. Organists. 3. Musical instruments, Electronic. 4. Musical instruments (Mechanical)

ISBN 1586481738

LC 2002037025

"Whitney extolls the organ's eclectic heritage at a time when the instrument seems poised for a return to the mainstream, and his glossary of its colorful terminology will help novices tell a windchest from a bombarde." The New Yorker.

787 Stringed instruments (Chordophones)

Seeger, Pete, 1919-2014

How to play the 5-string banjo : a manual for beginners / Pete Seeger. Hal Leonard Corporation, 2002. 72 p. : **787**

1. Banjo 2. Banjo -- History

ISBN 9781597731645

LC bl2014050878

Presents a history of the banjo, introduces strumming and fingering techniques, and offers advice on choosing and buying an instrument.

787.4 Cellos (Violoncellos)

Moskovitz, Marc

Beethoven's cello : five revolutionary sonatas and their world / Marc D. Moskovitz and R. Larry Todd. The Boydell Press, 2017. xxiv, 249 p. : **787.4**

1. Beethoven, Ludwig van, 1770-1827. Sonatas, cello, piano. 2. Sonata -- 19th century 3. Chamber music -- 19th century -- History and criticism

ISBN 9781783272372

LC 2017569147

"In 1796 the young Beethoven presented his first two cello sonatas at the court of Frederick William II, an avid cellist and the reigning Prussian monarch. Released in print the next year, these revolutionary sonatas forever altered the cello repertoire by fundamentally redefining the relationship between the cello and the piano and promoting their parity. Beethoven continued to develop the potential of the duo partnership in his three other cello sonatas--the lyrical and heroic Op. 69 and the two experimental sonatas Op. 102, No. 1 and No. 2, transcendent compositions conceived on the threshold of the composer's late style. In Beethoven's Cello, Marc D. Moskovitz and R. Larry Todd examine these seminal cornerstones of the cello repertoire and place them within their historical and cultural context. Also considered in a series of interludes are Beethoven's three variation sets, his cello-centric 'Triple' Concerto, and arrangements for cello and piano of other works. Two other interludes address the cellos owned by Beethoven and the changing nature of his pianos. Featuring a preface by renowned cellist Steven Isserlis and concluding with translated reviews of the composer's cello music published during his lifetime, Beethoven's Cello is the ideal companion for cellists, pianists, musicologists and chamber-music devotees desiring a comprehensive understanding of this beloved repertoire."--Jacket flap.

Siblin, Eric

The **cello** suites : J.S. Bach, Pablo Casals, and the search for a Baroque masterpiece / Eric Siblin. Atlantic Monthly Press, c2009. 319 p. ; **787.4**

1. Bach, Johann Sebastian, 1685-1750. Suites. 2. Casals, Pablo, 1876-1973. 3. Cellists -- Interviews. 4. Composers -- Germany. 5. Cello music. 6. Composition (Music) 7. Germany -- History -- 17th century. 8. Germany -- History -- 18th century. 9. Spain -- History -- 20th century.

ISBN 9780802119292

Governor General's Literary Awards, English-language Nonfiction finalist

Introduces Johann Sebastian Bach's "Cello Suites," discussing how the composition was lost in the eighteenth century and discovered by Pablo Casals in the late nineteenth century, and some of the historical questions remaining about the piece.

"Siblin's curiosity and passion for his subject is evident throughout, and his method of structuring the story according to the arrangement of the music is inspired. Meticulous in his research, as evidenced by copious notes and resources collected over his travels to several European countries, Siblin makes convincing connections and offers possible answers to the questions surrounding the suites. In the process, he sheds considerable light on the lives of Bach and Casals." Quill & Quire.

787.87 Guitars

Chapman, Richard

The **new** complete guitarist / Richard Chapman. DK, 2003. 208 p. : **787.87**

1. Guitar -- Instruction and study.
ISBN 9780789497017

LC 2004271630

Iintroduces a teach-yourself guitar program, complete with hundreds of step-by-step illustrations that include fingering charts, chords, notes, scales, modes, and sequences, as well as an annotated portfolio of more than one hundred makes and models of guitars.

Chappell, Jon

Guitar all-in-one for dummies / Jon Chappell, Mark Phillips, and Desi Serna. John Wiley & Sons, Inc., 2014 xvi, 628 p. : **787.87**

1. Guitar -- Methods 2. Guitar -- Self-instruction
ISBN 9781118872024

LC bl2014036815

"6 books in 1"--Cover.

Includes index.

Presents an easy-to-follow guide to the guitar, from the basics of the instrument to different guitar music styles, including guidance on purchasing and stringing guitars, chord and rhythm techniques, guitar theory, and chord exercises.

Fleming, Tom, 1975-

The **complete** guitar course : learn to play in 20 easy-to-follow lessons / Tom Fleming. Reader's Digest Association, c2006. 256 p. : **787.87**

1. Guitar
ISBN 9780762106622

LC 2006045420

At head of cover title: Reader's Digest.

Includes index.

A beginner's guide offers basic guitar instruction in twenty interlocking step-by-step lessons.

Port, Ian S

★The **birth** of loud : Leo Fender, Les Paul, and the guitar-pioneering rivalry that shaped rock 'n' roll / Ian S. Port. Scribner, [2019] 320 p. **787.87**

1. Fender, Leo, 1909-1991. 2. Paul, Les, 1915-2009 3. Gibson, Inc. 4. Fender Musical Instruments 5. Business competition 6. Electric guitar -- History. 7. Guitar -- History 8. Popular music
ISBN 9781501141652

LC 2018024537

Chronicles the rivalry between the two men who innovated the electric guitar's sound--Leo Fender and Les Paul--and their competition to convince rock stars like The Beatles, Jimi Hendrix, and Eric Clapton to play the instruments they built.

"This smartly written and genuinely exciting book walks us through the bitter rivalry between Fender and Gibson and, since there is no way to tell this story without telling the story of rock n roll itself, also provides a jaunty if necessarily abbreviated history of rock." Booklist.

790 Recreational and performing arts

Fletcher, Susan A., 1980-

Exploring the history of childhood and play through 50 historic treasures / Susan A. Fletcher. Rowman & Littlefield, 2020 xxvi, 299 p. : **790**

1. Toys -- United States -- History 2. Games -- United States -- History 3. Play -- United States -- History 4. Children -- United States -- History 5. United States -- Social life and customs.
ISBN 9781538118740

LC 2019049614

"Exploring The History of Childhood and Play in American History Through 50 Historic Treasures is a compilation of fifty iconic toys and games from American history. As the amount of leisure time available to children has increased in the United States, the number of toys available to them has also dramatically increased".-- Provided by publisher.

790.1 General kinds of recreational activities

Johnson, Steven, 1968-

Wonderland : how play made the modern world / Steven Johnson. Riverhead Books, 2016. 304 p. **790.1**

1. Technological innovations 2. Inventions -- Social aspects. 3. Technology -- Social aspects. 4. Amusements -- History.
ISBN 9780399184482

LC 2016035344

A history of popular entertainment explores the world-changing innovations humans have made while keeping themselves entertained and introduces the explorers, proprietors, showmen, and artists who became the innovators of leisure.

"This is a great book for all curious readers, especially the history-averse, who will enjoy the fast pace, topical diversity, and abundant trivia." Booklist.

Raab, Nathan, 1978-

The **hunt** for history : on the trail of the world's lost treasures - from the letters of Lincoln, Churchill, and Einstein to the secret recordings onboard JFK's Air Force One / Nathan Raab, with Luke Barr. Scribner, 2020. 288 p. **790.1**

1. Raab, Nathan, 1978- 2. Antique dealers 3. Collectors and collecting 4. Manuscripts -- Collectors and collecting 5. Historic documents
ISBN 9781501198908

LC 2019024822

Includes index.

A preeminent rare documents dealer recounts his years spent finding, authenticating and protecting important historical artifacts, from letters written by Alexander Hamilton to an American flag carried by Neil Armstrong to the moon and back.

"With several chill-inducing moments combined with engaging writing, this book will hold readers' interest until the last page. May be of particular interest to fans of Antiques Roadshow or American Pickers." Library Journal

791 Public performances

Moore, Rachel, 1964-

The **artist's** compass : the complete guide to building a life and a living in the performing arts / Rachel S. Moore, President and CEO of the Los Angeles Music Center. Touchstone, 2016.

xviii, 204 p. ; **791**

1. Performing arts 2. Performing arts -- Economic aspects 3. Vocational guidance
ISBN 9781501126642

LC 2015037025

Describes how to build and nurture a secure and successful career in the performing arts by approaching it like an entrepreneur.

"Moore is qualified to become a mentor to a whole new generation of artists, and they will benefit greatly from her advice." Publishers Weekly.

791.06 Organizations and management; amusement parks

Snow, Richard, 1947-

Disney's land : Walt Disney and the invention of the amusement park that changed the world / Richard Snow. Scribner, 2019. 432 p. **791.06**

1. Disney, Walt, 1901-1966. 2. Disneyland. 3. Walt Disney Company Buildings -- History. 4. Amusement parks 5. Entrepreneurs 6. Architecture and society. 7. Architecture, American. 8. California
ISBN 9781501190803

LC 2019024840

A history of the conception and development of the iconic California theme park chronicles how Walt and Roy Disney and a small group of artists endured innumerable setbacks to create one of the world's most popular destinations.

791.3 Circuses

Daly, Michael

Topsy : the startling story of the crooked tailed elephant, P.T. Barnum, and the American wizard, Thomas Edison / Michael Daly. Atlantic Monthly Press, 2013. 288 p. **791.3**

1. Edison, Thomas A. (Thomas Alva), 1847-1931 2. Barnum, P. T. (Phineas Taylor), 1810-1891 3. Westinghouse, George, 1846-1914 4. Animal welfare 5. Exploitation 6. Elephants 7. Electric currents 8. New York City 9. Animal biographies
ISBN 9780802119049

LC 2014466008

Describes how Forepaugh Circus' Topsy the elephant was electrocuted in Coney Island with 6600 volts of alternating current as proof that it was much more dangerous than direct current in an ongoing dispute between Thomas Edison and George Westinghouse.

791.43 Motion pictures

Arnold, Jeremy

Turner Classic Movies : the essentials : 52 must-see movies and why they matter / Jeremy Arnold ; foreword by Robert Osborne. Running Press, 2016. 288 p. : **791.43**

1. Motion pictures
ISBN 9780762459469

LC bl2016018038

Presents fifty-two films that everyone should see and explains why each film is such a classic, including such notable films as "Duck Soup," "Sunset Boulevard," and "The Graduate."

Barr, Patricia

Ultimate Star Wars / written by Patricia Barr, Adam Bray, Daniel Wallace, Ryder Windham. DK Publishing, 2015. 319 p. : **791.43**

1. Star Wars films
ISBN 9781465436016

LC 2015297170

"Characters, creatures, locations, technology, vehicles"--Cover.

"Foreword by Anthony Daniels, C-3PO"--Cover.

Includes index.

An in-depth, sumptuously illustrated survey of the characters and storylines from the Star Wars universe is chronologically organized and includes coverage of the films, and The Clone Wars and Rebels TV series. Movie tie-in.

"Some pages contain several photos of the same structure so that all angles can be seen. The book also contains a contributers page where each artist is given credit. Middle and high school librarians should definitely consider adding this volume to their collections. Creative teens will appreciate the addition." Voice of Youth Advocates.

Benson, Michael

Space Odyssey : Stanley Kubrick, Arthur C. Clarke, and the making of a masterpiece / Michael Benson. Simon & Schuster, April 2018. xii, 497 p., 16 unnumbered p. of plates : **791.43**

1. Kubrick, Stanley Criticism and interpretation. 2. Clarke, Arthur C. (Arthur Charles), 1917-2008. 2001, a space odyssey. 3. 2001, a space odyssey (Motion picture). 4. Filmmaking 5. Film producers and directors 6. Films -- History 7. Science fiction films
ISBN 9781501163937

LC 2017051254

"Published to coincide with the 50th anniversary of the film's release, this is the definitive story of the making of "2001: A Space Odyssey," acclaimed today as one of the greatest films ever made, and of director Stanley Kubrick and writer Arthur C. Clarke, who created this influential cinematic masterpiece".-- Provided by publisher.

Biskind, Peter

Easy riders, raging bulls : how the sex-drugs-and-rock-'n'-roll generation saved Hollywood / Peter Biskind. Simon & Schuster, 1999, c1998. 506 p. : **791.43**

1. Film producers and directors -- United States. 2. Films -- United States -- History. 3. Film industry and trade -- United States -- History.
ISBN 0684857081

LC BL 99003832

Examines the impact upon Hollywood of the generation of filmmakers from the 1960s to the 1980s.

Carlson, Erin, 1981-

I'll have what she's having : how Nora Ephron's three iconic films saved the romantic comedy / Erin Carlson. Hachette Books, 2017 304 p. **791.43**

1. Ephron, Nora. 2. When Harry met Sally... (Motion picture) 3. Sleepless in Seattle (Motion picture) 4. You've got mail (Motion picture) 5. Romantic comedy films 6. Film criticism 7. Films
ISBN 9780316353885

LC 2017014826

A backstage assessment of the making of Nora Ephron's revered trilogy, When Harry Met Sally, You've Got Mail and Sleepless in Seattle, shares an intimate portrait of the writer's life and her enduring influence on a generation of Hollywood women.

Cavalier, Stephen

The **world** history of animation / Stephen Cavalier. University of California Press, c2011. 416 p. : **791.43**

1. Animated films -- History and criticism. 2. Animation (Cinematography) 3. Animators. 4. Animated films.
ISBN 9780520261129

LC 2010931052

A lavishly illustrated volume with 250 color images traces the full history of animation from its very inception, looking at examples of the most groundbreaking work from around the globe and describing how animation technique has improved over the years.

Coppola, Francis Ford, 1939-

The **Godfather** notebook / Francis Ford Coppola. Regan Arts., 2016. 784 p. : **791.43**

1. Coppola, Francis Ford, 1939- Notebooks, sketchbooks, etc. 2. Puzo, Mario, 1920-1999 Film adaptations. 3. Godfather (Motion picture) 4. Creativity. 5. Filmmaking. 6. Film industry and trade. 7. Film producers and directors.
ISBN 9781682450741

LC bl2016049332

Presents Coppola's notes and annotations from the copy of "The Godfather" that he referred to while making the film, revealing the intense creative process behind the movie and complemented by exclusive images from on and off the set.

Corliss, Richard

Mom in the movies : the iconic screen mothers you love (and a few you love to hate) / Richard Corliss ; foreword by Debbie Reynolds and Carrie Fisher. Simon & Schuster, 2014. xxi, 231 p. : **791.43**

1. Mothers in motion pictures.
ISBN 1476738262

LC 2013044850

Featuring more than 100 photographs and film stills, this ultimate guide to mothers in film, presented by a film historian and critic and Turner Classic Movies, shows the many ways that Hollywood has celebrated, vilified and poked good fun at dear old Mom.

"A comprehensive retrospective of mothers as portrayed on film from the earliest Silent Moms...to the most recent figures." Library Journal.

Davis, Michael, 1952-

Street gang : the complete history of Sesame Street / Michael Davis. Viking, 2009. 379 p. **791.43**

1. Sesame Street (Television program) 2. Television programs for children -- History and criticism 3. Popular culture 4. Television and education 5. Television programs -- History 6. United States -- Social life and customs -- 20th century 7. United States -- Social life and customs -- 21st century
ISBN 9780670019960

LC 2008035498

A former family television editor for TV Guide traces the story of the landmark children's television show, from its origins at a dinner party by co-founder Joan Ganz Cooney and the creative achievements of Jim Henson to the Nixon administration's efforts to stop its funding and the advent of Elmo.

"Any grown-up fan will relish this account, gaining an even greater appreciation for the cultural contributions of Kermit, Big Bird, Oscar the Grouch and all their neighbors." Publishers Weekly.

Dixon, Wheeler W., 1950-

A **short** history of film / Wheeler Winston Dixon and Gwendolyn Audrey Foster. Rutgers University Press, 2018. xxxviii, 465 p., 16 unnumbered p. of plates : **791.43**

1. History. 2. Motion picture industry -- History. 3. Motion pictures -- History.
ISBN 0813595126

LC 2019296561

"With more than 250 images, new information on international cinema--especially Polish, Chinese, Russian, Canadian, and Iranian filmmakers--an expanded section on African-American filmmakers, updated discussions of new works by major American directors, and a new section on the rise of comic book movies and computer generated special effects..." - Back cover.

Frankel, Glenn

High Noon : the Hollywood blacklist and the making of an American classic / Glenn Frankel. Bloomsbury , 2017. 304 p. **791.43**

1. Foreman, Carl 2. United States. Congress. House. Committee on Un-American Activities. 3. High noon (Motion picture) 4. Communism -- United States. 5. Film industry and trade 6. Screenplay writing 7. Hollywood Blacklist.
ISBN 9781620409480

LC 2017000380

Beginning in 1947, Hollywood came [under] intense scrutiny by the House Committee on Un-American Activities (HUAC), which was looking into alleged communist influences in Hollywood; ultimately hundreds of directors, actors, and screenwriters were blacklisted or boycotted by risk-averse studios. In High Noon, author Glenn Frankel explores the era through the production of the film by the same name. During the shoot, screenwriter Carl Foreman came under fire from HUAC, but he wasn't the only one affected by the political climate. Check it out if you're interested in the link between film and politics.

"A comprehensive guide to both a classic film and the era that created it." Kirkus.

Gaines, Caseen, 1986-

We don't need roads : the making of the Back to the future trilogy / Caseen Gaines. Plume, 2015. 288 p. **791.43**

1. Back to the future films History and criticism. 2. Films 3. Filmmaking 4. Film industry and trade
ISBN 9780142181539

LC 2015007982

The cultural historian and award-winning author traces the story of the film-making partnership between Robert Zemeckis and Bob Gale that culminated in the blockbuster franchise.

Graham, Don, 1940-

Giant : Elizabeth Taylor, Rock Hudson, James Dean, Edna Ferber, and the making of a legendary American film / Don Graham. St. Martin's Press, 2018. 336 p. **791.43**

1. Giant (Motion picture). 2. Films -- History 3. Film producers and directors 4. Film actors and actresses 5. Texas -- History -- 20th century 6. The West (United States) 7. Hollywood, California
ISBN 9781250061904

LC 2017046287

A narrative of the making of the classic film discusses its production in the isolated wilds of Texas, the achievements of director George Stevens and other key contributors, and how the movie reflected America's rise as a superpower and the flowering of Texas culture as mythology.

"The book also features in-depth biographies of the film's three leads, because you can't tell the story of this classic film without telling the stories of its stars, who were as tortured as their characters in their own ways. A sharp, insightful look at a legendary film." Booklist.

Harris, Mark, 1963-
Pictures at a revolution : five movies and the birth of the new Hollywood / Mark Harris. Penguin Press, 2008. 496 p. **791.43**

1. Films, American -- History and criticism 2. Filmmaking. 3. Culture. 4. United States -- Social life and customs -- 20th century.
ISBN 1594201528

LC 2007032633

ALA Notable Book, 2009.

[Explores] the epic human drama behind the making of the five movies nominated for Best Picture in 1967--Guess Who's Coming to Dinner, The Graduate, In the Heat of the Night, Doctor Doolittle, and Bonnie and Clyde--and through them, the larger story of the cultural revolution that transformed Hollywood, and America, forever.

Hornaday, Ann
Talking pictures : how to watch movies / Ann Hornaday. Basic Books, 2017. 272 p. **791.43**

1. Filmmaking. 2. Film industry and trade. 3. Film music. 4. Film producers and directors.
ISBN 9780465094233

LC 2017009751

A veteran film critic, walking readers through the production of a typical movie, from the writing of the script to the final sound edit, presents an entertaining guide to thinking and talking about movies that features anecdotes and interviews with actors and filmmakers.

"Washington Post film critic Hornaday's new book gives the reader tools for watching films more intentionally and with more discerning taste." Publishers Weekly.

Jameson, A. D., 1976-
I find your lack of faith disturbing : Star Wars and the triumph of geek culture / A. D. Jameson. Farrar, Straus and Giroux, 2018. 272 p. **791.43**

1. Star Wars films -- Criticism and interpretation 2. Science fiction fandom 3. Fans (Persons) 4. Popular culture
ISBN 9780374537364

LC 2017038357

A lifelong geek invites readers on an irreverent journey through modern geek culture as he shines new light on well-loved movie classics in the science fiction, fantasy and superhero genres, and discusses why he thinks these films should be taken seriously.

Kael, Pauline, 1919-2001
The **age** of movies : selected writings of Pauline Kael / Pauline Kael ; edited by Sanford Schwartz. Library of America, 2011. 750 p. **791.43**

1. Film reviews 2. Film criticism 3. Film evaluation
ISBN 9781598531091

LC 2011923053

A compendium of top-selected, signature writings by the influential former critic of The New Yorker offers insight into her capacity for capturing cinematic details and includes her appraisals of such works as Bonnie and Clyde, The Godfather and Last Tango in Paris.

Karp, Josh
Orson Welles's last movie : the making of the other side of the wind / Josh Karp. St Martin's Press, 2015 352 p. **791.43**

1. Welles, Orson, 1915-1985. 2. Film producers and directors -- England 3. Filmmaking
ISBN 9781250007087

LC 2015002464

In the summer of 1970 legendary but self-destructive director Orson Welles returned to Hollywood from years of self-imposed exile in Europe and decided it was time to make a comeback movie. Coincidentally it was the story of a legendary self-destructive director who returns to Hollywood from years of self-imposed exile in Europe. Welles swore it wasn't autobiographical.

"A fascinating story, much more than your typical making-of book." Booklist.

Kenny, Glenn
Made men : the story of Goodfellas / Glenn Kenny. Hanover Square Press, 2020. 352 p. **791.43**

1. GoodFellas (Motion picture) 2. Film noir 3. Gangster films 4. Film criticism 5. Film producers and directors
ISBN 9781335016508

LC bl2020046755

When Goodfellas first hit the theatres in 1990, a classic was born. Few could anticipate the unparalleled influence it would have on pop culture, one that would inspire future filmmakers and redefine the gangster picture as we know it today. In the first ever behind-the-scenes story of Goodfellas, film critic Glenn Kenny chronicles the making and afterlife of the film that introduced America to the real modern gangster--brutal, ruthless, yet darkly appealing, the villain we can't get enough of. Featuring interviews with the film's major players, including Martin Scorsese and Robert De Niro, Made Men shines a light on the lives and stories wrapped up in the Goodfellas universe, and why its enduring legacy is still essential to charting the trajectory of American culture thirty years later.

"A must for any fan of Goodfellas, Scorsese, or movies in general." Library Journal

Klastorin, Michael, 1957-
Close encounters of the third kind : the ultimate visual history / Michael Klastorin ; foreword by Steven Spielberg. Harper Design, an imprint of HarperColinsPublishers, 2017. 188 p. : **791.43**

1. Close encounters of the third kind (Motion picture). 2. Art in motion pictures 3. Science fiction films
ISBN 9780062692993

LC bl2017043939

Explores the creation, production, and legacy of the science fiction film and offers never-before-seen imagery from the archives.

Larsen, Darl, 1963-
A **book** about the film Monty Python's Life of Brian : all of the references from Assyrians to Zeffirelli / Darl Larsen. Rowman & Littlefield, 2018. xxii, 473 p. **791.43**

1. Monty Python (Comedy troupe) 2. Life of Brian (Motion picture) 3. Films 4. Humorous writing 5. Film criticism 6. Films -- Appreciation
ISBN 9781538103654

LC 2017033575

This book identifies the plethora of cultural, historical, and topical references in the film Monty Python's Life of Brian. The author cites and explains virtually every allusion--from first-century Jerusalem through 1970s Great Britain, from terror groups ancient to modern, from Pontius Pilate to Margaret Thatcher--that appears in the film.

"American readers will benefit from definitions of uniquely British phenomena (e.g., anything associated with cricket). Along with explication, the essays on occasion look at the series within the cultural context of the late 1960s, touching on such topics as its treatment of homosexuality or women. Larsen ... is a devoted fan who exhaustively analyzes the series without ever obscuring its unique brand of humor." Library Journal.

Lumet, Sidney, 1924-2011

★**Making** movies / Sidney Lumet. Vintage Books, 1996, c1995. x, 220 p. ; **791.43**

1. Films -- Production and direction -- Handbooks, manuals, etc. 2. Filmmaking. 3. Film producers and directors 4. Cinematography.
ISBN 9780679756606

LC BL 99771663

Originally published: New York : Knopf, 1995.

The award-winning director journeys inside the world of film to illuminate the arduous process of creating movies, discussing the art and craft of directing, writers and actors, the camera, art direction, editing, sound tracks, and more.

"This is a book about the job of being a movie director. From the creation of the screeenplay to the final previews, Mr. Lumet explains every step in the process, drawing examples from his own career." New York Times Book Review.

Macek, Carl,

Film noir : the encyclopedia / edited by Alain Silver [and others] ; co-editor: Carl Macek ; designed by Bernard Schleifer. Overlook Duckworth, 2010. 511 p. : **791.43**

1. Film noir 2. Film noir -- History and criticism 3. Motion picture plays -- History and criticism 4. Motion pictures -- Plots, themes, etc
ISBN 9781590201442

LC 2016591749

A comprehensive overview and description of the characters, themes and motifs featured in film noir, includes films featuring Humphrey Bogart, Peter Lorre, James Cagney and Bette Davis, as well as contemporary contributions to the genre.

Mamet, David

On directing film / David Mamet. Penguin Books, 1992, c1991. xvi, 107 p. ; **791.43**

1. Motion pictures -- Production and direction.
ISBN 0140127224

LC BL 00007771

Originally published: New York : Viking, 1991.

"Noted playwright, screenwriter, and director Mamet offers his views on film directing taken, some in transcript form, from lectures and classes at Columbia. Refreshingly untheoretical, particularly regarding acting technique, this is fitfully interesting stuff." Library Journal.

Muir, John Kenneth, 1969-

The **encyclopedia** of superheroes on film and television / John Kenneth Muir. McFarland & Co., c2008. viii, 696 p. : **791.43**

1. Superhero films -- United States 2. Superhero television programs -- United States
ISBN 9780786437559

LC 2008019724

"This updated edition of 2004's award-winning encyclopedia traces developments in the popular genre; new shows; latest films; and covers more superheroes. Each entry includes a detailed history, cast and credits, episode and film descriptions, critical commentaries, and data on arch-villains, comic-book origins and super powers, while placing each production into its historical context".--Provided by publisher.

"Entries start with description and background of the hero. Live-action films are presented with reviewer comments and cast and crew. TV series also present reviewer comments and a description of the series. Episode guides include title, writer and director credits, and air dates as well as episode descriptions and guest casts. A good addition to the pop-culture collection." Booklist.

Nashawaty, Chris

Caddyshack : the making of a Hollywood Cinderella story and the remaking of American comedy / Chris Nashawaty. Flatiron Books, 2018. 288 p. **791.43**

1. Caddyshack (Motion picture). 2. Films 3. Comedy films.
ISBN 9781250105950

LC 2017051033

An anecdotal account of the making of Caddyshack shares profiles of the comedy pioneers behind it, citing the influence of Harvard's National Lampoon and the film, Animal House before stories from the country-club summer jobs of Bill and Brian Doyle Murray inspired the film's wacky production throughout a memorable Florida summer.

"Nashawatys prose is lively, and his exhaustive research is bolstered by interviews with many of the films principle players, including the famously elusive Murray. A wonderful celebration of a passionately loved film." Booklist.

Nichtern, Ethan

The **dharma** of The princess bride : what the coolest fairy tale of our time can teach us about Buddhism and relationships / Ethan Nichtern. North Point Press, 2017. 256 p. **791.43**

1. Princess bride (Motion picture). 2. Dharma (Buddhism) 3. Buddhism 4. Buddhists 5. Interpersonal relations
ISBN 9780865477766

LC 2016059269

"A Buddhist approach to navigating key relationships with lessons from the cult classic film." Kirkus.

Rabin, Nathan, 1976-

My year of flops : the A.V Club presents one man's journey deep into the heart of cinematic failure / Nathan Rabin and the A.V. Club. Scribner, 2010. 288 p. **791.43**

1. Film criticism 2. Films. 3. Essays.
ISBN 9781439153123

LC 2010018224

Draws on the author's work on the A.V. Club column in the satirical newspaper The Onion to provide a revisionist history of cinematic failure, collecting dozens of favorite entries complemented by such bonus features as interviews, illustrations and new entries on notorious failed movies.

"Follow Nathan Rabin on his quest to provide a sympathetic reappraisal of some of the most reviled films of all time, and what do you learn? Pennies From Heaven and Freddy Got Fingered are better than you might think, and Ishtar offers an exquisitely jaundiced take on American foreign policy. Mostly, though, Mr. Rabin sits slack-jawed watching the everlasting dreadfulness of Mame, Battlefield Earth and Exit to Eden (the mother of all unsexy sex films). Always glad to snark it up, Mr. Rabin can also be mournful when reflecting on how worthwhile failures like Heaven's Gate diminished Hollywood's ambitions, then and now. The book, which collects columns that first appeared on The Onion's pop-culture Web site, includes more bad movies and interviews with actors caught up in the cinematic wreckage." New York Times Book Review.

Resnick, Ira M.

Starstruck : vintage movie posters from classic Hollywood / Ira M. Resnick ; foreword by Martin Scorsese. Abbeville Press Publishers, 2010. 272 p. : **791.43**

1. Film posters, American.

ISBN 0789210193

LC 2009009337

Includes bibliographical references (p. 265) and index.

Samples posters and stills from Ira M. Resnick's extensive collection, covering actors ranging from Lillian Gish and the Marx Brothers to Marilyn Monroe and Audrey Hepburn.

Santopietro, Tom

The **Sound** of Music story : how one young nun, one handsome Austrian captain, and seven singing Von Trapp children inspired the most beloved film of all time / Tom Santopietro. St. Martin's Press, 2015. 288 p. **791.43**

1. Andrews, Julie. 2. Plummer, Christopher. 3. Trapp Family Singers. 4. Sound of music (Motion picture) 5. Musical films. 6. Folk music, Austrian. 7. Singers. 8. Musicals.

ISBN 9781250064462

LC 2014033795

Published to coincide with the film's 50th anniversary, an ultimate fan book shares behind-the-scenes facts about The Sound of Music's filming in Austria and Hollywood and incorporates new interviews with production insiders, including Johannes von Trapp.

"A fun-to-read book, perfect for musical-lovers, aspiring moviemakers, and film buffs." Booklist.

Schechter, Harold

★**Ripped** from the headlines! : the shocking true stories behind the movies most memorable crimes / Harold Schechter. Little A, 2020 374 p. **791.43**

1. Films -- History 2. Cult Films 3. Crime -- History 4. Film producers and directors 5. Essays

ISBN 9781542041805

LC bl2020016941

In this collection of revelatory essays, true-crime historian Harold Schechter takes a fascinating trip down the crossroads of fact and fiction to reveal the sensational real-life stories that are more shocking, taboo, and fantastic than even the most imaginative screenwriter can dream up.

"This fascinating look at the intersection of true crime and pop culture is a must." Library Journal

Schneider, Steven Jay,

1001 movies you must see before you die / General Editor, Steven Jay Schneider, Preface by Jason Solomons. Barron's, 2011. 960 p. : **791.43**

1. Film criticism -- History and criticism.

ISBN 9780764164224

LC bl2011027080

Includes indexes.

Lists "must-see" movies in a chronological arrangement, providing information on director, producer, screenplay writer, music, cast members, and awards, along with a detailed review of each.

Shepard, Jim

The **tunnel** at the end of the light : essays on movies and politics / Jim Shepard. Tin House Books, 2017. xxii, 261 p. ; **791.43**

1. Motion pictures -- Philosophy 2. Essays

ISBN 9781941040720

LC 2017010540

Argues that the movies shape some of America's most destructive political assumptions and culturally critiques certain films, including "Chinatown," "The Third Man," and "Badlands."

Stratton, W. K., 1955-

The **wild** bunch : Sam Peckinpah, a revolution in Hollywood, and the making of a legendary film / W.K. Stratton. Bloomsbury Publishing Inc., 2019. 352 p. **791.43**

1. Peckinpah, Sam, 1925-1984 2. Wild bunch (Motion picture) 3. Western films -- History and criticism 4. Film industry and trade 5. Film producers and directors 6. Filmmaking

ISBN 9781632862129

LC 2018024992

Chronicles the making of "The Wild Bunch," documenting the contributions of Mexican and Mexican-American actors and crew members and discussing how the film's dark, violent take on Western movies reflected the turbulent times in which it was created.

"Stratton's thorough research yields a fascinating perspective on how Peckinpah created a western of unparalleled realism and intensity." Publishers Weekly.

Szostak, Phil

The **art** of Star Wars, the last Jedi : The Last Jedi / written by Phil Szostak ; foreword by Rian Johnson. Abrams, 2017. 253 p. : **791.43**

1. Filmproduktion gnd 2. Star Wars, the last Jedi (Motion picture) Pictorial works. 3. Star wars: episode VIII - The last Jedi gnd 4. Cinematography -- Technique 5. Motion pictures -- Production and direction 6. Star Wars films

ISBN 9781419727054

LC 2017943326

Includes index.

Examines the development of the fantastic worlds, characters, and creatures of "The Last Jedi" through concept art, costume sketches, storyboards, blueprints, and exclusive interviews with the filmmakers.

Taylor, Chris, 1973-

How Star Wars conquered the universe : the past, present, and future of a multibillion dollar franchise / Chris Taylor. Basic Books, 2014. 488 p. **791.43**

1. Star wars (Motion picture) 2. Star Wars characters 3. Star Wars films. 4. Films -- History.

ISBN 9780465089987

LC 2014023580

In How Star Wars Conquered the Universe, veteran journalist Chris Taylor traces the series from the difficult birth of the original film through its sequels, the franchise's death and rebirth, the prequels, and the preparations for a new trilogy. Providing portraits of the friends, writers, artists, producers, and marketers who labored behind the scenes to turn Lucas' idea into a legend, Taylor also jousts with modern-day Jedi, tinkers with droid builders, and gets inside Boba Fett's helmet, all to find out how Star Wars has attracted and inspired so many fans for so long.

Thomson, David, 1941-

How to watch a movie / David Thomson. Alfred A. Knopf, 2015. 342 p. **791.43**

1. Film evaluation 2. Films 3. Film industry and trade 4. Popular culture

ISBN 9781101875391

LC 2014046757

A critic shares professional insights into how to derive more from a film experience, analyzing a range of iconic films to reveal metaphorical artistry techniques in the acting, filming, dialogue, and music.

"An enjoyably deep dive into the interaction between cinema and psyche." Kirkus.

Thorne, Kip S

The **science** of Interstellar / Kip Thorne. W.W. Norton & Company, 2014 x, 324 p. : **791.43**

1. Interstellar (Motion picture) 2. Science in motion pictures.
ISBN 0393351378

LC bl2014047435

Looks at the scientific aspects of the science fiction film directed by Christopher Nolan, delving into the theoretical physics that informed the making of the film from its inception onward due to the author's involvement as a consultant on the film.

Turan, Kenneth

Not to be missed : 54 favorites from a lifetime of film / Kenneth Turan. PublicAffairs, [2014] xix, 345 p. ; **791.43**

1. Films 2. Film industry and trade 3. Film reviews. 4. Actors and actresses.
ISBN 9781586483968

LC 2014007773

Includes index.

A film critic for the Los Angeles Times presents a list of his favorite films of all-time, from All About Eve to Spirited Away, and offers anecdotes on the cultural impact, controversies, and history surrounding each.

"Turans' illuminating reflections do what the best essays on film always do: send us to watch the movie, whether for the first time or the 20th." Publishers Weekly.

Wasson, Sam

The **big** goodbye : Chinatown and the last years of Hollywood / Sam Wasson. Flatiron Books, 2020. 336 p. **791.43**

1. Nicholson, Jack, 1937- 2. Polanski, Roman 3. Tate, Sharon, 1943-1969. 4. Dunaway, Faye, 1941- 5. Evans, Robert, 1930- 6. Towne, Robert, Chinatown. 7. Chinatown (Motion picture). 8. Films 9. Film industry and trade 10. Film criticism 11. Film producers and directors
ISBN 9781250301826

LC 2019045207

A revealing account of the making of the classic film Chinatown describes Jack Nicholson at the height of his career, his doomed love affair with Anjelica Huston and Roman Polanski, still reeling from the savage death of his wife.

"Inimitable Wasson (Fifth Avenue, 5 A.M.) examines the development of the iconic film Chinatown (1974), beginning with the months leading up to the murder of director Roman Polanski's wife, Sharon Tate, in 1969 ... On par with Wasson's exceptional Fosse, this portrait of a neonoir classic will weave a spell over cinephiles." Library Journal

Fifth Avenue, 5 a.m. : Breakfast at Tiffany's and the making of the modern American woman / Sam Wasson. Harpercollins 2010 304 p. **791.43**

1. Hepburn, Audrey, 1929-1993. 2. Breakfast at Tiffany's (Motion picture) 3. Women -- United States. 4. Women's role -- United States -- History -- 20th century 5. Transformations, Personal.
ISBN 9780061774157

LC 2009052439

"The author presents an irresistibly gossipy account of the production of Breakfast at Tiffany's (1961), charting the transformation of actress Audrey Hepburn into an icon of emerging sexual liberation--the good/bad girl, the lovable kook, independent and sexually experienced but sufficiently charming to bring home to mother. Rich in incident and set among the glitterati of America's most glamorous era, the book reads like a novel." Kirkus.

791.4302 Stock footage--motion pictures

Gora, Susannah

You couldn't ignore me if you tried : the Brat Pack, John Hughes, and their impact on a generation / Susannah Gora. Crown Publishers, c2010. xiv, 367 p. ; **791.4302**

1. Hughes, John, 1950-2009 Criticism and interpretation. 2. Teenagers' films -- United States -- History and criticism. 3. Film criticism 4. Teenagers in films 5. Popular culture -- History -- 20th century 6. United States -- Social life and customs -- 20th century 7. United States -- Popular culture
ISBN 9780307408433

LC 2009036246

"Though Gora discusses the work of Hughes's colleagues, she places the sharpest lens on the godfather of the genre himself. ... [p]erhaps it was his ability to relate to adolescents and his respect for their seemingly insignificant plights that allowed Hughes to capture coming-of-age so candidly. While a long and involved read, Gora's book offers an all-access pass to the Brat Pack, the films they starred in, and those behind the cameras of a movie era that is still relevant today." Paste

Harris, Mark, 1963-

★**Five** came back : a story of Hollywood and the Second World War / Mark Harris. The Penguin Press, 2014 480 p. **791.4302**

1. Ford, John, 1894-1973 2. Wyler, William, 1902-1981 3. Huston, John, 1906-1987 4. Capra, Frank, 1897-1991 5. Stevens, George, 1904-1975 6. World War II 7. Films 8. Film industry and trade 9. World War II films.
ISBN 9781594204302

LC 2013039983

Traces the World War II experiences of five legendary directors including John Ford, William Wyler, John Huston, Frank Capra and George Stevens to assess the transformative impact of the war and period beliefs on Hollywood.

"Narrative nonfiction that is as gloriously readable as it is unfailingly informative." Booklist.

Kazan, Elia

Kazan on directing / Elia Kazan. Alfred A. Knopf, 2009. xxiii, 341 p. **791.4302**

1. Kazan, Elia, 2. Film producers and directors 3. Films -- Production and direction 4. Theater -- Production and direction. 5. Screenplay writing 6. United States -- Social life and customs -- 20th century 7. United States -- Social life and customs -- 21st century
ISBN 9780307264770

LC 2008048345

From A Streetcar Named Desire to Death of a Salesman, from Cat on a Hot Tin Roof to On the Waterfront, Kazan's list of Broadway and Hollywood successes are among the twentieth-century's most profound productions, and the insights into these and other classic works are essential reading for anyone interested in American movies and theater.

Stevens, George, Jr

Conversations at the American Film Institute with the great moviemakers : the next generation / [edited and with an introduction by] George Stevens, Jr. Alfred A. Knopf, 2012. xxiii, 737 p. : **791.4302**

1. Motion picture producers and directors -- United States 2. Motion pictures -- Production and direction. 3. Interviews.
ISBN 0307273474

LC 2011043741

A companion to the Emmy and Peabody Award-winning author's well-received collection of American Film Institute seminars with film pioneers draws on AFI conversations with moviemakers from the 1950s to today, including Steven Spielberg, Nora Ephron and George Lucas.

Waxman, Sharon

Rebels on the backlot : six maverick directors and how they conquered the Hollywood studio system / Sharon Waxman. HarperEntertainment, c2005. xxi, 386 p. : **791.4302**

1. Film producers and directors 2. Film industry and trade -- Hollywood, California

ISBN 9780060540173

LC 2004059269

Draws on more than one hundred interviews and a decade's worth of reportage to chronicle the rise of six influential directors from the 1990s, including Quentin Tarantino, David Fincher, and Spike Jonze, in a portrait of contemporary Hollywood that focuses on the development, shooting, and release of each director's major film.

791.43079 Motion pictures--awards

Osborne, Robert, 1932-2017

85 years of the Oscar : the official history of the Academy Awards / Robert Osborne. Abbeville Press Publishers, 2013 472 p. : **791.43079**

1. Academy Awards (Motion pictures) 2. Motion pictures -- United States -- History

ISBN 9780789211422

LC 2013033021

Reaccounts the last eighty-five years of the Oscars, including over 750 pictures, information on the ceremonies, trends, developments, and events that occured in the film industry and within the academy.

791.43092 Motion pictures--Biography

Finch, Christopher

The **art** of Walt Disney : from Mickey Mouse to the Magic Kingdoms / Christopher Finch. Abrams, 2011. 503 p. : **791.43092**

1. Disney, Walt, 1901-1966. 2. Walt Disney Company. 3. Animators. 4. Animation (Cinematography) 5. Film industry and trade 6. Cartoonists.

ISBN 9780810998148

LC 2004010016

Includes index.

Traces the career of the beloved cartoonist while exploring the diverse artistic and cinematographic techniques used to make his animated and live action films.

791.430973 Motion pictures--United States

Longworth, Karina, 1980-

Hollywood frame by frame : the unseen silver screen in contact sheets, 1951-1997 / Karina Longworth. Princeton Architectural Press, 2014 208 p. : **791.430973**

1. Contact printing -- United States. 2. Motion pictures -- United States 3. Stills (Motion pictures) -- United States.

ISBN 1616892595

LC 2013051020

"A treasure trove for any fan of Hollywood's Golden Age, Frame by Frame: The Story of Hollywood in Contact Sheets, 1951-1997 is packed with images that have never before been published, offering a unique insight into the moments when movie history was made. Focusing on still photographers' contact sheets--a record of every shot they took--from the sets of some of the greatest films of the twentieth century, the book tells the story of Hollywood through images that have never been considered since the original shots were taken. The story of each movie's making--from King Kong to Some Like it Hot, from Taxi Driver to Pulp Fiction--is told in extended captions, providing insight into the art of moviemaking, the science of movie marketing, and the nature of stardom. Showing legends such as Woody Allen, Audrey Hepburn, Alfred Hitchcock, and Frank Sinatra at work and at repose, this book is the perfect gift for any movie enthusiast".-- Provided by publisher.

"Cinephiles will relish these moments captured from another era." Library Journal.

Schickel, Richard

Keepers : the greatest films and personal favorites of a moviegoing lifetime / Richard Schickel. Alfred A. Knopf, 2015 320 p. **791.430973**

1. Film evaluation 2. Films 3. Film industry and trade 4. Popular culture

ISBN 9780375424595

LC 2014034997

A film critic and movie historian who has been watching cinema for 70 years and has seen almost 19,000 films brings viewers on a tour of his favorite movies, highlighting forgotten treasures and explaining what makes a film a hit or a flop.

"Schickel, who posits in his introduction that movies are about both nothing and everything, wholly succeeds in making readers care about every film he's seen." Publishers Weekly.

Thomson, David, 1941-

The **big** screen : the story of the movies / David Thomson. Farrar, Straus and Giroux, 2012. 528 p. **791.430973**

1. Films -- Social aspects 2. Films -- History 3. Films -- Production and direction 4. Film actors and actresses

ISBN 9780374191894

LC 2012009140

Traces the rise, decline and influence of the film industry on the modern world, assessing its expressions in multiple media, its capacity for imitating and idealizing life and its role in the existences of everyday viewers. By the author of The New Biographical Dictionary of Film.

Urwand, Ben, 1977-

The **collaboration** : Hollywood's pact with Hitler / Ben Urwand. The Belknap Press of Harvard University Press, 2013. 320 p. **791.430973**

1. Films, American -- Germany -- History -- 20th century. 2. Film industry and trade -- Germany -- History -- 20th century. 3. Nazism. 4. World War II 5. Germany -- Civilization -- American influences.

ISBN 9780674724747

LC 2013013576

Argues that Hollywood studios collaborated with Hitler during the 1930s by agree to not make movies that disparaged Germany, investing in German newsreels and even financing the production of German armaments.

791.4372 Single films

Chaney, Jen

As if! : the oral history of Clueless as told by Amy Heckerling and the cast and crew / Jen Chaney. Touchstone Books, 2015 320 p. **791.4372**

1. Clueless (Motion picture) 2. Films 3. Popular culture 4. Screenplay writing. 5. Oral histories

ISBN 9781476799087

LC 2015943851

A 20th-anniversary oral history of the making of the cult-classic film offers behind-the-scenes insights into how the screenwriter was inspired by Jane Austen's Emma, how the cast was chosen, how costumes were designed and more.

791.4375 Two or more films

Revenson, Jody

Harry Potter magical places from the films : Hogwarts, Diagon Alley and beyond / Jody Revenson. Harper Design, an imprint of HarperCollinsPublishers, 2015. 205 p. : **791.4375**

1. Rowling, J. K. Settings. 2. Potter, Harry (Fictitious character) 3. Films -- Setting and scenery. 4. Filmmaking. 5. Fantasy films -- Miscellanea. 6. Franchise books.

ISBN 9780062385659

LC 2014957100

"An Insight Editions book."

A guide to the locations in the "Harry Potter" films includes detailed profiles of each location, concept art, behind-the-scenes photographs, and interviews from the cast and crew.

791.44 Radio

Dunning, John, 1942-

On the air : the encyclopedia of old-time radio / John Dunning. Oxford University Press, 1998. xvi, 822 p. ; **791.44**

1. Radio programs -- United States -- Dictionaries.

ISBN 0195076788

LC 96041959

Rev. ed. of: Tune in yesterday. c1976.

A comprehensive reference of the radio shows of the 1930s, 1940s, and 1950s has entries arranged in alphabetical order and includes each show's history, timeslot, network, advertisers, cast members, and much more.

"Dunning has compiled and organized a massive amount of research data on hundreds of radio shows aired from the 1920s through the 1960s. The entries, listed alphabetically by show title, each contain a treasure trove of information: broadcast dates, casts and personnel, anecdotes, special analyses, and a detailed overview of each show's background, format, and content." Library Journal.

Schwartz, A. Brad (Austin Bradley)

★**Broadcast** hysteria : Orson Welles's War of the worlds and the art of fake news / A. Brad Schwartz. Hill and Wang, 2015. 304 p. **791.44**

1. Welles, Orson, 1915-1985 Criticism and interpretation. 2. War of the worlds (Radio program) 3. Radio broadcasting -- United States -- History -- 20th century. 4. Deception 5. Hoaxes. 6. Mass media hoaxes

ISBN 9780809031610

LC 2014040510

"An entertaining assessment of a watershed moment in American life and its lasting effect on popular culture." Kirkus.

791.45 Television

Armstrong, Jennifer Keishin

Seinfeldia : how a show about nothing changed everything / Jennifer Keishin Armstrong. Simon & Schuster, 2015. 320 p. **791.45**

1. Seinfeld, Jerry 2. Seinfeld (Television program). 3. Television programs 4. Popular culture 5. Television -- Influence 6. Television writing 7. United States -- Social life and customs -- 20th century

ISBN 9781476756103

LC 2015023755

An uproarious behind-the-scenes account of the creation of the hit television series describes how comedians Larry David and Jerry Seinfeld dreamed up the idea for an unconventional sitcom over coffee and how, despite network skepticism and minimal plotlines, achieved mainstream success.

"Armstrong offers a masterly look at one of the greatest shows. The research involved makes this a boon to television scholars, but Seinfeld enthusiasts will also enjoy this funny, highly readable book." Library Journal.

Sex and the city and us : how four single women changed the way we think, live, and love / Jennifer Keishin Armstrong. Simon & Schuster, 2018. 288 p. **791.45**

1. Sex and the city (Television program). 2. Television programs 3. Popular culture 4. Television -- Influence 5. Television writing 6. United States -- Social life and customs -- 20th century

ISBN 9781501164828

LC 2018000333

A retrospective of the award-winning series features interviews from the cast and writers that further explore how the show changes the way women everywhere see themselves.

Fellowes, Jessica

The **wit** and wisdom of Downton Abbey / Jessica Fellowes. St. Martin's Griffin, 2015. 127 p. : **791.45**

1. Downton Abbey (Television program). 2. Quotations

ISBN 9781250093608

LC 2015953770

"Downton Abbey is loved the world over for its fabulous costumes, beautiful scenery, wonderful characters and intricate plot lines, but what keeps millions of us coming back time after time is the stellar quality of the writing. With each stroke of his pen Julian Fellowes seems to gift us with a cuttingly dry quip from the Dowager Countess, a perfectly timed word of wisdom from Mrs Patmore or a touchingly nostalgic pronouncement from Carson. Here in The Wit and Wisdom of Downton Abbey, Jessica Fellowes has gathered together her favorite quotes from the complete Downton Abbey oeuvre to take each of us back to the most memorable moments from the show and ensure we are armed with the very best ripostes should we ever need to chastise an impertinent lady's maid."--Provided by publisher.

Greene, Andy

The **office** : the untold story of the greatest sitcom of the 2000s :

an oral history / Andy Greene. Dutton, 2020. 336 p. **791.45**

1. Office (Television program : United States) 2. Television programs 3. Popular culture 4. Television -- Influence 5. Television -- Social aspects 6. United States -- Social life and customs -- 21st century 7. Oral histories
ISBN 9781524744977

LC 2019037591

The untold stories behind The Office, one of the most iconic television shows of the twenty-first century, told by its creators, writers, and actors.

"A fond, funny, informative trip down Memory Lane for series buffs and newcomers alike." Kirkus

Gross, Edward (Edward A.). 1960-

The **fifty** year mission : the first 25 years: the complete, uncensored, unauthorized oral history of Star trek / Edward Gross and Mark A. Altman Thomas Dunne Books, 2016. 544 p. **791.45**

1. Star trek (Television program). 2. Star Trek films.
ISBN 9781250065841

LC 2015051257

Includes index.

This 1st volume of an extensive oral history of Star Trek includes the uncensored and never-before-told stories of more than 200 people involved in creating the Star Trek franchise. Providing solid context for a bevy of quotes, the authors focus on the original series and the six movies that the show inspired -- and much of the entertainment comes from the different perspectives on the sometimes contentious relationships between contributors.

"Breathtaking in scope and depth, this is a must-read for Star Trek lovers as well as anyone who wants a better understanding of how television and film production works." Booklist.

Slayers & vampires : the complete uncensored, unauthorized oral history of Buffy and Angel / Edward Gross and Mark A. Altman. Tor Books, 2017. 576 p. **791.45**

1. Buffy, the vampire slayer (Television program) 2. Angel (Television program : 1999-2004) 3. Television programs 4. Characters and characteristics in television 5. Popular culture 6. Television industry and trade 7. Oral histories
ISBN 9781250128928

LC 2017297260

Featuring interviews with cast and crew members, an unauthorized chronicle of the story behind the making of two of the biggest cult television series includes coverage of how they were successfully spun from a failed movie, the network battle for their control and how their productions and storylines continue to influence television today.

"Filled with absorbing behind-the-scenes details, Altman and Gross illuminating celebration of Whedon's influential shows will thrill fans of Buffy and Angel and stand as invaluable primary TV history." Booklist.

Kaufman, Amy

Bachelor nation : inside the world of America's favorite guilty pleasure / Amy Kaufman. E.P. Dutton, 2018. 304 p. **791.45**

1. Bachelor (Television program) 2. Television programs 3. Popular culture 4. Television criticism
ISBN 9781101985908

LC 2017486601

Presents an unauthorized, behind-the-scenes cultural history of the Bachelor franchise.

"Essential for fans of pop culture, this book could play an important role in courses on feminism and gender studies. It's also a fascinating and fun read for anyone who wants to think about how and why viewers continue to tune into shows like The Bachelor." Library Journal.

Nussbaum, Emily, 1966-

I like to watch : arguing my way through the TV revolution / Emily Nussbaum. Random House, 2019. 365 p. **791.45**

1. Nussbaum, Emily, 1966- 2. Television programs 3. Television criticism 4. Popular culture 5. Media fandom
ISBN 9780525508960

LC 2018055067

Includes index.

Nussbaum writes about her passion for television, beginning with Buffy the Vampire Slayer, the show that set her on a fresh intellectual path. She explores the rise of the female screw-up, how fans warp the shows they love, the messy power of sexual violence on TV, and the year that jokes helped elect a reality-television president.

Peisner, David

Homey don't play that! : the story of In Living Color and the black comedy revolution / David Peisner. 37 INK/Atria, 2018. vii, 386 pages ; **791.45**

1. African American comedians 2. African Americans in television 3. Television comedies 4. Skits
ISBN 9781501143328

LC 2018285671

Engaging behind-the-scenes stories about the boundary-breaking sketch comedy show draw on interviews with cast members, writers, producers and network executives to celebrate its enduring influence on comedy, race relations and the careers of some of today's biggest stars.

Press, Joy, 1966-

Stealing the show : how women are revolutionizing television / Joy Press. Atria Books, 2018. 272 p. **791.45**

1. Television and women. 2. Women entertainers. 3. Women in television 4. Women television producers and directors.
ISBN 9781501137716

LC 2017032332

A leading cultural journalist traces the rise of the female showrunner and how women have become an integral part of today's television, sharing the stories of such boundary-breaking performers as Roseanne Barr, Diane English and Tina Fey.

Reiss, Mike, 1959-

Springfield confidential : jokes, secrets, and outright lies from a lifetime writing for the Simpsons / Mike Reiss, Mathew Klickstein ; foreword by Judd Apatow. HarperCollins 2018 320 p. **791.45**

1. Simpsons (Television program) 2. Television writing 3. Television writers 4. Television programs 5. Cartoons
ISBN 9780062748034

LC 2017279142

The Simpsons' longest-serving writer and producer offers a humorous look at the writing and making of the legendary Fox series that has become one of the most revered artistic achievements in television history.

"Always honest, playful, and engaging, the book will provide fans with deep insight into the show's history but also into its daily production and future." Kirkus.

Sepinwall, Alan, 1973-

TV (the book) : two experts pick the greatest American shows of all time / Alan Sepinwall & Matt Zoller Seitz. Grand Central Publishing, 2016. 352 p. **791.45**

1. Television criticism. 2. Television programs 3. Popular culture --

History 4. Mass media 5. Essays.
ISBN 9781455588190
LC 2016015540

Includes index.

While working at the Newark Star-Ledger, Matt Zoller Seitz and Alan Sepinwall created a popular column debating the merits of then-current television. Eventually they went on to successful careers as critics elsewhere, but the debate raged on and now comes to an epic conclusion in TV (THE BOOK).

"The great debate: how do you pick the best show of all time? -- The inner circle -- No-doubt-about-it classics -- Groundbreakers and workhorses -- Outlier classics -- Works in progress -- A certain regard -- Miniseries -- TV-movies -- Live plays made for television." Kirkus.

Shales, Tom

Live from New York : an uncensored history of Saturday Night Live / Tom Shales and James Andrew Miller. Little, Brown, 2014, c2002. 594 p., 16 p. of plates : **791.45**

1. Saturday night live (Television program) 2. Television -- History. 3. Television programs -- History. 4. Comedy -- History and criticism
ISBN 9780316295048
LC 2002072958

Includes index.

A history of the long-running television series draws on backstage anecdotes and uncensored reminiscences to create an oral history of "Saturday Night Live."

Smith, Chris

The **Daily** Show (the book) : an oral history as told by Jon Stewart, the correspondents, staff and guests / Chris Smith, foreword by Jon Stewart Grand Central Publishing, 2016. 304 p. **791.45**

1. Daily Show (Television program) 2. Comedians -- United States 3. Television writers 4. Television -- History. 5. Television programs -- History. 6. Oral histories
ISBN 9781455565382
LC 2016952042

An uncensored history of the Emmy and Peabody Award-winning The Daily Show With Jon Stewart as told by its correspondents, writers and host shares behind-the-scenes stories as well as observations about its blend of news reportage and comedy and its enduring cultural and professional influence.

791.4502 Stock footage--television

Kamp, David

Sunny days : the children's television revolution that changed America / David Kamp ; foreword by Questlove. Simon & Schuster, 2020. 320 p. **791.4502**

1. Sesame Street (Television program) 2. Television programs for children 3. Television programs -- Social aspects 4. Television and education 5. Inner city children 6. United States -- Social life and customs -- 20th century
ISBN 9781501137808
LC 2019059612

Tells the behind-the-scenes story of the creation of the children's TV programs Sesame Street, The Electric Company, Mister Rogers' Neighborhood and more, which transformed the American childhood for the better, teaching kids about diversity, the ABCs and feminism.

"This passionate, highly engaging media history will thrill pop culture buffs and those who remember these shows from their childhood." Publishers Weekly

791.4509 History, geographic treatment, biography

Martin, Brett, 1972-

Difficult men : behind the scenes of a creative revolution: from the Sopranos and the Wire to Mad Men and Breaking Bad / Brett Martin. Penguin, 2013 288 p. **791.4509**

1. Sopranos (Television program) 2. Breaking bad (Television program : 2008-) 3. Mad men (Television program) 4. The Wire (Television program) 5. Six Feet Under (Television program) 6. The Shield (Television program) 7. Television programs 8. Television industry and trade 9. Cable television 10. Television
ISBN 9781594204197
LC 2012047001

Since when have morally ambiguous "good" guys becomes so hot in TV? In a fascinating assessment of programs that have helped TV emerge as a legitimate creative art form over the last 15 years, author Brett Martin explores the unique writing and production choices that have place shows like The Wire, Deadwood, The Sopranos, and Mad Men a cut above. Full of both serious commentary and behind-the-scenes info, this is a great read for anyone interested in today's more challenging shows.

Thomson, David, 1941-

Television : a biography / David Thomson. Thanmes & Hidson, 2016 304 p. **791.4509**

1. Television -- History. 2. Television programs 3. Television criticism. 4. Popular culture
ISBN 9780500519165
LC 2016932145

A critical history of the first six decades of the television era, written by the acclaimed film critic and author of The Biographical Dictionary of Film, traces television's evolution from an immobile piece of furniture with limited sponsored programming to a diverse, on-demand content provider.

791.5 Puppetry and toy theaters

Blumenthal, Eileen, 1948-

★**Puppetry** : a world history / Eileen Blumenthal. Harry N. Abrams, 2005. 271 p. : **791.5**

1. Puppet theaters. 2. Puppetry -- History. 3. Puppets. 4. Puppeteers.
ISBN 0810955873
LC 2004029349

"This is a history of the puppet world, from prehistoric times to Tony-winning Broadway hit Avenue Q. This would be a welcome addition to the libraries of performing arts buffs who want to learn more about a lesser known form." Publishers Weekly.

791.6 Pageantry

Mifflin, Margot, 1960-

Looking for Miss America : a pageant's 100-year quest to define womanhood / Margot Mifflin. Counterpoint, 2020. 320

p. **791.6**

1. Miss America Pageant History. 2. Beauty contests -- History 3. Beauty contest industry and trade 4. Feminism 5. Racism in popular culture 6. United States
ISBN 9781640092235

LC 2019053730

Approaching its 100th anniversary, the pageant has survived scandal, protests, mockery, and the mutiny of a queen who got cold feet and skipped town the night she won. Looking for Miss America breaks down the blend of capitalism, patriotism, class anxiety and cultural mythology that has fueled the pageant, the racial biases it has perpetuated, and the social mobility it has enabled.

"This work offers a thought-provoking, balanced, and highly informative look at an institution that has perplexed and enticed Americans since its founding." Library Journal

791.8 Animal performances

Hemingway, Ernest, 1899-1961

Death in the afternoon / Ernest Hemingway. Scribner, 1999, c1932. 397 p. : **791.8**

1. Bullfights.
ISBN 9780684859224

LC 99231717

Originally published: 1932.

A fascinating look at the history and grandeur of bullfighting, Death in the Afternoon is also a deeper contemplation of the nature of cowardice and bravery, sport and tragedy, and is enlivened throughout by Hemingway's sharp commentary on life and literature. --From publisher description.

Peter, Josh

Fried twinkies, buckle bunnies, & bull riders : a year inside the professional bull riders tour / Josh Peter. Rodale, c2005. x, 246 p. : **791.8**

1. Professional Bull Riders, Inc. 2. Professional bull riders. 3. Bull riders. 4. Bull riding.
ISBN 9781594861192

LC 2005017297

Includes index.

An account of the 2004 Professional Bull Riders Tour describes how hundreds of cowboys risked life and limb throughout the course of twenty-nine major events to compete for a million-dollar prize.

"The argument can be made that the Professional Bull Riders Tour may be the most dangerous, least financially rewarding of all sporting endeavors. Skull fractures, punctured lungs, and destroyed knees are all relatively routine injuries. At least now there is a million-dollar payout for the overall champion each season, but even that is in deferred dollars. Peter, a sportswriter for the New Orleans Times-Picayune, spent the 2004 season with the PBR tour and offers a penetrating portrait of a sport that stands at that awkward stage between minor league and national acceptance. ... This is a tough book to walk away from." Booklist.

792 Stage presentations

Adler, Stella, 1902-1992

Stella Adler : the art of acting / compiled and edited by Howard Kissel. Applause Books, c2000. 271 p. : **792**

1. Acting
ISBN 9781557833730

LC 00108803

Drawing on an archive of notebooks, transcriptions, and audiotapes, the lessons and insights Stella Adler brought to the craft of acting are presented.

"In this collection of Adler's papers Kissel has taken tapes, transcriptions, notebooks, and other sources to reconstruct an acting course in 22 lessons. The lessons are graduated from very basic matters to quite complex issues of textual analysis and decorum. Though mostly monologs, they include enough exercises and student responses to get the flavor of Adler's work. This is required reading for anyone interested in theater practice." Library Journal.

Brockett, Oscar G. (Oscar Gross), 1923-2010

History of the theatre / Oscar G. Brockett, Franklin J. Hildy. Pearson, c2008. xii, 688 p. : **792**

1. Theater -- History 2. Drama -- History and criticism
ISBN 9780205511860

LC 2009291794

"40th anniversary edition"--Cover.

This 40th Anniversary Edition retains all of the traditional features that have made History of the Theatre the most successful text of its kind, including worldwide coverage, more than 530 photos and illustrations, useful maps, and the expertise of Oscar G. Brockett and Franklin J. Hildy, two of the most widely respected theatre historians in the field. As with every edition, the text reflects the current state of knowledge and brings the history of theatre up to the present. This tenth edition continues to provide the most thorough and accurate assessment of theatre history available.

"This edition, with its extensive bibliography and instructive images, ensures that this title will continue to be among the best resources on the market. This said, libraries that own the ninth edition may wish to pass on this one, since the information expanded in (and new to) the present volume is readily available elsewhere. " Choice.

Gillette, J. Michael

Designing with light : an introduction to stage lighting / J. Michael Gillette, Michael J. McNamara. McGraw-Hill Companies, 2013. 379 p. **792**

1. Stage lighting.
ISBN 0073514233

LC 2012034637

The authors approach stage lighting design as an art that integrates the vision of director, actor, and playwright, and as a craft that provides practical solutions for the manipulation of stage space. The sixth edition offers a wealth of new information on new trends in lighting design. --From publisher description.

Mamet, David

True and false : heresy and common sense for the actor / David Mamet. Pantheon Books, c1997. x, 127 p. ; **792**

1. Acting. 2. Actors and actresses. 3. Film actors and actresses. 4. United States -- Popular culture -- History -- 20th century. 5. Essays.
ISBN 0679442499

LC 97019336

Argues that the techniques taught in acting school, in particular the famous Stansilavsky Method, mislead aspiring actors and suggests ways for performers to remain true to the chararacters they represent.

"Mamet exhorts actors to show up early, have their lines down cold, and have a single objective for each scene. He contends that overthinking and too much emotional interpretation is not the actor's role. Essential reading for theater collections." Library Journal.

Moore, Sonia

★The **Stanislavski** system : the professional training of an actor : digested from the teachings of Konstantin S. Stanislavski / Sonia Moore. Penguin Books, 1984. xvi, 96 p. ; **792**

1. Method acting

ISBN 9780140466607

LC 84002855

Includes index.

Provides an explanation of the art and practice of acting as taught by Stanislavski and briefly describes the style and achievements of his disciple, Eugene Vakhtangov

792.01 Philosophy and theory

Brook, Peter, 1925-

The **empty** space / Peter Brook. Simon & Schuster, 1996, c1968. 141 p. ; **792.01**

1. Theater 2. Drama

ISBN 9780684829579

LC BL 99005347

"A Touchstone book."

Originally published: London : MacGibbon & Kee, 1968.

Discusses four types of theatrical landscapes; the deadly theatre, the holy theatre, the rough theatre, and the immediate theatre.

792.02 Miscellany

Essin, Christin

Stage designers in early twentieth-century America : artists, activists, cultural critics / Christin Essin. Palgrave Macmillan, 2012. xiii, 264 p. : **792.02**

1. Set designers -- United States. 2. Theaters -- Stage-setting and scenery -- United States -- History -- 20th century.

ISBN 0230115071

LC 2012043581

By casting designers as authors, cultural critics, activists, entrepreneurs, and global cartographers, Essin tells a story about scenic images on the page, stage, and beyond that helped American audiences see the everyday landscapes and exotic destinations from a modern perspective.

"All these treatments are enlivened with case studies of specific productions. Essin's research is thorough, her writing is engaging, and her insights are rewarding." Choice

Fischer, Jenna, 1974-

The **actor's** life : a survival guide / Jenna Fischer. BenBella Books, 2017 252 p. **792.02**

1. Acting -- Vocational guidance 2. Acting -- Handbooks, manuals, etc.

ISBN 9781944648220

LC 2017048157

An established actor and one of the stars of The Office, with amusing candor and wit and drawing on her own memorable and hilarious experiences, presents this handy guide for getting established as a professional actor, providing invaluable advice personally acquired from her many years of struggle.

Gillette, J. Michael

Theatrical design and production : an introduction to scene design and construction, lighting, sound, costume, and make-up / J. Michael Gillette. McGraw-Hill, c2013. xvi, 624 p. : **792.02**

1. Stage management. 2. Theater -- Production and direction. 3. Theaters -- Stage-setting and scenery.

ISBN 0073382221

LC 2012020022

"The author divides his standard text for undergraduate lighting design students into the two constituent elements of his craft--technology and design. He clearly and completely presents both technical and aesthetic design aspects." Library Journal.

Hagen, Uta, 1919-2004

★**Respect** for acting / Uta Hagen ; with Haskel Frankel. John Wiley & Sons, c2008. xiii, 226 p. ; **792.02**

1. Acting

ISBN 9780470228487

LC 2008016843

Includes index.

Originally published: New York : Macmillan, 1973.

"This classic treatise on the process and craft of acting has significantly benefited actors for three decades. Juxtaposed with Hagen's aesthetic is a wealth of practical information, creative ideas, and her uniquely useful object exercises." Library Journal.

Stanislavsky, Konstantin, 1863-1938

★An **actor's** work : a student's diary / Konstantin Stanislavski ; translated and edited by Jean Benedetti. Routledge, 2008. xxviii, 693 p. ; **792.02**

1. Method acting

ISBN 9780415422239

LC 2007045357

Presents a new translation of the author's incomplete works "An Actor Prepares" and " Building a Character" which provides a system for acting and developing a character.

"This translation by Benedetti of Stanislavski's famous works...will be greeted with excitement by actors everywhere." Library Journal.

Wasson, Sam

Improv nation : how we made a great American art / Sam Wasson. Houghton Mifflin Harcourt, 2017. 464 p. **792.02**

1. Second City (Theater company) 2. Compass Players. 3. Saturday night live (Television program) 4. Improvision (Acting) 5. Comedy. 6. Popular culture. 7. Women comedians. 8. United States -- Social life and customs -- 20th century.

ISBN 9780544557208

LC bl2017041789

A sweeping history of the uniquely American art form of improv, which has never been more popular--from its beginnings during the McCarthy Era through the rise of such institutions as Second City, the Groundlings and the Upright Citizens Brigade and such performers as Tine Fey, Steve Carell and Bill Murray.

"While comedians today take up a large space in public life, Wasson reminds us that a lot of hard work has been done for them to get there. An entertaining book, recommended for aspiring comedians who want to historicize their practice." Kirkus.

792.03 Theater--dictionaries

Kennedy, Dennis, 1940-

The **Oxford** companion to theatre and performance / edited by Dennis Kennedy. Oxford University Press, 2010. xii, 689 p. ; **792.03**

1. Theater -- Encyclopedias 2. Performing arts -- Encyclopedias 3. Encyclopedias
ISBN 9780199574193

LC 2010283468

Concise and updated version originally published in 2003, under title: Oxford encyclopedia of theatre & performance.

Features more than two thousand entries on theater and performance, covering styles and movements, buildings, organizations, and traditions--with a particularly strong focus on biographies of actors, playwrights, directors, and designers.

792.089 Ethnic groups--theater

Lane, Stewart F.

Black Broadway : African Americans on the great white way / Stewart F. Lane. Square One Publishers, 2015. 288 p. **792.089**

1. Theater 2. African Americans 3. African American entertainers 4. African Americans in the performing arts. 5. Broadway (New York, N.Y.) -- History.
ISBN 9780757003882

LC 2014006513

An entertaining, poignant history of a Broadway of which few are aware.

"In this wonderfully illustrated and researched book, Tony Award-winning producer Lane chronicles the evolution of black theater from the 1700s to today." Booklist

792.09 History, geographic treatment, biography

Cliff, Nigel

The **Shakespeare** riots : revenge, drama, and death in nineteenth-century America / Nigel Cliff. Random House, c2007. xxi, 312 p. : **792.09**

1. Forrest, Edwin, 1806-1872. 2. Macready, William Charles, 1793-1873. 3. Shakespeare, William, 1564-1616 Stage history -- 1800-4. Shakespeare, William, 1564-1616 Stage history New York City. 5. Astor Place Riot, New York City., 1849. 6. Theater -- New York City -- History. 7. New York City -- Social life and customs -- 19th century.
ISBN 0345486943

LC 2006049139

A social and cultural history of New York's 1849 Astor Place Riots describes how a feud between two Shakespearean actors of the era led to a violent public disturbance that resulted in the deaths of more than thirty people.

"Cliff argues persuasively that the Astor Place riot, as it came to be known, marked a turning point in America's search for a national identity. [This] is an intriguing, thought-provoking book." Washington Post Book World.

Riedel, Michael (Theater critic)

Razzle dazzle : the battle for Broadway / Michael Riedel. Simon & Schuster, 2015 352 p. **792.09**

1. Theater 2. Musicals 3. Cities and towns 4. Broadway, New York City
ISBN 9781451672169

LC 2015506947

"While not functioning as an introduction or a detailed history of the American commercial theater, this book articulates a neglected but historically essential point of view." Library Journal.

792.6 Musical plays

Bloom, Ken, 1949-

Broadway musicals : the 101 greatest shows of all time / Ken Bloom & Frank Vlastnik ; new preface by Broadway's leading ladies ; foreword by Jerry Orbach. Black Dog & Leventhal Publishers, 2010 344 p. : **792.6**

1. Musicals 2. Broadway, New York City Musicals
ISBN 9781579128494

LC 2012398655

Includes index.

Offers an alphabetical survey of the most popular Broadway musicals in history, with commentaries, synopses, behind-the-scenes information, and lists of songs and cast members for each musical.

792.609 Musical plays--History, geographic treatment, biography

Stempel, Larry

Showtime : a history of the Broadway musical theater / Larry Stempel. W.W. Norton & Co., c2010. xx, 826 p., 16 p. of plates : **792.609**

1. Musicals -- New York (State) -- New York -- History and criticism.
ISBN 0393067157

LC 2010019704

Presents the history of Broadway musicals over the past 150 years, examining their cultural context and historical significance, from the Astor Place Opera House riot of 1849 through the golden age of Show Boat and Oklahoma! and modern-day Rent.

"Theater buffs will be delighted to find that this scholarly, definitive work is also a hugely entertaining read." Publishers Weekly.

Viertel, Jack

The **secret** life of the American musical : how classic Broadway shows are built / Jack Viertel. Sarah Crichton Books, 2016. 336 p. **792.609**

1. Musicals -- United States -- History and criticism. 2. Theater 3. Musicals -- United States -- Analysis, appreciation. 4. Broadway, New York City
ISBN 9780374256920

LC 2015023713

Includes index.

How do musicals make it to Broadway? In this entertaining and informative book, Broadway veteran (producer, critic, professor, executive, etc.) Jack Viertel draws on a range of examples -- from The Music Man to Wicked to Hamilton -- and personal experiences to paint a picture of how the process works. Taking readers step-by-step through all the phases of a typical musical-theater story, from opening numbers to finales, Viertel offers a colorful exploration of Broadway. And for those who want to know what to listen to post-reading, Viertel provides a list of soundtracks.

792.7 Variety shows and theatrical dancing

Downer, Lesley

Women of the pleasure quarters : the secret history of the geisha / Lesley Downer. Broadway Books, 2002. xiv, 288 p., [16] p. of plates : **792.7**

1. Geishas. 2. Japan. 3. East Asia.
ISBN 0767904893

LC 00049409

Presents an authoritative account of geisha history, sharing the stories of some of Japan's most famous geishas and covering such areas as its training, rituals, customs, costumes, and private practices.

"The author skillfully intertwines her profiles of Kyoto personalities and tea-house customs with a fluidly written geisha history that's unabashedly aimed at a Western audience. Written in dynamic, highly readable prose, the book is supported by exhaustive research and a lengthy bibliography." Publishers Weekly.

Gold, Judy, 1962-

Yes I can say that : when they come for the comedians we're all in trouble / Judy Gold. Dey Street, 2020. 224 p. **792.7**

1. Comedians 2. Censorship 3. Freedom of speech 4. Political correctness (Concept)
ISBN 9780062953759

LC 2019054781

A comedy veteran, in 10 impassioned polemics, frames comedy as a tool of empowerment -- a way to reclaim hateful rhetoric and battle the democracy-crushing plight of censorship.

"A powerful, and powerfully funny, argument in support of how vital free speech is to comedy and comedy is to us." Booklist

Nesteroff, Kliph

The **comedians** : drunks, thieves, scoundrels, and the history of American comedy / Kliph Nesteroff. Grove Press, 2015. 512 p. **792.7**

1. Stand-up comedy. 2. Stand-up comedians. 3. Comedy -- History and criticism
ISBN 9780802123985

LC 2016479007

Explores and describes the history of stand-up comedy in America, beginning with vaudeville and moving through radio, late-night television, the counter-culture comedy icons of the 1960s, the first stand-up clubs in the 1970s and the cocaine-fueled boom of the 1980s.

"Both pop culture enthusiasts and entertainment scholars will relish this important history of American comedy." Library Journal.

Rosenfield, Stephen

Mastering stand-up : the complete guide to becoming a successful comedian / Stephen Rosenfield. Chicago Review Press, 2018 xiv, 256 p. ; **792.7**

1. Stand-up comedy -- Vocational guidance
ISBN 9781613736920

LC bl2017042209

Includes index.

An entertaining and sharply written guide--for both beginners breaking into comedy and professionals seeking to improve their sets and advance their careers--examines the work of great comedians such as Jerry Seinfeld, Eddie Izzard, Moms Mabley, Hannibal Buress, Sarah Silverman, Richard Pryor and more as a means of illustrating the most important techniques of performing and writing stand-up.

Seibert, Brian

What the eye hears : a history of tap dancing / Brian Seibert. Farrar, Straus and Giroux, 2015. 560 p. **792.7**

1. Tap dancing -- History. 2. Tap dancers 3. Culture 4. Dancing
ISBN 9780865479531

LC 2015005010

Includes index.

National Book Critics Circle Award for Nonfiction finalist, 2015.

The first authoritative history of tap dancing, one of the great art forms--along with jazz and musical comedy--created in America.

"Drawing on primary sources of every kind, from written accounts by slave traders in the early 17th century to personal interviews conducted in the 21st, the author breaks down not merely the origins art of tap dancing itself, but the racial and gender constructs that forced the industry--and its performers--to develop in the ways they did, while acknowledging his own white male privilege." Publishers Weekly.

Zemeckis, Leslie

Behind the Burly Q : the story of burlesque in America / Leslie Zemeckis. Skyhorse Publishing, 2013 xxiv, 360 p. : **792.7**

1. Burlesque 2. Stripteasers 3. Traveling theater 4. Dancers
ISBN 9781620876916

LC 2015302007

Featuring interviews by performers and other notables of the industry, presents the history of American burlesque theater from its golden age through its decline and its current renaissance.

792.8 Ballet and modern dance

Copeland, Misty

Ballerina body : dancing and eating your way to a leaner, stronger, and more graceful you / Misty Copeland, with Charisse Jones ; movement and dance photography by Henry Leutwyler, food photography by Amy Roth. Grand Central Life & Style, 2017. xii, 226 p. : **792.8**

1. Ballet dancers -- Nutrition 2. Ballet dancers -- Training of 3. Ballet dancing
ISBN 9781455569878

LC OC2018136608

Includes index.

The celebrated ballerina and role model, Misty Copeland, shares the secrets of how to reshape your body and achieve a lean, strong physique and glowing health.

Craine, Debra

The **Oxford** dictionary of dance / Debra Craine, Judith Mackrell. Oxford University Press, 2010. vi, 502 p. : **792.8**

1. Dance -- Dictionaries 2. Ballet -- Dictionaries 3. Dictionaries
ISBN 9780199563449

LC 2010930321

Previous ed.: 2000.

"Very affordable, it is well worth adding to a dance collection in any library and provides a compact, handy way to access dance facts quickly." Booklist

Homans, Jennifer

★**Apollo's** angels : a history of ballet / Jennifer Homans. Random House, 2010. 464 p. **792.8**

1. Ballet -- History. 2. Ballet dancers. 3. Dancing. 4. Dancers.
ISBN 9781400060603

LC 2010006945

ALA Notable Book, 2012.

National Book Critics Circle Award for Nonfiction finalist, 2010.

"A book of this breadth is going to have its own biorhythms: chapters that engage the author's mind and heart wholly, where everything clicks and the thinking is virtually kinetic, and chapters that don't come as easily. Ms. Homans is at her best when the ideological agenda at hand aspires to discipline, precision and refinement. Her French section is masterful, as are the chapters on the rise of the ballerina, the Danish style, Imperial Russian classicism, and British ballet." Wall Street Journal.

Jacobs, Laura

★**Celestial** bodies : how to look at ballet / Laura Jacobs. Basic Books, 2018. 272 p. **792.8**

1. Ballet 2. Ballet -- History 3. Choreography 4. Dancing
ISBN 9780465098477

LC 2017051470

In Celestial Bodies, dance critic Laura Jacobs makes the foreign familiar, providing a lively, poetic, and uniquely accessible introduction to the world of classical dance. Combining history, interviews with dancers, technical definitions, descriptions of performances, and personal stories, Jacobs offers an intimate and passionate guide to watching ballet and understanding the central elements of choreography.

"Ballet history, explanations of technique, interviews with dancers, first-person accounts of performances, and personal reflections on a variety of other related topics are presented in engaging prose, enhanced by Jessica Roux's delicate illustrations." Booklist.

Minden, Eliza Gaynor

The **ballet** companion : a dancer's guide to the technique, traditions, and joys of ballet / Eliza Gaynor Minden. Fireside Book/Simon & Schuster, c2005. xv, 331 p. : **792.8**

1. Ballet dancing
ISBN 9780743264075

LC 2005044102

"A Fireside book."

"A Lark production."

An illustrated reference for dancers at all levels shares advice about how to train safely, observe appropriate etiquette, and learn the techniques of accomplished dancers, in a volume complemented by historical information.

Morrison, Simon Alexander, 1964-

Bolshoi confidential : secrets of the Russian ballet from the rule of the tsars to today / Simon Morrison. Liveright Publishing Corporation, 2016. 512 p. **792.8**

1. Bolshoi Ballet Company. 2. Dance companies. 3. Ballet dancers. 4. Ballets. 5. Russia.
ISBN 9780871402967

LC 2016031665

A history of the Bolshoi Ballet from its beginnings in 1776 to today, describing the careers of those onstage and off, tracing its political ties to the varying Russian regimes, and detailing some of the best-loved ballets in its repertoire.

"A must for ballet buffs. Not the last word on the Bolshoi, but a look backstage that is both lively and learned." Kirkus.

Gottlieb, Robert, 1931-

Reading dance : a gathering of memoirs, reportage, criticism, profiles, interviews, and some uncategorizable extras / edited and with an introduction by Robert Gottlieb. Pantheon Books, 2009. 1360 p. **792.8**

1. Dancers -- Interviews 2. Dancing -- History 3. Choreography 4. Performing arts -- History
ISBN 9780375421228

LC 2008024392

Brings together a collection of seminal writings--including memoirs, letters, criticism, reportage, interviews, and profiles--that explore the art, history, and cultural influence of the dance, with contributions from notable dancers, choreographers, teachers, critics, and commentators from the nineteenth century to the present day.

792.809 Ballet and modern dance--History, geographic treatment, biography

Fuhrer, Margaret

American dance : the complete illustrated history / Margaret Fuhrer ; foreword by Alicia Graf Mack. Voyageur Press, 2014. 288 p. : **792.809**

1. Dance -- United States -- History. 2. Modern dance -- United States -- History.
ISBN 0760345996

LC 2014022261

"A lavishly illustrated history of American dance; covers more than four centuries, from Native American ceremonial dances to the early 21st century; written by journalist and dancer Margaret Fuhrer".-- Provided by publisher.

"A dance sampler that should prompt readers to further explore the multifaceted history of dance and maybe take a class!" Library Journal.

792.9 Stage productions

Dromgoole, Dominic

Hamlet globe to globe / Dominic Dromgoole. Grove Press, 2017. 320 p. **792.9**

1. Shakespeare, William, 1564-1616. Hamlet 2. Drama. 3. Acting. 4. Theater.
ISBN 9780802125620

LC 2017001313

From the artistic director of Shakespeare's Globe Theatre in London comes an account of the theater's extraordinary two-year tour bringing Hamlet to every country on Earth, and an exploration of the play's history, meaning and impact.

"Sly, witty, and delightfula glorious Shakespearean romp." Kirkus.

793.3 Social, folk, national dancing

Browar, Ken

The **art** of movement : NYC Dance Project / Ken Browar and Deborah Ory, NYC Dance Project. Black Dog & Leventhal Publishers, 2016. 1 volume (unpaged) : **793.3**

1. Dance 2. Dancers
ISBN 9780316318587

LC bl2016046027

Chiefly illustrations.

Celebrates movement and dance via hundreds of photographs of more than 70 dancers from American Ballet Theater, New York City Ballet, Alvin Ailey American Dance Theater, Martha Graham Dance Company, Boston Ballet, Royal Danish Ballet, the Royal Ballet and many more.

793.734 Word games

Merriam-Webster, Inc,

The **official** Scrabble players dictionary / Merriam-Webster. Merriam-Webster, Incorporated, 2018 12a, 736 p. ; **793.734**

1. Scrabble (Game) -- Glossaries, vocabularies, etc.
ISBN 9780877795964

LC bl2018183112

New Edition! A comprehensive book that millions of SCRABBLE players consider the only necessary resource for winning the game! More than 100,000 playable two-to-eight-letter words with hundreds of new words including facepalm, listicle, bitcoin, and emoji. Includes variant spellings with expanded coverage of Canadian and British words. Main entries include a brief definition, a part-of-speech label, and inflected forms for fast, easy word validation. Endorsed by the North American SCRABBLE Players Association for recreational and school use.

793.74 Mathematical games and recreations

Stewart, Ian, 1945-

Professor Stewart's casebook of mathematical mysteries / Ian Stewart. Basic Books, 2014 x, 307 p. : **793.74**

1. Mathematical recreations. 2. Mathematics 3. Essays
ISBN 9780465054978

LC bl2014045135

Offers mathematical games, puzzles, facts, and stories that tackle subjects ranging from prime numbers to Pi Day and other mathematical dates.

"Add a few jokes, a few serious applications, and plenty of references for further online exploration, and the result is another fine book from Stewart. Summing Up: Highly recommended. All levels/libraries." Choice.

793.8 Magic and related activities

Diaconis, Persi

Magical mathematics : the mathematical ideas that animate great magic tricks / Persi Diaconis and Ron Graham ; with a foreword by Martin Gardner. Princeton University Press, 2012. xii, 244 p. : **793.8**

1. Card tricks -- Mathematics
ISBN 9780691151649

LC 2011014755

"Magical Mathematics reveals the secrets of amazing, fun-to-perform card tricks--and the profound mathematical ideas behind them--that will astound even the most accomplished magician. Persi Diaconis and Ron Graham provide easy, step-by-step instructions for each trick, explaining how to set up the effect and offering tips on what to say and do while performing it. Each card trick introduces a new mathematical idea, and varying the tricks in turn takes readers to the very threshold of today's mathematical knowledge. For example, the Gilbreath principle--a fantastic effect where the cards remain in control despite being shuffled--is found to share an intimate connection with the Mandelbrot set. Other card tricks link to the mathematical secrets of combinatorics, graph theory, number theory, topology, the Riemann hypothesis, and even Fermat's last theorem. Diaconis and Graham are mathematicians as well as skilled performers with decades of professional experience between them. In this book they share a wealth of conjuring lore, including some closely guarded secrets of legendary magicians. Magical Mathematics covers the mathematics of juggling and shows how the I Ching connects to the history of probability and magic tricks both old and new. It tells the stories--and reveals the best tricks--of the eccentric and brilliant inventors of mathematical magic. Magical Mathematics exposes old gambling secrets through the mathematics of shuffling cards, explains the classic street-gambling scam of three-card monte, traces the history of mathematical magic back to the thirteenth century and the oldest mathematical trick--and much more".-- Provided by publisher.

Miles, Bryan

101 magic tricks : any time, any place / Bryan Miles. Quarry, 2016. 208 p. : **793.8**

1. Magic tricks
ISBN 9781631590726

LC 2015025881

Includes index.

Presents step-by-step instructions for over one hundred magic tricks.

794.1 Chess

Fischer, Bobby, 1943-

★**Bobby** Fischer teaches chess / Bobby Fischer, Stuart Margulies, Donn Mosenfelder. Bantam Books, 1972, c1966. 179 p. : **794.1**

1. Chess -- Programmed instruction
ISBN 9780553263152

LC BL 99788921

Originally published: New York : Xerox Learning Systems, 1966.

Programmed text offers experienced as well as beginning players the opportunity to develop chess skills.

Just, Tim

U.S. Chess Federation's official rules of chess / Tim Just, chief editor, National Tournament Director. Random House, 2014. xlii, 369 p. ; **794.1**

1. United States Chess Federation. 2. Chess -- Rules.
ISBN 9780375724008

LC 2014009874

Includes index.

"This is a book of the detailed rules for tournament chess".-- Provided by publisher.

794.6 Bowling

Mullen, Michelle, B.S.

Bowling fundamentals / Michelle Mullen. Human Kinetics, c2004. xiv, 127 p. : **794.6**

1. Bowling
ISBN 9780736051200

LC 2003013368

Discusses essential skills, tactics and fundamentals--grip, stance, footwork, arm swing, timing, and release--and provides a base for solid technique.

794.8 Electronic games

Bissell, Tom, 1974-

Extra lives : why video games matter / Tom Bissell. Pantheon Books, 2010. 240 p. **794.8**

1. Video Games -- Social aspects. 2. Popular culture -- Social aspects. 3. Electronic games. 4. Video games -- History.

ISBN 9780307378705

LC 2009039602

Includes index.

Millions of adults spend hours every week playing video games, and the industry itself now reliably out earns Hollywood. But the wider culture seems to regard video games as, at best, well designed if mindless entertainment. Extra Lives is an impassioned defense of this assailed and misunderstood art form. Bissell argues that we are in a golden age of gaming--but he also believes games could be even better. He offers a fascinating and often hilarious critique of the ways video games dazzle and, just as often, frustrate. Along the way, we get firsthand portraits of some of the best minds (Jonathan Blow, Clint Hocking, Cliff Bleszinski, Peter Molyneux) at work in video game design today, as well as a shattering and deeply moving final chapter that describes, in searing detail, Bissell's descent into the world of Grand Theft Auto IV, a game whose themes mirror his own increasingly self-destructive compulsions. -- Description from Random House via TS3.

Burak, Asi

Power play : how video games can save the world / Asi Burak and Laura Parker. St. Martin's Press, 2017. 256 p. **794.8**

1. Video games 2. Social change 3. Education 4. Nonprofit organizations

ISBN 9781250089335

LC 2016036716

Explores how the Games for Change movement, which uses games as a platform to engage players in current social issues, is spearheading humanitarian and educational efforts around the globe in collaboration with the White House, NASA, the World Bank and The United Nations.

"These compelling examples of games for change are sure to engage gaming enthusiasts, activists, and game studies scholars." Library Journal.

Grossman, Dave

Assassination generation : video games, aggression, and the psychology of killing / Lt. Col. Dave Grossman and Kristine Paulsen with Katie Miserany. Little, Brown and Company, 2016. 264 p. **794.8**

1. Violence -- Social aspects. 2. Children and violence. 3. Violence in video games. 4. Violence -- Psychological aspects.

ISBN 9780316265935

LC bl2016031885

Drawing on crime statistics, social research and studies of the teenage brain, the author, one of the world's foremost experts in the field of human aggression, the roots of violence and violent crime, reveals how violent video games have ushered in a new era of mass homicide--and what we must do about it.

Kearney, Kirsten

Block city : how to build incredible worlds in Minecraft® / Kirsten Kearney with Yazur Strovoz. Abrams, 2015. 256 p. : **794.8**

1. Minecraft (Game) 2. Computer games 3. Minecraft (Game) 4. Video games

ISBN 9781419716188

LC 2014945989

A collection of advanced Minecraft city prototypes by master gamers shares step-by-step tutorials for how to create high-creativity virtual structures and features.

McGonigal, Jane

Super better : a revolutionary approach to getting stronger, happier, braver, and more resilient* / Jane McGonigal. Penguin Press, 2015. xii, 466 p. ; **794.8**

1. Internet games -- Psychological aspects 2. Resilience (Personality trait)

ISBN 9781594206368

LC bl2015032053

"*Powered by the science of games."

A renowned game designer and author of the best-selling Reality Is Broken describes how she recovered from a debilitating concussion by turning her therapeutic process into a digital game that became the subject of a major NIH research study.

Parkin, Simon

An **illustrated** history of 151 video games : a detailed guide to the most important games / Simon Parkin. Lorenz Books, 2013 255 p. : **794.8**

1. Video games -- History

ISBN 9780754823902

LC bl2015000018

"Explore five decades of game evolution, includes 1000 photographs and screenshots"--Cover.

Includes index.

Examines the evolution of video games, chronicles the history of gaming, and profiles key titles across all platforms.

Quinn, Zoe, 1987-

Crash override : how Gamergate nearly destroyed my life, and how we can win the fight against online hate / Zoe Quinn. Public Affairs, 2017. 256 p. **794.8**

1. Cyberbullying 2. Sexism 3. Internet -- Social aspects. 4. Misogyny

ISBN 9781610398084

LC 2017017273

Informed by the game-designer author's highly publicized experience with online harassment, an exploration of the problems of Internet abuse offers solutions for lawmakers, police, parents, corporations and individuals.

"She elevates diverse voices in her engaging, often-humorous writing. Whether readers are Internet devotees or not, Quinn's writing provides important context for our increasingly online lives." Booklist.

World Video Game Hall of Fame,

A **history** of video games in 64 objects / World Video Game Hall of Fame. Dey St., 2018 ix, 341 p. : **794.8**

1. Video games -- History.

ISBN 9780062838698

LC bl2018087104

Visually chronicles the history and evolution of video games from Pong to Call of Duty through 64 unique objects in this reverential reference guide that pays homage to ITA History of the World in 100 Objects.

795.4 Card games

Ho, Oliver

The **ultimate** book of family card games / Oliver Ho. Sterling Children's Books, c2012. x, 118 p. : **795.4**

1. Card games 2. Games. 3. Amusements. 4. Playing cards.
ISBN 9781402750410

LC 2010026522

Includes index.

Presents a collection of fifty card games, organized by type and difficulty, and complete with instructions, rules, and strategies.

Hoyle, Edmond, 1672-1769

Hoyle's rules of games : descriptions of indoor games of skill and chance, with advice on skillful play : based on the foundations laid down by Edmond Hoyle, 1672-1769 / edited by Albert H. Morehead and Geoffrey Mott-Smith. Plume, 2001. xvii, 362 p. : **795.4**

1. Hoyle, Edmond, 1672-1769. 2. Card games
ISBN 9780452283138

LC 2002278550

Provides rules, strategies, and odds for card, board, parlor, and computer games including backgammon, blackjack, and Scrabble.

795.41 Games in which skill is a major element

Hellmuth, Phil

Play poker like the pros / Phil Hellmuth, Jr. Quill, c2003. xviii, 394 p. : A HarperResource book **795.41**

1. Poker
ISBN 9780060005726

LC 2002032703

Includes index.

Describes the rules and basic and advanced strategies for a variety of poker games and includes tips on reading other players and beating online poker games.

McManus, James

Positively Fifth Street : murderers, cheetahs, and Binion's World Series of Poker / James McManus. Farrar, Straus, Giroux, 2003. 422 p. : **795.41**

1. Binion, Ted, died 1998. 2. World Series of Poker. 3. Poker players. 4. Trials (Murder) 5. Gamblers -- United States 6. Card games -- Tournaments. 7. Las Vegas, Nevada.
ISBN 0374236488

LC 2002033882

A chronicle of life in Las Vegas investigates the murder of poker player Ted Binion, revealing a secret world of kinky sex, black magic, and science lurking at the heart of gambling's World Series of Poker.

"McManus went to Las Vegas in May 2000 on assignment for Harper's to cover the World Series of Poker. He was to throw in coverage of the trial of Sandy Murphy, an ex-stripper, and her boyfriend, Rick Tabish, accused of murdering Ted Binion, the tournament's host. To satisfy his own gambling urge, McManus enter the poker competition and spends 10 days immersed in the culture of Vegas and gambling, rendering a fast-paced, riveting account of his progress through the tournament. A delicious inside look." Booklist.

796 Athletic and outdoor sports and games

Crouse, Karen

Norwich : one tiny Vermont town's secret to happiness and excellence / Karen Crouse. Simon & Schuster, 2018. 272 p. **796**

1. Sports. 2. Olympic athletes. 3. Athletes. 4. Growing up. 5. Norwich, Vermont -- Social life and customs. 6. Vermont
ISBN 9781501119897

LC 2017012269

Traces the history and achievements of the small Vermont community that has likely produced more Olympians per capita than any other place in the country, assessing its model for achieving excellence and a well-rounded life based on the counterintuitive practices of moderate competition, inclusion regardless of talent, and emphasis on childhood fun.

"Short and sweet, this important book highlights what's wrong with youth sports by focusing on a community that gets it right." Publishers Weekly.

Halberstam, David

Summer of '49 / David Halberstam. Harper Perennial, 2006, c1989. 354 p. : **796**

1. Major League Baseball (Organization) 2. Boston Red Sox (Baseball team) -- History. 3. New York Yankees (Baseball team) -- History. 4. Cleveland Indians (Baseball team) -- History. 5. Baseball. 6. Baseball teams. 7. Professional baseball. 8. Professional baseball teams. 9. United States -- Social life and customs.
ISBN 0060884266

LC oc2007042254

Originally published: New York : W. Morrow, 1989.

Chronicles the 1949 pennant race between the Boston Red Sox and the New York Yankees, profiling the players, owners, and fans as major league baseball was poised on the brink of major changes.

"This book is ostensibly about the pennant race between the Yankees and Red Sox {in 1949} and the 'rivalry' between Joe DiMaggio and Ted Williams. It is a study of all the elements and personalities that influenced baseball that year and beyond. Halberstam brings them together in such an enjoyable, interesting, and informative manner that a reader needn't be a baseball fan to appreciate the book." Library Journal.

Pesca, Mike

Upon further review : the greatest what-ifs in sports history / Mike Pesca. Twelve, 2018. 320 p. **796**

1. Sports 2. Options, alternatives, choices 3. Athletes 4. Fans (Persons) 5. Essays
ISBN 9781455540365

LC 2017041897

Based on a podcast.

The host of The Gist podcast shares perspectives by some of history's greatest sports minds on how the world might have changed if iconic plays, trades, injuries or referee's calls had gone the other way.

Rhoden, William C.

$40 million slaves : the rise, fall, and redemption of the Black athlete / William C. Rhoden. Crown Publishers, c2006. xiii, 286 p. : **796**

1. African American athletes -- Social conditions. 2. Sports -- History -- 19th century 3. Racism in sports -- History -- 19th century 4. African American athletes -- History -- 19th century 5. United States -- Social life and customs -- 19th century. 6. United States

-- Social life and customs -- 20th century.
ISBN 0609601202

LC 2005034952

A critical analysis of race, politics, and the history of American sports traces the origins and evolution of the black athlete, arguing that every advance by black athletes has been countered by a definite setback and that black youngsters who are brought into big-time programs are cut off from their heritage and exploited by the media, team owners, and others.

796.01 Sports--philosophy

Afremow, James A.

The **champion's** mind : how great athletes think, train, and thrive / Jim Afremow, PhD ; foreword by Jim Craig, goalie for the 1980 U.S. "Miracle on Ice" hockey team. Rodale, 2013 xvi, 269 p. ; **796.01**

1. Physical education and training 2. Sports -- Psychological aspects
ISBN 9781623361488

LC 2013032605

"Even amongst the most elite performers, certain athletes stand out as a cut above the rest, able to outperform in clutch, game-deciding moments. These athletes prove that raw athletic ability doesn't necessarily translate to a superior on-field experience--it's the mental game that matters most. Sports participation--from the recreational to the collegiate Division I level--is at an all-time high. While the caliber of their game may differ, athletes at every level have one thing in common: they want to excel. In The Champion's Mind, sports psychologist Jim Afremow, PhD, LPC, now offers the same advice he uses with Olympians, Heisman Trophy winners, and professional athletes, including: Tips and techniques based on high-performance psychology research, such as how to get in a "zone," thrive on a team, and stay humble; How to progress within a sport and sustain excellence long-term; Customizable pre-performance routines to hit full power when the gun goes off or the puck is dropped. The Champion's Mind distills actionable advice into clear and concise steps for athletes looking to find confidence, concentration, and mental preparedness--the mental edge that sets champions apart".-- Provided by publisher.

Pilon, Mary,

Losers : dispatches from the other side of the scoreboard / edited by Mary Pilon and Louisa Thomas. Penguin Books, 2020. 304 p. **796.01**

1. Sports -- Psychological aspects 2. Defeat (Psychology) 3. Failure (Psychology) 4. Winning and losing 5. Essays 6. Anthologies
ISBN 9780143133834

LC 2019053006

Twenty-two notable writers--including Bob Sullivan, Abby Ellin, Mike Pesca, Sir Arthur Conan Doyle, Louisa Hall, and Gay Talese--examine the untold stories of the losers, and in doing so reveal something raw and significant about what it means to be human. Interweaving fourteen completely new and unpublished pieces alongside beloved classics of the genre, Losers turns the art of sports writing on its head and proves that there is inspiration to be found in stories of risk, resilience, and getting up after you've been knocked down.

"A fascinating look at another side of sports, emphasizing those who lost games, matches, and tournaments, along with the pressures they faced and the ramifications of their losses. A wonderful choice for sports enthusiasts." Library Journal

Rotella, Robert J.

How champions think : in sports and in life / Dr. Bob Rotella, with Bob Cullen. Simon & Schuster, 2015. 290 p. : **796.01**

1. Athletes -- Attitudes 2. Athletes -- Psychology 3. Sports -- Psychological aspects 4. Success -- Psychological aspects
ISBN 9781476788623

LC 2014044600

A preeminent sports psychologist shares his years of in-depth research and practical experience in a guide that aims to help readers achieve success in all aspects of their lives.

"Rotella's liberal use of sports anecdotes and an effective piece on a coach's perspective (Kentucky basketball coach John Calipari) further underscore the importance of the core set of philosophies and behaviors he promotes, although his frequent and distractive allusions to faith and religion as one of the linchpins to an athlete's or a team's success may not appeal to more secular readers. A solid motivational text for the sports-minded and those interested in the bridging of athletics and exceptionalism." Kirkus.

Wertheim, L. Jon

This is your brain on sports / L. Jon Wertheim and Sam Sommers. Crown Archetype, 2016 272 p. **796.01**

1. Sports -- Psychological aspects. 2. Professional sports 3. Athletes 4. Winning and losing -- Psychological aspects
ISBN 9780553447408

LC 2015021731

The executive editor of Sports Illustrated and a psychologist join forces to examine the behavior of those involved in professional sports, explaining how athletes can successfully put aside personal trauma on game day and why people love to root for a loser.

"If sports bring out the kooky, spooky, and creepy in us, Wertheim and Sommers give us a chance to understand ourselves and perhaps get a grip before we totally lose it." Kirkus.

Winston, Wayne L.

Mathletics : how gamblers, managers, and sports enthusiasts use mathematics in baseball, basketball, and football : with a new epilogue by the author / Wayne L. Winston. Princeton University Press, 2012. 372 p. **796.01**

1. Sports. 2. Applied mathematics. 3. Mathematics -- Social aspects. 4. Games.
ISBN 9780691154589

Describes how to use simple mathematics to analyze a range of statistical and probability-related questions in professional baseball, basketball, and football, and in sports gambling.

"Sports fans will learn much from probability theory and statistical models. A rare fusion of sports enthusiasm and numerical acumen." Booklist.

796.04 General kinds of sports and games

Nocera, Joseph

Indentured : the inside story of the rebellion against the NCAA / Joe Nocera and Ben Strauss. Portfolio, 2016 ix, 369 p. **796.04**

1. National Collegiate Athletic Association. 2. College sports. 3. College athletes.
ISBN 9781591846321

LC 2015044500

Includes index.

Asserts that the NCAA is a cartel that has acted to prevent college athletes from receiving any money for their labors, discussing the legal push to bring down this morally corrupt and hypocritical organization.

"Championship-level reporting on the boundaries of sport and business." Kirkus.

796.043 College sports

McIntire, Mike

Champions way : football, Florida, and the lost soul of college sports / Mike Mcintire. Norton, 2017. 256 p. **796.043**

1. National Collegiate Athletic Association. 2. Florida State Seminoles (Football team) -- History 3. College sports 4. Universities and colleges 5. College athletes 6. Corruption 7. Florida
ISBN 9780393292619

LC 2017017863

A searing expose of how the multibillion dollar college sports empire fails universities, students, and athletes.

"McIntire summarizes the history of college sports and the social and economic culture of football in American universities, particularly in the South, convincingly arguing that these transgressions are widespread." Publishers Weekly.

796.06 Organizations, facilities, management

Kohan, Rafi

The **arena** : inside the tailgating, ticket-scalping, mascot-racing, dubiously funded, and possibly haunted monuments of American sport / Rafi Kohan. Liveright Publishing Corporation, 2017. 416 p. **796.06**

1. Stadiums 2. Sports 3. Sports facilities 4. Arenas
ISBN 9781631491276

LC 2017015161

Rafi Kohan's The Arena is a vivid exploration of what it's like behind the scenes at a modern American sports stadium, from tailgating and ticket scalpers to halftime shows and local traditions. It also includes a look at the role that big-ticket sports plays in both U.S. culture and local economies. Mixing humor, hands-on research, and sociological analysis, this is an entertaining and edifying look at sports as entertainment -- and business.

"Kohan's curiosity and empathy are infectious as he demonstrates how human this corporate aspect of sports can be. He has created an immersive, informative work that will delight and enlighten a wide range of readers." Publishers Weekly.

796.07 Education, research, related topics

Davis, Seth

★**Getting** to us : how great coaches make great teams / Seth Davis. Penguin Group USA, 2018. 320 p. : **796.07**

1. Athletic coaches 2. Coaching (Athletics) 3. Sports
ISBN 9780735222724

LC 2018285542

The acclaimed sports commentator and author of the best-selling When March Went Mad presents a guide for coaching leadership that identifies the characteristics of exemplary coaches and how to implement the examples of such forefront individuals as Urban Meyer, Dabot Swinney and Brad Stevens.

"Each chapter includes interviews with the selected coach, along with relatives, mentors, assistants, and former players as Davis relates the subject's life, career, and method. Although the coaches' styles vary from Harbaugh's in-your-face intensity to Boeheim's aloof practicality to Swinney's loquacious empathy, the nine essays fit together with what Davis views as the common keys to successful coaching." Library Journal.

Walker, Sam (Newspaper editor)

The **captain** class : the hidden force that creates the world's greatest teams / Sam Walker. Random House Inc, 2017 304 p. **796.07**

1. Sports teams. 2. Athletes. 3. Sportsmanship. 4. Success (Concept)
ISBN 9780812997194

LC 2016054597

A former Wall Street Journal global sports editor reveals the essential contributions of unconventional players behind the world's highest-performing sports teams, explaining how their unofficial leadership examples and counterintuitive strategies helped enable remarkable, long-term successes.

"Written for serious sports fans in lively language that also speaks to aspiring athletes and business professionals, this book offers a compelling argument for the value of inspired leadership." Publishers Weekly.

796.08 Groups of people

Thomas, Etan

We matter : athletes and activism / Etan Thomas. Edge of Sports, [2018] 320 pages : **796.08**

1. Athletes 2. Social advocacy 3. African Americans -- Social conditions 4. Race relations 5. United States -- Race relations 6. Essays
ISBN 9781617755941

LC 2017936007

In interviews and essays, high-profile activist athletes explore the intersection of sports and politics.

"Recommended for not only high school and college students but all readers concerned with social activism and awareness. An excellent resource to spark discussions and motivate positive community expression and involvement." Library Journal.

796.083 Outdoor recreation -- Young people

Garlick, Hattie

Born to be wild : hundreds of free nature activities for families / Hattie Garlick ; photographs by Nancy Honey. Bloomsbury, 2016. 256 p. : **796.083**

1. Nature craft 2. Outdoor recreation for children
ISBN 9781472915337

LC bl2016019687

Includes index.

Shares instructions for over 250 free nature-based activities suitable for families, including building a butterfly feeder, making a weather vane, pressing flowers, and spotting clouds.

"Spring presents a wonderful opportunity to reconnect with the outdoors, and with this title nearby, even smartphone-obsessed kids will soon be clamoring to plan an outing." Library Journal.

796.0973 Sports--United States

Murphy, Cait, 1961-

A **history** of American sports in 100 objects / Cait Murphy. Basic Books, 2016 400 p. **796.0973**

1. Sports -- History.
ISBN 9780465097746

LC 2016012506

A sports historian describes 100 iconic objects that embody American sports, including Yogi Berra's glove, used to catch the only perfect game in World Series history, and the goggles Amelia Earhart wore in the first Women's Air Derby.

796.323 Basketball

Abrams, Jonathan P. D., 1984-

Boys among men : how the prep-to-pro generation redefined the NBA and sparked a basketball revolution / Jonathan Abrams. Crown Archetype, 2016 336 p. **796.323**

1. National Basketball Association. 2. Basketball draft. 3. Basketball players. 4. College basketball players -- Recruiting
ISBN 9780804139250

LC 2015027590

Explores the trend of teenage basketball stars skipping college and going right into playing professionally, resulting in the 2005 age limit requirement instituted by the NBA, mandating that all players must attend college or another developmental program for at least a year.

"[T]his essential, well-researched book will appeal to readers interested in basketball's business side as well as the factors that have helped shape the modern NBA." Library Journal.

Blais, Madeleine

In these girls, hope is a muscle / Madeleine Blais. Warner Books, 1996, c1995. vi, 266 p. ; **796.323**

1. Amherst Regional High School, Amherst, Massachusetts Basketball. 2. Basketball for girls -- Massachusetts -- Case studies. 3. High school basketball. 4. Lady Hurricanes (High school basketball team).
ISBN 0446672106

LC 95034477

Originally published: New York : Atlantic Monthly Press, c1995.

National Book Critics Circle Award for Nonfiction finalist, 1995.

A look at the trials and triumphs of high school girls' basketball chronicles one season of the Lady Hurricanes of Amherst, Massachusetts, as they learn loyalty and self-confidence on their way to a championship game.

"Alternately funny, exciting and moving, the book should be enjoyed not only by girls and women who have played sports but also those who wanted to but let themselves be discouraged." Publishers Weekly.

Bradburd, Rus, 1959-

All the dreams we've dreamed : a story of hoops and handguns on Chicago's West Side / Rus Bradburd. Lawrence Hill Books, 2018. 265 p. **796.323**

1. Harrington, Shawn 2. John Marshall High School (Chicago, Ill.) 3. Urban violence 4. African American basketball players 5. Basketball coaches 6. Basketball 7. West Side, Chicago, Illinois
ISBN 9781613739310

LC 2017054197

A tale of courage, endurance, and friendship in one of America's most violent neighborhoods follows the experiences of coach Shawn Harrington and his John Marshall High School team over a series of three years marked by murder, racism, and corruption.

Chansky, Art

Blue blood II : Duke-Carolina: the latest on the never-ending and greatest rivalry in college hoops / Art Chansky. St Martins Press 2018 320 p. **796.323**

1. Duke Blue Devils (Basketball team) -- History. 2. North Carolina Tar Heels (Basketball team) -- History. 3. Duke University Basketball 4. University of North Carolina Basketball 5. College basketball 6. Sports rivalry 7. College sports -- North Carolina -- History. 8. North Carolina
ISBN 9781250193278

LC 2018410335

This follow-up to Blue Blood, published 13 years after the first book, tells the recent history of the Duke-Carolina college basketball rivalry and is a must-have for Duke and UNC fans, as well as college basketball fans in general.

Colton, Larry

Counting coup : a true story of basketball and honor on the Little Big Horn / Larry Colton. Warner Books, 2000. 420 p. **796.323**

1. Hardin High School (Montana) Lady Bulldogs basketball team. 2. Basketball for women -- Hardin, Montana. 3. Native American athletes. 4. Teenage girls 5. Native American women 6. Hardin, Montana. 7. Pacific Northwest literature
ISBN 0446526835

LC 00024987

Includes index.

Profiles a Montana high-school girls' basketball team--made up of Crow Indian and white girls from a rural town--that carries on its shoulders the dreams and hopes of a Native American tribe during their winning season.

Dohrmann, George

★**Play** their hearts out : a coach, his star recruit, and the youth basketball machine / George Dohrmann. Balantine Books, c2010. 416 p. **796.323**

1. Keller, Joe. 2. Walker, Demetrius. 3. Basketball coaches. 4. Basketball. 5. Youth league basketball. 6. Basketball players.
ISBN 9780345508607

LC 2010015470

Pulitzer Prize-winning journalist George Dohrmann's remarkable debut offers an up-close and unforgettable narrative that reveals the gritty reality hiding behind the romanticized hoop dreams of America's basketball prodigies.

Feinstein, John

★The **back** roads to March : the unsung, unheralded, and unknown heroes of a college basketball season / John Feinstein. Doubleday, 2020 304 p. **796.323**

1. NCAA Basketball Tournament. 2. Basketball teams 3. College basketball players 4. College basketball 5. College basketball coaches
ISBN 9780385544481

LC 2019047926

Includes index.

Sports journalist John Feinstein returns to his first love--college basketball--with a fascinating and compelling journey through a landscape of unsung, unpublicized and often unknown heroes of Division-1 college hoops.

"Feinstein writes with warmth and enthusiasm of a beloved sport in a book that will grab any fan." Kirkus

A **march** to madness : the view from the floor in the Atlantic Coast Conference / John Feinstein. Little, Brown and Co., 1998. xvii, 464 p. : **796.323**

1. Atlantic Coast Conference. 2. Basketball 3. College basketball. 4. College sports. 5. Basketball teams.

ISBN 0316277401

LC 97031060

Includes index.

Follows the eventful 1996-1997 season in college basketball's most competitive league, the Atlantic Coast Conference, offering behind-the-scenes portraits of the nine top teams and coaches in action.

"Feinstein covers one year with all of the teams in the perennially powerful Atlantic Coast Conference. After introducing each of the schools, their teams, their coaches, and their expectations for the 1996/97 basketball season, the book describes their progress week by week, culminating with Dean Smith's run to the NCAA Final Four. Such a detailed accounting of a sports season could seem interminable to readers, but Feinstein has again produced a narrative that is not only interesting but often exciting." Library Journal.

★**Last** dance : behind the scenes at the Final Four / John Feinstein. Little, Brown, 2006. 375 p. ; **796.323**

1. NCAA Basketball Tournament History. 2. NCAA Basketball Tournament Anecdotes. 3. College basketball players. 4. College basketball. 5. Basketball tournaments -- United States -- History 6. Basketball teams.

ISBN 031616030X

LC 2005028478

Includes index.

A portrait of the NCAA Final Four competition is presented from the perspectives of schools, coaches, and players who have made it to college basketball's final weekend, in a collection that also includes accounts by officials, referees, and scouts.

"The author employs the 2005 [Final Four] weekend as the catalyst to discuss the history of the event, the key people, and, most significantly, the effect that involvement in the Final Four has had on participants' lives. The anecdotes are entertaining, and the insights into the tournament's logistics fascinating, but what will linger most are the remembrances of players, especially those who ended up on the losing side." Booklist.

Fury, Shawn

Rise and fire : the origins, science, and evolution of the jump shot --- and how it transformed basketball forever / Shawn Fury. Flatiron Books, 2016. 288 p. **796.323**

1. Basketball -- Shooting. 2. Basketball players 3. Basketball -- Offense. 4. Basketball -- History

ISBN 9781250062161

LC 2015040454

An analysis of the play that revolutionized baseball and has been a component in most of the game's top moments draws on in-depth research to cover the roles of equipment, the contributions of team rivalries and the achievements of legendary athletes.

Glockner, Andy

Chasing perfection : a behind-the-scenes look at the high-stakes game of creating an NBA champion / Andy Glockner. Da Capo Press, 2016. 288 p. **796.323**

1. National Basketball Association 2. Basketball 3. Professional basketball 4. Professional basketball players 5. Basketball teams

ISBN 9780306824029

LC bl2016008751

A tour of the multi-million-dollar world of analytics, player identification, talent development and other methods employed by NBA teams to make champions demonstrates how the 2014-2015 NBA season reflected key practices shaping the game today.

"Highly recommended for NBA junkies who scour box scores." Library Journal.

Goodman, Matthew

The **city** game : triumph, scandal, and a legendary basketball team / Matthew Goodman. Ballantine Books, 2019. ix, 350 p. : **796.323**

1. College sports 2. Basketball 3. Basketball teams 4. Scandals 5. New York City -- History -- 20th century

ISBN 9781101882832

LC bl2019027021

The powerful story of a college basketball team who carried an era's brightest hopes--racial harmony, social mobility, and the triumph of the underdog--but whose success was soon followed by a shocking downfall.

"Recommended for anyone interested in the history of post-World War II basketball; relevant to issues within amateur athletics today." Library Journal.

MacMullan, Jackie

★**Basketball** : a love story / Jackie MacMullan and Rafe Bartholomew. Crown Archetype, [2018] 448 p. **796.323**

1. Basketball 2. Basketball players 3. Basketball coaches 4. Professional basketball 5. Oral histories

ISBN 9781524761783

LC 2018023541

A revelatory history of basketball, published to coincide with a major ESPN and ABC series, draws on hundreds of interviews with leading athletes, coaches, executives and journalists from the NBA, WNBA, NCAA and international leagues.

"Professional basketball fans will go to the net for this exciting history." Publishers Weekly.

Malinowski, Erik

Betaball : how Silicon Valley and science built one of the greatest basketball teams in history / Erik Malinowski. Atria Books, 2017. 320 p. **796.323**

1. Golden State Warriors (Basketball team) 2. National Basketball Association 3. Professional basketball 4. Basketball teams 5. Professional sports teams -- Economic aspects. 6. Basketball

ISBN 9781501158193

LC bl2017039746

Describes how a venture capitalist and a Hollywood producer turned a declining franchise into one of the greatest teams in basketball, becoming a model organization for other professional sports teams for instilling workplace principles modeled after successful corporations.

"Much the way David Kaplan chronicled the creation of the 2016 champion Chicago Cubs in The Plan (2017), so free-lance sportswriter Malinowski has laid out the construction, piece by piece, of the powerhouse Golden State Warriors, who won NBA titles in 2015 and 2017, and in the 2016 regular season won a record-breaking 79 games... An insightful portrait of, yes, one of the all-time great NBA teams." Booklist.

McCallum, Jack, 1949-

Golden days : West's Lakers, Steph's Warriors, and the California dreamers who reinvented basketball / Jack McCallum. Ballantine Books, [2017] xxv, 308 pages ; **796.323**

1. West, Jerry, 1938- 2. Curry, Stephen, 1988- 3. Golden State Warriors (Basketball team) 4. Los Angeles Lakers (Basketball team) 5. National Basketball Association -- History 6. Basketball 7. Professional basketball 8. Professional basketball players 9. Basketball teams
ISBN 9780399179075

LC 2017038872

Tells the interconnected stories of today's Golden State Warriors and the early-1970s Los Angeles Lakers, two extraordinary teams playing in extraordinary times and linked by one extraordinary man: Jerry West.

Pearlman, Jeff

★**Three-ring** circus : Kobe, Shaq, Phil, and the crazy years of the Lakers dynasty / Jeff Pearlman. Houghton Mifflin Harcourt, 2020 xix, 426 p. **796.323**

1. Bryant, Kobe, 1978-2020 2. O'Neal, Shaquille, 1972- 3. Jackson, Phil 4. Los Angeles Lakers (Basketball team) -- History 5. Basketball teams 6. Basketball players 7. Interpersonal relations 8. Quarreling 9. Los Angeles, California
ISBN 9781328530004

LC 2019057830

Tells the story of the Lakers dynasty from 1996 through 2004, when Kobe Bryant and Shaquille O'Neal combined--and collided--to help bring the Lakers three straight championships and restore the franchise as a powerhouse.

"A must-read for all basketball fans." Library Journal

Powell, Michael (Michael H.)

★**Canyon** dreams : a basketball season on the Navajo Nation / Michael Powell. Blue Rider Press, [2019] 264 pages, 8 unnumbered pages of plates : **796.323**

1. Indians of North America 2. Navajo Indians 3. High school students 4. Basketball 5. Arizona
ISBN 9780525534662

LC 2019034479

The moving story of a Navajo high school basketball team, its members struggling with the everyday challenges of high school, adolescence, and family, and the great and unique obstacles facing Native Americans living on reservations.

Reynolds, Bill, 1945-

Hope : a school, a team, a dream / Bill Reynolds. St Martins Press, 2016. 272 p. **796.323**

1. Hope High School (Providence, R.I.) Basketball. 2. Basketball players 3. High school basketball 4. African Americans 5. Inner city 6. Providence, Rhode Island. 7. Rhode Island
ISBN 9781250080691

LC 2015037368

Recounts the inspirational story of inner-city Providence, Rhode Island's Hope High School basketball team, detailing the formidable obstacles faced by coach Dave Nyblom and a ragtag group of at-risk youths who overcame gang violence, drug problems and family disputes to reclaim their champion status.

"A basketball book but also a candid look at inner-city life that should garner it a broad audience." Booklist.

Serrano, Shea

★**Basketball** (and other things) : a collection of questions asked, answered, illustrated / Shea Serrano ; with illustrations by Arturo Torres. Abrams Image, 2017. 239 p. : **796.323**

1. National Basketball Association -- History. 2. Basketball -- Miscellanea. 3. Questions and answers. 4. Sports -- Humor. 5. Basketball fans.
ISBN 9781419726477

LC 2017930301

Shares lighthearted coverage of a wide range of fan debates about basketball history, from Kobe Bryant's actual league dominance to what rules are not permitted in pickup games.

"An original work that captures the spirit of basketball. Highly recommended for die-hard NBA fans." Library Journal.

Simmons, Bill, 1969-

The **book** of basketball : the NBA according to The Sports Guy / Bill Simmons. Ballantine/ESPN Books, 2009. xi, 715 p. : **796.323**

1. National Basketball Association 2. Basketball 3. Professional sports 4. Professional basketball. 5. Professional basketball teams
ISBN 9780345511768

LC 2009036006

A lively and opinionated tour of the past, present, and future of pro basketball, written by ESPN's "Sports Guy" columnist, shares provocative insights on everything from major NBA events and underrated players to how the author believes Hall of Famers should be selected.

"The true NBA fan will dive into this hefty volume and won't resurface for about a week, emerging from the man cave unshaven, smelling of beer and pizza, grinning, and armed with NBA history, insight, anecdotes, statistics, and a dozen new examples of Simmons' Unintentional Comedy Scale. This is just plain fun. Expect significant demand from hoops junkies." Booklist.

Smith, Sam, 1948-

Hard labor : the battle that birthed the billion-dollar NBA / Sam Smith. Triumph Books, 2017. 256 p. **796.323**

1. National Basketball Association 2. Professional basketball players 3. Labor unions 4. Negotiation 5. Basketball
ISBN 9781629372785

LC 2017026712

In Hard Labor, Sam Smith unearths this incredible and untold fight for players' rights and examines the massive repercussions for the NBA and sports in the United States in the 40 years since.

Thomsen, Ian

The **soul** of basketball : the epic showdown between LeBron, Kobe, Doc, and Dirk that saved the NBA / Ian Thomsen. Houghton Mifflin Harcourt, 2018. 288 p. **796.323**

1. James, LeBron 2. Bryant, Kobe, 1978-2020 3. Rivers, Glenn 4. Nowitzki, Dirk, 1978- 5. National Basketball Association -- History 6. Basketball -- History 7. Sports -- History 8. Professional basketball players 9. Professional basketball
ISBN 9780547746517

LC 2017046213

Includes index.

A narrative chronicle of the transformations throughout the NBA that played out most notably during the 2010-2011 season traces the particular stories of LeBron James, Kobe Bryant, Doc Rivers, Dirk Nowitzki and other stars who were at the forefront of significant league changes.

Weitzman, Yaron

Tanking to the top : the Philadelphia 76ers and the most audacious process in the history of professional sports / Yaron Weitzman. Grand Central Publishing, 2020. 288 p. **796.323**

1. Philadelphia 76ers (Basketball team) 2. Organizational change. 3. Trading and swapping 4. Professional basketball players 5.

Professional basketball 6. United States
ISBN 9781538749722

LC 2019041816

Includes index.

The story of how the Philadelphia 76ers employed a rebuilding strategy of trading short-term winning for long-term success through minimal spending and accumulating low-level talent that could be traded away for future draft picks.

"Readers interested in the business of basketball, and how it affects teams and players above all, will find this a must-read." Library Journal

796.332 American football

Anderson, Lars

Carlisle vs. Army : Jim Thorpe, Dwight Eisenhower, Pop Warner, and the forgotten story of football's greatest battle / Lars Anderson. Random House, c2007. 349 p. : **796.332**

1. United States Indian School (Carlisle, Pa.) Football. 2. Football -- History. 3. United States -- Social life and customs -- 20th century
ISBN 140006600X

LC 2007008410

Describes the November 1912 football matchup between college football powerhouse Army--which included cadet Dwight Eisenhower--and the Native American team from Carlisle, a team that was coached by the inventive Pop Warner and included Jim Thorpe.

"A forgotten football game in 1912, between Carlisle, led by Jim Thorpe and coached by the legendary Pop Warner, and Army, led by Dwight Eisenhower, becomes the launching point for a fascinating look at multiple levels of American popular culture." Booklist.

Benedict, Jeff

The **dynasty** / Jeff Benedict. Avid Reader Press, 2020. xii, 578 p. ; **796.332**

1. Belichick, Bill. 2. Brady, Tom, 1977- 3. Kraft, Robert 4. New England Patriots (Football team) -- History. 5. National Football League. 6. Football teams 7. Football 8. Success (Concept) 9. Football coaches
ISBN 9781982134105

LC bl2020019651

How was the Patriots dynasty built? And how did it last for two decades? In The Dynasty, acclaimed journalist Jeff Benedict provides richly reported answers in a sweeping account based on exclusive interviews with more than two hundred insiders, including team executives, coaches, players, players' wives, team doctors, lawyers, and more, as well as never-before-seen recordings, documents, and electronic communications.

"Smart, engaging sportswriting. . . . Good reading for organization builders as well as Pats fans." Kirkus

The **system** : the glory and scandal of big-time college football / Jeff Benedict, Armen Keteyian. Doubleday, 2013 336 p. **796.332**

1. College sports 2. College football 3. Football -- Corrupt practices 4. Universities and colleges
ISBN 9780385536615

LC 2013362311

A revelatory account based on the authors' unprecedented access to the NCAA's highest-level programs throughout the 2012 season describes its high-powered system of billion-dollar television deals, high-priced coaches, football "hostessing," castoff athlete-students and paid test takers.

"An overwhelming recommendation for all readers who love or hate college sports." Library Journal.

Bissinger, H. G.

★**Friday** night lights : a town, a team, and a dream / H.G. Bissinger. Da Capo Press, 2003, c1990. xiv, 367 p. : **796.332**

1. Permian High School, Odessa, Texas Football. 2. Football -- Social aspects -- Odessa, Texas. 3. High school football. 4. Football teams. 5. Small town life. 6. Texas -- Social life and customs. 7. Odessa, Texas -- Social life and customs.
ISBN 9780306812828

LC bl2006017196

Originally published: Reading, MA : Addison-Wesley Pub. Co., 1990.

Chronicles a football season in Odessa, Texas, a depressed All-American town that lives and dies with the fortunes of its high school football team.

"It is a tricky balancing act, but Mr. Bissinger carries it off: Friday Night Lights offers a biting indictment of the sports craziness that grips not only Odessa but most of American society, while at the same time providing a moving evocation of its powerful allure." New York Times Book Review.

Colt, George Howe

The **game** : Harvard, Yale, and America in 1968 / George Howe Colt. Scribner, 2018. x, 386 pages, 8 unnumbered pages of plates : **796.332**

1. Yale University. 2. Harvard University. 3. College sports 4. College football 5. Young men 6. College students 7. United States -- History -- 20th century
ISBN 9781501104787

LC 2018410267

Tells the story of the unforgettable group of young athletes who battled in the legendary Harvard-Yale football game of 1968 amidst the sweeping currents of one of the most transformative years in American history.

"First-rate reporting and writing that will appeal to gridiron fans and general readers as well." Kirkus.

Dawidoff, Nicholas

Collision low crossers : a year inside the turbulent world of NFL football / Nicholas Dawidoff. Little Brown & Co, 2013 496 p. **796.332**

1. New York Jets (Football team) 2. National Football League. 3. Football -- United States. 4. Professional football.
ISBN 9780316196796

LC 2013030013

An award-winning author and scholar describes what it was like to experience a year in the scouting department of the New York Jets and the time he spent with coach Rex Ryan, defensive player Darrelle Revis and quarterback Mark Sanchez.

Eatman, Nicholas

Friday, Saturday, Sunday in Texas : a year in the life of Lone Star football, from high school to college to the Cowboys / Nicholas Eatman. Dey Street Books, 2016 304 p. **796.332**

1. Dallas Cowboys (Football team) 2. National Football League 3. High school football 4. College football 5. Professional football 6. High school football players 7. Texas
ISBN 9780062433312

LC bl2016041583

A veteran Texas sports writer follows three teams in three leagues -- Plano Senior High School, Baylor University and the Dallas Cowboys -- throughout the 2015 season, blending their stories into a revealing chronicle of Lone Star Football and highlighting the ups and downs, and even the parallels, that these teams experienced over the course of a year.

"A realistic look at football as its played in Texas." Booklist.

Eisenberg, John, 1956-

The **League** : how five rivals created the NFL and launched a sports empire / John Eisenberg. Basic Books, [2018] 336 p. **796.332**

1. Bell, Bert, 1894-1959. 2. Mara, Tim 3. Marshall, George Preston, 1896-1969. 4. Rooney, Art, 1901-1988 5. Halas, George Stanley, 1895-1983 6. National Football League -- History. 7. Football -- United States -- History. 8. Professional football. 9. Sports team owners -- United States

ISBN 9780465048700

LC 2018012386

Part history of football, part extraordinary story of business ingenuity, a riveting story follows the five individuals who took an immense risk by investing in the professional game, shepherding the league through its rough early decades and building the most popular sport in America.

Feinstein, John

Quarterback : inside the most important position in the National Football League / John Feinstein. Doubleday, [2019] 357 pages : **796.332**

1. National Football League 2. Professional football 3. Quarterbacks (Football) 4. Professional football players 5. Professional athletes

ISBN 9780385543033

LC 2018031266

Dives deep into the most coveted and hallowed position in the NFL, exploring the stories of five top quarterbacks.

Gaul, Gilbert M.

Billion-dollar ball : a journey through the out-of-control money culture of college football / Gilbert Gaul. Viking Press, 2015 288 p. **796.332**

1. College football 2. Football -- Corrupt practices 3. Higher education 4. Hypocrisy

ISBN 9780670016730

LC 2015473475

A two-time Pulitzer Prize-winning journalist explores how college football has come to dominate some of the most prestigious universities, transforming athletic departments into wildly rich entertainment factories that put sports before education.

"Gaul's reporting is unassailable, but watch as his conclusions stir up a furor in the sports press. You don't even have to hate football to find this book valuable and certainly worth reading." Kirkus.

Horrigan, Joe

NFL century : the one-hundred-year rise of America's greatest sports league / Joe Horrigan. Crown Archetype, [2019] 364 p. **796.332**

1. National Football League -- History 2. Football -- United States -- History 3. Professional football 4. Sports organizations

ISBN 9781635653595

LC 2018057907

Includes index.

The NFL Hall of Fame executive director and host of the popular radio show, Pro Football Hall of Fame Radio, chronicles the history of the NFL through its founding in 1920 Ohio through its 100th anniversary season.

"This engagingly written chronicle of the most powerful and influential sports league in American history should be of wide interest." Library Journal.

Jaworksi, Ron

The **games** that changed the game : the evolution of the NFL in seven Sundays / Ron Jaworksi, with Greg Cosell and David Plaut. ESPN Books, c2010. 224 p. **796.332**

1. National Football League -- History. 2. Football -- United States -- History. 3. Professional football. 4. Football players

ISBN 9780345517951

LC 2010031008

Includes index.

A leading professional football analyst best known for his game tape breakdowns on Monday Night Football isolates seven historically significant games in which famous coaches demonstrated ideal executions of innovative strategies.

"Filled with anecdotes, player recollections, and other wonderful details, this should be the most popular football book of the season. Terrific reading." Booklist.

Leibovich, Mark

Big game : the NFL in dangerous times / Mark Leibovich. Penguin Group USA 2018 400 p. **796.332**

1. Brady, Tom, 1977- 2. National Football League 3. New England Patriots (Football team) 4. Professional football 5. Sports injuries 6. Scandals 7. Nationalism and sports

ISBN 9780399185427

LC 2018022700

The award-winning New York Times Magazine chief national correspondent, best-selling author of This Town and lifelong Patriots fan presents a scathing analysis of professional football in the present climate of high success, dangerous injuries and scandal.

Myers, Gary, 1954 July 1-

Brady vs. Manning : the untold story of the rivalry that transformed the NFL / Gary Myers. Crown/Archetype, 2015 272 p. **796.332**

1. Manning, Peyton 2. Brady, Tom, 1977- 3. Football players 4. Quarterbacks (Football) 5. Professional football 6. Sports rivalry

ISBN 9780804139373

LC 2015027579

An insider's account of the contrasting characters of Tom Brady and Peyton Manning explores how their rivalry has shaped their careers and the NFL overall, sharing insights into their actual opinions about each other and the factors that shaped them as men and athletes.

"Myers is a thorough professional with impeccable contacts to successfully tell this account, which will be of interest to all football fans." Library Journal.

The **catch** : one play, two dynasties, and the game that changed the NFL / Gary Myers. Crown Publishers, 2009. xiii, 252 p. **796.332**

1. San Francisco 49ers (Football team) -- History. 2. Dallas Cowboys (Football team) -- History. 3. National Football League 4. National Football League Championship Game (16th: 1982: San Francisco) 5. Professional football. 6. Football. 7. Football players.

ISBN 9780307409089

LC 2009014961

A behind-the-scenes retelling of the 1982 showdown between the Dallas Cowboys and the San Francisco 49ers explains its relevance to NFL history, drawing on interviews with leading figures to offer insight into the role of similar events on the rise and fall of franchises.

Oriard, Michael, 1948-

Brand NFL : making and selling America's favorite sport / Michael Oriard. University of North Carolina Press, c2007. 326 p. ; **796.332**

1. National Football League. 2. Football -- United States -- Management. 3. Corporate sponsorship. 4. Marketing. 5. Football -- United States -- Marketing.

ISBN 9780807831427

LC 2007008867

The evolution of how the NFL is marketed as entertainment rather than sport is detailed in a study that looks closely at the development of the sport and its unique place in American life.

Pearlman, Jeff

Boys will be boys : the glory days and party nights of the Dallas Cowboys dynasty / Jeff Pearlman. HarperCollins, 2008. ix, 406 p. : **796.332**

1. Dallas Cowboys (Football team) 2. National Football League 3. Professional football. 4. Professional football players. 5. Professional football coaches 6. Professional football teams 7. Dallas, Texas -- Social life and customs.

ISBN 9780061256806

Chronicles the rise and fall of the Dallas Cowboys during the 1990s, citing the contributions of owner Jerry Jones and coach Jimmy Johnson as well as the achievements of such players as Troy Aikman, Emmitt Smith, and Deion Sanders.

Football for a buck : the crazy rise and crazier demise of the USFL / Jeff Pearlman. Houghton Mifflin Harcourt, 2018. 320 p. **796.332**

1. Trump, Donald, 1946- 2. USFL (Organization) 3. Football -- United States 4. Football team owners 5. Professional football 6. Professional football players

ISBN 9780544454385

LC 2018006360

Traces the three seasons of existence of the United States Football League, revealing its early success, how it launched the careers of many football superstars, and how it ultimately crashed and failed due to the influence of Donald Trump and other teamowners.

Price, S. L., 1962-

Playing through the whistle : steel, football, and an American town / S.L. Price. Atlantic Monthly Press, 2016. 400 p. **796.332**

1. High school football 2. Working class 3. Steel towns 4. Steel industry and trade 5. Aliquippa, Pennsylvania 6. Pennsylvania

ISBN 9780802125644

LC 2018420187

A Sports Illustrated senior writer presents a moving epic of football in industrial America, tracing the story of Aliquippa, Pennsylvania's now-shuttered steel mill, and its legendary high school football team.

"From the rigidly stratified life in the 1920s and 30s during J&Ls 'despotic prime,' to the brief, postwar golden age, 'a moment of civic equipoise,' to today's 'company town without a company,' where the combination of unemployment, drugs, and crime crushes hope, Price's football story is really that of Americas Rust Belt in poignant miniature." Kirkus.

Roberts, Diane, 1959-

Tribal : college football and the secret heart of America / Diane Roberts. Harper, 2015. 304 p. **796.332**

1. Football -- United States -- History. 2. College sports -- United States -- History. 3. Universities and colleges. 4. College athletes

ISBN 9780062342621

LC 2015025010

"Both dispatch and dissertation, NPR contributor Diane Roberts, an English professor at Florida State University, gives a insider's account of a big time college football program in the midst of controversy, while examining the impact and legacy of the sport's popularity in America today".-- Provided by publisher.

"This volume seems to be aimed at readers who already hate the sport." Library Journal.

Savage, Phil

4th and goal every day : Alabama's relentless pursuit of perfection / Phil Savage with Ray Glier ; preface by Nick Saban ; foreword by Rece Davis. St Martin's Press, 2017. 320 p. **796.332**

1. Alabama Crimson Tide (Football team) 2. University of Alabama 3. Football players 4. College football 5. College sports 6. Alabama

ISBN 9781250130808

LC 2017016459

The former general manager of the Cleveland Browns and current game commentator for the Alabama Crimson Tide Sports Network discusses how the college football team rebuilt itself to win four national titles in eight seasons through commitment to recruiting, practice and fundamentals.

"A football lifer gives insight into how the Alabama Crimson Tide continue to be the most dominant force in college football." Kirkus.

Syken, Bill,

Sports illustrated football's greatest / Bill Syken, editor. Liberty Street, 2017 288 p. : **796.332**

1. Football -- United States -- Miscellanea 2. Football players -- Rating of -- United States

ISBN 9781683300038

LC bl2017043276

Polls experts to determine the top ten NFL quarterbacks, games, rivalries, linebackers, tight ends, coaches, wide receivers, stadiums, and teams.

796.334 Soccer (Association football)

Abbot, Sebastian

The **away** game : the epic search for soccer's next superstars / Sebastian Abbot. W W Norton & Company, 2018 336 p. **796.334**

1. Professional soccer 2. Soccer scouts. 3. Soccer 4. Soccer -- Scouting

ISBN 9780393292206

LC 2017052648

Traces the audacious scouting program known as Football Dreams that for the past decade has strategically recruited young African boys to become the sport's future elites, describing the experiences of a group of talented hopefuls who train, compete and pursue their fortunes at Europe's top clubs.

"Abbot's narrative features vivid profiles, engrossing play-by-play, and a sobering lesson: bad breaks and cold business calculations sometimes trump ability in the making of champions." Publishers Weekly.

Anderson, Christopher, 1966-

The **numbers** game : why everything you know about soccer is wrong / Chris Anderson and David Sally. Penguin Books, 2013. 384 p. **796.334**

1. Soccer. 2. Statistics. 3. Sports -- Statistics.
ISBN 9780143124566

LC 2013011448

A former professional goalkeeper turned soccer statistics guru, along with a behavioral analyst, presents this first book on soccer stats that reveals the numbers that truly count, exposing the sport's hidden rules.

Bass, Amy

One goal : a coach, a team, and the game that brought a divided town together / Amy Bass. Hachette Books, 2018. 288 p. **796.334**

1. Lewiston High School (Lewiston, Me.) Soccer -- History. 2. Soccer 3. Immigrants 4. Race relations 5. Small town life 6. Maine 7. Lewiston, Maine -- Social conditions.
ISBN 9780316396547

LC 2017034578

In the tradition of Friday Night Lights and Outcasts United, ONE GOAL tells the inspiring story of the soccer team in a town bristling with racial tension that united Somali refugees and multi-generation Mainers in their quest for state--and ultimately national--glory. When thousands of Somali refugees resettled in Lewiston, Maine, a struggling, overwhelmingly white town, longtime residents grew uneasy. Then the mayor wrote a letter asking Somalis to stop coming, which became a national story. While scandal threatened to subsume the town, its high school's soccer coach integrated Somali kids onto his team, and their passion began to heal old wounds.

"Basss effective portrayal of Lewiston as a microcosm of America's changing culture should be required reading for coaches, teachers, and those working with diverse populations." Publishers Weekly.

Bennett, Roger, 1970-

Men in Blazers present encyclopedia blazertannica : a suboptimal guide to soccer, America's "sport of the future" since 1972 / Roger Bennett, Michael Davies. Alfred A. Knopf, 2018. 240 p. **796.334**

1. Soccer. 2. Soccer players.
ISBN 9781101875988

LC 2017028596

Two popular British soccer experts who host a podcast and a television show fill in the gaps for newly minted fans of the sport with great moments in the sport's history.

Bensinger, Ken

★**Red** card : how the U.S. blew the whistle on the world's biggest sports scandal / Ken Bensinger. Simon & Schuster 2018 352 p. **796.334**

1. Federation internationale de football association 2. World Cup (Soccer) 3. Sports -- Corrupt practices 4. Scandals 5. Soccer 6. Corruption investigation
ISBN 9781501133909

LC bl2018063563

An award-winning journalist presents an account of the FIFA corruption scandal that implicated nearly every aspect of international soccer, sharing insights into the roles of key personalities while tracing the efforts of law officials to expose the truth.

"With the flair of a novelist, Bensinger meticulously chronicles the magnitude of corruption that permeates the world's most popular sport." Publishers Weekly.

Conn, David, 1965-

The **fall** of the house of FIFA : the multimillion-dollar corruption at the heart of global soccer / David Conn. Nation Books, [2017] 328 p. **796.334**

1. Federation internationale de football association Corrupt practices. 2. World Cup (Soccer) 3. Soccer. 4. Professional soccer. 5. Soccer tournaments. 6. Corruption.
ISBN 9781568585963

LC 2017905020

Chronicles the history and staggering scale of corruption at the center of FIFA and paints revealing portraits of the power brokers at the center of the scandal.

"Conn's meticulous research and smooth writing style bring this unseemly chapter in FIFA history to a close, with realistic hope for the future of the most popular sport on earth." Library Journal.

Galeano, Eduardo, 1940-2015

Soccer in sun and shadow / Eduardo Galeano ; translated by Mark Fried. Verso, 1998. viii, 228 p. ; **796.334**

1. Soccer -- History. 2. Soccer players. 3. Soccer -- Social aspects. 4. South America -- Social life and customs -- 20th century.
ISBN 9781568584942

LC 98006769

Presents observations and reflections on soccer showing both the tragedy and the triumph of the game throughout the years.

Goldblatt, David

★The **age** of football : soccer and the 21st century / David Goldblatt. W.W. Norton & Co., 2020, c2019. 624 p. **796.334**

1. Soccer -- Social aspects. 2. Soccer -- Political aspects. 3. Soccer -- Economic aspects. 4. Soccer -- History -- 21st century.
ISBN 9780393635119
Originally published: London : Macmillan, 2019.

The "Game of Our Lives" podcaster and author presents a wide-reaching exploration of soccer and society that charts the sport's global cultural ascent, economic transformation and deep politicization.

"Superb: Essential reading not just for fans of the sport, but also for students of geopolitics." Kirkus

Honigstein, Raphael, 1973-

Das reboot : how German soccer reinvented itself and conquered the world / Raphael Honigstein. Nation Books, [2015] 276 p. **796.334**

1. World Cup 2. Soccer -- Germany 3. Germany
ISBN 9781568585307

LC 2015947738

Guardian journalist and television pundit Raphael Honigstein charts the return of German soccer from the international wilderness of the late nineteen-nineties to Götze's moment of genius and asks, how did this come about? How did German soccer reinvent itself away from its efficient but unappealing and defensively-minded past to the free-flowing, attack-minded soccer that was on display in 2014? The answer takes him from California to Stuttgart, from Munich to the Maracanã, via Dortmund and Amsterdam. Packed with exclusive interviews with the key protagonists, Honigstein's book lifts the lid on the secrets of German soccer's success.

"Championship teams always have their books, but few are as thoughtful and edifying as this one." Booklist.

Hopcraft, Arthur

The **football** man : people and passions in soccer / Arthur Hopcraft ; with a new foreword by Michael Parkinson. Aurum,

2013. 253 p. ; **796.334**

1. Soccer -- England

ISBN 9781781311516

LC oc2014001408

Includes index.

Originally published: Harmondsworth: Penguin, 1971.

Written just two years after England's '66 triumph when the national game was at its zenith, Arthur Hopcraft's The Football Man is repeatedly quoted as the best book every written about the sport.

Kuper, Simon

Soccernomics : why England loses, why Germany and Brazil win, and why the U.S., Japan, Australia, Turkey and even Iraq are destined to become the kings of the world's most popular sport / Simon Kuper and Stefan Szymanski. Nation Books, c2009 336 p. **796.334**

1. Soccer -- Social aspects. 2. Economics. 3. Sports.

ISBN 9781568584256

LC 2009023502

A pair of award-winning journalists draw on analogies from a range of disciplines to consider why forefront soccer teams win or lose World Cup competitions, offering insight into the playing styles of leading national teams as well as overall factors that influence how the game is played.

"Whether analyzing the relationship of spending to winning or applying game theory to the penalty kick, the authors' delight in discovery proves both persuasive and contagious. It's a fascinating book with the potential to effect genuine change in the sport." Booklist.

Oxenham, Gwendolyn

Under the lights and in the dark : untold stories of women's soccer / Gwendolyn Oxenham. Icon Books, 2017. 272 p. **796.334**

1. Women soccer players 2. Professional athletes 3. Soccer 4. Women's sports

ISBN 9781785781537

LC bl2017040525

California-based writer Gwendolyn Oxenham presents an insider's look at women's soccer, following players across the world from Portland Thorns' Allie Long to FC Kansas City's Amy Rodriguez.

Vecsey, George

Eight world cups : my journey through the beauty and dark side of soccer / George Vecsey. Times Books, 2014 288 p. **796.334**

1. World Cup (Soccer) History. 2. Soccer. 3. Soccer players 4. Tournaments

ISBN 9780805098488

LC 2013042574

"As Americans increasingly embrace soccer, one of the country's most respected sports columnists has been covering the world's signature tournament for three decades. In Eight World Cups George Vecsey of The New York Times pulls back the curtain on the beautiful game. Blending witty travelogue with action on the field--and shady dealings in the back rooms--Vecsey offers an eye-opening, globetrotting account of the last eight World Cups, chronicling the United States team's slow, episodic rise while evidence of corruption grows in the sport's executive suites.

"Vecsey's insights offer a unique look at the grace of the game as well as the underside of world soccer." Library Journal.

Villoro, Juan, 1956-

God is round / Juan Villoro ; translated by Thomas Bunstead. Restless Books, 2016 240 p. **796.334**

1. Soccer 2. Soccer players 3. Sports 4. Essays

ISBN 9781632060587

LC bl2016016137

A brilliant and kaleidoscopic exploration of the world's favorite sport and the passion, hopes, rivalries, superstitions, and global solidarity soccer inspires from award-winning author and Mexico's leading sports journalist, Juan Villoro.

"For millions around the world, soccer is not just a game, but rather life itself and, as Villoro ably reveals, very much worth pursuing to the final whistle." Kirkus.

Wahl, Grant

★**Masters** of modern soccer : how the world's best play the twenty-first-century game / Grant Wahl. Crown Archetype, 2018 304 p. **796.334**

1. Soccer. 2. Soccer players.

ISBN 9780307408600

LC 2017053620

Includes index.

The forefront Sports Illustrated soccer journalist and best-selling author of The Beckham Experiment profiles master players in every key position to reveal how elite athletes and coaches strategize on and off the field and perform in high-pressure game situations.

"One of the best books on the sport, alongside Raphael Honigstein's Das Reboot and Simon Kuper and Stefan Szymanski's Soccernomics, this gem of a work will appeal to longtime soccer fans and budding enthusiasts." Library Journal.

West, Phil

I believe that we will win : the path to a US men's World Cup victory / Phil West. Overlook Press, 2018. 272 p. **796.334**

1. World Cup (Soccer) 2. Professional soccer 3. Professional soccer players 4. Soccer tournaments. 5. Soccer coaches. 6. United States -- History -- 20th century.

ISBN 9781468315196

LC bl2018070675

Drawing on interviews from past and current players, coaches and journalists, the author of The United States of Soccer and veteran soccer journalist, examining every aspect of the U.S. Men's National Team and their competition, presents an assessment of the history and future potential of American soccer on the international playing field.

"Recommended for all soccer fans and readers interested in a deep dive into the U.S. men's soccer team, specifically the developmental program. Casual sports fans or readers may have a difficult time owing to West's lack of narrative style, making for an occasionally dense read." Library Journal.

796.34 Racket games

Hinkson, Jim

Lacrosse for dummies / Jim Hinkson and Joe Lombardi. John Wiley & Sons Canada, Ltd., c2010. xxvi, 330 p. : **796.34**

1. Lacrosse

ISBN 9780470738559

LC 2010282483

Previous ed.: 2003.

The book offers everything the beginning player needs to know, from the necessary equipment to the basic rules of the game, with explanations of the women's game and the indoor game, too.

McAfee, Richard
Table tennis : steps to success / Richard McAfee. Human Kinetics, c2009. xx, 203 p. : **796.34**

1. Table tennis
ISBN 9780736077316

LC 2009004824

Combines the knowledge and experience of master instructor Richard McAfee with essential table tennis techniques and strategies for today's player.

McPhee, John, 1931-
Levels of the game / John McPhee. Farrar, Straus & Giroux, 1989, c1969. 149 p. ; **796.34**

1. Ashe, Arthur. 2. Graebner, Clark, 1943- 3. Sports journalism. 4. Tennis. 5. Tennis players. 6. Tennis tournaments
ISBN 9780374515263

"Levels of the game is a narrative of a tennis match played by Arthur Ashe and Clark Graebner at Forest Hills."--back cover.

The contents of this book originally appeared in The New Yorker.

Narrates the events surrounding the 1968 championship tennis match at Forest Hills, focusing on the psychological game played by each of the opposing players, Arthur Ashe and Clark Graebner.

796.342 Tennis (Lawn tennis)

Fisher, Marshall Jon
A **terrible** splendor : three extraordinary men, a world poised for war, and the greatest tennis match ever played / Marshall Jon Fisher. Crown, 2009. 336 p. **796.342**

1. Davis Cup. 2. Professional tennis -- Tournaments. 3. Tennis. 4. Tennis players. 5. Germany -- History -- 1933-1945.
ISBN 0307393941

LC 2008050527

"Richly detailed . the story moves from one nail-biting set to the next against a backdrop of improbably high personal and political stakes." Boston Globe.

Gallwey, W. Timothy
★The **inner** game of tennis / W. Timothy Gallwey. Random House, 1997. xx, 122 p. : **796.342**

1. Tennis -- Psychological aspects.
ISBN 0679778314

LC 97000895

Concentrates upon overcoming mental attitudes that adversely affect tennis performance, including learning to relax, effectively concentrating, and discarding bad habits.

Howard, Johnette
The **rivals** : Chris Evert vs. Martina Navratilova : their epic duels and extraordinary friendship / Johnette Howard. Broadway Books, 2005. 296 p. : **796.342**

1. Evert, Chris, 1955- 2. Navratilova, Martina, 1956- 3. Sports rivalry 4. Tennis players 5. Women tennis players -- United States 6. Women -- Sexuality 7. United States -- Social life and customs -- 20th century
ISBN 9780767918848

LC 2004061918

Follows the careers of tennis greats Chris Evert and Martina Navratilova, from their first match in 1973 through the dramatic changes that occurred in the world of sports and society.

"This work makes a fine contribution to the history of women in sports." Publishers Weekly.

Phillips, Rowan Ricardo
The **circuit** : a tennis odyssey / Rowan Ricardo Phillips. Farrar, Straus and Giroux, 2018. xvii, 256 p. **796.342**

1. ATP Tour (Organization) 2. Tennis tournaments 3. Tennis players 4. Professional tennis 5. Seasons
ISBN 9780374123772

LC 2018017728

An award-winning poet describes the historic 2017 tennis season, from the Australian Open, which pitted Roger Federer against rival Rafael Nadal to the U.S. Open which saw the shocking return of Maria Sharapova.

796.352 Golf

Feinstein, John
The **first** major : the inside story of the 2016 Ryder Cup / John Feinstein. Doubleday, 2017. 304 p. **796.352**

1. Ryder Cup (Golf) 2. Golf -- Tournaments -- History.
ISBN 9780385541091

LC 2017021758

A dramatic chronicle of the bitterly fought 2016 Ryder Cup discusses the multiple losses and recent death of Arnold Palmer that spurred a vengeful match between the American and European teams, citing the particular contributions of such figures as Phil Mickelson, Rory McIlroy and Patrick Reed.

"Golf fans will know what happened, of course, but Feinstein compellingly re-creates the excitement, sometimes shot by shot, especially in the classic McIlroy-Reed singles match, which has come to be a symbol of golf at its best, both for shotmaking and sportsmanship. A great moment in golf history, vividly captured." Booklist.

A **good** walk spoiled : days and nights on the PGA tour / John Feinstein. Little, Brown, 1995. xx, 475 p., 16 p. of plates : **796.352**

1. PGA Tour (Association) 2. Professional golfers. 3. Golf -- Tournaments. 4. Professional golf. 5. Golfers.
ISBN 9780316277204

LC 94049552

Includes index.

A study of men's professional golf follows a year on the PGA tour, sharing portraits of superstars and rising players, the pressures of a high-profile sport, and dramatic tournament moments

"Along with profiles of the game's big names--Norman, Price, Watson--Feinstein's sojourn through the 1994 PGA tour also offers remarkable glimpses of the marginal players who struggle to first qualify for the tour and then maintain their tenuous places on it. Golfers of all ages simply won't be able to put this book down." Booklist.

Frost, Mark, 1953-
★The **match** : the day the game of golf changed forever / Mark Frost. Hyperion, 2007. 272 p. **796.352**

1. Lowery, Eddie. 2. Golf -- Pebble Beach, California -- History. 3. Golfers -- California 4. Sports betting -- California 5. Pebble Beach, California -- Social life and customs -- 20th century
ISBN 9781401302788

LC 2007023325

In 1956, a casual bet between two millionaires eventually pitted two of the greatest golfers of the era--Byron Nelson and Ben Hogan--against top amateurs Harvie Ward and Ken Venturi. Frost recounts this dramatic tale from start to finish, detailing the match that vaulted golf out of the shadows and into the national spotlight.

"What makes this account so fresh and so exciting for golf fans is that--unlike any other re-creation of a great moment in sports history--Frost tells a story that, being virtually unknown, carries with it genuine suspense as to the outcome. Going well beyond the simple question of who will win, however, Frost makes us see this spur-of-the-moment match for what it was: the last hurrah of amateur golf. And, best of all, he captures one of those fleeting moments in sports when competing athletes reach a kind of transcendent perfection simultaneously. Superb narrative nonfiction." Booklist.

Hogan, Ben, 1912-1997

★**Five** lessons : the modern fundamentals of golf / Ben Hogan with Herbert Warren Wind ; drawings by Anthony Ravielli. Simon & Schuster, 1985. 127 p. : **796.352**

1. Golf.

ISBN 0671612972

LC 85014558

"A Fireside book."

Previously published in 1957.

The professional golfer provides tips on the grip, stance, and swing of successful golf shots.

"The basics of hitting a ball with a club haven't changed much since this debuted, so this still offers valuable advice from one of the greats." Library Journal.

Rotella, Robert J.

Golf is not a game of perfect / Bob Rotella with Bob Cullen. Simon & Schuster, c1995. 224 p. ; **796.352**

1. Golf -- Psychological aspects. 2. Golfers.

ISBN 068480364X

LC 95001120

A coach and sports psychologist presents anecdotes about the golfers he has worked with while offering advice on how to handle the mental aspects of golfing and accept personal potentials and limits

796.357 Baseball

Barry, Dan, 1958-

Bottom of the 33rd : hope and redemption in baseball's longest game / Dan Barry. Harper, 2011. 272 p. **796.357**

1. Pawtucket Red Sox (Baseball team) -- History. 2. Rochester Red Wings (Baseball team) -- History. 3. Baseball -- United States -- History. 4. Minor league baseball -- United States -- History. 5. Baseball -- Records 6. Ball games.

ISBN 9780062014481

LC 2010051656

Details the longest game in baseball history, a grueling minor-league matchup between the Pawtucket Red Sox and the Rochester Red Wings that lasted more than eight hours, with the last of the 33 innings being postponed until two months later.

"Barry exploits the power of memory and nostalgia with literary grace and journalistic exactitude. He blends a vivid, moment-by-moment recreation of the game with what happens to its participants in the next 30 years." New York Times Book Review.

Coffey, Wayne R.

They said it couldn't be done : the '69 Mets, New York City, and the most astounding season in baseball history / Wayne Coffey. Crown Publishing, 2019. 304 p. **796.357**

1. New York Mets (Baseball team) 2. World Series (Baseball) 3. Baseball 4. Baseball teams 5. Professional baseball 6. Sports -- History 7. New York City

ISBN 9781524760885

LC 2018043635

A 50th-anniversary group biography depicting the 1969 "Miracle Mets" season places their unlikely championship against a backdrop of the space race and the Vietnam War, sharing insight into the contributions of such individuals as Jerry Koosman, Gil Hodges and Ed Charles.

"A solid and rousing read that doesn't dive deep into baseball's minutia." Library Journal.

Cohen, Rich

The **Chicago** Cubs : story of a curse / Rich Cohen. Farrar, Straus and Giroux, [2017] 272 p. **796.357**

1. Chicago Cubs (Baseball team) -- History. 2. National League of Professional Baseball Clubs. 3. World Series (Baseball) 4. Professional baseball teams. 5. Baseball teams. 6. Baseball fans. 7. Chicago, Illinois.

ISBN 9780374120924

LC 2017025511

Combining reportage with memoir, the author chronicles the history of the Chicago Cubs and--drawing on interviews and travels with recent Cubs players, owners and coaching staff--tracks the famous curse that was placed on the team in 1945 by the owner of the Billy Goat Tavern.

"This is but one in what is already a succession of books on the Chicago Cubs historic 2016 World Series championship--books that include Scott Simons My Cubs and David Kaplans The Plan--but it might be the best, since its both a deeply satisfying historical account of that colorful franchise and a compelling, all-too-painful personal narrative of one longtime, besotted Cubs fan." Booklist.

Cook, Kevin, 1956-

Ten innings at Wrigley : the wildest ballgame ever, with baseball on the brink / Kevin Cook. Henry Holt and Company, [2019] 320 p. **796.357**

1. Chicago Cubs (Baseball team) -- History 2. Philadelphia Phillies (Baseball team) -- History 3. Wrigley Field (Chicago, Ill.) 4. Baseball teams 5. Professional baseball 6. Baseball players 7. Professional baseball players

ISBN 9781250182036

LC 2018047864

A recap of a wild 1979 baseball game at Wrigley Field between the Chicago Cubs and Philadelphia Phillies that featured 45 runs and 11 homers from legendary players such as Mike Schmidt, Bruce Sutter and Tug McGraw.

Diamond, Jared M.

Swing kings : the inside story of baseball's home run revolution / Jared Diamond. William Morrow & Co, 2020. 352 p. **796.357**

1. Baseball 2. Home runs (Baseball) 3. Baseball players 4. Baseball bats

ISBN 9780062872104

LC bl2020004928

The Wall Street Journal national baseball writer presents a narrative account of the "home run boom" that describes the pivotal contributions of such figures as J. D. Martinez, Aaron Judge and Justin Turner.

"This breezy and engaging history will be a hit with baseball aficionados and casual fans alike." Publishers Weekly

Eisenberg, John, 1956-

The **streak** : Lou Gehrig, Cal Ripken, and baseball's most historic record / John Eisenberg. Houghton Mifflin Harcourt, [2017] xii, 299 pages : **796.357**

1. Ripken, Cal, Jr., 1960- 2. Gehrig, Lou, 1903-1941. 3. Baseball Hall of Fame members. 4. Professional baseball players. 5. Baseball players. 6. Baseball -- Records.

ISBN 9780544107670

LC 2017000811

Discusses the historic, game-playing records by both Lou Gehrig and Cal Ripken Jr. and dissects who had the more difficult achievement through probing research, meticulous analysis and colorful parallel storytelling.

"Eisenberg examines one of baseball's most venerated records while exploring what it all means, providing a compelling, thought-provoking history for fans of America's grand game." Kirkus.

Feinstein, John

Where nobody knows your name : life in the minor leagues of baseball / John Feinstein. Doubleday, 2014 304 p. **796.357**

1. Minor league baseball. 2. Baseball 3. Minor league baseball players 4. Baseball players

ISBN 9780385535939

LC 2013030645

During the 2012 season, sportswriter John Feinstein dug into minor league baseball, spending his time with players, managers, and other members of the Triple-A International League. It's a very different world than the majors, which becomes clear as Feinstein focuses on eight men in particular, among a larger cast. Some of them have worked in the majors while others haven't -- but they all want to get there for good. From the Durham Bulls to the Lehigh Valley Iron Pigs, Where Nobody Knows Your Name offers a colorfully broad view of life in the minor leagues.

Geist, William

Little League confidential : one coach's completely unauthorized tale of survival / Bill Geist. Dell, 1999, c1992. 217 p. ; **796.357**

1. Little League baseball -- Humor

ISBN 9780440508779

LC BL 99003224

"A Dell trade paperback."

Originally published: New York : Macmillan, 1992.

A journalist tells of his experiences coaching his son's Little League team, with anecdotes about a ballerina batter, an unfair umpire uncle, and other stories that provide a fresh perspective on an American institution

"The author relates his decade of service as a little-league baseball coach. He admittedly distills his experiences--and those of others--into a season-long docudrama journal. He tells of pompous coaches lecturing their miniplayers on the subtleties of the infield fly rule; he addresses the question of positioning a player with a personal-injury lawyer for a dad. The book is a wonderful effort filled with empathy for kids, impatience for pushy parents, and a good sense of humor." Booklist.

Halberstam, David

The **teammates** : a portrait of friendship / David Halberstam. Hyperion, 2003. 217 p. : **796.357**

1. Williams, Ted, 1918-2002 2. Doerr, Bobby, 1918- 3. DiMaggio, Dom. 4. Pesky, Johnny, 1919- 5. Boston Red Sox (Baseball team) 6. Baseball players -- United States 7. Friendship. 8. Baseball. 9. Professional baseball players.

ISBN 140130057X

LC 2003042334

"This account of good people living full lives and appreciating the experience will move readers." Booklist.

Jaffe, Jay

The **Cooperstown** casebook : who's in the Baseball Hall of Fame, who should be in, and who should pack their plaques / Jay Jaffe. Thomas Dunne Books, 2017. 368 p. **796.357**

1. National Baseball Hall of Fame and Museum. 2. Baseball Hall of Fame members. 3. Professional baseball players. 4. Baseball -- Statistics -- History. 5. Baseball players. 6. Cooperstown, New York.

ISBN 9781250071217

LC 2017012016

Presenting his revolutionary method for electing players to the Hall of Fame, a contributing baseball writer for SI.com shares his popular and proprietary "JAWS" ranking system, which aims to ensure that the correct players are recognized, and shows why the Hall of Fame still matters in the 21st century.

Jamieson, David, 1946-

Mint condition : how baseball cards became an American obsession / David Jamieson. Atlantic Monthly Press, 2010. 320 p. **796.357**

1. Baseball cards. 2. Collectors and collecting. 3. Collectibles. 4. Sports cards.

ISBN 9780802119391

LC 2010282449

Explores the fascinating world of baseball-card collecting from its roots in the tobacco industry to its rise in popularity to its bubble bursting in the 90s, in a book that looks at mad-genius designers, professional "graders" who rate the cards and the "doctors" who secretly alter them.

"For much of his book, Jamieson seems to be saying that greed and grownups have spoiled card collecting forever. But there's comfort in knowing that the cards have always appealed to baseball lovers and bottom-line business types for their own reasons. Even Jamieson holds out hope that they will find their proper place again in American kids' lives even if it's only in their closets." Minneapolis Star Tribune

Kenny, Brian, 1963-

Ahead of the curve : inside the baseball revolution / Brian Kenny. Simon & Schuster, 2016 512 p. **796.357**

1. Baseball. 2. Statistics.

ISBN 9781501106330

LC 2015039474

The outspoken MLB Network commentator draws on stories from baseball's present and past to reveal the important role of analytical thinking in today's game, examining why baseball leaders have compromised teams by favoring traditional rather than logical strategies

"When Miguel Cabrera captured Major League Baseballs elusive Triple Crown in 2012, Kenny refused to join the adulatory journalists lauding his selection as the American Leagues Most Valuable Player. Convinced that two-thirds of the Crown's jewels (namely, batting average and runs batted in) poorly measure a players performance, Kenny argues that more-sophisticated metrics established Angels outfielder Mike Trout as a more deserving MVP...Recognizing Oakland's Moneyball transformation as a harbinger of things to come, Kenny predicts that as managers grow increasingly data-savvy, they will throw off the restraints of tradition when shifting infielders, setting a batting order, and using the bullpen. Perhaps unwelcome among fans who love the myth and nostalgia of the diamond, this bolt of analytical lightning will make sports talk shows crackle." Booklist.

Kepner, Tyler (Baseball writer)

K : a history of baseball in ten pitches / Tyler Kepner. Doubleday, 2019. 320 p. **796.357**

1. Pitching (Baseball) 2. Pitchers (Baseball) 3. Baseball -- United States -- History. 4. No-hitter (Baseball)
ISBN 9780385541015

LC 2018016158

A history of the national pastime as told through the craft of pitching draws on years of archival research and interviews with more than three hundred star athletes to reveal the colorful stories and folklore behind ten major pitches.

"From triumph to tragedy, readers trace the astonishingly diverse trajectories of the baseballs pitchers throw. Appreciative fans will keep this book zipping off library shelves " Booklist.

Knight, Molly

The **best** team money can buy : the Los Angeles Dodgers' wild struggle to build a baseball powerhouse / Molly Knight. Simon & Schuster, 2015 324 p. **796.357**

1. Los Angeles Dodgers (Baseball team) 2. Professional baseball teams. 3. Professional baseball players. 4. Baseball teams. 5. Baseball.
ISBN 9781476776293

LC 2015017287

Documents the lucrative 2012 purchase of a bankrupt Los Angeles Dodgers team and the ensuing high-conflict deals involving new owners, managers and players, including controversy-marked rookie Yasiel Puig.

"A must-read for fans of the Dodgers and all Los Angeles sports teams. Knight's undercover work is like none other. Dodger fanatics, this book is for you." Library Journal.

Kornhauser, Jacob, 1994-

The **cup** of coffee club : 11 players and their brush with baseball history / Jacob Kornhauser. Rowman & Littlefield, 2020. 208 p. **796.357**

1. Major League Baseball (Organization). 2. Baseball players -- United States 3. Minor league baseball -- United States.
ISBN 9781538130810

LC 2019038836

Most baseball players will never reach the major leagues. While many that do stay there for a long time, there are a select few that played in just one major league game. Cup of Coffee Club tells the stories of eleven of these players and their struggles to reach the major leagues, as well as their struggles to get back.

"This is one of the very best baseball books in years. Readers will put faces and names to what they knew on a subliminal level: major-league baseball is really, really hard, and a lot of fine young players get left behind." Booklist

Kurlansky, Mark

The **Eastern** stars : how baseball changed the Dominican town of San Pedro de Macoris / Mark Kurlansky. Riverhead Books, 2010. 288 p. **796.35707293**

1. Baseball. 2. Baseball players. 3. Sugar industry and trade 4. Migrant workers. 5. Dominican Republic.
ISBN 9781594487507

LC 2009041036

A history of San Pedro in the Dominican Republic traces its rise from a small and impoverished region to an area that has produced some of Major League Baseball's greatest talents, citing the influence of sugar industry migrant workers and the role of race in transforming the sport. By the best-selling author of Cod.

Law, Keith, 1973-

Smart baseball : the story behind the old stats that are ruining the game, the new ones that are running it, and the right way to think about baseball / Keith Law. William Morrow & Company, 2017. 304 p. **796.357**

1. Baseball -- History 2. Statistics 3. Forecasting 4. Big data
ISBN 9780062490223

LC bl2017016359

An ESPN senior baseball writer and statistical analyst looks at the numbers game of baseball, proving why some of the most trusted stats are surprisingly wrong, explaining what numbers actually work and exploring what the rise of Big Data means for the future of the sport.

"This book by ESPN sportswriter and analyst Law is both a primer on how sabermetrics are changing the way fans and professionals view baseball, as well as a thorough explanation of why traditional statistics are misleading or obsolete." Library Journal.

Lewis, Michael (Michael M.)

★**Moneyball** : the art of winning an unfair game / Michael Lewis. W. W. Norton, 2003. xv, 288 p. **796.357**

1. Oakland Athletics (Baseball team) 2. Baseball -- Statistics. 3. Professional baseball scouting. 4. Baseball players -- Salaries, etc. -- United States. 5. Professional sports teams -- Economic aspects.
ISBN 0393057658

LC 2003005089

Examines the fallacy behind the major league baseball refrain that the team with the biggest wallet is supposed to win. Over the past four years the Oakland Athletics, a major league team with a minor league payroll, have had one of the best records in the country.

"With so many baseball books to choose from, it is difficult to single out a few as must-haves, but this one comes pretty close." Booklist.

Lindbergh, Ben

The **only** rule is that it has to work : our wild experiment building a new kind of baseball team. / Ben Lindbergh, Sam Miller. Henry Holt & Co 2016 304 p. **796.357**

1. Sonoma Stompers (Baseball team) 2. Baseball -- Statistics. 3. Professional baseball scouting. 4. Statistics. 5. Minor league baseball
ISBN 9781627795647

LC 2016005561

Two statisticians describe what happened when they were given the chance to run the Sonoma Stompers, an independent minor-league team in California, according to the most advanced statistics.

"With honest and captivating prose, the authors compel readers to care about players that don't make a lot of money yet still have big league dreams and aspirations." Library Journal.

Megdal, Howard

The **Cardinals** way : how one team embraced tradition and Moneyball at the same time / Howard Megdal. Thomas Dunne Books/St. Martin's Press, 2016 304 p. **796.357**

1. Major League Baseball (Organization) 2. St. Louis Cardinals (Baseball team) 3. Baseball 4. Baseball teams. 5. Professional baseball teams. 6. Professional baseball.
ISBN 9781250058317

LC 2015039018

Includes index.

An inside portrait of the St. Louis Cardinals explores how their practices of developing homegrown talent and embracing analytics has rendered the team a successful model MLB organization, evaluating the strategies and contributors that have led to multiple World Series achievements.

Neyer, Rob

Power ball : anatomy of a modern baseball game / Rob Neyer. Harper, [2018] xii, 300 p. **796.357**

1. Major League Baseball (Organization) 2. Oakland Athletics (Baseball team) 3. Houston Astros (Baseball team) 4. Baseball 5. Professional baseball 6. Strategy 7. Winning and losing

ISBN 9780062853615

LC 2018027809

Includes index.

To show the many ways in which Major League Baseball has changed over the past 20 years, a former ESPN columnist and analytics pioneer dramatically recreates an action-packed 2017 game between the Oakland A's and eventual World Series Champion Houston Astros.

Nusbaum, Eric

Stealing home : Los Angeles, the Dodgers, and the lives caught in between / Eric Nusbaum. PublicAffairs, 2020. xiii, 331 p. **796.357**

1. Los Angeles Dodgers (Baseball team) -- History 2. Dodger Stadium (Los Angeles) -- History 3. Major League Baseball (Organization) 4. Mexican-Americans 5. Neighborhoods 6. Baseball fields 7. Municipal government 8. Chavez Ravine (Los Angeles, Calif.) 9. Los Angeles, California -- History -- 20th century

ISBN 9781541742215

LC 2019041742

"Dodger Stadium is an American icon. The oldest ballpark west of the Mississippi -- and the third oldest overall -- it is a shrine to baseball and an essential feature of the Los Angeles cityscape. Yet the story of how it was built has a dark side. To clear space for the stadium, the city tore down low-income, Hispanic-friendly housing, resulting in a dramatic confrontation between the County Sheriff and the one family -- the Arechigas -- who refused to yield their home. In Stealing Home, Eric Nusbaum -- a fluent Spanish-speaker, Dodgers fan, and lifelong Angeleno -- tells the stories of the people whose homes were destroyed, their conflict with the bureaucrats and money men of Los Angeles, and shows how their lives were overrun by the wheel of history.

"Provocative, essential reading for students of California history." Kirkus

Pessah, Jon

The **game** : inside the secret world of Major League Baseball's power brokers / Jon Pessah. Little, Brown and Company, 2015. 512 p. **796.357**

1. Major League Baseball (Organization) 2. Baseball 3. Professional baseball 4. Baseball players -- Salaries, etc. -- United States. 5. Baseball team owners

ISBN 9780316185882

LC 2015901927

The founding editor of ESPN the Magazine and Pulitzer Prize nominee presents the extraordinary inside story of baseball's last 20 years, during which the genius and struggle for power of three men saved the game from self-destruction.

"Labor strife and controversies over performance-enhancing drugs absolutely are essential to baseball's recent history, but the author presents them as virtually the only parts that matter. An important but incomplete picture of baseball's Bud Selig era." Kirkus.

Peta, Joe

Trading bases : a story about Wall Street, gambling, and baseball (not necessarily in that order) : Joe Peta. Dutton, c2013. 368 p. **796.357**

1. Baseball. 2. Statistics 3. Gambling. 4. Finance 5. Wall Street, New York City

ISBN 9780525953647

LC 2012043509

Includes index.

An ex-Wall Street trader improved on Moneyball's famed sabermetrics to place bets that would beat the Vegas odds on Major League Baseball games--with a 41 percent return in his first year. Trading Bases explains how he did it.

Rapp, David, 1951-

Tinker to Evers to Chance : the Chicago Cubs and the dawn of modern America / David Rapp. The University of Chicago Press, 2018. 325 p. **796.357**

1. Evers, Johnny. 2. Tinker, Joe, 1880-1948. 3. Chance, Frank L. (Frank Leroy), 1877-1924. 4. Chicago Cubs (Baseball team) -- History. 5. Baseball -- History. 6. Professional baseball players. 7. Professional baseball -- History. 8. Baseball players.

ISBN 9780226415048

LC 2017041630

"Tinker to Evers to Chance examines this pivotal moment in American history, when baseball became the game we know today. Each man came from a different corner of the country and brought a distinctive local culture with him: Evers from the Irish-American hothouse of Troy, New York; Tinker from the urban parklands of Kansas City, Missouri; Chance from the verdant fields of California's Central Valley. The stories of these early baseball stars shed unexpected light not only on the evolution of baseball and on the enthusiasm of its players and fans all across America, but also on the broader convulsions transforming the US into a confident new industrial society. With them emerged a truly national culture."--Inside dust jacket.

"The compelling narrative not only details the feats these three achieved in helping establish a Cubs dynasty but also chronicles the metamorphosis of the new twentieth-century nation that embraced baseball as a game that reflected the urban strength developed in modern industry while also offering green-field comfort to city dwellers nostalgic for a rural past." Booklist.

Reiter, Ben

Astroball : the new way to win it all / Ben Reiter. Crown Archetype, 2018 272 p. **796.357**

1. Houston Astros (Baseball team) 2. World Series (Baseball) (2017) 3. Baseball 4. Baseball teams 5. Professional baseball 6. Sports -- Statistics

ISBN 9780525576648

LC 2018019954

The Sports Illustrated writer who predicted the Houston Astros' unexpected rise to win the World Series three years before it happened offers an account of the team's breathtaking 2017 season.

Ripken, Bill

State of play : the old school guide to new school baseball / Bill Ripken. Diversion Books, 2020 xxix, 209 p. : **796.357**

1. Baseball -- Statistics 2. Sports -- Statistics

ISBN 9781635766592

"A well-written account by one of baseball's most influential players. Fans of America's pastime and die-hard sabermetrics devotees will savor this informed perspective." Library Journal

Ruck, Rob, 1950-

Raceball : how the Major Leagues colonized the Black and Latin game / Rob Ruck. Beacon Press, c2010. 288 p. **796.357**

1. Major League Baseball (Organization) -- History. 2. Baseball -- Social aspects -- United States. 3. Racism in sports 4. African

American baseball players 5. Hispanic American baseball players. 6. United States -- Social conditions. 7. Latin America -- Social conditions. 8. Caribbean Area -- Social conditions.
ISBN 9780807048054
LC 2010037079

Discusses the intricate relationship between race and baseball, from the integration of the Major Leagues to the resulting decline of the Negro League and contemporary prominence of baseball players from the Caribbean.

Sawchik, Travis

Big data baseball : math, miracles, and the end of a 20-year losing streak / Travis Sawchik. Flatiron Books, 2015 288 p. **796.357**

1. Pittsburgh Pirates (Baseball team) 2. Baseball -- Statistical methods 3. Baseball players -- United States -- Statistics 4. Baseball teams.
ISBN 9781250063502
LC 2015011231

A sports writer for the Pittsburgh Tribune-Review describes how the General Manager of the Pirates, tired of a 20-year losing streak, adopted the strategies of "big data," similar to those depicted in Moneyball, to help improve their game.

"Casual and hard-core baseball fans alike who enjoyed Moneyball are sure to be entertained and informed by this sort-of sequel." Library Journal.

Simon, Scott

My Cubs : a love story / Scott Simon. Blue Rider Press, 2017. 160 p. **796.357**

1. Simon, Scott Childhood and youth. 2. Chicago Cubs (Baseball team) -- History. 3. National League of Professional Baseball Clubs. 4. World Series (Baseball) 5. Baseball fans 6. Professional baseball teams. 7. Professional baseball 8. Baseball teams. 9. Chicago, Illinois
ISBN 9780735218031
LC 2017004698

The host of National Public Radio's Weekend Edition offers personal, heartfelt reflections on his beloved Chicago Cubs, replete with club lore, memorable anecdotes, frenetic fandom and wise and adoring intimacy that have made the world champion Cubbies baseball's most tortured--and now triumphant--franchise.

"There will be many books about the Cubs 2016 World Series win, but its doubtful any will surpass Simons for humor, poignancy, and, well, love." Booklist.

Stout, Glenn, 1958-

Fenway 1912 : the birth of a ballpark, a championship season, and Fenway's remarkable first year / Glenn Stout. Houghton Mifflin Harcourt, 2011. 256 p. **796.357**

1. Fenway Park (Boston, Mass.) -- History. 2. Boston Red Sox (Baseball team) -- History. 3. Baseball fields 4. Professional baseball. 5. Professional baseball teams. 6. Boston, Massachusetts.
ISBN 9780547195629
LC 2011016068

A centennial tribute to the beloved ballpark shares the behind-the-scenes story of its tumultuous origins and first year, sharing coverage of such topics as the unorthodox blueprint that belies the park's notorious quirks, the construction contributions of local citizens and the history-making World Series battle between the Red Sox and the Giants.

"While some sports histories are bone-dry and distant, Stout imbues his account with a unique vibrancy and a razor-sharp intelligence. A wonderful sports book." Booklist.

Svrluga, Barry

The **grind** : inside baseball's endless season / Barry Svrluga. Blue Rider Press, 2015. 192 p. **796.357**

1. Baseball -- United States. 2. Professional baseball 3. Baseball players 4. Baseball -- Psychological aspects.
ISBN 9780399176289
LC 2015016056

"What's it like to live through sports' longest season, the 162-game Major League Baseball schedule? THE GRIND captures the frustration, impermanence, and glory felt by the players, the staff, and their families from the start of spring training to the final game of the year; classy baseball writing in the Roger Angell or Tom Boswell tradition".-- Provided by publisher.

"A quick and enjoyable read for any baseball lover, not just Nationals fans." Library Journal.

Thorn, John, 1947-

Baseball in the Garden of Eden : the secret history of the early game / John Thorn. Simon & Schuster, c2011. 384 p. **796.357**

1. Baseball -- United States -- History -- 19th century. 2. Sports -- History 3. Popular culture -- History -- 19th century 4. Baseball betting. 5. United States -- History -- 19th century
ISBN 9780743294034
LC 2010045155

A revelatory history of the rise and fall of baseball in America challenges popular beliefs about the game's evolution while revealing how it reflects popular culture, citing the roles of such contributing factors as gambling and religion. By the co-author of Total Baseball.

"Thorn writes with authority, precision and humor." Minneapolis Star Tribune.

Turbow, Jason

The **baseball** codes : beanballs, sign stealing, and bench-clearing brawls : the unwritten rules of America's pastime / Jason Turbow with Michael Duca. Pantheon Books, 2010. 304 p. **796.357**

1. Baseball. 2. Baseball players. 3. Rules. 4. Baseball teams.
ISBN 9780375424694
LC 2009022253

A behind-the-scenes analysis of professional baseball's hidden rules reveals the impact of unwritten codes of conduct, retaliatory behaviors and cheating, providing dramatic examples as committed by such figures as Mickey Mantle, Willie Mays and Don Drysdale.

"The premise [of this book] is that ballplayers, managers, coaches and various other participants in the culture of baseball are all clued in to a value system, a mode of behavior that defines a gauzy ideal: the right way to play the game. [The authors] have collected dozens of stories from baseball history about situations that are not governed by the rule book but that pertain to the fuzzy notions of rightness and respect and that describe the contours of the so-called baseball codes. The stories the authors have unearthed to illustrate ballpark justice and morality are often delicious." New York Times Book Review.

They bled blue : Fernandomania, strike-season mayhem, and the weirdest championship baseball had ever seen: the 1981 Los Angeles Dodgers / Jason Turbow. Houghton Mifflin Harcourt, [2019] 320 p. **796.357**

1. Valenzuela, Fernando, 1960- 2. Lasorda, Tommy. 3. Los Angeles Dodgers (Baseball team) -- History 20th century. 4. World Series (Baseball) (1981) 5. Pitchers (Baseball) 6. Baseball managers. 7. Professional baseball teams. 8. Cy Young Award winners. 9. Los

Angeles, California.
ISBN 9781328715531

LC 2018043599

Recounts the 1981 season of the Los Angeles Dodgers, including the break out pitcher Fernando Venezuela, Tommy Lasorda's monologues about bleeding Dodger blue, and their unexpected World Series win.

"Fluidly written and expertly paced, this exciting look at a turbulent team will thrill baseball enthusiasts of all stripes. " Publishers Weekly.

Ward, Geoffrey C.

Baseball : an illustrated history / narrative by Geoffrey C. Ward ; based on a documentary filmscript by Geoffrey C. Ward and Ken Burns ; preface by Ken Burns and Lynn Novick ; with an introduction by Roger Angell ; contributions by John Thorn ... [et al.]. A. A. Knopf, 1994. xxv, 486 p. : **796.357**

1. Baseball -- United States -- History. 2. Baseball teams. 3. Baseball players. 4. Essays.

ISBN 9780679404590

LC 93039809

Rereleased to coincide with the PBS broadcast of a new two-part "Tenth Inning" episode, an updated edition features a new chapter on such topics as the 1994 strike, the home-run race of 1998, and recent steroid controversies.

"This lavishly produced, gorgeously illustrated history of the game rises far above the often dreary 'companion volume' genre." Booklist.

Wong, Stephen

Game worn : baseball treasures from the game's greatest heroes and moments / Stephen Wong and Dave Grob ; foreword by John Thorn ; photography by Francesco Sapienza. Smithsonian Books, 2016 320 p. : **796.357**

1. Smithsonian Institution. 2. Baseball uniforms -- United States -- History 3. Baseball uniforms -- United States -- History. 4. Baseball -- Collectibles -- United States 5. Baseball -- Collectibles -- United States.

ISBN 1588345718

LC 2016015599

"Game Worn: Treasures of Baseball's Greatest Heroes and Moments is a richly illustrated exploration and first-of-its-kind compendium study of the world's most coveted and precious baseball uniforms worn by Major League ballplayers during the twentieth century. This coffee-table book features many of the most historically significant uniforms, jackets, hats, as well as other treasured baseball collectibles that tell us as much about the history and soul of America as they do about the game and the players. Some of the extraordinary highlights featured in this book include: Babe Ruth's road jersey from his first season with the New York Yankees (1920), the sole surviving uniform from the infamous 1919 World Series, Joe DiMaggio's rookie uniform from 1936, the Boston Red Sox road uniform Ted Williams wore during his epic 1941 season, Jackie Robinson's Brooklyn Dodgers home jersey from the 1952 season, Bill Mazeroski's Pittsburgh Pirates home uniform worn to hit the game-winning home run in game 7 of the 1960 World Series, and a visual feast of rare uniform styles. Each of the 68 entries includes sumptuous photography of the uniform and associated memorabilia, as well as a poignant and lively narrative highlighting its significance. The book also featuresa first-of-its-kind illustrated compendium with elaborate definitions of relevant terms that every baseball fan and collector needs to know, ranging from the All Star Game Uniform to the Zig-Zag Stitch. This book is an absolute must-have for anyone who has ever loved the game of baseball".-- Provided by publisher.

"This rare look at the importance of baseball garments is a visually striking compilation that reads like a Ken Burns documentary. A book for all baseball lovers." Library Journal.

Smithsonian baseball : inside the world's finest private collections / Stephen Wong ; photographs by Susan Einstein. Smithsonian Books, c2005. x, 286 p. **796.357**

1. Smithsonian Institution. 2. Baseball -- Collectibles -- United States 3. Baseball -- Collectibles -- United States 4. Baseball -- Collectors and collecting

ISBN 9780060838515

LC 2006297206

An oversized volume showcases 350 full-color photographs of twenty-one of the best private collections of baseball memorabilia, featuring numerous historical and previously unseen artifacts and providing eight expert essays on how to build a personal collection.

796.3570973 Baseball--United States

Goldberger, Paul

Ballpark : baseball in the American city / Paul Goldberger. Alfred A. Knopf, 2019. 352 p. **796.3570973**

1. Baseball fields -- Design and construction 2. Stadiums. 3. Baseball -- United States -- History. 4. Historic buildings.

ISBN 9780307701541

LC 2018046223

This lavishly-illustrated look at the history of baseball through the lens of its ever-changing ballparks discusses the bond between American cities and the national pastime and how changes in the urban landscape have been reflected in stadium design.

Hample, Zack, 1977-

The **baseball** : stunts, scandals, and secrets beneath the stitches / Zack Hample. Anchor Books, c2011. ix, 356 p. : **796.3570973**

1. Baseball -- United States -- History. 2. Baseball fans. 3. Baseballs -- Collectors and collecting -- United States. 4. Professional baseball.

ISBN 9780307475459

LC 2010043551

"Anchor sports."

Includes index.

The best-selling author of Watching Baseball Smarter shares historical and modern stories about the ball at the center of America's favorite pastime while tracing the baseball's evolution from a string-wrapped walnut to today's invisible ink-stamped ball.

"The author covers basics such as what to watch for in pitchers, catchers, hitters, fielders and base runners; he also provides answers to such nagging questions as why spectators stretch in the seventh inning and why most ballplayers grab their crotches. Hample hits the equivalent of a reference book home run with his witty and loose style--taking a friendly for-a-fan-by-a-fan approach that doesn't hide his enormous depth of knowledge." Publishers Weekly.

Kurkjian, Tim

I'm fascinated by sacrifice flies : inside the game we all love / Tim Kurkjian. St. Martin's Press, 2016. 256 p. **796.3570973**

1. Sportscasters 2. Baseball -- Anecdotes.

ISBN 9781250077936

LC 2015048747

An ESPN baseball analyst offers hilarious and insightful tales from the world of Major League Baseball.

"Kurkjian's celebrity and the joyous contents within the covers merit the investment." Booklist.

796.3576 Specific types of baseball

Passan, Jeff

The **arm** : inside the billion-dollar mystery of the most valuable commodity in sports / Jeff Passan. HarperCollins, 2016 368 p. **796.3576**

1. Baseball 2. Pitchers (Baseball) 3. Pitching (Baseball) 4. Baseball players

ISBN 9780062400369

LC 2016303971

The Yahoo Sports lead columnist and author of Death to the BCS examines the franchise lifeblood role of pitchers in Major League Baseball and the considerable vulnerability of pitching arms, drawing on rare interviews with Daniel Hudson, Todd Coffey and Sandy Koufax to share insights into the impact of injuries on careers and teams.

"As Passan interviews professionals dealing with the problem--physicians, managers, trainers, pitchers, and even epidemiologists--he reports no magical breakthroughs. But he does give readers an insider's perspective on the threat hanging over every player who takes the mound." Booklist.

796.35764 Professional and semiprofessional baseball

Law, Keith, 1973-

The **inside** game : bad calls, strange moves, and what baseball behavior teaches us about ourselves / Keith Law. William Morrow, 2020. viii, 263 p. ; **796.35764**

1. Baseball 2. Professional baseball 3. Professional sports 4. Baseball players 5. United States -- Social life and customs

ISBN 9780062942722

Offers an era-spanning dissection of some of the best and worst decisions in modern baseball, explaining what motivated them, what can be learned from them, and how their legacy has shaped the game.

"Highly recommended for serious followers of baseball and readers interested in how statistical analysis and trends can be applied in any sport." Library Journal

796.357646 World series games

Cook, Kevin, 1956-

Electric October : seven world series games, six lives, five minutes of fame that lasted forever / Kevin Cook. Henry Holt and Company, 2017 320 p. **796.357646**

1. New York Yankees (Baseball team) -- History 20th century. 2. Brooklyn Dodgers (Baseball team) 3. World Series (Baseball) (1947) 4. World Series (Baseball) 5. Professional baseball 6. Baseball teams 7. Baseball players 8. Professional baseball players

ISBN 9781250116567

LC 2017008793

A chronicle of the dramatic 1947 World Series explores the roles of lesser-known but key contributors including journeyman pitcher Bill Bevens, batting champ Snuffy Stirnweiss and unlikely runner Bucky Harris, examining how their unsung victories reshaped perspectives about fame and heroism.

"Cook does an excellent job of weaving articles and interviews from that time with modern sabermetrics and perspectives to make athletes and moments more relatable to fans of the current game." Library Journal.

796.42 Track and field

Caesar, Ed

Two hours : the quest to run the impossible marathon / Ed Caesar. Simon & Schuster, 2015 288 p. **796.42**

1. Marathon running. 2. Marathons 3. Marathon runners 4. Marathon running -- Training.

ISBN 9781451685848

LC 2014043224

Delving into the science, physiology and psychology involved in running so fast, for so long, a first-of-its-kind book on marathons invites readers into the world of elite runners, showing us why this most democratic of races retains its savage, enthralling appeal--and why we are drawn to testing ourselves to the limit.

"Though the books are different in intent, readers might want to try David Epstein's The Sports Gene or Christopher McDougall's Born To Run." Library Journal.

Dixon, Matt

The **well-built** triathlete : turning potential into performance / Matt Dixon. VeloPress, 2014 xii, 356 p. : **796.42**

1. Triathletes. 2. Triathlon -- Training.

ISBN 1937715116

LC bl2014025090

Includes index.

A comprehensive, whole-body approach to training for triathletes identifies four pillars of performance--training, recovery, nutrition, and strength--and provides guidelines and advice for making improvements in each area.

Finn, Adharanand

The **way** of the runner : a journey into the fabled world of Japanese running / Adharanand Finn. Pegasus Books, 2016 326 p. **796.42**

1. Running 2. Runners 3. Long-distance running 4. National characteristics, Japanese 5. Japan

ISBN 9781681771212

LC 2017304780

The award-winning author of Running With the Kenyans turns his attention to Japan, the most running-obsessed country on earth, revealing a running culture that will fascinate and surprise anyone eager to explore why we run and how we might do it better.

"An elegant, well-written pleasure even for readers with no particular interest in foot racing." Kirkus.

Fitzgerald, Matt

Iron war : Dave Scott, Mark Allen & the greatest race ever run / Matt Fitzgerald with Bob Babbitt. VeloPress, c2011. 324 p., 24 p. of plates : **796.42**

1. Scott, Dave. 2. Allen, Mark, 1958- 3. Triathletes 4. Ironman triathlons. 5. Endurance sports 6. Biographies

ISBN 9781934030776

LC 2011027408

Weaving an examination of mental resolve into a gripping tale of athletic adventure, Iron War is a soaring narrative of two champions and the paths that led to their stunning final showdown.

"A true page-turner about a too-little-known great moment in sports." Booklist

Friel, Joe

★The **triathlete's** training bible : the world's most comprehensive training guide / Joe Friel. VeloPress, 2016 xv, 331 p.

: 796.42

1. Triathlon -- Training
ISBN 9781937715441

LC 2016034831

A comprehensive guide to triathlon training includes both power- and pace-based training, custom recovery plans, and techniques to build up speed and strength skills.

Higdon, Hal

Marathon : the ultimate training guide : advice, plans, and programs for half and full marathons / Hal Higdon. Rodale, c2011. x, 294 p. ; **796.42**

1. Marathon running -- Training
ISBN 9781609612245

LC 2011028075

Includes index.

A training guide for beginners, first-time marathoners, and women runners counsels readers on how to build speed and distance while maximizing one's performance and building on defensive running skills, in an updated edition by a senior writer for Runner's World magazine.

Karnazes, Dean

The **legend** of Marathon : retracing the ancient battle and epic run that inspired the world's greatest foot race / Dean Karnazes. Rodale Press, 2014. 304 p. **796.42**

1. Pheidippides, fl. 490 B.C. 2. Marathon, Battle of, Greece, 490 B.C. 3. Marathon running -- History. 4. Marathon runners 5. Marathons 6. Greece
ISBN 9781609614744

LC 2018300054

"This is a remarkable and inspiring memoir that will have casual and serious runners cheering." Publishers Weekly.

Magill, Pete

Build your running body : a total-body fitness plan for all distance runners, from milers to ultramarathoners' run farther, faster, and injury-free / Pete Magill, Thomas Schwartz, and Melissa Breyer ; photographs by Diana Hernandez. The experiment, 2014 xi, 434 p. : **796.42**

1. Long-distance running 2. Runners (Sports) 3. Running 4. Running -- Physiological aspects
ISBN 9781615191024

LC 2014010816

Includes index.

Draws on the latest research in running physiology to provide training programs and strategies for improving running mileage while preventing injuries, and includes nutrition guidance and beginner's guidelines.

McDougall, Christopher, 1962-

★**Born** to run : a hidden tribe, superathletes, and the greatest race the world has never seen / Christopher McDougall. Alfred A. Knopf, 2009. 287 p. **796.42**

1. Indians of Mexico 2. Ultramarathon running. 3. Runners. 4. Running. 5. Mexico
ISBN 9780307266309

LC 2009922861

ALA Notable Book, 2010.

McDougall reveals the secrets of the world's greatest distance runners--the Tarahumara Indians of Copper Canyon, Mexico--and how he trained for the challenge of a fifty-mile race through the heart of Tarahumara country pitting the tribe against an odd band of superathletic Americans.

"Implausibly difficult marathons, hundreds of miles long, and the ultra-elite competitive runners who tackle them for fun. A hidden, almost mythical, tribe in Mexico untouched by modern disease. Shoe manufacturers driven by corporate greed to sustain an industry that has created modern running injuries. An anthropological study of homo sapiens' physiology and the course we took to survive while Neanderthals died out. It may seem farfetched, but Born to Run entwines all those strands and even pop-culture references into an engaging and inspirational read." PopMatters.

Moore, Richard

The **Bolt** supremacy : inside Jamaica's sprint factory / Richard Moore. Pegasus Books, 2017. 336 p. **796.422097292**

1. Bolt, Usain, 1986- 2. Sprinting 3. Running 4. Runners 5. Track and field athletes 6. Jamaica
ISBN 9781681774077

LC bl2017019276

Beijing 2008: Usain Bolt slows down as he approaches the finish line of the the 100-meter finals. He beats his chest, well ahead of his nearest rival, his face filled with the euphoria of a young man utterly in thrall to his extraordinary physical talent. It is one of the greatest moments in sports history, and it is just the beginning.Of the ten fastest 100-meter times in history, eight belong to Jamaicans. How is it that a small Caribbean island has come to almost totally dominate the men's and women's sprint events?

"Fascinating reading for track fans." Booklist.

Romanov, Nicholas S.

The **running** revolution : how to run faster, farther, and injury-free--for life / Dr. Nicholas Romanov with Kurt Brungardt. Penguin Books, 2014. xv, 220 p. : **796.42**

1. Running -- Training
ISBN 9780143123194

LC 2014012161

Includes index.

Explains how to run more efficiently and with better biomechanics in order to minimize strain and injury, describing the best type of shoes, highlighting the safest type of foot strike, and outlining a four-week training program.

796.4252 Marathon

Keflezighi, Meb

Meb for mortals : how to run, think and eat like a champion marathoner / Meb Keflezighi with Scott Douglas. Rodale, 2015 xi, 196 p. : **796.4252**

1. Long-distance running -- Training 2. Marathon running -- Training
ISBN 9781623365479

LC 2016301845

Includes index.

Describes in unprecedented detail how three-time Olympian Keflezighi prepares to take on the best runners in the world. More important, the book shows everyday runners how to implement the training, nutritional, and mental principles that have guided him throughout his long career, which in addition to the 2014 Boston win includes an Olympic silver medal and the 2009 New York City Marathon title. --Publisher's description.

"The format is clean and the writing is simple and strong, all making this book a valuable tool for anyone with their sights set on running a marathon." Publishers Weekly.

Van Allen, Jennifer
The **Runner's** world big book of marathon and half-marathon training : winning strategies, inpiring stories, and the ultimate training tools / Jennifer Van Allen ... [et.al.]. Rodale, c2012. xiii, 290 p. : **796.4252**

1. Marathon running -- Training
ISBN 9781609616847

LC OC2018157655

Provides information about marathon training essentials, including workouts, nutrition, and injury prevention.

796.4809 Olympic Games--history

Goldblatt, David
The **games** : a global history of the Olympics / David Goldblatt. W. W. Norton & Company, 2016. 464 p. **796.4809**

1. Olympic games. 2. Sports -- History. 3. Social history. 4. Sports and state.
ISBN 9780393292770

LC 2016022203

The definitive sports and social history of the modern Olympic Games, by one of the most celebrated sportswriters of our time.

796.5 Outdoor life

Citro, Asia
150+ screen-free activities for kids : The Very Best and Easiest Playtime Activities from FunatHomeWithKids.com / Asia Citro, MEd, creator of Fun at Home with Kids. Adams Media, 2014 255 p. : **796.5**

1. Creative activities and seat work 2. Outdoor recreation for children
ISBN 9781440576157

LC 2014021922

Provides over one hundred fun and creative activities for children that take them away from screens and gadgets, including making "slime," crafting paints, and designing toys.

Coburn, Broughton, 1951-
Everest : mountain without mercy / Broughton Coburn ; introduction by Tim Cahill ; afterword by David Breashears. National Geographic Society, c1997. 256 p. : **796.5**

1. MacGillivray Freeman IMAX/IWERKS Expedition (1996 : Mount Everest) 2. Mountaineering -- Accidents -- Mount Everest 3. Mountaineering -- Mount Everest 4. Extreme sports. 5. Mount Everest
ISBN 9780792270140

LC 97010765

Includes index.

"Bringing an understated yet powerful Buddhist/Sherpa ethical perspective to the tragedy on Everest chronicled in Jon Krakauer's Into Thin Air, Coburn reports on the IMAX film crew who participated in the rescue effort when the May 1996 expeditions led by guides Rob Hall and Scott Fischer ended in death and crippling injury." Publishers Weekly.

796.51 Walking

Harvey, Mark W. T. (Mark William Thornton)
The **National** Outdoor Leadership School's wilderness guide : the classic handbook / Mark Harvey ; [illustrations by Rick Ruhman]. Simon & Schuster, c1999. 268 p. : **796.51**

1. National Outdoor Leadership School (U.S.). 2. Backpacking 3. Camping 4. Wilderness survival
ISBN 9780684859095

LC 99021875

"A Fireside book."

Rev. ed. of: The National Outdoor Leadership School's wilderness guide / Peter Simer. c1983.

A guide for backpackers, hikers, and other wilderness buffs offers information on equipment and techniques, search and rescue methods, cooking, and safety.

Lonely Planet Global Limited
Epic hikes of the world : explore the planet's most thrilling treks and trails. / Lonely Planet. Lonely Planet Global Limited, 2018. 328 p. : **796.51**

1. Hiking 2. Trails 3. Guidebooks.
ISBN 9781787014176

LC bl2018146646

At head of title: Lonely planet.

Includes index.

Highlights hiking routes in thirty countries worldwide, from New Zealand to Peru, discussing one-day jaunts, urban trails, and month-long hikes.

Solnit, Rebecca
Wanderlust : a history of walking / Rebecca Solnit. Viking, 2000. viii, 326 p. : **796.51**

1. Walking -- History. 2. Hiking -- History. 3. Voyages and travels.
ISBN 0670882097

LC 99041153

A cultural history of walking explores the ancient practice, from ancient Greece to the present, delving into Wordsworth, Gary Snyder, Rousseau, Jane Austen, and other cultural and literary icons to show how this basic activity has been imagined througout history.

"The author presents a look at how the act of walking...has influenced our history, our science, our literature, and the very way that we see ourselves as human beings. Drawing on a multitude of diverse disciplines, Solnit illustrates that walking has led to some of the best, and worst, incidents in all of history." Booklist.

Townsend, Chris, 1949-
The **backpacker's** handbook / Chris Townsend. McGraw-Hill , c2012. x, 468 p. : **796.51**

1. Backpacking
ISBN 9780071754897

LC 2011028816

Includes index.

Offers a handbook for all skill levels of hiking that covers a wide range of backbacking issues, including how to use a map and compass, survival skills, and tracking.

796.510973 Hiking--United States

Berger, Karen, 1959-
America's great hiking trails / Karen Berger ; photography by Bart Smith ; foreword by Bill McKibben. Rizzoli, 2014. 335 p.

: **796.510973**

1. Hiking -- United States 2. Guidebooks.
ISBN 9780789327413

LC oc2014124897

This lavishly illustrated celebration of more than 50,000 miles of America's most iconic trails celebrates the forty most important trails in America in forty-nine states and eight national parks.

Chamberlin, Silas

On the trail : a history of American hiking / Silas Chamberlin. Yale University Press, 2016. 243 p. **796.510973**

1. Hiking 2. Voyages and travels. 3. Travelers. 4. Trails
ISBN 9780300219111

LC 2016936121

The first history of the American hiking community and its contributions to the nation's vast network of trails.

"This winning, thought-provoking book offers insight into a relatively unknown aspect of environmental history." Library Journal.

796.5109756 Hiking--North Carolina

Spira, Timothy P.

Waterfalls and wildflowers in the Southern Appalachians : thirty great hikes / Timothy P. Spira. University of North Carolina Press, 2015 279 p. : **796.5109756**

1. Hiking -- Appalachian Region, Southern 2. Natural history -- Appalachian Region, Southern 3. Trails -- Appalachian Region, Southern 4. Waterfalls -- Appalachian Region, Southern 5. Appalachian Region, Southern Guidebooks. 6. Guidebooks.
ISBN 9781469622644

LC 2014044782

Includes index.

If you love waterfalls, here are some of the best hikes in the Southern Appalachians. And if you love plants--or simply would like to learn more about them--you will be in hiking heaven.

"Biologists will savor this handy hiking guide to a particularly beautiful region." Library Journal.

796.52 Walking and exploring by kind of terrain

Bukreev, Anatolii Nikolaevich, 1958-1997

The **climb** : tragic ambitions on Everest / Anatoli Boukreev and G. Weston DeWalt. St. Martin's Press, 1997. xi, 255 p. : **796.52**

1. Bukreev, Anatolii Nikolaevich, 1958-1997 2. Mountain Madness (Firm). Everest Expedition (1996) 3. Mountaineering accidents 4. Search and rescue operations. 5. Mount Everest Expedition, 1996. 6. Mountaineering -- Mount Everest. 7. Mount Everest.
ISBN 0312168144

LC 97023194

Relates the true story of what happened when a climbing expedition to Mount Everest was overcome by snow, wind, and lack of oxygen.

"This is a first-person account of the tragic climbing experience in May 1996 on Mount Everest that left eight hikers dead and several others struggling to stay alive. Fast-paced and easy to read, Boukreev's story of adventure and survival will remain in the reader's memory long after the book is finished." Library Journal.

Gutman, Matt, 1977-

The **boys** in the cave : deep inside the impossible rescue in Thailand / Matt Gutman Modern Library, 2018. 256 p. **796.52**

1. Caves 2. Search and rescue operations 3. Survival 4. Soccer teams 5. Thailand
ISBN 9780062909916

LC 2018054756

From award-winning ABC News Chief National Correspondent Matt Gutman, and written using exclusive interviews and information comes the definitive account of the dramatic story that gripped the world: the miracle rescue of twelve boys and their soccer coach trapped in a flooded cave miles underground for nearly three weeks; a pulse-pounding page-turner by a reporter who was there every step of their journey out.

Isserman, Maurice

Continental divide : a history of American mountaineering / Maurice Isserman. W.W. Norton & Co., 2016 416 p. **796.52**

1. Mountaineering.
ISBN 9780393068504

LC 2016000548

A history of the role of mountains and mountaineering in America is told through four centuries of landmark climbs and environmental activism, citing the contributions of notables ranging from Lewis and Clark to John Muir and Teddy Roosevelt.

"This broad sweep of American mountaineering history will satisfy general history readers and outdoor adventurers alike." Library Journal.

Krakauer, Jon

★**Into** thin air : a personal account of the Mount Everest disaster / Jon Krakauer. Villard, 1997. 293 p. : **796.52**

1. Krakauer, Jon. 2. Mount Everest Expedition, 1996. 3. Mountaineering accidents 4. Mountaineers -- Mount Everest. 5. Expeditions. 6. Mount Everest. 7. China. 8. Nepal. 9. First person narratives.
ISBN 9780679457527

LC 96030031

Map on lining papers.

ALA Notable Book, 1998.

National Book Critics Circle Award for Nonfiction finalist, 1997.

Pulitzer Prize for General Nonfiction finalist, 1998.

The author describes his spring 1996 trek to Mt. Everest, a disastrous expedition that claimed the lives of eight climbers, and explains why he survived.

"This tense, harrowing story is as mesmerizing and hard to put down as any well-written adventure novel." School Library Journal.

Tabor, James M.

Blind descent : the quest to discover the deepest place on earth / James M. Tabor. Random House, c2010. xv, 286 p. : **796.52**

1. Stone, W. C. (William C.) 2. Klimchuk, A. B. (Aleksandr Borisovich) 3. Caving. 4. Caves. 5. Underground areas.
ISBN 9781400067671

This is the story of the men and women who risked everything to find the deepest cave on Earth, earning their place in history beside the likes of Peary, Amundsen, Hillary, and Armstrong. Tabor focuses particularly on the heroic efforts of Bill Stone in the vast Cheve Cave of southern Mexico and Alexander Klimchouk in the supercave Krubera of the Republic of Georgia.

"The author examines the two polar opposites at the head of each of two major cave-diving expeditions: the win-at-all-costs, classic alpha-male, American Bill Stone, who led Mexican cave dives in Cheve and Huatula; and mild-mannered organization man, Ukrainian Alexander Klimchouk, who spearheaded the exploration of his country's notorious Krubera cave. Only one of these men came away with the distinction of having descended deeper into the earth's core than anyone else. Tabor expertly fashions a fly-on-the-wall narrative from the firsthand accounts of Stone, Klimchouk and their supporting casts of death-defying followers. A fascinating and informative introduction to the sport of cave diving, as well as a dramatic portrayal of a significant man-vs.-nature conflict." Kirkus.

Taylor, Joseph E.

Pilgrims of the vertical : Yosemite rock climbers and nature at risk / Joseph E. Taylor III. Harvard University Press, 2010. 384 p. **796.52**

1. Rock climbing. 2. Mountaineering. 3. Environmentalism. 4. Mountaineers. 5. Yosemite Valley.
ISBN 9780674052871

LC 2010021578

National Outdoor Book Award for History/Biography, 2010.

"Yosemite has been a climber magnet for decades, and it was here that many of rock climbing's highly ritualized set of norms and mores evolved. [This book] is at once a chronicle of how the sport evolved in Yosemite and a fascinating social history that considers climbing in the larger context of American life. For the general reader, the book makes a fine introduction to the history of climbing and Yosemite's special place in its development. For climbers, Pilgrims of the Vertical offers a somewhat idiosyncratic view of their sport." Wall Street Journal.

796.522 Mountains, hills, rocks

Burgman, John

High drama : the rise, fall, and rebirth of American competition climbing / John Burgman ; foreword by Kynan Waggoner. Triumph Books, 2020. 381 p. **796.522**

1. Rock climbing 2. Rock climbers 3. Competition 4. Free climbing
ISBN 1629377759

LC 2020040381

High Drama explores rock climbing's transformation from a pursuit of select anti-establishment vagabonds to a sport embraced by competitors of all ages, social classes, and backgrounds. Climbing magazine's John Burgman weaves a multi-layered story of traditionalists and opportunists, grassroots organizers and business-minded developers, free-spirited rebels and rigorously coached athletes.

"Leaving no stone unturned, this exhaustive history will find an audience with climbing enthusiasts." Library Journal

Conefrey, Mick

The **ghosts** of K2 : the epic saga of the first ascent / Mick Conefrey. Oneworld, 2015 336 p. **796.522**

1. Mountaineering 2. Mountains -- Description and travel 3. Expeditions 4. K2 (Mountain), Pakistan
ISBN 9781780745954

LC bl2015052047

National Outdoor Book Award for History/Biography, 2016.

Mick Conefrey tells the story of three extraordinary expeditions filled with riveting drama and unimaginable tragedy: Fritz Wiessener's controversial attempt of 1939, the disastrous American expedition of 1953, and the huge Italian expedition of 1954 on which K2 was first climbed.

"An absorbing chronicle of K2's early history that all fans of mountaineering will enjoy." Library Journal.

Cordes, Kelly

The **tower** : mountain of legends, spire of storms--Cerro Torre / Kelly Cordes. Patagonia Inc., 2014. 256 p. **796.522**

1. Mountains. 2. Mountaineers. 3. Mountaineering. 4. Extreme sports. 5. Torre Mountain (Argentina) 6. Argentina -- History.
ISBN 9781938340338

LC 2014947861

National Outdoor Book Award for Outdoor Literature, 2015.

Patagonia's Cerro Torre, considered by many the most beautiful peak in the world, draws the finest and most devoted technical alpinists to its climbing challenges. But controversy has swirled around this ice-capped peak since Cesare Maestri claimed first ascent in 1959. Since then a debate has raged, with world-class climbers attempting to retrace his route but finding only contradictions. This chronicle of hubris, heroism, controversies and epic journeys offers a glimpse into the human condition, and why some pursue extreme endeavors that at face value have no worth. --Publisher's description.

Ellsworth, Scott

The **world** beneath their feet : mountaineering, madness, and the deadly race to summit the Himalayas / Scott Ellsworth. Little Brown & Company, 2020 xix, 393 p. **796.522**

1. Mountaineering -- Himalaya Mountains. 2. Mountaineers 3. International competition 4. Adventure 5. Himalaya Mountains. 6. K2 (Mountain), Pakistan. 7. Mount Everest.
ISBN 9780316434867

LC bl2020004653

As tension steadily rose between European powers in the 1930s, a different kind of battle was already raging across the Himalayas. Teams of mountaineers from Great Britain, Nazi Germany, and the United States were all competing to be the first to climb the world's highest peaks, including Mount Everest and K2. Unlike climbers today, they had few photographs or maps, no properly working oxygen systems, and they wore leather boots and cotton parkas. Amazingly, and against all odds, they soon went farther and higher than anyone could have imagined.

"An excellent overview of mountaineering and exploration in the Himalayas and Karakoram, set against the backdrop of 20th-century history, that will appeal to mountaineers and armchair adventurers." Library Journal

Hall, Andy

Denali's howl : the deadliest climbing disaster on America's wildest peak / Andy Hall. Dutton Adult, 2014. 368 p. **796.522**

1. Mountaineering accidents 2. Mountaineering -- Alaska -- McKinley, Mount. 3. Search and rescue operations. 4. Mount Denali (Alaska) 5. Denali National Park and Preserve (Alaska) 6. Alaska.
ISBN 9780525954064

LC 2013047600

Denali's Howl is the white-knuckle account of one of the most deadly climbing disasters of all time. In 1967, twelve young men attempted to climb Alaska's Mount McKinley--known to the locals as Denali--one of the most popular and deadly mountaineering destinations in the world. Only five survived. Journalist Andy Hall, son of the park superintendent at the time, investigates the tragedy. He spent years tracking down survivors, lost documents, and recordings of radio communications. In Denali's Howl, Hall reveals the full story of an expedition facing conditions conclusively established here for the first time: At an elevation of nearly 20,000 feet, these young men endured an "arctic super blizzard," with howling winds of up to 300 miles an hour and windchill that freezes flesh solid in minutes. All this without the high-tech gear and equipment climbers use today. As well as the story of the men caught inside the storm, Denali's Howl is the story of those caught outside it trying to save them--Hall's father among them. The book gives readers a detailed look at the culture of climbing then and now and raises uncomfortable questions about each player in this tragedy. Was enough done to rescue the climbers, or were their fates sealed when they ascended into the path of this unprecedented storm?

Ralston, Aron

Between a rock and a hard place / Aron Ralston. Atria Books, 2004. xiii, 354 p. : **796.522**

1. Ralston, Aron. 2. Rock climbing accidents -- Bluejohn Canyon, Utah. 3. Rock climbing -- Bluejohn Canyon, Utah. 4. Desert survival -- Bluejohn Canyon, Utah. 5. Extreme sports. 6. Bluejohn Canyon, Utah.

ISBN 9780743492812

LC 2004303427

Book was adapted into a movie called 127 hours.

Later published: 127 hours. New York : Atria Books, 2010.

"With precious little water or food, his right arm pinned for nearly five days by a boulder in a narrow canyon shaft in central-eastern Utah, Ralston amputated the arm with his pocketknife, then rappelled and hiked his way to his own rescue. What makes his account of his ordeal extraordinary, too, is the detail and precision Ralston, a former mechanical engineer, brings to the telling, from the almost minute-by-minute chronology of his ordeal to topographical descriptions of the ground he's covered in his life as an outdoor adventurer." Booklist.

Zuckerman, Peter

Buried in the sky : the extraordinary story of the Sherpa climbers on K2's deadliest day / Peter Zuckerman and Amanda Padoan. W.W. Norton & Co., c2012. 320 p. **796.522**

1. Mountaineering -- K2 (Mountain), Pakistan 2. Sherpa (Nepalese people) 3. Mountaineers 4. Mountaineering accidents

ISBN 9780393079883

LC 2012008490

National Outdoor Book Award for History/Biography, 2012.

Presents the stories of the sharps who have acted as expert consultants to Westerners climbing the Himalayas, focusing in particular on Chhiring Dorje Sherpa and Pasang Lama, who survived when 11 other climbers died on K2 in August 2008.

796.54 Camping

White, Dan, 1967-

Under the stars : how America fell in love with camping / Dan White. Henry Holt and Co., 2016. 368 p. **796.54**

1. Camping. 2. Outdoor life.

ISBN 9781627791953

LC 2015042691

From the Sierras to the Adirondacks and the Everglades, from remote wildernesses to public campgrounds and RV meccas, Dan White travels across America, searching through its history and landscapes to tell the story of how camping took hold of the national imagination and evolved alongside a changing country.

"An adventurous, informative, and irreverent look at outdoor recreation." Booklist.

796.6 Cycling and related activities

Bambrick, Yvonne

The **urban** cycling survival guide : need-to-know skills & strategies for biking in the city / Yvonne Bambrick ; illustrated by Marc Ngui. ECW Press, 2015 xx, 203 p. : **796.6**

1. Cycling 2. City traffic

ISBN 9781770412187

LC bl2015010874

Presents a guide to cycling safely and understanding the rules of the road in urban areas, covering such topics as signals and communication, road-sharing, navigating obstacles, etiquette, and all-weather riding.

The **enlightened** cyclist : commuter angst, dangerous drivers, and other obstacles on the path to two-wheeled trancendence/ BikeSnobNYC. Chronicle Books, 2012. 240 p. **796.6**

1. Commuting 2. Bicycle commuting. 3. Bicycling.

ISBN 9781452105000

LC 2011041747

Addresses the trials of commuting by bicycle in a city, which include contending with careless drivers, pedestrians, and aggressive fellow cyclists.

Leonard, Max

Lanterne rouge : the last man in the Tour de France / Max Leonard. Pegasus, 2015 272 p. **796.6**

1. Tour de France (Bicycle race) 2. Bicycle racing 3. Bicyclists 4. Losers (Persons) 5. Bicycling

ISBN 9781605987866

LC bl2015021574

"Writer and amateur cyclist Leonard challenges what it means to achieve greatness through the mythos of the sport's underdogs. The author provides little information about the competitors we recognize as champions of the sport, instead populating the narrative with a strange sort of idol worship." Kirkus.

Moore, Tim 1964-

The **cyclist** who went out in the cold : adventures riding the Iron Curtain / Tim Moore. Pegasus Books, 2017. 368 p. **796.6**

1. Moore, Tim, 1964- Travel Europe. 2. Bicycle touring. 3. Travelers. 4. Voyages and travels 5. Iron Curtain. 6. Eastern Europe -- Description and travel.

ISBN 9781681772998

LC 2017302278

The author describes his bicycle tour through the old Iron Curtain territory, traveling 6,000 miles from the northern border between Russia and Norway to the Black Sea in Bulgaria while reflecting on what became of the Cold War Communist dream.

"An enjoyable account of an amazing human accomplishment." Kirkus.

Petersen, Grant

Just ride : a radically practical guide to riding your bike / Grant Petersen ; illustrations by Retsu Takahashi. Workman Pub., c2012. xi, 212 p. : **796.6**

1. Bicycles 2. Cycling

ISBN 0761155589

LC 2012001429

Includes index.

Questions and debunks over eighty myths to highlight bicycling's inherently enjoyable nature, addressing everything from clothing and accessories to health, fitness, and safety.

"Smell what Petersen is cooking*. *Except for this funny idea he has that the poncho is the ultimate cycling garment." Library Journal.

Weiss, Eben

The **ultimate** bicycle owner's manual : the universal guide to bikes, riding, and everything for beginner and seasoned cyclists / Eben Weiss, aka Bike Snob NYC. Black Dog & Leventhal Publishers, 2016. 240 p. : **796.6**

1. Cycling -- Handbooks, manuals, etc. 2. Bicycles -- Maintenance and repair -- Handbooks, manuals, etc.
ISBN 9780316352680

LC 2015041449

Includes index.

“"Everything you need to know to purchase, maintain, and ride a bike for recreation, commuting, competition, travel, and beyond! From the bike world's most beloved and trusted advocate." --Provided by the publisher.

796.72 Automobile racing

Baime, A. J. (Albert J.)

★**Go** like hell : Ford, Ferrari, and their battle for speed and glory at Le Mans / A. J. Baime. Houghton Mifflin Harcourt, 2009. xv, 304 p. : **796.72094417**

1. Ford, Henry, 1863-1947. 2. Iacocca, Lee A., 1924-2019. 3. Shelby, Carroll, 1923- 4. Ford Motor Company -- History. 5. Grand Prix racing -- History. 6. Sports cars -- United States -- History. 7. Industrialists -- United States -- History. 8. Automobile designers.
ISBN 9780618822195

LC 2008052948

Traces the story of how Henry Ford II competed against Enzo Ferrari for dominance in the speed- and style-driven 1960s automobile industry, revealing the contributions of visionary Lee Iacocca and former racing champion-turned-engineer Carroll Shelby.

"Baime tells an exciting story at a pace that manages to keep up with the drivers." Library Journal.

Hawley, Sam

Speed duel : the inside story of the land speed record in the sixties / Sam Hawley. Firefly Books Ltd, 2010. 360 p. **796.72097309**

1. Speed. 2. Record setting. 3. Dragsters. 4. Automobiles, Racing.
ISBN 9781554076338

LC 2012405437

"Even readers who don't know a spark plug from a gear shift will be transfixed by Hawley's white-knuckled account of the ever-escalating competition to hold the Land Speed Record in the '60s and early '70s. Drawing from countless articles, profiles, documentaries, and interviews with the men and women who were there, Hawley traces the sport's evolution from its first four-wheeled record of 39mph in 1898, to today's jet-propelled 700mph-plus, recounting the creation, testing, and repair of legendary cars like the humble Green Monster and the charismatic Spirit of America." Publishers Weekly.

796.7209 Automobile racing--history

Bascomb, Neal

Faster : how a Jewish driver, an American heiress, and a legendary car beat Hitler's best / Neal Bascomb. Houghton Mifflin Harcourt, 2020 304 p. **796.7209**

1. Dreyfus, Rene. 2. Schell, Lucy 3. Automobile racing -- History. 4. Automobile racing drivers 5. Discrimination in sports. 6. Grand Prix racing -- History.
ISBN 9781328489876

LC 2019033972

For fans of Boys in the Boat and In the Garden of Beasts, the pulse-pounding story of how a Jewish race car driver and an American speed queen triumphed over Hitler's fearsome Silver Arrows on the eve of World War II.

"This rousing popular history fires on all cylinders." Publishers Weekly

796.8 Combat sports

Lee, Shannon, 1969-

Be water, my friend : the teachings of Bruce Lee / Shannon Lee. Flatiron Books, 2020 240 p. **796.8**

1. Lee, Bruce, 1940-1973. 2. Martial arts -- Philosophy. 3. Personal conduct 4. Growth (Psychology) 5. Human body (Philosophy).
ISBN 9781250206688

LC 2020031675

The daughter of the legendary martial artist and president of the Bruce Lee Foundation shares insights into her father's life-shaping philosophies while demonstrating how the martial arts can be both a metaphor and tool of personal growth.

"This inspired guide will remind any reader that, while one cannot control external circumstance, how one responds is always a choice." Publishers Weekly

796.812 Wrestling

Kreidler, Mark

Four days to glory : wrestling with the soul of the American heartland / Mark Kreidler. Harper Collins, c2007. viii, 262, 8 p. of plates : **796.812**

1. Borschel, Jay 2. LeClere, Dan 3. Wrestlers -- Iowa 4. School sports -- Iowa. 5. Wrestling tournaments -- Iowa. 6. Iowa.
ISBN 9780060823184

LC 2007272997

Jay Borschel and Dan LeClere aspire to be four-time high school wrestling champions in Iowa.

"The author's deftness in Four Days is in turning a niche sport into one as accessible as baseball or basketball." New York Times Book Review.

Levi, Heather, 1962-

The **world** of lucha libre : secrets, revelations, and Mexican national identity / Heather Levi. Duke University Press, 2008. xxii, 265 p. **796.812**

1. Wrestling -- Mexico. 2. Wrestlers. 3. Mexico -- Social life and customs.
ISBN 9780822342328

LC 2008023166

Ethnography of Mexican professional wrestling by a female wrestler and scholar, showing how the sport is linked to national affirmations and counter-narratives.

"A small but fascinating part of Levi's book is the fieldwork she did while preparing the text. While living in Mexico, Levi trained as a luchadora with a former professional wrestler. The experience of training is not the focus of the work, however, but rather a tool the author used to further illuminate her research." PopMatters.

796.83 Boxing

Hauser, Thomas

Boxing is--- : reflections on the sweet science / Thomas Hauser. University of Arkansas Press, 2010. viii, 270 p. ; **796.83**

1. Boxing -- United States. 2. Boxers (Sports) -- United States. 3. Athletes. 4. Boxing trainers.

ISBN 9781557289421

LC 2010015354

"The collection begins with a detailed biographical examination of the career of Sugar Ray Robinson, considered by many to be the greatest pound-for-pound fighter ever. It's a sadly familiar tale of poverty, ascendancy, fame, and decline, related in a respectful, objective style. The rest of the book is focused on the boxing events of 2009, from the high-profile career of Manny Pacquiao to the progress of several relatively unknown young fighters learning the trade in New York's gyms. Hauser also explores the business end of boxing, especially its painful relationship with television, but above all, he is drawn to the people of the sport: the fighters, trainers, promoters, and hangers-on. Virtually every piece is notable for its carefully drawn characters who will linger on the edges of readers' minds long after the book has been shelved." Booklist.

Liebling, A. J. (Abbott Joseph), 1904-1963

The **sweet** science / A.J. Liebling ; foreword by Robert Anasi. North Point Press, 2004, c1956. xv, 267 p. ; **796.83**

1. Boxing -- United States -- History. 2. Boxers (Sports) 3. Essays.

ISBN 0374272271

LC 2004049509

Originally published: New York : Viking, 1956.

Here are the great events of boxing's American heyday: Sugar Ray Robinson's dramatic comeback, Rocky Marciano's rise to prominence, Joe Louis's unfortunate decline, brought so vividly to life that Sports Illustrated named The Sweet Science the best American sports book of all time.

796.830973 Boxing--United States

Lawton, James

A **ringside** affair : boxing's last golden age / James Lawton. Bloomsbury, 2017 viii, 296 p. **796.830973**

1. Boxing 2. Boxers (Sports)

ISBN 9781472945631

LC bl2017050972

Includes index.

Bringing the most compelling and climactic phase of boxing's long history to life, the chief sportswriter of the Daily Express and the Independent pays tribute to the epic quality of boxing's last years of glory, retracing arguably the richest inheritance bequeathed to any sport and pondering the possibility that we will never see such fighting again.

796.86 Fencing

Bennett, Alexander

Kendo : culture of the sword / Alexander C. Bennett. University of California Press, 2015 356 p. **796.86**

1. Kendo. 2. Martial arts 3. Swordplay -- Japan. 4. Military art and science.

ISBN 9780520284371

LC 2015004621

Kendo is the first book in English to provide an in-depth historical, cultural, and political account of the Japanese martial art of swordsmanship, from its beginnings in military training and arcane medieval schools to its widespread practice today as a global sport. Alexander Bennett shows how kendo evolved through a recurring process of 'inventing tradition', which served the changing ideologies and needs of Japanese warriors and governments over the course of history. Kendo follows the development of Japanese swordsmanship from the aristocratic pretensions of medieval warriors in the Muromachi period, to the samurai elitism of the Edo regime, and to the patriotism of the Meiji state.

"A highly recommended, useful resource for all readers interested in this popular sport." Library Journal.

796.93 Skiing and snowboarding

Vinton, Nathaniel

The **fall** line : how American ski racers conquered a sport on the edge / Nathaniel Vinton. W. W. Norton & Company, [2015] 384 p. **796.93**

1. Vonn, Lindsey 2. Miller, Bode, 1977- 3. Olympic Winter Games (21st : 2010 : Vancouver, B.C.) 4. Skiing -- United States -- History. 5. Skiers -- United States. 6. Skis -- United States -- History.

ISBN 9780393244779

LC 2014033594

Includes index.

A journey into the world's original extreme sport: downhill ski racing.

"As the season progresses, Vinton adds rich historical context to each race venue, documenting course changes and rule revisions, while profiling past skiing greats, including Austrians Franz Klammer and Hermann Maier. The subtitle is a bit of a misnomer as this is not simply a story of American skiers but, instead, a primer on the history and current state of Alpine skiing." Booklist.

796.962 Ice hockey

Coffey, Wayne R.

★The **boys** of winter : the untold story of a coach, a dream, and the 1980 U.S. Olympic hockey team / Wayne Coffey ; foreword by Jim Craig. Crown Publishers, 2005. xiii, 272 p. : **796.962**

1. Olympic Winter Games (13th : 1980 : Lake Placid, N.Y.) 2. Hockey -- History. 3. Hockey teams -- History. 4. Hockey players. 5. Olympic athletes -- United States.

ISBN 9781400047659

LC 2004014163

Looks back at one of the greatest moments of twentieth-century sports history, the victory of the U.S. hockey team over the Soviet Union, assessing the meaning of the triumph and the paths of the players and coaches on both sides since 1980.

"The author offers a nuanced portrait of the 1980 Olympics miracle on ice and the gold medal-winning U.S. hockey team." School Library Journal.

797.1 Aquatic sports

Sleight, Steve

★The **complete** sailing manual / Steve Sleight. DK/Penguin Random House Publishing, 2017 448 p. : **797.1**

1. Sailing

ISBN 9781465462572

LC 2017448422

"Foreword by Sir Ben Ainslie"--Front cover.

First American Edition: 2012.

Includes index.

An illustrated, step-by-step guide to sailing, reviewing the parts of the boat, equipment, controls, and other basics; and discussing dinghy sailing, cruiser sailing, navigation, weather, practical boat care, and safety.

797.12 Types of vessels

Brown, Daniel, 1951-

★The **boys** in the boat : nine Americans and their epic quest for gold at the 1936 Olympics / Daniel James Brown. Viking, 2013 432 p. **797.12**

1. University of Washington Rowing -- History. 2. Olympic Games (11th : 1936 : Berlin, Germany) 3. Rowing -- United States -- History. 4. Working class men 5. Friendship 6. Determination in men

ISBN 9780670025817

LC 2013001560

ALA Notable Book, 2014

Shortlisted for the James Tait Black Memorial Prize for Biography, 2013

The Boys in the Boat describes how a group of working class youths from the University of Washington rowing team emerged from obscurity to defeat a field of elite international rivals at the 1936 Berlin Olympics. Sports fans who love a good "Cinderella story" will cheer this fast-paced, emotionally charged account of the players' and coaches' struggles set against stark Depression-era realities.

797.122 Canoeing

Bennett, Jeff, 1961-

The **complete** whitewater rafter / Jeff Bennett. Ragged Mountain Press, c1996. xii, 196 p. : **797.122**

1. Rafting (Sports) -- Handbooks, manuals, etc

ISBN 9780070055056

LC 95049247

Rev. ed. of: Rafting! 1993.

With comprehensive step-by-step coverage starting with the first run, it includes tips from top guides, outfitters, and instructors, plus the most complete guide to Class V rafting techniques ever assembled.

Dillon, Pamela

Kayaking / editors, Pamela S. Dillon, Jeremy Oyen. Human Kinectics, c2009. ix, 237 p. : **797.122**

1. Kayaking -- Handbooks, manuals, etc.

ISBN 9780736067164

LC 2008032111

"American Canoe Association."

A kayaking handbook discusses equipment, fitness, water trail etiquette, and safety and survival skills, and offers step-by-step instructions on paddling techniques for flatwater, river and whitewater, and sea kayaking.

797.2 Swimming and diving

Checkoway, Julie

The **three-year** swim club : the untold story of Maui's Sugar Ditch Kids and their quest for Olympic glory / Julie Checkoway. Grand Central Pub., 2015 448 p. **797.2**

1. Swimming 2. Poor children. 3. Olympic games 4. Sugar plantations 5. Hawaii

ISBN 9781455523443

LC 2015947608

Offers an inspiring story of how a group of poor Japanese-American kids from Hawaii were transformed into Olympic-level swimming champions.

"Details about training, swim times, and the team's travels occasionally overwhelm Checkoway's tense, vivid, and inspiring narrative. Not without its flaws, but a good choice for fans of David Halberstam's The Amateurs (1985), Daniel Boyne's The Red Rose Crew (2000), and similar books." Kirkus.

Graver, Dennis

Scuba diving / Dennis K. Graver, EMT, SEI. Human Kinetics, 2017 ix, 245 p. : **797.2**

1. Scuba diving

ISBN 9781492525769

LC 2016018110

Packed with full-color photographs and illustrations, Scuba Diving offers step-by-step instruction on preparing for and managing a dive safely with information on the latest equipment, gear selection, recommended dive locations, technologies and techniques. Dennis Graver explains the basics of diving, including managing underwater emergencies, avoiding underwater hazards and equalizing pressure in the ears, sinuses and mask. The comprehensive content and world class photography of Scuba Diving make it the finest scuba title on the market!

Means, Howard B.

★**Splash!** : 10,000 years of swimming / Howard Means. Hachette Books, [2020] 336 p. **797.2**

1. Swimming -- History. 2. Olympic games (Ancient) 3. Olympic games -- History

ISBN 9780306845666

LC 2019056316

This history of 10,000 years of swimming from Ancient Egypt, Greece and Rome to today's Olympic games and backyard pools also looks its influence on religion, segregation and sex.

"For a sport generally underrepresented in library collections, this is a superb account of swimming's long and remarkable history." Library Journal

Nestor, James

Deep : freediving, renegade science, and what the ocean tells us about ourselves / James Nestor. Houghton Mifflin Harcourt, 2014. 272 p. **797.2**

1. Skin diving. 2. Marine biology 3. Marine animals.

ISBN 9780547985527

LC 2014002593

Surveys the achievements of adventurous scientists, athletes and explorers to reveal how new understandings about deep-sea life, from telepathic coral to shark navigation, are expanding what is known about the natural world and the human mind.

"[B]rimming with vivid portraits, lucid scientific explanations, gripping (and funny) first-person accounts, and urgent facts about the ocean's endangerment, Nestor's Deep is galvanizing, enlightening, and invaluable." Booklist.

Tsui, Bonnie

Why we swim / Bonnie Tsui. Algonquin Books, 2020, c2020. 277 p. **797.2**

1. Swimming. 2. Social history. 3. Well-being. 4. Swimmers.
ISBN 9781616207861

LC 2019042645

We swim in freezing Arctic waters and piranha-infested rivers to test our limits. We swim for pleasure, for exercise, for healing. But humans, unlike other animals that are drawn to water, are not natural-born swimmers. We must be taught. Sharing stories of Olympic champions, a Baghdad swim club, and modern-day Japanese samurai swimmers, a New York Times contributor investigates what about water--despite its dangers--draws us to it time and time again.

"A study of swimming as sport, survival method, basis for community, and route to physical and mental well-being. An absorbing, wide-ranging story of humans' relationship with the water." Kirkus

797.32 Surfing (Surf riding)

Mackinnon, Al

Epic surf breaks of the world : explore the planet's most thrilling waves / [authors, Al Mackinnon and others]. Lonely Planet, 2020 328 p. **797.32**

1. Surfing
ISBN 9781788686501

"The editors of this vibrant illustrated volume share tales of epic rides, advice on getting to the wave, and, most importantly, where to find the best breaks. . . . Surfers will immerse themselves in this bucket-list guidebook." Publishers Weekly

797.5 Air sports

Higgins, Matt

Bird dream : adventures at the extremes of human flight / Matt Higgins. Penguin Group USA, 2014 304 p. **797.5**

1. Wingsuit Landing Project 2. Flight. 3. Human flight 4. Extreme sports.
ISBN 9781594204654

LC 2014005399

Describes the participants and entries to the Wingsuit Landing Project, which includes groups from around the world as they embark on a quest to develop and pilot an outfit that will allow man to fly.

"A highflying, electrifying story of a treacherous sport in which every triumph is an eye blink away from becoming a disaster." Kirkus.

798.2 Horsemanship

Letts, Elizabeth

The **eighty-dollar** champion : Snowman, the horse that inspired a nation / Elizabeth Letts. Random House Inc, 2011. 288 p. **798.2**

1. Jumping (Equestrianism) 2. Show horses. 3. Equestrianism. 4. Humans and horses.
ISBN 9780345521088

LC 2010050993

The Eighty-Dollar Champion tells the dramatic odyssey of a horse called Snowman, saved from the slaughterhouse by a young Dutch farmer named Harry. Together, Harry and Snowman went on to become America's show-jumping champions, winning first prize in Madison Square Garden. Set in the mid to late 1950s, this book captures the can-do spirit of a Cold War immigrant who believed--and triumphed.

798.40092 Horse racing--Biography

Drape, Joe

American Pharoah : the untold story of the Triple Crown winner's legendary rise / Joe Drape. Hachette Books, 2016. x, 292 p. : **798.40092**

1. American Pharoah (Horse). 2. Race horses. 3. Horse racing. 4. Triple Crown, American (Horse racing)
ISBN 9780316268844

LC bl2016014449

Profiles the life and accomplishments of the Thoroughbred race horse American Pharoah, chronicling key events en route to him becoming the twelfth Triple Crown winner.

"A captivating story woven with an affectionate yet honest portrayal of the sometimes seedy sport of kings, this work will appeal to horse-racing fans and anyone who enjoys athlete biographies." Library Journal.

McGraw, Eliza

Here comes Exterminator! : the longshot horse, the great war, and the making of an American hero / Eliza Mcgraw. Thomas Dunne Books, 2016 320 p. **798.40092**

1. Exterminator (Race horse) 2. Horses 3. Horse racing 4. Race horses
ISBN 9781250065698

LC 2015048660

A New York Times and Washington Post contributor describes how a racehorse named Exterminator paved the way for equine celebrities like Seabiscuit, and showed Americans they could claim--and love--a famous racehorse as their own.

798.400929 Racehorses--Sports--Biography

Ours, Dorothy

Man o' War : a legend like lightning / Dorothy Ours. St. Martin's Press, 2006. viii, 342 p., 16 p. of plates : **798.400929**

1. Man o' War (Race horse) 2. Race horses -- United States 3. Horse racing -- United States -- History. 4. Horse racing -- Corrupt practices. 5. United States -- Social life and customs -- 20th century.
ISBN 9780312340995

LC 2006041631

The story of a legendary early twentieth-century racehorse offers insight into the sport during his career, describing the horse's rebellious early years, the rumors about race fixing that haunted his one defeat, and the role of arch-rival and Triple Crown winner Sir Barton.

"This book is clearly a labor of love, and it certifies Big Red's claim to immortality." New York Times Book Review.

798.4010973 Gambling--horse racing--United States

Lang, Arne K.

Sports betting and bookmaking : an American history / Arne K.

Lang. Rowman & Littlefield, 2016. xi, 293 p. **798.4010973**
1. Horse race betting 2. Sports betting. 3. Bookmaking (Betting) 4. Gambling
ISBN 9781442265530
LC 2015047132

This book is a sweeping overview of bookmaking in the United States, from the first thoroughbred meet at Saratoga in 1863 through the modern day. The cultural war between bookmakers and their adversaries is a recurrent thread, and the decline of horse racing--and concurrent rise of team sports--is examined at length.

799.1 Fishing

Bourne, Wade
Basic fishing : a beginner's guide / Wade Bourne. Skyhorse Pub., 2011. 159 p. : **799.1**
1. Fishing.
ISBN 1616082100
LC 2011017601

Includes index.

Offers advice for the beginner fisherman, including selecting the best fishing spots, choosing the right equipment, and how to clean and cook fish.

Cermele, Joe
The **total** fishing manual : 317 essential fishing skills / Joe Cermele and the editors of Field & Stream. Welden Owen, c2013. 314 p. ; **799.1**
1. Fishing -- Handbooks, manuals, etc.
ISBN 9781616286293
LC bl2013025585

Includes index.

A comprehensive guide to fishing, including information on the best lures for particular fish, picking the right rod, and how to troubleshoot a boat's motor.

799.12 Angling

Gierach, John, 1946-
All fishermen are liars / John Gierach. Simon & Schuster, 2014. 256 p. **799.12**
1. Fly fishing -- Anecdotes. 2. Fishing -- Anecdotes. 3. Fishers -- Anecdotes 4. Humans and fish. 5. Essays
ISBN 9781451618310
LC 2013012784

From the Pacific Northwest to the Upper Midwest to the Canadian Maritimes, "America's best fishing writer" shares insights, musings and countless stories he has collected over a lifetime of fishing, proving that life's most valuable lessons are found while fly-fishing.

"An engaging autobiographical introduction opens the book, which includes 22 perceptive and witty essays, recalling numerous fishing trips and offering insights on fly rods and fly patterns. These lyrical essays explode with descriptions of beautiful places, big fish, and beautiful fish." Booklist.

Gierach, John, 1946-
A **fly** rod of your own / John Gierach ; art by Glenn Wolff. Simon & Schuster, 2017. 256 p. **799.12**
1. Fly fishing. 2. Fishing. 3. Essays.
ISBN 9781451618341
LC 2016019507

National Outdoor Book Award for Outdoor Literature, 2017.

Called "the voice of the common angler" by The Wall Street Journal, and a member of the Fly Fishing Hall of Fame, the author travels to remote fishing locations, from Alaska to the Canadian Maritimes, where he, with his sharp sense of humor and keen eye for observation of the fishing life, scrutinizes the art of fly-fishing.

"A must for fisherman and outdoor enthusiasts, this book may also have wider appeal, as it is as much about travel, friendships, and navigating today's world as it is about fly-fishing." Library Journal.

Meyers, Charlie
The **little** red book of fly fishing : 250 tips to make you a better fisherman / Charlie Meyers and Kirk Deeter. Skyhorse Pub., c2010. xv, 201 p. : **799.12**
1. Fly fishing.
ISBN 1602399816
LC 2009046448

Kirk Deeter of Field & Stream and Charlie Meyers of the Denver Post, crack open their notebooks and share expert advice on flies, casting, reading the water, and much more.

Rosenbauer, Tom
The **Orvis** fly-fishing guide / Tom Rosenbauer. Lyons Press, 2017 vii, 400 p. : **799.12**
1. Fly fishing.
ISBN 1493025791
LC 2016048926

Presents a comprehensive guide to fly fishing, with information on rods, lines, reels, and leaders, advice for casting and fly selection, and tactics for stream, freshwater, and salt water fishing.

799.124 Fly fishing

Burke, Monte
Lords of the fly : madness, obsession, and the hunt for the world record tarpon / Monte Burke. Pegasus Books, 2020 xvii, 278 p. : **799.124**
1. Fishers 2. Fishing -- Anecdotes. 3. Tarpon fishing 4. Environmental degradation 5. Florida
ISBN 9781643135588

In the late 1970s and early 1980s, something unique happened in the quiet little town on the west coast of Florida known as Homosassa. The best fly anglers in the world gathered together to chase the same Holy Grail: The world record for the world's most glamorous and sought-after fly rod species, the tarpon.

"A fascinating look at the narrow but wild world of tarpon fishing. Burke constructs the rise and fall of this unique fishing tale with impressive narrative control and an obvious reverence for its vivid characters. Ably captures the swagger, attitudes, and angling derring-do of a golden age of fishing history." Kirkus

Gierach, John, 1946-
Dumb luck and the kindness of strangers / John Gierach. Simon & Schuster, 2020. 225 p. : **799.124**
1. Fly fishing. 2. Fishing. 3. Essays.
ISBN 9781501168581
LC 2020930580

"Gierach's inviting, down-to-earth, and humorous work shares a deep love of fly-fishing and the ways that it can be a metaphor for life." Publishers Weekly

799.2 Hunting

Huckelbridge, Dane

No beast so fierce : the terrifying true story of the Champawat Tiger, the deadliest animal in history / Dane Huckelbridge. William Morrow, 2019. 352 p. **799.2**

1. Corbett, Jim, 1875-1955. 2. Tiger attacks. 3. Tigers. 4. Wild cats. 5. Tiger hunting. 6. India. 7. Nepal. 8. Himalaya Mountains
ISBN 9780062678843

LC 2018024761

Provides a true account of the deadliest animal of all time, the Champawat Tiger--responsible for killing more than 400 hundred humans in northern India in the first decade of the 20th century--and the hunter who finally brought it down.

Rinella, Steven

The **complete** guide to hunting, butchering, and cooking wild game. Steven Rinella. Spiegel & Grau, 2015 xiii, 364 p. : **799.2**

1. Cooking (Game) 2. Fowling -- United States. 3. Game and game-birds, Dressing of. 4. Small game hunting -- United States.
ISBN 9780812987058

LC bl2015052507

Includes index.

Provides information on hunting, butchering, and cooking small game and fowl, discussing the equipment needed, basic and advanced hunting strategies, how to field dress animals, and recipes for indoor and outdoor cooking.

The **complete** guide to hunting, butchering, and cooking wild game : big game / Steven Rinella. Spiegel & Grau, 2015- 400 p. ; **799.2**

1. Big game hunting -- United States. 2. Cooking (Game) 3. Game and game-birds, Dressing of. 4. Hunting -- United States -- Equipment and supplies.
ISBN 081299406X

LC 2014013333

"A Spiegel & Grau trade paperback original."

Includes index.

This comprehensive guide to big game hunting, organized by animal, provides novices and experts alike with step-by-step instructions and photographs to help readers prep, track, hunt and prepare their kills.

"Rinella doesn't offer too many tips beyond the obvious grilled steaks and jerky, though wild pig hunters will appreciate his simple but flavorful recipe for smoked ham. Its a minor flaw in a book thats terrifically informative and is sure to inspire hunters to start poring over maps and readying themselves for their next hunt." Publishers Weekly.

801 Philosophy and theory

Chabon, Michael

Maps and legends / Michael Chabon. McSweeney's Books, 2008. 200 p. **801**

1. Books and reading. 2. Authors. 3. Readers. 4. Authors and readers. 5. Essays.
ISBN 9781932416893

LC bl2008009268

A series of linked essays about the enriching prospects of reading and writing argues for the importance of enjoying a diverse range of options rather than limiting oneself to studious or serious literature, in an anthology that also explores the Pulitzer Prize-winning author's own writings from a perspective of personal history.

Gardner, John, 1933-1982

On moral fiction / John Gardner. Basic Books, c1978. 214 p. ; **801**

1. Literature and morals 2. Arts and morals
ISBN 9780465052264

LC 77020409

A genuine classic of literary criticism, On Moral Fiction argues that "true art is by its nature moral."

Kundera, Milan

★The **curtain** : an essay in seven parts / Milan Kundera ; translated from the French by Linda Asher. HarperCollins Publishers, c2006. viii, 168 p. ; **801**

1. Fiction -- History and criticism. 2. Literature -- Philosophy.
ISBN 0060841869

LC 2006043420

Traces the author's personal view of the history and significance of the novel in western civilization, arguing that a novel's development crosses international and language boundaries while serving to reveal previously unknown aspects of a reader's existence.

"The immediacy of Kundera's evocative prose and the rich tapestry he weaves compel us to pick up and read, or reread, the bountiful literary treasures of Western literature. This could be a book from which to draw a summer reading list." Library Journal.

Mendelsohn, Daniel Adam, 1960-

Waiting for the barbarians : essays on the classics and pop culture / Daniel Mendelsohn. New York Review Books, c2012. 328 p. **801**

1. Books and reading 2. Popular culture 3. Essays
ISBN 9781590176078

LC 2012012240

A selection of 24 recent essays by a lauded modern critic includes pieces that explore his views on the lasting influence of classics, the appeal of pop-culture favorites and the art of fiction.

Moore, Lorrie

See what can be done : essays, criticism, & commentary / Lorrie Moore. Alfred A. Knopf, 2018. 416 p. **801**

1. Criticism 2. Modern literature -- History and criticism 3. Authors -- Criticism and interpretation 4. Political culture 5. United States -- Social conditions 6. Essays
ISBN 9781524732486

LC 2017006247

"This is a Borzoi book."

A treasury of more than 50 prose pieces by the cultural commentator and author of Bark reviews the literary achievements of her contemporaries, sharing perspectives on subjects ranging from the art of writing fiction and the historical imagination to terrorism and the continuing unequal state of race in America.

"Deft, graceful essays from a sharply incisive writer." Kirkus.

Moretti, Franco, 1950-

Distant reading / Franco Moretti. Verso, 2013. 244 p. : **801**

1. Criticism. 2. Literature -- History and criticism -- Theory, etc.
ISBN 1781681120

LC 2012047274

In ten essays, presents the author's philosophy of "distant reading" and challenges deep-rooted beliefs about world cultures and art, while applying economic and network theories to literature.

"Regardless of whether readers agree with Moretti's conclusions, they will find that his application of economic theory, network theory, and evolutionary models to literature and culture shows these subjects from fresh and often provocative new perspectives." Publishers Weekly.

Morrison, Toni, 1931-2019

Burn this book : PEN writers speak out on the power of the word / edited by Toni Morrison. HarperStudio, p2009. vi, 118 p. ; **801**

1. Censorship. 2. Literature and society.
ISBN 9780061774003

LC bl2009012805

Presents a collection of essays from a variety of authors, including John Updike, Russell Banks, and Salman Rushdie, on censorship and the power of literature on society.

"Published in conjunction with the PEN American Center, this slim collection of essays has an amazing list of contributors: Toni Morrison, John Updike, David Grossman, Francine Prose, Pico Iyer, Russell Banks, Paul Auster, Orhan Pamuk, Salman Rushdie, Ed Park, and Nadine Gordimer. [They] discuss the importance of writing from various views, political and social. They illustrate the need for freedom of speech and human rights, and they emphasize the target writers become in a tyranny. This is not an easy read, but it is a profound, absorbing, and moving collection of work." Library Journal.

Ozick, Cynthia, 1928-

Critics, monsters, fanatics, and other literary essays / Cynthia Ozick. Houghton Mifflin Harcourt, 2016. 224 p. **801**

1. Criticism. 2. Literature -- History and criticism 3. Essays.
ISBN 9780544703711

LC 2015037560

An essay collection by the National Book Critics Circle Award-winning critic includes a selection of new pieces as well as the author's gauntlet-throwing views on the essential role of critics in establishing a vibrant literary community

"This essay collection from novelist (Foreign Bodies) and literary critic Ozick takes a fresh look at renowned writers of the past and present." Publishers Weekly.

803 Dictionaries, encyclopedias, concordances

Baldick, Chris

★The **Oxford** dictionary of literary terms / Chris Baldick. Oxford University Press, 2015. x, 392 p. ; **803**

1. Literature -- Terminology 2. Criticism -- Terminology 3. English language -- Terms and phrases 4. Literary form -- Terminology 5. Dictionaries
ISBN 9780198715443

LC 2014960115

The bestselling Oxford Dictionary of Literary Terms provides clear and concise definitions of the most troublesome literary terms, from abjection to zeugma.

808 Rhetoric and collections of literary texts from more than two literatures

Conway, Jill K., 1934-2018

When memory speaks : reflections on autobiography / Jill Ker Conway. Alfred A. Knopf, 1998. 205 p. ; **808**

1. Autobiography 2. Memory. 3. Writing. 4. Biography.
ISBN 0679445935

LC 97049452

Focusing on writers over the centuries, the author explores the continuing popularity of autobiographies and accounts for the differences in form and style in men's and women's narratives.

"Conway's small gem is a landmark in eliciting fresh contemplation of the inchoate complexity of memory's manifold voices." Publishers Weekly.

Day, Robert A., 1924-

How to write and publish a scientific paper / Robert A. Day, Barbara Gastel. Greenwood Press, 2006. xv, 302 p. : **808**

1. Technical writing.
ISBN 9780313330278

LC 2005031621

Hay (emeritus, English, U. of Delaware) and Gastel (veterinary integrative biosciences and humanities in medicine, Texas A&M U.) describe the basic practical principles of scientific writing that are accepted in most disciplines in a straightforward "how-to" or "cookbook" format.

Fish, Stanley Eugene

Winning arguments : what works and doesn't work in politics, the bedroom, the courtroom, and the classroom / Stanley Fish. Harper, 2016. 212 p. ; **808**

1. Persuasion (Rhetoric). 2. Debates and debating. 3. Rhetoric.
ISBN 9780062226679

LC 2015046681

"Stanley Fish, the notoriously brash and brilliant English and Law professor, has authored dozens of academic books on subjects ranging from Milton to freedom of speech. In 2011, Fish turned his eye to a more popular subject, the art of writing great sentences. His short, wise book How to Write a Sentence became an instant New York Times Bestseller and continues to be read by students and aspiring writers. Adam Haslet called the book, "deeper and more democratic than The Elements of Style." If great sentences are, in effect, performances at the highest level, Fish acts as a lively sportscaster giving the reader a blow-by-blow. In Winning Arguments, Fish employs this same wit and observational prowess as he guides readers through the "greatest hits" of rhetoric including landmark legal cases, arguments drawn from popular film and TV, and even Fish's own career. The success of books like Jay Heinrich's Thank You For Arguing demonstrate a clear audience for fun, intellectually nourishing books that make youfeel just a little bit smarter for having read them. Like How to Write a Sentence, Winning Arguments will become a modern classic"-- Provided by publisher.

Garvey, Mark

Stylized : a slightly obsessive history of Strunk & White's The elements of style / Mark Garvey. Simon & Schuster, 2009. xxv, 208 p. : **808**

1. Strunk, William, 1869-1946. Elements of style. 2. Style manuals 3. Rhetoric 4. Writing. 5. English language -- Style.
ISBN 9781416590927

LC 2009007166

"A Touchstone book."

Published to coincide with the fiftieth anniversary of the classic guide, a story behind America's most beloved, and sometimes controversial, writing resource incorporates never-before-published letters and photos from the E. B. White archives alongside original interviews with modern writers.

hooks, bell, 1952-

Remembered rapture : the writer at work / bell hooks. Henry Holt, 1999. xvi, 237 p. ; **808**

1. hooks, bell, 1952- 2. Writing. 3. African American literature. -- History and criticism 4. Intellectual life -- United States -- 20th century 5. Intellectual life -- African American women 6. Essays.
ISBN 0805059091

LC 98007998

With grace and insight, celebrated writer bell hooks untangles the complex personae of women writers. Born and raised in the rural South, hooks learned early the power of the written word and the importance of speaking her mind. Her passion for words is the heartbeat of this collection of essays. Remembered Rapture celebrates literacy, the joys of reading and writing, and the lasting power of the book. Once again, these essays reveal bell hooks's wide-ranging intellectual scope; she is a universal writer addressing readers and writers everywhere.

Lamott, Anne

Bird by bird : some instructions on writing and life / Anne Lamott. Anchor Books, 1995, c1994. xxxi, 239 p. ; **808**

1. Writing. 2. Authors.
ISBN 0385480016

LC 95010225

Originally published: New York : Pantheon Books, 1994.

A step-by-step guide to writing and managing the writer's life covers each portion of a written project, addresses such concerns as writer's block and getting published, and offers awareness and survival tips.

Larimer, Kevin

The **poets** & writers complete guide to being a writer : everything you need to know about craft, inspiration, agents, editors, publishing, and the business of building a sustainable writing career / Kevin Larimer and Mary Gannon. Avid Reader Press, 2020. 416 p. **808**

1. Writing 2. Authors 3. Poets 4. Writing -- Handbooks, manuals, etc.
ISBN 9781982123079

LC bl2020010946

A Poets & Writers guide draws on the insights of published authors, literary agents and editors in an authoritative reference that includes coverage of pursuing an MFA, preparing submissions and marketing in today's digital world.

"A book of benefit to well-practiced as well as novice writers, full of useful advice, pointers, and prompts." Kirkus

Martin, Manjula,

Scratch : writers, money, and the art of making a living / edited by Manjula Martin. Simon & Schuster, 2017. 256 p. **808**

1. Authors and publishers. 2. Writing -- Marketing. 3. Books and reading. 4. Vocational guidance. 5. Essays.
ISBN 9781501134579

LC 2016024580

A collection of essays from some of today's most acclaimed authors on the realities of making a living in the writing world.

"Martin's collection removes the romantic veil surrounding the production of the written word and provides some solid counseling for aspirants on what it means to offer the labors of their heart for sale in the marketplace." Publishers Weekly.

O'Neil, Dennis, 1939-

The **DC** Comics guide to writing comics / Dennis O'Neil ; introduction by Stan Lee. Watson-Guptill, 2001. 128 p. : **808**

1. Comic book writing 2. Comic books, strips, etc. -- Technique. 3. Comic book illustration 4. Writing
ISBN 0823010279

LC 2001026101

Includes index.

Discusses the basic elements of comic book writing including script writing, story development, subplots, and character development.

Pinker, Steven, 1954-

The **sense** of style : the thinking person's guide to writing in the 21st century! / Steven Pinker. Viking, 2014. viii, 359 p. : **808**

1. English language -- Style. 2. English language -- Grammar.
ISBN 9780670025855

LC 2014004509

"Pinker has a lot of ideas and sometimes controversial opinions about writing and in this entertaining and instructive book he rethinks the usage guide for the 21st century. Don't blame the internet, he says, good writing has always been hard. It requires imagination, taking pleasure in reading, overcoming the difficulty we all have in imagining what it's like to not know something we do know".-- Provided by publisher.

Pollack, John

Shortcut : how analogies reveal connections, spark innovation, and sell our greatest ideas / John Pollack. Gotham, 2014. 256 p. **808**

1. Analogy. 2. Creative thinking. 3. Business communication. 4. English language
ISBN 9781592408498

LC 2014009895

"A presidential speechwriter for Bill Clinton explores the hidden power of analogy to fuel thought, connect ideas, spark innovation, and shape outcomes From the meatpacking plants that inspired Henry Ford's first moving assembly line to the "domino theory" that led America into Vietnam to the "bicycle for the mind" that Steve Jobs envisioned as the Macintosh computer, analogies have played a dynamic role in shaping the world around us--and still do today. Analogies are far more complex than their SAT stereotype and lie at the very core of human cognition and creativity. Once we become aware of this, we start seeing them everywhere--in ads, apps, political debates, legal arguments, logos, and euphemisms, to name just a few. At their very best, analogies inspire new ways of thinking, enable invention, and motivate people to action. Unfortunately, not every analogy that rings true is true. That's why, at their worst, analogies can deceive, manipulate, or mislead us into disaster. The challenge? Spotting the difference before it's too late. Rich with engaging stories, surprising examples, and a practical method to evaluate the truth or effectiveness of any analogy, Shortcut will improve critical thinking, enhance creativity, and offer readers a fresh approach to resolving some of today's most intractable challenges."-- Provided by publisher.

"Perhaps not all readers will be fully persuaded to the impact of analogies but most, especially those with an interest in language and psychology, will come away entertained and informed." Library Journal.

Prose, Francine, 1947-

★**Reading** like a writer : a guide for people who love books and for those who want to write them / Francine Prose. Harper Collins Publishers, 2006. 273 p. **808**

1. Prose, Francine, 1947- Books and reading. 2. Rhetoric 3. Creative writing. 4. Authors -- Books and reading

ISBN 0060777044

An insider's report on how professionals read and write instructs aspiring writers on the methods employed by such literary figures as Kafka, Austen, and Dickens, in a resource that draws on key examples to demonstrate the essentials of good plot and character development.

"This book should be greatly appreciated in and out of the classroom. Like the great works of fiction, it's a wise and voluble companion." New York Times Book Review.

Siegal, Allan M.

The **New** York Times manual of style and usage : the official style guide used by the writers and editors of the world's most authoritative news organization / Allan M. Siegal and William G. Connolly. Three Rivers Press, 2015 viii, 350 p. ; **808**

1. Journalism -- Style manuals.

ISBN 9781101905449

LC 2015431331

A revised and expanded edition of the classic reference tool includes hundreds of alphabetically arranged entries that provide guidelines and advice on questions of spelling, punctuation, English usage, grammar, syntax and style.

Strunk, William, 1869-1946

★The **elements** of style / William Strunk, Jr. ; with revisions, an introduction, and a chapter on writing by E.B. White ; [foreword by Roger Angell]. Allyn and Bacon, c1999. xviii, 105 p. ; **808**

1. English language -- Rhetoric 2. English language -- Style 3. Report writing

ISBN 9780205313426

LC 99016419

Includes index.

Offers advice on improving writing skills and promoting a style marked by simplicity, orderliness, and sincerity.

Woods, Geraldine

25 great sentences and how they got that way / Geraldine Woods. W.W. Norton & Company, 2020. 336 p. **808**

1. English language 2. Sentences (Grammar) 3. Writing 4. Rhetoric

ISBN 9781324004851

LC 2019047655

We all know the basic structure of a sentence: a subject/verb pair expressing a complete thought and ending with proper punctuation. But that classroom definition doesn't begin to describe the ways in which these elements can combine to resonate with us as we read, to make us stop and think, laugh or cry. Culled from fiction, nonfiction, drama, poetry, song lyrics, speeches, and even ads, these exemplary sentences are celebrated for the distinctive features--whether of structure, diction, connection/comparison, sound, or extremes--that underlie their beauty, resonance, and creativity. With dry humor and an infectious enjoyment that makes her own sentences a pleasure to read, Woods shows us the craft that goes into the construction of a memorable sentence.

"A practical, nonboring companion for writers aiming to hone their style." Kirkus

Zinsser, William Knowlton

Writing to learn / William Zinsser. Perennial Library, 1989, c1988. x, 256 p. ; **808**

1. English language -- Rhetoric -- Study and teaching 2. Interdisciplinary approach in education

ISBN 9780062720405

LC BL 99995954

Includes index.

Originally published: New York : Harper & Row, 1988.

The author demonstrates the importance of clear writing in every subject, discussing writing as a means to access knowledge, and surveys the growing emphasis on writing in American education

"Eschewing theory and philosophical breast-beating, Zinsser uses his own experience to reinforce the fact that clear, eloquent writing can be taught for every subject across the curriculum. A practical manual for teachers and a powerful reminder for everyone that good writing makes possible good thinking." American Libraries.

808.02 Authorship techniques, plagiarism, editorial techniques

D'Agata, John, 1974-

The **lifespan** of a fact / John D'Agata and Jim Fingal. W. W. Norton, c2012. 160 p. **808.02**

1. Essay writing. 2. Writing. 3. Truth.

ISBN 9780393340730

LC 2011042637

Depicts the arguments, negotiations and revisions that took place in extensive correspondence between an essayist and his fact-checker as they tried to determine the boundaries of literary nonfiction and offers a discussion on the correlation between "truth" and "accuracy."

Dreyer, Benjamin

Dreyer's English : an utterly correct guide to clarity and style / Benjamin Dreyer. Random House, 2019. xviii, 291 p. : **808.02**

1. English language -- Style 2. Writing 3. Grammar 4. Punctuation

ISBN 9780812995701

LC 2018027979

As Random House's copy chief, Dreyer has upheld the standards of the legendary publisher for more than two decades. Now he distills everything he has learned from the myriad books he has copyedited and overseen into a useful guide not just for writers but for everyone who wants to put their best prose foot forward.

"In this user-friendly guide, Random House copy chief Dreyer invites readers into his life's work, explaining how to navigate written communication through examples from years spent buried in unpublished manuscripts " Booklist.

Favilla, Emmy

A **world** without "whom" : the essential guide to language in the Buzzfeed age / Emmy J. Favilla, BuzzFeed CopyChief. Bloomsbury, 2017. vii, 392 p. : **808.02**

1. Authorship -- Style manuals 2. English language -- Style -- Handbooks, manuals, etc

ISBN 9781632867575

LC 2017018955

Builds on a premise that language in the Internet age is playful, flexible, and ethically aware to share observations that modern language has artistic qualities that should be assessed more for clarity than for adherence to grammatical rules.

Kidder, Tracy

Good prose : the art of nonfiction / Tracy Kidder and Richard Todd. Random House, c2013. 224 p. **808.02**

1. Kidder, Tracy 2. Todd, Richard, 1949- 3. Writing 4. Prose literature writing 5. Nonfiction novel writing
ISBN 9781400069750

LC 2012021165

The Pulitzer Prize and National Book Award-winning author and the editor of Atlantic Monthly share stories from their literary friendship and respective careers, offering insight into writing principles and mechanics that they have identified as elementary to quality prose.

Malcolm, Janet

Forty-one false starts : essays on artists and writers / Janet Malcolm. Farrar, Straus and Giroux, 2013. 352 p. **808.02**

1. Authors. 2. Artists. 3. Writing
ISBN 9780374157692

LC 2012034570

This collection of essays attempts to offer insight into the working minds of writers and artists including Edith Wharton, Edward Weston, Thomas Struth, and Sylvia Plath.

Maum, Courtney, 1978-

Before and after the book deal : a writer's guide to finishing, publishing, promoting, and surviving your first book / Courtney Maum. Catapult, 2020. xvii, 365 p. **808.02**

1. Writing 2. Authors and publishers 3. Publishers and publishing 4. Creative writing
ISBN 9781948226400

LC 2019941065

A candid and lighthearted guide for aspiring writers draws on the experiences of best-selling authors from all walks of the industry to discuss such topics as master's degrees, advances and how to navigate life before and after publishing.

"Maum's book should prove invaluable to new writers seeking advice and support in navigating their first publication." Publishers Weekly

McCann, Colum, 1965-

Letters to a young writer : some practical and philosophical advice / Colum McCann. Random House, [2017] xix, 166 pages : **808.02**

1. Creative writing 2. Writing 3. Authors 4. Books and reading 5. Essays
ISBN 9780399590801

LC 2016055256

A best-selling author and lecturer of creative writing at Hunter College in New York City presents a collection of essays featuring advice to writers just beginning to practice their craft.

"Pithy, wise, and gently encouraging advice from an acclaimed fiction writer." Kirkus.

McPhee, John, 1931-

Draft no. 4 : on the writing process / John McPhee. Farrar, Straus and Giroux, 2017. 208 p. **808.02**

1. Writing 2. Journalism 3. Creation (Literary, artistic, etc.) 4. Rhetoric 5. Essays
ISBN 9780374142742

LC 2016059416

A guide to writing long-form nonfiction, written by the legendary New Yorker author and teacher, is presented as a series of lighthearted essays that share insights into the lessons he has learned on the writing process during his years at Princeton University.

"The renowned writer offers advice on information-gathering and nonfiction composition. The book consists of eight instructive and charming essays about creating narratives, all of them originally composed for the New Yorker." Kirkus.

Modern Language Association of America

★**MLA** Handbook / Association of America, Modern Language. The Modern Language Association of America, 2016 xiv, 146 p. : **808.02**

1. Report writing -- Handbooks, manuals, etc. 2. Research -- Handbooks, manuals, etc.
ISBN 9781603292627

LC 2015040898

Previous title: MLA handbook for writers of research papers.

Provides guidelines and examples for handling research, outlining, spelling, punctuation, formatting, and documentation.

Rubin, Daniel Joshua

27 essential principles of story : master the secrets of great storytelling, from Shakespeare to South Park / Daniel Joshua Rubin. Workman Publishing Co., 2020 xi, 372 p. ; **808.02**

1. Storytelling 2. Plots (Drama, novel, etc.)
ISBN 9781523507160

LC 2020938343

A modern and actionable guide to the fundamentals of writing compelling, well-crafted, authentic stories in any medium, with lessons illustrated by novels, plays, films, music, video games, and TV, and writers from Shakespeare and Dostoevsky to Quentin Tarantino and Eminem.

"This is a no-brainer for both pro and would-be novelists." Publishers Weekly

Scalzi, John, 1969-

Don't live for your obituary : advice, commentary, and personal observations on writing / John Scalzi. Subterranean Press, 2017. 469 p. ; **808.02**

1. Science fiction writing 2. Authors 3. Writing 4. Books and reading 5. Essays
ISBN 9781596068582

LC 2017277896

A curated selection of that decade of advice, commentary and observations on the writing life, from one of the best-known science fiction authors working today. But more than that, it's a portrait of an era?ten years of drama, controversy and change in writing, speculative fiction and the world in general?from someone who was there when it happened? and who had opinions about it all.

"Above all [Scalzi] writes accessibly and so commonsensically that this book should appeal to writers in all disciplines, and even to SF readers who have no ambitions to write themselves." Publishers Weekly.

Shapiro, Susan

The **byline** bible : get published in 5 weeks / Susan Shapiro ; foreword by Peter Catapano. Writer's Digest Books, 2018. 267 p. ; **808.02**

1. Authorship -- Marketing. 2. Journalism -- Authorship. 3. Online authorship. 4. Creative nonfiction, American.
ISBN 9781440353680

LC 2018275842

Includes index.

Newspaper, magazine, and web editors are desperate for new voices, and anyone, in any field, can break in ... Over the last two decades, writing professor Susan Shapiro has taught more than 25,000 students of all ages and backgrounds at NYU, Columbia, Temple, the New School, and

Harvard University. Now in the BYLINE BIBLE she reveals the wildly popular "Instant Gratification Takes Too Long" technique she's perfected, sharing how to land impressive clips to start or re-launch your career. The author walks you through every stage of crafting and selling short nonfiction pieces. She shows you how to spot trendy subjects, where to start, finish, and edit, and divulges specific steps to submit work, have it accepted, get paid, and see your byline in your favorite publication in lightning speed.

Smith, Rebecca, 1966-

The **Jane** Austen Writers' Club : inspiration and advice from the world's best-loved novelist / Rebecca Smith ; illustrations by Sarah J. Coleman. Bloomsbury, 2016. xii, 336 p. : **808.02**

1. Austen, Jane, 1775-1817 Technique. 2. Austen, Jane, 1775-1817 Criticism and interpretation. 3. Austen, Jane, 1775-1817 Influence. 4. Austen, Jane, 1775-1817 Quotations. 5. Romance fiction, English -- History and criticism. 6. Fiction writing 7. Writing 8. Creative writing.

ISBN 9781632865885

"A worthy companion for writers and readers that entertains and enlightens." Kirkus.

Strand, Jessica

Upstairs at the Strand : writers in conversation at the legendary bookstore / edited by Jessica Strand & Andrea Aguilar. W. W. Norton & Co. Inc., 2016 240 p. **808.02**

1. Bookstores 2. Writing 3. Books and reading 4. Authors

ISBN 9780393352085

LC 2015051054

Offering candid and behind-the-scenes accounts of the ways leading writers work, think and live, a book based on a series of talks pairing writers of note at a beloved NYC bookstore features conversations with such celebrated novelists, playwrights and poets as Martin Amis, Patti Smith and Tea Obreht.

"An array of authors edifies their fans at the home of the flourishing last survivor of Gotham's grand old Book Row." Kirkus.

808.06 Rhetoric of specific kinds of writing

Jacob, Dianne, 1955-

Will write for food : the complete guide to writing cookbooks, blogs, memoir, recipes, and more / Dianne Jacob. Da Capo Lifeling, 2015 xii, 353 p. ; **808.06**

1. Food writing.

ISBN 9780738218052

LC 2015003915

Offers practical advice on how to achieve success in food writing, including information on self-publishing, creating and sustaining a food blog, and freelancing and reviewing.

Kephart, Beth

Handling the truth : on the writing of memoir / Beth Kephart. Gotham Books, 2013. 224 p. **808.06**

1. Autobiography 2. Writing. 3. Self-discovery

ISBN 9781592408153

LC 2012043517

A critically acclaimed National Book Award finalist offers writing lessons and examples for those interested in putting their memories down on paper and explains the difference between remembering and imagining and describes the language of truth.

Klein, Cheryl B., 1978-

★The **magic** words : writing great books for children and young adults / Cheryl B. Klein. W. W. Norton & Company, 2016 368 p. ; **808.06**

1. Children's literature -- Authorship 2. Young adult fiction -- Authorship

ISBN 9780393292244

LC 2016014423

Guides writers through the major elements of fiction for middle grade and young adult readers and provides exercises, questions, and rules of thumb to help jump-start the creative process.

Seuling, Barbara

How to write a children's book and get it published / Barbara Seulin. Wiley, c2004. v, 233 p. : **808.06**

1. Children's literature -- Authorship -- Marketing. 2. Children's literature -- Authorship.

ISBN 0471676195

LC 2004004691

"Presents five essential steps (from researching the current marketplace to submitting your manuscript) to publishing works for children." Library Journal.

Turabian, Kate L

Student's guide to writing college papers / Kate L. Turabian ; revised by Gregory G. Colomb, Joseph M. Williams, Joseph Bizup, William T. Fitzgerald, and the University of Chicago Press editorial staff. University of Chicago Press, 2019. xvii, 321 p. : **808.06**

1. Dissertations, Academic -- Handbooks, manuals, etc. 2. Academic writing -- Handbooks, manuals, etc. 3. Report writing -- Handbooks, manuals, etc.

ISBN 9780226430263

LC 2018060157

Friendly and authoritative, the fifth edition of Student's Guide to Writing College Papers combines decades of expert advice with new revisions based on feedback from students and teachers. Time-tested and teacher-approved, this book will prepare students to be better critical thinkers and help them develop a sense of inquiry that will serve them well beyond the classroom.

808.1 Rhetoric in specific literary forms

Abrams, M. H. (Meyer Howard), 1912-2015

The **fourth** dimension of a poem : and other essays / M.H. Abrams ; foreword by Harold Bloom. W. W. Norton & Co., c2012. xiv, 240 p. ; **808.1**

1. Poetics 2. Poetry -- History and criticism 3. Essays

ISBN 9780393058307

LC 2012020169

A literary critic, scholar and teacher presents a collection of nine new essays as he approaches his 100th birthday, including discussions of Kant, Keats and Hazlitt as well as piece on the pleasure of reading poems aloud.

Addonizio, Kim, 1954-

The **poet's** companion : a guide to the pleasures of writing poetry / Kim Addonizio and Dorianne Laux. W.W. Norton, c1997. 284 p. : **808.1**

1. Poetry -- Authorship.

ISBN 9780393316544

LC 96040451

Two accomplished poets and teachers offer a poetry primer that includes short essays on the elements of poetry, technique, and possible subjects for writing, along with writing exercises, tips on getting published, and examples of contemporary poetry.

Deutsch, Babette, 1895-

Poetry handbook : a dictionary of terms / Babette Deutsch. Barnes & Noble Books, 1981, c1974. xix, 203 p. ; **808.1**

1. Literature -- Terminology. 2. Poetics. 3. Poetry -- Study and teaching 4. Poetry -- Terminology.

ISBN 0064635481

LC BL 99922903

Previously published: New York : Funk & Wagnalls, 1974.

Terms relating to poetry written in the English language are defined and illustrated by means of complete poems and verse excerpts

Foster, Thomas C

How to read poetry like a professor : a quippy and sonorous guide to verse / Thomas C. Foster. Harper Perennial, 2018 212 p. ; **808.1**

1. Poetry -- Explication 2. Poetry -- Appreciation 3. Poetry -- Analysis

ISBN 9780062113788

LC 2018295084

"No literary form is as admired and feared as poetry. Admired for its lengthy pedigree--a line of poets extending back to a time before recorded history--and a ubiquitous presence in virtually all cultures, poetry is also revered for its great beauty and the powerful emotions it evokes. But the form has also instilled trepidation in its many admirers mainly because of a lack of familiarity and knowledge. Poetry demands more from readers--intellectually, emotionally, and spiritually--than other literary forms. Most of us started out loving poetry because it filled our beloved children's books from Dr. Seuss to Robert Louis Stevenson. Eventually, our reading shifted to prose, and later when we encountered poetry again, we had no recent experience to make it feel familiar. But reading poetry doesn't need to be so overwhelming. In an entertaining and engaging voice, Thomas C. Foster shows readers how to overcome their fear of poetry and learn to enjoy it once more."--Back cover.

Greene, Roland, 1957-

The **Princeton** encyclopedia of poetry and poetics / Roland Greene, editor in chief ; Stephen Cushman, general editor ; Clare Cavanagh, Jahan Ramazani, Paul Rouzer, associate editors ; Harris Feinsod, David Marno, Alexandra Slessarev, assistant editors. Princeton University Press, c2012. xxxvi, 1639 p. ; **808.1**

1. Poetry -- Dictionaries. 2. Poetics -- Dictionaries. 3. Poetry -- History and criticism.

ISBN 9780691154916

LC 2012005602

Rev. ed. of : The Princeton encyclopedia of poetry and poetics / Alex Preminger and T.V.F. Brogan, co-editors ; Frank J. Warnke, O.B. Hardison, Jr., and Earl Miner, associate editors. 1993.

Through three editions over more than four decades, The Princeton Encyclopedia of Poetry and Poetics has built an unrivaled reputation as the most comprehensive and authoritative reference for students, scholars, and poets on all aspects of its subject: history, movements, genres, prosody, rhetorical devices, critical terms, and more.

"The go-to resource for students doing research on poetry technique and terminology, the fourth edition of The Princeton Encyclopedia of Poetry & Poetics features many new and valuable updates from the third edition, in 1993." Booklist

Higginson, William J., 1938-

The **haiku** handbook : how to write, teach, and appreciate haiku / William J. Higginson and Penny Harter ; foreword by Jane Reichhold. Kodansha International, 2009. xix, 331 p. ; **808.1**

1. Haiku -- History and criticism 2. Haiku -- Technique

ISBN 9784770031136

LC 2009036628

Originally published: New York : McGraw-Hill, c1985.

In this groundbreaking and now-classic volume, the authors present haiku poets writing in English, Spanish, French, German, and five other languages on an equal footing with Japanese poets.

Hirsch, Edward, 1950-

How to read a poem : and fall in love with poetry / Edward Hirsch. Harcourt Brace & Co., 1999. xvi, 352 p. **808.1**

1. Poetry writing. 2. Poetry -- Explication. 3. Poetry -- History and criticism

ISBN 0151004196

LC 98050065

"Published by the Center for Documentary Studies in association with---."

ALA Notable Book, 2000.

An examination from an award-winning poet and critic of the reasons for and meanings of poetry offers an analysis of poems by Wordsworth, Plath, Neruda, and others to precisely delineate their unique power and their ineffable message.

"The author has gathered an eclectic group of poems from many times and places, with selections as varied as postwar Polish poetry, works by Keats and Christopher Smart, and lyrics from African American work songs. A prolific, award-winning poet in his own right, Hirsch suggests helpful strategies for understanding and appreciating each poem. The book is scholarly but very readable and incorporates interesting anecdotes from the lives of the poets." Library Journal.

A **poet's** glossary / Edward Hirsch. Houghton Mifflin Harcourt, 2014. vi, 730 p. ; **808.1**

1. Poetics. 2. Poetry

ISBN 0151011958

LC 2014011675

Includes index.

The poet and author of How to Read a Poem (And Fall in Love with Poetry) explores the traditions of poets throughout time and around the world and provides definitions of the art form's devices, movements, "isms" and aesthetics.

"Offering definitions, a discussion of poetic techniques, and an unalloyed spiritual quality to his work, Hirsch's...alphabetically arranged glossary includes historical explanations, quotes, interpretative material, usage in various languages, and references to additional terms for even more clarification." Library Journal.

Hirshfield, Jane, 1953-

Ten windows : how great poems transform the world / Jane Hirshfield. Knopf, 2015. 176 p. **808.1**

1. Poetry -- History and criticism. 2. Books and reading. 3. Essays

ISBN 9780385351058

LC 2014025430

"This is a Borzoi book."

"A collection of ten essays by the poet Jane Hirshfield, about reading and understanding poetry, and about the power of poetry".-- Provided by publisher.

"Hirshfield writes brilliantly of paradox in poetry, of what poets and stand-up comics have in common, and how poetry counters isolation and meaninglessness. The profound pleasure Hirshfield takes in delineating poetry's efficacy makes for a beautifully enlightening volume." Booklist.

Oliver, Mary, 1935-2019

A **poetry** handbook / Mary Oliver. Harcourt Brace & Co., c1994. viii, 130 p. ; **808.1**

1. English language -- Versification -- Handbooks, manuals, etc. 2. American poetry -- History and criticism -- Handbooks, manuals, etc. 3. English poetry -- History and criticism -- Handbooks, manuals, etc. 4. Poetry -- Authorship -- Handbooks, manuals, etc.
ISBN 9780156724005

LC 93049676

"A Harvest original."

Includes index.

Offers advice on reading and writing poetry, and discusses imitation, sound, the line, poem forms, free verse, diction, imagery, revision, and workshops.

Orr, David, 1974-

You, too, could write a poem : selected reviews and essays, 2000-2015 / David Orr. Penguin Books, 2017 ix, 384 p. ; **808.1**

1. Poetics.
ISBN 9780143128199

LC 2016040779

"A collection of reviews and essays by David Orr, the New York Times poetry columnist and one of the most respected critics in America today, his best work of the past fifteen years in one place. Poetry is never more vital, meaningful, or accessible than in the hands of David Orr. In the pieces collected here, most of them written originally for the New York Times, Orr is at his rigorous, conversational, and edifying best. Whether he is considering the careers of contemporary masters, such as Louise Gluck or Frederick Seidel, sizing up younger American poets, like Matthea Harvey and Matthew Zapruder, or even turning his attention to celebrities and public figures, namely Oprah Winfrey and Stephen Fry, when they choose to wade into the hotly contested waters of the poetry world, Orr is never any less than fully persuasive in arguing what makes a poem or poet great--or not."-- Provided by publisher.

Orr, Gregory

A **primer** for poets & readers of poetry / Gregory Orr. W. W. Norton & Company, 2018 325 p. ; **808.1**

1. Poetry writing 2. Poetry -- Appreciation.
ISBN 9780393253924

LC 2017052637

An award-winning poet and beloved professor, using such poems as Theodore Roethke's "My Papa's Waltz" and Robert Hayden's "Those Winter Sundays," guides young poets toward a deeper understanding of how poetry can function in their lives, while also introducing the art in an exciting new way.

Pinsky, Robert

Singing school : learning to write (and read) poetry by studying with the masters / Robert Pinsky. W. W. Norton & Company, 2013 xv, 221 p. ; **808.1**

1. Poetics. 2. Poetry -- Appreciation. 3. Poetry -- Authorship.
ISBN 0393050688

LC 2013022146

A former poet laureate provides informative introductions and sidebar notes for more than 80 poems by greats including William Butler Yeats, Emily Dickinson and George Herbert, in an effort to spark pleasure in reading and writing poems.

Sol, Adam, 1969-

How a poem moves : a field guide for readers afraid of poetry / Adam Sol. MisFit, 2019 200 p. **808.1**

1. Poetry -- Appreciation 2. Poetry -- Explication. 3. Poetry -- History and criticism
ISBN 9781770414563

LC bl2019005578

Developed from Adam Sol's popular blog, How a Poem Moves is a collection of 35 short essays that walks readers through an array of contemporary poems. Sol is a dynamic teacher, and in these essays, he has captured the humor and engaging intelligence for which he is known in the classroom. With a breezy style, Sol delivers essays that are perfect for a quick read or to be grouped together as a curriculum.

"His selections, largely derived from his time as a juror for the 2015 Griffin Poetry Prize, tend toward the relatively lesser-known, making this survey equally worthwhile for beginners who can learn from Sol's instruction and for more seasoned readers who will delight in the new discoveries contained within." Publishers Weekly.

Teicher, Craig Morgan, 1979-

We begin in gladness : how poets progress : essays / Craig Morgan Teicher. Graywolf Press, 2018. 164 p. ; **808.1**

1. Essays.
ISBN 9781555978211

LC 2018934489

An acclaimed poet and critic, through luminous essays, considers how poets start out, how they learn to hear themselves and how they create lasting work, tracing the poetic development of the works of Sylvia Plath, John Ashbery and Louise Gluck, among others.

808.2 Rhetoric of drama

Desberg, Peter

Now that's funny! : the art and craft of writing comedy / Peter Desberg ; Jeffrey Davis. Square One Publishers, 2017 viii, 376 p. ; **808.2**

1. Television comedies -- Authorship. 2. Comedy films -- Authorship. 3. Television comedy writers -- United States -- Interviews. 4. Screenwriters -- United States -- Interviews.
ISBN 9780757004452

LC 2016055985

"How 24 top Hollywood writers create comedy in real time"--Cover.

Previous edition, published in 2010, has other title information: at the writers' table with Hollywood's top comedy writers.

"The unique approach, combined with the in-depth interviews, makes this a solid go-to for aspiring comedy writers." Booklist.

Ellis, Sherry, 1950-

Now write! screenwriting : exercises by today's best writers and teachers / Sherry Ellis with Laurie Lamson. Jeremy P.

Tarcher/Penguin, 2010. 343 p. : **808.2**
1. Motion picture authorship 2. Motion picture authorship.
ISBN 1585428515
LC 2010029424

A handbook of previously unpublished writing exercises, contributed by the acclaimed screenwriters of such films as the Oscar-winning Raging Bull and the blockbuster Terminator 2, shares advice on such topics as character development, building ideas and overcoming psychological blocks.

Field, Syd
★**Screenplay** : the foundations of screenwriting / Syd Field. Delta Trade Paperbacks, 2005. 320 p. : **808.2**
1. Motion picture authorship.
ISBN 0385339038
LC 2005048491

Includes index.

Providing examples from well-known movies, a revised handbook explains the structural and stylistic elements as well as writing techniques basic to the creation of a successful film script and furnishes practical tips on script writing for original productions, sequels, novel adaptations, and adaptations by original authors.

Hauge, Michael
Writing screenplays that sell / Michael Hauge. Collins Reference, 2011 xxx, 349 p. ; **808.2**
1. Motion picture authorship. 2. Television authorship.
ISBN 0061791431
LC 2012450691

Includes index.

A new edition of a classic work, revised and updated for modern screenwriters, covers story concept, character development, theme, structure and scenes; analyzes a sample screenplay; and explains how to submit a manuscript, select an agent and market oneself.

"This book provides a discussion of the craftcharacters, story development, etc.and industry; lays out the all-important details of format; then tells how to market the finished product. Hauge's volume is a detailed manual offering a step-by-step methodology, a scriptual analysis of a hit film, The Karate Kid, and handy chapter summaries." Library Journal.

Venis, Linda,
Inside the room : writing TV with the pros at UCLA Extension Writers' Program / edited by Linda Venis, Director, UCLA Extension Department of the Arts and Writers' Program. Gotham Books, 2013 xvi, 256 p. ; **808.2**
1. Television authorship -- Vocational guidance.
ISBN 9781592408115
LC 2013004221

Includes index.

Provides aspiring professional television writers with industry insider information and explains how to write a spec script for dramas and sit-coms that will get noticed and provides a timeline for the steps involved in creating, selling and making a TV show.

808.3 Rhetoric of fiction

Cohen, Richard, 1952-
How to write like Tolstoy : a journey into the minds of our greatest writers / Richard Cohen. Random House, 2016. 336 p. **808.3**
1. Fiction writing 2. Fiction -- Technique. 3. Writing
ISBN 9780812998306
LC 2015018626

A critically acclaimed author, drawing on his illustrious career in publishing and a lifetime of reading, takes readers on a fascinating journey into the minds, techniques, concerns, tricks, flaws and obsessions of our greatest writers, including Ernest Hemingway and Gertrude Stein.

"Even readers with no intentions of writing a novel will relish the opportunity to join their favorite authors at the workbench." Booklist.

Gardner, John, 1933-
The **art** of fiction : notes on craft for young writers / John Gardner. Vintage Books, 1991. xii, 224 p. : **808.3**
1. Fiction writing 2. Essays
ISBN 9780679734031
LC BL 99723746

Includes index.

A guide to creative writing examines diverse facets of writing technique, and contains analyses of works by writers from Homer to Mark Twain.

George, Elizabeth, 1949-
Mastering the process : from idea to novel / Elizabeth George. Viking, 2020 318 p. : **808.3**
1. Fiction -- Authorship 2. Fiction -- Technique 3. Plots (Drama, novel, etc) 4. Creative writing
ISBN 9781984878311
LC 2019042814

"As the author of twenty-four novels, Elizabeth George is one of the most successful--and prolific--novelists today. In Mastering the Process, George offers readers a master class in the art and science of crafting a novel. For many writers, the biggest challenge is figuring out how to take that earliest glimmer of inspiration and shape it into a full-length novel. How do you even begin to transform a single idea to a complete book? Elizabeth George takes us behind the scenes and into each step of her writing process, revealing exactly what it takes to craft a novel. Drawing from her personal photos, early notes, character analyses, and rough drafts, George shows us every step of how she wrote her novel Careless in Red, from researching location to imagining plot to creating characters to the actual writing and revision process itself. George offers us an intimate look at the process she follows, while also providing invaluable advice for writers about what's worked for her--and what hasn't. Mastering the Process offers writers practical, prescriptive, and achievable tools to creating a novel, to editing a novel, and to problem solve when in the midst of a novel, from a master storyteller writing at the top of her game".-- Provided by publisher.

Johnson, Charles Richard, 1948-
The **way** of the writer : reflections on the art and craft of storytelling / Charles Johnson. Scribner, 2016. 256 p. **808.3**
1. Writing 2. Books and reading 3. Literature -- History and criticism 4. Advice 5. Essays
ISBN 9781501147210
LC 2016299742

The author of Middle Passage presents an inspiring guide to the craft and art of writing that examines the creative impulse while sharing lessons and exercises that reinforce the mechanical process of storytelling.

"All writers will welcome the useful tips and exercises, but the book will also appeal to readers interested in literature and the creative process. Johnson's wonderful prose will engage readers to think more deeply about how to tell a story and consider the truth-telling power of the arts." Library Journal.

Koch, Stephen, 1941-

★The **modern** library writer's workshop : a guide to the craft of fiction / Stephen Koch. Modern Library, 2003. 246 p. ; **808.3**

1. Fiction -- Authorship.
ISBN 9780375755583

LC 2002032593

Compiling wisdom and advice from such masters of the craft as Henry James, E. M. Forster, Eudora Welty, and Toni Morrison, this readerly guide to fiction writing provides helpful observations and techniques for would-be fiction writers, covering such topics as cultivating one's creative imagination, the mechanics of plot and character development, and narrative thinking.

Mattison, Alice

The **kite** and the string : how to write with spontaneity and control - and live to tell the tale / Alice Mattison. Viking, 2016 xx, 234 p. ; **808.3**

1. Fiction -- Technique. 2. Fiction -- Authorship.
ISBN 9780525428541

LC 2016286057

A targeted and insightful guide to the stages of writing fiction and memoir without falling into common traps, while wisely navigating the writing life, from an award-winning author and longtime teacher.

Moore, Dinty W., 1955-

The **story** cure : a book doctor's pain-free guide to finishing your novel or memoir / Dinty W. Moore. Ten Speed Press, 2017 181 p. : **808.3**

1. Fiction -- Authorship. 2. Fiction -- Technique. 3. Autobiography -- Authorship. 4. Creative writing.
ISBN 9780399578809

LC 2016036789

Drawing on his years of teaching at both the university level and at writing workshops across the country, the director of creative writing at Ohio University presents an authoritative guide to curing the issues that truly plague writers at all levels.

Mosley, Walter

Elements of fiction / Walter Mosley. Grove Press, 2019 xii, 115 p. ; **808.3**

1. Fiction -- Authorship. 2. Fiction -- Technique. 3. Creative writing. 4. Plots (Drama, novel, etc.)
ISBN 9780802147639

LC 2019033265

The award-winning author of the Easy Rawlins series presents a follow-up to This Year You Write Your Novel that offers conversational, instructive chapters demonstrating the essential elements of fiction, from character and plot development to context and description.

Percy, Benjamin

Thrill me : essays on fiction / Benjamin Percy. Graywolf Press, [2016] 174 p. **808.3**

1. Books and reading 2. Fiction writing 3. Writing. 4. Books 5. Essays
ISBN 9781555977597

LC 2016931536

In his first nonfiction book, the best-selling author challenges the notion that literary and genre fiction are somehow mutually exclusive through 15 essays on the craft of fiction that look to disparate sources such as Jaws, Blood Meridian and The Girl With the Dragon Tattoo.

"Percy's essays skillfully dissect the structure, mechanics, and concrete details of what makes good writing sparkle." Publishers Weekly.

Piercy, Marge

So you want to write : how to master the craft of writing fiction and memoir / Marge Piercy and Ira Wood. Leapfrog Press ; 2005. 324 p. ; **808.3**

1. Fiction -- Authorship 2. Autobiography -- Authorship
ISBN 9780972898454

LC bl2006016096

Includes index.

Describes the elements that are necessary to write novels, short stories, and memoirs.

Scofield, Sandra Jean, 1943-

The **last** draft : a novelist's guide to revision / Sandra Scofield. Penguin Books, 2017 xxviii, 240 p. ; **808.3**

1. Fiction -- Technique. 2. Fiction -- Authorship. 3. Manuscripts -- Editing. 4. Creative writing.
ISBN 9780143131359

LC 2017032030

Offering indispensable advice to both novice and experienced writers alike, a detailed, step-by-step guide illustrates how to reread a work of fiction with a view of its subject and vision, and how to take it apart and put it back together again so it is a stronger work that is deeper in meaning. By the author of The Scene Book.

Wheat, Carolyn

How to write killer fiction : the funhouse of mystery & the roller coaster of suspense / Carolyn Wheat. Perseverance Press, 2003. 191 p. : **808.3**

1. Detective and mystery stories -- Authorship 2. Suspense fiction -- Authorship
ISBN 9781880284629

LC 2002015588

Presents a guide to crafting mystery and suspense stories, defining the difference between the two genres and offering tips on subtly dispensing clues, constructing story arcs, and understanding the fundamentals of composition.

"Wheat begins with a discussion of the distinction between mystery and suspense...and then devotes a section to each genre. She offers up plenty of useful tips, such as how to dispense vital information in subtle ways and how to plant clues without being too obvious about it." Booklist.

Wood, James, 1965-

★**How** fiction works / James Wood. Farrar, Straus and Giroux, c2008. 208 p. **808.3**

1. Books and reading. 2. Literature 3. Literature -- History and criticism 4. Fiction -- 20th century -- History and criticism
ISBN 9780374173401

LC 2008010290

What makes a story a story? What is style? What's the connection between realism and real life? These are some of the questions James Wood answers in How Fiction Works, the first book-length essay by the preeminent critic of his generation. Ranging widely--from Homer to David Foster Wallace, from What Maisie Knew to Make Way for Ducklings--Wood takes the reader through the basic elements of the art, step by step.

808.5 Rhetoric of speech

Anderson, Chris, 1957 January 14-
TED talks : the official TED guide to public speaking / Chris Anderson. Houghton Mifflin Harcourt, 2016. xv, 269 p. ; **808.5**

1. Public speaking -- Handbooks, manuals, etc.
ISBN 9780544634497

LC 2015048798

Includes index.

Citing the powerful potential of short inspirational talks, an insider's guide by the successful TED curator draws insights from such popular associates as Sir Ken Robinson, Amy Cuddy and Bill Gates to explain how to tap and develop one's unique public-speaking and communication skills.

Linklater, Kristin
Freeing the natural voice / Kristin Linklater ; drawings by Douglas Florian. Drama Book Specialists, c1976. 210 p. : **808.5**

1. Voice training.
ISBN 9780896760714

LC 75028172

Describes the mechanics of the voice and obstacles of spontaneous, effective vocal expression and details exercises for developing and strengthening the voice as a human and actor's instrument.

"Predicated on the basic assumptions that everyone has a voice capable of expressing a full range of emotions within a normal two- to four-octave scale and that daily stress compromises the voice's natural abilities and power {the author} presents a simple and clear narrative, as well as a full set of exercises to cultivate and strengthen the voice." Library Journal.

Pinsky, Robert
The **sounds** of poetry : a brief guide / Robert Pinsky. Farrar, Straus and Giroux, 1999, c1998. 129 p. ; **808.5**

1. Oral interpretation of poetry.
ISBN 9780374526177

LC BL 99009766

Reprint. Originally published: c1998.

America's Poet Laureate offers a journey inside the world of poetry to explore the fundamental workings of this literary art, explaining how different sounds can be used to express meaning and images.

"By bringing his passion for the sound of language--so evident in his own poems--to his expert interpretations of the work of others, Pinsky cracks open the glass case that seems to separate poetry from everyday language, allowing the song of each poem to ring bright and clear." Booklist.

Rueckert, Veronica
Outspoken : why women's voices get silenced and how to set them free / Veronica Rueckert. HarperCollins, 2019. 304 p. **808.5**

1. Communication. 2. Interpersonal communication. 3. Men/women communication. 4. Career development.
ISBN 9780062879349

LC 2019016792

A Peabody Award-winning communications specialist and former host at Wisconsin Public Radio offers women practical tools, encouragement and advice for speaking with confidence and authority so that they will finally be heard.

"A practical and fascinating guide to liberating the female voice as a key to liberating the self." Kirkus.

808.8 Collections of literary texts from more than two literatures

The **Paris** Review book of heartbreak, madness, sex, love, betrayal, outsiders, intoxication, war, whimsy, horrors, God, death, dinner, baseball, travels, the art of writing, and everything else in the world since 1953 / the editors of the Paris review ; with an introduction by George Plimpton. Picador, 2003. xv, 751 p. ; **808.8**

1. Love. 2. Men/women relations. 3. Families 4. Family relationships. 5. Psychological fiction. 6. Domestic fiction
ISBN 0312422385

LC 2003045971

This anthology celebrates the 50th anniversary of The Paris Review. Includes short stories from 1953 to 2002.

An anthology celebrating the fiftieth anniversary of the "Paris Review" offers stories, poems, thoughts, and observations by such authors as W.H. Auden, William Faulkner, Jack Kerouac, and Ian McEwan.

Saba, Umberto, 1883-1957
Songbook : the selected poems of Umberto Saba / translated by George Hochfield and Leonard Nathan ; introduction, notes, and commentary by George Hochfield. Yale University Press, 2008. xxviii, 562 p. ; **808.8**

1. Italian poetry
ISBN 9780300136036

LC 2008017685

A beautifully translated selection of poems by one of the greatest Italian poets of the twentieth century.

808.81 Collections in specific forms

Chang, Tina
★**Language** for a new century : contemporary poetry from the Middle East, Asia, and beyond / edited by Tina Chang, Nathalie Handal, and Ravi Shankar. W.W. Norton, c2008. l, 734 p. ; **808.81**

ISBN 9780393332384

LC 2007049424

An extensive collection of contemporary Asian and Middle Eastern poetry includes the work of four hundred contributors from a variety of backgrounds, in a thematically organized anthology that is complemented by personal essays.

Dungy, Camille T., 1972-
Black nature : four centuries of African American nature poetry / edited by Camille T. Dungy. University of Georgia Press, c2009. xxxv, 387 p. ; **808.81**

1. Nature 2. African American poetry 3. American poetry
ISBN 9780820334318

LC 2009018528

The first anthology to focus on nature writing by African American poets, a genre that until now has not commonly been counted as one in which they participated. Dungy has selected 180 poems from 93 poets that provide unique perspectives on American social and literary history to broaden our concept of nature poetry and African American poetics.

"Expanding the realm of traditional nature poetry and African American writings, this work will appeal to readers of both genres." Library Journal

Ferlinghetti, Lawrence

City lights pocket poets anthology / edited by Lawrence Ferlinghetti. City Lights Books, c1995 ii, 259 p. ; **808.81**

ISBN 0872863115

LC 95031608

Includes writings by such individuals as Robert Duncan, Malcolm Lowry, Robert Nichols, Allen Ginsberg, and Kenneth Patchen.

"Drawing from the 52 volumes published in the Pocket Poets series since 1956, this selection provides a handy sampler of many of the prominent avant-garde and leftist poets of the post-WW II era. . . . The series' extensive international scope is highlighted in poems culled from German, Russian, Italian, Dutch, Nicaraguan and Spanish poets." Publishers Weekly.

Hirsch, Edward

Poet's choice / Edward Hirsch. Harcourt, c2006. xv, 432 p. ; **808.81**

1. Poetry -- History and criticism.
ISBN 015101356X

LC 2005026890

A collection of revised and expanded writings culled from the author's popular Washington Post Book World "Poet's Choice" column demonstrates how poetry responds to world challenges and introduces the work of more than 130 writers.

Housden, Roger

Risking everything : 110 poems of love and revelation / edited by Roger Housden. Harmony Books, c2003. xvi, 173 p. ; **808.81**

1. Love 2. Anthologies.
ISBN 9781400047994

LC 2002014410

Includes index.

Offers a collection of poems by world poets including Billy Collins, Seamus Heaney, Emily Dickinson, Naomi Shihab Nye, Rumi, and Chuang Tzu.

"This is an inspirational anthology sans inspirational chestnuts." Booklist.

Hulse, Michael, 1955-

The **20th** century in poetry / edited by Michael Hulse and Simon Rae. Pegasus Books, 2012, c2011. xviii, 860 p. ; **808.81**

1. Poetry -- 20th century
ISBN 9781605983646

LC bl2012027473

An anthology of poetry from the twentieth century features brief biographies and chronically arranged entries while providing insight into historical influences and the evolutions of various traditional and modernist forms.

Merwin, W. S. (William Stanley), 1927-2019

Selected translations : 1948-2011 / W.S. Merwin. Copper Canyon Press, c2013. vii, 407 p. ; **808.81**

1. Poetry
ISBN 1556594097

LC 2012025545

Includes index.

Selected Translations is the crowning achievement for one of the world's greatest and most prolific translators of poetry.

"And yet long works (like the Middle English Patience) and sophisticated moderns fit his gifts, too: if anyone can make a big hit out of a book of translations from all over, Merwin ought to be the one." Publishers Weekly

Milosz, Czeslaw

A **book** of luminous things : an international anthology of poetry / edited and with an introduction by Czeslaw Milosz. Harcourt Brace & Co., 1998, c1996. xx, 320 p. ; **808.81**

1. Poetry -- Collections.
ISBN 9780156005746

LC BL 98002295

"A Harvest book."

Includes indexes.

A collection of the world's greatest poetry from the past two thousand years brings together five hundred works by more than two hundred poets, along with commentary by the editor.

Moore, Gerald, 1924-

The **Penguin** book of modern African poetry / edited by Gerald Moore and Ulli Beier. Penguin Books, 2007, c1998. xxvi, 448 p. ; **808.81**

1. African poetry -- 20th century -- Translations into English. 2. Africa
ISBN 9780140424720

LC 2012387354

Reprint. Originally published: c1998.

Surveys the poetry of modern-day Africa, featuring the work of ninety-nine poets from twenty-seven countries, including Leopold Sedar Senghor, Augustinho Neto, and Christopher Okigbo.

Pinsky, Robert,

Americans' favorite poems : the Favorite Poem Project anthology / edited by Robert Pinsky and Maggie Dietz. Norton, 2000. xix, 327 p. **808.81**

1. Anthologies.
ISBN 9780393048209

LC 99031979

Includes index.

A collection of 200 poems by such authors as Margaret Atwood, Elizabeth Barrett Browning and John Keats, with comments by those Americans who chose them as their favorites.

"People across America, including many teens, share the poetry they love, and talk about what it means in their lives. Their choices--from John Keats to Lucille Clifton--defy stereotypes, and their comments are heartfelt." Booklist.

Poems to read : a new favorite poem project anthology / edited by Robert Pinsky and Maggie Dietz. W. W. Norton, c2002. xxv, 352 p. ; **808.81**

1. English poetry. 2. American poetry.
ISBN 9780393010749

LC 2002000321

Presents a collection of favorite poems sent in by thousands of Americans, with selections ranging from William Blake to Allen Ginsberg, includes comments from readers on how the poems affect them.

Rothenberg, Jerome, 1931-

Poems for the millennium : the University of California book of modern & postmodern poetry / edited by Jerome Rothenberg and Pierre Joris. University of California Press, c1995-c2009. 811 p. ; **808.81**

1. Poetry, Modern
ISBN 9780520072251

LC 93049839

Vol. 3 edited with commentaries by Jerome Rothenberg and Jeffrey C. Robinson.

"A centennial book"--Vol. 1, p. [v].

"Though its inclusions and exclusions will no doubt stimulate debate, this ambitious documentary history should take its place in most poetry collections, large and small." Library Journal

Stallworthy, Jon,

The **new** Oxford book of war poetry / chosen and edited by Jon Stallworthy. Oxford University Press, 2014. xl, 406 p. ; **808.81**

1. War and society. 2. War poetry.
ISBN 019870447X

LC 2013497520

"First edition published by Oxford University Press 1984"--Title page verso.

First edition published under title: The Oxford book of war poetry.

There can be no area of human experience that has generated a wider range of powerful feelings than war. Jon Stallworthy's classic and celebrated anthology spans centuries of human experience of war, from Homer's Iliad, through the First and Second WorldWars, the Vietnam War, and the wars fought since. This new edition, published to mark the centenary of the outbreak of the First World War, includes a new introduction and additional poems from David Harsent and Peter Wyton, amongst others. The new selection provides improved coverage of the two World Wars and the Vietnam War, and new coverage of the wars of the late twentieth and early twenty-first centuries. -- Publisher description.

Washburn, Katharine

World poetry : an anthology of verse from antiquity to our time / Katharine Washburn and John S. Major, editors ; Clifton Fadiman, general editor. W.W. Norton, c1998. xxii, 1338 p. ; **808.81**

ISBN 9780393041309

LC 97010879

An anthology of the best poetry ever written contains more than sixteen hundred poems, eighty percent of them originally written in languages other than English, spanning more than four millennia, from ancient Sumer and Egypt to the late twentieth century.

Young, Kevin

The **hungry** ear : poems of food & drink / [edited by] Kevin Young. Bloomsbury, 2012. xv, 319 p. ; **808.81**

1. Food 2. Beverages 3. Poetry -- Collections.
ISBN 9781608195510

LC bl2013002262

Includes index.

A collection of poetry celebrating the role of food and drink in everyday life, identity, and culture includes pieces by such writers as Elizabeth Bishop, Robert Frost, and Allen Ginsberg.

Young, Kevin

Jazz poems / selected and edited by Kevin Young. Alfred A. Knopf, 2006. 256 p. ; **808.81**

1. Jazz 2. African Americans 3. African American poetry 4. American poetry
ISBN 9781400042517

LC bl2006020783

A treasury of poetry inspired by the aethetic principles of jazz music and its performers captures the rhythms and energy of jazz in the words of such authors as Langston Hughes, William Carlos Williams, Frank O'Hara, Gwendolyn Brooks, Charles Simic, and Rita Dove.

808.82 Collections of drama

Clurman, Harold, 1901-

Nine plays of the modern theater / with an introd. by Harold Clurman. Grove Press, 1981. xiv, 896 p. ; **808.82**

1. Drama -- 20th century
ISBN 9780802150325

LC 79052121

Works by Brecht, Beckett, Genet, Pinter, Ionesco, and others explore the search for spiritual meaning in the modern world.

808.84 Collections of essays

Lopate, Phillip, 1943-

The **Art** of the personal essay : an anthology from the classical era to the present / selected and with an introduction by Phillip Lopate. Anchor Books, 1994. liv, 777 p. **808.84**

1. Essays.
ISBN 0385422989

LC 93029708

Contains over 75 essays written over a 400 year period.

"A Teachers & Writers Collaborative book."

"Not only are the selections a veritable feast, but Lopate's genre-defining introduction is not to be missed." Booklist.

808.86 Collections of letters

Mallon, Thomas, 1951-

Yours ever : people and their letters / Thomas Mallon. Pantheon Books 2009. 338 p. **808.86**

1. Letter writing. 2. Interpersonal communication. 3. Mail. 4. Letters.
ISBN 9780679444268

A tribute to the art of letter writing features the author's commentary on the circumstances and characters of famous accomplished practitioners, sharing the suicide letters, travel bulletins and other writings of figures ranging from F. Scott Fitzgerald to Lord Byron.

"This is an astute, exhilarating tour of the mailbag. [It] is nuanced, informed, full-blooded, a vigorous literary salute." New York Times Book Review.

Usher, Shaun

Letters of note : an eclectic collection of correspondence deserving of a wider audience/ compiled by Shaun Usher. Chronicle Books, 2014, c2013. xvi, 352 p. : Letters of note ; **808.86**

1. Letters
ISBN 9781452134253

LC 2013050330

"First published in Great Britain in 2013 by Canongate Books Ltd in conjunction with Unbound"--Title page verso.

Includes index.

"This collection of 125 letters offers a never-before-seen glimpse of the events and people of history--the brightest and the best, the most notorious, and the endearingly everyday. Letters are not ordered chronologically or thematically, but are artfully arranged for a discovery-rich reading experience. Each entry includes a transcript of the letter; a short contextual introduction; and, in 100 cases, a facsimile of the letter itself".-- Provided by publisher.

Letters of note : an eclectic collection of correspondence deserving of a wider audience/ compiled by Shaun Usher. Chronicle Books Llc, 2016 352 p. Letters of note ; **808.86**

1. Letters
ISBN 9781452153834

LC bl2016043167

Includes index.

The editor of the best-selling Letters of Note, Volume 1 presents a companion collection of 125 letters spanning history and cultures, complementing entries with letter transcripts, contextual introductions, archive photos and letter facsimiles.

"This fantastic collection of over 125 letters is endlessly entertaining." Publishers Weekly.

808.88 Collections of miscellaneous writings

Bartlett, John, 1820-1905

Bartlett's familiar quotations : a collection of passages, phrases, and proverbs traced to their sources in ancient and modern literature / John Bartlett ; Geoffrey O'Brien, general editor. Little, Brown, and Co., 2012. lxi, 1438 p. ; **808.88**

1. Quotations, English.
ISBN 0316017590

LC 2012019870

Includes indexes.

A completely revised and updated edition provides a sweeping overview of the cultural influence of inspirational language and includes new contributions by such authors as the Dalai Lama, Steve Jobs and Desmond Tutu.

809 History, description, critical appraisal of more than two literatures

Bird, Betsy

Wild things! : acts of mischief in children's literature / Betsy Bird, Julie Danielson, and Peter D. Sieruta. Candlewick Press, 2014. 277 p. : **809**

1. Children's literature authors. 2. Children's literature -- History and criticism 3. Children's literature writing 4. Authors.
ISBN 9780763651503

LC bl2014026608

Leading children's literature bloggers take readers behind the scenes of many beloved children's books, revealing secret lives, scandalous turns, and humorous surprises.

Bloom, Harold, 1930-2019

The **Western** canon : the books and school of the ages / Harold Bloom. Harcourt Brace, 1994. viii, 578 p. **809**

1. Books and reading 2. Literature -- History and criticism. 3. Books.
ISBN 9780151957477

LC 93043542

Includes index.

A study of twenty-six canonical writers details the qualities that make them literary essentials, and includes Shakespeare, Chaucer, Milton, Beckett, Tolstoy, and Freud.

"The book succeeds not as a polemic but as a passionate, erudite and highly idiosyncratic series of essays about the literature dearest to one of America's most influential academics." Publishers Weekly.

Calvino, Italo

Why read the classics? / Italo Calvino ; translated from the Italian by Martin McLaughlin. Vintage Books, 2000. x, 277 p. ; **809**

1. Canon (Literature) 2. Literature -- History and criticism 3. Essays
ISBN 9780679743491

LC BL2001000638

Includes index.

Originally published: London : Jonathan Cape, 1999.

In a collection of thirty-six wise, elegantly written essays, the late author of The Road to San Giovanni explores the the enduring significance of key authors and fine literature from the Western canon, discussing the works of Homer, Defoe, Galileo, Stendhal, Dickens, Hemingway, and many others.

"Calvino celebrates a wide range of great thinkers in these provocative essays. Here are writers from the ancient world, the Renaissance and recent times, and from the old and new worlds. [These essays] are a reminder to us that rereading the classics can amuse as well as reward." The New Scientist.

Canton, James,

The **literature** book / James Canton, consultant editor. DK Publishing, 2016. 352 p. : **809**

1. Literature -- History and criticism.
ISBN 9781465429889

LC 2015298134

Examines "the greatest works of world literature, from the Iliad to Don Quixote to The Great Gatsby. Around 100 ... articles explore landmark novels, short stories, plays, and poetry that reinvented the art of writing in their time, whether Ancient Greece, post-classical Europe, or modern-day Korea"--Amazon.com.

"The attractive presentation (not to mention price point) makes this suitable for the circulating collections of most libraries, where readers will find it as entertaining as it is informative." Booklist.

Carter, Graydon,

Vanity Fair's writers on writers / edited by Graydon Carter ; introduction by David Friend. Penguin Group USA, 2016. 432 p. **809**

1. Authors 2. Writing 3. Influence (Literary, artistic, etc.) 4. Creativity 5. Essays 6. Anthologies
ISBN 9780143111764

LC 2016031514

A collection features beloved authors discussing their favorite writers, including Martin Amis on Saul Bellow, Truman Capote on Willa Cather, Salman Rushdie on Christopher Hitchens and many more.

Damrosch, David

The **buried** book : the loss and rediscovery of the great Epic of Gilgamesh / David Damrosch. H. Holt, 2007. xi, 315 p. : **809**

1. Gilgamesh. 2. Books. 3. Middle East.
ISBN 0805080295

LC 2006049523

A critical study of the ancient Mesopotamian epic of Gilgamesh describes its composition around 1200 B.C., its loss in 600 B.C., its rediscovery and deciphering in the nineteenth century, and the fast-paced story itself of a great Middle Eastern hero and his exploits.

"Combining acuity about cultural contexts with wide-ranging knowledge, Damrosch's account is a superb and engrossing popular presentation." Booklist.

Danticat, Edwidge, 1969-

The **art** of death : writing the final story / Edwidge Danticat. Graywolf Press, [2017] 181 pages ; **809**

1. Danticat, Edwidge, 1969- 2. Death 3. Coping 4. Grief 5. Loss (Psychology)

ISBN 9781555977771

LC 2016951195

Edwidge Danticat's The Art of Death: Writing the Final Story is at once a personal account of her mother dying from cancer and a deeply considered reckoning with the ways that other writers have approached death in their own work.

"This slim volume wraps literary criticism, philosophy, and memoir into a gracefully circling whole, echoing the nature of grief as 'circles and circles of sorrow.'" Publishers Weekly.

Ghosh, Amitav, 1956-

The **great** derangement : climate change and the unthinkable / Amitav Ghosh. The University of Chicago Press, 2016. 176 p. **809**

1. Environmental protection in literature 2. Climate change 3. Global warming 4. Skeptics

ISBN 9780226323039

LC 2016018232

"Are we deranged? The acclaimed Indian novelist Amitav Ghosh argues that future generations may well think so. How else to explain our imaginative failure in the face of global warming? In his first major book of nonfiction since In an Antique Land, Ghosh examines our inability--at the level of literature, history, and politics--to grasp the scale and violence of climate change."--Provided by the publisher

"A slim but certainly significant contribution to the climate crisis dialogue sure to provoke discussion and increased awareness about our imperiled planet." Kirkus.

Handy, Bruce

Wild things : the joy of reading children's literature as an adult / Bruce Handy. Simon & Schuster, 2017. 272 p. **809**

1. Children's literature -- History and criticism. 2. Children's literature writing 3. Books and reading. 4. Literature -- History and criticism

ISBN 9781451609950

LC 2017003959

A nostalgic ramble through classic children's literature by a Vanity Fair contributing editor explores the stories of forefront authors and illustrators while revealing the wisdom that can be found in masterpieces ranging from The Cat in the Hat and Charlotte's Web to Goodnight Moon and The Very Hungry Caterpillar.

"As well-researched as it is seamlessly composed, this book entertains as it educates." Kirkus.

James, Henry, 1843-1916

Literary criticism. /Henry James. Literary Classics of the United States, c1984. 1484 p. ; The Library of America **809**

1. Literature, Modern -- 19th century -- History and criticism. 2. Literature.

ISBN 9780940450226

LC 84011241

Gathers James essays about fiction, literary criticism, and the works of Alcott, Emerson, Hawthorne, Howells, Stowe, Arnold, Browning, Byron, Trollope, and Stevenson.

Kirsch, Adam, 1976-

The **blessing** and the curse : the Jewish people and their books in the twentieth century / Adam Kirsch. W.W. Norton & Company, 2020 xiv, 279 p. ; **809**

1. Jewish literature -- 20th century -- History and criticism. 2. Judaism -- 20th century.

ISBN 9780393652406

LC 2020013974

"An erudite and accessible survey of Jewish life and culture in the twentieth century, as reflected in seminal texts. Following The People and the Books, which 'covers more than 2,500 years of highly variegated Jewish cultural expression' (Robert Alter, New York Times), formidable and perceptive literary critic Adam Kirsch now turns to the salient works of modern Jewish thought. From the vast emigration of Jews out of Eastern Europe to the Holocaust to the creation of Israel, the twentieth century transformed Jewish life. This was true, also, of writing: the novels, plays, poems, and memoirs of Jewish writers provided intimate access to new worlds of experience. Here Kirsch navigates four themes that shaped the twentieth century in Jewish literature and culture: Europe, America, Israel, and the endeavor to reconfigure Judaism as a modern faith. Reading writers ranging from Franz Kafka to Philip Roth, Anne Frank to Tony Kushner, Hannah Arendt to Judith Plaskow, Kirsch's scope is wide and his observations diverse. Insightful and engaging, The Blessing and the Curse brings the Jewish experience vividly to life." Provided by publisher.

"The focus throughout this illuminating and invaluable study is on secular modern Jewish writers from Central and Eastern Europe and their descendants. For all Jewish literature collections, and for informed general readers interested in modern Jewish secular literary culture." Library Journal

★The **people** and the books : 18 classics of Jewish literature / Adam Kirsch. W.W. Norton & Company, [2016] 432 p. **809**

1. Bible. Old Testament 2. Jewish literature -- History and criticism. 3. Judaism -- History 4. Jews -- History 5. Jewish way of life

ISBN 9780393241761

LC 2016024818

An anthology of Jewish literary classics stands as an essential exploration of a rich literary tradition spanning biblical through modern times and includes such entries as the books of Deuteronomy and Esther, the philosophy of Maimonides, the autobiography of Gluckel of Hameln and the Zionist manifestos of Theodor Herzl.

Kolbert, Elizabeth

The **ends** of the earth : an anthology of the finest writing on the Arctic and the Antarctic Bloomsbury USA, 2007. 560 p. : **809**

1. Arctic regions. 2. Antarctica

ISBN 9781596914438

LC 2009285278

A literary anthology explores the natural wonders of the frozen landscapes of the Arctic and Antarctic in a compilation of first-person narratives, cultural histories, science and nature writing, and fiction.

Kundera, Milan

Encounter / Milan Kundera ; translated from the French by

Linda Asher. Harper, 2010. 176 p. **809**

1. Modern literature -- 20th century -- History and criticism. 2. Music -- History and criticism. 3. Painting -- Appreciation. 4. Humanism. 5. Essays

ISBN 9780061894411

LC 2010004908

"Of specific interest are chapters comparing Francis Bacon to Samuel Beckett; Kundera's devilish mixing up of Roland Barthes with the dour theologian Karl Barth in a chance conversation; several discussions on the virtues of Rabelais as well as a restoration to prominence of Anatole France, who had been given the French intellectualist bum's rush; a powerful coupling of the bright birth of film with the sad death of Fellini; a scholar's relishing of Bertolt Brecht's body odor; the music of his fellow Czech Leos Janacek. Like the proverbial meal at the Chinese restaurant, the delicious musings of this book are filling at first. Two hours later, one craves more." Publishers Weekly.

Manglik, Gauri

★**Muslims** in story : expanding multicultural understanding through children's and young adult literature / Gauri Manglik and Sadaf Siddique. ALA Editions, 2018. xvi, 248 p. : **809**

1. Islam -- United States -- Bibliography. 2. Muslims -- United States -- Bibliography. 3. Children's literature -- Bibliography. 4. Children -- Books and reading.

ISBN 9780838917411

LC 2018023567

Includes index.

One of the key causes of Islamophobia is ignorance, often fueled by negative portrayals of Muslims in media and popular culture. Counter Islamophobia through Stories is a timely and proactive approach to tackling this issue, by engendering friendships and empathy through literature. Our goal is to facilitate a systemic long term change in understanding the diversity of the Muslim experience and to build bridges of understanding and empathy. Exposing children in their formative years to positive stories about Muslims can go a long way to creating a multicultural understanding, and cementing ideas of tolerance, respect and acceptance. Books also help achieve visual diversity by showcasing different foods, dress and traditions. The proposed book will equip librarians to expose all children to Muslim children's books around different themes. -- Provided by publisher.

"This timely and essential purchase for public and school libraries humanizes Muslims and gives Muslim children authentic mirrors while creating important windows for non-Muslim readers." School Library Journal

Manguel, Alberto

The **dictionary** of imaginary places / Alberto Manguel & Gianni Guadalupi ; illustrated by Graham Greenfield ; with additional illustrations by Eric Beddows ; maps and charts by James Cook. Harcourt Brace, c2000. xvi, 755 p. : **809**

1. Geomythology 2. Imaginary places

ISBN 9780151005413

LC 99046994

"This resource contains entries for more than 1,200 imaginary places from literature and folklore. Each entry describes the place, its locale, and history and provides citations to the source work or tale. More than 220 maps and illustrations are included." Booklist.

McKee, Robert, 1941-

Dialogue : the art of verbal action for page, stage, screen / Robert McKee. Twelve, 2016. xviii, 312 p. ; **809**

1. Dialogue. 2. Playwriting. 3. Fiction -- Technique. 4. Motion picture authorship.

ISBN 9781455591916

LC 2016001679

In a much anticipated follow-up to the best-selling writers' guide Story, a leading authority on story creation and design analyzes how characters speak on the screen, on the stage and on the page, and applies a framework of incisive thinking to instruct the prospective writer on how to create artful, impactful speech.

Miller, Laura, 1960-,

Literary wonderlands : a journey through the greatest fictional worlds ever created / edited by Laura Miller. Black Dog Publishing, 2016. 319 p. : **809**

1. Imaginary places 2. Setting (Literature)

ISBN 9780316316385

LC 2017287179

Includes index.

Meticulously researched, beautifully written and visually stunning, a collection, spanning 2,000 years of creative endeavors, explores the features of fiction's imagined worlds including everything from each writer's own life to the creation of a story, influential contemporary events and philosophies and the meaning that can be extracted from the details of the work

"An encyclopedic look at literary landscapes featuring an encyclopedias breadth and lack of depth." Kirkus.

Morrison, Toni, 1931-2019

★The **origin** of others / Toni Morrison ; foreword by Ta-Nehisi Coates. Harvard University Press, 2017. 116 p. **809**

1. Racism 2. Difference (Psychology) 3. Identity (Psychology) 4. Literature -- History and criticism 5. United States -- History -- 19th century 6. Essays

ISBN 9780674976450

LC bl2017036607

What is race and why does it matter? Why does the presence of Others make us so afraid? America's foremost novelist reflects on themes that preoccupy her work and dominate politics: race, fear, borders, mass movement of peoples, desire for belonging. Ta-Nehisi Coates provides a foreword to Toni Morrison's most personal work of nonfiction to date.

"Nobel laureate Morrison, long known for her penetrating exploration of race in the U.S., continues that examination with essays derived from a lecture series at Harvard." Booklist.

Nissley, Tom, 1967-

A **reader's** book of days : true tales from the lives and works of writers for every day of the year / Tom Nissley ; illustrated by Joanna Neborsky. W.W. Norton & Co., 2013. 416 p. **809**

1. Authors 2. Writing 3. Books 4. Reading

ISBN 9780393239621

LC 2013031250

"The book itself is guaranteed to occupy plenty of pleasant hours, but Nissley's recommended reading lists are a bibliophilic bonus." Kirkus.

Poe, Edgar Allan, 1809-1849

Essays and reviews / Edgar Allan Poe. Literary Classics of the U.S., c1984. 1544 p. : The Library of America **809**

1. Literature -- History and criticism -- Theory, etc 2. Books -- Reviews

ISBN 9780940450196

LC 83019923

"G.R. Thompson wrote the notes and selected the texts for this volume"--Prelim. p.

Gathers Poe's essays on the theory of poetry, the art of fiction, the role of the critic, leading nineteenth-century writers, and the New York literary world.

Puchner, Martin, 1969-

The **written** world : the power of stories to shape people, history, civilization / Martin Puchner. Random House, 2017. 416 p. **809**

1. Literature and society. 2. Literature -- History and criticism. 3. Books and reading. 4. Literature and history

ISBN 9780812998931

LC 2017002438

Includes index.

"The story of literature in sixteen acts, from Alexander the Great and the Iliad to ebooks and Harry Potter, this engaging book brings together remarkable people and surprising events to show how writing shaped cultures, religions, and the history of the world".-- Provided by publisher.

"By providing snapshots of key moments in the written words evolution, Puchner creates a gripping intellectual odyssey." Publishers Weekly.

Pullman, Philip, 1946-

Daemon voices : on stories and storytelling / Philip Pullman. Alfred A. Knopf, 2018. 416 p. **809**

1. Pullman, Philip, 1946- Books and reading 2. Storytelling 3. Fiction -- Appreciation 4. Books and reading -- Psychological aspects 5. Authors, English 6. Essays

ISBN 9780525521174

LC 2017049677

The internationally best-selling author of the His Dark Materials trilogy shares insights into the art of writing while exploring how education, religion and science, as well as his favorite classics, helped shaped his literary life.

" A collection of pieces infused with abundant wisdom, provocative notions, and illuminating insights." Kirkus.

Roiphe, Katie

The **violet** hour : great writers at the end / Katie Roiphe. The Dial Press, 2016. 320 p. **809**

1. Authors -- Death. 2. Artists -- Death. 3. Death. 4. Writing

ISBN 9780385343596

LC 2015014085

Examining the final days of five great writers and artists--Susan Sontag, Sigmund Freud, John Updike, Dylan Thomas and Maurice Sendak--a thought-provoking volume helps readers look boldly at death and be less afraid, in a wholly original meditation on mortality.

Roth, Philip, 1933-2018

Shop talk : a writer and his colleagues and their work / Philip Roth. Houghton Mifflin, 2001. 160 p. ; **809**

1. Authors 2. Essays 3. Interviews.

ISBN 9780618153145

LC 2001024523

In a look at the work of an international cast of writers, the author explores the significance of region, history, and politics on an author's work and the ways in which the broader conditions of life influence a writer's personal art.

"In this collection of encounters with distinguished minds--unguarded interviews with Primo Levi and Aharon Appelfeld, among others; an odd exchange of letters with Mary McCarthy; fondly contentious portraits of Bernard Malamud and the painter Philip Guston--Roth manages to tease from his subjects the convictions that fuel their work and the vulnerabilities that make them human." New York Times Book Review.

Smith, Ali, 1962-

Artful / Ali Smith. Penguin Press, 2013. 237 p. **809**

1. Storytelling 2. Loss (Psychology) 3. Creativity 4. Books and reading 5. Literary fiction 6. Metafiction 7. First person narratives

ISBN 9781594204869

Originally presented as four lectures for the Weidenfeld Visiting Professorship in European comparative literature at St Anne's College, Oxford, in January and February 2012.

A meditative collection of stories on the nature of art and storytelling as they evolved through her 2012 Weidenfeld lectures on European comparative literature at St. Anne's College, Oxford, in a volume that incorporates tribute elements to iconic writers and artists throughout history.

Wilde, Oscar, 1854-1900

The **artist** as critic : critical writings of Oscar Wilde / edited by Richard Ellmann. University of Chicago Press, 1982, c1969. xxviii, 446 p. ; **809**

1. Criticism 2. Books -- Reviews

ISBN 9780226897646

LC 82013361

Reprint. Originally published: New York : Random House, [1969]

Includes index.

Presents a collection of Oscar Wilde's book reviews.

Yagoda, Ben

Memoir : a history / Ben Yagoda. Riverhead Books, 2009. 291 p. ; **809**

1. Autobiography. 2. Literature -- History and criticism 3. Writing -- History

ISBN 9781594488863

LC 2009030859

Includes index.

An analysis of the memoir as a literary art form considers the hallmark stories written by some of the western world's most famous contributors while examining the controversial nature of the fraudulent memoir and its role in shaping collective memories. By the author of The Sound on the Page.

809.1 Poetry -- history and criticism

Gioia, Dana

Can poetry matter? : essays on poetry and American culture / Dana Gioia. Graywolf Press, c2002. xviii, 231 p. ; **809.1**

1. Literature and society -- United States. 2. Poetry -- History and criticism.

ISBN 1555973701

LC 2002102971

Originally published: Saint Paul, Minn. : Graywolf Press, 1992. With new introd.

Graywolf is pleased to re-issue this highly acclaimed collection in a handsome new edition, which includes a new Introduction by distinguished critic and poet, Dana Gioia.

Koch, Kenneth, 1925-

Making your own days : the pleasures of reading and writing poetry / Kenneth Koch. Simon & Schuster, 1999, c1998. 317 p. ; **809.1**

1. Poetry -- History and criticism. 2. Poetry -- Collections.

ISBN 9780684824383

LC BL 99003985

"A Touchstone book."

Includes index.
Originally published: New York : Scribner, c1998.
Selections from the work of sixty-five poets, from Homer and Ovid to Frank O'Hara and John Ashberry, accompany a discussion of poetry, including meter, line division, rhyme, and poetic forms.

Sato, Hiroaki, 1942-
On haiku / Hiroaki Sato. New Directions Publishing Corporation, 2018. 320 p. **809.1**
1. Haiku -- History and criticism 2. Japanese poetry -- History and criticism 3. Haiku, American -- History and criticism 4. American poetry -- Japanese influences 5. Essays
ISBN 9780811227414
LC 2018021511
"I would like to thank Jeffrey Yang for patiently, meticulously, editing these essays" -- Preface, page.
A collection of essays, some previously published, some given as speeches by the first president of the American Haiku Society, and including many haiku translated from the Japanese.
"An expert illumination of a poetic form, to read and reread." Booklist.

809.2 Drama (Literature)--history and criticism

Bentley, Eric, 1916-
The **life** of the drama / Eric Bentley. Applause Theatre Books, 1991. ix, 371 p. ; **809.2**
1. Drama -- History and criticism. 2. Theater.
ISBN 1557831106
LC 91028774
Originally published: New York : Atheneum, 1964.
"Eric Bentley's radical new look at the grammar of theatre...is a work of exceptional virtue... The book justifies its title by being precisely about the ways in which life manifests itself in the theatre...This is a book to be read again and again." The New York Review of Books.

809.3 Fiction--history and criticism

Hollands, Neil
Fellowship in a ring : a guide for science fiction and fantasy book groups / Neil Hollands. Libraries Unlimited, c2010. xiv, 300 p. ; **809.3**
1. Fantasy fiction -- Appreciation -- Handbooks, manuals, etc. 2. Science fiction -- Appreciation -- Handbooks, manuals, etc. 3. Book clubs (Discussion groups) -- Handbooks, manuals, etc. 4. Group reading -- Handbooks, manuals, etc.
ISBN 9781591587033
LC 2009046456
Provides guidance on successfully running a book club devoted to science fiction and fantasy titles, offering discussion questions, book lists for themes, recommended books, and a chronology of science fiction and fantasy history.

Moore, Steven
The **novel** : an alternative history : beginnings to 1600 / Steven Moore. Continuum, 2010. vi, 698 p. ; **809.3**
1. Fiction -- History and criticism 2. Literature -- History and criticism
ISBN 9781441177049
LC 2010279268
"Reveling in the most innovative and daring creations, Moore energetically evaluates tales fantastic, chilling, hilarious, erotic, and tragic, comparing centuries-old novels to those of Barth, Gaddis, Pynchon, and Vollmann. Destined for controversy, Moore's erudite, gargantuan, kaleidoscopic, and venturesome alternative history will leave readers feeling as though they've been viewing literature with blinders on." Booklist.

Nevala-Lee, Alec
Astounding : John W. Campbell, Isaac Asimov, Robert A. Heinlein, L. Ron Hubbard, and the golden age of science fiction / Alec Nevala-Lee. Dey Street Books, 2018 320 p. **809.3**
1. Campbell, John Wood, 1910-1971 2. Asimov, Isaac, 1920-1992. 3. Heinlein, Robert A. (Robert Anson), 1907-1988. 4. Hubbard, L. Ron (La Fayette Ron), 1911-1986 5. Science fiction -- History and criticism 6. Science fiction writing. 7. Authors, American -- 20th century 8. Science fiction -- History and criticism
ISBN 9780062571946
LC 2018275384
A comprehensive account of the creative partnership shared among literary visionaries Campbell, Heinlein, Asimov and Hubbard discusses how they invented modern science fiction and indelibly transformed world culture.
"The golden age of science fiction, spanning the years 1939 to 1950, gets an authoritative examination in this fascinating appraisal of its key players. The primary focus is John W. Campbell, editor of Astounding Science Fiction magazine, and the three very different writers who served him best: Isaac Asimov, Robert A. Heinlein, and L. Ron Hubbard." Publishers Weekly.

809.7 Humor -- Criticism

Dauber, Jeremy Asher
Jewish comedy : a serious history / Jeremy Dauber. W W Norton & Company, 2017 xviii, 364 p. **809.7**
1. Jewish wit and humor 2. Jews 3. Jokes 4. Joke writing
ISBN 9780393247879
LC 2017017864
An account of Jewish humor describes its nature, its development, and its vital role in the history of the Jewish people.
"Dauber takes in a wide swath of intellectual territory--from Kafka to Mad magazine--but he delicately mixes scholarship with comedy in what is an entertaining and even profound book." Booklist.

Jennings, Ken, 1974-
Planet funny : how comedy took over our culture / Ken Jennings. Simon & Schuster 2018 336 p. **809.7**
1. Comedy -- History and criticism 2. Humor -- History and criticism 3. Comedians 4. Jokes
ISBN 9781501100581
LC bl2018063558
From the witty and exuberant New York Times best-selling author comes a history of humor?from fart jokes on clay Sumerian tablets all the way up to the latest Twitter memes--that tells the story of how comedy came to rule the modern world.

810 Literatures of specific languages and language families

Cohen, Leonard, 1934-2016
The **flame** : poems and selections from notebooks / Leonard Cohen ; edited by Robert Faggen and Alexandra Pleshoya-

no. Farrar Straus & Giroux, 2018, c2018. 275 p. : **810**

1. Singers 2. Songwriters 3. Life 4. Canadian poetry

ISBN 9780374156060

Poems.

Originally published by Penguin Random House Canada, 2018.

An eloquent valedictory collection of lyrics, poems, notebook sketches and self-portraits maps the Rock and Roll Hall of Fame inductee's singular creative journey through the weeks just prior to his death.

"Poignant and brave, lit up with flashes of anger, this is a luminous collection and classic Cohen." Booklist.

Elliott, Emory, 1942-2009

Columbia literary history of the United States / Emory Elliott, general editor ; associate editors, Martha Banta ... [et al.] ; advisory editors, Houston A. Baker ... [et al.]. Columbia University Press, 1988. xxviii, 1263 p. ; **810**

1. American literature -- History and criticism 2. United States -- Intellectual life.

ISBN 9780231058124

LC 87014672

Includes index.

This comprehensive, up-to-date survey examines the literature of the United States, from prehistoric cave narratives to the radical movements of the sixties and the experimentation of the eighties.

Eliot, T. S. (Thomas Stearns), 1888-1965

★**Complete** poems and plays. 1909-1950 / T. S. Eliot. Harcourt, Brace, 1952 vii, 392 p. **810**

1. American poetry -- 20th century

ISBN 9780151211852

LC 52011346

This omnibus collection includes all of the author's early poetry as well as the Four Quartets, Old Possum's Book of Practical Cats, and the plays Murder in the Cathedral, The Family Reunion, and The Cocktail Party.

Evans, Mari

Black women writers (1950-1980) : a critical evaluation / edited by Mari Evans. Anchor Press/Doubleday, 1984, c1983. xxviii, 543 p. ; **810**

1. American literature -- African American authors -- History and criticism 2. Women and literature -- United States -- History -- 20th century 3. American literature -- Women authors -- History and criticism 4. American literature -- 20th century -- History and criticism

ISBN 9780385171250

LC 81043914

Critical interpretations, personal reflections, and literary works highlight an anthology focusing on the lives and works of Maya Angelou, Nikki Giovanni, and others.

McKibben, Bill,

★**American** Earth : environmental writing since Thoreau / edited by Bill McKibben; foreword by Al Gore. Library of America, 2008. xxxi, 1047 p. **810**

1. Environmental movement -- United States -- History 2. Nature. 3. Overpopulation -- Environmental aspects 4. Consumerism. 5. United States -- Environmental conditions 6. United States -- History -- 19th century 7. United States -- History -- 20th century 8. United States -- History -- 21st century 9. Essays

ISBN 9781598530209

LC bl2008019508

A provocative anthology of top-selected American environmental writings from the past two centuries considers their influence on the ways in which people view the natural world.

Poe, Edgar Allan, 1809-1849

Complete poems / Edgar Allan Poe ; edited by Thomas Ollive Mabbott. University of Ill. Press, 2000 xxx, 627 p. : **810**

1. Fantasy poetry, American.

ISBN 0252069218

LC 00038639

Originally published as v. 1 of: Collected works of Edgar Allan Poe. Cambridge, Mass. : Belknap Press of Harvard University Press, 1978.

101 poems by Edgar Allan Poe, as well as uncollected poems, fragments, and other content attributed to him. Illustrated and containing context and biographical background.

"Massive and important." American Literature

Salzman, Jack

The **Cambridge** handbook of American literature / edited by Jack Salzman, with Cameron Bardrick ... [et al.]. Cambridge University Press, 1986. 286 p. ; **810**

1. American literature

ISBN 9780521307031

LC 86002587

Comprising over 750 entries in a single alphabetical sequence, the Cambridge Handbook of American Literature offers a compact and accessible guide to the major landmarks of American literature from colonial times to the present day.

"Only the most comprehensive collections will need both books; the Handbook is a fine choice for libraries not able to pay extra dollars for the [Oxford Companion to American Literature]'s greater depth of coverage." Library Journal

Samet, Elizabeth D.

★**Soldier's** heart : reading literature through peace and war at West Point / Elizabeth D. Samet. Farrar, Straus and Giroux, 2007. x, 259 p. ; **810**

1. United States Military Academy 2. Literature and morals. 3. American literature -- Study and teaching 4. English literature -- Study and teaching 5. Literature -- Study and teaching 6. West Point, New York.

ISBN 9780374180638

LC 2007009159

"Like the best professors, Samet asks tough questions and offers no easy answers. Her book is filled with lively classroom discussions and poignant e-mails from former students now in Iraq, often writing about the books they're reading there. I know of no other new book that's a better choice for any reading group that loves to debate literature and politics." USA Today.

Wall, Cheryl A.

Women of the Harlem renaissance / Cheryl A. Wall. Indiana University Press, c1995. xx, 246 p. : **810**

1. Fauset, Jessie Redmon Criticism and interpretation. 2. Hurston, Zora Neale Criticism and interpretation. 3. Larsen, Nella Criticism and interpretation. 4. African American women in literature. 5. African American women -- New York (State) -- New York -- Intellectual life. 6. African Americans in literature. 7. American literature -- African American authors -- History and criticism. 8. Harlem (New York, N.Y.) -- Intellectual life.

ISBN 0253209803

LC 95003132

"Wall offers strong critiques of these women's work, uncovering certain similarities, including, most importantly, the travel motif as not only a reflection of the mass migrations of the day but also a larger dislocation." Publishers Weekly.

Wilson, Edmund, 1895-1972

Patriotic gore : studies in the literature of the American Civil War / Edmund Wilson. W.W. Norton, 1994, c1962. xxxii, 816 p. ; **810**

1. American literature -- 19th century -- History and criticism. 2. United States -- Intellectual life -- 19th century. 3. War in literature. 4. United States -- History -- Civil War, 1861-1865 -- Literature and the war.

ISBN 0393312569

LC BL 99782173

Includes index.

Originally published: New York : Farrar, Straus and Giroux, 1962.

Critical/biographical portraits of such notable figures as Harriet Beecher Stowe, Abraham Lincoln, Ulysses S. Grant, Ambrose Bierce, Mary Chesnut, William Tecumseh Sherman, and Oliver Wendell Holmes prove Wilson to be the consummate witness to the most eloquently recorded era in American history.

810.8 American literature (English)--collections

Chametzky, Jules

Jewish American literature : a Norton anthology / compiled and edited by Jules Chametzky ... [et al.]. Norton, c2001. xxiv, 1221 p. : **810.8**

1. Jewish Americans -- Literary collections 2. Jewish way of life 3. Jewish men 4. Jewish women 5. United States -- History 6. Anthologies 7. Essays 8. Short stories

ISBN 9780393048094

LC 00055393

Collects the work of 145 writers.

Selections cover three centuries of Jewish contributing voices to American letters, including those of Arthur Miller, Tillie Olsen, Bernard Malamud, Allen Ginsberg, Cynthia Ozick, and Philip Roth.

"The editors have attempted to encompass Jewish literature from 1654 to the present in this collection of poems, cartoons, sermons, diaries, letters, stories, speeches, plays, prayers, novel excerpts, and critical writings either translated from Hebrew or Yiddish or written in English. Major sections group the literature chronologically to help identify large movements. This great anthology is essential for Jewish studies and American literature collections." Library Journal.

Edim, Glory, 1982-

★**Well-read** black girl : finding our stories, discovering ourselves / curated by Glory Edim. Ballantine Books, 2018. xxv, 239 p. : **810.8**

1. African American women authors 2. Books and reading 3. Self-discovery 4. African American women 5. Essays 6. Anthologies

ISBN 9780525619772

The founder of the popular online book club curates a collection of original essays from today's best black female voices.

"Speaking directly to black women readers, this book contains a journey from which anyone can derive enjoyment and benefit." Publishers Weekly.

Friend, David, 1955-

Bohemians, bootleggers, flappers, and swells : the best of early Vanity Fair / introduction by Graydon Carter ; edited by David Friend. The Penguin Press, 2014. 352 p. **810.8**

1. American literature -- 20th century -- History and criticism. 2. Modern literature -- 20th century -- History and criticism. 3. Essays 4. Anthologies

ISBN 9781594205989

LC 2014009783

In honor of the 100th anniversary of Vanity Fair magazine, Bohemians, Bootleggers, Flappers, and Swells celebrates the publication's astonishing early catalogue of writers, with works by Dorothy Parker, Noel Coward, P. G. Wodehouse, Jean Cocteau, Colette, Gertrude Stein, Edna St. Vincent Millay, Sherwood Anderson, Robert Benchley, Langston Hughes, and many others. Vanity Fair editor Graydon Carter introduces these fabulous pieces written between 1913 and 1936, when the magazine published a murderers' row of the world's leading literary lights.

"These delightful period pieces reflecting the social mores of their time hold up in their innovation, style, and concern about modern life nearly a century later." Booklist.

Kimball, George, 1943-2011

At the fights : American writers on boxing / edited by George Kimball & John Schulian ; foreword by Colum McCann. Library of America : c2011. xxiv, 517 p. ; **810.8**

1. Boxing 2. Boxers (Sports) 3. Boxing in literature. 4. Sports. 5. Essays 6. Anthologies.

ISBN 9781598530926

LC bl2011012734

Features literary excerpts and articles written by sportswriters and authors that celebrate one hundred years of American boxing.

"The book's editors accomplish several things in At the Fights. They sample the work of devotees such as the incomparable A.J. Liebling and Gene Tunney on his defeat of Jack Dempsey, and of comparative outsiders such as James Baldwin and Joyce Carol Oates, whose novelistic fascination with violence, class and gender inevitably led her to ponder the boxing life. The collection plots a zigzag course through a century of boxing milestones, offering a striking range of approaches to the subject. It also throws open controversies racial, moral, legal and medical that have swirled around the sport since it first attained a sort of legitimacy. [This anthology] presupposes an interest in writing as much as in boxing. Many of its contributors, such as Baldwin, Vic Ziegel, Pete Hamill, Bill Barich and Katherine Dunn, pay as much or more attention to stories tributary to fights as to the ring contests themselves. Observations in many different registers form an engrossing counterpoint as the book proceeds." San Francisco Chronicle.

Montgomery, Sy

The **best** American science and nature writing 2019 / Sy Montgomery, editor Mariner Books, 2019. 336 p. Best American science and nature writing **810.8**

1. Science. 2. Nature. 3. Science writers -- United States 4. Nature writers -- United States 5. United States -- History -- 21st century. 6. Essays.

ISBN 9781328519009

LC bl2019028222

New York Times best-selling author of How to Be a Good Creature, The Soul of an Octopus, The Good Good Pig, and more, Sy Montgomery, selects the year's top science and nature writing from writers who balance research with humanity, and, in the process, uncover riveting stories of discovery across the disciplines

Mullane, Deirdre

Crossing the danger water : three hundred years of African-

American writing / edited and with an introduction by Deirdre Mullane. Anchor Books, 1993. xxii, 769 p. ; **810.8**

1. American literature -- African American authors. 2. African Americans -- Literary collections. 3. African Americans -- History.
ISBN 9780385422437

LC 93017194

A chronological history of African-American life and thought represents a broad written and oral tradition and includes evidence of an African presence in America predating Columbus, brief historical introductions to each piece, and biographical notes.

Stavans, Ilan

The **Norton** anthology of Latino literature / Ilan Stavans, general editor ; [editors, Edna Acosta-Belen ... [et al.]]. W. W. Norton, c2011. lxxi, 2489 p. : **810.8**

1. Hispanic Americans -- Literary collections. 2. Anthologies 3. Literary fiction
ISBN 9780393080070

LC 2010015108

Maps on lining papers.

Features the work of Latino writers from Chicano, Puerto Rican, and Cuban- and Dominican-American traditions and Spanish-speaking countries, from letters to the Spanish crown by conquistadors to modern-day cartoonists.

"With a great array of writers celebrated and too little known, and invaluable supporting materials, this grand and affecting treasury of culturally rich and aesthetically dynamic poems, fiction, drama, letters, diaries, and essays illuminates every aspect of Latino life." Booklist.

810.9 American literature (English)--history and criticism

Bader, Philip, 1969-

★**African-American** writers / Philip Bader ; revised by Catherine Reef. Facts On File, c2011. xii, 340 p. : **810.9**

1. American literature -- African American authors -- Biobibliography -- Dictionaries 2. African Americans -- Intellectual life -- Dictionaries 3. African American authors -- Dictionaries 4. African Americans in literature -- Dictionaries
ISBN 9780816081417

LC 2010005463

"Otherwise, African-American Writers does a good job in serving as a general resource and is recommended for high-school, public, and undergraduate libraries." Booklist

Burroway, Janet,

A **story** larger than my own : women writers look back on their lives and careers / edited by Janet Burroway. The University of Chicago Press, 2014. vii, 199 p. ; **810.9**

1. Women authors 2. Women. 3. Gender role 4. Authors, American 5. Essays
ISBN 9780226014104

LC 2013032197

Collects essays and poems by women authors discussing their writing lives and how they achieved success despite the status quo, offering advice for aspiring writers.

"In this engrossing volume edited by [Janet] Burroway...19 accomplished female authors reflect on their careers and offer insights on craft and life. The contributors, all of whom are 60 or older, came of professional age during second wave feminism, confronted the prejudice against women writers of the 1950's and 60's, and continue to publish in the digital age. The variety of voices and styles adds up to a mesmerizing tapestry of a generation, made up of both individual experiences and the commonalities between them." Publishers Weekly.

Flora, Joseph M.

★The **companion** to southern literature : themes, genres, places, people, movements, and motifs / edited by Joseph M. Flora and Lucinda H. MacKethan ; associate editor, Todd Taylor. Louisiana State University Press, c2002. xxvi, 1054 p. ; **810.9**

1. American literature -- Southern States -- Encyclopedias. 2. Authors, American -- Homes and haunts -- Southern States -- Encyclopedias. 3. Southern States -- Intellectual life Encyclopedias. 4. Southern States -- In literature Encyclopedias.
ISBN 9780807126929

LC 2001029959

"Solidly authoritative and comprehensive, The Companion to Southern Literature spans the genres, languages, ideologies, events, culture, literary history, works, and writers that comprise the literature of the South. From incest to grits, topics are wide-ranging and eclectic. It features alphabetical and topical tables of contents and a thorough index that allows users to find important names that may lack an entry. With more than 500 entries by 200 contributors, the book contains signed essays that are critical and complete with cross-references and a brief bibliography. This companion's affordability and comprehensiveness make it a value and a prized reference work."--"The Best of the Best Reference Sources," American Libraries, May 2003.

Ginsberg, Allen, 1926-1997

Best minds of my generation : a literary history of the beats / Allen Ginsberg ; edited by Bill Morgan ; introduction by Anne Waldman. Grove Press, 2017. 496 p. **810.9**

1. Beat generation 2. Beat poets 3. Literary movements 4. Poets, American
ISBN 9780802126498

LC 2017003026

A unique and compelling history of the Beats, in the words of the movement's most central member, Allen Ginsberg, based on a seminal series of his lectures.

Hart, James David, 1911-

★The **Oxford** companion to American literature / James D. Hart ; with revisions and additions by Phillip W. Leininger. Oxford University Press, 1995. ix, 779 p. ; **810.9**

1. American literature 2. Authors, American
ISBN 9780195065480

LC 94045727

Includes index.

A completely revised edition of a standard reference work covers the movements, authors, genres, critics, awards, and many other aspects of American literature, and includes nearly two hundred new entries, many covering female and ethnic writers.

Krstovic, Jelena O.

Black literature criticism : classic and emerging authors since 1950 / Jelena O. Krstovic, project editor ; foreword by Howard Dodson. Gale Cengage Learning, 2008. 3 volumes : **810.9**

1. American literature -- African American authors -- History and criticism. 2. English literature -- Black authors -- History and criticism. 3. African Americans -- Intellectual life. 4. African Americans in literature.
ISBN 9781414431703

LC 2009290893

Presents entries for eighty African American writers, featuring for each a biography, literary interests, summaries of major works, critical commentary, and reading lists.

Laing, Olivia

The **trip** to Echo Spring : on writers and drinking / Olivia Laing. Picador, 2013 352 p. **810.9**

1. Fitzgerald, F. Scott (Francis Scott), 1896-1940 2. Hemingway, Ernest, 1899-1961. 3. Williams, Tennessee, 1911-1983 4. Berryman, John, 1914-1972. 5. Cheever, John 6. Carver, Raymond, 1938-1988 7. Alcoholic authors. 8. Addiction and creativity. 9. Alcoholism. 10. Authors.
ISBN 9781250039569

LC 2013038323

Examines the connection between creativity and alcohol by traveling to locales well-loved by six of America's greatest writers, who were also alcoholics, including John Cheever's New York, Tennessee Williams' New Orleans and Ernest Hemingway's Key West.

"Intently observant, curious, and empathetic, Laing, with shimmering detail and arresting insights, presents a beautifully elucidating and moving group portrait of writers enslaved by drink and redeemed by 'the capacity of literature to somehow...make one feel less flinchingly alone.' " Booklist.

Marcus, Greil,

A **new** literary history of America / edited by Greil Marcus and Werner Sollors. Belknap Press of Harvard University Press, 2009. xxvii, 1095 p. : **810.9**

1. American literature -- History and criticism 2. United States -- Civilization. 3. Essays
ISBN 9780674035942

LC 2009014255

A volume of more than 200 original essays traces the dynamic expression of the American experience and how the nation's evolving sense of identity can offer alternate perspectives into history, in an anthology that also explores modern cultural creations in a broad range of disciplines.

"This is an adventurous, jazzily choral, and kaleidoscopic book of interpretations, illuminations, and revitalized history." Booklist.

Matthiessen, F. O. (Francis Otto), 1902-1950

★**American** renaissance : art and expression in the age of Emerson and Whitman / F. O. Matthiessen. Oxford University Press, 1968. xxiv, 678 p. **810.9**

1. Emerson, Ralph Waldo, 1803-1882 Knowledge United States. 2. Whitman, Walt, 1819-1892 Knowledge United States. 3. American literature -- 19th century -- History and criticism 4. United States -- Intellectual life -- 1783-1865.
ISBN 9780195007596

LC 68105842

Studies the views of 5 prominent mid-19th century writers on the function and nature of literature and how they applied these views to their works.

McClinton-Temple, Jennifer

Encyclopedia of American Indian literature / [edited by] Jennifer McClinton-Temple, Alan Velie. Facts on File, c2007. xii, 466 p. ; **810.9**

1. American literature -- Indian authors -- Encyclopedias. 2. Indians in literature -- Encyclopedias. 3. Indians of North America -- Intellectual life -- Encyclopedias.
ISBN 9780816056569

LC 2006023762

Presents alphabetical entries that cover major Native American works of literature; important Native American writers; and terms, themes, genres, and movements related to Native American literature.

Morgan, Bill, 1949-

The **typewriter** is holy : the complete, uncensored history of the Beat generation / Bill Morgan. Free Press, 2010. 352 p. **810.9**

1. Authors, American -- 20th century 2. Beat culture 3. American literature -- 20th century -- History and criticism. 4. Subcultures. 5. United States -- Social life and customs -- 20th century.
ISBN 9781416592426

LC 2009042224

A narrative account chronicles the lives of key contributors while offering insight into their lasting influence, featuring coverage of the stories surrounding such publications as Allen Ginsberg's Howl and Other Poems and Jack Kerouac's On the Road.

Morrison, Toni, 1931-2019

Playing in the dark : whiteness and the literary imagination / Toni Morrison. Harvard University Press, 1992. xiii, 91 p. ; **810.9**

1. Race relations 2. African Americans in literature. 3. Human skin color. 4. Race (Social sciences) 5. Essays.
ISBN 0674673778

LC 91039671

Examines the effect of a racially divided society on ninteenth century American writings, and discusses works by Poe, Hawthorne, Melville, and Twain.

"Novelist Morrison takes a turn as a literary critic, examining the American literary imagination and finding it obsessed with the white/black polarity." Publishers Weekly

Ostrom, Hans A.,

African American literature : an encyclopedia for students / Hans A. Ostrom and J. David Macey, editors. Greenwood, [2020] xxiv, 429 p. ; **810.9**

1. American literature -- African American authors -- Encyclopedias.
ISBN 9781440871504

LC 2019029439

"This essential volume provides an overview of and introduction to African American writers and literary periods, from the beginning of the 20th century into the 21st century".-- Provided by publisher.

"Entries on horror and children's fiction sit side by side with entries on postmodernism and lyric poetry; rap and hip-hop have their own entries, as do spirituals and performance poetry. . . . Highly recommended for high school and undergraduate libraries." Booklist

Parini, Jay

Promised land : thirteen books that changed America / Jay Parini. Doubleday, 2008. 400 p. **810.9**

1. American literature -- History and criticism 2. National characteristics, American, in literature. 3. Literature -- Moral and ethical aspects. 4. Literature and society -- United States -- History. 5. United States -- Historiography.
ISBN 9780385522762

LC 2008009990

Includes index.

An analysis of the thirteen books that changed America.

"This is a mind-expanding book of books guaranteed to provoke discussion and fuel reading groups." Booklist.

Pierpont, Claudia Roth

Passionate minds : women rewriting the world / Claudia Roth Pierpont. Knopf, 2000. xiii, 298 p. : **810.9**

1. Women and literature. 2. American literature -- 20th century -- History and criticism 3. English literature -- 20th century -- History and criticism 4. Authors, American -- 20th century 5. Essays.
ISBN 0679431063

LC 99033349

Includes index.

"A scintillating collection of brief lives of women writers, a book that sparkles with intelligence, wit and human interest. Unfolding with the dramatic elan of a novella, each one is exhaustively researched, sharply focused, convincingly opinionated." New York Times Book Review.

Porter, Joy, 1967-

The **Cambridge** companion to Native American literature / edited by Joy Porter and Kenneth M. Roemer. Cambridge University Press, 2005. xviii, 343 p. : **810.9**

1. American literature -- Indian authors -- History and criticism. 2. Indians of North America -- Intellectual life. 3. Indians in literature.
ISBN 9780521529792

LC 2005044298

Collects information on literature by Native Americans from the 1770s to the present day.

Roberts, Kim, 1961-

A **literary** guide to Washington, DC : walking in the footsteps of American writers from Francis Scott Key to Zora Neale Hurston / Kim Roberts. University of Virginia Press, 2018. x, 228 p. : **810.9**

1. American literature Bio-bibliography. -- Washington (D.C.). 2. Authors, American -- Homes and haunts -- Washington (D.C.) 3. Literary landmarks -- Washington (D.C.) 4. Washington (D.C.) -- Intellectual life. 5. Washington (D.C.) Guidebooks. 6. Guidebooks.
ISBN 0813941164

LC 2017059448

"The perfect accompaniment for a literature-inspired vacation in the U.S. capital. The compact size, clearly labeled maps, and succinct, informative text make this a handy guide to slip into your suitcase." Library Journal

Shields, David, 1956-

The **inevitable** : contemporary writers confront death / edited by David Shields and Bradford Morrow ; with an introduction by the editors. W. W. Norton & Co., 2011. 320 p. **810.9**

1. Authors, American -- 20th century -- Psychology. 2. Death -- Psychological aspects. 3. Fear of death. 4. Essays.
ISBN 9780393339369

LC 2010043479

"Often poetic and at times funny or gruesome while exposing raw grief, the writers...tackle the subject of death with honesty and courage." Publishers Weekly.

Showalter, Elaine,

★A **jury** of her peers : American women writers from Anne Bradstreet to Annie Proulx / Elaine Showalter. Alfred A. Knopf, 2009. 608 p. **810.9**

1. Women authors, American -- Criticism and interpretation 2. Women and literature -- United States -- History. 3. Intellectual life -- Women. 4. Women in literature.
ISBN 9781400041237

LC 2008042312

A comprehensive history of American women writers explores the contributions of more than 250 female authors--both famous and little-known--to every field of literary endeavor and reflects on their role in the evolution of our American literary heritage.

811 American poetry

Abdurraqib, Hanif, 1983-

★A **fortune** for your disaster / Hanif Abdurraqib. Tin House Books, 2019. 120 p. **811**

1. Violence 2. Racism 3. African Americans 4. Interpersonal relations
ISBN 9781947793439

LC 2019013318

In this follow-up to The Crown Ain't Worth Much, a poet, essayist, biographer and music critic presents a poetry collection about how one rebuilds oneself after heartbreak.

"This resonant second collection from cultural critic, essayist, and poet Abdurraqib grapples with physical and emotional acts of violence and their political context." Booklist

Addonizio, Kim, 1954-

Mortal trash : poems / Kim Addonizio. W. W. Norton & Company, 2016. 107 p. ; **811**

1. American poetry
ISBN 9780393249163

LC 2016008753

Explores the author's perspectives on contemporary situations of love, loss, and violence, through free verse and sonnets.

Akbar, Kaveh

Calling a wolf a wolf : poems / Kaveh Akbar. Alice James Books, 2017 89 p. ; **811**

1. Alcoholism 2. Alcoholics -- Rehabilitation 3. American poetry
ISBN 9781938584671

LC 2017015979

Poems confront craving, control, the constant battle of alcoholism and sobriety, and the questioning of the self and its instincts within the context of this never-ending fight. --From publisher description.

Alexander, Elizabeth, 1962-

Crave radiance : new and selected poems, 1990-2010 / Elizabeth Alexander. Graywolf Press, c2010. 255 p. ; **811**

1. African American poetry 2. American poetry
ISBN 9781555975685

LC bl2010033551

Features a collection of previously published poetry from the author along with some new material, including "Praise Song for the Day," which the author read during President Obama's inauguration.

Alvarez, Julia

The **woman** I kept to myself : poems / Julia Alvarez. Algonquin Books of Chapel Hill, 2004. 155 p. ; **811**

1. Dominican American women 2. Sisters 3. Women
ISBN 1565124065

LC 2003070807

"This collection of 75 poems is divided into three sections, and each poem has three stanzas, exactly . . . The poet, who is from the Dominican Republic, writes about being raised with her sisters in New York. The subjects are personal--love, marriage, rejection, divorce, death, religion--but also universal." School Library Journal.

American journal : fifty poems for our time / selected and with an introduction by Tracy K. Smith. Graywolf Press, in association with the Library of Congress, 2018 120 p. ; **811**

1. American poetry -- 21st century.
ISBN 9781555978389

LC 2018934514

Presents a poetry anthology that explores and celebrates the United States.

Ammons, A. R., 1926-2001

★The **complete** poems of A. R. Ammons. edited by Robert M. West ; introduction by Helen Vendler. W.W. Norton & Company, 2017 xlvii, 1102 p. ; **811**

1. American poetry -- 20th century
ISBN 9780393070132

LC bl2017051008

Collects the author's poems from 1955 to 1977, including his three book-length poems from that period.

★The **complete** poems of A. R. Ammons. edited by Robert M. West ; introduction by Helen Vendler. W.W. Norton & Company, 2017 liii, 1031 p. ; **811**

1. American poetry -- 20th century
ISBN 9780393254891

LC 2017047332

Collects the author's poems from 1978 on, including over one hundred and twenty previously uncollected poems dating from the 1950s to the late 1990s in two appendices, addressing such topics as loss, mortality, and the natural world.

Angelou, Maya

★The **complete** collected poems of Maya Angelou. / Maya Angelou. Random House, c1994. xiv, 273 p. ; **811**

1. American poetry 2. African American poetry
ISBN 9780679428954

LC 94014501

Presents a definitive collection of poetry from Angelou's previous anthologies

Armantrout, Rae, 1947-

Versed / Rae Armantrout. Wesleyan University Press, c2009. ix, 121 p. ; **811**

1. American poetry
ISBN 9780819568793

LC 2008043809

Provides an expanded view of the arc of the author's writing, collecting poems dealing with the perversity of human consciousness and the confrontation of the invisible experienced during the author's bout with cancer.

Wobble / Rae Armantrout. Wesleyan University Press, 2018. 128 p. **811**

1. Language and languages 2. Communication 3. Consciousness 4. Technology
ISBN 9780819578235

LC 2018002974

"This volume is marked by wry humor and striking self-awareness when considering writerly craft." Publishers Weekly.

Asghar, Fatimah

If they come for us : poems / Fatimah Asghar. One World, 2018 x, 106 p. **811**

1. American poetry -- 21st century
ISBN 9780525509783

LC 2019296383

ALA Notable Book, 2019.

In a debut poetry collection, the co-creator of the Emmy-nominated web series Brown Girls openly shares her experiences of being a young Pakistani Muslim woman in America by weaving together personal and marginalized people's histories.

Ashbery, John, 1927-2017

Commotion of the birds : new poems / John Ashbery. Ecco, 2016 100 p. ; **811**

1. American poetry
ISBN 9780062565099

LC 2017275703

"A crackling, moving new collection from one of America's greatest living poets. In over twenty-six original books, the poems of John Ashbery have long served as signposts guiding us through the delights, woes, hypocrisies, and uncertainties of living in the modern world. With language harvested from everyday speech, fragments of pop culture, objects and figures borrowed from art and literature, his work makes light out of darkness, playing with tone and style to show how even the seemingly frivolous stuff of existence can be employed to express the deepest levels of feeling. Commotion of the Birds showcases once again Ashbery's mastery of a staggering range of voices and his singular lyric agility: wry, frank, contemplative, resigned, bemused, and ecstatic. The poet in this new collection is at once removed from and immersed in the terrain of his examination. Disarmingly conversational, he invites the reader to join him in looking out onto the future with humor, curiosity, and insight. The lines of these poems achieve a low-humming, thrilling point of vibration, a jostling of feathers before flight."--Amazon.com

John Ashbery : collected poems, 1956-1987 / John Ashbery. Library of America, c2008. xx, 1042 p. : **811**

1. American poetry -- 20th century
ISBN 9781598530285

LC bl2008033577

Includes index.

A definitive volume of works by the preeminent American poet includes "Some Trees," as well as the complete texts of such collections as "Rivers and Mountains," "Self-Portrait in a Convex Mirror," and "Houseboat Days."

Notes from the air : selected later poems / John Ashbery. Ecco, c2007. xv, 364 p. ; **811**

1. American poetry
ISBN 9780061367175

LC 2008270813

Includes indexes.

A selection of key works from ten major collections by the influential American poet as written throughout the past two decades includes pieces from the critically acclaimed "April Galleons" and "Flow Chart," as well as the 2005 National Book Award finalist "Where Shall I Wander."

Selected poems / John Ashbery. Penguin Books, 1986,

c1985. 349 p. ; **811**

1. American poetry -- 20th century
ISBN 9780140585537

LC 86009521

"Elisabeth Sifton books."

Includes index.

A collection of works by the Pulitzer Prize-winning poet that includes "Some Trees," "The Tennis Court Oath," "The Double Dream of Spring," "Self Portrait in a Convex Mirror," and "A Wave".

Auden, W. H. (Wystan Hugh), 1907-1973

Collected poems / W.H. Auden ; edited by Edward Mendelson. Modern Library, 2007. xxxi, 928 p. ; **811**

1. British poetry -- 20th century
ISBN 9780679643500

LC 2006047163

Includes indexes.

In honor of the centennial of the poet's birth, a definitive anthology of works collects all of the poems Auden wished to preserve, in the versions he approved as final, providing the full range of the great poet's work between 1930 and 1974.

Austin, Derrick, 1989-

Trouble the water : poems / Derrick Austin ; foreword by Mary Szybist. BOA Editions Ltd., 2016. 96 p. ; **811**

1. African American poetry 2. American poetry 3. Religious poetry
ISBN 9781942683049

LC 2015046377

"Rich in religious and artistic imagery, Trouble the Water is an intriguing exploration of race, sexuality, and identity, particularly where self-hood is in constant flux. These intimate, sensual poems interweave pop culture and history--moving from the Bible through several artistic eras--to interrogate what it means to be, as Austin says, fully human as a "queer, black body" in 21st century America".-- Provided by publisher.

Baca, Jimmy Santiago, 1952-

Selected poems : = Poemas Selectos / Jimmy Santiago Baca. New Directions, 2009 285 p. **811**

1. American poetry 2. Bilingual materials English/Spanish
ISBN 9780811218160

LC 2009015089

The best of the award-winning Chicano poet is available for the first time in a completely bilingual edition, in a book with poems that draw on the author's experiences as a father and a prisoner and on the lush, and sometimes stark, landscape of the Rio Grande valley.

Spring poems along the Rio Grande / Jimmy Santiago Baca. New Directions Pub., 2007. 75 p. ; New Directions paperbook ; **811**

1. Poetry of places 2. Spring 3. Rio Grande Valley 4. Rio Grande
ISBN 9780811216852

LC 2006101678

Includes index.

A follow-up to Winter Poems Along the Rio Grande continues the poet's daily pilgrimages through the meadows, riverbanks, and bosques of the Rio Grande, where he finds reflections of his visions of love and loss, poverty and renewal, and redemption and war.

"The Rio Grande, as both setting and symbol of freedom and life, meanders through the poems, evoking a natural progression of time and the natural ebb and flow of feelings such as love, hope, and connection. The bosque along the river is home to birds both resident and migratory, trees, fish, bushes, insects, and encroaching urban life represented by power lines and interstate traffic noise. Jogging here, Baca evinces a love of his hometown of Albuquerque but, even more, reveals his well of poetic inspiration: Chicano, Catholic religiosity, Native American symbolism, and universal milestones. With its highly accessible language and thoughtful reflections on the natural world, readers will find Baca's poetry extremely inviting." Booklist.

Bang, Mary Jo

The **bride** of E : poems / Mary Jo Bang. Graywolf Press, c2009. 90 p. ; **811**

1. American poetry
ISBN 9781555975395

LC 2009926850

Presents one or more poems for every letter of the alphabet that deal with human existential problems.

A **doll** for throwing : poems / Mary Jo Bang. Graywolf Press, 2017. 76 p. : **811**

1. American poetry
ISBN 9781555977818

LC 2016951417

The author's eighth poetry collection explores the concepts of nostalgia, xenophobia, misogyny, and political extremism through the voice of a person who was once part of the German Bauhaus school, only to see it shuttered by the Nazis.

"With rich metaphors and abundant irony, these difficult prose poems serve as a portrait of the artist as a young woman whose work and reputation were stolen." Library Journal

Elegy : poems / Mary Jo Bang. Graywolf Press, 2007. 92 p. ; **811**

1. Elegiac poetry 2. American poetry
ISBN 9781555974831

LC 2007924768

Provides a collection of poems examining grief and loss of an adult child.

Barot, Rick, 1969-

The **galleons** : poems / Rick Barot. Milkweed Editions, 2020. 71 p. ; **811**

1. Identity (Psychology) 2. Postcolonialism 3. Immigrants
ISBN 9781571315236

LC 2019022928

For almost twenty years, Rick Barot has been writing some of the most stunningly crafted lyric poems in America, paying careful, Rilkean attention to the layered world that surrounds us. In The Galleons, he widens his scope, contextualizing the immigrant journey of his Filipino-American parents in the larger history and aftermath of colonialism.

"Important reading, especially for those interested in the issues of colonialism and immigration." Library Journal

Benfey, Christopher E. G., 1954-

A **summer** of hummingbirds : love, art, and scandal in the intersecting worlds of Emily Dickinson, Mark Twain, Harriet Beecher Stowe, and Martin Johnson Heade / Christopher Benfey. Penguin Press, 2008. xv, 287 p. : **811**

1. Dickinson, Emily, 1830-1886 Criticism and interpretation 2. Twain, Mark, 1835-1910 Criticism and interpretation 3. Stowe, Harriet Beecher, 1811-1896 Criticism and interpretation 4. Heade, Martin Johnson, 1819-1904 Criticism and interpretation. 5. Women and literature -- United States -- History -- 19th century. 6. Literature and society -- United States -- History -- 19th century. 7. Literature

and history -- United States -- History -- 19th century. 8. Florida in art. 9. United States -- History -- 1865-1898.
ISBN 9781594201608

"Benfey's subtitle neatly conveys the fascinating and sometimes tortuous complexities of this literary/historical snapshot of post-Civil War America. Benfey finds a common connection among these diverse characters through, improbably, hummingbirds, an intense interest in which seems to have taken hold of artists and writers throughout the late nineteenth century. Benfey's eclectic and original approach brings this period and these personalities vividly to life. He presents sensitive critiques of literature and art alongside tales of illicit love and broken, bent, or triumphant lives, all of which makes for compelling reading for specialist and nonspecialist alike." Booklist.

Berkson, Bill

★**Portrait** and dream : new and selected poems / Bill Berkson. Coffee House Press, 2009. 314 p. ; **811**

1. American poetry
ISBN 9781566892292

LC 2008052607

This collection spans nearly fifty years of Bill Berkson's poetry.

Bernstein, Charles, 1950-

All the whiskey in heaven : selected poems / Charles Bernstein. Farrar Straus Giroux, 2010. 300 p. ; **811**

1. American poetry
ISBN 9780374103446

LC 2009010187

Collects the poet's best work from the past 30 years--in which, through a series of poems of varied forms, he explores how language both limits and liberates thought.

Berry, Wendell, 1934-

New collected poems / Wendell Berry. Counterpoint, 2012. xvii, 391 p. ; **811**

1. American poetry
ISBN 9781582438153

LC 2016296610

Includes index.

This volume reprints the nearly two hundred pieces from his earlier Collected Poems, together with the poems from his most recent collections: Entries, Given, and Leavings, to create an expanded compilation. It contains all the poems from previous collections Mr. Berry wishes to collect, except no selections have been made from his ongoing sequence published as The Sabbath Poems.

A **timbered** choir : the sabbath poems, 1979-1997 / Wendell Berry. Counterpoint, c1998. xviii, 216 p. ; **811**

1. Nature 2. American poetry
ISBN 9781887178686

LC 98004925

A collection of poems written outdoors on Sunday mornings over a span of more than two decades explores the beauty and spirituality of the natural world.

"Berry has continued periodically to write poems out-of-doors on days of little other work. This book reprints Sabbaths, a collection of that writing, adding to it about one and a half times as much new work. Few other poets have such chaste and precise diction or manage line and stanza with such unaffected serenity." Booklist.

Berryman, John, 1914-1972

Collected poems, 1937-1971 / John Berryman ; edited and introduced by Charles Thornbury. Noonday Press, 1991, c1989. lxvii, 347 p. ; **811**

1. American poetry
ISBN 9780374522810

LC BL 99718107

Includes index.

Originally published: New York : Farrar Straus Giroux, c1989.

Presents Berryman's seven collections of short poems and offers a brief overview of his life, his career, and his poetics.

Berssenbrugge, Mei-mei, 1947-

A **treatise** on stars / Mei-mei Berssenbrugge. New Directions Books, 2020. 96 p. **811**

1. Poetry of places
ISBN 9780811229388

LC 2019047008

"A New Directions book."

"Mei-mei Berssenbrugge's A Treatise on Stars extends the intensely phenomenological poetics of 'The Star Field' in Empathy, which appeared over thirty years ago. The book is structured as a continuous enfolding of poems, each made up of numbered serial parts, their presiding poetic consciousness moving from the desert arroyo of New Mexico to the white-tailed deer of Maine and between conversations with daughter, husband, friends, pets (corn snake and poodle), and a woman, or star-visitor, beneath a tree who calls 'any spirit in matter ... star-walking.' These are poems of deep listening and patient waiting, open to the channeling of daily experience, to gestalt and angel, dolphins and extraterrestrials. Here, family is a type of constellation and 'thought is a form of organized light.' All our senses are activated by Berssenbrugge's light absorbing lines, lines that map a geography of interconnected intelligence--interdimensional intelligence--that exists in all sentient objects and sustains us. This is not new age poetry but poetry for a new age, rigorous of thought and grounded in the physical world where 'days fill with splendor, and earth offers its pristine beauty to an expanding present.'"-- Provided by publisher.

"Lovers of the constellations and abstraction, however, will find themselves at home in the lyrical language." Publishers Weekly

Bidart, Frank, 1939-

★**Half-light** : collected poems 1965-2016 / Frank Bidart. Farrar Straus Giroux, 2017. 718 p. ; **811**

1. American poetry
ISBN 9780374125950

LC 2015038552

The collected poems of the award winning American poet Frank Bidart.

"This collected poems is an almost overwhelming bounty, a permanent book." Publishers Weekly

Star dust / Frank Bidart. Farrar, Straus and Giroux, c2005. 84 p. ; **811**

1. American poetry
ISBN 9780374269739

LC 2004056293

A collection of poems illuminates the drive to create, not as reverie, pleasure, or afterthought, but as a task and a burden.

Watching the spring festival / Frank Bidart. Farrar, Straus and Giroux, 2008. vi, 61 p. ; **811**

1. American poetry
ISBN 9780374286033

LC 2007040513

A first collection of lyrics by the Bollingen Prize-winning author evaluates the role of imminent mortality in forcing the self to question the relation between actual life and the promise of transformation, in a volume that explores such subjects as Marilyn Monroe, the ballet Giselle, and the nature of tragedy.

Bishop, Elizabeth, 1911-1979
Edgar Allan Poe & the juke-box : uncollected poems, drafts, and fragments / Elizabeth Bishop ; edited and annotated by Alice Quinn. Farrar, Straus, and Giroux, 2006. xx, 367 p. : **811**
1. American poetry -- 20th century
ISBN 9780374146450
LC 2005011511

A collection of unpublished drafts and partial works by the author includes pieces that were started in her early adulthood about her love for Elizabethan verse and surrealist technique, dream fragments from the 1940s, and poems about her Canadian childhood.

Bitsui, Sherwin, 1975-
Dissolve / Sherwin Bitsui. Copper Canyon Press, [2019] vii, 67 p. ; **811**
1. Navajo Indians 2. Native American men. 3. Language and languages. 4. Identity (Psychology) 5. Southwest (United States) 6. Canadian poetry.
ISBN 9781556595455
LC 2018016188

Drawing upon Navajo traditions and language, Sherwin Bitsui composes a brutal and catastrophic passage through the American Southwest.

Blackburn, Paul
The **collected** poems of Paul Blackburn / edited, with an introduction, by Edith Jarolim. Persea Books, c1985. xxxv, 687 p. : **811**
1. American poetry
ISBN 9780892550869
LC 85009309

Includes index.

"Paul Blackburn wrote over 1200 poems, and Jarolim has rescued 523 of them, working mainly with out-of-print editions." Library Journal

Blount, Tommye
Fantasia for the man in blue / Tommye Blount. Four Way Books, 2020. 139 p. **811**
1. American poetry
ISBN 9781945588495
LC 2019031755

"An examination of a brutal America through the voices of its most vulnerable sons. In his debut collection, Fantasia for the Man in Blue, Tommye Blount orchestrates a chorus of distinct, unforgettable voices that speak to the experience of the black, queer body as a site of desire and violence. A black man's late-night encounter with a police officer--the titular "man in blue"--becomes an extended meditation on a dangerous, erotic fantasy. The late Luther Vandross, resurrected here in a suite of poems, addresses the contradiction between his public persona and a life spent largely in the closet: "It's a calling, this hunger / to sing for a love I'm too ashamed to want for myself." In "Aaron McKinney Cleans His Magnum," the convicted killer imagines the barrel of the gun he used to bludgeon Matthew Shepherd as an "infant's small mouth" as well as the "sad calculator" that was "built to subtract from and divide a town." In these and other poems, Blount viscerally captures the experience of the "other" and locates us squarely within these personae." Provided by publisher.

"A captivating, unrelenting collection of poetry composed of sharp-edged truths and beautiful complexities." Booklist

Bly, Robert
Collected poems / Robert Bly. W. W. Norton & Company, [2018] 528 p. **811**
1. Transcendentalism. 2. Mysticism. 3. Imagery (Psychology) 4. Intellectual life.
ISBN 9780393652444
LC 2018028547

Includes index.

An extraordinary culmination for Robert Bly's lifelong intellectual adventure, Collected Poems presents the full magnitude of his body of work for the first time. Influenced by Emerson and Thoreau alongside spiritual traditions from Sufism to Gnosticism, he is a poet moved by mysteries, speaking the language of images.

Eating the honey of words : new and selected poems / Robert Bly. HarperFlamingo, 1999. xvi, 270 p. ; **811**
1. American poetry -- 20th century
ISBN 0060175621
LC 98051152

"This volume is an appealing poetic sampler, although the ten new poems are unexciting. The poems celebrating discoveries Bly makes when alone and silent are always striking, and his imaginative prose poems radiate witty delight." Library Journal.

The **night** Abraham called to the stars : poems / Robert Bly. HarperCollins, 2001. 95 p. **811**
1. American poetry.
ISBN 9780060188818
LC 00066360

The author of Iron John returns with a poetic homage to Islamic poetry, offering a collection of poems inspired by the "ghazal" verse form popularized by Rumi and other Muslim writers.

Booth, Philip, 1925-2007
Selves : new poems / Philip Booth. Penguin Books, 1991. x, 75 p. ; **811**
1. American poetry
ISBN 9780140586466
LC 90007683

Illuminates the poet's visions of courage and sadness in the search for the meaning of human frailty.

Boruch, Marianne, 1950-
Eventually one dreams the real thing / Marianne Boruch. Copper Canyon Press, 2016 127 p. ; **811**
1. American poetry 2. Poetry of places
ISBN 9781556594915
LC 2015032450

Marianne Boruch's generous and gathering mind wanders through her poems -- taking in, then turning around, a curious world.

"In her meditative new collection, Boruch (Cadaver, Speak) writes at once with and against the cascade of information and fevered, restless attention that mark contemporary daily life." Publishers Weekly

Borzutzky, Daniel
Lake Michigan / Daniel Borzutzky. University of Pittsburgh

Press, 2018 81 p. ; **811**
1. Prisons 2. American poetry 3. Chicago (Ill.)
ISBN 9780822965220
LC bl2018187827

An imagined prison camp located on the beaches of Chicago is explored through nineteen lyrical poems that show the ways in which economic policy, racism, and militarized policing combine to shape the city.

The **performance** of becoming human / Daniel Borzutzky. Brooklyn Arts Press, 2016 89 p. ; **811**
1. American poetry
ISBN 9781936767465
LC 2015028529

The bay of Valparaiso merges into the western shore of Lake Michigan, where Borzutzky continues his poetic investigation into the political and economic violence shared by Chicago and Chile, two places integral to his personal formation. --From publisher description.

"This is one of contemporary poetry's most cogent documents of humanity and suffering in the 21st century, one born out of an impossible but necessary struggle to reconcile existence with destruction, excess with deprivation, and alienation with proximity." Publishers Weekly.

Boss, Todd

Tough luck : poems / Todd Boss. W. W. Norton & Company, 2017. xii, 100 p. ; **811**
1. American poetry
ISBN 9780393608625
LC 2016058733

"Readers may be drawn into this collection for the poems that touch on disaster and divorce, but they'll stay for the memorable verses on nature and memory." Library Journal.

Bowers, Edgar

Collected poems / Edgar Bowers. Knopf, 1999, c1997. ix, 168 p. ; **811**
1. American poetry
ISBN 9780679766070
LC BL 99001753

Reflecting some forty years of literary work, this poetry compilation encompasses both previously published works and new material.

Brock-Broido, Lucie

Stay, illusion / Lucie Brock-Broido. Alfred A. Knopf, 2013. viii, 100 p. ; **811**
1. American poetry
ISBN 9780307962027
LC 2013023978

Presents a collection of poems which explore imagination, myth, violence, the treament of animals, and the death penalty in America.

Bronk, William

Selected poems / William Bronk ; selected by Henry Weinfield. New Directions Pub., 1995. xii, 80 p. ; **811**
1. American poetry
ISBN 9780811213141
LC 95000290

Selected Poems is an indispensable collection, containing the most compelling and the most popular of Bronk's eloquent poems.

Brooks, Gwendolyn, 1917-2000

★The **essential** Gwendolyn Brooks : selected poems / Gwendolyn Brooks, Elizabeth Alexander, editor. Library of America, 2005. xxvi, 148 p. : American poets project ; **811**
1. American poetry 2. African American poetry
ISBN 9781931082877
LC 2005044162

A selection of the influential African-American poet's works reflects her modernist style and includes numerous definitive World War II poems as well as pieces about the social and political upheavals of the 1960s.

In Montgomery, and other poems / Gwendolyn Brooks. Third World Press, c2003. ix, 147 p. ; **811**
1. African Americans 2. African American poetry 3. American poetry
ISBN 9780883782323
LC 2003050749

Presents a collection of poems that provide monologues of a variety of voices, including urban children, Winnie Mandela, and Alabama civil rights workers.

Brown, Jericho

★The **tradition** / Jericho Brown. Copper Canyon Press, [2019] xiii, 77 p. **811**
1. Race (Social sciences) 2. Violence 3. Vulnerability 4. Anger
ISBN 9781556594861
LC 2018048965

ALA Notable Book, 2020.

The Tradition details the normalization of evil and its history at the intersection of the past and the personal. Brown's poetic concerns are both broad and intimate, and at their very core a distillation of the incredibly human: What is safety? Who is this nation? Where does freedom truly lie? Brown makes mythical pastorals to question the terrors to which we've become accustomed, and to celebrate how we survive. Poems of fatherhood, legacy, blackness, queerness, worship, and trauma are propelled into stunning clarity by Brown's mastery, and his invention of the duplex--a combination of the sonnet, the ghazal, and the blues--is testament to his formal skill.

"Brown's third collection (after The New Testament) pulsates with the acute anxieties of racial and sexual difference, the psychologically complex intersections of personal intimacy with social responsibility." Library Journal.

Budbill, David

Happy life / David Budbill. Copper Canyon Press, c2011. xii, 119 p. ; **811**
1. American poetry
ISBN 9781556593741
LC 2011010988

A favorite of Garrison Keillor, David Budbill continues his popular ruminations on a "chop wood, carry water" life in Vermont.

Burrows, Mark S., 1955-

The **Paraclete** poetry anthology, 2005-2016 : selected and new poems / edited and introduced by Mark S. Burrows ; foreword by Jon M. Sweeney. Paraclete Press, 2016. xxvii, 188 p. ; **811**
1. Christian poetry 2. Religious poetry
ISBN 9781612619064
LC 2016041812

"The range of poetic expression here encompasses spiritual journaling, prayer, legends and biography, visionary and ordinary mysticism, nature contemplation, and, of course, prayer as well as both formally relaxed and formally precise individual poems." Booklist.

Burt, Stephanie, 1971-

Don't read poetry : a book about how to read poems / Stephanie Burt. Basic Books, 2019. ix, 306 p. **811**

1. American poetry -- History and criticism 2. English poetry -- History and criticism 3. Poetry -- Appreciation 4. Poetry -- Explication

ISBN 9780465094509

LC 2018054504

Includes index.

"Award-winning poet and literary critic Stephanie Burt offers an accessible introduction to the seemingly daunting task of reading, understanding, and appreciating poetry. Burt dispels preconceptions about poetry and explains how poems speak to one another--and how they can speak to our lives. She shows readers how to find more poems once they have some poems they like, and how to connect the poetry of the past to the poetry of the present. Burt moves seamlessly from Shakespeare and other classics to the contemporary poetry circulated on Tumblr and Twitter. She challenges the assumptions that many of us make about "poetry," whether we think we like it or think we don't, in order to help us cherish--and distinguish among--individual poems."-- Provided by publisher.

"Burt's sweeping, insightful survey makes a great case that with wider exposure, people will discover how poems can be relevant to anyone who has 'ever felt unique, or confused, or confusing to others.'." Publishers Weekly.

Carruth, Hayden, 1921-2008

★**Toward** the distant islands : new & selected poems / Hayden Carruth ; edited and with an introduction by Sam Hamill. Copper Canyon Press, 2006. 150 p. **811**

1. Poetry of places -- New England.

ISBN 1556592361

LC 2005028705

Collects 79 poems.

"Carruth's books encompass Frostian tales of farm life with New England eccentrics, compilations of haiku, long and unguarded poems of erotic devotion, autobiographical laments, and sensitive odes to jazz greats. All sides of Carruth's oeuvre find a place in this welcome volume. The selection here gives just enough of everything Carruth has learned, and he has learned a lot, especially about the ways and landscapes of New England." Publishers Weekly.

Carson, Anne, 1950-

Autobiography of Red : a novel in verse / Anne Carson. A. A. Knopf, 1998. 149 p. **811**

1. Love triangles 2. Crushes (Interpersonal relations) 3. Red (Color) 4. Hercules (Roman mythology) 5. Novels in verse

ISBN 9780375401336

An award-winning poet bridges the gap between modernity and classism, prose and poetry, with an evocative journey into the soul of a winged red monster named Geryon, who retreats into the world of photography after losing a male lover.

Red doc> / Anne Carson. Alfred A. Knopf, 2013. 167 p. ; **811**

1. Stesichorus. Gryonis Adaptations. 2. Epic poetry, Greek -- Adaptations. 3. Monsters 4. Canadian poetry 5. Epic poetry

ISBN 9780307960580

LC 2012032322

"This is a Borzoi book."

G navigates the complex labyrinths of the modern age at the side of his war veteran lover Sad and the artist Ida while attending the death of his mother and tempering his hunger for flight with his longing for family and home.

Carver, Raymond, 1938-1988

All of us : the collected poems / Raymond Carver. Vintage Contemporaries, 2000, c1996. xxx, 386 p. ; **811**

1. American poetry

ISBN 9780375703805

LC BL 00011534

"Originally published in hardcover in Great Britain by the Harvill Press, London, in 1996"--T.p. verso.

A comprehensive anthology of more than three hundred poems, organized chronologically in order of their publication, features works from Fires, Where the Water Comes Together With Other Water, and A New Path to the Waterfall.

A **new** path to the waterfall : poems / Raymond Carver ; introduction by Tess Gallagher. Atlantic Monthly Press, c1989. xxxi, 126 p. ; **811**

1. American poetry

ISBN 9780871133748

LC 88034989

Poems deal with memories, loss of identity, childhood innocence, the past, and mortality.

Chang, Tina

Hybrida : poems / Tina Chang. W.W. Norton & Company, [2019] 133 p. **811**

1. Multiracial children 2. Motherhood 3. Violence 4. Ethnic identity 5. United States -- Race relations

ISBN 9781324002482

LC 2018056723

"A timely, stirring, and confident examination of mixed- race identity, violence, and history skillfully rendered through the lens of motherhood. In Hybrida, Tina Chang confronts the complexities of raising a mixed-race child during an era of political upheaval in the United States. She ruminates on the relationship between her son's blackness and his safety, exploring the dangers of childhood in a post-Trayvon Martin era by invoking racialized roles in fairy tales. Meditating on the lives of Michael Brown, Leiby Kletzky, and Noemi Alvarez Quillay--lost at the hands of individuals entrusted to protect them--Chang creates hybrid poetic forms that mirror her investigation of racial tensions."-- Provided by publisher.

"For academic holdings and public collections that include a political or own voices element." Library Journal

Chang, Victoria, 1970-

Obit : poems / Victoria Chang. Copper Canyon Press, 2020. x, 113 p. ; **811**

1. Obituaries

ISBN 9781556595745

LC 2019043837

"After her mother died, poet Victoria Chang refused to write elegies. Rather, she distilled her grief during a feverish two weeks by writing scores of poetic obituaries for all she lost in the world. In Obit, Chang writes of "the way memory gets up after someone has died and starts walking." These poems reinvent the form of newspaper obituary to both name what has died ("civility," "language," "the future," "Mother's blue dress") and the cultural impact of death on the living. Whereas elegy attempts to immortalize the dead, an obituary expresses loss, and the love for the dead becomes a conduit for self-expression. In this unflinching and lyrical book, Chang meets her grief and creates a powerful testament for the living." Provided by publisher.

"Often incorporating short declarative sentences, Chang's poems can veer toward being list-like but move forward quickly to endings that surprise and even amaze as they burrow deep into those grieving places all of us have experienced." Library Journal

Chavez, Felicia,

LatiNext / edited by Felicia Rose Chavez, Jose Olivarez, and Willie Perdomo. Haymarket Books, 2020. 326 p. **811**

1. Ethnic identity 2. Hispanic Americans 3. Hip-hop culture -- Influence 4. Sound 5. Anthologies

ISBN 9781642591293

LC 2019056428

In the dynamic tradition of the BreakBeat Poets anthology, The BreakBeat Poets Vol. 4: LatiNext celebrates the embodied narratives of Latinidad. Poets speak from an array of nationalities, genders, sexualities, races, and writing styles, staking a claim to our cultural and civic space. Like Hip-Hop, we honor what was, what is, and what's next.

"A phenomenal testament to emerging and enduring Latinx poetic excellence." Booklist

Charles, Jos, 1988-

feeld / Jos Charles. Milkweed Editions, 2018. 64 p. ; **811**

1. Gender identity 2. American poetry

ISBN 9781571315052

LC 2017058971

"Poetic exploration in Middle English about the body, physical space, ownership of space, gender, and transitioning genders."-- Provided by publisher.

Choi, Don Mee

Hardly war / Don Mee Choi. Wave Books, 2016 97 p. : **811**

1. Families

ISBN 9781940696232

LC 2015025698

"Far from lackadaisical, Choi's poetry operates within a tradition of Korean-American experimental poets that includes Theresa Hak Kyung Cha and Myung Mi Kim. Choi's zany take on militarism and the Korean diaspora may seem absurdist, but it is an inventive and daring waltz that upends what is commonly understood as the Forgotten War." Publishers Weekly

Ciardi, John, 1916-1986

The **collected** poems of John Ciardi / compiled and edited by Edward M. Cifelli. University of Arkansas Press, c1997. xxxii, 618 p. ; **811**

1. American poetry -- 20th century.

ISBN 9781557284495

LC 96046331

"Reprinted here are 450 poems by John Ciardi, over 62 percent of the verse that originally appeared in twenty individual volumes published between 1940 and 1993"--Foreword.

Includes index.

Presents a collection of 450 poems that originally appeared in twenty individual volumes published between 1940 and 1993.

Ciuraru, Carmela

Beat poets / selected and edited by Carmela Ciuraru. Alfred A. Knopf, 2002. 250 p. ; **811**

1. Beats (Persons) 2. American poetry -- 20th century.

ISBN 9780375413322

LC 2002510236

Includes index.

Complemented by commentary on Beat poetics and selections from the letters of Beat Generation writers, this collection of expressive and improvisational poetry features contributions from Allen Ginsberg, Jack Kerouac, Robert Creeley, Diane Di Prima, Gregory Corso, Denise Levertov, Lawrence Ferlinghetti, Peter Orlovsky, and other notables.

Clifton, Lucille, 1936-2010

Mercy : poems / Lucille Clifton. BOA Editions, 2004. 79 p. ; **811**

1. African American poets -- 20th century 2. Poetry, Modern -- 20th century

ISBN 9781929918546

LC 2004010396

A collection of poems by the African American poet focus on the stratification of American society, the power of Western materialism, and her concern for the world's children.

Cloud, Abigail

Sylph / Abigail Cloud ; selected by Dana Levin. Pleiades Press, 2014. 71 p. ; **811**

1. American poetry

ISBN 9780807156933

LC bl2014043844

Presents a collection of poetry inspired by nineteenth century European romantic ballets.

Cody, Anthony, 1981-

Borderland apocrypha / Anthony Cody. Omnidawn Publishing, 2020 159 p. **811**

1. Lynching -- Mexico

ISBN 9781632430762

LC 2019049154

"Borderland Apocrypha is centered around the collective histories of Mexican lynchings following the signing of the Treaty of Guadalupe Hidalgo in 1848, and the subsequent erasures, traumas, and state-sanctioned violences committed towards communities of color in the present day. Cody's debut collection responds to the destabilized, hostile landscapes and silenced histories via an experimental poetic that invents and shapeshifts in both form and space across the margin, the page, and the book's axis in a resistance, a reclamation and a re-occupation of what has been omitted. Part autohistoria, part docupoetic, part visual monument, part myth-making, Borderland Apocrypha exhumes the past in order to work toward survival, reckoning, and future-building." Provided by publisher.

Collins, Billy

180 more : extraordinary poems for every day / selected and with an introduction by Billy Collins. Random House Trade Paperbacks, c2005. xxiii, 373 p. ; **811**

1. American poetry

ISBN 9780812972962

LC 2005042798

Includes index.

Selected and introduced by America's former poet laureate, a second innovative anthology of 180 works by leading contemporary poets features the work of Robert Bly, Jane Kenyon, Galway Kinnell, Sharon Olds, Franz Wright, Paul Muldoon, Edward Hirsch, and other notable writers.

Collins, Billy

Poetry 180 : a turning back to poetry / selected and with an introduction by Billy Collins. Random House Trade Paperbacks, c2003. xxiv, 323 p. ; **811**

1. American poetry -- 21st century.
ISBN 9780812968873

LC 2002036949

Billy Collins compiles 180 poems, one for each day of the school year, for high school students to read so that they might learn the value of poetry in their daily lives.

The **trouble** with poetry and other poems / Billy Collins Random House, c2005. 88 p. ; **811**

1. American poetry
ISBN 9780375503825

LC 2005046562

An all-new collection of poetry by America's former Poet Laureate features witty, insightful, and simple poems dealing with the themes of jazz, the passage of time, love, boyhood, and writing.

Collins, Martha, 1940-

Admit one : an American scrapbook / Martha Collins. University of Pittsburgh Press, 2016 89 p. ; **811**

1. Racism 2. Eugenics 3. American poetry
ISBN 9780822964056

LC 2018276885

In this collection of poetry, Martha Collins relentlessly traces the history of scientific racism from the 1904 St. Louis World's Fair through the eugenics movement of the 1920s.

Cummings, E. E. (Edward Estlin), 1894-1962

★**Complete** poems, 1904-1962 / E.E. Cummings ; edited by George J. Firmage. Liveright, 1994, c1991. xxxii, 1102 p. ; **811**

1. American poetry -- 20th century
ISBN 9780871401526

LC BL 99789950

Originally published: New York : W.W. Norton, c1991.

A collection of the modern poet's work shows his use of satire and sentiment in unconventional verse.

"This volume has been prepared directly from the poet's original manuscripts, preserving the original typography and format. It includes all the previously published works, from Tulips (1922) to Etcetera (1983), as well as 36 uncollected poems that originally appeared in little magazines or anthologies." Library Journal.

Davis, Geffrey M., 1983-

Night angler / poems by Geffrey Davis. BOA Editions, Ltd., 2019. 96 p. **811**

1. Families 2. African American families 3. Fatherhood 4. African American poetry
ISBN 9781942683780

LC 2018050058

A book-length love letter of poems by a young black man seeking a new model of care for his family.

"Davis has written one of the most moving collections about fatherhood to come along in years." Publishers Weekly.

Dawson, Erica, 1979-

When rap spoke straight to God : a poem / Erica Dawson. Tin House Books, 2018. 50 p.; **811**

1. American poetry 2. African American poetry
ISBN 9781947793033

LC 2018021938

"A book-length poem navigating belief, black lives, the tragedies of Trump, and the boundaries of being a woman. A mix of traditional forms where sonnets mash up with sestinas morphing to heroic couplets, When Rap Spoke Straight to God insists that while you may recognize parts of the poem's world, you can't anticipate how it will evolve".-- Provided by publisher.

"For the poet, the scars of history are powerful reminders of how blackness rises above the cruelty of oppression, always reaching for the light." Publishers Weekly

Derricotte, Toi, 1941-

I : new and selected poems / Toi Derricotte. University of Pittsburgh Press, 2019. 298 p. **811**

1. Derricotte, Toi, 1941- 2. African American women 3. Wisdom 4. Purpose in life
ISBN 9780822945666

LC bl2020006994

"Derricotte's attention lingers on places of struggle where life is at its most vibrant, urgent, and surprising." Publishers Weekly.

Diaz, Natalie

Postcolonial love poem / Natalie Diaz. Graywolf Press, 2020. 105 p. **811**

1. Indigenous peoples 2. Hope. 3. Colonialism 4. Native Americans.
ISBN 9781644450147

LC 2019933473

Postcolonial Love Poem is an anthem of desire against erasure. Natalie Diaz's brilliant second collection demands that every body carried in its pages--bodies of language, land, rivers, suffering brothers, enemies, and lovers--be touched and held as beloveds.

"In this exquisite, electrifying collection, Diaz . . . continues to demonstrate her masterful use of language while reinventing narratives about desire." Publishers Weekly

Dickinson, Emily, 1830-1886

Dickinson : selected poems and commentaries / Helen Vendler. The Belknap Press of Harvard University Press, 2010. xiv, 535 p. ; **811**

1. Dickinson, Emily, 1830-1886 Criticism and interpretation. 2. American poetry
ISBN 9780674048676

LC 2010007090

Presents 150 selected poems of Emily Dickinson along with commentary on both the stylistic and imaginative features of the poems.

Dickman, Michael, 1975-

The **end** of the west / Michael Dickman. Copper Canyon Press, c2009. ix, 89 p. ; **811**

1. American poetry
ISBN 9781556592898

LC 2008039990

Poems describe growing up in the American West and life in a troubled family.

Donovan, Karen, 1956-

Your enzymes are calling the ancients : poems / Karen Donovan. Persea Books, 2016 87 p. ; **811**

1. American poetry
ISBN 9780892554768

LC 2016022139

"A Karen & Michael Braziller Book."

"Donovan expertly crafts a cohesive book from so many seemingly different parts of art and nature and weaves them through the loom and perspective of human experience." Booklist.

Doty, Mark

Deep lane : poems / Mark Doty. W.W. Norton & Company, 2015 93 p. ; **811**

1. American poetry

ISBN 9780393070231

LC 2015000660

A new collection of poems from the National Book Award-winning author features works that describe a series of descents before moving on to more uplifting possibilities.

"A somber, struggling, honest collection for Doty's many fans." Library Journal.

Fire to fire : new and selected poems / Mark Doty. Harper, c2008. x, 326 p. ; **811**

1. American poetry

ISBN 9780060752477

LC 2007044646

A collection of selected works and new poems features pieces that meditate on such topics as mortality, the instructive presence of animals, and art's ability to give shape to human life.

What is the grass : Walt Whitman in my life / Mark Doty. W. W. Norton & Company, 2020 272 p. **811**

1. Doty, Mark 2. Whitman, Walt, 1819-1892 Influence. 3. Whitman, Walt, 1819-1892 Appreciation. 4. Poets, American 5. Influence (Literary, artistic, etc.) 6. Homosexuality 7. Gay men

ISBN 9780393070224

LC 2019044569

The National Book Award-winning poet explores Walt Whitman's poetic themes of love, death and queer sexuality while reflecting on Whitman's complicated impact on his own work, his sense of self and the American imagination.

"Fans of Whitman will surely enjoy Doty's extensive passages of exegesis, and many readers will admire the author's occasional descriptions of his own revisions of his ideas about Whitman's diction and poetic design. Throughout, the author exudes an exuberance about life and words that rivals that of his subject. Also informative (and necessary) are Doty's evocations of 19th-century Brooklyn and New York City. A captivating paean to Whitman combined with an unblinking self-examination." Kirkus.

Dove, Rita

Selected poems / Rita Dove. Vintage Books, 1993. xxvi, 210 p. ; **811**

1. American poetry 2. African American poetry

ISBN 9780679750802

LC 93026112

Includes index.

Gathers poems about slavery and freedom, home and family, and the past by America's youngest poet laureate

"This volume places three previous collections under one cover. . . . The selection begins with The Yellow House on the Corner, Dove's first book, most notable for its poems derived from slave narratives. Museum, her second book, offers a potpourri of work that ranges over several continents and many millenia; Dove's tirelessly exact language illuminates the lives of saints, contemporary lifestyles, and Greek myths." Booklist.

Dove, Rita

Sonata mulattica : a life in five movements and a short play : poems / Rita Dove. W. W. Norton & Co., c2009. 231 p. ; **811**

1. Bridgetower, George Augustus Polgreen 2. Multiracial men 3. Musicians 4. African American poetry 5. American poetry

ISBN 9780393070088

LC 2008054281

A lyric narrative by a Pulitzer Prize-winning former U.S. poet laureate, inspired by the life of a nineteenth-century virtuoso violinist, traces the early years of George Polgreen Bridgetower as a son of a white woman and an "African prince," his acclaim in Vienna, and his break with Beethoven after a dispute over a woman.

Duncan, Robert, 1919-1988

Selected poems / Robert Duncan ; edited by Robert J. Bertholf. New Directions, 1993. xi, 147 p. ; **811**

1. American poetry -- 20th century

ISBN 9780811212274

LC 92035812

Includes index.

A collection of poetry deals with such topics as love, death, revelation, religion, humanity, and war.

"Duncan was one of the true masters of contemporary American poetry. His oeuvre is by turns lyrical, experimental, archaic, visionary and political. In Bertholf's brief, insightful introduction, he makes necessary connections between the often-neglected early work and the later masterpieces." Publishers Weekly.

Dunn, Stephen, 1939-

Local visitations : poems / Stephen Dunn. Norton, c2003. 96 p. ; **811**

1. American poetry

ISBN 9780393052008

LC 2002014204

A twelfth collection by the 2000 Pulitzer Prize winner for poetry finds a temporarily freed Sisyphus struggling through twenty-first century America and nineteenth-century novelists visiting the author's South Jersey towns.

New & selected poems : 1974-1994 / Stephen Dunn. W.W. Norton, 1995, c1994. xvii, 296 p. ; **811**

1. American poetry -- 20th century

ISBN 9780393313000

LC bl2007001363

Includes index.

Sixteen new poems and poems selected from the author's previous collections focus on the nuances of family and domestic life, as well as philosophical and metaphysical concerns.

Ellis, Thomas Sayers

Skin, Inc. : identity repair poems / Thomas Sayers Ellis. Graywolf Press, 2010. 181 p. ; **811**

1. African American poetry 2. American poetry

ISBN 9781555975678

LC 2010922920

Presents a collection of poetry that looks at the American identity.

Emerson, Ralph Waldo, 1803-1882

★**Collected** poems and translations : Collected Poems and Translations / Ralph Waldo Emerson ; [compiled by Harold Bloom and Paul Kane]. Library of America : c1994. 637 p. ;

The library of America ; 811
1. Poetry -- Translations into English
ISBN 9780940450288
LC 93040245

Contains Emerson's published poetry, plus selections of his unpublished poetry from journals and notebooks, and some of his translations of poetry from other languages, notably Dante's La vita nuova.

A comprehensive new volume that includes all of the poetry that Emerson published during his lifetime, demonstrates his skill and depth as a poet, and reveals his private, meditative, emotional side--a portrait of a freer, more unconventional Emerson.

Erdrich, Heid E. (Heid Ellen),
★**New** poets of Native nations / edited by Heid E. Erdrich. Graywolf Press, 2018 xvi, 284 p. ; 811
1. American poetry -- Native American authors. 2. Indians of North America 3. American poetry -- 21st century. 4. Anthologies
ISBN 9781555978099
LC bl2018180332

A landmark anthology celebrating twenty-one Native poets first published in the twenty-first century.

"An immensely important anthology that belongs in every library." Booklist

Evans, William, III (William H.)
We inherit what the fires left : poems / William Evans. Simon & Schuster, 2020. 149 p. 811
ISBN 9781982127398
LC 2019028078

"William Evans, the award-winning poet and cofounder of the popular culture website Black Nerd Problems, offers an emotionally vulnerable poetry collection exploring the themes of inheritances, dreams, and injuries that are passed down from one generation to the next and delving into the lived experience of a black man in the American suburbs today".-- Provided by publisher.

"This is a powerful, transformative book." Booklist

Ewing, Eve L.
1919 / Eve L. Ewing. Haymarket Books, 2019. 74 p. 811
1. Chicago Race Riot, Chicago, Ill., 1919 2. Racism -- United States -- History 3. Race Riots 4. Violence against African Americans 5. Chicago, Illinois -- History -- 20th century
ISBN 9781608466023

Ewing uses speculative and Afrofuturist lenses to recast history, and illuminates the thin line between the past and the present. --From publisher description.

"These clarion and haunting poems--some psalm-like, others percussive, even concussive, all technically brilliant and sure to galvanize adults and teens alike--incisively and resoundingly evoke the promise and betrayal of the Great Migration and the everyday struggles of Chicago's Black community against vicious and violent racism." Booklist.

Fagan, Deirdre J.
Critical companion to Robert Frost : a literary reference to his life and work / Deirdre Fagan. Facts On File, c2007. ix, 454 p. : 811
1. Frost, Robert, 1874-1963 Handbooks, manuals, etc.
ISBN 0816061823
LC 2006013269

A guide to the author's life and work presents a brief biography; offers synopses of his writings; and discusses important people, places, and themes in his life.

Faizullah, Tarfia
Registers of illuminated villages : poems / Tarfia Faizullah. Graywolf Press, 2018 96, 98 p. ; 811
1. American poetry -- 21st century.
ISBN 9781555978006
LC 2017938024

Faizullah's new work extends and transforms her powerful accounts of violence, war, and loss into poems of many forms and voices--elegies, outcries, self-portraits, and larger-scale confrontations with discrimination, family, and memory. --From publisher description.

"More than this collection's almost eponymous opener, Register of Eliminated Villages" is also the title of a sinister war document detailing the destruction of 397 Kurdish villages." And Faizullah's second collection--following the award-winning Seam (2014)--is itself a mesmerizing inventory." Booklist.

Fearing, Kenneth, 1902-1961
Selected poems / Kenneth Fearing ; Robert Polito, editor. Library of America, c2004. xxii, 183 p. : 811
1. American poetry
ISBN 9781931082570
LC 2003060482

Includes index.

Poems by the Depression-era poet, journalist, and crime novelist are featured here, presenting his depictions of fragmented urban life as well as his portrayal of the restlessness underpinning American life.

Ferlinghetti, Lawrence, 1919-
These are my rivers : new & selected poems, 1955-1993 / Lawrence Ferlinghetti. New Directions, 1994, c1993. v, 308 p. : 811
1. American poetry -- 20th century 2. African American poetry
ISBN 9780811212731
LC BL 99756912

Includes index.

Origially published: 1993.

Gathers poems from each period of the poet's career, including poems dealing with fame, memory, politics, love, travel, and poetry.

"Reading this hefty selection from 12 previous volumes, plus 50 pages of new poems, we realize how accurately the poet described himself in 1979: a man who 'thinks he's Dylan Thomas and Bob Dylan rolled together with Charlie Chaplin thrown in.' His style is recognizable throughout--phlegmatic poems running several pages, often lacking stanza breaks, with short lines at the left margin or moving across the page as hand follows eye... Essential." Library Journal.

Love child's hotbed of occasional poetry : poems & artifacts / Nikky Finney. Triquarterly Books, 2020. xvi, 237 p. 811
1. African Americans -- History 2. Memories 3. Social history 4. Social marginality
ISBN 9780810142015
LC 2019042370

National Book Award winner Nikky Finney's fifth collection contains light house poems, prosaic hot beds, and personal artifacts, copper coins struck from a new matrix for American poetry, one that testifies from the witness stand and punctuates the occasional lyric within a new language of "docu-poetry." The tenderness of a father's handwritten notes shadows the collection like a ghost, while the treasured, not-for-sale interiority of a black girl's fountainhead takes over every page. "One yellaw gal with an all-black tongue has gone missing." Finney has composed a new black spiritual, and one of the great voices of our time again stamps her singular sound into the new day.

"Finney's skillful, sweeping epic ambitiously connects personal and public history." Publishers Weekly

Flynn, Nick, 1960-

The **captain** asks for a show of hands : poems / Nick Flynn. Graywolf Press, 2011. 94 p. ; **811**

1. American poetry
ISBN 9781555975746

LC 2010937512

A meditation on love disintegrates into a collage of voices derived from media reports, overheard conversations, childhood memories, and other sources to highlight the storm of noise that permeates society.

Forche, Carolyn

Blue hour / Carolyn Forche. Perennial, 2004, c2003. 73 p. ; **811**

1. American poetry
ISBN 9780060099138

LC bl2008019681

Originally published: New York : HarperCollins, 2003.

A volume of poetry by the award-winning author of The Angel of History includes works that demonstrate her use of imagery, application of the elegy form, and considerable moral principles.

Ford, Katie (Poet)

Blood lyrics : poems / Katie Ford. Graywolf Press, 2014 62 p. ; **811**

1. American poetry
ISBN 9781555976927

LC 2014935705

In Katie Ford's third collection, she sets her music into lyrics wrung from the world's dangers. Blood Lyrics is a mother's song, one seared with the knowledge that her country wages long, aching wars in which not all lives are equal. --From publisher description.

"Her finely wrought paeans and laments complicate the possibility of total joy or total despair when personal pain is not projected externally or the existence of others' suffering is not apparent in our own daily lives." Publishers Weekly.

Forsythe, Kelly

Perennial / Kelly Forsythe. Coffee House Press, 2018. 66 p. ; **811**

1. American poetry -- 21st century 2. Poetry of places 3. Elegiac poetry
ISBN 9781566895170

LC 2018000107

The events of 1999's Columbine shooting preoccupy Forsythe in these poems, refracting her vision to encompass killer, victim, and herself as a girl, suddenly aware of the precarity of her own life and the porousness of her body to others' gaze, demands, violence. --From publisher description.

"Forsythe's moving catalogue of a horrific event becomes a diagram of senselessness where minutiae take on a stark and eerie resonance when read beside today's headlines." Publishers Weekly.

Gallagher, Tess

Dear ghosts, : poems / Tess Gallagher. Graywolf Press, c2006. 140 p. ; **811**

1. American poetry
ISBN 9781555974435

LC 2005938149

Conjures the spirits of the author's deceased parents, Holocaust victims, and others as relevant members of the present, in a volume in which the writer confronts her own illness and mortality while celebrating love and friendship.

Is, is not : poems / Tess Gallagher. Graywolf Press, 2019 147 p. **811**

ISBN 9781555978419

LC 2018958155

Is, Is Not upends our notions of linear time, evokes the spirit and sanctity of place, and hovers daringly at the threshold of what language can nearly deliver while offering alternative corollaries as gifts of its failures. Tess Gallagher's poems reverberate with the inward clarity of a bell struck on a mountaintop. Guided by humor, grace, and a deep inquiry into the natural world, every poem nudges us toward moments of awe. How else except by delight and velocity would we discover the miracle within the ordinary?

"Readers of quiet, thoughtful poetry will find much to savor." Library Journal.

Gander, Forrest, 1956-

★**Be** with / Forrest Gander ; with six photographs by Michael Flomen. New Directions Publishing Corporation, 2018 92 p. : **811**

1. John of the Cross, Saint, 1542-1591 2. Mothers -- Death 3. Mexican-American Border Region
ISBN 9780811226059

LC 2018002148

"First published as a New Directions Paperbook (NDP1408)" -- Verso title page.

"A New Directions Book."

"Drawing from his experience as a translator, Forrest Gander includes in the first, powerfully elegiac section a version of a poem by the Spanish mystical poet St. John of the Cross. He continues with a long multilingual poem examining the syncretic geological and cultural history of the U.S. border with Mexico. The poems of the third section--a moving transcription of Gander's efforts to address his mother dying of Alzheimer's--rise from the page like hymns, transforming slowly from reverence to revelation. Gander has been called one of our most formally restless poets, and these new poems express a characteristically tensile energy and, as one critic noted, 'the most eclectic diction since Hart Crane'".-- Provided by publisher.

"In the depths of grief, Gander conceives of a realm more real than life. ... Throughout, he traverses literal and figurative boundaries, probing languages limits in regards to aging, loss, and violence." Publishers Weekly.

Core samples from the world / Forrest Gander ; with photographs by Raymond Meeks, Graciela Iturbide and Lucas Foglia. New Directions, c2011. 95 p. : **811**

1. Haibun, American. 2. American poetry
ISBN 9780811218870

LC 2011001154

A compendium of poetry, photography and haibun (Japanese essay-poem).

Torn awake / Forrest Gander. New Directions, 2001. 95 p. ; **811**

1. American poetry
ISBN 9780811214865

LC 2001032657

"A New Directions paperbook original; NDP926.

A new collection by one of America's most respected young experimental poets.

Gay, Ross, 1974-
Catalog of unabashed gratitude / Ross Gay. University of Pittsburgh Press, 2015. 102 p. ; **811**
1. American poetry
ISBN 9780822963318
LC 2018276408
National Book Critics Circle Award for Poetry, 2015
Catalog of Unabashed Gratitude is a sustained meditation on that which goes away-- loved ones, the seasons, the earth as we know it -- that tries to find solace in the processes of the garden and the orchard.

Gerstler, Amy
Scattered at sea / Amy Gerstler. Penguin Books, 2015. 77 p. : **811**
1. POETRY / American / General. 2. American poetry
ISBN 9780143126898
LC 2015002411
"A dazzling new collection from an award-winning poet. Amy Gerstler has won acclaim for sly, sophisticated, and subversive poems that find meaning in unexpected places. The title of her new collection, Scattered at Sea, evokes notions of dispersion, diaspora, sowing one's wild oats, having one's mind expanded or blown, losing one's wits, and mortality. Making use of dramatic monologue, elegy, humor, and collage, these poems explore hedonism, gender, ancestry, reincarnation, bereavement, and the nature of prayer. Groping for an inclusive, imaginative, postmodern spirituality, they draw from an array of sources, including the philosophy of the ancient Stoics, diagnostic tests for Alzheimer's disease, 1950s recipes, the Babylonian Talmud, and Walter Benjamin's writing on his drug experiences".-- Provided by publisher.

Gibbons, Reginald
Creatures of a day : poems / Reginald Gibbons. Louisiana State University Press, c2008. 79 p. ; **811**
1. American poetry
ISBN 9780807133170
LC 2007034185
In Creatures of a Day, Reginald Gibbons presents intense encounters with everyday people amidst the historical and social contexts of everyday life.

Gibran, Kahlil, 1883-1931
And the prophet said : Kahlil Gibran's classic text with newly discovered writings / Kahlil Gibran ; edited by Dalton Hilu Einhorn ; with a foreword by Daniel Ladinsky. Hampton Roads Publishing, 2020, c1923. xxv, 147 p. **811**
1. Prophets 2. Prophecy 3. Wisdom 4. Immigrants 5. Anthologies 6. Classics
ISBN 9781642970166
LC 2019052619
Originally published in 1923 by Knopf, The Prophet is a teaching fable that is essentially a little book of life for all people at all times. In it, the author explores all of life's important issues--including love, marriage, the human condition, friendship, prayer, beauty, death, and much more. This edition is especially exciting because of the inclusion of newly discovered material--over 150 Kahlil Gibran poems, aphorisms, and sayings that have never been published.
"A rich collection for all interested in the work and ongoing legacy of Gibran." Library Journal

The **collected** works : with eighty-four illustrations by the author / Kahlil Gibran. Alfred A. Knopf, 2007. viii, 880 p. : **811**
ISBN 9780307267078
LC 2007028736
A collection of the major works of the celebrated poet, artist, and mystic features an array of stories, parables, prose poems, and essays that include "The Prophet," "The Wanderer," "Jesus the Son of Man," "Spirits Rebellious," and "The Gardens of the Prophet".

★The **prophet** / Kahlil Gibran. Knopf, 1995, c1923. 105 p. **811**
1. Prophets 2. Prophecy 3. Wisdom 4. Immigrants 5. Anthologies
ISBN 9780679440673
Presents the Lebanese poet and philosopher's inspirational essays on love, marriage, work, joy, sorrow, freedom, pain, teaching, friendship and death.

Gilbert, Jack, 1925-2012
Collected poems / Jack Gilbert. Alfred A. Knopf, 2012. xviii, 408 p. ; **811**
1. American poetry
ISBN 9780307269683
LC 2011025743
Includes indexes.
The Pulitzer Prize-nominated author presents a complete collection of his poetry as written over the course of more than 50 years including the periods when he withdrew from the literary world to establish his signature fierce and declarative style, in a volume that also features several previously unpublished works.

Ginsberg, Allen, 1926-1997
The **letters** of Allen Ginsberg / edited by Bill Morgan. Da Capo Press, 2008. xxii, 468 p. ; **811**
1. Ginsberg, Allen, 1926-1997 Correspondence. 2. Poets, American -- 20th century 3. Correspondence.
ISBN 9780306814631
LC 2008011054
Includes index.
This volume that showcases the author's correspondence with some of the most original and interesting artists of his time--including Jack Kerouac, William S. Burroughs, Lionel Trilling, Neal Cassady, Lawrence Ferlinghetti, Arthur Miller, and Ken Kesey--provides an intimate guide to understanding an entire creative generation.
"Morgan, Ginsberg's biographer (I Celebrate Myself) and archivist, studied 3700 letters left behind by the poet, selecting 165 of the most significant for this edition; over 125 appear here for the first time. Always intelligent, sometimes gossipy, and occasionally cranky and impatient, Ginsberg is accurately reflected in these letters taken together. Correspondents include Ginsberg's father, Louis, and brother, Eugene; the poet's longtime companion, Peter Orlovsky; fellow Beat writers Jack Kerouac, William Burroughs, and Gregory Corso; and a host of friends and acquaintances." Library Journal.

Gioia, Dana
99 poems : new & selected / Dana Gioia. Graywolf Press, 2016. 194 p. ; **811**
1. American poetry
ISBN 9781555977320
LC 2015953592
Includes index.

99 Poems: New & Selected for the first time gathers work from across his career, including a dozen remarkable new poems. Gioia has not ordered this selection chronologically. Instead, his great subjects organize this volume into broad themes of mystery, remembrance, imagination, place, stories, songs, and love. The result is a book we might live our lives alongside, and a reminder of the deep and abiding pleasures and reassurances that poetry provides us.

Disappearing ink : poetry at the end of print culture / Dana Gioia. Graywolf Press, c2004. xiv, 271 p. ; **811**

1. American poetry -- 20th century -- History and criticism. 2. American poetry -- 21st century -- History and criticism. 3. Oral interpretation of poetry -- History -- 20th century. 4. Oral interpretation of poetry -- History -- 21st century.
ISBN 1555974104

LC 2004104190

Presents a searching analysis of poetry that explores the line between traditional written poetry and the "looser" oral conventions of slam and hip hop.

Giovanni, Nikki

Blues : for all the changes : new poems / Nikki Giovanni. William Morrow, c1999. viii, 100 p. ; **811**

1. African American poetry 2. American poetry
ISBN 9780688156985

LC 98050996

A collection of fifty-one poems from a best-selling poet embodies her fearless passion and wit in outspoken odes to Jackie Robinson, space, illness, manners, the environment, and many other topics.

Chasing Utopia : a hybrid / Nikki Giovanni. William Morrow, 2013 xi, 143 p. ; **811**

1. African American poetry 2. American poetry
ISBN 9780688156978

LC 2013008776

One of America's most celebrated poets pays homage to gatherings of friends, family, and lovers where at the center is food as sustenance, as aphrodisiac, and as memory.

A **good** cry : what we learn from tears and laughter / Nikki Giovanni. William Morrow, 2017 xi, 111 p. ; **811**

1. African American poetry 2. American poetry -- 21st century.
ISBN 9780062399458

LC 2017275349

A celebrated American poet offers an intimate, affecting and revealing look at her personal history and the mysteries of her own heart, taking us into her confidence as she ruminates on her life and the people who have helped shape her into the woman she has become.

The **collected** poetry of Nikki Giovanni, 1968-1998 / chronology and notes by Virginia C. Fowler. William Morrow, c2003. xliii, 452 p. ; **811**

1. African American poetry 2. American poetry
ISBN 9780060541330

LC 2004302269

An omnibus of early works features pieces written between 1968 and 1998 and includes the contents of five previously published volumes.

Quilting the black-eyed pea : poems and not quite poems / Nikki Giovanni. William Morrow, c2002. xii, 110 p. ; **811**

1. African American women
ISBN 9780060099527

LC 2002066025

A collection of poems, sketches, and meditations on popular culture and life in America includes the author's writings on her personal battle with illness, the relationships between mothers and their children, the South, and other topics.

Girmay, Aracelis

The **black** Maria : poems / Aracelis Girmay. BOA Editions Ltd., 2016. 120 p. ; **811**

1. African American poetry 2. American poetry
ISBN 9781942683025

LC 2015043256

"Taking its name from the moon's dark plains, misidentified as seas by early astronomers, The Black Maria investigates African diasporic histories, the consequences of racism within American culture, and the question of human identity. Central to this project is a desire to recognize the lives of Eritrean refugees who have been made invisible by years of immigration crisis, refugee status, exile, and resulting statelessness. The recipient of a 2015 Whiting Award for Poetry, Girmay's newest collection elegizes and celebrates life, while wrestling with the humanistic notion of seeing beyond: seeing violence, seeing grace, and seeing each other better. "to the sea great storage house, history on which we rode, we touched the brief pulse of your fluttering pages, spelled with salt & life, your rage, your indifference your gentleness washing our feet, all of you going on whether or not we live, to you we bring our carnations yellow & pink, how they float like bright sentences atop your memory's dark hair." Aracelis Girmay is the author of two poetry collections, Teeth and Kingdom Animalia, which won the Isabella Gardner Award and was a finalist for the NBCC Award. The recipient of a 2015 Whiting Award, she has received grants and fellowships from the Jerome, Cave Canem, and Watson foundations, as well as Civitella Ranieri and the NEA. She currently teaches at Hampshire College's School for Interdisciplinary Arts and in Drew University's low residency MFA program. Originally from Santa Ana, California, she splits her time between New York and Amherst, Massachusetts".-- Provided by publisher.

Gloria, Eugene

Sightseer in this killing city / Eugene Gloria. Penguin Books, [2019] 96 p. Penguin poets **811**

1. Filipino American women 2. LGBTQIA persons 3. City life 4. Multiculturalism
ISBN 9780143133841

LC 2018055871

"Eugene Gloria's fourth collection of poetry captures the surreal and unreal feelings of the present. Through the voice of Nacirema, the central persona of the collection, who is a Filipina American woman with an ambiguous sexual identity, we are introduced to a character who chooses mystery and inhabits landscapes fraught with brutality and beauty. Flawed like America, Nacirema embodies ideas of wanderlust and self-discovery."-- Provided by publisher.

"A seriously outstanding collection." Booklist.

Gluck, Louise, 1943-

Averno / Louise Gluck. Farrar, Straus and Giroux, 2006. viii, 79 p. ; **811**

1. Persephone (Greek deity) 2. American poetry
ISBN 9780374107420

LC 2005042658

A collection of works by the Pulitzer Prize and National Book Critics Circle Award-winning writer takes its inspiration from a small crater lake in southern Italy and is an extended lamentation that evaluates Averno's existence in a winter landscape and role as a doorway between worlds.

Poems 1962-2012 / Louise Gluck. Ecco Press, 2012. xvii, 634 p. ; **811**
1. American poetry
ISBN 9780374126087
LC 2011051349

Includes index.

The collected works of the Pulitzer Prize and National Book Critics Circle Award-winning writer explores her transfigured landscapes and offers insight into her unique form created to reflect the human drive to release the past in order to realize the yet-unimagined.

Graham, Jorie, 1950-

The **dream** of the unified field : selected poems 1974-1994 / Jorie Graham. Ecco Press, c1995. 199 p. ; **811**
1. American poetry -- 20th century.
ISBN 9780880014380
LC 95016572

A major collection of poetry brings together works from the poet's first five works: Hybrids of Plants and Ghosts, Erosion, The End of Beauty, Region of Unlikeness, and Materialism.

"Combining great vision like Blake's, a Dickinsonian philosophical introspection, and a richly modern sensuality, this selection demonstrates the full range of Graham's poetic gifts." Booklist.

Fast / Jorie Graham. ECCO, 2017. 84 p. ; **811**
1. American poetry -- 21st century.
ISBN 9780062663481
LC 2017299626

In her first new collection in five years--her most exhilarating, personal, and formally inventive to date--Graham explores the limits of the human and the uneasy seductions of the post-human. Conjuring an array of voices and perspectives--from bots, to the holy shroud, to the ocean floor, to a medium transmitting from beyond the grave--these poems give urgent form to the ever-increasing pace of transformation of our planet and ourselves. As it navigates cyber life, 3D-printed "life," life after death, biologically, chemically, and electronically modified life, Fast lights up the border of our new condition as individuals and as a species on the brink.-- Book jacket.

From the new world : poems, 1976-2014 / Jorie Graham. Ecco, 2015 359 p. ; **811**
1. Poetry of places 2. Nature 3. American poetry
ISBN 9780062315403
LC bl2015005706

Offers poems selected from almost forty years of the author's works, as well as several new and revised poems, touching on a broad variety of topics explored during her career.

Overlord : poems / Jorie Graham. Ecco, c2005. xii, 93 p. ; **811**
1. American poetry
ISBN 9780060745653
LC 2004053681

A collection of the Pulitzer Prize-winning writer's most personal and passionate works considers such themes as the meaning of being fully present in a human life, one's vulnerability to mortal and transcendent forces, and the human capacity for being oneself. By the author of The Dream of the Unified Field.

Guest, Barbara

The **collected** poems of Barbara Guest / Barbara Guest ; edited by Hadley Haden Guest. Wesleyan University Press, c2008. xxxi, 525 p. : **811**
1. American poetry
ISBN 9780819568601
LC 2008020147

Includes bibliographical references and index.

The lifework of a preeminent New York School poet.

"This book, one of the year's essential releases, should be part of any library of 20th-century American poetry." Publishers Weekly

H. D. (Hilda Doolittle), 1886-1961

Collected poems, 1912-1944 / H.D. ; edited by Louis L. Martz. New Directions Book, 1986, c1983. xxxvi, 629 p. ; **811**
ISBN 9780811209717
LC BL 99958483

Previously published: 1983.

Gathers poems from each period of Hilda Doolittle's career and includes background information on her major works.

"The editor's textual notes offer valuable and illuminating scholarly commentary and present the most important of the textual variants. An informative and sensitively written introduction discusses aspects of the interpenetration of H.D.'s biography with her poetic sensibility. This volume is an impressive scholarly work." Choice.

Hacker, Marilyn, 1942-

Selected poems, 1965-1990 : 1965-1990 / Marilyn Hacker. W.W. Norton, c1994. xii, 250 p. ; **811**
1. Lesbians 2. Mothers and daughters 3. Women 4. African American poetry
ISBN 9780393036756
LC 94027507

Includes index.

Poems from five previous collections deal with feminism, politics, and human sexuality.

"Few poets have been as successful as Hacker in negotiating the boundary of the feminist and lesbian canon while generating a buzz around their early work. Iambic and readable, the pieces in Selected Poems--taken from five previous volumes use unique inversions to explore self and other through changing situations between friends, lovers, family, and one's surroundings. Often, these are poems of loss, of desire delayed, of pleasure deferred." Library Journal.

Hacker, Marilyn, 1942-

Squares and courtyards : Poems / Marilyn Hacker. W.W. Norton & Co., c2000. 107 p. ; **811**
1. American poetry
ISBN 9780393048308
LC 99039110

A ninth anthology of poetry by a winner of the National Book Award, Lenore Marshall Prize and Poets' Prize celebrates the diverse passages of life, along with the community of friends, the courage of those living with terminal illness, and the mysteries of life and death.

"With customary fortitude and intelligence, Hacker confronts such sobering subjects as the trauma of her own chemotherapy and the loss of friends, in poems that are at once clear-sighted and emotionally full." The New Yorker.

Hacker, Marilyn, 1942-

A **stranger's** mirror : new and selected poems, 1994-2014 / Marilyn Hacker. W. W. Norton & Company, 2015 xiv, 288 p. ; **811**

1. American poetry
ISBN 9780393244649

LC 2014037031

Includes index.

Draws on two decades of poetry by the author in a collection of twenty-five pieces that span different forms to explore international dilemmas while engaging poets from different ages.

Hall, Donald, 1928-2018

The **back** chamber / Donald Hall. Houghton Mifflin Harcourt, 2011. 82 p. ; **811**

1. American poetry
ISBN 9780547645858

LC 2011009152

"The first full-length volume of poems in a decade by former poet laureate of the United States Donald Hall. In The Back Chamber, Donald Hall illuminates the evocative, iconic objects of deep memory--'a cowbell,' 'a white stone perfectly round,' 'a three-legged milking stool'--that serve to foreground the rich meditations on time and mortality that run through his remarkable new collection. While Hall's devoted readers will recognize many of his long-standing preoccupations--baseball, the family farm, love, sex, and friendship--what will strike them as new is the fierce, pitiless poignancy he reveals as his own life's end comes into view. The Back Chamber is far from being death-haunted but rather is lively, irreverent, sexy, hilarious, ironic, and sly--full of the life-affirming energy that has made Donald Hall one of America's most popular and enduring poets".-- Provided by publisher.

★The **selected** poems of Donald Hall. / Donald Hall. Houghton Mifflin Harcourt 2015 x, 148 p. ; **811**

1. American poetry 2. Elegiac poetry
ISBN 9780544555600

LC 2015004341

A collection of signature works by the former poet laureate reflects the evolution of his literary career and shares insight into his use of humor, eros, and engaging simple language.

White apples and the taste of stone : selected poems, 1946-2006 / Donald Hall. Houghton Mifflin Co., 2007, c2006. xv, 431 p. ; **811**

1. American poetry
ISBN 9780618919994

LC bl2007029407

"A Mariner book."

Reprint. Originally published: 2006.

Spanning the entire career of the celebrated American poet, a collection of 226 works represents sixty years of poetic endeavor, including recent poems and a CD containing readings by the author.

Hardwick, Elizabeth

The **dolphin** letters, 1970-1979 : Elizabeth Hardwick, Robert Lowell and their circle / edited by Saskia Hamilton. Farrar, Straus and Giroux, 2019. 560 p. **811**

1. Hardwick, Elizabeth 2. Lowell, Robert, 1917-1977 3. Bishop, Elizabeth, 1911-1979. 4. Blackwood, Caroline. 5. McCarthy, Mary, 1912-1989. 6. Rich, Adrienne, 1929-2012 7. Poets 8. Authors 9. Letter writing 10. Marital conflict 11. Letters
ISBN 9780374141264

LC 2019016287

Collects correspondence between the famous literary couple and their circle of friends--including Elizabeth Bishop, Mary McCarthy and Adrienne Rich--during a time of personal crisis and the creation of Lowell's controversial poem The Dolphin.

Harjo, Joy

An **American** sunrise : poems / Joy Harjo. W. W. Norton & Company, 2019 xiii, 116 p. : **811**

1. Creek Indians -- History
ISBN 9781324003861

LC 2019021562

"Newly named poet laureate and Ruth Lilly prize-winner Harjo (Conflict Resolution for Holy Beings) intertwines verse with prose vignettes, oral histories, and flash memoirs in this expressive and generous book." Publishers Weekly

A **map** to the next world : poetry and tales / Joy Harjo. W.W. Norton, 2001, c2000. 137 p. ; **811**

1. American poetry
ISBN 9780393320961

LC bl2010034450

The poet draws on her own Native American heritage in a collection of lyrical poetry that explores the cruelties and tragedies of history and the redeeming miracles of human kindness.

Harper, Michael S., 1938-2016

Every shut eye ain't asleep : an anthology of poetry by African Americans since 1945 / edited by Michael Harper and Anthony Walton. Little, Brown, c1994. xiv, 327 p. ; **811**

1. African American poetry 2. American poetry -- 20th century.
ISBN 9780316347105

LC 93010788

A collection of postwar African American poetry showcases the works of such poets as Derek Walcott, Amiri Baraka, Ishmael Reed, Gwendolyn Brooks, Audre Lorde, and others.

Harris, Francine J.

Play dead / Francine J. Harris. Alice James Books, 2016 xii, 85 p. : **811**

1. African American poetry 2. American poetry
ISBN 9781938584251

LC 2015036404

"Though some poets revel in emotional chaos and seek an existential abyss, Harris (allegiance) works in her second collection to peel back the superficial aspects of subjects such as emerging girlhood, sex, romantic relationships, and love, exposing raw wounds and snarling demons." Publishers Weekly.

Harrison, Jim, 1937-2016,

The **essential** poems of Jim Harrison : The Essential Poems / edited by Joseph Bednarik. Copper Canyon Press, [2019] 200 p. **811**

ISBN 9781556595288

LC 2018049116

Includes indexes.

"The Essential Poems of Jim Harrison is distilled from nearly 1,000 poems that appeared in fourteen volumes--from visionary lyrics and meditative suites to shape-shifting ghazals and prose-poem letters. Teeming throughout these pages are Harrison's legendary passions and appetites, his meditations, rages, and love-songs to the natural world. The New York Times concluded a review from early in Harrison's career with a provocative quote: 'This is poetry worth loving, hating, and fighting over, a subjective mirror of our American days and needs.' That sentiment still holds true, as Jim Harrison's essential poems continue to call for our fiercest attention".-- Provided by publisher.

"Reading this essential volume, one might imagine that the gods are, indeed, staying up late, reading lights on, turning the pages." Booklist.

Songs of unreason / Jim Harrison. Copper Canyon Press, c2011. xi, 143 p. ; **811**

1. American poetry

ISBN 9781556593895

LC 2011025560

Jim Harrison's compelling and provocative Songs of Unreason explores what it means to inhabit the world in atavistic, primitive, and totemistic ways.

"Most readers of contemporary poetry will enjoy this work." Library Journal

Harrison, Leslie, 1962-

The **book** of endings / Leslie Harrison. The University of Akron Press, 2017 88 p. ; **811**

1. Elegiac poetry 2. American poetry

ISBN 9781629220628

LC 2016026149

The poems in The Book of Endings try to make sense of, or at least come to some kind of reckoning with absence: the death of the author's mother, the absence of the beloved, the absence of an accountable god, cicadas, the dead stars arriving, the dead moon aglow in the night sky. --From publisher description.

"Harrison (Displacement) reveals a psyche made strange through grieving in this luminous and musical collection. Here, the self is seen as other, an art object to behold at some degree of remove." Publishers Weekly.

Hass, Robert

The **apple** trees at Olema : new and selected poems / Robert Hass. Ecco, c2010. xv, 352 p. ; **811**

1. American poetry

ISBN 9780061923821

LC 2010281516

From the National Book Award-winning author of Time and Materials comes 20 new and selected poems, grounded in the beauty of the physical world, in the smaller details of natural, human life.

Time and materials : poems, 1997-2005 / Robert Hass. Ecco, c2007. 88 p. ; **811**

1. American poetry

ISBN 9780061349607

LC 2007030294

Reflects on the beauty and energy of the physical world as well as life in contemporary America, in a stylistically varied collection of poetry that includes the poem, "Envy of Other People's Poems."

Hayden, Robert, 1913-1980

Collected poems / Robert Hayden ; edited by Frederick Glaysher. Liveright, 1996. xxxiv, 205 p. ; **811**

1. African American poetry 2. American poetry

ISBN 9780871401595

LC 96142645

Originally published: New York : Liveright, c1985. With a new introduction by Arnold Rampersad.

Enhanced by a biographical portrait and a critical analysis of Hayden's poetry, an anthology featuring the work of one of the most important African-American poets of the twentieth century contemplates the black experience and deals with such themes as dreams, mortality, nature, travel, and memory.

Hayes, Terrance

American sonnets for my past and future assassin / Terrance Hayes. Penguin Poets, 2018. 91 p. ; **811**

1. American poetry -- 21st century

ISBN 9780143133186

ALA Notable Book, 2019.

One of America's most acclaimed poets presents 70 poems bearing the same title that, written during the first 200 days of the Trump presidency, are haunted by the country's past and future eras and errors, its dreams and nightmares.

How to be drawn / Terrance Hayes. Penguin Books, 2015. ix, 99 p. ; **811**

1. American poetry 21st century 2. African American poetry

ISBN 9780143126881

LC 2014045785

"Hayes writes far-reaching yet intimate monologues that are simultaneously subtle and hard-hitting; he unearths shards of shameful antebellum history and takes measure of the current state of moral and political paralysis." Booklist.

Lighthead / Terrance Hayes. Penguin Books, 2010. ix, 95 p. ; **811**

1. American poetry 21st century 2. African American poetry

ISBN 9780143116967

LC 2009053319

Investigates through verse how humans construct experience and combines the loftiness of dreams and the reality of everyday life into poetry that is both dark and buoyant.

"This collection is a celebration and castigation of American culture, one worthy of the term Americanist. The title references the light of inspiration and the fire that pours from the heads of two teenage lynching victims in one of the opening poems. The fact that the title can do both inspiration and elegy is indicative of how meaning is contested terrain in Hayes' work. [He] deftly quilts together different textures of language. Rants move into love poems and biting humor butts up against meditations. Sound is of primary importance to Mr. Hayes. Throughout the book he borrows from hip-hop, jazz, slang, lists, and T-shirt slogans. Content aside, his poems are full of pure pleasure of sound in his startling and sonically dense images." Pittsburgh Post-Gazette.

Hicok, Bob, 1960-

Elegy owed / Bob Hicok. Copper Canyon Press, 2013 ix, 111 p. ; **811**

ISBN 9781556594366

LC 2012043531

"Words have weight in Hicok's poems. They feel nailed in place, and the meter hits like the sure pounding of a hammer. Yet as heft, muscle, and precision draw you forward, Hicok evokes not solidity but, rather, shifting ground, flux, metamorphosis, and, most arrestingly, most unnervingly, death... This trenchant collections got heart and soul." Booklist.

Hirsch, Edward

Earthly measures : poems / Edward Hirsch. Alfred A. Knopf,

1994. x, 93 p. ; **811**

1. Religious poetry 2. American poetry

ISBN 9780679765660

LC 93026410

Judged the author's best work yet by his contemporaries, a collection of poems highlights a human being's struggle with the urgency of everyday emotions.

Gabriel : a poem / Edward Hirsch. Alfred A. Knopf, 2014. 78 p. ; **811**

1. Children -- Death 2. Grief 3. American poetry

ISBN 9780385353571

LC 2013049301

A poignant volume of works inspired by the author's son's tragic early death reflects on the young man's boisterous youth, his rebellious early adulthood, and the author's experiences of grief.

The **living** fire : new and selected poems, 1975-2010 / Edward Hirsch. Alfred A. Knopf, 2010. xii, 237 p. ; **811**

1. American poetry

ISBN 9780375415227

LC 2009024452

A volume of more than one hundred definitive and original pieces by the National Book Critics Circle Award-winning writer includes poems that critically assess his own works and explore such topics as insomnia, culture and the arts.

On love : poems / Edward Hirsch. Alfred A. Knopf, 2000, c1998. viii, 86 p. ; **811**

1. American poetry

ISBN 9780375702600

LC BL 00009058

Poems deal with separateness, autonomy, loneliness, and longing, and include soliloquies by a variety of historical figures on the meaning of love.

Special orders : poems / Edward Hirsch. Alfred A. Knopf, 2008. viii, 64 p. ; **811**

1. American poetry

ISBN 9780307266811

LC 2007040336

A new, deeply personal anthology of poetry by the award-winning author of Wild Gratitude and Earthly Measures provides a profound, often painful, self-examination in such works as "Self-Portrait," "The Sweetness," and "I Wish I Could Paint You."

Stranger by night : poems / Edward Hirsch. Alfred A. Knopf, 2020. 62 p. ; **811**

1. American poetry 2. Elegiac poetry 3. Poetry of places

ISBN 9780525657781

LC 2019022482

Prose that reflects on the distinctly beautiful moments in life and also acts as a lamentation for the dead appears side by side in this new collection of poems from the prolific and award-winning poet and MacArthur Fellow.

Hirshfield, Jane, 1953-

After : poems / Jane Hirshfield. HarperCollins, c2006. 97 p. ; **811**

1. American poetry

ISBN 9780060779160

LC 2005050260

Collects poetry that explores such diverse topics as global warming, sneezing, and our relationship to certainty, possibility, judgment, and grief, while reflecting on the influence of time on human life.

The **beauty** : poems / Jane Hirshfield. Alfred A. Knopf, 2015. 107 p. ; **811**

1. American poetry

ISBN 9780385351072

LC 2014025831

"This is a Borzoi Book"--Title page verso.

"A collection of original poems by Jane Hirshfield exploring the profundities and quirks of existence"-- Provided by publisher.

Ledger : poems / Jane Hirshfield. Alfred A. Knopf, 2020. 128 p. **811**

1. Social responsibility. 2. Environmentalism

ISBN 9780525657804

LC 2019022480

The internationally renowned power named "among the modern masters," in this book of personal, ecological and political reckoning, shares a collection of indispensable poems that are tuned toward issues of consequence to all who share this world's current and future fate.

"In her ninth book of poetry, Hirshfield, avidly read and justly celebrated with numerous prestigious awards, seeks to balance what we take with what we give, what we seek with what we find, what we observe with what we comprehend." Booklist

Hoagland, Tony

Priest turned therapist treats fear of God : poems / Tony Hoagland. Graywolf Press, 2018 74 p. ; **811**

1. American poetry -- 20th century 2. American poetry

ISBN 9781555978075

LC 2017953461

Tony Hoagland's poems interrogate human nature and contemporary culture with an intimate and wild urgency, located somewhere between outrage, stand-up comedy, and grief. His new poems are no less observant of the human and the worldly, no less skeptical,and no less amusing, but they have drifted toward the greater depths of open emotion. Over six collections, Hoagland's poetry has gotten bigger, more tender, and more encompassing. The poems in Priest Turned Therapist Treats Fear of God turn his clear-eyed vision toward the hidden spaces--and spaciousness--in the human predicament.

Unincorporated persons in the late Honda dynasty : poems / Tony Hoagland. Graywolf Press, 2010. 90 p. ; **811**

1. American poetry

ISBN 9781555975494

LC 2009933818

"Hoagland (What Narcissism Means to Me) has fun in these poems but always in service to a smart and insightful notion." Library Journal

What narcissism means to me / Tony Hoagland. Graywolf Press, c2003. 78 p. ; **811**

1. American poetry

ISBN 9781555973865

LC 2003101172

An eagerly awaited new collection of poems by contemporary favorite Tony Hoagland.

Hollander, John

A **draft** of light : poems / John Hollander. Alfred A. Knopf,

2008. viii, 109 p. ; **811**
1. American poetry
ISBN 9780307269119
LC 2008004751

"Like Shakespeare, Hollander fuses a somber tone with comic conventions, resulting in the poetic equivalent of the problem play." Library Journal

Figurehead & other poems / John Hollander. Knopf, 1999. vi, 89 p. : **811**
1. American poetry
ISBN 9780375704338
LC 98014208

A collection of poems that encompass a wide variety of subjects, from philosophy and personal reflections to meditations on paintings

Hong, Cathy Park

Engine empire / Cathy Park Hong. W.W. Norton & Co., 2012. 95 p. ; **811**
ISBN 0393082849
LC 2012000596

Poems.

A trilogy of three interconnected poems addresses prosperity in a nineteenth-century California mining town, present-day Shenzhen, China, and the far future.

Hopler, Jay, 1970-

★The **abridged** history of rainfall / Jay Hopler. McSweeney's, 2016 ix, 75 p. : Mcsweeney's Poetry **811**
1. Grief
ISBN 9781944211264
LC 2018295065

National Book Award Finalist, Poetry, 2016

Jay Hopler's second collection, a mourning song for his father, is an elegy of uproar, a careening hymn to disaster and its aftermath. In lyric poems, by turns droll and desolate, Hopler documents the struggle to live in the face of great loss, a task that sends him ranging through Florida's torrid subtropics, the mountains of the American West, the streets of Rome, and the Umbrian countryside.- Provided by the publisher.

Howard, Richard, 1929-

★**Inner** voices : selected poems, 1963-2003 / Richard Howard. Farrar, Straus and Giroux, c2004. x, 428 p. ; **811**
1. American poetry
ISBN 9780374258627
LC 2004040464

The first collection of poems to span the published work of the Pulitzer Prize-winning poet includes fine examples of lyric poetry and fascinating monologues and fictive conversations between famous figures.

Without saying : new poems / Richard Howard. Turtle Point Press, 2008. 108 p. **811**
1. American poetry -- 21st century
ISBN 9781933527147
LC 2007907229

In Richard Howard's new collection, voices of myth and memory prevail by means of prevarication.

"In these thoughtful new poems, Howard offers, and excels in, sophisticated verbal comedy, making his personae of all ages show and say more than they know." Publishers Weekly

Howe, Fanny

Second childhood / Fanny Howe. Graywolf Press, 2014 77 p. ; **811**
1. American poetry
ISBN 9781555976828
LC 2013958013

"Recipient of the 2009 Ruth Lilly Poetry Prize for lifetime achievement, Howe (Come and See) is masterfully lyrical in her newest collection, one marbled throughout with musings over identity." Publishers Weekly

Hughes, Langston, 1902-1967

★**Selected** poems of Langston Hughes / Langston Hughes. Vintage Books, 1990. 297 p.; Vintage classics **811**
1. American poetry 2. African American poetry
ISBN 9780679728184
LC 90050179

A collection of the author's favorite poetry from published books, private publications, and unpublished manuscripts

Hugo, Richard, 1923-1982

Making certain it goes on : the collected poems of Richard Hugo / Richard F. Hugo. Norton, c1984. xxi, 456 p. ; **811**
1. American poetry
ISBN 9780393307849
LC 83008016

Includes index.

Poems written over twenty years deal with nature, travel, art, the past, mortality, friendship, marriage, and memory

Hutchinson, Ishion

★**House** of lords and commons / Ishion Hutchinson. Farrar, Straus and Giroux, 2016. 81 p. ; **811**
1. American poetry
ISBN 9780374173029
LC 2015045801

"A stunning collection that traverses the borders of culture and time."-- Provided by publisher.

Ignatow, David, 1914-1997

I have a name / David Ignatow. University Press of New England, c1996. ix, 75 p. ; **811**
1. American poetry
ISBN 9780819522405
LC 96019350

Poems discuss such timeless subjects as loss, age, death, and the joy of fleeting moments.

Shadowing the ground / David Ignatow. Wesleyan University Press, c1991. ix, 68 p. ; **811**
1. American poetry
ISBN 9780819511973
LC 90020872

A collection of poems that deal with life and its various stages, including death.

Jackson, Major, 1968-

Holding company / Major Jackson. W.W. Norton & Co., c2010. 91 p. ; **811**
1. American poetry -- 21st century.
ISBN 9780393070804
LC 2010017728

A collection of poetry explores art, literature, and music as seductive forces in our lives.

Hoops : poems / Major Jackson. Norton, 2006. 125 p. ; **811**

1. American poetry
ISBN 9780393059373

LC 2005033320

Collects poetic meditations evaluating everyday life, from a grandfather gardening in a tenement backyard to a teacher who unconsciouly renames her black students after French painters.

Jarrell, Randall, 1914-1965

★The **complete** poems / Randall Jarrell Farrar, Strauss & Giroux, 1981 xvi, 507 p. ; **811**

1. American poetry -- 20th century
ISBN 9780374513054

LC bl2013032386

Originally published: 1969.

A definitive anthology represents four decades of writing and includes new poems and previously published ones.

Jeffers, Honoree Fanonne, 1967-

The **age** of Phillis / Honoree Fanonne Jeffers. Wesleyan University Press, 2020. 213 p. Wesleyan Poetry **811**

1. Wheatley, Phillis, 1753-1784 2. African American women authors 3. Women slaves 4. Slavery -- Massachusetts -- History -- 18th century
ISBN 9780819579492

LC 2019040204

"A collection of original poems speaking to the life and times of Phillis Wheatley, a Colonial America-era poet brought to Boston as a slave".-- Provided by publisher.

"A true and rounded life, told in elegant, sometimes ravishing verse." Library Journal

Jeffers, Robinson, 1887-1962

The **selected** poetry of Robinson Jeffers / edited by Tim Hunt. Stanford University Press, 2001. 758 p. : **811**

1. American poetry
ISBN 9780804741088

LC 00048490

Includes indexes.

To accompany his five-volume collected poetry of the American poet, to be completed this year, Hunt (English, Washington State U.) offers a one-volume selection.

"A volume for the core of American literature collections." Booklist

Johnson, James Weldon, 1871-1938

Complete poems / James Weldon Johnson ; edited with an introduction by Sondra Kathryn Wilson. Penguin Books, 2000. xxxiii, 202 p. ; **811**

1. African Americans 2. African American poetry 3. American poetry
ISBN 9780141185453

LC 00039969

The complete poems of James Weldon Johnson are collected in the centenary year of "Lift Every Voice and Sing," considered to be his most important work.

Johnson, Jenny, 1979-

In full velvet : poems / Jenny Johnson. Sarabande Books, 2017 68 p. ; **811**

1. American poetry
ISBN 9781941411377

LC 2016014117

"Sinuous and sensual, the poems of In Full Velvet interrogate the nuances of desire, love, gender, ecology, LGBTQ lineage and community, and the tension between a body's material limits and the forms made possible by the imagination. Characterized by formal poise, vulnerability, and compassion, Johnson's debut collection is one of resounding generosity and grace."-- Provided by publisher.

Jones, Saeed

★**Prelude** to bruise : poetry / Saeed Jones. Coffee House Press, 2014. xii, 103 p. ; **811**

1. African American poetry 2. American poetry 3. Love poetry
ISBN 9781566893749

LC 2014008086

Offers a collection of poems that explore questions of masculinity, sexuality, race, and shifting identity.

Jordan, June, 1936-2002

★**Directed** by desire : the collected poems of June Jordan / edited by Jan Heller Levi and Sara Miles. Copper Canyon Press, c2005. xxix, 649 p. ; **811**

1. American poetry -- 20th century
ISBN 1556592280

LC 2005011701

Includes indexes.

"Jordan's poems consistently display a loving devotion to black English and pride in her femininity, race, and individuality. Directed by Desire is an important addition to African American or feminist poetry collections." Booklist..

Justice, Donald, 1925-2004

★**Collected** poems / Donald Justice. Alfred A. Knopf, 2004. xii, 289 p. ; **811**

1. American poetry
ISBN 9781400042395

LC 2003065735

A collection of poems features the writer's theme of classic American melancholy and includes such pieces as "Bus Stop," "Men at Forty," "Crossing Kansas by Train," "The Small White Churches of the Small White Towns."

Kaminsky, Ilya, 1977-

Deaf republic : poems / Ilya Kaminsky. Graywolf Press, 2019. 96 p. **811**

1. Resistance to government 2. Deafness 3. Sign language 4. Political violence
ISBN 9781555978310

LC 2018947088

ALA Notable Book, 2020.

Deaf Republic opens in an occupied country in a time of political unrest. When soldiers breaking up a protest kill a deaf boy, Petya, the gunshot becomes the last thing the citizens hear--they all have gone deaf, and their dissent becomes coordinated by sign language. The story follows the private lives of townspeople encircled by public violence. At once a love story, an elegy, and an urgent plea, these poems confronts our time's vicious atrocities and our collective silence in the face of them.

Karr, Mary

Tropic of squalor : poems / Mary Karr. Harper, an imprint of HarperCollins Publishers, 2018 xiv, 75 p. ; **811**

1. American poetry 2. Religious poetry
ISBN 9780062699824

LC 2017279116

"Long before she earned accolades for her genre-defining memoirs, Mary Karr was winning poetry prizes. Now the beloved author returns with a collection of bracing poems as visceral, deeply felt, and hilarious as her memoirs. In Tropic of Squalor, Karr dares to address the numinous--that mystery some of us hope toward in secret, or maybe dare to pray to. The "squalor" of meaninglessness that every thoughtful person wrestles with sits at the core of human suffering, and Karr renders it with power--illness,death, love's agonized disappointments. Her brazen verse calls us out of our psychic swamplands and into that hard-won awareness of the divine hiding in the small moments that make us human. In a single poem she can generate tears, horror, empathy, laughter, and peace. She never preaches. But whether you're an adamant atheist, a pilgrim, or skeptically curious, these poems will urge you to find an inner light in the most baffling hours of darkness." --Front flap of dust jacket.

Kasischke, Laura, 1961-

Space, in chains / Laura Kasischke. Copper Canyon Press, 2011. xi, 113 p. ; **811**

1. Poetry, Modern -- 21st century. 2. American poetry
ISBN 9781556593338

LC 2010040037

"Space, in Chains speaks in ghostly voices, fractured narratives, songs, prayers, and dark riddles as it moves through contemporary tragedies of grief and the complex succession of generations. In her eighth book of poetry, Laura Kasischke has pared the construction of her verse to its bones, leaving haunting language and a visceral strangeness of imagery. By turns mournful and celebratory, Kasischke's poetry insists upon asking hard questions that are courageously left unanswered."--Cover, p. [4].

Kaur, Rupi

Milk and honey / Rupi Kaur. Andrews McMeel Publishing, [2015] 204 p. **811**

1. Growth (Psychology) 2. Coping 3. Self-fulfillment
ISBN 9781449496364

LC bl2018181271

Presents poems that deal with the bitter aspects of love, loss, abuse, violence, and trauma, and celebrates the unstoppable power of grace, healing, and feminine strength.

Kelly, Robert, 1935-

Lapis : poems / Robert Kelly. David R. Godine, c2005. 221 p. : **811**

1. American poetry
ISBN 9781574231861

LC 2004016724

"A Black Sparrow book."

"Poem after poem builds on razor-sharp textures that draw the eye to the obvious and to the hidden world behind it. Here again is poetry that gleams in the light of the numinous." The Bloomsbury Review

Kelly, Robert, 1935-

Red actions : selected poems, 1960-1993 / Robert Kelly. Black Sparrow Press, 1995. 398 p. : **811**

1. American poetry
ISBN 9780876859773

LC 95035351

A collection by Robert Kelly.

Kendall, Tim, 1970-

The **art** of Robert Frost / Tim Kendall. Yale University Press, c2012. xvi, 392 p. ; **811**

1. Frost, Robert, 1874-1963 Criticism and interpretation. 2. Frost, Robert, 1874-1963 Aesthetics. 3. American poetry
ISBN 9780300118131

LC 2011041416

Includes the entirety of Frost's North of Boston (1914); selections from A boy's will (1913); generous selections from Mountain Interval (1916) and New Hampshire (1923); and a selection of lyrics in the section titled Later poems, from West-running brook (1928), A further range (1936), A witness tree (1942), and Steeple bush (1947).

Offers detailed accounts of sixty-five poems that span Frost's writing career and assesses the particular nature of the poet's style, discussing how it changes over time and relates to the works of contemporary poets and movements.

Kenner, Hugh

The **Pound** era / Hugh Kenner. University of California Press, 1973, c1971. xiv, 606 p. : **811**

1. Pound, Ezra, 1885-1972 Criticism and interpretation. 2. Twentieth century
ISBN 9780520024274

LC BL 00003890

Reprint. Originally published: 1971.

Hugh Kenner's The Pound Era could as well be known as the Kenner era, for there is no critic who has more firmly established his claim to valuable literary property than has Kenner to the first three decades of the 20th century in England. --From publisher description.

Book of blues / Jack Kerouac ; [introduction by Robert Creeley]. Penguin, 1995. xiii, 273 p. ; **811**

1. Beats (Persons) 2. American poetry
ISBN 9780140587005

LC 94045902

"Like all of Kerouac's work, these choruses live or die with the poet's enthusiasm, sometimes sunk in navel-gazing, sometimes stunning in their inspired leaps between images or thoughts." Publishers Weekly

Kerouac, Jack, 1922-1969

Scattered poems / Jack Kerouac. City Lights Books 1971 76 p. **811**

1. Beats (Persons) 2. American poetry
ISBN 9780872860643

LC 71028511

Spontaneous poetry by the author of On the Road, gathered from underground and ephemeral publications; including "San Francisco Blues," the variant texts of "Pull My Daisy," and "American haiku."

Kinnell, Galway, 1927-2014

★**Collected** poems / Galway Kinnell ; introduction by Edward Hirsch. Houghton Mifflin Harcourt, 2017. xliv, 591 p. : **811**

1. American poetry
ISBN 9780544875210

LC 2017044904

Includes index.

"The first complete showcase of "one of the true master poets of his generation," Galway Kinnell (1927-2014): a lifetime's work and a deeply lived life reflected in over two hundred poems".-- Provided by publisher.

A **new** selected poems / Galway Kinnell. Houghton Mifflin, 2001. xi, 179 p. ; **811**

1. American poetry

ISBN 9780618154456

LC 2001039523

"A Mariner book."

The Pulitzer Prize- and National Book Award-winning author selects poetry from his eight collections spanning 1960 to 1994 for inclusion in this sweeping survey of his work.

Strong is your hold / Galway Kinnell. Houghton Mifflin, 2006. 69 p. ; **811**

1. American poetry

ISBN 9780618224975

LC 2006011292

Presents a new collection of poetry by the winner of the Pulitzer Prize and the National Book Award, including "When the Towers Fell," his requiem for the victims of the September 11 attacks.

Kirby, David, 1944-

Talking about movies with Jesus : poems / David Kirby. Louisiana State University Press, c2011. 70 p. ; **811**

1. American poetry

ISBN 9780807137727

LC 2010024229

Much like a traveling circus, Kirby's poems are equally defined by their transient nature and by their destination. --From publisher description.

Kleinzahler, August

Sleeping it off in Rapid City : poems, new and selected / August Kleinzahler. Farrar, Straus and Giroux, 2008. 234 p. ; **811**

1. American poetry

ISBN 9780374265830

LC 2007041926

Collects poems from the author's major works along with a selection of new works.

Klink, Joanna, 1969-

Raptus / Joanna Klink. Penguin Books, 2010. xii, 60 p. ; **811**

1. American poetry

ISBN 9780143117728

LC 2010008246

The third collection of poetry from Joanna Klink, looks at every aspect of failed relationships.

Koch, Kenneth, 1925-2002

On the edge : collected long poems / Kenneth Koch. Alfred A. Knopf, 2007. 411 p. ; **811**

1. American poetry

ISBN 9780307262844

LC 2007024041

A companion volume to the Collected Poems of Kenneth Koch brings together six longer poetic masterworks that include When the Sun Tries to Go On, The Duplications, Seasons on Earth, Impressions of Africa, On the Edge, and Ko, or A Season on Earth.

Komunyakaa, Yusef

The **chameleon** couch : poems / Yusef Komunyakaa. Farrar, Straus and Giroux, 2011. 115 p. : **811**

ISBN 9780374120382

LC 2010033148

A collection of poems by Yusef Komunyakaa that explores the complexities of culture and its relation to artifact and place.

"In this collection, the author shares unusually personal reflections steeped in his intimacy with ancestors, gods, and monsters. These finely formed lyrics are timeless in their shadows and wounds, and startlingly fresh in mood, metaphor, image, and such pairings as gargoyles and power lines, sugar and salt." Booklist.

Talking dirty to the gods : poems / Yusef Komunyakaa. Farrar Straus & Giroux, 2001 134 p. **811**

1. American poetry 2. African American poetry

ISBN 9780374527938

LC 00021277

The Pulitzer Prize-winning poet-author of the critically acclaimed Thieves of Paradise explores rituals that link humans, animals, and insects in this lively, often satirical collection of poems.

"Komunyakaa's mournful surrealism seems to have found a perfect mathematical embodiment in this...collection, which comprises a hundred and thirty-two poems of four four-line stanzas. These are poems about the uncontrollable human and natural mysteries, and they are made sharper and more mysterious by the eternal recurrence of the stanzaic structure." The New Yorker.

Warhorses : poems / Yusef Komunyakaa. Farrar, Straus and Giroux, 2008. viii, 86 p. ; **811**

1. War poetry. 2. Love poetry. 3. African American poetry 4. American poetry

ISBN 9780374286439

LC 2007051760

Poems reflecting on love and war.

A collection of poems evaluates themes of war and conflict as demonstrated by global battles, social uprisings, and sexual confrontations, in a volume that explores lengthier poetic forms and includes such works as "The Autobiography of My Alter Ego."

Kooser, Ted

Delights & shadows : poems / Ted Kooser. Copper Canyon Press, c2004. xii, 87 p. ; **811**

1. American poetry

ISBN 9781556592010

LC 2003018447

Presents a collection of poems that celebrate everyday life.

Kumin, Maxine, 1925-2014

Jack and other new poems / Maxine Kumin. W.W. Norton & Co., c2005. 112 p. **811**

1. American poetry

ISBN 9780393059564

LC 2004021762

A fourteenth collection by the writer of Bringing Together focuses on a central theme of death, in a volume that includes meditations on the social consequences of the Civil War two hundred years later, praise songs for beloved animals, and explorations of the memory's ability to both haunt and console.

"This collection of poetry focuses on three subjects the poet knows well: first, the fauna (wild and domestic) in and around her New Hampshire farm; second, the troubles and lessons of advancing age; third, large-scale political history, this century born in blood and bombs as this Jewish-American poet has known it. Most of her strongest work (the title poem included) concerns elderly or deceased animals, obvious analogues for Kumin's ill, deceased or grieving human beings." Publishers Weekly.

Kunitz, Stanley, 1905-2006

★The **collected** poems / Stanley Kunitz. Norton, c2000. 285 p. ; **811**

1. American poetry
ISBN 9780393050301

LC 00041130

The author celebrates a life in poetry, sharing his work--published and unpublished--in this single volume of his life's accomplishment.

"What makes this collection of a lifetime's work so valuable is the way it allows us to perceive the interconnectedness of all Kunitz has written. Each poem stands alone, but each also enriches the others." New York Times Book Review.

Kusnetz, Ilyse, 1966-2016,

Angel bones : poems / Ilyse Kusnetz. Alice James Books, [2019] 100 p. **811**

1. Death 2. People with terminal illnesses
ISBN 9781948579001

LC 2018044235

"Angel Bones has an introspective voice that maintains a bright understanding of the temporal. As we read, we are painfully aware the speaker is dying from cancer and death is imminent. The attempt to not only explain, but understand how to welcome and embrace death is a bittersweet calm. How can one leave willingly when there is so much left behind?"-- Provided by publisher.

"Rapturous and heartbreaking, Kusnetz's posthumous second collection (after Small Hours) grieves both her own impending death from cancer and the decay of Earth due to humanity's negligence. Kusnetz offers a masterful examination of the minute details and baffling unknowns that sculpt our lives, excavating the liminal and giving meaning to a bleak existence through beauty found between the physical universe and cosmic energy of the soul." Publishers Weekly.

Kyger, Joanne

About now : collected poems / Joanne Kyger. National Poetry Foundation, c2007. 798 p. : **811**

1. American poetry
ISBN 9780943373713

LC 2006048192

This latest collection may serve as the definitive one, highlighting an excellent sampling of her work. --From publisher description.

Laughlin, James, 1914-1997

The **collected** poems of James Laughlin / with an introduction by Hayden Carruth. Moyer Bell, c1994. xxxi, 574 p. : **811**

1. American poetry
ISBN 9781559210676

LC 91032232

Includes index.

This volume collects Laughlin's poems from 1935 to 1993.

"This comprehensive collection is a fine showcase for a poet who also happens to be one of the foremost American literary publishers of our time." Library Journal

Lax, Robert

Love had a compass : journals and poetry / Robert Lax ; edited by James J. Uebbing. Grove Press, c1996. xviii, 253 p. ; **811**

1. American poetry
ISBN 9780802115874

LC 96001255

A collection of the poems and writings of Trappist monk Robert Lax, detailing his experiences living among the poor people of Mediterranean countries.

Le Guin, Ursula K., 1929-2018,

So far so good : poems, 2014-2018 / Ursula K. Le Guin. Copper Canyon Press, [2018] 80 p. **811**

1. Aging. 2. Memory. 3. Identity (Psychology) 4. Poets.
ISBN 9781556595387

LC 2018016185

Redolent of myths, history, nursery rhymes, and the natural world, LeGuin bookends a long, daring, and prolific career.

Lee, Li-Young, 1957-

The **undressing** : poems / Li-Young Lee. W. W. Norton & Company, 2018 95 p. ; **811**

ISBN 039306543X

LC 2017051768

Drawing from different sources--including the Old Testament, the Dao De Jing and the music of the Wu Tang Clan--a collection of poems attempts to uncover things hidden since the dawn of the world, investigating human violence and dispossession increasingly prevalent around the world, as well as the horrors the poet grew up with as a child of refugees.

Leiter, Sharon

Critical companion to Emily Dickinson : a literary reference to her life and work / Sharon Leiter. Facts on File, c2007. xv, 448 p. : **811**

1. Dickinson, Emily, 1830-1886 Handbooks, manuals, etc. 2. Poets, American -- 19th century -- Biography 3. Women and literature -- United States -- History -- 19th century
ISBN 0816054487

LC 2005028123

An encyclopedic guide to the American poet includes biographical information, critical analyses of her poems, and important places and influential people in her life.

Leonard, Keith (Keith R.)

Ramshackle ode / Keith Leonard. Mariner Books/Houghton Mifflin Harcourt, 2016. 93 p. ; **811**

1. American poetry 2. Nature
ISBN 9780544649675

LC 2015046790

"A Mariner original"

A debut collection from a Pushcart Prize-nominated poet.

"Intriguing and triumphant, Leonard's collection embodies the subject matter it so aptly depicts, whether it's a storm or steeple or meadow." Booklist

Lerner, Ben, 1979-

Angle of yaw / Ben Lerner. Copper Canyon Press, c2006. 127 p. ; **811**

1. American poetry
ISBN 9781556592461

LC 2006014260

"A handful of the more fragmentary poems in this long collection lack the satisfying associative logic and punch that characterize the best of these, and could have been omitted, but overall this collection places Lerner (The Lichtenberg Figures , 2004) among the most promising young poets now writing." Publishers Weekly

Levertov, Denise, 1923-1997

Selected poems / Denise Levertov ; with a preface by Robert Creeley ; edited and with an afterword by Paul A. Lacey. New Directions Books, 2003 xvi, 220 p. ; **811**

ISBN 9780811215541

LC bl2015032377

Presents a collection of poems that reflect the author's childhood inspiration by T.S. Eliot, her experiences as a newcomer to post-World War II America, and her beliefs as an anti-war activist and environmentalist.

Levin, Phillis, 1954-

Mr. memory & other poems / Phillis Levin. Penguin, 2016 80 p. ; **811**

1. American poetry

ISBN 9780143128113

LC 2015042145

"Pathos and sweetness dominate the careful, information-rich book, which should appeal to readers who admire Robert Pinsky or Gjertrud Schnackenberg." Publishers Weekly.

Levine, Philip, 1928-2015

Breath : poems / Philip Levine. Knopf, 2004. 82 p. ; **811**

1. American poetry

ISBN 9781400042913

LC 2004040839

Looking back at his own life and the experiences of ancestors, family, and friends, this collection of poetry explores their diverse rites of passage in America in a celebration of the power of love, the strength of the human spirit, and the persistence of life in a world of challenge and pain.

Levine, Philip, 1928-2015

The **mercy** : poems / Philip Levine. Alfred A. Knopf, 1999. viii, 81 p. ; **811**

1. American poetry

ISBN 9780375701351

LC 98043353

A collection of poems on journeys--from innocence to experience, from youth to age, and from life to death.

Levine, Philip, 1928-2015

New selected poems / Philip Levine. Knopf, 1991. 292 p. ; **811**

1. American poetry

ISBN 9780679740568

LC 90053422

Poems portray the feelings and experiences of the author and explore themes such as age, faith, and death.

Levine, Philip, 1928-2015

The **simple** truth : poems / Philip Levine. Knopf, 1995, c1994. viii, 69 p. ; **811**

1. American poetry 2. Families

ISBN 9780679765844

LC bl 99778002

Offers thirty-three poems that interweave a complex web of myth, public and private history, family, memory, and invention as they explore the timeless truths of human existence

Levine, Philip, 1928-2015

What work is : poems / Philip Levine. A. A. Knopf : 1999, c1991. 77 p. ; **811**

1. American poetry

ISBN 9780679740582

LC BL 00003289

A collection of poems culled from the poet's twelve earlier books includes such pieces as "Fear and Fame," "Coming Close," "Every Blessed Day," and the title poem.

Levis, Larry

The **darkening** trapeze : last poems / Larry Levis ; edited with an afterword by David St. John. Graywolf Press, 2016 100 p. ; **811**

1. American poetry

ISBN 9781555977276

LC 2015952175

A collection of poems from the poet, including major unpublished works and a coda believed to be the last poem he wrote.

Lewis, Robin Coste

★**Voyage** of the Sable Venus and other poems / Robin Coste Lewis. Alfred A. Knopf, 2015. x, 142 p. ; **811**

1. African American poetry 2. American poetry

ISBN 9781101875438

LC 2014047762

"This is a Borzoi book."

A collection of poetry which analyzes the role of the black woman through time.

Lima, Frank, 1939-

Incidents of travel in poetry : new and selected poems / Frank Lima ; edited by Garrett Caples and Julien Poirier. City Lights Books, 2015 xxxvi, 279 p. : **811**

1. Poetry of places

ISBN 9780872866676

LC 2015035462

"Incidents of Travel in Poetry is the first collection by Latino New York School poet Frank Lima in almost 20 years. In addition to a generous selection of his published books, Incidents contains a wealth of previously unpublished new material, tracing his development from his early gritty portrayals of Spanish Harlem street life to his later abstractly lyrical mode".-- Provided by publisher.

Limon, Ada

Bright dead things : poems / Ada Limon. Milkweed Editions, 2015. 105 p. ; **811**

1. Identity (Psychology) 2. Memories 3. Loss (Psychology) 4. Mortality

ISBN 9781571314710

LC 2015000088

Bright Dead Things examines the chaos that is life, the dangerous thrill of living in a world you know you have to leave one day, and the search to find something that is ultimately "disorderly, and marvelous, and ours." -- from publisher description

"Recurring instances of anxiety about mortality in Limon's poems complicate experiences so richly written and felt." Publishers Weekly.

★The **carrying** : poems / Ada Limon. Milkweed Editions, 2018. 95 p. **811**

1. American poetry -- 21st century
ISBN 9781571315120

LC 2017061361

ALA Notable Book, 2019.

The Carrying continues further and deeper into the bloodstream, following the hard-won truth of what it means to live in an imperfect world. -- from publisher description.

Lindsay, Sarah, 1958-

Twigs & knucklebones / Sarah Lindsay. Copper Canyon Press, 2008. 117 p. ; **811**

1. American poetry
ISBN 9781556591648

LC 2008019578

Presents a collection of surreal poems that blend science and art.

Long Soldier, Layli

★**Whereas** : poems / Layli Long Soldier. Graywolf Press, 2017 101 p. ; **811**

1. Indians of North America, Treatment of 2. Lakota Indians 3. Government relations with indigenous peoples 4. Language and languages
ISBN 9781555979614

LC OC2018009514

Whereas confronts the coercive language of the United States government in its responses, treaties, and apologies to Native American peoples and tribes, and reflects that language in its officiousness and duplicity back on its perpetrators. Through a virtuosic array of short lyrics, prose poems, longer narrative sequences, resolutions, and disclaimers, Layli Long Soldier has created a brilliantly innovative text to examine histories, landscapes, her own writing, and her predicament inside national affiliations.

"A wickedly smart, necessarily solemn, and unmistakably urgent addition to a continually burgeoning canon of Native poetry." Booklist.

Longenbach, James

Earthling : poems / James Longenbach. W. W. Norton & Company, 2018 94 p. ; **811**

1. American poetry
ISBN 9780393353433

LC 2017015728

"Longenbach's language remains sparse, calm, and graceful even as his poems confront the finiteness of individual human lives." Publishers Weekly

Longfellow, Henry Wadsworth, 1807-1882

★**Poems** and other writings / Henry Wadsworth Longfellow. Library of America, c2000. xiv, 854 p. ; The Library of America ; **811**

1. American poetry 9th century 2. American literature 19th century
ISBN 9781883011857

LC 00026678

Selected poems, novels, and essays are included in a collection of the nineteenth-century American poet's works.

Lowell, Robert, 1917-1977

★**Collected** poems / Robert Lowell ; edited by Frank Bidart and David Gewanter ; with the editorial assistance of DeSales Harrison. Farrar, Straus and Giroux, 2003. xvii, 1186 p. : **811**

1. American poetry
ISBN 9780374126179

LC BL2003013769

The first full collection of Robert Lowell's work introduces readers to the literary genius of the nation's most important postwar poet, including several never-before-anthologized poems.

Selected poems / Robert Lowell. Farrar, Straus and Giroux, 1977. xvi, 255 p. ; **811**

ISBN 0374258694

LC 78104855

Includes indexes.

MacGowan, Christopher J. (Christopher John)

Twentieth-century American poetry / Christopher MacGowan. Blackwell Pub., 2004. xvi, 331 p. ; Blackwell guides to literature **811**

1. American poetry -- 20th century -- History and criticism.
ISBN 9780631220251

LC 2003012196

Provides guidance to the study of twentieth-century American poetry, including biographical, cultural, historical, and thematic influences.

MacLeish, Archibald, 1892-1982

Collected poems, 1917-1982 / Archibald MacLeish ; with a prefatory note to the newly collected poems by Richard B. McAdoo. Houghton Mifflin, 1985. 524 p. ; **811**

1. American poetry -- 20th century 2. Poetry, Modern -- 20th century
ISBN 0395395690

LC 85014392

Poems deal with space, birth, aging, death, writers, poetry, history, and travel.

Mackey, Nathaniel, 1947-

Splay anthem / Nathaniel Mackey. New Directions Book, 2006. xvi, 126 p. ; **811**

1. African American poetry 2. American poetry
ISBN 9780811216524

LC 2005035051

A new collection of poetry is divided into three sections including "Braid," "Fray," and "Nub" and features two ongoing serial poems that have evolved throughout more than twenty years, such as a West African spirit song and an exploration of a lost "we"tribe.

Majmudar, Amit

Dothead : poems / Amit Majmudar. Alfred A. Knopf, 2016 ix, 104 p. ; **811**

ISBN 1101947071

LC 2015020310

"This is a Borzoi book."

A poetry collection by the Indian-American author explores his sense of self and presents a cultural critique of "the other" in the United States.

Manning, Maurice, 1966-

The **common** man / Maurice Manning. Houghton Mifflin Harcourt, 2010. viii, 96 p. ; **811**

1. American poetry 2. Appalachian Region
ISBN 9780547249612

LC 2009029080

The poet offers a series of narratives celebrating the Kentucky mountain country of his youth and the hidden complexities of everyday people and experiences.

Matthews, Airea D.

Simulacra / Airea D. Matthews ; foreword by Carl Phillips. Yale University Press, 2017. xviii, 80 p. ; **811**

1. African American poetry 2. American poetry -- 21st century.
ISBN 9780300223965

LC 2016952569

Winner of the 2016 Yale Series of Younger Poets prize.

A fresh and rebellious poetic voice, Airea D. Matthews debuts in the acclaimed series that showcases the work of exciting and innovative young American poets. Matthews's superb collection explores the topic of want and desire with power, insight, and intense emotion. Her poems cross historical boundaries and speak emphatically from a racialized America, where the trajectories of joy and exploitation, striving and thwarting, violence and celebration are constrained by differentials of privilege and contemporary modes of communication. In his foreword, series judge Carl Phillips calls this book "rollicking, destabilizing, at once intellectually sly and piercing and finally poignant." This is poetry that breaks new literary ground, inspiring readers to think differently about what poems can and should do in a new media society where imaginations are laid bare and there is no thought too provocative to send out into the world.

Matthews, William, 1942-1997

Selected poems and translations, 1969-1991 / William Matthews. Houghton Mifflin, 1992. xii, 200p. ; **811**

1. American poetry -- 20th century
ISBN 9780395669938

LC 91045716

Includes index.

The author's poems deal with sports, music, wine, homes, pets, love, children, and literature, and are accompanied by poems translated from French, Latin, and Bulgarian.

May, Jamaal

Hum / Jamaal May. Alice James Books, 2013. 74 p. ; **811**

1. African American poetry 2. American poetry 3. Poetry of places
ISBN 9781938584022

LC 2013022185

"Linguistically acrobatic, these poems render the violence of a body's undoing--by war, by drugs--and the mind's in ways that are beautifully crafted, whether formal or free, and resistant to sentimentality." Publishers Weekly.

Mayer, Bernadette

Scarlet tanager / Bernadette Mayer. New Directions Book, 2005. 117 p. ; **811**

1. American poetry
ISBN 9780811215824

LC 2005005539

"A New Directions paperbook original, NDP1015"--p. [4] of cover.

New work from one of America's most original experimental poets. Comprised almost entirely of never-before-collected poems, Scarlet Tanager is Bernadette Mayer's first collection of new work in nearly a decade.

"Mayer should know that many young poets continue to read everything she writes; those readers will delight in the disarming appeal her capacious collection retains." Publishers Weekly

McClatchy, J. D., 1945-

Poets of the Civil War / J.D. McClatchy, editor. Library of America, c2005. xxvii, 211 p. ; **811**

1. American poetry -- 19th century 2. War poetry, American 3. American poetry 4. United States -- History -- Civil War, 1861-1865
ISBN 9781931082761

LC 2004061552

Collects poems inspired by the Civil War, including works by William Cullen Bryant, Henry Wadsworth Longfellow, Oliver Wendell Holmes, and Walt Whitman.

McCrae, Shane, 1975-

In the language of my captor / Shane McCrae. Wesleyan University Press, 2017 86 p. ; **811**

1. American poetry
ISBN 9780819577115

LC 2016035696

In the book's three sequences, McCrae explores the role mass entertainment plays in oppression, he confronts the myth that freedom can be based upon the power to dominate others, and, in poems about the mixed-race child adopted by Jefferson Davis in the last year of the Civil War, he interrogates the infrequently examined connections between racism and love. --From publisher description.

"With a raw honesty, McCrae refuses to shy away from the effects of oppression and faces up to those not willing to acknowledge their part in a history many want to forget." Publishers Weekly.

McGrath, Campbell, 1962-

Nouns & verbs : new and selected poems / Campbell McGrath. Ecco, [2019] xiii, 272 pages ; **811**

1. American poetry -- 21st century.
ISBN 9780062854148

LC 2018278470

Deeply personal but also expansive in its imaginative scope, Nouns & Verbs brings together thirty-five years of writing from Campbell McGrath, one of America's most highly lauded poets. Offering a hint of where he's headed while charting the territory already explored, McGrath gives us startlingly inventive new poems while surveying his previous work: lyric poems, prose poems, and a searing episodic personal epic, "An Odyssey of Appetite," exploring America's limitless material and spiritual hungers.

"McGrath is intelligent company, his poems exhibiting a curious, sometimes furious mind tuning into the literal noise of our culture, both violent and beautiful." Publishers Weekly.

McGrath, Thomas, 1916-1990

Letter to an imaginary friend / Thomas McGrath. Copper Canyon Press, 1998. iv, 405 p. ; **811**

1. American poetry -- 20th century 2. Epic poetry.
ISBN 9781556590771

LC 97033929

"Although McGrath, who died in 1990 at 74, published the poem's four parts separately, it appears here complete for the first time. A surprisingly accessible long poem in the Pound tradition of personal epics, Letter arrives helved, greaved, and garlanded and compels our intimate attention." Publishers Weekly.

McHugh, Heather, 1948-

Muddy matterhorn : poems 2009-2019 / Heather McHugh. Copper Canyon Press, [2020] 104 p. **811**

ISBN 9781556595967

LC 2019043664

"Heather McHugh's first book in a decade, Muddy Matterhorn, reclaims the mix of high and low that is her sensibility's signature, in matters practical and philosophical, semantic and stylistic, mortal and transitory, amorous and political, hilarious and heartbreaking. With fierce attacks on technology and social structures, McHugh finds a way to enjoy and empathize with humanity on her own terms. Ever the outsider, McHugh combines a strong sense of self with a determination to love people and the worlds they build without losing her biting criticism or witty rejection of societal norms and expectations. She is both pragmatic and theorizing, esoteric and identifiable. The joy and anger in these poems join to form an empowered and impassioned declaration of self in a chaotic time".-- Provided by publisher.

"McHugh's wordplay is peerless. . . . This is a high-impact book that is impossible to exhaust." Booklist

McLane, Maureen N.

This blue / Maureen N. McLane. Farrar, Straus and Giroux, 2014. 107 p. ; **811**

1. American poetry
ISBN 9780374275938

LC 2013033882

The National Book Critics Circle nominee presents her third poetry collection that contains songs for and of a new century, poems both archaic and wholly now.

McMichael, James, 1939-

Capacity / James McMichael. Farrar, Straus and Giroux, 2006 74 p. ; **811**

1. Nature 2. Human ecology 3. Natural resources 4. American poetry
ISBN 9780374118907

LC 2005051628

Collects poems that contemplate a planet Earth that supplies what people need in order to survive, and considers how such elements as water and shelter are taken for granted.

Mead, Jane, 1958-

World of made and unmade : a poem / Jane Mead. Alice James Books, 2016 65 p. ; **811**

1. Elegiac poetry 2. Families 3. American poetry
ISBN 9781938584329

LC 2016011688

"This accessible work will appeal to a wide range of readers." Library Journal

Millay, Edna St. Vincent, 1892-1950

Collected poems / Edna St. Vincent Millay. Harper & Row, 1981. 757 p. **811**

1. American poetry -- 20th century
ISBN 9780060908898

LC BL 99753230

A selection of poems which demonstrates Millay's technical ability and directness

"The poems in this collection are divided into two separate sections of lyrics and sonnets, arranged chronologically and printed in groups under the titles of the original volumes, ranging from Renascence of 1917 to Mine the harvest, published in 1954, four years after the poet's death." Booklist.

★**Selected** poems / Edna St. Vincent Millay ; J.D. McClatchy, editor. The Library of America, c2003. xxxiii, 231 p. ; **811**

1. American poetry
ISBN 9781931082358

LC 2002032126

Includes index.

Offers new insights into Millay's career, presenting both familiar favorites and lesser-known pieces including translations, a verse play, songs from her opera libretto "The King's Henchmen," and the complete sonnet sequence of "Fatal Interview."

Miranda, Lin-Manuel, 1980-

Gmorning, gnight! : little pep talks for me & you / Lin-Manuel Miranda ; Illustrations by Jonny Sun. Random House, 2018. 208 p. **811**

1. Self-esteem. 2. Personal conduct. 3. Motivation (Psychology) 4. Maxims.
ISBN 9781984854278

LC 2018029526

The creator and star of "Hamilton" presents an illustrated book of affirmations to provide inspiration at the beginning and end of each day.

Moore, Marianne, 1887-1972

New collected poems / Marianne Moore ; edited by Heather Cass White. Farrar, Straus and Giroux, 2017. xxvi, 453 p. ; **811**

1. American poetry
ISBN 9780374221041

LC 2017003857

The definitive collected edition of one of our most innovative and beloved poets, Marianne Moore.

★The **poems** of Marianne Moore / edited by Grace Schulman. Viking, 2003. xxx, 449 p. ; **811**

1. American poetry
ISBN 9780670031986

LC 2003050159

Includes index.

A complete posthumous collection of poems includes 120 previously unprinted works that were omitted from earlier definitive publications, as well as original notes, and is organized chronologically to enable readers to follow her development as a poet.

"The great modernist poet finally gets her due with this outstanding compilation." Library Journal.

Mosby, Rebekah Presson

Poetry speaks expanded : hear poets from Tennyson to Plath read their own work / Elise Paschen & Rebekah Presson Mosby, editors ; Charles Osgood, narrator. Sourcebooks, c2007. xiv, 384 p. : **811**

1. American poetry -- 20th century -- History and criticism. 2. American poetry -- 20th century. 3. English poetry -- 19th century -- History and criticism. 4. English poetry -- 19th century.
ISBN 1402210620

LC 2007037080

Includes index.

Rev. ed. of: Poetry speaks, 2001.

Offers brief biographies, critical interpretations, and selected poems by forty-seven American and English poets from 1809 to 1963, along with recordings of each of the authors reading the works aloud.

"Reluctant poetry readers may find themselves drawn to the printed page by the spoken work, and poetry fans are likely to find much to love here." Publishers Weekly.

Nadelberg, Amanda

Bright brave phenomena : poems / Amanda Nadelberg. Coffee House Press, 2012. 118 p. ; **811**

1. American poetry

ISBN 9781566893039

LC 2011029251

A collection of poems build a playful and heartbreaking universe from ordinary moments, weather, landscape, and memory.

Nguyen, Diana Khoi, 1985-

Ghost of / Diana Khoi Nguyen. Omnidawn Publishing, 2018. 83 p. ; **811**

1. American poetry

ISBN 9781632430526

LC 2017051224

A collection of poems focuses on the photographs the author's brother left behind before his death in which he cut himself out, detailing her experiences dealing with memory, physical voids, and her family captured around an empty space.

Nguyen, Hieu Minh

Not here / Hieu Minh Nguyen. Coffee House Press, 2018. 73 p. ; **811**

1. American poetry 2. Families 3. Love poetry

ISBN 9781566895095

LC 2017040746

"Nguyen follows up his debut, This Way to the Sugar (2014), with a collection that astounds in its intensity. Through elastic, creative form, Nguyen, a child of Vietnamese immigrants, explores Asian American identity and queer identity with acerbic wit and an open heart." Booklist.

Niatum, Duane, 1938-

Harper's anthology of 20th century Native American poetry / edited by Duane Niatum. Harper & Row, c1988. 396 p. ; **811**

1. Indians of North America

ISBN 9780062506658

LC 86045023

Includes indexes.

The rich, varied work of 36 contemporary Native American poets of stature is sampled in this welcome anthology.

"This collection contains the work of 36 native American poets, with hearty selections from each. ... This book belongs in every collection that claims to represent the multiple voices of American literature today." Booklist.

Niedecker, Lorine

Lorine Niedecker collected works / edited by Jenny Penberthy. University of California Press, c2002. xxiii, 471 p. : **811**

1. American poetry -- 20th century

ISBN 9780520224339

LC 2001005376

The important "Objectivist" poet finds full voice in this full collection of her poetry, plays, and creative prose from the 1930s and 1940s, organized into the sequence of their creation.

Norris, Kathleen, 1947-

Journey : new and selected poems, 1969-1999 / Kathleen Norris. University of Pittsburgh Press, c2001. 131 p. : **811**

1. American poetry

ISBN 9780822957614

LC 2001281180

The best-selling author of The Cloister Walk and other thought-provoking memoirs of faith presents a collection of her poetry, which explores the sacredness of life and the diverse landscapes of the spiritual world in works spanning three decades, including both new poems and selections from three previous anthologies.

Notley, Alice, 1945-

In the pines / Alice Notley. Penguin Books, 2007. xii, 131 p. ; **811**

1. American poetry

ISBN 9780143112549

LC 2007012076

Presents a collecton of narrative, prose, and free-verse poems.

Nye, Naomi Shihab

You & yours : poems / Naomi Shihab Nye. BOA Editions, 2005. 87 p. ; American poets continuum series ; **811**

ISBN 9781929918690

LC 2005011360

A collection of poems by the Palestinian-American poet looks at life in her inner-city Texas neighborhood, as well as the daily rituals of Jews and Palestinians who live in the war-torn Middle East.

"Part one covers Nye's personal experience, at home with her child in San Antonio or as a Frequent Frequent Flyer enjoying the sights of Scotland. . . . Part two covers the Middle East." Publishers Weekly.

O'Hara, Frank, 1926-1966

The collected poems of Frank O'Hara / edited by Donald Allen ; with an introduction by John Ashbery. University of California Press, 1995 xxix, 586 p. ; **811**

1. City and town life -- Poetry. 2. American poetry 3. New York (N.Y.) -- Poetry.

ISBN 9780520201668

LC 94024660

Reflects the poet's growth as an artist from the earliest experimental verses in the late 1940s to the years before his accidental death at forty.

Selected poems / Frank O'Hara ; edited by Mark Ford. Alfred A. Knopf, 2008. xix, 265 p. ; **811**

1. American poetry

ISBN 9780307268150

LC 2007042865

Includes index.

A compendium of selected works by the influential New York poet features poetry from "A City in Winter" and his six other collections of poems, accompanied by an overview of his work and influence on modern American literature.

Oliver, Mary, 1935-2019

★**Devotions** : the selected poems of Mary Oliver / Mary Oliver. Penguin Press, 2017. xx, 455 p. ; **811**

1. American poetry 2. Nature

ISBN 9780399563249

LC 2017025254

Includes index of titles and first lines.

"Pulitzer Prize-winning poet Mary Oliver presents a personal selection of her best work in this definitive collection spanning more than five decades of her esteemed literary career. Throughout her celebrated career, Mary Oliver has touched countless readers with her brilliantly crafted verse, expounding on her love for the physical world and the powerful bonds between all living things. Identified as "far and away, this country's best selling poet" by Dwight Garner, she now returns with a stunning and definitive collection of her writing from the last fifty years. Carefully curated, these 200 plus poems feature Oliver's work from her very first book of poetry, No Voyage and Other Poems, published in 1963 at the age of 28, through her most recent collection, Felicity, published in 2015. This timeless volume, arranged by Oliver herself, showcases the beloved poet at her edifying best. Within these pages, she provides us with an extraordinary and invaluable collection of her passionate, perceptive, and much-treasured observations of the natural world." Provided by publisher.

★**Dream** work / Mary Oliver. Atlantic Monthly Press, c1986. 90 p. ; **811**

1. American poetry
ISBN 9780871130693

LC 86007956

Presents poems that explore such themes as joy, self-awareness, and mankind's connection to the natural world.

★**New** and selected poems, Mary Oliver. Beacon Press, 2004, c1992. 272 p. ; **811**

1. American poetry -- 20th century
ISBN 9780807068779

LC 92007767

A collection of poems covering such topics as nature, writing, and art.

A **thousand** mornings / Mary Oliver. Penguin Press, 2012. 82 p. ; **811**

1. American poetry
ISBN 9781594204777

LC 2012027310

Presents a collection of poems that explore such themes as the wonder of nature, the power of attention, and the mysteries of the daily experience.

Oppen, George

★**New** collected poems / George Oppen ; edited with an introduction and notes by Michael Davidson ; preface by Eliot Weinberger. New Directions, 2002. xlv, 433 p. : **811**

1. American poetry
ISBN 9780811214889

LC 2001044048

George Oppen's New Collected Poems brings together all of the Objectivist poet's published work, together with a selection of his previously unpublished poems.

"Admirers of Oppen's foundational volumes should be very pleased with this update." Publishers Weekly

Ostriker, Alicia

No heaven / Alicia Suskin Ostriker. University of Pittsburgh Press, c2005. 136 p. ; **811**

1. American poetry
ISBN 9780822958758

LC 2005282457

A commentary on America, this book delves into major aspects of contemporary society and expounds upon the country's qualities, both positive and negative.

"Ostriker's tonic poems remind us that although we are the animal that kills out of rage and greed, we are also creatures of grace and harmony." Booklist

Padgett, Ron, 1942-

Collected poems / Ron Padgett. Coffee House Press, 2013. 810 p. ; **811**

1. American poetry
ISBN 9781566893428

LC 2013017190

Includes indexes.

Gathering the work of more than fifty years, Ron Padgett's Collected Poems is the record of one of the most dynamic careers in twentieth-century American poetry.

Pankey, Eric, 1959-

Trace : poems / Eric Pankey. Milkweed Editions, 2013. 68 p. ; **811**

1. American poetry 2. Religious poetry
ISBN 9781571314499

LC 2012028097

"Occasionally they are repetitive, recycled. But Pankey is a powerful poet, and not only because of his engagement: his best poems speak for themselves." Booklist

Pardlo, Gregory

Digest / Gregory Pardlo. Four Way Books, 2014 75 p. ; **811**

1. African American poetry 2. American poetry
ISBN 9781935536505

LC 2014011291

From Epicurus to Sam Cooke, the Daily News to Roots, Digest draws from the present and the past to form an intellectual, American identity.

Parker, Morgan

★**Magical** negro : poems / Morgan Parker. W W Norton & Co Inc 2019 112 p. **811**

1. African Americans 2. Civil Rights Movement 3. Racism
ISBN 9781947793187

LC 2018041653

A latest collection by the prizewinning author of There Are More Beautiful Things Than Beyoncé explores black American womanhood through evocative themes ranging from self-conception and loneliness to objectification and ancestral trauma.

"A searing indictment, an irreverent lampoon, and a desperately urgent work of poetry, to be read alongside the work of Eve L. Ewing, Tiana Clark, and Nicole Sealey." Booklist.

There are more beautiful things than Beyoncé / Morgan Parker. Tin House Books, 2017. 85 p. ; **811**

1. African American poetry 2. American poetry
ISBN 9781941040539

LC 2016049158

Morgan Parker stands at the intersectionsof vulnerability and performance, of desire and disgust,of tragedy and excellence. Unrelentingly feminist,tender, ruthless, and sequined, these poems are an altarto the complexities of black American womanhood inan age of non-indictments and deja vu, and a time ofwars over bodies and power. --From publisher description.

"Cheeky and luscious yet ever aching, this collection from Pushcart Prize winner Parker (Other People's Comfort Keeps Me Up at Night) uses a tough vernacular to unfold the story of a black woman." Library Journal.

Perillo, Lucia, 1958-2016

On the spectrum of possible deaths / Lucia Perillo. Copper

Canyon Press, 2012. x, 81 p. ; **811**

1. American poetry

ISBN 9781556593970

LC 2011050110

"In her sixth collection, this Pulitzer Prize finalist and winner of the Library of Congress' Rebekah Johnson Bobbitt Award stealthily combines earthy intimacy, wry deprecation, metaphysics, and acute observations expressed in exuberant yet piercing images." Booklist

Time will clean the carcass bones : selected and new poems / Lucia Perillo. Copper Canyon Press, 2016 ix, 239 p. ; **811**

1. POETRY / American / General. 2. American poetry

ISBN 9781556594731

LC 2015034497

A retrospective of the poet's work, as well as some new poems.

Petrosino, Kiki, 1979-

White blood : a lyric of Virginia / Kiki Petrosino. Sarabande Books, 2020 107 p. **811**

1. African American women 2. Women -- Identity 3. Families -- History 4. Slavery 5. Virginia 6. Southern States

ISBN 9781946448545

LC 2019032278

Kiki Petrosino turns her gaze to Virginia, where she digs into her genealogical and intellectual roots, while contemplating the knotty legacies of slavery and discrimination in the Upper South. Speaking to history, loss, and injustice with wisdom, innovation, and a scientific determination to find the poetic truth, White Blood plants Petrosino's name ever more firmly in the contemporary canon.

"The result of deep historical research, impressive formal dexterity, and savvy storytelling, this volume of poetry combines genealogy, history, and verse in a way that reflects many American experiences." ForeWord Magazine

Phillips, Rowan Ricardo

Heaven / Rowan Ricardo Phillips. Farrar, Straus and Giroux, 2015. 61 p. ; **811**

1. African American poetry 2. American poetry

ISBN 9780374168520

LC 2014039377

"A spectacularly vibrant and continually surprising collection from one of the poetry world's rising young stars 'Who the hell's heaven is this?' Rowan Ricardo Phillips offers many answers, and none at all, in Heaven, the piercing and revelatory encore to his award-winning debut, The Ground. Swerving elegantly from humor to heartbreak, from Colorado to Florida, from Dante's Paradise to Homer's Illiad, from knowledge to ignorance to awe, Phillips turns his gaze upward and outward, probing and upending notions of the beyond. 'Feeling, real feeling / with all its faulty / Architecture, is / Beyond a god's touch'--but it does not elude Phillips. Meditating on feverish boyhood, on two paintings by Chuck Close, on Shakespeare's Measure for Measure, on a dead rooster by the side of the road in Ohio, on an elk grazing outside his window, his language remains eternally intoxicating, full of play, pathos, and surprise. 'The end,' he writes, 'like / All I've ever told you, is uncertain.' Or, elsewhere: 'The only way then to know a truth / Is to squint in its direction and poke.' Phillips--who received a 2013 Whiting Writers' Award as well as the PEN/Joyce Osterweil Award--may not be certain, but as he squints and pokes in the direction of truth, his power of perception and elegance of expression create a place where beauty and truth come together and drift apart like a planet orbiting its star. The result is a book whose lush and wounding beauty will leave its mark on readers long after they've turned the last page".-- Provided by publisher.

Living weapon / Rowan Ricardo Phillips. Farrar, Straus and Giroux, 2020. 79 p. **811**

1. City life 2. Political culture -- United States 3. Violence 4. Human/computer interaction 5. New York City

ISBN 9780374191993

LC 2019038070

A revelation, a shoring up, a transposition: Rowan Ricardo Phillips's Living Weapon is a love song to the imagination, a new blade of light honed in on our political moment. A winged man plummets from the troposphere; four NYPD officers enter a cellphone store; concrete sidewalks hang overhead. Here, in his third collection of poems, Phillips offers us ruminations on violins and violence, on hatred, on turning forty-three, even on the end of existence itself. Living Weapon reveals to us the limitations of our vocabulary, that our platitudes are not enough for the brutal times in which we find ourselves. But still, our lives go on, and these are poems of survival as much as they are an indictment.

"Phillips's latest is lyrical, imaginative, and steeped in a keen understanding of current events." Publishers Weekly

Pico, Tommy

Feed / Tommy Pico. Tin House Books, 2019. 78 p. ; **811**

1. Love poetry 2. American poetry

ISBN 9781947793576

LC 2019013806

The American Book Award-winning author of IRL and Junk presents a conclusion to the Teebs Cycle in an irreverent epistolary collection that examines existential questions and the wild inconsistencies of life.

Pinsky, Robert

The **figured** wheel : new and collected poems, 1966-1996 / Robert Pinsky. Noonday Press, 1997, c1996. x, 308 p. ; **811**

1. American poetry

ISBN 9780374525064

LC BL 00006276

Originally published: New York : Farrar, Straus and Giroux, 1996.

Brings together the complete works from four previous books of poetry--Sadness and Happiness, An Explanation of America, History of My Heart, and The Want Bone--along with a dozen new poems and some of Pinsky's notable translations.

Plath, Sylvia

Ariel : the restored edition / Sylvia Plath ; foreword by Frieda Hughes. HarperCollins Publishers, c2004. xxi, 211 p. ; **811**

1. Plath, Sylvia. Ariel Criticism, Textual. 2. American poetry

ISBN 9780060732592

LC 2004047703

Seeking to restore the selection and arrangement originally intended by Plath at the time of her death, this edition of her final works features a facsimile of her complete working drafts of the title poem provided to offer insight into her creative process.

Pound, Ezra, 1885-1972

★**Poems** and translations / Ezra Pound. Library of America, 2003. xxiii, 1363 p. ; The Library of America ; **811**

1. American poetry

ISBN 9781931082419

LC 2003040142

Includes index.

A collected edition of the modernist writer's works includes previously out-of-print pieces and demonstrates his contributions to the Imagist and Vorticist movements, in a volume that includes "Hilda's Book" and "Lustra."

Powell, D. A. (Douglas A.)

Repast / D.A. Powell. Graywolf Press, 2014 xiv, 206 p. ; **811**

1. American poetry 2. Civil society
ISBN 9781555976965

LC 2014935838

Published together for the first time, D. A. Powell's landmark trilogy of Tea, Lunch, and Cocktails make up a three-course Divine Comedy for our day. With a new introduction by novelist David Leavitt, Repast presents a major achievement in contemporary poetry.

Useless landscape, : or, a guide for boys / D.A. Powell. Graywolf Press, 2012 108 p. ; **811**

1. American poetry
ISBN 9781555976057

LC 2011942041

Collects the author's newest poems in his fifth tome that explores the darker side of divisions and developments.

Raab, Lawrence, 1946-

Mistaking each other for ghosts : poems / Lawrence Raab. Tupelo Press, 2015 xi, 84 p. ; **811**

1. American poetry
ISBN 9781936797653

LC 2015017797

"A wonderful, mature, sweeping collection." Booklist

Rasmussen, Matt

Black aperture : poems / Matt Rasmussen. Louisiana State University Press, 2013 64 p. ; **811**

1. American poetry
ISBN 9780807150863

LC 2012038045

Destructive and redemptive, Black Aperture opens to the complicated entanglements of mourning: damage and healing, sorrow and laughter, and torment balanced with moments of relief. --From publisher description.

Reed, Ishmael, 1938-

New and collected poems, 1964-2007 / Ishmael Reed. Thunder's Mouth Press, 2007. xix, 490 p. ; **811**

1. American poetry
ISBN 9781568583419

LC 2008270117

First poetry collection in nearly twenty years. In language that is pointed, innovative and profoundly optimistic, Reed weaves politics and war with Nigerian poetry and jazz all in the service of his continual redefinition of American culture.

Reed, Justin Phillip

Indecency / Justin Phillip Reed. Coffee House Press, 2018 70 p. ; **811**

1. African American poetry 2. American poetry 3. Love poetry
ISBN 9781566895149

LC 2017039180

A collection of poems explores inequity and injustice while critiquing the culture of white supremacy and the dominant social order.

Rekdal, Paisley

Animal eye / Paisley Rekdal. University of Pittsburgh Press, c2012. 86 p. ; **811**

1. American poetry
ISBN 9780822961796

LC 2011277541

A collection of the author's poetry employs pastoral motifs to engage a discourse on life and love.

Rich, Adrienne, 1929-2012

Collected early poems, 1950-1970 / Adrienne Rich. W. W. Norton, 1995, c1993. xxi, 435 p. ; **811**

1. American poetry -- 20th century.
ISBN 9780393313857

LC BL 99768405

More than two hundred poems--including her first poem, published in the Yale Younger Poets--culled from Rich's earlier collections

The **school** among the ruins : poems, 2000-2004 / Adrienne Rich. W. W. Norton, c2004. 113 p. ; **811**

1. American poetry
ISBN 9780393059830

LC 2004008370

A collection of poetic works considers the impact of the twenty-first century's dislocations, upheavals, and public crises on individual lives, conveying in the title poem a young schoolteacher's evocation of the lessons learned by her students amid violence and hatred.

Ritvo, Max, 1990-2016

The **final** voicemails / Max Ritvo ; edited by Louise Gluck. Milkweed Editions, 2018. 81 p. **811**

1. Death 2. Mortality 3. Identity (Psychology)
ISBN 9781571315113

LC 2017058089

Diagnosed with terminal cancer at sixteen, Ritvo spent the next decade of his life writing with frenetic energy, culminating in the publication of Four Reincarnations. As with his debut, The Final Voicemails brushes up against the pain, fear, and isolation that accompany a long illness, but with all the creative force of an artist in full command of his craft and the teeming affection of a human utterly in love with the world.

"The Final Voicemails may conclude Ritvo's literary legacy, but it will stand as a testament to the salvation that is poetry, how it lives beyond the page and the poet." Booklist.

Four reincarnations : poems / Max Ritvo. Milkweed Editions, 2016. 79 p. ; **811**

1. American poetry 2. Elegiac poetry
ISBN 9781571314901

LC 2016030740

When Max Ritvo was diagnosed with cancer at age sixteen, he became the chief war correspondent for his body. The poems of Four Reincarnations are dispatches from chemotherapy beds and hospitals and the loneliest spaces in the home. They are relentlessly embodied, communicating pain, violence, and loss. --From publisher description.

"Slippery and terrifyingly urgent, funny yet despairingly so, Ritvo (1990--2016) hits all the right notes in an accomplished, surprising, and bizarrely erotic debut made more poignant by his death weeks before publication." Publishers Weekly.

Letters from Max : a book of friendship / Sarah Ruhl and Max Ritvo. Milkweed Editions, 2018. 336 p. **811**

1. Ritvo, Max, 1990-2016 Correspondence 2. Ruhl, Sarah, 1974-

Correspondence 3. Poets 4. People with cancer 5. Friendship 6. Women dramatists
ISBN 9781571313690
LC 2018007328

"Correspondence between playwright-teacher Sarah Ruhl and poet-cancer patient Max Ritvo, in which the student becomes the teacher" .-- Provided by publisher.

"This companion volume to The Final Voicemails (2018), a moving compilation of the late Ritvo's incandescent poems, takes readers behind the curtain of his writing to expose his hard-won, well-lived, if sadly brief life, including his painful struggle with cancer, evolving love and marriage, and the tree-bud-to-redwood maturation of an intimate friendship with award-winning playwright Ruhl." Booklist.

Robinson, Edwin Arlington, 1869-1935

Robinson : poems / selected and edited by Scott Donaldson. A.A. Knopf, 2007. 254 p. ; **811**

1. American poetry
ISBN 9780307265760
LC 2006048269

Includes index.

A compilation of poetry by the first great American modernist poet features his lyric portrait studies of vivid characters in such works as "Aunt Imogen," "Isaac and Archibald," "Miniver Cheevy," and "Richard Cory," as well as his poems set in the fictional Tilbury Town, based on his boyhood home in Gardiner, Maine.

Roethke, Theodore, 1908-1963

The **collected** poems of Theodore Roethke / Theodore Roethke. Anchor Books, 1991 xiii, 272 p. ; **811**

1. American poetry -- 20th century
ISBN 0385086016
LC 90048811

Includes index.

"Originally published in hardcover by Doubleday in 1966"-- T.p. verso.

Contains selections from Open House, The Lost Son and Other Poems, Praise to the End, Words for the Wind, The Waking, I Am! Says the Lamb, and The Far Field in addition to sixteen previously unpublished poems.

Rogers, Pattiann, 1940-

Quickening fields / Pattiann Rogers. Penguin Books, 2017 114 p. ; **811**

1. American poetry 2. Nature
ISBN 9780143131328
LC 2016053786

"A new collection by an award-winning poet who 'presents her apprehensions of the natural world with striking accuracy and emotional impact' (Orion Magazine). Denise Levertov has called Pattiann Rogers a 'visionary of reality, perceiving the material world with such intensity of response that impulse, intention, meaning, interconnections beyond the skin of appearance are revealed.' Quickening Fields gathers fifty-three poems that focus on the wide variety of life forms present on earth and their unceasing zeal to exist, their constant 'push against the beyond' and the human experience among these lives. Whether a glassy filament of flying insect, a spiny spider crab, a swath of switch grass, barking short-eared owls, screeching coyotes, or racing rat-tailed sperm, all are testifying to their complete devotion to being. Many of the poems also address celestial phenomena, the vision of the earth immersed in a dynamic cosmic milieu and the effects of this vision on the human spirit. While primarily lyrical and celebratory in tone, these poems acknowledge, as well, the terror, suffering, and unpredictability of the human condition. Advance Praise for Quickening Fields: 'No one better expresses the sensory world--its sublimity, and the flood of the tactile that so stirs us--than Pattiann Rogers. She is a virtuoso of exactitude, celebrating both the fabric of nature and its spiritual evocations. Her open-eyed love of the physical, indoors and out, is catching.' --Marvin Bell"-- Provided by publisher.

Ronk, Martha Clare

Ocular proof / Martha Ronk. Omnidawn Publishing, 2016. 75 p. ; **811**

1. American poetry
ISBN 9781632430250
LC 2016017043

Taking its title from Shakespeare's Othello, a play that questions the veracity of what eyes actually see, Ocular Proof explores not only what each of us sees, but also how photographs modify sight as they capture, distort, frame, and simultaneously encourage discovery.

"National Poetry Series winner Ronk (Vertigo) here offers an elegant, supremely intelligent investigation of photography both as document and as proof that we cannot fully capture the moment through art, memory, or any other means." Library Journal

Roripaugh, Lee Ann

Tsunami vs. the Fukushima 50 : poems / Lee Ann Roripaugh. Milkweed Editions, 2019. 98 p. **811**

1. Fukushima Nuclear Disaster, Japan, 2011. 2. Nuclear power plants -- Accidents 3. Tsunamis 4. Natural disasters
ISBN 9781571314857
LC 2018033636

In March 2011, a tsunami caused by an earthquake collided with nearby power plant Fukushima Daiichi, causing the only nuclear disaster in history to rival Chernobyl in scope. Those who stayed at the plant to stabilize the reactors, willing to sacrifice their lives, became known internationally as the Fukushima 50. In tsunami vs. the fukushima 50, Lee Ann Roripaugh takes a piercing, witty, and ferocious look into the heart of the disaster. Here we meet its survivors and victims, from a pearl-catcher to a mild-mannered father to a drove of mindless pink robots. And then there is Roripaugh's unforgettable Tsunami: a force of nature, femme fatale, and "annihilatrix." As humanity rebuilds in disaster's wake, Tsunami continues to wreak her own havoc, battling humans, self-appointed role as colonizer of Earth and its life-forms.

"From origin tale to glossary, anime battle to leisure ocean cruise, barbed wire that interns her to shoes that pinch and jeans that ride, Roripaugh's wave rises above tragedy and the shock of a real-life nightmare." Publishers Weekly.

Rowell, Charles H.

Angles of ascent : a Norton anthology of contemporary African American poetry / edited by Charles Henry Rowell. W.W. Norton & Co., c2013. liii, 617 p. ; **811**

1. African American poetry 2. American poetry
ISBN 9780393339406
LC 2011042967

Includes index.

A collection of poems from 1960 to the present highlights the political, social, economic, and personal struggles of African Americans, and features works from such poets as Gwendolyn Brooks, Rita Dove, and Major Jackson.

Ruefle, Mary, 1952-

Selected poems / Mary Ruefle. Wave Books, c2010. 154 p.

; **811**

1. American poetry
ISBN 9781933517452

LC 2010005808

Includes index.

A career-defining retrospective by a much-beloved contemporary master.

"This first retrospective collection from Ruefle, which selects from her nine previous books of poetry, the earliest of which first appeared in 1982, shows her to be a poet of visionary imagination, abiding sensitivity, and melancholy humor." Publishers Weekly

Rukeyser, Muriel, 1913-1980

Selected poems / Muriel Rukeyser ; Adrienne Rich, editor. Library of America, c2004. xxv, 180 p. : **811**

1. American poetry
ISBN 9781931082587

LC 2003060484

The poet, translator, and political activist is given full expression through poems selected by Adrienne Rich that feature musings on politics, geography, sexuality, and mythology, as well as observations of her own life.

Ryan, Kay

The **best** of it : new and selected poems / Kay Ryan. Grove Press, c2010. xiv, 270 p. ; **811**

1. American poetry
ISBN 9780802119148

LC bl2010014718

Includes index.

Presents a selection of more than two hundred poems from his previous works along with a collection of new poems.

Salter, Mary Jo

The **surveyors** : poems / Mary Jo Salter. Alfred A. Knopf, 2017. viii, 89 p. ; **811**

1. Love poetry 2. American poetry
ISBN 9781524732660

LC 2016042321

A beautiful new collection from Mary Jo Salter brings us poems of puzzlement and acceptance in the face of life's surprises.

"Essential not only for Salter's fans but for readers of poetry in general; Salter provides sane and long-lasting rewards." Library Journal

Sanchez, Erika L.

Lessons on expulsion : poems / Erika L. Sanchez. Graywolf Press, 2017 73 p. ; **811**

1. Immigrants 2. Women
ISBN 1555977782

LC 2016951419

"What is life but a cross / over rotten water?" Poet, novelist, and essayist Erika L. Sanchez's powerful debut poetry collection explores what it means to live on both sides of the border -- the border between countries, languages, despair and possibility, and the living and the dead. Sanchez tells her own story as the daughter of undocumented Mexican immigrants and as part of a family steeped in faith, work, grief, and expectations. The poems confront sex, shame, race, and an America roiling with xenophobia, violence, and laws of suspicion and suppression. With candor and urgency, and with the unblinking eyes of a journalist, Sanchez roves from the individual life into the lives of sex workers, narco-traffickers, factory laborers, artists, and lovers. What emerges is a powerful, multifaceted portrait of survival. Lessons on Expulsion is the first book by a vibrant, essential new writer now breaking into the national literary landscape.

Sandburg, Carl, 1878-1967

★The **complete** poems of Carl Sandburg / Carl Sandburg. Harcourt, 2003. xxxi, 797 p. ; **811**

1. American poetry
ISBN 0151009961

LC bl2005019694

Originally published: New York : Harcourt Brace Jovanovich, 1970.

A compilation of the American poet's works includes the contents of such acclaimed anthologies as "Chicago Poems," "Cornhuskers," and "Smoke and Steel."

Sarton, May, 1912-1995

Selected poems of May Sarton / edited and with an introd. by Serena Sue Hilsinger and Lois Brynes. Norton, c1978. 206 p. ; **811**

ISBN 9780393045123

LC 78014850

Includes index.

Ranging from pastoral and lyrical to polemical and dissonant, Sarton's poems written over a period of forty years explore private moments of erotic love, public events, and sources of the creative process.

"What May Sarton does is to follow the round of a woman's life. Her verse is traditional, warm, ripe with the wisdom of her years as a poet, novelist, autobiographer. She draws on the artifacts of the past for images to live by in the here and now." Christian Science Monitor.

Scenters-Zapico, Natalie

Lima : limon / Natalie Scenters-Zapico. Copper Canyon Press, 2019. 75 p. **811**

1. Boundaries 2. Gender identity 3. Femininity 4. Masculinity
ISBN 9781556595318

LC 2018048964

"A dazzling collection, it punches like spiked limonada; to be read alongside writers like Marcelo Hernandez Castillo and angel Garca." Booklist.

Schiff, Robyn

A **woman** of property / Robyn Schiff. Penguin Books, 2016 81 p. ; **811**

ISBN 9780143128274

LC 2015048702

"A new book from a poet whose work is 'wild with imagination, unafraid, ambitious, inventive' (Jorie Graham) Located in a menacing, gothic landscape, the poems that comprise A Woman of Property draw formal and imaginative boundaries against boundless mortal threat, but as all borders are vulnerable, this ominous collection ultimately stages an urgent and deeply imperiled boundary dispute where haunting, illusion, the presence of the past, and disembodied voices only further unsettle questions of material and spiritual possession. This is a theatrical book of dilapidated houses and overgrown gardens, of passageways and thresholds, edges, prosceniums, unearthings, and root systems. The unstable property lines here rove from heaven to hell, troubling proportion and upsetting propriety in the name of unfathomable propagation. Are all the gates in this book folly? Are the walls too easily scaled to hold anything back or impose self-confinement? What won't a poem do to get to the other side?"-- Provided by publisher.

"Few collections this year are likely to match the subtle intelligence in this third outing from Schiff." Publishers Weekly.

Schlegel, Rob

In the tree where the double sex sleeps / Rob Schlegel. University of Iowa Press, 2019. 60 p. **811**

1. Fatherhood 2. Nature 3. Sense of wonder 4. Identity (Psychology)
ISBN 9781609386450

LC 2018040183

With calm abandon, Rob Schlegel stands among the genderless trees to shake notions of masculinity and fatherhood. Schlegel incorporates the visionary into everyday life, inhabiting patterns of relation that do not rely on easy categories. Working from the premise that poetry is indistinguishable from the life of the poet, Schlegel considers how his relationship to the creative process is forever changed when he becomes something new to someone else. 'The meaning I'm trying to protect is,' Schlegel writes, "the heart is neither boy, nor girl.' In the Tree Where the Double Sex Sleeps is a tender search for the mother in the father, the poet in the parent, the forest in the human.

"This slim volume covers remarkable emotional terrain with perceptive insight into fatherhood and the inner workings of a poet's associative thought process. It is rich and complex but utterly accessible, with lyrical lines that beg to be read aloud." Publishers Weekly.

Schmidt, Elizabeth

The **poets** laureate anthology / edited and with introductions by Elizabeth Hun Schmidt ; foreword by Billy Collins. W.W. Norton & Co., c2010. liii, 762 p. : **811**

1. American poetry -- 20th century. 2. American poetry -- 21st century. 3. Poets laureate -- United States.
ISBN 9780393061819

LC 2010021692

At head of title: In association with the Library of Congress.

Poems by each of the forty-three poets who have been named our nation's Poet Laureate since the post (originally called Consultant in Poetry to the Library of Congress) was established in 1937.

Schultz, Philip

Luxury : poems / Philip Schultz. W. W. Norton & Company, 2018 xi, 76 p. ; **811**

1. American poetry
ISBN 9780393634686

LC 2017033688

"Not a perfect collection, but one that will provide revelations with each rereading." Library Journal

Schuyler, James

Collected poems / James Schuyler. Farrar, Straus, Giroux, 1993. 429 p. ; **811**

1. American poetry
ISBN 9780374524036

LC 92040977

Includes index.

Gathers all of the late writer's published poetry, and includes unpublished poems written in the last few years before his death.

Seidel, Frederick, 1936-

Poems 1959-2009 / Frederick Seidel. Farrar, Straus and Giroux, 2009. xv, 509 p. ; **811**

1. American poetry
ISBN 9780374126551

LC 2008047161

Includes indexes.

Presents a complete collection of the poems written to date by the National Book Critics Circle Award and Griffin Poetry Prize finalist, in a volume that encompasses his nine anthologies as well as new and previously uncollected works. By the author of Ooga-Booga.

Sexton, Anne

The **complete** poems / Anne Sexton ; foreword by Maxine Kumin. Houghton Mifflin Harcourt, 1999 624 p. **811**

1. American poetry -- 20th century
ISBN 9780395957769

LC BL 99009511

"This collection contains all the poems in the eight volumes published in Sexton's lifetime, the two published after her death, and seven poems never before in print." Library Journal.

Shapiro, Alan, 1952-

Reel to reel / Alan Shapiro. The University of Chicago Press, 2014 77 p. ; **811**

1. American poetry 2. Love poetry
ISBN 9780226110639

LC 2013016631

Reel to Reel, Alan Shapiro's twelfth collection of poetry, moves outward from the intimate spaces of family and romantic life to embrace not only the human realm of politics and culture but also the natural world, and even the outer spaces of the cosmos itself.

Shapiro, David, 1947-

New and selected poems, 1965-2006 / David Shapiro. Overlook Press, 2007. 267 p. ; **811**

1. American poetry
ISBN 9781585678778

LC 2006052718

A collection of definitive works by the modern intellectual poet offers insight into his observations about the chaos of postmodern life.

Shapiro, Harvey, 1924-

★**Poets** of World War II / Harvey Shapiro, editor. Library of America, 2003. xxxii, 262 p. **811**

1. World War II
ISBN 9781931082334

LC 2002032125

Contains 120 poems written during World War II by 62 American poets.

Shapiro, Karl, 1913-2000

★**Selected** poems / Karl Shapiro ; John Updike, editor. Library of America, c2003. xxxi, 197 p. : **811**

1. American poetry
ISBN 9781931082341

LC 2002032123

A reassessment of the poet explores the range of his work and considers his role as a key writer of the postwar period.

Sharif, Solmaz

Look : poems / Solmaz Sharif. Graywolf Press, 2016 98 p. ; **811**

1. American poetry
ISBN 9781555977443

LC 2015953717

A collection of poems uses words and phrases lifted from the "Department of Defense Dictionary of Military and Associated Terms" to highlight the cost of ongoing war and the dehumanization of conflict.

Shaughnessy, Brenda, 1970-

Human dark with sugar / Brenda Shaughnessy. Copper Canyon Press, c2008. viii, 77 p. ; **811**

1. American poetry -- 21st century.
ISBN 9781556592768

LC 2007052225

Presents a collection of poems that focus on women's lives and loves.

Sherman, Joan R.

African-American poetry of the nineteenth century : an anthology / edited by Joan R. Sherman. University of Illinois Press, c1992. 506 p. ; **811**

1. American poetry -- African American authors. 2. African Americans 3. American poetry -- 19th century.
ISBN 9780252062469

LC 91041709

Gathers poems by thirty-five Black, nineteenth-century poets, and, using a chronological arrangement, traces changes in theme from pre- to post-Civil War times

Shockley, Evie, 1965-

The **new** black / Evie Shockley. Wesleyan University Press, c2011. 104 p. : **811**

1. African American poetry 2. American poetry
ISBN 0819571407

LC 2010046345

Smart, grounded, and lyrical, Evie Shockley's the new black integrates powerful ideas about "blackness," past and present, through the medium of beautifully crafted verse.

"Full of surprising turnabouts and shaped by a deep quest for knowledge and understanding, Shockley's inviting and invigorating collection shimmers with positive creative energy." Booklist

Semiautomatic / Evie Shockley. Wesleyan University Press, 2017 110 p. ; **811**

1. African American poetry 2. American poetry
ISBN 9780819577443

LC 2016059299

"Poetry by Evie Shockley, critiquing daily life as well as responding to race- and gender-based violence".-- Provided by publisher.

Simic, Charles, 1938-

Come closer and listen : poems / Charles Simic. Ecco, 2019 xiii, 75 p. ; **811**

1. American poetry 2. Elegiac poetry
ISBN 9780062908469

LC bl2019019054

A new collection of poems from the Pulitzer Prize-winning poet of The World Doesn't End offers modern reflections on love, grief, the wonders of nature with a pithy, wry and cutting edge.

The **lunatic** : poems / Charles Simic. Ecco, 2015 xi, 84 p. ; **811**

1. American poetry
ISBN 9780062364746

LC bl2015014919

A collection of the author's poetry features a mix of wry melancholy and sardonic wit.

New and selected poems : 1962-2012 / Charles Simic. Houghton Mifflin Harcourt, 2013 355 p. ; **811**

1. American poetry
ISBN 9780547928289

LC 2012042188

Collects four hundred of the American writer's poems about such topics as folktales, marriage, war, life, and American blues.

"But, until now, Simic's body of work was split between two publishers and two separate 'Selected Poems' volumes. This books brings together, for the first time, poems from Simic's entire career." Publishers Weekly.

★The **voice** at 3:00 a.m. : selected late & new poems / Charles Simic. Harcourt, c2003. 177 p. ; **811**

1. American poetry
ISBN 0151008426

LC 2002038715

Offers a new collection of poems that plumbs the ordinary American experience for spiritual insights, wit, and historical relevance.

"This volume collects outstanding poems from six previous books ... and presents a sterling set of new poems, each moody, surprising, and tonic." Booklist.

Sinclair, Safiya

Cannibal / Safiya Sinclair. University of Nebraska Press, 2016 x, 111 p. ; **811**

1. Women -- Identity 2. Human body 3. Jamaican poetry
ISBN 9780803290631

LC 2016007774

"Colliding with and confronting The Tempest and postcolonial identity, the poems in Safiya Sinclair's Cannibal explore Jamaican childhood and history, race relations in America, womanhood, otherness, and exile. She evokes a home no longer accessible and a body at times uninhabitable, often mirrored by a hybrid Eve/Caliban figure. Blooming with intense lyricism and fertile imagery, these full-blooded poems are elegant, mythic, and intricately woven. Here the female body is a dark landscape; the female body is cannibal. Sinclair shocks and delights her readers with her willingness to disorient and provoke, creating a multitextured collage of beautiful and explosive poems".-- Provided by publisher.

Smith, Danez

★**Homie** : poems / Danez Smith. Graywolf Press, 2020. 96 p. **811**

1. Friendship 2. Communities 3. Prejudice 4. Racism
ISBN 9781644450109

LC bl2020045532

Rooted in the loss of one of Smith's close friends, this book comes out of the search for joy and intimacy within a nation where both can seem scarce and getting scarcer. In poems of rare power and generosity, Smith acknowledges that in a country overrun by violence, xenophobia, and disparity, and in a body defined by race, queerness, and diagnosis, it can be hard to survive, even harder to remember reasons for living. But then the phone lights up, or a shout comes up to the window, and family--blood and chosen--arrives with just the right food and some redemption.

"Smith is a visionary polyglot with a fearless voice." Publishers Weekly.

Smith, Patricia, 1955-

Shoulda been Jimi Savannah : poems / Patricia Smith. Coffee House Press, c2012. 115 p. ; **811**

1. African American poetry 2. American poetry
ISBN 9781566892995

LC 2011029282

A collection of poems explores the second wave of the Great Migration.

Smith, Tracy K.

The **body's** question / Tracy K. Smith ; selected and introduced by Kevin Young. Graywolf Press, c2003. xiv, 85 p. ; **811**

1. African American poetry 2. American poetry

ISBN 9781555973919

LC 2003101170

Winner of the Cave Canem Poetry Prize for best first book by an African-American poet, this compelling collection of poems gathers together stories from the intersection of race, family, adulthood, and childhood in search of herself, concluding that "I was anyone I wanted to be."

Duende : poems / Tracy K. Smith. Graywolf Press, c2007. 87 p. ; **811**

1. African American poetry 2. American poetry

ISBN 9781555974756

LC 2006938264

Calls on "duende," the source of artistic power described by Federico Garcia Lorca, in thirty poems that explore identity, marginalization, and the sources of pain in a variety of geographical and historical situations.

Life on Mars : poems / Tracy K. Smith. Graywolf Press, 2011. 75 p. ; **811**

1. African American poetry 2. American poetry

ISBN 9781555975845

LC 2011920674

With allusions to David Bowie and interplanetary travel, Life on Mars imagines a soundtrack for the universe to accompany the discoveries, failures, and oddities of human existence. --From publisher description.

"Hypnotic and brimming with irony, the poems in Smith's latest volume aren't so much about outer space as the interior life and the search for the divine." Library Journal.

Snyder, Gary, 1930-

No nature : new and selected poems / Gary Snyder. Pantheon Books, 1993, c1992. xv, 390 p. ; **811**

1. American poetry

ISBN 9780679742524

LC BL 00003305

Includes index.

Presents selections from the author's eight previous collections of poetry, as well as previously unpublished works.

Spicer, Jack

★**My** vocabulary did this to me : the collected poetry of Jack Spicer / edited by Peter Gizzi and Kevin Killian. Wesleyan University Press, c2008. xxxi, 465 p. : **811**

1. American poetry

ISBN 9780819568878

LC 2008024997

Presents a collection of poems taken from a variety of the author's books along with poems published for the first time.

Stallings, A. E. (Alicia Elsbeth), 1968-

Like : poems / A. E. Stallings. Farrar, Straus and Giroux, 2015. 137 p. **811**

1. Mythology, Greek 2. Families

ISBN 9780374187323

LC 2018010177

A new collection of poems on Classic and family themes.

"A classicist, translator of Lucretius, and MacArthur and Guggenheim fellow, Stallings is primarily a formalist poet. Her lines scan and rhyme." Booklist.

Stanford, Frank, 1949-1978

What about this : collected poems of Frank Stanford / edited by Michael Wiegers. Copper Canyon Press, 2015 xvi, 747 p. : **811**

1. American poetry

ISBN 9781556594687

LC 2014045989

Includes index.

Readers have dreamed about this collection for nearly four decades -- an energized presentation of Frank Stanford's raw-genius ungovernable oeuvre.

"In this comprehensive and essential retrospective, the body of work left behind by Stanford -- who took his own life in 1978, at age 29 -- more than makes good on his insistence that 'poetry busts guts.'" Publishers Weekly

Stevens, Wallace, 1879-1955

Collected poetry and prose / Wallace Stevens. Library of America, c1997. xxii, 1032 p. ; The library of America ; **811**

1. American poetry -- 20th century

ISBN 9781883011451

LC 97007023

Includes indexes.

Selected works celebrate the writer's poetic response to life.

"Having all of Stevens' poems--especially all the late poems--in one volume is a great thing (previously, one had to seek them out in three different books); the Adagia and his replies to questionnaires are marvelous; and even in the somewhat turgid prose pieces, he sometimes expresses himself with exemplary force and concision." New York Times Book Review.

Stone, Ruth

What love comes to : new & selected poems / Ruth Stone ; foreword by Sharon Olds. Copper Canyon Press, c2008. xxi, 359 p. ; **811**

1. American poetry

ISBN 9781556592713

LC 2007045832

"But the real news is found in the selections from Stone's earlier books -- beginning in 1959, but especially with Topography (1971) and Cheap (1975), which may stun younger readers with their sheer variety." Publishers Weekly

Strand, Mark, 1934-2014

Collected poems / Mark Strand. Alfred A. Knopf, 2014. xviii, 520 p. ; **811**

ISBN 9780385352512

LC 2013049034

"A collection of all of the poet Mark Strand's previously published poems".-- Provided by publisher.

"For all the streamlined sadness of his dreamlike domain, Strand remains aware of other poets, which is particularly evident in his homages, translations, and elegies. His recent string of short sardonic prose poems are all quite distinct from one another, but all are instantly, recognizably Strand, 'erasing the world and leaving instead/ The invisible lines of its calling: Out there, out there.'" Publishers Weekly.

Swenson, May, 1919-1989
Nature : poems old and new / May Swenson. Houghton Mifflin, 2000, c1994 240 p. **811**
1. American poetry 2. Nature
ISBN 9780618064083
"This collection of Swenson's poetry brings together poems from several earlier books, as well as poems published only in magazines, and introduces us to nine splendid poems published here for the first time. This collection . is brought together with special attention to poems describing the environment; poems of tides and the sea, of birds and gardens, of moods and seasons, of self and others. This is a collection to be treasured; it belongs in all libraries with even a modest selection of poetry." Library Journal.

Sze, Arthur
Compass Rose / Arthur Sze. Copper Canyon Press, 2014 viii, 75 p. ; **811**
1. American poetry
ISBN 9781556594670
LC 2013025678
"It's easy for readers to become lost in the intricacies, but the beauty of image and symmetry of ideas offer balance and direction." Library Journal

★**Sight** lines / Arthur Sze. Copper Canyon Press, 2019. viii, 69 p. ; **811**
1. Multiple perspectives
ISBN 9781556595592
LC 2018052007
Sze, in drawing connections between the pastoral and the catastrophic, speaks to a contemporary condition in which we are constantly fragmented and made whole again as we are presented with a saturation of narratives. In his scenes of the quotidian, musings on life and death, and traversals between the natural and the artificial, Sze opens us to multitudinous lines of sight.
"Finely crafted and philosophical, this is a book that rewards multiple careful readings." Publishers Weekly.

Tapahonso, Luci, 1953-
A **radiant** curve : poems and stories / Luci Tapahonso. University of Arizona Press, 2008. x, 93 p. ; **811**
1. Navajo Indians -- Literary collections. 2. American poetry
ISBN 9780816527083
LC 2008027223
An American Indian literary series
In this sixth collection of stories and verse, award-winning writer Luci Tapahonso finds sacredness in everyday life.
"In 2006, Tapahonso received a Lifetime Achievement Award from the Native Writers Circle of the Americas. " Library Journal

Tarn, Nathaniel
Selected poems : 1950-2000 / Nathaniel Tarn. Wesleyan University Press, c2002. xii, 335 p. ; **811**
ISBN 0819565415
LC 2002001701
"Nathaniel Tarn here provides samples from 19 of his 25 collections in Selected Poems 1950-2000." Publishers Weekly

Trethewey, Natasha D., 1966-
★**Monument** : poems : new and selected / Natasha Trethewey. Houghton Mifflin Harcourt, 2018. 224 p. **811**
1. Families -- History 2. African Americans 3. Interracial families 4. Race relations 5. Mississippi
ISBN 9781328507846
LC 2018012255
The two-term U.S. Poet Laureate and Pulitzer Prize-winning author of Native Guard poetically links the human struggles and resilience of African-American women throughout history to the collective trauma of national wounds.
"Monument is an essential volume of piercing wit, elegiac beauty, profound insights intimate and cultural, and the sustaining power of remembrance." Booklist.

Trinidad, David, 1953-
Dear Prudence : new and selected poems / David Trinidad. Turtle Point Press, c2011. 494 p. ; **811**
1. American poetry
ISBN 9781933527475
LC bl2011035013
Presents a compilation of previously published and new poems that explore such topics as the influence of pop culture on the author's life, revolutionary female poets from the past, and his obsession with feminine objects.

Twichell, Chase, 1950-
Horses where the answers should have been : new and selected poems / Chase Twichell. Copper Canyon Press, c2010. xii, 255 p. ; **811**
1. American poetry
ISBN 9781556593185
LC 2009048885
A collection of poems exhibit a deep and urgent love for the threatened natural world.

Updike, John
Collected poems, 1953-1993 / John Updike. Knopf, 1997, c1993. xxiv, 387 p. : **811**
1. American poetry
ISBN 9780679762041
LC BL 00006243
Includes index.
A varied anthology of poetry, representing some forty years of work, encompasses nearly every poem from five previously published collections, as well as sixty new poems and a selection of light verse.

Valentine, Jean
Door in the mountain : new and collected poems, 1965-2003 / Jean Valentine. Wesleyan University Press, c2004. xv, 285 p. ; Wesleyan poetry **811**
1. American poetry
ISBN 9780819567123
LC 2004016019
Presents a collection of the author's established works in addition to new poems, which deal with such topics as death, aging, and the passage of time.
"The defiant, angular, yet propulsively emotional recent poems that occupy the first and last parts of the book should please both fans of Valentine's earliest poetry and fans of her strongly feminist middle period." Publishers Weekly.

Vang, Mai Der, 1981-
Afterland : poems / Mai Der Vang. Graywolf Press, 2017. 94 p. ; **811**
1. Hmong (Asian people) 2. Refugees -- Laos 3. American poetry

4. Laos
ISBN 9781555977702

LC 2016938843

Mai Der Vang is telling the story of her own family, and by doing so, she also provides an essential history of the Hmong culture's ongoing resilience in exile. Many of these poems are written in the voices of those fleeing unbearable violence after U.S. forces recruited Hmong fighters in Laos in the Secret War against communism, only to abandon them after that war went awry. --From publisher description.

"Yet, amid bullets and bees, cyanide and stars, humpbacks and harvests, Vang imbues her imagery not only with loss but also with the remarkable resilience and crystalline spirituality of Hmong lore and language." Booklist.

Walcott, Derek

Omeros / Derek Walcott. Farrar, Straus and Giroux, 1992, c1990. 325 p. ; **811**

1. Saint Lucian poetry (English)
ISBN 9780374523503

LC bl2005011953

A poem in five books, of circular narrative design, titled with the Greek name for Homer, which simultaneously charts two currents of history: the visible history charted in events -- the tribal losses of the American Indian, the tragedy of African enslavement -- and the interior, unwritten epic fashioned from the suffering of the individual in exile.

"If you can buy only one Walcott title, get this Carribean epic." Library Journal

The **poetry** of Derek Walcott 1948-2013 / Derek Walcott ; selected by the poet Glyn Maxwell. Farrar, Straus and Giroux, 2014. xiii, 617 p. ; **811**

1. Saint Lucian poetry (English)
ISBN 9780374125615

LC 2013034997

Includes index.

A collection spanning the range of the Nobel Prize-winning writer's career includes his first published poem, "In My Eighteenth Year"; his first widely celebrated verses on the violence in Africa; his mature work from The Star-Apple Kingdom; and his late masterpieces from White Egrets.

The **prodigal** / Derek Walcott. Farrar, Straus and Giroux, 2004. 105 p. ; **811**

1. Saint Lucian poetry (English) 2. Exiles 3. Poetry of places
ISBN 9780374237431

LC 2004005147

The celebrated poet shares his sweeping vision of the ancient and the sublime in the Old World while never forgetting his roots in the New--particularly the Caribbean, which has served as a poetic backdrop throughout his career.

Waldrop, Keith

Transcendental studies : a trilogy / Keith Waldrop. University of California Press, c2009. 201 p. ; **811**

1. American poetry
ISBN 9780520258785

LC 2008025958

Presents a selection of recent work by the poet, including three related poem sequences that use collaged words out of context to take on new meanings.

Walker, Alice, 1944-

Hard times require furious dancing : new poems / Alice Walker ; foreword and illustrations by Shiloh McCloud. New World Library, c2010. xvi, 165 p. : **811**

1. American poetry 2. African American poetry
ISBN 1577319303

LC 2010029972

"A Palm of Her Hand project."

Includes index.

Presents a collection of poems that focus on both the joys and sorrows of life.

"In this poetry collection, the author writes of loss and disappointment, and the strength that rises from meeting them unflinchingly... These are powerful anthems of womanhood and age, although just as likely to be empowering to men and to the not-yet-old." Booklist.

Warren, Robert Penn, 1905-1989

★The **collected** poems of Robert Penn Warren / edited by John Burt ; with a foreword by Harold Bloom. Louisiana State University Press, 1998. xxvi, 830 p. ; **811**

1. American poetry -- 20th century
ISBN 9780807123331

LC 98026104

Includes index.

Works spanning sixteen years and sixteen volumes have been collated and revised according to the Poet Laureate's specifications

"This immense volume gathers 15 books of poetry--as well as uncollected verse from the beginning and end of his writing life--from a formidable American man of letters and our first poet laureate. . . . Scholars will especially cherish the careful, copious textual and explanatory notes provided by Warren's literary executor Burt . . . and fans of American poetry and literary history alike should welcome this opportunity to explore the prodigious oeuvre of one of the New Criticism's most forceful, convincing proponents." Publishers Weekly.

Wharton, Edith, 1862-1937

Selected poems / Edith Wharton ; Louis Auchincloss, editor. Library of America, c2005. 183 p. : **811**

1. American poetry
ISBN 9781931082860

LC 2005044163

Features a range of previously unpublished works as well as pieces written in response to World War I, in a comprehensive survey that sheds light on how Wharton used poetry to express the deeply emotional side of her nature.

Wheatley, Phillis, 1753-1784

The **poems** of Phillis Wheatley / edited with an introduction by Julian D. Mason, Jr. University of North Carolina Press, c1989. xvi, 235 p. ; **811**

1. African American poetry 2. American poetry
ISBN 9780807842454

LC 88023280

Collects poems by the young Black slave with critical commentaries on her short career.

Whitman, Walt, 1819-1892

★**Poetry** and prose / Walt Whitman. Library of America, 1996. 1407 p. ; **811**

1. American poetry -- 19th century.
ISBN 9781883011352

LC 95052466

Rev. ed. of: Complete poetry and collected prose. New York, N.Y. : Literary Classics of the United States, c1982.

Gathers the original 1855 edition of "Leaves of Grass," the 1891-92 edition--the last published in Whitman's lifetime--his writings on New York history and the Civil War, and other works, with a chronology and information on his work.

★**Selected** poems / Walt Whitman ; Harold Bloom, editor. The Library of America, c2003. xxxi, 221 p. ; **811**

1. American poetry

ISBN 9781931082327

LC 2002032124

Surveys Walt Whitman's significant poetic works, from early notebook fragments of "Song of Myself" to the late poems of "Good-bye my Fancy."

Whittier, John Greenleaf, 1807-1892

Selected poems / John Greenleaf Whittier ; Brenda Wineapple, editor. Library of America, ; c2004. 187 p. ; **811**

1. American poetry

ISBN 9781931082594

LC 2003060483

The work of the abolitionist poet is featured here, including his denunciation of the Fugitive Slave Law and his portraits of rural life that combine religion, politics, and rich narration.

Wicker, Marcus

Silencer / Marcus Wicker. Mariner Books/Houghton Mifflin Harcourt, 2017. 73 p. ; **811**

1. African American poetry 2. American poetry 3. Poetry of places 4. Religious poetry

ISBN 9781328715548

LC 2017014165

"Welcome to Marcus Wicker's Midwest, where the muzzle is always on and where silence and daily microaggressions can chafe away at the faith of a young man grieved by images of gun violence and police brutality in twenty-first-century America. Precisely contradictory, bittersweet, witty, and heartbreaking, Silencer is where the political and the personal collide. Driven by the sounds of hip-hop and reimagined forms and structures, Wicker's explosive second book is composed of poems at war with themselves, verses in which the poet questions his own faith in God, in hope, in the American Dream, and in himself. Pushing our ideas of traditions and expectations, these poems and queries work in concert towards creating a new dialectic".-- Provided by publisher.

Wilbur, Richard, 1921-2017

Anterooms : new poems and translations / Richard Wilbur. Houghton Mifflin Harcourt, 2010. 63 p. ; **811**

1. American poetry

ISBN 9780547358116

LC 2010005772

Celebrates the human condition through reflections on nature and love, while a series of translations bring other authors' poems and riddles into a new light.

★**Collected** poems, 1943-2004 / Richard Wilbur. Harcourt, c2004. xvi, 585 p. : **811**

1. American poetry

ISBN 9780151011056

LC 2004009228

Includes index.

A comprehensive collection of works written throughout the course of the National Book Award and two-time Pulitzer Prize-winning poet's more than sixty-year career includes "In Trackless Woods" and several new and previously unpublished pieces.

Williams, C. K. (Charles Kenneth), 1936-2015

★**Collected** poems / C.K. Williams. Farrar, Straus and Giroux, 2006. xx, 682 p. ; **811**

ISBN 9780374126520

LC 2005051867

Includes indexes.

Collects nearly four decades of the author's work, featuring peoms from "Tar," "With Ignorance," "Flesh and Blood," "A Dream of Mind," "Repair," and "The Singing."

"This weighty, even daunting, tome shows new and old readers the long arc of this Pulitzer Prize and National Book Award winner's career, from the morbid sanguinities of his apprentice work to the careful, moving, stanzaic focus evident in 21 new poems." Publishers Weekly.

Falling ill : last poems / C.K. Williams. Farrar Straus Giroux, 2017. 54 p. ; **811**

1. Death 2. Mortality 3. American poetry 4. Elegiac poetry

ISBN 9780374152208

LC 2016025612

Shares poems related to "the burden of being alive."

Williams, William Carlos, 1883-1963

Paterson / William Carlos Williams. New Directions Books, 1995. xv, 311 p. ; **811**

1. Poetry of places 2. American poetry -- 20th century. 3. New Jersey

ISBN 9780811212984

LC bl2015032612

Presents the American poet's extended lyrical work in which the life and history of a city become the symbol of humanity.

Wright, C. D., 1949-2016

One with others : [a little book of her days] / C.D. Wright. Copper Canyon Press, 2010. 168 p. : **811**

1. Civil rights movements 2. Civil rights movements -- Arkansas -- History -- 20th century. 3. American poetry

ISBN 9781556593246

LC 2010016789

Presents a collection of poems, along with a historical account, describing the 1969 "walk against fear" through a small Arkansas by a group of African Americans.

Wright, James Arlington, 1927-

Above the river : the complete poems / James Wright ; with an introduction by Donald Hall. Noonday Press, 1992, c1990. xxxvii, 387 p. ; **811**

1. American poetry

ISBN 9780374522827

LC BL 99726841

Includes indexes.

Poems deal with love, travel, myth, friendship, the past, the seasons, mortality, and language.

Xie, Jenny

Eye level : poems / Jenny Xie. Graywolf Press, 2018 79 p. ; **811**

1. American poetry -- Asian American authors -- 21st century. 2.

American poetry -- 21st century. 3. Identity (Psychology) 4. Travel
ISBN 1555978029

LC 2017938013

Walt Whitman Award of the Academy of American Poets, 2017.

"Jenny Xie's award-winning debut, Eye Level, takes us far and near, to Phnom Penh, Corfu, Hanoi, New York, and elsewhere, as we travel closer and closer to the acutely felt solitude that centers this searching, moving collection. Animated by a restless inner questioning, these poems meditate on the forces that moor the self and set it in motion, from immigration to travel to estranging losses and departures. The sensual worlds here--colors, smells, tastes, and changing landscapes--bring to life questions about the self as seer and the self as seen. As Xie writes, 'Me? I'm just here in my traveler's clothes, trying on each passing town for size.' Her taut, elusive poems exult in a life simultaneously crowded and quiet, caught in between things and places, and never quite entirely at home. Xie is a poet of extraordinary perception--both to the tangible world and to 'all that is untouchable as far as the eye can reach.'"--Amazon.com.

Young, Kevin, 1970-

Ardency : a chronicle of the Amistad rebels / compiled from authentic sources by Kevin Lowell Young. Alfred A. Knopf, 2011. xiii, 249 p. : **811**

1. Amistad (Schooner) 2. Slaves 3. Slave resistance and revolts -- United States -- History -- 19th century 4. Mutiny. 5. Slave trade 6. United States -- History -- 19th century
ISBN 9780307267641

LC 2010030007

"Being an epic account of the capture of the Spanish schooner Amistad, by the Africans on board; their voyage and capture near Long Island, New York; with phrenological studies of several of the surviving Africans."

A poetic epic written over the course of 20 years chronicles the story of the Africans who mutinied on board the slave ship Amistad through different voices, from an interpreter for the rebels to inmates in a New Haven jail who appealed to John Quincy Adams. By the National Book Award finalist author of Jelly Roll.

"This poetry collection chronicles the slave mutiny aboard the schooner Amistad in 1839. This three-part book focuses on the 53 Africans who rebelled against their would-be slave owners. Young expertly blends cultural and social history as well as religion to dramatize the lives of the rebels. His evocative use of language--punctuated with stunning metaphors--keeps the historical context clear while moving the gripping true story forward." Library Journal.

★The **art** of losing : poems of grief and healing / edited by Kevin Young. Bloomsbury USA, 2010. xxiv, 311 p. ; **811**

1. Grief 2. Bereavement
ISBN 9781608190331

LC 2009028888

A book that includes contributions from such poets as Dylan Thomas, John Ashbery, Emily Dickinson, Rita Dove, Anne Sexton, Robert Pinsky, and many more collects 150 contemporary elegies that embrace the pain, heartbreak, and healing stages of mourning.

"This book will provide solace for the bereaved. Both clergy and family members will use it to create meaningful memorial services, and all poetry lovers will find much to celebrate and ponder here." Library Journal

Brown : poems / Kevin Young ; photographs by Melanie Dunea. Alfred A. Knopf, 2018. vii, 161 p. : **811**

1. African Americans 2. Injustice 3. Race relations 4. Racism 5. United States
ISBN 9781524732547

LC 2017029270

"This is a Borzoi book"--Title page verso.

"James Brown. John Brown's raid. Brown v. the Topeka Board of Ed.: the recently National Book Award-longlisted author of Blue Laws meditates on all things 'brown' in this powerful new collection. A testament to Young's own--and our collective--experience, Brown offers beautiful, sustained harmonies from a poet whose wisdom deepens with time".-- Provided by publisher.

Yu, Josephine

Prayer book of the anxious / Josephine Yu. Elixir Press, 2016 x, 83 p. ; **811**

1. American poetry
ISBN 9781932418583

LC 2015048259

"With a perceptiveness and poise that serve as a curative balm, Yu brilliantly tackles the notion of healing in a society that can make its most aware citizens ill." Publishers Weekly

Zapruder, Matthew, 1967-

Come on all you ghosts / Matthew Zapruder. Copper Canyon Press, c2010. xi, 111 p. ; **811**

1. American poetry
ISBN 9781556593222

LC 2010016787

A third collection of poems mixes humor with themes of love and loss and draws upon past personal experiences in a search for self-revelation.

Zukofsky, Louis, 1904-1978

Selected poems / Louis Zukofsky ; Charles Bernstein, editor. Library of America, 2006. xxvii, 172 p. : **811**

1. American poetry
ISBN 9781931082952

LC 2006040808

A single-volume selection of the influential Objectivist poet's works includes several of his short pieces as well as excerpts from his twenty-four-part, "A," in a collection that offers insight into his experimentations with exacting literary details and use of musical language.

811.008 American poetry -- Collections

Giovanni, Nikki

The **100** best African American poems : (but I cheated) / edited by Nikki Giovanni. Sourcebooks MediaFusion, c2010. 228 p. ; **811.008**

1. African American poetry 2. American poetry
ISBN 9781402221118

LC bl2010029481

Includes index.

"Featuring performances on CD by Ruby Dee, Novella Nelson, Nikki Giovanni, Elizabeth Alexander, Sonia Sanchez, Robert Hayden, Marilyn Nelson, and many more friends."

Contains one hundred poems from classic and contemporary African American poets, as selected by an award-winning black poet and activist, including such writers as Robert Hayden, Mari Evans, Kevin Young, and Rita Dove.

Harjo, Joy, 1951-

★**When** the light of the world was subdued, our songs came through : a Norton anthology of Native Nations poetry / edited by Joy Harjo, with LeAnne Howe, Jennifer Elise Foerster, and contributing editors. W.W. Norton & Company, 2020. 496 p. **811.008**

1. Indians of North America 2. Indigenous peoples 3. Culture 4. Cultural relations 5. Anthologies
ISBN 9780393356809

LC 2020019323

United States Poet Laureate Joy Harjo gathers the work of more than 160 poets, representing nearly 100 indigenous nations, into the first historically comprehensive Native poetry anthology. This landmark anthology celebrates the indigenous peoples of North America, the first poets of this country, whose literary traditions stretch back centuries.

"Together with uncredited historical pieces and collectively authored verses, the anthology includes poems by established authors, such as N. Scott Momaday and Leslie Marmon Silko, and showcases emerging voices, like Layli Long Soldier and Natalie Diaz, and also introduces relative newcomers, such as Jake Skeets and Tommy Pico. If there's one poetry anthology that belongs on every bookshelf in this country called America, it's this one." Booklist

Harper, Michael S., 1938-2016

The **Vintage** book of African American poetry / edited and with an introduction by Michael S. Harper and Anthony Walton. Vintage Books, 2000. xxxiii, 403 p. ; **811.008**

1. American poetry -- African American authors. 2. African Americans 3. Anthologies
ISBN 9780375703003

LC 99039428

"A Vintage original"--T.p. verso.

An anthology representing more than two hundred years of African American creative poetic endeavors features the work of fifty-two poets.

"Included in chronological order here are over two centuries of poets, from Jupitor Hammon (1720-1800) to Reginald Shepherd (b.1963). . . . The editors' eloquent, outspoken vision provides a springboard for further examination of what constitutes the mainstream of American poetry." Library Journal.

Keillor, Garrison

Good poems / selected and introduced by Garrison Keillor. Viking, 2002. xxvi, 476 p. **811.008**

ISBN 9780670031269

LC 2002016881

Contains 350 poems featured on Garrison Keillor's radio segment entitled The Writer's Almanac.

Includes poems about lovers, work, failure, snow, everyday life, beasts, trips, death and transcendence, and the color yellow, written by classic poets, contemporary greats, and young writers.

"Keillor has put together a collection of close to 300 poems he has read during...[the] PBS broadcast, The Writer's Almanac. Poems are arranged by 19 general themes, such as Snow, Failure, and A Good Life. Authors range from well-known oldies like Emily Dickinson and Robert Frost to unknowns like C.K. Williams. An outstanding feature of this collection is that the selections are all so accessible--even folks who say they don't like poetry can find something here to enjoy." School Library Journal.

Lehman, David, 1948-

The **best** American poetry 2012 / series editor David Lehman ; guest editor Mark Doty. Scribner, 2012. 256 p. Best American poetry ; **811.008**

1. Anthologies
ISBN 9781439181522

LC bl 98010757

Edited by the National Book Award-winning author of Fire to Fire, an annual guide to contemporary American verse includes top-selected pieces that reflect high moral earnestness, humor and composition boundary testing by a range of eminent and lesser-known writers.

Young, Kevin, 1970-

★**African** American poetry : 250 years of struggle & song / edited by Kevin Young. Library of America, 2020 1150 p. Library of America ; **811.008**

1. African American poets 2. Racism 3. Slavery 4. Culture 5. Anthologies
ISBN 9781598536669

LC 2019954344

Only now, in the 21st century, can we fully grasp the breadth and range of African American poetry: a magnificent chorus of voices, some familiar, others recently rescued from neglect. Here, in this unprecedented anthology expertly selected by poet and scholar Kevin Young, this precious living heritage is revealed in all its power, beauty, and multiplicity.

"Vitality, beauty, anger, sorrow, humor, and hope all find original, resonant, and consummate expression throughout this expert gathering of works by both celebrated poets and many who will be new to readers. . . . A profound and affirming pleasure to read and an imperative resource." Booklist

811.009 American poetry--history and criticism

Parini, Jay

The **Columbia** history of American poetry / Jay Parini, editor, Brett C. Miller, Associate editor. Columbia University Press, c1993. xxxi, 894 p. ; **811.009**

1. American poetry -- History and criticism.
ISBN 9780231078368

LC 92029399

Essays look at important periods, movements, and writers

811.3 American poetry--1830-1861

Whitman, Walt, 1819-1892,

★**Leaves** of grass / Walt Whitman. William Collins, 2015. ix, 162 p. ; **811.3**

1. American poetry -- 19th century.
ISBN 9780008110604
First published: 1855.

Walt Whitman (1819--92) was an influential American poet and essayist, and is credited with being the founding father of free verse. He first published his culturally significant poetry collection 'Leaves of Grass' in 1855 from his own pocket, and revised and expanded it over thirty years. It is an essential element of America's literary tradition, much taught in schools and universities around the world. -- From publisher description

811.4 American poetry--1861-1899

Dickinson, Emily, 1830-1886

★The **complete** poems. Edited by Thomas H. Johnson. Little, Brown [1960] xiii, 770 p. **811.4**

1. American poetry
ISBN 9780316184137

LC 60011646

This volume, containing all of Emily Dickinson's lyrics, presents biographical data about the poet and information about previous collections of her works.

"Complete is the keyword here as this is the only edition currently available that contains all of Dickinson's poems. The works were originally gathered by editor Johnson and published in a three-volume set in 1955." Library Journal

811.5 American poetry--20th century

Gioia, Dana

Twentieth-century American poetry / edited by Dana Gioia, David Mason, Meg Schoerke. McGraw Hill, c2004. xlvi, 1143 p. : **811.5**

1. American poetry -- 20th century 2. Anthologies
ISBN 9780072400199

LC 2003061449

An anthology of twentieth-century American poetry spans the genre's development throughout the past one hundred years and is arranged by major movement to provide a comprehensive historical and cultural overview.

"Make room for this affordable, remarkable volume." Library Journal.

811.54 American poetry--1945-1999

Ginsberg, Allen, 1926-1997

★**Howl** : and other poems / Allen Ginsberg. City Lights Books, c1959. 57 p. ; **811.54**

1. American poetry -- 20th century 2. Beat generation 3. American poetry
ISBN 9780872860179

LC 56008587

Ginsberg's love for a man with whom he shared some of life's worst experiences is celebrated in poems which were once the subject of a prolonged court trial.

Gregg, Linda

All of it singing : new and selected poems / Linda Gregg. Graywolf Press, c2008. 213 p. ; **811.54**

1. American poetry
ISBN 9781555975074

LC 2008928247

"A Jane Kenyon book"--T.p. verso.

A single-volume anthology of definitive pieces reflects the career of the PEN/Voelcker Award-winning poet and combines pieces from her six previous collections with thirty new works.

Hecht, Anthony, 1923-2004

Collected later poems / Anthony Hecht. Knopf, 2005. 231 p. **811.54**

1. American poetry
ISBN 9780375710308

LC oc2007117319

In honor of his eightieth birthday, an omnibus edition brings together selections from the poet's three most recent collections--The Transparent Man, Flight Among the Tombs, and The Darkness and the Light--in which he contemplates the mortal fate of humankind with trademark wit, insight, and dark humor.

Myles, Eileen

I must be living twice : new & selected poems, 1975-2014 / Eileen Myles. Ecco, 2015 xii, 356 p. ; **811.54**

1. American poetry.
ISBN 9780062389084

LC 2016297462

"Readers will be thrilled not only that this old work is available again, but that the new work is as impressive as ever." Publishers Weekly.

Plath, Sylvia

The **letters** of Sylvia Plath : Volume 2: 1956-1963 / Sylvia Plath ; edited by Peter K. Steinberg and Karen V. Kukil. Harper, 2018. 1280 p. **811.54**

1. Plath, Sylvia Correspondence 2. Women poets 3. Women authors 4. Women college students 5. Marriage 6. Letters
ISBN 9780062740588

One of the most talented and beloved poets, Sylvia Plath continues to fascinate and inspire the modern literary imagination. The tragedy of her untimely death at age thirty, almost fifty-five years ago, has left much unknown about her creative and personal life. In this remarkable second volume of the iconic poet and writer's collected letters, the full range of Plath's ambitions, talents, fears, and perspective is made visible through her own powerful words.

Smith, Patricia, 1955-

★**Incendiary** art : poems / Patricia Smith. TriQuarterly Books/ Northwestern University Press, 2017. 132 p. ; **811.54**

1. Till, Emmett, 1941-1955 2. African Americans 3. African American poetry 4. American poetry
ISBN 9780810134331

LC 2016036601

A National Book Award finalist and the author of six critically acclaimed volumes of poetry presents a compelling new collection that envisions, re-envisions and ultimately reinvents the role of witness with an incendiary fusion of forms, including prose poems, ghazals, sestinas and sonnets.

811.5408 American poetry--1945-1999--collections

Moore, Honor, 1945-

Poems from the women's movement / edited by Honor Moore. Library of America, c2009. xxix, 238 p. ; **811.5408**

1. Feminist poetry 2. American poetry -- 20th century. 3. Women
ISBN 9781598530421

LC 2008943071

A volume of top-selected works representing definitive modes of thought during the women's movement of the 1960s, 1970s, and 1980s includes pieces by such writers as Adrienne Rich, Muriel Rukeyeser, and Judy Grahn.

811.6 American poetry -- 2000-

Browne, Mahogany L.

Black girl magic : a poem / Mahogany L. Browne ; art by Jess X. Snow. Roaring Brook Press, 2018, c2016. 40 p. **811.6**

1. African American teenage girls 2. Expectation (Psychology) 3. Success (Concept) 4. Values 5. African American poetry

ISBN 9781250173720

LC 2017944500

Much of what twenty-first century culture tells black girls is not pretty: Don't wear this; don't smile at that. Don't have an opinion; don't dream big. And most of all, don't love yourself. In response to such destructive ideas, internationally recognized poet Mahogany Browne challenges the conditioning of society by crafting an anthem of strength and magic undeniable in its bloom for all beautiful Black girls.

"These dense, entrancing, necessary works by more than 60 black women poets create a black-girl-centric world of their own...a well-rounded look at what it means to be a black woman and in the process serves as a platform for our voices and bodies, revealing our maneuvers through the world as deeply relevant to and deserving of literary space." Chicago Reader

Corral, Eduardo C., 1973-

Guillotine : poems / Eduardo C. Corral. Graywolf Press, 2020. 81 p. ; **811.6**

1. Borderlands 2. Immigrants 3. Grief 4. Rejection (Psychology)

ISBN 9781644450307

LC 2019949953

Guillotine traverses desert landscapes cut through by migrants, the grief of loss, betrayal's lingering scars, the border itself--great distances in which violence and yearning find roots. Through the voices of undocumented immigrants, border patrol agents, and scorned lovers, award-winning poet Eduardo C. Corral writes dramatic portraits of contradiction, survival, and a deeply human, relentless interiority. With extraordinary lyric imagination, these poems wonder about being unwanted or renounced.

"In his latest, corruscatingly brilliant collection, Yale Younger Poet Corral (Slow Lightning) communicates a sense of loss and betrayal along the Mexican-American border in a multivoiced narrative that becomes a single story, a single low wail. . . . The images rushing down these pages in tightly paced cadence take readers on a haunting journey, with Corral's impressionism delivering more than taut realism ever could." Library Journal

Kaur, Rupi

The **sun** and her flowers / Rupi Kaur. Andrews McMeel Publishing, 2017. 256 p. **811.6**

1. Grief 2. Loss (Psychology) 3. Coping 4. Self-fulfillment

ISBN 9781449486792

A collection of poetry about growth and healing, ancestry and honoring one's roots and expatriation and rising up to find a home within yourself, augmented by the author's own illustrations.

Seuss, Diane

Still life with two dead peacocks and a girl : poems / Diane Seuss. Graywolf Press, 2018 108 p. : **811.6**

1. Still-life in art 2. Ekphrasis 3. Authors and artists 4. Painting -- Themes, motives

ISBN 9781555978068

LC 2017953321

First Graywolf Printing.

This volume of poetry takes its title from Rembrandt's painting, a dark emblem of femininity, violence, and the viewer's troubled gaze. The collection shatters the notion of a still life, and presents the painting in pieces. With invention and irreverence, the poems escape their gilded frames and overturn traditional representations of gender, class, and luxury. Details from this gallery of lives in shards hide more than they reveal, like fragmented memories, waiting until they are reassembled into a whole.

Skaja, Emily

Brute / Emily Skaja. Graywolf Press, 2019. 74 p. **811.6**

1. Gender identity 2. Femininity 3. Violence 4. Self-discovery

ISBN 9781555978358

LC 2018947085

Emily Skaja's debut collection is a fiery, hypnotic book that confronts the dark questions and menacing silences around gender, sexuality, and violence. Brute arises, brave and furious, from the dissolution of a relationship, showing how such endings necessitate self-discovery and reinvention. The speaker of these poems is a sorceress, a bride, a warrior, a lover, both object and agent, ricocheting among ways of knowing and being known. Each incarnation squares itself up against ideas of feminine virtue and sin, strength and vulnerability, love and rage, as it closes in on a hard-won freedom.

"With relentless, driving energy, Skaja's poems seek brutal truths while searching for meaningful transformation. The mythological allusions and imagery, the violence, the honest and painful reflections all travel toward an awakening achieved by being fully rooted in dark, human soil." Publishers Weekly.

Smith, Danez

★**Don't** call us dead : poems / Danez Smith. Graywolf Press, [2017] 88 p. ; **811.6**

1. Identity (Psychology) 2. African Americans 3. Gay men 4. Racism 5. United States -- Race relations

ISBN 9781555977856

LC 2017930111

An award winning-poet presents a collection of works that opens with a heartrending sequence that imagines an afterlife for black men shot by police--a place where suspicion, violence and grief are forgotten and replaced with the safety, love and longevity they deserved here on earth.

"Poised at the bruising intersection of black and queer identity, poems such as "dear white america" ("I tried to love you, but you spent my brother's funeral making plans for brunch") lose no impact moving from spoken-word stage to page." Publishers Weekly

Smith, Tracy K.

★**Wade** in the water : poems / Tracy K. Smith. Graywolf Press, [2018] 83 p. ; **811.6**

1. Inequality 2. Social classes 3. Race relations 4. United States

ISBN 9781555978136

LC 2017951515

A Pulitzer Prize-winning poet, using her signature voice--inquisitive, lyrical and wry--mulls over what it means to be a citizen, a mother and an artist in a culture arbitrated by wealth, men and violence, boldly tying America's modern moment both to our nation's fraught founding history and to a sense of the spirit, the everlasting.

"The sacred and the malevolent are astutely juxtaposed in this beautifully formed, deeply delving, and caring volume." Booklist.

Youn, Monica

Blackacre / Monica Youn. Graywolf Press, 2016 85 p.

; **811.6**

1. American poetry
ISBN 9781555977504

LC 2016931136

In the title sequence, the poet gleans a second crop from the field of Milton's great sonnet on his blindness: a lyric meditation on her barrenness, on her own desire--her own struggle--to conceive a child. What happens when the transformative imagination comes up against the limits of unalterable fact? --From publisher description.

"Throughout, Youn's lawyerly analyses--of life, of herself, her feelings, and of language--cut through the poetic to a place that lies triangulated between poetry, lyric memoir, and textual analysis." Publishers Weekly.

812 American drama in English

Abbotson, Susan C. W., 1961-

Critical companion to Arthur Miller : a literary reference to his life and work / Susan C.W. Abbotson. Facts On File, c2007. x, 518 p. : **812**

1. Miller, Arthur, 1915-2005 Handbooks, manuals, etc. 2. Miller, Arthur, 1915-2005 Criticism and interpretation.
ISBN 0816061947

LC 2006022902

A guide to the playwright's life and work presents a brief biography; offers synopses and critical assessments of his writings; and discusses important people, places, and themes in his life.

Adler, Stella, 1902-1992

★**Stella** Adler on America's master playwrights : Eugene O'Neill, Clifford Odets, Tennessee Williams, Arthur Miller, Edward Albee, et al. / Stella Adler ; edited and with commentary by Barry Paris. Alfred A. Knopf, Inc., 2012. 320 p. **812**

1. O'Neill, Eugene, 1888-1953 Criticism and interpretation 2. Odets, Clifford, 1906-1963 Criticism and interpretation 3. Williams, Tennessee, 1911-1983 Criticism and interpretation 4. Miller, Arthur, 1915-2005 Criticism and interpretation 5. Albee, Edward, 1928- Criticism and interpretation 6. Drama -- Explication. 7. Dramatists. 8. Actors and actresses. 9. Essays
ISBN 9780679424437

LC 2012018983

"An exciting, inspiring and essential book for anyone interested in American theater." Kirkus.

Albee, Edward, 1928-

★**Who's** afraid of Virginia Woolf? / Edward Albee. Scribner Classics, 2003. 243 p. ; **812**

1. College teachers 2. Domestic drama. 3. Married people 4. New England Drama. 5. Drama.
ISBN 0743255259

LC 2003054206

Originally published: New York : Atheneum, 1962.

A social event becomes a personal challenge for two faculty members and their wives at a small New England college as their inner fears and desires are exposed.

Auburn, David, 1969-

Proof : a play / David Auburn. Faber and Faber, 2001. 83 p. ; **812**

1. Fathers -- Death 2. Man-woman relationships 3. Mathematicians 4. Drama.
ISBN 0571199976

LC 00050284

In a play portraying the uncertainties of trust, integrity, and genius, a woman claims authorship of a mathematical proof found among her late father's papers by one of his former students, who doubts her claim.

"Twenty-five-year-old Catherine, who sacrificed college to care for her mentally ill father (once a brilliant, much-admired mathematician), is left in a kind of limbo after his death. Socially awkward and a bit of a shut-in, she is gruff with Hal, a former student who shows up even before the funeral wanting to root through the countless notebooks her father kept in the years of his decline, hoping to find mathematical gold. On the heels of his arrival comes Claire, Catherine's cosmopolitan, blandly successful, and pushy sister, with plans to sell their father's house and take Catherine...with her back to New York." School Library Journal.

Butler, Isaac

The **world** only spins forward : the ascent of Angels in America / Isaac Butler and Dan Kois. St Martins Pr 2018 304 p. **812**

1. Kushner, Tony. Angels in America 2. Drama 3. Musicals 4. Homosexuality -- Public opinion 5. Performing arts and society 6. Broadway, New York City
ISBN 9781635571769

LC 2018003632

Commemorating the 25th anniversary of the show's Broadway premiere, an oral history of Angels in America, a generation-defining classic and moving account of the AIDS era, is told through nearly 200 voices in vibrant conversation and debate and is both a rollicking theater saga and an uplifting testament to one of the great works of art of the past century.

"Highly recommended for anyone interested in performance, cultural history, and theater." Library Journal.

Cruz, Nilo

Anna in the tropics / Nilo Cruz. Theatre Communications Group ; 2003. 84 p. ; **812**

1. Tolstoy, Leo, graf, 1828-1910 Appreciation Drama. 2. Cigar industry 3. Cuban American families 4. Depressions 5. Historical drama. 6. Tampa (Fla.) Drama. 7. Drama.
ISBN 1559362324

LC 2003015859

"2003 Pulitzer Prize for Drama"--Cover.

When a new "lector" arrives at a Cuban-American cigar factory in Florida, he begins to read aloud from "Anna Karenina," an act which becomes the catalyst in the lives of his listeners.

Edson, Margaret, 1961-

Wit : a play / Margaret Edson. Faber and Faber, 1999. 85 p. ; **812**

1. Cancer in women -- Drama. 2. English teachers -- Drama. 3. Women college teachers -- Drama.
ISBN 0571198775

LC 99011921

The Pulitzer Prize-winning drama explores the role of nurses in the care of terminally ill patients, as Professor Vivian Bearing endures eight months of experimental chemotherapy in a grueling effort to fight ovarian cancer.

Gibson, William, 1914-2008

★The **miracle** worker / William Gibson. Scribner, 2008. 112 p. ; **812**

1. Keller, Helen, 1880-1968 Drama. 2. Sullivan, Annie, 1866-1936

Drama. 3. Deafblind women 4. Teachers of deafblind people 5. Women teachers 6. Drama.
ISBN 1416590846

LC 2008275273

A text of the television play, intended for reading, of Anne Sullivan Macy's attempts to teach her pupil, Helen Keller, to communicate.

Goodrich, Frances

The **diary** of Anne Frank / Frances Goodrich and Albert Hackett ; newly adapted by Wendy Kesselman. Dramatists Play Service, c2000. 72 p. : **812**

1. Frank, Anne, 1929-1945 Drama 2. Holocaust, Jewish (1939-1945) -- Drama 3. Netherlands -- History -- German occupation, 1940-1945 Drama.
ISBN 9780822217183

LC bl2006027516

"Based upon 'Anne Frank: the diary of a young girl'"--T.p. verso.

A two-act play based on the diary of a Jewish girl who died in a Nazi concentration camp at the age of fifteen.

Guare, John

Six degrees of separation : a play / John Guare. Vintage Books, c1990. xiii, 120 p. ; **812**

ISBN 9780679734819

LC 90050588

A play about a young, black con man and the wealthy white family he fools, deals with liberal guilt, greed, loveless families, false aesthetics, and modern life in New York City.

Gurney, A. R. (Albert Ramsdell), 1930-2017

Love letters, and two other plays, The golden age and What I did last summer : The Golden Age and What I Did Last Summer / A.R. Gurney ; with an introduction by the playwright. Plume, c1990. xi, 209 p. ; **812**

ISBN 9780452265011

LC 90034177

Three plays look at love and the times of our lives.

Heintzelman, Greta

Critical companion to Tennessee Williams / Greta Heintzelman, Alycia Smith Howard. Facts On File, c2005. xi, 436 p. : **812**

1. Williams, Tennessee, 1911-1983 Encyclopedias 2. Dramatists, American -- 20th century -- Encyclopedias
ISBN 9780816048885

LC 2004007362

An encyclopedic guide to the dramatist includes entries on Tennessee William's works and characters, influential people in his life, important places, and literary terms.

Kushner, Tony

Angels in America : a gay fantasia on national themes / Tony Kushner. Theatre Communications Group, 2003 289 p. ; **812**

1. Cohn, Roy M. Drama. 2. AIDS (Disease) -- Patients 3. Angels 4. Gay men 5. Mormons 6. Drama.
ISBN 1559362316

LC 2003017904

Dramatizes the effects of AIDS on the United States through the experiences of lawyer Roy Cohn, a Mormon couple, and a young man called Prior Walter.

Lawrence, Jerome, 1915-2004

Inherit the wind / Jerome Lawrence and Robert E. Lee. Ballantine Books, 2007. 129 p. ; **812**

1. Evolution (Biology) -- Study and teaching -- Law and legislation -- Drama 2. Science teachers -- Drama 3. Historical drama 4. Dayton (Tenn.) Drama.
ISBN 9780345501035

LC 2007281039

Originally published: New York : Random House, c1955.

Dramatizes the famous Scopes "Monkey Trial," where William Jennings Bryan and Clarence Darrow clash over a teacher's right to teach evolution.

Mamet, David

Glengarry Glen Ross : a play / David Mamet. Grove Press, 1992, c1983. 108 p. ; **812**

ISBN 9780802130914

LC BL 99732734

A group of ruthless real estate salesmen try to sell worthless land in Florida to innocent buyers

Mamet, David

Speed-the-plow : a play / David Mamet. Grove Press, 1988, c1987. 82 p. ; **812**

ISBN 9780802130464

LC 87037252

Dramatizes the deal making that goes on behind the scenes in the movie industry.

O'Neill, Eugene, 1888-1953

Complete plays / Eugene O'Neill. Literary Classics of the United States, c1988. 3 vols. ; The Library of America ; **812**

ISBN 9780940450486

LC 88050685

"Travis Bogard wrote the notes and selected the texts for this volume"--5th prelim. p., v. 1-3.

Gathers all fifty of O'Neill's plays, lists the original cast for each play, and includes his only published short story.

Parks, Suzan-Lori

Topdog/underdog / Suzan-Lori Parks. Theatre Communications Group, 2001. 109 p. ; **812**

1. Brothers 2. Domestic drama. 3. Sibling rivalry 4. Drama.
ISBN 1559362014

LC 2001027316

"Underdog" in the title appears reversed and upside down on the t.p.

Brothers Lincoln and Booth--given their names by their father as a joke--share an obsession with three-card monte and act out a lifetime of sibling rivalry and resentment.

Rankine, Claudia, 1963-

The **white** card : a play in one act / Claudia Rankine. Graywolf Press, 2019 ix, 89 p. : **812**

1. African Americans 2. Art and race 3. Artists 4. Race relations 5. Drama.
ISBN 1555978398

LC 2018947087

A revealing drama about racial divisions is experienced in the white spaces of the living room, the art gallery, the theater and the imagination itself.

"Each act in this fast-paced, thought-provoking play reads like a swift conversation, inviting readers to experience the power of whiteness from Charlotte's perspective." Library Journal.

Rose, Reginald

Twelve angry men / Reginald Rose ; introduction by David Mamet. Penguin Books, 2006. xi, 73 p. ; **812**

1. Legal drama, American.
ISBN 0143104403

LC 2006046006

Originally published: U.S.A. :Dramatic Pub., 1955.

A new edition of the landmark American play presents a compelling courtroom drama revolving around the trial of a boy accused of killing his father, where one man, a single hold-out juror, stands between the accused and capital punishment.

Shanley, John Patrick

Doubt : a parable / John Patrick Shanley. Theatre Communications Group, 2005. x, 58 p. ; **812**

1. Nuns -- Drama. 2. Clergy -- Drama. 3. Catholics -- Drama. 4. Child sexual abuse -- Drama.
ISBN 9781559362764

LC 2005005284

Set in a Bronx Catholic school in 1964, a nun is faced with uncertainty as she has grave concerns for a male colleague.

Shepard, Sam, 1943-2017

Fool for love, and other plays / Sam Shepard ; introduction by Ross Wetzsteon. Dial Press Trade Paperbacks, 2006. 307 p. ; **812**

1. Drama
ISBN 9780553345902

LC 2006272011

Here are eight of Pulitzer-prizewinning Sam Shepard's most stunning plays with an introduction by Ross Wetzsteon.

Simon, Neil, 1927-2018

Brighton Beach memoirs / a play by Neil Simon. Plume, 1995. 130 p. ; **812**

1. Simon, Neil, 1927-2018 2. Brooklyn, New York City 3. Drama.
ISBN 9780452275287

LC bl2013056271

An autobiographical play based on the story of an extended family living in Brooklyn during the Depression, and their fifteen-year-old son, Eugene Jerome, who dreams of playing for the Yankees and becoming a writer.

Simon, Neil, 1927-2018

Lost in Yonkers / Neil Simon. Plume, c1991 120 p. ; **812**

ISBN 9780452268838

LC 92029111

Two young brothers living with their cold and cruel grandmother watch as their Aunt Bella, a warm woman hungry for experience, searches for love and enters into the ultimate showdown with her mother.

Wasserstein, Wendy

The **Heidi** chronicles and other plays / Wendy Wasserstein. Vintage Books, 1991. xi, 249 p. ; **812**

ISBN 0679734996

LC 90055681

Three plays deal with recent college graduates deciding what to do with their lives, a woman trying to be a successful executive and mother, and an art historian changing with the times from the sixties to the eighties.

Wilder, Thornton, 1897-1975

★**Our** town : a play in three acts / Thornton Wilder. HarperCollins, 2003. xx, 181 p. : **812**

1. City and town life 2. Death 3. Domestic drama. 4. Young women 5. New Hampshire Drama. 6. Drama.
ISBN 0060535253

LC 2004274063

Contains a foreword by Donald Margulies.

An illustrated hardcover edition of the Pulitzer Prize-winning drama, first produced in 1938, follows the changes that gradually occur in the lives of two early-twentieth-century New Hampshire families and their neighbors.

Wilder, Thornton, 1897-1975

Thornton Wilder : collected plays & writings on theater / [J.D. McClatchy, selected the texts and wrote the notes for this volume]. Library of America : c2007. x, 871 p. ; The library of America ; **812**

ISBN 1598530038

LC 2006048620

A volume of approximately three dozen plays includes "The Alcestiad," "Our Town," and a previously unpublished Alfred Hitchcock screenplay, "Shadow of a Doubt," in a collection that also restores to print a key selection of Wilder's theatrical essays.

Williams, Tennessee, 1911-1983

★**Plays,** 1937-1955 / Tennessee Williams. Library of America, c2000. 975 p. ; The Library of America ; **812**

ISBN 9781883011864

LC 00030190

Selection and notes by Mel Gussow and Kenneth Holditch.

"Editors Gussow (drama critic, New York Times) and Holditch (founder/editor, the Tennessee Williams Journal) have added detailed notes on the texts and a newly researched chronology of Williams's life. Highly recommended for public and academic American drama collections." Library Journal.

Williams, Tennessee, 1911-1983

★**Plays,** 1957-1980 / Tennessee Williams. Library of America, c2000. 975 p. ; The Library of America ; **812**

ISBN 9781883011871

LC 00030190

Selection and notes by Mel Gussow and Kenneth Holditch.

A second compilation of plays focuses on the dramatist's later works, icnluding The Night of the Iguana, Sweet Bird of Youth, Orpheus Descending, Suddenly Last Summer, The Eccentricities of a Nightingale, and the autobiographical Vieux Carre.

Williams, Tennessee, 1911-1983

★A **streetcar** named desire / Tennessee Williams ; with an introduction by Arthur Miller. New Directions, c2004. xv, 192 p. ; **812**

1. Domestic drama. 2. Married people 3. Rape 4. Sisters 5. New Orleans (La.) Drama. 6. Drama.
ISBN 0811216020

LC 2004011654

Tennessee Williams' classic drama studies the emotional disintegration of a Southern woman whose last chance for happiness is destroyed by her vindictive brother-in-law.

Wilson, August
Fences : a play / August Wilson ; introduction by Lloyd Richards. Plume, c1986. xviii, 101 p. ; **812**
1. African Americans -- History -- 20th century -- Drama.
ISBN 9780452264014
LC BL 99006429

Originally published: New York : New American Library, c1986.

During the 1950s Troy Maxson struggles against racism and tries to preserve his feelings of pride in himself.

Wilson, August
Jitney / August Wilson. Overlook Press, 2003, c2000. 96 p. ; **812**
1. African American neighborhoods 2. African Americans 3. Historical drama. 4. Taxicab drivers 5. Hill District (Pittsburgh, Pa.) Drama. 6. Pittsburgh (Pa.) Drama. 7. Drama.
ISBN 1585673706
LC oc2010019435

Reprint. Originally published: 2000.

Completely revised and reworked from the 1979 original, this play--the seventh in a series of ten about the black experience in the twentieth century--depicts gypsy cab drivers who serve the African-American community in Pittsburgh.

Wilson, August
Joe Turner's come and gone : a play in two acts / August Wilson. New American Library, c1988. 94 p. ; **812**
1. African Americans -- Drama 2. Historical drama
ISBN 9780452260092
LC 88001660

"A Plume book."

After seven years on a chain gang, Herald Loomis returns to Pittsburgh in search of his wife

Wilson, August
King Hedley II / August Wilson. Theatre Communications Group, 2005. xi, 103 p. ; **812**
1. African American men 2. Ex-convicts 3. Historical drama. 4. Pittsburgh (Pa.) Drama. 5. Drama.
ISBN 155936260X
LC 2005012535

King Hedley II is the eighth work in playwright August Wilson's 10-play cycle chronicling the history of the African American experience in each decade of the twentieth century. It's set in 1985 and tells the story of an ex-con in post-Reagan Pittsburgh trying to rebuild his life. --From publisher description.

Wilson, August
Ma Rainey's black bottom : a play / August Wilson. New American Library, c1985. xvi, 111 p. ; **812**
ISBN 9780452261136
LC BL 99701783

Ma Rainey, the legendary blues singer, is due to arrive with her entourage to cut new sides of old favorites. Waiting for her are her black musician sidemen, the white owner of the record company, and her white manager. What goes down in the session to come is more than music. --From publisher description.

Wilson, August
Seven guitars / August Wilson. Plume, 1997, c1996. 107 p. ; **812**
1. Afro-Americans -- History -- 20th century -- Drama. 2. Afro-Americans -- Pennsylvania -- Pittsburgh -- Drama. 3. Blues musicians -- Pennsylvania -- Pittsburgh -- Drama.
ISBN 0452276926
LC BL 99791011

Originally published: New York : Dutton, 1996.

Dramatizes the hopes and struggles of African Americans in 1940s Pittsburgh, as a group of neighbors gathers to talk, play cards, and listen to the blues.

"Pittsburgh, summer 1948. Five of his friends gather after the funeral of Floyd Barton, mysteriously murdered at 35, just as his first blues record had become a hit. The sixth play in Wilson's cycle concerned with twentieth-century African American lives is mostly a flashback. We learn what happened to Floyd, but before that horrifying climax, Wilson steeps us in the pathos that Floyd glimpsed a way to escape. As powerful as modern drama gets." Booklist.

Wilson, August
The **piano** lesson / August Wilson. Plume, c1990. 108 p. ; **812**
1. African Americans
ISBN 9780452265349
LC 90038735

When Boy Willie wants to sell the family's prized upright piano to purchase some land, the family must re-evaluate the piano's true worth.

"Feisty, ebullient, exuberant; Wilson is a consummate storyteller." Los Angeles Times.

Wilson, August
Two trains running : 1969 / August Wilson ; foreword by Laurence Fishburne. Theatre Communications Group, 2007. ix, 99 p. ; **812**
1. African American neighborhoods 2. African Americans 3. Historical drama. 4. Nineteen sixties 5. Hill District (Pittsburgh, Pa.) Drama. 6. Drama.
ISBN 1559363037
LC 2007022095

Set during the civil rights movement, at the lunch counter of Memphis Lee's diner. --From publisher description.

Wilson, Lanford, 1937-2011
Lanford Wilson : 21 short plays / [introduction by Frank Rich]. Smith and Kraus, 1993. x, 268 p. ; **812**
ISBN 1880399318
LC 93034434

"Contemporary playwrights series."

"This collection is an absorbing rendition of a playwright's voice, and the format is well suited to the reader's edification." Library Journal.

812.52 American drama--1900-1945

Hughes, Langston, 1902-1967
Five plays / edited with an introduction by Webster Smalley. Indiana University Press 1963 258 p. **812.52**
1. African Americans -- Drama
ISBN 9780253322302
LC 63007169

Tambourines to Glory, Soul Gone Home, Little Ham, Mulatto, and Simply Heavenly reflect the black author's concern with the position of the Negro in the United States.

813 American fiction in English

Bloom, Harold

Zora Neale Hurston / edited and with an introduction by Harold Bloom. Bloom's Literary Criticism, c2008. vii, 238 p. ; **813**

1. Hurston, Zora Neale Criticism and interpretation.
ISBN 0791096106

LC 2007049161

Presents critical analysis of the themes, symbols, and ideas that appear in the author's works.

Bernard, Emily, 1967-

Carl Van Vechten and the Harlem Renaissance : a portrait in black and white / Emily Bernard. Yale University Press, c2012. xiii, 358 p. : **813**

1. Van Vechten, Carl, 1880-1964 Criticism and interpretation. 2. Harlem Renaissance. 3. African American authors 4. African American arts -- Harlem, New York City 5. Intellectual life -- African Americans 6. New York City 7. Harlem, New York City -- 20th century
ISBN 9780300121995

LC 2011034190

Discusses the author's works and their significance to the Harlem Renaissance, focusing on the fiction, essays, and letters that Van Vechten wrote about black culture, and the interpersonal exchanges that inspired his works.

Bloom, Harold

J.D. Salinger / edited and with an introduction by Harold Bloom. Bloom's Literary Criticism, c2008. vii, 254 p. ; **813**

1. Salinger, J. D. (Jerome David), 1919-2010 Criticism and interpretation.
ISBN 9780791098134

LC 2007044662

Collects critical essays on the works of J.D. Salinger, including his novellas, short stories, and novels.

Bloom, Harold

John Steinbeck / edited and with an introduction by Harold Bloom. Bloom's Literary Criticism, c2008. vii, 176 p. ; **813**

1. Steinbeck, John, 1902-1968 Criticism and interpretation.
ISBN 9780791097878

LC 2007038676

Essays discuss the themes and techniques used by the author in his major works.

Bradbury, Ray, 1920-2012

Bradbury speaks : too soon from the cave, too far from the stars / Ray Bradbury. William Morrow, c2005. xi, 243 p. ; **813**

1. Science fiction writing 2. Writing 3. Celebrities 4. Essays
ISBN 0060585684

LC 2005041489

A collection of personal essays shares the writer's thoughts on such topics as Paris, Gene Kelly, and space travel, in a volume that offers insight into the events that influenced Bradbury's life and literary career.

"By turns whimsical, insightful, and unabashedly metaphoric, his prose is immediately accessible as well as thought-provoking. Fans and nonfans alike should enjoy." Booklist.

Ellison, Ralph

The **selected** letters of Ralph Ellison / edited by John F. Callahan and Marc C. Conner ; with introductory essays by John F. Callahan. Random House, 2019. 512 p. **813**

1. Ellison, Ralph Correspondence 2. Authors, American -- 20th century 3. African American authors 4. Letter writing 5. Interpersonal relations 6. Letters
ISBN 9780812998528

LC 2018020868

Over six decades (1933 to 1993), Ralph Ellison's extensive and revealing correspondence remarkably details his aspirations and anxieties, confidence and uncertainties throughout his personal and professional life. From early notes to his mother, as an impoverished college student; to debates with the most distinguished American writers and thinkers of his time, including Romare Bearden, Saul Bellow, Robert Penn Warren, Richard Wright, and Alfred Kazin, among others; to exchanges with friends and family from his hometown of Oklahoma City, whose influence would always be paramount, these letters communicate the immense importance of Ellison's life and work..

Fargnoli, A. Nicholas

Critical companion to William Faulkner : a literary reference to his life and work / A. Nicholas Fargnoli, Michael Golay, Robert W. Hamblin. Facts On File, c2008. xi, 562 p. : **813**

1. Faulkner, William, 1897-1962 Encyclopedias 2. Novelists, American -- 20th century -- Encyclopedias 3. Yoknapatawpha County (Imaginary place) -- Encyclopedias 4. Mississippi -- In literature Encyclopedias.
ISBN 9780816064328

LC 2007032361

Rev. ed. of: William Faulkner A to Z. c2002.

An encyclopedic guide to the American author includes critical entries on his works and characters, biographical information, and influential people and places in his life.

Farrell, Susan Elizabeth, 1963-

Critical companion to Kurt Vonnegut : a literary reference to his life and work / Susan Farrell. Facts On File, c2008. xi, 532 p. : **813**

1. Vonnegut, Kurt Handbooks, manuals, etc 2. Trout, Kilgore (Fictitious character)
ISBN 9780816065981

LC 2007037900

A guide to the American author includes critical entries on his works and characters, biographical information, and influential people and places in his life.

Freeman, John, 1974-

Tales of two Americas : stories of inequality in a divided nation / edited by John Freeman. Penguin Books, 2017. 304 p. **813**

1. Social problems. 2. Social justice. 3. Social conflict. 4. Race relations. 5. Essays 6. Anthologies
ISBN 9780143131038

LC 2017011506

In Tales of Two Americas, some of the literary world's most exciting writers look beyond numbers and wages to convey what it feels like to live in this divided nation. Their extraordinarily powerful stories, essays, and poems demonstrate how boundaries break down when experiences are shared, and that in sharing our stories we can help to alleviate a suffering that touches so many people.

"Urgent, worthy reportage from our fractious, volatile social and cultural moment." Kirkus.

Gillespie, Carmen
Critical companion to Toni Morrison : a literary reference to her life and work / Carmen Gillespie. Facts On File, c2008. xi, 484 p. : **813**

1. Morrison, Toni.
ISBN 9780816062768

LC 2006038231

A comprehensive guide to the American novelist includes a chronology of her life, summaries of each of her works, and entries on major characters, important places, and relevant literary terms.

Helbig, Alethea
Dictionary of American young adult fiction, 1997-2001 : books of recognized merit / Alethea K. Helbig and Agnes Regan Perkins. Greenwood Press, 2004. xxii, 558 p. ; **813**

1. American fiction -- 20th century 2. American fiction -- 20th century -- Bio-bibliography 3. Best books. 4. Young adult fiction in libraries. 5. Book lists.
ISBN 9780313324307

LC 2003056804

Looks at 290 award-winning books for young adults, using 750 alphabetical entries on individual works, authors, characters, and settings to provide plot summaries, critical assessments, and biographical information.

"[The information is collected] usefully for selectors of young adult fiction, reader's advisers, teachers, and libraries supporting young adult fiction teaching." Library Journal.

Kerouac, Jack, 1922-1969
Selected letters, 1940-1956 / Jack Kerouac ; edited with an introduction and commentary by Ann Charters. Penguin Books, 1996, c1995. xxvi, 629 p. ; **813**

1. Kerouac, Jack, 1922-1969 Correspondence. 2. Authors, American -- 20th century -- Correspondence 3. Beat generation
ISBN 9780140234442

LC BL 99776024

Originally published: New York : Viking, 1995.

Kirk, Connie Ann
Critical companion to Flannery O'Connor / Connie Ann Kirk. Facts on File, c2008. xiv, 415 p. : **813**

1. O'Connor, Flannery Handbooks, manuals, etc. 2. O'Connor, Flannery Criticism and interpretation. 3. Women and literature -- United States -- History -- 20th century.
ISBN 0816064172

LC 2007006512

An encyclopedic guide to the American author's life and works presents a brief biography, offers synopses of her writings, critical analysis of her characters and major themes, and discusses important people, places, and topics in her life.

Levy, Andrew
Huck Finn's America : Mark Twain and the era that shaped his masterpiece / Andrew Levy. Simon & Schuster 2014 304 p. **813**

1. Twain, Mark, 1835-1910. Adventures of Huckleberry Finn Influence 2. Race relations 3. Children 4. Innocence (Personal quality) 5. National characteristics 6. United States -- History -- 19th century
ISBN 9781439186961

LC 2014040482

A provocative, deeply researched investigation into Twain's writing of Huckleberry Finn challenges basic understandings to argue its reflection of period fears about youth violence, education, pop culture and parenting.

"Delving deeply into 19th-century sources, generations of readers' responses and a wide range of Twain's writing, Levy complicates the possibilities of what the novel meant for its contemporaries and what it might mean for readers." Kirkus.

Marrs, Suzanne,
Meanwhile there are letters : the correspondence of Eudora Welty and Ross Macdonald / edited and with an introduction by Suzanne Marrs and Tom Nolan. Arcade Publishing, 2015. 512 p. **813**

1. Welty, Eudora, 1909-2001 Correspondence. 2. Macdonald, Ross, 1915-1983 Correspondence. 3. Friendship 4. Authors, American -- 20th century -- Correspondence. 5. Letters
ISBN 9781628725278

LC 2015005957

"The moving portrait in letters of two American literary icons and their deeply loving friendship. Though separated by background, geography, genre, and his marriage, the two authors shared their lives in witty, wry, tender, and at times profoundly romantic letters, each drawing on the other for inspiration, comfort, and strength. The letters reveal the impact each had on the other's work, and they show the personal support Welty provided when Alzheimer's destroyed Macdonald's ability to communicate and write".-- Provided by publisher.

"An intimate, luminous portrait of a friendship." Kirkus.

Michener, James A. (James Albert), 1907-1997
Return to paradise / James A. Michener. Dial Press, 2015, c1951. xiv, 422 p. ; **813**

1. Michener, James A. (James Albert), 1907-1997 Travel South Pacific Ocean 2. Travelers -- United States 3. Island life -- South Pacific Ocean 4. South Pacific Ocean -- Description and travel 5. Oceania -- Description and travel. 6. Essays.
ISBN 9780812986778

LC 2015506621

Originally published: New York : Random House, 1951.

In factual essays Michener provides his impressions of the beautiful Pacific Islands. Fiction pieces are Mr. Morgan, Povenaaa's daughter, The mynah birds, The story, The good life, Until they sail, The jungle, The fossickers.

Murphy, Mary McDonagh
Scout, Atticus, and Boo : a celebration of fifty years of To kill a mockingbird / Mary McDonagh Murphy. Harper, 2010. 208 p. **813**

1. Lee, Harper. To kill a mockingbird. 2. American fiction -- History and criticism 3. Books and reading. 4. Writing. 5. Literature and society.
ISBN 9780061924071

LC 2010006739

"In celebration of the 50th anniversary of To Kill a Mockingbird (June 8, 2010), an American classic that sells almost a million copies per year, Scout, Atticus, and Boo features interview selections with prominent figures including Oprah Winfrey, Tom Brokaw, Wally Lamb, and Anna Quindlen on how the book has impacted their lives".-- Provided by publisher.

Nadel, Ira Bruce
Critical companion to Philip Roth : a literary reference to his life and

work / Ira B. Nadel. Facts On File, c2011. xii, 356 p. : **813**

1. Roth, Philip
ISBN 9780816077953

LC 2010022769

A concise but thorough biography of Roth.

"This user-friendly, comprehensive resource provides detailed coverage of Philip Roth's life and works." Booklist.

Philbrick, Nathaniel

Why read Moby-Dick? / Nathaniel Philbrick. Viking, 2011. 144 p. **813**

1. Melville, Herman, 1819-1891. Moby Dick. 2. Sea stories -- History and criticism. 3. Characters and characteristics in literature 4. Relevance 5. Literature -- History and criticism
ISBN 9780670022991

LC 2011019766

Shares expert guidelines on how to read and appreciate Herman Melville's classic work, offering insight into its history, characters, and themes while explaining its literary relevance in the modern world.

Pritchard, William H.

Updike : America's man of letters / William H. Pritchard. Steerforth Press, 2000. xiii, 351 p. **813**

1. Updike, John Criticism and interpretation 2. American literature -- 20th century -- History and criticism 3. Authors, American
ISBN 158642002X

LC 00033835

"All in all, Pritchard's book is a gentle and intelligent request for a little more thought and a little less cranky let's-move-on speed in judging the work of one of America's pre-eminent writers." New York Times Book Review.

Rehak, Melanie

Girl sleuth : Nancy Drew and the women who created her / Melanie Rehak. Harcourt, 2005. xviii, 364 p., 8 p. of plates : **813**

1. Wirt, Mildred A. (Mildred Augustine), 1905- Characters Nancy Drew. 2. Adams, Harriet Stratemeyer Characters Nancy Drew. 3. Keene, Carolyn (Publisher pseudonym) Characters Nancy Drew. 4. Stratemeyer Syndicate. 5. Mystery stories -- History and criticism 6. Women and literature -- United States -- History -- 20th century. 7. Women authors, American -- 20th century 8. Teenage fiction -- History and criticism
ISBN 0151010412

LC 2005009129

Agatha Award for Best Nonfiction, 2005.

Macavity Award for Best Non-Fiction, 2006.

Edgar Allan Poe Award for Best Critical/Biographical, 2006.

"Packed with revealing anecdotes, Rehak's meticulously researched account of the publishing phenomenon that survived the Depression and WWII . . . will delight fans of the beloved gumshoe whose gumption guaranteed that every reprobate got his due." Booklist.

Reynolds, David S., 1948-

Mightier than the sword : Uncle Tom's Cabin and the battle for America / David S. Reynolds. W W Norton & Co Inc, 2011. 352 p. **813**

1. Stowe, Harriet Beecher, 1811-1896. Uncle Tom's cabin. 2. Books. 3. Reading -- Social aspects. 4. Civil war 5. United States Civil War, 1861-1865 6. United States -- History -- Civil War, 1861-1865.
ISBN 9780393081329

LC 2011000702

"The powerful antislavery message of Uncle Tom's Cabin fueled the flames leading to the Civil War, making it the most influential novel in American history. Stowe claimed the novel came to her in a vision and God was its true author. Accordingly, her book is weighted with religious symbolism, which Reynolds interprets with typical English professor's zeal. He also examines its impacts not just on public attitudes toward slavery, but on women's rights, temperance, capitalism, minstrel shows, sexual customs and other aspects of mid-19th century American life. Reynolds dissects dozens of imitative novels, plays and minstrel shows--some against, others for slavery or segregation--and traces the influence of Stowe's novel into modern times, including film spin-offs. [This is] not easy reading, but it offers virtually everything you ever wanted to know about Uncle Tom's Cabin--and probably a lot more." Seattle Times.

Rioux, Anne Boyd

Meg, Jo, Beth, Amy : the story of Little women and why it still matters / Anne Boyd Rioux. W. W. Norton & Company, [2018] 352 p. **813**

1. Alcott, Louisa May, 1832-1888. Little women. 2. American literature -- History and criticism 3. Influence (Literary, artistic, etc.) 4. Women authors, American 5. Women in literature
ISBN 9780393254730

LC 2018006602

A 150th anniversary tribute describes the cultural significance of Louisa May Alcott's classic, exploring how its relatable themes and depictions of family resilience, community and female resourcefulness have inspired generations of writers.

Row, Jess

White flights : race, fiction, and the American imagination / Jess Row. Graywolf Press, 2019. 320 p. **813**

1. Row, Jess 2. European Americans -- Identity 3. American literature -- History and criticism 4. Race (Social sciences) 5. Race awareness in literature
ISBN 9781555978327

LC 2018958158

White Flights is a meditation on whiteness in American fiction and culture from the end of the civil rights movement to the present. At the heart of the book, Jess Row ties "white flight"--the movement of white Americans into segregated communities, whether in suburbs or newly gentrified downtowns?to white writers setting their stories in isolated or emotionally insulated landscapes, from the mountains of Idaho in Marilynne Robinson's Housekeeping to the claustrophobic households in Jonathan Franzen's The Corrections. Row uses brilliant close readings of work from well-known writers to examine the ways these and other writers have sought imaginative space for themselves at the expense of engaging with race.

Schultz, Jeffrey D.

Critical companion to John Steinbeck : a literary reference to his life and work / Jeffrey Schultz, Luchen Li. Facts On File, c2005. ix, 406 p. : **813**

1. Steinbeck, John, 1902-1968 Handbooks, manuals, etc 2. Novelists, American -- 20th century -- Handbooks, manuals, etc
ISBN 9780816043002

LC 2004026100

Presents a guide to the life and literary accomplishments of the American author, including analyses of the contents and characters of each of his works and discussions on places and events in his life which influenced his writing.

Silko, Leslie Marmon, 1948-

Storyteller / Leslie Marmon Silko. Seaver Books, 1981. 278 p. **813**

1. Indians of North America 2. Native American storytelling. 3. Laguna Pueblo Reservation, New Mexico 4. United States -- Social life and customs -- 20th century 5. Short stories 6. Literary fiction
ISBN 0394515897

LC 80020251

Collects short stories and poems.

A collection of stories focuses on contemporary Native American concerns--white injustice, the fragmenting of the Indian community, and the loss of tribal identity--and recalls Indian legends and tribal stories. --From publisher description.

Vap, Sarah

Viability / Sarah Vap. Penguin Books, 2016. 161 p. ; **813**

1. American poetry -- 21st century. 2. Women's poetry -- 21st century.
ISBN 9780143128281

LC 2015011853

"In her sixth collection ... Vap ... innovatively mediates language of the body--membranes, tonsils, embryos, and blood--through prose poems in an imaginative structure based on the rhizome." Publishers Weekly.

Vonnegut, Kurt

Kurt Vonnegut : letters / edited and with an introduction by Dan Wakefield. Delacorte, 2012. 464 p. **813**

1. Vonnegut, Kurt Correspondence 2. Authors, American -- 20th century 3. Authors, American -- 20th century -- Correspondence 4. United States -- Social life and customs -- 20th century 5. United States -- Social life and customs -- 21st century 6. Letters
ISBN 9780385343756

LC 2012001544

A compilation of personal correspondence written over a sixty-year period offers insight into the iconic American author's literary personality, his experiences as a German POW, his struggles with fame, and the inspirations for his famous books.

Wallace, David Foster

The **David** Foster Wallace reader. / David Foster Wallace. Little, Brown and Company, 2014. x, 963 p. ; **813**

1. LITERARY COLLECTIONS / American / General
ISBN 9780316182393

LC 2014032157

"Where do you begin with a writer as original and brilliant as David Foster Wallace? Here--with a carefully considered selection of his extraordinary body of work, chosen by a range of great writers, critics, and those who worked with him most closely. This volume presents his most dazzling, funniest, and most heartbreaking work--essays like his famous cruise-ship piece, "A Supposedly Fun Thing I'll Never Do Again," excerpts from his novels The Broom of the System, Infinite Jest, and The Pale King, and legendary stories like "The Depressed Person." Wallace's explorations of morality, self-consciousness, addiction, sports, love, and the many other subjects that occupied him are represented here in both fiction and nonfiction. Collected for the first time are Wallace's first published story, "The View from Planet Trillaphon as Seen In Relation to the Bad Thing" and a selection of his work as a writing instructor, including reading lists, grammar guides, and general guidelines for his students. A dozen writers and critics, including Hari Kunzru, Anne Fadiman, and Nam Le, add afterwords to favorite pieces, expanding our appreciation of the unique pleasures of Wallace's writing. The result is an astonishing volume that shows the breadth and range of "one of America's most daring and talented writers" (Los Angeles Times Book Review) whose work was full of humor, insight, and beauty".-- Provided by publisher.

Walton, Jo

What makes this book so great : re-reading the classics of Fantasy and SF / Jo Walton. Tor, 2014. 464 p. **813**

1. Science fiction -- History and criticism 2. Fantasy fiction -- History and criticism. 3. Books and reading -- United States. 4. Essays
ISBN 9780765331939

LC 2013028170

"A Tom Doherty Associates Book"

Locus Award for Best Nonfiction/Related/Reference Book, 2015.

A collection of more than 125 essays about past and present-day fantasy and science fiction.

"Walton shares not only her deep love for sf and fantasy in general and these novels in particular but the insights of a truly thoughtful reader." Library Journal.

Welty, Eudora, 1909-2001

What there is to say we have said : the correspondence of Eudora Welty and William Maxwell / edited by Suzanne Marrs. Houghton Mifflin Harcourt, 2011. 499 p. : **813**

1. Welty, Eudora, 1909-2001 Correspondence. 2. Maxwell, William, 1908-2000 Correspondence. 3. Authors, American -- 20th century -- Correspondence. 4. Letters
ISBN 9780547376493

LC 2010042105

Traces the celebrated literary friendship through their personal letters to each other, a correspondence that reflected their private struggles, literary opinions and major events while offering insight into their editorial relationships with their contemporaries.

"Letters between writers often have a lot of shop talk of interest to other writers and literary cultists, but this collection yields broader pleasures, too. In addition to being stellar writers, Welty and Maxwell were also accomplished critics, and one of the joys of the book is eavesdropping on their assessments of authors ... The title of the collection comes from Maxwell's conclusion, as he and Welty faced their mortality, that what there is to say we have said, in one way or the other. You know how much we love you. That love, a source of sustenance and strength between two great writers, is also a bright tonic for the readers of this volume." Christian Science Monitor.

813.009 American fiction -- History and criticism

Nafisi, Azar

★The **republic** of imagination : a portrait of America in three books / Azar Nafisi. Viking, 2014. 368 p. **813.009**

1. Twain, Mark, 1835-1910. Adventures of Huckleberry Finn. 2. Lewis, Sinclair, 1885-1951. Babbit. 3. McCullers, Carson, 1917-1967. Heart is a lonely hunter. 4. Literature and society -- United States. 5. Books and reading -- United States. 6. National characteristics, American. 7. Fiction and culture. 8. United States -- Social life and customs. 9. Autobiographies and memoirs.
ISBN 9780670026067

LC 2014022287

The best-selling author presents an impassioned tribute to the importance of fiction to democracy that blends memoir with close readings of The Adventures of Huckleberry Finn, Babbitt and The Heart Is a Lonely Hunter.

"The author's literary exegesis lightly moves through her own experiences as a student,teacher, friend and new citizen. Touching on myriad literary examples, from L.Frank Baum to James Baldwin, her work is both poignant and informative." Kirkus.

Town, Caren J., 1957-

LGBTQ young adult fiction : a critical survey, 1970s-2010s / Caren J. Town. McFarland & Company, 2017. vii, 197 p. ; **813.009**

1. Adolescence in literature. 2. Gays' writings, American -- History and criticism. 3. Gender identity in literature. 4. Homosexuality and literature -- United States.

ISBN 0786496940

LC 2017023518

"The author explores a selection of recent novels--many of which may be new to readers--and places them in the wider contexts of LGBTQ literature and history. Chapters discuss a range of topics, including the relationship of Queer Theory to literature, LGBTQ families, and recent trends in utopian and dystopian science fiction".-- Provided by publisher.

814 American essays in English

Angelou, Maya

Letter to my daughter / Maya Angelou. Random House, 2008. 176 p. **814**

1. Angelou, Maya. 2. Growing up. 3. Quality of life. 4. Essays.

ISBN 9781400066124

LC bl2008017958

A collection of short essays includes personal reminiscences, hard-won wisdom, and inspirational ideas.

"A slim volume packed with nourishing nuggets of wisdom." Kirkus.

Angelou, Maya

Wouldn't take nothing for my journey now / Maya Angelou. Random House, c1993. xiii, 141 p. ; **814**

1. Understanding (Personal quality) 2. Meditations. 3. Reminiscing in old age. 4. Essays.

ISBN 0679427430

LC 93005904

"A portion of this work was originally published in the December 1992 issue of Essence magazine"--T.p. verso.

A collection of wise and inspirational messages from the author distills her thoughtful insights into such topics as Friendship, Grace, Spirit, Family, and Healing.

"Angelou's prose is brisk, fluid, and entrancing. This work will provide a taste of wisdom to all who read it." Library Journal.

Arndt, Rachel Z.

Beyond measure : essays / Rachel Z. Arndt. Sarabande Books, 2018. 190 p. **814**

1. Sexism 2. Measurement 3. Women's role 4. Sleep disorders 5. Essays

ISBN 9781946448132

LC 2017032569

A fascinating inquiry into the metrics, rituals, routines, and expectations through which we attempt to quantify and comprehend our lives.

Baker, Nicholson, 1957-

The way the world works : essays / Nicholson Baker. Simon & Schuster, c2012. 304 p. **814**

1. Social criticism. 2. Popular culture 3. Political corruption 4. Essays

ISBN 9781416572473

LC 2011052741

A second collection of essays by the National Book Critics Circle Award-winning author explores what ails humanity, what eases pain and what brings joy in an anthology that considers subjects ranging from political controversies and the human fascination with video games to the forgotten heroes of pacifism and the intimacy of the author's own life.

Baldwin, James, 1924-1987

★Collected essays / James Baldwin. Library of America, 1998. 869 p. ; **814**

1. Racism. 2. Race relations 3. Civil rights 4. Civil Rights Movement. 5. United States -- Race relations. 6. United States -- History -- 1961-1969. 7. Essays.

ISBN 1883011523

LC 97023496

A comprehensive compilation of Baldwin's previously published, nonfiction writings encompasses essays on America's racial divide, the social and political turbulence of his time, and his insights into the poetry of Langston Hughes and the music of Earl Hines.

"Novelist Morrison's editing of this omnibus, which includes a chronology and notes, should help rekindle interest in Baldwin, whose recurrent themes--the African American search for identity, the hypocrisy of white America, the urgent necessity for love--make his work timely and challenging." Publishers Weekly

Berry, Wendell, 1934-

Imagination in place : essays / Wendell Berry. Counterpoint : c2010. viii, 196 p. ; **814**

1. Literature -- History and criticism 2. Essays

ISBN 9781582435626

LC 2009038104

"For those who've already come to admire Berry's moral clarity and closely argued critiques of contemporary society, Imagination in Place is a welcome chance to continue the conversation." Christian Science Monitor.

Capote, Truman, 1924-1984

★Portraits and observations : the essays of Truman Capote / Truman Capote. Random House, 2007. x, 518 p. ; **814**

1. Capote, Truman, 1924-1984 2. Authors, American -- 20th century 3. United States -- Social life and customs -- 20th century 4. Essays.

ISBN 1400066611

LC 2007036624

Includes index.

A definitive anthology containing all of the author's essays encompasses his early travel sketches of Brooklyn, New Orleans, and Hollywood; portraits of Isak Dinesen, Mae West, Humphrey Bogart, and Marilyn Monroe; accounts of the filming of "In Cold Blood;" autobiographical musings; and the recently discovered "Remembering Willa Cather."

"The featured works cover the artist's interests in travel, celebrities, the arts--both visual and literary, of passion, and himself. This collection offers the highest quality of writing from a genuine American stylist." Library Journal.

Cusk, Rachel, 1967-

Coventry : essays / Rachel Cusk. Farrar, Straus and Giroux, 2019. 288 p. **814**

1. Cusk, Rachel, 1967- 2. Women authors, English 3. Family

relationships 4. Writing 5. Creation (Literary, artistic, etc.) 6. Essays
ISBN 9780374126773

LC 2019020202

A collection of essays by the author of A Life's Work explores themes ranging from family and gender to politics and art, discussing her fictional stories while exploring the work of such writers as D. H. Lawrence and Elena Ferrante.

"An eloquent and engrossing selection of nonfiction writing that will enhance Cusk's stature in contemporary literature." Kirkus.

Daum, Meghan, 1970-

The **unspeakable** : and other subjects of discussion / Meghan Daum. Farrar, Straus and Giroux, 2014. 256 p. **814**

1. Culture 2. National characteristics, American 3. Popular culture 4. United States 5. Essays
ISBN 9780374280444

LC 2014014643

"Essays on American sentimentality and its impact on the way we think about death, children, patriotism, and other matters".-- Provided by publisher.

"This book will appeal to memoir enthusiasts seeking an insightful reading experience that will entertain as well as challenge." Library Journal.

Didion, Joan

We tell ourselves stories in order to live : collected nonfiction / Joan Didion ; with an introduction by John Leonard. Alfred A. Knopf, c2006. xxxvii, 1122 p. ; **814**

1. Didion, Joan 2. Popular culture. 3. Essays.
ISBN 0307264874

LC 2006041043

A compilation of essays and nonfiction writings spanning more than forty years includes the author's reflections on politics, lifestyle, place, and cultural figures, including such topics as Haight-Ashbury, the Manson family, the Black Panthers, California earthquakes, and Bill Clinton.

Dillard, Annie

The **abundance** : narrative essays old and new / Annie Dillard. Ecco Press, 2016 224 p. **814**

1. Nature. 2. Women and nature. 3. Life. 4. Spirituality 5. Essays
ISBN 9780062432971

LC bl2016003136

A landmark collection of author-curated pieces celebrates the master essayist's celebrated career and offers insight into her establishment of the "novelized nonfiction" form.

"This collection is an excellent entry point into Dillard's writing and would especially appeal to new readers, although Dillard devotees will also enjoy this kaleidoscopic retrospective, this new way of 'seeing' her prose." Library Journal.

Ehrenreich, Barbara

★**Had** I known : collected essays / Barbara Ehrenreich. Twelve, 2020. 352 p **814**

1. Social justice 2. United States 3. Essays
ISBN 9781455543670

LC bl2020004777

A selection of the best-selling writer and political activist's most provocative signature writings includes her groundbreaking undercover investigations, op-ed pieces, essays and reviews, including the award-winning "Welcome to Cancerland."

"A rewarding, illuminating tour de force." Booklist

Ellis, Bret Easton

White / Bret Easton Ellis. Alfred A. Knopf, 2019. 272 p. **814**

1. Ellis, Bret Easton 2. Social media 3. Online social networks. 4. Interpersonal relations 5. Censorship 6. Essays.
ISBN 9780525656302

LC 2018050947

Published in the UK by Pan Macmillan, 2019.

The author of Less Than Zero and American Psycho combines personal reflection and social observation in a first work of nonfiction that explores such subjects as self-inflicted censorship and the cult of likeability that has overshadowed the social-media age.

"Regardless of their opinions about social media, readers will be captivated by these provocative essays and then move on to rereading Less Than Zero and American Psycho." Library Journal.

Ellison, Ralph

The **collected** essays of Ralph Ellison / edited, with an introduction by John F. Callahan ; preface by Saul Bellow. Modern Library, 2003, c1995. xxix, 860 p. ; **814**

1. Ellison, Ralph Authorship. 2. African Americans in literature. 3. African Americans -- Literary collections 4. Essays.
ISBN 9780812968262

LC bl2008033155

A complete collection of essays, reviews, interviews, and criticism by the acclaimed author includes the collections Shadow and Act and Going to the Territory, along with newly discovered and previously uncollected works, covering such topics as literature, folklore, jazz, black culture, and the African-American experience.

Ephron, Nora

I feel bad about my neck : and other thoughts on being a woman / Nora Ephron. Knopf, 2006. viii, 137 p. **814**

1. Ephron, Nora. 2. Sexagenarians. 3. Aging. 4. Women -- Identity. 5. Middle-aged women -- Attitudes 6. Essays.
ISBN 0307264556

LC 2005057780

"While very little in the book is meant to be taken seriously, it is clever enough to qualify as more than just an assemblage of one-liners. Whether you agree with her observations or not, Ephron's perspective as an admittedly high-maintenance, New York-dwelling, successful screenwriter will keep you entertained." Christian Science Monitor.

Franzen, Jonathan

★The **end** of the end of the earth : essays / Jonathan Franzen. Farrar, Straus and Giroux, 2018. 288 p. **814**

1. Climate change 2. Interpersonal relations 3. Family relationships 4. Observation (Psychology) 5. Essays
ISBN 9780374147938

LC 2018017731

A provocative new essay collection by the award-winning author of Freedom and The Corrections includes an exploration of his complex relationship with his uncle, an assessment of the global seabird crisis and his young adulthood in New York.

"Whether observing the eerie beauty of Antarctica ('far from having melted,' he reports) or dispensing 'Ten Rules for the Novelist,' Franzen makes for an entertaining, sometimes prickly, but always quotable companion." Publishers Weekly.

Franzen, Jonathan

★**Farther** away : essays / Jonathan Franzen. Farrar, Straus and Giroux, 2012. 272 p. **814**

1. Self. 2. Literature. 3. Essays. 4. Speeches, addresses, etc.
ISBN 9780374153571

LC 2011046067

A collection of speeches and essays on a wide variety of topics.

Frazier, Ian

★**Hogs** wild : selected reporting pieces / Ian Frazier. Farrar, Straus and Giroux, 2016. 368 p. **814**

1. Essays
ISBN 9780374298524

LC 2015036372

A generous selection of Frazier's most sophisticated and uproarious feature stories.

"His celebrated humor glows rather than erupts in these more expository pieces. Pieces that show Frazier's ranging curiosity, lucent style, and capacious heart." Kirkus.

Gluck, Louise, 1943-

American originality : [essays] / Louise Gluck. Farrar, Straus and Giroux, 2017. 208 p. **814**

1. Creation (Literary, artistic, etc.) 2. American poetry -- History and criticism 3. Poets 4. Intellectual life 5. Essays.
ISBN 9780374299552

LC 2016026993

"A love of poetry--of the poet's life--infuses these essays and brings a glow to the theoretical and a bright flame to the personal." Kirkus.

Hamid, Mohsin, 1971-

Discontent and its civilizations : dispatches from Lahore, New York, and London / Mohsin Hamid. Riverhead Hardcover, 2015. 240 p. **814**

1. Essays.
ISBN 9781594633652

LC 2014027668

The author offers essays that discuss the similarities and differences in everyday living between the three countries he was able to call home at different periods of his life: America, Pakistan and England. By the author of The Reluctant Fundamentalist.

"Hamid is an intelligent and impassioned writer whose work deserves a wide readership. Those interested in memoirs, world politics, and cultural and religious differences will enjoy these essays." Library Journal.

Harrington, Walt, 1950-

The **beholder's** eye : a collection of America's finest personal journalism / edited and with an introduction by Walt Harrington. Grove Press, 2005. xxii, 256 p. ; **814**

1. Literary journalism. 2. Journalism -- United States. 3. Introspection. 4. Essays.
ISBN 0802142249

LC 2005046242

A collection of America's best contemporary first-person journalism selected by Walt Harrington, the award-winning former Washington Post reporter and author of two highly acclaimed works of personal nonfiction. Many great journalists have, at one time or another, been characters in their own stories--people with personalities that shaped what they saw and reported, who were touched and changed by the experiences about which they wrote, and who borrowed the storytelling techniques of fiction.

"These stories are amusing, insightful, and touching in a way that only something personal can be." Booklist.

Hitchens, Christopher, 1949-2011

Arguably : essays / Christopher Hitchens. Twelve, 2011. 384 p. **814**

1. Political science 2. Essays.
ISBN 9781455502776

LC 2011930917

Also published: Toronto : McClelland & Stewart, 2011.
ALA Notable Book, 2012.

Spanning four remarkable decades, a collection includes the author's early writings on civil rights, Vietnam and international incidents, as well as his inflammatory -- and now infamous -- columns on the Clintons, the Catholic Church, Mother Theresa, radical Islam and an array of meditations on contemporary politics and political figures.

"Goading, brilliant, funny, and caring, Hitchens is a voice of enlightenment in a wilderness of cant." Booklist.

Holt, Jim, 1954-

★**When** Einstein walked with Godel : excursions to the edge of thought / Jim Holt. Farrar Straus & Giroux, 2018 368 p. **814**

1. Quantum theory. 2. Mathematics. 3. Logic. 4. Essays
ISBN 9780374146702
Includes index.

An accessible guide introduces readers to some of science's least understood ideas, including the mysteries of quantum mechanics, the foundations of mathematics and the nature of logic and truth.

"A collection of incisive essays that make learning about science fun." Kirkus.

Houston, Pam

Deep Creek : finding hope in the high country / Pam Houston. W.W. Norton & Company, [2019] 288 p. **814**

1. Ranches 2. Women authors 3. Nature 4. Land stewardship 5. Colorado 6. Rocky mountains 7. Essays
ISBN 9780393241020

LC 2018037969

The author of Contents May Have Shifted draws on her travels and homestead life in the Colorado Rockies in an essay collection on her ties to nature that explores the symbiotic relationship between humans and the earth.

Hustvedt, Siri

Living, thinking, looking : essays / Siri Hustvedt. Picador, 2012. 384 p. **814**

1. Humans. 2. Thought and thinking. 3. Identity (Psychology) 4. Essays.
ISBN 9781250009524

LC 2011035714

"A Frances Coady book."

Essays that explore what it means to be a human being draw upon the author's personal experiences; thoughts on memory, emotion, and the imagination; and the visual arts.

A **woman** looking at men looking at women : essays on art, sex, and the mind / Siri Hustvedt. Simon & Schuster, 2016. 512 p. **814**

1. Sexism 2. Feminism 3. Neuroscience 4. Sexism in art 5. Essays
ISBN 9781501141096

LC 2016022677

A radical collection of essays on art, feminism, neuroscience, psychology and philosophy by the prize-winning author of The Blazing World reflects her explorations into the workings of human perception and how they are reflected by gender bias, the mind-body challenge and neurological disorders.

"A wide-ranging, irreverent, and absorbing meditation on thinking, knowing, and being." Kirkus.

Jamison, Leslie, 1983-

★**Make** it scream, make it burn : essays / Leslie Jamison. Little, Brown & Company, 2019. 272 p. **814**

1. Jamison, Leslie, 1983- 2. Identity (Psychology) 3. Loneliness 4. Belonging 5. Women authors 6. Essays

ISBN 9780316259637

LC 2019931414

With the virtuosic synthesis of memoir, criticism, and journalism for which she has become known, Leslie Jamison offers us fourteen new essays that are by turns ecstatic, searching, staggering, and wise. In its kaleidoscopic sweep, Make It Scream, Make It Burn creates a profound exploration of the oceanic depths of longing and the reverberations of obsession.

"Jamison's observational skills, genuine empathy, and lack of sentimentality create an intelligent blending of journalism, scholarship (she directs the graduate nonfiction program at Columbia Univ.), and memoir." Library Journal.

Kinsley, Michael E.

Old age : a beginner's guide / Michael Kinsley. Tim Duggan Books, 2016. 208 p. **814**

1. Kinsley, Michael E. 2. Aging -- United States. 3. Life change events -- Psychological aspects. 4. Baby boom generation 5. Life. 6. Essays

ISBN 9781101903766

LC 2015038958

"A collection of essays on aging, Parkinson's disease, fame, and the legacy of the Baby Boomer generation".-- Provided by publisher.

"Kinsley's superb prose and well-judged tone--both frustrated and hopeful for the future--make this a valuable book for anyone interested in exploring ideas around life, death, and legacy." Publishers Weekly.

Knapp, Cheston

Up up, down down : essays / Cheston Knapp. Scribner, 2018 320 p. **814**

1. Identity (Psychology) 2. Growing up 3. Self-acceptance 4. Eccentrics and eccentricities 5. Essays

ISBN 9781501161025

LC 2018285672

An anthology of seven linked essays by the managing editor of Tin House explores the nature of identity as it can be understood through eclectic venues, from a pro-wrestling ad that illuminates a complicated father-son relationship, to a UFO enthusiast group that reflects the nature and limits of religious faith.

"Knapp is a master of collage, both in subject and in tone...The essays are hyperarticulate, literary, and occasionally self-conscious, but Knapp uses these tendencies to masterful effect." Booklist.

Krakauer, Jon

Classic Krakauer : essays on wilderness and risk / Jon Krakauer. Anchor Books, 2019. 160 p. **814**

1. Mountaineering. 2. Extreme sports. 3. Mountaineers. 4. Eccentrics and eccentricities 5. Essays.

ISBN 9781984897695

LC 2019018697

"The gripping articles collected in Classic Krakauer--originally published in magazines such as The New Yorker, Outside, and Smithsonian--show why he is considered a standard-bearer of modern journalism. Spanning an extraordinary range of subjects and locations, these pieces take us from a horrifying avalanche on Mount Everest to a volcano poised to obliterate a big chunk of Seattle; from a wilderness teen-therapy program run by apparent sadists to an otherworldly cave in New Mexico, studied by NASA to better understand Mars; from the notebook of one Fred Beckey, who catalogued the greatest unclimbed mountaineering routes on the planet, to the last days of legendary surfer Mark Foo. Rigorously researched and vividly written, marked by an unerring instinct for storytelling and scoop, these pieces are unified by the author's ambivalent love affair with unruly landscapes and his relentless search for truth".-- Provided by publisher.

Krauthammer, Charles, 1950-2018

The **point** of it all : a lifetime of great loves and endeavors / Charles Krauthammer, edited by Daniel Krauthammer. Random House Inc., 2018. 368 p. **814**

1. Journalism 2. Columnists 3. Political culture -- United States 4. Democracy 5. United States -- Politics and government 6. Essays

ISBN 9781984825483

LC 2018050329

Compiled by Charles Krauthammer before his passing, an intimate collection of his most notable works and writings includes never-before-published speeches on his political philosophy and personal history and a major, new essay about the state of global democracy.

Le Guin, Ursula K., 1929-2018,

★**No** time to spare : thinking about what matters / Ursula K. Le Guin ; introduction by Karen Joy Fowler. Houghton Mifflin Harcourt, 2017. 192 p. **814**

1. Aging 2. Literature 3. Belief and doubt 4. Cats 5. United States -- Civilization 6. Essays

ISBN 9781328661593

LC 2017019808

Hugo Award for Best Related Non-Fiction Book, 2018.

Drawing on her blog, the author shares a collection of thoughts on aging, belief, the state of literature, and the state of the nation.

"Spirited, wry reflections on aging, literature, and America's moral life." Kirkus.

Leopold, Aldo, 1886-1948

A **Sand** County almanac & other writings on ecology and conservation : A Sand County Almanac & Other Writings on Conservation and Ecology / Aldo Leopold ; Curt Meine, editor. The Library of America, c2013. xv, 931 p. : **814**

1. Ecology -- United States. 2. Nature conservation -- United States. 3. Essays

ISBN 1598532065

LC bl2013009940

A volume of essential writings by the environmental pioneer includes previously unpublished and hard-to-find pieces and provides a relevant blueprint to environmental ethics, in a collection complemented by more than 100 letters and original images.

"The volume also includes a chronology of Leopold's life; extensive notes; an index to plants/animals, with a mixture of common and scientific nomenclature; and a general index." Choice.

Lethem, Jonathan

The **ecstasy** of influence : nonfictions, etc. / Jonathan Lethem. Doubleday, c2011. 592 p. **814**

1. Popular culture 2. Fiction writing 3. Essays 4. Anthologies

ISBN 9780385534956

LC 2011016248

A career-spanning anthology of fiction, memoir and commentary incorporates several new essays and includes numerous celebrity portraits as well as the author's musings on topics ranging from sex in cinema and drugs to cyberculture and graffiti.

More alive and less lonely : on books and writers / Jonathan Lethem ; edited and with an introduction by Christopher Boucher. Melville House, 2017 288 p. **814**

1. Literature -- History and criticism -- Theory, etc. 2. Authors and readers. 3. Books and reading. 4. Writing 5. Essays 6. Anthologies
ISBN 9781612196039

LC 2016036950

"Picking up where The Ecstasy of Influence left off, an NBCC prize-winning author collects more than a decade of his finest writing on writing, with new, previously unpublished material that inspires readers to dive back into their favorite books and then points them towards what to read next.

"One of America's most accomplished writers looks back between the pages of other writers' books." Kirkus.

Lorde, Audre, 1934-1992

★The **selected** works of Audre Lorde / edited and with an introduction by Roxane Gay. W. W. Norton & Company, 2020 382 p. **814**

1. Femininity 2. Queer theory 3. African American women 4. Intersectionality 5. Essays
ISBN 9781324004615

LC 2020020850

Includes index.

A definitive selection of prose and poetry from the self-described "black, lesbian, mother, warrior, poet," for a new generation of readers. Audre Lorde is an unforgettable voice in twentieth-century literature, one of the first to center the experiences of black, queer women. Her incisive essays and passionate poetry--alive with sensuality, vulnerability, and rage--remain indelible contributions to intersectional feminism, queer theory, and critical race studies.

"Readers new to Lorde's work couldn't ask for a better introduction, and those already familiar will find this an ideal collection of her greatest hits." Publishers Weekly

Lorde, Audre, 1934-1992

Sister outsider : essays and speeches / Audre Lorde ; [new foreword by Cheryl Clarke]. Crossing Press, 2007, c1984. 190 p. ; **814**

1. Feminism. 2. Lesbianism. 3. Social justice 4. Sexism 5. Essays
ISBN 9781580911863

LC 2008540402

Originally published in 1984.

The leader of contemporary feminist theory discusses such issues as racism, self-acceptance, and mother- and woman-hood.

"With her poet's command of language, she addresses sexism, racism, black women, black lesbians, eroticism, and more. Still powerful." Library Journal

Lurie, Alison

Words and worlds : from autobiography to zippers / Alison Lurie. Delphinium Books, 2019. 225 p. **814**

1. Lurie, Alison 2. Writing 3. Friendship 4. Feminism 5. Men/women relations 6. Essays
ISBN 9781883285784

LC bl2019014784

This engaging new collection of essays from the New York Times-bestselling novelist gathers together her reflections on the writing life; fond recollections of inspiring friends; and perceptive, playful commentary on preoccupations ranging from children's literature to fashion and feminism.

Malcolm, Janet

Nobody's looking at you : essays / Janet Malcolm. Farrar, Straus and Giroux, 2019. 256 p. **814**

1. Television personalities 2. Fashion designers 3. Russian literature -- History and criticism 4. Essays
ISBN 9780374279493

LC 2018031206

An eclectic collection of essays from the award-winning author of Forty-One False Starts: Essays on Artists and Writers features profiles of fashion designer, Eileen Fisher, TV personality Rachel Maddow, pianist Yuju Wang and discussions of Russian literature.

Martin, Steve, 1945-

Pure drivel / Steve Martin. Hyperion, c1998. 104 p. ; **814**

1. Comedians. 2. Essays.
ISBN 0786864672

LC 98028739

A collection of Martin's comic writings, some of which first appeared in the New Yorker.

"The short essays, conversations, and proclamations collected here are relayed in a slyly deadpan Valley voice that belies the coiled craziness of their content. Martin also brings his gift for comedic timing to these creations, setting a quirky beat that perfectly sets off their ironic wiles." Booklist.

Momaday, N. Scott, 1934-

Earth keeper : reflections on the American land / N. Scott Momaday. HarperCollins Publishers, 2020. 96 p. **814**

1. Kiowa Indians 2. Indians of North America 3. Humans -- Effect of environment on 4. Nature 5. North America
ISBN 9780063009332

LC 2020025782

A Pulitzer Prize-winning novelist and poet celebrates the oral tradition of his Native American culture as he recalls the stories of his childhood, passed down for generations, and their profound and sacred connection to the natural world.

"Widely acclaimed for his poetry, fiction, and folklore, Native American writer Momaday (The Death of Sitting Bear, 2020) delivers a profound reflection on humanity's relationship with its terrestrial home, the planet Earth. . . . Even readers unfamiliar with Momaday will appreciate the timeliness of this important call to care and revel in its poetry." Booklist

Morrison, Toni, 1931-2019

★The **source** of self-regard : selected essays, speeches, and meditations / Toni Morrison. Alfred A. Knopf, 2019. 336 p. **814**

1. Race (Social sciences) 2. Power (Social sciences) 3. Literature and society. 4. Identity (Psychology) 5. Speeches, addresses, etc.
ISBN 9780525521037

LC 2018023690

One of the most celebrated and revered writers of our time now gives us a new nonfiction collection--a rich gathering of her essays, speeches, and meditations on society, culture, and art, spanning four decades.

"Morrison is a master of the luminous thought, of the sense of outrage or compassion that makes readers feel as if they are in the presence of an author who deeply cares about literature and the themes that engage her. Topics include the author developing the openings of her novels and deciding what tone or turn of phrase was the perfect vehicle to convey her insights about humanity." Library Journal.

Notaro, Laurie

Housebroken : admissions of an untidy life / Laurie Notaro. Ballantine Books, 2016 270 p. **814**

1. Notaro, Laurie 2. Home (Social sciences) 3. Homemaking. 4. Essays

ISBN 9781101886083

A new collection of essays from the New York Times best-selling author describes her personal attempts at mastering the domestic arts, including manners, power outages and entertaining guests.

"Notaro, a humorist and novelist (It Looked Different on the Model) recounts her forays into the domestic realm with this latest collection of essays." Library Journal.

Oates, Joyce Carol, 1938-

★The **best** American essays of the century / Joyce Carol Oates, editor ; Robert Atwan, series editor. Houghton Mifflin, 2000. 596 p. Best American essays **814**

1. United States -- Social life and customs -- 20th century. 2. Essays

ISBN 0618043705

"Oates has assembled a provocative collection of masterpieces reflecting both the fragmentation and surprising cohesiveness of various American identities." Publishers Weekly.

Oates, Joyce Carol, 1938-

Soul at the white heat : inspiration, obsession, and the writing life / Joyce Carol Oates. Ecco, 2016. 320 p. **814**

1. Literature -- History and criticism 2. Books and reading 3. Writing 4. Authors 5. Essays

ISBN 9780062564504

LC bl2016040333

A new collection of critical and personal essays on writing, obsession, and inspiration from National Book Award-winning and New York Times bestselling author Joyce Carol Oates.

Oliver, Mary, 1935-2019

Upstream : selected essays / Mary Oliver. Penguin Press, 2016. 256 p. **814**

1. Oliver, Mary, 1935-2019 2. Poets. 3. Nature. 4. Women and nature. 5. Creativity. 6. Essays.

ISBN 9781594206702

LC 2016043612

A collection of essays with a new piece on Provincetown, follows the author as she contemplates the pleasure of artistic labor; her boundless curiosity for the flora and fauna that surround her; and the responsibility she has inherited from the great thinkers and writers of the past, to live thoughtfully, intelligently and to observe with passion.

"A lyrical, tender essay collection." Kirkus.

Park, Ed, 1970-,

Read harder / edited by Ed Park and Heidi Julavits. Believer Books/McSweeney's, 2014 294 p. : **814**

1. Readers 2. Books and reading. 3. Reading interests. 4. Essays

ISBN 9781940450186

LC 2015431367

"These pieces appeared between 2009 and 2013 in the 'Believer' magazine"--Title page verso.

As the Believer enters its second decade, Read Harder serves as both an essential primer for one of the finest, strangest magazines in the country, and an indispensable stand-alone volume. --From publisher description.

"Nineteen essays, often funny and sometimes poignant, from the journalists, essayists and novelists long admired by the editors at McSweeney's Believer magazine." Kirkus.

Passarello, Elena

Animals strike curious poses : essays / Elena Passarello. Sarabande Books, 2017 264 p. **814**

1. Famous animals 2. Human/animal relationships 3. Animal welfare 4. Animals 5. Essays

ISBN 9781941411391

LC 2016039498

With exuberant wit, Elena Passarello casts her gaze on famous historical animals, crafting an essay collection organized as medieval bestiary.

"The entire collection satisfies through a feast of surprising juxtapositions and gorgeous prose." Publishers Weekly.

Rankine, Claudia, 1963-

★**Citizen** : an American lyric / Claudia Rankine. Graywolf Press, [2014] 169 p. : **814**

1. Racism 2. Justice 3. African Americans 4. Violence 5. United States -- Race relations. 6. Essays

ISBN 9781555976903

LC 2014935702

Collects essays, poetry, and images that expose the racial tensions in twenty-first century life, highlighting the slights, slips of the tongue, and intentional offensives that pervade the home, school, and popular media.

"Accounts of racially charged interactions, insidious and flagrant, transpiring in private and in the public eye, distill the immediate emotional intensity of individual experience with tremendous precision while allowing ambiguity, ambivalence, contradiction, and exhaustion to remain in all their fraught complexity...Once again Rankine inspires sympathy and outrage, but most of all a will to take a deep look at ourselves and our society." Publishers Weekly

Reece, Erik

Practice resurrection : and other essays / Erik Reece. Counterpoint, 2017. 220 p. **814**

1. Faith (Christianity) 2. Men and nature 3. Environmentalism 4. Belief and doubt 5. Essays

ISBN 9781619026087

LC 2017004033

In a book written over 10 years--and revealing the author's continued obsession with religion, family and the natural world--one of our foremost religious and environmental thinkers presents a collection of essays that use ideas as the main characters.

Rich, Adrienne, 1929-2012

Essential essays : culture, politics, and the art of poetry / Adrienne Cecile Rich. W W Norton & Co Inc, 2018. 352 p. **814**

1. Essays

ISBN 9780393652369

LC 2018013156

Presents 25 essays--culled from the works of an award-winning poet, influential essayist, radical feminist and major intellectual voice of her generation--that unite the political, personal and poetical and demonstrate her revolutionary views on social justice.

Robinson, Marilynne

What are we doing here? : essays / Marilynne Robinson. Farrar, Straus and Giroux, 2018 272 p. **814**

1. Political culture 2. Faith 3. Beauty 4. Essays
ISBN 9780374282219

LC 2017038302

A new essay collection assesses today's political climate and the mysteries of faith, from the influence of intellectual minds on society's political consciousness to the way that beauty informs and disciplines daily life.

"Robinson's gorgeous, demanding, and enlightening essays, propelled by her intricate vision of unity, radiantly recharge both mind and soul." Booklist.

When I was a child I read books : essays / Marilynne Robinson. Farrar, Straus and Giroux, 2012. 336 p. **814**

1. Theology. 2. Ideology. 3. United States -- Civilization -- Philosophy. 4. United States -- Civilization -- European influences. 5. Essays.
ISBN 9780374298784

LC 2011041206

In this new collection of incisive essays, Robinson returns to the themes which have preoccupied her work: the role of faith in modern life, the inadequacy of fact, the contradictions inherent in human nature.

Robinson, Phoebe

Everything's trash, but it's okay / Phoebe Robinson ; foreword by Ilana Glazer. Plume, 2018. 320 p. **814**

1. African American women 2. Dating (Social customs) -- Humor 3. Work -- Humor 4. Social norms 5. Essays
ISBN 9780525534143

LC 2018025958

The star of 2 Dope Queens and best-selling author of You Can't Touch My Hair presents an uproarious essay collection that explores subjects ranging from intersectional feminism and today's destructive dating scene to our culture's obsession with work and beauty.

Ross, Lillian, 1918-2017

The **fun** of it : stories from The talk of the town, The New Yorker / edited by Lillian Ross ; introduction by David Remnick. Modern Library, 2001. xxi, 478 p. ; **814**

1. Essays
ISBN 9780375756498

LC 00068237

A selection of essays and articles from The New Yorker's "Talk of the Town" section features an entertaining selection of writings by E. B. White, John Updike, A. J. Liebling, Lillian Hellman, James Thurber, Harold Ross, Janet Flanner, Susan Orlean, and many other notable authors.

Russo, Richard, 1949-

★The **destiny** thief : essays on writing, writers, and life / Richard Russo. Alfred A. Knopf, 2018. 224 p. **814**

1. Authors 2. Books and reading 3. Writing 4. Friendship 5. Essays
ISBN 9781524733513

LC 2017024819

A collection of personal essays from the Pulitzer Prize-winning author of Everybody's Fool describes his broad interests and experiences, from an analysis on the value of Mark Twain, to accompanying a good friend on her pursuit of gender reassignment surgery.

"For aspiring writers, Russo's musings on the art and craft of the novel are a trove of knowledge and guidance. For adoring readers, they are a window into the imagination and inspiration for Russos beloved novels, screenplays, and short stories." Booklist.

Said, Edward W., 1935-2003

Reflections on exile and other essays / Edward W. Said. Harvard University Press, 2000. xxxv, 617 p. **814**

1. Politics and literature. 2. Politics and culture. 3. Criticism -- Political aspects. 4. Modern literature -- 20th century -- History and criticism 5. Essays.
ISBN 0674003020

LC 00044996

Contains 46 essays.

"Written between 1967 and the present by a literary critic and advocate for the Palestinian cause, these pieces often deal with the self-deceiving fictions of the colonizers about the people they oppress; others deplore some fashionable critical theories as unengaged with real life and history." New York Times Book Review.

Sedaris, David

Let's explore diabetes with owls / David Sedaris. Little Brown & Co, 2013 288 p. **814**

1. Voyages and travels. 2. Travel writing 3. Essays.
ISBN 9780316154697

LC 2013930473

Traces the author's offbeat world travel experiences, which involved surreal encounters with everything from French dentistry and Australian kookaburra eating habits to Beijing squat toilets and a wilderness Costco in North Carolina.

Solnit, Rebecca,

The **best** American essays 2019 / edited and with an introduction by Rebecca Solnit ; Robert Atwan, series editor. Mariner Books, 2019 xxvii, 226 p. ; Best American essays **814**

1. United States -- Social life and customs -- 21st century 2. United States -- Politics and government -- 21st century 3. Essays
ISBN 9781328465801

Edited by a Pulitzer Prize-winning and Guggenheim-honored author, this annual showcase presents the best essays from hundreds of magazines, journals and websites.

"The works in this year's collection are a mix of the disconcerting, the probing, and the self-reflective, and well-suited to challenging times." Publisher's Weekly.

The **faraway** nearby / Rebecca Solnit. Viking, 2013. 272 p. **814**

1. Empathy. 2. Storytelling. 3. Books and reading. 4. Death.
ISBN 9780670025961

LC 2013001563

ALA Notable Book, 2014

National Book Critics Circle Award for Autobiography/Memoir finalist

A companion to A Field Guide for Getting Lost explores the ways that people construct lives from stories and connect to each other through empathy, narrative and imagination, sharing illustrative anecdotes about historical figures and members of her own family.

Sontag, Susan, 1933-2004

★**At** the same time : essays and speeches / Susan Sontag ; edited by Paolo Dilonardo and Anne Jump ; foreword by David Rieff. Farrar, Straus, and Giroux, 2007. xvii, 235 p. ; **814**

1. Literature. 2. Political activists. 3. Social justice. 4. Injustice. 5. United States -- Politics and government. 6. Essays. 7. Speeches,

addresses, etc.
ISBN 9780374100728

LC 2006031179

A powerful compilation of sixteen essays, written in the last years of the author's life, offers a series of reflections on her commitment to the power of literature, political activism, the resistance to injustice as an ethical duty, the problems of post-9/11 America, and the work of such diverse writers as Soviet novelist Leonid Tsypkin and Nobel laureate Nadine Gordimer.

Talese, Gay

High notes : selected writings of Gay Talese / Gay Talese. Bloomsbury USA, 2017. 352 p. **814**

1. Talese, Gay 2. Essays
ISBN 9781632867469

LC 2016031081

High Notes draws from six decades of Talese's work, from his long-form pieces for Esquire to his more autobiographical writings of the eighties and nineties to his twenty-first-century reflections on New York, New Yorkers, and the institution of which he is the longtime chronicler, the New York Times.

"A worthy collection that would have benefitted from further effort from the book's editor and publisher." Kirkus.

Trillin, Calvin

Too soon to tell / Calvin Trillin. Farrar, Straus, Giroux, c1995. 292 p. ; **814**

1. United States -- Social life and customs -- 1989- Humor. 2. United States -- Politics and government -- 1993-2001 Humor. 3. Essays 4. Political satire.
ISBN 0374278466

LC 94024629

"In this collection of nearly 100 syndicated columns, Calvin Trillin holds forth on everything from the animal kingdom...to the possibility of being labeled a member of the cultural elite. Too Soon to Tell abounds with Mr. Trillin's self-deprecating humor and slyly acerbic insights, not to mention invaluable homespun wisdom." New York Times Book Review.

Updike, John

Due considerations : essays and criticism / John Updike. Alfred A. Knopf, 2007. xxii, 703 p. : **814**

1. Updike, John Criticism and interpretation 2. Authors, American 3. Book reviews 4. Modern literature -- History and criticism 5. Characters and characteristics. 6. United States -- Social life and customs -- 21st century 7. Essays.
ISBN 0307266400

LC 2007018665

John Updike's sixth collection of essays and literary criticism opens with a skeptical overview of literary biographies, proceeds to five essays on topics ranging from China and small change to faith and late works, and takes up, under the heading "General Considerations," books, poker, cars, and the American libido. The last, informal section of Due Considerations assembles more or less autobiographical pieces--reminiscences, friendly forewords, comments on the author's own recent works, responses to probing questions.--From publisher's description.

"A lush book to be savored over a long period of time." Booklist.

Vidal, Gore, 1925-2012

The **selected** essays of Gore Vidal / Gore Vidal ; edited by Jay Parini. Doubleday, c2008. 480 p. **814**

1. Vidal, Gore, 1925-2012 2. Essayists -- 21st century 3. Political science -- History and criticism 4. International relations -- History and criticism 5. Literature and society -- United States -- History -- 20th century 6. United States -- History 7. United States -- Social life and customs -- 20th century 8. United States -- Social life and customs -- 21st century 9. Essays.
ISBN 9780385524841

LC 2008013517

A definitive compilation of literary essays by a master of the form features twenty-three classic examples of his outstanding work, including political commentary, memoir, criticism, and literary reviews.

"Regardless of what one thinks of Vidal, what Vidal thinks is never in doubt in these 24 essays, divided here into two groups: literary criticism and historical or cultural commentary. His writing is clear, sharp, and disciplined, and his approbation of William Dean Howells and Italo Calvino are as finely tuned as his excoriation of John Updike and Herman Wouk." Library Journal.

Wallace, David Foster

Consider the lobster : and other essays / David Foster Wallace. Little, Brown, 2005. 343 p. : **814**

1. Essays. 2. Trivia and miscellaneous facts
ISBN 9780316156110

LC 2005010886

A collection of essays shares whimsical and biting observations about such topics as the Bush-Kerry presidential race, the pain experienced by lobsters while they are being prepared for the feast, and Franz Kafka's questionable sense of humor.

"Wallace's complex essays are written, and rightfully so, to be read more than once." Booklist.

String theory : David Foster Wallace on tennis / David Foster Wallace ; introduction by John Jeremiah Sullivan. Library of America, 2016 144 p. **814**

1. Tennis 2. Tennis players 3. Professional tennis players. 4. Sports 5. Essays
ISBN 9781598534801

LC 2015951697

Hailed as "the best tennis writer of all time" by The New York Times, an instant classic of American sportswriting contains David Foster Wallace's five famous essays on tennis that are some of the greatest and most innovative magazine writing in recent history.

Weinberger, Eliot

The **ghosts** of birds / Eliot Weinberger. W W Norton & Co Inc 2016 240 p. **814**

1. I ching. 2. Nature 3. Culture 4. Philosophy 5. Culture and globalization 6. Essays.
ISBN 9780811226189

LC 2016021273

"The Ghosts of Birds offers thirty-five essays by Eliot Weinberger: the first section of the book continues his linked serial-essay, An Elemental Thing, which pulls the reader into "a vortex for the entire universe" (Boston Review)."--Provided by the publisher.

"A new book of essays proves to be as erudite, compelling, and delightfully strange as we have come to expect from Weinberger (An Elemental Thing, 2007)." Booklist.

White, E. B. (Elwyn Brooks), 1899-1985

Essays of E.B. White / E.B. White. Perennial Classics, 1999. xi, 364 p. : **814**

1. Essays.
ISBN 0060932236

LC 98056019

Collects over 30 essays.

Presents essays written during all stages of the author's illustrious career that range in scope from his thoughts on the city of New York and its inhabitants to his preference for brown eggs over white eggs.

Williams, Terry Tempest

Erosion : essays of undoing / Terry Tempest Williams. Sarah Crichton Books/Farrar, Straus and Giroux, [2019] 320 p. **814**

1. Erosion 2. Environmentalism 3. Identity (Psychology) 4. Nature conservation 5. Bears Ears National Monument (Utah) 6. The West (United States) 7. United States 8. Essays

ISBN 9780374280062

LC 2019017871

Timely essays by the conservationist and author of The Hour of Land explore the concept of erosion, the paradox of desert landscapes and the environmental hazards of present-day American politics.

Mosaic : finding beauty in a broken world / Terry Tempest Williams. Pantheon Books, 2008. 432 p. **814**

1. Aesthetics. 2. Hope. 3. Beauty. 4. Mosaics.

ISBN 9780375420788

LC 2008007196

The naturalist author of Refuge and An Unspoken Hunger reflects on what it means to be human, the interconnection between the natural and human worlds, and how they combine to produce both tumult and peace, ugliness and beauty.

"Scientific in her exactitude, compassionate in her receptivity, and rhapsodic in expression, Williams has constructed a beautiful mosaic of loss and renewal that affirms, with striking lucidity, the need for reverence for all of life." Booklist.

814.54 American essays -- 1945-1999

Burt, Stephanie, 1971-

Close calls with nonsense : reading new poetry / Stephen Burt. Graywolf Press, c2009. xvi, 374 p. ; **814.54**

1. Poetry, Modern -- 20th century -- History and criticism.

ISBN 9781555975210

LC 2008935602

A volume of essays and critical writings by the Harvard University instructor and distinguished critic explores the works of such figures as Rae Armantrout, Paul Muldoon, and C. D. Wright, in a collection that accessibly introduces key works by modern poets.

Goldbarth, Albert

The **adventures** of form and content : essays / Albert Goldbarth. Graywolf Press, 2016. 272 p. **814.54**

1. Love 2. Loss (Psychology) 3. Self-discovery 4. Essays 5. Reversible books

ISBN 9781555977610

LC 2016938022

Albert Goldbarth's first book of essays in a decade, The Adventures of Form and Content is about the mysteries of dualities, the selves we all carry inside, the multiverses that we are.

"A nostalgic, rueful, and sometimes sweetly funny collection." Kirkus.

814.6 American essays -- 2000-

Als, Hilton

★**White** Girls / Hilton Als. McSweeneys Books 2013 300 p. **814.6**

1. African Americans -- Identity. 2. Gender role -- History 3. Race (Social sciences) 4. Essays

ISBN 9781936365814

LC 2014397324

Lambda Literary Award for LGBT Nonfiction

A collection of analyses on literature, art and music by the award-winning author of The Women shares cultural, meditative insights into race, gender and history that encompass a diverse range of subjects from Truman Capote and Louise Brooks to Malcolm X and Flannery O'Connor.

"Whether his subject is his mother, himself, or seminal artists, Als is a fine, piercing observer and interpreter, a writer of lashing exactitude and veracity." Booklist.

817 American humor and satire in English

Rosen, Michael J., 1954-

Mirth of a nation : the best contemporary humor / edited by Michael J. Rosen. HarperPerennial, c2000. xv, 619 p. ; **817**

1. American wit and humor. 2. Essays

ISBN 9780060953218

LC 99044293

Celebrates contemporary humor with a collection of stories, essays, and columns focusing on such topics as the Bill Clinton scandal, Baby Boomers, and sex education.

Twain, Mark, 1835-1910,

Mark Twain's library of humor / compiled by Mark Twain ; illustrated by E.W. Kemble ; introduction by Roy Blount ; series editor: Steve Martin. Modern Library, 2000, c1888. xl, 560 p. : **817**

1. Satirical fiction. 2. Short stories

ISBN 0679640363

LC 00025971

Selections from an anthology originally published in 1888 include twenty pieces by Mark Twain in addition to works by forty-three of his contemporaries, including Washington Irving, Harriet Beecher Stowe, and William Dean Howells.

818 American miscellaneous writings in English

Atwood, Margaret, 1939-

Writing with intent : essays, reviews, personal prose, 1983-2005 / Margaret Atwood. Carroll & Graf Publishers ; 2005. xvii, 427 p. ; **818**

1. Canadian literature -- History and criticism 2. Women's role. 3. Families 4. Literature -- History and criticism 5. Essays.

ISBN 9780786715350

LC 2005042086

"A different collection containing some of the essays in this book has been published under the title Moving targets in Canada by House of Anansi Press"--T.p. verso.

The first collection of nonfiction work by the author in more than two decades features fifty-seven essays and reviews on a wide range of topics, including John Updike, Toni Morrison, grunge, September 11th, and Gabriel García Márquez, among others.

"In these essays, the author comments on world events, fellow writers, and her own development. She reviews books by John Updike, Italo

Calvino, Antonia Fraser, and Dashiell Hammett, as well as the lesser-known Robert Bringhurst, Hilary Mantel, and H. Rider Haggard. This collection will not disappoint Atwood fans as her analyses both challenge and entertain." Library Journal.

Baraka, Amiri, 1934-2014

The **LeRoi** Jones/Amiri Baraka reader / Amiri Baraka ; edited by William J. Harris in collaboration with Amiri Baraka. Thunder's Mouth Press ; c2000. xxxiii, 586 p. ; **818**

1. African Americans 2. Literary collections.
ISBN 9781560252382

LC 99032364

Amiri Baraka -- dramatist, poet, essayist, orator, and fiction writer -- is one of the preeminent African-American literary figures of our time. The Leroi Jones/Amiri Baraka Reader provides the most comprehensive selection of Baraka's work to date, spanning almost 40 years of a brilliant, prolific, and controversial career, in which he has produced more than 12 books of poetry, 26 plays, eight collections of essays and speeches, and two books of fiction. This updated edition contains over 50 pages of previously unpublished work, as well as a chronology and full bibliography. -- From publisher description.

Barry, Dave

★**Lessons** from Lucy : the simple joys of an old, happy dog / Dave Barry. Simon & Schuster, October 2018. 224 p. **818**

1. Dogs. 2. Personal conduct. 3. Aging -- Humor. 4. Pets -- Humor.
ISBN 9781501161155

LC 2018003591

The popular humorist takes cues from his beloved and highly intelligent dog, Lucy, to navigate his later years with grace and face the absurdities of daily life.

"Even for those who are not as enamored by dogs as the author, his gentle wisdom seeps through the humor. He successfully pokes fun at the aging process without wallowing in overly long discussions of declining health and the wear and tear of body parts. Astute advice about growing older rolled into a blanket of classic Barry humor." Kirkus.

Berry, Wendell, 1934-

★The **world-ending** fire : the essential Wendell Berry / selected and introduced by Paul Kingsnorth. Counterpoint Press, 2018. 368 p. **818**

1. Berry, Wendell, 1934- 2. Agriculture 3. Farm life 4. Authors, American 5. Sustainable agriculture 6. United States -- Social life and customs 7. Essays 8. Diaries
ISBN 9781640090286

LC 2017060544

Celebrating our cultural heritage, our history and our home, an essayist, novelist and poet presents a collection of writings of a life spent farming the fields of rural Kentucky with mules and horses, and of the deeply personal knowledge of the land cultivated by this work.

"A great place to start for those who are not familiar with Berry's work; for those who are, it will be a nostalgic stroll down a rural, wooded Memory Lane. In this day and age, his writings are must-reads." Kirkus.

Blount, Roy

Alphabetter juice : or, the joy of text / Roy Blount. Farrar, Straus and Giroux, 2011. 283 p. ; **818**

1. Vocabulary -- Humor. 2. English language -- Dictionaries -- Humor. 3. Words 4. Alphabet.
ISBN 9780374103705

LC 2010039937

"Sarah Crichton books."

The NPR panelist and humorist author of Alphabet Juice presents a second helping of dexterous and lighthearted vocabulary factoids, fripperies and phenomena compiled to raise awareness about the relationship between words and their various definitions.

Bryson, Bill,

The **best** American travel writing 2016 / Bill Bryson, editor ; Jason Wilson, series editor. Houghton Mifflin Harcourt 2016. 336 p. Best American travel writing **818**

1. Voyages and travels. 2. Travelers. 3. Travel writing.
ISBN 9780544812093

LC bl2016042123

Collected by the best-selling author of A Short History of Nearly Everything, a far-ranging anthology of the best travel writing pieces published in 2015 captures the wonder, humor, fear and exhilaration that greets all of us when we journey to a new place.

Carlin, George

Napalm & silly putty / George Carlin. Hyperion, 2001. 269 p. ; **818**

1. Culture. 2. Comic routines 3. Comedians -- United States -- Anecdotes 4. Humorists -- United States -- 20th century -- Anecdotes 5. United States -- Social life and customs -- 20th century Humor
ISBN 0786864133

LC 00054055

George Carlin is back with another generous helping of notions, nonsense, assertions, assumptions, mockery, merriment, silliness, sarcasm, and, to be sure, plenty of disturbing references and toxic alienation.

"The comedian covers a wide range of issues from rape and religion to the homeless. And any topic is fair game: abortion, airport security, cars, funerals, language, organ donors, sports, technology, TV and war. Over 100 scintillating short pieces are interrupted by loony lists and hundreds of clever one-liners." Publishers Weekly.

Chabon, Michael

Bookends : collected intros and outros / Michael Chabon. Harper Perennial, 2019. 224 p. **818**

1. Literature -- History and criticism 2. Literature -- Appreciation 3. Books and reading 4. Book introductions 5. Essays
ISBN 9780062851291

LC bl2019001547

The Pulitzer Prize-winning author of Moonglow presents an idiosyncratic compilation of introductions, afterwords and liner notes from classic works of literature to explore how they influenced his literary life.

Choi, Don Mee

★**DMZ** colony / Don Mee Choi. Wave Books, 2020 132 p. : **818**

1. Korean War, 1950-1953 2. Korean American poetry
ISBN 9781940696966

LC 2019030061

"Woven from poems, prose, photographs, and drawings, Don Mee Choi's DMZ Colony is a tour de force of personal and political reckoning set over eight acts." Provided by publisher.

"Virtuosic in its range and empathy, this is a book that shifts the reader's understanding of historical narrative from one of war to one of flight." Publishers Weekly

Collins, Lauren (Journalist),

The **best** American travel writing 2017 / edited and with an introduction by Lauren Collins. Houghton Mifflin Harcourt,

2017 xxi, 295 p. ; Best American travel writing **818**

1. Voyages and travels. 2. Travelers. 3. Travel writing. 4. Essays
ISBN 9781328745736

LC bl2017037363

"A Mariner original."

Presents an anthology of the best travel writing published in 2017, selected from magazines, newspapers, and web sites.

Dick, Philip K.

The **exegesis** of Philip K. Dick / Philip K. Dick ; edited by Pamela Jackson and Jonathan Lethem. Houghton Mifflin Harcourt 2011 1056 p. **818**

1. Dick, Philip K. Philosophy. 2. Reality 3. Perception 4. Metaphysics
ISBN 9780547549255

LC 2011028561

Based on thousands of personal notes, letters, and other written sources, a definitive presentation of the late author's unpublished masterwork offers insight into his exploration of the nature of reality and the relationship between humanity and the divine.

Didion, Joan

South and West : from a notebook / Joan Didion. Knopf, 2017. 144 p. **818**

1. Didion, Joan 2. Walker, Percy, 1916- 3. Everyday life 4. Manners and customs 5. Race relations 6. Gulf Coast (United States) 7. Pacific Coast (United States) 8. Southern States 9. Essays.
ISBN 9781524732790

LC 2016962161

Two excerpts from never-before-seen notebooks by the National Book Award-winning author of The Year of Magical Thinking offer insights into her literary mind and process and includes notes on her Sacramento upbringing, her life in the Gulf states, her views on prominent locals and her experiences during a formative Rolling Stone assignment.

"Students of social history, fans of Didion, and those seeking a quick, engaging read will appreciate this work: the raw immediacy of unedited prose by a master has an urgency that more polished works often lack." Publishers Weekly.

Ehrlich, Gretel

The **future** of ice : a journey into cold / Gretel Ehrlich. Pantheon Books, 2004. 200 p. **818**

1. Ehrlich, Gretel Travel Cold regions. 2. Cold -- Psychological aspects. 3. Weather -- Physiological effect. 4. Environmental protection. 5. Ecology. 6. Polar regions -- Description and travel. 7. Polar region -- Description and travel.
ISBN 037542251X

LC 2004044666

"In this meditation on deep cold and its potential demise through global warming, Ehrlich...backpacks among the glaciers of the southern Andes, winters in a Wyoming cabin and sails with the research ship Noorderlicht to the Greenland ice pack. Her prose is as sharply observed as poetry and nearly as compressed, and her narrative favors short scenes as fragmented as the breaking ice sheets she encounters." Publishers Weekly.

Fuller, Alexandra,

The **best** American travel writing 2019 / Alexandra (EDT) Fuller. Houghton Mifflin Harcourt, 2019. 378 p. Best American travel writing **818**

1. Voyages and travels. 2. Travelers. 3. Travel writing. 4. Essays
ISBN 9780358094234

LC bl2019029302

An eclectic compendium of the best travel writing essays published in 2018, collected by Alexandra Fuller. Best American Travel Writing gathers together a satisfyingly varied medley of perspectives, all exploring what it means to travel somewhere new.

Hemingway, Ernest, 1899-1961

The **dangerous** summer / Ernest Hemingway ; introduction by James A. Michener. Scribner, 1985. ix, 228 p., 16 p. of plates : **818**

1. Hemingway, Ernest, 1899-1961 -- Travel -- Spain. 2. Ordonez Araujo, Antonio, 1932- 3. Dominguin, Luis Miguel, 1926- 4. Bullfights -- Spain. 5. Bullfighters -- Spain 6. Spain -- Description and travel.
ISBN 0684183552

LC 84027578

Includes index.

Originally published: New York : Scribner, 1960.

Describes the rivalry of two Spanish matadors, brothers-in-law, and their competition in one season of bullfights.

"A look at the personal and professional rivalry of the two greatest bullfighters since the death of Manolete in 1947: Luis Miguel Domingun and Antonio Ordez. The Dangerous Summer provides an insider's view based on extensive experience, mingles memory and desire, and is essential reading for anyone interested in the subject or the author." National Review.

Inman, Matthew

The **terrible** and wonderful reasons why I run long distances / Oatmeal, Matthew Inman. Andrews McMeel, 2014. 148 p. **818**

1. Long-distance running. 2. Runners. 3. Running. 4. Alternative comics 5. Satirical comics 6. Comics and Graphic novels 7. Webcomics.
ISBN 9781449459956

LC 2014937161

This is not just a book about running. It's a book about cupcakes. It's a book about suffering. It's a book about gluttony, vanity, bliss, electrical storms, ranch dressing, and Godzilla. It's a book about all the terrible and wonderful reasons we wake up each day and propel our bodies through rain, shine, heaven, and hell.

Jackson, Shirley, 1916-1965

Let me tell you : new stories, essays, and other writings / Shirley Jackson ; edited by Laurence Jackson Hyman and Sarah Hyman DeWitt. Random House Inc., 2015 496 p. **818**

1. Families 2. Family relationships 3. Short stories 4. Essays
ISBN 9780812997668

LC 2014036656

This volume of unpublished and uncollected works brings together Shirley Jackson's deliciously eerie short stories along with frank lectures on writing, comic essays about her large, boisterous family, and whimsical drawings. Jackson's landscape here is most frequently domestic, but this familiar setting is also her most subversive: She wields humor, terror, and the uncanny to explore the real challenges of marriage, parenting, and community -- the pressure of social norms, the veins of distrust in love, the constant lack of time and space.

Jacobson, Abbi

Carry this book / Abbi Jacobson. Viking, 2016 144 p. **818**

1. Popular culture 2. Handbags 3. Celebrities 4. Personal belongings

5. Comics and Graphic novels
ISBN 9780735221598

LC 2016044009

From the mind of one of the creators and stars of Broad City comes a wonderfully weird illustrated look at the world around us--all through the framework of the things we carry in a book that has illustrated looks at what could be inside Oprah's bag, Donald Trump's weekender, Martha Stewart's hand-knit fanny pack and much more.

"As an exercise in creativity or as a way of understanding history, this would make good inspiration for workshops for middle schoolers through adults." Library Journal.

Kerouac, Jack, 1922-1969

★**Book** of sketches, 1952-57 / Jack Kerouac ; introduction by George Condo. Penguin Poets, 2006. 496 p. **818**

1. Kerouac, Jack, 1922-1969 Diaries. 2. Notebooks. 3. Beat culture. 4. Beat authors. 5. Voyages and travels. 6. Autobiographical fiction
ISBN 0142002151

LC 2005044535

"Somewhere between diary, verbal sketchbook and play-by-play account of whatever passed before his eyes, this collection of poems transcribed from notebooks Kerouac kept in his pocket between 1952 and 1954 turns out to rank with his most interesting work. . . . Kerouac hits all the notes for which he and his fellow beats are known. While not everything here is golden, the immediacy and unpretentiousness of this off-the-cuff writing makes it an intimate glimpse into the consciousness of a man who simply couldn't stop observing." Publishers Weekly.

Kilgariff, Karen

★**Stay** sexy & don't get murdered : the definitive how-to guide / Karen Kilgariff and Georgia Hardstark. Forge Books, 2019. 304 p. **818**

1. Kilgariff, Karen. 2. Hardstark, Georgia 3. Human behavior 4. Podcasters 5. Murder -- Case studies 6. Advice
ISBN 9781250178954

LC bl2019009802

Tom Doherty Associates
Based on a podcast.

Sharing never-before-heard stories ranging from their struggles with depression, eating disorders, and addiction, Karen and Georgia irreverently recount their biggest mistakes and deepest fears, reflecting on the formative life events that shaped them into two of the most followed voices in the nation. The authors focus on the importance of self-advocating and valuing personal safety over being "nice" or "helpful." They delve into their own pasts, true crime stories, and beyond to discuss meaningful cultural and societal issues with fierce empathy and unapologetic frankness.

Knight, Sarah

The **life-changing** magic of not giving a f*ck : how to stop spending time you don't have with people you don't like doing things you don't want to do / Sarah Knight. Little, Brown and Company, 2015. xi, 208 p. ; **818**

1. Kond, Marie. Life-changing magic of tidying up Parodies, imitations, etc. 2. Kond, Marie. Life-changing magic of tidying up Parodies, imitations, etc. 3. Self-help techniques
ISBN 9780316270724

LC bl2015056603

Includes index.

A parody of The Life-Changing Magic of Tidying Up explains how to rid yourself of mental clutter--unwanted obligations, shame and guilt, and instead give your attention to people and things that make you happy.

Le Guin, Ursula K., 1929-2018

★**Words** are my matter : writings about life and books, 2000-2016 with a journal of a writer's week / Ursula K. Le Guin. Small Beer Press, 2016. 352 p. **818**

1. Le Guin, Ursula K., 1929-2018 Authorship. 2. Writing 3. Creative writing 4. Narration (Rhetoric) 5. Science fiction writing. 6. Essays.
ISBN 9781618731340

LC 2016029895

Hugo Award for Best Related Non-Fiction Book, 2017.

A brilliant collection showcases the essays, reviews, talks, book reviews and more from the National Book Foundation Medalist author and one of our foremost public literary intellectuals.

"The wide-ranging collection includes essays, lectures, introductions, and reviews, all informed by Le Guins erudition, offered without academic mystification, and written (or spoken) with an inviting grace." Publishers Weekly.

Leary, Denis

Why we don't suck : and how all of us need to stop being such partisan little bitches / Denis Leary. Crown Archetype, [2017] x, 304 pages : **818**

1. Politics and culture -- United States 2. Mass media 3. Popular culture 4. United States -- Social life and customs -- 21st century. 5. Satire 6. Political satire 7. Essays
ISBN 9781524762735

LC 2017299308

The actor, writer and comedian takes equal opportunity aim at both liberals and conservatives with his signature blend of biting sarcasm and common sense, in his latest humorous treatise and follow-up to the best-selling Why We Suck.

"A fun and thought-provoking romp through politics and popular culture." Kirkus.

Marx, Patricia (Patricia A.)

Why don't you write my eulogy now so I can correct it? : a mother's suggestions / Patricia Marx and Roz Chast. Celadon Books, 2019. xxiii, 81 p. : **818**

1. Marx, Patricia (Patricia A.) Family 2. Jokes 3. Advice 4. Mothers 5. Wisdom
ISBN 9781250301963

A gift collection of witty one-liners by the New Yorker writer and first woman elected to the Harvard Lampoon celebrates the universal advice of her mother and is accompanied by full-color illustrations by a New Yorker staff cartoonist.

"Here, New Yorker writer Marx collects her mother's sparkling witticisms, as exemplified by the title. The New Yorker staff cartoonist Chast, National Book Critics Circle Award winner for her immortally funny and insightful Can't We Talk About Something More Pleasant?, contributes her genius as illustrator." Library Journal.

McCammon, Ross

Works well with others : an outsider's guide to shaking hands, shutting up, handling jerks, and other crucial skills in business that no one ever teaches you / Ross McCammon. Dutton, 2015 xix, 263 p. ; **818**

1. Business -- Humor. 2. Business etiquette -- Humor.
ISBN 9780525955023

LC 2015009498

Includes index.

A former editor at Esquire and the current etiquette columnist at Entrepreneur offers practical advice for getting the small things right at the workplace from a simple business handshake to networking during a meeting at a bar.

McWilliams, Susan Jane, 1977-

A **political** companion to James Baldwin / edited by Susan J. McWilliams. University Press of Kentucky, 2017 426 p. **818**

1. Baldwin, James, 1924-1987 Political and social views. 2. Politics and literature -- United States -- History -- 20th century. 3. Politics in literature.

ISBN 9780813169910

LC 2017038157

In A Political Companion to James Baldwin, a group of prominent scholars assess the prolific author's relevance to present-day political challenges. Together, they address Baldwin as a democratic theorist, activist, and citizen, examining his writings on the civil rights movement, religion, homosexuality, and women's rights. --From publisher description.

"The individual contributions are uniformly excellent, but what the work as a whole does so effectively is establish the power of Baldwin's theoretical lens." Choice.

Poe, Edgar Allan, 1809-1849

★**Poetry** and tales : Poetry and Tales / Edgar Allan Poe. Literary Classics of the U.S. : c1984. 1408 p. ; The Library of America **818**

1. Fantasy poetry, American 2. Horror tales, American

ISBN 9780940450189

LC 83019931

"Patrick F. Quinn wrote the notes and selected the texts for this volume"--Prelim. p.

Gathers all of Poe's poetry, tales, short stories, and general essays in chronological order.

Roberson, Blythe

How to date men when you hate men / Blythe Roberson. Flatiron Books, 2019 224 p. **818**

1. Men/women relations 2. Dating (Social customs) 3. Feminism 4. Patriarchy 5. United States -- Social life and customs -- 21st century

ISBN 9781250193421

LC 2018046993

A humorous roadmap to modern dating draws on the author's own disastrous experiences with the opposite sex to share lighthearted counsel on what it means to date real men within the trappings of today's society.

"This is a perfect book for women of all ages who have found that, despite their best efforts, dating men rarely works out in their favor." Publishers Weekly.

Salter, James

Don't save anything : the uncollected writing of James Salter / James Salter. Counterpoint Press, 2017. 320 p. **818**

1. Voyages and travels 2. Writing 3. Books and reading 4. Essays

ISBN 9781619029361

LC 2017017393

The late award-winning author of Dusk and Other Stories presents a collection of literary essays gathering his thoughts on such topics as the writers who shaped his literary world, America's changing military life, mountain climbing and his travels to Europe and Asia.

"Crisp and razor sharp, Salter's work peels away illusions to reveal the matter-of-fact nuances of his and our lives." Publishers Weekly.

Scottoline, Lisa

I need a lifeguard everywhere but the pool / Lisa Scottoline and Francesca Serritella. St. Martin's Press, 2017. 336 p. **818**

1. Scottoline, Lisa 2. Serritella, Francesca Scottoline 3. Mothers and daughters 4. Women 5. Essays

ISBN 9781250059963

LC 2017004247

A lighthearted collection of stories by the mother-and-daughter team features warm and witty memoir tales for women, in an entry in the series that includes, I've Got Sand in All the Wrong Places.

I've got sand in all the wrong places / Lisa Scottoline & Francesca Serritella. St. Martin's Press, 2016. 272 p. **818**

1. Scottoline, Lisa. 2. Serritella, Francesca Scottoline. 3. Mothers and daughters. 4. Women. 5. Essays

ISBN 9781250059956

LC 2016003973

A best-selling mother-daughter duo present a new collection of witty, wise and heartwarming stories.

"More light, bright essays to delight fans of this mother-daughter writing team." Kirkus.

Smith, Larry, 1968-

The **moment** : wild, poignant, life-changing stories from 125 wrtiers and artists / edited by Larry Smith. Harper Perennial, c2012. 344 p. **818**

1. Life change events. 2. Memories. 3. Authors, American -- 21st century 4. Authors. 5. Essays.

ISBN 9780061719653

LC 2011033766

The creators of the best-selling Not Quite What I Was Planning present a collection of brief and moving personal stories about how a single instant, decision, accident, conversation or message prompted profound changes, in a treasury that includes contributions by such individuals as Melissa Etheridge, Justin Halpern and Jennifer Egan.

"Each author's ability to concisely describe such big moments pulls the reader in. Book and writing groups will have a lot to talk about after reading this first-rate collection." Library Journal.

Sontag, Susan, 1933-2004

Reborn : journals and notebooks, 1947-1963 / Susan Sontag ; edited by David Rieff. Farrar, Straus and Giroux, 2008. xiv, 318 p. ; **818**

1. Sontag, Susan, 1933-2004 Diaries 2. Sontag, Susan, 1933-2004 Notebooks, sketchbooks, etc. 3. Authors, American -- 20th century -- Diaries 4. Women authors -- 20th century -- Diaries 5. Women and literature -- United States -- History -- 20th century

ISBN 9780374100742

LC 2008034247

Presents excerpts from the early writings of the author, with reflections on her meetings with influential writers and intellectuals, her literary ambitions, and her criticisms of other writers.

Stein, Gertrude, 1874-1946

Writings, 1903-1932 : Writings 1903-1932 / Gertrude Stein. Library of America : c1998. x, 941 p. : The library of America ; **818**

ISBN 188301140X

LC 97028915

The first in a two-volume set of works combines fiction with the author's personal experiences in Paris and includes the play Four Saints in Three Acts and Lifting Belly, in which she documents her wonderful relationship with Alice B. Toklas.

★**Writings,** 1932-1946 / Gertrude Stein. Library of America, c1998. 844 p. ; **818**

1. Essays

ISBN 9781883011413

LC 97028916

The second in a two-volume set furnishes Stein's later literary masterpieces, including Stanzas in Meditation, Lectures in America, and The Geographical History of America, and details her relationship with Picasso and the public figures that inspired her works.

"In addition to theater pieces, fiction, and poetry memoir, philosophical speculation, literary criticism and theory, all sorts of briefer forms that are hard to account for but easy to marvel at and even to delight in, pack these volumes, and constitute, as the editors surely intended us to discover, the most consistently achieved representation of new ways of responding to life and new possibilities of getting experience into words that American literature has to show." New York Times Book Review.

Stein, Joel

In defense of elitism : why I'm better than you and you're better than someone who didn't buy this book / Joel Stein. Grand Central Publishing, 2019. xxiv, 308 p. ; **818**

1. Elite (Social sciences)

ISBN 9781455591473

LC 2019009317

The former staff writer for Time Magazine examines the anti-elitist shift that elected Donald Trump by spending a week in Roberts County, Texas, which had the highest percentage of Trump voters in the country.

Strayed, Cheryl, 1968-,

The **best** American travel writing 2018 / edited and with an introduction by Cheryl Strayed ; Jason Wilson, series editor. Houghton Mifflin Harcourt, 2018. 320 p. Best American travel writing **818**

1. Voyages and travels. 2. Travelers. 3. Travel writing. 4. Essays

ISBN 9781328497697

LC bl2018187047

"A Mariner original."

Presents an anthology of the best travel writing published in 2018, selected from magazines, newspapers, and web sites.

Thoreau, Henry David, 1817-1862

★**Collected** essays and poems / Henry David Thoreau. Library of America, c2001. xiv, 703 p. ; **818**

1. Essays

ISBN 9781883011956

LC 00046234

A collection of essential writings features Thoreau's poetry and essays on nature, materialism, conformity, and politics; including such works as "Slavery in Massachusetts," "Civil Disobedience," "A Winter Walk," and "Life Without Principle."

Thursby, Jacqueline S., 1940-

Maya Angelou : a literary reference to her life and work / Jacqueline S. Thursby. Facts On File, 2011. x, 430 p. ; **818**

1. Angelou, Maya Handbooks, manuals, etc. 2. African Americans in literature -- Handbooks, manuals, etc.

ISBN 9780816080939

LC 2010032716

Critical Companion to Maya Angelou is a comprehensive and up-to-date resource for students interested in this prolific poet. --From publisher description.

"The opening biography gives a clear, concise overview that references a number of secondary and primary works; these also are listed in valuable bibliographies contained in the appendixes. The section titled 'Works' divides Angelou's oeuvre into 'Autobiographies,' 'Essay Collections,' 'Poetry,' 'Children's Books,' and 'Major Essays.'" Choice.

Trethewey, Natasha D., 1966-

Beyond Katrina : a meditation on the Mississippi Gulf Coast / Natasha Trethewey. University of Georgia Press, 2010. 144 p. **818**

1. Trethewey, Natasha D., 1966- Homes and haunts. 2. Hurricane Katrina, 2005. 3. African Americans -- Social conditions. 4. Survival (after hurricanes) 5. Hurricanes. 6. Gulf Coast, Mississippi. 7. Mississippi.

ISBN 9780820333816

LC 2010011417

A collection of essays, poems, and letters, chronicling the effects of Hurricane Katrina on the Mississippi Gulf Coast.

"By looking at the vast devastation with sober and poetic eyes, Trethewey has written a hauntingly beautiful book." Publishers Weekly.

Updike, John

Higher gossip : essays and criticism / John Updike ; edited by Christopher Carduff. Alfred A. Knopf, 2011. 480 p. **818**

1. Authors. 2. Creativity. 3. Essays.

ISBN 9780307957153

LC 2011013586

Includes index.

A collection of the eloquent, insightful, and beautifully written prose works that Updike was compiling when he died in January 2009, this book opens with a self-portrait of the writer in winter--a Prospero who, though he fears his most dazzling performances are behind him, reveals himself in every sentence to be in deep conversation with the sources of his magic.

West, Lindy

Shrill : notes from a loud woman / Lindy West. Hachette Books, 2016. 272 p. **818**

1. West, Lindy 2. Women journalists -- United States 3. Feminists -- United States 4. Women -- Humor. 5. Personal conduct -- Humor 6. Books to TV

ISBN 9780316348409

LC 2016001577

The Guardian columnist and This American Life social commentator presents a series of essays about the qualities of a comedic feminist and her experiences of coming of age in a popular culture that is hostile to plus-sized women who speak their minds.

Wilson, Ronaldo V.

Farther traveler : poetry, prose, other / Ronaldo V. Wilson. Counterpath, 2014. 144 p. **818**

1. African American poetry 2. American poetry

ISBN 9781933996332

LC 2014034097

FARTHER TRAVELER by Ronaldo Wilson is an expansive, complex hybrid of poetry, prose, and memoir that engages with contemporary culture, race and sexuality. --From publisher description.

818.5403 Diaries--American literature--1945-1999

Sedaris, David

David Sedaris diaries : a visual compendium / introduction & design, Jeffrey Jenkins ; foreword, David Sedaris. Little, Brown and Company, 2017. 249 p. : **818.5403**

1. Sedaris, David Diaries. 2. Essayists -- United States -- Diaries 3. Humorists, American -- 20th century -- Diaries 4. Humorists, American -- 21st century -- Diaries 5. Illustrated books 6. Essays

ISBN 9780316431712

LC 2016955673

Includes facsimile items and memorabilia ; pocket on the back inside cover holds loose cards.

Includes index.

A vibrant compendium of artwork and images culled from decades of personal journals shares insight into his celebrations of the unexpected in the everyday and is complemented by an array of interactive components and postcards.

818.602 Jokes -- American literature -- -2000

Ajayi, Luvvie

I'm judging you : the do-better manual / Luvvie Ajayi. Henry Holt and Company, [2016] 224 p. **818.602**

1. Personal conduct -- Humor 2. Popular culture. 3. Social media 4. Misbehavior 5. Essays. 6. Anthologies.

ISBN 9781627796064

LC 2016009018

"A Holt paperback."

"Be prepared for some laughs, but also be prepared to think and confront tougher issues. Bits of humor help these occasionally hard-hitting essays go down." Kirkus.

820 English and Old English (Anglo-Saxon) literatures

Garner, Helen, 1942-

Everywhere I look / Helen Garner. The Text Publishing Company, 2016. 229 p. ; **820**

1. Garner, Helen, 1942- Criticism and interpretation. 2. Garner, Helen, 1942- Diaries. 3. Writing 4. Life. 5. Australian 6. Essays

ISBN 9781925355369

LC 2015463935

Everywhere I look is a collection of essays, diary entries and true stories spanning more than fifteen years of the work of one of Australia's greatest writers. Helen Garner takes us from backstage at the ballet to the trial of a woman for infanticide, from the significance of moving house to the pleasure of re-reading Pride and Prejudice. The collection includes her famous and controversial essay on the insults of age, her deeply moving tribute to her mother, and the story of her joy in discovering the ukulele. Everywhere I look is a multifaceted, profound portrait of life. It glows with insight and wisdom.

"Garner, one of Australia's most acclaimed writers (This House of Grief), gives her fans a captivating collection of personal essays and diary entries." Publishers Weekly.

Moran, Caitlin, 1975-

Moranifesto / Caitlin Moran. Harper Perennial, 2016. xiv, 329 p. **820**

1. Moran, Caitlin, 1975-. 2. Celebrities. 3. Women journalists. 4. Popular culture 5. Great Britain -- Social life and customs -- 21st century. 6. Essays

ISBN 9780062433756

Gathers columns originally from the "London Times," that celebrate celebrity, society, and culture in today's society, from Bendedict Cumberbatch and hangovers to printers and affordable housing.

"With her exuberant vocabulary full of Briticisms, Moran's wise, bracing observations about politics, pop culture, feminism, and nearly everything else are no-holds-barred, and made easy and fun to digest by her crackling humor." Booklist.

820.9 English literature--history and criticism

Batchelor, Jennie, 1976-

The **history** of British women's writing / [general editors, Jennie Batchelor and Cora Kaplan]. Palgrave Macmillan, 2010-2015 10 vols. **820.9**

1. English literature -- Women authors -- History and criticism. 2. Women and literature -- Great Britain -- History.

ISBN 9780230235106

LC 2010026127

Provides essays offering a critical analysis and describing the history of British women's literature, from 700 to the present day.

Coles, Robert

Handing one another along : literature and social reflection / Robert Coles ; edited by Trevor Hall and Vicki Kennedy. Random House, 2010. xxiv, 273 p. : **820.9**

1. Literature -- Moral and ethical aspects. 2. Character education 3. Literature and society

ISBN 9781400062034

Shares inspirational insights into how character, courage and moral understanding can be promoted by reflecting on the lives of others, drawing on the author's famous Harvard course to offer provocative assessments of the examples of famous writers.

Sage, Lorna

The **Cambridge** guide to women's writing in English / Lorna Sage ; advisory editors, Germaine Greer, Elaine Showalter. Cambridge University Press, 1999. viii, 696 p. : **820.9**

1. English literature -- Women authors -- Dictionaries 2. Women and literature -- English-speaking countries -- Dictionaries 3. Women and literature -- Great Britain -- Dictionaries

ISBN 9780521495257

LC 98050778

This Guide aims to consolidate and epitomise the re-reading of women's writing that has gone on in the last twenty-five years. This is an opportunity for stock-taking--a timely project, when so much writing has been rediscovered, reclaimed and republished. --From publisher description.

"A worthy addition to most reference collections, the volume will be useful for literature and women's studies collections in public and academic libraries. Though its style is fairly scholarly, it might also be of interest to high schools that have adopted curricula emphasizing multicultural literature and work by women writers." Booklist.

Sanders, Andrew, 1946-

The **short** Oxford history of English literature / Andrew Sanders. Oxford University Press, 2004. vii, 756 p. ; **820.9**

1. English literature -- History and criticism. 2. Great Britain --

Intellectual life.
ISBN 0199263388

LC 2004049555

The Short Oxford History of English Literature provides a comprehensive and authoritative introductory guide to the literature of the British Isles from the Anglo-Saxon period to the present day, including a full treatment of Irish, Scottish, and Welsh writing in English. --From publisher description.

"He skillfully introduces controversies about the development of an English literature canon and explains how writers got selected for burial in Poets' Corner of Westminster Abbey, arguing that English literature has always been rife with contradiction, 'both multiple and polarized, both popular and elite.'" Library Journal.

Vendler, Helen, 1933-

Coming of age as a poet : Milton, Keats, Eliot, Plath / Helen Vendler. Harvard University Press, 2003. 174 p. : **820.9**

1. Eliot, T. S. (Thomas Stearns), 1888-1965 Criticism and interpretation. 2. Keats, John, 1795-1821 Criticism and interpretation. 3. Milton, John, 1608-1674 Criticism and interpretation. 4. Plath, Sylvia Criticism and interpretation. 5. American poetry -- 20th century -- History and criticism 6. English poetry -- History and criticism 7. Maturation (Psychology) in literature 8. English-speaking countries -- Intellectual life.
ISBN 9780674010246

LC 2002027287

The author delves deeply into the lives of four poets--Milton, Keats, Eliot, and Plath--to shed light on the vital maturation process that turns minor talents into major poetic voices.

"Vendler succeeds in revealing the aesthetic power and technical beauty of great poetry. New York Times Book Review.

Welch, Robert, 1947-

The **Oxford** companion to Irish literature / edited by Robert Welch, assistant editor, Bruce Stewart. Clarendon Press, 1996. xxv, 614 p. : **820.9**

1. English literature -- Irish authors -- Dictionaries. 2. Authors, Irish -- Biography -- Dictionaries. 3. Irish literature -- Dictionaries. 4. Ireland -- In literature Dictionaries.
ISBN 9780198661580

LC 95044943

A comprehensive reference on the literature of Ireland encompasses more than two thousand entries that discuss the history of Irish poetry, drama, and fiction, from ancient times to the present, along with biographical profiles, historical events, and more.

821 English poetry

Blake, William, 1757-1827

The **complete** poetry and prose of William Blake / edited by David V. Erdman. University of California Press, 2008 xxviii, 990 p. : **821**

ISBN 9780520256378

LC 2008275592

Critical commentary illuminating Blake's allusions and references accompanies the texts of his poetic and prose works.

Boland, Eavan

New collected poems / Eavan Boland. W.W. Norton, 2008, c2005. 320 p. ; **821**

1. Irish poetry 2. Ireland
ISBN 9780393065794

LC 2007042554

Includes indexes.

A chronologically arranged selection of poems deals with the experiences of Irish women in love, marriage, motherhood, and modern society.

A **woman** without a country : poems / Eavan Boland. W.W. Norton & Company, 2014 xii, 81 p. ; **821**

1. American poetry
ISBN 9780393244441

LC 2014030073

A collection of poems explores themes of mother, daughter, and generation and how, even without country or settled identity, a legacy of love can endure.

Browning, Elizabeth Barrett, 1806-1861

★**Sonnets** from the Portuguese : a celebration of love / Elizabeth Barrett Browning. St. Martin's Press, c1986. 63 p. : **821**

1. Love poetry, English 2. Sonnets, English
ISBN 9780312745011

LC 86013755

Forty-four poems examine the depth and complexities of married love and shares a wife's feelings for her husband

Browning, Robert, 1812-1889

★**Robert** Browning's poetry : authoritative texts, criticism / selected and edited by James F. Loucks and Andrew M. Stauffer. W. W. Norton & Co., c2007. x, 689 p. ; **821**

1. Browning, Robert, 1812-1889 Criticism and interpretation. 2. British poetry -- 19th century
ISBN 9780393926002

LC 2006047308

Works by modern and Victorian critics are presented together with poems from each stage of Browning's literary career.

Bunting, Basil

Complete poems / Basil Bunting ; associate editor, Richard Caddel. New Directions Books, 2003. 239 p. ; **821**

1. English poetry
ISBN 9780811215633

LC 2003015465

As well as "Briggflatts" (long out of print in the US, and now only available in this edition), this new Complete Poems includes Bunting's other great sonatas, most notably Villon (1925) and The Spoils (1951), along with his two books of Odes, his vividly realized "Overdrafts" (as he called his free translations of Horace, Rudaki, and others), and his brilliantly condensed Japanese adaptation, Chomei at Toyama (1932). --From publisher description.

Burns, Robert, 1759-1796

Burns : poems / edited and introduced by Gerard Carruthers. Alfred A. Knopf , 2007. 255 p. ; **821**

1. Scottish poetry
ISBN 9780307266163

LC 2006047299

Includes index.

A selection of poetry and lyrics by Scotland's most famous poet features Tam o' Shanter, "Holy Willie's Prayer," "Auld Lang Syne," "To a Mouse," "A Red, Red Rose," and many others.

Byron, George Gordon Byron, Baron, 1788-1824
Selected poetry of Lord Byron / edited by Leslie A. Marchand ; introduction by Thomas Disch ; notes by Jeffrey Vail. Modern Library, 2001. xv, 745 p. ; **821**

1. English poetry
ISBN 9780375758140
LC 2001042771

Includes index.

Presents a collection of Lord Byron's poetry, including "Manfred," "Childe Harold," and "Don Juan."

Chaucer, Geoffrey, d. 1400
★The **complete** poetry and prose of Geoffrey Chaucer / edited by John H. Fisher. Holt, Rinehart, and Winston, c1989. xiii, 1040 p. : **821**

1. Chaucer, Geoffrey, d. 1400
ISBN 9780030286124
LC 88029400

This edition is intended to make Chaucer's texts accessible with a minimum of scholary interference. The critical, biographical, and linguistic essays are grouped at the end so as not to impede the approach to the text. --From publisher description.

Coleridge, Samuel Taylor, 1772-1834
The **complete** poems / Samuel Taylor Coleridge ; edited by William Keach. Penguin Books, 1997. xxx, 626 p. ; **821**

1. English poetry -- 18th century 2. English poetry -- 19th century 3. Romanticism in poetry
ISBN 9780140423532
LC 97208514

Contains all the poems published in the poet's lifetime, arranged chronologically, and includes important earlier versions of such poems as "The Eolian Harp" and "The Rime of the Ancient Mariner."

Constantine, David, 1944-
Collected poems / David Constantine. Bloodaxe, 2004. 384 p. ; **821**

1. English poetry
ISBN 9781852246679
LC 2007408546

Includes index.

"A superb writer on myth, middle age and marital love; a maker of odes and elegies in ancient style; a poet of seascapes and cityscapes; a taker of romantic risks: this English poet shows all his talents in this important (and bulky) collection, which folds in most or all of eight previous books, from A Brightness to Cast Shadows (1980) through Something for the Ghosts (2002)." Publishers Weekly.

Davis, Wes
An **anthology** of modern Irish poetry / edited by Wes Davis. Belknap Press of Harvard University Press, 2010. xxxiv, 976 p. ; **821**

1. Irish poetry -- 20th century 2. English poetry -- 20th century. 3. Anthologies.
ISBN 9780674049512
LC 2009037231

The editor's selection includes work by world-renowned poets, including a couple of Nobel Prize winners, as well as work by poets whose careers may be less well known to the general public; by poets writing in English; and by several working in the Irish language (Gaelic selections appear in translation). --From publisher description.

"Appealingly priced and impressively comprehensive, Davis's anthology should have a broad audience. Indeed, with its engaging introduction and comprehensive biographies introducing each poet, it is ideal for the classroom and the living room, as well as for the library." Choice.

Day-Lewis, Cecil, 1904-1972
The **complete** poems of C. Day Lewis / Cecil Day Lewis. Stanford University Press, 1995 745 p. **821**

1. British poetry -- 20th century
ISBN 9780804725859
LC 91068076

"The still lively fascination of his verse seems to depend on the variety of tones [Day Lewis] could pick up, change, and discard at will. His modesty was genuine and profound, giving his verse texture, its winning versatility, its air that 'tenure is not for me.' Nothing that Day Lewis wrote is lacking its own sort of ephemeral though rediscoverable effectiveness. He was well aware of this, and it was a part of his modesty, as Jill Balcon points out in her thoughtful and sensitive introduction. For anyone who likes poetry there is real interest here in [this] complete record." New York Review of Books.

Donne, John, 1572-1631
Poems and prose / John Donne. A. A. Knopf, 1995. 256 p. ; **821**

1. English poetry -- 17th century
ISBN 9780679444671
LC 95015330

Includes index.

Gathers songs, sonnets, elegies, satires, letters, and religious poetry by the seventeenth century English poet

Dryden, John, 1631-1700
John Dryden : the major works / edited with an introduction and notes by Keith Walker. Oxford University Press, 2003. xviii, 967 p. ; **821**

ISBN 0192840770
LC 2003270051

This authoritative edition brings together a unique combination of Dryden's poetry and prose--all the major poems in full, literary criticism, and translations--to give the essence of his work and thinking. --From publisher description.

Dunmore, Helen, 1952-2017
Inside the wave / Helen Dunmore. Bloodaxe Books, 2017. 63 p. ; **821**

1. English poetry -- 21st century
ISBN 9781780373584
LC 2017296582

"To be alive is to be inside the wave, always travelling until it breaks and is gone. These poems are concerned with the borderline between the living and the dead--the underworld and the human living world--and the exquisitely intense being of both. They possess a spare, eloquent lyricism as they explore the bliss and anguish of the voyage."--Publisher information.

Feldman, Paula R.
British women poets of the Romantic era : an anthology / edited by Paula R. Feldman. Johns Hopkins University Press, 1997. xxxvi, 879 p. ; **821**

1. Women poets -- England 2. English poetry -- History and criticism. 3. English poetry -- 19th century. 4. English poetry -- 18th century.

5. Anthologies
ISBN 9780801854309

LC 96047417

"An anthology of works by 62 British women poets writing between 1770 and 1840. The poets are presented in alphabetical order, with each entry including a brief biography with birth and death dates, sample poems, major works, selected works, and the source of the poetry. The result is a singular resource providing information found in no other reference work." Library Journal.

Fenton, James, 1949-

Selected poems / James Fenton. Farrar, Straus and Giroux, 2006. vii, 196 p. ; **821**

1. English poetry
ISBN 9780374260651

LC 2006002691

Originally published: London : Penguin Books, 2006.

Features selected poems from all of the author's published works and a few new, uncollected poems.

Fisher, Roy, 1930-2017

★**Selected** poems / Roy Fisher ; edited by August Kleinzahler. Flood Editions, 2011 158 p. **821**

1. British poetry
ISBN 9780981952062

Foulds, Adam, 1974-

The **broken** word : an epic poem of the British empire in Kenya, and the Mau Mau uprising against it / Adam Foulds. Penguin Books, 2011. 60 p. ; **821**

1. Epic poetry, English. 2. Kenya -- History -- Mau Mau Emergency, 1952-1960
ISBN 9780143118091

LC 2012462029

Offers a lyrical poem about Tom, a young man who gets caught up in the violent 1950s Mau Mau Uprising in Kenya protesting the British colonial control of that country.

Fuller, John, 1937 January 1-

The **Oxford** book of sonnets / edited by John Fuller. Oxford University Press, 2000. xxxiv, 362 p. ; **821**

1. Sonnets, American. 2. Sonnets, English.
ISBN 0192803891

LC 00036757

An anthology of more than three hundred sonnets, arranged by the birth date of the poets, features the work of Shakespeare, Donne, Milton, Wordsworth, the Brownings, Christina Rossetti, Frost, Millay, Walcott, Heaney, and others.

"Indisputable masterpieces appear plentifully, but Fuller's determination to present a large number of distinguished practitioners assures that there are also many superb poems by virtual unknowns. And Fuller's introduction is a sharp-witted miracle of concise comprehensiveness." Booklist.

Gunn, Thom

Boss Cupid : poems / Thom Gunn. Farrar, Straus, Giroux, 2000. vii, 111 p. ; **821**

1. Poetry
ISBN 9780374115579

LC 99057739

"Boss Cupid offers a splendid introduction for the uninitiated. Almost all of Gunn's virtues are on display here: his playful, metrical dexterity, his unflinching celebration both of beauty and of transience. Advancing age and the AIDS-related deaths of friends--my everpresent dead--figure prominently in these poems, but so does Gunn's humorous touch." Time.

Hardy, Thomas, 1840-1928

Thomas Hardy : the complete poems / edited by James Gibson. Palgrave, 2001. xxxvi, 1003 p. : **821**

ISBN 9780333949290

LC 2001032732

The Complete Poems , edited by James Gibson, includes all of Hardy's prolific output of more than nine hundred poems, complemented by a detailed notes section. Collected in this single volume are his eight books of verse, all the uncollected poems, 'Domicilium' and the songs from The Dynasts. --From publisher description.

Heaney, Seamus, 1939-2013

District and circle / Seamus Heaney. Farrar, Straus and Giroux, 2006. 78 p. ; **821**

1. Rural families -- Ireland. 2. Rural life -- Ireland. 3. Childhood -- Ireland. 4. Poets.
ISBN 9780374140922

LC 2005044687

A collection by the Nobel Prize-winning writer contains pieces that evince a childhood spent safe from the horrors of World War II, a journey on the Underground, and a melting glacier, in a volume that includes a number of prose poems and translations.

Human chain / Seamus Heaney. Farrar, Straus and Giroux, 2010. viii, 85 p. ; **821**

1. Irish poetry 2. Ireland
ISBN 9780374173517

LC 2010010274

Heaney's collection elicits continuities and solidarities, between husband and wife, child and parent, then and now, inside an intently remembered present--the stepping stones of the day, the weight and heft of what is passed from hand to hand, lifted and lowered.

Opened ground : selected poems, 1966-1996 / Seamus Heaney. Farrar, Straus and Giroux, 1998. 443 p. ; **821**

1. Ireland
ISBN 0374526788

LC 98004331

Includes index.

Selected poems by the Nobel Prize-winning Irish poet are taken from Heaney's twelve previous collections and includes work published since 1987.

Herbert, George, 1593-1633

Herbert : poems / George Herbert, Peter Washington. Alfred A. Knopf, 2004. 253 p. ; **821**

1. Christian poetry, English -- Early modern, 1500-1700.
ISBN 9781400043293

LC 2005273574

Poems selected by Peter Washington.

A collection of poetry by the renowned seventeenth-century English metaphysical poet captures his rich emotional voice, luminous precision of language, and technical brilliance in such works as "The Collar," "The Church-porch," "The Altar," and "Easter Wings," among others.

Heylin, Clinton

So long as men can breathe : the untold story of Shakespeare's Sonnets

/ Clinton Heylin. Da Capo Press, 2009. 304 p. **821**

1. Shakespeare, William, 1564-1616. Sonnets. 2. Sonnets -- History and criticism 3. Poetry -- Publishing. 4. Literature -- Publishing -- Great Britain -- History. 5. Poetry -- History and criticism 6. Great Britain -- History -- 17th century.

ISBN 9780306818059

LC 2009008999

"This is more of a literary detective story than a deep analysis of the sonnets themselves that will interest all lovers of Shakespeare and literature." Library Journal.

Hill, Geoffrey

★The **orchards** of Syon / Geoffrey Hill. Counterpoint, c2002. 72 p. ; **821**

1. Christian poetry, English.

ISBN 9781582431666

LC 2001047245

A stunning volume of poetry, which continues the remarkable series that began with Canaan, is a Dantean eclogue that examines the natural world and provides insight into Paradise, presenting a modern devotional poem.

Selected poems / Geoffrey Hill. Yale University Press, 2009. 276 p. ; **821**

1. English poetry -- 20th century 2. English poetry -- 21st century

ISBN 9780300121568

LC 2008930384

"After four decades with just five books, the past 10 years have seen Hill offer six more, including a trio of long works some liken to Dante and Blake. This first selected since 1994 ... should get instant critical attention (and sustained academic adoption) even though it contains no new work. Here, entire, is Mercian Hymns, with its gorgeously medievalized evocation of a rural English upbringing. Here, complete, are all three recent long poems, with their erudite mix of elegy and jeremiad. Here, too, are the descriptive beauties that sparkle through even Hill's most rebarbative works." Publishers Weekly.

The **triumph** of love / Geoffrey Hill. Houghton Mifflin, 2000, c1998. 82 p. ; **821**

1. English poetry

ISBN 9780618001835

LC BL 00005662

A book-length poem describes the author's slow coming-to-terms with the brutality, political idiocy, and ecclesiastic blindness of the twentieth century, and his own failings.

Hopkins, Gerard Manley, 1844-1889

Poems and prose / Gerard Manley Hopkins. Alfred A. Knopf, 1995. 256 p. ; **821**

1. Religious poetry

ISBN 9780679444695

LC 95015331

Includes poems, essays on poetry, and selections from the nineteenth century poet's letters and notebooks.

Housman, A. E. (Alfred Edward), 1859-1936

★**Collected** poems / A. E. Housman. Holt, Rinehart and Winston, 1965 254 p. : **821**

1. British poetry

ISBN 9780805005479

LC 65019348

Presents the texts, authorized in 1939, of the modern British writer's poems and classical translations, providing insight into his literary style and concerns.

Jonson, Ben, 1573?-1637

The **complete** poems / Ben Jonson ; edited by George Parfitt. Penguin Books, 1996. 634 p. ; **821**

1. English poetry -- 17th century

ISBN 9780140422771

LC bl2006012182

Includes bibliographical references (p. [481]-614) and indexes.

Presents the complete poems of the seventeenth century dramatist, poet, and wit.

Keats, John, 1795-1821

★The **complete** poems of John Keats / John Keats. Modern Library, 1994. xiv, 398 p. ; **821**

1. English poetry

ISBN 9780679601081

LC 94004339

Includes index.

Presents all of the English poet's verse, including his sonnets and odes, the allegorical romance "Endymion," and the five-act poetic tragedy "Otho the Great."

Poems / Keats ; [selected by Peter Washington]. A.A. Knopf, c1994. 253 p. ; **821**

1. British poetry 2. Romanticism in poetry.

ISBN 0679433198

LC 94002495

Cover Title: Keats.

Includes index.

A selection of poems by the English Romantic poet.

Kipling, Rudyard, 1865-1936

Complete verse : Definitive Edition / Rudyard Kipling. Anchor Press, 1989, c1940. xiv, 850 p. ; **821**

1. British poetry

ISBN 9780385260893

LC 88007364

Includes index.

A complete collection of Kipling's poetry.

Langland, William, 1330?-1400?

Piers Plowman : the Donaldson translation, select authoritative Middle English text, sources and backgrounds, criticism / William Langland ; edited by Elizabeth Robertson and Stephen H.A. Shepherd. W.W. Norton, c2006. xviii, 644 p. ; A Norton critical edition **821**

1. Langland, William, 1330?-1400? Piers Plowman. 2. Pilgrims and pilgrimages, Christian 3. Religious poetry 4. Visions 5. Dreams 6. Allegories

ISBN 9780393975598

LC 2004057578

William Langland's iconoclastic masterpiece is at once a historical relic and a deeply spiritual vision, probing not only the social and religious aristocracy but also the day-to-day realities of a largely voiceless proletariat class. E. Talbot Donaldson's translation of the text has been selected for this Norton Critical Edition because of its skillful emulation of the original poem's distinct alliterative verse.-- From publisher description.

Larkin, Philip

★**Collected** poems / Philip Larkin ; edited and with an introduction by Anthony Thwaite. Farrar, Straus and Giroux, 2004. 218 p. ; **821**

1. English poetry
ISBN 9780374529208

LC 2003060846

Includes index.

A new collection of Phillip Larkin's poetry combines all of his published collections--North Ship, The Less Deceived, The Whitsun Weddings, and High Windows--with his uncollected poems from 1940-1984.

The **complete** poems / Philip Larkin ; edited and with an introduction and commentary by Archie Burnett. Farrar, Straus and Giroux, 2012. xxx, 729 p. ; **821**

1. English poetry -- 20th century.
ISBN 9780374126964

LC 2011945978

This entirely new edition brings together all of Philip Larkin's poems. In addition to those that appear in Collected Poems (1988) and Early Poems and Juvenilia (2005), some unpublished pieces from Larkin's typescripts and workbooks are included, as well as verse--by turns scurrilous, satirical, affectionate, and sentimental--that had been tucked away in his letters. For the first time, Larkin's poems are given a comprehensive commentary. This draws critically upon, and substantially extends, the accumulated scholarship on Larkin, and covers closely relevant historical contexts, persons and places, allusions and echoes, and linguistic usage. Prominence is given to the poet's comments on his own poems, which often outline the circumstances that gave rise to a poem or state what he was trying to achieve. Larkin often played down his literariness, but his poetry enrichingly alludes to and echoes the writings of many others; Archie Burnett's commentary establishes him as a more complex and more literary poet than many readers have suspected.

Lawrence, D. H. (David Herbert), 1885-1930

The **complete** poems / D.H. Lawrence ; collected and edited with an introduction and notes by Vivian de Sola Pinto and Warren Roberts. Penguin Books, 1993. 1079 p. ; **821**

1. English poetry
ISBN 9780140186574

LC BL 00006352

This collection includes all the poems from the incomplete "Collected Poems" of 1929 and from the separate smaller volumes issued during Lawrence's lifetime; uncollected poems; an appendix of juvenilia and another containing variants and early drafts; and all Lawrence's critical introductions to his poems. --From publisher description.

Lear, Edward, 1812-1888

The **complete** verse and other nonsense : The Complete Verse and Other Nonsense / Edward Lear ; compiled and edited with an introduction and notes by Vivien Noakes. Penguin Books, 2002. li, 566 p. : **821**

1. Nonsense verses, English. 2. Nonsense literature, English.
ISBN 9780142002278

LC 2002028998

A comprehensive collection of Lear's poetry and other nonsense writings features an array of limericks, stories, letters, illustrated alphabets, and previously unpublished material, all accompanied by the poet's own line drawings and a detailed introduction to Lear's work.

Levin, Phillis, 1954-

The **Penguin** book of the sonnet : 500 years of a classic tradition in English / edited by Phillis Levin. Penguin Books, 2001. lxxvii, 448 p. ; **821**

1. Sonnets, English.
ISBN 9780140589290

LC 00062350

Features more than six hundred sonnets from notable poets representing the Elizabethan, Romantic, and Victoria eras, as well as writers from the Harlem Renaissance and contemporary authors.

Lowell, Amy, 1874-1925

Selected poems / Amy Lowell ; Honor Moore, editor. Library of America, c2004. xxxiii, 156 p. : **821**

1. American poetry
ISBN 9781931082709

LC 2004048505

Provides selections of the author's Imagist poems, polyphonic prose, and narrative poetry.

MacDiarmid, Hugh, 1892-1978

Selected poetry / Hugh MacDiarmid ; introduction by Eliot Weinberger ; edited by Alan Riach & Michael Grieve. New Directions Pub. Corp., 1993. xxv, 289 p. ; **821**

1. Scottish poetry 2. Scotland
ISBN 9780811212489

LC 93005312

Includes index.

A selection from 50 years of work by the great Scottish poet (1892-1978) who was both the author of an enormous body of poems in English and the man responsible for reviving Scots as a literary language. --From publisher description.

Marvell, Andrew, 1621-1678

Poems / Marvell ; [selected by Peter Washington]. Alfred A. Knopf, c2004. 256 p. ; **821**

1. English poetry -- 17th century
ISBN 9781400042524

LC 2004556267

A complete edition of English lyric pieces by the seventeenth-century metaphysical poet explores period issues, the inner life, and famous people from his era.

Maxwell, Glyn, 1962-

One thousand nights and counting : selected poems / Glyn Maxwell. Farrar, Straus and Giroux, 2011. 239 p. ; **821**

1. English poetry
ISBN 9780374226480

LC 2011005176

"Originally published in the United Kingdom in 2011 by Picador"--T.p. verso.

Presents a collection of poems that are influenced by history, fairy tales, and myths to create a parallel world.

Morrissey, Sinead, 1972-

Parallax : and selected poems / Sinead Morrissey. Farrar, Straus and Giroux, 2015. 211 p. ; **821**

1. POETRY / English, Irish, Scottish, Welsh.
ISBN 9780865478299

LC 2014043835

This edition of Parallax also includes Morrissey's own selection of her favorite poems from her previous collections, published for the first time in the United States. --From publisher description.

"Consisting of Morrissey's T.S. Eliot Prize-winning Parallax (2013) as well as selections from the latest three of her four other collections, this is a sprawling volume characterized by restlessness." Booklist.

Muldoon, Paul

Maggot : poems / Paul Muldoon. Farrar, Straus and Giroux, 2010. 134 p. ; **821**

1. Irish poetry

ISBN 9780374200329

LC 2010005700

"This first full-length outing since he took the poetry editorship at the New Yorker will certainly hold the attention of devotees, and individual poems, as always, shine: sestinas, monorhymed works and especially sonnets (including a fine translation of Baudelaire's "The Albatross" and a diptych entitled "Nope" and "Yup") make Muldoon's acrobatic technique serve his strikingly playful--yet grim--sensibility." Publishers Weekly.

Selected poems 1968-2014 / Paul Muldoon. Farrar, Straus and Giroux, 2016. 228 p. ; **821**

1. POETRY / English, Irish, Scottish, Welsh.

ISBN 9780374260828

LC 2016033242

Includes index.

"A selection of Muldoon's award-winning poetry, from his earliest work to his most recent collections".-- Provided by publisher.

Murray, Les A., 1938-

Poems the size of photographs / Les Murray. Farrar, Straus, and Giroux, 2003. x, 115 p. ; **821**

1. Australian poetry

ISBN 9780374235208

LC 2002192520

A collection by the award-winning Australian poet considers such topics as Australia's people, politics, and landscape as well as its history, myths, and symbolism.

Taller when prone : poems / Les Murray. Farrar, Straus and Giroux, 2011. ix, 82 p. ; **821**

1. Australian poetry -- 21st century

ISBN 9780374272371

LC 2010033150

A new collection by the T. S. Eliot Prize- and Gold Medal for Poetry-winning author of The Biplane Houses offers insight into his combination of the poetic form and Australian vernacular, in a volume that features pieces that reflect rural life and the observations of locals and travelers.

Ormsby, Frank, 1947-

The **darkness** of snow / Frank Ormsby. Wake Forest University Press, 2017 143 p. **821**

1. Irish poetry

ISBN 9781930630826

LC 2017931446

In his most recent volume, The Darkness of Snow, we see memories of his youth in Fermanagh as well as poems of adult years in Belfast, reflecting on the aftermath of the Troubles and the city's restoration while commemorating a life lived in poetry. This collection also includes a sequence that meditates on the art of Irish painters.

Oswald, Alice, 1966-

Falling awake : poems / Alice Oswald. W. W. Norton & Company, 2016. 81 p. ; **821**

1. English poetry

ISBN 9780393285284

LC 2016012940

"In an era in which most poetry is concerned with personality, prize-winning Oswald takes a different approach in her attention to phenomena. In the best known of her previous six collections, Memorial (2011), a brilliant, inimitable rendering of Homer's Iliad, the similes are as vivid as the heroes." Booklist.

Paterson, Don, 1963-

Rain : poems / Don Paterson. Farrar, Straus, and Giroux, 2010, c2009. 61 p. **821**

1. Scottish poetry

ISBN 9780374246297

LC 2009938696

London :

A collection of poems--addressed to the rain and the sea, to the poet's young sons or beloved friends--never shy from their inquiry into truth and lie and serve both to expose readers to the unsettling forces within the world and to offer some protection against them. By the award-winning poet behind Landing Light.

Pope, Alexander, 1688-1744

Selected poetry / Alexander Pope ; edited with an introduction and notes by Pat Rogers. Oxford University Press, 1998. xxiii, 226 p. ; **821**

1. Verse satire, English.

ISBN 9780192834942

LC 98230887

Pope's greatest works--which exhibit his astonishing human insight, his wide sympathies, and powers of social observation (displayed to greatest effect in his talent for satire)--are included in this selection of his poetry. It has been compiled by the distinguished Pope scholar and editor Pat Rodgers, who also provides an indispensable introduction that offers a new interpretation of Pope's poetry, and the philosophical ideas behind it. -- From publisher description.

Raine, Kathleen, 1908-2003

The **collected** poems of Kathleen Raine. / Kathleen Raine. Counterpoint, c2001. xvi, 368 p. ; **821**

1. Imagination

ISBN 9781582431352

LC 00064448

Known for writing mystical nature poetry immersed in the quiet air of solitude and imagination, the author offers a collection of poems celebrating the miracles of nature and mankind's place among them.

Riggs, Thomas, 1963-

★**Contemporary** poets / editor, Thomas Riggs ; with a preface by Diane Wakoski. St. James Press, c2001. xxiii, 1443 p. ; **821**

1. American poetry -- 20th century 2. English poetry -- 20th century 3. Poets, American -- 20th century 4. Poets, English -- 20th century

ISBN 9781558623491

LC 00045882

Ross, David A., 1970-

Critical companion to William Butler Yeats : a literary reference to his life and work / David A. Ross. Facts On File, c2009.

xix, 652 p. : **821**

1. Yeats, W. B. (William Butler), 1865-1939
ISBN 9780816058952

LC 2008013642

A guide to the Irish poet and playwright includes a chronology of his life, descriptions of the important personalities and issues of his day, and entries on his major works with discussions on themes, langauge, forms, and imagery.

Satyamurti, Carole

Mahabharata : a modern retelling / Carole Satyamurti. W. W. Norton & Company, [2015] 1200 p. **821**

1. Feuds. 2. Rulers. 3. Hinduism. 4. Spiritualism. 5. India -- History -- To 324 B.C. 6. Epic poetry.
ISBN 9780393081756

LC 2014033595

An English retelling of the 2,000-year-old epic Hindu poem that includes the Bhagavad Gita recounts the story of the feud over a kingdom ruled by royalty descended from the gods.

"Satyamurti's exquisitely lucid and involving retelling is bookended with expert commentary by Wendy Doniger (The Hindus: An Alternative History, 2009) and translator and scholar Vinay Dharwadker." Booklist.

Scarry, Elaine

Naming thy name : cross talk in Shakespeare's sonnets / Elaine Scarry. Farrar, Straus and Giroux, 2016. 291 p. ; **821**

1. Constable, Henry, 1562-1613. 2. Shakespeare, William, 1564-1616 Characters Men. 3. Shakespeare, William, 1564-1616. Sonnets. 4. Love poetry, English -- History and criticism. 5. Sonnets, English -- History and criticism.
ISBN 0374279934

LC 2016016700

" Shakespeare's sonnets are indisputably the most enigmatic and enduring love poems written in English. They also may be the most often argued-over sequence of love poems in any language to date. But what is it that continues to elude us? While it is in part the spellbinding incantations, the hide-and-seek of sound and meaning, it is also the mystery of the noble youth to whom he makes a promise -- the promise that he will survive in the breath and speech and minds of all of those who ever read these sonnets. 'How can such promises be fulfilled if no name is actually given?' Scarry asks, and this book is the answer. Naming Thy Name lays bare William Shakespeare's devotion to a beloved whom he not only names but names repeatedly in a love affair immortalized in the microtexture of the sonnets, in their overarching architecture, and in their deep fabric. By naming his name, Scarry enables us to hear clearly a lover's call and the beloved's response for the very first time. Here, over the course of many poems, are two poets in conversation, in love, speaking and listening, writing and writing back. In a true work of alchemy, Elaine Scarry, one of America's most innovative and passionate thinkers, brilliantly synthesizes textual analysis, literary criticism, and historiography in pursuit of the haunting call and recall of Shakespeare's verse, and that of his (now at last named) beloved friend."-- Provided by publisher.

Shelley, Percy Bysshe, 1792-1822

Shelley : poems / Percy Bysshe Shelley. Knopf, 1993. 250 p. ; **821**

1. English poetry
ISBN 9780679429098

LC 93078335

Includes index.

A classicist, a headlong visionary, a social radical, and a poet of serene artistry with a lyric touch second to none, Shelley personified the richly various--and contradictory--energies of his time. This compact yet comprehensive collection showcases all the extraordinary facets of Shelley's art. --From publisher description.

Shelley's poetry and prose : authoritative texts, criticism / selected and edited by Donald H. Reiman and Neil Fraistat. Norton, c2002. xxii, 786 p. : **821**

1. Shelley, Percy Bysshe, 1792-1822 Criticism and interpretation. 2. English poetry
ISBN 9780393977523

LC 2001030903

Annotated definitive texts of all of Shelley's greatest poetry as well as other poems frequently discussed and three prose works are combined with general critical studies of his art and thought and scholarly writings analyzing specific poems.

Sisson, C. H. (Charles Hubert), 1914-2003

Selected poems / C.H. Sisson ; foreword by M.L. Rosenthal. New Directions, 1996 94 p. ; **821**

1. English poetry -- 20th century
ISBN 9780811213271

LC 95047599

Starting with poems written on a troopship and ending on home ground in Somerset, England, Selected Poems provides a comprehensive selection of Sisson's work, including "Tristan," a sequence written in the poet's eighty-first year. --From publisher description.

"Individual poems--'On My 51st Birthday' and The Mappemonde'--are outstanding, but the collection overall has a one-note tone and seems somewhat dated and weighty." Publishers Weekly.

Smith, Stevie, 1902-1971

Collected poems / Stevie Smith ; edited with a preface by James MacGibbon. New Directions Pub. Corp., 1983. 591 p. : **821**

1. English poetry
ISBN 9780811208826

LC 83043008

Includes indexes.

The English author's lively, witty style and morbid and macabre themes are revealed in a complete collection illustrated with her unusual drawings.

Spark, Muriel

All the poems of Muriel Spark. / Muriel Spark. New Directions Books, c2004. 129 p. ; **821**

1. English poetry
ISBN 9780811215763

LC 2004000948

"A New Directions book."

Includes index.

A collection of the author's poems covers such topics as European cities and the literary world.

Spencer, Bernard, 1909-1963

Bernard Spencer : complete poetry : translations & selected prose / edited by Peter Robinson. Bloodaxe Books, 2011. 351 p. ; **821**

1. World War II 2. English poety
ISBN 9781852248918

LC 2011453820

Bernard Spencer's work has been out of print for many years. This new edition will be welcomed by readers and academics, and will help redress the recent neglect of his work. Publication was timed to coincide with a major conference on the work of Bernard Spencer at Reading University in 2011.

Tennyson, Alfred, 1809-1892

Poems / Tennyson. Alfred A. Knopf, 2004. 255 p. ; **821**

1. English poetry -- 19th century
ISBN 9781400041879

LC 2003049505

A collection of narrative and short lyrical works by the poet favored by Queen Victoria includes "The Lady of Shalott," extracts from "Idylls of the King," and the complete text of "Ulysses."

Thomas, Dylan, 1914-1953

The **poems** of Dylan Thomas / edited with an introduction and notes by Daniel Jones ; with a preface by Dylan Thomas. New Directions, 2003. xxix, 320 p. : **821**

1. Welsh poetry -- 20th century
ISBN 9780811215411

LC 2002155790

Thomas' lyrical prologue introduces this collection of his complete and unfinished poems and early works.

Tomlinson, Charles, 1927-2015

Selected poems : 1955-1997 / Charles Tomlinson. New Directions, 1997. xiv, 226 p. ; **821**

1. English poetry
ISBN 9780811213691

LC 97025373

Includes index.

A collection of the acclaimed English poet's work from 1955 to 1997 exhibits his sense of both tragedy and the possibility of growth, expressed through his reflections on the qualities of the things around us and the pressure of time.

Tomlinson, Charles, 1927-2015

Skywriting : and other poems / Charles Tomlinson. Ivan R. Dee, 2003. 93 p. ; **821**

1. English poetry
ISBN 9781566635417

LC 2003055504

Winner of the third annual New Criterion Poetry Prize, here is a triumphant book in which Tomlinson's unfailing sensitivity and decorum toward the visual world is brilliantly realized.

Yeats, W. B. (William Butler), 1865-1939

The **collected** poems of W.B. Yeats / edited by Richard J. Finneran. Scribner Paperback Poetry, 1996. xxv, 544 p. ; **821**

1. Irish poetry
ISBN 9780684807317

LC 96023314

Newly revised, a collection of every poem the Irish poet approved for publication during his lifetime, grouped according to the work in which each first appeared, includes a preface and notes by a world-renowned Yeats scholar.

821.008 English poetry--collections

Ellmann, Richard, 1918-1987

★The **Norton** anthology of modern and contemporary poetry / edited by Jahan Ramazani, Richard Ellmann, Robert O'Clair. W.W. Norton, c2003. 2 v. ; **821.008**

1. Anthologies
ISBN 0393977919

LC 2002037990

"This volume includes 1596 poems by 195 poets. The anthology includes the works of such masters as Walt Whitman, Ezra Pound, Dylan Thomas, Langston Hughes, Gertrude Stein, Lucille Clifton, Louise Erdrich, and Allen Ginsberg. Extensive, and beautifully composed introductions provide insight, observations, and historical context for the selections. This ambitious, highly successful work is a veritable tribute to the enduring power of literature and language." School Library Journal.

Hollander, John

Christmas poems / selected and edited by John Hollander and J.D. McClatchy. Knopf, 1999. 254 p. ; **821.008**

1. Christmas poetry.
ISBN 9780375407895

LC 99036265

An enchanting and witty compendium of Yuletide poetry includes the lyrics to familiar carols, Moore's "A Visit from St. Nicholas," and other great works by Langston Hughes, Emily Dickinson, Rudyard Kipling, Dorothy Parker, Robert Graves, and Philip Larkin.

Strand, Mark, 1934-

The **making** of a poem : a Norton anthology of poetic forms / edited by Mark Strand and Eavan Boland. Norton, 2001, c2000. xxxi, 366 p. : **821.008**

1. Literary form.
ISBN 9780393321784

LC BL2001004850

Reprint. Originally published: 2000.

Provides a detailed explanation of the different forms of poetry--sonnet, ballad, villanelle, sestina--and explains the origin, traces their history, and provides examples for each form.

821.009 English poetry--history and criticism

Paglia, Camille, 1947-

★**Break,** blow, burn / Camille Paglia. Pantheon Books, 2005. xvii, 247 p. **821.009**

1. English poetry -- History and criticism 2. American poetry -- History and criticism
ISBN 0375420843

LC 2004056573

Contains 43 poems with criticism.

"This work is vintage Paglia: bracing, opinionated, and deliciously enjoyable." National Review.

821.1 English poetry--1066-1400

Armitage, Simon, 1963-

Sir Gawain and the Green Knight : a new verse translation / translated by Simon Armitage. W.W. Norton, 2007. 198 p.

; **821.1**

1. Arthur, King 2. Knights and knighthood 3. Quests 4. Honor in men 5. Temptation 6. Arthurian legends 7. Classics
ISBN 9780393060485

LC 2007028520

Middle English text, parallel English translation.

The famous Middle English poem by an anonymous Northern England poet is beautifully translated by fellow poet Simon Armitage in this edition. "Sir Gawain and the Green Knight" narrates in crystalline verse the strange tale of a green knight who rudely interrupts the Round Table festivities one Yuletide, casting a pall of unease over the company and challenging one of their number to a wager. The virtuous Gawain accepts, and decapitates the intruder with his own axe. Gushing blood, the knight reclaims his head, orders Gawain to seek him out a year hence, and departs. Next Yuletide Gawain dutifully sets forth. His quest for the Green Knight involves a winter journey, a seduction scene in a dreamlike castle, a dire challenge answered, and a drama of enigmatic reward disguised as psychic undoing.

"Armitage clearly feels a special kinship with the Gawain poet. He captures his dialect and his landscape and takes great pains to render the tale's alliterative texture and drive. His vernacular translation isn't literal--sometimes he alliterates different letters, sometimes he foreshortens the number of alliterations in a line, sometimes he changes lines altogether and so forth--but his imitation is rich and various and recreates the gnarled verbal texture of the Middle English original, which is presented in a parallel text." New York Times Book Review.

821.3 English poetry -- 1558-1625

Adamson, Robert

★The **goldfinches** of Baghdad / Robert Adamson. Flood Editions, 2006 103 p. **821.3**

1. Australian poetry
ISBN 9780974690285

LC oc2007048573

Robert Adamson has long been recognized as one of Australia's major poets, from his early writing as a poet in Sydney through twenty books of verse and prose. In The Goldfinches of Baghdad he explores the landscape of the Hawkesbury River, sounding its waters and wildlife for psychological resonances.

821.8 English poetry--1837-1899

Browning, Robert, 1812-1889

Robert Browning : the major works / edited with notes by Adam Roberts ; with an introduction by Daniel Karlin. Oxford University Press, 2005. xxxii, 828 p. ; **821.8**

1. English poetry
ISBN 9780192806260

LC 2006277696

"Including Pippa passes and courtship correspondences" --Cover.

This selection and notes originally published: 1997.

A comprehensive selection includes over eighty shorter poems, the complete text of many longer poems, three books, critical writing, and correspondence.

Rossetti, Christina Georgina, 1830-1894

Christina Rossetti : the complete poems / text [edited] by R.W. Crump ; notes and introduction by Betty S. Flowers. Penguin, 2001. lv, 1221 p. ; **821.8**

1. English poetry
ISBN 9780140423662

LC 2002281810

Presents a complete collection of poems by the English author along with a chronology, further reading, and notes.

821.914 English poetry -- 1945-1999

Hill, Geoffrey

Without title / Geoffrey Hill. Yale University Press, 2007 81 p. ; **821.914**

1. English poetry
ISBN 9780300121766

LC 2006926124

"For much of Hill's five-decade career, his forbiddingly allusive and elliptical style, his sometimes peevish tone, his interest in English church history, and his rapt pastoralism have made him an unfashionable figure, but also a highly individual one. His latest collection exhibits typical erudition... Though the method is a magpie one, the impression that emerges is of absolute control and single-mindedness. And while Hill's outlook can seem willfully bleak ... there is genuine grace in his descriptions of natural beauty." The New Yorker.

Turnbull, Gael, 1928-2004

★**There** are words : collected poems / Gael Turnbull. Mariscat Press, 2006 496 p. **821.914**

1. Scottish poetry
ISBN 9780907562894

This Collected gathers almost all of Gael Turnbull's published poetry as well as a selection of uncollected and unpublished works. --From publisher description.

822 English drama

Baker, William, 1944-

The **Facts** on File companion to Shakespeare / William Baker and Kenneth Womack. Facts On File, c2012. 2156 p. ; **822**

1. Shakespeare, William, 1564-1616
ISBN 9780816078202

LC 2010054012

The Facts On File Companion to Shakespeare is the largest and most comprehensive student's guide to Shakespeare ever published. The primary goal of this new five-volume set is to make Shakespeare's poems and plays accessible and appealing to high school and college students. Written and edited by active Shakespearean scholars and critics who have a love of teaching and explaining Shakespeare, this landmark collection presents Shakespeare's poems and plays in a whole new light for anyone interested in fully comprehending this great writer's works.

"The whole formed by these many parts makes a serviceable introduction and study guide to Shakespeare's works. Libraries that conclude they offer insufficient Shakespeare reference sources can remedy that with this highly readable and insightful set." Booklist.

Bennett, Alan, 1934-

The **history** boys / Alan Bennett. Faber and Faber, 2006. xxvii, 109 p. ; **822**

1. Boarding schools 2. Education 3. Teacher-student relationships 4.

England Drama. 5. Drama.
ISBN 0571224644

LC 2005936593

"Originally published in 2004 by Faber and Faber Limited, Great Britain"--T.p. verso.

An unruly bunch of bright, funny sixth-form (or senior) boys in a British boys' school are, as such boys will be, in pursuit of sex, sport, and a place at a good university, generally in that order. --From publisher description.

Bloom, Harold, 1930-2019

Hamlet : poem unlimited / Harold Bloom. Riverhead Books, 2004, c2003. xviii, 156 p. ; **822**

1. Shakespeare, William, 1564-1616. Hamlet. 2. Hamlet (Legendary character) 3. Tragedy.
ISBN 9781573223775

LC bl2005007573

Reprint. Originally published: 2003.

In a study of "Hamlet," the author discusses mysteries surrounding the play and its central character, discussing how both break through theatrical conventions while analyzing major soliloquies, scenes, characters, and events.

"Far superior to existing theories of performance and worth yards of criticism for each well-wrought page." Library Journal.

Lear : the great image of authority / Harold Bloom. Scribner, 2018. xi, 160 p. ; **822**

1. Shakespeare, William, 1564-1616. King Lear. 2. Lear, King (Legendary character) -- Drama 3. Kings and rulers in literature.
ISBN 9781501164194

LC 2017061767

A Sterling Professor of Humanities at Yale University and noted Shakespeare scholar presents a portrait of King Lear, who is a classic example of the fall from majesty, and explores his own personal relationship with the character.

"Bloom's short, superb book has a depth of observation acquired from a lifetime of study, and the author knows when to let Shakespeare and his play speak for themselves." Publishers Weekly.

Shakespeare : the invention of the human / Harold Bloom. Riverhead Books, 1998. xx, 745 p. **822**

1. Shakespeare, William, 1564-1616 Characters. 2. Shakespeare, William, 1564-1616 Knowledge and learning Psychology. 3. Personality in literature. 4. Humanism in literature. 5. Human nature. 6. Characters and characteristics in literature.
ISBN 1573221201

LC 98021325

National Book Award for Nonfiction finalist, 1998

"The passion and obsessiveness of Bloom's approach are its greatest recommendation." New York Review of Books.

Bolt, Robert

A **man** for all seasons : a play in two acts / Robert Bolt. Vintage Books, 1990. xxv, 163 p. ; **822**

1. More, Thomas, Saint, 1478-1535 2. Great Britain -- History -- Henry VIII, 1509-1547 3. Drama.
ISBN 9780679728221

LC 89040518

Consciences of Sir Thomas More and Henry VIII are poles apart in the religious conflict over the king's marriage to Anne Boleyn.

Boyce, Charles

Critical companion to William Shakespeare : a literary reference to his life and works / Charles Boyce. Facts On File, c2005. 800 p. ; **822**

1. Shakespeare, William, 1564-1616 Dictionaries. 2. Dramatists, English -- Early modern, 1500-1700 -- Dictionaries.
ISBN 9780816053735

LC 2004025769

Rev. ed. of: Shakespeare A to Z. 1990.

More than three thousand entries provide information on Shakespeare's life and works.

Butler, Colin

The **practical** Shakespeare : the plays in practice and on the page / Colin Butler. Ohio University Press, c2005. 205 p. ; **822**

1. Shakespeare, William, 1564-1616 Dramatic production. 2. Shakespeare, William, 1564-1616 Technique. 3. Drama -- Technique. 4. Theater -- Production and direction.
ISBN 0821416227

LC 2004030580

"Butler writes for a broad readership, but he expects the reader to have a basic grasp of the canon. Those investigating Shakespeare in performance will find Butler's book not only practical but also a good read." Choice.

Churchill, Caryl

Mad forest : a play from Romania / Caryl Churchill. Theatre Communications Group, 1996. 87 p. ; **822**

1. Romania -- History -- 1944-1989 -- Drama.
ISBN 155936114X

LC 96012875

Caryl Churchill's play about the Romanian revolution was written after she, the director, and a group of students from London's Central School of Speech and Drama went to Romania to work with acting students there. The play was first performed in 1990, only three months after their return.

Coward, Noel, 1899-1973

Three plays : Blithe spirit, Hay fever, Private lives / Noel Coward ; introduction by Philip Hoare. Vintage Books, 1999. 254 p. ; **822**

ISBN 067978179X

LC 98047414

Filled with languid aristocrats trading witticisms as they wait for martinis, this collection of three Noel Coward plays encapsulates the qualities that made him one of the most popular playwrights of the 1930s and '40s and one of the great personalities of the century.

Falk, Dan

The **science** of Shakespeare : a new look at the playwright's universe / Dan Falk. Thomas Dunne Books, 2014. xv, 364 p. **822**

1. Shakespeare, William, 1564-1616. 2. Literature and science. 3. England -- History -- 17th century.
ISBN 9781250008770

LC 2013046842

Discusses the connections between William Shakespeare and the beginnings of the scientific revolution.

"This eminently readable book should prove fascinating to both lovers of science and bardolators." Library Journal.

Frye, Northrop

Northrop Frye on Shakespeare / Northrop Frye ; edited by Robert Sandler. Yale University Press, 1986. vi, 186 p. **822**

1. Shakespeare, William, 1564-1616 Criticism and interpretation. 2. Dramatists. 3. Literature -- History and criticism 4. Rites and ceremonies.
ISBN 0300037112

LC 86050485

"These lectures represent one-third of a course in Shakespeare taught at Victoria College ... University of Toronto."--P.v.

Governor General's Literary Award for English-Language Nonfiction, 1986.

"Frye's work is completely accessible, its style crisp and engaging. Most of all, it is full of basic good sense about our most abused literary figure." Library Journal.

Fugard, Athol

Blood knot, and other plays / Athol Fugard. Theatre Communications Group, 1991. 202 p. ; **822**

1. South Africa -- Drama.
ISBN 1559360194

LC 90029029

These three Port Elizabeth plays, which established South African playwright Athol Fugard's international reputation more than twenty years ago, examine with passion and grace close family relationships strained almost unendurably by the harshest of economic and political conditions.

Fugard, Athol

★**"Master** Harold"-- and the boys / Athol Fugard. Vintage Books, 2009. 60 p. ; **822**

1. Race relations 2. South Africa Drama. 3. Drama.
ISBN 9780307475206

LC 2010292381

An argument between Master Harold, a seventeen-year-old South African, and Sam, the black man employed at Harold's mother's restaurant, makes them reevaluate their friendship.

Garber, Marjorie B.

Shakespeare after all / Marjorie Garber. Anchor Books, 2005, c2004. xii, 989 p. ; **822**

1. Shakespeare, William, 1564-1616 Criticism and interpretation Handbooks, manuals, etc.
ISBN 0385722141

LC bl2007019649

Originally published: New York : Pantheon Books, 2004.

Presents an introduction to Shakespeare's life and times through an extended commentary and presentation of his plays in chronological order.

Shakespeare and modern culture / Marjorie Garber. Pantheon Books, c2008. xxxv, 326 p. : **822**

1. Shakespeare, William, 1564-1616 Criticism and interpretation. 2. Civilization, Western. 3. Culture 4. Popular culture. 5. Modern history
ISBN 9780307377678

LC 2008026802

Addressing the continued timeliness of Shakespeare's work, a leading Shakespearean scholar reassesses ten key plays to explore the interconnection between the playwright and the modern world.

"Writing on ten plays, [Garber] offers examples of their uncanny anticipation of present-day phenomena and our own appropriations of them, as in the now fashionable use of Henry V as a blueprint for success in business. (She quotes one manual that calls Bardolph's hanging the ultimate pink slip.) Garber's approach is eclectic, spanning Freud and evolutionary biology; occasionally, she gets caught up in secondary concerns, but she is an inspiring reader." The New Yorker.

Greenblatt, Stephen, 1943-

Tyrant / Stephen Greenblatt. W W Norton & Company, 2018 208 p. **822**

1. Shakespeare, William, 1564-1616 Characters. 2. Despotism 3. Personality in literature. 4. Human nature. 5. Characters and characteristics in literature.
ISBN 9780393635751

LC 2018002449

A world-renowned Shakespeare scholar from Harvard explores the bard's insight into history's controversial, often mentally unstable, rulers, illuminating how Shakespeare's plays reflected his investigations into the social causes, psychological roots and twisted consequences of tyranny.

"An incisive and instructive study of personality politics and the abuse of powertopical literary criticism with classical virtues." Kirkus.

Heaney, Seamus, 1939-2013

The **burial** at Thebes : a version of Sophocles' Antigone / Seamus Heaney. Farrar, Straus and Giroux, 2004. 79 p. ; **822**

1. Antigone (Mythological character) Drama. 2. Tragedies. 3. Thebes (Greece) Drama.
ISBN 9780374117214

LC 2004043986

An updated version of the ancient play by Sophocles retells the tragic story of Creon and his rebellious daughter Antigone, who disobeys her father's command to leave her dead brother unburied and thus incurs the full measure of his wrath.

Kells, Stuart

Shakespeare's library : unlocking the greatest mystery in literature / Stuart Kells. Counterpoint, 2019, c2018. 322 p. ; **822**

1. Shakespeare, William, 1564-1616. 2. Books and reading. 3. Libraries. 4. Literature and society. 5. Authors, English. 6. Great Britain -- History -- Tudors, 1485-1603.
ISBN 9781640091832

LC 2018050854

An exploration of the quest to find the personal library of William Shakespeare.

Kermode, Frank, 1919-2010

Shakespeare's language / Frank Kermode. Farrar, Straus, and Giroux, 2000. x, 324 p. **822**

1. Shakespeare, William, 1564-1616 Language. 2. Shakespeare, William, 1564-1616 Style. 3. Shakespeare, William, 1564-1616 Criticism and interpretation. 4. Literary style. 5. Rhyme. 6. English language -- Early modern, 1500-1700 7. English language -- Style.
ISBN 0374226369

LC 99055846

"Kermode devotes particular attention to the four great tragedies written at the height of Shakespeare's powers: Hamlet, Othello, King Lear and Macbeth. While Kermode's concern is with the Bard's verse, he betrays no simplistic notions about literary language operating in a vacuum. A careful, close analysis of passages in each play is informed by a breathtaking knowledge of Elizabethan history and culture, as well as by the entire history of Shakespeare criticism from Coleridge to Eliot and the new historicists." Publishers Weekly.

Lamb, Charles, 1775-1834

Tales from Shakespeare / Charles and Mary Lamb ; illustrated by Arthur Rackham. Folger Shakespeare Library, 1979. xi, 363 p. : **822**

1. Shakespeare, William, 1564-1616 Paraphrases, tales, etc. 2. Drama 3. Tragedy

ISBN 9780918016041

Shakespeare's fourteen comedies and six tragedies retold in prose.

"These stories remain excellent introductions for readers of all ages engaging with Shakespeare for the first time." Library Journal

Marlowe, Christopher, 1564-1593

The **complete** plays / Christopher Marlowe ; edited by Frank Romany and Robert Lindsey. Penguin Books, 2003. xliv, 702 p. ; **822**

1. Tragedies

ISBN 9780140436334

LC 2004268858

Accompanied by a critical introduction, a biographical chronology, incisive commentary, and a glossary, this definitive dramatic collection features all seven of the plays written by Christopher Marlowe--including Dido, Queen of Carthage, The Jew of Malta, Doctor Faustus, and The Massacre at Paris.

Norwich, John Julius, 1929-2018

Shakespeare's kings : the great plays and the history of England in the Middle Ages, 1337-1485 / John Julius Norwich. Scribner, 2000. 401 p. : **822**

1. Shakespeare, William, 1564-1616 Histories. 2. Drama -- History and criticism 3. Literature and history -- Great Britain. 4. Rulers in literature. 5. Medieval civilization in literature. 6. Great Britain -- History -- Medieval period, 1066-1485 -- Historiography.

ISBN 9780684814346

LC 99058271

Originally published: London : Viking, 1999.

Compares the historical kings with their portrayal in Shakespeare's plays.

"The author offers overviews of Edward III; Richard II; Henry IV, parts 1 and 2; Henry V; Henry VI, parts 1, 2, and 3; and Richard III, examining each play through the lens of history. In addition to providing the necessary historical commentary, he also fills in the gaps between the plays, enabling readers to thoroughly comprehend the entire series in the proper historical context." Booklist.

Nuttall, A. D. (Anthony David)

Shakespeare the thinker / A.D. Nuttall. Yale University Press, c2007. xi, 428 p. ; **822**

1. Shakespeare, William, 1564-1616 Knowledge and learning. 2. England -- Intellectual life -- 16th century. 3. England -- Intellectual life -- 17th century.

ISBN 9780300119282

LC 2006035179

Offers a critical analysis of the themes, ideas, and preoccupation exemplified in the body of Shakespeare's work, including the nature of motive, cause, personal identity and relation, the status of imagination, ethics and subjectivity, and language and its capacity to occlude and communicate, in a study that emphasizes the link between great literature and its social and historical matrix.

Orton, Joe

The **complete** plays : The Ruffain on the Stair, Entertaining Mr. Sloan, the Good and Faithful Servant, Loot, the Erpingham Camp, Funeral Games, What the Butler Saw / Joe Orton ; introduced by John Lahr. Grove Weidenfeld, 1990. 448 p. ; **822**

ISBN 0802132154

LC 90003069

An Evergreen book"--P. [4] of cover.

Originally published: London : E. Methuen, 1976.

This volume contains every play written by Joe Orton, who emerged in the 1960s as the most talented comic playwright in recent English history and was considered the direct successor to Wilde, Shaw, and Coward. --From publisher description.

Osborne, John, 1929-1994

Look back in anger / John Osborne. Penguin, 1982, c1957. 96 p. ; **822**

ISBN 9780140481754

LC 82009144

Reprint. Originally published: New York : Criterion Books, 1957.

The text of the play, first performed in London in 1956, depicts the despair of post-war youth.

Pinter, Harold, 1930-2008

Complete works. Harold Pinter Grove Weidenfeld, 1990. 248 pages ; **822**

1. English drama -- 20th century. 2. Dramas

ISBN 9780802132376

LC 90013933

Collects some of the author's most famous writings, including plays, short stories, and essays.

Rasmussen, Eric, 1960-

The **Shakespeare** thefts : in search of the first folios / Eric Rasmussen. Palgrave Macmillan, 2011. 212 p. : **822**

1. Shakespeare, William, 1564-1616 Folios. 1623 History. 2. Rare books. 3. Book collecting. 4. Quests. 5. Stealing.

ISBN 9780230109414

LC 2011028287

"The first edition of Shakespeare's collected works, the First Folio, published in 1623, is one of the most valuable books in the world and has historically proven to be an attractive target for thieves. Of the 160 First Folios listed in a census of 1902, 14 were subsequently stolen-and only two of these were ever recovered. In his efforts to catalog all these precious First Folios, renowned Shakespeare scholar Eric Rasmussen embarked on a riveting journey around the globe, involving run-ins with heavily-tattooed criminal street gangs in Tokyo, bizarre visits with eccentric, reclusive billionaires, and intense battles of wills with secretive librarians. He explores the intrigue surrounding the Earl of Pembroke, arguably Shakespeare's boyfriend, to whom the First Folio is dedicated and whose personal copy is still missing. He investigates the uncanny sequence of events in which a wealthy East Coast couple drowned in a boating accident and the next week their First Folio appeared for sale in Kansas. We hear about Folios that were censored, the pages ripped out of them, about a volume that was marked in red paint--or is it blood?--on every page; and of yet another that has a bullet lodged in its pages. Part literary detective story, part Shakespearean lore, The Shakespeare Thefts will charm the Bard's many fans".-- Provided by publisher.

Rosenbaum, Ron

The **Shakespeare** wars : clashing scholars, public fiascoes, palace coups / Ron Rosenbaum. Random House, c2006. xvii,

601 p. ; **822**

1. Shakespeare, William, 1564-1616 Appreciation. 2. Shakespeare, William, 1564-1616 Criticism and interpretation History -- 20th century. 3. Shakespeare, William, 1564-1616 Dramatic production. 4. Shakespeare, William, 1564-1616 Technique.

ISBN 0375503390

LC 2006042541

Cultural historian Rosenbaum gives readers a way of rethinking the greatest works of the human imagination, as he shakes up much that we thought we understood about a vital subject and renews our sense of excitement and urgency. Rather than raking over worn-out fragments of biography, Rosenbaum focuses on cutting-edge controversies about the true source of Shakespeare's enchantment and illumination--the astonishing language itself. He takes readers into the midst of fierce battles among the most brilliant Shakespearean scholars and directors over just how to delve deeper into the mind of Shakespeare. He makes ostensibly arcane textual scholarship seductive, and he shows us great directors as Shakespearean scholars in their own right. This book offers a thrilling opportunity to engage with Shakespeare's work at its deepest levels.--From publisher description.

Shaffer, Peter, 1926-2016

★**Equus** / Peter Shaffer. Scribner, 2005. x, 112 p. ; **822**

1. Psychotherapist and patient 2. Obsessive-compulsive disorder 3. Horses 4. Teenage boys

ISBN 9780743287302

LC 2005051600

Originally published: Great Britain: Andre Deutsch, 1973.

The Tony Award-winning drama deals with a psychiatrist's exploration of the psyche of a troubled seventeen-year-old boy who senselessly and systematically blinds six horses.

Shaffer, Peter, 1926-2016

★**Peter** Shaffer's Amadeus / with an introduction by the director Sir Peter Hall and a wholly new preface by the author. Perennial, c2001. xxxiv, 124 p. ; **822**

1. Mozart, Wolfgang Amadeus, 1756-1791 Drama. 2. Salieri, Antonio, 1750-1825 Drama.

ISBN 0060935499

LC 2001278382

Originating at the National Theatre of Great Britain, Amadeus was the recipient of both the Evening Standard Drama Award and the Theatre Critics Award. In the United States, the play won the coveted Tony Award and went on to become a critically acclaimed major motion picture winning eight Oscars, including Best Picture. --From publisher description.

Shakespeare, William, 1564-1616

★The **complete** works : The Complete Works / general editors, Stanley Wells and Gary Taylor ; editors Stanley Wells ... [et al.] ; with introductions by Stanley Wells. Clarendon Press ; 2005. lxxv, 1344 p. : **822**

ISBN 0199267170

LC 2005047272

Presents the works of William Shakespeare, along with an analysis of the nature and authority of the early documents, a list of the canon and chronological order of composition, an essay on Shakespeare's language, and a bibliography.

Shapiro, James, 1955-

Contested Will : who wrote Shakespeare? / James Shapiro. Simon & Schuster, 2010. 384 p. **822**

1. Shakespeare, William, 1564-1616 Authorship. 2. Shakespeare, William, 1564-1616 Authorship Baconian theory. 3. Shakespeare, William, 1564-1616 Authorship Oxford theory. 4. Writing. 5. Literary forgeries and hoaxes.

ISBN 9781416541622

LC 2009032710

Examines current debates about the actual authors of Shakespeare's plays, citing challenges from famous historical figures while discussing the sources of modern doubts and the author's own beliefs.

"A thorough, engaging work whose arguments would prove more persuasive were we not living in an era of such fierce anti-intellectualism and pervasive conspiracy theory." Kirkus.

Shakespeare in a divided America : what his plays tell us about our past and future / James Shapiro. Penguin Press, 2020. 320 p. **822**

1. Shakespeare, William, 1564-1616 Influence. United States. 2. Influence (Literary, artistic, etc.) 3. Literature and society. 4. Theater and society. 5. Politics and literature. 6. United States

ISBN 9780525522294

LC 2019026000

The award-winning author of The Year of Lear presents a scholarly examination of how American leaders have found wisdom in the works of Shakespeare, revealing the lessons that the Bard's plays can teach about the political turbulence of today.

"Written with broad appeal and expert insight, this sparkling account deserves to be widely read." Publishers Weekly

A **year** in the life of William Shakespeare, 1599 / James Shapiro. HarperCollins Publishers, 2005. xix, 394 p., 8 p. of plates : **822**

1. Shakespeare, William, 1564-1616. 2. Shakespeare, William, 1564-1616 Homes and haunts 3. Shakespeare, William, 1564-1616. As you like it. 4. Shakespeare, William, 1564-1616. Julius Caesar. 5. Shakespeare, William, 1564-1616. Henry V. 6. Shakespeare, William, 1564-1616. Hamlet. 7. Kemp, Will. 8. Globe Theatre (London, England : 1599-1644) 9. Dramatists, English -- Early modern, 1500-1700 10. Theater -- London, England -- History -- 16th century. 11. London, England -- Social life and customs -- 16th century. 12. Southwark (London, England) -- Social life and customs. 13. Ireland -- History -- 1558-1603. 14. Great Britain -- History -- 16th century. 15. Great Britain -- Politics and government -- 1558-1603.

ISBN 9780060088736

LC 2005043342

Samuel Johnson Prize for Nonfiction, 2006.

A detailed portrait of a year in the life of the bard traces his career in 1599, which marked the building of the Globe Theater, the English invasion of Ireland, and the creation of the plays, Henry V, Julius Caesar, As You Like It, and Hamlet.

Shaw, Bernard, 1856-1950

Arms and the man : a pleasant play / Bernard Shaw ; introduction by Rodelle Weintraub ; definitive text under the editorial supervision of Dan H. Laurence. Penguin Books, 2006. xxvi, 73 p. ; **822**

ISBN 0143039768

LC 2005056724

Raina, a young woman with romantic notions of war and an idealized view of her soldier fiancé is surprised one night by a Swiss mercenary soldier seeking refuge in her bedchamber. The pragmatic Captain

Bluntschli proceeds to puncture all of Raina's illusions about love, heroism, and class. In a second duel of sex, Louka, Raina's maid, uses her wiles in her attempt to gain power. --From publisher description.

Heartbreak House : a fantasia in the Russian manner on English themes / Bernard Shaw ; definitive text under the editorial supervision of Dan H. Laurence ; with an introduction by David Hare. Penguin Books, 2000. xii, 160 p. : **822**

ISBN 0140437878

LC 2001266517

Written at the height of the first World War in Europe, an impassioned satire of the late nineteenth and early twentieth-century bourgeoisie offers a scathing portrait of a household of independent eccentrics.

Major Barbara / Bernard Shaw ; definitive text under the editorial supervision of Dan H. Laurence ; with an introduction by Margery Morgan. Penguin Books, 2000. 156 p. ; **822**

1. Salvation Army Drama. 2. Children of the rich 3. Crime 4. Didactic drama 5. Fathers and daughters 6. Drama.

ISBN 9780140437904

LC 2002275028

An enthusiastic young woman in the Salvation Army is contrasted by her wealthy and greedy father who despises poverty.

Man and Superman : a comedy and a philosophy / Bernard Shaw ; definitive text under the editorial supervision of Dan H. Laurence ; with an introduction by Stanley Weintraub. Penguin, 2000. xiv, 264 p. ; **822**

ISBN 0140437886

LC 2001266518

In Shaw's classic battle of the sexes, John Tanner flees when Ann Whitefield declares her intention to marry him.

★**Pygmalion** : a romance in five acts / George Bernard Shaw. And My fair lady, based on Shaw's Pygmalion / adaptation and lyrics by Alan Jay Lerner ; music by Frederick Loewe. Signet Classics, 2006 xiii, 219 p. ; **822**

ISBN 0451530098

LC bl2007001519

Accompanied by the adaptation and lyrics of the Broadway play "My Fair Lady," this play follows Professor Henry Higgins as he transforms a rough-hewn girl into a sophisticated lady of society.

Saint Joan : a chronicle play in six scenes and an epilogue / Bernard Shaw ; definitive text under the editorial supervision of Dan H. Laurence ; with 'On playing Joan' by Imogene Stubbs ; and an introduction by Joley Wood. Penguin Books, 2001. 163 p. ; **822**

1. Joan, of Arc, Saint, 1412-1431 Drama. 2. Christian women saints 3. Historical drama, English 4. France -- History -- Charles VII, 1422-1461 Drama. 5. Drama.

ISBN 9780140437911

LC 2002275027

Dramatizes the trial, career, and execution of Joan of Arc.

Sheridan, Richard Brinsley, 1751-1816

The **school** for scandal and other plays / Richard Brinsley Sheridan ; edited with an introduction and notes by Eric Rump. Penguin Books, 1988. 284 p. ; **822**

ISBN 014043240X

LC 89132729

"A Penguin original"--Label on cover.

Offers three plays featuring witty repartee, farcial situations and flamboyant characters by the nineteenth-century playwright known for satirizing the manners of his age.

Smith, Emma (Emma Josephine)

Shakespeare's First Folio : four centuries of an iconic book / Emma Smith. Oxford University Press, 2016. xiv, 379 p. : **822**

1. Shakespeare, William, 1564-1616. Plays. First Folio. 2. Shakespeare, William, 1564-1616 Criticism and interpretation History. 3. Shakespeare, William, 1564-1616 Bibliography Folios 4. Early printed books -- England -- 17th century

ISBN 9780198754367

LC 2015945824

This is a biography of a book: the first collected edition of Shakespeare's plays printed in 1623 and known as the First Folio. It begins with the story of its first purchaser in London in December 1623, and goes on to explore the ways people have interacted with this iconic book over the four hundred years of its history. Throughout the stress is on what we can learn from individual copies now spread around the world about their eventful lives. From ink blots to pet paws, from annotations to wineglass rings, First Folios teem with evidence of its place in different contexts with different priorities. This study offers new ways to understand Shakespeare's reception and the history of the book. Unlike previous scholarly investigations of the First Folio, it is not concerned with the discussions of how the book came into being, the provenance of its texts, or the technicalities of its production. Instead, it reanimates, in narrative style, the histories of this book, paying close attention to the details of individual copies now located around the world--their bindings, marginalia, general condition, sales history, and location--to discuss five major themes: owning, reading, decoding, performing, and perfecting. This is a history of the book that consolidated Shakespeare's posthumous reputation: a reception history and a study of interactions between owners, readers, forgers, collectors, actors, scholars, booksellers, and the book through which we understand and recognize Shakespeare.

This is Shakespeare / Emma Smith. Pantheon Books, 2020, c2019. 349 p. **822**

1. Shakespeare, William, 1564-1616 Criticism and interpretation 2. Drama -- History and criticism 3. Theater and society 4. English drama 5. England -- Social life and customs -- 17th century 6. Essays

ISBN 9781524748548

LC 2019028316

Originally published: London : Pelican Books, 2019.

A genius and prophet whose timeless works encapsulate the human condition like no other. A writer who surpassed his contemporaries in vision, originality, and literary mastery. A man who wrote like an angel, putting it all so much better than anyone else. Is this Shakespeare? Well, sort of. But it doesn't tell us the whole truth. So much of what we say about Shakespeare is either not true, or just not relevant. In This Is Shakespeare, Emma Smith takes us into a world of politicking and copycatting, as we watch Shakespeare emulating the blockbusters of Christopher Marlowe and Thomas Kyd (the Spielberg and Tarantino of their day), flirting with and skirting around the cutthroat issues of succession politics, religious upheaval, and technological change.

"Smith wears her learning lightly and writes in an accessible, conversational style, making this an excellent work for those eager to brush up their Shakespeare, forsooth." Library Journal

Stoppard, Tom

Arcadia / Tom Stoppard. Faber and Faber, 1993. 97 p.

; **822**
1. Drama
ISBN 9780571169344
LC 94103754

Arcadia takes us back and forth between the nineteenth and twentieth centuries, ranging over the nature of truth and time, the difference between the Classical and the Romantic temperament, and the disruptive influence of sex on our orbits in life. --From publisher description.

The **invention** of love / Tom Stoppard. Grove Press, 1998. v, 102 p. ; **822**
1. Housman, A. E. (Alfred Edward), 1859-1936 Drama.
ISBN 0802135811
LC 98028331

It is 1936 and A. E. Housman is being ferried across the river Styx, glad to be dead at last. The river that flows through Tom Stoppard's The Invention of Love connects Hades with the Oxford of Housman's youth: High Victorian morality is under siege from the Aesthetic movement, and an Irish student named Wilde is preparing to burst onto the London scene. --From publisher description.

★**Rosencrantz** & Guildenstern are dead / Tom Stoppard. Grove Press, 1991, c1967. 126 p. **822**
1. Hamlet (Legendary character) 2. Families of murder victims. 3. Fathers -- Death 4. Princes 5. Denmark
ISBN 9780802130334
Presents the play of Hamlet as seen through the eyes of Rosencrantz and Guildenstern.

Stott, Andrew McConnell, 1969-
What blest genius? : the jubilee that made Shakespeare / Andrew McConnell Stott. W.W. Norton & Company, [2019] 208 p. **822**
1. Shakespeare, William, 1564-1616 Anniversaries, etc. 2. Garrick, David, 1717-1779. 3. Shakespeare, William, 1564-1616 Appreciation. 4. Stratford Jubilee (1769 : Stratford-upon-Avon, England) 5. Authors, English 6. Festivals 7. English literature -- Appreciation 8. Literature -- Appreciation
ISBN 9780393248654
LC 2018051189

Recounts the 1769 Jubilee celebrating William Shakespeares work in Stratford-upon-Avon, which culturally elevated his work despite unwelcoming locals and weather flooding the streets.

Synge, J. M. (John Millington), 1871-1909
Complete plays. / John Millington Synge. Vintage Books, 1960 268 p. **822**
1. Deirdre (Legendary character) -- Drama 2. Ireland -- Drama.
ISBN 9780394701783
LC 60050766

This volume includes the complete texts of all the plays by J.M. Synge. Produced at the Abbey Theater which Synge founded. Represents one of the major dramatic achievements of the 20th century. --From publisher description.

Thomas, Dylan, 1914-1953
Under milk wood : a play for voices / Dylan Thomas. New Directions 1954 xiv, 107 p. **822**
1. Wales Drama.
ISBN 9780811202091
LC 54009641

"Music for the songs": p. 100-107.

The inhabitants of a small Welsh town must defend their sanity in a court case.

Wilde, Oscar, 1854-1900
★The **importance** of being earnest and other plays : And Other Plays / Oscar Wilde ; introduction by Terrence McNally ; notes by Michael F. Davis. Modern Library, 2003. xvi, 257 p. ; **822**
ISBN 9780812967142
LC 2003044566

The Importance of Being Earnest is a farce, playing with love, religion, and truth as it tells the tale of two men, Jack Worthing and Algernon Moncrieff, who bend the truth in order to add excitement to their lives.

Wills, Garry, 1934-
Verdi's Shakespeare : men of the theater / Garry Wills. Viking, 2011. xi, 225 p. ; **822**
1. Operas -- Italy -- 19th century. 2. Theater -- Italy -- History -- 19th century. 3. Dramatists 4. Operas, Italian.
ISBN 9780670023042
LC 2011019768

Explores the writing and staging of the Italian Romantic composer's three Shakespearian operas, offering insight into Verdi's obsessive devotion to his productions and the ways in which his intense working relationships with performers and producers paralleled Shakespeare's own style.

Yoshino, Kenji
A **thousand** times more fair : what Shakespeare's plays teach us about justice / Kenji Yoshino. Ecco Press, 2011. 320 p. **822**
1. Shakespeare, William, 1564-1616 Criticism and interpretation 2. Justice 3. Drama -- History and criticism 4. Law -- History and criticism. 5. Fairness
ISBN 9780061769108
LC 2011456758

"Readers will find Yoshino provocative, often controversial, and Shakespeare, as always, entertaining." Publishers Weekly.

822.33 William Shakespeare

MacGregor, Neil, 1946-
Shakespeare's restless world : a portrait of an era in twenty objects / Neil MacGregor. Viking Press, 2013, c2012 336 p. **822.33**
1. Shakespeare, William, 1564-1616 Characters 2. Shakespeare, William, 1564-1616 Miscellanea. 3. Material culture 4. Excavations (Archaeology) 5. England -- Social conditions -- 16th century. 6. England -- Social conditions -- 17th century. 7. England -- Antiquities 8. Great Britain -- History -- Tudors, 1485-1603.
ISBN 9780670026340
LC 2014412281

Originally published: London : Allen Lane, 2012.

"Beautifully illustrated, MacGregor's history offers a vibrant portrait of Shakespeare's dramatic, perilous and exhilarating world." Kirkus.

823 English fiction

Ackroyd, Peter, 1949-

The **death** of King Arthur: the immortal legend / Sir Thomas Malory ; a retelling by Peter Ackroyd. Viking, 2011. 336 p. **823**

1. Arthur, King 2. Grail. 3. Knights and knighthood -- Great Britain 4. Rulers 5. Love triangles 6. Great Britain -- History -- Anglo-Saxon period, 449-1066 7. Arthurian legends

ISBN 9780670023073

LC 2011021800

A modern adaptation of the legendary epic by the author of The Canterbury Tales: A Retelling adds vivid dimensions to Malory's 15th-century work using contemporary prose that makes such events as the romance between Guinevere and Lancelot, the search for the Holy Grail and the treacherous betrayal of Mordred accessible to today's audiences.

"Ackroyd takes the daunting Middle English verse and retells the ancient legends in modern English prose. He also omits most of Malory's medieval tales as perhaps too creaky for modern minds, or maybe simply to make his retelling a niftier little book. All the essential stories are here ... Ackroyd tells these stories in such simple, vivid language that they seem as new as they must have when first heard around the peat fires of cold and gloomy England perhaps 1,000 years ago. And they're still a lot of fun." Dallas Morning News.

Baker, William, 1944-

Critical companion to Jane Austen : a literary reference to her life and work / William Baker. Facts On File, c2008. xii, 644 p. : **823**

1. Austen, Jane, 1775-1817.

ISBN 9780816064168

LC 2006102848

A comprehensive guide to the English novelist includes a chronology of her life, summaries of each of her works, and entries on major characters, important places, and relevant literary terms.

Braudy, Leo

Haunted : on ghosts, witches, vampires, zombies, and other monsters of the natural and supernatural worlds / Leo Braudy. Yale University Press, 2016 306 p. **823**

1. Monsters. 2. Fear 3. Supernatural. 4. Paranormal phenomena.

ISBN 9780300203806

LC 2016937700

Includes index.

This book explores how fear has been shaped into images of monsters and monstrosity. From the Protestant Reformation to contemporary horror films and fiction, he explores four major types: the monster from nature (King Kong), the created monster (Frankenstein), the monster from within (Mr. Hyde), and the monster from the past (Dracula). Drawing upon deep historical and literary research, Braudy discusses the lasting presence of fearful imaginings in an age of scientific progress, viewing the detective genre as a rational riposte to the irrational world of the monstrous.

Carlyle, Thomas, 1795-1881

Sartor resartus / Thomas Carlyle ; edited with an introduction and notes by Kerry McSweeney and Peter Sabor. Oxford University Press, 1999. xlii, 273 p. ; **823**

1. Clothing and dress 2. Conduct of life 3. Philosophers 4. Germany 5. Didactic fiction 6. Satirical fiction 7. Classics

ISBN 9780192836731

LC 2001277126

Carlyle's enigmatic work of fiction is presented as it originally appeared, with indications of the changes the author made to later editions.

Carson, Susannah

A **truth** universally acknowledged : 33 great writers on why we read Jane Austen / edited by Susannah Carson ; foreword by Harold Bloom. Random House, c2009. xx, 295 p. ; **823**

1. Austen, Jane, 1775-1817 Appreciation. 2. Austen, Jane, 1775-1817 Influence.

ISBN 9781400068050

LC 2009012904

A erudite collection of essays considers Jane Austen's lasting influence and popularity in literary circles as well as her work's reflection of humanity, in an anthology that includes pieces by such writers as Virginia Woolf, C. S. Lewis and E. M. Forster.

Dirda, Michael

On Conan Doyle : or, the whole art of storytelling / Michael Dirda. Princeton University Press, 2011. 232 p. **823**

1. Doyle, Arthur Conan, Sir, 1859-1930 Criticism and interpretation. 2. Books and reading. 3. Books. 4. Mystery stories -- History and criticism

ISBN 9780691151359

LC 2011020674

Edgar Allan Poe Award for Best Critical/Biographical, 2012.

"Dirda is at his best in his sensitive appreciation of Doyle's style, direct, fluent, and surprisingly flexible as he moves from genre to genre, and in his account of manly civic inspiration as the value Doyle aimed above all to inculcate in his writing...An endearing, well-balanced introduction to a writer the Strand Magazine called 'the greatest natural storyteller of his age.'" Kirkus.

Edwards, Martin, 1955-

The **golden** age of murder / Martin Edwards. HarperCollins 2015. 448 p. **823**

1. Christie, Agatha, 1890-1976 2. Sayers, Dorothy L. (Dorothy Leigh), 1893-1957 3. Berkeley, Anthony, 1893-1971 4. Detection Club 5. Mystery stories -- History and criticism 6. Cold cases (Criminal investigation) 7. Secrets 8. Murder

ISBN 9780008105969

LC bl2015037974

Agatha Award for Best Nonfiction, 2015.

Edgar Allan Poe Award for Best Critical/Biographical, 2016.

Macavity Award for Best Critical/Biographical, 2016.

Looks at how the authors in the Detection Club, which came to include such personalities as Agatha Christie, G.K. Chesterton, and Dorothy Sayers, changed the way mystery novels were conceived and written in 1920s and 1930s Britain.

Ford, Paul F.

Companion to Narnia / Paul F. Ford ; foreword by Madeleine L'Engle ; illustrated by Lorinda Bryan Cauley. Harper, 1994. xlii, 460 p. : **823**

1. Lewis, C. S. (Clive Staples), 1898-1963. Chronicles of Narnia Dictionaries. 2. Children's stories, English -- Dictionaries 3. Narnia (imaginary place) 4. Fantasy fiction

ISBN 006251136X

LC 94027063

An updated handbook on C. S. Lewis's magical world of Narnia encompasses hundreds of alphabetically arranged entries that include the characters, events, places, themes, and other aspects of the enchanting fantasy series.

French, Paul, 1966-

City of devils : the two men who ruled the underworld of old Shanghai / Paul French. Picador, 2018. xvi, 299 p., 16 unnumbered p. of plates : **823**

1. Criminals 2. Organized crime 3. Americans in China 4. Casinos 5. Shanghai, China 6. China -- History -- 20th century
ISBN 9781250170583

LC 2017060113

Traces the rags-to-riches story of self-made casino gangsters Jack Riley and Joe Farren, drawing on eyewitness accounts, letters and articles to trace their activities in the 1930s Shanghai underworld.

Greene, Graham, 1904-1991

Graham Greene : a life in letters / edited by Richard Greene. W.W. Norton, 2008, c2007. xxxiv, 446 p., 8 p. of plates : **823**

1. Greene, Graham, 1904-1991 Correspondence. 2. Novelists, English -- 20th century 3. Letters
ISBN 9780393066425

LC 2008040452

First published: London : Little, Brown, 2007.

An autobiographical account in letters offers insight into the late-twentieth-century author's political influence, espionage activities, and personal life, in a volume that also covers how his work was influenced by his humanitarian visits to Mexico, Vietnam, and Cuba.

"Greene is presented in these letters through the five main preoccupations of his life: Roman Catholicism, politics, love, travel and...the processes of writing and publishing. This well-thought-out collection newly reveals a remarkable activist-writer." Publishers Weekly.

Head, Dominic

★The **Cambridge** introduction to modern British fiction, 1950-2000 / Dominic Head. Cambridge University Press, 2002. viii, 307 p. ; **823**

1. English fiction -- 20th century -- History and criticism.
ISBN 0521660149

LC 2001043261

"Anyone with an interest in the contemporary novel, not just British fiction, will appreciate this outstanding survey and analysis. The quality of discussion is admirably consistent within and between each chapter, the prose as carefully crafted as the judgments are measured. This book should become a standard reference work for its subject." Choice.

Huxley, Aldous, 1894-1963

★**Brave** new world revisited / Aldous Huxley. Harper Perennial Modern Classics, 2006, c1958. 123, 14 p. ; **823**

1. Culture 2. Propaganda 3. Brainwashing
ISBN 9780060898526

LC bl2007012306

Originally published: New York : Harper, 1958. With additional material.

Written thirty years after his epic novel Brave New World, a thoughtprovoking sequel describes the shocking scientific devices and techniques available to any group in a position to manipulate society.

Iyer, Pico

The **man** within my head / Pico Iyer. Random House Inc, 2012. 240 p. **823**

1. Greene, Graham, 1904-1991. 2. Fathers and sons. 3. Books and reading. 4. Voyages and travels.
ISBN 9780307267610

LC 2011041285

Recounts the author's life-long obsession with Graham Greene's writings on the experiences of being an outsider, which informed both the author's travels and his private explorations of his relationship with his elusive father.

James, P. D.

Talking about detective fiction / P.D. James. Alfred A. Knopf, 2009. viii, 198 p. : **823**

1. Characters and characteristics in literature. 2. Detectives in literature. 3. Mystery story writing 4. Mystery stories -- History and criticism
ISBN 9780307592828

LC 2009038501

Anthony Award for Best Critical/Nonfiction, 2010.

Macavity Award for Best Non-Fiction, 2010.

To judge by the worldwide success of Arthur Conan Doyle's Sherlock Holmes and Agatha Christie's Poirot, it is not only the Anglo-Saxons who have an appetite for mystery and mayhem. Talking about the craft of detective writing and sharing her personal thoughts and observations on one of the most popular and enduring forms of literature, P.D. James examines the challenges, achievements and potential of a genre which has fascinated her for nearly fifty years as a novelist.

Jones, Wendy S.

Jane on the brain : exploring the science of social intelligence with Jane Austen / Wendy Jones. Pegasus Books, 2017. 336 p. **823**

1. Austen, Jane, 1775-1817. 2. Characters and characteristics in literature. 3. Psychology and literature. 4. Neuroscience. 5. Psychology.
ISBN 9781681775548

LC 2017277389

An Austen scholar and therapist reveals Jane Austen's intuitive ability to imbue her characters with hallmarks of social intelligence, and how these beloved works of literature can further illuminate the mind-brain connection.

"In a fascinating mash-up of literary analysis and neuroscience, psychotherapist and former English professor Jones attributes Jane Austen's everlasting appeal to her ability to empathize." Booklist.

Kelly, Helena, 1981-

Jane Austen, the secret radical / Helena Kelly. New York, 2017. 352 p. **823**

1. Austen, Jane, 1775-1817 Political and social views. 2. Social problems in literature. 3. Literature and society 4. Social change 5. Feminism
ISBN 9781524732103

LC 2016042656

An authority on Jane Austen invites readers to look deeper into the author's work and see her true, subversive nature which brought to life radical subjects including slavery, poverty, feminism, the Church and evolution between the pages of her demure drawing rooms.

"A fine-grained study that shows us how to read between the lines to discover the remarkable woman who helped transform the novel from trash to an absolute art form." Kirkus.

Kiberd, Declan

Ulysses and us : the art of everyday life in Joyce's masterpiece / Declan Kiberd. W.W. Norton & Co., 2009. 416 p. **823**

1. Joyce, James, 1882-1941. Ulysses Criticism and interpretation 2. Personal conduct in literature 3. Influence (Literary, artistic, etc.)
ISBN 9780393070996

LC 2009014101

Explores the lessons that modern readers can draw from Joyce's classic work, revealing how Ulysses offers a more humane vision of a more tolerant and decent society in which seemingly banal hero, Leopold Bloom, represents ordinary wisdom that can offer a model for living.

Lynskey, Dorian

The **ministry** of truth : the biography of George Orwell's 1984 / Dorian Lynskey. Doubleday, 2019. 256 p. **823**

1. Orwell, George, 1903-1950. Nineteen eighty-four 2. Authors, English -- 20th century 3. Literature -- History and criticism 4. Influence (Literary, artistic, etc.) 5. Political culture -- History -- 20th century

ISBN 9780385544054

LC 2019937137

The Ministry of Truth is the first book that fully examines the epochal and cultural event that is 1984 in all its aspects: its roots in the utopian and dystopian literature that preceded it; the personal experiences in wartime Great Britain that Orwell drew on as he struggled to finish his masterpiece in his dying days; and the political and cultural phenomena that the novel ignited at once upon publication and that far from subsiding, have only grown over the decades.

"Lynskey maps the vast influence of Nineteen Eighty-Four in discussions of its stage and screen adaptations, its language, from doublethink to Newspeak, thoughtcrime, unperson, and Big Brother, and the many novels it inspired, including." Booklist.

Malory, Thomas, Sir, 15th cent

Le morte Darthur, or, The hoole book of Kyng Arthur and of his noble knyghtes of the Rounde Table : authoritative text, sources and backgrounds, criticism / Sir Thomas Malory ; edited by Stephen H.A. Shepherd. Norton, c2004. lii, 954 p. ; **823**

1. Malory, Thomas, Sir, 15th cent. Le Morte d'Arthur 2. Knights and knighthood 3. Rulers 4. Arthurian legends

ISBN 9780393974645

LC 2002026534

A primary and secondary source to the 15th-century prose saga for students of English literature. The text includes footnotes explaining terms and references, and marginal references to manuscript pages. --From publisher description.

Miller, Laura, 1960-

The **magician's** book : a skeptic's adventures in Narnia / Laura Miller. Little, Brown and Co., 2008. 311 p. **823**

1. Lewis, C. S. (Clive Staples), 1898-1963 Criticism and interpretation. 2. Lewis, C. S. (Clive Staples), 1898-1963. Chronicles of Narnia. 3. Lewis, C. S. (Clive Staples), 1898-1963 Influence. 4. Authors -- 20th century 5. Books and reading. 6. Children's stories, English -- History and criticism 7. Fantasy fiction -- History and criticism

ISBN 9780316017633

LC 2008020629

Includes index.

Explores the meaning and influence of C. S. Lewis' Chronicles of Narnia series while revealing how Lewis's troubled childhood, unconventional love life, and friendship with J. R. R. Tolkien affected his writing.

Murdoch, Iris

Living on paper : letters from Iris Murdoch, 1934-1995 / Iris Murdoch and edited by Avril Horner and Anne Rowe. Princeton University Press, 2016, c2015. xx, 666 pages, 16 unnumbered pages of plates : **823**

1. Murdoch, Iris -- Correspondence. 2. Women authors, English -- 20th century -- Correspondence 3. Letters.

ISBN 9780691170565

LC 2015952098

"First published in 2015 by Chatto & Windus"--Title page verso.

"An impressively edited, sharply revealing life in letters." Kirkus.

Olsen, Kirstin

All things Austen : an encyclopedia of Austen's world / Kirstin Olsen. Greenwood Press, 2005. 2 v. (xxii, 804 p.) : **823**

1. Austen, Jane, 1775-1817 2. Novelists, English -- 19th century 3. Women and literature -- England -- History -- 19th century

ISBN 9780313330322

LC 2004028664

Alphbetically arranged entries on the world of the English author, covering the social customs and culture of her time and including such topics as etiquette, gentry, marriage, religion, travel, and servants.

"This well-written and meticulously researched work provides a convenient means for general readers, students, and scholars to gain a better understanding of the social, cultural, and political climate of Austen's time." Booklist.

Saler, Michael T., 1960-

As if : modern enchantment and the literary pre-history of virtual reality / Michael Saler. Oxford University Press, c2012. x, 283 p. : **823**

1. Fantastic, The, in literature. 2. Imaginary societies in literature. 3. Marvelous, The, in literature. 4. Virtual reality in literature.

ISBN 0195343174

LC 2011010276

From Lovecraft's Cthulhu Mythos and Tolkien's Middle-earth to the World of Warcraft and Second Life, As If provides a cultural history that reveals how we can remain enchanted but not deluded in an age where fantasy and reality increasingly intertwine. --From publisher description.

Standiford, Les

The **man** who invented Christmas : how Charles Dickens's "A Christmas carol" rescued his career and revived our holiday spirits / Les Standiford. Crown Publishers, 2008. 256 p. **823**

1. Dickens, Charles, 1812-1870. Christmas carol. 2. Christmas stories, English -- History and criticism 3. Christmas -- Great Britain -- History. 4. Christmas in literature. 5. Holidays. 6. England -- Social life and customs -- 19th century. 7. Great Britain -- Social life and customs -- 19th century.

ISBN 9780307405784

LC 2008014978

A study of the story behind "A Christmas Carol" describes how Charles Dickens self-published the holiday classic, revitalizing his failing literary career and reviving the celebration of Christmas amid the struggles of the Industrial Revolution.

Woolf, Virginia, 1882-1941

The **Virginia** Woolf reader / edited by Mitchell A. Leaska. Harcourt Brace Jovanovich, c1984. ix, 371 p. ; **823**

ISBN 9780156935906

LC 84004478

"A Harvest/HBJ book."

Presents five short stories, essays, correspondence, and selections from four novels by the prominent British author.

Zoob, Caroline

Virginia Woolf's garden : the story of the garden at Monk's house / Caroline Zoob with photography by Caroline Arber ; foreword by Cecil Woolf. Jacqui Small, 2013. 192 p. : **823**

1. Woolf, Virginia, 1882-1941 2. Woolf, Leonard, 1880-1969 3. Literary landmarks 4. Gardens 5. Orchards 6. Country homes 7. Sussex, England 8. England
ISBN 9781909342132

LC oc2013128344

This chronological account takes you through the key events in the lives of Virginia and Leonard Woolf through a history of their home, Monk's House in Sussex, where Virginia wrote most of her major novels. --From publisher description.

"Striking archival photographs mix well with Caroline Arber's radiant color shots, and Zoob is the best possible guide, having moved into Monk's House, which is owned by the National Trust, with her husband in 2000, and tended the garden for more than a decade." Booklist.

823.009 English fiction--history and criticism

Richetti, John J.

The **Columbia** history of the British novel / John Richetti, editor ; John Bender, Deirdre David, Michael Seidel, associate editors. Columbia University Press, c1994. xix, 1064 p. ; **823.009**

1. English fiction -- History and criticism. 2. Essays
ISBN 9780231078580

LC 92035749

Includes index.

Essays discuss the beginnings of the art form, the social background which produced "Tom Jones," Kipling's works, sexuality, eroticism, women's emancipation, and more.

824 English essays

Amis, Martin

★The **rub** of time : Bellow, Nabokov, Hitchens, Travolta, Trump: essays and reportage, 1986-2017 / Martin Amis. Alfred A. Knopf, 2018. 336 p. **824**

1. Literary journalism. 2. Essays
ISBN 9781400044535

LC 2017017321

"This is a Borzoi book"
Includes index.

The definitive collection of essays and reportage written during the past thirty years from one of most provocative and widely read writers--with new commentary by the author. For more than thirty years, Amis has turned his keen intellect and unrivaled prose loose on an astonishing range of topics--politics, sports, celebrity, America, and, of course, literature. Now, at last, these incomparable essays have been gathered together.

"Amis writes with buoyant and cutting authority. His vocabulary, cross-pollinated by his trans-Atlantic reading and life, is pinpointed and peppery; his syntax supple and ensnaring. The pleasure Amis takes in observation, cogitation, and composition is palpable, and he is acidly funny." Booklist.

Cole, Teju

★**Known** and strange things : essays / Teju Cole. Random House, 2016. 384 p. **824**

1. Travelers. 2. Men -- Psychology. 3. Voyages and travels. 4. Photography. 5. Essays
ISBN 9780812989786

LC 2015042074

The award-winning author of Open City and Every Day Is for the Thief presents a collection of more than 50 essays on politics, photography, travel, history and literature that provide a fresh new interpretation of art, people and historical moments.

"A bold, honest, and controversially necessary read." Kirkus.

Dyer, Geoff

White sands : experiences from the outside world / Geoff Dyer. Pantheon Books, [2016] 240 p. **824**

1. Voyages and travels 2. Travelers 3. Place (Philosophy) 4. Identity (Philosophical concept) 5. Essays
ISBN 9781101870853

LC 2015030019

In Geoff Dyer's latest thought-provoking book, a small volume of travel essays, he asks big questions: who are we? why are we here? Pondering them, he journeys to a variety of disparate locales, including Beijing to visit the Forbidden City, Tahiti to learn about the artist Gauguin, Norway to see the Northern Lights (though he didn't see them), New Mexico to see the land art installation "The Lightning Field," and Los Angeles to visit philosopher Theodor Adorno's former home. Photographs enhance the witty and astute observations by the sometimes persnickety Dyer, who also addresses his recent mild stroke in the final essay of this fascinating collection.

"A mesmerizing compendium that reflects on time, place, and just what, exactly, we are doing here." Kirkus.

Kermode, Frank, 1919-2010

★**Pieces** of my mind : essays and criticism, 1958-2002 / Frank Kermode. Farrar, Straus and Giroux, 2003. xii, 466 p. **824**

1. Criticism. 2. Essays.
ISBN 0809076012

LC 2003054727

"The author parses complicated, even esoteric aspects of story and text, metaphysics and poetry, and the link between social change and the evolution of the novel, yet he is unfailingly clear and cheerfully engaging, classy, and stimulating." Booklist.

O'Faolain, Nuala

A **radiant** life : the selected journalism of Nuala O'Faolain / Nuala O'Faolain ; [introduction by Fintan O'Toole]. Abrams Image, 2011. xiv, 302 p. ; **824**

1. Essays
ISBN 9780810998063

LC 2010037687

Selected columns previously published in the The Irish times, and other writings, from the 1980's through 2008.

Collects the columns of Irish journalist Nuala O'Faolain, who tackled a vast range of subjects--from Catholicism to feminism, from Sinatra to Africa, and from Irish American culture to Islam and the West.

Orwell, George, 1903-1950

Essays / George Orwell ; selected and introduced by John Carey. Alfred A. Knopf, 2002. xlv, 1369 p. ; **824**

1. English essays -- 20th century 2. Essays
ISBN 9780375415036

LC bl2013040560

In a varied compilation of essays, the author of Animal Farm and 1984 reflects on a wide range of social, political, and literary issues of his time, in selections that capture his firm belief in social justice, universal freedom and equality, and truth in language, in such pieces as "My Country Right or Left," "Shooting an Elephant," and "A Nice Cup of Tea."

"The real reason we read Orwell is because his own fault-line, his fundamental schism, his hybridity, left him exceptionally sensitive to the fissure--which is everywhere apparent--between what ought to be the case and what actually is the case. He says the unsayable." Financial Times.

Smith, Zadie

Changing my mind : occasional essays / Zadie Smith. Penguin Press, 2009. 320 p. **824**

1. Smith, Zadie. 2. Fiction writing. 3. Film reviews 4. Families 5. Authors -- Criticism and interpretation 6. Essays

ISBN 9781594202377

LC 2009023419

Zadie Smith offers a collection of essays penned between 1999 and 2009.

"The author has organized this collection of essays into sections on reading, being, seeing, feeling, and remembering to create a strong and piquant collection. As the title implies, Smith's thinking evolves before our eyes as she articulates her responses to art and life. Smith is a superb essayist of skill, candor, and caring." Booklist.

Smith, Zadie

★**Feel** free : essays / Zadie Smith. Penguin Press, 2018 448 p. **824**

1. Social media 2. Race relations 3. Political culture 4. Essays

ISBN 9781594206252

LC 2017478938

In a collection of essays arranged into five sections--In the World, In the Audience, In the Gallery, On the Bookshelf, and Feel Free--the best-selling author discusses important questions about our world that readers will immediately recognize.

"In this collection of conversational essays, novelist Smith (Swing Time) brings her precise observations and distinct voice to an expansive range of topics." Publishers Weekly.

Smith, Zadie

Intimations : six essays / Zadie Smith. Penguin Books, 2020. 97 p. **824**

1. Smith, Zadie 2. Social isolation 3. Epidemics 4. Current events 5. Violence against minorities 6. Essays

ISBN 9780593297612

LC 2020027444

Written during the early months of lockdown, Intimations explores ideas and questions prompted by an unprecedented situation. What does it mean to submit to a new reality--or to resist it? How do we compare relative sufferings? What is the relationship between time and work? In our isolation, what do other people mean to us? What is the ratio of contempt to compassion in a crisis? When an unfamiliar world arrives, what does it reveal about the world that came before it? Suffused with a profound intimacy and tenderness in response to these extraordinary times, Intimations is a slim, suggestive volume with a wide scope, in which Zadie Smith clears a generous space for thought, open enough for each reader to reflect on what has happened--and what should come next.

"In just under 100 pages, Smith intimately captures the profundity of our current historical moment. Quietly powerful, deftly crafted essays bear witness to the contagion of suffering." Kirkus

Young, Ashleigh

Can you tolerate this? : essays / Ashleigh Young. Riverhead Books, 2018, c2016. 256 p. **824**

1. Purpose in life. 2. Human behavior. 3. Identity (Psychology) 4. Misfits (Persons) 5. New Zealand -- Social life and customs. 6. Essays.

ISBN 9780525534037

LC 2017057498

Collects 21 essays.

Originally published: Wellington, NZ : Victoria University Press, 2016.

Ockham New Zealand Book Awards, General Nonfiction, 2017.

An already prize-winning collection of essays on youth and aging, ambition and disappointment, Katherine Mansfield tourism and New Zealand punk rock and the limitations of the body.

824.914 English essays -- 1945-1999

Dyer, Geoff

Otherwise known as the human condition : selected essays and reviews / Geoff Dyer. Farrar Straus & Giroux, 2011. 384 p. **824.914**

1. Culture. 2. Art. 3. Music. 4. Writing. 5. Essays.

ISBN 9781555975791

LC 2010937517

"A grab-bag of critical essays, reportage and personal stories from the irrepressibly curious Dyer. The title of this hefty tome, featuring pieces published in two United Kingdom-only collections, suggests ponderous philosophizing. But though Dyer takes his art seriously, his prose is as relaxed and self-effacing as it is informed. Though the book is wide-ranging, his command is consistent, whether he's writing about Richard Avedon or model airplanes." Kirkus.

828 English miscellaneous writings

DeGategno, Paul J.

Critical companion to Jonathan Swift : a literary reference to his life and works / Paul J. deGategno, R. Jay Stubblefield. Facts on File, c2006. vi, 474 p. : **828**

1. Swift, Jonathan, 1667-1745 Encyclopedias 2. Swift, Jonathan, 1667-1745 Handbooks, manuals, etc. 3. Church of Ireland Clergy Biography Handbooks, manuals, etc.. 4. Satire, English -- History and criticism -- Handbooks, manuals, etc. 5. Authors, Irish -- 18th century -- Biography -- Handbooks, manuals, etc.

ISBN 9780816050932

LC 2005025470

Presents a guide to the life and literary accomplishments of the Irish author, including analyses of the contents and characters of each of his works and discussions on places and events in his life which influenced his writing.

James, Clive, 1939-2019

As of this writing : the essential essays, 1968-2002 / Clive James. W.W. Norton, c2003. xix, 619 p. ; **828**

1. Modern literature -- 20th century -- History and criticism. 2. Authors -- 20th century -- Criticism and interpretation. 3. Political culture. 4. Film criticism. 5. Essays. 6. Anthologies.

ISBN 9780393051803

LC 2003041257

Includes index.

"James writes with fluent wit, remarkable warmth, deep knowledge, and an exhilarating sense of mission." Booklist.

Johnson, Samuel, 1709-1784
The **major** works : The Major Works / Samuel Johnson ; edited with an introduction and notes by Donald Greene. Oxford University Press, 2000. xxxii, 840 p. ; **828**
ISBN 0192840428
LC 2001277128

It brings together a unique combination of Johnson's poetry and prose--all the major poems, complemented by essays, criticism, and fiction--to give the essence of his work and thinking. --From publisher description.

Orwell, George, 1903-1950
★**Diaries** / George Orwell ; edited by Peter Davison ; introduction by Christopher Hitchens. Liveright, 2012. 608 p. **828**
1. Orwell, George, 1903-1950 Diaries. 2. Authors. 3. Writing. 4. Diaries.
ISBN 9780871404107
LC 2012009895

"The diaries will appeal to all -- literary scholars, historians, and students of 20th-century literature -- seeking the inner life of this profoundly influential writer. Strongly recommended." Library Journal.

Rosset, Barney
Dear Mr. Beckett : the Samuel Beckett file / Barney Rosset ; foreword by Edward Beckett ; preface by Paul Auster ; edited by Lois Oppenheim ; curated by Astrid Myers Rosset. Opus, 2017. 473 p. : **828**
1. Beckett, Samuel, 1906-1989. 2. Beckett, Samuel, 1906-1989 Correspondence. 3. Rosset, Barney. 4. Rosset, Barney Correspondence. 5. Grove Press -- History. 6. Dramatists -- 20th century. 7. Authors, French -- 20th century 8. Authors, Irish -- 20th century 9. Literature, Modern -- History and criticism. 10. Letters
ISBN 9781623160708

Through letters, contracts, photos, interviews, speeches, reviews, and memorabilia--most of which has never before been made public--a rare personal and professional friendship unfolds between these two oddly shy daredevils, shifting and turning the tide of literature in America. Barney Rosset, more than any other publisher, fiercely advocated for the most daring and influential writers of the 20th century. Through his Grove imprint, whole generations have embraced some of the greatest playwrights of our time, including Genet, Pinter, Mamet, Ionesco, D.H. Lawrence, and of course Samuel Beckett. Scholars, students, and fans of literary letters will find this volume beguiling reading.--Publisher.

829 Old English (Anglo-Saxon) literature

Delanty, Greg, 1958-
The **word** exchange : Anglo-Saxon poems in translation / edited by Greg Delanty, Michael Matto. W.W. Norton, c2011. xvii, 557 p. ; **829**
1. English poetry -- Old English, ca. 450-1100 -- Modernized versions. 2. English poetry -- Old English, ca. 450-1100.
ISBN 9780393079012
LC 2010028560

More than seventy of today's most celebrated poets, including Seamus Heaney, Robert Pinsky, and Molly Peacock, present new translations of Anglo-Saxon poetry that give life to medieval English voices ranging from weary sailors and forlorn wives to farmers and drunken louts.

Heaney, Seamus, 1939-2013
Beowulf / translated by Seamus Heaney. Farrar, Straus and Giroux, 1999 208 p. **829**
1. Beowulf 2. Heroes and heroines, Scandinavian 3. Monsters 4. Dragons 5. Epic poetry.
ISBN 0374111197
LC 99023209

Irish poet Seamus Heaney's award-winning translation of the Anglo-Saxon epic chronicling the heroic adventures of Beowulf, the Scandinavian warrior who saves his people from the ravages of the monster Grendel and Grendel's mother.

"He draws upon his own considerable skill as a poet and his love of the sound of language to effect this brilliant translation which, despite his predilection for "weighty distinctness," verges on melody. Overall, he has a tendency to avoid Old English's appositional syntax and prefers that a line make sense rather than adhere strictly to alliterative conventions. For the modern reader, these are improvements over earlier translations. Mr. Heaney does a most creditable job of stripping off the layers of venerable varnish and letting the classic tale resound in the "big voiced" style of its mortal heroes." Kirkus

830 German literature and literatures of related languages

Schiller, Friedrich, 1759-1805
Don Carlos ; and, Mary Stuart / Friedrich Schiller ; translated with notes by Hilary Collier Sy-Quia ; adapted in verse drama by Peter Oswald ; with an introduction by Lesley Sharpe. Oxford University Press, 2008. xxx, 359 p. : **830**
1. Carlos, Prince of Asturias, 1545-1568 Drama. 2. Mary, Queen of Scots, 1542-1587 Drama.
ISBN 0199540748
LC 2008275155

Don Carlos and Mary Stuart, two of German literature's greatest historical dramas, deal with the timeless issues of power, freedom, and justice. Dating from 1787 and 1800 respectively, one play was written immediately before the French Revolution, the other in its aftermath. --From publisher description.

831 German poetry

Celan, Paul
Breathturn into timestead : the collected later poetry : a bilingual edition / Paul Celan ; translated from the German and with commentary by Pierre Joris. Farrar, Straus and Giroux, 2014. lxxviii, 654 p. ; **831**
1. Bilingual materials English/German
ISBN 9780374125981
LC 2014020543

"A collection of the late poems of German-language poet Paul Celan".-- Provided by publisher.

"Celan's poetry focuses on a new (and very ancient) kind of light: the light of 'the other's Other,' the dark, invisible light beyond all fictions of the abyssal non-origin of being, time, and space. Poetry suffers from what Celan calls Lichtzwang, light duress, which has prevented poetry from 'darkening over' to its essence. Summing Up: Highly recommended. Upper-division undergraduates through faculty." Choice.

Goethe, Johann Wolfgang von, 1749-1832
Selected poetry / Johann Wolfgang von Goethe ; translated with an introduction and notes by David Luke. Penguin Books,

2005, c1999. xliv, 283 p. ; **831**

1. German poetry
ISBN 9780140424560

LC bl2007011896

Originally published: London : Libris, 1999.

Presents a collection of Goethe's best and most famous poems, in the original German with English translation.

Hofmann, Michael, 1957 August 25-

Twentieth-century German poetry : an anthology / edited by Michael Hofmann. Farrar, Straus and Giroux, 2006. xxvii, 511 p. ; **831**

1. German poetry -- 20th century
ISBN 9780374105358

LC 2006006873

Originally published as The Faber Book of 20th-Century German Poems: London : Faber and Faber, 2005.

A bilingual anthology features translations of works by major German poets ranging from Rilke and Brecht to Durs Gr|nbein and Jan Wagner and includes pieces that reflect Germany's history, the fear and dissent of its citizens, and its experiences with division and reunification.

Rilke, Rainer Maria, 1875-1926

Ahead of all parting : the selected poetry and prose of Rainer Maria Rilke / edited and translated by Stephen Mitchell. Modern Library, 1995. xiii, 615 p. ; **831**

1. Rilke, Rainer Maria, 1875-1926 2. German poetry
ISBN 9780679601616

LC 94043917

Includes indexes.

Presents a collection of the twentieth-century German poet's collected and uncollected works, as well as passages from his novel, "The Notebooks of Malte Laurids Brigge."

★**Duino** elegies / Rainer Maria Rilke ; translated from the German by David Young ; with an introduction and commentary. W. W. Norton, 2006. 202 p. ; **831**

1. Rilke, Rainer Maria, 1875-1926 Translations into English. 2. German poetry
ISBN 9780393328844

LC 2006009872

"This translation was originally published in Field, Contemporary Poetry and Poetics, issues 5 through 9. Reissued in Norton paperback editions 1992, 2006."

New poems / Rainer Maria Rilke ; selected and translated by Edward Snow. North Point Press, 2001. xii, 329 p. ; **831**

1. German poetry
ISBN 9780865476127

LC 2001042714

"The translations in this book were originally published in two separate volumes: New poems (Neue Gedichte) in 1984 and New poems: the other part ((Der neuen Gedichte anderer Teil) in 1987"--Pref.

Includes indexes.

Originally published in two volumes in 1907 and 1908, this collection of poetry, now available in a superlative new translation, by the acclaimed poet includes such works as "The Panther" and "Archaic Torso of Apollo."

★**Sonnets** to Orpheus / Rainer Maria Rilke ; translated from the German by M.D. Herter Norton. W.W. Norton, 2006, c1942. 160 p. ; **831**

1. German poetry
ISBN 9780393328851

LC oc2007045642

German and English on opposite pages.

832 German drama

Durrenmatt, Friedrich

The **visit;** a tragi-comedy. / Friedrich Durrenmatt ; translated from the German by Patrick Bowles. Grove Press, 1962 109 p. **832**

1. Tragicomedy
ISBN 9780802130662

LC 62016341

A millionairess returns to her home town to seek revenge on a man who wronged her in her youth.

Goethe, Johann Wolfgang von, 1749-1832

★**Goethe's** Faust / translated by by Walter Kaufmann. Anchor Books, 1989, c1961. 503 p. ; **832**

1. Faustian bargains 2. Devil 3. Contracts 4. Temptation 5. Classics
ISBN 9780385031141

LC 89018328

"Part one and sections from part two."

The best translation of Faust available, this volume provides the original German text and its English counterpart on facing pages. --From publisher description.

833 German fiction

Sebald, W. G. (Winfried Georg), 1944-2001

★**On** the natural history of destruction / W.G. Sebald ; translated by Anthea Bell. Modern Library, 2004. x, 202 p. : **833**

1. Bombing, Aerial -- Germany. 2. German literature -- 20th century -- History and criticism. 3. World War II -- Destruction and pillage -- Germany. 4. World War II -- Literature and the war.
ISBN 0375756574

LC 2004269961

"Originally published in German by Hanser as Luftkrieg und Literatur in 1999 and in slightly different form:--T.p. verso.

In a profound, thought-provoking meditation, the award-winning author of After Nature reflects on the topics of individual and collective guilt, the consequences of denying the past, and the need to reclaim history as he examines why Germans have maintained silence on World War II, the Allied bombing that destroyed German cities, and the resulting devastation.

838 German miscellaneous writings

Grass, Gunter, 1927-2015

Of all that ends / Gunter Grass ; translated from the German by Breon Mitchell. Houghton Mifflin Harcourt, 2016. 167 pages : **838**

1. Grass, Gunter, 1927-2015 2. Aging 3. Writing 4. Essays
ISBN 9780544785380

LC 2018295490

Contains fiction, poetry, and original artwork by the author.

A final major collection by the late Nobel Prize-winning author is comprised of lighthearted and elegiac meditations on writing, aging and the world.

"Fractured but elegant musings on dying and, most poignantly, living." Kirkus.

839 Other Germanic literatures

Smiley, Jane,

★The **sagas** of Icelanders: a selection / preface by Jane Smiley; introduction by Robert Kellogg. Viking, 2000. 782 p. : **839**

1. Heroes and heroines, Norse. 2. Epic poetry
ISBN 0670889903

LC 99044111

"The sagas and tales in this book are reprinted from the Complete sagas of Icelanders I-V, published 1997 by Leifur Eiriksson Publishing, Iceland, with minor alterations"--P. [lviii].

"The Icelandic Sagas are among the masterpieces of world literature whose composition stretches from about the year 1000 to 1500. Presenting the adventures of Norse and Viking heroes, the sagas are told with ritual simplicity and a realism that anticipate the modern novel." Library Journal.

839.7 Swedish literature

Strindberg, August, 1849-1912

Strindberg : five plays / August Strindberg ; translated from the Swedish, with an introduction, by Harry G. Carlson. University of California Press, c1983. 297 p. ; **839.7**

1. Strindberg, August, 1849-1912 Translations into English.
ISBN 9780520046986

LC 82015882

Strindberg's most important and most frequently performed plays--The Father, Miss Julie, A Dream Play, The Dance of Death, and The Ghost Sonata--are gathered together here in translations praised for their fluency and their elegance. --From publisher description.

839.71 Swedish poetry

Tranströmer, Tomas, 1931-2015

The **great** enigma : new collected poems / Tomas Tranströmer ; translated from the Swedish by Robin Fulton. New Directions Pub., 2006. xxii, 262 p. ; New Directions paperbook ; **839.71**

1. Transtromer, Tomas, 1931-2015
ISBN 9780811216722

LC 2006022551

"A New Directions paperbook original, NDP1050"--P. [4] of cover.

Includes index.

Firmly rooted in the natural world, his work falls between dream and dream; it probes "the great unsolved love" with the opening up, through subtle modulations, of "concrete words." --From publisher description.

"The major contemporary poet of Scandinavia, and a perennial Nobel Prize candidate (so rumor has it), Tranströmer and his compact, sometimes grim lyricism have long enjoyed a serious following in the United States. This version from the Scot Fulton (whose first Tranströmer selection appeared in 1987) contains everything Tranströmer has published in book form." Publishers Weekly.

839.8 Danish and Norwegian literatures

Ibsen, Henrik, 1828-1906

The **complete** major prose plays / Henrik Ibsen ; translated [from the Norwegian] and introduced by Rolf Fjelde. New American Library, 1978. vi, 1143 p. ; **839.8**

1. Ibsen, Henrik, 1828-1906 Translations into English.
ISBN 9780452262058

LC 78050714

Gathers the Norwegian writer's most important dramas, including A Doll's House, An Enemy of the People, Hedda Gabler, and Ghosts.

839.82 Norwegian literature

Knausgaard, Karl Ove, 1968-

Home and away : writing the beautiful game / Karl Ove Knausgaard and Fredrik Ekelund, translated by Don Bartlett, and San Kinsella. Farrar, Straus and Giroux, 2017, c2015 496 p. **839.82**

1. Knausgaard, Karl Ove, 1968- 2. Ekelund, Fredrik, 1953- 3. World Cup (Soccer) 4. Soccer. 5. Soccer teams. 6. Soccer fans. 7. Sports fans. 8. Letters
ISBN 9780374279837

LC 2016959056

Translation of: Hjemme - Borte

Originally published: Lindhardt og Ringhof, 2015

Two internationally acclaimed writers reveal themselves to be the ultimate soccer fans, in a collection of letters that use soccer and the World Cup in Brazil as the arena for reflections on life and death, art and politics and class and literature.

840.9 French literature--history and criticism

Levin Becker, Daniel

Many subtle channels : in praise of potential literature / Daniel Levin Becker. Harvard University Press, 2012. 296 p. **840.9**

1. Levin Becker, Daniel. 2. Oulipo (Association) 3. Literary form. 4. Authors, American -- 21st century 5. Writing. 6. Authors.
ISBN 9780674065772

LC 2011044577

Includes index.

The youngest member of the Paris-based experimental collective Oulipo, Levin Becker tells the story of one of literature's quirkiest movements--and the personal quest that led him to seek out like-minded writers, artists, and scientists who are obsessed with language and games, and who embrace formal constraints to achieve literature's potential. --From publisher description.

"In this intimate and informative book, Levin Becker explores the history of Oulipo (short for Ouvroir de Litterature Potentielle, or Workshop for Potential Literature), easily one of the most bizarre and charming literary movements of the 20th century." Publishers Weekly.

841 French poetry

Auster, Paul, 1947-

The **Random** House book of twentieth-century French poetry : with translations by American and British poets / edited by Paul Auster. Vintage Books, 1984, c1982. xlix, 635 p. ; **841**

1. French poetry -- 20th century -- Translations into English 2. French poetry -- 20th century
ISBN 9780394717487

LC 82017324

English and French.

Includes the original text and English translations for poems by Apollinaire, Cendrars, Breton, Tzara, Prevert, and Michaux.

Baudelaire, Charles, 1821-1867

Les fleurs du mal : the complete text of The flowers of evil / Charles Baudelaire ; in a new translation by Richard Howard ; illustrated with nine original monotypes by Michael Mazur. D.R. Godine, 1982. xxxii, 365 p. : **841**

1. French poetry -- 19th century
ISBN 9780879234621

LC 81013283

Includes index.

Presents the first American translation of the complete text of Baudelaire's 1857 masterwork and includes the complete original French texts for easy comparison.

"Howard puts the original's rhymed alexandrines primarily into iambic pentameter blank verse, which allows him to capture the immediate, concrete, visceral quality of Baudelaire's imagery." Choice.

Baudelaire, Charles, 1821-1867

Poems / Baudelaire. A.A. Knopf, 1993. 256 p. ; **841**

1. Baudelaire, Charles, 1821-1867 2. French poetry -- 19th century
ISBN 9780679429104

LC 93014363

Cover title: Baudelaire.

Includes index.

Modern poetry begins with Charles Baudelaire (1821-67), who employed his unequalled technical mastery to create the shadowy, desperately dramatic urban landscape -- populated by the addicted and the damned -- which so compellingly mirrors our modern condition. Deeply though darkly spiritual, titanic in the changes he wrought, Baudelaire looms over all the work, great and small, created in his wake. -- From publisher description

Beckett, Samuel, 1906-1989

Collected poems in English and French / Samuel Beckett. Grove Press, 1977. ix, 147 p. ; **841**

1. Irish poetry
ISBN 9780802130969

LC 77077855

Contains poems written by Beckett in English, and by Beckett in French, with translations in some cases, and bilingual versions of poems by Eluard, Rimbaud, Apollinaire, and Chamfort in Beckett's translations.

Gathers together the Nobel Prize-winning writer's English verses, English translations of poems by Eluard, Rimbaud, Apollinaire, and Chamfort, and poems in French, several of which are presented in translation.

Bloch, R. Howard

One toss of the dice : the incredible story of how a poem made us modern / R. Howard Bloch. Liveright Publishing Corporation, 2016. 320 p. **841**

1. Mallarme, Stephane, 1842-1898. Coup de des jamais n'abolira le hasard 2. Literature and society 3. Modernism (Literature) 4. Poets, French. 5. Poems.
ISBN 9780871406637

LC 2016023400

Includes an English translation of the French poem "Coup de des jamais n'abolira le hasard."

Explores how Stephane Mallarme's "One Toss of the Dice," an enigmatic twenty-page poem about a shipwreck, published in 1897, that could be read up and down, backward and forward, and even sideways, launched the modernist movement.

"Blochs analysis of the poem's verbal and syntactical acrobatics and its resonance with later works is enlightening." Publishers Weekly.

Hugo, Victor, 1802-1885

Selected poems of Victor Hugo : a bilingual edition / Victor Hugo ; translated from the French by E. H. and A. M. Blackmore. University of Chicago Press, 2004, c2001. xxx, 631 p. : **841**

1. Hugo, Victor, 1802-1885 Translations into English. 2. French poetry
ISBN 9780226359816

LC bl2007005468

Selected from the French writer's vast collection of verse, this bilingual collection introduces readers to the breadth of Hugo's poetic vision, which covered religion, love, politics, and other incisive themes.

Mallarme, Stephane, 1842-1898

Collected poems and other verse / Stephane Mallarme ; translated with notes by E.H. and A.M. Blackmore ; with an introduction by Elizabeth McCombie. Oxford University Press, 2006. xxxvii, 282 p. ; **841**

1. Mallarme, Stephane, 1842-1898 Translations into English.
ISBN 019280362X

LC 2006297077

This is the fullest collection of Mallarme's poetry ever published in English, and the only edition in any language that presents his Poesies in the last arrangement known to have been approved by the author. --From publisher description.

Merwin, W. S. (William Stanley), 1927-2019

★The **song** of Roland / translated, with an introduction, by W.S. Merwin. Modern Library, 2001. xv, 137 p. ; **841**

1. Roland (Legendary character) Romances. 2. Knights and knighthood 3. French poetry 4. Epic poetry
ISBN 9780375757112

LC 00048989

A translation of the medieval epic poem about Roland's adventures and death in Charlemagne's war against the pagans.

Rimbaud, Arthur, 1854-1891

The **illuminations** / Arthur Rimbaud ; translated from the French by Donald Revell. Omnidawn Pub., 2009. 119 p. ; **841**

1. Rimbaud, Arthur, 1854-1891 Translations into English. 2. French poetry
ISBN 9781890650360

LC 2009015569

Presents a new translation of the author's collection of prose poems, rendered for a contemporary audience.

Poems : Poems / Rimbaud ; [selected by Peter Washington].

A.A. Knopf, c1994. 288 p. ; **841**

1. Rimbaud, Arthur, 1854-1891 2. French poetry -- 19th century
ISBN 067943321X

LC 94002496

Cover title: Rimbaud.
Includes index.
A collection of works by the nineteenth-century French poet.

Rimbaud : complete works, selected letters : a bilingual edition / translated with an introduction and notes by Wallace Fowlie ; updated, revised and with a foreword by Seth Whidden. University of Chicago Press, c2005. xxxvi, 458 p. : **841**

1. Rimbaud, Arthur, 1854-1891 Translations into English. 2. Rimbaud, Arthur, 1854-1891 Correspondence. 3. Poets, French -- 19th century -- Correspondence. 4. French poetry
ISBN 9780226719771

LC 2005041859

Thoroughly revising Fowlie's edition, Seth Whidden has made changes on virtually every page, correcting errors, reordering poems, adding previously omitted versions of poems and some letters, and updating the text to reflect current scholarship; left in place are Fowlie's literal and respectful translations of Rimbaud's complex and nontraditional verse. --From publisher description.

Villon, Francois, 1431-1463
The **poems** of Francois Villon / translated with an introduction and notes by Galway Kinnell. University Press of New England, 1982. xxiii, 246 p. ; **841**

1. Villon, Francois, 1431-1463
ISBN 9780874512366

LC 81071907

Text of poems in English and French.
"Using standard academic texts of the medieval French poet, Kinnell exceeds a transliteration of the originals. Villon's ribaldry and humorous despair sparkle throughout." Booklist.

842 French drama

Bloom, Harold
Samuel Beckett's Waiting for Godot / edited and with an introduction by Harold Bloom. Bloom's Literary Criticism, c2008. vii, 172 p. ; **842**

1. Beckett, Samuel, 1906-1989. En attendant Godot.
ISBN 9780791097939

LC 2007049864

Presents a collection of critical essays on the play that analyze its structure, characters, and themes.

Camus, Albert, 1913-1960
Caligula & three other plays. Translated from the French by Stuart Gilbert. With a pref. written specially for this ed., and translated by Justin O'Brien. Knopf, 1958. x, 302 p. **842**

1. Camus, Albert, 1913-1960 2. Caligula, Emperor of Rome, 12-41 Drama. 3. Historical drama
ISBN 9780394702070

LC 58011227

Contains four plays:--Caligula.--The misunderstanding.--State of siege.--The just assassins

Genet, Jean, 1910-
The **maids** ; Death watch / two plays by Jean Genet ; with an introduction by Jean-Paul Sartre ; translated from the French by Bernard Frechtman. Grove Press, 1962. 166 p. ; **842**

1. Genet, Jean, 1910- Translations into English.
ISBN 9780802150561

LC BL 99792309

Presents two plays that attempt to analyze the mores of the bourgeois society:"The Maids" in which two domestic workers who resent their inferior position try to detroy their employer, and "Deathwatch," which depicts two convicts who try to gain legendary status in criminal circles.

Goldsby, Robert
Molière on stage : what's so funny? / Robert W. Goldsby. Anthem Press, 2012. xx, 202 p. : **842**

1. Moliere, 1622-1673 Dramatic production. 2. Moliere, 1622-1673 Stage history.
ISBN 0857284428

LC 2012001708

Molière on Stage takes the reader onstage, backstage and into the audience of Molière's plays, analyzing the performance of his works in both his own time and in ours. --From publisher description.

"Joy is what actors experience when they perform great theater, and joy is what theater lovers will feel when they read this fact-filled, elegantly written book on the incomparable comedic genius Molière." Choice.

Molière, 1622-1673
The **misanthrope** and other plays / Molière ; translated, and with an introduction by Donald M. Frame ; and a new afterword by Lewis C. Seifert. Signet Classics, c2005. 524 p. **842**

1. Moliere, 1622-1673 Translations into English.
ISBN 0451529871

LC 2006276841

This collection includes The Misanthrope, a comedy about Alceste, who openly champions morals, but is in love with Celimene, who embodies immorality, as well as The Doctor in Spite of Himself, The Imaginary Invalid, and other works by France's greatest playwright. Reissue.

Sartre, Jean-Paul, 1905-1980
★**No** exit, and three other plays / Jean-Paul Sartre. Vintage International, 1989. 275 p. ; **842**

1. Sartre, Jean-Paul, 1905-1980 Translations into English.
ISBN 9780679725169

LC 89040097

English translations of four plays which dramatize the theme of man's responsibility for his own actions, by the leader of French existentialism.

843 French fiction

Bellos, David
The **novel** of the century : the extraordinary adventure of Les Miserables / David Bellos. Farrar, Straus & Giroux, 2017. 352 p. **843**

1. Hugo, Victor, 1802-1885. Miserables 2. Authors 3. Writing 4. Books 5. Literature -- History and criticism 6. France -- History -- 19th century
ISBN 9780374223236

LC 2016049133

A narrative account of the story behind Victor Hugo's literary masterpiece describes how he wrote the book under violent conditions and during exile, the considerable measures that were required for its publication and its various stage and screen interpretations.

"Anyone who loves Hugo, France, and the French language will revel in this delightful book that explains all the intimacies of 19th-century French life." Kirkus.

Shattuck, Roger

Proust's way : a field guide to In search of lost time / Roger Shattuck. W.W. Norton, 2000. xxiv, 290 p. **843**

1. Proust, Marcel, 1871-1922. In search of lost time Criticism and interpretation. 2. Literature -- History and criticism

ISBN 0393049140

LC 99058472

A critical evaluation of Proust's "In Search of Lost Time" which is most traditionally translated as "Remembrance of Things Past."

"Shattuck is most helpful in placing Proust and the work in the context of his time, giving a balanced treatment to the novel as a whole. Written in a style that will appeal to both the scholar and the lay reader, Shattuck's field guide should be a standard for years to come." Library Journal

844 French essays

Camus, Albert, 1913-1960

The **myth** of Sisyphus and other essays / Albert Camus ; translated from the French by Justin O'Brien. Vintage Books, 1991. vi, 212 p. ; **844**

1. Essays

ISBN 9780679733737

LC 90050476

Originally published: New York : Knopf, 1955.

Essays deal with nihilism and the problem of suicide.

Resistance, rebellion, and death / Albert Camus ; translated from the French and with an introduction by Justin O'Brien. Vintage International, 1995. viii, 272 p. ; **844**

1. Good and evil 2. Europe -- Politics and government.

ISBN 9780679764014

LC 95215592

Essays selected by the author from his Actuelles and other works.

Originally published: New York : Knopf, 1960.

The author's personal beliefs and his reactions to the major issues of his lifetime are reflected in these selected writings.

Frampton, Saul

When I am playing with my cat, how do I know she is not playing with me? : Montaigne and being in touch with life / Saul Frampton. Pantheon Books, c2011. 288 p. **844**

1. Montaigne, Michel de, 1533-1592 Criticism and interpretation 2. Montaigne, Michel de, 1533-1592. Essais. 3. European Renaissance. 4. Grief. 5. Philosophers. 6. Authors

ISBN 9780375424717

LC 2010043642

An introduction to the life and works of the 16th-century literary master traces the impact of personal tragedies and war on such pieces as Les Essais, discussing the writer's reflections on myriad subjects and his enduring legacy.

"The author renders a rigorous history of ideas in this engaging account of the life and the work of Michel de Montaigne (1533--1592). Frampton tucks a good deal of biography into his tour of the evolution of the essays and the events that inspired them, but his extraordinary achievement is in conveying and inviting the reader to commune with Montaigne's unique sensibility and his take on death, sex, travel, friendship, kidney stones, the human thumb, and above all, the power of the ordinary and the unremarkable, the value of the here-and-now. This scholarly romp through the Renaissance is a jewel." Publishers Weekly.

848 French miscellaneous writings

Beckett, Samuel, 1906-1989

★The **letters** of Samuel Beckett, editors, Martha Dow Fehsenfeld, Lois More Overbeck ; associate editors, George Craig, Daniel Gunn. Cambridge University Press, 2009. 782 p. Letters of Samuel Beckett ; **848**

1. Beckett, Samuel, 1906-1989 Correspondence. 2. Authors, Irish -- 20th century -- Correspondence. 3. Authors, French -- 20th century -- Correspondence. 4. Letters.

ISBN 9780521867931

LC 2008025530

Correspondence chiefly written in English; letters written in French and German are accompanied by English translations.

"This is an extraordinary work of scholarship on the part of its main editors. What Fehsenfeld and Overbeck have produced is a revelatory triumph." Los Angeles Times Book Review.

Samuel Beckett : the Grove centenary edition / series editor, Paul Auster. Grove Press, c2006. 509 p. ; **848**

ISBN 0802118194

LC 2005055078

Edited by Paul Auster, this four-volume set of Beckett's canon has been designed by award winner Laura Lindgren. Available individually, as well as in a boxed set, the four hardcover volumes have been specially bound with covers featuring images central to Beckett's works. --From publisher description.

Coffin, Judith G., 1952-

Sex, love, and letters : writing Simone de Beauvoir / Judith G. Coffin. Cornell University Press, 2020 xiv, 310 p. **848**

1. Beauvoir, Simone de, 1908-1986 2. Beauvoir, Simone de, 1908-1986 Correspondence 3. Women authors, French -- 20th century 4. Letter writing 5. Authors and readers 6. Public opinion 7. Letters

ISBN 9781501750540

LC 2020005876

When Judith G. Coffin discovered a virtually unexplored treasure trove of letters to Simone de Beauvoir from her international readers, it inspired her to explore the intimate bond between the famed author and her reading public. This correspondence, at the heart of Sex, Love, and Letters, immerses us in the tumultuous decades from the late 1940s to the 1970s, from the painful aftermath of World War Two to the horror and shame of French colonial brutality in Algeria, through the dilemmas and exhilarations of the early gay liberation and feminist movements. It also provides a glimpse into the power of reading and the power of readers to seduce the authors of their favorite books.

"This beautifully written, frequently moving book is a crucial addition to the scholarship on Simone de Beauvoir." Kirkus

851 Italian poetry

Ariosto, Lodovico, 1474-1533

Orlando furioso = : The frenzy of Orlando : a romantic epic / Ludovico Ariosto ; translated with an introduction by Barbara Reynolds. Penguin, 1975. 827 pages : **851**

1. Roland (Legendary character) 2. Epic poetry, Italian -- Translations into English

ISBN 9780140443110

LC 75327748

One of the greatest epic poems of the Italian Renaissance, Orlando Furioso is an intricate tale of love and enchantment set at the time of the Holy Roman Emperor Charlemagne's conflict with the Moors. --From publisher description.

Dante Alighieri, 1265-1321

The **divine** comedy : Inferno, Purgatorio, Paradiso / Dante Alighieri ; translated by Allen Mandelbaum ; with an introduction by Eugenio Montale and notes by Peter Armour. Alfred A. Knopf, 1995. 798 p. : **851**

1. Italian poetry 2. Epic poetry

ISBN 9780679433132

LC BL 98005712

Dante Alighieri's epic poem travels through the endless agony of Hell, up the treacherous slopes of Purgatory, and on to the wondrous kingdom of Paradise--the realm of universal unity and eternal salvation.

Inferno / Dante Alighieri ; translated by Robert & Jean Hollander ; introduction & notes by Robert Hollander. Anchor Books, 2002. xl, 694 p. : **851**

1. Future life 2. Hell

ISBN 9780385496988

LC bl2015010141

In a new translation of the first part of Dante's epic poem about the Christian afterlife, presented with the original Italian and the English version on facing pages, Virgil leads a spiritual pilgrim through the circles of Hell.

"The heart of the Hollanders' edition is the translation itself, which nicely balances the precision required for a much-interpreted allegory and the poetic qualities that draw most readers to the work. The result is a terse, lean Dante with its own kind of beauty. The Hollanders' lines will satisfy both the poetry lover and scholar; they are at once literary, accessible and possessed of the seeming transparence that often characterizes great translations. The Italian text is included on the facing page for easy reference, along with notes drawing on some 60 Dante scholars, several indexes, a list of works cited and an introduction by Robert Hollander." Publishers Weekly.

The **paradiso** / Dante Alighieri ; translated by John Ciardi ; with an introduction by John Freccero and an afterword by Edward M. Cifelli. New American Library, 2009. 365 p. : **851**

1. Christianity. 2. Life after death. 3. Heaven. 4. Paradise. 5. Epic poetry.

ISBN 9780451531414

LC 2010668194

The final canticle of Dante's "The Divine Comedy" shares the ultimate goal of human striving: the merging of individual destiny with universal order. One of the towering creations of world literature, Dante's vision of universal harmony and eternal salvation is an immortal hymn to God, Nature, Eternity, and Love.

Paradiso / Dante Alighieri ; a verse translation by Robert & Jean Hollander ; introduction & notes by Robert Hollander. Anchor Books, 2008. xxix, 989 p. : **851**

1. Future life 2. Hell 3. Paradise 4. Italian poetry 5. Epic poetry

ISBN 9781400031153

LC bl2015010149

Follows the spiritual pilgrim as he puts behind him the horrors of Hell and the trials of Pugatory to ascend to Paradise, where he encounters his beloved Beatrice and meets the Heavenly Court and the Lord.

Purgatorio / Dante Alighieri ; a verse translation from the Italian by Jean Hollander & Robert Hollander ; introduction & notes by Robert Hollander. Doubleday, 2003. xxiv, 742 p. ; **851**

1. Sin 2. Repentance 3. Salvation 4. Purgatory 5. Epic poetry

ISBN 9780385496995

LC 2002067100

A verse translation of the second section of Dante's monumental epic, the Divine Comedy, chronicles the poet-narrator's odyssey, with the poet Virgil as his guide, up the Mount of Purgatory toward Paradise, in a version that includes a detailed introduction, extensive notes, and commentaries on each canto.

"These translations, honed over Robert Hollander's 35 years teaching Dante at Princeton, are touted as the U.S. English standard for rendering Dante's layered meanings." Publishers Weekly.

Montale, Eugenio, 1896-1981

The **collected** poems of Eugenio Montale 1925-1977 / translated from the Italian by William Arrowsmith ; edited by Rosanna Warren. W. W. Norton & Co., c2012. xxxiv, 793 p. ; **851**

1. Montale, Eugenio, 1896-1981 Translations into English. 2. Italian poetry -- 20th century

ISBN 9780393080636

LC 2011034993

An English-language translation of works by the late Nobel Prize winner offers insight into his role in influencing Italian poetry and international Modernism, as well as his views on such topics as modernity, fascism, and war.

854 Italian essays

Calvino, Italo

★**Collection** of sand / Italo Calvino ; translated by Martin McLaughlin. Mariner Books, 2014. 240 p. **854**

1. Calvino, Italo 2. Essays

ISBN 9780544146464

LC 2014001373

Published for the first time in English, a final collection of essays by the renowned fabulist writer tours the visual world through explorations of subjects ranging from cuneiform and antique maps to Mexican temples and Japanese gardens.

Eco, Umberto

How to travel with a salmon & other essays / Umberto Eco ; translated from the Italian by William Weaver. Harcourt, Brace, c1994. vii, 248 p. : **854**

1. Popular culture. 2. Essays

ISBN 9780151001361

LC 94010340

Translation of: Il secondo diario minimo.

These essays, written in the late eighties and early nineties, are his playful but unfailingly accurate takes on militarism, computer jargon, Westerns, art criticism, librarians, bureaucrats, meals on airplanes, Amtrak trains, bad coffee, maniacal taxi drivers, express mail, 33-function watches, fax machines and cellular phones, pornography, soccer fans, academia, and--last but definitely not least--the author's own self....

"In this collection of parodies, satires and whimsical mini-essays written over the last 30 years, Italian novelist/critic Eco...takes readers on a delightful romp through the absurdities of modern life." Publishers Weekly.

860.9 Spanish literature--history and criticism

Donoghue, Emma, 1969-
Inseparable : desire between women in literature / Emma Donoghue. Alfred A. Knopf, 2010. x, 271 p. : **860.9**

1. English literature -- History and criticism. 2. French literature -- History and criticism. 3. Lesbians in literature 4. Lesbianism.
ISBN 9780307270948
LC 2009048368

Stonewall Book Award for the Israel Fishman Non-fiction Award, 2011.

An admired literary critic and scholar and author of Life Mask illuminates the long-standing but little-known tradition of love between women in Western literature, citing examples from the works of Shakespeare, Agatha Christie, Charles Dickens and many more.

861 Spanish poetry

Aleixandre, Vicente, 1898-1984
A **longing** for the light : selected poems of Vicente Aleixandre / edited by Lewis Hyde. Copper Canyon Press, c2007. xxi, 279 p. ; **861**

1. Aleixandre, Vicente, 1898-1984 Translations into English. 2. Spanish poetry
ISBN 9781556592546
LC 2007000992

A comprehensive collection spans the entirety of Nobel Laureate Aleixandre's career, from his early surrealist work to his complex and fascinating "dialogues," as well as prose interludes.

Borges, Jorge Luis, 1899-1986
★**Selected** poems / Jorge Luis Borges ; edited by Alexander Coleman. Penguin Books, 2000, c1999. xii, 483 p. ; **861**

1. Borges, Jorge Luis, 1899-1986 2. Argentine poetry -- 19th century 3. Latin American poetry
ISBN 0140587217
LC bl2011001811

Originally published: New York : Viking, 1999.

A bilingual collection presents two hundred of the Argentine author's poems.

"Poetry is the heart of Borges' metaphysical, mythical, and cosmopolitan oeuvre. Editor Coleman commissioned a wealth of new translations for this unprecedented and invaluable collection, and the roster of translators includes such luminaries as Robert S. Fitzgerald, W.S. Merwin, Mark Strand, and John Updike." Booklist.

Cardenal, Ernesto, 1925-2020
Pluriverse : new and selected poems / Ernesto Cardenal ; edited by Jonathan Cohen ; with a foreword by Lawrence Ferlinghetti ; translations from the Spanish by Jonathan Cohen ... [et al.]. New Directions Pub., 2009. xxii, 249 p. ; **861**

1. Cardenal, Ernesto, 1925-2020 Translations into English.
ISBN 9780811218092
LC 2008040582

"Cardenal is political, of course, and much of the work presented here (translated by many illustrious hands, including Jonathan Cohen, Thomas Merton and Kenneth Rexroth) deals with the struggle and history of his country and Latin America at large. But he can sing lyrically too. Beautiful." Los Angeles Times Book Review.

Cohen, J. M. (John Michael), 1903-1989
The **Penguin** book of Spanish verse / introduced and edited by J.M. Cohen ; with plain prose translations of each poem. Penguin, 1988. xliii, 596 p. ; **861**

1. Spanish poetry
ISBN 9780140585704
LC 88166999

"New parallel text edition"--Cover.

Includes index.

Poems in the original Spanish are accompanied by English translations and represent each period of Spanish literature.

Cortazar, Julio
Save twilight : selected poems of / Julio Cortazar ; translated from the Spanish by Stephen Kessler. City Lights Books, 2016 xvii, 257 p. : **861**

1. Spanish poetry 2. Poetry of places
ISBN 9780872867093
LC 2016008225

"Originally published as Salvo el crepâusculo by Editorial Nueva Imagen, S.A., Mexico City, 1984" -- Title page verso.

"World renowned as one of the masters of contemporary fiction, Julio Cortazar was also a prolific poet, who in his final months in Paris, ill with leukemia, assembled what he wanted saved of his life's work in verse. This expanded edition of Save Twilight, offers a bilingual survey of Cortazar's enduring poetry ranging through his various voices, moods, and styles".-- Provided by publisher.

Garcia Lorca, Federico, 1898-1936
Collected poems / Federico Garcia Lorca ; revised edition, with an introduction and notes by Christopher Maurer ; translated from the Spanish by Catherine Brown ... [et al.]. Farrar, Straus and Giroux, 2002. lxiv, 990 p. : **861**

1. Garcia Lorca, Federico, 1898-1936 Translations into English. 2. Spanish poetry -- 19th century
ISBN 9780374526917
LC 2001018779

Rev. ed. of: Collected poems / Federico Garcia Lorca. 1991. (Poetical works of Federico Garcia Lorca ; v. 2)

Spain's greatest twentieth-century poet and most influencial modernist speaks to a new generation of readers in this revised edition of his complete poetical works.

Poet in New York : a bilingual edition / Federico Garcia Lorca ; translated from the Spanish by Greg Simon and Steven F. White ; edited and with an introduction and notes by Christopher Maurer. The Noonday Press, 1998. xxxv, 303 p. : **861**

1. Garcia Lorca, Federico, 1898-1936 Translations into English. 2. Spanish poetry -- 19th century
ISBN 9780374525408
LC 97049953

A collection of surrealistic poems with English translations reflect Lorca's response to New York City during a prolonged visit in 1930.

Juana Ines de la Cruz, Sister, 1651-1695
Selected works / Sor Juana Ines de la Cruz ; translated by

Edith Grossman ; introduction by Julia Alvarez. W. W. Norton & Company, 2014 xxiv, 216 p. ; **861**

1. Spanish poetry -- 17th century.
ISBN 9780393241754

LC 2014025634

A collection of best-known works from the seventeenth-century feminist poet showcases her intellect and range and highlights her belief in a woman's right to study and write.

Michael, Ian, 1915-

The **poem** of the Cid / translated by Rita Hamilton and Janet Perry ; with an introduction and notes by Ian Michael. Penguin, 1984, c1975. 242 pages : **861**

1. Spanish poetry 2. Epic poetry
ISBN 9780140444469

LC BL 99794084

Originally published in translation: Manchester : Manchester University Press, 1975.

The medieval epic poem is presented in parallel Spanish and English text with English introduction and notes.

Neruda, Pablo, 1904-1973

All the odes / Pablo Neruda ; edited by Ilan Stavans. Farrar, Straus and Giroux, 2013. xxiii, 861 p. ; **861**

1. Neruda, Pablo, 1904-1973 Translations into English. 2. Spanish poetry -- 20th century
ISBN 9780374115289

LC 2012009146

Includes index.

A career-spanning volume charting the Nobel laureate's work in the ode form is published in a dual-language format and includes English-language renderings by such accomplished translators as Philip Levine, Paul Muldoon and Mark Strand.

Book of twilight / Pablo Neruda ; translated from the Spanish by William O'Daly. Copper Canyon Press, 2017 xvi, 147 p. ; **861**

1. Neruda, Pablo, 1904-1973 Translations into English. 2. Spanish poetry -- 20th century
ISBN 9781556593987

LC 2017022735

A first English-language translation of the late Nobel Prize-winning poet's debut collection shares insight into his romantic early development as a literary master and his evolving explorations of such subjects as impurity, imperfection and banality.

Then come back : the lost Neruda poems / Pablo Neruda ; translated from the Spanish by Forrest Gander. Copper Canyon Press, 2016 xx, 165 p. ; **861**

1. Neruda, Pablo, 1904-1973 Translations into English. 2. Spanish poetry -- 20th century
ISBN 9781556594946

LC 2015048546

In a Spanish-English edition, the lost poems of one of the world's most beloved and best-selling poets--which were originally composed on napkins, playbills, receipts and notebooks--have been translated for the first time.

Paz, Octavio, 1914-1998

★The **collected** poems of Octavio Paz, 1957-1987 / edited and translated by Eliot Weinberger ; with additional translations by Elizabeth Bishop ... [et al.]. New Directions, 1991. xvii, 669 p. : **861**

1. Paz, Octavio, 1914-1998. Translations into English. 2. Bilingual materials English/Spanish
ISBN 9780811210379

LC bl2006006081

Poems, in both English translation and the original Spanish, deal with fate, nature, language, intimacy, love, friendship, and the senses.

"Dense, weighty, and miraculous, this bilingual edition compresses into one volume all the poems published in book form since 1957. Nearly 200 poems, some newly translated, many new to an English-language edition, conclusively demonstrate Paz's power." Library Journal.

Torre, Monica de la

Reversible monuments : contemporary Mexican poetry / edited by Monica de la Torre and Michael Wiegers. Copper Canyon Press, c2002. xvii, 675 p. ; **861**

1. Mexican poetry
ISBN 9781556591594

LC 2002006189

Includes indexes.

"Spacious and accommodating, this work presents a generous number of gracefully translated poems by each poet, a felicitous in-depth approach that makes this much more than a sampler, and a sound decision given the poets' propensity for long, dreamy poems." Booklist.

862 Spanish drama

Calderon de la Barca, Pedro, 1600-1681

Life's a dream / Pedro Calderon de la Barca ; a prose translation and critical introduction by Michael Kidd. University Press of Colorado, c2004. xii, 159 p. ; **862**

1. Calderon de la Barca, Pedro, 1600-1681. Vida es sueño.
ISBN 0870817779

LC 2004010260

Calderon's long life witnessed both the pinnacle and collapse of Spanish political power as well as the great flowering of Spanish classical literature. Michael Kidd's new prose translation renders Calderon's masterpiece into a transparent, modern American idiom that preserves the beauty and complexity of Calderon's Baroque Spanish. --From publisher description.

Vega, Lope de, 1562-1635

Fuente Ovejuna, The knight from Olmedo, Punishment without revenge : Fuente Ovejuna/The Knight from Olmedo/Punishment Without Revenge Lope de Vega ; translated with an introduction and notes by Gwynne Edwards. Oxford University Press, 2008 xli, 300 p. ; **862**

1. Spanish drama.
ISBN 0199540179

LC 2009291022

Lope de Vega (1562-1635), widely regarded as the architect of the drama of the Spanish Golden Age, created plots and characters notable for their energy, inventiveness, and dramatic power. This unique edition includes his most famous play, Fuente Ovejuna, as well as The Knight from Olmedo and Punishment without Revenge. --From publisher description.

864 Spanish essays

Borges, Jorge Luis, 1899-1986

★**Selected** non-fictions / Jorge Luis Borges ; edited by Eliot Weinberger ; translated by Esther Allen, Suzanne Jill Levine & Eliot Weinberger. Viking, 1999. xvi, 559 p. ; **864**

1. Borges, Jorge Luis, 1899-1986. 2. Literature. 3. Lectures and lecturing. 4. Time. 5. Eternity. 6. Essays.
ISBN 9780670849475

LC 99012386

A third and last volume in a centenary edition of the collected works in English of one of the century's most respected literary figures offers new translations of more than 150 of Borges's nonfiction works.

"Shifting effortlessly from Homer to Hitler, from Kafka to King Kong, these hundred and sixty-one essays, appreciations, prologues, and philosophical investigations are dizzying in scope and dazzling in execution. But it is Borges's dogged pursuit of familiar themes--infinity and eternity, reflexivity and recurrence--which gives this collection its unusual unity and depth." The New Yorker.

García Márquez, Gabriel, 1928-2014

The **scandal** of the century : and other writings / Gabriel García Márquez ; translated from the Spanish by Anne McLean. Alfred A. Knopf, 2019, c2018. 320 p. **864**

1. Columnists 2. Journalism
ISBN 9780525656425

LC 2019001736

Originally published: Barcelona : Literatura Random House, 2018.

A journalism anthology by the Nobel Prize-winning author of One Hundred Years of Solitude is comprised of selections Márquez considered the most important to his legacy, including his articles for international papers and his columns for Spain's El Pas.

"The text is elegantly translated...García Márquez fans will welcome these fresh and lively examples of his beautiful, lyrical writing." Kirkus.

Luiselli, Valeria, 1983-

Sidewalks / Valeria Luiselli ; translated from the Spanish by Christina MacSweeney. Coffee House Press, 2014, c2010. 120 p. **864**

1. City life 2. Cities and towns 3. Mexico (City) 4. New York City. 5. Venice, Italy. 6. Essays
ISBN 9781566893565

LC 2013035162

Originally published in Spanish in 2010 as Papeles falsos.

Valeria Luiselli is an evening cyclist; a literary tourist in Venice, searching for Joseph Brodsky's tomb; an excavator of her own artifacts, unpacking from a move. In essays that are as companionable as they are ambitious, she uses the city to exercise a roving, meandering intelligence, seeking out the questions embedded in our human landscapes.

865 Spanish speeches

García Márquez, Gabriel, 1928-2014

I'm not here to give a speech / Gabriel García Márquez ; translated by Edith Grossman. Vintage International, Vintage Books, a division of Penguin Random House LLC, 2019, c2010. 160 p. **865**

1. Garcia Marquez, Gabriel, 1928-2014 2. Speeches, addresses, etc.
ISBN 9781101911181

LC 2018032878

"This collection first published in Spanish by Grijalbo Mondadori 2010 (Yo no vengo a decir un discurso)."

Available in English for the first time, a collection of speeches from the notable author records key events throughout his life, from a farewell to his classmates delivered when he was only 17 to his Nobel Prize acceptance speech.

"These talks, so eloquently rendered by García Márquez's longtime translator Grossman, capture the novelists passion, genius, and energetic way of telling a story with a clear moral." Publishers Weekly.

868 Spanish miscellaneous writings

Biron, Rebecca E

Elena Garro and Mexico's modern dreams / Rebecca E. Biron. Bucknell University Press : 2013 xi, 261 p. ; **868**

1. Garro, Elena Criticism and interpretation. 2. Modernism (Literature) -- Mexico. 3. National characteristics, Mexican, in literature. 4. Mexico -- Civilization.
ISBN 1611484707

LC 2012042552

Blending cultural studies, literary analysis, and political history, this book shows how Elena Garro's life and work expose the impasses inherent to the concept of Mexican modernity. --From publisher description.

"A thought-provoking text that shows how this important Mexican author fits within the literary history of the 20th century, and that joins other explorations like Sandra Messinger Cypess's Uncivil Wars (CH, Dec'12)." Choice.

871 Latin poetry

Juvenal

The **sixteen** satires / Juvenal ; translated with an introduction and notes by Peter Green. Penguin Books, 1998. lxvii, 252 p. ; **871**

1. Juvenal Translations into English. 2. Verse satire, Latin 3. Rome
ISBN 9780140447040

LC 99187049

Translation is based on the Oxford classical text ed. of A. Persi Flacci et D. Iuni Iuvenalis saturae, edidit W.V. Clausen, 1959.

Green's celebrated translation is fully annotated and clarifies all references and allusions in the text, making it equally suitable for students and for continuous reading. For this new edition it has been substantially revised throughout to give it an even more contemporary flavour. --From publisher description.

Virgil, 70-19 B.C.

The **eclogues** of Virgil : a translation / David Ferry. Farrar Straus & Giroux 2000 xv, 101 p. ; 21 cm **871**

1. Pastoral poetry.
ISBN 9780374146344

LC 98052547

Text in Latin and English on facing pages.

872 Latin dramatic poetry and drama

Seneca, Lucius Annaeus, 4 B.C.?-65 A.D.

Thyestes; Phaedra; The Trojan women; Oedipus; with, Octavia

/ translated with an introduction by E. F. Watling. Penguin, 1972. 319 p. **872**

1. Seneca, Lucius Annaeus, 4 B.C.?-65 A.D. 2. Octavia, Empress, consort of Nero, Emperor of Rome, approximately 42-62 Drama 3. Mythology, Classical -- Drama 4. Tragedy
ISBN 9780140441741

LC 73158325

Cover title: Four tragedies, and Octavia.

Dramas by the classical playwright and philosopher are accompanied by a modern work to demonstrate the Roman's impact on the development of the tragedy.

Terence

Terence, the comedies : The Comedies / translations by Palmer Bovie, Constance Carrier, and Douglass Parker ; edited by Palmer Bovie. Johns Hopkins University Press, 1992. xxi, 398 p. ; **872**

1. Terence Translations into English.
ISBN 0801843545

LC 91033984

Originally published: The complete comedies of Terence. New Brunswick, N.J. : Rutgers University Press, 1974.

In English translations that achieve a lively readability without sacrificing the dramatic and comic impact of the original Latin, this volume presents all six comedies: The Girl from Andros (Andria), The Self-Tormentor (Heautontimorumenos), The Eunuch (Eunouchus), Phormios, The Brothers (Adelphoe), and Her Husband's Mother (Hecyra). -- From publisher description.

873 Latin epic poetry and fiction

Erasmus, Desiderius, -1536

Praise of folly ; and, Letter to Maarten Van Dorp, 1515 / Erasmus of Rotterdam ; translated by Betty Radice ; with an introduction and notes by A.H.T. Levi. Penguin Books, 1993. lvi, 188 p. ; **873**

1. Erasmus, Desiderius, -1536 Translations into English. 2. Folly 3. Folly -- Religious aspects -- Christianity
ISBN 9780140446081

LC 94142502

"Introduction and notes have been brought up to date ... the translation was revised"--P. [x].

The classic work of the Renaissance humanist satirizes the organized Christian Church of the sixteenth century.

Ovid, 43 B.C.-17 or 18 A.D.

Tales from Ovid / [translated by] Ted Hughes. Farrar, Straus and Giroux, 1997. x, 257 p. ; **873**

1. Metamorphosis -- Mythology 2. Epic poetry. 3. Classics
ISBN 0374228418

LC 97036061

Comprises 24 stories from Metamorphoses.

A translation of Ovid's narrative collection of tales from ancient Greek and Roman mythology tells the stories of Theseus, King Midas, Hercules, Daedalus, Icarus, and the Trojan War, among other legends.

"This is an inspired act of translation that stands as vigorous poetry in its own right." New York Times Book Review.

Virgil, 70-19 B.C.

★The **Aeneid** / Virgil ; translated by Robert Fagles ; introduction by Bernard Knox. Viking, 2006, 1826. 496 p. **873**

1. Aeneas (Legendary character) 2. Heroes and heroines, Roman. 3. Gods and goddesses, Roman. 4. Warriors. 5. Troy (Extinct city) 6. Carthage (Extinct city) 7. Rome 8. Italy 9. Epic poetry. 10. Classics
ISBN 0670038032

LC 2006047220

Previously published: Glasgow : J. Aitken & Co., 1826.

Robert Fagles is a highly celebrated poet and translator of ancient texts. He makes Virgil's wondrous epic feel utterly relevant and modern with this stunning treatment. It is the tale of Aeneas, who flees the smoldering ashes of Troy to found a new civilization--Rome.

Virgil, 70-19 B.C.

The **Aeneid** / Virgil ; translated from the Latin by Robert Fitzgerald. Knopf, 1992. xxvii, 483 p. ; **873**

1. Aeneas (Legendary character) 2. Epic poetry 3. Classics
ISBN 9780679413356

LC 91058698

Virgil's poem about the adventures of Aeneas after the fall of Troy

874 Latin lyric poetry

Catullus, Gaius Valerius

The **poems** of Catullus / translated by Charles Martin. Johns Hopkins University Press, c1990. xxv, 181 p. ; **874**

1. Catullus, Gaius Valerius Translations into English. 2. Elegiac poetry, Latin 3. Epigrams, Latin 4. Love poetry, Latin 5. Rome -- Poetry.
ISBN 0801839262

LC 89045486

"A limited edition of these poems was published by Abattoir Editions, the University of Nebraska at Omaha, in 1979"--T.p. verso.

Includes index.

Lyric poems, often inspired by the joy, pain, or disillusionment brought about by his love for Lesbia, demonstrate the evocative and satirical talents of the ancient Roman poet

"The introduction ranges through Martin's observations on Catullus' place among Roman lyricists, his virtuosity, acuity, irony, and appeal to modern poets. The translations themselves, while open to inevitable quibbling among Latinists, are remarkably true to the versification, denotations, and connotations of the original texts. Martin is particularly adept at shaping the English into approximations of the Latin meters." Choice.

Horace

★**Odes** and epodes / Horace ; edited and translated by Niall Rudd. Harvard University Press, 2004. ix, 350 p. ; The Loeb classical library ; **874**

1. Horace Translations into English. 2. Laudatory poetry, Latin 3. Verse satire, Latin 4. Rome
ISBN 0674996097

LC 2003065236

Includes index.

The poetry of Horace (born 65 BCE) is richly varied, its focus moving between public and private concerns, urban and rural settings, Stoic and Epicurean thought. Here is a new Loeb Classical Library edition of the great Roman poet's Odes and Epodes, a fluid translation facing the Latin text. --From publisher description.

875 Latin speeches

Cicero, Marcus Tullius

Political speeches / Cicero ; translated with introductions and notes by D.H. Berry. Oxford University Press, 2006. xl, 345 p. : **875**

1. Cicero, Marcus Tullius Translations into English. 2. Speeches, addresses, etc, Latin 3. Rome -- Politics and government -- 265-30 B.C. Sources.
ISBN 9780192832665

LC 2005020919

This book presents nine speeches which reflect the development, variety, and drama of his political career. They include two speeches from his prosecution of Verres, a corrupt and cruel governor of Sicily; four speeches against the conspirator Catiline; and the Second Philippic, the famous denunciation of Mark Antony which cost Cicero his life. --From publisher description.

Cicero, Marcus Tullius

Selected works / Cicero ; translated with an introduction by Michael Grant. Penguin, 2004. 272 p. ; **875**

1. Cicero, Marcus Tullius Translations into English.
ISBN 9780140440997

LC bl2012019000

Offers a selection of writings from the Roman orator and statesman.

878 Latin miscellaneous writings

Cicero, Marcus Tullius

On the good life : [selected writings of] Cicero / translated with an introduction by Michael Grant. Penguin, 1971. 382 p. **878**

1. Cicero, Marcus Tullius Translations into English. 2. Personal conduct -- Early works to 1800 3. Ethics -- Early works to 1800
ISBN 9780140442441

LC 77030399

This volume brings together a wide range of his reflections upon the importance of moral integrity in the search for happiness. In essays that are articulate, meditative and inspirational, Cicero presents his views upon the significance of friendship and duty to state and family, and outlines a clear system of practical ethics that is at once simple and universal. --From publisher description.

880 Classical Greek literature and literatures of related Hellenic languages

Howatson, M. C,

★The **Oxford** companion to classical literature. / M. C. () Howatson. Oxford University Press, 2011. vi, 632 p. : **880**

1. Classical literature -- Dictionaries 2. Classical dictionaries 3. Dictionaries
ISBN 9780199548545

LC bl2013035931

Provides a guide to the literature of ancient Greece and Rome, discussing the lives and works of the principal authors and placing them within the societal and political context of the day.

880.09 Classical literatures (Greek and Latin)--history

Jenkyns, Richard

★**Classical** literature : an epic journey from Homer to Virgil and beyond / Richard Jenkyns. Basic Books, 2016 xi, 270 p. ; **880.09**

1. Classical literature. 2. Greek literature. 3. Latin literature. 4. Literature, Ancient.
ISBN 9780465097975

LC bl2016007791

Introduces and discusses thousands of years of Greek and Roman literature, including Homer and the birth of epic poetry, how Aeschylus developed tragedy, and the love poems of Catullus.

"A rich, witty, perceptive, and brief account of the Greek and Latin classics and their importance, both in themselves and in their enduring influence on the Western world. One of the best introductions available to the general reader." Library Journal.

881 Classical Greek poetry

Davenport, Guy

7 Greeks / translations by Guy Davenport. New Directions, 1995. 241 p. ; **881**

1. Greek poetry
ISBN 9780811212885

LC 95004227

Here is a colorful variety of works by seven Greek poets and philosophers who lived from the eighth to the third centuries BC. Salvaged from shattered pottery vases and tattered scrolls of papyrus, everything decipherable from the remains of these ancient authors is assembled here. --From publisher description.

Hesiod

Works and days ; and Theogony / Hesiod ; translated by Stanley Lombardo ; with introduction, notes, and glossary by Robert Lamberton. Hackett Pub. Co., c1993. 128 p. ; **881**

1. Hesiod Translations into English. 2. Religious poetry, Greek -- History and criticism. 3. Didactic poetry, Greek -- History and criticism. 4. Agriculture -- Greece -- Poetry. 5. Gods, Greek -- Poetry.
ISBN 9780872201798

LC 93024545

"This is a translation of two ancient Greek poems. Theogony is a genealogy of the Greek gods and some of their myths, and the Works and Days is a meditation on work, justice, and the gods, together with a farmer's almanac of the ancient agricultural year. For a literal rendition of the Greek, readers should turn elsewhere, but those who want a translation that captures something of the spirit of an ancient Greek poetic voice and its cultural milieu and transmits it in an appealing, lively, and accessible style will now turn to Lombardo." Choice.

882 Classical Greek dramatic poetry and drama

Aeschylus

The **complete** Greek tragedies : Aeschylus / edited by David Grene and Richmond Lattimore. University of Chicago Press, 1992. vi, 352 pages ; **882**

1. Greek drama (Tragedy) 2. Tragedy.
ISBN 9780226307640

LC 91045936

All other volumes contain the translations of the tragedies of Aeschylus, Sophocles, and Euripides for the most part from the original versions first published in the 1940s and 1950s. These translations have been the choice of generations of teachers and students, selling in the past forty years over three million copies. -- From publisher description.

Aeschylus

The **oresteia** / Aeschylus ; translated by Alan Shapiro and Peter Burian. Oxford University Press, 2003. ix, 285 p. ; **882**

1. Aeschylus Translations into English. 2. Agamemnon (Greek mythology) Drama. 3. Orestes (Greek mythology) Drama. 4. Electra (Greek mythology) Drama. 5. Drama. 6. Classical tragedy.
ISBN 9780195135923

LC 2002066272

"The collaboration of poet and scholar ... produces a language that is easy to read and easy to speak." Library Journal.

Aristophanes

The **complete** plays / Aristophanes ; the new translations by Paul Roche. New American Library, c2005. xvii, 715 p. ; **882**

1. Aristophanes Translations into English 2. Comedies 3. Athens (Greece) Drama.
ISBN 9780451214096

LC 2004056681

Presents a lively new translation of the eleven surviving satirical plays of the great ancient Greek playwright, including such comedy classics as The Birds, Lysistrata, The Clouds, The Frogs, and The Wasps.

Grene, David

The **Complete** Greek tragedies : Euripides / edited by David Grene and Richmond Lattimore. University of Chicago Press, 1992. unpaged ; **882**

1. Greek drama (Tragedy) -- Translations into English 2. Mythology, Greek -- Drama
ISBN 9780226307671

LC 91045936

Grene, David

The **Complete** Greek tragedies : Euripides / edited by David Grene and Richmond Lattimore. University of Chicago Press, 1992. unpaged ; **882**

1. Greek drama (Tragedy) -- Translations into English 2. Mythology, Greek -- Drama
ISBN 9780226307664

LC 91045936

Grene, David

The **Complete** Greek tragedies : Sophocles / edited by David Grene and Richmond Lattimore. University of Chicago Press, 1992. unpaged ; **882**

1. Greek drama (Tragedy) -- Translations into English 2. Mythology, Greek -- Drama
ISBN 9780226307657

LC 91045936

Sophocles

The **Theban** plays of Sophocles / translated by David R. Slavitt. Yale University Press, c2007. 237 p. ; **882**

1. Antigone (Mythological character) Drama. 2. Oedipus (Greek mythological figure) Drama. 3. Sophocles Translations into English.
ISBN 0300117760

LC 2006026965

Slavitt chooses to present the plays not in narrative sequence but in the order in which they were composed--Antigone, Oedipus Tyrannos, Oedipus at Colonus--thereby underscoring the fact that the story of Oedipus is one to which Sophocles returned over the course of his lifetime. --From publisher description.

883 Classical Greek epic poetry and fiction

Alexander, Caroline, 1956-

The **war** that killed Achilles : the true story of Homer's Iliad / Caroline Alexander. Viking, 2009. 320 p. **883**

1. Homer. Iliad. 2. War in literature. 3. Trojan War in literature 4. Trojan War. 5. Achilles (Greek mythology) 6. Ancient Greece -- History.
ISBN 9780670021123

LC 2009020160

"In its bones and sinews, the book is a nobly bold, even rousing, venture, a read-through of the Iliad, from beginning to end, always with a sharp eye to half a century of revealing scholarship, by great Hellenists like Gregory Nagy, Jasper Griffin, M.L. West and many others. The book's best ideas won't be new to readers versed in this work, but it would be hard to find a faster, livelier, more compact introduction to such a great range of recent Iliadic explorations." New York Times Book Review.

Homer

The **Iliad** / Homer ; translated by Robert Fagles ; introduction and notes by Bernard Knox. Viking, 1990. xvi, 683 p. ; **883**

1. Achilles (Greek mythology) 2. Trojan War 3. Classics 4. Epic poetry.
ISBN 0670835102

LC 89070695

The centuries-old epic about the wrath of Achilles is rendered into modern English verse by a renowned translator.

"Fagles offers a new verse rendering of the Iliad. Maneuvering between the literal and the literary, he tries with varying degrees of success to suggest the vigor and manner of the original while producing readable poetry in English." Library Journal.

Homer

The **Iliad** / Homer ; translated by Robert Fitzgerald ; with an introduction by Gregory Nagy. Knopf, 1992. xxv, 594 p. ; **883**

1. Achilles (Greek mythology) 2. Trojan War 3. Classics 4. Epic poetry.
ISBN 0679410759

LC 91053222

Includes bibliographical references (p. xxiii-xxv).

"Fitzgerald has solved virtually every problem that has plagued translators of Homer. The narrative runs, the dialogue speaks, the military action is clear, and the repetitive epithets become useful text rather than exotic relics. Aside from the ability to write poetry, which is basic to the undertaking, Mr. Fitzgerald's success derives from the use of a predominantly Anglo-Saxon vocabulary, a concentration on specific meanings, and an occasional arbitrary, but highly effective, substitution of implication for literal sense." The Atlantic.

Homer
Iliad / Homer ; translated by Stanley Lombardo ; introduction by Sheila Murnaghan. Hackett Pub. Co., c1997. lvii, 516 p. : **883**

1. Achilles (Greek mythology) 2. Trojan War 3. Classics 4. Epic poetry.
ISBN 0872203522

LC 96053368

"Lombardo manages to be respectful of Homer's dire spirit while providing on nearly every page some wonderfully fresh refashioning of his Greek. The result is a vivid and sometimes disarmingly hard-bitten reworking of a great classic. Not all of Lombardo's gambles pay off, and his attention-grabbing colloquialisms sometimes undermine the force of the original. Still, the success of so many of Lombardo's choices more than makes up for the false notes." New York Times Book Review.

Homer
The **Odyssey** / Homer ; translated by Emily Wilson. W. W. Norton & Co., 2018. 582 p. **883**

1. Heroes and heroines, Greek 2. Adventurers 3. Ocean travel 4. Seafaring life 5. Ancient Greece 6. Epic poetry 7. Classics
ISBN 9780393089059

LC 2017027185

A new translation of the epic poem, and the first by a woman, brings alive Homer's tale of shipwrecks, monsters, and magic, and provides an introductory overview of the poem's major themes, controversial origin, and the scope of its influence.

"Wilson's goal is for the work to sound natural to the modern reader without falling into contemporizing anachronisms, such as those found in the translation of Stanley Lombardo." Library Journal.

Homer
The **Odyssey** / Homer ; translated by Robert Fagles ; introduction and notes by Bernard Knox. Viking, c1996. x, 541 p. ; **883**

1. Heroes and heroines, Greek 2. Adventurers 3. Voyages and travels 4. Odysseus (Greek mythology) 5. Troy (Extinct city) 6. Ancient Greece 7. Epic poetry. 8. Classics
ISBN 0670821624

LC 96017280

A new verse translation of the Greek classic describes the wanderings of Odysseus after the fall of Troy.

"Fagles' Odyssey is the one to put into the hands of younger, first-time readers, not least because of its paucity of notes, which, though sometimes frustrating, is a sign that translation has been used to do the work of explanation. Altogether, an outstanding piece of work." Booklist.

Homer
The **Odyssey** / Homer ; translated by Robert Fitzgerald ; introduction by D.S. Carne-Ross. Farrar, Straus and Giroux, 1998. lxx, 515 p. : **883**

1. Heroes and heroines, Greek 2. Gods and goddesses, Greek 3. Voyages and travels 4. Odysseus (Greek mythology) 5. Epic poetry. 6. Classics
ISBN 0374525749

LC 98-73703

Presents the classic poem concerning the wanderings of the hero Odysseus and his miraculous return to Ithaca and a faithful wife.

Homer
Odyssey / Homer ; translated by Stanley Lombardo ; introduction by Sheila Murnaghan. Hackett Pub. Co., c2000. lxiv, 414 p. : **883**

1. Adventurers 2. Gods and goddesses, Greek 3. Voyages and travels 4. Odysseus (Greek mythology) 5. Epic poetry. 6. Classics
ISBN 0872204855

LC 99054175

"Lombardo has brought his laconic wit and love of the ribald, as well as his clever use of idiomatic American slang, to his version of the Odyssey. His carefully honed syntax gives the narrative energy and a whirlwind pace. The lines, rhythmic and clipped, have the tautness and force of Odysseus' bow." New York Times Book Review.

Homer
The **Odyssey** / Homer ; translated, with an introduction and notes, by Stephen Mitchell. Atria Books, 2013. xlv, 375 p. : **883**

1. Epic poetry
ISBN 9781451674170

LC 2012050572

A new translation of Homer's epic adventure endeavors to instill the poetic nature of its original language while retaining accuracy, readability, and character vibrancy.

Manguel, Alberto
Homer's the Iliad and the Odyssey : a biography / Alberto Manguel. Atlantic Monthly Press, c2007. x, 285 p. ; **883**

1. Homer. Iliad. 2. Homer. Odyssey. 3. Odysseus, King of Ithaca (Mythological character). 4. Homer. Iliad. sears 5. Homer. Odyssey. sears 6. Epic poetry, Greek -- History and criticism 7. Trojan War
ISBN 9780871139764

LC 2013443263

An insightful analysis of the two great epic poems that have served as the cornerstone of Western literature traces the history of The Iliad and The Odyssey from their earliest origins, the colorful characters and events chronicling the Trojan War and its aftermath, and their important legacy for Western culture.

"A study of the influence of The Iliad and The Odyssey on Western literature. First describing the two epics and the Homer question, Manguel then compares various translations in English, Spanish, French, and German, a move that brings out the complexities and richness of Homer's language. Does the poet sing of the rage, wrath, anger, rancor, or mania of Achilles? Then, following a more or less chronological progression, Manguel surveys the various shifting interpretations of the epics from Plato and Virgil to the present, including extended discussions of Derek Walcott, Timothy Findley, and Jorge Luis Borges. Highly recommended for general readers." Library Journal.

Nicolson, Adam, 1957-
Why Homer matters / Adam Nicolson. Henry Holt and Company, 2014. 288 p. **883**

1. Homer Criticism and interpretation. 2. Homer Influence. 3. Homer. Odyssey. 4. Homer. Iliad. 5. Poets 6. Europe
ISBN 9781627791793

LC 2014006763

"A John Macrae book."

Taking readers on an extraordinary journey through mythical and modern landscapes, the author of a celebrated column for The Sunday Telegraph explores the places forever haunted by their Homeric heroes and reveals the real roots of Homeric consciousness.

"Nicholson writes in a clear, fluid prose with apparently effortless ease; his vivid descriptions of landscapes and archaeological remains and his passionate engagement with history make this book a page-turner. Classicists will no doubt find fault with some of Nicholson's statements, but they will also be grateful to the author for explaining to the larger public in such an appealing fashion why Homer is not only unique but also relevant and necessary today. Summing Up: Highly recommended. General readers." Choice.

885 Classical Greek speeches

Pindar

★The **complete** odes / Pindar ; translated by Anthony Verity ; with an introduction and notes by Stephen Instone. Oxford University Press, 2007. xxvii, 186 p. ; **885**

1. Pindar Translations into English. 2. Athletics -- Greece 3. Games -- Greece 4. Laudatory poetry, Greek -- Translations into English.
ISBN 0192805533

LC 2006039673

The Greek poet Pindar (c. 518-428 b.c.) composed victory odes for winners in the ancient Games, including the Olympics. He celebrated the victories of athletes competing in foot races, horse races, boxing, wrestling, all-in fighting, and the pentathlon, and his Odes are fascinating not only for their poetic qualities, but for what they tell us about the Games. --From publisher description.

889 Modern Greek literature

Cavafy, Constantine, 1863-1933

The **collected** poems / C.P. Cavafy ; translated by Evangelos Sachperoglou ; Greek text edited by Anthony Hirst ; with an introduction by Peter Mackridge. Oxford University Press, 2007. xlviii, 238 p. ; **889**

1. Cavafy, Constantine, 1863-1933 Translations into English. 2. Greek poetry
ISBN 9780199212927

LC 2007015833

The only bilingual edition of Cavafy's collected poems currently available, this volume presents the most authentic Greek text of every poem he ever published, together with a new English translation that beautifully conveys the accent and rhythm of Cavafy's individual tone of voice. --From publisher description.

Elytis, Odysseas, 1911-1996

The **collected** poems of Odysseus Elytis / translated by Jeffrey Carson and Nikos Sarris ; introduction and notes by Jeffrey Carson. Johns Hopkins University Press, 2004. xliv, 715 p. ; **889**

1. Elytēs, Odysseas, 1911-1996 Translations into English. 2. Greek poetry
ISBN 9780801880452

LC 2004013496

Included in this landmark volume were Elytis's early poems, influenced in equal parts by surrealism and the natural world; Song Heroic and Mourning for the Lost Second Lieutenant of the Albanian Campaign, his epic poem connecting Greece's--and his own--Second World War experience to the myth of the eternal Greek hero; his most ambitious work, The Axion Esti; and his mature poetry, from Maria Nephele to West of Sorrow. --From publisher description.

891 East Indo-European and Celtic literatures

Firdawsi

★**Shahnameh** : the Persian book of kings / Abolqasem Ferdowsi ; translated by Dick Davis; with a foreword by Azar Nafisi. Viking, 2006. xxxvii, 886 p. : **891**

1. Rulers 2. Fathers and sons. 3. Heroes and heroines 4. Inheritance and succession 5. Iran -- History -- To 640 A. D. 6. Epic fiction.
ISBN 9780670034857

LC 2005042352

Includes index.

A new translation of the late-tenth-century Persian epic follows its story of pre-Islamic Iran's mythic time of creation through the seventh-century Arab invasion, tracing ancient Persia's incorporation into an expanding Islamic empire.

Griswold, Eliza, 1973-

I am the beggar of the world : landays from contemporary Afghanistan / translated and presented by Eliza Griswold ; photographs by Seamus Murphy. Farrar, Straus and Giroux, 2014. 149 p. : **891**

1. Folk poetry 2. Pushto poetry
ISBN 9780374191870

LC 2013035179

Written by Afghan women, this illuminating collection of landays - ancient oral and anonymous forms created by and for mostly illiterate people - express rage, longing, separation and love and reflect on contemporary Pashtun life and the impact of three decades of war.

Ḥāfiẓ, active 14th century

The **gift** : poems by the great Sufi master / Hafiz ; translated from the Persian by Daniel James Ladinsky. Arkana, 1999. xvi, 333 p. ; **891**

1. Sufi poetry, Persian -- Translations into English. 2. Religious poetry 3. Persian poetry
ISBN 9780140195811

LC 99010920

Celebrates one of Islam's greatest poetic voices and renowned spiritual leaders with a collection of 250 mystical healing poems

Jalāl al-Dīn Rūmī, Maulana, 1207-1273

The **essential** Rumi / translated by Coleman Barks, with John Moyne, A.A. Arberry, Reynold Nicholson. Harper, 1995. 302 p. ; **891**

1. Jalāl al-Dīn Rūmī, Maulana, 1207-1273 Translations into English. 2. Sufi poetry, Persian -- Translations into English. 3. Persian poetry
ISBN 9780062509598

LC 94044995

A collection of poetry by the thirteenth century Sufi saint cover topics ranging from emptiness and silence to elegance and majesty.

Jall al-Dn Rm, Maulana, 1207-1273

Rumi : bridge to the soul : journeys into the music and silence of the heart / translations by Coleman Barks, with A.J. Arberry and Nevit Ergin. HarperOne, c2007. x, 148 p. : **891**

1. Sufi poetry, Persian -- Translations into English. 2. Religious poetry
ISBN 9780061338168

LC 2007018384

A new collection of poems by the great Sufi mystic, the majority of which have never been published previously, is in celebration of the master writer's eight hundredth birthday and is accompanied by a description of the interpreter's culturally rich visit to Iran at the side of the poet Robert Bly.

Jall al-Dn Rm, Maulana, 1207-1273

Rumi : the big red book : the great masterpiece celebrating mystical love and friendship / the collected translations of Coleman Barks, based on the work of John Moyne ... [et al.]. HarperOne, c2010. 492 p. ; **891**

1. Jall al-Dn Rm, Maulana, 1207-1273 Translations into English. 2. Persian poetry

ISBN 9780061905827

LC 2010007895

"Odes and Quatrains from The Shams."

"Rumi's "Divani Shamsi Tabriz" ("The Works of Shams of Tabriz"--Named in honor of Rumi's spiritual teacher and friend) is a collection of lyric poems that contain more than 40,000 verses by America's best-selling poet, and is a classic of Persian literature. Its most familiar form is as a big red book, hence the name. Coleman Barks is famous for his renderings of Rumi's poetry and his work on these particular poems has never been published anywhere. This book represents over thirty-three years on Rumi's seminal classic"-- Provided by publisher.

Omar Khayyam

★**Rubaiyat** of Omar Khayyam / rendered into English verse by Edward FitzGerald ; with illustrations by Edmund J. Sullivan. St. Martin's Press, c1983. 75 p. : **891**

1. Persian poetry -- Translations into English

ISBN 0312695276

LC 83009767

Translation of: Rubaiyat

Contains the English edition of the eleventh-century Persian poet's quatrains that express his philosophy of love and life

Tagore, Rabindranath, 1861-1941

Selected poems / Rabindranath Tagore ; translated from the Bengali by William Radice. Penguin Books, 2005. 202 p. ; **891**

1. Tagore, Rabindranath, 1861-1941 Translations into English. 2. Bengali poetry 3. Indic poetry

ISBN 9780140449884

LC oc2007026863

Poems such as 'Earth' and 'In the Eyes of a Peacock' present a picture of natural processes unaffected by human concerns, while others, as in 'Recovery - 14', convey the poet's bewilderment about his place in the world. --From publisher description.

Washington, Peter

Persian poets / selected and edited by Peter Washington. Alfred A. Knopf, 2000. 254 p. ; Everyman's library pocket poets **891**

1. Persian poetry -- Translations into English. 2. Anthologies.

ISBN 9780375411267

LC bl2008017337

Celebrating the accomplishments of the medieval Persian poets, this anthology of poetry from the era and home territory of Rumi includes the work of Hafiz, Attar, Jumi, Saadi, and other lesser-known one-name Persian literary heavyweights.

891.6 Celtic literatures

Kinsella, Thomas

The **Tain** : translated from the Irish epic Tain Bo Cualinge / Thomas Kinsella ; with brush drawings by Louis le Brocquy. Oxford University Press, 1970 282 p. : **891.6**

1. Epic literature, Irish -- Translations into English. 2. Heroes -- Ireland -- Legends. 3. Mythology, Celtic -- Ireland. 4. Tales -- Ireland.

ISBN 9780192803733

LC 2002726950

The Tain Bo Cuailnge is the centre-piece of the eight-century Ulster cycle of heroic tales. In this great epic tale Cuchulainn, the Hound of Ulster single-handedly resists the invading armies of the king and queen of Connacht, Ailill and Medb, who seek to carry off the great Brown Bull of Cuailnge. --From publisher description.

891.7 Russian literature and related East Slavic literatures

Batuman, Elif, 1977-

The **possessed** : adventures with Russian books and the people who read them / Elif Batuman. Farrar, Straus and Giroux, 2010. 304 p. **891.7**

1. Authors, Russian. 2. Writing. 3. Books and reading. 4. Readers. 5. Essays.

ISBN 9780374532185

LC 2009025416

"In this book, the author makes you look at Russian literature from a fresh perspective, using an unusual blend of memoir and travelogue as she delves into the lives and personalities of such Russian literary giants as Isaac Babel, Fyodor Dostoevsky and Leo Tolstoy. ... In a sense, the details of Batuman's essays are less significant than the tone. She cruises through minor crises with an air of detached amusement, eye focused on the little absurdities that make travel--and people--fun." Cleveland Plain Dealer.

891.709 Russian literature--history and criticism

Nabokov, Vladimir Vladimirovich, 1899-1977

Lectures on Russian literature / Vladimir Nabokov ; edited, with an introduction, by Fredson Bowers. Harcourt/Bruccoli Clark Layman, 2002, c1981. xvii, 324 p. : **891.709**

1. Russian literature -- 19th century -- History and criticism

ISBN 9780156027762

LC bl2011017735

Originally published: New York : Harcourt Brace Jaovanovich/ Bruccoli Clark, 1981.

Collects critical essays discussing Gogol, Turgenev, Dostoevski, Tolstoy, Chekhov, Gorki, and the nature of philistinism.

Terras, Victor

A **history** of Russian literature / Victor Terras. Yale University Press, c1991. x, 654 p. ; **891.709**

1. Russian literature -- History and criticism.

ISBN 0300049714

LC 91013337

Surveys Russian literature from the eleventh century to the present, set within the context of political, social, religious, and philisophical developments.

"The book's minor shortcomings are overshadowed by its numerous merits; its accuracy, keenness of observation, subtle comments, vivid quotations, erudition. Almost every page of the book invites one to read and re-read Russian literature." Times Literary Supplement.

891.71 Russian poetry

Akhmatova, Anna Andreevna, 1889-1966

The **complete** poems of Anna Akhmatova / translated by Judith Hemschemeyer ; edited by Roberta Reeder. Zephyr Press ; 1992. 908 p. : **891.71**

1. Akhmatova, Anna Andreevna, 1889-1966 Translations into English. 2. Russian poetry

ISBN 9780939010271

LC 92062648

The present edition adds 80 new poetic texts which came to light at the end of 1990, as well as numerous photographs, and a 16-page portfolio portraying the poet through the eyes of painters, sculptors, and other artists. --From publisher description.

Poems : Poems / Akhmatova ; translated from the Russian by D.M. Thomas. Knopf, c2006. 256 p. ; **891.71**

1. Akhmatova, Anna Andreevna, 1889-1966 Translations into English. 2. Russian poetry -- 20th century

ISBN 9780307264244

LC 2006297217

"This selection first published, under the title You will hear thunder, in Great Britain by Martin Secker & Warburg Ltd, 1985"--T.p. verso.

A definitive body of work by one of the great Russian poets of the twentieth century includes poetry from all of her major collections, including "Requiem," a memorial to the victims of Stalin's terror, as well as twenty poems that have been newly translated for this collection.

Pushkin, Aleksandr Sergeevich, 1799-1837

Eugene Onegin : and other poems / Pushkin ; translated from the Russian by Charles Johnston. Knopf, 1999. 240 p. ; **891.71**

1. Russian poetry

ISBN 9780375406720

LC BL 99006547

Two brief poems accompany a long narrative poem about a heartless fop who is the object of an ardent young woman's selfless love.

TSvetaeva, Marina, 1892-1941

Selected poems / Marina TSvetayeva ; translated from the Russian and introduced by Elaine Feinstein ; with literal versions provided by Angela Livingstone ... [et al.] Penguin Books, 1994, c1993. xviii, 131 p. ; **891.71**

1. TSvetaeva, Marina, 1892-1941 Translations into English. 2. Russian poetry

ISBN 9780140187595

LC BL 00003448

Originally published: Oxford ; New York : Oxford University Press, 1993. (Oxford poets)

An admired contemporary of Rilke, Akhmatova, and Mandelstam, Marina Tsvetaeva was a witness to the political turmoil and the social devastation wrought by the Russian Revolution and a powerfully inspired chronicler of a difficult life and exile sustained by poetry. --From publisher description.

Yevtushenko, Yevgeny

Selected poems / Yevgeny Yevtushenko ; translated from the Russian by Robin Milner-Gulland and Peter Levi. Penguin, 2008 90 p. **891.71**

1. Russian poetry.

ISBN 9780140424775

This volume contains a selection of early works by Yevgeny Alexandrovich Yevtushenko who blazed a trail for a generation of Soviet poets with a confident poetic voice that moves effortlessly between social and personal themes.

891.72 Russian drama

Chekhov, Anton Pavlovich, 1860-1904

The **complete** plays / Anton Chekhov ; translated, edited, and annotated by Laurence Senelick. W.W. Norton, 2007, c2006. lx, 1060 p. ; **891.72**

1. Chekhov, Anton Pavlovich, 1860-1904 Translations into English.

ISBN 0393330699

LC bl2008007029

Reprint. Originally published: c2006.

A single-volume, English-language collection of all of Chekhov's plays includes previously untranslated pieces including The Power of Hypnosis, a first version of Ivanov, and early humorous dialogues.

Chekhov : the four major plays / in new translations by Curt Columbus. Ivan R. Dee, c2005. 294 p. ; **891.72**

1. Chekhov, Anton Pavlovich, 1860-1904 Translations into English.

ISBN 1566636264

LC 2004048612

Curt Columbus endows these timeless dramas, Seagull, Uncle Vanya, Three Sisters and Cherry Orchard, with dialogue that is faithful to the Russian original but dazzlingly attuned to contemporary audiences. -- From publisher description.

Malcolm, Janet

Reading Chekhov : a critical journey / Janet Malcolm. Random House, 2001. 209 p. **891.72**

1. Chekhov, Anton Pavlovich, 1860-1904 Criticism and interpretation. 2. Russia in literature. 3. Russia -- Description and travel.

ISBN 0375506683

LC 2001019585

"The author's pilgrimage to Chekhov's Russia--Moscow, St. Petersburg, the gardens of his villa in Yalta--is a reunion with this most reticent of literary fathers. Malcolm analyzes the transformations that Chekhov grants his redeemable roués and guileless heroines, and illuminates the hidden surreality and waywardness of his realism." The New Yorker.

891.73 Russian fiction

Finn, Peter, 1962-

The **Zhivago** affair : the Kremlin, the CIA, and the battle over a forbidden book / Peter Finn and Petra Couvée. Pantheon Books, 2014. 352 p. ; **891.73**

1. Pasternak, Boris Leonidovich, 1890-1960. Doktor Zhivago. 2. Pasternak, Boris Leonidovich, 1890-1960 Censorship. 3. CIA -- History 4. Authors, Russian -- 20th century 5. Dissenters -- Soviet Union 6. Cold War 7. Banned books 8. Soviet Union -- Foreign relations United States. 9. United States -- Foreign relations Soviet

Union. 10. Soviet Union -- Politics and government -- 1953-1985.
ISBN 9780307908001

LC 2013033875

National Book Critics Circle Award for Nonfiction finalist, 2014.

Doctor Zhivago, a novel published in translation during the late 1950s by Russian author Boris Pasternak, created a sensation in the West with its negative depiction of the Russian Revolution. The CIA recognized that the book could promote anti-Communist sentiment within the Soviet Union, so they arranged to produce copies of the original Russian text and sneak them into Russia. The Zhivago Affair relates the exciting story of how the book-smuggling was accomplished, the severe consequences the Kremlin imposed on Pasternak and his family, and the international controversy aroused by the novel.

"Drawing on recently declassified CIA documents, Finn and Couvée present an engaging thriller, in which bureaucratic obstructions and Cold War politics threaten the publication of a controversial masterpiece of world literature." Booklist.

891.8 Slavic (Slavonic) literatures

Dimkovska, Lidija, 1971-

pH neutral history / Lidija Dimkovska ; translated from the Macedonian by Ljubica Arsovska and Peggy Reid. Copper Canyon Press, 2012. viii, 75 p. ; **891.8**

1. Dimkovska, Lidija, 1971- Translations into English. 2. Macdeonian poetry
ISBN 9781556593758

LC 2011044017

Poems explore the consequences of living in an era of contradictory ethics.

Havel, Vaclav

The **garden** party and other plays / Vaclav Havel. Grove Press, 1993. 273 p. ; **891.8**

1. Havel, Vaclav Translations into English.
ISBN 080213307X

LC 93008656

Herbert, Zbigniew

The **collected** poems, 1956-1998 / Zbigniew Herbert ; translated and edited by Alissa Valles ; with additional translations by Czeslaw Milosz and Peter Dale Scott ; introduction by Adam Zagajewski. Ecco, c2007. xviii, 600 p. ; **891.8**

1. Polish poetry -- 19th century
ISBN 9780060783907

LC 2006040856

Includes index.

A new translation of poetic works by the Polish Nobel Prize candidate includes pieces from his entire body of work, from String of Light to Epilogue of the Storm, in a volume that offers insight into his perspectives on such topics as imagination, art, and exile.

Milosz, Czeslaw

Legends of modernity : essays and letters from occupied Poland, 1942-43 / Czeslaw Milosz ; translated from the Polish by Madeline G. Levine ; introduction by Jaroslaw Anders. Farrar, Straus and Giroux, 2005. xvi, 266 p. ; **891.8**

1. Milosz, Czeslaw Correspondence. 2. Andrzejewski, Jerzy, 1909-1983 Correspondence. 3. Authors, Polish -- 20th century -- Correspondence. 4. World War II, Polish 5. Poland -- Social life and customs -- 20th century. 6. Letters. 7. Essays.
ISBN 0374184992

LC 2005040950

The Nobel Laureate reflects on his childhood in Nazi-occupied Poland and on the failure of Europe to avoid the catastrophic war and genocide of the 1930s and 1940s in a series of letters and essays that plumb the painful legacy of World War II.

"Written to the young intellectual Jerzy Andrejewski, the letters reveal Milosz's concern about the political climate of the era and the deterioration of religious influence owing to the chaos all across Europe and the rest of the world. The essays explore the ideas of William James, André Gide, Stendhal (Henri Beyle), Honor de Balzac, and others as they relate to religious faith, reason and rationalism, contradictions, doubting, and believing in a civilized world and its religious institutions. Reading Milosz is a demanding, rewarding, and ultimately powerful experience for the mind and the soul." Library Journal.

★**Milosz's** ABC's / Czeslaw Milosz ; translated from the Polish by Madeline G. Levine. Farrar, Straus and Giroux, 2001. 313 p. **891.8**

1. Milosz, Czeslaw 2. Authors, Polish -- 20th century. 3. Poland.
ISBN 0374199779

LC 00042176

Translation of selections from the author's Abecadlo Milosza and Inne abecadlo.

"The short prose entries in this quiet book take note of some of the people and places and ideas that contributed to the making of Milosz. The subjects of his sketches range from Alchemy and Curiosity to Rimbaud and Whitman, from childhood friends to Polish intellectuals little known in the West. But what could have been no more than a light memory work becomes almost a registry of gratitude: a meditation on the obligations of having lived a life and the responsibilities inherent in its particulars." The New Yorker.

Road-side dog / Czeslaw Milosz ; translated by the author and Robert Hass. Farrar, Straus and Giroux, 1999, c1998. xi, 208 p. ; **891.8**

ISBN 0374526230

LC BL 00001255

Reprint. Originally published: 1998.

A collection of poems, essays, aphorisms, and anecdotes which addresses such issues as youth, falling in love, beauty, and growing old.

To begin where I am : selected essays / Czeslaw Milosz ; edited and with an introduction by Bogdana Carpenter and Madeline G. Levine. Farrar, Straus and Giroux, 2001. xvi, 462 p. ; **891.8**

1. Milosz, Czeslaw 2. War -- Moral and ethical aspects. 3. Human nature. 4. Faith. 5. Communism. 6. Essays.
ISBN 0374258902

LC 2001033356

Five decades of essays by the revered writer are collected here, with writings on war, human nature, faith, communism, and Polish culture, among other topics.

Ristovi, Ana, 1972-

Directions for use : selected poems / Ana Ristovi ; translated from the Serbian by Steven Teref & Maja Teref. Zephyr Press,

2017 xv, 111 p. ; **891.8**

1. Ristovi, Ana, 1972- Translations into English. 2. Serbian poetry
ISBN 9781938890147

LC 2018295234

A rich embroidery of frank sexuality and lyric images from award-winning Serbian poet. -- From publisher description.

Sosnowski, Andrzej, 1959-

Lodgings : selected poems, 1987-2010 / Andrzej Sosnowski ; translated from the Polish by Benjamin Paloff. Open Letter, 2011. xi, 163 p. ; **891.8**

1. Polish poetry
ISBN 9781934824320

LC 2010052054

First collection in English of the foremost Polish poet of his generation. --From publisher description.

Szymborska, Wislawa

Here / Wislawa Szymborska ; translated from the Polish by Clare Cavanagh and Stanisław Baraczak. Houghton Mifflin Harcourt, 2010. 85 p. ; **891.8**

1. Polish poetry
ISBN 9780547364612

LC 2010018889

A collection of poems covering aspects of life as varied as Vermeer's "Milkmaid," miniseries, and the apocalypse.

"Szymborska writes pithy, mischievous, and wise poems that disarm, delight, and enlighten in a flash even as they illuminate hidden dimensions of existence. She writes of her teenage self, the earth's astounding bounty, accidents, nature's innocence, and time. Szymborska is sharply ironic and lithely philosophical, pondering the phenomenal precision of dreams and the elusiveness of meaning. The neat, prancing lyrics collected in this slender, piercing book are delectable and profound." Booklist.

Map : collected and last poems / Wislawa Szymborska ; translated from the Polish by Clare Cavanagh and Stanisław Baraczak ; edited by Clare Cavanagh. Houghton Mifflin Harcourt, 2015. xiv, 447 p. ; **891.8**

1. Polish poetry
ISBN 9780544126022

LC 2015297265

Includes index.

Collects translations of poems from throughout the author's career, including several new translations, including her entire final collection in English for the first time.

"Throughout, Szymborska considers loss and fragility, as when former lovers walk past each other and an aging professor is no longer allowed his vodka and cigarettes. She writes, too, of the imprecision of memory, and in the title poem, the discovery that maps 'give no access to the vicious truth.' This is a brilliant and important collection." Booklist.

Poems, new and collected, 1957-1997 / Wislawa Szymborska ; translated from the Polish by Stanisław Baranczak and Clare Cavanagh. Harcourt Brace, c1998. xvii, 273 p. ; **891.8**

1. Polish poetry -- 20th century.
ISBN 9780151003532

"Szymborska's work is ultimately wisdom literature, written in a first person that expresses a universal humanity that American poets--lockstep individualists all--haven't dared essay since early in this century." Booklist.

Zagajewski, Adam, 1945-

Eternal enemies / Adam Zagajewski ; translated from the Polish by Clare Cavanagh. Farrar, Straus and Giroux, 2008. 116 p. ; **891.8**

1. Zagajewski, Adam, 1945- Translations into English. 2. Polish poetry
ISBN 9780374216344

LC 2007042855

An anthology of poetry reflects on place, language, and history in a collection that includes tributes to such writers as Milosz, Sebald, Brodsky, and Blake, as well as portraits of family members and other loved ones.

Unseen hand / Adam Zagajewski ; translated from the Polish by Clare Cavanagh. Farrar, Straus and Giroux, 2011. 107 p. ; **891.8**

1. Zagajewski, Adam, 1945- Translations into English. 2. Polish poetry
ISBN 9780374280895

LC 2010046274

892 Afro-Asiatic literatures

Darwsh, Mahmoud

Unfortunately, it was paradise : selected poems / Mahmoud Darwish ; translated and edited by Munir Akash and Carolyn Forche ; with Sinan Antoon and Amira El-Zein. University of California Press, c2003. xix, 191 p. ; **892**

1. Arabic poetry
ISBN 9780520237544

LC 2002068454

Mitchell, Stephen, 1943-

★**Gilgamesh** : a new English version / Stephen Mitchell. Free Press, 2004. 304 p. **892**

1. Rulers. 2. Giants. 3. Companionship 4. Male friendship 5. Mesopotamia -- History -- To 330 B.C. 6. Adventure stories. 7. Epic poetry. 8. Classics
ISBN 074326164X

LC 2004050072

"Relying on existing translations (and in places where there are gaps, on his own imagination), Mitchell seeks language that is as swift and strong as the story itself. . . . This wonderful new version of the story of Gilgamesh shows how the story came to achieve literary immortality--not because it is a rare ancient artifact, but because reading it can make people in the here and now feel more completely alive." Publishers Weekly.

892.4 Hebrew literature

Amichai, Yehuda

Open closed open : poems / Yehuda Amichai ; translated from the Hebrew by Chana Bloch and Chana Kronfeld. Harcourt, c2000. vi, 184 p. ; **892.4**

1. Amichai, Yehuda Translations into English. 2. Hebrew poetry
ISBN 9780151003785

LC 00023537

A new anthology of poetry by Israel's leading poet offers meditative, lyrical, and playful observations on the language of love, Jerusalem, beauty, and the Jewish experience.

Poems of Jerusalem ; and, Love poems : a bilingual edition / Yehuda Amichai. Sheep Meadow Press, 1992 xi, 265 p. ; **892.4**

1. Amichai, Yehuda Translations into English. 2. Love poetry, Israeli -- Translations into English. 3. Love poetry, Israeli. 4. Jerusalem -- Poetry.
ISBN 1878818198

LC 92031558

English and Hebrew.

First work originally published: New York : Perennial Library, c1988; 2nd work originally published: New York : Harper & Row, c1981.

"This work is actually drawn from eight previous works and boasts an even larger array of translators (including Stephen Mitchell, David Rosenberg, Ted Hughes, and the poet himself). The thematic arrangement deftly emphasizes the Israeli poet's constant preoccupation with both Jerusalem and love." Library Journal.

Shabtai, Aharon

War & love, love & war : new and selected poems / Aharon Shabtai ; translated from the Hebrew by Peter Cole. New Directions, 2010. 175 p. ; **892.4**

1. Shabtai, Aharon Translations into English. 2. Israeli poetry 3. Hebrew poetry
ISBN 9780811218900

LC 2010010440

892.7 Arabic and Maltese literatures

Adunis, 1930-

Concerto al-Quds / Adonis ; translated from the Arabic by Khaled Mattawa. Yale University Press, 2017 85 p. **892.7**

1. Syrian poetry. 2. Jerusalem, Israel
ISBN 9780300197648

LC 2017941088

"In this stunning volume about Jerusalem (al-Quds in Arabic), Syrian poet Adonis, who has been hailed as a founding voice in Arabic-language modernism, envisions the poem as a space for dialogue between traditions, nations, and historical milieux." Publishers Weekly.

Darwsh, Mahmoud

If I were another / Mahmoud Darwish ; translated from the Arabic by Fady Joudah. Farrar, Straus and Giroux, 2009. xxviii, 201 p. ; **892.7**

1. Arabic poetry
ISBN 9780374174293

LC 2009011521

Contains translations of the popular Palestinian poet's work focusing on themes including loss and exile.

Handal, Nathalie, 1969-

The **poetry** of Arab women : a contemporary anthology / edited by Nathalie Handal. Interlink Books, 2001. xxi, 355 p. ; **892.7**

1. Arabic poetry
ISBN 9781566563741

LC 00058054

Irwin, Robert, 1946-

Night and horses and the desert : an anthology of classical Arabic literature / edited by Robert Irwin. Anchor Books, c2001. xviii, 462 p. ; **892.7**

1. Arabic literature -- History and criticism. 2. Anthologies
ISBN 9780385721554

LC 2001053721

Ranging from the fifth to sixteenth centuries, a comprehensive survey of Arabic poetry and literature covers the broad sweep of Arabic writing, from Afghanistan to Spain, including readings from the Koran, The Thousand and One Nights, and more with accompanying notes on genres and history.

"The chapter on the Qur'an is perhaps the most essential as it examines just how vital the dogma of Islam has been for the Arabic understanding of culture and art. This persuasive work will surely fill in the gap in the study of Arabic literature." Publishers Weekly.

894 Literatures of Altaic, Uralic, Hyperborean, Dravidian languages literatures of miscellaneous languages of south Asia

Pamuk, Orhan, 1952-

Other colors : essays and a story / Orhan Pamuk ; translated from the Turkish by Maureen Freely. Alfred A. Knopf, 2007. xi, 433 p. : **894**

1. Art. 2. Families 3. Love. 4. Writing. 5. Essays.
ISBN 0307266753

LC 2007021132

Includes index.

A compilation of essays spanning three decades of work presents an array of criticism, autobiographical writings, and meditations on such topics as the writing process, romantic and parental love, and differing attitudes toward art in the East and West.

"Whether he's writing wistfully about Andre Gide as the hero of Turkish intellectuals...or recalling how he used to collect Coca-Cola cans as a boy, from the trash cans of expat Americans, Pamuk is taking the world we thought we knew and making it fresh and alive." New York Times Book Review.

895 Literatures of East and Southeast Asia

Rexroth, Kenneth, 1905-1982

One hundred poems from the Japanese / Kenneth Rexroth. New Directions, 1955. 143 p. **895**

1. Japanese poetry 2. Ogura hyakunin Isshu.
ISBN 9780811201810

LC 56002557

A collection of Japanese poems accompanied by their English translations.

895.1 Chinese literature

Hinton, David, 1954-

Mountain home : the wilderness poetry of ancient China / selected and translated by David Hinton. New Directions Pub. Corp., 2005. xxi, 295 p. : **895.1**

1. Chinese poetry -- Translations into English. 2. Nature in literature. 3. Poetry of places -- China 4. Nature

ISBN 9780811216241

LC 2005000869

"A new directions book."

Originally published: Washington, D.C. : Counterpoint, 2002.

"Translator and scholar Hinton ensures that Western readers will experience this supreme collection of Chinese rivers-and-mountains (shan-shui) poetry at the deepest possible level by succinctly explaining the cosmology inherent in this vital and profoundly influential tradition. The keys to understanding the elegant poetry of such masters as T'ao Ch'ien (365-427), Li Po (701-762), and Lu Yu (1125-1210) are realizing that they perceive no divide between the human and what we call nature, or between being and nonbeing. Oneness with life at its purest is the desired mode for these thoughtful, yet often playful, poets, and dwelling within these meditative pages is the first step on the way there." Booklist.

Mair, Victor H., 1943-

The **Columbia** history of Chinese literature / Victor H. Mair, editor. Columbia University Press, c2001. xx, 1342 p. : **895.1**

1. Chinese literature -- History and criticism.

ISBN 9780231109840

LC 2001028236

Watson, Burton, 1925-

The **Columbia** book of Chinese poetry : from early times to the thirteenth century / translated and edited by Burton Watson. Columbia University Press, 1984. 385 p. : **895.1**

1. Chinese poetry -- Translations into English

ISBN 9780231056823

LC 83026182

Includes index.

Chinese poems exploring themes such as nature, death, and politics are accompanied by essays tracing the development of poetry in China.

895.6 Japanese literature

Carter, Steven D.

Haiku before haiku : from the Renga masters to Bash / translated, with an introduction, by Steven D. Carter. Columbia University Press, c2011. viii, 163 p. ; **895.6**

1. Haiku -- Translations into English. 2. Japanese poetry -- 1185-1600 -- Translations into English. 3. Japanese poetry -- Edo period, 1600-1868 -- Translations into English. 4. Renga -- Translations into English.

ISBN 9780231156479

LC 2010037030

Keene, Donald

The **pleasures** of Japanese literature / Donald Keene. Columbia University Press, c1988. xii, 133 p., 4 p. of plates : **895.6**

1. Japanese literature -- To 1868 -- History and criticism 2. Theater -- Japan -- History 3. Aesthetics, Japanese

ISBN 9780231067362

LC 88018069

Includes index.

Introduces Japanese culture, and discusses the aesthetics, poetry, fiction, and theater of Japan.

"If your library has no other introduction to the Japanese classics, nor any need for another, this is the one it ought to include." Booklist.

Seeds in the heart : Japanese literature from earliest times to the late sixteenth century / with a new preface by the author, Donald Keene. Columbia University Press, c1999. xii, 1265 p. ; **895.6**

1. Japanese literature -- To 1600 -- History and criticism

ISBN 9780231114417

LC 99025990

Originally published: New York : Henry Holt & Co., 1993.

"The first half of Seeds in the Heart encompasses everything from the myths, legends, songs and poems of the eighth-century Kojiki (Record of Ancient Matters) and Manyoshu, a collection of 4,500 poems, to The Tale of Genji and later works of fiction. During Japan's middle ages (1185-1600), Buddhism and popular (rather than aristocratic) forms of storytelling and theater generated a repertory of characters and genres that would eventually form the country's first broadly based, national culture. The literature of these centuries has rarely attracted the scholarly attention paid to the earlier high classical tradition. So Mr. Keene's attention to this period makes the second half of Seeds in the Heart especially valuable." New York Times Book Review.

895.8 Burmese literature

Szymborska, Wislawa

★**Monologue** of a dog : new poems / Wislawa Szymborska ; translated from the Polish by Clare Cavanagh and Stanislaw Baraczak. Harcourt, c2006. xiv, 96 p. ; **895.8**

ISBN 9780151012206

LC 2005016084

Featuring a foreword by former U.S. poet laureate Billy Collins, a collection of poetry by the Nobel Prize-winning writer explores such topics as unremembered love and keys mislaid in the grass, in a volume that reflects the author's humorous, compassionate, and contemplative nature and presents her poems in both English and their original Polish.

"In this volume, Nobel laureate Szymborska invites readers to linger over moments small, earthly, and sometimes life-altering. With characteristically simple language and imagery, wit and irony, she shows us how life can change at any moment. Hers are the politics of the everyday, little observations on the value of life." Library Journal.

901 Philosophy and theory of history

MacMillan, Margaret, 1943-

Dangerous games : the uses and abuses of history / Margaret MacMillan. Modern Library, 2009, c2008. xi, 188 p. ; **901**

1. Historiography. 2. History -- Philosophy. 3. Decision making. 4. History -- Errors, inventions, etc.

ISBN 9780679643586

Based on the Joanne Goodman lecture series of the University of Western Ontario.

Originally published : The uses and abuses of history. Toronto : Viking Canada, 2008.

Explores the ways in which history has been used to influence people and government, focusing on how reportage of past events has been manipulated to justify religious movements and political campaigns.

"This is a must read for anyone who wants to understand the importance of correctly understanding the past." Publishers Weekly.

Ortega y Gasset, Jose, 1883-1955

The **revolt** of the masses / Jose Ortega y Gasset. W.W. Norton, 1993. 190 p. ; **901**

1. Civilization 2. Proletariat 3. Europe -- Civilization.
ISBN 9780393310955

LC 93029295

Translation of: La rebelion de las masas.

902 Miscellany of history

Grun, Bernard, 1901-1972

★The **timetables** of history : a historical linkage of people and events / Bermard Grun. Simon & Schuster, 2005. 835 p. ; **902**

1. Chronology, Historical
ISBN 9780743270038

LC 2005049766

"A Touchstone book."
"Based on Werner Stein's Kulturfahrplan."
Includes index.

Updated to cover the years 1990 through 2004, this detailed historical reference provides a chronology of seven thousand years of significant moments in history, religion, science, technology, culture, and the arts in an accessible format designed for quick reference.

"This chronology includes material from 4500 BCE to 2004. . . . The information is listed by year in seven columns labeled History, Politics, Literature, Theater, Religion, Philosophy, Learning, Visual Arts, Music, Science, Technology, Growth, and Daily Life. . . . This work is an excellent chronological tool, and should be found in all libraries." Choice.

DK Publishing, Inc,

★**Timelines** of history. the ultimate visual guide to the events that shaped the world DK Publishing, 2018. 512 p. : **902**

1. Chronology, Historical.
ISBN 9781465470027

LC 2018302099

"The ultimate visual guide to the events that shaped the world"--Cover.

Includes index.

"This edition published in the United States in 2018 by DK Publishing"--Title page verso.

With easily accessible cross-references that build bite-size pieces of information into a narrative that leads readers back and forth through time, "Timelines of History" makes the past accessible to all families, students, and the general reader.

Kagan, Neil

National Geographic concise history of the world : an illustrated time line / edited by Neil Kagan. National Geographic Society, 2013. 416 p. : **902**

1. Chronology, Historical.
ISBN 9781426211782

LC 2015430064

Presents world history from an original international perspective to offer new insights to key events as they occurred simultaneously while providing innovative timelines and visual spreads that allow readers to scan single areas or compare multiple societies, offering complementary sidebars detailing milestones, personality portraits and major innovations.

Rosenberg, Daniel, 1966-

Cartographies of time / Daniel Rosenberg and Anthony Grafton. Princeton Architectural Press, 2009. 272 p. **902**

1. Maps. 2. Chronology, Historical. 3. Cartography. 4. History -- Philosophy.
ISBN 9781568987637

LC 2008052892

"The authors aim to provide the first full account of the development of the modern timeline, from its inauspicious beginnings in crude lists and tables, to the glorious, colorful artworks that convey the sweep of time with arresting visual drama. There's more to this story, however. The story of the timeline is also the story of how humanity's perception of time has evolved, and how the various representations of time can tell us much about the personality and proclivity of the era in which it was designed. Rosenberg and Grafton's text is crisp and informative, but the true stars of Cartographies of Time are the numerous illustrations and photographs of the chronologies themselves." PopMatters.

902.02 Chronologies

Berndl, Klaus

National Geographic visual history of the world / [authors, Klaus Berndl ... et al.]. National Geographic Society, 2005. 656 p. : **902.02**

1. World history -- Pictorial works.
ISBN 9780792236955

LC 2005541553

Includes index.

Looks at the important events and figures in world history, from 4000 B.C. to the present day.

903 Dictionaries, encyclopedias, concordances of history

Znamierowski, Alfred

The **world** encyclopedia of flags : an illustrated guide to international flags, banners, standards and ensigns / Alfred Znamierowski. Lorenz Books, 2019. 256 p. : **903**

1. Flags
ISBN 9780754834809

A comprehensive reference to flags including a fascinating history, with over 1400 illustrations and newly updated in a special large-format edition.

904 Collected accounts of events

Cassidy, Cody

Who ate the first oyster? : the extraordinary people behind the greatest firsts in history / Cody Cassidy. Penguin Books, 2020 208 p. **904**

1. Firsts (Events, inventions, etc.) 2. Inventions -- History 3. Scientific discoveries -- History 4. Civilization
ISBN 9780143132752

LC 2019030541

Who wore the first pants? Who painted the first masterpiece? Who first rode the horse? This madcap adventure across ancient history uses everything from modern genetics to archaeology to uncover the geniuses behind these and other world-changing innovations. Who invented the wheel? Who told the first joke? Who drank the first beer? Who was the murderer in the first murder mystery, who was the first surgeon, who sparked the first fire--and most critically, who was the first to brave the slimy, pale oyster? In this book, writer Cody Cassidy digs deep into the latest research to uncover the untold stories of some of these incredible innovators (or participants in lucky accidents).

"Cassidy embarks on a wide-ranging, far-flung journey of curiosity that easily engages the reader. Chapters are brimming with history that may surprise readers as well as compel them to further investigate." Booklist

Davis, Lee (Lee Allyn)

Man-made catastrophes / Lee Davis. Facts on File, c2002. xi, 402 p. : Facts on File science library **904**

1. Disasters.
ISBN 081604418X

LC 2001054324

A worldwide survey of man-made disasters describes fires, explosions, airplane crashes, maritime disasters, railway accidents, civil unrest, terrorism, space disasters, and nuclear and industrial accidents.

907 Education, research, related topics of history

Tuchman, Barbara W. (Barbara Wertheim), 1912-1989

Practicing history : selected essays / Barbara W. Tuchman. Ballantine Books, 1982, c1981. vi, 306 p. ; **907**

1. Historiography 2. Modern history 3. Essays
ISBN 9780345303639

LC 82008757

The noted historian's essays, written over thirty-five years, include comments on the writing of history, shorter historical and journalistic pieces, and essays on the importance of history and historical awareness.

907.2 Historical research

Bailyn, Bernard

Sometimes an art, never a science, always a craft : on history / Bernard Bailyn. Alfred A. Knopf, 2015. 288 p. **907.2**

1. History -- Philosophy. 2. Historiography -- Philosophy. 3. Great Britain -- Colonies -- Historiography. 4. United States -- Historiography. 5. Essays
ISBN 9781101874479

LC 2014022229

"This is a Borzoi book"--Title page verso.

Drawing on a career spanning more than five decades, a Pulitzer Prize-winning author and one of the most respected historians in America presents a new collection of essays that reflect on a lifetime of erudition and accomplishments in history.

"Another theme is the role of creativity in historical inquiry, and in one of this selection's more personal (yet unfailingly scholarly) essays, Bailyn pays tribute to historians whose innovative methods revealed 'hitherto submerged worlds' while also acknowledging the limitations inherent to such disruptions." Booklist.

Hamilton, Nigel

★**Biography** : a brief history / Nigel Hamilton. Harvard University Press, 2007. 345 p. : **907.2**

1. Biography. 2. Writing. 3. Books and reading.
ISBN 0674024664

LC 2006051132

"Hamilton has given readers a thought-provoking look at biography in its various forms; a fascinating and handy reference book for anyone wishing to know more about the history and art of biography." Library Journal.

909 World history

Barnavi, Elie

A **historical** atlas of the Jewish people : from the time of the patriarchs to the present / general editor, Eli Barnavi ; English edition editor, Miriam Eliav-Feldon ; cartography, Michel Opatowski ; new edition revised by Denis Charbit. Schocken Books, 2002. xi, 321 p. : **909**

1. Jews -- History. 2. Jews -- History -- Maps.
ISBN 9780805242263

LC 2003279553

Includes index.

A comprehensive overview of more than four thousand years of Jewish history includes maps, artwork, chronologies, and commentary.

Biale, David, 1949-

★**Cultures** of the Jews : a new history / edited by David Biale. Schocken Books, c2002 xxxiii, 1196 p. : **909**

1. Jews -- History. 2. Jews -- Civilization. 3. Judaism -- History.
ISBN 9780805241310

LC 2002023008

A collection of essays by twenty-three international scholars sheds new light on the history of the Jews from biblical times to the modern day and explores the fundamental question of Jewish culture and identity at each period in history, in three chronological sections--Mediterranean Origins, Diversities of Diaspora, and Modern Encounters.

Boorstin, Daniel J. (Daniel Joseph), 1914-2004

The **creators** / Daniel J. Boorstin. Random House, 1992. xiv, 811 p. : **909**

1. Civilization -- History. 2. Civilization, Western. 3. Arts -- History. 4. Art history
ISBN 0394543955

LC 91039948

Companion volume to: The discoverers.

"In this volume Boorstin undertakes an interpretive history of creativity in Western civilization. Packed with shrewd, entertaining profiles of Dante, Goethe, Benjamin Franklin and dozens of others, this stimulating synthesis sets the achievements of individual geniuses into a coherent narrative of humanity's advance from ignorance." Publishers Weekly.

Brown, Cynthia Stokes, 1938-

Big history : from the Big Bang to the present / Cynthia Stokes Brown. New Press : 2007. xvi, 288 p. : **909**

1. Science -- History 2. Human ecology. 3. Big Bang Theory

(Astronomy) 4. Cosmology -- History
ISBN 1595581960

LC 2007006741

"A Caravan book"--T.p. verso.

Identifies key links between the history of the universe and human history, drawing on cutting-edge science to illuminate the ecological impact of human life on the planet.

"In a multidisciplinary narrative subtly emphasizing the mutual impact of people and planet, Brown covers Earth's history from the big bang through the development of life and the growth of civilization. . . . This exciting saga crosses space and time to illustrate how humans, born of stardust, were shaped--and how they in turn shaped the world we know today." Publishers Weekly.

Cahill, Thomas

The **gifts** of the Jews : how a tribe of desert nomads changed the way everyone thinks and feels / Thomas Cahill. Nan A. Talese/ Doubleday, 1998. xii, 291 p. : Hinges of history ; **909**

1. Bible. Old Testament History of Biblical events 2. Judaism -- History -- To 70 A.D. 3. Jews -- History -- To 70 A.D. 4. Civilization -- Jewish influences.
ISBN 0385482485

LC 97045139

Includes indexes.

Presents a survey of the Jewish contributions to Western civilization, in a work exploring a pivotal period in human history.

"In this colloquial look at the influence of the Hebrew Bible on civilization, the author gives the Jews credit for revolutionizing the concepts of democracy, universal law, monotheism, linear time, personal vocation, destiny, self-improvement and the belief in the equality of all humans. He stumbles on the odd aside and occasionally is surprisingly insensitive. . . Still, his passion and breadth of knowledge are admirable." New York Times Book Review.

Sailing the wine-dark sea : why the Greeks matter / Thomas Cahill. Nan A. Talese, Doubleday, 2003. xiv, 304 p., 32 p. of plates : Hinges of history ; **909**

1. Civilization, Western -- Greek influences. 2. Philosophy, Ancient. 3. Ancient Greece -- Civilization -- To 146 B.C. 4. Ancient Greece -- History -- To 146 B.C.
ISBN 0385495536

LC 2003050725

Examines the remarkable legacy of the ancient Greeks, from the origins of Greek culture to the development of Western literature, drama, poetry, and philosophy to the Greek influence on human science, mathematics, and logic.

"This author begins with a discussion of Homer's Iliad and Odyssey and how these two epic poems relate to the history of Greece. He then focuses on such themes as the Greek alphabet, literature, and political system, and its playwrights, philosophers, and artists. A final chapter examines the effects that Greco-Roman and Judeo-Christian traditions had on each other." Booklist.

Christian, David, 1946-

Origin story : a big history of everything / David Christian. Little Brown & Company, 2018 320 p. **909**

1. Science -- History 2. Scientific discoveries 3. Cosmology
ISBN 9780316392006

LC 2017952230

Offers a captivating history of the universe--from before the dawn of time through the far reaches of the distant future.

Cliff, Nigel

Holy war : how Vasco da Gama's epic voyages turned the tide in a centuries-old clash of civilizations / Nigel Cliff. Harper, 2011. 480 p. **909**

1. Gama, Vasco da, 1469-1524. 2. Gama, Vasco da, 1469-1524 Influence. 3. East and West. 4. Discoveries (in geography) 5. Christianity -- Relations -- Islam. 6. Explorers 7. Africa -- Exploration -- Religious aspects. 8. India -- Exploration -- Religious aspects.
ISBN 9780061735127

LC 2011021331

Later published as The last crusade: New York : HarperCollins, 2012.

This radical new interpretation of Vasco da Gama's revolutionary voyages, which were seen as a turning point in the struggle between Christianity and Islam, presents the epic story of da Gama and his crew of adventurers that explores the tragic collision of cultures.

Cole, Juan Ricardo

The **new** Arabs : how the Millennial Generation is changing the Middle East / Juan Cole. Simon & Schuster, 2014. 288 p. **909**

1. Millennials 2. Young adults 3. Political culture 4. Protest movements 5. Middle East
ISBN 9781451690392

LC 2014005627

The Middle-East expert illuminates the role of today's Arab youth to reveal their motivations and growing influence on world politics, sharing the stories of activists in the "Arab Spring" while outlining the historical sources of dramatic regional changes.

Crowley, Roger, 1951-

Conquerors : how Portugal forged the first global empire / Roger Crowley. Random House, 2015. 384 p. **909**

1. Exploration. 2. Imperialism -- History. 3. Portugal -- Colonies -- History -- 16th century.
ISBN 9780812994001

LC 2015008152

In Conquerors, Crowley gives us the epic story of the emergence of Portugal, a small, poor nation that enjoyed a century of maritime supremacy thanks to the daring and navigational skill of its explorers--a tactical advantage no other country could match. Portugal's discovery of a sea route to India, campaign of imperial conquest over Muslim rulers, and domination of the spice trade would forever disrupt the Mediterranean and build the first global economy.

"An impressive history of global clashes, religious zealotry, and economic triumph." Kirkus.

Davidson, Peter (Peter Bruce), 1963-

Atlas of empires : the world's greatest powers from ancient times to today / Peter Davidson. CompanionHouse Books, 2018 240 p. : **909**

1. Imperialism -- History 2. Imperialism -- Maps
ISBN 9781620082874

LC 2017048739

"Tells the stories of imperial societies throughout human history and shows how they developed using labeled maps".-- Provided by publisher.

Davis, Jack E., 1956-

★The **Gulf** : the making of an American sea / Jack E. Davis. Liveright Publishing Corporation, 2017. x, 592 p. : **909**

1. Coastal ecology 2. Coasts -- United States 3. Humans -- Effect of

environment on 4. Environmentalism 5. Gulf of Mexico
ISBN 9780871408662

LC 2016051692

Kirkus Prize for Nonfiction, 2017.
Pulitzer Prize for History, 2018.
Longlisted for the Andrew Carnegie Medal for Excellence in Non-Fiction, 2018.
National Book Critics Circle Award for Nonfiction finalist, 2017
A comprehensive history of the Gulf of Mexico and its identity as a region marked by hurricanes, oil fields and debates about population growth and the environment demonstrates how its picturesque ecosystems have inspired and reflected key historical events.
"An elegant narrative braced by a fierce, sobering environmental conviction." Kirkus.

De Bellaigue, Christopher, 1971-
The **Islamic** enlightenment : the struggle between faith and reason, 1798 to modern times / Christopher de Bellaigue. Liveright Pub. Corp., 2017. 560 p. **909**
1. Intellectual life 2. Islam -- History 3. Modernization (Social sciences) 4. Faith (Islam) 5. Islamic countries -- History 6. Middle East -- History 7. Istanbul, Turkey 8. Cairo, Egypt 9. Tehran, Iran
ISBN 9780871403735

LC 2017000479

A revisionist history of the 19th and 20th centuries challenges current understandings about the Middle East and Islam, focusing on the stories of Istanbul, Cairo and Tehran to reveal the intellectual, cultural and political sophistication of their populations.
"Recommended for historians, religious scholars, or anyone interested in relations between the Middle East and the West." Library Journal.

Emmerson, Charles
The **future** history of the Arctic / Charles Emmerson. PublicAffairs, 2010. 448 p. **909**
1. Geopolitics -- Arctic regions. 2. Exploration. 3. Ecology 4. Arctic regions -- Exploration 5. Arctic regions -- Environmental conditions.
ISBN 9781586486365

LC 2009035094

An expert defines the forces that have shaped the Arctic's history and introduces the players in politics, business and science who are struggling to mold its future, in a book where the author shares--through the stories of those who live in the region, those who study it and those who determine its destiny--how the Arctic is coming of age.

Ferguson, Niall
Empire : the rise and demise of the British world order and the lessons for global power / Niall Ferguson. Basic Books, 2003. xxix, 392 p. : **909**
1. Civilization, Western -- British influences. 2. Imperialism. 3. World politics 4. Great Britain -- Colonies -- History. 5. Great Britain -- Foreign relations. 6. Commonwealth countries.
ISBN 0465023282

LC 2003041469

A narrative history profiles the British Empire as a "cradle of modernity," tracing the expansion of Britain's economy, population, and culture during the last four centuries and continuing with discussions of such topics as economic globalization, the communications revolution, the racial components of North America, humanitarianism, and democracy.
"Lively and thoughtful: provocative both as history and forecast." Kirkus

Frankopan, Peter
The **Silk** Roads : a new history of the world / Peter Frankopan. Alfred A. Knopf, 2016. xix, 645 p., 16 unnumbered p. of plates : **909**
1. Trade routes -- Asia -- History 2. Commerce -- History 3. Historic sites -- Asia 4. Silk Road -- History. 5. Eurasia -- Commerce -- History. 6. Central Asia -- History
ISBN 9781101946329

LC 2015013264

Looks at how the Asian Silk Roads have acted as a crucible of culture throughout history, capturing the importance of these networks that linked the Atlantic with the Pacific, the Mediterranean with India, and America with the Persian Gulf.
"A timely challenge to conventional thinking about a pivotal part of the globe." Booklist.

Galeano, Eduardo, 1940-2015
Mirrors : stories of almost everyone / Eduardo Galeano ; English translation by Mark Fried. Nation Books, c2009. 391 p. : **909**
1. History -- Miscellanea. 2. Civilization. 3. Social classes. 4. Social history.
ISBN 9781568584232

LC 2009004518

Translation of : Espejos.
Includes indexes.
"Each entry is an avatar of outrage over the depredations of power against its multifarious victims, those rendered helpless by poverty, religion, race, sexual identity or--as in the vignettes about Galileo and Isaac Babel--the simple accident of being right when the truth defined by the prevailing authority was wrong. As in his previous books, [Galeano] succeeds in capturing the bottomless horror of the state's capacity to inflict pain on the individual, offering as effective an act of political dissent as exists anywhere in contemporary literature." New York Times Book Review.

Gies, Joseph
Life in a medieval city / Joseph and Frances Gies. Harper & Row, 1981, c1969. xiii, 274 p. : **909**
1. Medieval cities and towns -- Europe. 2. Civilization, Medieval -- Europe
ISBN 0060908807

LC BL 99920289

Originally published: New York : Crowell, 1969.
Every aspect of life in a prosperous thirteenth-century city is explored in this representative study of Troyes in 1250 A.D.

Grant, R. G,
The **history** book / contributors, Reg Grant, consultant editor, Fiona Coward, Thomas Cussans, Joel Levy, Philip Parker, Sally Regan, Philip Wilkinson. DK Publishing, 2016. 352 p. : **909**
1. World history -- Juvenile literature.
ISBN 9781465445100

LC 2016429085

Presents a full-color global look at world-changing events in history and the themes that unite them.

Hansen, Valerie, 1958-
The **year** 1000 : when globalization began / Valerie Hansen. Scribner, 2020. xi, 308 p. **909**
1. Millennium (1000 A.D.) 2. Trade routes -- Asia -- History. 3.

International trade. 4. Civilization. 5. Silk Road -- History.
ISBN 9781501194108
LC 2019045048

The author draws on extensive research in a groundbreaking history of the explorations and trade commissions that connected the world's most advanced societies for the first time 1,000 years ago.

"The author covers a vast amount of territory in a concise, readable manner, making for a welcome contribution to the popular literature on early global trade and geopolitics. A thoroughly satisfying history of a distant era and people." Kirkus

Harari, Yuval N.

Sapiens : a brief history of humankind / Yuval Noah Harari. Harper, 2015 352 p. **909**

1. Humans 2. Evolution 3. Biology 4. Memory
ISBN 9780062316097
LC 2014028418

A narrative history of humanity's creation and evolution explores how biology and history have defined understandings of what it means to be human and details the role of modern cognition in shaping the ecosystem and civilizations.

"Although Harari's ideas may be controversial for some readers, those who are interested in history, anthropology, and evolution will find his work a fascinating, hearty read." Library Journal.

History of the world in 1,000 objects DK Publishing, 2014. 480 p. : **909**

1. World history -- Sources. 2. Material culture -- History.
ISBN 9781465422897
LC 2014497752

Includes index.

Offers an illustrated look at one thousand artifacts of human creation through history, from stone age tools to tablet computers, as well as an extensive timeline featuring key events in world history.

Hart-Davis, Adam

History : the definitive visual guide : from the dawn of civilization to the present day / editorial consultant, Adam Hart-Davis. Dorling Kindersley Limited, 2015, c2007. 620 p. : **909**

1. World history. 2. World history -- Pictorial works.
ISBN 9781465437976
LC 2015451995

"DK Smithsonian"--Cover.

Includes index.

Traces the course of human history from prehistoric times to the present day, analyzing the common themes, threads, forces, and factors that have shaped human life--including climate, ecology, disease, and geology--and examining human accomplishments, from the technological innovations that changed the world to key cultural, social, artistic, and intellectual achievements.

James, Clive, 1939-2019

Cultural amnesia : necessary memories from history and the arts / Clive James. W.W. Norton & Co., 2007. xxxii, 876 p. : **909**

1. Civilization, Western. 2. Intellectuals -- 20th century 3. Artists 4. Musicians
ISBN 9780393061161
LC 2006036398

Includes index.

"The author not only preserves culture and nurtures humanism but also revitalizes the beauty and power of the English language." Booklist.

Jasanoff, Maya, 1974-

Edge of empire : lives, culture, and conquest in the East, 1750-1850 / Maya Jasanoff. Knopf, 2005. ix, 404 p. : **909**

1. Collectors and collecting -- Great Britain -- Colonies -- History -- 18th century. 2. Collectors and collecting -- Great Britain -- Colonies -- History -- 19th century. 3. Material culture -- Great Britain -- Colonies -- History -- 18th century. 4. Material culture -- Great Britain -- Colonies -- History -- 19th century. 5. Great Britain -- Colonies -- History -- 18th century. 6. Great Britain -- Colonies -- History -- 19th century.
ISBN 1400041678
LC 2004060221

A dramatic history of the formative years of the British Empire captures the events of the time through the lives of individuals who played a key role in the era and the objects they chose as memorials to their experiences, including a Palladian mansion filled with Western artifacts in Calcutta, a French archive of letters by a Mughal emperor, and other unique objects.

"In graceful prose and with evocative illustrations, Jasanoff scores her points about conquest, collecting, and cultural crossing, offering a thoughtful and highly subtle study." Library Journal.

Johnson, Paul, 1928-

A **history** of the Jews / Paul Johnson. Harper & Row, 1987. x, 644 p. **909**

1. Jews -- History. 2. Judaism -- History.
ISBN 0060915331
LC 85042575

Spans four thousand years of Jewish history, detailing the Jews as a people, Judaism, Jewish ideas and culture, and Israel's history, providing a sweeping account of Jewish philosophy, history, ethics, and politics.

"This is an absorbing, provocative, well-written, often moving book, an insightful and impassioned blend of history and myth, story and interpretation." Christian Science Monitor.

Kwarteng, Kwasi

Ghosts of empire : Britain's legacies in the modern world / Kwasi Kwarteng. Public Affairs, 2012. 512 p. **909**

1. Imperialism, British -- History 2. Cultural imperialism, English 3. British in foreign countries 4. World politics 5. Great Britain -- Colonies
ISBN 9781610391207
LC 2011935845

An economic history scholar examines the impact and political, linguistic and cultural legacy left by the British Empire on its former overseas colonies and trading posts, from South-East Asia and India to Australia.

Lamb, David, 1940-

The **Arabs** : journeys beyond the mirage / David Lamb. Vintage Books, 2002. xvi, 348 p. : **909**

1. International relations. 2. Arabs -- Social life and customs 3. Arab countries -- Social life and customs 4. Middle East -- History
ISBN 1400030412
LC 2002524048

"Intelligent and incisive...Mr. Lamb has the first-rate reporter's tools, and he uses them to relate, with compelling detail, who the Arabs are." New York Times Book Review.

Marozzi, Justin, 1970-

Islamic empires : the cities that shaped civilization--from Mecca to Dubai / Justin Marozzi. Pegasus Books, 2020, c2019.

512 p. **909**
1. Civilization, Islamic 2. Islam -- History 3. Cities and towns 4. Middle East -- Civilization 5. Middle East -- Description and travel 6. Islamic countries
ISBN 9781643133065
LC bl2019037183

Originally published in the UK as Islamic empire : fifteen cities that define a civilization, Allen Lane, 2019.

Takes readers on a tour of the defining moments, diverse civilizations and the greatest cities in Islamic history over fifteen centuries, from Mecca in the seventh century to the rise of Doha in the twenty-first century.

"A rich foray into the history of Islam and the emergence of key cities as capitals of commerce, culture, and conquest." Kirkus

Martin, Richard C.

Encyclopedia of Islam and the Muslim world / Richard C. Martin, editor in chief. Macmillan Reference USA, a part of Gale, Cengage Learning, 2016. 1353 p. ; **909**
1. Islam -- Encyclopedias 2. Encyclopedias
ISBN 9780028662695
LC 2015015535

Covers the issues, countries, people, history, and cultures of the Muslim world.

Morris, Ian, 1960-

Why the West rules-- for now : the patterns of history, and what they reveal about the future / Ian Morris. Farrar, Straus and Giroux, 2010. 768 p. **909**
1. Civilization, Western. 2. Comparative civilization. 3. East and West. 4. Geopolitics.
ISBN 9780374290023
LC 2010005702

An archaeologist and historian offers his view on why the West has dominated the globe for the past two hundred years and whether or not its power will last, examining the past fifty thousand years of human history and predicting what the next one hundred years will bring.

"It may seem at first sight a little odd to recommend a history book as a guide to the future. But Morris' new book illustrates perfectly why one really scholarly book about the past is worth a hundred fanciful works of futurology." Foreign Affairs.

Morris, Lawrence, 1972-

Daily life through world history in primary documents : The Ancient World; the Middle Ages and Renaissance; the Modern World / Lawrence Morris, general editor. Greenwood Press, 2009. 1000 p. ; **909**
1. Civilization -- History 2. Manners and customs -- History 3. Social history
ISBN 9780313338984
LC 2008008925

Collects primary source documents from major world cultures throughout history that illustrate domestic, economic, intellectual, material, political, recreational, and religious life.

Mortimer, Ian, 1967-

Millennium : from religion to revolution: how civilization has changed over a thousand years / Ian Mortimer. Pegasus Books, 2016. 416 p. **909**
1. Civilization, Western. 2. Social change 3. Technology and civilization 4. Intellectual life
ISBN 9781681772431
LC 2018418421

An expansive journey through the last millennium of human innovation in the Western world profiles the pivotal discoveries, inventions, revolutions and perspective changes that have shaped the modern world.

"A quirky but always delightful social history that will convince most readers that social revolutions have been happening for a long time." Kirkus.

Pagden, Anthony

★**Peoples** and empires : a short history of European migration, exploration, and conquest, from Greece to the present / Anthony Pagden. Modern Library, 2003. xxv, 216 p. ; **909**
1. Immigration and emigration -- History. 2. Military occupation 3. Exploration -- History 4. Migrations of nations. 5. Mediterranean Region -- Civilization. 6. Rome -- History -- Germanic Invasions, 3rd-6th centuries. 7. Europe -- History. 8. Essays
ISBN 0812967615
LC 2003269730

"A Modern Library chronicles book."

Describes the history and influence of European contact with other regions of the world, discussing the role of migration, exploration, and conquest in shaping world political boundaries and culture.

"This overview of European empire building and colonization commences with the diffusion of Greek civilization and traces the subsequent evolution of the ensuing Roman, Spanish, French, and British empires. More interesting than how those empires physically expanded is the insightful discussion on what motivated individual men and entire nations to migrate and conquer." Booklist.

Parker, Geoffrey, 1943-

Global crisis : war, climate change, and catastrophe in the seventeenth century / Geoffrey Parker. Yale University Press, 2013 xxix, 871 p., 16 p. of plates : **909**
1. Climate change 2. Military history. 3. Civil war. 4. Revolutions.
ISBN 9780300153231
LC 2012039448

Argues that climate change was to blame for a global crisis in the seventeenth century that brought about war, revolution, and suffering, and suggests that advice about preparing for global warming's fallout can be gleaned from this era.

Roberts, Callum

The **unnatural** history of the sea / Callum Roberts. Island Press ; Shearwater Books, c2007. xvii, 435 p. : **909**
1. Marine biology. 2. Ocean and civilization. 3. Oceans -- History. 4. Oceanography.
ISBN 1597261025
LC 2007001841

Examines the history of the sea and the marine life it contains over centuries of human commercial exploitation.

"Starting with the eighteenth-century voyages of Vitus Bering, Roberts leads the reader through a wealth of maritime history revealing countless examples of overfishing. . . . Thoughtful, inspiring, devastating, and powerful, Roberts' comprehensive, welcoming, and compelling approach to an urgent subject conveys large problems in a succinct and involving manner. Readers won't be able to put it down." Booklist.

Roberts, J. M. (John Morris), 1928-2003

The **history** of the world / J.M. Roberts and O.A. Westad. Oxford University Press, 2013. xiv, 1,260 p. ; 909

1. History. 2. Civilization -- History. 3. Humans.

ISBN 9780199936762

Rogan, Eugene L.

The **Arabs** : a history / Eugene Rogan. Basic Books, 2009. 624 p. 909

1. Arab nationalism. 2. Oil industry and trade -- Arab countries 3. Islam and politics -- Arab countries. 4. Imperialism. 5. Arab countries -- History -- 1517-1918. 6. Arab countries -- History -- 20th century. 7. Palestine -- History -- Partition, 1947.

ISBN 9780465071005

LC 2009028575

An Oxford historian presents an authoritative account of five centuries of Arab history from the Ottoman conquests to the present while explaining that American policies are compromising the region's ability to protect its own interests.

"This is not a particularly happy story, but it is a fascinating one, and exceedingly well told. [Eugene] Rogan manoeuvres with skilful assurance, maintaining a steady pace through time, and keeping the wider horizon in view even as he makes use of a broad range of judiciously chosen primary sources to enrich the narrative." The Economist.

Schama, Simon

★The **story** of the Jews. Belonging, 1492-1900 / Simon Schama. Ecco Press, 2017. 790 p. 909

1. Jews -- History 2. Judaism. 3. History

ISBN 9780062339577

LC bl2017034048

A second volume of a sumptuously illustrated companion to the PBS and BBC series spans centuries and continents from the Iberian Peninsula and the shtetls of Russia to the streets of early Hollywood and the poetry written in concentration camps.

"This is a wonderful chronicle spanning centuries in the development of an enduring people." Booklist.

★The **story** of the Jews. Finding the words, 1000 BC-1492 AD / Simon Schama. Ecco Press, 2014 496 p., 24 unnumbered p. of plates : 909

1. Jews -- History 2. Judaism. 3. History

ISBN 9780060539184

LC 2014466181

Acclaimed author and historian Simon Schama explores the Jewish sense of identity, art, and religious teachings from 1000 B.C. to 1492 A.D., when Portugal expelled Jewish residents. Focusing on a specific object at the beginning of each chapter, Schama explores the item's context and its significance to the people associated with it, broadening his discussion to examine the Jewish community at each relevant geographical location and historical period. Schama's engaging approach draws readers into the settings and provides insight into the history of Jews and Judaism through the millennia.

"Schama has written an unconventional but masterful and deeply felt history of his people, which seamlessly integrates themes of art, religion, and ethnicity as he illustrates how Jews both influenced and were influenced by the other people they lived among for more than 1,500 years." Booklist.

Skolnik, Fred,

Encyclopaedia Judaica / Fred Skolnik, editor-in-chief ; Michael Berenbaum, executive editor. Macmillan Reference USA, c2007. 22 v. : 909

1. Jews -- Encyclopedias. 2. Judaism -- Encyclopedias.

ISBN 9780028659282

LC 2006020426

Alphabetically arranged entries cover Jewish history and culture.

Tinniswood, Adrian

Pirates of Barbary : corsairs, conquests, and captivity in the seventeenth-century Mediterranean / Adrian Tinniswood. Riverhead Books, 2010. 368 p. 909

1. Pirates. 2. Piracy. 3. Seafaring life. 4. Mediterranean Region -- History -- 1517-1789. 5. North Africa -- History -- 1517-1882.

ISBN 9781594487743

LC 2010023421

Adrian Tinniswood brings alive this dynamic chapter in history, where clashes between pirates of the East and governments of the West grew increasingly intense and dangerous. In vivid detail, Tinniswood recounts the brutal struggles, glorious triumphs, and enduring personalities of the pirates of the Barbary Coast, and how their maneuverings between the Muslim empires and Christian Europe shed light on the religious and moral battles that still rage today.

Treuer, Anton

Everything you wanted to know about Indians but were afraid to ask / Anton Treuer. Borealis Books, c2012. 184 p. 909

1. Indians of North America -- History. 2. Ojibwa Indians 3. Race relations 4. Interethnic relations

ISBN 9780873518611

LC 2011053026

Treuer, an Ojibwe scholar and cultural preservationist, answers the most commonly asked questions about American Indians, both historical and modern. He gives a frank, funny, and personal tour of what's up with Indians, anyway.

"Overall, this is a thoughtful and thought-provoking overview that serves to alleviate misconceptions and bridge knowledge gaps among cultures." School Library Journal.

Watson, Peter, 1943-

★The **great** divide : history and human nature in the old world and the new / Peter Watson. HarperCollins, 2012. 640 p. ; 909

1. Humans. 2. Civilization. 3. Nature and civilization. 4. Culture. 5. Western Hemisphere. 6. Eastern Hemisphere.

ISBN 9780061672453

LC 2012288077

Comparing and contrasting the development of humankind in the "Old World" and the "New" between 15,000 B.C. and 1500 A.D., a cultural historian ponders a vast array of questions central to the human story, providing uniquely revealing insight into what it means to be human.

Ideas : a history of thought and invention, from fire to Freud / Peter Watson. Harper Collins, c2005. xix, 822 p. ; 909

1. Civilization -- History. 2. Intellectual life -- History. 3. Inventions.

ISBN 006621064X

LC 2005050255

Traces the evolution of numerous schools of thought in the western intellectual and cultural communities, from the creation of language to the invention of mathematical principles.

Winchester, Simon

Pacific : silicon chips and surfboards, coral reefs and atom bombs, brutal dictators, fading empires, and the coming collision of the world's superpowers / Simon Winchester. Harper-

Collins, 2015 480 p. **909**

1. Oceans 2. Geopolitics 3. Geography 4. Pacific Ocean
ISBN 9780062315410

LC 2015020468

Kirkus Prize for Nonfiction finalist, 2015.

The New York Times best-selling author of The Men Who United the States traces the geological history of the Pacific Ocean to assess its relationship with humans and indelible role in the modern world.

"Winchester...does not do the expected: there is no chapter about the geological history of the ocean, followed by a slow chronology. Instead, realizing the difficulty of his own task, the author focuses on 10 aspects of the ocean and its inhabitants--islanders, those on the shores--and uses them to illustrate some historical points." Kirkus.

Worth, Robert Forsyth, 1965-

★A **rage** for order : the Middle East in turmoil, from Tahrir Square to ISIS / Robert F. Worth. Farrar, Straus and Giroux, 2016. 400 p. **909**

1. Arab Spring, 2010- 2. Civil rights -- Middle East. 3. Social movements -- Middle East. 4. Human rights -- Middle East. 5. Arab countries -- Politics and government -- 21st century.
ISBN 9780374252946

LC 2015041559

Lionel Gelber Prize (Canada), 2017.

A New York Times former Beirut bureau chief chronicles the events of the Arab Spring and its troubled aftermath, discussing the uprising of Middle Eastern revolutionaries whose efforts to end tyranny, corruption and poverty eventually succumbed to prior divisions under the oppression of terrorists and dictators.

"General readers and policymakers will find this timely volume enlightening." Library Journal.

909.04 History with respect to ethnic and national groups

Mackintosh-Smith, Tim, 1961-

Arabs : a 3,000-year history of peoples, tribes and empires / Tim Mackintosh-Smith. Yale University Press, 2019. xxvi, 630 p. : **909.04**

1. Civilization, Arabic 2. Arabic language 3. Language and languages 4. Nomads
ISBN 9780300180282

This kaleidoscopic book covers almost 3,000 years of Arab history and shines a light on the footloose Arab peoples and tribes who conquered lands and disseminated their language and culture over vast distances. Tracing this process to the origins of the Arabic language, rather than the advent of Islam, Tim Mackintosh-Smith begins his narrative more than a thousand years before Muhammad and focuses on how Arabic, both spoken and written, has functioned as a vital source of shared cultural identity over the millennia.

"Over the course of an extensive, consistently fascinating history, Mackintosh-Smith expertly picks and chooses his details and analyses, providing an admirably complete picture of a consistently misunderstood part of world history and culture." Kirkus.

909.07 General historical periods

Asbridge, Thomas S.

★The **crusades** : the authoritative history of the war for the Holy Land / Thomas Asbridge. Ecco Press, 2010 640 p. **909.07**

1. Crusades 2. Christianity -- Relations 3. Religious tolerance -- History -- To 1500. 4. Civilization, Medieval 5. Europe -- Church history -- 600-1500 6. Islamic Empire -- Foreign relations Europe 7. Europe -- Foreign relations Islamic Empire 8. Middle East -- History
ISBN 9780060787288

LC bl2010006562

"Covering the 200-year period of the Crusades in a single volume is a monumental task, but Asbridge...handles it well, presenting an even-handed view of the actions of Christian and Muslim forces and paying particular attention to the larger-than-life figures of Richard the Lionheart and Saladin. In addition to relating the facts of the expeditions, he explores both the motivations of the Crusaders...and the reasons that Christians eventually failed to retain any hold on conquered territory." Library Journal.

Catlos, Brian A.

Infidel kings and unholy warriors : faith, power, and violence in the age of crusade and jihad / Brian A. Catlos. Farrar, Straus and Giroux, 2014. 416 p. **909.07**

1. Crusades -- Influence. 2. Civilization, Medieval. 3. Religion and civilization. 4. Mediterranean Region -- History. 5. Mediterranean Region -- History -- 476-1517.
ISBN 9780809058372

LC 2013043160

In this fresh and vivid history of the Mediterranean region during the Middle Ages, author Brian Catlos depicts the relationships among Muslims and Christians as complex and subtle, arguing that the Crusades were motivated as much by economics and politics as by religion. Showing that accounts of certain heroes (such as el Cid) portrayed them as either Muslim or Christian, depending on who wrote the account, he also highlights internal violence within Christian and Muslim factions. Moreover, collaboration among Christians, Jews, and Muslims was common.

Cobb, Paul M., 1967-

The **race** for paradise : an Islamic history of the crusades / Paul M. Cobb. Oxford University Press, 2014 368 p. **909.07**

1. Crusades. 2. Islam -- Relations -- Christianity -- History -- To 1500. 3. Christianity -- Relations -- Islam -- History -- To 1500 4. Muslims -- Mediterranean Region -- History -- To 1500. 5. Middle East -- History
ISBN 9780199358113

LC 2013040040

"In The Race for Paradise, Paul M. Cobb offers an accurate and accessible representation of the Islamic experience of the Crusades during the Middle Ages. Cobb overturns previous claims and presents new arguments, such as the idea that the Frankish invasions of the Near East were something of a side-show to the broader internal conflict between Sunnis and Shi'ites in the region. The Race for Paradise moves along two fronts as Cobb stresses that, for medieval Muslims, the contemporaneous Latin Christian expansion throughout the Mediterranean was seen as closely linked to events in the Levant. As a consequence of this expanded geographical range, the book takes a broader chronological range to encompass the campaigns of Spanish kings north of the Ebro and the Norman conquest of Sicily (beginning in 1060), well before Pope Urban II's famous call to the First Crusade in 1095. Finally, The Race for Paradise brilliantly combats the trend to portray the history of the Crusades, particularly the Islamic experience, in simplistic or binary terms. Muslims did not solely experience the Crusades as fanatical warriors or as helpless victims, Cobb writes; as with any other human experience of similar magnitude, the Crusades were experienced in a great variety of ways, ranging from heroic martyrdom, to collaboration, to utter indifference".-- Provided by publisher.

"Cobb's multidisciplinary approach illuminates the experience of invaded societies in their chaotic and climactic contacts with the Other." Publishers Weekly.

Gertsman, Elina

The **Middle** Ages in 50 objects / Elina Gertsman, Barbara H. Rosenwein. Cambridge University Press, 2018. xvii, 233 p. : **909.07**

1. Civilization, Medieval
ISBN 1107150388

LC 2017037848

"Complex and varied, vibrant and intense, medieval objects demand to be examined closely, to be thought about deeply, to be approached kinesthetically. Extraordinary in the multiplicity of meanings that it harbors and engenders, the material culture of the Middle Ages offers its beholders a rich experience of looking, often multisensory, always rewarding. It offers, too, a glimpse of an equally rich society, or rather the many societies that were in constant flux and in intermittent conversations (and, at times, screaming matches) with one another. And yet, each object has its own history. So how do we write history through objects?" -- Provided by publisher.

Jones, Dan, 1981-

Crusaders : an epic history of the wars for the holy lands / Dan Jones. Viking, 2019 448 p. **909.07**

1. Crusades. 2. War -- Religious aspects -- Christianity. 3. Christianity -- Relations -- Islam. 4. Islam -- Relations -- Christianity. 5. Europe -- History -- 1000-1500. 6. Europe -- History, Military.
ISBN 9780525428312

LC 2019017922

The author presents a wide-ranging, narrative history of the Crusades that examines 8th-century Christian-Muslim relations from the perspectives of diverse people on all sides of the wars.

Phillips, Jonathan (Jonathan P.)

Holy warriors : a modern history of the crusades / Jonathan Phillips. Random House, 2010. 464 p. **909.07**

1. Crusades. 2. Religion. 3. Civilization, Medieval. 4. Christianity -- Relations -- Islam 5. Middle East -- History. 6. Europe -- Church history -- 600-1500.
ISBN 9781400065806

LC 2009033153

Draws on varied source material to offer insight into the Crusades and its complexities, tracing the experiences of leading figures while discussing such specific events as the origins of Saladin's jihad and the trial of the Knights Templar.

909.08 Modern history, 1450/1500

Aaronovitch, David

Voodoo histories : the role of the conspiracy theory in shaping modern history / David Aaronovitch. Riverhead Books, 2010. 400 p. **909.08**

1. Conspiracies. 2. Conspiracy theories. 3. History. 4. Conspiracies -- History.
ISBN 9781594488955

LC 2009037018

Our age is obsessed by the idea of conspiracy. We see it everywhere--from Pearl Harbor to 9/11, from the assassination of Kennedy to the death of Diana. In this age of terrorism, the idea of conspiracy can fuel radical or fringe elements to violence. The author, a journalist, sees a pattern among these inflammatory theories. They use similarly murky methods to insinuate their claims: they link themselves to the supposed conspiracies of the past; they carefully manipulate their evidence, to hide its holes; they rely on the authority of dubious academic sources. Most important, they elevate their believers to an elite, a group of people able to see beyond lies to a higher reality. In this book, the author carefully probes and explodes a dozen of the major conspiracy theories. He examines why people believe them, and makes an argument for a true skepticism: one based on a thorough knowledge of history and a strong dose of common sense.--From publisher description.

"The book is an evenhanded, lively, and fascinating look not just at the people who believe these theories but also at the people who promote them: the evidence manipulators, the liars, the con artists, and the almost pathetically gullible and uninformed." Booklist.

Tuchman, Barbara W. (Barbara Wertheim), 1912-1989

March of folly : from Troy to Vietnam / Barbara W. Tuchman. Ballantine Books, 1985. xvi, 447 p. : **909.08**

1. Modern history 2. History -- Errors, inventions, etc 3. Power (Social sciences) 4. Judgment
ISBN 9780345308238

LC 84045672

Examines the irrationalities of governments through analysis of four crises of history--the fall of Troy, the Renaissance popes' provocation of the Protestant Reformation, Britain's loss of the American colonies, and America's involvement in Vietnam

909.0971241 Commonwealth of Nations

Brendon, Piers

★The **decline** and fall of the British Empire, 1781-1997 / Piers Brendon. Alfred A. Knopf, 2008, c2007. 816 p. **909.0971241**

1. Imperialism -- History. 2. Commonwealth countries -- History. 3. Great powers. 4. Colonialism. 5. Great Britain -- Colonies -- History. 6. Great Britain -- Civilization.
ISBN 9780307268297

LC 2008014192

"Originally published in Great Britain by Jonathan Cape, London"--T.p. verso.

Chronicles Britain's rise to imperial might in the wake of the American Revolution, recording life in its diverse colonies and reflecting on the inherent weaknesses of the empire, its inevitable decline, and its legacy for the present.

"A richly detailed, lucid account of how the British Empire grew and grew--and then, not quite inexorably, fell apart." Kirkus.

909.8 World history--1800

Mishra, Pankaj

★**Age** of anger : a history of the present / Pankaj Mishra. Farrar Straus & Giroux, 2017. 192 p. **909.8**

1. Colonialism 2. Nationalism 3. Globalization 4. Xenophobia
ISBN 9780374274788

LC 2016050813

A columnist explores the rising tide of paranoid hatred in modern times and attributes it to our inability to fulfill the promises of a globalized economy.

909.82 World history--20th century, 1900-1999

Dallek, Robert

The **lost** peace : leadership in a time of horror and hope / Robert Dallek. Harper, 2010. 432 p. **909.82**

1. World politics -- 1945-1955. 2. World War II -- Peace. 3. Cold War. 4. Politicians.
ISBN 9780061628665

LC 2010005727

Dallek sheds new light on the post-war period of 1945-1953. After enduring over six years of combat, what drove the leaders of the world's great nations--the US, Britain, France, and the USSR--to employ tactics of traditional power politics in their international dealings? Here Dallek examines the fateful consequences of their actions and decisions.

"The author's interpretation of the thinking and actions of American, Chinese, European, and Soviet leaders is worth the book's reasonable price. This is solid historical scholarship from a master." Library Journal.

Emmerson, Charles

1913 : in search of the world before the Great War / Charles Emmerson. Perseus Books Group, 2013. 352 p. **909.82**

1. Capitals (Cities) 2. International relations. 3. World economy. 4. Globalization. 5. Europe -- History -- 1913.
ISBN 9781610392563

LC 2013935895

A Chatham House senior research fellow and author of The Future History of the Arctic presents an assessment of the year 1913 that is independent of an imminent World War I, drawing on visits to European capitals and other major cities to reveal how the world was more integrated and internationalized than previously understood.

"By staying so tightly focused on this single year, Emmerson is able to reveal causal mechanisms while simultaneously making readers wonder what could have been." Publishers Weekly.

Finder, Henry,

The **60s** : the story of a decade / New Yorker Magazine, edited by Henry Finder. Random House, 2016. 720 p. New Yorker decades ; **909.82**

1. National characteristics, American. 2. United States -- Civilization -- 1945-
ISBN 9780679644835

LC 2016013617

The third installment of a fascinating decade-by-decade series, this anthology collects historic New Yorker pieces from the most tumultuous years of the twentieth century--including pieces by James Baldwin, Pauline Kael, Sylvia Plath, Roger Angell, Muriel Spark, and John Updike--alongside new assessments of the 1960s by some of today's finest writers.

"Collectively, the essays provide a keen intellectual view of the 1960s while reintroducing readers to some of the best writers of the decade." Library Journal.

Gilbert, Martin, 1936-

A **history** of the twentieth century : the concise edition of the acclaimed world history / Martin Gilbert. Perennial, 2002, c2001. xv, 783 p. : **909.82**

1. History, Modern -- 20th century
ISBN 9780060505943

LC BL2003000787

Condensed version of the three-volume work first published 1997-1999; this ed. originally published by HarperCollins in Great Britain in 2001.

Chronicles the events, wars, disasters, cultural developments, religious and social movements, technological innovations, scientific advances, and personalities that shaped the twentieth century.

Gorman, Robert F.,

Great events from history : the 20th century, 1901-1940 / editor, Robert F. Gorman. Salem Press, c2007. 6 v. (dxiii, 3453, cxxx p.) : Great events from history **909.82**

1. Essays
ISBN 1587653249

LC 2007001930

Some of the essays in this work originally appeared in various Salem Press publications.

Presents essays arranged in chronological order on key world events that occurred in such areas as politics, science, medicine, communications, literature, music, philosophy, and international affairs during the first forty years of the twentieth century.

"This set provides access to clear, objective information, especially on topics in the sciences and mathematics." Library Journal.

Harari, Yuval N.

★**21** lessons for the 21st century / Yuval Noah Harari. Spiegel & Grau, [2018] 240 p. **909.82**

1. Civilization, Western -- 21st century 2. Technology and civilization 3. World politics 4. Forecasting
ISBN 9780525512172

LC 2018013856

Shares insights into such present-day issues as the role of technology in transforming humanity, the epidemic of false news, and the modern relevance of nations and religion.

"Magnificently combining historical, scientific, political, and philosophical perspectives, Harari (Sapiens and Homo Deus), a Hebrew University of Jerusalem history professor, explores 21 of what he considers to be today's greatest challenges." Publishers Weekly.

Hillstrom, Kevin, 1963-

The **Cold** War / Kevin Hillstrom ; foreword by Christian Ostermann. Omnigraphics, c2006. xx, 536 p. : **909.82**

1. Cold War. 2. Cold War -- Sources. 3. World politics -- 1945-1989. 4. World politics -- 1985-1995.
ISBN 9780780809345

LC 2006015330

"Examines the Cold War and its impact on America, the Soviet Union, and the world. Features include narrative overviews of key events and trends, 100+ primary source documents, chronology, glossary, bibliography, and subject index".--Provided by publisher.

Hochschild, Adam

Lessons from a dark time : and other essays / Adam Hochschild. University of California Press, 2018. 303 p. **909.82**

1. Social advocacy 2. Social justice 3. Political activists 4. Political persecution 5. Essays 6. Anthologies
ISBN 9780520297241

LC 2018009384

Includes index.

Hochschild shares the stories of people who took a stand against despotism, spoke out against unjust wars and government surveillance, and dared to dream of a better and more just world.

Huntington, Samuel P.

The **clash** of civilizations and the remaking of world order / Samuel P. Huntington. Simon & Schuster, 1996. 367 p.

: **909.82**

1. World politics -- 1989- 2. Post-communism. 3. Civilization -- 20th century. 4. Nationalism.

ISBN 0684811642

LC 96031492

Predicting greater future conflicts between Western and non-Western cultures, a political study argues for greater understanding of non-Western civilizations.

"The Huntington argument that the West should stop intervening in civilizational conflicts it doesn't understand makes a powerful claim that internationalists cannot easily ignore." New York Times Book Review.

Judt, Tony

Reappraisals : reflections on the forgotten twentieth century / Tony Judt. Penguin Press, 2008. 464 p. **909.82**

ISBN 1594201366

LC 2007030297

An historian and political intellectual shares a cautionary evaluation of profound differences between twentieth- and twenty-first-century culture as a result of globalization, citing sobering compromises to intellectual thought and social activism that the author believes have rendered the modern world more vulnerable to recurrences of past tragedies

Junger, Sebastian

Fire / Sebastian Junger. W.W. Norton, 2001. xv, 224 p. **909.82**

1. Disasters. 2. Survival. 3. World politics -- 1989- 4. Terrorism. 5. Essays.

ISBN 0393010465

LC 2001045236

Contains previously published magazine articles.

Junger brings his heart-pounding prose to bear on forest fires, terrorism, and war, in a collection of pieces that span a decade's worth of journalism. Junger's firsthand acounts of how people handle danger reveals both the awe and the terror evoked by desperate situations.

"The stories are all told with Junger's unfailing eye for detail, which often lends the pieces a disturbing authenticity." Library Journal.

Kennedy, Paul M., 1945-

The **rise** and fall of the great powers : economic change and military conflict from 1500 to 2000 / Paul Kennedy. Vintage Books, 1989, c1987. xxv, 677 p. : **909.82**

1. History, Modern 2. Economic history 3. Military history, Modern 4. Military readiness -- Economic aspects

ISBN 9780679720195

LC 88040123

Includes index.

Surveys global politics over the past five hundred years and discusses current problems facing the major powers.

Kurlansky, Mark

1968 : the year that rocked the world / Mark Kurlansky. Ballantine, 2004. xx, 441 p. : **909.82**

1. King, Martin Luther, Jr., 1929-1968 Assassination 2. Kennedy, Robert Francis, 1925-1968 Assassination. 3. Democratic Party. National Convention, Chicago, Illinois, 1968. 4. Radicalism -- History -- 20th century. 5. Modern history -- 1945-1989 6. Insurgency -- History -- 20th century. 7. Political violence -- History. 8. My Lai (4), Vietnam -- Massacre, 1968.

ISBN 0345455819

LC 2004299128

ALA Notable Book, 2005.

"This is an account of the global, social, and political upheaval, warfare, and assassinations that define one year in a tumultuous decade." Booklist.

Lukacs, John, 1924-

A **short** history of the twentieth century / John Lukacs. The Belknap Press of Harvard University Press, 2013. viii, 230 p. ; **909.82**

1. Modern history. 2. World leaders. 3. Great powers. 4. History.

ISBN 9780674725362

LC 2013007948

Offers a succinct chronicle of 20th century world history, focusing on the period from the beginning of World War I through the fall of the Soviet Union.

Sebestyen, Victor, 1956-

1946 : the making of the modern world / Victor Sebestyen. Pantheon Books, 2015. 464 p. **909.82**

1. World politics -- 1945-1955.

ISBN 9781101870426

LC 2015014902

A narrative account of the world-changing negotiations of the post-World War II era draws on new archival material and interviews to analyze the influences of discussions surrounding such events as the development of the atomic bomb, Britain's withdrawal from India and the creation of the Israeli state.

"Highly recommended for anyone interested in world history or for those seeking to understand why the world is as it is today." Library Journal.

Service, Robert, 1947-

The **end** of the Cold War 1985-1991 / Robert Service. Public Affairs, 2015 464 p. **909.82**

1. Cold War 2. World politics -- 1945-1990. 3. International relations. 4. East-West relations 5. United States -- Foreign relations Soviet Union 6. Soviet Union -- Foreign relations United States.

ISBN 9781610394994

LC 2015942161

A British historian and author investigates the final years of the Cold War from both sides of the Iron Curtain, discussing the relationship between Reagan and Gorbachev whose unprecedented, historic cooperation worked against the odds to end the arms race.

"A wholly satisfying, likely definitive, but not triumphalist account of the end of an era." Kirkus.

Tuchman, Barbara W. (Barbara Wertheim), 1912-1989

The **proud** tower : a portrait of the world before the war, 1890-1914 / Barbara W. Tuchman. Ballantine Books, 1996, c1966. xiii, 528 p. : **909.82**

1. Modern history. 2. Social history. 3. Europe -- History -- 1871-1918. 4. Europe -- Social conditions -- 1871-1918.

ISBN 9780345405012

LC 96096511

Originally published: New York : Macmillan, 1966.

Looks at the history of society and culture in the years leading up to World War I.

Tucker, Spencer, 1937-

The **encyclopedia** of the Cold War : a political, social, and military history / Spencer C. Tucker, volume editor. ABC-CLIO, c2008. 5 v. (xxxviii, 1969, I-21 p.) : **909.82**

1. Cold War 2. World politics -- 1945-1990 3. World politics -- 1985-

1995 4. Encyclopedias
ISBN 9781851097012

LC 2007009681

Documents volume editor, Priscilla Roberts.

Offers alphabetical entries on the ideologies, organizations, events, and prominent people associated with the Cold War, along with essays, primary documents, a chronology, a bibliography, and a glossary.

"The content gives a broad global view of an anxious period and provides useful background for some of today's conflicts." Booklist.

Vinen, Richard

1968 : radical protest and its enemies / Richard Vinen. HarperCollins 2018 224 p. **909.82**

1. Radicalism 2. Social advocacy 3. Protests, demonstrations, vigils, etc. 4. Civil Rights Movement 5. France -- History -- 20th century 6. United States -- History -- 20th century 7. Great Britain -- History -- 20th century 8. West Germany
ISBN 9780062458742

LC bl2018079926

A major new history of one of the seminal years in the postwar world describes how rebellion and disaffection broke out around the globe on an extraordinary scale.

"Although British historian Richard Vinen's rather academic examination lacks storytelling finesse, it is rich in distinct and acute observations. His subject is not the year per se but rather the long 68, that is, the radical movements and rebellion of the late 1960s and early 1970s." Booklist.

Von Tunzelmann, Alex, 1977-

Blood and sand : Suez, Hungary, and Eisenhower's campaign for peace / Alex Von Tunzelmann. Harper, 2016. xvi, 534 pages, 16 unnumbered pages of plates : **909.82**

1. Eisenhower, Dwight D. (Dwight David), 1890-1969. 2. International relations. 3. Cold War. 4. Diplomatic negotiations in international disputes. 5. Presidents -- United States. 6. Egypt -- History -- Intervention, 1956. 7. Suez Canal (Egypt) -- History. 8. United States -- Foreign relations -- 1953-1961. 9. Hungary
ISBN 9780062249241

LC bl2016043983

Describes the twin crises in 1956 involving Suez and Hungary that brought the world to the brink of nuclear war and discusses both events in the context of the resulting global Cold War, the ongoing Arab-Israeli conflict and the dangerous politics of oil.

"This is an outstanding reexamination of these sad, history-altering events." Booklist.

909.825 World history, 1950-1959

Westad, Odd Arne

The **Cold** War : a world history / Odd Arne Westad. Basic Books, 2017. 710 p. **909.825**

1. Cold War -- History. 2. World politics -- 20th century 3. International relations 4. Socialism 5. Soviet Union -- Politics and government 6. United States -- Politics and government
ISBN 9780465054930

LC 2017939229

The immediate historical roots of the Cold War sprouted after World War II, when Soviet-led countries faced off against the U.S. and its allies. Though the division of Germany into East and West, the Iron Curtain cutting off Eastern Europe, and the American anticommunist frenzy of the 1940s and '50s come readily to mind, award-winning historian Odd Arne Westad traces the Cold War's origins to the Industrial Revolution and illuminates its effects throughout the world.

"He ably synthesizes contemporary scholarship to produce an accessible narrative that provides a fresh perspective on the conflicts pervasive global influence." Publishers Weekly.

909.83 World history--21st century, 2000-2099

Bergen, Peter L., 1962-

The **longest** war : the enduring conflict between America and al-Qaeda / Peter L. Bergen. Free Press, 2011. xx, 473 p., 8 p. of plates : **909.83**

1. Qaida (Organization) 2. War on Terrorism, 2001-2009. 3. Terrorism -- United States -- Prevention. 4. Antiterrorist policy. 5. Terrorists.
ISBN 9780743278935

LC 2010015268

A forefront expert on al Qaeda draws on his unique first-hand interviews with Osama bin Laden, top-level jihadists and Washington officials to offer insight into the war on terror from both sides. By the author of The Osama bin Laden I Know.

"This is a broad, almost stereoscopic account that brings an array of sources together into an illuminating synthesis...If you want a solid, readable history of the Long War, this is a great place to start." Washington Monthly.

Gunderson, Jessica

Pivotal moments / Jessica Gunderson. Creative Education, c2012. 48 p. : War on terror **909.83**

1. Terrorism -- United States 2. War on Terrorism, 2001-2009 3. Iraq War, 2003-2011 4. Terrorists.
ISBN 9781608181025

LC 2010033845

"An examination of landmark events in the ongoing war against Islamic extremists, spotlighting such incidents as the 9/11 attacks, the invasion of Iraq, and the creation of new democracies".--Provided by publisher.

Harari, Yuval N.

Homo deus : a brief history of tomorrow / Yuval Noah Harari ; translated by the author. Harper, 2017, c2016 449 p. **909.83**

1. Forecasting. 2. Humans 3. Ethics 4. Evolution
ISBN 9780062464316

LC bl2017000348

"First published as The History of Tomorrow in Hebrew in Israel in 2015 by Kinneret Zmora-Bitan Dvir. Previously published in Great Britain in 2016 by Harvill Secker, a division of Penguin Random House Group Ltd."--Title page verso.

The best-selling author of Sapiens examines the civilized world's phenomenal achievements in the areas of famine, disease and war while making provocative predictions about the evolutionary goals of the 21st century, philosophy and every discipline in between.

"A relentlessly fascinating book that is sure to becomeand deserves to bea bestseller." Kirkus.

Klosterman, Chuck, 1972-

★**But** what if we're wrong : thinking about the present as if it were the past / Charles Klosterman. Blue Rider Press, 2016.

288 p. **909.83**

1. Popular culture. 2. National characteristics, American. 3. Essays

ISBN 9780399184123

LC 2016023103

The best-selling author of Sex, Drugs, and Cocoa Puffs explores the idea that today's mainstream beliefs about the world are fundamentally incorrect, drawing on original interviews with forefront intellectuals and experts to consider how the music, sports, literature and other present-day conventions may be perceived in future centuries.

Chuck Klosterman X : a highly specific, defiantly incomplete history of the early 21st century / Chuck Klosterman. Penguin Group USA, 2017. 400 p. **909.83**

1. Journalists 2. Popular culture 3. Popular music 4. Essays

ISBN 9780399184154

LC 2017004695

An anthology of articles, essays and columns by the cultural critic and best-selling author of Sex, Drugs, and Cocoa Puffs celebrates more than a decade of journalism and includes signature pieces, original drafts and previously unpublished passages on a wide range of subjects.

"This collection features his best pieces from the last ten years. Although a majority of the articles focus on music or sports, Klosterman also ruminates on literature, pop culture, death, and much more." Library Journal.

McKibben, Bill

Falter : has the human game begun to play itself out? / Bill McKibben. Henry Holt and Co., 2019. 291 p. **909.83**

1. Civilization, Western -- 21st century 2. Nature -- Effect of humans on 3. Technology and civilization 4. Human ecology

ISBN 9781250178268

LC 2018046452

Shares cautionary insights into how emerging technologies, including artificial intelligence and robotics, are being developed through fervent ideologies that are threatening the diversity of human experience.

910 Geography and travel

Allaby, Michael

The **encyclopedia** of Earth : a complete visual guide / [authors, Michael Allaby ... [et al.]]. University of Calif. Press, c2008. 608 p. : **910**

1. Earth (Planet)

ISBN 9780520254718

LC 2008006956

Includes index.

Statement of responsibility from p. [5].

Provides comprehensive information on the planet, including its geological history, physical composition, weather, and humankind's relationship with the Earth.

Butler, Daniel Allen

"Unsinkable" : the full story of the RMS Titanic / Daniel Allen Butler. Da Capo Press, 2003, c1998. xii, 292 p. : **910**

1. Titanic (Steamship) 2. Shipwrecks -- North Atlantic Ocean. 3. North Atlantic Ocean.

ISBN 0306811103

LC BL2003016651

Originally published: Mechanicsburg, PA : Stackpole Books, 1998.

Describes the construction and maiden voyage of the "unsinkable" Titanic, which sank after colliding with an iceberg in the North Atlantic in April 1912.

Fuller, Gary, 1941-

The **trivia** lover's guide to the world : geography for the lost and found / Gary Fuller. Rowman & Littlefield Publishers, Inc., c2012. xviii, 270 p. : **910**

1. Geography -- Miscellanea.

ISBN 9781442214033

LC 2011051863

Includes index.

Provides answers and explanations to one hundred fifty geography questions, addressing which of the U.S.'s contiguous states is most northerly and what the most recently settled country in the world is.

García Márquez, Gabriel, 1928-2014

The **story** of a shipwrecked sailor : who drifted on a life raft for ten days without food or water, was proclaimed a national hero, kissed by beauty queens, made rich through publicity, and then spurned by the government and forgotten for all time / Gabriel García Márquez ; translated from the Spanish by Randolph Hogan. Vintage Books, 1987, c1986. ix, 106 p. ; **910**

1. Velasco, Luis Alejandro. 2. Sailors -- Colombia. 3. Shipwrecks -- Caribbean Area -- History 4. Survival (after airplane accidents, shipwrecks, etc.) 5. Colombia -- Politics and government.

ISBN 067972205X

LC 86046175

Translation of: Relato de un naufrago.

Reprint. Originally published: New York : Knopf, 1986.

"In 1955 García Márquez was working as a reporter in Colombia. One of his stories was a serialized account of a sailor who was swept overboard with seven other crew members of a Colombian destroyer and who was the only one to survive. This book presents García Márquez's version of the sailor's first-person narrative." Booklist.

Heyerdahl, Thor, 1914-2002

Kon-Tiki : across the Pacific by raft / Thor Heyerdahl ; translated by F.H. Lyon. Washington Square Press, 1984, c1950. 240 p., 48 p. of plates : **910**

1. Heyerdahl, Thor, 1914-2002 2. Kon-Tiki Expedition, 1947 3. Ethnology -- Polynesia. 4. Pacific Ocean.

ISBN 9780671726522

LC 8442785

Translation of: Kon-Tiki ekspedisjonen.

Includes index.

Photographs illustrate the author's account of his voyage from Peru to Tahiti on a balsa raft to test a theory concerning the origins of the Polynesian race.

Lord, Walter, 1917-2002

★A **night** to remember / Walter Lord. Henry, Holt, and Co., 2005, c1955. xx, 182 p. : **910**

1. Titanic (Steamship) 2. Shipwrecks -- North Atlantic Ocean. 3. North Atlantic Ocean.

ISBN 0805077642

LC 2004059509

"A Owl Book."

"First published in hardcover in 1955 by Henry, Holt, and Company"--T.p. verso.

Recounts the demise of the "unsinkable" Titanic, the massive luxury liner that housed extravagances such as a French "sidewalk cafe" and a grand staircase, but failed to provide enough lifeboats for the 2,207 passengers on board.

"A detailed account of the tragic drama of that terrible night--April 4, 1912--when the Titanic, the unsinkable ship, struck an iceberg and went down in the icy waters of the Atlantic." Library Journal.

910.2 World travel guides

Boorman, Charley,

The **road** trip book : 1001 drives of a lifetime / general editor, Darryl Sleath ; foreword, Charley Boorman. Universe Publishing, 2018. 960 p. : **910.2**

1. Automobile travel 2. Travel 3. Voyages and travels 4. Voyages around the world 5. Guidebooks.

ISBN 9780789334251

LC 2017945497

Includes indexes.

"For anyone who has fallen under its spell, a car represents freedom and adventure. For decades, the American tradition of the road trip has been bound up with the idea of new possibilities and new horizons. This book is an indispensable guide to the most beautiful, breathtaking, extraordinary, and fun road trips the world has to offer. Complete with road trips varying in length and level of challenge, from an epic trans-global route inspired by Ewan McGregor and Charley Boorman's Long Way Round documentary series to a two-mile blast around Monaco's F1 street circuit, there is something for any adventurer. Each entry provides information about distance, start and finish points, road surfaces, must-see stop-offs, detours, and other details to plan an unforgettable trip. Entries are organized into three categories: Scenic, Adventure, and Culture. One can marvel at the views from Cape Town's scenic Chapman's Peak Drive or central California's Pacific Coast Highway, but the thrill seeker might opt for the hair-raising ride through Montenegro's coastal mountains to reach the medieval walled town of Sveti Stefan on the Adriatic. The culture category features routes inspired by film, literature, and history: re-create Thelma and Louise's heart-pounding joyride (minus the final leap), savor Japan's 'Romance Road' through unspoiled small towns, or follow Jack Kerouac's path from On the Road."-- Amazon.com.

Bray, Hiawatha

You are here : from the compass to GPS, the history and future of how we find ourselves / Hiawatha Bray. Basic Books, 2014. xiii, 258 p. ; **910.2**

1. Geographic information systems 2. Electronics in navigation 3. Geospatial data. 4. Maps

ISBN 9780465032853

LC 2014002731

"Filled with tales of scientists and astronauts, inventors and entrepreneurs, You Are Here tells the story of how humankind ingeniously solved one of its oldest and toughest problems--only to herald a new era in which it's impossible to hide. "-- Provided by publisher.

Howard, Alex

Secret marvels of the world : 360 Extraordinary Places You Never Knew Existed and Where to Find Them / written by Alex Howard, Alexis Averbuck, Amy Balfour, Amy Karafin, Anita Isalska, Anna Kaminski, Anthony Ham, Bailey Johnson, Brandon Presser, Brendan Sainsbury [and 42 others]. Lonely Planet Global Limited, 2017. 304 p. : **910.2**

1. Travel -- Guidebooks

ISBN 9781787010048

LC oc2018166569

Includes index.

Naghten, Catherine,

The **World** : a traveller's guide to the planet / product editors, Catherine Naghten, Tracy Whitmey. Lonely Planet Global Limited, 2017. 991 p. : **910.2**

1. Travel -- Guidebooks

ISBN 9781786576538

LC bl2017038455

Includes index.

Offers an A to Z guide to every country, providing maps and facts about each and highlighting the must see sites.

Unesco

World Heritage sites : a complete guide to 1,073 UNESCO World Heritage sites Firefly Books, 2018. 955 p. : **910.2**

1. World Heritage areas 2. Guidebooks.

ISBN 9780228101352

LC 2018933773

"Published jointly by the United Nations Educational Scientific and Cultural Organization (UNESCO) ..."--Title page verso.

Includes indexes.

910.3 Dictionaries, encyclopedias, concordances, gazetteers

Hill, Melissa Sue

Worldmark encyclopedia of the nations Gale, Cengage Learning, [2017] 5 volumes : **910.3**

1. United Nations 2. Geography 3. History 4. Economics 5. Political science

ISBN 9781410338983

LC 2016034911

Concise, informative word portraits of each country describe distinctive physical characteristics, populations, history, infrastructure, and (in less detail) cultural highlights. School Library Journal

910.4 Accounts of travel and facilities for travelers

Baggett, Jennifer

The **lost** girls : three friends, four continents, one unconventional detour around the world / Jennifer Baggett, Holly C. Corbett, and Amanda Pressner. HarperCollins, c2010. 560 p. **910.4**

1. Baggett, Jennifer Travel 2. Corbett, Holly C. Travel 3. Pressner, Amanda Travel 4. Women travelers. 5. Friendship. 6. Backpacking. 7. Twenties (Age)

ISBN 9780061689062

LC 2009054294

Three friends at a crossroads in their twenties quit their high pressure New York media jobs; leave their friends, boyfriends and everything familiar behind; and embark on a year-long backpacking adventure around the world.

"Friends Pressner, Baggett, and Corbett were all busy climbing the corporate ladder of Manhattan media when they realized that, in their late twenties, they weren't sure they wanted the golden handcuffs of New York success. Reprioritizing, they decide on a rebellious, extreme course of action: quit their jobs, abandon their boyfriends, and take a year-long trip around the world. In this group memoir, the three take turns chronicling a journey from Peru to Kenya to Vietnam to Australia, and everywhere in between. [The authors] provide passionate, vivid descriptions of their far-flung travels, bolstered by thoughtful insights and genuine intentions, making this an intensely enjoyable read for fans of travel writing." Publishers Weekly.

Bryson, Bill

World's best travel experiences : 400 extraordinary places / foreword by Andrew McCarthy ; [with recollections by Bill Bryson, Anna Quindlen, and more]. National Geographic, c2012. 319 p. : **910.4**

1. Travel photography 2. Voyages and travels
ISBN 9781426209598

LC 2012016594

Includes index.

An evocative travel gift book in the spirit of National Geographic Traveler's acclaimed "Places of a Lifetime" features sumptuously photographed coverage of some of the world's most transformative locales, from Norway's western fjords and Cambodia's Angkor Wat to Kyoto's Moss Garden and the urban surprises of Denver, Pittsburgh and Vancouver.

"Readers will dip into this book for inspiration for future travel as well as for fuel for beautiful daydreams." Library Journal.

Burgin, Robert

Going places : a reader's guide to travel narratives / Robert Burgin. Libraries Unlimited, c2013. xxx, 572 p. ; **910.4**

1. Travel writing. 2. Essays
ISBN 1598849727

LC 2012035744

Chaplin, Joyce E.

Round about the earth : circumnavigation from Magellan to orbit / Joyce E. Chaplin. Simon & Schuster, c2012. xxi, 535 p., 21 p. : **910.4**

1. Trips around the world. 2. Vehicles -- History. 3. Voyages and travels -- History. 4. Exploration.
ISBN 9781416596196

LC 2012016459

An account of the history of circumnavigation and how it has influenced the way people think about the Earth, profiling the early quests of famous historical figures, and the innovations that enabled world travel.

Cordingly, David

Seafaring women : an untold maritime history / David Cordingly. Random House, 2007, c2001. xv, 286 p. : **910.4**

1. Women and the sea. 2. Women sailors. 3. Seafaring life. 4. Sailors. 5. Europe -- History.
ISBN 0375500413

LC 00062762

Originally published under the title: Women sailors and sailors' women: an untold maritime history, 2001.

The author takes readers on a wild ride through three hundred years of maritime history in search of women pirates, captains, seafarers, and explorers who broke new ground in the male-dominated maritime world.

"A look at the lives of the intrepid women who went to sea during the great age of sail. Countless females set sail for reasons of adventure, romance, or duty in the seventeenth, eighteenth, and nineteenth centuries. Included among their numbers were the wives or mistresses of ships' officers, prostitutes, female pirates, and women disguised as male sailors. A significant contribution to both women's history and maritime scholarship." Booklist.

Under the black flag : the romance and the reality of life among the pirates / David Cordingly. Random House Trade Paperbacks, 2006, c1996. xxi, 296 p. : **910.4**

1. Pirates -- History. 2. Seafaring life -- History. 3. Pirate ships. 4. Piracy.
ISBN 081297722X

LC bl2006011709

Originally published: New York : Random House, 1996.

A revisionist history of the golden age of piracy draws on original archive records to provide a realistic study of pirates and their lives that refutes many of the myths about the era.

"This succinct history is full of unexpected revelations about the facts and myths of piracy; a typical seventeenth-century Western pirate vessel, for example, was run democratically long before the French Revolution, and one of the most successful pirates of all time was a nineteenth-century Chinese woman who controlled some fifty thousand seagoing outlaws." The New Yorker.

Engdal, Eskil, 1964-

Catching Thunder : the story of the world's longest sea chase / Eskil Engdal, Kjetil Saeter ; translated from the Norwegian by Diane Oatley. Zed Books, 2018. vii, 280 pages : **910.4**

1. Thunder (Fishing vessel) 2. Sea Shepherd Conservation Society 3. Organized crime 4. Fishing industry and trade 5. Poaching 6. Environmental degradation 7. Antarctica
ISBN 9781786990877

LC bl2018055791

December, 2014: In the forbidding waters off Antarctica, Captain Hammarstedt of the Bob Barker embarks on a voyage unlike any seen before. Across ten thousand miles of hazardous seas, Hammarstedt's crew will relentlessly pursue the Thunder--an infamous illegal fishing ship--for what will become the longest chase in maritime history.

Fagan, Brian M.

Beyond the blue horizon : how the earliest mariners unlocked the secrets of the oceans / Brian Fagan. New York, c2012. 384 p. **910.4**

1. Explorers. 2. Seafaring life -- History 3. Ocean travel -- History 4. Navigation -- History 5. Pacific Ocean -- Exploration.
ISBN 9781608190058

LC 2011045758

Looks at the early development of navigation, examining how ancient humans discovered the secrets of wind, tides, and stars that allowed them to make long voyages that profoundly changed human civilization.

Foer, Joshua

★**Atlas** Obscura / Joshua Foer, Dylan Thuras & Ella Morton. Workman Publishing, 2016. 480 p. **910.4**

1. Voyages and travels. 2. Curiosities and wonders. 3. Trivia and miscellaneous facts
ISBN 9780761169086

LC 2016041548

"Atlas Obscura is the bucket-list guide to over 700 of the most unusual, curious, bizarre, and mysterious places on earth".-- Provided by publisher.

"Featuring full-color illustrations, this hefty and gorgeously produced tome will be eagerly pored over by readers of many ages and fans of the original website." Booklist.

Heat Moon, William Least

Here, there, elsewhere : stories from the road / William Least Heat-Moon. Little, Brown & Co., 2013. 432 p. **910.4**

1. Heat Moon, William Least Travel 2. Travelers -- United States 3. Essays

ISBN 9780316110242

LC 2012953180

Though most famous for his road trips around the U.S., acclaimed travel writer William Least Heat-Moon ranges further in this collection of 30 essays written over the course of 30 years. Visiting Japan, England, Wales, Italy, New Zealand, and other distant locales as well as places closer to home, Heat-Moon once again offers readers thought-provoking observations and lyrical writing. A must-read for his many fans -- and a great introduction for those new to his writing.

Hoffman, Carl, 1960-

The **lunatic** express : discovering the world-- via its most dangerous buses, boats, trains, and planes / Carl Hoffman. Broadway Books, c2010. 286 p. : **910.4**

1. Hoffman, Carl, 1960- Travel 2. Voyages and travels. 3. Transportation -- Evaluation. 4. Trips around the world. 5. Travelers

ISBN 9780767929806

LC 2009021477

Documents the author's six-month effort to circumnavigate the globe by means of the statistically most dangerous methods, a journey that provides insight into the hazards that influence everyday life in a variety of cultures.

Johnson, Steven, 1968-

★**Enemy** of all mankind : a true story of piracy, power, and history's first global manhunt / Steven Johnson. Riverhead Books, 2020. 288 p. **910.4**

1. Avery, John, active 1695 2. Great Britain. Royal Navy -- History 3. Pirates 4. Corporations 5. Merchant ships 6. International trade -- History 7. Great Britain -- History -- 17th century 8. Indian Ocean

ISBN 9780735211605

LC 2019022493

Henry Every was the seventeenth century's most notorious pirate. The press published wildly popular--and wildly inaccurate--reports of his nefarious adventures. The British government offered enormous bounties for his capture, alive or (preferably) dead. But Steven Johnson argues that Every's most lasting legacy was his inadvertent triggering of a major shift in the global economy. Enemy of All Mankind focuses on one key event--the attack on an Indian treasure ship by Every and his crew--and its surprising repercussions across time and space. It's the gripping tale of one of the most lucrative crimes in history, the first international manhunt, and the trial of the seventeenth century.

"Consummate popular history: fast-paced, intelligent, and entertaining." Library Journal

King, Greg, 1964-

Lusitania : triumph, tragedy, and the end of the Edwardian age / Greg King and Penny Wilson. St. Martin's Press, 2015. 400 p. **910.4**

1. Lusitania (Steamship) 2. Shipwrecks -- History -- 20th century. 3. Ocean travel -- North Atlantic Ocean -- Anecdotes. 4. Upper class -- Social life and customs -- 20th century. 5. Shipwreck victims -- North Atlantic Ocean -- Anecdotes. 6. Europe -- History, Military -- 20th century

ISBN 9781250052544

LC 2014040843

A hundred years after her sinking, Lusitania remains an evocative ship of mystery. Was she carrying munitions that exploded? Did Winston Churchill engineer a conspiracy that doomed the liner? Lost amid these tangled skeins is the romantic, vibrant, and finally heartrending tale of the passengers who sailed aboard her. Lives, relationships, and marriages ended in the icy waters off the Irish Sea; those who survived were left haunted and plagued with guilt. Now, authors Greg King and Penny Wilson resurrect this lost, glittering world to show the golden age of travel and illuminate the most prominent of Lusitania's passengers. Rarely was an era so glamorous; rarely was a ship so magnificent; and rarely was the human element of tragedy so quickly lost to diplomatic maneuvers and militaristic threats.

"The authors devote inordinate portions of the text to biographies of passengers and still more to the lives of the survivors, but their exploration of the facts surrounding the mystery is the primary pleasure of the book. Those who relish tales of the rich and famous will appreciate this book, but the real joy is in the authors' detective work and attention to detail." Kirkus.

Konstam, Angus

The **history** of pirates / Angus Konstam. Globe Pequot Press, 2002, c1999. 192 p. **910.4**

1. Pirates -- History. 2. Piracy -- History. 3. Pirate ships -- History.

ISBN 1585745162

LC BL 00004083

"The author chronicles the evolution of piracy from antiquity to the present. Konstam profiles individual pirates, explores infamous vessels, and compares and contrasts various pirate regions and eras. He does a commendable job of separating fact from fiction." Booklist.

Lonely Planet Publications (Firm)

An **innocent** abroad : life-changing trips from 21 great writers / Lonely Planet Publications. Lonely Planet, 2014. 320 p. **910.4**

1. Voyages and travels 2. Travelers

ISBN 9781743603604

LC bl2015013153

"Most, but not all, of these vignettes effectively convey the sense of novelty, and sometimes wide-eyed wonder, that youthful travelers are often fortunate to experience." Booklist.

McPhee, John, 1931-

Looking for a ship / John McPhee. Farrar Straus Giroux, 1990. 241 p. ; **910.4**

1. Stella Lykes (Ship) 2. Merchant marine 3. Seafaring life. 4. Merchant sailors. 5. Merchant ships. 6. First person narratives.

ISBN 0374190771

LC 90003311

Pulitzer Prize for General Nonfiction finalist

"In this book McPhee focuses on the plight of the U.S. merchant marine. Accompanying Second Mate Andy Chase on a 42-day run down the west coast of South America aboard the S.S. Stella Lykes, McPhee provides the reader with stories and tales of modern seafaring life and the problems of making a living as a merchant mariner. An engrossing tale of the sea, with excellent detail and humanity." Library Journal.

Sides, Hampton

★**In** the kingdom of ice : the grand and terrible polar voyage of the U.S.S. Jeannette / Hampton Sides. Doubleday, [2014] 384 p. **910.4**

1. Bennett, James Gordon, 1841-1918. 2. De Long, George W. (George Washington), 1844-1881. 3. Jeannette (Steamer) -- History. 4. Shipwrecks -- Arctic Ocean -- History -- 19th century. 5. Survival (after airplane accidents, shipwrecks, etc.) -- Arctic Ocean -- History -- 19th century. 6. Polar expeditions 7. Survival 8. Arctic Ocean
ISBN 9780385535373

LC 2014004367

ALA Notable Book, 2015.

On his first Polar voyage in 1873, nothing in the frigid north appealed to Lieutenant George De Long, but he soon became obsessed. A few years later, leading an 1879 Arctic expedition and tasked with finding a mythical open-sea passage, De Long and his crew faced deadly trouble when their ship became trapped in the ice. Using letters, diaries, expedition records, newspaper reports, and other documents, bestselling author Hampton Sides provides a dramatic account of what happened to De Long and his crew in this gripping nautical tale.

"Sides...tapped amazing archival material, including diaries, letters, and the ship logs, to render a completely thrilling saga of survival in unbelievably harsh conditions." Booklist.

910.452 Shipwrecks

Mearns, David L.

The **shipwreck** hunter : a lifetime of extraordinary discovery and adventure in the deep seas / David L. Mearns. W W Norton & Company, 2018, c2017 xiii, 400 p., 32 unnumbered p. of plates : **910.452**

1. Mearns, David L. 2. Treasure troves. 3. Underwater exploration 4. Shipwrecks -- History. 5. Oceanography
ISBN 9781681777603

Originally published Australia, 2017

David Mearns, the man who discovered the wreck of HMAS Sydney, takes us on an extraordinary voyage through his amazing career as one of the world's most successful shipwreck hunters.

910.9 History, geographic treatment, biography

Adams, Simon (Transport consultant)

Journey : an illustrated history of travel / foreword, Michael Collins ; contributors, Simon Adams, R.G. Grant, Andrew Humphreys. DK, a division of Penguin Random House, 2017. 440 p. : **910.9**

1. Travel -- History 2. Emigration and immigration -- History
ISBN 9781465464149

LC 2017297217

Includes index.

At head of cover title: Smithsonian.

"An illustrated account of human movement, travel, exploration, and scientific discovery--from the first trade networks in ancient Sumer to the epic Voyager missions. Human journeys arise from all manner of impulses, from migration and the search for food, to pilgrimages, trade, scientific curiosity, or simply the quest for adventure. Journey traces each through lively accounts, alongside the biographies of conquerors, explorers, and travelers; stories of technological innovation; literary journals; and works of art. Themed spreads and feature panels capture the romance of travel with evocative accounts, archive images, historic maps, and artifacts, while catalog spreads add glamour and nostalgia, showcasing objects and documents associated with the rise of travel, such as postcards and passports. A textured cover with a picture-perfect image and shiny finishes make it ideal for gift-giving. Produced in association with the Smithsonian Institution." -- ONIX annotation.

Bellec, François

Unknown lands : the log books of the great explorers / Francois Bellec ; translated by Lisa Davidson and Elizabeth Ayre. Overlook Press, 2002, c2000. 213 p., 3 p. : **910.9**

1. Discoveries in geography. 2. Explorers -- History. 3. Navigation -- History. 4. Voyages and travels -- History.
ISBN 1585672017

LC 2001036800

A vividly illustrated celebration of the mapmakers and mythmakers from the European age of exploration features dozens of maps, paintings, and engravings detailing the European vision of lands beyond the horizon.

"Weaving together logs, correspondence, and stories of the ordinary and extraordinary men who explored the oceans and unknown lands over five centuries, Bellec offers a...snapshot of the cultural and political circumstances that set the stage for maritime adventures and New World discoveries. Eyewitness accounts retold alongside maps and drawings contribute to an enlightening view of the minds, hearts, and talents of adventurers such as Columbus, Vasco de Gama, and James Cook. This is simply a stunning book." Library Journal.

Rader, Andrew (Andrew Alan)

Beyond the known : how exploration created the modern world and will take us to the stars / Andrew Rader. Scribner, [2019] 352 p. **910.9**

1. Explorers 2. Exploration 3. Discoveries (in geography) 4. Scientific expeditions
ISBN 9781982123536

LC 2019002126

An examination of all the chief periods of discovery and rediscovery from classical times to our spacefaring future.

910.91 Geography of and travel in areas, regions, places in general

Bain, Andrew

Ultimate travel : our list of the 500 best places to see... ranked / written by, Andrew Bain, Anthony Ham, Emily Matchar, James Smart, Jessica Cole, Jessica Lee, Joe Bindloss, Joshua Samuel Brown, Karla Zimmerman, Karyn Noble [and 16 others]. Lonely Planet Publications Pty Ltd, 2015. 328 p. : **910.91**

1. Voyages and travels
ISBN 9781760342777

LC bl2015041554

At head of title: Lonely Planet.

Includes index.

Presents a guide to the five hundred most unmissable places around the globe, from the Eiffel Tower and the Taj Mahal to the Nazca lines and Uluru.

Blainey, Geoffrey

Sea of dangers : Captain Cook and his rivals in the South Pacific / Geoffrey Blainey. Ivan R. Dee, 2009. xi, 322 p., 8 p. of plates : **910.91**

1. Cook, James, 1728-1779. 2. Explorers -- Great Britain 3. Trips around the world -- History -- 18th century 4. Exploration -- History 5. Ocean travel -- History -- 18th century 6. Oceania -- Exploration 7. Pacific Ocean -- Exploration -- British
ISBN 9781566638258

LC 2008052623

Originally published: Camberwell, Vic. : Viking, 2008.

In 1769 two ships set out independently in search of a missing continent: a French merchant ship, the St. Jean-Baptiste, commanded by Jean de Surville, and a small British naval vessel, the Endeavour, commanded by Captain James Cook. That Christmas, in New Zealand waters, the two captains were almost within sight of each other, though neither knew of the other's existence. This is the stirring tale of these rival ships and the men who sailed in them.

"An excellent work of popular history that recounts the exploits of men who dramatically expanded our knowledge of the globe." Booklist.

Bown, Stephen R.

Island of the blue foxes : disaster and triumph on the world's greatest scientific expedition / Stephen R. Bown. Da Capo Press, 2017. 336 p. **910.91**

1. Bering, Vitus Jonassen, 1681-1741 2. Scientific expeditions. 3. Discoveries (in geography) 4. Explorers 5. Exploration 6. Bering Strait 7. Alaska
ISBN 9780306825194

LC bl2017046753

Shortlisted for The Charles Taylor Prize for Literary Non-Fiction, 2018

Discusses the Great Northern Expedition which was a scientific expedition envisaged by Peter the Great in the 1730s and led by Danish mariner Vitus Bering.

"Luckily for readers, diaries, letters, and official reports provide Bown ample material for a gripping account of 'the most extensive scientific expedition in history,' whose impressive results were certainly matched by its duration and miseries." Kirkus.

Brandt, Anthony

The **man** who ate his boots : the history of the search for the Northwest passage / Anthony Brandt. Alfred A. Knopf, c2010. 464 p. **910.91**

1. Explorers -- Northwest Passage -- History. 2. Survival. 3. Explorers -- Arctic regions -- History. 4. Northwest Passage -- Exploration -- History. 5. Arctic regions -- Exploration -- History.
ISBN 9780307263926

LC 2009038835

"A Borzoi book."

Documents the experiences of nineteenth-century adventurers who searched for the Northwest Passage, describing the sixteenth-century myths that inspired their pursuits and the ways in which many met tragic ends when confronting the harsh Arctic elements.

"Often witty in his approach, Brandt makes the absurdity of Arctic exploration and the quest for the Northwest Passage entertaining for the general reader. Highly recommended for fans of British or Arctic exploration history." Library Journal.

Dean, Josh

The **taking** of K-129 : how the CIA used Howard Hughes to steal a Russian sub in the most daring covert operation in history / Josh Dean. E.P. Dutton, 2017. 384 p. **910.91**

1. CIA History -- 20th century 2. Hughes, Howard, 1905-1976 3. Glomar Explorer (Ship) 4. K-129 (Submarine) 5. Soviet Union. Navy -- History 6. Jennifer Project. 7. Submarine disasters -- Soviet Union. 8. Intelligence service -- United States 9. Nuclear warfare
ISBN 9781101984437

LC 2017011991

A true story of Cold War espionage and engineering reveals how the CIA, the U.S. Navy and an eccentric billionaire spent six years and nearly a billion dollars to steal a nuclear-armed Soviet submarine after it sank in the Pacific Ocean.

"Dean delivers an engaging rendition of the high-profile espionage effort." Booklist.

Easter, Gerald, 1959-

The **tsarina's** lost treasure : Catherine the Great, a golden age masterpiece, and a legendary shipwreck / Gerald Easter, Mara Vorhees. Pegasus Books, 2020. xvii, 366 p.,16 unnumbered p. of plates : **910.91**

1. Catherine II, Empress of Russia, 1729-1796 2. Dou, Gerard, 1613-1675 3. Vrouw Maria (Ship) 4. Art -- Collectors and collecting 5. Shipwrecks 6. Underwater archeology 7. Artists -- Netherlands 8. Russia -- History -- Catherine II, 1762-1796 9. Russia
ISBN 9781643135564

A riveting history and maritime adventure about priceless masterpieces originally destined for Catherine the Great.

"Readers will covet this intriguing portrait of an art world mystery." Publishers Weekly

Kurson, Robert

Pirate hunters : treasure, obsession, and the search for a legendary pirate ship / Robert Kurson. Random House Inc, 2015. 336 p. **910.91**

1. Pirate ships 2. Voyages and travels 3. Underwater exploration 4. Explorers
ISBN 9781400063369

LC 2014020225

"An enjoyable read, especially if you've got a thing for pirates." Kirkus.

Levy, Buddy, 1960-

Labyrinth of ice : the triumphant and tragic Greely polar expedition / Buddy Levy. St. Martin's Press, 2019. 336 p. **910.91**

1. Greely, A. W. (Adolphus Washington), 1844-1935 2. Lady Franklin Bay Expedition, 1881-1884 3. Voyages and travels 4. Exploration 5. Adventure 6. Scientists 7. Arctic regions -- Exploration 8. Polar regions
ISBN 9781250182197

LC 2019034039

In July 1881, Lt. A.W. Greely and his crew of 24 scientists and explorers were bound for the last region unmarked on global maps. Their goal: Farthest North. What would follow was one of the most extraordinary and terrible voyages ever made. Labyrinth of Ice tells the true story of the heroic lives and deaths of these voyagers hell-bent on fame and fortune--at any cost--and how their journey changed the world.

O'Neill, Zora

All strangers are kin : adventures in Arabic and the Arab world / Zora O'Neill. Houghton Mifflin Harcourt, 2016. 336 p. **910.91**

1. O'Neill, Zora. 2. Women journalists 3. Travel writers 4. Arabic language -- Study and teaching -- Foreign speakers. 5. Manners and

customs 6. Arab countries -- Description and travel.
ISBN 9780547853185
LC 2015020508

A lively, often hilarious, and always warm-hearted exploration of Arabic language and culture, guided by a keen-eyed travel writer with twenty years of experience studying Arabic.

"What emerges is the idea of language as a connection, passion, and a reflection of the lives and history of diverse Arab peoples, a view which is lacking in the general news coverage of Middle Eastern conflict. Glimpses of daily life, particularly of Arab women, are intriguing and sometimes unexpected, including the rich assortment of Lebanese cursing while driving." Library Journal.

Russell, Gareth

The **ship** of dreams : the sinking of the Titanic and the end of the Edwardian era / Gareth Russell. Atria Books, 2019. 423 p. **910.91**

1. Titanic (Steamship). 2. Shipwrecks 3. Ship passengers. 4. Social classes 5. Social change
ISBN 9781501176722
LC 2019005535

"Originally published in Great Britain in 2019 as The Darksome Bounds of a Failing World by William Collins"-- T.p. verso.

A narrative history links the Titanic tragedy to unprecedented social, technological, political and economic changes in England and the United States.

Slade, Rachel

★**Into** the raging sea : thirty-three mariners, one megastorm, and the sinking of El Faro / Rachel Slade. Ecco Press, 2018. xiv, 391 p. **910.91**

1. SS El Faro (Ship) 2. Ships 3. Hurricanes 4. Shipwrecks 5. Sailors 6. Atlantic Ocean 7. Caribbean Sea
ISBN 9780062699701
LC 2018002800

On October 1, 2015, Hurricane Joaquin barreled into the Bermuda Triangle and swallowed the container ship El Faro whole, resulting in the worst American shipping disaster in thirty-five years. A richly reported account of a singular tragedy, Into the Raging Sea takes us into the heart of an age-old American industry, casting new light on the hardworking men and women who paid the ultimate price in the name of profit.

"A pulse-pounding, Perfect Storm-style tale of a shipping disaster. A taut, chilling, and emotionally charged retelling of a doomed ship's final days." Kirkus.

Turner, Steve, 1949-

The **band** that played on : the extraordinary story of the 8 musicians who went down with the Titanic / Steve Turner. Thomas Nelson, c2011. 259 p. **910.91**

1. Titanic (Steamship) 2. Musicians -- History -- 20th century. 3. Courage in men. 4. Drowning victims. 5. Shipwrecks
ISBN 9781595552198
LC 2010047182

When Titanic collided with an iceberg at 23:40 on April 14th, the eight members of the band had already retired for the evening. Still, they put on overcoats and mufflers came out to play in the lounge. When most of the First Class passengers had taken to their lifeboats, the musicians simply moved to the deck and continued to play, calming the passengers as the ship sank. Historian and biographer Steve Turner delves into the lives of these men, revealing eight unique portraits of bravery. --from publisher description

Vallely, Kevin

Rowing the Northwest Passage : adventure, fear, and awe in a rising sea / Kevin Vallely. Greystone Books, 2017. 224 p. **910.91**

1. Adventurers 2. Wilderness survival 3. Climate change -- Arctic regions 4. Boats 5. Northwest Passage -- Description and travel
ISBN 9781771641340
LC bl2017052646

Four men in a rowboat make an historic attempt on the Northwest Passage to focus global attention on an environmental catastrophe.

"A rousing combination of science and adventure in the Arctic." Booklist.

Williams, Glyndwr

Arctic labyrinth : the quest for the Northwest Passage / Glyn Williams. University of California Press, 2010, c2009. xix, 439 p., 16 p. of plates : **910.91**

1. Exploration. 2. Expeditions -- Arctic regions. 3. Discoveries (in geography) 4. Explorers. 5. Northwest Passage -- Exploration -- British. 6. Northwest Passage -- Description and travel. 7. Polar regions -- Exploration.
ISBN 9780520266278
LC 2009035546

Originally published: London : Allen Lane, 2009.

"If you read one book on the history of the mythic Northwest Passage, read this one. Williams deftly weaves together explorers' logbooks and diaries (published and unpublished) with a lifetime of research, and the result is a masterpiece." Library Journal.

910.911 Frigid zones -- Travel

Larson, Edward J. (Edward John)

To the edges of the Earth : 1909, the race for the three poles, and the climax of the age of exploration / Edward Larson. William Morrow & Co., 2018. 384 p. **910.911**

1. Voyages and travels 2. North Pole expeditions. 3. South Pole expeditions. 4. Discovery and exploration 5. North Pole -- Exploration. 6. Arctic regions -- Exploration. 7. Antarctica -- Exploration
ISBN 9780062564474
LC bl2018000736

National Outdoor Book Award for History/Biography, 2018.

The Pulitzer Prize-winning historian and author of The Return of George Washington presents an analysis of an exceptional year during the peak of exploration, 1909, that was marked by record-setting expeditions to the North and South Poles and the legendary K2 mountain in the Himalayas.

" A fascinating look at the adventures of remarkably resilient men, so well-related as to make you feel the chill." Kirkus.

Seaman, Camille, 1969-

Melting away : a ten-year journey through our endangered polar regions / Camille Seaman. Princeton Architectural Press, 2015 156 p. : **910.911**

1. Seaman, Camille, 1969- 1 Travel Polar regions. 2. Icebergs -- Polar regions -- Pictorial works 3. Animals -- Polar regions -- Pictorial works 4. Natural history -- Polar regions -- Pictorial works 5. Climatic changes -- Polar regions -- Pictorial works 6. Polar regions

Pictorial works.
ISBN 9781616892609

LC 2014018830

Streever, Bill
Cold : adventures in the world's frozen places / Bill Streever. Little, Brown, c2009. 320 p. **910.911**

1. Streever, Bill Travel Arctic Regions 2. Authors, American -- 21st century -- Travel 3. Ecology -- Arctic regions 4. Hibernation 5. Geography 6. Arctic regions -- Description and travel.
ISBN 9780316042918

LC 2008045350

A narrative account of the author's forays into some of the world's coldest regions describes his encounter with an Arctic swimming hole, investigations into ancient and more recent ice ages, and examinations of animal hibernation habits.

Welky, David
★A **wretched** and precarious situation : in search of the last Arctic frontier / David Welky. W.W. Norton & Company, 2016. 480 p. **910.911**

1. MacMillan, Donald Baxter, born 1874 Travel Arctic regions. 2. Borup, George, 1885-1912. 3. Crocker Land Expedition (1913-1917). 4. Explorers. 5. North Pole. 6. Arctic regions -- Discovery and exploration -- American.
ISBN 9780393254419

LC 2016023022

In 1906, from atop a snow-swept hill in the ice fields northwest of Greenland, Commander Robert E. Peary spotted a heretofore unknown land looming in the distance. He called it "Crocker Land." Scientists and explorers agreed that Peary had found a new continent. Several years later, two of Peary's disciples, George Borup and Donald MacMillan--with the sponsorship of the American Museum of Natural History--assembled a team of amateurs to investigate.

Wheeler, Sara
The **magnetic** north : notes from the Arctic circle / Sara Wheeler. Farrar, Strauss and Giroux, c2011. 336 p. **910.911**

1. Wheeler, Sara Travel Arctic regions. 2. Voyages and travels. 3. Arctic regions -- Description and travel. 4. Arctic regions -- History.
ISBN 9780374200138

LC 2010014576

"Originally published, in slightly different form, in 2009 by Jonathan Cape, Great Britain."

"With wry humor and extensive research, Wheeler captures a swiftly transforming region with which we all have a symbiotic relationship." New York Times Book Review.

Wilkinson, Alec, 1952-
The **ice** balloon : S.A. Andree and the heroic age of Arctic exploration / Alec Wilkinson. Alfred A. Knopf, c2011. 272 p. **910.911**

1. Andree, Salomon August, 1854-1897. 2. Explorers -- Sweden 3. Balloon ascensions. 4. Exploration. 5. Polar regions -- Exploration. 6. Arctic regions -- Exploration.
ISBN 9780307594808

LC 2011025434

Documents the dramatic 1897 flight of a visionary Swedish explorer who attempted to discover the North Pole in a hydrogen balloon, describing the formidable environmental conditions that challenged his efforts.

910.915 Regions by type of vegetation

Atkins, William (Editor)
The **immeasurable** world : journeys in desert places / William Atkins. Doubleday, 2018. 368 p. **910.915**

1. Atkins, William (Editor) Travel 2. Deserts 3. Voyages and travels 4. Natural history 5. Arid regions
ISBN 9780385539883

LC 2017053583

Recounts the author's travels through eight of the world's most extreme deserts, including the Gobi Desert and the Great Victoria Desert, in a literary tribute to their cultural relevance and allure.

"The subject is riveting, the gorgeous prose reminiscent of nature observers from Thoreau to Leopold. Lovers of good descriptive writing will eat up this book." Library Journal.

910.92 Geographers, travelers, explorers regardless of country of origin

Buisseret, David
The **Oxford** companion to world exploration / David Buisseret, editor in chief. Oxford University Press, 2007. 976 p. ; **910.92**

1. Discoveries in geography.
ISBN 9780195149227

LC 2006027968

"Published in association with the Newberry Library."

Eight hundred entries provide readers with information on influential explorers, national expeditions, and navigational science from exploration of ancient civilizations to the space exploration of today.

Macleod, Alasdair, 1963-
Explorers : great tales of adventure and endurance / Royal Geographical Society ; [written by Alasdair Macleod]. DK Pub., 2010. 360 p. : **910.92**

1. Discoveries in geography 2. Explorers -- History
ISBN 9780756667375

LC bl2010026183

Published in association with the Smithsonian Institution.

Includes index.

Presents an overview of the world's greatest explorers, revealing who they were, where they went, and how their expeditions shaped the course of human history.

Moore, Peter, 1983-
Endeavour : the ship that changed the world / Peter Moore. Farrar, Straus and Giroux, 2019, c2018. 432 p. **910.92**

1. Endeavour (Ship) 2. Ships 3. Navigation -- History 4. Exploration 5. Australia -- Exploration 6. New Zealand -- Exploration
ISBN 9780374148416

"Originally published in 2018 by Chatto & Windus, Great Britain, as Endeavour : the ship and the attitude that changed the world."

Originally published: London : Chatto & Windus, 2018

The Enlightenment was an age of endeavours. From Johnson's Dictionary to campaigns for liberty to schemes for measuring the dimensions of the solar system, Britain was consumed by the impulse for grand projects, undertaken at speed. 'Endeavour' was also the name given to a Whitby collier bought by the Royal Navy in 1768 for an expedition to the South Seas. A commonplace, coal-carrying vessel, no one could have guessed that Endeavour would go on to become the most significant ship in the history of British exploration.

"With an acute eye, Moore limns the conflicting human impulses in the first episodes of this epoch-making drama. Maritime history that opens onto much more." Booklist.

911 Historical geography

DK Publishing, Inc,

History of the world map by map / foreword by Peter Snow. DK Publishing, 2018. 440 p. : **911**

1. World history. 2. Historical geography.
ISBN 9781465475855

LC bl2019000495

Includes index.

Complemented by specially commissioned, storytelling maps and published in association with the Smithsonian Institution, a map representation of the history of the world features maps reflecting major explorations, conquests, colonies and advances.

Hayes, Derek, 1947-

Historical atlas of the American West : with original maps / Derek Hayes. University of Calif. Press, c2009. 1 atlas (288 p.) : **911**

1. The West (United States) -- Historical geography Maps. 2. The West (United States) -- History.
ISBN 9780520256521

LC oc2010000799

Presents a collection of more than six hundred maps that depict the history of the American West.

"More than 600 maps have been carefully selected and beautifully reproduced in full color. They provide the primary-source documentation for the historical narrative, written for the general reader, tracing the development of the Western United States from its indigenous inhabitants to European exploration, the migration of settlers, and 20th-century events. . . . A high quality publication at an amazingly low price, this atlas is highly recommended for all public and academic libraries, history buffs, and map enthusiasts." Library Journal.

Historical atlas of the United States : with original maps / Derek Hayes. University of Calif. Press, c2007. 1 atlas (280 p.) : **911**

1. United States -- Historical geography Maps.
ISBN 0520250362

LC bl2008002456

Originally published: Vancouver : Douglas & McIntyre, 2006.

Presents a collection of more than five hundred historical maps covering more than half a millennium and ranging from the earliest days of exploration to the transformation of the Gulf Coast following hurricane Katrina.

Hellmann, Paul T., 1949-

★**Historical** gazetteer of the United States / Paul T. Hellmann. Routledge, 2005. xvii, 865 p. ; **911**

1. U.S. states 2. United States Gazetteers. 3. United States -- Historical geography Dictionaries. 4. United States -- History, Local Dictionaries.
ISBN 0415939488

LC 2004011421

Includes index.

"Overall, this is an excellent counterpart to almanacs and atlases and a solid geographical and historical reference work for users in public and academic libraries." Booklist.

Hemming, John, 1935-

Atlas of exploration / foreword by John Hemming ; [cartography, Philip's]. Oxford University Press, c2008. 1 atlas (256 p.) : **911**

1. Explorers -- History -- Maps 2. Discoveries in geography -- History -- Maps 3. Voyages and travels -- History -- Maps 4. Atlases
ISBN 9780195343182

LC bl2010016404

At head of title: Oxford.

Includes index.

Covers over three thousand years of exploration, from the ancient Egyptians to the present, and examines the reasons, results, people, routes, and equipment behind expeditions on each continent.

912 Maps and plans of surface of earth and of extraterrestrial worlds

Aczel, Amir D.

The **riddle** of the compass : the invention that changed the world / Amir D. Aczel. Harcourt, 2002, c2001. xvii, 178 p. : **912**

1. Compass. 2. Inventions. 3. Navigation. 4. Ships.
ISBN 0156007533

LC bl2005007269

"A Harvest book."

Originally published: New York : Harcourt, 2001.

Discusses the twelfth-century invention of the compass, its dramatic influence on navigation and the rise of Italian sea power, and its impact on the development of world trade and the Age of Discovery.

American University in Cairo Press

The **new** atlas of the Arab world. / American University in Cairo Press (COR). American University in Cairo Press, 2010. 1 atlas (144 p.) : **912**

1. Arab countries Maps. 2. Middle East Maps.
ISBN 9774164199

LC bl2012012466

Includes index.

Presents profiles, photographs, satellite images, and maps for each country in the League of Arab States.

DK Publishing, Inc

Atlas A-Z. / Dorling Kindersley. DK Pub., 2012. 432 p. : **912**

1. Geography 2. Atlases 3. Reference books
ISBN 9780756689773

LC bl2013001192

Includes index.

A compact, timely cartographic reference of the world provides more than 6,500 cross-referenced geographical names and sixty clearly labeled maps, with a "country factfile" incorporating information on nearly two hundred nations.

George Philip & Son,

Oxford new concise world atlas / cartography by Philip's. Oxford University Press, 2015 1 atlas (288 p.) : **912**

1. World maps. 2. Atlases
ISBN 9780190265410

LC bl2015048969

Relief shown by shading, gradient tints, and spot heights. Depths shown by gradient tints.

Includes a quick-reference index; updated statistical information on world population, climate, and geography; in-depth mapping; and instructive charts and graphs.

Goode, J. Paul, 1862-1932

Goode's world atlas. / Christopher J., Ph.D. (EDT) Sutton. Rand McNally, 2016 1 atlas (xxi, 426 p.) : **912**

ISBN 0133864642

LC bl2017008087

"Formerly Goode's school atlas"--Title page verso.

At head of title: Rand McNally

Maps provide information on world politics, climate, population, industry, and agriculture.

Harmon, Katharine A., 1960-

You are here : personal geographies and other maps of the imagination / Katharine Harmon. Princeton Architectural Press, c2004. 191 p. : **912**

1. Cartography. 2. Orientation 3. Geography 4. Maps

ISBN 1568984308

LC 2003015044

"A wonderful treat for New Yorkers and for lovers of geography- and cartography-inspired looks at life in the past and today." Library Journal.

Lavin, Stephen J. (Stephen James)

Atlas of the Great Plains / Stephen J. Lavin, Fred M. Shelley, and J. Clark Archer ; foreword by David J. Wishart ; introduction by John C. Hudson. University of Nebraska Press, c2011. 1 atlas (xvi, 335 p.) : **912**

1. Great Plains -- History Maps.

ISBN 9780803215368

LC bl2012034827

Explores the history of the Great Plains through more than three hundred full-color maps and extensive explanatory text.

Lester, Toby

The **fourth** part of the world : the race to the ends of the Earth, and the epic story of the map that gave America its name / Toby Lester. Free Press, 2009 xii, 442 p. : **912**

1. Waldseemüller, Martin, 1470-1519 2. Paris, Matthew, 1200-1259. 3. Polo, Marco, 1254-1323? 4. Cartography -- History. 5. Names, Geographical -- United States 6. Exploration -- History 7. Voyages and travels -- History -- To 1500. 8. United States -- History Maps

ISBN 9781416535317

LC 2009001230

Lester spotlights Martin Waldseemuller's 1507 world map and recounts the epic tale of the mariners and scholars who facilitated this watershed of Western history.

"In 2003, the Library of Congress paid Library Journal.

National Geographic Society (U.S.),

National Geographic visual atlas of the world National Geographic, 2017 1 atlas (416 p.) : **912**

1. Atlases. 2. Oversize books -- Specimens.

ISBN 9781426218385

LC bl2017038302

Includes indexes.

Issued in slipcase.

A comprehensive, up-to-date atlas encompasses more than three hundred thematic maps, along with more than six hundred color photographs, illustrations, charts, and graphs, that document the world's natural and cultural wonders.

Times Books (Firm)

The **Times** comprehensive atlas of the world. Times Books, 2018 223 p. : **912**

1. World maps. 2. Atlases

ISBN 9780008293383

Previous edition published 2014.

The 15th edition contains over 200,000 place names, more than any other world atlas, which means even small villages are included in the index and on the maps. It is a benchmark of cartographic excellence, trusted by governments, media and international organisations as well as being a go to reference source for households across the country. It's independent--apolitical and neutral, elegant in an attractive slipcase, and endlessly fascinating. Produced by the world's leading atlas makers for over 100 years, it's bought by over 1 million people worldwide. -- From publisher description

912.09 History and biography of maps and map making

Brotton, Jerry

Great maps / Jerry Brotton. DK Publishing, 2014. 256 p. : **912.09**

1. Cartography 2. Maps

ISBN 9781465424631

LC bl2014033540

Includes index.

A guided tour of cartography through the ages provides the fascinating stories behind 55 historical maps, profiles the explorers whose expeditions and resident cartographers helped map out the world and discusses the map's unique influence on power, art and politics.

"The thematic maps are particularly interesting, including a 'Cholera Map' from 1854, a map depicting the slave population of the Southern states, and Dr. Livingstone's map of Africa." Booklist.

Mitchell, Rose (Archivist)

Maps : their untold stories : map treasures from The National Archives / Rose Mitchell and Andrew James. The National Archives : 2014. 254 p. : **912.09**

1. National Archives (Great Britain) Map collections. 2. Cartography -- History. 3. Maps -- History. 4. Map collections -- England -- London.

ISBN 9781408189672

LC bl2014044026

Includes index.

A history of maps and what they reveal about the times and places they were made, based on the collections of the British National Archives, features maps of cities and rural areas, military maps, naval charts, and other historic examples.

Reinhartz, Dennis

The **art** of the map : an illustrated history of map elements and embellishments / Dennis Reinhartz ; foreword by John Noble Wilford. Sterling, 2012 xix, 218 p. : **912.09**

1. Cartography -- History 2. Map drawing -- History

ISBN 9781402765926

LC bl2014034309

Presents an illustrated history of the golden age of cartography, exploring the embellishments on maps and what they reveal about the world in which they were created.

913 Geography of and travel in ancient world

Grant, Michael, 1914-2004

A **guide** to the ancient world : a dictionary of classical place names / Michael Grant. H.W. Wilson, 1986. 728 p. : **913**

1. Classical antiquities 2. Mediterranean Region -- Gazetteers. 3. Encyclopedias

ISBN 9780824207427

LC 86015785

Surveys ancient cities, excavation sites, and ruins of the Hellenistic world.

914 Geography of and travel in Europe

Adams, Max, 1961-

In the land of giants : a journey through the Dark Ages / Max Adams. W W Norton & Co., 2016. 416 p. **914**

1. Civilization, Medieval 2. Memorials 3. Churches 4. Landscape 5. Great Britain -- Description and travel

ISBN 9781681772189

LC 2017302598

Explores the medieval past of Britain through 10 walking narratives that explore paths through valleys, hills and fields and taking note of the remnants of forts, fyrds, crypts, crannogs, churches, causeways, holy wells and memorial stones.

"Myth and ancient magic meet with solid historical ground in Adam's voyage through a largely forgotten age." Kirkus.

Barber, Emily

London / Emily Barber. Blue Guides Limited, 2014 592 p. : **914**

1. London (England) Guidebooks.

ISBN 1905131631

LC bl2014039227

A guidebook to London with special focus on the city's history, art, and architecture.

Baxter, John, 1939-

Five nights in Paris : after dark in the City of Light / John Baxter. William Morrow, 2015. 334 p. : **914**

1. Baxter, John, 1939- Travel Paris, France. 2. Neighborhoods 3. Walking 4. Intellectual life. 5. Nightlife 6. Paris, France -- Description and travel. 7. Paris, France -- Social life and customs.

ISBN 9780062296252

LC 2015000100

Presents an off-the-beaten-path guide to exploring Paris at night, outlining five evening tours, each of which has a connection to one of the five senses.

"In closing, Baxter writes, each of us must, in our own way, as with a new lover, seduce, or allow ourselves to be seduced by the Paris night. This is not a walking guide to Paris, but it is most certainly a guide to seeing and knowing Paris, one no Francophile should be without." Kirkus.

A **year** in Paris : season-by-season in the City of Light / John Baxter. Harper Perennial, 2019. 352 p. **914**

1. Cities and towns 2. Seasons 3. Months 4. City life 5. Paris, France -- Social life and customs 6. Paris, France -- Description and travel 7. Paris, France -- History

ISBN 9780062846884

LC 2018277172

A melange of history, travel reportage, and myth, of high culture and low, A Year in Paris is vintage John Baxter: a vicarious thrill ride for anyone who loves Paris.

"Part history, part memoir, part travelog, this book has something for everyone. Of special interest to those who hope to visit Paris." Library Journal.

Bryson, Bill

Notes from a small island / Bill Bryson. Morrow, 1995. 324 p. : **914**

1. Bryson, Bill Travel England. 2. Voyages and travels. 3. Travelers. 4. National characteristics, British. 5. England -- Civilization -- 20th century. 6. England -- Description and travel.

ISBN 0688147259

LC 95043437

Before returning to America after spending twenty years in Britain, the author decided to tour his second home and presents a look at England's quirks and its endearing qualities,

★The **road** to Little Dribbling : adventures of an American in Britain / Bill Bryson Doubleday, 2016 400 p. **914**

1. Bryson, Bill 2. Travelers. 3. Voyages and travels. 4. National characteristics, British. 5. Americans in Great Britain. 6. England -- Civilization -- 21st century. 7. England -- Description and travel.

ISBN 9780385539289

LC 2015027450

"Anglophiles will find Bryson's field notes equally entertaining and educational." Kirkus.

Eichar, Donnie

Dead Mountain : the true story of the Dyatlov Pass incident / Donnie Eichar. Chronicle Books, 2013. 288 p. **914**

1. Eichar, Donnie Travel Ural Mountains Region (Russia) 2. Hiking -- Ural Mountains Region (Russia) 3. Mountaineering accidents -- Ural Mountains Region (Russia) -- 20th century. 4. Mountaineering 5. Tragedy 6. Ural Mountains Region (Russia) -- History -- 20th century. 7. Ural Mountains (Russia)

ISBN 9781452112749

LC 2013014843

"Eichar marries the short story of the students' lives with the procedural tale of the official investigation and then integrates his own amateur investigation. [A] well-told and accurate whodunit." Kirkus.

Gray-Durant, Delia

Paris / Delia Gray-Durant. Blue Guides Limited, a Somerset Books Company, 2015. 592 p. : **914**

1. Paris (France) Guidebooks.

ISBN 1905131674

LC bl2018028594

Includes index.

A guide to Paris presents information about each section of the city, recommends restaurants and accomodations, and provides a detailed map.

Greene, David, 1976-

Midnight in Siberia : a journey into the heart of Russia / David Greene. W W Norton & Co Inc 2014 320 p. **914**

1. Greene, David, 1976- 2. Trans-Siberian Railway 3. Railroad travel 4. Russia

ISBN 9780393239959

LC 2014029382

The co-host of NPR's "Morning Edition" describes his travels along the Trans-Siberian Railroad, from Moscow to Vladivostok, describing the people he met, from singing babushkas to entrepreneurial teens to political activists, and discusses the challenges faced by 21st-century Russia.

"With abundant interpersonal detail, Greene delivers a lively, tangible feeling of meeting modern Russians on one of the worlds famous railroads." Booklist.

Keahey, John

Sicilian splendors : discovering the secret places that speak to the heart / John Keahey. St. Martin's Press, 2018. 304 p. **914**

1. Keahey, John Travel Sicily 2. Villages 3. Travelers 4. Voyages and travels 5. Cooking, Sicilian 6. Sicily, Italy -- Description and travel. 7. Mediterranean Islands
ISBN 9781250104694

LC 2018022343

"Thomas Dunne Books."

"This insightful book, with its unique portraits of historically diverse small villages, should be a must-read for everyone interested in Sicily and Mediterranean Europe." Booklist.

Landmarks / Robert Macfarlane. Penguin UK, 2015. 400 p. **914**

1. Macfarlane, Robert, 1976- 2. Nature 3. Language and languages 4. Great Britain
ISBN 9780241146538

LC bl2017021022

Presents a joyous meditation on words, landscape and the relationship between the two. This is a field guide to the literature of nature, and a glossary containing thousands of remarkable words used in England, Scotland, Ireland and Wales to describe land, nature and weather.

Macfarlane, Robert, 1976-

The **old** ways : a journey on foot / Robert Macfarlane. Viking, 2012. 320 p. **914**

1. Macfarlane, Robert, 1976- Travel England. 2. Macfarlane, Robert, 1976- Travel Scotland. 3. Trails. 4. Walking. 5. Natural history. 6. Landscapes. 7. England -- Description and travel. 8. Scotland -- Description and travel.
ISBN 9780670025114

LC 2012005887

The acclaimed author of The Wild Places recounts his walking explorations through historical British territories, roads and sea paths, drawing on themes in natural history, cartography, archaeology and literature to illuminate such landscapes as the bird islands of the Scottish northwest and the sacred regions of the Himalayas.

The **wild** places / Robert Macfarlane. Penguin Books, 2008. 352 p. **914**

1. Macfarlane, Robert, 1976- Travel Great Britain. 2. Macfarlane, Robert, 1976- Travel Ireland. 3. Wilderness areas -- Great Britain. 4. Wilderness areas -- Ireland. 5. Nature 6. Great Britain -- Description and travel. 7. Ireland -- Description and travel.
ISBN 9780143113935

LC 2008017162

"Evocative and well-written, a delight for nature and travel buffs." Kirkus.

McGregor, James H. S.

Paris from the ground up / James H.S. McGregor. Belknap Press of Harvard University Press, 2009. 327 p., 10 p. of plates : **914**

1. Cities and towns -- France. 2. National characteristics, French. 3. Culture. 4. Paris, France -- Description and travel. 5. Paris, France -- History.
ISBN 9780674033160

LC 2008043696

"Readers can use this as a well-researched but accessible history of Paris, tracing the story of the City of Light from its earliest residents, the Gauls and the Parisii, to the present day. Travelers will use chapters on churches, cathedrals, museums, and neighborhoods; those interested in the history of a particular area or landmark will find the index excellent. The many illustrations enhance the text, and the ten historical and contemporary maps help pinpoint attractions both ancient and modern." Library Journal.

Meier, Andrew

Black earth : a journey through Russia after the fall / Andrew Meier. Norton, c2003. 511 p. : **914**

1. Meier, Andrew Travel Russia 2. Post-communism -- Russia. 3. Russia -- Description and travel. 4. Russia -- Social conditions -- 1991-
ISBN 0393051781

LC 2003006562

Takes readers on a tour of contemporary Russia, revealing a country in search of its post-Communist identity and offering insight to the political and economic challenges its people still face.

"After talking to scores of people--from survivors of the Aldy massacre to a harrowed Russian lieutenant colonel who runs the body-collection point closest to the Chechen battleground--Meier paints in this heartbreaking book a devastating picture of contemporary life in a country where, as one man put it, 'people have lived like the lowest dogs for more than eighty years.'" Publishers Weekly.

Rumiz, Paolo

The **fault** line : traveling the other Europe, from Finland to Ukraine / Paolo Rumiz, translated by Gregory Conti. Rizzoli Ex Libris, 2015, c2012 256 p. **914**

1. Rumiz, Paolo. 2. Cold War -- Influence. 3. Eastern Europe -- Description and travel.
ISBN 9780847845422

LC bl2015007121

Originally published in Italian as :Trans Europa Express, 2012

Paolo Rumiz traces the path that has twice cut Europe in two--first by the Iron Curtain and then by the artificial scaffolding of the EU--moving through vibrant cities and abandoned villages, some places still gloomy under the ghost of these imposing borders, some that have sought to erase all memory of it and jump with both feet into the West (if only the West would have them).

"Exploring the border between Russia and the European Union, Rumiz realized that he was traveling a seismic fault that's only apparently dormant because Russia, under Putin, is becoming a renewed threat. A richly detailed journey into Europe's dark past and vulnerable present." Kirkus.

914.04 Europe--travel

MacLean, Rory, 1954-,

Pravda ha ha : true travels to the end of Europe / Rory Maclean. Bloomsbury Publishing Plc, 2020. 353 p. **914.04**

1. Voyages and travels 2. Post-communism 3. Former Soviet

republics -- Description and travel 4. Eastern Europe -- Description and travel 5. Russia -- Description and travel
ISBN 9781408896525
LC bl2020000696

An unsettling, timely, and darkly comic exposé of Putin's Russia and European disintegration from highly acclaimed travel writer Rory MacLean.

"An engrossing travelogue that's both trenchantly observant and deeply felt." Publishers Weekly.

914.304 Germany -- Travel

Allen, Dan

Fodor's Germany / writers: Dan Allen, Christie Dietz, Lee A. Evans, Adam Groffman, Evelyn Kanter, Jeff Kavanagh, Giulia Pines, Clare Richardson, Leonie Schaumann, Juergen Scheunemann ... [and 3 others]. Fodor's Travel,, 2016 896 p. : **914.304**

1. Germany Guidebooks.
ISBN 110187970X
LC bl2016015119

Includes index.

Detailed and timely information on accommodations, restaurants and local attractions highlight these updated travel guides, which feature all-new covers, a dramatic visual design, symbols to indicate budget options, must-see ratings, multi-day itineraries, Smart Travel Tips, helpful bulleted maps, tips on transportation, guidelines for shopping excursions and other valuable features.

Egert-Romanowska, Joanna

Germany / main contributors, Joanna Egert-Romanowska and Małgorzata Omilanowska. DK Publishing, 2016 584 p. : **914.304**

1. Germany Guidebooks.
ISBN 1465440186
LC bl2016013494

Includes index.

Describes the history and architecture of Germany, and identifies the best hotels, restaurants, shops, sights, and cultural attractions each region of the country has to offer.

Gorra, Michael Edward

The **bells** in their silence : travels through Germany / Michael Gorra. Princeton University Press, c2004. xvii, 211 p. ; **914.304**

1. Travel writing -- History. 2. Americans in Germany 3. Voyages and travels. 4. Germany in literature. 5. Germany -- Social life and customs. 6. Germany -- Description and travel.
ISBN 0691117659
LC 2003056474

"Gorra's account of his travels through Germany is shaped--perhaps even haunted--by figures from the past: historical, literary, personal. A captivating, unique work of synthesis." Booklist.

914.404 France -- Travel

Ardagh, John, 1928-2008

France / main contributors, John Ardagh, Rosemary Bailey, Judith Fayard, Lisa Gerard-Sharp, Colin Jones, Alister Kershaw, Alec Lobrano, Anthony Roberts, Alan Tillier, Nigel Tisdall. DK Publishing, 2016 672 p. : **914.404**

1. France Guidebooks.
ISBN 1465440178
LC bl2016013496

Includes index.

Describes the architecture, culture, and history of France; explores the highlights of each region of the country; and recommends hotels, restaurants, shops, sights, and scenic routes.

Baxter, John, 1939-

The **most** beautiful walk in the world : a pedestrian in Paris / John Baxter. Harper Perennial, c2011. xv, 298 p. : **914.404**

1. Baxter, John, 1939- Travel Paris, France. 2. Walking -- Paris, France. 3. Voyages and travels. 4. Social history. 5. Australians in France. 6. Paris, France -- Description and travel -- Walking tours 7. Paris, France -- Social life and customs.
ISBN 9780061998546
LC 2010046259

In this breathtalking guided tour of the most beautiful walks through Paris, including the favorite walking routes of the many acclaimed artists and writers who have called this magical city home, the author recalls his many encounters and adventures in the City of Lights.

"The author knows Paris, both the modern, cosmopolitan city of today as well as the 1920s cultural mecca of expat American authors like Ernest Hemingway and F. Scott Fitzgerald. Baxter, in fact, lives in the same Paris building that once was a Jazz Age hangout for literary greats like James Joyce, Ezra Pound, Hemingway, and others. It's also the site of Sylvia Beach's famous bookstore, Shakespeare and Company. [He] takes us on a tour of the city's outdoor cafes, amazing restaurants, cabarets, and gorgeous architecture; he tells us about its history and its unique passion for art. Baxter gives us a Paris that is not just a place but an idea." Boston Globe.

914.5 Italy -- Geography

Macadam, Alta

Florence / Alta Macadam. Somerset, 2017 440 p. : **914.5**

1. Florence (Italy) Guidebooks.
ISBN 9781905131754
LC bl2017024033

Includes indexes.

Mayes, Frances

★**See** you in the piazza : new places to discover in Italy / Frances Mayes. Crown Publishing, 2019. xvii, 429 p. : **914.5**

1. Mayes, Frances 2. Voyages and travels 3. Women travelers 4. Recipes 5. Culture 6. Italy -- Description and travel
ISBN 9780451497697
LC 2018289932

Includes indexes.

Presents an evocative, recipe-complemented travel narrative through Italy's 20 regions, from Friuli to Calabria, that identifies the lesser-known cultural and historical gems enjoyed by locals.

"Accompanied by her husband, Ed, and sometimes by her precocious grandson, William, or by various friends, Mayes enthusiastically seeks out the highlights of small towns, usually in the off season." Booklist.

914.504 Italy -- Travel

Andrews, Rob

The **rough** guide to Italy / updated by Robert Andrews, Ros Belford, Jonathan Buckley, Agnes Crawford, Kiki Deere, Marc Di Duca, Natasha Foges, Charles Hebbert, Anthon Jackson and Tim Jepson. Rough Guides, 2016. 1038 p. : Rough Guide Italy **914.504**

1. Italy Guidebooks.
ISBN 9780241216224

LC bl2016013961

Explores Italian culture, history, architecture, art, music, politics, and customs while rating and reviewing accommodations, restaurants, attractions, shopping, and entertainment.

914.94 Switzerland

Bewes, Diccon, 1967-

Slow train to Switzerland : one tour, two trips, 150 years - and a world of change apart / Diccon Bewes. Nicholas Brealey, 2014 xviii, 301 p. : **914.94**

1. National characteristics, Swiss 2. Voyages and travels. 3. Mountains 4. Switzerland -- Description and travel.
ISBN 9781857886092

LC 2015451055

A travel diary from 1863 inspires author Diccon Bewes to retrace Thomas Cook's historic train trip that revolutionized tourism forever.

"Covering the development of tourism, rail travel, and hospitality, this account informs while providing an entertaining read for lovers of history and travel." Library Journal.

915 Geography of and travel in Asia

Ash, John, 1948-

A **Byzantine** journey / John Ash. Random House, c1995. xv, 330 p., [8] p. of plates : **915**

1. Antiquities. 2. Byzantine civilization. 3. Civilization, Medieval. 4. Voyages and travels 5. Byzantine Empire -- History. 6. Turkey -- Antiquities, Byzantine.
ISBN 0679409343

LC 94036159

The author shares his experiences traveling through Turkey, and discusses the history and culture of the Byzantine Empire.

Bowden, David, 1952-

Malaysia & Singapore / contributors, David Bowden, Ron Emmons, Andrew Forbes, Naiya Sivaraj, Richard Watkins. DK Publishing, 2016. 356 p. : **915**

1. Malaysia Guidebooks. 2. Singapore Guidebooks.
ISBN 1465440054

LC bl2015057857

Includes index.

Provides advice on acommodations, restaurants, shopping, and the sights of Malaysia and Singapore.

Chandler, David, 1962-

Cambodia & Laos / main contributors, David Chandler, Peter Holmshaw, Iain Stewart, Richard Waters. DK Publishing, 2016. 288 p. : **915**

1. Cambodia Guidebooks. 2. Laos Guidebooks.
ISBN 1465440062

LC bl2016047495

Includes index.

Describes the history, geography, and people of Cambodia and Laos, suggests itineraries for exploring the region, and recommends hotels, restaurants, transportation, attractions, and nature sights.

Elliot, Jason, 1965-

Mirrors of the unseen : journeys in Iran / Jason Elliot. St. Martin's Press, 2006. 415 p., 16 p. of plates : **915**

1. Elliot, Jason, 1965- Travel Iran. 2. Voyages and travels. 3. Travelers. 4. Iran -- Social life and customs. 5. Iran -- Description and travel.
ISBN 031230191X

LC 2006042918

Includes index.

A literary travelogue combining history, anecdote, and cultural analysis explores the rich heritage of Persian culture, offering a multifaceted portrait of the art, architecture, culture, and people of Iran.

"With Iran so central in the news, this is a good read for the armchair traveler and amateur geopolitical strategist alike." Publishers Weekly.

An **unexpected** light : travels in Afghanistan / Jason Elliot. Picador, 2001. 473 p. : **915**

1. Elliot, Jason, 1965- Travel Afghanistan 2. Voyages and travels. 3. Travelers. 4. Afghanistan -- Description and travel.
ISBN 0312274599

LC 2001050036

ALA Notable Book, 2002.

"This is an account of Elliot's two visits to Afghanistan. The first occurred when he joined the mujaheddin circa 1979 and was smuggled into Soviet-occupied Afghanistan; the second happened nearly ten years later, when he returned to the still war-torn land. The skirmishes that Elliot painstakingly describes here took place between the Taliban and the government of Gen. Ahmad Shah Massoud in Kabul. Elliot traveled widely in the hinterland, visiting Faizabad in the north and Herat in the west. The result is some of the finest travel writing in recent years." Library Journal.

Feiler, Bruce, 1964-

Walking the Bible : a journey by land through the five books of Moses / Bruce Feiler. Harper Perennial, 2005, c2001. 451 p. : **915**

1. Feiler, Bruce, 1964- Travel Middle East 2. Bible Antiquities 3. Bible. Pentateuch Geography 4. Pilgrims and pilgrimages. 5. Voyages and travels. 6. Travelers. 7. Middle East -- Description and travel.
ISBN 9780060838638

LC oc2007124492

The author recounts his ten-thousand-mile journey across the Middle East in search of the roots of the Bible to discover whether it was an abstraction or a living, breathing entity.

"Determined to connect more deeply with his religious roots, Feiler joined an archaeologist in a trek through the Middle East, visiting the sites mentioned in the Pentateuch, the first five books of the Hebrew Bible. A book full of wonder and awe and personal enlightenment." Booklist.

Gargan, Edward A.

The **river's** tale : a year on the Mekong / Edward A. Gargan.

Alfred A. Knopf, 2002. 332 p. : **915**

1. River life -- China. 2. Southeast Asia -- Description and travel. 3. Southeast Asia -- History -- 1945- 4. China -- Description and travel. 5. Mekong River -- Description and travel. 6. Mekong Delta, Vietnam.

ISBN 0375405844

LC 2001038056

"A chronicle of a year-long journey along the nearly 3,000 miles of the Mekong River as it descends from the Tibetan plateau through southern Asia, Gargan's book is a vivid look at the disparate peoples [that] settled the length of the river's path." Publishers Weekly.

Grange, Kevin

Beneath blossom rain : discovering Bhutan on the toughest trek in the world / Kevin Grange. University of Nebraska Press, c2011. 336 p. **915**

1. Grange, Kevin Travel Bhutan. 2. Mountaineering. 3. Mountaineers. 4. Trails. 5. Travelers. 6. Bhutan -- Description and travel.

ISBN 9780803234338

LC 2010028970

"For the armchair traveler, Grange does a fine job of showing readers the nature, history, and landscape of Bhutan, as well as taking us to remote villages and monasteries. He is equally open about what is essentially a personal search for meaning." Seattle Post-Intelligencer.

Houton, Jody

A **geek** in Thailand : discovering the land of golden buddhas, pad Thai and kickboxing / Jody Houton. Tuttle Publishing, 2016 159 p. : **915**

1. Popular culture -- Thailand 2. Thailand -- Description and travel. 3. Thailand -- Social life and customs.

ISBN 9780804844482

LC 2015949992

A Geek in Thailand is a lighthearted look at Thailand from a young foreign visitor and resident's perspective. This alternative guide to Thailand offers a smart and concise take on Thai culture, entertainment, daily life--covering all the classics--but also revealing the path less traveled. In short articles accompanied by sidebars and numerous, colorful photographs, it paints a revealing picture of Asia's most popular travel destination. A Geek in Thailand is for the holidaymakers who visit for two weeks every year and have a desire to learn about the culture, but are struggling to know where to begin. Sections on the food, drink, social scene, music, film and everyday Thai life are sure to appeal to them. It is also for those who wish to move to Thailand on a more permanent basis as it contains helpful information regarding purchasing property, setting up a company and applying for visas and work permits. Chapters on the Thai character and cultural dos and don'ts and faux pas will allow the reader to go beyond the Thai smile. Sections on politics, history, economy and the unique relationship between the Thai Nation, Religion and Monarchy will also be of interest to those who wish to delve into a deeper understanding of Thailand.

Jubber, Nicholas

Drinking arak off an ayatollah's beard : a journey through the inside-out worlds of Iran and Afghanistan / Nicholas Jubber. Da Capo Press, 2010. 320 p. **915**

1. Jubber, Nicholas Travel Iran. 2. Jubber, Nicholas Travel Afghanistan. 3. Firdawsi. Shahnamah. 4. Social conflict -- Iran. 5. Social conflict -- Afghanistan. 6. Iran -- Description and travel. 7. Afghanistan -- Description and travel. 8. Iran -- Social conditions -- 1997- 9. Afghanistan -- Social conditions -- 21st century.

ISBN 9780306818844

LC 2009048191

"The author took it upon himself to travel across Iran and Afghanistan, using as his window into the region's past the Shahnameh, a 1,000-year-old national epic of the Persian-speaking world. Jubber's travels take him from edgy underground parties in Tehran to facing the business end of a Kalashnikov in Afghanistan's Helmand province. Geographical, Jubber's account offers a full and satisfying panorama of the region with its rich paradoxes and complexities intact." Publishers Weekly.

Ma, Jian, 1953-

Red dust : a path through China / Ma Jian ; translated from the Chinese by Flora Drew. Pantheon Books 2001. 324 p. : **915**

1. Ma, Jian, 1953- Travel China. 2. Travelers. 3. China -- Description and travel.

ISBN 0375420592

LC 2001021575

Maps on endpapers.

"Faced with imprisonment, Jian fled to the Chinese countryside, eventually making his way to Tibet. His journey is presented as a combination travelogue and a narrative of sheer poetry and spirituality." Booklist.

Man, John, 1941-

Marco Polo : the journey that changed the world / John Man. William Morrow, 2014, c2009. 394 p. : **915**

1. Polo, Marco, 1254-1323? 2. Kublai Khan, 1216-1294. 3. Explorers -- Italy 4. Mongols -- History. 5. Ancient cities and towns. 6. Exploration. 7. China -- Description and travel. 8. China -- Rulers. 9. Books to TV

ISBN 9780062375070

LC 2010549618

Originally published in the UK by Transworld Publishers under the title Xanadu.

Originally published: 2009.

Draws on the author's own parallel journey and new archaeological findings to retrace the steps of the medieval Italian merchant who traveled from Venice, through the Middle East and Central Asia, to China and Xanadu, the summer capital of Kublai Khan.

Morris-Suzuki, Tessa

To the Diamond Mountains : a hundred-year journey through China and Korea / / Tessa Morris-Suzuki. Rowman & Littlefield Pub Inc, 2010. 201 p. **915**

1. Morris-Suzuki, Tessa 2. Kemp, E. G. (Emily Georgiana), b. 1860 3. Voyages and travels 4. China -- Description and travel. 5. North Korea -- Description and travel. 6. South Korea -- Description and travel. 7. Diamond Mountains (Korea)

ISBN 9781442205031

LC 2010023685

Includes bibliographical references.

"Morris-Suzuki, an Australian professor, recently traveled through northeast China and the two Koreas; she was retracing the route of Emily Kemp, an extraordinary writer, artist, and intrepid adventurer who wrote about her experiences a century ago. Morris-Suzuki, like her predecessor, is a keen observer and a fine writer; she has combined the disciplines of history and travel writing in an absorbing analysis of the past, present, and future of this volatile region." Booklist.

Polo, Marco, 1254-1323?

The **travels** of Marco Polo / edited and with an introduction by Milton Rugoff ; with a new afterword by Howard Mittelmark. Signet Classics, 2004. xxix, 297 p. ; **915**

1. Polo, Marco, 1254-1323? 2. Explorers 3. Voyages and travels. 4. Mongols -- History. 5. Asia -- Description and travel Early works to 1800.
ISBN 0451529510

LC 2004052535

Includes index.

This brilliant volume vividly brings to life the mysterious East in the Middle Ages by chronicling the author's journey from Venice to Asia, during which he met people from a wide range of cultures, and encountered a vast array of landscapes, plants, and animals.

Tang, Phillip

Vietnam, Cambodia, Laos & Northern Thailand / Phillip Tang, Tim Bewer, Greg Bloom, Austin Bush, Nick Ray, Richard Waters, China Williams. Lonely Planet Global Limited, 2017. 575 p. : **915**

1. Cambodia Guidebooks. 2. Laos Guidebooks. 3. Thailand, Northern Guidebooks. 4. Vietnam Guidebooks.
ISBN 1786570300

LC bl2017032532

At head of title: Lonely Planet.
Includes index.

Complemented by easy-to use, reliable maps, helpful recommendations, authoritative background information and up-to-date coverage of things to see and do, these popular travel guides cover in detail countries and regions around the world for travelers of every budget, along with extensive itineraries, maps with cross-referencing to the text, "Top 10" and "Top 5" lists and other practical features.

Theroux, Paul

The **great** railway bazaar : by train through Asia / Paul Theroux. Houghton Mifflin, 2006, c1975. 342 p. ; **915**

1. Theroux, Paul Travel Asia. 2. Americans in Asia. 3. Travelers -- United States 4. Railroad travel 5. Railroads 6. Asia -- Description and travel.
ISBN 9780618658947

LC 2006287162

Reprint. Previously published: Boston : Houghton Mifflin, 1975.

"I have seldom heard a train go by and not wished I was on it," confesses the author. Take the train with him through Europe and Asia.

"The author took a four-month solitary lecture tour of Asia in 1973, traveling by train wherever possible. His route was through Turkey, Iran, India, Southeast Asia, Japan, and back to London via the Soviet Union. He writes of conversations and impressions of the people encountered." Library Journal.

Riding the iron rooster : by train through China / Paul Theroux. Houghton Mifflin, 2006, c1988. 528 p. **915**

1. Theroux, Paul Travel China. 2. Americans in China. 3. Railroad travel -- China. 4. Authors, American -- 20th century 5. Trains -- China. 6. China -- Description and travel.
ISBN 0618658971

LC 2006028745

Originally published: New York : Putnam's, 1988.

"This is an account of the author's yearlong rail journey through China. For Theroux, traveling is both about people--their thoughts, customs, and peculiarities--and a form of autobiography, and here we learn as much about his own quirks and fancies as we do about the intriguing world of contemporary China." Library Journal.

Thubron, Colin, 1939-

Shadow of the Silk Road / Colin Thubron. Harper Collins, 2007, c2006. 363 p. : **915**

1. Thubron, Colin, 1939- Travel Silk Road. 2. Travelers -- England 3. Roads. 4. Voyages and travels. 5. Silk Road -- Description and travel.
ISBN 006123172X

LC 2006052142

Includes index.

Originally published: London : Chatto & Windus, 2006.

The author recounts his ambitious and dangerous trek along the legendary Silk Road, during which he ventured from the heart of China to the mountains of Central Asia, through northern Afghanistan, across the plains of Iran, and into Kurdish Turkey.

"An illuminating account of a breathtaking journey." Booklist.

Winchester, Simon

The **river** at the center of the world : a journey up the Yangtze and back in Chinese time / Simon Winchester. H. Holt, 1996. xx, 410 p. : **915**

1. Yangtze River Valley, China -- Description and travel. 2. China -- Description and travel. 3. China -- Social conditions. 4. China -- Social life and customs.
ISBN 0805038884

LC 96012399

ALA Notable Book, 1998.

"In 1994, the author followed the Yangtze's course from the East China Sea to Tibet by boat, car, train, plane, bus and foot; but this is more than an ordinary account of a traveler's pilgrimage, although it is a must for any visitor to China. Wryly humorous, gently skeptical, immensely knowledgeable as he wends his way along the 3900 miles of the great river, Winchester provides an irresistible feast of detail about the character of the river itself, the landscape, the cities, villages and people along its banks." Publishers Weekly.

915.204 Japan -- Travel

Denson, Abby

Cool Tokyo guide : adventures in the city of kawaii fashion, train sushi and Godzilla / Abby Denson. Tuttle Pub, 2018 128 p. **915.204**

1. Tourism 2. Voyages and travels 3. Tokyo, Japan 4. Japan -- Description and travel 5. Comics and Graphic novels
ISBN 9784805314418

LC bl2018029313

An informative and entertaining comic-book guide to Tokyo?a city for lovers of Japanese culture, fashion and great food, which is the anime, cosplay and manga capital of the world--takes readers on a personal tour of its coolest sites and helps them navigate everyday Tokyo life.

"The overall result is a love song to a city and an inspiration for prospective visitors." Booklist.

915.804 Central Asia -- Travel

Fatland, Erika, 1983-

Sovietistan : travels in Turkmenistan, Kazakhstan, Tajikistan, Kyrgyzstan, and Uzbekistan / Erika Fatland ; translated by Kari Dickson. Pegasus Books, 2020. 479 p. **915.804**

1. Fatland, Erika, 1983- 2. Voyages and travels 3. Women journalists 4. Manners and customs 5. Oil industry and trade 6. Central Asia -- Description and travel 7. Former Soviet republics 8. Turkmenistan 9. Kazakhstan 10. Tajikistan 11. Kyrgyzstan 12. Uzbekistan

ISBN 9781643133263

LC bl2019037376

Originally published: Oslo : Kagge, 2014.

Draws on the author's undercover visits in a report on the five Central Asian regions that established independent statehoods in 1991 that discusses how ancient history, cultural traditions and Soviet influences have shaped their government experiments in democracy and dictatorship.

"Her remarkable look at the region serves as a solid introduction to an area that remains little traveled by those from the West." Publishers Weekly.

916 Geography of and travel in Africa

Butcher, Tim

Chasing the devil : a journey through Sub-Saharan Africa in the footsteps of Graham Greene / Tim Butcher. Atlas Books, 2011. 336 p. **916**

1. Greene, Graham, 1904-1991 Journey without maps 2. Greene, Graham, 1904-1991 Travel 3. Voyages and travels 4. Travelers -- England 5. British in foreign countries. 6. Authors, English -- 20th century

ISBN 9781935633297

LC bl2011029108

Using the 75-year-old travel classic Journey Without Maps as a guide, an award-winning journalist and best-selling author visits Liberia and encounters masked sorcerers who get their powers from cannibalism and long-forgotten missionaries.

"While vividly describing the beauty of landscapes and the ugliness of derelict shantytowns, the author weaves in stories of freed slaves who settled both Sierra Leone and Liberia, and the tensions between settlers and indigenous people that have shaped the histories of both places. This engaging tale will leave many reaching for their Graham Greene." Kirkus.

Campbell, James T.

Middle passages : African American journeys to Africa, 1787-2005 / James Campbell. Penguin Press, 2006. xxvi, 513 p., [16] p. of plates : **916**

1. African Americans -- Travel -- Africa -- History. 2. African Americans -- Relations with Africans. 3. Africa -- Description and travel. 4. United States -- History -- 18th century.

ISBN 9781594200830

LC 2005058672

Mark Lynton History Prize, 2007.

Pulitzer Prize for History finalist, 2007.

A three-century history of African-American journeys back to Africa from an America where the profiled travelers or their ancestors were slaves traces the experiences of such people as W. E. B. Du Bois, Martin Luther King, Jr., and the founders of Liberia.

Grant, Richard, 1963-

Crazy river : a journey to the source of the Nile / Richard Grant. Free Press, 2011. 304 p. **916**

1. Grant, Richard, 1963- Travel East Africa 2. Burton, Richard Francis, Sir, 1821-1890 Travel East Africa 3. East Africa -- Description and travel 4. Tanzania -- Description and travel. 5. Malagarasi River (Burundi and Tanzania) -- Exploration

ISBN 9781439154144

LC 2011012168

"The Malagarasi River in Tanzania had not been fully traveled by either Westerners or Africans. So, in the tradition of 19th-century British explorers, first and foremost Richard Burton, who became his spectral travel companion, Grant set out to do so. But his adventures on the river--disease and disappointment, danger from crocs, hippos and bandits--became but part of his larger story about what Africa is and how to make sense of it. Dyspeptic, disturbing and brilliantly realized, Grant's account of Africa is literally unforgettable." Kirkus.

Langewiesche, William

Sahara unveiled : a journey across the desert / William Langewiesche. Vintage Books, 1997, c1996. 301 p. : **916**

1. Langewiesche, William Travel Sahara. 2. Desert life. 3. Sahara -- Description and travel.

ISBN 9780679429821

LC BL 99789183

Originally published: New York : Pantheon Books, c1996.

Blending history, anecdote, travelogue, and reportage, the author describes his journey across the Sahara, captures life in the region, and describes the unique character, history, and religious, cultural, and social aspects of North Africa.

"Besides evoking the Sahara's power, majesty, emptiness, heat, beauty and terrors and describing its ecology and meteorology, Langewiesche adds details that may astonish armchair travelers who still think of the desert as populated by camels and Bedouins. He is knowledgeable about the imprint of French colonialism on North African economy and politics, and about Muslim beliefs in practice. Throughout this vivid account, he scatters many charming native folktales." Publishers Weekly.

Shah, Tahir

In search of King Solomon's mines / Tahir Shah. Arcade Pub., 2003. x, 240 p., 16 p. of plates : **916**

1. Solomon, King of Israel. 2. Sheba, Queen of. 3. Shah, Tahir Travel Ethiopia. 4. Gold mines and mining -- Ethiopia -- History. 5. Adventurers. 6. Travels. 7. Quests. 8. Ethiopia -- Description and travel.

ISBN 1559706414

LC 2003045161

"This is an account of the author's search for the mysterious mines of Ophir, where King Solomon, the Bible's wisest king, was supposed to have buried a fortune in gold. According to his reckoning, the mines should be in modern-day Ethiopia, so he set out on an adventure of a lifetime with a shifty bookseller named (no kidding) Ali Baba. Along the way, readers are treated to his accounts of everything from the California gold rush to a sadistic Sultan." Library Journal.

Stothard, Peter

Alexandria : the last nights of Cleopatra / Peter Stothard. Overlook, 2013 304 p. **916**

1. Stothard, Peter Travel Egypt 2. Cleopatra, Queen of Egypt, 69-30 B.C. 3. Journalists -- Great Britain 4. Voyages and travels. 5. British in Egypt. 6. Women rulers. 7. Egypt -- History

ISBN 9781468303704

LC 2016498140

A Times Literary Supplement editor recounts his exploration of Hosni Mubarak-era South Africa, his reconnection to formative childhood experiences and his discouraged efforts to write a book on the history of Cleopatra.

Tayler, Jeffrey

Angry wind : through Muslim black Africa by truck, bus, boat, and camel/ Jeffrey Tayler. Houghton Mifflin, 2005. x, 252 p. : **916**

1. Tayler, Jeffrey Travel Sahel region. 2. Religion and politics -- Sahel region -- History -- 21st century 3. Islam -- Sahel region. 4. Christianity -- Relations -- Islam -- Sahel region. 5. Sahel region -- Description and travel.
ISBN 061833467X

LC 2004054066

Takes readers into one of the least Westernized and travel-friendly regions of the planet--the Sahel, the lower region of the Sahara and the belt where Islam meets Central Africa.

"This substantial and informative work is no mere travel tale--it is a firsthand account of the author's deeply personal quest for knowledge and understanding of a people and a region that continues to struggle with extreme poverty and unrest." Library Journal.

Theroux, Paul

Dark star safari : overland from Cairo to Cape Town / Paul Theroux. Houghton Mifflin, 2003. 472 p. : **916**

1. Theroux, Paul Travel Africa. 2. Hitchhiking -- Africa. 3. Voyages and travels. 4. Authors, American -- 20th century. 5. Reunions. 6. Africa -- Social life and customs. 7. Africa -- Description and travel.
ISBN 0618134247

LC 2002032710

"Where Theroux sees Africa uncluttered by preconceived notions, his writing can be brilliant. But where Theroux has traveled before--40 years ago, as first a Peace Corps teacher, then a lecturer at Uganda's Makerere University in the golden years just after the country's independence--he sees Africa not for what it is, but for what it might have been." Christian Science Monitor.

Wood, Levison, 1982-

Walking the Nile / Levison Wood. Atlantic Monthly Press, 2016. 352 p. **916**

1. Wood, Levison, 1982- 2. Walking. 3. Rivers -- Africa. 4. Voyages and travels. 5. British in Africa. 6. Nile River -- Description and travel.
ISBN 9780802124494

LC 2016301855

Includes index.

The former British paratrooper, photographer and explorer documents his nine-month, 4,000-mile journey by foot along the Nile, discussing his life-threatening natural and cultural encounters in six different nations and the loss of a colleague along the journey.

916.8 Southern Africa--geography

Theroux, Paul

★The **last** train to Zona Verde : my ultimate African safari / Paul Theroux. Houghton Mifflin Harcourt, 2013. 353 p. : **916.88104331**

1. Voyages and travels 2. Americans in Africa
ISBN 9780618839339

An acclaimed travel writer and novelist describes his journey across Africa, from Cape Town to Cape Province and into Namibia, riding elephants, meeting Bushmen and discussing the changes that have taken place since his first visit 50 years ago.

"The acclaimed travel writer and novelist chronicles his journey through Africa as tourist, adventure-seeker, thinker and hopeful critic... Reading this enlightening book won't only open a window into Theroux's mind, it will also impart a deeper understanding of Africa and travel in general." Kirkus.

917 Geography of and travel in North America

Ambrose, Stephen E.

★**Undaunted** courage : Meriwether Lewis, Thomas Jefferson, and the opening of the American West / Stephen E. Ambrose. Simon & Schuster, 1996. 511 p. : **917**

1. Lewis, Meriwether, 1774-1809. 2. Clark, William, 1770-1838. 3. Jefferson, Thomas, 1743-1826. 4. Lewis and Clark Expedition (1804-1806) 5. Explorers -- United States 6. Exploration -- History. 7. Overland journeys to the Pacific 8. Voyages and travels. 9. The West (United States) -- Exploration. 10. United States -- Exploration.
ISBN 0684811073

LC 95037146

ALA Notable Book, 1997.

Spur Award for Historical Nonfiction, 1997.

In 1803 President Thomas Jefferson selected his personal secretary, Captain Merriwether Lewis, to lead a voyage up the Missouri River to the Rockies, over the mountains, down the Columbia River to the Pacific Ocean and back. Lewis and his partner, Captain William Clark, endured incredible hardships and saw incredible sights.

"This treatment of the Lewis and Clark Expedition is essentially a biography of Lewis, although the bulk of it is a lively retelling of the journey of the two captains--together with their party of soldiers and frontiersmen, Clark's black slave, York, and the legendary Shoshone Indian woman, Sacagawea, and her infant son--conveyed with passionate enthusiasm by Mr. Ambrose and sprinkled liberally with some of the most famous and vivid passages from the travelers' journals. " New York Times Book Review.

Boissoneault, Lorraine

The **last** voyageurs : retracing La Salle's journey across America: sixteen teenagers on an adventure of a lifetime / Lorraine Boissoneault. Pegasus, 2016 368 p. **917**

1. Canoeing 2. Exploration 3. Voyages and travels 4. Rivers 5. Mississippi River
ISBN 9781605989761

LC 2016461056

In 1976, America's bicentennial, 24 young men set out to re-create French explorer La Salle's voyage down the entire length of the Mississippi River, abandoning their modern identities in order to live like the voyageurs of the 1600s.

"All the elements of an exciting adventure story are here. Boissoneault describes interesting, complicated people facing life-threatening perils, and in alternating Lewis's story with that of La Salle's journey, she makes fascinating historical comparisons." Publishers Weekly.

Bryson, Bill

A **walk** in the woods : rediscovering America on the Appalachian Trail / Bill Bryson. Broadway Books, c1998. 276 p. ; **917**

1. Bryson, Bill Travel Appalachian Trail. 2. Natural history -- Appalachian Trail. 3. Voyages and travels. 4. Hiking. 5. Travelers. 6. Appalachian Trail -- Description and travel.
ISBN 9780767902519

LC 97032627

Later published in an omnibus entitled: Walkabout.

Bryson shares his breath-taking adventures and the fascinating history of the 2,100-mile Appalachian Trail, as he travels slowly on foot.

"Bryson's breezy, self-mocking tone may turn off readers who hanker for another Into Thin Air or Seven Years in Tibet. Others, however, may find themselves turning the pages with increasing amusement and anticipation as they discover that they're in the hands of a satirist of the first rank, one who writes (and walks) with Chaucerian brio." New York Times Book Review.

Duncan, Dayton

Lewis and Clark : the journey of the Corps of discovery : an illustrated history / Dayton Duncan ; based on a documentary film by Ken Burns, written by Dayton Duncan ; with a preface by Ken Burns ; and contributions by Stephen E. Ambrose, Erica Funkhouser, William Least Heat-Moon. Knopf, 1997. xix, 248 p. : **917**

1. Lewis, Meriwether, 1774-1809. 2. Clark, William, 1770-1838. 3. Lewis and Clark Expedition (1804-1806) 4. Lewis and Clark Expedition (1804-1806) Pictorial works. 5. Explorers -- United States 6. Exploration. 7. Overland journeys to the Pacific. 8. Expeditions. 9. United States -- Exploration. 10. The West (United States) -- Exploration 11. The West (United States) -- Description and travel 12. Essays.

ISBN 0679454500

LC BL 99790330

Companion volume to the PBS TV series: Lewis & Clark: the journey of the Corps of Discovery.

The companion volume to the PBS film follows the epic odyssey of Meriwether Lewis and William Clark from St. Louis to the Pacific Ocean, documenting the varied spectrum of landscapes, people and cultures, and wildlife that they encountered. TV tie-in.

"An attractive book with a well-written text and an excellent presentation of historic paintings, photographs, maps, and original quotations from various of Lewis and Clark's journals." Science Books & Films.

Frazier, Ian

Great Plains / Ian Frazier. Picador USA, 2001, c1989. 290 p., 16 p. of plates : **917**

1. Frazier, Ian Travel Great Plains (United States) 2. Voyages and travels. 3. Americans. 4. Great Plains (United States) -- Description and travel. 5. Great Plains (United States) -- History. 6. Great Plains (United States) -- Social life and customs.

ISBN 0312278500

LC 2001032096

Includes index.

Originally published: New York : Farrar, Straus, Giroux, 1989.

Spur Award for Nonfiction, 1990.

"This is a colorful and engaging blend of travelogue, local color, geography and folklore." Publishers Weekly.

Freudenheim, Ellen

The **Brooklyn** experience : the ultimate guide to neighborhoods & noshes, culture & the cutting edge / Ellen Freudenheim. Rutgers University Press, 2016 xvi, 342 p. : **917**

1. Brooklyn (New York, N.Y.) Guidebooks. 2. New York (N.Y.) Guidebooks.

ISBN 9780813577432

LC 2015035672

Offering photos, itineraries and 40 neighborhood profiles from Coney Island to Williamsburg, the book showcases Brooklyn's remarkable culinary, cultural and artistic renaissance through interviews with 60 luminaries who capture Brooklyn today. (Travel)

Gimlette, John, 1963-

Theatre of fish : travels through Newfoundland and Labrador / John Gimlette. Knopf, 2005. xxii, 360 p. : **917**

1. Gimlette, John, 1963- Travel Newfoundland and Labrador Atlantic Coast. 2. Great-Grandfathers. 3. Atlantic Coast (Canada) 4. Newfoundland and Labrador -- Description and travel. 5. Newfoundland and Labrador -- History.

ISBN 1400043220

LC 2005044149

"Readers will be fascinated by Newfoundland's and Labrador's bizarre, often tragic pasts and equally strange presents, and they will be glad it was the eloquent Gimlette who made the trip so they don't have to." Publishers Weekly.

Gopnik, Adam

Through the children's gate : a home in New York / Adam Gopnik. Alfred A. Knopf, 2006. 318 p. ; **917**

1. Gopnik, Adam Family. 2. Home (Concept) -- Social aspects. 3. City life. 4. Families 5. Cities and towns. 6. New York City -- Description and travel. 7. New York City -- Social life and customs. 8. Essays.

ISBN 9781400041817

LC 2006045260

Describes the author's fall 2000 move from Paris back to New York with his family in a series of essays that profile the teachers, therapists, coaches, friends, adversaries, and others who make up their extended urban family and describe their new home, the impact of 9/11, real estate, and the meaning of life.

Hawke, David Freeman

Those tremendous mountains : the story of the Lewis and Clark expedition / David Freeman Hawke. W.W. Norton, 1998, c1980. xvi, 273 p. : **917**

1. Lewis, Meriwether, 1774-1809. 2. Clark, William, 1770-1838. 3. Lewis and Clark Expedition (1804-1806) 4. The West (United States) -- Description and travel. 5. Rocky Mountain Region -- Description and travel 6. The West (United States) -- History -- To 1848.

ISBN 0393317749

LC BL 98010499

Includes excerpts from the journals of Lewis and Clark, first published in 1904-5 under title: Original journals of the Lewis and Clark expedition, 1804-1806.

Reprint. Originally published: 1980.

Heat Moon, William Least

Blue highways : a journey into America / William Least Heat-Moon ; photographs by the author ; with a new afterword by the author. Back Bay Books, 1999, c1982. 429 p. : **917**

1. Heat Moon, William Least Travel United States 2. Automobile travel -- United States. 3. Cross-country automobile trips. 4. Travelers -- United States 5. Automobile driving on highways. 6. United States -- Description and travel.

ISBN 9780316353298

LC 00265444

Includes index.

Originally published: Boston : Little, Brown, c1982.

Hailed as a masterpiece of American travel writing, Blue Highways is an unforgettable journey along our nation's backroads. William Least Heat-Moon set out with little more than the need to put home behind him and a sense of curiosity about "those little towns that get on the map--if they get on at all--only because some cartographer has a blank space to fill: Remote, Oregon; Simplicity, Virginia; New Freedom, Pennsylvania; New Hope, Tennessee; Why, Arizona; Whynot, Mississippi." His adventures, his discoveries, and his recollections of the extraordinary people he encountered along the way amount to a revelation of the true American experience.

Heat Moon, William Least

Roads to Quoz : an American mosey / William Least Heat-Moon. Little, Brown, 2008. 592 p. **917**

1. Heat Moon, William Least Travel United States 2. Small town life -- United States. 3. Small towns -- United States. 4. States. 5. Americans. 6. United States -- Description and travel.
ISBN 9780316110259

LC 2008019375

Recounts the author's series of journeys into small-town America, visits during which he performed life-enhancing investigations into some of the nation's most incongruous regions.

"The author's journey is as meandering as the Ouachita itself, and readers will relish the experiences he and...[his wife] describe along their trip." Library Journal.

Hely, Steve

The **wonder** trail : true stories from Los Angeles to the end of the world / Steve Hely. Dutton, 2016. 320 p. **917**

1. Hely, Steve Travel Central America. 2. Hely, Steve Travel South America. 3. Curiosities and wonders -- Central America. 4. Curiosities and wonders -- South America. 5. Central America -- Description and travel. 6. South America -- Description and travel. 7. Central America -- Social life and customs. 8. South America -- Social life and customs.
ISBN 9780525955016

LC 2015038442

"Steve Hely, writer for The Office and American Dad! and recipient of the Thurber Prize for American Humor, presents a travel book about his journey through Central and South America. Part travel book, part pop history, part comic memoir, Hely's writing will make any reader want to reach for their backpack and hiking boots. The Wonder Trail is the story of Steve's trip from Los Angeles to the bottom of South America, presented in 102 short chapters. The trip was ambitious--Steve traveled through Mexico City, ancient Mayan ruins, the jungles and coffee plantations and remote beaches of Central America, across the Panama Canal, by sea to Colombia, to the wild Easter celebration of Popayan, to the Amazon rainforest, the Inca sites of Cuzco and Machu Picchu, to the Galapagos Islands, the Atacama Desert of Chile, and down to the jagged and wind-worn land of Patagonia, at the very end of the western hemisphere. Steve's plan was to discover the weird, wonderful, and absurd--not to ignore the challenges and problems in Central and South America--but to focus on the incredible, delightful people and experiences that came his way. And the book that resulted is just as fun. A blend of travel writing, history, and comic memoir, The Wonder Trail will inspire, inform,and delight".-- Provided by publisher.

"Hely's hilarious descriptions of the stunning sights and quirky people he encounters along the way will delight experienced globetrotters and armchair travelers alike." Library Journal.

Horwitz, Tony, 1958-

Spying on the South : an odyssey across the American divide / Tony Horwitz. Penguin Press, 2019. 496 p. **917**

1. Olmsted, Frederick Law, 1822-1903 Travel Southern States 2. Horwitz, Tony, 1958- Travel Southern States 3. Travelers 4. Voyages and travels 5. Cultural differences 6. Race relations 7. Southern States -- Description and travel 8. Southern States -- Social life and customs
ISBN 9781101980286

LC 2018056912

The Pulitzer Prize-winning New Yorker writer and author of Confederates in the Attic retraces Frederick Law Olmstead's epic journey across the pre-Civil War American South in search of common ground in today's dangerously divided nation.

Jenkins, Peter, 1951-

A **walk** across America / Peter Jenkins. Perennial, 2001, c1979. x, 290 p. : **917**

1. Jenkins, Peter, 1951- Travel United States. 2. Travelers -- United States 3. Walking. 4. Adventure travel. 5. Voyages and travels. 6. United States -- Description and travel. 7. United States
ISBN 006095955X

LC BL2004001132

Sequel: The walk west.

Originally published: New York : Morrow, 1979.

A young New Englander celebrates a rarely seen and almost forgotten America as he recalls the people he met and the situations he experienced during a journey in search of his country and himself.

Lopez, Barry Holstun, 1945-

Home ground : language for an American landscape / Barry Lopez, editor ; Debra Gwartney, managing editor. Trinity University Press, c2006. xxiv, 449 p. : **917**

1. American literature 2. Americanisms 3. Geography 4. Landscapes in literature
ISBN 1595340246

LC 2006019942

Over 850 terms for land and water--words like kiss tank, milk gap, goat prairie, basket-of-eggs relief, misfit river, swale, yazoo--are described by forty-five of our most respected writers, including Jon Krakauer, Terry Tempest Williams, Barbara Kingsolver, Charles Frazier, and Robert Hass. Home Ground is a language-lover's dream, a visionary and fresh reference work that combines geography, literature, and folklore, and represents tremendous research distilled in a single paragraph.

Muir, John, 1838-1914

Anywhere that is wild : John Muir's first walk to Yosemite / John Muir ; edited by Peter and Donna Thomas. Yosemite Conservancy, [2018] xv, 47 pages : **917**

1. Muir, John, 1838-1914. 2. National parks and reserves 3. Naturalists 4. Humans -- Effect of environment on 5. Conservation of natural resources 6. Yosemite National Park
ISBN 9781930238831

LC 2017956271

Gathered from John Muir's own writings, this fascinating compilation recounts his historic, first walk from the San Francisco bay to Yosemite.

National Geographic Society

Abroad at home : the 600 best international travel experiences in North America National Geographic Books, 2015. 286 p. : **917**

1. Canada -- Description and travel. 2. United States -- Description and travel.
ISBN 9781426214998

LC 2014037548

Includes index.

National Geographic Society
★**Guide** to national parks of the United States / National Geographic Society National Geographic, 2016. 494 p. : **917**
1. National parks and reserves -- United States -- Guidebooks 2. United States -- Description and travel Guidebooks
ISBN 9781426216510
LC bl2016000919

Includes index.

Offers descriptions, road maps, itineraries, travel tips, costs, and contact information for national parks ranging from Virginia's Shenandoah to Alaska's Glacier Bay.

"You can't do better than this guide. . . . Highly detailed and beautiful, this one is a must for all collections." Library Journal.

National Geographic Society (U.S.),
Guide to the state parks of the United States National Geographic, 2018. 479 p. : **917**
1. Parks -- United States -- Guidebooks. 2. United States Guidebooks.
ISBN 9781426218859
LC bl2018028824

At head of title: National Geographic.
Includes index.

Provides simple information about state parks in the United States, offers tips from parks staff, and suggests trails for biking, hiking, and flower gazing.

Sandoval-Strausz, A. K.
★**Hotel** : an American History / A. K. Sandoval-Strausz. Yale University Press, 2007. 375 p. **917**
1. Hotels -- United States -- History. 2. Hotels -- Social aspects -- United States.
ISBN 9780300106169
LC 2007010239

Presents a history of the nineteenth-century first-class hotel, of what hotels have meant to American business, culture, and racial politics.

"The author develops social, moral, economic, legal and political connections with originality and insight. His impassioned reading of our built environment is fascinating, his research prodigious. And the subject merits his talent as a historian." New York Times Book Review.

Satow, Julie
The **Plaza** : the secret life of America's most famous hotel / Julie Satow. Twelve, 2019. 352 p. **917**
1. Plaza Hotel, New York City. 2. Architecture. 3. Hotels 4. Historic buildings 5. Architecture, American. 6. New York City -- History.
ISBN 9781455566679
LC 2018048170

Recounts the wealthy history of the Plaza hotel, covering major scandals, tragedies, and some of the celebrities who have graced the rooms of the establishment.

"Readers will happily soak up period details and take notes on how the stalwart staff dealt with class snobbery, prohibition and gangsters, wartime privations, the turbulent 1960s, wealthy dowagers, blushing debutantes, persistent groupies, omnipresent prostitutes, and brawling Indian billionaires. This is social history at its best: thoughtful, engaging, and lots of fun." Booklist.

Savoy, Lauret E.
Trace : memory, history, race, and the American landscape / Lauren Edith Savoy. Counterpoint Press, 2015. 240 p. **917**
1. Savoy, Lauret E. Travel United States. 2. Place (Philosophy) 3. Memory -- Social aspects -- United States. 4. Landscape -- Social aspects -- United States. 5. Culture 6. United States -- Description and travel. 7. United States -- History -- Philosophy. 8. United States -- Race relations -- History. 9. United States -- Social conditions.
ISBN 9781619025738
LC 2015009588

In a mosaic of personal journeys and historical inquiry across a continent and time, the author explores how America's still unfolding history, and ideas of "race," have marked her and the land--from twisted terrain within the San Andreas Fault zone to a South Carolina plantation, from national parks to burial grounds, from the U.S.-Mexico Border to the U.S. capital.

"Springing from the literal Earth to metaphor, Savoy demonstrates the power of narrative to erase as easily as it reveals, yielding a provocative, eclectic exposé of the palimpsest historically defining the U.S. as much as any natural or man-made boundary." Kirkus.

Slaughter, Thomas P. (Thomas Paul)
Exploring Lewis and Clark : reflections on men and wilderness / Thomas P. Slaughter. Alfred A. Knopf, 2003. xviii, 231 p. : **917**
1. Lewis, Meriwether, 1774-1809. 2. Clark, William, 1770-1838. 3. Sacagawea. 4. York, ca. 1775-ca. 1815 5. Lewis and Clark Expedition (1804-1806) 6. Explorers -- The West (United States) 7. Indians of North America -- The West (United States) -- History -- 19th century. 8. Wilderness areas -- The West (United States) -- History -- 19th century. 9. The West (United States) -- Exploration 10. The West (United States) -- Description and travel.
ISBN 0375400788
LC 2002069376

A fascinating account of the famed expedition draws on the personal journals of the explorers themselves to re-examine their odyssey in light of the cultural prejudices and goals of Lewis and Clark, offers profiles of Sacajawea and York, Clark's slave, and discusses the meaning and impact of the journey.

Souders, Paul
Arctic solitaire : a boat, a bay, and the quest for the perfect bear / Paul Souders. Mountaineers Books, 2018 301 p. : **917**
1. Souders, Paul. 2. Polar bear -- Hudson Bay Region -- Anecdotes 3. Dories (Boats) -- Hudson Bay Region -- Anecdotes 4. Wildlife photographers 5. Hudson Bay -- Description and travel.
ISBN 9781680511048
LC 2018015726

"Professional photographer and amateur adventurer Paul Souders takes his C-Dory and his cameras to Hudson Bay to find and photograph polar bears over the course of three summers. He interacts with the people, animals, and history that he encounters and experiences life-threatening conditions on his solo expeditions."--Provided by publisher.

Theroux, Paul
The **old** Patagonian express : by train through the Americas / Paul Theroux ; maps by Richard Sanderson. Houghton Mifflin, 1997, c1979. xv, 404 p. : **917**
1. Theroux, Paul Travel South America. 2. Railroad travel -- South America. 3. Voyages and travels 4. Trains. 5. Culture conflict. 6. North America -- Description and travel. 7. South America -- Description and travel. 8. Latin America -- Description and travel.
ISBN 039552105X
LC 98162535

"A Mariner book."
Originally published: Boston : Houghton Mifflin, 1979.

Theroux's travels by train from Boston to Patagonia--a journey of selfdiscovery and uncommon encounters marked by startling contrasts in culture, climate, landscape, altitude, and attitude--are recounted.

On the plain of snakes : a Mexican journey / Paul Theroux. Houghton Mifflin Harcourt, [2019] 448 p. **917**

1. Theroux, Paul 2. Voyages and travels 3. Manners and customs 4. Travelers 5. Boundaries 6. Mexico -- Description and travel. 7. Mexican-American Border Region -- Description and travel.
ISBN 9780544866478

LC 2019004920

Includes index.

Legendary travel writer Paul Theroux fearlessly drives the entire length of the US-Mexico border, then goes deep into the hinterland, on the back roads of Chiapas and Oaxaca, to uncover the rich, layered world behind today's brutal headlines.

"This is a personal book, and Theroux does not hesitate to articulate his point of view on a number of topics, allowing for no sacred cows [cuidado con el realismo mágico!] as he unapologetically takes into consideration context, anecdotal evidence, and his on-the-road experiences to arrive at his prescription for improving the Mexican situation." Booklist.

Thoreau, Henry David, 1817-1862

The **Maine** woods / Henry David Thoreau ; introduction by Edward Hoagland. Penguin Books, 1988, c1864. xxxiii, 442 p. ; **917**

1. Thoreau, Henry David, 1817-1862 Travel Maine. 2. Authors, American -- 19th century. 3. Natural history -- Maine 4. Voyages and travels 5. Nature. 6. Piscataquis County, Maine -- Description and travel. 7. Maine -- Description and travel.
ISBN 0140170138

LC 88003644

Includes index.

Reprint, with new introd. Originally published: Boston : Ticknor & Fields, 1864.

Thoreau's narratives of his journeys into the Maine wilderness are presented.

Wallis, Michael, 1945-

Route 66 : the mother road / Michael Wallis. St. Martin's Griffin, 2001, c1990. xi, 276 p. : **917**

1. Roads. 2. United States Highway 66. 3. The West (United States) -- Description and travel.
ISBN 9780312281670

LC BL 00005386

"75th anniversary edition."

Updated and revised to coincide with the seventy-fifth anniversary of this American icon, a fascinating social history of Route 66, which spurred a revival of the dying American road, evokes the magic of the people and landscapes that surround it. A cultural history of America's most famous highway chronicles the road from its founding to its demise and unprecented revival, and celebrates the many sites and stops along its 2,400-mile route.

Waterman, Jonathan

★**National** Geographic atlas of the national parks / Jon Waterman ; foreword by Gary Knell, Chairman, National Geographic Partners. National Geographic, 2019 431 p. : **917**

1. National parks and reserves -- United States -- Guidebooks.
ISBN 9781426220579

LC 2019009040

Includes indexes.

"Profiles of 60 parks--from battlefields to national seashores--administered by the National Park Service, highlighting their diverse appeal and available outdoor activities. A brief glimpse is given of 29 additional parks, including the newly created Indiana Sand Dunes." --Provided by publisher.

Watson, Paul, 1959-

Ice ghosts : the epic hunt for the lost Franklin expedition / Paul Watson. W.W. Norton & Company, 2017. xxxii, 384 pages, 8 unnumbered pages of plates : **917**

1. John Franklin Arctic Expedition (1845-1851?) 2. Explorers -- Arctic regions 3. Salvage 4. Shipwrecks 5. Arctic regions -- Exploration 6. Northwest Passage -- Exploration -- British
ISBN 9780393249385

LC 2016054683

A Pulitzer Prize-winning journalist, author, and expedition member describes how an unlikely combination of marine science and Inuit knowledge helped solve the mystery of the lost Franklin expedition of 1845.

"A keen, entertaining chronicle of the various attempts to locate a sensationally doomed expedition." Kirkus.

Winter, Kathleen

Boundless : tracing land and dream in a new Northwest Passage / Kathleen Winter. House of Anansi Press, 2014. 264 p. : **917**

1. Winter, Kathleen. 2. Inuit -- Canada. 3. Climate change -- Arctic regions. 4. Northwest Passage -- Description and travel.
ISBN 9781619025677

Shortlisted for The Charles Taylor Prize for Literary Non-Fiction
Hilary Weston Writers' Trust Prize for Nonfiction finalist, 2014.

A chronicle of author Kathleen Winter's journey through the Northwest Passage, including vivid descriptions of the land and its people.

"Perceptive and thoughtful, Winter's ruminations on Arctic life and its continuous clashes with modern civilization are compelling and thought-provoking. The north is a place rarely visited and little understood, but it looms ever larger in our collective future, and to ignore it and its people would be an act of global arrogance." Booklist.

Wright, Carol V.

New York / Carol von Pressentin Wright. Blue Guides Limited, 2016. 623 p. : **917**

1. New York City Guidebooks.
ISBN 9781905131709

LC bl2018028600

Includes index.

A guide to New York presents information about each section of the city, recommends restaurants and accomodations, and provides a detailed map.

917.104 Canada -- Travel

Bishop, Bruce

Canada / contributors, Bruce Bishop, Eric and Katharine Fletcher, Paul Franklin, Sam Ion, Helena Katz, Philip Lee, Ffion Llywd-Jones, Cam Norton, Lorry Patton, Sandra Phinney, Geoffrey Roy, Michael Snook, Donald Telfer, Paul Waters. DK Publishing, 2018. 440 p. : **917.104**

1. Canada Guidebooks.
ISBN 9781465468246

LC bl2018056006

Includes index.

Describes the history, geography, and people of Canada; recommends hotels and restaurants; and surveys the attractions of each province.

917.91 Arizona -- Geography

Dolnick, Edward, 1952-

Down the great unknown : John Wesley Powell's 1869 journey of discovery and tragedy through the Grand Canyon / Edward Dolnick. Perennial, 2002, c2001. viii, 367 p. : **917.91**

1. Powell, John Wesley, 1834-1902 Travel Grand Canyon. 2. Explorers -- United States 3. Grand Canyon -- Exploration. 4. Grand Canyon -- Description and travel. 5. Colorado River -- Exploration.

ISBN 9780060196196

LC bl2004111079

Originally published: New York : HarperCollins, 2001.

Draws on the journals of the great explorer of the Grand Canyon to offer a detailed account of his meticulous, often perilous journey through the famous canyon.

"Dolnick, a science journalist who has rafted down the Grand, turns in a most estimable rendition of that storied expedition. It skillfully integrates the notes and journals of expedition members with technical insight about the perils of roiling whitewater." Booklist.

Fletcher, Colin

The **man** who walked through time / Colin Fletcher. Vintage Books, 1989. 247 p. : **917.91**

1. Fletcher, Colin Travel Grand Canyon. 2. Men and nature. 3. Hiking. 4. Backpacking. 5. Grand Canyon -- Description and travel. 6. Grand Canyon National Park -- Description and travel.

ISBN 0679723064

LC 89180305

The author recounts his two-month hiking tour of the Grand Canyon, which won him the honor of being the first man to traverse Colorado River's giant gorge.

Owen, David, 1955-

Where the water goes : life and death along the Colorado River / David Owen. Riverhead Books, 2017 272 p. **917.91**

1. Owen, David, 1955-. 2. Water-supply. 3. Stream ecology. 4. Colorado River.

ISBN 9781594633775

LC 2016039410

The author of The Conundrum presents a revelatory account of where our water comes from and where it goes, examining the complicated human-made ecosystem of waterways, reservoirs, power plants, fracking sites and farms that contribute to shortage issues in the western United States.

"With water shortages looming across the globe, Owen's work provides invaluable lessons on the rewards and pitfalls involved in managing an essential natural resource." Booklist.

917.98 Alaska -- Geography

McPhee, John, 1931-

Coming into the country / John McPhee. Farrar, Straus and Giroux, 1977. 438 p. : **917.98**

1. McPhee, John, 1931- Travel Alaska. 2. Natural history -- Alaska 3. Wilderness areas -- Alaska. 4. City life -- Alaska. 5. Animals -- Alaska. 6. Alaska -- Description and travel.

ISBN 0374126453

LC 77012249

National Book Critics Circle Award for Nonfiction finalist, 1977.

"This book is actually three lengthy bulletins about Alaska. The first describes a canoe trip that McPhee and four companions took. Second, McPhee tells of a helicopter ride with a committee looking for a site on which to build a new state capital. The last and longest section covers some wintry months spent in Eagle, a tiny settlement on the Yukon River." Time.

Raban, Jonathan

Passage to Juneau : a sea and its meanings / Jonathan Raban. Pantheon Books, 1999. 435 p. **917.98**

1. Vancouver, George, 1757-1798 Travel Northwest Coast of North America. 2. Raban, Jonathan, 1942- Travel Northwest Coast of North America. 3. Raban, Jonathan 4. Romanticism. 5. Boats. 6. Indians of North America -- Pacific Northwest -- Folklore. 7. Indians of North America -- Pacific Northwest -- Art. 8. Northwest Territories -- Description and travel. 9. Pacific Northwest -- Description and travel. 10. Inside Passage (Pacific Northwest) -- Description and travel. 11. Alaska -- Description and travel. 12. Pacific Northwest literature

ISBN 0679442626

LC 99028777

ALA Notable Book, 2000.

Acclaimed travel writer Jonathan Raban invites us aboard his boat, a floating cottage cluttered with books, curling manuscripts, and dead ballpoint pens. He's about to sail alone from Seattle to the Alaskan Panhandle, following an ancient sea route rich in history, riddles, and whirlpools. It's the perfect setting for Raban's prodigious intellect, eloquence, and eye for detail.

"Long fascinated by the Inside Passage (the protected waterway that runs from Washington State up to Alaska), Raban casts off in his 35'ketch from his home port in Seattle to follow in the wake of generations of salmon fishermen. He draws a rather dark portrait of the region as he fills out its history, through the cranky journals of Captain Vancouver and others, and meditates on the beautiful but threatening and lonesome landscape, with its struggling communities, submerged mountains, tricky waters, and names like Deception Pass and Desolation Sound." Library Journal.

918 Geography of and travel in South America

Chatwin, Bruce, 1940-1989

In Patagonia / Bruce Chatwin ; introduction by Nicholas Shakespeare. Penguin Books, 2003, c1977. xxiv, 204 p. : **918**

1. Chatwin, Bruce, 1940-1989 Travel Patagonia (Argentina and Chile) 2. Travelers -- England 3. Voyages and travels. 4. Argentines. 5. Chileans. 6. Patagonia (Argentina and Chile) -- Description and travel.

ISBN 0142437190

LC 2002045038

Originally published: New York : Summit Books, c1977. With new introd.

"This travelogue captures the exotic characters and scenery Chatwin encountered in the southern tip of South America on a search for an important prehistoric artifact." Booklist.

Stafford, Ed

Walking the Amazon : 860 days, one step at a time / Ed Stafford. Plume Books, c2012. 320 p. **918**

1. Stafford, Ed Travel Amazon Valley. 2. Hiking -- Amazon Valley. 3. Walking. 4. Men and nature. 5. Amazon Valley -- Description and travel. 6. Amazon River -- Description and travel.

ISBN 9780452298262

LC 2012010986

Describes the author's 860-day, 4,000 mile quest to walk the entire length of the Amazon River, offering details on the effects of deforestation and his encounters with both vicious animals and tribal members with machetes.

918.1 Brazil -- Geography

Grann, David

The **lost** city of Z : a tale of deadly obsession in the Amazon / David Grann. Doubleday, c2008. 352 p. **918.1**

1. Fawcett, Percy Harrison, 1867-1925? 2. Grann, David Travel Amazon River. 3. El Dorado (Legendary land) 4. Explorers -- Amazon River. 5. Exploration. 6. Voyages and travels. 7. Amazon River -- Description and travel. 8. Latin America -- Description and travel.

ISBN 9780385513531

LC 2008017432

ALA Notable Book, 2010.

Interweaves the story of British explorer Percy Fawcett, who vanished during a 1925 expedition into the Amazon to find an ancient civilization, with the author's own adventure-filled quest into the uncharted wilderness to uncover the mysteries surrounding Fawcett's final journey and the secrets of what really lies deep in the Amazon jungle.

"A colorful tale of true adventure, marked by satisfyingly unexpected twists, turns and plenty of dark portents." Kirkus.

Millard, Candice

River of doubt : Theodore Roosevelt's darkest journey / Candice Millard. Doubleday, 2005. ix, 416 p., 16 p. of plates : **918.1**

1. Roosevelt, Theodore, 1858-1919 Travel Brazil Roosevelt River. 2. Roosevelt-Rondon Scientific Expedition (1913-1914) 3. Rain forests -- Amazon Valley. 4. Natural history -- Amazon River Valley. 5. Presidents -- United States 6. Roosevelt River (Brazil) -- Description and travel. 7. Amazon Valley -- Description and travel.

ISBN 0385507968

LC 2005046541

Chronicles the 1914 expedition of Theodore Roosevelt into the unexplored heart of the Amazon basin to explore and map the region surrounding a tributary called the River of Doubt, detailing the perilous conditions they faced.

"The author turns this incredible story into one that easily matches an Indiana Jones screen adventure." Library Journal.

Robinson, Alex (Travel writer and photographer)

Top 10 Rio de Janeiro / Alex Robinson. DK Publishing, 2016 128 p. : **918.1**

1. Rio de Janeiro (Brazil) Guidebooks.

ISBN 1465440925

LC bl2016029745

Includes indexes.

Shares top ten lists that identify the city's best attractions, including museums, beaches, outdoor activities, restaurants, nightclubs, and shops, and suggests itineraries and walking tours.

919 Geography of and travel in Australasia, Pacific Ocean islands, Atlantic Ocean islands, Arctic islands, Antarctica and on extraterrestrial worlds

Alexander, Caroline, 1956-

The **Endurance** : Shackleton's legendary Antarctic expedition / Caroline Alexander. Knopf, 1998. 211 p. : **919**

1. Shackleton, Ernest Henry, Sir, 1874-1922 Travel 2. Imperial Trans-Antarctic Expedition, 1914-1917. 3. Endurance (Ship) 4. Explorers -- Great Britain 5. Exploration. 6. Survival (after airplane accidents, shipwrecks, etc.) -- Antarctica. 7. Photographs. 8. Antarctica -- Exploration

ISBN 0375404031

"In association with the American Museum of Natural History."

Recounts Sir Ernest Shackleton's expedition to cross Antarctica and the harrowing fight to survive for twenty months in freezing Antarctic conditions.

"Alexander, relying extensively on journals by crew members, some never published, as well as on myriad other sources, delivers a spellbinding story of human courage. . . . What makes this book especially exciting, however, are the 170 previously unpublished photos by the expedition's photographer, Frank Hurley." Publishers Weekly.

Bell, Jim, 1965-

The **interstellar** age : inside the forty-year Voyager mission / Jim Bell. Dutton, 2015. x, 324 p. : **919**

1. Project Voyager 2. Astronautics -- United States -- History. 3. Space exploration 4. Space probes.

ISBN 9780525954323

LC 2014031706

ALA Notable Book, 2016.

The story of the men and women who drove the Voyager spacecraft mission told by a scientist who was there from the beginning.

"A highly enjoyable read for anyone with an interest in popular science." Library Journal.

Bryson, Bill

In a sunburned country / Bill Bryson. Broadway Books, 2000. x, 307 p. : **919**

1. Bryson, Bill Travel Australia. 2. Voyages and travels. 3. Travelers. 4. National characteristics, Australian. 5. Australia -- Description and travel.

ISBN 9780767903851

LC 00025566

Also published as: Down under: travels in a sunburned country.

Later published in an omnibus entitled: Walkabout.

Bryson shares accounts of his travels in Australia, which has the friendliest inhabitants, the hottest weather, and the most peculiar and lethal wildlife on the planet.

"In this book, Bryson chronicles his exploration of Australia, he introduces us to a town that went without electricity until the early 1990s, a former high-ranking politician who hawks his own autobiography to passersby, an assortment of coffee shops and restaurants...a type of giant worm, and the world's most poisonous creature, the box jellyfish." Booklist.

Flannery, Tim F. (Tim Fridtjof), 1956-

Throwim way leg : tree-kangaroos, possums, and penis gourds--on the track of unknown mammals in wildest New Guinea / Tim Flannery. Atlantic Monthly Press, 1998. 326 p. : **919**

1. Indigenous peoples -- New Guinea. 2. Ethnology -- New Guinea.

3. Natural history -- New Guinea. 4. New Guinea -- Social life and customs. 5. New Guinea -- Description and travel.
ISBN 0871137313

LC 98038435

Includes index.

"This is more than an account of [the author's] fieldwork. It is an enthralling introduction to the mountain people of New Guinea." New York Times Book Review.

Griffiths, Tom, 1957-

Slicing the silence : voyaging to Antarctica / Tom Griffiths. Harvard University Press, 2007. 399 p. : **919**

1. Griffiths, Tom, 1957- Diaries. 2. Griffiths, Tom, 1957- Travel Antarctica 3. Voyages and travels. 4. Explorers -- Australia 5. Expeditions -- Antarctica 6. Antarctica -- Description and travel
ISBN 9780674026339

LC 2007006549

Simultaneously published in Australia by the UNSW Press.

Prime Minister's Prize for Australian History, 2008.

The author reflects on his experiences exploring Antarctica, the last true wilderness.

"Believing that to understand the experiences of explorers and the history of Antarctica one must experience its mighty winds, cold, danger, and silence, the author, in 2002, joined a ship delivering scientists and supplies to Casey Station. This book is part diary of that voyage and part history of that most southerly land. This enjoyable and highly readable book would be an excellent addition to any natural history, polar history, or adventure travel collection." Library Journal.

Larson, Edward J. (Edward John)

★An **empire** of ice : Scott, Shackleton, and the heroic age of Antarctic science / Edward J. Larson. Yale University Press, c2011. 360 p. **919**

1. Scott, Robert Falcon, 1868-1912. 2. Shackleton, Ernest Henry, Sir, 1874-1922. 3. Explorers -- Great Britain 4. Scientific expeditions -- Antarctica -- History -- 20th century. 5. Voyages and travels -- Antarctica 6. Discoveries (in geography) 7. Antarctica -- Exploration -- British. 8. Biographies
ISBN 9780300154085

LC 2010044396

Examines the pioneering Antarctic expeditions of the early twentieth century within their larger scientific, social, and geopolitical context.

McGonigal, David, 1950-

Antarctica : secrets of the southern continent / chief consultant, David McGonigal. Firefly Books, 2008. 400 p. : **919**

1. Physical geography -- Antarctica. 2. Geology -- Antarctica. 3. Biology -- Antarctica. 4. Antarctica -- Geography. 5. Antarctica -- History.
ISBN 9781554073986

LC 2009294127

Includes index.

A comprehensive guide filled with vibrant illustrations and detailed maps captures this wondrous and remote land of ice and snow, with up-to-date information on its climate, the nature of ice, its famous explorers, conservation issues, geology, geography, and the animals who call it home.

Riffenburgh, Beau, 1955-

Shackleton's forgotten expedition : the voyage of the Nimrod / Beau Riffenburgh. Bloomsbury : 2004. xxiv, 358 p. : **919**

1. Shackleton, Ernest Henry, Sir, 1874-1922 Travel Antarctica 2. British Antarctic Expedition (1907-1909) 3. Antarctica -- Exploration
ISBN 1582344884

LC 2004011999

"The author recounts Shackleton's voyage to the Antarctic from 1907 to 1909, during which he led a small group of men to within 97 miles of the South Pole. For those who thrilled to the Endurance saga, Riffenburgh offers an equally gripping adventure, which laid the foundations of Shackleton's capacity for brilliant leadership under pressure." Publishers Weekly.

Sagan, Carl, 1934-1996

Pale blue dot : a vision of the human future in space / Carl Sagan. Random House, c1994. xviii, 429 p. : **919**

1. Space exploration. 2. Space.
ISBN 0679438416

LC 94018121

Examines humankind's changing awareness of its place in the universe and the rich potential of human ventures into the world beyond Earth

"In a tour of our solar system, galaxy and beyond...Sagan meshes a history of astronomical discovery, a cogent brief for space exploration and an overview of life. His exploration of our place in the universe is illustrated with photographs, relief maps and paintings, including high-resolution images made by Voyager 1 and 2, as well as photos taken by the Galileo spacecraft, the Hubble Space Telescope and satellites orbiting Earth." Publishers Weekly.

Solomon, Susan, 1956-

The **coldest** March : Scott's fatal Antarctic expedition / Susan Solomon. Yale University Press, c2001. xxii, 383 p. : **919**

1. Scott, Robert Falcon, 1868-1912 Travel Antarctica. 2. British Antarctic ("Terra Nova") Expedition (1910-1913) 3. South Pole expeditions. 4. Antarctica -- Exploration 5. South Pole -- Exploration.
ISBN 0300089678

LC 00054996

Details the expedition of Robert Falcon Scott and his British team to the South Pole in 1912.

"In November 1911, Capt. Robert Falcon Scott and his British team set out to be the first to reach the South Pole. Battling the brutal weather of Antarctica, they reached the pole in January 1912 only to discover that a Norwegian team had beat them there by nearly a month. On their return from the Pole, Scott and four of his companions died in harsh conditions. Ever since, history has not known whether to label them heroes or bunglers. Solomon...analyzes all the factors present during Scott's expedition in an attempt to explain that his failure was due not to incompetence but to a combination of unpredictable weather, erroneous choices and bad luck." Library Journal.

Theroux, Paul

The **happy** isles of Oceania : paddling the Pacific / Paul Theroux. Houghton Mifflin Co., 2006, c1992. 528 p. : **919**

1. Theroux, Paul Travel Oceania. 2. Travelers -- United States 3. Americans in Oceania. 4. Authors, American -- 20th century. 5. Voyages and travels. 6. Oceania -- Description and travel. 7. Oceania -- History. 8. Pacific Ocean -- Description and travel.
ISBN 9780618658985

LC 91039687

Originally published: New York : G.P. Putnam's Sons, c1992.

The author recounts in vivid, exhilarating detail his journey--by kayak--through the diverse landscapes and wonders of New Zealand, Tahiti, Hawaii, Easter Island, and other islands of the Pacific.

"The author spent 18 months in a one-man collapsible kayak exploring such exotic Pacific islands as New Zealand, Australia, the Soloman and Cook Islands, Fiji, Samoa, Tahiti, Easter Island, and Hawaii. A brilliant storyteller with an eye for the absurd, Theroux takes the reader to little-known places where time seems to have stood still and people lead simple lives totally unrelated to 20th-century America." Library Journal.

919.4 Bolivia -- Geography

Chatwin, Bruce, 1940-1989

The **songlines** / Bruce Chatwin. Penguin Books, 1988, c1987. 295 p. ; **919.4**

1. Chatwin, Bruce, 1940-1989 Travel Australia. 2. Aboriginal Australians -- Social life and customs. 3. Wanderers and wandering. 4. Travelers -- England 5. Voyages and travels. 6. Australia -- Description and travel.

ISBN 0140094296

LC 87029204

Commonwealth Writers' Prize, South Asia and Europe: Best Book, 1988.

"This is an important book and a challenging one. It is full of odd characters, bizarre incidents, moments of poetry--some of them comic--that spring as much from the writer's own generosity of spirit as from the richness of things." Times Literary Supplement.

919.804 Arctic islands -- Travel

Beattie, Owen

Frozen in time : the fate of the Franklin Expedition / Owen Beattie, John Geiger. MJF Books/Fine Communications, 2007, c1988. 288 p. **919.804**

1. John Franklin Arctic Expedition (1845-1851?) 2. Explorers -- Great Britain 3. Exploration. 4. Missing persons. 5. Arctic regions -- Exploration -- British. 6. Northwest Passage.

ISBN 1567318630

LC 2007920415

Originally published: New York : Dutton, 1988.

Discusses the tragic fate of Sir John Franklin's failed expedition to find the Northwest Passage in 1845.

"The authors present a richly researched history of the expedition and the following relief expeditions and seamlessly merge the worlds of forensic anthropology and 19th-century history. Reading almost like a whodunit page-turner, Beattie and Geiger capture the thrill of making new scientific discoveries and finding important clues to solve a haunting mystery." Publishers Weekly.

Cookman, Scott, 1952-

★**Ice** blink : the tragic fate of Sir John Franklin's lost polar expedition / Scott Cookman. Wiley, c2000. xii, 244 p. : **919.804**

1. Franklin, John, Sir, 1786-1847 2. Explorers -- Great Britain. 3. Expeditions -- Arctic regions. 4. Food industry and trade -- Corrupt practices. 5. Canned foods. 6. Northwest Passage -- Exploration -- British 7. Arctic regions -- Exploration -- British.

ISBN 0471377902

LC 99047620

Follows the trail of the expedition by Sir John Franklin, which sailed north from Greenland in 1845 with two iron-plated ships and 128 men, only to be swallowed up by the ice and snow.

"In this account of the fabled 1845 Franklin expedition in search of the Northwest Passage, Cookman inculpates a novel malefactor in the tragedy: botulism. In the 1980s, three frozen corpses of expedition members were found and exhumed. Autopsies revealed lead, fingering lead-soldered cans from the provisions. Adventure readers will flock to this fine regaling of the enduring mystery surrounding the best-known disaster in Arctic exploration." Booklist.

Fleming, Fergus, 1959-

Ninety degrees north : the quest for the North Pole / Fergus Fleming. Grove Press, 2001. xxi, 470 p., 16 p. of plates : **919.804**

1. Expeditions -- Arctic regions. 2. Explorers. 3. Polar expeditions. 4. North Pole expeditions. 5. North Pole -- Exploration. 6. Arctic regions -- Exploration. 7. Polar regions -- Exploration

ISBN 0802117252

LC 2002021469

"The book is fascinating for how Fleming renders the haughty, post-Enlightenment brio of the principal adventurers and the extreme, often fatal ends toward which it pushed them." Publishers Weekly.

Kavenna, Joanna

The **ice** museum : in search of the lost land of Thule / Joanna Kavenna. Viking, 2006, c2005. 294 p. : **919.804**

1. Kavenna, Joanna Travel Arctic regions. 2. Geomythology. 3. Voyages and travels. 4. Women explorers. 5. Explorers. 6. Thule, Greenland. 7. Arctic regions -- Exploration. 8. Arctic regions -- Mythology.

ISBN 0670034738

LC bl2006007617

Traces the author's extensive research of the ancient ice civilization, describing her travels through Iceland, Greenland, the arctic wilderness, and other frozen terrains; her learning through the works of other writers and explorers; and her discoveries about the Thule Society.

"The author chronicles her personal journey into the myth and reality of the legendary Arctic land of Thule. [This book] transcends all genre description, and holds its own as a journey into a world that somehow vibrantly exists on paper and nowhere else." Booklist.

919.89 Antarctica -- Geography

Grann, David

★The **white** darkness / David Grann. Doubleday, [2018] 144 p. **919.89**

1. Worsley, Henry. 2. Shackleton, Ernest Henry, Sir, 1874-1922. 3. Explorers -- Great Britain 4. Obsession 5. Adventurers 6. Walking 7. Antarctica -- Exploration 8. Antarctica -- Description and travel

ISBN 9780385544573

LC 2018023450

Traces the South Pole expedition of a decorated British special forces officer, an admirer of Ernest Shackleton's expedition and descendant of one of Shackleton's crew, who in 2015 risked his life to walk across Antarctica alone.

"A modern-day hero dedicated to a goal is much needed in today's society." Library Journal.

McOrist, Wilson

Shackleton's heroes : the epic story of the men who kept the Endurance expedition alive / Wilson McOrist ; foreword by Sir Ranulph Fiennes. The Robson Press, 2015. xix, 362 p., 8 unnumbered p. of plates : **919.89**

1. Shackleton, Ernest Henry, Sir, 1874-1922 Travel Antarctica. 2. Imperial Trans-Antarctic Expedition, 1914-1917. 3. Endurance (Ship) 4. Polar expeditions. 5. Survival -- Antarctica. 6. Exploration. 7. Explorers. 8. Antarctica -- Exploration.
ISBN 9781510710757

LC 2014455778

Chronicles the lesser-known story of the Mount Hope Party, also known as the Ross Sea party, who faced extreme and life-threatening obstacles to provide food and supplies to Sir Ernest Shackleton's legendary Imperial Trans-Antarctic Expedition crew.

"All polar enthusiasts will be impressed anew by not only what the Ross Sea Party endured but also how hard McOrist has worked to share their words with the world." Booklist.

Smith, Roff Martin

Life on the ice : no one goes to Antarctica alone / Roff Smith. National Geographic, 2005, c2002. 208 p. ; **919.89**

1. Discoveries in geography. 2. Antarctica -- Description and travel
ISBN 0792293452

LC 2005298454

Originally published: Crows Nest, N.S.W. : Allen & Unwin, 2002.

"Smith is the most exceptional of travel writers: his portraits of people are deeply sympathetic, while his language is at once lyrical and knowledgeable. Not to be missed." Booklist.

Wood, Gillen D'Arcy

Land of wondrous cold : the race to discover Antarctica and unlock the secrets of its ice / Gillen D'Arcy Wood. Princeton University Press, 2020. 304 p. **919.89**

1. Ice caps -- Antarctica. 2. Explorers 3. Exploration 4. Expeditions 5. Antarctica -- Exploration 6. Antarctica -- Environmental conditions.
ISBN 9780691172200

LC 2019029836

"Outstanding history accompanied by outstanding popular science." Kirkus

920 Collective biographies

Abbott, Karen, 1973-

Liar, temptress, soldier, spy : four women undercover in the Civil War / Karen Abbott. Harper, 2014. 368 p. **920**

1. Boyd, Belle, 1844-1900. 2. Greenhow, Rose O'Neal, 1814-1864. 3. Van Lew, Elizabeth L., 1818-1900. 4. Bowser, Mary Elizabeth, approximately 1840- 5. Women spies 6. Women and war 7. Disguises 8. Deception 9. United States -- History -- Civil War, 1861-1865 10. Collective biographies
ISBN 9780062092892

LC 2014013602

Draws from primary source material and interviews to weave together the adventures of four courageous women who risked everything to become spies during the most tumultuous years of the Civil War.

"Remarkable, brave lives rendered in a fluidly readable, even romantic history lesson." Kirkus.

Acevedo, Carlos

Sporting blood : tales from the dark side of boxing / Carlos Acevedo ; foreword by Thomas Hauser. Hamilcar Publications, 2020. xiii, 211 p. : **920**

1. Boxing -- History 2. Boxers (Sports) 3. Competition 4. Fame 5. Essays 6. Collective biographies
ISBN 9781949590074

LC 2019953179

The essays that make up Sporting Blood include Carlos Acevedo's moving meditation on Muhammad Ali; his penetrating look at Ali's fearsome rival, the enigmatic heavyweight Charles "Sonny" Liston; and his profile of Mike Tyson, which brilliantly conjures the Boy King's late 1980s reign of terror. Acevedo offers many other unforgettable tales from boxing's dark side, featuring Jack Johnson, Joe Frazier, Roberto Duran, Aaron Pryor, Johnny Tapia, Evander Holyfield, Jake LaMotta, and more.

"One of the better books on boxing in recent years. An often engaging set of boxing profiles that packs a powerful punch and rarely misses its target." Kirkus

Ackmann, Martha

The **Mercury** 13 : the untold story of thirteen American women and the dream of space flight / Martha Ackmann. Random House, c2003. 239 p. : **920**

1. Project Mercury. 2. Women astronauts 3. Astronautics -- United States -- History. 4. Sexism. 5. United States -- Social conditions -- History -- 20th century. 6. Collective biographies.
ISBN 0375507442

LC 2002037118

"Mercury 13 is both an outstanding work of research and an exceptionally readable and well-told story. Readers will gain new perspectives on space, medicine, women, and American culture, and will appreciate the magnitude of what was lost when the women were grounded." School Library Journal.

Ahamed, Liaquat

Lords of finance : the bankers who broke the world / Liaquat Ahamed. Penguin Press, 2009. 576 p. **920**

1. Capitalists and financiers 2. Bankers 3. Economic history -- 1918-1945. 4. Gold standard -- History 5. United States -- Economic conditions -- 20th century 6. Biographies 7. Collective biographies.
ISBN 9781594201820

LC bl2008029148

Pulitzer Prize for History, 2010.

With penetrating insights for today, this vital history of the world economic collapse of the late 1920s offers unforgettable portraits of four men--Montagu Norman, Amile Moreau, Hjalmar Schacht, and Benjamin Strong--whose personal and professional actions as heads of their respective central banks changed the course of the twentieth century.

"A grand, sweeping narrative of immense scope and power." New York Times Book Review.

Ambrose, Stephen E.

★**Band** of brothers : E Company, 506th Regiment, 101st Airborne : from Normandy to Hitler's Eagle's nest / Stephen E. Ambrose. Simon & Schuster, 1992. 335 p. : **920**

1. United States. Army. Parachute Infantry Regiment, 506th. Company E 2. Courage in men. 3. Soldiers -- United States. 4. World War II 5. Military campaigns 6. Western Europe. 7. Collective biographies. 8. Books to TV
ISBN 0671769227

LC 91047684

Describes E Company's contributions to the campaigns in western Europe

"Here is the story of the daring E Company, which began the war by parachuting into France on D-Day and ended it by capturing Eagle's Nest, Hitler's outpost in Bavaria." Library Journal.

Andersen, Christopher P.

Game of crowns : Elizabeth, Camilla, Kate, and the throne / Christopher Andersen. Gallery Books, 2016. 320 p. **920**

1. Elizabeth II, Queen of Great Britain, 1926- 2. Catherine, Duchess of Cambridge, 1982- 3. Windsor, House of 4. Camilla, Duchess of Cornwall, 1947- 5. Women rulers 6. Inheritance and succession 7. Monarchy 8. Collective biographies
ISBN 9781476743950

LC 2015050619

Traces the family histories and controversies that have marked the lives of Queen Elizabeth, the Duchess of Cornwall, and the Duchess of Cambridge to illuminate their stark differences, their remarkable similarities, and their roles in an evolving monarchy.

"With gaspworthy and laugh-out-loud moments revealing scandalous and sympathetic details of the royal family, Andersen humanizes this privileged yet embattled group." Kirkus.

Anderson, Lars

The **Mannings** : the fall and rise of a football family / Lars Anderson. Ballantine, 2016. 256 p. **920**

1. Manning, Archie, 1949- 2. Manning, Peyton. 3. Manning, Eli, 1981- 4. Manning family. 5. Professional football players 6. Football players. 7. Quarterbacks (Football). 8. Football 9. Collective biographies.
ISBN 9781101883822

LC 2016018007

A biography of the first family of sports in the United States describes how an early tragedy that tested their faith ultimately led the Mannings to athletic greatness, producing three football stars over two generations.

"An expertly written impressionistic account of the first family of football that will be of wide interest." Library Journal.

Avrich, Paul

Sasha and Emma : the anarchist odyssey of Alexander Berkman and Emma Goldman / Paul Avrich and Karen Avrich. Belknap Press of Harvard University Press, c2012. 528 p. **920**

1. Berkman, Alexander, 1870-1936. 2. Goldman, Emma, 1869-1940. 3. Anarchists -- United States 4. Political activists. 5. Anarchism -- United States -- History. 6. Collective biographies.
ISBN 9780674065987

LC 2012008659

Offers a glimpse into the intertwined lives of the anarchist movement leaders who remained comrades despite separations caused by Berkman's fourteen-year imprisonment and Goldman's fame as the champion of revolutionary causes.

Bailey, Mark, 1968-

Nine Irish lives : the thinkers, fighters, and artists who helped build America / edited by Mark Bailey. Algonquin Books of Chapel Hill, 2018 xiv, 256 p. **920**

1. Irish Americans 2. Immigrants, Irish 3. Collective biographies 4. Essays
ISBN 9781616205171

LC 2017042933

Combining history with personal reflection, and written by nine contemporary Irish Americans, an anthology profiles nine incredible Irish immigrants, including Margaret Haughery, known as "Mother of Orphans"; muckraking journalist Samuel McClure, who not only became American but helped to shape the United States; actor Pierce Brosnan; and others.

"Readers interested in getting their Irish on will delight in this collection of essays detailing a variety of significant contributions by Irish immigrants to the history of the U.S." Booklist.

Baker, John F., 1962-

The **Washingtons** of Wessyngton Plantation : stories of my family's generational journey to freedom / John F. Baker, Jr. Atria, 2009. 432 p. **920**

1. Washington family. 2. Baker, John F., 1962- Family. 3. African American families 4. African Americans -- Genealogy. 5. African Americans -- Tennessee 6. Slaves -- Tennessee 7. Tennessee -- Antiquities. 8. Collective biographies.
ISBN 9781416567400

LC 2008018742

Traces the author's thirty-year research into his slave ancestry, describing the history of the massive tobacco plantation where his ancestors worked and his family's extensive genealogical legacy.

"Historians will find this book useful for its examination of rural life in the 19th-century South, and general readers will find a moving story of a family achieving freedom." Library Journal.

Bakewell, Sarah

★**At** the existentialist cafe : freedom, being, and apricot cocktails / Sarah Bakewell. Other Press, 2016. 304 p. **920**

1. Philosophers 2. Existentialism 3. Philosophy -- Political aspects 4. Freedom 5. Collective biographies
ISBN 9781590514887

LC 2015047824

"With Jean-paul Sartre, Simone De Beauvoir, Albert Camus, Martin Heidegger, Maurice Merleau-ponty and others".

ALA Notable Book, 2017.

Kirkus Prize for Nonfiction finalist, 2016.

Featuring not only philosophers, but also playwrights, anthropologists, convicts, and revolutionaries, At the Existentialist Cafe follows the existentialists' story, from the first rebellious spark through the Second World War, to its role in postwar liberation movements such as anticolonialism, feminism, and gay rights.

Ball, Edward, 1958-

The **sweet** hell inside : a family history / Edward Ball. William Morrow, c2001. xv, 384 p., [32] p. of plates : **920**

1. Harleston family. 2. African American families 3. Interracial marriage 4. Slaves -- South Carolina 5. African Americans 6. Charleston Region, South Carolina -- Race relations. 7. South Carolina. 8. Collective biographies.
ISBN 068816840X

LC 2001030880

The author continues the story of the Harleston family, focusing on a dynasty of cultural leaders during the Jazz Age and pioneers in art, music, and business whose power began to fade as black America was winning the right to vote.

"The Harlestons of South Carolina were descended from a slave woman and her master, the start of a line of fair-skinned blacks who rose to prominence in the state through commerce, social service, and the arts. [The author] was approached by Edwina Harleston Whitlock, a distant black relative (a sixth cousin, twice removed), to take a storehouse of genealogical material she had about her family and to write its history. The result is a stunning look at a fascinating family and the history of blacks in the U.S. from the 1800s to the 1960s." Booklist.

Barr, Luke

Ritz & Escoffier : the hotelier, the chef, and the rise of the leisure class / Luke Barr. Clarkson Potter, 2018 288 p. **920**

1. Ritz, Cesar, 1850-1918. 2. Escoffier, A. (Auguste), 1846-1935. 3. Savoy Hotel (London, England) -- History. 4. Hospitality industry and trade. 5. Leisure class. 6. Luxury. 7. Hotels. 8. Collective biographies

ISBN 9780804186292

LC 2017015344

Transports readers to turn-of-the-century London and Paris to discover how celebrated hotelier César Ritz and famed chef Auguste Escoffier joined forces at the Savoy Hotel to spawn the modern luxury hotel and restaurant, where women and American Jews mingled with British high society, signaling a new social order and the rise of the middle class.

"A well-researched, glitzy, and flawed history of conspicuous consumption." Kirkus.

Barrett, Duncan

GI brides : the wartime girls who crossed the Atlantic for love / Duncan Barrett & Nuala Calvi. William Morrow Paperbacks, 2014. 592 p. **920**

1. World War II -- Women. 2. War brides 3. Women immigrants. 4. British Americans 5. Collective biographies

ISBN 9780062328052

LC 2014010526

Worn down by years of war and hardship, girls like Sylvia, Margaret, and Gwendolyn were thrilled when American GI's arrived in Britain with their exotic accents, handsome uniforms and aura of Hollywood glamor. Others, like Rae, who distrusted the Yanks,were eventually won over by their easy charm. So when VE Day finally came, for the 70,000 women who'd become GI brides, it was tinged with sadness--it meant leaving their homeland behind to follow their husbands across the Atlantic. And the long voyage was just the beginning of an even bigger journey. Adapting to a new culture thousands of miles from home, often with a man they barely knew, was difficult--but these women survived the Blitz and could cope with anything. GI BRIDES shares the sweeping, compelling, and moving true stories of four women who gave up everything and crossed an ocean for love.

"Alternating among the women, the authors bring to light the joys and sorrows of each woman, but readers may find it easier to read each story in its entirety before switching to another one. Entertaining stories about four women who embraced life with American soldiers after the end of World War II." Kirkus.

Bates, Stephen, 1954-

Royalty Inc : Britain's best-known brand / Stephen Bates. Aurum Press, 2015. 358 p., 8 unnumbered p. of plates : **920**

1. Windsor, House of. 2. Elizabeth II, Queen of Great Britain, 1926- 3. Elizabeth II, Queen of Great Britain, 1926- Family. 4. Queens -- Great Britain 5. Monarchy -- Great Britain -- History 6. Great Britain -- History -- Elizabeth II, 1952- 7. Great Britain -- Kings and rulers. 8. Windsor, House of.

ISBN 9781781313565

LC 2015463235

Includes index.

Baum, Dan

Nine lives : death and life in New Orleans / Dan Baum. Spiegel and Grau, 2009. 288 p. **920**

1. City dwellers -- New Orleans, Louisiana -- Interviews 2. Hurricanes -- Louisiana 3. Subcultures 4. New Orleans, Louisiana -- Social life and customs -- 20th century 5. New Orleans, Louisiana -- Social life and customs -- 21st century 6. Collective biographies

ISBN 9780385523196

LC 2008031483

"Nine Lives" explores New Orleans through the lives of nine characters over 40 years, bracketed by two epic hurricanes. It brings back to life the doomed city, its wondrous subcultures, and the rich and colorful lives that played themselves out within its borders.

"Baum's in-depth reporting (he was on scene during Katrina, even turning himself in at the Convention Center to chronicle the out-of-sight outrages) is evident on every page." Booklist.

Beam, Alex

The **feud** : Vladimir Nabokov, Edmund Wilson, and the end of a beautiful friendship / Alex Beam. Pantheon, 2016. 224 p. **920**

1. Nabokov, Vladimir Vladimirovich, 1899-1977 Friends and associates. 2. Wilson, Edmund, 1895-1972 Friends and associates. 3. Authors 4. Friendship 5. Writing 6. Male friendship 7. Collective biographies

ISBN 9781101870228

LC 2016007056

Traces the ironic factors that contributed to the estrangement between intimate friends and literary colleagues Edmund Wilson and Vladimir Nabokov, describing their political differences and escalating disagreements about Nabokov's translation of Pushkin's Eugene Onegin.

"An outstanding and entertaining book that could have surprising appeal beyond its intended literary audience. Readers who give it a chance will soon find themselves unable to put it down." Library Journal.

The **Beatles** anthology Chronicle Books, c2000. 367 p. : **920**

1. Beatles (Musical group) 2. Rock musicians 3. Collective biographies

ISBN 0811826848

LC 00023685

Created in cooperation with the surviving members of the group and Yoko Ono, this unique anthology features more than 1,300 full-color and black-and-white images, including personal memorabilia, documents, photographs, and other items from personal archives, that chronicle the band's Liverpool origins, rise to fame, and breakup.

"The density of the text is daunting, but the book's browsability makes it as appealing to casual readers as it is indispensable to Beatlemaniacs." Library Journal.

Becker, Adam, 1984-

What is real? : the unfinished quest for the meaning of quantum physics / Adam Becker. Basic Books, 2018 288 p. **920**

1. Quantum theory -- History. 2. Physicists 3. Physics 4. Collective biographies

ISBN 9780465096053

LC 2017043844

Describes how a long line of physicists, beginning in the 1920s, persisted in seeking the true meaning of quantum mechanics despite the scientific community's favoring of Niels Bohr's Copenhagen interpretation that dismissed it as solipsism and poor reasoning.

"With his crisp voice, Becker lucidly relates the complicated history of quantum foundations." Publishers Weekly.

Bell, Eric Temple, 1883-1960

★**Men** of mathematics / E.T. Bell. Simon & Schuster, 1986, c1937. xvii, 590 p. ; **920**

1. Mathematicians. 2. Mathematicians 3. Mathematics -- History. 4.

Collective biographies.
ISBN 0671628186

LC 86010229

"A Touchstone book"
Includes index.
The achievements and lives of important world mathematicians prior to 1900.

Bell-Scott, Patricia

★The **firebrand** and the First Lady : portrait of a friendship : Pauli Murray, Eleanor Roosevelt, and the struggle for social justice / Patricia Bell-Scott. Alfred A. Knopf, 2016 480 p. **920**

1. Roosevelt, Eleanor, 1884-1962 Friends and associates. 2. Murray, Pauli, 1910-1985 Friends and associates. 3. Episcopal Church Clergy 4. Women social reformers 5. Presidents' spouses -- United States 6. African American women civil rights workers 7. African American intellectuals 8. Collective biographies.
ISBN 9780679446521

LC 2015033959

ALA Notable Book, 2017.
Andrew Carnegie Medal for Excellence in Non-Fiction Finalist, 2017
Describes the unlikely friendship between First Lady Eleanor Roosevelt and Pauli Murray, a lawyer and civil rights pioneer whose grandfather was a mixed race slave, and the important work they each did, taking stands for justice and freedom.
"Bell-Scott's groundbreaking portrait of these two tireless and innovative champions of human dignity adds an essential and edifying facet to American history." Booklist.

Berkin, Carol

Civil War wives : the lives and times of Angelina Grimke Weld, Varina Howell Davis, and Julia Dent Grant / Carol Berkin. Alfred A. Knopf, 2009. xiv, 361 p. : **920**

1. Grimke, Angelina Emily, 1805-1879. 2. Grimke, Angelina Emily, 1805-1879 Marriage. 3. Davis, Varina Howell, 1826-1906. 4. Davis, Varina Howell, 1826-1906 Marriage. 5. Grant, Julia Dent, 1826-1902. 6. Grant, Julia Dent, 1826-1902 Marriage. 7. Women -- United States 8. Married women -- United States 9. Civil war 10. United States Civil War, 1861-1865 11. United States -- History -- Civil War, 1861-1865 -- Women. 12. United States -- History -- Civil War, 1861-1865 13. Collective biographies
ISBN 9781400044467

LC 2009019476

Traces the vivid stories of the wives of Theodore Weld, Jefferson Davis, and Ulysses S. Grant to demonstrate how their personal beliefs were overshadowed by the supporting roles they played to their high-profile husbands before unique wartime and personal challenges brought their characters to the foreground.
"This finely nuanced, absorbing account makes an important contribution to both Civil War literature and the history of American women." Booklist.

Berlin, Leslie, 1969-

Troublemakers : how a generation of silicon valley upstarts invented the future / Leslie Berlin. Simon & Schuster 2017 448 p. **920**

1. Technological innovations. 2. Businesspeople 3. High technology industry and trade 4. Internet -- History. 5. Santa Clara Valley, California. 6. Silicon Valley, California 7. Collective biographies
ISBN 9781451651508

LC bl2017037748

A narrative history of the Silicon Valley generation that launched five major high-tech industries in seven years details the specific contributions of seven technical pioneers and how they established the foundation for today's tech-driven world.
"A sturdy, skillfully constructed work of business and technological history." Kirkus.

Bernstein, Andrea

American oligarchs : the Kushners, the Trumps, and the marriage of money and power / Andrea Bernstein. W W Norton & Co Inc 2020. 484 p. **920**

1. Kushner family 2. Trump family 3. Kushner, Jared, 1981- 4. Trump, Ivanka, 1981- 5. Trump, Donald, 1946- 6. Rich people 7. Ambition 8. Scandals 9. Rich families 10. Collective biographies
ISBN 9781324001874

LC bl2019038547

Bernstein traces how the two families ruthlessly harnessed New York and New Jersey machine politics to gain valuable tax breaks and grew rich on federal programs that bolstered the middle class.
"The author, who conducted hundreds of interviews and read more than 100,000 documents to create this damning portrait of two clearly unscrupulous families . . . [offers a] painstaking documentation of a relentless culture of corruption." Kirkus

Blight, David W.

A **slave** no more : two men who escaped to freedom : including their own narratives of emancipation / David W. Blight. Harcourt, c2007. 320 p. **920**

1. Washington, John, 1838-1918. 2. Turnage, Wallace, 1846-1916. 3. Fugitive slaves 4. Slaves. 5. African Americans 6. Working class -- United States -- History -- 19th century 7. United States -- History -- Civil War, 1861-1865 -- African Americans. 8. Virginia -- History -- 19th century 9. North Carolina -- History -- 19th century 10. Collective autobiographies and memoirs
ISBN 9780151012329

LC 2007014467

Two slave narratives that document the experiences of runaway slaves who managed to reach the protection of Union forces are accompanied by biographies of both men that reconstruct their childhoods, escape, Civil War service, and successful later lives.

Bond, Jenny

Who the hell is Pansy O'Hara? : the fascinating stories behind 50 of the world's best-loved books / Jenny Bond & Chris Sheedy. Penguin Books, 2008. xiii, 318 p. ; **920**

1. Writing 2. Books and reading 3. Authors 4. Authors, English -- 20th century 5. Collective biographies.
ISBN 9780143113645

An entertaining collection of the real-life stories behind fifty of the world's most popular books shares trivia, anecdotes, author details, inspiration, and other aspects of such volumes as Margaret Mitchell's Gone With the Wind, J. K. Rowling's Harry Potter series, War and Peace by Leo Tolstoy, and other literary masterworks.
"Between the engaging information and the range of popular texts ... this affectionate literary history should appeal to many readers." Publishers Weekly.

Borman, Tracy

The **private** lives of the Tudors : uncovering the secrets of Britain's greatest dynasty. / Tracy Borman. Grove Press, 2016. 464 p. **920**

1. Tudor, House of 2. Monarchy -- Great Britain -- History -- 16th

century 3. Royal houses. 4. Rulers. 5. Nobility -- Great Britain. 6. Great Britain -- History -- Tudors, 1485-1603. 7. Great Britain -- Rulers. 8. Collective biographies.
ISBN 9780802125996
LC 2017275637

An in-depth examination behind the public faces of the Tudor monarchs draws on original material from their most intimate courtiers to illuminate lesser-known details about their private worlds, from what they ate and the clothes they wore to how they practiced their faith and how they were treated while sick.

"This Downton Abbey-like peek into the everyday lives of these privileged yet cloistered rulers and their households will appeal to both serious scholars and Tudor enthusiasts." Booklist.

Bram, Christopher

Eminent outlaws : the gay writers who changed America / Christopher Bram. Twelve, 2012. 320 p. **920**

1. Gay men's writings -- History and criticism. 2. Authors, American -- 20th century. 3. Gay authors -- United States. 4. Collective biographies
ISBN 9780446563130
LC 2011029910

Describes the trailblazing, post-war gay literary figures, including Tennessee Williams, Gore Vidal, Truman Capote and Allen Ginsberg, who paved the way for newer generations including Armistead Maupin, Edmund White and Edward Albee.

Branch, John (Sports reporter)

The **last** cowboys : a pioneer family in the new West / John Branch. W W Norton & Company, 2018 304 p. **920**

1. Wright family 2. Ranchers 3. Rodeo performers. 4. Cowboys. 5. Cattle ranchers. 6. Utah 7. Collective biographies
ISBN 9780393292343
LC 2017061611

The Pulitzer Prize-winning reporter and award-winning author presents a portrait of the Wright family of Smith Mesa and their generations-long achievements as some of the world's most successful cattle ranchers and rodeo champions, tracing three generations of their battles against natural obstacles, federal regulation and injuries and how the changes of the 21st century are challenging their future.

Brands, H. W.

★The **zealot** and the emancipator : John Brown, Abraham Lincoln and the struggle for American freedom / H.W. Brands. Doubleday, 2020 464 p. **920**

1. Brown, John, 1800-1859. 2. Lincoln, Abraham, 1809-1865. 3. Abolitionists 4. Anti-slavery movements -- History -- 19th century 5. Presidents -- United States 6. Harper's Ferry, West Virginia -- History -- John Brown's Raid, 1859. 7. United States -- History -- 19th century. 8. United States -- History -- Civil War, 1861-1865 -- Causes. 9. Collective biographies
ISBN 9780385544009
LC 2019036370

Follows the epic struggle over slavery as embodied by John Brown and Abraham Lincoln--two men moved to radically different acts to confront our nation's gravest sin.

"A fascinating and wonderfully readable portrayal of the tensions between fiery militancy and determined but measured devotion in working toward a goal. Excellent for general readers, especially those with an interest in the Civil War." Library Journal

Brian, Denis

The **Curies** : a biography of the most controversial family in science / Denis Brian. Wiley, c2005. ix, 438 p. : **920**

1. Curie family. 2. Curie, Marie, 1867-1934. 3. Curie, Pierre, 1859-1906. 4. Chemists -- Poland 5. Physicists -- France 6. Women physicists -- France 7. Nobel Prize winners. 8. France -- History -- 19th century 9. France -- History -- 20th century 10. Poland -- History -- 19th century 11. Collective biographies.
ISBN 0471273910
LC 2005007001

An intimate look at the lives of this scientific family retraces the important work in radium by Pierre and Marie Curie, as well as the subsequent careers and scandals of their children, including Eve Curie, the writer and war correspondant.

"This book follows five generations of the Sklodowska-Curie-Joliot family. Beginning before Marie Sklodowska and Pierre Curie meet, Brian details their courtship and 11-year marriage, bringing the reader to the Curie dinner table and into the converted garden shed (replete with a leaking roof) where the Curies' work on polonium and radium transformed physics and won them two Nobel prizes. Extremely well-done and highly recommended." Publishers Weekly.

Brokaw, Tom

An **album** of memories : personal histories from the greatest generation / Tom Brokaw. Random House, 2001. x, 314 p. : **920**

1. Generations -- United States -- History -- 20th century. 2. World War II, American. 3. Depressions -- 1929-1941. 4. United States -- History -- 1933-1945. 5. Collective biographies.
ISBN 0375505814
LC 2001273436

Celebrates the "greatest generation" of Americans, from the Great Depression to the Bataan Death March and beyond, in a series of biographical profiles that chronicle the experiences of ordinary Americans who became caught up in historic twentieth-century events.

"This volume gathers letters written to Brokaw by Americans who lived through the Depression and World War II and, in some cases, letters written by their children. Brokaw provides a brief introduction and a time line for each chapter; these cover the Depression, the war in Europe and in the Pacific, and the wartime home front, closing with Reflections. The book is lavishly illustrated with reproductions of photographs, drawings, documents, and other memorabilia of the era." Booklist.

Broven, John

Record makers and breakers : voices of the independent rock 'n' roll pioneers / John Broven. University of Illinois Press, c2008. 592 p. **920**

1. Sound recording executives and producers -- United States 2. Sound recording industry and trade -- History. 3. Rock music. 4. Collective biographies
ISBN 9780252032905
LC 2008027204

Describes the history of the early independent rock 'n' roll industry, from its regional beginnings in the 1940s through its peak and decline in the 1960s, celebrating its contribution to modern music history.

Brower, Kate Andersen

First in line : presidents, vice presidents, and the pursuit of power / Kate Andersen Brower. HarperCollins 2018. 400 p. **920**

1. Presidents 2. Vice presidents 3. Politicians. 4. Washington, D.C. 5.

United States -- Politics and government. 6. Collective biographies
ISBN 9780062668943

LC 2018655046

From the author of the New York Times best-sellers First Women and The Residence comes an intimate, news-making look at the men who are next in line to the most powerful office in the world--the vice presidents of the modern era--from Richard Nixon to Joe Biden to Mike Pence.

"Notwithstanding the famous assessment that the vice presidency is not worth a bucket of warm spit, 14 of the 47 U.S. vice presidents have gone on to the presidency. CNN contributor Brower interviewed 200 people, including VPs and their families, to find out what the job is really like." Library Journal.

First women : the grace and power of America's modern First Ladies / Kate Andersen Brower. HarperCollins 2016 352 p. **920**

1. Presidents' spouses -- United States 2. Women and politics. 3. Washington, D.C. 4. Collective biographies
ISBN 9780062439659

LC 2016440928

The author of The Residence presents an intimate examination of the true influences of White House First Ladies from Jackie Kennedy to Michelle Obama, which draws on previous untapped and candid sources to document their stories.

"Brower writes with grace and ease and finely outlines the lives of these influential figures, providing deep insights into the experiences of each." Library Journal.

Brown, Craig, 1957-

150 glimpses of the Beatles / Craig Brown. Farrar, Straus and Giroux, 2020. 574 p. **920**

1. Lennon, John, 1940-1980. 2. McCartney, Paul. 3. Starr, Ringo, 1940- 4. Harrison, George, 1943-2001. 5. Beatles (Musical group) 6. Bands (Music) 7. Rock music. 8. Popular culture 9. Biographies 10. Collective biographies
ISBN 9780374109318

LC 2020022500

Originally published in 2020 by 4th Estate, Great Britain.

The author draws on previously unexamined lore and celebrity testimony in a kaleidoscopic group portrait of the Fab Four that reveals lesser-known examples of their indelible and enduring cultural impact.

"Brown presents a fresh take on a seemingly inexhaustible subject--Beatles people, you know you should be glad." Library Journal

Browne, David, 1960-

Crosby, Stills, Nash and Young : the wild, definitive saga of rock's greatest supergroup / David Browne. Da Capo Press, 2019. xiii, 465 p. **920**

1. Crosby, Stills, Nash & Young (Musical group) 2. Rock groups 3. Rock musicians 4. Fame 5. Artistic collaboration 6. Collective biographies
ISBN 9780306903281

LC 2018968044

Even in the larger-than-life world of rock and roll, it was hard to imagine four more different men. David Crosby, the opinionated hippie guru. Stephen Stills, the perpetually driven musician. Graham Nash, the tactful pop craftsman. Neil Young, the creatively restless loner. But together, few groups were as in sync with their times as Crosby, Stills, Nash and Young. But their story would rarely be as harmonious as their legendary and influential vocal blend. In the years that followed, these four volatile men would continually break up, reunite, and disband again--all against a backdrop of social and musical change, recurring disagreements and jealousies, and self-destructive tendencies that threatened to cripple them both as a group and as individuals.

Buckley, Gail Lumet, 1937-

★The **Black** Calhouns : from Civil War to civil rights with one African American family / Gail Lumet Buckley. Atlantic Monthly, 2016. 336 p. **920**

1. African American families 2. African Americans 3. African American civil rights workers 4. Social change. 5. New York City -- Race relations 6. Atlanta, Georgia -- Race relations 7. Collective biographies
ISBN 9780802124548

LC 2016304588

The daughter of actress Lena Horne traces the story of her family between two major human rights periods in America, sharing the stories of her house-slave-turned-businessman ancestor, the branches of her family that lived in the North and South and their experiences during the Jim Crow and wartime eras.

Burke, Carolyn

Foursome : Alfred Stieglitz, Georgia O'Keeffe, Paul Strand, Rebecca Salsbury / Carolyn Burke. Alfred A. Knopf, 2019. 432 p. **920**

1. O'Keeffe, Georgia, 1887-1986 2. Stieglitz, Alfred, 1864-1946 3. Strand, Paul, 1890-1976 4. James, Rebecca Salsbury, 1891-1968 5. Artists 6. Painters 7. Art, American -- 20th century 8. Photographers 9. Collective biographies
ISBN 9780307957290

LC 2018016794

A portrait of the intense relationship among Alfred Stieglitz, Georgia O'Keeffe, Paul Stand and Rebecca Salsbury explores how their strong personalities, passions and aesthetic ideals shaped their bonds and influenced 20th-century art. By the author of No Regrets.

Cadbury, Deborah

Princes at war : the bitter battle inside Britain's royal family in the darkest days of WWII / Deborah Cadbury. Public Affairs, 2015. 320 p. **920**

1. Windsor, Edward, Duke of, 1894-1972 Abdication, 1936. 2. George VI, King of Great Britain, 1895-1952. 3. Windsor, House of History -- 20th century 4. Princes 5. Royal houses 6. Rulers 7. Monarchy -- Great Britain -- History -- 20th century 8. Great Britain -- Rulers 9. Great Britain -- History -- Edward VIII, 1936. 10. Great Britain -- History -- George VI, 1936-1952. 11. Collective biographies
ISBN 9781610394031

LC 2014957933

"Bias aside, this is an engaging, well-told history of England and its royals during its most fragile period; conveying wartime tensions, worldwide scandals, and familial devotions and rivalries with equal vividness." Library Journal.

Cameron, Steve, 1981-

Hockey Hall of Fame book of players / edited by Steve Cameron. Firefly Books, 2018. 336 p. : **920**

1. Hockey Hall of Fame. 2. National Hockey League 3. Hockey players 4. Hockey -- History. 5. Collective biographies
ISBN 9781770855977

Includes index.

From early pioneers to women's hockey legends to modern NHL superstars, profiles every player who has been inducted into the Hockey Hall of Fame. Includes statistics and archival photos for each player.

Caroli, Betty Boyd

First ladies : the ever changing role, from Martha Washington to Melania Trump / Betty Caroli. Oxford University Press, 2019, c1987. 496 p. **920**

1. Presidents' spouses -- United States 2. Women -- United States 3. United States -- History. 4. Collective biographies

ISBN 9780190669133

LC 2019004676

Originally published: New York : Oxford University Press, 1987.

Betty Boyd Caroli's engrossing and informative First Ladies is both a captivating read and an essential resource for anyone interested in the role of America's First Ladies. Caroli observes the role as it has shifted and evolved from ceremonial backdrop to substantive world figure. This expanded and updated fifth edition presents Caroli's keen political analysis and astute observations of recent developments in First Lady history, including Melania Trump's reluctance to take on the mantle and former First Lady Hilary Clinton's recent run for president. Caroli here contributes a new preface and updated chapters. -- From publisher description

Lady Bird and Lyndon : the hidden story of a marriage that made a president / Betty Boyd Caroli. Simon & Schuster, 2015. 544 p. **920**

1. Johnson, Lady Bird, 1912-2007. 2. Johnson, Lyndon B., 1908-1973. 3. Married people. 4. Presidents' spouses. 5. Presidents. 6. Collective biographies

ISBN 9781439191224

LC 2015011027

A fresh look at Lady Bird Johnson that upends her image as a plain Jane who was married for her money and mistreated by Lyndon. This Lady Bird worked quietly behind the scenes through every campaign, every illness, and a trying presidency as a key strategist, fundraiser, barnstormer, peacemaker, and indispensable therapist.

"Caroli's suggestion and amplification of a virtual pact teased out of Lyndon and Bird's correspondence during a very brief courtship frames the story of this alliance. Recommended for history buffs and devotees of human behavior." Library Journal.

Carter, Alice A.

The **Red** Rose girls : an uncommon story of art and love / Alice A. Carter. H.N. Abrams, 2000. 216 p. : **920**

1. Smith, Jessie Willcox, 1863-1935. 2. Elliott, Elizabeth Shippen Green. 3. Oakley, Violet, 1874- 4. Women artists -- United States 5. Lesbian artists -- United States 6. Artists -- United States 7. Artists' studios -- Pennsylvania -- Philadelphia Region. 8. Collective biographies

ISBN 0810944375

LC 99039866

"Three of the first American women artists to achieve fame and fortune in the Victorian era--Jessie Willcox Smith, Elizabeth Shippen Green and Violet Oakley--lived unconventional lives marked by a remarkable degree of collaboration. In this study, Carter explores the trio's internecine artistic and romantic relations." Publishers Weekly.

Chaffin, Tom

Revolutionary brothers : Thomas Jefferson, the Marquis de Lafayette, and the friendship that helped forge two nations / Tom Chaffin. St. Martin's Press, 2019. 528 p. **920**

1. Jefferson, Thomas, 1743-1826 2. Lafayette, Marie Joseph Paul Yves Roch Gilbert Du Motier, marquis de, 1757-1834 3. Diplomats -- United States 4. Revolutionaries -- France 5. Alliances 6. Friendship 7. United States -- History -- Revolution, 1775-1783 -- Participation, French 8. France -- History -- Revolution, 1789-1799 9. United States -- Politics and government -- 18th century 10. United States -- Politics and government -- 19th century 11. Collective biographies

ISBN 9781250113726

LC 2019024564

The author offers a panoramic analysis of the four-decade friendship between Thomas Jefferson and the Marquis de Lafayette, drawing on primary sources to explore the role of their political strategies and interventions in two major revolutions.

Cheever, Susan

American Bloomsbury : Louisa May Alcott, Ralph Waldo Emerson, Margaret Fuller, Nathaniel Hawthorne, and Henry David Thoreau : their lives, their loves, their work / Susan Cheever. Simon & Schuster, c2006. xvi, 223 p., 8 p. of plates : **920**

1. Authors, American -- Homes and haunts -- Concord, Massachusetts. 2. Authors, American -- 19th century 3. Intellectual life -- Concord, Massachusetts -- 19th century. 4. Massachusetts in literature 5. Concord, Massachusetts. 6. Collective biographies

ISBN 0743264614

LC 2006045015

A portrait of five Concord, Massachusetts writers whose works were at the center of mid-nineteenth-century American thought and literature evaluates their interconnected relationships, influence on each other's works, and complex beliefs.

Cheney, Lynne V.

The **Virginia** dynasty : four presidents and the creation of the American nation / Lynne Cheney. Viking Press, 2020 576 p. **920**

1. Washington, George, 1732-1799. 2. Jefferson, Thomas, 1743-1826. 3. Madison, James, 1751-1836. 4. Monroe, James, 1758-1831. 5. Presidents -- United States 6. Politicians -- Virginia 7. Founding Fathers of the United States 8. United States -- Politics and government -- 1783-1865. 9. Virginia -- History -- 1775-1865 10. Collective biographies

ISBN 9781101980040

LC bl2020018419

A group portrait of America's first four Virginia Presidents focuses on a series of key historical episodes that illustrate how the myriad leadership roles of Washington, Jefferson, Madison and Monroe promoted transcendental, if contradictory, national views about freedom and equality

"Bringing these men together as a group draws attention to how their thought and action unfolded in response to new challenges and dispels any illusion that they were a monolithic bloc. Cheney is an adept writer who makes no wrong steps. Perfect for history buffs, though little new ground is tread." Library Journal

Chivers, C. J. (Christopher John)

The **fighters** : Americans in combat in Afghanistan and Iraq / C.J. Chivers. Simon & Schuster, 2018 xxiii, 374 p. : **920**

1. Iraq War, 2003-2011 2. Afghan War, 2001- 3. Soldiers 4. Pilots 5. United States -- Armed Forces 6. United States -- History, Military -- 21st century 7. Collective biographies

ISBN 9781451676648

LC 2018003987

The Pulitzer Prize-winning author traces the wars in Afghanistan and Iraq through its most at-risk participants, offering insights into such events as the hunt for bin Laden and counterguerilla warfare in the mountains of the Korengal Valley.

"Civilians will gain understanding of the military world. Prospective recruits will get an unvarnished look at what may await them: the challenges, the hardships, the glory, the camaraderie, and some of the things recruiters don't talk about." Booklist.

Clarke, Gemma

Soccerwomen : the icons, rebels, stars, and trailblazers who transformed the beautiful game / Gemma Clarke. Nation Books, [2019] 304 p. **920**

1. Women soccer players 2. Women and sports. 3. Women athletes. 4. Soccer players 5. Collective biographies
ISBN 9781568589213

LC 2018050633

Based on more than 50 interviews with current and former players and coaches, a British sports journalist celebrates the elite athletes of women's professional soccer, including profiles on Mia Hamm, Abby Wambach, Marta and Sun Wen.

"Similar to Gwendolyn Oxenham's recent Under the Lights and in the Dark, while offering more of a historical perspective on the women's game. Soccer fans will enjoy learning more about these athletes." Library Journal.

Clavin, Thomas

The **DiMaggios** : three brothers, their passion for baseball, their pursuit of the American dream / Tom Clavin. HarperCollins, 2013. 288 p. **920**

1. DiMaggio, Joe, 1914-1999. 2. DiMaggio, Vince. 3. DiMaggio, Dom. 4. New York Yankees (Baseball team) 5. Boston Red Sox (Baseball team) 6. Professional baseball players 7. Professional baseball. 8. Brothers 9. Popular culture -- History -- 20th century. 10. United States -- Popular culture -- History -- 20th century. 11. Collective biographies.
ISBN 9780062183774

LC 2013443409

Drawing from a vast of array of source materials, interviews with family members and teammates, and in-depth reporting, this Great American Story traces the DiMaggio brothers' rise to fame in American sports and popular culture.

Clavin, Thomas

Dodge City : Wyatt Earp, Bat Masterson, and the wickedest town in the American West / Tom Clavin. St. Martin's Press, 2017. 384 p. **920**

1. Earp, Wyatt, 1848-1929. 2. Masterson, Bat, 1853-1921. 3. Peace officers. 4. Outlaws. 5. Frontier and pioneer life. 6. Dodge City, Kansas -- History -- 19th century. 7. Kansas -- History -- 19th century. 8. Collective biographies
ISBN 9781250071484

LC 2016038741

Well known as an inspiration for many of Hollywood's Wild West shoot-em-ups, 1870s Dodge City, Kansas was a supply center, a railhead, and a host to gigantic stockyards. Attracting characters of all types, it existed on the fuzzy boundary between law and lawlessness, where tough and fearless men, among them Bat Masterson and Wyatt Earp, kept order. In this vivid portrait of the city and its denizens, award-winning journalist Tom Clavin traces Masterson's and Earp's careers, culminating with the final battle, called the Dodge City War, between lawmen and desperados. Wild West aficionados will find Dodge City un-put-downable.

"This is an enjoyable saga, appealing to both Old West aficionados and general readers." Booklist.

Clavin, Thomas

Tombstone : the Earp brothers, Doc Holliday, and the vendetta ride from hell / Tom Clavin. St. Martin's Press, 2020. 448 p. : **920**

1. Earp, Wyatt, 1848-1929. 2. Earp, Morgan, 1851-1882. 3. Holliday, John Henry, 1851-1887. 4. Gunfights 5. Frontier and pioneer life 6. Outlaws 7. Feuds 8. Arizona (Territory) -- History -- 19th century 9. Tombstone, Arizona -- History -- 19th century. 10. The West (United States) -- History -- 19th century 11. O. K. Corral, Arizona -- History 12. Collective biographies
ISBN 9781250214584

LC 2019035020

Chronicles the true story of Wyatt, Virgil and Morgan Earp and the famous Fight at the OK Corral.

"Readers who enjoyed the first two books in this popular history trilogy will look forward to this excellent and fitting conclusion on one famous town of the 'Wild West.'" Library Journal

Clay, Catrine

King, Kaiser, Tsar : three royal cousins who led the world to war / Catrine Clay. Walker, 2007, c2006. xiii, 416 p. : **920**

1. George V, King of Great Britain, 1865-1936 2. William II, German Emperor, 1859-1941 3. Nicholas II, Emperor of Russia, 1868-1918 4. Heads of state -- Europe. 5. World War I. 6. Rulers. 7. Europe -- Rulers. 8. Great Britain -- History -- George V, 1910-1936. 9. Germany -- History -- William II, 1888-1918. 10. Russia -- History -- Nicholas II, 1894-1917. 11. Collective biographies
ISBN 0802716237

LC bl2007016520

Originally published: London : John Murray, 2006.

Profiles three royal cousins--George V of England, Kaiser Wilhelm II of Germany, and Tsar Nicholas II of Russia--whose actions shaped the course of twentieth-century history, drawing on hitherto unpublished diaries and letters.

"This is a biography of not one but three significant men. King George V of England, Kaiser Wilhelm II of Germany, and Tsar Nicholas II of Russia (familiarly known as Georgie, Willy, and Nicky) were more than just the leaders of three of the most powerful countries in the world in the early 20th century--they were cousins who had grown up together, played together, and attended family functions together. [The author] provides an intimate look inside the lives of these boys as they grew into manhood and became king, kaiser, and tsar, bringing new pleasures and details to a well-known subject." Library Journal.

Clinton, Hillary Rodham

The **book** of gutsy women : favorite stories of courage and resilience / Hillary Rodham Clinton and Chelsea Clinton. Simon & Schuster, 2019. 464 p. **920**

1. Women 2. Resilience (Personal quality) 3. Courage 4. Determination in women 5. Collective biographies 6. Essays
ISBN 9781501178412

LC bl2019028632

Hillary Rodham Clinton and her daughter, Chelsea, share the stories of the gutsy women who have inspired them; women with the courage to stand up to the status quo, ask hard questions, and get the job done.

"A book to savor over multiple sittings, allowing readers to revisit well-known heroines or discover new ones among the pages." Library Journal

Cohan, William D.

Four friends : promising lives cut short / William D. Cohan. St Martins Pr 2019 400 p. **920**

1. Kennedy, John F. Jr., 1960-1999 2. Cohan, William D. 3. Phillips Academy, Andover, Massachusetts 4. Friends' death 5. Premature death 6. Loss (Psychology) 7. Violent deaths 8. Collective

biographies
ISBN 9781250070524

LC 2019002980

The award-winning author of The Last Tycoons shares a powerful portrait of four of his fellow Andover boarding-school graduates, including John F. Kennedy, Jr., whose lives were cut short by tragedy.

"The titular friends who serve as the subject of this latest from Cohan (The Last Tycoons) are linked by two experiences: their years at Phillips Andover Academy, MA, and the tragedy of early death." Library Journal.

Cohen, Lisa, 1962-

All we know : three lives / Lisa Cohen. Farrar, Straus and Giroux, 2012. 429 p. **920**

1. Murphy, Esther, 1898-1962. 2. Acosta, Mercedes de, 1893-1968. 3. Garland, Madge, 1896-1990. 4. Lesbians. 5. Women intellectuals. 6. Women 7. Glamour. 8. Collective biographies.
ISBN 9780374176495

LC 2011041055

National Book Critics Circle Award for Biography finalist, 2012.

A revelatory account of the lives of New York intellectual Esther Murphy, celebrity ephemera collector Mercedes de Acosta and British Vogue editor Madge Garland explores their glamorous but controversial lifestyles, influence on fashion and celebrity friendships.

Coll, Steve

The **Bin** Ladens: an Arabian family in the American century / Steve Coll. Penguin Press, 2008. 671 p., 8 p. of plates : **920**

1. Bin Laden, Osama, 1957-2011 2. Bin Laden family. 3. Terrorism 4. International relations 5. September 11 Terrorist Attacks, 2001 6. Saudi Arabia -- History -- 20th century. 7. Middle East -- History -- 20th century. 8. Collective biographies
ISBN 9781594201646

LC 2007042748

ALA Notable Book, 2009.

National Book Critics Circle Award for Biography finalist, 2008.

Pulitzer Prize for Biography or Autobiography finalist, 2009.

Traces the Bin Laden family's rise to power and privilege, describes the diverse lifestyles of the generation to which Osama bin Laden belongs, and discusses their attempts to recover from the effects of September 11.

Collins, Max Allan

Scarface and the Untouchable : Al Capone, Eliot Ness, and the battle for Chicago / Max Allan Collins, with A. Brad Schwartz. HarperCollins 2018 400 p. **920**

1. Capone, Al, 1899-1947 2. Ness, Eliot 3. Gangsters 4. Prohibition 5. Government investigators 6. Organized crime 7. Chicago, Illinois 8. Biographies 9. Collective biographies
ISBN 9780062441942

LC 2018024767

A groundbreaking dual biography of notorious gangster Al Capone and Prohibition agent Eliot Ness explores the violence and corruption of 1930s Chicago and the history-shaping raids and arrests made by the legendary Untouchables.

"The authors' intent is to take two men who have been mythologized over decades, strip away the fictions that have been piled on them, and leave us with a clearer sense of the true Ness and Capone. And they succeed admirably." Booklist.

Cook, Kevin, 1953-

Tommy's honor : the story of old Tom Morris and young Tom Morris, golf's founding father and son / Kevin Cook. Gotham Books, c2007. 327 p. : **920**

1. Morris, Old Tom, 1821-1908. 2. Morris, Tommy, 1851-1875. 3. Golfers -- Scotland 4. Golf -- Scotland -- History -- 19th century. 5. Fathers and sons 6. Scotland -- Social life and customs -- 19th century 7. Collective biographies
ISBN 1592402976

LC 2007008165

A tribute to the professional achievements of the father-and-son team of Tom and Tom Morris cites their pivotal contributions to the founding of golf in the 1800s, the differences in their athletic styles, and young Tom's tragic early death.

"In Cook's telling, the story of Tom Morris, winner of golf's first Open Championship in 1860, and his son, Tommy, who won the Open three years in a row, becomes a compelling saga of near-Homeric proportions." Booklist.

Cooney, Kara

When women ruled the world : six queens of Egypt / Kara Cooney. National Geographic, 2018. 400 p. **920**

1. Women rulers 2. Gender role 3. Leadership in women 4. Patriarchy 5. Ancient Egypt -- History -- To 332 B.C. 6. Ancient Egypt -- Civilization -- To 332 B.C. 7. Egypt -- Rulers 8. Collective biographies
ISBN 9781426219771

LC 2018377472

A professor of Egyptology at UCLA explores the lives of the queens of Egypt, including Hatshepsut, Nefertiti, and Cleopatra, who transcended traditional patriarchal obstacles and describes what the modern world can learn from example.

"Not since Leonard Cottrell's Lady of the Two Lands (1966) has such an engrossing, well-researched collective study of Egyptian power queens been available." Library Journal.

Cornejo Villavicencio, Karla

The **undocumented** Americans / Karla Cornejo Villavicencio. One World, 2020. xvii, 185 p. ; **920**

1. Cornejo Villavicencio, Karla 2. Undocumented immigrants 3. Undocumented workers 4. Immigrant families 5. Hispanic Americans 6. United States -- Immigration and emigration 7. United States -- Social conditions 8. Collective biographies
ISBN 9780399592683

LC 2018039595

An Ivy League-educated DACA beneficiary reveals the hidden lives of her fellow undocumented Americans, from the volunteers recruited for the 9/11 Ground Zero cleanup to the homeopathy botanicas of Miami that provide limited health care to non-citizens.

"A must-read indictment on what it means to be undocumented and what it means to be American." Library Journal

Cozzens, Peter, 1957-

★ **Tecumseh** and the prophet : the Shawnee brothers who defied a nation / Peter Cozzens. Alfred A. Knopf, 2020. 560 p. **920**

1. Tecumseh, Shawnee Chief, 1768-1813 2. Tenskwatawa, Shawnee Prophet 3. Shawnee Indians 4. Shawnee Indians -- History 5. Shawnee Indians -- Wars -- 1750-1815 6. Indians of North America -- Wars 7. Great Lakes region 8. Ohio River Valley 9. Collective biographies
ISBN 9781524733254

LC 2019052436

"This is a Borzoi book"--Title page verso.

The first biography of the great Shawnee leader in more than 20 years, and the first to make clear that his misunderstood younger brother,

Tenskwatawa, was an equal partner in the last great pan-Indian alliance against the United States. Detailed research of Native American society and customs provides a window into a world often erased from history books and reveals how both men came to power in different but no less important ways.

"Tecumseh's life and the wider struggle for the Great Lakes and Ohio River valley now has a current, solid work by an accomplished author." Library Journal

Crown, Sarah Rose

★**D-Day** girls : the untold story of the female spies who helped win World War Two / Sarah Rose Crown. Crown, [2019] 320 p. **920**

1. Odette, 1912-1995. 2. Baissac, Lise de, 1905-2004. 3. Borrel, Andree, 1919-1944. 4. Women spies -- Great Britain 5. Secret service 6. Spies 7. Intelligence service -- Great Britain -- History -- 20th century 8. Collective biographies

ISBN 9780451495082

LC 2018038372

"The dramatic, inspiring story of the extraordinary women recruited by Britain's elite spy agency to sabotage the Nazis, shore up the Resistance, and pave the way for Allied victory in World War II."--Provided by publisher.

"Thoroughly researched and written as smoothly as a good thriller, this is a mesmerizing story of creativity, perseverance, and astonishing heroism." Publishers Weekly.

Damrosch, Leopold

The **Club** : Johnson, Boswell, and the friends who shaped an age / Leo Damrosch. Yale University Press, 2019. 472 p. **920**

1. Johnson, Samuel, 1709-1784 2. Boswell, James, 1740-1795 3. Intellectuals 4. Authors 5. Clubs 6. Conversation 7. London, England -- History -- 18th century 8. Great Britain -- History -- 18th century 9. Collective biographies

ISBN 9780300217902

LC 2018952381

Brings to life a brilliant and eccentric cast of characters known simply as "the Club," a group of extraordinary writers, artists and thinkers who gathered weekly at a London tavern, whose friendship with Samuel Johnson and James Boswell stand at the heart of the narrative, conjuring the exciting, often brutal world of late 18th-century Britain.

"Enriched with well-chosen color plates and black-and-white illustrations, this is an excellent introduction to Johnson and his world for the novice and a pleasant retelling for the initiated." Library Journal.

Dance, Stanley, 1910-1999

The **world** of Earl Hines / Stanley Dance. Da Capo Press, 1983, c1977. ix, 324 p. : **920**

1. Jazz musicians 2. Jazz music. 3. Collective biographies

ISBN 0306801825

LC 82025252

Originally published: New York : Scribner, 1977. (The World of swing ; v. 2)

Includes index.

"This book consists of numerous tape-recorded and edited interviews with musicians and vocalists associated with Basie, and each gets to tell his own story. Many overlap and there are interesting confirmations and disputes over details. The language has been polished (and no doubt in some cases cleaned up), but Dance does not noticeably impose his own views on others. There are good photographs." Choice.

Davenport, Christian

The **space** barons : Jeff Bezos, Elon Musk, and the quest to colonize the cosmos / Christian Davenport. PublicAffairs, [2018] 320 p. **920**

1. Bezos, Jeffrey 2. Musk, Elon 3. Blue Origen (Firm). 4. SpaceX (Firm). 5. Space exploration 6. Space industrialization 7. Industrialists 8. Entrepreneurs 9. Space -- Civilian use 10. Collective biographies 11. Biographies

ISBN 9781610398299

LC 2017053089

Traces the historic quest to rekindle the human exploration of space as navigated by billionaire entrepreneurs, sharing insights into how professional rivalry and Silicon Valley innovations are lowering the cost of space travel and exceeding the achievements of NASA.

Davis, William C., 1946-

Crucible of command : Ulysses S. Grant and Robert E. Lee : the war they fought, the peace they forged / William C. Davis. Da Capo Pr., 2015. 448 p. **920**

1. Grant, Ulysses S., 1822-1885 Military leadership. 2. Lee, Robert E. (Robert Edward), 1807-1870 Military leadership. 3. Generals. 4. Civil War. 5. Command of troops. 6. Military strategy. 7. United States -- History -- Civil War, 1861-1865 8. Collective biographies. 9. Biographies.

ISBN 9780306822452

LC 2013497767

A dual biography sheds new light of the two iconic leaders--who determined the outcome of the Civil War and cast competing styles for the reunited nation--by exploring their personalities, character and their ethical, moral and political worlds.

De Courcy, Anne

The **husband** hunters : American heiresses who married into the British aristocracy / Anne De Courcy. St. Martin's Press, 2018, c2017. 368 p. **920**

1. Americans in Great Britain 2. Nouveaux riches 3. Aristocracy -- Great Britain 4. Heirs and heiresses 5. Great Britain -- Social conditions -- 19th century. 6. Great Britain -- Social conditions -- 20th century. 7. Collective biographies

ISBN 9781250164599

LC 2018013474

Originally published: London : Weidenfeld & Nicolson, 2017.

Describes the years between 1874 and 1904, a period that saw an unprecedented amount of young, American heiresses marrying into the British peerage, trading their New World wealth for Old World titles and sophistication.

De Semlyen, Nick

Wild and crazy guys : how the comedy mavericks of the '80s changed Hollywood forever / Nick De Semlyen. Crown Archetype, [2019] xvii, 331 pages, 8 unnumbered pages of plates : **920**

1. Aykroyd, Dan, 1952- 2. Belushi, John, 1949-1982 3. Candy, John, 1950-1994 4. Chase, Chevy, 1943- 5. Martin, Steve, 1945- 6. Murphy, Eddie, 1961- 7. Murray, Bill, 1950 September 21- 8. Saturday Night Live (Television program) 9. Comedians 10. Comedy films 11. Actors and actresses 12. Film industry and trade 13. Collective biographies

ISBN 9781984826640

LC bl2019014657

Featuring icons like Bill Murray, Steve Martin and Eddie Murphy--and covering films like Animal House, Caddyshack and Ghostbusters--the author tells the behind-the-scenes story of the comedy misfits who ruled 1980s Hollywood and the beloved films that made them famous.

"Children of the 1980s, take note: this is a fond, engrossing look back at the making of movies that became cultural touchstones, with plenty of behind-the-scenes details about the key male performers who brought them to life." Booklist.

DePalma, Anthony

The **Cubans** : ordinary lives in extraordinary times / Anthony DePalma. Viking, [2020] 368 p. **920**

1. Everyday life 2. Island life 3. Resilience (Personal quality) 4. Poverty 5. Havana, Cuba 6. Cuba -- History -- 1959-1990. 7. Cuba -- History -- 1990- 8. Collective biographies

ISBN 9780525522447

LC 2019052262

Includes index.

A foreign correspondent for the New York Times creates a snapshot of modern Cuba by focusing on a single neighborhood near Old Havana and describing their optimism towards the future as well as the huge challenges they still face.

"Overall, a rich, intimate, evenhanded narrative that reveals the Cuban people's resilience and resourcefulness amid oppression." Library Journal

DeWees, Shelley

Not just Jane : rediscovering seven amazing women writers who transformed British literature / Shelley DeWees. HarperCollins, 2016. 352 p. **920**

1. Women authors 2. Authors, English -- 19th century 3. Women authors, English 4. English literature -- 19th century -- History and criticism 5. Collective biographies 6. Biographies

ISBN 9780062394620

LC 2016001019

Weaving together history, biography and critical analysis, a vastly entertaining volume focuses on the creative contributions and personal stories of seven long-forgotten woman authors, including Charlotte Turner Smith and Mary Elizabeth Braddon, and realizes why, now more than ever, that it's vital we remember.

"In addition to being a lively read, this group biography is an important contribution to the scholarship of womens literature." Booklist.

Demick, Barbara

★**Nothing** to envy : ordinary lives in North Korea / Barbara Demick. Spiegel & Grau, 2009. 336 p. **920**

1. Kim, Chong-il, 1942-2011. 2. Kim, Il-song, 1912-1994. 3. Government services. 4. Dictatorship 5. Totalitarianism. 6. North Korea 7. North Korea -- Social conditions. 8. North Korea -- Economic conditions. 9. Collective biographies

ISBN 9780385523905

LC bl2009000139

ALA Notable Book, 2011.

BBC Samuel Johnson Prize for Non-Fiction, 2010.

National Book Award for Nonfiction finalist, 2010.

National Book Critics Circle Award for Nonfiction finalist, 2010.

Follows the lives of six North Koreans over fifteen years, a chaotic period that saw the rise to power of Kim Jong Il and the devastation of a famine that killed one-fifth of the population, illustrating what it means to live under the most repressive totalitarian regime today.

"Strongly written and gracefully structured, Demick's potent blend of personal narratives and piercing journalism vividly and evocatively portrays courageous individuals and a tyrannized state within a saga of unfathomable suffering punctuated by faint glimmers of hope." Booklist.

Doherty, Maggie

The **equivalents** : a story of art, female friendship, and liberation in the 1960s / Maggie Doherty. Alfred A. Knopf, 2020. 352 p. **920**

1. Radcliffe Institute for Independent Study 2. Women artists 3. Feminism 4. Self-fulfillment in women 5. Scholarships and fellowships 6. Cambridge, Massachusetts 7. Collective biographies

ISBN 9781524733056

LC 2019036686

The timely, never-before-told story of five brilliant, passionate women who, in the early 1960s, converged at the newly founded Radcliffe Institute for Independent Study and became friends as well as artistic collaborators, and who went on to shape the course of feminism in ways that are still felt today. Poets Anne Sexton and Maxine Kumin, painter Barbara Swan, sculptor Mariana Pineda, and writer Tillie Olsen--quickly formed deep bonds with one another that would inspire and sustain their most ambitious work. They called themselves "the Equivalents."

"Harvard University lecturer Doherty debuts with an elegant, novelistic history of the Radcliffe Institute for Independent Study and its influence on the lives and careers of five female artists and the women's movement at large. . . . This empathetic, wide-angled portrait will resonate with fans of the individual artists as well as feminists and readers of women's history." Publishers Weekly

Downing, Taylor

Secret warriors : the spies, scientists and code breakers of World War I / Taylor Downing. Pegasus Books, 2015. 464 p. **920**

1. World War I 2. Technology and war 3. Scientists 4. Inventors 5. Collective biographies

ISBN 9781605986944

LC 2016303544

Describes the scientists, engineers, doctors and mathematicians who were fighting World War I from the homefront, making positive and integral contributions in the areas of code-breaking, aeronautics and research that resulted in some of the century's most significant strides forward.

"This volume should be of interest to most readers, especially those interested in military history." Library Journal.

Dubbs, Chris (Military historian)

An **unladylike** profession : American women war correspondents in World War I / Chris Dubbs ; foreword by Judy Woodruff. Potomac Books, 2020. 336 p. **920**

1. World War I 2. Women war correspondents -- United States 3. Women journalists 4. War in the news media 5. Collective biographies

ISBN 9781640123069

LC 2019053513

Chris Dubbs tells the fascinating stories of Edith Wharton, Nellie Bly, and more than thirty other American women who worked as war reporters. As Dubbs shows, stories by these journalists brought in women from the periphery of war and made them active participants--fully engaged and equally heroic, if bearing different burdens and making different sacrifices. Women journalists traveled from belligerent capitals to the front lines to report on the conflict. But their experiences also brought them into contact with social transformations, political unrest, labor conditions, campaigns for women's rights, and the rise of revolutionary socialism.

"Delivers a rousing narrative of adventurous women, passionate about their careers, who broke free from oppressive gender norms to accomplish their goals. Hand this book to World War I aficionados and casual history buffs." Booklist

Duberman, Martin B.

Hold tight gently : Michael Callen, Essex Hemphill, and the Battlefield of AIDS / Martin Duberman. New Press, The, [2014] 368 p. **920**

1. Callen, Michael, 1955-1993. 2. Hemphill, Essex. 3. Gay men 4. AIDS (Disease) 5. People with AIDS 6. AIDS activists 7. Collective biographies

ISBN 9781595589453

LC 2013039158

Lambda Literary Award for LGBT Nonfiction

"This combination of cautionary tale, history, and dual biography of compelling, if obscure, artist-activists is fluidly written." Library Journal.

Duncombe, Laura Sook

Pirate women : the princesses, prostitutes, and privateers who ruled the Seven Seas / Laura Sook Duncombe. Chicago Review Press, Incorporated, [2017] 250 p. **920**

1. Women pirates 2. Piracy -- History. 3. Privateering -- History. 4. Seafaring life 5. Collective biographies

ISBN 9781613736012

LC 2016031175

"Duncombe's well-researched account will appeal to history and womens studies aficionados, lovers of myth and lore, and all interested in viewing the past through a new lens." Booklist.

Eig, Jonathan

★The **birth** of the pill : how four crusaders reinvented sex and launched a revolution / Jonathan Eig. W. W. Norton & Company, 2014 400 p. **920**

1. McCormick, Katherine Dexter, 1876-1967. 2. Pincus, Gregory, 1903-1967. 3. Rock, John, 1890-1984. 4. Sanger, Margaret, 1879-1966. 5. Oral contraceptives. 6. Birth control -- United States -- History. 7. Feminism. 8. Contraception. 9. Collective biographies

ISBN 9780393073720

LC 2014019355

ALA Notable Book, 2015.

We know it simply as "the pill", yet its genesis was anything but simple. Jonathan Eig's masterful narrative revolves around four principal characters: the fiery feminist Margaret Sanger, who was a champion of birth control in her campaign for the rights of women but neglected her own children in pursuit of free love; the beautiful Katharine McCormick, who owed her fortune to her wealthy husband, the son of the founder of International Harvester and a schizophrenic; the visionary scientist Gregory Pincus, who was dismissed by Harvard in the 1930s as a result of his experimentation with in vitro fertilization but who, after he was approached by Sanger and McCormick, grew obsessed with the idea of inventing a drug that could stop ovulation; and the telegenic John Rock, a Catholic doctor from Boston who battled his own church to become an enormously effective advocate in the effort to win public approval for the drug that would be marketed by Searle as Enovid.

Eilenberger, Wolfram, 1972-

Time of the magicians : Wittgenstein, Benjamin, Cassirer, Heidegger, and the decade that reinvented philosophy / Wolfram Eilenberger ; translated by Shaun Whiteside. Penguin Press, 2020, c2018. 432 p. **920**

1. Wittgenstein, Ludwig, 1889-1951 2. Cassirer, Ernst, 1874-1945 3. Benjamin, Walter, 1892-1940 4. Heidegger, Martin, 1889-1976 5. Philosophers 6. Intellectuals 7. Philosophy, Modern 8. Scholars and academics 9. Collective biographies

ISBN 9780525559665

LC 2019050893

Originally published: Stuttgart : Klett-Cotta, 2018.

A grand narrative of the intertwining lives of Walter Benjamin, Martin Heidegger, Ludwig Wittgenstein, and Ernst Cassirer, major philosophers whose ideas shaped the twentieth century. The year is 1919. The horror of the First World War is still fresh for the protagonists, each of whom finds himself at a crucial juncture. The stage is set for a great intellectual drama, which will unfold across the next decade. The lives and ideas of this extraordinary philosophical quartet will converge as they become world historical figures. But as the Second World War looms on the horizon, their fates will be very different.

"A readable, expert introduction to some of the most abstruse yet influential philosophical thought of the 20th century. . . . The book's special value lies in greatly advancing accessibility to these men's works and thought." Kirkus

Eisen, Norman L., 1961-

The **last** palace : Europe's turbulent century in five lives and one legendary house / Norman Eisen. Crown Publishing, 2018. 368 p. **920**

1. Eisen, Norman L., 1961- Family 2. Palaces 3. Mansions 4. Diplomatic and consular service 5. War 6. Prague, Czech Republic 7. Czechoslovakia -- History -- 20th century 8. Europe -- History -- 20th century 9. Collective biographies

ISBN 9780451495785

LC 2018014382

A former U.S. ambassador describes the prior occupants of his residence in Prague, including a Jewish financial baron and a Nazi general who carved swastikas into the furniture, and in the process creates a detailed history of Central Europe in the 20th century.

Emling, Shelley

Marie Curie and her daughters : the private lives of science's first family / Shelley Emling. Palgrave Macmillan, 2012. 272 p. **920**

1. Curie, Marie, 1867-1934. 2. Joliot-Curie, Irene, 1897-1956. 3. Curie, Eve, 1904-2007. 4. Women scientists. 5. Mothers and daughters 6. Women chemists. 7. Women philanthropists. 8. Collective biographies

ISBN 9780230115712

LC 2012005625

"Marie Curie was the first person to be honored by two Nobel Prizes and she pioneered the use of radiation therapy for cancer patients. But she was also a mother, widowed young, who raised two extraordinary daughters alone: Irene, a Nobel Prize winning chemist in her own right, who played an important role in the development of the atomic bomb, and Eve, a highly regarded humanitarian and journalist, who fought alongside the French Resistance during WWII. As a woman fighting to succeed in a male dominated-profession and a Polish immigrant caught in a xenophobic society, she had to find ways to support her research. Drawing on personal interviews with Curie's descendents, as well as revelatory new archives, this is a wholly new story about Marie Curie--and a family of women inextricably connected to the dawn of nuclear physics".-- Provided by publisher.

Emre, Merve

The **personality** brokers : the strange history of Myers-Briggs and the birth of personality testing / Merve Emre. Doubleday, 2018. 336 p. **920**

1. Briggs, Katharine Cook 2. Myers, Isabel Briggs 3. Myers-Briggs Type Indicator 4. Personality tests 5. Mothers and daughters 6. Women authors 7. Collective biographies

ISBN 9780385541909

LC 2018011977

An unprecedented history of the personality test conceived a century ago by a mother and her daughter--fiction writers with no formal training in psychology--and how it insinuated itself into our boardrooms, classrooms, and beyond

Evans, Claire Lisa

Broad band : the untold story of the women who made the Internet / Claire L. Evans. Portfolio, 2018. 272 p. **920**

1. Women computer scientists. 2. Internet -- History. 3. Women and technology 4. Women computer programmers 5. Collective biographies

ISBN 9780735211759

LC 2017054620

Includes index.

The YACHT lead singer and VICE reporter celebrates the lesser-known contributions of women to the history of technology, sharing brief profiles of such boundary-breaking innovators as Ada Lovelace, Grace Hopper, Elizabeth "Jake" Feinler and Stacy Horn.

"From COBOL and ARPANET to Silicon Valley and cyberfeminism, women have always played a major role in developing computer technology. Now their collective stories are finally being shared in Evan's fascinating and inspiring work of womens' history." Booklist.

Eyman, Scott, 1951-

★**Hank** and Jim : the fifty-year friendship of Henry Fonda and James Stewart / Scott Eyman. Simon & Schuster, 2017. 416 p. **920**

1. Fonda, Henry, 1905-1982 2. Stewart, James, 1908-1997 3. Film actors and actresses 4. Friendship 5. Interpersonal relations 6. Family relationships 7. New York City 8. Hollywood, California 9. Collective biographies

ISBN 9781501102172

LC 2017011527

Scott Eyman tells the story of the remarkable friendship of two Hollywood legends who, though different in many ways, maintained a close friendship that endured all of life's twists and turns. A fascinating portrait of an extraordinary friendship that lasted through war, marriages, children, careers, and everything else.

"An entertaining, richly documented biography that will be appreciated by film and theater scholars as well as fans of these memorable actors." Kirkus.

Fehrman, Craig

Author in chief : the untold story of our presidents and the books they wrote / Craig Fehrman. Avid Reader Press, 2020. 416 p. **920**

1. Presidents -- United States 2. Authors 3. Books 4. Autobiography. 5. Collective biographies

ISBN 9781476786391

LC bl2020000504

In Craig Fehrman's groundbreaking work of history, Author in Chief, the story of America's presidents and their books opens a rich new window into presidential biography. From volumes lost to history--Calvin Coolidge's Autobiography, which was one of the most widely discussed titles of 1929--to ones we know and love--Barack Obama's Dreams from My Father, which was very nearly never published--Fehrman unearths countless insights about the presidents through their literary works.

"Illustrations grace the text, and extensive bibliographic notes brim with intriguing facts. Both history buffs and politics enthusiasts will relish this." Booklist

Feldman, Noah, 1970-

Scorpions : the battles and triumphs of FDR's great Supreme Court justices / Noah Feldman. Twelve, 2010. 448 p. **920**

1. Frankfurter, Felix, 1882-1965. 2. Black, Hugo LaFayette, 1886-1971. 3. Jackson, Robert, 1911-1977. 4. Douglas, William O. (William Orville), 1898-1980. 5. United States. Supreme Court. 6. Judges -- United States 7. Liberalism. 8. Conservatism. 9. Judicial system. 10. Collective biographies

ISBN 9780446580571

LC 2010007788

Includes index.

"The author argues that the distinctive constitutional theories of Roosevelt's four greatest justices, all of whom began as New Deal liberals--Hugo Black, William O. Douglas, Felix Frankfurter, and Robert Jackson--have continued to cover the whole field of constitutional thought up to the present day. This is a first-rate work of narrative history that succeeds in bringing the intellectual and political battles of the post-Roosevelt Court vividly to life." Publishers Weekly.

Field, Kendra Taira

★**Growing** up with the country : family, race, and nation after the Civil War / Kendra Taira Field. Yale University Press, 2018. 224 p. **920**

1. Field, Kendra Taira Genealogy 2. African American families 3. Freed slaves 4. Migration, Internal 5. Slaves -- Emancipation 6. Southern states 7. Oklahoma 8. The West (United States) -- History -- 19th century 9. Collective biographies

ISBN 9780300180527

LC 2017932063

The masterful and poignant story of three African-American families who journeyed west after emancipation, by an award-winning scholar and descendant of the migrants.

"A masterpiece in the areas of personal narration, family genealogy, and African American historiography. Highly recommended for U.S. Civil War/Reconstruction and African American scholars and enthusiasts, genealogical specialists, and all readers." Library Journal.

Figes, Orlando

The **Europeans** : three lives and the making of a cosmopolitan culture / Orlando Figes. Metropolitan Books, 2019. xix, 562 p., 16 unnumbered p. of plates : **920**

1. Turgenev, Ivan Sergeevich, 1818-1883. 2. Viardot, Louis, 1800-1883 3. Viardot-Garcia, Pauline, 1821-1910 4. Culture and globalization 5. Cosmopolitanism. 6. Art and culture. 7. Art and globalization. 8. Europe -- Intellectual life -- 19th century. 9. Europe -- Social life and customs -- 19th century 10. Collective biographies

ISBN 9781627792141

LC 2019035029

Using documents, letters and archival materials an acclaimed historian and author describes the first age of cultural globalization in the 1800s that led to heightened cosmopolitanism across a Europe that freely shared ideas and artistic creations between nations.

Finkel, David, 1955-

★**Thank** you for your service / David Finkel. Sarah Crichton Books, 2013. 256 p. : **920**

1. Veterans -- Psychology. 2. Iraq War, 2003-2011 -- Psychological aspects. 3. Homecomings 4. Post-traumatic stress disorder 5. United States -- Social life and customs -- 21st century. 6. Essays 7. Collective biographies

ISBN 9780374180669

LC 2013021990

National Book Critics Circle Award for Nonfiction finalist, 2013.

An award-winning staff writer for The Washington Post discusses the hardships faced by soldiers who have come home from service by following the men of the 2-16 Infantry Battalion originally depicted in his book The Good Soldiers.

"It is impossible not to be moved, outraged, and saddened by these stories, and Finkel's deeply personal brand of narrative journalism is both heartbreaking and gut-wrenching in its unflinching honesty." Booklist.

Flanders, Judith

A **circle** of sisters : Alice Kipling, Georgiana Burne-Jones, Agnes Poynter and Louisa Baldwin / Judith Flanders. W.W. Norton & Co. 2005. xxiii, 392 p. ; **920**

1. Baldwin, Louisa, 1845-1925. 2. Burne-Jones, Georgiana, Lady, 1840-1920. 3. Kipling, Alice, 1837-1910. 4. Poynter, Agnes, 1843-1906. 5. McDonald family. 6. Women -- Great Britain 7. Sisters -- Great Britain 8. Women -- Great Britain -- Social conditions -- 19th century. 9. Gender role 10. Great Britain 11. Great Britain -- Social life and customs -- 19th century. 12. Collective biographies.

ISBN 0393052109

LC 2004065415

Traces the lives and influences of the four MacDonald sisters of nineteenth-century Britain, citing their origins in the poorly educated lower-middle class, their identities as the wives or mothers of famous artists and leaders, and the social changes that enabled their achievements.

"Offering perceptive commentary on the prescribed role of women in Victorian society to be mere helpmeets, Flanders' attentive, scholarly accuracy is enhanced by piquant observations that demonstrate both her professional talent and personal take on the lives of these remarkable, but unremarked upon, women." Booklist.

Fox, James, 1945-

Five sisters : the Langhornes of Virginia / James Fox. Simon & Schuster, 2000, c1998. 496 p. : **920**

1. Langhorne family. 2. Astor, Nancy Witcher Langhorne, 1879-1964. 3. Brand, Phyllis, 1880-1937. 4. Americans in Great Britain 5. Gibson girls. 6. Sisters. 7. United States -- Social life and customs -- 20th century. 8. Virginia 9. Great Britain -- Social life and customs -- 20th century. 10. Collective biographies

ISBN 0684808129

LC 99041815

Originally published as The Langhorne sisters: London : Granta Books, 1998.

"Fox brings intimacy to these semi-public personalities, elevating a century's gossip and legend into absorbing history." The New Yorker.

Fox, Margalit

★The **riddle** of the labyrinth : the quest to crack an ancient code / Margalit Fox. HarperCollins, 2013. 400 p. **920**

1. Kober Alice, 1906-1950. 2. Ventris, Michael, 1922-1956. 3. Evans, Arthur, Sir, 1851-1941. 4. Women linguists. 5. Writing methods and systems. 6. Excavations (Archaeology) -- Crete. 7. Archaeology -- History. 8. Ancient Greece -- Antiquities. 9. Knossos, Crete (Extinct city) 10. Collective biographies.

ISBN 9780062228833

LC 2013404394

ALA Notable Book, 2014

William Saroyan International Prize for Writing, Nonfiction category, 2014.

An award-winning journalist presents a gripping, intellectual detective story set in the 1900s that follows the three men who were driven to unlock one of the great secrets of human history--the decipherment of an unknown script from the Aegean Bronze Age.

"This exciting linguistic adventure, intended for the nonspecialist, is recommended to anyone interested in archaeological mysteries--and even to crossword puzzle enthusiasts!" Library Journal.

Fraser, Antonia, 1932-

The **wives** of Henry VIII / Antonia Fraser. Knopf, 1992. ix, 479 p., 48 p. of plates : **920**

1. Catharine, of Aragon, Queen, consort of Henry VIII, King of England, 1485-1536. 2. Anne Boleyn, Queen, consort of Henry VIII, King of England, 1507-1536. 3. Jane Seymour, Queen, consort of Henry VIII, King of England, 1509?-1537. 4. Anne, of Cleves, Queen, consort of Henry VIII, King of England, 1515-1557. 5. Catherine Howard, Queen, consort of Henry VIII, King of England, d. 1542. 6. Catharine Parr, Queen, consort of Henry VIII, King of England, 1512-1548. 7. Henry VIII, King of England, 1491-1547 Marriage. 8. Marriages of royalty and nobility -- Great Britain -- History -- 16th century. 9. Women rulers -- Great Britain 10. Monarchy -- Great Britain 11. Great Britain -- History -- Henry VIII, 1509-1547 12. Collective biographies.

ISBN 9780394585383

LC 92052950

"Originally published in Great Britain in 1992 as: The six wives of Henry VIII by George Weidenfeld and Nicholson Limited"--T.p. verso.

Presents a provacative study of the diverse and complex characters of the the six wives of Henry VIII and their impact on the world.

Fraser, Flora

Princesses : the six daughters of George III / Flora Fraser. Knopf, 2005, c2004. xv, 478 p., [8] p. of plates : **920**

1. George III, King of Great Britain, 1738-1820 Family. 2. Charlotte, Queen, Consort of Frederick I, King of Wurttemberg, 1766-1828. 3. Augusta Sophia, Princess, daughter of George III, King of Great Britain, 1768-1840. 4. Elizabeth, Princess of England, 1770-1840. 5. Mary, Duchess of Gloucester, 1776-1857. 6. Sophia, Princess, daughter of George III, King of Great Britain, 1777-1848. 7. Amelia, Princess, daughter of George III, King of Great Britain, 1783-1810. 8. Princesses -- Great Britain 9. Collective biographies

ISBN 0679451188

Originally published: London : John Murray, 2004.

"This is a rich and richly hued Regency tale. Fraser is splendidly at home in the 18th century, adroit at teasing history out from between guarded lines." New York Times Book Review.

Fraser, Flora

The **Washingtons** : "join'd by friendship, crown'd by love" / Flora Fraser Alfred A. Knopf, 2015 448 p. **920**

1. Washington, George 1732-1799 2. Washington, Martha 1731-1802 3. Presidents' spouses 4. Presidents 5. Generals 6. Husband and wife 7. Collective biographies

ISBN 9780307272782

LC 2014045521

A full-scale portrait of the marriage of the father and mother of our country--and of the struggle for Independence that he led.

"Fraser's prose flows well with the voices of her 18th-century subjects. However, the impression that emerges from the copious details of plantation management, children's tutoring, and relatives born and dying is of two busy lives on parallel courses; their devotion to each other is clearly evident, but so are several potential sources of sharp conflict between them. Fraser provides no sense of how these shoals were negotiated or how these formidable individuals actually got on with each other when they could be together. A difficult task crowned with mixed success." Kirkus.

Freeman, Sally Mott

The **Jersey** brothers : a missing naval officer in the Pacific and his family's quest to bring him home / Sally Mott Freeman. Simon & Schuster, 2017. 576 p. **920**

1. Cross, Barton, 1918-1945 Family 2. Brothers 3. Missing in action 4. World War II -- Philippines 5. Soldiers 6. Biographies 7. Collective biographies

ISBN 9781501104145

LC 2016021592

Documents the extraordinary story of three brothers in World War II who found themselves at the epicenter of three of the war's most crucial moments, describing the rescue mission launched by the elder two when their youngest brother was declared missing in action in the Philippines. A first book.

"A grieving family ultimately finds closure in this meticulously researched and compelling history." Kirkus.

Frieda, Leonie

The **deadly** sisterhood : a story of women, power, and intrigue in the Italian Renaissance, 1427-1527 / Leonie Frieda. Harper Collins, 2013 448 p. **920**

1. Gonzaga family 2. Este family 3. Borgia family 4. Medici, House of. 5. Sforza family 6. Power (Social sciences) 7. Women rulers 8. European Renaissance -- Italy. 9. Italy -- Civilization -- 1268-1559. 10. Collective biographies

ISBN 9780061563089

LC 2013474176

Tells the story of the famous and infamous women of the late Italian Renaissance, tied together by political marriages and bloodlines, and reassesses the reputations of such figures as Isabella d'Este and Lucrezia Borgia.

Funk, Mason

★The **book** of pride : LGBTQ heroes who changed the world / Mason Funk. HarperOne, 2019. 288 p. **920**

1. LGBTQIA rights 2. Gay activists 3. Gay and Lesbian Movement 4. Gay men -- Rights 5. Collective biographies

ISBN 9780062571700

LC 2019006758

Paying tribute to more than 50 extraordinary and influential leaders who sparked the worldwide LGBTQ-rights movement, this important volume tells stories of dedication and triumph through never-before-published original interviews.

"Funk serves up a generous offering of 75 interviews with individuals whom the book's subtitle accurately calls LGBTQ Heroes Who Changed the World. Culled from the Outwords Archive, an oral-history project, these interviews represent an invaluable contribution to American LGBTQ+ history." Booklist.

Gabriel, Mary, 1955-

Love and capital : Karl and Jennie Marx and the birth of a revolution / Mary Gabriel. Little, Brown and Company, 2011. 800 p. **920**

1. Marx, Karl, 1818-1883. 2. Marx, Jenny, 1814-1881. 3. Revolutionaries. 4. Socialists. 5. Communists. 6. Husband and wife. 7. Collective biographies.

ISBN 9780316066112

LC 2010044021

National Book Award for Nonfiction finalist, 2011

National Book Critics Circle Award for Biography finalist, 2011.

Pulitzer Prize for Biography or Autobiography finalist, 2012.

An acclaimed biographer tells the story of the Karl and Jenny Marx's marriage, painting a unique and human picture of the revolutionary German socialist as a protective father, loving husband and a jokester.

Gabriel, Mary

★**Ninth** Street women : Lee Krasner, Elaine De Kooning, Grace Hartigan, Joan Mitchell, and Helen Frankenthaler: five painters and the movement that changed modern art / Mary Gabriel. Little Brown & Co, 2018. 568 p. **920**

1. Women artists 2. Creativity in women 3. Abstract expressionism 4. Nonconformists 5. New York City -- Social life and customs -- 20th century 6. United States -- Social life and customs -- 20th century. 7. Collective biographies

ISBN 9780316226189

LC bl2018185097

A National Book Award finalist describes the lives and careers of five pioneering women artists who entered the male-dominated world of mid-20th century abstract painting and changed their field and American society in the process.

"Biographer Gabriel corrects long-standing misperceptions about New York's abstract-expressionism movement by telling the dramatic, often traumatic stories of the five gifted and courageous women painters at the center of that radical flowering." Booklist.

Garcia, Mayte, 1973-

The **most** beautiful : my life with Prince / Mayte Garcia. Hachette Books, 2017. 304 p. **920**

1. Prince 2. Garcia, Mayte, 1973- 3. Rock musicians -- United States 4. Dancers -- United States 5. Couples 6. Love 7. Collective biographies 8. Autobiographies and memoirs

ISBN 9780316468978

LC 2016054437

A candid assessment of the iconic musician's personal and professional life by his first wife traces their long-distance courtship, marriage, and creative partnership as well as the challenges that compromised their romance.

"A genial, candid portrait of Prince's ill-fated turn as a family man." Kirkus.

Garrett, Kent

★The **last** negroes at Harvard : the class of 1963 and the 18 young men who changed Harvard forever / Kent Garrett and Jeanne Ellsworth. Houghton Mifflin Harcourt, 2020. 288 p. **920**

1. Garrett, Kent 2. Harvard University -- Students 3. Harvard University -- History 4. African American college students 5. African American men 6. Discrimination in universities and colleges -- United States. 7. Racism 8. Cambridge, Massachusetts 9. United States -- Race relations -- History -- 20th century. 10. United States -- Social life and customs -- 20th century. 11. Collective biographies 12. Interviews

ISBN 9781328879974

LC 2019014973

A Harvard graduate who attended as one of 18 African-American recruits in an early affirmative-action program describes how he reconnected with his fellow graduates half a century later to learn their remarkable stories.

"Essential reading for those interested in civil rights, racial identity, and higher education." Library Journal

Gelwicks, Andrew

The **queer** advantage : conversations with LGBTQ+ leaders on the power of identity / Andrew Gelwicks Hachette Go, 2020. 528 p. **920**

1. LGBTQIA persons 2. Identity (Psychology) 3. Success (Concept) 4. Gay men 5. Collective biographies 6. Interviews
ISBN 9780306874628

LC 2020940814

Collecting incisive, deeply personal conversations with LGBTQ+ trailblazers about how they leveraged the challenges and insights they had as relative outsiders to succeed in the worlds of business, tech, politics, Hollywood, sports and beyond, The QueerAdvantage celebrates the unique, supercharged power of queerness.

"The result is a book that is both informative and inspirational." Booklist

Ghez, Didier

The **hidden** art of Disney's golden age : the 1930s / Didier Ghez ; foreword by Pete Docter. Chronicle Books, 2015 207 p. : **920**

1. Horvath, Ferdinand, 1891-1973. 2. Hurter, Albert. 3. Majolie, Bianca. 4. Tenggren, Gustaf, 1896-1970. 5. Walt Disney Productions -- History 20th century. 6. Animated films -- United States -- History -- 20th century 7. Animation (Cinematography) -- United States -- History -- 20th century 8. Animators -- United States 9. Cartoon characters 10. Collective biographies
ISBN 9781452137438

LC 2016439270

Introducing new biographical material about the artists and including largely unpublished artwork from the depths of the Walt Disney Archives and the Disney Animation Research Library, this volume offers a window into the most inspiring work created by the best Disney artists during the studio's early golden age.

Goldberg, Dan C., 1984-

The **golden** thirteen : how black men won the right to wear Navy gold / Dan C. Goldberg. Beacon Press, 2020. 288 p. **920**

1. United States. Navy African Americans 2. United States. Navy Officers 3. African American men 4. Social integration 5. World War II 6. Racism 7. United States -- Armed Forces -- African Americans 8. United States -- History, Naval -- 20th century 9. United States -- Race relations -- History -- 20th century 10. Collective biographies
ISBN 9780807021583

LC 2019059058

An award-winning journalist, through oral histories and original interviews with surviving family members, recounts the story of 13 courageous black men--the first to wear gold stripes--who integrated the officer corps of the US Navy during World War II.

"This stirring portrait shines a well-deserved spotlight on a little-known victory in the fight for civil rights." Publishers Weekly

Goldstein, Bill

The **world** broke in two : Virginia Woolf, T. S. Eliot, D. H. Lawrence, E. M. Forster and the year that changed literature / Bill Goldstein. Henry Holt and Co., 2017. 352 p. **920**

1. Eliot, T. S. (Thomas Stearns), 1888-1965. 2. Woolf, Virginia, 1882-1941. 3. Lawrence, D. H. (David Herbert), 1885-1930. 4. Forster, E. M. (Edward Morgan), 1879-1970. 5. Bloomsbury group. 6. Modernism (Literature) 7. Authors. 8. English fiction -- 20th century -- History and criticism. 9. Collective biographies
ISBN 9780805094022

LC 2017001569

"A literary history of the year 1922 in the lives of Virginia Woolf, D.H. Lawrence, E.M. Forster, and T.S. Eliot".-- Provided by publisher.

"Goldstein's ardently detailed, many-faceted story of a pivotal literary year illuminates all that these tormented visionaries had to overcome to 'make the modern happen.'" Booklist.

Goldstone, Lawrence, 1947-

★**Birdmen** : the Wright brothers, Glenn Curtiss, and the battle to control the skies / Lawrence Goldstone. Ballantine, 2014. 448 p. **920**

1. Wright, Orville, 1871-1948. 2. Wright, Wilbur, 1867-1912. 3. Curtiss, Glenn Hammond, 1878-1930. 4. Flight 5. Aviation -- United States -- History 6. Competition 7. Inventors 8. Collective biographies
ISBN 9780345538031

LC 2014001424

"A superbly crafted retelling of a story familiar to aviation buffs, here greatly strengthened by fresh perspectives, rigorous analyses, comprehensible science, and a driving narrative." Library Journal.

Goldstone, Nancy Bazelon

Daughters of the Winter Queen : four remarkable sisters, the crown of Bohemia, and the enduring legacy of Mary, Queen of Scots / Nancy Goldstone. Little, Brown and Company, 2018. 464 p. **920**

1. Elizabeth, Queen, consort of Frederick I, King of Bohemia, 1596-1662. 2. Elisabeth, Countess Palatine, 1618-1680. 3. Louise Hollandine, Countess Palatine, Abbess of Maubuisson, 1622-1709. 4. Sophia, Electress, consort of Ernest Augustus, Elector of Hanover, 1630-1714. 5. Women rulers. 6. Princesses. 7. Collective biographies
ISBN 9780316387910

LC bl2018003653

Documents how a betrayed Elizabeth Stuart, the daughter of James I, raised her four daughters in exile during the Dutch Golden Age, tracing how their stories shaped a three-decade war and fulfilled the promises of their great-grandmother, Mary Queen of Scots.

Goodwin, Doris Kearns

No ordinary time : Franklin and Eleanor Roosevelt : the home front in World War II / Doris Kearns Goodwin. Simon & Schuster, 1994. 759 p., 32 p. of plates : **920**

1. Roosevelt, Franklin D. (Franklin Delano), 1882-1945 2. Roosevelt, Eleanor, 1884-1962. 3. World War II -- United States. 4. Presidents -- United States 5. Women and politics. 6. Presidents' spouses -- United States 7. United States -- History -- 1933-1945. 8. Collective biographies
ISBN 0671642405

LC 94028565

ALA Notable Book, 1995.
Pulitzer Prize for History, 1995.

Presents a social history of the United States in 1940, along with a moment-by-moment account of Roosevelt's leadership and the private lives of the president and first lady.

Gopal, Anand, 1980-

No good men among the living : America, the Taliban, and the war through Afghan eyes / Anand Gopal. Metropolitan Books, 2014. 272 p. American Empire Project **920**

1. Taliban. 2. Afghan War, 2001, Afghani. 3. Soldiers 4. Warlords 5.

Homemakers 6. Afghanistan. 7. United States -- Military policy. 8. Collective biographies
ISBN 9780805091793
LC 2014001384

Includes index.
Pulitzer Prize for General Nonfiction finalist, 2015.
National Book Award for Nonfiction finalist, 2014

Following three Afghans--a Taliban commander, a US-backed warlord and a housewife trapped in the middle of the fighting--through years of US missteps, this dramatic narrative reveals the workings of America's longest war and the truth behind its prolonged agony.

"Policymakers and informed readers will benefit immensely from this illuminating book." Library Journal.

Gopnik, Adam

Angels and ages : a short book about Lincoln, Darwin, and modern life / Adam Gopnik. Alfred A. Knopf, 2009. 224 p. **920**

1. Lincoln, Abraham, 1809-1865 Influence. 2. Darwin, Charles, 1809-1882 Influence. 3. Presidents -- United States 4. Naturalists -- England 5. Civilization, Western 6. Liberalism. 7. Collective biographies
ISBN 9780307270788
LC 2008036224

Written 200 years after Charles Darwin and Abraham Lincoln shared a birthday on February 12, 1809, this account sheds new light on two men who changed the way we think about the meaning of life and death. Adam Gopnik's unique perspective, combined with previously unexplored stories and figures, reveals two men planted firmly at the roots of modern views and liberal values.

"The book is worth reading for the author's unquestioned skill as a craftsman and the light he sheds on what has become, for many, settled history." Bookmarks.

Gordon, Charlotte

Romantic outlaws : the extraordinary lives of Mary Wollstonecraft and her daughter Mary Shelley / Charlotte Gordon. Random House, 2015 640 p. **920**

1. Wollstonecraft, Mary, 1759-1797. 2. Shelley, Mary Wollstonecraft, 1797-1851. 3. Authors, English. 4. Women authors, English. 5. Feminists 6. Women authors 7. Biographies 8. Collective biographies.
ISBN 9781400068425
LC 2014014841

ALA Notable Book, 2016.
National Book Critics Circle Award for Biography, 2015.

Mary Wollstonecraft and her daughter Mary Shelley were ardent feminists long before feminism was cool -- actually, it was considered morally suspect. In Romantic Outlaws, author Charlotte Gordon relates their lives in alternating chapters, demonstrating the parallels between their philosophical and socially conscious outlooks. Wollstonecraft, who penned the revolutionary Vindication of the Rights of Women, died just two weeks after her daughter's 1797 birth, but Shelley (author of Frankenstein), who led a similarly tumultuous life, found inspiration in her mother's writings. Viewing the remarkable women's biographies in parallel provides unexpected insights and enriched appreciation of their achievements.

"Gordon's prose is compelling and her scholarship meticulous; her contention that both women led 'lives as memorable as the words they left behind' is brilliantly supported." Library Journal.

Gordon, Lyndall

Outsiders : five women writers who changed the world / Lyndall Gordon. Johns Hopkins University Press, 2019, c2018. 352 p. **920**

1. Authors 2. Women authors 3. Books and reading 4. Women's role 5. Great Britain -- History 6. Collective biographies
ISBN 9781421429441
LC bl2019004257

Shares the lives and novels of five legendary female writers--Mary Shelley, Emily Bronte, George Eliot, Olive Schreiner, and Virginia Woolf--showing how their unique creativity was due to their lives as outsiders.

Gordon-Reed, Annette

★The **Hemingses** of Monticello : an American family / Annette Gordon-Reed. W.W. Norton & Co., 2008. 608 p. **920**

1. Hemings family. 2. Hemings, Sally, 1773-1835? Family 3. Jefferson, Thomas, 1743-1826 Family 4. Monticello (Va.) 5. African American families. 6. Multiracial persons 7. Slaves 8. Slaveholders. 9. Virginia -- History. 10. United States -- History -- 19th century 11. Collective biographies.
ISBN 9780393064773
LC 2008014642

ALA Notable Book, 2009.
National Book Award for Nonfiction, 2008.
Pulitzer Prize for History, 2009.
National Book Critics Circle Award for Biography finalist, 2008.

Traces the history of the Hemings family from early eighteenth-century Virginia to their dispersal after Thomas Jefferson's death in 1826, and describes their family ties to the third president against a backdrop of Revolutionary America and the French Revolution.

Gray, Charlotte, 1948-

★**Reluctant** genius : Alexander Graham Bell and the passion for invention / Charlotte Gray. Arcade Pub. : c2006. 466 p. : **920**

1. Bell, Alexander Graham, 1847-1922. 2. Bell, Mabel Hubbard, 1857-1923. 3. Inventors -- United States 4. Hearing -- Experiments 5. Telephones -- History 6. Husband and wife 7. United States -- Social life and customs -- 19th century 8. United States -- Social life and customs -- 20th century 9. Collective biographies.
ISBN 1559708093
LC 2005029609

Draws on new research to offer insight into the inventor's private life, as well as his passionate drive for new innovations, discussing the influence of his speech therapist father and deaf mother on his work, his tempestuous relationship with his wife, and his avoidance of fame and fortune.

"The author recounts both the inventor of the telephone's creation of the device and the projects he pursued once his future was secured. . . . Combining the household history of the Bells with that of Alexander's successive enthusiasms (Helen Keller, kites, airplanes, hydrocraft), Gray fairly portrays the attractions and exasperations of Bell's life." Booklist.

Grescoe, Taras

Shanghai grand : forbidden love and international intrigue in a doomed world / Taras Grescoe. St. Martin's Press, 2016. 352 p. **920**

1. Hahn, Emily, 1905-1997. 2. Sassoon, Elias Victor, 1881-1961. 3. Cathay Hotel (Shanghai, China) -- History. 4. Americans in Shanghai, China. 5. Love triangles 6. Sino-Japanese Conflict, 1937-1945. 7. Shanghai, China -- Social life and customs. 8. Collective biographies
ISBN 9781250049711
LC 2016001124

"First published in the United Kingdom by Macmillan, an imprint of Pan Macmillan"--Title page verso.

Tells the true story of a British aristocrat, an American flapper and a Chinese poet, who found themselves trapped in an unlikely love triangle amid the decadence of Jazz Age Shanghai.

"Grescoe (Straphanger, 2012) interweaves a cast of intriguing international characters into this seductive biography of a time, a place, a poet, and a girl." Booklist.

Groom, Winston, 1944-2020

The **aviators** : Eddie Rickenbacker, Jimmy Doolittle, Charles Lindbergh, and the epic age of flight / Winston Groom. National Geographic, 2013. 448 p. **920**

1. Rickenbacker, Eddie, 1890-1973. 2. Doolittle, James Harold, 1896-1993. 3. Lindbergh, Charles A. (Charles Augustus), 1902-1974. 4. Pilots -- United States 5. Military pilots -- United States 6. Heroes and heroines, American 7. Adventurers -- United States 8. United States -- History, Military -- 20th century. 9. Collective biographies
ISBN 9781426211560

LC 2013015171

"A gripping document of a brilliant era in our history and a few of the men who helped make it so." Kirkus.

The **generals** : Patton, Macarthur, Marshall, and the winning of World War II / Winston Groom. National Geographic, 2015. 464 p. **920**

1. MacArthur, Douglas, 1880-1964. 2. Marshall, George C., (George Catlett), 1880-1959 3. Patton, George S., 1885-1945 4. United States. Army 5. Generals -- United States 6. World War II. 7. Military campaigns. 8. Military strategy 9. United States -- History, Military -- 20th century 10. Collective biographies.
ISBN 9781426215490

LC 2015021562

"There is much material on the battle tactics of both World Wars, which should appeal to military buffs, while general readers will welcome a review of the facts about these men conveyed through felicitous prose." Library Journal.

Gross, Michael, 1952-

Focus : the secret, sexy, sometimes sordid world of fashion photographers / Michael Gross. Atria Books, 2016 416 p. **920**

1. Fashion photographers. 2. Fashion models 3. Fashion photography. 4. Fashion merchandising -- Social aspects. 5. Collective biographies
ISBN 9781476763460

LC 2015045564

Shares chronological anecdotes tracing the golden age of fashion photography to explore the drama and achievements of leading visionaries.

"The subject matter will be historically significant to those who are concerned with the photo artist's role in the golden age of modern fashion photography." Library Journal.

Guinn, Jeff

The **vagabonds** : the story of Henry Ford and Thomas Edison's ten-year road trip / Jeff Guinn. Simon & Schuster, 2019. 320 p. **920**

1. Ford, Henry, 1863-1947 2. Edison, Thomas A. (Thomas Alva), 1847-1931 3. Automobile designers 4. Businesspeople 5. Inventors 6. Automobile travel 7. United States -- Description and travel 8. Collective biographies 9. Biographies
ISBN 9781501159305

LC 2018053698

Explains how two American business giants--Henry Ford and Thomas Edison--and their annual summer sojourns introduced the road trip to American culture and made the automobile an essential part of modern life, even as their own relationship altered dramatically.

"An arresting account of America's auto-camping movement and its incipient motivators. Highly recommended, especially for social historians, travel and camping enthusiasts, automotive specialists, naturalists, and also for general readers." Library Journal.

Guralnick, Peter

Looking to get lost : adventures in music and writing / Peter Guralnick. Little Brown & Company, 2020 448 p. **920**

1. Music 2. Creativity 3. Musicians 4. Creativity in music 5. Essays 6. Collective biographies
ISBN 9780316412629

LC 2020937314

Includes index.

This new book of profiles is not so much a summation as a culmination of Peter Guralnick's remarkable work, which from the start has encompassed the full sweep of blues, gospel, country, and rock 'n' roll. It covers old ground from new perspectives, offering deeply felt, masterful, and strikingly personal portraits of creative artists, both musicians and writers, at the height of their powers.

"A wide-ranging vision and appreciation of American musical creativity from a writer who is himself an essential voice." Library Journal

Guy, John

The **children** of Henry VIII / John Guy. Oxford University Press, 2013 272 p. **920**

1. Henry VIII, King of England, 1491-1547 2. Tudor, House of 3. Royal houses 4. Great Britain -- History -- Tudors, 1485-1603 5. Collective biographies
ISBN 9780192840905

LC 2012277518

Gwynne, S. C. (Samuel C.), 1953-

The **perfect** pass : American genius and the reinvention of football / S. C. Gwynne. Scribner, 2016 320 p. **920**

1. Mumme, Hal 2. Leach, Mike, 1961- 3. Football coaches 4. Football 5. Passing (Football) 6. Collective biographies
ISBN 9781501116193

LC 2016012980

As brutal as football can be today, it was much worse in the past -- and one of the reasons was that forward passing was not permitted. When it was eventually legalized thanks to the efforts of those looking to make the game safer, it was still rarely used, as passing continued to be seen as a sissy move. In the 1980s, football coaches Hal Mumme and Mike Leach started developing a pass-centric strategy that came to be known as the Air Raid -- and transformed the sport into a faster, more dynamic game.

"That makes his subtitle all the more fitting, for undeniably, the two coaches changed the game--and brought glory to their institutions. A superb treat for all gridiron fans." Kirkus.

Halberstam, David

The **amateurs** / David Halberstam. Fawcett Columbine, 1996, c1985. 221 p. : **920**

1. Olympic Games (23rd : 1984 : Los Angeles, Calif.) 2. Rowers -- United States 3. Olympic games. 4. Rowing. 5. Athletes. 6. Collective biographies
ISBN 0449910032

LC BL 99791675

Originally published: New York : Morrow, c1985.

The Pulitzer Prize-winning journalist profiles the struggles of four unknown young men who compete to represent the U.S. as its lone single sculler in the 1984 Olympics.

Hall, Jacquelyn Dowd

★**Sisters** and rebels : a struggle for the soul of America / Jacquelyn Dowd Hall. W.W. Norton & Company, 2019. 704 p. **920**

1. Lumpkin, Katharine Du Pre, 1897-1988. 2. Lumpkin, Grace, 1891-1980. 3. Glenn, Elizabeth Elliott Lumpkin, 1880 or 1881-1963. 4. Sisters 5. White supremacists 6. Women political activists -- United States 7. Women authors, American 8. Georgia 9. Southern States -- Race relations. 10. Southern States -- Civilization. 11. Southern States -- History. 12. Collective biographies.
ISBN 9780393047998

LC 2018057931

Traces the parallel lives of the three Lumpkin sisters, describing how one remained a believer in the white-supremacy culture of their Southern upbringing, while the others became progressive supporters of race and labor initiatives.

"These admirably crafted biographies of the Lumpkins, their cohorts, and their causes opens a fascinating window on America's social and intellectual history." Publishers Weekly.

Halpern, Paul, 1961-

Einstein's dice and Schrödinger's cat : how two great minds battled quantum randomness to create a unified theory of physics / Paul Halpern. Basic Books, 2015 288 p. **920**

1. Einstein, Albert, 1879-1955 2. Schrodinger, Erwin, 1887-1961. 3. Quantum theory -- History. 4. Physicists 5. Physics 6. Collective biographies
ISBN 9780465075713

LC 2014041325

Includes index.

A physics professor and popular science author describes the quests of two great physicists who both balked at the randomness of quantum mechanics and sought to explain it, at first as collaborators but then as competitors.

"Einstein's life feels familiar and true; Schrödinger emerges as someone scarred by envy and not a little opportunistic--e.g., when he composed a 'statement of support for the Anschluss.' Halpern ably explores the clashing personalities and worldviews that had physics in churning ferment during the early part of the 20th century." Kirkus.

Hardesty, Von, 1939-

Black wings : courageous stories of African Americans in aviation and space history / Von Hardesty. Collins, 2008. x, 180 p. : **920**

1. United States. Air Force. 2. United States. National Aeronautics and Space Administration. 3. African-American pilots 4. African-American astronauts 5. Pilots -- United States 6. Astronauts -- United States 7. United States -- History. 8. Collective biographies
ISBN 9780061261381

LC 2007021270

"In association with the Smithsonian National Air and Space Museum."

A history of African Americans in aviation and space cites the efforts of black men and women to promote integration by entering the military, breaking transcontinental records, and joining the space program.

Hargittai, Istvan

The **Martians** of Science : five physicists who changed the twentieth century / Istvan Hargittai. Oxford University Press, 2006. xxiv, 313 p., 32 p. of plates : **920**

1. Szilard, Leo. 2. Teller, Edward, 1908-2003. 3. Von Karman, Theodore, 1881-1963. 4. Von Neumann, John, 1903-1957. 5. Wigner, Eugene Paul, 1902-1995. 6. Physicists -- United States 7. Science -- United States -- History -- 20th century. 8. Collective biographies.
ISBN 9780195178456

LC 2005029427

"This is a presentation of the lives of five scientists (physicists and engineers) from Hungary who went to Germany and then to the United States. They . . . [are] Theodore von Karman, Leo Szilard, Eugene P. Wigner, John von Neumann, and Edward Teller. . . . [This book is an] extremely valuable account of the lives of these five brilliant and interesting Hungarian physicists." Science Books & Films.

Harris, M. A., 1908-

The **Black** book : 35th Anniversary Edition / Middleton A. Harris ; with the assistance of Morris Levitt, Roger Furman, Ernest Smith ; with a new foreword by Toni Morrison ; including the original introduction by Bill Cosby. Random House, 2009. 198 p. : **920**

1. African Americans -- History -- Miscellanea
ISBN 9781400068487

LC 2010292662

"35th anniversary ed."

"Originally published in hardcover and trade paperback in the United States by Random House ... in 1974"--T.p. verso.

Now in a deluxe 35th anniversary hardcover edition, The Black book remains a breathtaking testament to the legendary wisdom, strength, and perseverance of Black men and women intent on freedom; features a new foreword and original poem by Toni Morrison.

Haskins, James, 1941-

African-American religious leaders / Jim Haskins and Kathleen Benson. John Wiley & Sons, c2008. 168 p. Black stars series **920**

1. Religious leaders 2. African American leadership. 3. African Americans 4. Christian leadership. 5. Collective biographies.
ISBN 0471736325

LC 2007027347

Explores the role and importance of African Americans as religious leaders through the profiles of significant personalities from the Revolutionary era through modern times, including Absalom Jones, Sojourner Truth, and Al Sharpton.

Heilbroner, Robert L.

★The **worldly** philosophers : the lives, times, and ideas of the great economic thinkers / Robert L. Heilbroner. Simon & Schuster, c1999. 365 p. ; **920**

1. Economists 2. Economics -- History. 3. Collective biographies
ISBN 068486214X

LC 99014050

"A Touchstone book."

Defines the world's greatest economic thinkers and explores the philosophies that motivate them

Hibbert, Christopher, 1924-2008

The **Borgias** and their enemies : 1431-1519 / Christopher Hibbert. Harcourt, Inc., 2008. 336 p. **920**

1. Borgia family. 2. European Renaissance -- Italy. 3. Nobility -- Italy 4. Italy -- History -- 15th century. 5. Italy -- History -- 1492-

1559. 6. Collective biographies
ISBN 9780151010332

LC 2008003076

"Lucrezia Borgia, on hearing that her father, Pope Alexander VI, was choosing her third husband, noted that her first two had been very unlucky. Luck had little to do with it, as Hibbert shows in this vivid chronicle of the notoriously corrupt Renaissance family. One husband was killed on the orders of her brother Cesare, whose ruthlessness made him the model for Machiavelli's The Prince; the other was discarded after ceasing to be politically useful to the Pope. Hibbert ably traces the web of alliances through which the Spanish-born Alexander hoped to secure his hold on Italy and his family's place in power." The New Yorker.

The **House** of Medici : its rise and fall / Christopher Hibbert. Morrow Quill Paperbacks, 1980, c1974. 364 p., 12 leaves of plates : **920**

1. Medici, House of. 2. Florence, Italy -- History -- 1421-1737. 3. Italy -- History. 4. Collective biographies
ISBN 0688053394

LC 79026508

First published in 1974 under title: The rise and fall of the House of Medici.

Includes index.

An account of the fortunes and influences of the great Florentine banking family, covering over three hundred years of soldiers, art patrons, collectors, builders, popes, statesmen, and scholars

"This book is concerned with heads of the Medici family {who} directed the government of the Florentine state from 1434, with Cosimo's return from exile, until the death of the Grand Duke Giovanni Gastone in 1737." Times Literary Supplement.

Hoffman, Adina

Till we have built Jerusalem : architects of a new city / Adina Hoffman. Farrar, Straus and Giroux, 2016 192 p. **920**

1. Mendelsohn, Erich, 1887-1953. 2. Harrison, Austen St . Barbe, 1891-1976 3. Houris, Spyro 4. Architects -- Jerusalem 5. Architecture -- Jerusalem, Israel 6. Jerusalem, Israel -- History -- 20th century 7. Jerusalem, Israel -- Buildings 8. Collective biographies
ISBN 9780374289102

LC 2015034650

Includes index.

Part biographical puzzle, architectural meditation and probing detective story, a portrait of the three architects who helped build modern Jerusalem is also a riveting examination of the ways in which politics and aesthetics clash in a place of constant conflict.

Hoffman, Carl, 1960-

The **last** wild men of Borneo : a true story of death and treasure / Carl Hoffman. William Morrow & Company, 2018. 336 p. **920**

1. Manser, Bruno, 1954- 2. Palmieri, Michael 3. Explorers 4. Adventurers 5. Indigenous peoples 6. Penan (Bornean people) 7. Borneo 8. Collective biographies
ISBN 9780062439024

LC 2017033692

Traces the parallel stories and impact of two very different men, Swiss environmentalist Bruno Manser and American art dealer Michael Palmieri, on the land, culture and legacy of Borneo.

"An expertly wrought tale of exploration, adventure, and mischief by Hoffman...who returns to the South Pacific island of Borneo to tell it." Kirkus.

Hollingsworth, Mary, 1947-

★The **family** Medici : the hidden history of the Medici dynasty / Mary Hollingsworth. Pegasus, 2018. 528 p. **920**

1. Medici, House of 2. European Renaissance. 3. Power (Social sciences) 4. Florence, Italy -- History -- 1421-1737. 5. Collective biographies
ISBN 9781681776484

LC bl2018020480

A fresh, revelatory, and shockingly revisionist narrative of the rise and fall of the House of Medici, by the acclaimed author of The Cardinal's Hat and The Borgias.

"A vital acquisition for anyone who studies the Renaissance and seeks the true role of the Medici in the history of Florence." Kirkus.

Holt, Nathalia, 1980-

The **queens** of animation : the untold story of the women who transformed the world of Disney and made cinematic history / Nathalia Holt. Little, Brown and Company, 2019. xiv, 379 p., 8 unnumbered p. of plates : **920**

1. Walt Disney Company. 2. Gender role 3. Women artists 4. Animated films -- History and criticism 5. Women cartoonists 6. Collective biographies
ISBN 9780316439152

The best-selling author draws on extensive research to trace the role of women employees at Walt Disney Studios, who endured sexism, domestic abuse and workplace intimidation to create iconic films.

"This groundbreaking work laments the discrimination these artists endured while celebrating the verve, creativity, and resiliency they drew on to bring beautiful art and three-dimensional characters to the big screen." Booklist.

Howard, Hugh, 1952-

Architecture's odd couple : Frank Lloyd Wright and Philip Johnson / Hugh Howard. Bloomsbury Press, 2016. 320 p. **920**

1. Wright, Frank Lloyd, 1867-1959 2. Johnson, Philip, 1906-2005 3. Architecture. 4. Collective biographies
ISBN 9781620403754

LC 2015042135

In architectural terms, the twentieth century can be largely summed up with two names: Frank Lloyd Wright and Philip Johnson. Wright (1867-1959) began it with his romantic prairie style; Johnson (1906-2005) brought down the curtain with his spare postmodernist experiments. Between them, they built some of the most admired and discussed buildings in American history. Differing radically in their views on architecture, Wright and Johnson shared a restless creativity, enormous charisma, and an outspokenness that made each man irresistible to the media. Often publicly at odds, they were the twentieth century's flint and steel; their repeated encounters consistently set off sparks. Yet as acclaimed historian Hugh Howard shows, their rivalry was also a fruitful artistic conversation, one that yielded new directions for both men.

"Written with wit and flair and supported by solid research, this thoughtful and well-built book will delight architecture buffs." Booklist.

Howley, Kerry

Thrown / Kerry Howley. Sarabande Books, [2014] 240 p. **920**

1. Martial artists -- United States. 2. Mixed martial arts. 3. Sports spectators. 4. Martial arts -- Psychological aspects. 5. Collective biographies
ISBN 9781936747924

LC 2014010165

"Acclaimed journalist Kerry Howley infiltrates the world of mixed martial arts and the lives of aspiring cage fighters. For three years, Howley follows these fighters as they tear ligaments and lose a third of their body mass to make weight, and is drawn deeply into this riveting culture of violence"--Provided by publisher.

"Howley's brilliant prose is as dexterous and doughty as the fighters she trails, torquing into philosophy, parody, and sweat-soaked poetry. At times, the narrative is difficult to follow, while the contrast between her highbrow analysis and the aggressive MMA subculture can be disorienting. Her year-long immersion in the sport, however, proves as captivating as any blood-spattered spectacle." Publishers Weekly.

Huang, Yunte

Inseparable : the original Siamese twins and their rendezvous with American history / Yunte Huang. Liveright Publishing Corporation, a Division of W.W. Norton & Company, [2018] 416 p. **920**

1. Bunker, Chang, 1811-1874. 2. Bunker, Eng, 1811-1874. 3. Conjoined twins 4. Celebrities 5. Brothers 6. Freaks (Entertainers) 7. United States -- History -- 19th century 8. United States -- Social life and customs -- 19th century 9. Collective biographies

ISBN 9780871404473

LC 2017055799

National Book Critics Circle Award for Biography finalist, 2018

A wryly whimsical dual portrait of famous 19th-century conjoined twins Chang and Eng Bunker shares an Asian-American perspective on their improbable lives, describing their rise from savvy side-show celebrities to wealthy Southern gentry, their large family and how their experiences reflected America's historical penchant for objectifying differences.

"Huang offers a vivid portrait of two men who did the best they could to live ordinary lives, and a revealing look at a somewhat scandalous side of the prim-and-proper Victorian Era." Booklist.

Hutchison, Kay Bailey, 1943-

American heroines : the spirited women who shaped our country / Kay Bailey Hutchison. Harper, 2006. xx, 372 p. : **920**

1. Heroes and heroines, American 2. Women -- United States 3. Collective biographies

ISBN 0060566361

LC 2005055129

"This paperback is almost the same as the hardback; a few omissions, a few additions, a few changes"--Foreword.

Explores the lives of women who have made significant contributions to American history and society, including Red Cross founder Clara Barton and aviation pioneer Amelia Earhart.

"Hutchinson's lively, personal writing makes this an accessible and important volume." Booklist.

Ignotofsky, Rachel, 1989-

Women in science : 50 fearless pioneers who changed the world / written and illustrated by Rachel Ignotofsky. Ten Speed Press, [2016] 127 p. **920**

1. Women scientists 2. Scientists 3. Collective biographies 4. Illustrated books

ISBN 9781607749769

LC 2015050246

Illustrated by the author.

A collection of artworks inspired by the lives and achievements of fifty famous women in science, technology, engineering, and mathematics, from the ancient world to the present, profiles each notable individual.

Jackson, Jeffrey H., 1971-

Paper bullets : two artists who risked their lives to defy the Nazis / Jeffrey H. Jackson. Algonquin Books of Chapel Hill, 2020 326 p. **920**

1. Cahun, Claude, 1894-1954 2. Malherbe, Suzanne, 1892-1972 3. Women artists 4. Anti-Nazi movement 5. World War II -- Underground movements 6. Avant-garde (Aesthetics) 7. Channel Islands -- History -- German occupation, 1940-1945 8. Collective biographies

ISBN 9781616209162

LC 2020018040

Paper Bullets is the first book to tell the history of an audacious anti-Nazi campaign undertaken by an unlikely pair: two French women, Lucy Schwob and Suzanne Malherbe, who drew on their skills as Parisian avant-garde artists to write and distribute "paper bullets"--wicked insults against Hitler, calls to rebel, and subversive fictional dialogues designed to demoralize Nazi troops occupying their adopted home on the British Channel Island of Jersey.

"Drawing on archival and genealogical sources, the women's own writings, and histories of the period, Jackson creates a vivid picture of the tense, fearsome atmosphere of Jersey under Nazi occupation and the perils of resistance. A unique WWII history and absorbing story of two bold, unconventional women." Kirkus.

Jeal, Tim

Explorers of the Nile : the triumph and tragedy of a great Victorian adventure / Tim Jeal. Yale University Press, 2011. 592 p. **920**

1. Burton, Richard F., 1821-1890 2. Speke, John Hanning, 1827-1864 3. Explorers -- Africa. 4. Explorers -- Great Britain 5. Nile River -- Exploration -- British 6. Central Africa -- Exploration 7. Congo (Democratic Republic) -- Exploration 8. Collective biographies

ISBN 9780300149357

LC 2011933872

Examines the journeys of the six men and one woman, who risked their lives, to solve the mystery of the source of the White Nile, between 1856 and 1876, and discusses the consequences the search has had on Uganda and the Sudan.

Jenkins, Steve, 1982-

Happily ever Esther : two men, a Wonder Pig, and their life-changing mission to give animals a home / Steve Jenkins, Derek Walter, and Caprice Crane ; foreword by Alan Cumming. Grand Central Publishing, 2018. 224 p. **920**

1. Jenkins, Steve, 1982- 2. Walter, Derek, 1981- 3. Pigs as pets 4. Animal sanctuaries 5. Pet owners 6. Misadventures 7. Ontario 8. Canada 9. Collective autobiographies and memoirs

ISBN 9781538728147

LC 2017046608

The authors of Esther the Wonder Pig share the riotous story of how after leaving the city to open their farm sanctuary, they tackled the unexpected realities of farm life and eventually accepted dozens of animals.

Johnson, Marilyn, 1954-

Lives in ruins : archaeologists and the seductive lure of human rubble / Marilyn Johnson. Harper Collins, c2014. 272 p. **920**

1. Archaeologists 2. Archaeology 3. Archaeological sites 4. Archaeological thefts 5. Ireland 6. Collective biographies

ISBN 9780062127181

"Without glitz, the author has created a very enjoyable work that will be appreciated by experts in the field and casual readers alike. Well suited to anyone contemplating archaeology as a career, those curious about what the profession is like, lovers of history and science, and readers who enjoy and are grateful for the lure of prehistory and discovery as a mental process." Library Journal.

Johnson, Mindy

Ink & paint : the women of Walt Disney's animation / Mindy Johnson ; foreword by June Foray. Disney Editions, 2017. 384 p. : **920**

1. Walt Disney Company. 2. Women cartoonists 3. Women animators 4. Animated films -- History and criticism 5. Animation (Cinematography) 6. Collective biographies

ISBN 9781484727812

LC bl2017042093

From the earliest black-and-white Alice Comedies to the advent of CAPS and digital animation, meet the pioneering women who brought hand-rendered animated stories to vibrant, multicolored life at Walt Disney Studios and beyond.

Jordan, Jonathan W., 1967-

American warlords : how Roosevelt's high command led America to victory in World War II / Jonathan W. Jordan. NAL Caliber, 2015 576 p. **920**

1. Roosevelt, Franklin D. (Franklin Delano), 1882-1945 Military leadership. 2. Eisenhower, Dwight D. (Dwight David), 1890-1969. 3. Stimson, Henry L. (Henry Lewis), 1867-1950. 4. Marshall, George C. (George Catlett), 1880-1959. 5. Presidents -- United States 6. Generals -- United States 7. Command of troops -- United States 8. World War II -- United States. 9. United States -- Politics and government -- 1933-1945. 10. Collective biographies

ISBN 9780451414571

LC 2014036427

Takes readers behind closed doors where President Franklin D. Roosevelt--when war in Europe and Asia threatened America's shores, and his friends became his foes, his enemies his allies--turned to one of history's most remarkable triumvirates to lead America from isolation to the summit of global power.

"Jordan's wonderful new insight into the leaders shows how lucky we were regarding Stimson's prescient warnings about nuclear war, Marshall's long-suffering, self-effacing loyalty, and King's rough-and-ready fighting abilities. In addition to World War II buffs, other readers will enjoy the intrigue, back-stabbing, action, and diplomacy in this well-written book." Kirkus.

Kaiser, Charles

The **cost** of courage / Charles Kaiser. Other Press, 2015. 300 p. **920**

1. Audibert-Boulloche, Christiane. 2. Katlama, Jacqueline Boulloche, 1918-1994. 3. Boulloche, Andre. 4. French Resistance (World War II) 5. Guerrillas -- France 6. Military occupation 7. Spies. 8. France -- History -- German occupation, 1940-1945 9. Collective biographies

ISBN 9781590516140

LC 2015008560

Describes how the heroism of three siblings, who took over and lead the French Resistance during World War II after their older brother was betrayed, wounded and arrested by the Gestapo surviving three concentration camps.

"Kaiser's account of a family's devotion and resilience in the face of horrific tyranny tells a highly recommended story of resolve and bravery that can't help but feel romantic in its selfless and profound obligation, but this is not gloss nor ungrounded canonization." Library Journal.

Kalb, Claudia

Andy Warhol was a hoarder : inside the minds of history's great personalities / Claudia Kalb. National Geographic Books, 2016. 288 p. **920**

1. Fame -- Psychological aspects. 2. Celebrities -- Psychology 3. Mental illness 4. Eccentrics and eccentricities 5. Collective biographies

ISBN 9781426214660

LC 2015024370

In this surprising, inventive, and meticulously researched look at the evolution of mental health, acclaimed health and science journalist Claudia Kalb gives readers a glimpse into the lives of high-profile historic figures through the lens of modern psychology, weaving groundbreaking research into biographical narratives that are deeply embedded in our culture.

"In all, Kalb's well-written exercise in applying modern psychiatric theory to historical figures, from Marilyn Monroe to Albert Einstein to Charles Darwin, certainly makes for some very entertaining armchair speculation." Booklist.

Kaplan, Janice

The **genius** of women : from overlooked to changing the world / Janice Kaplan. E.P. Dutton, 2020. 320 p. **920**

1. Genius 2. Gifted women 3. Creativity in women 4. Intellectuals 5. Collective biographies

ISBN 9781524744212

LC 2019027361

A look at the history of women geniuses and how they have historically not been recognized to the same degree as their male counterparts in a variety of fields including science and the performing arts.

"Expect this well-reasoned account to generate a lot of interest and conversation." Booklist

Kashner, Sam

The **fabulous** Bouvier sisters : the tragic and glamorous lives of Jackie and Lee / Sam Kashner and Nancy Schoenberger. Harper, an imprint of HarperCollinsPublishers, 2018. 400 p. **920**

1. Onassis, Jacqueline Kennedy, 1929-1994 2. Radziwill, Lee Bouvier, 1933- 3. Sisters -- United States 4. Presidents' spouses -- United States 5. Celebrities -- United States 6. Sibling rivalry 7. Collective biographies 8. Biographies

ISBN 9780062364982

LC bl2018134487

Draws on candid interviews with Jackie Kennedy Onassis' sister, Lee, to share dramatic insights into the complicated relationship the two shared, discussing their artistic interests and the rivalries that complicated their bond.

Katz, Catherine Grace

The **daughters** of Yalta : the Churchills, Roosevelts, and Harrimans: a story of love and war / Catherine Grace Katz. Houghton Mifflin Harcourt, 2020 400 p. **920**

1. Roosevelt, Anna, 1906-1975 2. Churchill, Sarah, 1914-1982 3. Mortimer, Kathleen Lanier Harriman, 1917-2011 4. Yalta Conference, 1945 5. World War II -- Diplomatic history 6. Alliances 7. Summit meetings 8. Women and politics 9. IAlta, Ukraine 10. Collective biographies

ISBN 9780358117858

LC 2020004935

"The story of the fascinating and fateful 'daughter diplomacy' of Anna Roosevelt, Sarah Churchill, and Kathleen Harriman, three glamorous young women who accompanied their famous fathers to the Yalta

Conference with Stalin in the waning days of World War II".-- Provided by publisher.

"Katz effectively shows how these three often overlooked women proved to be indispensable in a variety of ways. Engaging, multilayered history of the best kind, grounded in telling detail and marvelous personalities." Kirkus

Kearse, Bettye

★The **other** Madisons : the lost history of a president's black family / Bettye Kearse. Houghton Mifflin Harcourt, 2020. x, 253 p. **920**

1. Kearse, Bettye Family 2. Madison, James, 1751-1836 Family 3. Madison, James, 1751-1836 relations with African Americans 4. Madison family 5. Mandy, active 18th century 6. Coreen, active 18th century 7. African American families 8. Presidents -- United States -- Family 9. Multiracial persons 10. Founding fathers of the United States 11. Virginia 12. Texas 13. United States 14. Collective biographies

ISBN 9781328604392

LC 2019024941

For thousands of years, West African griots (men) and griottes (women) have recited the stories of their people. Without this tradition Bettye Kearse would not have known that she is a descendant of President James Madison and his slave, and half-sister, Coreen. In 1990, Bettye became the eighth-generation griotte for her family. Their credo--"Always remember--you're a Madison. You come from African slaves and a president"--was intended to be a source of pride, but for her, it echoed with abuses of slavery, including rape and incest. Confronting those abuses, Bettye embarked on a journey of discovery--of her ancestors, the nation, and herself.

"Poignant and eye-opening, this is a must-read." Booklist

Kennedy, John F. (John Fitzgerald), 1917-1963

★**Profiles** in courage / John F. Kennedy. Harper Collins, 2003, c1956. xxii, 245 p. **920**

1. United States. Congress. Senate 2. Legislators -- United States 3. Courage in men. 4. Politicians. 5. United States -- Politics and government. 6. Collective biographies.

ISBN 0060530626

LC 2003040676

Originally published: New York : Harper & Brothers, 1956.

Pulitzer Prize for Biography or Autobiography, 1957.

Profiles eight historical figures who demonstrated particular integrity in the face of opposition, including John Quincy Adams, Daniel Webster, Thomas Hart Benton, and Robert A. Taft.

Kerrison, Catherine, 1953-

Jefferson's daughters : three sisters, white and black, in a young America / Catherine Kerrison. Ballantine Books, 2018 432 p. **920**

1. Randolph, Martha Jefferson, 1772-1836. 2. Eppes, Maria, 1778-1804. 3. Hemings, Harriet, 1801- 4. Jefferson, Thomas, 1743-1826 Family. 5. Fathers and daughters 6. Gender role 7. Women and politics 8. Half sisters 9. Collective biographies

ISBN 9781101886243

LC 2017043540

A portrait of the divergent lives of Thomas Jefferson's three daughters reveals how his white daughters struggled with the realities of lives they were ill-prepared to manage, while the daughter he fathered with a slave did not achieve freedom until adulthood.

"Incisive and elegant, Kerrison's book is at once a fabulous family story and a stellar work of historical scholarship." Publishers Weekly.

Khan, Mahvish

My Guantanamo diary : the detainees and the stories they told me / Mahvish Khan. PublicAffairs, 2008. xv, 302 p. **920**

1. Detention of persons -- Guantanamo Bay Naval Base (Cuba) 2. Prisoners of war -- Legal status, laws, etc. -- Guantanamo Bay Naval Base (Cuba) 3. Combatants and noncombatants (International law) 4. Due process of law. 5. Guantanamo Bay Naval Base (Cuba) 6. Collective biographies

ISBN 9781586484989

LC bl2008011526

An American attorney born to immigrant Afghan parents describes her outrage over the detainments at Guantanamo, her volunteer role as an interpreter for prisoners, and the plight of those who have been detained for years without trial.

Khilnani, Sunil, 1960-

Incarnations : a history of India in fifty lives / Sunil Khilnani. Farrar, Straus and Giroux, 2016, c2016 384 p. **920**

1. Human geography. 2. Intellectual life. 3. India -- Civilization. 4. India -- Social life and customs. 5. India -- History. 6. India 7. Collective biographies

ISBN 9780374175498

LC 2016007101

"Originally published, in somewhat different form, in 2016 by Allen Lane, an imprint of Penguin Books, Great Britain"--Title page verso.

The author of The Idea of Indian presents an entertaining and provocative account of India's past via a series of portraits of emperors, warriors, philosophers, film stars and corporate titans -- some famous, some unjustly forgotten, but all important in the country's rich history.

"Khilnani's essays are provocative and serious, a worthy rebuttal to the image of Indian history as 'curiously unpeopled.'" Publishers Weekly.

King, Charles, 1967-

Gods of the upper air : how a circle of renegade anthropologists reinvented race, sex, and gender in the twentieth century / Charles King. Doubleday, 2019. xii, 431 p. **920**

1. Boas, Franz, 1858-1942 2. Anthropologists 3. Sociocultural anthropology 4. Women anthropologists 5. Non-industrial societies 6. Collective biographies

ISBN 9780385542197

LC 2019014081

National Book Critics Circle Award for Biography finalist, 2019

A dazzling group portrait of Franz Boas, the founder of cultural anthropology, and his circle of women scientists, who upended American notions of race, gender, and sexuality in the 1920s and 1930s--a sweeping chronicle of how our society began to question the basic ways we understand other cultures and ourselves.

"Rich in ideas, the book also abounds in absorbing accounts of friendships, animosities, and rivalries among these early anthropologists. This superb narrative of debunking scientists provides timely reading for our great-again era." Kirkus.

Koch, Bea

Mad and bad : real heroines of the Regency / Bea Koch. Grand Central Publishing, 2020. viii, 261 p. **920**

1. Women -- Great Britain -- History -- 19th century 2. Women -- Great Britain -- Social conditions -- 19th century 3. Women intellectuals 4. Lesbians 5. England -- Social life and customs -- 19th century. 6. Great Britain -- History -- George IV, 1820-1830 7. Collective biographies

ISBN 9781538701010

LC 2019049246

A feminist pop history explores the achievements of iconoclastic women from the Regency era, from Dido Elizabeth Belle and Caroline Herschel to Anne Lister and Judith Montefiore, who broke barriers to live on their own terms.

"This fun and informative account will be treasured by readers of Jane Austen and contemporary Regency romance novelists, as well as fans of feminist history." Publishers Weekly

Koehn, Nancy F. (Nancy Fowler), 1959-

Forged in crisis : the making of five legendary leaders / Nancy F. Koehn. Scribner, 2017. ix, 517 p. : **920**

1. Lincoln, Abraham, 1809-1865 2. Douglass, Frederick, 1818-1895 3. Carson, Rachel, 1907-1964 4. Bonhoeffer, Dietrich, 1906-1945 5. Shackleton, Ernest Henry, Sir, 1874-1922 6. Leadership in business 7. Leadership 8. Collective biographies

ISBN 9781501174445

LC 2017297073

Presents a portrait of five extraordinary figures--Ernest Shackleton, Abraham Lincoln, Frederick Douglass, Dietrich Bonhoeffer, and Rachel Carson--to illuminate how great leaders are made in times of adversity and the diverse skills they summon in order to prevail.

"Wise, thoughtful, and valuable, this book will foster a new appreciation for effective leadership and prompt many readers to lament the lack of it in the world today." Kirkus.

Koertge, Noretta

New dictionary of scientific biography / Noretta Koertge, editor in chief. Charles Scribner's Sons/Thomson Gale, c2008. 8 volumes : **920**

1. Scientists 2. Collective biographies

ISBN 9780684313207

LC 2007031384

Offers profiles covering the lives and careers of a variety of prominent scientists.

Kolker, Robert

★**Hidden** Valley Road : inside the mind of an American family / Robert Kolker. Doubleday, 2020 352 p. **920**

1. Galvin family. 2. People with schizophrenia 3. Schizophrenia -- Genetic aspects. 4. Schizophrenia -- Treatment 5. People with schizophrenia -- Family relationships 6. Collective biographies

ISBN 9780385543767

LC 2019028466

Tells the heartrending story of a midcentury American family with 12 children, 6 of them diagnosed with schizophrenia, that became science's great hope in the quest to understand the disease.

"An exceptional, unforgettable, and significant work that must not be missed." Booklist

Koppel, Lily

The **astronaut** wives club : a true story / Lily Koppel. Grand Central Publishing, 2013 288 p. **920**

1. Women in public life. 2. Astronauts -- United States 3. Married women -- United States 4. Public opinion -- United States -- History -- 20th century. 5. Houston, Texas -- Social life and customs -- 20th century. 6. United States -- Social life and customs -- 20th century. 7. Collective biographies. 8. Books to TV

ISBN 9781455503254

LC 2012045976

With selection of the first crew members of the Mercury space program in 1959, a small group of women who had been ordinary military wives became celebrities. As role models and representatives of the space program, NASA demaneded their perfection, from their clothing to the meals they served at home.This intimate, informative group portrait chronicles how they formed a support group (after extending to the wives the Gemini and Apollo astronauts) and became an essential resource behind the scenes of the space program's early years.

Krauss, Erich, 1971-

Wave of destruction : the stories of four families and history's deadliest tsunami / Erich Krauss. Rodale, 2006. xi, 244 p. : **920**

1. Indian Ocean Tsunami, 2004. 2. Tsunamis -- Indian Ocean. 3. Tsunamis -- Nam Keam, Thailand. 4. Survival (after airplane accidents, shipwrecks, etc.) 5. Thailand 6. India. 7. Collective biographies

ISBN 1594863784

LC 2005024531

Four tsunami survival stories offer insight into the experiences of people who endured devastating odds in their determination to stay alive, recounting their painful losses of families, friends, and homes and their subsequent efforts to rebuild.

"The author provides an account of four families in a Thai village devastated by the tsunami of December 26, 2004. Passionately told, this tragic story portrays the full human cost of natural devastation." Publishers Weekly.

Kreisler, Harry

Political awakenings : conversations with history / Harry Kreisler. New Press : 2010. xi, 286 p. ; **920**

1. Political activists -- Interviews. 2. World politics -- 1945-1990 3. Modern history -- 1945-1989 4. World politics -- 1989- 5. Oral histories.

ISBN 9781595583406

LC 2009036808

"Interviews with twenty of the world's most influential writers, thinkers, and activists."

History archive is maintained by the Institute of International Studies of the University of California, Berkeley.

Collects interviews with a diverse group of influential writers and activists and showcases their reflections on the experiences that shaped their political commitments.

Krist, Gary

The **mirage** factory : illusion, imagination, and the invention of Los Angeles / Gary Krist. Crown Publishing, 2018 432 p. **920**

1. Mulholland, William, 1855-1935. 2. Griffith, D. W. (David Wark), 1875-1948. 3. McPherson, Aimee Semple, 1890-1944. 4. Social history 5. Los Angeles, California 6. Collective biographies

ISBN 9780451496386

LC 2017049682

Describes how the visions of three people: William Mulholland, an engineer; D.W. Griffith, an early filmmaker; and Aimee Semple McPherson, an evangelist and faith healer combined to turn sleepy, near-desert farmland into the city of Los Angeles.

Kroger, Lisa

Monster, she wrote : the women who pioneered horror and speculative fiction / Lisa Kroger and Melanie R. Anderson. Qurik Books, 2019. 352 p. **920**

1. Women authors 2. Books and reading 3. Women science fiction authors 4. Women fantasy fiction authors 5. Collective biographies

ISBN 9781683691389

LC 2019930321

Bram Stoker Award for Best Nonfiction, 2019.

Locus Award for Best Nonfiction/Related/Reference Book, 2020.

Frankenstein was just the beginning: horror stories and other weird fiction wouldn't exist without the women who created it. From Gothic ghost stories to psychological horror to science fiction, women have been primary architects of speculative literature of all sorts. And their own life stories are as intriguing as their fiction. Part biography, part reader's guide, the engaging write-ups and detailed reading lists will introduce you to more than a hundred authors and over two hundred of their mysterious and spooky novels, novellas, and stories.

"Straddling the divide between highly useful reference and compulsively readable stories about the writing lives of the women of horror, this book will keep you up all night (one way or another)." Booklist.

Kyle, Taya, 1974-

American spirit : profiles in resilience, courage, and faith / Taya Kyle, Jim DeFelice. William Morrow, [2019] xi, 348 pages ; **920**

1. Resilience (Personal quality) 2. Purpose in life. 3. Despair. 4. Courage. 5. Essays 6. Collective biographies.

ISBN 9780062683717

LC bl2019006330

"Kyle follows up American Wife, about her Navy SEAL husband Chris Kyle (author of American Sniper), with this moving and passionate collection of essays in which she shares her experiences with people she has met as a public speaker...Once again, Kyle and DeFelice inspire with touching stories of compassion." Publishers Weekly.

Lahr, John, 1941-

Joy ride : show people and their shows / John Lahr. W. W. Norton & Company, 2015. 512 p. **920**

1. Theatrical producers and directors. 2. Dramatists, American. 3. Theater. 4. Collective biographies

ISBN 9780393246407

LC 2015013987

Collection of profiles and reviews originally published in The New Yorker.

Includes index.

This collection of profiles and reviews from New Yorker columnist John Lahr reveals the details of the lives of contemporary dramatists as well as their sources of solace and inspiration, including Arthur Miller, Wallace Shawn, Harold Pinter and David Mamet.

"Faithful readers of The New Yorker will enjoy revisiting these articles. Anyone interested in the history of the American theater and contemporary drama will applaud these thoughtful and critical pieces." Library Journal.

Lamb, Brian, 1941-

Booknotes : life stories : notable biographers on the people who shaped America / [compiled by] Brian Lamb. Three Rivers Press, 2000, c1999. xxiii, 471 p. : **920**

1. Biography.

ISBN 9780812933390

LC BL 00010548

Collection of essays by various biographers based on interviews originally held on the television program Booknotes.

Includes index.

Originally published: New York : Times Books, c1999.

Interviews with some of the world's foremost biographers explore the lives and achievements of the people who have shaped the modern world, from Winston Churchill and Thomas Jefferson to Martin Luther King, Jr., and FDR.

Landdeck, Katherine Sharp

The **women** with silver wings : the inspiring true story of the women airforce service pilots of World War II / Katherine Sharp Landdeck. Crown, 2020 368 p. **920**

1. Women Airforce Service Pilots (U.S.). 2. World War II -- Women's participation 3. Military pilots 4. Women pilots -- United States 5. Sexism 6. Collective biographies

ISBN 9781524762810

LC 2019059114

Includes index.

Tells the true story of the daring female aviators who helped the United States win World War II--only to be forgotten by the country they served.

"Based on hundreds of oral histories with surviving WASP women, along with letters, diaries, and government documents, Landdeck explains the women's vital role ferrying planes, the group's disbandment, and their fight decades later to be rightfully recognized as veterans ... A must-read for those interested in women's and World War II history." Library Journal

Larson, Edward J. (Edward John)

★**Franklin** & Washington : the founding partnership / Edward J. Larson. William Morrow & Company, 2020. 352 p. **920**

1. Franklin, Benjamin, 1706-1790 2. Washington, George, 1732-1799 3. Founding Fathers of the United States 4. Politicians -- United States 5. Presidents -- United States 6. Diplomats 7. United States -- Politics and government -- 18th century 8. United States -- History -- 18th century 9. United States -- History -- Revolution, 1775-1783 10. Collective biographies

ISBN 9780062880154

LC bl2020000418

The historian and author of Summer for the Gods presents a dual biography of the two Founding Fathers to illuminate in fresh detail how their underexplored relationship forged the United States.

"Based on primary and secondary sources, this well-researched work tells the story of a significant relationship of the era." Library Journal

Lascher, Bill

Eve of a hundred midnights : the star-crossed love story of two WWII correspondents and their epic escape across the Pacific / Bill Lascher. William Morrow, 2016. 288 p. **920**

1. Jacoby, Melville Jack, 1916-1942. 2. Jacoby, Annalee, 1916-2002. 3. World War II -- Journalists 4. World War II -- Press coverage -- United States. 5. War correspondents -- United States 6. Islands of the Pacific 7. Collective biographies

ISBN 9780062375209

LC 2015046489

Documents the story of two married journalists who toured the Pacific islands after the fall of Manila during World War II, describing how they had many near-brushes with the Japanese and risked their lives to cover the war in the Pacific Theater.

"From interviews and archival documents, Lascher creates a seamless narrative of daring and dedication." Kirkus.

Laskas, Jeanne Marie, 1958-

★**Hidden** America : from coal miners to cowboys, an extraordinary exploration of the unseen people who make this country work / Jeanne Marie Laskas. G.P. Putnam's Sons, 2012. 304 p. **920**

1. Laskas, Jeanne Marie, 1958- Travel United States. 2. Working class -- United States 3. Work -- Social aspects 4. Subcultures 5. United States -- Social life and customs -- 1971- 6. United States

-- Social conditions -- 1980- 7. Collective biographies
ISBN 9780399159008

LC 2012025457

Five hundred feet underground, Jeanne Marie Laskas asked a coal miner named Smitty, "Do you think it's weird that people know so little about you?" He replied, "I don't think people know too much about the way the whole damn country works"...Hidden America intends to fix that.

Leach, William, 1944-
Butterfly people : an American encounter with the beauty of the world / William R. Leach. Pantheon Books, 2012. 416 p. **920**

1. Butterflies -- United States 2. Entomology 3. Collectors and collecting 4. Industrial revolution -- United States 5. Collective biographies
ISBN 9780375422935

LC 2012000389

The historian author of the National Book Award finalist, Land of Desire presents a chronicle of 19th-century America's fascination with butterflies that traces the achievements of six naturalists who identified countless new species and unveiled the mysteries of their existence.

Leamer, Laurence
The **Kennedy** men : 1901-1963 : the laws of the father / Laurence Leamer. Wm. Morrow, c2001. 882 p. : **920**

1. Kennedy, Joseph P. (Joseph Patrick), 1888-1969 2. Kennedy, Joseph P. (Joseph Patrick), 1888-1969 Family 3. Kennedy, John F. (John Fitzgerald), 1917-1963. 4. Kennedy family. 5. Politicians -- United States 6. Collective biographies.
ISBN 9780688163150

LC 2001031689

Presents a multigenerational portrait of the Kennedy men and their rise to the heights of American politics, beginning in 1901 with twelve-year-old Joseph P. Kennedy and ending in 1963 with the assassination of President John F. Kennedy.

"Leamer's writing is impressive throughout, regularly catching the reader up with a felicitous phrase or a surprising insight." Booklist.

Lee, Hermione
Virginia Woolf's nose : essays on biography / Hermione Lee. Princeton University Press, 2005. 141 p. ; **920**

1. Shelley, Percy Bysshe, 1792-1822. 2. Woolf, Virginia, 1882-1941. 3. Pepys, Samuel, 1633-1703. 4. Austen, Jane, 1775-1817. 5. Authors, English 6. Collective biographies 7. Essays.
ISBN 0691120323

LC 2004058457

"Lee's immensely enjoyable study will energize debate among thoughtful readers and should become essential reading for aficionados of literary biography." Publishers Weekly.

Lees, Gene
You can't steal a gift : Dizzy, Clark, Milt, and Nat / Gene Lees ; foreword by Nat Hentoff. Yale University Press, c2001. xvii, 269 p. : **920**

1. Gillespie, Dizzy, 1917-1993. 2. Terry, Clark. 3. Hinton, Milt, 1910-2000. 4. Cole, Nat "King," 1919-1965. 5. Jazz musicians 6. United States -- Race relations -- History. 7. Collective biographies
ISBN 0300089651

LC 2001003444

Includes index.

"The author has a natural ease with words and a graceful prose style that captures the reader's attention." Booklist.

Lehr, Dick
Dead reckoning : the story of how Johnny Mitchell and his fighter pilots took on Admiral Yamamoto and avenged Pearl Harbor / Dick Lehr. Harper, 2020 xi, 399 p. : **920**

1. Mitchell, John W., 1914-1995 2. Yamamoto, Isoroku, 1884-1943 3. Fighter pilots 4. Admirals 5. World War II -- Aerial operations, American 6. Enemies 7. Collective biographies
ISBN 9780062448514

The definitive and dramatic account of what became known as "Operation Vengeance" -- the targeted kill by U.S. fighter pilots of Japan's larger-than-life military icon, Admiral Isoroku Yamamoto, the naval genius who had devised the devastating attack on Pearl Harbor.

"Anyone interested in World War II, and especially the war in the Pacific, will find this account fascinating." Library Journal

Levingston, Steven
Kennedy and King : the president, the pastor, and the battle over civil rights / Steven Levingston. Hachette Books, 2017. 352 p. **920**

1. King, Martin Luther, Jr., 1929-1968 2. Kennedy, John F. (John Fitzgerald), 1917-1963 3. Civil Rights Movement 4. Presidents -- United States 5. Civil rights workers 6. Political science 7. Collective biographies 8. Biographies
ISBN 9780316267397

LC bl2017015720

A revelatory account of the contentious relationship between the 35th President and Martin Luther King, Jr. throughout the tumultuous early years of the Civil Rights movement shares insights into their profound influence on one another and the important decisions that were inspired by their rivalry.

"A dual biography chronicles three years of upheaval in the civil rights movement." Kirkus.

Lewis, Andrew B., 1967-
The **shadows** of youth : the remarkable journey of the civil rights generation / Andrew B. Lewis. Hill and Wang, 2009. 368 p. **920**

1. Student Nonviolent Coordinating Committee (U.S.) 2. African American civil rights workers 3. African American college students 4. Civil Rights Movement 5. African Americans -- Civil rights -- History -- 20th century. 6. United States -- Race relations -- History -- 20th century. 7. Southern States -- Race relations -- History -- 20th century. 8. Collective biographies.
ISBN 9780809085989

LC 2009009980

A group portrait of leading civil rights activists who comprised the Student Nonviolent Coordinating Committee draws on original sources to illuminate their challenges to American perspectives on human rights, politics, and moral obligation.

Lewis, Michael (Michael M.)
★The **undoing** project : a friendship that changed our minds / Michael Lewis. W W Norton & Company, 2016. 362 p. ; **920**

1. Kahneman, Daniel, 1934- 2. Tversky, Amos 3. Cognitive neuroscience 4. Neuroscience 5. Decision-making 6. Male friendship 7. Collective biographies
ISBN 9780393254594

Examines the history of behavioral economics, discussing the theory of Israeli psychologists who wrote the original studies undoing assumptions about the decision-making process and the influence it has had on evidence-based regulation.

Lewis-Jones, Huw

Explorers' sketchbooks : the art of discovery & adventure / Huw Lewis-Jones, Kari Herbert ; foreword by Robert Macfarlane. Chronicle Books, 2017. 320 p. : **920**

1. Explorers -- Archives. 2. Notebooks. 3. Exploration -- History. 4. Expeditions. 5. Collective biographies.

ISBN 9781452158273

LC bl2016048901

Showcases material from the sketchbooks of seventy explorers from all over the world, including Charles Darwin, Sir Edmund Hillary, and Gertrude Bell.

Livingstone, Natalie

The **mistresses** of Cliveden : three centuries of scandal, power, and intrigue in an English stately home / Natalie Livingstone. Ballantine Books, 2016. 512 p. **920**

1. Shrewsbury, Anna Maria Brudenell Talbot, Countess of, 1642-1702. 2. Villiers, Elizabeth, Countess of Orkney, 1657?-1733. 3. Augusta, Princess of Wales, 1719-1772. 4. Sutherland, Harriet Elizabeth Georgiana Leveson-Gower, Duchess of, 1806-1868. 5. Astor, Nancy Witcher Langhorne Astor, Viscountess, 1879-1964. 6. Cliveden (England) -- History. 7. Cliveden (England) 8. Women -- England 9. Nobility -- England 10. Rich people -- England 11. Mansions 12. England 13. Collective biographies

ISBN 9780553392074

LC 2015049927

"Originally published in hardcover in the United Kingdom by Hutchinson, a member of Penguin Random House, London, in 2015"--Title page verso.

The latest mistress of the 17th-century rural mansion Cliveden traces its history through the stories of some of its most noteworthy women, including an aristocrat-turned-adulteress, a best friend of Queen Victoria, a German royal who nearly became the Queen of England and a first woman member of Parliament.

"In her debut book, Livingstone ably avoids tabloidlike gossip to profile five remarkable women, and she provides a helpful cast of characters at the beginning of the story. Readers who enjoy English history will be happy to have this in their libraries." Kirkus.

Lord, Bette

Legacies : a Chinese mosaic / Bette Bao Lord. Knopf, 1990. viii, 245 p. **920**

1. Tiananmen Square Massacre, Beijing, China, June 3-4, 1989. 2. Revolutions -- China. 3. Political prisoners. 4. State-sponsored terrorism 5. China -- History -- Cultural Revolution, 1966-1976. 6. China -- Social life and customs -- 1976- 7. Beijing, China. 8. Collective biographies.

ISBN 9780394583259

LC 89043452

ALA Notable Book, 1991.

"A vivid and startling mosaic of the political struggles that foreshadowed the Tiananmen Square uprising." Time.

MacMillan, Margaret, 1943-

History's people : personalities and the past / Margaret MacMillan. House of Anansi Press, 2015 304 p. **920**

1. History 2. Celebrities 3. Collective biographies

ISBN 9781487000059

LC bl2015042855

Internationally acclaimed historian Margaret MacMillan gives her own personal selection of the great figures of the past, women and men, who have changed the course of history and even directed the currents of their times--and sometimes with huge consequences, as in the cases of Hitler, Stalin, and Thatcher.

Mackrell, Judith

Flappers : six women of a dangerous generation / Judith Mackrell. Farrar, Straus and Giroux, 2014. 512 p. **920**

1. Cooper, Diana, 1892-1986. 2. Cunard, Nancy, 1896-1965. 3. Bankhead, Tallulah, 1902-1968. 4. Fitzgerald, Zelda, 1900-1948. 5. Baker, Josephine, 1906-1975. 6. Lempicka, Tamara de, 1898-1980. 7. Feminism 8. Femininity 9. Flappers. 10. Sex customs -- United States -- History -- 20th century. 11. Collective biographies

ISBN 9780374156084

LC 2013035397

The forefront British dance critic and award-nominated author of Bloomsbury Ballerina presents a revisionist assessment of the movement that shattered the boundaries of conventional femininity through the lives of six figures that exemplified it, including Lady Diana Cooper, Nancy Cunard, Tallulah Bankhead, Zelda Fitzgerald, Josephine Baker and Tamara de Lempicka.

"Avidly researched and deeply inquisitive, Mackrell's prodigious group portrait is spectacularly dramatic and thought-provoking." Booklist.

Mahoney, Richard D.

Sons & brothers : the days of Jack and Bobby Kennedy / Richard D. Mahoney. Arcade Pub., c1999. xvii, 441 p. : **920**

1. Kennedy, John F. (John Fitzgerald), 1917-1963. 2. Kennedy, Robert Francis, 1925-1968 3. Kennedy family. 4. United States. Congress. Senate 5. Presidents -- United States 6. Legislators -- United States 7. Brothers -- United States 8. United States -- Politics and government -- 1961-1963. 9. United States -- Politics and government -- 1963-1969. 10. Collective biographies

ISBN 1559704802

LC 99025681

An intimate and powerful portrait of the Kennedy brothers details their extraordinary bond based on their shared belief of tragic destiny.

"Writing in a steady, almost relentlessly elegiac tone, Mahoney proves that the lives and deaths of John F. and Robert F. Kennedy remain as compelling now as they were throughout the turbulent 1960s." Publishers Weekly.

Maier, Thomas, 1956-

When lions roar : the Churchills and the Kennedys / Thomas Maier. Crown Publishers, 2014. 784 p. **920**

1. Churchill, Winston, 1874-1965. 2. Kennedy, John F. (John Fitzgerald), 1917-1963. 3. Churchill family. 4. Kennedy family. 5. Great Britain -- Relations United States. 6. United States -- Relations Great Britain. 7. Great Britain -- Politics and government -- 20th century. 8. United States -- Politics and government -- 20th century. 9. Collective biographies

ISBN 9780307956798

LC 2014007201

A far-reaching history of the intertwined personal and public lives of the Churchills and the Kennedys discusses their respective family views, how they overcame bitter differences to unite against Hitler and the enduring influence of their collaborations.

"An excellent work for all history collections, especially those devoted to 20th-century political history." Library Journal.

Makos, Adam

Devotion : an epic story of heroism, friendship, and sacrifice / Adam Makos. Ballantine Books, 2015 400 p. **920**

1. Brown, Jesse Leroy 2. Hudner, Tom 3. United States. Navy Aviation. 4. Korean War, 1950-1953. 5. African American men 6. Racism in the military 7. Search and rescue operations. 8. Collective biographies

ISBN 9780804176583

LC 2015023955

Traces the inspirational story of famous Navy aviator duo Tom Hudner and Jesse Brown, recounting how they defied period conventions to serve their country, overcome racial barriers and protect one another on a daring Korean War mission.

Malek, Cate,

Palestine speaks : narratives of life under occupation / edited by Cate Malek and Mateo Hoke. Voice of Witness, 2014. 346 p. : **920**

1. Arab-Israeli conflict 2. Palestinians -- Politics and government -- 1993- 3. West Bank (Jordan River) 4. Gaza Strip 5. Middle East. 6. Israeli-occupied territories 7. Interviews 8. Oral histories 9. Collective autobiographies and memoirs

ISBN 9781940450247

LC 2015452323

The occupation of the West Bank and Gaza has been one of the world's most widely reported yet least understood human rights crises for over four decades. In this oral history collection, men and women from Palestine -- including a fisherman, a settlement administrator, and a marathon runner -- describe in their own words how their lives have been shaped by the historic crisis.

"An absolute must for anyone interested in the Arab-Israeli conflict or with an interest in human rights. This book, similar to the other titles in the series, is an excellent way of developing a deeper understanding of people living the encounters about which we read in the papers and watch on the news." Library Journal.

Mann, James

The **great** rift : Dick Cheney, Colin Powell, and the broken friendship that defined an era / James Mann. Henry Holt and Company, 2020. 416 p. **920**

1. Cheney, Richard B. 2. Powell, Colin, 1937- 3. Vice-presidents -- United States 4. Cabinet officers -- United States 5. Friendship 6. Disagreement 7. United States -- Politics and government 8. Collective biographies

ISBN 9781627797559

LC 2019038052

The Great Rift is a sweeping history of the intertwined careers of Dick Cheney and Colin Powell, whose rivalry and conflicting views of U.S. national security color our political debate to this day.

"A significant work of American history." Kirkus

Mann, William J.

The **wars** of the Roosevelts : the ruthless rise of America's greatest political family / William J. Mann. Harper, 2016. x, 609 pages, 32 unnumbered pages of plates : **920**

1. Roosevelt family 2. Roosevelt, Franklin D. (Franklin Delano), 1882-1945 3. Roosevelt, Eleanor, 1884-1962. 4. Roosevelt, Theodore, 1858-1919 5. Sibling rivalry 6. Ambition 7. Power (Social sciences) 8. Jealousy 9. Collective biographies

ISBN 9780062383334

LC bl2016046398

A provocative group biography of the Roosevelt family draws on lesser-known family secrets and complex rivalries to argue that the Roosevelts' rise to power was driven by a series of inside competitions that were witnessed firsthand by an increasingly begrudging Eleanor Roosevelt.

"Perhaps best known for his popular film biographies and histories, and thus no stranger to tales of scandal and coverup, feuds and intrigue, Mann writes sympathetically about all the Roosevelts but particularly the black sheep, the nonconformists whose births into this powerful family imposed special burdens." Kirkus.

Markel, Howard

The **Kelloggs** : the battling brothers of Battle Creek / Howard Markel. Pantheon Books, 2017. 352 p. **920**

1. Kellogg, John Harvey, 1852-1943. 2. Kellogg, W. K. (Will Keith), 1860-1951 3. Kellogg Company -- History 4. Battle Creek Sanitarium (Battle Creek, Mich.) -- History. 5. Holistic medicine 6. Cereal products 7. Physicians. 8. Businesspeople 9. Collective biographies

ISBN 9780307907271

LC 2016053946

National Book Critics Circle Award for Biography finalist, 2017

Brothers John Harvey and Will Kellogg made Battle Creek, Michigan famous for their work in promoting health (and healthy breakfast cereal) from the 1870s to the mid-20th century. Ironically, they hated each other! In The Kelloggs, Dr. Howard Markel, a professor of the history of medicine, details the brothers' lives, careers, and intra-family warfare.

Markham, Lauren

★The **far** away brothers : two young migrants and the making of an American life / Lauren Markham. Crown Publishing, 2017. 352 p. **920**

1. Flores, Ernesto, 1997- 2. Flores, Raúl, 1997- 3. Twin brothers 4. Undocumented immigrants. 5. Teenagers 6. Immigration policy 7. El Salvador 8. Oakland, California 9. California 10. Collective biographies

ISBN 9781101906187

LC 2017000952

Author Lauren Markham was working as a counselor in an Oakland, California school district when she met identical twins Raúl and Ernesto Flores. The teenagers had fled El Salvador to escape deadly gang violence, knowing no English and unprepared for American society. Markham traces their harrowing journey to the U.S. and their struggles to survive in a strange land, illuminating the difficulties of undocumented minors; she also offers details on migrant shelters, the Texas border wall, and court proceedings in immigration cases.

"This is a timely and thought-provoking exploration of a international quagmire. Markham provides a sensitive and eye-opening take on whats at stake for young immigrants with nowhere else to go." Publishers Weekly.

Martin, Justin

Rebel souls : Walt Whitman and America's first bohemians / Justin Martin. Da Capo Press, 2014. 368 p. **920**

1. Whitman, Walt, 1819-1892. 2. Ward, Artemus, 1834-1867. 3. Booth, Edwin, 1833-1893. 4. Ludlow, Fitz Hugh, 1836-1870. 5. Menken, Adah Isaacs, 1839?-1868 6. Bohemianism -- New York City. 7. Beat culture 8. Intellectual life 9. Bars (Drinking

establishments). 10. New York City 11. Collective biographies
ISBN 9780306822261

LC 2014008822

"This book is a lively and entertaining read for students of American literature, history, and culture." Choice.

Marton, Kati

The **great** escape : nine Jews who fled Hitler and changed the world / Kati Marton. Simon & Schuster, c2006. 271 p. : **920**

1. Jews 2. Refugees, Jewish 3. Exiles -- Hungary 4. Budapest, Hungary -- History -- 20th century. 5. Collective biographies
ISBN 0743261151

LC 2006049162

Traces the early twentieth century journey of nine prominent men from Budapest who fled fascism to seek sanctuary in America, where they made pivotal contributions to science, film, and photojournalism.

"By looking at these nine lives salvaged, and crucial--Marton provides a moving measure of how much was lost." The New Yorker.

Massing, Michael

Fatal discord : Erasmus, Luther, and the fight for the Western mind / Michael Massing. Harper, 2018 xvi, 987 pages, 16 unnumbered pages of plates : **920**

1. Erasmus, Desiderius, died 1536 2. Luther, Martin, 1483-1546 3. Catholic Church 4. Theologians 5. Academic rivalry 6. Religious reformers 7. Christian philosophy 8. Collective biographies 9. Biographies
ISBN 9780060517601

LC 2018304707

The Harvard-educated author presents an intellectual assessment of the rivalry between Desiderius Erasmus and Martin Luther that examines their respective characters and belief systems, sharing insights into their enduring influence and proper historical roles in western tradition.

"As we commemorate the 500th anniversary of the Protestant Reformation, this engaging tale of the contentious relationship between two precursors of the modern world--one who remained a Catholic, the other whose teaching spawned the various Protestant denominations--provides much-needed historical background and reflection on a major period in church and world history." Library Journal.

Matteson, John

Eden's outcasts : the story of Louisa May Alcott and her father / John Matteson. W.W. Norton, 2007. 528 p. **920**

1. Alcott, Louisa May, 1832-1888 Family. 2. Authors, American -- Family relationships. 3. Fathers and daughters -- United States 4. Transcendentalism (New England) 5. United States -- Social life and customs -- 20th century 6. Collective biographies.
ISBN 0393059642

LC 2007013707

Pulitzer Prize for Biography or Autobiography, 2008.

Evaluates the relationship between Louisa May Alcott and her idealistic father, discussing how Louisa's exuberant personality often challenged Bronson's child-rearing philosophies and how Louisa eventually came to support her family through writing.

"Matteson's lucid, commanding biography casts new light on an unusual father-daughter bond and a new land at war with itself." Booklist.

McCluskey, Audrey Thomas

A **forgotten** sisterhood : pioneering Black women educators and activists in the Jim Crow South / Audrey Thomas McCluskey. Rowman & Littlefield Pub Inc, 2014. 181 p. **920**

1. Laney, Lucy Craft 2. Bethune, Mary McLeod, 1875-1955 3. Brown, Charlotte Hawkins, 1883-1961. 4. Burroughs, Nannie Helen, 1879-1961. 5. African American women teachers 6. African American women political activists 7. African American women social reformers 8. African American women 9. United States 10. Collective biographies
ISBN 9781442211384

LC 2014025293

"McCluskey's well-researched account articulates the importance of this particular movement in education, appropriately and skillfully, to memorialize the four pioneering women at the forefront." Publishers Weekly.

McCullough, David G.

★The **greater** journey : Americans in Paris, 1830-1900 / David McCullough. Simon & Schuster, 2011. 544 p. **920**

1. Americans in France. 2. Intellectual life. 3. Americans in Paris, France. 4. Intellectuals. 5. Paris, France -- History -- 19th century. 6. France -- Relations United States. 7. United States -- Foreign relations France.
ISBN 9781416571766

LC 2010053001

Relates the story of the American artists, writers, and doctors who traveled to Paris in the nineteenth century, fell in love with the city and its people, and changed America through what they learned there.

"An account of young Americans, driven by wanderlust, setting out in search of greener Parisian pastures. Well-known figures such as James Fenimore Cooper, Oliver Wendell Holmes Sr., and Mary Cassat, and long-forgotten entities like Elizabeth Blackwell and William Wells Brown, all walked along the Avenue des Champs-lyses, went to the Muse du Louvre, ate wonderful meals, and became inspired. Their life-changing adventures played a vital role in transforming the course of US history." Christian Science Monitor.

★The **pioneers** : the heroic story of the settlers who brought the American ideal west / David McCullough. Simon & Schuster, 2019. 320 p. **920**

1. Pioneers 2. Pioneer families 3. Frontier and pioneer life 4. Ohio River Valley 5. United States -- Territorial expansion 6. United States -- History -- 1783-1815 7. Collective biographies
ISBN 9781501168680

LC 2018057066

"Simon & Schuster nonfiction original hardcover."

Best-selling author David McCullough chronicles the lesser-known settling of the Northwest Territory by dauntless pioneers whose community ideals shaped a fledgling America.

"Drawing on little-known archives, acclaimed popular historian McCullough offers a unique chronicle of the settlement of the Ohio River Valley that emphasizes the courage and tenacity of early pioneers and the precedents they set for further westward expansion." Booklist.

Mehr, Bob

Trouble boys : the true story of the Replacements / Bob Mehr. Da Capo Press, 2015 304 p. **920**

1. Replacements (Musical group). 2. Rock musicians -- United States 3. Rock groups 4. Collective biographies. 5. Biographies
ISBN 9780306818790

LC 2015026791

The definitive biography of The Replacements, told with the cooperation of the band and those closest to them.

Meyer, G. J., 1940-

The **Tudors** : the complete story of England's most notorious dynasty / G.J. Meyer. Delacorte Press, c2010. 640 p. **920**

1. Tudor, House of. 2. Monarchy -- Great Britain -- History -- 16th century 3. Royal houses. 4. Rulers 5. Great Britain -- History -- Tudors, 1485-1603. 6. Great Britain -- Politics and government -- 1485-1603. 7. Collective biographies.
ISBN 9780385340762

LC 2009040032

A single-volume history of Henry VIII and his three heirs offers new insights into the dynasty's precarious position in world politics and culture while evaluating the role of religion in 16th-century government.

Mezrich, Ben, 1969-

Once upon a time in Russia : the rise of the oligarchs / Ben Mezrich. Atria Books, 2015. 288 p. **920**

1. Abramovich, Roman Arkadievich, 1966- 2. Berezovskii, B. A. (Boris Abramovich), 1946-2013. 3. Elite (Social sciences) 4. Power (Social sciences) 5. Political corruption 6. Ambition in men 7. Russia 8. Collective biographies
ISBN 9781476771892

LC 2015295889

The best-selling author of Bringing Down the House and The Accidental Billionaires delivers an epic drama of wealth, rivalry and betrayal among mega-wealthy Russian oligarchs--and its international repercussions.

"Mezrich's ability to tell a true (and well-documented) story, in a way that makes it look and feel like the most involving of narratives, is nearly unparalleled. He is one of the few writers whose name on a piece of nonfiction guarantees not only quality but also interest, no matter the subject, and this fine book is one more example of just how talented a storyteller he is." Booklist.

Michaelis, Arno

The **gift** of our wounds : a Sikh and a former white supremacist find forgiveness after hate / Arno Michaelis and Pardeep Singh Kaleka, with Robin Gaby Fisher. St. Martin's Press, 2018. 240 p. **920**

1. Michaelis, Arno 2. Kaleka, Pardeep 3. Race relations 4. Violence against minorities 5. Social advocacy 6. Hate crimes 7. Collective autobiographies and memoirs
ISBN 9781250107541

LC 2017053392

Documents the story of the unlikely and powerful friendship between a Sikh and a former white supremacist in the aftermath of Wade Michael Page's murderous 2012 attack on a Wisconsin Sikh Temple, describing how they launched the Serve 2 Unite organization to promote community inclusion and fight hate crimes.

Middleton, William, 1961-

Double vision : the unerring eye of art world avatars Dominique and John de Menil / William Middleton. Alfred A. Knopf, 2018. 800 p. **920**

1. Menil, John de. 2. Menil, Dominique de. 3. Art -- Collectors and collecting. 4. Collectors and collecting. 5. Intellectual life. 6. Art patronage. 7. Collective biographies
ISBN 9780375415432

LC 2017027976

A dual portrait of celebrated collectors Dominique and John de Menil draws on unprecedented access to family archives to trace how they became one of the leading cultural forces of the 20th century through their groundbreaking exhibits, artistic scholarship, the creation of innovative galleries and museums and work on behalf of civil rights.

"This exhaustively researched, satisfying slab of a book offers a thorough look into the lives and influence of an extraordinary couple." Publishers Weekly.

Midorikawa, Emily

A **secret** sisterhood : the literary friendships of Jane Austen, Charlotte Bronte, George Eliot, and Virginia Woolf / Emily Midorikawa and Emma Claire Sweeney, foreword by Margaret Atwood. Houghton Mifflin Harcourt, 2017 288 p. **920**

1. Austen, Jane, 1775-1817. 2. Bronte, Charlotte, 1816-1855 3. Eliot, George, 1819-1880 4. Woolf, Virginia, 1882-1941. 5. Women authors 6. Intellectual life 7. Female friendship 8. Friendship 9. Letters 10. Collective biographies
ISBN 9780544883734

LC 2017044906

Draws on previously unpublished letters and diaries to reveal the lesser-known friendships of female literary masters, from the influence of feminist Mary Taylor on Charlotte Bronte's writings to the erotically charged, love-hate associations between Virginia Woolf and Katherine Mansfield.

"The authors (who are themselves close friends) astutely explain that the friendships they depict became lost to cultural memory due to prevailing stereotypes of female authors as solitary eccentrics or isolated geniuses. It is a delight to learn about them here, as related by two talented authors." Publishers Weekly.

Moorehead, Caroline

A **bold** and dangerous family : the remarkable story of an Italian mother, her two sons, and their fight against Fascism / Caroline Moorehead. HarperCollins, 2017. 384 p. **920**

1. Mussolini, Benito, 1883-1945 2. Rosselli family 3. Anti-fascism 4. Political activists 5. Intellectuals 6. Courage 7. Italy -- Politics and government -- 1922-1945 8. Italy -- History -- 1918-1945 9. Collective biographies
ISBN 9780062308306

LC 2017470659

Examines the lives of Amelia, Carlo, and Nello Rosselli, an Italian family from Florence who opposed Mussolini and became leaders of an anti-fascist movement.

"Based in part on letters preserved by the family and secret police files, Moorehead's account tells an extremely personal and engaging story about the price one family paid for its political resistance." Library Journal.

Mordden, Ethan, 1947-

Love song : the lives of Kurt Weill and Lotte Lenya / Ethan Mordden. St. Martin's Press, 2012. 304 p. **920**

1. Weill, Kurt, 1900-1950 2. Lenya, Lotte, 1898-1981. 3. Composers 4. Singers 5. Husband and wife 6. Actors and actresses 7. Collective biographies
ISBN 9780312676575

LC 2012028287

Includes index.

A noted Broadway musical historian traces the romance shared by composer Kurt Weill and stage performer Lotte Lenya against a backdrop of tumultuous 20th-century events, tracing the impact of their backgrounds on their careers and relationship while evaluating their role in shaping the history of Western music.

Morgan, Edmund S. (Edmund Sears), 1916-2013

★**American** heroes : profiles of men and women who shaped early America / Edmund S. Morgan. W.W. Norton & Co., c2009. 352 p. **920**

1. Heroes and heroines, American 2. Courage. 3. Revolutions -- United States 4. American Revolution, 1775-1783 5. United States -- History -- Colonial period, 1600-1775 6. United States -- History -- Revolution, 1775-1783 7. United States -- History -- 1783-1825 8. Collective biographies.

ISBN 9780393070101

LC 2009000714

Historian Edmund S. Morgan delivers 17 stirring essays about heroic Americans. John Winthrop's unpopular stand saves Massachusetts Bay Colony. William Penn's principles forge a Philadelphia miracle. George Washington's strategy stuns the British. And Anti-Federalist opposition fosters the Bill of Rights.

"This book is a perfect gem. Both specialists and general readers will find this book both authoritative and fun to read." Library Journal.

Mortimer, Gavin

The **great** swim / Gavin Mortimer. Walker & Company, 2008. 325 p. : **920**

1. Women swimmers -- United States 2. Swimmers -- United States 3. Marathon swimming -- English Channel. 4. Extreme sports. 5. United States -- History -- 1919-1933. 6. English Channel -- History -- 1919-1933. 7. Collective biographies

ISBN 0802715958

LC 2008000256

Draws on primary sources, diaries, and family interviews to document the story of four American athletes who in 1926 became the first women to swim the English Channel, in an account that also cites the media frenzy that surrounded their achievement.

Mosley, Charlotte,

The **Mitfords** : letters between six sisters / editedy by Charlotte Mosley. Harper, 2007. 832 p. **920**

1. Mitford family. 2. Sisters -- Correspondence. 3. Family relationships. 4. United States -- History -- 20th century. 5. Europe -- History -- 20th century.

ISBN 9780061373640

LC bl2007029548

Collects the correspondence of the six Mitford sisters--Nancy, Pamela, Diana, Unity, Jessica, and Deborah--to shed light on their private lives and the broader British aristocracy, offering vivid insights into such factors as their career and lifestyle choices, the impact of World War II on their political beliefs, and their high-profile marriages.

"The lost art of letter writing is splendidly portrayed in this massive volume of correspondence among the six Mitford sisters: Nancy, Pamela, Diana, Unity, Jessica, and Deborah." Library Journal.

Mulley, Clare

The **women** who flew for Hitler : a true story of soaring ambition and searing rivalry / Clare Mulley. St. Martin's Press, 2017. 400 p. **920**

1. Reitsch, Hannah 2. Stauffenberg, Melitta, Grafin, 1903-1945 3. Nazi Party (Germany) 4. Germany. Air Force 5. Women pilots 6. World War II 7. Gender role 8. Aeronautical engineers 9. Germany -- History -- 1933-1945 10. Collective biographies 11. Biographies

ISBN 9781250063670

LC 2017011483

A dual biography of the first two women flight captains for the Nazis describes how, in spite of Hitler's dictates against women in the military, Aryan poster girl Hanna Reitsch and Jewish aeronautical engineer Melitta Schenk Gräfin von Stauffenger were awarded the Iron Cross.

"Absolutely gripping, Mulley's double portrait is a reminder that there are many more stories to tell from this oft-examined time." Booklist.

Myers, Paul, 1960-

The **Kids** in the Hall : one dumb guy / Paul Myers. House of Anansi Press, 2017. 320 p. **920**

1. McCulloch, Bruce. 2. Foley, Dave, 1963- 3. McDonald, Kevin, 1961- 4. McKinney, Mark, 1963- 5. Thompson, Scott, 1959- 6. Kids in the Hall (Comedy group) 7. Kids in the Hall (Television program) 8. Comedians -- Canada 9. Comedy sketches. 10. Television writing. 11. Television comedies 12. Collective biographies

ISBN 9781487001834

LC oc2017014199

The definitive, authorized story of legendary sketch comedy troupe The Kids in the Hall by critically acclaimed biographer and comedy aficionado Paul Myers.

"A terrific account of a truly unique sensation, best accompanied by pulling up corresponding sketches on YouTube." Kirkus.

Napoli, Lisa, 1963-

Ray and Joan : the man who made the McDonald's fortune and the woman who gave it all away / Lisa Napoli. Penguin Random House LLC, 2016 320 p. **920**

1. Kroc, Joan B. 2. Kroc, Ray, 1902-1984. 3. McDonald's Corporation. 4. Women philanthropists. 5. Businesspeople. 6. Husband and wife 7. Philanthropy 8. Collective biographies

ISBN 9781101984956

LC 2016023340

A portrait of the relationship between McDonald's chairman Ray Croc and his wife, Joan, describes how he helped establish an international brand and amassed a considerable estate before his impassioned wife gave most of the family fortune away to philanthropic pursuits.

"Napoli's energetic, slightly tabloidesque narrative style make this a must-read for anyone who loves a good love story behind a business success." Publishers Weekly.

Napoli, Philip F., 1960-

Bringing it all back home : oral histories of New York's Vietnam veterans / Philip F. Napoli. Hill and Wang, 2012. 272 p. **920**

1. Vietnam War, 1961-1975, American. 2. Vietnam veterans 3. Veterans -- Psychology. 4. Self-sacrifice. 5. New York City -- History -- 20th century. 6. Collective biographies. 7. Oral histories

ISBN 9780809073184

LC 2012034731

A collection of oral histories challenges the prejudices surrounding the veterans of the Vietnam War, surveying the experiences of soldiers who in spite of traumatizing experiences returned home to serve productive lives of public service.

Neff, James

Vendetta : Bobby Kennedy versus Jimmy Hoffa / James Neff. Little Brown & Co, 2014. 384 p. **920**

1. Kennedy, Robert Francis, 1925-1968. 2. Hoffa, Jimmy, 1913-1975? 3. International Brotherhood of Teamsters. 4. Enemies 5. Labor union officials and employees. 6. Politicians 7. Organized crime. 8. Collective biographies

ISBN 9780316738347

LC 2015939408

Based on newly released documents, sheds a new light on the historic and ongoing battle between U.S. Attorney General Robert Kennedy and Teamsters leader Jimmy Hoffa during the Senate Rackets Committee hearings and beyond during 1957 to 1964.

"This enthralling account, based mostly on archival research, will appeal to Kennedy followers, true crime fans, and students and scholars of modern American history." Library Journal.

Newton, David E.

Latinos in science, math, and professions / David E. Newton. Facts on File, c2007. xiv, 274 p. : **920**

1. Hispanic-American scientists 2. Scientists 3. Hispanic Americans 4. Collective biographies

ISBN 9780816063857

LC 2006016769

Presents alphabetically arranged biographical profiles of Latino scientists and mathematicians who have influenced and continue to impact the Latino community, the United States, and the world.

"Among the figures profiled in this biographical dictionary are sociology expert Maxine Baca Zinn; Ellen Ochoa, the first Latina in space; and research entomologist Fernando E. Vega." Library Journal.

Nicolson, Adam, 1957-

The **making** of poetry : Coleridge, the Wordsworths, and their year of marvels / Adam Nicolson ; with woodcuts and paintings by Tom Hammick. Farrar, Straus and Giroux, 2020, c2019. 390 p. : **920**

1. Coleridge, Samuel Taylor, 1772-1834 2. Wordsworth, Dorothy, 1771-1855 3. Wordsworth, William, 1770-1850 4. Poetry -- History and criticism 5. Poets, English -- 18th century 6. Romanticism in poetry 7. Nature (Aesthetics) 8. England 9. Collective biographies

ISBN 9780374200213

LC 2019951670

Originally published: London : William Collins, 2019.

Celebrates the poems that the two English poets composed within a space of one year in which they challenged the accepted ideas of their time and presented a new vision of hope and possibility.

"An astonishingly rich re-creation of the months that the Wordsworths and Coleridges lived near each other in southwest England." Kirkus

Nimura, Janice P.

Daughters of the samurai : a journey from east to west and back / Janice P. Nimura. W.W. Norton & Company, [2015] 336 p. : **920**

1. Japanese in the United States 2. Cultural differences 3. Culture conflict 4. Collective biographies

ISBN 9780393077995

LC 2014046933

In the years after 1853, when Japan opened its harbors to trade with the U.S., the Japanese government realized that its citizens would need to understand Western culture as it pursued commerce with the rest of the world. Since they viewed women as essential to the preparation of future leaders, they decided to send some girls to the U.S. so they could learn American ways and return to Japan as educators. Daughters of the Samurai presents complete biographies of three of the five girls who were chosen, tracing their foreign experiences and following their adult lives in Japan.

Nordland, Rod

The **lovers** : Afghanistan's Romeo and Juliet, the true story of how they defied their families and escaped an honor killing / Rod Nordland. Ecco, 2016. 336 p. **920**

1. Forbidden love. 2. Islamic law 3. Women's rights -- Afghanistan. 4. Men/women relations. 5. Afghanistan 6. Collective biographies

ISBN 9780062378828

LC bl2015053793

An account illuminating the ongoing debate about women's rights in the Muslim world documents the true story of how two people from different Afghani tribes pursued marriage against Islamic law and remain in hiding from relatives who would kill them to restore family honor.

"Nordland offers a stark, eye-opening look at the deplorable state of womens rights in Afghanistan through the travails of a brave, determined young couple." Booklist.

Nutt, Amy Ellis

Becoming Nicole : the transformation of an American family / Amy Ellis Nutt. Random House, 2015. 336 p. **920**

1. Identical twins 2. Transgender persons 3. Adoption 4. Transgender persons -- Rights 5. Collective biographies

ISBN 9780812995411

LC 2015031162

Stonewall Non-Fiction Honor Book, 2016

The inspiring true story of a transgender girl, her identical twin brother, and an ordinary American family's extraordinary journey to understand, nurture, and celebrate the right to be different--from the Pulitzer Prize-winning science reporter for The Washington Post.

"This poignant account of a transgender girl's transition offers a heartfelt snapshot of a family whose only objective is to protect their daughter. Tackling the subject from a biological, social, and psychological viewpoint, Pulitzer-winning reporter Nutt weaves complex elements of what being transgender means into a compelling narrative about a young woman who has identified as female since early childhood. Writing in a very journalistic tone, Nutt succeeds in placing Nicole's individual story within the more general narrative of transgender rights in the United States and humanizes the issues currently at play." Publishers Weekly.

O'Brien, Keith, 1973-

★**Fly** girls : how five daring women defied all odds and made aviation history / Keith O'Brien. Houghton Mifflin Harcourt 2018 xiv, 338 p. ; **920**

1. Elder, Ruth, 1902-1977 2. Earhart, Amelia, 1897-1937 3. Nichols, Ruth, 1901-1960 4. Thaden, Louise McPhetridge, 1905-1979 5. Klingensmith, Florence 6. Aviation 7. Women pilots 8. Airplane racing 9. Air shows 10. Biographies 11. Collective biographies

ISBN 9781328876645

An award-winning journalist traces the lesser-known story of five women, including Amelia Earhart, who successfully fought to compete against men in the high-stakes national air races of the 1920s and 1930s.

"Highly recommended for readers with an interest in aviation history, women's history, cultural history, and 20th-century history." Library Journal.

O'Hagan, Andrew, 1968-

The **secret** life : three true stories of the digital age / Andrew O'Hagan. Farrar, Straus and Giroux, 2017. 224 p. **920**

1. Assange, Julian 2. Wright, Craig Steven 3. Nakamoto, Satoshi. 4. Pinn, Ronald 5. Online identities. 6. Secrets 7. Identity (Psychology) 8. Internet 9. Collective biographies 10. Essays

ISBN 9780374277918

LC 2017001315

An essayist and novelist presents three essays that explore identity and the Internet, taking readers to the weirder fringes of life in a digital world through the eyes of unforgettable characters who question the reality of selfhood in the digital age.

O'Meara, Mallory

The **lady** from the Black Lagoon : Hollywood monsters and the lost legacy of Milicent Patrick / Mallory O'Meara. Hanover Sqaure Press, 2019. 307 p. : **920**

1. Patrick, Milicent, 1915-1998 2. O'Meara, Mallory 3. Creature from the Black Lagoon (Motion picture) 4. Filmmaking 5. Women animators 6. Special effects (Cinematography) 7. Women artists
ISBN 9781335937803

LC 2019299927

The story of Millicent Patrick, a feminist trailblazer in the horror film industry who never received proper credit for creating the classic monster from Creature from the Black Lagoon.

"This is a fascinating slice of Hollywood history with a feminist slant, correcting a sexist wrong from decades ago and restoring Patrick to her rightful place of esteem." Publishers Weekly.

Oppenheimer, Jerry

The **Kardashians** : an American drama / Jerry Oppenheimer. St. Martin's Press, [2017] xxii, 313 pages, 8 unnumbered pages of plates : **920**

1. Reality television programs 2. Kardashian family 3. Kardashian, Kourtney, 1979- 4. Kardashian, Kim, 1980- 5. Kardashian, Khloe, 1984- 6. Rich families 7. Popular culture 8. Collective biographies
ISBN 9781250087140

LC 2017017721

An unauthorized family biography dissects the scandals and secrets of the infamous reality TV clan, from the overshadowed life of patriarch Robert Kardashian to "momager" Kris Jenner's top-secret plan for the future.

Pappu, Sridhar

The **year** of the pitcher : Bob Gibson, Denny McLain, and the end of baseball's golden age / Sridhar Pappu. Houghton Mifflin Harcourt, 2017 320 p. **920**

1. Gibson, Bob, 1935- 2. McLain, Denny 3. Pitching (Baseball) 4. Pitchers (Baseball) 5. Baseball. 6. Baseball players. 7. Collective biographies
ISBN 9780547719276

LC bl2017039163

The story of the remarkable 1968 baseball season: an epic battle of pitchers, Bob Gibson and Denny McClain, which culminated in one of the greatest World Series of all time

"The author effectively interweaves the stories of McLain and Gibson in an engaging fashion, engrossing readers with the rivalry of Detroit and St. Louis." Library Journal.

Paul, Richard, 1959-

We could not fail : the first African Americans in the Space Program / Richard Paul and Steven Moss. University of Texas Press, [2015] 274 p. **920**

1. United States. National Aeronautics and Space Administration Officials and employees 2. United States. National Aeronautics and Space Administration Officials and employees -- History. 3. African American engineers 4. African American astronauts 5. Discrimination in employment 6. Racism 7. Collective biographies
ISBN 9780292772496

LC 2014030513

Profiles ten pioneer African American space workers whose stories illustrated the role NASA and the space program played in promoting civil rights.

"Vital and of interest to all Americans, from history and space buffs to students, researchers, and casual readers." Library Journal.

Pawel, Miriam, 1958-

The **Browns** of California : the family dynasty that transformed a state and shaped a nation / Miriam Pawel. St Martins Pr 2018 400 p. **920**

1. Brown family 2. Brown, Jerry, 1938- 3. Brown, Edmund G. (Edmund Gerald), 1905-1996 4. Families 5. Governors 6. States -- History 7. State governments 8. California -- History 9. Collective biographies 10. Biographies
ISBN 9781632867339

LC 2018011464

The Pulitzer Prize-winning author of The Crusades of Cesar Chavez presents a panoramic history of California and its impact on the nation from the Gold Rush to Silicon Valley, told through the lens of Governor Jerry Brown's family dynasty.

Pearl, Nancy,

The **writer's** library : the authors you love on the books that changed their lives / edited by Nancy Pearl and Jeff Schwager. Harper One, 2020 320 p. **920**

1. Authors -- Interviews 2. Books and reading 3. Writing 4. Influence (Literary, artistic, etc.) 5. Interviews 6. Collective biographies
ISBN 9780062968500

LC 2020010253

Interviews with 23 of today's most accomplished authors reveal the books that inspired their literary careers, in an illustrated volume.

"Readers of this delightful compendium will relish the chance to find many of those shared loves, as well as discover new ones." Publishers Weekly

Penn, Thomas

The **brothers** York : a royal tragedy / Thomas Penn. Simon & Schuster, 2020, c2019. xxiii, 660 p. **920**

1. York, House of. 2. Edward IV, King of England, 1442-1483. 3. Richard III, King of England, 1452-1485. 4. Clarence, George, Duke of, 1449-1478. 5. Royal houses 6. Political corruption 7. Great Britain -- History -- Wars of the Roses, 1455-1485. 8. Great Britain -- Rulers 9. Collective biographies
ISBN 9781451694178

LC 2019045050

Originally published in Great Britain in 2019 by Penguin Random House UK.

Fascinating, dramatic, and filled with vivid historical detail, The Brothers York is a brilliant account of a conflict that fractured England for a generation. Riven by internal rivalries, jealousy, and infighting, the three York brothers failed to sustain their power and instead self-destructed. It is a rich and bloody tale as gripping as any historical fiction.

"Penn's latest is a treat for dedicated readers of English history who know the outlines of the story covered but wish to learn more." Library Journal

Plutarch, 46?-120?

The **age** of Caesar : five Roman lives / Plutarch ; translated by Pamela Mensch ; edited, with preface and notes, by James Romm.. W. W. Norton & Company, 2017 xxxviii, 393 p. **920**

1. Plutarch, 46?-120? 2. Scholars -- Rome 3. Rulers -- Rome 4. Civilization, Ancient. 5. Rome -- Civilization. 6. Collective

biographies.
ISBN 9780393292824

LC 2016035735

A new edition of Plutarch, the inventor of biography, focused on five lives that remade the Roman world. Pompey, Caesar, Cicero, Brutus, Antony: the names still resonate across thousands of years. Major figures in the civil wars that brutally ended the Roman republic, they haunt us with questions of character and authority: how to safeguard a republic from the flaws of its leaders.

"For those with a serious interest in Roman history. As this is an ancient primary source, it is helpful if readers come at this work with a general understanding of the events and people of the first century BCE Roman world." Library Journal.

Popova, Maria

Figuring / Maria Popova. Pantheon Books, 2019. 544 p. **920**

1. Artists. 2. Authors 3. Women scientists -- History. 4. Women and art -- History. 5. Collective biographies.
ISBN 9781524748135

LC 2018027009

Andrew Carnegie Medal for Excellence in Non-Fiction Finalist, 2020

Explores the search for truth and meaning through the interconnected lives of historical figures from four centuries--artists, writers, and scientists, most of them women, who changed the way humans understand, experience, and appreciate the universe.

"Writing with an ardor for language and musing on chance, affinity, and our fear of change, Popova constructs an intricate biographical cosmos that is intellectually scintillating, artistically wondrous, and deeply affecting." Booklist.

Porter, Cecelia Hopkins

Five lives in music : women performers, composers, and impresarios from the baroque to the present / Cecelia Hopkins Porter. University of Ill. Press, c2012. xiv, 244 p. : **920**

1. Sophie Elisabeth, Duchess, consort of August, Duke of Braunschweig-Luneburg, 1613-1676. 2. Bach, Maria, 1896-1978. 3. Jacquet de La Guerre, Elisabeth-Claude, 1665-1729. 4. Lang, Josephine, 1815-1880. 5. Schein, Ann, 1939- 6. Composers 7. Musicians 8. Women composers 9. Women musicians 10. Collective biographies
ISBN 0252037014

LC 2011051102

Examines the lives of five women musicians from the seventeenth century to the twentieth century, discussing the personal experiences of each to provide insight into each woman's general and musical culture.

Quinn, Bridget

Broad strokes : 15 women who made art and made history, in that order / Bridget Quinn ; with illustrations by Lisa Congdon. Chronicle Books, 2017. 192 p. **920**

1. Women artists 2. Women artists -- History. 3. Art history 4. Collective biographies
ISBN 9781452152363

LC 2016023856

Shares the lives and careers of fifteen female artists, including Artemisia Gentileschi, Edmonia Lewis, and Susan O'Malley.

"Quinn skillfully examines the lives of an eclectic group of artists and the treatment of their work over time, mixing in comments from art historians and her own personal anecdotes." Publishers Weekly. Annex

Rader, Peter

Playing to the gods : Sarah Bernhardt, Eleonora Duse, and the rivalry that changed acting forever / Peter Rader. Simon & Schuster 2018 256 p. **920**

1. Duse, Eleonora, 1858-1924 2. Bernhardt, Sarah, 1844-1923 3. Actors and actresses 4. Competition 5. Acting 6. Drama 7. Europe -- Social life and customs -- 19th century 8. Collective biographies 9. Biographies
ISBN 9781476738376

LC 2017046516

Traces the infamous rivalry between two renowned 19th-century actresses, credited with popularizing the natural style of acting that is celebrated today, sharing insights into their personalities, ambitions and relationships with each others' lovers.

"This entertaining chronicle illustrates how both women captivated audiences and made a lasting impact on the theater." Publishers Weekly.

Rappaport, Helen

The **Romanov** sisters : the lost lives of the daughters of Nicholas and Alexandra / Helen Rappaport. St. Martin's Press, 2014. 512 p. **920**

1. Nicholas II, Emperor of Russia, 1868-1918 Assassination. 2. Nicholas II, Emperor of Russia, 1868-1918 Family Assassination. 3. Romanov, House of History -- 20th century. 4. Anastasia Nikolaevna, Grand Duchess, daughter of Nicholas II, Emperor of Russia, 1901-1918 5. Olga, Grand Duchess of Russia, 1895-1918 6. Marie, Grand Duchess of Russia, b. 1890. 7. Tatiana Nikolaevna, Grand Duchess, daughter of Nicholas II, Emperor of Russia, 1897-1918 8. Alexandra, Empress, consort of Nicholas II, Emperor of Russia, 1872-1918. 9. Princesses -- Russia. 10. Sisters. 11. Royal houses. 12. Russia -- History -- Nicholas II, 1894-1917. 13. Collective biographies
ISBN 9781250020208

LC 2014003159

Draws on personal writings and private sources to challenge common misperceptions and illuminate the daily lives and vibrant personalities of the four Russian Grand Duchesses from their own perspectives, revealing their awareness of family turmoil and the approach of the Russian Revolution.

"A gossipy, revealing story of the doomed Russian family's fairy tale life told by an expert in the field." Kirkus.

Reeder, Lydia

Dust Bowl girls : the inspiring story of the team that barnstormed its way to basketball glory / Lydia Reeder. Algonquin Books, 2017. 336 p. **920**

1. Babb, Sam, 1891-1937 2. Harris, Doll, 1913-2001 3. Basketball coaches 4. Women athletes 5. Gender role 6. Women basketball players 7. Oklahoma 8. Collective biographies
ISBN 9781616204662

LC 2016016234

"Published simultaneously in Canada by Thomas Allen & Son Limited."

At the height of the Great Depression, Sam Babb, the charismatic basketball coach of tiny Oklahoma Presbyterian College, began dreaming. Traveling from farm to farm, he recruited talented, hardworking young women and offered them a chance at a better life: a free college education if they would come play for his basketball team, the Cardinals.

"Author Reeder, Babb's grandniece, had access to such primary materials as player diaries, which reveal the players' relationships to one another and their coach, and to a dust-bowl era and region marked by serious hardship." Booklist.

Remnick, David,

Life stories : profiles from The New Yorker / edited by David Remnick. Random House, c2000. xii, 530 p. ; **920**

1. Celebrities 2. Authors 3. Criminals 4. Politicians 5. United States -- Social life and customs -- 20th century. 6. Collective biographies
ISBN 0375503552

LC 99053712

An anthology of biographical profiles from "The New Yorker" covers some of the most influential and infamous people of the century, from Ernest Hemingway and Legs Diamond to Adolf Hitler and Edith Wharton.

"An assemblage of 25 biographical profiles spanning the years 1927 to 1999 with subjects ranging from Ernest Hemingway and Marlon Brando to a fake prince, a pair of eccentric mathematicians, and Biff the show dog." Booklist.

Ribowsky, Mark

In the name of the father : family, football, and the Manning dynasty / Mark Ribowsky. Liveright Publishing Corporation, A division of W.W. Norton & Company Independent Publishers since 1923, [2018] 448 p. **920**

1. Manning, Archie, 1949- 2. Manning, Cooper. 3. Manning, Peyton. 4. Manning, Eli, 1981- 5. Manning family. 6. Quarterbacks (Football) 7. Football players 8. Fathers and sons 9. Family relationships 10. Collective biographies 11. Biographies
ISBN 9781631493096

LC 2018008749

A portrait of the Manning family traces their story against a backdrop of American football history and the fading traditions of Southern Christian manhood, illuminating the scandals and rivalries that have overshadowed their achievements.

"Ribowsky relies too heavily on game detail, but it's worth it for the insight he provides into the very different personalities and approaches to the game of each of the Mannings. A fascinating account of a football family." Booklist.

Ricca, Brad

Super boys : the amazing adventures of Jerry Siegel and Joe Shuster---the creators of Superman / Brad Ricca. St. Martin's Press, 2013. xxi, 423 p., 16 unnumbered p. of plates : **920**

1. Siegel, Jerry, 1914-1996. 2. Shuster, Joe. 3. Superman (Fictitious character) 4. Cartoonists -- United States 5. Comic books, strips, etc. -- History and criticism. 6. Cartooning. 7. Collective biographies.
ISBN 9780312643805

LC 2013004046

A biography of Jerry Siegel and Canadian-born Joe Shuster, two best friends who, created Superman, one of the most iconic superheroes in popular culture.

Richardson, Peter, 1959-

No simple highway : a cultural history of the Grateful Dead / Peter Richardson. St. Martin's Press, 2015. 320 p. **920**

1. Garcia, Jerry, 1942-1995. 2. Grateful Dead (Musical group) 3. Jam bands 4. Rock musicians -- United States 5. Rock music -- Social aspects. 6. Music and society. 7. United States -- Popular culture -- History -- 20th century. 8. Collective biographies. 9. Biographies.
ISBN 9781250010629

LC 2014036345

"For almost three decades, the Grateful Dead was America's most popular touring band. No Simple Highway is the first book to ask the simple question of why--and attempt to answer it. Drawing on new research, interviews, and a fresh supply of material from the Grateful Dead archives, author Peter Richardson vividly recounts the Dead's colorful history, adding new insight into everything from the acid tests to the band's formation of their own record label to their massive late career success, while probing the riddle of the Dead's vast and durable appeal. Arguing that the band successfully tapped three powerful utopian ideals--for ecstasy, mobility, and community--it also shows how the Dead's lived experience with these ideals struck deep chords with two generations of American youth and continues today. Routinely caricatured by the mainstream media, the Grateful Dead are often portrayed as grizzled hippy throwbacks with a cult following of burned-out stones. No Simple Highway corrects that impression, revealing them to be one of the most popular, versatile, and resilient music ensembles in the second half of the twentieth century. The band's history has been well-documented by insiders, but its unique and sustained appeal has yet to be explored fully. At last, this legendary American musical institution is given the serious and entertaining examination it richly deserves"-- Provided by publisher.

Ricks, Thomas E.

Churchill and Orwell : the fight for freedom / Thomas E. Ricks. Penguin Group USA, 2017. 320 p. **920**

1. Orwell, George, 1903-1950. 2. Churchill, Winston, 1874-1965 3. Authors, English 4. Anti-fascism 5. Politicians 6. Ideology 7. Collective biographies 8. Biographies
ISBN 9781594206139

LC 2016056757

A dual portrait of Winston Churchill and George Orwell focuses on the pivotal years from the mid-1930s through the 1940s, describing how both suffered nearly fatal injuries before their vision and campaigns inspired action to preserve democracy throughout the world.

"In vivid prose, Ricks entwines the biographies of two figures who fought in strikingly different ways to achieve similar goals." Publishers Weekly.

Roberts, Andrew, 1963-

Leadership in war : essential lessons from those who made history / Andrew Roberts. Viking, 2019. 256 p. **920**

1. Leadership -- Case studies 2. Command of troops 3. World leaders 4. Military strategy 5. Collective biographies
ISBN 9780525522386

LC 2019025070

Taking us from the French Revolution to the Cold War, Andrew Roberts presents us with a bracingly honest and deeply insightful look at nine major figures in modern history: Napoleon Bonaparte, Horatio Nelson, Winston Churchill, Adolf Hitler, Joseph Stalin, George C. Marshall, Charles de Gaulle, Dwight D. Eisenhower, and Margaret Thatcher.

Roberts, Cokie, 1943-2019

Capital dames: the Civil War and the women of Washington, 1848-1868 / Cokie Roberts. HarperCollins 2015 400 p. **920**

1. Women and war 2. Women and politics. 3. Independence in women 4. Women -- Political activity. 5. United States -- History -- Civil War, 1861-1865 6. Collective biographies
ISBN 9780062002761

LC 2015001049

Documents the experiences, influence and contributions of women during the American Civil War.

"An enlightening account detailing how the Civil War changed the nation's capital while expanding the role of women in politics, health care, education, and social services." Kirkus.

★**Founding** mothers: the women who raised our nation / Cokie Roberts. William Morrow, 2004. xx, 359 p. : **920**

1. Women -- United States 2. Women and politics. 3. Women -- Political activity -- History. 4. Revolutions -- United States 5. United States -- History -- Colonial period, 1600-1775. 6. United States -- History -- Revolution, 1775-1783 7. United States -- History -- Revolution, 1775-1783 -- Women. 8. United States -- History -- 1783-1815. 9. Collective biographies

ISBN 0060090251

Explores the lives of women who helped shape the United States, profiling such key figures as Abigail Adams, Eliza Pinkney, Dolley Payne Madison, Deborah Read Franklin, and Catherine Littlefield Greene.

"In addition to telling wonderful stories, Roberts also presents a very readable, serviceable account of politics--male and female--in early America. If only our standard history textbooks were written with such flair!" Publishers Weekly.

Ladies of liberty : the women who shaped our nation / Cokie Roberts. HarperCollins, 2007. 336 p. **920**

1. Women and politics. 2. Women -- Political activity. 3. United States -- History -- 1783-1825. 4. Collective biographies

ISBN 9780060782344

LC 2008298367

A sequel to Founding Mothers shares the stories of remarkable women who shaped American history between 1796 and 1828, including Dolley Madison, Theodosia Burr, and Sacajawea.

"While Roberts' aim is to see the period from her subjects' point of view, she is not uncritical; for instance, Roberts casts blame on Mrs. Adams's uncompromising partisanship in the undoing of her husband. With a little-seen perspective and fascinating insight into the culture of the day, this is popular history done right." Publishers Weekly.

Roberts, Randy, 1951-

Blood brothers : the fatal friendship between Muhammad Ali and Malcolm X / Randy Roberts, Johnny Smith. Basic Books, 2016 400 p. **920**

1. Malcolm X, 1925-1965 2. Ali, Muhammad, 1942-2016 3. Nation of Islam 4. Male friendship 5. Boxers (Sports) 6. Political activists 7. Former friends. 8. Collective biographies

ISBN 9780465079704

LC 2015043982

Draws on previously untapped sources to illuminate the secret friendship and disastrous estrangement between Cassius Clay and Malcolm X, sharing insights into Malcolm's alleged role in shaping Clay's double life as a patriotic athlete and Islamic reformer.

"A page-turning tale from the 1960s about politics and sports and two proud, extraordinary men whose legacies endure." Kirkus.

Rocca, Mo

Mobituaries : great lives worth reliving / Mo Rocca and Jonathan Greenberg. Simon & Schuster, 2019. 384 p. **920**

1. Obituaries 2. Biography 3. Humorous writing 4. Celebrities 5. Collective biographies

ISBN 9781501197628

LC 2019949306

Based on a podcast.

A popular TV correspondent and writer offers an irreverent and rigorously researched book that celebrates the dead people who made life worth living.

Roe, Sue

In Montmartre : Picasso, Matisse and the birth of Modernist art / Sue Roe. Penguin Group USA, 2015 352 p. **920**

1. Picasso, Pablo, 1881-1973. 2. Matisse, Henri, 1869-1954 3. Derain, Andre, 1880-1954 4. Vlaminck, Maurice de, 1876-1958 5. Braque, Georges, 1882-1963. 6. Modigliani, Amedeo, 1884-1920. 7. Brancusi, Constantin, 1876-1957 8. Stein, Gertrude, 1874-1946. 9. Modernism (Art) 10. Artists 11. Paris, France 12. Montmartre, Paris, France. 13. Collective biographies

ISBN 9781594204951

LC bl2015009983

Beginning about 1900, the Paris suburb of Montmartre became one of the trendiest artists' enclaves in history. Pablo Picasso, Georges Braque, Amedeo Modigliani, Constantin Brancusi, Gertrude Stein, and many other painters, sculptors, writers, musicians, and dancers lived and worked there. Author Sue Roe engagingly and vividly creates a portrait of the time, place, and people while exploring modernist movements such as Fauvism and Cubism.

The **private** lives of the Impressionists / Sue Roe. Harper Collins Publishers, 2006. viii, 356 p., 8 p. of plates : **920**

1. Impressionism (Art) -- France. 2. Painters -- France -- 19th century 3. Artists -- France 4. Collective biographies

ISBN 0060545585

LC 2006043621

A group portrait of the Impressionist artists traces how the movement's early leaders met in the studios of Paris and lived and worked together closely for several years, supporting one another through a series of emotional and financial difficulties.

Roper, Robert, 1946-

Now the drum of war : Walt Whitman and his brothers in the Civil War / Robert Roper. Walker & Co., 2008. 432 p. **920**

1. Whitman, Walt, 1819-1892. 2. Whitman, George Washington, 1829-1901. 3. Whitman family. 4. Poets, American -- 19th century 5. Civil war 6. Brothers. 7. Family relationships. 8. United States -- History -- Civil War, 1861-1865. 9. Collective biographies

ISBN 9780802715531

LC bl2008020569

A profile of the Whitman family evaluates how their war experiences reflected the progression of the Civil War, in an account that traces Walt's work as a nurse, his brother George's military service, and their correspondence with other family members.

Rose, Alexander, 1971-

Empires of the sky : zeppelins, airplanes, and two men's epic duel to rule the world / Alexander Rose. Random House, 2020. 592 p. **920**

1. Eckener, Hugo, 1868-1954 2. Trippe, J. T. (Juan Terry), 1899-1981 3. Zeppelin, Ferdinand, Graf von, 1838-1917 4. Aviation -- History 5. Inventors 6. Competition 7. Commercial aviation 8. Collective biographies

ISBN 9780812989977

LC 2019024115

At the dawn of the twentieth century, when human flight was still considered an impossibility, Germany's Count Ferdinand von Zeppelin vied with the Wright Brothers to build the world's first successful flying machine. As the Wrights labored to invent the airplane, Zeppelin fathered the remarkable airship, sparking a bitter rivalry between the two types of aircraft and their innovators that would last for decades, in the quest to control one of humanity's most inspiring achievements.

"A dense yet exhilarating history of the dawn of modern air travel." Publishers Weekly

Rubenhold, Hallie

The **five** : the untold lives of the women killed by Jack the Ripper / Hallie Rubenhold. Houghton Mifflin Harcourt, 2019. viii, 333 p. : **920**

1. Jack, the Ripper. 2. Women murder victims 3. Working class women -- London, England. 4. Whitechapel murders, 1888 5. Women -- Social conditions -- 19th century. 6. Whitechapel (London, England) -- History -- 19th century. 7. London, England -- History -- 19th century. 8. Collective biographies

ISBN 9781328663818

LC 2018038562

Researched portraits of the five women murdered by Jack the Ripper in 1888 reveal each victim's historically relevant and diverse background while discussing the cultural and gender disadvantages that made them vulnerable.

"A lively if morbid exercise in Victorian social history essential to students of Ripperiana." Kirkus.

Rubin, Louis Decimus, 1923-

My father's people : a family of Southern Jews / Louis D. Rubin Jr. Louisiana State University Press, 2002. 139 p. : **920**

1. Rubens family. 2. Jewish Americans -- Charleston, South Carolina. 3. Charleston, South Carolina. 4. Collective biographies.

ISBN 0807128082

LC 2002000454

"The author tells the stories of Hyman and Fannie Rubin, his grandparents, and their seven children. Rubin's descriptions are affectionate, yet he doesn't gloss over their flaws, and as a result, those he knows best come alive for readers." Publishers Weekly.

Russo, Frank, 1959-

The **Cooperstown** chronicles : baseball's colorful characters, unusual lives, and strange demises / Frank Russo. Rowman & Littlefield, 2014 272 p. **920**

1. Baseball players -- United States 2. Baseball -- United States -- History. 3. Collective biographies

ISBN 9781442236394

LC 2014019500

"Fans of baseball, in particular baseball history, will enjoy this work for the multitude of players (various teams, various years) that are documented in its pages." Library Journal.

Ryan, Mike, 1974-

Tennis' greatest stars / Mike Ryan. Firefly Books, 2014. 216 p. **920**

1. Tennis players 2. Tennis -- History. 3. Collective biographies

ISBN 177085293X

LC oc2014012018

Includes index.

"This is a good purchase for any tennis collection and is recommended for the circulating collections of public libraries." Booklist.

Sakamoto, Pamela Rotner

Midnight in broad daylight : a Japanese American family caught between two worlds / Pamela Rotner Sakamoto. Harper, 2016 400 p. **920**

1. Fukuhara, Harry K., 1920-2015 2. Fukuhara, Pierce, 1922-2008 3. Fukuhara, Frank, 1924-2015 4. World War II -- Japanese Americans. 5. Pearl Harbor, Attack on, 1941. 6. Japanese American families. 7. Translators 8. Hiroshima, Japan -- Atomic bombing, 1945 9. Collective biographies

ISBN 9780062351937

LC 2015017943

Describes the true story of three Japanese American brothers, two of whom move to their mother's ancestral home in Hiroshima after their father's death, and find themselves on opposite sides of the world and the war as Pearl Harbor unfolds

"A beautifully rendered work wrought with enormous care and sense of compassionate dignity." Kirkus.

Samaha, Albert

Never ran, never will : boyhood and football in a changing American inner city / Albert Samaha. PublicAffairs, 2018. xiv, 343 p. **920**

1. Mo Better Jaguars (Football team) 2. Football 3. African American neighborhoods 4. Inner city 5. Sports -- Social aspects 6. Brownsville, Brooklyn, New York City -- Social conditions 7. Brooklyn, New York City 8. Collective biographies

ISBN 9781610398688

LC 2018000983

Describes the history and impact of the Mo Better Jaguars, a football team in a poor Brooklyn neighborhood and the people who have had their lives shaped for the better by playing and participating. Football isn't everybody's ideal way to find the American dream, but for some kids it's the surest road there is.

Sankovitch, Nina

American rebels : how the Hancock, Adams, and Quincy families fanned the flames of revolution / Nina Sankovitch. St. Martin's Press, 2020. 384 p. **920**

1. Hancock family. 2. Adams family. 3. Quincy family. 4. Quincy, Josiah, 1744-1775. 5. Adams, John, 1735-1826 6. Adams, Abigail, 1744-1818. 7. Hancock, John, 1737-1793 8. Hancock, Dorothy Quincy, 1747-1830 9. Revolutionaries 10. Founding Fathers of the United States. 11. Families 12. Friendship 13. Massachusetts 14. United States -- History -- Revolution, 1775-1783. 15. Collective biographies

ISBN 9781250163288

LC 2019043211

Explores, for the first time, the intertwined lives of the Hancock, Quincy, and Adams families, and the role each person played in sparking the American Revolution.

"Sankovitch has woven a compelling, potent chronicle of members of three principal American families that will be valued by readers of American history at all levels." Library Journal

Schatz, Kate

Rad women worldwide : artists and athletes, pirates and punks, and other revolutionaries who shaped history / Kate Schatz ; illustrated by Miriam Klein Stahl. Ten Speed Press, 2016. 112 p. **920**

1. Women 2. Women's rights -- History 3. Intersectionality 4. Collective biographies

ISBN 9780399578861

LC 2016012179

"From the authors of the New York Times bestselling book Rad American Women A-Z, comes a bold new collection of 40 biographical profiles, each accompanied by a striking illustrated portrait, showcasing extraordinary women from around the world."-- Provided by publisher.

"Readers of either gender could well find a role model in the India-born U.S. astronaut Kalpana Chawla, or in Wangari Maathai, whose

Green Belt Movement in Africa resulted in the planting of more than 30 million environment-reviving trees." Booklist.

Schell, Orville, 1940-

★**Wealth** and power : China's long march to the twenty-first century / Orville Schell & John Delury. Random House, 2013. 288 p. **920**

1. Intellectual life -- China 2. Economic development -- China 3. Political science -- China 4. China -- History -- 20th century 5. China -- History -- 21st century 6. China -- Politics and government -- 20th century. 7. China -- Politics and government -- 21st century. 8. Collective biographies
ISBN 9780679643470

LC 2013002596

"An astute, knowledgeable and nicely accessible history and assessment of China for all readers." Kirkus.

Schiff, Karenna Gore

Lighting the way : nine women who changed modern America / Karenna Gore Schiff. Miramax Books/Hyperion, 2005. xv, 528 p. : **920**

1. Women -- United States 2. Social reformers -- United States 3. Women social reformers -- United States 4. United States -- Social conditions -- 20th century. 5. Collective biographies
ISBN 1401352189

LC 2005056247

Provides a study of nine women who transformed modern America through their battle against inequity and social injustice, including Ida B. Wells-Barnett, Mother Jones, Alice Hamilton, Frances Perkins, Virginia Durr, and Septima Clark.

"This is an inspirational collection of biographies of women of various social, ethnic, and racial backgrounds fighting for social justice." Booklist.

Schmidt, Michael, 1947-

★**Lives** of the poets / Michael Schmidt. Knopf, 1999, c1998. xii, 975 p. **920**

1. English poetry -- History and criticism 2. American poetry -- History and criticism 3. Poets, American 4. Poets, English 5. Collective biographies
ISBN 0375406247

LC 98051913

Originally published: London : Weidenfeld & Nicolson, 1998.

"In this survey of poetry in English, Schmidt ... enthuses about more than 250 poets whose work dates from the 14th century to 1998. More than a critical essay, this friendly and accessible history embodies the life of poetry and conveys its changeable, subjective beauty." Library Journal.

Schoenberger, Nancy

Wayne and Ford : the films, the friendship, and the forging of an American hero / Nancy Schoenberger. Nan A. Talese Doubleday, 2017. 320 p. **920**

1. Ford, John, 1894-1973 2. Wayne, John, 1907-1979 3. Actors and actresses 4. Film producers and directors 5. Western films -- History and criticism 6. Mentors 7. Collective biographies
ISBN 9780385534857

LC 2016057903

A dual portrait of Western film titans John Ford and John Wayne shares insights into their productive collaborations and often turbulent relationship, providing details about the makings of their iconic films while discussing each star's enduring legacy and influence.

Schultz, Kevin Michael

Buckley and Mailer : the difficult friendship that shaped the Sixties / Kevin M. Schultz. W. W. Norton & Company, Inc., 2015. 400 p. **920**

1. Buckley, William F., Jr., 1925-2008. 2. Mailer, Norman. 3. Journalists -- United States 4. Authors, American -- 20th century 5. United States -- History -- 1961-1969. 6. Collective biographies
ISBN 9780393088717

LC 2015001553

A lively chronicle of the 1960s through the incredibly contentious and surprisingly close friendship of its two most colorful characters. Norman Mailer and William F. Buckley, Jr., were towering figures who argued publicly about every major issue of the1960s: the counterculture, Vietnam, feminism, civil rights, the Cold War. Behind the scenes, the two were close friends and trusted confidantes who lived surprisingly parallel lives. In Buckley and Mailer, historian Kevin M. Schultz delves into their personal archives to tell the rich story of their friendship, arguments, and the tumultuous decade they did so much to shape.

"By contextualizing the friendship, this volume, in addition to its considerable virtues as quasi-biography, is also a provocative and thorough, if not quite comprehensive (it's pretty much all East Coast, and there's no music), social and political history of the sixties, among the very best we have had." Booklist.

Seagrave, Sterling

The **Yamato** dynasty : the secret history of Japan's imperial family / Sterling Seagrave and Peggy Seagrave. Broadway Books, 2001, c1999. xvii, 394 p. : **920**

1. Meiji, Emperor of Japan, 1852-1912. 2. Meiji, Emperor of Japan, 1852-1912 Family. 3. Taisho, Emperor of Japan, 1879-1926. 4. Taisho, Emperor of Japan, 1879-1926 Family. 5. Hirohito, Emperor of Japan, 1901-1989. 6. Hirohito, Emperor of Japan, 1901-1989 Family. 7. Japan -- Rulers 8. Japan -- History -- Meiji period, 1868-1912. 9. Japan -- History -- Taisho period, 1912-1926. 10. Japan -- History -- Showa period, 1926-1989. 11. East Asia. 12. Collective biographies
ISBN 0767904974

LC BL2001009783

Reprint. Originally published: 1999.

A portrait of the world's longest-reigning dynasty offers a look at the shoguns, emperors, and financiers who have controlled Japan.

"This history of Japan from the mid-19th century to the present weaves together an iconoclastic historical narrative with a mostly caustic view of Japan's imperial family. The Seagraves depict modern Japan as a country consistently dominated by a closed financial oligarchy in league with politicians, bureaucrats, the imperial family, and underworld bosses." Library Journal.

Sears, Stephen W.

Lincoln's lieutenants : the high command of the Army of the Potomac / Stephen W. Sears. Houghton Mifflin Harcourt, 2017. 640 p. **920**

1. Lincoln, Abraham, 1809-1865 Military leadership 2. United States. Army. Army of the Potomac 3. Civil War 4. Command of troops 5. Generals 6. Armies 7. Collective biographies 8. Biographies
ISBN 9780618428250

LC 2017288442

The award-winning author of Landscape Turned Red presents a multilayered group portrait of the commanders who led the Army of the Potomac to explore how interpersonal tensions and their disagreements with Washington politics rendered them pawns to a vindictive Congress.

"A staggering work of research by a masterly historian." Kirkus.

Secrest, Meryle

The **mysterious** affair at Olivetti : IBM, the CIA, and the Cold War conspiracy to shut down production of the world's first desktop computer / Meryle Secrest. Alfred A. Knopf, [2019] 352 p. **920**

1. Olivetti, Adriano 2. Olivetti, Camillo, 1868-1943 3. Ing. C. Olivetti & C. Divisione elettronica 4. Computer industry and trade 5. Computer science 6. Personal computers 7. Business competition 8. Italy -- History -- 20th century. 9. Collective biographies

ISBN 9780451493651

LC 2018059556

Shares the previously undisclosed story of the design and development of the first desktop computer by the high-styled typewriter company, exploring the influences of visionary Adriano Olivetti, two world wars and the space race.

Seward, Desmond 1935-

The **demon's** brood : a history of the Plantagenet dynasty / Desmond Seward. Pegasus Books, 2014. xxix, 322 p., 16 unnumbered p. of plates : **920**

1. Plantagenet, House of. 2. Royal houses -- Great Britain 3. Civilization, Medieval 4. Rulers 5. Great Britain -- Rulers. 6. Great Britain -- Politics and government -- 1154-1399 7. Great Britain -- History -- Plantagenets, 1154-1399 8. Collective biographies

ISBN 9781605986180

LC bl2014039899

Based on major contemporary sources and recent research, an acclaimed historian presents a complete history of the most dominant royal dynasty in English history, from Richard the Lionheart and Edward the Black Prince to Henry IV and Richard III.

"Seward is a good author to turn to for ease in reading history; his writing style is quick, vibrant and delightfully pithy in its simplicity of phrase." Kirkus.

Seymour, Miranda

★**In** Byron's wake : the turbulent lives of Lord Byron's wife and daughter : Annabella Milbanke and Ada Lovelace / Miranda Seymour. Simon & Schuster, 2018. 544 p. **920**

1. Byron, George Gordon Byron, Baron, 1788-1824. 2. Byron, Anne Isabella Milbanke Byron, Baroness, 1792-1860. 3. Lovelace, Ada King, Countess of, 1815-1852. 4. Byron family. 5. Social reformers. 6. Resourcefulness in women. 7. Gender role. 8. Women mathematicians. 9. England -- Social life and customs -- 19th century. 10. Collective biographies.

ISBN 9781681778723

The only legitimate daughter of Lord Byron, Ada Lovelace was to become a pioneer of the computer revolution. This masterful new biography is a portrait of two remarkable women, Ada and her mother Annabella, haunted by the mercurial spirit of the notorious poet.

"Seymour's great achievement is the resourcefulness and diligence she brings to both Annabella and Ada, complex figures who alternately invite and test readers' sympathies. Their inner and outer lives--along with those of dozens of others who populate this tragic farce--are told with singular narrative skill." Kirkus.

Shapiro, Laura

What she ate : six remarkable women and the food that tells their stories / Laura Shapiro. Viking, 2017. 320 p. **920**

1. Women celebrities 2. Diet 3. Food 4. Cooking 5. Collective biographies

ISBN 9780525427643

LC 2016057055

A culinary historian's short takes on six famous women through the lens of food and cooking explore what these women ate and how their attitudes toward food offer surprising new insights into their lives, in a book that covers Dorothy Wordsworth, Rosa Lewis, Eleanor Roosevelt, Eva Braun, Barbara Pym and Helen Gurley Brown.

"A unique and delectable work that sheds new light on the lives of women, food, and men." Kirkus.

Showalter, Dennis E.

★**Patton** and Rommel : men of war in the twentieth century / Dennis Showalter. Berkley Caliber, c2005. 441 p. ; **920**

1. Patton, George S., 1885-1945. 2. Rommel, Erwin, 1891-1944. 3. United States. Army Officers 4. Germany. Army Officers 5. Generals 6. World War II. 7. Command of troops 8. Collective biographies.

ISBN 9780425193464

LC 2004057464

Includes index.

Examines the influence of Erwin Rommel and George S. Patton, renowned World War II generals from opposite sides of the conflict, by analyzing the paths taken, decisions made, and their influence on military tactics and history.

"This is a parallel biography of George Patton and Erwin Rommel. The research is thorough, the quality of the writing superb. [The author] ranks as a scholar who has done them justice, making two complex men and a vast panorama of military history remarkably accessible for experts and lay readers alike." Publishers Weekly.

Shulman, Aaron

The **age** of disenchantments : the epic story of Spain's most notorious literary family and the long shadow of the Spanish Civil War / Aaron Shulman. Ecco Press, 2019. 496 p. **920**

1. Panero family 2. Panero, Leopoldo 3. Families 4. Poets 5. Dictatorship 6. Patriarchs 7. Spain -- History -- Civil War, 1936-1939 8. Spain -- History -- 20th century 9. Collective biographies

ISBN 9780062484192

LC bl2019001090

A narrative history of the Paneros literary family places their story against a backdrop of the Spanish Civil War and explores how their lives intersected with those of the period's most storied figures in culture and politics. Weaving memoir with cultural history and biography, and brought together with vivid storytelling and striking images, The Age of Disenchantments sheds new light on the romance and intellectual ferment of the era while revealing the profound and enduring devastation of the war, the Franco dictatorship, and the country's transition to democracy.

"Prodigiously researched and beautifully written, Shulman's work reveals a remarkable family of refreshing weirdness, poetic obsessions, and sacrilegious taste for destruction as a microcosm of Spain's tortured 20th century." Publishers Weekly.

Sigmund, Karl, 1945-

Exact thinking in demented times : the Vienna Circle and the epic quest for the foundations of science / Karl Sigmund. Basic Books, 2017 384 p. **920**

1. Science -- Philosophy. 2. Vienna circle. 3. Logical positivism. 4. Intellectual life. 5. Collective biographies

ISBN 9780465096954

LC 2017037770

A group portrait of the early 20th-century intellectuals who transformed the way the world regarded math and science examines the collective stories of such forefront minds as Kurt Gödel, Rudolph Carnap, Ludwig Wittgenstein and Karl Popper.

"Many readers will agree that we are currently living in demented times, and Sigmund adeptly lays out a history that has great relevance for today." Kirkus.

Singer, Mark

Character studies : encounters with the curiously obsessed / Mark Singer. Houghton Mifflin, 2005. 256 p. ; **920**

1. Characters and characteristics. 2. Eccentrics and eccentricities -- United States 3. Nonconformists. 4. United States -- Social life and customs. 5. Essays.

ISBN 9780618197255

LC 2004062757

"This is a mix of ... [the author's] portraits from The New Yorker, gathered in book form for the first time. ... It's quite a cast of characters, and Singer lavishly gives them all their due." Library Journal.

Smith, Andrew, 1961-

Moondust : in search of the men who fell to Earth / Andrew Smith. Fourth Estate, 2005. 372 p. : **920**

1. United States. National Aeronautics and Space Administration 2. Project Apollo (U.S.) 3. Astronauts -- United States 4. Space exploration -- History 5. United States -- History -- 20th century 6. Collective biographies

ISBN 0007155417

LC 2005040081

Originally published: Great Britain : Bloomsbury, 2005.

The Apollo Moon landings have been called the last optimistic act of the twentieth century. Twelve astronauts made this greatest of all journeys, and all were indelibly marked by it. Journalist Smith reveals the stories of the nine still living men caught between the gravitational pull of the Moon and the Earth's collective dreaming: we relive the flashbulbs, the first shocking glimpse of Earth from space, the sense of euphoria and awe. This was the first global media event, and the astronauts were its superstars. They had been schooled by NASA for deep space but were completely unprepared for fame. Marriages crumbled under the strain. The wild and happy sixties gave way to the cynicism and self-doubt of the seventies, and the Moonwalkers faced their greatest challenge: how to find meaning in life when the biggest adventure you could possibly have was a memory.--From publisher description.

"In an artful blend of memoir and popular history, Smith makes flesh-and-blood people out of icons and reveals the tenderness of his own heart." Publishers Weekly.

Snyder, Laura J.

Eye of the beholder : Johannes Vermeer, Antoni van Leeuwenhoek, and the reinvention of seeing / Laura J. Snyder. W.W. Norton & Company, 2015. 416 p. **920**

1. Vermeer, Johannes, 1632-1675 Knowledge Science. 2. Leeuwenhoek, Anthony van, 1632-1723. 3. Science and art 4. Painters 5. Scientists 6. Art 7. Netherlands -- History -- 17th century 8. Collective biographies.

ISBN 9780393077469

LC 2014038143

Taking readers to 17th-century Holland, where artists and scientists gathered, an extraordinary story reveals how two geniuses--a self-taught natural philosopher and an artist--transformed the way we see the world by coming to the realization that there is more than meets the eye.

"Though it is only speculation that these great thinkers knew each other personally, Snyder expertly brings to life their shared social milieu of artists and scientists, all seeking new ways to investigate nature. These intertwined biographies weave a story of two men whose insistence on daring to see revolutionized our understanding of perception itself." Booklist.

The **philosophical** breakfast club : four remarkable men who transformed science and changed the world / Laura Snyder. Broadway Books, 2011. 439 p. : **920**

1. Babbage, Charles, 1791-1871. 2. Herschel, John Frederick William, 1792-1871. 3. University of Cambridge. 4. Intellectual life -- 19th century. 5. College students. 6. Science. 7. Scientists. 8. Cambridge, England. 9. Collective biographies

ISBN 9780767930482

LC 2010025790

Traces the influential friendship of William Whewell, Charles Babbage, John Herschel and Richard Jones, citing their pivotal contributions to a significant array of scientific achievements throughout the mid-19th century.

"This book gives a unique view of the background and times in which these men lived, and a peek at the implications that their work and philosophy had on today's modern science." Science Books & Films.

Sobel, Dava

★The **glass** universe : how the ladies of the Harvard Observatory took the measure of the stars / Dava Sobel. Viking, 2016. 336 p. **920**

1. Fleming, Willielmina 2. Cannon, Annie Jump, 1863-1941 3. Payne-Gaposchkin, Cecilia, 1900-1979 4. Harvard College Observatory. 5. Women scientists 6. Astronomy -- History 7. Gender role 8. Women mathematicians 9. Collective biographies

ISBN 9780670016952

LC 2016029496

The little-known true story of the unexpected and remarkable contributions to astronomy made by a group of women working in the Harvard College Observatory from the late 1800s through the mid-1900s.

"With grace, clarity, and a flair for characterization, Sobel places these early women astronomers in the wider historical context of their field for the very first time." Publishers Weekly.

Spring, Justin, 1962-

The **gourmands'** way : six Americans in Paris and the birth of a new gastronomy / Justin10 Spring. Farrar, Straus and Giroux, [2017] 448 p. **920**

1. Food writers -- United States 2. Cooks -- United States 3. Cooking, French 4. Americans in France 5. France -- Social life and customs -- 20th century 6. France -- History -- 1945- 7. Collective biographies

ISBN 9780374103156

LC 2017001319

A biography of six writers on food and wine whose lives and careers intersected in mid-twentieth-century France.

"A literary meal both luscious and lively--and essential to understanding our vacillating love affair with the French." Kirkus.

Starkey, David

Six wives : the queens of Henry VIII / David Starkey. Harper Collins Publishers, 2003. xxvii, 852 p. : **920**

1. Henry VIII, King of England, 1491-1547 Wives. 2. Catharine, of Aragon, Queen, consort of Henry VIII, King of England, 1485-1536. 3. Anne Boleyn, Queen, consort of Henry VIII, King of England, 1507-1536. 4. Anne, of Cleves, Queen, consort of Henry VIII, King of England, 1515-1557. 5. Marriages of royalty and nobility -- Great Britain -- History -- 16th century. 6. Women rulers -- Great Britain 7. Divorce -- England -- History. 8. Great Britain -- History -- Henry VIII, 1509-1547. 9. Collective biographies

ISBN 069401043X

LC 2004556138

"Solidly researched and delightfully told, this is highly recommended." Library Journal.

Stein, Sarah Abrevaya

Family papers : a Sephardic journey through the twentieth century / Sarah Abrevaya Stein. Farrar, Straus and Giroux, [2019] 288 p. **920**

1. Levy family. 2. Sephardim 3. Family history 4. Jewish families 5. Jews 6. Greece -- History 7. Collective biographies

ISBN 9780374185428

LC 2019020324

An award-winning historian uses the letters and correspondence of one Sephardic family to tell the story of their journey from Salonica, Greece, through their migration across the continents and how they were almost eradicated by the Holocaust.

Stewart, Ian, 1945-

Significant figures : the lives and work of great mathematicians / Ian Stewart. Basic Books, 2017. vi, 303 pages : **920**

1. Mathematicians 2. Collective biographies

ISBN 9780465096121

LC bl2017037604

A mathematician spotlights the lives of twenty-five legendary people in his field and examines the impact they had on shaping today's mathematics, including Archimedes, Benoit Mandelbrot, Muhammad ibn Musa al-Khwarizmi and Augusta Ada King.

Stillman, Deanne

Blood brothers : the story of the strange friendship between Sitting Bull and Buffalo Bill / Deanne Stillman. Simon & Schuster, 2017. 288 p. **920**

1. Buffalo Bill, 1846-1917 Friends and associates. 2. Sitting Bull, 1831-1890 Friends and associates. 3. Buffalo Bill's Wild West Show 4. Entertainers. 5. Dakota Indians. 6. Wild west shows. 7. The West (United States) -- History. 8. Collective biographies

ISBN 9781476773520

LC 2017006041

Documents the unlikely friendship between Buffalo Bill Cody and Sitting Bull, tracing the events of their brief but important collaboration during Cody's 1880s Wild West Show and the impact of Little Big Horn, the contributions of Annie Oakley and Sitting Bull's assassination in 1890.

"Thoughtful and thoroughly well-told--just the right treatment for a subject about which many books have been written before, few so successfully." Kirkus.

Symmes, Patrick, 1964-

The **boys** from Dolores : Fidel Castro's schoolmates from revolution to exile / Patrick Symmes. Pantheon Books, c2007. 352 p. ; **920**

1. Castro, Fidel, 1926-2016 Childhood and youth 2. Symmes, Patrick, 1964- Travel Cuba. 3. Colegio de Dolores (Cuba) 4. Cuba -- Description and travel. 5. Cuba -- History -- 20th century 6. Collective biographies

ISBN 0375422838

LC 2006030323

Includes index.

Draws on interviews with Fidel Castro's former classmates at the Colegio de Dolores, an elite Jesuit school in Santiago, Cuba, to provide a close-up look at a little-known period in Castro's life and the effects of the Cuban Revolution on his classmates, many of whom left Cuba in its wake.

"The author writes of Castro's schoolmates from Dolores, the private Jesuit academy in Santiago de Cuba on the island's eastern end, and he visits several of them. Among the Dolores students were Castro's brothers Raul and Ramon and a future star in North American television, Desi Arnaz. But it is Cuban intellectuals like Lundy Aguilar to whom Symmes turns for insights into Cuba before and after Castro's revolution. The result is a remarkable account of the country and its people." Library Journal.

Taraborrelli, J. Randy

The **Kennedy** heirs : John, Caroline, and the new generation ; a legacy of triumph and tragedy / J. Randy Taraborrelli. St. Martin's Press, 2019. 480 p. **920**

1. Kennedy family. 2. Politicians' families 3. Children of politicians 4. Rich families 5. Fame 6. Collective biographies

ISBN 9781250174062

LC 2018055445

Explores the lives of the third generation of Kennedys, from undisclosed facts about the deaths of John Kennedy, Jr., and Carolyn Bessette to Joseph Kennedy III's compelling response to Trump's State of the Union.

Jackie, Janet & Lee : the secret lives of Janet Auchincloss and her daughters, Jacqueline Kennedy Onassis and Lee Radziwill / J. Randy Taraborrelli. St. Martin's Press, 2018. 544 p. **920**

1. Onassis, Jacqueline Kennedy, 1929-1994 2. Auchincloss, Janet Lee, 1907-1989. 3. Radziwill, Lee Bouvier, 1933- 4. Mothers and daughters 5. Presidents' spouses 6. Celebrities 7. Marriage 8. Collective biographies

ISBN 9781250128010

LC 2017036190

A portrait of Jacqueline Bouvier Kennedy Onassis; her mother, Janet Lee Auchincloss; and her sister, Princess Lee Radziwill, discusses their ambitions, status-seeking marriages, illicit liaisons and psychological profiles as based on interviews with close friends and family members.

Taylor, Yuval

Zora and Langston : a story of friendship and betrayal / Yuval Taylor. W.W. Norton & Company, [2019] 304 p. **920**

1. Hurston, Zora Neale 2. Hughes, Langston, 1902-1967 3. African American authors -- 20th century 4. Friendship 5. Collaboration 6. Disagreement 7. Collective biographies

ISBN 9780393243918

LC 2018050513

Traces the story of the literary friendship of Harlem Renaissance figures Zora Neale Hurston and Langston Hughes, tracing their folklore-collecting journeys through the 1920s South, their influential creative collaborations and their passionate but mysterious falling out.

"Fascinating in their own rights as major literary figures, Langston Hughes and Zora Neale Hurston are also fascinating for their complicated relationship, which ended in a spectacular clash." Booklist.

Teitel, Amy Shira

Fighting for space : two pilots and their historic battle for female spaceflight / Amy Shira Teitel. Grand Central Publishing, 2020. 448 p. **920**

1. Cochran, Jacqueline 2. Cobb, Jerrie 3. United States. National Aeronautics and Space Administration -- History 4. Women pilots 5. Women astronauts 6. Gender equity 7. Gender role 8. United States -- History 9. Collective biographies

ISBN 9781538716045

LC bl2020000072

The spaceflight historian and creator of YouTube's "Vintage Space" traces the engaging story of female pilots Jackie Cochran and Jerrie Cobb, who battled personal and patriarchal challenges to pursue their dream of becoming astronauts.

"A well-researched contribution to women's and aviation history." Kirkus

Terkel, Studs, 1912-2008

Working : people talk about what they do all day and how they feel about what they do / Studs Terkel. The New Press, 1997, c1974. xlix, 589 p. ; **920**

1. Working class -- United States -- Interviews. 2. Occupations. 3. Work. 4. Working class -- United States -- Attitudes. 5. Collective biographies

ISBN 9781565843424

LC 73018037

Originally published: New York : Pantheon Books, 1974.

Men and women representing a variety of occupations, describe the daily routine of their jobs and express their grievances, aims, and dreams.

Thomas, Dana, 1964-

Gods and kings : the rise and fall of Alexander McQueen and John Galliano / Dana Thomas Penguin Books, 2014 384 p. **920**

1. Galliano, John 2. McQueen, Alexander, 1969-2010 3. Fashion designers 4. Couture clothing 5. Clothing industry and trade 6. Luxury. 7. Collective biographies

ISBN 9781594204944

LC 2015460559

In her groundbreaking work, Gods and Kings, acclaimed journalist Dana Thomas tells the true story of McQueen and Galliano. In so doing, she reveals the relentless world of couture--and the price it demanded of the very ones who saved it.

Thomas, Gordon, 1933-2017

Defying Hitler : the Germans who resisted Nazi rule / Gordon Thomas, Greg Lewis. Dutton, 2019 560 p. **920**

1. Scholl, Sophie, 1921-1943. 2. Harnack-Fish, Mildred, 1902-1943. 3. Bonhoeffer, Dietrich, 1906-1945. 4. Gerstein, Kurt, 1905-1945. 5. Baum, Herbert, 1912-1942 6. Oster, Hans 7. Stauffenberg, Claus von 1907-1944. 8. Schulze-Boysen Harro, 1909-1942 9. Rote Kapelle (Resistance group) 10. Nazism. 11. Anti-Nazis 12. Anti-Nazi movement 13. World War II 14. Germany -- Politics and government -- 1933-1945 15. Collective biographies

ISBN 9780451489043

LC 2018021073

A vivid chronicle of the underground resistance efforts of everyday Germans who thwarted Nazi rule shares the stories of heroes who risked or lost their lives to speak out, smuggle intelligence, defy wrongful laws and help Jewish escapees.

"Highly recommended for those wishing to comprehend life in Nazi Germany and what courage it took not to surrender to authority." Library Journal.

Thomas, Robert McG. (Robert McGill), 1940-2000

52 McGs. : the best obituaries from legendary New York Times writer Robert McG. Thomas Jr. / edited by Chris Calhoun ; foreword by Thomas Mallon. Scribner, c2001. 192 p. : **920**

1. Obituaries. 2. Obituary writing. 3. Obituary writers.

ISBN 9781416598275

LC 2001042952

An unusual compilation of obituaries by the late New York Times reporter presents his intriguing accounts of the lives of unsung heroes, eccentrics, and underachievers.

"This highly browsable collection of 52 obits shows Thomas at his deadline best." Publishers Weekly.

Thompson, Laura, 1964-

The **six** : the lives of the Mitford sisters / Laura Thompson. St. Martin's Press, 2016, c2015 480 p. **920**

1. Mitford, Nancy, 1904-1973. 2. Mitford, Pamela, 1907-1994. 3. Mosley, Diana, 1910-2003. 4. Mitford, Unity, 1914-1948. 5. Mitford, Jessica, 1917-1996. 6. Devonshire, Deborah Vivien Freeman-Mitford Cavendish, Duchess of, 1920-2014. 7. Mitford family. 8. Sisters. 9. Great Britain. 10. Collective biographies

ISBN 9781250099532

LC 2016024061

Previously published: Take Six Girls. London : Head of Zeus, 2015.

The eldest was a razor-sharp novelist of upper-class manners; the second was loved by John Betjeman; the third was a fascist who married Oswald Mosley; the fourth idolized Hitler and shot herself in the head when Britain declared war on Germany; the fifth was a member of the American Communist Party; the sixth became Duchess of Devonshire. They were the Mitford sisters: Nancy, Pamela, Diana, Unity, Jessica, and Deborah. Born into country-house privilege in the early years of the 20th century, they became prominent as "bright young things" in the high society of interwar London. Then, as the shadows crept over 1930s Europe, the stark--and very public--differences in their outlooks came to symbolize the political polarities of a dangerous decade.

"Appreciators of biography and social history will find much to engage their interest here." Booklist.

Thompson-Hernandez, Walter

The **Compton** Cowboys : the new generation of cowboys in America's urban Heartland / Walter Thompson-Hernandez. William Morrow & Co, 2020. 304 p. **920**

1. African Americans 2. Cowboys 3. Horses 4. Ranch life 5. California 6. Compton, California 7. Collective biographies

ISBN 0062910604

LC bl2020011729

Tells the story of The Compton Cowboys, a group of African-American men and women who defy stereotypes and continue the proud, centuries-old tradition of black cowboys.

"A year in the lives of 10 inner-city men fighting to keep black cowboy culture alive and well even as their personal lives are in disarray. A gritty and somber chronicle of an often overlooked community." Kirkus

Tisch, Andrew

Journeys : an American story / Andrew Tisch, Mary Skafidas. RosettaBooks, 2018. 272 p. **920**

1. Immigrants. 2. Immigration and emigration. 3. Second chances. 4. Freedom. 5. United States -- Immigration and emigration. 6. Collective biographies.

ISBN 9781948122016

LC 2017958682

Every family has a story of how they arrived in America, whether it was a few months, years, decades, or centuries ago. Celebrating the vastness and variety of immigration tales in America, this is a collection of family lore, whether it has been passed down through many generations or is being created right now.

"A collection of pieces by immigrants in America (and some by their descendants), essays that coalesce to counter the narrative of fear offered by the loud anti-immigrant voices throughout the country." Kirkus.

Toibin, Colm, 1955-

Mad, bad, dangerous to know : the fathers of Wilde, Yeats and Joyce / Colm Toibin. Scribner, 2018. 240 p. **920**

1. Wilde, Oscar, 1854-1900 Family 2. Yeats, W. B. (William Butler) 1865-1939 Family 3. Joyce, James, 1882-1941 Family 4. Family relationships 5. Poets, Irish 6. Authors, Irish 7. Fathers and sons 8. Ireland 9. Collective biographies

ISBN 9781476785172

LC 2018037024

The New York Times best-selling author of Brooklyn offers an intimate study of Irish culture, history and literature told through the lives of William Wilde, John Butler Yeats and John Stanislaus Joyce--and the complicated relationships they had with their literary-legend sons.

Tuchman, Barbara W. (Barbara Wertheim), 1912-1989

The **Zimmermann** telegram / Barbara W. Tuchman. Ballantine Books, 1985, c1966. xii, 244 p., 8 p. of plates : **920**

1. Codes (Communication) 2. Cryptography. 3. World War I -- Military intelligence -- Great Britain. 4. Diplomats -- Germany 5. Collective biographies.

ISBN 0345324250

LC BL 99948559

Originally published: Rev. ed. New York : Macmillan, 1966.

"In the dark winter of 1917, as World War I was deadlocked, Britain knew that Europe could be saved only if the United States joined the war. But President Wilson remained unshakable in his neutrality. Then, with a single stroke, the tool to propel America into the war came into a quiet British office. One of countless messages intercepted by the crack team of British decoders, the Zimmermann telegram was a top-secret message from Berlin inviting Mexico to join Japan in an invasion of the United States: Mexico would recover her lost American territories while keeping the U.S. occupied on her side of the Atlantic. How Britain managed to inform America of Germany's plan without revealing that the German codes had been broken makes for an incredible, true story of espionage, intrigue, and international politics as only Barbara W. Tuchman could tell it."--Publisher's description.

Walsh, Jim, 1959-

The **Replacements** : all over but the shouting : an oral history / Jim Walsh. MBI Pub. Co. and Voyageur Press, 2007. 304 p. **920**

1. Replacements (Musical group) 2. Rock musicians -- United States 3. Rock music -- History and criticism 4. United States -- Social life and customs -- 20th century 5. Oral histories

ISBN 076033062X

LC 2007022576

"In this loving, appropriately ramshackle tribute to one of the most beloved rock-and-roll bands of the 1980s, Walsh gives his subjects the oral history treatment, assembling a wide range of associates, friends and famous fans to put their memories on the record." Publishers Weekly.

Ward-Royster, Willa, 1922-

How I got over : Clara Ward and the world-famous Ward Singers / Willa Ward-Royster ; as told to Toni Rose ; foreword by Horace Clarence Boyer. Temple University Press, c1997. xiii, 263 p. : **920**

1. Ward-Royster, Willa, 1922- 2. Clara Ward Singers. 3. Gospel musicians -- United States 4. African American gospel singers. 5. United States -- Social life and customs -- 20th century 6. Collective biographies.

ISBN 1566394899

LC 96005943

Includes index.

The author recounts the experiences of her family who began singing gospel music for goodwill in rural South Carolina and eventually became the world-famous Ward Singers.

"Ward-Royster relates the rise of her family's world-renowned gospel group, formed by her mother and headlined by her sister. The book contains details on everything from successful performances on the stage of the Apollo, major TV variety shows, and international tours to top sales of hit recordings and friendships with such luminaries as Mahalia Jackson." Library Journal.

Ware, Susan, 1950-

Why they marched : untold stories of the women who fought for the right to vote / Susan Ware. Harvard University Press, 2019. viii, 345 p. **920**

1. Suffrage 2. Women's rights 3. Suffragists 4. Voting 5. United States -- History 6. Collective biographies

ISBN 9780674986688

LC 2018039670

For far too long, the history of how American women won the right to vote has been told as the tale of a few iconic leaders, all white and native-born. But Susan Ware uncovered a much broader and more diverse story waiting to be told. Why They Marched is a tribute to the many women who worked tirelessly in communities across the nation, out of the spotlight, protesting, petitioning, and insisting on their right to full citizenship.

"This text brings to light fascinating stories underrepresented in traditional looks at women's suffrage in the United States, providing just the right amount of detail in each chapter before moving on to yet another enthralling tale." Library Journal.

Weber, Caroline, 1969-

Proust's duchess : how three celebrated women captured the imagination of fin de siècle Paris / Caroline Weber. Alfred A. Knopf, 2018. 736 p. **920**

1. Proust, Marcel, 1871-1922 2. Straus, Genevieve, 1849-1926. 3. Chevigne, Laure de, 1859-1936. 4. Greffulhe, Elisabeth, comtesse, 1860-1952. 5. Aristocracy 6. Intellectual life 7. Authors 8. Women intellectuals -- Europe. 9. Paris, France -- Social life and customs -- 19th century. 10. France -- History -- 19th century. 11. Collective biographies

ISBN 9780307961785

LC 2017038855

Pulitzer Prize for Biography or Autobiography finalist, 2019.

Describes the glittering lives and fabled salons of three members of fin-de-siecle Parisian high society who acted as muses to several generations of writers, artists, composers, designers and journalists, ultimately influencing a composite character in The Remembrance of Things Past.

Weber, Nicholas Fox, 1947-

The **Bauhaus** group : six masters of modernism / Nicholas Fox Weber. Alfred A. Knopf, 2009. 544 p. **920**

1. Bauhaus 2. Artists -- Germany 3. Designers -- Germany 4. Avant-garde (Aesthetics) -- Germany -- History -- 20th century. 5. Art, German. 6. Germany -- Social life and customs. 7. Collective biographies.

ISBN 9780307268365

LC 2009028729

"A Borzoi book."

A collective biography brings to life the Bauhaus geniuses and the community of the pioneering art school in Germany's Weimar and Dessau in the 1920s and early 1930s.

Weintraub, Stanley, 1929-

15 stars : Eisenhower, MacArthur, Marshall : three generals who saved the American century / Stanley Weintraub. Free Press, c2007. xvi, 541 p. : **920**

1. MacArthur, Douglas, 1880-1964. 2. Marshall, George C., (George Catlett), 1880-1959 3. Eisenhower, Dwight D. (Dwight David), 1890-1969. 4. United States. Army 5. Generals -- United States 6. Presidents -- United States 7. World War II 8. Military campaigns. 9. United States -- History -- 20th century 10. Collective biographies.
ISBN 0743275276

LC 2007016018

Profiles three five-star generals who were pivotal to the evolution of World War II, describing their wartime and peacetime achievements, from MacArthur's and Marshall's respective efforts to rebuild Japan and Europe to Eisenhower's presidency.

"The author provides a detailed and absorbing gloss on the relationships among three extraordinary leaders." Library Journal.

Weir, Alison, 1951-

★**Queens** of the conquest / Alison Weir. Ballantine Books, 2017. 448 p. England's medieval queens ; **920**

1. Plantagenet, House of 2. Women rulers 3. Rulers 4. Civilization, Medieval 5. England -- History -- Medieval period, 1066-1485 6. Collective biographies
ISBN 9781101966662

LC 2018303412

Vivid profiles of five powerful Norman queens examine their enduring influence and the myths and prejudices that obscured their achievements, in a first joint biography that includes portraits of Matilda of Flanders; William the Conqueror's wife; and Empress Matilda, the mother of King Henry II.

Weller, Sheila

Girls like us : Carole King, Joni Mitchell, and Carly Simon--and the journey of a generation / Sheila Weller. Atria Books, c2008. 592 p. **920**

1. King, Carole, 1942- 2. Mitchell, Joni, 1943- 3. Simon, Carly. 4. Singers 5. Women singers 6. Rock musicians 7. Women rock musicians 8. Collective biographies
ISBN 0743491475

LC 2007043445

Joni Mitchell, Carole King, and Carly Simon remain among the most enduring and important women in popular music. Each woman is distinct: King is the product of outer-borough, middle-class New York City; Mitchell is a granddaughter of Canadian farmers; and Simon is a child of the Manhattan intellectual upper crust. They collectively represent, in their lives and their songs, a great swath of American girls who came of age in the late 1960s.

"A must-read for any fan of these artists, this bio will prove an absorbing, eye-opening tour of rock (and American) history for anyone who's appreciated a female musician in the past thirty years." Publishers Weekly.

The **news** sorority : Diane Sawyer, Katie Couric, Christiane Amanpour and the (ongoing, imperfect, complicated) triumph of women in tv news / Sheila Weller. The Penguin Press, 2014. 496 p. **920**

1. Sawyer, Diane, 1945- 2. Couric, Katie, 1957- 3. Amanpour, Christiane. 4. Women television newscasters and commentators. 5. Television news. 6. Women in the mass media industry and trade 7. Women in mass media. 8. Collective biographies
ISBN 9781594204272

LC 2014009725

For decades, women battered the walls of the male fortress of television journalism, until finally three--Diane Sawyer, Katie Couric, and Christiane Amanpour--broke through, definitively remaking America's nightly news. Drawing on exclusive interviews with their colleagues and intimates from childhood on, bestselling author Sheila Weller crafts a lively and eye-opening narrative, revealing the combination of ambition, skill, and character that enabled these three singular women to infiltrate the once impenetrable "boys club" and become cultural icons.

"News junkies and fans will love all of the insider details on the media and the lives of these women." Library Journal.

West, Cornel,

Black prophetic fire / in dialogue with and edited by Christa Buschendorf. Beacon Press, 2014. 248 p. **920**

1. Douglass, Frederick, 1818-1895 Political and social views. 2. Du Bois, W. E. B. (William Edward Burghardt), 1868-1963 Political and social views. 3. King, Martin Luther, Jr., 1929-1968 Political and social views. 4. Baker, Ella, 1903-1986 Political and social views. 5. Malcolm X, 1925-1965 Political and social views 6. Wells-Barnett, Ida B., 1862-1931 Political and social views. 7. West, Cornel, 1953- Interviews. 8. African Americans 9. Revolutionaries -- United States 10. Political activists 11. Collective biographies
ISBN 9780807003527

LC 2014010359

A prominent activist and democratic thinker along with a distinguished scholar examine the legacies of African American leaders from the past two centuries and discuss their passion, vision and commitment.

Whipple, Chris

The **spymasters** : how the CIA directors shape history and the future / Chris Whipple. Scribner, 2020. 384 p. **920**

1. CIA 2. Directors of Central Intelligence 3. Presidents -- United States 4. Intelligence service -- United States 5. United States 6. United States 7. Collective biographies
ISBN 1982106409

LC bl2020045525

The best-selling author of The Gatekeepers presents a behind-the-scenes tour of the inner workings of the CIA and how it often operates as an essential counterforce against presidents who would overstep the powers of the executive office.

"Whipple makes excellent use of insider accounts and provides enough color to keep readers turning the pages. This well-written and accessible survey illuminates a neglected role in American history." Publishers Weekly

Wideman, John Edgar

Writing to save a life : the Louis Till file / John Edgar Wideman. Scribner, 2016 224 p. **920**

1. Till, Louis 2. Till, Emmett, 1941-1955. 3. Injustice 4. Racism 5. Civil rights 6. Discrimination 7. Southern States -- Race relations. 8. Multiple perspectives 9. Collective biographies
ISBN 9781501147289

National Book Critics Circle Award for Nonfiction finalist, 2016

An award-winning writer traces the lesser-known story of Louis Till, the father of iconic civil rights martyr Emmet Till, tying their fates together to reveal how the father was wrongly convicted for rape and murder before being executed by the Army a decade before his son's murder.

"A book seething with the passion and sense of outrage behind the Black Lives Matter movement that also traces specific roots of the movement's genealogy." Kirkus.

Wides-Munoz, Laura

The **making** of a dream : how a group of young undocumented immigrants helped change what it means to be American / Laura Wides-Munoz. HarperCollins, 2018. 304 p. **920**

1. Immigration and emigration 2. Undocumented immigrants. 3. Child immigrants 4. Teenagers 5. Collective biographies

ISBN 9780062560124

LC bl2017048622

A journalist chronicles the next chapter in civil rights--the story of a movement and a nation, witnessed through the poignant and inspiring experiences of five young undocumented activists who are transforming society's attitudes toward one of the most contentious political matters roiling America today: immigration.

"This inspiring, well-written, well-documented account is an important read for Americans on all sides of this lingering issue." Library Journal.

Wieland, Karin

Dietrich & Riefenstahl : Hollywood, Berlin, and a century in two lives / Karin Wieland ; Translated from the German by Shelley Frisch. Liveright Pub Corp, 2015. vii, 612 p. **920**

1. Actors and actresses -- Germany 2. Film industry and trade -- History. 3. World War II -- Women. 4. Silent film actors and actresses. 5. Collective biographies. 6. Biographies.

ISBN 9780871403360

LC 2015026548

Translation of Dietrich & Riefenstahl : der Traum von der neuen Frau, originally published by Carl Hanser in 2011.

National Book Critics Circle Award for Biography finalist, 2015.

"Wieland deftly traces both lives through their many ups and downs. A sweeping, revelatory dual biography." Kirkus.

Wiggins, Arthur W.

The **human** side of science : Edison and Tesla, Watson and Crick, and other personal stories behind science's big ideas / Arthur W. Wiggins and Charles M. Wynn Sr. ; with cartoon commentary by Sidney Harris. Prometheus Books, 2016. 364 p. **920**

1. Science. 2. Scientific discoveries 3. Scientists. 4. Collective biographies

ISBN 9781633881563

LC 2016007462

This book focuses attention on the fact that science is a human enterprise. The reader learns about the foibles and quirks as well as the admirable ingenuity and impressive accomplishments of famous scientists who made some of the greatest discoveries of the past and present.

"A good addition to any popular-science collection." Booklist.

Wills, Shomari

Black fortunes : the story of the first six African Americans who escaped slavery and became millionaires / Shomari Wills. Amistad Press, 2018. 320 p. **920**

1. African Americans 2. Freed slaves. 3. Millionaires 4. Success (Concept) 5. United States -- Race relations. 6. Collective biographies

ISBN 9780062437594

LC bl2018002424

The astonishing untold history of America's first black millionaires--former slaves who endured incredible challenges to amass and maintain their wealth for a century, from the Jacksonian period to the Roaring Twenties--self-made entrepreneurs whose unknown success mirrored that of American business heroes such as Henry Ford, John D. Rockefeller, and Thomas Edison.

"Wills' storytelling is infectious, his subjects are irresistible, and his broad coverage invites readers to venture further into the events and historical context he so vividly introduces." Booklist.

Witcover, Jules

America's vice presidents : from irrelevance to power / Jules Witcover. Smithsonian Books, 2014. 592 p. **920**

1. Vice-Presidents -- United States. 2. Politicians. 3. United States -- Politics and government. 4. Collective biographies

ISBN 9781588344717

LC 2014004242

Profiles each of the forty-seven vice presidents, providing an examination of the role throughout American history, revealing the maneuvering that transformed this office from consolation prize to de facto assistant presidency.

Wolff, Daniel J.

Grown-up anger : the connected mysteries of Bob Dylan, Woody Guthrie, and the Calumet massacre of 1913 / Daniel Wolff. Harper, 2017. 304 p. **920**

1. Dylan, Bob, 1941- 2. Guthrie, Woody, 1912-1967. 3. Popular music -- Political aspects 4. Folk music 5. Injustice 6. Strikes 7. United States -- Social life and customs -- 20th century 8. Collective biographies

ISBN 9780062451699

LC 2017003018

After researching a 1913 tragedy described in a Woody Guthrie song, a lifelong Bob Dylan fan discusses the historical details of the event and how rage at the injustice inspired both musicians to create art from loss and fury.

"Wolff has crafted a fascinating and relevant whirlwind examination of music, economic injustice, and two American icons." Booklist.

★**How** Lincoln learned to read : twelve great Americans and the educations that made them / Daniel Wolff. Bloomsbury, 2009. 345 p. **920**

1. Education -- United States -- History 2. United States 3. Collective biographies

ISBN 9781596912908

LC 2008024695

Wolff presents an engaging, provocative history of American ideas, told through the educations (both in and out of school) of 12 great figures, from Benjamin Franklin to Elvis Presley.

"This provocative book is not only an important addition to the history of education in America, but also a valuable contribution to the history and understanding of the country's ideas and culture." School Library Journal.

Wood, Gordon S.

Friends divided : John Adams and Thomas Jefferson / Gordon S. Wood. Penguin Press, 2017 512 p. **920**

1. Jefferson, Thomas, 1743-1826 Friends and associates 2. Adams, John, 1735-1826 Friends and associates 3. Politicians 4. Male friendship 5. Political parties 6. Presidents 7. United States -- Politics and government. 8. Collective biographies

ISBN 9780735224711

LC 2017025116

A dual portrait of the second and third U.S. presidents shares insights into their disparate backgrounds, the partnership decisions that helped establish America's foundation and the unexpected ways their subsequent falling out and reconciliation corrected the course of a young republic.

"Wood glides through the political intricacies and intrigues of the times, offering incisive analyses, especially of the ongoing debate over slavery, finely illuminating the minds of Adams and Jefferson." Publishers Weekly.

Wulf, Andrea

The **brother** gardeners : botany, empire, and the birth of an obsession / Andrea Wulf. Knopf, 2009, c2008. 368 p. **920**

1. Horticulturists. 2. Plant collectors. 3. Gardening -- Great Britain. 4. Plant collecting 5. England -- History -- 18th century. 6. Great Britain -- History -- 18th century. 7. Collective biographies.
ISBN 9780307270238

LC bl2009000183

Originally published: London : William Heinemann, 2008.

Follows the lives of six men who shared a passion for plants and a love of gardening in eighteenth-century London, who made Britain the epicenter of horticulture, and transformed gardening from an aristocratic pastime to a national obsession.

"A garden will never look quite the same after you've read this book. Wulf's book will be of interest to anyone with a garden, even if it's on a windowsill." Library Journal.

Wyllie, James

Nazi wives : the women at the top of Hitler's Germany / James Wyllie. St. Martin's Press, 2020, c2019. 288 p. **920**

1. Hitler, Adolf, 1889-1945 Friends and associates 2. Nazi women 3. Nazism and women 4. Nazis 5. World War II -- Germany 6. Germany -- Politics and government -- 1933-1945 7. Collective biographies
ISBN 9781250271563

LC 2020028410

Originally published: Cheltenham, UK : The History Press, 2019.

Goering, Goebbels, Himmler, Heydrich, Hess, Bormann--names synonymous with power and influence in the Third Reich. Perhaps less familiar are Carin, Emmy, Magda, Margarete, Lina, Ilse and Gerda... These are the women behind the infamous men, complex individuals with distinctive personalities who were captivated by Hitler and whose everyday lives were governed by Nazi ideology. Throughout the rise and fall of Nazism these women loved and lost, raised families and quarreled with their husbands and each other, all the while jostling for position with the Fuhrer himself. James Wyllie explores these women in detail for the first time, skillfully interweaving their stories through years of struggle, power, decline and destruction into the post-war twilight of denial and delusion.

"Wyllie sets a brisk pace through colorful material drawn from primary and secondary sources, though it's sometimes difficult to keep track of the large cast. Still, this is an evenhanded and comprehensive account of an underexamined aspect of Nazi Germany." Publishers Weekly

Yaffa, Joshua

Between two fires : truth, ambition, and compromise in Putin's Russia / Joshua Yaffa. Tim Duggan Books, 2020 356 p. ; **920**

1. Putin, Vladimir Vladimirovich, 1952- 2. Power (Social sciences) -- Russia 3. Investigative journalism 4. Dissenters 5. Public opinion -- Russia 6. Russia -- Politics and government -- 1991- 7. Collective biographies
ISBN 9781524760595

LC 2019025918

Between Two Fires chronicles the lives of eight ambitious Russians--from politicians and entrepreneurs to artists and historians--who have built their careers and constructed their identities in the shadow of the Putin system, where astonishingly, Putin's approval rating remains at 80%. Torn between their own ambitions and the omnipresent demands of the state, some muster cunning and cynicism to extract privileges from those in power while others are broken or demoralized. For each, the question of compromise--where to bend, how much, and in the service of what goal--is ever-present. The result is an intimate and probing portrait of the way citizens shape their lives around the demands of a capricious and repressive state, which offers urgent lessons about the nature of modern authoritarianism.

"This superb portrait of contemporary Russia is full of insight and moral drama." Publishers Weekly.

Zwonitzer, Mark

Will you miss me when I'm gone? : the Carter Family and their legacy in American music / Mark Zwonitzer with Charles Hirshberg. Simon & Schuster, 2002. xii, 417 p. : **920**

1. Carter Family (Musical group) 2. Country musicians -- United States 3. Music, American -- History and criticism 4. Virginia 5. Collective biographies
ISBN 9780684857633

LC 2002022395

Includes index.

National Book Critics Circle Award for Biography finalist, 2002.

Traces the bluegrass country music achievements of the Carter family, from their discovery by a New York record maker to their rise to stardom and eventual breakup, noting their influence on the careers of top performers.

"The author follows the Carter family's history from the 1891 birth of A.P. Carter, the musical founder, up through the late 1970s, offering background on the social, economic and technological developments that spawned American folk, country and rock music. Zwonitzer writes with flair, weaving anecdotes into a compelling study that will intrigue historians and music lovers alike." Publishers Weekly.

Smith, Jessie Carney, 1930-

Notable Black American women / Jessie Carney Smith, editor. Gale Research, c1992-c2003. 3 volumes : **920**

1. African American women 2. Collective biographies
ISBN 9780810347496

LC 91035074

Vol. 3 has Shirelle Phelps as a contributing editor.

Provides brief biographies of business executives, writers, journalists, lawyers, physicians, actresses, singers, musicians, artists, educators, religious leaders, civil rights activists, politicians, aviators, athletes, and scientists

920.71 Men

Gates, Henry Louis, 1950-

Thirteen ways of looking at a Black man / Henry Louis Gates, Jr. Random House, c1997. xxvi, 226 p. ; **920.71**

1. African American men 2. African Americans 3. Race relations. 4. Essays
ISBN 0679457135

LC 96033138

Includes index.

A leading Black scholar interviews famous African Americans, including Colin Powell, Louis Farrakhan, and Harry Belafonte, exploring their views on America and the significance of their lives in terms of race relations.

"Mr. Gates's strong suit is finding the common man in uncommon figures, without losing sight of the ways in which race, class and personal experience have shaped each life." New York Times Book Review.

920.72 Women

Livingston, Sonja

Ladies night at the Dreamland / Sonja Livingston. The University of Georgia Press, 2016. 200 p. **920.72**

1. Women. 2. Essays
ISBN 9780820349138

LC 2015032665

"Wise, fresh, captivating essays." Kirkus.

Ware, Susan, 1950-

Letter to the world : seven women who shaped the American century / Susan Ware. W.W. Norton, c1998. xxiv, 344 p. : **920.72**

1. Women -- United States 2. Biography -- 20th century.
ISBN 0393046524

LC 97045923

A portrait of the public and private lives of women who had a profound impact on American culture in the twentieth century offers profiles of Eleanor Roosevelt, Margaret Mead, Dorothy Thompson, and Marian Andersen.

"The author considers the lives of seven women who had an exceptional impact on 20th-century American culture and society's perception of the role of women: Eleanor Roosevelt, Dorothy Thompson, Margaret Mead, Katharine Hepburn, Babe Didrikson Zaharias, Martha Graham, and Marian Anderson. In addition to focusing on outstanding achievements in their chosen fields, Ware looks at their often unconventional private lives." Library Journal.

929 Genealogy, names, insignia

Frank, Michael, 1959 June 2-

The **mighty** Franks : a family memoir / Michael Frank. Farrar, Straus and Giroux, 2017. 320 p. **929**

1. Frank, Michael, 1959 June 2- Family. 2. Journalists 3. Aunt and nephew 4. Family relationships 5. Screenwriters 6. Hollywood, California -- History -- 20th century
ISBN 9780374210120

LC 2016041346

A Los Angeles Times book critic chronicles his upbringing and education in an insular family of Hollywood screenwriters, describing how his once-beloved aunt's psychological illness forced him to reconstruct his senses of self and family.

Franklin, John Hope, 1915-2009

★**In** search of the promised land : a Black family and the Old South / John Hope Franklin, Loren Schweninger. Oxford University Press, 2006. xvii, 286 p. : **929**

1. Thomas, Sally, 1787-1850 Family. 2. Thomas family 3. Rapier family. 4. Slaves 5. African Americans -- Nashville, Tennessee 6. African American families -- Southern States 7. Slavery 8. Nashville, Tennessee -- History. 9. Nashville, Tennessee -- Race relations. 10. Southern states
ISBN 0195160878

LC 2004061666

"The authors trace the history of the Thomas-Rapier family during the antebellum and Civil War eras. Starting with matriarch Sally Thomas, born a slave in 1787, the book enables readers to distinguish the various complex modes within which slavery operated. The resulting family history also traces the evolution of race relations in diverse locations from New Orleans to New York City, Canada, Minnesota, and the Caribbean." Library Journal.

Kemp, Thomas Jay

International vital records handbook / Thomas Jay Kemp. Genealogical Pub., c2009. xiv, 587 p. : **929**

1. Marriage records 2. Marriage records -- United States 3. Registers of births, etc. 4. Registers of births, etc. -- United States
ISBN 0806317930

LC bl2010006873

Provides application forms and ordering information for birth, marriage, and death certificates from every state in the United States, the provinces of Canada, and most other countries in the world.

Leepson, Marc, 1945-

Flag : an American biography / Marc Leepson. Thomas Dunne Books/St. Martin's Press, 2005. xviii, 334 p. : **929**

1. Flags -- United States -- History. 2. American flag -- History. 3. Signs and symbols, American. 4. Nationalism. 5. United States -- History.
ISBN 9780312323080

LC 2004065920

This history of the American flag traces its evolution from the colonial period to its present-day role as a symbol of American resolve, discussing such topics as the myths surrounding Betsy Ross, the stars-and-stripes design, and the impact of war on the flag's appearance.

"From reverence to kitsch, Americans' attitudes to their flag and its mythology have changed over the years, and Leepson does a creditable job of recounting those changes." Publishers Weekly.

McCarthy, Andrew, 1962-

Journeys home : inspiring stories, plus tips and strategies to find your family history / featuring Andrew McCarthy, Joyce Maynard, Pico Iyer, Diane Johnson & the National Geographic travel team ; foreword by Dr. Spencer Wells, National Geographic explorer-in-residence National Geographic, 2015. 287 p. : **929**

1. Genealogy -- Anecdotes. 2. Voyages and travels -- Anecdotes. 3. Celebrities -- Travel -- Anecdotes. 4. Celebrities United States Genealogy Anecdotes. 5. United States Genealogy Anecdotes. 6. United States -- Genealogy Handbooks, manuals, etc.
ISBN 9781426213816

LC 2014033593

An actor and award-winning travel writer describes his quest to uncover his family's history in Ireland and is joined by other writers who tell the stories of their trips to various locales around the globe in search of their roots.

Minahan, James

The **complete** guide to national symbols and emblems / James Minahan. Greenwood Press, c2010. 2 v. (xxi, 977 p.) : **929**

1. Emblems, National -- Encyclopedias. 2. National characteristics -- Encyclopedias.
ISBN 9780313344961

LC 2009036963

Provides information about the official and unofficial symbols of all two hundred nations, including flags, national seals, mottoes, national colors, flowers, animals, national anthems, festivals, holidays, and cultural symbols.

Neighbors, Joy

The **Family** Tree cemetery field guide : how to find, record, & preserve your ancestors' graves / Joy Neighbors. Family Tree Books, 2017 239 p. : **929**

1. Cemeteries -- United States. 2. Cemeteries. 3. Genealogy. 4. Registers of births, etc. 5. United States -- Genealogy Handbooks, manuals, etc.

ISBN 1440352127

LC 2017276788

"Unearth clues to your past. Not all research can be done from home--sometimes you have to head into the field. Cemeteries are crucial for any genealogist's search, and this book will show you how to search for and analyze your ancestors' graves. Discover tools for locating tombstones, tips for traipsing through cemeteries, an at-a-glance guide to frequently used gravestone icons, and practical strategies for on-the-ground research. And once you've returned home, learn how to incorporate gravestone information into your research, as well as how to upload grave locations to BillionGraves and record your findings in memorial pages on Find A Grave. The Family Tree Cemetery Field Guide features: Detailed step-by-step guides to finding ancestor's cemeteries using websites like Find A Grave, plus how to record and preserve death and burial information; tips and strategies for navigating cemeteries and finding individual tombstones in the field, plus an at-a-glance guide to tombstone symbols and iconography; resources and techniques for discovering other death records and incorporating information from cemeteries into genealogical research".--Back cover.

"Cemeteries are crucial for genealogy research, and this solid, compact, one-stop book shows how to search for and analyze ancestors graves." Booklist.

Shane, Neala, 1948-

Inspired baby names from around the world : 6,000 international names and the meaning behind them / Neala Shane. New World Library, 2015 701 p. ; **929**

1. Names, Personal -- Dictionaries.

ISBN 9781608683208

LC 2014042449

Includes indexes.

"More than 6,000 baby names and their meanings, with each name accompanied by an inspiring quotation. Includes naming customs, guided meditations for selecting a name, and indexes of names by meaning and ethnicity. Also includes popular names by decade, terms for grandparents, and popular pet names".--Provided by publisher.

Testi, Arnaldo

Capture the flag : the stars and stripes in American history / Arnaldo Testi ; translated by Noor Giovanni Mazhar. New York University Press, 2010, c2003 165 p. **929**

1. Flags -- United States -- History. 2. National characteristics, American. 3. Patriotism -- United States -- History. 4. Political culture -- United States -- History. 5. United States -- History.

ISBN 9780814783221

LC 2009039278

Originally published in Italian by Bollati Boringhieri Editore in 2003.

"From our July 4th celebrations to the iconic images from 9/11, the American flag is an all-pervasive, definitive symbol of American national identity. [Testi] provides readers with an engaging and fresh perspective that can only be provided by an outsider standing above the fray. Whether discussing the evolution of flag etiquette or its relationship to the U.S. Constitution, Testi deftly explores the shifting cultural meanings of the American symbol, from 1776 through the growth of the American empire to the contentious debates occurring today." Library Journal.

Weil, Francois

Family trees : a history of genealogy in America / Francois Weil. Harvard University Press, 2013. 304 p. **929**

1. Genealogy. 2. National characteristics, American. 3. Group identity 4. Ancestors. 5. United States -- History.

ISBN 9780674045835

LC 2012044769

Traces the history of genealogy in the United States, from its early preoccupation with social status and lineage, to a nineteenth-century search for Anglo-Saxon roots, to a twentieth-century acceptance of diversity and the introduction of DNA technology.

929.1 Genealogy

Jacobs, A. J., 1968-

It's all relative : adventures up and down the world's family tree / A.J. Jacobs. Simon & Schuster, 2017. 416 p. **929.1**

1. Jacobs, A. J., 1968- Family. 2. Jacobs family. 3. Genealogy 4. Ancestors 5. Families 6. Genetic genealogy

ISBN 9781476734491

LC bl2017036988

Traces the author's three-year investigation into what constitutes family, describing how, after receiving an e-mail from a stranger who claimed to be a distant cousin, he embarked on an effort to build the biggest family tree in history.

"A delightful, easy-to-read, informative book." Kirkus.

Pennavaria, Katherine, 1959-

Genealogy : a practical guide for librarians / Katherine Pennavaria. Rowman & Littlefield, 2015. xxii, 167 p. : **929.1**

1. Genealogy.

ISBN 9780810893252

LC 2014032466

929.4 Personal names

Ciuraru, Carmela

Nom de plume : a (secret) history of pseudonyms / Carmela Ciuraru. Harper, c2011. 288 p. **929.4**

1. Anonyms and pseudonyms 2. Names, Personal. 3. Closet writers. 4. Authors.

ISBN 9780061735264

LC 2010053603

Part detective story, part exposé and part literary history, this fascinating exploration reveals writers throughout history who hoarded secret identities-- sometimes playfully, and sometimes with tragic consequences--including Mark Twain, George Eliot and Lewis Carroll.

930 History of ancient world (to ca. 499)

Allan, Tony

Life, myth, and art in Ancient Rome / Tony Allan. J. Paul Getty Museum, c2005. 144 p. : **930**

1. Art, Roman. 2. Mythology -- History and criticism 3. Rome --

Civilization. 4. Rome -- Antiquities.
ISBN 0892368217
LC 2004114326

Bahn, Paul G,

Archaeology : the essential guide to our human past / general editor: Paul Bahn ; foreword by Brian Fagan. Smithsonian Books, 2017 576 p. : **930**

1. Archaeology.
ISBN 9781588345912
LC 2017025534

Includes index.

An illustrated guide explores the entire history of human civilization through tours of every site of key archaeological significance, from the prehistoric cave paintings of Lascaux to the city of Pompeii and from China's Terracotta Army to the Gbekli Tepe in Turkey.

Bass, George F.,

Beneath the seven seas : adventures with the Institute of Nautical Archaeology / edited by George F. Bass. Thames & Hudson, 2005. 256 p. : **930**

1. Underwater archaeology. 2. Shipwrecks. 3. Extinct cities.
ISBN 9780500051368
LC oc2007030542

A collection of first-hand accounts by archaeologist from all over the world provides vivid descriptions of historical shipwrecks, from Cemal Pulak's exploration of a royal ship that sank more than 3,300 years ago off the Aegean coast of Turkey, to Donny Hamilton's report about the infamous pirate stronghold of Port Royal, Jamaica, to Robert Ballard's undersea discovery of the Titanic.

"This book features accounts by many distinguished archaeologists associated with the INA [Institute of Nautical Archaeology]. They tell of the discovery, excavation, and preservation of more than 40 shipwrecks--and one sunken city--the world over, from ancient times through the Byzantine, medieval, and Renaissance eras and on through World War II. . . . This book will appeal to general readers and specialists alike in nautical archaeology." Library Journal.

Beard, Mary, 1955-

Confronting the classics : traditions, adventures, and innovations / Mary Beard. Liveright Publishing Corporation, 2013. 320 p. **930**

1. Civilization, Classical. 2. Classical antiquities. 3. Classical literature -- History and criticism. 4. Classical antiquities in art.
ISBN 9780871407160
LC 2013016133

An internationally recognized historian takes us on an eye-opening tour of the Ancient World, shedding new light on the Greek and Roman history, and combines the epic with the everyday, which forces us to reexamine the assumptions we held as gospel.

The **fires** of Vesuvius : Pompeii lost and found / Mary Beard. Belknap Press of Harvard University Press, 2008. 360 p., 16 p. of plates : **930**

1. City life. 2. Ancient cities and towns -- Rome. 3. Pompeii (Extinct city) 4. Rome -- History 5. Rome -- Social life and customs.
ISBN 9780674029767
LC 2008027513

From its political and religious systems to slavery and attitudes toward sex, the ruins of this ancient Roman city are explored in a study that brings to light new facts about the way the people of Pompeii lived prior to meeting their devastating end in 79 CE.

S.P.Q.R. : a history of ancient Rome / Mary Beard. Liveright Publishing Corporation, 2015. 606 p., [16] leaves of plates : **930**

1. Ancient history. 2. Roman law. 3. Romans. 4. Civilization, Classical. 5. Rome -- History
ISBN 9780871404237
LC 2015036060

National Book Critics Circle Award for Nonfiction finalist

"Since the author is a well-known popularizer of classical studies, it is no surprise that this is a humorous and accessible work, but it is also extremely rigorous in its questioning of standard conclusions and methods. At all points, her approaches are easy to follow." Library Journal.

Berry, Joanne, 1971-

The **complete** Pompeii / Joanne Berry. Thames & Hudson, 2007. 256 p. : **930**

1. Pompeii (Extinct city) 2. Pompeii (Extinct city) -- Civilization. 3. Pompeii (Extinct city) -- History.
ISBN 050005150X
LC 2007922095

A comprehensive visual survey of the ancient city draws on cutting-edge architectural research to reconstruct the latest beliefs about Pompeii's history, discussing such topics as the lives and deaths of its citizens, its political and religious structures, and its destruction by the eruption of AD 79.

"This book covers the origins and evolution of the city, the daily life of its residents, the geography of the region, and the eruption of Mt. Vesuvius, as well as a history of the excavation of the site. Easy to read and with full color pictures of the excavation, along with maps, time lines, diagrams, and vivid art reproductions, this book gives a broad and comprehensive introduction to the Pompeian world. . . . High school libraries should be advised that there is a section on eroticism that contains visually and verbally explicit sexual material." Library Journal.

Bunson, Matthew

Encyclopedia of ancient Rome / Matthew Bunson. Facts On File, c2012. xxxvii, 788 p. : **930**

1. Civilization, Ancient 2. Ancient history 3. Rome -- History -- Empire, 30 B.C.-476 A.D.
ISBN 9780816082179
LC 2011038366

Expanded ed. of: Encyclopedia of the Roman Empire. Rev. ed. c2002.

Provides information on the key places, people, events, and culture of more than seven hundred years of Roman history, from the legendary founding of the city by Aeneas to the fall of the last Roman emperor in 476 A.D.

Caesar, Julius

The **Gallic** War / with an English translation by H. J. Edwards. Harvard University Press, 1958. xxii, 619 p. **930**

1. Gaul -- History -- 58 B.C.-511 A.D.
ISBN 9780674990807
LC BL 99914782

Caesar's commentaries are presented in Latin and English with background notes and maps.

Cartledge, Paul

Ancient Greece : a history in eleven cities / Paul Cartledge.

Oxford University Press, 2009. xv, 261 p., 16 p. of plates : **930**

1. Ancient history. 2. Greek civilization -- To 146 B.C. 3. Byzantine civilization. 4. Civilization, Ancient. 5. Greece. 6. Byzantine Empire.
ISBN 9780199233380

LC 2009026999

Introduces major topics in ancient Greek civilization through the development of eleven characteristic city states, ranging from prehistoric Cnossos through Byzantion, and including the future Marseilles as well as Athens and Sparta.

Thebes : the forgotten city of Ancient Greece / Paul Cartledge. Abrams Press, 2020 xxxi, 304 p., 16 unnumbered leaves of unnumbered plates : **930**

1. Ancient cities and towns 2. City-states 3. Greek civilization -- To 146 B.C. 4. Mythology, Greek -- History and criticism 5. Ancient Greece -- History 6. Thebes, Greece -- History
ISBN 9781468316063

LC 2020932371

Includes bibliographical references (pages 278-286) and index.

Among the extensive writing available about the history of ancient Greece, there is precious little about the city-state of Thebes. At one point the most powerful city in ancient Greece, Thebes has been long overshadowed by its better-known rivals, Athens and Sparta. Acclaimed classicist and historian Paul Cartledge brings the city vividly to life and argues that it is central to our understanding of the ancient Greeks' achievements--whether politically or culturally--and thus to the wider politico-cultural traditions of western Europe, the Americas, and indeed the world.

"Diving deep into centuries' worth of scholarship, Cartledge manages to make the ancient world accessible to modern readers. This deeply informed and richly detailed chronicle restores Thebes to its rightful place in history." Publishers Weekly

Ceram, C. W., 1915-

Gods, graves & scholars : the story of archaeology / C.W. Ceram ; translated from the German by E.B. Garside and Sophie Wilkins. Wings Books, 1994, c1951. xiv, 441, xiv p. : **930**

1. Archaeology -- History. 2. Archaeologists. 3. Archaeological expeditions. 4. Archaeological sites.
ISBN 0517119811

LC 94015215

Originally published: New York : Knopf, 1951.

A highly readable introduction to archeology that details the expeditions and work of individuals who made such important discoveries as Troy, Pompeii, Teotihuacan, and the Tower of Babel.

Childs, Craig

Finders keepers : a tale of archaeological plunder and obsession / Craig Childs. Little, Brown and Co., 2010. 288 p. **930**

1. Archaeology -- Moral and ethical aspects. 2. Pillage. 3. Archaeological thefts 4. Professional ethics
ISBN 9780316066426

LC 2009051921

"Childs treks the canyon-incised Colorado Plateau in search of pre-Columbian artifacts. Their legal regulation collides with collectors' obsessions to possess them. Childs, though, does not remove what he finds, an ethic that vies with other precepts for the proper preservation of antiquities. For every stand he takes on archaeological morality in this narrative mix of his backcountry experiences and conversations with collectors, curators, dealers, and an occasional looter, Childs engages their justifications for taking custody of ancient objects. Alternating romantic and practical moods, Childs hunts virtue as much as baskets in this engaging discourse." Booklist.

David, A. Rosalie (Ann Rosalie)

Handbook to life in Ancient Egypt / Rosalie David. Oxford University Press, 2007 xiv, 417 p. : **930**

1. Ancient Egypt -- Civilization
ISBN 9780195366716

In this new edition, the author discusses the latest findings in areas that are currently at the forefront of Egyptological research. A new chapter on Egyptology describes the history of the field, the results of the latest excavations, and the techniques involved in new scientific studies, such as DNA analysis and the tracing of disease patterns. This newly revised edition takes into account the discoveries of the last few years that have led Egyptologists to change their perspective on some aspects of life in ancient Egypt, including a reevaluation of the purpose and functions of the Egyptian temples, the role of the Great Royal Wife, and the possible date and nature of the Biblical Exodus.

Everitt, Anthony

The **rise** of Athens : the story of the world's greatest civilization / Anthony Everitt. Random House, 2016. 512 p. **930**

1. Greek civilization -- To 146 B.C. 2. Mythology -- History and criticism. 3. Architecture, Greek. 4. Mythology -- History and criticism. 5. Ancient Greece -- History -- To 146 B.C. 6. Athens, Greece -- History.
ISBN 9780812994582

LC 2016014843

Presents a magisterial account of how Athens became the world's most influential civilization, charting the characteristics, flaws and unique intellectual accomplishments of the ambitious city-civilization and how it helped establish the foundations of today's world.

"Everitt has a gift for making ancient history accessible. Highly recommended to anyone with an interest in world history, Western civilization, philosophy, or political science." Library Journal.

The **rise** of Rome : the making of the world's greatest empire / Anthony Everitt. Random House, c2012. 416 p. **930**

1. Romans. 2. Imperialism -- History 3. Civilization, Classical. 4. Civilization, Ancient. 5. Rome -- History -- Empire, 30 B.C.-476 A.D.
ISBN 9781400066636

LC 2011048318

The best-selling author of Cicero traces the rise of Rome as an unlikely evolution from a market village to the world's most powerful empire, offering insight into its political clashes, military strategies, leading figures and internal corruptions.

Felch, Jason

Chasing Aphrodite : the hunt for looted antiquities at the world's richest museum / Jason Felch and Ralph Frammolino. Houghton Mifflin Harcourt, 2011. 384 p. **930**

1. J. Paul Getty Museum. Department of Antiquities 2. Classical antiquities 3. Pillage. 4. Cultural property 5. Art smuggling. 6. Italy 7. Malibu, California
ISBN 9780151015016

LC 2010025835

A dramatic account of the recent voluntary surrender of priceless pieces of art by American museums to the governments of Italy and Greece reveals the illegal antiquities trade at the Getty museum, the roles played by various contributors and the aftershocks being experienced throughout the art world.

Fletcher, Joann

The **story** of Egypt : the civilization that shaped the world / Joann Fletcher. Pegasus Books, 2016. 496 p. **930**

1. Civilization, Ancient. 2. Ancient history. 3. Ancient Egypt -- Civilization -- To 332 B.C. 4. Egypt -- Antiquities.

ISBN 9781681771342

LC 2017304511

Ancient Egyptian civilization lasted for 4,000 years and produced a dazzling array of monumental architecture, art, and religious writings. In The Story of Egypt, archaeologist Joann Fletcher provides a comprehensive and accessible summary of those millennia. Fletcher pays more attention to female rulers than do many other historians, and she emphasizes the importance in Egyptian cosmology of balancing female and male elements. She provides fascinating details of distinct cultures in the Lower and Upper Nile regions, describes technological developments that enabled Egypt to flourish, and provides historical context from the wider region. While Fletcher addresses general readers, her authoritative scholarship backs up her animated narrative.

"The authoritative author imparts her vast knowledge in an orderly chronology and lively, intimate history. A perfect choice for budding Egyptologists." Kirkus.

Fowler, Brenda

Iceman : uncovering the life and times of a prehistoric man found in an alpine glacier/ Brenda Fowler. Random House, c2000. xv, 313 p., [16] p. of plates : **930**

1. Otzi (Ice mummy) 2. Copper age -- Hauslabjoch Pass, Italy 3. Stone age -- Hauslabjoch Pass, Italy 4. Copper age -- Alps. 5. Hauslabjoch Pass, Italy -- Antiquities. 6. Alps -- Antiquities.

ISBN 9780679431671

LC 99039878

Tells the story of the international scientific investigation launched to uncover the mystery behind a well-preserved 5,000-year-old body found frozen in a glacier.

"Fowler ... offers a brisk and easy-to-follow narrative, first of the great discovery, then of the personal and political struggles for control of the frozen body." Publishers Weekly.

Fox, Robin Lane, 1946-

The **classical** world : an epic history from Homer to Hadrian / Robin Lane Fox. Basic Books, 2006. 656 p. **930**

1. Civilization, Classical. 2. Civilization, Greco-Roman. 3. Mediterranean Region -- Civilization.

ISBN 0465024963

LC 2006020247

"A portrait of Greek and Roman culture over a period of roughly 900 years. Although he utilizes a broadly chronological approach, Fox goes well beyond the usual, dreary narrative of battles, dynastic changes, and political conflicts that often characterize surveys of the period. Instead, Fox focuses on the gradual development and transformation of various cultural aspects of Greek and Roman societies, and he discusses in often fascinating detail topics that are normally given short shrift in general histories." Booklist.

Freeman, Charles, 1947-

★**Egypt,** Greece, and Rome : civilizations of the ancient Mediterranean / Charles Freeman. Oxford University Press, 2014. 759 p. **930**

1. Mediterranean Region -- Civilization.

ISBN 9780199651917

LC 2013951730

Covering more than four thousand years of ancient history, from the early Egyptians to the dawn of Byzantium, an illustrated introduction to the Mediterranean's three major civilizations examines their links and traces their influence up to the present day.

Freisenbruch, Annelise, 1977-

Caesars' wives : sex, power, and politics in the Roman Empire / Annelise Freisenbruch. Free Press, 2010. 336 p. **930**

1. Rulers' spouses -- Rome. 2. Women rulers -- Rome. 3. Married women 4. Mothers. 5. Rome -- History 6. Rome -- Politics and government -- 30 B.C.-476 A.D.

ISBN 9781416583035

LC 2010019368

Documents the true stories of eight wives of Roman rulers to assess their historical contributions and cultural influence, drawing parallels between modern first ladies and the lives of such ancient-world figures as Livia, Helena and Julia.

"Providing well-chosen, scintillating details--e.g., enemies being boiled alive, familial bonds savagely snapped in an instant--alongside careful historical analysis, the author breathes new life into these overlooked subjects. A captivating look at imperial Rome's roots in the making of the modern stateswoman." Kirkus.

Garland, Robert, 1947-

Athens Burning : The Persian Invasion of Greece and the Evacuation of Attica / Robert Garland, Colgate University. Johns Hopkins University Press, 2017. viii, 170 p. : **930**

1. Civilians in war -- Greece -- Athens -- History -- To 1500. 2. Athens (Greece) -- History -- Siege, 480 B.C. 3. Greece -- History -- Persian Wars, 500-449 B.C. -- Campaigns. 4. Greece -- History -- Persian Wars, 500-449 B.C. -- Social aspects.

ISBN 142142195X

LC 2016022026

"In this next offering for the Witness to Ancient History series, Robert Garland writes about the Persian invasion of Greece in the 5th century BC. After introducing the reader to the contextual background of the Greco-Persian Wars, including the famous Battle of Marathon, Garland describes the various stages of the invasion from both the Persian and Greek point of view. He focuses on the Greek evacuation of Attica (the peninsular region of Greece that includes Athens), the siege of the Acropolis, the eventual defeat of the Persians by Athenian and Spartan armies, and the return of the Greek people to their land. Coming off his 2014 PUP book on the experience of diaspora in ancient Greece, Garland is well placed to speak authoritatively on this important time in ancient history when the Greeks had to flee their homeland. Garland is an experienced and productive writer whose experience producing video lecture courses for The Great Courses company makes him an ideal author for this introductory volume".--Provided by publisher.

"This book is by far the best basic introduction to its subject now available in English." Choice.

Gibbon, Edward, 1737-1794

★The **decline** and fall of the Roman empire / Edward Gibbon ; edited, abridged, and with a critical introduction by Hans-Friedrich Mueller ; introduction by Daniel J. Boorstin ; illustrations by Giovanni Battista Piranesi. Modern Library, 2003. xxxvii, 1258 p. : **930**

1. Civilization, Ancient 2. Rome -- History -- Empire, 30 B.C.-476

A.D. 3. Byzantine Empire -- History.
ISBN 0375758119

LC 2002032585

Recounts the events that led to the fall of the Roman Empire, from the second century A.D. to the fifteenth century A.D.

Goldsworthy, Adrian Keith

Pax Romana : war, peace and conquest in the roman world / Adrian Goldsworthy. Yale University Press, 2016. 528 p. **930**

1. Ancient history. 2. Civilization, Ancient 3. Military history. 4. Culture. 5. Rome -- History -- Empire, 30 B.C.-476 A.D. 6. Rome -- Civilization.
ISBN 9780300178821

LC 2016941493

"An engrossing account of how the Roman Empire grew and operated." Kirkus.

Green, Peter, 1924-

The **Hellenistic** age : a history / Peter Green. Modern Library, 2007. 240 p. **930**

1. Hellenism. 2. Mediterranean Region -- History -- To 476. 3. Ancient Greece -- History -- To 146 B.C. 4. Ancient Greece
ISBN 067964279X

LC 2006046657

Covering three centuries of history, from the age of Alexander the Great to the rise of Rome, an engaging study of the Hellenistic period traces the influence of Greek culture on the ancient world with the establishment of Alexander's empire, the establishment of new political dynasties in the wake of his death, and the cultural, social, philosophical, and intellectual contributions of the era.

"This study traces the unfolding of Hellenistic civilization in a linear fashion, while at the same time drawing connections between successive alterations in the political, economic and social landscape of the Hellenistic East and the appearance of new cultural and intellectual perspectives. [The book] provides an interesting and well-written overview of a historical period that Green aptly describes as covering some of the most crucial and transformational history of the ancient world. The changes are lasting and fundamental. If only for this, students of world history are in Green's debt." Philadelphia Inquirer.

Harper, Kyle, 1979-

The **fate** of Rome : climate, disease, and the end of an empire / Kyle Harper. Princeton University Press, 2017. 420 p. **930**

1. Climate change 2. Droughts 3. Diseases 4. Regression (Civilization) 5. Rome -- History -- Empire, 30 B.C.-476 A.D. 6. Rome -- Civilization
ISBN 9780691166834

LC 2017952241

A sweeping chronicle of the role of climate change and disease in the fall of the Roman Empire interweaves historical narrative with cutting-edge climate science and genetic discoveries to trace 500 years of volcanic eruptions, solar cycles, climate instability and devastating illnesses that combined in catastrophic ways.

"There is much to absorb in this significant scholarly achievement, which effectively integrates natural, social, and humanistic sciences to show how the fall of the empire caused the decline of Rome." Kirkus.

Hawass, Zahi A.

Hidden treasures of ancient Egypt : unearthing the masterpieces of Egyptian history / Zahi Hawass ; photographs by Kenneth Garrett. National Geographic, 2004. 239 p. : **930**

1. Excavations (Archaeology) -- Egypt. 2. Art, Egyptian. 3. Egypt -- Antiquities.
ISBN 9780792263197

LC 2004044845

Includes index.

A world famous Egyptologist presents the stories of the fabulous ancient treasures contained within Cairo's Egyptian Museum, many of which have never been seen outside of Egypt, complete with beautiful color photographs of the masterpieces.

Herodotus, 484-420? B.C.

The **histories** / Herodotus ; translated by Tom Holland ; introduction and notes by Paul Cartledge. Viking, 2014. xxxix, 833 p. : **930**

1. Ancient history 2. Civilization, Ancient. 3. Ancient Greece -- History -- To 146 B.C. 4. Ancient Greece -- History -- Persian Wars, 500-449 B.C.
ISBN 9780670024896

LC bl2014020136

Recounts the causes and history of the wars between the Greek city-states and Persia.

"This ancient Greek historian could easily be called the father of humor; he irreverently describes events, players and their countless harebrained schemes." Kirkus.

★The **Landmark** Herodotus : the histories / a new translation by Andrea L. Purvis with maps, annotations, appendices, and encyclopedic index; edited by Robert B. Strassler ; with an introduction by Rosalind Thomas. Pantheon Books, c2007. lxiv, 953 p. : **930**

1. History, Ancient. 2. Greece -- History -- To 146 B.C.
ISBN 0375421092

LC 2007024149

Offers a definitive new translation of the historical works by the fifth-century B.C. Greek historian, which includes a chronicle of the war between Greece and the Persian empire, accompanied by maps, detailed textual annotations, and twenty-two appendixes covering such topics as Athenian government, Persian arms and tactics, religion, Sparta, and more.

"A major theme of the Histories is the way in which time can effect surprising changes in the fortunes and reputations of empires, cities, and men; all the more appropriate, then, that Herodotus' reputation has once again been riding very high. In the academy, his technique, once derided as haphazard, has earned newfound respect, while his popularity among ordinary readers will likely get a boost from the publication of perhaps the most densely annotated, richly illustrated, and user-friendly edition of his Histories ever to appear: The Landmark Herodotus, edited by Robert B. Strassler and bristling with appendices, by a phalanx of experts, on everything from the design of Athenian warships to ancient units of liquid measure." The New Yorker.

Higgins, Charlotte, 1972-

Under another sky : journeys in Roman Britain / Charlotte Higgins. The Overlook Press, 2015, c2013 304 p. **930**

1. Romans in Great Britain 2. Great Britain -- History -- Roman period 55 B.C.-449 A.D.
ISBN 9781468310894
Originally published in 2013 (London : Jonathan Cape, 2013).

"A thoroughly researched, elegantly written history." Kirkus.

Hornblower, Simon

The **Oxford** classical dictionary / general editors, Simon Hornblower and Antony Spawforth ; assistant editor, Esther Eidinow. Oxford University Press, 2012. lv, 1592 p. ; **930**

1. Classical dictionaries.

ISBN 9780199545568

LC 2012009579

"Completely revised and updated, the fourth edition of this established dictionary offers entries on all aspects of the classical world. With reception and anthropology as new focus areas and numerous new entries, it is an essential reference work for students, scholars, and teachers of classics and for anyone with an interest in the classical era".-- Provided by publisher.

Hunt, Patrick

Ten discoveries that rewrote history / Patrick Hunt. Plume, c2007. xiii, 226 p. ; **930**

1. Archaeology -- History. 2. Excavations (Archaeology) -- History. 3. Antiquities. 4. Historic sites.

ISBN 0452288770

LC 2007019808

A renowned archaeologist offers a close-up look at the ten most important ancient archaeological discoveries and what they have revealed about human history, examining the Rosetta Stone, Troy, King Tut's Tomb, Machu Picchu, the Dead Sea Scrolls, Pompeii, Thera, Ninevah's Assyrian Library, Olduvai Gorge, and the Tomb of 10,000 Warriors.

"The author has produced a wonderful volume of archaeological history. In doing so, he has provided a seldom seen look at some of the most important scientific developments in the field." Science Books & Films.

Kagan, Donald

The **Peloponnesian** War / Donald Kagan. Viking, c2003. xxvii, 511 p. : **930**

1. Peloponnesian War, 431-404 B.C. 2. Military history. 3. Ancient Greece -- History -- Peloponnesian War, 431-404 B.C. 4. Sparta (Extinct city) -- History 5. Athens, Ancient Greece -- History.

ISBN 0670032115

LC 2002193377

The classical scholar takes a new look at the war between Athens and Sparta, examining the conflict that devastated Ancient Greece in the fifth century B.C.E.

"This is a study of the conflict between Athens and Sparta in the fifth century B.C.E. {Kagan's} primary source is, of course, Thucydides' epic history, but {he} draws on Aristotle, Xenophon, and others to provide an objective, nuanced perspective on the military drama. And it's quite a drama: the clash of democracy and oligarchy, the testing of great leaders, the innovative military tactics, and the unprecedented human cost." Booklist.

Kapuscinski, Ryszard

Travels with Herodotus / Ryszard Kapuscinski ; translated from the Polish by Klara Glowczewska. A.A. Knopf, 2007. viii, 275 p. ; **930**

1. Herodotus, 484-420? B.C. History. 2. Kapuscinski, Ryszard Travel 3. China -- Description and travel. 4. India -- Description and travel. 5. Iran -- Description and travel. 6. Africa -- Description and travel.

ISBN 1400043387

LC 2006039565

A Polish journalist describes his earliest odysseys into the world beyond the Iron Curtain, detailing his journeys of discovery to China, India, Iran, Africa, and beyond, accompanied by a volume of Herodotus, a gift from his first boss.

"A work of art: so eloquent, so simple, that you find yourself marveling at its prose, its gentle observation and the rhythm of the words. And you find yourself applauding such good translation as well." Washington Post Book World.

Kemp, Barry J.

The **city** of Akhenaten and Nefertiti : Amarna and its people / Barry Kemp. Thames & Hudson, c2012. 320 p. : **930**

1. Rulers. 2. Cities and towns. 3. History. 4. Amarna, Egypt -- Antiquities

ISBN 9780500051733

LC 2011945993

The ancient site of Tell el-Amarna in Middle Egypt was the capital city of the heretic pharaoh Akhenaten and his chief consort, Nefertiti. Occupied for just sixteen or so years in the fourteenth century BC, the city lay largely abandoned and forgotten until excavations over the last hundred years brought it back into prominence. Based on more than three decades of research and excavation by Barry Kemp, this account provides new insight into Amarna and its people. The author brings to life the royal family--and their offspring, including Tutankhamun, as well as prominent citizens such as the high priest Panehsy, the vizier Nakht, the general Ramose, and the sculptor Thutmose.

MacGregor, Neil, 1946-

A **history** of the world in 100 objects / Neil MacGregor. Allen Lane, 2010. xxvi, 707 p. : **930**

1. British Museum. 2. Civilization -- History. 3. Material culture -- History. 4. Antiquities. 5. Antiquities, Prehistoric.

ISBN 9781846144134

"Based on the celebrated BBC Radio 4 series" - front cover.

Neil MacGregor's radio series 'A History of the World in 100 Objects' has been a unique event that has set a benchmark for public service broadcasting in the UK and across the world. This book is the tie-in to that event, reproducing the scripts describing the objects that made us who we are.

Mertz, Barbara

Temples, tombs, & hieroglyphs : a popular history of ancient Egypt / Barbara Mertz. William Morrow, 2007. xxvi, 324 p. : **930**

1. Temples -- Egypt -- History 2. Tombs -- Egypt 3. Egyptian hieroglyphics 4. Ancient Egypt -- History -- To 332 B.C.

ISBN 006125276X

LC 2007029118

An updated classic history of ancient Egypt draws on archaeological reporting, historical speculation, and other sources, in an account that provides coverage of professional discoveries from the past quarter century.

"This is an introduction to the history of ancient Egypt and Egyptology. . . . Mertz gives special attention to such topics as the kingship (yes) of Queen Hatshepsut, the exploits of Thutmose III, and the Amarna Period with its intriguing players Akhenaten, Nefertiti, and Tutankhamen. Presenting both pros and cons of current theories, Mertz also explains in simple language archaeological techniques such as carbon 14 dating and historical chronology. . . . [This is] an excellent introduction for patrons interested in the land of the pharaohs." Library Journal.

Naunton, Chris

Searching for the lost tombs of Egypt / Chris Naunton. Thames & Hudson, 2018. 288 p. : **930**

1. Excavations (Archaeology) -- Egypt. 2. Funeral rites and ceremonies -- Egypt. 3. Tombs -- Egypt. 4. Egypt -- Antiquities. 5. Egypt -- History -- 332-30 B.C.

ISBN 0500051992

LC 2018932306

An Egyptologist examines the famous pharaohs of Egypt, highlights their achievements and speculates on why archeologists haven't found their tombs yet and what treasures and historic artifacts may await archeologists in these lost tombs.

O'Connell, Robert L.

The **ghosts** of Cannae : Hannibal and the darkest hour of the Roman republic / Robert L. O'Connell. Random House, 2010. 320 p. **930**

1. Hannibal, 247 B.C.-182 B.C. 2. Scipio, Africanus 236?-183 B.C. 3. Cannae, Battle of, 216 B.C. 4. Punic War, 2nd, 218-201 B.C. 5. Military campaigns 6. Military strategy. 7. Carthage (Extinct city) -- History. 8. Rome -- Army. 9. Rome -- History, Military -- 265-30 B.C.

ISBN 9781400067022

LC 2009040006

An account of the slaughter at Cannae traces the massive defeat of the huge but inexperienced Roman army by Hannibal's forces, interpreting the larger course of the Second Punic War and the often-disastrous ways in which the battle has been imitated throughout history.

"The distinctive edge of The Ghosts of Cannae is Robert L. O'Connell's consistently professional instinct for the behavior of men and units on the battlefield. He is able to put himself and his reader on the ground at Cannae, gagging in the heat of a southern Italian midsummer, assailed by an overload from every one of the five senses." New York Times Book Review.

Parcak, Sarah H

Archaeology from space : how the future shapes our past / Sarah Parcak. Henry Holt and Company, 2019. 288 p. **930**

1. Archaeology 2. Remote sensing 3. Space photography. 4. Artificial satellites

ISBN 9781250198280

LC 2018040565

The National Geographic Fellow and TED Prize winner tours the modern world of satellite-driven "space archaeology" and its role in significantly advancing human discoveries and understandings about the ancient world.

Pellegrino, Charles R.

★**Ghosts** of Vesuvius : a new look at the last days of Pompeii, how towers fall, and other strange connections / Charles Pellegrino. W. Morrow, c2004. 489 p. : **930**

1. Excavations (Archaeology) -- Pompeii (Extinct city) 2. Vesuvius -- Eruption -- 79. 3. Pompeii (Extinct city) 4. Rome -- History -- Empire, 30 B.C.-284 A.D.

ISBN 0380973103

LC 2003071055

An examination of the disasters at Pompeii and Herculaneum discusses what forensic archaeology and new findings in volcano physics reveal about modern events, including the "collapse column" at the World Trade Center.

"In August A.D. 79, Mt. Vesuvius erupted and famously buried the city of Pompeii and, less famously, the city of Herculaneum. From this node of history, Pellegrino goes off on a...search for the connections and ruptures that have shaped not only human civilization but the very course of life on Earth and the universe at large. This is a book to be savored, reread and passed along to future generations." Publishers Weekly.

Redford, Donald B.

The **Oxford** encyclopedia of ancient Egypt / Donald B. Redford, editor in chief. Oxford University Press, 2001. 3 vols. : **930**

1. Egypt -- Civilization -- To 332 B.C. Encyclopedias. 2. Egypt -- Civilization -- 332 B.C.-638 A.D. Encyclopedias. 3. Egypt -- Antiquities Encyclopedias.

ISBN 9780195102345

LC 99054801

"Until now, there has been no comprehensive, scholarly English-language encyclopedia covering ancient Egypt. This beautifully constructed work fills that gap with more than 600 academic, but accessible, articles on all aspects of Egyptology. The coverage is interdisciplinary, combining history, archaeology, economics, science, and literary and religious studies. A stunning piece of scholarship."--"Outstanding Reference Sources," American Libraries, May 2002.

Roberts, Jennifer Tolbert, 1947-

The **plague** of war : Athens, Sparta, and the struggle for ancient Greece / Jennifer T. Roberts. Oxford University Press, 2017. 448 p. **930**

1. Peloponnesian War, 431-404 B.C. 2. City-states 3. War and society 4. Strategic alliances (Military) 5. Ancient Greece -- History -- To 146 B.C. 6. Ancient Greece -- History -- Peloponnesian War, 431-404 B.C. 7. Athens, Ancient Greece 8. Sparta (Extinct city) -- History

ISBN 9780199996643

LC 2016012098

"Tracing the conflict among the city-states of Greece over several generations, this book argues that the Peloponnesian War did not entirely end in 404 with the capture of the Athenian fleet at Aegospotami in 404 B.C. but rather continued in one form or another well into the fourth century."--Provided by publisher.

"Literate and lucid--a fine complement and corrective to the ancient sources." Kirkus.

Romer, John

A **history** of ancient Egypt : from the first farmers to the Great Pyramid / John Romer. Thomas Dunne Books, 2013 512 p. **930**

1. Ancient history 2. Civilization, Ancient 3. Ancient Egypt -- History -- To 332 B.C.

ISBN 9781250030115

LC 2013012485

A first volume of a history of the earliest days of ancient Egypt challenges popular archaeological understandings to chronicle the ancient world's first agricultural practices through the construction of the pyramids.

Silberman, Neil Asher, 1950-

The **Oxford** companion to archaeology / editor in chief, Neil Asher Silberman ; editors, Alexander A. Bauer ... [et al.]. Oxford University Press, c2012. 3 vols. : **930**

1. Archaeology -- Dictionaries.

ISBN 9780199735785

LC 2011051893

Spawforth, Antony

The **story** of Greece and Rome / Tony Spawforth. Yale University Press, [2018] x, 375 pages, 16 unnumbered pages of plates : **930**

1. Civilization, Ancient 2. Greek civilization 3. Rome -- Civilization 4. Ancient Greece

ISBN 9780300217117

LC 2018939477

The extraordinary story of the intermingled civilizations of ancient Greece and Rome, spanning more than six millennia from the late Bronze Age to the seventh century.

"In a time when education in the classics is ever scarcer, this is an attractive and learned introduction to a history that reverberates in present events." Kirkus.

Thompson, Erin L

Possession : the curious history of private collectors from antiquity to the present / Erin L. Thompson. Yale University Press, 2016 vii, 224 p. : **930**

1. Classical antiquities -- Collectors and collecting -- Europe -- History. 2. Collectors and collecting -- Psychological aspects. 3. Classical antiquities thefts. 4. Classical antiquities -- Forgeries.

ISBN 9780300208528

LC bl2016033227

From ancient Greek and Roman times to the present day, delves into the seedy underworld of forgery, smuggling, and theft that underlies many museum and private art collections.

Thucydides, 460?-395? B.C.E.

The **landmark** Thucydides : a comprehensive guide to the Peloponnesian War / edited by Robert B. Strassler ; introduction by Victor Davis Hanson. Free Press, c1996. xxxiii, 711 p. : **930**

1. Thucydides, 460?-395? B.C.E. 2. Ancient history 3. Civilization, Ancient 4. Historians 5. Peloponnesian War, 431-404 B.C. 6. Ancient Greece -- History -- To 146 B.C. 7. Ancient Greece -- History -- Peloponnesian War, 431-404 B.C.

ISBN 0684828154

LC 96024555

"A newly revised edition of the Richard Crawley translation with maps, annotations, appendices, and encyclopedic index."

The Peloponnesian War, 431 to 404 b.c., pitted the all-powerful Spartan infantry against the supremely powerful Athenian navy. Thucydides actually participated in this war and realized it would have an unparalleled influence on the history of Greece. He vividly narrates exciting episodes and carefully describes tactical aspects of the war as well as provides various illuminating character profiles.

"Strassler, an unaffiliated scholar of classical studies, has remedied many of the flaws of Richard Crawley's 1874 translation of The Peloponnesian War. He has added descriptive paragraph-by-paragraph synopses, topic headers on every page, numerous maps keyed to the adjoining text, explanatory footnotes, an extensive index, an excellent introduction by Victor Davis Hanson . . . , and 11 appendixes (by various scholars) on politics, warfare, and society in the Greece of the fifth century B.C.E." Library Journal.

Valavanēs, Panos

Great moments in Greek archaeology / academic coordinator, Panos Valavanis ; translated by David Hardy ; foreword by Angelos Delivorrias ; essays by George F. Bass ... [et al.]. J. Paul Getty Museum, 2007. 379 p. : **930**

1. Excavations (Archaeology) -- Greece. 2. Greece -- Antiquities.

ISBN 9780892369102

LC 2007016609

"First published in Greek and English by Kapon Editions"--P. [4].

Watts, Edward Jay, 1975-

Mortal republic : how Rome fell into tyranny / Edward J. Watts. Basic Books, 2018. 352 p. **930**

1. Ancient history 2. Romans 3. Civilization, Classical 4. Civilization, Greco-Roman 5. Rome -- Politics and government -- 265-30 B.C. 6. Rome -- History -- Republic, 265-30 B.C.

ISBN 9780465093816

LC 2018018024

The prize-winning historian and author of The Final Pagan Generation offers a revisionist history of the Roman Republic that explains why it transitioned from freedom to autocracy, triggering civil wars and the imperial reign of Augustus.

"The author traverses the period stretching from Rome's rise to preeminence during the second Punic War (21802 BCE) to the end of the republic, detailing key developments, particularly focusing on the abandonment of compromise and traditional norms that held Roman politics together and fostered centuries of stability." Library Journal.

Wilkinson, Toby A. H.

★The **rise** and fall of ancient Egypt / Toby Wilkinson. Random House, c2011. 656 p. **930**

1. Ancient history. 2. Civilization, Ancient. 3. Ancient Egypt -- History -- To 332 B.C. 4. Ancient Egypt -- History -- 332-30 B.C.

ISBN 9780553805536

LC 2009047322

An authoritative history of a 3,000-year period from the birth of the world's first nation-state to its absorption into the Roman Empire includes comprehensive coverage of such topics as its government, the influence of religion and the roles of women.

"The author offers a revisionist view of the ugly life hidden by the splendors and dazzling treasures of pharaonic Egypt. He shows in rich detail that it was a brutal society where life was cheap, royal power absolute and established through fear and coercion. This is a penetrating and authoritative overview of a violent ancient civilization often revered by contemporary scholars and enthusiasts." Publishers Weekly.

A **world** beneath the sands : the golden age of Egyptology / Toby Wilkinson. W.W. Norton & Company, 2020 528 p. **930**

1. Egyptology 2. Excavations (Archaeology) -- Egypt 3. Egyptologists 4. Archaeologists 5. Egypt -- Antiquities 6. Egypt -- History -- 19th century 7. Nile Valley

ISBN 9781324006893

LC 2020010916

From the decipherment of hieroglyphics in 1822 to the discovery of Tutankhamun's tomb by Howard Carter and Lord Carnarvon a hundred years later, the uncovering of Egypt's ancient past took place in an atmosphere of grand adventure and international rivalry. In A World Beneath the Sands, the acclaimed Egyptologist Toby Wilkinson chronicles the ruthless race between the British, French, Germans and Americans to lay claim to its mysteries and treasures.

"The result is an essential portrait of how the rediscovery of 'ancient past paved the way for its modern rebirth.'" Publishers Weekly

Xenophon

★The **Landmark** Xenophon's Hellenika : a new translation / John Marincola ; with maps, annotations, appendices, and encyclopedic index edited by Robert B. Strassler ; with an introduction by David Thomas. Pantheon Books, c2009. 579 p. **930**

1. Ancient history. 2. Civilization, Ancient. 3. Greek civilization. 4. Ancient Greece -- History -- To 146 B.C. 5. Ancient Greece -- History -- Peloponnesian War, 431-404 B.C.

ISBN 9780375422553

LC 2009020970

Documents the years between 411 and 362 B.C.E.--which were marked by dynamic political alliances among Athens, Sparta, Thebes and Persia--in an annotated and visually enhanced volume that includes the relevant texts of Diordorus Siculus and the Oxyrhynchus historian.

933 Palestine to 70

Hoyland, Robert G., 1966-

The **Oxford** illustrated history of the Holy Land / edited by Robert G. Hoyland, H.G.M. Williamson. Oxford University Press, 2018. vi, 402 p. : **933**

1. Palestine -- History. 2. Palestine -- Historical geography. 3. Middle East -- History. 4. Middle East -- Historical geography.

ISBN 9780198724391

LC bl2019000538

includes bibliographical references (pages 373-385) and index.

Covering the 3,000 years which saw the rise of Judaism, Christianity and Islam, an illustrated history begins with the origins of the people who became the "Israel" of the Bible to the time when the Ottoman Empire succumbed to British and French rule at the end of the First World War.

Garfinkel, Yosef

In the footsteps of King David : revelations from an ancient biblical city / Yosef Garfinkel, Saar Ganor, Michael G. Hasel. Thames & Hudson, [2018] 240 p. **933**

1. David, King of Israel 2. Bible. Old Testament History of Biblical events 3. Extinct cities 4. Archaeology 5. Excavations (Archaeology) 6. Anthropology 7. Qeiyafa Site (Israel) 8. Israel

ISBN 9780500052013

LC bl2018087239

Offers an account of how years of investigating the excavation of Khirbet Qeiyafa in the Valley of Elah have uncovered a city dating back to the time of the Biblical King David, and how these findings shed light on his kingdom and defend the historicity of the Bible.

"This is a worthwhile work on a number of counts. Though sometimes a bit technical, the book is a fascinating glimpse into the methods, rigors, and rewards of archaeology. On another level, the authors add to a larger conversation about the historicity of the Bible while describing a find of true significance. An engaging glimpse into the ancient past." Kirkus.

Goodman, Martin, 1953-

Rome and Jerusalem : the clash of ancient civilizations / Martin Goodman. Alfred A. Knopf, 2007. xiv, 598 p., 16 p. of plates : **933**

1. Jews -- History -- 168 B.C.-135 A.D. 2. Judaism -- History -- Post-exilic period, 586 B.C.-210 A.D. 3. Palestine -- Rulers. 4. Rome -- History 5. Jerusalem, Israel -- History

ISBN 0375411852

LC 2007005267

"Originally published in Great Britain by Allen Lane"--T.p. verso.

A leading scholar of the ancient Roman and Jewish worlds explains how the first generation of Christians distanced themselves from their Jewish origins and then became hostile to Jews as their influence spread within the empire, in a critical study that examines the origins of anti-Semitism.

"For scholars of Roman and Jewish history as well as well-informed general readers, this work provides a definitive account." Booklist.

Korb, Scott

Life in year one : what the world was like in first-century Palestine / Scott Korb. Riverhead Books, 2010. 256 p. **933**

1. Palestinians. 2. Sociology. 3. Palestine -- History -- To 70 A.D. 4. Palestine -- Social life and customs -- To 70 A.D. 5. Rome -- History -- Empire, 30 B.C.-476 A.D.

ISBN 9781594488993

LC 2010000146

An energetic portrait of the Middle East during the time of Jesus draws on primary and scholarly sources to reveal everyday routines, customs and traditions that governed people, providing additional coverage of the politics of the Roman Empire and the birth of Christianity. By the author of The Faith Between Us.

"The author calls his retrospective a lively romp through the land of Palestine, circa 5 B.C.E.70 C.E., but the picture he draws from archeology, ancient historical accounts, and religious texts is anything but lighthearted. Korb's vivid, breezy prose makes accessible a mountain of scholarship that illuminates the past." Publishers Weekly.

935 Mesopotamia to 637 and Iranian Plateau to 637

Kriwaczek, Paul

Babylon : Mesopotamia and the birth of civilization / Paul Kriwaczek. Thomas Dunne Books/St. Martin's Press, 2012, 2010. 320 p. **935**

1. Hammurabi, King of Babylonia 2. Ancient cities and towns 3. Civilization, Ancient 4. Mesopotamia -- Civilization 5. Iraq -- History -- To 634 6. Babylonia -- History

ISBN 9781250000071

LC 2012003104

A history of the ancient city credited with establishing the foundations of modern civilization documents its rise and fall over thousands of years and includes coverage of its politics, social systems and technical innovations. By the award-winning author of Yiddish Civilisation.

936.2 England to 410 and Wales to 410

Hill, Rosemary

Stonehenge / Rosemary Hill. Harvard University Press, 2008. 242 p. : **936.2**

1. Megalithic monuments -- Wiltshire, England 2. Historic preservation 3. Monuments 4. Theories 5. Stonehenge, England 6. Wiltshire, England -- Antiquities. 7. Stonehenge, England -- Historiography.

ISBN 9780674031326

LC 2008012024

Looks at the expert studies recorded of this historic monument, the numerous theories and speculations about its purpose and creators, the modern replicas made of it across the globe, and the cultural significance it has had during different periods in history.

"Many books seek to tell the truth about Stonehenge, ranging from exact measurements of its various stones to theories about its original use. Hill's is less concerned with some inarguable truth than with the history of various interpretations of Stonehenge." Booklist

Parker Pearson, Michael, 1957-

Stonehenge : a new understanding : solving the mysteries of the greatest stone age monument / Mike Parker Pearson and the Stonehenge Riverside Project. The Experiment, [2013] 410 p. : **936.2**

1. Megalithic monuments -- England. 2. Archaeology. 3. Stonehenge (England) -- History. 4. England -- Antiquities. 5. Stonehenge World Heritage Site (England)

ISBN 9781615190799

LC 2012047688

"First published in Great Britain in 2012 as Stonehenge : exploring the greatest stone age mystery by Simon & Schuster, a division of Simon & Schuster UK Ltd."--T.p. verso.

"Renowned archaeologist Pearson...presents the findings of the most ambitious and scientifically informed investigation of Stonehenge thus far. Filled with maps, drawings, photographs and diagrams, the book details the group's findings in a well-organized, absorbing manner." Kirkus.

Pryor, Francis

★**Stonehenge** : the story of a sacred landscape / Francis Pryor. Pegasus Books, 2018. 207 p. **936.2**

1. Megalithic monuments 2. Prehistoric humans -- England 3. Monuments -- History 4. Archaeology 5. Stonehenge, England

ISBN 9781681776408

Describes the nature and history of one of the world's most well-known and mysterious places, discussing how it was constructed in phases over 1,500 years and examining the enigmatic prehistoric monument in a wider cultural context.

"A renowned archaeologist chronicles the remarkable changes in our knowledge of the builders of Stonehenge and other, equally important and connected henges throughout Britain." Kirkus.

937 Italian Peninsula to 476 and adjacent territories to 476

Stothard, Peter

The **last** assassin : the hunt for the killers of Julius Caesar / Peter Stothard. Oxford University Press, 2020, c2021. 224 p. **937**

1. Cassius Parmensis, Gaius, (73-31 a.C.). 2. Caesar, Julius, 100-44 B.C. Assassination. 3. Augustus, Emperor of Rome, 63 B.C.-14 A.D. 4. Assassination. 5. Rulers. 6. Civilization, Ancient 7. Assassins 8. Rome -- Politics and government -- 265-30 B.C. 9. Rome -- History -- 53-44 B.C.

ISBN 9780197523353

Many men killed Julius Caesar. Only one man was determined to kill the killers. From the spring of 44 BC through one of the most dramatic and influential periods in history, Caesar's adopted son, Octavian, the future Emperor Augustus, exacted vengeance on the assassins of the Ides of March. The last assassin left alive was one of the lesser-known: Cassius Parmensis was a poet and sailor who chose every side in the dying Republic's civil wars except the winning one, a playwright whose work was said to have been stolen and published by the man sent to kill him. Parmensis was in the back row of the plotters, many of them Caesar's friends, who killed for reasons of the highest political principles and lowest personal piques. For fourteen years he was the most successful at evading his hunters but has been barely a historical foot note--until now.

"A deep immersion in a bloody era of ancient Rome, perfect for readers of Mary Beard and Tom Holland." Kirkus

939 Other parts of ancient world

Wood, Michael, 1948-

In search of the Trojan War / Michael Wood. University of California Press, c1998. 288 p. : **939**

1. Trojan War. 2. Bronze age -- Turkey. 3. Civilization, Homeric. 4. Battles -- History 5. Troy (Extinct city) 6. Turkey -- Antiquities.

ISBN 0520215990

LC 98004958

Originally published: New York : Facts on File, c1985.

"This is a first-rate book. The book makes a readable and clear approach to some of the knottiest problems of Bronze Age archaeology." Choice. [review of 1985 edition]

MacLennan, Julio

Europa : how Europe shaped the modern world / Julio MacLennan. Pegasus Books, 2018. 336 p. **940**

1. Civilization, Western 2. Influence (Literary, artistic, etc.) 3. Culture 4. Europe

ISBN 9781681777566

LC 2018276307

An original and innovative examination of the continent--and its culture--that was the epicenter of the world for almost five centuries.

"Why, as the U.S. wrestles with China for global advantage, do both rely heavily on ideas originally forged in Europe? MacLennan answers this question in an epic narrative exceptional in interpretive breadth." Booklist.

940 History of Europe

Spector, Shmuel

The **Encyclopedia** of Jewish life before and during the Holocaust / editor in chief, Shmuel Spector ; consulting editor, Geoffrey Wigoder ; foreword by Elie Wiesel. Yad Vashem ; 2001. 3 v. (1769 p.) : **940**

1. Jews -- Europe -- History -- Encyclopedias. 2. Jews -- Africa, North -- Encyclopedias. 3. Holocaust, Jewish (1939-1945) -- Encyclopedias. 4. Europe -- History, Local. 5. Africa, North -- History, Local.

ISBN 9780814793565

LC 2001030771

"These three volumes are an abridgment of the multi-volume Encyclopedia of Jewish Communities published in Hebrew by Yad Vashem"--T.p. verso.

Stokes, Gale, 1933-

The **walls** came tumbling down : the collapse of communism in Eastern Europe / Gale Stokes. Oxford University Press, 1993. viii, 319 p. ; **940**

1. Europe, Eastern -- History -- 1945-

ISBN 0195066456

LC 92044862

Looks at the forces that helped defeat communism in Eastern Europe, including Solidarity and Charter 77, a group of Czech intellectuals who demanded that their government obey its own laws.

Wells, Colin, 1960-

Sailing from Byzantium : how a lost Empire shaped the world / Colin Wells. Delacorte Press, 2006. xxx, 335 p. : **940**

1. Civilization, Slavic -- Byzantine influences. 2. Civilization, Islamic -- Byzantine influences. 3. Civilization, Western -- Byzantine influences. 4. Byzantine Empire -- History -- 1081-1453.

ISBN 0553803816

LC 2006042665

A history of the Byzantine Empire describes the cultural, artistic, religious, and scientific heritage of Byzantium that was preserved in the wake of the empire's 1453 fall to enemy conquerors, and its influence on Western civilization.

"The author considers how Byzantium, the Eastern, Greek-language Roman Empire of the Middle Ages, influenced three successor civilizations Western Europe, Islam, and the eastern Slavic world of the Balkans and Russia. This history is a needed reminder of the debt that three of our major civilizations owe to Byzantium." Library Journal.

940.1 History of Europe--Early history to 1453

Bouchard, Constance Brittain,

Knights : in history and in legend / chief consultant Constance Brittain Bouchard. Firefly Books, 2009. 304 p. : **940.1**

1. Knights and knighthood -- Europe -- History. 2. Military art and science -- History -- Medieval, 500-1500. 3. Civilization, Medieval 4. Knights and knighthood -- Europe -- Social life and customs. 5. Europe -- History -- 476-1492
ISBN 9781554074808

LC 2010292451

The history of knights, from their everyday lives to their clothing, training, heraldry and orders, as well as their role in literature and film, and the decline of traditional knighthood.

"Aimed at history and art history lovers, this work would be excellent reading for medieval history enthusiasts and should be welcomed as a library reference resource." Library Journal.

Freeman, Charles, 1947-

The **closing** of the Western mind : the rise of faith and the fall of reason / Charles Freeman. Vintage Books, 2005, c2002. xxiii, 432 p. : **940.1**

1. Civilization, Western. 2. Christianity -- Influence. 3. Church and state -- Europe -- History. 4. Church history -- Primitive and early church, ca. 30-600. 5. Europe -- History -- To 476. 6. Europe -- History -- 476-1492.
ISBN 1400033802

LC bl2006008192

Originally published: London : Heineman, 2002.

Describes the first alliance of church and state in the fourth century, marked by the Roman emperor Constantine's conversion to Christianity, and how this decision irrevocably compromised the Roman Empire's intellectual tradition of rationalism.

"This is one of the best books to date on the development of Christianity. Beautifully written and impressively annotated, this is an indispensable read for anyone interested in the roots of Christianity and its implications for our modern worldview." Choice.

Gies, Joseph

Life in a medieval castle / Joseph Gies and Frances Gies. Harper & Row, 1979, c1974. xv, 272 p. : **940.1**

1. Chepstow, Castle. 2. Castles. 3. Courts and courtiers. 4. Castles -- Great Britain. 5. Europe -- History, Military -- 476-1492. 6. Great Britain -- Court and courtiers -- History -- To 1500. 7. Wales -- History -- To 1536.
ISBN 9780060906740

LC 79103901

Describes the evolution, architecture, and historical function of the medieval castle and the daily life, habits, and relationships of its inhabitants through a detailed study of England's thirteenth-century Chepstow Castle.

"Using Chepstow Castle on the Welsh border as a model, the authors provide descriptions of the medieval world where the castle was household, feudal center, and military target, and by concentrating on Anglo-Norman examples illustrate what existence was like as the dark ages began to brighten." Booklist.

Herlihy, David

The **black** death and the transformation of the west / David Herlihy ; edited and with an introduction by Samuel K. Cohn, Jr. Harvard University Press, 1997. 117 p. ; **940.1**

1. Black Death -- Europe 2. Civilization, Medieval 3. Diseases and history 4. Renaissance
ISBN 9780674076136

LC 96054637

"These essays redefine the historical study of the Black Death. Herlihy's contention is that we can learn from this 'devastating natural disaster': for example, parallels can be drawn to today's pandemic of AIDS, especially in the resultant bigotries that both engendered. Cohn introduces the lectures, admirably setting the scene. This book, which opens a new chapter on the history and implications of the plague, is essential for all readers of medieval history." Library Journal.

Pye, Michael, 1946-

The **edge** of the world : a cultural history of the North Sea and the transformation of Europe / Michael Pye. Pegasus Books, 2015. 360 p. **940.1**

1. Civilization, Medieval 2. North Sea 3. Europe
ISBN 9781605986999

LC 2016303224

In a lost history of a thousand years, an award-winning author, taking readers on an epic adventure rife with saints, spies, pirates, philosophers, artists and intellectuals, tells the extraordinary story of how modernity emerged on the shores of the North Sea.

Reston, James, Jr., 1941-

The **last** apocalypse : Europe at the year 1000 A.D. / James Reston, Jr. Anchor Books, 1999, c1998. 299 p. : **940.1**

1. Europe -- History -- 476-1492.
ISBN 9780385483360

LC BL 99002813

Originally published: New York : Doubleday, c1998.

Traces the victories of the kings and popes of Christendom against the seemingly invincible Vikings, Moors, and Hungarian Magyars, shaking the world and confirming the popular belief that history was about to end.

Tyerman, Christopher

The **world** of the crusades / Christopher Tyerman. Yale University Press, 2019. 517 p. **940.1**

1. Crusades. 2. Material culture. 3. War and society. 4. Crusaders (Middle Ages) 5. Europe -- History -- 476-1492.
ISBN 9780300217391

LC 2019931656

Examines crusader artifacts in a reimagining of medieval warfare that reveals what the things they made and used, from art and architecture to weapons and manuscripts, tell us about crusader beliefs and military strategies.

"Historians and lay readers interested in the history of European conquest in the Middle East will relish this investigation into the grist of the Crusaders journey." Publishers Weekly.

Wickham, Chris, 1950-

★The **inheritance** of Rome : illuminating the Dark Ages, 400-1000 / Chris Wickham. Viking, c2009. 400 p. **940.1**

1. Civilization, Medieval 2. History. 3. Culture. 4. Rome -- Civilization -- Influence. 5. Europe -- History -- 476-1492
ISBN 9780670020980

LC 2009015169

"Wickham's achievement contributes richly to our picture of this often narrowly understood period." Publishers Weekly.

940.2 History of Europe--1453-

Barbero, Alessandro

The **battle** : a new history of Waterloo / Alessandro Barbero ; translated from the Italian by John Cullen. Walker, 2006, c2005. xii, 340 p. : **940.2**

1. Waterloo, Battle of, 1815. 2. Napoleonic Wars, 1800-1815 3. Military campaigns 4. Belgium. 5. Europe -- History, Military -- 19th century. 6. Europe -- History -- 19th century.

ISBN 0802715001

LC bl2006030201

Reprint. Originally published: 2005.

Published to coincide with the 190th anniversary of the battle, this reconstruction of the Battle of Waterloo narrates the story of this historic conflict between Napoleon Bonaparte and the Duke of Wellington, which changed the face of nineteenth-century Europe, from the point of view of all combatants.

"The author's narrative flows smoothly, making readers feel part of the battle's events. The chapters are short--never more than a few pages--and they pull the reader along with the action." Choice.

Barzun, Jacques, 1907-2012

From dawn to decadence : 500 years of western cultural life : 1500 to the present / Jacques Barzun. Harper Collins, 2000. xviii, 877 p. **940.2**

1. Civilization, Western. 2. Intellectual life -- Europe. 3. Learning and scholarship -- History. 4. Europe -- Civilization. 5. Europe -- History.

ISBN 0060175869

LC 99016194

ALA Notable Book, 2001.

National Book Award for Nonfiction finalist, 2000

Showcases the triumphs and defeats of five hundred years of Western cultural history, highlighting the contributions of women and arguing that decadance is required in order to spark creativity in the next era.

"Encyclopedic without being discontinuous, the book hardly seems as long, as carefully constructed or as densely packed as it is. Though the ideas it explains are often complicated, the explanations it offers are limpidly clear, sparkling with biographical anecdote and counter-canonical observations." New York Times Book Review.

Blanning, T. C. W.

★The **pursuit** of glory : Europe, 1648-1815 / Tim Blanning. Viking, 2007. 736 p. **940.2**

1. Europe -- History -- 1648-1789. 2. Europe -- History -- 1789-1815. 3. Europe -- Civilization.

ISBN 0670063207

LC 2006037324

Includes index.

An accessible chronicle of European history from the end of the Thirty Years' War to the Battle of Waterloo features vivid coverage of such events as the Enlightenment period, the French Revolution, and the Napoleonic era.

"The author thoroughly covers the politics and endless wars of the period. The Pursuit of Glory is history writing at its glorious best." New York Times.

Blom, Philipp

The **vertigo** years : Europe, 1900-1914 / Philipp Blom. Perseus Books Group, 2008. 512 p. **940.2**

1. Europeans. 2. World War I -- Causes. 3. Disorientation. 4. Prejudice -- Europe. 5. Europe -- History -- 1900-1914.

ISBN 9780465011162

LC 2008935053

"Offers a look at how the changes from the Industrial Revolution prior to World War I brought about radical transformation in society that resulted in a new world order, changes in education, and massive migration in population that led to one of the bloodiest events in history in later years.

Coote, Stephen

Napoleon and the Hundred Days / Stephen Coote. DaCapo Press, 2005. 308 p. : **940.2**

1. Napoleon I, Emperor of the French, 1769-1821 Elba and the Hundred Days, 1814-1815. 2. Command of troops 3. France -- History -- Consulate and First Empire, 1799-1815 4. France -- History -- Restoration, 1814-1830. 5. Europe -- History -- 19th century.

ISBN 0306814080

LC 2004065505

An unforgettable portrait of the legendary general and self-made emperor, who in 1815 escaped captivity and fought his way across Europe for one hundred days, until meeting his match at Waterloo, a journey chronicled in a complete recreation of the rise and fall of an Empire.

"This history of the 100 days between Napoleon's escape from Elba and his capitulation after Waterloo uses the period as a lens through which to examine his character in general. This accessible work is reminiscent of the finest classical Roman histories and biographies." Publishers Weekly.

Cornwell, Bernard

Waterloo : the history of four days, three armies, and three battles / Bernard Cornwell. HarperCollins 2015. 352 p. **940.2**

1. Napoleon I, Emperor of the French, 1769-1821 Military leadership. 2. Wellington, Arthur Wellesley, Duke of, 1769-1852 Military leadership. 3. Waterloo, Battle of, 1815. 4. Napoleonic Wars, 1800-1815 5. Military campaigns 6. Belgium. 7. Germany -- History, Military -- 19th century. 8. France -- History, Military -- 1789-1815

ISBN 9780062312051

LC 2015487235

In his first work of nonfiction, Bernard Cornwell combines his storytelling skills with a meticulously researched history to give a riveting chronicle of every dramatic moment, from Napoleon's daring escape from Elba to the smoke and gore of the three battlefields and their aftermath. Through quotes from the letters and diaries of Emperor Napoleon, the Duke of Wellington, and the ordinary officers and soldiers, he brings to life how it actually felt to fight those famous battles--as well as the moments of amazing bravery on both sides that left the actual outcome hanging in the balance until the bitter end.

Corrigan, Gordon

Waterloo : a new history / Gordon Corrigan. Pegasus, 2014 368 p. **940.2**

1. Napoleon I, Emperor of the French, 1769-1821 Military leadership. 2. Wellington, Arthur Wellesley, Duke of, 1769-1852. 3. Waterloo, Battle of, 1815. 4. Napoleonic Wars, 1800-1815 -- Influence. 5. Command of troops. 6. Military strategy. 7. Belgium 8.

Europe -- History -- 1789-1900
ISBN 9781605986524

LC 2014466225

A veteran historian presents a bicentennial history of the campaign and battle that profiles its armies, commanders and other key contributors against a backdrop of warn-torn future Belgium to share new insights into the conflict's relevance and legacy. By the author of A Great and Glorious Adventure.

"Those interested in military history, particularly that of England or France, will love the detail in this volume. Corrigan keeps things exciting by blending his own brand of wit with historical fact." Library Journal.

Crane, David, 1942-

Went the day well? : witnessing Waterloo / David Crane. Alfred A. Knopf, 2015. 400 p. **940.2**

1. Waterloo, Battle of, 1815. 2. Napoleonic Wars, 1800-1815 3. Military campaigns 4. War and society. 5. Belgium 6. Europe -- History, Military -- 19th century. 7. Europe -- History -- 19th century.
ISBN 9780307594921

LC 2014044143

Chronicles the battle of Waterloo through interwoven narratives drawn from the diaries, letters, reminiscences, and great novels of participants and witnesses.

"History buffs will relish both of these works. Readers should also consider Brendan Simms's The Longest Afternoon." Library Journal.

Crowley, Roger, 1951-

Empires of the sea : the siege of Malta, the Battle of Lepanto, and the contest for the center of the world / Roger Crowley. Random House Inc, 2008 256 p. **940.2**

1. Lepanto, Battle of, 1571. 2. Christianity -- Relations -- Islam. 3. Islam -- Relations -- Christianity. 4. Civilization, Islamic -- Western influences. 5. Mediterranean Islands 6. Mediterranean Region. 7. Malta -- History -- Siege, 1565. 8. Rhodes, Greece -- History -- Siege, 1522.
ISBN 9781400066247

LC 2007033794

A study of the fifty-year conflict between Islam and Christianity for control of the Mediterranean discusses the decisive sixteenth-century battles at Malta and Lepanto that permanently ended Muslim expansion in the region.

Esdaile, Charles J.

Napoleon's wars : an international history, 1803-1815 / Charles Esdaile. Penguin Group USA, 2008. 656 p. **940.2**

1. Napoleon I, Emperor of the French, 1769-1821 2. France. Army -- History Napoleonic Wars, 1800-1815. 3. Napoleonic Wars, 1800-1815. 4. Command of troops. 5. Generals -- France 6. Ambition in men. 7. France -- History, Military -- 19th century.
ISBN 9780670020300

LC bl2008023324

An account of the European wars during the rise and fall of Napoleon challenges popular conceptions about his ambitions and achievements while posing an alternative view on the circumstances that motivated long-standing armed conflicts throughout Europe.

"Recapturing the flux of international diplomacy and Napolon's congenital rejection of compromise, Esdaile persuasively places the diplomatic foundation to popular military histories about the Napoleonic wars." Booklist.

Evans, Richard J.

The **pursuit** of power : Europe 1815-1914 / Richard J. Evans. Viking, 2016 928 p. **940.2**

1. World War I -- Causes. 2. Europe -- Politics and government -- 1871-1918.
ISBN 9780670024575

LC 2016044050

Covers the century between the fall of Napoleon to the outbreak of World War I, discussing events ranging from the crumbling of the Spanish, Ottoman and Mughal empires and the rise of British imperial ambition to the violent revolution in Spain and the unifications of Germany and Italy.

"An immensely readable work that considers incremental continental developments up to the outbreak of war in 1914." Kirkus.

Grayling, A. C.

★The **age** of genius : the seventeenth century and the birth of the modern mind / A.C. Grayling. Bloomsbury USA, 2016 352 p. **940.2**

1. Intellectual life 2. Individualism 3. Human rights 4. Europe
ISBN 9781620403440

LC 2016429801

The Age of Genius explores the eventful intertwining of outward event and inner intellectual life to tell, in all its richness and depth, the story of the 17th century in Europe. It was a time of creativity unparalleled in history before or since, from science to the arts, from philosophy to politics. Acclaimed philosopher and historian A.C. Grayling points to three primary factors that led to the rise of vernacular (popular) languages in philosophy, theology, science, and literature; the rise of the individual as a general and not merely an aristocratic type; and the invention and application of instruments and measurement in the study of the natural world.

"Grayling does a fantastic job of proving his assertion that the 17th century saw a dramatic shift in Western thought. Readers with an interest in the history of philosophy and scientific discovery will enjoy this highly engaging book." Library Journal.

Greenblatt, Stephen, 1943-

★The **swerve** : how the world became modern / Stephen Greenblatt. W. W. Norton & Co., 2011. 320 p. **940.2**

1. European Renaissance. 2. Humanism (14th-16th centuries) 3. Intellectual life. 4. Intellectuals. 5. Europe -- History -- 1492-1782.
ISBN 9780393064476

LC 2011019765

ALA Notable Book, 2012.

National Book Award for Nonfiction, 2011.

Pulitzer Prize for General Nonfiction, 2012.

A humanities professor describes the impact had by the translation of the last remaining manuscript of On the Nature of Things by Roman philosopher Lucretius, which fueled the Renaissance and inspired artists, great thinkers and scientists.

"A fascinating, intelligent look at what may well be the most historically resonant book-hunt of all time." Booklist.

Hobsbawm, E. J. (Eric J.), 1917-2012

The **age** of revolution 1789-1848 : 1789-1848 / Eric Hobsbawm. Vintage Books, 1996. x, 356 p. : **940.2**

1. Industrial revolution 2. Europe -- History -- 1789-1900.
ISBN 9780679772538

LC 96007765

King, David, 1970-

Vienna 1814 : how the conquerors of Napoleon

made war, peace, and love at the Congress of Vienna / David King. Harmony Books, 2008. 448 p. **940.2**

1. Congress of Vienna, 1814-1815. 2. Napoleonic Wars, 1800-1815 -- Treaties 3. Politicians -- Europe -- History -- 19th century. 4. Europe -- Politics and government -- 1789-1815.

ISBN 9780307337160

LC 2007024680

Details the 1814 Congress of Vienna, offering portraits of the participants and discussing the political intrigues, illicit affairs, tangled alliances, and bitter rivalries that marked the occasion that transformed the face of nineteenth-century Europe.

"The conquerors of Napoleon were in a festive mood when they met in Vienna in the fall of 1814 to decide the fate of Europe. [The author] does a superb job of evoking the bedazzling social scene that served as the backdrop to the Congress of Vienna. His characterizations of such luminaries as Czar Alexander, Metternich, Talleyrand, and Castlereagh are lucid and thoroughly grounded in primary sources. This is a worthy contribution to the study of a critical historical event long neglected by historians." Library Journal.

Lieven, Dominic

Russia against Napoleon : the true story of the campaigns of War and peace / Dominic Lieven. Viking, 2010. 640 p. **940.2**

1. Tolstoy, Leo, graf, 1828-1910. War and Peace. 2. Napoleonic Wars, 1800-1815 3. Military campaigns 4. Military history. 5. Russia -- History -- Alexander I, 1801-1825.

ISBN 9780670021574

LC 2009042564

A revisionist history of the Russian conflict immortalized in Tolstoy's War and Peace challenges popular myths and imbalances in British and French interpretations while covering such topics as the treaty between Alexander I and Napoleon and the challenges of supplying Russian troops.

Manchester, William, 1922-2004

A **world** lit only by fire : the medieval mind and the Renaissance : portrait of an age / William Manchester. Little, Brown, 1993, c1992. xvii, 322 p. : **940.2**

1. European Renaissance. 2. Civilization, Medieval 3. Europe -- History.

ISBN 0316545562

LC BL 99738239

Originally published: Boston, MA : Little, Brown, 1992.

Chronicles the historical transition from the Middle Ages to the Renaissance, profiling the age's leading figures and noting key events and accomplishments.

"The author covers the tumultuous span from the Dark Ages to the dawn of the Renaissance. He delineates an age when invisible spirits infested the air, when tolerance was seen as treachery and 'a mafia of profane popes desecrated Christianity.' Besides re-creating the arduous lives of ordinary people...{Manchester} peoples his tapestry with such figures as Leonardo, Machiavelli, Lucrezia Borgia, Erasmus, Luther, Henry VIII and Anne Boleyn." Publishers Weekly.

Mostert, Noel

Line upon a wind : the great war at sea, 1793-1815 / Noel Mostert. W W Norton & Co Inc, 2008. 800 p. **940.2**

1. Napoleonic Wars, 1800-1815 -- Naval operations. 2. Seafaring life -- History -- 19th century. 3. Naval battles 4. Military history 5. Europe -- History, Naval -- 19th century. 6. Europe -- History, Naval -- 18th century. 7. France -- History -- Revolution, 1789-1799. 8. Great Britain -- History.

ISBN 9780393066531

LC 2007039313

Traces the twenty-two-year conflict between France and Britain, profiling the war as one of history's longest and most devastating while profiling the new naval tactics and weapons it brought into action, in a narrative account that covers a range of topics, from the contributions of Napoleon and Nelson to ship-construction strategies and related land battles.

"This is a vast, fast-moving chronicle that ranges across great distances while examining a host of characters, both well known and relatively obscure. Mostert does justifiably place great emphasis on Admiral Nelson and the critical battle at Trafalgar. He also offers useful and interesting descriptions of less-prominent aspects of the wars, including conflicts with the Barbary pirates and the British struggles against the rise of American naval power. This is an outstanding survey of a prolonged struggle that helped shape world history." Booklist.

O'Keeffe, Paul

Waterloo : the aftermath / Paul O'Keeffe. Overlook Press, 2015. 400 p. **940.2**

1. Waterloo, Battle of, 1815. 2. Napoleonic Wars, 1800-1815 3. Military campaigns 4. War and society 5. Europe -- History -- 19th century

ISBN 9781468311303

LC 2015010800

A 200th anniversary account of the last days of the Napoleonic Wars traces the events and aftermath of the battle of Waterloo, as well as the perspective of Napoleon as he considered his surrender, exile and captivity.

Pagden, Anthony

The **Enlightenment** : and why it still matters / Anthony Pagden. Random House, 2013. 448 p. **940.2**

1. Enlightenment (European intellectual movement) 2. Intellectual life -- Europe -- 18th century. 3. Philosophy and science. 4. Reason. 5. Europe -- History -- 18th century.

ISBN 9781400060689

LC 2012043848

An assessment of the Enlightenment period as an influential intellectual movement reveals how it laid the foundation of today's government, philosophy, science and society, noting the pivotal contributions of scholars ranging from Hume and Diderot to Voltaire and Rousseau. By the award-winning author of Worlds at War.

Pocock, Tom

The **terror** before Trafalgar : Nelson, Napoleon, and the secret war / Tom Pocock. W.W. Norton, 2003. xiii, 255 p. : **940.2**

1. Nelson, Horatio Nelson, Viscount, 1758-1805 Adversaries. 2. Napoleon I, Emperor of the French, 1769-1821 Adversaries. 3. Napoleonic Wars, 1800-1815 4. Military campaigns 5. Great Britain -- History -- Invasions. 6. Europe -- History -- 19th century.

ISBN 9780393057768

LC 2003001969

Napoleon's threatened invasion of England is examined, revealing a "secret war" being waged between the two powers employing spies and new weapons.

"The author retells the story of the four years in which the French confidently prepared to invade Britain, overrun its army, take out its armaments and replace the government with something easier to control. Pocock's little book...gives a chilling insight into ineffectual undercover operations and groundbreaking weaponry: rockets, torpedos, submarines, airships and the construction of an undersea tunnel, all so far ahead of their time that none turned out in the end to be much use in practical terms to either side." New York Times Book Review.

Reston, James, Jr., 1941-

Defenders of the faith : Charles V, Suleyman the Magnificent, and the battle for Europe, 1520-1536 / James Reston, Jr. Penguin Press, 2009. 384 p. **940.2**

1. Charles V, Holy Roman Emperor, 1500-1558. 2. Suleyman I, Sultan of the Turks, 1494 or 1495-1566. 3. Religion and civilization -- Europe. 4. Rulers -- History 5. Islam -- History 6. Christianity -- History 7. Holy Roman Empire -- History -- Charles V, 1519-1556. 8. Turkey -- History -- Suleyman I, 1520-1566. 9. Holy Roman Empire -- Foreign relations Turkey. 10. Turkey -- Foreign relations Holy Roman Empire. 11. Holy Roman Empire -- Religion -- 16th century. 12. Turkey -- Religion -- 16th century. 13. Vienna, Austria -- History -- Siege, 1529 -- Religious aspects.
ISBN 9781594202254

LC 2008054655

Describes the events surrounding the clash between Charles V, the Holy Roman Emperor, and Suleyman I, the Sultan of the Turks and their battle for supremacy in Europe.

"Fast-paced and engaging, this is excellent reading for popular audiences." Library Journal.

Roberts, Andrew, 1963-

Waterloo : June 18, 1815: the battle for modern Europe / Andrew Roberts. Harper Collins, c2005. 143 p., 16 p. of plates : **940.2**

1. Waterloo, Battle of, 1815. 2. Napoleonic Wars, 1800-1815 3. Military campaigns 4. Belgium. 5. Europe -- History, Military -- 19th century.
ISBN 0060088664

LC 2005282517

An exploration of the conflict that ended the reign of Napoleon draws on new evidence about how the battle was lost, offering extensive background information about the political, strategic, and historical factors of the time while sharing new insights into the tactics employed by the French cavalry.

"The author instills an appreciation for Waterloo as a horrific experience saturated with alternative possible outcomes. A must for the military shelf." Booklist.

Simms, Brendan

The **longest** afternoon : the 400 men who decided the Battle of Waterloo / Brendan Simms. Basic Books, 2015 192 p. **940.2**

1. Napoleon I, Emperor of the French, 1769-1821 Military leadership. 2. Wellington, Arthur Wellesley, Duke of, 1769-1852. 3. Napoleonic Wars, 1800-1815 4. Military campaigns 5. Waterloo, Battle of, 1815. 6. Command of troops. 7. Belgium 8. Europe -- History -- 1789-1900
ISBN 9780465064823

LC 2015451024

"This thoroughly engrossing account will thrill all history lovers." Library Journal.

Talty, Stephan

The **illustrious** dead : the terrifying story of how typhus killed Napoleon's greatest army / Stephan Talty. Crown Publishers, 2009. 336 p. **940.2**

1. Napoleon I, Emperor of the French, 1769-1821 Military leadership. 2. France. Army -- History Napoleonic Wars, 1800-1815 3. Napoleonic Wars, 1800-1815 4. Military campaigns 5. Typhus fever -- History 6. Military history -- 19th century 7. Russia -- History, Military -- 1801-1917.
ISBN 9780307394040

LC 2008050646

In a dual narrative that pits the heights of human ambition and achievement against the supremacy of nature, Stephan Talty tells the story of a mighty ruler and a tiny microbe, antagonists whose struggle would shape the modern world. -- from publisher description

Wilson, Peter H. (Peter Hamish)

The **Thirty** Years War : Europe's tragedy / Peter H. Wilson. Belknap Press of Harvard University Press, 2009. 1040 p. **940.2**

1. Thirty Years' War, 1618-1648. 2. War. 3. Europe -- History, Military -- 1492-1648.
ISBN 9780674036345

LC 2009011266

"This is a history of prodigious erudition that manages to corral the byzantine complexity of the Thirty Years War into a coherent narrative." Wall Street Journal.

Zamoyski, Adam

Rites of peace : the fall of Napoleon & the Congress of Vienna / Adam Zamoyski. Harper Collins, 2007. xviii, 634 p. : **940.2**

1. Congress of Vienna, 1814-1815. 2. Napoleonic Wars, 1800-1815 -- Peace. 3. Napoleonic Wars, 1800-1815 -- Diplomatic history. 4. Diplomacy -- History 5. Europe -- History -- 1789-1815.
ISBN 0060775181

LC bl2007010398

Originally published: London : HarperPress, 2007.

Traces the epic events following Napoleon's exile in 1814 and the subsequent Treaty of Paris, examining how the eight-month Viennese carnival brought thousands of aristocrats to the Austrian capital and established the Congress of Vienna.

940.21 History of Europe--Renaissance period, 1453-1517

Campbell, Gordon, 1944-

The **Oxford** illustrated history of the Renaissance / edited by Gordon Campbell. Oxford University Press, 2019. viii, 506 p. : **940.21**

1. Renaissance.
ISBN 019871615X

LC 2018939297

The Renaissance is one of the most celebrated periods in European history. But when did it begin? When did it end? And what did it include? Traditionally regarded as a revival of classical art and learning, centred upon fifteenth-century Italy, views of the Renaissance have changed considerably in recent decades. The glories of Florence and the art of Raphael and Michelangelo remain an important element of the Renaissance story, but they are now only a part of a much wider story which looks beyond an exclusive focus on high culture, beyond the Italian peninsula, and beyond the fifteenth century. The Oxford Illustrated History of the Renaissance tells the cultural history of this broader and longer Renaissance: from seminal figures such as Dante and Giotto in thirteenth-century Italy, to the waning of Spain's 'golden age' in the 1630s, and the closure of the English theatres in 1642, the date generally taken to mark the end of the English literary Renaissance. Geographically, the story ranges from Spanish America to Renaissance Europe's encounter with the Ottomans--and far beyond, to the more distant cultures of China and Japan. And thematically, under Gordon Campbell's expert editorial guidance, the volume covers the whole gamut of Renaissance civilization, with chapters on humanism and the classical tradition; war and the state; religion; art and architecture; the performing arts; literature; craft and technology; science and medicine; and travel and cultural exchange.

"This single volume offers advanced readers a thorough understanding of the history, politics, religious and cultural influences, art, architecture, science, and technology from the fifteenth century and into the seventeenth century in Europe." Booklist.

940.27 History of Europe--Period of French Revolution and Napoleon I, 1789-1815

Adkin, Mark

The **Trafalgar** companion : a guide to history's most famous sea battle and the life of Admiral Lord Nelson / Mark Adkin ; with illustrations by Clive Farmer. Aurum Press, 2005. 560 p. : **940.27**

1. Nelson, Horatio Nelson, Viscount, 1758-1805 Military leadership. 2. Napoleonic Wars, 1800-1815. 3. Trafalgar, Battle of, 1805. 4. France -- History, Naval -- 19th century. 5. Great Britain -- History, Naval -- 19th century.

ISBN 1845130189

LC 2006389181

"Beginning with a prologue that describes the wounding and death of Vice-Admiral Horatio Nelson, the book introduces readers to the history of the campaign from 1802 to 1805 and to...information about the men and ships of the Royal Navy, in alternate chapters. It will long stand as the definitive one-volume study of Great Britain's foremost naval hero and his times." Choice.

940.3 World War I, 1914-1918

Audoin-Rouzeau, Stephane

14-18, understanding the Great War / Stephane Audoin-Rouzeau and Annette Becker ; translated from the French by Catherine Temerson. Hill and Wang, 2002. v, 280 p. ; **940.3**

1. World War I -- Psychological aspects. 2. World War I -- Social aspects. 3. Nationalism -- Europe -- History -- 20th century. 4. Bereavement -- Europe -- History -- 20th century.

ISBN 9780809046423

LC 2002111422

Translation originally published: Great Britain : Profile Books, 2002.

"The authors take an anthropological approach to the cataclysm that engulfed Europe in 1914 and examine three significant aspects of the war: violence, crusade, and mourning. Supported by contemporary documentation, this unique work will become a classic study." Library Journal.

Carter, Miranda, 1965-

George, Nicholas and Wilhelm : three royal cousins and the road to World War I / Miranda Carter. Alfred A. Knopf, 2010, c2009. xxv, 498 p., 32 p. of plates : **940.3**

1. William II, German Emperor, 1859-1941. 2. Edward VII, King of Great Britain, 1841-1910. 3. Nicholas II, Emperor of Russia, 1868-1918 4. World War I -- Causes. 5. Rulers. 6. World politics. 7. Europe -- Politics and government -- 1871-1918. 8. Germany -- History -- William II, 1888-1918. 9. Great Britain -- History -- Edward VII, 1901-1910. 10. Russia -- History -- Nicholas II, 1894-1917.

ISBN 9781400043637

LC 2009037690

Originally published as The three emperors: London : Fig Tree, 2009.

Draws on correspondence and diaries to trace the parallel stories of monarchs William II of Germany, George V of Britain, and Nicholas II of Russia, who at the onset of World War I wrongly counted on their shared family relationship to safeguard European interests.

Clark, Christopher M.

★The **sleepwalkers** : how Europe went to war in 1914 / Christopher Clark. Harper, 2013. 400 p. **940.3**

1. World War I -- Causes. 2. Diplomacy 3. International relations -- History 4. Europe -- Politics and government -- 1871-1918.

ISBN 9780061146657

LC 2012038473

"First published in Great Britain in 2012 by Allen Lane, an imprint of Penguin Books."

Cundill Prize in Historical Literature finalist

Illustrated with dozens of black-and-white photos, this authoritative chronicle, drawing on new research on World War I, traces the paths to war in a minute-by-minute, fast-paced narrative that examines the decades of history that informed the events of 1914.

"Emphasizing the human element, Clark bestows a tragic sensibility on a magisterial work of scholarship." Booklist.

Clarke, Peter

The **locomotive** of war : money, empire, power, and guilt / Peter Clarke. Bloomsbury, 2017 432 p. **940.3**

1. Wilson, Woodrow, 1856-1924. 2. Lloyd George, David, 1863-1945. 3. Churchill, Winston, 1874-1965 4. Keynes, John Maynard, 1883-1946. 5. War 6. Politics and war. 7. Nationalism. 8. Modern history

ISBN 9781620406601

LC 2017027577

Twentieth-century warfare, based on new technologies and vast armies, saw the locomotive power of war heightened to an unprecedented level. Through the unique prism of this vast tragedy, Peter Clarke examines some of the most influential figures of the day, on both sides of the Atlantic.

Gilbert, Martin, 1936-2015

The **First** World War : a complete history / Martin Gilbert. H. Holt, 1996, c1994. xxiv, 615 p. : **940.3**

1. World War I 2. War. 3. World War I -- Economic aspects. 4. Europe -- History, Military -- 20th century

ISBN 0805076174

LC bl 00004313

"An Owl book."

Reprint. Originally published: 1994.

Recounts the course of World War I, the enormity of its cost, the advances it brought in technology, and its effect on European society.

"What Mr. Gilbert seeks to do, and frequently succeeds in doing, is to humanize, indeed to personalize, World War I. His effort and accomplishment make this a rewarding and significant book." New York Times Book Review.

Grant, R. G

World War I : the definitive visual history : from Sarajevo to Versailles / R.G. Grant. DK Publishing, 2018. 372 p.

: **940.3**

1. World War I. 2. World War I -- Pictorial works.
ISBN 9781465470010

LC bl2018004158

At head of title: DK Smithsonian.

Includes index.

A guide to the first World War features timelines, maps, and accounts of the action to bring to life the world leaders, key players, and soldiers who fought the battles with weapons and new technologies that changed history.

Hastings, Max

Catastrophe 1914 : Europe goes to war / Max Hastings. Alfred A. Knopf, 2013. 640 p. **940.3**

1. World War I -- Causes. 2. Military history. 3. Europe -- History -- July Crisis, 1914.
ISBN 9780307597052

LC 2013027865

A history of the early phase of World War I traces the breakdown of diplomatic measures and the dramatic battles that occurred throughout the first year.

"Readers accustomed to Hastings' vivid battle descriptions, incisive anecdotes from all participants, and shrewd, often unsettling opinions will not be disappointed. Among the plethora of brilliant accounts of this period, this is one of the best." Kirkus.

Herman, Arthur, 1956-

1917 : Lenin, Wilson, and the birth of the new world disorder / Arthur Herman. Harper, 2017. 256 p. **940.3**

1. Wilson, Woodrow, 1856-1924 Influence. 2. Lenin, Vladimir Il'ich, 1870-1924 Influence. 3. World War I -- Influence. 4. Social change 5. World politics 6. Soviet Union -- History -- Revolution, 1917-1921 -- Influence. 7. United States -- Foreign relations -- 1913-1921.
ISBN 9780062570888

LC 2017021669

Chronicles the intertwined stories of Woodrow Wilson and Vladimir Lenin, revealing how their crucial decisions changed world politics and spread disruptive ideologies that continue to influence the modern world.

"Mixing both real events and a few moments of speculation, a fine account of a climacteric year." Kirkus.

Hochschild, Adam

To end all wars : a story of loyalty and rebellion, 1914-1918 / Adam Hochschild. Houghton Mifflin Harcourt, 2011. 480 p. **940.3**

1. World War, I -- Great Britain. 2. Soldiers -- Great Britain 3. Loyalty -- Case studies. 4. World War, I -- Social aspects -- Great Britain. 5. Great Britain -- History, Military -- 20th century
ISBN 9780618758289

LC 2010025836

National Book Critics Circle Award for Nonfiction finalist, 2011.

Presents a history of World War I, focusing on the moral conflict between the proponents of the war and its critics in Great Britain.

"An ambitious narrative that presents a teeming worldview through intimate, human portraits." Kirkus.

Hughes-Wilson, John

The **First** World War in 100 objects / John Hughes-Wilson ; IWM consultant, Nigel Steel ; editor, Mark Hawkins-Dady. Firefly Books, 2014. 448 p. : **940.3**

1. World War I -- Antiquities. 2. Material culture.

LC bl2014019027

Tells the story of World War I through one hundred events and developments, each of which is visualized through an object or artifact drawn in large part from the collections of the Imperial War Museums in the United Kingdom.

"The text packs in an impressive amount of detail, making it seem fussy at times, but the explanations of facts and events are always clear. Altogether, this is a stunning read that is exciting in its depth, scope and personal feel. After seeing and reading about objects touched, used, cherished and hated by those who experienced the war, it will be impossible not to gain a greater understanding and appreciation of the struggle that 'truly... still shapes the world in which we live.' " Publishers Weekly.

Jeffery, Keith

1916 : a global history / Keith Jeffery. Bloomsbury USA, 2016 512 p. **940.3**

1. World War I
ISBN 9781620402696

LC bl2016001948

A broad-scale assessment of World War I, told through the significant global events of 1916, includes coverage of such pivotal factors as the Gallipoli campaign, the Easter Rising in Ireland, the war in East Africa and the November U.S. presidential race.

"A brilliant compendium of everything-you-didn't-know-about World War I, which, for many readers, will be a great deal." Kirkus.

Kazin, Michael, 1948-

War against war : the American fight for peace, 1914-1918 / Michael Kazin. Simon & Schuster, 2017. 400 p. **940.3**

1. Addams, Jane, 1860-1935 2. Eastman, Crystal, 1881-1928 3. La Follette, Robert (Robert Marion), 1855-1925 4. Kitchin, Claude, 1869-1923 5. Peace activists 6. World War I 7. Peace movements -- United States -- History -- 20th century. 8. Neutrality -- History -- 20th century 9. United States -- Politics and government -- 1913-1921.
ISBN 9781476705903

LC 2016005355

This book is about the Americans who tried to stop their nation from fighting in one of history's most destructive wars and then were hounded by the government when they refused to back down. In the riveting War Against War, Michael Kazin brings us into the ranks of the largest, most diverse, and most sophisticated peace coalition up to that point in US history.

"A valuable history suitable for all audiences and an important addition to American history and World War I literature." Library Journal.

MacMillan, Margaret, 1943-

Paris 1919 : six months that changed the world / Margaret MacMillan. Random House, 2002, c2001. xxxi, 570 p., 16 p. of plates : **940.3**

1. Wilson, Woodrow, 1856-1924. 2. Lloyd George, David, 1863-1945. 3. Clemenceau, Georges, 1841-1929. 4. League of Nations -- History. 5. Paris Peace Conference, 1919-1920. 6. Versailles, Treaty of, June 28, 1919 (Germany) 7. World War I -- Peace. 8. Treaties -- History. 9. Nationalism. 10. Reparations. 11. Paris, France -- History -- 20th century. 12. Germany -- History -- 1918-1933. 13. Germany -- Boundaries. 14. Europe -- History -- 1918-1945.
ISBN 0375508260

LC 2002023707

Originally published as Peacemakers : the Paris Peace Conference of 1919 and its attempt to end war: London : J. Murray, 2001.

Governor General's Literary Award for English-Language Nonfiction, 2003.

Samuel Johnson Prize for Nonfiction, 2002.

Describes the six months following the end of the First World War when leaders of the great powers, as well as men and women from all over the world, all with their own agendas, converged on Paris to shape the peace.

"MacMillan's lucid prose brings her participants to colorful and quotable life, and the grand sweep of her narrative encompasses all the continents the peacemakers vainly carved up." Publishers Weekly.

McMeekin, Sean, 1974-

★The **Berlin-Baghdad** express : the Ottoman Empire and Germany's bid for world power / Sean McMeekin. Belknap Press of Harvard University Press, 2010. xv, 460 p., 16 p. of plates : **940.3**

1. Geopolitics -- Germany -- History. 2. Jihad. 3. World War I -- Islamic countries. 4. World War I -- Turkey. 5. Germany -- Foreign relations -- 1888-1918. 6. Germany -- Foreign relations Turkey. 7. Turkey -- Foreign relations Germany.

ISBN 0674057392

LC 2010019199

"First published in the United Kingdom by Penguin Books Ltd. 2010"--T.p. verso.

"The subject matter is fresh, and the style is engaging--a worthwhile read and acquisition." Choice Reviews.

★**July** 1914 : countdown to war / Sean McMeekin. Basic Books, 2013. xviii, 461 p. : **940.3**

1. Militarism. 2. Diplomacy. 3. World War I -- Causes. 4. War -- Causes. 5. Europe -- History -- July Crisis, 1914.

ISBN 9780465031450

LC 2012049777

The award-winning author of The Russian Origins of the First World War traces the efforts of a small group of influential statesmen who used the largely ignored assassination of Archduke Franz Ferdinand to trigger World War I, drawing on new archival evidence to reveal the roles of duplicitous figures in Russia and France in setting the stage for the conflict.

"McMeekin's work is a fine diplomatic history of the period, a must-read for serious students of WWI, and a fascinating story for anyone interested in modern history." Publishers Weekly.

Meyer, G. J., 1940-

The **world** remade : America in World War I / G.J. Meyer. Bantam, 2017. 688 p. **940.3**

1. Wilson, Woodrow, 1856-1924. 2. Presidents -- United States. 3. World War I -- Diplomatic history 4. Isolationism 5. Intervention (International relations)

ISBN 9780553393323

LC 2016036502

An indispensable, sharply drawn account of America's pivotal--and still controversial--intervention in World War I, enlivened by fresh insights into the key issues, events, and personalities of the period.

"A refreshing look at this still-much-debated world debacle." Kirkus.

Stone, Norman, 1941-2019

★**World** War One : a short history / Norman Stone. Basic Books, 2009 xiv, 226 p. : **940.3**

1. World War I 2. Military campaigns 3. Military history 4. War -- History -- 20th century 5. Europe

ISBN 9780465013685

Originally published: London : Allen Lane, 2007.

"Stone is as unconventional as he is brilliant, and this provocative interpretation of the Great War combines impressive command of the literature with a telling eye for relevant facts and a sensitive ear for telling epigrams." Publishers Weekly.

Strachan, Hew

The **First** World War / Hew Strachan. Viking, 2004. xviii, 364 p. : **940.3**

1. World War I

ISBN 0670032956

LC 2003062191

A history of the Great War explores the causes and consequences of this global conflict, while tracing its continual reverberations throughout world history almost a century later.

"Readers already familiar with the sequence of events in strict order will benefit most. But all readers will eventually be gripped, and even the most seasoned ones will praise the insights and the original choice of illustrations." Publishers Weekly.

Thompson, Mark, 1959-

The **white** war : life and death on the Italian front, 1915-1919 / Mark Thompson. Basic Books, 2009. 464 p. **940.3**

1. World War I 2. Military campaigns 3. Soldiers -- History -- World War I 4. Military history -- 20th century 5. Italy

ISBN 9780465013296

LC 2008934425

"Penetrating study of one of the forgotten fronts of the Great War. A much-needed addition to the literature of World War I." Kirkus.

Tooze, J. Adam

★The **deluge** : the Great War and the remaking of global order, 1916-1931 / Adam Tooze. Viking Adult, 2014. 640 p. **940.3**

1. World War I -- Economic aspects. 2. World politics -- 1919-1932. 3. Balance of power. 4. Economic history -- 1918-1945.

ISBN 9780670024926

LC 2014005314

Kirkus Prize for Nonfiction finalist, 2015.

An analysis of World War I and its aftermath explores how the conflict fundamentally changed the world, shifting financial systems to America while transforming economic and political strategies in numerous countries.

"Tooze's grand economic history is stimulating, persuasive, and surprisingly accessible." Publishers Weekly.

Woodward, David R., 1939-

World War I almanac / David R. Woodward. Facts On File, c2009. vi, 554 p. : **940.3**

1. World War I -- Almanacs. 2. World War I -- Chronology. 3. World War I 4. Almanacs, American.

ISBN 9780816071340

LC 2008041575

Chronologically records European history and American military involvement beginning in 1871 and ending in 1923, with profiles of key individuals.

940.309 History of Europe--History, geographic treatment, biography

Englund, Peter, 1957-

★The **beauty** and the sorrow : an intimate history of the First World War / Peter Englund. Alfred A. Knopf, 2011, c2009. 560 p. **940.309**

1. World War, I 2. Military history -- 20th century 3. War -- History. 4. History
ISBN 9780307593863

LC 2011020828

Includes index.

"Originally published in Sweden as Stridens Skonhet Och Sorg by Atlantis, Stockholm, in 2009" [i.e. 2008].--T.p. verso.

A revelatory narrative history of World War I explores its impact on everyday men and women, drawing on diaries and letters by 20 individuals from various countries to present an international mosaic of less-represented perspectives.

"Mr. Englund's book is a deviation from standard history books. It is a corrective too to the notion that World War I was only about the dire trench warfare on the Western Front. [It] expertly pans across other theaters of war: the Alps, the Balkans, the Eastern Front, Mesopotamia, East Africa." New York Times Book Review.

Englund, Will

March 1917 : on the brink of war and revolution / Will Englund. W.W. Norton & Company, 2017. 416 p. **940.309**

1. Wilson, Woodrow, 1856-1924. 2. World War I 3. Social change 4. Suffragist movement 5. Soviet Union -- History -- Revolution, 1917-1921 6. United States -- History -- 1913-1921 7. Europe -- History -- 20th century
ISBN 9780393292084

LC 2016046272

A history of a pivotal month on the eve of World War I describes the abdication of Russian Tsar Nicholas II and America's declaration of war on Germany as part of the Wilson administration's decision to establish the U.S. as a global power.

"Recommended for those eager to learn about watershed moments in history and all readers interested in World War I." Library Journal.

940.4 Military history of World War I

Bascomb, Neal

The **escape** artists : a band of daredevil pilots and the grandest escape of the Great War / Neal Bascomb. Houghton Mifflin Harcourt, 2018. 320 p. **940.4**

1. Prisoners of war. 2. Escaped prisoners of war -- Great Britain. 3. World War I -- Prisoners and prisons. 4. Airmen -- Great Britain.
ISBN 9780544937116

LC 2017058527

Presents the story of a group of downed Allied airmen who masterminded a courageous and ingenious breakout from Germany's Holzminden POW camp.

Carroll, Andrew

My fellow soldiers : General John Pershing and the Americans who helped win the Great War / Andrew Carroll. Penguin Group USA 2017 400 p. **940.4**

1. Pershing, John Joseph, 1860-1948 2. United States. Army. American Expeditionary Forces 3. World War I -- American participation 4. Soldiers -- United States 5. War and society
ISBN 9781594206481

LC 2016056754

The best-selling author of War Letters presents a 100th anniversary account of the American experience during World War I, centering on an intimate portrait of General Pershing while drawing on a rich trove of newly uncovered letters to convey the grassroots realities of everyday workers, soldiers, medics and families.

"Carroll uses the personal correspondence of Gen. Pershing...as a means of establishing the war timeline. Varied American perspectives of the war are included, and the letters of African-Americans and women figure prominently in the work." Publishers Weekly.

Davenport, Matthew J.

First over there : the attack on Cantigny, America's first battle of World War I / Matthew J. Davenport. Thomas Dunne Books, St. Martin's Press, 2015. 360 p. **940.4**

1. United States. Army. Infantry Division, 1st. 2. Cantigny, Battle of, 1918. 3. World War I 4. Military campaigns 5. Soldiers -- United States 6. France
ISBN 9781250056443

LC 2015012154

Relying on letters, diaries and reports by the "doughboys" themselves, the author describes the events that took place on May 28, 1918, when the United States fought and won its first battle of World War I in Cantigny.

"From the 'creeping barrage' of artillery to the eventual American victory, the reader will hear every explosion, feel each bullet whiz past, and sometimes cry at the loss of a comrade." Library Journal.

Dyer, Geoff

The **missing** of the Somme / Geoff Dyer. Vintage Books, 2011. 176 p. **940.4**

1. World War I 2. War -- Moral and ethical aspects
ISBN 9780307742971

LC 2012450530

Weighs the significance of World War I as it is reflected in memories, works of art, cemeteries, and traditions that illuminate humanity's understanding of and relationship to the conflict.

Eisenhower, John S. D., 1922-

Yanks : the epic story of the American Army in World War I / John S.D. Eisenhower with Joanne Thompson Eisenhower. Free Press, c2001. xiv, 353 p. : **940.4**

1. United States. Army -- History World War I. 2. United States. Army. American Expeditionary Forces -- History. 3. Western Front (World War I) 4. World War I 5. Military campaigns
ISBN 9780684863047

LC 2001023124

Provides a detailed overview of the role of the United States during World War I, from the selection of Pershing as commanding general, to the buildup of troops, to American intervention in Europe.

"This is an important work that should help alter the historical picture of the American role in the conflict." Booklist.

Farwell, Byron

Over there : the United States in the Great War, 1917-1918 / Byron Farwell. Norton, c1999. 336 p. : **940.4**

1. World War I -- United States. 2. United States -- History -- 1913-1921.
ISBN 0393046982

LC 98035705

Chronicles the rise of the American military and the role it played in winning World War I, from the declaration of war in 1917 to the social changes that occurred on the home front.

"This title does provide good coverage on the intervention in Russia and the role of women in the war, notably the Hello Girls." Library Journal.

Flood, Charles Bracelen

First to fly : the story of the Lafayette Escadrille, the American heroes who flew for France in World War I / Charles Bracelen Flood. Atlantic Monthly, 2015. 256 p. **940.4**

1. Fighter pilots -- United States 2. World War I 3. Volunteers

ISBN 9780802123657

LC 2016303710

Tells the story of the men who were at the forefront of aviation during World War I--the daredevil Americans of the Lafayette Escadrille, who flew in French planes, wore French uniforms and showed the world an American brand of heroism before the United States entered the Great War.

Harries, Meirion, 1951-

The **last** days of innocence : America at war, 1917-1918 / Meirion and Susie Harries. Vintage Books, 1998, c1997. xiii, 573 p. : **940.4**

1. World War I -- United States. 2. United States -- History, Military

ISBN 0679743766

LC BL 98013976

Originally published: New York : Random House, 1997.

Traces the unprecedented, massive mobilization of American society between April 1917 and November 1918 to fight Germany in World War I and its profound effects on Americans' attitudes toward their government.

"This is an excellent study of US participation in WWI. The research is in far greater depth than the usual 'popular history,' the analysis is sharp and informative, and the writing is clear and a pleasure to read. The authors strike an even balance between necessity for condensation and the accuracy that comes from detailed treatment." Choice.

Hart, Peter, 1955-

The **Somme** : the darkest hour on the Western front / Peter Hart. Pegasus Books : 2008, c2005. 589 p. : **940.4**

1. Somme, 1st Battle of the, 1916. 2. Battles -- History -- 20th century. 3. World War I 4. Military campaigns 5. France -- History -- 1914-1940.

ISBN 9781605980164

LC bl2009003386

Originally published: London : Weidenfeld & Nicolson, 2005.

Traces the 1916 "Big Push" confrontation between English, French, and German forces during which the British lost more than twenty thousand soldiers in the first day, in an account drawn from letters, diaries, and first-person testimonies.

Hernon, Peter, 1947-

The **great** rescue : American heroes, an iconic ship, and the race to save Europe in WWI / Peter Hernon. HarperCollins Publishers, 2017. 368 p. **940.4**

1. Leviathan (Steamship). 2. Steamships. 3. Naval tactics. 4. World War I -- Naval operations, American.

ISBN 9780062433862

LC 2017012596

Published in commemoration of America's centennial entry into World War I, the story of the legendary liner-turned-warship Leviathan traces its multiple voyages carrying tens of thousands of soldiers, crewpeople, Spanish flu victims and more.

"An intriguing work of World War I research resurrects the little-known history of a massive German luxury liner that was confiscated and retooled for the American war effort." Kirkus.

Herwig, Holger H.

The **Marne,** 1914 : the opening of World War I and the battle that changed the world / Holger H. Herwig. Random House, 2009. 416 p. **940.4**

1. Marne, 1st Battle of the, France, 1914. 2. World War I. 3. Battles. 4. France -- History, Military -- 20th century. 5. Germany -- History, Military -- 20th century.

ISBN 9781400066711

LC 2009005687

Evaluates the Battle of the Marne as what the author believes to be the most important land battle of the 20th century, in an account that analyzes the strategies of German's plan to capture France and how its failure culminated in a catastrophic trench war.

"This fine history of World War I's opening battle argues persuasively that it was decisive in setting the pattern for the war, a pattern that made World War II inevitable. Herwig's research has been exhaustive, including of archives long since thought destroyed that help him fill in a great many details about the German side. As fine an addition to scholarly World War I literature as has been seen in some time." Booklist.

Hynes, Samuel, 1924-

The **unsubstantial** air : American fliers in the First World War / Samuel Hynes. Farrar, Straus and Giroux, 2014. 352 p. **940.4**

1. World War I -- Aerial operations, American. 2. Fighter pilots -- United States. 3. Aviation -- History.

ISBN 9780374278007

LC 2014008673

The Unsubstantial Air is the gripping story of the Americans who fought and died in the aerial battles of World War I, told through the words and voices of the aviators themselves.

"The reader quickly becomes aware of the acute danger pilots faced--the narratives Haynes utilizes to tell the story often end abruptly with a terse account of a death due to a training accident, mechanical failure, or combat. It is a must read for anyone interested in aviation history, military history, and the American experience in the Great War." Publishers Weekly.

Larson, Erik, 1954-

★**Dead** wake : the last crossing of the Lusitania / Erik Larson. Crown Publishers, 2015 464 p. **940.4**

1. Lusitania (Steamship) 2. World War I -- Naval operations, German. 3. Shipwrecks -- History -- 20th century. 4. Shipping -- Government policy -- Great Britain -- History -- 20th century. 5. Passenger ships. 6. Europe -- History, Military -- 20th century

ISBN 9780307408860

LC 2014034182

ALA Notable Book, 2016.

The author of In the Garden of Beasts presents a 100th-anniversary chronicle of the sinking of the Lusitania that discusses the factors that led to the tragedy and the contributions of such figures as President Wilson, bookseller Charles Lauriat and architect Theodate Pope Riddle.

"Reader engrossment is tightly sustained as we move back and forth between the Lusitania on its return from New York City to its home port of Liverpool under a black cloud of warnings that the imperial German government considered the waters around Britain to be a war zone, and the rapacious German submarine U-20, stalking the seas for prey like a lion on the Serengeti. Factual and personal to a high degree, the narrative reads like a grade-A thriller." Booklist.

Laskin, David, 1953-

The **long** way home : an immigrant generation and the crucible of war / David Laskin. Harper, 2010. 416 p. **940.4**

1. United States. Army 2. World War I 3. Soldiers -- United States 4. Immigrants -- United States 5. Immigration and emigration.
ISBN 9780061233333

LC 2009028191

"Narrative account of how twelve immigrant soldiers became Americans through fighting in World War I".--Provided by publisher.

"The author follows the lives of 12 American doughboys who had been born in Europe and who then returned there to fight for their adopted country in World War I. It's an imaginative concept, and Laskin mines family legends and official documents to tell the stories of these ordinary foot soldiers from Italy and Ireland, Poland and Russia, Slovakia and Norway." Washington Post.

Massie, Robert K., 1929-2019

Castles of steel : Britain, Germany, and the winning of the Great War at sea / Robert K. Massie. Random House, 2003. xii, 865 p., 16 p. of plates : **940.4**

1. Great Britain. Royal Navy -- History 20th century. 2. Germany. Navy -- History World War I 3. World War I -- Naval operations, British. 4. Naval history. 5. Jutland, Battle of, 1916. 6. World War I -- Naval operations, German. 7. North Sea.
ISBN 0679456716

LC 2003041373

Sequel to: Dreadnought.

"The author makes a coherent if long narrative out of a sequence of events familiar to students of naval history but probably not to many other potential readers." Publishers Weekly.

Millman, Chad

The **detonators** : the secret plot to destroy America and an epic hunt for justice / Chad Millman. Little, Brown, 2006. xviii, 330 p., 8 p. of plates : **940.4**

1. Mixed Claims Commission, United States and Germany. 2. World War I -- Black Tom Island, New Jersey. 3. Explosions. 4. Sabotage -- Black Tom Island, New Jersey -- History -- 20th century. 5. Spies -- Germany 6. United States Claims. 7. Germany Claims.
ISBN 0316734969

LC 2005024401

In July 1916, a spit of land in New York Harbor called Black Tom Island exploded, pelting the Statue of Liberty with shrapnel, devastating much of lower Manhattan, and casting a fiery orange glow over New York City. The attack, so massive that people as far away as Maryland felt the ground shake, had been shockingly easy. America was riddled with networks of German saboteurs .... Three lawyers--John McCloy, Amos Peaslee, and Harold Martin--made it their mission to solve the Black Tom mystery. With the pace of a legal thriller and the detail of the richest history, The Detonators is the first full accounting of a crime and a cover-up that resonate strongly in a post-9/11 America.

"With its obvious contemporary resonance, Millman's able account of an earlier foreign attack on America should draw the espionage audience and more." Booklist.

Moore, Wendy, 1952-

No man's land : the trailblazing women who ran Britain's most extraordinary military hospital during World War I / Wendy Moore. Basic Books, 2020. 336 p. **940.4**

1. Murray, Flora. 2. Anderson, Louisa Garrett, 1873-1943. 3. Women physicians 4. World War I 5. Suffragists 6. Women's rights 7. Great Britain -- History -- 20th century
ISBN 9781541672727

LC 2019041778

Documents the story of how two pioneering suffragette doctors transformed modern medicine, broke boundaries and raised standards for patient care in World War I-era London before founding Endell Street's highly respected Suffragette's Hospital.

"Drawing on diaries, letters, and newspaper accounts, Moore narrates with verve and precision, highlighting the pressures and obstacles these women and their staff faced. Readers interested in medical, military, and women's histories will savor this sterling account." Publishers Weekly

Mosier, John, 1944-

The **myth** of the Great War : a new military history of World War I / John Mosier. Harper Collins, 2001. xiv, 381 p. : **940.4**

1. World War I 2. Military campaigns 3. France -- History, Military.
ISBN 0060196769

LC 00046103

A controversial new history of the "Great War" challenges traditional views of World War I and argues that the Germans beat the French and British decisively and were rescued by American intervention in 1918.

"After dissecting the major campaigns on the western front, Mosier concludes that Germany's ultimate defeat was the direct result of the influx of American soldiers into France in 1917 and 1918. . . . This is revisionist history that convincingly smashes the myths that Allied governments, leaders, and propagandists worked so hard to promulgate. Mosier's masterful account is a welcome addition." Booklist.

Neiberg, Michael S.

★**Fighting** the Great War : a global history / Michael S. Neiberg. Harvard University Press, 2005. xx, 395 p. : **940.4**

1. World War I -- History.
ISBN 9780674016965

LC 2004054330

Presents an analysis of the events and strategies of World War I.

"Readers interested in a general overview of WW I can do no better than Neiberg's excellent account." Choice.

Ousby, Ian, 1947-2001

The **road** to Verdun : World War I's most momentous battle and the folly of nationalism / Ian Ousby. Doubleday, 2002. ix, 393 p., [16] p. of plates : **940.4**

1. Verdun, Battle of, 1916. 2. World War I 3. Military campaigns 4. Nazism -- Europe -- History -- 20th century. 5. Europe -- History, Military -- 20th century. 6. France -- History, Military -- 20th century. 7. Verdun, France.
ISBN 0385503938

LC 2002019475

In a radical, iconoclastic reexamination of one of the bloodiest battles of World War I, the author of Occupation: The Ordeal of France 1940-1944 sheds new light on the devastating engagement, its impact on the soldiers who fought, and its long-term implications for the history of the twentieth century and Franco-German relations.

"This is a study of the Battle of Verdun which killed 700,000 French and German soldiers, 10% of all those killed in the war. Yet a sense of glory was maintained, however inappropriately, amid the gore: the road leading to the battlefield was called the Sacred Way, and the French General Neville gained immortality by his brave statement, 'They {the Germans} shall not pass.'" Publishers Weekly.

Paice, Edward

World War I : the African front: an imperial war on the African continent / Edward Paice. Pegasus, 2008. 544 p. **940.4**

1. World War I 2. Military campaigns 3. Combat. 4. Imperialism. 5. Africa.

ISBN 9781933648903

LC bl2008026945

Documents the lesser-known course of World War I as it was fought in Africa, tracing Britain's elimination of German naval bases in the region, the tragic and costly land war that extended beyond the signing of the Armistice in Europe, and the role of imperialism in East Africa.

"An authoritative summing-up of a grim, complex and little-known part of World War I." Kirkus.

Philpott, William James

Three armies on the Somme : the first battle of the twentieth century / William Philpott. Alfred A. Knopf, 2010. 544 p. **940.4**

1. Great Britain. Army -- History World War I. 2. France. Army -- History World War I. 3. Germany. Army -- History World War I. 4. Somme, 1st Battle of the, 1916. 5. World War I. 6. Battles. 7. Military strategy.

ISBN 9780307265852

LC 2010004070

"A Borzoi book"--T.p. verso.

A provocative reinterpretation of a defining World War I battle argues that it provided crucial information to British and French forces to ending the war by shaping period understandings of such emerging technologies as the tank and machine gun.

"The Battle of the Somme is branded in British memory as the exemplar of WWI: a months-long cataclysm that, at the cost of monumental casualties, repelled the Germans from a few square miles of shell-blasted French countryside. This account by a descendant of an artillerist in the battle has two aims: to narrate the battle from its initial strategic concept to its sputtering-out in late 1916 and to refute historical and popular opinion about the battle. Comprehensive research and convention-bucking arguments qualify Philpott for the WWI shelf." Booklist.

Preston, Diana, 1952-

A **higher** form of killing : six weeks in World War I that forever changed the nature of warfare / Diana Preston. Bloomsbury Press, 2015 340 p. **940.4**

1. World War I 2. Weapons of mass destruction. 3. Airships 4. Torpedoes.

ISBN 9781620402122

LC 2014019999

An acclaimed historian chronicles the birth of weapons of mass destruction during World War I, including the use of poison gas by the Germans at Ypres, the torpedoes that sunk the Lusitania and an aerial bombardment of London by a zeppelin.

"In what is often difficult but necessary reading, Preston provides haunting descriptions of the effects of poison gas. A harrowing--and, in this era of drones, absolutely pertinent--look at the rapacious reaches of man's murderous imagination." Kirkus.

Sacco, Joe

The **Great** War : July 1, 1916 : the first day of the Battle of the Somme : an illustrated panorama / Joe Sacco. W. W. Norton & Company, 2013. 54 p. **940.4**

1. Great Britain. Army -- History World War I. 2. Somme, 1st Battle of the, 1916 3. World War I 4. Military campaigns 5. Battles 6. Great Britain -- History, Military -- 20th century. 7. France -- History, Military -- 20th century. 8. Somme River, France. 9. Stories without words 10. Comics and Graphic novels

ISBN 9780393088809

LC 2013010710

Describes the battle on the first day of World War I, which saw 20,000 British soldiers killed and another 40,000 injured, on the banks of the French river as they mounted a joint offensive against the German army.

Scott, R. Neil

★**Many** were held by the sea : the tragic sinking of HMS Otranto / R. Neil Scott ; foreword by Lord George Islay MacNeill Robertson. Rowman & Littlefield, c2012. xxx, 249 p. : **940.4**

1. Otranto (Troopship) 2. Kashmir (Troopship) 3. World War I -- Naval operations, British. 4. Marine accidents -- Great Britain -- History -- 20th century. 5. Shipwrecks -- Islay, Scotland. 6. Transportation -- Great Britain -- History -- 20th century.

ISBN 9781442213425

LC 2012003033

"Highly recommended to all who love crackerjack sea chronicles and can bear the heartbreak; and all readers of wartime naval histories." Library Journal

Sebag-Montefiore, Hugh

Somme : into the breach / Hugh Sebag-Montefiore. Harvard Univ Pr., 2016. 650 p. **940.4**

1. Somme, 1st Battle of the, 1916 2. World War I 3. Military campaigns 4. Battles 5. France 6. Europe -- History, Military -- 20th century

ISBN 9780674545199

LC 2016025276

A noted military historian and the author of the critically acclaimed Enigma: The Battle for the Code takes readers to the front lines of the Battle of the Somme, revealing the Somme campaign in all its glory as well as its misery, and giving voice to the relatives of the many forgotten heroes whose bravery has been overlooked.

"A beautifully crafted, blow-by-blow account with deep insight into the lives of these diverse young men." Kirkus.

Slotkin, Richard, 1942-

Lost battalions : the Great War and the crisis of American nationality / Richard Slotkin. H. Holt, 2005. xii, 639 p. : **940.4**

1. United States. Army. Infantry Regiment, 369th 2. United States. Army Recruiting, enlistment, etc. 3. United States. Army African-American troops. 4. World War I -- Regimental histories -- United States. 5. World War -- African-American troops. 6. African American soldiers -- History -- 20th century. 7. Minorities -- United States. 8. United States -- Interethnic relations.

ISBN 0805041249

LC 2005046312

Examines the United States' history of ethnic assimilation and racial strife through the experience of World War I regiments, the fabled Harlem Hell Fighters of the 369th infantry and the legendary "lost battalion" of the 77th division.

"This is a history of the African-American 369th Infantry, known as the Harlem Hellfighters, and the 77th Division, dubbed the Melting Pot for its ranks of Italians, Jews and other eastern Europeans. Slotkin smoothly telescopes from the trenches to the political and social implications for decades to come in this insightful, valuable account." Publishers Weekly.

Tuchman, Barbara W. (Barbara Wertheim), 1912-1989
★The **guns** of August / Barbara W. Tuchman ; with a new foreword by Robert K. Massie. Ballantine, 1994, c1962. xxiv, 511 p. : **940.4**

1. World War I 2. Military campaigns 3. Western Front (World War I) 4. Europe -- History -- 1900-1914.
ISBN 034538623X

LC 93090461

Originally published: New York : Macmillan, 1962.

Pulitzer Prize for General Nonfiction, 1963.

Barbara Tuchman has brought to life again the people and events that led up to World War I. With attention to fascinating detail, and an intense knowledge of her subject and its characters, Ms. Tuchman reveals, for the first time, just how the war started, why, and why it could have been stopped but wasn't.

Walker, William T., Jr
Betrayal at Little Gibraltar : a German fortress, a treacherous American general, and the battle to end World War I / William T. Walker. Scribner, 2016. 352 p. **940.4**

1. Bullard, Robert Lee, 1861-1947 Military leadership. 2. United States. Army. Infantry Division, 79th -- History World War I. 3. Argonne, Battle of the, France, 1918 4. World War I 5. Military campaigns 6. Battles 7. France -- History, Military 8. Montfaucon (Meuse, France) -- History, Military -- 20th century.
ISBN 9781501117893

LC 2015044665

A painstakingly researched account of World War I's violent Meuse-Argonne Offensive and the 100-year-old cover-up at its center traces the efforts of AEF Commander-in-Chief John J. Pershing to capture the near-impregnable German Montfaucon and the inside betrayal that cost untold lives.

"He creates a convincing argument for a postwar cover-up of Bullard's actions. A military history for all libraries." Library Journal.

Wawro, Geoffrey
A **mad** catastrophe : the outbreak of World War I and the collapse of the Habsburg Empire / Geoffrey Wawro. Basic Books, 2014. 472 p. **940.4**

1. Habsburg, House of. 2. World War I -- Austria. 3. Austro-Hungarian Empire 4. Austria -- History -- 1900-1945
ISBN 9780465028351

LC 2013039393

The Austro-Hungarian army that marched east and south to confront the Russians and Serbs in the opening campaigns of World War I had a glorious past but a pitiful present. Speaking a mystifying array of languages and lugging outdated weapons, the Austrian troops were hopelessly unprepared for the industrialized warfare that would shortly consume Europe. As prizewinning historian Geoffrey Wawro explains in A Mad Catastrophe, the doomed Austrian conscripts were an unfortunate microcosm of the Austro-Hungarian Empire itself--both equally ripe for destruction. After the assassination of the Austrian Archduke Franz Ferdinand in June 1914, Germany goaded the Empire into a war with Russia and Serbia. With the Germans massing their forces in the west to engage the French and the British, everything--the course of the war and the fate of empires and alliances from Constantinople to London--hinged on the Habsburgs' ability to crush Serbia and keep the Russians at bay. However, Austria-Hungary had been rotting from within for years, hollowed out by repression, cynicism, and corruption at the highest levels. Commanded by a dying emperor, Franz Joseph I, and a querulous celebrity general, Conrad von Hotzendorf, the Austro-Hungarians managed to bungle everything: their ultimatum to the Serbs, their declarations of war, their mobilization, and the pivotal battles in Galicia and Serbia. By the end of 1914, the Habsburg army lay in ruins and the outcome of the war seemed all but decided. Drawing on deep archival research, Wawro charts the decline of the Empire before the war and reconstructs the great battles in the east and the Balkans in thrilling and tragic detail. A Mad Catastrophe is a riveting account of a neglected face of World War I, revealing how a once-mighty empire collapsed in the trenches of Serbia and the Eastern Front, changing the course of European history.

"Wawro's authoritative account is a damning analysis of an empire and a people unready for war." Publishers Weekly.

Yockelson, Mitchell A., 1962-
Forty-seven days : how Pershing's warriors came of age to defeat the German Army in World War I / Mitchell Yockelson. New American Library, 2016. 432 p. **940.4**

1. Pershing, John Joseph, 1860-1948 2. United States. Army. American Expeditionary Forces. 3. World War I 4. Military campaigns 5. Western Front (World War I)
ISBN 9780451466952

LC 2015039121

The Battle of the Meuse-Argonne stands as the deadliest clash in American history: more than a million untested American soldiers went up against a better-trained and -experienced German army, costing more than twenty-six thousand deaths and leaving nearly a hundred thousand wounded. Yet in forty-seven days of intense combat, those Americans pushed back the enemy and forced the Germans to surrender, bringing the First World War to an end--a feat the British and the French had not achieved after more than three years of fighting.

"An accessible, elucidating study by a knowledgeable expert." Kirkus.

940.5 Europe--1918

Gerwarth, Robert
The **vanquished** : why the First World War failed to end / Robert Gerwarth. Farrar, Straus and Giroux, 2016. 416 p. **940.5**

1. World War I -- Influence. 2. War and society. 3. Interethnic conflict 4. Political violence 5. Europe -- Ethnic relations -- History -- 20th century. 6. Europe -- Politics and government -- 1918-1945. 7. Europe -- Social conditions -- 20th century.
ISBN 9780374282455

LC 2016032496

"Originally published in 2016 by Allen Lane, an imprint of Pengin Books, Great Britain"--Title page verso.

An account of the ethnic and state violence that followed the end of World War I and shaped the course of the 20th century explores how countries on both sides of the original conflict suffered revolutions, pogroms, mass expulsions and major military clashes that cost millions of lives.

Jarausch, Konrad Hugo
Out of ashes : a new history of Europe in the twentieth century / Konrad H. Jarausch. Princeton University Press, 2015. 744 p. **940.5**

1. Social change -- Europe. 2. Europe -- History -- 20th century. 3. Europe -- Politics and government -- 20th century. 4. Europe -- Social conditions -- 20th century.
ISBN 9780691152790

LC 2014031328

A sweeping history of twentieth-century Europe, Out of Ashes tells the story of an era of unparalleled violence and barbarity yet also of humanity, prosperity, and promise. Konrad Jarausch describes how the European nations emerged from the nineteenth century with high hopes for continued material progress and proud of their imperial command over the globe, only to become embroiled in the bloodshed of World War I, which brought an end to their optimism and gave rise to competing democratic, communist, and fascist ideologies. He shows how the 1920s witnessed renewed hope and a flourishing of modernist art and literature, but how the decade ended in economic collapse and gave rise to a second, more devastating world war and genocide on an unprecedented scale.

"The work isn't designed to be encyclopedic, yet it should be on the shelf of everyone seeking a panoramic, narrative guide to history's most violent century. This comprehensive history of 20th-century Europe is bound to become the standard work on its subject: a bold, major achievement." Publishers Weekly.

Kershaw, Ian

To hell and back : Europe 1914-1949 / Ian Kershaw. Penguin Group, 2015 608 p. **940.5**

1. World War I 2. World War II 3. World politics 4. History 5. Europe -- History -- 20th century

ISBN 9780670024582

LC 2015040523

The long continuous period from 1914 to1949, was unprecedented in human history--an extraordinarily dramatic, often traumatic, and endlessly fascinating period of upheaval and transformation. This new volume in the Penguin History of Europe series offers comprehensive coverage of this tumultuous era. Beginning with the outbreak of World War I through the rise of Hitler and the aftermath of the Second World War, award-winning British historian Ian Kershaw combines his characteristic original scholarship and gripping prose as he profiles the key decision makers and the violent shocks of war as they affected the entire European continent and radically altered the course of European history.

"Kershaw concludes with a somewhat less successful appraisal of the vastly altered geopolitical landscape following WWII, the social and economic disruptions, the physical ruin of the continent, and the responses to the devastation offered by the Christian churches, leading intellectuals, and popular entertainments. An ambitious, dense , sometimes-difficult treatment of a vast topic." Kirkus.

Mak, Geert

★**In** Europe : travels through the twentieth century / Geert Mak ; translated from the Dutch by Sam Garrett. Pantheon Books, c2007. xvi, 976 p. : **940.5**

1. Mak, Geert Travel Europe. 2. Journalists -- Netherlands -- Diaries. 3. Historians -- Netherlands -- Diaries. 4. Europe -- History -- 20th century. 5. Europe -- Description and travel.

ISBN 0375424954

LC 2007009260

Includes index.

Translation of : In Europa.

A Dutch journalist crisscrosses Europe in search of the evidence of and eyewitnesses to the turbulent events of the twentieth century, drawing on interviews, diaries, newpaper reports, and other sources to explore the people and places that transformed Europe.

940.53 World War II, 1939-1945

Aleksievich, Svetlana, 1948-

Last witnesses : an oral history of the children of World War II / Svetlana Alexievich ; translated by Richard Pevear and Larissa Volokhonsky. Random House, 2019, c1985. 320 p. **940.53**

1. Children and war 2. Child soldiers 3. Child war victims 4. World War II -- Children. 5. Soviet Union -- History -- 20th century 6. Europe -- History -- 20th century

ISBN 9780399588754

LC 2018034984

Translation of: Poslednie svideteli : kniga nedetskikh rasskazov.

Originally published: Moscow : Molodaia gvardiia, 1985.

A Nobel Prize-winning author presents an oral history of children's experiences in WWII across Europe and Russia, providing a kaleidoscopic portrait of the human consequences of the war.

"As usual, Alexievich shines a bright light on those who were there; an excellent book but not for the faint of heart." Kirkus.

The **unwomanly** face of war : an oral history of women in World War II / Svetlana Alexievich. Random House, 2017, c1985. 384 p. **940.53**

1. World War II -- Women's participation. 2. Women soldiers 3. Women's role 4. Soviet Union -- History -- 20th century 5. Europe -- History -- 20th century

ISBN 9780399588723

LC 2016036099

Originally published by Mastatskaya litaratura in 1985.

This absorbing oral history, a Nobel Prize-winning author compiles firsthand reports of Russian women in military service during World War II. Many were reluctant to discuss their experiences; while they often performed similar duties as men (for example, as snipers or tank drivers) their perceptions and experiences differed significantly. Weaving their accounts into a vivid tapestry, The Unwomanly Face of War spotlights previously unnoticed ordeals and historical achievements.

"A worldwide best seller when it was originally published in Russian in 1985, this work by Nobel Prize winner Alexievich...combines hundreds of oral history accounts with the author's own reflections. Alexievich conducted these interviews between 1978 and 1985, intending to capture 'women's history of war.'" Library Journal.

Allport, Alan, 1970-

Britain at bay : the epic story of the Second World War, 1938-1941 / Alan Allport. Alfred A. Knopf, 2020. xviii, 590 p. **940.53**

1. World War II -- Great Britain. 2. Military campaigns 3. World War II -- Social aspects -- Great Britain. 4. Great Britain -- Politics and government -- 1936-1945. 5. Great Britain -- Social conditions -- 20th century.

ISBN 9780451494740

LC 2020028530

Here is the many-faceted, world-historically significant story of Britain at war. In looking closely at the military and political dimensions of the conflict's first crucial years, Alan Allport tackles questions such as: Could the war have been avoided? Could it have been lost? Were the strategic decisions the rights ones? How well did the British organize and fight? How well did the British live up to their own values? What difference did the war make in the end to the fate of the nation?

"Expertly researched and marvelously written, this sterling history casts an oft-studied subject in a new light." Publishers Weekly

Baier, Bret

Three days at the brink : FDR's daring gamble to win World War II / Bret Baier, with Catherine Whitney. William Morrow & Company, 2019. 448 p. **940.53**

1. Roosevelt, Franklin D. (Franklin Delano), 1882-1945 2. Churchill, Winston, 1874-1965 3. Stalin, Joseph, 1879-1953 4. Teheran

Conference (1943) 5. World War II 6. Heads of state 7. Alliances 8. Military strategy 9. Tehran, Iran
ISBN 9780062905680

LC bl2019023566

November 1943: World War II teetered in the balance. The Nazis controlled nearly all of the European continent. Japan dominated the Pacific. That same month in Tehran, with the fate of the world in question, the "Big Three"--Franklin D. Roosevelt, Winston Churchill, and Joseph Stalin--secretly met for the first time to chart a strategy for defeating Hitler. Over three days, this trio--strange bedfellows united by their mutual responsibility as heads of the Allied powers--made essential decisions that would direct the final years of the war and its aftermath.

Barr, Niall

Eisenhower's armies : the American-British alliance during World War II / Niall Barr. Pegasus Books, 2015. 400 p. **940.53**

1. United States. Army. 2. Great Britain. Army. 3. World War II. 4. Strategic alliances (Military) 5. International relations. 6. United States -- Foreign relations Great Britain. 7. Great Britain -- Foreign relations United States.
ISBN 9781605988160

LC 2016429702

An authoritative behind-the-scenes history of World War II's "Atlantic Alliance" draws on considerable archival research to share insights into how its unprecedented level of cooperation led to victory in spite of considerable tensions and controversies.

"This dramatic work isn't just for military historians or World War II scholars. It is also highly recommended for students of World War II and of the Atlantic Alliance of the mid-20th century and is a great read for anyone interested in leadership, decision making, international relations and diplomacy, and 20th-century history." Library Journal.

Berenbaum, Michael, 1945-

The **world** must know : the history of the Holocaust as told in the United States Holocaust Memorial Museum / Michael Berenbaum ; Arnold Kramer, editor of photographs. United States Holocaust Memorial Museum, c2006. xxi, 250 p. : **940.53**

1. United States Holocaust Memorial Museum Exhibitions. 2. Holocaust (1933-1945)
ISBN 9780801883583

LC bl2006005031

Draws on eyewitness accounts, artifacts, and photographs to tell the story of the perpetrators, bystanders, rescuers, and victims of the Holocaust.

Berthon, Simon

Warlords : an extraordinary re-creation of World War II through the eyes and minds of Hitler, Churchill, Roosevelt, and Stalin / Simon Berthon and Joanna Potts. Da Capo Press, 2006. ix, 358 p., 16 p. of plates : **940.53**

1. Hitler, Adolf, 1889-1945. 2. Churchill, Winston, 1874-1965. 3. Roosevelt, Franklin D. (Franklin Delano), 1882-1945. 4. Stalin, Joseph, 1879-1953 5. World War II. 6. Politicians. 7. International relations.
ISBN 9780306814679

LC 2008299408

First published in the United Kingdom by Methhuen Publishing Limited.

Looks at the events of World War II by detailing the day-to-day actions of Hitler, Stalin, Churchill, and Roosevelt as they grapple with the war's events and plot strategy.

"This book focuses on the day-to-day actions of Hitler, Stalin, Churchill, and Roosevelt as they grapple with the war's events and plot strategy. For anyone interested in how these four leaders engaged in the war, here is a great place to start." Library Journal.

Beschloss, Michael R.

★The **conquerors** : Roosevelt, Truman, and the destruction of Hitler's Germany, 1941-1945 / Michael Beschloss. Simon & Schuster, 2002. xiv, 377 p., 16 p. of plates : **940.53**

1. Roosevelt, Franklin D. (Franklin Delano), 1882-1945 2. Truman, Harry S., 1884-1972. 3. Morgenthau, Henry, 1891-1967. 4. Churchill, Winston, 1874-1965 5. Stalin, Joseph, 1879-1953. 6. World War II -- Germany. 7. Reconstruction (1939-1951) -- Germany. 8. Geopolitics. 9. World War II -- Diplomatic history. 10. United States -- Foreign relations -- 1933-1945. 11. United States -- Politics and government -- 1933-1945.
ISBN 0684810271

LC 2002030331

Based on recently released documents, one of the nation's most celebrated historians reveals one of the little-known secrets of World War II--FDR's and Truman's sometimes shocking plans for a postwar Germany.

"As German forces were driven back in 1943-45, American leaders were anxious that in 20 years, just as it had done after its defeat in 1918, a vengeful Germany would start another world war. To prevent this, two schools of thought flowed through DC's salons of power: punishment or rehabilitation. Beschloss covers the meeting-by-meeting, memo-by-memo political battle between the two approaches. Beschloss' comprehensive research and narration into every nuance opens a significant perspective on bureaucratic politics' effect on the Germany that eventually formed in the early cold war." Booklist.

Boehm, Philip,

★A **woman** in Berlin : eight weeks in the conquered city : a diary / Anonymous ; translated by Philip Boehm. Metropolitan Books/Henry Holt, 2005, c2003 xxi, 261 p. **940.53**

1. World War II -- Berlin, Germany. 2. Women and war. 3. Rape as a weapon -- History -- World War II. 4. Berlin, Battle of, 1945 5. Berlin, Germany. 6. Diaries.
ISBN 0805075402

LC 2005041984

Originally published as Eine frau in Berlin: Frankfurt am Main : Eichborn, 2003.

ALA Notable Book, 2006.

A wartime journal by a reporter living through the Russian occupation of Berlin includes her observations of survival under harsh conditions; the mass rapes endured by the city's women; and the corruption of Berlin's citizens.

"This is one of the most important documents to emerge from World War II." New York Times Book Review.

Buruma, Ian

Year zero : 1945 and the aftermath of war / Ian Buruma. Penguin Press, 2013. 384 p. **940.53**

1. World War II -- Peace. 2. Modern history -- 1945-1989 3. Cold War 4. History
ISBN 9781594204364

LC 2013007702

ALA Notable Book, 2014

A history professor describes the events during the year World War II ended, beginning a new era of prosperity in America, rebirth and rebuilding in Europe and the start of the Cold War era.

Cahan, Richard

Un-American : the incarceration of Japanese Americans during World War II / Richard Cahan and Michael Williams ; images by Dorothea Lange, Ansel Adams, and other government photographers. CityFiles Press, 2016. 240 p. : **940.53**

1. Japanese Americans -- Evacuation and relocation, 1942-1945 2. Japanese Americans -- Evacuation and relocation, 1942-1945. 3. World War II -- Concentration camps -- United States 4. World War II -- Concentration camps -- United States.

ISBN 0991541863

LC bl2016055107

Photographs captured by U.S. government photographers relate the experiences of Japanese Americans and those of Japanese ancestry throughout their internment during World War II.

Carley, Michael Jabara

1939 : the alliance that never was and the coming of World War II / Michael Jabara Carley. I.R. Dee, 1999. xxv, 321 p. : **940.53**

1. World War II -- Diplomatic history. 2. World War II -- Causes. 3. Europe -- History -- 20th century.

ISBN 1566632528

LC 99024873

Explores the failed diplomacy that led to World War II, and describes secret negotiations between Britain, France, and the Soviet Union to document the failure to form a united front against Nazi Germany.

"The author provides a detailed and fascinating perspective on one of the major causes of World War II." Library Journal.

Churchill, Winston, 1874-1965

Closing the ring / Winston S. Churchill. Houghton Mifflin, 1985, c1951. xxii, 673 p. : **940.53**

1. Churchill, Winston, 1874-1965 2. Military strategy. 3. Military campaigns 4. World War II -- Diplomatic history. 5. Italy -- History -- Allied occupation, 1943-1947. 6. Europe -- History -- 1918-1945.

ISBN 0395410592

LC bl 99959218

Includes index.

Reprint. Originally published: 1951.

An account of World War II from 1943 to June 5, 1944 tracing the liberation of France and the slow collapse of Nazi Germany.

The **gathering** storm / Winston S. Churchill. Houghton Mifflin, 1985, c1948. xxiii, 724 p. : **940.53**

1. Churchill, Winston, 1874-1965 2. World War II -- Causes. 3. International relations. 4. Diplomacy. 5. World War II -- Diplomatic history. 6. Europe -- Politics and government -- 1918-1945. 7. Europe -- History -- 1918-1945.

ISBN 039541055X

LC 86144242

Studies the events from 1919-1939, stressing the allied errors that led to World War II and analyzes the first months of the war.

The **hinge** of fate / Winston S. Churchill. Houghton Mifflin, 1985, c1950. xxii, 917 p., 4 leaves of plates : **940.53**

1. Churchill, Winston, 1874-1965 2. Military strategy. 3. World War II -- Diplomatic history. 4. Military campaigns 5. North Africa. 6. East Asia. 7. Europe -- History -- 1918-1945.

ISBN 0395410584

LC 86144267

Includes index.

A chronicle of the period from January 1942 through May 1943 during which the fortunes of the Allies turned from disaster to success.

Cohen, Rich

The **Avengers** : a Jewish war story / Rich Cohen. A.A. Knopf, 2000. 261 p. : **940.53**

1. Kovner, Abba, 1918-1987. 2. Korchak, Reizl, 1921-1988 3. Kempner, Vitka. 4. World War II 5. Jewish resistance and revolts 6. Resistance to military occupation 7. Holocaust (1933-1945) 8. Europe -- History, Military -- 20th century

ISBN 0375705295

LC 00021062

Describes the World War II accomplishments of a daring team of Jewish guerrillas, their struggle in the ghetto and in the Baltic forests, and their efforts to build new lives for themselves as part of the new state of Israel.

"Cohen is a skilled writer. His language is spare and muscular, his descriptions evocative, his technique suspenseful." New York Times Book Review.

Collingham, E. M. (Elizabeth M.)

The **taste** of war : World War Two and the battle for food / Lizzie Collingham. Penguin Press, 2012, c2011. xv, 634 p. : **940.53**

1. Hunger. 2. Genocide -- Eastern Europe. 3. Food supply -- History 4. Food as a weapon. 5. Eastern Europe -- History -- 20th century

ISBN 9781594203299

Originally published: London : Allen Lane, 2011.

A history of the role of food in World War II reveals how more than twenty million people died from starvation, malnutrition and related diseases during the war and traces the interaction between food and strategy.

Cooke, Alistair, 1908-2004

The **American** home front, 1941-1942 / Alistair Cooke. Atlantic Monthly Press : c2006. xx, 327 p. : **940.53**

1. Cooke, Alistair, 1908- Travel United States. 2. World War II -- United States. 3. United States -- Social life and customs -- 1918-1945. 4. United States -- Social conditions -- 1933-1945. 5. United States -- History -- 1933-1945.

ISBN 0871139391

LC 2005058860

Includes index.

Map on lining papers.

The famed BBC correspondent furnishes an incisive, firsthand portrait of America on the homefront during the early days of World War II, describing the dramatic changes that were occurring throughout the nation during the period as it was transformed from a civilian society to a wartime one, as seen through the eyes of ordinary citizens.

"Crisscrossing the American continent from east to west and north to south, stopping in diners and bus stations and newly humming industrial plants, Mr. Cooke brings to life an America stepping into the unknown, committing its muscle and blood to an enterprise that most citizens could barely articulate, in places most of them had never heard of." New York Times.

Costigliola, Frank, 1946-

Roosevelt's lost alliances : how personal politics helped start the Cold War / Frank Costigliola. Princeton University Press, c2012. 440 p. **940.53**

1. Roosevelt, Franklin D. (Franklin Delano), 1882-1945. 2. Stalin, Joseph, 1879-1953. 3. Churchill, Winston, 1874-1965. 4. Cold war -- Diplomatic history. 5. Politicians. 6. Diplomacy. 7. Interpersonal relations. 8. United States -- Foreign relations -- 1933-1945. 9. United States -- Foreign relations -- 1945-1953. 10. United States --

Foreign relations Soviet Union. 11. Soviet Union -- Foreign relations United States. 12. United States -- Foreign relations Great Britain. 13. Great Britain -- Foreign relations United States.
ISBN 9780691121291

LC 2011025271

Shows how Franklin D. Roosevelt alienated his inner circle of advisors as he built an alliance between him, Winston Churchill and Joseph Stalin, an alliance that eroded when Harry Truman took the presidency after Roosevelt's death, eventually leading to the Cold War.

Daniels, Roger

Prisoners without trial : Japanese Americans in World War II / Roger Daniels. Hill and Wang, c2004. 162 p. : A Critical issue **940.53**

1. Japanese Americans -- Evacuation and relocation, 1942-1945. 2. Japanese Americans -- Pacific States -- History -- 20th century. 3. World War II -- United States.
ISBN 0809078961

LC 2004047328

Part of Hill and Wang's Critical Issues Series and well established on college reading lists, Prisoners Without Trial presents a concise introduction to a shameful chapter in American history: the incarceration of nearly 120,000 Japanese Americans during World War II. With a revised final chapter and expanded recommended readings, Roger Daniels's updated [2004] edition examines a tragic event in our nation's past and thoughtfully asks if it could happen again.

"An account of the relocation of Japanese Americans during World War II, an injustice prompted not by military necessity but by political and racial motivations. The purpose of this volume is to tell the story in light of the redress legislation enacted in 1988." Library Journal [review of 1993 edition].

Dawidowicz, Lucy S.

The **war** against the Jews : 1933-1945 / Lucy S. Dawidowicz. Seth Press, 1986, c1975. xxxx, 466 p. : **940.53**

1. Holocaust (1933-1945) 2. Antisemitism -- Germany. 3. World War II 4. Jewish resistance and revolts 5. Germany -- History -- 20th century.
ISBN 055334532X

LC 86006516

Originally published: New York : Holt, Rinehart, and Winston, 1975. With new introd. and supplementary bibliography.

Details the origins, growth and implementation of Nazi Germany's plan to annihilate European Jewry and the various responses of individual Jews and organized Jewish communities to the Holocaust in its several stages in ghettos and death camps.

Dobbs, Michael, 1948-

Six months in 1945 : FDR, Stalin, Churchill, Truman, and the birth of the modern world / Michael Dobbs. Alfred A. Knopf, 2012. 416 p. **940.53**

1. Roosevelt, Franklin D. (Franklin Delano), 1882-1945. 2. Stalin, Joseph, 1879-1953. 3. Churchill, Winston, 1874-1965. 4. Truman, Harry S., 1884-1972. 5. World War II -- Diplomatic history 6. World politics -- 1945-1955. 7. Cold War -- Diplomatic history. 8. World War II -- Peace 9. United States -- Foreign relations Soviet Union. 10. Soviet Union -- Foreign relations United States.
ISBN 9780307271655

LC 2012021747

The author of the best-selling One Minute to Midnight presents a dramatic account of the final six months of World War II through the beginning of the Cold War, analyzing the events and legacy of the 1945 Yalta meeting by Roosevelt, Churchill and Stalin as well as the geopolitical ramifications of the atomic bomb and the fall of the Iron Curtain.

Dower, John W.

★**Ways** of forgetting, ways of remembering : Japan in the modern world / John W. Dower. New Press, c2012. 324 p. **940.53**

1. World War II -- Japan. 2. Collective memory. 3. Social change. 4. International relations. 5. Japan -- History -- 1945- 6. Japan -- Politics and government -- 1945- 7. Japan -- Social conditions -- 1945-
ISBN 9781595586186

LC 2011033861

"Scrupulously researched and bravely presented scholarship." Kirkus.

Edsel, Robert M.

The **monuments** men : allied heros, Nazi thieves, and the greatest treasure hunt in history / Robert M. Edsel with Bret Witter. Center Street, 2009. 496 p. **940.53**

1. Allied Forces. Supreme Headquarters. Monuments, Fine Arts and Archives Section -- History. 2. Art thefts 3. World War II -- Confiscations and contributions -- Germany. 4. Nazi plunder. 5. Art and war 6. Germany -- History -- 20th century.
ISBN 9781599951492

LC 2009012255

Film adaptation by the same name (2013).

The previously untold story of a little-known WWII Allied division whose mission was to track down European art and treasures that had been looted by the Nazis at Hitler's command.

Evans, Richard J.

★The **Third** Reich at war / Richard J. Evans. Penguin Press, 2008. 800 p. **940.53**

1. World War II -- Germany. 2. Military history. 3. War. 4. Germany -- Armed Forces -- History -- World War II 5. Germany -- History -- 1933-1945.
ISBN 9781594202063

LC 2008044765

A final volume in a trilogy on the history of Nazi Germany traces the rise and fall of the military, the ways in which the Nazis gained compliance and support from the private sector, and Hitler's campaign of racial subjugation and genocide. By the author of The Coming of the Third Reich.

"Perhaps the best of an impressive series, this book is recommended for all libraries." Library Journal.

Faber, David

Munich, 1938 : appeasement and World War II / David Faber. Simon & Schuster, 2009. 520 p., 16 p. of plates : **940.53**

1. Munich Four-Power Agreement, 1938 2. World War II -- Causes 3. Military history -- 20th century 4. World War II -- Diplomatic history 5. Europe -- Politics and government -- 1918-1945
ISBN 9781439132333

LC 2008044896

David Faber pens a dramatic, detailed, and essential narrative account of the 1938 Munich appeasement crisis.

"Faber's account of the preparation for and actual unfolding of the conference is comprehensive, engrossing, and depressing, like viewing a slow-motion train wreck. He does a masterful job of recounting the political maneuvers and infighting within both the British and German camps." Booklist.

Fleming, Gerald

Hitler and the final solution / Gerald Fleming ; with an introduction by Saul Friedlander. University of California Press, 1984. xxxvi, 219 p., 16 p. of plates : **940.53**

1. Hitler, Adolf, 1889-1945. 2. Holocaust (1933-1945) 3. Germany -- Interethnic relations.

ISBN 0520051033

LC 83024352

Translation of: Hitler und die Endlosung.

Friedlander, Saul, 1932-

Nazi Germany and the Jews : The years of extermination, 1939-1945 / Saul Friedlander. Harper, 2007. 896 p. **940.53**

1. Jews -- Persecutions. 2. World War II 3. Holocaust (1933-1945) 4. Germany.

ISBN 9780060190439

Pulitzer Prize for General Nonfiction, 2008.

An authoritative account of the Holocaust goes beyond usual historical studies to include coverage of the reactions of period world authorities, religious groups, and social groups, in a volume that draws on more than thirty years of research.

Nazi Germany and the Jews : The years of persecution, 1933-1939 / Saul Friedlander. HarperCollins, 1997. xii, 436 p. **940.53**

1. Jews, German -- History -- 1933-1945. 2. Jews -- Persecutions -- Germany. 3. Holocaust (1933-1945) -- Germany. 4. Germany -- Interethnic relations.

ISBN 9780060190422

"Not the least impressive aspect of Friedlnder's book is the skill with which he juxtaposes different levels of reality within an overall chronological frame, moving from high-level Nazi debates on Jewish policy to the routine brutalities of the SA and SS, and from the perceptions of the average German citizen to those of the victims." New York Review of Books.

Fritzsche, Peter, 1959-

An **iron** wind : Europe under Hitler / Peter Fritzsche. Basic Books, 2016 352 p. **940.53**

1. Hitler, Adolf, 1889-1945 Influence. 2. Military occupation. 3. World War II -- Social aspects -- Europe. 4. Civilians in war. 5. Violence -- Social aspects. 6. Europe -- Social conditions -- 20th century.

ISBN 9780465057740

LC 2016018828

A prize-winning historian, drawing on first-person accounts, pieces together the broken words of World War II's witnesses and victims to show how civilians in occupied Europe desperately tried to make sense of the horrors around them as Germany targeted Europe's Jews for deportation and death.

Gilbert, Martin, 1936-2015

Kristallnacht : prelude to destruction / Martin Gilbert. Harper Collins, 2006. 314 p. : **940.53**

1. Kristallnacht, 1938 2. Jews -- Persecutions -- Germany. 3. Jews, German -- History -- 1933-1945. 4. Antisemitism -- Germany -- History -- 20th century. 5. Germany -- History -- 1933-1945.

ISBN 0060570830

Drawing on eyewitness testimonies and period accounts of the event, a distinguished British historian offers a compelling account of Kristallnacht, the November 1938 rampage by Nazi storm troopers and Hitler Youth through Jewish neighborhoods throughout Germany, a nationwide destruction that ignited the devastation of the Holocaust.

The **Second** World War : a complete history / Martin Gilbert. H. Holt, 1991. xviii, 846 p., [64] p. of plates : **940.53**

1. World War II. 2. Military history 3. Europe -- History -- 20th century.

ISBN 0805017887

LC 91028255

"First owl book revised edition"--T.p. verso.

"An owl book"--P. [4] of cover.

"The author begins this study with the invasion of Poland. Gilbert's flowing narrative is spiced with anecdotal details culled from diaries, memoirs and official documents. He is especially skillful at interweaving summaries of military strategy with vignettes of civilian suffering--the genocide of the Jews is never far from view." Newsweek

Goldhagen, Daniel Jonah

Hitler's willing executioners : ordinary Germans and the Holocaust / Daniel Jonah Goldhagen. Vintage Books, 1997, c1996. x, 634 p. : **940.53**

1. Holocaust (1933-1945) -- Causes. 2. Antisemitism -- Germany. 3. War criminals -- Germany -- Psychology 4. Nazism -- Moral and ethical aspects.

ISBN 0679772685

LC BL 99782641

Originally published: New York : Knopf, 1996.

National Book Critics Circle Award for Nonfiction finalist, 1996.

A revisionist study of Nazi Germany and the Holocaust reveals why ordinary Germans from all walks of life participated willingly in the extermination of the Jews

"The author endeavors to show that the common apologia for the Germans--that Hitler brainwashed them--is nonsense and that most Germans gave their active assent to genocide. An ordinary German commander, for example, might feel himself bound by a strict code of conduct yet not be at all averse to murdering Jews. The book ends with a detailed notes section and an appendix that explains the correct methodology for studying the Nazi period." Library Journal.

Groom, Winston, 1944-2020

★**1942** : the year that tried men's souls / Winston Groom. Atlantic Monthly Press, 2005. xiv, 459 p. : **940.53**

1. World War II. 2. Military strategy.

ISBN 0871138891

LC 2004062779

An account of perseverance, innovation, tactics, tragedy, and triumphs vividly recreates the story of America's first year in World War II and portrays 1942 as the defining act in the great drama of the war.

"In this military history of one year during World War II, the author delivers the traditional worshipful portrait of General MacArthur while admitting he made several key blunders that doomed the Philippines in the year's early months. He adds that brains and luck win more battles than courage, providing a perfect illustration in Midway, fought in June 1942. Groom has written a page-turner; readers needing an introduction will love it." Publishers Weekly.

Gross, Jan Tomasz

Neighbors : the destruction of the Jewish community in Jedwabne, Poland / Jan T. Gross. Princeton University Press, c2001. x, 261 p. : **940.53**

1. Jews, Polish 2. Jews -- Persecutions -- Poland. 3. Holocaust (1933-1945) -- Poland. 4. Interethnic relations. 5. Jedwabne, Poland

6. Poland
ISBN 9780691086675

LC 2003286412

National Book Award for Nonfiction finalist, 2001

National Book Critics Circle Award for Nonfiction finalist, 2001.

Documents the brutal 1941 massacre of 1,600 Jewish men, women, and children by their own neighbors in the Polish town of Jedwabne, offering additional examinations of the period's Jewish-Polish relations, the Holocaust, and human responses to occupation and totalitarianism.

Guttenplan, D. D.

The **Holocaust** on trial / D.D. Guttenplan. Norton, c2001. xiv, 328 p. : **940.53**

1. Irving, David, 1938- Trials, litigation, etc. 2. Lipstadt, Deborah E., 1947- Trials, litigation, etc. 3. Trials (Libel) -- London, England 4. Holocaust Revisionism -- Great Britain. 5. Holocaust (1933-1945) -- Historiography.
ISBN 0393020444

LC 2001030370

Based on exclusive access to many of the participants, the inside story of the trial that made headlines around the world by questioning the existence of the Nazi death camps during World War II urges readers to question what we can and do know about history.

"The author chronicles the libel trial in Britain brought by historian David Irving. Irving, widely viewed as an apologist for Hitler, sued American scholar Deborah Lipstadt, whose Denying the Holocaust (1993) had labeled Irving as a right-wing extremist. Interspersing essayistic diversions, the author presents a thoughtful work as well as a courtroom thriller." Booklist.

Hamilton, Nigel

Commander in chief : FDR's battle with Churchill, 1943 / Nigel Hamilton. Boston, 2016. 480 p. **940.53**

1. Churchill, Winston, 1874-1965. 2. Roosevelt, Franklin D. (Franklin Delano), 1882-1945. 3. World War II -- United States. 4. Command of troops -- United States. 5. Great Britain -- Foreign relations United States. 6. United States -- Foreign relations Great Britain.
ISBN 9780544279117

LC 2015037253

Describes the yearlong battle between Roosevelt and Churchill during World War II to decide whether the Allies should carry out the planned invasion of Normandy, or take on disastrous fighting in Italy.

"This is an outstanding contribution to understanding the wartime alliance and Roosevelt's role in it." Booklist.

Hackett, David A.

The **Buchenwald** report / translated, edited, and with an introduction by David A. Hackett ; foreword by Frederick A. Praeger. Westview Press, c1995. xviii, 397 p. : **940.53**

1. Buchenwald (Concentration camp) -- History 2. Holocaust, Jewish (1939-1945) -- Germany
ISBN 9780813317779

LC 94039714

Original report was produced by the Intelligence Team of the Psychological Warfare Division of the Supreme Headquarters of the Allied Forces.

Includes interviews with prisoners of the Nazi concentration camp describing their mistreatment and torture and details of the camp's history, function, and how it was run.

War and peace : FDR's final odyssey, D-Day to Yalta, 1943-1945 / Nigel Hamilton. Houghton Mifflin Harcourt, [2019] 528 p. **940.53**

1. Roosevelt, Franklin D. (Franklin Delano), 1882-1945. 2. World War II -- Diplomatic history. 3. World War II -- United States. 4. Military strategy 5. Command of troops -- United States. 6. Great Britain -- Foreign relations United States. 7. United States -- Foreign relations Great Britain.
ISBN 9780544876804

LC 2018043601

Draws from previously unpublished documents and interviews to recount how the terminally-ill president championed the successful D-Day landings but did not live long enough to see victory in World War II.

"Drawing from primary documents that President Franklin D. Roosevelt planned to use to write his memoirs, as well as diaries from people close to the major figures involved in planning D-Day and the end of World War II, Hamilton presents the final installment of his bibliographic trilogy, after The Mantle of Command and Commander in Chief, tracing an engaging and eye-opening series of events from the Tehran Summit through the Yalta Conference and finally Roosevelt's untimely death in 1945." Library Journal.

Hayes, Peter, 1946 September 7-

Why? : explaining the Holocaust / Peter Hayes. W.W. Norton & Company, 2017. 400 p. **940.53**

1. Holocaust (1933-1945) -- Causes. 2. Antisemitism -- Germany -- History -- 20th century. 3. Jews -- Persecutions -- Europe -- History -- 20th century. 4. Religious persecution 5. Germany -- History -- 1933-1945. 6. Germany -- Interethnic relations
ISBN 9780393254365

LC 2016031588

A timely exploration of the most commonly asked questions about the Holocaust challenges common misconceptions and discusses how no single theory fully explains the tragedy, drawing on a wealth of scholarly research and experience to offer new insights to future generations.

Helm, Sarah

★**Ravensbruck** : life and death in Hitler's concentration camp for women / Sarah Helm. Nan A. Talese/Doubleday, [2014] 656 p. **940.53**

1. Ravensbruck (Concentration camp) 2. World War II 3. Women concentration camp inmates 4. Concentration camps
ISBN 9780385520591

LC 2014014974

Includes index.

"This book deserves significant attention, both for Helm's notable interviews of aging witnesses and as a beautifully written history of events that offers additional insight into Nazism and those caught in its path." Publishers Weekly.

Henderson, Bruce B., 1946-

Rescue at Los Baños : the most daring prison camp raid of World War II / Bruce Henderson. William Morrow, 2015 352 p. **940.53**

1. Los Banos Internment Camp 2. World War II 3. Military campaigns 4. Prisoners of war. 5. Military history 6. Philippines
ISBN 9780062325068

LC 2015007141

Draws on personal interviews, diaries, correspondences, memoirs and archival research to document the bold 1945 World War II prison camp raid at Los Baños in The Philippines that freed more than 2,000 brutalized men, women and children.

"This narrative of one event depicting the horrors of war and its resolution should broaden the perspective of general readers of 20th-century military history. Although a monument, a ceremony, and a joint U.S.

congressional resolution honored this liberation on its 60th anniversary, the event was underpublicized at the time since Joe Rosenthal's iconic photograph of the raising of the American flag on Iwo Jima taken the same day received more media coverage." Library Journal.

Herman, Arthur, 1956-

Freedom's forge : how American business built the arsenal of democracy that won World War II / Arthur Herman. Random House, c2012. 400 p. **940.53**

1. World War II -- Economic aspects -- United States 2. Industrial mobilization -- United States -- History -- 20th century. 3. Economic policy -- 1933-1945 4. Industrial management -- United States -- History -- 20th century. 5. United States -- Economic conditions -- 1933-1945
ISBN 9781400069644

LC 2011040661

Herman pens this look at how two businessmen turned the U.S. into a military powerhouse during World War II. In 1940, FDR asked General Motors CEO William Knudsen to oversee the production of guns, tanks, and planes needed for the war. Meanwhile, industrialist Henry J. Kaiser presided over the building of "Liberty ships"--vessels that came to symbolize America's great wartime output.

Hett, Benjamin Carter

The **Nazi** menace : Hitler, Churchill, Roosevelt, Stalin, and the road to war / Benjamin Carter Hett. Henry Holt and Company, 2020. 416 p. **940.53**

1. Hitler, Adolf, 1889-1945. 2. Churchill, Winston, 1874-1965. 3. Roosevelt, Franklin D. (Franklin Delano), 1882-1945. 4. Stalin, Joseph, 1879-1953 5. World War II -- Diplomatic history 6. Anti-Nazi movement 7. Nazism 8. World War II. 9. Germany -- Politics and government -- 1933-1945.
ISBN 9781250205230

LC 2020002916

The author of The Death of Democracy presents a narrative account of the years leading up to World War II, examining the racial conflicts and challenges to democracy that compromised Europe's early response to growing Nazi extremism.

"An excellent read for anyone who wants a deeper understanding of the thinking behind World War II." Kirkus

Hoffman, Eva, 1945-

After such knowledge : memory, history, and the legacy of the Holocaust / Eva Hoffman. Public Affairs, 2004. xv, 301 p. **940.53**

1. Children of Holocaust survivors. 2. Holocaust survivors. 3. Memory. 4. Holocaust (1933-1945) -- Historiography. 5. Essays.
ISBN 1586480464

LC 2003066443

Contains 7 essays.

"The author focuses on the consciousness and experience of the Holocaust's second generation--the children of survivors. The book considers such diverse concepts as how the trauma of the Holocaust is constructed, the role of emigration and national identity in shaping the second generation's narratives of their lives. Hoffman writes with a subdued but vibrant passion." Publishers Weekly.

Holden, Wendy, 1961-

Born survivors : three young mothers and their extraordinary story of courage, defiance, and hope / Wendy Holden. HarperCollins 2015 320 p. **940.53**

1. Holocaust survivors 2. Jewish women 3. Concentration camps 4. Pregnant women.
ISBN 9780062370259

LC bl2015016220

In a true account, three pregnant women meet in Auschwitz where they, managing to conceal their pregnancies from the infamous Nazi doctor Josef Mengele, fight for their survival as well as the survival of their newborns as they embark on a treacherous journey to freedom.

"An engrossing, intense, and highly descriptive narrative chronicling the ghastly conditions three pregnant women suffered through at the hands of the Nazis." Kirkus.

Horwitz, Gordon J.

Ghettostadt : Lodz and the making of a Nazi city / Gordon J. Horwitz. The Belknap Press of Harvard University Press, 2008. 416 p. **940.53**

1. Jews -- Persecutions -- Lodz, Poland 2. Ghettoes, Jewish -- Lodz, Poland. 3. Holocaust (1933-1945) -- Lodz, Poland. 4. Nazism -- Lodz, Poland -- History 5. Lodz, Poland -- Ethnic relations. 6. Lodz, Poland -- History -- 20th century
ISBN 9780674027992

LC 2007050934

An examination of the Jewish ghetto's place in the Nazi worldview deftly maneuvers between the perspectives and actions of Lodz's Jewish community, the Germans who oversaw and administered the ghetto's affairs, and the ordinary inhabitants of the once Polish city.

Jones, Michael K.

After Hitler : the last ten days of World War II in Europe / Michael Jones. NAL Caliber, 2015. 400 p. **940.53**

1. World politics 2. Diplomacy -- History 3. World War II -- Diplomatic history. 4. World War II -- Peace.
ISBN 9780451477019

LC 2015018149

Originally published: London : John Murray, 2015.

"Unlike connoisseurs of military history, casual readers may not be concerned with martial unit designations and some of the gritty details of battle formation, but the exploits of the men and women they represented are engrossing, sometimes even heartbreaking. A skillful historian demonstrates how courage and hope characterized the last act of the great campaign to bring peace to Europe 70 years ago." Kirkus.

Klein, Maury, 1939-

A **call** to arms : mobilizing America for World War II / Maury Klein. Bloomsbury Press, 2013. 560 p. **940.53**

1. Industrial mobilization -- United States -- History -- 20th century. 2. World War II -- Economic aspects -- United States. 3. Armed forces. 4. Military history. 5. United States -- Armed Forces -- Mobilization -- History -- 20th century.
ISBN 9781596916074

LC 2012039497

"The colossal scale of World War II required a mobilization effort greater than anything attempted in all of the world's history. The United States had to fight a war across two oceans and three continents--and to do so it had to build and equip a military that was all but nonexistent before the war began. Never in the nation's history did it have to create, outfit, transport, and supply huge armies, navies, and air forces on so many distant and disparate fronts.The Axis powers might have fielded better trained soldiers, better weapons, better tanks and aircraft. But they could not match American productivity. America buried its enemies in aircraft, ships, tanks, and guns; in this sense, American industry, and American workers, won World War II. The scale of effort was titanic, and the result historic. Not only did it determine the outcome of the war, but it transformed the American economy and society. Maury Klein's A

Call to Arms is the definitive narrative history of this epic struggle, told by one of America's greatest historians of business and economics, and renders the transformation of America with a depth and vividness never available before".-- Provided by publisher.

Klingaman, William K.

The **darkest** year : the American home front 1941-1942 / William K. Klingaman. St. Martin's Press, 2019 320 p. **940.53**

1. World War II -- United States 2. War and society 3. Social history 4. War -- Psychological aspects 5. United States -- History -- 1933-1945

ISBN 9781250133175

LC 2018045704

A psychological history of the American home front at the peak of World War II argues that class and partisan divides of the mid-20th century as well as Roosevelt administration blunders had rendered the United States vulnerable to losing the war.

"This thoroughly researched and accessible text will prove elucidating to anyone curious about social history, World War II, or the rhetoric of a country in crisis." Library Journal.

Langer, Lawrence L.,

Art from the ashes : a Holocaust anthology / edited by Lawrence L. Langer. Oxford University Press, 1995. 689 p. : **940.53**

1. Holocaust (1933-1945) 2. Holocaust (1933-1945) -- Literary collections.

ISBN 0195075595

LC 94011446

Includes index.

A collection of art, drama, poetry, and prose about the Holocaust offers a somber portrait of its human realities and includes the works of unknown writers as well as those of Elie Wiesel, Paul Celan, and Joshua Sobol.

Levi, Primo,

The **drowned** and the saved / Primo Levi ; translated from the Italian by Raymond Rosenthal. Vintage International, 1989, c1988. 203 p. ; **940.53**

1. Levi, Primo, 2. Auschwitz (Concentration camp) 3. Holocaust (1933-1945) 4. Authors, Italian -- 20th century.

ISBN 067972186X

LC 88040375

Translation of: I Sommersi e i salvati.

Reprint. Originally published: New York : Summit Books, 1988.

A meditation on the meaning of the Nazi exterminations after the passing of forty years reveals how memories of the Holocaust have been filtered and rearranged by both the oppressor and the victims.

"If the unending tragedy of the Holocaust can ever be said to make sense, then it does so in these pages." The New Yorker.

Lewy, Guenter, 1923-

★**Perpetrators** : the world of the Holocaust killers / Guenter Lewy. Oxford University Press, 2017 ix, 195 p. : **940.53**

1. Holocaust (1933-1945) 2. Jews -- Persecutions -- Germany 3. War crimes -- History -- 20th century 4. Nazism -- Moral and ethical aspects 5. Germany -- History -- 20th century

ISBN 9780190661137

LC 2016053104

Explores the dynamics of participation in large-scale atrocities, offering a thought-provoking and timely reflection on individual responsibility for collective crimes.

Lipstadt, Deborah E., 1947-

Denying the Holocaust : the growing assault on truth and memory / Deborah E. Lipstadt. Free Press, 1993. ix, 278 p. ; **940.53**

1. Holocaust Revisionism. 2. Antisemitism -- United States -- History -- 20th century. 3. Holocaust (1933-1945) -- Historiography.

ISBN 9780029192351

LC 93009952

"Lipstadt has written a disturbing book that deserves a wide readership." Library Journal.

★**History** on trial : my day in court with David Irving / Deborah E. Lipstadt. Ecco, c2005. xxi, 346 p. : **940.53**

1. Irving, David, 1938- Trials, litigation, etc. 2. Lipstadt, Deborah E., 1947- Trials, litigation, etc. 3. Penguin (Firm) Trials, litigation, etc. 4. Trials (Libel) -- London, England 5. Holocaust (1933-1945) -- Historiography. 6. Holocaust Revisionism.

ISBN 9780060593766

LC 2004057533

National Jewish Book Award, 2005.

Chronicles the author's legal battle with David Irving, a prolific supporter of Holocaust denial, and describes how the author and a team of experts defended against Irving's libel suit while exposing his distortions of history.

"No one who cares about historical truth, freedom of speech or the Holocaust will avoid a sense of triumph from Gray's decision--or a sense of dismay that British libel laws allowed such intimidation by Irving of a historian and a publisher in the first place." Publishers Weekly.

Lower, Wendy

Hitler's furies : German women in the Nazi killing fields / Wendy Lower. Houghton Mifflin Harcourt, 2013 288 p. **940.53**

1. World War II -- Women. 2. Nazism and women. 3. Women -- Germany 4. Holocaust (1933-1945) 5. Europe

ISBN 9780547863382

LC 2013026081

National Book Award for Nonfiction finalist, 2013

A revelatory history of the role of German women in the Holocaust reveals their lesser-known roles as plunderers, witnesses and actual executioners on the Eastern front, describing how period nurses, teachers, secretaries and wives responded to what they believed to be Nazi opportunities only to perform brutal duties.

"Lower, a consultant for the Holocaust Memorial Museum in Washington, D.C., sheds some much-needed light on an aspect of WWII history that has remained in the shadows for decades. The consensus in Holocaust and genocide studies, the author writes, is that the systems that make mass murder possible would not function without the broad participation of society, and yet nearly all histories of the Holocaust leave out half of those who populated that society, as if women's history happens somewhere else. Based on two decades of research and interviews, the book looks at the role of women in Nazi Germany, in particular women who participated in the Nazi extermination of the Jews...Lower writes about horribly violent female concentration-camp guards; of young girls trained in the use of firearms; of brutality that would rival anything perpetrated by their male counterparts. Surprising and deeply unsettling, the book is a welcome addition to the literature on the Holocaust." Booklist.

Lukacs, John, 1924-

Five days in London, May 1940 / John Lukacs. Yale University Press, c1999. xvi, 236 p. : **940.53**

1. Halifax, Edward Frederick Lindley Wood, Earl of, 1881-1959.

2. Churchill, Winston, 1874-1965 Military leadership 3. World War II -- Diplomatic history. 4. World War II -- Great Britain. 5. Great Britain -- Politics and government -- 1936-1945. 6. Great Britain -- History, Military -- 20th century

ISBN 0300080301

LC 99027583

"This work focuses on the chaotic few days during which, according to the author, Hitler came closest to winning the war. Lukacs concentrates on the struggle within the British War Cabinet, which pitted the Prime Minister, Winston Churchill, against the Foreign Secretary, Lord Halifax, a Tory idol and a friend of the King. The point of contention was Halifax's belief that England should attempt to negotiate a general European settlement with Hitler. Churchill's stubborn refusal won out. The author's equally stubborn digging uncovered a stunning amount of defeatism and intrigue against Churchill by contemporary statesmen." The New Yorker.

Manbo, Bill T., 1908-1992

★**Colors** of confinement : rare Kodachrome photographs of Japanese American incarceration in World War II / edited by Eric L. Muller ; with photographs by Bill Manbo. University of North Carolina Press ; c2012. xi, 122 p. : **940.53**

1. Manbo, Bill T., 1908-1992. 2. Heart Mountain Relocation Center (Wyo.) Pictorial works. 3. Japanese Americans -- Evacuation and relocation, 1942-1945 4. World War II -- Concentration camps -- Wyoming

ISBN 0807835730

LC 2011052817

Presents a collection of rare photographs depicting the Japanese camps in the Midwest to which Japanese Americans were confined during World War II.

Mazower, Mark

Hitler's empire : how the Nazis ruled Europe / Mark Mazower. Penguin Press, 2008. 768 p. **940.53**

1. World War II -- Germany. 2. Nazis. 3. Political leadership. 4. Nazism. 5. Germany -- History -- 1933-1945. 6. Europe -- History -- 1918-1945.

ISBN 9781594201882

LC 2008026997

Profiles the Reich's pre-World War II plans for transforming Eastern Europe, describing the considerable resources that were amassed for the endeavor while explaining how Nazi brutality and short-sightedness ultimately cost Germany its victories.

McConahay, Mary Jo

The **tango** war : the struggle for the hearts, minds and riches of Latin America during World War II / Mary Jo McConahay. St. Martin's Press, 2018. 320 p. **940.53**

1. World War II 2. International relations 3. Political intrigue 4. War and society 5. Latin America -- History

ISBN 9781250091239

LC 2018011523

Traces the lesser-known story of the fight for the allegiance of Latin America during World War II, tracing the region's essential role in supplying important materials, providing military support and negotiating prisoner exchanges.

McDougall, Christopher, 1962-

Natural born heroes : how a daring band of misfits mastered the lost secrets of strength and endurance / Christopher McDougall. Alfred A. Knopf, 2015 368 p. **940.53**

1. Pheidippides, fl. 490 B.C. 2. Marathon, Battle of, Greece, 490 B.C. 3. Marathon running -- History. 4. Endurance sports 5. Running

ISBN 9780307594969

LC 2014047459

The author of the best-selling Born to Run describes his investigation into ancestral training techniques that have enabled Mediterranean athletes to achieve extraordinary levels of strength and fitness.

Moorehead, Caroline

A **house** in the mountains : the women who liberated Italy from fascism / Caroline Moorehead. HarperCollins, 2020, c2019. 432 p. **940.53**

1. Gobetti, Ada, 1902-1968 2. Malan, Frida 3. Pons, Silvia, 1919-1958 4. Guidetti Serra, Biana 5. World War II 6. World War II -- Underground movements 7. Resistance to military occupation 8. Anti-Nazi movement 9. Italy -- History -- German occupation, 1943-1945. 10. Turin, Italy

ISBN 9780062686350

LC bl2019037375

Drawing on previously untranslated sources, a prize-winning historian tells the little-known story of the women of the Italian-partisan movement and their fight for freedom against fascism in all its forms, while Europe collapsed in ruins around them.

A **train** in winter : an extraordinary story of women, friendship, and resistance in occupied France / Caroline Moorehead. Harpercollins, 2011. 352 p. **940.53**

1. Women and war. 2. Concentration camps. 3. French Resistance (World War II) 4. World War II 5. France -- History -- German occupation, 1940-1945.

ISBN 9780061650703

LC bl2011033120

In January 1943, the Gestapo hunted down 230 women of the French Resistance and sent them to Auschwitz. This is their story, told in full for the first time--a searing and unforgettable chronicle of terror, courage, defiance, survival, and the power of friendship to transcend evil that is an essential addition to the history of World War II.

Moorhouse, Roger

The **Devils'** alliance : Hitler's pact with Stalin, 1939-1941 / Roger Moorhouse. Basic Books, 2014. 432 p. **940.53**

1. Nazi-Soviet Pact, 1939. 2. World War II -- Diplomatic history. 3. Treaties. 4. Germany -- Foreign relations Soviet Union. 5. Soviet Union -- Foreign relations Germany

ISBN 9780465030750

LC 2012278241

In The Devils' Alliance, acclaimed historian Roger Moorhouse explores the causes and implications of the Nazi-Soviet Pact, an unholy covenant whose creation and dissolution were crucial turning points in World War II. Forged by the German foreign minister, Joachim von Ribbentrop, and his Soviet counterpart, Vyacheslav Molotov, the nonaggression treaty briefly united the two powers in a brutally efficient collaboration. Together, the Germans and Soviets quickly conquered and divided central and eastern Europe--Poland, the Baltic States, Finland, and Bessarabia--and the human cost was staggering: during the two years of the pact hundreds of thousands of people in central and eastern Europe caught between Hitler and Stalin were expropriated, deported, or killed. Fortunately for the Allies, the partnership ultimately soured, resulting in the surprise June 1941 German invasion of the Soviet Union. Ironically, however, the powers' exchange of materiel, blueprints, and technological expertise during the period of the Pact made possible a far more bloody and protracted war than would have otherwise been conceivable.

"Moorhouse's accessible prose and clear explication make this a great story for history readers, and his extensive research and documentation help create a critical text for academics focusing on World War II, German history, and Soviet history." Library Journal.

Mortimer, Gavin

The **longest** night : the bombing of London on May 10, 1941 / Gavin Mortimer. Berkley Caliber, 2005. x, 356 p. : **940.53**

1. World War II -- Aerial operations, German. 2. Bombing. 3. Bombing victims. 4. London, England -- History -- Bombardment, 1940-1945 5. Europe -- History, Military -- 20th century

ISBN 0425205576

LC 2005045281

Includes index.

Numerous eyewitness accounts, survivor testimony, and previously classified documents inform a close-up look at a devastating bombing raid by the Luftwaffe on London on May 10, 1941, revealing the near catastrophoic results of the raid in terms of the ultimate fate of the British during World War II.

"This account is given special power and poignancy by using the recollections of surviving men and women who endured that terrible night. An outstanding addition to World War II collections." Booklist.

Muller, Melissa, 1967-

Lost lives, lost art : Jewish collectors, Nazi art theft, and the quest for justice / Melissa Muller, Monika Tatzkow ; with contributions from Thomas Blubacher and Gunnar Schnabel : foreword by Ronald S. Lauder. Vendome Press, 2010. 248 p. : **940.53**

1. Art thefts 2. Art -- Collectors and collecting 3. Intellectual life -- 20th century. 4. World War II -- Confiscations and contributions -- Europe. 5. Europe -- History -- 20th century.

ISBN 9780865652637

LC 2010015337

Relates the tragic stories of fifteen Jewish art collectors whose art and lives were stolen by the Nazis, as well as the drama of their heirs' convoluted and lengthy legal battles to recover their inheritance.

"The authors cover 15 Jewish/possibly Jewish families with vast art collections looted by the Nazis. Jewish collectors either had to sell their treasures for a pittance or had them seized. The Bloch-Bauer family's story is famous, but the unknown histories of other prominent families are compellingly told here, and there is a final historical-legal commentary by expert Gunnar Schnabel on Nazi-looted art and the German laws that perpetuated these crimes. Richly illustrated with excellent art reproductions and family photographs." Library Journal.

Nagorski, Andrew

The **Nazi** hunters / Andrew Nagorski. Simon & Schuster, 2016. 400 p. **940.53**

1. Nazi hunters -- History. 2. World War II 3. Atrocities. 4. War criminals 5. Germany -- History -- 20th century

ISBN 9781476771861

LC 2015027334

Describes the small group of men and women who sought out former Nazis all over the world after the Nuremberg trials, refusing to let their crimes be forgotten or allowing them to quietly live inconspicuous, normal lives.

"A detailed look at the grim work of tracking Nazis over the decades since World War II." Kirkus.

Nasaw, David

★The **last** million : Europe's displaced persons from World War to Cold War / David Nasaw. Penguin Press, 2020. 651 p. **940.53**

1. United Nations Relief and Rehabilitation Administration. 2. International Refugee Organization. 3. World War II -- Refugees -- Europe. 4. Concentration camp survivors, 5. Prisoners of war 6. Political prisoners 7. Europe -- Immigration and emigration 8. United States -- Immigration and emigration

ISBN 9781594206733

LC 2020016888

Documents the experiences and fates of the one million concentration camp survivors, POWs, slave laborers and political prisoners left in Germany after World War II who spent years as displaced refugees in unsupported, segregated, and poorly converted buildings while the world's nations refused shelter.

"A thought-provoking, highly recommended perspective on a complex and largely overlooked people and period of modern history." Library Journal

Neiberg, Michael S.

Potsdam : the end of World War II and the remaking of Europe / Michael Neiberg. Basic Books, 2015 320 p. **940.53**

1. Potsdam Conference, 1945 2. World War II -- Peace 3. International relations 4. World politics 5. Military history

ISBN 9780465075256

LC 2015007545

"A must-have account for everyone from students of world history at the undergraduate and graduate levels to knowledgeable recreational readers." Library Journal.

O'Reilly, Bill

Killing the SS : the hunt for the worst war criminals in history / Bill O'Reilly and Martin Dugard. Henry Holt and Company, [2018] 307 pages : **940.53**

1. S. S. 2. Nazis 3. War criminals 4. War crime trials 5. Nazi hunters

ISBN 9781250165541

LC 2018017242

Traces the daring of Nazi hunters after World War II, revealing the contributions of legal experts, intelligence agents and concentration-camp survivors in tracking down and capturing high-profile Nazis. By the #1 New York Times best-selling authors of Killing the Rising Sun.

Ohler, Norman

★The **Bohemians** : the lovers who led Germany's resistance against the Nazis / Norman Ohler ; translated from the German by Tim Mohr and Marshall Yarbrough. Houghton Mifflin Harcourt, 2020, c2019. 320 p. **940.53**

1. Schulze-Boysen, Harro, 1909-1942. 2. Schulze-Boysen, Libertas, 1913-1942. 3. Die Rote Kapelle 4. Anti-Nazi movement -- Germany 5. World War II -- Underground movements -- Germany 6. Military intelligence -- Soviet Union 7. Spies -- History -- 20th century 8. Germany -- History -- 1933-1945.

ISBN 9781328566300

LC 2019057794

Originally published: Koin : Kiepenheuer & Witsch, 2019.

The author draws on unpublished diaries, letters and Gestapo files to trace the remarkable story of idealistic lovers Harro Schulze-Boysen and Libertas Haas-Heye, the leaders of the anti-Nazi resistance in 1930s Berlin's bohemian underworld.

"This deeply researched and stylishly written account unearths an appealing yet overlooked chapter in WWII history. Espionage enthusiasts will be riveted." Publishers Weekly

Olson, Lynne

Last Hope Island : Britain, occupied Europe, and the brotherhood that helped turn the tide of war / Lynne Olson. Random House, [2016] 576 p. **940.53**

1. Heads of state 2. Political refugees 3. World War II -- Diplomatic history 4. Resistance to government 5. Europe -- Politics and government -- 1918-1945 6. Great Britain -- Politics and government -- 1936-1945

ISBN 9780812997354

LC 2016019187

Chronicles how Britain became an island of refuge for Europeans who escaped the Nazi juggernaut, exploring how royals, soldiers, government leaders, and resistance fighters found safety and established bases of operations to reclaim their homelands.

"The many individuals are finely drawn, major developments... are well covered, and the book provides an unusual and very insightful angle on the war." Booklist.

Those angry days : Roosevelt, Lindbergh, and America's fight over World War II, 1939-1941 / Lynne Olson. Random House, c2013. 608 p. **940.53**

1. Roosevelt, Franklin D. (Franklin Delano), 1882-1945 Political and social views. 2. Lindbergh, Charles A. (Charles Augustus), 1902-1974 Political and social views. 3. World War II -- Diplomatic history 4. Isolationism -- United States -- History -- 20th century 5. Intervention (International law) -- History -- 20th century 6. Political culture -- United States -- History -- 20th century 7. United States -- Politics and government -- 1933-1945 8. United States -- Foreign relations -- 1933-1945 9. United States -- Military policy

ISBN 9781400069743

LC 2012025381

From the acclaimed author of Citizens of London comes the definitive account of the debate over American intervention in World War II -- a bitter, sometimes violent clash of personalities and ideas that divided the nation and ultimately determined the fate of the free world.

Orbach, Danny

The **plots** against Hitler / Danny Orbach. Houghton Mifflin Harcourt, 2016 432 p. **940.53**

1. Hitler, Adolf, 1889-1945 Attempted assassination. 2. Anti-Nazi movement. 3. Assassination plots. 4. Opposition (Political science). 5. Assassins. 6. Germany -- Politics and government -- 1933-1945.

ISBN 9780544714434

LC 2015043037

A deeply researched historical account of the anti-Nazi underground in Germany and its numerous efforts to assassinate Hitler explores the activities of unlikely conspirators who supported local efforts to dismantle Nazism.

"Likely to become the definitive general history of the subject and the starting place for all future research, Orbach's work is a fascinating story of courage and an excellent study of the struggle of individuals to act morally and honorably." Publishers Weekly.

Overy, Richard, 1947-

The **New** York Times complete World War 2 : all the coverage from the battlefields and the home front / Richard Overy. Black Dog & Leventhal Pub., 2013. 612 p. **940.53**

1. New York Times. 2. World War II 3. Journalism 4. War in the news media. 5. War propaganda.

ISBN 9781579129446

LC 2015300116

A respected historian guides readers through hundreds of the most riveting World War II Era New York Times articles, putting every major battle into historical context, in a book that includes hundreds of maps and photos, as well as a DVD that gives access to even more day-by-day coverage.

"This is a book to lose yourself in, to witness the war transmuted into print for the masses of readers living through it and anxious to follow its twists and turns." Library Journal.

Why the allies won / Richard Overy. W.W. Norton, c1995. xiv, 396 p., 16 p. of plates : **940.53**

1. World War II 2. Strategy.

ISBN 039331619X

LC 95052444

Explains how the Allies regained military superiority after 1942, and discusses important campaigns, naval battles, industrial strength, fighting ability, leadership, and moral issues.

"Eschewing the belief that the Allies won solely because of their prodigious production of weapons and equipment, Mr. Overy points out that in the early stages of the war, before the Allies were fully mobilized, the Axis countries held the production advantage, yet failed to achieve victory because Germany's management of supply logistics was far inferior to that of the Allies--frequently as a result of Hitler's wrongheaded interference. . . . Assiduously researched and concisely written, this is a highly perceptive study. " New York Times Book Review.

Pelt, R. J. van (Robert Jan), 1955-

Auschwitz : not long ago. not far away / edited by Robert Jan van Pelt, with Luis Ferreiro and Miriam Greenbaum. Abbeville Press Publishers, 2019 240 p. **940.53**

1. Auschwitz (Concentration camp) Exhibitions Catalogs.

ISBN 9780789213310

LC 2019014483

This catalogue of the first-ever traveling exhibition about the Auschwitz concentration camp tells the stories behind the more than 280 objects and images, providing an encompassing history of Auschwitz, which has become a powerful site of remembrance.

Plokhy, Serhii, 1957-

Yalta : the price of peace / S.M. Plokhy. Viking, 2010. 448 p. **940.53**

1. Yalta Conference, 1945. 2. World War II -- Diplomatic history. 3. World politics -- 1945-1990 4. Military history. 5. Peace.

ISBN 9780670021413

LC 2009026833

A history of the eight-day peace conference in 1945 between FDR, Churchill, and Stalin offers insight into the strained political forces that influenced peace talks, challenging popular opinions about Yalta's role in triggering the Cold War.

"Plokhy has produced a colorful and gripping portrait of the three aging leaders at their historic encounter." Wall Street Journal.

Preston, Diana, 1952-

Eight days at Yalta : how Churchill, Roosevelt and Stalin shaped the post-war world / Diana Preston. Atlantic Monthly Press, 2020. 416 p. **940.53**

1. Churchill, Winston, 1874-1965 2. Roosevelt, Franklin D. (Franklin Delano), 1882-1945 3. Stalin, Joseph, 1879-1953 4. Yalta Conference, 1945. 5. World War II -- Diplomatic history. 6. World politics -- 1945-1990 7. Military history. 8. World War II -- Peace. 9. Europe -- Foreign relations United States. 10. United States --

Foreign relations Europe.
ISBN 9780802147653
LC 2019045231

Presents a 75th-anniversary account of the historic conference, discussing its role in strategizing the end of World War II, the restructuring of Germany and the constitution of a nascent United Nations.

"Colorful personalities, piquant details, and a diverse array of perspectives make this a satisfying introduction to the subject." Publishers Weekly

Prose, Francine, 1947-

Anne Frank : the book, the life, the afterlife / Francine Prose. HarperCollins, 2009. 288 p. **940.53**

1. Frank, Anne, 1929-1945. 2. Holocaust (1933-1945) -- Amsterdam, Netherlands 3. Creative writing. 4. Diary writing. 5. Writing.
ISBN 9780061430794
LC 2009017703

Francine Prose argues that the diary of Anne Frank is as much a deliberate work of art as it is an historical record, noting its literary merits and thoroughly investigating the diary's unique afterlife as one of the world's most read, and banned, books.

"In this definitive, deeply moving inquiry into the life of the young, imperiled artist, and masterful literary exegesis of The Diary of a Young Girl, Prose tells the crushing story of the Frank family, performs a revelatory analysis of Anne's exacting revision of her coming-of-age memoir, and assesses her father's editorial decisions as he edited his murdered daughter's manuscript for publication. . . . Extraordinary testimony to the power of literature and compassion." Booklist.

Rees, Laurence, 1957-

Auschwitz : a new history / Laurence Rees. Public Affairs, 2005. xxii, 327 p. **940.53**

1. Eichmann, Adolf, 1906-1962. 2. Auschwitz (Concentration camp) 3. Concentration camps -- Poland. 4. Nazis -- Germany. 5. Holocaust (1933-1945) -- Poland. 6. Holocaust survivors -- Interviews. 7. Poland -- History -- 1918-1945.
ISBN 158648303X
LC 2004043196

"For this history of the concentration camp, the author interviewed 100 former Nazi perpetrators and survivors from the camp and drew on hundreds of interviews conducted for his previous research on the Third Reich, many with former members of the Nazi Party. This is a significant contribution to our understanding of the intricacies of Nazi racial and ethnic policy that resulted in this ultimate abomination." Booklist.

★The **Holocaust** : a new history / Laurence Rees. Public Affairs, 2017 xv, 509 p. **940.53**

1. Holocaust (1933-1945) 2. Jews -- Persecutions 3. Persecution by Nazis 4. Political persecution
ISBN 9781610398442
LC 2017933355

Includes index.

A historian who has an unrivaled archive of firsthand testimony from both the perpetrators and victims of the Holocaust presents almost all of this evidence for the first time in an authoritative and accessible account of the greatest crime against humanity.

"Historian Rees ... combines thorough scholarship of the Nazi era with his own vast archive of interviews with survivors, perpetrators, and bystanders to create a comprehensive, chilling, and readable history of the Holocaust." Library Journal.

Reeves, Richard, 1936-

Infamy : the shocking story of the Japanese American internment in World War II / Richard Reeves. Henry Holt and Company, 2015. 384 p. **940.53**

1. Japanese Americans -- Forced removal and incarceration, 1942-1945 2. World War II -- Japanese Americans. 3. Concentration camps.
ISBN 9780805094084
LC 2014033329

In Infamy, the story of this appalling chapter in American history is told more powerfully than ever before. Acclaimed historian Richard Reeves has interviewed survivors, read numerous private letters and memoirs, and combed through archives to deliver a sweeping narrative of this atrocity. Men we usually consider heroes--FDR, Earl Warren, Edward R. Murrow--were in this case villains, but we also learn of many Americans who took great risks to defend the rights of the internees. Most especially, we hear the poignant stories of those who spent years in "war relocation camps," many of whom suffered this terrible injustice with remarkable grace.

"Reeves mixes intimate narratives with historical documents to give an authoritative account of one of the darkest periods in American history." Library Journal.

Reynolds, David, 1952-

In command of history : Churchill fighting and writing the Second World War / David Reynolds. Random House, 2005. xxiv, 631 p. : **940.53**

1. Churchill, Winston, Sir, 1874-1965. Second World War. 2. World War II -- Historiography. 3. World War II -- Personal narratives, British -- History and criticism
ISBN 0679457437
LC 2004051087

Provides an anaylsis of the dual roles that Winston Churchill played in World War II, as a stateman who led his country during the war, and as an historian who chronicled the events of the era in six epic volumes of memoirs.

"Packed with detail and vivid characterizations...[this book is] a different take on one of the few men capable of both making history and writing it." Publishers Weekly.

Rosenfeld, Oskar, 1884-1944

In the beginning was the ghetto : notebooks from Lodz / Oskar Rosenfeld ; edited and with an introduction by Hanno Loewy ; translated from the German by Brigitte M. Goldstein. Northwestern University Press, c2002. xxxviii, 313 p. ; **940.53**

1. Rosenfeld, Oskar, 1884-1944 Diaries. 2. Jews, Polish 3. Holocaust (1933-1945) -- Lodz, Poland 4. Interethnic relations. 5. Lodz, Poland
ISBN 0810114887
LC 2001006691

Translation of : Wozu noch Welt.

"These entries from Rosenfeld's diary contain vivid descriptions of daily life in the ghetto, including details about deportations, forced labor, hunger, diseases, cold, terror, and the struggle to maintain human dignity. This book is one of the most important and lasting works documenting the horrors of the Holocaust." Booklist.

Russell, Jan Jarboe, 1951-

The **train** to Crystal City : FDR's secret prisoner exchange program and America's only family internment camp during World War II / Jan Jarboe Russell. Scribner 2015 416 p. **940.53**

1. Italian Americans -- Evacuation and relocation, 1942. 2. Japanese Americans -- Forced removal and incarceration, 1942-1945 3. World War II -- Prisoners and prisons, American. 4. German Americans -- Evacuation and relocation, 1941-1948. 5. United States -- History

-- 20th century.
ISBN 9781451693669

LC 2014030862

A little-known episode in World War II history appears in The Train to Crystal City, which details how the U.S. incarcerated thousands of civilians in a Texas facility. Italian, Japanese, and German immigrants were sent there with their spouses and children, many of whom were U.S. citizens. Relying in part on personal interviews, author Jan Russell portrays life in the camp, the struggles of those who were sent abroad in prisoner exchanges, and post-war expulsion of foreign nationals.

"Based in part on interviews with camp survivors, Russell documents in chilling detail a shocking story of national betrayal." Kirkus.

Ryan, Mark

Hornet's sting : the amazing untold story of second World War spy Thomas Sneum / Mark Ryan. Skyhorse Pub., c2009. xi, 386 p. **940.53**

1. Sneum, Thomas 2. Spies. 3. World War II 4. Intelligence service. 5. Nazis. 6. Europe -- History -- 20th century.
ISBN 9781602397101

LC 2009006210

Traces the career of the late Danish-born spy, drawing on extensive first-person interviews to recount some of his more dramatic missions, which involved such activities as the refueling of a homemade plane in midair, the dual seduction of a mother and daughter, and a crossbow assassination.

Smith, Lyn, 1934-

Remembering : voices of the Holocaust : a new history in the words of the men and women who survived / Lyn Smith. Carroll & Graf Publishers ; 2006, c2005. xvi, 351 p. : **940.53**

1. Holocaust (1933-1945) 2. World War II, Jewish. 3. Concentration camps.
ISBN 0786716401

LC bl2006007388

Originally published: Forgotten voices of the Holocaust. London : Ebury Press, 2005.

Presents paragraph-long remembrances of over one hundred people persecuted by the Nazis, primarily European Jews, of what their experiences were prior to, during, and after the Holocaust.

"The author, who has recorded the experiences of survivors for London's Imperial War Museum, weaves together more than 100 accounts to construct a narrative of Nazi persecutions from the first anti-Semitic measures in 1933 through the liberation of the concentration camps. This is an extraordinary work of scholarship and a reminder of the power of individual stories, which can bring home the horrors of WWII more forcefully than abstract numbers." Publishers Weekly.

Snyder, Timothy

Black earth : the holocaust as history and warning / Timothy Snyder. Crown, 2015 464 p. **940.53**

1. Genocide 2. Holocaust (1933-1945) -- Causes 3. World War II -- Jews -- Rescue 4. Holocaust (1933-1945) -- Moral and ethical aspects
ISBN 9781101903452

LC 2015016818

The award-winning author of Bloodlands presents a history of the Holocaust that offers insights into Hitler's genocidal views and the partisan groups who supported Jewish targets, arguing that wrong conclusions about the Holocaust are compromising the world's future. Map(s).

"Snyder brings two fresh elements to his dizzying, harrowing tale. The first is his extraordinarily wide and deep research into the remarkable stories, many unknown, of individual Holocaust survivors, the subject of the last half of his book. The second element, likely to be controversial, is his argument, asserted and reasserted, that, at its roots, the Holocaust was made possible by the failure of national states." Publishers Weekly.

Stargardt, Nicholas

The **German** war : a nation under arms / Nicholas Stargardt. Basic Books, 2015 768 p. **940.53**

1. Hitler, Adolf, 1889-1945. 2. World War II. 3. Germans 4. Germany -- Politics and government -- 1933-1945. 5. Germany -- History -- 1933-1945. 6. Germany -- History, Military -- 20th century.
ISBN 9780465018994

LC 2015945013

Drawing on a range of primary source materials--personal diaries, court records and military correspondence--the author explores the German psyche during World War II, specifically why they prolonged the war when their defeat was all but assured as early as 1941.

"A well-researched, unsettling social history of war that will prove deeply thought-provoking--even worrying--for readers who wonder what they might have done under the same circumstances." Kirkus.

Witnesses of war : children's lives under the Nazis / Nicholas Stargardt. Vintage Books, 2007, c2005. xvi, 491 p. : **940.53**

1. Nazi Party (Germany) 2. World War II -- Children. 3. Child witnesses. 4. Germany -- History -- 1933-1945.
ISBN 9781400033799

LC 2007271285

Originally published: London : Jonathan Cape, 2005.

An in-depth examination of the lives and fates of children of all nationalities under the Nazi regime draws on a host of primary material--diaries; letters from reformatories, asylums, and camps, and to fathers at the front; accounts of children's games; and reminscences--to share the personal stories of a generation of European youngsters.

"An absorbing study of Nazi-era childhood, drawing on diaries, interviews and other primary sources... Fascinating and often unsettling; an illuminating companion to firsthand accounts such as Irmgard Hunt's On Hitler's Mountain and The Diary of Anne Frank." Kirkus.

Takaki, Ronald T., 1939-2009

Double victory : a multicultural history of America in World War II / Ronald Takaki. Back Bay Books, 2001, c2000. vi, 281 p. : **940.53**

1. World War II -- United States. 2. Racism -- United States. 3. Race relations. 4. United States -- Race relations.
ISBN 0316831565

LC BL2001013368

Originally published: Boston : Little, Brown, 2000.

Arguing that many Americans fought in World War II for a "double victory"--one against fascism abroad, the other against racism at home--the author captures the voices of people who are often overlooked in traditional narratives of the conflict.

United States Military Academy

The **West** Point history of World War II. The United States Military Academy ; Editors: Clifford J. Rogers, Ty Seidule, and Steve R. Waddell. Simon & Schuster, 2015. 432 p. **940.53**

1. World War II 2. Battles. 3. Military history. 4. War.
ISBN 9781476782737

LC 2015031711

Complete in two volumes.

"An astonishing, important book that will inform and entertain all readers, this is an essential purchase. Fans of military history, strategy, warfare, and human conflict will reap the benefits of this work." Library Journal.

United States Military Academy
The **West** Point history of World War II. The United States Military Academy ; Timothy Strabbing, editor. Simon & Schuster, 2016. 352 p. **940.53**
1. World War II 2. Battles 3. Military history 4. War
ISBN 9781476782775
LC bl2016048321

Complete in two volumes.

The definitive, must-have military history of World War II--spanning 1942 until the end of the war--packed with the same expert analysis, exclusive tactical maps, unique graphics, and historical images used by The United States Military Academy at West Point to teach the art of war to its own cadets.

"An astonishing, important book that will inform and entertain all readers, this is an essential purchase. Fans of military history, strategy, warfare, and human conflict will reap the benefits of this work." Library Journal.

Wachsmann, Nikolaus
KL : a history of the Nazi concentration camps / Nikolaus Wachsmann. Farrar, Straus and Giroux, 2015 896 p. **940.53**
1. Concentration camp inmates 2. Concentration camps 3. World War II -- Prisoners and prisons, German. 4. Holocaust (1933-1945)
ISBN 9780374118259
LC 2014031269

Mark Lynton History Prize, 2016.

While many accounts of Nazi concentration camps have focused on particular facilities or described the effects on prisoners, historian Nicolaus Wachsmann is the first to analyze the entire system of labor camps and extermination centers. This gripping, revelatory study draws on massive collections of documents, some of which have only become available over the past 25 years. KL doesn't just detail Nazi Germany's methodology of slave labor and genocide: it reveals how it was integral to the Third Reich's economic and political system.

"A comprehensive, encyclopedic work that should be included in the collections of libraries, schools and other institutions." Kirkus.

Wallace, Max
In the name of humanity : the secret deal to end the Holocaust / Max Wallace. Allen Lane, 2017. 486 p. : **940.53**
1. Auschwitz (Concentration camp) 2. Holocaust (1933-1945) 3. World War II. 4. Concentration camps. 5. Negotiation.
ISBN 0670069590

Canadian Jewish Book Award, 2018.

Shortlisted for The Charles Taylor Prize for Literary Non-Fiction, 2018

Discusses the secret negotiations of three people, a former fascist President of Switzerland, an Orthodox Jewish woman, and Himmler's Finnish osteopath, to end the Holocaust, assisted by Swedish and American intelligence efforts. The author recounts their efforts to deceive Heinrich Himmler who was considering the possibility of entering into an alliance with the West against the Soviet Union as Germany's defeat approached. By exploiting that idea and convincing Himmler to betray Hitler's orders, the group helped to save tens of thousands of Jews during the last months of the Second World War.

Ward, Geoffrey C.
The **war** : an intimate history, 1941-1945 / Geoffrey C. Ward and Ken Burns. A.A. Knopf, 2007. 480 p. **940.53**
1. World War II -- United States. 2. Concentration camps 3. Soldiers 4. Civilians 5. United States -- History, Military -- 20th century.
ISBN 0307262839
LC 2007003640

Based on Burns' documentary, The war.

Chronicles the American experience of World War II, both on the battlefields and on the home front, as chronicled in the voices and experiences of ordinary men and women from four towns across the country, from 1941 to 1945.

Weinberg, Gerhard L.
★A **world** at arms : a global history of World War II / Gerhard L. Weinberg. Cambridge University Press, 2005, c1994. xix, 1178 p. : **940.53**
1. World War II 2. Military history.
ISBN 9780521853163
LC BL 99776740

Reprint. Originally published: 1994.

Provides an overview of the entire war from a global perspective, looking at diplomatic actions, military strategy, economic developments, and pressures from the home front

"Weinberg's unrivaled command of archival sources combine with a smooth writing style to produce a definitive one-volume history of World War II." Library Journal. [review of 1994 edition]

Winik, Jay, 1957-
1944 : FDR and the year that changed history / Jay Winik. Simon & Schuster, 2015. 512 p. **940.53**
1. Roosevelt, Franklin D. (Franklin Delano), 1882-1945 Influence. 2. World War II 3. Political leadership -- United States -- History -- 20th century. 4. Holocaust (1933-1945) 5. Presidents
ISBN 9781439114087
LC 2015013912

The best-selling author of April 1865 chronicles the events of 1944 to reveal how nearly the Allies lost World War II, citing the pivotal contributions of FDR, Churchill and Stalin.

"An accomplished popular historian unpacks the last full year of World War II and the excruciatingly difficult decisions facing Franklin Roosevelt. A complex history rendered with great color and sympathy." Kirkus.

Wittman, Robert K.
The **devil's** diary : Hitler's high priest and the hunt for the lost papers of the Third Reich / Robert K. Wittman, David Kinney. HarperCollins, 2016. 420 p. **940.53**
1. Rosenberg, Alfred, 1893-1946. 2. Wittman, Robert K. 3. Nazi Party (Germany) 4. Nazism. 5. Nazis. 6. Holocaust (1933-1945) -- Germany. 7. World War II -- Germany. 8. Germany -- History -- 1933-1945.
ISBN 9780062319012
LC 2015036609

Alfred Rosenberg laid the philosophical foundations of the Third Reich; his diary provides an inside narrative of the Nazi rise to power, the Holocaust, and Hitler's post-invasion plans for Russia. Lost after the Nuremberg Trials, this is also the story of the hunt for the diary and its recovery decades afterwards.

Wyman, David S.
The **world** reacts to the Holocaust / David S. Wyman, editor ; Charles H. Rosenzveig, project director. Johns Hopkins univer-

sity Press, 1996. xxiii, 981 p. ; **940.53**

1. Holocaust, Jewish (1939-1945) -- Public opinion. 2. Holocaust, Jewish (1939-1945) -- Influence.
ISBN 9780801849695
LC 96015395

Offers a country-by-country breakdown of the impact the Holocaust had on world history, through politics, economics, and culture, covering twenty-two member states of the United Nations.

Yellin, Emily, 1961-

Our mothers' war : American women at home and at the front during World War II / Emily Yellin. Free Press, 2004. xiv, 447 p. : **940.53**

1. World War II -- Women -- United States. 2. World War II -- Women's participation. 3. Women -- United States -- History -- 20th century.
ISBN 0743245148
LC 2004040496

"Yellin reveals all of the responsibilities held by women, including helping to manufacture aircraft, ships, and other munitions; and, in the process, outproducing all of America's allies and enemies, by far. Readers see war brides who worked hard to maintain the morale of their husbands while surviving long separation, fear, and shortages of virtually everything necessary to support a family. . . . [This book] is an important book because the role played by women in World War II has been regularly ignored." School Library Journal.

Zuccotti, Susan, 1940-

Under his very windows : the Vatican and the Holocaust in Italy / Susan Zuccotti. Yale University Press, c2000. 408 p. : **940.53**

1. Pius XII, Pope, 1876-1958 Relations with Jews. 2. Catholic Church Relations Judaism. 3. Jews -- Persecutions -- Italy. 4. Holocaust (1933-1945) -- Italy. 5. World War II -- Religious aspects -- Catholic Church. 6. Judaism -- Relations -- Catholic Church. 7. Italy -- History -- 1914-1945.
ISBN 0300084870
LC 00043307

"Zuccotti's aim is to show that whatever help was given to the Jews by the Catholic Church during the war resulted almost entirely from spontaneous acts by courageous individuals--priests, monks and nuns, and occasionally prelates--and not from any interventions by the Vatican. Zuccotti makes her case strongly. This is a serious and well-researched book." New York Times Book Review.

940.5308 World War II, 1939-1945--Groups of people

Brock, Julia

Beyond Rosie : a documentary history of women and World War II / edited by Julia Brock, Jennifer W. Dickey, Richard J.W. Harker, and Catherine M. Lewis. The University of Arkansas Press, 2015. xxxvi, 262 p. : **940.5308**

1. World War II -- Participation, Female. 2. World War II -- War work -- United States. 3. World War II -- Women -- United States. 4. Women -- Employment -- United States -- History -- 20th century.
ISBN 9781557286703
LC 2014949011

"More so than any war in history, World War II was a woman's war. Women, motivated by patriotism, the opportunity for new experiences, and the desire to serve, participated widely in the global conflict. Within the Allied countries, women of all ages proved to be invaluable in the fight for victory. Rosie the Riveter became the most enduring image of women's involvement in World War II. What Rosie represented, however, is only a small portion of a complex story. As wartime production workers, enlistees in auxiliary military units, members of voluntary organizations or resistance groups, wives and mothers on the home front, journalists, and USO performers, American women found ways to challenge traditional gender roles and stereotypes. Beyond Rosie offers readers an opportunity to see the numerous contributions women made to the fight against the Axis powers and how American women's roles changed during the war. The primary documents (newspapers, propaganda posters, cartoons, excerpts from oral histories and memoirs, speeches, photographs, and editorials) collected here represent cultural, political, economic, and social perspectives on the diverse roles women played during World War II."--Page 4 of cover.

Henderson, Bruce B., 1946-

Sons and soldiers : the untold story of the Jews who escaped the Nazis and returned with the U.S. Army to fight Hitler / Bruce Henderson. William Morrow, 2017. 384 p. **940.5308**

1. World War II 2. Jews -- History 3. Military interrogation 4. Refugees 5. United States -- History -- 20th century 6. Europe -- History -- 20th century
ISBN 9780062419095
LC bl2017020900

Drawing on veteran interviews and archival research, an account of the lesser-known contributions of the German-born Jewish-American soldiers known as the Ritchie Boys describes how they risked their lives to join major combat units and gather crucial intelligence from German POWs.

"A gripping addition to the literature of the period and an overdue tribute to these unique Americans." Kirkus.

Shephard, Ben, 1948-

The **long** road home : the aftermath of the Second World War / Ben Shephard. Alfred A. Knopf, 2011, c2010. 496 p. **940.5308**

1. Repatriation -- Europe -- History -- 20th century. 2. Refugees. 3. World War II -- Refugees. 4. World War II -- Forced repatriation. 5. Eastern Europe -- History 6. Europe -- History.
ISBN 9781400040681
LC 2010023894

"Originally published in Great Britain in slightly different form by The Bodley Head, London, 2010"--T.p. verso.

"This is a Borzoi book published by Alfred A. Knopf"--T.p. verso.

A controversial reassessment of World War II's legacy evaluates the unique challenges of reconstructing an entire continent of holocaust survivors and starving refugees, in an account that draws on memoirs, essays and oral histories to discuss lesser-known aspects of the massive postwar relief efforts. By the author of After Daybreak.

940.5309 World War II, 1939-1945--History, geographic treatment, biography

Gilbert, Martin, 1936-

The **Routledge** atlas of the Holocaust : the complete history / Martin Gilbert. Routledge, 2009. 286 p. **940.5318**

1. Holocaust, Jewish (1939-1945)
ISBN 9780415484817
LC oc2009005891

Previous ed.: 2002.

940.5322 World War II, 1939-1945--Diplmatic history--Allies

Roberts, Andrew, 1963-

Masters and commanders : how four titans won the war in the west, 1941-1945 / Andrew Roberts. Harper, 2009, c2008. xl, 673 p. : **940.5322**

1. Roosevelt, Franklin D. (Franklin Delano), 1882-1945 Military leadership. 2. Churchill, Winston, 1874-1965 Military leadership 3. Marshall, George C., (George Catlett), 1880-1959 4. Alanbrooke, Viscount, 1883-1963. 5. World War II -- Diplomatic history. 6. Command of troops 7. Military history 8. Combined operations (Military science)
ISBN 9780061228575

Previous ed. has subtitle: how Roosevelt, Churchill, Marshall, and Alanbrooke won the war in the West.

Originally published: London : Allen Lane, 2008.

A joint profile of Winston Churchill, Franklin D. Roosevelt, and their armed forces commanders Alan Brooke and George C. Marshall evaluates the pivotal ways in which they determined the strategies of allied forces during World War II, in an account that reveals their divergent agendas and tense efforts to collaborate or outmaneuver each other.

940.54 Military history of World War II

Alperovitz, Gar

The **decision** to use the atomic bomb / Gar Alperovitz ; with the assistance of Sanho Tree ... [et al.]. Vintage Books, 1996, c1995. xiv, 847 p. ; **940.54**

1. Strategy. 2. Atomic bomb. 3. World War II 4. Military campaigns 5. Hiroshima, Japan -- Atomic bombing, 1945. 6. United States -- Foreign relations -- 1945-1953. 7. United States -- Foreign relations Soviet Union. 8. Soviet Union -- Foreign relations United States.
ISBN 067976285X

LC BL 99776416

Originally published: New York : Knopf, 1995.

Reconstructs the events leading up to the bombing of Hiroshima in 1945.

"Alperovitz is the dean of revisionist scholars who argue that the nuclear bombing of Japan was unnecessary and that America bears a hefty responsibility for the cold war. His main and probably most controversial contention is that certain documents pertaining to the decision were doctored, some by none other than Truman himself. Further, Alperovitz sees James Byrnes, Truman's Mephistophelian secretary of state, as a furtive player who nixed such alternative plans as modifying the unconditional-surrender demand and encouraging a Russian declaration of war." Booklist.

Ambrose, Stephen E.

Citizen soldiers : the U.S. Army from the Normandy beaches to the Bulge to the surrender of Germany, June 7, 1944-May 7, 1945 / Stephen E. Ambrose. Simon & Schuster, 1997. 512 p. : **940.54**

1. United States. Army -- History World War II. 2. Western Front (World War II) 3. Soldiers -- United States -- History -- 20th century. 4. World War II 5. Military campaigns 6. Europe -- History -- 1939-1945.
ISBN 0684815257

LC 97023876

Citizen Soldiers opens on June 7, 1944, on the Normandy beaches, and ends on May 7, 1945. From the high command on down to the enlisted men, Stephen E. Ambrose draws on hundreds of interviews and oral histories from men on both sides who were there. He recreates the experiences of the individuals who fought the battles, the women who served, and the Germans who fought against us.

"These events have all been well documented, but in Ambrose's capable hands, the bloody and dramatic battles fought in northwest Europe in 1944-45 come alive as never before." New York Times Book Review.

D-Day, June 6, 1944 : the climactic battle of World War II / Stephen E. Ambrose Simon & Schuster, 1995, c1994. 655 p. : **940.54**

1. World War II 2. Normandy Invasion, June 6, 1944 3. Military campaigns 4. Battles. 5. Normandy -- History, Military -- 20th century. 6. France.
ISBN 068480137X

LC BL 99763163

"A Touchstone book."

"Appendix A: Veterans who contributed oral histories or written memoirs to the Eisenhower Center as of August 13, 1993": p. 617-632.

Originally published: New York : Simon & Schuster, 1994.

Chronicles the events, politics, and personalities of this pivotal day in World War II, shedding light on the strategies of commanders on both sides and the ramifications of the battle.

"Mr. Ambrose wonderfully illuminates the mind of the very young soldier of any nation anywhere who has never been in fighting before. " New York Times Book Review.

The **wild** blue : the men and boys who flew the B-24s over Germany / Stephen E. Ambrose. Simon & Schuster, 2001. 299 p., 8 p. of plates : **940.54**

1. McGovern, George S., 1922- 2. United States. Army Air Forces. Squadron, 741st 3. United States. Army Air Forces 4. Dakota Queen (Bomber) 5. B-24 bomber. 6. World War II -- Aerial operations, American. 7. Bomber pilots -- United States 8. Germany.
ISBN 0743203399

LC 2001020563

The stories of the Army Air Forces' B24 pilots and crews who were stationed in Italy and flew combat missions over Germany during World War II.

"Ambrose's narrative flows smoothly, even as he manages to cover each man's story." Library Journal.

Atkinson, Rick

★An **army** at dawn : the war in North Africa, 1942-1943 / Rick Atkinson. Henry Holt & Co., 2002. xiii, 681 p., 32 p. of plates : Liberation trilogy ; **940.54**

1. World War II 2. Operation Torch. 3. Military campaigns 4. Military history. 5. North Africa -- History, Military -- 20th century. 6. Tunisia -- History.
ISBN 0805062882

LC 2002024130

Pulitzer Prize for History, 2003.

Atkinson tells the story of the war in North Africa in this first volume of a trilogy about the liberation of Europe in World War II.

"This volume covers the conception of Operation Torch through the German surrender in Tunisia in May 1943. An exemplary work that feeds anticipation of the succeeding volumes." Booklist.

★The **day** of battle : the war in Sicily and Italy, 1943-1944 / Rick Atkinson. H. Holt, 2007. 816 p. Liberation trilogy ; **940.54**

1. World War II 2. Military history. 3. Military campaigns 4. Armed

forces. 5. Italy -- History, Military -- 1914-1945. 6. Europe -- History -- 20th century.
ISBN 0805062890
LC 2007007653

The second volume in a trilogy chronicling the liberation of Europe during World War II focuses on the Allied campaigns in Sicily and Italy, detailing the bloody battles at Salerno, Anzio, and Monte Cassino, as well as the June 1944 liberation of Rome.

"The second volume of...[the author's] Liberation trilogy, which began with the Pulitzer Prizewinning An Army at Dawn: The War in North Africa, 1942-1943, this is probably the most eagerly awaited World War II book of the year. Atkinson's clear prose, perceptive analysis, and grasp of the personalities and nuances of the campaigns make his book an essential purchase." Library Journal.

The **guns** at last light : the war in Western Europe, 1944-1945 / Rick Atkinson. Henry Holt and Co., c2013. 896 p. Liberation trilogy ; **940.54**

1. Western Front (World War II) 2. Military history 3. World War II 4. Military campaigns
ISBN 9780805062908
LC 2012034312

"[L]ively, occasionally lyric prose brings the vast theater of battle, from the beaches of Normandy deep into Germany, brilliantly alive." Publishers Weekly.

Ballard, Robert D.

Return to Midway : the quest to find the Yorktown and the other lost ships from the pivotal battle of the Pacific War / Robert D. Ballard and Rick Archbold ; principal photography by David Doubilet ; additional photography by Mark Thiessen, Keith Morehead, and Glen Marullo ; underwater paintings by Ken Marschall ; technical and historical consultation by Robert J. Cressman, Charles Haberlein, Jr., and John Lundstrom. National Geographic, 1999. 191 p. : **940.54**

1. Midway, Battle of, 1942. 2. Shipwrecks 3. Naval battles. 4. World War II -- Naval operations, American. 5. Pacific Ocean.
ISBN 0792275004
LC 99010831

Provides an account of the 1942 battle of Midway and the high-tech hunt for the lost ships fifty-six years later.

"In this narrative, Ballard intersperses chapters on the Battle of Midway with a fascinating account of his search for the U.S.S. Yorktown, which was sunk by a Japanese destroyer on June 7, 1942. Period photographs from the battle are combined with those of the Yorktown as she rests today, and paintings by marine artist Ken Marschall add detail to complete the record. The lively narrative is punctuated with two Japanese and two American oral history accounts of the battle." Library Journal.

Bascomb, Neal

The **winter** fortress : the epic mission to sabotage Hitler's atomic bomb / Neal Bascomb. Houghton Mifflin Harcourt, 2016. 352 p. **940.54**

1. Commando operations. 2. Sabotage. 3. World War II 4. Resistance to military occupation 5. Norway
ISBN 9780544368057
LC 2015042716

Documents the Allied raid against occupied Norway's Vermork hydroelectric plant, the world's only supplier of an essential ingredient needed by the Nazis to build an atomic bomb, citing the teamwork of British Special Ops, a brilliant scientists and refugee Norwegian commandos that foiled Hitler's nuclear ambitions.

"Parts of the book read like an adventure novel, others like straightforward history, but the combination will appeal to readers of both WWII fiction and nonfiction." Booklist.

Beevor, Antony, 1946-

Ardennes 1944 : Hitler's last gamble / Antony Beevor. Viking, 2015 xix, 451 p. **940.54**

1. Ardennes, Battle of the, 1944-1945. 2. World War II 3. Battles 4. Military history
ISBN 9780670025312
LC 2015490442

Reconstructs the Battle of the Bulge in riveting detail to discuss the surprise counter--offensive by German forces, the numerous casualties on both sides and the strategies that enabled an Allied victory.

"Beevor skewers the pretensions and weaknesses of generals and details atrocities and mistreatment of both civilians and surrendering enemies by both sides. The author takes for granted more knowledge of the battle, the terrain, and the German language than general readers may possess, and he occasionally repeats information attentive readers will recall from previous mentions. But these are small quibbles. On the whole, this is a treasure of memorable portraits, striking details, fascinating revelations, and broad insights; likely to be the definitive account of the battle for years to come. Essential reading for anyone interested in World War II." Kirkus.

The **battle** of Arnhem : the deadliest airborne operation of WWII, 1944 / Antony Beevor. Viking, [2018] 480 p. **940.54**

1. Arnhem, Battle of, 1944. 2. Military campaigns. 3. Parachute troops. 4. Airborne troops. 5. Arnhem, Netherlands -- History.
ISBN 9780525429821

The prize-winning historian and author of "D-Day" reconstructs the devastating airborne battle of Arnhem.

D-day : the Battle for Normandy / Antony Beevor. Viking, 2009. 608 p. **940.54**

1. World War II 2. Normandy Invasion, June 6, 1944 3. Military history. 4. Military campaigns 5. Normandy -- History.
ISBN 9780670021192
LC 2009023574

Presents an account of the Normandy invasion that offers insight into the experiences of soldiers and French civilians, documenting the heavy casualties suffered on all fronts and the ways in which the war influenced relations between America and Europe.

"This is a vibrant work of history that honors the sacrifice of tens of thousands of men and women." Time.

The **Second** World War / Antony Beevor. Little, Brown and Co., 2012. 704 p. **940.54**

1. World War II 2. War and society -- History -- 20th century 3. War -- History -- 20th century 4. War -- Moral and ethical aspects
ISBN 9780316023740
LC 2012007028

The British historian and author presents a single volume history of the world's largest conflict, from Manchuria in 1939 to the Soviet invasion of northern China six years later, describing the human drama of soldiers, civilians and political leaders.

Beevor, Antony, 1946-

The **fall** of Berlin, 1945 / Antony Beevor. Viking, 2002. xxxvii, 489 p., 24 p. of plates : **940.54**

1. Berlin, Battle of, 1945 2. World War II -- Berlin, Germany. 3. World War II -- Destruction and pillage -- Germany. 4. Berlin (Germany) -- History.

ISBN 0670030414

LC 2002510674

"The author relies on material from American, German, British, French, and Swedish archives and documents from former Soviet files, making the book an invaluable and meticulous account." Booklist.

Stalingrad / Antony Beevor. Viking, 1998. xvii, 493 p., 16 p. of plates : **940.54**

1. Stalingrad, Battle of, 1942-1943. 2. Operation Barbarossa. 3. Soviet Union -- History -- German occupation, 1941-1944.

ISBN 9780670870950

LC 98019346

Samuel Johnson Prize for Nonfiction, 1999.

Hawthornden Prize, 1999.

"Beevor has composed a history of Stalingrad unlikely to be bettered." Booklist.

Blume, Lesley M. M.

Fallout : the Hiroshima cover-up and the reporter who revealed it to the world / Lesley M. M. Blume. Simon & Schuster, 2020. 288 p. **940.54**

1. Hersey, John, 1914-1993. 2. Hersey, John, 1914-1993. Hiroshima 3. World War II -- Japan 4. Journalists -- United States 5. Atomic bomb -- History 6. Hibakusha 7. Hiroshima, Japan -- Atomic bombing, 1945 8. Japan -- History -- 20th century

ISBN 9781982128517

LC 2020000055

Just days after the United States decimated Hiroshima and Nagasaki with nuclear bombs, the Japanese surrendered unconditionally. But even before the surrender, the US government and military had begun a secret propaganda and information suppression campaign to hide the devastating nature of these experimental weapons. The cover-up intensified as Occupation forces closed the atomic cities to Allied reporters, preventing leaks about the horrific long-term effects of radiation which would kill thousands during the months after the blast. For nearly a year the cover-up worked--until New Yorker journalist John Hersey got into Hiroshima and managed to report the truth to the world. When the magazine published "Hiroshima" in August 1946, it became an instant global sensation, and inspired pervasive horror about the hellish new threat that America had unleashed.

"Journalist Blume (Everybody Behaves Badly) delivers a thrilling behind-the-scenes account of John Hersey's seminal 1946 report on the atomic bombing of Hiroshima. . . . This enthralling, fine-grained chronicle reveals what it takes to cut through 'dangerously anesthetizing' statistics and speak truth to power." Publishers Weekly

Borneman, Walter R., 1952-

Brothers down : Pearl Harbor and the fate of the many brothers aboard the USS Arizona / Walter R. Borneman. Little, Brown & Companyh, 2019. 343 p. **940.54**

1. United States. Navy -- History World War II 2. Pearl Harbor, Attack on, 1941 3. USS Arizona Memorial (Hawaii) 4. Brothers 5. Sailors

ISBN 9780316438889

LC 2019932184

The surprise attack at Pearl Harbor on December 7, 1941 remains one of the most traumatic events in American history. America's battleship fleet was crippled, thousands of lives were lost, and the United States was propelled into a world war. Few realize that aboard the iconic, ill-fated USS Arizona were an incredible 79 blood relatives. In Brothers Down, acclaimed historian Walter R. Borneman returns to that critical week of December, masterfully guiding us on an unforgettable journey of sacrifice and heroism, all told through the lives of these brothers and their fateful experience.

"An excellent popular history, this intimately researched text will appeal to anyone with interest in military or maritime history as well as those who enjoy personal narratives." Library Journal.

Breitman, Richard, 1947-

Official secrets : what the Nazis planned, what the British and Americans knew / Richard Breitman. Hill and Wang, 1998. viii, 325 p. ; **940.54**

1. World War II -- Atrocities. 2. Holocaust (1933-1945) 3. Genocide -- Germany. 4. United States -- Foreign relations Great Britain. 5. Great Britain -- Foreign relations United States. 6. Germany -- Politics and government -- 1933-1945.

ISBN 0809038196

LC 98007997

Examines evidence of Nazi war crimes gathered by British intelligence

"This is a remarkable study, concise yet carefully nuanced." New York Times Book Review.

Burleigh, Michael, 1955-

Moral combat : good and evil in World War II / Michael Burleigh. Harpercollins, 2011. 608 p. **940.54**

1. World War II. 2. War -- Moral and ethical aspects. 3. Good and evil. 4. Ethics.

ISBN 9780060580971

LC bl2011007916

Examines the Second World War in terms of the moral and ethical decisions made by the leaders of both sides and their consequences, including the effects it had on the civilian populations in both theaters.

"Burleigh examines the concessions of collaborators, real and supposed, the bravery of the depressingly small local resistance movements, the moral dilemmas accompanying secret warfare, the unspeakable Nazi extermination camps and the inverted moral universe within them, and the statistically insignificant acts of rescue (e.g., Schindler, Wallenberg)." Kirkus.

Caddick-Adams, Peter, 1960-

Sand and steel : the D-Day invasions and the liberation of France / Peter Caddick-Adams. Oxford University Press, 2019. 1072 p. **940.54**

1. Normandy Invasion, June 6, 1944 2. World War II 3. Operation Overlord 4. Military campaigns 5. Normandy 6. France

ISBN 9780190601898

LC 2018055471

Sand and Steel gives us D-Day, arguably the greatest and most consequential military operation of modern times, beginning with the years of painstaking and costly preparation, through to the pitched battles fought along France's northern coast, from Omaha Beach to the Falaise and the push east to Strasbourg.

Clark, Lloyd, 1967-

Blitzkrieg : myth, reality, and Hitler's lightning war: France 1940 / Lloyd Clark. Atlantic Monthly Press, 2016. 384 p. **940.54**

1. Lightning war 2. Bombings. 3. World War II -- Aerial operations, German.

ISBN 9780802125132

LC 2017276501

A leading military historian from the UK presents a controversial reassessment of the infamous German warfare tactic and its role in the fall of France to the Nazis in 1940, arguing that better Allied competence may have prevented German success.

"A solid, well-documented military history, Clark's newest work will appeal to anyone interested in World War II and early operations on the western front." Library Journal.

Conant, Jennet

The **irregulars** : Roald Dahl and the British spy ring in wartime Washington / Jennet Conant. Simon & Schuster, 2008. 416 p. **940.54**

1. Dahl, Roald Career in espionage. 2. Great Britain. British Security Coordination. 3. Influence (Psychology) 4. Secrecy in government. 5. Spies -- Great Britain 6. Intelligence officers -- Great Britain. 7. Great Britain -- Politics and government -- 20th century. 8. United States -- Politics and government -- 20th century.

ISBN 9780743294584

LC 2008012483

Includes index.

Describes the covert intelligence operations of allied forces during World War II as experienced by wounded RAF pilot Roald Dahl, a patriot who used his charm and wits to infiltrate the upper reaches of Georgetown society and influence U.S. policy in favor of England.

"Entertaining social history that also reveals a little-known aspect of an important literary figure's life." Kirkus.

The **lotus** eaters : the adventures of Julia Child and Paul Child in the OSS / Jennet Conant. Simon & Schuster, 2011. 448 p. **940.54**

1. Child, Julia. 2. Child, Paul, 1902-1994. 3. McCarthy, Joseph, 1908-1957. 4. United States. Office of Strategic Services 5. Intelligence service -- United States. 6. Spies. 7. World War II. 8. Secret service. 9. United States -- History -- 1945-1953

ISBN 9781439163528

LC 2011002875

Also published as A Covert Affair.

Chronicles the iconic chef's contributions as a member of the OSS during World War II and her efforts at the side of her husband to support an agent accused of being a spy, describing how their wartime experiences shaped their characters, relationships, and ambitions.

Corera, Gordon

Operation Columba : the Secret Pigeon Service : the untold story of World War II resistance in Europe / Gordon Corera. William Morrow, 2018. viii, 334 p., 16 unnumbered p. of plates : **940.54**

1. Intelligence service -- Great Britain 2. Homing pigeons 3. Espionage 4. World War II 5. Great Britain -- History -- 20th century 6. Europe -- History -- 1939-1945

ISBN 9780062667076

The author of Intercept traces the lesser-known story of how British intelligence secretly used homing pigeons as part of a clandestine espionage operation in support of the Resistance in occupied Europe during World War II.

Costello, John, 1943-

The **Pacific** War / John Costello. Quill, 1982, c1981. xi, 742 p., 20 leaves of plates : **940.54**

1. World War II -- Pacific Ocean

ISBN 9780688016203

LC 82015054

Includes index.

Originally published: New York : Rawson, Wade, 1981.

An incisive history of World War II in the Pacific traces the campaigns and strategies from before the attack on Pearl Harbor to the surrender of Japan and analyzes the causes of the war.

Cross, Robin

Operation Dragoon : the allied liberation of the south of France: 1944 / Robin Cross. Pegasus Books, 2019. 304 p. **940.54**

1. United States. Army -- History World War II 2. France. Army -- History World War II 3. Military history 4. Military campaigns 5. Soldiers 6. World War II 7. French Riviera 8. France

ISBN 9781681778600

LC bl2019001101

The best-selling author of We'll Meet Again presents a narrative account of the 1944 Operation Dragoon Allied liberation of the South of France, chronicling major campaign stages while exploring the pivotal contributions of the French.

Curtis, Brian, 1971

Fields of battle : Pearl Harbor, the Rose Bowl, and the boys who went to war / Brian Curtis. Flatiron Books, 2016. 320 p. **940.54**

1. Duke University Football 2. Oregon State University Football 3. College football. 4. Pearl Harbor, Attack on, 1941 5. Military recruiting and enlistment 6. Rose Bowl Game, Durham, North Carolina

ISBN 9781250059581

LC 2016020829

Tells the tale of the boys who played in the 1942 Rose Bowl and then served on the World War II battlefields.

"A fine sports book with a stirring extra dimension." Kirkus.

Dando-Collins, Stephen

The **big** break : the greatest American WWII POW escape story never told / Stephen Dando-Collins. St Martin's Press, 2017 272 p. **940.54**

1. Oflag 64 (Concentration camp) 2. World War II -- Prisoners and prisons. 3. Prisoners of war, American 4. Prisoner-of-war escapes. 5. Escapes 6. Schubin, Poland 7. Poland

ISBN 9781250087560

LC 2016037566

In The Big Break, we follow famous POWs, such as General Eisenhower's personal aide, General Patton's son-in-law, and Ernest Hemingway's eldest son, as the first American escapes via a tunnel in a stinking latrine, with almost 250 US officers following closely behind in a mass break. The Schubin escapes are by far the largest Allied POW escape of the second World War, surpassing even The Great Escape of 1944.

"An exciting account from a passionate author who has done the necessary research." Kirkus.

David, Saul, 1966-

The **force** : the legendary special ops unit and WWII's mission impossible / Saul David. Hachette Books, 2019. 336 p. **940.54**

1. First Special Service Force 2. World War II 3. Commando operations 4. Special forces 5. Elite operatives 6. Italy

ISBN 9780316414531

LC 2019000521

Details the true story of a group of elite North American soldiers from humble backgrounds who were tasked with skiing, rock climbing, and parachuting in order to capture a crucial Nazi stronghold in the cliffs of Italy.

Daws, Gavan

Prisoners of the Japanese : POWs of World War II in the Pacific / Gavan Daws. W. Morrow, c1994. 462 p. : **940.54**

1. World War II -- Prisoners and prisons, Japanese. 2. Prisoners of war -- Pacific Area -- History -- 20th century. 3. Japan -- History -- 1926-1945. 4. Japan -- History, Military -- 20th century.
ISBN 0688118127

LC 93049363

Map on lining paper.

Survivors of the notorious Bataan death march, members of slave labor teams, soldiers in Douglas MacArthur's army in the Philippines, and other prisoners of war tell the stories of their capture, stories often ignored in official accounts.

"Daws offers a well-written thoroughly researched account of these POWs. . . . An exceptionally worthwhile addition to the literature on the war in the Pacific." Booklist.

Dickson, Paul

The **rise** of the G.I. Army 1940-1941 : the forgotten story of how America forged a powerful army before Pearl Harbor / Paul Dickson. Atlantic Monthly Press, 2020 384 p. **940.54**

1. United States. Army. 2. United Service Organizations (U.S.) 3. World War II 4. Soldiers -- United States -- History -- World War II. 5. Military education 6. Infantry 7. United States -- History -- 20th century. 8. United States -- History, Military
ISBN 9780802147677

LC bl2020019435

This important addition to American history presents the gripping, untold story of the extraordinary transformation of America's military in a little more than 18 months, which turned them into a disciplined and mobile fighting force that helped win World War II.

"One of the best treatments to date of America's rapid transition from the Depression to the wartime power it became." Kirkus

Dimbleby, Jonathan

The **Battle** of the Atlantic : how the allies won the war / Jonathan Dimbleby. Oxford University Press, 2016. 560 p. **940.54**

1. United States. Navy -- History World War II. 2. World War II 3. Military campaigns 4. Submarine warfare. 5. Naval battles 6. Atlantic Ocean.
ISBN 9780190495855

LC 2015032726

Though often overlooked, the Battle of the Atlantic was crucial to both sides. Had Germany succeeded in cutting off the supply of American ships, England would have likely not held out; the outcome of the war -- as well as the future of Europe and the world -- would have been remarkably different.

"The history of the battle for the Atlantic is well documented, but Dimbleby's work, with its emphasis on the strategic importance of the battle, is an excellent addition to the story, and expert historians as well as general readers can enjoy this effort." Publishers Weekly.

Doyle, William, 1957-

PT 109 : an American epic of war, survival, and the destiny of John F. Kennedy / William Doyle. William Morrow, 2015. 368 p. **940.54**

1. Kennedy, John F. (John Fitzgerald), 1917-1963. 2. PT-109 (Torpedo boat). 3. World War II 4. Military campaigns 5. Naval history 6. Shipwrecks 7. Solomon Islands
ISBN 9780062346582

LC 2015021575

A moment-by-moment account of the sinking of PT-109 shares detailed perspectives into a future 35th President's heroic contributions, sharing insights into his leadership over a small band of survivors while awaiting rescue.

Duffy, James P., 1941-

War at the end of the world : Douglas MacArthur and the forgotten fight for New Guinea, 1942-1945 / James P. Duffy. NAL Caliber, 2016. 448 p. **940.54**

1. MacArthur, Douglas, 1880-1964. 2. World War II 3. Military campaigns 4. Military strategy 5. Military history 6. New Guinea
ISBN 9780451418302

LC 2015019828

An account of General Douglas MacArthur's four-year effort to defend New Guinea from Japanese would-be occupiers details how the campaign involved some of history's most brutal warfare and was complicated by tropical disease, violent weather and unforgiving terrain.

"Duffy's portrait of the South Pacific is an entertaining and well-researched war history that will satisfy intrigued novices and devoted students alike." Kirkus.

Felton, Mark, 1974-

Zero Night : the untold story of World War Two's greatest escape / Mark Felton. Thomas Dunne Books, St. Martin's Press, 2015. 320 p. **940.54**

1. Oflag VI B (Concentration camp). 2. Prisoner-of-war escapes 3. Escapes. 4. Prisoners of war. 5. World War II -- Prisoners and prisons
ISBN 9781250073747

LC 2015017591

"First published in Great Britain by Icon Books Ltd"--Title page verso.

On August 30, 1942--Zero Night--40 Allied officers staged the most audacious mass escape of World War II. Months of meticulous planning and secret training hung in the balance during three minutes of mayhem as the officers boldly stormed the huge doublefences at Oflag Prison. Employing wooden ladders and bridges previously disguised as bookshelves, the highly coordinated effort succeeded and set 36 men free into the German countryside. Later known as the 'Warburg Wire Job', fellow prisoner and fighter ace Douglas Bader once described the attempt as "the most brilliant escape conception of this war."

"The author grippingly tracks the evaders' trek to freedom, an event that would warrant a book in itself. Even the epilogue will bring a smile. In this exciting book, Felton has captivatingly captured the bravery of the prisoners." Kirkus.

Frank, Richard B., 1947-

★**Downfall** : the end of the Imperial Japanese Empire / Richard B. Frank. Random House, 1999. 484 p. : **940.54**

1. World War II 2. Military campaigns 3. Air warfare 4. B-29 bomber. 5. Japan -- History -- Bombing, 1944-1945 6. Japan -- History -- 1926-1945.
ISBN 067941424X

LC 99011838

A chronicle of the months leading up to the dropping of the atomic bomb in 1945 includes information from recently declassified documents and offers insight into the reasons behind the decision.

Geroux, William

The **Mathews** men : seven brothers and the war against Hitler's

U-boats / William Geroux. Viking, 2016. 400 p. **940.54**

1. Submarines, German 2. Merchant marine 3. World War II 4. Military campaigns 5. Atlantic Ocean. 6. Virginia 7. Mathews County, Virginia

ISBN 9780525428152

LC bl2016007304

The Mathews Men shows us the war far beyond traditional battlefields--often the U.S. merchant mariners' life-and-death struggles took place just off the U.S. coast--but also takes us to the landing beaches at D-Day and to the Pacific. "When final victory is ours," General Dwight D. Eisenhower had predicted, "there is no organization that will share its credit more deservedly than the Merchant Marine." Here, finally, is the heroic story of those merchant seamen, recast as the human story of the men from Mathews County, Virginia.

"Geroux presents an unflinching, inspiring, and long-delayed tribute to the sacrifice of these men." Booklist.

Giangreco, D. M., 1952-

Hell to pay : Operation Downfall and the invasion of Japan, 1945-47 / D.M. Giangreco. Naval Institute Press, c2009. xxiii, 362 p. : **940.54**

1. World War II 2. Military campaigns 3. Military history. 4. Operation Downfall, 1945-1946. 5. United States -- Armed Forces -- History -- World War II. 6. Japan.

ISBN 9781591143161

LC 2009027766

"Illustrative of just how much the war with Japan was a close-run thing, this is essential reading." Library Journal.

Glass, Charles, 1951-

The **deserters** : a hidden history of World War II / Charles Glass. The Penguin Press, 2013. 400 p. **940.54**

1. World War II 2. War -- Psychological aspects. 3. Military desertion 4. Deserters

ISBN 9781594204289

LC 2012046881

A narrative history of World War II from the perspective of deserters reveals how desertion was often experienced as a natural part of conflict, sharing the stories of a decorated soldier-turned-gangster and a three-time deserter who eventually lost his legs in combat.

Grayling, A. C.

Among the dead cities : the history and moral legacy of the WWII bombing of civilians in Germany and Japan / A.C. Grayling. Walker & Co., 2006. xii, 361 p. : **940.54**

1. World War II -- Aerial operations, American -- Moral and ethical aspects. 2. World War II -- Aerial operations, British -- Moral and ethical aspects. 3. World War II -- Moral and ethical aspects. 4. World War II -- Casualties -- Germany. 5. Germany -- History, Military -- 1939-1945. 6. Japan -- History, Military -- 20th century.

ISBN 9780802714718

Presents an analysis of the miltary rationale used by Britain and the United States for bombing civilian targets in Germany and Japan during World War II, discussing the reasons why such tactics were both largely ineffective and morally reprehensible.

"Was it wrong for the Allies to bomb German and Japanese civilians in World War II? In this book, . . . [the author] attends to one of the twentieth-century's largest unexploded moral conundrums. . . . Grayling's book builds careful, generous cases for and against the bombing, admitting as evidence both the experience of the bombed as well as the bombers." Booklist.

Ham, Paul

Hiroshima Nagasaki : the real story of the atomic bombings and their aftermath / Paul Ham. Thomas Dunne Books, St. Martin's Press, 2014, c2011. ix, 629 p., 8 unnumbered p. of plates : **940.54**

1. Atomic bomb 2. World War II -- Atrocities 3. Hibakusha 4. Hiroshima, Japan -- Atomic bombing, 1945. 5. Nagasaki, Japan -- Atomic bombing, 1945.

ISBN 9781250047113

LC 2014008489

Originally published: Pymble, N.S.W. : HarperCollins, 2011.

A comprehensive history drawn from eyewitness accounts challenges the belief that the nuclear attacks on Hiroshima and Nagasaki brought the war in the Pacific to an end, arguing that the bombings were unnecessary to the war's outcome, especially because they cost tens of thousands of human lives.

"A valuable contribution to the literature of World War II that asks its readers to rethink much of what they've been taught about America's just cause." Kirkus.

Hamilton, Nigel

The **mantle** of command : FDR at war, 1941/1942 / Nigel Hamilton. Houghton Mifflin Harcourt, 2014 528 p. **940.54**

1. Roosevelt, Franklin D. (Franklin Delano), 1882-1945. 2. World War II -- United States. 3. Command of troops -- United States. 4. Great Britain -- Foreign relations United States. 5. United States -- Foreign relations Great Britain.

ISBN 9780547775241

LC 2013045586

An in-depth analysis of FDR's leadership during the Second World War reveals how he assumed control over key decisions to launch a successful trial landing in North Africa to shift the war in favor of Allied forces.

"Though it's a weighty tome, and is based extensively on Roosevelt's own notes, Hamilton keeps a brisk pace throughout to produce what will likely be seen as a definitive volume on this aspect of Roosevelt's career." Publishers Weekly.

Hammel, Eric M.

Two flags over Iwo Jima : solving the mystery of the U.S. Marine Corps' proudest moment / Eric Hammel. Casemate Publishing 2018. 222 p. **940.54**

1. United States. Marine Corps. Marine Regiment, 28th 2. Iwo Jima, Battle of, 1945 3. World War II 4. Military campaigns 5. Photographs 6. Iwo Jima, Japan -- History, Military -- World War II

ISBN 9781612006291

LC bl2018192337

The saga of the flags on Iwo Jima has fascinated America for decades. Not only is the full story behind one of the most iconic photographs ever taken revealed, but also the real heroism and stories of the men behind this most fervent expression of American patriotism.

Hampton, Dan

Operation vengeance : the astonishing aerial ambush that changed World War II / Dan Hampton. William Morrow and Company, 2020 448 p. : **940.54**

1. Mitchell, John W., 1914-1995 2. Yamamoto, Isoroku, 1884-1943 3. Fighter pilots 4. Admirals 5. World War II -- Aerial operations, American 6. Enemies

ISBN 9780062938091

LC bl2020015968

The best-selling author of Viper Pilot presents a narrative account of America's secret World War II mission to assassinate Isoroku Yamamoto, the Japanese commander who masterminded the Pearl Harbor attacks.

"Although this history is well documented in World War II literature, the accessible storytelling by Hampton will likely be of interest for aficionados of the period." Library Journal

Hanson, Victor Davis

The **second** world wars : how the first global conflict was fought and won / Victor Davis Hanson. Basic Books, 2017. 688 p. **940.54**

1. World War II 2. War and civilization 3. Military power 4. Weapons
ISBN 9780465066988

LC 2017024227

A noted military historian presents a definitive account of World War II and a dramatic reinterpretation the most lethal conflict in human history.

"An ingenious, always provocative analysis of history's most lethal war." Kirkus.

Hastings, Max

Armageddon : the battle for Germany, 1944-45 / Max Hastings. A.A. Knopf, 2004. xxiii, 584 p. : **940.54**

1. World War II 2. Military campaigns 3. Germany -- History -- 1933-1945.
ISBN 9780375414336

LC 2004046468

A sweeping history of the final eight months of World War II on the European front draws on interviews with survivors and the archives of the major combatants to raise provocative questions about the pact between the Allies and the Soviet Union, the role of strategic bombing, the combat abilities of soldiers on all sides of the conflict, and the roles of such leaders as Eisenhower, Roosevelt, Churchill, Montgomery, and others.

"The author tells the grim tale of the final collapse of the Third Reich. It does so from the viewpoints of the upper millstone (the Western Allies), the lower millstone (the Russians) and the grain being ground in between (the Germans). The research includes previously untapped Russian archives (particularly in the accounts of Soviet veterans) and leads to a gripping and horrifying story that serious students of military history will find almost impossible to put down." Publishers Weekly.

Hastings, Max

Inferno : the world at war, 1939-45 / Max Hastings. Alfred A. Knopf, 2011, c2010. 672 p. **940.54**

1. World War II. 2. Soldiers.
ISBN 9780307273598

LC 2011013890

Originally published: London : HarperPress, 2010.

Here, for the first time, Max Hastings gives us a magnificent, single-volume history of World War II in its entirety. Through his strikingly detailed stories of everyday people, he provides an intimate portrait of the world at war. Remarkably informed and wide-ranging, Inferno is both elegantly written and cogently argued. Above all, it is a new and essential understanding of one of the greatest and bloodiest events of the twentieth century.

Hastings, Max

Operation Chastise : the RAF's most brilliant attack of World War II / Max Hastings. HarperCollins, 2020. 416 p. **940.54**

1. Great Britain. Royal Air Force 2. World War II. 3. Air warfare. 4. Bombers -- History -- World War II. 5. Dams 6. Europe -- History, Military -- 20th century 7. Germany -- History -- 20th century
ISBN 9780062953636

LC bl2020000366

One of the most lauded historians of our time returns to the Second World War in this magnificent retelling of the awe-inspiring raid on German dams conducted by the Royal Army Force's 617 Squadron.

"The master of military history takes on Britain's celebrated May 1943 Dam Buster air attack . . . showing once again that the preparations, participants, and consequences of a military action are as fascinating as the fireworks." Kirkus

Hastings, Max

Retribution : the battle for Japan, 1944-45 / Max Hastings. Alfred A. Knopf, 2008. xxv, 615 p., 32 p. of plates : **940.54**

1. Military history -- 20th century. 2. World War II veterans. 3. World War II 4. Military campaigns 5. Japan -- History -- 20th century 6. Japan -- History, Military -- 20th century 7. Pacific Area.
ISBN 0307263517

LC 2007034202

A definitive chronicle of the final year in the Pacific war of World War II offers insightful portraits of key figures in the efforts to defeat Japan--MacArthur, Nimitz, Mountbatten, Mao, and Chiang Kai-shek--and discusses such topics as the road to Allied victory, the war's bloody campaigns, Japan's war against China, and the decision to bomb Hiroshima and Nagasaki.

"Encompassing the British, Chinese, and Soviet roles in vanquishing Japan, Hastings is both comprehensive and finely acute in this masterful interpretive narrative." Booklist.

Hastings, Max

The **secret** war : spies, ciphers, and guerrillas, 1939-1945 / Max Hastings. HarperCollins, 2016 640 p. **940.54**

1. Secret service. 2. Commando operations. 3. World War II 4. Military intelligence.
ISBN 9780062259271

LC bl2016012661

A sweeping examination of one of the most important yet underexplored aspects of World War II--intelligence--showing how espionage successes and failures by the United States, Britain, Russia, Germany and Japan influenced the course of the war and its final outcome.

"This wide-ranging account is filled with compelling characters, some admirable, others morally dubious. Hastings also illustrates that even great intelligence coups can be wasted by politicians who fail to properly utilize the information." Booklist.

Haynes, Fred

The **lions** of Iwo Jima / Fred Haynes and James A. Warren. Henry Holt, 2008. x, 272 p., [16] p. of plates : **940.54**

1. Haynes, Fred 2. Veterans 3. Iwo Jima, Battle of, 1945 4. Military history -- 20th century 5. Marines -- Iwo, Jima, Japan -- World War II 6. Iwo Jima, Japan -- History, Military -- World War II 7. Pacific Area
ISBN 9780805083255

LC 2007042245

A narrative account of the battle of Iwo Jima by Combat Team 28 captain offers insight into the conflict's brutality and high death toll, discussing the team's battlefield performance and their grueling daily experiences throughout the confrontation.

"The account focuses on the experience of Combat Team 28, a unit of 4,500 marines; their best-known accomplishment was the raising of the flag atop Mount Suribachi. However, that event, immortalized by the classic photograph, occurred only four days into the month-long battle. Ahead lay a cauldron of merciless slaughter, with marines inching forward against Japanese troops entrenched in a series of interlocking caves and tunnels. The authors capture the horror of their advance as close-range combat in confined areas became the norm. This is a disturbing, sometimes sickening chronicle, but the harsh face of war in the Pacific theater has rarely been portrayed so effectively." Booklist.

Hellbeck, Jochen

Stalingrad : the city that defeated the Third Reich / Jochen Hellbeck, translated by Chrisopher Tauchen and Dominic Bonfiglio. PublicAffairs, 2015, c2012. viii, 500 p. **940.54**

1. Stalingrad, Battle of, 1942-1943 2. World War II 3. Military campaigns 4. Soviet Union -- History -- 1925-1953.
ISBN 9781610394963

LC 2015002880

"First published in Germany in 2012 by S. Fischer Verlag GmbH"--Title page verso.

Collected by Moscow's Historical Commission, candid accounts by Red Army combatants at the Battle of Stalingrad share harrowing insights into the lives lived and lost during the Second World War's turning point.

Hersey, John, 1914-1993

Hiroshima / John Hersey. Vintage Books, 1989, c1946. 152 p. ; **940.54**

1. World War II -- Hiroshima, Japan. 2. Atomic bomb -- Blast effect. 3. Bombs. 4. Bombing. 5. Hiroshima, Japan -- Atomic bombing, 1945.
ISBN 0679721037

LC 88040016

"A new edition with a final chapter written forty years after the explosion."

Reprint. Originally published: New York : A.A. Knopf, 1985.

The classic tale of the day the first atom bomb was dropped offers a haunting evocation of the memories of survivors and an appeal to the conscience of humanity.

Hervieux, Linda

Forgotten : the untold story of D-Day's Black heroes, at home and at war / Linda Hervieux. HarperCollins Publishers, 2015 368 p. **940.54**

1. United States. Army. Anti-Aricraft Barrage Balloon Battalion, 320th -- History. 2. World War II 3. African American soldiers 4. Normandy Invasion, June 6, 1944 5. Race relations 6. Normandy
ISBN 9780062313799

LC 2015017941

Drawing on newly uncovered military records and original interviews with surviving members of the 320th Barrage Balloon Battalion--a unit of African-American soldiers that has been overlooked by history--and their families, the author tells the story of these heroic men charged with manning armed balloons meant to deter enemy aircraft on D-Day.

"Recommended for aviation buffs, chroniclers of World War II, and anyone who wants a nondense military read." Library Journal.

Hicks, George L.

The **comfort** women : Japan's brutal regime of enforced prostitution in the Second World War / George Hicks. W.W. Norton, 1997, c1994. 303 p. : **940.54**

1. Comfort women. 2. Service, Compulsory non-military. 3. World War II -- Women -- Asia. 4. Sexual slavery 5. Asia
ISBN 0393316947

LC BL 98006670

Originally published: St. Leonards, NSW : Allen & Unwin, 1994.

"The author begins his report with a historical survey of wartime sexual exploitation of women, then narrows the focus to the comfort women system developed by the Japanese. The copious testimony of victims is shockingly graphic. This significant addition to the poor record of mankind to womankind, especially in war, properly approaches the subject as a human-rights issue tied to the rise of feminism in Asia." Publishers Weekly.

Holland, James, 1970-

Battle of Britain : five months that changed history, May-October 1940 / James Holland. St. Martin's Press, 2011. 704 p. **940.54**

1. Britain, Battle of, 1940 2. Battles. 3. World War II 4. Military history.
ISBN 9780312675004

LC 2010040646

"First published in Great Britain by Bantam Press"--T.p. verso.

The historian author of Italy's Shadow presents an account of the pivotal World War II battle based on extensive interviews with people on both sides, offering insight into how the fight was won and the potential of alternate scenarios.

"This massive volume is informative, enthralling, and moving--often all three at once. It effectively combines narrative and analysis to tell the story of the confrontation between the Luftwaffe and RAF Fighter Command from May through October 1940." Booklist.

Normandy '44 : D-day and the epic 77-day battle for France / James Holland. Atlantic Monthly, 2019 649 p. **940.54**

1. Normandy Invasion, June 6, 1944 2. World War II 3. Operation Overlord 4. Military campaigns 5. Normandy 6. France
ISBN 9780802129420

LC bl2019016622

Uses archival knowledge and eyewitness testimonies to reexamine D-Day, including the extraordinary planning, the brutal landings, and the strategic decisions of the commanders.

"From Omaha Beach to the Falaise Gap, this is thoughtful, crisply written military history." Booklist.

The **rise** of Germany, 1939-1941 : the war in the west. James Holland. Grove/Atlantic, 2015 512 p. **940.54**

1. World War II 2. Nazis 3. World politics 4. Germany
ISBN 9780802123978

LC bl2015034780

The first segment in a three-part history of World War II in Europe, North Africa, and the Atlantic draws on original testimony and new research to discuss events from the outbreak of war in 1939 to the eve of the invasion of the Soviet Union.

"Holland skillfully integrates the broad political, diplomatic, economic, and military narrative with stories of individuals, civilians, and soldiers from all the belligerents." Library Journal.

Sicily '43 : the first assault on fortress Europe / James Holland. Atlantic Monthly Press, 2020 592 p. **940.54**

1. Operation Husky, 1943. 2. World War II 3. Military campaigns 4. Allied forces 5. Sicily, Italy -- History
ISBN 9780802157188

LC 2020038631

Based on his own battlefield studies in Sicily and on much new research, James Holland's Sicily '43 offers a vital new perspective on a major turning point in World War II and a chronicle of a multi-pronged campaign in a uniquely diverse and contained geographical location.

"An excellent and accessible telling of the invasion that will be enjoyed by military history and World War II enthusiasts alike." Library Journal

Holmes, Richard, 1946-2011

World War II : the definitive visual history : from Blitzkrieg to the atom bomb / editorial consultant, Richard Holmes. DK, 2015. 372 p. : **940.54**

1. World War II. 2. World War II -- Pictorial works.

ISBN 9781465436023

LC bl2015016265

Includes index.

A 70th anniversary edition looks at this epic war from every angle, tracing the course of military, strategic and political events across the globe and documenting the experiences of combatants and civilians.

Hopkins, William B.

The **Pacific** War : the strategy, politics, and players that won the war / William B. Hopkins. MBI Pub. Co., 2008. 400 p. **940.54**

1. World War II -- Pacific Area. 2. Strategy. 3. Military history. 4. War. 5. United States -- Military policy -- 20th century. 6. United States -- Politics and government -- 1933-1945.

ISBN 9780760334355

LC 2008038157

Hotta, Eri, 1971-

Japan 1941 : countdown to infamy / Eri Hotta. Alfred A. Knopf, 2013. 320 p. **940.54**

1. World War II -- Japan. 2. Military planning -- Japan -- History -- 20th century. 3. War -- Decision making. 4. Pearl Harbor, Attack on, 1941 5. Japan -- Politics and government -- 1926-1945.

ISBN 9780307594013

LC 2013014781

A history of the attack on Pearl Harbor from a Japanese perspective argues that the nation's leaders largely understood they were destined to lose the war, offering insight into the tradition-obscured belief system that prompted the country to place its citizens in harm's way.

Jacobsen, Annie

Operation Paperclip : the secret intelligence program to bring Nazi scientists to America / Annie Jacobsen. Little Brown & Co., 2014 680 p. **940.54**

1. World War II -- Technology 2. Nazis -- History -- 20th century. 3. Brain drain -- Germany -- History -- 20th century. 4. Scientists -- Germany -- Recruiting -- History -- 20th century.

ISBN 9780316221047

LC 2013028255

Details how the U.S. government embarked on a covert operation to recruit and employ Nazi scientists in the years following World War II in an effort to prevent their knowledge and expertise from falling into the hands of the Soviet Union.

"Built upon archival records, court transcripts, declassified documents, and interviews, Jacobsen's impressive book plumbs the dark depths of this postwar recruiting and shows the historical truths behind the space race and postwar U.S. dominance." Library Journal.

Jones, Michael K.

The **retreat** : Hitler's first defeat / Michael Jones. Thomas Dunne Books/St. Martin's Press, 2010, c2009 328 p. **940.54**

1. Moscow, Battle of, 1941-1942 2. World War II 3. Military campaigns 4. Battles. 5. Soviet Union

ISBN 9780312628192

LC 2010034784

Originally published: London : John Murray, 2009.

A dramatic account of a World War II turning point introduces the military tradition of the ubermensch iron-willed fighter while documenting how Moscow was saved from German forces during an arduous Soviet retreat supported by tanks and ski battalions. By the author of Stalingrad.

Kaplan, Alice Yaeger

The **interpreter** / Alice Kaplan. Free Press, 2005. xii, 240 p. : **940.54**

1. Hendricks, James E. Trials, litigation, etc. 2. Whittington, George P, 1913-1996 Trials, litigation, etc. 3. Guilloux, Louis, 1899-1980. 4. United States. Army Officers. 5. World War II -- African Americans 6. African American soldiers 7. Courts-martial and courts of inquiry -- France. 8. Trials (Murder) -- France. 9. France -- History -- 20th century.

ISBN 9780743254243

LC 2005040099

Draws on the account of World War II French court interpreter Louis Guilloux, who witnessed general Patton's example-setting executions of seventy American troops, many of whom he believed were condemned because of their race.

"Inventive, moving, and beautifully written, this is a major contribution to investigative history." Library Journal.

Karnad, Raghu

Farthest field : an Indian story of the Second World War / Raghu Karnad. W.W. Norton & Company, 2015. 240 p. **940.54**

1. Mugaseth, Bobby, 1919-1944 Family. 2. Great Britain. Army. British Indian Army 3. World War II -- India. 4. Soldiers -- India 5. Social change -- India -- History -- 20th century. 6. War and society -- India -- History -- 20th century. 7. India

ISBN 9780393248098

LC 2015018733

Bobby Mugaseth, a young man from the sleepy south Indian coast, sensing adventure and opportunity, follows his brothers-in-law into the army and onto the front lines of India's Second World War. His army fights for the British empire, even as his countrymen fight for freedom from it, and Indian soldiers end up on both sides of the vast conflict. The Farthest Field reveals how the war transformed India, its army, and the British empire that had ruled the country for so long and would, barely two years after the end of the war, abandon it to the horrors of partition.

"An appealing, if necessarily fictionalized in places, portrait of three officers who did their best fighting a war widely opposed by many countrymen and that provided little benefit to the nation and was quickly forgotten after Indian independence in 1947." Kirkus.

Katz, Robert, 1933-

The **battle** for Rome : the Germans, the allies, the partisans and the Pope, September 1943-June 1944 / Robert Katz. Simon & Schuster, 2003. xviii, 418 p. : **940.54**

1. World War II -- Rome, Italy. 2. Rome, Italy -- History -- 1870-1945.

ISBN 0743216423

LC 2003045677

"This narrative history describes the Eternal City at a key time of struggle: the dark year of German occupation between the overthrow of Mussolini in 1943 and liberation by the Allies in 1944. Four parties wrestle for Rome: the ruthless yet wary German occupiers, the Holy See in self-preservation mode, a gutsy band of patriotic students with homemade explosives, and the U.S. Fifth Army under Mark Clark. This is challenging research presented fluidly, and Katz's fascination with a key moment for a fascinating city shines through." Booklist.

Kennedy, Paul, 1945-

Engineers of victory : the problem solvers who turned the tide in the Second World War / Paul Kennedy. Random House Inc, 2013. 224 p. **940.54**

1. Military strategy. 2. Military tactics. 3. Soldiers. 4. World War II.
ISBN 9781400067619

LC 2012024284

The renowned historian analyzes previously unexplored strategic factors he believes to be responsible for the Allied victory in World War II, sharing behind-the-scenes assessments of ambitious goals successfully pursued by FDR, Churchill and other attendees at the Casablanca Conference.

Kershaw, Alex

Escape from the deep : a legendary submarine and her courageous crew / Alex Kershaw. Perseus Books Group, 2008. 288 p. **940.54**

1. United States. Navy Submarine forces 2. Tang (Submarine : SS-306) 3. Submarines, American -- History -- World War II 4. Submarine warfare -- History -- World War II 5. Submarine disasters. 6. Prisoners of war, American
ISBN 0306815192

LC 2008298762

In this harrowing war saga, Kershaw recounts the incredible story of the U.S. Navy's deadliest World War II submarine, the USS Tang. Across the Pacific theater, dodging mines and depth charges, the 80 men of the Tang became legends. By 1944, they had sunk more Japanese ships than any other Allied submarine.

"The author has researched exhaustively, including interviewing the last two living survivors, and written compactly the portrait of nine Americans who rose to heroism and of a ship that well deserved its status as a legend in the naval history of World War II." Booklist.

The **first** wave : the D-Day warriors who led the way to victory in World War II / Alex Kershaw. Dutton Caliber, [2019] 464 p. **940.54**

1. Normandy Invasion, June 6, 1944 2. World War, 1939-1945 -- Campaigns -- France -- Normandy 3. Combat 4. Soldiers
ISBN 9780451490056

LC 2018057388

"Beginning in the predawn darkness of June 6, 1944, The First Wave follows the remarkable men who carried out D-Day's most perilous missions. The first to fight when the stakes were highest and the odds longest, these men would determine the fate of the invasion of Hitler's Fortress Europe--and the very history of the twentieth century."-- Provided by publisher.

"Kershaw presents war in all of its ugliness and horror even as he emphasizes the commitment of the young fighters to their comrades. The First Wave, a welcome and fresh take on one of the greatest and most significant of WWII missions, marks D-Day's 75th anniversary." Booklist.

Kershaw, Robert J., 1950-

Landing on the edge of eternity : twenty-four hours at Omaha Beach / Robert Kershaw. Pegasus Books, 2018. xl, 376 p., 24 unnumbered p. of plates : **940.54**

1. Normandy Invasion, June 6, 1944 2. Soldiers 3. Battles 4. World War II 5. Normandy -- History, Military -- 20th century
ISBN 9781681778662

A visceral narrative of the first 24 hours of D-Day on the Allied landing site on Omaha Beach draws on soldier accounts to examine the formidable natural obstacles and German resistance that cost more than 2,400 lives.

Korda, Michael, 1933-

★**Alone** : Britain, Churchill, and Dunkirk : defeat into victory / Michael Korda. Liveright Publishing Company, a division of W. W. Norton & Company, [2017] 564 p. **940.54**

1. Korda, Michael, 1933- Childhood and youth. 2. Dunkirk, France, Battle of, 1940. 3. War and society 4. World War II -- Great Britain. 5. World War II -- France.
ISBN 9781631491320

LC 2017017244

Author and former editor-in-chief of Simon & Schuster Michael Korda was born in England in 1933; his family went to the US in 1941 for the duration of World War II. In Alone, Korda weaves his childhood memories of Britain with a thoroughly researched history of the early months of the war up through the 1940 evacuation from Dunkirk. This detailed history presents an engaging review of military tactics and international politics, illuminated by Korda's personal recollections.

"Korda succeeds in infusing straight history with the accessible tone of narrative nonfiction." Booklist.

With wings like eagles : a history of the Battle of Britain / Michael Korda. Harper, 2009. 336 p. **940.54**

1. Great Britain. Royal Air Force -- History World War II 2. Britain, Battle of, 1940 3. World War II -- Aerial operations, British. 4. Battles. 5. Military history. 6. Great Britain -- History -- 20th century.
ISBN 9780061125355

LC 2008009293

"This is a skillful, absorbing, often moving contribution to the popular understanding of one of the few episodes in history to live on untarnished and undiminished in the collective memory and to deserve the description heroic." Washington Post.

Larson, Erik, 1954-

★The **splendid** and the vile : a saga of Churchill, family, and defiance during the Blitz / Erik Larson. Crown, 2020. 464 p. **940.54**

1. Churchill, Winston, 1874-1965. 2. Prime ministers -- Great Britain 3. World War II -- Great Britain. 4. World War II -- Social aspects -- Great Britain. 5. London, England -- History -- Bombardment, 1940-1941 6. Great Britain -- History -- Bombing, 1940-1945 7. England -- History -- 20th century
ISBN 9780385348713

LC 2019045028

Draws on personal diaries, archival documents and declassified intelligence in a portrait of Winston Churchill that explores his day-to-day experiences during the Blitz and his role in uniting England.

"Blending a gripping narrative and a well-researched examination of personal and news archives, Larson's distinctive history of Britain's 'darkest hour' offers a new angle for those already familiar with this era, while attracting readers who wish to learn more about the notable leader." Library Journal

Leckie, Robert, 1920-

Okinawa : the last battle of World War II / Robert Leckie. Penguin Books, 1996, c1995. x, 220 p. : **940.54**

1. World War II 2. Military campaigns 3. Okinawa -- History. 4.

Japan.
ISBN 0140173897

LC BL 99775455

Includes index.
Originally published: New York : Viking, 1995.
A retelling of the April Fool's Day invasion of Japan in 1945 by a U.S. Marine veteran offers a perspective of the eighty-three-day battle from American and Japanese viewpoints.
"In this history of the Battle of Okinawa Leckie supplies an accessible historical overview of a perplexing war tactic, the kamikaze attack." Booklist.

Letts, Elizabeth
The **perfect** horse : the daring U.S. mission to rescue the priceless stallions kidnapped by the Nazis / Elizabeth Letts. Ballantine, 2016. 368 p. **940.54**
1. Patton, George S., 1885-1945. 2. Thoroughbred horses 3. Lipizzaner horse. 4. Nazi propaganda. 5. Horse breeding.
ISBN 9780345544803

LC 2016010501

Traces the lesser-known efforts of Hitler to build a master race of the finest purebred horses and the heroic achievements of American soldiers to rescue imperiled stolen equines from a hidden Czechoslovakian farm during a 1945 battle between Third Reich and Allied forces.
"The author's elegant narrative conveys how the love for these amazing creatures transcends national animosities." Kirkus.

Lifton, Robert Jay, 1926-
Hiroshima in America : a half century of denial / Robert Jay Lifton, Greg Mitchell ; with a new afterword by the authors. Avon Books, 1996, c1995. xviii, 427 p. ; **940.54**
1. Hibakusha. 2. Atomic bomb. 3. World War II -- United States. 4. Hiroshima, Japan -- Atomic bombing, 1945 -- Influence. 5. Hiroshima, Japan -- Atomic bombing, 1945 -- Moral and ethical aspects.
ISBN 0380727641

LC BL 99776169

Originally published: New York : Putnam's Sons, c1995.
Argues that information and debate about President Truman's decision to drop the bomb on Japan have been suppressed.

The **Nazi** doctors : medical killing and the psychology of genocide / Robert Jay Lifton. Basic Books, c1986. xiii, 561 p. ; **940.54**
1. Human experimentation in medicine -- Germany -- Psychological aspects. 2. Medical scientists 3. Holocaust (1933-1945) -- Germany -- Psychological aspects. 4. World War II 5. Germany
ISBN 0465049052

LC 85073874

Includes index.
National Jewish Book Award, 1987.
Explores the psychological conditions that promote the human potential for evil, relating medical killing to broader principles of doubling and genocide.
"How could German physicians trained as scientist-healers carry out Nazi orders for mass killings? Lifton, an American Jewish physician, seeks answers through interviews with surviving doctors, family members, and victims and by painstakingly gleaning Holocaust archives." Science Books & Films.

Lineberry, Cate
The **secret** rescue : an untold story of American nurses and medics behind Nazi lines / Cate Lineberry. Little, Brown and Co., 2013. 288 p. **940.54**
1. United States. Army Medical service. 2. World War II 3. Airplane accidents 4. Survival. 5. Nurses.
ISBN 9780316220224

LC 2013934814

Lukacs, John, 1924-
Escape from Davao : the forgotten story of the most daring prison break of the Pacific war / John D. Lukacs. Simon & Schuster, 2010. 384 p. **940.54**
1. Prisoners of war, American 2. Prisoner-of-war escapes 3. Escaped prisoners of war 4. World War II 5. Philippines -- History -- Japanese occupation, 1942-1945.
ISBN 9780743262781

LC 2010003238

Draws on primary source material and survivor interviews to document the escape of ten American POWs from a World War II Japanese prison camp in the Philippines, describing the inhumane conditions they endured and the international political struggle that influenced their return home.
"The author is a gifted stylist and storyteller. He doesn't flinch at the grim or the gruesome. At bottom, Escape From Davao is a morality tale, not unlike the war movies of the 1940s and '50s, about pluck, luck, courage, comradeship, Yankee humor, ingenuity, and religious faith." Pittsburgh Post-Gazette

Lulushi, Albert
Donovan's Devils : OSS commandos behind enemy lines : Europe, World War II / Albert Lulushi. Arcade Pubishing, 2016. 336 p. **940.54**
1. Donovan, William J. (William Joseph), 1883-1959. 2. Holohan, William V. 3. United States. Office of Strategic Services -- History. 4. Secret service. 5. World War II 6. Commando operations.
ISBN 9781628725674

LC 2015037691

Based on declassified OSS records, personal collections, and oral histories of participants from both sides of the conflict, Donovan's Devils provides the most comprehensive account to date of the Operational Group activities, including a detailed narrative of the ill-fated Ginny mission, which resulted in the one of the OSS's gravest losses of the war.
"A proficient, well-wrought work that emphasizes the actual fighting men, their deeds, and their fates." Kirkus.

Marston, Daniel,
The **Pacific** War companion : from Pearl Harbor to Hiroshima / edited by Daniel Marston. Osprey, 2005. 272 p. : **940.54**
1. World War II 2. Naval battles -- History -- 20th century 3. Military campaigns 4. Pacific Area -- History, Military. 5. Pacific Area -- History, Naval
ISBN 1841768820

LC bl2005021034

Offers an introduction to the Pacific War, including such topics as the opening amphibious operations and Japanese naval strategy after Midway.
"These essays on the Pacific theater of WW II, written by a group of international scholars representing Australia, Great Britain, Japan, and the US, cover the wellknown events at Pearl Harbor, the Coral Sea, and Midway; MacArthur's push to the Philippines; Nimitz's island campaign in the central Pacific; Okinawa; and the dropping of the atomic bomb on Hiroshima and Nagasaki. A chronology, detailed maps, and

photographs greatly enhance this excellent volume on the Pacific phase of WW II." Choice.

Macintyre, Ben, 1963-

Operation Mincemeat : how a dead man and a bizarre plan fooled the Nazis and assured an Allied victory / Ben MacIntyre. Harmony Books, 2010. x, 400 p., [16] p. of plates : **940.54**

1. Montagu, Ewen, 1901-1985. 2. Great Britain. Royal Navy -- History World War II 3. Military deception. 4. Military intelligence 5. Operation Mincemeat. 6. World War II 7. England -- History -- 20th century

ISBN 9780307453273

LC 2009047562

Chronicles World War II's pivotal deception by two British naval officers who successfully fed false intelligence to the Nazis about where Allied forces were planning an attack in southern Europe.

"A true WWII tale that reads like something by Ian Fleming. In fact, two of Fleming's fellow British intelligence officers hatched the title operation. They dressed a corpse in uniform and arranged for it to wash up on a Nazi-friendly stretch of the Spanish coast bearing a suitcase with false war plans. Against all odds, Operation Mincemeat succeeded and helped convince the Germans that the Allies planned to invade Sardinia and Greece in 1943 instead of their real target, Sicily. Relying on a cache of once-classified documents, Macintyre provides the fullest account yet of this curious episode and enlivens his yarn with quirky details." Entertainment Weekly.

★**Rogue** heroes : The history of the SAS, Britain's secret special forces unit that sabotaged the Nazis and changed the nature of war / Ben MacIntyre. Crown, 2016. 352 p. **940.54**

1. Great Britain. Army. Special Air Service. 2. Special forces 3. Commando troops 4. World War II 5. Sabotage

ISBN 9781101904169

LC bl2016035969

A history of Great Britain's Special Air Service or SAS that fought against the Nazis during World War II.

"He demonstrates that even in a global war, a few uniquely talented, imaginative, and bold individuals of relatively junior rank can have a major impact. Macintyre delivers a solid history and an enjoyable read that will appeal to those interested in military history as well as readers who enjoy real-life tales of adventure." Publishers Weekly.

Maslov, Sasha

Veterans : faces of World War II / Sasha Maslov. Princeton Architectural Press, 2017 142 p. : **940.54**

1. World War II 2. World War II -- Veterans -- Pictorial works 3. World War II -- Veterans -- Interviews

ISBN 9781616895785

LC 2016038694

"Since 2010, Ukrainian-born photographer Sasha Maslov has traveled to more than twenty countries, interviewing participants in World War II and taking richly detailed photographs of them in their homes. Soldiers, support staff, and resistance members candidly discuss wartime experiences and their lifelong effects. We meet Ichiro Sudai, who trained to be a kamikazi; Urszula Hoffmann, who taught young children as a member of the Polish resistance; Roscoe Brown, a commander in the Tuskegee Airmen, the first African American military aviators; Charin Singh, a farmer from Delhi who spent seven years as a Japanese prisoner of war, returning home only in 1949; and Uli John, who lost an arm while serving in the German Army and ultimately befriended former enemy soldiers as part of a network of veterans--"people who fought in the war and know what war really means." Veterans is a record of a cataclysmic time in world history and a tribute to the members of an indomitable generation; it is also a meditation on memory, human struggle, and the passage of time. Its portraits are indelible."--Provided by publisher.

McKay, Sinclair

The **fire** and the darkness : the bombing of Dresden, 1945 / Sinclair McKay. St. Martin's Press, 2020. 400 p. **940.54**

1. World War II -- Germany 2. Bombings 3. Fires 4. World War II -- Aerial operations 5. Dresden, Germany -- Bombing, 1945 6. Germany -- History -- 1933-1945

ISBN 9781250258014

LC 2019044455

On February 13th, 1945 at 10:03 PM, British bombers began one of the most devastating attacks of WWII: the bombing of Dresden. The first contingent killed people and destroyed buildings, roads, and other structures. The second rained down fire, turning the streets into a blast furnace, the shelters into ovens, and whipping up a molten hurricane in which the citizens of Dresden were burned, baked, or suffocated to death. Early the next day, American bombers finished off what was left. Sinclair McKay's The Fire and the Darkness is a pulse-pounding work of history that looks at the life of the city in the days before the attack, tracks each moment of the bombing, and considers the long period of reconstruction and recovery.

"McKay's extensive research and animated prose capture the terror and tragedy of the bombing. Readers won't soon forget this devastating account." Publishers Weekkly

The **secret** lives of codebreakers : the men and women who cracked the Enigma code at Bletchley Park / Sinclair McKay. Penguin Group, 2012. 352 p. **940.54**

1. Great Britain. Government Communications Headquarters -- History. 2. World War II -- Cryptography. 3. Cryptography 4. Intelligence service 5. World War II -- Electronic intelligence -- Great Britain. 6. England 7. Bletchley Park (Milton Keynes, England) -- History.

ISBN 9780452298712

LC 2012018408

Previous ed.: The secret life of Bletchley Park : the WWII codebreaking centre and the men and women who worked there / Sinclair McKay, 2010.

A remarkable look at the day-to-day lives of the codebreakers whose clandestine efforts helped win World War II.

Merridale, Catherine, 1959-

★**Ivan's** war : life and death in the Red Army, 1939-1945 / Catherine Merridale. Metropolitan Books, 2006. xii, 462 p. : **940.54**

1. Soviet Union. Army -- History World War II 2. Eastern Front (World War II) 3. World War II 4. Military campaigns 5. Soldiers -- Soviet Union -- Social conditions -- 20th century. 6. Soviet Union -- Social conditions -- 1917-1945 7. Soviet Union -- History, Military -- German occupation, 1941-1944

ISBN 0805074554

LC 2005050457

Drawing on previously closed military and secret police archives and interviews with veterans, a comprehensive history of the Red Army rank and file follows the soldiers from the shock of the German invasion to their costly triumph in Stalingrad.

Miller, Nathan, 1927-

War at sea : a naval history of World War II / Nathan Miller. Scribner, c1995. 592 p., 16 p. of plates : **940.54**

1. World War II -- Naval operations. 2. Naval battles
ISBN 0684803801

LC 95008484

"A Lisa Drew book."

Covers each of the sea battles of World War II as recorded in ship logs, intelligence documents, official reports, and servicemen interviews.

"Miller's research--primarily on the Royal Navy--and a reading of hundreds of pertinent monographs has enabled him to fashion a briskly paced narrative that will both inform and entertain." Choice.

Milton, Giles

Churchill's ministry of ungentlemanly warfare : the mavericks who plotted Hitler's defeat / Giles Milton. Picador USA, 2017. 368 p. **940.54**

1. Churchill, Winston, 1874-1965 Military leadership 2. World War II 3. Subversive activities. 4. Special forces 5. Guerrilla warfare.
ISBN 9781250119025

LC 2016039180

Documents the top-secret guerilla campaign founded in London to orchestrate spectacular acts of sabotage against Hitler's war machine, profiling the six remarkable men behind the campaign and how they changed the course of World War II.

"An exciting, suspenseful tale of international intrigue." Kirkus.

Soldier, sailor, frogman, spy, airman, gangster, kill or die : how the Allies won on D-day / Giles Milton. Henry Holt & Company, 2019. 489 p. **940.54**

1. Normandy Invasion, June 6, 1944. 2. Military campaigns 3. World War II 4. Battles
ISBN 9781250134929

LC bl2019001163

A chronicle of the first 24 hours of the D-Day invasion shares the perspectives of a diverse range of Allied, German and French contributors to explore the conflict's strategic mastery and human realities. Map(s).

"Highly recommended for World War II aficionados and those seeking a great read in military history." Library Journal.

Morris, Jan, 1926-2020

Battleship Yamato : of war, beauty and irony / Jan Morris. Liveright Publishing Corporation, 2017 111 p. : **940.54**

1. Yamato (Battleship). 2. World War II -- Naval operations, Japanese.
ISBN 1631493426

LC 2017035438

An illustrated assessment of the meaning of war by the author of the Pax Britannia trilogy traces the dramatic story of the Imperial Japanese Navy battleship "Yamato" and how it represents turning points in both World War II and the warrior traditions of the Japanese samurai.

Mueller, Gordon H., 1940-

Everything we have : D-Day 6.6.44 / Gordon H. "Nick" Mueller ; foreword by Tom Brokaw. Andre Deutsch, 2019. 255 p. **940.54**

1. Normandy Invasion, June 6, 1944. 2. Operation Overlord 3. Military campaigns 4. World War II 5. Oral histories
ISBN 9780233005812

LC bl2019031427

"Produced in association with the US National World War II Museum to commemorate the 75th anniversary of D-Day"

June 6, 1944--D-Day--is a date that will live forever in history. More than 150,000 troops landed on five beaches, with over 20,000 reported casualties on both sides. Rather than looking at the big picture, recounted so often, Everything We Have: D-Day 6.6.'44 tells the personal stories of the people involved, in their own words. Rare documents, artifacts, and firsthand accounts from The National WWII Museum's official archives provide rare and poignant insight into the thoughts and feelings of those soldiers who fought on the beaches of Normandy.

"This superbly illustrated work of military and oral history is both a defining introduction and a vivid refresher to D-Day." Booklist.

Mundy, Liza, 1960-

Code girls : the untold story of the American women code breakers who helped win World War II / Liza Mundy. Hachette Books, 2017. 500 p. **940.54**

1. World War II -- Cryptography 2. World War II -- Women's participation. 3. Women -- Employment -- United States. 4. Cryptographers
ISBN 9780316439893

LC 2017020069

Recruited by the U.S. Army and Navy from small towns and elite colleges, more than ten thousand women served as codebreakers during World War II. While their brothers and boyfriends took up arms, these women moved to Washington and learned the meticulous work of code-breaking. Their efforts shortened the war, saved countless lives, and gave them access to careers previously denied to them. A strict vow of secrecy nearly erased their efforts from history; now, through dazzling research and interviews with surviving code girls, bestselling author Liza Mundy brings to life this riveting and vital story of American courage, service, and scientific accomplishment.

"A well-researched, compellingly written, crucial addition to the literature of American involvement in World War II." Kirkus.

Neiberg, Michael S.

The **blood** of free men : the liberation of Paris, 1944 / Michael Neiberg. Basic Books, 2012. 352 p. **940.54**

1. World War II 2. Military campaigns 3. War 4. Paris, France.
ISBN 9780465023998

LC 2012016282

Describes the operation involving Resistance fighters, Allied commanders, and French citizens that resulted in the liberation of Paris in 1944 from German occupation and ultimately helped shape the outcome of World War II.

Neitzel, Sonke

Soldaten : on fighting, killing, and dying / Sonke Neitzel and Harald Welzer ; translated from the German by Jefferson Chase. Alfred A. Knopf, 2012. 496 p. **940.54**

1. Military intelligence -- Great Britain. 2. World War II -- Prisoners and prisons, British. 3. Prisoners of war, German 4. Prisoners of war, British 5. Germany -- Armed Forces -- History -- 20th century
ISBN 9780307958129

LC 2012005744

A compendium of previously unpublished, transcribed conversations among German POWs, secretly recorded by the Allies and recently declassified, offers insight into the mindset of World War II German soldiers.

Nelson, Craig, 1955-

The **first** heroes : the extraordinary story of the Doolittle Raid-- America's first World War II victory / Craig Nelson. Viking, 2002. xviii, 430 p., 16 p. of plates : **940.54**

1. Doolittle, James Harold, 1896-1993. 2. United States. Army Air Forces 3. United States. Army Air Forces -- History World War II. 4. Bombing -- Tokyo, Japan. 5. World War II -- Aerial operations, American. 6. Tokyo, Japan -- History -- Bombardment, 1942.

ISBN 0670030872

LC 2002028092

An account of the Doolittle Raid against Tokyo explores this seminal event in the early stages of World War II, discusses its ramifications in terms of the Allied war effort, and profiles the men who took part in the raid.

"The most interesting part of the book is the harrowing story of survival as crew members are forced to ditch their planes on the Asian mainland. This is a thrilling real-life saga that both informs and inspires." Booklist.

Pearl Harbor : from infamy to greatness / Craig Nelson. Scribner, an imprint of Simon & Schuster, 2016 384 p. **940.54**

1. Pearl Harbor, Attack on, 1941 2. United States -- History, Military -- 20th century

ISBN 9781451660494

LC 2016018490

Published to commemorate the 75th anniversary of the attack, an account based on years of research and new information illuminates less-understood aspects of how and why Japan targeted America, sharing additional details about the experiences of survivors.

"Nelsons well written history of Pearl Harbor will be enjoyed by the general reader and appropriately highlights the battles historical significance." Publishers Weekly.

Norman, Michael, 1947 October 2-

★**Tears** in the darkness : the story of the Bataan Death March and its aftermath / Michael Norman and Elizabeth M. Norman. Farrar, Straus, and Giroux, 2009. 480 p. **940.54**

1. Bataan Death March, 1942. 2. World War II -- Prisoners and prisons, Japanese. 3. Prisoners of war. 4. Military history.

ISBN 9780374272609

LC 2008047163

ALA Notable Book, 2010.

"This book is authoritative history. Ten years in the making, it is based on hundreds of interviews with American, Filipino and Japanese combatants. But it is also a narrative achievement. The book seamlessly blends a wide-angle view with the stories of many individual participants." New York Times.

Parkin, Simon

★A **game** of birds and wolves : the ingenious young women whose secret board game helped win World War II / Simon Parkin. Little, Brown and Company, 2020. 309 pages, 16 unnumbered pages of plates : **940.54**

1. Women and war 2. Military strategy 3. Submarines, German 4. Young women

ISBN 9780316492096

LC 2019954676

Tells the triumphant story of a group of young women who helped devise a winning strategy to defeat the Nazi U-boats and deliver a decisive victory in the Battle of the Atlantic.

"An informative, satisfying, and overall great read." Booklist

Peffer, Randall S.

Where divers dare : the hunt for the last U-boat / Randall Peffer. Berkley Calibre, 2016. 320 p. **940.54**

1. U-550 (Submarine). 2. Naval battles 3. World War II 4. Submarine warfare 5. Military campaigns 6. North Atlantic Ocean.

ISBN 9780425276365

LC 2015028313

An exciting story of the 20-year quest to find the tanker SS Pan Pennsylvania--which was torpedoed and sunk by the U-550 on April 16, 1944--follows the courageous men who dived on the last sunken U-Boat off the Eastern Seaboard.

"Peffer conveys the tension, fear, and exhilaration of deep wreck diving in this uncomfortable true story of bravery, compassion, and death that characterized the violent last hours of U-550." Publishers Weekly.

Pellegrino, Charles R.

To hell and back : the last train from Hiroshima / Charles Pellegrino. Rowman & Littlefield, 2015. 424 p. **940.54**

1. Hibakusha 2. Atomic bomb -- Blast effect. 3. Radiation victims. 4. Hiroshima, Japan -- Atomic bombing, 1945. 5. Japan -- History -- 1945- 6. Essays.

ISBN 9781442250581

LC 2015014341

Originally published under title: The last train from Hiroshima. New York : Henry Holt and Co., 2010.

"This is horrifying, painful, and necessary reading." Kirkus.

Pleshakov, Konstantin

★**Stalin's** folly : the tragic first ten days of World War II on the Eastern front / Constantine Pleshakov. Houghton Mifflin, 2005. 326 p. **940.54**

1. Stalin, Joseph, 1879-1953. 2. Eastern Front (World War II) 3. World War II 4. Military campaigns 5. Europe -- History, Military -- 20th century

ISBN 0618367012

LC 2004065133

Reassessing the Soviet response to the Nazi invasion of Russia, the author portrays Stalin as an ineffective military leader who allowed hundreds of thousands of his soldiers to be slaughtered in the first ten days of the invasion.

"This book belongs in every World War II collection." Library Journal.

Prados, John

Storm over Leyte : the Philippine invasion and the destruction of the Japanese Navy / John Prados. New American Library, [2016] 400 p. **940.54**

1. United States. Navy. 2. World War II 3. Military campaigns 4. Leyte Gulf, Battle of, Philippines, 1944. 5. Naval battles 6. Philippines 7. Pacific Ocean. 8. Leyte Island (Philippines) -- History, Military.

ISBN 9780451473615

LC 2015047067

As Allied ships prepared for the invasion of the Philippine island of Leyte, every available warship, submarine and airplane was placed on alert while Japanese admiral Kurita Takeo stalked Admiral William F. Halsey's unwitting American armada. It was the beginning of the epic Battle of Leyte Gulf--the greatest naval battle in history. Prados gives readers an unprecedented look at both sides of this titanic naval clash, demonstrating that, despite the Americans' overwhelming superiority in firepower and supplies, the Japanese achieved their goal, inflicting grave damage on U.S. forces. And for the first time, readers will have access to the naval intelligence reports that influenced key strategic decisions on both sides.

"The work is exceedingly balanced and provides detailed portraits of the personalities of the Japanese commanders, their understanding of events, and their decision-making processes." Publishers Weekly.

Prange, Gordon W., 1910-1980

At dawn we slept : the untold story of Pearl Harbor / Gordon W. Prange in collaboration with Donald M. Goldstein and Katherine V. Dillon. Penguin Books, 2001, c1981. xvi, 889 p. : **940.54**

1. Pearl Harbor, Attack on, 1941. 2. World War II. 3. Hawaii.
ISBN 0140157344

LC 2001276551

Originally published: New York : McGraw-Hill, 1981.

Records the planning and execution of the Japanese attack on Pearl Harbor, and looks at what it reveals about American leadership.

"The author offers a comprehensive account of Japanese preparations for the attack, the origins and extent of American unpreparedness, and the aftermath of the attack on both sides." Booklist.

Raghavan, Srinath

India's war : World War II and the making of modern South Asia / Srinath Raghavan. Basic Books, 2016 512 p. **940.54**

1. Soldiers -- India 2. Social change -- India -- History -- 20th century. 3. War and society -- India -- History -- 20th century. 4. India
ISBN 9780465030224

LC 2016933273

Between 1939 and 1945 India underwent irreversible change when Indians suddenly found themselves fighting in World War II, and the author paints a picture of battles abroad and life on the home front, arguing that the war is crucial to explaining why colonial rule ended in South Asia.

"This book will be appreciated by scholars and general readers alike who wish to discover more answers to India's role in World War II." Library Journal.

Read, Anthony

The **fall** of Berlin / Anthony Read and David Fisher. Da Capo Press, 1995, c1992. 513 p. : **940.54**

1. Berlin, Battle of, 1945 2. World War II -- Germany. 3. Nazism. 4. Germany -- History -- 1933-1945. 5. Berlin (Germany) -- History.
ISBN 0306806193

LC 94047998

Originally published: London : Hutchinson, 1992.

A narrative of the fall of Berlin chronicles the history of the city from the pomp and glitter of the 1936 Olympic games, through the rise of the Nazis, to World War II and the Allied conquest.

"The result is a highly readable and, at the same time, sophisticated and reliable narrative history." Library Journal.

Reid, Anna

Leningrad : the epic siege of World War II, 1941-1944 / Anna Reid. Walker & Co., 2011. xv, 492 p., 16 p. of plates : **940.54**

1. Siege warfare. 2. Operation Barbarossa. 3. Bombardment. 4. World War II. 5. St. Petersburg, Russia -- Siege, 1941-1944
ISBN 9780802715944

LC bl2011021728

A narrative account of the siege of Leningrad reveals the Nazi decision to starve Leningrad into surrender and related Soviet leadership failures, describing the harrowing experiences of residents within the blockaded city.

Roberts, Andrew, 1963-

The **storm** of war : a new history of the Second World War / Andrew Roberts. Harpercollins, 2011 608 p. **940.54**

1. Hitler, Adolf, 1889-1945 Military leadership 2. World War II. 3. Military campaigns. 4. Military strategy -- Germany
ISBN 9780061228599

LC bl2011011949

Analyzing the factors that affected the war's outcome and presenting stories of many little-known individuals whose experiences are the epitome of remarkable courage and self-sacrifice, the New York Times best-selling author of Masters and Commanders tells the story of World War II like never before.

Scott, James (James M.)

Rampage : Macarthur, Yamashita, and the Battle of Manila / James M. Scott. W.W. Norton & Company, 2018. 635 p., 16 unnumbered p. of plates : **940.54**

1. MacArthur, Douglas, 1880-1964 2. Yamashita, Tomobumi, 1885-1946 3. Atrocities 4. World War II -- Philippines 5. Military occupation 6. Violence 7. Manila, Philippines 8. Philippines
ISBN 9780393246940

LC 2018289656

Presents a history of the Battle of Manila that traces the capture of the Philippine capital by Japanese forces, the massacre of an estimated 100,000 civilians and liberation campaign that ultimately destroyed the city.

Target Tokyo : Jimmy Doolittle and the raid that avenged Pearl Harbor / James M. Scott. W.W. Norton & Company, 2015. 640 p. **940.54**

1. Doolittle, James Harold, 1896-1993. 2. World War II -- Aerial operations, American. 3. Bombing 4. Air defenses 5. Military history 6. Tokyo, Japan -- Bombing, 1942
ISBN 9780393089622

LC 2014043257

Pulitzer Prize for History finalist, 2016.

Presents a gripping account of the Doolittle Raid, a top-secret bombing mission and ambitious counterstrike against Tokyo in 1941, that was led by daredevil Lieutenant Colonel Jimmy Doolittle and turned the tide of the *war/but* came at a horrific cost.

"This popular history will appeal to fans of Laura Hillebrand's Unbroken and is comparable to other histories of the Tokyo Raid including Craig Nelson's The First Heroes and Carroll V. Glines's The Doolittle Raid." Library Journal.

Sebag-Montefiore, Hugh

Enigma : the battle for the code / Hugh Sebag-Montefiore. J. Wiley, c2000. x, 422 p. : **940.54**

1. ULTRA (Military intelligence) 2. Enigma machine. 3. World War II -- Cryptography. 4. World War II -- Electronic intelligence.
ISBN 0471490350

LC 00043920

Recounts a true tale of espionage, retracing the successful Allied effort to break the German "Enigma" code.

"Describing the breaking of the German naval code during World War II, is both engrossing and exciting. Much of the information presented here is based on recently declassified documents." Booklist.

Sheftall, Mordecai G.

Blossoms in the wind : the human legacy of the Kamikaze / M.G. Sheftall. NAL Caliber, c2005. x, 480 p. : **940.54**

1. Japan. Navy. Kamikaze Corps. 2. World War II 3. Kamikaze

airplanes. 4. Kamikaze pilots. 5. Air warfare 6. Japan -- History, Military -- 20th century. 7. Pacific Ocean.
ISBN 0451214870

LC 2004027356

Drawing on firsthand, intimate interviews with the few remaining survivors of Japan's kamikaze corps, a thought-provoking study offers a revealing glimpse into the lives, attitudes, beliefs, and mindsets of former kamikaze pilots who never completed their suicidal missions.

"The author has produced a superior addition to the literature on Japan's tokko, or suicide, warriors." Publishers Weekly.

Sides, Hampton

Ghost soldiers : the forgotten epic story of World War II's most dramatic mission / Hampton Sides. Doubleday, 2001. 342 p., 16 p. of plates : **940.54**

1. United States. Army. Rangers. 2. Military campaigns 3. Concentration camps -- Cabanatuan, Philippines. 4. World War II -- Prisoners and prisons, Japanese. 5. Atrocities. 6. Cabanatuan, Philippines -- History, Military -- 20th century.
ISBN 0385495641

LC 2001017337

Maps of Route of death march and Ranger raid on Cabanatuan on end pages.

Chronicles the daring mission of the elite U.S. Army Sixth Ranger Battalion to slip behind enemy lines in the Phillipines and rescue the 513 American and British POWs who had spent over three years in a hellish, Japanese-run camp near Cabanatuan.

"The author's excellent grasp of human emotions and bravery makes this a compelling book hard to put down." Publishers Weekly.

Smith, Jean Edward

The **liberation** of Paris : how Eisenhower, De Gaulle, and Von Choltitz saved the City of Light / Jean Edward Smith. Simon & Schuster, 2019. 256 p. **940.54**

1. Eisenhower, Dwight D. (Dwight David), 1890-1969. 2. DeGaulle, Charles 1890-1970 3. Choltitz, Dietrich von 4. Resistance to military occupation 5. World War II -- Paris, France 6. Nazism 7. Paris, France -- History -- German occupation, 1940-1944. 8. France -- History -- German occupation, 1940-1945.
ISBN 9781501164927

LC 2018036260

"Simon & Schuster nonfiction original hardcover."

"The liberation of Paris tells the dramatic story of the Allied decision in World War II to divert from the strategic plan in order to save the City of Light from chaos and assist de Gaulle's efforts to become France's new leader even as the German general in charge of the occupation defied his orders to destroy the city as the Allies closed in".-- Provided by publisher.

"A succinctly instructive historical narrative by a top-notch historian and author." Kirkus.

Smith, Larry (Larry Earl),

Iwo Jima : World War II veterans remember the greatest battle of the Pacific / edited by Larry Smith. W.W. Norton, 2008. 320 p. **940.54**

1. Iwo Jima, Battle of, 1945, American 2. World War II, American.
ISBN 0393062341

LC 2008001301

Smith offers a new and unrivaled perspective on the events that took place in Iwo Jima in 1945. Officers and enlisted men tell their stories in this collection of twenty-two oral histories.

"This is a superb collection of 22 oral histories from Iwo Jima veterans, including two Medal of Honor winners, a Navajo Code-Talker, the last surviving flag raiser from the first flag raising on Mount Suribachi, a war correspondent, and an African American marine who served in an ammo company." Library Journal.

Smyth, Denis

Deathly deception : the real story of Operation Mincemeat / Denis Smyth. Oxford University Press, 2010. 320 p. **940.54**

1. Great Britain. Royal Marines. 2. World War II. 3. Military deception. 4. Operation Mincemeat. 5. Military strategy. 6. Mediterranean Region.
ISBN 9780199233984

LC 2010923437

Provides details on Operation Mincemeat, an incredible plot to mislead the German High Command about the Allies' impending Mediterranean invasion.

Snyder, Timothy

Bloodlands : Europe between Hitler and Stalin / Timothy Snyder. Basic Books, 2010. 432 p. **940.54**

1. Stalin, Joseph, 1879-1953. 2. Hitler, Adolf, 1889-1945. 3. Genocide -- Eastern Europe. 4. Massacres. 5. Holocaust (1933-1945) 6. World War II -- Atrocities. 7. Eastern Europe -- History -- 1918-1945. 8. Soviet Union -- History -- 1917-1936. 9. Germany -- History -- 1933-1945.
ISBN 9780465002399

LC 2010016816

Cundill Prize in Historical Literature finalist

Describes how fourteen million people were murdered by Hitler's and Stalin's regimes in the area between Germany and Russia during the time when both men were in power and examines the motives and methods behind the mass murders.

"Mr. Snyder's book is revisionist history of the best kind: in spare, closely argued prose, with meticulous use of statistics, he makes the reader rethink some of the best-known episodes in Europe's modern history." The Economist.

Spector, Ronald H., 1943-

Eagle against the sun : the American war with Japan / Ronald H. Spector. Vintage Books, c1985. xvi, 589 p., 16 p. of plates : **940.54**

1. World War II 2. Military campaigns 3. United States -- History -- 1933-1945. 4. Japan -- History -- 1912-1945. 5. Pacific Area.
ISBN 0394741013

LC 85040140

Includes index.

Traces the war in the Pacific from Pearl Harbor to the atomic bombing of Hiroshima and Nagasaki, and examines the major battles and campaigns.

"While policy, strategy and military operations are emphasized...Mr. Spector makes a real attempt to give readers some idea of what the war was like for the men and women who fought it. It is here that the book is at its best." New York Times Book Review.

Summers, Anthony

A **matter** of honor : Pearl Harbor: betrayal, blame, and a family's quest for justice / Anthony Summers & Robbyn Swan. HarperCollins, 2016. 544 p. **940.54**

1. Kimmel, Husband Edward, 1882-1968. 2. Roosevelt, Franklin D. (Franklin Delano), 1882-1945. 3. Pearl Harbor, Attack on, 1941 4. Intelligence service -- United States. 5. Military cover-ups 6. World

War II -- Diplomatic history. 7. Pearl Harbor, Hawaii. 8. Hawaii.
ISBN 9780062405517

LC 2017304855

Draws on unprecedented access to documents, letters and diaries to explore claims of high-ranking duplicity and exonerate scapegoated admiral Husband Kimmel and President Roosevelt.

"This sad story reads like a thriller, thanks to the author's evocative prose and careful use of detail." Publishers Weekly.

Symonds, Craig L.

★**World** War II at sea : a global history / Craig L. Symonds. Oxford University Press, 2018. 792 p. **940.54**

1. Naval art and science -- History -- 20th century. 2. Naval history -- 20th century. 3. Sailors -- History -- 20th century. 4. World War II -- Naval operations
ISBN 9780190243678

LC 2017032532

"A veteran maritime historian delivers a satisfying one-volume history of 'the impact of sea services from all nations on the overall trajectory and even the outcome' of World War II." Kirkus.

Takaki, Ronald T., 1939-2009

Hiroshima : why America dropped the atomic bomb / Ronald Takaki. Little, Brown, and Co., c1995. 193 p., 8 p. of plates : **940.54**

1. Atomic bomb -- History. 2. Military strategy -- History -- World War II 3. Nuclear weapons -- History -- 20th century 4. World War II -- United States. 5. United States -- Politics and government -- 1945-1953. 6. Hiroshima, Japan -- Atomic bombing, 1945
ISBN 9780316831222

LC 95013546

Explores the decision to drop the bomb on Hiroshima through a study of the personalities involved.

"Right or wrong, the study is a provocative addition to the unresolved debate over the dropping of the atomic bombs." Publishers Weekly.

Terkel, Studs, 1912-2008

The **good** war : an oral history of World War Two / Studs Terkel. Pantheon Books, 1984. 587 p. **940.54**

1. World War II. 2. War and society. 3. World War II, American. 4. United States -- History -- 1939-1945. 5. Oral histories.
ISBN 9780394531038
Pulitzer Prize for General Nonfiction, 1985.

Oral history evokes the innocent idealism, as well as the terror and horror, of ordinary Americans at home and abroad during World War II.

Thomas, Evan, 1951-

★**Sea** of thunder : four commanders and the last great naval campaign, 1941-1945 / Evan Thomas. Simon & Schuster, c2006. 415 p. : **940.54**

1. Halsey, William Frederick, 1882-1959 2. Evans, Ernest Edwin, 1908-1944. 3. Kurita, Takeo, 1889-1977. 4. Ugaki, Matome, 1890-1945. 5. Leyte Gulf, Battle of, 1944 6. Naval battles. 7. Command of troops. 8. World War II 9. Philippines. 10. Pacific Ocean. 11. United States -- History, Military -- 20th century.
ISBN 0743252217

LC 2006047511

An account of the Battle of Leyte Gulf in October 1944 is told through the commands of four naval leaders, including two American commanders and two Japanese admirals, and offers insight into how the war reflected profound cultural differences.

"This is an account of the Battle of Leyte Gulf, October 1944, one of history's largest naval battles, where Admiral William Bull Halsey, the commander of the U.S. Third Fleet, and his commander, Ernest Evans, met the forces of Japanese admirals Takeo Kurita and Matome Ugaki. Thomas paints compelling portraits of these men, offering insight into their characters and actions throughout the war in the Pacific." Library Journal.

Toll, Ian W.

The **conquering** tide : war in the Pacific Islands, 1942/1944 / Ian W. Toll. W. W. Norton & Company, 2015. 672 p. **940.54**

1. Japan. Navy. 2. United States. Navy. 3. Naval tactics. 4. Naval battles. 5. World War II 6. Military campaigns 7. Pacific Area.
ISBN 9780393080643

LC 2015009591

Presents an account of the Allied effort to reclaim thousands of Japanese-occupied islands, detailing the campaign's technical innovations, logistic complications, and human and economic costs.

Pacific crucible : war at sea in the Pacific, 1941-1942 / Ian W. Toll. W W Norton & Co Inc., 2011. 544 p. **940.54**

1. Japan. Navy. 2. United States. Navy. 3. Naval tactics. 4. Naval battles. 5. World War II 6. Military campaigns 7. Pacific Ocean
ISBN 9780393068139

LC 2011028907

"The author makes vast quantities of technological and tactical concepts intelligible to all but the rankest beginner--for whom this book is not remotely suitable. A particular gift of the author is intelligent character portraits: Yamamoto, MacArthur, Halsey, and Nimitz (clearly one of the author's favorites). Add to all these other attributes a thorough scholarly apparatus, and it is difficult to think of a recent book on this subject that is of such consistently outstanding value." Booklist.

★**Twilight** of the Gods : war in the Western Pacific, 1944-1945 / Ian W. Toll. W. W. Norton & Company, 2020 864 p. **940.54**

1. MacArthur, Douglas, 1880-1964 2. Naval battles. 3. Military campaigns 4. World War II 5. Military strategy 6. Pacific Area.
ISBN 9780393080650

LC 2020009619

A conclusion to the trilogy that began with Pacific Crucible is based on the final year of World War II and follows MacArthur's pledge to the Philippines, the kamikaze attacks on Allied fleets and the bombing of Hiroshima and Nagasaki.

"Written with flair and chock-full of stories both familiar and fresh, this monumental history fires on all cylinders. WWII aficionados will be enthralled." Publishers Weekly

Twomey, Steve

Countdown to Pearl Harbor : the twelve days to the attack / Steve Twomey. Simon & Schuster, 2016 416 p. **940.54**

1. Pearl Harbor, Attack on, 1941 2. World War II 3. Hawaii
ISBN 9781476776460

LC 2016019080

A Pulitzer Prize-winning reporter chronicles the 12 days leading up to the Japanese attack on Pearl Harbor, examining the miscommunications, clues, missteps and racist assumptions that may have been behind America's failure to safeguard against the tragedy.

"A well-researched study of an infamous moment that is still fascinating and controversial." Kirkus.

Vincent, Lynn

★**Indianapolis** : the true story of the worst sea disaster in U.S. naval history and the fifty-year fight to exonerate an innocent man / Lynn Vincent and Sara Vladic. Simon & Schuster, [2018] 320 p. **940.54**

1. McVay, Charles Butler, III, 1898-1968 Trials, litigation, etc. 2. Indianapolis (Cruiser) 3. United States. Navy Search and rescue operations Pacific Ocean 4. Shipwrecks 5. Government cover-ups 6. World War II -- Naval operations, American 7. Courts-martial and courts of inquiry

ISBN 9781501135941

LC 2018015537

An account of the sinking of the USS "Indianapolis" during World War II draws on original research and new reporting to trace the half-century battle to exonerate Captain Charles McVay after a wrongful court martial.

"Recommended for readers interested in the final days of World War II, particularly naval activity in the Pacific theater, and anyone curious about McVay and his vessel." Library Journal.

Wallace, Chris

Countdown 1945 : the extraordinary story of the atomic bomb and the 116 days that changed the world / Chris Wallace, with Mitch Weiss. Avid Reader Press, 2020. 312 p. **940.54**

1. Truman, Harry S., 1884-1972. 2. Presidents -- United States 3. Atomic bomb 4. World War II -- Japan 5. World War II -- Aerial operations, American 6. Hiroshima, Japan -- Atomic bombing, 1945 7. Nagasaki, Japan -- Atomic bombing, 1945 8. United States -- History -- 1933-1945 9. Japan -- History -- 1926-1945

ISBN 9781982143343

LC bl2020012971

April 12, 1945: After years of bloody conflict in Europe and the Pacific, America is stunned by news of President Franklin D. Roosevelt's death. In an instant, Vice President Harry Truman, who has been kept out of war planning and knows nothing of the top-secret Manhattan Project to develop the world's first atomic bomb, must assume command of a nation at war on multiple continents--and confront one of the most consequential decisions in history. Countdown 1945 tells the gripping true story of the turbulent days, weeks, and months to follow, leading up to August 6, 1945, when Truman gives the order to drop the bomb on Hiroshima.

"A brisk work of history that weaves together the various factions responsible for the deployment of the first nuclear bombs." Kirkus

Weale, Adrian

Army of evil : a history of the SS / Adrian Weale. New American Library, 2012. 496 p. **940.54**

1. Waffen-SS -- History. 2. S. S. 3. World War II -- Regimental histories -- Germany. 4. Nazism 5. World War II -- Germany. 6. Germany -- Politics and government -- 1933-1945.

ISBN 9780451237910

LC 2012014170

Describes how the Nazi enforcers of the Third Reich began as a small group of politically-motivated thugs and grew to take control of all the police and security positions in Germany and ultimately became the Waffen SS with more than 800,000 members.

Williams, A. Susan

Spies in the Congo : America's atomic mission in World War II / Susan Williams. PublicAffairs, [2016] xxiv, 369 pages, 32 unnumbered pages of plates : **940.54**

1. Espionage 2. Spies 3. World War II 4. Intelligence officers 5. Congo (Democratic Republic)

ISBN 9781610396547

LC 2016936154

First published in the United Kingdom in 2016 by C. Hurst & Co.

Documents the lesser-known work of the Belgian Congo secret intelligence mission to prevent uranium from being smuggled into Germany during World War II, drawing on recently released archival materials to illuminate the contributions of intelligence heroes from the founding generation of America's covert warriors.

"While there are numerous books on the Manhattan Project, this is the first to focus on operations related to the origins of the uranium used." Library Journal.

Wilson, Kevin, 1942-

Blood and fears : how America's bomber boys of the 8th Air Force saved World War II / Kevin Wilson. Pegasus Books, 2017, c2016. 560 p. **940.54**

1. United States. Air Force. Air Force, 8th 2. Bomber pilots 3. Pilots -- United States 4. World War II -- England 5. MIlitary history 6. Great Britain -- History -- 20th century

ISBN 9781681773193

LC bl2017005016

Originally published in 2016 by W&N under the title Blood and fears: how America's bomber boys and girls in England won their war.

Describes the heroism of the US 8th Air Force during World War II, from Operation Argument, which targeted German airplane production plants, to battling the Luftwaffe over Berlin and finally to their joint effort with the Royal Air Force in Normandy.

"A well-researched and well-written history of a significant aspect of World War II." Library Journal.

Wortman, Marc (Marc Josef)

1941 : fighting the shadow war: a divided America in a world at war / Marc Wortman. Atlantic Monthly Press, 2016. 416 p. **940.54**

1. Roosevelt, Franklin D. (Franklin Delano), 1882-1945 2. World War II 3. United States -- Foreign relations.

ISBN 9780802125118

LC 2016440842

Describes how Franklin D. Roosevelt quietly used his power and all the tools he had to assist Winston Churchill in fighting the Axis long before the United States' official entry into World War II.

"The author displays a nice sense of the dramatic scene and a solid ear for telling quotes, and ample documentation gives readers the opportunity to look further into the history." Kirkus.

Wukovits, John F., 1944-

Hell from the heavens : the epic story of the USS Laffey and World War II's greatest kamikaze attack / John Wukovits. Da Capo Press, 2015. 320 p. **940.54**

1. Laffey (Ship) 2. Kamikaze pilots 3. Naval battles 4. Military campaigns 5. World War II 6. Pacific Area

ISBN 9780306823244

LC 2014042127

"For WWII buffs, surely, but also for general readers looking to understand the damage inflicted and the terror inspired by the Japanese suicide squadrons." Kirkus.

Zuckoff, Mitchell

Lost in Shangri-la : the epic true story of a World War II plane crash into the Stone Age / Mitchell Zuckoff. HarperCollins, c2011. 448 p. **940.54**

1. United States. Army Air Forces. 2. Search and rescue operations 3. World War II -- Missing in action. 4. Survival (after airplane accidents, shipwrecks, etc.) 5. Airplane accidents. 6. New Guinea.
ISBN 9780061988349

LC 2010034508

"On May 13, 1945, an American transport plane carrying 24 servicemen and women crashed into a mountain in the tropical jungles of Dutch New Guinea (now Papua), leaving three survivors. Learning about the event while researching another subject, the author recognized the ingredients of a terrific tale: a beautiful young WAC, a hidden valley reminiscent of the Shangri-La in James Hilton's Lost Horizon, primitive tribal people and a daring air rescue. In this well-crafted book, Zuckoff turns the long-forgotten episode into an unusually exciting narrative. Drawing on the young WAC survivor Margaret Hastings' diary as well as journals and interviews, the author hones in on life at the U.S. military base in Hollandia, on the northern coast of uncharted New Guinea; a soldier's chance discovery a year earlier of Baliem Valley, a verdant area about 150 miles into the interior, with its hundreds of native villages surrounded by gardens; and the doomed flight of officers and enlisted personnel out on a joy ride to view this much-talked-about land of Stone Age people from the air." Kirkus.

940.54012 Military history of World War II--Strategy--Allies

Olson, Lynne

Citizens of London : the Americans who stood with Britain in its darkest, finest hour / Lynne Olson. Random House, 2010 448 p. **940.54012**

1. Murrow, Edward R., 1908-1965 2. Harriman, William Averell, 1891-1986 3. Churchill, Winston, 1874-1965 Military leadership 4. World War II -- Diplomatic history. 5. Strategic alliances (Military) 6. Military history. 7. Great Britain -- Foreign relations United States 8. United States -- Foreign relations Great Britain
ISBN 9781400067589

LC 2010278653

ALA Notable Book, 2011.

The behind-the-scenes story of how the United States forged its wartime alliance with Britain, told from the perspective of three key American players in London: Edward R. Murrow, Averell Harriman, and John Gilbert Winant.

"A nuanced history that captures the intensity of life in a period when victory was not a foregone conclusion." Kirkus.

940.5426 Military history of World War II--Pacific Ocean theater

Cleaver, Thomas McKelvey

I will run wild : the Pacific war from Pearl Harbor to Midway / Thomas McKelvey Cleaver. Osprey Publishing, 2020. 320 p. **940.5426**

1. Pearl Harbor, Attack on, 1941 2. World War II -- Aerial operations 3. Military aircraft 4. Military aviation
ISBN 9781472841339

Drawing on extensive first-hand accounts and a new analysis, this history of the early stages of the Pacific War tells the story of Americans, British, Dutch, Australians and New Zealanders taken by surprise from Pearl Harbor to Singapore that first Sunday of December 1941.

"Authoritative and colorful--a must-read account of the initial phase of the war in the Pacific." Kirkus

940.55 History of Europe--1945-1999

Judt, Tony

Postwar : a history of Europe since 1945 / Tony Judt. Penguin Press, 2005. xv, 878 p., 24 p. of plates : **940.55**

1. Postwar life 2. World War II -- Post-war aspects 3. International relations 4. Cold War. 5. Europe -- Foreign relations. 6. Europe -- Politics and government -- 1945- 7. Europe -- Economic conditions -- 1945- 8. Europe -- Social life and customs -- 1945- 9. Europe -- History -- 1945-
ISBN 9781594200656

LC 2005052126

Pulitzer Prize for General Nonfiction finalist

Covering 34 countries and 60 years of history, Tony Judt chronicles the rebuilding of Europe after the devastation and havoc of World War II. Here, Judt takes listeners through the Holocaust, Stalinism's spread through the eastern continent, the dramatic changes of the 1960s, and the fall of Communism.

"This is the best history we have of Europe in the postwar period and not likely to be surpassed for many years." Publishers Weekly.

Kershaw, Ian

★The **global** age : Europe 1950-2017 / Ian Kershaw. Penguin Group, 2019. 656 p. **940.55**

1. World politics. 2. Economic development. 3. International cooperation. 4. Peace.
ISBN 9780735223981

LC 2019023176

Traces the latter half of the twentieth century to the present and covers the impact of nuclear threat, accelerating globalization, and the post-2008 financial crises.

"The second installment of the eminent English historian's comprehensive overview of modern European history." Kirkus.

Lowe, Keith, 1970-

Savage continent : Europe in the aftermath of World War Two / Keith Lowe. St. Martin's Press, 2012. 400 p. **940.55**

1. World War II. 2. Winning and losing. 3. Reconstruction (1939-1951) -- Europe. 4. Crime. 5. Europe -- History -- 1945-
ISBN 9781250000200

LC 2011279703

An account of the period of violent disorder that racked Europe after World War II describes the brutal acts against Germans and collaborators, the anti-Semitic beliefs that reemerged and the Allied-tolerated expulsions of millions of citizens from their ancestral homelands. By the author of Inferno.

Mazower, Mark

Dark continent : Europe's twentieth century / Mark Mazower. A.A. Knopf, 1999, c1998 xvi, 487 p. : **940.55**

1. Europe -- History -- 20th century. 2. Europe -- Politics and government -- 20th century.
ISBN 9780679438090

LC 98015886

First published: London : Allen Lane, 1998.

A study of the twentieth-century history of Europe explores the struggle for control among liberal democracy, communism, and fascism, tracing the ideological, economic, political, and military factors that transformed the face of Europe since the end of World War I.

"The author's relative unconcern with international and great-power politics probably accounts for a rather intra-European perspective...just as it contributes to some exaggeration of the points of comparison and convergence in East and West European economic history. But these are minor defects, the price to be paid for a confident and unconventional work of historical interpretation." New York Times Book Review.

941 British Isles

Burns, William E., 1959-

A **brief** history of Great Britain / William E. Burns. Facts On File, c2009. 320 p. Brief history (Facts on File) **941**

1. Great Britain -- History. 2. Ireland -- History. 3. Scotland

ISBN 9780816077281

LC 2009008217

Surveys the history of Great Britain and Ireland from the earliest settlements to the prime ministership of Gordon Brown, covering social, economic, and religious developments along with political changes and international conflicts.

Fraser, Rebecca

★The **story** of Britain : from the Romans to the present : a narrative history / Rebecca Fraser. W.W. Norton & Co., 2005, c2003. xvii, 829 p. : **941**

1. Great Britain -- History Anecdotes. 2. Great Britain -- Social life and customs.

ISBN 0393060101

LC 2004026049

"Originally published in Great Britain under the title A People's history of Britain"--T.p. verso.

An anecdotal account about the men and women who helped found Britain's national institutions discusses how their achievements reflected such historical endeavors as liberty, the rule of law, and parliamentary democracy, in an epic volume that features such individuals as Thomas More, William Wilberforce, and Winston Churchill.

"The author's narrative advances with the emphasis on the roles of a litany of historical icons, from Queen Boudica to Margaret Thatcher. For those readers who are primarily interested in the who, what, when, where, why of British history, this is a valuable general study." Booklist.

Hunt, Tristram, 1974-

Cities of empire : the British colonies and the creation of the urban world / Tristram Hunt. Metropolitan Books, 2014. 448 p. **941**

1. Cities and towns -- Case studies. 2. Metropolitan areas -- Case studies. 3. Imperialism -- History -- Case studies. 4. Great Britain -- Colonies -- History

ISBN 9780805093087

LC 2014030024

"Originally published in England in 2014 under the title Ten Cities that Made an Empire by Allen Lane, London."

A history of the colonial creation of the city is told through the stories of 10 influential urban centers left in the wake of the British Empire, drawing on historical scholarship, cultural criticism and personal reportage to trace the rise of such cities as Boston, Hong Kong and New Delhi.

"A book to be enjoyed by an array of readers, including historians of various stripes, particularly those who have traveled to any of the book's cities." Library Journal.

Lacey, Robert

Great tales from English history: 2 : Joan of Arc, the princes in the Tower, Bloody Mary, Oliver Cromwell, Sir Isaac Newton, and more / Robert Lacey. Little, Brown and Co., 2005, c2004. xvi, 271 p. : **941**

1. Great Britain -- History -- Medieval period, 1066-1485 Anecdotes. 2. Great Britain -- History -- Stuarts, 1603-1714 Anecdotes. 3. Great Britain -- History -- Tudors, 1485-1603 Anecdotes.

ISBN 031610924X

LC 2004063351

"First published in Great Britain by Little, Brown and Company, 2004"--T.p. verso.

A second collection of historical accounts from the England of Chaucer and Shakespeare covers the period between 1387 and 1687, and features influential figures including Henry VIII, Mary, Queen of Scots, and Sir Francis Drake.

"The author's second volume on English history opens in 1348, the year of the Black Plague, which wiped out half of England's five million people, and proceeds through the astonishing scientific discoveries of Sir Isaac Newton in 1687. Lacey's animated prose, energetic storytelling and spirited approach to British history bring the past to life." Publishers Weekly.

★**Great** tales from English history: 3 : Captain Cook, Samuel Johnson, Queen Victoria, Charles Darwin, Edward the Abdicator, and more / Robert Lacey. Little, Brown, 2006. ix, 305 p. : **941**

1. Great Britain -- History Anecdotes. 2. Great Britain -- Social life and customs.

ISBN 0316114596

LC 2006931723

"First published in Great Britain by Little, Brown and Company, 2006"--T.p. verso.

A third compilation of historical accounts covers English history from 1690 to 1953 and captures the pivotal events and characters of England's modern age, including Samuel Johnson, Mary Wollstonecraft, Charles Darwin, and Winston Churchill.

"The third volume in Lacey's series of edifying and entertaining stories from English history abounds in fascinating profiles. Industrial and agricultural pioneers such as Jethro Tull, James Hargreaves and Isambard Kingdom Brunel abide alongside human rights protestors such as Thomas Clarkson, who founded the British antislavery movement; feminist philosopher Mary Wollstonecraft; and journalist Annie Besant, who initiated a successful 1888 match girls' strike." Publishers Weekly.

Morgan, Kenneth O.

The **Oxford** history of Britain / edited by Kenneth O. Morgan. Oxford University Press, 2010. xiv, 821 p. : **941**

1. Great Britain -- History.

ISBN 9780199579259

LC 2010279308

Previous ed.: 2001.

Schama, Simon

A **history** of Britain. Simon Schama. Hyperion, 2000. 416 p. : **941**

1. Great Britain -- Civilization. 2. Great Britain -- History. 3. Great Britain -- Foreign relations.

ISBN 9780786866755

LC 00061442

A comprehensive history of Britain chronicles battles waged by the British, both at home and abroad, details its role as a global power, and examines key events and personalities that shaped more than two centuries of history.

"Schama writes wonderfully, in an easygoing yet elegant manner, with an eye for the telling aesthetic detail, and throughout brimming with intelligence and passion." New York Times Book Review.

A **history** of Britain. Simon Schama. Hyperion, 2001. 544 p. : **941**

1. Great Britain -- Civilization. 2. Great Britain -- History. 3. Great Britain -- Foreign relations.

ISBN 9780786867523

LC 00061442

A comprehensive history of Britain chronicles battles waged by the British, both at home and abroad, details its role as a global power, and examines key events and personalities that shaped more than two centuries of history.

"Schama writes wonderfully, in an easygoing yet elegant manner, with an eye for the telling aesthetic detail, and throughout brimming with intelligence and passion." New York Times Book Review.

A **history** of Britain. Simon Schama. Hyperion, 2002. 576 p. : **941**

1. Great Britain -- Civilization. 2. Great Britain -- History. 3. Great Britain -- Foreign relations.

ISBN 9780786868995

LC 00061442

A comprehensive history of Britain chronicles battles waged by the British, both at home and abroad, details its role as a global power, and examines key events and personalities that shaped more than two centuries of history.

"Schama writes wonderfully, in an easygoing yet elegant manner, with an eye for the telling aesthetic detail, and throughout brimming with intelligence and passion." New York Times Book Review.

Strong, Roy

The **story** of Britain : from the Romans to the present day / Roy Strong. Pegasus Books, 2019, c2018. xviii, 590 p., 16 unnumbered p. of plates : **941**

1. History 2. Geography 3. Culture 4. Great Britain -- History

ISBN 9781643130132

Originally published: London : J. MacCrae, 1996.

Revised and updated in the UK: London : Weidenfeld & Nicolson, 2018.

Revised for a new generation of readers, an authoritative history of Britain from the Romans to the present day incorporates into the new edition coverage of the Blair years and the current Brexit decisions.

"Strong succeeds in making British history a page-turner for general readers in this excellent introduction to the grand sweep of British history." Library Journal.

941.009 British Isles -- Areas, regions places in general

Tinniswood, Adrian

Behind the throne : a domestic history of the British royal household / Adrian Tinniswood. Basic Books, [2018] xii, 402 p. **941.009**

1. Royal houses -- Great Britain 2. Rulers 3. Household employees 4. Great Britain -- History

ISBN 9780465094028

LC 2018008384

In Behind the Throne, historian Adrian Tinniswood uncovers the reality of five centuries of life at the English court, taking the reader on a remarkable journey from one Queen Elizabeth to another and exploring life as it was lived by clerks and courtiers and clowns and crowned heads. A masterful and witty social history of five centuries of royal life, Behind the Throne offers a grand tour of England's grandest households.

941.0099 Great Britain--collected biography

Cannon, John, 1926-2012

The **kings** & queens of Britain / John Cannon & Anne Hargreaves. Oxford University Press, 2009. xii, 404 p. : **941.0099**

1. Great Britain -- Kings and rulers 2. Great Britain -- History.

ISBN 9780199559220

LC 2009278738

941.06 House of Stuart and Commonwealth periods, 1603-1714

Ackroyd, Peter, 1949-

Rebellion : the history of England from James I to the glorious revolution / Peter Ackroyd. St Martins Pr., 2014. 528 p. History of England ; **941.06**

1. James I, King of England, 1566-1625. 2. Charles I, King of England, 1600-1649 3. Cromwell, Oliver, 1599-1658. 4. Civil war -- England. 5. Regicide -- Great Britain. 6. Royal houses. 7. English Civil War, 1642-1649 8. Great Britain -- History -- Stuarts, 1603-1714.

ISBN 9781250003638

LC 2014026045

A latest volume in the award-winning author's series covers the Stuart dynasty during a turbulent 17th century marked by three civil wars, citing the roles of such figures as James VI, Charles I and Oliver Cromwell.

"Although general readers in the U.S. may find some of the names and places unfamiliar, this masterful work of popular history will remind them that the ideas that launched our own revolution were forged during this seminal period of English history." Booklist.

Jordan, Don, 1948-

The **king's** revenge : Charles II and the greatest manhunt in British history / Don Jordan and Michael Walsh. Pegasus Books, 2016. 400 p. **941.06**

1. Charles I, King of England, 1600-1649 Death and burial. 2. Charles II, King of England, 1630-1685 3. Regicide -- Great Britain. 4. English Civil War, 1642-1649 5. Great Britain -- History -- Charles II, 1660-1685.

ISBN 9781681771687

LC bl2016030845

Set in an age of intrigue and espionage, this is the story of the greatest manhunt in British history: the quest for retribution upon the traitors who brought about the death of Charles I.

"Crafted like a spy novel as Charles II set about to find the living regicides, this work will intrigue readers with the breadth and ruthlessness of the king's search." Library Journal.

Mortimer, Ian, 1967-

The **time** traveler's guide to Restoration Britain : a handbook for visitors to the seventeenth century: 1660-1699

/ Ian Mortimer. Pegasus Books, 2017. 416 p. **941.06**

1. Charles II, King of England, 1630-1685 2. Civilization, Western. 3. History 4. Great Britain -- History -- Charles II, 1660-1685. 5. Great Britain -- History -- Restoration, 1660-1688.
ISBN 9781681773544

LC bl2017013557

An up-close-and-personal look at Britain between the Restoration of King Charles II in 1660 and the end of the century delves into the nuances of daily life to paint a vibrant and detailed picture of society at the dawn of the modern world. By the author of The Time Traveler's Guide to Medieval England.

"This is a sure bet for history lovers and readers with a penchant for unusual travelogues." Booklist.

Woolley, Benjamin

The **king's** assassin : the secret plot to murder King James I / Benjamin Woolley. St Martins Pr 2018 368 p. **941.06**

1. James I, King of England, 1566-1625 2. Assassination plots 3. Favorites, Royal 4. Rulers -- Death 5. Murder 6. Great Britain -- History -- James I, 1603-1625
ISBN 9781250125033

LC 2018006541

Draws on new historical scholarship to validate centuries of theories that James I may have been murdered by his gentleman of the royal bedchamber and lover, George Villiers.

"Woolley presents an engrossing portrait of an ambitious man trusted by two kings that both casual readers and Stuart history fans can enjoy." Publishers Weekly.

941.07 Period of House of Hanover, 1714-1837

Ackroyd, Peter, 1949-

Revolution : the history of England from the Battle of the Boyne to the Battle of Waterloo / Peter Ackroyd. Thomas Dunne Books/St. Martin's Press, 2017, c2016. 416 p. History of England ; **941.07**

1. William III King of Great Britain 1650-1702. 2. Mary II, Queen of Great Britain, 1662-1694. 3. Anne, Queen of Great Britain, 1665-1714. 4. George I, King of Great Britain, 1660-1727. 5. George II King of Great Britain 1683-1760. 6. George III, King of Great Britain, 1738-1820. 7. George IV, King of Great Britain, 1762-1830. 8. Stuart, House of 9. Hanover, House of 10. Industrial revolution 11. Economic development 12. Napoleonic Wars, 1800-1815 13. Royal houses 14. England -- History -- 17th century 15. England -- History -- 18th century 16. England -- History -- 19th century
ISBN 9781250003645

LC 2017027329

Originally published: 2016.

The award-winning novelist, broadcaster, biographer and historian behind Thames: Sacred River offers the fourth volume in his sweeping history of England, covering the events from William of Orange's accession to the defeat of Napoleon at Waterloo.

Fraser, Antonia, 1932-

The **King** and the Catholics : England, Ireland, and the fight for religious freedom, 1780-1829 / Antonia Fraser. Nan A. Talese, 2018. 336 p. **941.07**

1. Catholic Church 2. Great Britain. Parliament 3. Gordon Riots, 1780 4. Catholics 5. Social change 6. Law 7. London, England 8. Ireland 9. Great Britain -- History -- 18th century 10. Great Britain -- History -- 19th century
ISBN 9780385544528

LC 2018015523

The award-winning author of Marie Antoinette traces the high-suspense story of how the Gordon Riots of the late-18th century helped secure key protections for Catholics after two centuries of legal discrimination.

Morrison, Robert, 1961-

The **Regency** years : during which Jane Austen writes, Napoleon fights, Byron makes love, and Britain becomes modern / Robert Morrison. W. W. Norton & Company, [2019] 416 p. **941.07**

1. National characteristics, English -- History -- 19th century. 2. English literature -- 19th century -- History and criticism 3. Arts -- Great Britain -- History -- 19th century. 4. Modern arts -- 19th century 5. England -- Civilization -- 19th century. 6. Great Britain -- History -- George III, 1760-1820. 7. Great Britain -- Civilization -- 19th century. 8. Great Britain -- Social life and customs -- 19th century. 9. Great Britain -- Social conditions -- 19th century.
ISBN 9780393249057

LC 2018053659

Also published in the UK under the title, The regency revolution

Examines the complex history of the Regency era, exploring the social, religious, scientific, and artistic movements of the period that helped shape the modern world.

"An intriguing discussion on the finer and more fascinating aspects of the Regency period that will appeal to history buffs, particularly those curious about European and British history." Library Journal.

941.08 Period of Victoria and House of Windsor, 1837

McKillop, A. B.

The **spinster** & the prophet : Florence Deeks, H.G. Wells, and the mystery of the purloined past / A.B. McKillop. Four Walls Eight Windows, 2002, c2000. xvi, 477 p. : **941.08**

1. Wells, H. G. (Herbert George), 1866-1946. Outline of history. 2. Deeks, Florence Amelia. 3. Plagiarism -- Great Britain -- History -- 20th century. 4. Historiography. 5. Suing (Law) -- England.
ISBN 9781568582368

Originally published: Toronto : Macfarlane Walter & Ross, 2000.

Arthur Ellis Award for Nonfiction, 2001.

Governor General's Literary Awards, English-language Nonfiction finalist

"When, in 1920, Florence Deeks finally received her rejected manuscript--a feminist history of the world--from Macmillan after eight months, she couldn't understand why it appeared in such bad condition. Later that year, when she read H.G. Wells's new book, The Outline of History, published by Macmillan, she felt a chill. There were so many similarities to her own work: shared themes, organization, word choice, even the same mistakes. Florence made a dramatic decision: she would sue Wells and his publisher for plagiarism. The author handles the dual story line brilliantly, weaving together two opposing characters into one altogether gripping tale of literary theft." Publishers Weekly.

941.081 British Isles--Reign of Victoria, 1837-1901

Murphy, Paul Thomas, 1957-

Shooting Victoria : madness, mayhem, and the rebirth of the British monarchy / Paul Thomas Murphy. W W Norton & Co

Inc, 2012. 512 p. **941.081**

1. Victoria, Queen of Great Britain, 1819-1901. 2. Attempted assassination. 3. Monarchy -- Great Britain 4. Royal houses -- Great Britain. 5. Women rulers. 6. Great Britain -- History -- Victoria, 1837-1901.

ISBN 9781605983547

LC 2013387369

ALA Notable Book, 2013

From a hunchbacked dwarf to a paranoid poet-assassin, a history of Victorian England as seen through the numerous assassination attempts on Queen Victoria.

Wilson, A. N., 1950-

The **Victorians** / A.N. Wilson. W.W. Norton, 2004, c2002. xii, 724 p. : **941.081**

1. Great Britain -- History -- Victoria, 1837-1901. 2. Great Britain -- Civilization -- 19th century.

ISBN 0393325431

LC bl2004004601

Originally published: London : Hutchinson, 2002.

A revisionist panorama of the nineteenth century examines the era's material and spiritual changes in the wake of emerging British capitalism and imperialism.

"Even to fastidious readers, Wilson's failings are minor, and the colorful tapestry he presents of a smoky world peopled with the likes of Carlyle, Mill, Marx, Ruskin, and Darwin can hardly fail to enthrall. Both professional scholars and laypeople will love to relax with this book, although some knowledge of the age is a must." Choice.

941.084 British Isles--Period of Victoria and House of Windsor--1936-1945

Morton, Andrew, 1953-

17 carnations : the royals, the Nazis and the biggest cover-up in history / Andrew Morton. Grand Central Publishing, 2015 368 p. **941.084**

1. Windsor, Edward, Duke of, 1894-1972. 2. Windsor, Wallis Warfield, Duchess of, 1896-1986. 3. World War II 4. Nazis 5. Royal houses 6. Government cover-ups

ISBN 9781455527113

LC 2014957815

Tells the story of the feckless Edward VIII, Duke of Windsor, and his wife Wallis Simpson, whose affair with Joachim von Ribbentrop embroiled the duke in a German plot to use him as a puppet king during their takeover of the British Empire. Although we know that the war ended with Hitler's defeat, Edward's story was far from over. The Duke's collaboration with Hitler had resulted in piles of correspondence between them; this damning correspondence, now hidden in a German castle that had fallen to American soldiers, could forever tarnish the reputation of the royal family.

941.1 Scotland

Herman, Arthur, 1956-

How the Scots invented the modern world : the true story of how western Europe's poorest nation created our world & everything in it / Arthur Herman. Crown Publishers, c2001. viii, 392 p. ; **941.1**

1. Civilization, Western -- Scottish influences. 2. National characteristics, Scottish. 3. Scots in foreign countries. 4. Enlightenment (European intellectual movement) -- Scotland. 5. Scotland -- Civilization.

ISBN 0609606352

LC 2001028951

Explores the seminal contributions of Scotland to the development of modern Western civilization, discussing the impact of such ideals as democracy, freedom of speech, equal opportunity, and a commitment to education.

"This is a worthwhile book for the general reader." Publishers Weekly.

Nicolson, Adam, 1957-

Sea room : an island life in the Hebrides / Adam Nicolson. North Point Press, 2002, c2001. 391 p. : **941.1**

1. Nicolson, Adam, 1957- Homes and haunts Hebrides. 2. Natural history -- Hebrides. 3. Hebrides -- Social life and customs. 4. Scotland -- Description and travel. 5. Hebrides -- Description and travel.

ISBN 0865476365

LC 2002019816

Originally published: London, HarperCollins Publishers, 2001.

Documents the author's experiences with and love for three Outer Hebrides islands he inherited as a young man, tracing the area's rich and sometimes violent history of hermits, legendary ghosts, farmers, fishermen, and Bronze Age gold.

"Magnificent and poetic, this is a literary and ecological masterpiece." Booklist.

941.105 Scotland--Reformation period, 1542-1603

Weir, Alison, 1951-

Mary, Queen of Scots, and the murder of Lord Darnley / Alison Weir. Ballantine Books, 2003. xvii, 670 p., [16] p. of plates ; **941.105**

1. Darnley, Henry Stuart, Lord, 1545-1567 Death and burial. 2. Mary, Queen of Scots, 1542-1587 Marriage. 3. Murder -- Scotland -- History -- 16th century. 4. Women rulers -- Scotland. 5. Scotland -- History -- Mary Stuart, 1542-1567.

ISBN 9780345436580

LC 2002034467

The best-selling author of Henry VIII reexamines an array of source material to describe the relationship between Mary, Queen of Scots, and her ambitious second husband, Lord Darnley, and to investigate the 1567 murder of Lord Darnley, to assess the potential involvement of Mary, and to provide a solution to this four-hundred-year-old mystery.

"No stone is left unturned in {Weir's} investigation, and despite its detail, her book is as dramatic as witnessing firsthand the most riveting court case." Booklist.

941.1072 Scotland--1727-1760

Royle, Trevor, 1945-

★**Culloden** : Scotland's last battle and the forging of the British Empire / Trevor Royle. Pegasus Books, 2016. 420 p. **941.1072**

1. Culloden, Battle of, 1746 2. Jacobite Rebellion, 1745-1746 3. Scotland -- History -- 18th century 4. Great Britain -- History, Military -- 18th century

ISBN 9781681772363

LC bl2016044522

An authoritative history of the last major battle fought between Scottish and English forces on British soil traces events on both sides of the conflict, evaluating how it permanently ended the Stuart claim to the throne and ignited Royal Army campaigns in America and India.

"Culloden's importance to Scotland's fortunes has never been doubted; Royle now demonstrates that its relevance to decades of British global supremacy cannot be questioned." Publishers Weekly.

941.3 Southeastern Scotland

Robb, Graham, 1958-

The **debatable** land : the lost world between Scotland and England / Graham Robb. Picador, 2018. x, 334 p., 16 unnumbered p. of plates : **941.3**

1. Ptolemy, active 2nd century. 2. Robb, Graham, 1958- Travels. 3. Maps. 4. Archaeology. 5. Boundaries. 6. Borderlands. 7. Scotland -- History. 8. Scottish Borders (England and Scotland) -- History. 9. Great Britain -- History.

ISBN 9780393285321

LC 2017054854

A biographer and historian describes his firsthand investigation into the 2,000-year-old map of Ptolemy, which led him to more than one discovery of major historical significance in the once-hotly contested Debatable Land territory.

Stewart, Rory

The **marches** : a borderland journey between England and Scotland / Rory Stewart. Houghton Mifflin Harcourt, 2016 304 p. **941.3**

1. Borderlands. 2. Landscape 3. Walking 4. Boundaries 5. England 6. Scotland 7. Great Britain -- History

ISBN 9780544108882

LC bl2016030217

The New York Times best-selling author of The Places in Between explores the landscape of his home on the borderland between England and Scotland--known as the Marches--and the history, people and conflicts that have shaped it.

941.5 Ireland

State, Paul F., 1950-

A **brief** history of Ireland / Paul F. State. Facts On File, 2009. 432 p. Brief history (Facts on File) **941.5**

1. History 2. World politics. 3. Ireland -- History. 4. Western Europe -- History

ISBN 9780816075164

LC 2008029243

Follows the political, economic, and social development of Ireland from the pagan past to the contemporary religious strife and hope for reconciliation.

941.501 Early history to 1086

Cahill, Thomas

How the Irish saved civilization : the untold story of Ireland's heroic role from the fall of Rome to the rise of medieval Europe / Thomas Cahill. Nan A. Talese, Doubleday, 1995. x, 246 p. : Hinges of history ; **941.501**

1. Learning and scholarship -- History -- Medieval, 500-1500. 2. Civilization, Medieval -- Ireland 3. Manuscripts -- Ireland -- History. 4. Books -- Ireland -- History -- 400-1400. 5. Ireland -- Civilization -- To 1172. 6. Europe Civilization -- Irish influences.

ISBN 0385418485

LC 94028130

Presents an accessible and revealing portrait of medieval times. As Europe reaches intellectual stagnation and decline, Ireland bursts forth as a vigourous haven of scholarship.

"Highly literate and affectionate, if somewhat rambling and indulgent. As a freewheeling, witty popular history of Irish Christianity in the Dark Ages, this will amuse and enlighten." Library Journal.

941.505 Period under House of Tudor, 1485-1603

Ekin, Des

The **last** armada : Queen Elizabeth, Juan del Aguila, and the 100-day invasion of England / Des Ekin. Pegasus, 2016 420 p. **941.505**

1. Aguila, Juan del, 1545-1602 2. Naval history 3. Sieges 4. Ireland -- History -- 1558-1603. 5. Kinsale (Ireland) -- History -- Siege, 1601-1602. 6. Great Britain -- History, Military -- 1485-1603. 7. Spain -- History, Military -- 17th century.

ISBN 9781605989440

LC 2016440004

A tale inspired by the great 1601 naval battle between England and Spain depicts a vengeful General Juan del Aguila, who would seize control of a bridgehead in Elizabeth I's England, while strategist Charles Blount works to escape treason charges and insurgent Hugh O'Neill struggles to free Ireland from English control.

"The author explains the terrain, battles, siege construction, and weaponry well enough to please any military historian, but the real prizes here are the author's discussions of the effect of the battle on Spain as its empire died and England's colonies grew, the end of Spain's religious wars, the shift of power in England, and the cataclysm as Gaelic Ireland declined and died. A fantastic book that finally assigns Kinsale its rightful place in history." Kirkus.

941.5081 Ireland--1800-1899

Kelly, John, 1945-

The **graves** are walking : the great famine and the saga of the Irish people / John Kelly. Henry Holt and Co., 2012. 304 p. **941.5081**

1. Famines. 2. Nation-building. 3. British in Ireland. 4. Hunger. 5. Ireland -- History -- Famine, 1845-1852.

ISBN 9780805091847

LC 2012011493

Describes the Great Irish Potato Famine that began in 1845 and discusses how the combined forces of bacterial infection, political greed and religious intolerance started a disaster that killed twice as many people as died during the American Civil War.

941.5082 Ireland--1900-1999

Ferriter, Diarmaid, 1972-

The **transformation** of Ireland / Diarmaid Ferriter. Overlook

Press, 2005, c2004. 884 p. **941.5082**

1. Ireland -- History -- 20th century. 2. Ireland -- Civilization -- 20th century.

ISBN 1585676810

LC 2005049849

Originally published: London : Profile Books, 2004.

"This book isn't a political history of 20th-century Ireland; it's more a chronicle of the social reaction to the events that shaped that century. [The author] has written an informative, funny, at times derisive book that takes a fresh approach to 20th-century Ireland." Publishers Weekly.

Nic Dhiarmada, Briona

The **1916** Irish Rebellion / Briona Nic Dhiarmada ; foreword by Mary McAleese. University of Notre Dame Press, 2016. ix, 205 p. : **941.5082**

1. Irish Republican Army. 2. Anglo-Irish relations 3. Revolutions -- History -- 20th century. 4. Irish resistance and revolts 5. World politics -- 1919-1932. 6. Ireland -- History -- Easter Rising, 1916. 7. Ireland -- History -- 1910-1921. 8. Ireland -- History -- Easter Rising, 1916

ISBN 9780268036140

LC 2015042508

"Rich in fascinating historical photographs and informative and poignant documents that capture each phase of the struggle and its inevitable and tragic outcome, this striking volume tells the complex tale of a singular chapter in the long war against colonialism in plain and ringing language." Booklist.

Walsh, Maurice

Bitter freedom : Ireland in a revolutionary world / Maurice Walsh. Liveright Publishing Corporation, a division of W.W. Norton & Company, 2016. 544 p. **941.5082**

1. Irish Republican Army. 2. Revolutions -- History -- 20th century. 3. Irish resistance and revolts 4. World politics -- 1919-1932. 5. Easter Rising 1916 6. Ireland -- History -- Civil War, 1922-1923 7. Ireland -- History -- 1910-1921. 8. Ireland -- History -- Easter Rising, 1916

ISBN 9781631491955

LC 2016002970

"First published in Great Britain by Faber & Faber Ltd. under the title Bitter freedom : Ireland in a revolutionary world, 1918-1922"--Title page verso.

In the tradition of Margaret MacMillan's Paris 1919 comes this groundbreaking history of the Irish Revolution.

"An excellent history, but more importantly, a sharply written portrait of a people and their long struggle to survive." Kirkus.

941.6 Northern Ireland; Donegal County, Monaghan County, Cavan County of Republic of Ireland

Campbell, Julieann

Setting the truth free : the inside story of the Bloody Sunday Justice Campaign / Julieann Campbell. Liberties Press, 2012. 219 p. : **941.6**

1. Bloody Sunday Justice Campaign. 2. Bloody Sunday, Derry, Northern Ireland, 1972. 3. Massacres. 4. Northern Ireland -- History -- 20th century.

ISBN 9781907593376

LC 2012379691

"Foreword by Gareth Peirce"--Cover.

Explores the forty-year struggle for justice for those who were killed on Bloody Sunday, detailing how twenty-eight families came together to demand that Britain launch an inquiry into its cover-up of events surrounding the massacre.

Coogan, Tim Pat, 1935-

The **troubles** : Ireland's ordeal, 1966-1995 and the search for peace / Tim Pat Coogan. Robert Rinehart Pub., 1996, c1995. 460 p. **941.6**

1. Peace movements -- Northern Ireland 2. Violence -- Northern Ireland. 3. Northern Ireland -- History -- 1969-1994.

ISBN 1570980926

LC 96067091

Originally published: London : Hutchinson, 1995.

Drawing on rare interviews with his sources on both sides of the conflict, the author traces the causes, effects, and dimensions of the ongoing conflict in Northern Ireland, up to and beyond the unstable cease-fire of 1994.

"In this political history the author examines all parties to the struggle. He reconstructs the past 30 years, from the 1969 marching and riots to the H-Block protests, the MacBride Principles, the Anglo-Irish agreement, and the recent paramilitary cease-fire. Coogan traces the current peace process, stalled by Great Britain's insistence that the IRA hand in its weapons, to the 1979 visit of Pope John Paul II." Library Journal.

941.7 Republic of Ireland (Eire)

Gibney, John, 1976-

A **short** history of Ireland, 1500-2000 / John Gibney. Yale University Press, 2017 xiv, 281 p. : **941.7**

1. Ireland -- History.

ISBN 0300208510

LC 2017941374

942 England and Wales

Castor, Helen

She-wolves : the women who ruled England before Elizabeth / Helen Castor. Harpercollins, 2011. 480 p. **942**

1. Women rulers. 2. Rulers. 3. Great Britain -- Rulers. 4. England -- Rulers.

ISBN 9780061430763

LC 2010013263

Explores women and power in England, as witnessed through the lives of six females who exercised power against the odds--and one who never got the chance.

"The author recounts the lives of six women who exercised--or tried to exercise--political power in England prior to Elizabeth I: Matilda, granddaughter of William the Conqueror; Eleanor of Aquitaine; Isabella of France; Margaret of Anjou; Jane Grey; and Mary Tudor. Readers of popular history of British royals will enjoy their immensely human stories and applaud the indomitable will of these strong protofeminists." Library Journal.

Gott, Richard, 1938-

Britain's empire : resistance, repression and revolt / Richard Gott. Verso Books, 2011. vii, 568 p. : **942**

1. Government, Resistance to -- Commonwealth countries -- History. 2. Government, Resistance to -- Great Britain -- Colonies -- History.

3. Imperialism -- History. 4. Commonwealth countries -- History. 5. Great Britain -- Civilization. 6. Great Britain -- Colonies -- History.
ISBN 1844677389
LC 2011456112

Tombs, Robert

The **English** and their history / Robert Tombs. Alfred A. Knopf, 2015. 1024 p. **942**

1. History 2. National characteristics, British 3. Great Britain -- History.
ISBN 9781101874769
LC 2014048390

"This is a Borzoi Book."

Presents the story of England, examining the language, literature, law, religion, politics, and more while investigating the sources of England's collective memory and belief..

"All readers will benefit from a history that reveals the connections and disconnections, the continuities and discontinuities that make the English who they think they are. Summing Up: Essential. All levels/libraries." Choice.

942.01 England--Early history to 1066

Lacey, Robert

Great tales from English history: 1 : the truth about King Arthur, Lady Godiva, Richard the Lionheart, and more / Robert Lacey. Little, Brown, 2004. xvi, 254 p. : **942.01**

1. Great Britain -- History -- To 1485.
ISBN 031610910X
LC 2003115660

"First published in Great Britain by Little, Brown, 2003"--T.p. verso.

This is the same as the British title: Great tales from English history : Cheddar Man to the Peasants' Revolt--per pub. of 2nd book; there will be three books in total in this "series."

Vivid retellings of forty-three classic English tales include the 7150 BC life and death of Cheddar Man, the infamous adventures of Hobbehod, and the Peasants' Revolt of 1381.

942.02 England--Norman period, 1066-1154

Morris, Marc, 1973-

★The **Norman** Conquest : the Battle of Hastings and the fall of Anglo-Saxon England / Marc Morris. Pegasus Books, 2013, c2012 440 p. **942.02**

1. Hastings, Battle of, England, 1066 2. Normans 3. Battles. 4. Great Britain -- History -- William I, 1066-1087. 5. Great Britain -- History -- Norman period, 1066-1154 6. Great Britain -- History -- Anglo-Saxon period, 449-1066
ISBN 9781605984513
LC 2013431768

Originally published: London : Hutchinson, 2012.

Explains why the Norman conquest was the most significant event in English history, assessing the historical circumstances of the battle and how language, law, philosophy, and other aspects of society were permanently altered by the conquest.

942.03 England--Period of House of Plantagenet, 1154-1399

Picard, Liza, 1927-

Chaucer's people : everyday lives in Medieval England / Liza Picard. W. W. Norton & Company, [2019] 368 p. **942.03**

1. Chaucer, Geoffrey, d. 1400 Characters. 2. Everyday life. 3. Working class. 4. Civilization, Medieval. 5. Manners and customs. 6. Great Britain -- History -- Medieval period, 1066-1485. 7. England -- Civilization -- 1066-1485.
ISBN 9781324002291
LC 2018044655

Originally published: Great Britain : Weidenfeld & Nicolson, 2017.

Uses the characters from Chaucer's "The Canterbury Tales" to illustrate how the people of medieval England lived and worked.

"Writing in the same detailed yet readable style as her Elizabeth's London, Picard uses Chaucer's descriptions of common occupations to delve into the smells, grit, and rituals of medieval life in the burgeoning city of London." Publishers Weekly.

942.03092 England--Period of House of Plantagenet, 1154-1399--biography

Jones, Dan, 1981-

★The **Plantagenets** : the warrior kings and queens who made England / Dan Jones. Viking, 2013. 560 p. **942.03092**

1. Plantagenet, House of 2. Royal houses -- Great Britain 3. Civilization, Medieval 4. Rulers. 5. Great Britain -- History -- Plantagenets, 1154-1399 6. Great Britain -- Rulers
ISBN 9780670026654
LC 2012039998

An epic history of the Plantagenet royal dynasty traces its first king's inheritance of a violence-stricken realm through the family's growth of a powerful empire that stretched from Scotland to Jerusalem, citing the enduring influences of such figures as Eleanor of Aquitaine, Richard II and King John.

"The great battles against the Scots and French and the subjugation of the Welsh make for thrilling reading but so do the equally enthralling struggles over succession, the Magna Carta, and the Provisions of Oxford...Written with prose that keeps the reader captivated throughout accounts of the span of centuries and the not-always-glorious trials of kingship, this book is at all times approachable, academic, and entertaining." Booklist.

942.04 England--Period of Houses of Lancaster and York, 1399-1485

Bicheno, Hugh

Blood royal : the Wars of the Roses, 1462-1485 / Hugh Bicheno. Pegasus Books, 2017. 416 p. Wars of the Roses (Hugh Bicheno) ; **942.04**

1. Wars of the Roses, 1455-1485 2. Civil war 3. Civilization, Medieval 4. Great Britain -- History -- Wars of the Roses, 1455-1485. 5. Great Britain -- History -- Lancaster and York, 1399-1485.
ISBN 9781681774282
LC 2017448714

The concluding volume to this rousing two-part history of the Wars of the Roses, England's longest and bloodiest civil war, narrated by a master historian.

Jones, Dan, 1981-

The **Wars** of the Roses : the fall of the Plantagenets and the rise of the Tudors / Dan Jones. Viking, 2014. 416 p. **942.04**

1. Tudor, House of. 2. Plantagenet, House of. 3. Margaret of Anjou, Queen of England, 1430-1482. 4. Beaufort, Margaret, Countess of Richmond and Derby, 1443-1509. 5. Elizabeth, Queen, consort of Edward IV, King of England, 1437?-1492 6. Wars of the Roses, 1455-1485 7. Great Britain -- History -- Wars of the Roses, 1455-1485.

ISBN 9780670026678

LC 2014010099

Traces the fifteenth-century civil wars that irrevocably shaped the British crown, particularly evaluating the roles of strong women including Margaret of Anjou, Elizabeth Woodville, and Margaret Beaufort in shifting power between two ruling families.

"This excellent and fairly accessible contribution to the history of the Wars of the Roses serves as a helpful corrective to previous mythologized versions. It is highly recommended for studies of British royal history and for readers of popular narrative nonfiction." Library Journal.

Jones, Michael K.

Bosworth 1485 : the battle that transformed England: the rise of the Tudor Dynasty / Michael K. Jones. Pegasus Books, 2015. 259 p. : **942.04**

1. Richard III, King of England, 1452-1485. 2. Henry VII, King of England, 1457-1509. 3. Tudor, House of. 4. Civil war 5. Rulers 6. Wars of the Roses, 1455-1485 7. Bosworth Field, Battle of, England, 1485. 8. Great Britain -- History -- Tudors, 1485-1603.

ISBN 9781605988597

LC 2016303507

A lively and authoritative reinterpretation of the Battle of Bosworth Field, where the Wars of the Roses ended and the Tudor dynasty began.

"Jones recounts the actual battle in easily understood terms for laymen and offers unusual insights into the role of foreign fighters. This is a well-done reexamination of the conflict that truly altered the course of history." Booklist.

Weir, Alison, 1951-

The **Wars** of the Roses / Alison Weir. Ballantine Books, 1995. xvii, 462 p., 12 p. of plates : **942.04**

1. Richard II, King of England, 1367-1400. 2. Henry VI, King of England, 1421-1471. 3. Wars of the Roses, 1455-1485 4. Great Britain -- History -- Wars of the Roses, 1455-1485. 5. Great Britain -- History -- Plantagenets, 1154-1399. 6. Great Britain -- History -- Tudors, 1485-1603.

ISBN 9780345391179

Originally published: London : J. Cape, 1995.

Chronicles the struggles of the Lancaster and York families to control the British monarchy, while offering profiles of such figures as Katherine of Valois, Elizabeth Wydville, and Margaret of Anjou.

"No history collection should do without this perfectly focused and beautifully unfolded account." Booklist.

942.04092 England--Period of Houses of Lancaster and York, 1399-1485--biography

Gristwood, Sarah

Blood sisters : the women behind the Wars of the Roses / Sarah Gristwood. Basic Books, 2013. 384 p. **942.04092**

1. Plantagenet, House of. 2. Margaret of Anjou, Queen of England, 1430-1482. 3. York, Cecily, Duchess of, 1415-1495. 4. Elizabeth, Queen, consort of Edward IV, King of England, 1437?-1492. 5. Anne, Queen, consort of Richard III, King of England, 1456-1485. 6. Margaret, of York, Duchess, consort of Charles the Bold, Duke of Burgundy, 1446-1503. 7. Elizabeth, Queen, consort of Henry VII, King of England, 1465-1503. 8. Beaufort, Margaret, Countess of Richmond and Derby, 1443-1509. 9. Wars of the Roses, 1455-1485 10. Inheritance and succession -- England -- History 11. Rulers 12. Civil war 13. Great Britain -- History -- Lancaster and York, 1399-1485. 14. Great Britain -- History -- Wars of the Roses, 1455-1485. 15. Great Britain -- History -- Henry VII, 1485-1509.

ISBN 9780465018314

LC 2012044813

A historian describes the drama and family feuding within the Plantagenets, England's fifteenth-century ruling family, from the perspective of the mothers, wives and daughters who wove a web of loyalty and betrayal that ultimately gave way to the Tudors.

942.05 England--Period of House of Tudor, 1485-1603

Ackroyd, Peter, 1949-

Tudors : the history of England from Henry VIII to Elizabeth I / Peter Ackroyd. Thomas Dunne Books/St. Martin's Press, 2013, c2012. 512 p. History of England ; **942.05**

1. Reformation -- England 2. Royal houses. 3. Great Britain -- History -- Tudors, 1485-1603.

ISBN 9781250003621

LC 2013024573

Originally published: London : Macmillan, 2012.

A chronicle of the English Reformation, the making of the Anglican Church, and the age of the Tudors follows Henry VIII's relentless pursuit of both the perfect wife and the perfect heir, the brief reign of teenage king Edward VI, and the long reign of Elizabeth I.

De Lisle, Leanda

The **sisters** who would be queen : Katherine, Mary, and Lady Jane Grey: a Tudor tragedy / Leanda De Lisle. Ballantine Books, 2009. 352 p. **942.05**

1. Grey, Jane, Lady, 1537-1554 2. Hertford, Katherine Seymour, Countess of, 1540-1568. 3. Keys, Mary Grey, 1545?-1578. 4. Gray family 5. Sisters -- Great Britain 6. Nobility -- Great Britain 7. Women rulers -- Great Britain 8. Royal houses -- Great Britain -- History -- 16th century 9. Great Britain -- History -- Tudors, 1485-1603.

ISBN 9780345491350

LC 2009031074

Mary, Katherine and Jane Grey--sisters whose mere existence nearly toppled a kingdom and altered a nation's destiny are three women, who were victimized by the vicious Tudor power struggle and whose heirs would otherwise probably be ruling England today. Exploding the many myths of Lady Jane Grey's life, unearthing the details of Katherine's and Mary's dramatic stories, and casting new light on Elizabeth's reign, the author gives voice and resonance to the lives of the Greys and offers perspective on their place in history and on a time when a royal marraige could gain a woman a kingdom or cost her everything.

Fletcher, Catherine, 1975-

The **divorce** of Henry VIII : the untold story from inside the Vatican / Catherine Fletcher. Palgrave Macmillan, 2012. 288 p. **942.05**

1. Henry VIII, King of England, 1491-1547 Divorce. 2. Henry VIII, King of England, 1491-1547 Relations with popes. 3. Catholic

Church Foreign relations Great Britain. 4. Church and state -- Great Britain -- History -- 16th century. 5. Reformation -- England. 6. Religion -- History 7. Great Britain -- Foreign relations -- Catholic Church. 8. Great Britain -- Politics and government -- 1509-1547.
ISBN 9780230341517
LC 2011050335

"In 1533 the English monarch Henry VIII decided to divorce his wife of twenty years Catherine of Aragon in pursuit of a male heir to ensure the Tudor line. He was also head over heels in love with his wife's lady in waiting Anne Boleyn, the future mother of Elizabeth I. But getting his freedom involved a terrific web of intrigue through the enshrined halls of the Vatican that resulted in a religious schism and the formation of the Church of England. Henry's man in Rome was a wily Italian diplomat named Gregorio Casali who drew no limits on skullduggery including kidnapping, bribery and theft to make his king a free man. In this absorbing narrative, winner of the Rome Fellowship prize and University of Durham historian Catherine Fletcher draws on hundreds of previously-unknown Italian archive documents to tell the colorful tale from the inside story inside the Vatican".-- Provided by publisher.

Goodman, Ruth, 1963-

How to be a Tudor : a dawn-to-dusk guide to Tudor life / Ruth Goodman. Liveright Publishing Corporation, 2016. 464 p. **942.05**

1. Tudor, House of 2. Manners and customs. 3. Historical reenactments 4. Great Britain -- Social life and customs -- 16th century. 5. Great Britain -- History -- Tudors, 1485-1603. 6. Great Britain -- Social conditions -- 16th century.
ISBN 9781631491399
LC 2015038420

On the heels of her triumphant How to Be a Victorian, Ruth Goodman travels even further back in English history to the era closest to her heart, the dramatic period from the crowning of Henry VII to the death of Elizabeth I. Drawing on her own adventures living in re-created Tudor conditions, Goodman serves as our intrepid guide to sixteenth-century living.

"Throughout, Goodman's palpable enthusiasm and clear appreciation for the resourcefulness of the eras people make these men and women entirely relatable and yet full of surprises." Publishers Weekly.

Goodman, Ruth, 1963-

★**How** to behave badly in Elizabethan England : a guide for knaves, fools, harlots, cuckolds, drunkards, liars, thieves, and braggarts / Ruth Goodman. Liveright Publishing, A Division of W. W. Norton & Company, 2018 320 p. **942.05**

1. Etiquette 2. Manners and customs -- History 3. Great Britain -- Social life and customs -- 16th century
ISBN 9781631495113
LC 2018032705

"First published in Great Britain under the title How to behave badly in Renaissance Britain."

Drawing from period-specific advice manuals, court cases, and sermons the author celebrates one of the naughtiest eras of British history through the troublemakers, drunkards, snooty needlers and boors present in Elizabethan England.

Lipscomb, Suzannah

The **king** is dead : the last will and testament of Henry VIII / Suzannah Lipscomb. Pegasus Books, 2016. 336 p. **942.05**

1. Henry VIII, King of England, 1491-1547. 2. Inheritance and succession 3. Wills. 4. Legacies. 5. Church and state 6. Great Britain -- History -- Henry VIII, 1509-1547
ISBN 9781681772547
LC 2018300499

The author of 1536 and co-presenter of the History Channel documentary Inside the World of Henry VIII, presents an expert interpretation of the Tudor king's highly contested last will and testament against the backdrop of his glittering world.

"A delightful story of intrigue and manipulation that shows how Henry really couldn't control his kingdom." Kirkus.

Mortimer, Ian, 1967-

The **time** traveler's guide to Elizabethan England / Ian Mortimer. Viking, 2013. 384 p. **942.05**

1. European Renaissance. 2. Civilization, Western. 3. England -- Social life and customs -- 16th century. 4. Great Britain -- History -- Elizabeth I, 1558-1603 5. England -- Social conditions -- 16th century.
ISBN 9780670026074
LC 2013001566

Mortimer explores the reign of Queen Elizabeth I. A golden age of maritime heroes like Sir Walter Raleigh and writers such as Shakespeare, Elizabethan England was also an era of violence, famine, and religious persecution. But for all these trials, Elizabeth's subjects settled America, circumnavigated the globe, and laid the groundwork for the modern world.

942.06 England--House of Stuart and Commonwealth periods to present, 1603

Fraser, Antonia, 1932-

Faith and treason : the story of the Gunpowder Plot / Antonia Fraser. Doubleday, 1996. xxxv, 347 p. : **942.06**

1. Fawkes, Guy, 1570-1606. 2. Great Britain. Parliament -- History. 3. Gunpowder Plot, 1605. 4. Insurgency. 5. Conspiracy theories. 6. Rebels. 7. Great Britain -- Politics and government -- 1603-1625. 8. Great Britain -- History -- James I, 1603-1625.
ISBN 9780385471909

Later republished in England as The Gunpowder Plot : terror & faith in 1605.

Gold Dagger Award for Best Nonfiction of the Year, 1996.

Recounts one of the most famous conspiracies in British history, the attempt in 1605, led by Guy Fawkes, to blow up the House of Parliament and King James I.

"The Gunpowder Plot was both cruel and crackpot, but Fraser does a wonderful job of conveying to the modern reader just why a few Catholics felt that it was justified and also was likely to succeed." The New Yorker.

942.07 England--1714-1837

Brewer, John, 1947-

The **pleasures** of the imagination : English culture in the eighteenth century / John Brewer. University of Chicago Press, 2000. xxx, 721 p. : **942.07**

1. England -- Civilization -- 18th century. 2. England -- Intellectual life -- 18th century. 3. England -- Social life and customs -- 18th century.
ISBN 9780226074191
LC 99057059

Originally published: United Kingdom : HarperCollins and by New York : Farrar, Straus and Giroux, 1997.

942.081 England--1837-1901

Ackroyd, Peter, 1949-

Dominion : the history of England from the Battle of Waterloo to Victoria's Diamond Jubilee / Peter Ackroyd. Thomas Dunne Books, 2018. 416 p. History of England ; **942.081**

1. George IV, King of Great Britain, 1762-1830. 2. William IV, King of Great Britain, 1765-1837 3. Victoria, Queen of Great Britain, 1819-1901 4. Royal houses 5. War and society 6. Manners and customs 7. Battles 8. Great Britain -- History -- 19th century.
ISBN 9781250003652

LC 2018019772

First published in Great Britain by Macmillan as a set, complete in 6 volumes, under the common title: The history of England; Dominion is volume 5 in that series.

In this fifth installment of the History of England series, a historian and award-winning author starts in the year of 1815 as national glory following the Battle of Waterloo gives way to a post-war depression and ends with the death of Queen Victoria in January 1901.

"With a large cast of historic figures, a chronicling of the coalescence of the middle class and changing labor concerns, the rise of secularism, and the expanse of the British empire, Ackroyd's deep and broad canvas is rich in informative details and will appeal to all readers interested in British history while especially pleasing those fascinated by this era." Booklist.

942.083 England--1910-1936

Nicolson, Juliet

The **perfect** summer : England 1911, just before the storm / Juliet Nicolson. Grove Press, c2006. xiii, 290 p., 16 p. of plates : **942.083**

1. Social classes 2. Social structure 3. Great Britain -- Social life and customs -- 20th century. 4. Great Britain -- History -- George V, 1910-1936. 5. Great Britain -- Social conditions -- 20th century.
ISBN 9780802118462

LC 2006048854

Originally published: London : John Murray, 2006.

Chronicling four months during 1911, an evocative portrait of an English society on the brink of turbulent change describes such milestones as the crowning of a new king, strikes that paralyzed British industry, and the first London appearance of the Ballets Russes, from the viewpoints of a debutante, a suffragette, a trade unionist, a butler, a politician, the queen, and others.

"With her sparkling social history about Edwardian society on the brink of World War I, Nicolson has created the perfect beach reading for Anglophiles." Christian Science Monitor.

942.1 London (England)

Ackroyd, Peter, 1949-

London : the biography / Peter Ackroyd. Nan A. Talese, c2000. xxvi, 801 p. : **942.1**

1. London, England -- Social life and customs. 2. London, England -- History.
ISBN 9780385497701

LC 2001326868

Originally published: London : Chatto & Windus, 2000.

Bestselling British author Peter Ackroyd draws upon everything from ballads and folk tales to court records and newspaper accounts to create a book about London that's as diverse and enthralling as the city itself. Ackroyd portrays this amazing place as a living entity and organizes his chapters thematically, writing about such topics as the city's inhabitants, crime, theater, street life, and waste disposal practices over time.

"A sweeping, highly readable account of London's colorful and complicated history." Library Journal.

Alexander, Eileen, 1917-1986

Love in the Blitz : the long-lost letters of a brilliant young woman to her beloved on the front / Eileen Alexander. Harper, 2020. xx, 474 p., 16 unnumbered p. of plates : **942.1**

1. Alexander, Eileen, 1917-1986 Correspondence 2. Young women 3. Lovers 4. World War II -- Great Britain 5. Soldiers 6. London, England -- History -- Bombardment, 1940-1945 7. Great Britain -- History -- George VI, 1936-1952 8. Letters
ISBN 9780062888808

"Originally published as 'Love in the blitz: the greatest lost love letters of the second World War' in Great Britain in 2020 by William Collins, an imprint of HarperCollins Publishers."--Title page verso.

This extraordinary glimpse of life in London during World War II is told through recently discovered letters written by a young woman to her university beau as she tries to carve a place for herself in a time of uncertainty, providing a vivid and personal account of this historic era.

"This treasure trove of love letters, cultural history, and memoir should make a wonderful addition to all World War II collections." Library Journal

Flanders, Judith

The **Victorian** city : everyday life in Dickens' London / Judith Flanders. St. Martins Press, 2014 544 p. **942.1**

1. Street life 2. England -- Social life and customs -- 19th century. 3. England -- Social conditions -- 19th century.
ISBN 9781250040213

LC 2014007566

A meticulously researched portrait of everyday life in Dickensian London evaluates the Victorian era as a time of unprecedented transformation marked by rapid construction, railways, street lighting and a population boom at every economic level.

"This is a superb portrait of an exciting, thriving, and dangerous city." Booklist.

Hollis, Leo

London rising : the men who made modern London / Leo Hollis. Walker & Co., 2008. x, 390 p., 8 p. of plates : **942.1**

1. Wren, Christopher, Sir, 1632-1723 2. Locke, John, 1632-1704. 3. Evelyn, John 1620-1706. 4. Hooke, Robert, 1635-1703. 5. Barbon, Nicholas, d. 1698. 6. St. Paul's Cathedral, London, England -- History 17th century. 7. Urban planning -- London, England -- History. 8. Urban renewal -- London, England. 9. Buildings -- Repair and reconstruction -- London, England -- History. 10. London, England -- History -- 17th century.
ISBN 0802716326

LC 2008000179

Traces the contributions of five individuals to restore London after the English Civil War, plague, and the Great Fire of 1666 all but decimated the city, in a historical account that cites their pivotal influence on subsequent cultural, scientific, and architectural advances.

"London in the mid-17th century remained a medieval city. The civil war, a plague that claimed 100,000 lives and the Great Fire of 1666 would have been sufficient to send it back to the Dark Ages. Instead, London was transformed into a modern metropolis. Hollis controls the narrative by focusing on the five figures who best represent the spirit of the age. John Locke, the philosopher, outlined a daring theory of universal natural rights; social observer John Evelyn grappled with the specific meaning of Englishness; real estate developer and speculator Nicholas Barbon rebuilt the center of London (with designs by the scientific polymath Robert Hooke); and lastly, Christopher Wren, who created St. Paul's Cathedral, eternal symbol of the glittering city." Publishers Weekly.

Jenkins, Simon

The **city** on the Thames : the creation of a world capital: a history of London / Simon Jenkins. Pegasus Books, 2020, c2019 xvi, 393 p. **942.1**

1. Cities and towns -- History 2. Capitals (Cities) 3. London, England -- History 4. Great Britain -- Civilization

ISBN 9781643135526

Originally published: London : Viking, 2019.

London: a settlement founded by the Romans, occupied by the Saxons, conquered by the Danes, and ruled by the Normans. This transformative place became a medieval maze of alleys and courtyards, later to be checkered with grand estates of Georgian splendor. It swelled with industry and became the center of the largest empire in history. And having risen from the rubble of the Blitz, it is now one of the greatest cities in the world. From the prehistoric occupants of the Thames Valley to the preoccupied commuters of today, Simon Jenkins brings together the key events, individuals and trends in London's history to create a matchless portrait of the capital.

"In addition to providing an enjoyable urban history that accurately and affectionately captures the fabric and character of London history, this account also serves as an optimal guide for armchair travelers." Library Journal

Jones, Nigel H.

Tower : an epic history of the Tower of London / Nigel Jones. St. Martin's Press, 2012, c2011 464 p. **942.1**

1. Tower of London (London, England) -- History. 2. Forts 3. Prisons -- London, England -- History. 4. Castles. 5. Towers. 6. London, England -- Buildings, structures, etc. 7. London, England -- History.

ISBN 9780312622961

LC 2012028273

Originally published : London : Hutchinson, 2011.

A dramatic history of the Tower of London places its story in a context of national and international events, drawing on primary sources to explore its diverse functions as a British symbol, epicenter for violent events and modern tourist attraction. By the author of Through a Glass Darkly.

Jordan, Don,

The **king's** city : a history of London during the Restoration; the city that transformed a nation / Don Jordan. Pegasus Books, [2018] xvii, 526 pages, 8 unnumbered pages of plates : **942.1**

1. London, England -- History -- 17th century. 2. England -- History -- 17th century. 3. Great Britain -- History -- Restoration, 1660-1688.

ISBN 9781681776385

LC bl2018029259

A tantalizing and thrilling history of London at the time of King Charles II.

"A wonderful picture of 17th-century England, replete with the excitement of ideas and discoveries and the beginnings of the empire." Kirkus.

Sinclair, Iain, 1943-

The **last** London : true fictions from an unreal city / Iain Sinclair. Oneworld Publications, 2017. 336 p. **942.1**

1. Sinclair, Iain, 1943- -- Travel -- England. 2. Human geography. 3. Walking. 4. Cities and towns. 5. City life. 6. London, England -- Description and travel.

ISBN 9781786071743

LC bl2018001637

Sinclair strikes out on a series of solitary walks and collaborative expeditions to make a final reckoning with a capital stretched beyond recognition. Travelling from the pinnacle of the Shard to the outer limits of the London Overground system at Croydon and Barking, from the Thames Estuary to the future ruins of Olympicopolis, the author reflects on where London begins and where it ends.

"An unconventional, atmospheric exploration of London from one its most unique chroniclers." Kirkus.

942.901 Historical periods

Charles-Edwards, T. M.

Wales and the Britons, 350-1064 / T.M. Charles-Edwards. Oxford University Press, 2013. xx, 795 p. : **942.901**

1. Wales -- History -- To 1063.

ISBN 0198217315

LC 2012376060

943 Germany and neighboring central European countries

Coy, Jason Philip, 1970-

A **brief** history of Germany / Jason Philip Coy. Facts On File, c2011. xvi, 288 p. : Brief history (Facts on File) **943**

1. Germany -- History.

ISBN 9780816081424

LC 2010023139

Covering more than 2,000 years of history, A Brief History of Germany provides a concise account of the events, people, and special customs and traditions that have shaped Germany from ancient times to the present. -- from publisher description.

Harding, Thomas, 1968-

The **house** by the lake : one house, five families, and a hundred years of German history / Thomas Harding. Picador, 2016, c2015. 464 p. : **943**

1. Houses 2. Families 3. Communities 4. War and society 5. Germany -- Social life and customs -- 20th century 6. Germany -- History -- 20th century

ISBN 9781250065063

LC 2015044339

Originally published: London : William Heinemann, 2015.

Tells the story of Germany through the inhabitants of one small wooden building: a nobleman farmer, a prosperous Jewish family, a renowned Nazi composer, a widow and her children, a Stasi informant.

"This personal saga centered on a family home will appeal to enthusiasts of German history, especially post-World War II division and reunification." Library Journal.

MacGregor, Neil, 1946-

Germany : memories of a nation / Neil MacGregor. Alfred A. Knopf, 2015. 644 p. **943**

1. Culture 2. National characteristics, German 3. Germany -- History. 4. Germany -- Civilization.
ISBN 9781101875667

LC 2014048396

"Germany is unlike any other country in the world. But how much do we really know about it, and how do its people understand themselves? In Germany: Memories of a Nation, Neil MacGregor -- director of the British Museum and author of A History of the World in 100 Objects -- presents the stories of a nation through a collection of thirty objects and touchstones. From coins and crowns to fairytales and philosophers, MacGregor presents the inventions, ideas, and icons that comprise the many identities of the German people. Germany: Memories of a Nation is a view of this complex and fascinating country like no other".-- Provided by publisher.

"Most importantly, the author finds post-World War II Germany hyperattuned to the need for memorials to victims of terror and oppression--e.g., via the work of painter and printmaker Kathe Kollwitz. A comprehensive record jam-packed with visuals." Kirkus.

Mitchell, Greg, 1947-

The **tunnels** : escapes under the Berlin Wall and the historic films the JFK White House tried to kill / Greg Mitchell. Crown Publishing, 2016. 390 p. **943**

1. National Broadcasting Company -- History. 2. Columbia Broadcasting System, inc. -- History. 3. Berlin Wall 4. Cold War. 5. Censorship 6. Tunnels. 7. Berlin, Germany 8. East Germany.
ISBN 9781101903858

LC 2016013452

A dramatic Cold War narrative of two harrowing attempts to rescue East Germans by tunneling beneath the Berlin Wall also describes the financial contributions of two U.S. television networks who would document the stories and the efforts of the Kennedy administration to suppress both films.

"Mitchell's tense, fascinating account reveals how the U.S. undermined a freedom struggle for the sake of diplomacy." Publishers Weekly.

Moorhouse, Roger

Berlin at war / Roger Moorhouse. Basic Books, c2010. 432 p. **943**

1. World War II -- Berlin, Germany. 2. Bombardment. 3. Sieges. 4. Rationing. 5. Berlin, Germany -- History -- 1918-1945. 6. Berlin, Germany -- Social conditions -- 20th century. 7. Germany -- History -- 1933-1945.
ISBN 9780465005338

LC bl2010027837

"Election results in the fading days of the Weimar Republic indicate that Berliners were not particularly sympathetic to Hitler or his movement. Yet Berlin endured horrible physical destruction, deprivation, and death. This included intense Allied bombings by day and night, and a siege and eventual ravaging by the Russian army. [Moorhouse] begins with an almost idyllic scene as huge crowds in Berlin witness the celebration of Hitler's birthday in April 1939; at the time, of course, Germany seemed to have achieved its foreign-policy goals without firing a shot. As the fortunes of Germany and Berlin deteriorate, Moorhouse uses the testimonies of a variety of Berliners to describe some memorable scenes and struggles.This is a hard, unrelenting saga of the effects of total warfare on citizens just hoping to survive." Booklist.

Nelson, Anne, 1954-

Red Orchestra : the story of the Berlin underground and the circle of friends who resisted Hitler / Anne Nelson. Random House, 2009. 416 p. **943**

1. Die Rote Kapelle 2. Anti-Nazi movement -- Berlin, Germany -- History 3. World War II -- Underground movements -- Berlin, Germany 4. Spies -- History -- 20th century 5. War -- History -- 20th century 6. Berlin, Germany -- History -- 1918-1945.
ISBN 9781400060009

LC 2008023465

Relates the story of the Rote Kapelle, or Red Orchestra, a group of German artists, intellectuals, and bureaucrats who conspired to bring down the Nazi regime and whose acts of resistance resulted in capture and execution.

"The author documents the wartime journey of Greta Kuckhoff, a young German, and her valiant colleagues who formed a potent resistance to the Hitler regime in its glory days. Nelson's riveting book speaks proudly of Greta...and all of the nearly three million Germans who resisted Hitler's iron will, and gives the reader a somber view of hell from the inside." Publishers Weekly.

Reeves, Richard, 1936-

Daring young men : the heroism and triumph of the Berlin Airlift, June 1948-May 1949 / Richard Reeves. Simon & Schuster, c2010. xvii, 316 p., 8 p. of plates : **943**

1. Military pilots -- United States -- History -- 20th century. 2. Military history. 3. Military pilots -- Great Britain -- History -- 20th century. 4. Berlin, Germany -- History -- Blockade, 1948-1949.
ISBN 9781416541196

LC 2009015333

Documents the contributions of western pilots, navigators and air-traffic controllers to bring food, medicine and other survival supplies to Berlin during the Soviet blockade, drawing on hundreds of interviews to describe the effort's dangerous and politically charged risks. By the award-winning author of President Reagan.

"The American people will not allow the German people to starve, Colonel Frank Howley, one of the top American commanders in Berlin, said in June, 1948, after the Soviets cut off all supply routes except an air corridor to the Western sectors of the city. But when the blockade began, as Reeves notes in his appealing account, almost no one believed that food and fuel for an urban population of more than two million could be delivered by air, and many American officials thought the question was how Berlin could be abandoned with the least embarrassment. Ten and a half months and a quarter-million American and British flights later--an unmatched act of politico-logistical bravado--the Soviets abandoned their blockade." The New Yorker.

Smith, Helmut Walser, 1962-

Germany, a nation in its time : before, during, and after Nationalism, 1500-2000 / Helmut Walser Smith. Liveright Publishing Corporation, 2020 xvi, 590 p. **943**

1. Nationalism -- Germany. 2. National characteristics. 3. Maps. 4. Germany -- History -- 1517-1871. 5. Germany -- History -- 1871-1933. 6. Germany -- History -- 1933-1945. 7. Germany -- History -- 1945-
ISBN 9780871404664

LC 2019050560

The first major history of Germany in a generation, a work that presents a five-hundred-year narrative that challenges our traditional perceptions of Germany's conflicted past.

"This new perspective on German history should be welcomed by all libraries." Library Journal

Watson, Peter, 1943-

The **German** genius : Europe's third renaissance, the second scientific revolution, and the twentieth century / Peter Watson. Harper, 2010. xix, 964 p. **943**

1. Intellectual life -- Germany. 2. Germany -- Civilization. 3. Germany -- History.

ISBN 9780060760229

LC 2010006738

"This is a panoramic review of German cultural and intellectual development from 1750 to the present. Examining the contributions of literally hundreds of German thinkers and doers and mapping the conceptual connections between them, the author demonstrates the breadth, volume, and influence of German output in philosophy, science, industry, art, literature, and all forms of scholarly activity. But Watson's true focus is the cultural crucible, forged in the eighteenth and nineteenth centuries and informed by notions of Bildung and inwardness, that gave rise to such accomplishments but also set the stage for the evil actions of the Third Reich. To some extent an effort to untether our understanding of German history from the conflicts of the twentieth century, this study is also a reminder that our modern Western worldview has deep German roots." Booklist.

943.08 Germany since 1866

Barth, Rudiger

The **last** winter of the Weimar Republic : the rise of the Third Reich / Rudiger Barth, Hauke Friederichs ; translated by Caroline Waight. Pegasus Books, 2020, c2018. 384 p. **943.085**

1. Hitler, Adolf, 1889-1945 2. Nazi Party (Germany) 3. Politicians -- Germany. 4. Nazism 5. World War II -- Causes. 6. Political corruption 7. Germany -- History -- 1918-1933. 8. Germany -- Politics and government -- 1918-1933. 9. Germany -- Economic conditions -- 1918-1945.

ISBN 9781643133331

LC bl2020005873

Originally published: Frankfurt : S. Fischer, 2018.

An extensively researched, day-by-day account of the final months of the Weimar Republic examines the economic and political factors that shaped the collapse of democracy in Germany and Hitler's frightening rise to power.

"A sharply focused study of the many poor decisions that ended with Hitler's taking power. . . . An expert and highly disheartening history of a dictator's early rise." Kirkus

Craig, Gordon Alexander, 1913-2005

Germany, 1866-1945 / Gordon A. Craig. Oxford University Press, 1980, c1978. xv, 825 p. ; **943.08**

1. Germany -- History -- 1866-1871. 2. Germany -- History -- 1871-1918. 3. Germany -- History -- 1918-1933. 4. Germany -- History -- 1933-1945.

ISBN 9780195027242

LC BL 99736808

Evans, Richard J.

★The **coming** of the Third Reich / Richard J. Evans. The Penguin Press, 2004. xi, 622 p. : **943.08**

1. Hitler, Adolf, 1889-1945. 2. Nazi Party (Germany) -- History 3. Nazism -- History. 4. Germany -- History -- 1871-1918. 5. Germany -- History -- 1918-1933.

ISBN 1594200041

LC 2003063205

A history of Adolf Hitler's rise to power and the collapse of democracy in Nazi Germany explains why Nazism's ideology of hatred flourished in a country embittered by military defeat and economic disaster following World War I.

"This is a first-rate narrative history that informs and educates and may inspire readers to delve even deeper into the subject." Booklist.

943.085 Period of Weimar Republic, 1918-1933

Hett, Benjamin Carter

The **death** of democracy : Hitler's rise to power and the downfall of the Weimar Republic / Benjamin Carter Hett. Henry Holt & Company, 2018. 288 p. **943.085**

1. Hitler, Adolf, 1889-1945 2. Nazi Party (Germany) 3. Politicians 4. Nazism.

ISBN 9781250162502

LC bl2018003982

A timely account of how the Nazi party came to power argues that failures throughout the Weimar Republic and the shortsightedness of German politicians who were trying to co-opt populist insurgencies inadvertently secured the tools that Hitler needed to get elected and establish a genocidal dictatorship.

943.086 Germany--Period of Third Reich, 1933-1945

Aycoberry, Pierre

The **social** history of the Third Reich : 1933-1945 / Pierre Aycoberry ; translated from the French by Janet Lloyd. New Press : c1999. 380 p. ; **943.086**

1. Nazism. 2. National characteristics, German. 3. Political culture -- Germany. 4. Germany -- Politics and government -- 1933-1945. 5. Germany -- Social conditions -- 1933-1945. 6. Germany -- Social life and customs -- 1933-1945.

ISBN 1565845498

LC 99014059

Examines all aspects of German life under Hitler, including the roles that economics and social class played in shaping German life during the Third Reich

"In examining the actions of individuals and social groups, {the author} illustrates that German citizens' response to the Nazi regime varied wildly. Some resisted bravely; others saw an opportunity for advancement. Most people sought merely to survive. In fact, what is extremely unsettling is how so many could maintain a semblance of normalcy in their lives. Aycoberry does not attempt to answer the unanswerable questions posed by the Nazi era, but his disturbing, brutally honest, and scrupulously fair work may be a landmark in the field." Booklist.

Bailey, Catherine, 1960-

A **castle** in wartime : one family, their missing sons, and the fight to defeat the Nazis / Catherine Bailey. Viking, 2019. ix, 461 p., 16 unnumbered p. of plates : **943.086**

1. Pirzio-Biroli, Detalmo, 1916- 2. Hassell, Ulrich von, 1881-1944 Family 3. Anti-Nazi movement 4. World War II -- Underground movements 5. Husband and wife 6. Diplomatic and consular service 7. Italy -- History -- 1922-1945.

ISBN 9780525559290

Originally published in Great Britain as The lost boys: a family ripped apart by war by Viking, London, 2019.

The author documents the experiences of ambassador's daughter Fey von Hassell, whose family made the brave decision to forfeit their privileged existences to resist the Nazis during the occupation of northern Italy.

Burleigh, Michael, 1955-

The **Third** Reich : a new history / Michael Burleigh. Hill and Wang, 2001, c2000. xxv, 965 p. : **943.086**

1. Hitler, Adolf, 1889-1945. 2. Nazi Party (Germany) 3. World War II -- Germany. 4. Ethics. 5. Religion and politics. 6. War -- Moral and ethical aspects. 7. Germany -- History -- 1933-1945.

ISBN 0809093251

LC 00031838

Samuel Johnson Prize for Nonfiction, 2001.

Argues that the Germans' acceptance of Hitler's totalitarianism and Nazi philosophies stemmed from their desire for economic prosperity and a national identity, which slowly developed into a collective conscience and religious fervor.

"Burleigh has produced an important work of synthesis that recapitulates an impressive array of sources. It deserves to become the jumping-off point for scholars who want to take their studies of this uniquely horrible era in new directions." Publishers Weekly

Childers, Thomas, 1946-

★The **third** reich : a history of Nazi Germany / Thomas Childers. Simon & Schuster, 2017. 651 p. : **943.086**

1. Nazis 2. World War II -- Causes. 3. Holocaust (1933-1945) 4. Atrocities 5. Germany -- History -- 1933-1945. 6. Germany -- Politics and government -- 1933-1945. 7. Germany -- Social conditions -- 1933-1945.

ISBN 9781451651133

LC 2016019506

"Based in part on documents seldom used by previous historians, this history of the Third Reich shows how the dramatic, improbable rise of the Nazis happened because of tragic miscalculations and blunders, then documents what life was like for ordinary Germans as the Nazis precipitated the horrors of World War II and the Holocaust".-- Provided by publisher.

"A riveting study delves deeply into the conditions of the perfect storm that allowed Hitler and his Nazi party to seize and wield unprecedented power." Kirkus.

Evans, Richard J.

★The **Third** Reich in power, 1933-1939 / Richard J. Evans. Penguin Press, 2005. xvii, 941 p. : **943.086**

1. Hitler, Adolf, 1889-1945. 2. Nazi Party (Germany) -- History 3. Nazism -- History. 4. State-sponsored terrorism -- Germany -- History -- 20th century 5. Jews -- Persecutions -- Germany. 6. Germany -- History -- 1933-1945. 7. Germany -- Politics and government -- 1933-1945. 8. Germany -- Economic policy -- 1933-1945.

ISBN 1594200742

LC 2005052128

Documents the radical transformation of Germany under Nazi rule, exploring how virtually every area of life was reordered to comply with the regime's preparations for war, and describes the increasing brutality towards marginalized groups.

"This is a major achievement. No other recent synthetic history has quite the range and narrative power of Evans's work." Publishers Weekly.

Fritzsche, Peter, 1959-

★**Hitler's** first hundred days : when Germans embraced the Third Reich / Peter Fritzsche. Basic Books, 2020. 496 p. **943.086**

1. Hitler, Adolf, 1889-1945 2. Nazi Party (Germany) 3. Nazism 4. Elections -- Germany. 5. Nationalism -- Germany. 6. Social classes 7. Germany -- Politics and government -- 1933-1945.

ISBN 9781541697430

LC 2019041776

A history professor and author describes how the deep division between political extremes in early 1930s Germany led to the pivotal moments that allowed the majority of Germans to join the Nazis and create the Third Reich.

"Everyone concerned about the rise of nationalism, the impact of extreme partisanship, and preserving democracy should read this insightful book." Library Journal

Life and death in the Third Reich / Peter Fritzsche. Belknap Press of Harvard University Press, 2008. viii, 368 p. ; **943.086**

1. Nazism 2. Collective memory 3. Ideology -- Germany. 4. Holocaust (1933-1945) -- Causes 5. Germany -- Ethnic relations -- History -- 20th century. 6. Germany -- History -- 1933-1945. 7. Germany -- Social conditions -- 1918-1933. 8. Germany -- Politics and government -- 1933-1945.

ISBN 9780674027930

LC 2007040552

Cundill Prize in Historical Literature finalist

A scholar deciphers the puzzle of Nazism's ideological grip in a critical analysis that examines the efforts of Germans to adjust to new racial identities, to believe in the necessity of war, and to accept the dynamic of unconditional destruction.

Garson, Paul

Album of the damned : snapshots from the Third Reich / Paul Garson. Academy Chicago Publishers, 2008. xiii, 408 p. : **943.086**

1. National socialism 2. World War II 3. Germany -- History -- 1933-1945

ISBN 9780897335768

LC bl2009017893

Presents a collection of photographs, many taken by soldiers, of life in Germany during World War II.

Gellately, Robert, 1943-

The **Oxford** illustrated history of the Third Reich / edited by Robert Gellately. Oxford University Press, 2018. 384 p. **943.086**

1. World War II. 2. Military history 3. Nazism 4. Nazis 5. Germany -- History -- 1933-1945 6. Europe -- History -- 20th century. 7. Essays

ISBN 9780198728283

LC 2017939066

A look at the Third Reich covers the history of Germany from the Nazi rise to power in 1933 to the end of World War II in 1945.

Johnson, Eric A. (Eric Arthur), 1948-

What we knew : terror, mass murder and everyday life in Nazi Germany : an oral history / interviews conducted by Eric A. Johnson and Karl-Heinz Reuband. Basic Books, 2005. xxiii, 434 p. **943.086**

1. Holocaust (1933-1945) 2. World War II -- Atrocities. 3. Nazism

-- Psychological aspects. 4. Germany -- History -- 1933-1945.
ISBN 0465085717

LC 2005544069

"The authors posit that far from living in a state of constant fear and discontent, most Germans led happy and even normal lives in Nazi Germany. They believe that the Holocaust could not have been possible without the complicity of the majority of the German population. This scholarly work is a major contribution to the understanding of life in Nazi Germany and a compelling narrative that is certain to be the standard work on the subject." Booklist.

O'Donnell, Svenja

Inge's war : a German woman's story of family, secrets, and survival under Hitler / Svenja O'donnell. Viking, 2020. 256 p. **943.086**

1. Single mothers. 2. Soldiers. 3. Refugees. 4. Grandmothers. 5. Konigsberg, Germany. 6. Kaliningrad, Russia. 7. Paris, France.
ISBN 9781984880215

LC bl2020007326

An award-winning political correspondent shares the long-secret story of her German grandmother, who endured the brutal Nazi regime and postwar years before the advancing Red Army separated her from the father of her baby.

"The author, a graceful, eloquent writer, follows a trail that sometimes takes her through deeply troubling terrain, and she amply reveals the cruelty and compassion that characterize times of war. Haunting family stories that serve as a metaphor for human suffering everywhere." Kirkus

Shirer, William L. (William Lawrence), 1904-1993

The **rise** and fall of the Third Reich : a history of Nazi Germany / William L. Shirer. Simon & Schuster, 1981, c1960. xii, 1249 p. ; **943.086**

1. Hitler, Adolf, 1889-1945. 2. Nazi Party (Germany) 3. Nazism -- Germany 4. Germany -- History -- 1933-1945.
ISBN 0671728687

LC BL 99788949

"A Touchstone book."
Originally published: New York : Simon and Schuster, 1960.
National Book Award for Nonfiction, 1961.

The rise and fall of the Third Reich offers an examination of how Adolf Hitler nearly succeeded in conquering the world. Shirer's account of the pivotal characters and events of that critical era benefits from his many years as a reporter and his own personal recollections, as well as from the mass of historical documents retrieved from the German Foreign Office. The result is this account of how Hitler wrested political control of Germany and managed to take the country with him on his mad six-year quest for world domination, only to see it go down in flames in the end.

Tubach, Frederic C.

German voices : memories of life during Hitler's Third Reich / Frederic C. Tubach with Sally Patterson Tubach. University of California Press, c2011. xvii, 273 p. : **943.086**

1. National socialism -- Social aspects 2. World War II -- Social aspects -- Germany 3. World War II, German 4. Germany -- History -- 1933-1945. 5. Germany -- Social conditions -- 1933-1945. 6. Germany -- Social life and customs -- 20th century. 7. Germany -- History -- 1933-1945
ISBN 9780520269644

LC 2010051218

Turner, Henry Ashby

Hitler's thirty days to power : January 1933 / Henry Ashby Turner, Jr. Basic Books, 2001, c1996. 300 p. **943.086**

1. Hitler, Adolf, 1889-1945. 2. Nazi Party (Germany) 3. Nazism. 4. Heads of state -- Germany 5. Political culture -- Germany. 6. Political parties -- Germany -- History -- 20th century. 7. Germany -- Politics and government -- 1918-1933. 8. Germany -- History -- 1918-1945.
ISBN 0201328003

Originally published: Reading, Mass. : Addison-Wesler, 1996.

"The author explores the fateful 30 days before Hitler became chancellor of Germany in January 1933. Although many of the facts are known, this study reveals that the Nazi dictator did not come to power as the result of 'impersonal forces.' The slender, analytical volume indicates that rather, at a time of mortal peril for Germany--and the world--intrigue was the order of the day in Berlin. Students of German history and extremist movements should enjoy this fast-paced narrative." Publishers Weekly.

943.086092 Germany--1933-1945--Biography

Bascomb, Neal

Hunting Eichmann : how a band of survivors and a young spy agency chased down the world's most notorious Nazi war criminal / Neal Bascomb. Houghton Mifflin Harcourt, 2009. 400 p. **943.086092**

1. Eichmann, Adolf, 1906-1962. 2. War criminals -- Germany 3. Fugitives -- Argentina 4. Secret service -- Israel. 5. Nazis.
ISBN 9780618858675

LC 2008035757

"The author recounts the pursuit, capture, and abduction of Nazi war criminal Adolf Eichmann. Bascomb spread a wide net in researching the 15-year hunt, and he fills his book with previously unknown or neglected details, utilizing the remembrances of former Mossad agents, German and American intelligence operatives, and Argentine Nazi sympathizers who tried to find Eichmann after his seizure. This is an outstanding account of a sustained and worthy manhunt." Booklist.

943.087 Germany--1945-1990

Bessel, Richard

Germany 1945 : from war to peace / Richard Bessel. HarperCollins, c2009. 448 p. **943.087**

1. Reconstruction (1939-1951) -- Germany. 2. World War II 3. Germany -- History -- 1945-1955. 4. Germany -- History -- 1933-1945.
ISBN 9780060540364

LC 2010275629

Originally published: Great Britain : Simon & Schuster UK, 2009.

"The author does an excellent job of evoking the blasted landscape of a conquered Germany--the homelessness and the hunger, the rubble and the mass rape." The New Yorker.

Sarotte, Mary Elise

The **collapse** : the accidental opening of the Berlin Wall / Mary Elise Sarotte. Basic Books, 2014. 320 p. **943.087**

1. Berlin Wall 2. Cold War. 3. German reunification. 4. Bureaucracy -- Germany -- History. 5. Berlin, Germany -- Politics and government -- 1945-1990. 6. Germany -- History -- 20th century.
ISBN 9780465064946

LC 2014026435

In The Collapse historian Mary Elise Sarotte shows that the opening of the Berlin Wall on November 9, 1989, was not, as is commonly believed, the East German government's deliberate concession to outside influence. It was an accident. A carelessly worded memo written by mid-level bureaucrats, a bumbling press conference given by an inept member of the East German Politburo, the negligence of government leaders, the bravery of ordinary people in East and West Berlin--these combined to bring about the end of nearly forty years of oppression, fear, and enmity in divided Berlin. Drawing on evidence from archives in multiple countries and languages, along with dozens of interviews with key actors, The Collapse is the definitive account of the event that brought down the East German Politburo and came to represent the final collapse of the Cold War order.

"Amply researched and emotive, this work shares the full narrative of events leading to the fall of the Berlin Wall in a way that both academics and lay readers will appreciate. Those already familiar with the subjects and time frames involved will definitely benefit from the author's extensive research and emphasis on personal narratives." Library Journal.

Taylor, Fred, 1947-

Exorcising Hitler : the occupation and denazification of Germany / Frederick Taylor. Bloomsbury Press, 2011. 480 p. **943.087**

1. Hitler, Adolf, 1889-1945 Influence 2. Denazification -- History. 3. Reconstruction (1939-1951) -- Germany. 4. Nazis. 5. Germany -- History -- 1945-1955. 6. Germany -- Social conditions -- 1945-1955. 7. Germany -- Politics and government -- 1945-1990. 8. Germany -- Economic conditions -- 1945-1990.

ISBN 9781596915367

LC 2010046282

A comprehensive history of the origins of democracy in Germany offers insight into the magnitude of the Third Reich's 1945 collapse and the challenges faced by the Allies in their efforts to construct a humane and democratic nation against formidable Nazi resistance.

943.71 Czech Republic

Demetz, Peter, 1922-

Prague in black and gold : scenes from the life of a European city / Peter Demetz. Hill and Wang, 1997. xviii, 411 p. : **943.71**

1. Prague, Czech Republic -- History. 2. Czech Republic -- History.

ISBN 0809078430

LC 96052216

"The author presents an account of the city's history and culture by focusing on epic events as well as heroes, villains and martyrs throughout the millennia of its existence. A highly literate panorama of a focal point of European culture." Publishers Weekly.

943.8 Poland

Dobroszycki, Lucjan

The **chronicle** of the Lodz ghetto, 1941-1944 / edited by Lucjan Dobroszycki ; translated by Richard Lourie, Joachim Neugroschel, and others. Yale University Press, c1984. lxviii, 551 p., 58 p. of plates : **943.8**

1. Jews -- Persecutions -- Lodz, Poland -- History -- Sources. 2. Holocaust (1939-1945) -- Lodz, Poland -- Sources. 3. Lodz, Poland -- Ethnic relations -- Sources.

ISBN 9780300039245

LC 84003614

Translation of: Kronika getta łodzkiego.

Includes index.

A firsthand record of life in the Lodz ghetto from 1941 to its 1944 liquidation provides a devastating look at the Jewish community and the impact of the Holocaust

Swan, Oscar E.

Kaleidoscope of Poland : a cultural encyclopedia / Oscar E. Swan with Ewa Kołaczek-Fila ; with a foreword by Adam Zamoyski. University of Pittsburgh Press, [2015] xxvii, 366 p. : **943.8**

1. Poland Encyclopedias. 2. Poland -- History Encyclopedias. 3. Poland -- Social life and customs Encyclopedias.

ISBN 9780822944386

LC 2015013694

Includes indexes.

Highlights the contributions to history and culture and the accomplishments of the people of Poland for more than 1,000 years, including bagels, Chopin, Madame Curie, as well as customs, folklore, historic events, phrases, places and geography.

"A balanced, splendidly illustrated survey of Polish history and culture." Booklist.

943.9 Hungary

Michener, James A. (James Albert), 1907-1997

The **bridge** at Andau / James A. Michener. Random House, 1957. 270 p. **943.9**

1. Refugees, Hungarian. 2. Hungary -- History -- Revolution, 1956.

ISBN 9780394417783

LC 57008158

By a trick of fate, the Andau Bridge becomes a lifeline to freedom for Hungarians fleeing the Russians in 1956.

944 France and Monaco

Baxter, John, 1939-

Saint-Germain-des-Pres : Paris's rebel quarter / John Baxter. Harper Perennial, 2016 xi, 235 p. : **944**

1. Paris (France) -- History. 2. Paris (France) -- Intellectual life. 3. Saint-Germain-des-Pres (Paris, France : Quarter) -- Description and travel. 4. Saint-Germain-des-Pres (Paris, France : Quarter) -- History. 5. Saint-Germain-des-Pres (Paris, France : Quarter) -- Intellectual life.

ISBN 0062431900

LC bl2016048676

Includes index.

A narrative portrait of one of Paris' great communities celebrates Saint-Germain-des-Pres as a center of artistic, intellectual, and revolutionary activity and culture.

Caro, Ina

Paris to the past : traveling through French history by train / Ina Caro. W.W. Norton & Co., c2011. 416 p. **944**

1. Caro, Ina Travel France. 2. Railroad travel -- France. 3. Historic sites -- France. 4. France -- Description and travel. 5. Paris, France

-- Description and travel. 6. France -- History, Local.
ISBN 9780393078947

LC 2011003060

"One single Paris Metro line can take you through a dazzling panoply of history: the Chateau de Vincennes, Charles V's 14th-century fortress; Francis I's Hotel de Ville; the Place de la Concorde, constructed by Louis V in the mid-18th century; the Palais-Royal, fashioned by Philippe Egalite in the late 18th century; and the 21st-century neighborhood of La Defense. Take another Metro line, Caro discovered gleefully, and you can descend to the period of the Romans, on the Ile-de-la-Cite, then arrive glamorously in the 19th century, at the Opera Garnier. Moreover, you can manage day trips to sites as far away as Tours (90 minutes by TGV) in one day, returning to Paris. In this cheerful, logical, easy-to-follow narrative (which includes favorite restaurants and hotels), Caro builds on previous trips to France and presents her timeline through history chronologically, from the 12th-century Basilica of Saint-Denis, where nearly all of the French kings and queen are buried, to the Gare d'Orsay, now fabulously converted into a museum of 19th-century art." Kirkus.

Christiansen, Rupert

City of light : the making of modern Paris / Rupert Christiansen. Basic Books, 2018. 206 p. **944**

1. Haussmann, Georges Eugene, Baron, 1809-1891 Influence 2. Urban renewal 3. Public works 4. Urban planning 5. Public officials 6. Paris, France -- History -- 1848-1870
ISBN 9781541673397

LC 2018012387

Describes the ambitious public works program initiated in 1853 by Napoleon that transformed of the old medieval Paris of squalor and slums into the "City of Light" encompassing wide boulevards, apartment blocks, parks, squares and public monuments.

Green, David, 1969-

The **Hundred** Years War : a people's history / David Green. Yale University Press, 2014 xvi,339 p. **944**

1. Hundred Years' War, 1339-1453. 2. Medieval military history 3. France -- History, Military -- 1328-1589. 4. Great Britain -- History, Military -- Medieval period, 1066-1485 5. France -- Foreign relations Great Britain. 6. Great Britain -- Foreign relations France.
ISBN 9780300134513

LC 2014014233

The Hundred Years War (1337-1453) dominated life in England and France for well over a century. It became the defining feature of existence for generations. This sweeping book is the first to tell the human story of the longest military conflict in history. Historian David Green focuses on the ways the war affected different groups, among them knights, clerics, women, peasants, soldiers, peacemakers, and kings. He also explores how the long war altered governance in England and France and reshaped peoples' perceptions of themselves and of their national character.

"This impressive survey ought to be included in any collection on the Middle Ages or the history of England and France. Summing Up: Highly recommended. All levels/libraries." Choice.

Horne, Alistair, 1925-

★**La** belle France : a short history / Alistair Horne. Knopf, 2005, c2004. xvii, 485 p. **944**

1. Civilization, Western -- French influences. 2. France -- Civilization. 3. France -- Social life and customs. 4. France -- History.
ISBN 1400041406

LC 2004042329

Originally published under the title: Friend or Foe: An Anglo-Saxon History of France. London : Weidenfeld & Nicolson, 2004.

A concise history of France profiles the lives of the great leaders, artists, and others who helped shape Western culture and thought, and examines the impact of important events, social movements, and military campaigns.

"This compelling narrative belongs in any public library needing an excellent, current one-volume history of France." Booklist.

Seven ages of Paris / Alistair Horne. A.A. Knopf, 2002. xvii, 458 p., 24 p. of plates : **944**

1. Paris, France -- History.
ISBN 0679454810

LC 2002029653

In this luminous portrait of Paris, the celebrated historian gives us the history, culture, disasters, and triumphs of one of the world's truly great cities. While Paris may be many things, it is never boring. With a keen eye for the telling anecdote and pivotal moment, he portrays an array of vivid incidents to show us how Paris endures through each age, is altered but always emerges more brilliant and beautiful than ever.

"The author traces the history of Paris through seven periods, beginning in the 12th century and ending with the death of Charles de Gaulle in 1969. Each section includes fascinating insights into the social and cultural life of the age, fashions in clothing, architectural developments, leading personalities, and lifestyles of rich and poor alike. With the verve of a master storyteller, Horne captures Parisians' zest for living." Library Journal.

Jones, Colin, 1947-

Paris : biography of a city / Colin Jones. Viking, 2005. xxv, 566 p. : **944**

1. Cities and towns -- France. 2. Paris, France -- Social life and customs. 3. Paris, France -- History.
ISBN 0670033936

LC 2004053608

A history of the Paris covers such events as its settlement at the end of the Stone Age, its role in numerous social and political revolutions, and the cultural and architectural achievements of the Impressionist era.

"Moving from prehistoric tribal habitation through Roman times, medieval uncertainty and splendor, early modern religious wars, Enlightenment, revolution, and two world wars, Jones examines how rulers, economy, religion and violence have shaped the city. Anyone who loves Paris will find connections and revelations here, a Paris of the mind that resonates through the centuries." Publishers Weekly.

Versailles / Colin Jones. Perseus Books Group 2018 240 p. **944**

1. Louis XIV, King of France, 1638-1715 2. Palaces 3. Historic buildings 4. Historic preservation 5. Rulers -- France 6. Versailles, France 7. France -- History
ISBN 9781541673380

LC bl2018192527

An account of the vivid creation, renovation and enduring legacy of the palace of Versailles traces its history as well as the debates surrounding the question of if and how to restore it.

"Francophiles, architecture buffs, monarchists, and history readers will appreciate this compact, comprehensive work." Library Journal.

Mayle, Peter

Encore Provence : new adventures in the south of France / Peter Mayle. Knopf, 1999. 226 p. : **944**

1. Mayle, Peter Homes and haunts Provence, France. 2. British in France. 3. Voyages and travels. 4. Tourists. 5. Tourism 6. France

-- Social life and customs. 7. Provence, France -- Social life and customs.
ISBN 0679441247

LC 99062335

"Mayle's book is all about the renewal of his acquaintance with the land he so loves. Essays range widely over Provecal life. His observations and commentaries are laced with humor but encompass true respect and admiration for his adopted homeland." Booklist.

A **year** in Provence / Peter Mayle ; illustrations by Judith Clancy. Knopf, 1990, c1989. 207 p. ; **944**

1. Mayle, Peter Homes and haunts Provence, France. 2. Voyages and travels. 3. British in France. 4. Moving, Household. 5. Moving to a new country. 6. France -- Social life and customs. 7. Provence, France -- Social life and customs.
ISBN 0394572300

LC 89038475

"Originally published in Great Britain by Hamish Hamilton, Ltd., London, in 1989"--T.p. verso.

The author describes his experiences when he and his wife moved to a two-hundred-year-old French farmhouse, and shares his observations on the people and culture of Provence.

Moorehead, Caroline

Village of secrets : defying the Nazis in Vichy France / Caroline Moorehead HarperCollins, 2014, c2014. 384 p. **944**

1. French Resistance (World War II) 2. Anti-Nazi movement 3. Righteous Gentiles in the Holocaust. 4. Hidden children (Holocaust) 5. Le Chambon-sur-Lignon, France. 6. France -- History -- German occupation, 1940-1945 7. Le Chambon-sur-Lignon, France -- History -- German occupation, 1940-1945
ISBN 9780062202475

LC 2014497785

Originally published in Canada (Toronto : Random House Canada, 2014)

A small mountain village in France, Le Chambon-sur-Lignon, has a long heritage of dealing with religious persecution because of its Huguenot roots. During World War II, Protestant Pastor Andre Trocme inspired the villagers to shelter Resistance fighters, Jews, and escaped POWs. Their efforts included such activities as forging ration books (so the hidden population could eat), warning of the arrival of Nazi officials, and guiding refugees through the mountains into Switzerland. Author Caroline Moorehead draws on interviews with survivors as well as archival records to bring this heroic tale to life, producing a riveting account of World War II survival.

"Moorehead not only recounts the heroics but also the everyday ordinariness of those involved, busting the embellished mythology while emphasizing the essential humanity of the entire operation." Booklist.

Norwich, John Julius, 1929-2018

A **history** of France / John Julius Norwich. Atlantic Monthly Press, 2018. 400 p. **944**

1. Rulers. 2. Political intrigue. 3. Politicians. 4. Battles. 5. France -- History. 6. Gaul -- History -- 58 B.C.-511 A.D.
ISBN 9780802128904

LC 2018026531

With his trademark stylistic panache and expert command of detail, a world-renowned historian presents this ode to France, filled with heroes and villains, battles and rebellion.

Riding, Alan

And the show went on : cultural life in Nazi-occupied Paris / Alan Riding. Alfred A. Knopf, 2010. xiii, 399 p., 16 p. of plates : **944**

1. Military occupation. 2. Artists. 3. Nazis. 4. Anti-Nazi movement. 5. Paris, France -- History -- German occupation, 1940-1944.
ISBN 9780307268976

LC 2010016841

An account of artistic life in Nazi-occupied Paris traces how cultural centers were reopened shortly after Germany captured the city, describing the circumstances of artists who fled, collaborated with, or resisted German forces.

"This engrossing work, rich in detail, should appeal to French historians and serious readers interested in 20th-century cultural history." Library Journal.

Robb, Graham, 1958-

Parisians : an adventure history of Paris / Graham Robb. W. W. Norton & Co., c2010. 496 p. **944**

1. Cities and towns -- History. 2. City dwellers. 3. Social history. 4. Paris, France -- History.
ISBN 9780393067248

LC 2009054279

Reveals the historical secrets of the City of Light from the Revolution to the present, including how Marie Antoinette was unable to flee the city because she lacked a reliable map.

"Robb has the passion of a naturalist displaying a wall of rare butterflies or a cabinet of exotic corals, but his specimens are all human and walked the streets of Paris at some point between the French revolution and now. [A] generous and humane book." Times (London).

Rowlands, Penelope,

Paris was ours : thirty-two writers reflect on the city of light / edited by Penelope Rowlands. Algonquin Books of Chapel Hill, 2011. 288 p. **944**

1. Visitors. 2. City life -- Paris, France. 3. Expatriates. 4. Paris, France -- Description and travel. 5. Paris, France -- Social life and customs. 6. Essays.
ISBN 9781565129535

LC 2010030560

"In this anthology Penelope Rowlands culled 32 essays, stories and poems, some original, some previously published, from writers who include professors, single mothers, gay men, a homeless woman, a wealthy Iranian and a poor young Cuban. The collection takes some of the shine off Paris but not the allure--not unlike the pull of a troubled but passionate lover who could never be more than a fling. Ultimately, the writers fall in love with Paris, a city that embraces sorrow, depression, snarkiness, human frailty and living in the moment no matter the menial task that entails. In dismantling the dream of Paris, they reveal an infinitely more complex city and people." Minneapolis Star Tribune.

Sante, Luc

The **other** Paris : the people's city, nineteenth and twentieth centuries / Luc Sante. Farrar, Straus and Giroux, 2015. 320 p. : **944**

1. City life 2. Poor people 3. Working class 4. Criminals 5. Paris, France -- Social life and customs -- 19th century. 6. Paris, France -- Social life and customs -- 20th century. 7. Paris, France -- Social conditions. 8. Paris, France -- Description and travel.
ISBN 9780374299323

LC 2015004988

"A vivid investigation into the seamy underside of nineteenth and twentieth century Paris".-- Provided by publisher.

"A fascinating stroll through a vanished, wild past. Recommended for general readers." Library Journal.

Tuchman, Barbara W. (Barbara Wertheim), 1912-1989

A **distant** mirror : the calamitous 14th century / Barbara W. Tuchman. Ballantine Books, 1979, c1978. xx, 677 p., 20 leaves of plates : **944**

1. Coucy, Enguerrand de, 1340-1397. 2. Civilization, Medieval. 3. France -- History -- 14th century. 4. France -- Nobility.

ISBN 0345349571

LC BL 99917028

National Book Critics Circle Award for Nonfiction finalist, 1978.

The prize-winning historian traces the major currents of the fourteenth century, revealing the century's great historical rhythms and events and the texture of daily life at all levels of European society.

"The author traces the history of the fourteenth century by following the career of a feudal lord, Enguerrand de Coucy VII, the seigneur of some 150 towns and villages in Picardy. He was born in 1340, and he died in captivity in 1397, having been made a prisoner by the Turks." Time.

White, Edmund, 1940-

The **flaneur** : a stroll through the paradoxes of Paris / Edmund White. Bloomsbury, 2001. 211 p. : **944**

1. White, Edmund, 1940- Homes and haunts Paris, France. 2. Voyages and travels. 3. Travelers. 4. Paris, France -- Description and travel. 5. Paris, France -- Social life and customs.

ISBN 1582341354

LC 00046812

"White is richly informed, and his evocative writing should appeal to both armchair travelers and visitors to Paris." Library Journal.

944.02542 France and Monaco--Land operations--Hundred Years' War

Fiennes, Ranulph, 1944-

Agincourt : the fight for France / Ranulph Fiennes. Pegasus Books, 2015. 336 p. **944.02542**

1. Agincourt, Battle of, 1415. 2. Medieval military history 3. France -- History, Military -- 1328-1589. 4. Great Britain -- History, Military -- Medieval period, 1066-1485.

ISBN 9781605989150

LC 2016301600

Written by the OBE-awarded leader of the first polar circumnavigation of the globe, a dynamic account of the Battle of Agincourt shares new perspectives into the battle to illuminate the lesser-known roles of the author's English knight ancestors.

"Despite its shortcomings, Fiennes's strong narrative style pulls readers along quickly, leaving plenty of time to tackle another more authoritative book on Agincourt such as Juliet Barker's Agincourt: Henry V and the Battle That Made England." Library Journal.

944.04 France since 1789

Burke, Edmund, 1729-1797

★**Reflections** on the revolution in France / Edmund Burke. Oxford University Press, 2009, c1999. 352 p. **944.04**

1. Revolutions. 2. French Revolution, 1789-1799 3. Military history. 4. Public opinion -- Great Britain -- History -- 18th century 5. France -- History -- Revolution, 1789-1799 -- Causes. 6. France -- Politics and government -- 1789-1799.

ISBN 9780199539024

LC oc2009000560

This ed. originally published: 1999.

Reflections on the Revolution in France is a slashing attack on the French Revolution by one of Britain's most famous statesmen. Liberty and social order, Burke argues, are maintained by the traditional rights and duties embedded in custom and law. And when these traditions are overthrown in revolutions, society is threatened with chaos, bloodshed and despotism.

McPhee, Peter, 1948-

★**Liberty** or death : the French Revolution, 1789-1799 / Peter McPhee. Yale University Press, 2016. 480 p. **944.04**

1. French Revolution, 1789-1799 2. France -- History -- Revolution, 1789-1799.

ISBN 9780300189933

LC 2015040677

A strikingly new account of the impact of the French Revolution in Paris, across the French countryside, and around the globe.

"McPhee (emeritus, history, Univ. of Melbourne; Robespierre: A Life) has written on many aspects of the French Revolution but never more beneficially than in this articulate and perceptive volume. McPhee's revolution is truly national in scope; Paris interacting with the hinterlands rather than a case of Paris playing the dog and the rest of France the tail. The author also makes solid use of primary source materials from outside France. Numerous histories of the French Revolution exist; while many are good, none is so current on the literature and lucidly presented as this. Scholars and history lovers will rejoice." Library Journal.

Popkin, Jeremy D., 1948-

A **new** world begins : the history of the French Revolution / Jeremy D. Popkin. Basic Books, [2019] 640 p. **944.04**

1. French Revolution, 1789-1799 2. Social change 3. Political violence 4. Regime change 5. France -- History -- Revolution, 1789-1799.

ISBN 9780465096664

LC 2019019101

A comprehensive analysis of the principles, events and influences of the French Revolution examines the roles of such contributors as Mirabeau and Robespierre while explaining the violent debates that led to modernism and the rise of Napoleon.

Schama, Simon

★**Citizens** : a chronicle of the French Revolution / Simon Schama. Alfred A. Knopf, 1989. xx, 948 p. : **944.04**

1. Louis XVI, King of France, 1754-1793 2. Revolutions -- France 3. Revolutionaries. 4. Nationalism. 5. France -- History -- Revolution, 1789-1799. 6. France -- History -- 18th century. 7. France -- Social conditions -- 18th century.

ISBN 9780394559483

LC 88045320

Explores the roots and fruition of the French Revolution in terms of the vitality and infatuation with technology that motivated French citizenry toward change and the conflicting strained economics frustrating their visions for France.

"The author offers a narrative in the form of a nineteenth-century chronicle that delves into the events and meaning of that momentous series of historical events." Booklist.

944.05 Period of First Empire, 1804-1815

Schom, Alan

One hundred days : Napoleon's road to Waterloo / Alan Schom. Atheneum, 1992. xv, 398 p. : **944.05**

1. Napoleon I, Emperor of the French, 1769-1821 Elba and the Hundred Days, 1814-1815 2. Generals. 3. Waterloo, Battle of, 1815. 4. Napoleonic Wars, 1800-1815. 5. France -- Rulers

ISBN 9780689120978

LC 92004249

A full-scale reconstruction of the eventful one hundred days following Napoleon's escape from exile on Elba examines his march across France, the rebuilding of his army, and his epic confrontation with Wellington at Waterloo.

"This is an account of Napoleon's escape from Elba in February 1815 and his return...to France. Rallying the nation behind him, he mustered his army and marched off to meet Wellington at Waterloo. This is a first-class reconstruction of Napoleon's final campaign." Publishers Weekly.

944.081 Period of Third Republic, 1870-1945

Brown, Frederick, 1934-

For the soul of France : culture wars in the age of Dreyfus / Frederick Brown. Alfred A. Knopf, 2010. 336 p. **944.081**

1. Nationalism -- France -- History -- 19th century. 2. Secularism -- France -- History -- 19th century. 3. Church and state -- France -- History -- 19th century. 4. National characteristics, French. 5. France -- History -- Third Republic, 1870-1940. 6. France -- Civilization -- 19th century.

ISBN 9780307266316

LC 2009030912

Sequel The embrace of unreason

An analysis of the events following the Franco-Prussian war of 1870-1871 includes coverage of France's forced relinquishment of the border states of Alsace and Lorraine, Napoleon III's defeat during the civil war and the circumstances that led to the Dreyfus affair.

"Brown recounts the history of France, following its 1789 revolution, as an ongoing contest between the champions and foes of the Enlightenment. The humiliating defeat of the Franco-Prussian War of 1870-71 was followed by the economic crash of 1882 and the Panama Company bribery scandal of 1893, both of which were reputedly executed by Jewish masters. In 1894, an opportunity for revenge presented itself in the person of Alfred Dreyfus, a 34-year-old Jewish army officer. Accused of espionage on the flimsiest of evidence--fabrications, and forgeries--Dreyfus was twice tried and convicted. Dreyfus was eventually freed in 1906, one year after a law requiring the separation of church and state had passed. Secularism seemed to hold sway. But, as Brown demonstrates in his brilliant study, religious fervor and bellicose patriotism combined in World War I to shift the balance yet again." Boston Globe.

Derfler, Leslie

★The **Dreyfus** affair / Leslie Derfler. Greenwood Press, 2002. xxii, 167 p., 10 p. of plates : **944.081**

1. Dreyfus, Alfred, 1859-1935. 2. France -- Politics and government -- 1870-1940.

ISBN 0313317917

LC 2001038365

"The blend of reference material and essays that provide background and context is particularly helpful when applied to topics that may be unfamiliar or are not heavily covered elsewhere. This new series should be useful in high-school, college, and large public libraries." Booklist.

Read, Piers Paul, 1941-

The **Dreyfus** affair : the scandal that tore France in two / Piers Paul Read. Bloomsbury Press, 2012. 408 p. **944.081**

1. Dreyfus, Alfred, 1859-1935. 2. Dreyfus, Alfred, 1859-1935 Influence. 3. Scandals -- History. 4. Trials (Treason) 5. Antisemitism -- France -- History -- 19th century. 6. Religion and politics. 7. France -- Politics and government -- 1870-1940. 8. France -- History -- Third Republic, 1870-1940.

ISBN 9781608194322

LC 2011034456

The award-winning historian documents the late 19th-century case of a successful Jewish captain in the French artillery command who was wrongly convicted of high treason, chronicling the 12-year effort to secure his freedom and describing the roles of colorful contributors and period anti-Semitism.

944.9 Provence-Côte d'Azur, Monaco, Corsica

De Courcy, Anne

Chanel's Riviera : glamour, decadence, and survival in peace and war, 1930-1944 / Anne de Courcy. St. Martin's Press, 2020, c2019. 304 p. **944.9**

1. Chanel, Coco, 1883-1971 2. Socialites 3. World War II 4. Women fashion designers 5. Fashion designers -- France 6. French Riviera 7. France -- Social life and customs -- 20th century.

ISBN 9781250177070

Originally published: London : Weidenfeld & Nicolson, 2019.

"This will be popular with royal watchers, fashionistas, and readers who relish the international social scene, and should cover new territory for most." Booklist

Lovell, Mary S.

The **Riviera** set : glitz, glamour, and the hidden world of high society / Mary S. Lovell. Pegasus Books, 2017. 448 p. **944.9**

1. Upper class 2. Socialites 3. Rich people 4. Celebrities 5. French Riviera

ISBN 9781681775159

LC bl2017030263

The author of the bestselling The Sisters: The Saga of the Mitford Family brings her trademark brio and relish to the charming and fascinating world of the Chateau de l'Horizon on the French Riviera.

"Lovell bridges the Edwardian age and postwar Europe, as cultural and political shifts brought more Americans and money usurped style as the most valuable currency in the region." Publishers Weekly.

945 Italy, San Marino, Vatican City, Malta

Berendt, John, 1939-

The **city** of falling angels / John Berendt. Penguin Press, 2005. 414 p. ; **945**

1. Teatro La Fenice Fire, 1996. 2. Fires. 3. Fire investigation. 4. Opera houses -- Italy. 5. Arson. 6. Venice, Italy -- Description and travel. 7. Venice, Italy -- Social life and customs. 8. Italy -- Social life and customs.

ISBN 1594200580

LC 2005047661

Map of Venice on endpapers.

Traces the aftermath of the 1996 Venice opera house fire, an event that devastated Venetian society and was investigated by the author, who through interviews with local figures learned about the region's rich cultural history.

"Berendt delivers an urbane, beautifully fashioned book with much exotic charm. [The author] makes erudite, inquisitive, nicely skeptical company as he leads the reader through the shadows of what was heretofore better known as a tourist attraction." New York Times.

Crowley, Roger, 1951-

★**City** of fortune : how Venice ruled the seas / Roger Crowley. Random House, 2011. xxix, 432 p. : **945**

1. Sea power. 2. Military history. 3. International trade. 4. Merchants. 5. Venice, Italy -- History -- 697-1508 6. Venice, Italy -- Economic conditions -- To 1797 7. Mediterranean Region -- Commerce -- History

ISBN 9781400068203

LC 2011005529

"An action-packed political and military history that will remind readers of the Italian sea power that prevailed for centuries before Western European nations arrived on the scene." Kirkus.

Keahey, John

Seeking Sicily : a cultural journey through myth and reality in the heart of the Mediterranean / John Keahey. Thomas Dunne Books/St. Martin's Press, 2011. 320 p. **945**

1. Keahey, John Travel Sicily. 2. Culture 3. Travelers 4. Island life 5. Cooking, Sicilian 6. Sicily, Italy -- Description and travel 7. Mediterranean Islands

ISBN 9780312597054

LC 2011026786

"The author takes a meandering and inspiring tour through the history, culture, and landscape of Sicily, an island that has been a crossroads for the various peoples of the Mediterranean for millennia. Keahey's thoroughly researched book will inspire any traveler to look past the Sicily of the traditional tourist's guide and appreciate its diverse, layered, and sometimes dark history." Library Journal.

Lee, Alexander (Historian)

The **ugly** Renaissance : sex, greed, violence and depravity in an age of beauty / Alexander Lee. Doubleday, 2013 416 p. **945**

1. European Renaissance -- Italy 2. Degeneration. 3. Corruption. 4. Italy -- History -- 16th century

ISBN 9780385536592

LC 2013015480

A survey of the darker cultural elements that shaped the works of Renaissance-era master artists reveals the power politics, bigotry and corruption that overshadowed period Italy.

"This highly inviting history should appeal widely to both scholars and casual readers." Library Journal.

Madden, Thomas F.

Venice : islands of honor and profit : a new history / Thomas F. Madden. Viking, 2012. 480 p. **945**

1. Architecture, Italian. 2. Civilization, Western -- Italian influences. 3. Art, Renaissance (Europe) -- Venice, Italy. 4. Performing arts -- History. 5. Venice, Italy -- History.

ISBN 9780670025428

LC 2012005304

An all-encompassing history of Venice draws on rare archival material and newly translated documents to chronicle the city's rise from a humble lagoon refuge, to its apex as a maritime empire and Renaissance epicenter, to its rebirth as a modern tourist hub.

Strathern, Paul, 1940-

The **artist,** the philosopher, and the warrior : the intersecting lives of Da Vinci, Machiavelli, and Borgia and the world they shaped / Paul Strathern. Bantam Books, 2009. 480 p. **945**

1. Leonardo, da Vinci, 1452-1519. 2. Machiavelli, Niccolo, 1469-1527. 3. Borgia, Cesare, 1476?-1507. 4. European Renaissance -- Italy. 5. Artists -- Italy -- 16th century 6. Philosophers -- Italy 7. Soldiers -- Italy 8. Italy -- History -- 1492-1559.

ISBN 9780553807523

LC 2009006950

Originally published: London : Johathan Cape, 2009.

A comparative profile of three Italian Renaissance icons evaluates them as products and complements of their times, in an account that considers how events in early sixteenth-century Italy as well as their relationships with each other profoundly affected their legacies. By the Somerset Maugham-winning author of Napoleon in Egypt.

"Strathern does for Machiavelli and da Vinci what he does for Borgia: creates a flesh-and-blood portrait for each that defies historical stereotype. Using his novelist's eye and a historian's sweep, Strathern conveys the emotional subtleties that animated their lives. It's no small feat that he makes you care deeply for these complex figures who lived half a millennium ago." Washington Post.

Death in Florence : the Medici, Savonarola, and the battle for the soul of a Renaissance city / Paul Strathern. Pegasus Books, 2015 464 p. **945**

1. Medici, Lorenzo de', 1449-1492. 2. Savonarola, Girolamo, 1452-1498. 3. Renaissance -- Italy. 4. Florence, Italy -- History. 5. Politicans -- Florence, Italy 6. Intellectuals -- Florence, Italy

ISBN 9781605988269

LC bl2015030446

Describes the Renaissance-era battle that took place in Florence between Lorenzo de' Medici, a generous patron of the arts, progressive humanist and a diplomat and Savonarola, a fire-and-brimstone-preaching monk who tried to establish a "City of God."

"Strathern brings his two opponents to life by including a great deal about their physicality (Lorenzo was plagued by gout and arthritis; Savonarola had a plain face but eyes that burned with intensity). The juxtaposition of Lorenzo's and Savonarola's lives and approaches to life adds to the sense of a 'cat and mouse game' throughout this riveting narrative history." Booklist.

Taylor, Benjamin, 1952-

Naples declared : a walk around the bay / Benjamin Taylor. G.P. Putnam's Sons, c2012. 240 p. **945**

1. Taylor, Benjamin, 1952- Travel 2. Cities and towns 3. City life 4. Voyages and travels 5. Italy -- Description and travel 6. Naples, Italy -- Description and travel 7. Naples, Italy -- History 8. Naples, Italy -- Social life and customs.

ISBN 9780399159176

LC 2011049450

"A Marian Wood book."

A personal tour through the beauty and squalor of Naples profiles the city's natural and human-made characteristics around its bay while sharing insights into the ancient city and its culture.

945.06 Italy, San Marino, Vatican City, Malta--1494-1527

Strathern, Paul, 1940-

The **Borgias** : power and fortune / Paul Strathern. Pegasus

Books, 2019. xvi, 383 p. : **945.06**

1. Borgia family. 2. Alexander VI, Pope, 1431-1503. 3. Borgia, Lucrezia, 1480-1519. 4. Borgia, Cesare, 1476?-1507. 5. Political corruption. 6. Ambition. 7. Power (Social sciences) 8. Nobility -- Italy. 9. Italy -- History -- 1492-1559.
ISBN 9781643130835

LC 2020275788

Corruption, incest, ruthless megalomania, avarice and vicious cruelty-- all have been associated with the name Borgia. But the family which produced corrupt popes, depraved princes and poisoners would also produce a saint. Strathern believes that, in order to understand the Borgias, one must understand the world which enabled them to flourish: the Renaissance. -- adapted from jacket

"Highly recommended for readers interested in the drama surrounding the Borgias that spurred a number of scandalous rumors that continue to circulate today." Library Journal.

945.091 Reign of Victor Emmanuel III, 1900-1946

Bosworth, R. J. B.

Mussolini's Italy : life under the dictatorship, 1915-1945 / R.J.B. Bosworth. Penguin Books, 2006. xxvi, 692 p. : **945.091**

1. Mussolini, Benito, 1883-1945 2. Fascism -- Italy. 3. Dictatorship. 4. Totalitarianism. 5. Fascists. 6. Italy -- History -- 1914-1945.
ISBN 1594200785

LC 2005052127

Includes bibliographical references (p. [xvii]) and index.

NSW Premier's History Awards, General History Prize, 2006.

An evaluation of Italy's notorious Fascist period under dictator Benito Mussolini considers its violence and demands for obedience, noting how it served as a model for other twentieth-century dictatorships while arguing that the nation's largely undeveloped country and tribal family structures helped Italians to devise creative survival and resistance methods.

"Bosworth combines prodigious research with a clear writing style that will appeal to all readers interested in the Italy of Il Duce." Library Journal.

Corner, Paul

The **Fascist** Party and popular opinion in Mussolini's Italy / Paul Corner. Oxford University Press, 2012. x, 302 p. ; **945.091**

1. Partito nazionale fascista (Italy). 2. Fascism -- Italy -- History 3. Fascism -- Italy -- Public opinion 4. Public opinion -- Italy -- History -- 20th century
ISBN 9780198730699

LC 2012462711

945.093 Italy, San Marino, Vatican City, Malta--2000-

Hooper, John, 1950-

The **Italians** / John Hooper. Viking Press, 2015. 336 p. **945.093**

1. Italians. 2. National characteristics, Italian. 3. Italy
ISBN 9780525428077

LC 2014038474

If you love all things Italian and wish you knew more about the country and its people, The Italians makes an offer you can't refuse. This entertaining book explains what makes Italians unique, and it covers a wide range of topics well, from Italy's storied beginnings, ties to religion, and the roots of the mafia to its beautiful land, delicious food, and intriguing regional differences. Written by British journalist John Hooper, who's lived in Italy for years, this book may prove especially intriguing for those of Italian ancestry.

"Few countries,' writes the author, 'are as comprehensively associated with happiness as Italy. Just the mention of its name brings to mind sunny days, blue skies, glittering seas; delicious, comforting food; good-looking, well-dressed people; undulating hills topped with cypress trees; museums crammed with much of the best of Western art.' What's not to love? A thoroughly researched, well-written, ageless narrative of a fascinating people." Kirkus.

945.5 Tuscany (Toscana) region

Capponi, Niccolo

The **day** the Renaissance was saved : the battle of Anghiari and Da Vinci's lost masterpiece / Niccolo Capponi ; translated by Andre Naffis-Sahely. Melville House, 2015 240 p. **945.5**

1. European Renaissance 2. Military history 3. Italy -- History
ISBN 9781612194608

LC 2015955589

Meticulously researched, a thrilling account of the little-known battle of Anghiari in 1440 combines a narrative of battle with the mystery of a famous painting by Leonardo da Vinci gone missing, intricately weaving together military history, art history and political history.

"A significant survey of an important battle and its outcomes as retold by an expert of Italian Renaissance military and political history, this book will be of interest mostly to scholars, graduate students, and some general readers of the subject. For both large public and academic libraries." Library Journal.

Strathern, Paul, 1940-

The **Medici** : power, money, and ambition in the Italian Renaissance / Paul Strathern. Pegasus Books, 2016 464 p. **945.5**

1. Medici, House of 2. European Renaissance. 3. Art patrons 4. Art, Italian 5. Artists -- Italy
ISBN 9781605989662

LC 2017304214

One of the most influential families in history, the Medici dominated Florence and much of Europe for several generations, promoting the arts and sciences at the height of the Renaissance and transforming the economy through their banking system. In this detailed and engaging book, author Paul Strathern traces the origins, rise, and eventual collapse of this dynasty. He recounts the lives of individual family members, both great and inconsequential, as well as the artists and scientists they sponsored. If you enjoy fiction or nonfiction about the Renaissance, give this enthralling history a try.

"A fantastically comprehensive history covering the breadth of the great learning, art, politics, and religion of the period." Kirkus.

945.6 Central Italy and Vatican City

Addis, Ferdinand

The **eternal** city : a history of Rome / Ferdinand Addis. Pegasus Books, 2018. 648 p. **945.6**

1. Capitals (Cities) 2. Rome -- Civilization 3. Rome -- History
ISBN 9781681775425

LC bl2018188542

A historian describes the history of Rome through its most dramatic moments, including the city's mythic founding in 753 BC, the murder of Caesar, the coronation of Charlemagne and the painting of the Sistine Chapel.

"The author's methodical yet swiftly flowing presentation yields an excellent and valuable one-volume treatment of the many-faceted tale of the Eternal City, a widely appealing achievement that deserves a place in all public libraries." Booklist.

Failmezger, Victor

Rome : city in terror : the Nazi occupation 1943-44 / Victor Failmezger. Osprey Publishing, 2020. 496 p., 32 unnumbered p. of plates : **945.6**

1. Gestapo. 2. Resistance to military occupation 3. Military occupation 4. Nazis. 5. World War II 6. Rome, Italy -- History -- German occupation, 1943-1945. 7. Italy -- History -- German occupation, 1943-1945

ISBN 9781472841285

From the street fighting that heralded the German occupation to the Gestapo repression that followed, this is the gripping story of the German occupation of Rome from the Italian armistice in September 1943 until the Allied liberation of the city on June 5, 1944.

"Failmezger presents fascinating stories and characters from a dramatic period of the war on the Italian front. Highly recommended for anyone interested in World War II history." Kirkus

Hughes, Robert, 1938-2012

Rome : a personal, visual and cultural history / Robert Hughes. Weidenfeld & Nicolson, 2011. 534 p., 32 p. of plates : **945.6**

1. Rome, Italy -- History 2. Rome, Italy -- Civilization 3. Rome -- Civilization 4. Rome -- History

ISBN 9780297844648

LC oc2009059681

"The author gives us a guided tour through the city in its many incarnations, excavating the geologic layers of its cultural past and creating an indelible portrait of a city in love with spectacle and power...The reader need not agree with Mr. Hughes's acerbic assessments or even be interested in Rome as a destination on the map to relish this volume, so captivating is his narrative. Although his book is a biography of Rome, it is also an acutely written historical essay informed by his wide-ranging knowledge of art, architecture and classical literature, and a thought-provoking meditation on how gifted artists (like Bernini and Michelangelo) and powerful politicians and church leaders (like Augustus, Mussolini and Pope Sixtus V) can reshape the map and mood of a city." New York Times Book Review.

Kneale, Matthew, 1960-

Rome : a history in seven sackings / Matthew Kneale. Simon & Schuster, 2018. 432 p. **945.6**

1. Military art and science 2. Natural disasters 3. Military campaigns 4. Battles 5. Rome, Italy -- History 6. Rome, Italy -- History, Military 7. Italy -- History

ISBN 9781501191091

LC 2017045287

A novelist offers a nonfiction history of the Eternal City by focusing on seven moments of crisis and catastrophe, including fires, floods, earthquakes and most epically, attacks and invasions from roving armies.

945.8 Sicily and adjacent islands

Norwich, John Julius, 1929-2018

Sicily / John Julius Norwich. Random House, 2015. 416 p. **945.8**

1. Sicily, Italy -- History.

ISBN 9780812995176

LC 2015007371

A history of Sicily analyzes its influence on world events and culture, profiling its remarkable leaders, its Crusades-era rise to a multicultural trading hub and the evolution of the Mafia.

"This excellent, informative source on natural features, art and architecture, and regional lifestyles is not to be missed by armchair travelers, history lovers, and fans of Norwich's previous works." Library Journal.

946 Spain, Andorra, Gibraltar, Portugal

Hughes, Robert, 1938-2012

Barcelona / Robert Hughes. Knopf, 1992. xi, 573 p. : **946**

1. Arts -- Spain. 2. Architecture -- Barcelona, Spain. 3. Barcelona, Spain -- Civilization. 4. Barcelona, Spain -- Buildings, structures, etc.

ISBN 0394580273

LC 91053179

"The great distinction of Hughes' approach is that he can move, commandingly, from a Mir canvas to transvestite hookers in the street without missing a beat--and bring to both the same kind of rigorous attention and full-bodied sensibility." Time.

Kurlansky, Mark

The **Basque** history of the world / Mark Kurlansky. Walker, 1999. xii, 387 p. : **946**

1. Basques. 2. Basque language. 3. Ethnic groups. 4. Basques -- History. 5. Basque Provinces. 6. Spain.

ISBN 9780802713490

LC 99026808

A history of the Basque people of Spain speculates on the origins of this enigmatic group of Europeans whose language and culture have long baffled anthropologists.

"This book traces the history of the Basques from their mysterious origins to their politically fraught existence in this century. Kurlansky shows how Basques, famed for their geographic and linguistic isolation, have played significant roles in world history--as mercenaries in ancient Greece, whalers in the Middle Ages, explorers in the Americas, and even cautious supporters of modern European integration." The New Yorker.

Lowney, Chris

A **vanished** world : medieval Spain's golden age of enlightenment / Chris Lowney. Free Press, 2005. 320 p. : **946**

1. Toleration -- Spain -- History. 2. Muslims -- Spain -- History. 3. Christians -- Spain -- History. 4. Jews, Spanish -- History. 5. Spain -- Civilization -- 711-1516. 6. Spain -- Interethnic relations. 7. Spain -- Religion.

ISBN 0743243595

LC 2004056362

A history of Spain's medieval period cites its unique position as a multi-religious society that enabled a progression of art and science far beyond the achievements of other pre-Renaissance nations.

"The author successfully brings the story of medieval Spain to a wider audience and draws out of this rich history important lessons for the post-9/11 world." Christian Science Monitor.

Preston, Paul, 1946-

★A **people** betrayed : a history of corruption, political incompetence and social division in modern Spain / Paul Preston. Liveright Publishing Corporation, 2020. 752 p. **946**

1. Franco, Francisco, 1892-1975. 2. Political corruption -- Spain -- History 3. Fascism 4. Spain -- History -- Civil War, 1936-1939 5. Spain -- Politics and government -- 20th century 6. Spain -- History -- 20th century

ISBN 9780871408686

LC 2020012133

Nowhere does the ceaseless struggle to maintain democracy in the face of political corruption come more alive than in Paul Preston's magisterial history of modern Spain.

"Likely to be the go-to history of modern Spain for many years to come." Kirkus

Stewart, Chris, 1950-

Driving over lemons : an optimist in Spain / Chris Stewart. Vintage Departures, 2001, c1999. 249 p. : **946**

1. Stewart, Chris, 1950- Homes and haunts Alpujarra Region, Spain 2. Rural life -- Spain. 3. Sheep ranches 4. Families 5. Interpersonal relations 6. Spain -- Social life and customs. 7. Andalusia, Spain -- Social life and customs. 8. Alpujarra Region, Spain -- Social life and customs.

ISBN 0375709150

LC bl2006027328

Originally published: New York : Pantheon Books, c1999.

A bestseller in England, this warm, funny account of a British family's attempt to make a home in southern Spain follows the first drummer for the rock band Genesis as he heads for Andalucia with his wife and kids.

"The ability to write hilarious travelogues featuring excruciating scenes of discomfort may well be a {British} national characteristic. It's certainly possessed by Chris Stewart." New York Times Book Review.

946.04 Spain--Period of House of Habsburg, 1516-1700

Goodwin, Robert, 1969-

Spain : the center of the world 1519-1682 / Robert Goodwin. Bloomsbury Publishing, 2015. 528 p. **946.04**

1. Spain -- History -- House of Austria, 1516-1700. 2. Spain -- Civilization -- 1516-1700

ISBN 9781620403600

LC 2014415759

Describes the Golden Age of the Spanish Empire, which saw discovery, adventure and sweeping political and social changes and was populated by legendary scholars, artists and soldiers--including the Duke of Alba, El Greco, Miguel de Cervantes and Diego Velazquez.

"Anyone wanting a better idea of the feel of this phase of Spanish history will be well served by this title. Accompanying maps and a genealogical chart are helpful." Library Journal.

946.08 Spain--1931-

Tremlett, Giles

Ghosts of Spain : travels through Spain and its silent past / Giles Tremlett. Walker & Co., 2007, c2006. 386 p. ; **946.08**

1. Tremlett, Giles Travel Spain. 2. National characteristics, Spanish. 3. Spain -- Social life and customs -- 20th century. 4. Spain -- History -- Civil War, 1936-1939 -- Influence. 5. Spain -- Description and travel.

ISBN 0802715745

LC bl2006029008

Includes index.

Originally published: London : Faber and Faber, 2006.

An odyssey through Spain's painful recent past examines the causes and consequences of the Spanish Civil War, as well as its repercussions in the lives of modern-day Spaniards, and offers observations on other elements of Spanish life.

946.081 Period of Second Republic, 1931-1939

Hochschild, Adam

Spain in our hearts : Americans in the Spanish Civil War, 1936/1939 / Adam Hochschild. Houghton Mifflin Harcourt, 2016 448 p. **946.081**

1. Revolutions -- Spain. 2. Civil war -- Spain 3. Dictatorship -- Spain. 4. Democracy -- Spain. 5. Spain -- History -- Civil War, 1936-1939. 6. Spain -- Politics and government -- 1931-1939.

ISBN 9780547973180

LC 2015037244

From 1936-39, news about the Spanish Civil War fired the imaginations of young men and women in other parts of the world, especially the U.S. and Britain. Thousands went to Spain to fight with the underdog Republicans, who were backed by the Soviet Union but ill-equipped and underfunded. Germany, Italy, and anti-Communist businessmen guaranteed the eventual success of Generalissimo Francisco Franco's Nationalists. In Spain in Our Hearts, acclaimed historian Adam Hochschild highlights the war's complexities and explores the personal perspectives of Americans who participated in the fighting.

Lewis, Norman

The **tomb** in Seville / Norman Lewis. Carroll & Graf, 2004, c2003. 160 p. **946.081**

1. Lewis, Norman Travel Spain. 2. Seville, Spain -- Description and travel. 3. Spain -- Description and travel.

ISBN 0786714395

LC oc2007113793

Originally published: London : Jonathan Cape, 2003.

The final book by the master travel writer recalls the author's journey to war-torn Spain in 1934, recounting nights spent sleeping in caves and days spent dodging sniper fire as he traversed the Iberian peninsula.

"Reading the author's account of his travels in a country on the brink of war is almost as satisfying as being there." Booklist.

Rhodes, Richard, 1937-

Hell and good company : the Spanish Civil War and the world It made / Richard Rhodes. Simon & Schuster, 2015. 384 p. **946.081**

1. Art movements 2. Democracy. 3. Ideology. 4. Spain -- History -- Civil War, 1936-1939.

ISBN 9781451696219

LC 2015300015

From the life of John James Audubon to the invention of the atomic bomb, readers have long relied on Richard Rhodes to explain, distill, and dramatize crucial moments in history. Now, he takes us into battlefields and bomb shelters, into the studios of artists, into the crowded wards of war hospitals, and into the hearts and minds of a rich cast of characters to show how the ideological, aesthetic, and technological developments that emerged in Spain changed the world forever.

"Despite the inclusion of a superb bibliography, the author's interpretation seems stuck in 1936. Other recent histories offer a more complicated and, in many instances, a more nuanced understanding of events and the actions of key personalities and groups. Summing Up: Recommended. General and undergraduate libraries." Choice.

946.8 Andalusia autonomous community and Gibraltar

Adkins, Roy (Roy A.)

★**Gibraltar** : the greatest siege in British history / Roy Adkins and Lesley Adkins. Viking, 2018. 448 p. **946.8**

1. Military campaigns 2. Forts 3. Weapons 4. Battles 5. Great Britain -- Foreign relations 6. Gibraltar

ISBN 9780735221628

LC 2018303986

Describes the four-year siege against the British on the small territory of Gibraltar by Spanish and French forces that put soldiers, civilians and families through bombardments, starvation and disease in a fortress on 2 square miles of rock.

" This intense account portrays the heroism and sufferings of the defenders while offering interesting vignettes that cover intriguing personalities on both sides. The Adkinses have created an absorbing examination of an important episode in British and European history." Booklist.

947 Russia and neighboring east European countries

Applebaum, Anne, 1964-

★**Iron** curtain : the crushing of Eastern Europe, 1945-1956 / Anne Applebaum. Doubleday, c2012. 640 p. **947**

1. Political culture -- Eastern Europe -- History -- 20th century. 2. Political persecution 3. Communist countries -- Politics and government. 4. Communist countries -- Social conditions. 5. Eastern Europe -- Foreign relations Soviet Union 6. Soviet Union -- Foreign relations Eastern Europe. 7. Eastern Europe -- Politics and government -- 1945-1989. 8. Eastern Europe -- Social conditions -- 20th century.

ISBN 9780385515696

LC 2012022086

Cundill Prize in History, 2013.

National Book Award for Nonfiction finalist, 2012

"A dark but hopeful chronicle that shows how even humanity's worst can fracture and fall." Kirkus.

Figes, Orlando

The **Crimean** War : a history / Orlando Figes. Metropolitan Books/Henry Holt and Co., c2011. 592 p. **947**

1. Crimean War, 1853-1856. 2. War.

ISBN 9780805074604

LC 2010023152

"Published simultaneously in the United Kingdom by Penguin Books, London"--T.p. verso.

"This is a complex tale, told vividly by Mr Figes. Perhaps it should serve as a healthy cold shower for any modern civilisational warrior who sets out to present the course of history as a simple tug-of-war between Christianity and Islam." The Economist.

Garrels, Anne, 1951-

Putin country : a journey into the real Russia / Anne Garrels. Farrar, Straus and Giroux, 2015. 288 p. **947**

1. Garrels, Anne, 1951- Travel Russia 2. Putin, Vladimir Vladimirovich, 1952- Influence. 3. Interviews -- Russia 4. Political culture 5. Subcultures 6. Russia -- Description and travel. 7. Russia -- Social conditions. 8. Russia -- Social life and customs. 9. Chelyabinsk, Russia

ISBN 9780374247720

LC 2015034644

What is life in Russia really like and why do Russians love Vladimir Putin? Anne Garrels, formerly an NPR correspondent based in Moscow, answers these complicated questions using a variety of people (from taxi drivers to doctors) in the Chelyabinsk region as a microcosm. Having visited the area (which is located far from Moscow) for two decades, she not only offers a journalistic collection that documents the differences in everyday lives over time, but also describes how growing freedoms have not always been beneficial, and shares what Russians really think of the West.

"This book will be of interest to general readers seeking to learn more about the country that exists beyond Moscow and St. Petersburg, as well as those wanting to gain better insight into its interior political and social conditions." Library Journal.

Hosking, Geoffrey A.

Russia : people and empire, 1552-1917 / Geoffrey Hosking. Harvard University Press, 1997. xxviii, 548 p. : **947**

1. National characteristics, Russian. 2. Nationalism -- Russia. 3. Russia -- History -- 1533-1613. 4. Russia -- History -- 1613-

ISBN 067478118X

LC 97005069

"The author explores the question of how and why the Russians never developed a sense of nation. He argues that the Russian monarchy and aristocracy were always more interested in building an expansive empire than in promoting the belief in nationhood, something understood by the powerless peasantry. The expensive and inefficient bureaucracy that emerged over the centuries weighed against any possibility of community, and in the end this tottering edifice was unable to withstand the cataclysm of World War I. Hosking has brought a powerful intellect and great erudition to this work." Library Journal.

★**Russia** and the Russians : a history / Geoffrey Hosking. Belknap Press of Harvard University Press, 2001. xiii, 718 p., 32 leaves of plates : **947**

1. Russia -- History. 2. Soviet Union -- History. 3. Russia -- Civilization.

ISBN 9780674004733

LC 00065085

Chronicles the history of the Russian Empire from the Mongol Invasion, through the Bolshevik Revolution, to the aftereffects of the Cold War.

"This is a high-quality overview, suitable for all libraries." Booklist.

Kotkin, Stephen

Uncivil society : 1989 and the implosion of the communist establishment / Stephen Kotkin ; with a contribution by Jan T. Gross. Modern Library, 2009. xxiii, 197 p., 16 p. of plates : **947**

1. Social change -- Soviet Union -- History. 2. State (Political science) -- Soviet Union -- History 3. Social change -- Eastern Europe -- History -- 20th century. 4. State (Political science) -- Eastern Europe -- History -- 20th century. 5. Soviet Union -- Politics and government -- 1985-1991. 6. Eastern Europe -- Politics and government -- 1989- 7. Soviet Union -- Social conditions -- 1970-1991. 8. Eastern Europe

-- Social conditions -- 20th century.
ISBN 9780679642763

LC 2009012903

Documents the peaceful collapse of communism following the falling of the Berlin Wall, drawing on case studies to illuminate the factors that deconstructed communist establishments.

Pleshakov, Konstantin

There is no freedom without bread! : 1989 and the civil war that brought down communism / Constantine Pleshakov. Farrar, Straus and Giroux, 2009. 289 p. ; **947**

1. Berlin Wall 2. Communism -- Eastern Europe -- History. 3. Anticommunist movements -- Eastern Europe -- History. 4. Political reform. 5. Eastern Europe -- Politics and government -- 1945-1989. 6. Soviet Union -- Politics and government -- 1945-1991. 7. Poland -- Politics and government -- 1945-1980. 8. Poland -- Politics and government -- 1980-1989.
ISBN 9780374289027

LC 2009010185

A revisionist analysis of the end of the Cold War reasons that contributing factors were much more complex than commonly understood, citing national civil wars and internal power struggles.

"The author's explanation of the 1989 collapse respects the complexity of Eastern Europe, yet his account is both clear and beautifully lyrical. His greatest strength lies in not being burdened by doctrine; he finds worth in communists and in Reagan. Pleshakov writes history with a human face." Washington Post Book World.

Polonsky, Rachel

Molotov's magic lantern : travels in Russian history / Rachel Polonsky. Farrar, Straus and Giroux, 2011, c2010. 416 p. **947**

1. Polonsky, Rachel Travel Russia (Federation) 2. Molotov, Vyacheslav Mikhaylovich, 1890-1986 Homes and haunts Russia (Federation) Moscow. 3. Molotov, Vyacheslav Mikhaylovich, 1890-1986 Library. 4. Authors, Russian -- 20th century -- Homes and haunts. 5. Communism and literature -- Soviet Union -- History. 6. Voyages and travels. 7. Authors, Russian -- 20th century -- Political and social views. 8. Russia (Federation) -- Description and travel. 9. Moscow (Russia) -- Description and travel. 10. Moscow (Russia) -- History. 11. Soviet Union -- Intellectual life.
ISBN 9780374211974

LC 2010023037

"Originally published in 2010 by Faber and Faber Ltd., Great Britain as Molotov's magic lantern : a journey in Russian history"--T.p. verso.

"After moving into a Moscow apartment building, British journalist Rachel Polonsky discovered that Vyacheslav Molotov, Stalin's infamous henchman, once lived there...and that some of his belongings still did, including hundreds of books. Using Molotov's library to propel her exploration of the country, British journalist Rachel Polonsky visited Siberia, Rostov-on-Don, and more. For an intelligent, elegant look at Russia's past and present, pick up this combination literary travelogue, history, and biography."--Description by Dawn Towery.

"Polonsky has produced a spectacular and enjoyable display of intellectual fireworks for the general reader. Her finely drawn literary travelogues on Taganrog, Murmansk, Vologda, Irkutsk and other places depict squalor, pomp, misery, exhilaration, heroism and brutishness, each cameo framed in its historical, cultural and physical context. She has a knack for putting herself into other people's shoes with empathy and skill. The author has grit, charm and style--and a gift for traveller's tales." The Economist.

Riasanovsky, Nicholas V. (Nicholas Valentine), 1923-2011

A **history** of Russia / Nicholas V. Riasanovsky, Mark D. Steinberg. Oxford University Press, 2018. xx 658 p. : **947**

1. Russia -- History. 2. Soviet Union -- History. 3. Russia -- Social life and customs.
ISBN 9780190645588

LC 98056640

Maps on lining papers.

Now extensively revised in this ninth edition, A History of Russia covers the entire span of the country's history, from ancient times to the post-communist present. Keeping with the hallmark of the text, Riasanovsky and Steinberg examine all aspects of Russia's history--political, international, military, economic, social, and cultural--with a commitment to objectivity, fairness, and balance, and to reflecting recent research and new trends in scholarly interpretation. In the ninth edition, this includes expanded attention to the experiences of ordinary men and women and to imperial expansion and diversity.

Sebag Montefiore, Simon, 1965-

★The **Romanovs** : 1613-1918 / Simon Sebag Montefiore. Alfred A. Knopf, 2016. 816 p. **947**

1. Romanov, House of. 2. Rulers 3. Royal houses 4. Monarchy -- Russia 5. Russia -- Rulers 6. Russia -- History -- 1613-1917.
ISBN 9780307266521

LC 2015046026

"This is a Borzoi Book."

The acclaimed author of Young Stalin and Jerusalem gives readers an accessible, lively account--based in part on new archival material--of the extraordinary men and women who ruled Russia for three centuries.

"Montefiore's compassionate and incisive portraits of the Romanov rulers and their retinues, his liberal usage of contemporary diaries and correspondence, and his flair for the dramatic produce a narrative that effortlessly holds the reader's interest and attention despite its imposing length." Publishers Weekly.

Volkov, Solomon

St. Petersburg : a cultural history / Solomon Volkov ; translated by Antonina W. Bouis. Free Press Paperbacks, 1997, c1995. xxiv, 598 p. : **947**

1. Saint Petersburg (Russia) -- Civilization.
ISBN 0684832968

LC BL 99784391

Originally published: New York : Free Press, 1995.

A Russian emigre draws a panoramic view of the cosmopolitan culture that thrived over three centuries in Russia's "Gateway to the West," producing such figures as Stravinsky, Nabokov, Balanchine, and Chagall.

947.08 Russia since 1855

Figes, Orlando

A **people's** tragedy : the Russian Revolution, 1891-1924 / Orlando Figes. Viking, 1997. 960 p. **947.08**

1. Lenin, Vladimir Il'ich, 1870-1924. 2. Kerensky, Alexander, 1881-1970. 3. Communist Party of the Soviet Union. 4. Revolutions. 5. Revolutionaries. 6. Social change. 7. Russia -- History -- Nicholas II, 1894-1917. 8. Soviet Union -- History -- Revolution, 1917-1921. 9. Soviet Union -- History -- 1917-1936.
ISBN 9780670859160

LC 96036761

ALA Notable Book, 1998.

Covers Russian history from the end of the nineteenth century to the death of Lenin, and explores how Russian pre-revolution social forces were violently erased and replaced.

"The author has produced an engagingly written and well-researched book that will leave few readers with any doubts that the Bolsheviks, and especially their leader, Lenin, were ruthless killers, willing to sacrifice millions of lives for the sake of power and their own personal ambitions." New York Times Book Review.

Kurth, Peter

Tsar : the lost world of Nicholas and Alexandra / Peter Kurth ; photographs by Peter Christopher ; introduction by Edvard Radzinksy. Little, Brown and Co., 1995. 229 p. : **947.08**

1. Nicholas II, Emperor of Russia, 1868-1918 2. Alexandra, Empress, consort of Nicholas II, Emperor of Russia, 1872-1918. 3. Russia -- Rulers 4. Russia -- History -- Nicholas II, 1894-1917.

ISBN 0316507873

LC 95012820

"A Madison press book."

"A large format and a profusion of illustrations ostensibly mark it a picture book; instead it is a remarkably comprehensive overview of the reign of the last czar and his consort. Kurth sensitively documents the imperial family's suffering as prisoners of the Bolsheviks and their eventual execution." Booklist.

Massie, Robert K., 1929-2019

Nicholas and Alexandra / Robert K. Massie. Ballantine Books, 2000. 613 p. : **947.08**

1. Nicholas II, Emperor of Russia, 1868-1918 2. Alexandra, Empress, consort of Nicholas II, Emperor of Russia, 1872-1918. 3. Romanov, House of 4. Royal houses. 5. Rulers. 6. Nobility. 7. Russia -- History -- 1801-1917.

ISBN 9780345438317

LC 99091507

An incisive account of the last of the Romanov dynasty details the love affair of Tsar Nicholas II and his wife, Alexandra, their family, their involvement with Rasputin, and the revolution that transformed imperial Russia.

"This book, solid with research, reads as lightly as a novel, as authoritatively as a textbook. Dialogue and lively description lend a sense of immediacy, but his notes, discreetly relegated to the back of the book, show how carefully he has avoided slipping into fiction." Christian Science Monitor.

The **Romanovs** : the final chapter / Robert K. Massie. Random House, 1995. 308 p. : **947.08**

1. Nicholas II, Emperor of Russia, 1868-1918 Assassination. 2. Alexandra, Empress, consort of Nicholas II, Emperor of Russia, 1872-1918. 3. Romanov, House of. 4. Olga, Grand Duchess of Russia, 1895-1918. 5. Marie, Grand Duchess of Russia, b. 1890. 6. Tatiana Nikolaevna, Grand Duchess, daughter of Nicholas II, Emperor of Russia, 1897-1918 7. Anastasia Nikolaevna, Grand Duchess, daughter of Nicholas II, Emperor of Russia, 1901-1918. 8. Forensic osteology -- Russia. 9. Royal pretenders -- Russia. 10. Royal houses. 11. Russia -- History -- Nicholas II, 1894-1917.

ISBN 0394580486

LC 95004718

The story behind the Romanov murders and the investigation to find their hidden bodies describes Lenin's cover-up and the roles played by such figures as James Baker, Boris Yeltsin, and Prince Philip.

"With memorable sketches of the main participants and a skillful discussion of the scientific evidence, Massie pulls together a sprawling theme and infuses it with quiet drama." Kirkus.

Rappaport, Helen

The **race** to save the Romanovs : the truth behind the secret plans to rescue the Russian imperial family / Helen Rappaport. St Martins Pr 2018 464 p. **947.08**

1. Romanov, House of 2. Royal houses 3. Massacres 4. Rescues 5. Murder

ISBN 9781250151216

LC 2018005136

Published to mark the 100th anniversary of the massacre, a heavily researched investigation into the international efforts to save the Romanov family explores why every measure failed and who was responsible.

"Relying on fresh archival material, Rappaport dispels some mystery about secret Western rescue plans--that is to say, she clarifies that they were nonexistent. Regarding myriad Russian monarchist rescue plots, she admits that rumors and misinformation make unraveling the truth an impossible task. This is a well-researched account of a colorful, suspenseful, and tragic series of events." Publishers Weekly.

Zygar, Mikhail, 1981-

The **empire** must die : Russia's revolutionary collapse, 1900-1917 / Mikhail Zygar. PublicAffairs, 2017. 256 p. **947.08**

1. Romanov, House of 2. Liberalism 3. Intellectual life 4. Financial crises 5. Elite (Social sciences) 6. Russia -- History -- Nicholas II, 1894-1917 7. Russia -- Politics and government -- 1894-1917

ISBN 9781610398312

LC bl2017045807

A vivid portrayal of Russia's brief and exotic experiment with liberalism and cultural openness in the years before the Communist Revolution and the deaths of the Tsar and his family reveals how the period marked a blossoming of artistic expression and open political views.

"A vivid, character-driven reconstruction of the period leading up to the overthrow of the Romanovs and the birth of modern Russia." Kirkus.

947.084 Soviet Union -- 1917-1991

Amis, Martin

Koba the dread : laughter and the twenty million / Martin Amis. Vintage International, 2003, 2002. viii, 306 p. : **947.084**

1. Terrorism -- Soviet Union. 2. State-sponsored terrorism -- Soviet Union 3. Political persecution 4. Soviet Union -- Politics and government -- 1917-1936. 5. Soviet Union -- Politics and government -- 1936-1953.

ISBN 1400032202

LC 2003053764

Includes index.

Originally published: New York : Talk Miramax Books, 2002.

The author describes the role of communism in mid-twentieth-century thought and its influence on his own family as he reflects on Stalin, his impact on the Soviet Union, and his legacy.

"Amis create{s} a compelling narrative, summarizing vast amounts of information and presenting it in a lucid, accessible form.New York Times.

Brent, Jonathan

Stalin's last crime : the plot against the Jewish doctors, 1948-1953 / Jonathan Brent and Vladimir P. Naumov. Harper Collins, c2003. xi, 399 p. ; **947.084**

1. Stalin, Joseph, 1879-1953. 2. Jews, Soviet. 3. Jews -- Persecutions -- Soviet Union. 4. Physicians -- Soviet Union. 5. Soviet Union --

History -- 1925-1953.
ISBN 006019524X

LC 2002191930

A study based on KGB documents and classified archives discusses the conspiracy known as "The Doctor's Plot," exploring the theory that Stalin was responsible for its engineering as part of his intent to start a holocaust in the Soviet Union.

"This book points out suspicious inconsistencies in official accounts of Stalin's death and fingers chief of secret police Beria as a likely assassin. Brent and Naumov link Stalin's famously anti-Semitic Doctors' Plot, in which Jewish doctors were unjustly accused of conspiring to murder important politicians, to the ridiculous plan of the internal blow, another alleged conspiracy of officials supposedly aiding an American plan to nuke the Kremlin itself. The authors argue that these Stalin-engineered plots were to be used by the paranoid dictator as justification for nuclear war. Tales of Stalin's paranoia are nothing new, but rarely are his subtle, yet relentless, machinations laid out in such intricate detail." Booklist.

Gellately, Robert, 1943-

Stalin's curse : battling for communism in war and Cold War / Robert Gellately. Alfred A. Knopf, 2013. 464 p. : **947.084**

1. Stalin, Joseph, 1879-1953. 2. Cold war. 3. War -- Causes. 4. Communism -- Europe -- History. 5. Stalinism. 6. Soviet Union -- Politics and government -- 1936-1953.
ISBN 9780307269157

LC 2012028768

Draws on newly released Russian documentation to explore Stalin's commitment to expanding the Soviet empire and his seeming collaboration with Roosevelt and Churchill, offering insight into his true motives and role in triggering the Cold War.

Hickey, Michael, 1929-

Competing voices from the Russian Revolution / edited by Michael C. Hickey. Greenwood, c2011. xiii, 599 p. : **947.084**

1. Social conflict. 2. Revolutions. 3. Revolutionaries. 4. Soviet Union -- History -- Revolution, 1917-1921.
ISBN 9780313385230

LC 2010039676

This new collection of documents helps students understand the complex texture of Russian public rhetoric and popular debate during World War I and the 1917 Revolution.

Hochschild, Adam

The **unquiet** ghost : Russians remember Stalin / Adam Hochschild. Viking, 1994. xxvii, 304 p. : **947.084**

1. Stalin, Joseph, 1879-1953. 2. Disappeared persons -- Soviet Union. 3. Soviet Union -- History -- 1925-1953.
ISBN 0670840912

LC 93027473

Explores how Russians--prison survivors, historians, concentration camp guards, and others--are healing the wounds inflicted by long-repressed memories of the former leader and recounts the efforts of many to locate or find out what happened to relatives who disappeared during Stalin's tyrannical tenure.

"In this look at Stalin's legacy the author visits the ruins of the old prison camps of Kazakhstan and Kolyma, digs through the K.G.B. archives and spends a night at Stalin's seaside retreat. Most important, he interviews camp survivors, camp guards and the children of both. The questions he asks are of universal significance. By asking these questions while traveling through today's Russia, Mr. Hochschild effectively places Stalinism in a modern context." New York Times Book Review.

McMeekin, Sean, 1974-

The **Russian** Revolution : a new history / Sean McMeekin. Basic Books, 2017. 384 p. **947.084**

1. Revolutions 2. Communism 3. Social classes 4. Marxism 5. Soviet Union -- History -- Revolution, 1917-1921
ISBN 9780465039906

LC 2016058361

Discusses how the Russian Revolution changed the course of world history in the early part of the 20th century, describing how the Bolsheviks came into power, ending Romanov rule and killing over 20 million Russians in the process.

"McMeekin effectively shows how easily one man could undermine the foundations of a nation, and he makes the revolution comprehensible as he exposes the deviousness of its leader." Kirkus.

Medvedev, Roy Aleksandrovich, 1925-

★**Let** history judge : the origins and consequences of Stalinism / Roy Medvedev. Columbia University Press, c1989. xxi, 903 p. ; **947.084**

1. Stalin, Joseph, 1878-1953. 2. Political atrocities -- Soviet Union. 3. Soviet Union -- Politics and government -- 1917-1936. 4. Soviet Union -- Politics and government -- 1936-1953.
ISBN 9780231063500

LC 89000758

A translation of the Soviet scholar's definitive study of Stalin and his era.

"Never have Stalin's crimes against humanity been more forcefully or more thoroughly documented than in...{this book, which} distills firsthand testimonies of the mass arrests, torture, imprisonment and executions that befell millions of innocent Soviet citizens." Publishers Weekly.

Mieville, China

October : the story of the Russian Revolution / China Mieville. Verso, 2017. 304 p. **947.084**

1. Lenin, Vladimir Il'ich, 1870-1924 2. Trotsky, Leon, 1879-1940 3. Kerensky, Alexander, 1881-1970 4. Kornilov, Lavr Georgievich, 1870-1918 5. Revolutionaries 6. Communism 7. Socialists 8. Rebels 9. Soviet Union -- History -- Revolution, 1917-1921 10. Russia -- History -- 20th century
ISBN 9781784782771

LC 2016051217

A new account of the Russian Revolution explores how the ongoing consequences of the political event created a story of drama, passion, and strangeness.

"Miville is an ideal guide through this complex historical moment, giving agency to obscure and better-known participants alike, and depicting the revolution as both a tragically lost opportunity and an ongoing source of inspiration." Publishers Weekly.

Nelson, James Carl

The **Polar** Bear expedition : the heroes of America's forgotten invasion of Russia / James Carl Nelson. William Morrow, [2019] 384 p. **947.084**

1. United States. Army. Infantry Regiment, 339th -- History. 2. Polar Bear Expedition (1918-1919) 3. World War I -- Regimental histories -- United States. 4. Military history -- 20th century. 5. International relations. 6. Soldiers -- History -- 20th century. 7. Soviet Union -- History -- Allied intervention, 1918-1920. 8. Soviet Union -- History -- Revolution, 1917-1921. 9. Michigan -- History, Military -- 20th century. 10. United States -- Military relations Soviet Union. 11.

Soviet Union -- Military relations United States.
ISBN 9780062852779

LC 2018037597

An unforgettable human drama deep with contemporary resonance, award-winning historian James Carl Nelson's The Polar Bear Expedition draws on an untapped trove of firsthand accounts to deliver a vivid, soldier's-eye view of an extraordinary lost chapter of American history--the Invasion of Russia one hundred years ago during the last days of the Great War.

Pipes, Richard

A **concise** history of the Russian Revolution / Richard Pipes. Knopf, 1995. xvii, 431 p. : **947.084**

1. Revolutions. 2. War. 3. World politics. 4. Soviet Union -- History -- Revolution, 1917-1921. 5. Russia -- History -- Nicholas II, 1894-1917.
ISBN 0679422773

LC 95003127

Abridged version of The Russian Revolution.

"Forcefully showing why the 70-year-old Communist experiment failed {Pipes} provides the nonacademic reader with accurate historical events in a highly readable format." Library Journal.

Russia under the Bolshevik regime / Richard Pipes. A.A. Knopf, 1993. xviii, 587 p. : **947.084**

1. Lenin, Vladimir Ilich, 1870-1924. 2. Communist Party of the Soviet Union. 3. Revolutionaries -- Soviet Union. 4. Despotism in men. 5. Dictatorship. 6. Soviet Union -- History -- Revolution, 1917-1921. 7. Soviet Union -- History -- 1917-1936.
ISBN 9780394502427

LC 92042710

Explores the formative years of the Soviet Union under communism, ranging from the Bolshevik takeover in 1918 to the 1924 death of Lenin, and examines the impact of Bolshevik leaders and period events on the USSR.

"In this sequel to The Russian Revolution, Pipes persuasively argues that Lenin's one-party dictatorship, through its terrorizing, suppression of the press, censorship and monopolistic control of cultural organizations, set the stage for Stalin's genocidal totalitarianism. Pipes shows how both Hitler and Mussolini drew on Lenin's tyrannical methods, and he perceptively analyzes the mindset of Western fellow-travelers who wove fantasies of the U.S.S.R. as an egalitarian Eden while rationalizing its evils." Publishers Weekly.

The **Russian** Revolution / Richard Pipes. Vintage Books, 1991. xxiv, 944 p. : **947.084**

1. Russia -- History -- Nicholas II, 1894-1917. 2. Soviet Union -- History -- Revolution, 1917-1921.
ISBN 0679736603

LC 91050008

Includes index.

Originally published: New York : Knopf, 1990.

Looks at the decay of the Czarist regime and the causes of the Revolution, discusses the aims of the Bolshevik party, and recounts the major events of the conflict.

Reed, John, 1887-1920

Ten days that shook the world / John Reed. Penguin Books, 2007, c1977. xix, 351 p. ; **947.084**

1. Soviet Union -- History -- Revolution, 1917-1921
ISBN 9780141442129

LC 78305844

Originally published: New York : Boni & Liveright, 1919.

Chronicles the events in Petrograd in November 1917, when Lenin and the Bolsheviks finally seized power, including speeches by leaders and quotes from everyday bystanders.

Smith, Douglas, 1962-

The **Russian** job : the forgotten story of how America saved the Soviet Union from ruin / Douglas Smith. Farrar Straus & Giroux, 2019 320 p. **947.084**

1. American Relief Administration -- History. 2. Food relief -- Soviet Union -- History. 3. Famines -- Soviet Union -- History. 4. Humanitarian assistance 5. Soviet Union -- History -- Famine, 1921-1922. 6. Soviet Union -- Foreign relations United States. 7. United States -- Foreign relations Soviet Union.
ISBN 9780374252960

LC 2019017677

The award-winning historian and author of Rasputin traces the little-known story of Herbert Hoover's American Relief Administration and its 1921 effort to save the newly formed Soviet Union from a devastating famine.

947.085 Soviet Union -- 1953-1991

Gorbachev, Mikhail Sergeevich, 1931-

On my country and the world : On My Country and the World / Gorbachev. Columbia University Press, c2000. 300 p. ; **947.085**

1. Gorbachev, Mikhail Sergeevich, 1931- Political and social views. 2. World politics -- 1989- 3. Russia (Federation) -- History -- 1991- -- Philosophy. 4. Soviet Union -- History -- Philosophy.
ISBN 0231115148

LC 99031273

Includes index.

Looks at the October Revolution, the Cold War, Lenin, Stalin, Yeltsin, and the future of Russia, and argues that the development of socialism was cut short by Stalin.

Remnick, David

★**Lenin's** tomb : the last days of the Soviet Empire / David Remnick. Random House, 1993. xii, 576 p., 16 p. of plates : **947.085**

1. Gorbachev, Mikhail, 1931- 2. Yeltsin, Boris Nikolayevich, 1931-2007 3. Sakharov, Andrei, 1921-1989. 4. Glasnost. 5. Perestroika. 6. Economic policy -- Soviet Union -- 1985-1991. 7. Governmental reform -- Soviet Union. 8. Soviet Union -- Politics and government -- 1985-1991.
ISBN 0679423761

LC 92056841

Sequel: Resurrection.

ALA Notable Book, 1994.

Pulitzer Prize for General Nonfiction, 1994.

National Book Critics Circle Award for Nonfiction finalist, 1993.

"This book is a record of almost four years beginning in 1988 when David Remnick, a Washington Post reporter, was assigned to Moscow. He argues convincingly that what did in the old Soviet leadership, right down through Mikhail Gorbachev, was its unending assault not only on people but on memory. By making a secret of history, it made its people increasingly distracted, and desperate, until they overthrew it." New York Times Book Review.

Sebestyen, Victor, 1956-

Revolution 1989 : the fall of the Soviet empire / Victor Sebestyen. Pantheon Books, 2009. 480 p. **947.085**

1. Cold War -- History 2. Democracy -- Soviet Union. 3. Communism -- Soviet Union 4. Socialism -- Soviet Union 5. Soviet Union -- Politics and government -- 1985-1991
ISBN 9780375425325

LC 2009023045

Documents the collapse of the Soviet Union's European empires and the transition of each to independent states, drawing on interviews with everyday people and newly uncovered archival material to offer insight into 1989's rapid changes and the USSR's minimal resistance.

"Numerous books have come out that attempt to synthesize the compelling story of the fall of communism, but Revolution 1989 comes closest to being the essential volume. Sebestyen's elegant narrative lays out in crisp episodes what was happening in Russia, Bulgaria, East Germany, Hungary, Czechoslovakia, and Afghanistan throughout the tumultuous 1980s. His portrait of Gorbachev is particularly sharp, and asks us to reconsider the Soviet leader's surprising role 20 years ago. As a refugee from Hungary in 1956, Sebestyen brings a personal touch to these historic moments." Daily Beast.

947.086 Russia--1991-

Aleksievich, Svetlana, 1948-

★**Secondhand** time : the last of the Soviets / Svetlana Alexievich ; translated by Bela Shayevich. Random House, 2016. 512 p. **947.086**

1. Communism 2. Post-communism -- Russia 3. Soviet Union 4. Russia -- Social conditions -- 1991- 5. Soviet Union -- Social conditions. 6. Oral histories
ISBN 9780399588808

LC 2016005925

First published in Russian in 2013.

"Though it's too late to travel to the Soviet Union, which broke up in 1991, you can still visit via this moving oral history collection that provides an eye-opening look at the (pre- and post-) Soviet soul. Sharing the stories of a wide variety of people from across the vast country -- ranging from before the end of communism to the beginnings of the new Russia and the rise of Putin -- 2015 Nobel Prize winner Svetlana Aleksievich provides a thorough, fascinating look at war, freedom, family, and more, giving voice to those who've seen so much upheaval."--Description by Dawn Towery.

"Journalist Alexievich (Voices from Chernobyl), who won the 2015 Nobel Prize in Literature, captures the heartache, excitement, and harsh realities of life at the end of the Soviet era and the birth of modern Russia. A collection of oral histories linked by topic, theme, and the author's own musings, this impassioned and critical study, originally published in Russian in 2013, documents the immense changes the Russian people underwent in the 1990s and 2000s. A must for historians, lay readers, and anyone who enjoys well-curated personal narratives. All readers will appreciate the revelations about Russia's turbulent transition and present cultural and political status." Library Journal.

Baker, Peter, 1967-

Kremlin rising : Vladimir Putin's Russia and the end of revolution / Peter Baker and Susan Glasser. Scribner, c2005. 453 p. : **947.086**

1. Putin, Vladimir Vladimirovich, 1952- 2. Russia -- Politics and government -- 1991- 3. Russia -- Social conditions -- 1991-
ISBN 0743264312

LC 2005044157

"A Lisa Drew book."

Two journalists for "The Washington Post" examine modern-day Russia, assessing the ways in which Vladimir Putin and his former KGB associates have shaped the country and threatened Russia's chances for long-term democracy.

"Well written, well reported and well organized, the book consists of freestanding chapters that touch on the most important events and trends in contemporary Russia, from the war in Chechnya to the spread of AIDS and the dire state of the Russian judicial system." New York Times.

Brent, Jonathan

Inside the Stalin archives : discovering the new Russia / Jonathan Brent. W. W. Norton & Co. Inc., 2008. 304 p. **947.086**

1. Archives -- Russia. 2. Communism and culture -- Soviet Union. 3. Antisemitism -- Russia. 4. Capitalism -- Russia. 5. Russia -- History -- 1991- 6. Soviet Union -- Influence.
ISBN 9780977743339

LC bl2008023011

"A provocative assessment of modern Russia based on the personal archives of Stalin charges the country with failing to deal with past events that contributed to its collapse, in a report that covers such topics as the tolerance of anti-Semitism, governme

"This work, which draws upon the author's fifteen years of unprecedented access to high-level Soviet Archives, reveals as much about the grim realities of post-Soviet life and bureaucracy as it does about the archives themselves. Equipped with little Russian and few contacts, but with an almost palpable sense of decency and honest intentions that illuminate his book, Brent explains for the general reader as well as for specialists how he went about his work in the new Russia." New York Times Book Review.

Buettner, Dan

Sovietrek : a journey by bicycle across Russia / written and photographed by Dan Buettner. Lerner Publications, c1994. 104 p. : **947.086**

1. Buettner, Dan. 2. Bicyclists. 3. Bicycle touring. 4. Voyages and travels. 5. Southern Russia -- Description and travel.
ISBN 0822529505

LC 94005449

Includes index.

"Readers seeking a healthier lifestyle will appreciate this warm and encouraging book." Library Journal.

Dawisha, Karen

Putin's kleptocracy : who owns Russia? / Karen Dawisha. Simon & Schuster, 2014. vii, 445 p. : **947.086**

1. Putin, Vladimir Vladimirovich, 1952- 2. Political corruption -- Russia 3. Organized crime 4. World politics 5. Politicians 6. Russia -- Politics and government -- 1991-
ISBN 9781476795195

LC 2014948969

The raging question in the world today is who is the real Vladimir Putin and what are his intentions. Karen Dawisha's brilliant work provides an answer, describing how Putin got to power, the cabal he brought with him, the billions they have looted, and his plan to restore the Greater Russia.

"A rich and exhaustive account of Putin and his regime that supports a forecast of its 'hard authoritarian' drift and dependence on 'European public goods' for survival." Library Journal.

Gessen, Masha

★The **future** is history : how totalitarianism reclaimed Russia / Masha Gessen. Riverhead Books, 2017 400 p. **947.086**

1. Despotism 2. Totalitarianism 3. Political persecution. 4. Russia

-- Politics and government -- 1991- 5. Russia -- Social conditions -- 1991- 6. Russia -- Moral conditions.
ISBN 9781594634536
LC 2017014363

National Book Award for Nonfiction, 2017.
National Book Critics Circle Award for Nonfiction finalist, 2017

The award-winning Russian-American journalist and author of the best-selling The Man Without a Face traces how within the space of a generation, Russia has succumbed to a more virulent and resistant strain of autocracy as demonstrated by the experiences of four prototype individuals born at the once-presumed dawn of Russian democracy.

"A superb, alarming portrait of a government that exercises outsize influence in the modern world, at great human cost." Kirkus.

Judah, Tim, 1962-

In wartime : stories from Ukraine / Tim Judah. Tim Duggan Books, 2016. 240 p. **947.086**

1. Judah, Tim, 1962- Travel Ukraine. 2. War and society 3. International relations. 4. Ukraine Conflict, 2014- 5. National liberation movements. 6. Ukraine -- Foreign relations Russia 7. Russia -- Foreign relations Ukraine 8. Former Soviet republics
ISBN 9780451495471
LC 2016000368

Drawing on interviews with Russian agents, weary historians, desperate civil servants and retirees from the villages that dot the country's famous farmland, one of the best journalists of his generation presents a definitive, first-hand account from the front lines of the conflict in Ukraine, creating a sweeping portrait of a disintegrating nation.

"Judah's special and timely book will provide lay readers with an apt introduction to Ukraine, and specialists will appreciate its atypical yet enlightening approach and its insights into the social aspects of ongoing conflicts." Publishers Weekly.

Ostrovsky, Arkady, 1971-

The **invention** of Russia : from Gorbachev's freedom to Putin's war / Arkady Ostrovsky. Viking Press, 2016 384 p. **947.086**

1. World politics 2. Political leadership 3. International relations 4. Russia -- History
ISBN 9780399564161
LC 2016008393

Orwell Prize, 2016.

An original narrative history by the Moscow Bureau Chief for The Economist traces Russia's evolution from the Cold War through its breakup and recent rise as a fiercely nationalistic, anti-American police state, introducing readers to the propagandists, oligarchs and fixers behind the nation's current status.

"A troubling and superbly documented book that will make readers wonder what comes next for Russia and its propagandists." Booklist.

Politkovskaya, Anna

A **Russian** diary : a journalist's final account of life, corruption, and death in Putin's Russia / Anna Politkovskaya ; translated by Arch Tait ; foreword by Scott Simon. Random House, 2007. 369 p. **947.086**

1. Putin, Vladimir Vladimirovich, 1952- 2. Journalists -- Russia. 3. Political corruption -- Russia. 4. Russia -- Social conditions -- 1991- 5. Russia -- Politics and government -- 1991-
ISBN 1400066824
LC bl2007014787

National Book Critics Circle Award for Autobiography/ Memoir finalist

Written in the form of a diary, a stark account of life in twenty-first-century Russia offers an unflinching account of the plight of millions of Russian citizens and the corruption of the Putin presidency, in a final work by the acclaimed Russian journalist, murdered in October 2006.

Remnick, David

Resurrection : the struggle for a new Russia / David Remnick. Random House, 1997. xiii, 398 p. **947.086**

1. Politics and culture 2. Political corruption -- Russia 3. Russia -- Politics and government -- 1991- 4. Russia -- Economic conditions -- 1991- 5. Russia -- Social conditions -- 1991-
ISBN 9780679423775
LC 96047360

Sequel to: Lenin's tomb.

Offers a study of the Soviet Union in the aftermath of communism, tracing Russia's search for stability following the chaotic elections of 1996.

"In this companion volume to Lenin's tomb, Remnick concentrates on the post-Soviet scene and its prospects. Chaotic uncertainty, massive corruption, and crime are notoriously present, yet the possibility of a different, better life also beckons. This is an interesting, highly informative portrait of a country struggling toward a fateful future." Library Journal.

Seierstad, Asne, 1970-

Angel of Grozny : orphans of a forgotten war / Asne Seierstad. Perseus Books Group, 2008. 384 p. **947.086**

1. Orphans. 2. Civil war -- Russia. 3. War and society. 4. Abandonment (Psychology) 5. Chechnya, Russia -- Social conditions -- 1994- 6. Chechnya, Russia -- History -- Civil War, 1994- 7. Russia -- History -- 1991-
ISBN 9780465011223
LC 2008925222

"Seierstad's searing, evocative recounting brings Chechnya to life, especially the unimaginable suffering and strength of the Chechen people. Powerful, painful, and raw...[this] is essential reading." Booklist.

Szablowski, Witold, 1980-

Dancing bears : true stories of people nostalgic for life under tyranny / Witold Szablowski ; translated by Antonia Lloyd-Jones. Penguin Books, 2018, c2014. 233 p. **947.086**

1. Post-communism 2. Social change 3. Former Communists 4. Bulgaria 5. Eastern Europe 6. Cuba
ISBN 9780143129745
LC 2017043107

Originally published: Warsaw : Agora S.A., 2014.

An award-winning Polish journalist, in the tradition of Ryszard Kapuscinski, presents the extraordinary stories of people throughout Eastern Europe and in Cuba who, like Bulgaria's dancing bears, are now free but who seem nostalgic for the time when they were not.

"A surprising look at societies grappling with profound change." Kirkus.

Treisman, Daniel

The **return** : Russia's journey from Gorbachev to Medvedev / Daniel Treisman. Free Press, 2011. 352 p. **947.086**

1. Post-communism. 2. Democratization. 3. International relations. 4. Russia -- Politics and government -- 1991-
ISBN 9781416560715
LC 2010011520

The author of Without a Map assesses modern-day Russia to consider such topics as whether the collapse of the Soviet Union was preventable, Yeltsin's impact on political order and Putin's public popularity.

"The politics and economics of post-Communist Russia occupy this survey of the past two decades. Treisman...works commentary about Russia's successive leaders--Gorbachev, Yeltsin, Putin, and Medvedev--into the problems they confronted. Encompassing foreign policy and Russian public opinion, Treisman's knowledgeable presentation is a reliable current-affairs source for Russia's economic revival and reassertion in international affairs." Booklist.

Walker, Shaun (Journalist)
★The **long** hangover : Putin's new Russia and the ghosts of the past / Shaun Walker. Oxford University Press, 2018. 278 pages : **947.086**

1. Putin, Vladimir Vladimirovich, 1952- 2. Presidents. 3. Political culture. 4. International relations 5. Post-communism. 6. Russia -- Politics and government -- 1991-
ISBN 9780190659240

LC 2017015739

A deeply reported, bottom-up explanation of Russia's resurgence under Putin. By cleverly exploiting the memory of the Soviet victory over fascism in World War II, Putin's regime has made ordinary Russians feel that their country is great again.

"Intelligent and ambitious, Walker's book succeeds in providing insight into the recent history of a nation at the center of world attention." Publishers Weekly.

Zygar, Mikhail, 1981-
All the Kremlin's men : inside the court of Vladimir Putin / Mikhail Zygar. PublicAffairs, 2016 336 p. **947.086**

1. Putin, Vladimir Vladimirovich, 1952- 2. Kremlin, Moscow. 3. Political consultants 4. Charismatic political leadership. 5. Manipulation (Social sciences) 6. Russia -- Politics and government -- 1991-
ISBN 9781610397391

LC 2016018443

In an account based on first-hand interviews with Vladimir Putin's inner circle, the author asserts that Putin is actually a weary leader controlled by the many men who advise and deceive him and that many of the Kremlin's decisions have been nothing more than tactical responses to external events, devoid of logic or objective.

"This excellent book contains a continuous account of Putin's years in power seasoned with details that are poorly known to most readers, if known at all." Library Journal.

947.6 Moldova

Zipperstein, Steven J., 1950-
Pogrom : Kishinev and the tilt of history / Steven J. Zipperstein. Liveright Publishing, [2018. 352 p. **947.6**

1. Kishinev Massacre, Chisinau, Moldova, 1903 2. Massacres 3. Jews -- Persecutions 4. Genocide 5. Moldova 6. Eastern Europe
ISBN 9781631492693

LC 2017055798

Explores the history of the 1903 Kishinev Massacre, in which Jews were murdered, assaulted, raped, and saw their property destroyed, using new evidence to shed light on the event and its profound effect on twentieth-century history.

947.7 Ukraine

King, Charles, 1967-
Odessa : genius and death in a city of dreams / Charles King. W.W. Norton & Co., 2011. 352 p. **947.7**

1. Multiculturalism 2. Cosmopolitanism. 3. Cities and towns. 4. Genius. 5. Odesa, Ukraine -- History.
ISBN 9780393070842

LC 2010038000

Describes the vibrant Black Sea port city of Odessa and the thriving Jewish population that included Alexander Pushkin, Isaac Babel, Zionist activist Vladimir Jabotinsky and immunologist Ilya Mechnikov and the mass murders of the Romanian occupation during World War II.

"This is a finely written and evocative portrait of the city. [Its] detail, coupled with a fine feel for the sweep of history...makes this book a worthy tribute to one of Europe's greatest and least-known cities." The Economist.

947.708 Ukraine--1855-

Applebaum, Anne, 1964-
Red famine : Stalin's war on Ukraine / Anne Applebaum. Doubleday, 2017 384 p. **947.708**

1. Famines 2. Collectivization of agriculture 3. Atrocities 4. Genocide 5. Ukraine -- History -- Famine, 1932-1933. 6. Soviet Union -- History 7. Eastern Europe.
ISBN 9780385538855

LC 2017029952

Lionel Gelber Prize (Canada), 2018.

According to Pulitzer Prize-winning historian Anne Applebaum, Soviet dictator Joseph Stalin deliberately created famine conditions in Ukraine as an act of genocide from 1931-34. Making effective use of previously published and newly available sources, Red Famine documents the effects of collectivization, removal of food to other regions, and other oppressive measures that resulted in the deaths of four million Ukrainians. Applebaum concludes that Stalin aimed to replace ethnic Ukrainians with Russians to achieve a more compliant populace. Though her analysis may be controversial, it sheds light on current tensions between Russia and Ukraine.

"An authoritative history of national strife from a highly knowledgeable guide." Kirkus.

947.98086 Estonia--1991-

Theroux, Alexander
Estonia : a ramble through the periphery / [Alexander Theroux]. Fantagraphics Books, c2011. 351 p., 12 p. of plates : **947.98086**

1. Theroux, Alexander Travel Estonia. 2. Estonia -- Description and travel. 3. Estonia -- History. 4. Essays
ISBN 1606994654

LC 2012289396

Statement of responsibility from spine.

A travelogue of the author's nine-month sojourn in Estonia relates his fascination with the history and culture of a country that appears to outsiders as distanced from the modern world.

948 Scandinavia and Finland

Ferguson, Robert, 1948-

Scandinavians : in search of the soul of the North / Robert Ferguson. Overlook Press, 2017, c2016. xxiii, 455 p. **948**

1. Manners and customs 2. Vikings. 3. Northmen and Northwomen. 4. Civilization, Viking 5. Scandinavia 6. Norway 7. Denmark 8. Sweden 9. Finland 10. Iceland

ISBN 9781468314823

LC bl2017025105

Originally published: London : Head of Zeus, 2016.

Chronicles the history of Scandinavia, from the Vendel era of prehistoric Sweden, to the Vikings and the Christian conversion and unified state of the Middle Ages, through the world wars of the past century, discussing the region's society, politics and culture.

"In a free-wheeling love letter to the essence of Scandinavia, Ferguson (Life Lessons from Kierkegaard) takes readers on a leisurely jaunt through the collective, interconnected histories of Norway, Denmark, and Sweden." Publishers Weekly.

Price, Neil S.

Children of ash and elm : a history of the Vikings / Neil Price. Basic Books, 2020. 608 p. **948**

1. Vikings. 2. Northmen and Northwomen. 3. Civilization, Viking. 4. Vikings -- Antiquities

ISBN 9780465096985

LC 2020001863

A distinguished archaeologist with decades of expertise offers a full history of the Vikings--from arts and culture to politics and cosmology.

"Readers interested in Viking culture should consider this monumental history a must-read." Publishers Weekly

Roesdahl, Else

The **Vikings** / Else Roesdahl ; translated by Susan M. Margeson and Kirsten Williams. Penguin Books, 1998. xix, 324 p., 16 p. of plates : **948**

1. Vikings. 2. Northmen and Northwomen. 3. Scandinavia -- History.

ISBN 0140252827

LC 99178674

Translation of: Vikingernes verden.

"About one-third of the book deals with Viking expansion into Russia, Normandy, the British Isles, Iceland, Greenland, etc. Most of the book surveys the geography, people, society, religion, art, etc., of the Vikings' Scandinavian homelands." Library Journal.

Sawyer, P. H.

The **Oxford** illustrated history of the Vikings / edited by Peter Sawyer. Oxford University Press, 1997. xv, 298 p. : **948**

1. Vikings -- Pictorial works. 2. Vikings.

ISBN 0198205260

LC 97016649

Covers the different geographical areas of the Viking world, and traces the Viking story from the first raids on isolated coastal communities toward the end of the eighth century to the establishing of permanent settlements.

948.022 Scandinavia and Finland--Viking period, ca. 800-ca. 1050

Ferguson, Robert, 1948-

The **Vikings** : a history / Robert Ferguson. Viking, 2009. 480 p. **948.022**

1. Civilization, Viking 2. Warriors. 3. Explorers. 4. Seafaring life. 5. Europe -- History -- 476-1492.

ISBN 9780670020799

LC 2009026818

"Ferguson's scholarly study requires close attention, but the intellectual rewards are plentiful. Provides a significant deepening of our knowledge of the Vikings." Kirkus.

948.071 Scandinavia and Finland--2000-2019

Booth, Michael

The **almost** nearly perfect people : behind the myth of the Scandinavian utopia / Michael Booth. Picador, 2015. 448 p. **948.071**

1. National characteristics 2. Social policy 3. Economic policy 4. Taxation 5. Scandinavia 6. Norway 7. Denmark 8. Sweden 9. Finland

ISBN 9781250061966

LC 2015413295

Journalist Michael Booth has lived among the Scandinavians for more than ten years, and he has grown increasingly frustrated with the rose-tinted view of this part of the world offered up by the Western media. In this timely book he leaves his adopted home of Denmark and embarks on a journey through all five of the Nordic countries to discover who these curious tribes are, the secrets of their success, and, most intriguing of all, what they think of one another.

"Thanks to Booth's good-natured description of his adventures--and his honest admiration--we may head for Scandinavia after all (bringing some elf-off spray, just in case)." Booklist.

948.9703 Finland--1917-1999

Edwards, Robert, 1955-

The **Winter** War : Russia's invasion of Finland, 1939-1940 / Robert Edwards. Pegasus Books, 2008, c2006. 319 p., 8 unnumbered p. of plates : **948.9703**

1. World War II 2. Finland -- History -- 1939- 3. Russia -- Armed Forces -- History -- 20th century.

ISBN 9781933648507

Originally published: London: Weidenfeld & Nicolson, 2006.

Discusses the background, nature, effect, and events of the war that occured after the Soviet Union invaded Finland in 1939.

"A brisk, efficient account of one of the most overlooked episodes of World War II. Highly readable and informative." Kirkus.

949.12 Iceland

Gudni Th. Johannesson, 1968-

The **history** of Iceland / Gudni Thorlacius Johannesson. Greenwood, 2013. xv, 172 p. : **949.12**

1. Iceland -- History.

ISBN 9780313376207

LC 2012031759

949.2 Netherlands

Schama, Simon

The **embarrassment** of riches : an interpretation of Dutch culture in the Golden Age / Simon Schama. Alfred A. Knopf, 1987. xiii, 698 p. : **949.2**

1. Identity (Psychology) 2. Nationalism. 3. Netherlands -- Civilization -- 17th century. 4. Netherlands -- History -- 17th century.
ISBN 0394510755

LC 86045418

The author of Citizens presents an exhaustive, lively history of life in seventeenth-century Holland, the height of Dutch influence, culture, and affluence, accompanied by more than one hundred black-and-white reproductions and illustrations.

"Delving into customs, beliefs, popular art and quirks of behavior, Schama has fashioned a tour de force, a profound, unconventional and rewarding portrait of a people." Publishers Weekly.

Shorto, Russell

Amsterdam : a history of the world's most liberal city / Russell Shorto. Doubleday, [2013] 357 p., [24] p. of plates : **949.2**

1. Liberalism 2. City life 3. Canals 4. Coasts 5. Amsterdam, Netherlands
ISBN 9780385534574

LC 2013003544

A historical portrait of Amsterdam and the ideas that make it unique explores the ongoing efforts of its citizens to navigate its seaside challenges and democratic philosophies, revealing the influence of the liberal ideals that evolved there.

949.5 Greece

Brownworth, Lars

Lost to the west : the forgotten Byzantine Empire that rescued western civilization / Lars Brownworth. Random House, 2009. 352 p. **949.5**

1. Byzantine civilization. 2. Civilization, Medieval 3. Civilization, Ancient. 4. Byzantine Empire -- Social life and customs 5. Rome -- Civilization. 6. Byzantine Empire -- Civilization -- To 527. 7. Byzantine Empire -- Civilization -- 527-1081.
ISBN 9780307407955

LC 2009279520

A portrait of the lesser-known Byzantine Empire reveals how it endured as Christianity's capital for a long period following the fall of the Roman Empire and shaped the Renaissance in the west, in an account that includes vivid coverage of the deliverance of numerous adversaries to Constantinople's throne.

Mazower, Mark

Salonica, city of ghosts : Christians, Muslims, and Jews, 1430-1950 / Mark Mazower. Alfred A. Knopf, 2005, c2004. xv, 490 p., 32 p. of plates : **949.5**

1. Thessalonike, Greece -- History. 2. Greece -- History.
ISBN 0375412980

LC 2004057690

Originally published: London : HarperCollins, 2004.

National Jewish Book Award, 2005.

Presents a history of Salonica, from its heyday as a Byzantine port, through its role as a progressive center of the Ottoman Empire, to its occupation during World War II by the Nazis and their deportation of its Jewish inhabitants.

"The author's graceful, evocative prose, his deft attention to details and his empathetic presentation of all sides of the story add up to a magnificent tale of this unique city." Publishers Weekly.

Norwich, John Julius, 1929-

Byzantium : the apogee / John Julius Norwich. Knopf, 1992. xxiv, 389 p. : **949.5**

1. Byzantine Empire -- History -- 527-1081.
ISBN 0394537793

LC 91053119

"Originally published in the United Kingdom by Viking Penguin, London"--T.p. verso.

Describes Byzantium's battles against foreign threats, its internal conflicts, the return of iconoclasm in the ninth century, and the struggles between Anatolia's military aristocracy and the eunuchs of the capital.

Byzantium : the decline and fall / John Julius Norwich. Knopf, 1996. xxxvii, 488 p. : **949.5**

1. Byzantine Empire -- History -- 1081-1453.
ISBN 9780679416500

LC BL 99788137

The third and final volume of a trilogy that also includes Byzantium: The Early Centuries and Byzantium: The Apogee describes the final days of the city of Constantinople and its fall in May 1453.

949.61 Turkey in Europe (Eastern Thrace)

Hughes, Bettany

Istanbul : a tale of three cities / Bettany Hughes. Da Capo Press, 2017. 416 p. **949.61**

1. Cities and towns 2. Capitals (Cities) 3. Geopolitics 4. Commerce 5. Istanbul, Turkey
ISBN 9780306825842

LC 2017937000

A historian describes the history of one of the world's greatest and oldest cities, which has held three different names and has played host to Phoenicians, Genoese, Venetians, Jews, Vikings and Azeris who all called it home.

"Hughes balances especially well a study of one city with the commentary of greater time periods and historic events taking place simultaneously around the world; the rich, cultural, religious, and social presence of Istanbul's complex tale lends itself as an excellent focus." Library Journal.

949.7 Serbia, Croatia, Slovenia, Bosnia and Hercegovina, Montenegro, Macedonia

Rieff, David

Slaughterhouse : Bosnia and the failure of the West / David Rieff. Simon & Schuster, 1995. 240 p. **949.7**

1. Rieff, David. 2. United Nations Bosnia and Hercegovina 3. Genocide -- Bosnia and Hercegovina 4. Serbs. 5. Muslims -- Bosnia and Hercegovina 6. Yugoslav War, 1991-1995 -- Bosnia and Hercegovina. 7. Bosnia and Hercegovina -- History -- 1991-
ISBN 9780671881184

LC 94040148

Includes index.

Discusses the war in Bosnia, the U.N. contingents "standing by" as the genocide continues, and aid workers risking their lives to help victims.

"Slaughterhouse is perhaps the most powerful, passionate, and penetrating dissection of a Westerner of the ongoing Bosnian tragedy." Booklist.

949.702 Yugoslavia, 1918-1991

Maass, Peter, 1960-

Love thy neighbor : a story of war / Peter Maass. Alfred A. Knopf, 1996. 305 p. : **949.702**

1. Maass, Peter, 1960- 2. Milosevic, Slobodan, 1941-2006 3. Serbs. 4. Muslims -- Bosnia and Hercegovina 5. Genocide -- Bosnia and Hercegovina 6. Interethnic relations. 7. Bosnia and Hercegovina -- Politics and government 8. Bosnia and Hercegovina -- History -- 1991-

ISBN 9780679444336

LC 95039250

A foreign correspondent offers a portrait of the conflict in Bosnia, from the battlefield of Sarajevo, to the atrocities that have been reported, to the lives of those caught in the crossfire.

949.703 Period as sovereign nations, 1991

Clark, Wesley K.

★Waging modern war : Bosnia, Kosovo, and the future of combat / Wesley K. Clark. Public Affairs, 2001. xxxi, 479 p., 8 p. of plates : **949.703**

1. Clark, Wesley K. 2. Yugoslav War, 1991-1995, American 3. Yugoslav War, 1991-1995 -- Bosnia and Hercegovina 4. Genocide 5. Kosovo, Serbia -- History -- Civil War, 1998, American

ISBN 9781586480431

LC 2001019717

Maps on lining papers.

Includes index.

A behind-the-scenes look at contemporary warfare recounts the author's experiences at the head of NATO forces in Kosovo, explaining why the lessons of Kosovo are applicable to the war against terrorism.

Rohde, David, 1967-

Endgame : the betrayal and fall of Srebrenica, Europe's worst massacre since World War II / David Rohde. Westview Press, 1998. xvi, 450 : **949.703**

1. Yugoslav War, 1991-1995 -- Campaigns -- Bosnia and Herzegovina -- Srebrenica. 2. Yugoslav War, 1991-1995 -- Atrocities. 3. Srebrenica (Bosnia and Herzegovina) -- History, Military.

ISBN 9780813335339

LC 98026127

949.7103 Serbia--1991-

McAllester, Matthew, 1969-

Beyond the mountains of the damned : the war inside Kosovo / Matthew McAllester. New York University Press, 2002. ix, 227 p., [8] p. of plates : **949.7103**

1. Kosovo, Serbia -- History -- Civil War, 1998 2. Pec, Serbia -- History, Military -- 20th century.

ISBN 0814756603

LC 2001004370

"McAllester's spare, understated prose...is potent, as is his exploration of the human side of geopolitics and war." Publishers Weekly.

949.8 Romania

Kaplan, Robert D., 1952-

In Europe's shadow : two cold wars and a thirty-year journey through Romania and beyond / Robert D. Kaplan. Random House, 2015. 320 p. **949.8**

1. Kaplan, Robert D., 1952- 2. Romania -- Description and travel. 3. Romania -- History

ISBN 9780812996814

LC 2015012726

A history of Romania traces the author's intellectual development throughout his extensive visits to the country, sharing his observations about its reflection of European politics, geography and key events while exploring the indelible role of Vladimir Putin.

"Despite the lack of a clear focus and the somewhat incoherent organization, this is a well-written, intriguing, and informative book." Publishers Weekly.

949.9 Bulgaria

Kassabova, Kapka

Border : a journey to the edge of Europe / Kapka Kassabova. Granta, 2017. xviii, 379 p. : **949.9**

1. Borderlands 2. Boundaries 3. Refugees 4. Culture 5. Balkan Peninsula 6. Mediterranean Region 7. Bulgaria 8. Thrace 9. Greece 10. Turkey

ISBN 9781555977863

LC 2016436902

National Book Critics Circle Award for Nonfiction finalist, 2017

Bulgarian-born poet and writer Kapka Kassabova lives in Scotland, but in Border she describes return visits to Eastern Europe between 2013-2015. In the complex, magical area where Bulgaria, Turkey, and Greece meet, Kassabova traveled through mountains, villages, and forests and spoke with former border guards, people who tried to escape Communist Bulgaria, villagers who live near the countries' edges, and incoming refugees fleeing Syria. Clever, lyrical, and acutely observed, this book is a fascinating examination of Eastern European borderlands.

"Wild animals abound, myths mingle with reality, and Kassabova proves to be a penetrating and contemplative guide through rough terrain." Publishers Weekly.

950 History of Asia

Amrith, Sunil S., 1979-

Unruly waters: how rains, rivers, coasts and seas have shaped Asia's history / Sunil Amrith. Basic Books, 2018. 416 p. **950**

1. Water 2. Bodies of water 3. Water and civilization 4. Asian civilization 5. Asia

ISBN 9780465097722

LC 2018020666

Explores Asia's history through the stories of its rains, rivers and seas, demonstrating how efforts to control water shaped regional politics, economics and foreign relations.

Said, Edward W., 1935-2003

Orientalism / Edward W. Said. Vintage Books, 1979, c1978. xi, 368 p. ; **950**

1. Orientalism. 2. Imperialism. 3. Art and society 4. East and West. 5. Middle East -- Study and teaching. 6. Middle East -- Foreign opinion, Occidental. 7. Asia -- Foreign opinion, Occidental.
ISBN 9780394740676

LC 79010497

A provocative critique of Western attitudes about the Orient, this history examines the ways in which the West has discovered, invented, and sought to control the East from the 1700s to the present.

950.4 History of Asia--1905-

Mishra, Pankaj

From the ruins of empire : the intellectuals who remade Asia / Pankaj Mishra. Farrar Straus & Giroux, 2012. 320 p. **950.4**

1. Intellectuals. 2. Intellectual life. 3. Asia -- Social life and customs.
ISBN 9780374249595

LC 2012940483

Provides an overview of the great thinkers and philosophical leaders from across Asia who helped change and shape the modern continent, including Tagore and Gandhi in India, Liang Qichao in China and Abdurreshi al Ibrahim in the Ottoman Empire.

951 China and adjacent areas

Clunas, Craig,

Ming : 50 years that changed China / edited by Craig Clunas and Jessica Harrison-Hall. University of Washington Press, 2014 312 p. : **951**

1. Art, Chinese -- Ming-Qing dynasties, 1368-1912 -- Exhibitions 2. Art objects, Chinese -- Ming-Qing dynasties, 1368-1912 -- Exhibitions 3. China -- Civilization -- 960-1644 Exhibitions. 4. China -- History -- Ming dynasty, 1368-1644 Exhibitions.
ISBN 9780295994505

LC bl2015026208

Published to accompany a major exhibition at the British Museum, September 18, 2014-January 5, 2015.

Showcases some of the most significant art objects created during the time of the Ming dynasty from all aspects of Chinese culture, including government, literature, religious life, the imperial court, and commerce.

Dalai Lama

My appeal to the world : in quest of truth and justice on behalf of the Tibetan people, 1961-2010 / Dalai Lama. Tibet House, 2015. 400 p. **951**

1. Peace-building 2. Tibetans 3. Military occupation. 4. National liberation movements. 5. Tibet -- History -- Chinese occupation, 1950- 6. Speeches, addresses, etc.
ISBN 9780967011561

LC 2014034290

Every March 10th, from 1961 until 2011, in commemoration of the greatest uprising of the Tibetan people against the Chinese military occupation, the Dalai Lama delivered an appeal to the world on behalf of his people. Each statement is a heartfelt call to recognize the truth and the factual reality of Tibet's history and situation; a cry for help, a plea for justice, and a pledge of determination to withstand the worst and to overcome. In these annual addresses, he began to articulate and fully express his overarching appeal to humanity. All of the Dalai Lama's March 10th speeches, at their most poignant and eloquent, are collected here, introduced and historically contextualized by Sofia Stril-Rever, an author and scholar of Tibetan history and culture and Buddhist spirituality who has long served as his French translator.

"Those who wish to learn more about the late 20th-century history of Sino-Tibetan relations will find this a respectable resource, but it should be noted that this set of writings does not offer Chinese perspectives on the thorny issue." Publishers Weekly.

My Tibet / text by His Holiness the Fourteenth Dalai Lama of Tibet ; photographs and introduction by Galen Rowell. University of California Press, 1990. 162 p. : **951**

1. Dalai Lama XIV, 1935- 2. Peace. 3. Environmentalism. 4. Tibet Pictorial works. 5. Central Asia. 6. Essays.
ISBN 0520071093

LC 90010868

"A Mountain Light Press book."
Includes index.

The fourteenth Dalai Lama of Tibet offers his views on world peace and environmental responsibility in a collection of essays accompanied by photographs of his beloved Tibet.

Demick, Barbara

★**Eat** the Buddha : life and death in a Tibetan town / Barbara Demick. Random House, 2020. 352 p. **951**

1. Tibetans 2. Resistance to government 3. Culture conflict 4. Social change 5. Tibet 6. China -- Social conditions 7. China -- History
ISBN 9780812998757

LC 2019044133

Eat the Buddha spans decades of modern Tibetan and Chinese history, as told through the private lives of Demick's subjects, among them a princess whose family is wiped out during the Cultural Revolution, a young Tibetan nomad who becomes radicalized in the storied monastery of Kirti, an upwardly mobile entrepreneur who falls in love with a Chinese woman, a poet and intellectual who risks everything to voice his resistance, and a Tibetan schoolgirl forced to choose at an early age between her family and the elusive lure of Chinese money. All of them face the same dilemma: Do they resist the Chinese, or do they join them? Do they adhere to Buddhist teachings of compassion and nonviolence, or do they fight?

"Taking a compelling approach to documenting Ngaba's history through the eyes of its own people, this wonderfully written book will leave readers with a stronger appreciation for why the movement to support the Tibetan people deserves so much more attention." Library Journal

Hessler, Peter, 1969-

★**Oracle** bones : a journey between China's past and present / Peter Hessler. HarperCollins, 2006. xi, 491 p. : **951**

1. Language and culture. 2. Economic development. 3. East and West 4. China -- Social life and customs. 5. China -- Description and travel. 6. China -- Civilization.
ISBN 9780060826581

LC 2005052607

ALA Notable Book, 2007.
National Book Award for Nonfiction finalist, 2006

Chronicles the author's 7,000-mile drive across northern China, following the Great Wall, during which he investigated a historically important rural region being abandoned as young people migrate to jobs in the southeast; his five-year stay in a small farming village; and his three years of research in Lishui, a small city slated to become a major industrial center.

"The author has a marvelous sense of the intonations and gestures that give life to the moment; he knows when to join in the action and when simply to wait for things to happen." New York Times Book Review.

Leibovitz, Liel

Fortunate sons : the 120 Chinese boys who came to America, went to school, and revolutionized an ancient civilization / Liel Leibovitz & Matthew Miller. W.W. Norton, 2011. 288 p. **951**

1. Yung, Wing, 1828-1912. 2. Chinese Educational Commission -- History. 3. Students -- China. 4. Exchange students. 5. Modernization (Social sciences) 6. War. 7. China -- History -- 1861-1912. 8. China -- Politics and government -- 19th century. 9. China -- Education -- 19th century.

ISBN 9780393070040

LC 2010037724

At the twilight of the nineteenth century, China sent a detachment of boys to America in order to learn the ways of the West, modernize the antiquated empire, and defend it from foreigners invading its shores. After spending a decade in New England's finest schools, the boys returned home, driven by a pioneering spirit of progress and reform. Their lives in America influenced not only their thinking but also their nation's endeavor to become a contemporary world power, an endeavor that resonates powerfully today.

"A curious, little-known episode of Sino-American history vividly told." Kirkus.

Meyer, Michael J., 1972-

The **last** days of old Beijing : life in the backstreets of a changing city / Michael Meyer. Walker & Company, c2008. 368 p. **951**

1. Meyer, Michael J., 1972- 2. Travel writers 3. Alleys 4. Streets 5. Urban renewal 6. Beijing, China -- Social life and customs -- 20th century 7. Beijing, China -- Social life and customs -- 21st century

ISBN 9780802716521

LC 2008015546

An intimate portrait of Beijing by an award-winning travel writer, Peace Corps volunteer, and long-time resident describes his life on a hutong in the region's oldest neighborhood, a historically rich community that is being compromised by modern development and technologies.

Platt, Stephen R.

Autumn in the Heavenly Kingdom : China, the West, and the epic story of the Taiping Civil War / Stephen R. Platt. Alfred A. Knopf, 2012. 480 p. **951**

1. Interethnic conflict -- China -- History -- 19th century. 2. Manchus -- History -- 19th century. 3. Civil war 4. Europeans in China -- History -- 19th century. 5. China -- History -- Taiping Rebellion, 1850-1864. 6. China -- Foreign relations Western countries. 7. Western countries -- Foreign relations China. 8. China -- History -- Taiping Rebellion, 1850-1864 -- Participation, Foreign. 9. China -- Ethnic relations -- History -- 19th century.

ISBN 9780307271730

LC 2011035137

"This is a Borzoi book"--T.p. verso.

Cundill Prize in History, 2012.

A narrative history of China's 19th-century Taiping Rebellion traces an 1850s revolution led by a failed civil servant who claimed divine ties, citing the roles played by the United States and Britain as well as the contributions of such figures as military strategist Zeng Guofan and Taiping leader Hong Rengan.

Platt, Stephen R.

Imperial twilight : the Opium War and the end of China's last golden age / Stephen R. Platt. Alfred A. Knopf, 2018. 592 p. **951**

1. International trade 2. Colonialism 3. East and West 4. Opium industry and trade 5. China -- History -- Opium War, 1840-1842 6. China -- History -- Qing dynasty, 1644-1912

ISBN 9780307961730

LC 2017028172

"A Borzoi book."

Describes how 19th-century British efforts to "open" China to trade set in motion the fall of the Qing dynasty and started a war that allowed for the rise of nationalism and communism in the 20th century.

Preston, Diana, 1952-

The **boxer** rebellion : the dramatic story of China's war on foreigners that shook the world in the summer of 1900 / Diana Preston. Walker, 2000. xxvii, 436 p. : **951**

1. Boxer Rebellion, 1899-1901 2. China -- Social life and customs. 3. China -- History -- Boxer Rebellion, 1899-1901.

ISBN 9780802713612

LC 00039243

"First published, in somewhat different form, as Besieged in Peking in Great Britain in 1999 by Constable and Company, Ltd."--T.p. verso.

Later published as: A brief history of the Boxer Rebellion

Portrays the dramatic human experience of the Boxer Rebellion from both a Western and Chinese perspective, drawing on diaries, memoirs, and letters of those who lived through this pivotal time in the history of China.

"Preston's account, compiled from the many letters, diaries, and memoirs by European survivors of the siege, captures an odd strain of mordant humor." New York Times Book Review.

Schmitz, Rob

Street of Eternal Happiness : big city dreams along a Shanghai road / Rob Schmitz. Crown Publishers, 2016. 336 p. **951**

1. Streets. 2. Neighborhoods. 3. City life 4. China 5. Shanghai, China

ISBN 9780553418088

LC 2015041162

A narrative account profiling the ordinary men and women who live, work, and dream on the author's street in Shanghai, inspired by his enormously popular Marketplace series of the same name.

"Probing human-interest stories that mine the heart of today's China." Kirkus.

Spence, Jonathan D.

God's Chinese son : the Taiping Heavenly Kingdom of Hong Xiuquan / Jonathan D. Spence. W.W. Norton, 1997, c1996. xxvii, 400 p. : **951**

1. Hung, Hsiu-Chuan, 1814-1864. 2. Revolutions -- China. 3. China -- History -- Taiping Rebellion, 1850-1864. 4. China -- Religion. 5. China -- History -- 19th century. 6. East Asia.

ISBN 0393315568

LC BL 99783519

Reprint. Originally published: 1996.

A history of the Taiping Heavenly Kingdom in mid-nineteenth-century China profiles a period of extreme violence, during which a massive uprising, led by religious visionary Hong Xiuquan, cost some twenty million lives.

"In 1836, twenty-two-year-old Hong Xiuquan failed the civil-service examinations in Canton and came across some Christian tracts. When he later fell sick and had visions, he became convinced that he was the Christian God's second son, destined to rule a 'heavenly kingdom' on earth. Many were attracted to Hong's egalitarian policies--despite his enforced separation of the sexes--and his sect prospered. But its attempts to overthrow the Qing dynasty resulted in unprecedented bloodshed: twenty million people died before the uprising was defeated, in 1864. Spence's present-tense narrative is riveting." The New Yorker.

The **search** for modern China / Jonathan D. Spence. Norton, c1990. xxv, 876 p., 136 p. of plates : **951**

1. China -- History -- Qing dynasty, 1644-1912 2. China -- History -- 20th century.

ISBN 0393307808

LC 89009241

Lionel Gelber Prize (Canada), 1990.

Covering more than four centuries of Chinese history, this work chronicles the various dynasties, the ideas of reformist Confucian scholars, and China's poets, novelists, artists, students, and leaders.

"Beginning with the decline of the Ming dynasty and ending with the Tiananmen Square massacre, Spence chronicles the cultural and social transformations of the country, concentrating on the many wars and rebellions." Booklist.

Spence's own sense of China's past is so vivid, his understanding so sure and his writer's skill so powerful that the reader apprehends distant events as if they were contemporary. New Statesman (1913)

Treason by the book / Jonathan D. Spence. Viking, 2001. xvi, 300 p. : **951**

1. Zeng, Jing, 1679-1736. 2. Yongzheng, Emperor of China, 1677-1735. 3. Revolutionaries -- China 4. China -- History -- 18th century. 5. China -- History -- Qing dynasty, 1644-1912

ISBN 9780670892921

LC 00043805

An acclaimed historian delves deeply into a famous 1728 plot to overthrow the Manchu dynasty, in a fascinating study of the intrigues, political and legal systems, and key personalities of eighteenth-century China.

"Spence's story of emperor, officials, and conspirators is both rousingly unlikely and highly informative." Library Journal.

Tsering Shakya

The **dragon** in the land of snows : a history of modern Tibet since 1947 / Tsering Shakya. Columbia University press, c1999. xxix, 574 p. : **951**

1. Tibet -- History -- 20th century.

ISBN 0231118147

LC 99014020

Provides a history of modern Tibet from 1947, providing Chinese and Tibetan versions of events in many cases and critiquing Tibets's leadership strategy as well as China's.

"Drawing on Tibetan, Chinese, British, Indian and American sources, Shakya weaves an authoritative and easily readable narrative. 'The Dragon in the Land of Snows' is likely to be the definitive history of modern Tibet for a generation or more." New York Times Book Review.

Xinran, 1958-

China witness : voices from a silent generation / Xinran ; translated from Chinese by Esther Tyldesley, Nicky Harman and Julia Lovell. Pantheon Books, c2009. 448 p. **951**

1. Chinese -- Interviews 2. Modern history 3. Communism -- China -- History 4. Generations -- China 5. China -- History 6. China -- Social life and customs -- 21st century

ISBN 9780375425479

LC 2008035840

"Originally published in 2008 in Great Britain by Chatto & Windus, The Random House Group Limited, London."

Includes index.

"The author, traveling across the expanse of the Chinese Republic over the years, sought out those who had witnessed the rise of communism more than half a century ago. The result is this stirring, startlingly honest account of life under Chairman Mao and the current reformers revamping the socialist state." Publishers Weekly.

951.04 China--Period of Republic, 1912-1949

Chang, Iris

★The **rape** of Nanking : the forgotten holocaust of World War II / Iris Chang. BasicBooks, 1997. xi, 290 p. : **951.04**

1. Rabe, John, 1882-1949. 2. Sino-Japanese Conflict, 1937-1945. 3. Nanking Massacre, Nanjing, Jiangsu Sheng, China, 1937. 4. Massacres. 5. Genocide 6. Nanking, China -- History -- 1937-1945. 7. China -- History -- 1937-1945.

ISBN 9780465068357

LC 97024137

Relates an account of the 1937 massacre of 250,000 Chinese civilians in Nanking by the invading Japanese military, a carnage for which the Japanese government has never admitted responsibility.

"Chang's book is a memorial to the victims of Nanking, a damning indictment of Japanese political historiography, a valuable addition to Pacific war literature, and a literary model of how to speak about the unspeakable." Booklist.

Kurtz-Phelan, Daniel

The **China** mission : George Marshall's unfinished war, 1945-1947 / Daniel Kurtz-Phelan. W W Norton & Co Inc, 2018 416 p. **951.04**

1. Marshall, George C., (George Catlett), 1880-1959. 2. United States. Secretary of State. 3. Political leadership. 4. Communism. 5. World politics. 6. China -- History -- Civil War, 1945-1949. 7. United States -- Foreign relations China 8. China -- Foreign relations United States

ISBN 9780393240955

LC 2017053909

Presents a narrative account of General George Marshall's high-stakes mission to broker peace among rival Chinese leaders, establish a Chinese democracy and prevent a Communist takeover while navigating threats of another war.

Schoppa, R. Keith, 1943-

In a sea of bitterness : refugees during the Sino-Japanese War / R. Keith Schoppa. Harvard University Press, 2011. 360 p. **951.04**

1. Sino-Japanese Conflict, 1937-1945. 2. Refugees. 3. Migration, Internal.

ISBN 9780674059887

LC 2011022421

Sun, Shuyun

The **Long** March : the true history of Communist China's founding myth / Sun Shuyun. Doubleday, c2006. 270 p.

: 951.04

1. Mao, Zedong, 1893-1976. 2. Communist Party of China. 3. Communism -- China. 4. Communists 5. Ideology. 6. Propaganda. 7. China -- Politics and government -- 20th century. 8. China -- History -- Long March, 1934-1935.

ISBN 0385520247

LC 2006052132

Retracing the events and personalities of China's Long March, a colorful narrative describes the epic odyssey of thousands of Chinese Communist followers from their bases to the remote north of China, going behind the myth to recount the stories behind the March, including ruthless purges, hunger and disease, desertions, mistreatment of women, and more.

"In 1934, surrounded by Chiang Kai-shek's forces in the south, Mao's Red Army marched more than eight thousand miles to a new base, in the northwest. The march, completed by only a fifth of the original army, was a defeat in all ways but one: it returned Mao from the political wilderness to power. Mao transformed the march into the founding myth of modern China and, in doing so, created a new narrative around victories that never happened. Shuyun, a Chinese-born BBC documentary producer, retraces the route and interviews the few remaining survivors, in an account that shows the human cost of Mao's revisionism." The New Yorker.

Zia, Helen

Last boat out of Shanghai : the epic story of the Chinese who fled Mao's revolution / Helen Zia. Ballantine Books, [2019] 496 p. **951.04**

1. Refugees. 2. Civil war -- China. 3. Immigration and emigration. 4. Exiles. 5. Shanghai, China -- History -- 20th century. 6. China -- History -- Civil War, 1945-1949. 7. China -- Emigration and immigration -- History -- 20th century.

ISBN 9780345522320

LC 2018036197

A rare English-language account traces the dramatic true stories of four young people caught up in the mass exodus of Shanghai in the wake of China's 1949 Communist Revolution.

"In this enthralling, heartfelt narrative, journalist Zia (Asian American Dreams) tells the stories of four people during the 1949 mass exodus from Shanghai following Chinas Communist takeover." Publishers Weekly.

951.05 China--Period of People's Republic, 1949

Dikotter, Frank

Mao's great famine : the history of China's most devastating catastrophe, 1958-1962 / Frank Dikotter. Walker & Co., 2010. 448 p. **951.05**

1. Famines -- China. 2. Forced labor. 3. Agricultural policy. 4. Industrial policy. 5. China -- Economic policy -- 1949-1976.

ISBN 9780802777683

LC 2010013141

BBC Samuel Johnson Prize for Non-Fiction, 2011.

"The author parses this study of the Great Leap Forward into three components: Mao Zedong's bloody-minded resolve to implement the accelerated collectivization of the countryside, and the stifling of all opposition; the effects of these devastating policies on agriculture, industry, trade, housing and nature; and the catastrophic human toll (at least 45 million people died unnecessarily between 1958 and 1962)." Kirkus.

Palmer, James, 1978-

Heaven cracks, Earth shakes : the Tangshan earthquake and the death of Mao's China / James Palmer. Basic Books, 2012. ix, 273 p. : **951.05**

1. Chou En-lai, 1898-1976. 2. Mao, Zedong, 1893-1976. 3. Communist Party of China. 4. Earthquakes. 5. Revolutions -- China. 6. Communism. 7. Communists. 8. China -- History -- Cultural Revolution, 1966-1976.

ISBN 9780465014781

LC 2011934180

Documents the tumultuous years in China surrounding the death of Chairman Mao, providing coverage of contributing factors ranging from the death of popular premier Zhou Enlai and growing anger towards the Gang of Four to the 1976 earthquake in Tangshan and resistance to the Cultural Revolution.

Pomfret, John

Chinese lessons : five classmates and the story of the new China / John Pomfret. H. Holt, 2006. xii, 315 p. : **951.05**

1. Pomfret, John. 2. American students in China. 3. Foreign correspondents -- United States 4. Americans in China 5. China -- History -- 1976-2002 6. China -- History -- Cultural Revolution, 1966-1976.

ISBN 0805076158

LC 2006041211

Includes index.

A journalist for the "Washington Post" offers an eyewitness account of the changes in China over the past forty years as he recalls his stint as a twenty-year-old exchange student from Stanford at China's Nanjing University and the lives of his Chinese classmates, in a study of the human cost of China's development.

"This is a highly personal, honest, funny and well-informed account of China's hyperactive effort to forget its past and reinvent its future." New York Times Book Review.

951.056 China, 1960-1969

Dikotter, Frank

The **Cultural** Revolution : a people's history, 1962-1976 / Frank Dikotter. St. Martin's Press, 2016 400 p. **951.056**

1. Political leadership. 2. Communism. 3. World politics. 4. Revolutions -- China 5. China -- History -- Cultural Revolution, 1966-1976

ISBN 9781632864215

LC 2019303176

Drawing on hundreds of previously classified party documents, from secret police reports to unexpurgated versions of leadership speeches, the author sheds new light on China's most tumultuous era, during which the country descended into violent purges and entrenched fear.

"Dikotter tells a harrowing tale of unbelievable suffering. A potent combination of precise history and moving examples, plus a useful chronology of events." Kirkus.

951.06 China and adjacent areas--2000-

Osnos, Evan, 1976-

★**Age** of ambition : chasing fortune, truth, and faith in the new China / Evan Osnos. Farrar, Straus and Giroux, 2014. 416 p. **951.06**

1. Social change -- China. 2. Economic development -- China. 3.

Individualism -- China. 4. Authoritarianism -- China. 5. China -- Civilization -- 2002- 6. China -- Social conditions -- 2000- 7. China -- Politics and government -- 2000-
ISBN 9780374280741

LC 2013041338

Includes index.
National Book Award for Nonfiction, 2014.
Pulitzer Prize for General Nonfiction finalist

A Beijing correspondent for The New Yorker documents the political, economic and cultural changes occurring in today's China, examining a transition from Communist to personal power while addressing key questions about national freedom, generational identity and the influence of the West.

"Osnos combines scintillating reportage with an eye for telling ironies that illuminate broader trends; without downplaying the uniqueness of Chinese society, he makes its tensions feel achingly familiar for Western readers." Publishers Weekly.

951.9 Korea

Breen, Michael, 1952-

The **Koreans** : who they are, what they want, where their future lies / Michael Breen. Thomas Dunne Books, 2004. xii, 286 p. ; **951.9**

1. National characteristics, Korean. 2. South Korea -- History 3. Korea -- History.
ISBN 0312326092

LC 2004268667

"Revised and updated"--Front cover.

Updated to incorporate information on the growing unrest with North Korea, an incisive look at Korea, the history of its people, and the country itself examines how far the Koreans have come and where their advances will take them in the future, as well as how they will effect the world.

"In this survey of Korea's culture, the author probes such diverse topics as the status of civil liberties, generational social strains within families, and the massive corruption that permeates Korean society. He writes with a snappy, readable style." Booklist.

Peterson, Mark, 1946-

A **brief** history of Korea / Mark Peterson with Phillip Margulies. Facts On File, c2009. 318 p. Brief history (Facts on File) **951.9**

1. Korea -- History. 2. South Korea -- History 3. North Korea -- History 4. East Asia.
ISBN 9780816050857

LC 2009018889

An introduction to the history of Korea that covers its past from prehistoric times, to the medieval period, to the country's status as a Japanese colony prior to World War II, to its present day division into North and South Korea.

951.904 Korea--1945-1999

Cumings, Bruce, 1943-

★**Korea's** place in the sun : a modern history / Bruce Cumings. W. W. Norton, 2005. 542 p. : **951.904**

1. Korean War, 1950-1953 2. South Korea 3. Korea -- History -- 20th century 4. Korea -- History -- 1864-1910. 5. Korea -- History -- Japanese occupation, 1910-1945
ISBN 0393327027

LC 2006276040

Previous ed.: 1997.

A narrative chronicle of modern Korea focuses on the country's turbulent twentieth-century history, discussing its 1910 loss of independence, its years under Japanese rule, its division and the Korean War, and its postwar recovery and economic growth.

"Mr. Cumings has pored over the historical documents and he argues intelligently. His book is important precisely because he marshals considerable evidence to challenge conventional understanding." New York Times Book Review.

The **Korean** War : a history / Bruce Cumings. Modern Library, 2010. xix, 288 p. : **951.904**

1. Korean War, 1950-1953. 2. United States -- History -- 1945-1953
ISBN 9780679643579

LC 2010005629

A revisionist account of the controversial war examines perspectives on both sides of the conflict while assessing its cultural contradictions and lasting influence, placing particular focus on the roles of McCarthyism and the media.

Halberstam, David

★The **coldest** winter : America and the Korean War / David Halberstam. Hyperion, 2007. 736 p. **951.904**

1. Korean War, 1950-1953 -- United States. 2. Soldiers. 3. Military policy. 4. War. 5. United States -- History -- 20th century.
ISBN 1401300529

LC 2007001635

Pulitzer Prize for History finalist, 2008.

Explores the lesser-known elements of heroism and pathos that marked the Korean War and evaluates political decisions and miscalculations on both sides of the conflict.

Hanley, Charles J.

Ghost flames : life and death in a hidden war, Korea 1950-1953 / Charles J. Hanley. PublicAffairs, 2020. 528 p. **951.904**

1. Korean War, 1950-1953 2. Oral histories
ISBN 9781541768178

LC 2019036790

Drawing on newly discovered material, this vivid and emotional history of the Korean war details the events as they happened through the eyes of 20 different people, from a North Korean refugee girl to an American nun.

"A top-notch addition to the literature on the Korean War." Kirkus

Hickey, Michael, 1929-

The **Korean** War : the West confronts communism / Michael Hickey. Overlook Press, 2000. xii, 397 p. : **951.904**

1. United Nations Armed Forces Korea. 2. Korean War, 1950-1953. 3. War. 4. Korea.
ISBN 9781585670352

LC 00027692

Written for the fiftieth anniversary of the Korean War, this chronicle of the United Nation's first war takes an international look at the combatants and the conflict.

"An analysis of both the military and political factors that caused the war and the conduct on all sides. The author does not mince words when criticizing General MacArthur and other UN commanders. Using declassified documents as well as regimental and personal diaries, he wades through political intrigue and military disasters and triumphs to give us a memorable account." Library Journal.

Hutton, Robin L.

Sgt. Reckless : America's war horse / Robin Hutton. Regnery Publishing, [2014] 256 p. **951.904**

1. Sergeant Reckless (War horse), approximately 1948-1968. 2. United States. Marine Corps. Marine Regiment, 5th 3. United States. Marine Corps -- History 20th century. 4. Korean War, 1950-1953 5. Military campaigns 6. Horses -- History. 7. Human/animal relationships 8. Korea
ISBN 9781621572633

LC 2014019750

Describes the small Mongolian mare and celebrated hero of the Korean War who helped the American war effort by carrying wounded soldiers and making multiple trips across combat zones to deliver supplies.

"Hutton's passion and admiration for her subject (she also heads an effort to create a monument to Reckless) shines through in this sparkling and engaging portrait of a most remarkable and courageous animal." Publishers Weekly.

Oberdorfer, Don

The **two** Koreas : a contemporary history / Don Oberdorfer. Addison Wesley, c1997. xvii, 472 p. : **951.904**

1. South Korea -- History 2. North Korea -- History
ISBN 0201409275

LC 97019302

Details the near war between the U.S. and Korea in 1994 during a nuclear crisis, potential future dilemmas, the troops poised at the demilitarized zone, and other important facts, drawn from twenty-five years of extensive research.

Sides, Hampton

★**On** desperate ground : the Marines at the reservoir, the Korean War's greatest battle / Hampton Sides. Doubleday, [2018] 368 p. **951.904**

1. United States. Marine Corps. Marine Division, 1st 2. Korean War, 1950-1953 3. Military campaigns 4. Marines. 5. Korean War, 1950-1953 -- Regimental histories -- United States. 6. Chosin Reservoir, Korea -- History. 7. Korea.
ISBN 9780385541152

LC 2018010543

"A chronicle of the extraordinary feats of heroism by Marines called on to do the impossible during the greatest battle of the Korean War."--Provided by publisher.

"The result is a masterpiece of storytelling about a war that is often given short shrift in American history. Readers will feel the fierce cold, the constant threat of death, and the desperation of being trapped and under siege felt by the U.S. Marines in Sides' vivid and invaluable history. " Booklist.

Weintraub, Stanley, 1929-

A **Christmas** far from home : an epic tale of courage and survival during the Korean War / Stanley Weintraub. Da Capo Press, a member of the Perseus Books Group Press, 2014. 320 p. **951.904**

1. United States. Army. Corps, 10th 2. Korean War, 1950-1953 3. Military campaigns 4. Marines -- United States -- History -- 20th century. 5. Soldiers -- United States -- History -- 20th century. 6. Chosin Reservoir, Korea -- History 7. North Korea
ISBN 9780306822322

LC 2014011944

The epic story of the 1950 Christmas season, when American troops faced extreme cold, a determined enemy, and long odds.

"The tragic tale of how the arrogance of a general led to disastrous consequences for the American troops in North Korea in 1950... Weintraub expertly delineates the unraveling disaster for the entrapped, frozen, dispirited troops on the ground." Kirkus.

951.93 North Korea (People's Democratic Republic of Korea)

Cha, Victor D., 1961-

The **impossible** state : North Korea, past and future / Victor Cha. Ecco, 2012. 544 p. **951.93**

1. Kim, Chong-il, 1942-2011. 2. Kim, Il-song, 1912-1994. 3. Kim, Chong-un, 1984- 4. Kim family. 5. Dictatorship 6. International relations. 7. Political culture -- North Korea -- History. 8. Isolationism. 9. North Korea -- Politics and government. 10. United States -- Foreign relations North Korea.
ISBN 9780061998508

LC 2012009517

"A useful, pertinent work for understanding the human story behind the headlines." Kirkus.

Tudor, Daniel

North Korea confidential : private markets, fashion trends, prison camps, dissenters and defectors / Daniel Tudor, James Pearson. Tuttle Publishing, 2015. 192 p. **951.93**

1. Totalitarianism 2. Dictatorship 3. North Korea -- Social life and customs -- 21st century 4. North Korea -- Social conditions -- 21st century
ISBN 9780804844581

LC 2016469265

"Rather than describing a gray, economically stagnant, and totalitarian society dominated by dictator Kim Jong Un, veteran journalists and coauthors Tudor and Pearson paint a vivid portrait of how North Korea functions by opportunistic entrepreneurism abetted by bribery." Library Journal.

951.9304 North Korea (People's Democratic Republic of Korea)--1945-1994

Lankov, A. N. (Andrei Nikolaevich)

The **real** North Korea : life and politics in the failed Stalinist utopia / Andrei Lankov. Oxford University Press, 2013. 304 p. **951.9304**

1. Kim, Il-song, 1912-1994. 2. Kim, Chong-un, 1984- 3. Communism -- North Korea. 4. Political culture -- North Korea. 5. Social forecasting -- North Korea. 6. Dictators. 7. North Korea -- Politics and government -- 1994-
ISBN 9780199964291

LC 2012046992

After providing an accessible history of the nation, the author turns his focus to what North Korea is, what its leadership thinks and how its people cope with living in such an oppressive and poor place, arguing that North Korea is not irrational, but rather a nation that has survived against all odds.

951.9305 North Korea (People's Democratic Republic of Korea)--1994-

Sweeney, John, 1958-

North Korea undercover : inside the world's most secret state. / John Sweeney. Pegasus Books, 2015. 336 p. **951.9305**

1. Kim, Chong-il, 1942-2011. 2. Kim, Il-song, 1912-1994. 3. Kim, Chong-un, 1984- 4. Kim family. 5. Dictatorship 6. Totalitarianism 7. Isolationism. 8. Political leadership. 9. North Korea -- Social conditions. 10. North Korea -- Politics and government

ISBN 9781605988023

LC 2016303460

An authoritative and, at times, frightening investigation into the dark side of North Korean society.

952 Japan

Gordon, Andrew, 1952-

A **modern** history of Japan : from Tokugawa times to the present / Andrew Gordon. Oxford University Press, 2003. xiv, 384 p. : **952**

1. Japan -- History -- 1868- 2. Japan -- History -- Tokugawa period, 1600-1868.

ISBN 0195110609

LC 2002070916

"The author examines Japan's political, economic, social, and cultural inventions of its modernity in evolving international contexts, incorporating inside viewpoints and debates. Beyond identifying the national stages (feudalism, militarism, democracy), the author innovatively emphasizes how labor unions, cultural figures, and groups in society (especially women) have been affected over time and have responded." Library Journal.

Jansen, Marius

★The **making** of modern Japan / Marius B. Jansen. Belknap Press of Harvard University Press, 2000. 871 p. : **952**

1. Japan -- History -- Tokugawa period, 1600-1868. 2. Japan -- History -- Meiji period, 1868-1912.

ISBN 0674003349

LC 00041352

A sweeping history of modern Japan begins in 1600 and retraces the three major upheavals in Japanese history that have helped shape it into a modern Asian nation.

"Jansen has produced what is sure to become the standard narrative history of modern Japan. In every way this is a remarkable book...and no reference collection on Japan can pretend to be complete without it." Choice.

Perez, Louis G.

The **history** of Japan / Louis G. Perez. Greenwood Press, 2009. xvii, 266 p. : **952**

1. Japan -- History.

ISBN 9780313364426

LC 2008052242

952.03 Japan--1868-1945

Buruma, Ian

Inventing Japan, 1853-1964 / Ian Buruma. The Modern Library, 2003. 194 p. **952.03**

1. Japan -- History -- 1868- 2. Japan -- History -- Restoration, 1853-1870.

ISBN 0679640851

LC 2002026346

"A Modern Library chronicles book."

Traces the history of Japan from the country's nineteenth-century feudal isolation, to its rise to military power and defeat during World War II, to its rebirth as a global economic and working democracy in the postwar era.

"Buruma traces the remarkable metamorphosis that transformed an isolated island shogunate into an expansive military empire and then into a pacified and prosperous democracy. . . . An excellent introductory study." Booklist.

McClain, James

Japan : a modern history / James L. McClain. W.W. Norton & Co., c2002. xxiii, 632, 92 p. : **952.03**

1. Japan -- History -- 1868- 2. Japan -- History -- Tokugawa period, 1600-1868.

ISBN 0393041565

LC 2001034545

A definitive and compelling history of Japan details the tumultuous political, economic, and social change, over four centuries, that molded Japan into a modern world power by bringing to life the many historical figures who helped build a successful and strong nation.

"This is a well-written, well-researched, and easily readable survey of the modern history of a fascinating and important nation." Booklist.

Pleshakov, Konstantin

The **tsar's** last armada : the epic journey to the Battle of Tsushima / Constantine Pleshakov. Basic Books, 2002. xx, 396 p. : **952.03**

1. Russia. Navy -- History. 2. Japan. Navy -- History. 3. Tsushima, Battle of, 1905. 4. Japan -- History -- 20th century. 5. Russia -- History -- 1904-1914.

ISBN 0465057926

LC 2004270583

"A compulsively readable account told from the Russian viewpoint." Booklist.

952.04 Japan--1945-1999

Dower, John W.

Embracing defeat : Japan in the wake of World War II / John W. Dower. W.W. Norton & Co., 1999. 676 p. : **952.04**

1. Hirohito, Emperor of Japan, 1901-1989 2. Tojo, Hideki, 1884-1948. 3. MacArthur, Douglas, 1880-1964. 4. War crime trials. 5. World War II -- Japan. 6. Japan -- History -- Allied Occupation, 1945-1952. 7. Japan -- History -- 1945- 8. Japan -- Politics and government -- 1945- 9. Japan -- Social life and customs -- 1945-

ISBN 0393046869

LC 98022133

ALA Notable Book, 2000.
Mark Lynton History Prize, 2000.
National Book Award for Nonfiction, 1999.
Pulitzer Prize for General Nonfiction, 2000.

National Book Critics Circle Award for Nonfiction finalist, 1999.

Dower illuminates how shattering defeat, followed by years of American military occupation, affected every level of Japanese society in ways that neither the victor nor the vanquished could anticipate. The book vividly portrays the countless ways the Japanese met the challenge of starting over.

"Dower demonstrates an impressive mastery of voluminous sources, both American and Japanese, and he deftly situates the political story within a rich cultural context." Publishers Weekly.

952.05 Japan--2000-

Iyer, Pico

A **beginner's** guide to Japan : observations and provocations / Pico Iyer. Alfred A. Knopf, 2019. 240 p. **952.05**

1. Iyer, Pico 2. Manners and customs 3. Culture 4. Voyages and travels. 5. Japan -- Description and travel. 6. Essays

ISBN 9780451493958

LC 2018038539

A lyrical guide to the enigma of contemporary Japan by the author of The Art of Stillness draws on more than three decades of residence and his local friendships to share unexpected, incisive glimpses into Japan's regional culture and landmarks.

Parry, Richard Lloyd

Ghosts of the tsunami : death and life in Japan's disaster zone / Richard Lloyd Parry. Farrar, Straus and Giroux, 2017. 352 p. **952.05**

1. Tsunamis. 2. Natural disasters. 3. Tohoku Earthquake and Tsunami, Japan, 2011 4. Fukushima Nuclear Disaster, Japan, 2011 5. Japan -- History -- 21st century

ISBN 9780374253974

LC 2017021678

The award-winning correspondent and author of In the Time of Madness presents an account of the events and fallout of the 2011 tsunami in Japan that explores reports of ghosts and hauntings in a community tormented by devastating secrets.

"A sobering and compelling narrative of calamity." Kirkus.

953 Arabian Peninsula and adjacent areas

Filiu, Jean-Pierre

Gaza : a history / Jean-pierre Filiu. Oxford University Press, 2014 440 p. **953**

1. Fatah. 2. Hamas 3. Arab-Israeli conflict. 4. Gaza Strip. 5. West Bank (Jordan River) 6. Israeli-occupied territories 7. Middle East. 8. Palestinian State (Proposed)

ISBN 9780190201890

LC 2013497342

"While the chronological account leaves out some significant discussions, such as everyday politics in Gaza, as in Asef Bayat's Life as Politics: How Ordinary People Change the Middle East (CH, Aug'10, 47-7167), Filiu is at his best when he engages with various sources in uncovering histories mostly ignored or even unknown to many. A must read for students and scholars of the modern Middle East, and anyone who wants to understand Palestinian history. Summing Up: Essential. All public and academic libraries." Choice.

Kennedy, Hugh (Hugh N.)

When Baghdad ruled the Muslim world : the rise and fall of Islam's greatest dynasty / Hugh Kennedy. Perseus Books Group 2006, c2005. 326 p. **953**

1. Islam -- History. 2. Baghdad, Iraq -- History. 3. Islamic Empire -- History -- 661-750. 4. Islamic Empire -- History -- 750-1258. 5. Middle East -- History.

ISBN 0306814803

LC bl2014006703

Originally published in the United Kingdom under as The Court of the Caliphs.

Presents a history of the Abbasid dynasty, the founders of Baghdad, and discusses the politics, military conquests, court life, palace bureacracy, culture, and arts which characterized the era.

"The author has written an informative and sobering lesson for those who idolize the past." Choice.

953.8 Saudi Arabia

House, Karen Elliot

On Saudi Arabia : its people, past, religion, fault lines - and future / Karen Elliot House. Random House Inc, 2012. 336 p. **953.8**

1. National characteristics, Saudi Arabian. 2. Islam and state. 3. Saudi Arabia -- Social life and customs. 4. Saudi Arabia -- Social conditions.

ISBN 9780307272164

LC 2012018977

A Pulitzer Prize-winning journalist from The Wall Street Journal draws on three decades of firsthand experience to profile the Saudi Arabia of today, offering insight into its leaders, citizens, cultural complexities and international prospects.

Wynbrandt, James

A **brief** history of Saudi Arabia / James Wynbrandt, Fawaz A. Gerges. Facts On File, 2010. 368 p. Brief history (Facts on File) **953.8**

1. History. 2. World politics. 3. Saudi Arabia -- History. 4. Middle East -- History.

ISBN 9780816078769

LC 2010005466

953.805 Saudi Arabia--1926-

Lacey, Robert

Inside the Kingdom : kings, clerics, modernists, terrorists, and the struggle for Saudi Arabia / Robert Lacey. Viking, 2009. 432 p. **953.805**

1. Lacey, Robert Travel Saudi Arabia. 2. Islam -- Saudi Arabia. 3. Royal houses -- Saudi Arabia. 4. Saudi Arabia -- History -- 1932- 5. Middle East -- Civilization. 6. Saudi Arabia -- Politics and government -- 1982- 7. Saudi Arabia -- Social conditions. 8. Saudi Arabia -- Description and travel.

ISBN 9780670021185

LC 2009008367

Sequel to: The Kingdom: New York : Harcourt Brace Jovanovich, 1982, c1981.

Tracing a path through the Persian Gulf War and the events of 9/11 to the oil market convulsions of today, this gives readers a modern history of the Saudis in their own words, revealing a people attempting to reconcile life under religious law with the demands of a rapidly changing world.

"The author's eye for sweeping trends and the telling detail combined with the depth, breadth and evenhandedness of his research makes for an indispensable guide." Publishers Weekly.

954 India and neighboring south Asian countries

Black, George, 1949-

On the Ganges : encounters with saints and sinners on India's mythic river / George Black. St Martins Pr., 2018 352 p. **954**

1. Rivers 2. Sacred space 3. Voyages and travels 4. Hinduism 5. Ganges River -- Description and travel 6. India 7. Bangladesh 8. South Asia

ISBN 9781250057358

LC 2018003985

The author of Empire of Shadows presents an extraordinary tour of the Ganges that explores its major regions as well as the eclectic populations that worship the river, pollute it or visit it from all world regions. Map(s).

"Black is a great storyteller, putting scenarios--some familiar, others verging on the surreal--into context. Never condescending or sensationalized, but always interesting, his vignettes capture Indias continuing dependence on Ma Ganga, the great Ganges River." Booklist.

Dalrymple, William

White Mughals : love and betrayal in the eighteenth-century India / William Dalrymple. Viking, 2003. xlvii, 459 p. : **954**

1. East India Company (English) -- History. 2. British in India -- History -- 18th century. 3. Interethnic relations. 4. Men/women relations. 5. India -- Social life and customs -- 1500-1765. 6. India -- History -- 18th century. 7. India -- History -- British occupation, 1765-1947

ISBN 0670031844

LC 2002191082

Shortlisted for the James Tait Black Memorial Prize for Biography, 2003

Traces the practice by British colonizers in India to assume local customs and religious practices, offering a particular focus on James Kirkpatrick, who converted to Islam and spied on the East India Company while having an affair with the great-niece of the region's prime minister.

"This book, ambitious in scope and rich in detail, demonstrates that a century before Kipling's never the twain--and two centuries before neocons and radical Islamists trumpeted the clash of civilizations--the story of the Westerner in Muslim India was one not of conquest but of appreciation, adaptation, and seduction." The New Yorker.

Lapierre, Dominique

The **City** of Joy / Dominique Lapierre ; translated from the French by Kathryn Spink. Warner Books, 1986, c1985. 464 p. ; **954**

1. Personal conduct 2. Altruism. 3. Refugees -- Calcutta, India 4. Calcutta, India -- Description and travel 5. Calcutta, India -- Social conditions.

ISBN 0446355569

LC BL 99963471

Translation of: La Cite de la joie.

Originally published: Garden City, N.Y. : Doubleday, 1985.

Depicts the efforts of four people to improve the harsh conditions of life in the impoverished and over-populated area of Calcutta, India.

Mehta, Suketu

★**Maximum** city : Bombay lost and found / Suketu Mehta. Vintage Books, 2005, c2004. xii, 542 p. : **954**

1. Mehta, Suketu Travel Mumbai, India. 2. City life -- Mumbai, India 3. Mumbai, India -- Description and travel 4. Mumbai, India -- Social life and customs 5. India -- Social life and customs

ISBN 9780375703409

LC bl2005021325

Originally published: New York : Alfred A. Knopf, 2004.

Pulitzer Prize for General Nonfiction finalist

A portrait of Bombay, India, and its people chronicles the everday life of the city and its inhabitants, from the criminal underworld of rival Muslim and Hindu gangs to the diverse people who come from the villages in search of a better life.

"The author explores various aspects of Bombay life, from setting up residence to exploring the hugely successful domestic film industry; from detailing Bombay's sex industry to profiling the reasons behind India's own September 11, the 1993 riots and bombings that exposed a vast enmity between extremist Hindus and Muslims. Mehta delivers a fresh and unblinking look at contemporary Bombay." Booklist.

Miller, Sam, 1962-

Delhi : adventures in a megacity / Sam Miller. St. Martin's Press, 2010. ix, 291 p. : **954**

1. Miller, Sam, 1962- Travel Delhi 2. Journalists -- England 3. City life -- Delhi 4. Megacities 5. Travel writing 6. Delhi -- Description and travel 7. Delhi -- Social life and customs

ISBN 9780312612375

LC 2010013043

"First published in Great Britain by Jonathan Cape"--T.p. verso.

Includes index.

A BBC World Service Trust member and former correspondent presents a provocative and lighthearted portrait of Delhi as viewed by everyday residents from all walks of life that goes beyond tourist perspectives to offer insight into its cultural significance and modern potential.

"The author presents a highly entertaining and witty account of a walking tour of Delhi. He describes 12 walks that begin in the center of the city and proceed outward to the satellite towns at the outskirts. Miller's portrayal of the changing landscape and street life is engrossing." Library Journal.

Sen, Amartya

The **argumentative** Indian : writings on Indian history, culture, and identity / Amartya Sen. Farrar, Straus and Giroux, 2005. xx, 409 p. : **954**

1. India -- Civilization. 2. India -- Social life and customs.

ISBN 0374105839

LC 2005049460

"Sen's lucid reasoning and thoroughgoing humanism...ensure a lively and commanding defense of diversity and dialogue." Publishers Weekly.

Singh, Patwant, 1925-

The **Sikhs** / Patwant Singh. Knopf, 2000. xvii, 276 p., 8 p. of plates : **954**

1. Sikhs -- History. 2. Sikhs -- India -- History. 3. India -- History.

ISBN 0375407286

LC 99031807

A comprehensive history of the Sikh people and religion traces the origins of the sect five centuries ago in India and discusses its current, sometimes violent, role in Indian politics.

"The author traces Sikh history from its origins in the 15th century through Indira Gandhi's 1984 storming of the Golden Temple. Sikhs, he argues, have for centuries been an embattled people because their culture and religion defy the predominant religions in the region, as well as the Indian caste system with its ruling elite." Publishers Weekly.

954.04 India and neighboring south Asian countries--1947-1971

French, Patrick, 1966-

India : a portrait / Patrick French. Random House Inc, 2011. 416 p. **954.04**

1. India -- Social conditions. 2. India -- Politics and government.
ISBN 9780307272430

LC 2011003921

"This work combines deep research about the country's history with a series of vignettes culled from French's street-level reporting. Taken together, his reading of seminal texts and his interviews with politicians, pimps, businessmen, laborers, farmers, scholars and people from all levels of India's caste system result in a fittingly vigorous and colorful book about what it means to live in India six decades after the nation freed itself from British rule." San Francisco Chronicle.

Guha, Ramachandra

India after Gandhi : the history of the world's largest democracy / Ramachandra Guha. Ecco, c2007. xviii, 893 p. : **954.04**

1. India -- History -- 1947- 2. India -- Social life and customs.
ISBN 0060198818

LC 2006052180

Documents the conflicts that have shaped modern India while evaluating the factors that have helped maintain stability and democracy throughout the region.

Hajari, Nisid

Midnight's furies : the deadly legacy of India's partition / Nisid Hajari. Houghton Mifflin Harcourt, 2015. 304 p. ; **954.04**

1. Jinnah, Mahomed Ali, 1876-1948. 2. Nehru, Jawaharlal, 1889-1964. 3. India-Pakistan Conflict, 1947-1949. 4. World politics 5. Colonialism 6. India -- History -- Partition, 1947. 7. Pakistan -- History -- 20th century.
ISBN 9780547669212

LC 2014034426

The author describes how a few bloody months in South Asia during the summer of 1947--the Partition of India, which led to the creation of Pakistan--largely explain the world that troubles us today.

954.05 India and neighboring south Asian countries--1971-

Giridharadas, Anand

India calling : an intimate portrait of a nation's remaking / Anand Giridharadas. Henry Holt & Co, 2011. 288 p. **954.05**

1. East Indian Americans 2. India -- Description and travel.
ISBN 9780805091779

LC 2010018447

"This is a fine book, elegant, self-aware and unafraid of contradictions and complexity. Giridharadas captures fundamental changes in the nature of family and class relationships and the very idea of what it means to be an Indian." New York Times Book Review.

Mishra, Pankaj

★**Temptations** of the West : how to be modern in India, Pakistan, Tibet and beyond / Pankaj Mishra. Farrar, Straus, and Giroux, 2006. 323 p. **954.05**

1. Mishra, Pankaj Travel South Asia. 2. Voyages and travels. 3. Travelers. 4. South Asia -- Description and travel. 5. South Asia -- Western influences. 6. South Asia -- Civilization. 7. Essays.
ISBN 0374173214

LC 2006011987

Essays first appearing in slightly different forms in The New York Review of Books, Granta, The New York Times Magazine, and the Guardian Weekend Magazine.

"A worthwhile read given this region's increasing importance on the world stage, but be braced for discouragement. Suitable for larger public libraries." Library Journal.

954.91 Pakistan

Inskeep, Steve

Instant city : life and death in Karachi / Steve Inskeep. Penguin Group USA, 2011. 288 p. **954.91**

1. City life. 2. Migration, Internal. 3. Prejudice. 4. Pakistan -- Social life and customs.
ISBN 9781594203152

LC 2011020673

Analyzes the growing metropolis of Karachi, Pakistan, including the importance of regional stability to American security interests, the terrorist bombing of a Shia religious procession, and the challenging religious, ethnic, and political divides.

954.9105 Pakistan--1971-

Gul, Imtiaz

The **most** dangerous place : Pakistan's lawless frontier / Imtiaz Gul. Viking, 2010, c2009. xxx, 282 p. : **954.9105**

1. Qaida (Organization) 2. Terrorism -- Pakistan. 3. Terrorism -- Religious aspects -- Islam. 4. Pakistan. 5. Federally Administered Tribal Areas (Pakistan)
ISBN 9780670022250

LC 2010001898

Originally published: The al Qaeda connection. New Delhi : Penguin Books India, 2009.

Explains how Pakistani jihadists have now incorporated suicide bombing into their arsenal and are no longer targeting their enemies but are instead attacking their own country, killing Muslim soldiers and civilians alike.

Lieven, Anatol

Pakistan : a hard country / Anatol Lieven. Perseus Books Group, 2011. 560 p. **954.9105**

1. Politics and culture. 2. International relations. 3. Pakistan.
ISBN 9781610390217

LC 2011921821

Explores nearly every facet of Pakistan--from its regions, ethnicities and religious traditions to its violent history and political tensions, as well as its periods of surprising stability. By the author of Chechnya: Tombstone of Russian Power.

"Lieven breaks down his study by specific region; considers the structures of justice, religion, the military and politics in turn; and, finally, in a skillful, insightful synthesis, addresses the history of and issues concerning the Taliban, both Pakistani and Afghani. A well-reasoned, welcome resource for Western experts and lay readers alike." Kirkus.

954.96 Nepal

Twigger, Robert, 1964-

★**White** mountain : a cultural adventure through the Himalayas / Robert Twigger. Pegasus Books, 2017. 458 pages : **954.96**

1. Mountains 2. Wilderness areas 3. Explorers 4. Exploration 5. Himalaya Mountains 6. Himalaya Mountains region

ISBN 9781681775357

LC bl2017039317

A sweeping biography of the Himalayas by the acclaimed author of Angry White Pyjamas.

955 Iran

Housden, Roger

Saved by beauty : an American romantic in Iran / Roger Housden. Broadway Books, c2011. 320 p. **955**

1. Housden, Roger Travel Iran. 2. Rumi, Jalal al-Din, 1207-1273 3. Hafiz, 1320-1389. 4. Americans in Iran. 5. Intellectual life. 6. Voyages and travels. 7. Travelers 8. Iran -- Description and travel. 9. Iran -- Social life and customs.

ISBN 9780307587732

LC 2011003323

The author of Ten Poems to Change Your Life challenges popular misconceptions about Iran's youth culture, describing his visits to regions that inspired Rumi and Hafez, where he learned about the rich histories, cuisines and arts that comprise everyday life.

"The author documents his travels to Iran in late 2008 and early 2009. The narrative flows seamlessly as the author visits Tehran, paradise gardens in Shiraz, the Pasargadae archaeological site where Cyrus the Great is buried, Persepolis, the Jewish quarter in Yazd, Esfaha-n, Sanandaj, Mashhad, Neysha-bur, Tu-s, Kermanshah, Ahvaz, and Turkey's Bursa and Konya, as well as surrounding settlements, plains, deserts, and mountainous areas. Poetry lovers and adventurers alike will appreciate this work." Library Journal.

Polk, William Roe, 1929-

Understanding Iran : everything you need to know, from Persia to the Islamic Republic, from Cyrus to Ahmadinejad / William R. Polk. Palgrave Macmillan, 2011. xvii, 247 p. : **955**

1. Iran -- History.

ISBN 023010343X

LC oc2011003750

Originally published: 2009.

An accessible history of Iran predicts its eventual cultural and military dominance in the Middle East while illuminating many factors that are commonly misunderstood by the West, including the oppression of citizens under current leadership and their negative regard of western policy.

955.05 Iran--1906-2005

Abrahamian, Ervand, 1940-

The **coup** : 1953, the CIA, and the roots of modern U.S.-Iranian relations / Ervand Abrahamian. The New Press, 2013. 304 p. **955.05**

1. CIA 2. Anglo-Iranian Oil Company 3. Intervention (International relations) 4. Coups d'etat. 5. Oil industry and trade -- Political aspects 6. Iran -- History -- 20th century 7. Iran -- Foreign relations United States. 8. United States -- Foreign relations Iran. 9. Iran -- Foreign relations Great Britain. 10. Great Britain -- Foreign relations Iran.

ISBN 9781595588265

LC 2012031402

"A history of the CIA's 1953 coup in Iran and its aftermath".--Provided by publisher.

Buchan, James

Days of God : the revolution in Iran and its consequences / James Buchan. Simon & Schuster, 2013, c2012. 272 p. **955.05**

1. Khomeini, Ruhollah, 1902-1989 2. Political violence -- Iran -- History -- 20th century. 3. Revolutions. 4. Islam 5. Iran -- History -- Islamic revolution, 1979-1997.

ISBN 9781416597773

LC 2013008890

"Originally published in Great Britain in 2012 by John Murray Publishers"--Title page verso.

An insider's account of the 1979 Iranian Revolution challenges popular beliefs while drawing on a wealth of memoirs, diaries and newspaper reports to discuss such topics as the rise of Ayatollah Khomeini, the establishment of Saddam Hussein's Iraq and the development of Al-Qaida. By the award-winning author of Heart's Journey in Winter.

Cooper, Andrew Scott

The **fall** of heaven : the Pahlavis and the final days of imperial Iran / Andrew Scott Cooper. Henry Holt and Co., 2016. 352 p. **955.05**

1. Mohammed Reza Pahlavi, Shah of Iran, 1919-1980 2. Farah, Empress, consort of Mohammad Reza Pahlavi, Shah of Iran, 1938- 3. Iran -- History -- Mohammed Reza Pahlavi, 1941-1979.

ISBN 9780805098976

LC 2015046095

Describes the rise and fall of the glamorous Pahlavi dynasty in Iran, which began when Mohammad Reza Pahlavi took the throne in 1941 and ended during the Iranian Revolution in 1979 led by the Ayatollah Khomeini.

"A thorough new appraisal of an enigmatic ruler who died believing his people still loved him." Kirkus.

Ghattas, Kim

Black wave : the Saudi-Iran wars on religion and culture that destroyed the Middle East / Kim Ghattas. Henry Holt and Co., 2020. 368 p. **955.05**

1. Islam and politics -- Middle East 2. Social conflict -- Religious aspects. 3. Sunni Islam -- Iraq. 4. Shiites -- Iraq. 5. Middle East -- History -- 1979- 6. Iran -- History -- Islamic revolution, 1979-1997 7. Saudi Arabia

ISBN 9781250131201

LC 2019024945

Chronicles decades of rivalry between Saudia Arabia and Iran, linking the 1979 Iranian revolution, American policy changes, distortions in religious expression and the rise of sectarian violence to present-day perceptions about the Middle East.

"Essential for all who follow world events." Kirkus

Mackey, Sandra, 1937-

The **Iranians** : Persia, Islam, and the soul of a nation, with a new afterword by the author / Sandra Mackey ; W. Scott Harrop, research assistant. Plume Book, 1998, c1996. xxii, 442 p. : **955.05**

1. Islam and politics. 2. Iran -- Politics and government -- 20th century.

ISBN 0452275636

LC 98167695

Provides a portrait of the troubled nation of Iran and the complex religious, historical, political, and cultural forces--especially the dichotomy between Islam and the culture of ancient Persia--that continue to shape it

"The author presents information on Iranian civilization from Cyrus the Great to the present. Throughout this turbulent history of invasions and conquerors, the Persian soul, with its foundations in the Zoroastrian concept of justice overlaid with Shia Islam, has steadfastly endured. Since many Westerners had little familiarity with Iran until the overthrow of the Shah in 1979, this very readable book provides a perspective on what led up to those events, what is happening in Iran today, and how the current situation is likely to affect the future of Iran and its relationship with the West." Library Journal.

Mendez, Antonio J.

Argo : how the CIA and Hollywood pulled off the most audacious rescue in history / Antonio J. Mendez and Matt Baglio. Viking, 2012. 352 p. **955.05**

1. Mendez, Antonio J. 2. CIA 3. Former CIA agents 4. Iran Hostage Crisis, 1979-1981. 5. Diplomats -- United States -- History 6. Undercover operations 7. Canada -- Foreign relations Iran. 8. Iran -- Foreign relations Canada

ISBN 9780670026227

LC 2012014991

An account of the Iran Hostage Crisis and how the United States Central Intelligence Agency and the Government of Canada rescued six American diplomats.

Secor, Laura

Children of paradise : the struggle for the soul of Iran / Laura Secor. Riverhead Books, 2016. 336 p. **955.05**

1. Theocracy. 2. Islam and politics. 3. Iran -- History -- Islamic revolution, 1979-1997. 4. Iran -- Social life and customs.

ISBN 9781594487101

LC 2015509831

Chronicles the events that rendered Iran the first revolutionary theocracy of the modern world, tracing its symbolism as a barometer of Eastern culture and upheaval while exploring the contributions of religion, politics, artists, journalists and activists in shaping the country's present-day circumstances.

Wright, Robert A. (Robert Anthony), 1960-

Our man in Tehran : Ken Taylor and the Iran Hostage crisis / Robert Wright. Other Press, 2011, c2009. 406 p. **955.05**

1. Taylor, Kenneth, 1934- 2. Iran Hostage Crisis, 1979-1981. 3. Diplomats. 4. Intelligence service. 5. Hostages. 6. Iran -- History -- Islamic revolution, 1979-1997.

ISBN 9781590514139

LC 2010020376

Originally published: Toronto ; HarperCollins Canada, c2009.

In November 1979, the American embassy in Tehran was invaded by a group of radical students who took 54 workers hostage. However, six diplomats secretly escaped. Here, author Robert Wright chronicles the escapees' harrowing ordeal and the men and women who were working undercover in Tehran to bring the hostage crisis to an end.

955.06 Iran--2005-

Orth, Stephan, 1979-

Couchsurfing in Iran : revealing a hidden world / Stephan Orth. Greystone Books, 2018, c2015. 240 p. **955.06**

1. Culture 2. Voyages and travels 3. Europeans in the Middle East 4. Stereotypes (Social psychology) 5. Middle East -- Description and travel 6. Iran -- Description and travel

ISBN 9781771642804

LC bl2018179650

Originally published in 2015 by Malik.

The author recounts the sixty-two days he spent traveling around Iran, providing a behind-the-scenes look at life in one of the world's most closed societies, including what he calls the "two Irans" that coexist side by side.

956 Middle East

Barr, James, 1976-

A **line** in the sand : the Anglo-French struggle for the Middle East, 1914-1948 / James Barr. W. W. Norton & Co., 2012. 352 p. **956**

1. Balfour Declaration 2. Zionism 3. Imperialism 4. Middle East -- Politics and government -- 1914-1945 5. Middle East -- Foreign relations 6. Great Britain -- Foreign relations 7. France -- Foreign relations

ISBN 9780393070651

LC 2011038037

Uses recently declassified French and British government documents to describe how the two countries secretly divided the Middle East during World War I and the effect these mandates had on local Arabs and Jews.

Collins, Larry

O Jerusalem! / Larry Collins and Dominique Lapierre. Simon & Schuster, 1988, c1972. 635 p. : **956**

1. Israel-Arab War, 1948-1949 -- Jerusalem, Israel. 2. Jerusalem, Israel -- History -- 1948-1949.

ISBN 0671662414

LC 87038121

An account of the bitter 1948 dispute between the Arabs and Jews over Jerusalem, highlights the role of the British as well as prominent individuals in the struggle.

Lambert, Malcolm (Malcolm D.)

God's armies : crusade and jihad: origins, history, aftermath / Malcolm Lambert. WW Norton & Co Inc., 2016. 352 p. **956**

1. Jihad. 2. Crusades. 3. War -- Religious aspects. 4. Islam -- Relations -- Christianity. 5. Middle East -- History

ISBN 9781681772240

LC 2017275409

Chronicling the Christian and Islamic struggle to control the sacred places of Palestine and the Middle East between the 7th and 13th century, a dynamic new history, placing equal emphasis on the inner histories of Christianity and Islam, traces the origins and development of the crusade and jihad.

"An all-encompassing introduction to the Christian-Islamic struggle for the armchair history buff." Kirkus.

Lewis, Bernard, 1916-

The **Middle** East : a brief history of the last 2,000 years / Bernard Lewis. Simon & Schuster, 1997, c1995. xii, 433 p. : **956**

1. Middle East -- History.

ISBN 0684832801

LC BL 99790901

"A Touchstone book."

Originally published: New York : Scribner, 1995.

National Book Critics Circle Award for Nonfiction finalist, 1996.

A popular history of the Middle East traces the rise and spread of Islam throughout this volatile region, the impact of Western ideas and technology, and Islamic fundamentalism and its struggle to control the spread of Western thought.

"Lewis has chosen to accentuate the social, economic, and cultural changes that have occurred over 20 centuries. He ranges from seemingly trivial concerns (changes in dress and manners in an Arab coffeehouse) to earth-shaking events (the Mongol conquest of Mesopotamia) in painting a rich, varied, and fascinating portrait of a region that is steeped in traditionalism while often forced by geography and politics to accept change." Booklist.

Lust, Ellen,

★The **Middle** East / Ellen Lust, editor Sage/CQ Press, 2017 xxxiii, 1020 p. : **956**

1. Middle East -- Politics and government -- 1979-

ISBN 9781506329284

LC 2015045140

Morris, Benny, 1948-

Righteous victims : a history of the Zionist-Arab conflict, 1881-1999 / Benny Morris. Knopf, 1999. xiv, 751 p. **956**

1. Arab-Israeli conflict. 2. Arab-Israeli relations -- 1917- 3. Israeli-Palestinian relations. 4. Oslo Accords, 1993. 5. Israel -- History -- 20th century. 6. Palestine -- History -- 20th century.

ISBN 0679421203

LC 98042774

"The author displays a remarkable grasp of the history of the Zionist-Arab conflict and an analytical style that is devoid of the polemics that have characterized so many books on this subject." Library Journal.

956.04 Middle East--1945-1980

Fisk, Robert

The **great** war for civilisation : the conquest of the Middle East / Robert Fisk. Alfred A. Knopf, 2005. xxii, 1107 p. : **956.04**

1. War and society -- Middle East. 2. Middle East -- History, Military -- 20th century. 3. Middle East -- History, Military -- 21st century. 4. Middle East -- Colonization. 5. United States -- Foreign relations Middle East. 6. Middle East -- Foreign relations United States.

ISBN 1400041511

LC 2005049813

National Book Critics Circle Award for Nonfiction finalist, 2005.

A journalist in the Middle East for more than thirty years brings his intimate knowledge of the region to address the recent historical and political events in Iraq, Iran, Afghanistan, Algeria, Israel, and Lebanon.

Friedman, Thomas L.

From Beirut to Jerusalem : updated with a new chapter / Thomas L. Friedman. Anchor Books, 1995, c1989. xv, 588 p. **956.04**

1. Friedman, Thomas L. Travel Middle East. 2. Arab-Israeli conflict. 3. Palestinians -- History. 4. Jews -- Arab countries. 5. Middle East -- Politics and government -- 1979- 6. Lebanon -- History -- Israeli intervention, 1982-1985 7. Lebanon -- Politics and government -- 1975-1990 8. Israel -- Politics and government -- 1978- 9. Middle East -- Foreign relations. 10. Israel -- Foreign relations Lebanon. 11. Lebanon -- Foreign relations Israel.

ISBN 0385413726

LC 95001665

Includes index.

Originally published: New York : Farrar, Straus, Giroux, 1989.

ALA Notable Book, 1990.

National Book Award for Nonfiction, 1989.

The New York Times Middle East correspondent profiles this troubled region, describing the everyday horrors of Beirut, the intricacies of Arab politics, Arab-Israeli relations, and American perceptions of the region.

"When recounting his frequently harrowing experiences in that troubled region, Friedman can be absolutely riveting; similarly, his historical insights, his explanation of the root causes of the Arab-Israeli conflict, and his impressions of people and places in the Holy Land never fail to fascinate." Booklist.

Gandt, Robert L.

Angels in the sky : how a band of volunteer airmen saved the new state of Israel / Robert Gandt. W.W. Norton & Company, 2017 320 p. **956.04**

1. Israel. Hel ha-avir -- History. 2. Israel-Arab War, 1948-1949 -- Aerial operations. 3. Fighter pilots. 4. Military aviation 5. Military pilots 6. Israel -- History -- 20th century

ISBN 9780393254778

LC 2017028807

Explains how an all-volunteer air force helped defeat five Arab nations and protect the fledgling Jewish state of Israel during the 1948 Arab-Israeli War.

"An exciting military chronicle packed with well-documented, intimate portraits of a group of brave pilots." Kirkus.

Meyer, Karl E. (Karl Ernest), 1937-

Kingmakers : the invention of the modern Middle East / Karl E. Meyer and Shareen Blair Brysac. Norton, 2008. 480 p. **956.04**

1. Britons in the Middle East -- History 2. Americans in the Middle East -- History 3. Middle East -- History -- 20th century.

ISBN 9780393061994

LC 2008007378

"The authors have written a timely and engrossing study of the men and women who were instrumental in giving birth to some of the nations, institutions, and chronic problems of the area." Booklist.

Oren, Michael B., 1955-

Six days of war : June 1967 and the making of the modern Middle East / Michael B. Oren. Oxford University Press, 2002. xv, 446 p., 16 p. of plates : **956.04**

1. Arab-Israeli relations -- 1967-1973. 2. Israel-Arab War, 1967. 3. Military occupation. 4. West Bank (Jordan River) -- History. 5. Gaza Strip -- Politics and government 6. Israel -- History -- 1948-1967. 7.

Israel -- Politics and government -- 1948-
ISBN 0195151747

LC 2001058823

Relates the events of the six-day Arab-Israeli War of June, 1967, discussing it in the context of regional and international politics and examining its consequences for the Middle East.

"What makes this book important is the breadth and depth of the research. Oren draws on archives, newly declassified documents, memoirs and interviews from Israel, America, Britain and what was then the Soviet Union." New York Times Book Review.

Sacco, Joe

Footnotes in Gaza / Joe Sacco. Metropolitan Books, 2009. 432 p. **956.04**

1. Arab-Israeli conflict. 2. Arab-Israeli relations. 3. Violence -- Gaza Strip. 4. Massacres. 5. Gaza Strip. 6. Egypt -- History -- Intervention, 1956 7. Comics and Graphic novels

ISBN 9780805073478

LC 2009028433

"From the great cartoonist-reporter, a sweeping, original investigation of a forgotten crime in the most vexed of places. Rafah, a town at the bottommost tip of the Gaza Strip, is a squalid place. Raw concrete buildings front trash-strewn alleys. The narrow streets are crowded with young children and unemployed men. On the border with Egypt, swaths of Rafah have been bulldozed to rubble. Rafah is today and has always been a notorious flashpoint in this bitterest of conflicts. Buried deep in the archives is one bloody incident, in 1956, that left 111 Palestinians dead, shot by Israeli soldiers. Seemingly a footnote to a long history of killing, that day in Rafah-- cold-blooded massacre or dreadful mistake-- reveals the competing truths that have come to define an intractable war. In a quest to get to the heart of what happened, Joe Sacco immerses himself in daily life of Rafah and the neighboring town of Khan Younis, uncovering Gaza past and present. Spanning fifty years, moving fluidly between one war and the next, alive with the voices of fugitives and schoolchildren, widows and sheikhs, Footnotes in Gaza captures the essence of a tragedy".-- from publisher's web site.

Shlaim, Avi

The **iron** wall : Israel and the Arab world / Avi Shlaim. W.W. Norton, c2000. xxv, 670 p. : **956.04**

1. Arab-Israeli conflict. 2. Israel -- Foreign relations. 3. Middle East -- History.

ISBN 9780393048162

LC 99023121

Challenging the consequences of the political, social, and military miracles of the modern State of Israel, the author argues that the "Iron Wall" strategy of making Israel the dominant state in the region has not produced large-scale peace or prosperity in the Middle East.

"A thorough analysis of Israel's relationships with the West as well as its neighbors from a controversial but thoughtful point of view." Booklist.

Wright, Lawrence, 1947-

★**Thirteen** days in September : Carter, Begin, and Sadat at Camp David / Lawrence Wright. Alfred A. Knopf, 2014. 360 p. **956.04**

1. Carter, Jimmy, 1924- 2. Begin, Menachem, 1913-1992. 3. Sadat, Anwar, 1918-1981 4. Arab-Israeli conflict. 5. Israel-Arab War, 1973 6. Camp David Accords, 1978

ISBN 9780385352031

LC 2013497329

Andrew Carnegie Medal for Excellence in Non-Fiction finalist, 2015.

In September 1978, President Jimmy Carter brought representatives of Israel and Egypt together at Camp David (the U.S. president's retreat in Maryland) and persuaded them to sign a peace treaty. This detailed, authoritative account provides a compelling day-by-day chronicle of the two weeks in which President Carter, Israeli Prime Minister Menachem Begin, and Egyptian President Anwar Sadat negotiated a historic agreement that paved the way for subsequent progress toward Middle Eastern peace. Character profiles of the participants and commentary on how Judaism, Islam, and Christianity influenced the negotiations, this study vividly dramatizes and humanizes the momentous conference.

956.05 Middle East (Near East)--1980-

Bacevich, Andrew J.

★**America's** war for the greater Middle East : a military history / Andrew J. Bacevich. Random House, 2016 480 p. **956.05**

1. Military policy. 2. Military history. 3. International relations. 4. Intervention (International relations) 5. United States -- Foreign relations Middle East. 6. Middle East -- Foreign relations United States. 7. United States -- History, Military.

ISBN 9780553393934

LC 2015038868

A critical assessment of America's foreign policy in the Middle East throughout the past four decades evaluates and connects regional engagements since 1990 while revealing their massive costs

Miller, Aaron David

The **much** too promised land : America's elusive search for Arab-Israeli peace / Aaron David Miller. Bantam Books, 2008. 416p. **956.05**

1. Arab-Israeli conflict -- 1973-1993. 2. Arab-Israeli conflict -- 1993- -- Peace. 3. Palestins -- Politics and government -- 1993- 4. United States -- Foreign relations Middle East. 5. Middle East -- Foreign relations United States. 6. Israel -- Politics and government -- 1973-1993. 7. Israel -- Politics and government -- 1993-

ISBN 0553804901

LC 2007038982

A Middle East advisor examines efforts to broker peace between Israel and its Arab neighbors; tackles complex issues of history, religion, culture, domestic politics, national security, and foreign policy; and offers practical solutions for the future.

Said, Edward W., 1935-2003

The **end** of the peace process : Oslo and after / Edward W. Said. Pantheon Books, 2000. xxi, 345 p. **956.05**

1. Israel-Arab War, 1993. 2. Arab-Israeli relations -- 1993- -- Peace. 3. Arab-Israeli conflict. 4. Israeli-Palestinian relations. 5. Essays.

ISBN 0375409300

LC 99044765

Includes index.

Contains 50 essays on life in Israel and Palestine as a result of the 1993 Oslo Accords.

"The author provides analysis of the pitfalls of the Oslo agreement. Most of the essays in this collection have appeared in Cairo's al-Ahram Weekly and al-Hayat, London's Arabic-language daily. Each essay is Said's reflection on a dimension of the Palestinian predicament. He is as critical of the corruption, incompetence, and authoritarianism of the Palestinian Authority as he is of American and Israeli postures." Library Journal.

Shavit, Ari

My promised land : the triumph and tragedy of Israel / Ari Shavit. Spiegel & Grau, 2013. 480 p. **956.05**

1. Arab-Israeli conflict. 2. Zionism 3. Arab-Israeli relations. 4. Jews, Israeli 5. Israel -- Interethnic relations. 6. Israel -- Politics and government.

ISBN 9780385521703

LC 2012046122

National Jewish Book Award, 2013.

Presents an examination of Israel that traces the events that led the country to its current state of conflict through the stories of everyday citizens to illuminate the importance of lesser-known historical events.

Wright, Robin B., 1948-

Dreams and shadows : the future of the Middle East / Robin Wright. Penguin Press, 2008. 480 p. **956.05**

1. Middle East -- History. 2. Middle East -- Politics and government -- 21st century.

ISBN 1594201110

LC 2007046267

A field report by a renowned regional specialist documents the major crises that have overshadowed the Middle East throughout the past thirty years, offering insight into the decisive events that are reshaping the region.

956.054 Middle East, 2000-

Weiss, Michael

ISIS : inside the army of terror / Michael Weiss and Hassan Hassan. Regan Arts, 2015. 288 p. **956.054**

1. ISIS (Islamic State of Iraq and Syria) 2. Terrorism -- Religious aspects -- Islam. 3. Terrorists -- Iraq. 4. Fundamentalism 5. Violence 6. Middle East -- History -- 21st century.

ISBN 9781941393574

LC 2015930621

"How did a group of religious fanatics, clad in black pajamas and armed to the teeth, manage to carve out a violent, fundamentalist "Islamic state" in wide swaths of Syria and Iraq? How did the widely celebrated revolution against Syrian dictator Bashar Assad descend into a movement led by a psychopathically violent band of jihadists dedicated to the destruction of America? And just who are these brutal Islamic militants--many speaking unaccented English and holding European passports--beheading Western hostages in slickly produced videos? In Isis: Inside the Army of Terror, Syrian journalist Hassan Hassan and American analyst Michael Weiss explain how the terrorists of ISIS evolved from a nearly defeated insurgent group into a jihadi army--armed with American military hardware and the capability to administer a functioning state. Weiss and Hassan, who have both been on the frontlines of the Syrian revolution, have interviewed dozens of experts, American military and intelligence officials, and ISIS fighters to paint the first comprehensive picture of the rise and expansion of America's most formidable terrorist enemy. ISIS: Inside the Army of Terror is destined to become the standard text on a terror group that, unfortunately, shows no signs of going away".-- provided by publisher.

956.1 Turkey

Finkel, Caroline

★**Osman's** dream : the story of the Ottoman Empire, 1300-1923 / Caroline Finkel. Basic Books, 2006, c2005. xix, 660 p. : **956.1**

1. Osman I, Sultan of the Turks, 1258-1326. 2. Rulers. 3. Empires. 4. Civilization, Islamic. 5. Turkey -- History -- Ottoman Empire, 1288-1918.

ISBN 9780465023967

LC bl2006029375

Originally published: London : John Murray Publishers, 2005.

An account of the epic story of the Ottoman empire, from its origins in the thirteenth century through its destruction on the battlefields of World War I.

"This history makes a riveting and enjoyable read for all audiences." Publishers Weekly.

Goodwin, Jason, 1964-

Lords of the horizons : a history of the Ottoman Empire / Jason Goodwin. H. Holt, 1999, c1998. xv, 351 p. : **956.1**

1. Islam and state. 2. Religion and culture. 3. Culture. 4. Turkey -- History -- Ottoman Empire, 1288-1918.

ISBN 9780805040814

LC 98041601

"A John Macrae book."

Originally published: London : Chatto & Windus, 1998.

An evocation of the lost world of the Ottoman Empire traces the rise of the Turks, showing their early world dominance, which touched Europe, Africa, and India, and exploring the Empire's long degeneration and fall.

"A history of distinctive originality, Goodwin's account imbibes deeply of traveler's impressions and seeks to see and describe, rather than explain and judge. A valuable synthesis." Booklist.

Kinzer, Stephen

Crescent and star : Turkey between two worlds / Stephen Kinzer. Farrar, Straus and Giroux, 2001. xi, 252 p. **956.1**

1. Islam 2. Islam and politics. 3. Islam and state. 4. State (Political science) 5. Turkey -- Politics and government -- 20th century. 6. Turkey -- Interethnic relations -- History -- 20th century. 7. Turkey -- Armed Forces -- Political activity -- History -- 20th century. 8. Turkey -- Social life and customs -- 20th century.

ISBN 9780374131432

LC 2001023298

Includes index.

Examining the glories of its past and its hopes for the future, the author explores Turkey's unrealized potential as a nation poised between Europe and Asia.

"The author gives a concise introduction to Turkey: Kemal Atatrk's post-WWI establishment of the modern secular Turkish state; the odd makeup of contemporary society, in which the military enforces Atatrk's reforms. In stylized but substantive prose, he devotes chapters to the problems he sees plaguing Turkish society: Islamic fundamentalism, frictions regarding the large Kurdish minority and the lack of democratic freedoms." Publishers Weekly.

Ureneck, Lou

The **great** fire : one American's mission to rescue victims of the 20th century's first genocide / Lou Ureneck. Ecco Press, 2015 320 p. **956.1**

1. Jennings, Asa Kent, 1877-1933 2. Armenian genocide, 1915-1923. 3. Genocide. 4. War crimes 5. Refugees, Armenian. 6. Turkey -- History -- 20th century. 7. Izmir, Turkey.

ISBN 9780062259882

LC bl2015016238

In 1922, Asa Jennings, a YMCA worker from upstate New York, arrives in Smyrna to teach sports to boys, but instead works tirelessly to help rescue more than 250,000 refugees during the genocide of Armenian and Greek Christians with the help of a principled American naval officer and a handful of others.

"This account is written with fans of popular narrative history in mind. Despite the muddled material, many will find this a worthwhile read. Students of this dark part of history, however, will most appreciate Ureneck's research." Library Journal.

956.103 Turkey--1950-1999

Mango, Andrew

The **Turks** today / Andrew Mango. Overlook Press, 2004. xii, 292 p. : **956.103**

1. Turks. 2. Turkey -- History. 3. Turkey -- Politics and government. 4. Middle East -- History.
ISBN 1585676152

LC 2004058339

"This fascinating ... survey is both a political history and a cultural examination of a diverse, dynamic society." Booklist.

956.6 Eastern Turkey

Akcam, Taner, 1953-

A **shameful** act : the Armenian genocide and the question of Turkish responsibility / Taner Akcam ; translated by Paul Bessemer. Metropolitan Books, 2006. x, 483 p. : **956.6**

1. Armenian genocide, 1915-1923. 2. Genocide. 3. War crimes. 4. Turkey -- History -- 20th century.
ISBN 0805079327

LC 2005058401

"Originally published in Turkey in 1999 under the title Insan hakları ve Ermeni sorunu : Ittihat ve Terakki'den Kurtulus Savası'na"--T.p. verso.

A study of the Armenian genocide draws on Ottoman sources, including parliamentary minutes, letters, military and court records, and eyewitness accounts, to lay responsibility for the event on Turkish authorities, revealing a systematic orchestration of the killings by the military, ruling political parties, and the Ottoman state.

Balakian, Peter, 1951-

★The **burning** Tigris : the Armenian genocide and America's response / Peter Balakian. Harper Collins, 2003. xx, 475 p. : **956.6**

1. Armenians in Turkey -- History -- 20th century. 2. Armenian genocide, 1915-1923. 3. Genocide -- Turkey -- History -- 20th century. 4. Human rights. 5. Turkey -- History -- 1909-
ISBN 0060198400

LC 2003044986

"The book's real power derives from the eyewitness accounts of the genocide itself. The sheer volume of outsiders' testimony that Balakian compiles, and the horrifying similarity of their observations of men, women and children beaten, tortured, burned to death in churches or sent out into the desert to starve, is an overwhelmingly convincing retort to genocide deniers." New York Times Book Review.

Suny, Ronald Grigor

They can live in the desert but nowhere else : a history of the Armenian genocide / Ronald Grigor Suny. Princeton Univ Pr., 2015. 408 p. **956.6**

1. Armenian genocide, 1915-1923. 2. Crimes against humanity. 3. Atrocities. 4. Genocide. 5. Turkey -- History -- Ottoman Empire, 1288-1918.
ISBN 9780691147307

LC 2014041347

"Suny weaves this complex story into a nuanced, meticulously researched, and compellingly argued book. Summing Up: Highly recommended. Advanced undergraduate and graduate collections." Choice.

956.7 Iraq

Polk, William R. (William Roe), 1929-

★**Understanding** Iraq : the whole sweep of Iraqi history, from Genghis Khan's Mongols to the Ottoman Turks to the British mandate to the American occupation / William R. Polk. Harper Collins, 2005. xviii, 221 p. : **956.7**

1. Iraq War, 2003-2011 2. Iraq -- History. 3. United States -- Foreign relations Iraq. 4. Iraq -- Foreign relations United States.
ISBN 0060764686

LC 2005281319

A historical explanation of the U.S.'s decision to intervene in Iraq explains the Middle-Eastern nation's potential future role in the face of the world's growing energy needs, offering insight into the economic and political forces shaping the region and the events that will affect U.S.-Iraqi relations.

"This is a sober and informed account of Iraq's history, culminating in a compelling critique of the U.S. intervention there." Foreign Affairs.

Robertson, John F.

Iraq : a short history / John F. Robertson. Oneworld, 2015. 336 p. **956.7**

1. Iraq -- History
ISBN 9781851685868

LC bl2015041248

John Robertson canvases the entirety of Iraq's rich history, from the seminal advances of its Neolithic inhabitants to the aftermath of the American-led invasion and Iraq today. Grounded in extensive research, this balanced account of a country and its people explores the greatness and grandeur of Iraq's achievements, the brutality and magnificence of its ancient empires, its contributions to the emergence of the world's enduring monotheistic faiths, and the role the great Arab caliphs of Baghdad played in the medieval cultural flowering that contributed so much to the European Renaissance and the eventual rise of the West.

"Few books in English cover Iraq's entire history in such a holistic manner. This highly readable and informative book will be a valuable tool in teaching and research for informed general readers and Middle East specialists." Library Journal.

Sky, Emma

The **unraveling** : high hopes and missed opportunities in Iraq / Emma Sky. Public Affairs, 2015. 496 p. **956.7**

1. Iraq War, 2003-2011. 2. Women and the military. 3. Postwar reconstruction. 4. Militarism.
ISBN 9781610395939

LC 2015932207

A British civilian who became the unlikely confidante of American General Odierno tells the story of the U.S.'s strategic failures and efforts to rebuild Iraq, the ongoing catastrophe there, and the people at the center of it all.

"At once informative and emotional, this book will find a wide audience of adult readers, especially those interested in global politics and current events." Library Journal.

956.704 Iraq--1920-

Tripp, Charles

A **history** of Iraq / Charles Tripp. Cambridge University Press, 2000. xvii, 311 p. : **956.704**

1. Iraq -- History -- 1921- 2. Middle East -- History.
ISBN 9780521554046

LC 2001274022

Tripp's book traces Iraq's political history from its nineteenth-century roots in the Ottoman empire, to the development of the state, its transformation from monarchy to republic and the rise of the Ba'th party and the ascendancy and current rule of Saddam Husain. This is a story of social conflict, of power struggles between rival clans, of hostility and wars with neighboring states, as well as of their aftermath, and Iraq's deteriorating relations with the West.

956.7044 Iraq--1979-

Allawi, Ali A., 1947-

The **occupation** of Iraq : winning the war, losing the peace / Ali A. Allawi. Yale University Press, 2007. xxiv, 518 p. : **956.7044**

1. Iraq War, 2003-2011 2. Iraq -- Politics and government -- 2003-
ISBN 9780300110159

LC 2006039445

The former Iraqi Defense Minister examines what the United States did and didn't know at the time of the invasion, the reasons for the confused and contradictory polices, and the emergence of the Iraqi political class during the transition process.

"This scholarly yet immensely readable exposition of Iraqi society and politics will likely become the standard reference on post-9/11 Iraq." Publishers Weekly.

Atkinson, Rick

Crusade : the untold story of the Persian Gulf War / Rick Atkinson. Houghton Mifflin, 1993. xii, 575 p. : **956.7044**

1. Persian Gulf War, 1991. 2. Military history. 3. Armed forces. 4. United States -- History, Military -- 20th century.
ISBN 0395710839

LC 93014388

Integrating interviews with individuals ranging from senior policymakers to frontline soldiers, a look at the Persian Gulf War shows how the conflict transformed modern warfare

"The author provides an account of the actions and utterances of those who directed and fought in the Persian Gulf War. He also provides a thorough analysis of diplomatic and political aspects of the conflict. Rich in pertinent details, the powerful narrative leaps nimbly from Washington to Riyadh, from Baghdad to Kuwait City, and to various battle sites across the sands. Expectedly, the book's dominant personality is General H. Norman Schwarzkopf." Publishers Weekly.

In the company of soldiers : a chronicle of combat / Rick Atkinson. Henry Holt, 2005, c2004. xi, 322 p. : **956.7044**

1. United States. Army. Airborne Division, 101st 2. United States. Army Military life. 3. Iraq War, 2003-2011 4. Armed forces. 5. Military campaigns 6. Military history.
ISBN 0805077731

LC bl2005003694

Reprint. Originally published: 2004.
Includes index.

The author provides an eyewitness account of life on the front lines in Iraq with a portrait of the remarkable soldiers and leaders of the 101st Airborne Division.

"In the spring of 2003, the author accompanied combat units to Iraq. He spent two months embedded with the 101st Airborne Division's headquarters staff, sharing their daily experiences from initial deployment out of Fort Campbell, KY, to overseas staging areas in Kuwait, and ultimately bearing witness to the unit's march on Baghdad. His view of the war was from a vantage point that permitted scrutiny of strategy, planning, and decision making at the senior command level." School Library Journal.

Bolger, Daniel P., 1957-

Why we lost : a general's inside account of the Iraq and Afghanistan Wars / Daniel P. Bolger. Houghton Mifflin Harcourt, 2014. 400 p. **956.7044**

1. Iraq War, 2003-2011 2. Afghan War, 2001- 3. National security 4. Military strategy 5. United States -- Military policy
ISBN 9780544370487

LC 2014026908

A three-star general offers a gripping insider account of the U.S. wars in Iraq and Afghanistan, and how it all went wrong.

"Bolger does a fine job of delineating the technical aspects of military workings (while making good fun of the euphemistic names of the various operations labeled by the 'guys in the Pentagon basement') and candidly describes America's efforts after a decade of attrition as 'global containment of Islamic threats.' With vigorous, no-nonsense prose and an impressive clarity of vision, this general does not mince blame in this chronicle o f failure." Kirkus.

Chandrasekaran, Rajiv

Imperial life in the Emerald City : inside Iraq's green zone / Rajiv Chandrasekaran. Alfred A. Knopf, 2006. x, 320 p. : **956.7044**

1. Coalition Provisional Authority. 2. Postwar reconstruction -- Iraq. 3. Iraq War, 2003-2011 4. Political corruption. 5. Iraq -- History -- 2003- 6. United States -- Politics and government -- 2001-2009 7. First person narratives
ISBN 1400044871

LC 2006041014

Book made into a movie called Green zone.
Samuel Johnson Prize for Nonfiction, 2007.
National Book Award for Nonfiction finalist, 2006

A journalist and former Baghdad bureau chief for The Washington Post furnishes a revealing look at life in Baghdad's Green Zone, the headquarters for the American occupation in Iraq, criticizing the follies and foibles of L. Paul Bremer and others in the invasion and reconstruction of Iraq.

"This is a clearly written, blessedly undidactic book. It should be read by anyone who wants to understand how things went so badly wrong in Iraq." New York Times Book Review.

Draper, Robert

★**To** start a war : how the Bush administration took America into Iraq / Robert Draper. Penguin Press, 2020. xiv, 480 p. **956.7044**

1. Bush, George W. (George Walker), 1946- Military leadership 2. Iraq War, 2003-2011 -- Causes 3. Presidents -- United States 4.

Cabinet officers -- United States 5. Military intelligence 6. United States -- Politics and government -- 2001-2009 7. United States -- History -- 21st century

ISBN 9780525561040

LC 2020001715

From the author of Dead Certain comes the definitive, revelatory reckoning with arguably the most consequential decision in the history of American foreign policy--the decision to invade Iraq. Even now, after more than fifteen years, it is hard to see the these events through the cool, considered gaze of history. For too many people, the damage is still too palpable, and still unfolding. Robert Draper's prodigious reporting has yielded scores of consequential new revelations, from the important to the merely absurd. As a whole, the book paints a vivid and indelible picture of a decision-making process that was fatally compromised by a combination of post-9/11 fear and paranoia, rank naivete, craven group-think, and a set of actors who gamed the process relentlessly.

"Although exhaustive details might discourage general audiences, informed readers and foreign policy specialists will be engaged in what is likely the definitive contemporary account of the origins of the War in Iraq." Library Journal

Filkins, Dexter

★The **forever** war / Dexter Filkins. Alfred A. Knopf, 2008. 384 p. **956.7044**

1. Taliban 2. Iraq War, 2003-2011 3. War on Terrorism, 2001-2009 4. World politics. 5. Terrorism. 6. Middle East -- Politics and government.

ISBN 9780307266392

LC 2008011761

National Book Critics Circle Award for Non-Fiction, 2008.

ALA Notable Book, 2009.

Provides a firsthand account of the battle against Islamic fundamentalism, from the rise of the Taliban in the 1990s, to the terrorist attacks of 9/11, to the wars in Afghanistan and Iraq, offering a study of the people involved from all sides of the conflict.

Finkel, David, 1955-

The **good** soldiers / David Finkel. Farrar, Straus and Giroux, 2009. 304 p. **956.7044**

1. United States. Army Military life. 2. Iraq War, 2003-2011 3. Military campaigns 4. Battles 5. Soldiers -- United States 6. Iraq -- History -- 2003-

ISBN 9780374165734

LC 2009019391

J. Anthony Lukas Book Prize, 2010.

ALA Notable Book, 2010.

Relates the author's experiences as an embedded reporter with Battalion 2-16, telling the story of the surge from the perspective of the someone who worked with the soldiers every day.

Frederick, Jim, 1971-

Black hearts : one platoon's plunge into madness in the triangle of death and the American struggle in Iraq / Jim Frederick. Harmony Books, c2010. 352 p. **956.7044**

1. United States. Army. Airborne Division, 101st 2. Iraq War, 2003-2011 -- Atrocities -- Mahmudiyah, Iraq 3. War crimes -- Mahmudiyah, Iraq 4. Murder -- Mahmudiyah, Iraq 5. Rape -- Mahmudiyah, Iraq 6. Iraq -- Social life and customs -- 21st century 7. Mahmudiyah, Iraq

ISBN 9780307450753

LC 2009035537

Documents the events surrounding the tragic rape of a 14-year-old Iraqi girl and the executions of her family members by members of the 502nd Infantry Regiment, citing contributing factors while examining the event's relevance in shaping future military initiatives.

Gordon, Michael R., 1951-

The **end** game : the hidden history of America's struggle to build democracy in Iraq / Michael R. Gordon and Gen. Bernard E. Trainor. Random House, 2012. xix, 779 p., 24 p. of plates : **956.7044**

1. Democracy 2. Nation-building 3. Iraq War, 2003-2011 4. Politicians 5. United States -- Armed Forces -- History 6. Iraq -- Politics and government 7. United States -- Foreign relations Middle East

ISBN 9780307377227

LC 2012024746

Also published under the title The endgame : the inside story of the struggle for Iraq, from George W. Bush to Barack Obama.

An inside account based on extensive reporting from Iraq between 2006 and 2011 as well as highly classified military and diplomatic information offers insight into the political struggles shaping the war in Iraq.

Gordon, Michael R., 1951-

The **generals'** war : the inside story of the conflict in the Gulf / Michael R. Gordon and Bernard E. Trainor. Back Bay Books, 1995. xv, 551 p. : **956.7044**

1. Persian Gulf War, 1991. 2. Military strategy -- United States. 3. Command of troops. 4. Leadership in men. 5. Iraq -- History -- 1991-2003.

ISBN 0316321001

LC BL 99769186

An account of the war in the Persian Gulf takes readers behind the scenes at the Pentagon and the White House to provide portraits of the top military commanders and to discuss what worked and what did not.

"This cogent analysis provides several disturbing answers worthy of our attention." Library Journal.

Gourevitch, Philip, 1961-

Standard operating procedure / Philip Gourevitch and Errol Morris. Penguin Press, 2008. 288 p. **956.7044**

1. Abu Ghraib Prison. 2. Iraq War, 2003-2011, American 3. Iraq War, 2003-2011, Iraqi. 4. Iraq War, 2003-2011 -- Prisoners and prisons, American 5. Iraq War, 2003-2011 -- Atrocities

ISBN 1594201323

LC bl2008000199

Later published under the title: The ballad of Abu Ghraib: 2009.

Collects the stories of the American soldiers who took and appeared in the controversial digital photographs from Abu Ghraib, in a collaborative account of Iraq's occupation that reveals how it is being experienced by both guards and prisoners.

"This deft piece of reportage will stir readers' anger, at both the actions and the consequences. A thorough, terrifying account of an American-made bedlam." Publishers Weekly.

Haass, Richard N.

War of necessity : war of choice / Richard N. Haass. Simon & Schuster, c2009. 336 p. **956.7044**

1. Bush, George W. (George Walker), 1946- Political and social views. 2. Bush, George, 1924-2018 Political and social views. 3. Iraq War, 2003-2011 -- Causes 4. Persian Gulf War, 1991 -- Causes. 5. War. 6. Iraq War, 2003-2011 -- Political aspects. 7. United States -- Politics and government -- 1989- 8. United States -- Foreign relations Middle East. 9. Middle East -- Foreign relations United

States. 10. United States -- Military policy.
ISBN 9781416549024

LC 2009004495

A president of the Council on Foreign Relations compares the reasons behind the two middle-east wars during the Bush administrations, drawing on senior-level interviews to argue that the first war was warranted while the second was not; in a critical assessment that examines U.S. policy today and what the author believes that policy should seek.

Hoyt, Mike,

★**Reporting** Iraq : an oral history of the war by the journalists who covered it / edited by Mike Hoyt, John Palattella, and the staff of the Columbia Journalism Review. Melville House Publishing, 2007. 191 p. : **956.7044**

1. Iraq War, 2003-2011 2. War correspondents. 3. Middle East -- Politics and government. 4. Oral histories
ISBN 9781933633381

LC 2014498067

"44 reporters casually and directly discuss all angles of the War in Iraq, including their own shock, fear and incomprehension, in this compilation of interviews conducted by The Columbia Journalism Review. This vital, breathtaking collection may be the closest contemporary reporting gets to cutting through the fog of war." Publishers Weekly.

McDonell, Nick

The **bodies** in person : an account of civilian casualties in American wars / Nick McDonell. Penguin Group USA 2018 352 p. **956.7044**

1. War casualties 2. Civilians in war 3. Military history 4. War 5. United States -- Military relations
ISBN 9780735211575

LC bl2018135365

A best-selling novelist and internationally acclaimed reporter investigates the true price of America's wars to innocents on the ground.

Packer, George, 1960-

The **assassins'** gate : America in Iraq / George Packer. Farrar, Straus and Giroux, 2005. 467 p. **956.7044**

1. Military policy. 2. Iraq War, 2003-2011 3. Insurgency -- Iraq. 4. Civil war -- Iraq 5. Iraq -- Politics and government -- 2003- 6. United States -- Foreign relations Iraq. 7. Iraq -- Foreign relations United States. 8. United States -- Politics and government -- 2001-2009
ISBN 0374299633

LC 2005011521

ALA Notable Book, 2006.

Pulitzer Prize for General Nonfiction finalist

The Assassins' Gate, dubbed so by American soldiers, is the entrance to the American zone in the city of Baghdad. In 2003, the United States blazed into Iraq to depose dictator Saddam Hussein. But after three years and unknown thousands killed, that country faces an escalating civil war and an uncertain fate. How did it get to this point? George Packer describes the players and ideas behind the Bush administration's war policy. He also provides first-hand accounts of the men and women--both civilian and military, coalition and Iraqi--who are caught in the middle of the conflict.

"This book rests on three main pillars: analysis of the intellectual origins of the Iraq war, summary of the political argument that preceded and then led to it, and firsthand description of the consequences on the ground. The Iraq debate has long needed someone who is both tough-minded enough, and sufficiently sensitive, to register all its complexities. In George Packer's work, this need is answered." Publishers Weekly.

Ricks, Thomas E.

Fiasco : the American military adventure in Iraq / Thomas E. Ricks. Penguin Press, 2006. xiv, 482 p., 16 unnumbered p. of plates : **956.7044**

1. Iraq War, 2003-2011 2. Military strategy. 3. Decision-making. 4. United States -- Armed Forces 5. Iraq -- Foreign relations United States. 6. United States -- Foreign relations Iraq.
ISBN 9780143038917

Pulitzer Prize for General Nonfiction finalist

An assessment of America's role in the Iraq War as viewed from the perspectives of senior military officers argues that the guerrilla insurgency after the fall of Saddam Hussein was avoidable and that officers who spoke against the war did so at the cost of their careers.

"The author critically assesses the Bush administration's decision to invade Iraq and its management of the war and the occupation. New York Times.

This book is not a political rant nor is it shrill. But in its low-key, extraordinarily well-sourced, highly-detailed portrait of the run-up to and conduct of the war it is devastating." Christian Science Monitor.

Shadid, Anthony

Night draws near : Iraq's people in the shadow of America's war / Anthony Shadid. Henry Holt, 2005. xiv, 424 p. : **956.7044**

1. Iraq War, 2003-2011 2. War. 3. Iraq -- Social life and customs-
ISBN 0805076026

LC 2005040348

National Book Critics Circle Award for Nonfiction finalist, 2005.

An Arab-American journalist looks at the Iraq War from the perspective of ordinary Iraqi citizens confronted by the dislocations, hardships, tragedies, and harsh realities of the conflict.

"Evenhanded and keenly observed, containing just enough (and no more) of the author to suggest a decent man worthy of our trust...[this book] is written for the inexpert but has fresh material for scholars." The Economist.

Sheeler, Jim

Final salute : a story of unfinished lives / Jim Sheeler. Penguin Press, 2008. 320 p. **956.7044**

1. Death notification 2. Military ceremonies, honors, and salutes 3. Iraq War, 2003-2011 -- Casualties 4. Death -- Psychological aspects.
ISBN 159420165X

LC 2007044130

National Book Award for Nonfiction finalist, 2008

A survey of the way America honors fallen soldiers follows the experiences of a Marine major whose duties include casualty notification, a responsibility involving unexpected and untrained acts of compassion.

Thorpe, Helen, 1965-

Soldier girls : the battles of three women at home and at war / Helen Thorpe. Scribner, [2014] 384 p. **956.7044**

1. United States. Army Women 2. Indiana. National Guard 3. Women soldiers -- United States 4. Afghan War, 2001- 5. Iraq War, 2003-2011 6. Military campaigns 7. Afghanistan 8. Iraq
ISBN 9781451668100

LC 2014000658

Describes the experiences of three women soldiers deployed to Afghanistan and Iraq to reveal how their military service has affected their friendship, personal lives and families, detailing the realities of their work on bases and in war zones and how their choices and losses shaped their perspectives.

"Thorpe fills this gripping tale with the women's own words, texts, and letters (from friends and their children, as well), and the story is engrossing and heartbreaking at once. Thorpe notes in the acknowledgments that the women's full-bore contributions to the book were not just to enlighten readers but also to let other war veterans know that they are not alone in their struggle to put their lives back together after a deployment." Booklist.

Woodward, Bob, 1943-

★**Plan** of attack / Bob Woodward. Simon & Schuster, 2004. xi, 467 : **956.7044**

1. Bush, George W. (George Walker), 1946- Interviews. 2. Iraq War, 2003-2011 -- Causes 3. Presidents -- United States. 4. Leadership in men. 5. Antiterrorist policy. 6. United States -- Officials and employees Interviews. 7. United States -- Foreign relations -- 2001-2009 8. United States -- Politics and government -- 2001-2009

ISBN 074325547X

LC 2004351204

Includes index.

Sequel to: Bush at war.

Sequel: State of denial.

Details the sixteen months of planning and decision making between President Bush, his war council, and key foreign leaders leading up to the 2003 war in Iraq and the toppling of Saddam Hussein's regime.

"The author delivers an engrossing blow-by-blow of the run-up to war in Iraq. With this book, Woodward...has delivered his most important and impressive work in years. Ultimately, this first-class work of contemporary history will be remembered for shedding needed light on the Iraq War." Publishers Weekly.

Wright, Evan

Generation kill : Devil Dogs, Iceman, Captain America, and the new face of American war / Evan Wright. G.P. Putnam's Sons, 2004. 354 p. : **956.7044**

1. Marines. 2. Guerrilla warfare. 3. War -- Psychological aspects. 4. Soldiers -- United States -- Psychology. 5. Iraq -- History -- 2003-

ISBN 0399151931

LC 2004044682

J. Anthony Lukas Book Prize, 2005.

Wright rode into Iraq on March 20, 2003, with a platoon of First Reconnaissance Battalion Marines, the Marine Corps' special operations unit whose motto is "Swift, Silent, Deadly." These highly trained and highly motivated First Recon Marines were the leading unit of the American-led invasion force. Wright wrote about that experience in a three-part series in Rolling Stone that was hailed for its evocative, accurate war reporting.

"This account is a personality-driven, readable and insightful look at the Iraq War's first month from the Marine grunt's point of view." Publishers Weekly.

956.70443 Iraq--1991-

Seierstad, Asne, 1970-

A **hundred** and one days : a Baghdad journal / Asne Seierstad ; translated by Ingrid Christophersen. Basic Books, 2005, c2003. 321 p. : **956.70443**

1. Seierstad, Asne, 1970- 2. Journalists 3. Iraq War, 2003-2011, Norwegian. 4. Iraq War, 2003-2011 -- Journalists 5. Iraq -- Social conditions 21st century. 6. Iraq -- Social life and customs 21st century.

ISBN 9780465076000

Originally published in Norwegian as Hundre og en dag: Oslo, Norway : J.W. Cappelen, 2003.

Provides a narrative of life in Iraq just before, during, and after the American invasion of March 2003, presenting the opinions and experiences of ordinary Iraquis attempting to carry on some semblance of normal life.

"The author writes about her stay as a reporter for Scandinavian, Dutch, and German media in Baghdad in the days before the war in Iraq through the fall of Baghdad. . . . Seierstad puts a human face to and provides insight into the mosaic of the people of Iraq, the Bath party supporters, the dissidents, and the average person caught in the nightmare of the Saddam regime and the horrors of war." School Library Journal.

956.9104 Syria--1920-

Erlich, Reese W., 1947-

Inside Syria : the backstory of their civil war and what the world can expect / Reese Erlich ; foreword by Noam Chomsky. Prometheus Books, 2014. 287 p. **956.9104**

1. Assad, Bashar, 1965- 2. Protest movements -- Syria -- History -- 21st century. 3. Political violence -- Syria -- History -- 21st century. 4. Arab Spring, 2010- 5. Civil war 6. Syria -- History -- Civil War, 2011- 7. Syria -- Politics and government -- 2000-

ISBN 9781616149482

LC 2014015840

Based on first-hand reporting from Syria and Washington, journalist Reese Erlich unravels the complex dynamics underlying the Syrian civil war. Through vivid, on-the-ground accounts and interviews with both rebel leaders and Syrian President Bashar al-Assad, Erlich gives the reader a better understanding of this momentous power struggle and why it matters. Through his many contacts inside Syria, the author reveals who is supporting Assad and why; he describes the agendas of the rebel factions; and he depicts in stark terms the dire plight of many ordinary Syrian people caught in the cross-fire. The book also provides insights into the role of the Kurds, the continuing influence of Iran, and the policies of US leaders who seem interested only in protecting US regional interests. As Erlich shows, current events in Syria can be best understood by looking at Syria's recent history, especially the roles of key historic figures. Several chapters are devoted to these influential leaders--including T.E. Lawrence (Lawrence of Arabia), journalist Lowell Thomas, Muslim brotherhood founder Hassan al Banna, Zionist leader Chaim Weizmann, Ayatollah Ruhollah Khomeini, Saddam Hussein, and Hafez al-Assad. Disturbing and enlightening at once, this timely book shows you not only what is happening inside Syria but why it is so important for the Middle East, the US, and the world.

"A timely, immediate description and explanation of social and political disintegration at huge human cost in war-torn Syria." Library Journal.

Minoui, Delphine

The **book** collectors : a band of Syrian rebels and the stories that carried them through a war / Delphine Minoui ; translated from the French by Lara Vergnaud. Farrar, Straus and Giroux, 2020, c2020. 160 p. **956.9104**

1. Books and reading 2. Libraries and community 3. Young men 4. Libraries 5. Syria -- Social life and customs. 6. Syria -- History -- Civil War, 2011- 7. Damascus, Syria.

ISBN 9780374115166

LC 2020023646

"Originally published in French in 2017 by Editions du Seuil, France, as 'Les passeurs de livres de Daraya.' "

An extraordinary account of a band of young men in a besieged Damascan suburb who find books in the rubble and create a secret library.

"This compassionate portrayal of an engaging group of rebels serves as a testament to both the resilience of the human spirit and to the power of story. Highly recommended for those interested in current events, Middle East history and politics, and personal accounts of war." Library Journal

Seierstad, Asne, 1970-

Two sisters : a father, his daughters, and their journey into the Syrian jihad / Asne Seierstad ; translated from the Norwegian by Sean Kinsella. Farrar, Straus and Giroux, 2018, c2016. vi, 418 p. **956.9104**

1. ISIS (Islamic State of Iraq and Syria) 2. Teenagers. 3. Runaways. 4. Fathers and daughters. 5. Women terrorists. 6. Norway. 7. Syria.
ISBN 9780374279677

LC 2017047949

Describes the true story of how two Somali immigrants living in Norway discovered that their teenage twin daughters had been radicalized and had run away to Syria to join the Islamic State and recounts their harrowing attempt to find them.

"Seierstad's scrupulous reporting shines a revealing new light on the phenomenon of young Westerners becoming fervent supporters of terror." Publishers Weekly.

Warrick, Joby

★**Black** flags : the rise of ISIS / Joby Warrick. Doubleday, 2015 416 p. **956.9104**

1. ISIS (Islamic State of Iraq and Syria) 2. Terrorism -- Middle East 3. Fundamentalism 4. Terrorists 5. Terrorism -- Religious aspects -- Islam 6. Middle East -- Politics and government -- 21st century
ISBN 9780385538213

LC 2015020949

Pulitzer Prize for General Nonfiction, 2016.

The Pulitzer Prize-winning author of The Triple Agent traces how the strain of militant Islam behind ISIS first arose in a remote Jordanian prison and spread with the unwitting aid of two American presidents.

"The author focuses on dramatic flashpoints and the roles of key players, creating an exciting tale with a rueful tone, emphasizing how the Iraq invasion's folly birthed ISIS and created many missed opportunities to stop al-Zarqawi quickly. Warrick stops short of offering policy solutions, but he provides a valuable, readable introduction to a pressing international security threat." Kirkus.

956.94 Palestine; Israel

Armstrong, Karen, 1944-

Jerusalem : one city, three faiths / Karen Armstrong. Ballantine Books, 2005, c1996. xxi, 482 p. : **956.94**

1. Monotheism. 2. Religion -- History. 3. Christianity. 4. Judaism. 5. Jerusalem, Israel -- History. 6. Jerusalem, Israel -- Religion. 7. Jerusalem, Israel -- Interfaith relations. 8. Jerusalem, Israel -- Interethnic relations. 9. Jerusalem, Israel -- Politics and government.
ISBN 0345391683

LC 2005281886

Originally published: New York : A.A. Knopf, 1996.

A comprehensive history of Jerusalem, the holy city venerated by the Christian, Jewish, and Muslim faiths, explains how the city became a defining site for the three religions, following its development from its earliest origins to the present day.

"Armstrong's overarching theme, that Jerusalem has been central to the experience and sacred geography of Jews, Muslims and Christians and thus has led to deadly struggles for dominance, is a familiar one, yet she brings to her sweeping, profusely illustrated narrative a grasp of sociopolitical conditions seldom found in other books." Publishers Weekly.

Blincoe, Nicholas

Bethlehem : biography of a town / Nicholas Blincoe. Nation Books, 2017. viii, 271 pages : **956.94**

1. Bible History of Biblical events 2. Bible History of Biblical events 3. Ancient history 4. Interethnic conflict 5. Cities and towns -- Israel 6. Bethlehem 7. Israel -- History
ISBN 9781568585833

LC 2017297281

Tells the town's history through the visceral experience of living there, taking readers through its stone streets and desert wadis, its monasteries, aqueducts, and orchards to show the city from every angle and era. His portrait of Bethlehem sheds light on one of the world's most intractable political problems, and he maintains that if the long thread winding back to the city's ancient past is severed, the chances of an end to the Palestine-Israel conflict will be lost with it.

"Deftly written, this narrative has something to offer a wide variety of readers, whether interested in history, archaeology, religious connection, or the Israeli-Palestinian conflict." Library Journal.

Bregman, Ahron

A **history** of Israel / Ahron Bregman. Palgrave Macmillan, 2002. 352 p. **956.94**

1. Zionism -- History. 2. Palestine -- History -- 1799-1917. 3. Palestine -- History -- 1917-1948. 4. Israel -- History.
ISBN 0333676327

LC 2002072304

"Bregman takes into account all the major issues involving Israel's history." Booklist.

Carroll, James, 1943-

Jerusalem, Jerusalem : how the ancient city ignited our modern world / James Carroll. Houghton Mifflin Harcourt, 2011. 432 p. **956.94**

1. Israeli-Palestinian relations 2. Religions -- History 3. Cultural differences 4. Jerusalem, Israel -- History 5. Jerusalem, Israel -- Description and travel 6. Jerusalem, Israel -- Religion 7. Jerusalem, Israel -- Interethnic relations
ISBN 9780547195612

LC 2010043034

Traces the evolution of the belief that Jerusalem is the center of the Christian, Jewish, and Muslim religious worlds and argues that this fixation is a main cause of the modern-day Israeli-Palestinian conflict.

"Carroll examines the enigma that is Jerusalem--the holiest and most blood-soaked spot on earth. While various religions flourished all over the ancient world, it was in Jerusalem that God emerged. Not just a god, but God, one who recognizes how both the need for violence and the hatred of violence reside within the human spirit. These conflicting impulses are the subthemes that propel Carroll's story across the ages, through Jerusalem's wreckages and rebirths, as the three Abrahamic religions claim the city as its own. Carroll's writing is so compelling, so beautifully constructed, that, ironically, the book can be a very slow read. There is something on almost every page that makes the reader want to stop and contemplate." Booklist.

Cohen, Rich

Israel is real / Rich Cohen. Farrar, Straus, and Giroux, c2009.

400 p. **956.94**

1. Cohen, Rich Travel Israel. 2. Judaism and state -- Israel 3. Jews -- History. 4. Zionism 5. Religion and state -- Israel 6. Israel -- Description and travel.

ISBN 9780374177782

LC 2008049223

A history of the idea of Israel offers insight into the views of people behind the polemics and politics of today's Israel, exploring how Israel was transformed sixty years ago from an idea into a place that is once again subject to destruction.

"The author explains the history of a people and its religion from the time Zealots revolted against their Roman occupiers to the rise of the Zionists, who helped build the current republic. A must-read for those who want to understand the context of the modern Jewish state." Kirkus.

Gilbert, Martin, 1936-2015

Jerusalem in the twentieth century / Martin Gilbert. J. Wiley & Sons, 1996. xvi, 412 p., 16 p. of plates : **956.94**

1. Jerusalem, Israel -- History. 2. Palestine -- History -- 1917-1948. 3. Israel -- History.

ISBN 0471163082

LC 96018458

A modern history of Jerusalem, from its 1917 liberation from the Turks by the British to present-day uneasy peace accords with the Palestinians, covers every political, cultural, religious, intellectual, architectural, and social facet of the city.

"Gilbert's history is heavily Zionist...nevertheless, despite his tilt, Gilbert is well worth reading. He has an unrivalled ability to tell a story through the eyes of (some of) those taking part and his book is good popular history." London Review of Books

Herzog, Chaim, 1918-1997

The **Arab-Israeli** wars : war and peace in the Middle East from the 1948 War of Independence to the present / Chaim Herzog ; updated by Shlomo Gazit ; introduction by Isaac Herzog and Michael Herzog. Vintage Books, 2005, c1982. 476 p. : **956.94**

1. Arab-Israeli conflict. 2. Arab-Israeli relations. 3. Israel -- History, Military. 4. Israel -- History. 5. Palestine -- History.

ISBN 1400079632

LC 2005280207

A Knesset member and former Director of Military Intelligence for Israel chronicles the series of wars that commenced with the 1948 War of Independence, highlighting the personal and political struggles that have shaped Israeli history and includes an updated section that recounts the events of the past twenty years.

"This book traces the Arab-Israeli wars and military conflicts from the 1948 War of Independence through the 1973 Yom Kippur War." Library Journal.

Hoffman, Bruce

Anonymous soldiers : the struggle for Israel, 1918-1947 / Bruce Hoffman. Alfred A. Knopf, 2015. 532 p. **956.94**

1. Lohame herut Yisrael. 2. Irgun "Ahenu" (Jerusalem) 3. Jews -- History -- 20th century. 4. World War II -- Palestine. 5. Unconventional warfare -- Palestine -- History -- 20th century. 6. Zionism -- Palestine -- History -- 20th century. 7. Palestine -- Politics and government -- 1917-1948. 8. Palestine -- History -- 1917-1948. 9. Middle East 10. Great Britain -- Politics and government -- 20th century.

ISBN 9780307594716

LC 2014018177

Draws on newly available documents from the National Archives in Britain to chronicle the historical events and key campaigns that led to the creation of Israel. By the author of Inside Terrorism.

"A must-read for anyone interested in the origins of the State of Israel." Library Journal.

Laqueur, Walter, 1921-2018

A **history** of Zionism : from the French Revolution to the establishment of the state of Israel / Walter Laqueur ; with a new preface by the author. Schocken Books, c2003. xxviii, 639 p., 16 p. of plates : **956.94**

1. Zionism -- History

ISBN 9780805211498

LC 2003269536

Reprint, with new introd. Originally published: New York : Holt, Rinehart, and Winston, 1972.

LeBor, Adam

City of oranges : an intimage history of Arabs and Jews in Jaffa / Adam LeBor. Norton & Company, 2007. 384 p. **956.94**

1. Jewish way of life 2. Jews 3. Arabs -- Social life and customs. 4. Jaffa (Tel Aviv, Israel) -- Social life and customs. 5. Jaffa (Tel Aviv, Israel) -- History. 6. Tel Aviv, Israel -- Social life and customs. 7. Israel -- History -- 20th century

ISBN 0393329844

LC 2007002389

An account of the Israeli-Palestinian conflict through the perspectives of three Arab and three Jewish families is drawn from personal interviews, generations-old memoirs, letters, and diaries, and offers insight into the intersection of Muslim, Jewish, and Christian communities in Tel Aviv.

Sachar, Howard Morley, 1928-2018

A **history** of Israel : from the rise of Zionism to our time / Howard M. Sachar. Knopf, 2007. 1296 p. **956.94**

1. Zionism -- History. 2. Israel -- History. 3. Palestine -- History -- 1917-1948.

ISBN 0375711325

LC 2006101970

"This is a Borzoi book"--T.p. verso.

A comprehensive account of the origins, establishment, development, and struggles of the modern Jewish state describes the men and women who helped or hindered Israel's survival, in an updated history that covers the 1995 Oslo II agreement, the assassination of Rabin and rise of Shimon Peres, the rise of the Palestinian state, and more.

"This is a history of the state of Israel. When first published in 1976, this truly monumental history was hailed as a definitive work. As extraordinarily stimulating as the first edition." Booklist.

Sebag-Montefiore, Simon, 1965-

Jerusalem : the biography / Simon Sebag Montefiore. Alfred A. Knopf, 2011. 672 p. **956.94**

1. Interfaith relations. 2. Jews -- Civilization. 3. Civilization, Islamic. 4. Religion and culture. 5. Jerusalem, Israel -- History

ISBN 9780307266514

LC 2011020827

"This Is a Borzoi Book"--T.p. verso.

"If, as some have maintained, the word Jerusalem means city of peace, it is a grand historical irony. For, as this beautifully written, absorbing, but often grim account shows, there are few stones of the city that have not been stained with the blood of its inhabitants during the past 3,000 years. Acclaimed historian and biographer Montefiore views Jerusalem as a living, breathing organism bearing the genetic imprint of many conquerors, including Jews, Greeks, Arabs, crusading Franks, Turks, and the British. While sometimes painful to read, this is an essential book for those who wish to understand a city that remains a nexus of world affairs." Booklist.

956.9405 Palestine; Israel--1948-

Bregman, Ahron

Cursed victory : a history of Israel and the occupied territories 1967 to the present / Ahron Bregman. Pegasus Books, 2015 416 p. **956.9405**

1. Military occupation 2. Arab-Israeli conflict 3. Palestinians -- History 4. Israel -- History 5. Arab countries -- History 6. Middle East -- History

ISBN 9781605987804

LC 2015509822

A former Israeli soldier discusses what led up to 1967's Six Day War--the fight itself and the troubled results of that conflict, which continue five decades later--and advocates for an end to his country's occupation of Arab territory.

Brenner, Michael, 1964-

In search of Israel : the history of an idea / Michael Brenner. Princeton University Press, 2018. xv, 372 p. : **956.9405**

1. Arab-Israeli conflict. 2. Zionism 3. Jews -- History. 4. Jewish way of life. 5. Israel -- Politics and government -- 20th century. 6. Israel -- Interethnic relations.

ISBN 9780691179285

"This edition is a substantially revised translation of Israel: Traum und Wirklichkeit des Jèudischen Staates by Michale Brenner, Ã Verlag C.H. Beck oHG, Munchen 2016"--Title page verso.

Seventy years after its founding, Israel has achieved much, but for a state widely viewed as either a paragon or a pariah, Brenner argues, the goal of becoming a state like any other remains elusive. If the Jews were the archetypal "other" in history, ironically, Israel--which so much wanted to avoid the stamp of otherness--has become the Jew among the nations.

"A lucid, valuable text about a homeland that may not yet be a light unto the nations but is surely unique." Kirkus.

Di Cintio, Marcello, 1973-

Pay no heed to the rockets : Palestine in the present tense / Marcello Di Cintio. Counterpoint, [2018] 272 p. **956.9405**

1. Di Cintio, Marcello, 1973- Travel 2. Arabic literature -- History and criticism 3. Literature and society 4. Palestinians 5. Intellectual life 6. Jerusalem, Israel 7. West Bank (Jordan River) -- Social conditions 8. Gaza Strip -- Social conditions

ISBN 9781640090811

LC 2018007702

Marcello Di Cintio first visited Palestine in 1999, and as with most outsiders, the narrative he knew was one defined by unending struggle, a near-Sisyphean curse of stories of oppression, exile, and occupation. In Pay No Heed to the Rockets, he reveals a more complex story: the Palestinian experience as seen through the lens of authors, books, and literature. Using the form of a political-literary travelogue, he explores what literature means to modern Palestinians and how Palestinians make sense of the conflict between a rich imaginative life and the daily tedium and violence of survival.

"Interweaving history and politics, the book introduces Western readers to the modern Palestinian literary scene while celebrating the rich diversity of voices that comprise it." Kirkus.

Ephron, Dan

Killing a king : the assassination of Yitzhak Rabin and the remaking of Israel / Dan Ephron. W.W. Norton & Company, 2015 352 p. **956.9405**

1. Rabin, Yitzhak, 1922-1995 Assassination. 2. Amir, Yigal 3. Assassination. 4. Political violence -- Israel 5. Right-wing extremists -- Israel -- History. 6. Orthodox Judaism -- Israel -- Political aspects 7. Israel -- Politics and government.

ISBN 9780393242096

LC 2015025695

Traces the parallel stories of Israeli Prime Minister Yitzhak Rabin and his stalker, Yigal Amir, to explore the assassination's fundamental and wrenching impact on the conflict between Israel and Palestine.

"Fascinating characterizations of real people and intrigue make this book appealing to readers of both fiction and nonfiction thrillers and anyone interested in the history of Israel." Library Journal.

Gordis, Daniel

Israel : a concise history of a nation reborn / Daniel Gordis. Ecco Press, 2016 256 p. **956.9405**

1. Jews -- History 2. Arab-Israeli conflict -- 1993- 3. Israel 4. Middle East

ISBN 9780062368744

LC 2017303760

Presenting a brief but thorough account of the cultural, economic and political history of the state of Israel, a public intellectual sheds light on the past of this complex nation, one rife with conflict, so that readers can understand its future.

"A readable, concise history that effectively captures the sense of grand ideas in Israel's identity." Kirkus.

Gorenberg, Gershom

The **accidental** empire : Israel and the birth of settlements, 1967-1977 / Gershom Gorenberg. Times Books, 2006. xvii, 454 p. : **956.9405**

1. Arab-Israeli conflict. 2. Land settlement. 3. Israelis. 4. Jews -- Colonization -- Palestine. 5. Israel -- Politics and government. 6. Israeli-occupied territories. 7. Palestine -- Politics and government.

ISBN 080507564X

LC 2005052988

Discusses the creation of Jewish settlements in territories seized following the 1967 Six-Day War, the actions and inactions that led to the move into occupied regions, and the long-term implications of the move.

Khalidi, Rashid

The **hundred** years' war on Palestine : a history of settler colonialism and resistance, 1917-2017 / Rashid Khalidi. Metropolitan Books, 2019. 352 p. **956.9405**

1. Palestinian Arabs -- Politics and government 2. Arab-Israeli conflict. 3. Arab-Israeli relations. 4. Military occupation. 5. Palestine -- History

ISBN 9781627798556

LC 2019008933

A history of the Israeli/Palestinian conflict told from the Palestinian perspective, arguing the period since the Balfour Declaration of 1917 has amounted to a hundred years of colonial war against the Palestinians.

"Highly recommended as a valuable and accurate presentation of a century of struggle between Jews and Palestinians seeking to build a nation on the same territory, vastly unequal in resources and efficacy." Library Journal.

La Guardia, Anton

War without end : Israelis, Palestinians, and the struggle for a promised land / Anton La Guardia. Thomas Dunne Books/St. Martin's Griffin, 2003. xxii, 436 p., 16 p. of plates : **956.9405**

1. Arab-Israeli conflict. 2. Arab-Israeli conflict -- 1993- -- Influence. 3. National characteristics, Israeli. 4. Jews, Israeli -- Identity. 5. Israel -- History -- 20th century.

ISBN 031231633X

LC 2003041288

Updated ed. of: Holy Land, unholy war : Israelis and Palestinians. Great Britain : John Murray, 2001.

The struggles of the Israelis and Palestinians, with their terrible histories of disaster and redemption, command the obsessive attention of the world. Statesmen tinker with peace plans for the Middle East and generals worry about future wars there. Religious leaders stoke the violent passions of the devout while pilgrims flock to find God and archaeologists dig to find the origins of His revelations. All this goes on under the watchful eye of an army of reporters, observers, diplomatic envoys, and aid workers. Between the Mediterranean and the Jordan River, dreams and ideals collide with the reality of violent nationalist struggle, and God's name is invoked in defense of the jealousies of men. The author offers an intimate look into the Israelis as they come to terms with the "post-Zionist" demolition of national myths, and the Palestinians as they try to build their own state.

"This is fundamentally an examination of two wounded peoples, neither of whom seems capable of surmounting national myths and past hatreds to forge a new future. La Guardia is evenhanded in his criticism of both Israeli and Palestinian leaders, but he does not spare ordinary people. This is an absorbing but heartbreaking examination of a seemingly endless tragedy that continues to unfold before our eyes." Booklist. [review of 2002 edition]

Lozowick, Yaacov

Right to exist : a moral defense of Israel's wars / Yaacov Lozowick. Doubleday, 2003. 326 p. : **956.9405**

1. Arab-Israeli conflict. 2. Jews -- Public opinion. 3. Public opinion -- Arab countries. 4. War -- Moral and ethical aspects. 5. Palestine -- History -- 20th century. 6. Israel -- Public opinion. 7. Israel -- History, Military. 8. Arab countries.

ISBN 0385509057

LC 2003048477

Includes index.

Provides an unbiased analysis of the Arab-Israeli conflict, tracing the history of Israel from the roots of the Zionist enterprise though the second Palestinian intifada, examining Israel's major conflicts and leaders to challenge the nation's internal and external identities.

"The author asserts that Israel is now, as before, struggling against opponents whose goal is the eventual destruction of the Jewish state. In examining the entire history of the Zionist enterprise, he illustrates both the moral justification of that enterprise and of the wars Israelis have been compelled to fight to preserve their independence. {This} is an eloquent and necessary justification of Israel's right to defend itself." Booklist.

Miller, Jennifer, 1980-

★**Inheriting** the Holy Land : an American's search for hope in the Middle East / Jennifer Miller. Ballantine Books, c2005. xxxiii, 261 p. : **956.9405**

1. Miller, Jennifer, 1980- 2. Arab-Israeli conflict -- 1993- 3. Arab-Israeli relations. 4. Middle East -- Politics and government.

ISBN 0345469240

LC 2004066349

Examines the Israeli-Palestinian conflict from the perspective of young Middle Eastern men and women who are coming of age, and offers an optimistic view of the possibility for peace.

"The author is the daughter of one of the chief American negotiators in the Israeli-Palestinian conflict and a longtime participant in the Seeds of Peace program, bringing together Israeli and Palestinian children. Using the many contacts that she has made, from the highest leaders to the children on the street, Miller explores...the many different viewpoints and preconceptions of the people involved in the conflict, not excluding her own. This is a superb book on a crucial issue of our time." School Library Journal.

Mitchell, George J., 1933-

A **path** to peace : a brief history of Israeli-Palestinian negotiations and a way forward in the Middle East / George J. Mitchell, Alon Sachar. Simon & Schuster, 2016. 192 p. **956.9405**

1. Arab-Israeli conflict. 2. Peace -- Middle East. 3. Palestinians -- Politics and government. 4. Israel -- Politics and government -- 1993-

ISBN 9781501153914

LC 2016027278

A former Democratic senator from Maine and the primary architect of the 1998 Good Friday Agreement for peace in Northern Ireland offers an insider's account of how the Palestinians and Israelis have progressed and regressed in their talks for peace in the region.

"Mitchell's careful statements may simply seem inconclusive to the more casual reader, but this is only a testament to the level of nuance in this scrupulous book." Publishers Weekly.

O'Malley, Padraig

The **two-state** delusion : Israel and Palestine : a tale of two narratives / Padraig O'Malley. Viking, 2015. 352 p. **956.9405**

1. Arab-Israeli conflict -- Causes. 2. Jews -- Identity. 3. Palestinians -- Politics and government 4. Arab-Israeli conflict -- 1993- -- Peace. 5. Israel -- Politics and government -- 21st century. 6. Israel -- History -- 21st century.

ISBN 9780670025053

LC 2014038545

Arguing that a two-state solution is no longer a viable path to lasting peace, a controversial assessment of the Israeli-Palestine conflict by the author of Biting at the Grave addresses key issues while outlining a framework for action.

"If O'Malley's out-of-the-box advice lacks a comprehensive one-state solution, it could galvanize readers to engage in the discussion in new and more creative ways." Booklist.

Rubin, Barry

Israel : an introduction / Barry Rubin. Yale University Press, c2012. ix, 340 p. : **956.9405**

1. Nation-building. 2. Zionism. 3. Judaism and state -- Israel. 4. Israel.

ISBN 9780300162301

LC 2011028927

956.95 Jordan and West Bank

Ehrenreich, Ben

The **way** to the spring : life and death in Palestine / Ben Ehrenreich. Penguin, 2016 352 p. **956.95**

1. Arab-Israeli conflict 2. Israeli West Bank Barrier. 3. Farmers 4. Palestinians 5. West Bank (Jordan River) 6. Israel -- Boundaries.
ISBN 9781594205903

LC 2016287137

The award-winning journalist and author of The Suitors describes his immersion into the lives and struggles of everyday Palestinians along the West Bank, sharing firsthand insights into their resistance and resilience in the face of occupation by the Israeli military.

"Ehrenreich's journal conveys how the Israeli-Palestinian conflict truly plays out at ground level, where normal might include the sounds of screaming, being arrested and questioned for hours, or simply being shot at." Booklist.

Grossman, David

The **yellow** wind / David Grossman ; translated from the Hebrew by Haim Watzman. Picador USA/Farrar, Straus and Giroux, 2002. xii, 222 p. : **956.95**

1. Grossman, David Travel West Bank (Jordan River). 2. Arab-Israeli conflict. 3. Palestinians -- West Bank (Jordan River). 4. Israelis -- West Bank (Jordan River). 5. Israeli-Palestinian relations. 6. West Bank (Jordan River) -- Description and travel.
ISBN 0312420986

LC 2002067325

A prominent Israeli writer's report on the Israeli-Arab situation describes what he observed on the West Bank in early 1987, from the miserable condition of the Palestinian refugees and their hatred of the Israelis to the costs of occupation for both occupier and occupied.

"Grossman was assigned to report for a weekly newspaper on life for both occupied and occupier on the West Bank during the 20th anniversary of its conquest. With an eye and ear for revealing detail, he argues that the Jews are now doing to Palestinians what has been done to them through the ages." Library Journal.

957 Siberia (Asiatic Russia)

Frazier, Ian

Travels in Siberia / Ian Frazier. Farrar, Straus and Giroux, 2010. 560 p. **957**

1. Frazier, Ian Travel Siberia. 2. Voyages and travels. 3. Travelers. 4. Siberia -- Description and travel 5. Siberia -- History 6. Siberia -- Social life and customs.
ISBN 9780374278724

LC 2010005784

ALA Notable Book, 2011.

"Did you know that Siberia doesn't officially exist? Or that there's a city that was once known as the "Paris of Siberia"? Or that...well, we could go on and on. And you'll be able to, too, if you read author and humorist Ian Frazier's Travels in Siberia. Frazier's taken five trips to the region, and he describes his various travels across the vast, remote area (including long road trips in both winter and summer) and discusses Siberian geography, people, culture, and history."--Description by Dawn Towery.

"A dense, challenging, dazzling work that will leave readers exhausted but yearning for more." Kirkus.

Gessen, Masha

Where the Jews aren't : the sad and absurd story of Birobidzhan, Russia's autonomous region / Masha Gessen. Nextbook/ Schocken, 2016 208 p. **957**

1. Jews, Russian 2. Social history. 3. Jews -- History. 4. Ethnic policy -- Soviet Union 5. Birobidzhan, Russia. 6. Soviet Union -- Social conditions -- 1917-
ISBN 9780805242461

LC 2015049370

An account of the lesser-known story of the 20th-century Jewish-Russian experience reveals the complex, unconventional and wrenching truths behind pogrom and emigration activities, detailing the waves of Jewish influxes in the Birobidzhan homeland before its already dispossessed citizens were silenced by state-sanctioned purges.

"Gessen ably tells one of the 20th centurys most chilling stories of struggle, perseverance, and despair." Publishers Weekly.

Thubron, Colin, 1939-

In Siberia / Colin Thubron. Harper Collins, 1999. 286 p. **957**

1. Thubron, Colin, 1939- Travel Siberia. 2. Russians in Siberia. 3. Voyages and travels. 4. Travelers. 5. Siberia -- Description and travel. 6. Siberia -- Peoples. 7. Siberia -- Social life and customs.
ISBN 0060195436

LC 99041346

Includes index.

ALA Notable Book, 2001.

"Thubron elegantly encompasses both awe-inspiring landscapes and their dark histories as well as immersing himself in local eccentricities." Times Literary Supplement.

958.1 Afghanistan

Dalrymple, William

The **return** of a king : the battle for Afghanistan, 1839-42 / William Dalrymple. Alfred A. Knopf, 2013. 384 p. **958.1**

1. Shah Shuja, Amir of Afghanistan, 1780?-1842 2. Colonialism -- History -- 19th century. 3. Imperialism, British. 4. Intervention (International relations) 5. Defeat (Military science) 6. Afghanistan -- History -- British Intervention, 1838-1842.
ISBN 9780307958280

LC 2012040998

Examines the mid-19th-century Afghan war as a tragic result of neo-colonial ambition, cultural collision and hubris, drawing on previously untapped primary sources to explore such topics as the reestablishment of a puppet-leader Shah, the conflict's brutal human toll and the similarities between the war and present-day challenges.

Ewans, Martin

Afghanistan : a short history of its people and politics / Martin Ewans. Perennial, 2002. 338 p. : **958.1**

1. Afghanistan -- History.
ISBN 0060505087

LC 2002024954

Examines the history, people, politics, religion, geography, and culture of Afghanistan, offering a revealing portrait of the war-ravaged nation and the Taliban regime and including new information covering events up to spring 2002.

"This is a fascinating story and the best book-length examination of Afghanistan's history we're likely to have for some time." Booklist.

Wahab, Shaista

★A **brief** history of Afghanistan / Shaista Wahab and Barry Youngerman. Facts on File, 2010. 368 p. Brief history (Facts on File) **958.1**

1. Afghanistan -- History. 2. South Asia 3. Islamic countries.
ISBN 9780816082186

LC 2010019656

"This work is a good choice for those wanting to familiarize themselves with the roots of the current conflict, and a handy reference for basic information on Afghanistan." Choice Reviews

958.104 Afghanistan--1919

Coll, Steve

★**Directorate** S : the C.I.A. and America's secret wars in Afghanistan and Pakistan / Steve Coll. Penguin Press, 2018. xxiii, 757 p., 8 unnumbered p. of plates : **958.104**

1. CIA. 2. Qaida (Organization) 3. Taliban -- History 4. International relations 5. Terrorism 6. Afghanistan. 7. Pakistan
ISBN 9781594204586
National Book Critics Circle Award for Non-Fiction, 2018.

A follow-up to the Pulitzer Prize-winning Ghost Wars traces America's intelligence, military and diplomatic efforts to defeat Al Qaeda and the Taliban in Afghanistan and Pakistan in the years since 9/11.

"With his evenhanded approach, gift for limning character, and dazzling reporting skills, he has created an essential work of contemporary history." Booklist.

Ghost wars : the secret history of the CIA, Afghanistan, and bin Laden, from the Soviet invasion to September 10, 2001 / Steve Coll. Penguin Press, 2004. xvii, 695 p. : **958.104**

1. Bin Laden, Osama, 1957-2011 2. CIA. 3. Qaida (Organization) 4. Taliban -- History 5. International relations 6. Terrorism 7. Afghanistan -- History -- Soviet occupation, 1979-1989. 8. Afghanistan -- History -- 1973- 9. Afghanistan -- Politics and government -- 1989-2001. 10. United States -- Foreign relations Afghanistan.
ISBN 1594200076

LC 2003058593

Lionel Gelber Prize (Canada), 2004.
Pulitzer Prize for General Nonfiction, 2005.

To what extent did America's best intelligence analysts grasp the rising threat of Islamist radicalism? Who tried to stop bin Laden and why did they fail? Comprehensively and for the first time, this Pulitzer Prize-winning work by journalist Steve Coll recounts the history of the covert wars in Afghanistan that fueled Islamic militancy and sowed the seeds of the September 11 attacks. Based on scrupulous research and firsthand accounts by key government, intelligence, and military personnel both foreign and American, Ghost Wars details the secret history of the CIA's role in Afghanistan, the rise of the Taliban, the emergence of bin Laden, and the efforts by US forces to find and assassinate bin Laden in Afghanistan.

"The author has given us what is certainly the finest historical narrative so far on the origins of Al Qaeda in the post-Soviet rubble of Afghanistan." New York Times Book Review.

Darack, Ed

The **final** mission of Extortion 17 : special ops, helicopter support, SEAL Team Six, and the deadliest day of the U.S. war in Afghanistan / Ed Darack. Smithsonian Books, [2017] 256 p. **958.104**

1. United States. Navy. SEALs -- History 21st century. 2. United States. Naval Special Warfare Development Group -- History. 3. United States. Army. Ranger Regiment, 75th -- History 21st century. 4. Afghan War, 2001- -- Aerial operations, American. 5. Military helicopters 6. Military aircraft 7. Chinook (Military transport helicopter).
ISBN 9781588345899

LC 2017001110

Uncovering the truth behind the mysterious tragedy of Extortion 17, a helicopter shot down while on a mission to reinforce American and coalition special operations troops during the war in Afghanistan, a gripping volume recounts the brave pilots, crew and passengers of Extortion 17 and the events of that fateful day.

"Darack delivers a respectful salute to the dead amid detailed exemplification of the bravery of those fighting America's protracted war in Afghanistan." Booklist.

Farwell, Matt

American cipher : Bowe Bergdahl and the U.S. tragedy in Afghanistan / Matt Farwell and Michael Ames. Penguin Press, 2019. 320 p. **958.104**

1. Bergdahl, Bowe, 1986- Trials, litigation, etc. 2. Taliban. 3. Soldiers -- United States 4. Afghan War, 2001- 5. Courts-martial and courts of inquiry. 6. Trials. 7. Afghanistan.
ISBN 9780735221048

LC 2018046632

Draws on exclusive reporting and military, government, and family sources in a narrative account of the life, captivity, and trial of the Taliban-abducted soldier whose story has become a symbol of America's foundering war in Afghanistan.

"The engrossing narrative intertwines Bergdahl's odyssey with an effective critique of U.S. policy in Afghanistan under both Republican and Democratic administrations. Readers looking for a nontechnical history of America's longest war and a nuanced look at Bergdahl's story will find that here." Publishers Weekly.

Feifer, Gregory

The **great** gamble : the Soviet war in Afghanistan / Gregory Feifer. Harper, 2009. 336 p. **958.104**

1. Military occupation. 2. Military history. 3. Afghanistan -- History -- Soviet occupation, 1979-1989. 4. Soviet Union -- History, Military.
ISBN 9780061143182

LC 2008022594

The Soviet war in Afghanistan was a grueling debacle that has striking lessons for the 21st century. Parallels between the Soviet invasion of Afghanistan and the U.S. invasions of Afghanistan and Iraq are impossible to ignore. The Soviet Union sent some of its most elite troops to unfamiliar lands to fight a vaguely defined enemy, which eventually defeated their superior numbers with unconventional tactics. Although the Soviet leadership initially saw the invasion as a victory, many Russian soldiers came to view the war as a demoralizing and devastating defeat, the consequences of which had a substantial impact on the Soviet Union and its collapse. NPR Moscow correspondent Gregory Feifer examines the conflict from the perspective of the soldiers on the ground. His extensive research includes eye-opening interviews with participants from both sides of the conflict, vividly depicting the invasion of a volatile country that no power has ever successfully conquered.--From publisher description.

Gall, Carlotta

The **wrong** enemy : America in Afghanistan, 2001/2014 / Carlotta Gall. Houghton Mifflin Harcourt, 2014 352 p. **958.104**

1. Taliban. 2. Pakistan. Inter Services Intelligence. 3. Qaida (Organization) 4. Afghan War, 2001- 5. War on Terrorism, 2001-2009 6. Pakistan -- Politics and government. 7. Afghanistan -- Politics and government. 8. United States -- Foreign relations Pakistan. 9. Pakistan -- Foreign relations United States. 10. United States -- Foreign relations Afghanistan. 11. Afghanistan -- Foreign relations United States.

ISBN 9780544046696

LC 2013044257

A veteran journalist for the New York Times describes the toll taken on the U.S., Afghanistan and Pakistan since September 11 through ordinary citizens' accounts of fighting and first-hand descriptions from Taliban warlords, intelligence thugs, American generals and Afghani politicians.

"The author offers a compelling account of the attack on bin Laden's compound, the repercussions of which are still being felt. Gall admirably never loses sight of the human element in this tragedy." Kirkus.

Junger, Sebastian

War / Sebastian Junger. Twelve, c2010. 320 p. **958.104**

1. United States. Army. Airborne Brigade, 173rd 2. War. 3. Soldiers 4. Battles 5. Coping. 6. Afghanistan.

ISBN 9780446556248

LC 2009049493

Includes index.

Offers an on-the-ground account of a single platoon during its fifteen-month tour of duty in the most dangerous outpost in Afghanistan's Korengal Valley.

"The war in Afghanistan contains brutal trauma but also transcendent purpose in this riveting combat narrative. Junger spent 14 months in 2007-2008 intermittently embedded with a platoon of the 173rd Airborne brigade in Afghanistan's Korengal Valley, one of the bloodiest corners of the conflict. Junger experiences everything they do--nerveracking patrols, terrifying roadside bombings and ambushes, stultifying weeks in camp when they long for a firefight to relieve the tedium. The result is an unforgettable portrait of men under fire." Publishers Weekly.

Lamb, Christina

Farewell Kabul : / Christina Lamb. HarperCollins 2016, c2015. 640 p. **958.104**

1. Afghan War, 2001- 2. Terrorism -- Causes. 3. Military policy -- United States -- 2001- 4. Consequences. 5. Afghanistan -- Foreign relations United States. 6. United States -- Foreign relations Afghanistan.

ISBN 9780008171520

LC bl2016019208

"Lamb's focus on the facts... provides an intense primer to the various sides of a complicated war that readers intrigued by foreign policy and curious about the region will certainly find well worth their time." Booklist.

Partlow, Joshua

★A **kingdom** of their own : the family Karzai and the Afghan disaster / Joshua Partlow. Knopf, 2016. 304 p. **958.104**

1. Karzai, Hamid, 1957- 2. Military strategy. 3. Afghan War, 2001- 4. Warlords. 5. Strategic alliances (Military) 6. Afghanistan -- Foreign relations United States. 7. United States -- Foreign relations Afghanistan.

ISBN 9780307962645

LC 2016007281

A former Washington Post Kabul bureau chief examines the ultimately failed relationship between the powerful Karzai family and the United States.

"American military and political arrogance butts up against deep-rooted cultural customs and family networks throughout this excellent account of a vastly difficult topic." Publishers Weekly.

Romesha, Clinton

★**Red** Platoon : a true story of American valor / Clinton Romesha. E P Dutton, 2016 368 p. **958.104**

1. Romesha, Clinton 2. Taliban 3. Battles 4. Afghan War, 2001- 5. Military campaigns 6. Unconventional warfare. 7. Afghanistan 8. Combat Outpost Keating (Afghanistan)

ISBN 9780525955054

LC 2016498127

A comprehensive account of the 13-hour firefight at the Battle of Keating by a Medal of Honor recipient describes the harrowing events of the October 3, 2009 attack and how the sacrifices and victories of heroic men raised questions about whether the strategically vulnerable outpost should ever have been built.

Schroen, Gary C.

First in : an insider's account of how the CIA spearheaded the war on terror in Afghanistan / Gary C. Schroen. Presidio Press/Ballantine Books, 2005. xiii, 379 p. : **958.104**

1. Schroen, Gary C. 2. CIA. 3. Afghan War, 2001-, American. 4. Afghan War, 2001- -- Secret service -- United States.

ISBN 0891418725

LC 2005043171

Includes index.

"The author describes his experiences after he was tapped to lead the effort to establish contact with the Northern Alliance in the days following 9/11; the 35-year CIA veteran commanded the first American team on the ground in Afghanistan. Schroen delivers what he advertises: a powerful account that takes the reader inside war councils and 19th-century- style cavalry charges in the months just after 9/11." Publishers Weekly.

Smith, Graeme, 1979-

The **dogs** are eating them now : our war in Afghanistan / Graeme Smith. Counterpoint, 2015, c2013. xvi, 298 p. : **958.104**

1. Taliban. 2. Afghan War, 2001- -- Social aspects. 3. Insurgency -- Afghanistan -- History -- 21st century. 4. War correspondents -- Canada 5. War and society. 6. Afghanistan -- Social conditions -- 21st century.

ISBN 9781619024793

LC 2014034083

Previously published in 2013 (Toronto : Knopf Canada, c2013.

Hilary Weston Writers' Trust Prize, 2013.

Shortlisted for The Charles Taylor Prize for Literary Non-Fiction

A highly personal narrative of the war in Afghanistan by the Emmy Award-winning foreign correspondent behind Talking With the Taliban shares poignant stories that identify key reasons why he believes the mission has failed to promote peace and democracy.

"Recommended for readers of battlefield accounts and those seeking a better understanding of the Afghani people. For another excellent journalistic account, see Edward Giradet's Killing the Cranes." Library Journal.

West, Francis J.

The **wrong** war : grit, strategy, and the way out of Afghanistan

/ Bing West. Random House Inc, 2011. 448 p. **958.104**

1. Afghan War, 2001- 2. Military strategy. 3. Soldiers. 4. Afghanistan.
ISBN 9781400068739

LC 2010043107

Takes a look the war that has dominated America's military attention the nearly 10 years after the September 11 attacks and offers a plan for withdrawing troops.

"This is a crushing and seemingly irrefutable critique of the American plan in Afghanistan. It should be read by anyone who wants to understand why the war there is so hard." New York Times Book Review.

959 Southeast Asia

Somers Heidhues, Mary F.

Southeast Asia : a concise history / Mary Somers Heidhues. Thames & Hudson, c2000. 192 p. : **959**

1. Southeast Asia -- History.
ISBN 0500251177

LC 99066014

"This history ranges from Southeast Asia's prehistoric times to the most recent political developments in Indonesia. Heidhues...divides her study into seven well-balanced chapters, touching on the political history, economics, society, and culture of Burma, Thailand, Cambodia, Vietnam, Malaysia, Singapore, Brunei, Indonesia, and the Philippines." Library Journal.

959.1 Myanmar

Thant Myint-U

The **river** of lost footsteps : histories of Burma / Thant Myint-U. Farrar, Straus and Giroux 2006 xiv, 361 p., 8 p. of plates : **959.1**

1. Burma -- History -- 1824-1948. 2. Burma -- History -- 1948-
ISBN 0374163421

LC 2006009199

Retraces the complex and turbulent story of Burma, from the time of Portuguese pirates to the sixty-year-old civil war that continues today, in a narrative that portrays Burma's rise and decline through the stories of the author's family and others.

"This readable, reflective history will support revived interest in Burma." Booklist.

959.105 Myanmar--1948-

Larkin, Emma

Everything is broken : a tale of catastrophe in Burma / Emma Larkin. Penguin Press, 2010. 288 p. **959.105**

1. Larkin, Emma Travel Burma 2. Cyclones -- Burma 3. Disaster relief -- Burma 4. Social control. 5. Totalitarianism 6. Burma -- Description and travel 7. Burma -- Politics and government -- 1988-
ISBN 9781594202575

LC 2010004029

A deeply reported account of life inside Burma in the months following the disastrous Cyclone Nargis and an analysis of the brutal totalitarian regime that clings to power in the devastated nation.

"Larkin is such a facile observer and writer, she tempts comparisons to Orwell, and certainly ranks with Ryszard Kapuscinski as a lyric writer of reportage." Cleveland Plain Dealer.

Thant Myint-U

The **hidden** history of Burma : race, capitalism, and the crisis of democracy in the 21st century / Thant Myint-U. W. W. Norton & Company, [2020] 272 p. **959.105**

1. Aung San Suu Kyi 2. War crimes 3. Crimes against humanity. 4. Genocide. 5. Refugees 6. Burma -- History -- 1988-
ISBN 9781324003298

LC 2019026007

The award-winning historian, former diplomat and presidential advisor shares first-person insights into the recent election of Nobel Laureate Aung San Suu Kyi and the war crimes, inequalities and expulsions that have decimated Burma in less than a decade.

959.604 Cambodia--1949-

Brinkley, Joel, 1952-

Cambodia's curse : the modern history of a troubled land / Joel Brinkley. PublicAffairs, c2011. 416 p. **959.604**

1. Pol Pot, 1928-1998. 2. Democracy. 3. Social change. 4. Genocide -- Cambodia. 5. Cambodian genocide, 1975-1979 6. Cambodia -- History -- 1979- 7. Cambodia -- Politics and government -- 1979- 8. Cambodia -- Social conditions -- 21st century.
ISBN 9781586487874

LC 2010044806

A Pulitzer Prize-winning reporter who covered the fall of the Khmer Rouge in Cambodia returns 30 years later to discover a people plagued by the effects of PTSD and examines how genocide can affect later generations.

"Brinkley cuts a clear narrative path through the bewildering, cynical politics and violent social life of one of the worlds most brutalized and hard-up countries." Foreign Affairs.

959.7 Vietnam

Goscha, Christopher E.

Vietnam : a new history / Christopher Goscha. Basic Books, [2016] 592 p. **959.7**

1. Vietnam -- History. 2. Vietnam -- Colonization.
ISBN 9780465094363

LC 2016017630

Cundill History Prize finalist, 2017.

Tells the full history of the events that created the modern state of Vietnam, from antiquity to the present day.

"A vigorous, eye-opening account of a country of great importance to the world, past and future." Kirkus.

959.704 Vietnam--1945-

Appy, Christian G.

American reckoning : the Vietnam War and our national identity / Christian G. Appy. Viking, 2015 416 p. **959.704**

1. Vietnam War, 1961-1975 -- Social aspects. 2. Nationalism 3. Political culture -- United States -- History -- 20th century. 4. Popular culture 5. United States -- Civilization -- 1970- 6. United States -- Foreign relations
ISBN 9780670025398

LC 2014038477

The critically acclaimed author of Patriots draws on sources ranging from movies and songs to official documents and news stories to analyze the role of the Vietnam War in shaping America's national identity, popular culture and post-war foreign policy.

"Appy paints with a broad brush and may interpret our national security needs too narrowly. Still, his assertion that our current policies could guarantee constant warfare deserves to be seriously considered." Booklist.

Bowden, Mark, 1951-

★**Hue** 1968 : the turning point of the American war in Vietnam / Mark Bowden. Atlantic Monthly Press, 2017. 394 p. **959.704**

1. Hue, Battle of, 1968. 2. Tet Offensive, 1968. 3. Urban warfare 4. Vietnam War, 1961-1975 5. United States -- History, Military -- 20th century. 6. Vietnam -- History, Military -- 20th century. 7. Hue, Vietnam -- History 8. United States -- Foreign relations Vietnam. 9. Vietnam -- Foreign relations United States.

ISBN 9780802127006

LC 2017022809

ALA Notable Book, 2018.

Longlisted for the Andrew Carnegie Medal for Excellence in Non-Fiction, 2018.

Interviews with participants from both sides of the conflict and materials from Vietnamese and American archives provide multiple points of view on each stage of the Battle of Hue.

"One of the best books on a single action in Vietnam, written by a tough, seasoned journalist who brings the events of a half-century past into sharp relief." Kirkus.

Burrows, Larry

Vietnam / Larry Burrows ; introduction by David Halberstam. A.A. Knopf, 2002. 243 p. : **959.704**

1. Photojournalism -- United States -- History -- 20th century. 2. Vietnam War, 1961-1975 -- Pictorial works. 3. War photography. 4. War. 5. Vietnam Pictorial works.

ISBN 037541102X

LC 2002019100

"This confirms that {Burrows} was an artist as well as a journalist, capable of arousing the great tragic emotions, pity and terror." Booklist.

Clarke, Thurston

Honorable exit : how a few brave Americans risked all to save our Vietnamese allies at the end of the war / Thurston Clarke. Doubleday, [2019] 448 p. **959.704**

1. Vietnam War, 1961-1975 2. Evacuation of civilians 3. Refugees 4. Rescues 5. Vietnam -- Foreign relations United States 6. United States -- Foreign relations Vietnam

ISBN 9780385539647

LC 2018029232

A revisionist history of the end of the Vietnam War reveals how American evacuees helped more than 100,000 South Vietnamese civilians to escape execution or concentration-camp incarceration by North Vietnamese invaders. By the author of The Last Campaign.

"Fans of military and U.S. history will revel in Clarke's expert storytelling, well-crafted re-creations, and research." Library Journal.

FitzGerald, Frances, 1940-

Fire in the lake : the Vietnamese and the Americans in Vietnam / Frances Fitzgerald ; [with a new afterword by the author]. Little, Brown, 2002. xii, 500 p. : **959.704**

1. Vietnam War, 1961-1975 -- United States. 2. Vietnam -- Politics and government -- 1945-1975. 3. United States -- Foreign relations Vietnam. 4. Vietnam -- Foreign relations United States. 5. Vietnam -- History -- 20th century.

ISBN 9780316159197

LC 2003543944

Originally published: Boston, MA : Little, Brown, 1972.

Pulitzer Prize for General Nonfiction, 1973.

Presents a study of Vietnamese society and politics and the effects of American intervention, based on the journalist's stay in South Vietnam from February through November of 1966.

Glasser, Ronald J.

365 days / Ronald J. Glasser. George Braziller, 2003. xii, 292 p. **959.704**

1. Vietnam War, 1961-1975.

ISBN 9780807615270

LC 2003063579

Assigned to Zama, an Army hospital in Japan in September 1968, Glasser arrived as a pediatrician in the U.S. Army Medical Corps to care for the children of officers and high-ranking government officials. The hospital's main mission, however, was to support the war and care for the wounded. At Zama, an average of six to eight thousand patients were attended to per month, and the death and suffering were staggering. The soldiers counted their days by the length of their tour--one year, or 365 days--and they knew, down to the day, how much time they had left. Glasser tells their stories of lives shockingly interrupted by the tragedies of war. --From publisher description.

Hampton, Dan

The **hunter** killers : the extraordinary story of the first Wild Weasels, the band of maverick aviators who flew the most dangerous missions of the Vietnam War / Dan Hampton. William Morrow, 2015 352 p. **959.704**

1. Vietnam War, 1961-1975 2. Electronic warfare aircraft -- United States -- History -- 20th century. 3. Military campaigns 4. Military aviation 5. Vietnam

ISBN 9780062375131

LC 2015007013

The New York Times best-selling author of Viper Pilot presents a gripping chronicle of the band of maverick fighter pilots who signed on for the extremely dangerous top-secret Iron Hand| program during the Vietnam War--which used revolutionary tactics to combat Soviet missile technology.

"Hampton uses a lot of military terminology, some of which might be difficult for the lay reader to understand, but his overall writing style is excellent; in particular, his vivid, fast-paced combat narratives. His latest work will appeal to military history fans or anyone looking for an absorbing read." Library Journal.

Hastings, Max

Vietnam : an epic tragedy, 1945-1975 / Max Hastings. HarperCollins, 2018. 512 p. **959.704**

1. Vietnam War, 1961-1975. 2. War and society 3. War -- Psychological aspects 4. Military history 5. Vietnam

ISBN 9780062405661

LC bl2018168524

The best-selling author of The Secret War draws on survivor interviews from both sides in a modern history of the Vietnam War that discusses its hotly debated political divides, major and lesser-known battles and brutal human costs.

"This isn't an easy read, but it is an essential one to comprehend the totality of the wars in that long-besieged country." Booklist.

Hendrickson, Paul, 1944-

The **living** and the dead : Robert McNamara and five lives of a lost war / Paul Hendrickson. Alfred A. Knopf, 1996. ix, 427 p. : **959.704**

1. McNamara, Robert S., 1916- 2. United States. Secretary of Defense. 3. Vietnam War, 1961-1975 -- United States. 4. United States -- Military policy. 5. United States -- Politics and government -- 1961-1969.
ISBN 9780679427612

LC 96007445

National Book Award for Nonfiction finalist, 1996

"Exhaustively researched, probing, important contribution to the annals of American history." Publishers Weekly.

Karnow, Stanley

Vietnam, a history / Stanley Karnow. Penguin Books, 1997. xv, 768 p. : **959.704**

1. Vietnam War, 1961-1975 -- United States. 2. Vietnam War, 1961-1975. 3. United States -- History -- 1945- 4. Vietnam -- History -- 1858-1945. 5. Vietnam -- History -- 1945-1975.
ISBN 0140265473

LC 97197160

Originally published: New York : Viking, 1983.

A study of American involvement in Vietnam, from French domination to the final withdrawal of American forces, discusses the historical background, politics, military campaigns, participants, and consequences of American involvement.

"A summation of over two centuries of conflict in Indochina. Chronicling a tragic history, Karnow presents a balanced and sympathetic view of Vietnamese aspirations and the mishaps that led to American involvement in a war nobody won." Voice of Youth Advocates. [review of 1983 edition]

Kissinger, Henry, 1923-

Ending the Vietnam War : a history of America's involvement in and extrication from the Vietnam War / Henry Kissinger. Simon & Schuster, 2003. 635 p. : **959.704**

1. Vietnam War, 1961-1975 -- United States. 2. Vietnam War, 1961-1975 -- Diplomatic history.
ISBN 074321532X

LC 2002017996

The former Secretary of State describes America's involvement in Southeast Asia, the events of the war, the peace negotiations, the domestic unrest over the war, and the diplomats, politicians, military leaders, and others who became part of history.

"Readers interested in the Vietnam period but unfamiliar with Kissinger's previous books will find this new volume worthwhile. Kissinger's account of America's venture in Vietnam and his role in that shipwreck is factually accurate, eminently informed and masterfully crafted." Publishers Weekly.

Langguth, A. J., 1933-

Our Vietnam : the war, 1954-1975 / A.J. Langguth. Simon & Schuster, 2002, c2000. 766 p. : **959.704**

1. Vietnam War, 1961-1975. 2. Politicians. 3. Politics and war. 4. Vietnam -- Politics and government -- 1945-1975. 5. United States -- History -- 1945-
ISBN 0743212312

LC bl2006003516

"A Touchstone book."

Originally published: New York : Simon and Schuster, 2000.

Presents the Vietnam War as a series of missteps, misunderstandings, and mistakes by leaders including Defense Secretary Robert McNamara and the heads of the CIA, and explains the origins of those errors.

"This book is unique in its perspective of the major players on both sides." Booklist.

Lee, Heath Hardage

The **League** of Wives : the untold story of the women who took on the U.S. Government to bring their husbands home / Heath Hardage Lee. St. Martin's Press, [2019] 288 p. **959.704**

1. National League of Families of American Prisoners and Missing in Southeast Asia. 2. Military spouses. 3. Prisoners of war, American. 4. Missing in action. 5. Vietnam War, 1961-1975 -- Prisoners and prisons, North Vietnamese. 6. Hanoi, Vietnam. 7. United States -- Politics and government -- 1969-1974.
ISBN 9781250161109

LC 2018041164

Describes how a fierce band of military wives transformed themselves from convention-ruled married women into national lobbyists, advocates, international human-rights figures, and spies in their efforts to bring their POW husbands home from Vietnam.

"Lee addresses the stringent societal constraints the wives struggled under, rules that demanded they defer to the military in all matters regarding threats to their husbands careers and livelihoods." Booklist.

Lind, Michael, 1962-

Vietnam, the necessary war : a reinterpretation of America's most disastrous military conflict / Michael Lind. Free Press, 1999. xix, 314 p. **959.704**

1. Cold War. 2. Vietnam War, 1961-1975 -- United States. 3. United States -- Foreign relations -- 1963-1969. 4. United States -- Foreign relations -- 1969-1974. 5. United States -- Foreign relations Vietnam. 6. Vietnam -- Foreign relations United States.
ISBN 9780684842547

LC 99028449

Offering what is sure to be a controversial perspective on America's most painful war, the author proposes that Vietnam should have been fought, but with different tactics.

"Lind's arguments, if not always persuasive, are always provocative." Publishers Weekly.

Logevall, Fredrik, 1963-

★**Embers** of war : the fall of an empire and the making of America's Vietnam / Fredrik Logevall. Random House, c 2012. 880 p. **959.704**

1. Imperialism, French -- Vietnam 2. Cold War 3. International relations 4. Indochina -- History -- War for national liberation, 1946-1954 5. France -- Colonies Asia. 6. Vietnam -- Politics and government -- 1945-1975. 7. United States -- Foreign relations Vietnam.
ISBN 9780375504426

LC 2011034971

Pulitzer Prize for History, 2013.

Cundill Prize in Historical Literature finalist

"Logevall's exhaustive study shows chapter and verse why not--and why the ensuing American war was doomed to fail." Kirkus.

Maraniss, David

They marched into sunlight : war and peace, Vietnam and America, October 1967 / David Maraniss. Simon & Schuster, 2003. xvii, 572 p., 16 p. of plates : **959.704**

1. United States. Army. Infantry, 28th 2. University of Wisconsin,

Madison. 3. Vietnam War, 1961-1975 -- Protest movements. 4. Protest movements. 5. Ambushes and surprises. 6. United States -- Politics and government -- 1963-1969. 7. Madison, Wisconsin.
ISBN 0743217802

LC 2003052885

J. Anthony Lukas Book Prize, 2004.

Pulitzer Prize for History finalist, 2004.

The epic story of Vietnam and the sixties is told through the events of a few tumultuous days in 1967, bringing that catastrophic time back to life while examining questions about the meaning of dissent and the official manipulation of the truth.

"This is a narrative by a reporter who juxtaposes a ghastly little battle in Vietnam with an antiwar and anti-Dow demonstration at the University of Wisconsin, Madison, on the same day; it captures moral ambiguity everywhere, without stereotyping or condescension. " New York Times Book Review.

McNamara, Robert S., 1916-

In retrospect : the tragedy and lessons of Vietnam / Robert S. McNamara with Brian VanDeMark. Times Books, 1995. xviii, 414 p. : **959.704**

1. Vietnam War, 1961-1975 -- United States. 2. Military policy. 3. Military history. 4. United States -- Military policy. 5. United States -- Politics and government -- 1961-1963. 6. United States -- Politics and government -- 1963-1969.
ISBN 9780812925234

LC 94040088

Maps on lining papers.

The Secretary of Defense for the Kennedy and Johnson administrations provides an account of how and why America became involved in Vietnam and discusses the legacy of decisions made during the 1960s.

"Former defense secretary McNamara seeks to put Vietnam in context and counter the cynicism and even contempt with which so many people view our political institutions and leaders. He identifies eleven major causes for our disaster in Vietnam and six points when the U.S. could legitimately have withdrawn. Certainly not the last word on this still-controversial subject but an essential acquisition for most libraries." Booklist.

Moore, Harold G., 1922-

We are soldiers still : a journey back to the battlefields of Vietnam / Harold G. Moore, Joseph L. Galloway. Harper, 2008. 304 p. **959.704**

1. Moore, Harold G., 1922- 2. Galloway, Joseph L., jt. author 3. Vietnam veterans 4. Ia Drang Valley, Battle of, 1965. 5. Vietnam War, 1961-1975 6. Military campaigns 7. Vietnam -- Description and travel
ISBN 9780061147760

LC 2008011034

To honor fallen comrades, a journalist and a soldier return to Vietnam battlefields more than 30 years later.

Moore, Harold G., 1922-

We were soldiers once -and young : Ia Drang, the battle that changed the war in Vietnam / Harold G. Moore and Joseph L. Galloway. Random House, 1992. xvi, 412 p., 20 p. of plates : **959.704**

1. Ia Drang Valley, Battle of, 1965. 2. Vietnam War, 1961-1975. 3. Battles. 4. Soldiers.
ISBN 0679411585

LC 92053642

A definitive study of the 1965 battle of Ia Drang, in the central highlands of South Vietnam, provides a blow-by-blow account of the battle and the implications of this key confrontation.

"On Nov. 14, 1965, the 1st Battalion of the 7th Cavalry, commanded by Col. Moore and accompanied by UPI reporter Galloway, helicoptered into Vietnam's remote Ia Drang Valley and found itself surrounded by a numerically superior force of North Vietnamese regulars. Moore and Galloway here offer a detailed account, based on interviews with participants and on their own recollections, of what happened during the four-day battle." Publishers Weekly.

Morgan, Ted, 1932-

Valley of death : the tragedy at Dien Bien Phu that led America into the Vietnam War / Ted Morgan. Random House, c2010. 752 p. **959.704**

1. Dien Bien Phu, Vietnam, Battle of, 1954. 2. War. 3. Military history. 4. Indochinese War, 1946-1954 -- Causes. 5. United States -- Foreign relations -- 1945-1953. 6. United States -- Foreign relations Vietnam. 7. Vietnam -- Foreign relations United States.
ISBN 9781400066643

LC 2009019714

A Pulitzer Prize-winning author presents a history of the onset of the Vietnam War that documents the contributions of Senior General V Nguyñ Giṗ and the pivotal 1954 defeat of French forces that ended colonial rule in Indochina.

Nguyen, Viet Thanh, 1971-

Nothing ever dies : Vietnam and the memory of war / Viet Thanh Nguyen. Harvard University Press, 2016. 310 p. **959.704**

1. Vietnam War, 1961-1975 -- Social aspects. 2. Memory -- Sociological aspects. 3. War and society. 4. Art and war.
ISBN 9780674660342

LC 2015037444

National Book Critics Circle Award for Nonfiction finalist, 2016

"Nothing Ever Dies, Viet Thanh Nguyen writes. All wars are fought twice, the first time on the battlefield, the second time in memory. From the author of the bestselling novel The Sympathizer comes a searching exploration of a conflict that lives on in the collective memory of both the Americans and the Vietnamese.

"Essentially a critical study, Nguyen's work is a powerful reflection on how we choose to remember and forget." Kirkus.

Reston, James, Jr., 1941-

A **rift** in the Earth : art, memory, and the fight for a Vietnam War memorial / James Reston, Jr. Arcade Publishing, 2017. 224 p. **959.704**

1. Lin, Maya Ying. 2. Hart, Frederick, 1943- 3. Vietnam Veterans Memorial (Washington, D.C.) -- History. 4. Vietnam War, 1961-1975 -- Monuments -- Washington, D.C. 5. Vietnam veterans 6. Soldiers' monuments -- Washington, D.C. 7. Washington, D.C. -- Buildings
ISBN 9781628728569

LC 2017012314

"A gripping history of the fights over how to memorialize the Vietnam War." Kirkus.

Sallah, Michael

Tiger Force : a true story of men and war / Michael Sallah and Mitch Weiss. Little, Brown, 2006. xi, 403 p., 8 p. of plates : **959.704**

1. United States. Army. 2. Vietnam War, 1961-1975.
ISBN 9780316159975

LC 2005020921

Written by a pair of Pulitzer Prize-winning investigative reporters, an account of the tragic massacres of countless innocent Vietnamese citizens at the hands of the U.S. Army's Tiger Force unit documents how its members spun out of control over a seven-month period.

Shultz, Richard H., 1947-

The **secret** war against Hanoi : the untold story of spies, saboteurs, and covert warriors in North Vietnam / Richard H. Shultz, Jr. Perennial, 2000, c1999. xvii, 408 p. : **959.704**

1. Vietnam War, 1961-1975 -- Military intelligence -- United States. 2. Spies 3. Psychological warfare 4. Deception 5. Vietnam -- Politics and government. 6. United States -- Politics and government -- 1961-1963. 7. United States -- Politics and government -- 1963-1969. 8. United States -- Covert operations

ISBN 0060932538

LC BL2001000308

Originally published: New York : HarperCollins, 1999.

The largest covert operation of the Cold War is laid bare in this fascinating account of the eight-year Pentagon-run espionage campaign against North Vietnam--a program initiated in 1963 by JFK to replace the CIA's ineffectual effort.

"Schultz was given access to SOG archives and veterans and has produced a professional volume on how SOG originated and operated over its eight-year existence." Booklist.

Stanton, Doug

The **odyssey** of Echo Company : The 1968 Tet Offensive and the epic battle to survive the Vietnam War / Doug Stanton. Scribner, 2017. 416 p. **959.704**

1. Viet Cong 2. Vietnam War, 1961-1975. 3. Military campaigns 4. Guerrilla warfare. 5. Tet Offensive, 1968. 6. United States -- History -- 1961-1969. 7. Vietnam -- History -- 1945-1975.

ISBN 9781476761916

LC bl2017030704

A portrait of the American recon platoon of the 101st Airborne Division describes their 60-day fight for survival during the early 1968 attack by North Vietnamese soldiers on dozens of South Vietnam cities, tracing their postwar difficulties with acclimating into a peacetime America that did not want to hear their story.

Talty, Stephan

Saving Bravo : the greatest rescue mission in Navy SEAL history / Stephan Talty. Houghton Mifflin Harcourt, 2018. 304 p. **959.704**

1. Hambleton, Gene (Iceal Eugene), 1918-2004. 2. United States. Navy. SEALs Search and rescue operations 3. Vietnam War, 1961-1975 -- Search and rescue operations. 4. Search and rescue operations -- Vietnam. 5. Easter Offensive, 1972 6. United States -- History, Military -- 20th century.

ISBN 9781328866721

LC 2018006365

The untold story of the most important rescue mission not just of the Vietnam War, but the entire Cold War: one American aviator, who knew our most important secrets, crashed behind enemy lines and was sought by the entire North Vietnamese and Russian military machines. One Navy SEAL and his Vietnamese partner had to sneak past them all to save him.

Ward, Geoffrey C.

★The **Vietnam** War : an intimate history / Geoffrey C. Ward ; based on a documentary film by Ken Burns & Lynn Novick ; with a preface by Ken Burns & Lynn Novick. Alfred A. Knopf, 2017. 528 p. **959.704**

1. Vietnam War, 1961-1975. 2. War. 3. Military history. 4. United States -- History -- 1969- 5. Vietnam -- History -- 1945-1975.

ISBN 9780307700254

LC 2017015686

More than forty years after it ended, the Vietnam War continues to haunt our country. We still argue over why we were there, whether we could have won, and who was right and wrong in their response to the conflict. When the war divided the country, it created deep political fault lines that continue to divide us today.

"Accompanying the PBS series to be aired in September 2017, this is an outstanding, indispensable survey of the Vietnam War." Kirkus.

Wright, James Edward, 1939-

★**Enduring** Vietnam : an American generation and its war / James Wrigh. Thomas Dunne Books, an imprint of St. Martin's Press, 2017. 352 p. **959.704**

1. Vietnam War, 1961-1975. 2. Soldiers 3. Families of military personnel. 4. War

ISBN 9781250092489

LC 2016038762

Depicts the cruelty of the Vietnam war through interviews with those who served and the families of those who served and never returned, discussing why they joined the military, what they thought of the war and what it was like to serve.

"Wrights worthy effort is a tribute to Americans who saw the worst that the Vietnam War offered, combined with a broad look at the domestic and geopolitical factors that led to the U.S. getting involved in the long, controversial conflict." Publishers Weekly.

959.7043 Vietnamese War, 1961-1975

Lawrence, Mark Atwood

The **Vietnam** War / editor, Mark Lawrence ; introduction by David K. Shipler. Fitzroy Dearborn Publishers, 2001. 2 v. (xvii, 922 p.) : **959.7043**

1. Vietnam War, 1961-1975 -- Sources. 2. Vietnam War, 1961-1975 -- United States -- Sources.

ISBN 9781579583682

LC 2002726953

Includes indexes.

959.9 Philippines

Jones, Gregg R.

Honor in the dust : Theodore Roosevelt, war in the Philippines, and the rise and fall of America's imperial dream / Gregg Jones. New American Library, c2012. 400 p. **959.9**

1. Waller, Littleton Waller Tazewell, 1856-1926. 2. Roosevelt, Theodore, 1858-1919. 3. Imperialism, American -- Philippines. 4. Leadership in men. 5. Philippine-American War, 1896-1902 6. Philippines -- History

ISBN 9780451229045

LC 2011033386

Describes the life of Teddy Roosevelt from his time as a Rough Rider at San Juan Hill to being charged with military misconduct in the Philippines and through his presidency which forever changed the United States' position in global affairs.

Karnow, Stanley
In our image : America's empire in the Philippines / Stanley Karnow. Random House, 1989. xii, 494 p., 24 p. of plates : **959.9**

1. Imperialism, American -- Philippines. 2. Elitism. 3. Philippines -- History -- Colonial period (American), 1898-1946. 4. Philippines -- History. 5. United States -- Foreign relations Philippines.
ISBN 9780394549750

LC 88042676

Pulitzer Prize for History, 1990.

Traces the history of the Philippines, discusses the influence of Spain and the United States, and looks at the problems facing the Philippines.

"The author's treatment of the indecisiveness of President McKinley over the issue of empire and of the egotistical General MacArthur make the work a definite purchase for libraries. Those who love swashbuckling history will enjoy this work." Library Journal.

960 History of Africa

Appiah, Anthony
Africana : the encyclopedia of the African and African American experience / editors, Kwame Anthony Appiah, Henry Louis Gates, Jr. Oxford University Press, 2005. 5 volumes : **960**

1. African Americans 2. African diaspora 3. Africa -- Civilization
ISBN 9780195170559

LC 2004020222

Meredith, Martin
Born in Africa : the quest for the origins of human life / Martin Meredith. PublicAffairs, c2011. 608 p. **960**

1. Humans -- Origin. 2. Human evolution. 3. Human remains (Archaeology) 4. Evolution. 5. Africa -- Antiquities. 6. Olduvai Gorge, Tanzania
ISBN 9781586486631

LC 2010043985

Chronicles the efforts of anthropologists, archeologists and other scientists to uncover the many mysteries of human origins.

Meredith, Martin
The **fortunes** of Africa : a 5000-year history of wealth, greed, and endeavor / Martin Meredith. Public Affairs, 2014. 784 p. **960**

1. African civilization. 2. Africa 3. Africa -- Social life and customs.
ISBN 9781610394598

LC 2014939816

In this vast and vivid panorama of history, Martin Meredith follows the fortunes of Africa over a period of 5,000 years. With compelling narrative, he traces the rise and fall of ancient kingdoms and empires; the spread of Christianity and Islam; the enduring quest for gold and other riches; the exploits of explorers and missionaries; and the impact of European colonization. He examines, too, the fate of modern African states and concludes with a glimpse of their future.

"A gripping tale of insatiable greed--personal and collective." Booklist.

Soyinka, Wole
Of Africa / Wole Soyinka. Yale University Press, 2012. 224 p. **960**

1. Postcolonialism. 2. Religion and politics. 3. Culture. 4. Civil rights. 5. Africa -- History. 6. Essays.
ISBN 9780300140460

LC 2012013544

The first African recipient of a Nobel Prize in Literature offers a thought-provoking analysis of Africa's current crises while making recommendations for cultural and political renewal, exploring the region's history as it relates to the histories of other nations and critically assessing Africa's stances on race and religious tolerance.

960.3 History of Africa--1885-

Pakenham, Thomas, 1933-
The **scramble** for Africa, 1876-1912 / Thomas Pakenham. Random House, c1991. xxv, 738 p. : **960.3**

1. Africa -- History -- To 1884. 2. Africa -- History -- 1884-1918. 3. Africa -- Colonization -- History -- 19th century 4. Africa -- Colonization -- History -- 20th century. 5. Europe -- Colonies Africa -- History -- 19th century. 6. Europe -- Colonies Africa -- History -- 20th century.
ISBN 0394515765

LC 91052681

"This is a sweeping narrative, refreshingly old fashioned in its appreciation of the fact that imperialism did have some virtues, which offers as good an introduction to the scramble as has ever been written." Library Journal.

961.205 Libya--2011-

Wehrey, Frederic M.
★The **burning** shores : inside the battle for the new Libya / Frederic Wehrey. Farrar, Straus and Giroux, 2018. 352 p. **961.205**

1. Revolutions 2. Civil war 3. Terrorism 4. Nation-building 5. Libya -- History -- Civil War, 2011- 6. Libya -- Politics and government 7. Middle East
ISBN 9780374278243

LC 2017049275

The death of Colonel Muammar Qadhafi freed Libya from forty-two years of despotic rule, raising hopes for a new era. But in the aftermath, the country descended into bitter rivalries and civil war, paving the way for the Islamic State and a catastrophic migrant crisis. Middle East scholar Frederic Wehrey chronicles the American and international missteps after the dictator's death that hastened the country's unraveling.

"A searing tale of violence, chaos, and unintended consequences in post-Gadhafi Libya. Essential reading for anyone interested in the facts of the Benghazi attacks and in the future of a definitively troubled region." Kirkus.

962 Egypt, Sudan, South Sudan

Strathern, Paul, 1940-
Napoleon in Egypt / Paul Strathern. Bantam Dell, 2008. 368 p. **962**

1. Napoleon I, Emperor of the French, 1769-1821 2. Civilization -- Egyptian influences. 3. History. 4. Leadership. 5. Generals. 6. Egypt -- History -- French occupation, 1798-1801. 7. France -- History --

1789-1815.
ISBN 9780553806786
LC 2008028135

Describes Napoleon Bonaparte's invasion of Egypt in 1798, the first attack on a Middle Eastern country by a Western power in modern times, examining Napoleon's military victories and the legacy of his expedition.

962.05 Egypt since 1922

Hessler, Peter, 1969-

The **buried** : an archaeology of the Egyptian Revolution / Peter Hessler. Penguin Press, 2019. 463 p. : **962.05**

1. Hessler, Peter, 1969- Travel Egypt 2. Journalists -- United States 3. Ancient Cities and towns 4. Revolutions 5. Social change 6. Cairo, Egypt -- Social life and customs 7. Cairo, Egypt -- Social conditions 8. Egypt -- Politics and government -- 21st century
ISBN 9780525559566
LC 2018050659

National Book Critics Circle Award for Nonfiction finalist, 2019

"This is writing at its best and highly recommended for anyone interested in Egypt, modern or ancient." Library Journal.

Khalil, Ashraf

Liberation Square : inside the Egyptian revolution and the rebirth of a nation / Ashraf Khalil. St. Martin's Press, 2012. 320 p. **962.05**

1. Mubarak, Muhammad Husni, 1928- 2. Revolutions -- Egypt 3. Social conflict -- Egypt 4. Political persecution 5. Egypt -- Politics and government -- 1970- 6. Egypt -- History -- Protests, 2011-2013
ISBN 9781250006691
LC 2011038194

A Cairo-based journalist presents an account of the Egyptian Revolution based on the author's witness to the demise of Mubarak and the country's first efforts to build a democracy, documenting the violent 18-day revolt during which protestors of all ages united for specific political and social goals.

Morrison, Dan

The **black** Nile : one man's amazing journey through peace and war on the world's longest river / Dan Morrison. Viking, 2010. 304 p. **962.05**

1. Morrison, Dan Travel Nile River. 2. War and society. 3. Canoes. 4. Rivers. 5. Oil industry and trade. 6. Nile River -- Description and travel.
ISBN 9780670021987
LC 2010004709

A foreign correspondent traces the four-thousand-mile plank-board boat journey he took with an inexperienced childhood friend along the Nile River from Lake Victoria to the Mediterranean Sea, during which he surveyed regional culture and politics.

"Morrison's account transcends the travel genre to provide authentic and timely information on a complicated part of the world." Library Journal.

Deng, Alephonsion

They poured fire on us from the sky : the true story of three lost boys from Sudan / Alephonsion Deng, Benson Deng, Benjamin Ajak ; with Judy A. Bernstein. Public Affairs, c2005. xxiii, 311 p. : **962.404**

1. Deng, Benson. 2. Deng, Alephonsion. 3. Ajak, Benjamin. 4. Refugees, Sudanese 5. Genocide -- Sudan -- History -- 20th century. 6. Civil war -- East Africa -- History -- 20th century 7. Atrocities -- East Africa -- History -- 20th century 8. Sudan -- History -- Civil War, 1983-2005 9. Sudan -- History -- Civil War, 1983-2005 -- Atrocities
ISBN 2005042566

As gunshots, flames, and screams engulfed their village, three cousins fled into the cover of the forest. Every step led the boys away from their peaceful, agrarian world--a traditional world were spear-toting fathers protected their huts from the lions that roamed by night. With each footstep they were drawn deeper into the horrific violence of Sudan's civil war: a world of bombed-out villages, mine-sown roads, and relentless desert, a world where starving adults would snatch the grain from a weak child's fingers. Across Sudan, between 1987 and 1989, tens of thousands of young boys took flight from these massacres. Their journey led them first to Ethiopia and then, driven back into Sudan, toward Kenya. They walked nearly one thousand miles, sustained only by the sheer will to live. This book is the three boys' account of that unimaginable journey.--From publisher description.

"This collection is moving in its depictions of unbelievable courage." Publishers Weekly.

964 Morocco, Ceuta, Melilla, Western Sahara, Canary Islands

Shah, Tahir

The **Caliph's** house / Tahir Shah. Bantam Books, c2006. 349 p. : **964**

1. Shah, Tahir. 2. Travel writers -- England 3. British in Morocco. 4. Historic buildings -- Casablanca, Morocco. 5. Houses -- Conservation and restoration. 6. Casablanca, Morocco. 7. Morocco -- Description and travel.
ISBN 0553803999
LC 2005053656

Describes the author's and his family's experiences after purchasing a run-down palace in the Moroccan city of Casablanca, as they work to renovate the house, exorcise the jinns haunting the structure, and cope with the house's human guardians.

"Shah's picture of Moroccan society, its deeply held Islamic faith, its primitive superstition, and its raucous economy makes for endlessly fascinating reading." Booklist.

965 Algeria

Camus, Albert, 1913-1960

Algerian chronicles / Albert Camus ; translated by Arthur Goldhammer ; with an introduction by Alice Kaplan. Harvard University Press, 2013, c1958. 154 p. **965**

1. Algeria -- Politics and government -- 20th century. 2. Algeria -- Social conditions -- 20th century. 3. Algeria -- History -- Revolution, 1954-1962.
ISBN 9780674072589
LC 2012036100

Originally published in French: Paris : Gallimard, 1958.

More than 50 years after its original publication in French, Albert Camus' controversial look at the Algerian War for independence--and his opinions on terrorism--is published in English for the first time.

Evans, Martin, 1964-

Algeria : France's undeclared war / Martin Evans. Oxford

University Press, 2012. xxi, 457 p. : **965**

1. Algeria -- History -- Revolution, 1954-1962. 2. Algeria -- History -- Revolution, 1954-1962 -- Causes. 3. France -- Colonies Africa. 4. France -- Foreign relations Algeria. 5. Algeria -- Foreign relations France. 6. France -- Foreign relations -- 1945- 7. Algeria -- Foreign relations.

ISBN 9780192803504

965.04 Middle East (Near East)--1945-1980

MacFarquhar, Neil

The **media** relations department of Hizbollah wishes you a happy birthday : unexpected encounters in the changing Middle East / Neil MacFarquhar. PublicAffairs, c2009. 400 p. **965.04**

1. MacFarquhar, Neil Travel Middle East. 2. Social change -- Middle East. 3. Political culture -- Middle East. 4. Middle East -- Description and travel. 5. Middle East Anecdotes. 6. Middle East -- Social life and customs. 7. Middle East -- Politics and government -- 1979-

ISBN 9781586486358

LC 2009002004

"The author offers something fresh and unexpected for readers steeped in a decade of news reports about suicide bombers, absolutist imams and tyrannical despots. [This book] is MacFarquhar's effort to write a funny (yet penetrating) account about real Arabs--and a few Persians--struggling against long odds to bring their societies into the modern age. For those who care about the Middle East and want to start listening to weak but growing voices calling for reform and modernization on local rather than Western terms, MacFarquhar's account is a fine place to begin." New York Times Book Review.

966.23 Mali

English, Charlie

The **storied** city : the quest for Timbuktu and the fantastic mission to save its past / Charlie English. Riverhead Books, 2017. 432 p. **966.23**

1. Libraries -- Destruction and pillage -- Mali 2. Manuscripts. 3. Cultural property -- Protection. 4. Islam 5. Mali -- History -- Tuareg Rebellion, 2012- -- Destruction and pillage. 6. Tombouctou, Mali 7. West Africa

ISBN 9781594634284

LC 2016039192

Recounts how a team of librarians and archivists in Timbuktu, Mali started a high-stakes smuggling operation to save hundreds of thousands of ancient manuscripts from advancing Al Qaeda jihadists in 2012.

"With a clear-eyed and straightforward approach, English thoroughly dispels the myths about Timbuktu to reveal a truth that is, in many ways, even more remarkable." Booklist.

966.905 Nigeria--1960-

Maier, Karl, 1957-

This house has fallen : midnight in Nigeria / Karl Maier. PublicAffairs, 2000. xxxvii, 327 p. **966.905**

1. Islam -- Relations -- Christianity. 2. Nigeria -- History. 3. Nigeria -- Politics and government -- 1993-2007

ISBN 1891620606

LC 00028199

Introduces readers to the people and problems threatening Nigeria's existence, discussing the abject poverty despite hefty foreign aid, military coups, political corruption, and conflicts between Christians and Muslims over Islamic law.

"The author explores the promise and paradox of Nigeria. {He}... recounts the history of this nation cobbled together from British colonial interests in its formative years and dominated by international oil interests in more recent years." Booklist.

967.031 Central Africa--1885-1945

Harms, Robert W., 1946-

Land of tears : the exploration and exploitation of equatorial Africa / Robert Harms. Basic Books, 2019. 336 p. **967.031**

1. Rain forests 2. Environmental degradation 3. Colonialism 4. Jungles 5. Central Africa 6. Congo River 7. Africa -- History 8. Africa -- Colonization

ISBN 9780465028634

LC 2019021576

In just three decades at the end of the nineteenth century, the heart of Africa was utterly transformed. Virtually closed to outsiders for centuries, by the early 1900s the rainforest of the Congo River basin was one of the most brutally exploited places on earth. The author of The Diligent presents an epic account of the scramble to control equatorial Africa that discusses the brutal exploitation of the Congo River basin rainforest by Western ivory and rubber markets.

"Essential reading for serious students of modern African history." Library Journal.

967.51 Democratic Republic of the Congo

Hochschild, Adam

★**King** Leopold's ghost : a story of greed, terror, and heroism in Colonial Africa / Adam Hochschild. Houghton Mifflin, 1998. 366 p. : **967.51**

1. Leopold II, King of the Belgians, 1835-1909. 2. Forced labor 3. Indigenous peoples -- Congo (Democratic Republic) 4. Human rights -- History 5. Mass murder -- Africa. 6. Congo (Democratic Republic) -- Politics and government 7. Congo (Democratic Republic) -- Race relations -- History -- 19th century. 8. Congo (Democratic Republic) -- Race relations -- History -- 20th century. 9. Belgium -- Colonies Africa.

ISBN 9780395759240

LC 98016813

ALA Notable Book, 1999.

Lionel Gelber Prize (Canada), 1999.

Mark Lynton History Prize, 1999.

National Book Critics Circle Award for Nonfiction finalist, 1998.

A provocative study of King Leopold II of Belgium's genocidal plunder of the Congo in the 1880s, as the European powers were colonizing Africa, reveals the heroic efforts that led to the first international human rights movement.

"Hochschild's impressively researched history records the roles of the famous and obscure, missionaries, journalists, opportunists, politicians, and royalty in this long-forgotten drama." Booklist.

967.5103 Democratic Republic of the Congo--1960-

Stearns, Jason K.

Dancing in the glory of monsters: the collapse of the Congo and the great war of Africa / Jason K. Stearns. PublicAffairs, c2011. 400 p. **967.5103**

1. Political violence 2. Interethnic conflict 3. War and society 4. Genocide -- Congo (Democratic Republic) 5. Congo (Democratic Republic) -- History -- 1997- 6. Congo (Democratic Republic) -- Politics and government -- 1997-

ISBN 9781586489298

LC 2010043075

Chronicles the horrors of the years-long war still raging in the Congo by focusing on the personal stories of those most affected by the conflict.

"A look at the war that began in Congo in 1996 and that eventually involved nine countries and 20 different rebel movements, resulting in the deaths of more than five million people. In sheer brutality, this mostly unremarked upon cataclysm ranks with the two world wars, the Great Leap Forward and the Cambodia genocide. Mr. Stearns has spoken to everyone: villagers, child soldiers, Mobutu's commanders, Kabila's ministers, Rwandan intelligence officers. In these conversations he found gold, bringing clarity--and humanity--to a place that usually seems inexplicable and barbaric. Dancing in the Glory of Monsters is riveting and certain to become essential reading for anyone looking to understand Central Africa." Wall Street Journal.

967.57104 Rwanda--1962-

Hatzfeld, Jean

The **antelope's** strategy : living in Rwanda after genocide / a report by Jean Hatzfeld ; translated from the French by Linda Coverdale. Farrar, Straus and Giroux, 2009, c2007. 256 p. **967.57104**

1. Reconciliation -- Social aspects -- Rwanda. 2. Tutsi (African people) -- Rwanda -- History. 3. Hutu (African people) -- Rwanda. 4. Genocide -- Rwanda -- History -- 20th century. 5. Rwanda -- History -- Civil War, 1994 -- Atrocities. 6. Rwanda -- History -- Civil War, 1994 7. Rwanda -- Interethnic relations -- History -- 20th century.

ISBN 9780374271039

LC 2008052489

Translation of: La strategie des antilopes. Paris : Seuil, 2007.

A follow-up to "Liberation" and "Machete Season" continues the author's research into genocidal activities in Rwanda, exploring how former Hutu killers were re-acclimating to life after prison and how formerly victimized Tutsis were tolerating their Hutu neighbors.

"This is a book that illustrates vividly the thorny realities that accompany survival and appeasement." Washington Post.

Machete season : the killers in Rwanda speak : a report / Jean Hatzfeld ; translated from the French by Linda Coverdale ; preface by Susan Sontag. Farrar, Straus and Giroux, 2005, c2003. xiv, 253 p. : **967.57104**

1. Tutsi (African people) -- Rwanda -- History. 2. Hutu (African people) -- Rwanda. 3. Genocide -- Rwanda -- History -- 20th century. 4. Rwanda -- History -- Civil War, 1994 -- Atrocities. 5. Rwanda -- History -- Civil War, 1994 6. Rwanda -- Interethnic relations -- History -- 20th century.

ISBN 0374280827

LC 2004061600

Originally published in French as Saison de machettes: Paris : Seuil, 2003.

A veteran foreign correspondent shares a collection of interviews with ten Hutu men--all tried, convicted and sentenced for the genocidal killings of their Tutsi neighbors--as they describe their participation in the heinous crimes and their reasons for the murders, in a study that considers the roots of human morality and ethics.

"Steering clear of politics, this important book succeeds in offering the reader some grasp of how such unspeakable acts unfolded." Publishers Weekly.

967.5710431 Rwanda--Civil War of 1994

Hatzfeld, Jean

Blood Papa : Rwanda's new generation / Jean Hatzfeld ; translated from the French by Joshua David Jordan. Farrar, Straus and Giroux, 2018 240 p. **967.5710431**

1. Tutsi (African people) 2. Tutsi (African people) -- Rwanda. 3. Genocide 4. War 5. Rwanda -- History -- Civil War, 1994 6. Interviews

ISBN 9780374279783

LC 2018007632

Originally published: Paris : Gallimard, 2015.

Provides first-person accounts of what life is like for today's Rwandan teenagers and what they have learned from their parents, one generation removed from the ethnic-based genocide in 1994 when the Hutu killed 800,000 Tutsis.

"This book, more of an ethnography than a history, exposes the effects of the genocide's stubborn legacy on the next generation, but is not an introduction to the events of 1994. Readers approaching it without prior knowledge of the genocide or Hutu-Tutsi relations will have a hard time fully understanding it, but those who have context will find this an illuminating update." Publishers Weekly.

967.6 Uganda and Kenya

Chretien, Jean-Pierre

★The **great** lakes of Africa : two thousand years of history / Jean-Pierre Chretien ; translated by Scott Straus. Zone Books ; 2003. 503 p. : **967.6**

1. East Africa -- History. 2. Central Africa -- History. 3. Rwanda -- History. 4. Burundi -- History. 5. Uganda -- History.

ISBN 189095134X

LC 2002191001

"This is an impressive and important book surveying 2,000 years of history. The preeminence accorded Rwanda and Burundi...leads to the book's most significant contribution: to demonstrate that the region's recent interrelated conflicts claiming over four million lives are not based on ancient, unchanging ethnic cleavages, most notably between Tutsi and Hutu." Choice.

967.6104 Uganda--1962-

David, Saul, 1966-

Operation Thunderbolt : Flight 139 and the raid on Entebbe Airport, the most audacious hostage rescue mission in history / Saul David. Little, Brown, & Co., 2015 416 p. **967.6104**

1. Entebbe Airport Raid, 1976. 2. Terrorists. 3. Hijacking of aircraft 4. Hostages. 5. Israel -- Foreign relations Uganda. 6. Uganda --

Foreign relations Israel.
ISBN 9780316245418

LC bl2015046579

The author presents an account of the Raid of Entebbe that covers the 1976 hijacking of a Air France flight by Arab and German terrorists and the rescue of hostages by Israeli commandos at the expense of the operation's leader.

"A definitive history of the Entebbe operation, likely to be popular among readers of military and terrorism works." Library Journal.

Rice, Andrew, 1975-

The **teeth** may smile but the heart does not forget : murder and memory in Uganda / Andrew Rice. Metropolitan Books, Henry Holt and Co., 2009. 384 p. **967.6104**

1. Laki, Eliphaz, d. 1972. 2. Laki, Duncan. 3. Gowon, Yusuf Trials, litigation, etc. 4. Amin, Idi, 1925-2003. 5. Extrajudicial executions -- Uganda. 6. Atrocities -- Uganda. 7. Uganda -- Politics and government -- 1971-1979. 8. Uganda -- Politics and government -- 1979-
ISBN 9780805079654

LC 2008041984

An analysis of Uganda's formidable national challenges in the aftermath of Idi Amin's tyrannical reign focuses on the unsolved murder of Eliphaz Laki and the country's polarizing efforts to simultaneously move on from past conflicts and provide justice for victims.

"At the core of the book is an unsolved disappearance: Eliphaz Laki, a local leader with ties to the anti-Amin opposition, vanished in the early days of the Amin regime. When his son, Duncan, uncovered a clue to his father's disappearance 30 years later, the investigation eventually implicated Amin's second-in-command, Maj. Gen. Yusuf Gowon. With Amin living out his years safely in Saudi Arabia, the trial of Gowon forced Uganda to confront its brutal past. Treating the Lakis' story as a microcosm of Uganda's own, the author weaves together the family's search for truth and justice with Uganda's history." Publishers Weekly.

967.62 Kenya

Anderson, David, 1957-

Histories of the hanged : the dirty war in Kenya and the end of empire / David Anderson. W.W. Norton, 2005. viii, 406 p., 16 p. of plates : **967.62**

1. Mau Mau Movement and Revolt, 1946-1960. 2. Kenya -- History.
ISBN 0393059863

LC 2004024804

A history of the war between the colonial government and the insurrectionist Mau Mau between 1952 and 1960 casts Gikuyu rebels in a more sympathetic light and profiles the British as the conflict's aggressors, in a volume that also discusses the contributions of such figures as Winston Churchill and Harold MacMillan.

"This is vital reading for any student of British colonial and African history." Publishers Weekly.

967.7305 Somalia--1960-

Bowden, Mark, 1951-

Black Hawk down : a story of modern war / Mark Bowden. Atlantic Monthly Press, 1999. 386 p. : **967.7305**

1. Aidid, Mohammed Farah, 1934- 2. United States. Army. Task Force Ranger -- History 3. Green Berets. Delta Force. 4. Black Hawk (Military transport helicopter) 5. Rescue work. 6. Military strategy. 7. Adventure 8. Somalia 9. Mogadishu, Somalia.
ISBN 0871137380

LC 98046688

"Portions of this book were originally published as a series in The Philadelphia inquirer."

ALA Notable Book, 2000.

National Book Award for Nonfiction finalist, 1999

A group of elite U.S. soldiers is sent into Mogadishu in 1993 on a U.N. peacekeeping operation, and for eighteen harrowing hours they are trapped, facing overwhelming odds in hostile territory.

"The author describes both sides of the October 1993 raid into the heart of Mogadishu, Somalia, a raid that quickly became the most intensive close combat Americans have engaged in since the Vietnam War. But Bowden's gripping narrative of the fighting is only a framework for an examination of the internal dynamics of America's elite forces and a critique of the philosophy of sending such high-tech units into combat with minimal support." Publishers Weekly.

Rawlence, Ben

★**City** of thorns : nine lives in the world's largest refugee camp / Ben Rawlence. Picador, [2016] 400 p. **967.7305**

1. Refugee camps 2. Refugees, Somali. 3. Human rights 4. Interpersonal relations 5. Kenya. 6. Somalia -- History -- 1960-1991
ISBN 9781250067630

LC 2015029505

A researcher for Human Rights Watch describes the refugee camp in Dabaab, home to those fleeing civil war in Somalia, and highlights the life of various residents, including a former child soldier, a schoolgirl and a youth leader.

967.73053 Somalia--1991-2000

Fergusson, James, 1966-

The **world's** most dangerous place : inside the outlaw state of Somalia / James Fergusson. Da Capo Press, 2013. 405 p., 16 unnumbered p. of plates : **967.73053**

1. Shabaab (Organization) 2. War -- Somalia. 3. War and society. 4. Militias and irregular armies. 5. Civil war 6. Somalia -- Social conditions. 7. Islamic countries.
ISBN 9780306821172

LC 2013933566

An authoritative account of the Somali region, its history and the story of the Islamic extremists operating there today cites the high human cost of the region's clan-based civil war while explaining how current activities are directly threatening world security.

968.04 Republic of South Africa--1814-1910

Meredith, Martin

Diamonds, gold, and war : the British, the Boers, and the making of South Africa / Martin Meredith. PublicAffairs, 2007. xi, 570 p. : **968.04**

1. Boer War, 1899-1902. 2. Diamond industry and trade -- South Africa -- History -- 19th century. 3. Nonferrous metal industry and trade -- South Africa -- History -- 19th century. 4. Afrikaners -- South Africa -- History. 5. Great Britain -- Colonies Africa -- Administration. 6. Great Britain -- Foreign relations -- 19th century 7. South Africa -- History -- 19th century 8. South Africa -- Politics

and government -- 19th century
ISBN 1586484737

LC 2007034540

"First published in Great Britain in 2007 by Simon & Schuster UK Ltd."--T.p. verso.

A history of the tumultuous period leading up to the 1910 founding of the modern state of South Africa explores how the discovery of vast diamond and gold deposits led to a fierce struggle between the British and the Boers for control of the region.

"Meredith thoroughly involves us in this gripping history. Highly recommended for all libraries." Library Journal.

968.06 South Africa--Period as Republic, 1961

Carlin, John, 1956-

Playing the enemy : Nelson Mandela and the game that made a nation / John Carlin. Penguin Group, 2008. 304 p. **968.06**

1. Mandela, Nelson, 1918-2013 2. Springboks (Rugby team) 3. Presidents -- South Africa 4. Postcolonialism -- South Africa 5. Rugby football -- South Africa 6. Segregation in sports. 7. South Africa -- Politics and government -- 1994- 8. South Africa -- Race relations -- History -- 20th century
ISBN 9781594201745

LC 2008298721

Book made into a movie called Invictus.

"Deftly sketched characters make up both an audience for the big game and a gallery of South Africa, through which Carlin will recount the absorbing story of a country emerging from its cruelly absurd racist experiment." New York Times Book Review.

Duke, Lynne

Mandela, Mobutu, and me : a newswoman's African journey / Lynne Duke. Doubleday, 2003. x, 294 p. ; **968.06**

1. Mandela, Nelson, 1918-2013 2. Mobutu Sese Seko, 1930-1997 3. Duke, Lynne. 4. Women journalists 5. Voyages and travels 6. Africa -- Politics and government
ISBN 0385503989

LC 2002073365

Includes index.

"The author covers some of the bloodier postcolonial wars of southern Africa as well as one of the most constructive struggles: the shaping of a postapartheid government. Her interviews with Mandela and Mobutu bookend...conversations with common folk: township women struggling for clean water, AIDS nurses battling superstitious villagers and even a quiet old Zulu man impressed to meet his first foreign black folk. A consummate journalist, Duke gives readers concise but thorough background briefings on a country's relevant history before cutting to the chase: who's taken control now, why, and what that means for the balance of power. She deftly combines solid information and personal perspective to produce a powerful, readable chronicle." Publishers Weekly.

Tutu, Desmond

No future without forgiveness / Desmond Mpilo Tutu. Doubleday, 1999. 287 p. ; **968.06**

1. South Africa. Truth and Reconciliation Commission. 2. Forgiveness (Christianity) 3. Reconciliation -- Religious aspects -- Christianity. 4. South Africa -- Race relations.
ISBN 9780385496896

LC 99034451

The chairman of South Africa's Truth and Reconciliation Commission explains the healing power of his country's investigation into the wrongdoing of white leaders and citizens against blacks under apartheid.

"The author reflects on his role as chairman of the Truth and Reconciliation Commission. Tutu speaks frankly of...the struggle that preceded it and of the betrayals and jubilations of this unique commission. The TRC's work was unprecedented not only in its emphasis on restorative over retributive justice but in the spirituality that permeated its work, the bulk of which constituted hearings from the victims and perpetrators of apartheid." Publishers Weekly.

Tutu, Desmond

The **rainbow** people of God : the making of a peaceful revolution / Desmond Tutu ; edited by John Allen. Doubleday, 1994. xxii, 281 p. : **968.06**

1. Church of the Province of South Africa. 2. Sermons, South African. 3. Anglican Communion -- South Africa -- Clergy -- Sermons. 4. South Africa -- Race relations.
ISBN 9780385475464

LC 94016011

"This collection of Tutu's speeches, letters, and sermons--from the time of the 1976 Soweto Uprising, through the long years of repression and defiance, up to the triumph of the democratic election--serves as an immediate contemporary history of South Africa. Tutu's media secretary, John Allen, provides a general historical introduction and a connecting narrative that places the individuals pieces in dramatic context." Booklist.

Waldmeir, Patti

Anatomy of a miracle : the end of apartheid and the birth of the new South Africa / Patti Waldmeir. Rutgers University Press, 1998, c1997. xiv, 289 p. ; **968.06**

1. South Africa -- Politics and government -- 1978-1989. 2. South Africa -- Politics and government -- 1989-1994. 3. South Africa -- Race relations.
ISBN 0813525829

LC 98015628

Originally published: New York : W.W. Norton & Co., c1997.

"Although Mandela attributes greatness to de Klerk for his courage, it is Mandela's own character that dominates this history. Engrossing in its sweep, this account also describes the obstacles facing the regime." Publishers Weekly.

968.06092 South Africa--1961---biography

Mandela, Nelson, 1918-2013

The **prison** letters of Nelson Mandela / Nelson Mandela ; edited by Sahm Venter, with foreword by Zamaswazi Dlamini-Mandela. Liveright Publishing Corporation, 2015. 592 p. **968.06092**

1. Mandela, Nelson, 1918-2013 2. Anti-apartheid Movement South Africa 3. Presidents -- South Africa 4. Human rights 5. Justice 6. Anti-apartheid activists 7. South Africa -- Politics and government -- 1948-1994. 8. Letters
ISBN 9781631491177

LC 2018009933

Published on the centenary of his birth, a selection of 255 of the anti-apartheid champion's letters, written during his incarceration, convey his intimate perspectives on such subjects as his wife's imprisonment, the death of his son and human rights.

968.9105 Zimbabwe

Godwin, Peter, 1957-

The **fear** : Robert Mugabe and the martyrdom of Zimbabwe / Peter Godwin. Little, Brown and Co., 2011. 304 p. **968.9105**

1. Mugabe, Robert Gabriel, 1924- 2. World politics. 3. Dictators 4. Fear. 5. Journalists. 6. Zimbabwe -- Politics and government -- 1980- 7. Zimbabwe -- Economic conditions -- 1980- 8. Zimbabwe -- Social conditions -- 1980-

ISBN 9780316051736

LC 2010041557

Born in what's now called Zimbabwe, journalist Peter Godwin returns to his homeland in 2008 after three decades of Robert Mugabe's brutal economic and human destruction. Hoping to "dance on Mugabe's political grave" in the wake of the tyrant's defeat at the polls, Godwin instead risks his life to secretly chronicle Mugabe's ruthless backlash of torture and terror locals call "The Fear."

"Godwin's work serves as an invaluable, urgent dispatch from a country in the throes of an international humanitarian crisis. The author's return to his beloved homeland transformed by violence and no longer familiar proves heart-wrenching and extremely moving." Kirkus.

Lamb, Christina

House of stone : the true story of a family divided in war-torn Zimbabwe / Christina Lamb. Lawrence Hill Books, 2007. 320 p. **968.91051**

1. Hough, Nigel. 2. Aqui, 1962- 3. Land tenure -- Zimbabwe. 4. Europeans in Zimbabwe 5. Violence against farmers -- Zimbabwe. 6. Zimbabwe -- Race relations. 7. Zimbabwe -- Politics and government -- 1980- 8. Zimbabwe -- Social conditions -- 1980- 9. Zimbabwe -- History -- Chimurenga War, 1966-1980

ISBN 9781556527357

LC 2007019814

Describes the lives of two very different Zimbabweans--Nigel Hough, a wealthy white farmer, and Aqui, his poor black nanny--from the 1970s to 2002, focusing how both were affected by Zimbabwe's brutal civil war and its aftermath.

"Through the parallel accounts of two people in Zimbabwe, one a poor black maid, one a rich white farmer, . . . Lamb tells the compelling story of a country ravaged first by colonial settlers and now by brutal civil war. . . . The anguished personal detail, true to the changing viewpoints, makes for a gripping read." Booklist.

970 History of North America

Keegan, John, 1934-

Fields of battle : the wars for North America / John Keegan. Vintage Books, 1997, c1995. xii, 348 p. : **970**

1. Keegan, John, 1934- Travel North America. 2. Battles -- History. 3. Battlefields -- North America. 4. Military history. 5. Military geography. 6. United States -- Armed Forces -- History. 7. North America -- History, Military.

ISBN 0679746641

LC 96046868

Includes index.

Originally published: Warpaths. London : Hodder and Stoughton, 1995.

A definitive survey of the military history of North America explains how geography has shaped America's military heritage and discusses every major fortification and battle site on the continent.

Milton, Giles

Big chief Elizabeth : the adventures and fate of the first English colonists in America / Giles Milton. Farrar, Straus and Giroux, 2000. x, 358 p. : **970**

1. Elizabeth I, Queen of England, 1533-1603 Relations with Americans. 2. Indians of North America 3. Indians of North America, Treatment of. 4. Government relations with indigenous peoples 5. First contact (Anthropology) 6. Great Britain -- Colonies North America -- History -- 16th century. 7. Great Britain -- Foreign relations United States. 8. Western Hemisphere -- Exploration -- British.

ISBN 0374265011

LC 00031522

"First published in Great Britain by Hodder & Stoughton"-- T.p. verso.

A historical account of England's relations with the Native American tribes of North America examines the fate of one hundred English colonists who arrived in the new world in 1587 and then disappeared into the wilderness.

"Nearly 500 years ago, a small group of white men landed on the shores of North America and named it Virginia (for the Virgin Queen [Elizabeth]). Their purpose was to capture some natives and bring them to England to learn their language and everything else they could about the country they wished to colonize. [Milton] chronicles the century-long battle to establish a permanent settlement in Virginia." Christian Science Monitor.

Richter, Daniel K.

Facing east from Indian country : a Native history of early America / Daniel K. Richter. Harvard University Press, 2001. x, 317 p. : **970**

1. First contact of indigenous peoples with Europeans 2. Colonists. 3. Indians of North America -- History -- Colonial period, 1600-1775. 4. Indians of North America, Treatment of -- United States -- History. 5. United States -- History -- Colonial period, 1600-1775

ISBN 9780674006386

LC 2001024997

Pulitzer Prize for History finalist, 2002.

In the beginning, North America was Indian country. But only in the beginning. After the opening act of the great national drama, Native Americans yielded to the westward rush of European settlers. Or so the story usually goes. Yet, for three centuries after Columbus, Native people controlled most of eastern North America and profoundly shaped its destiny. In Facing East from Indian Country, Daniel K. Richter keeps Native people center-stage throughout the story of the origins of the United States. Viewed from Indian country, the sixteenth century was an era in which Native people discovered Europeans and struggled to make sense of a new world.

"The author recasts early American history from the Native American point of view and in doing so illuminates as much about the Europeans as about the original Americans. Exploring the varying complexities of different native people's relationships with England, France and Spain, he argues that the Native Americans were safer during the colonial era than after the Revolution. Gracefully written and argued, Richter's compelling research and provocative claims make this an important addition to the literature for general readers of both Native American and U.S. studies." Publishers Weekly.

970.004 North American native peoples

Dunbar-Ortiz, Roxanne, 1939-

An **indigenous** peoples' history of the United States / Roxanne Dunbar-Ortiz. Beacon Press, 2014 296 p. **970.004**

1. Indians of North America -- Colonization. 2. Indians of North America, Treatment of 3. Intersectionality 4. United States -- Colonization.

ISBN 9780807000403

LC 2013050262

Challenges the founding myth of the United States and shows how policy against the indigenous peoples was genocidal and imperialist, designed to crush the original inhabitants. Spanning more than 300 years, a classic bottom-up history significantly reframes how we view our past. Told from the viewpoint of the indigenous, it reveals how Native Americans, for centuries, actively resisted expansion of the U.S. empire.

Gulbrandsen, Don

Edward Sheriff Curtis : visions of the first Americans / Don Gulbrandsen. Chartwell Books, 2010. 256 p. : **970.004**

1. Curtis, Edward S., 1868-1952. 2. Curtis, Edward S., 1868-1952. North American Indian. 3. Indians of North America -- Pictorial works. 4. Indians of North America -- Social life and customs -- Pictorial works. 5. Indians of North America -- Portraits.

ISBN 9780785826507

LC bl2017008407

Includes index.

Presents photographs selected from each volume of Edward Sheriff Curtis' "The North American Indian" that provide insight into the lifestyles of numerous Native American tribes.

Hogeland, William

Autumn of the Black Snake : the creation of the U.S. Army and the invasion that opened the West / William Hogeland. Farrar Straus & Giroux, 2017 448 p. **970.004**

1. Wayne, Anthony, 1745-1796 2. United States. Army -- History 3. Indians of North America -- Wars. 4. Wayne's Campaign, 1794 5. United States -- History, Military

ISBN 9780374107345

LC 2016052193

An account of how the U.S. Army was created to fight a crucial Native American war describes how George Washington and other early leaders organized the Legion of the United States under General "Mad" Anthony Wayne in response to a 1791 militia defeat in the Ohio River Valley.

"This is a scrupulously balanced account of a formative period in westward expansion." Booklist.

Johnson, Michael, 1937 April 22-

Ojibwa : people of forests and prairies / Michael G. Johnson. Firefly Books, 2016. 160 p. : **970.004**

1. Ojibwa Indians -- History. 2. Indians of North America -- Great Lakes region 3. First Nations (Canada) 4. Ojibwa Indians -- Social life and customs.

ISBN 9781770858008

A look at the history, demography, culture, and material culture of the Ojibwa of North America.

"This study will appeal to anyone interested in First Nations people and would make a great addition to reference libraries." Publishers Weekly.

Josephy, Alvin M., 1915-2005

The **longest** trail : writings on American Indian history, culture, and politics / Alvin M. Josephy, Jr. ; edited by Marc Jaffe and Rich Wandschneider. Vintage Books, A Division of Penguin Random House LLC, 2015. 544 p. **970.004**

1. Indians of North America -- History. 2. Indians of North America -- Social life and customs. 3. Indians of North America -- Politics and government. 4. Essays

ISBN 9780345806918

LC 2015010197

Alvin Josephy Jr.'s groundbreaking, popular books and essays advocated for a fair and true historical assessment of Native Americans, and set the course for modern Native American studies.This collection, which includes magazine articles, speeches, a white paper, and introductions and chapters of books, gives a generous and reasoned view of five hundred years of Indian history in North America from first settlements in the East to the long trek of the Nez Perce Indians in the Northwest.

"Essential for anyone interested in contemporary Native American history and culture and should be read alongside Josephy's autobiography A Walk Toward Oregon: A Memoir." Library Journal.

Nabokov, Peter,

★**Native** American testimony : a chronicle of Indian-white relations from prophecy to the present, 1492-2000 / edited by Peter Nabokov ; with a foreword by Vine Deloria, Jr. Penguin Books, 1999. xxiii, 506 p. : **970.004**

1. Indians of North America -- History -- Sources. 2. Government relations with indigenous peoples. 3. United States -- History

ISBN 0140281592

LC BL 00004382

Presents a history of native American and white relations from the earliest encounters to the present day.

"A collection of primary-source material, grouped by key issues that arose during 500 years of Indian and white encounters in North America. Nabokov uses traditional narratives, old government transcripts, reservation newspapers, and firsthand interviews to highlight this chronological volume. Photographs appear throughout." School Library Journal. {review of 1991 edition}

Rajtar, Steve, 1951-

Indian war sites : a guidebook to battlefields, monuments, and memorials, state by state with Canada and Mexico / Steve Rajtar. McFarland, c1999. v, 330 p. ; **970.004**

1. Battlefields -- North America 2. Historic sites -- North America 3. Indians of North America -- History 4. Indians of North America -- Wars 5. North America Guidebooks. 6. Guidebooks.

ISBN 9780786407101

LC 99025893

"This is a reference to hundreds of conflicts, both major and minor, between American Indians and Europeans. Divided alphabetically by state and then chronologically within each, entries include name and date, a nonspecific location (e.g., Spring River), a brief description, and bibliographic sources. If the battle was a part of a larger war Rajtar also gives the name of the war; and if there is a monument, he tells its location and briefly describes what's there." Library Journal.

Robbins, Catherine C.

All Indians do not live in teepees (or casinos) / Catherine C. Robbins. University of Nebraska Press, c2011. xvi, 385 p. : **970.004**

1. Indians of North America -- Social life and customs. 2. Kinship-

based society 3. Indians of North America -- Material culture.
ISBN 9780803239739

LC 2011011320

Both a tribute to the unique experiences of individual Native Americans and a celebration of the values that draw American Indians together, All Indians Do Not Live in Teepees (or Casinos) explores contemporary Native life.

Treuer, Anton

Atlas of Indian nations / Anton Treuer. National Geographic, c2013. 1 atlas (319 p.) : **970.004**

1. Indians of North America -- Maps 2. Indians of North America -- History -- Maps 3. Atlases
ISBN 9781426211607

LC 2013036634

Examines the history, beliefs, traditions, languages, and lifestyles of indigenous peoples of North America, in a text organized by eight geographical regions.

Treuer, David

★The **heartbeat** of Wounded Knee : Native America from 1890 to the present / David Treuer. Riverhead Books, 2019. 512 p. : **970.004**

1. Indians of North America -- History -- 20th century 2. Indians of North America -- Identity 3. Indians of North America, Treatment of 4. Native American resistance and revolts
ISBN 9781594633157

National Book Award for Nonfiction finalist, 2019.

Andrew Carnegie Medal for Excellence in Non-Fiction Finalist, 2020

An anthropologist's chronicle of Native American life from the Wounded Knee massacre to the present traces the unprecedented resourcefulness and reinvention of distinct tribe cultures that assimilated into mainstream life to preserve Native identity.

"Treuer takes on a bold task: a history of Native America from the Paleolithic to the Standing Rock Reservation protest against the Dakota Access Pipeline in 2017. Peoples from all regions of North America are included. Unlike other works that depict the 'vanishing Indian' narrative, Treuer's does not end at the 1890 Wounded Knee massacre. Rather, he uses Wounded Knee as a springboard to discuss the Native American experience as it has adapted and persisted since." Library Journal.

Wilson, James, 1949-

The **Earth** shall weep : a history of Native America / James Wilson. Atlantic Monthly Press, 1999. xxix, 466 p. : **970.004**

1. Indians of North America -- History. 2. Indians of North America, Treatment of. 3. Government relations with indigenous peoples
ISBN 0871137305

LC 99013098

Originally published: London : Picador, 1998.

Provides a Native American perspective on the history of North America.

"Employing elegiac prose and steady narrative momentum, Wilson has written a richly informative history that places Native Americans 'at the center of the historical stage.'" Publishers Weekly.

Woodard, Colin, 1968-

American nations : a history of the eleven rival regional cultures of North America / Colin Woodard. Viking, c2011. 320 p. **970.004**

1. Regionalism -- North America -- History 2. Race relations 3. Culture conflict 4. Indians of North America 5. North America -- Race relations.
ISBN 9780670022960

LC 2011015196

Includes index.

A history of North America's 11 rival cultural regions challenges popular perceptions about the red state-blue state conflict, tracing lingering tensions stemming from disparate intranational values that have shaped every major event in history. By the author of Ocean's End.

"The author's take on American history identifies the original cultural settlements that became the United States, and proceeds with the thesis that these regional and cultural divisions are responsible for clashes stretching back to Revolutionary times. The 11 nations don't follow state or even country territory lines, but rather the paths taken by the earliest settlers of these areas; while later immigrants added to the mix, they didn't change the fundamental culture. The book's compelling explanations and apt descriptions will fascinate anyone with an interest in politics, regional culture, or history." Publishers Weekly.

970.00497 American native peoples

Johnson, Michael, 1937 Apr. 22-

Encyclopedia of native tribes of North America / Michael Johnson ; illustrator, Richard Hook. Compendium, 2007. 320 p. : **970.00497**

1. Indians of North America
ISBN 190557374X

LC 2008360036

Previous ed.: Oxford: Compendium, 2001.

Respected researcher Michael G. Johnson meticulously details every aspect of each American Indian tribe's history, arts, crafts and material culture

"The maps, photographs, and beautiful illustrations by Hook, combined with concise, accurate entries, make this volume a good purchase, especially for libraries that lack the 2007 edition." Choice

970.01 North America--Early history to 1599

Adovasio, J. M.

The **first** Americans : in pursuit of archaeology's greatest mystery / J. M. Adovasio with Jake Page. Random House, c2002. xii, 328 p. : **970.01**

1. Indians of North America -- Origin. 2. Paleo-Indians. 3. Clovis culture. 4. Archaeology. 5. Western Hemisphere -- Antiquities.
ISBN 0375505520

LC 2002069766

A leading archaeologist addresses the complex puzzle about the origins of the first humans to settle in America, reassessing common myths about early human migration and lifestyle.

"Readers get a lively, close-up view of how archaeologists study America's original discoverers." Booklist.

Butman, John

New World, Inc. : the making of America by England's merchant adventurers / John Butman and Simon Targett. Little, Brown & Company, 2018. 432 p. **970.01**

1. Entrepreneurs 2. Businesspeople 3. Colonies 4. Adventurers 5. North America -- History -- Colonial period, 1600-1775 6. England -- History -- 17th century 7. Great Britain -- History -- 17th century
ISBN 9780316307888

LC bl2018001081

Three generations of English merchant adventurers--not the Pilgrims, as we have so long believed--were the earliest founders of America, with profit, not piety, as their primary motive.

"An eye-opening and thoroughly enjoyable look at the roots of American ambition." Booklist.

Horwitz, Tony, 1958-

★A **voyage** long and strange : rediscovering the new world / Tony Horwitz. Henry Holt and Co., 2008. 448 p. **970.01**

1. Explorers -- Western Hemisphere -- History. 2. Exploration. 3. Explorers -- North America -- History. 4. Western Hemisphere -- Exploration 5. North America -- Exploration.

ISBN 9780805076035

LC 2007045883

ALA Notable Book, 2009.

A chronicle of the period in American history between Columbus's discovery of the new world and Jamestown's founding evaluates the voyages and first-contact experiences of numerous European adventurers.

"Realizing that his knowledge of American history between Columbus's discovery and Plymouth Rock over 100 years later was sketchy at best, . . . [the author] sets out to educate himself with his own explorations. He intertwines his experiences retracing the early conquistadors, adventurers, and entrepreneurs through such regions as Newfoundland, the Dominican Republic, and the American South, Southwest, and New England with thoroughly researched accounts of the territories themselves, the natives who were historically affected, and the motives of the explorers. . . . This readable and vastly entertaining history travelog is highly recommended for public libraries." Library Journal.

Mann, Charles C.

1491 : new revelations of the Americas before Columbus / Charles C. Mann. Knopf, 2005. xii, 465 p. : **970.01**

1. Civilization, Pre-Columbian 2. Indians of Central America. 3. Indians of South America. 4. Indians of North America. 5. United States -- Antiquities.

ISBN 140004006X

LC 2004061547

National Academies Communication Award, 2006.

An analysis of America prior to 1492 describes how the research of archaeologists and anthropologists has transformed myths about the Americas, revealing that the cultures were far older and more advanced than previously known.

"Mann navigates adroitly through the controversies. He approaches each in the best scientific tradition, carefully sifting the evidence, never jumping to hasty conclusions, giving everyone a fair hearing: the experts and the amateurs; the accounts of the Indians and their conquerors. And rarely is he less than enthralling." New York Times Book Review.

970.5 Atlantic Provinces

Redniss, Lauren

★**Oak** Flat : a fight for sacred land in the American West / Lauren Redniss. Random House, 2020. 288 p. **970.5**

1. Apache Indians -- Land rights 2. Government relations with indigenous peoples 3. Nature conservation 4. Indians of North America -- Southwest (United States) 5. Arizona 6. San Carlos Indian Reservation, Arizona 7. Illustrated books 8. Multiple perspectives

ISBN 9780399589720

Illustrated by the author.

Three generations of an Apache family struggle to protect sacred land from a multinational mining corporation.

"As a work of advocacy, the book is compelling and convincing; as a work of art, it is masterful." Kirkus

971 Canada

Black, Conrad

Rise to greatness : the history of Canada from the Vikings to the present / Conrad Black. McClelland & Stewart, 2014 xiii, 1106 p. : **971**

1. Canada -- History.

ISBN 077101354X

LC 2014944153

Financier and columnist Conrad Black presents a history of Canada from 874 to 2014, beginning with Canada's first inhabitants and early explorers and running to the present day.

Elliott, Alicia

A **mind** spread out on the ground / Alicia Elliott. Melville House, 2020, c2019. 256 p. **971**

1. Colonization -- Social aspects -- Canada. 2. Indigenous peoples -- Social conditions 3. Psychic trauma 4. Racism -- Canada. 5. Canada -- Race relations.

ISBN 9781612198668

Originally published: Toronto : Doubleday Canada, 2019.

Hilary Weston Writers' Trust Prize for Nonfiction finalist, 2019.

A personal meditation on trauma, legacy, oppression and racism in North America, in an urgent and visceral work that asks essential questions about Native people in North America.

"A bicultural, binational writer examines racial justice, mental illness, cultural appropriation, and other issues in this powerful set of essays. . . . An impressive debut from a welcome new voice in Native letters." Kirkus

971.01 Early history to 1763

MacLeod, D. Peter, 1955-

Northern Armageddon : the Battle of the Plains of Abraham and the making of the American Revolution / Peter MacLeod. Alfred A. Knopf, 2016 384 p. **971.01**

1. Quebec Campaign, 1759 2. Plains of Abraham, Battle of the, Quebec, 1759. 3. Seven Years' War, 1756-1763 4. Canada -- History -- To 1763 (New France).

ISBN 9780307269898

LC 2015015893

A re-creation of the 18th-century Battle of the Plains of Abraham discusses its critical roles in the Seven Years' War, the colonial War of Independence and the establishment of Canada. By the author of The Canadian Iroquois and the Seven Years'

"This is a superbly researched and written account of a seminal episode in world history." Booklist.

971.2 Prairie Provinces

Sacco, Joe

★**Paying** the land / Joe Sacco. Metropolitan Books, 2020. 256 p. **971.2**

1. Chipewyan Indians 2. Indians of North America, Treatment of 3. First Nations (Canada) 4. Racism 5. Comics and Graphic novels 6.

Historical comics
ISBN 9781627799034

LC 2019053376

Chiefly illustrated.

Joe Sacco travels the frozen North to reveal a people in conflict over the costs and benefits of development. The mining boom is only the latest assault on indigenous culture: Sacco recounts the shattering impact of a residential school system that aimed to "remove the Indian from the child;" the destructive process that drove the Dene from the bush into settlements and turned them into wage laborers; the government land claims stacked against the Dene Nation; and their uphill efforts to revive a wounded culture.

"Harrowing and enlightening, Sacco presents another solemn, resonating dispatch." Booklist

971.6 Nova Scotia

Bacon, John U., 1964-

The **great** Halifax explosion : a World War I story of treachery, tragedy, and extraordinary heroism / John U. Bacon. William Morrow & Co., 2017. ix, 418 p., 16 unnumbered p. of plates : **971.6**

1. Halifax Explosion, December 6, 1917. 2. Explosions. 3. World War I 4. Halifax, Nova Scotia -- History -- 20th century.
ISBN 9780062666536

LC 2017276263

A gripping account of the world's largest man-made explosion before the atomic bomb describes the events that led to the catastrophic igniting of the French freighter Mont-Blanc in 1917 Halifax, killing and wounding thousands while leading to advances in medicine and weapons science.

"An absorbing history of disaster and survival." Kirkus.

MacDonald, Laura, 1963-

Curse of the Narrows : the Halifax Disaster of 1917 / Laura M. MacDonald. Walker & Co., 2005. 350 p. **971.6**

1. Mont Blanc (Freighter) 2. Imo (Steamer) 3. Halifax Explosion, December 6, 1917. 4. Explosions -- Halifax, Nova Scotia -- History -- 20th century. 5. Halifax, Nova Scotia -- History -- 20th century. 6. Halifax, Nova Scotia
ISBN 0802714587

LC 2005044255

Traces the 1917 disaster in Nova Scotia during which two ships collided and one exploded and devastated the city under circumstances that would later be studied for the making of the atomic bomb, in an account that also describes the subsequent relief mission and trial of the ship's captain.

"This book captures in vivid detail the history of this catastrophe." Booklist.

971.9 Northern territories

Gray, Charlotte, 1948-

Gold diggers : striking it rich in the Klondike / Charlotte Gray. Counterpoint, c2010. 413 p. : **971.9**

1. Gold rush -- Klondike River Valley, Yukon Territory. 2. Frontier and pioneer life. 3. Gold miners. 4. Mines and mineral resources. 5. Dawson, Yukon Territory. 6. Klondike River Valley, Yukon Territory -- History -- 19th century. 7. Yukon Territory -- History -- 19th century. 8. Canada -- History -- 19th century.
ISBN 9781582436111

LC 2010017805

Also published: Toronto : HarperCollins Canada, 2010.

Presents the story of the Klondike gold rush, told through the lives of six different people: miner William Haskell, priest Father Judge, businesswoman Belinda Mulrooney, writer Jack London, British journalist Flora Shaw, and Mountie Sam Steele.

"This is an enchanting recitation of lives--and deaths--in the Klondike during the gold rush over 100 years ago. Combining a keen eye for detail and firsthand histories of contemporary witnesses, Gray sets forth the lives of six stampeders." Library Journal.

972 Mexico, Central America, West Indies, Bermuda

Crutchfield, James A., 1938-

Revolt at Taos : the New Mexican and Indian insurrection of 1847 / James A. Crutchfield. Westholme, [2015] 400 p. **972**

1. Indians of North America 2. Mexican-American War, 1845-1848 3. Insurgency 4. Manifest destiny, 5. Taos Pueblo, New Mexico 6. New Mexico
ISBN 9781594162237

LC 2015451017

"This broad treatment of the Taos Revolt is a sincere attempt to view events and consequences from the perspectives of all peoples involved. Recommended for the examination of civil rights during the forced Americanization of established residents of New Mexico territory." Library Journal.

Diaz del Castillo, Bernal, 1496-1584

The **discovery** and conquest of Mexico, 1517-1521 / Bernal Diaz del Castillo ; edited from the only exact copy of the original MS (and published in Mexico) by Genaro Garcia ; translated with an introduction and notes by A.P. Maudslay ; new introduction by Hugh Thomas. Da Capo Press, 1996. xxxi, 478 p. : **972**

1. Cortes, Hernan, 1485-1547. 2. Mexico -- History -- Conquest, 1519-1540.
ISBN 0306806975

LC 95045871

Originally published: New York : Farrar, Straus, and Cudahy, 1956.
Includes index.

"The memoirs of an old man, who began to write of his experiences half a century after they occurred and completed his account at the age of 84, they are not free from minor inaccuracies, but they are the most reliable narrative that exists." Chicago Sunday Tribune.

Foster, Lynn V.

★A **brief** history of Mexico / Lynn V. Foster. Facts On File, c2009. 336 p. Brief history (Facts on File) **972**

1. History. 2. Culture. 3. Mexico -- History. 4. Central America -- History.
ISBN 9780816074051

LC 2009018298

An introduction to the history of Mexico covers such topics as indigenous peoples, the environment, the North American Free Trade Agreement, and current law enforcement efforts against the drug cartels.

Fuentes, Carlos

A **new** time for Mexico / Carlos Fuentes ; translated from the Spanish by Marina Gutman Castaneda and the author. University of California Press, 1997. xiv, 226 p. ; **972**

1. Freedom. 2. Political corruption. 3. Political science. 4. Chiapas, Mexico (State) -- History -- Peasant uprising, 1994. 5. Mexico -- Politics and government -- 1988- 6. Latin America -- History -- 1980-
ISBN 0520211839

LC 97008427

Originally published: New York : Farrar, Straus & Giroux, 1996. With new pref.

Includes index.

"In these essays Fuentes calls on Mexican president Ernesto Zedillo to take definitive steps toward a full democracy: electoral reform; equal access of candidates to the media; independent, aggressive labor unions; and, above all, true separation between the ruling party and the government. Offering lapidary, lyrical meditations on Mexico as a land of continual metamorphosis, Fuentes nostalgically reminisces about his home in Veracruz, whose port his father defended against a Yankee invasion in 1914." Publishers Weekly.

Henderson, Timothy J.

The **Mexican** Wars for Independence / Timothy J. Henderson. Hill and Wang, 2009. 272 p. **972**

1. National liberation history. 2. Social reformers. 3. Revolutionaries -- Mexico -- 19th century. 4. Mexico -- History -- Wars of Independence, 1810-1821. 5. Mexico -- History -- 1821-1867 6. Latin America -- History -- Wars of Independence, 1806-1830
ISBN 9780809095094

LC 2008048141

A chronicle of Mexico's war for independence explains how the conflict's revolutionaries were more intent on implementing social reforms than achieving political independence, in an account that also examines the roles of Miguel Hidalgo and José María Morelos.

Kirkwood, Burton

The **history** of Mexico / Burton Kirkwood. Greenwood Press/ ABC-CLIO, c2010. xix, 258 p. : **972**

1. Mexico -- History. 2. Latin America -- History. 3. Mexico -- History.
ISBN 9780313366017

LC 2009036964

This sweeping introduction unveils the fascinating, complex, and evolving history of Mexico--from its earliest settlement to the first decade of the 21st century.

"In a brief overview ranging from prehistoric times to 1999, Kirkwood offers a basic chronology of major events and outstanding personalities that have helped to shape Mexico's colorful and often convoluted history." Choice.

Meyer, Michael C.

The **Oxford** history of Mexico / edited by Michael C. Meyer and William H. Beezley. Oxford University Press, c2000. xii, 709 p. : **972**

1. Mexico -- History.
ISBN 9780195112283

LC 99056044

Fully illustrated, with black-and-white photos throughout and a sixteen page color insert, suggestions for future reading, an index, and a glossary, this is the fullest and most engaging history of Mexico available today. --From publisher description.

Restall, Matthew, 1964-

When Montezuma met Cortes : the true story of the meeting that changed history / Matthew Restall. Ecco, 2018. 256 p. **972**

1. Montezuma II, Emperor of Mexico, ca. 1480-1520 2. Cortes, Hernan, 1485-1547. 3. Aztecs -- History -- 16th century. 4. Indians of Mexico -- History -- 16th century. 5. Mexico -- History -- Conquest, 1519-1540.
ISBN 9780062427267

LC bl2018002433

An extensively researched account of the early 16th-century encounter between Montezuma and Hernando Cortes that overturns what is popularly understood about the natures of both men and the Spanish conquest of the Americas.

"Blending erudition with enthusiasm, Restall has achieved a rare kind of work: serious scholarship that is impossible to put down." Publishers Weekly.

Townsend, Richard F.

The **Aztecs** / Richard F. Townsend. Thames & Hudson, 2009. 256 p. : **972**

1. Aztecs -- History. 2. Indians of Mexico. 3. Civilization, Ancient. 4. Mexico -- Civilization.
ISBN 9780500287910

LC 2010549825

Examines the history of these accomplished people through a review of the monuments and artifacts they left behind; exploring how their water-control projects worked, the purposes of their ceremonial centers, and the way they built their incredible ancient structures that still stand today.

972.81 Guatemala

Carlsen, William

Jungle of stone : the true story of two men, their extraordinary journey, and the discovery of the lost civilization of the Mayans / William Carlsen. William Morrow, 2016 464 p. **972.81**

1. Stephens, John L., 1805-1852. 2. Catherwood, Frederick. 3. Carlsen, William 4. Archaeological expeditions -- Central America 5. Explorers 6. Mayas 7. Expeditions 8. Central America
ISBN 9780062407399

LC 2016429951

Documents the true story of the 19th-century rediscovery of the Mayan civilization by American ambassador John Lloyd Stephens and British architect Frederick Catherwood, illuminating how their findings profoundly changed Western understandings about human history.

"A captivating history of two men who dramatically changed their contemporaries' view of the past." Kirkus.

Coe, Michael D

Royal cities of the ancient Maya / text by Michael D. Coe ; photographs by Barry Brukoff. The Vendome Press, 2012. 223 p. : **972.81**

1. Maya architecture. 2. Mayas -- Antiquities. 3. Central America -- Antiquities.
ISBN 0865652848

LC 2011051139

Witschey, Walter Robert Thurmond, 1941-

Encyclopedia of the Ancient Maya / edited by Walter R. T.

Witschey. Rowman & Littlefield, 2016 xxxv, 538 p. : **972.81**

1. Mayas -- Encyclopedias.

ISBN 9780759122840

LC 2015032712

Encyclopedia of the Ancient Maya provides an A-to-Z overview of the ancient Maya culture from its inception to the Spanish Conquest. Exploring Maya society, celebrations, and achievements, as well as new insights into Maya culture and collapse, this is a sophisticated yet accessible introduction suitable for students and general readers.

972.87 Panama

McCullough, David G.

★The **path** between the seas : the creation of the Panama Canal, 1870-1914 / David McCullough. Simon and Schuster, c1977 698 p. : **972.87**

1. Lesseps, Ferdinand Marie, comte de, 1805-1894. 2. Roosevelt, Theodore, 1858-1919. 3. Canals -- Design and construction. 4. Imperialism, American -- Panama -- History. 5. Civil engineering. 6. Panama Canal -- History. 7. Canal Zone.

ISBN 9780743262132

LC 00266235

National Book Critics Circle Award for Nonfiction finalist

Describes all the events and personalities involved in the monumental undertaking which precipitated revolution, scandal, economic crisis, and a new Central American republic.

"Not only is this a well-told story of the building of the Panama Canal but it also supplies welcome background for the . . . debate on the canal's role in inter-American relations." Booklist.

972.9 West Indies (Antilles) and Bermuda

Gibson, Carrie, 1976-

Empire's crossroads : a history of the Caribbean from Columbus to the present day / Carrie Gibson. Atlantic Monthly Press, 2014. 448 p. **972.9**

1. Sugar industry and trade 2. Caribbean Area -- History

ISBN 9780802126146

LC 2015430678

Traces the story of the coveted area from the northern rim of South America up to Cuba, exploring its history from discovery through colonialism to today, offering a vivid, panoramic view of this complex region.

"Alongside her stark descriptions of the slave economies, Gibson recounts geopolitical events that have periodically wracked the Caribbean Sea, from wars galore in the 1700s to the Cold War, as well as the supplanting of European suzerainty by American influence, expressed today more by cruise ship than by gunboat. Sympathetically attuned to the hard actualities of life in ostensibly paradisaical tropics, Gibson delivers a fine, faceted history for general-interest readers." Booklist.

Jelly-Schapiro, Joshua

Island people : the Caribbean and the world / Joshua Jelly-Schapiro. Knopf, 2016. 384 p. **972.9**

1. Colonized peoples 2. Intellectual life 3. Culture 4. West Indians. 5. West Indies 6. Caribbean Area -- History. 7. Cuba 8. Jamaica 9. Puerto Rico 10. Trinidad and Tobago 11. Haiti 12. Barbados

ISBN 9780385349765

LC 2016010673

A kaleidoscopic portrait of the societies, cultures, and politics of Cuba, Jamaica, Puerto Rico, Trinidad, Haiti, Barbados and their interspersed islands seeks to connect the region's common heritage to its fierce grip on the world's imagination.

"Though his arguments about the relationship between modernity, tourism, and branding are not always clear, Jelly-Schapiro writes joyfully about music and literature and how these arts reflect the Caribbean's hybrid and evolving culture." Publishers Weekly.

Von Tunzelmann, Alex, 1977-

Red heat : conspiracy, murder, and the Cold War in the Caribbean / Alex von Tunzelmann. Henry Holt, 2011. 432 p. **972.9**

1. Castro, Fidel, 1926-2016 2. Castro Ruz, Raul, 1930- 3. Guevara, Che, 1928-1967. 4. Trujillo Molina, Rafael Leonidas, 1891-1961. 5. Duvalier, Francois, 1907-1971. 6. Cold War. 7. International relations. 8. Great powers. 9. Politicians. 10. Caribbean Area -- History -- 1945- 11. Dominican Republic -- History -- 1930-1961. 12. Cuba -- History -- 1959-1990. 13. Haiti -- History -- 1934-1986. 14. United States -- Foreign relations Caribbean Area. 15. Caribbean Area -- Foreign relations United States.

ISBN 9780805090673

LC 2010037585

Includes index.

"Three dictators, circa 1960--Castro in Cuba, Fracois Duvalier in Haiti, and Rafael Trujillo in the Dominican Republic--are the principals in von Tunzelmann's political history. Recounting alarms that trio set off in Washington, she ponders how well the Eisenhower and Kennedy administrations understood situations on the islands of Cuba and Hispaniola. Not very realistically, runs the tenor of von Tunzelmann's narrative. Punctuated by accounts of such major incidents as the Bay of Pigs, the assassination of Trujillo, the Cuban missile crisis, and LBJ's 1965 intervention in the Dominican Republic, von Tunzelmann's diligent work will widen the eyes of cold war buffs." Booklist.

972.91 Cuba

Cooke, Julia

The **other** side of paradise : life in the new Cuba / Julia Cooke. Seal Press, 2014. 248 p. **972.91**

1. Castro, Fidel, 1926-2016 2. Social change. 3. Young adults. 4. Cubans. 5. Havana, Cuba 6. Cuba

ISBN 9781580055314

LC 2013044413

Over a period of five years, beginning when Fidel Castro stepped down from his presidency after almost a half-century of reign, journalist Julia Cooke embedded herself in Cuba, gaining access to a dynamic Havana--one that she found populated with twenty-five-year-old Marxist philosophy students, baby-faced anarchists, children of the whiskey-drinking elite, Santeria trainees, pregnant prostitutes, and more. Combining intimate storytelling with in-depth reportage, The Other Side of Paradise weaves together stories of the Cubans whom Cooke encountered, providing a vivid and unprecedented look into the daily lives and future prospects of young people in Cuba today. From ambitious Lucia, a recent university graduate with an acerbic sense of humor and plans to leave Cuba for the first country to give her a visa, if she can just get the roadblocks out of the way--to a crew of mohawk-wearing teenage anarchists who toss bricks at police cars and cite lyrics by The Clash (but don't know the lead singer's name), the characters of The Other Side of Paradise paint a captivating portrait of Cuban culture and the emerging legacy of Fidel Castro's failed promises. Eye-opening and politically prescient, The Other Side of Paradise is sure to linger in readers' minds long after they've finished reading.

"An absorbing and educational read about contemporary Cuba, the love of its people for their country, and their hope for opportunity." Library Journal.

Kurlansky, Mark

Havana : a subtropical delirium / Mark Kurlansky. Bloomsbury USA, 2017. 224 p. **972.91**

1. Kurlansky, Mark Travel 2. Americans in Cuba 3. City life 4. Havana, Cuba -- History. 5. Havana, Cuba -- Description and travel.
ISBN 9781632863911

LC 2016041072

Award-winning author Mark Kurlansky, who wrote the bestesellers Salt and Cod, here turns his keen eye to the beloved city he's been visiting for 30 years: Havana, Cuba. In this adoring travelogue/history, Kurlansky shares personal stories and offers details about the 500-year-old Caribbean city's past and present, people, culture, sports, and music, as well as its appearances in art and literature (yes, Hemingway is discussed). Havana is a complex place, and if you want a talented guide to help you understand this elegant yet downtrodden city, pick up Havana, which includes not only recipes but pen-and-ink drawings by the talented author.

"An affectionate, richly detailed, brief biography of a unique city." Kirkus.

Perez, Louis A., 1943-

Cuba : between reform and revolution / Louis A. Perez, Jr. Oxford University Press, 2006. xvii, 442 p. : **972.91**

1. Nationalism -- Cuba -- History. 2. Cuba -- History.
ISBN 9780195179125

LC 2004065477

Suchlicki, Jaime

Cuba : from Columbus to Castro and beyond / James Suchlicki. Brassey's, c2002. xiii, 285 p. ; **972.91**

1. Cuba -- History.
ISBN 9781574884364

LC 2002003953

Surveys Cuban history, focusing on the twentieth century and the revolution led by Castro.

972.9106 Cuba--1899-

Dobbs, Michael, 1950-

★**One** minute to midnight : Kennedy, Khrushchev, and Castro on the brink of nuclear war / Michael Dobbs. Alfred A. Knopf, 2008. 448 p. **972.9106**

1. Cuban Missile Crisis, 1962 2. Cold War -- History 3. Ballistic missiles 4. Missiles 5. Soviet Union 6. Cuba -- History -- 20th century 7. United States -- History -- 20th century
ISBN 9781400043583

LC 2007052250

A study of the 1962 Cuban missile crisis chronicles the standoff between the U.S. and the Soviet Union over the placement of missiles in Cuba, analyzing the events and personalities involved to reveal how close the world came to all-out nuclear war.

"This book is filled with...insights that will change the views of experts and help inform a new generation of readers." New York Times Book Review.

Rasenberger, Jim

The **brilliant** disaster : JFK, Castro, and America's doomed invasion of Cuba's Bay of Pigs / Jim Rasenberger. Simon & Schuster, 2011. 352 p. **972.9106**

1. Kennedy, John F. (John Fitzgerald), 1917-1963. 2. Castro, Fidel, 1926-2016 3. Bay of Pigs Invasion, 1961. 4. Communism. 5. United States -- Foreign relations Cuba. 6. Cuba -- Foreign relations United States.
ISBN 9781416596509

LC 2011004178

Rasenberger delivers the definitive account of one of the most ill-fated blunders in U.S. history. Trained by the CIA, 1,400 Cuban expats planned to invade Cuba, trigger a popular revolt, and topple Castro's communist regime. But when Castro was tipped off and U.S. air support was cancelled, the would-be liberators were sacrificed in a crossfire of betrayal.

"On Apr., 17, 1961, a CIA-trained brigade of 1,400 Cuban exiles, mostly students and former soldiers, made an unsuccessful amphibious assault on the Bay of Pigs, in southern Cuba, hoping to spur a popular revolt and overthrow the Castro regime. Fifty years later, Rasenberger succeeds admirably in offering a nuanced view of the entire botched operation, from its planning in two U.S. administrations to the Cuban armed forces' quick defeat of the exiles, whose attack lacked air cover and the element of surprise." Kirkus.

Sherwin, Martin J.

Gambling with armageddon : nuclear roulette from Hiroshima to the Cuban Missile Crisis, 1945-1962 / Martin J. Sherwin. Alfred A. Knopf, 2020. 624 p. **972.9106**

1. Kennedy, John F. (John Fitzgerald), 1917-1963. 2. Cuban Missile Crisis, 1962. 3. Nuclear crisis control. 4. Arms race -- History -- 20th century. 5. World politics -- 1945-1955.
ISBN 9780307266880

LC 2019057322

"A Borzoi Book."

In this groundbreaking look at the Cuban Missile Crisis, Martin Sherwin not only gives us a riveting sometimes hour-by-hour explanation of the crisis itself, but also explores the origins, scope, and consequences of the evolving place of nuclear weapons in the post-World War II world.

"Intricately detailed, vividly written, and nearly Tolstoyan in scope, Sherwin's account reveals just how close the Cold War came to boiling over. History buffs will be enthralled." Publishers Weekly

972.9107 Cuba--2008-

Craig, William, 1929-

Yankee come home : on the road from Guantanamo to San Juan Hill / William Craig. Walker & Co., 2011. 288 p. **972.9107**

1. Spanish-American War, 1898 2. Imperialism, American -- History -- 19th century 3. Imperialism, American -- Cuba 4. Families -- History 5. United States -- Foreign relations Cuba 6. Cuba -- Foreign relations United States
ISBN 9780802710932

LC bl2012027963

Contends that events from the Spanish-American war set the stage for troubled present-day relations between the United States and Cuba, arguing that America's 1898 intervention was an act of hubris and avarice that has culminated in a regional abandonment of defining ideals.

972.92 Jamaica and Cayman Islands

Kincaid, Jamaica

A **small** place / Jamaica Kincaid. Farrar, Straus and Giroux, 2000, c1988. 81 p. : **972.92**

1. Kinkaid, Jamaica Homes and haunts 2. Authors -- 20th century 3. Postcolonialism 4. Power (Social sciences) 5. Tourism 6. West Indies -- Description and travel 7. Antigua and Barbuda -- Social conditions 8. Essays

ISBN 9780374527075

Antigua--a ten-by-twelve-mile island in the British West Indies and the author's birthplace--is the setting of a lyrical, sardonic, and forthright essay that offers an insider's eye-opening view of the lives and ways of her people.

972.94 Haiti

Dubois, Laurent, 1971-

Haiti : the aftershocks of history / Laurent Dubois. Metropolitan Books, 2012. 434 p. : **972.94**

1. Autonomy -- Haiti. 2. Democracy -- Haiti. 3. Postcolonialism. 4. Nation-building 5. Haiti -- History. 6. Haiti -- Civilization. 7. Haiti -- Politics and government -- 1804-

ISBN 9780805093353

LC 2011020162

Challenges popular misconceptions to link Haiti's troubled current state to its turbulent history, documenting how the 1804 slave rebellion placed Haiti at odds with the rest of the world, in an account that also illuminates the country's lesser-known cultural successes.

973 United States

Andersen, Kurt, 1954-

★**Fantasyland** : how America went haywire: a 500-year history / Kurt Andersen. Random House, 2017. 480 p. **973**

1. Reality 2. Empiricism 3. Belief and doubt 4. Public opinion 5. United States -- Social conditions

ISBN 9781400067213

LC 2017016052

The author of Heyday explains how the influences of dreamers, zealots, hucksters and superstitious groups shaped America's tendency toward a rich fantasy life, citing the roles of contributors ranging from P. T. Barnum and Billy Graham to Disney and Donald Trump in perpetuating conspiracy theories, self-delusion and magical thinking.

Anderson, Fred, 1949-

The **dominion** of war : empire and liberty in North America, 1500-2000 / Fred Anderson and Andrew Cayton. Penguin Books, 2005. xxiv, 520 p. : **973**

1. Imperialism -- History. 2. Republicanism -- United States -- History. 3. War and society -- History. 4. National characteristics, American. 5. United States -- History, Military. 6. United States -- Territorial expansion. 7. North America -- History, Military.

ISBN 0143036513

LC bl2006007432

Originally published: New York : Viking, 2005.

A reinterpretation of the development of the United States argues that warfare has played a leading role in shaping North America throughout the past five hundred years, in a history that focuses on the lives of eight men, including George Washington, Ulysses S. Grant, and Colin Powell.

"The authors provide an account of the U.S. rise to global preeminence over five centuries. Central to their thesis is the assertion that military conflict has been essential in determining the cultural and political evolution of North America. Anderson and Cayton have provided a well-written and important reinterpretation of our past." Booklist.

Ashby, Ruth

The **great** American documents. Ruth Ashby, Ernie Colon. Hill and Wang, 2014. 151 p. Great American documents ; **973**

1. Historic documents. 2. Legislation -- United States. 3. Speeches, addresses, etc. -- History and criticism. 4. United States -- Politics and government. 5. Historical comics 6. Comics and Graphic novels

ISBN 9780809094608

LC 2013956401

A graphically illustrated history of America through its major speeches, laws, proclamations, court decisions and essays introduces through the narrative character of "Uncle Sam" each influential document's origins, creation and impact.

"Colon uses well-designed, full-color panel layouts to eloquently blend charts and other informative graphics with straightforward images of events, clothing, and customs as well as clear, concise metaphors, all with an eye toward promoting a solid understanding of the basic facts and their impact." Booklist.

Ashby, Ruth

The **great** American documents. Ruth Ashby, illustrated by Ernie Colon. Hill and Wang, 2019. 159 p. Great American documents ; **973**

1. Historic documents. 2. Legislation -- United States. 3. Speeches, addresses, etc. -- History and criticism. 4. Books 5. United States -- Politics and government. 6. Historical comics 7. Comics and Graphic novels

ISBN 9780809094592

LC 2013956401

The second volume begins where the first left off. Uncle Sam returns to take us through numerous major documents, ranging from the Texas Declaration of Independence from Mexico in 1836 to Jacob Riis's seminal exposé of slum life in New York City, How the Other Half Lives, published in 1900. Each document gets its own chapter, in which Uncle Sam explains not only its key passages but its origins, how it came to be written, and its impact.

Berlin, Ira, 1941-

The **making** of African America : the four great migrations / Ira Berlin. Viking, 2010. 320 p. **973**

1. African Americans -- History. 2. Slave trade -- United States -- History 3. Migration, Internal. 4. Immigrants. 5. United States -- Immigration and emigration -- History.

ISBN 9780670021376

LC 2009028366

A 400-year history of the African-American experience traces four pivotal migrations including the violent relocation of one million slaves to the antebellum South, the movement of millions to industrial cities a century later and the arrivals of black immigrants since the 1960s.

"Berlin's neat synthesis offers the sharp insights and provocative commentary of one of the foremost historians of black America. Essential for library collections, general readers, and scholars of African American history." Library Journal.

Boorstin, Daniel J. (Daniel Joseph), 1914-2004

The **Americans:** the democratic experience / Daniel J. Boorstin. Cardinal, 1988, c1973. 717 p. **973**

1. Democracy -- United States -- History -- 19th century. 2.

Americanization. 3. United States -- Civilization. 4. United States -- Economic conditions. 5. United States -- History -- 1865-1898.
ISBN 0747401160
LC 95152524

Sequel to: The Americans: the national experience
Originally published: New York : Random House, 1973.
Pulitzer Prize for History, 1974.

Boorstin, Daniel J. (Daniel Joseph), 1914-2004

The **Americans:** the national experience / Daniel J. Boorstin. Random House, 1965. 517 p. **973**

1. National characteristics, American. 2. United States -- Civilization -- 1783-1865. 3. United States -- History -- 1783-1865. 4. United States -- Social life and customs -- 1783-1865.
ISBN 0394703588
LC 95153525

Sequel to: The Americans: the colonial experience.
Sequel: The Americans: the democratic experience.

A view of American life and dominant figures from the Revolution to the Civil War

"A cultural interpretation of American history, this book traces the roots of contemporary American life to the years between the Revolution and the Civil War." Booklist.

Cahan, Richard,

★**River** of blood : American slavery from the people who lived it : interviews & photographs of formerly enslaved African Americans / edited by Richard Cahan and Michael Williams ; foreword by Adam Green. CityFiles Press, 2020 240 p. : **973**

1. Slavery -- United States -- History. 2. Slavery -- United States 3. African Americans -- History. 4. Reconstruction (U.S. history, 1865-1877). 5. United States -- History -- 19th century
ISBN 9780991541850
LC bl2020002482

An updated edition of the Slave Narratives, collected in the 1930s by the federal government's Works Progress Administration, incorporates hundreds of photographs that were omitted from the original interviews documenting the slave experience before and during the American Civil War. (United States history).

Conwill, Kinshasha,

Dream a world anew : the African American experience and the shaping of America / introduction by Lonnie G. Bunch III ; edited by Kinshasha Holman Conwill Smithsonian Books, 2016 287 p. ; **973**

1. African Americans -- History. 2. United States -- Civilization -- African American influences.
ISBN 9781588345684
LC 2016015596

"In association with the National Museum of African American History and Culture."

Includes index.

Marking the opening of the Smithsonian National Museum of African American History and Culture, a visual history of the African-American experience combines informative narratives from leading scholars, curators and authors with objects from the museum's collection to present a thorough exploration of African-American history and culture.

Colbert, David,

Eyewitness to America : 500 years of America in the words of those who saw it happen / edited by David Colbert. Pantheon Books, c1997. xxx, 599 p. ; **973**

1. United States -- History Sources. 2. Diaries. 3. Interviews 4. Letters.
ISBN 0679442243
LC 96024150

Gathered from five hundred years of diaries and memoirs, letters and reporting, an entertaining and fascinating collection of firsthand accounts offers new perspectives on familiar and not so familiar events from American history.

"This volume contains a panorama of first-person accounts of moments in the country's story that stretch from an October 10, 1492, diary entry by one of Columbus's crewmen to a 1994 e-mail message from Bill Gates. The nearly 300 entries tend to be short, preceded by informative introductions. The result is a feeling for history that is both immediate and dramatic." Publishers Weekly.

Curtis, Nancy C.

Black heritage sites : an African American odyssey and finder's guide / Nancy C. Curtis. American Library Association, 1996. viii, 677 p. : **973**

1. African Americans -- History. 2. Historic sites -- United States
ISBN 0838906435
LC 95005788

Lists historic sites related to African American history, organized geographically, and discusses the significance of each site.

Davis, Thomas J. (Thomas Joseph)

History of African Americans : exploring diverse roots / Thomas J. Davis. Greenwood, an imprint of ABC-CLIO, LLC, 2016 xxxiii, 271 p. : **973**

1. African Americans -- History. 2. African Americans -- Race identity. 3. African Americans -- Social conditions. 4. Racism -- United States -- History.
ISBN 0313385408
LC 2016025200

"Over the centuries Black peoples in America have nurtured distinctive attitudes, beliefs, characters, folkways, and manners. They have shared common circumstances and conditions that have distinguished them in America beyond reference to the continent of their ancestral origins or their physical appearance. Yet African Americans have never been singular in experience or outlook. They have ever been diverse peoples. Time, temperament, talents, opportunities, place, and interpersonal relations, among myriad elements of life, have invariably set Blacks apart from one another as individuals and as groups, even as pronounced racial distinction and discrimination have invariably set Blacks as a group apart from others in America. African American history is thus not singular or simple; it has many facets and layers; it spreads across time and place and personalities."--Provided by publisher.

"Davis's book is mandatory reading for undergraduates and the general public, who tend to have only the most superficial understanding of African American history." Choice.

Deloria, Vine

Custer died for your sins : an Indian manifesto / Vine Deloria, Jr. University of Oklahoma Press, 1988. xiii, 278 p. ; **973**

1. Indians of North America -- Government relations -- 1934- 2. Indians, Treatment of -- United States
ISBN 9780806121291
LC 87040561

Reprint. Originally published: New York : Macmillan, 1969. With new pref.

Includes index.

The author speaks for his people in this witty confutation of almost everything the white man "knows" about Native Americans

Du Bois, W. E. B. (William Edward Burghardt), 1868-1963
★The **souls** of black folk / W.E.B. Du Bois ; edited with an introduction and notes by Brent Hayes Edwards. Oxford University Press, 2007, c1903. 223 p. **973**

1. African Americans 2. Racism -- United States. 3. Intersectionality 4. United States -- Race relations. 5. Essays.
ISBN 9780192806789

LC 2006035193

Published together with Up from slavery and The autobiography of an ex-colored man, as Three negro classics, 1965.

Originally published: Chicago, IL : A.C. McClurg & Co., 1903.

Personal recollections are included in this work depicting the spirit, status, and problems of African Americans since emancipation and reflecting on the history of race and democracy in America.

Du Bois, W. E. B. (William Edward Burghardt), 1868-1963
★**Writings** : The Suppression of the African Slave-Trade : The Souls of Black Folk : Dusk of Dawn : Essays : Articles from the Crisis / W.E.B. Du Bois ; [Nathan Huggins, editor]. Library of America : 1996, c1986. 1334 p. ; **973**

1. African Americans
ISBN 9781883011314

LC BL 00016300

Originally published: New York, N.Y. : Literary Classics of the United States, 1986.

Gathers writings, articles, and essays revealing Du Bois's views on racial inequality and oppression.

Franklin, John Hope, 1915-2009
★**From** slavery to freedom : a history of African Americans / John Hope Franklin, Evelyn Higginbotham. McGraw-Hill, c2011. xxv, 710 p. : **973**

1. African Americans -- History. 2. Slavery -- History. 3. Slaves. 4. Free African Americans 5. United States -- History -- To 1865.
ISBN 9780072963786

LC 2005299886

Documents the African American experience, from their origin in Africa to slavery in the Western Hemisphere and their successful struggle for freedom.

Gates, Henry Louis, 1950-
100 amazing facts about the Negro / Henry Louis Gates. Pantheon Books, 2017 288 p. **973**

1. African Americans -- History 2. Racism 3. Race relations
ISBN 9780307908711

LC 2016024453

The first edition of Joel Augustus Rogers's now legendary 100 Amazing Facts About the Negro with Complete Proof, published in 1957, was billed as "A Negro 'Believe It or Not.'" Rogers's little book was priceless because he was delivering enlightenment and pride, steeped in historical research, to a people too long starved on the lie that they were worth nothing. For African Americans of the Jim Crow era, Rogers's was their first black history teacher. But Rogers was not always shy about embellishing the "facts" and minimizing ambiguity; neither was he above shock journalism now and then. With élan and erudition--and with winning enthusiasm--Henry Louis Gates, Jr. gives us a corrective yet loving homage to Roger's work.

Gates, Henry Louis, 1950-
In search of our roots : how 19 extraordinary African Americans reclaimed their past / Henry Louis Gates, Jr. Crown Publishers, c2008. 448 p. **973**

1. African Americans -- Genealogy. 2. Genealogy. 3. Generations. 4. Families 5. United States Genealogy. 6. Africa Genealogy.
ISBN 9780307382405

LC 2008011860

The distinguished scholar examines the origins and history of African-American ancestry as he profiles nineteen noted African Americans and illuminates their individual family sagas throughout U.S. history.

Gates, Henry Louis, 1950-
Life upon these shores : looking at African American history, 1513-2008 / Henry Louis Gates, Jr. Knopf, 2011. 416 p. **973**

1. African Americans -- History 2. United States -- Civilization -- African-American influences.
ISBN 9780307593429

LC 2011014277

A director of the W. E. B. Du Bois Institute at Harvard presents a sumptuously illustrated chronicle of more than 500 years of African-American history that focuses on defining events, debates and controversies as well as important achievements of famous and lesser-known figures, in a volume complemented by reproductions of ancient maps and historical paraphernalia.

"With nearly 900 illustrations (formal portraits, news photos, historic lithographs, broadsides, flyers, posters, newspaper clippings, advertisements) complemented by a succinct but informing text, Harvard professor Gates (Black in Latin America) provides a visual sojourn through African-American history, a generally upbeat march from Juan Garrido, accompanying Cortés in 1519, to Barack Obama taking the presidential oath in 2008. Gathered in this chronologically arranged compendium, with its focus on the accomplishments and moments of achievement in the African-American community, is a wealth of materials about the historical, political, social, literary, and scientific events influencing American social and political culture." Publishers Weekly.

Gates, Henry Louis, 1950-
★**Stony** the road : Reconstruction, white supremacy, and the rise of Jim Crow / Henry Louis Gates, Jr. Penguin Press, 2019. 320 p. **973**

1. Racism 2. African Americans -- Segregation -- History. 3. Reconstruction (United States history) 4. African Americans -- History -- 1863-1877. 5. United States -- Race relations.
ISBN 9780525559535

LC 2018056211

This book is published with the companion PBS documentary, Reconstruction: America after the Civil War.

The NAACP Image Award-winning creator of The African Americans: Many Rivers to Cross presents a revisionist chronicle of America's post-Civil War struggle for racial equality and the violent counterrevolution that resubjugated black Americans throughout the 20th century.

"This fresh, much-needed inquiry into a misunderstood yet urgently relevant era will appear in conjunction with Gates new PBS documentary, Reconstruction: America after the Civil War, scheduled for broadcast in April." Booklist.

Glass, Brent D
50 great American places : essential historic sites across the U.S. / Brent D. Glass ; foreword by David McCullough. Si-

mon & Schuster Paperbacks, 2016 xxiv, 293 p. : **973**

1. Historic sites -- United States 2. Guidebooks.
ISBN 9781451682038

LC 2015031714

A one-of-a-kind guide to 50 of the most important cultural and historic sites in the United States is guaranteed to fascinate, educate and entertain, and is selected and described by the former director of the Smithsonian's National Museum of American History.

"This book will whet the appetite of history buffs interested in possible destinations, or anybody who would like to learn American history through the places where it happened." Library Journal.

Grandin, Greg, 1962-

The **end** of the myth : from the frontier to the wall in the mind of America / Greg Grandin. Metropolitan Books, 2019. 224 p. **973**

1. Turner, Frederick Jackson, 1861-1932 Criticism and interpretation. 2. Populism. 3. Nationalism -- United States -- History -- 20th century. 4. National characteristics, American. 5. Frontier thesis. 6. United States -- History.
ISBN 9781250179821

LC 2018027790

Pulitzer Prize for General Nonfiction, 2020.
Pulitzer Prize for History finalist, 2020.
Longlisted for the National Book Award for Nonfiction, 2019.

Examines how the identity-shaping idea of an open and ever-expanding American frontier has evolved from early westward expansion into the reactionary populism of Donald Trump's border-wall proposals.

"In a broad and sweeping history stretching from the founding of the nation through the election of Donald Trump, Bancroft Prize winner Grandin . . . examines what he calls the 'expansionist imperative' of the frontier and what happens when that expansion comes to a halt." Library Journal

Gregory, Dick

Defining moments in Black history : reading between the lies / Dick Gregory. Amistad Press, 2017. 240 p. **973**

1. African Americans -- History 2. African Americans -- Social life and customs 3. Race (Social sciences) 4. Racism 5. United States -- Race relations 6. Essays
ISBN 9780062448699

LC bl2017036957

The activist and social satirist who trail-blazed a new form of racial commentary in the 1960s examines 100 key events in Black History through this collection of essays which examine Middle Passage, the creation of Jheri Curl and the Black Lives Matter movement.

"Gregory's devotion to civil rights and his global recognition add to his appealing writing style and clever sense of humor to make this a book for a wide audience." Kirkus.

Hilgers, Lauren

★**Patriot** number one : American dreams in Chinatown / Lauren Hilgers. Crown Publishing, 2018. 336 p. **973**

1. American dream 2. Immigration and emigration 3. Immigrants, Chinese 4. Chinese Americans 5. Queens, New York City 6. New York City
ISBN 9780451496133

LC 2017043609

A deeply reported analysis of the Chinese immigrant community in the United States offers revisionist insights into how their experiences in China and America have reflected and transformed the American dream.

"This book is hard to put down. It would be easy to say that it is recommended for readers interested in Chinese-American communities, but at its heart is a highly readable story about starting over in a new land; a must-read for all." Library Journal.

Hoffer, Peter Charles, 1944-

Seven fires : the urban infernos that reshaped America / Peter Charles Hoffer. PublicAffairs, c2006. xii, 460 p. : **973**

1. Fires -- United States -- History -- Anecdotes. 2. Cities and towns -- United States -- History -- Anecdotes. 3. United States -- History Anecdotes. 4. United States -- History, Local Anecdotes.
ISBN 1586483552

LC 2005055345

Discusses how urban fires have impacted American history, from the emergence of the modern skyscraper after Chicago's fire to the realization that modern emergency services need revamping after the attacks of September 11, 2001.

Horton, James Oliver

Slavery and the making of America / James Oliver Horton and Lois E. Horton. Oxford University Press, c2005. 254 p. : **973**

1. Slavery -- History. 2. African Americans -- History -- To 1863. 3. Anti-slavery movements -- History -- 19th century. 4. United States -- History -- 19th century
ISBN 019517903X

"The oft-told tale is made fresh through up-to-date slavery scholarship, the extensive use of slave narratives and archival photos and, especially, a focus on individual experience." Publishers Weekly.

Immerwahr, Daniel, 1980-

How to hide an empire : a history of the greater United States / Daniel Immerwahr. Farrar, Straus and Giroux, 2019. 560 p. **973**

1. Imperialism. 2. Globalization. 3. Citizenship. 4. Civil rights. 5. United States -- Territories and possessions -- History. 6. Philippines. 7. Puerto Rico. 8. Guam. 9. Virgin Islands of the United States. 10. United States -- Colonies.
ISBN 9780374172145

LC 2018020388

Traces the stories of the U.S. territories outside the mainland, including the Guano Islands, the Philippines, and Puerto Rico, to offer insights into how America has transitioned from colonialism to technological innovation.

Lee, Erika

★The **making** of Asian America : a history / Erika Lee. Simon & Schuster, 2015. 416 p. **973**

1. Asian Americans -- History. 2. Asians in the United States -- History. 3. Racism -- United States -- History. 4. Immigration and emigration 5. United States -- Immigration and emigration -- History. 6. South Asia -- Immigration and emigration -- History. 7. United States -- Interethnic relations -- History. 8. United States -- Race relations -- History.
ISBN 9781476739403

LC 2015010372

Asian Pacific American Award for Literature: Adult Nonfiction, 2016.

Describes the lasting impact and contributions Asian immigrants have had on America, beginning with sailors who crossed the Pacific in the 16th century, through the ordeal of internment during World War II and to their current status as "model minorities."

"An impressive work that details how this diverse population has both swayed and been affected by the United States." Library Journal.

Lepore, Jill, 1966-

★The **mansion** of happiness : a history of life and death / Jill Lepore. Alfred A. Knopf, 2012. 304 p. **973**

1. Popular culture 2. Intellectual life -- United States 3. Happiness -- Social aspects 4. Life 5. United States -- Social life and customs. 6. United States -- History

ISBN 9780307592996

LC 2011050566

"This is a Borzoi book"--T.p. verso.

"Parts of this book originally appeared in The New Yorker"--T.p. verso.

Andrew Carnegie Medal for Excellence in Non-Fiction finalist, 2013.

"A superb examination of the never-ending effort to enhance life, as well as the commensurate refusal to ever let it go." Kirkus.

The **story** of America : essays on origins / Jill Lepore. Princeton University Press, 2012. 448 p. **973**

1. United States -- History -- Sources. 2. United States -- Politics and government -- Sources. 3. Essays

ISBN 9780691153995

LC 2012016854

A New Yorker staff writer examines the origins of dozens of writings, speeches and other printed pieces from American history--from paper ballots and I.O.U.s to the Constitution and Thomas Paine's Common Sense to Edgar Allan Poe's "The Raven" to Barack Obama's 2009 inaugural address.

★**These** truths : a history of the United States / Jill Lepore. W. W. Norton & Co., 2018 xx, 932 p. : **973**

1. Political values 2. Social values -- United States 3. Slavery 4. Nation-building 5. United States -- History

ISBN 9780393635249

In the most ambitious one-volume American history in decades, award-winning historian and New Yorker writer Jill Lepore offers a magisterial account of the origins and rise of a divided nation, an urgently needed reckoning with the beauty and tragedy of American history.

"Lepore is a historian with wide appeal, and this comprehensive work will answer readers' questions about who we are as a nation." Booklist.

Loewen, James W.

Lies across America : what our historic sites get wrong / James W. Loewen. The New Press, 2019, c1999. 480 p. : **973**

1. Historic sites -- United States. 2. Monuments -- United States. 3. History. 4. Errors 5. United States -- History -- Errors, inventions, etc.

ISBN 9781620975060

LC 00061215

Examines more than one hundred sites that promote incorrect interpretations of history and raises questions about what Americans choose to commemorate.

"The book consists of 95 brief commentaries on specific sites from Alaska to Florida to Maine, sandwiched between essays that offer advice on how to interpret what you read or are told at historic sites." New York Times Book Review. [review of 1999 edition]

Marable, Manning, 1950-2011

★**Freedom** on my mind : the Columbia documentary history of the African American experience / Manning Marable, general editor ; Nishani Frazier and John McMillian, assistant editors. Columbia University Press, c2003. xviii, 734 p. ; **973**

1. African Americans -- History -- Sources.

ISBN 9780231108904

LC 2003051605

McCullough, David G.

The **American** spirit : who we are and what we stand for / David McCullough. Simon & Schuster, 2017 176 p. **973**

1. National characteristics, American 2. American dream 3. Patriotism -- United States 4. Citizenship 5. United States -- Civilization 6. Essays

ISBN 9781501174216

LC 2017002640

A timely collection of speeches by David McCullough, the most honored historian in the United States--winner of two Pulitzer Prizes, two National Book Awards, and the Presidential Medal of Freedom, among many others--that reminds us of fundamental American principles.

"Historian McCullough...presents this collection of 15 inspiring speeches in which he celebrates America's talent for curiosity, intelligence, goodwill, and humanity." Library Journal.

McLoughlin, William Gerald

After the Trail of Tears : the Cherokees' struggle for sovereignty, 1839-1880 / William G. McLoughlin. University of North Carolina Press, c1993. xv, 439 p. : **973**

1. Cherokee Indians -- History -- 19th century. 2. Trail of Tears, 1838-1839. 3. Cherokee Indians -- Politics and government. 4. Government relations with indigenous peoples

ISBN 080782111X

LC 93018532

"The author recounts the tragedy that continued to afflict the Cherokee Nation after their forced removal from their traditional home to Oklahoma during the 1820s and 1830s. In Oklahoma the Cherokee Nation set out to reconstruct their society, reestablishing their newspaper, which published in the Cherokee language, and governing themselves according to a constitution modeled on that of the United States. McLoughlin vividly depicts the conflicts between full-bloods, who sought to live by more traditional ways, and Cherokees of mixed ancestry who favored assimilation into the dominant culture." Publishers Weekly.

Meacham, Jon

★The **soul** of America : the battle for our better angels / Jon Meacham. Random House, [2018] xii, 402 p. : **973**

1. National characteristics, American 2. Presidents -- United States 3. Democracy 4. United States -- History 5. United States -- Politics and government

ISBN 9780399589812

LC 2018010451

While the American story has not always been heroic, we have been sustained by a belief in progress even in the gloomiest of times. In this inspiring book, Meacham reassures us, "The good news is that we have come through such darkness before"--as, time and again, Lincoln's better angels have found a way to prevail.

"An excellent work by a skilled historian and worthy of all library collections." Library Journal.

Voices in our blood : America's best on the civil rights movement / edited by Jon Meacham. Random House Trade Paperbacks, 2003, c2001. ix, 561 p. ; **973**

1. African Americans -- Civil rights -- History -- 20th century -- Sources. 2. Civil Rights Movement 3. Race relations. 4. Civil rights.

5. United States -- Race relations Sources. 6. Essays.
ISBN 037575881X

LC BL2003000287

Originally published: New York : Random House, 2001.

Includes index.

Essays by such authors as Maya Angelou, Richard Wright, David Halberstam, and Eurdora Welty trace the history of America's civil rights movement, its leaders, and its implications for affirmative action and racial relations.

"A collection of acclaimed voices narrating the environment, origin, and progress of the Civil Rights movement, as told by reporters, artists, novelists, historians, and authors such as Maya Angelou, Eudora Welty, James Baldwin, Richard Wright, Willie Morris, Robert Penn Warren, Alice Walker, Murray Kempton, E. B. White, William Faulkner, Ralph Ellison, and Rebecca West." Library Journal.

Morris, Edmund

This living hand : and other essays / Edmund Morris. Random House Inc., 2012. 320 p. **973**

1. Music 2. Culture 3. History 4. Essays
ISBN 9780812993127

LC 2012013612

A wide-ranging collection of essays by a National Book Award-winning contemporary critic and historian traces four decades of writing and considers such diverse topics as Beethoven, Kilimanjaro and Britain's Imperial War Museum.

Proenza-Coles, Christina

American founders : how people of African descent established freedom in the new world / Christina Proenza-Coles ; Foreword by Edward L. Ayers. NewSouth Books, [2019] 450 p. **973**

1. African Americans -- History. 2. Multiculturalism. 3. Equality. 4. Freedom. 5. United States -- History.
ISBN 9781588383310

LC 2018047640

Examines American history as inexorably intertwined with its black and white counterparts contributing equally to the development and freedom of the nation.

"Lucid prose and straightforward structure make this easy to read, and the unearthing of so many lesser-known figures offers new perspectives to those with deeper knowledge of American history. " Publishers Weekly.

Prothero, Stephen R.

The **American** Bible : how our words unite, divide, and define a nation / Stephen Prothero. HarperCollins, 2012. 480 p. **973**

1. National characteristics, American. 2. Rhetoric -- Political aspects -- United States -- History 3. Literature and society -- United States -- History 4. Language and culture -- United States 5. United States -- Civilization 6. Speeches, addresses, etc.
ISBN 9780062123435

LC 2012005054

"The New York Times best-selling author of Religious Literacy identifies the most crucial texts written by Americans and published in America, which have profoundly shaped our national identity, including the speeches of Lincoln, Kennedy and Reagan, and the novels of Melville, Salinger and Rand."

Roberts, David, 1943-

Once they moved like the wind : Cochise, Geronimo, and the Apache wars / David Roberts. Simon & Schuster, c1993. 368 p. : **973**

1. Cochise, Apache chief, died 1874. 2. Geronimo, Apache chief, 1829-1909 3. Apache Indians 4. Indians of North America -- History. 5. Frontier and pioneer life. 6. Interethnic relations. 7. United States -- History -- 19th century.
ISBN 0671702211

LC 93007112

Recounts the days of the Indian wars when the U.S. Cavalry repeatedly tried to subdue the great warriors led by Cochise and, later, Geronimo.

"The book is history at its most engrossing." Publishers Weekly.

Schama, Simon

The **American** future : a history / Simon Schama. Ecco Press, 2009, c2008. xii, 400 p., [16] p. of plates : **973**

1. Presidential election, 2008 2. Politicians -- United States. 3. United States -- Politics and government -- 2001-2009 4. United States -- History -- 21st century. 5. United States -- History -- 20th century. 6. United States -- Foreign relations -- 2001-2009 7. United States -- History -- Philosophy.
ISBN 9780060539238

LC 2009455821

Originally published: London : Bodley Head, 2008.

"Schama has begun wandering through the literature of the American past to snap up unconsidered trifles. The result is a book of mixed genre-history, memoir and journalism--and none the worse for that. In four successive chapters, Schama considers the American relationship to war, religion, immigration and prosperity. Within each, he moves between historical narratives and vignettes from the contemporary scene, usually involving his own presence. So the book's architecture is crisp, even as its rationale is mysterious." Times Literary Supplement.

Stewart, Dianne M.

Black women, black love : America's war on African American marriage / Dianne M. Stewart. Seal Press, 2020 320 p. **973**

1. African American families 2. African American women 3. African American marriage 4. Racism 5. United States -- Social conditions
ISBN 9781580058186

LC 2019052810

According to the 2010 US census, more than seventy percent of Black women in America are unmarried. Black Women, Black Love reveals how four centuries of laws, policies, and customs have created that crisis. Prodigiously researched and deeply felt, Black Women, Black Love reveals how white supremacy has systematically broken the heart of Black America, and it proposes strategies for dismantling the structural forces that have plagued Black love and marriage for centuries.

"A professor of religion and African American studies offers a compelling look at Black women's love relationships through a historical lens. . . . A beautiful, strikingly original work that is both scholarly and deeply moving." Kirkus

Sullivan, Patricia, 1950-

Lift every voice : the NAACP and the making of the Civil Rights Movement / Patricia Sullivan. New Press : 2009. xii, 514 p., 16 p. of plates : **973**

1. National Association for the Advancement of Colored People -- History. 2. Civil Rights Movement. 3. Civil rights -- United States -- History -- 20th century. 4. African Americans -- Civil rights -- History -- 20th century. 5. Race relations. 6. United States -- Race relations.
ISBN 9781595584465

LC 2009009473

Delivers a solidly researched examination of the NAACP's growth and influence, from its inception in 1909 to the present.

Takaki, Ronald T., 1939-2009

Strangers from a different shore : a history of Asian Americans / Ronald Takaki. Little, Brown, 1998, c1989. xv, 591 p., 16 p. of plates : **973**

1. Asian Americans -- History. 2. Asian Americans -- Social conditions. 3. Immigrants. 4. Immigration and emigration.
ISBN 0316831301

LC 98218270

Originally published: Boston, MA : Little, Brown, 1989.
ALA Notable Book, 1990.

Including individuals from the first wave of immigrants in the 1840s, the author tells the story of some of the Asian-Americans who came to this country and the obstacles they faced here.

Urdang, Laurence

The **timetables** of American history / Laurence Urdang, editor ; with an introduction by Henry Steele Commager and a new foreword by Arthur Schlesinger, Jr. Simon & Schuster, 2001, 1996. 534 p. : **973**

1. History, Modern -- Chronology -- Tables. 2. America -- History Chronology Tables.
ISBN 9780743202619

LC BL2002002058

"A Touchstone book."
Includes index.

Updated to includes events through December 31, 2000, a single volume history chronicles American happenings in politics, the arts, science, and technology while relating them to the international scene.

Walker, Jesse, 1970-

The **United** States of paranoia : a conspiracy theory / Jesse Walker. Harper, 2013. 304 p. **973**

1. National characteristics, American. 2. Paranoia -- Political aspects -- United States. 3. Conspiracy theories -- United States. 4. Paranoia -- Social aspects -- United States. 5. United States -- Politics and government. 6. United States -- Civilization.
ISBN 9780062135551

LC 2013011426

Includes bibliographical references and index.

Explores the origins, evolution, legacy, and impact of paranoia in American politics and culture by discussing five conspiracy narratives that keep recurring throughout history.

Weatherford, J. McIver

Native roots : how the Indians enriched America / Jack Weatherford. Fawcett Columbine, 1992, c1991. 310 p. : **973**

1. Indians of North America. 2. United States -- Civilization -- Native American influences. 3. North America -- Civilization -- Native American influences.
ISBN 0449907139

LC BL 99732737

Originally published: New York : Crown, 1991.

An in-depth study of North American Indians shows how they made foreigners into Americans and how foreigners added European society, language, and culture onto an ancient system

"A valuable corrective to the sentimentality with which we regard the first U.S. settlers and developers." Booklist.

Weingarten, Gene

One day : the extraordinary story of an ordinary 24 hours in America / Gene Weingarten. Blue Rider Press, 2019. 384 p. **973**

1. Days 2. Life change events 3. United States -- Social conditions 4. United States -- Social life and customs Anecdotes 5. United States Anecdotes
ISBN 9780399166662

LC 2019001936

On New Year's Day 2013, two-time Pulitzer Prize--winner Gene Weingarten asked three strangers to, literally, pluck a day, month, and year from a hat. That day--chosen completely at random--turned out to be Sunday, December 28, 1986, by any conventional measure a most ordinary day. Weingarten spent the next six years proving that there is no such thing. One Day asks and answers the question of whether there is even such a thing as "ordinary" when we are talking about how we all lurch and stumble our way through the daily, daunting challenge of being human.

White, Shane

The **sounds** of slavery : discovering African American history through songs, sermons, and speech / Shane White and Graham White. Beacon Press, c2005. xxii, 241 p. ; 23 cm + **973**

1. Slavery -- Songs and music. 2. Slaves 3. Language and languages. 4. Songs -- History and criticism 5. Southern States -- Social life and customs. 6. United States -- History -- 19th century
ISBN 0807050261

LC 2004021447

Collects songs, speeches, and sermons that provide a revealing window into the sufferings of slaves, as well as some of the most revealing of such documents from the 1700s through the 1850s.

Wilsey, Sean,

State by state : a panoramic portrait of America / edited by Sean Wilsey, Matt Weiland. Harpercollins, 2008. 608 p. **973**

1. Federal Writers' Project. 2. Writers' Program. 3. Americans. 4. States. 5. United States -- Description and travel. 6. Essays.
ISBN 9780061470905

LC bl2008024139

The editors of The Thinking Fan's Guide to the World Cup collects original writings on all fifty states by leading novelists, journalists, and essayists, in a volume that includes such examples as Anthony Bourdain on New Jersey, Dave Eggers on Illinois, and Louise Erdrich on North Dakota.

"Taking as their inspiration the state guides published by the Federal Writers' Project during and shortly after the Great Depression, Weiland and Wilsey assembled 50 of America's finest writers and asked them to contribute essays on the same general theme: why my state is special--or not. The result is a funny, moving, rousing collection, greater than the sum of its excellent parts, a convention of literary super-delegates, each one boisterously nominating his or her piece of the Republic." New York Times Book Review.

Zinn, Howard, 1922-2010

★A **people's** history of the United States : 1492-present / Howard Zinn. Harper Perennial Modern Classics, 2005, c2003. 729, 16 p. ; **973**

1. Resistance to government 2. Protest movements 3. Social movements 4. Imperialism, American -- History 5. United States

-- History.
ISBN 0060838655

LC bl2005016609

Originally published: New York : HarperCollins, 2003.

Presents the history of the United States from the point of view of those who were exploited in the name of American progress.

Zoellner, Tom

The **national** road : dispatches from a changing America / Tom Zoellner. Counterpoint Press, 2020. 272 p. **973**

1. Migration, Internal -- United States. 2. Social change -- United States. 3. Nationalism 4. Roads -- United States. 5. United States -- Economic conditions -- 21st century. 6. United States -- Social conditions -- 21st century. 7. United States -- Social life and customs -- 21st century. 8. Essays

ISBN 9781640092907

LC 2020001055

The National Road is a collection of essays about American places, each dealing with contentious matters: religion, politics, sex, race, poverty, loss and the stubborn persistence of national pride, despite abundant reasons for cynicism. An important question lies at the heart of this collection: what does it mean to "belong" in America in the midst of an era when rootedness to a particular piece of ground means less than at any time during our history?

"Zoellner will acquaint you with byways, and mores, you never knew existed." Kirkus

973.04 United States -- Ethnic and national groups

Bruchac, Joseph, 1942-

Our stories remember : American Indian history, culture, & values through storytelling / Joseph Bruchac. Fulcrum Pub., c2003. 192 p. **973.04**

1. Indians of North America -- History. 2. Indians of North America -- Social life and customs. 3. Folklore, Native American -- History and criticism

ISBN 1555911293

LC 2002151236

Retells traditional Native American stories drawn from throughout the country, providing insights into Native American history, culture, values, and wisdom.

"This important volume includes a wealth of traditional stories and solid information." School Library Journal.

Philip, Neil

The **great** circle : a history of the First Nations / Neil Philip ; foreword by Dennis Hastings. Clarion Books, c2006. 153 p. : **973.04**

1. Indians of North America -- History. 2. Government relations with indigenous peoples. 3. Indians of North America -- Social life and customs. 4. Indians of North America -- Relations with European-Americans. 5. United States -- Race relations. 6. United States -- Interethnic relations.

ISBN 9780618159413

LC 2005032743

Offers a look at the long history of the Native American tribes in North America, the culture, their struggles against the white immigrants, and the resurgence of their customs, enhanced with source notes, index, and archival photographs.

"Philip takes on a huge challenge here: to present a unified narrative that explains the complex and confrontational relationships between Native Americans and white settlers. . . . He pulls it off, however, thanks to solid research, an engaging writing style, and a talent for making individual stories serve the whole. . . . Top marks, too, for the volume's photographs and historical renderings, which so intensely illustrate the pages." Booklist.

973.09 United States -- History, geographic treatment, biography

Goodwin, Doris Kearns

★**Leadership** in turbulent times / Doris Kearns Goodwin. Simon & Schuster, [2018] 352 p. **973.09**

1. Lincoln, Abraham, 1809-1865 2. Roosevelt, Theodore, 1858-1919 3. Roosevelt, Franklin D. (Franklin Delano), 1882-1945 4. Johnson, Lyndon B., 1908-1973 5. Presidents -- United States 6. Political leadership -- United States 7. Character 8. Crisis management 9. United States -- Politics and government Case studies

ISBN 9781476795928

LC 2018020283

Draws on five decades of scholarship to offer an illuminating exploration of the early development, growth, and exercise of leadership as demonstrated by Presidents Abraham Lincoln, Theodore Roosevelt, Franklin Roosevelt, and Lyndon Johnson.

"Goodwin draws on 50 years of scholarship in this strong and resonant addition to the literature of the presidency." Booklist.

Kane, Joseph Nathan, born 1899

★**Facts** about the presidents : a compilation of biographical and historical information / Joseph Nathan Kane, Janet Podell. H.W. Wilson Co., 2009. vii, 801 p. : **973.09**

1. Presidents -- United States -- History -- Miscellanea. 2. United States -- Politics and government

ISBN 9780824210878

LC 2008056016

Includes indexes.

"The eighth edition offers one-stop access to consistently formatted text, facts, and comparative data, and it remains a staple of the ready-reference shelf." Booklist.

Schneider, Dorothy

★**First** ladies: a biographical dictionary / Dorothy Schneider, Carl J. Schneider. Facts On File, c2010. xii, 436 p. : **973.09**

1. Presidents' spouses -- United States -- Dictionaries

ISBN 9780816077243

LC 2009009047

973.2 United States--Colonial period, 1607-1775

Bailyn, Bernard

★The **barbarous** years : the peopling of British North America: the conflict of civilizations, 1600-1675 / Bernard Bailyn. Alfred A. Knopf, 2012. 656 p. **973.2**

1. Immigration and emigration. 2. Immigrants. 3. Colonists

ISBN 9780394515700

LC 2012034223

Pulitzer Prize for History finalist, 2013.

"An extraordinary work of profound seriousness, characteristic of its author." Publishers Weekly.

The **peopling** of British North America : an introduction. / Bernard Bailyn. Vintage Books, 1988, c1986. xiii, 177 p. ; **973.2**

1. United States -- History -- Colonial period, 1600-1775.
ISBN 0394757793

LC 87045916

Includes index.

Previously published: 1st ed. New York : Knopf, c1986. (The Curti lectures ; 1985)

This book focuses on the beginnings of the peopling of America, from 1500 to the advent of the Industrial Revolution, taking into account such aspects as settlement, social patterns, and groups and races.

"In this introductory volume of a projected multivolume work, the author gives first airing to his overall argument on settling patterns in history. Though designed to introduce the subsequent volumes, this superbly articulate study is understandable on its own." Booklist.

Boorstin, Daniel J. (Daniel Joseph), 1914-2004

The **Americans:** the colonial experience / Daniel J. Boorstin. Random House, 1958. 434 p. ; **973.2**

1. National characteristics, American. 2. United States -- Civilization -- To 1783. 3. United States -- History -- Colonial period, 1600-1775 4. United States -- Social life and customs -- Colonial period, 1600-1775.
ISBN 0394705130

LC 58009884

Sequel: The Americans: the national experience.

"This study of colonial America attempts to show that it was not merely an offshoot of the mother country, but a new civilization. The author centers his highly informative work on colonial education, the special qualities of American speech, and the growth of a distinct culture." Booklist.

Demos, John

The **unredeemed** captive : a family story from early America / John Demos. Vintage Books, 1995, c1994. xiii, 315 p. : **973.2**

1. Williams, Eunice, 1696-1786. 2. Williams, John, 1664-1729. 3. Williams family. 4. Indian captivities -- Massachusetts. 5. Mohawk Indians -- Captivities. 6. Deerfield (Mass.) -- History -- Colonial period, ca. 1600-1775. 7. Massachusetts 8. United States -- History -- Queen Anne's War, 1702-1713.
ISBN 0679759611

LC bl2006000155

Originally published: New York : Alfred A. Knopf, 1994.

Describes the 1704 French and Indian attack on Deerfield, Massachusetts, and the capture of Puritan minister John Williams and his five children.

"This is a lively introduction to an authentically multicultural colonial North America." New York Times Book Review.

Lepore, Jill, 1966-

The **name** of war : King Philip's War and the origins of American identity / Jill Lepore. Knopf, 1998. xxviii, 337 p. : **973.2**

1. King Philip's War, 1675-1676. 2. Indians of North America -- Wars -- 1600-1750. 3. Wampanoag Indians -- History 4. Great Britain -- Colonies North America. 5. United States -- Politics and government -- 1600-1775.
ISBN 0679446869

LC 97002820

Examines how the American colonists interpreted the brutal war that erupted between them and Native Americans in New England in 1675, showing how they looked to it during the Revolution and used it to justify nineteenth-century Indian removals.

"This is a powerful book that doesn't shy away from depicting the sheer horror of what must be termed a race war." Booklist.

Philbrick, Nathaniel

★**Mayflower** : a story of courage, community, and war / Nathaniel Philbrick. Viking, 2006. xvii, 461 p. : **973.2**

1. Bradford, William, 1590-1657 2. Church, Benjamin, 1639-1718. 3. Massasoit, Wampanoag Indian Chief, 1590?-1661. 4. Mayflower (Ship) 5. Pilgrims (New England settlers) 6. Indians of North America -- Wars -- 1600-1750. 7. Colonists. 8. Wampanoag Indians -- History -- 17th century. 9. Massachusetts -- History -- New Plymouth, 1620-1691. 10. Plymouth, Massachusetts -- History.
ISBN 9780670037605

LC 2005058470

ALA Notable Book, 2007.

Pulitzer Prize for History finalist, 2007.

A history of the Pilgrim settlement of New England discusses such topics as the diseases of European origin suffered by the Wampanoag tribe, the relationship between the Pilgrims and their Native American neighbors, and the impact of King Philip's War.

"The author has written a judicious, fascinating work of revisionist history. Mayflower is a surprise-filled account of what are supposed to be some of the best-known events in this country's past but are instead an occasion for collective amnesia." New York Times.

Schultz, Eric B., 1957-

King Philip's War : the history and legacy of America's forgotten conflict / Eric B. Schultz, Michael J. Tougias. Countryman Press, 1999. xv, 416 p. : **973.2**

1. King Philip's War, 1675-1676. 2. Indians of North America -- New England -- History. 3. Government relations with indigenous peoples. 4. Wampanoag Indians -- History 5. New England -- History -- Colonial period, 1600-1775
ISBN 0881504343

LC 99023481

"The first part of this volume provides a chronological retelling of the war. The second part, organized geographically and the heart of the volume, takes readers through New England to various sites associated with the conflict. The third part offers three contemporary narratives reflecting the significance of the war on the people of the era. Useful maps assist the reader throughout." Library Journal.

973.3 United States--Periods of Revolution and Confederation, 1775-1789

Allen, Danielle S., 1971-

Our Declaration : a reading of the Declaration of Independence in defense of equality / Danielle Allen. Liveright Publishing Corporation, 2014. 288 p. **973.3**

1. United States. Declaration of Independence Criticism, Textual. 2. Equality -- United States. 3. Freedom
ISBN 9780871406903

LC 2014009825

A social science professor from Princeton University describes what she learned about freedom and equality when she and her students read the text of the Declaration of Independence from start to finish.

"As if conducting a friendly conversation, sentence by sentence, [Allen] takes readers through all the text's words, and she proves a patient, informed and friendly guide." Kirkus.

Allison, David K., 1950-

The **American** Revolution : a world war / edited by David K. Allison and Larrie D. Ferreiro. Smithsonian Books, [2018] 272 p. **973.3**

1. American Revolution, 1775-1783 2. United States -- History -- Revolution, 1775-1783 -- Participation, Foreign 3. United States -- Foreign relations -- 1775-1783 4. Great Britain -- Colonies -- History 5. Essays

ISBN 9781588346339

LC 2018009738

"An illustrated collection of essays that explores the international dimensions of the American Revolution and its legacies in both America and around the world."--Provided by publisher.

Atkinson, Rick

★The **British** are coming : the war for America, Lexington to Princeton, 1775-1777 / Rick Atkinson. Henry Holt & Company, 2019. 800 p. **973.3**

1. American Revolution, 1775-1783 2. War 3. Military history 4. Revolutionaries 5. United States -- History -- Revolution, 1775-1783 6. United States -- Colonies 7. Great Britain -- History, Military

ISBN 9781627790437

LC 2018029510

The Pulitzer Prize-winning author of the Liberation Trilogy presents the first volume in a new series on the American Revolution that draws on perspectives from both sides to chronicle the first 21 months of America's violent war for independence.

"This graphic account will especially appeal to military history enthusiasts but is accessible for all readers seeking to experience the realities of the revolution." Library Journal

Beck, Derek W.

The **war** before independence : 1775-1776 / Derek W. Beck. Sourcebooks, 2016. 528 p. **973.3**

1. Bunker Hill, Battle of, 1775 2. Revolutions -- United States 3. American Revolution, 1775-1783 4. United States -- History -- Revolution, 1775-1783 -- Causes.

ISBN 9781492633099

LC 2015049006

The War Before Independence transports readers into the violent years of 1775 and 1776, with the infamous Battle of Bunker Hill a turning point in the Revolution and the snowy, wind-swept march to the frozen ground at the Battle of Quebec, ending with the exciting conclusion of the Boston Campaign.

"Beck writes exceptionally vividly, and as such, even readers slow to respond to battleground to-and-fro will be fully engaged." Booklist.

Beeman, Richard R.

Our lives, our fortunes and our sacred honor : the forging of American independence, 1774-1776 / Richard R. Beeman. Basic Books, 2013. 384 p. **973.3**

1. United States. Continental Congress. 2. Politicians -- United States 3. Revolutionaries -- United States 4. American Revolution, 1775-1783 5. United States -- History -- Revolution, 1775-1783. 6. United States -- Politics and government -- 1775-1783.

ISBN 9780465026296

LC 2013001875

Describes the political, diplomatic, and military challenges faced by the delegates from the 13 colonies at the Continental Congress and how they came together to agree to free themselves from British rule and forge independence for America.

Berkin, Carol

A **brilliant** solution : inventing the American Constitution / Carol Berkin. Harcourt, c2002. 310 p. ; **973.3**

1. United States. Constitutional Convention (1787) 2. United States. Constitution Signers. 3. Politicians -- United States -- History -- 18th century. 4. Constitutional history. 5. United States -- Politics and government -- 1783-1789.

ISBN 0151009481

LC 2002005648

Includes index.

Shares the story of the Constitutional Convention in 1787 Philadelphia, detailing the human side of the considerable ideas, arguments, issues, and compromises that shaped the formation of the U.S. Constitution and government.

"This history of the 1787 Constitutional Convention emphasizes the importance of the delegates' anxieties, showing how they insinuated themselves into some of the compromises, such as the equality of the states in the Senate. Shrewd at integrating biographical detail on the delegates into their debates, Berkin fares well in comparison with previous historians on the topic." Booklist.

Blumrosen, Alfred W.

Slave nation : how slavery united the colonies & sparked the American Revolution / Alfred W. Blumrosen and Ruth G. Blumrosen ; introduction by Eleanor Holmes Norton. Sourcebooks, 2005. xv, 336 p., [16] p. of plates : **973.3**

1. Slavery -- History -- 18th century. 2. African Americans -- History -- To 1863. 3. Revolutions -- United States 4. American Revolution, 1775-1783 5. United States -- History -- Revolution, 1775-1783 -- Causes.

ISBN 1402204000

LC 2004027271

Bobrick, Benson, 1947-

Angel in the whirlwind : the triumph of the American Revolution / Benson Bobrick. Simon & Schuster, 1997. 553 p. : **973.3**

1. Revolutions -- United States. 2. Colonists. 3. Revolutionaries. 4. American Revolution, 1775-1783 5. United States -- History -- Revolution, 1775-1783.

ISBN 0684810603

LC 97011320

Explores the frequently overlooked fact that, despite charismatic leadership and eventual success, the revolutionary movement never garnered the support of more than half of the American colonists.

"Many of the stories are familiar--Paul Revere's ride, Arnold's descent into infamy--but the book's strength lies in its many lesser-known details on the battlefield and beyond. Though the format demands only brief treatment of complicated issues, what emerges is a highly impressive show of exhaustive research and engaging storytelling." Publishers Weekly.

Breen, T. H.

American insurgents, American patriots : the revolution of the people before independence / T.H. Breen. Hill and Wang, 2010. 384 p. **973.3**

1. Revolutionaries. 2. Insurgency. 3. Patriotism. 4. Militia movement. 5. United States -- History -- Revolution, 1775-1783 -- Social aspects. 6. United States -- Militia -- History -- 18th century.
ISBN 9780809075881

LC 2009042496

"Breen uses correspondence, diaries, outtakes from clergy sermons and newspaper reports to build a mosaic representation of the popular mood, and the escalating willingness to take up arms. [The] book shows an energetic and necessarily untidy process of invention on the part of a people, and captures well its improvisatory nature." Chicago Tribune.

Bunker, Nick

★An **empire** on the edge : how Britain came to fight America / Nick Bunker. Alfred A. Knopf, 2014 448 p. **973.3**

1. Boston Tea Party, 1773 2. American Revolution, 1775-1783 3. United States -- History -- Revolution, 1775-1783 -- Causes. 4. United States -- Foreign relations Great Britain. 5. Great Britain -- Foreign relations United States.
ISBN 9780307594846

LC 2014001032

Pulitzer Prize for History finalist, 2015.

A British-perspective chronicle of the Boston Tea Party and other events that led up to the American Revolution traces three years of volatile politics, personalities and economics on both sides of the conflict.

"Bunker's book argues that, for the British, America was 'a continent she did not comprehend and could not hope to rule.' The author is particularly attuned to economic context and concerned with how events unfolded in practice, rather than what was said in theory." Library Journal.

Daughan, George C.

Lexington and Concord : the battle heard round the world / George C. Daughan. W.W. Norton & Company, 2018. 368 p. **973.3**

1. American Revolution, 1775-1783 2. Lexington, Battle of, 1775 3. Concord, Battle of, 1775 4. Minutemen (Militia) 5. United States -- History -- Revolution, 1775-1783 -- Causes
ISBN 9780393245745

LC 2017060269

The award-winning historian and author of If By Sea reinterprets the battle that launched the American Revolution, arguing that the war was based as much in economic concerns as political ones and that most militiamen volunteered on behalf of their livelihoods and in protest of serf-like living conditions.

Drury, Bob

★**Valley** Forge / Bob Drury and Tom Clavin. Simon & Schuster, 2018. 432 p. **973.3**

1. Washington, George, 1732-1799 Headquarters Valley Forge, Pennsylvania 2. United States. Continental Army 3. American Revolution, 1775-1783 4. Generals 5. Command of troops 6. Determination in men 7. Valley Forge, Pennsylvania -- History -- Revolution, 1775-1783. 8. United States -- History -- Revolution, 1775-1783 -- Campaigns
ISBN 9781501152719

LC 2018022453

An account of Valley Forge, the Continental Army winter camp where George Washington turned the tide of the American Revolution.

"A fluent, readable story that corrects mythmaking errors and provides a more nuanced narrative in their place." Kirkus.

Duval, Kathleen

★**Independence** lost : lives on the edge of the American Revolution / Kathleen Duval. Random House, 2015 416 p. **973.3**

1. Indians of North America 2. International relations 3. American Revolution, 1775-1783 4. United States -- History -- Revolution, 1775-1783
ISBN 9781400068951

LC 2014042511

Depicts the American Revolution from the eyes of outsiders who just happened to be present, including an Irish trader, Scottish plantation owners and Creek leader Alexander McGillivray, exploring how their lives were affected and how they determined which side to support.

"By describing these lives and how the revolution affected them, DuVal accurately theorizes that independence was lost by many, and that the idea of 'empire' was often a place of security and affluence." Library Journal.

Ellis, Joseph J.

American creation : triumphs and tragedies at the founding of the republic / Joseph J. Ellis. A. A. Knopf, 2007. 304 p. **973.3**

1. Politicians -- United States -- History -- 18th century. 2. Political culture -- United States -- History -- 18th century. 3. Federal government. 4. National characteristics, American. 5. United States -- History -- Revolution, 1775-1783. 6. United States -- History -- 1783-1815. 7. United States -- Politics and government -- 1775-1783. 8. United States -- Politics and government -- 1783-1809.
ISBN 030726369X

LC 2007005273

"This is a Borzoi book"--T.p. verso.

An examination of the early years of the American Republic analyzes the eventful last quarter of the eighteenth century, the accomplishments of the American founders, and the triumphs and failures that shaped the early nation and the American character.

"The author selects certain propitious moments from the American Revolution and early republic, dramatizes them, and analyzes their crucial ramifications for America's future. . . . A history bound for phenomenal popularity." Booklist.

★**American** dialogue : the Founding Fathers and us / Joseph J. Ellis. Alfred A. Knopf, 2018. 304 p. **973.3**

1. Political culture -- United States -- History 2. Founding Fathers of the United States 3. Law 4. Political science -- Philosophy 5. United States -- Politics and government -- 18th century 6. United States -- Politics and government -- 21st century
ISBN 9780385353427

LC 2017050340

The story of history is a ceaseless conversation between past and present, and in American Dialogue, Joseph Ellis uses the perspective of the present to shed light on the views of the Founding Fathers. Examining four of the most seminal historical figures through the prism of particular topics, he makes clear how their now centuries-old ideas illuminate the disturbing impasse of today's political conflicts. Through these juxtapositions--and in his hallmark dramatic and compelling narrative voice--Ellis illuminates the obstacles and pitfalls paralyzing contemporary discussions of these fundamentally important issues"-- Provided by publisher.

"Drawing from his intimate knowledge of the Founding Fathers, Ellis addresses four 21st-century obstacles to reveal truths from their writings that should infuse wisdom into present-day debate: Thomas Jefferson's inconsistency on slavery and race; John Adams's warnings about financial aristocracy and economic inequality; James Madison's politically expedient concessions and the idea of original intent; and George Washington's approach to national and foreign policy, and the incompatibility of American imperialism with revolutionary ideals." Library Journal.

★**Revolutionary** summer : the birth of American independence / Joseph J. Ellis. Alfred A. Knopf, 2013. 240 p. **973.3**

1. Colonies 2. Battles 3. Politicians 4. American Revolution, 1775-1783 5. United States -- History -- Revolution, 1775-1783.
ISBN 9780307701220

LC 2012026140

"This thought-provoking, well-documented historical narrative is packed with insightful analysis. It will attract general and academic readers." Library Journal.

Ferling, John E.

Whirlwind : the American Revolution and the war that won it / John Ferling. Bloomsbury, 2015. 416 p. **973.3**

1. Revolutions -- United States 2. Colonists 3. Identity (Psychology) 4. War and society 5. United States -- History -- Revolution, 1775-1783. 6. United States -- History -- Revolution, 1775-1783 -- Campaigns.
ISBN 9781620401729

LC 2014033315

Kirkus Prize for Nonfiction finalist, 2015.

"Ferling has created another accessible yet scholarly work on the American Revolution. While its primary appeal is to history buffs, academics looking for an introductory survey history should also find this work useful." Library Journal.

Fischer, David Hackett, 1935-

Paul Revere's ride / David Hackett Fischer. Oxford University Press, 1994. xviii, 445 p. : **973.3**

1. Revere, Paul, 1735-1818. 2. Lexington, Battle of, 1775. 3. Concord, Battle of, 1775. 4. Revolutions -- United States. 5. Revolutionaries. 6. Massachusetts -- History -- Revolution, 1775-1783.
ISBN 0195088476

LC 93025739

"Fischer's solid study of Paul Revere and his infamous ride debunks the myths surrounding the event, reconstructing the circumstances leading to the Battle of Lexington and Concord. Fischer's extensive use of primary sources affords an intimate glimpse of the participants' thoughts and feelings." Booklist.

Washington's crossing / David Hackett Fischer. Oxford University Press, 2004. x, 564 p. : **973.3**

1. Washington, George, 1732-1799 Headquarters Valley Forge, Pennsylvania. 2. Generals -- United States -- 18th century. 3. Military strategy. 4. Command of troops. 5. Soldiers -- United States -- 18th century. 6. Delaware River. 7. Delaware River Valley -- History -- Revolution, 1775-1783. 8. United States -- History -- Revolution, 1775-1783 -- Campaigns 9. United States -- History -- Revolution, 1775-1783 -- British forces. 10. Trenton, New Jersey.
ISBN 9780195170344

LC 2003019858

ALA Notable Book, 2005.
Pulitzer Prize for History, 2005.
National Book Award for Nonfiction finalist, 2004

Provides a colorful and dramatic account of a pivotal moment in American history--the Christmas night crossing of the Delaware River to mount a sneak attack on British and Hessian troops at Trenton, New Jersey--an event that marked a turning point in America's battle for independence.

"This is Fischer's strong suit: he tells stories and gives details that bring history alive. In the hands of such a thorough researcher and talented writer, this is powerful stuff." School Library Journal.

Hogeland, William

Declaration : the nine tumultuous weeks when America became independent, May 1-July 4, 1776 / William Hogeland. Simon & Schuster, 2010. 320 p. **973.3**

1. United States. Declaration of Independence 2. United States. Constitution 3. United States. Continental Congress. 4. Revolutionaries -- United States -- History -- 18th century. 5. Revolutions -- United States 6. American Revolution, 1775-1783 7. United States -- History -- Revolution, 1775-1783 -- Causes. 8. United States -- Politics and government -- 1775-1783. 9. Great Britain -- Politics and government -- 1760-1820 10. United States -- History -- Colonial period, 1600-1775.
ISBN 9781416584094

LC 2010003239

"The author forges a compelling narrative from the dozens of intricate political imbroglios that culminated with the signing of the Declaration of Independence. By casting a light on the daily interests of colonial Americans, particularly those whose homes and businesses patterned the spaces of bustling 18th-century Philadelphia, the author animates the discontents of the soon-to-be independent citizenry. With charming detail, the narrative brings together the diverse political players working during the nine weeks prior to the signing of the Declaration." Kirkus.

Hoock, Holger

Scars of independence : America's violent birth / Holger Hoock. Random House Inc 2017 480 p. **973.3**

1. Violence 2. War crimes 3. American Revolution, 1775-1783 4. Political violence 5. United States -- History -- Revolution, 1775-1783
ISBN 9780804137287

LC 2016031348

According to historian Holger Hoock, the American Revolution wasn't only a conflict over principles, but also a violent civil war whose legacy historians have only recently recognized. In Scars of Independence, he carefully assesses how this violence affected everyone: Patriot and Loyalist civilians, military personnel on all sides, Native Americans, and free and enslaved blacks. Hoock's balanced and accessible historical analysis includes explicit descriptions of atrocities, which may be disturbing to some readers.

"An accomplished, powerful presentation of the American Revolution as it was, rather than as we might wish to remember it." Kirkus.

Jasanoff, Maya, 1974-

Liberty's exiles : American loyalists in the revolutionary world / Maya Jasanoff. Alfred A. Knopf, 2011. 480 p. **973.3**

1. Loyalists (United States history) 2. Exiles -- United States -- History -- 18th century. 3. Refugees -- United States -- History. 4. Colonists -- United States -- History. 5. United States -- History -- Revolution, 1775-1783 -- Refugees. 6. United States -- History -- Revolution, 1775-1783 -- Social aspects. 7. United States -- History -- Revolution, 1775-1783 -- Influence. 8. Great Britain -- Colonies -- History -- 18th century. 9. Great Britain -- Colonies -- History -- 19th century.
ISBN 9781400041688

LC 2010023514

National Book Critics Circle Award for Non-Fiction, 2011.

Cundill Prize in Historical Literature finalist

"The author examines the effects of the American Revolution on those whose loyalty to the Crown compelled them to flee the new United States." Kirkus.

Jefferson, Thomas, 1743-1826

Writings : autobiography notes on the State of Virginia public and private papers addresses letters / Thomas Jefferson. Literary Classics of the U.S., c1984. 1600 p. : The Library of America ; **973.3**

1. Jefferson, Thomas, 1743-1826. 2. United States -- Politics and government -- 1775-1783. 3. United States -- Politics and government -- 1783-1809. 4. Virginia. 5. Letters 6. Essays

ISBN 9780940450165

LC 83019917

"Merrill D. Peterson wrote the notes and selected the texts for this volume"--Prelim. p. 5.

Folded map in pocket.

Gathers Jefferson's letters to politicians, scientists, and family members, public speeches, travel essays, and political writings

"This is the largest and most skillfully edited single-volume Jefferson ever published." New York Times Book Review.

Ketchum, Richard M., 1922-2012

Saratoga : turning point of America's Revolutionary War / Richard M. Ketchum. H. Holt, 1997. xii, 545 p. : **973.3**

1. Saratoga Campaign, 1777. 2. Revolutions -- United States 3. American Revolution, 1775-1783 4. Saratoga Springs, New York -- History. 5. United States -- History -- Revolution, 1775-1783 -- Campaigns

ISBN 9780805046816

LC 97002773

The diaries and letters of soldiers under General Horatio Gates offer a view of the pivotal victory against the British in the Saratoga campaign.

"A narrative account of the Saratoga campaign of 1777. Ketchum provides the full political context within which the fighting took place while penning dozens of colorful portraits of the principal characters. The author also succeeds in his goal of telling the story from the perspective of the participants, illustrating what the American Revolution in upstate New York meant for soldiers and civilians alike." Library Journal.

Lockhart, Paul Douglas, 1963-

The **whites** of their eyes : Bunker Hill, the first American Army, and the emergence of George Washington / Paul Lockhart. Harper, 2011. 352 p. **973.3**

1. Washington, George, 1732-1799. 2. United States. Continental Army -- History. 3. Bunker Hill, Battle of, 1775 4. Revolutions -- United States 5. American Revolution, 1775-1783 6. United States -- History -- Revolution, 1775-1783

ISBN 9780061958861

LC 2010043033

"Lockhart's shrewd, well-judged interpretation corrects myths about the battle and the men who fought it while doing full justice to their achievement in creating an army--and a nation--out of chaos." Publishers Weekly.

Maier, Pauline, 1938-

American scripture : making the Declaration of Independence / Pauline Maier. Knopf, 1997. xxi, 304 p. : **973.3**

1. Jefferson, Thomas, 1743-1826. 2. United States. Declaration of Independence 3. Revolutions -- United States 4. American Revolution, 1775-1783 5. United States -- History -- 1775-1783. 6. United States -- History -- Revolution, 1775-1783 -- Causes. 7. United States -- Politics and government -- 1775-1783.

ISBN 0679454926

LC 97002769

ALA Notable Book, 1998.

National Book Critics Circle Award for Nonfiction finalist

Reveals the origins of the Declaration's ideas and phrases, unravels the story of its drafting, and explores the implications of its treatment as a sacred text

"In the spring of 1776, with a British invasion fleet on its way, the Second Continental Congress appointed a committee to compose a statement explaining America's decision to seek independence. Thomas Jefferson was the principal drafter of the statement, but Maier makes it clear that his task was to express the sentiments of the Congress, not his personal views, and she shows that when the congressmen edited his draft they improved it greatly (rather than mangling it, as Jefferson ever after maintained). The Declaration of Independence is, she argues, a profoundly collective document, both in its origins and in our still-evolving interpretation of its self-evident truths." The New Yorker.

McCullough, David G.

1776 / David McCullough. Simon & Schuster, 2005. 386 p. : **973.3**

1. Washington, George, 1732-1799. 2. George III, King of Great Britain, 1738-1820. 3. Militias and irregular armies -- United States -- History. 4. Rebels -- United States 5. Revolutionaries -- United States. 6. Revolutions -- United States. 7. United States -- History -- Revolution, 1775-1783. 8. United States -- History -- Revolution, 1775-1783 -- Causes.

ISBN 9780743287708

LC 2005042505

Draws on personal correspondence and period diaries to present a history of the American Revolution that ranges from the siege of Boston, to the American defeat at Brooklyn and retreat across New Jersey, to the American victory at Trenton.

"This is a narrative tour de force, exhibiting all the hallmarks the author is known for: fascinating subject matter, expert research and detailed, graceful prose." Publishers Weekly.

Middlekauff, Robert

The **glorious** cause : the American Revolution, 1763-1789 / Robert Middlekauff. Oxford University Press, 2005, c1982. xiv, 736 p. : **973.3**

1. Revolutions -- United States 2. American Revolution, 1775-1783 3. United States -- History -- Revolution, 1775-1783. 4. United States -- History -- Confederation, 1783-1789.

ISBN 0195162471

LC 2004016295

Previous ed. published as v. 2 in series: The Oxford history of the United States.

Originally published: New York : Oxford University Press, 1982.

Pulitzer Prize for History finalist, 1983.

"This is narrative history at its best, written in a conversational and engaging style." Library Journal.

Norton, Mary Beth

★**1774** : the long year of Revolution / Mary Beth Norton. Alfred A. Knopf, 2020. 400 p. **973.3**

1. United States. Continental Congress. 2. Boston Tea Party, 1773 3. Lexington, Battle of, 1775 4. Concord, Battle of, 1775 5. Loyalists (United States history) 6. United States -- History -- Colonial period,

1600-1775. 7. United States -- History -- Revolution, 1775-1783.
ISBN 9780385353366

LC 2019021556

"This is a Borzoi book."

A book on the American Revolution that looks at the critical "long year" of 1774, and the revolutionary change that took place from December 1773 to mid-April 1775, from the Boston Tea Party and the first Continental Congress to the Battle of Lexington and Concord.

"Norton makes a good case for considering 1774 and not 1776 to be the foundational year of the new republic." Kirkus

O'Donnell, Patrick K., 1969-

Washington's immortals : the untold story of an elite regiment who changed the course of the revolution / Patrick K. O'Donnell. Atlantic Monthly Press, 2016 xiv, 463 p., 16 unnumbered p. of plates : **973.3**

1. Washington, George, 1732-1799. 2. United States. Continental Army 3. Long Island, Battle of, 1776 4. Battles 5. Military history 6. American Revolution, 1775-1783 7. United States -- History -- Revolution, 1775-1783.
ISBN 9780802124593

LC bl2016003122

A best-selling military historian, drawing on extensive original sources, from letters to diaries to pension applications, pieces together the lives of the 256 brave men "who fell in the Battle of Brooklyn" in August 1776, saving General George Washington and his army, revealing their friendships, loves, defeats and triumphs.

"Using primary sources from both sides of the Atlantic, O'Donnell effectively traces the story of Maryland's immortals, describing the battles authentically along with the precariousness of the American cause." Library Journal.

Philbrick, Nathaniel

Bunker Hill : a city, a siege, a revolution / Nathaniel Philbrick. Viking, 2013. 400 p. **973.3**

1. Bunker Hill, Battle of, 1775 2. Military history 3. Military tactics -- United States 4. Siege warfare. 5. United States -- History -- Revolution, 1775-1783 6. Boston, Massachusetts -- History -- Revolution, 1775-1783
ISBN 9780670025442

LC 2013001534

Traces the experiences of Patriot leader Dr. Joseph Warren, a newly recruited George Washington, and British General William Howe.

★**In** the hurricane's eye : the genius of George Washington and the victory at Yorktown / Nathaniel Philbrick. Penguin Group USA 2018 448 p. **973.3**

1. Washington, George, 1732-1799 Military leadership 2. Lafayette, Marie Joseph Paul Yves Roch Gilbert Du Motier, marquis de, 1757-1834 3. France. Navy 4. American Revolution, 1775-1783 5. Command of troops 6. Naval battles 7. Strategic alliances (Military) 8. United States -- History -- Revolution, 1775-1783 9. France -- History, Military
ISBN 9780525426769

LC 2018029041

A narrative chronicle of the Battle of the Chesapeake traces the maneuvers by Lafayette and Washington that are credited with America's Revolutionary War victory.

"All readers interested in the Revolutionary War, and especially fans of naval history, will find Philbrick's fresh account rewarding, right through the epilogue describing what happened to many of the key figures going forward." Booklist.

★**Valiant** ambition : George Washington, Benedict Arnold, and the fate of the American Revolution / Nathaniel Philbrick. Viking Press, 2016 416 p. **973.3**

1. Washington, George, 1732-1799. 2. Arnold, Benedict, 1741-1801. 3. United States. Continental Army 4. Generals -- United States 5. Command of troops 6. Military history 7. Politicians 8. United States -- History -- Revolution, 1775-1783
ISBN 9780525426783

LC 2016303785

ALA Notable Book, 2017.

The National Book Award-winning author of In the Heart of the Sea presents an account of the complicated middle years of the American Revolution that shares lesser-known insights into the tragic relationship between George Washington and Benedict Arnold.

"Philbrick weaves exciting accounts of Arnold's impulsive battlefield exploits with the activities of self-interested military and civil associates into the demythified story of the circumstances of a tragic betrayal." Library Journal.

Phillips, Kevin, 1940-

1775 : a good year for revolution / Kevin Phillips. Viking, c2012. 640 p. **973.3**

1. Paine, Thomas, 1737-1809. Common sense. 2. United States. Continental Congress. 3. Lexington, Battle of, 1775 4. Concord, Battle of, 1775 5. Revolutions -- United States 6. American Revolution, 1775-1783 7. United States -- History -- Revolution, 1775-1783. 8. United States -- Politics and government -- 1775-1783. 9. Boston, Massachusetts -- History -- Revolution, 1775-1783 10. Fort Ticonderoga (N.Y. : Fort) -- Capture, 1775.
ISBN 9780670025121

LC 2012001786

An unconventional assessment of the American Revolution by the author of the Pulitzer Prize finalist The Cousins' War assesses the events, politics, economic factors and military preparations of 1775 that he believes ignited the war and established patriot control over American governance and key territories.

Rakove, Jack N., 1947-

Revolutionaries : a new history of the invention of America / Jack Rakove. Houghton Mifflin Harcourt, 2010. 487 p. ; **973.3**

1. Revolutionaries -- United States -- History -- 18th century. 2. Politicians -- United States -- History -- 18th century 3. Nation-building 4. Intellectual life -- United States -- 18th century 5. United States -- History -- Revolution, 1775-1783. 6. United States -- Politics and government -- 1775-1783.
ISBN 9780618267460

LC 2009047557

Spans the most crucial decades of the country's birth, from 1772 to 1792, using the stories of famous (and not-so-famous) men to capture the intensely creative period of the Republic's founding.

"The author reflects on how a group of lawyers and planters came to wage the American Revolution. Instead of focusing on the battlefield, the author examines what might be called a revolution of the mind, that is, how the early Founding Fathers' ideas developed and took hold. An ambitious, intelligent exploration into the intellectual underpinnings of the Revolution." Kirkus.

Raphael, Ray

★A **people's** history of the American Revolution : how common people shaped the fight for independence / Ray Raphael.

Perennial, 2002, c2001. xiv, 506 p. **973.3**

1. Revolutions -- United States 2. American Revolution, 1775-1783 3. United States -- History -- Revolution, 1775-1783. 4. United States -- History -- Revolution, 1775-1783 -- Social aspects. 5. United States -- History -- Revolution, 1775-1783

ISBN 0060004401

LC 2002016992

Originally published: New York : The New Press, 2001.

Presents a history of the American Revolution from the perspective of farmers, soldiers, laborers, and other common folk by using personal letters, diaries, and other primary source material.

"Moving from broad overviews to stories of small groups or individuals, Raphael's study is impressive in both its sweep and its attention to the particular." Publishers Weekly.

Tuchman, Barbara W. (Barbara Wertheim), 1912-1989

The **first** salute / Barbara W. Tuchman. Ballantine Books, 1989, c1988. xiii, 347 p., 16 p. of plates : **973.3**

1. Revolutions -- United States. 2. American Revolution, 1775-1783 3. United States -- History -- Revolution, 1775-1783 -- Naval operations. 4. United States -- History -- Revolution, 1775-1783 -- Campaigns

ISBN 0345336674

LC BL 99700019

Originally published: New York : Knopf, 1988.

Tuchman takes a fresh look at the men and events that produced and decided America's struggle for independence. At its climax is the 500-mile march undertaken by Washington and his combined army of 7000 American and French troops. Its destination was Yorktown; the resolve of its general unshakeable.

"The book is a tightly woven narrative, ingeniously structured. It is not a blow-by-blow account of the conflict; familiarity with issues and events is assumed. Instead, Tuchman takes a specific incident and through it elucidates the course and outcome of the war." Christian Science Monitor.

Unger, Harlow G., 1931-

American tempest : how the Boston Tea Party sparked a revolution / Harlow Giles Unger. Da Capo Press, 2011. 288 p. **973.3**

1. Boston Tea Party, 1773. 2. Protests, demonstrations, vigils, etc. 3. Revolutionaries. 4. Revolutions -- United States 5. Boston, Massachusetts -- History -- Revolution, 1775-1783. 6. United States -- History -- Revolution, 1775-1783 -- Causes.

ISBN 9780306819629

LC 2010047734

Describes the events of the Boston Tea Party on December 16, 1773, the turmoil it initiated in Boston and other cities, and the social, political, and economic consequences that eventually led to the Declaration of Independence and the birth of the United States.

"As Unger makes clear, the true impact of the Boston Tea Party came from Britain's ill-advised overreaction to the symbolic act of vandalism. It was exactly the response [Sam] Adams had dreamed of, with an enraged British government closing the port of Boston, sending more troops, imposing martial law, and requiring permits for any large Boston meetings. These Coercive Acts, along with Adams's constant drumbeat of anti-British propaganda, helped unify the colonies around the idea of independence. Unger ends the book with British soldiers marching out to Lexington and Concord hoping to arrest Adams and Hancock (who, tipped off by Paul Revere, had fled). The rest, as they say, is history, and Unger has brought it brilliantly to life." Boston Globe.

Weintraub, Stanley, 1929-

Iron tears : America's battle for freedom, Britain's quagmire, 1775-1783 / Stanley Weintraub. Free Press, 2005. xviii, 375 p., 16 p. of plates : **973.3**

1. Public opinion -- Great Britain -- History -- 18th century. 2. Revolutions -- United States. 3. Soldiers -- Great Britain. 4. War and society. 5. United States -- History -- Revolution, 1775-1783 -- Foreign public opinion, British. 6. Great Britain -- Politics and government -- 1760-1789.

ISBN 0743226879

LC 2004056363

"Weintraub's fast-paced narrative and impeccable historical research provide a stimulating challenge to conventional histories of the Revolutionary War that focus exclusively on the heroism of American forces." Publishers Weekly.

Winik, Jay, 1957-

★The **great** upheaval : America and the birth of the modern world, 1788-1800 / Jay Winik. Harper Collins, 2007. 688 p. **973.3**

1. Modern history. 2. World politics. 3. Revolutions. 4. United States -- History -- 1783-1815. 5. France -- History -- Revolution, 1789-1799. 6. Russia -- History -- Catherine II, 1762-1796.

ISBN 0060083131

LC bl2007015098

Documents the final years of the eighteenth century as a period of tumultuous change marked by Russia's imperial power, the revolution in France, and America's near-collapse, events that the author reveals to be intricately related.

"An outstandingly wide-ranging account of this vital era in world history." Booklist.

Wood, Gordon S.

The **radicalism** of the American Revolution / Gordon S. Wood. A.A. Knopf, 1992. x, 447 p. **973.3**

1. Radicalism -- United States -- History -- 18th century. 2. Political culture -- United States -- History -- 18th century. 3. Democracy -- United States -- History. 4. Commercialization. 5. United States -- History -- Revolution, 1775-1783 -- Social aspects. 6. United States -- Politics and government -- 1775-1783.

ISBN 0679404937

LC 91019719

Pulitzer Prize for History, 1993.

Examines colonial society and the transformations in colonial life that resulted from the republican tendencies brought to the surface by the Revolution.

"Under the broad categories of monarchy, republicanism, and democracy, Wood explains how the US was transformed from a society that took for granted a nonworking elite and a dependent servile underclass to one in which the free-standing individualist, who worked for a living, became the norm. {A} readable book based on hundreds of primary and secondary sources." Choice.

Wren, Christopher S. (Christopher Sale), 1936-

Those turbulent sons of freedom : Ethan Allen's Green Mountain boys and the American Revolution / Christopher S. Wren. Simon & Schuster, 2018. 320 p. **973.3**

1. Allen, Ethan, 1738-1789 2. Warner, Seth, 1743-1784 3. Sherwood, Justus, 1747-1798 4. Green Mountain Boys 5. Revolutionaries 6. Soldiers 7. Militias and irregular armies. 8. Vermont -- History -- Revolution, 1775-1783 9. New England 10. United States -- History

-- Revolution, 1775-1783
ISBN 9781416599555

LC 2017053023

Chronicles the exploits of Ethan Allen and the much-loved Green Mountain Boys of Vermont and their role in the American Revolution--both the myth and the reality.

973.4 United States--Constitutional period, 1789-1809

Adams, Abigail, 1744-1818

Abigail Adams : letters / Edith Gelles, editor. The Library of America, 2016 xxxix, 1180 p. ; **973.4**

1. Adams, Abigail, 1744-1818 Correspondence. 2. American letters 3. Presidents' spouses -- United States 4. United States -- History -- 1783-1815 Sources. 5. United States -- History -- Revolution, 1775-1783 Sources. 6. Correspondence.
ISBN 9781598534658

LC 2015935694

Includes index.

Chronicles the life of the first lady through her correspondence with her husband and other notable figures, covering her courtship and marriage, the American Revolution, her travels in Europe, and her time in the White House.

Adams, John, 1735-1826

★**My** dearest friend : letters of Abigail and John Adams / edited by Margaret A. Hogan and C. James Taylor. Belknap Press of Harvard University Press, 2007. xx, 508 p., [20] p. of plates : **973.4**

1. Adams, John, 1735-1826 Correspondence. 2. Adams, Abigail, 1744-1818 Correspondence. 3. Presidents -- United States -- Correspondence. 4. Presidents' spouses -- United States -- Correspondence 5. Married people -- United States -- Correspondence. 6. Couples -- United States -- Correspondence. 7. United States -- History -- Revolution, 1775-1783 Sources. 8. United States -- History -- 1783-1815 Sources. 9. Love letters 10. Letters
ISBN 0674026063

LC 2007004380

Includes index.

"This is a treasure, for general readers and scholars alike." Booklist.

Avlon, John P.

Washington's farewell : the founding father's warning to future generations / John Avlon. Simon & Schuster, 2017. 320 p. **973.4**

1. Washington, George, 1732-1799. Farewell address. 2. Washington, George, 1732-1799 Influence. 3. National characteristics, American. 4. Presidents -- United States -- History. 5. Political leadership -- United States -- History 6. Political parties -- United States 7. United States -- History -- 1783-1815
ISBN 9781476746463

LC 2016045258

In Washington's Farewell, Avlon offers important insight into Washington's final public days, presenting not only a startling description of the perilous state of the new nation but a rare view of the man behind the usual face of a tranquil First Father.

"A solid analysis of our first president and his farewell to the American people." Library Journal.

Dunbar, Erica Armstrong

Never caught : the Washingtons' relentless pursuit of their runaway slave, Ona Judge / Erica Armstrong Dunbar. 37 INK, 2017. 256 p. **973.4**

1. Washington, George, 1732-1799 2. Judge, Oney, 1773-1848 3. Washington, Martha, 1731-1802 4. Presidents -- United States 5. African Americans -- History 6. Fugitive slaves 7. Slavery 8. Mount Vernon 9. Philadelphia, Pennsylvania 10. Southern States -- History
ISBN 9781501126390

LC 2017932249

National Book Award for Nonfiction finalist, 2017

A revelatory account of the actions taken by the first president to retain his slaves in spite of Northern laws profiles one of the slaves, Ona Judge, describing the intense manhunt that ensued when she ran away.

"A startling, well-researched slave narrative that seriously questions the intentions of our first president." Kirkus.

Ellis, Joseph J.

Founding brothers : the revolutionary generation / Joseph J. Ellis. Alfred A. Knopf, 2000. xi, 288 p. **973.4**

1. Republican Party 2. Federal government. 3. Politicians -- United States 4. Presidents -- United States 5. Revolutionaries. 6. United States -- History -- 1783-1815 Anecdotes. 7. United States -- Politics and government -- 1783-1809 Anecdotes.
ISBN 0375405445

LC 99059304

Pulitzer Prize for History, 2001.

An analysis of the intertwined careers of the founders of the American republic documents the lives of John Adams, Aaron Burr, Benjamin Franklin, Alexander Hamilton, Thomas Jefferson, James Madison, and George Washington.

"Ellis' essays are angled, fascinating, and perfect for general-interest readers." Booklist.

Gaines, James R.

For liberty and glory : Washington, Lafayette, and their revolutions / James R. Gaines. W.W. Norton & Co., c2007. 512 p. **973.4**

1. Washington, George, 1732-1799. 2. Washington, George, 1732-1799 Influence. 3. Lafayette, Marie Joseph Paul Yves Roch Gilbert Du Motier, marquis de, 1757-1834. 4. Lafayette, Marie Joseph Paul Yves Roch Gilbert Du Motier, marquis de, 1757-1834 Influence. 5. Presidents -- United States. 6. Politicians -- France. 7. Revolutions -- United States 8. American Revolution, 1775-1783 9. United States -- History -- Revolution, 1775-1783. 10. France -- History -- Revolution, 1789-1799.
ISBN 0393061388

LC 2007022449

A narrative account of the "sister revolutions" of France and America reveals the lesser-known agendas that intertwined the conflicts, discussing the close but complex relationship between Washington and the Marquis de Lafayette.

"This is a fresh and engaging new look at the pair. Gaines has a dry sense of humor and an appreciation for human foibles. The American founding fathers, in particular, come across as extraordinary men with ordinary obsessions and--surprise!--senses of humor." Christian Science Monitor.

Hogeland, William

★The **Whiskey** Rebellion : George Washington, Alexander Hamilton, and the frontier rebels who challenged America's newfound sovereignty / William Hogeland. Scribner, 2006.

vii, 302 p. : **973.4**

1. Whiskey Rebellion, Pennsylvania, 1794.
ISBN 0743254902

LC 2005056340

"A Lisa Drew book."

A history of the 1790s insurrection that pitted America's founding fathers against Appalachian settlers offers insight into the devastating impact of the whiskey tax on rural economies.

"In a fast-paced, blow-by-blow account of this primal national drama, journalist Hogeland energetically chronicles the skirmishes that made the Whiskey Rebellion from 1791 to 1795 a symbol of the conflict between republican ideals and capitalist values." Publishers Weekly.

Kilmeade, Brian

George Washington's secret six : the spy ring that saved the American Revolution / Brian Kilmeade and Don Yaeger. Sentinel, 2013. 288 p. **973.4**

1. Washington, George, 1732-1799 Friends and associates. 2. Townsend, Robert, 1753-1838. 3. Spies -- United States -- History -- 18th century. 4. Secret service. 5. Spies -- New York (State) -- History -- 18th century. 6. American Revolution, 1775-1783 7. United States -- History -- Revolution, 1775-1783 -- Secret service. 8. New York (State) -- History -- Revolution, 1775-1783 -- Secret service.
ISBN 9781595231031

LC 2013032285

The co-host of Fox & Friends shares the true story of an anonymous group of spies who played lesser-known, important roles in winning the Revolutionary War, documenting how they risked their lives to obtain crucial intelligence for General Washington using sophisticated tactics and complex codes.

"While Kilmeade and Yaeger don't provide deep analysis, the narrative should please enthusiastic fans of the upheaval surrounding the founding of the United States. In a slim, quick-moving book, the authors bring attention to a group that exerted an enormous influence over events during the Revolutionary War." Kirkus.

Kukla, Jon, 1948-

A **wilderness** so immense : the Louisiana Purchase and the destiny of America / Jon Kukla. A. A. Knopf, 2003. x, 430 p. : **973.4**

1. Louisiana Purchase. 2. United States -- Territorial expansion.
ISBN 0375408126

LC 2002027395

A history of the Louisiana Purchase takes readers through events that transpired throughout the United States and its territories as well as Great Britain, France, Spain, and Haiti.

"This judicious, aptly illustrated work will gratify all its readers. Rarely does a work of history combine grace of writing with such broad authority." Publishers Weekly.

Meltzer, Brad

★The **first** conspiracy : the secret plot to kill George Washington / Brad Meltzer and Josh Mensch. Flatiron Books, 2019. 432 p. **973.4**

1. Washington, George, 1732-1799 2. United States. Continental Army. Commander-in-Chief's Guard 3. Presidents -- United States -- Assassination plots 4. Assassination plots 5. Treason 6. Military intelligence 7. United States -- History -- Revolution, 1775-1783
ISBN 9781250130334

LC 2018037886

The author of The Inner Circle presents the lesser-known story of an assassination attempt against pre-Revolutionary War George Washington by some of his own bodyguards, exploring how the plot catalyzed the creations of the CIA and FBI.

"What Meltzer and Mensch do bring out is how the scheme helped to inspire American innovations in defensive spycraft, eventually known as counterintelligence, by their juxtaposing the Hickey attempt with the ad hoc nature of the political and military leadership seeking to control the city and prosecute the war. Readers who like their histories full of twists, turns, and cliff-hangers will enjoy this romp through the Revolution." Booklist.

O'Connell, Robert L.

Revolutionary : George Washington at war / Robert L. O'Connell. Random House, [2019] xxviii, 368 pages : **973.4**

1. Washington, George, 1732-1799 Military leadership 2. Generals 3. Command of troops 4. American Revolution, 1775-1783 5. Soldiers -- Psychology 6. United States -- History -- Revolution, 1775-1783
ISBN 9780812996999

LC 2018013009

The military historian and author presents a bold reappraisal of George Washington as a young soldier of destiny whose Revolutionary War leadership came to define the American character.

Sedgwick, John, 1954-

War of two : Alexander Hamilton, Aaron Burr, and the duel that stunned the nation / John Sedgwick. Berkley Books, 2015. 432 p. **973.4**

1. Hamilton, Alexander, 1757-1804. 2. Burr, Aaron, 1756-1836. 3. Burr-Hamilton Duel, Weehawken, N.J., 1804. 4. Dueling -- United States -- History -- 19th century. 5. Politicians 6. Enemies. 7. United States -- Politics and government -- 1801-1809.
ISBN 9781592408528

LC 2015014275

In the summer of 1804, two of America's most eminent statesmen squared off, pistols raised, on a bluff along the Hudson River. That two such men would risk not only their lives but the stability of the young country they helped forge is almost beyond comprehension. Yet we know that it happened. The question is why. In War of Two, John Sedgwick explores the long-standing conflict between Founding Father Alexander Hamilton and Vice President Aaron Burr.

"A fine rendition of a storied episode in American history." Booklist.

Stewart, David O.

American emperor : Aaron Burr's challenge to Jefferson's America / David O. Stewart. Simon & Schuster, c2011. 352 p. **973.4**

1. Jefferson, Thomas, 1743-1826. 2. Burr, Aaron, 1756-1836. 3. Presidential election, 1800 4. Vice-presidents 5. Ambition in men. 6. Politicians. 7. United States -- Politics and government -- 1797-1801.
ISBN 9781439157183

LC 2011002647

Stewart traces the canny and charismatic Aaron Burr from the threshold of the presidency in 1800 to his duel with Alexander Hamilton. Stewart recounts Burr's efforts to carve out an empire, taking listeners across the American West as the renegade vice president schemes with foreign ambassadors, the U.S. general-in-chief, and future presidents.

"A persuasive, engaging examination of the post-political career of a shadowy and much-maligned figure from the era of the Founders." Kirkus.

Taylor, Alan, 1955-

Thomas Jefferson's education / Alan Taylor. W.W. Norton & Company, [2019] xiv, 426 p. **973.4**

1. Jefferson, Thomas, 1743-1826 Political and social views. 2. University of Virginia -- History 3. Higher education -- United States -- History -- 19th century 4. State universities and colleges 5. Former presidents -- United States 6. Elite (Social sciences) 7. Virginia 8. United States -- History -- 19th century

ISBN 9780393652420

LC 2019014796

"From the Pulitzer Prize- winning historian, a brilliant, absorbing study of Jefferson and his campaign to save Virginia through education. By turns entertaining and tragic, this beautifully crafted history reveals the origins of a great university in the dilemmas of Virginia slavery. Thomas Jefferson shares center stage with his family and fellow planters, all dependent on the labor of enslaved black families. With a declining Virginia yielding to commercially vibrant northern states, Jefferson in 1819 proposed to build a university to educate and improve the sons of the planter elite. They, he hoped, might one day lead a revitalized Virginia free of slavery-- and free of the former slaves. Jefferson's campaign to build the university was a contest for the future of a state and the larger nation. Although he prevails, Jefferson's vision of reform through education is hobbled by the actions of genteel students whose defiant sense of honor derived from owning slaves. It is the women of this hypermasculine society-- particularly Jefferson's granddaughters--who redeem the best elements of his legacy".-- Provided by publisher.

Wiencek, Henry

★An **imperfect** god : George Washington, his slaves, and the creation of America / Henry Wiencek. Farrar, Straus and Giroux, 2003. 404 p. : **973.4**

1. Washington, George, 1732-1799. 2. Washington, George, 1732-1799 Relations with African-Americans. 3. Presidents -- United States 4. Slavery -- Political aspects 5. United States -- Politics and government -- 1775-1783. 6. United States -- Race relations.

ISBN 0374175268

LC 2003006984

An analysis of how the life of George Washington was impacted by slavery discusses his blood ties to the slave community, childhood in a mixed-race neighborhood, activities as a slave owner, realization of the evils of slavery during the Revolutionary War, and political efforts on behalf of slaves.

"This work of stylish scholarship and genealogical investigation makes Washington an even greater and more human figure than he has seemed before." Publishers Weekly.

Wiencek, Henry

★**Master** of the mountain : Thomas Jefferson and his slaves / Henry Wiencek. Farrar, Straus and Giroux, 2012. 416 p. **973.4**

1. Jefferson, Thomas, 1743-1826 Relations with slaves 2. Hemings, Sally, 1773-1835? Family 3. Slaves 4. Slavery -- Economic aspects 5. Plantation life -- Virginia -- History 6. Virginia -- History -- 18th century 7. Monticello (Va.) -- History

ISBN 9780374299569

LC 2011052231

A controversial reassessment of the third President draws on new archaeological studies and previously disregarded personal records, assessing his contradictory views on slavery while examining what is revealed by his monetary records.

"Wiencek's insightful and engaging account is recommended to both the illustrious Virginian's detractors and to his devotees." Library Journal.

Wood, Gordon S.

Empire of liberty : a history of the early Republic, 1789-1815 / Gordon S. Wood. Oxford University Press, 2009. xix, 778 p., 32 p. of plates : **973.4**

1. Politicians -- United States. 2. Presidents -- United States. 3. United States -- Civilization -- 1783-1865. 4. United States -- Politics and government -- 1789-1815.

ISBN 9780195039146

LC 2009010762

American History Book Prize, 2009.

Pulitzer Prize for History finalist, 2010.

Integrating all aspects of life, from politics and law to the economy and culture, "Empire of Liberty" offers a marvelous account of this pivotal era when America took its first unsteady steps as a new and rapidly expanding nation.

973.5 United States--1809-1845

Brands, H. W.

★**Heirs** of the founders : the epic rivalry of Henry Clay, John Calhoun and Daniel Webster, the second generation of American giants / H. W. Brands. Doubleday, a division of Penguin Random House LLC, [2018] 432 p. **973.5**

1. Calhoun, John C., 1782-1850 2. Clay, Henry, 1777-1852. 3. Webster, Daniel, 1782-1852. 4. Politicians -- United States 5. Constitutional history 6. Nation-building 7. Politicians 8. United States -- Politics and government -- 1801-1815. 9. United States -- Politics and government -- 1815-1861.

ISBN 9780385542531

LC 2018010542

Chronicles the efforts of three second-generation political giants who at the beginning of the nineteenth century battled to complete the unfinished initiatives of the Founding Fathers.

"Requiring of readers no prior knowledge of the period or the players, this fascinating history illuminates rifts that still plague the country today." Publishers Weekly.

Daughan, George C.

1812 : the navy's war / George C. Daughan. Basic Books, c2011. 400 p. **973.5**

1. United States. Navy -- History War of 1812. 2. Naval battles. 3. Naval tactics. 4. War of 1812 5. United States -- History -- War of 1812 -- Naval operations.

ISBN 9780465020461

LC 2011020923

"Daughan narrates the story of the War of 1812, focusing on the tiny, 20-ship U.S. Navy. In doing so, from the poorly conducted chase of HMS Belvidera by Commodore John Rogers in June 1812 to the capture of HMS Penguin by USS Hornet in March 1815, Daughan also traces the development of the U.S. Navy." Library Journal.

Groom, Winston, 1944-2020

Patriotic fire : Andrew Jackson and Jean Laffite at the Battle of New Orleans / Winston Groom. Alfred A. Knopf, 2006. xxiv, 292 p., 8 p. of plates : **973.5**

1. Jackson, Andrew, 1767-1845. 2. Laffite, Jean. 3. New Orleans, Battle of, 1815. 4. Generals -- United States 5. Pirates -- Louisiana 6.

Battles. 7. New Orleans, Louisiana -- History -- 19th century.
ISBN 1400044367

LC 2005051001

A chronicle of the January, 1815 Battle of New Orleans describes how the American general, Andrew Jackson, unexpectedly joined forces with raffish French buccaneer, Jean Laffite, to repel an invasion of British troops from the Louisiana city.

Howe, Daniel Walker

★**What** hath God wrought : the transformation of America, 1815-1848 / Daniel Walker Howe. Oxford University Press, 2007. xviii, 904 p., 16 p. of plates : **973.5**

1. Social change -- United States -- History -- 19th century. 2. United States -- History -- 1815-1861. 3. United States -- Foreign relations -- 1815-1861. 4. United States -- Politics and government -- 1815-1861. 5. United States -- Economic conditions -- To 1865.
ISBN 0195078942

LC 2007012370

American History Book Prize, 2007.
Pulitzer Prize for History, 2008.
National Book Critics Circle Award for Nonfiction finalist, 2007.

A panoramic history of the United States ranges from the 1815 Battle of New Orleans to the end of the Mexican-American War and chronicles the dramatic changes that took place in America during the period, interweaving political and military events with social, economic, and cultural history to address such issues as women's rights, religion, slavery and abolition, education, literature, and more.

"The author narrates a crucial period in U.S. history--a time of territorial growth, religious revival, booming industrialization, a recalibrating of American democracy and the rise of nationalist sentiment. Supported by engaging prose, Howe's achievement will surely be seen as one of the most outstanding syntheses of U.S. history published this decade." Publishers Weekly.

Langguth, A. J., 1933-

Driven West : Andrew Jackson's trail of tears to the Civil War / A.J. Langguth. Simon & Schuster, 2011. 384 p. **973.5**

1. Trail of Tears, 1838-1839 2. Indian Removal, 1813-1903 3. North-South relations (United States) 4. Territorial expansion. 5. United States -- History -- 1815-1861.
ISBN 9781416548591

LC 2010020455

In this major work of narrative history, A.J. Langguth portrays four of the most turbulent decades in the growth of the American nation. After the War of 1812, Presidents Monroe, Jackson, Van Buren, and Polk led the country to its Manifest Destiny across the continent, but the forces and hostility unleashed by that expansion led inexorably to Civil War.

Lincoln, Abraham, 1809-1865

Speeches and writings, 1832-1858 : speeches, letters, and miscellaneous writings, the Lincoln-Douglas debates / Abraham Lincoln. Literary Classics of the United States : 1989. xix, 898 p. ; The Library of America ; **973.5**

1. Lincoln, Abraham, 1809-1865 Political career before 1861. 2. Lincoln-Douglas Debates, Ill, 1858 3. Illinois -- Politics and government -- To 1865. 4. United States -- Politics and government -- 1849-1861.
ISBN 9780940450431

LC 88082723

"First printing"--P. [iv].

The texts are selected (from The collected works of Abraham Lincoln / edited by Roy Basler, c1953 and its supplement, c1974) and annotated by Don E. Fehrenbacher.

"Don E. Fehrenbacher wrote the notes and selected the texts for this volume."

Includes index.

The President's writings trace his involvement in Illinois politics, his opposition to slavery, and his political debates with Stephen Douglas.

Reynolds, David S., 1948-

Waking giant : America in the age of Jackson / David S. Reynolds. Harper, c2008. 480 p. **973.5**

1. Jackson, Andrew, 1767-1845 Influence. 2. Politicians. 3. Political leadership. 4. United States -- History -- 1815-1861. 5. United States -- Politics and government -- 1815-1861. 6. United States -- Social conditions -- To 1865.
ISBN 9780060826567

LC 2007051751

A chronicle of political events between 1815 and 1848 evaluates their role in shaping American culture, covering such topics as the slavery controversy, the rise of capitalism, and the birth of urbanization.

"This is a terrific introduction of succinct length to...a time when the foundations of much of modern America were laid." New York Times.

Taylor, Alan, 1955-

The **civil** war of 1812 : American citizens, British subjects, Irish rebels, and Indian allies / Alan Taylor. Alfred A. Knopf, 2010. 640 p. **973.5**

1. Nationalism. 2. Loyalty. 3. Border disputes. 4. National territory. 5. United States -- History -- War of 1812. 6. Ontario -- History -- War of 1812. 7. Northern boundary of the United States -- History -- 19th century.
ISBN 9781400042654

LC 2010012783

In a world of double identities, slippery allegiances, and porous borders, the leaders of the American Republic and the British Empire struggled to control their own diverse peoples. Taylor's narrative of an often brutal--sometimes farcical--war reveals much about the tangled origins of the United States and Canada.

"Instead of a traditional narrative of the war from its beginnings in June 1812 to its end in early 1815, [this] book is structured topically. Such a neat and methodical organization helps Taylor bring the confused and chaotic events of the war under control. It also allows him to present an enormous amount of material--on persons, events, and stories--without overwhelming the reader. And the amount of material is enormous." New York Review of Books.

Vogel, Steve, 1960-

Through the perilous fight : six weeks that saved the nation / Steve Vogel. Random House, 2013. 448 p. **973.5**

1. Cockburn, George, Sir, 1772-1853. 2. Key, Francis Scott, 1779-1843. 3. Star-spangled banner (Song) 4. Military campaigns 5. Military history 6. Battles -- History 7. Baltimore, Battle of, Baltimore, Md., 1814. 8. Washington (D.C.) -- History -- Capture by the British, 1814. 9. Maryland -- History -- War of 1812 10. United States -- History -- War of 1812
ISBN 9781400069132

LC 2012039797

In a rousing account of one of the critical turning points in American history, Through the Perilous Fight tells the gripping story of the burning of Washington and the improbable last stand at Baltimore that helped save the nation and inspired its National Anthem.

Wilentz, Sean

The **rise** of American democracy : Jefferson to Lincoln

/ Sean Wilentz. Norton, c2005. xxiii, 1044 p. : **973.5**

1. Presidents -- United States -- History -- 18th century. 2. Presidents -- United States -- History -- 19th century. 3. Politicians -- United States -- History -- 18th century. 4. Politicians -- United States -- History -- 19th century. 5. United States -- Politics and government -- 1783-1865.

ISBN 0393058204

LC 2004029466

Pulitzer Prize for History finalist, 2006.

"This is a magnificent chronicle, the life of an idea that, although it is mentioned nowhere in the Constitution, nevertheless slowly elbowed its way into the heart of American life. Wilentz shows what [the] fight has cost, and why it's worth it." Newsweek.

973.56 Administration of Andrew Jackson, 1829-1837

Inskeep, Steve

Jacksonland : President Andrew Jackson, Cherokee Chief John Ross, and a great American land grab / Steve Inskeep. Penguin Group, 2015 480 p. **973.56**

1. Jackson, Andrew, 1767-1845 Relations with Indians 2. Ross, John, 1790-1866 3. Government relations with indigenous peoples 4. Cherokee Indians 5. Creek War, 1813-1814. 6. Creek Indians. 7. United States -- Politics and government -- 1829-1837. 8. United States -- Race relations.

ISBN 9781594205569

LC 2015300789

A renowned journalist and cohost of NPR's Morning Edition presents a thrilling narrative history of President Andrew Jackson and Cherokee Chief John Ross--two heroic yet tragically opposed men whose actions decided the fate of states and Indian nations in America at a moment of transition.

"This superb book is highly recommended for readers interested in Native American studies or Southern history. For more on Catherine Beecher and her movement, see Alisse Portnoy's Their Right To Speak: Women's Activism in the Indian and Slave Debates." Library Journal.

973.6 United States--1845-1861

Bordewich, Fergus M.

America's great debate : Henry Clay, Stephen A. Douglas, and the compromise that preserved the Union / Fergus M. Bordewich. Simon & Schuster, 2012. 448 p. **973.6**

1. Clay, Henry, 1777-1852. 2. Douglas, Stephen A. (Stephen Arnold), 1813-1861 3. Compromise of 1850. 4. Slavery -- History -- 19th century. 5. Debates and debating 6. United States Civil War, 1861-1865 7. United States -- Politics and government -- 1815-1861. 8. United States -- History -- Civil War, 1861-1865 -- Causes.

ISBN 9781439124604

LC 2011029547

Chronicles the heated debates surrounding the 1850s appeals of California and other territories to join the Union as slave or free states, profiling tenacious period balances in the Senate, Henry Clay's attempts at compromise and the explosive boundary crisis between New Mexico and Texas.

Guelzo, Allen C.

Lincoln and Douglas : the debates that defined America / Allen C. Guelzo. Simon & Schuster, 2008. 416 p. **973.6**

1. Lincoln, Abraham, 1809-1865 Political and social views. 2. Douglas, Stephen A. (Stephen Arnold), 1813-1861 Political and social views 3. Lincoln-Douglas Debates, 1858. 4. Politicians. 5. Presidential debates. 6. Debates and debating. 7. United States -- Politics and government -- 1857-1861. 8. Illinois -- Politics and government -- To 1865.

ISBN 0743273206

LC 2007044254

An account of the famous open-air 1858 Senate election debates between Stephen A. Douglas and Abraham Lincoln provides insight into their political rivalry while gauging mid-nineteenth-century issues and how they affected local and presidential campaigns.

"This Lincoln-Douglas rendition will engage every interest in Civil War and Black history." Booklist.

Lincoln, Abraham, 1809-1865

Speeches and writings, 1859-1865 : speeches, letters, and miscellaneous writings, presidential messages and proclamations / Abraham Lincoln. Literary Classics of the United States, c1989. xxxiii, 787 p. ; The Library of America ; **973.6**

1. Republican Party (U.S. : 1854-) -- History 19th century. 2. United States -- Politics and government -- 1857-1861. 3. United States -- Politics and government -- 1861-1865. 4. Speeches, addresses, etc.

ISBN 9780940450639

LC 89045349

The texts are selected (from The collected works of Abraham Lincoln / edited by Roy Basler, c1953 and its supplement, c1974) and annotated by Don E. Fehrenbacher.

"Don E. Fehrenbacher wrote the notes and selected the texts for this volume"--P. [v].

Includes index.

The President's writings trace his opposition to slavery, share his appraisal of the presidential election, and document his leadership during the Civil War.

Wineapple, Brenda

Ecstatic nation : confidence, crisis, and the end of compromise, 1848-1877 / Brenda Wineapple. Harper, 2013. 544 p. **973.6**

1. Slavery -- History -- 19th century. 2. Antislavery movements -- United States -- History -- 19th century. 3. Reconstruction (United States history) 4. United States Civil War, 1861-1865 5. United States -- History -- 1849-1877. 6. United States -- Territorial expansion -- History -- 19th century. 7. United States -- History -- Civil War, 1861-1865 -- Causes. 8. United States -- History -- Civil War, 1861-1865.

ISBN 9780061234576

LC 2012051538

Documents the rise of America during the heart of the 19th century, starting with the end of the Mexican-American War and moving through the complexities of Reconstruction and women's equality, the displacement of the Indians and the transformation of a confederation into one nation.

973.7 Administration of Abraham Lincoln, 1861-1865

Ash, Stephen V.

Firebrand of liberty : the story of two Black regiments that changed the course of the Civil War / Stephen V. Ash. W.W. Norton & Co., 2008. 320 p. **973.7**

1. United States. Army. South Carolina Volunteers, 1st (1862-1864) 2. United States. Army. South Carolina Volunteers, 2nd (1863-1864)

3. African American soldiers -- History -- 19th century. 4. Military history -- 19th century 5. United States Civil War, 1861-1865 6. Union soldiers 7. United States -- History -- Civil War, 1861-1865 -- African American troops 8. United States -- History -- Civil War, 1861-1865 -- Regimental histories. 9. Jacksonville, Florida -- Military history -- 19th century. 10. Florida -- History -- Civil War, 1861-1865 -- Campaigns. 11. United States -- History -- Civil War, 1861-1865 -- Campaigns. 12. United States -- Army -- African-American troops -- History -- 19th century.
ISBN 9780393065862

LC 2008002503

Traces the March 1863 invasion of African-American Union troops in Jacksonville, Florida, in a campaign led by prominent abolitionist Thomas Wentworth Higginson that was mysteriously called off but still influenced Lincoln's full-scale recruitment of free black soldiers.

"The titular firebrand in this revealing history is not an individual but a curious and ambitious project: the establishment, in March 1863, of a permanent Union outpost in Florida to serve as a haven for fugitive slaves and to help ignite the destruction of Southern slavery from within. In readable prose and relying exclusively on primary sources, historian Ash...tells the little-known but crucial story of how 900 newly freed slaves, under the leadership of white abolitionist officers, captured Jacksonville." Publishers Weekly.

Berg, Scott W.

★**38** nooses : Lincoln, Little Crow, and the beginning of the frontier's end / Scott W. Berg. Pantheon Books, c2012. 336 p. **973.7**

1. Lincoln, Abraham, 1809-1865 Relations with Dakota Indians. 2. Little Crow, died 1863 3. Dakota Indians -- Wars, 1862-1865. 4. Indian Removal, 1813-1903 5. Battles. 6. Executions and executioners. 7. United States -- History -- 19th century.
ISBN 9780307377241

LC 2012002807

"A captivating tale of an oft-overlooked, morally ambiguous moment in American history." Kirkus.

Blanton, DeAnne, 1964-

They fought like demons : women soldiers in the American Civil War / DeAnne Blanton and Lauren M. Cook. Louisiana State University Press, 2002. xiii, 277 p. : **973.7**

1. Women soldiers 2. Union soldiers 3. Civil war 4. United States Civil War, 1861-1865 5. United States -- History -- Civil War, 1861-1865 -- Women's participation. 6. United States -- History -- Civil War, 1861-1865 -- Women.
ISBN 9780807128060

LC 2002004441

A study of the hundreds of women who disguised themselves as male soldiers to fight on both sides of the Union and Confederate conflict chronicles the stories of Jennie Hodgers, Frances Clayton, and Loreta Velazquez, among others.

"The authors reconstruct the reasons why women entered the armed forces: many were simply patriotic, while others followed their husbands or lovers and yet others yearned to break free from the constraints that Victorian society had laid on them as women. Blanton and Cook detail women soldiers in combat, on the march, in camp and in the hospital, where many were discovered after getting sick. Some even wound up in grim prisons kept by both sides, while a few hid pregnancies and were only discovered after giving birth. Solid research by the authors, including a look at the careers of a few women soldiers after the war, makes this a compelling book that belongs in every Civil War library." Publishers Weekly.

Blight, David W.

American oracle : the Civil War in the civil rights era / David W. Blight. Belknap Press of Harvard University Press, c2011. 290 p. **973.7**

1. Warren, Robert Penn, 1905-1989. 2. Catton, Bruce, 1899-1978. 3. Wilson, Edmund, 1895-1972. 4. Baldwin, James, 1924-1987. 5. Civil rights. 6. Race relations. 7. Civil war 8. United States Civil War, 1861-1865 9. United States -- History -- Civil War, 1861-1865 -- Influence.
ISBN 9780674048553

LC 2011006653

"This book is a set of critical reflections on the racial attitudes and historical views of four great American writers--James Baldwin, Bruce Catton, Robert Penn Warren, and Edmund Wilson (and in an epilogue, Ralph Ellison)--around the time of the Civil War centennial 50 years ago." Publishers Weekly.

Bordewich, Fergus M.

★**Bound** for Canaan : the underground railroad and the war for the soul of America / Fergus M. Bordewich. Amistad, 2005. xv, 540 p., 16 p. of plates : **973.7**

1. Underground railroad. 2. Anti-slavery movements -- History -- 19th century. 3. Fugitive slaves 4. Abolitionists -- United States -- History -- 19th century.
ISBN 0060524308

LC 2004052082

ALA Notable Book, 2006.

Offers insight into the Underground Railroad and the role played by westward expansion, the spiritual beliefs that motivated each side of the conflict, and the efforts of black and white citizens to save tens of thousands of lives.

"The men and women of this remarkable account will remain with readers for a long time to come." Publishers Weekly.

Brewster, Todd

Lincoln's gamble : the tumultuous six months that gave America the Emancipation Proclamation and changed the course of the Civil War / Todd Brewster. Scribner, 2014. 320 p. **973.7**

1. Lincoln, Abraham 1809-1865 2. Emancipation Proclamation 3. Slaves -- Emancipation 4. Presidents -- United States 5. Anti-slavery movements -- History. 6. Political leadership. 7. United States -- Politics and government -- 19th century. 8. United States -- History -- Civil War, 1861-1865.
ISBN 9781451693867

LC 2013497336

On July 12, 1862, Abraham Lincoln spoke for the first time of his intention to free the slaves. On January 1, 1863, Lincoln signed the Emancipation Proclamation, doing precisely that. In between, however, was perhaps the most tumultuous six months of his presidency, an episode during which the sixteenth president fought bitterly with his generals, disappointed his cabinet, and sank into painful bouts of clinical depression. Most surprising, the man who would be remembered as "The Great Emancipator" did not hold firm to his belief in emancipation. He agonized over the decision and was wracked by private doubts almost to the moment when he inked the decree that would change a nation.

"Featuring vignettes of figures who met Lincoln during his formulation of the proclamation, Brewster's work illuminates Lincoln's lines of thought during this turning point in American history." Booklist.

Colaiaco, James A., 1945-

Frederick Douglass and the Fourth of July / James A. Colaiaco. Palgrave Macmillan, 2006. 247 p. ; **973.7**

1. Douglass, Frederick, 1818-1895 2. African American abolitionists 3. Fourth of July 4. Constitutional history 5. African Americans -- Civil rights -- History -- 19th century 6. United States -- History -- 19th century

ISBN 1403970335

LC 2005051520

An account of America's pre-Civil War conflict between its ideals and practices evaluates Douglass's famous Fourth of July speech and considers his lifelong dedication to refuting misconceptions about the Constitution's alleged support of slavery and the rights granted to black Americans by the phrase, "all men are created equal."

"Colaiaco's careful study recaptures Douglass' reputation as one of America's greatest orators." Booklist.

Daniel, Larry J., 1947-

Shiloh : the battle that changed the Civil War / Larry J. Daniel. Simon & Schuster, 1998, c1997. 430 p. : **973.7**

1. Shiloh, Battle of, 1862.

ISBN 0684838575

LC BL 98005353

"A Touchstone book."

Reprint. Originally published: 1997.

A reexamination of the most crucial battle of the Civil War explores the broader campaign and political decisions made in the White House and in the Executive Mansion in Richmond.

"The author has crafted a superbly researched volume that will appeal to both the beginning Civil War reader as well as those already familiar with the course of fighting in the wooded terrain bordering the Tennessee River." Publishers Weekly.

Davis, Burke, 1913-

Sherman's march / Burke Davis. Vintage Books, 1988, c1980. viii, 335 p. : **973.7**

1. Sherman, William Tecumseh, 1820-1891. 2. Sherman's March to the Sea. 3. Sherman's March through the Carolinas.

ISBN 0394757637

LC 87045927

Includes index.

Originally published: New York : Random House, 1980.

Weaving together hundreds of eyewitness accounts, a noted historian recreates Sherman's devastating sweep through Georgia and the Carolinas in 1864 and 1865 and narrates the experiences of soldiers and civilians.

"The author reconstructs Sherman's infamous, but vastly consequential march through Georgia and the Carolinas, which sent the Confederacy into its death throes. Basing his narrative on eyewitness accounts, Davis brings the event down to a personal level." Booklist.

Delbanco, Andrew, 1952-

The **war** before the war : fugitive slaves and the struggle for America's soul from the Revolution to the Civil War / Andrew Delbanco. Penguin Press, 2018. 384 p. **973.7**

1. Slaves 2. Fugitive slaves 3. Civil war 4. Constitutional history 5. United States -- History -- Civil War, 1861-1865 6. United States -- History -- 19th century

ISBN 9781594204050

LC 2018419007

Mark Lynton History Prize, 2019.

Argues that issues surrounding fugitive slaves is what truly drove the North and South to Civil War and explains the history behind how this happened.

"This well-documented and valuable work makes clear how slavery shaped the early American experience with effects that reverberate today." Publishers Weekly.

DK Publishing, Inc

The **Civil** War : a visual history / [produced in association with the Smithsonian Institution]. DK Pub., c2011. 360 p. : **973.7**

1. Confederate States of America 2. Confederate States of America -- History, Military 3. United States -- History -- 1815-1861 4. United States -- History -- Civil War, 1861-1865

ISBN 9780756671853

LC 2011281338

Presents a pictorial history of the Civil War that includes artifacts, maps, personal narratives, and historical timelines for each year of the war.

"Espionage, the home front, and politics get a nod, but this book is for those wanting to smell the sulfur and hear the thunder of guns." Library Journal.

Doyle, Don Harrison, 1946-

The **cause** of all nations : an international history of the American Civil War / Don H. Doyle. Basic Books, 2014. 384 p. **973.7**

1. International relations. 2. Democracy -- History. 3. United States Civil War, 1861-1865 4. United States -- History -- Civil War, 1861-1865 -- Influence.

ISBN 9780465029679

LC bl2014050392

In The Cause of All Nations, distinguished historian Don H. Doyle explains that the Civil War was viewed abroad as part of a much larger struggle for democracy that spanned the Atlantic Ocean, and had begun with the American and French Revolutions. While battles raged at Bull Run, Antietam, and Gettysburg, a parallel contest took place abroad, both in the marbled courts of power and in the public square. Foreign observers held widely divergent views on the war--from radicals such as Karl Marx and Giuseppe Garibaldi who called on the North to fight for liberty and equality, to aristocratic monarchists, who hoped that the collapse of the Union would strike a death blow against democratic movements on both sides of the Atlantic.

Egerton, Douglas R.

Thunder at the gates : the black Civil War regiments that redeemed America / Douglas R. Egerton. Basic Books, 2016. 448 p. **973.7**

1. United States. Army. Massachusetts Infantry Regiment, 54th (1863-1865). 2. United States. Army. Massachusetts Infantry Regiment, 55th (1863-1865). 3. United States. Army. Massachusetts Cavalry Regiment, 5th (1864-1865). 4. United States. Army African American troops -- History 19th century. 5. African American soldiers 6. African Americans -- History -- Civil War, 1861-1865 7. Civil war 8. United States Civil War, 1861-1865 9. United States -- History -- Civil War, 1861-1865 -- Participation, African American. 10. Massachusetts -- History -- Civil War, 1861-1865 -- Participation, African American. 11. United States -- History -- Civil War, 1861-1865 -- Campaigns.

ISBN 9780465096640

LC 2016032057

Illuminates the public responses, debates and dangers that shaped the entry of black regiments into the Civil War after the 1863 Emancipation Proclamation, chronicling the formation and battlefield triumphs of key regiments while discussing their role in shaping public opinion and promoting full citizenship for blacks.

Year of meteors : Stephen Douglas, Abraham Lincoln, and the election that brought on the Civil War / Douglas R. Egerton. Bloomsbury Press, 2010. 399 p. : **973.7**

1. Lincoln, Abraham, 1809-1865 Political and social views 2. Douglas, Stephen A. (Stephen Arnold), 1813-1861 Political and social views 3. Lincoln, Abraham, 1809-1865 Political career before 1861. 4. Presidential election, 1860 5. Elections -- United States -- History -- 19th century 6. United States Civil War, 1861-1865 7. United States -- Politics and government -- 1857-1861 8. United States -- History -- Civil War, 1861-1865 -- Causes

ISBN 9781596916197

LC 2010004965

Describes the events that led up to Abraham Lincoln outmaneuvering prominent Republicans and his biggest rival, Stephen Douglas, to win the presidency with a record-low percent of the popular vote.

"The author examines the importance of race in the presidential election of 1860, when a relatively unknown candidate came from behind to be elected to the nation's highest office. Following the fortunes of Democrat Stephen Douglas, Republican Abraham Lincoln, and a host of others significant to the election, Egerton highlights the central role played by race in the dynamics of political party, sectionalism, and politics generally in the election after which the nation was plunged into Civil War. Heavily documented, relying on substantial primary and manuscript sources, this book sheds new light on an often researched topic. All those with an interest in the importance of race in the nation's history will want to acquire this highly readable work." Library Journal.

Faust, Drew Gilpin

Mothers of invention : women of the slaveholding South in the American Civil War / Drew Gilpin Faust. University of North Carolina Press, c1996. xvi, 326 p. : The Fred W. Morrison series in Southern studies **973.7**

1. Women -- Confederate States of America -- History. 2. Confederate States of America -- History. 3. United States -- History -- Civil War, 1861-1865 -- Women.

ISBN 9780807822555

LC 95008896

Details how well-bred Confederate women tried to retain their social standing

"Faust's provocative analysis of a complex subject merits a place in all collections of U.S. history." Publishers Weekly.

★**This** republic of suffering : death and the American Civil War / Drew Gilpin Faust. Alfred A. Knopf, 2008. 346 p. : **973.7**

1. Death. 2. Burial. 3. Civil war 4. Loss (Psychology) 5. United States -- History -- Civil War, 1861-1865 -- Psychological aspects. 6. Books to TV

ISBN 9780375404047

LC 2007014658

The TV movie Death and the Civil War is based on this book.

ALA Notable Book, 2009.

American History Book Prize, 2008.

National Book Award for Nonfiction finalist, 2008

National Book Critics Circle Award for Nonfiction finalist, 2008.

Pulitzer Prize for History finalist, 2009.

Assesses the impact of the enormous carnage of the Civil War on every aspect of American life from a material, political, intellectual, cultural, social, and spiritual perspective.

"The result is an insightful, often moving portrait of a people torn by grief." Publishers Weekly.

Foner, Eric, 1943-

★**Gateway** to freedom : the hidden history of the Underground Railroad / Eric Foner. W. W. Norton & Co., 2015 288 p. **973.7**

1. Underground Railroad 2. Slavery -- History 3. Fugitive slaves 4. Anti-slavery movements 5. United States -- History -- 19th century

ISBN 9780393244076

LC 2014036993

American History Book Prize, 2015.

Traces the workings of the underground railroad in slave-dependent New York by three lesser-known heroes who coordinated with black dockworkers and counterparts in other states to help thousands of fugitive slaves between 1830 and 1860.

"The author eschews the common approach of documenting the phenomenon from the South, instead centering his monograph on New York City. Through individuals such as abolitionist Sydney Howard Gay and minister Charles Ray, he demonstrates that ferrying escaped slaves from the city's waterfront to other locales throughout the North was fraught with extreme danger." Library Journal.

Foote, Shelby

The **Civil** War : a narrative / Shelby Foote. Vintage Books, 1986, c1958-c1974. 3 v. : **973.7**

1. Civil war 2. United States Civil War, 1861-1865 3. United States -- History -- Civil War, 1861-1865.

ISBN 0394746236

LC 86040135

Follows the course of the war from 1862 to 1864, discusses the strategies of both sides in major battles, and assesses the performance of the Union generals.

Stars in their courses : the Gettysburg campaign, June-July 1863 / Shelby Foote. Modern Library, 1994. viii, 290 p. : **973.7**

1. Gettysburg Campaign, 1863.

ISBN 0679601120

LC 94196068

Series statement from jacket.

"Originally published by Random House, Inc., as volume II of The Civil War, a narrative : Fredericksburg to Meridian"--T.p. verso.

Recreates the Battle of Gettysburg from both the Confederate and Union perspectives.

Ford, Lacy K.

Deliver us from evil : the slavery question in the old south, 1787-1840 / Lacy K. Ford. Oxford University Press, 2009. 688 p. **973.7**

1. Slavery -- Southern States -- History -- 18th century. 2. European Americans -- Attitudes -- History -- 19th century 3. Slavery. 4. Slaveholders. 5. Southern States -- History.

ISBN 9780195118094

LC 2008047533

"This book provides an intricate, textured argument about the intellectual, social, and political interests shaping the slavery question, as well as a reminder that Southern white commitment to a hardened proslavery position was not preordained or one-dimensional. Essential for all students of this subject." Library Journal.

Foreman, Amanda, 1968-

A **world** on fire : Britian's crucial role in the American Civil War / Amanda Foreman. Random House, 2011, c2010. xxxix,

958 p., [39] p. of plates : **973.7**

1. British in the United States. 2. Confederate soldiers 3. Civil war 4. United States Civil War, 1861-1865 5. United States -- History -- Civil War, 1861-1865.

ISBN 9780375504945

Originally published: London : Allen Lane, 2010. Subtitle varies.

National Book Critics Circle Award for Nonfiction finalist, 2011.

"Ranging from the drawing rooms of Washington and London to the battlefields of Gettysburg and Antietam, to the high seas, and to Confederate and Union home fronts, Foreman has written a diplomatic, military, and social kaleidoscope of the Civil War. She superbly conveys the horror, pathos, and chaos of battle, the political and moral ambiguities, and the devotion of those who fought. She has also restored an international dimension missing from many histories." Boston Globe.

Freeman, Joanne B., 1962-

The **field** of blood : violence in Congress and the road to civil war / Joanne B. Freeman. Farrar, Straus & Giroux, 2018. 384 p. **973.7**

1. United States. Congress. House 2. United States. Congress. Senate 3. Legislators 4. Politicians 5. Violence 6. Hand-to-hand fighting 7. United States -- Politics and government

ISBN 9780374154776

LC 2018010176

Documents the lesser-known violence that marked legislative sessions in the decades before the American Civil War, detailing acts of physical fighting, duels and mortal threats over disagreements about key issues, particularly slavery. By the award-winning author of Affairs of Honor. Bibliography. Appendix. Index.

Goldfield, David R., 1944-

America aflame : how the Civil War created a nation / David Goldfield. Bloomsbury Press, c2011. 640 p. **973.7**

1. National characteristics, American. 2. Reconstruction (United States history) 3. War -- History -- 19th century 4. Civil war 5. United States -- History -- Civil War, 1861-1865 -- Influence. 6. United States -- History -- Civil War, 1861-1865 -- Causes. 7. United States -- History -- Civil War, 1861-1865 -- Campaigns 8. United States -- History -- Civil War, 1861-1865 -- Social aspects.

ISBN 9781596917026

LC 2010025241

A narrative history of the Civil War era argues that the conflict occurred as a result of a breakdown induced by the infusion of evangelical religion into the public sphere, causing citizens to regard political differences as matters of good and evil to be fought at any cost.

Goodheart, Adam

★**1861** : the Civil War awakening / Adam Goodheart. Alfred A. Knopf, c2011. 496 p. : **973.7**

1. War -- History -- 19th century 2. Military history -- 19th century 3. Intellectual life -- United States -- 19th century 4. Slavery -- History -- 19th century 5. United States -- History -- Civil War, 1861-1865 -- Causes. 6. United States -- Politics and government -- 1861-1865.

ISBN 9781400040155

LC 2010051326

Includes index.

Chronicles the revolution of ideas that preceded--and led to--the start of the Civil War, looking at a diverse cast of characters and the actions of citizens throughout the country in their efforts to move beyond compromise and end slavery.

"Goodheart leads us on a journey through the frenzied, frightening months between Abraham Lincoln's election to the presidency in 1860 followed with breakneck speed by the secession of the Confederate States and the outbreak of war and July 4, 1861, when President Lincoln delivered his first message to Congress, laying out the case not only for the necessity of war, but for a more democratic vision of the United States. The election of Lincoln and the secession crisis is, of course, familiar terrain. But Goodheart's version is at once more panoramic and more intimate than most standard accounts, and more inspiring. This is fundamentally a history of hearts and minds, rather than of legislative bills and battles." New York Times Book Review.

Goodwin, Doris Kearns

★**Team** of rivals : the political genius of Abraham Lincoln / Doris Kearns Goodwin. Simon & Schuster, 2005. xix, 916 p. : **973.7**

1. Lincoln, Abraham, 1809-1865 Friends and associates. 2. Seward, William Henry, 1801-1872. 3. Chase, Salmon Portland, 1808-1873. 4. Political leadership -- United States -- Case studies. 5. Political consultants. 6. Presidents -- United States. 7. Genius -- Case studies. 8. United States -- Politics and government -- 1861-1865.

ISBN 9780684824901

LC 2005044615

American History Book Prize, 2005.

National Book Critics Circle Award for Biography finalist, 2005.

An analysis of Abraham Lincoln's political talents identifies the character strengths and abilities that enabled his successful election, in an account that also describes how he used the same abilities to rally former opponents in winning the Civil War.

"The knowledge gained here about these three significant figures who well attended Lincoln gain for the reader an even keener appreciation of the rare individual that he was." Booklist.

Groom, Winston, 1944-2020

Shiloh, 1862 : the first great and terrible battle of the Civil War / Winston Groom. Random House Inc, 2012. 512 p. **973.7**

1. Shiloh, Battle of, 1862. 2. Battles. 3. Civil war. 4. United States Civil War, 1861-1865 5. United States -- History -- Civil War, 1861-1865 -- Campaigns

ISBN 9781426208744

LC 2012372339

Offers a detailed account of the Battle of Shiloh, a turning point when both the Union and the Confederacy realized the grand scale of the conflict, the large number of casualties to be expected, and that the war would not end quickly.

Vicksburg, 1863 / Winston Groom. Alfred A. Knopf, 2009. 496 p. **973.7**

1. Sieges. 2. Battles. 3. Military strategy. 4. Civil war. 5. Vicksburg, Mississippi -- History -- Siege, 1863. 6. United States -- History -- Civil War, 1861-1865.

ISBN 9780307264251

LC 2008045984

Recreates the 1863 siege of Vicksburg, Mississippi, that changed the direction of the Civil War and severely damaged the Confederacy.

Guelzo, Allen C.

Gettysburg : the last invasion / Allen C. Guelzo. Alfred A. Knopf, 2013. 688 p. **973.7**

1. Gettysburg, Battle of, 1863 2. Civil war 3. Battles -- History 4. United States Civil War, 1861-1865 5. United States -- History -- Civil War, 1861-1865

ISBN 9780307594082

LC 2012047013

"This is a Borzoi book"--Title page verso.

The award-winning author of Lincoln's Emancipation Proclamation presents a vivid 150th anniversary account of the legendary Civil War battle from the perspectives of ordinary soldiers to offer insight into 19th-century military practices, the pivotal influence of politics on the battle's course and the unique characters of artillery units.

Gwynne, S. C. (Samuel C.), 1953-

Hymns of the Republic : the story of the final year of the American Civil War / S.C. Gwynne. Scribner, [2019] 352 p. **973.7**

1. Grant, Ulysses S., 1822-1885 2. Lee, Robert E. (Robert Edward), 1807-1870 3. Lincoln, Abraham, 1809-1865 4. Barton, Clara, 1821-1912. 5. Military strategy 6. United States Civil War, 1861-1865 7. Civil war 8. United States -- History -- Civil War, 1861-1865.
ISBN 9781501116223

LC 2019017038

An epic account of the dramatic conclusion of the American Civil War.

Holzer, Harold

The **Civil** War in 50 objects / Harold Holzer and the New-York Historical Society ; with an introduction by Eric Foner. Viking, 2013. 416 p. **973.7**

1. New-York Historical Society. 2. Civil war 3. Material culture 4. War -- History -- 19th century 5. United States Civil War, 1861-1865 6. United States -- History -- Civil War, 1861-1865
ISBN 9780670014637

LC 2013001532

A companion to A History of the World in 100 Objects offers a visual perspective on the Civil War as reflected by artifacts ranging from a soldier's footlocker and the Emancipation Proclamation to leaves from Abraham Lincoln's bier and Grant's handwritten terms of surrender at Appomattox, in a reference featuring an introduction by a Pulitzer Prize-winning writer.

Horwitz, Tony, 1958-

Confederates in the attic : dispatches from the unfinished Civil War / Tony Horwitz. Pantheon Books, 1998. ix, 406 p. : **973.7**

1. Horwitz, Tony, 1958- Travel Southern States. 2. Historical reenactments. 3. Civil war 4. United States Civil War, 1861-1865 5. Confederate States of America. 6. United States -- History -- Civil War, 1861-1865 -- Influence. 7. United States -- History -- Civil War, 1861-1865 -- Campaigns -- Reenactment.
ISBN 9780679439783

LC 97026759

Includes index.

A journalist leads readers on a journey through the Old South, tangling with the forces of white rage, rebel grit, and regional pride in places where the Civil War is more than a memory.

"This is the work of a skilled journalist looking at how--and why--the War Between the States continues to live in so many issues still with us." Library Journal.

Jordan, Brian Matthew

Marching home : Union veterans and their unending Civil War / Brian Matthew Jordan. Liveright Publishing Corporation, A Division of W.W. Norton & Company, 2015. 416 p. **973.7**

1. Civil War veterans 2. War and society. 3. Union soldiers 4. Unionists (United States Civil War) 5. United States -- History -- Civil War, 1861-1865
ISBN 9780871407818

LC 2014032544

Pulitzer Prize for History finalist, 2016.

For well over a century, traditional Civil War histories have concluded in 1865, with a bitterly won peace and Union soldiers returning triumphantly home. In a landmark work that challenges sterilized portraits accepted for generations, Civil War historian Brian Matthew Jordan creates an entirely new narrative. These veterans--tending rotting wounds, battling alcoholism, campaigning for paltry pensions--tragically realized that they stood as unwelcome reminders to a new America eager to heal, forget, and embrace the freewheeling bounty of the Gilded Age.

Kagan, Neil

Atlas of the Civil War : a comprehensive guide to the tactics and terrain of battle / edited by Neil Kagan ; narrative by Stephen G. Hyslop ; introduction by Harris J. Andrews. National Geographic Society, c2009. 1 atlas (255 p.) : **973.7**

1. United States -- History -- Civil War, 1861-1865 -- Campaigns Maps. 2. United States -- History -- Civil War, 1861-1865 Maps.
ISBN 9781426203473

LC bl2010006772

Charts the ebb and flow of the war between the North and the South with 110 maps, both vintage battle maps and vivid recreations, and includes over 320 documentary photos, battlefield sketches, paintings, and artifacts that bear eyewitness testimony to the Civil War.

Keegan, John, 1934-

The **American** Civil War : a military history / John Keegan. Alfred A. Knopf, c2009. 416 p. **973.7**

1. Military geography -- United States -- History -- 19th century. 2. Military history. 3. Military strategy 4. Civil war 5. United States -- History -- Civil War, 1861-1865 -- Campaigns 6. United States -- Strategic aspects. 7. United States -- Geography.
ISBN 9780307263438

LC 2009019469

Analyzes many puzzling aspects of the Civil War, from its mismatched sides to the absence of decisive outcomes for dozens of skirmishes, and offers insight into the war's psychology, ideology, and economics while discussing the pivotal roles of leadership and geography.

"The author provides the single best one-volume assessment of the military character and conduct of America's ordeal by fire." Library Journal.

Levine, Bruce C., 1949-

The **fall** of the house of Dixie : how the Civil War remade the American South / Bruce Levine. Random House, c2013. 464 p. **973.7**

1. Elite (Social sciences) -- United States -- History -- 19th century. 2. Slavery -- Southern States -- Social aspects. 3. War and society. 4. Social classes. 5. Confederate States of America -- Social conditions. 6. United States -- History -- Civil War, 1861-1865 -- Social aspects.
ISBN 9781400067039

LC 2011048310

Told in the words of the people who lived it, The Fall of the House of Dixie illuminates the radical transformation of the American South during and after the Civil War. Award-winning author Bruce Levine employs a wealth of primary sources -- diaries, letters, newspaper articles, government documents, and more -- to vividly bring to life the perspectives of slaves, shopkeepers, soldiers, and others in a stellar history of the South's social, political and economic deconstruction and rebuilding.

Manning, Chandra

Troubled refuge : struggling for freedom in the Civil War / Chandra Manning. Alfred A. Knopf, 2016. 416 p. **973.7**

1. Slaves -- Emancipation 2. Freed slaves 3. African Americans -- Civil rights 4. United States Civil War, 1861-1865 5. United States -- History -- Civil War, 1861-1865 -- African Americans. 6. United States -- History -- Civil War, 1861-1865 -- Social aspects.
ISBN 9780307271204
LC 2015039724

In a riveting examination of the escaped-slave refugee camps at the end of the Civil War, the author, drawing on first-hand accounts, reveals what these camps were really like and how former slaves and Union soldiers warily united there, shaping the course of emancipation and black citizenship.

"An essential contribution to the history of the Civil War and its aftermath." Booklist.

Masur, Louis P.

The **Civil** War : a concise history / Louis P. Masur. Oxford University Press, c2011. xiv, 118 p. : **973.7**

1. United States -- History -- Civil War, 1861-1865.
ISBN 9780199740482
LC 2010019460

A year-by-year chronicle of the Civil War, highlighting major political, social, and military events, and looking at the causes and consequences of the conflict.

"The author provides a concise but compelling narrative of the Civil War era, packing in the critical information to track the trajectory of secession, war, emancipation, and Reconstruction. He focuses on the political and the military, with Lincoln, Jefferson Davis, and the generals especially getting their due." Library Journal.

McPherson, James M.

Battle cry of freedom : the Civil War era / James M. McPherson. Oxford University Press, 1988. xix, 904 p., 16 p. of plates : **973.7**

1. Civil war 2. Military history 3. United States Civil War, 1861-1865 4. United States -- History -- Civil War, 1861-1865 -- Campaigns 5. United States -- History -- Civil War, 1861-1865 -- Causes. 6. United States -- History -- Civil War, 1861-1865.
ISBN 9780195038637
LC 87011045

Includes index.

Pulitzer Prize for History, 1989.

National Book Critics Circle Award for Nonfiction finalist, 1988.

Abraham Lincoln wondered whether "in a free government the minority have the right to break up the government." Jefferson Davis felt "forced to take up arms" to guarantee his states' rights. McPherson merges the words of these men and other political luminaries, housewives, and soldiers from both armies with his own concise analysis of the war to create a story as compelling as any novel.

"This volume is comprehensive yet succinct, scholarly without being pedantic, eloquent but unrhetorical. It is compellingly readable. " New York Times Book Review.

Drawn with the sword : reflections on the American Civil War / James M. McPherson. Oxford University Press, 1996. xiv, 258 p. ; **973.7**

1. Lincoln, Abraham, 1809-1865. 2. Civil war 3. Military history. 4. United States Civil War, 1861-1865 5. United States -- History -- Civil War, 1861-1865. 6. Essays.
ISBN 0195096797
LC 95038107

Shares a collection of thought-provoking essays on the Civil War, discussing the leaders of the era, the international impact of the war, slavery, the problems with the modern study of history, and other topics.

"These pieces provide a lively reminder that the best scholarship is also often a pleasure to read." New York Times Book Review.

For cause and comrades : why men fought in the Civil War / James M. McPherson. Oxford University Press, 1997. xviii, 237 p. ; **973.7**

1. United States. Army -- History Civil War, 1861-1865. 2. Confederate States of America. Army 3. Combat -- Psychological aspects -- History -- 19th century. 4. Military history. 5. United States Civil War, 1861-1865 6. Civil war 7. United States -- History -- Civil War, 1861-1865 -- Psychological aspects.
ISBN 0195090233
LC 96024760

Drawing on thousands of letters and diaries by soldiers on both sides, the Pulitzer Prize-winning author shows how the soldiers remained firmly committed to their ideals throughout the Civil War.

"Volumes have been written on the causes of the Civil War, but less has been written on what caused soldiers to risk their lives on the battlefield. McPherson . . . fills the gap. After studying thousands of letters and diaries, he discusses what really led soldiers to enlist, what kept them in the army, and what led them to the front lines." Library Journal.

Hallowed ground : a walk at Gettysburg / James M. McPherson. Crown Journeys, 2003. 141 p. : **973.7**

1. Gettysburg, Battle of, 1863. 2. Walking -- Gettysburg, Pennsylvania. 3. Civil war 4. Battles 5. United States -- History -- Civil War, 1861-1865 -- Campaigns
ISBN 0609610236
LC 2002035154

"If it were only a pointer to the physical ground and commemorative markers, this guide would be ordinary, but McPherson so articulately injects reminders--as of a free black farmer who fled the approaching battle lest Confederates enslave him--of what the Civil War was about as to display the crystalline style that has made him one of our finest Civil War historians." Booklist.

★**This** mighty scourge : perspectives on the Civil War / James M. McPherson. Oxford University Press, 2007. 272 p. **973.7**

1. Civil war 2. Military history 3. War 4. United States Civil War, 1861-1865 5. United States -- History -- Civil War, 1861-1865. 6. Essays
ISBN 0195313666
LC 2006035523

Includes bibliographical references and index.

A collection of essays offers a fresh perspective on diverse facets of the Civil War, with profiles of such figures as Harriet Tubman and Jesse James, analyses of Confederate and Union military strategy, and studies on such topics as presidential power and the myths and realities of the Confederacy.

"These essays stand as a remarkably elegant and clarifying narrative exploration of the most basic questions concerning the Civil War, issues over which scholars and activists still contend. This Mighty Scourge, in fact, is an exemplary exercise in the contribution a great historian and eloquent writer can make to a people's understanding of themselves." Los Angeles Times.

The **war** that forged a nation : why the Civil War still matters

/ James M. McPherson. Oxford University Press, 2015 224 p. **973.7**

1. War and society 2. Social change 3. National characteristics, American 4. Civil war 5. United States -- History -- Civil War, 1861-1865 -- Influence. 6. United States -- History -- Civil War, 1861-1865 -- Psychological aspects 7. United States -- History -- Civil War, 1861-1865 -- Social aspects 8. Essays

ISBN 9780199375776

LC 2014018008

"In a discussion of Lincoln and slavery, the author agrees with Eric Foner that the president was anti-slavery (deeming it a violation of natural rights) but not an abolitionist (he expected slavery would eventually die out). These authoritative essays, most of which appeared previously in various formats, will appeal mainly to serious students and specialists." Kirkus.

Meyer, Eugene L.

Five for freedom : the African American soldiers in John Brown's army / Eugene L. Meyer. Lawrence Hill Books, [2018] 304 p. **973.7**

1. Anderson, Osborne P. (Osborne Perry), 1830-1872. 2. Copeland, John A. (John Anthony), 1834-1859. 3. Green, Shields, approximately 1836-1859. 4. Leary, Lewis Sheridan, 1835-1859. 5. Newby, Dangerfield, 1815-1859. 6. Brown, John, 1800-1859. 7. African American abolitionists. 8. Anti-slavery movements -- History -- 19th century. 9. Race relations. 10. Abolitionists. 11. United States -- History -- 19th century. 12. Harper's Ferry, West Virginia -- History -- John Brown's Raid, 1859.

ISBN 9781613735718

LC 2017045333

On October 16, 1859, John Brown and his integreted band of raiders descended on Harpers Ferry attempting to incite a slave insurrection; they seized the federal arsenal, took hostages, and retreated to a fire engine house where they barricaded themselves until soldiers forced their way in two days later. One of the few survivors later published an insider account of the event that was a catalyst to the catastrophic American Civil War that followed.

Miller, Donald L., 1944-

Vicksburg : Grant's campaign that broke the Confederacy / Donald L. Miller. Simon & Schuster, 2019. 640 p. **973.7**

1. Grant, Ulysses S., 1822-1885 2. Strategy. 3. Civil war 4. Gettysburg, Battle of, 1863. 5. United States Civil War, 1861-1865 6. Vicksburg, Mississippi -- History -- Siege, 1863. 7. United States -- History -- Civil War, 1861-1865

ISBN 9781451641370

LC 2019010269

The author of Masters of the Air presents an account of the decisive Civil War military campaign that split the Confederacy, freed tens of thousands of slaves and rendered Grant the war's most celebrated general.

Murray, Williamson

A **savage** war : a military history of the Civil War / Williamson Murray and Wayne Hsieh. Princeton University Press, 2016. 552 p. **973.7**

1. Grant, Ulysses S., 1822-1885 2. Battles 3. Military history 4. United States -- History -- Civil War, 1861-1865 -- Campaigns. 5. Confederate States of America 6. France -- History -- Revolution, 1789-1799 -- Influence

ISBN 9780691169408

LC 2016008730

"This expertly written narrative will draw in anyone with an interest in the Civil War at any knowledge level. A great resource for public and academic libraries." Library Journal.

Oakes, James

Freedom national : the destruction of slavery in the United States, 1861-1865 / James Oakes. W W Norton & Co Inc, 2012. 384 p. **973.7**

1. Slavery. 2. Freedom. 3. Abolitionists. 4. Civil war. 5. United States -- History -- Civil War, 1861-1865.

ISBN 9780393065312

LC 2012035601

Traces the history of emancipation and its impact on the Civil War, discussing how Lincoln and the Republicans fought primarily for freeing slaves throughout the war, not just as a secondary objective in an effort to restore the country.

Paludan, Phillip S., 1938-

The **presidency** of Abraham Lincoln / Phillip Shaw Paludan. University Press of Kansas, c1994. xx, 384 p. ; **973.7**

1. Lincoln, Abraham, 1809-1865. 2. Presidents -- United States. 3. Civil war 4. United States Civil War, 1861-1865 5. United States -- Politics and government -- 1861-1865. 6. United States -- History -- Civil War, 1861-1865.

ISBN 0700606718

LC 93046830

"The author traces the year-by-year chronology of a Presidency engaged with recruiting, placating, appeasing and coercing the various and competing factions of the war years, and sees in Lincoln 'a commitment to the political-constitutional system that would itself move the nation toward its highest ambitions....Equally interesting is Mr. Paludan's depiction of how the war transformed the national Government, not only establishing the foundations for the Gilded Age but more subtly strengthening and enriching the role of government." New York Times Book Review.

Sarna, Jonathan D.

Lincoln and the Jews : a history / Jonathan Sarna and Benjamin Shapell. St Martins Pr., 2015. 256 p. **973.7**

1. Lincoln, Abraham, 1809-1865 Relations with Jews. 2. Jewish Americans 3. Immigrants, Jewish 4. Jews -- Relations with Gentiles. 5. Civil War. 6. United States -- History -- Civil War, 1861-1865 -- Jews.

ISBN 9781250059536

LC 2014033453

A private collection of original manuscripts documents the 16th President's unpopular friendship with and advocacy of Jewish people at a time of rising anti-Semitism. Co-written by the award-winning author of American Judaism. Map(s).

"The authors provide extensive discussion of Lincoln's efforts to restrain anti-Semitic attitudes in the army, most notably General Ulysses Grant's infamous expulsion order, and extensive prejudice by General Benjamin Butler. This attractive volume featuring a plethora of primary documents highlights the political contributions of numerous Jews to Lincoln's decisions both small and momentous." Choice.

Sears, Stephen W.

★**Chancellorsville** / Stephen W. Sears. Houghton Mifflin, 1998, c1996. x, 593 p. : **973.7**

1. Chancellorsville, Battle of, 1863. 2. Military campaigns 3. Civil war 4. United States Civil War, 1861-1865 5. Virginia -- History --

Civil War, 1861-1865
ISBN 039587744X

LC BL 98006846

"A Mariner book."

Originally published: Boston, MA : Houghton Mifflin, 1996.

Recounts the Civil War battle at Chancellorsville where Robert E. Lee scored his greatest victory.

"In this history of the campaign that ended in Chancellorsville, the author argues that a chain of errors, assumptions, and communications failures combined with the genuine brilliance and good luck of the Confederates to lead to a stinging if indecisive Union defeat." Booklist.

★**Gettysburg** / Stephen W. Sears. Houghton Mifflin, 2003. xiv, 623 p. : **973.7**

1. Gettysburg, Battle of, 1863. 2. Civil war 3. United States Civil War, 1861-1865 4. United States -- History -- Civil War, 1861-1865 -- Campaigns 5. Gettysburg, Pennsylvania. 6. Pennsylvania -- History -- Civil War, 1861-1865.
ISBN 0395867614

LC 2002191259

Drawing on years of research, Sears focuses on the big picture, capturing the entire essence of the momentous three-day struggle while offering fresh insights that will surprise even the best-versed Civil War buffs, from Robert E. Lee's decision to bring the war north, to Joshua L. Chamberlain's brilliant defense of Little Round Top, to George Pickett's fateful charge.

"This is an assessment of the battle of Gettysburg and the events leading up to it. . . . Sears examines several turning points during the battle's buildup and three-day duration. The resulting insights add to the excellent and dramatic narrative flow. . . . For all Civil War collections and academic libraries." Library Journal.

★**Landscape** turned red : the Battle of Antietam / Stephen W. Sears. Houghton Mifflin, 2003, c1983. xii, 431 p. : **973.7**

1. Antietam, Battle of, Md., 1862. 2. Military campaigns 3. Civil war 4. United States Civil War, 1861-1865 5. Virginia -- History -- Civil War, 1861-1865
ISBN 9780618344192

LC BL2003011305

Originally published: New Haven, CT : Ticknor & Fields, 1983.
"A Mariner book."

A definitive study of the climactic and pivotal battle of Antietam offers a vivid account of the two armies, the soldiers and officers, and the bitter, bloody campaign and analyzes the impact of Antietam on the Civil War as a whole.

"This account of the Battle of Antietam, the bloodiest day of the Civil War, is wide-ranging, detailed, and copiously documented. Stephen Sears...describes the tension-filled days preceding September 17, 1862, especially the political climate of Union pessimism and Confederate optimism. The battle itself is then exhaustively recounted." Booklist.

Simpson, Brooks D.,

★The **Civil** War : the first year told by those who lived it / edited by Brooks D. Simpson, Stephen W. Sears, Aaron Sheehan-Dean. Library of America : c2011. xxv, 814 p. : **973.7**

1. United States Civil War, 1861-1865 2. Union soldiers 3. Confederate soldiers 4. Civil war 5. United States -- History -- Civil War, 1861-1865. 6. United States -- History -- Civil War, 1861-1865 7. United States -- History -- Civil War, 1861-1865 Sources.
ISBN 9781598530889

LC bl2011002792

Maps on lining papers.

Collects diaries, letters, and eyewitness accounts of individuals from all walks of life on such topics as Lincoln's election, the firing on Fort Sumter, and the battle at Shiloh.

"Drawing on diaries, letters, speeches, newspaper reports and editorials, memoirs, songs, poems, and other sources, the editors bring together a rich variety of voices relating or remembering the crisis of the Union from Lincoln's election in 1860 through the first year of war. . . . Readable and riveting, this you-are-there collection makes real the sense of urgency that gripped Americans as the nation came apart and as the war began, 175 years ago. An excellent primer on why the Civil War mattered to those living it." Library Journal.

Slotkin, Richard, 1942-

The **long** road to Antietam : how the Civil War became a revolution / Richard Slotkin. Liveright Publishing Corporation, 2012. 480 p. : **973.7**

1. Lincoln, Abraham, 1809-1865 Military leadership. 2. McClellan, George Brinton, 1826-1885 Military leadership. 3. Emancipation Proclamation. 4. Slavery 5. Civil war. 6. Politics and war. 7. Antietam, Battle of, Md., 1862. 8. United States -- History -- 19th century
ISBN 9780871404114

LC 2012007795

An award-winning author and historian describes the political challenges faced by President Lincoln during the summer after the Emancipation Proclamation, including his conflicts with General George McClellan, that ultimately gave General Robert E. Lee his best opportunity to win the war.

Snodgrass, Mary Ellen

The **Underground** Railroad : an encyclopedia of people, places, and operations / Mary Ellen Snodgrass. M.E. Sharpe, 2008. 746 p. ; **973.7**

1. Abolitionists -- United States 2. Antislavery movements -- United States -- History 3. Fugitive slaves 4. Slavery -- History 5. United States -- History -- 19th century
ISBN 9780765680938

LC 2007009199

Offers more than fifteen hundred alphabetically arranged entries covering the key people, routes, events, documents, organizations, and publications related to slave liberation, along with genealogical histories of participating families, passenger data, and detailed passenger maps.

"The author has compiled an important and extensively researched encyclopedia of the Underground Railroad. Beginning with a concise, informative general introduction, this ambitious two-volume set neatly identifies the key people, places, documents, organizations, and publications of the Underground Railroad movement, along with significant actions, events, and ideas underlying it in the US and Canada. Offering photographs, bookplates, sketches, and handbills, the set is visually attractive." Choice.

Snow, Richard, 1947-

Iron dawn : the Monitor, the Merrimack, and the Civil War sea battle that changed history / Richard Snow. Scribner, 2016. 384 p. **973.7**

1. Monitor (Ironclad). 2. Virginia (Ironclad). 3. Merrimack (Frigate) 4. Naval battles -- History -- 19th century. 5. Military history -- 19th century. 6. Hampton Roads, Battle of, 1862. 7. Battles -- History -- 19th century. 8. United States -- History -- Civil War, 1861-1865 -- Campaigns 9. United States -- History -- Civil War, 1861-1865

-- Naval operations.
ISBN 9781476794181

LC 2016006965

A popular historian describes the exciting naval battle that changed the course of the Civil War, when the North built a complicated, innovative warship out of iron, the Monitor, in record time, to combat the Merrimack.

"A thorough and enthusiastic treatment, Snow's account will capture the naval-history and Civil War readership." Booklist.

Tobin, Jacqueline, 1950-

From midnight to dawn : the last tracks of the underground railroad / Jacqueline Tobin with Hettie Jones. Doubleday, 2007. xi, 272 p. : **973.7**

1. Underground railroad. 2. Fugitive slaves. 3. African Americans. 4. Land settlement -- Ontario -- History -- 19th century. 5. Ontario -- History -- 19th century. 6. Detroit Region, Michigan -- History -- 19th century.
ISBN 038551431X

LC 2006046304

Map on lining papers.

A history of the Underground Railroad brings together portraits of the men and women who established the escape organization for runaway slaves, as well as the people who traveled it to find new lives in Canada.

"There's an enlightening portrait of Josiah Henson (the model for Stowe's Uncle Tom) as a political activist, a fascinating look at the pioneering journalist and early feminist Mary Ann Shadd and an intriguing section on the deep Canadian connection to Harpers Ferry, as John Brown meets with the fugitives in Chatham. Accessible and fluidly written, the book will appeal to general readers." Publishers Weekly.

Tobin, Jacqueline, 1950-

Hidden in plain view : the secret story of quilts and the underground railroad / Jacqueline L. Tobin and Raymond G. Dobard. Doubleday, 1999. x, 208 p. : **973.7**

1. Underground Railroad. 2. Fugitive slaves 3. African American quilts -- Social aspects -- History -- 19th century. 4. Codes (Communication) -- History -- 19th century. 5. United States -- History -- 1815-1866.
ISBN 0385491379

LC 98049804

Reveals the secret codes woven by African American slaves into quilts they used to navigate their escape on the Underground Railroad.

"This is a needed and valuable contribution to the literature of African American culture." Library Journal.

United States Military Academy

The **West** Point history of the Civil War / The United States Military Academy ; contributors, Timothy Strabbing, Colonel Ty Seidule, Clifford Roger. Simon & Schuster, 2014. 352 p. **973.7**

1. Battles. 2. Civil War. 3. Military history. 4. War. 5. United States -- History -- Civil War, 1861-1865.
ISBN 9781476782621

LC 2015304127

An authorized military account of the Civil War incorporates the same exclusive images, tactical maps and expert analysis commissioned by The United States Military Academy to teach history of the art of war to West Point cadets.

Waller, Douglas C.

Lincoln's spies : their secret war to save a nation / Douglas Waller. Simon & Schuster, 2019. 624 p. **973.7**

1. Van Lew, Elizabeth L., 1818-1900. 2. Lincoln, Abraham, 1809-1865. 3. Sharpe, George H. (George Henry), 1828-1900. 4. Baker, La Fayette C. (La Fayette Curry), 1826-1868. 5. Pinkerton, Allan, 1819-1884. 6. Espionage. 7. Spies. 8. Intelligence service. 9. Women spies. 10. United States -- History -- Civil War, 1861-1865.
ISBN 9781501126840

LC 2018277647

Describes the lives of three men and one woman who served as secret agents for the North who informed Lincoln's generals with crucial information on enemy positions and helped foil assassination attempts during the Civil War.

"For those wanting to see spying through both a wide-angle lens in terms of patterns of espionage and a microscopic one in terms of personalities, Waller's book is the one to read." Library Journal.

Walters, Kerry S.

The **underground** railroad : a reference guide / Kerry Walters. ABC-CLIO, 2012. x, 223 p. : **973.7**

1. Underground Railroad. 2. Anti-slavery movements -- History -- 19th century 3. Fugitive slaves 4. Abolitionists -- United States -- History -- 19th century. 5. United States -- Race relations -- History -- 19th century.
ISBN 9781598846478

LC 2011041517

Full of true stories more dramatic than any fiction, The Underground Railroad: A Reference Guide offers a fresh, revealing look at the efforts of hundreds of dedicated persons--white and black, men and women, from all walks of life--to help slave fugitives find freedom in the decades leading up to the Civil War. --from publisher description

Ward, Andrew, 1946-

★The **slaves'** war : the Civil War in the words of former slaves / Andrew Ward. Houghton Mifflin Co., 2008. 400 p. **973.7**

1. Slaves -- Southern States 2. Freed slaves 3. African Americans 4. Civil war 5. United States -- History -- Civil War, 1861-1865 6. United States -- History -- Civil War, 1861-1865 -- African-Americans. 7. United States -- History -- Civil War, 1861-1865 -- Social aspects.
ISBN 9780618634002

LC 2008001532

Includes index.

The Slaves' War delivers an unprecedented vision of the nation's bloodiest conflict, told from the perspective of those whose destiny it decided. Woven together from interviews, diaries, letters, and memoirs, here is the Civil War as seen not only from battlefields and camps but also from slave quarters, kitchens, roadsides, and fields. Speaking in a quintessentially American language of biblical power and intensity, body servants, army cooks and launderers, runaways, teamsters, and gravediggers bring the war to life--from theories about the war's causes to frank assessments of such figures as Lincoln, Davis, Lee, and Grant; from searing memories of the carnage of battle to often startling attitudes toward masters and liberators alike; and from initial jubilation at the Yankee invasion of the slave South to the crushing disappointment of freedom's promise unfulfilled.

"The author has provided a . . . narrative that gives voice to the experiences and attitudes of slaves who endured the conflict. Ward utilizes testimonials, diaries, and letters, and organizes them in chronological order from the months before the commencement of hostilities to the aftermath of the surrender at Appomattox. . . . This is a work that will interest both scholars and general readers." Booklist.

Ward, Geoffrey C.

The **Civil** War : an illustrated history / narrative by Geoffrey C. Ward ; based on a documentary filmscript by Geoffrey C. Ward, Ric Burns, and Ken Burns ; with contributions by Don E. Fehrenbacher [et al.]. Knopf, 1990. xix, 425 p. : **973.7**

1. Civil war 2. Slavery 3. Military history 4. Race relations 5. United States -- History -- Civil War, 1861-1865.
ISBN 0394562852

LC 89043475

Portrays the lives of politicians, soldiers, and slaves during the Civil War

"A companion to a nine-part Public Broadcasting System documentary, this superbly designed book easily stands on its own." New York Times Book Review.

Williams, David, 1959-

Bitterly divided : the South's inner Civil War / David Williams. New Press, 2008. 352 p. **973.7**

1. Social conflict 2. Social classes 3. Secession. 4. Public opinion -- Southern States 5. Confederate States of America -- Social conditions. 6. United States -- History -- Civil War, 1861-1865 -- Social aspects. 7. Southern States -- History -- 19th century
ISBN 9781595581082

LC 2007045285

A revisionist account of the American Confederacy's lesser-known internal divisions reveals how Civil War-era white southerners were divided about the issue of secession, in a volume that considers how southern resistance was significantly responsible for the Confederacy's ultimate collapse.

"Williams marshals abundant evidence to demonstrate that the Confederacy also lost an internal civil war during 1861-65. This firm repudiation of the myth of the solid Confederate South is absolutely essential Civil War reading." Booklist.

Willis-Braithwaite, Deborah, 1948-

Envisioning emancipation : Black Americans and the end of slavery / Deborah Willis and Barbara Krauthamer. Temple University Press, 2013. 248 p. **973.7**

1. African Americans -- History -- 1863-1877 -- Pictorial works. 2. Documentary photography -- United States. 3. Historiography and photography -- United States. 4. Slaves. 5. United States -- History -- Civil War, 1861-1865.
ISBN 9781439909850

LC 2012032600

Wills, Garry, 1934-

Lincoln at Gettysburg : the words that remade America / Garry Wills. Simon & Schuster, 1992. 317 p. **973.7**

1. Lincoln, Abraham, 1809-1865. Gettysburg address. 2. Lincoln, Abraham, 1809-1865 Oratory. 3. Presidents -- United States -- Messages. 4. Rhetoric -- Political aspects -- United States -- History -- 19th century. 5. Political leadership. 6. Civil war 7. United States -- History -- Civil War, 1861-1865. 8. Gettysburg, Pennsylvania. 9. Speeches, addresses, etc.
ISBN 9780671769567

LC 92003546

Pulitzer Prize for General Nonfiction, 1993.
ALA Notable Book, 1993.
National Book Award for Nonfiction finalist, 1992.
Pulitzer Prize for History finalist, 1993.

"This is a tour de force that will cause much discussion and argument." Library Journal.

Winik, Jay, 1957-

April 1865 : the month that saved America / Jay Winik. Harper Collins, 2001 xviii, 461 p. **973.7**

1. Lincoln, Abraham, 1809-1865 Assassination. 2. Appomattox Campaign, 1865. 3. Civil war 4. United States Civil War, 1861-1865 5. Richmond, Virginia -- History -- Siege, 1864-1865. 6. United States -- History -- Civil War, 1861-1865 -- Peace.
ISBN 9780060187231

LC 2001336531

Jay Winik explores the end of the Civil War in a panoramic narrative that takes readers on a journey through the tumultuous month of April 1865, showing that America's future rested on a few crucial decisions and twists of fate.

"Winik has written a provocative account. . . . He suggests that the assassination of Lincoln could have triggered a coup in the North, and his insights into the on-again, off-again 'peace' negotiations are incisive. Scholars and Civil War buffs may disagree with some of his assertions, but this fast moving, well-written chronicle will highlight obscure aspects of the war and stimulate further controversy." Booklist.

973.7092 United States--1861-1865--biography

Craughwell, Thomas J., 1956-

Stealing Lincoln's body / Thomas J. Craughwell. Harvard University Press, 2007. ix, 250 p. : **973.7092**

1. Lincoln, Abraham, 1809-1865 Tomb. 2. Lincoln, Abraham, 1809-1865 Family. 3. Grave robbing. 4. Body snatching. 5. Crime and the press. 6. Dead. 7. Illinois -- History -- 19th century. 8. Springfield, Illinois -- History -- 19th century.
ISBN 0674024583

LC 2006050842

Details a bizarre, little-known historical event in which a gang of Chicago counterfeiters attempted to steal the entombed, embalmed body of Abraham Lincoln on the night of the 1876 presidential election, discussing the planning and execution of the crime, the resulting investigation, the reaction of Lincoln's family, and the aftermath.

"Summoning the raw spirit of crime novels and horror stories, as well as the forensic detail of a coroner's inquest, Thomas J. Craughwell has turned the eerie final chapter of the Lincoln story into a guilty pleasure." Washington Post Book World.

Foner, Eric, 1943-

The **fiery** trial : Abraham Lincoln and American slavery / Eric Foner. W. W. Norton & Co., 2010. xxi, 426 p., 16 p. of plates : **973.7092**

1. Lincoln, Abraham, 1809-1865. 2. Presidents -- United States. 3. Slavery. 4. Racism. 5. Politicians -- United States. 6. United States -- Politics and government -- 1861-1865.
ISBN 9780393066180

LC 2010023425

Pulitzer Prize for History, 2011.

In this landmark work of deep scholarship and insight, Eric Foner gives the definitive history of Abraham Lincoln and the end of slavery in America. Foner's Lincoln emerges as a leader, one whose greatness lies in his capacity for moral and political growth through real engagement with allies and critics alike. This powerful work will transform our understanding of the nation's greatest president and the issue that mattered most.

"In the vast library on Lincoln, Foner's book stands out as the most sensitive and sensible reading of Lincoln's lifetime involvement with slavery and the most insightful assessment of Lincoln's--and indeed America's--imperative to move toward freedom lest it be lost. An essential work for all Americans.

Holzer, Harold

Lincoln president-elect : Abraham Lincoln and the great secession winter 1860-1861 / Harold Holzer. Simon & Schuster, 2008. 640 p. **973.7092**

1. Lincoln, Abraham, 1809-1865. 2. Lincoln, Abraham, 1809-1865 Political career before 1861. 3. Presidents -- United States -- History -- 19th century. 4. Secession -- United States. 5. North-South relations (United States) 6. Slavery -- History. 7. United States -- Politics and government -- 1857-1861. 8. United States -- History -- Civil War, 1861-1865 -- Causes.

ISBN 9780743289474

LC 2008021520

A chronicle of the four months between Lincoln's election and inauguration evaluates the period decisions he made regarding slavery, secession, and the possibility of a Civil War, in an account that also offers insight into the selections of his cabinet members.

"This excellent study fills a gap about which not much has been written in Lincoln's presidential career." Choice.

Kaplan, Fred, 1937-

Lincoln and the abolitionists : John Quincy Adams, slavery, and the Civil War / Fred Kaplan. HarperCollins, 2017. 352 p. **973.7092**

1. Adams, John Quincy, 1767-1848 Views on slavery 2. Lincoln, Abraham, 1809-1865 Views on slavery 3. Presidents -- United States 4. Abolitionists 5. Slavery 6. Equality 7. United States -- Race relations

ISBN 9780062440006

LC bl2017017854

Explores how the differing experiences and viewpoints of two Presidents shaped slavery and race relations in America for more than a century.

"A fresh look at John Quincy Adams, Abraham Lincoln, the Civil War, abolitionism, and other related American history." Kirkus.

McPherson, James M.

★**Tried** by war : Abraham Lincoln as commander in chief / James M. McPherson. Penguin Press, 2008. 384 p. **973.7092**

1. Lincoln, Abraham, 1809-1865 Military leadership. 2. Executive power -- United States -- History -- 19th century. 3. Presidents -- United States 4. Political leadership. 5. Civil war 6. United States -- History -- Civil War, 1861-1865. 7. United States -- Politics and government -- 1861-1865.

ISBN 9781594201912

LC 2008025229

Evaluates Lincoln's talents as a commander in chief in spite of limited military experience, tracing the ways in which he worked with, or against, his senior commanders to defeat the Confederacy and reshape the presidential role.

Meltzer, Brad

The **Lincoln** conspiracy : the secret plot to kill America's 16th president--and why it failed / Brad Meltzer and Josh Mensch. Flatiron Books, 2020. 416 p. **973.7092**

1. Lincoln, Abraham, 1809-1865 Attempted assassination, 1861 2. Pinkerton, Allan, 1819-1884. 3. Pinkerton's National Detective Agency 4. Presidents -- United States -- Attempted assassination 5. Proslavery movements 6. Assassination plots 7. Conspiracies 8. United States -- History -- Civil War, 1861-1865 9. Baltimore, Maryland -- History -- 19th century

ISBN 9781250317476

LC 2020006774

The best-selling authors of The First Conspiracy share the lesser-known story of the 1861 assassination attempt on the 16th President by a secret pro-Southern society that organized an elaborate plot targeting a newly elected Lincoln on his inaugural train journey.

"In short, energetic chapters, Meltzer and Mensch . . . fashion a brisk political thriller centered on a nefarious plot to murder Lincoln before his inauguration." Kirkus

973.8 United States--Reconstruction period, 1865-1901

Connell, Evan S., 1924-2013

Son of the morning star / Evan S. Connell. North Point Press, 1984. 441 p. : **973.8**

1. Custer, George A. (George Armstrong), 1839-1876. 2. United States. Army. Cavalry, 7th 3. United States. Army. Cavalry, 7th 4. Little Big Horn, Battle of the, 1876. 5. Generals -- United States 6. Cheyenne Indians -- History -- 19th century. 7. Dakota Indians -- History -- 19th century. 8. Montana -- History -- 19th century.

ISBN 0865471606

LC 84060681

Maps on lining papers.

Includes index.

National Book Critics Circle Award for Nonfiction finalist, 1984.

"This book is impressive in its massive presentation of information, and in the conclusions it draws about the probable events that led to the fracas on the banks of the Little Bighorn. But its strength lies in the way the author has shaped his material." New York Times Book Review.

Donovan, Jim, 1954-

A **terrible** glory : Custer and the Little Bighorn : the last great battle of the American West / James Donovan. Little, Brown and Co., c2008. 544 p. **973.8**

1. Custer, George A. (George Armstrong), 1839-1876. 2. United States. Army -- History 19th century 3. Little Big Horn, Battle of the, 1876. 4. Indians of North America. 5. Government relations with indigenous peoples 6. The West (United States) -- History, Military -- 19th century. 7. United States -- Military policy.

ISBN 9780316155786

LC 2007026156

In June of 1876, on a desolate hill above a winding river called "the Little Bighorn," George Armstrong Custer and all 210 men under his command were annihilated by almost 2,000 Sioux and Cheyenne. The news caused a public uproar, and those in positions of power promptly began to point fingers in order to avoid responsibility. Custer, who was conveniently dead, took the brunt of the blame. The truth, however, was far more complex.

"The author collects the multiple threads that led to the 1876 massacre at Little Big Horn. . . . Exhaustive research, lively prose and fresh interpretation make for a valuable addition to literature on this otherwise well-trodden historical event." Publishers Weekly.

Douglass, Frederick, 1818-1895

★**Frederick** Douglass : selected speeches and writings / edited by Philip S. Foner ; abridged and adapted by Yuval Taylor. Lawrence Hill Books, 1999. xviii, 789 p. ; The library of Black

America 973.8

1. Antislavery movements -- United States -- History -- 19th century 2. Slaves -- United States -- Social conditions -- 19th century 3. African Americans -- Civil rights -- History -- 19th century 4. Speeches, addresses, etc, American 5. United States -- History -- 19th century

ISBN 9781556523526

LC 99023180

Collects the abolitionist's ideas on slavery, feminism, electoral politics, and peace

Dray, Philip

Capitol men : the epic story of Reconstruction through the lives of the first black congressmen / Philip Dray. Houghton Mifflin Co., 2008. 480 p. **973.8**

1. United States. Congress. House 2. Reconstruction (United States history) 3. African American legislators 4. African American politicians 5. Social justice -- United States. 6. United States -- Race relations -- Political aspects. 7. Southern States -- Race relations -- Political aspects. 8. United States -- Politics and government -- 1865-1900. 9. Southern States -- Politics and government -- 1865-1950.

ISBN 9780618563708

LC 2008011292

A history of the Reconstruction era viewed from the perspective of America's first black members of Congress examines their key role in promoting such reforms as public education for all children, equal rights, and protection from Klan violence.

Foner, Eric, 1943-

Forever free : the story of emancipation and Reconstruction / Eric Foner ; illustrations edited and with commentary by Joshua Brown. Knopf, 2005. xxx, 268 p. : **973.8**

1. Reconstruction (United States history) 2. Slaves -- Emancipation 3. Civil war 4. United States Civil War, 1861-1865 5. United States -- History -- Civil War, 1861-1865 -- African Americans. 6. United States -- Race relations -- History -- 19th century. 7. United States -- Politics and government -- 1865-1900.

ISBN 0375402594

LC 2005040706

"Forever Free project : Stephen B. Brier, Peter O. Almond, executive editors/producers ; Christine Doudna, editor."

Analyzes the post-Civil War era of emancipation and Reconstruction with an emphasis on discovering the larger political and cultural meaning for contemporary America of the lives of the newly freed slaves and the rise of the Ku Klux Klan.

★**Reconstruction** : America's unfinished revolution, 1863-1877 / Eric Foner. Harper & Row, 1988. xxvii, 690 p., 16 p. of plates : **973.8**

1. Ku-Klux Klan -- History 19th century. 2. Reconstruction (United States history) 3. African Americans -- History -- 1863-1877. 4. Democracy. 5. Civil rights. 6. United States -- Politics and government -- 1865-1877. 7. United States -- History -- 1865-1877.

ISBN 9780060158514

LC 87045615

National Book Award for Nonfiction finalist, 1988

National Book Critics Circle Award for Nonfiction finalist, 1988.

Pulitzer Prize for History finalist, 1989.

"This invaluable, definitive history re-creates the post-Civil War period as a pivotal drama in which ordinary people get equal billing with politicians and wheelers and dealers." Publishers Weekly.

Langguth, A. J., 1933-

After Lincoln : how the north won the Civil War and lost the peace / A. J. Langguth. Simon & Schuster, 2014. 464 p. **973.8**

1. Republican Party 2. African Americans -- History -- 1863-1877. 3. Reconstruction (United States history) 4. United States -- Politics and government -- 1865-1877.

ISBN 9781451617320

LC 2013051340

A latest historical chronicle by the author of Patriots examines the Reconstruction era, covering such topics as the impeachment of Andrew Johnson, Ulysses Grant's efforts to quash a rising KKK and Rutherford Hayes' agreement to remove troops from the South.

"The power of the Ku Klux Klan to strike fear was very real, no matter how foreign it seems today. This is a cogent, well-researched, well-told history of that important period. Langguth shows rather than explains, and the result is a rich history of an understudied period of American history." Kirkus.

Miller, Scott, 1960-

The **president** and the assassin : McKinley, terror, and empire at the dawn of the American century / Scott Miller. Random House Inc., 2011. 464 p. **973.8**

1. McKinley, William, 1843-1901 Assassination. 2. Czolgosz, Leon F., 1873?-1901 3. Presidents -- United States -- Assassination. 4. Anarchism -- United States -- History. 5. Blue collar workers 6. United States -- Politics and government -- 1897-1901.

ISBN 9781400067527

LC 2010038857

An account of the 25th President's assassination places events against a backdrop of a rapidly changing, newly industrial nation that McKinley regarded as increasingly great while his assassin, Czolgosz, became obsessed with his views on poverty, injustice and social revolution.

Philbrick, Nathaniel

★The **last** stand : Custer, Sitting Bull, and the Battle of the Little Bighorn / Nathaniel Philbrick. Viking, 2010. 480 p. **973.8**

1. Sitting Bull, 1831-1890 2. Custer, George A. (George Armstrong), 1839-1876 3. Little Big Horn, Battle of the, 1876 4. Dakota Indians -- Wars, 1876. 5. Indians of North America -- Wars. 6. Native American resistance and revolts. 7. Montana -- History -- 19th century.

ISBN 9780670021727

LC 2009047209

ALA Notable Book, 2011.

Analyzes the characters and contributions of the Plains Indians leader and one of the Union's greatest cavalry officers while explaining how the conflict forged a Native American alliance and set the stage for the confinement of major tribal leaders on reservations.

"The author writes a lively narrative that brushes away the cobwebs of mythology to reveal the context and realities of Custer's unexpected 1876 defeat at the hands of his Indian enemies under Sitting Bull, and the character of each leader. Judicious in his assessments of events and intentions, Philbrick offers a rounded history of one of the worst defeats in American military history, a story enhanced by his minute examination of the battle's terrain and interviews with descendants in both camps." Publishers Weekly.

Tuccille, Jerome

The **roughest** riders : the untold story of the Black soldiers in the Spanish-American War / Jerome Tuccille. Chicago Review

Press, 2015. 304 p. **973.8**

1. Spanish American War, 1898 -- African-American troops. 2. African American soldiers -- History -- 19th century. 3. African American soldiers -- History.
ISBN 9781613730461

LC 2015001414

Americans have long heard the story of Teddy Roosevelt and the Rough Riders charging up San Juan Hill during the Spanish-American War. But often forgotten in the great swamp of history is that Roosevelt's success was ensured by a dedicated corps of black soldiers--the so-called Buffalo Soldiers--who fought by Roosevelt's side during his legendary campaign. Roosevelt admitted that the black troops actually spearheaded the charge, beating him to the top of Kettle Hill ahead of San Juan Hill, but later changed his story, claiming their performance was due to the superior white officers under whom the black troops served.

"Tuccille's excellent descriptions give readers a graphic feel for the vicissitudes of jungle warfare and the grim racial and social realities that these men endured." Publishers Weekly.

Wineapple, Brenda

The **impeachers** : the of trial of Andrew Johnson and the dream of a just nation / Brenda Wineapple. Random House, [2019] 512 p. **973.8**

1. Johnson, Andrew, 1808-1875 Impeachment. 2. Impeachments -- United States. 3. Trials (Impeachment) 4. Reconstruction (United States history) 5. United States -- Politics and government -- 1865-1869.
ISBN 9780812998368

LC 2018034980

ALA Notable Book, 2020.

An account of the impeachment of Andrew Johnson shares insights into the 17th President's disregard of Congress, opposition to civil rights and anti-Reconstruction stance, exploring the roles of such impeachment contributors as Ulysses S. Grant and Thaddeus Stevens.

"Complementing but not replacing David Stewart's Impeached, this volume offers a skillfully crafted and useful history." Library Journal.

973.9 United States--1901-

Allen, Frederick Lewis, 1890-1954

Only yesterday : an informal history of the 1920's / Frederick Lewis Allen. Perennial Classics, 2000, c1931. x, 338 p. : **973.9**

1. United States -- History -- 1919-1933. 2. United States -- Social conditions -- 1918-1932. 3. United States -- Economic conditions -- 1918-1945.
ISBN 0060956658

LC 00028345

Sequel: Since yesterday.

Originally published: Harper & Row, 1931.

Recreates the social, political, and economic scene of the 1920s in America.

Auster, Paul, 1947-

I thought my father was God and other true tales from NPR's National Story Project / edited and introduced by Paul Auster ; Nelly Reifler, assistant editor. Henry Holt, 2001. xxi, 383 p. : **973.9**

1. United States -- Social life and customs -- 20th century Anecdotes. 2. United States -- Social conditions -- 1945- Anecdotes. 3. United States Anecdotes. 4. Oral histories.
ISBN 0805067140

LC 00054397

Includes index.

"These are stop-you-in-your-tracks stories about hair-raising coincidences, miracles, tragedies, redemption, and moments of pure hilarity." Booklist.

Boorstin, Daniel J. (Daniel Joseph), 1914-2004

The **image** : a guide to pseudo-events in America / Daniel J. Boorstin. Harper & Row, 1964, c1961. iv, 315 p. ; **973.9**

1. National characteristics, American. 2. Popular culture -- History -- 20th century 3. United States -- Civilization -- 1945-
ISBN 9780679741800

LC 95152428

Discusses news gathering, celebrity, travel, prestige, and the American dream.

Churchwell, Sarah Bartlett, 1970-

Behold, America : the entangled history of "America first" and "the American dream" / Sarah Churchwell. Basic Books, 2018. viii, 348 p. **973.9**

1. National characteristics, American 2. American Dream 3. Nationalism -- United States -- History 4. Isolationism 5. United States -- History -- 20th century 6. United States -- Social conditions -- 20th century
ISBN 9781541673403

LC 2018020585

Discusses the history of the "America First" movement, which was linked with white supremacy, and compares it with the "American Dream," which promotes economic equality, through the various historical events of the twentieth century.

Frank, Robert, 1924-

The **Americans** / photographs by Robert Frank ; introduction by Jack Kerouac. Steidl ; 2008. 180 p. ; **973.9**

1. United States Pictorial works. 2. United States -- Social life and customs -- 1945-1970 Pictorial works.
ISBN 386521584X

LC bl2008020869

Originally published as: Les Americains. Paris : R. Delpire, 1958.

Grunwald, Lisa,

Letters of the century : America, 1900-1999 / edited by Lisa Grunwald & Stephen J. Adler. Dial Press, 1999. 741 p. : **973.9**

1. United States -- Civilization -- 20th century Sources. 2. United States 3. Letters
ISBN 0385315902

LC 99016808

Letters chronicle a century of life in the United States, from Mark Twain's humorous letter to the head of Western Union to Einstein's warning to Roosevelt about atomic warfare and a young Bill Gates begging hobbyists not to share software.

"This is one of the most original literary tributes to the closing century." Publishers Weekly.

973.91 United States--1901-1953

Bryson, Bill

One summer : America, 1927 / Bill Bryson. Doubleday, 2013. 544 p. **973.91**

1. Popular culture -- History -- 1920-1929 2. United States -- History -- 1919-1933. 3. United States -- Social conditions -- 1918-1932. 4. United States -- Social life and customs -- 1918-1945.
ISBN 9780767919401

LC 2013016041

Recounts the story of a pivotal cultural year in the United States when mainstream pursuits and historical events were marked by contributions by such figures as Charles Lindbergh, Babe Ruth, and Al Capone.

Cooper, John Milton

The **warrior** and the priest : Woodrow Wilson and Theodore Roosevelt / John Milton Cooper, Jr. Belknap Press of Harvard University Press, 1983. xiv, 442 p., 18 p. of plates : **973.91**

1. Wilson, Woodrow, 1856-1924. 2. Roosevelt, Theodore, 1858-1919. 3. Presidents -- United States. 4. United States -- Politics and government -- 1901-1909. 5. United States -- Politics and government -- 1913-1921.
ISBN 0674947517

LC 83006021

Compares the presidencies and accomplishments of Wilson and Roosevelt.

"The author's distinctions are sharp, his insights original, his judgments balanced and his narrative unfailingly graceful." New York Times Book Review.

Fraser, Steve, 1945-

The **age** of acquiescence : the life and death of American resistance to organized wealth and power / Steve Fraser. Little, Brown and Company, 2015. 432 p. **973.91**

1. Elite (Social sciences) -- United States -- History. 2. Power (Social sciences) -- United States -- History. 3. Social conflict. 4. Protest movements -- United States -- History. 5. United States -- Politics and government -- 1945-
ISBN 9780316185431

LC 2014020466

Investigates how and why, from the 18th century to the present day, Americans' resistance to their ruling elites has vanished.

Gardner, Mark L.

Rough riders : Theodore Roosevelt, his cowboy regiment, and the immortal charge up San Juan Hill / Mark Lee Gardner. William Morrow, 2016. 320 p. **973.91**

1. Roosevelt, Theodore, 1858-1919 Military leadership. 2. United States. Army. Volunteer Cavalry, 1st 3. Spanish-American War, 1898 4. Command of troops. 5. Military history. 6. San Juan Hill, Battle of, Cuba, 1898.
ISBN 9780062312082

LC 2015046230

From the author of To Hell on a Fast Horse comes a definitive account of this legendary U.S. fighting force during the Spanish-American War and its extraordinary leader, Theodore Roosevelt.

"Gardner provides some terrifying, exhilarating stories of the battle, including the valiant charge up San Juan Hill through enemy gunfire. Throughout, Gardner celebrates Roosevelt, who as a postwar commander-in-chief never forgot the lesson of war and the heroic sacrifices of the fighters." Publishers Weekly.

Goodwin, Doris Kearns

★The **bully** pulpit : Theodore Roosevelt, William Howard Taft, and the golden age of journalism / Doris Kearns Goodwin. Simon & Schuster, 2013. 848 p. **973.91**

1. Roosevelt, Theodore, 1858-1919. 2. Taft, William H. (William Howard), 1857-1930. 3. Republican Party -- History 20th century 4. Progressivism (United States politics) -- History -- 20th century. 5. Press and politics -- United States -- History -- 20th century. 6. Presidents. 7. United States -- Politics and government -- 1901-1909. 8. United States -- Politics and government -- 1909-1913.
ISBN 9781416547860

LC 2013032709

Andrew Carnegie Medal for Excellence in Non-Fiction, 2014.

Focusing on the broken friendship between Teddy Roosevelt and his chosen successor, William Howard Taft, a Pulitzer Prize-winning historian revisits the Progressive Era during which Roosevelt wielded the Bully Pulpit to challenge and triumph over abusive monopolies, political bosses and corrupt money brokers only to see it compromised by Taft.

"By shining a light on a little-discussed President and a much-discussed one, Goodwin manages to make history very much alive and relevant." Publishers Weekly.

Kennedy, David M.

★**Freedom** from fear : the American people in depression and war, 1929-1945 / David M. Kennedy. Oxford University Press, 1999. xviii, 936 p., 32 p. of plates : **973.91**

1. Depressions -- 1929-1941. 2. New Deal, 1933-1939. 3. Stock market crash, October 1929. 4. World War II -- United States. 5. United States -- History -- 1919-1933. 6. United States -- History -- 1933-1945.
ISBN 0195038347

LC 98049580

Pulitzer Prize for History, 2000.

Examines the forces and people that shaped United States history between the Great Depression and the end of World War II.

"Rarely does a work of historical synthesis combine such trenchant analysis and elegant writing. For its scope, its insight and its purring narrative engine, Kennedy's book will stand for years to come as the definitive account of the critical decades of the American century." Publishers Weekly.

Schlesinger, Arthur M. (Arthur Meier), 1917-2007

The **crisis** of the old order, 1919-1933 : the age of Roosevelt / Arthur M. Schlesinger, Jr. Houghton Mifflin, 2003, c1957. xiv, 557 p. ; **973.91**

1. Roosevelt, Franklin D. (Franklin Delano), 1882-1945. 2. Depressions -- 1929-1941 3. Recession (Economics) 4. Politicians. 5. United States -- History -- 1919-1933. 6. United States -- Politics and government -- 1919-1933.
ISBN 0618340858

LC 2003047884

"A Mariner book."

Originally published: Boston : Houghton Mifflin, 1957. With new foreword.

Shlaes, Amity

The **forgotten** man : a new history of the Great Depression / Amity Shlaes. Harper Collins Publishers, c2007. x, 464 p., 16 p. of plates : **973.91**

1. Depressions -- 1929-1941 2. New Deal, 1933-1939. 3. Economics -- History -- 20th century 4. United States -- History -- 1919-1933.

5. United States -- History -- 1933-1945. 6. United States -- Social conditions -- 1933-1945. 7. United States -- Economic conditions -- 1918-1945.
ISBN 0066211700
LC 2006049761

A reinterpretation of the Great Depression seeks to demonstrate how the failures of Hoover and Roosevelt to understand the prosperity of the 1920s directly contributed to massive national burdens that marginalized everyday citizens, in an account that shares the survival stories of lesser-known historical figures from the period.

"Reminding readers that the reputedly do-nothing Hoover pulled hard on the fiscal levers (raising tariffs, increasing government spending), Shlaes nevertheless emphasizes that his enthusiasm for intervention paled against the ebullient FDR's glee in experimentation. She focuses closely on the influence of his fabled Brain Trust, her narrative shifting among Raymond Moley, Rexford Tugwell, and other prominent New Dealers. Businesses that litigated their resistance to New Deal regulations attract Shlaes' attention, as do individuals who coped with the despair of the 1930s through self-help, such as Alcoholics Anonymous cofounder Bill Wilson. The book culminates in the rise of Wendell Willkie, and Shlaes' accent on personalities is an appealing avenue into her skeptical critique of the New Deal." Booklist.

Smith, Hedrick

Who stole the American dream? Can we get it back? / Hedrick Smith. Random House, 2012. 448 p. **973.91**

1. Political culture. 2. Polarization (Social sciences) 3. Income distribution. 4. Middle class -- United States -- Economic conditions. 5. United States -- Politics and government -- 1945-1989. 6. United States -- Politics and government -- 1989-
ISBN 9781400069668
LC 2012005865

The Pulitzer Prize-winning author of The New Russians presents a step-by-step account of how the American Dream has been dismantled throughout the past four decades by a series of landmark legislative, electoral and corporate decisions that have compromised the middle class and minimized individual economic and political power.

Terkel, Studs, 1912-2008

★**Hard** times : an oral history of the great depression / Studs Terkel. New Press, 2000, c1970. xvii, 462 p. ; **973.91**

1. Depressions -- 1929-1941 2. United States -- History -- 1933-1945. 3. United States -- History -- 1919-1933. 4. United States -- Social conditions -- 1933-1945. 5. Oral histories.
ISBN 9781565846562
LC 2003389318

Originally published: New York : Pantheon Books, 1970.

"Persons of all ages, occupations, and classes scattered across the U.S. remember what they experienced or were told about the economic crisis of the 1930's. The result is a social document of immense interest." Booklist.

973.91092 United States--1901-1953--biography

Schlesinger, Arthur M. (Arthur Meier), 1917-2007

Journals, 1952-2000 / Arthur M. Schlesinger, Jr. ; edited by Andrew Schlesinger and Stephen Schlesinger. Penguin Press, 2007. xvi, 894 p. ; **973.91092**

1. Schlesinger, Arthur M. (Arthur Meier), 1917-2007 Diaries. 2. Historians -- United States -- Diaries. 3. Authors, American -- 21st century 4. Politics and culture -- United States -- History -- 20th century 5. United States -- History -- 1945- 6. United States -- Social life and customs -- 1945-1970. 7. United States -- Social life and customs -- 1971- 8. United States -- Politics and government -- 1945-1989. 9. United States -- Politics and government -- 1989-
ISBN 1594201420
LC bl2007021482

Includes index.

The distinguished political historian's journals provide an intimate history of post-war America, the writer's contributions to multiple presidential administrations, and his relationships with numerous cultural and intellectual figures.

"This book contains juicy morsels on every one of its [pages]. The book contains not just his witty apercus, but those of hundreds of A-list friends, some of whom are still alive and will blanch at seeing private lunches in print. The presidential scuttlebutt is prime. The private score-settling is fun reading." Newsweek.

973.911 Administration of Theodore Roosevelt, 1901-1909

Egan, Timothy

★The **big** burn : Teddy Roosevelt and the fire that saved America / Timothy Egan. Houghton Mifflin Harcourt, c2009. 336 p. **973.911**

1. Roosevelt, Theodore, 1858-1919. 2. Pinchot, Gifford, 1865-1946. 3. United States. National Park Service -- History. 4. Forest fires -- Montana -- History. 5. Forest conservation -- United States -- History. 6. National parks and reserves -- United States -- History. 7. Presidents -- United States
ISBN 9780618968411
LC 2009021881

Narrates the struggles of the overmatched rangers against the implacable fire of August, 1910, and Teddy Roosevelt's pioneering conservation efforts that helped turn public opinion permanently in favor of the forests, though it changed the mission of the forest service with consequences felt in the fires of today.

973.917 Administration of Franklin Delano Roosevelt, 1933-1945

Finder, Henry

The **40s** : the story of a decade / New Yorker Magazine, edited by Henry Finder. Random House, 2014. 720 p. New Yorker decades ; **973.917**

1. National characteristics, American. 2. United States -- Civilization -- 1945-
ISBN 9780679644798
LC 2013047082

A cultural and political history of a watershed decade as reflected in the pages of New Yorker magazine includes coverage of topics ranging from the Nuremberg Trials and the statehood of Israel to the bombing of Hiroshima and the publication of Shirley Jackson's "The Lottery."

"Readers are certain to enjoy the beautiful writing, clever thinking and insightful thoughts across a vast range of topics." Kirkus.

Katznelson, Ira

Fear itself : the New Deal and the origins of our time / Ira Katznelson. Liveright Publishing Corporation, A Division of W.W. Norton & Company, 2013. 512 p. **973.917**

1. Roosevelt, Franklin D. (Franklin Delano), 1882-1945. 2. New Deal, 1933-1939 3. World politics -- 1933-1945 4. Political culture -- United States -- History -- 20th century 5. Depressions -- 1929-

1941. 6. United States -- Politics and government -- 1933-1945
ISBN 9780871404503

LC 2012041794

Brings to life the New Deal era of American history, highlighting the politicians and pundits of the time, many of whom argued for positions that modern citizens would find questionable, including advocating for separation of the races and an American dictatorship.

Schlesinger, Arthur M. (Arthur Meier), 1917-2007

The **coming** of the New Deal, 1933-1935 : the Age of Roosevelt / Arthur M. Schlesinger, Jr. Houghton Mifflin, 2003, c1958. xiv, 669 p. ; **973.917**

1. Roosevelt, Franklin D. (Franklin Delano), 1882-1945. 2. New Deal, 1933-1939. 3. Depressions -- 1929-1941. 4. Recession (Economics) 5. Politicians. 6. United States -- History -- 1933-1945.
ISBN 0618340866

LC 2003047859

"A Mariner Book."

Originally published: c1958. With new foreword.

"This second volume of 'The Age of Roosevelt' continues the work begun with 'The Crisis of the Old Order, 1919-1933'. The dramatic story of how representative democracy began the battle to conquer economic collapse is followed through the first two years of the New Deal." Library Journal.

973.917092 United States--1933-1945--biography

Fullilove, Michael, 1972-

Rendezvous with destiny : how Franklin D. Roosevelt and five extraordinary men took America into the war and into the world / Michael Fullilove. The Penguin Press, 2013. 480 p. **973.917092**

1. Roosevelt, Franklin D. (Franklin Delano), 1882-1945. 2. Roosevelt, Franklin D. (Franklin Delano), 1882-1945 Friends and associates. 3. Welles, Sumner, 1892-1961. 4. Donovan, William J. (William Joseph), 1883-1959. 5. Hopkins, Harry L. (Harry Lloyd), 1890-1946. 6. Willkie, Wendell L. (Wendell Lewis), 1892-1944. 7. Harriman, W. Averell (William Averell), 1891-1986. 8. World War II -- United States. 9. Diplomacy -- United States -- History -- 20th century 10. International relations -- History -- 20th century 11. United States -- Foreign relations -- 1933-1945.
ISBN 9781594204357

LC 2012047003

Documents the lesser-known role of the 32nd President and five influential diplomats in overturning American isolationist beliefs and pulling the country into World War II, citing the pivotal reports that led to America's support of an inundated Great Britain and Russia.

Persico, Joseph E.

Franklin and Lucy : an intimate portrait of Franklin D. Roosevelt, Mrs. Rutherford, and the other remarkable women who shaped FDR's life / Joseph E. Persico. Random House, 2008. 576 p. **973.917092**

1. Roosevelt, Franklin D. (Franklin Delano), 1882-1945 Relations with women. 2. Roosevelt, Franklin D. (Franklin Delano), 1882-1945 Friends and associates. 3. Roosevelt, Franklin D. (Franklin Delano), 1882-1945 Marriage. 4. Rutherfurd, Lucy Mercer. 5. Roosevelt, Eleanor, 1884-1962. 6. Roosevelt, Eleanor, 1884-1962 Marriage. 7. Presidents -- United States 8. Social secretaries -- United States 9. Presidents' spouses -- United States
ISBN 9781400064427

LC 2007036851

"The author engagingly and eloquently narrates the tangled relationships between Franklin and the various women to whom he became close. Persico offers what will prove an important, lasting addition to the literature of the Roosevelts." Publishers Weekly.

Simon, James F.

FDR and Chief Justice Hughes : the president, the Supreme Court, and the epic battle over the New Deal / James F. Simon. Simon & Schuster, c2012. 368 p. **973.917092**

1. Roosevelt, Franklin D. (Franklin Delano), 1882-1945 2. Hughes, Charles Evans, 1862-1948. 3. United States. Supreme Court -- History 20th century. 4. New Deal, 1933-1939 5. Political questions and judicial power -- United States -- History -- 20th century. 6. Executive power -- United States -- History -- 20th century 7. Depressions -- 1929-1941 8. United States -- Politics and government -- 1933-1945
ISBN 9781416573289

LC 2011028825

Documents the political clashes between the 32nd President and the Supreme Court under Chief Justice Hughes regarding the New Deal, providing coverage of the President's proposed legislative remedies, the constitutional challenges posed by a conservative bloc on the Court and FDR's efforts to undermine the abilities of opposing justices.

973.918092 United States--1945-1953--biography

Brands, H. W.

The **general** vs. the president : MacArthur and Truman at the brink of nuclear war / H.W. Brands. Doubleday, 2016 416 p. **973.918092**

1. Truman, Harry S., 1884-1972 Political and social views. 2. MacArthur, Douglas, 1880-1964 Political and social views. 3. Nuclear warfare -- Government policy. 4. Presidents. 5. Generals. 6. World War II -- Influence.
ISBN 9780385540575

LC 2016021412

Traces the story of how President Harry Truman and General Douglas MacArthur confronted each other's oppositional stances for America's future in the aftermath of World War II.

"An exciting, well-written comparison study of two American leaders at loggerheads during the Korean War crisis." Kirkus.

973.92 United States--1953-2001

Bryson, Bill

I'm a stranger here myself : notes on returning to America after twenty years away / Bill Bryson. Broadway Books, c1999. xiii, 288 p. : **973.92**

1. Bryson, Bill Anecdotes. 2. Bryson, Bill Travel United States. 3. National characteristics, American. 4. Small town life. 5. Moving to a new country. 6. United States -- Description and travel Anecdotes 7. United States -- Social life and customs -- 1971- Anecdotes.
ISBN 9780767903813

LC 99018074

The author describes his return to America after two decades of living abroad and his disconcerting reunion with his homeland as he discusses motels, tax-return instructions, and hardware stores.

"The author collects columns on America he wrote weekly, while living in New Hampshire in the mid-to-late 1990s, for a British Sunday newspaper. Although he happily describes himself as dazzled by American ease, friendliness and abundance, Bryson has no trouble finding comic targets, among them fast food, computer efficiency and, ironically, American friendliness and putative convenience." Publishers Weekly.

Finder, Henry,

The **50s** : the story of a decade / New Yorker Magazine, edited by Henry Finder. Random House, 2015 720 p. New Yorker decades ; **973.92**

1. National characteristics, American. 2. United States -- Civilization -- 1945-

ISBN 9780679644811

LC 2015030067

A one-of-kind look back at the 1950s, as told by some of The New Yorker's most notable contributors, chronicles the tensions and innovations that lay behind the decade's more placid surface during a time of prosperity and contradiction.

Halberstam, David

The **best** and the brightest / David Halberstam ; foreword by John McCain. Modern Library, 2001, c1972. xxviii, 780 p. ; **973.92**

1. Vietnam War, 1961-1975 -- United States. 2. Military policy. 3. Presidents -- United States. 4. Politicians -- United States. 5. United States -- Politics and government -- 1961-1963. 6. United States -- Politics and government -- 1963-1969.

ISBN 0679640991

LC 2001031261

Originally published: New York : Random House, 1972.

An account of American power and politics in the 1950s and 1960s highlights the political and military figures who shaped domestic and foreign policy and who orchestrated America's involvement in Vietnam.

"The author describes analytically rather than narratively, how the Kennedy-Johnson intellectual (McNamara, Bundy, Rusk, Ball, Taylor, et al.) men praised as 'the best and the brightest' men of this century, became the architects of the disastrous American policy of Indochina." Library Journal.

The **fifties** / David Halberstam. Villard Books, 1993. xi, 800 p. : **973.92**

1. United States -- Social life and customs -- 1945-1970. 2. United States -- Politics and government -- 1945-1989. 3. United States -- Economic conditions -- 1945- 4. United States -- Popular culture -- History -- 1950-1959.

ISBN 9780679415596

LC 92056815

The Pulitzer Prize-winning journalist examines the social, political, economic, and cultural history of the 1950s, from McCarthy to I Love Lucy.

"The author's sources are secondary and derivative, but his instinct for the revealing anecdote, his ear for the memorable quote, and his awesome powers of organization add up to a variegated overview that moves seamlessly between the serious shenanigans of Chief Justice Earl Warren and the frivolous ones of...Grace Metalious." National Review.

Kennedy, Robert Francis, 1925-1968

RFK : his words for our times / edited and introduced by Edwin O. Guthman & C. Richard Allen. William Morrow, 2018. xxxiii, 442 pages, 16 unnumbered pages of plates : **973.92**

1. Kennedy, Robert Francis, 1925-1968 2. Civil rights 3. Social justice 4. Politicians 5. Social change 6. Speeches, addresses, etc.

ISBN 9780062834102

LC bl2018045295

Published to commemorate the 50th anniversary of his assassination and featuring commentary by notable historians and public figures, an inspiring collection of Bobby Kennedy's most famous speeches shares intimate perspectives into his views on such subjects as civil rights, social justice, foreign policy, poverty and the Vietnam War.

"Rich background information on policy and historical context introduces each chapter and frames each speech, which reveal Kennedy's appeal to Democrats and Republicans, minorities and the middle class." Library Journal.

Klosterman, Chuck, 1972-

Eating the dinosaur / Chuck Klosterman. Scribner, 2009. 256 p. **973.92**

1. Popular culture. 2. Consumer economics -- Social aspects. 3. Sports -- Social aspects -- United States. 4. National characteristics, American. 5. United States -- Civilization -- 1970-

ISBN 9781416544203

LC 2009018719

The best-selling author of Downtown Owl and Sex, Drugs, and Cocoa Puffs takes a humorous look at expectations versus reality in pop culture, sports, and media, in a book that explores such questions as: Why is pop culture obsessed with time travel?; What do Kurt Cobain and David Koresh have in common?; and much more.

Kruse, Kevin Michael, 1972-

Fault lines : a history of the United States since 1974 / Kevin M. Kruse, Julian E. Zelizer. W.W. Norton & Company, 2019. 400 p. **973.92**

1. Political culture 2. Polarization (Social sciences) 3. Right and left (Political science) 4. Income distribution 5. United States -- History

ISBN 9780393088663

LC 2018035645

Two historians trace the origins of today's divided America to pivotal events in 1974, from Watergate to the energy crisis, to explore how long-standing disputes over income inequality, racial division, and gender roles fueled a polarized political landscape.

"Their survey constitutes a valuable road map for readers seeking to understand why the U.S. is the way it is and ends with the hopeful message that the wear-and-tear inflicted on the country has inspired new institutions before and may do so again " Booklist.

Schulman, Bruce J.

The **seventies** : the great shift in American culture, society, and politics / Bruce J. Schulman. Free Press, 2001. xvii, 334 p., 8 p. of plates : **973.92**

1. United States -- Civilization -- 1970- 2. United States -- Social life and customs -- 1970-1979. 3. United States -- Politics and government -- 1969-1981.

ISBN 0684828146

LC 2001023238

"This is an important contribution to modern American social history and the literature of popular culture." Publishers Weekly.

Thompson, Nicholas, 1975-

The **hawk** and the dove : Paul Nitze, George Kennan, and the history of the Cold War / Nicholas Thompson. Henry Holt, c2009. 416 p. **973.92**

1. Nitze, Paul H. 2. Kennan, George F. (George Frost), 1904-2005. 3. Cold War. 4. National security -- United States -- History -- 20th

century. 5. Anti-communist movements -- United States -- History -- 20th century. 6. Ambassadors -- United States 7. United States -- Foreign relations -- 1945-1989. 8. United States -- Officials and employees
ISBN 9780805081428
LC 2009009225

ALA Notable Book, 2010.

Only two Americans held positions of great influence throughout the Cold War; ironically, they were the chief advocates for the opposing strategies in that harrowing conflict. Both came to power during World War II, reached their professional peaks during the Cold War's most frightening moments, and fought epic political battles that spanned decades. Yet despite their very different views, Paul Nitze and George Kennan remained good friends all their lives. Nitze--the hawk--believed that the best way to avoid a nuclear clash was to prepare to win one. More than any other American, he was responsible for the arms race. Kennan--the dove--persuasively argued that we should contain the Soviet Union while waiting for it to collapse from within. In following these two rivals and friends from the beginning of the Cold War to its end, Nicholas Thompson tells the story of our nation during the most dangerous half century in history.--From publisher description.

"This dual biography of Nitze and Kennan focuses on their careers as statesmen, policy makers and public intellectuals. " New York Times Book Review.

This book does an inspired job of telling the story of the Cold War through the careers of two of its most interesting and important figures. Washington Monthly

Woodward, Bob, 1943-

Shadow : five presidents and the legacy of Watergate / Bob Woodward. Simon & Schuster, 1999. 592 p. : **973.92**

1. Nixon, Richard M. (Richard Milhous), 1913-1994 Influence. 2. Ford, Gerald R., 1913-2006 3. Carter, Jimmy, 1924- 4. Reagan, Ronald 5. Bush, George, 1924-2018 6. Clinton, Bill, 1946- 7. Presidents -- United States -- History -- 20th century. 8. Mass media -- Political aspects. 9. Impeachments -- United States. 10. Politicians. 11. United States -- Politics and government -- 1945-1989. 12. United States -- Politics and government -- 1989-
ISBN 0684852624
LC 99037045

Examines the legacy of Watergate in terms of how Nixon's disgrace forever altered American politics and culture.

973.92092 United States--1953-2001--biography

Gibbs, Nancy, 1960-

★The **presidents** club : inside the world's most exclusive fraternity / Nancy Gibbs and Michael Duffy. Simon & Schuster, 2012. 416 p. **973.92092**

1. Presidents -- United States -- History. 2. Former presidents -- United States. 3. Brotherhoods. 4. Politicians.
ISBN 9781439127704
LC 2011042047

Traces the history of the presidential fraternity conceived by Harry Truman and Herbert Hoover during Eisenhower's inauguration, exploring the ways in which the nation's presidents depended on, sabotaged, and formed alliances that had world-changing impacts.

Whipple, Chris (Christopher C.)

The **gatekeepers** : how the White House Chiefs of Staff define every presidency / Chris Whipple. Crown, 2017. 384 p. **973.92092**

1. White House chiefs of staff 2. Presidents -- United States -- Staff 3. Political culture -- United States -- History -- 20th century 4. United States -- Politics and government
ISBN 9780804138246
LC 2016046233

Examines how the American presidency has hinged on the effectiveness of the White House chiefs of staff, drawing on interviews with all seventeen living chiefs of staff and two former presidents to reveal how their decisions have influenced the nation.

"In this page-turner of a history, readers will discover new facets of historical events that they felt they already knew." Publishers Weekly.

973.921092 United States--1953-1961--biography

Thomas, Evan, 1951-

Ike's bluff : president Eisenhower's secret battle to save the world / Evan Thomas. Little, Brown and Co., c2012. 432 p. **973.921092**

1. Eisenhower, Dwight D. (Dwight David), 1890-1969. 2. Presidents. 3. Cold War. 4. National security -- United States -- History -- 20th century. 5. Nuclear weapons. 6. United States -- Foreign relations -- 1953-1961.
ISBN 9780316091046
LC 2012019640

Examines the White House years of Dwight Eisenhower and reveals the former president, often viewed as a doddering lightweight, as a brilliant, intellectual tactician who could be patient and ruthless, and generous and self-serving.

973.922 Administration of John Fitzgerald Kennedy, 1961-1963

Matthews, Christopher, 1945-

Kennedy & Nixon : the rivalry that shaped postwar America / Christopher Matthews. Simon & Schuster, c1996. 377 p. : **973.922**

1. Kennedy, John F. (John Fitzgerald), 1917-1963. 2. Nixon, Richard M. (Richard Milhous), 1913-1994 3. United States -- Politics and government -- 1945-1989.
ISBN 9780684810300
LC 96015677

Traces the rivalry between John Kennedy and Richard Nixon, whose 1960 presidential contest set America's Cold War political course.

973.922092 United States--1961-1963--biography

Coleman, David G.

The **fourteenth** day : JFK and the aftermath of the Cuban Missile Crisis / David G. Coleman. W.W. Norton & Co., c2012. 192 p. **973.922092**

1. Kennedy, John F. (John Fitzgerald), 1917-1963 2. Khrushchev, Nikita, 1894-1971 3. Cuban Missile Crisis, 1962 4. Nuclear weapons -- History 5. Ballistic missiles 6. Missiles 7. United States -- Politics and government -- 1961-1963. 8. United States -- Foreign relations -- 1961-1963. 9. United States -- Foreign relations Soviet Union. 10. Soviet Union -- Foreign relations United States. 11. United States -- Foreign relations Cuba. 12. Cuba -- Foreign relations United States.

13. United States -- Foreign relations Cuba. 14. Cuba -- Foreign relations United States.
ISBN 9780393084412

LC 2012025397

Describes what was going on in the Oval Office as the highly-charged events leading up the Cuban Missile Crisis unfolded, as well as the immediate aftermath, based on secret recordings made by President Kennedy.

Lattin, Don

The **Harvard** Psychedelic Club : how four visionaries killed the fifties and ushered in a new age for America / Don Lattin. HarperCollins Publishers, 2010. 272 p. **973.922092**

1. Smith, Huston, 1919- 2. Ram Dass 3. Weil, Andrew. 4. Leary, Timothy, 1920-1996. 5. Harvard University. Department of Social Relations 6. Hallucinogenic drugs -- Research. 7. Religion -- Social aspects. 8. Hallucinogenic drug use. 9. Research. 10. United States -- Social conditions -- 1960-1980.
ISBN 9780061655937

LC 2009026323

A Pulitzer Prize-nominated author explains how three brilliant scholars and one ambitious freshman crossed paths in Cambridge, Massachusetts, in the winter of 1960-61, and how their experiences in a psychedelic drug-research project transformed their lives and much of American culture in the 60s and 70s.

"Mr. Lattin does a lovely, gently humorous job of setting the scene and bringing these men together. This groovy story unfurls...like a ready-made treatment for a sprawling, elegiac and crisply comic movie, let's say Robert Altman by way of Wes Anderson." New York Times.

Minutaglio, Bill

Dallas 1963 : politics, treason, and the assassination of JFK / Bill Minutaglio, Steven L. Davis. Grand Central Pub 2013 272 p. **973.922092**

1. Kennedy, John F. (John Fitzgerald), 1917-1963 Assassination 2. Presidents -- United States 3. Assassination -- United States 4. Hate groups. 5. Right and left (Political science) 6. Dallas, Texas. 7. United States -- History -- 20th century
ISBN 9781455522095

LC 2013939303

Presents an explosive and unsettling account of the radicals, reactionaries and extremists who turned Dallas into a city infamous for the assassination of JFK.

Oliphant, Thomas

★The **road** to Camelot : inside JFK's five-year campaign / Thomas Oliphant and Curtis Wilkie. Simon & Schuster, 2017. 432 p. **973.922092**

1. Kennedy, John F. (John Fitzgerald), 1917-1963. 2. Democratic Party -- History 20th century 3. Presidential election, 1960 4. Presidential candidates 5. Elections -- United States -- History -- 20th century 6. Political campaigns 7. United States -- Politics and government -- 1953-1961. 8. United States -- Politics and government -- 1961-1963.
ISBN 9781501105562

LC 2016050682

"Simon & Schuster nonfiction original hardcover"--Title page verso.

A behind-the-scenes account of the 35th President's journey to the White House includes coverage of his failed vice presidential nomination in 1956, the ways his Catholic faith challenged his campaigns and the successful efforts of his team of young advisors to reinvent the traditional party.

"The authors add a new perspective to literature on Kennedy by focusing on his electioneering efforts rather than his persona and policy outcomes." Library Journal.

Sherman, Casey, 1969-

Above and beyond : John F. Kennedy and America's most dangerous Cold War spy mission / Casey Sherman and Michael Tougias. PublicAffairs, 2018. 352 p. **973.922092**

1. Kennedy, John F. (John Fitzgerald), 1917-1963 2. Cold war 3. Presidents -- United States -- History 4. Cuban Missile Crisis, 1962 5. Spy planes 6. United States 7. Soviet Union 8. Cuba
ISBN 9781610398046

LC 2018002748

The New York Times best-selling authors of The Finest Hours presents the gripping firsthand account of three war heroes--President John F. Kennedy and two U-2 pilots, Rudy Anderson and Chuck Maultsby--who were all brought together during Cuban Missile Crisis and risked their lives to save the United States.

Swanson, James L. 1959-

End of days : the assassination of John F. Kennedy / James L. Swanson. HarperCollins 2013 304 p. **973.922092**

1. Kennedy, John F. (John Fitzgerald), 1917-1963 Assassination. 2. Presidents -- Assassination. 3. Assassination. 4. United States -- History -- 20th century. 5. Dallas, Texas -- History -- 20th century. 6. United States -- Politics and government -- 1961-1963.
ISBN 9780062083487

The New York Times best-selling author of Manhunt: The 12-Day Chase for Lincoln's Killer presents a complete account of the day Kennedy was killed, following the event hour-by-hour, from the Kennedys' arrival in Texas through the shooting in Dealey Plaza to the shocking aftermath.

"Drawing on the decades of technological advances that have deepened the knowledge of the assassination, the author presents the stunning unfolding of the event in punchy, poignant vignettes, following one character after another to the inexorable conclusion." Kirkus.

973.923 Administration of Lyndon Baines Johnson, 1963-1969

Johnson, Lyndon B., 1908-1973

Taking charge : the Johnson White House tapes, 1963-1964 / edited and with commentary by Michael R. Beschloss. Simon & Schuster, 1997. 592 p. **973.923**

1. Johnson, Lyndon B., 1908-1973 Archives. 2. Presidents. 3. Tape recorders and players. 4. United States -- Politics and government -- 1963-1969 Sources.
ISBN 0684804077

Portrays the thirty-sixth president as a man who struggled to surpass JFK on civil rights, guided the country into Vietnam, and twisted the arms of friends and enemies alike.

"There are no stunning revelations and no recorded moments of epochal importance. But Taking Charge is a riveting book nevertheless. This is partly because it has been superbly edited and annotated by the historian Michael R. Beschloss, who has made everything--even the most arcane references--accessible to ordinary readers." New York Times Book Review.

973.924 Administration of Richard Milhous Nixon, 1969-1974

Packer, George, 1960-

★The **unwinding** : an inner history of the new America / George Packer. Farrar, Straus and Giroux, 2013. 432 p. **973.924**

1. Social problems -- United States. 2. National characteristics, American 3. Middle class -- United States -- Economic conditions -- 21st century. 4. Economic policy -- United States -- 21st century 5. United States -- History -- 1969- 6. United States -- Social conditions -- 1980- 7. United States -- Politics and government -- 1989-
ISBN 9780374102418

LC 2013004431

National Book Award for Nonfiction, 2013.
National Book Critics Circle Award for Nonfiction finalist, 2013.

Through an examination of the lives of several Americans and leading public figures over the past three decades, Packer portrays a superpower in danger of coming apart at the seams, its elites no longer elite, its institutions no longer working, its ordinary people left to improvise their own schemes for success and salvation.

Perlstein, Rick

The **invisible** bridge : the fall of Nixon and the rise of Reagan / Rick Perlstein. Simon & Schuster 2014 800 p. **973.924**

1. Nixon, Richard M. (Richard Milhous), 1913-1994 2. Reagan, Ronald 3. Conservatism -- United States -- History -- 20th century. 4. Ideology. 5. Presidents -- United States 6. United States -- History -- 20th century
ISBN 9781476782416

LC 2014381509

The best-selling author of Nixonland presents a portrait of the United States during the turbulent political and economic upheavals of the 1970s, covering events ranging from the Arab oil embargo and the era of Patty Hearst to the collapse of the South Vietnamese government and the rise of Ronald Reagan.

"Although the book only goes up to Reagan's loss of the 1976 Republican nomination to President Gerald Ford, the scope of the work never feels limited. A compelling, astute chronicle of the politics and culture of late-20th-century America." Kirkus.

★**Nixonland** : America's second Civil War and the divisive legacy of Richard Nixon, 1965-1972 / Rick Perlstein. Scribner, 2008. 640 p. **973.924**

1. Nixon, Richard M. (Richard Milhous), 1913-1994 2. Presidents -- United States 3. Elections -- United States -- History -- 20th century 4. United States -- History -- 20th century
ISBN 0743243021

LC 2008273706

An account of the thirth-seventh presidency sets Nixon's administration against a backdrop of the tumultuous civil rights movement while offering insight into how key events in the 1960s set the stage for today's political divides.

Zinn, Howard, 1922-2010

The **historic** unfullfilled promise / Howard Zinn ; introduction by Mathew Rothschild. City Lights Books, 2012. 184 p. **973.924**

1. World politics -- 20th century. 2. International relations. 3. United States -- History -- 1969- 4. United States -- Foreign relations -- 1981-1989. 5. United States -- Foreign relations -- 1989- 6. United States -- Politics and government -- 1981-1989. 7. United States -- Politics and government -- 1989- 8. Essays.
ISBN 9780872865556

LC 2012007955

Zinn's feature articles penned for the Progressive from 1980 to 2009.
Includes index.

Collects articles penned by the author for "Progressive" magazine from 1980 to 2009, offering critiques of the government, encouragement for citizens to organize, and a voice on behalf of the working class.

973.924092 United States--1969-1974--biography

Brinkley, Douglas,

The **Nixon** tapes : 1973 / edited and annotated by Douglas Brinkley and Luke A. Nichter. Houghton Mifflin Harcourt, 2015. 392 p. **973.924092**

1. Nixon, Richard M. (Richard Milhous), 1913-1994 Political and social views. 2. Presidents -- United States 3. Watergate Scandal. 4. United States -- Politics and government -- 1945-1989. 5. United States -- Foreign relations -- 1969-1974
ISBN 9780544610538

LC 2015028189

A conclusion to the revelatory translations published in The Nixon Tapes: 1971-1972 includes coverage of Nixon and Kissinger's private knowledge of flaws in the 1973 Vietnam peace agreement and the early warnings about the Yom Kippur War in the Middle East.

"General readers might prefer earlier transcription efforts, such as Watergate principal John Dean's 2014 The Nixon Defense, since the excerpts in that book are shorter and more context is given. Even so, these longer excerpts resemble an oddly fascinating reality show, and historians will like that Brinkley and Nichter worked with the most complete body of recordings and used audio equipment of the highest quality to ensure transcription accuracy." Library Journal.

Dean, John W. (John Wesley), 1938-

The **Nixon** defense : what he knew and when he knew it / John W. Dean. Viking, 2014 416 p. **973.924092**

1. Nixon, Richard M. (Richard Milhous), 1913-1994 2. Political corruption -- United States -- History -- 20th century 3. Watergate Scandal 4. Presidents -- United States
ISBN 9780670025367

LC 2014020821

A former White House Counsel and one of the last surviving major figures from Watergate uses his own transcripts from hundreds of conversations as well as documents in the archives to definitively determine what Nixon knew and when he knew it.

"[O]ne of the best and fullest accounts of the Watergate cover-up, one that conveys in Nixon's own voice the casual criminality of his troubled presidency." Publishers Weekly.

Feldstein, Mark Avrom

Poisoning the press : Richard Nixon, Jack Anderson, and the rise of Washington's scandal culture / Mark Feldstein. Farrar, Straus and Giroux, 2010. 480 p. **973.924092**

1. Nixon, Richard M. (Richard Milhous), 1913-1994 2. Anderson, Jack, 1922-2005. 3. Press and politics. 4. Presidents -- United States -- Press relations. 5. Political corruption -- United States -- History -- 20th century. 6. Political culture -- United States -- History -- 20th century. 7. United States -- Politics and government -- 1969-1974.
ISBN 9780374235307

LC 2010010272

Profiles the relationship between the 37th president and a reviled Pulitzer Prize-winning columnist, citing Anderson's shady investigative pursuits of revelatory information and Nixon's retaliatory campaign of bogus evidence and discrediting smears.

Hughes, Ken, 1964-

Chasing shadows : the Nixon tapes, the Chennault affair, and the origins of Watergate / Ken Hughes. University of Virginia Press, 2014. x, 228 p. ; **973.924092**

1. Nixon, Richard M. (Richard Milhous), 1913-1994. 2. Johnson, Lyndon B., 1908-1973. 3. Chennault, Anna. 4. Watergate Scandal. 5. Presidential tapes 6. United States -- Politics and government -- 1969-1974.

ISBN 9780813936635

LC 2014013429

This book, based on research on and transcripts of the Nixon, Johnson, and Kennedy White House presidential recordings as well as other contemporary sources, reveals for the first time the origins of the 'Plumbers' (the Special Investigations Unit) and Nixon's policy of illegal break-ins for partisan political gain, which led to Watergate, its cover-up, and Nixon's resignation.

"Through its foremost practitioners in Johnson and Nixon, Hughes reveals the realities of see American politics as a blood sport." Publishers Weekly.

Reston, James, Jr., 1941-

The **conviction** of Richard Nixon : the untold story of the Frost/Nixon interviews / James Reston, Jr. Harmony Books, c2007. 207 p. ; **973.924092**

1. Nixon, Richard M. (Richard Milhous), 1913-1994 Interviews. 2. Frost, David 3. Reston, James, Jr., 1941- 4. Presidents -- United States -- Interviews. 5. Former presidents -- United States -- Interviews. 6. Watergate Scandal 7. Interviews 8. United States -- Politics and government -- 1969-1974.

ISBN 0307394204

LC 2007001238

Drawing on his experiences spearheading the research team that prepared David Frost for his 1977 interviews with former president Richard Nixon, offers a dramatic perspective of the Watergate scandal and its aftermath.

"In 1977, three years after his resignation, Richard Nixon returned to the public eye in a series of interviews with British television journalist David Frost, for which Nixon received Publishers Weekly.

973.925092 United States--1974-1977--biography

Rumsfeld, Donald, 1932-

When the center held : Gerald Ford and the rescue of the American presidency / Donald Rumsfeld. Free Press, 2018. 352 p. **973.925092**

1. Ford, Gerald R., 1913-2006 2. Rumsfeld, Donald, 1932- 3. Presidents -- United States 4. Politicians 5. Watergate Scandal 6. Legislators 7. United States -- Politics and government -- 1974-1977

ISBN 9781501172939

LC 2018001411

A revealing political memoir of the presidency of Gerald Ford is seen through the eyes of Donald Rumsfeld--a New York Times best-selling author and Ford's former secretary of defense, chief of staff and longtime personal confidant.

"A few flaws aside, this is an engrossing and informative tribute to a man whom Jimmy Carter rightfully thanked in his inaugural address for all he has done to heal our land." Kirkus. Reviews

973.926 Administration of Jimmy (James Earl) Carter, 1977-1981

Perlstein, Rick, 1969-

★**Reaganland** : America's right turn 1976-1980 / Rick Perlstein. Simon & Schuster, 2020 1120 p. **973.926**

1. Reagan, Ronald. 2. Carter, Jimmy, 1924- 3. Conservatism -- United States 4. Presidents -- United States 5. Elections -- United States -- History -- 20th century 6. Right and left (Political science) 7. United States -- History -- 20th century 8. United States -- Politics and government -- 1977-1981.

ISBN 9781476793054

LC bl2020016082

Backed by a reenergized conservative Republican base, Reagan ran on the campaign slogan "Make America Great Again," and prevailed. Reaganland is the story of how that happened, tracing conservative's cutthroat strategies to gain power and explaining why they endure four decades later.

"Political historian Perlstein (The Invisible Bridge) concludes the saga of right-wing insurgency he started in Before the Storm, his magisterial account of the 1964 Goldwater presidential campaign, with this chronicle of intensifying 1970s political clashes. . . . The result is an insightful and entertaining analysis of a watershed era in American politics." Publishers Weekly

973.927092 United States--1981-1989--biography

Mann, Jim, 1946-

The **rebellion** of Ronald Reagan : a history of the end of the Cold War / James Mann. Viking, 2009. 432 p. **973.927092**

1. Reagan, Ronald Political and social views. 2. Nixon, Richard M. (Richard Milhous), 1913-1994 Influence. 3. Massie, Suzanne Influence. 4. Reagan, Ronald Speeches 5. Cold War. 6. Political leadership -- United States -- Case studies. 7. Presidents -- United States 8. International relations -- History -- 20th century 9. United States -- Foreign relations -- 1981-1989. 10. United States -- Foreign relations Soviet Union. 11. Soviet Union -- Foreign relations United States.

ISBN 9780670020546

LC 2008029029

Analyzes the fortieth president's role in ending the Cold War, in a report that challenges popular beliefs, reveals lesser-known aspects of the Reagan administration's foreign policy, and cites the contributions of such figures as Nixon, Kissinger, and Gorbachev.

"Ronald Reagan did not win the Cold War, nor was he just historically lucky, as two contrasting viewpoints would sometimes have it. Instead...[the author writes,] after a career of hard line anticommunism Reagan proved more flexible and visionary than many other leaders of American foreign policy and more opportunistic and insightful into the motives of Mikhail Gorbachev when the Soviet leader signaled change in the USSR's own conventional hard-line position. Mann bases his argument upon impressive original research, including interviews with principals who range from George Shultz, to Colin Powell, to Helmut Kohl, to Nancy Reagan." Library Journal.

973.928 Administration of George Bush, 1989-1993

Bush, George, 1924-2018

All the best, George Bush : my life in letters and other writings / George Bush. Scribner, c1999. 640 p. : **973.928**

1. Bush, George, 1924-2018 Correspondence. 2. Presidents -- United States -- Correspondence.

ISBN 068483958X

LC 99040440

"George Bush" in the title appears as his signature.

"A Lisa Drew book."

Includes index.

The former president shares his life in correspondence, diary entries, memos, and other writings, from his letter home as an eighteen-year-old Navy pilot during World War II to one written to his children on the eve of Desert Storm.

"This work is refreshing and, in many ways, will shed more light on the man's personal character and public persona than any memoir or biography could. It offers an intriguing picture of a man who takes fierce pride in his modesty." Publishers Weekly.

973.929 Administration of Bill Clinton, 1993-2001

Gates, Robert Michael, 1943-

★**Exercise** of power : American failures, successes, and a new path forward in the post-Cold War world / Robert M. Gates. Alfred A. Knopf, 2020. 256 p. **973.929**

1. International relations 2. Great powers 3. Military policy 4. Geopolitics 5. United States -- Foreign relations -- 1989- 6. United States -- Politics and government -- 1989- 7. United States -- Military relations.

ISBN 9781524731885

LC 2019057305

The former Secretary of Defense and author offers a candid, sweeping examination of American executive powers and how they have been exercised with positive and negative results by American Presidents throughout the post-Cold War era.

"This important work dives deep into the past three decades of American foreign policy to provide a realistic picture of how key policy decisions were crafted. Highly recommended for those wanting an examination of America's role within the global community." Library Journal

973.93 United States--2001-

Caputo, Philip, 1941-

The **longest** road : overland in search of America from Key West to the Arctic Ocean / Philip Caputo. Henry Holt and Company, 2013. 352 p. **973.93**

1. National characteristics, American. 2. Automobile travel 3. Voyages and travels 4. United States -- Description and travel. 5. United States -- Social life and customs -- 21st century. 6. United States -- Social conditions -- 21st century.

ISBN 9780805094466

LC 2012050451

What really unites (and divides) the large and diverse populations of the United States? With his wife and two dogs in a truck pulling an Airstream trailer, author Philip Caputo poses this question to the people he meets on an epic, all-American road trip beginning at the southernmost point of the continental U.S. (Key West, FL) and ending at the northernmost point reachable by road: Deadhorse, Alaska on the Arctic Ocean. Caputo's smart (but never stuffy) wit brings to light the pithy, enlightening, and inspiring "home truths" of everyday Americans from the road.

Gill, A. A., 1954-

To America with love / A. A. Gill. Simon & Schuster, 2013. 272 p. **973.93**

1. Gill, A. A., 1954- Travel 2. Voyages and travels 3. United States -- Description and travel 4. United States -- Social life and customs

ISBN 9781416596219

LC bl2013031371

Originally published in Great Britain in 2012 by Weidenfeld & Nicolson under title: The Golden door.

Presents a tribute to America that traces the history and logic of the nation's habits while sharing illuminating anecdotes reflecting the nation's diverse culture as experienced by everyday people.

Tolentino, Jia

★**Trick** mirror : reflections on self-delusion / Jia Tolentino. Random House, 2019. 256 p. **973.93**

1. Social networks. 2. Internet. 3. Identity (Psychology) 4. Self-deception. 5. United States -- Civilization -- 21st century. 6. Essays.

ISBN 9780525510543

LC 2019000446

Presents nine original essays examining the fractures at the center of culture today, offering insights into the conflicts, contradictions, incentives, and changes related to the rise of toxic social networking.

"Tolentino brings a preternaturally aware millennial sensibility and exceptional literary skills to her keenly inquisitive and complexly involving essays." Booklist.

973.931 Administration of George W. Bush, 2001-2009

Eichenwald, Kurt, 1961-

500 days : secrets and lies in the terror wars / Kurt Eichenwald. Touchstone, c2012. 640 p. **973.931**

1. September 11 Terrorist Attacks, 2001. 2. War on Terrorism, 2001-2009. 3. Terrorism -- Prevention. 4. World politics -- 21st century.

ISBN 9781451669381

LC 2012001214

Presents an account of the first five hundred days after September 11 that reveals previously undisclosed information about the terror wars, warrantless wiretapping, and the anthrax attacks.

Farmer, John J.

The **ground** truth : the untold story of America under attack on 9/11 / John Farmer. Riverhead Books, 2009. 384 p. **973.931**

1. September 11 Terrorist Attacks, 2001. 2. Terrorism -- United States. 3. National security. 4. Bureaucracy -- United States -- History 5. United States -- History -- 21st century.

ISBN 9781594488948

LC 2009023297

A senior counsel to the 9/11 Commission draws on recordings, transcripts, and recently declassified records to reveal aspects of the attacks that have not been previously disclosed, arguing that the day's events were predictable and that the nation is still at risk.

Graff, Garrett M., 1981-

★The **only** plane in the sky : an oral history of 9/11 / Garrett M. Graff. Avid Reader Press, 2019. 512 p. **973.931**

1. September 11 Terrorist Attacks, 2001 2. Witnesses 3. Tragedy 4. First responders 5. New York City 6. Washington, D.C. 7. United

States -- History -- 21st century 8. Oral histories
ISBN 9781501182204

LC bl2019021009

A panoramic oral history of the September 11 attacks draws on hundreds of interviews with government officials, first responders, survivors, friends and family members to recount events from the perspectives of firsthand witnesses.

"This excellent oral history provides a much-needed perspective of the events and aftermath." Library Journal

Jacobson, Sidney

The **9-11** report : a graphic adaptation / Sid Jacobson ; illustrated by Ernie Colon ; with a foreword by Thomas H. Kean and Lee H. Hamilton. Hill and Wang, 2006. x, 117 p. : **973.931**

1. World Trade Center, New York City. 2. Qaida (Organization) 3. September 11 Terrorist Attacks, 2001 4. Hijacking of aircraft -- United States 5. War on Terrorism, 2001-2009 6. Terrorism 7. Comics and Graphic novels
ISBN 9780809057382

LC 2006924343

"Based on the final report of the National Commission on Terrorist Attacks upon the United States"--Cover.

A graphic novel of the report of the 9/11 Commission reveals the Commission's findings regarding the terrorist attacks on the United States and its recommendations concerning what the United States government needs to do in its wake.

"The book aims to make . . . [The 9/11 Commission Report] more accessable to all readers and draw in young adults. . . . This graphic adaptation is an important and necessary part of any collection" Library Journal.

Mayer, Jane

The **dark** side : the inside story of how the War on Terror turned into a war on American ideals / Jane Mayer. Doubleday, 2008. 392 p. : **973.931**

1. Abu Ghraib Prison. 2. Antiterrorist policy -- United States. 3. Torture -- Political aspects. 4. National security -- United States. 5. Terrorists -- Arab countries 6. United States -- Politics and government -- 21st century.
ISBN 9780385526395
ALA Notable Book, 2009.
J. Anthony Lukas Book Prize, 2009.
Robert F. Kennedy Book Award, 2009.
National Book Award for Nonfiction finalist, 2008
National Book Critics Circle Award for Nonfiction finalist, 2008.

Examines how the U.S. made self-destructive decisions in pursuit of terrorism in the wake of 9/11 and reveals how these actions violated the Constitution, hampered efforts to bring down Al Qaeda, and damaged the nation's moral and political standing in the world.

"This is a brilliantly researched and deeply unsettling book." New York Times Book Review.

National Commission on Terrorist Attacks upon the United States

★The **9/11** Commission report : final report of the National Commission on Terrorist Attacks upon the United States / National Commission on Terrorist Attacks upon the United States. Norton, 2004. xviii, 567 p. : **973.931**

1. Qaida (Organization) 2. September 11 Terrorist Attacks, 2001. 3. Terrorism -- United States -- Prevention. 4. Intelligence service -- United States -- Evaluation. 5. National security -- United States. 6. United States -- Politics and government -- 2001-2009
ISBN 9780393326710

LC 2004057564

"Authorized edition."
ALA Notable Book, 2005.
National Book Award for Nonfiction finalist, 2004

"This book reads like a Shakespearean drama. . . . This multi-author document produces an absolutely compelling narrative intelligence, one with clarity, a sense of shared mission and an overriding desire to do something about the situation." Publishers Weekly.

Woodward, Bob, 1943-

State of denial / Bob Woodward. Simon & Schuster, 2006. xiv, 560 p., 16 p. of plates : **973.931**

1. Bush, George W. (George Walker), 1946- 2. Military policy -- Decision-making. 3. National security -- United States -- Decision making. 4. Iraq War, 2003-2011 5. Antiterrorist policy -- United States. 6. United States -- Military policy. 7. United States -- Officials and employees. 8. United States -- Politics and government -- 2001-2009
ISBN 0743272234

LC 2006285190

Sequel to: Plan of attack.

A secret Pentagon assessment sent to the White House in May 2006 forecasted a more violent 2007 in Iraq, contradicting the repeated optimistic statements of President Bush. This book examines how the Bush administration avoided telling the truth about Iraq to the public, to Congress, and often to themselves. In this detailed inside story of a war-torn White House, Woodward answers the core questions: What happened after the invasion of Iraq? Why? How does Bush make decisions and manage a war that he chose to define his presidency? And is there an achievable plan for victory?--From publisher description.

"If journalism is the first page of history, then Woodward's opus will be required reading for any would-be historians of the time." Publishers Weekly.

Wright, Lawrence, 1947-

★The **looming** tower : Al-Qaeda and the road to 9/11 / Lawrence Wright. Knopf, 2006. 469 p., 16 p. of plates : **973.931**

1. Qaida (Organization) 2. September 11 Terrorist Attacks, 2001. 3. Terrorism -- History -- 20th century. 4. Militants. 5. Antiterrorist policy -- United States. 6. Books to TV
ISBN 037541486X

LC 2006041032

This title was adapted into a 10-episiode TV miniseries of the same name airing on Hulu. This miniseries stars Alec Baldwin, Jeff Daniels, Tahar Rahim, and Peter Sarsgaard.
Pulitzer Prize for General Nonfiction, 2007.
J. Anthony Lukas Book Prize, 2007.
Lionel Gelber Prize (Canada), 2007.
National Book Award for Nonfiction finalist, 2006

"This book is not just a detailed, heart-stopping account of the events leading up to 9/11, written with style and verve, and carried along by villains and heroes that only a crime novelist could dream up. It's an education, too . a thoughtful examination of the world that produced the men who brought us 9/11, and of their progeny who bedevil us today." New York Times Book Review.

Zuckoff, Mitchell

★**Fall** and rise : the story of 9/11 / Mitchell Zuckoff. HarperCollins 2019. 592 p. **973.931**

1. September 11 Terrorist Attacks, 2001. 2. Terrorism -- United States. 3. United Airlines Flight 93 Hijacking Incident, 2001. 4.

Terrorism.
ISBN 9780062275646

LC bl2019008366

Weaves together the events in New York, at the Pentagon, and in Shanksville, Pennsylvania to create a complete narrative of the terrorist attacks of September 11, 2001, offering stories of the people most affected by the attacks and their immediate aftermath.

"Though difficult to read, this emotional compilation will find a place with other 9/11 histories for its thorough recounting of the human cost of political violence." Library Journal.

973.932 Administration of Barack Obama, 2009-2017

Balz, Daniel J.

The **battle** for America, 2008 : the extraordinary election of 2008 / Dan Balz and Haynes Johnson. Viking, c2009. 432 p. **973.932**

1. Obama, Barack 2. McCain, John, 1936-2018 3. Presidential candidates -- 2008. 4. Presidential election, 2008 5. Political campaigns -- United States -- History -- 21st century. 6. Elections -- United States -- History -- 21st century. 7. United States -- Politics and government -- 2001-2009
ISBN 9780670021116

LC 2009017129

"A James H. Silberman book."

In an account of an election during a most critical time, two political journalists cover the whole saga, from the earliest stages of the nominees' campaigns through a thorough analysis of what actually happened at the polls and why.

"Although we all know how things turned out, the authors know how to work a cliffhanger, and, as they effectively demonstrate, things could have turned out differently at any number of turns. Essential for watchers of politics and a model for similar electoral analyses in the future." Kirkus.

Mayer, Jane

★**Dark** money : the hidden history of the billionaires behind the rise of the radical right / Jane Mayer. Doubleday, 2016 xii, 449 p. ; **973.932**

1. Koch, David H., 1940- 2. Koch, Charles G. (Charles de Ganahl), 1935- 3. Conservatism -- United States. 4. Political culture -- United States. 5. Radicalism -- United States. 6. United States -- Politics and government -- 2009-2017
ISBN 9780385535595

LC bl2016000369

National Book Critics Circle Award for Nonfiction finalist, 2016

An investigation into the growing radical right reveals a network of wealthy people with extreme Libertarian views, led by the Koch brothers, that has been systematically influencing and controlling academic institutions, the courts, and the United States government.

Souza, Pete

Obama : an intimate portrait / Pete Souza ; foreword by Barack Obama. Little, Brown and Company, 2017. 349 p. : **973.932**

1. Obama, Barack. 2. Presidents -- United States 3. United States -- History -- 21st century.
ISBN 9780316512589

LC bl2017044934

A visual biography of Barack Obama's historic presidency, captured in unprecedented detail by his White House photographer, includes images documenting the most consequential hours of the Obama administration as well as the 44th President's encounters with world leaders, cultural figures and family members. (This book was listed in a previous issue of Forecast.)

"In addition to being a collection of masterfully crafted images, the volume is a time capsule, capturing an era in pictures--one still fresh in collective memory." Publishers Weekly.

Taibbi, Matt

Griftopia : bubble machines, vampire squids, and the long con that broke America / Matt Taibbi. Random House Inc, 2010. 288 p. **973.932**

1. Financial crises. 2. Financial institutions. 3. Business and politics. 4. Political corruption.
ISBN 9780385529952

LC 2010015067

Examines American financial, political, and media power and argues that the dramatic series of events that led to the financial crisis also resulted in a complete shift of power to the self-interested elite.

"Taibbi's glib prose is punctuated with just enough irreverence and wit to allow him to appeal to more casual readers while providing sufficient detail to satisfy those looking for a serious discussion of the high-level manipulation of the economy. Recommended for anyone interested in understanding the economy and how it got that way." Library Journal.

973.932092 United States--2009-2017--biography

Chait, Jonathan

Audacity : how Barack Obama defied his critics and transformed America / Jonathan Chait. Custom House, 2017 256 p. **973.932092**

1. Obama, Barack 2. Political leadership 3. Presidents 4. International relations 5. United States -- Politics and government 6. United States -- Foreign relations
ISBN 9780062426970

LC 2016038527

An analysis of Barack Obama's considerable accomplishments in the face of critics from both parties explains why the author believes he will be considered one of history's greatest leaders on major policy fronts ranging from economics and the environment to health care and civil rights.

Souza, Pete

Shade : a tale of two presidents / Pete Souza. Little, Brown and Company, 2018. 235 p. : **973.932092**

1. Obama, Barack Pictorial works. 2. Obama, Barack Political and social views. 3. Trump, Donald, 1946- Quotations. 4. Trump, Donald, 1946- Political and social views. 5. Political leadership -- United States 6. Presidents -- United States
ISBN 9780316421829

LC 2018946890

The former official White House photographer compares the most recent two administrations via photos of Barack Obama side-by-side with tweets, headlines and quotes from the Trump administration.

973.933 Administration of Donald Trump, 2017-

Gessen, Masha

Surviving autocracy / Masha Gessen. Riverhead Books, 2020.

xvi, 270 p. **973.933**

1. Trump, Donald, 1946- 2. Presidential election, 2016 3. Democracy -- United States 4. Leadership 5. Political culture -- United States 6. United States -- Politics and government -- 2017-
ISBN 9780593188934

LC 2020003180

An analysis of the destruction the Trump administration has waged on our institutions, the cultural norms we hoped would save us, and our very sense of identity. This incisive book provides an indispensable overview of the calamitous trajectory of the past few years. Gessen not only highlights the corrosion of the media, the judiciary, and the cultural norms we hoped would save us but also tells us the story of how a short few years have changed us, from a people who saw ourselves as a nation of immigrants to a populace haggling over a border wall, heirs to a degraded sense of truth, meaning, and possibility.

"Many writers have chronicled the Trump administration's missteps and crimes, but few as concisely as Gessen, and her book belongs on the shelf alongside Timothy Snyder's On Tyranny and Amy Siskind's The List as a record of how far we have fallen." Kirkus

Hoffman, Carl, 1960-

Liar's circus : a strange and terrifying journey into the upside-down world of Trump's MAGA rallies / Carl Hoffman. Custom House, 2020. xii, 249 p. **973.933**

1. Trump, Donald, 1946- 2. Personality and politics 3. Political culture -- United States. 4. Identity (Psychology) -- Political aspects 5. Social psychology -- United States. 6. United States -- Politics and government -- 2017-
ISBN 9780063009769

LC 2020017022

Fear and Loathing on the Campaign Trail meets a work of daring and immersive contemporary anthropology: Carl Hoffman, who has written about the most dangerous and remote corners of the world, journeys deep inside President Trump's rallies, seeking to understand the strange and powerful tribe that forms the president's base.

"A valuable portrait of authoritarianism in action and its more-than-willing adherents." Kirkus

Johnston, David Cay, 1948-

It's even worse than you think : what the Trump administration is doing to America / David Cay Johnston. Simon & Schuster, 2018. 320 p. **973.933**

1. Trump, Donald, 1946- 2. Political culture -- United States 3. Presidents 4. United States -- Politics and government -- 2017-
ISBN 9781501174162

LC bl2017046348

Examines the Trump administration's policies in its first one hundred days to reveal how its policies are affecting the daily lives of Americans and how the actions of federal government agencies have been quietly approved by the administration without drawing attention from the media.

"Thoroughly depressing--but urgent, necessary reading, at least for those who aren't true believers in the Trumpite cause." Kirkus.

Nance, Malcolm W.

The **plot** to betray America : how team Trump embraced our enemies, compromised our security, and how we can fix it / Malcolm Nance. Hachette Books, 2019. ix, 358 p. ; **973.933**

1. Trump, Donald, 1946- 2. Putin, Vladimir Vladimirovich, 1952- 3. Political corruption -- United States. 4. Democracy 5. Treason 6. Hacking 7. United States -- Politics and government -- 2017- 8. Russia -- Foreign relations United States 9. United States -- Foreign relations Russia
ISBN 9780316535762

LC bl2019027708

The counterterrorism analyst, whistleblower and best-selling author of The Plot to Hack America presents a searing investigation into the American officials who he believes have been complicit in the Trump-Russia conspiracy

Rohde, David, 1967-

In deep : the FBI, the CIA, and the truth about America's "Deep State" / David Rohde. W.W. Norton & Company, 2020. 352 p. **973.933**

1. FBI 2. CIA 3. Presidents -- United States 4. Politicians -- United States 5. Secrecy in government 6. Government conspiracies 7. United States -- Politics and government
ISBN 9781324003540

LC bl2020007688

A revelatory investigation into the alleged "deep state" that draws on dozens of interviews with career spymasters, covert CIA operatives and FBI agents to determine if they are working in America's democratic best interests.

"Pulitzer Prize-winner Rohde (Beyond War) delivers an illuminating history of the often tense relationship between U.S. presidents and the career civil servants who enact--or, by some accounts, thwart--their policies. . . . Political junkies and generalists alike will relish this deeply informed account." Publishers Weekly

Sharpton, Al

Rise up : confronting a country at the crossroads / Reverend Al Sharpton ; foreword by Michael Eric Dyson. Hanover Square Press, 2020. 304 p. **973.933**

1. Sharpton, Al 2. African American political activists 3. Baptists -- Clergy 4. African American politicians 5. Progressivism (United States politics) 6. United States -- Politics and government
ISBN 9781335966629

LC bl2020018644

A rousing call to action for today's turbulent political moment, drawing on lessons learned from Reverend Sharpton's unique experience as a politician, television and radio host, and civil rights leader. In Rise Up, Sharpton revisits the highlights of the Obama administration, the 2016 election and Trump's subsequent hold on the GOP, and draws on his decades-long experience with other key players in politics and activism, including Shirley Chisholm, Hillary Clinton, Dr. Martin Luther King Jr. and more.

"The outspoken civil rights leader sees a nation in peril. Baptist minister, former presidential candidate, and founder of the National Action Network, Sharpton mounts an impassioned call for activism." Kirkus

Smith, Mychal Denzel, 1986-

Stakes is high : life after the American dream / Mychal Denzel Smith. Bold Type Books, 2020. 208 p. **973.933**

1. Equality -- United States 2. American dream 3. Patriotism 4. Social justice 5. United States -- Social conditions 6. United States -- Politics and government 7. Essays
ISBN 9781568588735

LC 2020001915

Growth only happens when we confront our deceptions and our own complicity in them. In Stakes Is High, Smith exposes the contradictions at the heart of American life - between patriotism and justice, between freedom and inequality, incarceration, police violence. In a series of incisive essays, Smith holds us to account individually and as a nation. He examines his own shortcomings, grapples with the anxiety of feeling stuck, and looks in new directions for the tools to build a just America.

"This is not always easy book, but it is one that sees the United States for what it is. A searing combination of memoir and commentary that makes for essential reading." Library Journal

Toobin, Jeffrey

★**True** crimes and misdemeanors : the investigation of Donald Trump / Jeffrey Toobin. Doubleday, 2020. 432 p. **973.933**

1. Trump, Donald, 1946- Impeachment 2. Presidents -- United States -- Impeachment 3. Impeachments -- United States 4. Misconduct in office 5. Political corruption 6. United States -- Politics and government -- 2017-

ISBN 9780385536738

LC 2020017608

The CNN chief legal analyst and author presents a behind-the-scenes account of the Mueller investigation to explain how in spite of associate convictions and an impeachment, Donald Trump has survived to run for reelection.

"CNN legal analyst Toobin (American Heiress) delivers a vivid and doggedly reported rundown of special counsel Robert Mueller's investigation into Russian interference in the 2016 election and the impeachment of Donald Trump over the Ukraine affair. . . . The result is a definitive behind-the-scenes portrait of what these investigations accomplished, and why they didn't bring Trump down." Publishers Weekly

973.933092 United States--2017---biography

Carpenter, Amanda B.

Gaslighting America : why we love it when Trump lies to us / Amanda Carpenter. Harper, [2018] 224 p. **973.933092**

1. Trump, Donald, 1946- Language. 2. Deception 3. Communication in politics 4. Mass media -- Political aspects 5. Social media 6. United States -- Politics and government -- 2017-

ISBN 9780062748003

LC 2017047193

A CNN political commentator and former senior staffer to Senator Ted Cruz breaks down the formula behind Trump's fake narratives and conspiracy theories, which seem to enthrall his supporters and play his victims and detractors.

Frum, David, 1960-

Trumpocracy : the corruption of the American republic / David Frum. Harper, an imprint of HarperCollinsPublishers, 2018. 240 p. **973.933092**

1. Trump, Donald, 1946- 2. Authoritarianism. 3. Political culture. 4. United States -- Politics and government -- 2017-

ISBN 9780062796738

LC bl2017046357

Builds on the author's March 2017 "How to Build an Autocracy" column in "The Atlantic" to explain how Donald Trump has undermined America's most important institutions as part of a carefully crafted plan to institute authoritarianism.

"Highly recommended for anyone who cares about the republic and its future." Library Journal.

Hennessey, Susan, 1985-

Unmaking the presidency : Donald Trump's war on the world's most powerful office / Susan Hennessey and Benjamin Wittes. Farrar, Straus and Giroux, 2020. viii, 418 p. **973.933092**

1. Trump, Donald, 1946- 2. Presidents -- United States 3. Political leadership 4. Executive power -- United States 5. Presidents -- United States -- History 6. United States -- Politics and government

ISBN 9780374175368

LC 2019028858

The extraordinary authority of the U.S. presidency has no parallel in the democratic world. Today that authority resides in the hands of one man, Donald J. Trump. But rarely if ever has the nature of a president clashed more profoundly with the nature of the office. Unmaking the Presidency tells the story of the confrontation between a person and the institution he almost wholly embodies. By setting Trump in the light of history, Hennessey and Wittes provide a crucial and durable account of a presidency like no other.

"Serious political readers and presidential studies scholars will derive much from this cogent appraisal." Library Journal.

Karl, Jonathan, 1968-

Front row at the Trump show / Jonathan Karl. Dutton, [2020] xxvi, 340 p., 16 unnumbered p. of plates ; **973.933092**

1. Trump, Donald, 1946- 2. Karl, Jonathan, 1968- 3. Political journalists 4. Presidential election, 2016 5. Presidents -- Press coverage -- United States -- History -- 21st century. 6. Press and politics 7. United States -- Politics and government -- 2017-

ISBN 9781524745622

LC 2019046582

The ABC News chief White House correspondent and host of the Powerhouse Politics podcast reveals how Donald Trump wages a public campaign against the truth and orchestrates deliberate attacks against people and organizations that disagree with him

"No one's mind will be changed by Karl's book, but it's a valuable report from the scene of an ongoing train wreck." Kirkus

Kurtz, Howard, 1953-

Media madness : Donald Trump, the press, and the war over the truth / Howard Kurtz. Regnery Publishing, 2018 256 p. **973.933092**

1. Trump, Donald, 1946- 2. Mass media bias. 3. Political culture 4. Journalists 5. Mass media -- Political aspects 6. United States -- Politics and government -- 2017-

ISBN 9781621577263

LC 2018286477

A former media critic for The Washington Post argues that Donald Trump's criticism is, at least partially, justified and explains how he believes most journalists have gone from neutral truth-tellers to pure pundits.

"Alongside Kurtz's lively, entertaining narrative of vitriolic news cycles is a penetrating critique of a liberal news establishment that, he contends, has abandoned objectivity for a hysterical partisanship that galvanizes Trumps support among the conservative voters it disdains." Publishers Weekly.

Petri, Alexandra

Nothing is wrong and here is why : essays / Alexandra Petri. W. W. Norton & Company, 2020. 240 p. **973.933092**

1. Trump, Donald, 1946- 2. Presidents -- United States 3. Political corruption 4. Current events 5. Foreign interference in elections 6. United States -- Politics and government -- 2017- 7. Essays 8. Satire

ISBN 9781324006459

LC 2020007461

Adapted from the author's viral Post columns, a riotous essay collection on the normalized horrors of today's world outlines logical and reassuring reasons behind the seemingly inexplicable changes in American politics and culture throughout the past four years.

"Acidic and spot-on, Petri's work captures the surreal quality of Trump's tenure as perhaps no other book has." Publishers Weekly

Wilson, Rick, (Political consultant)

Running against the devil : a plot to save America from Trump -- and Democrats from themselves / Rick Wilson. Crown Forum, 2020. 272 p. **973.933092**

1. Trump, Donald 1946- 2. Presidential election, 2020 3. Political campaigns 4. Strategy 5. Democrats. 6. United States -- Politics and government -- 2009-2017 7. United States -- Politics and government -- 2017-

ISBN 9780593137581

LC 2019042005

The veteran Republican strategist and best-selling author of Everything Trump Touches Dies outlines the mistakes made by both parties during throughout the 2016 presidential campaign, identifying the challenges that must be overcome to prevent Trump's reelection.

"A caustically funny, outraged, and deadly serious analysis." Kirkus.

Wolff, Michael, 1953-

★**Fire** and fury : inside the Trump White House / Michael Wolff. Henry Holt & Co 2018 321 p. **973.933092**

1. Trump, Donald, 1946- 2. White House, Washington, D.C. Staff. 3. Presidents -- United States 4. Political leadership 5. Political culture 6. Political intrigue 7. Washington, D.C.

ISBN 9781250158062

LC 2017050324

"While Wolff's use of anonymous 'deep background' sources may give readers reservations about the accuracy of every detail, this explosive account will undoubtedly remain a topic of conversation for the near future." Publishers Weekly.

Woodward, Bob, 1943-

★**Fear** : Trump in the White House / Bob Woodward. Simon & Schuster, 2018 xxii, 420 p., 16 unnumbered p. of plates : **973.933092**

1. Trump, Donald, 1946- 2. Political culture. 3. Presidents 4. Political leadership. 5. Political intrigue. 6. Washington, D.C. 7. United States -- Politics and government -- 2017-

ISBN 9781501175510

LC 2019462344

Draws on interviews with firsthand sources, meeting notes, personal diaries, and other documents to depict life in the Trump White House, focusing on Trump's decision-making process for foreign and domestic policies.

"The title of the book comes from an interview in which the president states that true power comes through fear. Well, this look inside the Trump White House is pretty scary." Booklist.

974 Specific states of United States

Vowell, Sarah, 1969-

The **wordy** shipmates / Sarah Vowell. Riverhead Books, 2008. 272 p. **974**

1. Puritans -- New England -- History -- 17th century. 2. Religion and politics -- New England -- History -- 17th century. 3. Religion. 4. Christianity. 5. New England -- Politics and government -- To 1775.

ISBN 9781594489990

LC 2008030491

A cultural profile of Puritan life covers a wide range of topics, from their covenant communities and deep-rooted ideologies to their beliefs about church and state and their perspectives on other faiths, in an account that also evaluates their legacy.

"Focusing on the Puritans who settled in 1692 in the Massachusetts Bay Colony, Vowell laments their image as 'boring killjoys' when in fact they were 'fascinating killjoys.' A book dense with detail, insight, and humor." Booklist.

974.4 Massachusetts

Bradford, William, 1590-1657

Of Plymouth Plantation, 1620-1647 / William Bradford ; the complete text, with notes and an introduction by Samuel Eliot Morison. A.A. Knopf, 2001. 385 p. : **974.4**

1. Pilgrims (New England settlers) 2. Massachusetts -- History -- New Plymouth, 1620-1691.

ISBN 9780394438955

LC 2002514421

First ed. published in 1856 under title: History of Plymouth Plantation.

Includes index.

Bunker, Nick

★**Making** haste from Babylon : the Mayflower Pilgrims and their world : a new history / Nick Bunker. Alfred A. Knopf, 2010. 400 p. **974.4**

1. Mayflower (Ship) 2. Pilgrims (New England settlers) 3. Colonists. 4. Colonies. 5. Evangelicalism. 6. Massachusetts -- History -- New Plymouth, 1620-1691. 7. Plymouth, Massachusetts -- History -- Colonial period, 1600-1775.

ISBN 9780307266828

LC 2009038520

Explores the complexities of Pilgrim character from their radical sectarian beliefs to their entrepreneurial capabilities, drawing on previously untapped sources to offer insight into how they established a thriving New Plymouth settlement in spite of formidable circumstances.

Junger, Sebastian

★The **perfect** storm : a true story of men against the sea / Sebastian Junger. Norton, 1997. xii, 227 p. : **974.4**

1. Andrea Gail (Boat) 2. Shipwrecks -- North Atlantic Ocean. 3. Storms -- North Atlantic Ocean. 4. Natural disasters. 5. Halloween Nor'easter, 1991. 6. Northeastern States. 7. Atlantic Ocean.

ISBN 039304016X

LC 96042412

ALA Notable Book, 1998.

Presents a vivid account of a history-making storm that hit the New England coast in October 1991 and the lives it changed, weaving together the history of the fishing industry, the science of storms, and personal accounts.

"Junger's fine dramatic style is complemented by a wealth of details that flesh out the story: wave physics and water thermoclines; what it means if you see whitewater outside your porthole; where the terms mayday, ill-wind, and down East came from. Reading this gripping book is likely to make the would-be sailor feel both awed and a little frightened by nature's remorseless power." Kirkus.

Kidder, Tracy

Home town / Tracy Kidder. Random House, 1999. xiv, 349 p. **974.4**

1. Police -- Northampton, Massachusetts. 2. Small town life -- United States -- Case studies. 3. Small towns. 4. Northampton, Massachusetts. 5. Northampton, Massachusetts -- Social conditions.

6. Northampton, Massachusetts -- History.
ISBN 9780679455882

LC 99013614

Explores what life is really like in contemporary small-town America, focusing on the people of Northampton, Massachusetts, to assess how individuals in a community transform a place into a home.

A remarkably detailed, accomplished, and empathic portrait of a town, from its most basic workings to its most shameful failings, absurd prejudices, and heroic achievements. Kidder's acutely observed, crisply written, and utterly absorbing documentary proves that there is nothing on this spinning earth more amazing and full of grace than everyday life.

Manegold, Catherine S.

Ten Hills Farm : the forgotten history of slavery in the North / C.S. Manegold. Princeton University Press, 2010. 344 p. **974.4**

1. Slavery -- Massachusetts -- History. 2. Slave trade -- History 3. Slaves. 4. Race relations. 5. Massachusetts -- History. 6. Ten Hills Farm (Mass.) -- History.
ISBN 9780691131528

LC 2009030875

"Ten Hills Farm tells the powerful saga of five generations of slave owners in colonial New England. Settled in 1630 by John Winthrop, governor of the Massachusetts Bay Colony, Ten Hills Farm, a six-hundred-acre estate just north of Boston, passed from the Winthrops to the Ushers, to the Royalls--all prominent dynasties tied to the Native American and Atlantic slave trades. In this mesmerizing narrative, C. S. Manegold exposes how the fortunes of these families--and the fate of Ten Hills Farm--were bound to America's most tragic and tainted legacy. Manegold follows the compelling tale from the early seventeenth to the early twenty-first century, from New England, through the South, to the sprawling slave plantations of the Caribbean. John Winthrop, famous for envisioning his 'city on the hill' and lauded as a paragon of justice, owned slaves on that ground and passed the first law in North America condoning slavery. Each successive owner of Ten Hills Farm--from John Usher, who was born into money, to Isaac Royall, who began as a humble carpenter's son and made his fortune in Antigua--would depend upon slavery's profits until the 1780s, when Massachusetts abolished the practice. In time, the land became a city, its questionable past discreetly buried, until now. Challenging received ideas about America and the Atlantic world, Ten Hills Farm digs deep to bring the story of slavery in the North full circle--from concealment to recovery." -- from publisher's website.

Masur, Louis P.

The **soiling** of Old Glory : the story of a photograph that shocked America / Louis P. Masur. Bloomsbury Press, 2008. 240 p. **974.4**

1. Flags -- Desecration -- United States -- Pictorial works. 2. Protest movements -- Boston, Massachusetts -- History -- 20th century. 3. Busing (School integration) -- Boston, Massachusetts -- History -- 20th century. 4. African Americans -- Boston, Massachusetts -- Interviews. 5. Boston, Massachusetts -- Race relations -- History -- 20th century. 6. United States -- Race relations -- History -- 20th century.
ISBN 9781596913646

LC 2007031215

"On April 5, 1976, an antibusing rally in Boston grew violent when African American lawyer Ted Landsmark was attacked by some of the protesters. News photographer Stanley Forman captured the ruckus on film; one photo gained international attention and is the subject of this . . . study by Masur. . . . Masur writes descriptively about the photo while creating an ethnographic history of 1970s Boston, with diversions into the political and cultural uses of the American flag and the history of photojournalism in the United States. He also describes the aftermath of the photo's front-page publication. . . . A compelling story; highly recommended for all high school, public, and academic libraries." Library Journal.

Roberts, Randy, 1951-

War fever : Boston, baseball, and America in the shadow of the Great War / Randy Roberts and Johnny Smith. Basic Books, 2020. xix, 344 p. **974.4**

1. Muck, Karl 2. Ruth, Babe, 1895-1948 3. Whittlesey, Charles White, 1884-1921 4. United States. Army. Division, 77th -- History 5. World War I home front 6. World War I -- Social aspects 7. Xenophobia 8. Baseball players 9. Boston, Massachusetts -- History -- 20th century
ISBN 9781541672666

LC 2019045871

In the fall of 1918, a fever gripped Boston. The streets emptied as paranoia about the deadly Spanish flu spread. Newspapermen and vigilante investigators aggressively sought to discredit anyone who looked or sounded German. War Fever explores this delirious moment in American history through the stories of three men: Karl Muck, the German conductor of the Boston Symphony Orchestra, accused of being an enemy spy; Charles Whittlesey, a Harvard law graduate who became an unlikely hero in Europe; and the most famous baseball player of all time, Babe Ruth, poised to revolutionize the game he loved. Together, they offer a gripping narrative of America at war and American culture in upheaval.

"A compelling look at a tumultuous moment in U.S. history through the lives of three extraordinary individuals. Fans of 20th-century American culture as well as Boston and World War I history will rejoice." Library Journal

Silverman, David J., 1971-

★**This** land is their land : the Wampanoag Indians, Plymouth Colony, and the troubled history of Thanksgiving / David J. Silverman. Bloomsbury Publishing, 2019. 432 p. **974.4**

1. Rowlandson, Mary White, approximately 1635-1711. 2. Thanksgiving Day. 3. Wampanoag Indians. 4. Pilgrims (New England settlers) 5. Alliances 6. Plymouth, Massachusetts -- History -- Colonial period, 1600-1775. 7. United States -- History -- Colonial period, 1600-1775.
ISBN 9781632869241

LC 2019022966

Ahead of the 400th anniversary of the first Thanksgiving, a new look at the Plymouth colony's founding events, told for the first time with Wampanoag people at the heart of the story.

"Silverman's reconstruction of the world of the Wampanoag provides fascinating insights for both general readers and scholars into the early years of the colonization of Massachusetts, situating not only Thanksgiving within the nation's history but also the tragedy of King Philip's War." Library Journal.

Whittock, Martyn

Mayflower lives : Pilgrims in a new world and the early American experience / Martyn Whittock. Pegasus Books, 2019. 416 p. **974.4**

1. Bradford, William, 1590-1657 2. Standish, Myles, 1584?-1656 3. Howland, John, 1592?-1672. 4. Hopkins, Stephen, 1581-1644 5. Squanto 6. Mayflower (Ship) 7. Plimoth Plantation, Inc., Plymouth, Massachusetts. 8. Pilgrims (New England settlers) 9. Colonists. 10. Massachusetts -- History -- New Plymouth, 1620-1691. 11. Plymouth, Massachusetts -- History. 12. United States -- History --

Colonial period, 1600-1775.
ISBN 9781643131320

LC bl2019021741

A 400th anniversary tribute to the Mayflower voyage draws on the lives of 14 diverse individuals, from Myles Standish and Squanto to Mary Chilton and Stephen Hopkins, to illuminate the human realities of one of America's most seminal events.

"This accessible book, among several that have demythologized Mayflower history, will appeal to readers at all levels." Library Journal.

974.5 Rhode Island

Warren, James A.

God, war, and providence : the epic struggle of Roger Williams and the Narragansett Indians against the Puritans of New England / James A. Warren. Scribner, 2018. 352 p. **974.5**

1. Williams, Roger, 1604?-1683 2. Indians of North America -- Wars 3. Narragansett Indians 4. Colonists 5. Puritans 6. New England -- History -- Colonial period, 1600-1775
ISBN 9781501180415

LC bl2018100313

The tragic and fascinating history of the first epic struggle between white settlers and Native Americans in the early seventeenth century: a fresh look at the aggressive expansionist Puritans in New England and the determined Narragansett Indians, who refused to back down and accept English authority over people and their land.

974.7 New York

Alexiou, Alice Sparberg, 1951-

Devil's mile : the rich, gritty history of the Bowery / Alice Sparberg Alexiou. St. Martin's Press, 2018. 288 p. **974.7**

1. Streets 2. City life 3. Urban problems 4. Gentrification of cities 5. Bowery, New York City 6. New York City -- History
ISBN 9781250021380

LC 2018003989

The author of The Flatiron presents a cultural history of New York City's oldest street, contrasting the despairing conditions that rendered it the 20th century's "Mile of Hell" against the thriving hipster redevelopments of today.

"New York buffs, especially those nostalgic for a grittier time, will find this a learned pleasure." Kirkus.

Anbinder, Tyler

★**City** of dreams : the 400-year epic history of immigrant New York / Tyler Anbinder. Houghton Mifflin Harcourt, 2016 672 p. **974.7**

1. Immigration and emigration. 2. Immigrants 3. City life 4. New York City
ISBN 9780544104655

LC 2016286135

Mark Lynton History Prize, 2017.

A history of immigration in New York shares the poignant stories of individuals ranging from bodybuilder Charles Atlas to couture artist Oscar de la Renta to trace the essential role of foreign-born innovators and revolutionaries in the city's evolution.

Brenwall, Cynthia S

The **Central** Park : original designs for New York's greatest treasure / Cynthia S. Brenwall, New York City Municipal Archives ; foreword by Martin Filler. Abrams, 2019. 229 p. : **974.7**

1. Landscape architecture -- New York (State) -- New York 2. Central Park (New York, N.Y.) Streets 2. City life 3. Urban problems 4. Gentrification, N.Y.) -- History.
ISBN 9781419732324

LC bl2019029377

Brown, Phil,

In the Catskills : a century of Jewish experience in "the mountains" / edited by Phil Brown. Columbia University Press, 2002. xvi, 415 p. : **974.7**

1. Jewish Americans -- Catskill Mountains Region, New York State -- Social life and customs. 2. Jewish Americans -- Catskill Mountains Region, New York -- History 3. Catskill Mountains Region, New York -- Social life and customs 4. New York (State) -- Social life and customs.
ISBN 0231123604

LC 2001042319

"This is a great look at the history of Catskill culture for readers new to the material, but those looking for more depth will be disappointed." Publishers Weekly.

Burns, Cherie

The **great** hurricane--1938 / Cherie Burns. Atlantic Monthly Press, 2005. 238 p. : **974.7**

1. New England Hurricane, 1938. 2. Hurricanes -- New England -- History -- 20th century. 3. Natural disasters. 4. Hurricanes -- Long Island, New York -- History -- 20th century. 5. New England -- History -- 20th century. 6. Long Island, New York -- History -- 20th century.
ISBN 087113893X

LC 2005041211

Examines one of the worst natural disasters in the nation's history--the 1938 Hurricane that struck the coast of New England at 186 miles per hour causing devastation throughout the region--and the personal stories of survivors of the catastrophe.

Calhoun, Ada

St. Marks is dead : the many lives of America's hippest street / Ada Calhoun. W. W. Norton & Company, [2016] 304 p. **974.7**

1. Streets 2. Counterculture. 3. Neighborhoods. 4. Radicals. 5. Manhattan, New York City -- Social life and customs -- 20th century. 6. New York City -- Social life and customs -- 20th century.
ISBN 9780393240382

LC 2015028040

A vibrant narrative history of three hallowed Manhattan blocks--the epicenter of American cool.

"As Calhoun traces the neighborhood's evolution from wealthy and respectable to gritty and poverty-stricken and back again, she shows how one street can become a microcosm of Americas political and cultural history." Publishers Weekly.

Clark, Mary Marshall,

★**After** the fall : New Yorkers remember September 2001 and the years that followed / edited by Mary Marshall Clark ... [et al.]. New Press : 2011. xxiii, 263 p. ; **974.7**

1. September 11 Terrorist Attacks, 2001 -- Social aspects. 2. Life change events. 3. Essays.
ISBN 9781595586476

LC 2011012833

Collects accounts of the events and aftermath of the terrorist attacks of September 11, 2001.

"The Columbia Center for Oral History (CCOH) is committed to building repositories of living memory, and after 9/11 began to gather narratives from a variety of New York survivors and witnesses, eventually collecting over 600 histories. The skilled interviewers...are trained in oral history methods and richly summon forth from interviewees the repercussions of the attack on individuals, families, and communities. Those interviewed reflect a variety of perspectives, including both professional and unskilled workers in the Twin Towers, neighbors, first responders, and many of New York's immigrant groups, including Muslims." Library Journal.

Daughan, George C.

Revolution on the Hudson : New York City and the Hudson River Valley in the American War of Independence / George C. Daughan. W. W. Norton & Co., 2016. 432 p. **974.7**

1. American Revolution, 1775-1783 2. Revolutions -- United States 3. Hudson Valley. 4. United States -- History -- Revolution, 1775-1783 5. New York (State) -- History -- Revolution, 1775-1783.

ISBN 9780393245721

LC 2016007017

Traces the lesser-known story of the fight for the Hudson River Valley during the American Revolution, explaining the conflict's essential role in the outcome of the war and the political, military, economic and social strategies that influenced both sides.

"A stimulating look at the American Revolution by a diligent historian and talented writer." Kirkus.

Dwyer, Jim, 1957-

102 minutes : the unforgettable story of the fight to survive inside the Twin Towers / Jim Dwyer and Kevin Flynn. Times Books, 2011, c2005. xxiv, 353 p. **974.7**

1. World Trade Center, New York City. 2. September 11 Terrorist Attacks, 2001. 3. Victims of terrorism -- New York City. 4. Buildings -- Evacuation -- New York City. 5. Rescue work -- New York City. 6. New York City.

ISBN 9780805094213

LC 2006272620

Originally published: New York : Times Books, 2005.

Includes index.

National Book Award for Nonfiction finalist, 2005

"Dwyer and Flynn have given us a fitting tribute to the people caught up in one of the great dramas of our time. And for people still haunted by the events of that day, reading 102 Minutes provides a cathartic release." New York Times Book Review.

Friend, David, 1955-

Watching the world change : the stories behind the images of 9/11 / David Friend. Farrar, Straus and Giroux, 2006. xix, 435 p., 24 p. of plates : **974.7**

1. World Trade Center, New York City. 2. September 11 Terrorist Attacks, 2001. 3. September 11 Terrorist Attacks, 2001 -- Pictorial works. 4. Terrorism -- New York City. 5. Documentary photography.

ISBN 0374299331

LC 2005036158

Tells the stories behind the photographs of 9/11, discusses the controversy over whether the images are exploitative or redemptive, and shows how photographs help us witness, grieve, and understand the unimaginable.

"In this analysis of how images of 9/11 and the war on terror have altered our understanding of power, world politics, religion and identity... [the author] successfully merges reportage and analysis as he interprets the images of falling towers, panic in Manhattan streets and prisoners at Abu Ghraib that have been burned into our brains." Publishers Weekly.

Gage, Beverly

The **day** Wall Street exploded : a story of America in its first age of terror / Beverly Gage. Oxford University Press, 2009. viii, 400 p., 16 p. of plates : **974.7**

1. Terrorism -- New York City -- History. 2. Bombings -- New York City. 3. Bombing investigation -- New York City. 4. Wall Street, New York City -- History. 5. New York City -- History -- 20th century.

ISBN 9780195148244

LC 2008022074

Offers a factual account of the worst terrorist act in United States history up until 1920 when a cart packed with dynamite blew up on a corner near Wall Street, killing many, injuring hundreds, and putting in motion a four-year global manhunt to track down the perpetrators.

Gill, Jonathan

Harlem : the four hundred year history from Dutch village to capital of Black America / Jonathan Gill. Grove Press, 2011 448 p. **974.7**

1. African Americans -- New York City -- History -- 20th century. 2. Community life 3. African Americans -- History 4. Harlem, New York City. 5. New York City -- History.

ISBN 9780802119100

LC 2011283059

"Comprehensive and compassionate--an essential text of American history and culture." Kirkus.

Goodman, Matthew

The **Sun** and the moon : the remarkable true account of hoaxers, showmen, dueling journalists, and lunar man-bats in nineteenth-century New York / Matthew Goodman. Basic Books, c2008. ix, 350 p. : **974.7**

1. Day, Benjamin Henry, 1810-1889. 2. Sun (New York, N.Y. : 1833) 3. Science fraud. 4. Mass media hoaxes. 5. Newspapers -- New York City -- History. 6. Journalism -- Corrupt practices. 7. New York City -- History -- 19th century 8. Moon Miscellanea

ISBN 9780465002573

LC 2008023617

A study of a nineteenth-century journalistic hoax describes how a series of articles appearing in the "New York Sun" in 1835 purported to reveal lunar discoveries made by a noted British astronomer concerning life on the moon.

"The focus of this work concerns a series of 1835 New York Sun articles that convinced many of that newspaper's readers that the moon was inhabited. Goodman...gives the context of the time while also providing a look at the life of Richard Adams Locke, who wrote and published these stories." Library Journal.

Griswold, Mac K.

The **manor** : three centuries at a slave plantation on Long Island / Mac Griswold. Farrar, Straus and Giroux, 2013. 304 p. **974.7**

1. Slavery -- Long Island, New York -- History. 2. Plantations -- Long Island, New York -- History. 3. Plantation life -- Long Island, New York -- History. 4. Excavations (Archaeology) -- Long Island, New York. 5. Sylvester Manor Plantation Site (N.Y.) 6. Shelter Island, New York -- History. 7. Long Island, New York -- History.

ISBN 9780374266295

LC 2013005463

A compelling history of a Long Island plantation, spanning three centuries and eleven generations, reveals the extensive but little-known story of Northern slavery.

Khan, Yasmin Sabina

Enlightening the world : the creation of the Statue of Liberty / Yasmin Sabina Khan. Cornell University Press, 2010. 240 p. **974.7**

1. Bartholdi, Frederic Auguste, 1834-1904. 2. Monuments -- United States. 3. Statues. 4. Sculptors. 5. Symbolism in architecture. 6. New York City -- Buildings -- History. 7. United States -- Foreign relations France. 8. France -- Foreign relations United States.
ISBN 9780801448515

LC 2009035711

"This is a lucid account connecting France's widespread grief over Abraham Lincoln's 1865 assassination with that country's own struggles to establish a lasting democracy. Khan shows how Edouard-Reen Lefebvre de Laboulaye, a legal scholar and celebrant of French-American friendship, led others to design and construct what was officially called Liberty Enlightening the World. . . . An important book for general audiences." Publishers Weekly.

Langewiesche, William

American ground : unbuilding the World Trade Center / William Langewiesche. North Point Press, 2002. 205 p. **974.7**

1. World Trade Center, New York City. 2. September 11 Terrorist Attacks, 2001. 3. Wrecking. 4. Disaster relief -- United States. 5. Skyscrapers -- Manhattan, New York City -- Design and construction. 6. New York City.
ISBN 0865475822

LC 2002075153

National Book Critics Circle Award for Nonfiction finalist, 2002.

American Ground is the story--until now untold--of the people who responded to the destruction of the World Trade Center on September 11, 2001. Within days, William Langewiesche made his way into the innermost recesses of the collapse. By virtue of the integrity and excellence of his previous work, he quickly secured unique, unrestricted, around-the-clock access to the site, the rescue workers and laborers there, and the meetings of city officials, engineers, construction companies, and consultants.

"This is a genuinely monumental story, told without melodrama, an intimate depiction of ordinary Americans reacting to grand-scale tragedy at their best--and sometimes their worst." Publishers Weekly.

LeBlanc, Adrian Nicole

Random family : love, drugs, trouble, and coming of age in the Bronx / Adrian Nicole LeBlanc. Scribner, 2003. 408 p. **974.7**

1. Urban poor people -- New York City. 2. Teenagers -- New York City. 3. Teenagers -- Drug use. 4. Welfare recipients 5. Bronx, New York City -- Social conditions 6. New York City -- Social conditions.
ISBN 0684863871

LC 2002026673

ALA Notable Book, 2004.

National Book Critics Circle Award for Nonfiction finalist, 2003.

"A painstaking feat of reporting and empathy that resulted from 10 years of hanging out with a hard-pressed, loosely defined family in the Bronx." New York Times Book Review.

Lepore, Jill, 1966-

New York burning : liberty, slavery, and conspiracy in eighteenth-century Manhattan / Jill Lepore. Alfred A. Knopf, 2005. xx, 323 p. : **974.7**

1. Slave resistance and revolts -- New York City. 2. Fires -- New York City. 3. African Americans -- New York City -- History -- 18th century. 4. New York City -- History. 5. New York City -- Race relations. 6. New York City -- History -- Colonial period, 1600-1775.
ISBN 1400040299

LC 2004057625

ALA Notable Book, 2006.

Pulitzer Prize for History finalist, 2006.

The untold story of the little-known Manhattan slave rebellion of 1741 and the white hysteria that resulted in thirty black men hanged or burned at the stake, over a hundred black men and women thrown into the dungeon beneath City Hall, and many more shipped into bone-crushing slavery on Caribbean plantations. Was this a brutal and audacious rebellion prevented just in time or a far more horrible and unjust version of the Salem witch trials?

"In this first-rate social history, Lepore not only adroitly examines the case's travesty, questioning whether such a conspiracy ever existed, but also draws a splendid portrait of the struggles, prejudices and triumphs of a very young New York City in which fully one in five inhabitants was enslaved." Publishers Weekly.

MacColl, Gail, 1954-

To marry an English Lord / Gail MacColl and Carol McD. Wallace. Workman Pub., c1989. x, 403 p. : **974.7**

1. Upper class -- New York City -- History -- 19th century. 2. Nobility -- England -- History -- 19th century. 3. Marriage -- England -- History -- 19th century. 4. Wealth. 5. New York City -- Social life and customs. 6. England -- Social life and customs -- 19th century. 7. United States -- Social life and customs -- 1865-1918. 8. Great Britain -- Social life and customs -- Victoria, 1837-1901.
ISBN 0894809393

LC 85040529

Tells the stories of wealthy nineteenth-century American heiresses who married British nobleman.

McCurry, Steve

New York September 11 / Magnum photographers, Steve McCurry ... [et al.] ; additional photographs by Evan Fairbanks, Adam Wiseman, Ann-Marie Conlon ; introduction by David Halberstam. PowerHouse Books, 2001. 140 p. : **974.7**

1. World Trade Center (New York, N.Y.) Pictorial works. 2. September 11 Terrorist Attacks, 2001 -- Pictorial works. 3. Terrorism -- New York (State) -- New York -- Pictorial works. 4. Disasters -- New York (State) -- New York -- Pictorial works. 5. Rescue work -- New York (State) -- New York -- Pictorial works.
ISBN 9781576871300

LC 2001052330

Offers a photographic chronicle of the destruction of the World Trade Center in the terrorist attacks of September 11, 2001, and includes classic photographs of the Twin Towers taken over the twenty-five years of their existence.

Miller, Donald L., 1944-

★**Supreme** city : how Jazz Age Manhattan gave birth to Modern America / Donald L. Miller. Simon & Schuster, 2014. 672 p. **974.7**

1. Ambition 2. City life 3. Manhattan, New York City -- Social life and customs -- 20th century. 4. New York City -- Social life and customs -- 20th century. 5. Manhattan, New York City -- History -- 20th century. 6. New York City -- History -- 20th century. 7. Manhattan, New York City -- Social conditions -- 20th century. 8.

New York City -- Social conditions -- 20th century.
ISBN 9781416550198
LC 2013020154

Miller surveys the astonishing cast of characters who helped turn Manhattan into the world capital of commerce, communication and entertainment.

"Conveying the panoramic sweep of the era with wit, illuminating details, humor, and style, Miller illustrates how Midtown Manhattan became the nation's communications, entertainment, and commercial epicenter." Publishers Weekly.

Reid, David, 1946-

The **brazen** age : New York City and the American empire : politics, art, and bohemia / David Reid. Pantheon Books, 2016 384 p. **974.7**

1. Bohemianism -- New York City. 2. Manhattan, New York City -- History -- 20th century. 3. New York City -- History -- 1898-1951. 4. Greenwich Village, New York City -- History -- 20th century.
ISBN 9780394572376
LC 2015024900

Chronicles the vibrant and thriving history, culture and politics of mid-1900s Manhattan and the effect that Thomas Dewey, Henry Wallace, Harry Truman and James Forrestal had on focusing the attention of the world on the city.

"Reid delivers his opinion in a score of unrelated but brilliant chapters on iconic New York individuals (Berenice Abbott, Weegee), groups (returning soldiers, homosexuals), politics (the 1948 elections, leftist magazines), and bohemia (Greenwich village again and again). A historical tour de force." Kirkus.

Schneider, Paul, 1962-

The **Adirondacks** : a history of America's first wilderness / Paul Schneider. H. Holt and Co., 1997. xiii, 368 p. : **974.7**

1. Nature conservation. 2. Adirondack Mountains, New York -- History. 3. Adirondack Park, New York -- History 4. Adirondack Mountains region -- Social life and customs.
ISBN 0805034900
LC 96039844

"A John Macrae book."

A history of the Adirondack Mountains of New York describes the sometimes checkered history of the region, the creation of America's largest natural park, and its role in promoting the American romance with the wilderness as a place of solace and recreation.

"The author presents a history of New York State's Adirondack region. He relates here the life and lore of these scenic mountains and lakes (Whiteface, Mt. Marcy, Fulton Chain Lakes) from the region's earliest inhabitants (Haudenosaunce/Iroquois) through the advent of Henry Hudson (1609), the Revolutionary War, abolitionists (John Brown), 19th-century homesteaders, Hudson River School artists, tuberculosis patients to Melville Dewey's Lake Placid Club, the Adirondack Mountain Club, and the present environmental conservation efforts." Library Journal.

Smith, Dennis, 1940-

A **decade** of hope : stories of grief and endurance from 9/11 families and friends / Dennis Smith. Viking Adult, 2011. 256 p. **974.7**

1. September 11 Terrorist Attacks, 2001 2. Terrorism -- United States 3. Terrorism victims' families 4. Healing -- Psychological aspects
ISBN 9780670022939
LC 2011023325

Draws on a series of interviews with the heroes and families of those most affected by 9/11 to offer a ten-year look at the tragedy's lasting effects.

"The author, a former firefighter, collects 25 moving personal narratives in this significant addition to the literature of September 11. Featuring notable figures such as NYPD Commissioner Ray Kelly and Congressman Peter King alongside rescue workers and victims' family members and loved ones, Smith's interviewees offer their experiences of that tragic day, illustrating how the pain and losses are still acutely felt. With restraint and pathos, Smith's book provides powerful tribute and testimony." Publishers Weekly.

Report from ground zero : the story of the rescue efforts at the World Trade Center / Dennis Smith. Viking, 2002. vii, 366 p., 16 p. of plates : **974.7**

1. World Trade Center, New York City. 2. September 11 Terrorist Attacks, 2001. 3. Fire departments -- New York City. 4. Rescue work -- New York City. 5. Firefighters -- New York City. 6. Multiple perspectives 7. First person narratives.
ISBN 067003116X
LC 2002019840

In a tribute to the fallen heroes of September 11, 2001, a former firefighter provides an eyewitness record of events at Ground Zero and the extraordinary efforts of police, fire, and emergency medical teams.

Stanton, Brandon

Humans of New York / Brandon Stanton. St. Martin's Press, 2013. 304 p. **974.7**

1. Street photography 2. City life 3. Artistic photography 4. Portrait photography 5. New York City Pictorial works.
ISBN 9781250038821

A photographic census of New York City, inspired by the blog of the same name, showcases four hundred photos and stories that capture the outsized personalities of New York and pay tribute to the human side of a great city.

"There's the Yugoslavian janitor who studied for 12 years to earn his classics degree; Banana George, the worlds oldest barefoot water-skier who's now in a wheelchair; Muslims in prayer; and shots of adorable kids, crazy fashionistas, and young lovers, all paired with a comment from Stanton or from the subjects themselves. There's no judgment, just observation and in many cases reverence, making for an inspiring reading and visual experience." Publishers Weekly.

Humans of New York: stories / Brandon Stanton. St. Martin's Press, 2015. 432 p.. **974.7**

1. Photography. 2. City dwellers. 3. Humans. 4. Biography. 5. New York City Pictorial works. 6. Interviews.
ISBN 9781250058904
LC 2015025568

A follow-up to "Humans of New York" shares the frank and intimate human stories of some of the individuals depicted in the author's acclaimed photographic census.

Strausbaugh, John

The **Village** : 400 years of beats and bohemians, radicals and rogues, a history of Greenwich Village / John Strausbaugh. HarperCollins, 2013. xiv, 624 p. : ill. ; **974.7**

1. City life -- History. 2. Popular culture -- History. 3. City dwellers -- New York City. 4. Counterculture -- History. 5. Greenwich Village, New York City -- History. 6. United States -- Popular culture

-- History.
ISBN 9780062078193

LC 2013431528

From its origins as a rural frontier of New Amsterdam in the 1600s to its current status as an affluent bedroom community and tourist magnet, this engaging narrative reveals how Greenwich Village become the pinnacle of culture, politics, and social movements in America and around the world.

Taylor, Alan, 1955-

The **divided** ground : Indians, settlers and the northern borderland of the American Revolution / Alan Taylor. Alfred A. Knopf, 2006. 542 p. : **974.7**

1. Brant, Joseph, Mohawk chief, 1742-1807. 2. Iroquois Indians -- History -- 18th century. 3. Property rights. 4. Land tenure. 5. Government relations with indigenous peoples 6. United States -- History -- Revolution, 1775-1783 -- Native American participation 7. Northern boundary of the United States -- History -- 18th century. 8. New York (State) -- History -- 19th century 9. New York (State) -- History -- 18th century. 10. Ontario -- History -- 18th century. 11. Northern boundary of the United States -- Interethnic relations. 12. New York (State) -- Interethnic relations. 13. Ontario -- Interethnic relations.
ISBN 0679454713

LC 2005043582

The changing relationship of Joseph Brant, a young Mohawk, and Samuel Kirkland, the son of a colonial clergyman is set against the role of the Native American peoples in North America during the American Revolution.

"Taylor's exquisite writing and thorough research in both Canadian and US archives and manuscript collections make this a major work." Choice.

Von Drehle, Dave

★**Triangle** : the fire that changed America / David Von Drehle. Atlantic Monthly Press, 2003. 340 p. : **974.7**

1. Triangle Shirtwaist Company, Inc., New York City Fire, 1911. 2. Fires -- New York City. 3. Factories -- Safety measures. 4. Labor laws and legislation. 5. New York City -- History -- 1898-1951. 6. New York City
ISBN 9780871138743

LC 2003041835

ALA Notable Book, 2004.

Describes the 1911 fire that destroyed the Triangle Shirtwaist factory in New York's Greenwich Village, the deaths of 146 workers in the fire, and its implications for twentieth-century politics and labor relations.

"Von Drehle's engrossing account, which emphasizes the humanity of the victims and the theme of social justice, brings on of the pivotal and most shocking episodes of American labor history to life." Publishers Weekly.

Wallace, Mike, 1942-

Greater Gotham : a history of New York City from 1898 to 1919 / Mike Wallace. Oxford University Press, 2017. 1200 p. **974.7**

1. City life 2. New York City -- History. 3. Wall Street, New York City. 4. Broadway, New York City
ISBN 9780195116359

LC 2017005224

In Greater Gotham Mike Wallace, co-author of GOTHAM, picks up the story of New York at the critical juncture of 1898 and carries it forward during the period when it became not just the country's greatest urban center but a megapolis on an international scale, and with global reach. Between consolidation and the end of World War One, New York was transformed and transforming, mirroring the juggernauting dynamism of the country at large--and largely fueling it. The names of two its streets encapsulate the degree of the city's preeminence: Wall Street and Broadway.

"Wallace shapes this sprawl into a coherent, engrossing narrative thats nicely balanced between historical sweep and colorful detail. The result sets a standard for urban history, capturing both New Yorks particularities and its protean dynamism." Publishers Weekly.

974.8 Pennsylvania

Longman, Jere

Among the heroes : United Flight 93 and the passengers and crew who fought back / Jere Longman. Harper Collins, 2002. xiv, 288 p. : **974.8**

1. September 11 Terrorist Attacks, 2001. 2. Hijacking of aircraft -- United States. 3. Victims of terrorism -- United States. 4. Airplane accident victims.
ISBN 0060099089

LC 2002068530

"This book gives us an incredibly detailed and personal tale of that horrific episode." Booklist.

Miller, Randall M.,

Pennsylvania : a history of the Commonwealth / edited by Randall M. Miller and William Pencak. Pennsylvania State University Press ; c2002. xxxi, 654 p. : **974.8**

1. Pennsylvania -- History. 2. Pennsylvania -- Civilization.
ISBN 0271022140

LC 2002005457

"A keystone book."

"More than half of this book is an unusual and inspired hybrid of history and nine other disciplines from geography to literature. The editors profess to discover the sources of Pennsylvania's greatness and significance but also expose its faults and declining significance in the 20th century. They succeed at both." Choice.

Roker, Al, 1954-

Ruthless tide : the tragic epic of the Johnstown flood / Al Roker. William Morrow, 2018. vi, 305 pages, 8 unnumbered pages of plates : **974.8**

1. Natural disasters 2. Floods 3. Dams 4. Pennsylvania -- History -- 19th century
ISBN 9780062445513

LC bl2018045324

Presents a gripping narrative history of the 1889 Johnstown Flood to chronicle key events, the damage that rendered the flood one of America's worst disasters and the pivotal contributions of key period figures, from dam engineer John Parke to American Red Cross founder Clara Barton.

"Roker is especially adept at focusing on key individuals--residents, politicians, movers and shakers, rescue workers--and letting their stories represent the myriads of others. An exciting, tragic story seasoned with sensitive social analysis and criticism." Kirkus.

975 Southeastern United States (South Atlantic states)

Blount, Roy

Long time leaving : dispatches from up South / Roy Blount, Jr.

Alfred A. Knopf, 2007. xii, 383 p. ; **975**

1. Blount, Roy 2. Group identity -- Southern States. 3. North and south. 4. National characteristics, American. 5. Group identity -- Northeastern States. 6. Southern States -- Civilization. 7. Northeastern States -- Civilization. 8. Essays.

ISBN 0307266184

LC 2007006799

"Hard-working humorist Roy Blount Jr. lives in the North but he's from the South, a delicious tension that has always informed and shaped his work. In this new collection, he directs his acerbic wit and finely-tuned insight toward the persistent and colorful differences between the two. His essays treat every conceivable topic on which North and South misunderstand each other, from music to sports, eating, education, politics, child-rearing, religion, race, and language ("remember when there was lots of discussion of 'ebonics'?"). In this eminently quotable collection, Blount does justice to the charming, funny, infuriating facets of Southern tradition and their equally odd Northern counterpoints".-- from publisher's web-site.

"This delightful collection is not only fun and funny but insightful as well." Library Journal.

Bragg, Rick

Where I come from : stories from the deep South / Rick Bragg. Alfred A. Knopf, 2020. 256 p. **975**

1. Bragg, Rick 2. Identity (Psychology) 3. Men -- Southern states 4. Southern States 5. Southern States -- Social life and customs 6. Essays

ISBN 9780593317785

LC 2020005021

From his love of Tupperware ("My Affair with Tupperware") to the decline of country music, from the legacy of Harper Lee to the metamorphosis of the pick-up truck, the best way to kill fire ants, the unbridled excess of Fat Tuesday, and why any self-respecting Southern man worth his salt should carry a good knife, Where I Come From is an ode to the stories and the history of the deep south, written with tenderness, wit, and deep affection--a book that will be treasured by fans old and new.

"Bragg's longtime fans will enjoy the piquant one-liners they've come to expect, but new readers looking for meaningful insight into the South should look to his previous works." Publishers Weekly

Genovese, Eugene D., 1930-2012

★**Roll**, Jordan, roll : the world the slaves made / Eugene D. Genovese. Vintage Books, 1976, c1974. xxii, 823 p. ; **975**

1. Slaves -- United States -- Social conditions. 2. United States -- History -- 19th century

ISBN 9780394716527

LC 75026906

A definitive account of slave life in the Old South and the role of the slaves in fashioning a Black national culture.

"The most profound, learned, and detailed analysis of slavery to appear since World War II. It covers an incredible range of topics and offers fresh insights on nearly every page. . . . Genovese's great gift is his ability to penetrate the minds of both slaves and masters, revealing not only how they viewed themselves and each other, but also how their contradictory perceptions interacted." New York Times

Hahn, Steven, 1951-

A **nation** under our feet : black political struggles in the rural South, from slavery to the great migration / Steven Hahn. Belknap Press of Harvard University Press, 2003. 610 p., 16 p. of plates : **975**

1. African Americans -- Political activity -- Southern States -- 19th century 2. African Americans -- Southern States -- Politics and government -- 20th century. 3. African Americans -- Social conditions -- To 1964. 4. Slavery -- Southern States -- History -- 1775-1865. 5. Southern States -- Politics and government -- 1865-1950. 6. Southern States -- Race relations. 7. Southern States -- Rural conditions.

ISBN 0674011694

LC 2003045326

Pulitzer Prize for History, 2004.

Emphasizing the role of kinship, labor, and networks in the African-American community, the author retraces six generations of black struggles since the end of the Civil War, revealing a "nation" under construction throughout this entire period.

Lemann, Nicholas

Redemption : the last battle of the Civil War / Nicholas Lemann. Farrar, Straus and Giroux, 2006. xi, 257 p. **975**

1. Ames, Adelbert, 1835-1933. 2. Segregation -- United States -- History. 3. African Americans -- Civil rights -- Southern States -- History. 4. Violence against African-Americans -- History -- 19th century. 5. Reconstruction (United States history) -- Southern States 6. Southern States -- Race relations -- History -- 19th century. 7. Southern States -- History -- 1865-1950. 8. Southern States -- Politics and government -- 1865-1950.

ISBN 0374248559

LC 2006000091

A study of the campaign of organized racial violence that followed the Civil War describes efforts on the part of white Southern Democrats to prevent the rise of black political power.

"This book offers a vigorous, necessary reminder of how racist reaction bred an American terrorism that suppressed black political activity and crushed Reconstruction in the South." New York Times Book Review.

Luess, Valerie Fraser,

Southern Living 50 years : a celebration of people, places, and culture / introduction by Sid Evans ; by the editors of Southern Living with Valerie Fraser Luesse. Time Inc. Books, 2015 320 p. : **975**

1. Southern living History. 2. Southern living. 3. Recipes 4. Southern States -- Social life and customs. 5. Cookbooks

ISBN 9780848744144

LC bl2015040876

Includes index.

A tribute to Southern culture, published to mark the magazine's fiftieth anniversary, combines evocative photography with regionally inspired essays, tours of representative buildings and gardens, and forty all-time favorite recipes.

Theroux, Paul

Deep South : four seasons on back roads / Paul Theroux. Houghton Mifflin Harcourt, 2015. 384 p. **975**

1. Theroux, Paul Travel Southern States. 2. Scenic byways -- Southern States. 3. Seasons -- Southern States. 4. Voyages and travels 5. Southern States -- Description and travel. 6. Southern States -- Social life and customs. 7. Southern States -- Social conditions.

ISBN 9780544323520

LC 2015006631

For over 50 years, acclaimed novelist and travel writer Paul Theroux has traveled all over the world. But in his latest journey, he turned his eyes to a region of his home country he wanted to know better. Traveling to various Southern states (including Alabama, Arkansas, Mississippi, Louisiana, Georgia, and South Carolina) on a variety of road trips, Theroux bypassed the big cities and gleaming towns. Instead, he focused his keen eye on smaller, rural towns, where he visited with people in churches, restaurants, corner stores, farms, and gun shows, and explored the culture and paradoxes of the region.

"Therouxs books always appear on the best-seller list, and his latest may prove to be his most popular book yet." Booklist.

975.004 Southeastern United States -- Ethnic and national groups

Sedgwick, John, 1954-

Blood moon : an American epic of war and splendor in the Cherokee Nation / John Sedgwick. Simon and Schuster, 2018. 416 p. **975.004**

1. Ridge, Major, approximately 1771-1839. 2. Ross, John, 1790-1866. 3. Cherokee Indians. 4. Trail of Tears, 1838-1839. 5. Government relations with indigenous peoples 6. Forced relocations -- History.

ISBN 9781501128714

LC 2017041911

A history of the nineteenth-century rivalry between Cherokee chiefs The Ridge and John Ross contends that though initially allies, they and their followers became divided on key tenets of peace talks and devastated the Cherokee Nation with division, war,and forced migrations.

975.2 Maryland

Giorgione, Michael

Inside Camp David : the private world of the presidential retreat / Michael Giorgione. Little, Brown and Company, 2017 320 p. **975.2**

1. Presidents 2. Retreat centers. 3. Camp David, Maryland.

ISBN 9780316509619

LC 2017936280

Celebrates the 75th anniversary of the president's peaceful country retreat with an insider's account of how the leaders of the free world spent their time there, from horseback riding to jumping on a trampoline with their children and hosting diplomatic summits.

975.3 District of Columbia (Washington)

Bordewich, Fergus M.

Washington : making the American capital / Fergus M. Bordewich. Harper Collins Publishers, 2008. 320 p. **975.3**

1. Urban planning -- Washington, D.C. -- History -- 18th century. 2. Local government -- Planning. 3. Metropolitan government -- Planning. 4. Municipal government -- Planning. 5. Washington, D.C -- History -- 18th century. 6. Washington, D.C -- Politics and government -- To 1878.

ISBN 0060842385

LC 2007052053

A history of the nation's capital city reveals the role of slavery in its construction, the political and financial obstacles that were faced by the founding fathers, and the back-room deals and shifting alliances that were to shape the region's influence.

"The author explains how the city's site was chosen and how political scheming, personal conflicts, and greed almost doomed the project of designing and constructing a capital city from scratch. Two themes are woven throughout his narrative: the important but often overlooked role played by slaves and former freed slaves and the constant North-South debate at the root of the bitter dispute over the capital's locale." Library Journal.

Brower, Kate Andersen

The **residence** : inside the private world of the White House / Kate Andersen Brower. Harper, 2015 320 p. **975.3**

1. White House, Washington, D.C. 2. Presidents -- United States 3. Presidents' spouses 4. Children of presidents 5. Household employees 6. United States -- History

ISBN 9780062305190

LC 2014040404

An intimate account of White House life from the perspectives of the service staffs of the Kennedys through the Obamas details their friendships, marriages, everyday activities and elaborate state dinners.

"Fans of Downton Abbey will find this look into the secret world of the White House fascinating. History buffs who would like to learn more about the personal lives of the presidents and their families will definitely enjoy all the intriguing vignettes." Library Journal.

Euchner, Charles C.

Nobody turn me around : a people's history of the 1963 march on Washington / Charles Euchner. Beacon Press, c2010. 256 p. **975.3**

1. March on Washington for Jobs and Freedom, 1963 2. Civil Rights Movement. 3. Civil rights demonstrations. 4. African Americans -- Civil rights -- History -- 20th century. 5. United States -- History -- 20th century.

ISBN 9780807000595

LC 2009046943

Draws on the oral histories of more than one hundred participants to provide a behind-the-scenes look at the historic 1963 March on Washington that culminated in Martin Luther King Jr.'s "I Have a Dream" speech.

Gordon, John Steele

Washington's monument : and the fascinating history of the obelisk / John Steele Gordon. Bloomsbury USA, 2016. 288 p. **975.3**

1. Washington, George, 1732-1799 Monuments, etc. 2. Washington Monument (Washington, D.C.) -- History. 3. Monuments 4. Obelisks 5. Antiquities 6. Washington, D.C. -- Buildings

ISBN 9781620406502

LC 2015036462

Conceived soon after the American Revolution ended, the great monument to George Washington was not finally completed until almost a century later; the great obelisk was finished in 1884, and remains the tallest stone structure in the world at 555 feet.The story behind its construction is a largely untold and intriguing piece of American history, which acclaimed historian John Steele Gordon relates with verve, connecting it to the colorful saga of the ancient obelisks of Egypt.

"Filled with fascinating facts and interesting anecdotes, this is a book that will delight history and architecture buffs and enrich both past and planned visits to Washington, D.C., and its sights." Booklist.

Graham, Katharine, 1917-2001

Katharine Graham's Washington / selected by Katharine Graham. Vintage Books, 2003, c2002. xii, 813 p. : **975.3**

1. Washington, D.C. -- Social life and customs. 2. Washington, D.C. -- History -- 20th century. 3. United States -- Politics and government

-- 20th century. 4. Essays.
ISBN 1400030595
LC BL2003016744

Originally published: New York : Knopf, 2002.

Presents a collection of more than one hundred articles, essays, and excerpts about Washington, D.C., from 1917 to 2001, including selections by Will Rogers, David Brinkley, Harry Truman, Art Buchwald, P.J. O'Rourke, and Russell Baker.

"The late newspaper publisher's posthumous legacy is a delightful and insightful anthology of writings on the city that formed so much of her personality and her professional life. She draws from her personal collection of writings by a range of writers, many of them personal friends." Booklist.

Gugliotta, Guy

Freedom's cap : the United States Capitol and the coming of the Civil War / Guy Gugliotta. Hill and Wang, 2012. 512 p. **975.3**

1. United States Capitol (Washington, D.C.) -- History. 2. Buildings. 3. Architecture. 4. Washington, D.C. -- Buildings. 5. United States -- History -- 1849-1877.
ISBN 9780809046812
LC 2011025750

Traces lesser-known events in the history of the modern U.S. Capitol building before and during the American Civil War while revealing the significant contributions of Confederacy president Jefferson Davis, Union quartermaster general Montgomery Meigs and architect Thomas U. Walter.

Kendrick, Kathleen M

Official guide to the Smithsonian National Museum of African American History & Culture / National Museum of African American History and Culture ; writer: Kathleen M. Kendrick. Smithsonian Books, 2017 175 p. : **975.3**

1. National Museum of African American -- History and Culture (U.S.) Guidebooks. 2. TRAVEL / United States / South / South Atlantic (DC, DE, FL, GA, MD, NC, SC, VA, WV)
ISBN 9781588345936
LC 2016038059

"A colorful guide introducing the newest Smithsonian museum, the National Museum of African American History and Culture".-- Provided by publisher.

Lusane, Clarence, 1953-

The **Black** history of the White House / Clarence Lusane. City Lights Books, c2011. 200 p. **975.3**

1. White House (Washington, D.C.) -- History. 2. African Americans -- Washington, D.C. -- History 3. Presidents -- United States -- Staff -- History. 4. Slavery -- Washington, D.C. -- History. 5. African Americans -- Washington, D.C. -- Social conditions. 6. United States -- Race relations -- Political aspects.
ISBN 9780872865327
LC 2010036925

Presents a history of the White House from an African American perspective, with information on such topics as slavery, the abolitionist movement, and African-American White House staff.

Smith, Michael S. (Michael Sean), 1964-

Designing history : the extraordinary art & style of the Obama White House / Michael S. Smith with Margaret Russell ; foreword by Michelle Obama. Rizzoli International Publications, 2020 303 p. : **975.3**

1. Obama, Barack 2. Obama, Michelle, 1964- 3. White House, Washington, D.C. -- History 4. Presidents -- United States -- Homes and haunts
ISBN 9780847864799

Created for design enthusiasts, political aficionados, and students of Americana, Designing History documents Michael Smith's extraordinary collaboration with President Barack Obama and First Lady Michelle Obama. Not since Jacqueline Kennedy's iconic work on the White House has a designer of Michael Smith's stature been commissioned to bring a new design spirit to the mansion. Through extensive photography, behind-the-scenes stories, and rich archival material, the book places the Obama White House within the context of the building's storied past and its evolution over the past two centuries. The book beautifully documents the process of updating the country's most symbolic residence, revealing how Smith's collaboration on the decoration, showcasing of artworks, and style of entertaining reflected the youthful spirit of the First Family and their vision of a more progressive, inclusive American society. Provided by publisher

Snow, Peter, 1938-

When Britain burned the White House : the 1814 invasion of Washington / Peter Snow. Thomas Dunne Books, St. Martin's Press, 2014. 320 p. **975.3**

1. War of 1812. 2. Military history. 3. Military campaigns 4. Washington (D.C.) -- History -- Capture by the British, 1814. 5. United States -- History -- War of 1812 6. Maryland -- History -- War of 1812
ISBN 9781250048288
LC 2014010743

A 200th anniversary tribute chronicles the burning of a fledgling America's capital through the anthem-inspiring Battle of Fort McHenry, documenting the near-escape of the First Family while sharing eyewitness perspectives by forefront figures on both sides of the conflict.

"Although the author ultimately tells a riveting true story, he offers little new about the campaign, which is disappointing. Summing Up: Recommended. Public libraries/general collections." Choice.

975.5 Virginia

Ayers, Edward L., 1953-

★The **thin** light of freedom : the Civil War and emancipation in the heart of America / Edward L. Ayers. W. W. Norton & Company, 2017. xxiii, 576 p. : **975.5**

1. War and society 2. Postwar life 3. Civilians in war 4. War -- Psychological aspects 5. United States -- History -- Civil War, 1861-1865. 6. United States -- History -- 1865-1877.
ISBN 9780393292633
LC 2017021653

A landmark Civil War history told from a fresh, deeply researched ground-level perspective.

"Ayers focuses on the thoughts, fears, and hopes of normal people struggling to stay alive and make sense of the murderous events taking place around them. The result is a superb, readable work of history." Publishers Weekly.

Horn, James P. P.

Land as God made it : Jamestown and the birth of America / James P. P. Horn. Perseus Books Group, 2006. 337 p. **975.5**

1. Smith, John, 1580-1631. 2. Powhatan Indians -- Virginia --

Relations with European-Americans. 3. Indians of North America -- Relations with European-Americans. 4. European Americans -- Relations with Indians -- Jamestown, Virginia 5. United States -- History -- Colonial period, 1600-1775. 6. Jamestown, Virginia -- History.
ISBN 0465030955

LC bl2010021668

Chronicles the experiences of the first English settlers that colonized the future United States, and explains how Jamestown set the precedent for North American slavery, Native American conflicts, and representative government.

"Possessing Jamestown's inherent drama, this is a solid rendition of the saga." Booklist.

Kelly, Joseph, 1962-

Marooned : Jamestown, shipwreck, and the epic story of the first Americans / Joseph Kelly. Bloomsbury Publishing, 2018. 400 p. **975.5**

1. Hopkins, Stephen, 1581-1644 2. Virginia Company of London 3. Mayflower (Ship) 4. Frontier and pioneer life 5. Colonists 6. Colonies 7. Democracy 8. Jamestown, Virginia -- History -- Colonial period, 1600-1775 9. Virginia -- History -- Colonial period, 1600-1775
ISBN 9781632867773

LC 2018003587

A revisionist account of the history of Jamestown challenges popular beliefs to reveal how the Jamestown colonists were essentially marooned by the British caste system and were arguably responsible for America's founding beliefs about government by the people.

"Discovering seeds of democracy in Massachusetts' zealots or Virginia's autocratic patricians has never been easy, but Kelly's lively, heavily researched, frequently gruesome account gives a slight nod to Jamestown as the 'better place to look for the genesis of American ideals.'" Kirkus.

Lingan, John

Homeplace : a Southern town, a country legend, and the last days of a mountaintop honky-tonk / John Lingan. Houghton Mifflin Harcourt, 2018. 288 p. **975.5**

1. Mountain people 2. Country music 3. Small towns 4. Poor families 5. Winchester, Virginia 6. Virginia
ISBN 9780544932531

LC 2017050068

"In the tradition of Joe Bageant's Deer Hunting With Jesus and J. D. Vance's Hillbilly Elegy, an intimate account of social change, country music, and a vanishing way of life as a Shenandoah town collides with the twenty-first century".-- Provided by publisher.

"Readers interested in Patsy Cline and the Shenandoah Valley will appreciate the history and in-depth details of various localities." Library Journal.

McElya, Micki, 1972-

The **politics** of mourning : death and honor in Arlington National Cemetery / Micki McElya. Harvard University Press, 2016. 395 p. **975.5**

1. Arlington National Cemetery (Arlington, Va.) 2. Military history. 3. Memorials. 4. Cemeteries. 5. Funerals 6. Arlington, Virginia -- Buildings, structures, etc. 7. United States -- History, Military Miscellanea.
ISBN 9780674737242

LC 2016008043

Pulitzer Prize for General Nonfiction finalist, 2017.

Shares the history of Arlington National Cemetery and discusses its place in American culture and self-conception.

"McElya diligently unravels the American desire to honor the dead, preserve history and custom, and devise symbols of what the cemetery should represent in the minds of its citizens." Library Journal.

Poole, Robert M.

Section 60 : Arlington National Cemetery : where war comes home / Robert M. Poole. Bloomsbury, [2014] 304 p. **975.5**

1. Arlington National Cemetery (Arlington, Va.) 2. Families of military personnel. 3. Memorial Day. 4. Afghan War, 2001- -- Casualties. 5. Iraq War, 2003-2011 -- Casualties. 6. Arlington, Virginia.
ISBN 9781620402931

LC 2014017528

The acclaimed author of On Hallowed Ground, using Section 60 of the Arlington National Cemetery as a window into the latest wars, recounts stories of courage and sacrifice by fallen heroes and how they are honored and remembered by those they left behind.

"Nonfiction enthusiasts will appreciate this work; it will especially satisfy those with an interest in the human condition. It is a book that will linger in the reader's mind." Library Journal.

Price, David A. (David Andrew), 1961-

★**Love** and hate in Jamestown : John Smith, Pocahontas, and the heart of a new nation / David A. Price. Knopf, 2003. 305 p. : **975.5**

1. Smith, John, 1580-1631. 2. Pocahontas, d. 1617. 3. Indians of North America -- Relations with European-Americans. 4. Indians of North America -- Relations with Europeans -- History 5. First contact of indigenous peoples with Europeans. 6. Powhatan Indians -- Jamestown, Virginia -- History -- 17th century. 7. Jamestown, Virginia -- History -- Colonial period, 1600-1775. 8. Virginia -- History -- Colonial period, 1600-1775. 9. United States -- History -- Colonial period, 1600-1775.
ISBN 0375415416

LC 2002043437

"For those general readers who wish to move beyond the myths and obtain a better understanding of them and the early years of the colony, this book will be an enjoyable and valuable tool." Booklist.

Taylor, Alan, 1955-

★The **internal** enemy : slavery and war in Virginia, 1772-1832 / Alan Taylor. W. W. Norton & Company, 2013. 624 p. **975.5**

1. Slavery. 2. Slaves. 3. Freed slaves. 4. African American soldiers. 5. Virginia. 6. United States -- History -- War of 1812.
ISBN 9780393073713

LC 2013009643

Pulitzer Prize for History, 2014.

National Book Award for Nonfiction finalist, 2013

Drawn from new sources, a Pulitzer Prize-winning historian presents a gripping narrative that recreates the events that inspired hundreds of slaves to pressure British admirals into becoming liberators by using their intimate knowledge of the countryside to transform the war.

"This is a well-written and scrupulously researched examination of an important aspect of the struggle against American slavery." Booklist.

975.6 North Carolina

Horn, James P. P.

A **kingdom** strange : the brief and tragic history of the lost colony of Roanoke / James Horn. Basic Books, 2010. 304 p. **975.6**

1. Colonies. 2. Colonists. 3. Indians of North America. 4. Interethnic marriage. 5. Roanoke Island, North Carolina -- History 6. Roanoke Colony -- History.

ISBN 9780465004850

LC 2010000563

"The author creates an engaging, you-are-there feel to the narrative, with rich descriptions of European politics, colonists' daily struggles and the vagaries of relations between Native American tribes. A satisfying recounting of some of the earliest American history." Kirkus.

Kiernan, Denise

The **last** castle : the epic story of love, loss, and American royalty in the nation's largest home / Denise Kiernan. Touchstone, 2017. 384 p. **975.6**

1. Vanderbilt family Homes and haunts 2. Biltmore Estate (Asheville, N.C.) 3. Mansions 4. Rich people 5. Architecture 6. Buildings 7. Asheville, North Carlolina 8. North Carolina -- History -- 19th century 9. United States -- History -- 19th century

ISBN 9781476794044

LC 2017015229

Documents the story of the Gilded Age mansion Biltmore, tracing George Vanderbilt's construction of his spectacular European-style estate with the help of two famed architects and the efforts of his bride, Edith Stuyvesant Dresser, to become its mistress and protector in the face of changing fortunes and times.

"Kiernan (The Girls of Atomic City) presents an intriguing history of the largest private U.S. residence: the Biltmore House." Library Journal.

Lawler, Andrew

The **secret** token : myth, obsession, and the search for the lost colony of Roanoke / Andrew Lawler. Doubleday, [2018] 352 p. **975.6**

1. Dare, Virginia, 1587- 2. Colonialism 3. Colonies 4. Colonists 5. Archaeology and history 6. Roanoke Colony -- History 7. Roanoke Island, North Carolina -- History -- 16th century 8. North Carolina -- History -- Colonial period, 1600-1775

ISBN 9780385542012

LC 2017045395

Documents the events surrounding the unsolved 1587 disappearance of the Roanoke Island colony, tracing major investigations from the past 400 years as well as the author's own findings about how the Lost Colony is tied to today's America.

"This detailed historical inquiry will powerfully intrigue early American history buffs." Booklist.

975.7 South Carolina

Ball, Edward, 1958-

Slaves in the family / Edward Ball. Farrar, Straus and Giroux, 1998. 504 p. : **975.7**

1. Ball family. 2. Interracial families. 3. Slaves -- South Carolina 4. Slaveholders 5. Plantation life -- Charleston, South Carolina -- History. 6. Charleston, South Carolina -- Race relations. 7. Charleston, South Carolina -- History.

ISBN 9780374265823

LC 97034640

National Book Award for Nonfiction, 1998.

Explores the slave-holding dynasty of Elias Ball, a South Carolina plantation owner, the history of slave uprisings, and the memories of the descendants of those slaves.

"For nearly a hundred and seventy years before the Civil War, members of the Ball family owned a string of plantations worked by slaves along South Carolina's Cooper River. After the war, the author's ancestors lost or sold their land and scattered to make new lives, but he wondered what happened to the slaves. This book, a brilliant blend of archival research and oral history, tells what he found." The New Yorker.

Harris, J. William, 1946-

The **hanging** of Thomas Jeremiah : a free Black man's encounter with liberty / J. William Harris. Yale University Press, 2009. 223 p. : **975.7**

1. Jeremiah, Thomas, d. 1775 Trials, litigation, etc. 2. Laurens, Henry, 1724-1792. 3. Campbell, William, 1745-1781. 4. Free African Americans -- Social conditions. 5. Freedom -- History -- 18th century 6. Slavery -- History -- 18th century. 7. Charleston, South Carolina -- Race relations -- 18th century. 8. Charleston, South Carolina -- Social conditions -- 18th century. 9. United States -- History -- 19th century

ISBN 9780300152142

Describes the trial and execution of Thomas Jeremiah, a freeman falsely accused by whites of supporting insurrection among slaves, and reflects upon the political and social implications of his trial in pre-Revolutionary America.

Kytle, Ethan J.

Denmark Vesey's garden : slavery and memory in the cradle of Confederacy / Ethan J. Kytle and Blain Roberts. The New Press, [2018] 384 p. **975.7**

1. Vesey, Denmark, approximately 1767-1822. 2. Emanuel AME Church (Charleston, S.C.). 3. Slavery -- History. 4. Memory -- Social aspects 5. Collective memory 6. Charleston, South Carolina -- History -- Slave Insurrection, 1822. 7. United States -- History -- 19th century

ISBN 9781620973653

LC 2017041546

Striking at the heart of the recent flare-ups over Confederate symbols in Charlottesville, New Orleans and elsewhere, the authors reveal the deep roots of these controversies and trace them to the heart of slavery in the U.S.--Charleston, South Carolina--providing competing histories of how slavery is remembered in this city.

975.8 Georgia

Berendt, John, 1939-

Midnight in the garden of good and evil : a Savannah story / John Berendt. Random House, 1994 388 p. **975.8**

1. Williams, Jim, d. 1990. 2. Trials (Murder) 3. Eccentrics and eccentricities. 4. Murder 5. Murderers 6. Southern States -- Social life and customs. 7. Savannah, Georgia -- Social life and customs.

ISBN 0679429220

LC 93003955

Lambda Literary Award for Gay Men's Mystery, 1994.

Pulitzer Prize for General Nonfiction finalist

Tells the true story of the murder of the local bad boy in the opulent mansion of a gay antiques dealer in charming Old South Savannah, Georgia.

"Berendt has fashioned a Baedeker to Savannah that, while it flirts with condescension, is always contagiously affectionate. Few cities have been introduced more seductively." Newsweek.

Hudgins, Phil,

Travels with Foxfire : stories of people, passions, and practices from Southern Appalachia / Phil Hudgins and Foxfire student Jessica Phillips. Anchor Books, 2018 xv, 314 p. : **975.8**

1. Country life -- Appalachian Region 2. Country life -- Southern States 3. Handicraft -- Appalachian Region 4. Handicraft -- Southern States 5. Appalachian Region -- Civilization. 6. Southern States -- Civilization. 7. Appalachian Region -- Social life and customs. 8. Southern States -- Social life and customs.
ISBN 9780525436294

LC 2017056227

A rich compendium of the collected wisdom of artists, craftsmen, musicians, and moonshiners, Travels with Foxfire is a joyful tribute to the history, the geography, and the traditions that define Appalachian living.

Jones, Jacqueline, 1948-

Saving Savannah : the city and the Civil War / Jacqueline Jones. Alfred A. Knopf, 2008. 528 p. **975.8**

1. Freed slaves. 2. Elite (Social sciences) -- Georgia -- History -- 19th century. 3. Social classes -- Georgia -- History -- 19th century. 4. Slavery -- Georgia -- History -- 19th century. 5. Savannah, Georgia -- History -- 19th century. 6. Georgia -- History -- Civil War, 1861-1865. 7. Savannah, Georgia -- Race relations -- History -- 19th century. 8. Savannah, Georgia -- Social conditions -- 19th century.
ISBN 9781400042937

LC 2008011508

Drawing on diaries, letters, newspaper articles, memoirs, and military records, an in-depth study of the city of Savannah before, during, and in the aftermath of the Civil War describes the African-American struggle for equality and freedom in the midst of war, political turmoil, and social upheaval.

"Synthesizing the perspectives of the mercantile elite, the aristocratic upper crust and the downtrodden...[the author has] fashioned a compelling social and political history." Washington Post Book World.

Pressly, Paul M.

★**On** the rim of the Caribbean : colonial Georgia and the British Atlantic world / Paul M. Pressly. University of Georgia Press, c2013. xii, 354 p. : **975.8**

1. Plantations -- Georgia -- History -- 18th century. 2. Georgia -- Commerce West Indies, British -- History -- 18th century. 3. Georgia -- Economic conditions -- 18th century. 4. Georgia -- History -- Colonial period, ca. 1600-1775. 5. West Indies, British -- Commerce Georgia -- History -- 18th century.
ISBN 0820335673

LC 2012033964

"This richly documented, analytically complex, and well-written book is a major contribution to the study of Colonial Georgia and the 18th-century Atlantic world." Choice.

975.9 Florida

Barry, Dave

Best state ever : a Florida man defends his homeland / Dave Barry. G.P. Putnam's Sons, 2016. 256 p. **975.9**

1. States 2. Local history 3. Eccentrics and eccentricities 4. Stereotypes (Social psychology) 5. Florida -- Description and travel. 6. Essays.
ISBN 9781101982600

LC 2016027545

We've all seen the headlines: Florida Man [Does Something Bizarre]. Of late, the state has become a bit of a joke according to Dave Barry, the Pulitzer Prize-winning humorist who's lived in Florida for decades, so he feels he needs to defend his adopted home. In this lighthearted examination of the Sunshine State, he travels to an assortment of typically Florida places that aren't as well known as Disney World, including Gatorland (reptiles!), Cassadaga (psychics!), and Weeki Wachee Springs (mermaids!), offering informative yet funny insights into Florida as a place of history and fun. Our headline? "Proud Florida Man Writes Hilarious Book."

"Readers may not embrace Florida the way the author has, but they will understand why a humorist loves it." Kirkus.

Douglas, Marjory Stoneman, 1890-1998

The **Everglades** : river of grass / Marjory Stoneman Douglas ; illustrated by Robert Fink ; [update by Michael Grunwald]. Pineapple Press, 2007, c1947. 447 p. : **975.9**

1. Natural history -- Everglades, Florida. 2. Wilderness areas. 3. Nature 4. Everglades, Florida -- Description and travel. 5. Everglades, Florida -- History. 6. Everglades, Florida -- Environmental conditions. 7. Florida -- History.
ISBN 9781561643943

LC 2007028384

Original ed.: New York : Rinehart, 1947.

Gaines, Steven S.

Fool's paradise : players, poseurs, and the culture of excess in South Beach / Steven Gaines. Crown Publishers, c2009. 304 p. **975.9**

1. Upper class -- Miami Beach, Florida. 2. Celebrities -- Miami Beach, Florida. 3. South Beach (Miami Beach, Fla.) -- Social life and customs. 4. Miami Beach, Florida -- Social life and customs.
ISBN 9780307346278

LC 2008036067

"This is a terrific social history buffet. [Gaines is] a gifted storyteller. He fills the book with telling anecdotes and bons mots, but the narrative never gets off track. It would be easy to focus on the drug-and-sleaze aspect of South Beach. But Gaines lets a little bit go a long way. He could fill the book with stupid celebrity tricks. But again, less is more. This book succeeds not because of star power but because of story power. The centerpiece of the book is a war of dueling architects and builders fighting to build the iconic Fontainebleau hotel and then to destroy it out of spite." St. Petersburg Times

Grunwald, Michael, 1970-

The **swamp** : the Everglades, Florida, and the politics of paradise / Michael Grunwald. Simon & Schuster, 2006. 450 p. : **975.9**

1. Environmental protection -- Everglades, Florida -- History. 2. Drainage 3. Ecosystem management. 4. Everglades, Florida -- History. 5. Everglades, Florida -- Environmental conditions.
ISBN 0743251059

LC 2005056329

A history of the Everglades traces its emergence from the sea after the last ice age to its modern role as the world's largest ecosystem restoration project, an account marked by such events as Napoleon Bonaparte Borward's 1904 gubernatorial campaign, railroad and agricultural developments by the Army Corps of Engineers, and numerous political challenges.

"[This] is a riveting tale of ambition versus ecological reality, politics versus science, and, on the upside, our gradual awakening to the true nature of nature." Booklist.

976 South central United States

Dyson, Michael Eric

Come hell or high water : Hurricane Katrina and the color of disaster / Michael Eric Dyson. Basic Civitas, c2006. xii, 258 p. ; **976**

1. Bush, George W. (George Walker), 1946- Relations with African-Americans. 2. African Americans -- Civil rights -- History -- 21st century. 3. Hurricane Katrina, 2005 -- Political aspects. 4. African Americans -- Social conditions -- 21st century. 5. Hurricane Katrina, 2005 -- Social aspects. 6. United States -- Race relations -- Political aspects.

ISBN 9780465017614

A searing assessment of the meaning of Hurricane Katrina combines interviews with survivors of the disaster and the author's knowledge of black migrations and government policy over decades, and explores the legacy of black suffering in America since slavery.

"This book on Hurrican Katrina not only chronicles what happened when, it also argues that the nation's failure to offer timely aid to Katrina's victims indicates deeper problems in race and class relations. . . . [The author's] contention that Katrina exposed a dominant culture pervaded not only by active malice toward poor blacks but also by a long history of passive indifference to their problems is both powerful and unsettling." Publishers Weekly.

Van Heerden, Ivor

The **storm** : what went wrong and why during Hurricane Katrina--the inside story from one Louisiana scientist / Ivor van Heerden, Mike Bryan. Penguin Group USA, 2007. 326 p. **976**

1. United States. Federal Emergency Management Agency. 2. Hurricane Katrina, 2005. 3. Hurricanes -- Louisiana. 4. Disasters -- Prevention. 5. Emergency planning. 6. New Orleans, Louisiana.

ISBN 0143112139

A disaster specialist explains why he had been predicting a tragedy similar to hurricane Katrina's destruction for a decade, and outlines his plans for preventing a similar catastrophe from occurring in the future.

"This serious, scientific explanation of what exactly happened in the hours--and years--leading up to Hurricane Katrina's devestation of New Orleans brings a fresh perspective to a tragedy that has generated remarkably similar news accounts over the past eight months." Publishers Weekly.

976.1 Alabama

Agee, James, 1909-1955

★**Cotton** tenants : three families / James Agee ; [photographs by] Walker Evans ; edited by John Summers ; preface by Adam Haslett. Melville House, 2013. 224 p. : **976.1**

1. Depressions -- 1929-1941. 2. Sharecropping. 3. Sharecroppers. 4. Families -- United States. 5. United States -- Economic conditions -- 20th century.

ISBN 9781612192123

LC 2013370909

"Accessible, hard-hitting, moving, and still thematically relevant. Highly recommended for all collections." Library Journal.

Agee, James, 1909-1955

Let us now praise famous men : three tenant families / James Agee, Walker Evans ; with an introduction to the new edition by John Hersey. Houghton Mifflin, 1988, c1941. liv, 471 p., 61 p. of plates : **976.1**

1. Agee, James, 1909-1955 Travel Alabama. 2. Farm life 3. Poverty 4. Tenant farmers 5. Depressions -- 1929-1941 6. Alabama -- Rural conditions. 7. Alabama -- Description and travel.

ISBN 0395489016

LC 88018110

Originally published: Boston, MA : Houghton Mifflin, 1941.

An illustrated portrayal of three Alabama sharecropper families in 1936, examining their everyday existence in poverty.

McWhorter, Diane

Carry me home : Birmingham, Alabama, the climactic battle of the civil rights revolution / Diane McWhorter. Simon & Schuster, 2001. 701 p., 16 p. of plates : **976.1**

1. Wallace, George, 1919-1998. 2. Connor, Eugene, 1897-1973. 3. Ku-Klux Klan Alabama. 4. African Americans -- Civil rights -- Birmingham, Alabama -- History -- 20th century. 5. Freedom Riders (Civil rights movement) 6. White supremacists -- Alabama. 7. Civil Rights Movement -- Birmingham, Alabama 8. Birmingham, Alabama -- Race relations.

ISBN 0684807475

LC 00053827

Maps on lining papers.

J. Anthony Lukas Book Prize, 2002.

Pulitzer Prize for General Nonfiction, 2002.

"A daughter of Birmingham's privileged elite, McWhorter weaves a personal narrative through this startling account of the history, events, and major players on both sides of the civil rights battle in that city." Booklist.

976.2 Mississippi

Grant, Richard

The **deepest** South of all : true stories from Natchez, Mississippi / Richard Grant. Simon & Schuster, 2020. 288 p. **976.2**

1. Cities and towns 2. Race relations 3. Inequality 4. Eccentrics and eccentricities 5. Natchez, Mississippi -- Social life and customs 6. Natchez, Mississippi -- History

ISBN 9781501177828

LC bl2020018825

An engaging portrait of Natchez, Mississippi traces its rich cultural heritage and remarkable contradictions, sharing the stories of history-shaping locals, from FBI informant and brothel madam Nellie Jackson to enslaved West African prince Abd al Rahman Ibrahima.

"Readers will be enthralled by Grant's lively prose and the colorful contradictions of this unique and haunted place." Publishers Weekly

Welty, Eudora, 1909-2001

One time, one place : Mississippi in the Depression : a snapshot album / Eudora Welty. University Press of Mississippi, c1996. xiv, 115 p. : **976.2**

1. Depressions -- 1929 -- Mississippi -- Pictorial works. 2. Documentary photography -- Mississippi. 3. Mississippi -- Pictorial works.
ISBN 0878058664

LC 95046057

Originally published: New York : Random House, 1971.

Collects photographs of Mississippians that Welty took in the 1930s when she worked for the Works Progress Administration

"This is a collection of photographs of Mississippians that Welty took in the 1930s, when she worked for the Works Progress Administration (WPA). This Silver Anniversary Edition contains a great foreword by William Maxwell that absolutely nails the importance of the book for many readers." Booklist.

976.3 Louisiana

Berry, Jason

City of a million dreams : a history of New Orleans at year 300 / Jason Berry. The University of North Carolina Press, [2018] 424 p. **976.3**

1. New Orleans, Louisiana -- History
ISBN 9781469647142

LC 2018020837

Jason Berry delivers a character-driven history of New Orleans at its tricentennial. Chronicling cycles of invention, struggle, death, and rebirth, Berry reveals the city's survival as a triumph of diversity, its map-of-the-world neighborhoods marked by resilience despite hurricanes, epidemics, fires, and floods.

Brinkley, Douglas

The **great** deluge : Hurricane Katrina, New Orleans, and the Mississippi Gulf Coast / Douglas Brinkley. Morrow, 2006. xix, 716 p. : **976.3**

1. Hurricane Katrina, 2005. 2. Hurricanes -- New Orleans, Louisiana. 3. Disaster victims -- New Orleans, Louisiana. 4. Disaster relief -- United States. 5. New Orleans, Louisiana.
ISBN 9780061124235

LC 2006043338

Robert F. Kennedy Book Award, 2007.

A deeply personal account of hurricane Katrina and the devastation it left in New Orleans and across the Gulf Coast documents the events and repercussions of the tragedy and its aftermath, the historical roots of the terrible storm, and the ongoing crisis confronting the region.

"The author captures the human toll of Katrina as graphically as the most vivid newspaper and television accounts did, and by pulling together a huge, choral portrait of what happened during that first week of havoc and distress ... he gives the reader a richly detailed timeline of disaster--a timeline in which the sheer cumulative power of details impresses upon us, again, just how abysmally inept relief efforts were on every level, from FEMA to the Red Cross to the New Orleans police department, from the federal government to state and local authorities." New York Times.

Codrescu, Andrei, 1946-

New Orleans, mon amour : twenty years of writings from the city / Andrei Codrescu. Algonquin Books of Chapel Hill, 2006. 273 p. ; **976.3**

1. Codrescu, Andrei, 1946- Homes and haunts New Orleans, Louisiana Anecdotes. 2. City life -- New Orleans, Louisiana -- Anecdotes. 3. Cities and towns. 4. New Orleans, Louisiana -- Social life and customs Anecdotes. 5. Louisiana -- Social life and customs. 6. Essays.
ISBN 1565125053

LC 2005053599

"In this collection of short essays Codrescu sketches portraits of a fabled city and its equally fabled inhabitants. The author, who has called the Big Easy home for two decades, shows how, like some gigantic bohemian magnet, New Orleans attracts some of the world's most talented, self-indulgent freaks. Codrescu finds himself quite at home there. He expertly weaves pages of New Orleans history through his stories of personal discovery and debauchery. The last few essays, written post-Katrina, radiate simultaneous anger and clarity. Full of pride and defensiveness, Codrescu closes the collection ruminating about rebuilding the city and his longing to return to its rhythms and eccentricities. Despite Codrescu's frustrations, this collection is, in the end, gentle and sweet." Publishers Weekly.

Horne, Jed, 1948-

★**Breach** of faith : Hurricane Katrina and the near death of a great American city / Jed Horne. Random House, 2006. 432 p. **976.3**

1. Hurricane Katrina, 2005. 2. Disasters -- New Orleans, Louisiana. 3. Hurricanes -- New Orleans, Louisiana. 4. Floods -- New Orleans, Louisiana. 5. New Orleans, Louisiana.
ISBN 9781400065523

LC 2006046468

ALA Notable Book, 2007.

A journalist and resident of New Orleans offers a firsthand, eyewitness account of Hurricane Katrina, its devastating impact on New Orleans, and its terrifying aftermath, arguing that the origins of the disaster lie in the culture and politics of a troubled city and in the national politics of poverty, homeland security, and race relations.

"The New Orleans Times-Picayune's staff (including metro editor Horne) won Pulitzer Prizes for its coverage of Katrina. Such esteem is deserved, as Horne here demonstrates. His on-the-ground narrative emphasizes his ear for local idiom and his sharp eye for compelling detail." Library Journal.

Johnson, Walter, 1967-

Soul by soul : life inside the antebellum slave market / Walter Johnson. Harvard University Press, c1999. 283 p. : **976.3**

1. Slaves. 2. Slave trade -- New Orleans, Louisiana -- History -- 19th century. 3. African Americans -- New Orleans, Louisiana -- Social conditions -- 19th century. 4. Slaveholders 5. New Orleans, Louisiana -- Race relations. 6. New Orleans, Louisiana -- Social conditions -- 19th century.
ISBN 0674821483

LC 99046696

"This is an examination of the antebellum slave market. Using slave narratives, court records, planters' letters, and more, Johnson enters the slave pens and showrooms of the New Orleans slave market to observe how slavery turned men and women into merchandise and how slaves resisted such efforts to steal their humanity." Library Journal.

Krist, Gary

Empire of sin : a story of sex, jazz, murder, and the battle for modern New Orleans / Gary Krist. Crown, 2014. 432 p. **976.3**

1. Anderson, Thomas Charles, 1858-1931. 2. Political corruption 3. Police chiefs 4. Race relations 5. Crime 6. New Orleans, Louisiana -- History -- 20th century 7. Storyville (New Orleans, Louisiana)
ISBN 9780770437060

LC 2014003191

"Krist's lively book is only marred by an overlong section devoted to a series of axe murders that plagued the city. A wild, well-told tale." Kirkus.

Lane, Charles, 1961-

The **day** freedom died : the Colfax massacre, the Supreme Court, and the betrayal of Reconstruction / Charles Lane. Henry Holt, 2008. 352 p. **976.3**

1. Beckwith, James, 1832-1912. 2. United States. Supreme Court -- History 19th century. 3. Crimes against African-Americans -- Colfax, Louisiana -- History -- 19th century. 4. Massacres -- Colfax, Louisiana -- History -- 19th century. 5. Violence -- Colfax, Louisiana -- History -- 19th century. 6. Racism -- Colfax, Louisiana -- History -- 19th century. 7. Colfax, Louisiana -- Race relations -- History -- 19th century.

ISBN 0805083421

LC 2007037514

Describes the 1873 Colfax, Louisiana, massacre of sixty former slaves by former Confederate soldiers, and the efforts to bring the perpetrators to justice that ended with a Supreme Court verdict that left Southern blacks at the mercy of violent racists for generations.

"The Colfax Massacre...took place on an Easter Sunday afternoon in 1873. Within four hours, at least eighty black American men had been brutally murdered by white vigilantes in Colfax, La. Journalist Lane's groundbreaking and persuasive work illustrates this pivotal event in the political and constitutional history of post-Civil War America and its social, political and judicial aftermath. Students of American and African-American history will find it particularly valuable; fans of American history will find it a moving and instructive drama." Publishers Weekly.

Neufeld, Josh

A.D. : New Orleans after the deluge / Josh Neufeld. Pantheon Books, c2009. 193 p. : **976.3**

1. Natural disasters. 2. Hurricane Katrina, 2005 -- Social aspects. 3. Disaster victims -- New Orleans, Louisiana 4. Wind damage. 5. New Orleans, Louisiana -- History -- 21st century Comic books, strips, etc. 6. Comics and Graphic novels

ISBN 9780307378149

LC 2008055687

Uses graphic novel format to depict the events of Hurricane Katrina through six true stories of New Orleanians who survived the storm, including Denise, who experienced the chaos of the Superdome, and a doctor whose French Quarter home was unscathed.

"Graphic artist Neufeld paints an emotive portrait of New Orleans during and after Hurricane Katrina, as seen through the eyes of seven of the city's citizens. The opening panels coalesce into a long cinematic pan, a thrumming setup for the disaster. The half-page and quarter-page panels--satellite views of weather patterns and close inspections of neighborhoods--are crisp, and the two-page spreads are softly focused. Neufeld's words and images are commensurable and rhythmic, and the vernacular is sharp. Bristling with attitude and pungent with social awareness." Kirkus.

Rasmussen, Daniel, 1987-

American uprising : the untold story of America's largest slave revolt / Daniel Rasmussen. Harper, 2011. 288 p. **976.3**

1. Slave resistance and revolts. 2. Slavery. 3. Revolutions. 4. African Americans 5. New Orleans, Louisiana -- History -- 19th century. 6. New Orleans, Louisiana -- Race relations.

ISBN 9780061995217

LC 2010017855

The author, a historian reveals the long forgotten history of America's largest slave uprising, the New Orleans slave revolt of 1811 that nearly toppled New Orleans and changed the course of American history.

"This is an account of a large-scale, three-day slave revolt on the sugar plantations near New Orleans during the 1811 Carnival (Mardi Gras) season. The author argues that the slave-rebels, who had learned warfare tactics in their native Africa, were inspired by the successful Haitian revolution. This is a welcome addition to popular history and an engaging read for anyone interested in this important chapter in the tragic story of American slavery." Library Journal.

Rivlin, Gary

Katrina : after the flood / Gary Rivlin. Simon & Schuster, 2015. 416 p. **976.3**

1. Hurricane Katrina, 2005. 2. Urban renewal 3. Urban planning 4. City life 5. New Orleans, Louisiana

ISBN 9781451692228

LC 2015431412

Ten years after Hurricane Katrina made landfall in southeast Louisiana--on August 29, 2005--journalist Gary Rivlin traces the storm's immediate damage, the city of New Orleans's efforts to rebuild itself, and the storm's lasting effects not just on the city's geography and infrastructure--but on the psychic, racial, and social fabric of one of this nation's great cities.

"Rivlin captures the snark, the bellyaching, and the outright denial of those in charge--and many aimed to be in charge (while many dodged responsibility as well). A fascinating lesson in urban planning in the face of calamity and financial shenanigans about what has been deemed 'the most expensive disaster in history.' " Booklist.

976.4 Texas

Donovan, Jim, 1954-

The **blood** of heroes : the 13-day struggle for the Alamo -- and the sacrifice that forged a nation / James Donovan. Little, Brown and Co., 2012. 544 p. **976.4**

1. Alamo Siege, 1836. 2. Alamo -- History. 3. Sieges. 4. Courage in men. 5. Battles. 6. Texas -- History -- 19th century.

ISBN 9780316053747

LC 2011050067

The author describes the valiant fight by 200 Americans in an abandoned mission near San Antonio, Texas, against the Mexican army.

Harrigan, Stephen, 1948-

Big wonderful thing : a history of Texas / Stephen Harrigan. University of Texas Press, 2019. 925 p. : **976.4**

1. States. 2. Texas -- History. 3. United States -- History.

ISBN 9780292759510

Stephen Harrigan brings to life with novelistic immediacy the generations of driven men and women who shaped Texas, all of them taking their part in the creation of a place that became not just a nation, not just a state, but an indelible idea.

Hodge, Roger D., 1967-

Texas blood : seven generations among the outlaws, ranchers, Indians, missionaries, soldiers, and smugglers of the borderlands / Roger D. Hodge. Alfred A. Knopf, 2017. 352 p. **976.4**

1. Hodge, Roger D., 1967- 2. Ranchers 3. Borderlands 4. Families -- History 5. Local history 6. Texas -- History 7. Mexican-American

Border Region
ISBN 9780307961402

LC 2016053188

"A Borzoi Book."

A history of the Texas borderlands by the author of The Mendacity of Hope illuminates subjects ranging from colonization and conquest through the war on drugs and regional genocide, offering additional perspectives based on the experiences of the author's seven-generation ranching family.

McCollom, James P.

The **last** sheriff in Texas : a true tale of violence and the vote / James P. McCollom. Counterpoint Press, [2017] 272 p. **976.4**

1. Ennis, Vail 2. Sheriffs 3. Police misconduct 4. Small towns 5. Elections -- Texas 6. Texas
ISBN 9781619029965

LC 2017024770

"Of interest to students of Texas history as well as aspiring law enforcement officers, who should read it as an example of how not to conduct themselves." Kirkus. Reviews

Roker, Al, 1954-

The **storm** of the century : tragedy, heroism, survival, and the epic true story of America's deadliest natural disaster : the great Gulf hurricane of 1900 / Al Roker. William Morrow, [2015] 320 p. **976.4**

1. Survival (after hurricanes) 2. Natural disasters. 3. Hurricanes -- Texas -- History -- 20th century. 4. Galveston, Texas -- History -- 20th century. 5. Gulf Coast (United States) -- History.
ISBN 9780062364654

LC 2015007009

An award-winning meteorologist presents an account of the legendary hurricane to assess its destruction of Galveston, role in thousands of deaths and influence on American history and culture.

"Roker's account will interest readers who previously knew nothing about the Galveston hurricane. However, Isaac's Storm is not out of date and deserves its place as the recommended version." Kirkus.

Valby, Karen

Welcome to Utopia : notes from a small town / Karen Valby. Spiegel & Grau, 2010. 238 p. : **976.4**

1. Small town life -- Texas 2. Texas -- Social life and customs.
ISBN 9780385522861

LC 2009037970

"Entertainment Weekly magazine sent intrepid reporter Karen Valby into the great flyover zone in 2006 in search of a small town somewhere in America without popular culture. She found Utopia, a town of a few hundred souls 90 miles west of the nation's seventh-largest city, San Antonio. Utopia is not exactly off the grid, and one suspects that its name appealed to Valby more than its isolation. Her book...is a pleasant moment-in-time postcard of a typical U.S. town." Minneapolis Star Tribune.

976.6 Oklahoma

Anderson, Sam, 1977-

Boom town : the fantastical saga of Oklahoma city, its chaotic founding... its purloined basketball team, and the dream of becoming a world-class metropolis / Sam Anderson. Crown, 2018. 304 p. **976.6**

1. Oklahoma City Thunder (Basketball team) 2. Social history 3. Urban planning 4. Sports -- Social aspects 5. CIties and towns -- Growth 6. Oklahoma City, Oklahoma
ISBN 9780804137317

LC 2017054583

An award-winning journalist documents the idiosyncratic mix of history, sports, urban studies and more reflected in Oklahoma City, tracing its chaotic origins through the near-instant metropolis of today through the stories of creative innovators.

"Andersons lively and empathetic saga captures the outsize ambitions, provincial realities, and vibrant history of a quintessentially American city." Publishers Weekly.

Grann, David

★**Killers** of the Flower Moon : the Osage murders and the birth of the FBI / David Grann. Doubleday, 2017. x, 338 p. : **976.6**

1. FBI Case studies 2. Osage Indians 3. Serial murders 4. Murder investigation -- Case studies 5. Racism 6. Oklahoma 7. Osage County, Oklahoma
ISBN 9780385534246

LC 2016021407

Maps on endpapers.

ALA Notable Book, 2018.

Anthony Award for Best Critical/Nonfiction, 2018.

Edgar Allan Poe Award for Best Fact Crime, 2018.

Spur Award for Historical Nonfiction, 2018.

Andrew Carnegie Medal for Excellence in Non-Fiction finalist, 2018.

National Book Award for Nonfiction finalist, 2017

Presents a true account of the early 20th-century murders of dozens of wealthy Osage and law-enforcement officials, citing the contributions and missteps of a fledgling FBI that eventually uncovered one of the most chilling conspiracies in American history.

"Grann employs you-are-there narrative effects to set readers right in the action, and he relays the humanity, evil, and heroism of the people involved. His riveting reckoning of a devastating episode in American history deservedly captivates." Booklist.

Hirsch, James S.

Riot and remembrance : America's worst race riot and its legacy / James S. Hirsch. Houghton Mifflin, 2002. viii, 358 p. : **976.6**

1. African Americans -- Tulsa, Oklahoma -- History -- 20th century. 2. Racism -- Tulsa, Oklahoma -- History -- 20th century. 3. Riots -- Tulsa, Oklahoma -- History -- 20th century. 4. Violence -- Tulsa, Oklahoma -- History -- 20th century. 5. Tulsa, Oklahoma -- Race relations.
ISBN 0618108130

LC 2001051615

Drawing on period documents and interviews with survivors and their descendants, the author of Hurricane offers a definitive account of the 1921 race riot that destroyed the Greenwood section of Tulsa, Oklahoma, leaving hundreds of black residents dead, and describes the battle for belated justice and reparations to the victims.

"Hirsch unearths an important episode in U.S. history with verve, intelligence and compassion." Publishers Weekly.

976.7 Arkansas

Hill, David

The **Vapors** : a southern family, the New York mob, and the rise and fall of Hot Springs, America's forgotten capital of vice / David Hill. Farrar, Straus & Giroux, 2020. 368 p. **976.7**

1. Hill, David Family 2. Madden, Owney, 1891-1980 3. Organized crime 4. Resort towns 5. Casinos 6. Gangsters 7. Hot Springs, Arkansas 8. Arkansas -- History -- 20th century

ISBN 9781250086112

LC bl2020019326

Back in the days before Vegas was big, when the Mob was at its peak and neon lights were but a glimmer on the horizon, a little Southern town styled itself as a premier destination for the American leisure class. Hot Springs, Arkansas was home to healing waters, Art Deco splendor, and America's original national park--as well as horse racing, nearly a dozen illegal casinos, and some of the country's most bald-faced criminals. It was a place where small-town hustlers and bigtime high-rollers could make their fortunes, and hide from the law. The Vapors is the extraordinary story of three individuals--spanning the golden decades of Hot Springs, from the 1930s through the 1960s--and the lavish casino whose spectacular rise and fall would bring them together before blowing them apart.

"More than a simple crime story, this is a forgotten history of Arkansas in the mid-20th century. Recommended for readers interested in antiheroes, self-made men, and survivor stories." Library Journal

976.8 Tennessee

Kiernan, Denise

The **girls** of Atomic City : the untold story of the women who helped win World War II / Denise Kiernan. Simon & Schuster 2013. 320 p. **976.8**

1. Manhattan Project (U.S.) -- History 2. World War II -- Women. 3. Women and war. 4. Atomic bomb. 5. Secrecy. 6. Tennessee -- History. 7. Oak Ridge, Tennessee.

ISBN 9781451617528

LC 2013431175

The town of Oak Ridge, Tennessee, boomed on U.S military-owned acreage between 1942-1944. Its electricity usage matched that of New York City, and its population reached 75,000--yet it didn't appear on a single map during World War II. Many new residents were women, recruited at top-dollar wages for positions from chemists to couriers. Sworn to strict secrecy protocols, they were told only that their work would ensure a swift, final World War II victory. The nuclear blast at Hiroshima at last revealed their hidden roles. The Girls of Atomic City brilliantly illuminates a long-overlooked chapter of both World War II and women's history.

Lauterbach, Preston

Beale Street dynasty : sex, song, and the struggle for the soul of Memphis / Preston Lauterbach. W. W. Norton & Co. Inc., 2015. 320 p. **976.8**

1. Church, Robert Reed, 1839-1912 2. Cities and towns 3. African American families 4. Multiracial men 5. Race relations. 6. Beale Street (Memphis, Tennessee) 7. Memphis, Tennessee -- Streets

ISBN 9780393082579

LC 2014039928

Documents the rise and fall of the legendary Memphis thoroughfare that indelibly shaped American culture, documenting its story through the life of former slave and first black millionaire Robert Church. By the award-winning author ofThe Chitlin' Circuit.

"While sex and song (as promised in the book's subtitle) are present at times, this account is really about politics and power in a major Southern city. Recommended for all readers interested in Memphis or in African American history." Library Journal.

976.9 Kentucky

Snyder, Christina

Great Crossings : Indians, settlers, and slaves in the age of Jackson / Christina Snyder. Oxford Univ Pr., 2017. 408 p. **976.9**

1. Jackson, Andrew, 1767-1845 2. Social history 3. African Americans 4. Indians of North America 5. Racism 6. Kentucky -- History -- 19th century

ISBN 9780199399062

LC 2016024418

"Great Crossings features Indians from across the continent seeking new ways to assert anciently-held rights, and people of African descent who challenged the United States to live up to its ideals. These diverse groups met in an experimental community in central Kentucky called Great Crossings, home to the first federal Indian school and a famous interracial family."--Provided by the publisher.

"This is a well-researched, engagingly written, and remarkable work of scholarship." Publishers Weekly.

977 North central United States

Barry, John M., 1947-

Rising tide : the great Mississippi flood of 1927 and how it changed America / John M. Barry. Simon & Schuster, 1997. 524 p. : **977**

1. Humphreys, Andrew Atkinson, 1810-1883. 2. Eads, James Buchanan, 1820-1887. 3. Percy family. 4. Floods -- Mississippi Valley -- History -- 20th century. 5. Flood control -- Mississippi River -- History. 6. Survival (after floods) 7. Race relations. 8. Mississippi Valley -- History -- 1865-

ISBN 0684810468

LC 96040077

In 1927, the Mississippi River swept across an area roughly equal in size to Massachusetts, Connecticut, New Hampshire, and Vermont combined, leaving water as deep as thirty feet on the land stretching from Illinois and Missouri south to the Gulf of Mexico. Close to a million people -- in a nation of 120 million -- were forced out of their homes. Some estimates place the death toll in the thousands. The Red Cross fed nearly 700,000 refugees for months. Rising Tide tells how the flood changed the face of American and laid the groundwork for the New Deal.

"This is the story of human defeat by a savage, unpredictable river. The flood of 1927, three times greater than the flood of 1993, was an unprecedented disaster that spurred a political innovation. Congress's agreement to rebuild the Mississippi's shattered flood-control system marked the federal government's first assumption of full financial responsibility for a regional calamity. Much of the book recounts how the greed of New Orleans bankers and Delta planters increased the sufferings of the rural poor. Barry's book is a virtuoso piece of exposition." The New Yorker.

Cox, Anna-Lisa

The **bone** and sinew of the land : America's forgotten black pioneers and the struggle for equality / Anna-Lisa Cox. PublicAffairs, [2018] 336 p. **977**

1. African Americans -- History -- 19th century. 2. Race relations. 3. Racism 4. Frontier and pioneer life 5. Ohio -- History -- 19th century. 6. Indiana -- History -- 19th century. 7. Old Northwest (United States) -- History -- 1775-1865
ISBN 9781610398107

LC 2017056938

A revealing story of America's black pioneers discusses how thousands of free African Americans built hundreds of settlements in the Northern Territory, where slavery was banned and equal voting rights to all men were guaranteed.

Dennis, Jerry

The **living** Great Lakes : searching for the heart of the inland seas / Jerry Dennis. Thomas Dunne Books, 2003. viii, 296 p. : **977**

1. Dennis, Jerry Travel Great Lakes region. 2. Natural history -- Great Lakes. 3. Marine biology -- United States 4. Great Lakes region. 5. Great Lakes -- History. 6. Great Lakes -- Environmental conditions.
ISBN 9780312251932

LC 2002032500

Map on lining papers.

Provides a history of the Great Lakes as told by the biologists, fishermen, sailors, and others who have experienced them firsthand and traces the author's experiences as a local resident and schooner crewperson.

Erdrich, Louise

Books and islands in Ojibwe country / Louise Erdrich. National Geographic, 2003. 143 p. : **977**

1. Erdrich, Louise Travel 2. Ojibwa Indians 3. Island life. 4. Indians of North America -- Rites and ceremonies. 5. Mothers and daughters 6. Lake of the Woods. 7. Minnesota -- Description and travel 8. Ontario -- Description and travel
ISBN 0792257197

LC 2003045906

"Fans of Erdrich's bestselling fiction will recognize her signature combination of the sacred and the ordinary in this lively traveler's memoir, and many will enjoy the rare glimpse of her personal life as well as the physical facts of her journey from her home in Minneapolis to the lakes and islands of her Ojibwe ancestors in Ontario and Minnesota." Booklist.

Laskin, David, 1953-

The **children's** blizzard / David Laskin. Harper Perennial 2005, c2004. ix, 307, 16 p. : **977**

1. Blizzards -- History. 2. Prairies -- Middle West. 3. Children -- Death. 4. Hypothermia. 5. Middle West -- History -- 19th century.
ISBN 0060520760

LC bl2006029012

Originally published: New York : HarperCollins, 2004.

Describes the deadly 1888 snowstorm in the Great Plains that killed more than five hundred people including numerous schoolchildren, describing how the storm devastated immigrant families and dramatically affected pioneer advancement.

977.1 Ohio

Gup, Ted, 1950-

A **secret** gift : how one man's kindness--and a trove of letters--revealed the hidden history of the Great Depression / Ted Gup. Penguin Press, 2010. 368 p. **977.1**

1. Stone, Samuel, 1887-1981. 2. Benefactors. 3. Benevolence. 4. Depressions -- 1929-1941. 5. Rich men. 6. Canton, Ohio -- Economic conditions -- 20th century. 7. Canton, Ohio -- History -- 20th century.
ISBN 9781594202704

LC 2010017302

The author explains how the discovery of a cache of letters revealed his grandfather's offer of cash gifts to seventy-five families in distress in Depression-scarred Canton, Ohio, in 1933, and explores the profound effects the gifts had on their recipients.

977.3 Illinois

Dyja, Tom

The **third** coast : when Chicago built the American dream / Thomas Dyja. The Penguin Press, 2013. 384 p. **977.3**

1. City life. 2. Cities and towns -- Illinois. 3. Chicago, Illinois -- History. 4. Illinois -- History.
ISBN 9781594204326

LC 2012039710

A cultural history of mid-20th-century Chicago traces the emergence of mass-marketing practices, technological advances and artistic development that profoundly influenced modern America, offering additional insight into the role of racial divisions, housing projects and migration.

"A readable, richly detailed history of America's second city." Kirkus.

Miller, Donald L., 1944-

City of the century : the epic of Chicago and the making of America / Donald Miller. Simon & Schuster, 1997, c1996. 704 p. : **977.3**

1. Chicago, Illinois -- History.
ISBN 0684831384

LC BL 99785489

"A Touchstone book."

Originally published: New York : Simon & Schuster, 1996.

A chronicle of the coming of the Industrial Age to one American city traces the explosive entrepreneurial, technological, and artistic growth that converted Chicago from a trading post to a modern industrial metropolis by the 1890s.

"In this account of Chicago's history in the nineteenth century Miller tells of Chicago's historical and literary figures, reform leaders, architects, industrialists, and entrepreneurs." Library Journal.

Tintori, Karen

Trapped : the 1909 Cherry mine disaster / Karen Tintori. Atria Books, 2003, c2002. xiv, 273 p. : **977.3**

1. Cherry Mine Disaster, Cherry, Ill., 1909. 2. Coal mine accidents 3. Mine accidents. 4. Illinois -- History.
ISBN 0743421957

LC BL2003016242

Reprint. Originally published: 2002.

The granddaughter of a survivor recounts the tragedy that killed 259 miners, describing the fire that devastated a coal mine in Cherry, Illinois, the trial that followed, and the implications for workers' compensation laws.

"On November 13, 1909, a fire trapped 480 coal miners . 400 feet below ground in a mine at Cherry, Illinois. Only 221 escaped. Tintori describes the life-and-death struggle of the miners below ground and the terror of the women and children gathered at the mine's entrance. Tintori's graphic account of this tragedy is a sad but gripping story." Booklist.

977.4 Michigan

Boyd, Herb

Black Detroit : a people's history of self-determination / Herb Boyd. Amistad, 2017. xii, 416 pages, 16 unnumbered pages of plates : **977.4**

1. African Americans -- Social conditions 2. Urban economics 3. Urban economic development 4. Cities and towns 5. Detroit, Michigan -- Economic conditions 6. Detroit, Michigan -- Social conditions.
ISBN 9780062346629

LC 2017302465

The author looks at the evolving culture, politics, economics, and spiritual life of Detroit--a blend of memoir, love letter, history, and clear-eyed reportage that explores the city's past, present, and future and its significance to the African American legacy and the nation's fabric.

"An inspiring, illuminating book that will interest students of urban history and the black experience." Kirkus.

Maraniss, David

Once in a great city : a Detroit story / David Maraniss. Simon & Schuster, 2015 512 p. **977.4**

1. Automobile industry and trade 2. Detroit, Michigan.
ISBN 9781476748382

LC 2015017134

Robert F. Kennedy Book Award, 2016.

Despite everything that made Detroit great--from the auto industry visionaries, to influential labor leaders, to the hit-makers of Motown--shows how there were hints of the city's tragic collapse decades before the riot, years of civic corruption and neglect took their toll.

Martelle, Scott, 1958-

Detroit : a biography / Scott Martelle. Chicago Review Press, c2011. 288 p. **977.4**

1. African Americans -- Detroit, Michigan. 2. Automobile industry and trade 3. Economic development 4. Urbanization 5. Detroit, Michigan -- History
ISBN 9781569765265

LC 2011041173

Explains the history of Detroit from its beginnings as a French outpost, to its status as a major industrial city in the mid-twentieth century, to its recent economic collapse.

McDonnell, Michael

Masters of empire : Great Lakes Indians and the making of America / Michael McDonnell. Hill & Wang Pub., 2015 336 p. **977.4**

1. Indians of North America -- Relations with European Americans 2. Ottawa Indians 3. Kinship-based society 4. Lake Huron region 5. Great Lakes region 6. United States -- History -- Colonial period, 1600-1775
ISBN 9780809029532

LC 2015022331

Describes and chronicles the important historical role the native people of the Great Lakes had in the history of North America, highlighting the Anishinaabeg tribe's experiences with other native Americans, as well as with the newcomer Europeans.

"McDonnell's scholarly yet compelling history will be a valuable addition to American history and Native American collections." Booklist.

Miles, Tiya, 1970-

The **dawn** of Detroit : a chronicle of slavery and freedom in the city of the straits / Tiya Miles. The New Press, 2017. 288 p. **977.4**

1. Slavery. 2. Slave trade 3. Race relations. 4. Fur industry and trade 5. Detroit, Michigan -- History
ISBN 9781620972311

LC 2017018381

Hurston/Wright Legacy Award: Nonfiction, 2018.

From the MacArthur genius grant winner, a beautifully written and revelatory look at the slave origins of a major northern American city.

"Diligently researched and well written, this provocative exploration of slavery in frontier-era Detroit proves illuminating." Choice.

977.6 Minnesota

Brown, Daniel, 1951-

Under a flaming sky : the great Hinckley firestorm of 1894 / Daniel James Brown. Lyons Press, 2006. xi, 256 p. : **977.6**

1. Forest fires -- Minnesota. 2. Natural disasters. 3. Hinckley, Minnesota -- History. 4. Hinckley, Minnesota -- Fire, 1894.
ISBN 1592288634

Describes the devastating events of September 1894, when two forest fires converged on the town of Hinckley, Minnesota, and surrounding communities, trapping more than two thousand people and ultimately costing more than four hundred lives.

"On September 1, 1894, a firestorm consumed timber-boomtown Hinckley, Minnesota, and three nearby hamlets. Brown, grandson of an 11-year-old survivor, makes riveting, affecting, white-knuckle reading of that horrifying, internationally reported day's lethal passage." Booklist.

978 Western United States

Brands, H. W.

★**Dreams** of El Dorado : a history of the American West / H. W. Brands. Basic Books, 2019. 544 p. **978**

1. Pioneers 2. Indians of North America -- History 3. Frontier and pioneer life 4. Businesspeople 5. The West (United States) -- History 6. United States -- History
ISBN 9781541672529

LC 2018048887

H. W. Brands tells the thrilling, panoramic story of the settling of the American West. He takes us from John Jacob Astor's fur trading outpost in Oregon to the Texas Revolution, from the California gold rush to the Oklahoma land rush. He shows how the migrants' dreams drove them to feats of courage and perseverance that put their stay-at-home cousins to shame--and how those same dreams also drove them to outrageous acts of violence against indigenous peoples and one another. The West was where riches would reward the miner's persistence, the cattleman's courage, the railroad man's enterprise; but El Dorado was at least as elusive in the West as it ever was in the East.

"This broad but clearly structured study, with its many well-chosen illustrations, is likely to have wide appeal." Publishers Weekly.

Brown, Dee, 1908-2002

The **American** West / Dee Brown ; photos edited by Martin F.Schmitt. Scribner, 1994. 448 p. **978**

1. Pioneers -- The West (United States) -- History -- 19th century. 2. Ranches -- The West (United States) -- History. 3. The West (United States) in literature. 4. Wild West shows -- History. 5. The West (United States) -- History.
ISBN 0025174215

LC 94037444

An epic account of the American West depicts the tragic destruction of the Native American way of life and covers major events and key figures.

"This narrative history of westward expansion paints a vivid portrait of the settlers, pioneers, entrepreneurs, and Native Americans of the old West. Useful as collateral research material and for recreational reading." Booklist.

★**Bury** my heart at Wounded Knee : an Indian history of the American West / Dee Brown. H. Holt, 2001, c1971. xix, 487 p. : **978**

1. Indians of North America -- Wars -- The West (United States) 2. Battles. 3. Indians of North America -- The West (United States) -- History. 4. The West (United States) -- History -- 19th century.
ISBN 0805066349

LC 00040958

Originally published: New York : Holt, Rinehart & Winston, 1971.

The systematic destruction of the American Indians, told in the words of those who were there.

Buck, Rinker, 1950-

The **Oregon** Trail : an American journey / Rinker Buck. Simon & Schuster, 2015. 432 p. **978**

1. Buck, Rinker, 1950- 2. Brothers 3. Frontier and pioneer life -- The West (United States) 4. Covered wagons 5. Oregon Trail 6. The West (United States)
ISBN 9781451659160

LC 2015001159

Road trip, old-school style! Though the Oregon Trail fell out of favor with travelers after the transcontinental railroad was finished in 1869, it's still possible to travel the trail from Missouri to Oregon (though some parts are now paved roads). Over 100 years after the last known crossing, journalist Rinker Buck, his brother, and his brother's Jack Russell terrier set out in a covered wagon pulled by mules. Along with riveting details about their four-month, 2,000-mile trip (Terrible thunderstorms! Broken wagon wheels! Helpful strangers!), Buck describes the rich history of the trail and the pioneers who made the journey before him. Funny and touching, this book should especially please those interested in American history.

"Recommended for folk interested in the Oregon Trail, pioneer history, or mules." Library Journal.

Calloway, Colin G. (Colin Gordon), 1953-

One vast winter count : the Native American West before Lewis and Clark / Colin G. Calloway. University of Nebraska Press, 2003. xvii, 631 p. : **978**

1. Indians of North America -- The West (United States) -- History. 2. Government relations with indigenous peoples 3. Indians of North America -- Relations with Europeans -- History. 4. Indians of North America -- Relations with European-Americans -- History.
ISBN 0803215304

LC 2003044757

Spur Award for Historical Nonfiction, 2004.

"Calloway concentrates on the Indian experience from the Appalachians to the Pacific, in a time frame from prehistory to the 18th century. The scope is staggering, but Calloway masters it, demonstrating a remarkable command of a broad spectrum of historical, ethnographic and archeological sources including printed material and oral traditions." Publishers Weekly.

Cozzens, Peter, 1957-

The **earth** is weeping : the Indian wars for the American West, 1866-1891 / Peter Cozzens. Alfred A. Knopf, 2016. 576 p. **978**

1. Indians of North America -- Wars -- 1866-1895. 2. Government relations with indigenous peoples. 3. The West (United States) 4. United States -- History -- 19th century. 5. United States -- Interethnic relations -- Political aspects.
ISBN 9780307958044

LC 2015044077

"This is a Borzoi Book."

A history of the struggle between white forces and Native Americans over the fate of the post-Civil War West details the deconstruction of tribal culture to establish the modern U.S., covering such topics as the conditions endured by frontier soldiers and the ethical quandaries of military officials who sympathized with Native adversaries.

Egan, Timothy

The **worst** hard time : the untold story of those who survived the great American dust bowl / Timothy Egan. Houghton Mifflin Co., 2006. x, 340 p. : **978**

1. Droughts -- Great Plains (United States) -- History -- 20th century. 2. Depressions -- 1929-1941 -- Great Plains (United States) 3. Dust Bowl Era, 1931-1939. 4. Farms -- United States. 5. United States -- History -- 1929-1939. 6. Middle West -- Economic conditions. 7. Middle West -- Social conditions. 8. Great Plains (United States) -- History -- 20th century. 9. Great Plains (United States) -- Social conditions. 10. Dust Bowl (South Central United States)
ISBN 061834697X

LC 2005008057

ALA Notable Book, 2007.

National Book Award for Nonfiction, 2007.

Western Heritage Award for Outstanding Nonfiction Book, 2007.

Presents an oral history of the dust storms that devastated the Great Plains during the Depression, following several families and their communities in their struggle to persevere despite the devastation.

Estes, Nick

Our history Is the future : Standing Rock versus the Dakota Access Pipeline, and the long tradition of indigenous resistance / Nick Estes. Verso Books, 2019. 310 p. : **978**

1. Indigenous peoples 2. Indians of North America, treatment of 3. Resistance to government 4. Protests, demonstrations, vigils, etc.
ISBN 9781786636720

Traces the traditions of indigenous resistance that led to the #NoDAPL movement.

"An honest and passionate voice of Indigenous power that needs to be included in contemporary political discourse." Library Journal

Faulkner, Steven

Bitterroot : a memoir; echoes of beauty & loss / Steven Faulkner. Beaufort Books, 2016. 384 p. **978**

1. Smet, Pierre-Jean de, 1801-1873 2. Lewis and Clark Expedition (1804-1806) 3. Voyages and travels 4. Missouri -- Description and travel.
ISBN 9780825307928

LC 2017275863

Using the letters of the 19th-century explorer Pierre Jean De Smet, Steven Faulkner and his eighteen-year-old son, Alex, follow De Smet across the High Plains to the fur trappers' rendezvous on the Green River, then on to the Lewis and Clark Trail. Lewis and Clark take them over the Rockies (a part of their journey that almost killed the explorers) into the homeland of the Nez Perce whose fate (recorded by a young warrior named White Thunder) is strangely tied to these emissaries from the east.

"Faulkner's verbs vivify, his quotes enlarge his experience, and his poetic descriptions exploit all five senses colorfully; still, keener editing would have pared the backwoods baroque." Publishers Weekly.

Hyde, Anne Farrar, 1960-

Empires, nations, and families : a new history of the North American West, 1800-1860 / Anne F. Hyde. University of Nebraska Press, c2011. xv, 628 p. : **978**

1. Exploration. 2. Families 3. Frontier and pioneer life. 4. Pioneers. 5. The West (United States) -- History

ISBN 9780803224056

Pulitzer Prize for History finalist, 2012.

Morgan, Robert, 1944-

Lions of the West : heroes and villains of the westward expansion / Robert Morgan. Algonquin Books of Chapel Hill, 2011. 508 p. **978**

1. Pioneers -- The West (United States) 2. Explorers. 3. Presidents -- United States 4. United States -- Territorial expansion. 5. The West (United States) -- History -- To 1848.

ISBN 9781565126268

LC 2011023832

"A Shannon Ravenel Book."

Chronicles the lives of Americans who influenced the development of the Western frontier, including Thomas Jefferson, Kit Carson, and Sam Houston.

"This is a collection of biographical sketches of 10 men largely limited to the pivotal roles each played in America's westward expansion. Included are four U.S. presidents: Thomas Jefferson, Andrew Jackson, James K. Polk, and John Quincy Adams; orchardist and naturalist John Johnny Appleseed Chapman; frontier legends Davy Crockett and Kit Carson; statesmen Sam Houston and Nicholas Trist; and General Winfield Scott. This collective biography provides a digestible introduction to American expansion, Manifest Destiny, and the larger-than-life men who led the inexorable charge westward." Booklist.

Nelson, Megan Kate, 1972-

The **three-cornered** war : the Union, the Confederacy, and native peoples in the fight for the West / Megan Kate Nelson. Scribner, [2019] 320 p. **978**

1. Confederate States of America. Army 2. United States. Army 3. Frontier and pioneer life -- The West (United States) 4. Migration, Internal -- United States -- History -- 19th century. 5. Federal government -- The West (United States) 6. Indians of North America 7. New Mexico (Territory) 8. The West (United States) -- History -- Civil War, 1861-1865 9. The West (United States) -- History, Military -- 19th century. 10. United States -- Military policy.

ISBN 9781501152542

LC 2019018824

A deeply-researched, dramatic, and character-driven narrative account of the violent struggle between Union and Confederate forces to claim the American West during the Civil War.

"Nelson effectively blends military history with a fresh look at a region typically obscured in accounts of the Civil War. American history buffs will relish this entertaining and eye-opening portrait." Publishers Weekly

Raban, Jonathan

Bad land : an American romance / Jonathan Raban. Pantheon Books, 1996. 324p. : **978**

1. Frontier and pioneer life -- The West (United States) 2. Homesteaders -- The West (United States) 3. Homesteading -- Dakota Territory. 4. Prairie life. 5. The West (United States) -- History. 6. The West (United States) -- Description and travel. 7. Montana -- History. 8. North Dakota -- History. 9. South Dakota -- History. 10. Pacific Northwest literature

ISBN 0679442545

LC 96013432

ALA Notable Book, 1998.

National Book Critics Circle Award for Non-Fiction, 1996.

Journeys beyond the myth of the American West to reveal the harsh and desperate realities of the homesteaders' lives, offering an incisive portrait of the American heartland that redefines the essence of the American dream.

Sides, Hampton

Blood and thunder : an epic of the American West / Hampton Sides. Doubleday, 2006. xi, 460 p. : **978**

1. Carson, Kit, 1809-1868. 2. United States. Army -- History 19th century. 3. Military history -- 19th century. 4. Frontier and pioneer life -- The West (United States) 5. Indians of North America -- Wars. 6. Indians of North America -- The West (United States) -- History -- 19th century. 7. Southwest (United States) -- History -- 1848- 8. The West (United States) -- History -- 19th century. 9. United States -- Territorial expansion.

ISBN 9780385507776

LC 2006016579

Maps on endpapers.

Spur Award for Historical Nonfiction, 2007.

Examines America's westward expansion, describing the forcible subjugation of Native American tribes, including the fierce battles against the Navajo which ended with a brutal siege at Canyon de Chelly and the "Long Walk" migration.

"This book will surely capture readers, and it ought to. It's a riveting account of a vast swath of history with which few Americans are familiar." The New Yorker.

Wallis, Michael, 1945-

The **best** land under heaven : the Donner Party in the age of manifest destiny / Michael Wallis. Liveright Publishing Corporation, 2017. 320 p. **978**

1. Donner Party. 2. Frontier and pioneer life 3. Overland journeys to the Pacific 4. Pioneers. 5. The West (United States) -- Description and travel.

ISBN 9780871407696

LC 2017012937

Longlisted for the Andrew Carnegie Medal for Excellence in Non-Fiction, 2018.

An account of the 1846 Donner-Reed Party expedition parses fact from fiction to reveal the true events surrounding the tragedy, profiling the adventurous, business-savvy and adventurous characters who shaped the group and how various interpersonal factors led to their harrowing experiences.

"Solid Western history that enhances the understanding of a tragic tale by highlighting the strong human dimension through the accounts of participants before, during, and after the expedition." Kirkus.

Ward, Geoffrey C.
The **West** : an illustrated history / narrative by Geoffrey C. Ward ; based on a documentary film script by Geoffrey C. Ward and Dayton Duncan ; with a preface by Stephen Ives and Ken Burns ; and contributions by Dayton Duncan ... [et al.]. Back Bay Books, 2003, c1996. xvii, 445 p. : **978**

1. Frontier and pioneer life -- The West (United States) 2. Pioneers -- The West (United States) 3. Indians of North America -- The West (United States) 4. The West (United States) -- History.
ISBN 9780316735896

LC 96004323

Originally published: Boston : Little, Brown, 1996.

Based on the popular PBS-television series, the narrative from the landmark chronicle of the American West is accompanied by essays from seven renowned writers and historians on various aspects of western history.

"The book's eight chapters, each written by a different historian, are arranged according to the corresponding PBS series. Beginning with Western America in the 1500s, the work presents all aspects of Western culture from the reality to the myth, moving chronologically from the Spanish exploration of the West, Native Americans, Hispanic Westerners, women in the West, and the Gold Rush, and ending with Buffalo Bill's Wild West Show. If one is looking for an in-depth, comprehensive history of the westward movement, this is not it, but as an introduction, this work is an enjoyable and interesting place to start." Library Journal.

978.1 Kansas

Frank, Thomas, 1965-
What's the matter with Kansas? : how conservatives won the heart of America / Thomas Frank. Metropolitan Books, 2004. 306 p. : **978.1**

1. Republican Party 2. Conservatism -- United States. 3. Conservatives 4. Kansas -- Politics and government -- 1951-
ISBN 0805073396

LC 2004044824

Reveals how conservatism became the preferred national political ideology, exploring the origins of this philosophy in the upper classes and tracing its recent popularity within the middle class.

978.3 South Dakota

Mort, T. A. (Terry A.)
Thieves' road : the Black Hills betrayal and Custer's path to Little Bighorn / Terry Mort. Random House, 2015. 340 p. **978.3**

1. Culture conflict. 2. Gold rush. 3. Dakota Indians. 4. Gold mines and mining. 5. Black Hills. 6. South Dakota. 7. United States -- History -- 1865-1898.
ISBN 9781616149604

LC 2014035457

Describes a little-known exploratory mission by General Custer in 1874, who took 1,000 troops deep into the Black Hills of South Dakota where he found gold and started a chain of events that led up to the end of Sioux territorial independence.

"This highly readable and insightful work is recommended as an essential backstory to Custer's subsequent downfall at the aforementioned battle." Library Journal.

978.7 Wyoming

Black, George, 1949-
Empire of shadows : the epic story of Yellowstone / George Black. St. Martin's Press, c2012. 576 p. **978.7**

1. National parks and reserves. 2. Wilderness areas. 3. Natural areas. 4. Yellowstone National Park -- History.
ISBN 9780312383190

LC 2011041351

A reinterpretation of the 19th-century West documents the exploration of an uninhabited Yellowstone region after the Civil War, evaluating the roles of key contributors while providing coverage of the pioneer era, the Indian wars and period efforts to "civilize" the frontier. By the author of The Trout Pool Paradox.

Meyer, Judith L., 1956-
The **spirit** of Yellowstone / Judith L. Meyer ; photographs by Vance Howard. Roberts Rinehart, c2003. xii, 145 p. : **978.7**

1. Nature -- Effect of humans on 2. National parks and reserves -- Wyoming 3. Nature conservation -- Yellowstone National Park 4. Yellowstone National Park -- Description and travel.
ISBN 157098395X

LC 2002156320

"The author pays tribute to the park and all its glories, covering the park's history, its prime landmarks, and its prominence in art. The photographs are truly striking and not the typical landscape fare. Howard plays with light and texture to capture images that will amaze even those already familiar with the park's unprecedented beauty." Library Journal.

978.9 New Mexico

Childs, Craig
House of rain : tracking a vanished civilization across the American Southwest / Craig Childs. Little, Brown and Co., 2007. xiv, 496 p. : **978.9**

1. Pueblo Indians -- Southwest (United States) 2. Anasazi Culture -- History. 3. Indians of North America 4. Chaco Culture National Historical Park, New Mexico. 5. Southwest (United States) -- Description and travel. 6. Southwest (United States) -- Antiquities. 7. Chaco Canyon, New Mexico -- History
ISBN 0316608173

LC 2006019112

The greatest unsolved mystery of the American Southwest is the fate of the Anasazi, the native peoples who in the eleventh century converged on Chaco Canyon (in today's northwestern New Mexico) and built a flourishing cultural center that attracted pilgrims from far and wide, a vital crossroads of the prehistoric world. The Anasazis' accomplishments--in agriculture, art, commerce, architecture, and engineering--were astounding, as remarkable in their way as those of Mayans in distant Central America. By the thirteenth century, however, the Anasazi were gone from the region. What brought about the rapid collapse of their civilization? Was it drought? pestilence? war? Naturalist Childs draws on the latest scholarly research, as well as on a lifetime of adventure and exploration in the most forbidding landscapes of the American Southwest , to shed new light on this compelling mystery.--From publisher description.

"Beginning at the monumental cultural center of Chaco Canyon, where the Anasazi flourished, Childs's quest to understand their apparent disappearance leads him to the numerous great houses of New Mexico, such as Pueblo Bonito, to the Four Corners area of northeastern Arizona, southern Colorado and Utah, and beyond to northern Mexico. In these places, he identifies features that had not appeared prior to the apparent abandonment of Chaco (thus implying that the Anasazi migrated to these areas). Childs vividly weaves his personal narrative, imbued with a deep respect for the geography and cultural landscape, with scientific research and numerous interactions with foremost scholars." Library Journal.

979 Great Basin and Pacific Slope region of United States

Hutton, Paul Andrew, 1949-

The **Apache** wars : the hunt for Geronimo, the Apache Kid, and the captive boy who started the longest war in American history / Paul Andrew Hutton. Crown, 2016. 400 p. **979**

1. Mickey Free 2. Geronimo, Apache chief, 1829-1909. 3. Apache Kid, approximately 1860- 4. Apache Indians -- Wars, 1872-1873. 5. Multiracial men 6. Indians of North America 7. War 8. Southwest (United States) -- History -- 19th century

ISBN 9780770435813

LC 2015050712

Spur Award for Historical Nonfiction, 2017.

"What happened to Felix Ward is less important to the larger historical picture than how the situation with the Apaches was resolved, but Hutton provides an unexpected twist that keeps the story fresh until the end." Publishers Weekly.

Neely, Nick

Coast range : a collection from the Pacific edge / Nick Neely. Soft Skull Press, an imprint of Counterpoint Press, [2016] 200 p. **979**

1. Neely, Nick. 2. Nature 3. Men and nature 4. Nature conservation 5. Natural areas 6. Pacific Northwest 7. Oregon 8. Essays

ISBN 9781619028364

LC 2016020226

A collection of essays explores the lush and varied landscapes, sights and sounds of the Pacific Northwest, taking readers through the journey of salmon, on a tour of a casino kitchen, a tribal coming-of-age ceremony and a trip following hummingbirds.

"Neely capably explores the complexity of his subjects with polish and finesse, looking carefully and thinking deeply." Kirkus.

979.1 Arizona

Brooks, James, 1955-

Mesa of sorrows : a history of the Awat'ovi massacre / James F. Brooks. W.W. Norton & Company, [2016] 224 p. **979.1**

1. Indians of North America 2. Massacres -- Southwest (United States) 3. Hopi Indians -- Arizona 4. Excavations (Archaeology) -- Arizona 5. Arizona -- History. 6. Southwest (United States)

ISBN 9780393061253

LC 2015037504

Draws on oral traditions, archival accounts and archaeological research to investigate the reasons behind the 1700 slaughter of the Hopi community of Awat'ovi by their kinsmen, examining theories about their welcome of Franciscan missionaries, sorcery practices, political crises and beliefs about ritual bloodshed.

Iverson, Peter

Dine : a history of the Navajos / Peter Iverson ; featuring photographs by Monty Roessel. University of New Mexico Press, 2002. xii, 386 p. : **979.1**

1. Navajo Indians -- History. 2. Indians of North America -- Identity. 3. Navajo Indians -- Identity. 4. Navajo Indians -- Social life and customs. 5. Southwest (United States)

ISBN 0826327141

LC 2002006407

Spur Award for Contemporary Nonfiction, 2003.

Pasternak, Judy, 1956-

Yellow dirt : an American story of a poisoned land and a people betrayed / Judy Pasternak. Free Press, 2010. 336 p. **979.1**

1. Navajo Indians 2. Government relations with indigenous peoples 3. Uranium mines and mining. 4. Radiation. 5. Navajo Indian Reservation 6. Southwest (United States) -- History -- 20th century.

ISBN 9781416594826

LC 2010005546

Describes how the Navajo worked for the U.S. government unprotected in the uranium mines that fueled the Cold War, and how the abandoned mines remained on the Navajo reservation, causing cancer rates and birth defects to soar.

979.2 Utah

Walker, Ronald W., 1939-

★**Massacre** at Mountain Meadows / Ronald W. Walker, Richard E. Turley, Jr., Glen M. Leonard. Oxford University Press, 2008. xvi, 430 p. : **979.2**

1. Mountain Meadows Massacre, 1857. 2. Mormons 3. Massacres. 4. Violence. 5. Utah -- History -- 19th century.

ISBN 9780195160345

LC 2008014451

Map on lining papers.

This account of the most infamous event in Mormon history, the tragic massacre of the overland emigrants at Mountain Meadow, Utah, paints finely drawn portraits of the key players in the drama and their roles in the tragedy.

979.3 Nevada

D'Agata, John, 1974-

About a mountain / John D'Agata. W.W. Norton, 2010. 236 p. ; **979.3**

1. Radioactive waste sites. 2. Radioactive wastes. 3. Suicide. 4. Conservation of natural resources. 5. Las Vegas, Nevada -- Social life and customs. 6. Yucca Mountain radioactive waste site, Nevada.

ISBN 9780393068184

LC 2009039295

The author's investigation into all facets of Yucca Mountain, a desert range near Las Vegas slated to be a federal nuclear waste storage facility, turns personal when his research unearths a report of a teenager's suicidal plunge off the roof of the Stratosphere Hotel, a boy the author believes he spoke with before his suicide.

"D'Agata uses the federal government's highly controversial (and recently rejected) proposal to entomb the U.S.'s nuclear waste located in Yucca Mountain, near Las Vegas, as his way into a spiraling and subtle examination of the modern city, suicide, linguistics, Edvard Munch's The Scream, ecological and psychic degradation, and the gulf between information and knowledge. Acting as a counterpoint to Yucca is the story of a teenager named Levi who leapt to his death off Las Vegas' Stratosphere Motel. A sublime reading experience, aesthetically rewarding and marked by moral courage and humility." Publishers Weekly.

Denton, Sally

The **money** and the power : the making of Las Vegas and its hold on America, 1947-2000 / Sally Denton and Roger Morris. Alfred A. Knopf, 2001. x, 479 p. : **979.3**

1. Celebrities -- Las Vegas, Nevada -- History -- 20th century. 2. Politicians -- Las Vegas, Nevada -- History -- 20th century. 3. Organized crime -- Las Vegas, Nevada -- History -- 20th century. 4. Political corruption -- History -- 20th century. 5. Las Vegas, Nevada -- Civilization -- 20th century. 6. Las Vegas, Nevada -- Economic conditions -- 20th century. 7. Las Vegas, Nevada.
ISBN 9780375401305

LC 00062011

A study of the past, present, and future of Las Vegas traces the history of the city; the roles of organized crime, politics, and business; and the implications of Las Vegas in terms of both mirroring and shaping America's changing values.

"The idea of Las Vegas as the epitome of crass American pop culture has become at least a surface truism in most circles. But Denton and Morris . go much deeper than the surface in this sobering account of the famous Nevada resort town." Booklist.

979.4 California

Brands, H. W.

The **age** of gold : the California Gold Rush and the new American dream / H.W. Brands. Doubleday, 2002. 547 p., [16] p. of plates : **979.4**

1. Migration, Internal -- United States -- History -- 19th century. 2. Gold rush -- California -- Social aspects. 3. States -- History. 4. Prospectors. 5. United States -- Social conditions -- To 1865. 6. United States -- Territorial expansion 7. California -- History -- 19th century.
ISBN 0385502168

LC 2002023776

A history of the people and commercial imperatives that contributed to the California gold rush discusses the massive influx of hundreds of thousands of people to the area, which became a state in record time, in a volume set against the political climate and national issues of the period.

"Combining this wealth of ideas with vivid biographies of actors great and small in the expansionist drama, Brands has produced a work that stands far above the tide of mostly forgettable titles that accompanied the 150th anniversary of the Gold Rush three years ago. A lucid, literate survey of events that transformed the nation, for better and worse." Kirkus.

Kipen, David,

Dear Los Angeles : the city in diaries and letters 1542 to 2018 / edited by David Kipen. The Modern Library, 2018 320 p. **979.4**

1. Authors 2. Pioneers 3. Celebrities 4. City life 5. Los Angeles, California 6. Diaries 7. Letters
ISBN 9780812993981

LC 2018018940

Includes index.

A rich mosaic of diary entries and letters by famous residents and visitors draws on three centuries of writing and includes pieces by such notables as Marilyn Monroe, Cesar Chavez, Susan Sontag and Albert Einstein.

Lunenfeld, Peter

City at the edge of forever : Los Angeles reimagined / Peter Lunenfeld. Viking, [2020] 336 p. **979.4**

1. Cities and towns 2. Community development 3. Popular culture 4. Architecture 5. Los Angeles, California -- Social life and customs -- 20th century 6. Los Angeles, California -- Civilization -- 20th century 7. Los Angeles, California -- History -- 20th century
ISBN 9780525561934

LC 2020013210

How did Los Angeles start the 20th century as a dusty frontier town and end up a century later as one of the globe's supercities - with unparalleled cultural, economic, and technological reach? In City at the Edge of Forever, Peter Lunenfeld constructs an urban portrait, layer by layer, from serendipitous affinities, historical anomalies, and uncanny correspondences. Lunenfeld weaves together the city's art, architecture, and design, juxtaposes its entertainment and literary histories, and moves from restaurant kitchens to recording studios to ultra-secret research and development labs. In the process, he reimagines Los Angeles as simultaneously an exemplar and cautionary tale for the 21st century.

"UCLA digital media scholar Lunenfeld (coauthor, Digital_Humanities) draws surprising links between the artistic, economic, and political milieus of Los Angeles in this immersive cultural history. . . . Richly detailed and evocatively written, this highly original account unearths L.A. stories." Publishers Weekly

Menuez, Doug

Fearless genius : the digital revolution in Silicon Valley, 1985-2000 / Doug Menuez ; foreword by Elliott Erwitt ; introduction by Kurt Andersen. Atria Books, 2014 xix, 171 p. : **979.4**

1. Documentary photography -- California -- Santa Clara Valley (Santa Clara County). 2. High technology -- California -- Santa Clara Valley (Santa Clara County) -- History. 3. Microelectronics industry -- California -- Santa Clara Valley (Santa Clara County) -- History. 4. Santa Clara Valley (Santa Clara County, Calif.) Pictorial works.
ISBN 1476752699

LC 2013045228

An award-winning documentary photographer presents a striking visual history of the Silicon Valley technology boom that reflects key moments in the careers of Steve Jobs, Bill Gates and other leading innovators.

"Menuez even makes the innovators' solitude--sequestered behind drawn blinds for days or cordoned off from the rest of the pack in lonely cubicles--surprisingly compelling. The accompanying text is both complementary and instructive." Kirkus.

Muir, John, 1838-1914

The **Yosemite** / John Muir ; [foreword by David Brower]. Sierra Club Books, c1988. xx, 215 p. ; **979.4**

1. Yosemite National Park (Calif.) 2. Yosemite Valley (Calif.)
ISBN 9780871567826

LC 87023573

Includes index.

Reprint. Originally published: Boston : Houghton Mifflin, 1914.

The naturalist and founder of the Sierra Club recounts his experiences exploring Yosemite Valley and shares his observations on the local wildlife.

Ross, Steven Joseph

★**Hitler** in Los Angeles : how Jews foiled Nazi plots against Hollywood and America / Steven J. Ross. Bloomsbury Press, 2017 320 p. **979.4**

1. Lewis, Leon L.. 2. Roos, Joseph, 1908-1999. 3. Jewish Federation Council of Greater Los Angeles Political activity. 4. Nazis 5. Films, American -- Political aspects. 6. Spies. 7. Jews. 8. Los Angeles, California.

ISBN 9781620405628

LC 2017012324

Pulitzer Prize for History finalist, 2018.

An acclaimed historian presents a gripping, little-known story of the rise of Nazism in Los Angeles during which attorney Leon Lewis ran a spy operation to stop the Nazis from killing the city's Jews and sabotaging the nation's military installations.

"Ross puts his experience in film history to good use, and he creates lively portraits of the men and women whom Lewis recruited as spies and who succeeded in putting some dangerous Nazis behind bars." Kirkus.

Stein, Jean

West of Eden : an American place / Jean Stein. Random House, 2016. 320 p. **979.4**

1. Oral history -- Los Angeles, California 2. Popular culture 3. Los Angeles, California -- History. 4. Hollywood, California -- History. 5. Beverly Hills, California -- History. 6. Los Angeles, California -- Social life and customs. 7. Los Angeles, California -- Social conditions.

ISBN 9780812998405

LC 2015022411

An oral history of five outsider families who rose to power and fortune in Hollywood and Los Angeles traces their humble origins, the dreams that inspired their ambitions, the setbacks that challenged their achievements and their enduring legacies..

"Stein's exhaustive research and brand-new interviews make this an invaluable resource for any student of pop culture, or indeed of 20th-century American history." Publishers Weekly.

Winchester, Simon

A **crack** in the edge of the world : America and the great California earthquake of 1906 / Simon Winchester. Harper Collins, 2005. xiv, 462 p. : **979.4**

1. Earthquakes -- San Francisco, California -- History -- 20th century. 2. Disasters. 3. Natural disasters. 4. Fires -- San Francisco, California -- History -- 20th century 5. San Francisco, California -- History -- 20th century. 6. California -- History -- 20th century.

ISBN 0060571993

LC 2005046009

The definitive account of the San Francisco earthquake and a fascinating exploration of a legendary event that changed the way we look at the planet on which we live.

"In this brawny page-turner...[the author] has crafted a magnificent testament to the power of planet Earth and the efforts of humankind to understand her." Publishers Weekly.

979.5 Oregon

Sharfstein, Daniel J.

★**Thunder** in the mountains : Chief Joseph, Oliver Otis Howard, and the Nez Perce War / Daniel J. Sharfstein. W.W. Norton & Company, 2017. 384 p. **979.5**

1. Howard, O. O. (Oliver Otis), 1830-1909. 2. Joseph, Nez Perce Chief, 1840-1904. 3. Nez Perce Indians -- Wars, 1877. 4. Government relations with indigenous peoples. 5. Indians of North America -- Relations with European-Americans. 6. Indians of North America -- Civil rights. 7. United States -- Race relations. 8. The West (United States) -- History -- 19th century.

ISBN 9780393239416

LC 2016055352

Chronicles the epic clash between General Oliver Otis Howard, who took on a mission in the Pacific Northwest to force Native Americans onto reservations, and the Nez Perce leader Chief Joseph, who refused to leave his ancestral land.

"Sharfstein has provided a scrupulously researched and detailed revisiting of one of the most moving and saddest sagas in American history." Booklist.

Stark, Peter, 1954-

Astoria : John Jacob Astor and Thomas Jefferson's lost Pacific empire: a story of wealth, ambition, and survival / Peter Stark. Ecco Press, 2014. 384 p. **979.5**

1. Astor, John Jacob, 1763-1848. 2. Expeditions 3. Overland journeys to the Pacific 4. Ocean travel 5. Fur industry and trade

ISBN 9780062218292

LC bl2014004837

Drawing on original source material, this gripping true story, filled with high adventure and incredible hardship, documents the 3-year expedition, from 1810 to 1813, to establish Fort Astoria, a trading post on the Columbia River in the Pacific Northwest.

"A fast-paced, riveting account of exploration and settlement, suffering and survival, treachery and death." Kirkus.

979.7 Washington

Harmon, Alexandra, 1945-

Indians in the making : ethnic relations and Indian identities around Puget Sound / Alexandra Harmon. University of California Press, c1998. xii, 393 p. : **979.7**

1. Indians of North America -- Relations with European-Americans. 2. Indians of North America -- Washington (State) 3. Puget Sound area -- History. 4. Washington (State) -- History.

ISBN 0520211766

LC 98017665

"The author examines how both the federal government and the native peoples of western Washington were constantly redefining Indian identity to their advantage over a 150-year period. Harmon's examination of the native fishing rights controversy of the 1960s and 1970s is particularly useful." Library Journal.

Krist, Gary

The **white** cascade : the Great Northern Railway disaster and America's deadliest avalanche / Gary Krist. Henry Holt and Company, 2007. xii, 315 p., 16 p. of plates : **979.7**

1. Great Northern Railway -- History 20th century. 2. Avalanches -- Washington (State) -- History -- 20th century. 3. Railroad accidents -- Washington (State) -- History -- 20th century. 4. Railroad travel. 5. Blizzards. 6. Washington (State) -- History -- 20th century.

ISBN 0805077057

LC 2006049047

"In February 1910, a monstrous blizzard hit Washington State. High in the Cascade Mountains near the tiny town of Wellington, two trainloads of cold, hungry passengers and their crews found their railcars buried in rising drifts, parked precariously on the edge of a steep ravine. An army of the Great Northern Railroad's men worked round-the-clock to rescue the trains, but the storm was unrelenting. Suddenly the earth shifted and a colossal avalanche tumbled, sweeping the trains and their sleeping passengers over the steep slope and down the mountainside."--From source other than the Library of Congress

"This is a tale in which snow falls, a mountain looms, and most of the protagonists simply sit. The outcome is predetermined. Mr. Krist does wonders with this unpromising material, however. Adopting a restrained, documentary tone, he slowly builds a picture of massing natural forces and helpless humanity, brought closer and closer to catastrophe with each tick of the clock. The pacing is expertly judged, and the potentially confusing narrative threads, involving multiple actors in scattered locations, are tied together neatly." New York Times.

979.8 Alaska

Borneman, Walter R., 1952-

★**Alaska** : saga of a bold land / Walter R. Borneman. Harper Collins, c2003. xiv, 608 p. : **979.8**

1. Frontier and pioneer life. 2. Alaska -- History.
ISBN 9780060503062

LC 2002027271

A comprehensive history of Alaska provides coverage of such topics as the area's native culture, its exploration and mountaineering, the mining rushes, its railroads and aviation, its military operations, the conservation versus development conflict, and the ANWR oil drilling debate.

"Separated into nine chronologically based chapters, the text explores a recurring theme in Alaska's development: conflict among disparate groups over how the land would be used for personal enrichment. Engaging chapters detail the important events and those who helped shape Alaska's history. This expansive, comprehensive history is recommended for all libraries." Library Journal.

Heacox, Kim

Rhythm of the wild : a life inspired by Alaska's Denali National Park / Kim Heacox. Lyons Press, 2015. 256 p. **979.8**

1. Heacox, Kim Travel Denali National Park and Preserve. 2. Natural history. 3. Nature conservation. 4. Landscape protection. 5. Wildlife conservation. 6. Denali National Park and Preserve -- History. 7. Alaska -- Description and travel.
ISBN 9781493003891

LC 2014048442

A compelling memoir about Kim Heacox's more than thirty-year relationship with the most iconic landscape in Alaska

"The park's wildlife--moose, eagles, red fox, sandhill cranes, grizzly bears, porcupines and wolves--share the stage with human actors in Heacox's chronicle. Top-notch environmental writing to shelve alongside George Perkins Marsh, Aldo Leopold, Robert Marshall and Barry Lopez." Kirkus.

Jenkins, Peter, 1951-

Looking for Alaska / Peter Jenkins. St. Martin's Press, 2001. 434 p. : **979.8**

1. Jenkins, Peter, 1951- Travel Alaska. 2. Indians of North America -- Alaska -- Social life and customs. 3. Travelers -- United States 4. Adventure travel. 5. Voyages and travels. 6. Alaska -- Description and travel. 7. Alaska -- Social life and customs. 8. Alaska -- History, Local.
ISBN 0312261780

LC 2001048871

"This book sparkles with adventure, quirky characters, unbelievable hardships, and indescribable beauty." Library Journal.

980 History of South America

Chasteen, John Charles, 1955-

Americanos : Latin America's struggle for independence / John Charles Chasteen. Oxford University Press, 2008. 240 p. **980**

1. National liberation movements -- Latin America -- History. 2. Latin America -- History -- Wars of Independence, 1806-1830. 3. Latin America -- History -- 1830-1898.
ISBN 0195178815

LC 2007028595

"This is a beautiful, vibrant ... book; it may also be one of the more socially important books to appear in some time." Booklist.

Born in blood and fire : a concise history of Latin America / John Charles Chasteen. W.W. Norton & Company, 2016. xiii, 356, A50 p. : **980**

1. History. 2. Latin Americans. 3. National characteristics, Latin American. 4. Latin America -- History.
ISBN 9780393283051

LC 2016014210

Includes index.

"Chasteen focuses on major political, social and economic topics and trends that helped shape Latin America, including liberalism, the caste system, the mixing of races, nationalism and the Western notion of Progress; he also examines the role that Europe and the United States played in the development of these phenomena. Also refreshing is Chasteen's examination of the periods he covers from the perspective of women." Publishers Weekly. [review of 2000 edition]

Thomas, Hugh, 1931-

Rivers of gold : the rise of the Spanish Empire, from Columbus to Magellan / Hugh Thomas. Random House, 2003. xxi, 696 p. : **980**

1. Western Hemisphere -- Exploration -- Spanish. 2. Spain -- Colonies Western Hemisphere -- History. 3. Spain -- History -- Ferdinand and Isabella, 1479-1516. 4. Spain -- History -- Charles I, 1516-1556. 5. Caribbean Area -- Exploration -- Spanish.
ISBN 0375502041

LC 2003069316

"Engagingly presented, this book clearly shows the author's passion for his subject." Booklist.

Williamson, Edwin

The **Penguin** history of Latin America / Edwin Williamson. Penguin Books, 2009. viii, 705 p. : **980**

1. Latin America -- History.
ISBN 9780141034751

LC bl2015033163

"Fully updated with a new chapter"--Cover.

Details the history of Latin America and explores the political, social, economic, and cultural elements that have shaped the region, in an edition updated to discuss the impact of globalization and other issues since 1990.

980.03 History of South America -- 1830-1999

Casey, Michael, 1967-

Che's afterlife : the legacy of an image / Michael Casey. Vintage Books, 2009. 400 p. **980.03**

1. Korda, Alberto, 1928-2001. Che Guevara. 2. Guevara, Che, 1928-1967 Portraits 3. Guevara, Che, 1928-1967 Influence. 4. Revolutionaries -- South America -- History -- 20th century 5. Art -- Marketing 6. Radicalism -- History -- 20th century 7. Graphic design 8. South America -- History -- 20th century

ISBN 9780307279309

LC 2008032186

In 1960, Cuban photographer Alberto Korda captured fabled revolutionary Ernesto "Che" Guevara in what has become history's most reproduced photo. Now Michael Casey tells the remarkable story of this image, detailing its evolution from a casual snapshot to an omnipresent graphic--plastered on everything from T-shirts to vodka to condoms--and into a copyrighted brand.

"Casey has written a book that is not only a cultural history of an image, but also a sociopolitical study of the mechanisms of fame. It is a book about how ideas travel and mutate in this age of globalization, how concepts of political ideology have increasingly come to be trumped by notions of commerce and cool and chic, and how the historical Che Guevara gave way, postmortem, to a host of other Ches." New York Times.

Vargas Llosa, Mario, 1936-

Sabers and utopias : visions of Latin America / Mario Vargas Llosa ; translated from the Spanish by Anna Kushner. Farrar, Straus and Giroux, 2018, c2009. xxiii, 275 p. **980.03**

1. Latin American literature -- History and criticism. 2. Arts, Latin American. 3. Latin America -- Politics and government.

ISBN 9780374253738

LC 2017038306

Includes index.

"Originally published in Spanish in 2009 by Santillana Ediciones Generales, Spain, as Sables y Utopias."

A collection of essays from the winner of the 2010 Nobel Prize in Literature offers criticisms and meditations on issues affecting Latin America, including recent history with political groups like FARC and Sendero Luminoso and also the legacies of Papa Doc Duvalier and Fidel Castro.

"After nearly a half century of literary output, Vargas Llosa still has few equals when it comes to power of expression and clearheaded conviction." Booklist.

981 Brazil

Reel, Monte

The **last** of the tribe : the epic quest to save a lone man in the Amazon / Monte Reel. Scribner, 2010. ix, 273 p. : **981**

1. Indians of South America -- Brazil -- Social conditions. 2. Wild men. 3. Indigenous peoples -- Brazil 4. Brazil. 5. Guapore River Valley (Brazil and Bolivia)

ISBN 9781416594741

LC 2009037974

"In the opening scene of Monte Reel's The Last of the Tribe, Brazilian government workers approach the deep jungle hideout of an Amazonian Indian they suspect to be the last living member of his tribe. The Indian sits in his hut, cornered, an arrow drawn on his bow, and waits. After two hours, the standoff ends. The government workers leave; the Indian disappears into the jungle. Again. The Last of the Tribe is the story of the 20-year pursuit of that solitary Indian by aid workers who want to contact and protect him, and by loggers and miners who want him dead or moved before he gives the government a reason to protect more land from resource extraction. Reel's tale is expertly told: perfectly timed, thoroughly researched and descriptively written." San Francisco Chronicle.

Skidmore, Thomas E.

Brazil : five centuries of change / Thomas E. Skidmore. Oxford University Press, 2010. xv, 285 p. : **981**

1. Brazil -- History.

ISBN 9780195374551

LC 2009011669

Wallace, Scott, 1954-

The **unconquered** : in search of the Amazon's last uncontacted tribes / Scott Wallace. Crown Publishers, c2011. 512 p. **981**

1. Wallace, Scott Travel Amazon River Region. 2. Indians of South America -- Amazon River Region -- Social life and customs. 3. Expeditions -- Amazon River Region 4. Voyages and travels 5. Indigenous peoples 6. Amazon River Region -- Description and travel.

ISBN 9780307462961

LC 2011006717

A "National Geographic" writer describes his journey with thirty-four other people into the depths of the Amazon rain forest in an attempt to track one of the last uncontacted tribes on the planet, the "People of the Arrow."

982 Argentina

Parrado, Nando, 1949-

★**Miracle** in the Andes : 72 days on the mountain and my long trek home / Nando Parrado with Vince Rause. Crown Publishers, 2006. 291 p., 32 p. of plates : **982**

1. Parrado, Nando, 1949- 2. Airplane accidents -- Andes. 3. Cannibalism -- Andes. 4. Airplane accident victims. 5. Rugby football players. 6. Andes Region.

ISBN 1400097673

A survivor of the horrific 1972 plane crash that stranded his rugby team in the Andes for seventy-two days--popularized in the best-selling Alive--provides his own chilling account of the ordeal and of his desperate expedition across seventy miles of frozen wilderness to find help.

"Rugby team member Parrado has written a beautiful story of friendship, tragedy and perseverance." Publishers Weekly.

Read, Piers Paul, 1941-

★**Alive** : the story of the Andes survivors / Piers Paul Reed. Avon Books, 2002, c1974. xiv, 398 p. : **982**

1. Rugby football players -- Uruguay. 2. Survival (after airplane accidents, shipwrecks, etc.) 3. Airplane accidents -- Andes. 4. Cannibalism -- Andes. 5. Andes. 6. Andes Region.

ISBN 038000321X

LC 2003269866

Originally published: Philadelphia, PA : Lippincott, 1974.

Records the struggles and sufferings of the young Uruguayans during the ten weeks following an airplane crash in the Andes.

985 Peru

Adams, Mark, 1967-

Turn right at Machu Picchu : rediscovering the lost city one step at a time / Mark Adams. Dutton, c2011. 352 p. **985**

1. Adams, Mark, 1967- Travel Machu Picchu, Peru 2. Bingham, Hiram, 1875-1956. 3. Cultural property -- Protection -- Machu Picchu, Peru 4. Voyages and travels. 5. Exploration. 6. Material culture 7. Machu Picchu, Peru 8. Peru.
ISBN 9780525952244

LC 2011010211

Includes index.
ALA Notable Book, 2012.

Traces the author's recreation of Hiram Bingham III's discovery of an ancient Andes Mountains cloud city, describing the author's struggles with rudimentary survival tools and his experiences at the sides of local guides. By the author of Mr. America.

"While some readers may prefer a more straightforward version of Bingham's exploits... those favoring a quirkier retelling will relish Mr. Adams's wry, revealing romp through the Andes." Wall Street Journal.

Bingham, Hiram, 1875-1956

★**Lost** city of the Incas : the story of Machu Picchu and its builders / Hiram Bingham. Greenwood Press, 1981, c1948. xviii, 263 p., 64 p. of plates : **985**

1. Bingham, Hiram, 1875-1956 Travel Peru. 2. Yale Peruvian Expedition (1911) 3. Peruvian Expeditions (1912-1915) 4. Incas -- Antiquities. 5. Indians of South America 6. Machu Picchu, Peru 7. Peru -- Antiquities. 8. Peru -- Description and travel. 9. Latin America -- Description and travel.
ISBN 0313229503

LC 81007196

Originally published: New York : Duell, Sloan and Pearce, 1948.

"In 1911 Bingham, an American explorer, found the Inca city of Machu Picchu, which had been lost for 300 years. In this volume he tells of its origin, how it came to be lost and how it was finally discovered." Library Journal.

Thomson, Hugh

The **white** rock : an exploration of the Inca heartland / Hugh Thomson. Overlook Press, 2003, c2001. xviii, 316 p.,24 p. of plates : **985**

1. Thomson, Hugh Travel Peru Cuzco (Province) 2. Incas -- History. 3. Indians of South America 4. Incas -- Architecture. 5. Incas -- Antiquities. 6. Cuzco Region, Peru -- Antiquities. 7. Vilcabamba Mountains, Peru -- Exploration 8. Vilcabamba Mountains, Peru -- Antiquities. 9. Peru -- Description and travel.
ISBN 1585673552

LC 2002034606

Originally published: London : Weidenfeld & Nicolson, 2001.

"So entertaining and appealing is Thomson's story of his exploration of the Inca empire that readers will wish they could take off and follow in his footsteps. Thomson's wit, eye for detail and reverence for humanity set him apart from the average travel-adventure writer--he is as good a companion as a traveler could hope for." Publishers Weekly.

986.1 Colombia

Davis, Wade

Magdalena : river of dreams / Wade Davis. Alfred A. Knopf, 2020. 433 p. **986.1**

1. Rivers -- History 2. River travel 3. River life 4. Magdalena River (Colombia) 5. Colombia -- History. 6. Colombia -- Description and travel.
ISBN 9780375410994

LC 2019022605

The award winning writer, photographer, filmmaker, and ethnographer--a longtime Explorer-in-Residence at the National Geographic Society--recounts an enthralling journey down Colombia's Magdalena River that illuminates the country's rebirth after decades of political violence, drug cartels, and guerrilla warfare.

"In this deeply inquisitive, dazzlingly fluent scientific, cultural, and spiritual investigation, Davis illuminates the natural and human history of Rio Magdalena, 'the Mississippi River of Colombia'. . . . A far-reaching, centuries-encompassing river biography." Booklist

994 Australia

Clendinnen, Inga

Dancing with strangers : Europeans and Australians at first contact / Inga Clendinnen. Cambridge University Press, 2005, c2003. 324 p., 8 p. of plates : **994**

1. Assimilation (Sociology) 2. Immigrants -- Australia -- History. 3. Aboriginal Australians -- New South Wales -- History 4. National characteristics, Australian. 5. Australia -- Immigration and emigration -- History. 6. Great Britain -- Immigration and emigration -- History. 7. Europe -- Immigration and emigration -- History. 8. Australia -- Colonization. 9. Australia -- History -- 1788-1851.
ISBN 9780521851374

LC 2005011523

Originally published: Melbourne, Vic. : Text Pub., 2003.

Story of the first British settlers of Australia and the people they found living there.

Hughes, Robert, 1938-2012

The **fatal** shore / Robert Hughes. Vintage Books, 1988, c1986. xviii, 628 p., 40 p. of plates : **994**

1. Exiles -- Australia -- History. 2. Penal colonies -- Australia -- History. 3. Australia -- History -- 1788-1900.
ISBN 9780394753669

LC 87040089

"This epic account chronicles the history of Australia during the 80 years (1788-1868) of England's convict transportation system, when some 160,000 convicts reached 'the fatal shore.' Interweaving his own lucid narrative with untapped original sources--including the diaries and letters of the prisoners themselves--Hughes shows the evolution of the system and of the fledgling nation that emerged from the brutal penal colony." Library Journal.

995.1 Western New Guinea (Irian Barat)

Hoffman, Carl, 1960-

★**Savage** harvest : a tale of cannibals, colonialism, and Michael Rockefeller's tragic quest for primitive art / Carl Hoffman. HarperCollins, 2014 304 p. **995.1**

1. Rockefeller, Michael Clark Death and burial. 2. Missing persons. 3. Cannibalism. 4. Ethnology -- New Guinea. 5. Art -- Collectors and collecting. 6. New Guinea.
ISBN 9780062116154

LC 2015452225

In 1961, a scion of the powerful Rockefeller family, 23-year-old Michael, disappeared during an expedition to Dutch New Guinea where he planned to study a primitive tribe and gather art for a museum that his father -- the governor of New York -- had founded. Michael's body was never found, and officials ruled that he had drowned...but rumors swirled that he was actually killed and eaten by natives. In search of the truth, avid traveler and author Carl Hoffman recently retraced Michael's path, immersing himself in the world of former headhunters and cannibals to solve this historical whodunit.

"[An] unforgettable story of a soothing and politically expedient cover-up and a brutal and tragic collision of cultures." Booklist.

996.1 Southwest central Pacific, and isolated islands of southeast Pacific

Alexander, Caroline, 1956-

The **Bounty** : the true story of the mutiny on the Bounty / Caroline Alexander. Viking, 2003. 491 p. : **996.1**

1. Bligh, William, 1754-1817 Travel Oceania. 2. Christian, Fletcher, 1764-1793 Travel Oceania. 3. Bounty (Ship) 4. Courts-martial and courts of inquiry. 5. Mutiny -- History. 6. Bounty Mutiny, 1789. 7. Navigation. 8. Oceania -- Description and travel.

ISBN 9780670031337

LC 2003050158

National Book Critics Circle Award for Nonfiction finalist, 2003.

An account of the events surrounding the conflict aboard the HMS Bounty focuses on the court-martial of its ten mutineers, citing the breakdown and exile of Fletcher Christian and Lieutenant Bligh's navigation talents.

"A rollicking sea adventure told with enormous confidence and style." Booklist.

Severin, Timothy

In search of Robinson Crusoe / Tim Severin. Basic Books, 2002. 333 p. **996.1**

1. Defoe, Daniel, 1661?-1731. Robinson Crusoe Sources. 2. Defoe, Daniel, 1661?-1731 Knowledge History. 3. Selkirk, Alexander, 1676-1721. 4. Wafer, Lionel, 1660?-1705? 5. Pitman, Henry. 6. Survival (after airplane accidents, shipwrecks, etc.) 7. Literature and history -- Great Britain -- History. 8. Castaways. 9. Castaways in literature.

ISBN 9780465076987

LC 2002071661

Retraces the journeys of castaways and pirates to discover the inspiration for Daniel Defoe's classic, describing his undertaking of a perilous sea voyage and search for the Miskutu Indians in Nicaragua and Honduras.

"The work is energetic and Severin is an ideal guide to the world behind the word. This will surely appeal to the lovers of maritime history." Publishers Weekly.

996.18 Isolated islands of southeast Pacific

Preston, Diana, 1952-

Paradise in chains : the Bounty mutiny and the founding of Australia / Diana Preston. Bloomsbury USA, 2017. xii, 333 p. **996.18**

1. Bligh, William, 1754-1817. 2. Bounty Mutiny, 1789. 3. Transportation of prisoners 4. Prisoners 5. Escapes 6. Australia -- History -- 1788-1851.

ISBN 9781632866103

LC 2017002518

Celebrated historian Diana Preston presents betrayals, escapes, and survival at sea in her account of the mutiny of the Bounty and the flight of convicts from the Australian penal colony. The story of the mutiny of the Bounty and William Bligh and his men's survival on the open ocean for 48 days and 3,618 miles has become the stuff of legend. But few realize that Bligh's escape across the seas was not the only open-boat journey in that era of British exploration and colonization. Indeed, 9 convicts from the Australian penal colony, led by Mary Bryant, also traveled 3,250 miles across the open ocean and some uncharted seas to land at the same port Bligh had reached only months before.

"A wonderful look into the beginnings of Australia and the remarkable strength of the survivors of these dangerous voyages." Kirkus.

Treister, Kenneth

Easter Island's silent sentinels : the sculpture and architecture of Rapa Nui / Kenneth Treister, Patricia Vargas Casanova, and Claudio Cristino ; foreword by Daniel Libeskind ; maps and illustrations by Roberto Izaurieta and Kenneth Treister. University of New Mexico Press, 2013. xv, 144 p. : **996.18**

1. Easter Island -- Antiquities. 2. Easter Island -- History.

ISBN 9780826352644

LC 2013013728

"This richly illustrated book of the history, culture, and art of Easter Island is the first to examine in detail the island's vernacular architecture, often overshadowed by its giant stone statues".--Provided by publisher.

996.9 Hawaii and neighboring north central Pacific

Haley, James L.

Captive paradise : the United States and Hawai'i / James L. Haley. St. Martin's Press, 2014. 448 p. **996.9**

1. Hawaii -- History. 2. Hawaii -- Annexation to the United States. 3. United States -- Territorial expansion.

ISBN 9780312600655

LC 2014026108

A narrative history of Hawaii profiles its former state as a royal kingdom, recounting the wars fought by European powers for control of its position, its adoption of Christianity and its eventual annexation by the United States. By the author of Passionate Nation.

"Haley underscores how remarkable it was that the islands were able to withstand coercion by French, British and American forces for as long as they did. A pertinent work of keen understanding of the complex Hawaiian story." Kirkus.

Moore, Susanna

Paradise of the Pacific : approaching Hawaii / Susanna Moore. Farrar, Straus and Giroux, 2015. 352 p. **996.9**

1. Social change. 2. Culture conflict. 3. Acculturation 4. Legends -- Hawaii. 5. Hawaii -- History -- 18th century.

ISBN 9780374298777

LC 2015002967

The history of Hawaii may be said to be the story of arrivals--from the eruption of volcanoes on the ocean floor 18,000 feet below, the first hardy seeds that over millennia found their way to the islands, and the confused birds blown from their migratory routes, to the early Polynesian adventurers who sailed across the Pacific in double canoes, the Spanish galleons en route to the Philippines, and the British navigators in search of a Northwest Passage, soon followed by pious Protestant missionaries, shipwrecked sailors, and rowdy Irish poachers escaped from Botany Bay--all wanderers washed ashore, sometimes by accident. This is true of many cultures, but in Hawaii, no one seems to have left. And in Hawaii, a set of myths accompanied each of these migrants--legends that shape our understanding of this mysterious place.

"Moore's background in storytelling radiates throughout this work, creating a quick-paced and well-crafted narrative. Highly recommended for the armchair historian and those intrigued by Hawaiian history, maritime exploration, and the history of Christian missionaries. For readers with a continued fascination in the development of the Hawaiian Islands, perusing Julia Flynn Siler's Lost Kingdom might also prove a rewarding endeavor." Library Journal.

Vowell, Sarah, 1969-

Unfamiliar fishes / Sarah Vowell. Riverhead Books, 2011. 256 p. **996.9**

1. Americanization -- History. 2. Imperialism -- History. 3. Missionaries 4. Hawaii -- History. 5. Hawaii -- Annexation to the United States. 6. Hawaii -- Colonization. 7. United States -- Territorial expansion. 8. United States -- Foreign relations -- 1897-1901.

ISBN 9781594487873

LC 2010047943

An irreverent analysis of late-nineteenth-century imperialism in the United States focuses on the annexation of Hawaii as a defining historical milestone, covering such contributing factors as the missionary overthrow of the Hawaiian monarchy and the activities of whaling fleets.

"While Vowell's take on Hawaii's Americanization is abbreviated, it's never bereft of substance--her repartee manages to be filling, her insights astute and comprehensive." New York Times Book Review.

998 Arctic islands and Antarctica

Turney, Chris, 1973-

1912 : the year the world discovered Antarctica / Chris Turney. Counterpoint Press, 2012. 320 p. **998**

1. Discoveries (in geography) 2. Explorers 3. Expeditions 4. Antarctica -- Exploration. 5. Polar regions -- Exploration

ISBN 9781582437897

LC bl2012038688

Shares the stories behind the sensational newspaper headlines about the expeditions and discoveries in Antarctica a century ago, tracing the scientific achievements of five international teams who also made painful sacrifices to establish foundations for modern exploration.

998.2 Greenland

Ehrlich, Gretel

This cold heaven : seven seasons in Greenland / Gretel Ehrlich. Pantheon Books, 2001. xv, 377 p. : **998.2**

1. Ehrlich, Gretel Travel Greenland. 2. Rasmussen, Knud Johan Victor, 1879-1933 Travel Greenland. 3. Women and nature. 4. Men and nature. 5. Loneliness. 6. Inuit -- Greenland. 7. Greenland -- Exploration. 8. Greenland -- Description and travel. 9. Greenland -- Social life and customs.

ISBN 0679442006

LC 00069277

"Ehrlich began traveling to Greenland during her recovery from a nearly fatal lightning strike, and her keen, often poetic responses to the beauty of the frigid landscape and the warmth of Inuit families, combined with a profound immersion in Greenland history, infuse her captivating account with both drama and reflection." Booklist.

Zuckoff, Mitchell

Frozen in time : an epic story of survival and a modern quest for lost heroes of World War II / Mitchell Zuckoff. HarperCollins, 2013. 432 p. **998.2**

1. Search and rescue operations 2. World War II 3. Survival (after airplane accidents, shipwrecks, etc.) 4. Airplane accidents. 5. Arctic regions

ISBN 9780062133434

LC 2012532376

Drawing on intensive research and a firsthand account of the dangerous 2012 expedition, this thrilling true story of survival, which moves between World War II and today, follows the survivors of a U.S. cargo plane crash in 1942 and their 148 days spent fighting for their lives during a brutal Arctic winter.

"Zuckoff's...complex narrative involves the fates of three downed missions to Greenland in late 1942, juxtaposed with the events of the modern-day search effort, led by an exploration company in August 2012 and joined by the author. As a result of the many competing strands and characters, some confusion in the details ensues--though maps and a cast of characters are included to help orient readers... An exhaustively layered but exciting account involving characters of enormous courage and stamina." Kirkus.

92 Biography B

50 Cent (Musician)

50 Cent (Musician) **From** pieces to weight : once upon a time in Southside Queens / 50 Cent. Pocket Books/MTV Books, 2006. 223 p. **B**

ISBN 0743488040

1. Rap musicians -- United States 2. African American men 3. Drug dealers -- Queens, New York City. 4. Mothers and sons -- Queens, New York City. 5. Queens, New York City. 6. Autobiographies and memoirs

Street Lit Book Award Medal: Adult Non-Fiction, 2006

The rap artist recounts the story of how he abandoned his dangerous life of crime to pursue a hip-hop career, the confontation with a rival drug lord that nearly ended his life, and his rise to success in the music business.

Aaron, Hank, 1934-

Bryant, Howard, 1968- The **last** hero : a life of Henry Aaron / Howard Bryant. Pantheon Books, 2010. xvi, 600 p., 16 p. of plates : **B**

ISBN 9780375424854

1. African American baseball players 2. Baseball players -- United States 3. Baseball -- United States -- History -- 20th century. 4. Professional baseball players. 5. Biographies

LC 2009040573

Chronicles the baseball star's on-field achievements and explains how the dignity and determination with which Aaron stood against racism helped transform the role and significance of the professional black athlete and turn Aaron into a national icon.

Abbey, George, 1932-

Cassutt, Michael The **astronaut** maker : how one mysterious engineer ran human spaceflight for a generation / Michael Cassutt. Chicago Review Press Incorporated, 2018. 416 p. **B**

ISBN 9781613737002

1. United States. National Aeronautics and Space Administration 2. Aerospace engineers 3. Government executives -- United States 4. Space programs -- United States 5. Space flight 6. Biographies

LC 2017060552

"One of the most elusive and controversial figures in NASA's history, George W. S. Abbey was called "the Dark Lord," "the Godfather," and "UNO" (unidentified NASA official) by those within NASA. From young pilot and wannabe astronaut to engineer, bureaucrat, and finally director of the Johnson Space Center ("mission control"), Abbey's story has never been fully told--until now. This fascinating account takes readers inside NASA to learn the real story of how Abbey rose to power and wielded it out of the spotlight. Informed by countless hours of interviews with Abbey and his family, friends, adversaries, and former colleagues, The Astronaut Maker is the ultimate insider's account of ambition and power politics at NASA".-- Provided by publisher.

Abbott, Alysia

Abbott, Alysia **Fairyland** : a memoir of my father / Alysia Abbott. W. W. Norton & Company, 2013. 272 p. **B**

ISBN 9780393082524

1. Abbott, Alysia Family. 2. Gay fathers 3. Fathers and daughters. 4. Growing up 5. Gay men 6. San Francisco, California 7. Autobiographies and memoirs

LC 2013011614

A woman describes her life being raised by her widowed, bi-sexual father in the liberating cultural mecca of San Francisco in the 1970s and 1980s and how AIDS began claiming the lives of their friends and eventually her father.

Abbott, Berenice, 1898-1991

★Van Haaften, Julia **Berenice** Abbott: a life in photography / Julia Van Haaften. W.W. Norton & Company, 2018. 544 p. **B**

ISBN 9780393292787

1. Abbott, Berenice, 1898-1991. 2. Photographers. 3. Women photographers 4. Photography. 5. Biographies

LC 2017056400

Berenice Abbott is to American photography as Georgia O'Keeffe is to painting or Willa Cather to letters. She was a photographer of astounding innovation and artistry, a pioneer in both her personal and professional life. Abbott's sixty-year career established her not only as a master of American photography, but also as a teacher, writer, archivist, and inventor.

"Van Haaftens expert foundational biography brings Abbott into sharp focus as a photographer able to express deep feeling through technical mastery." Booklist.

Abdul-Jabbar, Kareem, 1947-

Abdul-Jabbar, Kareem, 1947- **Coach** Wooden and me : our 50-year friendship on and off the court / Kareem Abdul-Jabbar. Grand Central Publishing, 2017 288 p. **B**

ISBN 9781455542277

1. Wooden, John, 1910-2010. 2. Basketball coaches. 3. Mentoring. 4. Personal conduct. 5. Athletic coaches 6. Autobiographies and memoirs

LC 2018459432

In 1965, 18-year old Lew Alcindor played basketball for Coach John Wooden at UCLA. It was the beginning of what was to become a 50-year long relationship. On the court, they broke basketball records. Off the court, they transcended their athletic achievements to gain even wider recognition and tremendous national respect.

"Abdul-Jabbar and Wooden shared a priceless friendship, and this sensitive, sharply written account brings it to full, vivid life." Booklist.

★Abdul-Jabbar, Kareem, 1947- **On** the shoulders of giants : my journey through the Harlem Renaissance / Kareem Abdul-Jabbar with Raymond Obstfeld. Simon & Schuster, 2007. 274 p. : **B**

ISBN 1416534881

1. New York Renaissance (Basketball team) 2. Harlem Renaissance -- Influence. 3. Jazz music 4. African American basketball players 5. Basketball players. 6. Autobiographies and memoirs

LC 2006051776

A personal account by the basketball star traces his childhood in Harlem and the influence of the Harlem Renaissance on black culture in the United States, featuring interviews with Magic Johnson, Quincy Jones, Spike Lee, and Denzel Washington.

"By mixing personal anecdotes with traditional research and reporting, . [Abdul-Jabbar] acts as a knowledgeable, passionate tour guide through the artistic and social history of one America's most dynamic creative eras." New York Times Book Review.

Abdullahi, Asad

Steinberg, Jonny, 1970- A **man** of good hope / Jonny Steinberg. Alfred A. Knopf, 2014. 336 p. **B**

ISBN 9780385352727

1. Abdullahi, Asad. 2. Refugees, Somali. 3. Interethnic conflict. 4. Children of murder victims 5. Somali Americans 6. Somalia -- Interethnic relations -- History -- 20th century. 7. Mogadishu, Somalia -- Interethnic relations -- History -- 20th century. 8. Biographies.

LC 2013046388

"This is a Borzoi book"--T.p. verso.

Drawing on interviews with Asad Abdullahi himself and with people in Europe and the U.S. who knew his parents, one of South Africa's most distinguished journalists tells the story of Asad Abdullahi, a Somali man who, after witnessing his mother's murder by Somali militiamen, moved from place to place searching for peace and stability. Includes 6 maps.

"Steinberg's solid prose is perfect for the task of sharing Asad's history. He probes the darkest moments of his subject's life without ever becoming maudlin, telling the story starkly and bluntly." Kirkus.

Abouzeid, Rania

Abouzeid, Rania **No** turning back : life, loss, and hope in wartime Syria / Rania Abouzeid. W. W. Norton & Company, 2018. 384 p. **B**

ISBN 9780393609493

1. Assad, Bashar, 1965- 2. Civil war 3. Revolutions 4. Insurgency 5. Jihad 6. Syria -- History -- Civil War, 2011- 7. Middle East 8. Autobiographies and memoirs

LC 2017052698

Shortlisted for the RSL Ondaatje Prize, 2019.

Chronicles the tragedy of the Syrian War through the dramatic stories of four young people, including a creator of online video protests, a father who hides his radical beliefs, an unlikely poet commander in a Free Syrian Army militia and a child who opened her family's door to a military raid that forced her father to flee.

"A brilliant, detailed work on a devastating topic. For readers interested in narrative nonfiction, the Syrian war, the Middle East, and personal accounts." Library Journal.

Abrams, Stacey

Abrams, Stacey **Lead** from the outside : how to build

your future and make real change / Stacey Abrams. Picador, Henry Holt and Company, 2019. xxx, 226 p. ; **B**

ISBN 9781250214805

1. Abrams, Stacey. 2. African American women politicians -- Georgia 3. Politicians -- Georgia 4. Legislators -- Georgia 5. African American legislators -- Georgia

LC bl2019009214

Includes index.The Georgia politician describes her own experiences working in business and politics and offers guidance for people outside of traditional social groups to pursue success by recognizing their passion and pursuing it with their special perspective and strengths.

"Abrams offers a handbook for the dispossessed, disenfranchised, and underrepresented for rising to our rightful place at the table, in the boardroom, and eventually, in office. Calling her book the outsider's version of The Art of War, the author reveals herself to be a worthy successor to Sun Tzu." Kirkus.

Abrams, Stacey **Minority** leader : how to lead from the outside and make real change / Stacey Abrams. Henry Holt and Company, 2018. xxiv, 226 p. ; **B**

ISBN 9781250191298

1. African American women politicians -- Georgia 2. Politicians -- Georgia 3. Legislators -- Georgia 4. African American legislators -- Georgia

LC 2017058438

Includes index.

A guide to harnessing the strengths of being an outsider by the political activist slated to become America's first black woman governor shares the story of her own humble origins and rise through educational and political arenas, counseling women of color on how to overcome self-sabotaging beliefs while highlighting the strengths of their differences to gain a competitive edge in the real world.

Abu-Jaber, Diana

Abu-Jaber, Diana **Life** without a recipe : a memoir / Diana Abu-Jaber. W. W. Norton & Co., 2016. 256 p. **B**

ISBN 9780393249095

1. Abu-Jaber, Diana. 2. Women authors 3. Arab American women 4. Self-discovery in women 5. Parenting 6. Autobiographies and memoirs

LC bl2016004269

A follow-up to "The Language of Baklava" continues the story of the author's struggles with cross-cultural values and how they shaped her coming of age and her culinary life, tracing her three marriages, her literary ambitions, and her midlife decision to become a parent.

Aburedwan, Ramzi

Tolan, Sandy **Children** of the stone : the power of music in a hard land / Sandy Tolan. Bloomsbury USA, 2015. 356 p. **B**

ISBN 9781608198139

1. Aburedwan, Ramzi. 2. Violists. 3. Music and society 4. Refugees, Palestinian. 5. Conservatories of music. 6. West Bank -- International status. 7. Israel -- Boundaries. 8. Biographies.

LC 2014032528

Middle East Book Award, Honorable Mention, 2015

Children of the Stone is the unlikely story of Ramzi Hussein Aburedwan, a kid from a Palestinian refugee camp who confronts an occupying army, gets an education, masters an instrument, dreams of something much bigger than himself, and then, through his charisma and persistence, inspires scores of others to work with him to make that dream real. That dream: a music school in the midst of a refugee camp, a school to transform the lives of thousands of children-as Ramzi's life was transformed-through music.

"This is an engrossing and powerful story, moving skillfully amid the failure of the never-ending battles and 'peace' talks between Israel and Palestine and the determination of one brave young man to change his world." Booklist.

Achebe, Chinua

Achebe, Chinua The **education** of a British-protected child : essays / Chinua Achebe. Alfred A. Knopf, 2009. 208 p. **B**

ISBN 9780307272553

1. Authors, Nigerian -- 20th century 2. Writing. 3. Authors, African -- 20th century 4. Nigeria. 5. Autobiographies and memoirs 6. Essays.

LC 2009017480

A latest volume of autobiographical essays by the Man Booker International Prize-winning author of Things Fall Apart includes such pieces as "African-American Visitations," "What Is Nigeria to Me?" and "Politics of the Politicians of Language."

"With African literature emerging as a world force, it's good to have Achebe back after more than 20 years, offering 17 sterling essays." Library Journal.

Achebe, Chinua **Home** and exile / Chinua Achebe. Anchor Books, 2001. x, 115 p. ; **B**

ISBN 0385721331

1. Achebe, Chinua. 2. Authors, Nigerian -- 20th century 3. Exiles -- Nigeria 4. Nigerians -- United States 5. Africa -- Civilization -- Western influences. 6. Nigeria -- Intellectual life. 7. Essays

LC 2001022599

In three powerful essays, the acclaimed, Nigerian-born novelist and author of Things Fall Apart explores the complexities of African culture and discusses the devastating impact of European cultural imperialism on the African experience.

"This slim volume--told in Achebe's subtle, witty and gracious style--is one of those small gems of literary and historical analysis that readers will treasure and reread over the years." Publishers Weekly.

Achebe, Chinua **There** was a country : a personal history of Biafra / Chinua Achebe. Penguin Press, 2012. 352 p. **B**

ISBN 9781594204821

1. Achebe, Chinua. 2. Authors, Nigerian -- 20th century 3. Civil war -- Nigeria 4. Nigeria -- History -- Civil War, 1967-1970 5. Autobiographies and memoirs

LC 2012005603

A world-renowned novelist describes what it was like living through the Biafran War in Nigeria from 1967-1970, detailing the horror of those terrible years and discussing what that time has come to mean for him as a writer.

Acheson, Dean, 1893-1971

Chase, James **Acheson** : the Secretary of State who created the Ameircan world / James Chase. Simon & Schuster, 2007. 512 p. : **B**

ISBN 1416548653

1. Acheson, Dean, 1893-1971. 2. United States. Department of State 3. Cabinet officers -- United States 4. Statesmen -- United States 5. United States -- Foreign relations -- 1945-1989. 6. Biographies

LC bl2014018671

A definitive biography describes the personal and political life of Dean Acheson, who, in tandem with President Harry S. Truman, created the American force that won the Cold War and established a world order still in existence today.

"Dean Acheson was Truman's Secretary of State from 1949 to 1953, and today's world, as Chace shows in this lucid biography, was shaped in no small degree by his efforts." The New Yorker.

Achterberg, Cara Sue

Achterberg, Cara Sue **Another** good dog : one family and fifty foster dogs / Cara Sue Achterberg. W W Norton & Co Inc 2018 304 p. **B**

ISBN 9781681777931

1. Women and dogs 2. Dog adoption 3. Empty nesters 4. Volunteers 5. Autobiographies and memoirs

LC bl2018109824

The best-selling author of <I>Girls' Weekend</I> describes her decision to convert her Pennsylvania farm into a foster home for dogs, recounting her experiences with dozens of remarkable canines throughout her first two years.

"Witty and full of love, her memoir beautifully captures the personalities of the dogs shes helped save and recounts the concurrent struggles in her family life, particularly watching her teenagers fly the nest. This easy read is a must for animal lovers and those interested in volunteering with animals and a good choice for reluctant readers." Booklist.

Adam, David, 1972-

Adam, David, 1972- The **man** who couldn't stop : OCD and the true story of a life lost in thought / David Adam. Sarah Crichton Books, 2014. 324 p. **B**

ISBN 9780374223953

1. Obsessive-compulsive disorder 2. Coping 3. Journalists 4. Compulsive behavior 5. Great Britain 6. Autobiographies and memoirs

LC 2014017387

Originally published in UK

An intimate look at the power of intrusive thoughts, how our brains can turn against us, and living with obsessive compulsive disorder.

"For all the impressive marshaling of information, it is Adams own story of his struggles with the condition, which his infant daughter forced him to confront instead of uneasily accepting, that is the most captivating aspect of this impressive work." Booklist.

Adams, Abigail, 1744-1818

Holton, Woody **Abigail** Adams : a life / Woody Holton. Free Press, 2009. 512 p. **B**

ISBN 9781416546801

1. Adams, Abigail, 1744-1818. 2. Adams, John, 1735-1826. 3. Presidents' spouses -- United States 4. Women and politics. 5. Independence in women. 6. Husband and wife. 7. United States -- History -- 1783-1825. 8. Biographies

LC 2009016288

A narrative based on previously un-mined documents reveals that the popular "Founding Mother" was willing to disagree with her husband, shrewd when investing the family fortune, and eager to correspond about men's subjugation of women.

Adams, Ansel, 1902-1984

Alinder, Mary Street, 1946- **Ansel** Adams : a biography / Mary Street Alinder. H. Holt, 1996. xx, 489 p., [32] p. of plates : **B**

ISBN 0805041168

1. Adams, Ansel, 1902-1984. 2. Sierra Club 3. Photographers -- United States 4. Environmentalists 5. Nature photography. 6. Yosemite Valley. 7. Biographies.

LC 95044741

Traces the life and career of Ansel Adams, including his early years in San Francisco, his relationship with the Native Americans of Yosemite, and the influences on his photography and painting of western landscapes.

"As Alinder traces the straightforward course of Adams' dazzling career . she emphasizes the connection between his stunning landscape photography and his zealous work with the Sierra Club. Alinder is as lucid on the topic of Adams' technical mastery as on his environmentalism and aesthetics, and she also tackles the muddle of his contentious private life with aplomb and candor." Booklist.

Szarkowski, John **Ansel** Adams at 100 / John Szarkowski. Little, Brown and Co., c2001. 191 p. : **B**

ISBN 0821225154

1. Adams, Ansel, 1902-1984 Exhibitions 2. Artistic photography -- Exhibitions 3. Landscape photography -- Exhibitions 4. Picture books for adults.

LC 00069941

"In association with the San Francisco Museum of Modern Art."

Commemorates the art of the late landscape photographer and accompanies an international exhibit by showcasing 114 photographic images complemented by a critical essay on Adams' contributions to modern art.

Adams, Henry, 1838-1918

Adams, Henry, 1838-1918 The **education** of Henry Adams : an autobiography / Henry Adams ; with a new introduction by Donald Hall. Houghton Mifflin, 2000, c1918. xviii, 517 p. **B**

ISBN 0618056661

1. Adams, Henry, 1838-1918. 2. Historians -- United States 3. Self-acceptance in men. 4. Autobiographies and memoirs

LC 00026235

"A Mariner Book."Includes index.Originally published: Boston, MA : Houghton Mifflin, 1918.Pulitzer Prize for Biography or Autobiography, 1919.The American historian reflects on his own life and educational experiences and illuminates events in the nineteenth century.

Adams, John, 1735-1826

★Grant, James, 1946- **John** Adams : party of one / James Grant. Farrar, Straus and Giroux, c2005. 530 p., 16 p. of plates : **B**

ISBN 0374113149

1. Adams, John, 1735-1826. 2. Presidents -- United States 3. Social reformers -- United States 4. Founding Fathers of the United States 5. United States -- History -- 18th century 6. United States -- History -- 19th century 7. Biographies

LC 2004010863

A biography of the revolutionary, founding father, and second president of the United States explores his origins as a son of Massachusetts who crafted himself into an uncompromisingly ethical politician and social reformer.

"The author is excellent at developing Adams' devotion to liberty, honed by British policies that affronted him and turned him into a revolutionary. In Grant's fine synthesis, Adams on the page is the pious, ambitious, and loving man he was in life." Booklist.

Isenberg, Nancy The **problem** of democracy : the Presidents Adams confront the cult of personality / Nancy Isenberg and Andrew Burstein. Viking, [2019] 544 p. **B**

ISBN 9780525557500

1. Adams, John, 1735-1826 Political and social views. 2. Adams, John Quincy, 1767-1848 Political and social views. 3. Presidents -- United States 4. Democracy -- United States -- History. 5.

Elite (Social sciences) 6. Populism. 7. United States -- Politics and government -- 1783-1865. 8. United States -- Politics and government -- Philosophy. 9. Biographies.

LC 2018039232

A recasting of the second and sixth presidents, father and son John and John Quincy Adams, explores how they worked to partially protect a fledgling American democracy from its vulnerabilities to popularity-driven elections and an elite ruling class.

"To make sense of Americas twenty-first-century political discontents, Isenberg and Burstein turn to the nations second and sixth presidents, a father-son pair of one-term chief executives often dismissed as elitists, out of touch with their countrys democratic spirit." Booklist.

McCullough, David G. **John** Adams / David McCullough. Simon & Schuster, 2001. 751 p., 40 p. of plates : **B**

ISBN 0684813637

1. Adams, John, 1735-1826. 2. Presidents -- United States 3. Lawyers -- Massachusetts 4. Politicians -- United States. 5. Founding Fathers of the United States. 6. United States -- Politics and government -- 1775-1783. 7. United States -- Politics and government -- 1783-1809. 8. Massachusetts -- History. 9. Washington, D.C. -- History. 10. Biographies 11. Books to TV

LC 2001027010

ALA Notable Book, 2002.Pulitzer Prize for Biography or Autobiography, 2002.Chronicles the life of America's second president, including his youth, his career as a Massachusetts farmer and lawyer, his marriage to Abigail, his rivalry with Thomas Jefferson, and his influence on the birth of the United States.

"This is a wonderfully stirring biography; to read it is to feel as if you are witnessing the birth of a country firsthand." Booklist.

Adams, John, 1947-

Adams, John, 1947- **Hallelujah** junction : composing an American life / John Adams. Farrar, Straus and Giroux, 2008. 352 p. **B**

ISBN 9780374281151

1. Composers -- United States 2. Music. 3. Creativity. 4. United States -- Social life and customs -- 20th century. 5. Autobiographies and memoirs

LC 2008017922

Includes index.

An eminent composer shares the story of his life, from his childhood and early studies in classical composition to his minimalist and "docu-opera" achievements, in an account that evaluates his professional relationships and the social movements that inspired his creative process.

"Readers will enjoy the candor and completeness of the book, which serves as a gateway to an accomplished body of work. Like the author's music: carefully considered, deliberate and often exciting, gathering together many disparate elements of American life." Kirkus.

Adams, John Quincy, 1767-1848

Cook, Jane Hampton **American** phoenix : John Quincy and Louisa Adams, the War of 1812, and the exile that saved American independence / Jane Hampton Cook. Thomas Nelson, 2013. 496 p. **B**

ISBN 9781595555410

1. Adams, John Quincy, 1767-1848. 2. Adams, Louisa Catherine, 1775-1852. 3. Diplomats -- United States 4. Husband and wife 5. War of 1812 6. Presidents' spouses -- United States 7. United States -- History -- War of 1812 -- Peace. 8. United States -- Foreign relations Russia. 9. Russia -- Foreign relations United States. 10. Biographies

LC 2012039898

Draws from diaries and correspondence to chronicle John Quincy Adams's experience serving as U.S. envoy to Russia and his role in ending the War of 1812, while also detailing his wife Louisa's trials as a diplomatic spouse.

Cooper, William J., Jr. (William James), 1940- The **lost** founding father : John Quincy Adams and the transformation of American politics / William J. Cooper. Liveright, a division of W.W. Norton & Co., 2017. 512 p. **B**

ISBN 9780871404350

1. Adams, John Quincy, 1767-1848. 2. United States. Constitution Signers 3. Founding Fathers of the United States 4. Politicians -- United States 5. Presidents -- United States 6. United States -- History -- Revolution, 1775-1783. 7. United States -- Politics and government -- 1783-1789. 8. Biographies

LC 2017036932

"Coopers balanced, well-sourced, and accessible work focuses on a rarely examined yet pivotal period in American history." Publishers Weekly.

Kaplan, Fred, 1937- **John** Quincy Adams : American visionary / Fred Kaplan. HarperCollins Publishers, 2014. 672 p. **B**

ISBN 9780061915413

1. Adams, John Quincy, 1767-1848. 2. Monroe Doctrine. 3. Presidents -- United States 4. Biographies

LC 2013035334

A brilliant combination of literary analysis and historical detail, this masterfully written biography of the much misunderstood sixth president of the United States reveals the many sides of this forward-thinking man whose progressive vision helped shape the course of America.

"Kaplan sees not an inadequate man in a position he could not manage. He sees instead a visionary, who stood for a united American republic free of the divisiveness of slavery." Booklist.

Nagel, Paul C. **John** Quincy Adams : a public life, a private life / Paul C. Nagel. Knopf, 1997. xi, 432 p., 16 p. of plates : **B**

ISBN 9780679404446

1. Adams, John Quincy, 1767-1848. 2. United States. Secretary of State. 3. United States. Congress. House 4. Monroe Doctrine. 5. Presidents -- United States 6. Politicians -- United States 7. Men with depression 8. Biographies

LC 96049640

Traces the life and accomplishments of the sixth president of the United States, and attempts to depict his complex personality.

"The author traces the life and career of the sixth president of the United States utilizing diary entries to provide keen insight into this extraordinary man, who often suffered from severe depression. The result is a fascinating psychobiography." Library Journal.

Remini, Robert Vincent, 1921-2013 **John** Quincy Adams / Robert V. Remini. Times Books, 2002. xvi, 172 p. ; American presidents series (Times Books) **B**

ISBN 0805069399

1. Adams, John Quincy, 1767-1848. 2. Presidents -- United States 3. United States -- Politics and government -- 1825-1829. 4. United States -- Politics and government -- 1789-1815. 5. Biographies

LC 2002024210

"The author's judicious, eloquent survey of the sixth president's life and career intends not to proffer new and explosive ideas but to fashion recent scholarship into a highly readable overview for the general reader." Booklist.

Traub, James **John** Quincy Adams : militant spirit / James Traub. Basic Books, [2016] 560 p. **B**

ISBN 9780465028276

1. Adams, John Quincy, 1767-1848. 2. Adams family. 3. Presidents -- United States 4. Politicians 5. Political leadership 6. United States -- History -- 1783-1865. 7. United States -- Politics and government -- 1783-1865. 8. United States -- Foreign relations -- 1783-1865. 9. Biographies

LC 2015030745

Drawing on Adams' diary, letters and writings, a scholar and journalist chronicles the diplomat and president's numerous achievements--and equally numerous failures--that both stand as testaments to his unwavering moral convictions, revealing a brilliant, flinty and unyielding man whose life exemplified political courage.

"An impassioned biography of 'a coherent and consistent thinker who adhered to his core political convictions across his decades of public service.'" Kirkus.

Unger, Harlow G., 1931- **John** Quincy Adams : a life / Harlow Giles Unger. Da Capo Press, 2012. 400 p. **B**

ISBN 9780306821295

1. Adams, John Quincy, 1767-1848. 2. Presidents -- United States 3. Politicians. 4. Diplomats. 5. United States -- Politics and government -- 1789-1815. 6. United States -- Politics and government -- 1825-1829. 7. Biographies

LC 2012009399

Examines the role of the sixth U.S. president in helping form the nation, from negotiating the end of the War of 1812 to winning the Supreme Court case that freed the Amistad's African captives.

Adams, Louisa Catherine, 1775-1852

O'Brien, Michael, 1948 April 13- **Mrs.** Adams in winter : a journey in the last days of Napoleon / Michael O'Brien. Farrar, Straus and Giroux, 2010. 384 p. **B**

ISBN 9780374215811

1. Adams, Louisa Catherine, 1775-1852. 2. Adams, John Quincy, 1767-1848 Family. 3. Travelers. 4. Voyages and travels. 5. Coaching (Transportation) 6. Europe -- Description and travel. 7. Europe -- History -- 1789-1815. 8. Russia -- Description and travel. 9. Baltic States -- Description and travel. 10. Germany -- Description and travel. 11. France -- Description and travel.

LC 2009025437

Pulitzer Prize for Biography or Autobiography finalist

Chronicles a trip made by Louisa Catherine Adams with her young son from St. Petersburg, Russia, to Paris, France, to meet her husband, John Quincy Adams, providing a portrait of the state in which Napoleon's wars had left the European landscape.

"The author pursues Louisa Adams's 40-day trek through a Europe in the process of transformation. The Mrs. Adams in question is not to be confused with Abigail Adams, the Colonial matriarch and wife of the second president. Rather, Louisa Catherine Adams was her London-born daughter-in-law, the wife to Abigail's son John Quincy Adams. O'Brien's narrative is richly contextual, encompassing not only the great personalities of the age, whom Mrs. Adams met, but penetrating the secrets of a complicated marriage. A wide-sweeping historical survey and original intellectual journey." Kirkus.

★Thomas, Louisa **Louisa** : the extraordinary life of Mrs. Adams / Louisa Thomas. Penguin Press, 2016. 480 p. **B**

ISBN 9781594204630

1. Adams, Louisa Catherine, 1775-1852. 2. Adams, John Quincy, 1767-1848. 3. Presidents' spouses -- United States 4. Women and politics 5. Determination in women 6. Role models. 7. Biographies

LC 2015510022

ALA Notable Book, 2017.

An intimate portrait of the British-born wife of John Quincy Adams details her significantly different upbringing from her husband, their tempestuous marriage, their wide range of residences and her efforts to forge her own sense of self.

"Thomas has written an excellent account of the life of this woman, who certainly merits greater attention and praise." Booklist.

Adams, Mark, 1967-

Adams, Mark, 1967- **Tip** of the iceberg : my 3,000-mile journey around wild Alaska, the last great American frontier / Mark Adams. Dutton, 2018 336 p. **B**

ISBN 9781101985106

1. Harriman Alaska Expedition (1899) 2. Voyages and travels 3. Alaska -- Description and travel. 4. Autobiographies and memoirs

LC 2017039007

A fascinating and funny journey into Alaska, America's last frontier, retracing the historic 1899 Harriman Expedition.

"Tourists will certainly enjoy reading about both the past and the present, and the breezy, self-deprecating tone makes for an obvious vacation diversion." Booklist.

Addario, Lynsey

Addario, Lynsey **It's** what I do : a photographer's life of love and war / Lynsey Addario. The Penguin Press, 2015. 384 p. **B**

ISBN 9781594205378

1. Addario, Lynsey. 2. Women and war. 3. Women photojournalists 4. Women war correspondents 5. Photojournalists 6. Autobiographies and memoirs

LC 2014036653

Includes index.If you've ever wondered why war photographers risk their lives for photos, this heartfelt, powerful memoir will provide some insight. Pulitzer Prize-winning photojournalist Lynsey Addario touches on her quirky childhood in Connecticut before diving into how she went from taking pictures as a hobby to shooting in conflict zones for days on end, including Afghanistan just after 9/11, Lebanon, Iraq, Sudan, Congo, and Libya (where she was kidnapped).

"A brutally real and unrelentingly raw memoir that is as inspiring as it is horrific." Kirkus.

Addario, Lynsey **Of** love & war / Lynsey Addario. Penguin Press, 2018. 272 p. **B**

ISBN 9780525560029

1. Addario, Lynsey Travel. 2. War and society. 3. Photojournalists. 4. Human rights. 5. Women photojournalists. 6. Afghanistan. 7. Congo (Democratic Republic) 8. Sudan. 9. Middle East -- Social conditions. 10. Africa -- Social conditions. 11. Autobiographies and memoirs.

LC 2018006212

The photojournalist presents a curated selection of images from her work in the Middle East, South Asia, and Africa, in a collection that features essays by such contributors as Dexter Filkins, Suzy Hansen, and Christy Turlington.

Agassi, Andre, 1970-

Agassi, Andre, 1970- **Open** : an autobiography / Andre Agassi. A. A. Knopf, 2009. 400 p. **B**

ISBN 9780307268198

1. Tennis players. 2. Professional tennis. 3. Tennis. 4. Professional

tennis players. 5. Autobiographies and memoirs

LC 2009024004

"By sharing an unvarnished, at times inspiring story in an arresting, muscular style, Agassi may have just penned one of the best sports autobiographies of all time. Open's one of the better memoirs out there, period. Fans will devour Agassi's juicy revelations about both himself and other tennis luminaries.". Time

Agassiz, Louis, 1807-1873

Irmscher, Christoph **Louis** Agassiz : creator of American science / Christoph Irmscher. Houghton Mifflin Harcourt, 2013. 320 p. **B**

ISBN 9780547577678

1. Agassiz, Louis, 1807-1873 Influence. 2. Naturalists -- United States 3. Natural history -- United States -- History -- 19th century. 4. Science -- Influence 5. Zoology 6. United States -- History -- 19th century 7. Biographies

LC 2012014225

Traces the life and achievements of the famous 19th-century natural scientist who discovered how glaciers form and refuted the ideas of Darwin, describing how he enlisted the American public to collect natural specimens for his museum of comparative zoology, his work training a generation of scientists and his staunchly racist views.

Agee, James, 1909-1955

Wranovics, John **Chaplin** and Agee : the untold story of the tramp, the writer, and the lost screenplay / John Wranovics. Palgrave Macmillan, 2005. xxx, 256 p. : **B**

ISBN 1403968667

1. Agee, James, 1909-1955. 2. Chaplin, Charlie, 1889-1977. 3. Authors, American -- 20th century 4. Screenplay writing -- United States.

LC 2004062807

"A double biography of two of the 20th century's most talented artists. Wranovic's hook is a lost screenplay titled The Tramp's New World, which Agee wrote for Chaplin after the detonation of the atomic bomb over Hiroshima. Using personal correspondence and critical reviews, Wranovics re-creates the fascinating historical backdrop of the Agee/Chaplin friendship, interweaving into the stunning tapestry the colorful lives of such luminaries as Brecht, Auden, Ed Sullivan, and John Huston." Choice.

Agrippina, Minor, 15-59

Southon, Emma **Agrippina** : the most extraordinary woman of the Roman world / Emma Southon. Pegasus Books, 2019. 352 p. **B**

ISBN 9781643130781

1. Claudius I, Emperor of Rome, 10 B.C.-54 A.D. 2. Nero Emperor of Rome 37-68 3. Women rulers. 4. Ancient history. 5. Political intrigue 6. Ambition in women 7. Rome -- History -- Julio-Claudians, 30 B.C.-68 A.D. 8. Rome -- Social life and customs. 9. Rome -- Politics and government -- 30 B.C.-476 A.D. 10. Rome -- History -- Empire, 30 B.C.-476 A.D. 11. Biographies

LC bl2019021742

A portrait of the influential matriarch who played a major role throughout three generations of the Julio-Claudia dynasty includes coverage of her relationship with her brother, Caligula, her marriage to her uncle, Claudius, and her assassination by her son, Nero.

Ahmad, Aeham, 1988-

Ahmad, Aeham, 1988- The **pianist** from Syria : a memoir / Aeham Ahmad, as told to Sandra Hetzl and Ariel Hauptmeier ; translated by Emanuel Bergmann. Atria Books, 2019, c2018. 276 p. : **B**

ISBN 9781501173493

1. Pianists 2. Refugees, Palestinian 3. War -- Psychological aspects 4. Arab-Israeli conflict 5. Damascus, Syria 6. Syria -- History -- Civil War, 2011- 7. Germany 8. Palestine 9. Autobiographies and memoirs Originally published in the UK as The Pianist of Damascus.

The prize-winning human-rights activist and celebrated pianist traces the story of his escape from war-torn Syria, drawing on first-person perspectives to offer urgent insights into the Palestinian refugee crisis.

"Well-rendered and affecting, this is a fine delineation of the plight of an unwitting protagonist in the Syrian conflagration." Kirkus.

Aitkenhead, Decca

Aitkenhead, Decca **All** at sea : a memoir / Decca Aitkenhead. Nan a Talese, 2016. 224 p. **B**

ISBN 9780385540650

1. Aitkenhead, Decca. 2. Journalists -- Great Britain 3. Bereavement. 4. Grief in women 5. Recovering drug abusers. 6. Autobiographies and memoirs

LC 2016006847

A memoir from an award-winning journalist at The Guardian describes how her life changed forever when her boyfriend was swept out to sea attempting to save her 4-year old son from a rogue wave in Jamaica.

"While her grief is nearly incapacitating, readers will appreciate the frank manner in which she shares it. Intense and surprising from start to finish." Booklist.

Akhmatova, Anna Andreevna, 1889-1966

★Feinstein, Elaine **Anna** of all the Russias : the life of Anna Akhmatova / Elaine Feinstein. Knopf, 2006. 352 p. **B**

ISBN 1400040892

1. Women poets -- Russia -- 20th century 2. Poets, Russian -- 20th century 3. Russia -- History. 4. Soviet Union -- History. 5. Biographies

LC 2005044542

"Feinstein's magisterial translations of Akhmatova's poetry further enrich this portrait of a mythic personality as vulnerable as she was implacable. A window to a dazzling lost age." Kirkus.

Al Sa'ud, Muhammad bin Salman bin Abd al-Aziz, Crown Prince of Saudi Arabia, 1985-

★Hope, Bradley **Blood** and oil : Mohammed bin Salman's ruthless quest for global power / Bradley Hope and Justin Scheck. Hachette Books, 2020 xvii, 346 p. **B**

ISBN 9780306846663

1. Al Sa'ud, Muhammad bin Salman bin Abd al-Aziz, Crown Prince of Saudi Arabia, 1985- Family 2. Al Sa'ud, House of 3. Princes 4. Royal houses 5. Wealth 6. Ambition 7. Saudi Arabia -- Politics and government -- 21st century 8. Saudi Arabia -- Foreign relations 9. Biographies

LC 2020015477

A revelatory look at the inner workings of the world's most powerful ruling family, the royal family of Saudi Arabia, revealing how a rift within that family produced Crown Prince Mohammed bin Salman, aka MBS, a charismatic leader with charm, ambition, and a ruthless streak.

"A thorough delineation of the rapacious, ambitious new economic plan for Saudi Arabia by the heir apparent to the throne, Mohammed bin Salman. . . . An excellent work of impressive research on a dangerous world leader." Kirkus

Al Samawi, Mohammed

Al Samawi, Mohammed The **Fox** Hunt : A Refugee's Memoir of Coming to America / Mohammed Al Samawi. William Morrow & Company, 2018. 352 p. **B**

ISBN 9780062678195

1. Muslim men 2. Civil war 3. Escapes 4. Interfaith friendship 5. Yemen (Republic) 6. Arabian Peninsula 7. Autobiographies and memoirs

LC bl2018003717

The son of middle-class Shiite doctors in Yemen shares his moving story of love, war and hope that describes his harrowing escape from regional fanaticism and civil unrest through a daring plan engineered on social media by a small group of Western interfaith activists.

"Gracious and generous, this personal account of a remarkable life is a reminder of how peace comes in small increments as the result of the work of committed individuals." Kirkus.

Al Zamel, Doaa

Fleming, Melissa A **hope** more powerful than the sea : one refugee's incredible story of love, loss, and survival / Melissa Fleming. Flatiron Books, 2017. 320 p. **B**

ISBN 9781250105998

1. Refugees 2. Immigration and emigration 3. Resilience (Personal quality) 4. Families 5. Syria 6. Biographies

LC 2016044107

Recounts the powerful experiences of Syrian refugee Doaa Zamel, who was cast adrift in a frigid sea with the children of drowned parents after their dangerously overcrowded ship sank, in an account that details what their experiences reveal about an ongoing international crisis.

"This book amply demonstrates why she has since become a symbol of hope for other refugees. Fleming should be congratulated for bringing Al Zamels inspiring and illuminating story to the page." Publishers Weekly.

Alaric I, King of the Visigoths, -410

Boin, Douglas **Alaric** the Goth : an outsider's history of the fall of Rome / Douglas Boin. W. W. Norton & Company, 2020 272 p. **B**

ISBN 9780393635690

1. Alaric I, King of the Visigoths, -410. 2. Barbarians 3. Visigoths 4. Rulers 5. Romans. 6. Rome -- History -- Empire, 30 B.C.-476 A.D. 7. Rome -- History -- Germanic Invasions, 3rd-6th centuries. 8. Biographies

LC 2019050501

Alaric the Goth offers a deeply researched look at the end of the Roman Empire but from a surprising point-of-view. Offering the first full-length biography of Alaric, a talented and frustrated immigrant, it reveals the lasting contributions Goths made to legal history, to the values of religious toleration, and to modern ideas of citizenship. By moving this man from the borders to the center of Rome's story, it asks readers to think deeply and differently about the lives of marginalized people too often invisible in our history books.

"This invigorating rehash of ancient times speaks clearly to the modern world." Publishers Weekly

Albee, Edward, 1928-

Gussow, Mel **Edward** Albee : a singular journey : a biography / Mel Gussow. Simon & Schuster, 1999. 448 p. : **B**

ISBN 0684802783

1. Dramatists, American -- 20th century 2. Gay men 3. Alcoholic men 4. Biographies

LC 99026558

"Albee regained his position as one of America's greatest playwrights with the 1994 production of Three Tall Women, achieving a level of theatrical mastery and critical acclaim that he hadn't seen since Who's Afraid of Virginia Woolf and A Delicate Balance, almost two decades earlier. The years in between were marked by excessive drinking, outrageous behavior, inferior work, and a diminished career, but Gussow, with a light and generous touch, shows us the strengths of an artist whose core of resilience ultimately insured his survival." The New Yorker.

Albertine, Viv, 1954-

Albertine, Viv, 1954- **Clothes,** clothes, clothes. music, music, music : boys, boys, boys : a memoir / Viv Albertine. Thomas Dunne Books, 2014. 432 p. **B**

ISBN 9781250065995

1. Vicious, Sid 2. Jones, Mick 3. Slits (Musical group) 4. Punk rock musicians -- Great Britain 5. Women musicians 6. Self esteem 7. Gender role 8. England -- Popular culture -- History -- 20th century 9. Autobiographies and memoirs

LC 2014029971

As lead guitarist and songwriter for the seminal band The Slits, she influenced a future generation of artists including Kurt Cobain and Carrie Brownstein. She formed a band with Sid Vicious and was there the night he met Nancy Spungeon. She tempted Johnny Thunders, toured America with the Clash, dated Mick Jones, and inspired the classic Clash anthem "Train in Vain." But Albertine was no mere muse. In Clothes, Clothes, Clothes. Music, Music, Music. Boys, Boys, Boys., Albertine delivers a unique and unfiltered look at a traditionally male-dominated scene.

"This pioneer and pivotal punk rocker discusses her relationships/friendships with fellow musicians Joe Strummer, Johnny Rotten, Sid Vicious, and Johnny Thunders in this fascinating insiders look at the punk scene from a female perspective." Booklist.

Albom, Mitch, 1958-

Albom, Mitch, 1958- **Finding** Chika : a little girl, an earthquake, and the making of a family / Mitch Albom. HarperCollins, 2019. 256 p. **B**

ISBN 9780062952394

1. Jeune, Chika. 2. Orphans 3. Survival (after earthquakes) 4. Children with terminal illnesses 5. Families 6. Haiti

LC bl2019025255

The author traces the inspirational story of a child from The Have Faith Haiti Orphanage, whose short life of poverty and incurable illness prompted her loving adoption into his family.

Albracht, William

Albracht, William **Abandoned** in hell : the fight for Vietnam's Fire Base Kate / Captain William Albracht (Ret.) and Captain Marvin J. Wolf (Ret.). NAL Caliber, 2015. 400 p. **B**

ISBN 9780451468086

1. Albracht, William. 2. Vietnam War, 1961-1975, American. 3. Escapes -- Vietnam 4. Soldiers -- United States 5. Green Berets -- History -- Vietnam War, 1961-1975. 6. Fire Base Kate (Vietnam) 7. Autobiographies and memoirs

LC 2014028501

In October 1969, William Albracht, the youngest Green Beret captain in Vietnam, took command of a remote hilltop outpost called Fire Base Kate, held by only 27 American soldiers and 150 Montagnard militiamen. At dawn the next morning, three North Vietnamese Army regiments -- some 6,000 men -- crossed the Cambodian border and attacked. Albracht's men held off repeated ground assaults with fierce hand-to-hand fighting, air support and a dangerously close B-52 strike. After five days, Kate's defenders were out of ammo and water. Albracht led his troops, including many wounded, off the hill and on a daring night march through enemy lines.

"This fast-paced narrative encapsulates Vietnam War themes, significantly the bravery of grunts and company grade officers and their loyalty to one another, and also bureaucratic mistakes with tragic consequences made by inexperienced officers and government officials too far removed from front-line action. Ultimately, Firebase Kate, as Albracht says, was built in a vulnerable location and its men were written off when they could no longer defend it. Readers of such excellent battlefield works as Harold Moore and Joseph Galloway's We Were Soldiers OnceAnd Young will delve into this one." Library Journal.

Albright, Madeleine Korbel

Albright, Madeleine Korbel **Hell** and other destinations : a 21st-century memoir / Madeleine Albright. HarperCollins, 2020. xi, 370 p. **B**

ISBN 9780062802255

1. United States. Department of State 2. Women cabinet officers 3. Women politicians 4. Diplomatic and consular service 5. Diplomacy -- United States 6. United States -- Foreign relations 7. Autobiographies and memoirs

LC bl2020007191

The bestselling author and former Secretary of State?one of the world's most admired and tireless public servants?reflects on the final stages of her career and how she has blazed her own trail in her later years.

"This passionately told account of Albright's 'afterlife' will inspire readers to become involved in the issues meaningful to them. Recommended for all interested in politics, leadership, and women's studies." Library Journal

Albright, Madeleine Korbel **Prague** winter : a personal story of remembrance and war, 1937-1948 / Madeleine Albright. Harper, 2012. 352 p. **B**

ISBN 9780062030313

1. Albright, Madeleine Korbel Family. 2. Albright, Madeleine Korbel Childhood and youth. 3. World War II -- Prague, Czech Republic 4. Jewish families -- Prague, Czech Republic 5. Childhood -- Czechoslovakia 6. Memories 7. Prague, Czech Republic -- History -- 20th century 8. Czechoslovakia -- History -- 1938-1945. 9. Prague (Czech Republic) -- History -- 20th century. 10. Autobiographies and memoirs

LC 2011049416

"Set against the backdrop of occupied Czechoslovakia and World War II, the former Secretary of State paints a vivid portrait of her early life from 1937 to 1948 during which she witnessed the Nazi invasion of her native Prague, the Holocaust, the defeat of fascism, the rise of communism and the onset of the Cold War."

Alcott, Louisa May, 1832-1888

Reisen, Harriet **Louisa** May Alcott : the woman behind Little women / Harriet Reisen. Henry Holt, 2009. 384 p. **B**

ISBN 9780805082999

1. Alcott, Louisa May, 1832-1888. 2. Authors, American -- 19th century 3. Women authors -- 19th century 4. Writing. 5. Military nurses -- United States -- History -- Civil War, 1861-1865. 6. United States -- History -- 1849-1877. 7. Biographies

LC 2009010637

"A John Macrae book."

Explores Alcott's life in the context of her works, in a modern take on a remarkable and prolific writer--who secretly authored pulp fiction, harbored radical abolitionist views, and served as a Civil War nurse--that is also a story of how the beloved classic Little Women came to be.

"In this biography of the American author, Reisen analyzes Louisa's great pleasure in writing lucrative pulp fiction, her sacrifices, adventures, and brilliant career. Here . . . is Alcott whole, a trailblazing woman grasping freedom in a time of sexual inequality and war, a survivor of cruel tragedies, a quintessential American writer." Booklist.

Seiple, Samantha **Louisa** on the front lines : Louisa May Alcott in the Civil War / Samantha Seiple. Seal Press, 2019. 320 p. **B**

ISBN 9781580058049

1. Military nurses 2. United States Civil War, 1861-1865 3. Women authors, American -- 19th century 4. Women authors 5. United States -- History -- Civil War, 1861-1865 6. Biographies

LC 2018032967

An examination of Little Women author Louisa May Alcott's service as a Civil War nurse reveals how her experiences shaped her writing and activism, from her commitment to abolitionism to the creation of her book, Hospital Sketches.

"While other biographies may provide a more complete picture of Alcotts life, Seiples version is laser-focused on this particular period, convincingly making the unique argument that Alcotts difficult trials forged her personality and informed virtually every facet of her work." Publishers Weekly.

Alderson, Sandy

Kettmann, Steve **Baseball** maverick : how Sandy Alderson revolutionized baseball and revived the Mets / Steve Kettmann. Atlantic Monthly Press, 2015 320 p. **B**

ISBN 9780802119988

1. Alderson, Sandy. 2. New York Mets (Baseball Team) 3. Oakland Athletics (Baseball Team) 4. Baseball -- Management 5. Baseball teams 6. Professional baseball 7. Biographies

LC 2016301464

Taking readers behind-the-scenes of a Major League team, a best-selling author follows Sandy Alderson's transformation of baseball over the last 30 year and his attempts to turn the Mets back into a winning team.

"Kettmann has written a worthy biography of a compelling figure, but the author's desire to produce his own version of Moneyball has caused him to overstate his case." Kirkus.

Alderton, Dolly

Alderton, Dolly **Everything** I know about love : a memoir / Dolly Alderton. HarperCollins, 2020, c2018. 360 p. **B**

ISBN 9780062968784

1. Women journalists 2. Growing-up 3. Interpersonal relations 4. Friendship 5. England 6. Autobiographies and memoirs

First published in 2018 by Fig Tree, an imprint of Penguin Random House UK.

The award-winning Sunday Times columnist and co-host of The High Low podcast presents a U.S. release of her internationally best-selling memoir about growing up, aging and learning to navigate relationships and a career.

"A poignant breath of fresh air for those who struggled?or are struggling?with the dramedy of early adulthood." Kirkus

Aldridge, John

Aldridge, John A **speck** in the sea : a story of survival and rescue / John Aldridge and Anthony Sosinski. Weinstein Books, [2017] x, 262 pages, 8 unnumbered pages of plates : **B**

ISBN 9781602863286

1. Aldridge, John. 2. Sosinski, Anthony 3. Marine accidents 4.

Fishing boats. 5. Sea survival 6. Fishers. 7. Atlantic Ocean 8. Autobiographies and memoirs

LC 2017289284

Two veteran sailors who co-own and operate a Montauk lobster boat recount the 2013 search-and-rescue mission for co-author John Aldridge, describing how his partner, their families, the local fishing community and the U.S. Coast Guard in three states mobilized an unprecedented and ultimately successful operation.

"Told from multiple viewpoints, the book takes readers into the water with Aldridge as he shares first-person accounts of shark encounters and the mind games he played while clinging to his rubber boots to stay afloat." Publishers Weekly.

Aldrin, Buzz

Aldrin, Buzz **No** dream is too high / Buzz Aldrin with Ken Abraham. National Geographic Society, 2016. 223 p. **B**

ISBN 9781426216497

1. Project Apollo (U.S.) 2. Astronauts -- United States 3. Space flight to the moon 4. Apollo 11 (Spacecraft) 5. Space exploration -- History 6. Autobiographies and memoirs

LC 2015037069

The American astronaut shares the wisdom and guiding principles he has gleaned throughout his historical career, sharing accompanying anecdotes and memories on such topics as his initial rejection as an astronaut and his eightieth-birthday Galapagos dive.

"Aldrin's journey will engage space exploration enthusiasts, and his motivational advice will connect especially well with young adults." Library Journal.

Alexander, Elizabeth, 1962-

Alexander, Elizabeth, 1962- The **light** of the world : a memoir / Elizabeth Alexander. Grand Central Publishing, 2015. 224 p. **B**

ISBN 9781455599875

1. African American women poets 2. Loss (Psychology) 3. Self-discovery 4. Self-fulfillment 5. Autobiographies and memoirs

LC 2014020884

National Book Critics Circle Award for Autobiography/ Memoir finalist

Finalist for the Hurston/Wright Legacy Awards for Nonfiction, 2016

Pulitzer Prize for Biography or Autobiography finalist, 2016.

In THE LIGHT OF THE WORLD, Elizabeth Alexander--poet, mother, and wife--finds herself at an existential crossroads after the sudden death of her husband, who was just 49. She examines the journey we take in life through the lens of her own emotional and intellectual evolution, taking stock of herself at the midcentury mark. This book is for anyone who has loved and lost. It's about being strong when you want to collapse, about being grateful when someone has been stolen from you--it's discovering the truth in your life's journey: the good, the bad, and the ugly. It's Elizabeth Alexander's story but it is all of our stories because it is about discovering what matters.

"Fashioning her mellifluous narrative around the beauty she found in Ghebreyesus, Alexander is grateful, patient, and willing to pursue a fit of magical thinking that he might just return." Publishers Weekly.

Alexander, Jane, 1939-

Alexander, Jane, 1939- **Wild** things, wild places : adventurous tales of wildlife and conservation on planet Earth / Jane Alexander. Alfred A. Knopf, 2016. 352 p. **B**

ISBN 9780385354363

1. Environmentalists 2. Wildlife conservation. 3. Rare and endangered animals 4. Nature -- Effect of humans on 5. Autobiographies and memoirs

LC 2016007803

"A Borzoi book."

The author writes of her steady and fervent immersion into the worlds of wildlife conservation, of her coming to know the scientists throughout the world and her travels with them to save many species from extinction.

"Highly recommended for all interested in travel, natural history, and environmental issues." Library Journal.

Alexander, the Great, 356-323 B.C.

Everitt, Anthony **Alexander** the Great : his life and his mysterious death / Anthony Everitt. Random House, 2019. 496 p. **B**

ISBN 9780425286524

1. Rulers 2. Leadership 3. Command of troops 4. Determination (Personal quality) 5. Ancient Greece -- Rulers 6. Ancient Greece -- History -- Macedonian expansion, 359-323 B.C. 7. Biographies

LC 2018059885

A reconstruction of the life of the ancient Greek conqueror highlights his contradictory depictions throughout history, placing his achievements against a backdrop of his own historical time to discuss his growing empire, respect for regional traditions and mysterious death.

Alexie, Sherman, 1966-

Alexie, Sherman, 1966- **You** don't have to say you love me : a memoir / Sherman Alexie. Little, Brown & Company, 2017. 320 p. **B**

ISBN 9780316270755

1. Growing up 2. Indian reservations 3. Mothers and sons 4. Dysfunctional families 5. Washington (State) 6. Autobiographies and memoirs

LC 2016958327

ALA Notable Book, 2018.

The author of The Absolutely True Diary of a Part-Time Indian presents a literary memoir of poems, essays and intimate family photos that reflect his complicated feelings about his disadvantaged childhood on a Native American reservation with his siblings and alcoholic parents.

"Presented as a series of vignettes, some in prose, others in poetry, about Alexie's life and family, the narrative transitions between styles, which feels natural as Alexie searches for the best way to present complex memories and stories." Library Journal.

Alford, Henry, 1962-

Alford, Henry, 1962- **And** then we danced : a voyage into the groove / Henry Alford. Simon & Schuster, 2018. 224 p. **B**

ISBN 9781501122255

1. Dance -- Social aspects. 2. Dancers 3. Manners and customs 4. Misadventures 5. Essays 6. Autobiographies and memoirs

LC 2017044367

A journalist and humorist's story about Zumba leads him to a journey through many forms of dance, including ballet, hip-hop, jazz and ballroom, and how this new passion changed his life.

Ali, Muhammad, 1942-2016

★Eig, Jonathan **Ali** : a life / Jonathan Eig. Houghton Mifflin Harcourt, 2017 623 p. **B**

ISBN 9780544435247

1. Ali, Muhammad, 1942-2016. 2. African American boxers 3. Boxers (Sports). 4. Black Muslims 5. Race relations

LC bl2017033332

Shortlisted for the James Tait Black Memorial Prize for Biography, 2017

Presents an unauthorized portrait of the iconic champion fighter, arguing that race was a central theme in Muhammad Ali's career, faith, and advocacy work and that his political beliefs and neurological health shaped his complex character.

"Eig does a fine job of covering all the bases, and though the book is occasionally overwritten, it's only out of enthusiasm for his undeniably great subject, about whom the author is now working with Ken Burns to develop a documentary. An exemplary life of an exemplary man who, despite a few missteps, deserves to be remembered long in to the future." Kirkus.

Montville, Leigh **Sting** like a bee : Muhammad Ali vs. the United States of America, 1966-1971 / Leigh Montville. Doubleday, 2017. 320 p. **B**

ISBN 9780385536059

1. Ali, Muhammad, 1942-2016. 2. African American boxers 3. Boxers (Sports) -- United States 4. Black Muslims 5. Vietnam War, 1961-1975 -- Conscientious objectors. 6. Biographies

LC 2016056528

The best-selling author of At the Altar of Speed presents an insightful portrait of the iconic heavyweight champion and activist that examines the cultural and political implications of Ali's refusal to serve in the military after converting to Islam.

Remnick, David **King** of the world : Muhammad Ali and the rise of an American hero / David Remnick. Random House, 1998. xvii, 326 p. : **B**

ISBN 0375500650

1. Nation of Islam. 2. Boxers (Sports) -- United States 3. African American men 4. Boxing. 5. Biographies

LC 98024539

ALA Notable Book, 2000.National Book Critics Circle Award for Biography finalist, 1998."

This is the best book ever on Muhammad Ali and one of the best on America in the 1960s." Booklist.

Ali, Nujood

Ali, Nujood **I** am Nujood, age 10 and divorced / Nujood Ali, with Delphine Minoui ; translated by Linda Coverdale. Three Rivers Press, c2010. 188 p. ; **B**

ISBN 9780307589675

1. Ali, Nujood. 2. Child marriage -- Yemen (Republic) 3. Forced marriage -- Yemen (Republic) 4. Women's rights 5. Partner abuse 6. Yemen (Republic) -- Social conditions. 7. Autobiographies and memoirs

LC 2009033063

The true story of Yemen's heroic first child bride to win a divorce describes her forced marriage to an abusive husband three times her age, her daring pursuit of the marriage's dissolution and the cultural factors that place girls at risk in Yemeni society.

"One of 16 children living in squalor in Yemen, Nujood was married off at about age 10. Though her husband vowed he'd wait for sex until she reached puberty, he rapes her on their first night together. After months of abuse, Nujood goes to the courthouse, where with heartbreaking naiveté, she tells a judge she wants a divorce. Supported by the legal system, Nujood gets her wish. People,This is a shocking book that captures the social challenges facing Yemen better than any scholarly work could hope to do." Washington Post.

Ali, Taha Muhammad

★Hoffman, Adina **My** happiness bears no relation to happiness : a poet's life in the Palestinian century / Adina Hoffman. Yale University Press, 2009. vii, 454 p. : **B**

ISBN 9780300141504

1. Poets, Palestinian Arab 2. Poetry writing. 3. Israeli-Palestinian relations. 4. Arabs in Israel. 5. Palestine -- Social conditions. 6. Palestine -- Social life and customs. 7. Biographies

LC 2008037298

"An exceptional introduction to a literary world that has, until now, been little known to English-language readers, this is highly recommended for all libraries." Library Journal.

Alien (Hacker)

Smith, Jeremy N. **Breaking** and entering : the extraordinary story of a hacker called "Alien" / Jeremy N. Smith. Houghton Mifflin Harcourt, 2019. 320 p. **B**

ISBN 9780544903210

1. Alien (Hacker). 2. Hackers 3. Computer security 4. Hacking 5. Women hackers 6. Biographies

LC 2018024873

"An Eamon Dolan Book."

Portrays the career of an accomplished hacker--a woman known only as Alien--describing her experiences at MIT, cybersecurity firms, and with a boutique hacking outfit that caters to banks, retailers, and government agencies.

Alinizhad, Masih, 1976-

Alinizhad, Masih, 1976- The **wind** in my hair : my fight for freedom in modern Iran / Masih Alinejad. Little Brown & Company, 2018 352 p. **B**

ISBN 9780316548915

1. Social advocates 2. Hijab (Islamic clothing) 3. Women journalists 4. Women exiles. 5. Iran 6. Autobiographies and memoirs

LC bl2018029726

An Iranian journalist in exile discusses leaving her country, challenging tradition and sparking an online movement against compulsory hijab.

"Alinejad's journey both within and outside of Iran depicts her resilience and determination to lead a full life amid an often repressive society. For all readers interested in women's memoirs and women's rights." Library Journal.

Alkhanshali, Mokhtar

★Eggers, Dave The **monk** of Mokha / Dave Eggers. Alfred A. Knopf, 2018. 368 p. **B**

ISBN 9781101947319

1. Alkhanshali, Mokhtar. 2. Coffee industry and trade. 3. Businesspeople. 4. Yemeni Americans. 5. Determination in men 6. Biographies

LC 2017032893

Traces the story of Mokhtar Alkhanshali, a Yemeni-American in San Francisco, and his dream of resurrecting the ancient art of cultivating, roasting, and importing Yemeni coffee, an endeavor that is challenged by the brutal realities of Yemen's 2015 civil war.

"Eggerss book works as both a heartwarming success story with a winning central character and an account of real-life adventures that read with the vividness of fiction." Publishers Weekly.

Allen, Ray, 1975-

Allen, Ray, 1975- **From** the outside : my journey through life and the game I love / Ray Allen, with Michael Arkush. Dey Street Books, 2018. 288 p. **B**

ISBN 9780062675477

1. National Basketball Association. 2. Professional basketball

players 3. Basketball 4. Athletes 5. Autobiographies and memoirs
LC 2017278398

A record-holding, two-time NBA champion reflects on his work ethic, on-the-court friendships and rivalries and what he has learned about what is needed for a long and successful career, in a memoir that includes coverage of his military upbringing and his unforgettable 2013 Game Six three-pointer.

Allen, Richard, 1760-1831

Newman, Richard S. **Freedom's** prophet : Bishop Richard Allen, the AMR Church, and the Black founding fathers / Richard S. Newman. New York University Press, 2008. 368 p. **B**

ISBN 0814758266

1. Allen, Richard, 1760-1831. 2. African Methodist Episcopal Church Bishops 3. African Methodist Episcopal Church -- History. 4. Bishops -- United States 5. African American clergy 6. Biographies
LC 2007043259

Looks at the life of the first black pamphleteer, abolitionist, and founder of the African Methodist Episcopal Church.

Allen, Samantha, (Journalist)

Allen, Samantha, (Journalist) **Real** queer America : LGBT stories from red states / Samantha Allen. Little, Brown and Company, 2019. 307 pages : **B**

ISBN 9780316516037

1. Gay communities 2. Transgender persons 3. LGBTQIA rights 4. Homosexuality 5. Southern States
LC bl2019005340

A transgender reporter's narrative tour through the surprisingly vibrant queer communities sprouting up in red states, offering a vision of a stronger, more humane America.

Allen, Sandy, 1987-

Allen, Sandy, 1987- A **kind** of mirraculas paradise : a true story about schizophrenia / Sandra Allen. Scribner, 2018. 288 p. **B**

ISBN 9781501134036

1. People with schizophrenia 2. Family and mental illness. 3. Mental illness. 4. Family relationships. 5. Autobiographies and memoirs
LC 2017034690

A first book by a Brown-educated former BuzzFeed editor stands as cautionary tribute to life with schizophrenia and describes her relationship with her afflicted uncle and how he was marginalized and labeled throughout his formative years before embarking on an adulthood shaped by the limitations, prejudices and ignorances of mental healthcare in America.

"A page-turning biography and family history along the lines of Bryan Mealer's The Kings of Big Spring. Don't be put off by the subjectalthough Allen includes bits of medical history, this is a deeply personal story about an enigmatic person living the only way he knows how: by trial and error. In that, many can relate." Library Journal.

Allen, Tina Alexis

Allen, Tina Alexis **Hiding** out : a memoir of drugs, deception, and double lives / Tina Alexis Allen. Dey Street Books, 2018. 288 p. **B**

ISBN 9780062565679

1. Gay fathers 2. Lesbians 3. Fathers and daughters 4. Children of LGBTQIA parents 5. Autobiographies and memoirs
LC bl2017050049

The actress reveals her struggle growing up as a gay woman in a strict Catholic family until the age of eighteen, when her father discovered the truth about her sexuality and revealed that he too was gay, leading them to live their double lives together without their family's knowledge.

"A writer candidly confronts her personal truth in her quest for transformation, transcendence, and redemption." Kirkus.

Allen, Woody

Lax, Eric **Start** to finish : Woody Allen and the art of moviemaking / Eric Lax. Alfred A. Knopf, 2017. 320 p. **B**

ISBN 9780385352499

1. Allen, Woody. 2. Film producers and directors -- United States 3. Filmmaking 4. Biographies
LC 2017002887

Includes index.

The award-winning author of Conversations With Woody Allen shares behind-the-scenes insights into how the iconic filmmaker creates his productions, from shaping a screenplay and preparing scenes to working with engaged actors and crewmembers.

"The book succeeds simultaneously as biographical snapshot, primer on filmmaking, and documentary of an artworks creation." Publishers Weekly.

Allende, Isabel

Allende, Isabel **My** invented country : a nostalgic journey through Chile / Isabel Allende ; translated from the Spanish by Margaret Sayers Peden. Perennial, 2004, c2003. 224 p. **B**

ISBN 0060545674

1. Allende, Isabel. 2. Authors, Chilean -- 20th century 3. Exiles -- Chile 4. Immigrants 5. Writing. 6. Chile -- History -- Coup d'etat, 1973. 7. South America -- History -- 20th century. 8. Autobiographies and memoirs
LC bl2004004873

Originally published: New York : HarperCollins, 2003.

The author explores the landscapes and people of her native country; recounts the 1973 assassination of her uncle, which caused her to go into exile; and shares her experiences as an immigrant in post-September 11 America.

"In this memoir-cum-study of her home ground, the author delves into the history, social mores and idiosyncrasies of Chile, where she was raised, showing, in the process, how that land has served as her muse. This is a reflective book, lacking the pull of Allende's fiction but unearthing intriguing elements of the author's captivating history." Publishers Weekly.

★Allende, Isabel **Paula** / Isabel Allende ; translated from the Spanish by Margaret Sayers Peden. Harper Collins, 1995, c1994. 330 p. **B**

ISBN 9780060172534

1. Allende, Isabel Family. 2. Allende family. 3. Mother and adult daughter. 4. Death. 5. Coping in women. 6. Daughters -- Death. 7. Chile -- History. 8. Venezuela. 9. California. 10. Autobiographies and memoirs
LC 95002452

Originally published in Spanish with the same title: Barcelona : Plaza & Janes, 1994.ALA Notable Book, 1996.

Written next to the hospital bedside of her critically ill daughter, the acclaimed author presents the story of her ancestors and youth, reflecting on the challenges and achievements of one family during a turbulent era in Chilean history.

"Allende interweaves the story of her own life with the slow dying of her 28-year-old daughter, Paula." Publishers Weekly.

Allende, Isabel The **sum** of our days : a memoir / Isabel Allende ; translated from the Spanish by Margaret Sayers Peden.

Harper Collins, 2007. 320 p. **B**

ISBN 9780061551833

1. Allende, Isabel. 2. Authors, Chilean -- 20th century 3. Coping in women. 4. Writing. 5. Autobiographies and memoirs

LC 2007033251

Translation of : Suma de los dias.

Sequel to: Paula.

A narrative memoir of the author's life in the wake of her daughter's tragic death describes the idiosyncratic network of friends she has gathered around herself and the realizations she has formed about such topics as love, parenthood, and addiction.

"In this sequel to her memoir Paula (1995), about the yearlong coma suffered by her daughter, Chilean novelist Allende tells of the difficult years following Paula's death. . . . Surprisingly candid, frequently funny, and highly aware of her own failings, Allende is a person fully engaged in life, and readers will find her eloquent memoir inspirational reading." Booklist.

Allilueva, Svetlana, 1926-2011

Sullivan, Rosemary, 1947- **Stalin's** daughter : the extraordinary and tumultuous life of Svetlana Alliluyeva / Rosemary Sullivan. Harper, 2015. 416 p. **B**

ISBN 9780062206107

1. Allilueva, Svetlana, 1926-2011. 2. Stalin, Joseph, 1879-1953 Family. 3. Stalin, Joseph, 1879-1953 Influence. 4. Children of heads of state -- Soviet Union 5. Freedom 6. Communism -- History 7. Immigrants, Russian 8. Soviet Union -- History -- 1925-1953 9. Biographies

LC 2014045982

ALA Notable Book, 2016.

Charles Taylor Prize for Literary Non-Fiction (Canada), 2016.

Hilary Weston Writers' Trust Prize, 2015.

National Book Critics Circle Award for Biography finalist, 2015.

A painstakingly researched, revelatory portrait of the Soviet dictator's daughter traces her formative years in the Kremlin, the losses of numerous loved ones and her controversial defection to the United States.

"Svetlana's letters and family photographs enhance the portrait of a woman tortured by the secrets, lies, and intrigues at the center of her early life as a Kremlin princess and in later years as the object of fascination and scorn as the daughter of the feared Russian dictator." Booklist.

Alpert, Karen (Blogger)

Alpert, Karen (Blogger) **I** want my epidural back : adventures in mediocre parenting / Karen Alpert. William Morrow, 2016. 272 p. **B**

ISBN 9780062427083

1. Motherhood 2. Parenting 3. Mother and child 4. Essays 5. Autobiographies and memoirs

LC bl2016014228

A blogger and New York Times best-selling author of I Heart My Little A-Holes offers a dose of reality through her hilarious stories, essays and commentary on her experiences raising her children.

"Alpert is honest, humbling, and crass in this irreverent account on parenting." Publishers Weekly.

Alpeyrie, Jonathan

Alpeyrie, Jonathan The **shattered** lens : a war photographer's 81 days of captivity in Syria -- a story of survival / Jonathan Alpeyrie with Stash Luczkiw and Bonnie Timmermann. Atria Books, 2017. 256 p. **B**

ISBN 9781501146503

1. Alpeyrie, Jonathan Kidnapping, 2013. 2. Photojournalists. 3. Kidnapping victims 4. Torture victims 5. Survival. 6. Syria -- History -- Civil War, 2011- 7. Autobiographies and memoirs

LC 2017016403

A harrowing account co-written by a celebrated French-American war journalist who was held hostage by Syrian rebels in 2013 describes how he was betrayed by his fixer and bound, beaten and blindfolded by captors who introduced him to their language and culture, inadvertently helping him discover within himself a faith that helped him to survive.

Alterman, Ira

Alterman, Sara Faith **Let's** never talk about this again : a memoir / Sara Faith Alterman. Grand Central Publishing, 2020. 288 p. **B**

ISBN 9781538748671

1. Alterman, Ira Mental health. 2. Alterman, Sara Faith. 3. People with Alzheimer's disease. 4. Alzheimer's disease. 5. Authors. 6. Autobiographies and memoirs

LC 2019058222

Based on a podcast.

The producer of the Mortified series describes the innocence of her youth in suburban New England before her discovery that her father was a campy sex writer whose career she assumed when he developed early onset Alzheimer's.

"Entertaining, moving, and at times uncomfortable, this will especially resonate with those caring for an aging parent." Publishers Weekly

Alvarenga, Salvador, approximately 1977

Franklin, Jonathan **438** days : an extraordinary true story of survival at sea / Jonathan Franklin. Atria Books, 2015 304 p. **B**

ISBN 9781501116292

1. Alvarenga, Salvador, approximately 1977. 2. Marine accidents 3. Sea survival 4. Shipwrecks. 5. Fishers. 6. Chiapas, Mexico (State) 7. Biographies

LC 2015030740

Based on interviews with the man who survived alone and adrift at sea longer than anyone in recorded history and interviews with his colleagues, an epic tale of survival chronicles Salvador Alvarenga's 14 months at sea during which he imagined a method of survival that kept his body and mind intact until he was rescued.

"Franklin sprinkles the story with expert opinions to give it depth and context, but the most striking details are those offered by Alvarenga himself about the challenges he faced day in and day out. A spectacular triumph of grit over adversity, 438 Days is an intense, immensely absorbing read." Booklist.

Alvarez, Julia

Alvarez, Julia A **wedding** in Haiti / Julia Alvarez. Algonquin Books of Chapel Hill, 2012. 304 p. **B**

ISBN 9781616201302

1. Alvarez, Julia Friends and associates. 2. Alvarez, Julia Travel Haiti. 3. Dominican-American authors -- 21st century 4. Friendship 5. Weddings -- Haiti 6. Promises. 7. Autobiographies and memoirs

LC 2012000452

"Shannon Ravenel book."

The author writes about three personal relationships, those she has with her parents, her husband, and a young Haitian boy, and explores the bounds of human love and frailty.

Alvarez, Noe

Alvarez, Noe **Spirit** run : a 6,000-mile marathon through North America's stolen land / Noe Alvarez. Catapult, 2020.

xvii, 218 p. **B**

ISBN 9781948226462

1. Children of immigrants 2. Distance running 3. Immigrants, Mexican 4. Long distance runners 5. United States 6. Canada 7. Mexico 8. Guatemala 9. North America 10. Central America 11. Autobiographies and memoirs

A debut memoir by the son of working-class Mexican immigrants describes his upbringing in Washington State, membership in the Peace and Dignity Journeys movement and competition in the Native American cultural marathon from Canada to Guatemala.

"This is a powerful American coming-of-age story about a Mexican American who seeks to embrace his heritage while forging his own path forward. Certain to make a lasting impression on readers across generations and backgrounds, all of whom will be inspired by the young Álvarez." Booklist

Ames, Robert

Bird, Kai The **good** spy : the life and death of Robert Ames / Kai Bird. Crown Publishers, 2014 448 p. **B**

ISBN 9780307889751

1. CIA 2. Hizballah (Lebanon) 3. Spies 4. CIA agents. 5. Intelligence officers 6. Arab-Israeli conflict. 7. Beirut, Lebanon 8. United States -- Foreign relations Middle East. 9. Middle East -- Foreign relations United States. 10. Biographies

LC 2013049480

In The Good Spy, author Kai Bird builds a comprehensive profile of CIA intelligence officer Robert Ames, who died in 1983 when the American Embassy in Beirut, Lebanon, was bombed. Ames specialized in Arabic language and Arab history and politics, becoming a recognized expert who served as a key policy advisor to U.S. decision makers. Committed to finding solutions to the Israeli-Palestinian conflict and other sources of unrest in the Middle East, Ames emphasized fact-finding and rational policy analysis despite American partisan political pressures and decreasing stability in Lebanon and Iran. This absorbing portrait of a family man and dedicated professional also offers a compelling account of the region's history up to 1983.

"A low-key, respectful life of a decent American officer whose quietly significant work helped lead to the Oslo Accords." Kirkus.

Amis, Martin

Amis, Martin **Experience** : a memoir / Martin Amis. Talk Miramax Books, 2000. 406 p. : **B**

ISBN 9780786866526

1. Amis, Kingsley, 1922-1995 Family. 2. Authors, English -- 20th century 3. Fathers and sons. 4. Family relationships. 5. Autobiographies and memoirs

LC 00699777

James Tait Black Memorial Prize for Biography, 2000."

This is a portmanteau of personal history, ancestor worship and promiscuous opinionizing, and a piata of literary gossip that Amis beats with a stick, causing many names to drop. And if we stay put till the last 100 pages, it will break our heart." New York Times Book Review.

Amos, Tori, 1963-

Amos, Tori, 1963- **Resistance** : a songwriter's story of hope, change, and courage / Tori Amos. Atria Books, 2020. 261 p. : **B**

ISBN 9781982104153

1. Patriarchy 2. Social advocacy 3. Feminism 4. Environmentalism 5. Autobiographies and memoirs

LC bl2020011939

The Grammy-nominated music artist reflects on how her career has reflected her political views on toxic patriarchal power structures, urging readers for active engagement in protecting the environment and supporting the #MeToo movement.

"In this thoughtful book, Amos shares the inspiration for many of her songs, beginning with her teenage gig playing piano at a gay bar in Washington, DC, and weaving through years of touring, writing, successes, and setbacks." Booklist

Amundsen, Roald, 1872-1928

Bown, Stephen R. The **last** Viking : the life of Roald Amundsen / Stephen R. Bown. Da Capo Press, c2012. 320 p. **B**

ISBN 9780306820670

1. Amundsen, Roald, 1872-1928. 2. Explorers -- Norway 3. Exploration. 4. Voyages and travels. 5. Northwest Passage -- Exploration -- Norwegian. 6. Antarctica -- Exploration -- Norwegian. 7. North Pole -- Exploration -- Norwegian. 8. Arctic regions -- Exploration -- Norwegian. 9. Biographies

LC 2012012126

A biography of Roald Amundsen, the Norwegian explorer who was the first person to sail the Northwest Passage, the first to reach the South Pole, and possibly the first to set a flag on the North Pole.

Andalibian, Rahimeh

Andalibian, Rahimeh The **rose** hotel : a memoir of secrets, loss, and love from Iran to America / Rahimeh Andalibian. National Geographic, 2015. 368 p. **B**

ISBN 9781426214790

1. Andalibian, Rahimeh. 2. Political refugees 3. Iranians in the United States 4. Muslims 5. Moving to a new country 6. Iran -- History -- 20th century 7. California 8. Autobiographies and memoirs

LC 2014037952

"In this searing memoir, Iran-born author Rahimeh Andalibian tells the story of her family: their struggle to survive the 1979 revolution, their move to California, and their attempts to acculturate in the face of teenage rebellion, murder, addiction, and new traditions."-- Provided by publisher.

"A powerful and uplifting memoir of tragedy and healing." Kirkus.

Andersen, H. C. (Hans Christian), 1805-1875

Andersen, Jens, 1955- **Hans** Christian Andersen : a new life / Jens Andersen ; translated from the Danish by Tiina Nunnally. Overlook Press, c2005. 624 p. : **B**

ISBN 158567737X

1. Authors, Danish -- 19th century 2. Denmark -- Social life and customs -- 19th century 3. Biographies

LC 2004065985

A portrait published to coincide with the two hundredth anniversary of the writer's birth evaluates his role as a critical journalist and supporter of the scientific community, citing his travel writings, his achievements as a cut-paper artist, and his struggles with hypochondria.

"The author examines Andersen's considerable gifts as an oral storyteller; his eccentric, often annoying public habits; his ambivalent sexuality; his bouts of narcissism; his painfully slow transformation from rough-hewn provincial and awkward melodramatist into brilliant, internationally famous writer-celebrity. The biography is best and most moving when it is frank about formerly suppressed aspects of Andersen's life." Booklist.

Wullschlager, Jackie **Hans** Christian Andersen : the life of a storyteller / Jackie Wullschlager. A.A. Knopf, 2001, c2000.

viii, 489 p. : B

ISBN 0679455086

1. Authors, Danish -- 19th century 2. Biographies

LC 00062003

Originally published: London : Allen Lane, 2000.

Describes Andersen's turbulent and difficult life, from his birth in 1805, through his success as a writer in mid-nineteenth-century Europe, to his desperate search for love, ambition, and meaning.

"Wullschlager succeeds brilliantly at portraying Andersens inner mind and uncovering his hopes and fears and details the historical context that served to produce such a grand body of literature. [This biography] will be a standard study for years to come." Library Journal.

Anderson, Alice, 1966-

Anderson, Alice, 1966- **Some** bright morning, I'll fly away : a memoir / Alice Anderson. St Martin's Press, 2017 224 p. B

ISBN 9781250094964

1. Violence in men 2. Abused women 3. Hurricane Katrina, 2005 4. Divorce 5. Autobiographies and memoirs

LC 2017297026

A full-time wife and mother who left a lucrative career up north for her doctor husband in New Orleans, discusses his post-Katrina spiral into madness and the epic battle she faced trying to keep herself and her children safe.

"Anderson is a gifted writer who vividly describes both settings and emotions. Her powerful story gives voice and hope to women caught in similarly terrible conditions." Booklist.

Anderson, Clayton C., 1959-

Anderson, Clayton C., 1959- The **ordinary** spaceman : from boyhood dreams to astronaut / Clayton C. Anderson ; foreword by Nevada Barr. University of Nebraska Press, 2015. 376 p. B

ISBN 9780803262829

1. United States. National Aeronautics and Space Administration 2. International Space Station. 3. Astronauts -- United States 4. Space walking. 5. Space flight 6. Space exploration 7. Autobiographies and memoirs

LC 2014048858

A memoir chronicling Clayton Anderson's quest to become an astronaut. From his childhood to working for NASA, and then eventually becoming an astronaut.

Anderson, Marian, 1897-1993

Keiler, Allan **Marian** Anderson : a singer's journey / Allan Keiler. Scribner, 2000. 447 p. : B

ISBN 9780684807119

1. Anderson, Marian, 1897-1993. 2. Women singers -- United States 3. African American women singers 4. African American singers 5. Racism -- United States. 6. Biographies

LC 99043319

"A Lisa Drew book."

A definitive biography of one of America's greatest singers and a seminal figure in the American civil rights movement uncovers the life of the first African American soloist at the Met and the first African American singer to perform at the White House.

"The author's clear, succinct prose, initially lacking narrative coherence, gains strength and momentum as his subject matures from a young and struggling artist into one of the enduring voices of our century." Publishers Weekly.

Anderson, Sulome

Anderson, Sulome The **hostage's** daughter : a story of family, madness, and the Middle East / Sulome Anderson. Dey Street Books, 2016. 256 p. B

ISBN 9780062385499

1. Anderson, Terry A., 1949- -- Captivity, 1985-1991. 2. Anderson, Sulome Relations with hostages. 3. Hostages -- United States 4. Americans in Lebanon. 5. Fathers and daughters 6. Lebanon. 7. Autobiographies and memoirs

LC bl2016034972

A journalist and daughter of famous hostage Terry Anderson shares an intimate portrait of her father's captivity during the Lebanese Hostage Crisis and the surrounding political firestorm on both her family and the United States, sharing additional views about the role of the crisis in Middle East politics today.

"Through these dual narratives, Anderson creates a compelling depiction of the collateral damage of terrorism and a remarkable piece of investigative journalism with a surprise twist." Publishers Weekly.

Anderson, Tim

Anderson, Tim **Sweet** tooth / Tim Anderson. Lake Union Press, 2014 319 p. B

ISBN 9781477818077

1. Growing up 2. Identity (Psychology) 3. Gay teenagers 4. Homophobia 5. North Carolina 6. Autobiographies and memoirs

LC 2013919514

Sweet Tooth is Tim Anderson's uproarious memoir of life after his hormones and blood sugar both went berserk at the age of fifteen. With Morrissey and The Smiths as the soundtrack, Anderson self-deprecatingly recalls love affairs with vests and donuts, first crushes, coming out, and inaugural trips to gay bars. What emerges is the story of a young man trying to build a future that won't involve crippling loneliness or losing a foot to his disease --and maybe even one that, no matter how unpredictable, can still be pretty sweet.

"Staying true to his experiences, Anderson evokes the juvenile tendency toward self-destruction in a way that is simultaneously funny and frustrating. The combination gives readers a visceral taste of the rollercoaster ride that was his young adulthood." Publishers Weekly.

Andre, Christophe

Delisle, Guy **Hostage** / Guy Delisle. Drawn & Quarterly, 2017, c2016. 432 p. : B

ISBN 9781770462793

1. Andre, Christophe Kidnapping, 1997 2. Hostages 3. Kidnapping 4. Kidnapping victims 5. Biographical comics 6. Comics and Graphic novels

LC bl2017016554

Chiefly illustrations.

Originally published in 2016 as S'enfuir by Dargaud.

Recounts, in graphic novel format, the harrowing story of Christophe Andre, an administer with Doctors without Borders who was kidnapped and held by armed men while working in the Caucasus region.

"Delisle brings the reader so fully into Andre's world that a simple change in his routine becomes either harrowing or hopeful, and the mundane details of his daily existence, saving a piece of bread from his morning meal for a snack, enjoying some music drifting through the wall into his cell, become heroic acts of defiance." Library Journal

Andrews, Julie

Andrews, Julie **Home** : a memoir of my early years / Julie Andrews. Hyperion, 2008. 352 p. B

ISBN 0786865652

1. Film actors and actresses -- Great Britain 2. Singers -- Great Britain 3. Women singers -- Great Britain 4. Growing up. 5.

Autobiographies and memoirs

LC bl2008001661

A personal account of the iconic actress's pre-fame life traces the time between her birth in 1935 and her discovery by Walt Disney during her 1962 Broadway performance in "Camelot."

"Spanning events from her 1935 birth to the early 1960s, . [the author] covers her rise to fame and ends with Walt Disney casting her in Mary Poppins (1963). The heart of her book documents the rehearsals, tryouts and smash 1956 opening of My Fair Lady. Readers will rejoice, since Andrews is an accomplished writer who holds back nothing while adding a patina of poetry to the antics and anecdotes throughout this memoir of bittersweet backstage encounters and theatrical triumphs." Publishers Weekly.

★Andrews, Julie **Home** work : a memoir of my Hollywood years / Julie Andrews, with Emma Walton Hamilton. Hachette Books, 2019. 352 p. **B**

ISBN 9780316349253

1. Andrews, Julie. 2. Actors and actresses 3. Fame 4. Marriage 5. Family relationships 6. Autobiographies and memoirs

LC 2019947243

In a follow-up to the critically acclaimed Home, the beloved performing artist reflects on her Hollywood career and the creations of three of her most iconic films, Mary Poppins, The Sound of Music and Victor/Victoria.

Angel, Katherine

Angel, Katherine **Unmastered** : a book on desire, most difficult to tell / Katherine Angel. Farrar, Straus and Giroux, 2013, c2012. 304 p. **B**

ISBN 9780374280406

1. Desire 2. Women -- Sexuality 3. Identity (Psychology) 4. Sex customs 5. Autobiographies and memoirs

LC 2012048072

"Originally published, in slightly different form, in 2012 by Allen Lane, Great Britain."

Originally published: London : Allen Lane, 2012.An examination of the paradox at the core of female sexuality argues that public-life requirements often directly contrast with intimate desires.

Angell, Roger,

Angell, Roger, **This** old man : all in pieces / Roger Angell. Doubleday, 2015. 352 p. **B**

ISBN 9780385541138

1. Aging 2. Senior men 3. Essays.

LC 2015018255

The nonagenarian "New Yorker" writer and editor presents a selection of essays, letters, light verse, book reviews, and other pieces culled from the tenth decade of his vibrant life, including the title work, in which he surveys the limits and discoveries of great and abundant age.

"While essays such as the titular 'This Old Man' and 'Over the Wall' grab and hold tighter than others, fans of The New Yorker (and of baseball, one of Angell's most beloved subjects), will take pleasure in digging into this rich collection culled from an extraordinary career." Library Journal.

Angelou, Maya

★Angelou, Maya **I** know why the caged bird sings / Maya Angelou. Bantam Books, 1993, c1970. 289 p. ; **B**

ISBN 0553279378

1. Angelou, Maya. 2. Authors, American -- 20th century 3. African American authors 4. African American women authors -- 20th century 5. Intersectionality 6. United States -- Social life and customs 7. Autobiographies and memoirs

LC bl 00012436

Sequel: Gather Together In My Name.

Originally published: New York : Random House, 1970.

A Black woman recalls the anguish of her childhood in Arkansas and her adolescence in northern slums.

"Angelou is a skillful writer; her language ranges from beautifully lyrical prose to earthy metaphor, and her descriptions have power and sensitivity." Library Journal.

Angelou, Maya **Mom** & me & mom / Maya Angelou. Random House Inc., 2013. 224 p. **B**

ISBN 9781400066117

1. Angelou, Maya. 2. Authors, American -- 20th century 3. African American authors 4. African American women authors -- 20th century 5. Mothers and daughters 6. United States -- Social life and customs 7. Autobiographies and memoirs

LC 2012022257

In Mom & Me & Mom we learn of poet and author Maya Angelou's reunion at age 13 with her mother, Vivian Baxter, in San Francisco. Though at first Angelou resented her mother for having left her with her grandmother, she gradually began to recognize Baxter's efforts to provide for her daughter and to understand how much she loved her. Angelou captures the complexity and the depth of their relationship, and its effects on her as a young woman.

Angelou, Maya A **song** flung up to heaven / Maya Angelou. Random House, c2002. 212 p. ; **B**

ISBN 0375507477

1. Angelou, Maya. 2. African American women authors -- 20th century 3. Civil Rights Movement 4. Authors, American -- 20th century 5. African American authors 6. United States -- Social life and customs 7. Autobiographies and memoirs

LC 2001034914

Sequel to: All God's Children Need Traveling Shoes."

This sixth installment in Angelou's autobiographical works begins in 1964 as Angelou returned to the U.S. from Ghana. She worked in Watts at the time of the riots, and Malcolm X and Martin Luther King Jr. were both assassinated just before she was to begin working with them. She moved to New York, where she rejoined a vibrant group of famous writers, intellectuals, and friends; worried about her young-adult son; and understood the humor and heartache of a painful love affair. Spiced with her mother's aphorisms, her often-poetic prose is best at the end, as she muses on the condition of black women and sitting at her mother's table, begins to write I Know Why the Caged Bird Sings." Booklist.

Gillespie, Marcia **Maya** Angelou : a glorious celebration / Marcia Ann Gillespie, Rosa Johnson Butler and Richard A. Long ; foreword by Oprah Winfrey. Doubleday, c2008. 191 p. : **B**

ISBN 9780385511087

1. Angelou, Maya. 2. Authors, American 3. African American women authors 4. African American women poets 5. African Americans 6. Biographies

LC 2007031301

An unusual and irresistible look at Maya Angelou's life as well as her myriad interests and accomplishments by the people who know her best--her longtime friends Marcia Ann Gillespie and Richard Long, and her niece Rosa Johnson Butler. Features over 150 sepia portraits, family photographs, and letters.

Ankiel, Rick

Ankiel, Rick The **phenomenon** : pressure, the yips, and the pitch that changed my life / Rick Ankiel and Tim Brown. PublicAffairs, 2017. 320 p. **B**

ISBN 9781610396868

1. Ankiel, Rick. 2. Pitchers (Baseball) -- United States 3. Baseball players -- United States 4. Outfielders (Baseball) 5. Performance anxiety (Psychology) 6. Autobiographies and memoirs

LC 2016050707

The star St. Louis Cardinal pitcher describes his career-shaping battle with a devastating slump and how he learned to conquer it, sharing the profound lessons he learned about anxiety, pressure and adversity along the way.

"A solid sports memoir that explores more than just sports." Kirkus.

Annan, Kofi A. (Kofi Atta)

Annan, Kofi A. (Kofi Atta) **Interventions** : a life in war and peace / Kofi Annan with Nader Mousavizadeh. Penguin Press, 2012. 512 p. **B**

ISBN 9781594204203

1. United Nations 2. World politics -- 1989- 3. Politicians -- Ghana 4. Politicians -- Ghana 5. Nobel Prize winners 6. Autobiographies and memoirs

LC 2012008173

Includes index.

A former secretary-general of the United Nations shares his unique perspectives on the terrorist attacks of September 11; the American invasions of Iraq and Afghanistan; the wars among Israel, Hezbollah and Lebanon; the humanitarian tragedies of Somalia, Rwanda and Bosnia; and the geopolitical transformations following the Cold War.

Anne Boleyn, Queen, consort of Henry VIII, King of England, 1507-1536

Weir, Alison, 1951- The **lady** in the tower : the fall of Anne Boleyn / Alison Weir. Ballantine Books, 2009. 384 p. **B**

ISBN 9780345453211

1. Anne Boleyn, Queen, consort of Henry VIII, King of England, 1507-1536. 2. Henry VIII, King of England, 1491-1547. 3. Political prisoners. 4. Imprisonment. 5. Married women -- Death. 6. Rulers. 7. England -- History -- 16th century. 8. Great Britain -- History -- 16th century. 9. Biographies

LC 2009042748

An account of Henry VIII's second wife's final days seeks to vindicate her from popular negative perceptions while offering insight into additional nuances that affected her character and marriage to the infamous monarch.

Anne, Queen of Great Britain, 1665-1714

Somerset, Anne, 1955- **Queen** Anne : the politics of passion / Anne Somerset. Knopf, 2013, c2012. xii, 621 p., [8] p. of plates **B**

ISBN 9780307962881

1. Women rulers -- Great Britain 2. Great Britain -- History -- Stuarts, 1603-1714. 3. Great Britain -- History -- Anne, 1702-1714. 4. Biographies

LC 2012035334

Originally published: London : HarperPress, 2012.

Elizabeth Longford Prize for Historical Biography, 2013.

A sympathetic assessment of the rule of the early 18th-century monarch recounts how during her short 12-year reign she effectively united England and Scotland as a sovereign state to create the Kingdom of Great Britain, offering additional insight into the military victories that laid the foundations for Britain's future naval and colonial supremacy.

"Anne's natural reserve and her instinct for discretion has led historians to believe that she was weak and dominated by women of stronger character. Somerset's impressive scholarship debunks that belief and shows Anne as a masterful, even authoritative, queen who survived the influence of her 'friends.'" Kirkus.

Annigoni, Tony

McCumber, David **Playing** off the rail : a pool hustler's journey / David McCumber. Random House, 1996. 367 p. **B**

ISBN 0679423745

1. Annigoni, Tony. 2. Billiard players 3. Swindlers and swindling 4. Pool players 5. Pool (Game)

LC 95006955

A journalist chronicles his cross-country journey with ace pool player Tony Annigoni, documenting their zany odyssey from New York to Seattle, his role as a "stakehorse," the fascinating places they visited, and the colorful characters they encountered.

Ansary, Mir Tamim

Ansary, Mir Tamim **West** of Kabul, east of New York : an Afghan American story / Tamim Ansary. Farrar, Straus and Giroux, 2002. 292 p. **B**

ISBN 0374287570

1. Ansary, Mir Tamim. 2. Growing up. 3. Family relationships. 4. Afghan Americans 5. Muslims -- United States 6. Islamic countries -- Description and travel. 7. Autobiographies and memoirs

LC 2002102958

An Afghan American writer, most recently known for an e-mail on reprisals against Afghanistan, shares his experiences of Islam and the West, his feelings on Islamic militant fundamentalism, and his hopes for reconciliation.

"While Ansary's political insights can be detached or perhaps purposefully aloof his descriptions of having lived in and identified alternately with the West and the Islamic world are utterly compelling." Publishers Weekly.

Anselmo, Lisa

Anselmo, Lisa **My** (part-time) Paris life : how running away brought me home / Lisa Anselmo. Thomas Dunne Books/St. Martin's Press, 2016. 240 p. **B**

ISBN 9781250067470

1. Anselmo, Lisa. 2. Americans in France. 3. Self fulfillment 4. Mothers and daughters. 5. Grief 6. Paris, France -- Description and travel 7. Autobiographies and memoirs

LC 2016007864

Lisa Anselmo wrapped her entire life around her mother, a strong-woman who was a defining force in her daughter's life--maybe too defining. When her mother dies from breast cancer, Lisa realizes she hadn't built a life of her own, and struggles to find her purpose. Who is she without her mother--and her mother's expectations? Desperate for answers, she reaches for a lifeline in the form of an apartment in Paris, refusing to play it safe for the first time. What starts out as a lurching act of survival sets Lisa on a course that reshapes her life in ways she never could have imagined.

"In the end, this is a sweet and inspiring account of one womans taxing yet rewarding search for peace, happiness, and contentment in the City of Light." Publishers Weekly.

Antonius, Marcus, 83 B.C.?-30 B.C.

Goldsworthy, Adrian Keith **Antony** and Cleopatra / Adrian

Goldsworthy. Yale University Press, 2010. vi, 470 p., 16 p. of plates : col. ill., maps ; 24 cm. **B**

ISBN 9780300165340

1. Cleopatra, Queen of Egypt, 69-30 B.C. 2. Generals -- Rome 3. Politicians 4. Women rulers -- Egypt 5. Suicide -- History 6. Ancient Egypt -- History -- 332-30 B.C. 7. Rome -- History -- Republic, 265-30 B.C. 8. Biographies

In this dual biography of the two great lovers of antiquity, historian Adrian Goldsworthy goes beyond myth and romance to create a portrait of his subjects--who were first and foremost political animals.

"Narrating [Antony] and Cleopatra's parts in the tumultuous end of the Roman Republic, Goldsworthy skillfully integrates the partial and partisan source material into an accessible presentation of a classic tale from classical times." Booklist.

Antunes, Antonio Lobo, 1942-

Antunes, Antonio Lobo, 1942- The **fat** man and infinity : and other writings / Antonio Lobo Antunes ; translated with an introduction by Margaret Jull Costa. W. W. Norton, c2009. 396 p. : **B**

ISBN 9780393061987

1. Authors, Portuguese 2. Fiction writing 3. Portugal 4. Lisbon, Portugal 5. Autobiographies and memoirs

LC 2008041551

Written in chronicle form over the course of more than three decades, an account of the Nobel Prize short-listed candidate's life explores his childhood in class-minded, mid-twentieth-century Lisbon; the ways in which war shaped his writings; and his losses of loved ones.

"His bite-size essays contain no political ruminations and almost nothing about sports, or popular culture, or literary criticism or run-ins with the great and good. Instead they are interior diaries of a kind, most of them imbued with a deep nostalgia for the author's youth." New York Times Book Review.

Apatow, Judd, 1967-

Apatow, Judd, 1967- **Sick** in the head : conversations about life and comedy / Judd Apatow. Random House, 2015. 368 p. **B**

ISBN 9780812997576

1. Comedians -- United States -- Interviews. 2. Stand-up comedy -- United States. 3. Television actors and actresses -- United States -- Interviews. 4. Film actors and actresses -- United States -- Interviews. 5. Autobiographies and memoirs 6. Interviews

LC 2015008155

Presents a collection of conversations with some of today's most popular comedians, drawing on the author's teenage radio hosting days to include pieces from the early years, and including interviews with such names as Jerry Seinfeld, Jay Leno, and Sandra Bernhard.

"An exceptional volume; in a field where shallowness is a hallmark, these artists reveal an unexpected depth. For all libraries." Library Journal.

Apess, William, 1798-1839

Gura, Philip F., 1950- The **life** of William Apess, Pequot / Philip F. Gura. The University of North Carolina Press, 2015. 216 p. **B**

ISBN 9781469619989

1. Apess, William, 1798-1839. 2. Pequot Indians. 3. Itinerant preachers. 4. Methodist Church -- Clergy 5. Indians of North America, Treatment of 6. New England 7. Biographies

LC 2014026609

The Pequot Indian intellectual, author, and itinerant preacher William Apess (1798?1839) was one the most important voices of the nineteenth century. Here, Philip F. Gura offers the first book-length chronicle of Apess's fascinating and consequential life.

Appleseed, Johnny, 1774-1845

Means, Howard **Johnny** Appleseed : the man, the myth and the American story / Howard Means. Simon & Schuster, 2011. 320 p. **B**

ISBN 9781439178256

1. Appleseed, Johnny, 1774-1845. 2. Legends, American -- History and criticism. 3. Apple growers -- United States. 4. Frontier and pioneer life -- Middle West. 5. Faith in men. 6. Middle West -- History 7. United States -- History -- 1783-1865. 8. Biographies.

LC 2011000665

A profile of the real Johnny Appleseed goes behind his folk-legend persona to reveal his contributions as an animal whisperer, vegetarian and pacifist at a time when such practices were virtually non-existent, offering insight into his additional work as an evangelist and land speculator.

Arana, Marie

Arana, Marie **American** chica : two worlds, one childhood / Marie Arana. Dial Press, 2001. 309 p. **B**

ISBN 0385319622

1. Journalists -- United States 2. Hispanic-American women journalists 3. Growing up. 4. Multiracial girls 5. United States. 6. Peru. 7. Autobiographies and memoirs

LC 00047529

ALA Notable Book, 2002.

National Book Award for Nonfiction finalist, 2001

A journalist describes her efforts to come to terms with her dual heritage as a Hispanic American and offers a portrait of her family members, including her talented American mother and her brilliant Peruvian father.

"Arana blends a journalist's dedication to research with a style that sings with humor. Her memoir is an outstanding contribution to the growing shelf of Latina literature." Publishers Weekly.

Araton, Harvey

Araton, Harvey **Our** last season : a writer, a fan, a friendship / Harvey Araton. Penguin Press, 2020. 256 p. **B**

ISBN 9781984877987

1. Araton, Harvey Friends and associates. 2. Araton, Harvey. 3. Musler, Michelle, 1936-2018. 4. New York Knicks (Basketball team) 5. Friendship. 6. Sportswriters 7. Basketball fans 8. Mentors 9. United States 10. Autobiographies and memoirs

LC 2019053128

Includes index.

The moving story of a bond between sportswriter and fan that was forged in a shared love of basketball and grew over several decades into an extraordinary friendship that sees both through the trials of their later years.

"A wonderful and engaging book, not only for basketball and Knicks fans, but also a meaningful look about the importance of friendship." Library Journal

Arbus, Diane, 1923-1971

Lubow, Arthur **Diane** Arbus : portrait of a photographer / Arthur Lubow. Ecco Press, 2016 320 p. **B**

ISBN 9780062234322

1. Arbus, Diane, 1923-1971. 2. Photographers. 3. Women photographers. 4. Biographies

LC bl2016015617

The definitive biography of the beguiling Diane Arbus, one of the most influential and important photographers of the twentieth century, a brilliant and absorbing exposition that links the extraordinary arc of her life to her iconic photographs.

"Lubows portrait is the most sharply focused, encompassing, and incisive to date." Booklist.

Arceneaux, Michael

Arceneaux, Michael **I** can't date Jesus : love, sex, family, race, and other reasons I've put my faith in Beyonce / Michael Arceneaux. Simon & Schuster, 2018. 256 p. **B**

ISBN 9781501178856

1. African American gay men 2. Homophobia in Christianity 3. Intersectionality 4. Writing 5. Houston, Texas -- Social life and customs 6. Essays

LC 2018005087

This collection of humorous and contemplative essays from one of today's boldest writers on social issues discusses coming out to his mother, growing up in Houston, fire ants, fleas and being approached to join the priesthood.

Archimedes, 287?-212 B.C.

Hirshfeld, Alan **Eureka** man : the life and legacy of Archimedes / Alan Hirshfeld. Walker, 2009. 256 p. **B**

ISBN 9780802716187

1. Scientists -- Greece. 2. Inventors. 3. Inventions. 4. Buoyancy. 5. Ancient Greece. 6. Biographies

LC 2009005608

A portrait of the eminent scientist goes beyond popular recognition of his discovery about volume to explore both his mathematical achievements and his military contributions, revealing the engineering feats that prompted his considerable fame in the ancient world.

Arena, Bruce

Arena, Bruce **What's** wrong with US? : a coach's blunt take on the state of American soccer after a lifetime on the touchline / Bruce Arena, with Steve Kettmann. HarperCollins, 2018. 288 p. **B**

ISBN 9780062803948

1. United States Men's National Soccer Team 2. World Cup (Soccer) 3. Soccer coaches 4. Professional soccer 5. Professional sports 6. United States 7. Autobiographies and memoirs

LC 2017278899

Timed for publication just prior to the 2018 World Cup in Russia, a revealing memoir by a leading American soccer coach shares insights into how the USMNT has prepared to compete in the past.

"No surprise that Arena differs strongly from his predecessor, Jrgen Klinsmann, in an MLS-first approach, urging our top league to work together with U.S. Soccer for better development of American players. That and other suggestions informed by hard work and long experience will make this of interest to U.S. fans still wondering how to make things right." Booklist.

Arkin, Alan

Arkin, Alan An **improvised** life : a memoir / Alan Arkin. Da Capo Press, c2011. 224 p. **B**

ISBN 9780306819667

1. Arkin, Alan. 2. Film actors and actresses -- United States 3. Film industry and trade 4. Filmmaking. 5. Actors and actresses 6. Autobiographies and memoirs

LC 2010045034

Includes index."

An Improvised Life" is Oscar winner Alan Arkin's wise and unpretentious recollection of the process--artistic and personal--of becoming an actor, and a revealing look into the creative mind of one of the best practitioners on stage or screen.

"Arkin looks back on his career as an actor, but this memoir forgoes the backstage gossip and star-studded anecdotes readers might expect. In fact, the author largely ignores his accomplishments in favor of charting his inner evolution as an artist, focusing on intellectual and spiritual epiphanies that have shaped his approach to acting. . . . Earnest, intelligent and well-observedless a celebrity memoir than a serious consideration of the principles of acting and improvisation." Kirkus.

Armstrong, Karen, 1944-

Armstrong, Karen, 1944- The **spiral** staircase : my climb out of darkness / Karen Armstrong. Alfred A. Knopf, 2004. xxii, 305 p. ; **B**

ISBN 0375413189

1. Former nuns 2. Women with depression 3. Coping in women. 4. Faith in women. 5. England -- Religious life and customs -- 21st century 6. Autobiographies and memoirs

LC 2003047550

The author relates her decision to leave her convent after failing to find religious fulfillment, her struggles with depression and epilepsy, her realization of her calling, and her career working with sacred texts.

"Even among readers who embrace doctrines Armstrong dismisses (such as the reality of a personal God), this candid memoir will clarify thinking about the search for the sacred." Booklist.

Armstrong, Louis, 1901-1971

Armstrong, Louis, 1901-1971 **Louis** Armstrong, in his own words : selected writings / Louis Armstrong ; edited and with an introduction by Thomas Brothers. Oxford University Press, 1999. xxvii, 255 p. : **B**

ISBN 0195119584

1. Armstrong, Louis, 1901-1971. 2. Jazz musicians 3. African American jazz musicians 4. Jazz music -- History and criticism 5. New Orleans, Louisiana 6. New Orleans, Louisiana -- Social life and customs. 7. Biographies

LC 99017040

"In this collection Armstrong recounts episodes from his childhood in New Orleans, pays tribute to other musicians, and extolls the virtues of marijuana, laxatives, and rice and beans while speaking candidly about race relations, the music business, and his extramarital affairs. The joy he took in expressing himself on paper is abundantly evident." The New Yorker.

★Brothers, Thomas David **Louis** Armstrong, master of modernism / Thomas Brothers. W. W. Norton, 2014. 720 p. **B**

ISBN 9780393065824

1. Jazz musicians 2. African American jazz musicians 3. Racism 4. Jazz music -- New Orleans, Louisiana -- History and criticism 5. Biographies

LC 2013037726

Pulitzer Prize for Biography or Autobiography finalist

Picking up where "Louis Armstrong's New Orleans" left off, this biographical account of the legendary jazz trumpet virtuoso highlights the historical role Armstrong played in the creation of modern music and also his encounters with racism.

"A monumental follow-up to Louis Armstrongs New Orleans (2006). Brothers work, covering an astonishingly creative decade, is comprehensive and firmly grounded in musicology and in the racial and cultural climate of the 1920s. It is voluminously researched, compellingly written, and supported by a valuable discography and bibliography." Booklist.

Teachout, Terry **Pops** : a life of Louis Armstrong / Terry Teachout. Houghton Mifflin Harcourt, 2009. 496 p. **B**
ISBN 9780151010899
1. Armstrong, Louis, 1900-1971. 2. Jazz musicians 3. African American jazz musicians 4. Jazz music. 5. Jazz trumpeters. 6. Biographies
LC 2009006035

"The author makes an eloquent case for Armstrong's status as a pioneer, not just in jazz but in the broader context of 20th-century art. A rewarding jazz biography and a revealing look at a broad swath of American cultural history." Kirkus.

Armstrong, Neil, 1930-2012

Barbree, Jay **Neil** Armstrong : a life of flight / Jay Barbree. Thomas Dunne Books, 2014. 320 p. **B**
ISBN 9781250040718
1. Armstrong, Neil, 1930-2012. 2. Project Apollo (U.S.) -- History. 3. United States. National Aeronautics and Space Administration 4. Astronauts -- United States 5. Space flight to the moon -- History. 6. Space programs -- United States. 7. Pilots -- United States 8. Biographies
LC 2014008696

Published to coincide with the 45th anniversary of the Apollo 11 launch, a definitive portrait of the pioneering astronaut draws on personal notes and interviews with the Armstrong family and includes previously unshared photos and mission details.

"The author paints a detailed and colorful picture of his subject and an unbiased depiction of the period in which he lived, while also demonstrating reverence for Armstrong as a confidant." Library Journal.

Arney, Tommy

Swift, Earl, 1958- **Auto** biography : a classic car, an outlaw motorhead, and 57 years of the American dream / Earl Swift. It books, 2014 320 p. **B**
ISBN 9780062282668
1. Antique and classic cars 2. American Dream 3. Second chances 4. Restoration. 5. North Carolina 6. Biographies.
LC bl2014018802

Determined to restore a rusted out wreck of an old Chevy to its former glory in one last attempt to salvage his business and stay out of jail, Tommy Arney finds himself once again on the wrong side of the law, in this wise, funny and heartbreaking true story of man, machine and the rise, fall and rebirth of the American dream.

"A big, weird, heartfelt book about a badass who could give a damn whether you root for him or not." Kirkus.

Aron, Nina Renata

Aron, Nina Renata **Good** morning, destroyer of men's souls : a memoir of women, addiction, and love / Nina Renata Aron. Crown, 2020 288 p. **B**
ISBN 9780525576679
1. Aron, Nina Renata. 2. Codependency. 3. Drug addiction 4. Enabling (Psychology) 5. Drug addicts -- United States 6. California 7. Autobiographies and memoirs
LC 2020003061

A woman vividly recounts her love affair with an ex-addict who began using again and tries to make sense of drug abuse, codependency and obsession in this intense memoir of love and addiction.

"Aron's dark, gorgeously narrated memoir of destructive codependency will captivate readers." Publishers Weekly

Arsenault, Kerri

Arsenault, Kerri **Mill** town : reckoning with what remains / Kerri Arsenault. St. Martin's Press, 2020. 368 p. **B**
ISBN 9781250155931
1. Arsenault, Kerri Family 2. Rumford Mill 3. Paper mills 4. Small towns 5. Blue collar workers 6. Blue collar families 7. Maine -- Social life and customs 8. Maine -- Social conditions 9. Autobiographies and memoirs
LC 2020019303

Kerri Arsenault grew up in the rural working class town of Mexico, Maine. For over 100 years the community orbited around a paper mill that employs most townspeople, including three generations of Arsenault's own family. Years after she moved away, Arsenault realized the price she paid for her seemingly secure childhood. The mill, while providing livelihoods for nearly everyone, also contributed to the destruction of the environment and the decline of the town's economic, physical, and emotional health in a slow-moving catastrophe, earning the area the nickname "Cancer Valley."

"She writes urgently about the dire effects the mill's toxic legacy had on Mexico's residents and the area's ecology while evocatively mining the emotional landscape of caretaking for aging parents and rediscovering the roots of her childhood. Bittersweet memories and a long-buried atrocity combine for a heartfelt, unflinching, striking narrative combination." Kirkus

Ashbery, John, 1927-2017

Roffman, Karin The **songs** we know best : John Ashbery's early life / Karin Roffman. Farrar, Straus and Giroux, 2017. 496 p. **B**
ISBN 9780374293840
1. Poets, American. 2. Biographies
LC 2016045038

Drawing on unpublished correspondence, juvenilia and childhood diaries as well as more than 100 hours of conversation with the poet, a first comprehensive biography of the early life of the winner of nearly every major American literary award reveals how he drew on the details of his youth to populate the poems that made him an unpredictable literary force.

"This tender, youth-focused biography will be most enjoyed by Ashberys fans and readers interested in a remarkable gay artists midcentury coming-of-age story." Booklist.

Astaire, Fred, 1899-1987

Riley, Kathleen, 1974- The **Astaires** : Fred & Adele / Kathleen Riley. Oxford University Press, c2012. 272 p. **B**
ISBN 9780199738410
1. Astaire, Adele. 2. Dancers -- United States 3. Actors and actresses -- United States 4. Dancing 5. Brothers and sisters 6. Biographies
LC 2011018462

Traces siblings Fred and Adele Astaire's rise to fame, from humble Midwestern origins and early days as child performers on small-time vaudeville stages, to their 1917 debut on Broadway, to star billings on both sides of the Atlantic.

Athill, Diana, 1917-2019

Athill, Diana, 1917-2019 **Alive,** alive oh! and other things that matter / Diana Athill. W. W. Norton & Company, 2016, c2015.

192 p. **B**

ISBN 9780393253719

1. Aging. 2. Seniors 3. Life. 4. Women authors, English -- 20th century 5. England -- Social life and customs -- 20th century. 6. Essays

LC 2015042206

"First published in Great Britain by Granta Publications" [2015] -- Verso title page.

The award-winning author provides luminous, wise and joyful insight into what really matters at the end of a long life.

Atkins, Vera, 1908-2000

Helm, Sarah A **life** in secrets : Vera Atkins and the missing agents of WWII / Sarah Helm. Nan A. Talese, 2006, c2005. xxviii, 493 p., 16 p. of plates : **B**

ISBN 9780385508452

1. Atkins, Vera, 1908-2000. 2. Great Britain. Special Operations Executive 3. Secret service -- Great Britain 4. French Resistance (World War II) 5. World War II 6. Missing in action 7. France -- History -- 20th century. 8. Biographies

LC 2005056870

Originally published: London : Little, Brown, 2005.

Describes the life and espionage career of Vera Atkins, a talented agent who rose to the top of the Special Operations Executive (SOE), a British secret service dedicated to aiding resistance efforts throughout Nazi-occupied Europe.

"Helm has produced a memorable portrait of a woman who knowingly sent other women to their deaths and a searing history of female courage and suffering during WWII." Publishers Weekly.

Atlas, James

Atlas, James The **shadow** in the garden : a biographer's tale / James Atlas. Pantheon, 2017 384 p. **B**

ISBN 9781101871690

1. Biographers 2. Biography 3. Autobiographies and memoirs

LC 2016057846

A biographer describes what it's like to document the lives of other, more famous people and revisits the experiences and work of the classical biographers who brought the lives of Samuel Johnson and James Boswell to life.

"Atlas expert, provocative, and enlightening 'biographers tale' is a work of both depth and radiance." Booklist.

Atleework, Kendra, 1989-

Atleework, Kendra, 1989- **Miracle** country : a memoir / Kendra Atleework. Algonquin Books of Chapel Hill, 2020 368 p. **B**

ISBN 9781616209988

1. Growing up 2. Deserts 3. Mothers -- Death. 4. Climate change 5. California 6. Southern California. 7. Sierra Nevada Mountains 8. Autobiographies and memoirs

LC 2019053878

Describes how the author's thriving childhood in the natural desert landscape of the Eastern Sierra Nevada was upended by her mother's tragic early death and how the region of her youth has been ravaged by climate change.

"Essayist Atleework recalls her family roots and explores the history of California's arid Eastern Sierras in her ambitious, beautiful debut. . . . Atleework's remarkable prose renders the ordinary wondrous and firmly puts this overlooked region of California onto the map." Publishers Weekly

Attenborough, David, 1926-

Attenborough, David, 1926- **Adventures** of a young naturalist : the zoo quest expeditions / David Attenborough. Quercus, 2018, c2017. 400 p. **B**

ISBN 9781635060690

1. Wildlife 2. Nature study 3. Zoology 4. Zoos 5. Autobiographies and memoirs

LC 2017048329

Originally published: London: Hodder & Stoughton, 2017."

In 1954, David Attenborough, a young television presenter was offered the opportunity of a lifetime -- to travel the world finding rare and elusive animals for London Zoo's collection, and to film the expedition for the BBC for a new show called Zoo Quest".-- Provided by publisher.

Atwood, Margaret, 1939-

Atwood, Margaret, 1939- **In** other worlds : SF and the human imagination / Margaret Atwood. Nan A. Talese/Doubleday, 2011. 208 p. **B**

ISBN 9780385533966

1. Atwood, Margaret, 1939- Criticism and interpretation. 2. Science fiction -- History and criticism 3. Science fiction writing 4. Essays 5. Biographies

LC 2011013776

In this collection of essays Margaret Atwood contemplates the nature and history of science fiction and her relationship with it.

"A clever, thoughtful investigation that will appeal to science fiction readers and Atwood's loyal fans." Library Journal.

Augustine, Saint, Bishop of Hippo

Augustine, Saint, Bishop of Hippo **Confessions** / Augustine ; a new translation by Sarah Ruden. The Modern Library, 2017 xli, 484 p. ; **B**

ISBN 9780812996562

1. Catholic Church Bishops 2. Religion. 3. Christianity. 4. Faith (Christianity) 5. Christian saints 6. Autobiographies and memoirs

LC 2016033647

Translation of Confessiones.

The Christian theologian describes his sinful youth, his conversion to Christianity, his struggle against his sexuality, and his renunciation of secular ambition and marriage.

Augustine, Saint, Bishop of Hippo **Confessions** / Saint Augustine ; translated from the Latin by Henry Chadwick. Oxford University Press, 2008. xxviii, 311 p. ; Oxford world's classics (Oxford University Press) **B**

ISBN 9780199537822

1. Catholic Church Bishops 2. Religion. 3. Christianity. 4. Faith (Christianity) 5. Christian saints 6. Autobiographies and memoirs

LC 2008491261

Wills, Garry, 1934- **Saint** Augustine / Garry Wills. Viking, 1999. xx, 152 p. **B**

ISBN 0670886106

1. Christian saints -- Algeria -- Biography. 2. Bishops 3. Biographies

LC 98050317

"Wills begins by addressing centuries of misconceptions. Though his admiration for the saint is occasionally tainted by defensiveness, his account of Augustine's search for a faith and a philosophy engages our sympathy. He also conveys the turbulence of the era, when the Roman Empire was beleaguered by barbarians and the Catholic Church by heretics, and shows how Augustine's responses to the troubles of his time have shaped Christianity down to our own." The New Yorker.

Augustus, Emperor of Rome, 63 B.C.-14 A.D.

★Everitt, Anthony **Augustus** : the life of Rome's first emperor / Anthony Everitt. Random House, 2006. xxxviii, 377 p. : **B**

ISBN 1400061288

1. Roman emperors 2. Rome -- Rulers 3. Rome -- History -- Augustus, 30 B.C.-14 A.D. 4. Rome -- History -- Empire, 30 B.C.-476 A.D. 5. Rome -- History -- Empire, 30 B.C.-284 A.D. 6. Biographies

LC 2006041735

A biography of Rome's first emperor follows Augustus Caesar as he transformed the Roman Republic into the world's greatest empire, consolidating and expanding Roman power into every aspect of the known world of his time.

"This is a biography of Caesar Augustus (Octavian), first emperor of Rome." Library Journal.

Goldsworthy, Adrian Keith **Augustus** : first emperor of Rome / Adrian Goldsworthy. Yale University Press, 2014. 624 p. **B**

ISBN 9780300178722

1. Roman emperors 2. Rome -- History -- Augustus, 30 B.C.-14 A.D. 3. Biographies

LC 2014940657

In this highly anticipated biography Goldsworthy puts his deep knowledge of ancient sources to full use, recounting the events of Augustus' long life in greater detail than ever before. Goldsworthy pins down the man behind the myths: a consummate manipulator, propagandist, and showman, both generous and ruthless. Under Augustus' rule the empire prospered, yet his success was never assured and the events of his life unfolded with exciting unpredictability. Goldsworthy captures the passion and savagery, the public image and private struggles of the real man whose epic life continues to influence western history.

"Goldsworthy tells the story well. A commendable book. Summing Up: Highly recommended. General and undergraduate readers." Choice.

Aung San Suu Kyi

Aung San Suu Kyi **Freedom** from fear : and other writings / Aung San Suu Kyi ; foreword to the first edition by Vaclav Havel ; foreword to the second edition by Archbishop Desmond Tutu ; edited with an introduction by Michael Aris. Penguin Books, 1995, c1991. xxxi, 374 p., 12 p. of plates : **B**

ISBN 0140253173

1. Aung San Suu Kyi. 2. Women prisoners. 3. Nobel Prize winners. 4. Burma -- Politics and government. 5. Burma -- Social life and customs. 6. Southeast Asia. 7. Autobiographies and memoirs

LC 96103255

Originally published: New York : Penguin Books, 1991.

The winner of the 1991 Nobel Peace Prize shares essays about her father, Burma's cultural heritage, and the need for democracy

"Mrs. Aung San Suu Kyi's excellent book offers inspiration to many other peoples in the region as much as it reflects Myanmar's own desire for change." New York Times Book Review. {review of 1991 edition}

Wintle, Justin **Perfect** hostage : a life of Aung San Suu Kyi, Burma's prisoner of conscience / Justin Wintle. Skyhorse Pub., c2007. xxxi, 464 p., 16 p. of plates : **B**

ISBN 1602392668

1. Aung San Suu Kyi. 2. On Chan, Buil khyup, 1915-1947. 3. National League for Democracy (Burma) 4. Women political activists -- Burma 5. Women political prisoners -- Burma 6. Political activists -- Burma -- 20th century. 7. Nationalists -- Burma 8. Burma -- Politics and government -- 1988- 9. Burma -- Politics and government -- 1824-1948. 10. Biographies

LC 2007051031

A portrait of the Burmese activist minister and non-violence advocate describes the factors that contributed to her house arrest in 1989, her work to promote non-aggressive civil resistance, and her receipt of the Nobel Peace Prize in 1991.

"The author writes with a snarling wit, firm grasp of Burma's horrors, and penetrating respect for this tenacious and composed prisoner of conscience, detailing her genius for connecting with people, the threats against her life, and her devotion to peace." Booklist.

Austen, Jane, 1775-1817

Harman, Claire **Jane's** fame : how Jane Austen conquered the world / Claire Harman. Henry Holt and Co., 2010, c2009. 304 p. **B**

ISBN 9780805082586

1. Austen, Jane, 1775-1817 Appreciation. 2. Austen, Jane, 1775-1817 Influence. 3. Authors, English -- 19th century 4. Writing. 5. Biographies

LC 2009022291

Originally published: Edinburgh : Canongate, 2009.

In Jane's Fame, Claire Harman gives us the complete biography--of both the author and her lasting cultural influence--making this essential listen for anyone interested in Austen's life, works, and remarkably potent fame.

Nokes, David **Jane** Austen : a life / David Nokes. Farrar, Straus, and Giroux, 1997. xiv, 578 p. : **B**

ISBN 9780374113261

1. Austen, Jane, 1775-1817. 2. Authors, English -- 19th century 3. Single women 4. Family relationships. 5. Emotions in women. 6. Biographies

LC 97024768

Drawing on unpublished sources, the author offers an intimate, psychological portrait of the novelist, revealing the truth behind many disturbing Austen family secrets.

"Eschewing the biographer's usual perspective of omniscient foreknowledge in favor of a novelistic perspective of ambiguous immediacy, Nokes allows us to see Austen's talent as a mystery unfolding, not a fact explained. We thus witness the emergence of a personality sufficiently subtle and complex to produce Sense and Sensibility, Pride and Prejudice, and Emma. Readers of Austen's fiction will rejoice at having a biography so carefully nuanced, so refreshingly candid." Booklist.

Shields, Carol **Jane** Austen / Carol Shields. Viking, 2001. 185 p. ; **B**

ISBN 0670894885

1. Austen, Jane, 1775-1817. 2. Authors, English -- 19th century 3. Biographies

LC 00043807

"A Lipper/Viking book."

Charles Taylor Prize for Literary Non-Fiction (Canada), 2002.

Reveals Austen's private life and identity, including her family life, broken engagement, relationship with her sister Cassandra, and her writing process behind such novels as "Pride and Prejudice" and "Sense and Sensibility."

"In chronicling her subject's life and personality, Shields emphasizes Austen's keen ability to listen, observe, and capture clearly the social mores of her time and explore human nature in her writing. Shields contends that historical references are behind many of the scenes and characters in Austen's novels, and as a way of more clearly personalizing Austen's experiences or feelings, she interjects commentary regarding writing and publishing that is presumably based on personal experience." Library Journal.

Tomalin, Claire **Jane** Austen : a life / Claire Tomalin. Knopf, 1997. xiv, 341 p. : **B**

ISBN 9780679446286

1. Austen, Jane, 1775-1817. 2. Authors, English -- 19th century 3. Women authors -- England -- 19th century 4. Family relationships. 5. Biographies

LC 97036887

Recounts the life of the English novelist, and reveals how her works both reflected her times and differed from the world she experienced.

"The author has produced a portrait of remarkable subtlety. The light Ms. Tomalin casts on her subject is strong but oblique: the profile of the novelist appears surrounded by her friends and neighbours and by her energetic and beloved family." The Economist.

Worsley, Lucy **Jane** Austen at home : a biography / Lucy Worsley. St. Martin's Press, 2017. 400 p. **B**

ISBN 9781250131607

1. Women authors 2. Houses 3. Home (Concept) 4. Boarding schools 5. England 6. Biographies

LC 2017009308

A profile of the life and times of Jane Austen by the author of Courtiers tours the classic author's childhood home, schools, holiday accommodations and grand and small family estates to reveal lesser-known aspects of Austen's character and inspirations.

"Worsley (If Walls Could Talk) writes with a historian's acumen and a Janeite's passion, using these skills to unlock the doors of the many houses of Jane Austen (1775-1817)." Library Journal.

Auster, Paul, 1947-

Auster, Paul, 1947- **Report** from the interior / Paul Auster. Henry Holt and Company, 2013. 352 p. **B**

ISBN 9780805098570

1. Authors, American -- 20th century 2. Memory 3. Identity (Philosophical concept) 4. Childhood. 5. Autobiographies and memoirs

LC 2013002417

Evoking the sounds, scents and tactile sensations that marked his early life, the best-selling author of Winter Journal, in four parts, recalls his development from within through the encounters of his interior self with the outer world.

Austin, Nefertiti

Austin, Nefertiti **Motherhood** so white : a memoir of race, gender, and parenting in America / Nefertiti Austin. Sourcebooks, 2019. 304 p. **B**

ISBN 9781492679011

1. African American single mothers 2. Adoptive mothers 3. Adoption 4. African American parents 5. Autobiographies and memoirs

A literary diversity activist draws on her personal experiences as an African-American adoptive mother to reveal the virtual absence of Black representation in today's parenting culture and the challenges that diverse families encounter from the adoption community.

Austin, Paul, 1955-

Austin, Paul, 1955- **Beautiful** eyes : a father transformed / Paul Austin. W.W. Norton & Company, 2014 320 p. **B**

ISBN 9780393082449

1. Children with Down syndrome 2. Father and child. 3. Parents of children with disabilities 4. Autobiographies and memoirs

LC 2014025600

A father describes his experiences caring for and raising a daughter with Down syndrome, describing how he learned to see past her disability and helped her navigate through cultural assumptions and prejudices.

"This tender, bright and flawed child showed how being different enhanced her humanity rather than detracted from it. A poignant and candid father's memoir." Kirkus.

Autry, Gene, 1907-1998

George-Warren, Holly **Public** cowboy no. 1 : the life and times of Gene Autry / Holly George-Warren. Oxford University Press, 2007. 406 p., 64 p. of plates : **B**

ISBN 9780195177466

1. Autry, Gene, 1907-1998. 2. Country musicians -- United States 3. Film actors and actresses -- United States 4. Singers -- United States 5. Biographies

LC 2006036369

The only performer to earn five stars on the Hollywood Walk of Fame--for film, recordings, television, radio, and live performance--Gene Autry was the singing cowboy king. Journalist George-Warren offers the first serious biography, tracing Autry's climb from farm boy to multimillionaire. Autry's loving mother died on the brink of her son's success, while his ne'er-do-well father married five times and wandered the West. Autry battled his own demons but emerges here as one of America's most charitable benefactors, known for his boundless generosity, and a patriot who enlisted during World War II. The book provides colorful details of Autry's lengthy radio and recording career; his movie career, where he breathed new life into the Western genre; and his role in early television, the first movie star to develop his own TV shows. Along the way, he invested shrewdly, becoming the only entertainer listed among 1990's Fortune 400.--From publisher description.

"This colorful study is much more than a biography of Autry; it also tells the story of country-western music, singing cowboys, radio and early television, and celebrity." Choice.

Auvinen, Karen

★Auvinen, Karen **Rough** beauty : forty seasons of mountain living / Karen Auvinen. Simon & Schuster 2018 320 p. **B**

ISBN 9781501152283

1. Mountain life 2. Solitude 3. Cabins 4. Poets 5. Rocky Mountains 6. Autobiographies and memoirs 7. Essays

LC 2017061755

A memoir by an award-winning poet describes her retreats to a wilderness cabin to write in solitude and find answers to life's big questions, describing how a catastrophic fire forced her to reconcile her conflicting needs for isolation and community.

"This breathtaking memoir honors the wildness of the Rockies and shows readers how they might come to rely on their animal companions." Publishers Weekly.

Avedon, Richard

Gefter, Philip **What** becomes a legend most : a biography of Richard Avedon / Philip Gefter. HarperCollins, 2020 xv, 644 p. **B**

ISBN 9780062442710

1. Avedon, Richard. 2. Photographers. 3. Photography 4. Fashion photographers 5. Jewish men 6. United States -- Social life and customs -- 20th century 7. Biographies

A portrait of the twentieth-century photographer examines how Avedon endured intense personal and professional discrimination to join an influential group of artists who transformed women's culture.

"Gefter does a remarkable job of situating Avedon within the broader art scene, though the level of detail he goes into may overwhelm readers with a more casual interest in the subject. Nonetheless, this work serves as a definitive and insightful look into one of the titans of 20th century photography." Publishers Weekly

Stevens, Norma **Avedon** : something personal / Norma Stevens and Steven M.L. Aronson. Spiegel & Grau, 2017. 704 p. **B**

ISBN 9780812994438

1. Avedon, Richard. 2. Photographers. 3. Photography 4. Artists 5. Biographies

LC bl2017036562

A candid portrait of the famed photographer, co-written by his long-time business partner and confidante, traces Avedon's life from his humble New York childhood to his death during a shoot in 2004.

Avery, Sean, 1980-

Avery, Sean, 1980- **Ice** capades : a memoir of fast living and tough hockey / Sean Avery, with Michael McKinley. Blue Rider Press, 2017 320 p. **B**

ISBN 9780399575754

1. National Hockey League 2. Hockey players 3. Professional athletes 4. Celebrities 5. Hockey 6. Autobiographies and memoirs

LC 2017289448

Published in Canada under the title: Offside : my life crossing the line

Also published: Toronto : Viking, 2017

The controversial hockey star describes how he broke the bland set of rules that governed players for years and during the off-season and became an intern at Vogue, an advertising executive, a bar owner and a political activist.

Axelrod, David, 1955-

Axelrod, David, 1955- **Believer** : my forty years in politics / David Axelrod. Penguin, 2015 416 p. **B**

ISBN 9781594205873

1. Democratic Party. 2. Political consultants. 3. Former journalists 4. Autobiographies and memoirs

LC 2015302608

The man who masterminded Obama's historic election campaigns opens up about his years as a young journalist, political consultant, and ultimately senior adviser to the president.

"Axelrod's careful connection of the dots provides an illuminating study in how political power moves from generation to generation. The book-closing call to remake politics would sound like so much cheerleading in other hands, but Axelrod's connecting of Obama to JFK makes it work. Obama has been profiled many times but seldom with so practical an outlook. An excellent view of politics from the inside." Kirkus.

Axelrod, Howard, 1973-

Axelrod, Howard, 1973- The **point** of vanishing : a memoir of two years in solitude / Howard Axelrod. Beacon Press, 2015. 224 p. **B**

ISBN 9780807075463

1. Solitude -- Psychological aspects. 2. People with visual disabilities. 3. Living alone. 4. Self-perception. 5. Vermont 6. Autobiographies and memoirs

LC 2015004216

The author discusses his challenges after losing vision in one eye in college, and later retreating to a small house in the Vermont woods, where he lived without human contact for two years.

"This memoir is a keeper, touching and eloquent, full of hard lessons learned. Readers will hope for more from first-time-author Axelrod." Booklist.

Ayers, Nathaniel Anthony

Lopez, Steve The **soloist** : a lost dream, an unlikely friendship, and the redemptive power of music / Steve Lopez. G. P. Putnam's Sons, c2008. ix, 273 p. ; **B**

ISBN 0399155066

1. Ayers, Nathaniel Anthony. 2. African-American violinists 3. Men with schizophrenia 4. Homeless persons -- Los Angeles, California. 5. Skid row -- Los Angeles, California. 6. Los Angeles, California -- Social life and customs -- 21st century 7. Biographies

LC 2007046314

A portrait of gifted violinist Nathaniel Ayers traces his education at Juilliard, his struggles with schizophrenia, the factors that led to his homelessness in Los Angeles, his friendship with the author, and the author's efforts to improve the musician's life.

"With self-effacing humor, fast-paced yet elegant prose and unsparing honesty, Lopez tells an inspiring story of heartbreak and hope." Publishers Weekly.

B., David, 1959-

B., David, 1959- **Epileptic** / David B. Pantheon Books, 2005. 368 p. **B**

ISBN 0375423184

1. Brothers. 2. Growing up 3. Artists 4. Boy artists 5. Autobiographical comics 6. Comics and Graphic novels 7. Autobiographies and memoirs

LC 2004053419

Originally published: Paris : L'Association, 2002.

A personal memoir told in the form of a graphic novel chronicles the author's experiences growing up with an older brother suddenly afflicted with epilepsy and the effects of the disease on the family, and the roots of his career as a cartoonist.

"The author's artwork is magnificentgorgeously bold, impressionistic representations of the world not as it is but as he's taught himself to perceive it. . . . B.'s illustrations constantly underscore his writing's wrenching psychological depth; readers can literally see how the chaos of his childhood shaped his vision and mind." Publishers Weekly.

Baartman, Sarah

Holmes, Rachel **African** queen : the real life of the Hottentot Venus / Rachel Holmes. Random House, c2007. xiv, 161 p., 16 p. of plates : **B**

ISBN 1400061369

1. Baartman, Sarah. 2. Women, Khoikhoi 3. Women, Khoikhoi -- Europe -- History -- 19th century. 4. Women, Khoikhoi -- Europe -- Social conditions. 5. South Africans in England 6. Europe -- Social life and customs -- 19th century 7. Biographies

LC 2006045166

Profiles Saartjie Baartman, a South African woman shipped to England, where she became known as the Hottentot Venus and became the focus for late Georgian attitudes toward sex, race, colonialism, exploitation, prurience, and science.

"This is a probing look at historical racism and sexual exploitation presented through the life of an extraordinary woman." Booklist.

Babitz, Eve

Anolik, Lili **Hollywood's** Eve : Eve Babitz and the secret history of L.A. / Lili Anolik. Scribner, 2019. x, 277 p. ; **B**

ISBN 9781501125799

1. Babitz, Eve. 2. Women authors, American -- 20th century 3. Women artists -- United States 4. Hollywood, California -- Social life and customs -- 20th century. 5. Biographies.

LC 2018035881

A portrait of the Hollywood artist details the iconic photograph that catapulted Eve Babitz to notoriety, her high-profile affairs, her unheralded literary achievements, her years in seclusion and her recent re-emergence.

Bacall, Lauren, 1924-2014

Bacall, Lauren, 1924-2014 **By** myself and then some / Lauren Bacall. Harper, 2006, c2005. 506 p. : B

ISBN 0061127914

1. Film actors and actresses -- United States 2. Celebrities -- Anecdotes 3. Film acting 4. Entertainment industry and trade 5. Autobiographies and memoirs

LC bl2007014842

Rev. ed. of: Lauren Bacall by myself. 1st ed. 1979.

Originally published: New York : HarperEntertainment, c2005.

The star's memoir chronicles events since her story's original publication, from her appearances on Broadway to her latest film achievements and relationships with such individuals as Katharine Hepburn and Humphrey Bogart.

"Certainly more intelligently written than your average celebrity autobiography, this memoir tells a fascinating story of one woman's journey through life with an intimacy that's sure to engage legions of readers." Booklist.

Bach, Johann Sebastian, 1685-1750

Gardiner, John Eliot **Bach** : music in the castle of heaven / John Eliot Gardiner. Alfred A. Knopf, 2013. 640 p. B

ISBN 9780375415296

1. Bach, Johann Sebastian, 1685-1750. 2. Composers -- Germany 3. Classical music. 4. Classical musicians. 5. Biographies

LC 2013030398

National Book Critics Circle Award for Biography finalist, 2013.

A revisionist assessment of the life and achievements of the 18th-century master composer, written by one of the modern world's leading conductors and interpreters, shares scholarly insights into how Bach worked, how his effects are achieved and how his music reflects the man.

"Although Gardiner celebrates Bach's accomplishments through this dense, demanding but rewarding work, he reminds readers continually that the composer was no saint. [T]he author's focus is not so much on the man but on the music." Kirkus.

★Geck, Martin **Johann** Sebastian Bach : life and work / Martin Geck ; translated from the German by John Hargraves ; [foreword by Kurt Masur]. Harcourt, c2006. 738 p. : B

ISBN 0151006482

1. Bach, Johann Sebastian, 1685-1750 Criticism and interpretation 2. Composers -- Germany 3. Music, German -- History and criticism 4. Germany -- History -- 17th century 5. Germany -- History -- 18th century 6. Biographies

LC 2006012390

Discusses Bach's musical accomplishments through the stages of his life, from his humble origins as a self-taught court musician to his role as kapellmeister and cantor of St. Thomas's Church.

"This book adds original scholarship to an exhaustive study of other studies of Bach. And although it is often dense with information, it is just as often entertaining: rich in anecdotes and scintillating in its conjectures." New York Times.

Wolff, Christoph **Johann** Sebastian Bach : the learned musician / Christoph Wolff. W.W. Norton, 2001, c2000. xvii, 599 p. : B

ISBN 0393322564

1. Bach, Johann Sebastian, 1685-1750. 2. Composers -- Germany 3. Biographies

LC BL2001010688

Reprint. Originally published: 2000.

Pulitzer Prize for Biography or Autobiography finalist

Chronicles the life, work, and legacy of the inventive musician, composer, performer, scholar, and teacher.

"This work is likely to be the standard one-volume Bach biography for some time to come. It is a solid, richly informative treatment, presenting the copious details of Bach's life in a coherent, readable narrative." New York Review of Books.

Backman, Fredrik, 1981-

Backman, Fredrik, 1981- **Things** my son needs to know about the world / Fredrik Backman ; translated by Alice Menzies. Atria Books, 2019. 208 p. B

ISBN 9781501196867

1. Authors, Swedish 2. Fatherhood 3. Fathers and sons 4. Advice 5. Essays

LC 2018054900

Originally published: Stockholm : Forum, 2012."

Things My Son Needs to Know About the World collects the personal dispatches from the front lines of one of the most daunting experiences any man can experience: fatherhood. As he conveys his profound awe at experiencing all the "firsts" that fill him with wonder and catch him completely unprepared, Fredrik Backman doesn't shy away from revealing his own false steps and fatherly flaws, tackling issues both great and small, from masculinity and mid-life crises to practical jokes and poop. In between the sleep-deprived lows and wonderful highs, Backman takes a step back to share the true story of falling in love with a woman who is his complete opposite, and learning to live a life that revolves around the people you care about unconditionally."-- Provided by publisher.

"Each chapter is filled with Backmans dry wit and brutal honesty, but behind all of the humor is real, heartfelt sentiment and poignant advice." Booklist.

Badkhen, Anna, 1976-

Badkhen, Anna, 1976- **Walking** with Abel : journeys with the nomads of the African savannah / Anna Badkhen. Riverhead Books, 2015. 288 p. B

ISBN 9781594632488

1. Fula (African people). 2. Nomads. 3. Humans -- Migrations. 4. Migration, Internal. 5. Autobiographies and memoirs

LC 2015004476

An intrepid journalist joins the planet's largest group of nomads on an annual migration that, like them, has endured for centuries. Anna Badkhen has forged a career chronicling life in extremis around the world, from war-torn Afghanistan to the border regions of the American Southwest. In Walking with Abel, she embeds herself with a family of Fulani cowboys--nomadic herders in Mali's Sahel grasslands--as they embark on their annual migration across the savanna. It's a cycle that connects the Fulani totheir past even as their present is increasingly under threat--from Islamic militants, climate change, and the ever-encroaching urbanization that lures away their young. The Fulani, though, are no strangers to uncertainty--brilliantly resourceful and resilient, they've contended with famines, droughts, and wars for centuries.

"Readers with hectic lives may find the pace a bit slow, but the poetry in Badkhen's prose demands that readers slow down and savor her gentle, elegant story." Kirkus.

Bagehot, Walter, 1826-1877

Grant, James, 1946- **Bagehot** : the life and times of the greatest Victorian / James Grant. W.W. Norton & Company, [2019] 368 p. **B**

ISBN 9780393609196

1. Economist (London, England : 1843) History 2. Bankers 3. Journalists 4. Essayists 5. Intellectuals 6. Great Britain -- Politics and government -- 1837-1901 7. Great Britain -- Economic conditions -- 19th century 8. Biographies

LC 2019004287

Drawing on a wealth of historical documents, correspondences and publications, a vivid portrait of the 19th-century author of Lombard Street and inventor of the Treasury bill discusses his prolific writings, controversial politics and enduring economic influence. In James Grant's colorful and groundbreaking biography, Bagehot appears as both an ornament to his own age and a muse to our own.

Bailey, Blake, 1963-

Bailey, Blake, 1963- The **splendid** things we planned : a family portrait / Blake Bailey. W.W. Norton & Co., 2014. 254 p. **B**

ISBN 9780393239577

1. Bailey, Blake, 1963- Childhood and youth. 2. Bailey, Blake, 1963- Family. 3. Bailey family. 4. Authors, American 5. Biographers -- United States 6. Brothers 7. Family relationships. 8. Autobiographies and memoirs

LC 2013039720

National Book Critics Circle Award for Autobiography/Memoir finalist, 2014.

Presents a darkly humorous account of growing up in a prosperous, eccentric family with an older brother whose erratic and increasingly dangerous behavior threatens them all.

"A haunting portrait of more than one tortured soul and a heartfelt probing of the limits of brotherly love." Booklist.

Bailey, Elisabeth

Bailey, Elisabeth The **sound** of a wild snail eating / Elisabeth Bailey. Algonquin Books, 2010. 224 p. **B**

ISBN 9781565126060

1. Bailey, Elisabeth. 2. Companionship 3. Bonding (Human/animal) 4. Snails. 5. Women with terminal illnesses 6. Autobiographies and memoirs

LC 2010018603

National Outdoor Book Award for Natural History Literature, 2010.

William Saroyan International Prize for Writing, Nonfiction category, 2012."A small, short book filled with an enormous amount of natural history and science about snails; also, an acknowledgment of an individual's determination to recover and regain life with humor and insight. Highly recommended." Library Journal.

Bailey, Issac J.

Bailey, Issac J. **My** brother Moochie : regaining dignity in the face of crime, poverty, and racism in the American South / Issac J. Bailey. Other Press, 2018. 304 p. **B**

ISBN 9781590518601

1. Bailey, Issac J. Family 2. African American men 3. African American prisoners 4. African American families 5. Journalists 6. Southern states 7. Autobiographies and memoirs

LC 2017049799

A rare first-person account that combines a journalist's skilled reporting with the raw emotion of a younger brother's heartfelt testimony of what his family endured after his eldest brother killed a man and was sentenced to life in prison.

"Moochie and his tragic story have profoundly shaped Baileys life and deeply sensitized him to the pressures and traumas facing people of color, and the consequences." Booklist.

Bailey, Lily

Bailey, Lily **Because** we are bad : OCD and a girl lost in thought / Lily Bailey. HarperCollins, 2018 320 p. **B**

ISBN 9780062696168

1. Obsessive-compulsive disorder 2. Teenage girls with mental illnesses 3. Mental illness 4. Autobiographies and memoirs

LC bl2018053368

By the age of thirteen, Lily Bailey was convinced she was bad. She had killed someone with a thought, spread untold disease, and ogled the bodies of other children. Only by performing an exhausting series of secret routines could she make up for what she'd done. But no matter how intricate or repetitive, no act of penance was ever enough.

Bair, Deirdre

Bair, Deirdre **Parisian** lives : Samuel Beckett, Simone de Beauvoir, and me : a memoir / Deirdre Bair. Nan A. Talese/ Doubleday, 2019. 368 p. **B**

ISBN 9780385542456

1. Beckett, Samuel, 1906-1989 2. Beauvoir, Simone de, 1908-1986 3. Authors, American -- 20th century 4. Women authors 5. Women biographers 6. Intellectuals 7. Paris, France 8. Autobiographies and memoirs

LC 2019006879

Pulitzer Prize for Biography or Autobiography finalist, 2020.

The biographer explores her 15-year relationship with Samuel Beckett and Simone de Beauvoir, sharing insights into the biographical nature of their achievements and their long-standing feud against a backdrop of Parisian culture.

Baker, James Addison, 1930-

Baker, Peter, 1967- The **man** who ran Washington : the life and times of James A. Baker III / Peter Baker and Susan Glasser. Doubleday, 2020 688 p. **B**

ISBN 9780385540551

1. Cabinet officers -- United States 2. Politicians -- United States 3. Ambition in politicians. 4. Negotiation 5. United States -- Politics and government -- 1981-1989. 6. United States -- Politics and government -- 1989- 7. Biographies

LC 2019038715

A portrait of the influential White House Chief of Staff and Secretary of State includes coverage of the family tragedy that spurred his political career, his brokering of the reunification of Germany and his indelible role in the Gulf War.

"The authors interviewed Baker, and talked with numerous friends and associates to present a well-documented, engaging read. . . . Indispensable reading for anyone interested in late 20th-century U.S. politics." Library Journal

Baker, Nicholson, 1957-

Baker, Nicholson, 1957- **Substitute** : going to school with a thousand kids / Nicholson Baker. Penguin Group USA, 2016 416 p. **B**

ISBN 9780399160981

1. Substitute teachers 2. Classroom management. 3. Curriculum planning. 4. Teaching 5. Autobiographies and memoirs

LC bl2016032188

Describes how the National Book Critics Circle Award-winning author became an on-call substitute teacher in pursuit of the realities of American public education, describing his complex difficulties with helping educate today's students in spite of flawed curriculums and interpersonal challenges.

"An affecting (long-exposure) snapshot revealing real-life concerns." Kirkus.

Balanchine, George

Gottlieb, Robert, 1931- **George** Balanchine : the ballet maker / Robert Gottlieb. Harper Collins Atlas Books, c2004. 216 p. : Eminent lives **B**

ISBN 0060750707

1. Balanchine, George. 2. New York City Ballet -- History 3. Choreographers -- United States 4. Ballet dancers -- Russia 5. United States -- Social life and customs -- 20th century 6. Biographies

LC 2004048856

Documents the life and achievements of the foremost contemporary ballet choreographer, discussing how he founded what would become the New York City Ballet and choreographed major stage and movie productions.

"This loving tribute captures Balanchine's legacy: his energy, confidence, lack of pretension and, most important, his joy in creation." Publishers Weekly.

Teachout, Terry **All** in the dances : a brief life of George Balanchine / Terry Teachout. Harcourt, c2004. xv, 185 p. : **B**

ISBN 0151010889

1. Balanchine, George. 2. New York City Ballet -- History 3. Choreographers -- United States 4. Marriages -- History 5. Dancers -- United States 6. Ballet dancers -- Russia 7. United States -- Social life and customs -- 20th century 8. Biographies

LC 2004009226

Documents the late ballet magnate's Russian heritage, love for American culture, four marriages, and ongoing legacy that has caused his works to be danced by prestigious companies continuously since 1948.

"Balanchine's ballets are modern masterpieces, and Teachout, moving chronologically from work to work, uses them as stepping stones to tell Balanchine's own story. This is highly recommended as a first book on the life and art of George Balanchine for students and the general reader." Publishers Weekly.

Baldwin, Alec, 1958-

Baldwin, Alec, 1958- **Nevertheless** : a memoir / Alec Baldwin. HarperCollins, 2017. 400 p. **B**

ISBN 9780062409706

1. Actors and actresses 2. Film actors and actresses 3. Recovering addicts 4. Acting 5. Autobiographies and memoirs

LC 2017299664

The actor highlights parts of his life that he's long kept private, from his troubled childhood and efforts to make it as young actor to his struggles with addiction and his failings as a husband and parent.

Baldwin, James, 1924-1987

Glaude, Eddie S., Jr., 1968- **Begin** again : James Baldwin's America and its urgent lessons for our own / Eddie S. Glaude. Crown Pub, 2020 304 p. **B**

ISBN 9780525575320

1. Racism 2. Race relations 3. Civil Rights Movement 4. African Americans -- Identity 5. United States -- Race relations 6. Biographies

LC 2019059122

James Baldwin grew disillusioned by the failure of the Civil Rights movement to force America to confront its lies about race; in the era of Trump, what can we learn from his struggle?

"A penetrating study of how the words of James Baldwin (1924-1987) continue to have (often painful) relevance today." Kirkus

Baldwin, Rosecrans

Baldwin, Rosecrans **Paris,** I love you but you're bringing me down / Rosecrans Baldwin. Farrar, Straus and Giroux, 2012. 288 p. **B**

ISBN 9780374146689

1. Baldwin, Rosecrans. 2. Americans in Paris, France. 3. Americans in France. 4. Advertising agencies. 5. Bureaucracy. 6. Paris, France -- Description and travel. 7. Paris, France -- Social life and customs.

LC 2011045886

An account of a Francophile's haphazard relocation to Paris in spite of his lack of French fluency describes how the region considerably differed from his expectations and the ways in which he tapped his American optimism to overcome cultural challenges. By the author of You Lost Me There.

Ball, Lucille, 1911-1989

Ball, Lucille, 1911-1989 **Love,** Lucy / Lucille Ball with Betty Hannah Hoffman ; foreword by Lucie Arnaz. G. P. Putnam's Sons, c1996. xiv, 286 p., 32 p. of plates : **B**

ISBN 0399142053

1. Ball, Lucille, 1911-1989. 2. Arnaz, Desi, 1917-1986 3. Television actors and actresses -- United States 4. United States -- Social life and customs -- 20th century 5. Autobiographies and memoirs

LC 96020751

The comedienne's recently discovered memoirs, penned more than thirty years ago, recounts her career, including her marriage to Desi Arnaz and their life on and off the TV screen

Ballard, J. G., 1930-2009

Ballard, J. G., 1930-2009 **Miracles** of life : Shanghai to Shepperton : an autobiography / J.G. Ballard. Fourth Estate, 2008. 288 p. **B**

ISBN 0007270720

1. Authors, British -- 20th century. 2. World War II -- China. 3. Concentration camps -- China. 4. British in China. 5. China -- History -- 1937-1945. 6. Great Britain -- History. 7. Autobiographies and memoirs

LC 2008399727

Published for the first time in the United States, "the most original English writer of the last century," who authored such novels as Empire of the Sun and Crash, recalls his childhood, his first attempts at science fiction and his life as a single father after the premature death of his wife.

Balzac, Honore de, 1799-1850

Robb, Graham, 1958- **Balzac** : a life / Graham Robb. Norton, 1994. xvii, 521 p. : **B**

ISBN 0393036790

1. Authors, French -- 19th century 2. France -- Social life and customs -- 19th century. 3. Biographies

LC 94018614

A portrait of the self-destructive French novelist follows Balzac's early literary disappointments, impractical money-making schemes, love affairs, correspondences, and achievements

"Balzac's life was more cause for incredulity than anything he wrote, and Robb compellingly sets out the documentable facts against and within the world Balzac created from them. The result is nearly a novel, although Robb does not fictionalize with re-created dialogs and hypothetical events. He has in fact produced an extensive traditional biography...not a critical reassessment." Library Journal.

Bamberger, Louis, 1855-1944

Forgosh, Linda B. **Louis** Bamberger : department store innovator and philanthropist / Linda B. Forgosh. Brandeis University Press, [2016] 296 p. **B**

ISBN 9781611689815

1. Bamberger, Louis, 1855-1944. 2. Jews 3. Businesspeople 4. Philanthropists 5. Department stores 6. Newark, New Jersey -- History

LC 2016004971

"This biography is the first comprehensive examination of Bamberger's life, and it is long overdue." Library Journal.

Banks, Ernie, 1931-2015

Rapoport, Ron **Let's** play two : the legend of Mr. Cub, the life of Ernie Banks / Ron Rapoport. Hachette Books, 2019 384 p. **B**

ISBN 9780316318631

1. Banks, Ernie, 1931-2015. 2. Chicago Cubs (Baseball team) -- History 3. Baseball players 4. African American baseball players 5. Baseball 6. Men with depression 7. Chicago, Illinois -- Race relations 8. Biographies 9. Interviews

LC 2018044409

This biography of the baseball Hall of Famer examines his early years battling poverty and racism, his career with the Chicago Cubs and who, despite facing depression and loneliness, was known for his enthusiasm for the game.

"Regardless if readers are interested in Banks's psychological makeup, those who grew up baseball fans in the 1950s and 1960s will not want to miss this account of him and his midcentury Cubs." Kirkus.

Banville, John

★Banville, John **Time** pieces : a Dublin memoir / John Banville ; photographs by Paul Joyce. Alfred A. Knopf, 2018, c2016. 224 p. **B**

ISBN 9781524732837

1. Banville, John. 2. Authors, Irish 3. Dublin, Ireland 4. Autobiographies and memoirs

LC bl2017050209

Originally published by Hachette Books Ireland, 2016

Presents a memoir of the author's life near Dublin, a city that inspired his imagination and literary life and served as a backdrop for the dissatisfactions of adult years shaped by Dublin's cultural, political, architectural, and social history.

" Featuring excellent photographs by Paul Joyce, the short tome resembles a whimsical, funnier version of W. G. Sebalds meditative style. A richly rewarding and personal work of Irish history and culture." Booklist.

Barbarisi, Daniel

Barbarisi, Daniel **Dueling** with kings : high stakes, killer sharks, and the get-rich promise of daily fantasy sports / Daniel Barbarisi. Touchstone, 2017 304 p. **B**

ISBN 9781501146176

1. Winning and losing. 2. Fantasy sports. 3. Fantasy football (Game) 4. Gambling 5. Autobiographies and memoirs

LC 2016052642

An assessment of the influential world of Daily Fantasy Sports describes the author's decision to quit his reporter job and embark on a quest to join the top percent of DFS shark players, describing the fierce billion-dollar industry of FanDuel, DraftKings and online juggernauts who wager millions every day.

Bard, Elizabeth

Bard, Elizabeth **Lunch** in Paris : a love story, with recipes / Elizabeth Bard. Little, Brown and Co., 2010. 336 p. **B**

ISBN 9780316042796

1. Bard, Elizabeth. 2. Cooking, French. 3. Americans in France. 4. Husband and wife. 5. Men/women relations. 6. Autobiographies and memoirs

LC 2009022064

"Documents how the author fell in love and discovered the excellence of French cuisine during a life-changing lunch, recounting her decision to leave her fast-paced New York life to build a life abroad marked by bustling marketplaces, bad-tempered butchers and decadent chocolate shops."

"Falling in love with a Frenchman was not in Elizabeth Bard's master plan, but then he took her to a local canteen: Not to minimize Gwendal's many charms, but he was halfway to home base as soon as I cut into that marvelous steak, she writes. Culture shock set in as she learned to shop and cook in Paris, standing in line here for the best green beans, going there for the best walnuts. I thought the recipes were a cutesy touch until I made a few of them: chicken tagine with two kinds of lemon, spiced apricots, chouquettes. Forget the narrative you could just buy this as a cookbook." Entertainment Weekly.

Baret, Jeanne, 1740-1807

Ridley, Glynis The **discovery** of Jeanne Baret : a story of science, the high seas, and the first woman to circumnavigate the globe / Glynis Ridley. Crown Publishers, 2010. 352 p. **B**

ISBN 9780307463524

1. Baret, Jeanne, 1740-1807. 2. Commerson, Philibert, 1727-1773. 3. Bougainville, Louis-Antoine de, comte, 1729-1811. 4. Explorers -- France 5. Women explorers 6. Botanists. 7. Women botanists. 8. Biographies

LC 2010016778

Documents the pioneering round-the-world journey of the woman adventurer, tracing how she disguised herself as a boy to accompany her lover, botanist Philibert Commerson, on his 18th-century voyage before her true gender was exposed. By the award-winning author of Clara's Grand

"This is a biography of Jeanne Baret. Born in 1740 in France's Loire valley, Baret became an expert herb woman who proved to be indispensable to the ambitious botanist Philibert Commerson, accompanying him as his assistant when Commerson was appointed naturalist for France's first expedition to circumnavigate the globe. But women were forbidden, so Baret dressed as a man. Woven throughout this gripping story are Ridley's piquant insights into eighteenth-century exploration, botany, taxonomy, biopiracy, and sexism. Baret could not have asked for a more exacting and expressive champion. Ridley is incandescent in her passion for the truth." Booklist.

Barkan, Ady

Barkan, Ady **Eyes** to the wind : a memoir of love and death, hope and resistance / Ady Barkan ; foreword by Alexandria Ocasio-Cortez. Atria Books, 2019. 304 p. **B**

ISBN 9781982111540

1. Barkan, Ady. 2. Political activists 3. Political participation 4. People with amyotrophic lateral sclerosis 5. Grassroots movement 6. Autobiographies and memoirs

LC 2019019264

In this inspirational and moving memoir, activist Ady Barkan explores his life with ALS and how his diagnosis gave him a profound new understanding of his commitment to social justice for all.

"Barkans powerful narrative gives great insight into the nuts and bolts of political activism at work." Publishers Weekly.

Barlow, John Perry, 1947-2018

Barlow, John Perry, 1947-2018 **Mother** American night : my life and crazy times / John Perry Barlow with Robert Greenfield. Crown Archetype, [2018] 304 p. **B**

ISBN 9781524760182

1. Grateful Dead (Musical group) 2. Songwriters 3. Cattle ranchers 4. Political activists 5. Musicians 6. Autobiographies and memoirs

LC 2017050430

Traces the remarkable life story of the lyricist and political campaign manager, describing his upbringing among elite Wyoming ranchers, his vigorous advocacy of internet freedoms and his relationships with figures ranging from Jerry Garcia to Steve Jobs.

Barnard, Anne Lindsay, Lady, 1750-1825

Taylor, Stephen, 1948- **Defiance** : the extraordinary life of Lady Anne Barnard / Stephen Taylor. W. W. Norton & Company, 2017. 416 p. **B**

ISBN 9780393248173

1. Independence in women 2. Women artists 3. Women intellectuals 4. Women painters 5. England -- Social life and customs -- 18th century 6. England -- Social life and customs -- 19th century 7. South Africa

LC 2017011470

Having been given access to the private papers of Lady Anne Barnard, including six volumes of unpublished memoirs, the author chronicles the amazing life of this 18th- and 19th-century poet and painter, who lived on her own terms and defied the conventions of her day.

"This is a page-turning introduction to a fascinating life." Publishers Weekly.

Barnes, Julian

Barnes, Julian **Levels** of life / Julian Barnes. Alfred A. Knopf, 2013, c2013. 117 p. **B**

ISBN 9780385350778

1. Barnes, Julian. 2. Grief 3. Loss (Psychology) 4. Widowers 5. Depression 6. Autobiographies and memoirs 7. Essays.

Originally published: Toronto : Random House Canada, 2013.

A collection of essays by Julian Barnes.

Barnes, Julian **Nothing** to be frightened of / Julian Barnes. Alfred A. Knopf, 2008. 243 p. **B**

ISBN 9780307269638

1. Death. 2. Mortality. 3. Fear of death. 4. Authors, English -- 20th century. 5. Autobiographies and memoirs

LC 2008019603

'I don't believe in God, but I miss him. Julian Barnes new book is, among many things, a family memoir, an exchange with his brother (a philosopher), a meditation on mortality and the fear of death, a celebration of art, an argument with and about God, and a homage to the French writer Jules Renard. Though he warns us that 'this is not my autobiography', the result is like a tour of the mind of one of our most brilliant writers. When Angela Carter reviewed Barnes' first novel, Metroland, she praised the mature way he wrote about death. Now, nearly thirty years later, he returns to the subject in a wise , funny and constantly surprising book, which defies category and classification - except as Barnesian.

Barnett, Brittany K.

★Barnett, Brittany K. A **knock** at midnight : a story of hope, justice, and freedom / Brittany K. Barnett. Crown, 2020. 304 p. **B**

ISBN 9781984825780

1. Jones, Sharanda -- Trials, litigation, etc. 2. Buried Alive Project. 3. African American women defense attorneys. 4. Criminal justice system. 5. Racism in the criminal justice system. 6. Judicial system. 7. Texas. 8. United States. 9. Autobiographies and memoirs.

LC 2020007214

Presents an urgent call for justice-system reform in the story of a disadvantaged, African-American single mother from the rural South who was separated from her young daughter and sentenced to life in prison for a first-time offense.

"Recommended for readers who enjoyed Bryan Stevenson's Just Mercy, this is an essential read for anyone seeking to understand the devastating effects of mandatory drug sentencing and looking for inspiration to seek change." Library Journal

Barnett, Erica C.

Barnett, Erica C. **Quitter** : a memoir of drinking, relapse, and recovery / Erica C. Barnett. Viking, 2020. 322 p. **B**

ISBN 9780525522324

1. Alcoholic women 2. Addicts 3. Alcoholism 4. Drug abuse -- Treatment 5. Autobiographies and memoirs

LC 2019052898

An award-winning political reporter and recovering alcoholic shares her story, describing her repeated recoveries and lapses, discussing how Alcoholics Anonymous didn't correspond to her experience and actually was detrimental and highlighting the lack of rehabilitation options available to addicts.

"Emotionally devastating and self-aware, this cautionary tale about substance abuse is a worthy heir to Cat Marnell's How to Murder Your Life." Publishers Weekly

Barnett, Jacob, 1998-

Barnett, Kristine The **spark** : raising a genius / Kristine Barnett. Random House, 2013. 288 p. **B**

ISBN 9780812993370

1. Barnett, Jacob, 1998- Mental health 2. Children with autism -- Rehabilitation 3. Mothers of children with autism 4. Children with autism 5. Mothers and sons 6. Autobiographies and memoirs

LC 2012032774

Kristine Barnett, the mother of an autistic child, shares the strategies she utilized for tapping her son's potential.

"Barnett even runs a day-care center, takes in foster kids, and starts a sports program for autistic kids. Jake is unusual, but so is his superhuman mom." Booklist.

Barnum, P. T. (Phineas Taylor), 1810-1891

Wilson, Robert, 1951 February 21- **Barnum** : an American life / Robert Wilson. Simon & Schuster, 2019. 384 p. **B**

ISBN 9781501118623

1. Barnum, P. T. (Phineas Taylor), 1810-1891. 2. Circus 3. Circus owners 4. Entrepreneurs 5. Businesspeople 6. United States 7. Biographies

LC 2019000245

A biography of P.T. Barnum, nearly 125 years after his death, captures the full genius, infamy and allure of the forefather of American entertainment, and makes the case for his place among the icons of American history.

Barr, Nevada

Barr, Nevada **Seeking** enlightenment-- hat by hat : a skeptic's path to religion / Nevada Barr. G. P. Putnam's Sons, 2003. 222

p. ; **B**

ISBN 0399150579

1. Barr, Nevada. 2. Barr, Nevada Religion. 3. Women authors, American -- 20th century 4. Spiritual life -- United States 5. Purpose in life 6. Women and religion 7. United States -- Social life and customs 8. Autobiographies and memoirs

LC 2003043101

The author recounts her spiritual quest for meaning in her life, describing her experiences as an actor, writer, and adventure-seeker, and sharing her transition from atheism toward a sense of being part of something greater than herself.

"The author charts the course of her spiritual evolution, how she sought to understand the many aspects of spiritual life, from forgiveness (a sigh of relief on which the memory of evil is breathed out) to pain (it is a duty to relieve our own pain) to commitment (not a contract with the world but with the self). Barr's account of her transformation from nonbeliever to committed churchgoer--but one who maintains a healthy sense of doubt even as she prays and attends Bible studiesis moving but never saccharine." Booklist.

Barthelme, Donald

Daugherty, Tracy **Hiding** man : a biography of Donald Barthelme / Tracy Daugherty. St. Martin's Press, 2008. viii, 581 p., 16 p. of plates : **B**

ISBN 9780312378684

1. Authors, American -- 20th century 2. Postmodernism -- United States 3. United States -- Social life and customs -- 20th century. 4. Biographies

LC 2008029881

A detailed account of the life of the post-modern New Yorker writer evaluates the dynamic relationship he shared with his father that influenced many of his accomplishments, his creations of such stories as "Me and Miss Mandible" and "A Shower of Gold," and his friendships with such contemporaries as Thomas Pynchon, Kurt Vonnegut, and Tom Wolfe.

"Not dwelling on Barthelme's dark soul or his uneven work, Daugherty has created a convincing narrative from a life that was engaged, passionate and maybe even fulfilled." New York Times Book Review.

Bartolo, Pietro, 1956-

Bartolo, Pietro, 1956- **Tears** of salt : a doctor's story / Pietro Bartolo and Lidia Tilotta, translated by Chenxin Jiang. W.W. Norton & Company, 2018. 224 p. **B**

ISBN 9780393651287

1. Physicians. 2. Undocumented immigrants. 3. Asylum, Right of. 4. Civil rights. 5. Autobiographies and memoirs

LC bl2017045625

Translation of: Lacrime di sale: la mia storia quotidiana di medico di Lampedusa fra dolore e speranza

Originally published: Italy : Mondadori, 2016

A doctor at the lone medical clinic on the Italian island of Lampedusa chronicles his efforts to rescue, welcome, and care for many of the hundreds of thousands of desperate migrants from the Middle East and Africa who have washed up on the island's shores.

"In this moving account of attending to victims of war, Italian physician Bartolo makes an impassioned plea for more public awareness of and effective humanitarian solutions for refugees from Africa and the Middle East." Publishers Weekly.

Basie, Count, 1904-1984

Basie, Count, 1904-1984 **Good** morning blues : the autobiography of Count Basie / as told to Albert Murray. Random House, c1985. xiv, 399 p. : **B**

ISBN 9780394548647

1. Basie, Count, 1904-1984. 2. Jazz musicians 3. Autobiographies and memoirs

LC 85002439

Includes index.

Presents the life and times of the great jazz musician and band leader as told by the man himself, from his early days playing pickup at local social events, through his arrival--and eventual triumph--in New York.

"Basie pays tribute to his colleagues and managers (and to John Hammond for discovering him), but does not hesitate to discuss their weaknesses and short-comings; his language is direct and earthy. Although some of the book reads more like a catalogue or itinerary than an autobiography, it will have strong appeal for jazz buffs and fans of the late bandleader." Publishers Weekly.

Bass, Rick, 1958-

Bass, Rick, 1958- The **traveling** feast : on the road and at the table with America's finest writers / Rick Bass. Little Brown & Company, 2018. 448 p. **B**

ISBN 9780316381239

1. Authors, American 2. Voyages and travels 3. Dinners and dining 4. Writing 5. Autobiographies and memoirs

LC 2018933125

A transformative journey written in gratitude to the award-winning author's mentors describes his midlife attempt to recapture the passions of his youth, an effort marked by encounters with famous contemporaries and a variety of colorful mishaps.

"Bass reflective, funny, and generous chronicle of culinary adventures and nourishing literary encounters will renew readers appreciation for stories and storytellers and how literature guides us back to some deeper, older place." Booklist.

Bass, Rick, 1958- **Why** I came West / Rick Bass. Houghton Mifflin Co., 2008. 288 p. **B**

ISBN 9780618596751

1. Bass, Rick, 1958- Homes and haunts Montana 2. Authors, American -- 20th century 3. Writing 4. Montana 5. Autobiographies and memoirs 6. Pacific Northwest literature.

LC 2007030660

National Book Critics Circle Award for Autobiography/Memoir finalist"

Bass tells the tale of his apprenticeship to literature and the place that has defined his life for the past two decades, Montana's Yaak Valley. Bass looks back to his Houston childhood, Utah college years, and work as an oil geologist in Mississippi, searching for clues to his love-at-first sight response to the Yaak. As he describes his deep immersion in this bountiful land as a hunter, hiker, artist, and environmentalist, he . shares his anguish over the clear-cutting of woods, and chronicles the hard work of wilderness advocacy and the virulent hatred it arouses. Versed in paradox, Bass is bracing in his candor about how difficult it will be to change our destructive ways, and incandescent in his reasoned call to preserve the few remaining unspoiled places." Booklist.

Bastianich, Lidia

Bastianich, Lidia **My** American dream : a life of love, family, and food / Lidia Matticchio Bastianich. Alfred A. Knopf, 2018. 304 p. **B**

ISBN 9781524731618

1. Cooks. 2. Cooking, Italian. 3. Growing up. 4. Refugees 5. Autobiographies and memoirs

LC 2017045478

"This is a borzoi book."

The host of "Lidia's Kitchen" shares a memoir that traces her impoverished but loving upbringing under Tito's communist regime in Yugoslavia, her years as a refugee while trying to enter the United States, and her early start as a restaurant worker.

"A warm story of a life buoyed by resilience, determination, love of family, and food." Kirkus.

Baszile, Jennifer Lynn, 1969-

Baszile, Jennifer Lynn, 1969- The **Black** girl next door : a memoir / Jennifer Baszile. Simon & Schuster, 2009. 320 p. **B**

ISBN 9781416543275

1. Baszile, Jennifer Lynn, 1969- Childhood and youth. 2. African American women 3. African Americans 4. Race relations. 5. Suburban life. 6. Palos Verdes Estates, California. 7. California -- Race relations 8. Autobiographies and memoirs

LC 2008012867

"A Touchstone Book."

A powerful, beautifully written memoir about coming of age as a black girl in an exclusive white suburb in "integrated," post-Civil Rights California in the 1970s and 1980s.

Batali, Mario

Buford, Bill **Heat** : an amateur's adventures as kitchen slave, line cook, pasta-maker, and apprentice to a Dante-quoting butcher in Tuscany / Bill Buford. Alfred A. Knopf, 2006. 318 p. **B**

ISBN 9781400041206

1. Batali, Mario. 2. Cooking, Italian -- Tuscan style. 3. Restaurants. 4. Cooks. 5. Food. 6. Autobiographies and memoirs

LC 2006024646

A staff writer for The New Yorker offers an exuberant account of his entry into the world of a professional cook-in-training, documenting his experiences in the kitchen of Mario Batali's acclaimed restaurant Babbo, his apprenticeships with Batali's former teachers, his relationship with Batali, and his immersion in the world of food

Bauermeister, Erica

Bauermeister, Erica **House** lessons : renovating a life / Erica Bauermeister. Sasquatch Books, 2020. 224 p. **B**

ISBN 9781632172440

1. Women authors, American 2. Houses -- Conservation and restoration. 3. Families 4. Home (Concept) 5. Washington (State) 6. Port Townsend, Washington 7. Essays 8. Autobiographies and memoirs

LC 2020003113

In this mesmerizing memoir-in-essays, Erica Bauermeister renovates a trash-filled house in eccentric Port Townsend, Washington, and in the process takes readers on a journey to discover the ways our spaces subliminally affect us.

"This will resonate with any readers who love words and old houses." Booklist

Baylor, Elgin

Baylor, Elgin **Hang** time : my life in basketball / Elgin Baylor with Alan Eisenstock. Houghton Mifflin Harcourt, [2018] 336 p. **B**

ISBN 9780544617056

1. Basketball players 2. African American basketball players 3. Professional basketball 4. Racism 5. Autobiographies and memoirs

LC 2017045607

Includes index.

The 11-time NBA All-Star and 2006 NBA Executive of the Year traces his career in professional basketball, touching on such subjects as the vertical-versus-horizontal strategies that shaped him as both a player and a general manager, his battles against racism and his relationship with the notorious Donald Sterling.

Beah, Ishmael, 1980-

★Beah, Ishmael, 1980- A **long** way gone : memoirs of a boy soldier / Ishmael Beah. Farrar, Straus and Giroux, 2007. 229 p. : **B**

ISBN 0374105235

1. Child soldiers -- Sierra Leone 2. Civil war 3. Soldiers 4. Violence. 5. Sierra Leone -- History -- Civil War, 1991- 6. Sierra Leone -- History -- Civil War, 1991- -- Participation, Juvenile. 7. Sierra Leone -- Social conditions -- 1961- 8. Autobiographies and memoirs

LC 2006017101

Children's Africana Book Awards Honor Book, Older Readers, 2008.

A human rights activist offers a firsthand account of war from the perspective of a former child soldier, detailing the violent civil war that wracked his native Sierra Leone and the government forces that transformed a gentle young boy into a killer as a member of the army.

"Told in clear, accessible language by a young writer with a gifted literary voice, this memoir seems destined to become a classic firsthand account of war and the ongoing plight of child soldiers in conflicts worldwide." Publishers Weekly.

Beard, Amanda

Beard, Amanda **In** the water they can't see you cry : a memoir / Amanda Beard, with Rebecca Paley. Simon & Schuster, 2012. 256 p. **B**

ISBN 9781451644371

1. Beard, Amanda. 2. Swimmers. 3. Olympic athletes. 4. Women with depression 5. Women with anorexia 6. Autobiographies and memoirs

LC 2012006464

In this candid and ultimately uplifting memoir, Olympic medalist Amanda Beard reveals the truth about coming of age in the spotlight, the demons she battled along the way, and the newfound happiness that has proven to be her greatest victory.

Beard, James, 1903-1985

Birdsall, John The **man** who ate too much : the life of James Beard / John Birdsall. W. W. Norton & Company, 2020. 464 p. **B**

ISBN 9780393635713

1. Beard, James, 1903-1985. 2. Cooks -- United States 3. Gay men -- United States 4. Cooking, American 5. Biographies

LC 2020015582

After World War II, a newly affluent United States reached for its own gourmet culture, one at ease with the French international style of Escoffier, but also distinctly American. Enter James Beard, authority on cooking and eating, his larger-than-life presence and collection of whimsical bow ties synonymous with the nation's food for decades, even after his death in 1985.

"Highly recommended, this book offers new insight into Beard's life and time. It also helps another generation of foodies appreciate how Beard shaped American cuisine and helps all of us better understand the struggles LGBQT people faced in the mid-20th century." Library Journal

Beasley, Sandra

Beasley, Sandra **Don't** kill the birthday girl : tales from an allergic

life / Sandra Beasley. Crown Publishers, 2011. 240 p. **B**
ISBN 9780307588111
1. Beasley, Sandra Health. 2. Children with food allergies. 3. Food allergy 4. Allergic reaction 5. Food safety 6. United States -- Social life and customs -- 20th century 7. United States -- Social life and customs -- 21st century 8. Autobiographies and memoirs
LC 2010043724

The award-winning author of describes the impact of her anaphylactic food allergies on her childhood while tracing the cultural history of food allergies, relating such experiences as her short-lived job as a restaurant reviewer and dates that ended in trips to the emergency room.

Beatty, Warren, 1937-

Biskind, Peter **Star** : how Warren Beatty seduced America / Peter Biskind. Simon & Schuster, 2010. 640 p. **B**
ISBN 9780743246583
1. Film actors and actresses -- United States 2. Actors and actresses 3. Celebrities 4. Biographies
LC 2009022225

Drawing on interviews with Warren Beatty's colleagues and intimates, as well as the star himself, the author offers a tell-all biography of the Hollywood legend responsible for such classics as "Bonnie and Clyde," "Heaven Can Wait," and "Reds."

Beaumarchais, 1732-1799

Lever, Maurice **Beaumarchais** : a biography / Maurice Lever. Farrar, Straus and Giroux, 2008. 432 p. **B**
ISBN 9780374113285
1. Beaumarchais, 1732-1799. 2. Dramatists, French -- 18th century 3. France -- History -- 18th century. 4. Biographies
LC 2008055449

A portrait of the colorful eighteenth-century writer and public figure describes his unlikely fame as the author of The Marriage of Figaro at a time when self-fashioning was nearly impossible, his open support of American revolutionaries, and his advocacy of intellectual property rights.

"Best known as the author of the comedies that became Mozart's The Marriage of Figaro and Rossini's The Barber of Seville, Beaumarchais was a high-spirited adventurer for whom writing plays was only an honest relaxation. This erudite and wry biography covers the full range of his occupations, including watchmaking, espionage, pamphleteering, and transatlantic trade." The New Yorker.

Beauvoir, Simone de, 1908-1986

Bair, Deirdre **Simone** de Beauvoir : a biography / Deirdre Bair. Summit Books, c1991, c1990. 718 p. : **B**
ISBN 0671741802
1. Sartre, Jean Paul, 1905-1980 2. Authors, French -- 20th century 3. Women authors, French -- 20th century 4. Feminists -- France 5. Women philosophers -- France 6. France -- Social life and customs -- 20th century 7. Biographies
LC BL 99727632

Originally published: New York : Simon and Schuster, 1990.

Chronicles the life of the French writer, examining her roles as author, philosopher, feminist, and companion to Jean-Paul Sartre.

"Bair's biography of the French author, philosopher, and feminist aims to restore the balance between interest in de Beauvoir's personal lifeas the lifelong companion of Jean-Paul Sartre and sometime lover of Nelson Algrenand the question of her achievements as a writer and thinker." Booklist.

Beavan, Colin

Beavan, Colin **No** impact man : the adventures of a guilty liberal who attempts to save the planet, and the discoveries he makes about himself and our way of life in the process / Colin Beavan. Farrar, Straus, and Giroux, c2009. 288 p. **B**
ISBN 9780374222888
1. Authors, American -- 21st century 2. Environmental protection -- Citizen participation 3. Sustainable living. 4. Environmentalism 5. Autobiographies and memoirs
LC 2009010188

Includes index.

The author of Fingerprints describes his one-year experiment with minimizing his impact on the earth, an effort for which he eschewed technology, processed foods, and other negative-impact products while evaluating the plausibility and actual value of sustainable living.

"An inspiring, persuasive argument that individuals are not helpless in the battle against environmental degradation and global warming." Kirkus.

Bechtel, Warren A., 1872-1933

Denton, Sally The **profiteers** : Bechtel and the men who built the world / Sally Denton. Simon & Schuster 2016 384 p. **B**
ISBN 9781476706467
1. Bechtel family 2. Bechtel, Warren A., 1872-1933. 3. Bechtel Corporation. 4. Contractors 5. Building 6. Engineering 7. Infrastructure 8. Hoover Dam 9. Channel Tunnel
LC 2015510596

The tale of the Bechtel family dynasty is a classic American business story. It begins with Warren A. "Dad" Bechtel, who led a consortium that constructed the Hoover Dam. From that auspicious start, the family and its eponymous company would go on to "build the world," from the construction of airports in Hong Kong and Doha, to pipelines and tunnels in Alaska and Europe, to mining and energy operations around the globe.

"However readers view the company, Dentons extensively researched work informs readers about the firms maintenance as a privately held concern during its growth into a huge, multinational enterprise." Booklist.

Beckett, Samuel, 1906-1989

Gordon, Lois The **world** of Samuel Beckett, 1906-1946 / Lois Gordon. Yale University Press, c1996. ix, 250 p. : **B**
ISBN 0300064098
1. Beckett, Samuel, 1906-1989. 2. World War II -- Literature and the war. 3. Authors, Irish -- 20th century 4. Authors, French -- 20th century 5. Biographies
LC 95022851

"Gordon examines the first 40 years of the playwright/novelist's 83-year life, which includes periods in Ireland, where he was born; in Paris, where he spent much of his life; and in London, Germany, and other parts of France. Gordon has been thorough in her research and careful in her presentation." Choice.

Beecher, Henry Ward, 1813-1887

★Applegate, Debby The **most** famous man in America : the biography of Henry Ward Beecher / Debby Applegate. Doubleday, 2006. ix, 529 p., 16 p. of plates : **B**
ISBN 9780385513968
1. Beecher, Henry Ward, 1813-1887. 2. Congregational Church Clergy 3. Abolitionists 4. Clergy -- United States 5. Christianity -- United States -- History -- 19th century. 6. Men/women relations. 7. Biographies
LC 2005054842

Pulitzer Prize for Biography or Autobiography, 2007.

National Book Critics Circle Award for Biography finalist, 2006.

Presents the life of the nineteenth century orator, noted for his support of the abolition of slavery and the suffrage of women, as well as his friendships with some of the century's most famous writers such as Henry Thoreau, Mark Twain, and Walt Whitman.

Beethoven, Ludwig van, 1770-1827

Lockwood, Lewis **Beethoven** : the music and the life / Lewis Lockwood. W.W. Norton, c2003. xix, 604 p. : **B**

ISBN 0393050815

1. Beethoven, Ludwig van, 1770-1827. 2. Beethoven, Ludwig van, 1770-1827 Criticism and interpretation 3. Composers -- Austria 4. Biographies

LC 2002075397

Pulitzer Prize for Biography or Autobiography finalist

A portrait of the life, career, and milieu of the master composer describes the special challenges he faced as a gifted artist in the face of personal, historical, political, and cultural factors, in a volume that shares insight into his compositional methods through recreations of his sketchbooks and autograph manuscripts.

"Lockwood's study offers a new and authoritative interpretation of a prodigiously gifted and complex man and artist." Library Journal.

Morris, Edmund **Beethoven** : the universal composer / Edmund Morris. Atlas Books, 2005. 243 p. : **B**

ISBN 0060759747

1. Beethoven, Ludwig van, 1770-1827. 2. Composers -- Austria 3. Classical music. 4. Classical musicians 5. Musicians who are deaf 6. Biographies

LC 2006274925

Bashful with women and a stranger to romance, Beethoven was an abrasive, egotistical, and unsightly little man. Yet he was also a musical genius whose greatest works flowed from his deepest woes. His raging alcoholism and brooding psychosis seemed to stimulate not stifle his muse. But it wasn't until he lost the precious gift of hearing that he composed masterpieces whose grandeur and beauty tower above all others.

"The author clearly admires his subject not only for the work but also for his constant fight against the odds, and he has written an ideal biography for the general reader." Publishers Weekly.

Suchet, John, 1944- **Beethoven** : the man revealed / John Suchet. Atlantic Monthly Press, 2013 xv, 389 p. : **B**

ISBN 080212206X

1. Beethoven, Ludwig van, 1770-1827. 2. Composers -- Germany 3. Biographies

LC bl2013043813

Includes index.Drawing on the latest research as well as using source material, a leading authority on the life and works of Ludwig van Beethoven reveals the man behind the legend, painting a complete portrait of one of the greatest composers who ever lived.

"For the many readers lacking the proper background in musical theory, British broadcaster and Beethoven authority Suchet's explanations of Beethoven's music sing to us almost as if we could hear it." Kirkus.

★Swafford, Jan **Beethoven** : anguish and triumph : a biography / Jan Swafford. Houghton Mifflin Harcourt, 2014 xxi, 1077 p. : **B**

ISBN 9780618054749

1. Beethoven, Ludwig van, 1770-1827. 2. Composers -- Austria 3. Music, German -- History and criticism 4. Enlightenment (European intellectual movement) 5. Germany 6. Austria 7. Bonn, Germany. 8. Biographies

An esteemed music historian provides a rich, detailed overview of the life of Ludwig van Beethoven, traveling from Enlightenment-era Bonn to the musical capital of Europe, Vienna, to vividly describe the composer's career, ill health and romantic rejections.

"Rich in biographical detail, the volume contains revealing excerpts from many of Beethovens letters and from the written observations of his visitors and family; it also contains detailed analyses of many of his most notable works." Kirkus.

Begin, Menachem, 1913-1992

Shilon, Avi **Menachem** Begin : a life / Avi Shilon ; translated from the Hebrew by Danielle Zilberberg and Yoram Sharett. Yale University Press, 2012. 584 p. **B**

ISBN 9780300162356

1. Begin, Menachem, 1913-1992. 2. Prime ministers -- Israel 3. Revisionist Zionists -- Israel 4. Israel -- Politics and government -- 20th century. 5. Biographies

LC 2012012189

A full-scale portrait of the enigmatic Israeli leader draws on wide-ranging archival research and testimonials by his closest advisors to explore such topics as Begin's antagonistic relationship with David Ben-Gurion, his controversial role in the 1982 Lebanon War, his leadership style and his changing ideologies.

Belafonte, Harry, 1927-

Belafonte, Harry, 1927- **My** song : a memoir / Harry Belafonte with Michael Shnayerson. Alfred A. Knopf, Inc., 2011. 448 p. **B**

ISBN 9780307272263

1. Singers -- United States 2. African American singers -- United States 3. Autobiographies and memoirs

LC 2011014602

The National Medal of Arts recipient and former UNICEF Goodwill Ambassador shares the story of his life and career, from his impoverished childhood in Harlem and Jamaica and his racial barrier-breaking career to his commitment to numerous civil causes and his relationships with such figures as Eleanor Roosevelt, Martin Luther King, Jr. and Fidel Castro.

"The author covers his public career as an American entertainment icon (which solidified with his 1956 album, Calypso) and his interactions with many politicians and celebrities, e.g., Paul Robeson, Poitier, Marlon Brando, and Robert Kennedy, among many others. How these different strands interweavethe anger generated by the poverty and racial discrimination of his early years, the socially conscious reformer, and the well-respected entertainermake for a potent memoir of our times." Library Journal.

Belcourt, Billy-Ray

★Belcourt, Billy-Ray A **history** of my brief body : essays / Billy-Ray Belcourt. Two Dollar Radio, 2020. 142 p. **B**

ISBN 9781937512934

1. Belcourt, Billy-Ray. 2. Young gay men 3. First Nations (Canada) 4. Cree indians 5. Growing up 6. Autobiographies and memoirs 7. Essays

LC bl2020052265

A memoir of Canadian poet Billy-Ray Belcourt from the Driftpile Cree Nation.

"At the nexus of critical race and queer thought, this should become a timeless interdisciplinary resource for students, educators, and social justice activists." Kirkus

Belichick, Bill

O'Connor, Ian **Belichick** : the making of the greatest football coach of all time / Ian O'Connor. Houghton Mifflin Harcourt, 2018. 416 p. **B**

ISBN 9780544785748

1. National Football League 2. New England Patriots (Football team) 3. Football coaches -- United States 4. Football teams 5. Football -- United States 6. Coaching (Athletics) 7. United States -- Social life and customs

LC 2018017251

A biography of the NFL's most enigmatic, controversial, and yet successful coach follows his life in football, from watching Naval Academy games with his father to his success as head coach of the New England Patriots.

"...detailed look at Belichick's successful and controversial life." Library Journal.

Bell, Gertrude Lowthian, 1868-1926

Howell, Georgina **Gertrude** Bell : queen of the desert, shaper of nations / Georgina Howell. Farrar, Straus and Giroux, 2007, c2006. xix, 481 p., 16 p. of plates : **B**

ISBN 0374161623

1. Bell, Gertrude Lowthian, 1868-1926. 2. Women travelers. 3. Women archaeologists. 4. Colonial administrators -- Great Britain 5. Middle East -- History -- 20th century. 6. Biographies

LC 2006029994

"Originally published in 2006 by Macmillan, Great Britain, as Daugher of the desert"--T.p. verso.

ALA Notable Book, 2008.

An account of the adventure-filled life of Gertrude Bell describes how a woman transcended the restrictions of her gender, class, and era to become a renowned world traveler, archaeologist, spy, Arabist, linguist, author, poet, photographer, and mountaineer, and played a key role in the history of the Middle East.

"Bell's role in the creation of Iraq and the placement of Faisal upon the throne, is fully detailed. . . . But the strength and delight of Howell's superb biography is in the fullness with which Bell's character is drawn." Publishers Weekly.

Wallach, Janet, 1942- **Desert** queen : the extraordinary life of Gertrude Bell, adventurer, adviser to kings, ally of Lawrence of Arabia / Janet Wallach. Anchor Books, 2005. xxii, 425 p. : **B**

ISBN 1400096197

1. Bell, Gertrude Lowthian, 1868-1926. 2. Colonial administrators -- Great Britain 3. Women travelers. 4. Women archaeologists. 5. Middle East -- History -- 20th century. 6. Great Britain -- History -- 20th century 7. Biographies

LC 2005277878

Turning her back on her privileged life in Victorian England, Gertrude Bell journeyed the world and became fascinated with all things Arab. Traveling the length and breadth of the Arab region, armed with a love for its language and its people, she not only produced several enormously popular books based on her experiences, but became instrumental to the British foreign office. Janet Wallach reveals a woman whose achievements and independent spirit were especially remarkable for her times.

"High-spirited, outspoken, and self-reliant, . {Bell} was the first woman to earn a degree in history at Oxford, a skilled mountain climber and equestrienne, and an avid and fearless traveler who found her spiritual home in the deserts of Iraq and Arabia. Fluent in Arabic and on good terms with powerful men, Bell became an invaluable asset to British intelligence and was drafted as a spy during World War I. Wallach . brings the resolute Bell and her complex world vividly to life." Booklist.

Bell, Laura, 1954-

Bell, Laura, 1954- **Claiming** ground / Laura Bell. Alfred A. Knopf, 2010. 256 p. **B**

ISBN 9780307272881

1. Ranch life -- Wyoming. 2. Solitude. 3. Women and nature. 4. Social isolation. 5. Wyoming -- Social life and customs. 6. Autobiographies and memoirs

LC 2009029644

"After college, a Kentucky girl spends a summer in Wyoming to find herself and regroup. Thirty years later, she's still there. In this memoir, Bell vividly depicts her life out West, starting with her first job herding sheepan occupation usually done by men. She goes on to write about her life as a ranch hand, masseuse, housewife, stepmother, and forest ranger, mixing work experiences with touching and poignant accounts of family and friends. Bell here turns in satisfying reading for ranching enthusiasts, memoir fanatics, and anyone who likes to get lost in stories about rural life and nature's beauty." Library Journal.

Bellamy, Richard

Stein, Judith E. **Eye** of the sixties : Richard Bellamy and the transformation of modern art / Judith Stein. Farrar, Straus and Giroux, 2016. 320 p. **B**

ISBN 9780374151324

1. Bellamy, Richard. 2. Art dealers. 3. Art and society 4. Biographies

LC 2015036468

A portrait of the founder of the fabled Green Gallery explores such topics as his mixed heritage, advocacy of pop art and other less-represented forms and influential relationships with such figures as Norman Mailer, Yoko Ono and Diane Arbus.

Belle, Dido Elizabeth, 1761-1804

Byrne, Paula **Belle** : the slave daughter and the Lord Chief Justice / Paula Byrne. Perennial, 2014 192 p. **B**

ISBN 9780062310774

1. Belle, Dido Elizabeth, 1761-1804. 2. Lindsay, John, Sir, 1737-1788 3. Multiracial women 4. Illegitimacy 5. Civil rights 6. Equality 7. England -- History -- 18th century. 8. England -- Social life and customs -- 18th century 9. Biographies

LC 2014007447

This tells the story of Lord Mansfield, Lord Chief Justice, one of the most powerful men in the 18th century, and his highly controversial adoption of a mixed race girl, which resonated with the public as a campaign against slavery.

"Byrne brings to this brief history an eye for telling details of daily life, slaveholders' unthinkable cruelty, and the fervent work of a few good men and women who changed their world." Kirkus.

Bellow, Saul

Atlas, James **Bellow** : a biography / James Atlas. Random House, 2000. xiv, 686 p., 32 p. of plates : **B**

ISBN 0394585011

1. Authors, American -- 20th century 2. Men/women relations. 3. Biographies

LC 00042529

Chronicles the life of the Nobel Prize-winning writer, focusing on the period between 1944 and 1976 that saw the creation of such modern classics as "The Adventures of Augie March" and "Humbolt's Gift."

"Atlas shares his subject's devotion to literature, intimacy with Chicago (the city Bellow immortalized), and Jewishness, and he succeeds brilliantly in chronicling and interpreting Bellow's very full life, difficult personality, and powerful work." Booklist.

Bellow, Saul **Saul** Bellow : letters / edited by Benjamin Taylor. Viking, 2010. xxxvi, 571 p., 16 p. of plates : **B**
ISBN 9780670022212
1. Bellow, Saul Correspondence 2. Authors, American -- 20th century -- Correspondence
LC 2010022395
Includes index."
Saul Bellow wrote marvelously acute, unsparing, tender, ferocious, hilarious, and wise letters throughout his long life (1915-2005). Friends, lovers, wives, colleagues, and fans all cross these pages.This self-portrait shows the influences at work in the man and illuminates his enduring legacy: the novels and stories that earned him a Nobel Prize and the admiration of readers the world over."-Back cover.

Leader, Zachary, The **life** of Saul Bellow: love and strife, 1965-2005 / Zachary Leader. Alfred A. Knopf, [2018] 784 p. **B**
ISBN 9781101875162
1. Bellow, Saul. 2. Authors, American -- 20th century 3. Literature and society. 4. Literary prizes. 5. Senior men. 6. Biographies.
LC 2017053381
The second volume of the biography of the storied author describes how he expanded his collection of awards in his later years and continued to lead a dramatic, volatile love life, fathering his fourth child in his eighties.
"This is biography at its best and will appeal widely." Library Journal.

Benavidez, Roy P.

Blehm, Eric **Legend** : a harrowing story from the Vietnam War of one Green Beret's heroic mission to rescue a Special Forces team caught behind enemy lines / Eric Blehm. Crown Publishing, 2015. 288 p. **B**
ISBN 9780804139519
1. Green Berets. 2. United States. Army Special Operations Forces. 3. Rescues. 4. Vietnam War, 1961-1975. 5. Americans in Vietnam 6. Biographies
LC 2015451022
In May 1968, a 12-man US Special Forces team entered the jungles of Cambodia on a covert mission to uncover evidence that communists were using the area as a major conduit for supplying the North Vietnamese Army. Little did they know they had infiltrated a section of jungle that concealed numerous enemy bases. They soon found themselves surrounded by enemy, low on ammunition, and using the bodies of their dead comrades as cover. Roy Benavidez, a Green Beret, heard the distress call and climbed onboard the next helicopter bound for the combat zone. What followed was one of the most daring one-man rescue missions in military history, in which Benevidez rescued eight soldiers, while fending off heavy enemy fire and sustaining extensive injuries himself.
"Overall, the narrative seems a good magazine article pulled into book length, with some slipshod moments (e.g., one doesn't get a master's degree in Shakespeare) and too many draggy stretches. In the hands of a Junger or Krakauer, this story might have taken more memorable form. Still, Vietnam War completists will be interested." Kirkus.

Benedict, Saint, 480?-547?

Butcher, Carmen Acevedo **Man** of blessing : a life of St. Benedict / Carmen Acevedo Butcher. Paraclete Press, c2006. vi, 180 p. : **B**
ISBN 1557254850
1. Montecassino (Monastery) 2. Christian saints -- Italy 3. Italy -- Religious life and customs -- 6th century 4. Biographies
LC 2005035827
"This is the story of the life of St. Benedict of Nursia, who founded Western monasticism in the sixth century and later became the patron saint of Europe. . . . The book's readability will make it easy for patrons to escape into late Roman culture and find peace in a monastic simplicity." Library Journal.

Benincasa, Sara

Benincasa, Sara **Real** artists have day jobs : and other awesome things they don't teach you in school / Sara Benincasa. William Morrow, 2016 272 p. **B**
ISBN 9780062369819
1. Personal conduct 2. Autobiographies and memoirs
LC bl2016017566
Including 52 funny, yet thought-provoking, essays on how to live like a real adult, a comedian and author helps readers figure out who they are and where they fit in the world as they deal with the practical aspects of new adulthood. By the author of Agorafabulous.
"Outspoken and matter of fact, Benincasa points self-deprecatingly to her own failures to emphasize just how important they are to living a full, happy, and meaningful life. It's hard to imagine an actual self-help book could be more inspirational." Library Journal.

Benjamin, A. K.

Benjamin, A. K. **Let** me not be mad : my story of unravelling minds / A. K. Benjamin. Dutton, 2019. ix, 291 p. ; **B**
ISBN 9781524744380
1. Psychiatric hospitals 2. Psychiatric hospital patients 3. Psychologist and patient 4. Neuropsychology 5. London, England 6. Autobiographies and memoirs
LC 2018050850
Inspired by the author's years spent working as a clinical neuropsychologist at a London hospital, a multilayered personal account reveals the impact of his relationships with mentally disordered patients on his own perceptions of reality, sanity and healthcare.
"A well-conceived and -written exploration of the traps hidden in the art of mental healing." Kirkus.

Benmosche, Bob, 1944-2015

Benmosche, Bob, 1944-2015 **Good** for the money : my fight to pay back America / Bob Benmosche ; with Peter Marks and Valerie Hendy. St. Martin's Press, 2016. 304 p. **B**
ISBN 9781250072184
1. Benmosche, Bob, 1944-2015. 2. American International Group, Inc. 3. Chief executive officers. 4. Insurance companies. 5. Financial crises -- History -- 21st century. 6. Global Financial Crisis, 2008-2009. 7. Autobiographies and memoirs
LC 2015044720
In 2009, at the peak of the financial crisis, AIG - the American insurance behemoth - was sinking fast. It was the peg upon which the nation hung its ire and resentment during the financial crisis: the pinnacle of Wall Street arrogance and greed. When Bob Benmosche climbed aboard as CEO, it was widely assumed that he would go down with his ship. In mere months, he turned things around, pulling AIG from the brink of financial collapse and restoring its profitability. Before three years were up, AIG had fully repaid its staggering debt to the U.S. government - with interest.

"This is a definite must-read for anyone who wants to learn about the financial crisis, turnarounds in business, or leadership." Publishers Weekly.

Bennett, Alan, 1934-

Bennett, Alan, 1934- **Keeping** on keeping on / Alan Bennett. Farrar, Straus and Giroux, 2017 736 p. **B**

ISBN 9780374181055

1. Authors, English 2. Diaries 3. Autobiographies and memoirs

LC 2017034577

"A collection of Bennett's diaries and essays (2005 to 2015)."

Includes index.

The diary entries from one of England's leading dramatists from 2005 to 2015 include everything from his irreverent comedy pieces, reviews and celebrated essays to his personal reflections on his four major theatre premieres and two films during that time.

Berg, Elizabeth

Berg, Elizabeth **I'll** be seeing you : a memoir / Elizabeth Berg. Random House, 2020 224 p. **B**

ISBN 9780593134672

1. Berg, Elizabeth Family 2. Berg family 3. Children of aging parents 4. People with Alzheimer's disease 5. Husband and wife 6. Family relationships 7. Minnesota 8. Autobiographies and memoirs

LC 2019041943

The bestselling author shares her experiences caring for her parents in their final years, charting the passage from the anguish of loss to the understanding that even in the most fractious of times, love can heal.

"Berg's fans will be touched by her disclosures, and readers caring for an aging parent will see themselves in Berg's painfully honest, beautifully written account, and be comforted by her insights." Booklist

Berg, Ryan, 1974-

Berg, Ryan, 1974- **No** house to call my home : love, family, and other transgressions / Ryan Berg. Nation Books, 2015. 320 p. **B**

ISBN 9781568585093

1. Gay teenagers. 2. Group homes for teenagers. 3. Counselors. 4. Sexual minority youth. 5. Autobiographies and memoirs

LC 2015011424

"Underemployed and directionless, Ryan Berg took a job in a group home for disowned and homeless LGBTQ (lesbian, gay, bisexual, transgender and questioning) teenagers. His job was to help these teens discover their self worth, get them back on their feet, earn high school degrees, and find jobs. But he had no idea how difficult it would be, and the complexities that were involved with coaxing them away from dangerous sex work and cycles of drug and alcohol abuse, and helping them heal from years of abandonment and abuse. In No House to Call My Home, Ryan Berg tells profoundly moving, intimate, and raw stories from the frontlines of LGBTQ homelessness and foster care. I

"Through their compelling stories, Berg looks at inequalities suffered by LGBTQ youth in housing, public safety, health care, prison, immigration, employment, poverty, and homelessness." Booklist.

Bergen, Candice, 1946-

Bergen, Candice, 1946- A **fine** romance / Candice Bergen. Simon & Schuster, 2015. 368 p. **B**

ISBN 9780684808277

1. Actors and actresses -- United States 2. Husband and wife 3. Mothers and daughters 4. Widows 5. Hollywood, California -- History -- 20th century 6. Autobiographies and memoirs

LC 2014029293

"Witty and poignant and touching upon the many phases and challenges of daily existence, this book will appeal to a wide audience, especially those who are familiar with Bergen's work. For circulating libraries and entertainment collections." Library Journal.

Bergh, Henry, 1811-1888

Freeberg, Ernest A **traitor** to his species : Henry Bergh and the birth of the animal rights movement / Ernest Freeberg. Basic Books, 2020. 336 p. **B**

ISBN 9780465093861

1. Bergh, Henry, 1811-1888. 2. American Society for the Prevention of Cruelty to Animals. 3. Animal rights advocates 4. Animal welfare 5. Animal rights 6. Human/animal relationships

LC bl2020052174

An award-winning historian, in the revelatory social history, tells the story of an extraordinary man who gave voice to the voiceless and shaped our modern relationship with animals.

"Freeberg marshals a wealth of detail in tracking Bergh's campaigns and paints a vivid picture of Gilded Age America. Animal lovers and history buffs will savor this immersive account." Publishers Weekly

Bergman, Ingrid, 1915-1982

Thomson, David, 1941- **Ingrid** Bergman / David Thomson ; photo research by Lucy Gray. Faber and Faber, Inc., 2010. 118 p. **B**

ISBN 9780865479340

1. Bergman, Ingrid, 1915-1982. 2. Actors and actresses -- Sweden 3. Film actors and actresses -- Sweden 4. Film industry and trade 5. Hollywood, California -- History. 6. Biographies

LC 2009041757

"In this biography, the author describes Bergman's Hollywood-like rise, seemingly both unexpected and preordained, from talented Swedish actress to Hollywood goddess. He reserves his harshest criticism not for her increasingly chaotic private life but for how, after her brilliance in the 1940s--Casablanca, Gaslight, and the Hitchcock masterpieces Spellbound and Notorious, and more--she settled into a kind of unsatisfying mediocrity in the 1950s and 1960s. Thomson speculates that her fortunes faded with her legendary beauty." Booklist.

Berlin, Lucia

★Berlin, Lucia, **Welcome** home : a memoir with selected photographs and letters / Lucia Berlin. Farrar, Straus and Giroux, 2018. 160 p. **B**

ISBN 9780374287597

1. Women authors 2. Marriage 3. Voyages and travels 4. Women travelers 5. Autobiographies and memoirs

LC 2018017727

A compilation of previously unpublished sketches, photos, and letters from the late American short story writer depict and describe the places and people she met in Alaska, Argentina, Kentucky, Mexico, Chile, and New York City.

"An excellent start to understanding a writer and her work." Kirkus. Reviews

Bernard, Emily, 1967-

Bernard, Emily, 1967- **Black** is the body : stories from my grandmother's time, my mother's time, and mine / Emily Bernard. Alfred A. Knopf, 2019. 192 p. **B**

ISBN 9780451493026

1. African American women 2. African Americans -- Social conditions -- 21st century. 3. Race relations 4. Ethnic identity 5. United States -- Race relations. 6. Essays. 7. Autobiographies and

memoirs

LC 2018022594

"This is a Borzoi book."

A collection of personal essays explores the complexities and paradoxes of growing up black in the South with a white surname as well as the author's experiences with interracial marriage, international adoption, and teaching at a Northern white college.

"Bernard's honesty and vulnerability reveal a strong voice with no sugarcoating, sharing her struggle, ambivalence, hopes, and fears as an individual within a web of relationships black and white. Highly recommended." Library Journal.

Berner, David W.

Berner, David W. **Walks** with Sam : a man, a dog, and a season of awakening / David W. Berner. Roundfire Books, 2020. x, 157 p. ; **B**

ISBN 9781789044980

1. Authors 2. Leaves of absence 3. Dogs 4. Men and dogs 5. Essays

LC 2019949663

During a summer of hiking, the author finds that it is his beloved pet that allows him to awaken to a new spirit of mindfulness.

"It isn't profound, but Berner's plainspoken manner reveals moments of true enlightenment. Dog lovers and spiritualists will adore this." Publishers Weekly

Bernini, Gian Lorenzo, 1598-1680

Mormando, Franco **Bernini** : his life and his Rome / Franco Mormando. University of Chicago Press, 2011. xix, 429 p. : **B**

ISBN 9780226538525

1. Bernini, Gian Lorenzo, 1598-1680. 2. Sculptors -- Italy 3. Art, Baroque. 4. Artists -- Italy 5. Sculpture, Baroque. 6. Rome, Italy -- History. 7. Biographies

LC 2011023774

"In this biography of Baroque sculptor Gian Lorenzo Bernini since his death in 1680, . Mormando constructs a comprehensive, extraordinarily vivid portrait of the sculptor known as the Michelangelo of his age. Of great interest to general readers seeking a well-researched, highly readable portrait of the sculptor and those interested in the cultural history of baroque Rome." Publishers Weekly.

Bernstein, Jamie, 1952-

Bernstein, Jamie, 1952- **Famous** father girl : a memoir of growing up Bernstein / Jamie Bernstein. Harper, 2018. 352 p. **B**

ISBN 9780062641359

1. Bernstein, Leonard, 1918-1990. 2. Fathers and daughters. 3. Family relationships 4. Musicians -- United States. 5. Composers -- United States -- 20th century. 6. Autobiographies and memoirs

LC bl2018055502

Leonard Bernstein's oldest daughter presents a deeply intimate memoir of life with her father that shares insights into his complex personality, sense of humor, artistic influence and erratic creative process.

Bernstein, Leonard, 1918-1990

★Bernstein, Burton **Leonard** Bernstein : American original / Burton Bernstein and Barbara B. Haws. Collins, 2008. 240 p. **B**

ISBN 9780061537868

1. Bernstein, Leonard, 1918-1990. 2. New York Philharmonic. 3. Musicians -- United States 4. Conductors (Music) -- United States 5. Composers -- United States -- 20th century. 6. Music, American. 7. Broadway, New York City. 8. Biographies 9. Essays.

LC 2008013702

Includes index.

A visual tribute to the life and career of the pioneering conductor evaluates his role as a first American-born and trained conductor of a major orchestra, in an account that evaluates his contributions in a range of venues as well as his part in opening doors for women musicians.

"A flat-out wonderful book." Booklist.

Harmon, Charlie **On** the road & off the record with Leonard Bernstein : my years with the exasperating genius / Charlie Harmon ; foreword by Harold Prince. Charlesbridge, 2018. xi, 259 p. : **B**

ISBN 9781623545277

1. Bernstein, Leonard, 1918-1990. 2. Musicians -- United States 3. Personal assistants 4. Overdoing things 5. Drinking 6. Autobiographies and memoirs

LC 2017059790

A celebratory, intimate, and detailed look at the public and private life of Leonard Bernstein written by his former assistant.

Berra, Yogi, 1925-2015

★Barra, Allen **Yogi** Berra : eternal Yankee / Allen Barra. W. W. Norton & Co., c2009. 480 p. **B**

ISBN 9780393062335

1. New York Yankees (Baseball team) 2. Baseball players -- United States 3. Baseball coaches -- United States 4. Baseball. 5. United States -- Social life and customs -- 20th century. 6. Biographies

LC 2008045799

Allen Barra presents the life story of baseball's most successful player, Yogi Berra. From his rough-and-tumble childhood in St. Louis to the baseball Hall of Fame, Yogi has seen his share of triumphs, as well as defeats. As the most quoted, funniest athlete of all time, Yogi's story becomes complete in this larger-than-life biography.

"Barra brings to his sporting version of the Everyman story an encyclopedic knowledge and warm understanding of the game of baseball; meticulous research into business, sociology, and history; and a fluid writing style. Baseball biography taken to a higher level." Booklist.

Pessah, Jon **Yogi** : a life behind the mask / Jon Pessah. Little, Brown, & Company, 2020. viii, 566 p. : **B**

ISBN 9780316310994

1. Berra, Yogi, 1925-2015. 2. Baseball players -- United States

LC bl2020046716

A portrait of the 13-time World Series champion traces his rise to one of baseball's most accomplished athletes, discussing such topics as his experiences as an impoverished first-generation immigrant, his heroic war service and his paradoxical quotes.

Betjeman, John, 1906-1984

Wilson, A. N., 1950- **Betjeman** : a life / A.N. Wilson. Farrar, Straus and Giroux, 2006. 375 p. : **B**

ISBN 0374111987

1. Betjeman, John, 1906-1984. 2. Poets, English -- 20th century 3. England -- Social life and customs -- 20th century 4. Biographies

LC bl2006029420

Originally published: London : Hutchinson, 2006.

Based on an archive of personal material, chronicles the life of popular twentieth-century English poet John Betjeman, including his marriage to Penelope Chetwode, his love affair with Elizabeth Cavendish, and his role as a writer.

"Wilson's biography of the British Poet Laureate is a sharp-edged triumph of honest hero worship. Amazingly, he has found a real-life character whom he can love and admire. Brushing aside hundreds of chatty anecdotes and conversations that might have happened, Wilson has tied his primary source material around a subtle analysis of the ultimate first sources, the poems themselves. This, it is safe to say, should be the final biography." Times Literary Supplement.

Bettencourt, Liliane

Sancton, Thomas (Thomas Alexander), 1949- The **Bettencourt** affair : the world's richest woman and the scandal that rocked Paris / Tom Sancton. Dutton, 2017. 400 p. **B**

ISBN 9781101984475

1. Bettencourt, Liliane. 2. Banier, Francois-Marie. 3. Sarkozy, Nicolas, 1955- 4. L'Oreal (Firm) 5. Senior women. 6. Scandals -- Paris, France. 7. Swindlers and swindling. 8. Heirs and heiresses. 9. Biographies.

LC 2016058788

Part courtroom drama, part upstairs-downstairs tale, and part character-driven story of a complex, fascinating family and the intruder who nearly tore it apart, the Bettencourt affair started as a family drama but quickly became a massive scandal in France. As L'Oreal's shadowy corporate history and buried World War II secrets were uncovered, all of Paris was shaken by the blockbuster case, the shocking reversals, and the surprising final victim.

"A well-researched, crisply written, and entertaining story of family, greed, wealth, and the complex relations among them." Kirkus.

Betz-Hamilton, Axton

Betz-Hamilton, Axton The **less** people know about us : a mystery of betrayal, family secrets, and stolen identity / Axton Betz-Hamilton. Grand Central Publishing, [2019] 288 p. **B**

ISBN 9781538730287

1. Betz-Hamilton, Axton Family 2. Deception 3. Identity theft 4. Families 5. Betrayal 6. Autobiographies and memoirs

LC 2019011217

Edgar Allan Poe Award for Best Fact Crime, 2020.

Describes the impact of identity theft on the author's family at a time when banks and authorities were unwilling to help, revealing how her parents and she endured nightmarish victimization at the hands of a loved one.

Beyonce, 1981-

Chambers, Veronica, **Queen** Bey : a celebration of the power and creativity of Beyonce Knowles-Carter / edited by Veronica Chambers. St. Martin's Press, 2019. 240 p. **B**

ISBN 9781250200525

1. African American women -- Sexuality 2. African American women singers 3. Feminism 4. United States -- Social life and customs -- 21st century 5. Essays

LC 2018050716

The editor of the best-selling, The Meaning of Michelle, honors the career of the 22-time Grammy Award-winning music artist, sharing insights into Beyonce's record-setting achievements, her family life and her activist contributions..

"With such a dynamic ensemble of opinions and reflections, the collection will be sweet reading not just for Beyonc's superfans, but also for activists, feminists, and budding vocalists. An uplifting and resounding ovation." Kirkus.

Bialosky, Jill

Bialosky, Jill **Poetry** will save your life : a memoir / Jill Bialosky. Atria Books, 2017. 208 p. **B**

ISBN 9781451693201

1. Bialosky, Jill. 2. Poets, American. 3. American poetry -- 21st century. 4. Poetry -- History and criticism. 5. Growing up 6. Autobiographies and memoirs

LC 2016056306

The critically acclaimed author of The Prize presents a coming-of-age memoir organized around poems by such classic writers as Robert Frost, Emily Dickinson and Sylvia Plath, pairing each poem with key events that shaped her life, from the first time she fell in love and her sister's suicide to September 11 and the birth of a child.

"With brief poet biographies, this is a resplendent and invaluable anthology and an involving, richly illuminating narrative." Booklist.

Bianchi, Anna

Bianchi, Anna **Becoming** an ally to the gender expansive child : a guide for parents and carers / Anna Bianchi. Jessica Kingsley Publishers, 2017. 247 p. : **B**

ISBN 9781785920516

1. Gender identity. 2. Gender fluid 3. Parenting 4. Grandparent and child. 5. Autobiographies and memoirs

Includes index.

School Library Journal (March 2018)

How can parents and care-givers best support their gender expansive children? Drawing on the author's own experience with her grandchild, this book encourages adults to redefine their understanding of gender in order to understand and support their child more fully.

"Bianchi walks a graceful path, seamlessly exploring her own experience, that of her grandchild, the politics of society, and the human conditions of fear and love." Library Journal.

Biden, Jill

Biden, Jill **Where** the light enters : building a family, discovering myself / Jill Biden. Flatiron Books, 2019. 224 p. **B**

ISBN 9781250182326

1. Biden, Joseph R., 1942- Family 2. Vice-Presidents' spouses -- United States 3. Family relationships 4. Marriage 5. Teachers 6. Autobiographies and memoirs

LC 2019000561

The former Second Lady describes her marriage to Joe Biden and the role of politics in her life and teaching career, sharing intimate insights into the traditions, resilience and love that have helped her family establish balance and endure tragedy.

Biden, Joseph R., 1942-

Biden, Joseph R., 1942- **Promise** me, Dad : a year of hope, hardship, and purpose / Joe Biden. Flatiron Books, 2017. 272 p. **B**

ISBN 9781250171672

1. Biden, Beau, 1969-2015 Health. 2. Vice-Presidents -- United States 3. Fathers and sons 4. Coping 5. People with terminal illnesses -- Family relationships 6. Autobiographies and memoirs

LC bl2017036907

The former vice-president of the United States chronicles the difficult final year of his son's battle with cancer, his efforts to balance his responsibilities to the country and his family, and the lessons he learned.

"Written without an ounce of self-pity, it serves instead as an homage to a man Biden admired above all others and offers a passionate ray of hope to those who have suffered the loss of a loved one with the reassuring message that there is, indeed, a way through their grief." Booklist.

Bierce, Ambrose, 1842-1914?

Morris, Roy **Ambrose** Bierce : alone in bad company / Roy Morris, Jr. Crown Publishers, c1995. 306 p. ; **B**

ISBN 0517596466

1. Authors, American -- 19th century 2. Journalists -- United States 3. Disillusionment 4. Veterans 5. Biographies

LC 95030281

Includes index.Chronicles the life and career of the acerbic author, from his youth, through his experiences during the Civil War, to his 1913 disappearance in revolution-torn Mexico.

"Mr. Morris's disturbing, vividly realized biography brings to life a haunted writer whose private torments mirrored a turbulent era." New York Times Book Review.

Bilal, Wafaa

Bilal, Wafaa **Shoot** an Iraqi : life, art and resistance under the gun / Wafaa Bilal and Kari Lydersen. City Lights Books, 2008. xxii, 177 p. : **B**

ISBN 9780872864917

1. Bilal, Wafaa. 2. Artists -- Iraq 3. Iraqis in the United States 4. Conceptual art 5. Iraq War, 2003-2011 -- Art and the war. 6. United States -- Social life and customs -- 21st century 7. Iraq -- Social life and customs -- 21st century 8. Autobiographies and memoirs

LC 2008020487

The creator of "Domestic Tension," an unsettling interactive performance piece that speaks to the horrors of life in a conflict zone, reveals his experiences growing up under Saddam Hussein's rule.

"A powerful and demanding read, that is, frankly, a literary punch to the gut." Booklist.

Billings, J. Todd

Billings, J. Todd **Rejoicing** in lament : wrestling with incurable cancer and life in Christ / J. Todd Billings. Brazos Press, 2015. 224 p. **B**

ISBN 9781587433580

1. Billings, J. Todd. 2. People with cancer -- Psychology. 3. Cancer -- Religious aspects -- Christianity. 4. Suffering -- Religious aspects -- Christianity. 5. Clergy. 6. Autobiographies and memoirs.

LC 2014040099

"His poignant insight into the role of lament in faithful Christian living makes this a work of both astute scholarship and powerful testimony." Publishers Weekly.

Billy, the Kid

Gardner, Mark L. **To** hell on a fast horse : Billy the Kid, Pat Garrett, and the epic chase to justice in the Old West / Mark Lee Gardner. William Morrow, c2010 325 p. : **B**

ISBN 9780061368271

1. Billy, the Kid. 2. Garrett, Pat F. (Pat Floyd), 1850-1908. 3. Outlaws. 4. Sheriffs. 5. Frontier and pioneer life. 6. Criminals. 7. The West (United States) -- History -- 1860-1890. 8. Southwest (United States) -- History -- 1848- 9. Biographies

LC 2009025467

Draws on primary sources to recreate Sheriff Pat Garrett's manhunt for Billy the Kid, the Wild West's most notorious outlaw, and offers a dual biography of the two legendary larger-than-life figures.

"A double biography of the iconic western outlaw Billy the Kid and Sheriff Pat Garrett. Maintaining an objective perspective on both men in a narrative closely tied to historic source materials, Gardner's quick-moving story follows events of the civil war in Lincoln County, New Mexico Territory in 187778, and the Kid's death-by-shooting at the hands of Garrett in 1881. The final chapters describing Garrett as an old-style lawman in a postfrontier society, with interactions with President Theodore Roosevelt, serve to distinguish this book from other recent Kid biographies." Library Journal.

★Wallis, Michael, 1945- **Billy** the Kid : the endless ride / Michael Wallis. W.W. Norton & Co., c2007. xvii, 328 p., 16 p. of plates : **B**

ISBN 0393060683

1. Billy, the Kid Pictorial works. 2. Outlaws -- Southwest (United States) 3. Frontier and pioneer life -- Southwest (United States) 4. Southwest (United States) 5. Biographies

LC 2006101364

Historian Wallis has spent several years re-creating the rich, anecdotal saga of Billy the Kid (1859-1881), a deeply mythologized young man who became a legend in his own time and yet remains an enigma to this day. With the Gilded Age in full swing and the Industrial Revolution reshaping the American landscape, "the Kid," who was gunned down by Sheriff Pat Garrett in the New Mexico Territory at the age of 21, became a new breed of celebrity outlaw. He arose amid the mystery and myth of the swiftly vanishing frontier and, sensationalized beyond recognition by the tabloids and dime-store romances of the day, emerged as one of the most enduring icons of the American West--not to mention one of Hollywood's most misrepresented characters. This new biography, filled with dozens of rare images and period photographs, separates myth from reality in its portrait of this brief and violent life.--From publisher description.

"Drawing on archival sources and interviews as well as documents and secondary works, Wallis digs beneath the surface, clearly identifying what is known or probable and presenting the reasonable alternatives for what is conjecture." Library Journal.

Bin Laden, Osama, 1957-2011

Levy, Adrian, 1965- The **exile** : the stunning inside story of Osama bin Laden and Al Qaeda in flight / Cathy Scott-Clark and Adrian Levy. Bloomsbury USA, 2017. 400 p. **B**

ISBN 9781620409848

1. Qaida (Organization) 2. Terrorists 3. Terrorism 4. Fugitives 5. Antiterrorists 6. Biographies

LC 2017008379

Documents the inside story of Al Qaeda and its post-September 11 activities, drawing on interviews with the wives, military associates, spiritual advisors and radical followers of Osama bin Laden to trace his gradual loss of power and eventual defeat.

"This extensively researched, eminently readable work greatly enhances public knowledge of these dramatic years and will be welcomed by specialists and general readers alike." Publishers Weekly.

Scheuer, Michael **Osama** bin Laden / Michael Scheuer. Oxford University Press, 2011. 288 p. **B**

ISBN 9780199738663

1. Terrorists -- Saudi Arabia 2. Terrorism -- Religious aspects -- Islam. 3. Fundamentalists 4. Islam 5. Western bloc -- Foreign relations Islamic countries 6. Islamic countries -- Foreign relations -- Western bloc 7. Biographies

LC 2010021715

The author draws on his experience as the head of the CIA's bin Laden unit to argue that the terrorist leader is still relevant, still making decisions and still planning to put innocent people in harm's way.

Bingham, Hiram, 1875-1956

Heaney, Christopher **Cradle** of gold : the story of Hiram Bingham, a real-life Indiana Jones, and the search for Machu Picchu / Christopher Heaney. Palgrave Macmillan, 2010. 304 p. **B**

ISBN 9780230611696

1. Bingham, Hiram, 1875-1956. 2. Incas -- History. 3. Indians of South America -- Peru. 4. Cultural property 5. Incas -- Antiquities. 6. Machu Picchu, Peru 7. Peru -- History -- Conquest, 1522-1548. 8. Machu Picchu, Peru -- Exploration -- American. 9. Biographies

LC 2009038535

In 1911, a young Peruvian boy led an American explorer and Yale historian named Hiram Bingham into the ancient Incan citadel of Machu Picchu. Hidden amidst the breathtaking heights of the Andes, this settlement of temples, tombs and palaces was the Incas' greatest achievement. Tall, handsome, and sure of his destiny, Bingham believed that Machu Picchu was the Incas' final refuge, where they fled the Spanish Conquistadors. Bingham made Machu Picchu famous, and his dispatches from the jungle cast him as the swashbuckling hero romanticized today as a true Indiana Jones-like character. But his excavation of the site raised old specters of conquest and plunder, and met with an indigenous nationalism that changed the course of Peruvian history.

"On an archaeological trip to Peru on July 24, 1911, Hiram Bingham, an American explorer and history professor at Yale, happened upon the ruins of the Inca city of Machu Picchu. Although the site was already known to the local native people, Bingham made the Machu Picchu ruins famous and received acclaim as their discoverer. Heaney presents a well-researched and very readable biography of Bingham from his childhood in Hawaii as the son of missionaries, through his education and careers as historian, educator, explorer, and finally politician. He probes the depths of Bingham's work and character, examining setbacks, scandals, and achievements and skillfully unraveling Bingham's role in the controversy that still exists today between the government of Peru and Yale University over the ownership of the Machu Picchu burials and artifacts." Library Journal.

Birbiglia, Mike

Birbiglia, Mike The **new** one : painfully true stories from a reluctant dad / Mike Birbiglia ; with poems by J. Hope Stein. Grand Central Publishing, 2020. 256 p. **B**

ISBN 9781538701515

1. Birbiglia, Mike Family 2. Comedians 3. Fatherhood -- Humor 4. Parent and child -- Humor 5. Families

LC 2019049244

The comedian and author of the memoir Sleepwalk with Me shares laugh-out-loud observations on the haphazard journey of parenting as experienced by him and his poet wife that inspired a Broadway production.

"Hilarious, relatable, cringeworthy, and effortlessly entertaining, particularly for new parents or those in contemplation." Kirkus

Birdseye, Clarence, 1886-1956

Kurlansky, Mark **Birdseye** : the adventures of a curious man / Mark Kurlansky. Doubleday, c2012. 304 p. **B**

ISBN 9780385527057

1. Birdseye, Clarence, 1886-1956. 2. Frozen foods industry and trade 3. Inventors -- United States 4. Businesspeople 5. Biographies

LC 2011044891

A profile of eccentric genius inventor Clarence Birdseye chronicles how his innovative fast-freezing process revolutionized the food industry and American agriculture.

Bishop, Elizabeth, 1911-1979

Marshall, Megan **Elizabeth** Bishop : a miracle for breakfast / Megan Marshall. Houghton Mifflin Harcourt, 2017 368 p. **B**

ISBN 9780544617308

1. Bishop, Elizabeth, 1911-1979. 2. Poets, American -- 20th century 3. Women poets. 4. Women authors 5. Biographies

LC 2016043922

The Pulitzer Prize-winning author of Margaret Fuller traces the private life of revered American poet Elizabeth Bishop, drawing on insights from a newly discovered cache of letters to her psychiatrist and three lovers to illuminate her dark childhood and secret passions.

Travisano, Thomas J., 1951- **Love** unknown : the life and worlds of Elizabeth Bishop / Thomas Travisano. Viking, 2019. 432 p. **B**

ISBN 9780525428817

1. Bishop, Elizabeth, 1911-1979. 2. Poets, American -- 20th century 3. Women poets, American -- 20th century 4. Poetry -- History and criticism 5. Women poets 6. Biographies

LC 2019016018

An illuminating new biography of one of the greatest American poets of the twentieth century, Elizabeth Bishop.

Bismarck, Otto, Furst von, 1815-1898

Steinberg, Jonathan **Bismarck** : a life / Jonathan Steinberg. Oxford University Press, 2011. 544 p. **B**

ISBN 9780199782529

1. Bismarck, Otto, Furst von, 1815-1898. 2. Politicians -- Germany 3. Leadership in men. 4. Germany -- Politics and government -- 1871-1888. 5. Biographies

LC 2010045387

"The author delves into Bismarck's life as both an individual and a statesman, drawing on observations from his friends, colleagues, and enemies to advance the idea that much of Bismarck's power came from his magnetic, larger-than-life personality." Library Journal.

Bizot, Francois

Bizot, Francois The **gate** / Francois Bizot ; translated from the French by Euan Cameron ; with a foreword by John Le Carre. Knopf, 2003, c2000. xv, 275 p. **B**

ISBN 037541293X

1. Bizot, Francois. 2. Khmer Rouge. 3. Communism -- Cambodia. 4. Atrocities -- Cambodia. 5. Genocide 6. Cambodia -- History -- 1949-1975. 7. Cambodia -- History -- 1975- 8. Cambodia -- Politics and government -- 1975- 9. Autobiographies and memoirs

LC 2002069428

Originally published in French as Portail: Paris : Table ronde, 2000."

Bizot's tale of his experiences, both in the camp and as translator at the gate of the French embassy, leaves readers with haunting images of the doomed." Booklist.

Black Elk, 1863-1950

Black Elk, 1863-1950 **Black** Elk speaks : being the life story of a holy man of the Oglala Sioux / John G. Neihardt ; foreword by Vine Deloria, Jr. ; with illustrations by Standing Bear ; essays by Alexis N. Petri and Lori Utecht. University of Nebraska Press, 2004, c1932. xxix, 270 p. : **B**

ISBN 0803283857

1. Oglala Indians -- Religion. 2. Indians of North America 3. Healers 4. Spiritual life 5. Autobiographies and memoirs

LC 2004012692

Includes index.

Originally published: New York : W. Morrow, 1932.

Reveals the life of Lakota healer Nicholas Black Elk as he led his tribe's battle against white settlers who threatened their homes and buffalo herds, and describes the victories and tragedies at Little Bighorn and Wounded Knee.

Jackson, Joe, 1955- **Black** Elk : the life of an American visionary / Joe Jackson. Farrar, Straus and Giroux, [2016] 576 p. **B**

ISBN 9780374253301

1. Black Elk, 1863-1950. 2. Native American men 3. Spiritual life 4. Healers 5. Oglala Indians 6. Biographies

LC 2016016695

Spur Award for Biography, 2017.

National Book Critics Circle Award for Biography finalist, 2016

Describes the life of the Native American holy man who fought at Little Big Horn, witnessed the death of his cousin Crazy Horse, traveled to Europe as part of Buffalo Bill's Wild West show and became a traditionalist in the Ghost Dance movement.

Black, Derek

Saslow, Eli **Rising** out of hatred : the awakening of a former white nationalist / Eli Saslow. Doubleday, a division of Penguin Random House LLC, 2018. 288 p. **B**

ISBN 9780385542869

1. Stormfront (White nationalist organization) 2. New College of Florida (Sarasota, Fla.) 3. White supremacy movements 4. White nationalism 5. White supremacists 6. European Americans -- Attitudes 7. United States -- Race relations 8. Florida -- Race relations 9. Biographies

LC 2017061173

Traces the story of prominent white supremacist Derek Black and how his college and adult encounters with diverse perspectives changed his heart and mind.

"The heart of this book is the impact we do and can have on one another through meaningful, respectful interaction. Anyone looking to learn more about the history of white nationalism, and gain clarity of the arguments against it, will appreciate this compelling biography." Library Journal.

Black, Dustin Lance

★Black, Dustin Lance **Mama's** boy : a story from our Americas / Dustin Lance Black. Alfred A. Knopf, 2018. 336 p. **B**

ISBN 9781524733278

1. Gay men 2. Mothers and sons 3. Growing up 4. Screenwriters 5. Texas 6. California 7. Autobiographies and memoirs

LC 2018036767

"This is a Borzoi book.""

From the Academy Award-winning screenwriter and political activist, a candid, vivid, powerfully resonant memoir about growing up as a gay Mormon in Texas that is, as well, a moving tribute to the mother who taught him about surviving against all odds Dustin Lance Black wrote the Oscar-winning screenplay for Milk and helped overturn California's anti-gay marriage Proposition 8, but as an LGBTQ+ activist he has unlikely origins. Mama's Boy is a stirring celebration of the connections between mother and son, Redstates and Blue, and the spirit of optimism and perseverance that can create positive change in the world".-- Provided by publisher.

"Black provides a wholly en g rossing account of how a mother and son evolved beyond their potentially divisive religious and political beliefs to uncover a source of strength and unity through their enduring bond. A terrifically moving memoir of the myriad complexities of family dynamics." Kirkus.

Black, Michael Ian, 1971-

Black, Michael Ian, 1971- A **better** man : a (mostly serious) letter to my son / Michael Ian Black. Algonquin Books of Chapel Hill, 2020 304 p. **B**

ISBN 9781616209117

1. Personal conduct 2. Fathers and sons. 3. Masculinity. 4. Men -- Identity 5. Autobiographies and memoirs

LC 2019051609

The comedian, writer and actor discusses modern masculinity through a heartfelt letter to his college-bound son that will resonate with any parent looking to navigate complex gender issues and be or raise a better man.

"In this extended letter to his college-bound son, author and comedian Black (You're Not Doing Right) offers advice for navigating adulthood and masculinity, toxic or otherwise. . . . Both thoughtful and lighthearted, this work will appeal to anyone interested in masculinity and modern gender roles." Library Journal

Blackmun, Harry A., 1908-1999

Greenhouse, Linda **Becoming** Justice Blackmun : Harry Blackmun's Supreme Court journey / Linda Greenhouse. Times Books, 2005. xiii, 268 p. : **B**

ISBN 9780805077919

1. Blackmun, Harry A., 1908-1999. 2. United States. Supreme Court Justices. 3. Judges -- United States 4. Constitutional history. 5. Biographies

LC 2004063772

Includes index."

The author's achievement in her meticulous narrative history is to provide new ammunition for Justice Blackmun's critics as well as his admirers. And readers who are unfamiliar with the inner workings of the court could not hope for a more engrossing introduction." New York Times.

Blair, Tony, 1953-

Blair, Tony, 1953- A **journey** : my political life / Tony Blair. Alfred A. Knopf, 2010. xvi, 700 p., 32 p. of plates : **B**

ISBN 9780307269836

1. Labour Party (Great Britain) 2. Prime ministers -- Great Britain 3. Leadership in men. 4. Conservatism. 5. Politicians -- Great Britain 6. Great Britain -- Politics and government -- 1997-2007. 7. Great Britain -- Foreign relations -- 1997- 8. Autobiographies and memoirs

LC 2010028262

"This is a Borzoi book"--T.p. verso."

Without delving too deeply into his personal life, . [Blair] gives the reader a good sense of his role not just as a public figure but also as a son, husband, and father. Particulars of British party politics might elude some American readers, but the narrative keeps flowing. Essential for readers of current British politics." Library Journal.

Blake, William, 1757-1827

Bentley, G. E. (Gerald Eades), 1930- The **stranger** from paradise : a biography of William Blake / G.E. Bentley, Jr. Published for the Paul Mellon Centre for Studies in British Art by Yale University Press, 2003, c2001. 512 p. : **B**

ISBN 0300100302

1. Blake, William, 1757-1827. 2. Artists -- Great Britain 3. Poets, English -- 18th century 4. Poets, English -- 19th century 5. Biographies

LC bl2011001690

Reprint. Originally published: 2001.

Bentley traces Blake from his natal landscape, youth, marriage, and apprenticeship through to his later years as a working engraver, poet, and radical visionary. Bentley is academic and thorough

"The author traces Blake from his natal landscape, youth, marriage, and apprenticeship through to his later years as a working engraver, poet, and radical visionary. Bentley is academic and thorough, and this is more of a straight biography than an analysis." Library Journal.

Blanco, Richard, 1968-

Blanco, Richard, 1968- The **prince** of Los Cocuyos : a Miami childhood / Richard Blanco. Ecco Press, 2014. 288 p. **B**

ISBN 9780062313768

1. Poets 2. Gay men 3. Immigrants 4. Culture conflict 5. Autobiographies and memoirs

LC 2014501685

Lambda Literary Award for Gay Memoir/Biography"

Filled with colorful characters, often poignant and sometimes melancholy, Blancos episodic memoir is a meditation on belonging, on self-acceptance, and on his familys almost mystical connection to Cuba." Booklist.

Blazer, Chuck, 1945-

Papenfuss, Mary **American** huckster : how Chuck Blazer got rich from-and sold out-the most powerful fiefdom in world sports / Mary Papenfuss and Teresa Thompson. HarperCollins Publishers, 2016 272 p. **B**

ISBN 9780062449672

1. Soccer -- Economic aspects. 2. White collar crime 3. Corruption 4. Sports -- Corrupt practices

LC 2015050617

In a gripping true account of white-collar crime and betrayal at the highest levels of international business, two investigative reporters, drawing on sources in U.S. law enforcement, recount how Chuck Blazer, a stay-at-home New York soccer dad, illegally made millions from FIFA and became an unlikely FBI whistleblower.

"This grim, always entertaining cautionary tale of greed and runaway ego is a worthy addition to any reader's collection of business fantasies gone awry." Publishers Weekly.

Block, Francesca Lia

Block, Francesca Lia The **thorn** necklace : healing through writing and the creative process / Francesca Lia Block ; foreword by Grant Faulkner. Seal Press, 2018. 256 p. **B**

ISBN 9781580057516

1. Block, Francesca Lia. 2. Writing. 3. Authors. 4. Creativity. 5. Creative writing. 6. Autobiographies and memoirs.

LC 2017043732

The award-winning author of the Weetzie Bat series presents a memoir-driven guide to healing through the craft of writing, discussing such subjects as finding inspiration, organizing chaos and ignoring one's inner critic while exploring therapeutic exercises for processing pain and adversity.

"With every tip, Block provides examples from classic literature and exercises for writers, such as making characters mood boards, keeping updated lists of current obsessions, and writing scenes of backstory that may never appear in the final product. Wise and inspiring, this is a must-read for artists of all stripes." Booklist.

Bogart, Humphrey, 1899-1957

Thomson, David, 1941- **Humphrey** Bogart / David Thomson ; photo research by Lucy Gray. Faber and Faber, Inc., 2010, c2008. 127 p. : **B**

ISBN 9780865479333

1. Bogart, Humphrey, 1899-1957. 2. Film actors and actresses -- United States 3. Actors and actresses -- United States 4. Film industry and trade 5. Hollywood, California -- History. 6. Biographies

LC 2009041758

"Originally published in 2009 by Penguin Books, Great Britain"-- T.p. verso.

Presents the life and career of the motion picture actor, focusing on his inner doubts and contradictions, his most important films, and his personal life.

Boggs, Belle

★Boggs, Belle The **art** of waiting : on fertility, medicine, and motherhood / Belle Boggs. Graywolf, 2016. 224 p. **B**

ISBN 9781555977498

1. Fertility. 2. Motherhood 3. Conception. 4. Reproduction. 5. Autobiographies and memoirs 6. Essays

LC bl2016037260

The author describes her struggle to conceive a child and in the process explores the natural, medical, psychological and political facets of fertility.

"Readers struggling with infertility may find reassurance and comfort in Boggs's experiences; their loved ones will gain insight into the painful experience of infertility. All readers will appreciate the engaging prose and thought-provoking information." Library Journal.

Bolick, Kate

Bolick, Kate **Spinster** : making a life of one's own / Kate Bolick. Crown, 2015 304 p. **B**

ISBN 9780385347136

1. Bolick, Kate. 2. Authors, American -- 21st century 3. Single women -- Psychology 4. Women 5. Culture 6. Autobiographies and memoirs.

LC 2014037871

A celebration of the pleasures and possibilities of unmarried womanhood discusses the examples of such figures as Edna St. Vincent Millay, Edith Wharton, and Ganna Walska while charting the slowly changing societal attitudes toward women and marriage.

"Smartly written, intimate, and heartfelt, Spinster challenges readers to reconsider what a successful life feels like for women and gifts them with a wondrous group of historic figures to immerse themselves in. A brilliant and timely narrative for twenty-first-century bluestockings, and book groups shall rejoice from all the wonders it has to offer." Booklist.

Bolivar, Simon, 1783-1830

Arana, Marie **Bolivar** : American liberator / Marie Arana. Simon & Schuster, 2013. 603 p., 8 p. of plates : **B**

ISBN 9781439110195

1. Bolivar, Simon, 1783-1830. 2. Leadership. 3. Heads of state -- South America 4. Revolutionaries -- South America 5. National liberation movements. 6. South America -- History -- Wars of Independence, 1806-1830. 7. Biographies

LC 2012034661

An authoritative portrait of the Latin-American warrior-statesman draws on a wealth of primary documents to set his life against a backdrop of the explosive tensions of 19th-century South America, providing coverage of such topics as his role in the 1813 campaign for Colombian and Venezuelan independence, his legendary love affairs and his achievements as a strategist, abolitionist and diplomat.

"Drawing on Bolvar's voluminous correspondence and political writings, Arana assembles a chronological narrative that does justice to both Bolvar's august achievements and his human imperfections. This well-rounded work reveals not just an accomplished military tactician but also an able statesman." Library Journal.

Bolz-Weber, Nadia

Bolz-Weber, Nadia **Accidental** saints : confessions from a religious (but not so spiritual) life / Nadia Bolz-Weber. Convergent Books, 2015. 224 p. **B**

ISBN 9781601427557

1. Bolz-Weber, Nadia. 2. House for All Sinners and Saints (Denver, Colorado) 3. Lutheran Church 4. Toleration 5. God (Christianity) 6. Faith (Christianity) 7. Autobiographies and memoirs

LC 2015012506

A standup comic-turned-pastor describes her experiences with "accidental saints"--individuals with whom she has found the meaning of grace--including a drag queen, a felonious bishop, and a gun-toting member of the NRA.

"Recommended for readers who enjoyed Bolz-Webers previous books or authors such as Anne Lamott and Brian McClaren. An entertaining, reality-based alternative to the polished professional Christian memoir." Library Journal.

Bonaparte, Paolina, 1780-1825

Fraser, Flora **Pauline** Bonaparte : Venus of Empire / Flora Fraser. Alfred A. Knopf, 2009. xvi, 287 p. : **B**

ISBN 9780307265449

1. Bonaparte, Paolina, 1780-1825. 2. Napoleon I, Emperor of the French, 1769-1821 3. Princesses -- France 4. Brothers and sisters 5. Men/women relations 6. Extramarital affairs 7. France -- History -- Consulate and First Empire, 1799-1815 8. Biographies

LC 2008028639

Examines the life of Napoleon's favorite sister, Pauline Bonaparte Borghese, renowned at the turn of the nineteenth century as one of Europe's most beautiful women, who shocked the continent with her scandalous love affairs and opulent lifestyle.

"Fraser's narrative provides insight into the permissive culture of the French Empire and glimpses into Napoleon as a protective and exasperated older brother while simultaneously engaged in politics, invasions and his eventual fall from power." Publishers Weekly.

Bonhoeffer, Dietrich, 1906-1945

Marsh, Charles, 1958- **Strange** glory : a life of Dietrich Bonhoeffer / Charles Marsh. Alfred A Knopf, 2014 528 p. **B**

ISBN 9780307269812

1. Bonhoeffer, Dietrich, 1906-1945. 2. Thought and thinking 3. Faith in men. 4. Germans in the United States 5. Christian martyrs -- Germany 6. Biographies

LC 2013045873

A portrait of the German pastor-theologian draws on new research to cover the 1930 visit to America that shaped his perspectives on faith and moral responsibility, his achievements as an anti-Nazi activist and the plot against Hitler that would result in his execution.

"Marsh's portrait is of a spoiled, materialistic, and selfish young man who develops, over time, into a German hero. The writing is clear and concise, the endnotes extensive, and the index generous." Library Journal.

Metaxas, Eric **Bonhoeffer** : pastor, martyr, prophet, spy: a righteous Gentile vs. the Third Reich / Eric Metaxas ; foreword by Timothy J. Keller. Thomas Nelson, 2010. 591 p. **B**

ISBN 9781595551382

1. Bonhoeffer, Dietrich, 1906-1945. 2. Hitler, Adolf, 1889-1945 Attempted assassination, July 20, 1944 3. Righteous Gentiles in the Holocaust -- Germany 4. Martyrs. 5. Anti-Nazi movement. 6. Faith in men. 7. Germany -- History -- 1933-1945. 8. Biographies

LC 2010922204

ECPA Christian Book Awards, Christian Book of the Year, 2011.
ECPA Christian Book Awards, Non-Fiction, 2011.

Traces the life of the Christian theologian whose faith led him to speak out against Nazism and join in unsuccessful attempts to assassinate Hitler, discussing the personalities and experiences that shaped him and detailing his role in the religious resistance to Nazism.

"Insightful and illuminating, this tome makes a powerful contribution to biography, history and theology." Publishers Weekly.

Bonner, Betsy

Bonner, Betsy The **book** of Atlantis Black : the search for a sister gone missing / Betsy Bonner. Tin House Books, 2020. 280 p. **B**

ISBN 9781947793774

1. Black, Atlantis, 1976-2008 2. Missing women 3. Murder investigation 4. Sisters 5. Adult child abuse victims 6. Autobiographies and memoirs

LC 2020004078

A young woman is found dead on the floor of a Tijuana hotel room. An ID in a nearby purse reads "Atlantis Black." The police report states that the body does not seem to match the identification, yet the body is quickly cremated and the case is considered closed.

So begins Betsy Bonner's search for her sister, Atlantis, and the unraveling of the mysterious final months before Atlantis's disappearance, alleged overdose, and death. Through a history only she and Atlantis shared--a childhood fraught with abuse and mental illness, Atlantis's precocious yet short rise in the music world, and through it all an unshakable bond of sisterhood--Bonner finds questions that lead only to more questions and possible clues that seem to point in no particular direction. In this haunting memoir and piercing true crime account, Bonner must decide how far she will go to understand a sister who, like the mythical island she renamed herself for, might prove impossible to find.

"A haunting, profound investigative memoir that will resonate with readers as both a compelling true crime story and an affecting literary work. Bonner creates a sense of closeness with readers that makes this book a challenge to put down or forget." Library Journal

Bontinck, Dimitri, 1973-

Bontinck, Dimitri, 1973- **Rescued** from ISIS : the gripping true story of how a father saved his son / Dimitri Bontinck. St Martins Press, 2017 288 p. **B**

ISBN 9781250147585

1. Bontinck, Jejoen , 1995- 2. ISIS (Islamic State of Iraq and Syria) 3. Terrorism 4. Terrorists -- Recruiting 5. Radicalism 6. Fundamentalism 7. Syria -- History -- Civil War, 2011- 8. Autobiographies and memoirs

LC 2017297023

Documents the gripping true story of how the author rescued his son from a radical mosque that brainwashed him into becoming a jihadist soldier, describing the months of unassisted work that were required and how his success reverberated throughout the world, triggering pleas from other families whose children were similarly indoctrinated.

"A moving personal account that offers profound insights into Islamic terrorism and the struggle against it." Kirkus.

Boogaard, Derek, 1982-2011

Branch, John (Sports reporter) **Boy** on ice : the life and death of Derek Boogaard / John Branch. W.W. Norton & Company, 2014 384 p. **B**

ISBN 9780393239393

1. Boogaard, Derek, 1982-2011. 2. Hockey players -- Canada 3. Violence in sports. 4. Hockey. 5. Violence in hockey. 6. Biographies

LC 2014015731

The tragic death of hockey star Derek Boogaard at twenty-eight was front-page news across the country in 2011 and helped shatter the silence about violence and concussions in professional sports. Widely regarded as the toughest man in the NHL, Boogaard was a gentle man off the ice but a merciless fighter on it. But, as Branch reveals, behind the scenes Boogaard's injuries and concussions were mounting and his mental state was deteriorating, culminating in his early death from an overdose of alcohol and painkillers.

Boone, Daniel, 1734-1820

Morgan, Robert, 1944- **Boone** : a biography / Robert Morgan. Algonquin Books of Chapel Hill, 2007. 576 p. **B**

ISBN 1565124553

1. Boone, Daniel, 1734-1820. 2. Pioneers -- Kentucky 3. Explorers -- Kentucky 4. Frontier and pioneer life -- Kentucky. 5. Kentucky -- Social life and customs. 6. Kentucky -- Exploration. 7. Biographies

LC 2007014204

Often obscured by myth and folklore, Daniel Boone is as fascinating a character as any other American son. Here, Robert Morgan chronicles the life life of the frontier legend.

"This is an absorbing and stirring chronicle of the great frontiersman." Booklist.

Booth, John Wilkes, 1838-1865

Alford, Terry **Fortune's** fool : the life of John Wilkes Booth / Terry Alford. Oxford University Press, 2015 454 p. : **B**

ISBN 9780195054125

1. Booth, John Wilkes, 1838-1865. 2. Lincoln, Abraham, 1809-1865 Assassination. 3. Biographies

National Book Critics Circle Award for Biography finalist, 2015.

In Fortune's Fool, Terry Alford provides the first comprehensive look at the life of an enigmatic figure whose life has been overshadowed by his final, infamous act.

Borges, Jorge Luis, 1899-1986

Williamson, Edwin **Borges** : a life / Edwin Williamson. Viking, 2004. xviii, 574 p. : **B**

ISBN 0670885797

1. Borges, Jorge Luis, 1899-1986. 2. Authors, Argentine -- 20th century 3. Argentina -- Social life and customs -- 20th century 4. Biographies

LC 2004041290

A portrait of the Latin American writer and poet draws on interviews and previously unavailable sources to cover such topics as Borges' ancestry in Argentina, the challenges that marked his life, and the evolution of his political ideas.

"This is a richly psychological, dynamically intellectual, and deeply affecting portrait of an often anguished and inhibited man who, through heroic perserverance and spiritual conviction, found salvation in writing and transformed literature for all time." Booklist.

Borgia, Lucrezia, 1480-1519

Bradford, Sarah, 1938- **Lucrezia** Borgia : life, love and death in Renaissance Italy / Sarah Bradford. Viking, 2004. xxiv, 421 p. : **B**

ISBN 0670033537

1. Borgia, Lucrezia, 1480-1519. 2. Alexander VI, Pope, 1431-1503 Family. 3. Nobility -- Papal States 4. Italy -- History -- 1492-1559. 5. Ferrara, Italy -- History -- 16th century. 6. Biographies

LC 2004054881

Neither a vicious monster nor a seductive pawn, Lucrezia Borgia was a shrewd, determined woman who used her beauty and intelligence to secure a key role in the political struggles of her day. Drawing from a trove of contemporary documents and fascinating firsthand accounts, Bradford brings to life the art, the pageantry, and the dangerous politics of the Renaissance world Lucrezia Borgia helped to create.

"The author presents Lucrezia as an intelligent noblewoman, powerless to defy her family's patriarchal order, yet an enlightened ruler in her own right as Duchess of Ferrara. As a project designed to distinguish the historical Lucrezia Borgia from the legend, Bradford's readable biography resoundingly succeeds." Publishers Weekly.

Born, Max, 1882-1970

Greenspan, Nancy Thorndike The **end** of the certain world : the life and science of Max Born : the Nobel physicist who ignited the quantum revolution / Nancy Thorndike Greenspan. Basic Books, c2005. x, 374 p., 16 p. of plates : **B**

ISBN 9780738206936

1. Born, Max, 1882-1970. 2. Physicists -- Germany 3. Nobel Prize winners 4. Quantum theory -- History. 5. Biographies

LC 2004021809

A biography of Nobel Prize-winning physicist Max Born reveals the great scientist's struggle with morality, politics, war, and obscurity and reassesses his contributions to the world of twentieth-century physics and science..

Bosker, Bianca

Bosker, Bianca **Cork** dork : a wine-fueled adventure among the obsessive sommeliers, big bottle hunters, and rogue scientists who taught me to live for taste / Bianca Bosker. Penguin Group, 2017. 352 p. **B**

ISBN 9780143128090

1. Wine tasting 2. Lifestyle change 3. Wine and wine making 4. Senses and sensation 5. Autobiographies and memoirs

LC 2016029203

A tech reporter describes her introduction to the world of master sommeliers and her in-depth investigation into the source of their interests and skills, an effort marked by work with elite tasting groups, encounters at exclusive New York restaurants, visits to California winemakers and more.

"An interesting look at those with an unquenchable thirst for those unique bottles of vinicultural perfection." Booklist.

Boston, Sarah

Boston, Sarah **Lucky** dog : how being a veterinarian saved my life / Dr. Sarah Boston. Anansi, 2014. 288 p. **B**

ISBN 9781770893511

1. Boston, Sarah. 2. Women with cancer 3. Veterinarians 4. Cancer -- Diagnosis. 5. Human/animal relationships. 6. Florida 7. Autobiographies and memoirs

LC bl2014024704

Dr. Sarah Boston discusses her experience with thyroid cancer and how her training as a veterinarian helped her with her own diagnosis even after doctors repeatedly tried to convince her otherwise.

"Readers will count themselves fortunate, too, as they accompany Boston on her unexpected journey and spend time with some wonderful dogs along the way." Publishers Weekly.

Boswell, James, 1740-1795

★Martin, Peter, 1940- A **life** of James Boswell / Peter Martin. Yale University Press, 2000. x, 613 p. : **B**

ISBN 9780300084894

1. Boswell, James, 1740-1795. 2. Authors, Scottish -- 18th century 3.

Biographers -- Great Britain 4. Family relationships. 5. Biographies

LC 00102885

"Martin has written the best biography of the greatest biographer in the English language. One of the many virtues of Martin's work is his successful synthesis of Boswell's life story with a keen analysis of Boswell's artistry." The Atlantic.

Sisman, Adam **Boswell's** presumptuous task : the making of the life of Dr. Johnson / Adam Sisman. Farrar, Straus, and Giroux, 2001, c2000. xxii, 351 p. : **B**

ISBN 9780142001752

1. Boswell, James, 1740-1795. Life of Samuel Johnson. 2. Johnson, Samuel, 1709-1784. 3. Authors, English -- History and criticism. 4. Biography. 5. Male friendship 6. London, England -- History -- 18th century. 7. Biographies

LC 00067699

Originally published: London : Penguin, 2000.

National Book Critics Circle Award for Biography, 2001.

Follows James Boswell's seven-year struggle to chronicle the life of his friend and mentor, Dr. Samuel Johnson, and examines his efforts to become well-respected in the literary community despite his reputation as a drunk and a lecher.

"Mr. Sisman's book is illuminating both of Boswell's character and of all aspects of his authorship." The Economist.

Bourbaki, Nicolas

Aczel, Amir D. The **artist** and the mathematician : the story of Nicolas Bourbaki, the genius mathematician who never existed / Amir D. Aczel. Thunder's Mouth Press, 2006. 239 p. : **B**

ISBN 1560259310

1. Bourbaki, Nicolas. 2. Mathematicians -- France 3. Mathematics -- History -- 20th century. 4. Social change. 5. Impostors. 6. France -- Social life and customs -- 20th century 7. France -- History -- 20th century

LC bl2006025096

Traces the intellectual prank through which the character of a fictional 1930s genius mathematician was devised and promoted throughout the American education system, describing how he was credited with originating the modern mathematical proof and the emergence of "new math."

"Writing in an accessible, conversational style that excludes mathematical proofs, Aczel paints a clear picture of the Bourbaki movement and how it has influenced the way mathematics should be discussed and learned." Library Journal.

Bourdain, Anthony

Bourdain, Anthony **Kitchen** confidential : adventures in the culinary underbelly / Anthony Bourdain. Bloomsbury, c2000. x, 307 p. ; **B**

ISBN 9781582340821

1. Bourdain, Anthony. 2. Cooks -- United States 3. Cooking. 4. Food. 5. Food industry and trade. 6. New York City -- Social life and customs. 7. Autobiographies and memoirs

LC 2003267610

A New York City chef recounts his experiences in the restaurant business, and exposes abuses of power, sexual promiscuity, drug use, and other secrets of life behind kitchen doors.

"This is one bitter, nasty, searing, hard-to-swallow piece of work. But if you can choke the thing down, you'll probably wake up grinning in the middle of the night. In a style partaking of Hunter S. Thompson, Iggy Pop and a little Jonathan Swift, Bourdain gleefully rips through the scenery to reveal private backstage horrors little dreamed of by the trusting public. To a world infested with synthesized romance, candlelit illusions and sentimental piety, Kitchen Confidential offers a nice palate-clearing taste of poison." New York Times Book Review.

Bourdain, Anthony **Medium** raw : a bloody Valentine to the world of food and the people who cook / Anthony Bourdain. Ecco, 2010. xviii, 281 p. ; **B**

ISBN 0061718947

1. Bourdain, Anthony. 2. Cooks -- United States 3. Cooking. 4. Food. 5. Food industry and trade. 6. New York City -- Social life and customs. 7. Autobiographies and memoirs

LC bl2010014257

Tracking his own strange and unexpected voyage from journeyman cook to globe-traveling professional eater and drinker, and even to fatherhood, Bourdain takes no prisoners as he dissects what he's seen, pausing along the way for a series of confessions, rants, investigations, and interrogations of some of the most controversial figures in food.

"This book mixes personal memoir with travelogues and ruminations on such matters as the degradation of the American hamburger, the dumbing down of the Food Network, the tedium of multicourse tasting menus and the rise of food gurus such as David Chang. Mr. Bourdain is a vivid, bawdy and often foul-mouthed writer. He thrills in the attack, but he is also an enthusiast who writes well about things he holds dear. His detailed reporting on the backroom lives of restaurant employees is terrific." Wall Street Journal.

Bouton, Katherine, 1947-

★Bouton, Katherine, 1947- **Shouting** won't help : why I - and 50 million other Americans - can't hear you / Katherine Bouton. Sarah Crichton Books/Farrar, Straus, and Giroux, 2013. 288 p. **B**

ISBN 9780374263041

1. Women who are deaf 2. Deafness. 3. People who are deaf 4. Hearing disorders 5. Autobiographies and memoirs

LC 2012029096

A former senior editor at The New York Times traces her own experiences of hearing loss while evaluating a growing epidemic of hearing impairment in America, drawing on medical and specialist insights to identify possible causes while sharing perspective on how hearing loss affects everyday life.

"By interspersing her story with those of many others--both those suffering with hearing loss and the medical experts working to find a cure--the author provides a relatable, inspiring narrative of taking control, going public and finding comfort and empowerment in connecting with others facing similar difficulties. A well-written, powerful book." Kirkus.

Bowdler, Michelle

★Bowdler, Michelle **Is** rape a crime? : a memoir, an investigation, and a manifesto / Michelle Bowdler. Flatiron Books, 2020. 304 p. **B**

ISBN 9781250255631

1. Rape 2. Rape victims 3. Women social advocates 4. Violent crimes 5. Autobiographies and memoirs

LC 2019060188

Writer and public health executive Michelle Bowdler's memoir indicts how sexual violence has been addressed for decades in our society, asking whether rape is a crime given that it is the least reported major felony, least successfully prosecuted, and fewer than 3% of reported rapes result in conviction. Cases are closed before they are investigated and DNA evidence sits for years untested and disregarded. In 1984, the Boston Sexual Assault Unit was formed as a result of a series of break-ins and rapes that terrorized the city, of which Michelle's own horrific rape was the last. Twenty years later, after a career of working with victims like herself, Michelle decides to find out what happened to her case and why she never heard from the police again after one brief interview.

"This is a brilliant study of how society views rape." Publishers Weekly

Bowie, David, 1947-2016

Jones, Dylan, 1960- **David** Bowie : a life / Dylan Jones. Crown Archetype, 2017. 400 p. **B**

ISBN 9780451497833

1. Rock musicians -- England 2. Rock music. 3. Popular culture 4. Celebrities 5. Biographies 6. Interviews 7. Oral histories

LC 2017010571

Dylan Jones's engrossing, magisterial biography of David Bowie is unlike any Bowie story ever written. Drawn from over 180 interviews with friends, rivals, lovers, and collaborators, some of whom have never before spoken about their relationship with Bowie, this oral history weaves a hypnotic spell as it unfolds the story of a remarkable rise to stardom and an unparalleled artistic path.

"In this comprehensive oral history, GQ editor Jones delves deeply into the details of rock icon David Bowies fame, financial problems, drug use, sexuality, Buddhist practices, and romantic entanglements." Publishers Weekly.

Egan, Sean, **Bowie** on Bowie : interviews and encounters with David Bowie / edited by Sean Egan. Chicago Review Press, 2015. 434 p. **B**

ISBN 9781569769775

1. Rock musicians -- England 2. Autobiographies and memoirs

LC 2014042080

Bowie on Bowie presents some of the best interviews David Bowie has granted in his near five-decade career. Each featured interview traces a new step in his unique journey, successively freezing him in time in all of his various incarnations, from a young novelty hit-maker and Ziggy Stardust to plastic soul player, 1980s sell-out, and the artistically reborn and beloved elder statesman of challenging popular music. In all of these iterations he is remarkably articulate and also preternaturally polite as almost every interviewer remarks upon his charm. The features in this book come from outlets both prestigious--Melody Maker, MOJO, New Musical Express, Q, Rolling Stone--and less well-known--the Drummer, Guitar, Ikon, Mr. Showbiz--but no matter the renown of the magazine, newspaper, or website, Bowie lets us approach the nerve center of his notoriously creative output.

"Egan's curation places each interview in context, though the editorial language is choppy, giving helpful social reference points and highlighting the musician's notable remarks. Documented identities include Bowie as the brassy, bright-eyed newcomer, the rakish bisexual glam star, the evocative ambient artist using music as rehab, well into his later years as the reserved family man who has little use for the press. this is a fascinating journey through the mind of a musician many people claim to know but who proves time and again that his own essence is often foreign to himself. An asset for Bowie fans." Library Journal.

Morley, Paul The **age** of Bowie : how David Bowie made a world of difference / Paul Morley. Gallery Books, 2016. 304 p. **B**

ISBN 9781501151156

1. Rock musicians -- England 2. Influence (Literary, artistic, etc.) 3. Music -- Recording and reproducing 4. Rock music. 5. Biographies

LC 2017561198

An author and cultural critic describes the greatest moments of the life of pioneering musician David Bowie and explores how he worked, played, aged, structured his ideas, influenced others, invented the future and became someone who will never be forgotten.

"There is a great deal of cultural history to enjoy in this personal, engaged and slyly scholarly biography. Morley's triumph is to know there is no such thing as the definitive story: new generations of fans will continue to make it up as they go along." New Statesman.

Bown, Mike Spencer

Bown, Mike Spencer The **world's** most travelled man : a twenty-three-year odyssey to and through every country on the planet / Mike Spencer Bown. Douglas & McIntyre, 2017 viii, 372 p. : **B**

ISBN 1771621427

1. Bown, Mike Spencer. 2. Voyages and travels. 3. Trips around the world. 4. Autobiographies and memoirs

An account of the author's experiences travelling through each of the world's 195 countries spanning more than two decades.

Boyd, Gerald M.

Boyd, Gerald M. **My** Times in black and white : race and power at the New York Times / Gerald M. Boyd. Chicago Review Press, 2010. 402 p. **B**

ISBN 9781556529528

1. New York Times. 2. Journalists -- United States 3. African American journalists 4. Ambition in men. 5. Journalism 6. United States -- Race relations. 7. Autobiographies and memoirs

LC 2009035506

Includes index.Documents the life and career of the first black managing editor of the "New York Times" who was forced to resign during the Jayson Blair scandal, describing his rise from urban poverty and his struggles in a white-dominated media.

Boyer, Anne, 1973-

Boyer, Anne, 1973- The **undying** : pain, vulnerability, mortality, medicine, art, time, dreams, data, exhaustion, cancer, and care / Anne Boyer. Farrar, Straus and Giroux, 2019. 192 p. **B**

ISBN 9780374279349

1. Boyer, Anne, 1973- Health 2. Women with cancer 3. Women authors 4. Poets 5. Breast cancer

LC 2019000373

Pulitzer Prize for General Nonfiction, 2020.

A week after her forty-first birthday, the acclaimed poet Anne Boyer was diagnosed with highly aggressive triple-negative breast cancer. For a single mother living paycheck to paycheck who had always been the caregiver rather than the one needing care, the catastrophic illness was both a crisis and an initiation into new ideas about mortality and the gendered politics of illness.

"Boyers gorgeous language elevates this artful, piercing narrative well above the average medical memoir." Publishers Weekly.

Boylan, Jennifer Finney, 1958-

Boylan, Jennifer Finney, 1958- **Good** boy : my life in seven dogs / Jennifer Finney Boylan. Celadon Books, 2020. 288 p. **B**

ISBN 9781250261878

1. Authors, American -- 20th century 2. Dog owners 3. Dogs 4. Human-animal relationships 5. Autobiographies and memoirs

LC 2019037746

The best-selling author, New York Times opinion columnist and human rights activist offers a memoir of the transformative power of loving dogs.

"Intimate and insightful glimpses into Boylan's life and the dogs that have helped her learn more about love." Kirkus

Boylan, Jennifer Finney, 1958- **I'm** looking through you : growing up haunted / Jennifer Finney Boylan. Broadway Books, 2008. 288 p. **B**

ISBN 0767921747

1. Boylan, Jennifer Finney, 1958- Childhood and youth. 2. Authors, American -- 20th century 3. Ghosts. 4. Autobiographies and memoirs

LC 2007019199

The author describes growing up in a haunted Pennsylvania house, the influence of her experiences on her own transgender life, and how to make peace with our ghosts, our loved ones, and the boundaries between men and women in our society.

"The author, a male-to-female transgendered person, uses the metaphor of being haunted throughout to illustrate not only her boyhood experiences but also the memories that have shaped her as a person as she struggled with her gender identity throughout most of her life. Her writing style is witty, self-deprecating, entertaining, and often poignant, especially when describing family and friends who have passed away. An adventure to read, this is highly recommended for all libraries." Library Journal.

Bradbury, Ray, 1920-2012

Eller, Jonathan R., 1952- **Becoming** Ray Bradbury / Jonathan R. Eller. University of Illinois Press, c2011. xiii, 324 p., 16 p. of plates : **B**

ISBN 9780252036293

1. Authors, American -- 20th century 2. Science fiction -- History and criticism 3. Books and reading. 4. Authors. 5. Biographies

LC 2011008562

Sequel: Ray Bradbury unbound

Weller, Sam, 1967- The **Bradbury** chronicles : the life of Ray Bradbury / Sam Weller. William Morrow, c2005. x, 384 p. : **B**

ISBN 006054581X

1. Science fiction -- History and criticism 2. Authors, American -- 20th century 3. Science fiction writing. 4. United States -- Social life and customs -- 20th century 5. Biographies

LC 2004059491

An authorized portrait of the renowned science-fiction author's life draws on hundreds of hours of interviews with editors, family members, friends, and the writer himself, in an account that discusses his creative process and the inspirations for such works as The Martian Chronicles and Fahrenheit 451.

"Weller's research--based on interviews with Bradbury as well as family members and colleagues--is almost exhaustive in its detail, and he does a fine job of presenting the facts of his subject's unique life. The lively, conversational prose brings out the writer's winning personality and turns his struggles and successes into a highly readable story." School Library Journal.

Braddock, James J., 1906-

Schaap, Jeremy **Cinderella** Man : James J. Braddock, Max Baer, and the greatest upset in boxing history / Jeremy Schaap. Houghton Mifflin, 2005. xii, 324 p. : **B**

ISBN 0618551174

1. Baer, Max, 1909-1959. 2. Boxers (Sports) -- United States 3. Irish American men. 4. Sports rivalry 5. Depressions -- 1929-1941 6. United States -- Social life and customs -- 20th century 7. Biographies

LC 2004066085

Offers a portrait of an American icon, boxer James J. Braddock, who staged a remarkable comeback during the Depression that captured the imagination of millions of working-class Americans.

"The author goes into detail on the brawny, reserved Braddock, who, at his lowest moments, was reduced to living off government relief and doing grueling work on the Hoboken, N.J., docks. But the story is as much about Max Baer, the lovably clownish and handsome heavyweight Braddock defeated as a 10-to-one underdog. Boxing enthusiasts will be more than satisfied by Schaap's meticulous account, which includes round-by-round details of the fight, as well as profiles of other fighters of the era." Publishers Weekly.

Brady, James, 1928-2009

Brady, James, 1928-2009 The **coldest** war : a memoir of Korea / James Brady. St. Martin's Griffin, 2000, c1990. 256 p. **B**

ISBN 0312265115

1. United States. Marine Corps 2. Korean War, 1950-1953, American 3. Soldiers -- United States 4. Marines 5. Armed forces 6. Autobiographies and memoirs

LC BL 00010554

Includes index.

Originally published: New York : Orion Books, 1990.

A personal account of the Korean War, as chronicled by a young Marine lieutenant, describes the harsh realities of war, the pressures of command, the struggle for survival, and the tragic impact of the war on all Americans.

"From November 1951 to July 1952, the author was a marine lieutenant who frequently found himself called upon to fight and kill Chinese and North Korean soldiers on the battlefields of Korea. His memoir of that experience is a well-crafted piece told in a voice that skillfully mixes the sardonic insight of an older man looking back on a highly extraordinary episode of his past with the naivete of the young warrior he once was." Booklist.

Brady, Mathew B., ca. 1823-1896

Wilson, Robert, 1951 February 21- **Mathew** Brady : portraits of a nation / Robert Wilson. Bloomsbury, 2013 320 p. **B**

ISBN 9781620402030

1. Photographers -- United States 2. Photography -- History -- 19th century. 3. War photography -- United States -- History -- Civil War, 1861-1865. 4. Photojournalists. 5. United States -- History -- 19th century 6. United States -- History -- Civil War, 1861-1865 7. Biographies

LC 2013016928

A narrative portrait of the Civil War visual historian illuminates his pivotal role in establishing photography as a valued documenting tool, analyzing his portraits of period dignitaries and his self-sacrificing effort to capture images of the Civil War.

Bragg, Rick

★Bragg, Rick The **best** cook in the world : tales from my Momma's table / Rick Bragg. Alfred A. Knopf, 2018 512 p. **B**

ISBN 9781400040414

1. Bragg, Rick. 2. Families 3. Mothers and sons 4. Cooking, American -- Southern style 5. Autobiographies and memoirs

LC 2017024979

Includes recipes.

Presents a food memoir, cookbook, and tribute to the author's mother, sharing classic family recipes--many of them pre-dating the Civil War--and preparation secrets for such traditional fare as short ribs, biscuits, and perfect mashed potatoes.

"For readers who crave soul with their recipes (some 75 here), this is a fitting tribute to foodways that are fast slipping away." Library Journal.

Bragg, Rick The **prince** of Frogtown / Rick Bragg. Alfred A. Knopf, 2008. 288 p. **B**

ISBN 9781400040407

1. Bragg, Rick Childhood and youth. 2. Fathers and sons. 3. Parent and child. 4. Stepfathers 5. Journalists -- United States 6. Southern States -- Social life and customs. 7. Alabama -- Social life and customs. 8. Autobiographies and memoirs

LC 2007038884

"A Borzoi book."

The author details his quest to uncover the truth about the father he had never known and his unseen influence on the author's life and the choices he has made, inspired by his own relationship with his ten-year-old stepson.

"The author merges his father's history of severe hardships and simple joys with a tale from the present: his own relationship with his 10-year-old stepson. . . . [This book] is lush with narratives about manhood, fathers and sons, families and the changing face of the rural South." Publishers Weekly.

Brahms, Johannes, 1833-1897

Swafford, Jan **Johannes** Brahms : a biography / Jan Swafford. Alfred A. Knopf, 1997. xxii, 699 p. : **B**

ISBN 9780679422617

1. Brahms, Johannes, 1833-1897. 2. Composers -- Germany -- 19th century 3. Biographies

LC 97029308

A biography of the nineteenth-century German composer looks at his daily life, his associates--including his relationships with Robert Schumann, Clara Shumann, Richard Wagner, and Eduard Hanslick--and his achievements as a composer

"Swafford's study, clearly a labor of profound affection, is a model biography: eloquent, clear-sighted and often moving." Publishers Weekly.

Brandeis, Gayle

Brandeis, Gayle The **art** of misdiagnosis : surviving my mother's suicide / Gayle Brandeis. Beacon Press, 2017 240 p. **B**

ISBN 9780807044865

1. Brandeis, Gayle. 2. People with schizophrenia 3. Suicide victims. 4. Mother and child. 5. Suicide 6. Autobiographies and memoirs

LC 2017002002

Gayle Brandeis's mother disappeared just after Gayle gave birth to her youngest child. Several days later, her body was found: she had hanged herself in the utility closet of a Pasadena parking garage. In this searing, formally inventive memoir, Gayle describes the dissonance between being a new mother, a sweet-smelling infant at her chest, and a grieving daughter trying to piece together what happened, who her mother was, and all she had and hadn?t understood about her.

Brandeis, Louis Dembitz, 1856-1941

Urofsky, Melvin I. **Louis** D. Brandeis : a life / Melvin I. Urofsky. Pantheon Books, 2009. 976 p. **B**

ISBN 9780375423666

1. Brandeis, Louis Dembitz, 1856-1941. 2. United States. Supreme Court Justices. 3. Judges -- United States 4. Lawyers 5. Federal judges. 6. Law reform. 7. United States -- Politics and government -- 20th century. 8. Biographies

LC 2009003992

A full-scale portrait of the early twentieth-century Supreme Court justice seeks to distinguish his personal life from his achievements as a reformer and jurist, offering additional insight into his role in the development of pro bono legal services, the creations of the Federal Reserve Act and other key legislations, and his contributions to American-Jewish affairs as a practicing Zionist.

"This is a monumental, authoritative and appreciative biography of the man Franklin D. Roosevelt called Isaiah." New York Times Book Review.

Brando, Marlon, 1924-2004

Mann, William J. The **contender** : the story of Marlon Brando / William J. Mann. Harper360, 2019. 718 p. **B**

ISBN 9780062427649

1. Brando, Marlon, 1924-2004. 2. Actors and actresses -- United States 3. Acting 4. United States -- Social life and customs -- 20th century. 5. Biographies

LC 2019022978

Based on new and revelatory material from Brando's own private archives, an award-winning film biographer presents a deeply-textured, ambitious, and definitive portrait of the greatest movie actor of the twentieth century, the elusive Marlon Brando, bringing his extraordinarily complex life into view as never before.

Branum, Guy, 1975-

Branum, Guy, 1975- **My** life as a goddess : a memoir through (un)popular culture / Guy Branum ; foreword by Mindy Kaling. Atria Books, 2018. 272 p. **B**

ISBN 9781501170225

1. Comedians 2. Self-discovery 3. Actors and actresses 4. Gay men 5. Autobiographies and memoirs

LC 2018016385

Traces the author's path from a California farm town to success as a stand-up comic, and the inspiration he received from pop culture to accept himself as he truly was.

"Keenly observant and intelligent, Branum's book not only offers uproarious insights into walking paths less traveled, but also into what self-acceptance means in a world still woefully intolerant of difference. Wickedly smart, funny, and witty." Kirkus

Braun, Eva

Gortemaker, Heike B., 1964- **Eva** Braun : life with Hitler / Heike B. Görtemaker ; translated from the German by Damion Searls. Alfred A. Knopf, 2011, c2010. 320 p. **B**

ISBN 9780307595829

1. Braun, Eva. 2. Hitler, Adolf, 1889-1945 Friends and associates. 3. Hitler, Adolf, 1889-1945 Family. 4. Mistresses. 5. Women and politics. 6. Paramours. 7. Germany -- History -- 1933-1945. 8. Biographies

LC 2011009551

"This is a Borzoi book"--T.p. verso.

Originally published in Germany as Eva Braun : Leben mit Hitler, by Verlag C.H. Beck, Munich, in 2010.

A comprehensive portrait of Hitler's long-time mistress challenges popular depictions while profiling the bourgeois existence she shared with the F'hrer out of the public eye, drawing on newly discovered documents and anecdotal accounts to discuss such topics as her role as his trusted confidante, her position in his entourage and their double suicide two days after their marriage.

Braun, Wernher von, 1912-1977

Biddle, Wayne **Dark** side of the moon : Wernher von Braun, the Third Reich, and the space race / Wayne Biddle. W. W. Norton, 2009. 240 p. **B**

ISBN 9780393059106

1. Braun, Wernher von, 1912-1977. 2. Rocketry -- Research --

Germany -- History. 3. Space programs -- International competition. 4. Cold War. 5. World War II -- Science. 6. Germany -- Politics and government -- 1933-1945. 7. United States -- History -- 1945-

LC 2009015572

An investigation into the origins of the first moon landing evaluates ideas sparked by the modernism of the Third Reich while tracing the life of scientist Wernher von Braun, describing how his driving ambitions directly contributed to weapons development, the early space program, and Cold War culture.

★Neufeld, Michael J., 1951- **Von** Braun : dreamer of space, engineer of war / Michael J. Neufeld. Alfred A. Knopf, in association with the National Air and Space Museum, Smithsonian Institution, 2007. xiii, 587 p. : **B**

ISBN 0307262928

1. Scientists -- Germany 2. Rocketry -- Research -- United States -- History 3. Rocketry -- Research -- Germany -- History 4. Astronautics -- United States -- History 5. Germany -- Social life and customs -- 20th century 6. United States -- Social life and customs -- 20th century 7. Biographies

LC 2007005711

Offers a multifaceted portrait of the visionary German scientist who became the chief rocket engineer of the Third Reich, creator of the V-2 rocket, reluctant SS officer, and one of the fathers of the U.S. space program.

"This is a meticulously researched and technically accurate biography of von Braun." New York Review of Books.

Braverman, Blair

Braverman, Blair **Welcome** to the goddamn ice cube : chasing fear and finding home in the great white north / Blair Braverman. Ecco Press, 2016 288 p. **B**

ISBN 9780062311566

1. Self-reliance in women. 2. Wilderness survival 3. Women's role 4. Sled dogs. 5. Norway 6. Alaska 7. Autobiographies and memoirs

LC 2017304761

A revelatory memoir of the author's efforts to develop the strength and resilience to survive in the demanding landscapes of Norway and Alaska describes her physically exhausting survival endeavors on a ruthless arctic tundra marked by violent natural and human threats.

"Her external experiences are extraordinary in the frigid north that so few have experienced, but it's what happens internally that both sets this memoir apart and gives it universal resonance. Indelible characters, adventurous spirit, and acute psychological insight combine in this multilayered debut." Kirkus.

Brennan, Thomas J. (Thomas James)

Brennan, Thomas J. (Thomas James) **Shooting** ghosts : a U.S. Marine, a combat photographer, and their journey back from war / Thomas J. Brennan and Finbarr O'Reilly. Viking Press, 2017 336 p. **B**

ISBN 9780399562549

1. O'Reilly, Finbarr 2. Afghan War, 2001-, American. 3. Post-traumatic stress disorder 4. Friendship 5. Marines 6. Autobiographies and memoirs

LC 2017019760

In Shooting Ghosts, Marine veteran Thomas Brennan and battle photographer Finbarr O'Reilly team up to offer insight into their experiences in Afghanistan. Both of them were psychologically traumatized by their ordeals -- Brennan by his wounds from an explosion and O'Reilly's from the intensity of what he witnessed. Though civilian O'Reilly found help relatively easily, Brennan had to negotiate the complex military bureaucracy as well as the Marine culture of machismo. In this account, they defy the tradition that psychological trauma is a source of shame and make an appeal for mental health treatment for veterans.

"A courageous breaking of the code of silence to seek mental health for veterans and the war-scarred." Kirkus.

Brennan-Jobs, Lisa, 1978-

Brennan-Jobs, Lisa, 1978- **Small** fry / Lisa Brennan-Jobs. Grove Press, 2018. 304 p. **B**

ISBN 9780802128232

1. Jobs, Steve, 1955-2011 Family. 2. Brennan, Chrisann Family. 3. Mothers and daughters. 4. Father-separated girls. 5. Manipulation by men. 6. Dysfunctional families. 7. Santa Clara Valley, California 8. Autobiographies and memoirs.

LC 2018026614

The daughter of Steve Jobs offers a firsthand account of the difficult relationship she had with her father and the poignant story of a childhood spent between two imperfect but extraordinary homes.

"Brennan-Jobs skillfully relays her past without judgement, staying true to her younger self. It is a testament to her fine writing and journalistic approach that her memoir never turns maudlin or gossipy. Rather than a celebrity biography, this is Brennan-Jobs' authentic story of growing up in two very different environments, neither of which felt quite like home." Booklist.

Brierley, Saroo

Brierley, Saroo A **long** way home : a memoir / Saroo Brierley with Larry Buttrose. G.P. Putnam's Sons, 2014. 272 p. **B**

ISBN 9780399169281

1. Brierley, Saroo. 2. Adopted children. 3. Birthparents -- Identification 4. International adoption. 5. East Indians -- Australia 6. Hobart, Tasmania 7. Kolkata, India 8. Autobiographies and memoirs

LC 2014003745

Published in 2016 under the title Lion

An account of the author's inspirational effort to find his India birthplace describes how he was accidentally separated from his family in the mid-1980s, his survival on the streets of Calcutta, his adoption by an Australian family, and his headline-making Google Earth search.

Briggs, Arthur, 1901-1991

Atria, Travis **Better** days will come again : the life of Arthur Briggs, jazz genius of Harlem, Paris, and a nazi prison camp / Travis Atria. Chicago Review Press, 2020. 336 p. **B**

ISBN 9780914090106

1. Briggs, Arthur, 1901-1991. 2. Trumpet players 3. Jazz musicians 4. Concentration camp inmates -- France 5. World War II 6. Paris, France -- History -- 20th century 7. Biographies

LC 2019029238

Describes the life story of the legendary jazz musician who was regarded as the greatest trumpeter in Europe, but who failed to heed warnings to leave Paris before the Nazi takeover and was sent to a prison camp.

"A fascinating story and valuable reclamation of an overlooked musician." Booklist

Briggs, Kate

Briggs, Kate **This** little art / Kate Briggs. Fitzcarraldo Editions, 2017. 365 pages ; **B**

ISBN 9781910695456

1. Translating and interpreting 2. Reading 3. Translators 4. Essays. 5. Autobiographies and memoirs

LC bl2018125872

"Lucid and engaging, Briggs's book is essential, not just for translators, but anyone who has felt the magic of reading." Publishers Weekly.

Britten, Benjamin, 1913-1976

Powell, Neil, 1948- **Benjamin** Britten : a life for music / Neil Powell. Henry Holt and Company, 2013. 400 p. **B**

ISBN 9780805097740

1. Britten, Benjamin, 1913-1976. 2. Composers -- England 3. Gay men 4. England -- Social life and customs -- 20th century. 5. United States -- Social life and customs -- 20th century. 6. Biographies

LC 2012051536

Documents the life of the famous British composer, focusing on his relationship with tenor Peter Pears, who became the inspirational center of his emotional and musical life.

Brodak, Molly

★Brodak, Molly **Bandit** : a daughter's memoir / Molly Brodak. Black Cat, 2016. 240 p. **B**

ISBN 9780802125637

1. Brodak, Molly. 2. Brodak, Molly Family. 3. Fathers and daughters 4. Children of criminals 5. Bank robbers 6. Poets, American -- 20th century 7. Michigan 8. Autobiographies and Memoirs

LC 2016017971

Raw and powerful, the author, whose father was a con man and bank robber, recounts her childhood and attempts to make sense of her complicated relationship with the man she only half knew, who led a double life, and make peace with the parts of herself that she inherited from him.

"An intelligent, disturbing, and profoundly honest memoir." Kirkus.

Broder, Melissa

Broder, Melissa **So** sad today : personal essays / Melissa Broder. Grand Central Publishing, 2016, c2015 256 p. **B**

ISBN 9781455562725

1. Anxiety 2. Self-acceptance 3. Sadness 4. Autobiographies and memoirs 5. Essays

LC 2015039433

An acclaimed poet presents a darkly humorous collection of essays that describe in unstinting detail her lifetime struggles with anxiety and the 2012 cycle of panic attacks that inspired her popular Twitter account by the same name.

"Broders central insight is clear: it is okay to be sad, and our problems cant be reduced to a single diagnosis. All of the essays are linked together by the art of learning to love oneself, sadness and all." Publishers Weekly.

Brokaw, Tom

Brokaw, Tom The **fall** of Richard Nixon : a reporter remembers Watergate / Tom Brokaw. Random House, 2019 224 p. **B**

ISBN 9781400069705

1. Brokaw, Tom. 2. Nixon, Richard M. (Richard Milhous), 1913-1994. 3. Impeachments -- United States. 4. Journalists 5. Watergate Scandal -- Press coverage. 6. Press and politics 7. United States -- Politics and government -- 1969-1974. 8. Autobiographies and memoirs

LC 2019029798

Includes index.

The last year of the Nixon presidency was filled with power politics, legal jiu-jitsu and high-stakes showdowns, with head-shaking surprises every day. Tom Brokaw, the NBC News White House correspondent during the final year of Watergate, gives us a close-up, personal account of the players, the strategies, and the highs and lows of the scandal that brought down a president.

Brokaw, Tom A **long** way from home : growing up in the American heartland / Tom Brokaw. Random House, c2002. xii, 233 p. : **B**

ISBN 9780375507632

1. Television newscasters and commentators -- United States 2. Television journalists -- United States 3. Journalists -- United States 4. Journalists 5. United States -- Social life and customs -- 20th century. 6. Autobiographies and memoirs

LC 2002031865

The television journalist describes life growing up in the heart of the American Midwest and his early journalism career in the 1960s, reflecting on the people, places, culture, and values that shaped him and continue to shape him today.

"Peppered with photographs . . . this tribute to an idyllic childhood should please Brokaw's loyal fans." Publishers Weekly.

Brokaw, Tom A **lucky** life interrupted : a memoir of hope / Tom Brokaw. Random House, 2015. 240 p. **B**

ISBN 9781400069699

1. Television newscasters and commentators -- United States 2. Television journalists -- United States 3. People with cancer 4. Cancer 5. Autobiographies and memoirs

LC 2015008653

A best-selling author and former NBC anchorman chronicles a year spent battling cancer and reflects on his long, lucky life.

"Brokaw's account lacks the depth and fire of Christopher Hitchens' Mortality (2013), but it belongs on the same shelf as a wise and oddly comforting look at the toughest news of all." Kirkus.

Bromfield, Louis, 1896-1956

Heyman, Stephen The **planter** of modern life : Louis Bromfield and the seeds of a food revolution / Stephen Heyman. W.W. Norton & Company, 2020 340 p. : **B**

ISBN 9781324001898

1. Bromfield, Louis, 1896-1956 Homes and haunts Ohio. 2. Authors, American -- 20th century 3. Authors, American -- Homes and haunts -- Ohio 4. Agriculture -- Ohio -- History -- 20th century 5. Farm life -- Ohio -- History -- 20th century 6. Ohio -- Intellectual life -- 20th century.

LC 2019044443

"How a literary idol of the Lost Generation launched America's organic and sustainable food movement. In interwar France, Louis Bromfield was equally famous as a writer and as a gardener. He pruned dahlias with Edith Wharton, weeded Gertrude Stein's vegetable patch, and fed the starving artists who flocked to his farmhouse outside Paris. His best-selling novels earned him a Pulitzer-and the jealousy of friends like Ernest Hemingway. But his radical approach to the soil has aged better than his books, inspiring a wave of farmers, foodies, and chefs to rethink how they should grow and consume their food. In 1938, Bromfield returned to his native Ohio, an expat novelist now reinvented as the squire of 1,000-acre Malabar Farm. Transplanting ideas from India and Europe, he created a mecca for forward- thinking agriculturalists and a rural retreat for celebrities like Humphrey Bogart and Lauren Bacall (who were married there in 1945). Bromfield's untold story is a fascinating history of people and places-and of deep-rooted concerns about the environment and its ability to sustain our most basic needs and pleasures"-- Provided by publisher.

Bronte, Charlotte, 1816-1855

Gaskell, Elizabeth Cleghorn, 1810-1865 The **life** of Charlotte Bronte / Elizabeth Gaskell ; edited with an introduction by Angus Easson. Oxford University Press, 1996, c1857. xxxvi, 587 p. ; **B**

ISBN 0192828096

1. Authors, English -- 19th century 2. England -- Social life and customs -- 20th century. 3. Biographies

LC 95000491

Originally published: London: Smith, Elder & Co., 1857.

Gordon, Lyndall **Charlotte** Bronte : a passionate life / Lyndall Gordon. Norton, 1995. xiv, 418 p., 16 unnumbered p. : **B**

ISBN 9780393037227

1. Bronte, Charlotte, 1816-1855. 2. Authors, English -- 19th century 3. Women authors -- 19th century 4. Gender role 5. Women -- Social conditions -- 19th century. 6. England -- Social life and customs -- 19th century. 7. Biographies

Originally published: London : Chatto & Windus, 1994.

Searches for the real Charlotte Bronte behind the loneliness, loss, and unrequited love--a strong woman with a fierce belief in herself, creative energy, and powerful ambition, who shaped her life and transformed it into art.

"The author dismantles once and for all the image of Charlotte Bronte as a figure of pathos and presents, instead, a courageous survivor, a determined writer, and a woman of volcanic emotion. Gordon, as skilled at literary analysis as at chronicling a life, approaches Bronte's tragic and enduringly relevant story from several angles, carefully identifying all the autobiographical elements of her novels and contrasting her commitment to writing and her independent spirit to her era's strict and pitiless code of behavior for women." Booklist.

Harman, Claire **Charlotte** Bronte : a fiery heart / Claire Harman. Alfred A. Knopf, 2016. 384 p. **B**

ISBN 9780307962089

1. Authors, English -- 19th century 2. Women authors, English -- 19th century 3. Biographies

LC 2015028359

"This is a Borzoi book."

Charlotte Brontë wrote one of the most enduring novels of her era, Jane Eyre. More often portrayed jointly with her sisters Anne and Emily, her individual life story receives a thorough review in this biography by writer and literary critic Claire Harman, whose chronicle traces Charlotte's love life, connecting it with the romantic passion she depicts in her novels. This account brings Charlotte to life, offering a thoughtful consideration of her character both for her novels' fans and for readers generally interested in British literature.

Brookins, Cara

Brookins, Cara **Rise** : how a house built a family / Cara Brookins. St Martins Press, 2017. 320 p. **B**

ISBN 9781250095664

1. Determination in women 2. Abused women 3. Family violence 4. House construction 5. Autobiographies and memoirs

LC 2016036419

Tells the amazing story of a woman who, having escaped an abusive marriage but having no home to live in, enlisted the help of a small bank loan and a work crew consisting only of her and her four children to build a family home from the ground up, in the amazing story of a broken family's healing.

"Brookings deftly narrates the extreme learning curve the family experienced during the construction process, while putting a family back together again." Publishers Weekly.

Brooks, Gwendolyn, 1917-2000

Jackson, Angela, 1951- A **surprised** queenhood in the new black sun : the life & legacy of Gwendolyn Brooks / Angela Jackson. Beacon Press, 2017. 204 p. **B**

ISBN 9780807025048

1. Brooks, Gwendolyn, 1917-2000. 2. Black Aesthetic Movement 3. Writing 4. Poets, American -- 20th century 5. African American poets 6. Biographies

LC 2017001533

A look back at the cultural and political force of Pulitzer Prize?winning poet Gwendolyn Brooks, in celebration of her hundredth birthday

"Jackson presents an incisive portrait of poet Gwendolyn Brooks (19172000), sharing with her subject the experiences of an African American woman poet in Chicago." Booklist.

Brooks, Mel, 1926-

McGilligan, Patrick **Funny** man : Mel Brooks / Patrick McGilligan. HarperCollins 2019 832 p. **B**

ISBN 9780062560995

1. Comedians -- United States 2. Film actors and actresses -- United States 3. Film producers and directors -- United States 4. Filmmaking. 5. United States -- Social life and customs -- 20th century 6. Biographies

LC bl2019007786

A biography of a comic legend traces his life and career?from his childhood in Williamsburg tenements to becoming an actor, writer, and director responsible for such comedy classics as The Producers, Blazing Saddles, and Young Frankenstein.

"McGilligan's exhaustive biography will be essential reading for anyone interested in Brooks or, more broadly, how Hollywood functioned during the second half of the 20th century." Publishers Weekly.

Broom, Sarah M.

★Broom, Sarah M. The **yellow** house / Sarah M. Broom. Grove Press, [2019] 304 p. **B**

ISBN 9780802125088

1. Broom, Sarah M.. 2. African American women authors 3. African Americans 4. African American families 5. Home (Concept) 6. New Orleans, Louisiana 7. Autobiographies and memoirs

LC 2019009107

ALA Notable Book, 2020.

National Book Award for Nonfiction, 2019.

Describes the author's upbringing in a New Orleans East shotgun house as the unruly 13th child of a widowed mother, tracing a century of family history and the impact of class, race and Hurricane Katrina on her sense of identity.

"Broom's lyrical style celebrates her family bonds, but a righteous fury runs throughout the narrative at New Orleans' injustices, from the foundation on up. A tribute to the multitude of stories one small home can contain, even one bursting with loss." Kirkus.

Brosh, Allie

Brosh, Allie **Hyperbole** and a half : unfortunate situations, flawed coping mechanisms, mayhem, and other things that happened / Allie Brosh. Simon & Schuster 2013 288 p. **B**

ISBN 9781451666175

1. Brosh, Allie. 2. Comedians -- United States 3. Women with depression 4. Personal conduct -- Humor 5. Growing up -- Humor

6. Comics and Graphic novels 7. Webcomics 8. Autobiographical comics 9. Autobiographies and memoirs

LC 2013025527

In a four-color, illustrated collection of stories and essays, Allie Brosh's debut chronicles the many "learning experiences" Brosh has endured as a result of her own character flaws, and the horrible experiences that other people have had to endure because she was such a terrible child. Possibly the worst child. For example, one time she ate an entire cake just to spite her mother.

Brousse, Amy Elizabeth Thorpe, 1910-1963

Blum, Howard The **last** goodnight : a World War II story of espionage, adventure, and betrayal / Howard Blum. Harper Collins Publishers, 2016. 432 p. **B**

ISBN 9780062307675

1. Brousse, Amy Elizabeth Thorpe, 1910-1963. 2. Hyde, H. Montgomery (Harford Montgomery), 1907-1989. 3. World War II. 4. Secret service. 5. Espionage, American. 6. Women spies. 7. Biographies

LC 2015019329

Presents a portrait of American debutante and World War II spy Betty Pack that draws on recently declassified files to explore her MI-6 career and key role in successful Allied missions.

"Occasionally breathless and torrid in description, this is a well-documented work that certainly never bores." Kirkus.

Brown, Austin Channing

★Brown, Austin Channing **I'm** still here : Black dignity in a world made for whiteness / Austin Channing Brown. Convergent Books, 2018. 185 p. ; **B**

ISBN 9781524760854

1. Racism 2. Race relations 3. African Americans -- Social conditions 4. Race (Social sciences) 5. United States -- Race relations 6. Autobiographies and memoirs

Austin Channing Brown's first encounter with a racialized America came at age 7, when she discovered her parents named her Austin to deceive future employers into thinking she was a white man. Growing up in majority-white schools, organizations, and churches, Austin writes, "I had to learn what it means to love blackness," a journey that led to a lifetime spent navigating America's racial divide as a writer, speaker and expert who helps organizations practice genuine inclusion.

"An eloquent argument for meaningful reconciliation focused on racial injustice rather than white feelings." Booklist.

Brown, Carolyn, 1927-

Brown, Carolyn, 1927- **Chance** and circumstance : twenty years with Cage and Cunningham / Carolyn Brown. Alfred A. Knopf, 2007. vi, 645 p., 40 p. of plates : **B**

ISBN 0394401913

1. Cunningham, Merce, 1919-2009 2. Cage, John, 1912-1992 3. Merce Cunningham Dance Company 4. Dancers -- United States 5. Choreographers 6. Dance companies 7. Interpersonal relations 8. United States -- Social life and customs -- 20th century. 9. Autobiographies and memoirs

LC 2006048799

This long-awaited memoir is an intimate chronicle of a crucial era in modern dance: the story of Brown's own remarkable career, of the formative years of the Merce Cunningham Dance Company, and of the two brilliant, iconoclastic, and forward-thinking artists at its center--Merce Cunningham and John Cage. From its inception in the 1950s until her departure in the 1970s, Brown was a major dancer in the company and part of the vibrant artistic community of downtown New York. She describes the exhilaration--and dire financial straits--of the company's early days, when composer Cage was musical director and Robert Rauschenberg designed lighting, sets and costumes; and the struggle for acceptance of their controversial, avant-garde dance. She explores Cunningham's technique, choreography, and experimentation with compositional procedures influenced by Cage. And she probes the personalities of these two men: the reticent, moody, often secretive Cunningham, and the effusive, fun-loving, enthusiastic Cage.--From publisher description.

"The author traces the trajectory of her modern dance career with that organization during its crawling stages in the 1950s and 1960s, when composer John Cage was musical director and artist Robert Rauschenberg was set and costume designer. Brown documents the company's early struggles for acceptance (it was considered avant-garde), various tours, and eventual world recognition. This book will appeal to modern dance buffs and memoir readers." Library Journal.

Brown, Claude, 1937-

Brown, Claude, 1937- **Manchild** in the promised land / Claude Brown. Touchstone, 1999, c1965. 415 p. ; **B**

ISBN 9780684864181

1. African American men 2. Street life 3. African American teenage boys 4. African American gangs. 5. Harlem, New York City -- Social conditions. 6. New York City -- Social conditions. 7. Autobiographies and memoirs

Traces the author's experiences as a first-generation African American raised in the Northern ghettos of Harlem in the mid-twentieth century, an upbringing marked by violence, drugs, and devastating urban disadvantages.

Brown, Helen Gurley

Hirshey, Gerri **Not** pretty enough : the unlikely triumph of Helen Gurley Brown / Gerri Hirshey. Sarah Crichton Books ; Farrar, Straus and Giroux, 2016. 336 p. **B**

ISBN 9780374169176

1. Brown, Helen Gurley. 2. Periodical editors 3. Independence in women 4. Self-sufficency in women 5. Editors 6. Biographies

LC 2016007143

A portrait of the famed author of "Sex and the Single Girl" examines her role in advancing civil-rights feminism and traces her rags-to-riches story, transformation of "Cosmopolitan," and relationships with such figures as Liz Smith, Gloria Vanderbilt, and Barbara Walters.

Brown, James, 1933-2006

★McBride, James, 1957- **Kill** 'em and leave : searching for the real James Brown / James McBride. Spiegel & Grau, [2016] 256 p. **B**

ISBN 9780812993509

1. Brown, James, 1933-2006. 2. Soul musicians 3. Soul music. 4. African American musicians 5. Musicians 6. United States -- Social life and customs -- 20th century. 7. Biographies

LC 2015026358

Prompted by a comment from James Brown's grandson, author James McBride decided to look into the complex life and legacy of the Godfather of Soul. With input from Brown's friends, family members, and colleagues, McBride paints a picture not just of the founder of funk but of the world that made him; musings on race, identity, influence, and the American South abound. While there are other, more traditional biographies of James Brown available, this one is unique as it adds cultural history, context, and a personal perspective.

"An unconventional and fascinating portrait of Soul Brother No. 1 and the significance of his rise and fall i n American culture." Kirkus.

Sullivan, James, 1965 November 7- The **hardest** working man : how James Brown saved the soul of America : live at the Boston Garden, 1968 / James Sullivan. Gotham Books, 2008. 256 p. **B**

ISBN 9781592403905

1. Brown, James, 1933-2006. 2. Soul musicians 3. Civil Rights Movement. 4. Soul music. 5. Musicians 6. Boston, Massachusetts -- Social conditions -- 20th century. 7. United States -- Social life and customs -- 20th century. 8. Biographies

LC 2008013670

Documents the lesser-known story of the legendary soul performer's stirring Boston Garden concert in the wake of Martin Luther King, Jr.'s assassination, describing how he fought to prevent the concert's cancellation and his role in preventing riots in Boston.

"Sullivan examines James Brown's role in saving Boston from the fires and riots that swept the U.S. after Martin Luther King Jr.'s assassination. Booked into Boston Garden the night of April 5, 1968, Brown agreed to put the show on live local TV to give would-be rioters reason to stay home. Garden management wanted to cancel, doubtless to avoid rioting in the Garden, but Brown and Boston's first black city councillor interceded with Mayor Kevin White to prevent cancellation. Sullivan goes further in crediting Brown for keeping the peace than others have, and so doing, he also examines the Godfather of Soul's life and career in the context of the Civil Rights movement. A good record of a pivotal event and a serviceable Brown bio, to boot." Booklist.

Brown, James, 1957-

Brown, James, 1957- The **Los** Angeles diaries : a memoir / James Brown. William Morrow, c2003. 200 p. ; **B**

ISBN 0060521511

1. Drug abuse. 2. Dysfunctional families. 3. Drug addicts. 4. Drug use. 5. Los Angeles, California -- Social life and customs. 6. Autobiographies and memoirs

LC 2003048779

"Brown's revelations have no smugness or self-congratulation; they reek of remorse and desire, passion and futility. The result is a grimly exquisite memoir that reads like a noir novel but grips unrelentingly like the hand of a homeless drunk begging for help." Publishers Weekly.

Brown, Jim, 1936-

Zirin, Dave **Jim** Brown : last man standing / Dave Zirin. Blue Rider Press, 2018 320 p. **B**

ISBN 9780399173448

1. National Football League 2. Football players. 3. Civil rights workers. 4. African American film actors and actresses 5. Biographies

LC 2017035828

Jim Brown is recognized as perhaps the greatest football player to ever live. But his phenomenal nine-year career with the Cleveland Browns is only part of his remarkable story, the opening salvo to a much more sprawling epic. Brown parlayed his athletic fame into stardom in Hollywood, where it was thought that he could become "the black John Wayne." He was an outspoken Black Power icon in the 1960s, and he formed Black Economic Unions to challenge racism in the business world. For this and for his decades of work as a truce negotiator with street gangs, Brown--along with such figures as Muhammad Ali, Bill Russell, and Billie Jean King--is revered as a socially conscious athlete.

Brown, John, 1800-1859

★Horwitz, Tony, 1958- **Midnight** rising : John Brown and the raid that sparked the Civil War / Tony Horwitz. Henry Holt and Co., 2011 384 p. **B**

ISBN 9780805091533

1. Brown, John, 1800-1859. 2. Abolitionists -- United States -- History 3. Anti-slavery movements -- History -- 19th century. 4. Militants 5. United States -- History -- 19th century. 6. Harper's Ferry, West Virginia -- History -- John Brown's Raid, 1859 7. Biographies

LC 2011015659

Chronicles the 1859 raid by radical abolitionist John Brown on Harpers Ferry, revealing how his acts, deemed terrorism by the South, prompted a counterattack by Robert E. Lee and galvanized Northern supporters during Lincoln's election campaign.

"The author presents a narrative of Brown and the raid on Harpers Ferry that in many ways set the stage for Southern secession and civil war. . . . Horwitz's Brown did not die in vain. By recalling the drama that fired the imagination and fears of Brown's time, Midnight Rising calls readers to account for complacency about social injustices today. This is a book for our time." Library Journal.

Reynolds, David S., 1948- **John** Brown, abolitionist : the man who killed slavery, sparked the Civil War, and seeded civil rights / David S. Reynolds. Alfred A. Knopf, 2005. x, 578 p. : **B**

ISBN 0375411887

1. Brown, John, 1800-1859. 2. Abolitionists -- United States -- History 3. Anti-slavery movements -- History -- 19th century. 4. Militants 5. United States -- History -- 19th century. 6. Harper's Ferry, West Virginia -- History -- John Brown's Raid, 1859 7. Biographies

LC 2004048864

ALA Notable Book, 2006."

Almost every page forces you to think hard, and in new ways, about American violence, American history, and what used to be called the American character." The New Yorker.

Brown, Margaret Wise, 1910-1952

Gary, Amy **In** the great green room : the brilliant and bold life of Margaret Wise Brown / Amy Gary ; introduction by James Stillman Rockefeller Jr. Flatiron Books, 2017. 288 p. **B**

ISBN 9781250065360

1. Brown, Margaret Wise, 1910-1952. 2. Authors, American -- 20th century 3. Women authors, American -- 20th century 4. Children's literature writing 5. Children's literature authors, American -- 20th century 6. Biographies

LC 2016037634

Captures the exceptional life, imagination and passion of the author of Goodnight Moon, in a book that draws from unpublished manuscripts, songs, personal letters and diaries that the author discovered in Margaret Wise Brown's sister's attic.

"Brown's complicated personal life included numerous romantic adventures, most notably a ten-year relationship with poet/playwright/actress Blanche Oelrichs, former wife of John Barrymore." Library Journal.

Brown, Molly McCully, 1991-

Brown, Molly McCully, 1991- **Places** I've taken my body : essays / Molly McCully Brown. Persea Books, [2020] 215 p. **B**

ISBN 9780892555130

1. Brown, Molly McCully, 1991- Travel. 2. Brown, Molly McCully, 1991- Religion. 3. Women poets, American -- 21st century 4. Cerebral palsy 5. Women with cerebral palsy 6. Human body 7. Autobiographies and memoirs 8. Essays

LC 2019044336

"In sixteen intimate essays, poet Molly McCully Brown explores living within and beyond the limits of a body-in her case, one shaped since birth by cerebral palsy.

"Brown is a writer to watch. Heartfelt and wrenching, a significant addition to the literature of disability." Kirkus

Brown, Robert J. (Robert Joe), 1935-

Brown, Robert J. (Robert Joe), 1935- **You** can't go wrong doing right : how a child of poverty rose to the White House and helped change the world / Robert J. Brown. Convergent, 2019 xiii, 237 p. ; **B**

ISBN 9781524762780

1. Business consultants -- United States 2. Grandmothers -- United States 3. Grandparent and child -- United States 4. Political consultants -- United States 5. Autobiographies and memoirs.

LC bl2018192314

The highly sought power broker, presidential advisor and founder of global business-management consulting firm B&C International describes how the lessons of his impoverished childhood and wise grandmother informed his perspectives about a life in service and major historical events.

Brown, Theresa

Brown, Theresa The **shift** : one nurse, twelve hours, four patients' lives / Theresa Brown. Algonquin Books of Chapel Hill, 2015. 204 p. ; **B**

ISBN 9781616203207

1. Brown, Theresa. 2. Nurse and patient. 3. Nurses. 4. Intensive care nursing. 5. Intensive Care Units. 6. Autobiographies and memoirs

LC 2015010992

A moving story unfolds in real time as practicing nurse and New York Times columnist Theresa Brown reveals the individual struggles as well as the larger truths about medicine in this country. She lets us experience all the life that happens in just one day in a busy teaching hospital's oncology ward. In the span of twelve hours, lives can be lost, life-altering treatment decisions made, and dreams fulfilled or irrevocably stolen. Every day, Theresa Brown holds these lives in her hands. On this day there are four.

"At its best, Browns memoir increases empathy for nurses, who work hard and often must care for difficult patients and cope with a caste system that gives them less respect than MDs. This account also raises important ethical questions, such as just how fully informative healthcare workers should be when the prognosis isnt good." Booklist.

Brown, Tina

Brown, Tina The **Vanity** fair diaries : 1983-1992 / Tina Brown. Henry Holt & Co., 2017. 400 p. **B**

ISBN 9781627791366

1. Brown, Tina. 2. Vanity fair (New York, N.Y.). 3. Fashion periodicals 4. British in the United States 5. Women periodical editors -- United States 6. New York City 7. Diaries

LC 2017028578

The diaries of the author's years as editor-in-chief of "Vanity Fair" provide a portrait of the 1980s in New York and Hollywood, describing her summons from London to save Conde Nast's troubled periodical and her experiences within the cutthroat world of glamour magazines.

"High and low, perceptive and prescient (in 1987, she speculated that the American public wont be able to resist the crassness of Donald Trump), this is a wildly entertaining, essential look at print journalism before the fall. Let us all pray that Brown also kept diaries of her years in the 1990s as editor of the New Yorker." Booklist.

Brownstein, Carrie, 1974-

Brownstein, Carrie, 1974- **Hunger** makes me a modern girl : a memoir / Carrie Brownstein. Riverhead Books, 2015. 336 p. **B**

ISBN 9781594486630

1. Sleater-Kinney (Musical group) 2. Punk rock music 3. Sexism 4. Women musicians 5. Riot grrrl movement 6. United States -- Social life and customs -- 20th century 7. Olympia, Washington 8. Autobiographies and memoirs 9. Pacific Northwest literature

LC 2015024629

"A strong, engaging pop culture memoir: personal detail, a little dish, and a well-written look at what made the music, and the culture that spawned it, matter." Library Journal.

Bruni, Frank

Bruni, Frank **Born** round : the secret history of a full-time eater / Frank Bruni. Penguin Press, 2009. 384 p. **B**

ISBN 9781594202315

1. Bruni, Frank Childhood and youth. 2. New York Times 3. Food writers -- United States 4. Compulsive eating -- Case studies 5. Dieting -- Case studies 6. Overweight men 7. United States -- Social life and customs -- 21st century 8. Autobiographies and memoirs

LC 2009009532

A memoir from the "New York Times" restaurant critic traces his unlikely path to his profession and offers an honest exploration of his lifelong struggle with food.

"The book does not contain paeans to the glories of locavorism. It's not a tale of bawdy kitchen exploits, or of finding your true self over a bowl of pasta in Rome . His memoir tells a story of food addiction, eating disorders, and a lifelong struggle with his voracious appetite . Born Round makes for a breezy read. Even at its darkest, it goes down easy." Village Voice.

Bryant, Kobe, 1978-2020

Bryant, Kobe, 1978-2020 The **Mamba** mentality : how I play / Kobe Bryant ; photography by Andrew D. Bernstein. Farrar Straus & Giroux, 2018. 208 p. **B**

ISBN 9780374201234

1. Los Angeles Lakers (Basketball team) 2. National Basketball Association. 3. Professional basketball players. 4. African American basketball players. 5. Success (Concept) 6. Basketball. 7. Autobiographies and memoirs.

LC bl2018180038

In the wake of his retirement from professional basketball, the NBA great nicknamed "The Black Mamba" has decided to share his vast knowledge and understanding of the game to take readers on an unprecedented journey to the core of his legendary "Mamba mentality."

"He offers plenty of anecdotes about teammates and opponents, which will satisfy fans interested mainly in the memoir aspect; but what sets this book apart from the competition is Bernsteins photography. It's wonderful." Booklist.

Lazenby, Roland **Showboat** : the life of Kobe Bryant / Roland Lazenby. Little, Brown and Company, 2016. 352 p. **B**

ISBN 9780316387248

1. Los Angeles Lakers (Basketball team) 2. Basketball players. 3. Basketball 4. Professional basketball players. 5. Biographies

LC 2016016821

Seventeen-time all-star; scorer of 81 points in a game; MVP and a shooting guard second only to Jordan in league history: Kobe Bryant is one of basketball's absolute greatest players, a fascinating and complicated character who knew when he was a mere boy that he would be better than Jordan on the court. The debate about whether he achieved that is a furious one--but Kobe has surpassed Jordan on the all-time scoring list and has only one less championship than Jordan (5 to Jordan's 6).

Bryson, Bill

Bryson, Bill The **life** and times of the thunderbolt kid : a memoir / Bill Bryson. Broadway Books, c2006. x, 270 p. : **B**

ISBN 076791936X

1. Bryson, Bill. 2. Travel writers 3. Popular culture -- History -- 20th century. 4. Growing up. 5. Authors, American 6. Iowa. 7. Des Moines, Iowa. 8. Autobiographies and memoirs

LC 2006043859

Also published: Toronto : Anchor Canada, 2007, c2006.

The author describes his all-American childhood growing up as a member of the baby boom generation in the heart of Iowa, detailing his rich fantasy life as a superhero known as the Thunderbolt Kid and his remarkably normal 1950s family life.

Buber, Martin, 1878-1965

Friedman, Maurice S. **Encounter** on the narrow ridge : a life of Martin Buber / Maurice Friedman. Paragon House, 1991. xi, 496 p. : **B**

ISBN 1557784531

1. Buber, Martin, 1878-1965. 2. Jewish philosophers -- Germany 3. Jewish philosophers -- Israel 4. Jewish philosophy. 5. Zionists 6. Biographies

LC 90044502

Traces the life of the renowned Jewish religious philosopher, discussing his youth, his education in turn-of-the-century Vienna, his Zionism, and the impact of world politics on his life and thought

Buck, Joan Juliet

Buck, Joan Juliet The **price** of illusion : a memoir / Joan Juliet Buck. Atria Books, 2017. 432 p. **B**

ISBN 9781476762944

1. Vogue (Paris, France) 2. Vogue (New York, N.Y.) 3. Women editors 4. Fashion periodicals 5. Clothing industry and trade 6. Fathers and daughters 7. Autobiographies and memoirs

LC 2016032072

"Atria non fiction original hardcover" -- Verso title page.

A former editor-in-chief of Paris Vogue presents an account of her four decades spent in the creative heart of London, New York, Los Angeles and Paris, a vocation that enabled her to learn key differences about illusion versus substance and the qualities of genuine happiness.

"Buck includes a brilliant amount of detail in this memoir." Publishers Weekly.

Buck, Joe

Buck, Joe **Lucky** bastard : my life, my dad, and the things I'm not allowed to say on TV / Joe Buck, with Michael Rosenberg. Dutton, 2016. 320 p. **B**

ISBN 9781101984567

1. Sportscasters 2. Television sportscasters. 3. Autobiographies and memoirs

LC 2016011271

The famed Super Bowl sportscaster shares stories from his life and career, describing his work in and out of the shadow of his legendary sportscaster father Jack Buck, his marriage to sportscaster Michelle Beisner and more.

"With a comic yet reverent approach to his life and broadcasting, Buck effectively captures the merging of his career and the popularity of American sports." Publishers Weekly.

Buck, Leslie, 1965-

Buck, Leslie, 1965- **Cutting** back : my apprenticeship in the gardens of Kyoto / Leslie Buck. Timber Press, 2017. 280 p. **B**

ISBN 9781604697933

1. Gardening 2. Apprenticeship 3. Cultural differences 4. Gender role 5. Kyoto, Japan 6. Japan 7. Autobiographies and memoirs

LC 2016045504

This debut memoir recounts an American gardener's grueling apprenticeship with the most prestigious gardening firm in Kyoto.

"This is an absorbing read about the formative interplay of humans, cultures, and gardens." Publishers Weekly.

Buck, Pearl S., 1892-1973

Spurling, Hilary **Pearl** Buck in China : journey to the good Earth / Hilary Spurling. Simon & Schuster, 2010. xii, 304 p., 8 p. of plates : **B**

ISBN 9781416540427

1. Buck, Pearl S., 1892-1973 Homes and haunts China. 2. Authors, American -- 20th century 3. Identity (Psychology) 4. Americans in China 5. Women authors -- 20th century 6. China -- History -- 20th century 7. Biographies

James Tait Black Memorial Prize for Biography, 2010.

Presents a tribute to the life and work of the Pulitzer-winning author known for such works as The Good Earth, covering such topics as her fundamentalist upbringing, witness to the Boxer Revolution and two marriages.

"The author's account of Buck's rootless and fractured existence provides a fascinating dissection of the tortured relationships between a man of God, the hapless wife sucked into supporting his mission and their increasingly sceptical daughter, Pearl, who, in 1933, publicly turned her back on her late father's church. It is also just as revealing about the no less tortured relationship between the West and China in the early part of the last century." The Economist.

Buckley, Christopher, 1952-

Buckley, Christopher, 1952- **Losing** Mum and Pup : a memoir / Christopher Buckley. Twelve, 2009. 336 p. **B**

ISBN 9780446540940

1. Buckley, Christopher, 1952- Family. 2. Buckley, William F. (William Frank), 1925-2008 Last years. 3. Buckley, William F. (William Frank), 1925-2008 Death and burial. 4. Authors, American -- 20th century -- Family relationships. 5. Parents -- Death -- Psychological aspects. 6. Death. 7. Family relationships. 8. Autobiographies and memoirs

LC 2008043532

Includes index."

Christopher Buckley has not written a Mommie Dearest for the Evelyn Waugh set. Losing Mum and Pup is a subtle, fond and, above all, honest chronicle of his celebrated parents. Buckley has pulled off what eludes many writers: he has written candidly but not unkindly about people whose vices and virtues he sees clearly." Newsweek.

Buckley, William F. (William Frank), 1925-2008

Bogus, Carl T. **Buckley** : William F. Buckley Jr. and the rise of American conservatism / Carl T. Bogus. Bloomsbury Press, 2011. x, 405 p., 8 p. of plates : **B**

ISBN 9781596915800

1. Buckley, William F. (William Frank), 1925-2008. 2. Journalists -- United States 3. Conservatism -- United States 4. Ideology -- United States. 5. United States -- Politics and government -- 20th century 6. Biographies

LC 2011012734

Documents the story and legacy of a leading architect of the American conservative movement throughout the past half century, tracing his 1955 launch of the influential National Review and his television show Firing Line as well as his role in promoting modern values about the free market, religion and an aggressive foreign policy.

"This is an insightful book that will please anyone interested in mid-century American history and politics. Anyone serious about political philosophy will learn from it. Highly recommended." Library Journal

Buckley, William F. (William Frank), 1925-2008 **Nearer,** my God : an autobiography of faith / William F. Buckley, Jr. Doubleday, 1997. xx, 313 p. : **B**

ISBN 9780385478182

1. Catholic Church. 2. Journalists -- United States 3. Catholic men 4. Faith in men. 5. Religion and politics. 6. Autobiographies and memoirs

LC 97006219

The author and journalist describes his Catholic childhood in England and the United States, and how his Christianity has shaped his political and social views.

Hendershot, Heather **Open** to debate : how William F. Buckley put liberal America on the firing line / Heather Hendershot. Broadside, 2016 xxii, 357 p. **B**

ISBN 9780062430458

1. Journalists -- United States. 2. Right and left (Political science) 3. Conservatives -- United States. 4. Conservatism -- United States. 5. Biographies

LC 2016015903

Offers a portrait of William F. Buckley as the champion of conservative ideas in an age of liberal dominance, taking on the smartest adversaries he could find while singlehandedly reinventing the role of public intellectual in the network-TV era.

Buffalo Bill, 1846-1917

Warren, Louis S. **Buffalo** Bill's America : William Cody and the Wild West Show / Louis S. Warren. Alfred A. Knopf, 2005. xvi, 652 p. : **B**

ISBN 0375412166

1. Buffalo Bill, 1846-1917. 2. Buffalo Bill's Wild West Show 3. Wild West shows -- History. 4. Pioneers -- The West (United States) 5. Frontier and pioneer life -- The West (United States) 6. Entertainers -- United States 7. The West (United States) 8. Biographies

LC 2004063280

Spur Award for Historical Nonfiction, 2006."

This book is well written and exhaustively researched, the weightiest and surely the most ambitious book ever published about Cody and his times." New York Times Book Review.

Buffett, Jimmy

White, Ryan (Journalist) **Jimmy** Buffett : a good life all the way / Ryan White. Touchstone, [2017] 336 p. **B**

ISBN 9781501132551

1. Rock music 2. Rock musicians -- United States 3. Singers 4. Biographies

LC 2016052808

The acclaimed music critic and author of Springsteen: Album by Album explores the life, achievements and legacy of the iconic music artist and writer, tracing the experiences that shaped Buffett's career while celebrating the enduring culture he inspired.

"A thorough, well-researched, and fully dimensional portrait of a multitalented and wildly popular and influential music and entrepreneurial star." Booklist.

Buffett, Warren

Hagstrom, Robert G., 1956- The **Warren** Buffett way / Robert G. Hagstrom. Wiley, 2014 xxxvii, 281 p. ; **B**

ISBN 9781118503256

1. Buffett, Warren. 2. Capitalists and financiers -- United States 3. Investments -- United States 4. Biographies

LC 2013023887

"The bestselling book on Warren Buffett returns, with new insights on his continued success. Often described as the greatest investor of all time, Warren Buffett grew a $100 investment in the late 1950s into an investment empire. In the process, he has become one of the wealthiest individuals in the world, and the foremost authority on investing of our generation.With over one million copies sold, The Warren Buffett Way is the definitive book on "The Oracle of Omaha's" investment methods. Completely revised and updated, the Third Edition of The Warren Buffett Way focuses on the timeless principles and strategies behind Buffett's extraordinary investment success. This edition contains new chapters on the important distinctions between investing and trading, as well as an examination of the most successful disciples of Warren Buffett. Throughout the book, fresh examples and case studies are used and Buffett's successful formula is distilled in a way that will provide value to readers for decades to come. This edition represents the totality of Buffett's investment career and focuses on his timeless investing principles Companion website contains "Buffett Investment Calculators," which you can use to calculate the value and investment potential of companies Written by foremost Buffett expert Robert Hagstrom Engaging and informative, the Third Edition of The Warren Buffett Way is a must read--not just for avid Buffett fans, but for anyone who wants to know what it takes to make the best investment decisions possible".--Provided by publisher.

Schroeder, Alice The **snowball** : Warren Buffett and the business of life / Alice Schroeder. Bantam Books, 2008. 864 p. **B**

ISBN 0553805096

1. Buffett, Warren. 2. Capitalists and financiers -- United States 3. Brokers 4. Investment banking. 5. Stock market. 6. Biographies

LC bl2008002450

A portrait of the life and career of investment guru Warren Buffett sheds new light on the man, as well as on the work, ideas, business principles, strategies, and no-nonsense insights that have guided his phenomenally successful business endeavors.

"In a book that is dominated by unstinting descriptions of Buffett's appetitesfor profit, women (particularly nurturing maternal types), food (Buffett maintained his and his family's weight by dangling money)it is refreshing that Schroeder keeps her tone free of judgment or awe; Buffett's plain-speaking suffuses the book and renders his public and private successes and failures wonderfully human and universal. Inspiring managerial advice abounds and competes with gossipy tidbits . in this rich, surprisingly affecting biography." Publishers Weekly.

Buford, Bill

★Buford, Bill **Dirt** : adventures in Lyon as a chef in training, father, and sleuth looking for the secret of French cooking / Bill Buford. Alfred A. Knopf, 2020. 412 p. **B**

ISBN 9780307271013

1. Buford, Bill Travel 2. Cooks -- United States 3. Cooking -- Study and teaching 4. Cooking, French 5. Gourmet cooking 6. Lyon, France 7. France 8. Autobiographies and memoirs

LC 2019039927

Bill Buford turns his inimitable attention from Italian cuisine to the food of France. Baffled by the language, but convinced that he can master the art of French cooking--or at least get to the bottom of why it is so revered--he begins what becomes a five-year odyssey by shadowing the esteemed French chef Michel Richard, in Washington, D.C. But when Buford (quickly) realizes that a stage in France is necessary, he goes--this time with his wife and three-year-old twin sons in tow--to Lyon, the gastronomic capital of France.

"Buford (Heat) delivers a vivid and often laugh-out-loud account of the tribulations, humblings, and triumphs he and his family endured in the five years they lived in France. . . . It's a remarkable book, and even readers who don't know a sabayon from a Sabatier will find it endlessly rewarding." Publishers Weekly

Bui, Thi

★Bui, Thi The **best** we could do : an illustrated memoir / Thi Bui. Harry N Abrams Inc., 2017. 336 p. : **B**

ISBN 9781419718779

1. Bui, Thi Family. 2. Child immigrants 3. Immigrant families 4. Immigrants, Vietnamese 5. Immigration and emigration 6. Vietnam -- History -- 20th century 7. Autobiographical comics 8. Comics and Graphic novels

LC bl2017000643

ALA Notable Book, 2018.

National Book Critics Circle Award for Autobiography/Memoir finalist, 2017

The debut graphic novel memoir from Thi Bui is an intimate look at one family's journey from their war-torn home in Vietnam to their new lives in America. Exploring the anguish of immigration and the lasting effects that displacement has on a child and her family, Bui documents the story of her family's daring escape after the fall of South Vietnam in the 1970s, and the difficulties they faced building new lives for themselves."--Provided by the publisher

"In creatively telling a complicated story with the kind of feeling words alone rarely relay, The Best We Could Do does the very best that comics can do." Booklist.

Bulger, Whitey, 1929-

Cullen, Kevin (Journalist) **Whitey** Bulger : America's most wanted gangster and the manhunt that brought him to justice / Kevin Cullen and Shelley Murphy. W.W. Norton & Co., 2013. viii, 478 p., 16 unnumbered p. of plates : **B**

ISBN 9780393087727

1. Gangsters. 2. Organized crime. 3. Political corruption. 4. Murderers 5. Biographies

LC 2012050752

National Book Critics Circle Award for Nonfiction finalist, 2013.

Chronicles the criminal career of the gangster who provided a protection racket against drug lords, ran illegal gambling, robbed banks, and served as an informant for the FBI until going into hiding for sixteen years.

Sherman, Casey, 1969- **Hunting** Whitey : the inside story of the capture & killing of America's most wanted crime boss / Casey Sherman and Dave Wedge. William Morrow, 2020. 340 p. **B**

ISBN 9780062972545

1. Crime bosses 2. Organized crime 3. Fugitives 4. Assassins 5. Boston, Massachusetts 6. Biographies

LC bl2020012645

For the first time, Boston reporters Casey Sherman and Dave Wedge draw on exclusive interviews and exhaustive investigative reportage to tell the complete story of Whitey Bulger, one of the most notorious crime bosses in American history, and a longtime FBI informant. The leader of Boston's Winter Hill Gang and #1 on the FBI's Most Wanted list, Bulger was indicted for nineteen counts of murder, racketeering, narcotics distribution, and extortion. But it was his sixteen-year flight from justice on the eve of his arrest that made him a legend and exposed deep corruption within the FBI. Granted access to exclusive prison letters and interviews with dozens of people connected to the case on both sides, Sherman and Wedge offer a trove of fascinating new stories and create an incomparable portrait of one of the most infamous criminals in American history.

"A deeply unpleasant but highly readable story of crime and punishment." Kirkus

Bullard, Eugene Jacques, 1895-1961

Keith, Phil, 1946- **All** blood runs red : the legendary life of Eugene Bullard-Boxer, pilot, soldier, spy / Phil Keith and Tom Clavin. Hanover Square Press, [2019] 350 pages, 16 unnumbered pages of plates : **B**

ISBN 9781335005564

1. African American men 2. Military pilots 3. Civil rights 4. Social advocates 5. Europe -- History -- 20th century 6. United States -- History -- 20th century 7. Biographies

LC bl2019032891

A biography of the first African American fighter pilot to fly in combat, Eugene Bullard, who served France in World War One and World War Two.

Bunch, Robert

Dickey, Christopher **Our** man in Charleston : Britain's secret agent in the Civil War South / Christopher Dickey. Crown Pub 2015 336 p. **B**

ISBN 9780307887276

1. British in the United States 2. Diplomatic and consular service. 3. Slave trade 4. Deception 5. South Carolina 6. Confederate States of America

LC 2015016637

Documents the contributions of American-born Englishman Robert Bunch to negotiating fragile relations between the Confederate South and Britain while hiding his secret work as a determined abolitionist.

"A great book explaining the workings of what Dickey calls an erratic, cobbled-together coalition of ferociously independent states. It should be in the library of any student of diplomacy, as well as Civil War buffs." Kirkus.

Bundrum, Charlie, died 1958

Bragg, Rick **Ava's** man / Rick Bragg. Knopf, 2001. viii, 259 p. : **B**

ISBN 0375410627

1. European American working class -- Southern States 2. Rural families -- Southern States. 3. Poor families. 4. Depressions -- 1929-1941 -- Southern States. 5. Southern States -- Social life and customs -- 1865- 6. Alabama -- Social life and customs -- 1865- 7. Georgia -- Social life and customs -- 1865- 8. Biographies

LC 2001032677

"In this account of his maternal grandfather's life as a roofer and bootlegger in Appalachia, the author creates a soulful, poignant portrait of working-class Southern life." Publishers Weekly.

Bundy, Ted, 1946-1989

Rule, Ann The **stranger** beside me / Ann Rule. Norton, 2000. 456 p. : **B**

ISBN 0393050297

1. Bundy, Ted, 1946-1989. 2. Criminals -- United States. 3. Serial

murderers. 4. Serial murders. 5. Murder.

LC 00040224

From the perspective of the former policewoman, crime writer, and unknowing personal friend, tells the story of Ted Bundy, a brilliant law student executed for killing three women, who confessed to killing thirty-five others.

Burgin, R. V.

Burgin, R. V. **Islands** of the damned : a Marine at war in the Pacific / R.V. Burgin with William Marvel. New American Library, 2010. 296 p. **B**

ISBN 9780451229908

1. United States. Marine Corps 2. United States. Marine Corps. Regiment, 5th. Battalion, 3rd 3. World War II. 4. Military campaigns. 5. Marines -- United States 6. World War II, American. 7. Pacific area. 8. Autobiographies and memoirs

LC 2009040454

An eyewitness account of some of the most savage and brutal fighting in the war against Japan is told from the point of view of a young Marine who left Texas to escape life as a traveling salesman.

"As this well-written, excellently detailed personal narrative makes clear, some Marines who fought alongside him did not make it home alive. They and thousands more died amid war's confusing and unspeakable horrors. Sometimes they were killed by the enemy, sometimes by friendly fire, sometimes by accidents, and sometimes by shocking, split-second decisions where one life was sacrificed to save others. Time is thinning the ranks of America's Pacific War veterans. But Islands of the Damned is a taut, engrossing, haunting book that will help keep their accomplishments and enormous sacrifices alive." Dallas Morning News.

Burke, Edmund, 1729-1797

Norman, Jesse **Edmund** Burke : the first conservative / Jesse Norman. Basic Books, 2013. 325 p. : **B**

ISBN 9780465058976

1. Philosophers 2. Conservatives. 3. Political scientists -- Great Britain 4. Diplomats -- Great Britain 5. Great Britain -- Politics and government -- 1760-1820 6. Biographies.

Published in the UK as Edmund Burke : philosopher, politician, prophet (2013) and Edmund Burke : the visionary who invented modern politics (2014).

Examines the life of the great Irish philosopher, statesman and political thinker, who supported abolition, free markets, Catholic equality in Ireland in the eighteenth century while warning of ideological extremism and the dangers of a corporate state.

Burnett, Carol

Burnett, Carol **In** such good company : eleven years of laughter, mayhem, and fun in the sandbox / Carol Burnett. Crown Archetype, 2016. 288 p. **B**

ISBN 9781101904657

1. Burnett, Carol. 2. Carol Burnett Show (Television program : 1967-1978). 3. Women comedians. 4. Television comedies. 5. Autobiographies and memoirs

LC 2016008433

Comedy legend Carol Burnett tells the hilarious behind-the-scenes story of her iconic weekly variety series, The Carol Burnett Show. Who but Carol Burnett herself has the timing, talent, and wit to pull back the curtain on the Emmy-Award winning show that made television history for eleven glorious seasons? In Such Good Company delves into little-known stories of the guests, sketches and antics that made the show legendary, as well as some favorite tales too good not to relive again.

"Burnett watched every episode afresh to research this book, and that attention to detail shows in her exhaustive accounts of major sketches. However, even nonfans will enjoy the nuggets of intrigue Burnett scatters throughout, in which she shines a light on the sexism she faced during her tenure as a leading lady of the small screen." Publishers Weekly.

Burningham, Lucy

Burningham, Lucy **My** beer year : adventures with hop farmers, craft brewers, chefs, beer sommeliers & fanatical drinkers as a beer master in training / Lucy Burningham. Roost Books, 2016. vii, 278 p. ; **B**

ISBN 9781611802719

1. Burningham, Lucy. 2. Beer 3. Brewing 4. Brewing industry and trade 5. Brewers 6. Autobiographies and memoirs

LC 2016010941

A love note to beer--appreciating the history, craftsmanship, and taste of craft beer as told by a woman striving for beer-expert status.

"As Burningham shares the successes, failures, and stresses of her journey, readers will be drawn more and more into the bubbly, exciting, deliciously intoxicating world of beer." Booklist.

Burns, Mike, 1865?-1934

★Burns, Mike, 1865?-1934 The **only** one living to tell : the autobiography of a Yavapai indian / Mike Burns ; edited by Gregory McNamee. University of Arizona Press, c2012. 179 p. **B**

ISBN 9780816501205

1. Burns, Mike, 1865?-1934. 2. United States. Army Scouts. 3. Yavapai Indians. 4. Indians of North America. 5. Orphans. 6. Southwest (United States) -- History -- 1848- 7. Autobiographies and memoirs

LC 2011046513

"Essential reading for anyone interested in the history of the Southwest and its native peoples as conveyed by a native writer." Library Journal

Burns, Robert, 1759-1796

Crawford, Robert, 1959- The **bard** : Robert Burns, a biography / Robert Crawford. Princeton University Press, c2009. xii, 465 p. : **B**

ISBN 9780691141718

1. Burns, Robert, 1759-1796. 2. Poets, Scottish -- 18th century 3. Romanticism in poetry. 4. Men -- Personal conduct 5. Romanticism 6. Scotland -- History -- 18th century 7. Scotland -- Social life and customs -- 18th century. 8. Biographies

LC bl2009006738

"Crawford's Burns, merrily mixing high and low culture, seems eerily contemporary. He shares with great hip-hop artists a genius for catchy, sexy, and memorable rhymes gloriously liberated from the hegemony of standard English." The New Yorker.

Burns, William J. (William Joseph), 1956-

Burns, William J. (William Joseph), 1956- The **back** channel : a memoir of American diplomacy and the case for its renewal / William J. Burns. Random House, [2019] 288 p. **B**

ISBN 9780525508861

1. Diplomacy 2. International relations 3. World politics 4. Diplomats -- United States 5. United States -- Foreign relations -- 1945-1989. 6. United States -- Foreign relations -- 1989- 7. Autobiographies and memoirs

LC 2018042715

America's highest-ranking Foreign Service career ambassador and president of the Carnegie Endowment for International Peace presents a memoir of his career in service while outlining an impassioned case for diplomacy in today's increasingly volatile world.

Burroughs, Augusten

Burroughs, Augusten **Lust** & wonder / Augusten Burroughs. St. Martin's Press, 2016. 304 p. **B**

ISBN 9780312342036

1. Burroughs, Augusten. 2. Authors, American -- 20th century 3. Gay men 4. Interpersonal relations 5. Lust 6. New York City. 7. Autobiographies and memoirs

LC 2015041615

In chronicling the development and demise of the different relationships he's had while living in New York, Augusten Burroughs examines what it means to be in love, what it means to be in lust, and what it means to be figuring it all out. With Augusten's unique and singular observations and his own unabashed way of detailing both the horrific and the humorous, Lust and Wonder is an intimate and honest memoir that his legions of fans have been waiting for.

"His brutal honesty about himselfand othersis as sharp and surprising as ever, and how Burroughs manages to effortlessly convey so much of his complicated histories, such as a lifelong need to bury his fears in the purchase of jewelry, is a lesson in the elegant use of narrative as a vehicle for truth." Booklist.

★Burroughs, Augusten **Running** with scissors : a memoir / Augusten Burroughs. Picador, 2006, c2002. 331 p. ; **B**

ISBN 0312938853

1. Burroughs, Augusten Childhood and youth. 2. Burroughs, Augusten Homes and haunts Amherst, Massachusetts 3. Authors, American -- 20th century 4. Adopted teenagers -- Family relationships. 5. Growing up 6. Adoptive families. 7. Amherst, Massachusetts -- Social life and customs. 8. Autobiographies and memoirs

LC bl2006018788

Originally published: New York : St. Martin's Press, 2002.

The author describes his bizarre coming-of-age years after his adoption by his mother's psychiatrist, during which he witnessed such misadventures as a fake suicide attempt and front-lawn family/patient sleepovers.

"Burroughs tempers the pathos with sharp, riotous humor in stories that are self-deprecating, raunchy, sexually explicit." Booklist.

★Burroughs, Augusten **Toil** & trouble / Augusten Burroughs. St. Martin's Press, 2019. 304 p. **B**

ISBN 9781250019950

1. Authors, American 2. Gay couples 3. Witchcraft 4. Precognition 5. Autobiographies and memoirs

LC 2019018100

Master memoirist Augusten Burroughs delivers a hilarious and spooky account of his life as the descendant of witches. The author of Running with Scissors documents his lifelong capacity for causing impossible manifestations, exploring his mother's revelations about their witch ancestry and his efforts to understand himself and his powers.

"Although scientifically unsound, this book's allegorical evidence for the belief in witchcraft will appeal to casual memoir readers, particularly those interested in the lighter side of religion and psychology." Library Journal.

Burroughs, William S., 1914-1997

Burroughs, William S., 1914-1997 **Rub** out the words : the letters of William S. Burroughs, 1959-1974 / edited and with an introduction by Bill Morgan. Ecco, c2012. xxxv, 444 p., 16 p. of plates : **B**

ISBN 9780061711428

1. Burroughs, William S., 1914-1997 Correspondence. 2. Authors, American -- 20th century 3. Correspondence.

LC 2012371022

Presenting a glimpse into the private life of the misunderstood writer, this collection of letters from the 1960s and 1970s reveals the era in which Burroughs became an influential artistic and cultural leader beyond the literary world.

Miles, Barry, 1943- **Call** me Burroughs : a life / Barry Miles. Twelve, 2014. 736 p. **B**

ISBN 9781455511952

1. Burroughs, William S., 1914-1997. 2. Authors, American -- 20th century 3. Counterculture. 4. Beat authors. 5. Beat poets. 6. Biographies

LC 2013032565

An acclaimed biographer presents an overview of the life and cultural legacy of the American novelist who was an original member of the Beat Movement and became a countercultural icon in the 1960s after the publication of his seminal novel, Naked Lunch.

"A dense, detailed, yet wonderfully readable and entertaining narrative that illuminates, without sensationalizing, Burroughs's manifold peculiarities." Publishers Weekly.

Burton, Susan, 1973-

Burton, Susan, 1973- **Empty** : a memoir / Susan Burton. Random House, [2020] 288 p. **B**

ISBN 9780812992847

1. Burton, Susan, 1973- Health. 2. Eating disorders. 3. Food. 4. Food habits. 5. Compulsive eating. 6. Autobiographies and memoirs.

LC 2019037475

An award-winning This American Life documentary producer shares the story of her battles with anorexia and a binge-eating disorder, describing the painful compulsions that shaped her education, career and relationships.

"A powerful picture of anorexia and binge-eating disorder that would benefit from being shorter and more targeted." Kirkus

Bush, Barbara, 1925-2018

★Page, Susan, 1951- The **matriarch** : Barbara Bush and the making of an American dynasty / Susan Page. Twelve, 2019. viii, 418 p., 16 unnumbered p. of plates : **B**

ISBN 9781538713648

1. Bush family 2. Presidents' spouses -- United States 3. Matriarchs 4. Families 5. Social advocacy 6. United States -- Politics and government -- 1989- 7. Biographies

Drawing on diary access and more than 100 interviews, a vibrant portrait of the former first lady by the Washington bureau chief of USA Today includes coverage of Barbara Bush's private struggles and remarkable political achievements.

" While the work is not officially authorized, Page interviewed Bush many times before her death in 2018 and had access to her voluminous diaries that no other historian has seen." Library Journal.

Bush, George, 1924-2018

Bush, George W. (George Walker), 1946- **41** : a portrait of my father / George W. Bush. Crown Publishing, 2014. 288 p. **B**

ISBN 9780553447781

1. Presidents -- United States 2. Father and son 3. Biographies

LC 2014469972

Forty-three men have served as President of the United States. Countless books have been written about them. But never before has a President told the story of his father, another President, through his own eyes and in his own words. A unique and intimate biography, the book covers the entire scope of the elder President Bush's life and career, including his service in the Pacific during World War II, his pioneering work in the Texas oil business, and his political rise as a Congressman, U.S. Representative to China and the United Nations, CIA Director, Vice President, and Presiden

★Meacham, Jon **Destiny** and power : the American odyssey of George Herbert Walker Bush / Jon Meacham Random House, 2015 848 p. **B**

ISBN 9781400067657

1. Republican Party 2. Presidents -- United States 3. Politicians -- United States 4. United States -- Politics and government -- 1981- 5. Biographies

LC 2015016550

Based on rigorous research, hours of private interviews, and extraordinary access to Bush's diaries and to his family, Destiny and Power paints a vivid and affecting portrait of the distinctive American life of a man from the Greatest Generation: his childhood in Connecticut, his heroic service in World War II, his entry into the Texas oil business, and his storied rise in politics from congressman to U.N. ambassador to head of the CIA to forty-first president of the United States.

"In Zelig-like fashion, George H. W. Bush was present at many of the most important events of the last 65-plus years, and the remarkable story of his life and times comes vividly alive in the words of this highly skilled writer." Booklist.

Updegrove, Mark K. The **last** Republicans : inside the extraordinary relationship between George H.W. Bush and George W. Bush / Mark K. Updegrove. Harper, 2017. 304 p. **B**

ISBN 9780062654120

1. Bush, George W. (George Walker), 1946- 2. Bush family. 3. Republican Party 4. Presidents -- United States 5. Fathers and sons -- United States 6. Politicians -- United States 7. United States -- Politics and government -- 1989- 8. Biographies

LC 2017034575

Written with the full cooperation of Presidents George H. W. Bush and George W. Bush, a major biographical examination of their relationship as presidents and as father and son draws on exclusive interviews with the pair and close family members.

"A thoughtful political biography of two dynasts of a now-receding generation of politicians." Kirkus.

Bush, George W. (George Walker), 1946-

Bush, George W. (George Walker), 1946- **Decision** points / George W. Bush. Random House Inc, 2010. xii, 497 p., 32 p. of plates : **B**

ISBN 9780307590619

1. Republican Party. 2. Presidents -- United States 3. Republicans. 4. Politicians -- United States 5. Decision-making. 6. United States -- Politics and government -- 2001-2009 7. Autobiographies and memoirs

LC 2010513034

Includes index.

Many readers are interested in why George W. Bush made the choices he did while in office. Here, he offers a candid journey through his decisions, discussing the hotly contested 2000 election, his selection of key appointees, 9/11, the Iraq War, and his controversial choices during the financial crisis and Hurricane Katrina. Getting personal, he also addresses his decision to quit drinking as well as his faith and relationship with his family.

"Critics on both the left and right are challenged to walk in his shoes, and may come away with a new view of the former presidentor at least an appreciation of the hard and often ambiguous choices he was forced to make. Honest, of course, but also surprisingly approachable and engaging." Kirkus.

Smith, Jean Edward **Bush** / Jean Edward Smith. Simon & Schuster, 2016. 816 p. **B**

ISBN 9781476741192

1. Presidents 2. Faith (Christianity) 3. Decision-making 4. United States -- Politics and government -- 2001-2009. 5. Biographies

LC 2015034690

Examines the role of the forty-third president's deep religious faith in his controversial decisions, exploring his inclinations to ignore advisors and make fateful independent decisions, most significantly the invasion of Iraq, in ways that have had profound consequences.

"This is a superb recap and critical analysis of Bush's controversial administration." Publishers Weekly.

Butler, Brin-Jonathan

Butler, Brin-Jonathan The **domino** diaries : my decade boxing with Olympic champions and chasing Hemingway's ghost in the last days of Castro's Cuba / Brin-Jonathan Butler. Picador, 2015. 320 p. **B**

ISBN 9781250043702

1. Butler, Brin-Jonathan. 2. Boxing. 3. Athletes -- Cuba 4. Journalists 5. Cuba 6. Autobiographies and memoirs

LC 2015012698

Brin-Jonathan Butler's story of his time chasing the American dream through Cuba Whether he's hustling his way into Mike Tyson's mansion for an interview, betting his life savings on a boxing match, becoming romantically entangled with one of Fidel Castro's granddaughters, or simply manufacturing press credentials to go where he wants-Brin-Jonathan Butler has always been the "act first, ask permission later" kind of journalist. This book is the culmination of Butler's decade spent in the trenches of Havana, trying to understand a culture perplexing to Westerners: one whose elite athletes regularly forgo multimillion-dollar opportunities to stay in Cuba and box for their country, while living in penury. Butler's fascination with this distinctly Cuban idealism sets him off on a remarkable journey, training with, befriending, and interviewing the champion boxers that Cuba seems to produce more than any other country. In the process, though, Butler gets to know the landscape of the exhilaratingly warm Cuban culture-and starts to question where he feels most at home.

"Focusing on Dickensian characters as well as boxing, Butler's gonzo journalism should have broad appeal." Library Journal.

Butler, Marcia

Butler, Marcia The **skin** above my knee / Marcia Butler. Little Brown & Co, 2017 272 p. **B**

ISBN 9780316392280

1. Family violence 2. Musicians 3. Adult child abuse victims. 4. Child prodigies. 5. Autobiographies and memoirs

LC 2015960626

A musical prodigy relates how she sought refuge from an abusive family by immersing herself in the oboe, describing how as an adult her memories of trauma led to dangerous relationships and self-destructive habits until she returned to music as a primary source of therapy.

Buttigieg, Pete, 1982-

★Buttigieg, Pete, 1982- **Shortest** way home : one mayor's challenge and a model for America's future / Pete Buttigieg. W W Norton & Co Inc., 2019. 352 p. **B**

ISBN 9781631494369

1. Mayors 2. Politicians 3. Urban renewal 4. Political science 5. South Bend, Indiana 6. Indiana 7. Autobiographies and memoirs

LC 2018044991

An Afghanistan veteran and two-term mayor of South Bend, Indiana, traces the inspirational story of how the city, once an industrial wasteland, became a shining model of urban reinvention and anti-gun violence.

"First and foremost a great, engaging read, this is also an inspiring story of a millennial making a difference." Booklist.

Byron, Anne Isabella Milbanke Byron, Baroness, 1792-1860

Markus, Julia, 1939- **Lady** Byron and her daughters / Julia Markus. W.W. Norton & Company, 2015 384 p. **B**

ISBN 9780393082685

1. Byron, George Gordon Byron, Baron, 1788-1824. 2. Lovelace, Ada King, Countess of, 1815-1852. 3. Byron, Medora Gordon 4. Poets, English -- 19th century -- Family relationships. 5. Women social advocates. 6. Biographies

LC 2015022540

A rebel against fashionable snobbery of her class, Lady Byron, after her tumultuous marriage to Lord Byron, founded the first Infants School and Co-Operative School in England and was lauded as a pioneer of computer science, in a never-before-told story of a remarkable woman who made a life for herself and a progressive force in her century.

Byron, George Gordon Byron, Baron, 1788-1824

Eisler, Benita **Byron** : child of passion, fool of fame / Benita Eisler. Alfred A. Knopf, 1999. xii, 837 p. : **B**

ISBN 0679412999

1. Byron, George Gordon Byron, Baron, 1788-1824. 2. Poets, English -- 19th century 3. Men/women relations. 4. Bisexual men 5. Biographies

LC 98035261

Discusses the traumatic childhood, adventures, love affairs, and stardom of the nineteenth-century poet, and explores his relationships with friends and family as revealed in letters and poetry.

"This is a splendidly readable biography of a perpetually fascinating genius." The Atlantic.

Cadillac Man

Cadillac Man **Land** of the lost souls : my life on the streets / Cadillac Man. Bloomsbury, c2009. 304 p. **B**

ISBN 9781596914063

1. Cadillac Man. 2. Homeless persons -- New York City 3. Homelessness. 4. Social classes. 5. New York City.

LC 2008041111

A New York City homeless man recounts his sixteen-year experience on the streets as recorded in a series of spiral-bound notebooks, a life marked by periods of humor, colorful characters, and his struggles with myriad challenges and unexpected freedoms.

"A surprising find, Cadillac lets readers in on a rarely seen community, revealing the compassionate hearts that beat even in the most despairing circumstances." Publishers Weekly.

Caesar, Julius, 100-44 B.C.

★Goldsworthy, Adrian Keith **Caesar** : life of a colossus / Adrian Goldsworthy. Yale University Press, 2006. 583 p. : **B**

ISBN 9780300120486

1. Heads of state -- Rome 2. Politicians -- Rome 3. Generals -- Rome 4. Rome -- History -- Republic, 265-30 B.C. 5. Biographies

LC 2006922060

The first major biography in decades examines the full complexity of Julius Caesar's character in an incisive portrait that shows why his political and military leadership continues to resonate two thousand years following his death.

"This biography draws together Julius Caesar's personal, political, and military history into a single volume. This is an engaging and well-drawn resource for those who wish to be introduced to the man who was Caesar." Library Journal.

Strauss, Barry S. The **death** of Caesar : the story of history's most famous assassination / Barry Strauss. Simon & Schuster, 2015. 352 p. **B**

ISBN 9781451668797

1. Caesar, Julius, 100-44 B.C. Assassination. 2. Assassination. 3. Rulers. 4. Civilization, Ancient 5. Ancient history. 6. Rome -- Politics and government -- 265-30 B.C. 7. Rome -- History -- 53-44 B.C. 8. Biographies

LC 2014032045

Thanks to William Shakespeare, the death of Julius Caesar is the most famous assassination in history. But what actually happened on March 15, 44 BC is even more gripping than Shakespeare's play. In this thrilling new book, Barry Strauss tells the real story.

"The author explains how Caesar's funeral was even more dramatic than Shakespeare's versionespecially Mark Antony's eulogy. Once again, Strauss takes us deep into the psyche of ancient history in an exciting, twisted tale that is sure to please." Kirkus.

Cage, John, 1912-1992

Larson, Kay **Where** the heart beats : John Cage, Zen Buddhism, and the inner life of artists / Kay Larson. Penguin Press, 2012. 384 p. **B**

ISBN 9781594203404

1. Cage, John, 1912-1992 Criticism and interpretation. 2. Cage, John, 1912-1992 Influence. 3. Postmodernism. 4. Zen Buddhism -- Influence. 5. Composers -- United States 6. Biographies

LC 2011044714

A first book by a Zen Buddhist practitioner and leading art critic assesses the influence of Zen Buddhism on the work of composer John Cage, exploring the ways in which Zen transformed Cage's troubled psyche, his relationship with partner Merce Cunningham and his often indefinable music.

Cagney, James, 1899-1986

McCabe, John, 1920- **Cagney** / John McCabe. Knopf, 1997. xvi, 439 p. : **B**

ISBN 0679446079

1. Cagney, James, 1899-1986. 2. Film actors and actresses -- United States 3. Biographies

LC 97005067

"The author traces Cagney's life from his poor beginnings with an alcoholic father but fiercely determined mother through his unexpected drift into vaudeville and the theater to his slow but inevitable rise to film stardom." Library Journal.

Cahalan, Susannah

Cahalan, Susannah **Brain** on fire : my month of madness / Susannah Cahalan. Free Press, 2012. 288 p. **B**

ISBN 9781451621372

1. Cahalan, Susannah Health. 2. Diagnostic errors 3. Epidemic encephalitis 4. Memory 5. Identity (Psychology) 6. United States 7.

Autobiographies and memoirs

LC 2012012670

"Cahalan expertly weaves together her own story and relevant scientific and medical information about autoimmune diseases, which are about two-thirds environmental and one-third genetic in origin. So, she writes, an external trigger, such as a sneeze or a toxic apartment, probably combined with a genetic predisposition toward developing aggressive antibodies to create her problem. A compelling health story." Booklist.

Cahun, Claude, 1894-1954

Shaw, Jennifer Laurie **Exist** otherwise : the life and works of Claude Cahun / Jennifer L. Shaw. Reaktion Books, 2017 326 p. : **B**

ISBN 9781780237282

1. Artists 2. Surrealism -- France 3. Avant-garde (Aesthetics) 4. Art 5. Biographies

In the turmoil of the 1920s and ?30s, Claude Cahun challenged gender stereotypes with her powerful photographs, montages, and writings, works that appear to our twenty-first-century eyes as utterly contemporary, or even from the future. She wrote poetry and prose for major French literary magazines, worked in avant-garde theater, and was both comrade of and critical outsider to the Surrealists. Exist Otherwise is the first work in English to the tell the full story of Claude Cahun's art and life, one that celebrates and makes accessible Cahun's remarkable vision.

Caine, Michael

Caine, Michael **Blowing** the bloody doors off : and other lessons in life / Michael Caine. Hachette Books, 2018. 304 p. **B**

ISBN 9780316451192

1. Caine, Michael. 2. Film actors and actresses -- Great Britain 3. Film industry and trade. 4. Storytelling. 5. Success (Concept) 6. Autobiographies and memoirs

LC bl2018167870

The Hollywood legend reveals the wisdom, stories, insights and skills that life has taught him in his rise from humble origins to the pinnacle of success.

Cairo (Dog)

Chesney, Will, 1984- **No** ordinary dog : my partner from the Seal Teams to the Bin Laden raid / Will Chesney, with Joe Layden. St. Martin's Press, 2019 352 p. **B**

ISBN 9781250176950

1. Cairo (Dog). 2. Chesney, Will, 1984- 3. United States. Naval Special Warfare Development Group 4. Dogs -- War use. 5. Afghan War, 2001- 6. Afghan War veterans 7. Service dogs 8. Autobiographies and memoirs

LC 2019031697

The true story of a SEAL Team Operator and military dog handler, and the dog that saved his life.

"Touching on the power of the human-animal bond, the effects of PTSD, and the legacy of the 'war on terror,' this earnest account delivers many memorable moments. Dog lovers and fans of military history will be enthralled." Publishers Weekly

Calcaterra, Regina

Calcaterra, Regina **Etched** in sand : a true story of five siblings who survived an unspeakable childhood on Long Island / Regina Calcaterra. William Morrow & Co., 2013. 320 p. **B**

ISBN 9780062218834

1. Child abuse. 2. Brothers and sisters. 3. Abandoned children. 4. Childhood. 5. Long Island, New York 6. Autobiographies and memoirs

LC bl2013035608

In this real-life rags-to-riches story, a tenacious lawyer, state official and activist recounts her childhood in foster homes and on the streets with her four siblings, revealing a life of horrible abuse in the shadows between Manhattan and the Hamptons.

Calder, Alexander, 1898-1976

Perl, Jed **Calder** : the conquest of space : the later years : 1940-1976 / Jed Perl. Alfred A. Knopf, 2020. vi, 669 p. : **B**

ISBN 9780451494115

1. Calder, Alexander, 1898-1976. 2. Sculptors -- United States 3. Artists. 4. Modernism (Aesthetics) 5. Biographies

LC 2019025621

"The concluding volume of the first authorized biography of one of the most important, influential, and beloved of 20th century sculptors, and one of the greatest artists in the cultural history of America--a vividly written, illuminating account of his triumphant later years. The concluding volume of this magnificent biography begins during World War II, when Calder--known to all as Sandy--and his wife, Louisa, opened their home to the stream of artists and writers in exile from Europe. In the postwar decades, they divided their time between the United States and France, as Sandy made his first monumental public sculptures and received blockbuster commissions that included Expo '67 in Montreal, and the 1968 Olympics in Mexico City. Jed Perl makes clear how Sandy's radical sculptural imagination shaped the minimalist and kinetic art movements that emerged in the 1960s. And we see, as well, that through everything--their ever-expanding friendships with artists and writers of all stripes; working to end the war in Viet Nam; hosting riotous dance parties at their Connecticut home; seeing "mobile," Sandy's essential artistic invention, find its way into Webster's' dictionary--Sandy and Louisa remained the risk-taking, singularly bohemian couple they had been-since first meeting at the end of the Roaring Twenties. The biography ends with Sandy's death in 1976 at the age of seventy-eight--only weeks after an encyclopedic retrospective of his work opened at the Whitney Museum in New York--but leaves us with a new, clearer understanding of both the artist and the man"-- Provided by publisher.

★Perl, Jed **Calder** : the conquest of time: the early years 1898-1940 / Jed Perl. Alfred A. Knopf, 2017. 768 p. **B**

ISBN 9780307272720

1. Sculptors 2. Artists. 3. Modernism (Aesthetics) 4. Biographies

LC 2016054731

The first biography of America's greatest twentieth-century sculptor, Alexander Calder: an authoritative and revelatory achievement, based on a wealth of letters and papers never before available, and written by one of our most renowned art critics.

"Not only an essential record of the first 40 years of Calder's life, but an exceptional chronicle of the genesis of modernism." Kirkus.

Caldwell, Gail, 1951-

Caldwell, Gail, 1951- **Bright** precious thing : a memoir / Gail Caldwell. Random House, 2020. 193 p. **B**

ISBN 9780525510055

1. Women authors 2. Critics 3. Feminists 4. Senior women 5. Autobiographies and memoirs

LC 2019026880

In a voice as candid as it is evocative, Gail Caldwell traces a path from her west Texas girlhood through her emergence as a young daredevil, then as a feminist - a journey that reflected seismic shifts in the culture itself. Caldwell's travels took her to California and Mexico and dark country roads, and the dangers she encountered were rivaled only by the personal demons she faced. Bright Precious Thing is the captivating story of a woman's odyssey, her search for adventure giving way to something more profound: the evolution of a writer and a woman, a struggle to embrace one's life as a precious thing.

"Caldwell's fourth memoir sings. It's a song for the ages, but it sounds especially resonant in the #MeToo era." Kirkus

★Caldwell, Gail, 1951- **Let's** take the long way home : a memoir of friendship / Gail Caldwell. Random House, 2010. 208 p. **B**

ISBN 9781400067381

1. Knapp, Caroline, 1959-2002 Friends and associates. 2. Caldwell, Gail, 1951- Friends and associates. 3. Friendship 4. People with lung cancer 5. Women authors, American 6. Journalists -- United States 7. Autobiographies and memoirs

LC 2009029384

In this gorgeous, moving memoir, Pulitzer Prize-winning author Gail Caldwell reflects on her own coming-of-age in midlife, as she learns to open herself to the power and healing of sharing her life with a best friend.

"This is a book you'll want to share with your own necessary pillars of life, as Caldwell refers to her nearest and dearest. Her memoir, a tribute to the enduring power of friendship, is a lovely gift to readers." Washington Post.

Calhoun, Ada

Calhoun, Ada **Wedding** toasts I'll never give / Ada Calhoun. W W Norton & Company, 2017 256 p. **B**

ISBN 9780393254792

1. Married people. 2. Marriage. 3. Marital conflict 4. Love 5. Essays 6. Autobiographies and memoirs

LC 2017005487

A collection of poignant essays on the beautiful complexity of marriage, inspired by the author's wildly popular New York Times essay, weaves intimate moments from her own married life with the frank insights of experts, clergy and friends to challenge perceptions and depict more realistic views of married life.

"This realistic, empathetic book of advice is worthy of a spot on any newlyweds bookshelf." Publishers Weekly.

Campbell, Bruce, 1958-

Campbell, Bruce, 1958- **Hail** to the chin : further confessions of a B movie actor / Bruce Campbell, Craig Sanborn. Thomas Dunne Books\, c2017. 352 p. **B**

ISBN 9781250125606

1. Film actors and actresses -- United States 2. Cult films 3. Popular culture 4. Entertainment industry and trade 5. Autobiographies and memoirs

LC 2017016460

A raucous follow-up to If Chins Could Kill shares all-new confessions by the actor best known from the Evil Dead movies and the Ash vs. Evil Dead and Burn Notice TV series, covering the past decade of his experiences in acting and on the Wizard World convention circuit.

"Campbell sheds further light on the (decidedly unglamorous) existence of a B-list actor, and fans of his work will undoubtedly be excited to read more from the enigmatic movie star." Library Journal.

Campbell, Deborah, 1970-

Campbell, Deborah, 1970- A **disappearance** in Damascus : a story of friendship and survival in the shadow of war / Deborah Campbell. St Martin's Press, 2016. 341 p. **B**

ISBN 9781250147875

1. Mahmood, Ahlam A. 2. Political prisoners. 3. Iraq War, 2003-2011. 4. Refugees. 5. Journalists. 6. Iraq 7. Syria 8. Autobiographies and memoirs

Hilary Weston Writers' Trust Prize, 2016.

The true story of an amazing friendship between 2 women--the award-winning Canadian journalist Deborah Campbell and Ahlam, an Iraqi woman who worked as a "fixer" for Western media in Syria as it plunged into war.

"Campbells captivating writing allows readers to see inside the life of a foreign correspondent and the bonds forged and broken through investigative reporting." Booklist.

Camus, Albert, 1913-1960

Kaplan, Alice Yaeger **Looking** for The stranger : Albert Camus and the life of a literary classic / Alice Kaplan. The University of Chicago Press, 2016. 288 p. **B**

ISBN 9780226241678

1. Camus, Albert, 1913-1960. 2. Authors, French 3. Philosophers -- France 4. Biographies

LC 2016008498

"A compelling companion to a novel that has stayed strange." Kirkus.

Todd, Olivier **Albert** Camus: a life / Olivier Todd; translated by Benjamin Ivry. Alfred A. Knopf, 1997, c1996. x, 434 p. : **B**

ISBN 0679428550

1. Camus, Albert, 1913-1960. 2. Authors, French -- 20th century 3. Algerians in France. 4. Anti-Nazi Movement -- France. 5. Paris, France 6. Biographies

LC 97002991

Originally published in French with the same title: Paris : Gallimard, 1996.

Includes index."

Todd's exhaustive biography, which aimsand succeedsin presenting the man and not just the writer, has been shortened for its English translation, which refers readers to the French edition for notes, sources and bibliography." Publishers Weekly.

Cantu, Francisco (Essayist)

Cantu, Francisco (Essayist) The **line** becomes a river : dispatches from the border / Francisco Cantú. Riverhead Books, 2018. 256 p. **B**

ISBN 9780735217713

1. Cantu, Francisco (Essayist). 2. U.S. Border Patrol Officials and employees 3. Border patrol agents. 4. Undocumented immigrants. 5. Mexican Americans 6. Immigration and emigration. 7. Mexican-American Border Region. 8. Autobiographies and memoirs

LC 2017014247

Spur Award for First Nonfiction Book, 2019.

Spur Award for Contemporary Nonfiction, 2019.

National Book Critics Circle Award for Nonfiction finalist, 2018

Andrew Carnegie Medal for Excellence in Non-Fiction Finalist, 2019

A former agent for the U.S. Border Patrol describes his upbringing as the son of a park ranger and grandson of a Mexican immigrant, who upon joining the Border Patrol encountered the violence and political rhetoric that overshadows life for both migrants and the police.

"An exBorder Patrol agent finds himself on both sides of the battle over illegal immigration in this fraught memoir of his time patrolling the Arizona, New Mexico, and Texas borders from 2008 to 2012, an experience that roiled his emotions and shook his sense of his own part-Mexican identity. " Publishers Weekly.

Capone, Al, 1899-1947

Bair, Deirdre **Al** Capone : his life, legacy, and legend / Deirdre Bair. Nan A. Talese, 2016. 432 p. **B**

ISBN 9780385537155

1. Organized crime 2. Crime bosses 3. Criminals 4. Gangsters 5. Chicago, Illinois -- History -- 20th century 6. United States -- History -- 20th century 7. Biographies

LC 2016009367

"Bair has written perhaps the last word on Capone. Highly recommended." Library Journal.

Balsamo, William **Young** Al Capone : the untold story of Scarface in New York, 1899-1925 / William Balsamo and John Balsamo. Skyhorse Pub., c2010. 320 p. **B**

ISBN 9781616080853

1. Capone, Al, 1899-1947. 2. Criminals 3. Gangsters 4. Crime. 5. Crime bosses 6. Biographies

LC 2010034682

Includes index."

With insider facts and spare narrative, the authors show us not only how Capone got his scarred face; they deliver a scathing portrait of a power-mad predator coming up through the criminal ranks." Publishers Weekly.

Eig, Jonathan **Get** Capone : the real story of America's legendary gangster / Jonathan Eig. Simon & Schuster, 2010. 480 p. cm. **B**

ISBN 9781416580591

1. Capone, Al, 1899-1947. 2. Criminals. 3. Arrest. 4. Gangsters. 5. Organized crime. 6. Chicago, Illinois. 7. Biographies

LC 2009033949

Traces the criminal investigation of the notorious mobster, documenting his rise during the Prohibition era, the legal strategy that enabled his prosecution, and the possibility that he was innocent of the St. Valentine's Day massacre.

"The author rescues the narrative of Al Capone from the realm of pop melodrama, offering vibrant historical storytelling and a nuanced, enigmatic portrait of Capone and his Chicago milieu. An impressive, accessible history of a troubled time." Kirkus.

Capote, Truman, 1924-1984

★Capote, Truman, 1924-1984 **Too** brief a treat : the letters of Truman Capote / edited by Gerald Clarke. Random House, 2004. xvi, 487 p. : **B**

ISBN 0375501339

1. Capote, Truman, 1924-1984 Correspondence. 2. Authors, American -- 20th century -- Correspondence. 3. Writing. 4. Friendship.

LC 2004050313

"Capote's untrammeled personality fairly falls off the pages of these letters, and rather than being irritating, his disregard of reticence is especially poignant in this day of sterile e-mailing. Ideal for devotees to dip into here and there instead of reading from start to finish." Booklist.

Long, Robert Emmet **Truman** Capote, enfant terrible / Robert Emmet Long. Continuum, 2008. 192 p. **B**

ISBN 0826427634

1. Capote, Truman, 1924-1984. 2. Authors, American -- 20th century 3. Authors, American -- 20th century 4. United States -- Social life and customs -- 20th century 5. Biographies

LC 2008004957

"Long recounts Capote's early life, highlighting his tragic childhood and the relationships the eccentric author maintained with various members of New York's elite. Long draws heavily from Capote's unpublished papers and from Gerald Clarke's Capote: A Biography. This brief sketch, however, sets the stage for a compelling analysis of the effect of the author's tragic life on the gothic nature of his prose. Long brilliantly places each piece in the context of the author's life and of the culture at the time of its release. The book ends with a retrospective contemplation of Capote's influence and place in American letters. Each chapter represents a cogent and concise snapshot of Capote's genius in a specific period, while the entire book becomes a journey through Capote's life, work, and demons placed within the context of American literary culture." Library Journal.

Plimpton, George, 1927- **Truman** Capote : in which various friends, enemies, acquaintances, and detractors recall his turbulent career / George Plimpton. Nan A. Talese, Doubleday, 1997. xiv, 498 p. : **B**

ISBN 0385232497

1. Capote, Truman, 1924-1984 Friends and associates. 2. Authors, American -- 20th century 3. Biographies

LC 97014792

Katherine Graham, Lauren Bacall, Gore Vidal, John Huston, and many other familiars of the writer follow his life and career, from his Southern childhood to his precipitate decline.

"The book is an intoxicating swirl of contradictory stories, serious analysis and rumors, adroitly edited in chapters arranged like those of a picaresque novel." Publishers Weekly.

Caputo, Philip, 1941-

★Caputo, Philip, 1941- A **rumor** of war / Philip Caputo. Henry Holt and Co., 1996. xxi, 356 p. ; **B**

ISBN 0708958648

1. United States. Marine Corps 2. Vietnam War, 1961-1975, American. 3. Soldiers -- United States 4. Marines. 5. Autobiographies and memoirs

LC 96019314

"An Owl book".

Reprinted in 2017 as a 40th anniversary edition

Originally published: New York : Holt, Rinehart and Winston, 1977."

These are the combat recollections of a very young Marine officer in Vietnam in 1965-1966. Caputo later became a newspaperman. . . . He remembers himself as a patriotic youngster, eager to prove his manhood, and then . . . he takes us through his step-by-step discovery that war and manhood and their interrelation are more complicated than he had dreamed." The New Yorker.

Caravaggio, Michelangelo Merisi da, 1573-1610

Graham-Dixon, Andrew **Caravaggio** : a life sacred and profane / Andrew Graham-Dixon. W.W. Norton, 2011, c2010. xxviii, 514 p., [40] p. of plates : **B**

ISBN 9780393081497

1. Caravaggio, Michelangelo Merisi da, 1573-1610. 2. Artists -- Italy 3. Painters -- Italy -- 16th century 4. Painters -- Italy -- 17th century 5. Painting, Baroque 6. Biographies.

LC 2010497954

Originally published: London : Allen Lane, 2010.

A British art critic and historian describes the painter's artistic achievements and volatile life during the Counter-Reformation in Italy which included public brawls, murder, sexual escapades, and imprisonment in Malta.

Prose, Francine, 1947- **Caravaggio** : painter of miracles / Francine Prose. Atlas Books, c2005. 149 p. : Eminent lives **B**

ISBN 0060575603

1. Caravaggio, Michelangelo Merisi da, 1573-1610. 2. Painters -- Italy 3. Italy -- Social life and customs. 4. Biographies

LC 2005040203

A National Book Award finalist presents the story of the tumultuous life of the Baroque Italian artist, offering insight into how he defined the aesthetic conventions of his time to create realistic portraits of everyday people and natural subjects.

"A contemporary of Shakespeare, Caravaggio was belligerent, contemptuous, and competitive, a revered artist and a notorious street fighter wanted for murder who died at 39 under tragic circumstances. Much has been written about Caravaggio and his dramatic paintings, especially his daringly earthy depictions of biblical scenes, but somehow Prose's concentrated interpretation has a stronger impact. Not only does she cover all the biographical essentials but she also more clearly and descriptively explicates the pioneering painter's unique perception of the miraculous in everyday life. Prose also reveals, with both subtlety and flourish, how Caravaggio's frank interpretations of violence and pain, fear and grief, dignity and transcendence are matched with a brilliant subversion of our sense of reality." Booklist.

Cardano, Girolamo, 1501-1576

Brooks, Michael, 1970- The **quantum** astrologer's handbook : a history of the Renaissance mathematics that birthed imaginary numbers, probability, and the new physics of the universe / Michael Brooks. Scribe Publications, 2019. 256 p. **B**

ISBN 9781947534810

1. Physicians 2. European Renaissance 3. Quantum theory 4. Probabilities 5. Milan, Italy 6. Biographies

LC bl2019029290

Who is Jerome Cardano? A gambler and blasphemer, inventor and schemer, plagued by demons and anxieties, astrologer to kings, emperors, and popes. This stubborn and unworldly man was the son of a lawyer and a brothel keeper, but also a gifted physician and the unacknowledged discoverer of the mathematical foundations of quantum physics.

Cardwell, Diane, 1964-

Cardwell, Diane, 1964- **Rockaway** : surfing headlong into a new life / Diane Cardwell. Houghton Mifflin Harcourt, 2020. 272 p. **B**

ISBN 9780358067788

1. Women surfers 2. African American surfers 3. Surfing 4. Women journalists 5. Rockaway Beach (New York, N.Y.) 6. New York City 7. Autobiographies and memoirs

LC 2019045702

This wonderful story of one women's reinvention follows the author as she dives headlong into surfing off of New York City's eccentric Rockaway Beach, finding a true home among her fellow passionate longboarders.

"In this eloquent narrative, the author offers a moving portrait of a woman in search of herself as well as a joyful celebration of physicality, friendship, and the art of surfing. A bighearted and uplifting memoir." Kirkus

Carew, Keggie

Carew, Keggie **Dadland** / Keggie Carew. Atlantic Monthly Press, 2017, c2016. 432 p. **B**

ISBN 9780802125149

1. Carew, Tom (Thomas Arthur) 2. Carew, Keggie. 3. World War II veterans 4. Fathers and daughters 5. Former spies 6. People with dementia 7. Great Britain 8. Autobiographies and memoirs

LC 2016058365

Originally published: London: Chatto & Windus, 2016.

Costa Biography Award, 2016.

A family memoir about the author's race to document her father's story as a World War II paratrooper before his mind succumbed to dementia relates how he overcame formidable obstacles and maverick impulses to join an elite special ops unit that was a first collaboration between the American and British Secret Services.

"Carew is as vicious in her portrayal of this possessive, controlling stepmother as she is empathetic to her father's loss of his adventuresome past and, more tragically, sense of identity. A tender evocation of an extraordinary life." Kirkus.

Carhart, Thaddeus

Carhart, Thaddeus **Finding** Fontainebleau : an American boy in France / Thad Carhart. Viking, 2016. 304 p. **B**

ISBN 9780525428800

1. Carhart, Thaddeus. 2. Chateau de Fontainebleau (Fontainebleau, France). 3. Americans in France 4. Growing up 5. Boys. 6. Fontainebleau, France. 7. France -- Description and travel. 8. Autobiographies and memoirs

LC 2016008395

The best-selling author of The Piano Shop on the Left Bank chronicles the wonders of his childhood as an American in post-war France, bringing to life France in the 50s, from the parks and museums of Paris to the rigors of French schooling to the vast Chateau of Fontainebleau and its village, built, piece by piece, over many centuries.

"Carharts meandering, warmly evocative anecdotes register both the quirkiness of Frances traditions and the civilizing, humanizing influence they exert." Publishers Weekly.

Carl, Polly K.

Carl, Polly K. **Becoming** a man : the story of a transition / P. Carl. Simon and Schuster, 2020. 256 p. **B**

ISBN 9781982105099

1. Trans men 2. Transgender persons 3. Transitioning (Gender identity) 4. Gender identity 5. Autobiographies and memoirs

LC 2019027789

The author explores his gender transition in his 50s, from a woman to a man amid the rise of the Trump administration and the #MeToo movement.

"Carl's thoughts about sexuality and his compassionate feelings for sexual assault survivors will captivate readers from the first page to the last." Publishers Weekly.

Carlin, Kelly, 1963-

Carlin, Kelly, 1963- A **Carlin** home companion : growing up with George / Kelly Carlin. St. Martin's Press, 2015. 336 p. **B**

ISBN 9781250058256

1. Carlin, George. 2. Television producers and directors -- United States 3. Actors and actresses -- United States 4. Radio broadcasters 5. Comedians -- United States 6. Autobiographies and memoirs

LC 2015017795

The popular radio host and star of the acclaimed solo show by the same name recounts her experiences as the daughter of comedian, voice actor and social critic George Carlin, describing his early tours, drug use and renaissance in the years before his death.

"A funny, honest, and compassionate account of growing up with a master of comedy." Kirkus.

Carlson, Gretchen, 1966-

Carlson, Gretchen, 1966- **Be** fierce : stop harassment and take your power back / Gretchen Carlson. Center Street, 2017. 304 p. **B**

ISBN 9781478992172

1. Women television newscasters and commentators. 2. Sexual harassment 3. Sexism in employment 4. Sex discrimination 5. Autobiographies and memoirs

LC 2017289389

The former Miss America, mother of two and star news anchor recalls her career-risking decision to speak out against sexual harassment in the workplace, shares the stories of women who have faced similar challenges and outlines recommendations from lawyers, psychologists and other professionals on how to resist injustice.

Carlyle, Jane Baillie Welsh, 1801-1866

Chamberlain, Kathy **Jane** Welsh Carlyle and her Victorian world : a story of love, work, marriage, and friendship / Kathy Chamberlain. Overlook Press, 2017. 400 p. **B**

ISBN 9781468314205

1. Authors' spouses 2. Letter writing 3. Women's role 4. England -- History -- 19th century 5. Biographies

LC 2017295229

Describes the life of the wife of popular Victorian writer Thomas Carlyle, who had her own literary dreams despite living in an oppressive time period and is revered for her letter-writing and diaries and her passionate relationship with feminist author Geraldine Jewsbury.

Carnegie, Andrew, 1835-1919

Krass, Peter **Carnegie** / Peter Krass. John Wiley & Sons, c2002. xi, 612 p. : **B**

ISBN 0471386308

1. Carnegie, Andrew, 1835-1919. 2. Industrialists -- United States 3. Philanthropists -- United States 4. Steel industry and trade -- United States -- History. 5. Biographies

LC 2002010162

An account of the legendary industrialist and philanthropist discusses his rise from a life of poverty, uncanny sense of destiny, work for literacy and world peace, public persona as a ruthless empire builder, and struggles with internal conflict.

"From bobbin boy in a cotton mill to one of American history's most famous characters, Carnegie's life was one of contradictions. In his lifetime, Carnegie gave away a staggering 350 million, setting a standard for social conscience. Krass used original sources such as letters, diaries, and other writings by primary and peripheral characters in Carnegie's life to penetrate the public persona and show the man who crusaded for universal literacy and world peace." Booklist.

Nasaw, David **Andrew** Carnegie / David Nasaw. Penguin Press, 2006. xiv, 878 p. : **B**

ISBN 1594201048

1. Carnegie, Andrew, 1835-1919. 2. Industrialists -- United States 3. Philanthropists -- United States 4. Rich men -- United States 5. Men/women relations. 6. Biographies

LC 2006044840

American History Book Prize, 2006.

Pulitzer Prize for Biography or Autobiography finalist"

Highly readable despite it's length, Andrew Carnegie shows signs of prodigious original research on almost every page." New York Times.

Wall, Joseph Frazier, 1920-1995 **Andrew** Carnegie / Joseph Frazier Wall. University of Pittsburgh Press, 1989, c1970. xiii, 1137 p., 16 p. of plates : **B**

ISBN 0822959046

1. Carnegie, Andrew, 1835-1919. 2. Philanthropists -- United States 3. Industrialists -- United States 4. Steel industry and trade -- United States. 5. Business -- United States -- History -- 19th century 6. United States -- Social life and customs -- 19th century 7. United States -- Social life and customs -- 20th century 8. Biographies

LC 88038160

Originally published: New York : Oxford University Press, 1970. Includes index.

Authoritative portrait of the industrial magnate focuses on his contributions to industry, education, politics, and philanthropy

Carnegie, Dale, 1888-1955

Watts, Steven, 1952- **Self-help** Messiah : Dale Carnegie and success in modern America / Steven Watts. Other Press, 2013. 592 p. **B**

ISBN 9781590515020

1. Carnegie, Dale, 1888-1955. 2. Writing -- Vocational guidance. 3. Success (Concept) 4. Authors, American -- 20th century 5. Biographies

LC 2013003227

A full-scale portrait of the famed author of How to Win Friends and Influence People traces his humble origins in rural Mississippi and the early failures that inspired his career, describing how he wrote his best-selling book to promote interpersonal relations, effective communication skills and psychological insights. By the author of Mr. Playboy.

"A fascinating portrait of the father of self-help and incisive analysis of the mercurial era that produced him." Kirkus.

Caro, Robert A.

★Caro, Robert A. **Working** : researching, interviewing, writing / Robert A. Caro. Alfred A. Knopf, 2019. 240 p. **B**

ISBN 9780525656340

1. Authors 2. Biographers 3. Journalists 4. Writing 5. Autobiographies and memoirs 6. Essays

LC 2018055999

"This is a Borzoi book published by Alfred A. Knopf."

The author of The Power Broker and The Years of Lyndon Johnson provides an unprecedented gathering of vivid, candid and deeply revealing recollections about his experiences researching and writing his acclaimed books.

"Caro's skill as a biographer, master of compelling prose, appealing self-deprecation, and overall generous spirit shine through on every page." Kirkus.

Carr, David, 1956-2015

★Carr, David, 1956-2015 The **night** of the gun : a reporter investigates the darkest story of his life, his own / David Carr. Simon & Schuster, 2008. vii, 389 p. : **B**

ISBN 9781416541523

1. Drug addicts 2. Cocaine abuse -- Case studies 3. Journalists -- New York City 4. Drug abuse. 5. Minneapolis, Minnesota -- Social life and customs. 6. New York City -- Social life and customs. 7. Autobiographies and memoirs

LC 2008012178

A confessional account of the author's struggles with addiction traces his rise from a crack house regular to a columnist for "The New

York Times," describing his experiences with rehabilitation, cancer, and single parenthood.

"Carr takes a detailed inventory of his years of drug addiction, chronicling the slide from drinking and marijuana use during his teen years in Minneapolis to shooting cocaine and smoking crack while trying to maintain his life as a reporter and the father of twin girls. Carr is meticulous in the investigation of his past, reconstructing events with the aid of police reports, magazine rejection letters, and more than sixty interviews with friends, former dealers, and fellow-addicts. His journalistic skills are on full display as he works to excavate the truth from his often hazy memories. He evinces genuine remorse for his frequently reprehensible behavior and succeeds in creating something more than merely another entry in what he terms the growing pile of junkie memoirs." The New Yorker.

Carr, Erin Lee

Carr, Erin Lee **All** that you leave behind : a memoir / Erin Lee Carr. Ballantine Books, [2019] 272 p. **B**

ISBN 9780399179716

1. Carr, David, 1956-2015 2. Journalists 3. Recovering addicts 4. Fathers and daughters 5. Sobriety 6. Autobiographies and memoirs

LC 2018059597

A celebrated journalist, bestselling author (The Night of the Gun), and recovering addict, David Carr was in the prime of his career when he suffered a fatal collapse in the newsroom of The New York Times in 2015. Shattered by his death, his daughter Erin Lee Carr, at age twenty-seven an up-and-coming documentary filmmaker, began combing through the entirety of their shared correspondence--1,936 items in total--in search of comfort and support.

"Erin writes honestly about her relationship with her father...as she delivers a clear-eyed view into multigenerational substance abuse and simultaneously celebrates the redemption of a fathers love. Readers cant help but get caught up in Erins tragic and ultimately transformative story." Publishers Weekly.

Carroll, Diahann

Carroll, Diahann The **legs** are the last to go : aging, acting, marrying, mothering, and other things I learned along the way / Diahann Carroll. Amistad Press, 2008. 288 p. **B**

ISBN 9780060763268

1. Carroll, Diahann. 2. Actors and actresses -- United States 3. Singers -- United States 4. Marriage. 5. Aging. 6. Autobiographies and memoirs

LC bl2008020148

The barrier-breaking actress best known for her roles in "Julia" and "Grey's Anatomy" discusses her four marriages, the racial and sexual politics that shaped her roles in Hollywood and on Broadway, and the personal cost of her career.

"Carroll looks back on a groundbreaking career: the first black actress to star in her own television show and, more recently, the first black actress to play the role of Norma Desmond in Sunset Boulevard. In between, Carroll has racked up a breathtaking list of achievements on stage, in film, and on television. She's also racked up four failed marriages and a life full of the kind of mistakes a driven woman will make climbing to the top of a show-business career during a period when women and African Americans had few opportunities. Carroll is candid about the trials and tribulationsas well as the joys and triumphsin her public and private life." Booklist.

Carroll, Lewis, 1832-1898

Cohen, Morton Norton, 1921- **Lewis** Carroll : a biography / Morton N. Cohen. Vintage Books, 1996, c1995. xxiii, 577 p. : **B**

ISBN 0679745629

1. Authors, English -- 19th century 2. Mathematics teachers -- Great Britain 3. England -- Social life and customs -- 19th century 4. Biographies

LC BL 99782565

Originally published: New York : A.A. Knopf, 1995.

Includes index.

Examines the life of the enigmatic author of "Alice's Adventures in Wonderland," who was an Oxford don, pioneering photographer, shy bachelor, and humorist.

"Delightfully illustrated with photographs and Carroll's drawings woven throughout, this extraordinary, meticulous biography gives us a sharper and deeper picture of Carroll than any before, presenting a many-sided man." Publishers Weekly.

Carson, Rachel, 1907-1964

Lytle, Mark H. The **gentle** subversive : Rachel Carson, Silent spring, and the rise of the environmental movement / Mark Hamilton Lytle. Oxford University Press, 2007. x, 277 p. : **B**

ISBN 0195172469

1. Carson, Rachel, 1907-1964. 2. Biologists -- United States 3. Women environmentalists -- United States 4. Science writers -- United States 5. Environmentalists -- United States 6. United States -- Social life and customs -- 20th century. 7. Biographies

LC 2006049350

Examines the life of Rachel Carson in terms of the birth of the modern environmental movement, tracing the evolution of her ideas about nature, her career as a biologist, and her development as a writer of profound moral and ecological vision, especially in light of her most famous and controversial work, Silent Spring.

"The author examines the life of Rachel Carson, founder of today's environmental movement and antithesis of the stereotypical 1950s woman. Carson was educated in the sciences, worked full time, and was her family's primary provider and caregiver. Genteel in appearance, she was firmly committed to her goal of preserving nature. Using a lyrical, narrative style, Lytle probes Carson's interests and her purposes in writing a series of wellknown books that include The Sea Around Usand her most famous, Silent Spring." Library Journal.

Souder, William, 1949- **On** a farther shore : the life and legacy of Rachel Carson / William Souder. Crown Publishing Group, c2012. 496 p. **B**

ISBN 9780307462206

1. Carson, Rachel, 1907-1964. 2. Women naturalists -- United States 3. Women environmentalists -- United States 4. Marine biologists -- United States 5. Naturalists -- United States 6. Biographies

LC 2012003077

Published to commemorate the 50th anniversary of Silent Spring, an in-depth portrait of the biologist and reformer examines how she helped to raise awareness of the natural world, the importance of conservation and the dangers of synthetic pesticides.

Carter, Angela, 1940-1992

Gordon, Edmund The **invention** of Angela Carter : a biography / Edmund Gordon. Oxford University Press, 2017. 504 p. **B**

ISBN 9780190626846

1. Carter, Angela, 1940-1992. 2. Authors, English -- 20th century 3. Women authors 4. Biographies

LC 2016042329

Somerset Maugham Award, 2017.

National Book Critics Circle Award for Biography finalist, 2017

Angela Carter is widely considered one of the best loved and most highly acclaimed English writers of the last hundred years. Dozens of books have been written about Carter's work, but only a few have considered the author's life. Gordon takes readers through Carter's childhood in England, her struggling years as an apprentice writer, her breakthroughs in fiction, as well as insights into her private life.

"Written with grace and assurance, this volume will long stand as the definitive biography of Carter." Choice.

Carter, Eunice Hunton, 1899-1970

★Carter, Stephen L., 1954- **Invisible** : the forgotten story of the black woman lawyer who took down America's most powerful mobster / Stephen L. Carter. Henry Holt and Company, 2018. 336 p. **B**

ISBN 9781250121974

1. Carter, Eunice Hunton, 1899-1970. 2. African American women lawyers 3. Public prosecutors. 4. Organized crime. 5. African American authors 6. New York City.

LC 2017050088

Includes index.

Finalist for the Hurston/Wright Legacy Awards for Nonfiction, 2019.

Traces the story of his grandmother, an African-American attorney who, in spite of period barriers, devised the strategy that sent mafia chieftain Lucky Luciano to prison in the 1930s.

"With artful storytelling and a narrative-like delivery, Carter tells Eunice's story in the best way possible, offering a compelling, unputdownable read with as much value in social history as legal appeal. Not to be missed." Library Journal.

Carter, Jimmy, 1924-

Alter, Jonathan **His** very best : Jimmy Carter, a life / Jonathan Alter. Simon & Schuster, 2020. 672 p. **B**

ISBN 9781501125485

1. Presidents -- United States 2. Political leadership 3. Social advocacy 4. Biographies

An intimate portrait of the 39th President draws on fresh archival material to trace Jimmy Carter's improbable rise from a humble peanut farmer and complex man of faith to an American President and Nobel Prize-winning humanitarian.

"Alter's fluidly written account adds depth and nuance to the popular understanding of Carter's presidency, yet his post-White House career gets short shrift. Still, this is an illuminating and persuasive reevaluation of Carter's legacy." Publishers Weekly

Carter, Jimmy, 1924- **Everything** to gain : making the most of the rest of your life / Jimmy and Rosalynn Carter. University of Arkansas Press, 1995. xv, 176 p. ; **B**

ISBN 9781557283887

1. Carter, Jimmy, 1924- Philosophy. 2. Carter, Rosalynn Philosophy. 3. Emory University. Carter Center. 4. Life skills -- United States 5. Personal conduct 6. Presidents -- United States 7. Presidents' spouses -- United States

LC 95024257

Originally published: New York : Random House, c1987. With appropriate amendments to cover a few changed circumstances.

A dual account of the former president and first lady describes their post-White House careers and highlights such topics as midlife marriage, America's health-care issues, the efforts of the Carter Center, and more.

Carter, Jimmy, 1924- A **full** life : reflections at ninety / Jimmy Carter. Simon & Schuster, 2015. 256 p. **B**

ISBN 9781501115639

1. Presidents -- United States 2. Humanitarianism 3. Former presidents -- United States. 4. Politicians 5. United States -- Politics and government -- 1977-1981. 6. Autobiographies and memoirs

LC 2015007489

Includes index.

The 39th president and Nobel Peace Prize winner reflects on his full and happy life with pride, humor|and a few second thoughts.

"The drawings and poems by the author add even more of a personal touch, though crises in his marriage and his estrangement from the Obama presidency offer the most noteworthy revelations. A memoir that reads like an epilogue to a life of accomplishment." Kirkus.

Carter, Jimmy, 1924- An **hour** before daylight : memories of a rural boyhood / Jimmy Carter. Simon & Schuster, 2001. 284 p. : **B**

ISBN 0743211936

1. Carter, Jimmy, 1924- Childhood and youth. 2. Carter family. 3. Farm life. 4. Growing up. 5. Presidents -- United States 6. Farmers -- Plains, Georgia 7. Georgia. 8. Plains, Georgia -- Social life and customs -- 20th century. 9. Plains, Georgia -- Rural conditions. 10. Autobiographies and memoirs

LC 00048248

Includes index.

Pulitzer Prize for Biography or Autobiography finalist

In vivid detail and with "an appealingly gritty honesty" (Kirkus Reviews), former president Jimmy Carter relives his experiences growing up on a Georgia farm during the Depression in the time of segregation. In the process, he shares the difficulties of farm life and profiles the people who shaped his life, including his parents, his eccentric relatives, and his African-American friends.

"This is social and agricultural history as plain and honest as one of the tables the author makes in his workshop--an American classic." The New Yorker.

Carter, Jimmy, 1924- **Keeping** faith : memoirs of a president / Jimmy Carter. Bantam Books, 1982. xiv, 622 p. : **B**

ISBN 9780553050233

1. Presidents -- United States 2. United States -- Politics and government -- 1977-1981. 3. Autobiographies and memoirs

LC 82090323

Includes index.

In Keeping Faith, originally published in 1982, President Carter provides a candid account of his time in the Oval Office, detailing the hostage crisis in Iran, his triumph at the Camp David Middle East peace summit, his relationships with world leaders, and even glimpses into his private world.

"These memoirs treat such matters as improving relations with China; enacting energy legislation; negotiating the second Strategic Arms Limitation treaty (SALT II); concluding the Panama Canal treaties; and convincing Menachem Begin and Anwar Sadat to reach agreement at Camp David. Carter also devotes more than a quarter of the book to the frustrations arising from the capture of hostages in Tehran." New York Review of Books.

Carter, Jimmy, 1924- **Sharing** good times / Jimmy Carter. Simon & Schuster, 2005. xii, 174 p. ; **B**

ISBN 0743270681

1. Carter, Jimmy, 1924- Family. 2. Carter, Jimmy, 1924- Philosophy. 3. Sharing. 4. Families -- Miscellanea. 5. Family relationships. 6.

Interpersonal relations. 7. Autobiographies and memoirs
LC 2004051351

Includes index.

The former president recalls some of the simple joys that he has experienced throughout the years, especially those that he has shared with members of his family, friends, and colleagues.

"The author recalls various occasions in his life that became lasting sources of pleasure. [These remembrances] include his personal reasons for seeing his father as a hero, watching minor and major-league baseball games growing up, his days in the navy, road trips with his wife and children, his entry into politics, taking vacations while in the White House, his famous volunteer work, and even his hobbies." Booklist.

Carter, Jimmy, 1924- **White** House diary / Jimmy Carter. Farrar, Straus and Giroux, 2010. xv, 570 p., 24 p. of plates : **B**

ISBN 9780374280994

1. Carter, Jimmy, 1924-. 2. Presidents -- United States -- Diaries. 3. Executive power -- United States -- History -- 20th century 4. Politicians -- United States -- History -- 20th century 5. Political leadership 6. United States -- Politics and government -- 1977-1981. 7. United States -- Social conditions -- 1960- 8. Autobiographies and memoirs
LC 2010015544

Includes index.

The edited, annotated diary of President Jimmy Carter--filled with insights into his presidency, his relationships with friends and foes, and his lasting impact on issues that still preoccupy America and the world.

"That the language is blunt and occasionally a little un-Christian may come as a surprise. But the writings here reflect the Mr. Carter we know: boastful and painfully confessional, sanctimonious and callous, insightful and un-self-aware. These are the thoughts of a secular preacher and calculating politician, surrounded by friends and yet often alone." New York Times.

★Eizenstat, Stuart **President** Carter : the White House years / Stuart E. Eizenstat. Thomas Dunne Books, St. Martin's Press, 2018. 528 p. **B**

ISBN 9781250104557

1. Presidents -- United States 2. Political leadership 3. Cabinet officers -- United States 4. United States -- Politics and government -- 1977-1981 5. BIographies
LC 2017043521

The former U.S. Ambassador and author of Imperfect Justice presents an insider's history of the Carter Administration that shares insights into the 39th President's admirable character and the achievements that positively reshaped the country and the world long after Carter's single term.

"A compelling reassessment of an oft-maligned chief executive." Booklist.

Carter, Robert, 1728-1804

Levy, Andrew, 1962- The **first** emancipator : the forgotten story of Robert Carter, the founding father who freed his slaves / Andrew Levy. Random House, c2005. xviii, 310 p. ; **B**

ISBN 0375508651

1. Carter, Robert, 1728-1804. 2. Plantation owners -- Virginia 3. Slaveholders -- Virginia 4. Gentry -- Virginia 5. Revolutionaries -- United States 6. Virginia -- History -- Colonial period, 1600-1775. 7. Virginia -- History -- 18th century
LC 2004054054

An account of a landmark event in American history describes how, in 1791, Robert Carter III, one of Virginia's wealthiest planters, freed more than 450 slaves, revealing how and why Carter made his extraordinary gesture.

"This well-written and thoroughly engaging book will certainly appeal to readers interested in the history of 18th- and 19th-century Virginia, but also to those interested in the history of slavery and racism in America and in historical biography." Publishers Weekly.

Cartier family

Brickell, Francesca Cartier The **Cartiers** : the untold story of the family behind the jewelry empire / Francesca Cartier Brickell. Ballantine Books, 2019. 352 p. **B**

ISBN 9780525621614

1. Cartier (Firm) -- History 2. Jewelers 3. Rich families 4. Jewelry making 5. Luxury 6. Paris, France 7. London, England 8. New York City
LC bl2019029788

A Cartier great-granddaughter with exclusive access to long-lost family archives tells the story of the three brothers who turned their grandfather's humble Parisian jewelry store into a global luxury icon.

Case, Molly

Case, Molly **How** to treat people : a nurse's notes / Molly Case. W.W. Norton & Company, 2019. 272 p. **B**

ISBN 9781324003465

1. Nurses 2. Nursing 3. Father and adult daughter 4. Caregivers 5. Autobiographies and memoirs

The nurse behind the popular "Nursing the Nation" video poem presents an engaging memoir of the human body and its care that describes the teen surgery that inspired her career and the intricate experiences of patients being tended by strangers.

Cash, Johnny, 1932-2003

Beck, Richard Allan, 1967- **Trains,** Jesus, and murder : the gospel according to Johnny Cash / Richard Beck. Fortress Press, 2019. x, 205 p. ; **B**

ISBN 9781506433769

1. Cash, Johnny, 1932-2003 Faith 2. Singers 3. Country musicians 4. Faith (Christianity) 5. Christian values 6. Biographies
LC 2020302685

Johnny Cash sang about and for people on the margins. He famously played concerts in prisons, where he sang both murder ballads and gospel tunes in the same set. It's this juxtaposition between light and dark, writes Richard Beck, that makes Cash one of the most authentic theologians in memory. Beck explores the theology of Johnny Cash by investigating a dozen of Cash's songs. In reflecting on Cash's lyrics, and the passion with which he sang them, we gain a deeper understanding of the enduring faith of the Man in Black.

Hilburn, Robert **Johnny** Cash : the life / Robert Hilburn. Little Brown & Co 2013 608 p. **B**

ISBN 9780316194754

1. Country musicians -- United States 2. Country music -- History and criticism 3. Biographies
LC 2013941828

ALA Notable Book, 2014

In cooperation with the Johnny Cash estate, a noted music critic who knew the icon tells the unvarnished truth about Cash, whose personal life was far more troubled and his artistry much more profound than even his most devoted fans have realized.

"The personal knowledge aided by extensive archival research and always compelling, accessible writing make this an instant-classic music biography with something to offer all generations of listeners." Kirkus.

★Kleist, Reinhard, 1970- **Johnny** Cash : I see a darkness : a graphic novel / Reinhard Kleist. Abrams ComicArts, 2009, c2006. 221 p. : **B**

ISBN 9780810984639

1. Country musicians -- United States 2. Comics and Graphic novels 3. Biographical comics 4. Biographies

Originally published: Hamburg : Carlsen, 2006.

Presents a unique biography of the most famous country singer of all time, depicting Johnny Cash's eventful life from his early sessions with Elvis Presley (1956), through the concert in Folsom Prison (1968), his spectacular comeback in the 1990s and the final years before his death on September 12, 2003.

Light, Alan **Johnny** Cash : the life and legacy of the Man in Black / Alan Light ; foreword by Brad Paisley. Smithsonian Books, 2018. 224 p. **B**

ISBN 9781588346391

1. Cash, Johnny. 2. Country musicians 3. Fame 4. Family relationships 5. Marriage 6. Biographies

LC 2018011525

Includes index.

Describes the life of Johnny Cash, from rural Arkansas to his first recordings with Sun Records, to his battles with drugs and romance with June Carter through unpublished materials and memorabilia from his family, including handwritten notes and personal photos.

"The author draws on Cash's autobiographies, music history and criticism, interviews, and writings by Cash's family to produce an intimate and engaging portrait. By far the greatest strength of the book, though, are the illustrations: memorabilia from family archives and abundant photographs that capture Cash's undeniable charisma." Kirkus.

Cash, Rosanne

★Cash, Rosanne **Composed** : a memoir / Rosanne Cash. Viking, 2010. 288 p. **B**

ISBN 9780670021963

1. Singers -- United States 2. Songwriters 3. Country music. 4. Country musicians. 5. Autobiographies and memoirs

LC 2010010327

"The moving chapters about Roseanne Cash's glorious career--and the moments of great tenderness and tension with her legendary family--are like exquisite album tracks: Individually they are great reads, but together they add up to something cohesive and powerful. Composed provides no bombshell confessions about her failed marriage to Rodney Crowell or her wonderfully complicated relationship with her dad, Johnny. (Though she does dismiss the biopic Walk the Line as an egregious oversimplification of our family's private pain.) Instead, Cash delivers writerly meditations on what it means to be an artist and a public person and, yes, a daughter. Rare is the celebrity memoir that is so full of self-awareness and dignity." Entertainment Weekly.

Cassatt, Mary, 1844-1926

Mathews, Nancy Mowll **Mary** Cassatt : a life / Nancy Mowll Mathews. Yale University Press, 1998. ix, 383 p. : **B**

ISBN 9780300077544

1. Cassatt, Mary, 1844-1926. 2. Painters -- United States 3. Biographies

LC 98008028

Originally published: 1st ed. New York : Villard Books, 1994.

A biography of the American artist renowned for her portraits of mothers and children offers new insight into Cassatt's artistic and emotional odyssey from Pennsylvania to Belle Epoque Paris.

"This is an evenly written, well-documented, and sympathetic--but not patronizing--biography that should be acquired by most libraries." Library Journal.

Cassidy, Butch, 1866-1908

★Leerhsen, Charles **Butch** Cassidy : the true story of an American outlaw / Charles Leerhsen. Simon & Schuster 2020 304 p. **B**

ISBN 9781501117480

1. Thieves 2. Outlaws -- The West (United States) 3. Bank robberies 4. Train robberies 5. The West (United States) 6. Biographies

LC 2019034980

A portrait of the notorious Wild West outlaw separates facts from folklore to discuss Robert Leroy Parker's impoverished early life, humane approaches to crime, partnership with Harry "The Sundance Kid" Longabaugh and flight from the Pinkerton Agency.

"Perhaps the most successful of the frontier outlaws, Cassidy receives an entertaining and likely definitive account." Kirkus

Casso, Gaspipe, 1942-

Carlo, Philip **Gaspipe** : confessions of a Mafia boss / Philip Carlo. William Morrow, c2008. 368 p. **B**

ISBN 9780061429842

1. Gangsters 2. Organized crime 3. Mafia 4. Criminals 5. Autobiographies and memoirs

LC 2008002683

A look into the world of a convicted Mafia head covers such topics as the order he received to murder John Gotti, the intricate relationship between La Cosa Nostra and the Russian mafia, and the Mafia's role in America's unions and drug networks.

"This powerful story is required reading for anyone with a yen for the Mafia, the criminal underworld and a law enforcement system struggling to keep up." Publishers Weekly.

Castelli, Leo

Cohen-Solal, Annie, 1948- **Leo** & his circle : the life of Leo Castelli / Annie Cohen-Solal. Alfred A. Knopf, 2010. 384 p. **B**

ISBN 9781400044276

1. Castelli, Leo. 2. Castelli, Leo Friends and associates. 3. Art dealers -- United States 4. Art. 5. Jewish men 6. Biographies

LC 2009034454

Traces the life and career of the influential art dealer, from his Jewish-Italian heritage and midlife entry into the art world to his name-making exhibition of an unknown Jasper Johns and emergence as a cultivator of period masters. By the author of Sartre.

"This biography fleshes out not only a fascinating portrait of Castelli but also the excitement of the developing American art world to which he was so central." Publishers Weekly.

Castner, Brian

Castner, Brian **All** the ways we kill and die : an elegy for a fallen comrade and the hunt for his killer / Brian Castner. Arcade Pub., 2016 336 p. **B**

ISBN 9781628726541

1. Schwartz, Matthew, 1977-2012. 2. Castner, Brian. 3. United States. Air Force Officers 4. Afghan War, 2001-, American. 5. Improvised explosive devices. 6. Bomb squads 7. Afghanistan 8. Autobiographies and memoirs

LC 2015040029

When Brian Castner, an Iraq War vet, learns that his friend and EOD brother Matt has been killed by an IED in Afghanistan, he goes to console Matt's widow, but he also begins a personal investigation. Is the bomb maker who killed Matt the same man American forces have been hunting since Iraq, known as the Engineer?

"Castner's writing is evocative and engaging, completely absorbing from beginning to end. A must-read for military buffs and a should-read for anyone who has given even a cursory thought to the U.S. efforts in Afghanistan and Iraq." Kirkus.

Castner, Brian **Disappointment** river : finding and losing the Northwest Passage / Brian Castner. Doubleday, 2018 336 p. **B**

ISBN 9780385541626

1. Mackenzie, Alexander, 1764-1820. 2. Voyages and travels 3. Overland journeys to the Pacific 4. Canoeing 5. Mackenzie River Delta (Northwest Territories and Yukon) 6. Northwest Passage -- Description and travel. 7. Autobiographies and memoirs

LC 2017033495

A decorated Iraq War veteran and author of The Long Walk describes his journey in the footsteps of 18th-century explorer Alexander Mackenzie and his discovery of the fabled Northwest Passage that Mackenzie never realized he had found.

"A vital addition to the library of the far north and of exploration. " Kirkus.

Castner, Brian The **long** walk : a story of war and the life that follows / Brian Castner. Doubleday, c2012. 224 p. **B**

ISBN 9780385536202

1. United States. Air Force Officers 2. Iraq War, 2003-2011, American. 3. Bomb squads 4. Veterans 5. Explosives -- Detection 6. Autobiographies and memoirs

LC 2011052419

A memoir by a bomb-disposal veteran of the Iraq War traces his three tours of duty in the Middle East and his team's daily life-threatening efforts to stop roadside bombers, and shares the challenges he faced while reacclimating to civilian life.

Castro, Fidel, 1926-2016

★Castro, Fidel, 1926-2016 **Fidel** Castro : my life : a spoken autobiography / Fidel Castro and Ignacio Ramonet ; translated by Andrew Hurley. Scribner, 2008, c2007. 723 p. : **B**

ISBN 1416553282

1. Castro, Fidel, 1926-2016 Interviews. 2. Revolutionaries -- Cuba 3. Heads of state -- Cuba 4. International relations 5. Cuba -- History -- 20th century 6. Autobiographies and memoirs

LC bl2007014874

"English translation originally published in Great Britain in 2007 by Allen Lane"--T.p. verso.

In a series of interviews with a European journalist and scholar, the Cuban leader describes his early life, the Cuban Revolution, and his experiences ruling Cuba, and discusses his views on socialism, international affairs, and the future.

Coltman, Leycester The **real** Fidel Castro / Leycester Coltman ; with a foreword by Julia E. Sweig. Yale University Press, 2003. x, 335 p. : **B**

ISBN 0300101880

1. Heads of state -- Cuba 2. Cuba -- History -- 1933-1959. 3. Cuba -- History -- 1959-1990 4. Biographies

LC 2003012942

The former British ambassador to Cuba provides an intimate look at the life of the Cuban dictator.

"In a remarkably evenhanded and illuminating biography, Coltman (former British ambassador to Cuba) reveals how Fidel Castro repeatedly has frustrated his foes." Booklist.

Catharine Parr, Queen, consort of Henry VIII, King of England, 1512-1548

Porter, Linda, 1947- **Katherine** the queen : the remarkable life of Katherine Parr, the last wife of Henry VIII / Linda Porter. St. Martin's Press, 2010. 464 p. **B**

ISBN 9780312384388

1. Catharine Parr, Queen, consort of Henry VIII, King of England, 1512-1548. 2. Henry VIII, King of England, 1491-1547. 3. Husband and wife. 4. Rulers. 5. Royal houses. 6. Great Britain -- History -- Henry VIII, 1509-1547. 7. Biographies

LC 2010035251

Originally published: London : Macmillan, 2010."

Although often depicted by the Victorians as a matronly nurse to an elderly king, Katherine Parr (1512-1548), according to Porter, was a stylish trendsetter of 30, sensual, confident, dynamic, exceptionally educated and cultured, and able to perform with aplomb on both an English and international stage. Rich, perceptive, nuanced and creative, this first full-scale biography gives one of Britain's best but least-known queens her due." Publishers Weekly.

Cather, Willa, 1873-1947

Cather, Willa, 1873-1947 The **selected** letters of Willa Cather / edited by Andrew Jewell and Janis Stout. Alfred A. Knopf, 2013. xxiii, 715 p. : **B**

ISBN 9780307959300

1. Cather, Willa, 1873-1947 Correspondence. 2. Novelists, American -- 20th century 3. Correspondence.

LC 2012036882

"This is a Borzoi book."

A collection of the writer's personal correspondences includes teenage reports of her 1880s Red Cloud life, letters written during her early journalism years, and the exchanges penned in observation of World War II and her own struggles with aging.

Woodress, James Leslie **Willa** Cather : a literary life / James Woodress. University of Nebraska Press, 1989, c1987. xx, 583 p. : **B**

ISBN 9780803297081

1. Cather, Willa, 1873-1947. 2. Novelists, American -- 20th century

LC bl2005010011

Reprint. Originally published: 1987."

Bison books"--Spine.

Drawing on letters, interviews, speeches, and reminiscences, looks at the life and career of the American novelist.

Catherine II, Empress of Russia, 1729-1796

★Catherine The **memoirs** of Catherine the Great / a new translation by Mark Cruse and Hilde Hoogenboom. Modern Library, 2006. 247 p. : **B**

ISBN 9780812969870

1. Catherine II, Empress of Russia, 1729-1796. 2. Women rulers -- Russia 3. Russia -- History -- Catherine II, 1762-1796. 4. Autobiographies and memoirs

LC 2006278906

A definitive translation of the memoirs by the powerful Russian queen describes Catherine's youth, her unhappy marriage and life prior to taking the Russian throne, her dealing with the intrigues and betrayals of Russian court life, and her ultimate rise to power.

Jaques, Susan The **empress** of art : Catherine the Great and the transformation of Russia / Susan Jaques. Pegasus Books,

2016 384 p. **B**

ISBN 9781605989723

1. Catherine II, Empress of Russia, 1729-1796. 2. Hermitage Museum, St. Petersburg, Russia 3. Women rulers -- Russia 4. Art -- Collectors and collecting 5. Russia -- History -- Catherine II, 1762-1796. 6. Biographies

LC 2016440930

Traces the remarkable history of Catherine the Great's influential art collection and creation of the Hermitage, discussing how her cultural goals were part of a long-term plan to modernize and westernize Russia.

"An absorbing account of a fascinating figure and her legacy." Booklist.

Massie, Robert K., 1929-2019 **Catherine** the Great : portrait of a woman / Robert K. Massie. Random House, c2011. 544 p. **B**

ISBN 9780679456728

1. Catherine II, Empress of Russia, 1729-1796. 2. Women rulers. 3. Rulers. 4. Leadership in women. 5. Nobility. 6. Russia -- Rulers. 7. Russia -- History -- Catherine II, 1762-1796. 8. Biographies

LC 2011015279

Andrew Carnegie Medal for Excellence in Non-Fiction, 2012.

Presents a reconstruction of the eighteenth-century empress's life that covers her efforts to engage Russia in the cultural life of Europe, her creation of the Hermitage, and her numerous scandal-free romantic affairs.

"Massie delivers a fascinating account of dog-eat-dog politics in 18th-century Europe and the larger-than-life Russian empress who gave as good as she got." Kirkus.

Rounding, Virginia **Catherine** the Great : love, sex, and power / Virginia Rounding. St. Martin's Press, 2007, c2006. xxv, 566 p. : **B**

ISBN 0312328877

1. Catherine II, Empress of Russia, 1729-1796. 2. Women rulers -- Russia 3. Russia -- Rulers 4. Russia -- History -- Catherine II, 1762-1796. 5. Biographies

LC 2006047084

Originally published: London : Hutchinson, 2006.

A portrait of the late eighteenth-century Russian ruler discusses how she seized and kept the throne in spite of her illegitimate claim and a series of wars, rebellions, and plagues, tracing how she rendered Russia a major European power.

"The author relies on memoirs, private letters and previous monographs as she details how, after dissolution of the unhappy marriage that brought Catherine (1729-1798) to Russia from Germany, the empress juggled her relationships with men as she attempted to thrust Russia into the modern era and make it a European power. [This] work will appeal to Catherine-philes and those interested in women's history." Publishers Weekly.

Catherine de Medicis, Queen, consort of Henry II, King of France, 1519-1589

Goldstone, Nancy Bazelon The **rival** queens : Catherine De' Medici, her daughter Marguerite de Valois, and the betrayal that ignited a kingdom. / Nancy Goldstone. Little Brown & Co 2015 432 p. **B**

ISBN 9780316409650

1. Catherine de Medicis, Queen, consort of Henry II, King of France, 1519-1589. 2. Marguerite, Queen, consort of Henry IV, King of France, 1553-1615 3. Women rulers -- France 4. Rulers. 5. Ambition 6. Competition 7. France -- History -- 16th century. 8. Biographies

LC 2014955135

The author documents the turbulent mother-daughter relationship between Catherine de' Medici and Marguerite de Valois to explore the court politics, assassinations, espionage and betrayals that shaped their time.

"This highly accessible account is recommended for general but serious readers interested in European history and royal biography." Library Journal.

Catherine, Duchess of Cambridge, 1982-

Nicholl, Katie **Kate** : the future queen / Katie Nicholl. Weinstein Books, [2013] 320 p. **B**

ISBN 9781602862265

1. William, Prince, Duke of Cambridge, 1982- 2. Princesses -- Great Britain 3. Royal houses -- Great Britain 4. Great Britain -- Social life and customs -- 21st century 5. Biographies

LC 2013387679

Delivers the story of Kate Middleton's early life, first romances and love with Prince William.

Catlin, George, 1796-1872

Eisler, Benita The **red** man's bones : George Catlin, artist and showman / Benita Eisler. W.W. Norton & Company, 2013. 384 p. **B**

ISBN 9780393066166

1. Catlin, George, 1796-1872. 2. Painters -- United States 3. Indians of North America in art 4. The West (United States) in art 5. Artists 6. The West (United States) -- History -- 19th century 7. Biographies

LC 2013013973

"A welcome new evaluation of a significant American artist honed by the Wild West spirit and hucksterism of the age. Biographer of Byron, Chopin, George Sand and others (Naked in the Marketplace: The Lives of George Sand, 2007, etc.), Eisler now turns her considerable research talents to fleshing out the life and work of Pennsylvania-born artist George Catlin (1796-1892), whose sympathetic portraits of the Native Americans he sought out and lived among render an incalculable record of (and tribute to) a vanished people." Kirkus.

Catron, Mandy Len

Catron, Mandy Len **How** to fall in love with anyone : essays / Mandy Len Catron. Simon & Schuster, 2017 256 p. **B**

ISBN 9781501137440

1. Interpersonal relations 2. Love 3. Intimacy (Psychology) 4. Essays 5. Autobiographies and memoirs

LC 2017000307

A memoir by the author of the popular New York Times essay, "To Fall in Love with Anyone, Do This," shares the love stories that impacted her life and explores the romantic myths people create, explaining how implausible fantasies limit one's ability to achieve and sustain real intimacy.

"Personal musings and reminiscences paired with solid research provide an interesting stroll through an abstract topic." Kirkus.

Cavendish, Georgiana Spencer, Duchess of Devonshire, 1757-1806

Foreman, Amanda, 1968- **Georgiana,** Duchess of Devonshire / Amanda Foreman. Modern Library, 2001, c1998. xx, 456 p. : **B**

ISBN 0375753834

1. Cavendish, Georgiana Spencer, Duchess of Devonshire, 1757-1806. 2. Devonshire, William Cavendish, Duke of, 1748-1811 3.

Great Britain Politics and government -- 1789-1820. 4. Women politicians -- Great Britain 5. Nobility -- Great Britain 6. Great Britain -- History -- George III, 1760-1820. 7. Great Britain -- Social life and customs -- 18th century. 8. Biographies

LC 00064579

Book made into a movie called The Duchess.

Originally published as Duchess: London : HarperCollins, 1998.

Whitbread Book Award for Biography, 1998.

Amanda Foreman, a Londoner, freelance journalist, and Oxford graduate, presents the captivating story of Lady Georgiana Spencer, the Duchess of Devonshire. In 1774, Georgiana married wealthy aristocrat and fifth duke of Devonshire, William Cavendish. The marriage spoiled immediately, and Georgiana, noted for her style and political involvement, yet limited as a woman by law, dealt with her adulterous and cold husband through secret substance and gambling addictions as well as illicit romances.

"Georgiana was the society leader of her day. Daughter of the fabulously wealthy Earl Spencer (and ancestor of the late princess of Wales) and married to the even more wealthy duke of Devonshire, Georgiana was watched, adored, and imitated. But she evolved herself into more than just a fashionable hostess; she got involved in Whig politics, to an extent unprecedented for women. The tenor of the subject's time and placein this instance, aristocratic Britain in the late 1700s and early 1800sis both colorfully and meaningfully realized." Booklist.

Cayton-Holland, Adam

Cayton-Holland, Adam **Tragedy** plus time : a tragi-comic memoir / Adam Cayton-Holland. Touchstone, 2018. 288 p. **B**

ISBN 9781501170164

1. Comedians 2. Suicide victims 3. Brothers and sisters 4. Grief 5. Denver, Colorado 6. Autobiographies and memoirs

LC 2017049067

A memoir about the touring comic author's beautiful, funny and ultimately heartbreaking relationship with his younger sister describes their activist upbringing and the mental illness and depression that culminated in her suicide.

"This is Cayton-Holland's heartbreaking work of genius: his story of Lydia, his best friend and closest confidant, and her tragic suicide at 28. He writes with candor and care of Lydias bright light and his own darkest hour, making for an unforgettable read." Booklist.

Cercas, Javier, 1962-

Cercas, Javier, 1962- **Lord** of all the dead : a nonfiction novel / Javier Cercas ; translated from the Spanish by Anne McLean. Alfred A. Knopf, [2019] 288 p. **B**

ISBN 9780525520900

1. Cercas, Javier, 1962- Family 2. Family history 3. Shame 4. War 5. Forgiveness 6. Ibahernando, Spain -- History -- 20th century 7. Spain -- History -- Civil War, 1936-1939 8. Autobiographies and memoirs

LC 2019016660

"A Borzoi book"--Title page verso.

Originally published in the Spanish language as El monarca de las sombras by Javier Cercas, Penguin Random House Grupo Editorial, S. A. U. in 2017.

The award-winning author of Soldiers of Salamis explores the life of his enigmatic great-uncle, a Spanish Civil War soldier whose early battlefield death shaped family perspectives on heroism, morality, legacy and the historical relevance of everyday individuals.

"Cercas is a marvelous writer, and his character studies of the elusive Mena are masterly." Kirkus.

Cezanne, Paul, 1839-1906

Danchev, Alex **Cezanne** : a life / Alex Danchev. Pantheon, 2012. 608 p. **B**

ISBN 9780307377074

1. Cezanne, Paul, 1839-1906. 2. Painters -- France 3. Artists. 4. Art, French. 5. Impressionism (Art) 6. Provence (France) -- Civilization. 7. Biographies

LC 2012007182

A comprehensive assessment of the considerable work and restless life of Paul Cžanne offers insight into his far-reaching views about an artist's role and his self-doubt about his own capabilities, demonstrating how his beliefs revolutionized the ways subsequent artists would see and depict the world.

Chabon, Michael

Chabon, Michael **Manhood** for amateurs : the pleasures and regrets of a husband, father, and son / Michael Chabon. Harper, c2009. 320 p. **B**

ISBN 9780061490187

1. Chabon, Michael Marriage. 2. Chabon, Michael Family. 3. Married men 4. Fathers -- United States 5. Sons -- United States 6. Marriage -- United States. 7. Autobiographies and memoirs

LC 2009004749

The author questions what it means to be a man today in a series of interlinked autobiographical reflections, regrets, and reexaminations, each sparked by an encounter, in the present, that holds some legacy of the past.

"For the most part in these pages [Chabon] manages to write about himself, his family and his generation with humor and introspective wisdom. As in his novels, he shifts gears easily between the comic and the melancholy, the whimsical and the serious, demonstrating once again his ability to write about the big subjects of love and memory and regret without falling prey to the Scylla and Charybdis of cynicism and sentimentality." New York Times.

★Chabon, Michael **Pops** : fatherhood in pieces / Michael Chabon. Harper, 2018 127 p. **B**

ISBN 9780062834621

1. Fathers 2. Fatherhood 3. Father and child 4. Growing up 5. Essays 6. Autobiographies and memoirs

LC 2017279681

The Pulitzer Prize-winning author presents a full-length collection of essays on fatherhood, including his viral 2016 GQ piece about his 13-year-old son's immersion in Paris Men's Fashion Week.

"The author combines perfect pitch of tone with an acute eye for detail, whether reporting on his 13-year-old son's unlikely emergence as a fashion savant...or trying to navigate his way through reading Huckleberry Finn aloud to his children without repeating a word that makes him recoil. Even when he's driving at cruising speed, Chabon takes his readers for an enjoyable ride." Kirkus.

Chagall, Marc, 1887-1985

★Wullschlager, Jackie **Chagall** : a biography / Jackie Wullschlager. Alfred A. Knopf, 2008. 608 p. **B**

ISBN 9780375414558

1. Chagall, Marc, 1887-1985. 2. Artists -- Russia 3. Art. 4. Painters -- Russia 5. Painting. 6. Russia -- Social life and customs. 7. Biographies

LC 2008006162

Shortlisted for the James Tait Black Memorial Prize for Biography, 2008

An insightful portrait of the Russian-born modernist artist describes his stunning studies of the lost world of Eastern European Jewry in his paintings of the shtetl life of his childhood, his pioneering role in twentieth-century art, his colorful personal life, and his lasting artistic legacy, in a study highlighted by more than forty reproductions of important paintings.

Chambers, Julius L. (Julius LeVonne), 1936-2013

Rosen, Richard A., 1947- **Julius** Chambers : a life in the legal struggle for civil rights / Richard A. Rosen and Joseph Mosnier. The University of North Carolina Press, 2016 400 p. **B**

ISBN 9781469628547

1. Chambers, Julius L. (Julius LeVonne), 1936-2013. 2. Civil rights lawyers. 3. African American lawyers. 4. African Americans. 5. Civil Rights Movement 6. North Carolina 7. Biographies

LC 2016020980

A powerful biography of the nation's leading African American civil rights attorney in the 1960s and 1970s connects the details of his life to the wider struggle to secure racial equality through the development of modern civil rights law.

"Essential reading for those interested in African American history; the civil rights movement; and legal history, especially relating to North Carolina." Library Journal.

Champlain, Samuel de, 1567-1635

★Fischer, David Hackett, 1935- **Champlain's** dream / David Hackett Fischer. Simon & Schuster, 2008. 608 p. **B**

ISBN 9781416593324

1. Champlain, Samuel de, 1567-1635. 2. Explorers -- United States 3. Explorers -- France 4. Colonialism -- Canada. 5. Diplomacy. 6. Canada -- Exploration -- French. 7. New France -- Exploration -- French. 8. United States -- Exploration -- French. 9. Canada -- History -- To 1763 (New France) 10. Quebec (Province) -- History. 11. Biographies

LC 2008016286

Cundill Prize in Historical Literature finalist

Traces the story of Quebec's founder while explaining his influential perspectives about peaceful colonialism, in a profile that also evaluates his contributions as a soldier, mariner, and cultural diplomat.

Champollion, Jean-Francois, 1790-1832

Robinson, Andrew, 1957- **Cracking** the Egyptian code : the revolutionary life of Jean-Francois Champollion / Andrew Robinson. Oxford University Press, 2012. 272 p. **B**

ISBN 9780199914999

1. Champollion, Jean-Francois, 1790-1832. 2. Egyptologists 3. Egyptian hieroglyphics 4. Egyptian hieroglyphic texts 5. Rosetta Stone inscription 6. Biographies

LC 2011046769

Chan, Jackie, 1954-

Chan, Jackie, 1954- **Never** grow up / Jackie Chan, with Zhu Mo ; translated by Jeremy Tiang. Gallery Books, 2018, c2015. 352 p. **B**

ISBN 9781982107215

1. Film actors and actresses 2. Martial artists 3. Celebrities 4. Film producers and directors 5. Hong Kong 6. United States 7. Autobiographies and memoirs

LC 2018035059

"Originally published in China in 2015 by Jiangsu Literature and Art Publishing House as Never Grow Up, Only Get Older"-- T.p. verso.

The martial artist, actor, director and stuntman from Rush Hour and The Karate Kid reflects on his life, including his childhood at the China Drama Academy, his lucky breaks, setbacks and near death experiences both on and off movie sets.

Chandler, Raymond, 1888-1959

Hiney, Tom, 1970- **Raymond** Chandler : a biography / Tom Hiney. Atlantic Monthly Press, 1997. x, 310 p. : **B**

ISBN 9780871136909

1. Chandler, Raymond, 1888-1959. 2. Authors, American -- 20th century 3. Mystery story writing. 4. Oil executives 5. Alcoholic men 6. Biographies

LC 97000264

Drawing on never-before-seen personal papers and previously unrecorded remembrances of Chandler, a biographer portrays a man who was writer, oil executive, poet, recluse, charmer, gentleman, and alcoholic.

"Hiney traces the writer's nomadic childhood from pre-Mafia Chicago to pre-telephone Nebraska, from Quaker Ireland and Edwardian England to his education south of London at Dulwich College and his 19 Publishers Weekly.

Chanel, Coco, 1883-1971

Garelick, Rhonda K., 1962- **Mademoiselle** : Coco Chanel and the pulse of history / Rhonda Garelick. Random House, 2014. 608 p. **B**

ISBN 9781400069521

1. Fashion designers -- France 2. Women fashion designers -- France -- History -- 20th century 3. Fashion design -- France -- History -- 20th century 4. France -- Social life and customs -- 20th century. 5. Biographies

LC 2014006844

Little black dresses. Fake pearls. Jersey knit. Blazers. Ballet flats. Today--and for nearly the last hundred years--we all see some version of Gabrielle "Coco" Chanel every time we pass a woman on the street. But few among us realize that Chanel's role in the events of the twentieth century was as pervasive as her influence on fashion, or how deeply she absorbed and then brilliantly reimagined the historical currents around her. Here, with unprecedented detail and ambition--and through fascinating, thoroughly researched portraits of Chanel's lovers and friends--Rhonda Garelick shows us the Chanel who conquered the world . . . a woman who thirsted to create others in her image, who ruthlessly and innovatively borrowed from her famous (and infamous) intimates, who understood the idea of branding and image well ahead of her time, who created "wearable personality." This is Chanel at the nexus of history: a woman of daring, passion, and legendary vision, in a wonderful biography that gives her long-awaited due.

"Garelick pursues the catalog of Chanel's subsequent ill-fated lovers, her work with the Ballets Russes, her vast earnings from Chanel No. 5 and her fraught partnership with the Wertheimer brothers while frankly discussing her relentless, social-climbing attraction to right-wing, reactionary and racist elements. Certainly a definitive portrait, especially considering Garelicks intriguing venture into modern 'branding.'" Kirkus3

Chaney, Lon, Sr., 1883-1930

Dorian, Pat **Lon** Chaney speaks / Pat Dorian. Pantheon Books, 2020 160 p. **B**

ISBN 9781524747435

1. Film actors and actresses 2. Silent films 3. Silent film actors and actresses 4. Stage craft 5. Biographical comics 6. Comics and Graphic novels 7. Biographies

LC 2020000913

Illustrated by the artist

A stunning graphic debut: the life of the legendary silent-film actor Lon Chaney (the original Phantom of the Opera and Hunchback of Notre Dame), as imagined by an artist whose work recalls the style and skill of early-era New Yorker cartoonists.

"This spirited homage honors Chaney's life, as well as the silent film era in which he formed his legacy, appealing to cinema and comics fans alike." Publishers Weekly

Chang, David, 1977-

Chang, David, 1977- **Eat** a peach : a memoir / David Chang with Gabe Ulla. Clarkson Potter/Publishers, 2020. 448 p. ; **B**

ISBN 9781524759216

1. Restaurateurs. 2. Cooking 3. Belonging 4. Self-acceptance 5. Autobiographies and memoirs

LC 2019052985

The star of Ugly Delicious traces his upbringing as a youngest son in a deeply religious Korean-American family, his search for identity, his struggles with manic depression and his unlikely rise as one of his generation's most influential chefs.

"Culinary-minded readers will find much instruction here (including a section on 33 rules for becoming a chef), as well as the intimate self-portrait of a chef who works hard not to be at the top of his game, but instead always growing." Booklist

Chang, Jung, 1952-

Chang, Jung, 1952- **Wild** swans : three daughters of China / Jung Chang ; [with a new introduction by the author]. Touchstone, 2003. 524 p., 16 p. of plates : **B**

ISBN 9780743246989

1. Mothers and daughters 2. Communism. 3. Women -- China 4. China. 5. Collective autobiographies and memoirs

LC 91020696

Includes index.

Originally published : New York : Simon & Schuster, 1991.

Traces three generations of a family in twentieth-century China, during which a warlord's concubine, a powerful Communist Party member, and a Cultural Revolution survivor witness Mao's impact on their nation and their livelihoods.

"The author tells the harrowing life stories of her maternal grandmother, her mother, and herself. Their tales span a period of radical change in China that has touched every aspect of life." Booklist.

Chapin, Sasha

Chapin, Sasha **All** the wrong moves : a memoir about chess, love, and ruining everything / Sasha Chapin. Doubleday, [2019] 224 p. **B**

ISBN 9780385545174

1. Chess 2. Chess players 3. Obsession in men 4. Journalists 5. Autobiographies and memoirs

LC 2019000510

An award-winning journalist explores the consequences of obsessive addiction through his experiences as an amateur chess enthusiast, revealing how the game consumed his life, compelling two years of international travels in search of grandmaster challenges.

Chaplin, Charlie, 1889-1977

Ackroyd, Peter, 1949- **Charlie** Chaplin : a brief life / Peter Ackroyd. Doubleday, 2014 304 p. **B**

ISBN 9780385537377

1. Chaplin, Charlie, 1889-1977. 2. Film actors and actresses -- United States 3. Comedians -- United States 4. Biographies

LC 2014013009

A concise portrait of the iconic film star traces his humble theatrical beginnings through his honorary Academy Award win, sharing engaging anecdotes about his lesser-known antics and associations. By the award-winning author of Albion: The Origins of the English Imagination.

"Readers are left with an understanding of Chaplin's background, the biographical details of his long and troubled life, and some idea of the hellish conditions on the exacting filmmaker's sets, but conclusions about his significance as an artist, his work's relationship to the culture at large, and the internal forces that engendered such personal misery and creative transcendence fail to cohere. A comprehensive look at Chaplin the man but lacking as a portrait of the artist and his legacy." Kirkus.

Chapman, Eddie

Macintyre, Ben, 1963- **Agent** Zigzag : a true story of Nazi espionage, love, and betrayal / Ben MacIntyre. Harmony Books, 2007. 364 p. **B**

ISBN 9780307353405

1. Chapman, Eddie. 2. World War II 3. Secret service. 4. Spies 5. Intelligence service. 6. Germany -- History -- 20th century. 7. Great Britain -- History -- 20th century. 8. Biographies

"Meticulously researchedrelying extensively on recently released wartime files of Britain's Secret Intelligence ServiceMacintyre's biography often reads like a spy thriller." Publishers Weekly.

Chapo, 1957-

Feuer, Alan, 1971- **El** Jefe : the stalking of Chapo Guzman / Alan Feuer. Flatiron Books, 2020. 304 p. **B**

ISBN 9781250254504

1. Drug control 2. Drug dealers 3. Fugitives 4. Drug lords 5. Mexico 6. Mexican-American Border Region

LC 2020006743

The definitive account of the rise and fall of the ultimate narco, "El Chapo," from the New York Times reporter whose coverage of his trial went viral.

"Fast-paced tale of the decadeslong quest to capture a notorious drug kingpin. . . . Fans of Don Winslow's fiction and Mark Bowden's nonfiction alike will be eager to read Feuer's blood-spattered tale." Kirkus

Charlemagne, 742-814

Wilson, Derek, 1935- **Charlemagne** / Derek Wilson. Doubleday : 2006. xxv, 226 p. : **B**

ISBN 0385516703

1. France -- Rulers 2. Holy Roman Empire -- Rulers 3. France -- History -- To 987. 4. Holy Roman Empire -- History -- To 1517. 5. Biographies

LC 2005048483

A portrait of the powerful Holy Roman Emperor describes how Charlemagne served as a bridge between the ancient world and modern Europe, detailing his life, character, and military and political accomplishments.

"The author writes with clarity and passion, and his thesis is food for thought for both general readers and students." Library Journal.

Charles II, King of England, 1630-1685

Uglow, Jennifer S. A **gambling** man : Charles II's Restoration game / Jenny Uglow. Farrar, Straus and Giroux, 2009. 592 p. **B**

ISBN 9780374281373

1. Rulers 2. Secrecy in government. 3. Great Britain -- History -- Charles II, 1660-1685. 4. Great Britain -- History -- Restoration, 1660-1688. 5. Great Britain -- Rulers 6. Biographies

LC 2009025469

Analyzes the reign of Charles II during the first decade of the Restoration, assessing influences ranging from plague and court licentiousness to intolerance and war, in an account that describes the king's daring secret deal with his cousin, Louis XIV. By the PEN International Prize for History-winning author of The Lunar Men.

"When Charles II became King of England, in 1660, his task was daunting: to restore the authority of the monarchy while courting a fractious parliament. Uglow's vivid history of the first decade of his reign shows how boldly Charles embraced the openness and experimentation of the Age of Reason." The New Yorker.

Charles, Prince of Wales, 1948-

Mayer, Catherine **Born** to be king : Prince Charles on planet Windsor / Catherine Mayer. Henry Holt & Co., 2015. 272 p. **B**

ISBN 9781627794381

1. Windsor, House of 2. Princes -- Great Britain 3. Royal houses 4. Nobility -- Great Britain -- History -- 20th century 5. Great Britain -- History -- 20th century. 6. Biographies

LC 2014042418

Based on exclusive interviews with members of Prince Charles' inner circle and on rare access to the prince himself, the author looks at court life, Charles' struggles, his achievements as a philanthropist and activist and his popular marriage to Princess Diana.

"Though far from comprehensive, Mayer's intriguing snapshot of Prince Charles reveals the often overlooked intricacies of his personality." Kirkus.

Smith, Sally Bedell, 1948- **Prince** Charles : the passions and paradoxes of an improbable life / Sally Bedell Smith. Random House, 2017. 528 p. **B**

ISBN 9781400067909

1. Windsor, House of 2. Princes. 3. Marriages of royalty and nobility -- Great Britain. 4. Great Britain -- History -- 20th century 5. Europe -- History -- 20th century 6. Biographies

LC 2016031117

The best-selling author of Elizabeth the Queen presents a revelatory portrait of the crown royal that offers new insights into his lonely childhood, intellectual quests, entrepreneurial pursuits and marriages.

"In this biography, historian and frequent biographer Smith . presents a multidimensional portrait of a complex, sensitive, and often visionary man . who has carved out a dynamic public role as he waits his turn to govern." Library Journal.

Chast, Roz

★Chast, Roz **Can't** we talk about something more pleasant? : a memoir / Roz Chast. St Martins Pr., 2014. 224 p. : **B**

ISBN 9781608198061

1. Parent and adult child 2. Aging parents 3. Children of aging parents 4. Life change events 5. Autobiographical comics 6. Comics and Graphic novels 7. Autobiographies and memoirs

LC bl2014017757

Kirkus Prize for Nonfiction, 2014.

National Book Critics Circle Award for Autobiography, 2014.

National Book Award for Nonfiction finalist, 2014

Celebrates the final years of the author's aging parents' lives through cartoons, family photos, and documents that reflect the author's struggles with caregiver challenges.

"Chast brings her parents and herself to life in the form of her characteristic scratchy-lined, emotionally expressive characters, making the story both more personal and universal." Publishers Weekly.

Chatwin, Bruce, 1940-1989

Shakespeare, Nicholas, 1957- **Bruce** Chatwin / Nicholas Shakespeare. Nan A. Talese, 2000. xiv, 618 p. : **B**

ISBN 0385498292

1. Chatwin, Bruce, 1940-1989. 2. Authors, English -- 20th century 3. Art -- Collectors and collecting. 4. Bisexual men 5. Travelers -- England 6. Biographies

LC 99036474

ALA Notable Book, 2001."

This life of the author of The Songlines, who died of AIDS in 1989, portrays a man, beset with an almost biological lust for loneliness, whose singular genius was for passionate transitory connection." New York Times Book Review.

Chaucer, Geoffrey, d. 1400

Ackroyd, Peter, 1949- **Chaucer** / Peter Ackroyd. Nan A. Talese, Doubleday, 2005, c2004. xviii, 188 p. : **B**

ISBN 0385507976

1. Chaucer, Geoffrey, d. 1400. 2. Poets, English -- Middle English, 1100-1500 3. England -- History -- 14th century. 4. Biographies

LC 2004049796

"First published in Great Britain in 2004 by Chatto & Windus"--T.p. verso."

This account of the life of Geoffrey Chaucer (1343?-1400) [is also] a consideration of his role in shaping England's national identity. The poet is hailed as the progenitor of a national style, and deft literary analysis explicates Chaucer's innovations while acknowledging the influence of other poets. Much is made of Chaucer's position in the royal court, which provided the financial means to live comfortably while writing his verse." Publishers Weekly.

Rossignol, Rosalyn **Critical** companion to Chaucer : a literary reference to his life and work / Rosalyn Rossignol. Facts On File, c2007. viii, 648 p. : **B**

ISBN 0816061939

1. Chaucer, Geoffrey, -1400 Encyclopedias. 2. Civilization, Medieval, in literature 3. Poets, English -- Middle English, 1100-1500 4. Great Britain -- History -- 14th century Encyclopedias. 5. Biographies

LC 2006000099

An encyclopedic guide to the English author and poet includes critical entries on his works and characters, biographical information, and influential people and places in his life.

Chavez, Cesar, 1927-1993

Pawel, Miriam, 1958- The **crusades** of Cesar Chavez : a biography / Miriam Pawel. Bloomsbury, 2014. 548 p. : **B**

ISBN 9781608197101

1. Chavez, Cesar, 1927-1993. 2. United Farm Workers Union -- History. 3. Human rights activists 4. Labor leaders -- United States 5. Labor movement -- United States -- History -- 20th century 6. Labor unions -- Political activity -- California -- History 7. United States -- History -- 20th century 8. United States -- Race relations 9. California -- Race relations. 10. Biographies

Robert F. Kennedy Book Award, 2015.

National Book Critics Circle Award for Biography finalist, 2014.

The Pulitzer Prize-winning author draws on thousands of documents and interviews to examine the myths and achievements marking the life of the iconic labor leader and civil rights activist, portraying him as a flawed but brilliant strategist who was often at odds with himself.

"Pawel's clear, accessible prose befits a subject famous for his plain rhetoric, ensuring a broad readership can appreciate this valuable exploration of Chavez's unique legacy." Publishers Weekly.

Cheever, John

Bailey, Blake, 1963- **Cheever** : a life / Blake Bailey. Alfred A. Knopf, 2009. x, 770 p., 32 p. of plates : **B**

ISBN 9781400043941

1. Authors, American -- 20th century 2. Anxiety in men. 3. Alcoholics -- United States 4. Bisexual men 5. United States -- Social life and customs -- 20th century 6. Biographies

LC 2008042277

"This is a Borzoi book"--T.p. verso.

National Book Critics Circle Award for Biography, 2009.

Pulitzer Prize for Biography or Autobiography finalist, 2010.

Shortlisted for the James Tait Black Memorial Prize for Biography, 2009

A portrait of the life of John Cheever reveals a soul in conflict, describing his life as a high-school dropout, alcoholic, secret bisexual, and a man who concealed his deeply-rooted anxieties while becoming one of the most iconic literary figures of our time.

"The author plunges deeply into the murky, sometimes fetid stew of John Cheever's life (1912-82). ... [This is a] superb work that shows Cheever wrestling with dark angels, but wresting from those encounters some celestial prose." Kirkus.

Chekhov, Anton Pavlovich, 1860-1904

Chekhov, Anton Pavlovich, 1860-1904 **Anton** Chekhov's life and thought : selected letters and commentary / translated from the Russian by Michael Henry Heim, in collaboration with Simon Karlinsky ; selection, introduction, and commentary by Simon Karlinsky. Northwestern University Press, 1997. xiv, 494 p. ; **B**

ISBN 0810114607

1. Chekhov, Anton Pavlovich, 1860-1904 Correspondence. 2. Authors, Russian -- 19th century -- Correspondence.

LC 96041240

Originally published: Letters of Anton Chekhov. New York : Harper & Row, 1973."

Karlinsky's extended commentary and detailed notes amount to a first-rate critical biography, with much unfamiliar information and arrows pointing us toward further investigation." Newsweek.

Chen, Da, 1962-2019

Chen, Da, 1962-2019 **Colors** of the mountain / Da Chen. Random House, 1999. 310 p. **B**

ISBN 0375502882

1. Chen, Da, 1962-2019 Childhood and youth. 2. China 3. China -- History -- Cultural Revolution, 1966-1976. 4. China -- Social life and customs -- 1949- 5. Autobiographies and memoirs

LC 00698913

"Despite the devastating circumstances of his childhood and adolescence, Chen recounts his coming of age with arresting simplicity." Publishers Weekly.

Chen, Pauline W, 1964-

Chen, Pauline W., 1964- **Final** exam : a surgeon's reflections on mortality / Pauline W. Chen. Alfred A. Knopf, 2007. xv, 267 p. ; **B**

ISBN 9780307263537

1. Surgeons. 2. Death -- Moral and ethical aspects. 3. Terminal care -- Moral and ethical aspects.

LC 2006049361

"A graceful, precise, and empathetic writer enthralled by her work, Chen imparts much about medical schooling and surgery, too." Booklist.

Cheng, Nien, 1915-

Cheng, Nien, 1915- **Life** and death in Shanghai / Nien Cheng. Grove Press, 1987, c1986. ix, 547 p. ; **B**

ISBN 0394555481

1. Revolutions -- China. 2. Intellectual life -- China. 3. Communism -- China. 4. Loss (Psychology) 5. China -- History -- Cultural Revolution, 1966-1976. 6. Autobiographies and memoirs

LC 86045254

This account of the horrors faced by the author during China's Cultural Revolution tells of her arrest, the failed attempts to make her confess to spying, her imprisonment, and the story of her survival

"This is a volume that belongs on the shelf alongside the writings of Primo Levi, Elie Wiesel, Dith Pran, and other chroniclers of ideological fanaticism, its dehumanizing consequences, and its all too rare resisters." Christian Science Monitor.

Chesterton, G. K. (Gilbert Keith), 1874-1936

Ker, I. T. (Ian Turnbull) **G.K.** Chesterton : a biography / Ian Ker. Oxford University Press, 2011. xx, 747 p., 12 p. of plates : **B**

ISBN 0199601283

1. Chesterton, G. K. (Gilbert Keith), 1874-1936. 2. Authors, English -- 20th century 3. Biographies

LC 2010940318

Chiang, Kai-shek, 1887-1975

Taylor, Jay, 1931- The **generalissimo** : Chiang Kai-shek and the struggle for modern China / Jay Taylor. Belknap Press of Harvard University Press, 2009. 736 p. **B**

ISBN 9780674033382

1. Chiang, Kai-shek, 1887-1975. 2. Presidents -- China 3. Civil war -- China 4. Nationalism -- China 5. Presidents -- Taiwan 6. China -- History -- Republic, 1912-1949. 7. Taiwan -- History -- 1945- 8. Biographies.

LC 2008040492

Lionel Gelber Prize (Canada), 2010."

Taylor's fact-based chronological presentation of Chiang should temper the preexisting opinions of him that history readers may take into reading the book. An important biography, essential to the Chinese history shelves." Booklist.

Chiang, May-ling Soong, 1897-2003

Pakula, Hannah The **last** empress : Madame Chiang Kai-Shek and the birth of modern China / Hannah Pakula. Simon & Schuster, 2009. xix, 787 p., 32 p. of plates : **B**

ISBN 9781439148938

1. Chiang, May-ling Soong, 1897-2003. 2. Chiang, Kai-shek, 1887-1975. 3. Presidents' spouses -- China 4. Monarchy 5. Royal houses 6. Political leadership. 7. China -- History -- Republic, 1912-1949. 8. Taiwan -- History -- 1945- 9. Biographies

LC 2009017576

With the powerful Madame Chiang Kai-Shek at the center of one of the great dramas of the 20th century, the story of the founding of modern China ranges from the revolution that swept away the monarchy to the eventual loss to the communists and exile in Taiwan.

"A winning combination of measured, balanced research and critical evaluationthe definitive account of an important figure in 20th-century Chinese politics." Kirkus.

Child, Julia

Child, Julia **My** life in France / Julia Child with Alex

Prud'homme. Alfred A. Knopf, 2006. xi, 317 p. : **B**

ISBN 9781400043460

1. Child, Julia. 2. Cooks -- United States 3. Cooking, French. 4. Americans in France. 5. Cooking 6. Paris, France. 7. Autobiographies and memoirs

LC 2005044727

Includes index.

IACP Cookbook Awards, Literary Food Writing, 2007.

A memoir begun just months before Child's death describes the legendary food expert's years in Paris, Marseille, and Provence and her journey from a young woman from Pasadena who cannot cook or speak any French to the publication of her legendary Mastering cookbooks and her winning the hearts of America as "The French Chef."

Prud'homme, Alex The **French** chef in America : Julia Child's second act / Alex Prud'homme. Alfred A. Knopf, 2016. 320 p. **B**

ISBN 9780385351751

1. Child, Julia. 2. Women cooks -- United States 3. Television programs 4. Cooking, French 5. Television cooking shows 6. Massachusetts 7. United States -- Social life and customs -- 20th century

LC 2015043441

Alex Prud'homme recounts Julia Child's life during the late sixties to the early eighties when, after the success of her book Mastering the art of French cooking brought her fame, she struggled to re-find herself and create her legacy in America.

"Kelsey provides as much information as possible about all of the participants in these journeys and manages to keep it interesting." Publishers Weekly.

★Spitz, Bob **Dearie** : the remarkable life of Julia Child / Bob Spitz. Random House Inc, 2012. 432 p. **B**

ISBN 9780307272225

1. Child, Julia. 2. Cooks -- United States 3. Cooking. 4. Businesspeople 5. Family relationships. 6. United States -- Social life and customs. 7. Biographies

LC 2012019632

Draws on the iconic culinary figure's personal diaries and letters to present a one-hundredth birthday commemoration that offers insight into her role in shaping women's views and influencing American approaches to cooking.

"An engrossing biography of a woman worthy of iconic status." Kirkus.

Chirac, Jacques, 1932-

Chirac, Jacques, 1932- **My** life in politics / Jacques Chirac, with Jean-Luc Barre, translated by Catherine Spencer. Palgrave Macmillan 2012, c2009 344 p. **B**

ISBN 9780230340886

1. European Union. 2. Presidents -- France 3. Politicians -- France. 4. France -- Politics and government -- 1958- 5. Biographies

LC 2012018097

Includes index

Originally published in French as Memoires in 2009 by Nil.

A personal account by the two-time president of France traces his half-century political career and includes coverage of his efforts to maintain stability during the 1968 riots in Paris, controversial decision to sell Iraq its first nuclear reactor and role in establishing the European Union.

Cho, Catherine (Author of Inferno)

Cho, Catherine (Author of Inferno) **Inferno** : a memoir of motherhood and madness / Catherine Cho. Henry Holt & Company, 2020. 256 p. **B**

ISBN 9781250623713

1. Psychoses 2. Motherhood -- Psychological aspects 3. Postpartum -- Psychological aspects 4. Postpartum mental illness 5. London, England 6. United States 7. Autobiographies and memoirs

LC 2019042964

When Catherine Cho and her husband set off from London to introduce their newborn son to family scattered across the United States, she could not have imagined what lay in store. Before the trip's end, she develops psychosis, a complete break from reality, which causes her to lose all sense of time and place, including what is real and not real. In desperation, her husband admits her to a nearby psychiatric hospital, where she begins the hard work of rebuilding her identity. The result is a powerful exploration of psychosis and motherhood, at once intensely personal, yet holding within it a universal experience ? of how we love, live and understand ourselves in relation to each other.

"In an eerie, unsettling debut memoir about postpartum psychosis, Cho delves into her 2018 breakdown after the birth of her son, Cato. . . . This piercing narrative about motherhood and a fraying human mind will slowly and creepily pull the reader in and leave a chill." Publishers Weekly

Chopin, Frederic, 1810-1849

Eisler, Benita **Chopin's** funeral / Benita Eisler. Alfred A. Knopf, 2003. 230 p. : **B**

ISBN 9780375409455

1. Chopin, Frederic, 1810-1849 Death and burial. 2. Chopin, Frederic, 1810-1849 Last years. 3. Sand, George, 1804-1876. 4. Composers -- Poland 5. Pianists -- Poland 6. Funerals 7. Death. 8. Biographies

LC 2002073097

An intimate portrait of the great composer provides a close-up look at his final years, his legendary affair with novelist George Sand, his life as an artist in exile, and his decline and destitute final days.

"Eisler is a compelling storyteller, sweeping the reader into the exhilarating milieu of Paris in the 1820s and 1830s." Library Journal.

Kildea, Paul Francis **Chopin's** piano : in search of the instrument that transformed music / Paul Kildea. W. W. Norton & Company, 2018. xiv, 353 pages : **B**

ISBN 9780393652222

1. Chopin, Frederic, 1810-1849. 2. Pianos 3. Romanticism 4. Composers 5. Classical music. 6. Biographies

LC 2018027829

The captivating story of Frederic Chopin and the fate of both his Mallorquin piano and musical Romanticism from the earlynineteenth to the mid-twentieth century.

"Densely written and packed with details, this title will appeal not only to readers who enjoy Chopin but also those interested in piano history." Library Journal.

LaFarge, Annik **Chasing** Chopin : a musical journey across three centuries, four countries, and a half-dozen revolutions / Annik LaFarge. Simon & Schuster, 2020. 240 p. **B**

ISBN 9781501188718

1. Chopin, Frederic, 1810-1849. Sonatas, piano, no. 2, op. 35 2. Sand, George, 1804-1876 3. Composers 4. Pianists 5. Classical music 6. Revolutions 7. France -- History -- 19th century 8. Spain -- History -- 19th century 9. Poland -- History -- 19th century 10. Biographies

LC 2019049711

The Frederic Chopin Annik LaFarge presents here is not the melancholy, sickly, romantic figure so often portrayed. The artist she discovered is, instead, a purely independent spirit: an innovator who created a new musical language, an autodidact who became a spiritually generous, trailblazing teacher, a stalwart patriot during a time of revolution and exile. In Chasing Chopin she follows in his footsteps during the three years, 1837-1840, when he composed his iconic "Funeral March," using its composition story to illuminate the key themes of his life: a deep attachment to his Polish homeland; his complex relationship with writer George Sand; their harrowing but consequential sojourn on Majorca; the rapidly developing technology of the piano, which enabled his unique tone and voice; social and political revolution in 1830s Paris; and his friendship with other artists.

"This slender but wide-ranging volume is impeccably researched, with copious notes and a bibliography, but never seems overly scholarly and will appeal to a variety of general readers. . . . Well recommended to anyone with an interest in Chopin, though those seeking a definitive study of the composer's life and music are directed to Alan Walker's Fryderyk Chopin: A Life and Times." Library Journal

Walker, Alan, 1930- **Fryderyk** Chopin : a life and times / Alan Walker. Farrar, Straus and Giroux, 2018. xxix, 727 pages : **B**

ISBN 9780374159061

1. Chopin, Frederic, 1810-1849. 2. Composers 3. Pianists 4. Biographies

LC 2017046936

One of the world's leading authorities on Chopin and his time presents this groundbreaking biography in which the great Polish composer's dramatic life is examined and the many myths and legends that continue to surround Chopin are dispelled.

"General readers should find this accessible as well as engrossing, despite the abundant scholarly apparatus--annotated contents, list of works, illustrations, musical notations, and genealogical charts. Heartily recommended to everyone with an interest in the subject." Library Journal.

Christensen, Kate, 1962-

Christensen, Kate, 1962- **Blue** plate special : an autobiography of my appetites / Kate Christensen. Doubleday, 2013. 240 p. **B**

ISBN 9780385536264

1. Comfort food. 2. Growing up 3. Change (Psychology) 4. Mothers and daughters -- United States 5. Autobiographies and memoirs

LC 2012048556

Builds on the author's popular food-centric blog to recount her unconventional upbringing and her unusually happy and occasionally sorrowful life of literary and culinary sensuality.

Christie, Agatha, 1890-1976

Thompson, Laura, 1964- **Agatha** Christie : an English mystery / Laura Thompson. Headline Review, 2008. 534 p., 16 p. of plates : **B**

ISBN 9780755314881

1. Christie, Agatha, 1890-1976. 2. Women authors, English -- 20th century 3. Mystery story writing 4. Writing 5. Authors, English -- 20th century 6. Biographies

LC 2009291204

Reprinted by W. W. Norton in 2018 under the title Agatha Christie: a mysterious life

The award-winning author of The Six offers a portrait of the iconic mystery writer that shares insights into her Edwardian youth, her marriages, her relationship with her daughter and her mysterious 11-day disappearance in 1926.

"A tour-de-force, this thorough and eminently readable book will delight current Christie fans while also engaging new ones. Ideal for all collections." Library Journal.

Chu, Jeff

Chu, Jeff **Does** Jesus really love me? : a gay Christian's pilgrimage in search of God in America / Jeff Chu. Harper, 2013 256 p. **B**

ISBN 9780062049735

1. Chu, Jeff. 2. Christianity and homosexuality 3. Christianity 4. Homosexuality 5. Christian gay men and lesbians 6. Autobiographies and memoirs

LC bl2013011143

Tired of the homophobic image of Christianity in America, writer and editor Jeff Chu (a gay man, raised Southern Baptist) went on the road to talk to Christians about their views on whether God loves homosexuals. Most of the people he interviewed expressed accepting -- even welcoming -- attitudes on topics like same-sex marriage and the full inclusion of gay church members. Even those less accepting still didn't express hostility. This word-on-the-street memoir offers informative reading at the intersection of Christianity and American culture today.

"[T]he book brings complexity and humanity to a discourse often lacking in both." Publishers Weekly.

Chu, Lenora

Chu, Lenora **Little** soldiers : an American boy, a Chinese school, and the global race to achieve / Lenora Chu. HarperCollins, 2017. 368 p. **B**

ISBN 9780062367853

1. Chu, Lenora Family 2. Public education 3. Learning 4. Early childhood education 5. Education -- China 6. Shanghai, China 7. China 8. Autobiographies and memoirs

LC 2017276381

A hard-hitting exploration of China's widely acclaimed yet insular education system shares insights into how their examples are shaping the future of American parenting and education.

"Little Soldiers offers fascinating peeks inside the worlds largest educational system and at the future intellectual 'soldiers' American kids will be facing." Booklist.

Chua, Amy

Chua, Amy **Battle** hymn of the tiger mother / Amy Chua. Penguin Press, 2011. 256 p. **B**

ISBN 9781594202841

1. Chua, Amy. 2. Chinese American women 3. Parenting 4. High achievement. 5. Mothers -- United States 6. United States -- Social life and customs -- 21st century 7. Autobiographies and memoirs

LC 2010029623

Traces the rewards and pitfalls of a Chinese mother's exercise in extreme parenting, describing the exacting standards applied to grades, music lessons, and avoidance of Western cultural practices.

Chung, Nicole

★Chung, Nicole **All** you can ever know / Nicole Chung. Catapult, 2018 240 p. **B**

ISBN 9781936787975

1. Adoptees -- Identity 2. Korean American women 3. Interracial adoption 4. Identity (Psychology) 5. Autobiographies and memoirs

LC 2018938840

National Book Critics Circle Award for Autobiography/Memoir finalist, 2018

A Korean adoptee who grew up with a white family in Oregon discusses her journey to find her identity as an Asian American woman and a writer after becoming curious about her true origins.

"Chung's clear, direct approach to her experience, which includes the birth of her daughter as well as her investigation of her family, reveals her sharp intelligence and willingness to examine difficult emotions." Booklist.

Chura, David, 1948-

Chura, David, 1948- **I** don't wish nobody to have a life like mine : tales of kids in adult lockup / David Chura. Beacon Press, c2010. xxiii, 216 p. ; **B**

ISBN 9780807000649

1. Juvenile delinquents -- Education -- New York (State) 2. Teenage prisoners -- Education -- New York (State) 3. Prisons -- New York (State) 4. Corrections -- New York (State)

LC 2009027664

Profiles juvenile prisoners, sharing deeply personal stories of young men and women who are drug barons and reading tutors, foster children and poets, repeat offenders and animal lovers.

Churchill, Clementine, 1885-1977

Purnell, Sonia **Clementine** : the life of Mrs. Winston Churchill / Sonia Purnell. Viking Press, 2015. 448 p. **B**

ISBN 9780525429777

1. Churchill, Winston, 1874-1965. 2. Churchill, Clementine, 1885-1977. 3. Prime ministers' spouses 4. World War II -- Great Britain. 5. Great Britain -- History -- George VI, 1936-1952. 6. Great Britain -- History -- 20th century. 7. Biographies

LC 2015373202

A portrait of Winston Churchill's extraordinary wife and her lesser-known role in World War II discusses her relationship with political mentor Eleanor Roosevelt, her role in safeguarding Churchill's health throughout key historical events and her controversial family priorities.

Churchill, Winston, 1874-1965

Clarke, P. F. **Mr.** Churchill's profession : the statesman as author and the book that defined the 'special relationship' / Peter Clarke. Bloomsbury Press, 2012. 352 p. **B**

ISBN 9781608193721

1. Prime ministers -- Great Britain 2. Politicians -- England -- 20th century 3. Leadership in men. 4. Great Britain -- Politics and government -- 20th century. 5. Biographies

LC 2011044274

Looks at the Prime Minister's writing career over the course of his life, culminating in his four-volume "History of the English-Speaking Peoples."

D'Este, Carlo, 1936- **Warlord** : a life of Winston Churchill at war, 1874-1945 / Carlo D'Este. Harper, 2008. 864 p. **B**

ISBN 9780060575731

1. Churchill, Winston, 1874-1965 Military leadership 2. Prime ministers -- Great Britain. 3. Command of troops -- Great Britain -- History -- 20th century. 4. Military strategy -- Great Britain. 5. World War I -- Great Britain. 6. Great Britain -- History, Military -- 20th century. 7. Great Britain -- History, Military -- 19th century.

LC 2008009272

A biography of Winston Churchill's astonishing military career from his youth through World War II.

"D'Este has produced an outstanding work that should take its rightful place alongside the dozens of other studies of this most remarkable statesman." Library Journal.

Johnson, Paul, 1928- **Churchill** / Paul Johnson. Viking, 2009. 192 p. **B**

ISBN 9780670021055

1. Prime ministers -- Great Britain 2. Politicians -- Great Britain 3. Leadership in men. 4. Great Britain -- Politics and government -- 20th century. 5. Biographies

LC 2009008326

Shares unconventional and revelatory analyses of key moments in the twentieth-century prime minister's career, exploring his early achievements and subsequent leadership while providing anecdotal insights into the experiences and qualities that enabled his successes.

Manchester, William, 1922-2004 The **last** lion, Winston Spencer Churchill. William Manchester. Little, Brown, c1983-2012. 992 p. Last lion (William Manchester) ; **B**

ISBN 9780316545037

1. Churchill, Winston, 1874-1965. 2. Aristocracy. 3. Soldiers. 4. Politicians -- Great Britain -- 20th century. 5. Prime ministers -- Great Britain 6. England -- History -- 20th century. 7. Great Britain -- Politics and government -- 20th century. 8. Biographies

LC 82024972

Describes the early life and political career of the British prime minister Winston Churchill.

Manchester, William, 1922-2004 The **last** lion, Winston Spencer Churchill. William Manchester. Little, Brown, c1988. 816 p. Last lion (William Manchester) ; **B**

ISBN 9780316545129

1. Churchill, Winston, 1874-1965. 2. Politicians -- Great Britain -- 20th century. 3. Prime ministers -- Great Britain 4. Ambition in men. 5. England -- History -- 20th century. 6. Great Britain -- Politics and government -- 20th century. 7. Biographies

Details the life and times of one of the world's most powerful leaders.

★Manchester, William, 1922-2004 The **last** lion, Winston Spencer Churchill. William Manchester and Paul Reid. Little, Brown, and Company, 2012. 1232 p. Last lion (William Manchester) ; **B**

ISBN 9780316547703

1. Churchill, Winston, 1874-1965. 2. Politicians -- Great Britain -- 20th century. 3. Prime ministers -- Great Britain 4. World War II. 5. International relations. 6. England -- History -- 20th century. 7. Great Britain -- Politics and government -- 20th century. 8. Biographies

Details the life and times of Winston Churchill, one of the world's most powerful leaders.

McCarten, Anthony, 1961- **Darkest** hour : how Churchill brought England back from the brink / Anthony McCarten. HarperCollins, 2017 256 p. **B**

ISBN 9780062749512

1. World War II -- Diplomatic history. 2. Diplomacy. 3. Military strategy. 4. Britain, Battle of, 1940. 5. Europe -- History -- 1918-1945. 6. Biographies

LC bl2017034059

Presents an account of the period immediately following Winston Churchill's ascendancy to Prime Minister and how he met the challenges of the Blitzkrieg.

"A fresh, readable look at events and players that, though well-known to history, deserve to be studied for some time to come." Kirkus.

★Millard, Candice **Hero** of the empire : the Boer war, a daring escape, and the making of Winston Churchill / Candice Millard. Doubleday, a division of Penguin Random House LLC, 2016. 352 p. **B**

ISBN 9780385535731

1. Churchill, Winston, 1874-1965 Military leadership. 2. Prisoners of war. 3. Boer War, 1899-1902. 4. Escaped prisoners of war. 5. Survival. 6. South Africa -- Foreign relations Great Britain -- History -- 19th century. 7. Great Britain -- Foreign relations South Africa -- History -- 19th century. 8. Biographies

LC 2015049806

The best-selling author of Destiny of the Republic presents a narrative account of Churchill's lesser-known heroics during the Boer War, describing his daring escape from rebel captors, trek through hundreds of miles with virtually no supplies and eventual return to South Africa to liberate the soldiers captured with him.

"Here the author documents the equally risky adventures of Winston Churchill (1874-1965) during the Second Boer War, in which Churchill and his fellow soldiers were captured upon arriving in South Africa. Churchill managed an escape, eventually returning to South Africa to free the men with whom he was imprisoned. Enjoyable for all readers, especially fans of Churchill, military and world history, narrative nonfiction, and survival stories." Library Journal.

Roberts, Andrew, 1963- **Churchill** : walking with destiny / Andrew Roberts. Viking, 2018. 704 p. **B**

ISBN 9781101980996

1. Churchill, Winston, 1874-1965. 2. Prime ministers -- Great Britain 3. World War II -- Great Britain. 4. Leadership 5. Politicians -- Great Britain 6. Great Britain -- Politics and government -- 1936-1945. 7. Great Britain -- Politics and government -- 20th century. 8. Biographies

LC bl2018183334

Draws on extensive new materials, from private letters to transcripts of war cabinet meetings, to present a portrait of the iconic war leader that discusses Churchill's motivations and unwavering faith in the British Empire.

"This biography is exhaustively researched, beautifully written and paced, deeply admiring but not hagiographic, and empathic and balanced in its judgmentsa magnificent achievement." Publishers Weekly.

Toye, Richard, 1973- **Churchill's** empire : the world that made him and the world he made / Richard Toye. Henry Holt, 2010. 368 p. **B**

ISBN 9780805087956

1. Imperialism 2. Prime ministers -- Great Britain 3. Politicians -- Great Britain 4. Leadership 5. Great Britain -- Colonies -- History -- 20th century. 6. Biographies

LC 2010001427

Focuses on the British prime minister's career from less-remembered imperial aspects, contending that Churchill believed the English to be a superior race on whose behalf he promoted discriminating or morally questionable political agendas.

"In this biography, the author stresses that Churchill (1874-1965), a Victorian aristocrat, assumed white superiority but regularly proclaimed that nonwhites deserved equal rights and, eventually, independence once they discarded their primitive ways and achieved European levels of culture. This work is a valuable contribution to greater understanding of a historical icon." Booklist.

Cicero, Marcus Tullius

Everitt, Anthony **Cicero** : the life and times of Rome's greatest politician / Anthony Everitt. Random House, 2001. xv, 359 p. : **B**

ISBN 0375507469

1. Cicero, Marcus Tullius. 2. Rome. Senate. 3. Consuls 4. Politicians -- Rome 5. Roman orators 6. Rhetoric -- Political aspects. 7. Rome -- Politics and government -- 265-30 B.C. 8. Rome -- History -- Republic, 510-30 B.C. 9. Biographies

LC 2001048531

Originally published: John Murray Publishers, Great Britain, 2001.

A portrait of the Roman politician describes the life and times of the ancient statesman, based on the witty and candid letters that Cicero wrote to his friend Atticus in which he described the events and personalities that shaped the final days of Republican Rome.

"This masterful biography draws on Cicero's letters to his friend Atticus to give a clear picture of the famous Roman orator, noting both his brilliance and his faults." Booklist.

Ciezadlo, Annia

Ciezadlo, Annia **Day** of honey : a memoir of food, love, and war / Annia Ciezadlo. Free Press, 2011. 304 p. **B**

ISBN 9781416583936

1. Ciezadlo, Annia. 2. Journalists -- United States 3. Food -- Social aspects -- Iraq -- Baghdad. 4. Iraq War, 2003-2011 -- Social aspects 5. Food -- Social aspects -- Lebanon -- Beirut. 6. Baghdad, Iraq -- Social life and customs. 7. Beirut, Lebanon -- Social life and customs. 8. Autobiographies and memoirs

LC 2010019739

"There are many good reasons to read Day of Honey. It's a carefully researched tour through the history of Middle Eastern food. It's filled with adrenalized scenes from war zones, scenes of narrow escapes and clandestine phone calls and frightening cultural misunderstandings. These things wouldn't matter much, though, if her sentences didn't make such a sensual, smart, wired-up sound on the page." New York Times Book Review.

Cixi, Empress dowager of China, 1835-1908

Chang, Jung, 1952- **Empress** Dowager Cixi : the concubine who launched modern China / Jung Chang. Alfred A. Knopf, 2013. 352 p. **B**

ISBN 9780307271600

1. Cixi, Empress dowager of China, 1835-1908. 2. Women rulers -- China 3. Mistresses 4. China -- Politics and government -- 19th century. 5. China -- History -- 1861-1912. 6. Biographies

LC 2013020766

Shortlisted for the James Tait Black Memorial Prize for Biography, 2013

Chosen as one of the Emperor's concubines at age 16, Empress Dowager Cixi (1835?1908) ruled China for decades and brought a medieval empire into the modern age. Upon the Emperor's death in 1861, their 5-year-old son ascended to the throne; Cixi overthrew the appointed regents, to become the true power behind the throne (a silk screen literally separated her from her all-male advisors during briefings). She abolished tortuous punishements, inaugurated women's liberation, moved China toward more egalitarian means of rulership.

"Chang uses the work of revisionist scholars to paint a largely plausible portrait of a ruthless, farsighted politician who welcomed change and restructured the state." Library Journal.

Clancy, Tara, 1980-

Clancy, Tara, 1980- The **Clancys** of Queens : a memoir / Tara Clancy. Crown Publishers, 2016. 240 p. **B**

ISBN 9781101903117

1. Clancy, Tara, 1980- Childhood and youth. 2. Clancy, Tara, 1980- Family. 3. Clancy family. 4. Women authors 5. Family relationships. 6. Working class families 7. Social classes 8. Queens, New York City -- Social life and customs 9. New York City -- Social life and customs. 10. Coming-of-age stories 11. Autobiographies and memoirs

LC 2016003555

" The varied settings of her childhood, like the nautical-themed bar with regulars, including English Billy and a tall, mustachioed man known as Daisy, are full-fledged characters in themselves. As Clancy whirls with feverish tomboy energy from one escapade to the next, she gives a fantastically vivid view into her many worlds." Booklist.

Clapper, James R. (James Robert), 1941-

Clapper, James R. (James Robert), 1941- **Facts** and fears : hard truths from a life in intelligence / James R. Clapper with Trey Brown. Viking, [2018] 424 pages : **B**

ISBN 9780525558644

1. Intelligence service 2. National security 3. Intelligence officers 4. Surveillance 5. Autobiographies and memoirs

LC 2018023679

The former director of National Intelligence and senior advisor to Barack Obama traces his five-decade career, detailing his relationships with multiple presidents, the truth about Russia's alleged role in the election of Donald Trump, his efforts to make intelligence more transparent and his decision to step down in January 2017.

"If Clapper's revelations undermine the support of an irrational Trump among voters, he will consider the book a success, however limited. However, if the book fails to contribute to the halting of Trump's widespread corruption, Clapper makes clear he will do whatever he can from his retirement to protect what is left of American democracy." Kirkus.

Clapton, Eric

Clapton, Eric **Clapton** : the autobiography / Eric Clapton. Broadway Books, 2007. 343 p. : **B**

ISBN 038551851X

1. Rock musicians -- England 2. Musicians -- England 3. Guitarists 4. Autobiographies and memoirs

LC 2007015482

The legendary guitarist recounts the story of his life and his career, recalling his work with the Yardbirds, Cream, and as a solo artist; years of drug and alcohol abuse; failed marriage to Patti Boyd; and the accidental death of his young son.

"As he retraces every step of his career, from the early stints with the Yardbirds and Cream to his solo successes, Clapton also devotes copious detail to his drug and alcohol addictions, particularly how they intersected with his romantic obsession with Pattie Boyd. Both the youthful excesses and the current calm state are narrated with an engaging tone that nudges Clapton's story ahead of other rock 'n' roll memoirs." Publishers Weekly.

★Norman, Philip, 1943- **Slowhand** : the life and music of Eric Clapton / Philip Norman. Little, Brown and Company, 2018. 352 p. **B**

ISBN 9780316560436

1. Clapton, Eric. 2. Yardbirds (Musical group) 3. Cream (Musical group) 4. Derek and the Dominos (Musical group) 5. Rock musicians -- Great Britain 6. Musicians. 7. Rock music. 8. Guitarists. 9. Great Britain 10. Biographies.

LC bl2018183662

Chronicles the life of the rock legend and guitar virtuoso, including his scandalous childhood, early musical success, struggles with addiction in the 1960s and 1970s, marriage to Pattie Boyd, and the death of his son.

"Extremely knowledgeable about the rock music scene, Norman tells Clapton's story with verve and insight." Kirkus.

Clare, John, 1793-1864

Bate, Jonathan **John** Clare : a biography / Jonathan Bate. Farrar, Straus, and Giroux, 2003. xix, 16 plates, 648 p. : **B**

ISBN 0374179905

1. Clare, John, 1793-1864. 2. Poets, English -- 19th century 3. Psychiatric hospital patients -- Great Britain 4. People with mental illnesses -- Great Britain 5. Agricultural laborers. 6. Northamptonshire, England 7. Biographies

LC 2003044063

Hawthornden Prize, 2004.

James Tait Black Memorial Prize for Biography, 2004.

The first literary biography of the "poets' poet" chronicles his birth into poverty, his work as an agricultural laborer, his relationship with John Keats, and his career as a writer.

"This biography succeeds splendidly . not only making generous use of Clare's own wonderful prose and verse but adding historical perspective and a constant, intelligent probing which amount almost to a dialogue with Clare's view of himself." Times Literary Supplement.

Clark, Jim, 1944-

Lewis, Michael (Michael M.) The **new** new thing : a Silicon Valley story / Michael Lewis. W. W. Norton, 2000. 268 p. **B**

ISBN 0393048136

1. Businesspeople -- United States 2. Entrepreneurs 3. Computer software industry and trade -- United States -- History 4. Internet industry and trade 5. Biographies

LC 99043412

The strange, unlikely story of Silicon Valley is told through the life of one of it's greatest achievers--Jim Clark, who founded Silicon Graphics and Netscape and may be on the verge of another trillion-dollar miracle company.

"This is a splendid, entirely satisfying book, intelligent and fun and revealing and troubling in the correct proportions, resolutely skeptical but not at all cynical, brimming with fabulous scenes as well as sharp analysis." New York Times Book Review.

Clark, Kenneth, 1903-1983

Stourton, James **Kenneth** Clark : life, art and civilisation / James Stourton. Alfred A. Knopf, 2016. 304 p. **B**

ISBN 9780385351171

1. Clark, Kenneth, 1903-1983. 2. National Gallery (Great Britain) 3. Art historians. 4. Museum curators. 5. Biographies

LC bl2016047148

The first and definitive biography of this brilliant polymath--director of the National Gallery, author, patron of the arts, social lion, and singular pioneer of television--that also tells the story of the arts in the twentieth century through his astonishing life.

"A sparkling, thoroughly entertaining portrait of a brilliant popularizer who brought art to the masses." Kirkus.

Clarke, Rachel (Physician)

Clarke, Rachel (Physician) **Dear** life : a doctor's story of love and loss / Rachel Clarke. Thomas Dunne Books, 2020. 336 p. **B**

ISBN 9781250764515

1. Physicians -- England 2. Terminal care. 3. Palliative treatment 4. Quality of life. 5. Autobiographies and memoirs

LC 2020016411

Originally published: London : Little, Brown, 2020.

An NHS palliative medicine expert identifies an industry gap in guidelines for qualitative end-of-life care, sharing career-based insights into how loved ones and professional caregivers can more compassionately assist patients through the final stages of life.

"Clarke's message is especially timely as we continue to face a global pandemic, and she also includes practical advice on end-of-life preparations and helpful notes about relevant resources. Death comes to all of us; these authentic stories show how it can be met with strength and grace instead of fear." Kirkus

Clay, Henry, 1777-1852

Heidler, David Stephen, 1955- **Henry** Clay : the essential American / David S. Heidler and Jeanne T. Heidler. Random House, 2010. 384 p. **B**

ISBN 9781400067268

1. Clay, Henry, 1777-1852. 2. United States. Congress 3. United States. Secretary of State. 4. Legislators -- United States 5. Politicians -- United States 6. Presidential candidates. 7. United States -- Politics and government -- 1815-1861. 8. Biographies

LC 2009027872

Documents the life and career of Henry Clay from the founding of America through the eve of the Civil War, providing coverage of such topics as his infamous rivalry with Andrew Jackson, transformation of the office of Speaker of the House, and five unsuccessful runs for the presidency.

Cleage, Pearl

Cleage, Pearl **Things** I should have told my daughter : lies, lessons & love affairs / Pearl Cleage. Atria Books, 2014. 320 p. **B**

ISBN 9781451664690

1. Cleage, Pearl. 2. Women authors, American. 3. Self-fulfillment in women 4. Motherhood. 5. Autobiographies and memoirs

LC 2013034164

When author Pearl Cleage was going through boxes full of her journals, her daughter suggested burning them. Fortunately for readers, Cleage instead drew from them to compile Things I Should Have Told My Daughter. This memoir, which presents diary excerpts without added context, provides a compelling view of the African American experience from 1970 to 1988. Cleage is a highly regarded writer who was a civil rights activist, wrote speeches for Maynard Jackson, Atlanta's first black mayor, experimented with drugs, avidly followed cinema and popular music, and had numerous lovers.

Cleaver, Eldridge, 1935-1998

Cleaver, Eldridge, 1935-1998 **Soul** on ice / Eldridge Cleaver. Delta Trade Paperbacks, 1999, c1968. 242 p. ; **B**

ISBN 038533379X

1. African American authors -- 20th century 2. African Americans 3. African Americans -- Psychology. 4. Civil rights -- United States -- History -- 20th century 5. United States -- Social life and customs -- 20th century 6. United States -- Race relations -- History -- 20th century 7. Autobiographies and memoirs 8. Essays

LC BL 99004710

Originally published: New York : McGraw-Hill, 1968.

Eldridge Cleaver's letters from Folsom Prison in which he reveals his sensibility and his literary prowess.

Cleaver, Eldridge, 1935-1998 **Target** zero : a life in writing / Eldridge Cleaver ; edited by Kathleen Cleaver ; foreword by Henry Louis Gates, Jr. ; afterword by Cecil Brown. Palgrave Macmillan, 2006. xxvi, 336 p. : **B**

ISBN 1403962375

1. Cleaver, Eldridge, 1935-1998. 2. Black Panther Party. 3. African Americans 4. African American political activists 5. Political activists -- United States 6. African Americans -- Political activity 7. United States -- Race relations. 8. United States -- Politics and government. 9. Autobiographies and memoirs

LC 2005051252

Traces the controversial life story of the Black Panther information minister through a series of essays, short stories, letters, interviews, and poems, charting his quiet childhood, prison-marked youth, emergence as a Black Panther leader, seven-year exile, and religious and political conversion following his return to the U.S.

"The book's four parts chart Cleaver's life trhough his essays, short stories, letters, interviews, and poems, many previously unpublished. This well-crafted reader . is a rich experience." Choice.

Cleese, John

Cleese, John **So,** anyway... / John Cleese. Crown, 2014 416 p. **B**

ISBN 9780385348249

1. Monty Python (Comedy troupe) 2. Comedians -- Great Britain 3. Film actors and actresses -- Great Britain 4. Television actors and actresses -- Great Britain 5. Great Britain -- Social life and customs -- 20th century 6. Autobiographies and memoirs

LC bl2014043108

A rollicking memoir by the legendary Monty Python comic traces his ascent in the entertainment world, from his humble origins and early collaborations with Graham Chapman through his uproarious achievements in multiple venues.

Cleland, Max, 1942-

Cleland, Max, 1942- **Heart** of a patriot : how I found the courage to survive Vietnam, Walter Reed, and Karl Rove / Max Cleland, with Ben Raines. Simon & Schuster, 2009. 272 p. **B**

ISBN 9781439126059

1. United States. Congress. Senate 2. United States. Veterans Administration Officials and employees 3. Legislators -- United States 4. Disabled veterans -- United States 5. Vietnam veterans 6. Veterans -- Civil rights -- United States. 7. Autobiographies and memoirs

LC 2009011620

A former U.S. Senator and head of the Veterans Administration describes the challenges of recovering from war, detailing his own experiences as a soldier in the Vietnam War, where he became a triple amputee, and his subsequent battles with recovery and PTSD.

Clemente, Roberto, 1934-1972

Maraniss, David **Clemente** : the passion and grace of baseball's last hero / David Maraniss. Simon & Schuster, 2006. 401 p., 16 p. of plates : **B**

ISBN 0743217810

1. Clemente, Roberto, 1934-1972. 2. Pittsburgh Pirates (Baseball team) 3. Baseball players -- Puerto Rico 4. Athletes -- Puerto Rico 5. Professional baseball players. 6. Puerto Ricans in the United States 7. United States -- Social life and customs -- 20th century. 8. Biographies

On New Year's Eve 1972, following eighteen magnificent seasons in the major leagues, Roberto Clemente died a hero's death, killed in a plane crash as he attempted to deliver food and medical supplies to Nicaragua after a devastating earthquake.

"The author has produced a baseball-savvy book sensitive to the social context that made Clemente, a black Puerto Rican, a leading indicator of baseball's future." New York Times Book Review.

Santiago, Wilfred **"21"** : the story of Roberto Clemente : a graphic novel / Wilfred Santiago. Fantagraphics, 2011. 148 p. : **B**

ISBN 9781560978923

1. Clemente, Roberto, 1934-1972. 2. Professional baseball players 3. Athletes -- Puerto Rico 4. Baseball players -- Puerto Rico 5. Puerto Ricans in the United States 6. Biographies 7. Comics and Graphic novels 8. Biographical comics

LC 2012289663

A graphic tale inspired by the life of baseball star Roberto Clemente includes coverage of a wide range of topics from the ways in which prejudice challenged his career and his personal responsibilities to his achievements with the Pittsburgh Pirates and his triumphant 3,000th hit before his tragic fatal plane crash.

"Santiago skitters around formative scenes from Clemente's childhood--striking a complex chord of family, homeland, and a driving passion for baseball--before tracing significant moments from his professional career: staring down racism with the same resolute demeanor with which he faced a high heater, snagging batting championships and fans' hearts many times over, and always looking for ways to honor his heritage." Booklist.

Clemmons, Francois S.

Clemmons, Francois S. **Officer** Clemmons : more than a song / Francois S. Clemmons. Catapult, 2020. 268 p. : **B**

ISBN 9781948226707

1. Rogers, Fred 2. Mister Rogers' neighborhood (Television program) 3. Television personalities 4. African American men 5. Gay men 6. Spiritual life 7. Autobiographies and memoirs

LC bl2020010609

An intimate debut memoir by the Grammy Award-winning artist who famously played "Officer Clemmons" on Mister Rogers? Neighborhood traces his Oberlin College music studies, his embrace of his sexual orientation and his life-changing chance encounter with Fred Rogers.

"Clemmons's thoroughly delightful, inspiring story will speak particularly to artists in marginalized communities." Publishers Weekly

Cleopatra, Queen of Egypt, 69-30 B.C.

Fletcher, Joann **Cleopatra** the great : the woman behind the legend / Joann Fletcher. Harpercollins, 2011. 320 p. **B**

ISBN 9780060585587

1. Women rulers. 2. Rulers. 3. Leadership in women. 4. Ancient Egypt -- History -- 332-30 B.C. 5. Biographies

LC 2011283067

A world-renowned Egyptologist tells the real story, one that is not obscured by Roman propaganda, Shakespearean tragedy and Hollywood, of the extraordinary woman who realized what was necessary for Egypt's continued prosperity and allowed nothing to stand in her way of achieving it.

★Schiff, Stacy **Cleopatra** / Stacy Schiff. Little, Brown and Co., 2010. 368 p., 16 p. of plates : **B**

ISBN 9780316001922

1. Women rulers 2. Civilization, Ancient. 3. Inheritance and succession 4. Leadership in women 5. Ancient Egypt -- History -- 332-30 B.C. 6. Biographies

LC 2010006988

Separates fact from fiction to reconstruct the life of the most influential woman of her era, revealing Cleopatra as a complex woman and shrewd monarch whose life and death reshaped the ancient world.

"It's dizzying to contemplate the thicket of prejudices, personalities and propaganda Schiff penetrated to reconstruct a woman whose style, ambition and audacity make her a subject worthy of her latest biographer. After all, Stacy Schiff's writing is distinguished by those very same virtues." New York Times Book Review.

Cleveland, Grover, 1837-1908

Graff, Henry F. (Henry Franklin), 1921- **Grover** Cleveland : The American Presidents / Henry F. Graff. Times Books, 2002. xviii, 154 p. : **B**

ISBN 0805069232

1. Cleveland, Grover, 1837-1908. 2. Presidents -- United States 3. Biographies

LC 2002020315

An examination of the political contributions of the nineteenth-century president traces his rags-to-riches personal story and his efforts to restore stature to the office in the wake of several weak administrations.

"This volume is a valuable addition to the literature on the Presidency and is a compelling argument for taking Cleveland seriously as a President." Library Journal.

Cleveland, Pat

Cleveland, Pat **Walking** with the muses : a memoir / Pat Cleveland (with Lorraine Glennon). 37 INK, [2016] 320 p. **B**

ISBN 9781501108228

1. Cleveland, Pat. 2. African American models 3. Fashion -- United States. 4. Fashion designers -- United States. 5. African American women 6. Autobiographies and memoirs

LC 2015041692

An exciting account of the international adventures of fashion model Pat Cleveland--one of the first black supermodels during the wild sixties and seventies.

"Some readers will be particularly interested in her discussion of Bill Cosby, but Cleveland is the real star of her own story of passion, strength, and elegance above all." Publishers Weekly.

Clinton, Bill, 1946-

Branch, Taylor The **Clinton** tapes : wrestling history with the President / Taylor Branch. Simon & Schuster, 2009. x, 707 p., 8 p. of plates : **B**

ISBN 9781416543336

1. Presidents -- United States 2. Politicians. 3. Leadership in men. 4. United States -- Politics and government -- 1993-2001. 5. United States -- History -- 20th century 6. Biographies

LC 2009502213

Recounts the intimate talks the author shared with the forty-second president during the latter's two terms in office, sharing his perspective on Clinton's private torments, family life at the White House, and presidential challenges.

"Not everyone who begins it will finish Branch's book, yet Clinton's remarks . contribute critically to the historical record and accordingly merit a place in most library collections." Booklist.

Clinton, Bill, 1946- **My** life / Bill Clinton. Knopf, 2004.

957, xliii p. : **B**

ISBN 0375414576

1. Clinton, Bill, 1946- Family. 2. Clinton family 3. Clinton, Bill, 1946- Childhood and youth. 4. Presidents -- United States 5. Politicians -- United States 6. Arkansas. 7. Washington, D.C. 8. United States -- Politics and government -- 1993-2001. 9. Autobiographies and memoirs

LC 2004107564

Includes index.

The former president looks back on his life and career, discussing his youth and education, his early public service, his years as governor of Arkansas, and his accomplishments during two terms in the White House.

"Clinton's memoir has the raw material for a blockbuster book." Publishers Weekly.

Clinton, Hillary Rodham

Bernstein, Carl, 1944- A **woman** in charge : the life of Hillary Rodham Clinton / Carl Bernstein. Alfred A. Knopf, 2007. 628 p. : **B**

ISBN 0375407669

1. Clinton, Hillary Rodham Childhood and youth 2. United States. Congress. Senate 3. Presidents' spouses -- United States 4. Legislators -- United States 5. Women legislators -- United States 6. Presidential candidates 7. United States -- Social life and customs -- 21st century 8. Biographies

LC 2007017472

Traces the childhood, college years, and political accomplishments of the controversial 2008 presidential candidate.

"The author offers a three-dimensional portrait of a person with enduring strengths (discipline, tenacity, a sustaining religious faith) and weaknesses (excessive secrecy, a tendency to self-righteousness and a habit of nursing grudges). Bernstein almost always finds new facts and telling details. [His] account benefits enormously from remarkably candid on-the-record assessments of both Clintons by intimates such as close friend Jim Blair and Betsey Wright, Clinton's gubernatorial chief of staff in Arkansas." Los Angeles Times Book Review.

Chozick, Amy **Chasing** Hillary : ten years, two presidential campaigns, and one intact glass ceiling / Amy Chozick. HarperCollins, 2018 352 p. **B**

ISBN 9780062413598

1. Presidential election, 2016 2. Elections 3. Presidential candidates. 4. Political campaigns 5. United States -- Politics and government -- 21st century 6. Biographies

LC bl2018029362

Trailing Hillary Clinton through all of the highs and lows of the most noxious and wildly dramatic presidential election in American history, the author came to understand what drove Clinton, how she accomplished what no woman had before and why she ultimately failed.

Clinton, Hillary Rodham **Hard** choices / Hillary Rodham Clinton. Simon & Schuster, 2014. 688 p. **B**

ISBN 9781476751443

1. Clinton, Hillary Rodham. 2. United States. Congress. Senate 3. Cabinet officers -- United States 4. Women cabinet officers. 5. Presidents' spouses -- United States 6. Women legislators -- United States 7. United States -- Foreign relations -- 2009- 8. Autobiographies and memoirs

LC bl2014013685

The former secretary of state, senator, and first lady shares candid reflections about the key moments of her service in the Obama Administration as well as her thoughts about how to navigate the challenges of the 21st century.

"Hillary Clinton follows the well-trod path of possible presidential candidates: a few years out, write a book. Unlike the authors of a lot of these tomes, Clinton actually has an interesting story to tell, ... Written engagingly (and some will say with calculation), the book also offers Clinton the opportunity to get certain issues out of the way..." Booklist.

Clinton, Hillary Rodham **Living** history / Hillary Rodham Clinton. Simon & Schuster, 2003. xi, 562 p. : **B**

ISBN 0743222245

1. Clinton, Bill, 1946- 2. United States. Congress. Senate 3. Presidents' spouses -- United States 4. Women legislators -- United States 5. Legislators -- United States 6. Politicians -- United States 7. United States -- Politics and government -- 1993-2001. 8. United States -- Politics and government -- 2001-2009 9. Autobiographies and memoirs

LC 2003276264

The author chronicles her eight years as First Lady of the United States, looking back on her husband's two administrations, the challenges she faced during the period, the impeachment crisis, and her own political work.

"This book is important not because of the history Senator Clinton records, but because of the history she doesn't record, and what that airbrushing tells us about the history she aspires to shape." New York Times Book Review.

★Clinton, Hillary Rodham **What** happened / Hillary Rodham Clinton. Simon & Schuster, 2017 352 p. **B**

ISBN 9781501175565

1. Women presidential candidates. 2. Presidential election, 2016 3. Political campaigns. 4. Elections. 5. United States -- Politics and government -- 2017- 6. Essays 7. Biographies.

LC bl2017031097

A book of essays by the former secretary of state includes entries describing her experiences in the 2016 presidential campaign and incorporates hundreds of inspirational quotes that have shaped her life and work.

"Writing in her smart, sometimes self-deprecating voice, Clinton brings much-needed perspective to the election, especially for her millions of supporters, who also want to know what happened and why." Booklist.

D'Antonio, Michael The **hunting** of Hillary : the forty-year campaign to destroy Hillary Clinton / Michael D'Antonio. Thomas Dunne Books, 2020 336 p. **B**

ISBN 9781250154606

1. Clinton, Hillary Rodham. 2. Sexism in politics and government. 3. Misogyny 4. Women politicians -- United States 5. Sexism 6. United States -- Politics and government -- 2009-2017.

LC 2020010750

The Pulitzer Prize-winning journalist and author of A Consequential President explores the right-wing conspiracy that operated for decades to continually discredit Hillary Clinton, sharing insight into the unique opposition she encountered behind the scenes.

"This galvanizing exposé will stand as a key resource in the study of sexism and politics." Booklist

Close, Jessie

Close, Jessie **Resilience** : two sisters and a story of mental illness / Jessie Close with Pete Earley. Grand Central Publishing,

2015. 288 p. **B**
ISBN 9781455548828
1. Close, Jessie. 2. Close, Glenn, 1947- 3. People with mental illnesses -- Family relationships 4. Sisters. 5. Women with bipolar disorder 6. Bipolar disorder 7. Autobiographies and memoirs
LC 2014024743

Featuring chapters by the author's Tony Award-winning sister, Glenn Close, an account of the author's experiences with severe bipolar disorder discusses their parents' membership in the Moral Re-Armament (MRA) cult, her struggles with addiction and her later-in-life diagnosis.

"Closes story alternates with brief corroborative vignettes written by her sister in a belabored and grim memoir that will nonetheless reach its intended audience thanks to the authors famous sister and their shared nonprofit group geared toward mental health, Bring Change 2 Mind." Publishers Weekly.

Coates, Ta-Nehisi

Coates, Ta-Nehisi The **beautiful** struggle : a father, a son, and an unlikely road to manhood / Ta-Nehisi Coates. Spiegel & Grau, 2008. 240 p. **B**
ISBN 0385520360
1. Coates, Ta-Nehisi. 2. African American authors -- Baltimore, Maryland 3. African Americans -- Baltimore, Maryland -- Social conditions. 4. Fathers and sons -- Baltimore, Maryland 5. African American young men -- Family relationships 6. Baltimore, Maryland Social life and customs -- 20th century 7. Autobiographies and memoirs
LC 2007052166

A memoir of growing up in the tough world of Baltimore in the 1980s chronicles the relationship between the author and his father, a Vietnam vet and Black Panther affiliate, and his campaign to keep his sons from falling victim to the temptations of the streets.

Cobain, Kurt, 1967-1994

Cross, Charles R. **Heavier** than heaven : a biography of Kurt Cobain / Charles R. Cross. Hyperion, 2002, c2001. xi, 399 p. : **B**
ISBN 0786884029
1. Cobain, Kurt, 1967-1994. 2. Rock musicians -- United States 3. Biographies
LC BL2002009922
Reprint. Originally published: 2001.

Based on extensive research, more than four hundred interviews, and Kurt Cobain's unpublished diaries, a portrait of the late rock star traces his rise to fame, his relationship with wife Courtney Love, and his tragic suicide.

"Cross followed the Nirvana juggernaut from the beginning, and though he nearly bludgeons the reader with tales of Cobain's debauched excesses, one is still drawn to the artist's foreceful personality." Library Journal.

★Goldberg, Danny, 1950- **Serving** the servant : remembering Kurt Cobain / Danny Goldberg. Ecco, [2019] 294 pages : **B**
ISBN 9780062861504
1. Nirvana (Musical group) 2. Grunge music 3. Suicide 4. Executives 5. Men with depression 6. Autobiographies and memoirs
LC bl2019004131

Published to commemorate the 25th anniversary of Cobain's death, a biographical portrait by Nirvana's music manager shares unique insights into such subjects as the meteoric success of Nevermind, Cobain's marriage to Courtney Love and his industry-changing suicide.

"Goldberg, Nirvana's manager from 1990 to 1994, when their iconic album Nevermind was released, has written a thoughtful and oftentimes revelatory memoir of his relationship with the bands charismatic but troubled leader, Kurt Cobain." Booklist.

Cobb, Ty, 1886-1961

Stump, Al **Cobb** : a biography / Al Stump ; with a foreword by Jimmie Reese. Algonquin Books of Chapel Hill, 1994. xvii, 436 p. : **B**
ISBN 0945575645
1. Cobb, Ty, 1886-1961. 2. Baseball players 3. People with cancer 4. Alcoholic men 5. Family relationships. 6. Biographies
LC 94026122

As a boy in the 1890s, he went looking for thrills in a rural Georgia that still burned with the humiliation of the Civil War. As an old man in the 1960s, he dared death, picked fights, refused to take his medicine, and drove off all his friends and admirers. He went to his deathbed alone, clutching a loaded pistol and a bag containing millions of dollars worth of cash and securities. During the years in between, he was, according to Al Stump, "the most shrewd, inventive, lurid, detested, mysterious, and superb of all baseball players." He was Ty Cobb. Al Stump tells how the dying Cobb hired him in 1960 to ghostwrite his autobiography, giving him a fascinating window into the life and times of the Georgia Peach.

Coetzee, J. M., 1940-

Attwell, David **J. M. Coetzee** and the life of writing : face-to-face with time / David Attwell. Viking Press, 2015. 256 p. **B**
ISBN 9780525429616
1. Authors, South African -- 20th century 2. Nobel Prize winners 3. Authors, Australian -- 20th century 4. Fiction writing. 5. Biographies
LC 2016479778

An authoritative biography of the Nobel Prize-winning author traces the passage from confession to detachment in each of his novels, shedding new light on his personal papers that reveal him to be more autobiographical than readers would have imagined.

Coffin, Jaed

Coffin, Jaed **Roughhouse** Friday : a memoir / Jaed Coffin. Farrar, Straus and Giroux, 2019. 256 p. **B**
ISBN 9780374251956
1. Boxing 2. Fathers and sons 3. Masculinity 4. Identity (Psychology) 5. Alaska 6. Autobiographies and memoirs
LC 2018045292

While lifting weights in the Seldon Jackson College gymnasium on a rainy autumn night, Jaed Coffin heard the distinctive whacking sound of sparring boxers down the hall. That evening, Coffin joined a ragtag boxing club. Deeply honest and vulnerable, Roughhouse Friday is a meditation on violence and abandonment, masculinity, and our inescapable longing for love. It suggests that sometimes the truth of what's inside you comes only if you push yourself to the extreme.

"Coffins lyrical account of his eventful initiation into the world of amateur boxing takes readers to southeast Alaska. This is a powerful, wonderfully written exploration of ones sense of manhood." Publishers Weekly.

Cohen, Leonard, 1934-2016

Cohen, Leonard, 1934-2016 **Leonard** Cohen on Leonard Cohen : interviews and encounters / edited by Jeff Burger. Chicago Review Press, 2014. 608 p. **B**
ISBN 9781613747582
1. Cohen, Leonard, 1934-2016 Interviews. 2. Poets, Canadian -- 20th century -- Interviews. 3. Singers -- Canada -- Interviews. 4.

Composers -- Canada -- Interviews. 5. Autobiographies and memoirs

LC 2013034568

Includes index.Canadian singer, songwriter and poet, Leonard Cohen, tells his story using more then fifty interviews conducted world wide between 1966 and 2012.

"Burger's discerning editorial hand selects those conversations with Cohen that offer insights into his music." Publishers Weekly.

★Simmons, Sylvie **I'm** your man : the life of Leonard Cohen / Sylvie Simmons. Ecco Press, 2012. 384 p. **B**

ISBN 9780061994982

1. Songwriters 2. Musicians 3. Men/women relations 4. Buddhism 5. Biographies

LC 2013560061

Exploring the many facets of Cohen's life, this intimate portrait of one of the most important and influential songwriters of our time draws upon his private archives and a wealth of interviews with many of his closest associates, colleagues and other artists whose work he has inspired.

Cohen, Rich

Cohen, Rich **Sweet** and low : a family story / Rich Cohen. Farrar, Straus and Giroux, 2006. 272 p. **B**

ISBN 9780374272296

1. Eisenstadt family. 2. Eisenstadt, Benjamin Family. 3. Cohen family. 4. Cohen, Rich Family 5. Cumberland Packing Corporation. 6. Sweet 'N Low (Trademark) 7. Businesspeople -- United States 8. Brooklyn Bridge, New York City 9. Biographies

LC 2005015730

Traces the story of the creator of the sugar packet and Sweet'N Low, documenting how he converted his Brooklyn cafeteria into a factory and amassed a considerable fortune that would eventually destroy his family, in a portrait that places his life against a backdrop of post-World War II immigration and the late-twentieth century's health and diet craze.

Cohen, Richard M. (Richard Martin), 1941-

Cohen, Richard M. (Richard Martin), 1941- **Israel** : is it good for the Jews? Can it survive? / Richard Cohen. Simon & Schuster, 2014. 336 p. **B**

ISBN 9781416575689

1. Jewish Americans 2. Jews -- History. 3. Zionism. 4. Growing up 5. Israel 6. Autobiographies and memoirs

LC 2014021062

Part reportage, part memoir, a nationally syndicated columnist for The Washington Post since 1976 takes readers on a intimate journey through the history of Europe's Jews, while delving into his own Jewish history and sharing stories of his own relatives and his American boyhood.

"A thoughtful study recommended for both general and academic readers of history." Library Journal.

Cole, Nat King, 1919-1965

Friedwald, Will, 1961- **Straighten** up and fly right : the life and music of Nat King Cole / Will Friedwald. Oxford University Press, 2020. 560 p. **B**

ISBN 9780190882044

1. Cole, Nat King, 1919-1965. 2. Jazz musicians 3. Pianists 4. Jazz music 5. African American musicians 6. Biographies

LC 2019049935

"One of the most popular and memorable American musicians of the 20th century, Nat King Cole (1919-65) is remembered today as both a pianist and a singer, a feat rarely accomplished in the world of popular music. Now, in this complete life and times biography, author Will Friedwald offers a new take on this fascinating musician, framing him first as a bandleader and then as a star. "-- Provided by publisher.

"Though needlessly exaggerating its subject's considerable accomplishments and sometimes mired in details, this well-researched, comprehensive work should became a standard biography along with Daniel Mark Epstein's Nat King Cole." Library Journal

Cole, Natalie, 1950-

Cole, Natalie, 1950- **Angel** on my shoulder : an autobiography / Natalie Cole ; written with Digby Diehl. Warner Books, 2000. ix, 353 p. : **B**

ISBN 0446527467

1. Singers -- United States 2. Women singers. 3. Faith in women. 4. Fathers and daughters. 5. Autobiographies and memoirs

LC 00061455

The singer shares her tale of trijmph over drugs, depression, divorce, and all the worst celebrity can bring.

"Although she concentrates mostly on the good times, Cole isn't shy about the bad times, which makes this intriguing, engaging, and inspirational life story worthy of attention." Booklist.

Colletti, Ned

★Colletti, Ned The **Big** Chair : the smooth hops and bad bounces from the inside world of the acclaimed Los Angeles Dodgers general manager / Ned Colletti, with Joseph A. Reaves. G.P. Putnam's Sons, [2017] 436 p. **B**

ISBN 9780735215726

1. Colletti, Ned. 2. Los Angeles Dodgers (Baseball team) 3. Major League Baseball (Organization) 4. Baseball 5. Professional baseball players 6. Sports -- Management 7. Baseball general managers 8. Autobiographies and memoirs

LC 2017021965

An unprecedented, behind-the-scenes look at the career of famed former Los Angeles Dodgers General Manager (a position also known as "The Big Chair"), whose tenure spanned nine of the most exciting and turbulent years in the franchise's history.

Collins, Judy, 1939-

Collins, Judy, 1939- **Cravings** : how I conquered food : a memoir / Judy Collins. Nan A. Talese, 2017. 288 p. **B**

ISBN 9780385541312

1. Collins, Judy, 1939- Health. 2. Compulsive eating. 3. Overeating. 4. Eating disorders. 5. People with bulimia. 6. Autobiographies and memoirs

LC 2016009368

The platinum-selling folk music artist reveals her lifelong struggle with compulsive eating, describing how after decades of suffering she discovered her addiction to unhealthy ingredients and how embracing a strict diet of careful portions and unprocessed foods has restored her health and sense of wellness.

Collins, Lauren (Journalist)

Collins, Lauren (Journalist) **When** in French : love in a second language / Lauren Collins. Penguin Press, 2016. 256 p. **B**

ISBN 9781594206443

1. Women journalists 2. French language 3. Husband and wife 4. American women in foreign countries 5. Geneva, Switzerland 6. France -- Social life and customs. 7. Autobiographies and memoirs

LC 2016017611

An Anglophone American in London falls in love with a Frenchman and moves to Francophone Geneva, Switzerland. Once there, she decides to learn French; not only does she want to be able to buy things, but she wants to become closer to her new husband and, when the time comes, not be "a Borat of a mother." Chronicling her amusing adventures overseas and her attempts to communicate in a new tongue, talented New Yorker writer Lauren Collins serves up a funny, romantic, intelligent memoir.

"Throughout, the author ably weaves together the personal and the historical. A memoir filled with pleasing passages in every chapter." Kirkus.

Colon, Fernando, 1488-1539

★Wilson-Lee, Edward The **catalogue** of shipwrecked books : Christopher Columbus, his son, and the quest to build the world's greatest library / Edward Wilson-Lee. Scribner, 2019 384 p. **B**

ISBN 9781982111397

1. Columbus, Christopher, 1451-1506 2. Libraries 3. Exploration -- History. 4. Books and reading 5. Archives 6. Western Hemisphere -- Exploration. 7. Biographies

LC 2019934427

Shortlisted for the James Tait Black Memorial Prize for Biography, 2018

A vividly rendered account of the lesser-known quest by Christopher Columbus' illegitimate son, Hernando, to create a multicultural library details his world travels to collect thousands of books.

"An elegantly written, absorbing portrait of a visionary man and his age." Kirkus.

Colonna, Vittoria, 1492-1547

Targoff, Ramie **Renaissance** woman : the life of Vittoria Colonna / Ramie Targoff. Farrar, Straus and Giroux, 2018. 304 p. **B**

ISBN 9780374140946

1. Poets 2. Women poets 3. Authors, Italian 4. Women's role 5. Biographies

LC 2017036978

Describes the story of Vittoria Colonna, Marches of Pescara, the daughter of an incredibly powerful family who became a critical political activist and negotiator, was the first woman to publish a book of poems in Italy and was the best friend of Michelangelo.

Colt, Samuel, 1814-1862

Rasenberger, Jim **Revolver** : Sam Colt and the six-shooter that changed America / Jim Rasenberger. Scribner, 2020 x, 436 p. : **B**

ISBN 9781501166389

1. Colt revolver -- History 2. Guns 3. Gunsmiths 4. Industrialists -- United States 5. Biographies

LC bl2020013073

A sweeping portrait of the inventor of the legendary Colt revolver shares engaging insights into the role of the six-shooter in triggering the industrial revolution and the resettlement of the American West.

"This rollicking and informative account will delight American history buffs." Publishers Weekly

Coltrane, John, 1926-1967

Ratliff, Ben **Coltrane** : the story of a sound / Ben Ratliff. Farrar, Straus and Giroux, 2007. 272 p. **B**

ISBN 0374126062

1. Coltrane, John, 1926-1967. 2. Jazz musicians 3. Saxophonists -- United States 4. Jazz music. 5. United States -- Social life and customs. 6. Biographies

LC 2007004362

A study of jazz saxophonist John Coltrane and his musical development looks for the sources of power in Coltrane's music and examines his important influence and legacy in shaping the course of modern jazz music.

"This is an engaging study of the jazz saxophonist's artistic influence. . . . Ratliff patiently explicates Coltrane's legend, writing in short, aphoristic bursts, often as elliptically as his subject played tenor saxophone, but never less than lucidly. " New York Times Book Review.

Columbus, Christopher, 1451-1506

Morison, Samuel Eliot, 1887-1976 **Admiral** of the ocean sea : a life of Christopher Columbus / Samuel Eliot Morison ; maps by Erwin Raisz ; drawings by Bertram Greene. Little, Brown, 1991, c1942. xx, 680 p. : **B**

ISBN 9780316584784

1. Explorers -- Spain 2. Exploration -- History. 3. Western Hemisphere -- Exploration. 4. Biographies

Originally published: Boston, MA : Little, Brown, 1942.

Pulitzer Prize for Biography or Autobiography, 1943.

Admiral of the Ocean Sea is Samuel Eliot Morison's biography of the greatest sailor of them all, Christopher Columbus. It is written with the insight, energy, and authority that only someone who had himself sailed in Columbus's path to the New World could muster. Morison undertook this expedition in a 147-foot schooner and a 47-foot ketch, the dimensions of these craft roughly matching those of Columbus's Santa Maria and Niña. The result is this biography, detailing the voyages that, for better or worse, changed the world.

"An authoritative biography of Columbus which is also decidedly original in its emphasis on the ability of Columbus as seaman and navigator and in the amount of space given to tracing the routes of the voyages and landings." Library Journal.

Colvin, Marie

★Hilsum, Lindsey **In** extremis : the life and death of the war correspondent Marie Colvin / Lindsey Hilsum. Farrar, Straus and Giroux, 2018. 400 p. **B**

ISBN 9780374175597

1. War correspondents 2. Foreign correspondents 3. Journalists 4. Women war correspondents 5. Biographies

LC 2018022908

Includes index."Originally published in 2018 by Chatto & Windus, Great Britain."

James Tait Black Memorial Prize for Biography, 2018

Describes the life and tragic death of the accomplished war correspondent, who lost an eye reporting in Sri Lanka during its civil war, interviewed Gaddafi twice, and covered conflicts in Chechnya, Kosovo and Zimbabwe in her fearless and iconoclastic style.

"Hilsum has created something truly worthy of her subject, a biography that reads like high adventure, a masterwork that will draw well-deserved attention to a heroic witness." Booklist.

Colwell, Rita R., 1934-

Colwell, Rita R., 1934- A **lab** of one's own : one woman's personal journey through sexism in science / Rita Colwell and Sharon Bertsch McGrayne. Simon & Schuster, 2020 288 p. **B**

ISBN 9781501181276

1. Women scientists 2. Sex discrimination 3. Women microbiologists 4. Sexual harassment 5. Autobiographies and memoirs

LC bl2020017518

A Lab of One's Own shares the sheer joy a scientist feels when moving toward a breakthrough, and the thrill of uncovering a whole new generation of female pioneers. But it is also the science book for the

#MeToo era, offering an astute diagnosis of how to fix the problem of sexism in science and a celebration of the women pushing back.

"In this beautifully written memoir, Colwell, a leading microbiologist whose many accolades include being the first female director of the National Science Foundation, exposes 'a deep-seated bias against women in science [that] has been documented at almost every level, from Nobel Prize winners down to undergraduates.'... An unforgettable tell-all that's rife with details of insurrection, scientific breakthrough, and overcoming the odds." Kirkus

Comey, James B., Jr., 1960-

Comey, James B., Jr., 1960- A **higher** loyalty : truth, lies and leadership / James Comey. Flatiron Books, 2018. 416 p. **B**

ISBN 9781250192455

1. FBI 2. Leadership 3. Criminal investigation 4. Presidential elections 5. Organized crime 6. United States -- Politics and government -- 2009-2017. 7. Autobiographies and memoirs 8. Books to TV

LC bl2018012238

This book was adapted in 2020 to a TV miniseries under the title, The Comey rule, starring Jeff Daniels and Brendan Gleeson.The former FBI director shares his experiences over the past two decades working in the American government and explores ethical leadership and how it drives sound decision-making.

Common (Musician)

Common (Musician) **One** day it'll all make sense : a memoir / Common with Adam Bradley. Atria Books, c2011. 256 p. **B**

ISBN 9781451625875

1. Rap musicians -- United States 2. Childhood -- Chicago, Illinois 3. Family relationships 4. Acting 5. United States -- Social life and customs -- 20th century 6. United States -- Social life and customs -- 21st century 7. Autobiographies and memoirs

LC 2011021691

Street Lit Book Award Medal: Adult Non-Fiction, 2012The Grammy Award-winning recording artist, actor and friend to President Obama shares the story of his life, from his youth on Chicago's South side and rise in the hip-hop industry to his performances in such movies as Just Wright and the lessons he has learned as a son and a father.

Conant, James, 1893-1978

Conant, Jennet **Man** of the hour : James B. Conant, warrior scientist / Jennet Conant. Simon & Schuster, 2017. 416 p. **B**

ISBN 9781476730882

1. Manhattan Project (U.S.) 2. Scientists 3. Atomic bomb 4. Educators 5. Technology and war 6. United States -- History -- 20th century 7. Biographies

LC 2017033241

A portrait of the wartime scientist, Harvard University president and presidential advisor, written by his granddaughter, places his life against a backdrop of key historical events to offer particular insights into his oversight of the Manhattan Project and subsequent campaigns in support of atomic weapon control at the international level.

"Including frank portrayals of family situations and problems, Jennet Conants capable, informative portrait should be included in collections about the history of American science." Booklist.

Cone, David, 1963-

Cone, David, 1963- **Full** count : the education of a pitcher / David Cone and Jack Curry. Grand Central Pub 2019 320 p. **B**

ISBN 9781538748848

1. Professional baseball players 2. Baseball players -- United States 3. Pitchers (Baseball) 4. Baseball. 5. United States -- Social life and customs -- 20th century 6. Autobiographies and memoirs

LC bl2019008196

A Mets and Yankees All-Star pitcher shares lessons from the World Series and beyond in this essential memoir for baseball fans everywhere.

"For baseball fans, especially those who remember Cone's career, this is a must-read. While younger audiences may not recall Cole's significant role in the Yankees dynasty or even his perfect game, anyone wishing to learn what made him a successful pitcher will find this a rewarding read." Library Journal.

Connell, John, 1986-

Connell, John, 1986- The **farmer's** son : calving season on a family farm / John Connell. Houghton Mifflin Harcourt, 2019. 256 p. **B**

ISBN 9781328577993

1. Farm life 2. Family relationships 3. Cattle 4. Family farms 5. Ireland 6. Autobiographies and memoirs

LC 2018042556

First published, titled "The cow book : a story of life on an Irish family farm", in Great Britain by Granta Books, 2018.

Traces a calving season on the author's family farm in Ireland, where, after a decade's absence, he found hope and healing in his family, routines, faith, and community.

Connors, Philip

Connors, Philip **Fire** season : field notes from a wilderness lookout / Philip Connors. Ecco, 2011. 246 p. **B**

ISBN 9780061859366

1. Connors, Philip. 2. Fire lookouts. 3. Fire lookout stations. 4. Wilderness areas. 5. Men and nature. 6. Gila National Forest 7. New Mexico

LC bl2011005835

National Outdoor Book Award for Outdoor Literature, 2011.

The author discusses his time spent 10,000 feet above ground as a fire lookout in a remote part of New Mexico, a job where he witnessed some of the most amazing phenomena nature has to offer.

Connors, Philip A **song** for the river / Philip Connors. Cinco Puntos Press, [2018] 246 p. **B**

ISBN 9781941026908

1. Connors, Philip. 2. Wildfires. 3. Outdoor life. 4. Grief. 5. Loss (Psychology) 6. Gila National Forest. 7. New Mexico. 8. The West (United States) 9. Autobiographies and memoirs.

LC 2017057947

In a follow-up to the award-winning Fire Season, the author, interweaving colorful characters and beautiful evocations of the landscape, makes a plea to save the Gila Wilderness of New Mexico--a vital piece of our national and cultural heritage.

"This slim but potent volume of essays from Connors (Fire Season) beautifully examines themes of fire and water, life and death, and wonder and grief in the Gila Wilderness of New Mexico." Publishers Weekly.

Conroy, Pat

Conroy, Pat A **lowcountry** heart : reflections on a writing life / Pat Conroy. Nan A. Talese, 2016 304 p. **B**

ISBN 9780385530866

1. Authors, American 2. Writing 3. Friendship 4. Autobiographies and memoirs 5. Essays

LC 2016026695

A collection of letters, interviews and magazine articles spanning The Prince of Tides author's long literary career is supplemented by touching pieces from the beloved author's many friends.

Conroy, Pat **My** losing season / Pat Conroy. Nan A. Talese, 2002. 402 p. ; **B**

ISBN 0385489129

1. Citadel, the Military College of South Carolina. 2. Failure (Psychology) 3. Basketball players. 4. Authors, American -- 20th century 5. College sports. 6. Charleston, South Carolina 7. Autobiographies and memoirs

LC 2002066212

The author reflects on the place of sports in his own life, describing his love of basketball, the role of the athlete for young men searching for their own identity and place in the world, his education at the Citadel, his relationship with his coach, and his journey to best-selling writer.

"A wonderfully rich, informative, and well-researched reminiscence." Library Journal.

Conway, Jill K., 1934-2018

Conway, Jill K., 1934-2018 **True** north : a memoir / Jill Ker Conway. Alfred A. Knopf, 1994. xiii, 250 p. ; **B**

ISBN 9780679420996

1. Smith College Presidents 2. Australians in the United States 3. Women historians 4. Women scholars and academics 5. Feminists. 6. Autobiographies and memoirs

LC 93045302

The author recalls her arrival in the United States from Australia, her years at Harvard, marriage, and career in Toronto, and her acceptance of the presidency of Smith College

Cook, James, 1728-1779

Hough, Richard Alexander, 1922-1999 **Captain** James Cook / Richard Hough. W.W. Norton & Co., 1995, c1994. xviii, 398 p., [16] p. of plates : **B**

ISBN 9780393036800

1. Cook, James, 1728-1779. 2. Explorers -- Great Britain 3. Biographies

LC 2002113757

Originally published: London : Hodder & Stoughton, 1994.

Traces the life of the British explorer, recounts how he rose from the lowest ranks of the merchant marine, and describes his voyages to North America, the North and South Pacific, the Arctic, and the Antarctic.

"Hough's easygoing, thorough treatment ... spotlights a proud, determined man." Booklist.

Cooke, Sam

★Guralnick, Peter **Dream** boogie : the triumph of Sam Cooke / Peter Guralnick. Little, Brown, 2005. xv, 750 p. : **B**

ISBN 0316377945

1. Cooke, Sam. 2. Soul musicians. 3. African American gospel singers 4. Rhythm and blues musicians 5. African American sound recording executives and producers 6. Biographies

LC 2005000077

"For those who only know the singer through his pop hitsYou Send Me; Twistin' the Night Awaythe extensive account of his childhood background in gospel music will prove fascinating, and the evocation of the harsh realities faced by African-American musicians touring the South a powerful reminder of just how explosive this music could be." Publishers Weekly.

Coolidge, Calvin, 1872-1933

Shlaes, Amity **Coolidge** / Amity Shlaes. HarperCollins, 2012. 480 p. **B**

ISBN 9780061967559

1. Coolidge, Calvin, 1872-1933. 2. Public opinion. 3. Presidents -- United States 4. Popularity. 5. Prosperity. 6. Washington, D.C. -- History -- 20th century. 7. New England -- History -- 20th century. 8. Biographies

LC 2012032098

Examines America's thirtieth president, revealing a man who restored national trust in government, lived by example, suffered great tragedy, emphasized the importance of presidential humility, and inspired optimism.

Cooper, Alex, 1994-

Cooper, Alex, 1994- **Saving** Alex : when I was fifteen I told my Mormon parents I was gay, and that's when my nightmare began / Alex Cooper and Joanna Brooks HarperOne, 2016. 304 p. **B**

ISBN 9780062374608

1. Mormons 2. Lesbian teenagers 3. Abused women 4. Lesbians 5. Utah 6. Autobiographies and memoirs

LC 2015031520

After 15-year-old Alex Cooper told her Mormon parents she was a lesbian, they sent her to a family in Utah who promised to reorient her to "normal" sexuality. Using a combination of physical and emotional torture and intensive lessons in Mormon orthodoxy, they abused her for eight months until she contacted closeted gay people in the community, who helped her obtain legal assistance. In this troubling but inspiring memoir, Cooper relates how she persevered in seeking the right to make her own choices while striving to maintain her personal sense of faith.

"Alex's horrifying story is one that needs to be heard, and her book is an eloquent testament to that. It is encouraging proof that, as Alex is told, things do get better." Booklist.

Cooper, Anderson

Cooper, Anderson The **rainbow** comes and goes : a mother and son talk about life, love, and loss / Anderson Cooper and Gloria Vanderbilt. HarperCollins Publishers, 2016. 224 p. **B**

ISBN 9780062454942

1. Cooper, Anderson. 2. Vanderbilt, Gloria, 1924-2019 3. Television journalists -- United States 4. Celebrities -- United States 5. Mothers and sons -- United States -- Correspondence. 6. Aging 7. Letters

LC 2016000369

A poignant correspondence between the CNN journalist and his iconic designer mother, exchanged in the aftermath of the latter's brief illness, shares a rare window into their relationship and the life lessons imparted by an aging mother to her adult son.

"Vanderbilt and her son, Cooper, relate the touching story of how an epistolary exchange created new emotional intimacy between them." Publishers Weekly.

Cooper, Brittney C., 1980-

Cooper, Brittney C., 1980- **Eloquent** rage : a black feminist discovers her superpower / Brittney Cooper. St. Martin's Press, 2018. 288 p. **B**

ISBN 9781250112576

1. African American feminists. 2. Feminism. 3. Intersectionality 4. Autobiographies and memoirs

LC 2017036275

Finalist for the Hurston/Wright Legacy Awards for Nonfiction, 2019.

A leading young black feminist illuminates how organized anger, friendship and faith can be powerful sources of positive feminist change, explaining how targeted rage has shaped the careers of such African-American notables as Serena Williams, Beyoncé and Michelle Obama.

"Deftly blending the conversational tone of a memoir with pointed critique, Cooper offers a comprehensive and accessible analysis of topics from the Bible to pop music to U.S. politics past and present." Library Journal.

Cooper, Elisha

Cooper, Elisha **Falling** : a daughter, a father, and a journey back / Elisha Cooper. Pantheon, 2016. 192 p. **B**

ISBN 9781101871232

1. Cooper, Elisha. 2. Authors, American. 3. Fathers and daughters. 4. Parents of children with cancer 5. Illustrators. 6. Autobiographies and memoirs

LC 2015042319

An award-winning children's book author is forced to confront a whole new world after he discovers a lump in his 5-year-old daughter's midsection that changes everything and forces him to balance his desire to be a protective parent against the increasing helplessness he feels for his child's wellbeing--and his own.

"The children's book author shows masterful control in this memoir of a life careening beyond his control." Kirkus.

Cooper, Gary, 1901-1961

Thomson, David, 1941- **Gary** Cooper / David Thomson ; photo reseach by Lucy Gray. Faber and Faber, 2010. 129 p. : **B**

ISBN 9780865479326

1. Cooper, Gary, 1901-1961. 2. Film actors and actresses -- United States 3. Actors and actresses -- United States 4. Film industry and trade 5. Hollywood, California -- History. 6. Biographies

LC 2009041759

"Originally published in 2009 by Penguin Books, Great Britain"--T.p. verso."

In this biography of the actor, Cooper is presented as a hapless, weak-willed adulterer whose lean body, rugged handsomeness and preternatural stillness translated on camera as a quintessentially American rectitude and heroic stoicism. Thomson is wickedly funny and startlingly poetic in his observations." Kirkus.

Cooper, Gwen, 1971-

Cooper, Gwen, 1971- **Homer's** odyssey : a fearless feline tale, or how I learned about love and life with a blind wonder cat / Gwen Cooper. Delacorte Press, 2009. 304 p. **B**

ISBN 9780385343855

1. Women and cats. 2. Blind cats. 3. Human/animal relationships 4. Autobiographies and memoirs

LC 2009017602

"This tender and affecting book reveals Homer's lessons about love and acceptanceand how he transformed Cooper into the woman she had always wanted to be." Publishers Weekly.

Cooper, Helene

Cooper, Helene The **house** at Sugar Beach : a memoir / Helene Cooper. Simon & Schuster, 2008. 320 p. **B**

ISBN 0743266242

1. Cooper, Helene. 2. Liberia -- Politics and government. 3. Liberia -- History. 4. Autobiographies and memoirs

LC 2008277249

National Book Critics Circle Award for Autobiography/ Memoir finalist

The author traces her childhood in war-torn Liberia and her reunion with a foster sister who had been left behind when her family fled the region.

"A coming-of-age story told with unremitting honesty. With her pedigree and her freedom from internalized racism, Cooper is liberated to enjoy a social universe that is a fluid mix of all things American and African. . . . While Cooper's memoir is mesmerizing in its portrayal of a Liberia rarely witnessed, its description of the psychological devastationand coping mechanismsbrought on by profound loss is equally captivating. " New York Times Book Review.

Cooper, James Fenimore, 1789-1851

Franklin, Wayne **James** Fenimore Cooper : the early years / Wayne Franklin. Yale University Press, 2007. xxxiv, 708 p., 16 p. of plates : **B**

ISBN 0300108052

1. Cooper, James Fenimore, 1789-1851. 2. Cooper, James Fenimore, 1789-1851 Childhood and youth. 3. Authors, American -- 19th century 4. Biographies

LC 2006031247

"Published with assistance from the Louis Stern Memorial Fund"--T.p. verso."

This volume profoundly enriches our understanding of how the young writer helped forge our national mythology in works such as The Last of The Mohicans and The Pioneers." Booklist.

Cope, Alan Ingram, 1925-1999

Guibert, Emmanuel **Alan's** war : the memories of G.I. Alan Cope / Emmanuel Guibert ; translation, Kathryn Pulver ; lettering, Celine Merrien. First Second, 2008. 304 p. : **B**

ISBN 9781596430969

1. United States. Army 2. World War II 3. Military campaigns 4. Soldiers -- United States 5. Europe 6. France -- Social life and customs. 7. Comics and Graphic novels 8. Biographical comics 9. Biographies 10. Biographical comics

LC 2007046190

Translated from the French: Guerre d'Alan.

A graphic-novel biography presents the life of Alan Cope, an American World War II veteran, from being drafted at eighteen, through his war-time experiences, to his decision to return to France after the war was over.

"This is a poignant and frank graphic memoir of young soldier who was told to serve his country in WWII and how it changed him forever. . . . Cope and Guibert forge a story that resonates with humanity." Publishers Weekly.

Copeland, Misty

Copeland, Misty **Life** in motion : an unlikely ballerina / Misty Copeland. Touchstone Books, 2014 288 p. **B**

ISBN 9781476737980

1. American Ballet Theatre. 2. Ballet 3. Ballet dancers -- United States 4. Women ballet dancers. 5. African American ballet dancers. 6. Autobiographies and memoirs

LC 2014002922

Documents the author's emotionally dynamic effort to become the third African-American soloist in the history of the American Ballet Theatre, describing the harsh family difficulties she overcame including her mother's highly publicized custody battle to halt her career.

"Her story is an inspiration to anyone--man or woman, black or white--who has ever chased a dream against the odds, and the grace with which she triumphs is an example for us all." Booklist.

Copernicus, Nicolaus, 1473-1543

Sobel, Dava A **more** perfect heaven : how Copernicus revolutionized the cosmos / Dava Sobel. Walker Pub., 2011. 272 p. **B**

ISBN 9780802717931

1. Copernicus, Nicolaus, 1473-1543 Influence. 2. Copernicus,

Nicolaus, 1473-1543. De revolutionibus orbium caelestium. 3. Rhaticus, Georg Joachim, 1514-1576. 4. Astronomy. 5. Astronomers. 6. Mathematicians. 7. Solar system. 8. Varnia, Poland. 9. Biographies
LC 2011024772

The best-selling author of Galileo's Daughter traces the story of the reclusive 16th-century cleric who introduced the revolutionary idea that the Earth orbits the sun, in an account that describes the dangerous forces and complicated personalities that marked the publication of Copernicus's findings.

Vollmann, William T. **Uncentering** the Earth : Copernicus and the revolutions of the heavenly spheres / William T. Vollmann. Norton, c2006. 295 p. : **B**

ISBN 0393059693

1. Copernicus, Nicolaus, 1473-1543. 2. Astronomy -- Early works to 1800 3. Orbits. 4. Astronomers. 5. Solar system.
LC 2005025864

"Atlas books."

An analysis of the astronomer's pivotal sixteenth-century work traces how his challenge to beliefs about an Earth-centric solar system had a profound influence on the ways in which humanity understands itself and the universe.

"Readers who want to understand the significance of Copernicus's book in both his own time and ours will find this the next best thing to reading it." Publishers Weekly.

Copley, John Singleton, 1738-1815

Kamensky, Jane A **revolution** in color : the world of John Singleton Copley / Jane Kamensky. W.W. Norton & Company, 2016. 352 p. **B**

ISBN 9780393240016

1. Copley, John Singleton, 1738-1815. 2. Painters. 3. Artists 4. Intellectual life -- United States -- 19th century 5. Loyalists (United States history) 6. United States -- History -- Revolution, 1775-1783 -- Social aspects. 7. Biographies
LC 2016019022

American History Book Prize, 2016.

Looks at the American Revolution as seen through the eyes of Boston-born painter John Singleton Copley.

"There may never be a better biography of Copley than this sumptuous, exquisitely told story of a man and his time." Kirkus.

Corrigan, Kelly, 1967-

Corrigan, Kelly, 1967- **Glitter** and glue : a memoir / Kelly Corrigan. Ballantine Books, 2014. 240 p. **B**

ISBN 9780345532831

1. Mothers and daughters 2. Consolation 3. Motherhood 4. Nannies 5. Australia 6. Autobiographies and memoirs
LC 2013041936

Presents an account of the author's perspectives on motherhood, which have been shaped by her job as a nanny for a grieving Australian family and her character-testing experiences with her daughters.

"Written in a breezy style with humor and heart, the book reminds us how rewarding it can be to see a parent outside the context of our own needs." Kirkus.

Corrigan, Kelly, 1967- The **middle** place / Kelly Corrigan. Voice/Hyperion, 2007. 272 p. **B**

ISBN 1401303366

1. Family relationships 2. People with breast cancer 3. Motherhood 4. Breast cancer. 5. Philadelphia, Pennsylvania. 6. San Francisco, California. 7. Autobiographies and memoirs
LC 2007015316

Traces a San Francisco newspaper columnist's life experiences as evaluated during her late thirties, describing her relationships with her husband, children, and Irish-American father before and during her battle with breast cancer.

"Corrigan's story could have been unbearably depressing had she not made it clear from the start that she came from sturdy stock. Those learning to accept their own adulthood might find strength--and humor--in Corrigan's feisty memoir." Publishers Weekly.

Corrigan, Kelly, 1967- **Tell** me more : stories about the 12 hardest things I'm learning to say / Kelly Corrigan. Random House, 2018. 240 p. **B**

ISBN 9780399588372

1. Interpersonal communication. 2. Conversation. 3. Interpersonal relations. 4. Personal conduct. 5. Autobiographies and memoirs
LC bl2017045653

The best-selling author of Glitter and Glue assesses seven phrases that can lead to more qualitative adult lives, sharing poignant and whimsical stories of growth surrounding such expressions as "I don't know," "You got this" and "I was wrong."

"Moving and deeply personal, Corrigan's portraits of love and loss urge readers to speak more carefully and hold on tighter to the people they love." Kirkus.

Coscarelli, Don

Coscarelli, Don **True** indie : life and death in filmmaking / Don Coscarelli. St. Martin's Press, 2018. 352 p. **B**

ISBN 9781250193247

1. Film producers and directors 2. Independent filmmakers 3. Horror films 4. Cult films 5. Autobiographies and memoirs
LC 2018022134

The award-winning creator of Phantasm and other cult classics describes how he set a record upon selling his first feature film at age 19, an achievement that launched his haphazard journey of celebrity encounters and battles over creative control.

"Not just a fine life story, this is also one of the best books youll ever read about indie filmmaking." Booklist.

Cosell, Howard, 1918-1995

Ribowsky, Mark **Howard** Cosell : the man, the myth, and the transformation of American sports / Mark Ribowsky. W.W. Norton & Co., c2012. 496 p. **B**

ISBN 9780393080179

1. Cosell, Howard, 1918-1995. 2. Sportscasters -- United States 3. Sports -- History 4. United States -- Social life and customs -- 20th century. 5. Biographies
LC 2011027501

Describes the life of one of the most recognizable, colorful figures in American sports history and offers a behind-the-scenes look at Monday Night Football and the commercialization of sports based on more than forty interviews with colleagues and athletes.

"The sportscaster Howard Cosell erupted onto the national stage in the 1960s and quickly became a pop-culture icon. His raspy, heavily New York-accented voice, a sharp mind, an expansive vocabulary and a photographic memory were packaged into a larger-than-life and sometimes abrasive figure. Whether his audience loved him, hated him or loved to hate him, they tuned in, and he turned them on. He was impossible to ignore. Mr. Ribowsky's book is an entertaining read and a thought-provoking portrayal of the multifaceted Howard Cosell in all his glory and enmity. It is based on voluminous, well-sourced research into print and electronic material, coupled with numerous interviews with Cosell's contemporaries." Wall Street Journal.

Costello, Elvis

Costello, Elvis **Unfaithful** music & disappearing ink / Elvis Costello. Blue Rider Press, 2015. 674 p. : **B**

ISBN 9780399167256

1. Costello, Elvis. 2. Rock musicians -- England 3. Rock music 4. Fame 5. Musicians 6. Autobiographies and memoirs

LC 2015032865

A personal introspective by the influential pop songwriter and performer traces his Liverpool upbringing, artistic influences, creative pursuit of original punk sounds and emergence in the MTV world.

"Costello comes across as the perennial outsider, as someone who is surprised that he has been invited to the party. A must for Costello fans everywhere." Booklist.

Cote, Andrew

Cote, Andrew **Honey** and venom : confessions of an urban beekeeper / Andrew Cote. Ballantine Books, 2020 256 p. **B**

ISBN 9781524799045

1. Cote, Andrew. 2. Honeybee. 3. Beekeeping 4. Urban beekeeping -- New York City 5. Honeybee -- Effect of human beings on 6. New York City 7. Autobiographies and memoirs

LC bl2020013709

A fourth-generation beekeeper describes the work of the Bees Without Borders organization, the quirky personalities he has encountered throughout his career and the remarkable apiaries he maintains on iconic buildings throughout New York City.

"Honey and Venom is best read as a memoir--and a sweet one at that." Booklist

Cousteau, Jacques Yves

Cousteau, Jacques Yves The **human,** the orchid, and the octopus : exploring and conserving our natural world / Jacques Cousteau and Susan Schiefelbein. Bloomsbury USA : c2007. 320 p. **B**

ISBN 1596914173

1. Cousteau, Jacques Yves. 2. Oceanographers -- France. 3. Nature conservation. 4. Nature -- Effect of humans on 5. Nature.

LC 2007018824

The last book by the legendary explorer, activist, filmmaker, and oceanographer offers a call for action to preserve our world, its wildlife, and its natural wonders for future generations, looking at the impact of human action on our precarious environment.

"Cousteau's reverence for life's miracles . shines through in this eloquent testimony on the importance of pursuing higher ideals, particularly the preservation of the oceans and the natural world for future generations." Publishers Weekly.

Coutts, Marion

Coutts, Marion The **Iceberg** : a memoir / Marion Coutts. Black Cat, 2016, c2014. 294 p. **B**

ISBN 9780802124609

1. Lubbock, Tom 2. People with terminal illnesses 3. Husband and wife 4. Brain -- Tumors 5. Art critics 6. Autobiographies and memoirs

LC bl2016000441

Originally published in London in 2014 (London : Atlantic Books, 2014)

National Book Critics Circle Award for Autobiography/Memoir finalist, 2016

Meditates on family, love and language as experienced in the two years leading up to the artist author's Independent art critic husband's death from a brain tumor.

"A poetic and moving chronicle of loss." Kirkus.

Coviello, Peter

Coviello, Peter **Long** players : a love story in eighteen songs / Peter Coviello. Penguin Books, 2018. 272 p. **B**

ISBN 9780143132332

1. Divorce 2. Middle-age 3. Popular music 4. Loneliness in men 5. Autobiographies and memoirs

LC 2017037330

We follow Peter Coviello through his happy marriage, his blindsiding divorce, and his fumbling post marital forays into sex and romance. Above all we travel with him as he calibrates, mix by mix and song by song, his place in the lives of two little girls, his suddenly ex-stepdaughters. In his grief, he considers what keeps us alive (sex, talk, dancing) and our many interwoven ways of falling in love: with books and bands and records, with friends, with lovers, with the families we make.

Cox, Lynne, 1957-

Cox, Lynne, 1957- **Swimming** to Antarctica : tales of a long-distance swimmer / Lynne Cox. A.A. Knopf, 2004. ix, 323 p. **B**

ISBN 0375415076

1. Swimmers -- United States 2. Women athletes 3. Women swimmers 4. Athletes -- Health. 5. Autobiographies and memoirs

LC 2003047577

noted long-distance swimmer with a love for cold water describes her eventful career in the sport, from her record-breaking English Channel crossing and her 1987 swim across the Bering Strait from America to the Soviet Union to her exploits in the Straits of Magellan, Lake Baikal, and Antarctica.

"Cox is a pleasure. . . . Many passages are grip-the-page exciting, whether she's dodging Antarctic icebergs or Nile River sewage." Booklist.

Cox, Tom, 1975-

Cox, Tom, 1975- **Close** encounters of the furred kind : new adventures with my sad cat & other feline friends / Tom Cox. Thomas Dunne Books, St Martin's Press, 2016 304 p. **B**

ISBN 9781250077325

1. Cats 2. Cat owners 3. Pets 4. Cats as pets 5. England 6. Norfolk, England. 7. Autobiographies and memoirs

LC 2016003326

This Sunday Times bestselling memoir about a man at the mercy of his unpredictable, demanding and endlessly lovable cats is sure to become an instant hit with American readers and petlovers.

"Cox is endlessly funny, speaking for his cats and poking good-natured fun at every human he encounters, including himself." Booklist.

Coxeter, H. S. M. (Harold Scott Macdonald), 1907-2003

★Roberts, Siobhan **King** of infinite space : Donald Coxeter, the man who saved geometry / Siobhan Roberts. Walker & Co., 2006. xv, 399 p. : **B**

ISBN 9780802714992

1. Mathematicians -- Canada 2. Geometry. 3. Biographies

"The author is to be congratulated on the book's simplicity; completeness; excellent use of diagrams, figures, and photographs; appendixes of mathematical notes; and reams of endnotes. A significant work for mathematicians at all levels; recommended for both academic and public libraries." Library Journal.

Coyne, Tom

Coyne, Tom A **course** called Scotland : searching the home of golf for the secret to its game / Tom Coyne. Simon & Schuster,

2018. 336 p. **B**

ISBN 9781476754284

1. Authors 2. Golfers 3. Golf -- History 4. Voyages and travels 5. Scotland 6. Autobiographies and memoirs

LC 2018015536

Describes the author's visit to Scotland, the birthplace of golf, playing on over 100 of the oldest and most-revered courses in the world, including St. Andrews, Turnberry, Dornoch and Troon.

"In this witty and charming follow-up to A Course Called Ireland, Coyne continues living a golfers dream by playing every links course in Scotland, golfs birthplace." Publishers Weekly.

Coyote, Ivan E. (Ivan Elizabeth), 1969-

Coyote, Ivan E. (Ivan Elizabeth), 1969- **Tomboy** survival guide / Ivan Coyote. Arsenal Pulp Press, 2016 239 p. : **B**

ISBN 1551526565

1. Transgender persons 2. Tomboys. 3. Gender identity 4. Entertainers 5. Yukon Territory. 6. Autobiographies and memoirs

Hilary Weston Writers' Trust Prize for Nonfiction finalist, 2017.

An autobiography of transgender person and tomboy Ivan E. Coyote.

"Stylishly illustrated with sketches of tools and enriched with poems and stories others have shared with Coyote, this book is highly recommended for transgender readers as well as those exploring their own gender identities or wanting to better understand non-binary experiences of a gendered world." Publishers Weekly.

Crabapple, Molly

Crabapple, Molly **Drawing** blood / Molly Crabapple. HarperCollins, 2015. 352 p. : **B**

ISBN 9780062323644

1. Women journalists 2. Women artists 3. Autobiographies and memoirs

LC bl2015044785

The underground artist and journalist presents a memoir of her years between September 11 and the Occupy movement in New York City to discuss the impact of historical events on her work and her decision to become a witness journalist.

"Lavishly illustrated, the book offers a candid portrayal of an artist's journey to self-knowledge and fulfillment." Kirkus.

Crais, Clifton C.

Crais, Clifton C. **History** lessons : a memoir of madness, memory, and the brain / Clifton Crais. Overlook Press, 2014 288 p. **B**

ISBN 9781468303681

1. Alcoholic mothers 2. Amnesia 3. Chronic diseases 4. Child neglect victims 5. New Orleans, Louisiana 6. Autobiographies and memoirs

LC bl2014012646

An Emory University professor and co-author of Sara Baartman and the Hottentot Venus draws on his expertise as a historian to better understand his traumatic early life in New Orleans, marked by an alcoholic mother who tried to drown him, an absent father, his chronic childhood amnesia and long-buried family secrets.

"The ambiguities of a life only half recalled are fully illuminated in this chronicle of trying to understand what has been forgotten." Library Journal.

Crane, Hart, 1899-1932

Mariani, Paul L., The **broken** tower : a life of Hart Crane / Paul Mariani. W.W. Norton, 1999. 492 p. : **B**

ISBN 9780393047264

1. Crane, Hart, 1899-1932. 2. Poets, American -- 20th century 3. Gay men 4. Men with depression 5. Suicide 6. New York City 7. Biographies

LC 98037726

Shortlisted for the James Tait Black Memorial Prize for Biography, 2000"

Using unpublished letters, manuscripts, and photographs [Mariani] pieces together the life and passions of this brilliant yet tormented man whose creative genius left us The Bridge and whose influence still reverberates among poets today." Library Journal.

Crane, Leon, 1919-2002

Murphy, Brian, 1959- **81** days below zero : the incredible survival story of a World War II pilot in Alaska's frozen wilderness / Brian Murphy. Da Capo Press, 2015. 256 p. **B**

ISBN 9780306823282

1. Crane, Leon, 1919-2002. 2. Military pilots 3. World War II -- Aerial operations, American. 4. Airplane accidents. 5. Survival (after airplane accidents, shipwrecks, etc.) 6. Alaska 7. Biographies

LC 2015003484

Shortly before Christmas in 1943, five Army aviators left Alaska's Ladd Field on a test flight. Only one ever returned: Leon Crane, a city kid from Philadelphia with little more than a parachute on his back when he bailed from his B-24 Liberator before it crashed into the Arctic. Alone in subzero temperatures, Crane managed to stay alive in the dead of the Yukon winter for nearly twelve weeks and, amazingly, walked out of the ordeal intact. Murphy recounts, for the first time, the full story of Crane's remarkable saga.

Crawford, Lacy

Crawford, Lacy **Notes** on a silencing : a memoir / Lacy Crawford. Little, Brown & Company, 2020. 391 p. ; **B**

ISBN 9780316491556

1. St. Paul's School, Concord, New Hampshire -- History 2. Private schools 3. Teenage girls 4. Rape 5. Teenage sexual abuse 6. New Hampshire 7. Autobiographies and memoirs

LC 2019947036

The author traces her healing journey after a traumatizing sexual assault at infamous St. Paul's boarding school, describing how she helped police uncover proof of the school's institutionalized mandate of silence.

"Crawford's teenage assault is, as she writes 'not a remarkable story.' Teens who are ready may find powerful truths and a sympathetic perspective." Booklist

Crazy Horse, approximately 1842-1877

McMurtry, Larry **Crazy** Horse / Larry McMurtry. Viking, 1999. 148 p. **B**

ISBN 0670882348

1. Oglala Indians 2. Warriors 3. Indians of North America -- Relations with European-Americans 4. Forced relocations 5. Black Hills -- History -- 19th century 6. Biographies

LC 98026644

"A Lipper/Viking book."

Strips away the tall tales of legend to reveal the essence of Crazy Horse, profiling him as a brilliant and ascetic warrior-hero whose life exemplified Native American tragedy and the end of the untamed West

"Though essentially a loner and devoid of political ambition, Crazy Horse was a respected military tactician, equally feared and admired for the strength and the intensity of his convictions. Rather than merely attempting to sort out fact from fiction, McMurtry incorporates conjecture and legend into this philosophical portrait of both the man and the myth." Booklist.

Powers, Thomas, 1940 December 12- The **killing** of Crazy Horse / Thomas Powers. Alfred A. Knopf, 2010. 576 p. **B**

ISBN 9780375414466

1. Oglala Indians. 2. Indians of North America. 3. Death. 4. Rulers.

LC 2010016842

Spur Award for Historical Nonfiction, 2011.

National Book Critics Circle Award for Biography finalist, 2010.

Investigates the enigmatic Native American figure, assessing critical battles attributed to his leadership within a context of the Great Sioux Wars, exploring the relationships between the Lakota Sioux and other tribes and analyzing the subjugation of North Plains Native Americans.

"Despite the title, this beautifully written and absorbing work is less about the death of Crazy Horse and more about the personality and life of the Native American icon. It is also an insightful and scrupulously fair examination of the culture of Plains Indian bands and their interaction with advancing white civilization in the nineteenth century." Booklist.

Cregan, Mary,

Cregan, Mary The **scar** : a personal history of depression and recovery / Mary Cregan. W.W. Norton & Company, 2019 256 p. **B**

ISBN 9781324001720

1. Cregan, Mary, Mental health. 2. Women with depression 3. Depression -- Treatment 4. Suicidal behavior 5. Infant death 6. Autobiographies and memoirs

LC 2018050858

"While there are quite a few memoirs on depression, Cregan's debut stands out for its personal and profound insights into a subject that can be difficult to grasp." Library Journal.

Cregar, Laird, 1913-1944

Mank, Gregory W **Laird** Cregar : a Hollywood tragedy / Gregory William Mank. McFarland & Company, Inc., Publishers, 2018. 325 p. **B**

ISBN 9780786449569

1. Cregar, Laird, 1913-1944. 2. Actors and actresses. 3. Films 4. Biographies

LC 2017048598

In 1944, Laird Cregar played Jack the Ripper in The Lodger, giving one of the most haunting performances in Hollywood history. This first biography of Cregar tells the heartbreaking story of the brilliant but doomed actor. Appendices cover his film, theatre, and radio work. Many never before published photographs are included.

"Like the actors and actresses who died from too much alcohol or too many drugs, Cregar's obsession with becoming a success wound up killing him, and yet Mank finds joy as well as tragedy in Cregar's attempt to live his dream. Many showbiz biographies reduce the lives of stars to formula; this one gives rich life to an unknown Hollywood story." Booklist.

Crews, Harry, 1935-2012

Geltner, Ted **Blood,** bone, and marrow : a biography of Harry Crews / Ted Geltner. The University of Georgia Press, 2016 414 p. **B**

ISBN 9780820349237

1. Crews, Harry, 1935-2012. 2. Authors, American 3. Biographies

LC 2015032701

The first full-length biography of one of the most unlikely figures in twentieth-century American literature, a writer who emerged from a dirt-poor South Georgia tenant farm and went on to create a singularly unique voice of fiction.

"An absorbing but sad chronicle of a tormented writer." Kirkus.

Cromwell, Thomas, Earl of Essex, 1485?-1540

Borman, Tracy **Thomas** Cromwell : the untold story of Henry VIII's most faithful servant / Tracy Borman. Atlantic Monthly Press 2015. 336 p. **B**

ISBN 9780802123176

1. Henry VIII, King of England, 1491-1547 2. Prime ministers -- England 3. Reformation -- England 4. Bribery -- History 5. Politicians -- Great Britain -- 16th century 6. Great Britain -- History -- Henry VIII, 1509-1547 7. England -- History -- 16th century 8. Biographies

LC 2015431316

A sympathetic portrait of the architect of the English Reformation describes Cromwell's lesser-known experiences as a devoted family man, fiercely loyal servant and revolutionary who helped transform England into a modern state

"Neglecting neither the public persona nor the private man, Borman provides an insightful biography of a much-maligned historical figure." Booklist.

MacCulloch, Diarmaid **Thomas** Cromwell : a revolutionary life / Diarmaid MacCulloch. Viking, 2018. 640 p. **B**

ISBN 9780670025572

1. Politicians 2. Rulers 3. Courts and courtiers 4. Great Britain -- History -- Henry VIII, 1509-1547 5. Biographies

LC bl2018167915

Examines the life of Henry VII's right-hand man, who did everything he could to secure the future of a son he loved dearly, but who ultimately could not control the unpredictable monarch.

"A must-read biography of a man whose role in shaping English and Protestant history has long been misunderstood." Library Journal.

Cronkite, Walter

★Brinkley, Douglas **Cronkite** / Douglas Brinkley. Harper, 2012. 400 p. **B**

ISBN 9780061374265

1. Television journalists -- United States 2. Journalists -- United States 3. Broadcasting 4. Biographies

LC 2011051467

The author of The Quiet World offers a candid look at the renowned, yet fiercely private, journalist and news anchor who reported on some of the biggest news of the 20th century.

"The best portrait of Cronkite--that legendary journalist, certainly worthy of a big biography--that we have." Kirkus.

Cronkite, Walter A **reporter's** life / Walter Cronkite. A.A. Knopf, 1996. viii, 384 p. : **B**

ISBN 0394578791

1. Cronkite, Walter. 2. Journalists -- United States 3. Journalists -- United States 4. Autobiographies and memoirs

LC 96021053

"Cronkite's memoir is a short course on the flow of events in the second half of this centuryevents the world knows more about because of Walter Cronkite's work, and some of which might not have happened without it." New York Times Book Review.

Crosby, Bing, 1904-1977

Giddins, Gary **Bing** Crosby : a pocketful of dreams: the early years, 1903-1940 / Gary Giddins. Little, Brown, 2001. 736 p.

: Bing Crosby (Gary Giddins) ; **B**
ISBN 0316881880
1. Crosby, Bing, 1904-1977. 2. Singers -- United States 3. Radio actors and actresses 4. Crooning 5. United States -- Popular culture -- History -- 20th century. 6. Hollywood, California -- Social life and customs -- 20th century 7. Biographies
LC 00044403

Traces the rise of Bing Crosby from his early successes as a radio star to his initial foray into Hollywood.

"Giddins has contributed a landmark study of popular singing in the first half of the twentieth century." Booklist.

★Giddins, Gary **Bing** Crosby : swinging on a star: the war years, 1940-1946 / Gary Giddins. Little Brown & Co 2018 736 p. Bing Crosby (Gary Giddins) ; **B**
ISBN 9780316887922
1. Crosby, Bing, 1904-1977. 2. Singers -- United States 3. Radio actors and actresses 4. Crooning 5. World War II 6. United States -- Popular culture -- History -- 20th century. 7. Hollywood, California -- Social life and customs -- 20th century 8. Biographies
LC bl2018190537

In a much-anticipated follow-up to the universally acclaimed first volume of a comprehensive Bing Crosby biography, an NBCC Winner and preeminent cultural critic focuses on Crosby's most memorable period, the war years and the origin story of White Christmas.

"For a twenty-first-century audience, the idea of Bing Crosby as both a swoonworthy movie idol and an inspiration to battle-hardened soldiers may seem difficult to comprehend, but that is the brilliance of Giddins work: he makes us see how, in a very different time, Crosby's easygoing, waggish style was just what the country craved, on records and radio, at the movies, and in person." Booklist.

Crosby, Christina, 1953-

Crosby, Christina, 1953- A **body,** undone : living on after great pain / Christina Crosby. New York University Press, 2016 208 p. **B**
ISBN 9781479833535
1. People with quadriplegia 2. Paralysis. 3. Chronic pain 4. Autobiographies and memoirs
LC 2015034127

In the early evening on October 1, 2003, Christina Crosby was three miles into a seventeen mile bicycle ride, intent on reaching her goal of 1,000 miles for the riding season. She was a respected senior professor of English who had celebrated her fiftieth birthday a month before. As she crested a hill, she caught a branch in the spokes of her bicycle, which instantly pitched her to the pavement. Her chin took the full force of the blow, and her head snapped back. In that instant, she was paralyzed.

"A potent memoir that rips open a most human heart." Kirkus.

Crosley, Sloane

Crosley, Sloane **I** was told there'd be cake / Sloane Crosley. Riverhead Books, c2008. 320 p. **B**
ISBN 159448306X
1. Crosley, Sloane. 2. Autobiographies and memoirs 3. Essays
LC 2007033228

A debut compilation of literary essays offers a revealing and humorous look at human fallibility and the vagaries of modern urban life as the author details the despoiling of an exhibit at the Natural History Museum, the provocation of her first boss, siccing the cops on her mysterious neighbor, and other offbeat situations.

★Crosley, Sloane **Look** alive out there : essays / Sloane Crosley. MCD/Farrar, Straus and Giroux, 2018. 272 p. **B**
ISBN 9780374279844
1. Women authors 2. Everyday life 3. Misadventures 4. Middle-age 5. Essays 6. Autobiographies and memoirs
LC 2017038323

A collection of essays shares the author's trademark observations on subjects ranging from scaling active volcanoes and crashing shivas to assisted fertility and playing herself on "Gossip Girl."

"A smart, droll essay collection that is all over the map but focused by Crosley's consistently sharp eye." Kirkus.

Crowell, Rodney

★Crowell, Rodney **Chinaberry** sidewalks / Rodney Crowell. Alfred A. Knopf, 2011. 288 p. **B**
ISBN 9780307594204
1. Crowell, Rodney. 2. Alcoholic fathers. 3. Growing up. 4. Families 5. Country musicians -- United States 6. Houston, Texas 7. Autobiographies and memoirs
LC 2010035996

Recounts the author's experiences growing up in Houston in the 1950s as the only child of an alcoholic father and epileptic mother, describing a coming-of-age marked by barroom brawls, apocalyptic hurricanes, and wild improvisations in the face of unpaidbills.

"Crowell is among the best storytellers to emerge from Nashville. Up to now, he told his stories in song, but with this heartfelt memoir, he can now be called a writer of the first order. Houston, where Crowell grew up in the 1950s and early 1960s, was a city full of characters found in stereotypical country songs: hard-drinking fathers and longsuffering mothers singing along to the beer-soaked ballads of Hank Williams. But this is not fiction; Crowell actually lived the life, soaking up its exhilarating and disturbing atmosphere. Crowell is unsparingly honest, yet there is an admirable restraint here, too." Booklist.

Crump, Benjamin, 1969-

Crump, Benjamin, 1969- **Open** season : legalized genocide of colored people / Ben Crump. Amistad, 2019. 272 p. **B**
ISBN 9780062375094
1. African American lawyers 2. Civil rights lawyers 3. Civil rights 4. Racism 5. United States -- Race relations 6. Autobiographies and memoirs

The president of the National Bar Association and a civil rights attorney chronicles his most memorable legal battles, including Trayvon Martin and Michael Brown, and describes the hidden and systemic injustices minorities face in the U.S. legal system.

Crystal, Billy, 1947-

Crystal, Billy, 1947- **Still** foolin' 'em : where I've been, where I'm going, and where the hell are my keys? / Billy Crystal. Henry Holt and Company, 2013. 256 p. **B**
ISBN 9780805098204
1. Comedians -- United States 2. Aging. 3. Actors and actresses 4. Baby Boom generation 5. Autobiographies and memoirs
LC 2013012238

Nearing age 65, Billy Crystals acknowledges his accomplishments -- hosting major award shows, appearances on TV series like Soap and Saturday Night Live, and roles in blockbusters like When Harry Met Sally, and more -- with all the wry and quirky charm for which he is famed. Fans will find that Crystal still sparkles as he shares private disappointments along with details of those public successes, and fellow baby boomers will relate to Crystal's humorously catalog of the indignities of aging.

"Avoiding the trappings--excess schmaltz, laundry list of famous friends, boozy party log--of so many celebrity memoirs, Crystal delivers a funny and genuinely moving chronicle of his life inside and outside Hollywood." Publishers Weekly.

Crystal, David, 1941-

Crystal, David, 1941- **By** hook or by crook : a journey in search of English / David Crystal. Overlook Press, 2008, c2007. 336 p. **B**

ISBN 9781590200612

1. Crystal, David, 1941- Travel 2. Linguists -- England 3. English language -- Dialects -- Great Britain. 4. Language and languages. 5. Linguistics. 6. Great Britain -- Social life and customs -- 20th century 7. Europe -- Social life and customs -- 20th century 8. United States -- Social life and customs -- 20th century 9. Autobiographies and memoirs

LC bl2008006385

Originally published: London : HarperPress, 2007.

Combines personal reflections, historical allusions, and traveler's observations about the author's encounters with language and its users throughout the English-speaking world.

"In a conversational style that includes plenty of quirky facts, Crystal captures the exploratory, seductive, teasing, quirky, tantalizing nature of language study, and in doing so illuminates the fascinating world of words in which we live." Publishers Weekly.

Cummings, E. E. (Edward Estlin), 1894-1962

Rosenblitt, J. Alison (Jennifer Alison) The **beauty** of living : E. E. Cummings in the Great War / J. Alison Rosenblitt. W.W. Norton & Company, 2020 320 p. **B**

ISBN 9780393246964

1. Poets, American -- 20th century 2. World War I -- Literature and the war. 3. Authors, American -- 20th century 4. Literature and history. 5. Biographies

LC 2019058084

Using letters, journal entries, sketches and analyses of his work, describes the period of time the poet known for his intentionally fractured and fun prose was unjustly imprisoned in France during World War I.

"Rosenblitt breathes new life back into poems too often anthologized and too little read. Highly recommended." Library Journal

★Sawyer-Laucanno, Christopher, 1951- **E.E.** Cummings : a biography / Christopher Sawyer-Laucanno. Sourcebooks, 2004. xvi, 606 p., 32 p. of plates : **B**

ISBN 1570717753

1. Poets, American -- 20th century 2. Authors, American -- 20th century 3. Biographies

LC 2004012234

Presents the life of E.E. Cummings, his childhood in Cambridge, Massachusetts, his early attempts to establish himself as a poet, his marriages, his travels, and his eventual great success and world recognition.

"This is a responsible, adept, and necessary contribution to the body of secondary work about one of America's greatest poets." Christian Science Monitor.

Cummings, Elijah

★Cummings, Elijah **We're** better than this : my fight for the future of our democracy / Elijah Cummings, with James Dale ; foreword by Speaker Nancy Pelosi. HarperCollins, 2020. 272 p. **B**

ISBN 9780062992260

1. African American legislators 2. African American politicians 3. Democracy 4. Justice 5. Maryland 6. United States -- Politics and government 7. Autobiographies and memoirs

LC bl2020012969

A memoir by the late Congressman details how his experiences as a sharecroppers? son in volatile South Baltimore shaped his life in activism, explaining how government oversight can become a positive part of a just American collective.

"Excellent political memoir by the late Democratic representative from Baltimore, one of the sitting president's most vocal opponents. . . . A thoughtful and inspiring exhortation to do better by a much-missed leader." Kirkus

Cunningham, William J.

★Cunningham, William J. **Fashion** climbing : a memoir with photographs / Bill Cunningham ; preface by Hilton Als. Penguin Press, 2018. 256 p. **B**

ISBN 9780525558705

1. Fashion designers 2. Photographers 3. Fashion 4. Portrait photography 5. New York City 6. Autobiographies and memoirs

LC 2018024955

The iconic "New York Times" photographer presents a sophisticated, visual account of his early education in New York City's high-fashion circles.

"It documents his unparalleled eye and appreciation for fashions magic, mystery, and illusions; styles potential to invent and transform. As both the very personal autobiography of an icon and a valuable social history, this wins." Booklist.

Curie, Marie, 1867-1934

Dry, Sarah **Curie** / Sarah Dry ; with an essay by Sabine Seifert. Haus Pub., 2003. 170 p. : **B**

ISBN 9781904341291

1. Curie, Marie, 1867-1934. 2. Chemists -- Poland 3. Women chemists -- Poland

LC bl2007024702

Presents the life of the Polish scientist, including her childhood, her marriage and collaboration with Pierre Curie, and her research which led to the discovery of polonium and radium, for which she was awarded two Noble Prizes.

Curtis, Edward S., 1868-1952

★Egan, Timothy **Short** nights of the shadow catcher : the epic life and immortal photographs of Edward Curtis / Timothy Egan. Houghton Mifflin Harcourt, 2012. 352 p. **B**

ISBN 9780618969029

1. Curtis, Edward S., 1868-1952. 2. Photographers -- United States 3. Indians of North America -- Pictorial works. 4. United States -- History -- 19th century 5. United States -- History -- 20th century 6. Biographies

LC 2012022390

ALA Notable Book, 2013

Andrew Carnegie Medal for Excellence in Non-Fiction, 2013.

Recounts the pioneering photographer's life-risking effort to document the disappearing North American Indian nation, offering insight into the danger and resolve behind his venture, his elevation to an impassioned advocate, and the posthumous discovery of his achievements.

Cushman, Charlotte, 1816-1876

Wojczuk, Tana **Lady** Romeo : the radical and revolutionary life of Charlotte Cushman, America's first celebrity / Tana Wojczuk. Avid Reader Press, 2020. viii, 226 p. : **B**

ISBN 9781501199523

1. Cushman, Charlotte, 1816-1876. 2. Actors and actresses -- United States 3. Gender role 4. Lesbians 5. Social norms 6. Biographies

LC bl2020014811

A portrait of the less-remembered 19th-century queer actress draws on rare correspondence to trace the radical formative years, glittering performances and professional affiliations that shaped the cultural landscapes of 19th-century New York City.

"This enthralling history restores Cushman to her rightful place in the spotlight." Publishers Weekly

Cusk, Rachel, 1967-

★Cusk, Rachel, 1967- **Aftermath** : on marriage and separation / Rachel Cusk. Farrar, Straus and Giroux, c2012. 160 p. **B**

ISBN 9780374102135

1. Marriage -- Psychological aspects. 2. Divorce -- Psychological aspects. 3. Divorced women. 4. Authors, English -- 20th century

LC 2012003807

aA well-known memoirist and novelist presents an intense study on divorce and its place in modern society, discussing the pain that accompanies ending a relationship but also the new opportunities it presents.

Custer, George A. (George Armstrong), 1839-1876

McMurtry, Larry **Custer** / Larry McMurtry. Simon & Schuster, 2012. 256 p. **B**

ISBN 9781451626209

1. Custer, George A. (George Armstrong), 1839-1876. 2. United States. Army 3. Generals -- United States 4. Little Big Horn, Battle of the, 1876 5. Indians of North America -- Great Plains (United States) -- Wars -- 1866-1895 6. United States Civil War, 1861-1865 7. United States -- History -- Civil War, 1861-1865 8. Biographies

LC 2012012374

A lavishly illustrated portrait of the 19th-century cavalry commander traces his rise from an unpromising West Point graduate to a distinguished military leader, providing coverage of such topics as his complicated marriage, mythologized defeat at Little Big Horn and enduring legacy.

Stiles, T. J. **Custer's** trials : a life on the frontier of a new America / T. J. Stiles. Alfred A. Knopf, [2015] 352 p. **B**

ISBN 9780307592644

1. Custer, George A. (George Armstrong), 1839-1876. 2. United States. Army 3. Generals -- United States 4. Little Big Horn, Battle of the, 1876. 5. Indians of North America 6. Frontier and pioneer life -- The West (United States) 7. United States -- History -- Civil War, 1861-1865. 8. The West (United States) -- History -- 19th century 9. Biographies

LC 2015002070

Pulitzer Prize for History, 2016.

Spur Award for Biography, 2016.

National Book Critics Circle Award for Biography finalist, 2015.

Pulitzer Prize for Biography or Autobiography finalist, 2016."

Stiles ably points out [Custer's] many defining flaws: his heroic style didn't work in an era of tact and skill, and there is no doubt that he was self-serving, generally assuming that rules weren't made for him and never showing remorse. In addition to examining Custer's life, the author also introduces his cook, the fascinating Eliza Brown, an escaped slave who deserves a biography of her own." Kirkus.

Wert, Jeffry D. **Custer** : the controversial life of George Armstrong Custer / Jeffry D. Wert. Simon & Schuster, c1996. 462 p., [16] p. of plates : **B**

ISBN 0684810433

1. Custer, George A. (George Armstrong), 1839-1876. 2. United States. Army 3. Generals -- United States 4. Command of troops 5. United States -- History -- 19th century. 6. Biographies

LC 96007290

"Focusing on Custer's Civil War actions, Wert methodically examines a man often considered an enigma in American history. Clear writing and excellent use of primary source materials demonstrate how history should be written." Booklist.

D'Alessandro, Emilio

D'Alessandro, Emilio **Stanley** Kubrick and me : thirty years at his side / Emilio D'Alessandro with Filippo Ulivieri ; translated by Simon Marsh. Arcade Publishing, 2016. 352 p. **B**

ISBN 9781628726695

1. Kubrick, Stanley, 1928-1999 2. D'Alessandro, Emilio. 3. Film producers and directors 4. Filmmaking 5. Filmmakers 6. Film industry and trade 7. Biographies

LC 2015050645

This intimate portrait by his former personal assistant and confidante reveals the man behind the legendary filmmaker--for the first time.

"Hard-core Kubrick devotees won't learn much, but this easy-going and likable memoir humanizes an eccentric titan of cinema." Library Journal.

D'Annunzio, Gabriele, 1863-1938

Hughes-Hallett, Lucy **Gabriele** d'Annunzio : poet, seducer and preacher of war / Lucy Hughes-Hallett. Alfred A. Knopf, 2013. 608 p. **B**

ISBN 9780307263933

1. Poets. 2. Nationalists. 3. Celebrities 4. Authors, Italian. 5. Italy 6. Biographies.

LC 2012033943

Published simultaneously in Canada.

Published as The Pike in the UK"A Borzoi book"--Title page verso.

Costa Biography Award, 2013.

Samuel Johnson Prize for Non-Fiction, 2013.

A profile of the controversial Italian poet and nationalist is set against a backdrop of early 20th-century Italy's transition from Romantic idealism to fascism and war and includes coverage of such topics as his contradictory literary subjects, pivotal roles in World War I and status as a role model for Mussolini.

Dahl, Roald

Sturrock, Donald **Storyteller** : the life of Roald Dahl / Donald Sturrock. Simon & Schuster, 2010. 655 p., 16 p. of plates : ill., ports. ; 24 cm. **B**

ISBN 9781416550822

1. Dahl, Roald. 2. Authors, British -- 20th century 3. Children's literature writing 4. Self in literature. 5. Storytelling. 6. Great Britain 7. Biographies

This authorized biography, written by a BBC producer and director who knew Dahl and worked with the cooperation of the author's adult children and both wives--one of whom was film star Patricia Neal--covers the man and his reputation.

Dalai Lama XIV, 1935-

★Dalai Lama **Freedom** in exile : the autobiography of the Dalai Lama. / Dalai Lama XIV. Harper Collins, 1990. xiv, 288 p. : **B**

ISBN 0060987014

1. Dalai lamas 2. Buddhism -- Tibet. 3. Buddhists. 4. Tibet. 5. Central Asia 6. Autobiographies and memoirs

LC 89046523

"A Cornelia & Michael Bessie book."

Includes index.

Tibet's exiled spiritual and secular leader describes his childhood, the Chinese invasion of Tibet, and how exiled Tibetans have rebuilt their lives and explains Tibetan Buddhism along with his philosophy of peace

"The Dalai Lama's story is, in part, a chapter in the 2,500-year history of Buddhism as well as a testament to the mendacity and barbarity of Communist China. He shares the details of his amazing life, a glimpse at some of the mysteries of Tibetan Buddhism, and his unshakable belief in the basic good of humanity." Booklist.

Iyer, Pico The **open** road : the global journey of the fourteenth Dalai Lama / Pico Iyer. Alfred A. Knopf, 2008. 288 p. **B**

ISBN 9780307267603

1. Buddhism. 2. Religious leaders. 3. Buddhists.

LC 2007043991

"The combination of Iyer's exacting observations, incisive analysis, and frank respect for the unknowable results in a uniquely internalized, even empathic portrait of one of the world's most embraced and least understood guiding lights." Booklist.

Dana, Richard Henry 1815-1882

Dana, Richard Henry, 1815-1882 **Two** years before the mast : a personal narrative of life at sea / Richard Henry Dana ; introduction by Gary Kinder ; notes by Duncan Hasell. Modern Library, c2001. xxiv, 516 p. : **B**

ISBN 9780375757945

1. Pilgrim (Brig) 2. Alert (Brig) 3. Seafaring life 4. Voyages and travels -- 19th century 5. Sailors -- Diaries 6. California -- Description and travel -- 19th century 7. Cape Horn -- Description and travel -- 19th century 8. Autobiographies and memoirs

LC 2001031243

A personal narrative of life aboard an American merchant ship in the 1830s.

Daniels, J. D., 1974-

Daniels, J. D., 1974- The **correspondence** : essays / J. D. Daniels. Farrar, Straus and Giroux, 2017. 128 p. **B**

ISBN 9780374535940

1. Civilization, Western. 2. Books and reading 3. Personal conduct 4. Essays 5. Autobiographies and memoirs

LC 2016017824

Can civilization save us from ourselves? That is the question J. D. Daniels asks in his first book, a series of six letters written during dark nights of the soul. Working from his own highly varied experience--as a janitor, a night watchman, an adjunct professor, a drunk, an exterminator, a dutiful son--he considers how far books and learning and psychoanalysis can get us, and how much we're stuck in the mud.

Daniels, Jesse Delbert, 1938-

King, Gilbert **Beneath** a ruthless sun : a true story of violence, race, and justice lost and found / Gilbert King. Riverhead Books, 2018. 416 p. **B**

ISBN 9780399183386

1. Malicious accusation 2. People with developmental disabilities 3. Police misconduct 4. Frameups 5. Florida

LC 2017053110

ALA Notable Book, 2019.

The author of the Pulitzer Prize-winning Devil in the Grove documents the mid-20th-century case of a gentle, developmentally challenged youth who was falsely accused of raping a wealthy woman, in an account that traces the efforts of a crusading journalist to uncover the virulent racism and class corruption that led to his incarceration without a trial.

"From the opening pages, King's narrative barrels forward, leaving readers wondering what it will take for justice to prevail. By turns sobering, frightening, and thrilling, this meticulous account of the power and tenacity of officially sanctioned racism recalls a dark era that America is still struggling to leave behind." Kirkus.

Danler, Stephanie

Danler, Stephanie **Stray** : a memoir / Stephanie Danler. Alfred A. Knopf, 2020. 240 p. **B**

ISBN 9781101875964

1. Danler, Stephanie. 2. Authors, American -- 21st century 3. Children of alcoholics 4. Children of drug abusers 5. Coping in women 6. California 7. Southern California. 8. Autobiographies and memoirs

LC 2019055034

After selling her first novel--a dream she'd worked long and hard for--Stephanie Danler knew she should be happy. Instead, she found herself driven to face the difficult past she'd left behind a decade ago: a mother disabled by years of alcoholism, further handicapped by a tragic brain aneurysm; a father who abandoned the family when she was three, now a meth addict in and out of recovery. After years in New York City she's pulled home to Southern California by forces she doesn't totally understand, haunted by questions of legacy and trauma. Here, she works toward answers, uncovering hard truths about her parents and herself as she explores whether it's possible to change the course of her history. Lucid and honest, heart-breaking and full of hope, Stray is an examination of what we inherit and what we don't have to, of what we have to face in ourselves to move forward, and what it's like to let go of one's parents in order to find peace--and a family--of one's own.

"Danler knits together the stories of her long-divorced parents and the effects of their addictions on her self-formation. . . . Acknowledging both the tribute of memory and the mercy of forgetting with one distinctive voice, this is a rare and skillfully structured view of an artist's love, grief, and growth." Booklist

Danticat, Edwidge, 1969-

★Danticat, Edwidge, 1969- **Brother,** I'm dying / Edwidge Danticat. Alfred A. Knopf, 2007. x, 272 p. ; **B**

ISBN 1400041155

1. Danticat, Edwidge, 1969- Family. 2. Authors, American -- 20th century 3. Immigration and emigration 4. Family relationships 5. Uncles -- Haiti 6. Haiti -- Social conditions -- 20th century. 7. Autobiographies and memoirs

LC 2007006887

National Book Critics Circle Award for Autobiography, 2007.

Hurston/Wright Legacy Award: Nonfiction, 2008.

National Book Award for Nonfiction finalist, 2007

In a personal memoir, the author describes her relationships with the two men closest to her--her father and his brother, Joseph, a charismatic pastor with whom she lived after her parents emigrated from Haiti to the United States.

"The author has written a fierce, haunting book about exile and loss and family love, and how that love can survive distance and separation, loss and abandonment and somehow endure, undented and robust." New York Times.

Danticat, Edwidge, 1969- **Create** dangerously : the immigrant artist at work / Edwidge Danticat. Princeton University Press, 2010. 189 p. **B**

ISBN 9780691140186

1. Authors, American -- 20th century 2. Immigration and emigration.

3. Expatriate artists. 4. Artists -- Haiti. 5. Haiti -- Social conditions -- 20th century.

LC 2010010302

"This tender . book about loss and the unquenchable passion for homeland makes us remember the powerful material from which most fiction is wrought: it comes from childhood, and place. No matter her geographic and temporal distance from these, Danticat writes about them with the immediacy of love." New York Times Book Review.

Darling, Ron

Darling, Ron The **complete** game : reflections on baseball, pitching, and life on the mound / Ron Darling with Daniel Paisner. Alfred A. Knopf, 2009. 288 p. **B**

ISBN 9780307269843

1. Darling, Ron. 2. Baseball players -- United States 3. Baseball. 4. Pitchers (Baseball) -- United States 5. Pitching (Baseball) 6. Autobiographies and memoirs

LC 2008055706

"Darling, the stalwart ex-Mets starter and incumbent Mets broadcaster . offers pitches and outcomes (but no box scores) from ten selected games in his career, including a successful World Series start against the Red Sox at Fenway Park in 1986, a gruesome windy-day thumping suffered at Wrigley Field, and his celebrated extra-inning near-no-hitter back when he was pitching for Yale. Among them are enough oddities and thrilling turns of baseball to make a reader glad to be here andwell, not out there." The New Yorker.

Darrow, Clarence, 1857-1938

Farrell, John A. (John Aloysius) **Clarence** Darrow : attorney for the damned / John A. Farrell. Doubleday, c2011. 576 p. **B**

ISBN 9780385522588

1. Darrow, Clarence, 1857-1938. 2. American Civil Liberties Union -- History 3. Lawyers -- United States 4. Progressivism (United States politics) 5. Defense attorneys 6. Social advocacy 7. United States -- Politics and government -- 20th century 8. Biographies

LC 2010046273

A portrait of the legendary defense attorney and progressive covers his decision to leave a promising career to advocate on behalf of disadvantaged groups, his campaign against Jim Crow policies, and his achievements in headline-making trials.

"Farrell gleans from previously undisclosed material to offer a completely engaging portrait of a flawed man of noble ideals." Booklist.

Darwin, Charles, 1809-1882

Browne, E. J. (E. Janet), 1950- **Charles** Darwin : a biography. Janet Browne. Knopf, 1995. xiii, 605 p., 32 unnumbered p. of plates : **B**

ISBN 9780394579429

1. Beagle Expedition, 1831-1836 2. Naturalists -- England 3. Evolution -- History -- 19th century. 4. Natural history -- History. 5. Family relationships. 6. England -- History -- 19th century. 7. Biographies

LC 94006598

The first of a two-volume biography of Charles Darwin follows the great nineteenth-century scientist from his youth, through his scientific apprenticeship at sea, to his refinement of the ideas that he presented in Origin of Species.

"The author captures the spirit of a quietly revolutionary scientist whose ingrained Victorian prejudices were at odds with his radical ideas." Publishers Weekly.

Browne, E. J. (E. Janet), 1950- **Charles** Darwin : a biography. Janet Browne. Knopf, 2002. 591 p., 24 unnumbered p. of plates : **B**

ISBN 9780679429326

1. Naturalists -- England 2. Evolution -- History -- 19th century. 3. Natural history -- History. 4. Family relationships. 5. England -- History -- 19th century. 6. Biographies

James Tait Black Memorial Prize for Biography, 2003.

National Book Critics Circle Award for Biography, 2002.

The second volume in a definitive biography of Charles Darwin, following Charles Darwin: Voyaging, begins in 1858 when, against his better judgment, Darwin was forced to publicly reveal his theory of evolution in a world that held to the biblical creation ideal, and examines the fierce controversy that resulted from his work.

"This second volume of Browne's biography of Darwin begins a year before the publication of On the Origin of Species, with the arrival of a package from Alfred Russel Wallace, whose own ideas on natural selection virtually mirrored Darwin's, forcing him to go public. Browne's subject is monumental, but her writing style is never overburdened by the weight. Rather, her prose is elegant in its clarity of thought, her craftsmanship impeccable in the way it weaves a coherent whole from the innumerable threads of thought, experience and persona that comprised this colossal life." Publishers Weekly.

Byrne, Eugene **Darwin** : a graphic biography / Eugene Byrne and illustrated by Simon Gurr. Smithsonian Institute Press, 2013 104 p. **B**

ISBN 9781588343529

1. Naturalists -- England 2. Evolution -- History -- 19th century. 3. Natural history -- History. 4. England -- History -- 19th century. 5. Comics and Graphic novels 6. Biographies

LC bl2013046169

Depicts the life and adventures of a young Charles Darwin in graphic novel form, following the intrepid scientist on an expedition to discover new specimens of beetles and describing the world of the 1800s.

Johnson, Paul, 1928- **Darwin** : portrait of a genius / Paul Johnson. Viking, 2012. 176 p. **B**

ISBN 9780670025718

1. Darwin, Charles, 1809-1882. 2. Naturalists -- England 3. Evolution. 4. Scientists. 5. Biographies

LC 2012003433

Includes index.

The author of Socrates: A Man for Our Times presents a richly detailed account of the life and career of the evolutionary scientist that places his achievements against a backdrop of his time and includes coverage of such topics as his voyage aboard the Beagle and the long-delayed publication of Origin of Species.

Wesson, Rob **Darwin's** first theory : exploring Darwin's quest for a theory of Earth / Rob Wesson. W. W. Norton & Co., 2017. 384 p. **B**

ISBN 9781681773162

1. Darwin, Charles, 1809-1882. 2. Plate tectonics. 3. Natural history. 4. Geology. 5. Geologists. 6. Biographies.

LC 2017446462

A geologist traces Darwin's footsteps through the Andes, Scotland and Wales and discusses the importance of his theory of plate tectonics and the huge impact created by imperceptibly slow change.

"In this recovery of Darwin's early adulthood, Wesson reminds readers that the great naturalist began his scientific career as a geologist framing his first daring hypotheses in geological, not biological, terms." Booklist.

David, King of Israel

Pinsky, Robert The **life** of David / Robert Pinsky. Nextbook : 2005. 209 p. ; **B**

ISBN 0805242031

1. David, King of Israel. 2. Bible. Old Testament. 3. Rulers. 4. Israel

LC 2005041696

Profiles one of the most important and complex figures of the Old Testament, describing the eventful life, triumphs and failures, divine destiny, and lasting influence of the poet, warrior, and king.

"The author considers the peculiarities, paradoxes, and timeless significance of David's often baffling story from his golden days as a handsome upstart confronting King Saul in gangsterish encounters to David's wild years as a desert Robin Hood and ascension to the throne. Witty, frank, skeptical, and clearly moved by mercurial David's chutzpah and losses, Pinsky brings remarkable lucidity, depth, and creativity to his dynamic and poetic reading of a legendary figure who has become emblematic of both destructive and heroic aspects of human nature." Booklist.

Davidman, Joy, 1915-1960

Santamaria, Abigail **Joy** : poet, seeker, and the woman who captivated C. S. Lewis / Abigail Santamaria. Houghton Mifflin Harcourt, 2015. 432 p. **B**

ISBN 9780151013715

1. Davidman, Joy, 1915-1960. 2. Lewis, C. S. (Clive Staples), 1898-1963. 3. Women poets. 4. Authors' spouses. 5. Converts to Christianity from Judaism 6. Biographies

LC 2014034506

The first full biography of Joy Davidman, known primarily as C.S. Lewis's late-in-life bride, but who here receives her much deserved rescue from that shadow.

"With access to unpublished documents and family papers, Santamaria has fashioned a compelling narrative, remaining cleareyed about her subject's many personal failings." Kirkus.

Davies, Dawn (Dawn S.)

Davies, Dawn (Dawn S.) **Mothers** of Sparta : a memoir in pieces / Dawn Davies. Flatiron Books, 2018. 288 p. **B**

ISBN 9781250133700

1. Davies, Dawn (Dawn S.). 2. Mothers of children with autism 3. Sjogren's syndrome. 4. Personal conduct. 5. Growing up. 6. Autobiographies and memoirs 7. Essays

LC 2017041747

A debut memoir by a Pushcart Special Mention recipient shares a series of autobiographical stories tracing her misfit teens and early adulthood before her three difficult pregnancies, struggles with post-partum depression, divorce, a loving if jaded early parenting life and a growing awareness that one of her children is deeply troubled.

"Davies first book is magnetic attraction in memoir form: it will pull readers in with stories that are funny, insightful, and bordering on farce while also pushing them away with darker pieces about loss, mental illness, and an immense amount of physical pain. Davies uses her oodles of talent to remind readers that human beings are never just one thing, and in her essays, we see a whole life revealed." Booklist.

Davis, Bette, 1908-1989

Thomson, David, 1941- **Bette** Davis / David Thomson ; photo research by Lucy Gray. Faber and Faber, Inc., 2010. 144 p. **B**

ISBN 9780865479319

1. Davis, Bette, 1908-1989. 2. Film actors and actresses 3. Actors and actresses 4. Film industry and trade 5. Hollywood, California. 6. Biographies

LC 2009041760

"Chronicling Davis' life and evolution in Hollywood, Thomson illustrates how changes in her often-disappointing private life (she had a habit of marrying the wrong men) influenced and often deepened her onscreen persona. Reading of how Davis bounced from one bad movie to the next in the early years of her career, it's hard not to share Thomson's enthusiasm for her talent, drive, and will. And it is hard not to feel Thomson's disappointment when Davis' major, artistic breakthroughs (The Little Foxes, All About Eve) are followed by lapses into forgettable mediocrity (The Man Who Came to Dinner, Payment on Demand)." Booklist.

Davis, Jennifer Pharr

Davis, Jennifer Pharr **Called** again : a story of love and triumph / Jennifer Pharr Davis. Beaufort Books, 2013. 298 p. **B**

ISBN 9780825306938

1. Davis, Jennifer Pharr. 2. Hikers -- United States 3. Hiking. 4. Self-discovery. 5. Christian women 6. Appalachian Trail 7. Autobiographies and memoirs

LC 2013002077

"A serviceably written yet inspired exploration of the meaning of commitment." Kirkus.

★Davis, Jennifer Pharr The **pursuit** of endurance : harnessing the record-breaking power of strength and resilience / Jennifer Pharr Davis. Penguin Group USA, 2018 320 p. **B**

ISBN 9780735221895

1. Long distance runners. 2. World records. 3. Endurance sports. 4. Running -- Psychological aspects. 5. Autobiographies and memoirs

LC 2018013087

Jennifer Pharr Davis, a record holder of the FKT (fastest known time) on the Appalachian Trail, reveals the secrets and habits behind endurance as she chronicles her incredible accomplishments in the world of endurance hiking, backpacking, and trail running.

"A captivating narrative guidebook that will inspire readers to test their own limits, on the trail and off." Kirkus.

Davis, Miles

Cook, Richard, 1957-2007 **It's** about that time : Miles Davis on and off record / Richard Cook. Oxford University Press, 2007. ix, 373 p. : **B**

ISBN 0195322665

1. Davis, Miles Criticism and interpretation 2. Jazz musicians. 3. Jazz music -- History and criticism 4. Biographies

LC 2006050694

An engaging portrait of the life and work of jazz great Miles Davis traces his career through the window of fourteen important albums recorded by Davis, illuminating each in terms of their contribution to Davis's evolution as a musician, composer, and group leader, as well as relating them to wider currents in contemporary music and the events in Davis's life.

"Cook's thoughtful, illuminating criticism and boundless knowledge of his subject make this a rich and satisfying read for jazz aficionados and novices alike." Publishers Weekly.

Davis, Miles **Miles,** the autobiography / Miles Davis with Quincy Troupe. Simon and Schuster, c1989. 431 p., [30] p. of plates : **B**

ISBN 9780671635046

1. Davis, Miles. 2. Jazz musicians 3. Autobiographies and memoirs

LC 89019652

Includes index.

In discussing his legendary forty-year career, Davis discusses music's "cool" era and fusion movement and offers candid views on fellow musicians, promoters, producers, critics, and his personal life.

Dawkins, Richard, 1941-

Dawkins, Richard, 1941- An **appetite** for wonder : the making of a scientist / Richard Dawkins. Ecco Press, 2013. 320 p. **B**

ISBN 9780062225795

1. Biologists 2. Evolution 3. Scientists 4. Atheism 5. Autobiographies and memoirs

LC bl2013035860

Famous for his radical new vision of Darwinism, Richard Dawkins paints a colorful, richly textured canvas of his early life from innocent child to charismatic world-famous scientist.

Dawkins, Richard, 1941- **Brief** candle in the dark : my life in science / Richard Dawkins. Ecco, 2015 320 p. **B**

ISBN 9780062288431

1. Biologists -- Great Britain 2. Ethologists -- Great Britain 3. Intellectual life 4. Scientists 5. Autobiographies and memoirs

LC bl2015029707

A sequel to An Appetite for Wonder candidly explores the influences of fame on the author's career, shares memories about his intellectual peers and evaluates the events and ideas that have shaped his beliefs.

"Though the narrative could have used some pruning, the author provides an entertaining portrait of his life and times, including the quaint cus t oms still in practice at Oxford. An impressive overview of Dawkins' life's work, written with the freshness of youthful vigor." Kirkus.

Day, Daniel R.

Day, Daniel R. **Dapper** Dan : made in Harlem : a memoir / Daniel R. Day with Mikael Awake. Random House, [2019] 304 p. **B**

ISBN 9780525510512

1. Day, Daniel R.. 2. African American fashion designers 3. Fashion 4. City life 5. Hip hop culture 6. Harlem, New York City 7. New York City 8. Autobiographies and memoirs

LC 2018036839

BCALA Literary Award for Nonfiction, 2020.A memoir by the legendary designer who pioneered high-end streetwear traces his rise from an early-1980s Harlem storefront to the red carpet in Hollywood, working with such celebrities as Salt-N-Pepa and Beyonce. Illustrations.

"Day is a natural storyteller with a distinct point of view that clearly comes through in this enjoyable memoir." Booklist.

Day, Dorothy, 1897-1980

Hennessy, Kate, 1960- **Dorothy** Day : the world will be saved by beauty :an intimate portrait of my grandmother / Kate Hennessy. Scribner, 2017. 352 p. **B**

ISBN 9781501133961

1. Social reformers -- United States 2. Catholic women. 3. Catholic Worker Movement. 4. Catholics -- United States 5. Biographies

LC bl2016052573

The youngest grandchild of controversial Catholic and social activist Dorothy Day shares personal insights into her life and work that describe Day's experiences before and after conversion, her prolific writings and her sometimes radical perspectives.

"Hennessy has created an amazing tapestry of Day's life and the memories she left with her loved ones." Publishers Weekly.

Day, Felicia, 1979-

Day, Felicia, 1979- **You're** never weird on the internet (almost) : a memoir / Felicia Day. Touchstone, 2015 288 p. **B**

ISBN 9781476785653

1. Actors and actresses 2. Geeks (Computer enthusiasts) 3. Internet personalities 4. Introverts 5. Autobiographies and memoirs

LC 2015506836

The entertainment artist best known for her web videos shares stories of her homeschooled childhood, her rags-to-riches professional successes, and her thoughts on such topics as creativity, video games, and feminism.

Day, John D., Dr

Day, John D., Dr The **longevity** plan : seven life-transforming lessons from ancient China / Dr. John D. Day and Jane Ann Day with Matthew LaPlante Harper, an imprint of HarperCollinsPublishers, 2017 288 p. **B**

ISBN 9780062319814

1. Day, John D., Dr. 2. Longevity 3. Aging 4. Centenarians. 5. Personal conduct 6. China -- Social life and customs 7. Autobiographies and memoirs

LC bl2017027411

A doctor shares his story and findings about the time he spent in Longevity Village, a mountainous region in China where most people live past 100 in very good health, and reveals the seven principles that work together to create health, happiness and longevity.

"Practical, applicable health guidance validated by a remarkable collective of revered Chinese elders." Kirkus.

Day, Thomas, 1748-1789

★Moore, Wendy, 1952- **How** to create the perfect wife : Britain's most ineligible bachelor and his enlightened quest to train the ideal mate / Wendy Moore. Basic Books, 2013. vii, 351 p. : **B**

ISBN 9780465065745

1. Day, Thomas, 1748-1789. 2. Rousseau, Jean-Jacques, 1712-1778. Emile Influence. 3. Authors, English -- 18th century. 4. Radicalism -- England -- History -- 18th century. 5. Marriage -- Great Britain -- History -- 18th century. 6. Enlightenment (European intellectual movement) 7. Great Britain -- History -- 18th century. 8. Biographies.

LC 2012048149

The award-winning author traces the efforts of Georgian man Thomas Day to create an ideal wife after failing to find a woman who reflected his views about subservience, describing how he adopted two young orphans and raised them according to the extreme principles of Jean-Jacques Rousseau and the Enlightenment.

"A darkly enlightening tale--thoroughly researched, gracefully written--about Enlightenment thought, male arrogance and the magic of successful matrimony." Kirkus.

Dayan, Mosheh, 1931-1979

Bar-On, Mordechai, 1928- **Moshe** Dayan : Israel's controversial hero / Mordechai Bar-On. Yale University Press, 2012. 224 p. **B**

ISBN 9780300149418

1. Dayan, Mosheh, 1931-1979. 2. Generals -- Israel 3. Arab-Israeli conflict. 4. Leadership in men. 5. Zionists. 6. Biographies

LC 2012000595

This intimate portrait of one of Israel's most charismatic--and controversial--personalities discusses Dayan's private life, public career and political controversies set against an original analysis of Israel's political environment from pre-Mandate Palestine through the early 1980s.

De Quincey, Thomas, 1785-1859

De Quincey, Thomas, 1785-1859 **Confessions** of an English opium-eater and other writings / Thomas De Quincey ; edited with an introduction and notes by Barry Milligan. Penguin Books, 2003, c1821. xliv, 296 p. ; **B**

ISBN 0140439013

1. De Quincey, Thomas, 1785-1859. 2. Drug addicts -- Great Britain 3. Authors, English -- 19th century 4. Opium addiction -- England. 5. Great Britain -- Social life and customs -- 19th century. 6. Autobiographies and memoirs

LC 2003286414

Originally published in the London magazine for September & October, 1821, the Appendix in December, 1822.

This classic work was first published in book form in 1822. Thomas De Quincey, who was a friend of William Wordsworth and Samuel Taylor Coleridge, discusses his life, including estrangements from his family, the ailments that led to his eventual daily use of opium, and the addiction that followed.

De Vries, Hendrika

De Vries, Hendrika **When** a toy dog became a wolf and the moon broke curfew : a memoir / Hendrika de Vries. She Writes Press, 2019. xiii, 215 p. : **B**

ISBN 9781631526589

1. Mothers and daughters 2. Courage in women 3. Prisoner-of-war camps 4. Fathers 5. Netherlands 6. Amsterdam, Netherlands 7. Autobiographies and memoirs

LC 2019934428

Hendrika is "Daddy's little girl," but when Nazis occupy Amsterdam and her father is deported to a POW labor camp, she must bond with her mother--who joins the Resistance after her husband's deportation--and learn about female strength in order to discover the strong woman she can become.

DeMille, Cecil B., 1881-1959

★Eyman, Scott, 1951- **Empire** of dreams : the epic life of Cecil B. Demille / Scott Eyman. Simon & Schuster, 2010. 576 p. **B**

ISBN 9780743289559

1. DeMille, Cecil B., 1881-1959. 2. Film producers and directors 3. Film industry and trade 4. Filmmakers. 5. Silent film industry and trade 6. Hollywood, California. 7. Biographies

LC 2010027710

"Eyman's evocative prose and exhaustive research makes this an engaging and authoritative biography." Publishers Weekly.

DeRoche, Torre

DeRoche, Torre The **worrier's** guide to the end of the world : love, loss, and other catastrophes -- through Italy, India, and beyond / Torre DeRoche. Seal Press, 2017. xxi, 259 p. **B**

ISBN 9781580056854

1. DeRoche, Torre Travel 2. Vapnitchnaia, Masha Travel 3. Women travelers 4. Walking 5. Female friendship 6. Fear 7. India -- Description and travel 8. Italy -- Description and travel 9. Autobiographies and memoirs

LC 2017025963

A funny and heartwarming story of one woman's attempt to walk off a lifetime of fear--with a soulmate, bad shoes, and lots of wine.

"This page-turning memoir is a thoughtful and entertaining addition to the minigenre of grief-induced travelogues like Cheryl Strayeds Wild (2012) and Shannon Leone Fowlers Traveling with Ghosts (2017)." Booklist.

DeVita, Vincent T., Jr., 1935-

★DeVita, Vincent T., Jr., 1935- The **death** of cancer : after fifty years on the front lines of medicine, a pioneering oncologist reveals why the war on cancer is winnable--and how we can get there / Vincent T. DeVita, Jr., M.D., and Elizabeth DeVita-Raeburn. Sarah Crichton Books/Farrar, Straus and Giroux, 2015. 400 p. **B**

ISBN 9780374135607

1. Cancer -- History. 2. Oncologists. 3. Autobiographies and memoirs

LC 2015011104

Includes index.

In The Death of Cancer, Dr. Vincent T. DeVita Jr.--former director of the National Cancer Institute, former physician-in-chief at Memorial Sloan Kettering, director of the Yale Cancer Center, former president of the American Cancer Society, and developer of the first successful chemotherapy treatment for Hodgkin's lymphoma, which first demonstrated that advanced cancers of a major organ system in adults could be cured by chemotherapy--provides a personal history of one of the greatest science stories of our time, covering our fight against cancer from a man who's seen it all.

DeWoskin, Rachel

DeWoskin, Rachel **Foreign** babes in Beijing : behind the scenes of a new China / Rachel DeWoskin. W. W. Norton, c2005. 332 p. ; **B**

ISBN 0393059022

1. DeWoskin, Rachel Travel China. 2. Americans in China 3. Culture conflict 4. Soap operas 5. Television actors and actresses 6. China -- Social life and customs -- 1976- 7. Autobiographies and memoirs

LC 2005000939

Traces the author's decision to broaden her cultural horizons by working as a Beijing consultant for an American PR firm in China for five years, a period during which she starred in a popular Chinese-western soap opera, experienced a cross-cultural private life, and witnessed numerous changes throughout the country.

"Ms DeWoskin's portrait of the complexities of urban China is not uncritical. But her book is written with enormous warmth for its people. And it is all the better for avoiding neat conclusions." The Economist.

Dean, James, 1931-1955

★Gehring, Wes D. **James** Dean : rebel with a cause / Wes D. Gehring. Indiana Historical Society Press, 2005. xix, 303 p. : **B**

ISBN 0871951819

1. Dean, James, 1931-1955. 2. Dean, James, 1931-1955 Childhood and youth 3. Dean, James, 1931-1955 Filmography 4. Dean, James, 1931-1955 Death and burial 5. Film actors and actresses -- United States 6. Gay film actors 7. Bisexual men -- United States 8. Fatal traffic accidents -- California 9. United States -- Social life and customs -- 20th century 10. Biographies

LC 2005041440

Aided by the cooperation of Dean's family members and friends, chronicles the life of the actor who died in a car accident at the age of twenty-four and is known for his roles in "East of Eden" and "Rebel without a Cause."

"This is a study of Dean's entire life and an appreciation of his rightful place in film history. Gehring makes the point that audiences have confused the actor with his troubled-teenager roles, and he counters that misimpression with a fuller portrait." Booklist.

Dean, Margaret Lazarus, 1972-

Dean, Margaret Lazarus, 1972- **Leaving** orbit : notes from the last days of American spaceflight / Margaret Lazarus Dean.

Graywolf Pr., 2015. 240 p. **B**

ISBN 9781555977092

1. United States. National Aeronautics and Space Administration 2. Space flight 3. Space programs 4. Space centers 5. Space vehicles 6. Autobiographies and memoirs

LC bl2015019660

The winner of the Graywolf Press Nonfiction Prize, exploring Florida's Space Coast and the history of NASA, takes measure of what American spaceflight has achieved and gathers possible answers to the question: What does it mean that a spacefaring nation won't be going to space anymore?

"Dean deftly captures the thrill and discovery of American space exploration, as well as the disappointment and outrage she believes everyone should feel at its ending." Publishers Weekly.

Debussy, Claude, 1862-1918

★Walsh, Stephen, 1942- **Debussy** : a painter in sound / Stephen Walsh. Random House Inc 2018 336 p. **B**

ISBN 9781524731922

1. Debussy, Claude, 1862-1918. Piano music. 2. Piano music. 3. Composers -- France 4. Classical music 5. Biographies

LC 2017058738

Claude Debussy (1862-1918) was that rare creature, a composer who reinvented the language of music without alienating the majority of music lovers. The creator of such classics as La Mer and Clair de Lune, of Pelleas et Melisande and his magnificent, delicate piano works, he is the modernist everybody loves, the man who drove French music into entirely new regions of beauty and excitement at a time when old traditions--and the overbearing influence of Wagner--threatened to stifle it. As a central figure at the birth of modernism, Debussy's influence on French culture was profound. Yet at the same time his own life was complicated and often troubled by struggles over money, women, and ill-health.

"Walsh uses the musical compositions of French composer Achille-Claude Debussy (18621918) as a framework to tell the story of his short life in this richly descriptive biography." Publishers Weekly.

Dederer, Claire, 1967-

Dederer, Claire, 1967- **Love** and trouble : a primer / Claire Dederer. Alfred A. Knopf, 2017. 256 p. **B**

ISBN 9781101946503

1. Motherhood 2. Midlife crisis 3. Middle-aged persons 4. Midlife crisis in women 5. Autobiographies and memoirs

LC 2016035870

The best-selling author of Poser describes the erotic reawakening she experienced at midlife that completely derailed her family life and career, recounting how she attempted to reconnect with her husband and reconcile her teen past with the woman she became.

"In her frank and frankly hilarious new memoir, Dederer (Poser, 2011) explores the female midlife crisis in all its glorious, tear-streaked, and hormone-crazed inconvenience." Booklist.

Deford, Frank

Deford, Frank **Over** time : my life as a sportswriter / Frank Deford. Atlantic Monthly Press, 2012. 288 p. **B**

ISBN 9780802120151

1. Sportswriters -- United States 2. Sports 3. Career development 4. Journalism 5. Essays 6. Autobiographies and memoirs

LC 2012285460

Frank Deford went straight from college to Sports Illustrated. In the decades since, he's become an iconic in sports commentary, covering events and athletes in a multitude of disciplines. Here, he meshes insights from his career into a warm, sincere anecdotal history of American sports writing in general. Deford pays homage to writers like Ring Lardner and Jim Murray, all while addressing personal topics like his stint with The National Sports Daily, his visit to apartheid South Africa with Arthur Ashe, and marking his 1,500th commentary on NPR's "Morning Edition."

Del Giocondo, Lisa, 1479-

Hales, Dianne R., 1950- **Mona** Lisa : a life discovered / Dianne Hales. Simon & Schuster, 2014. 336 p. **B**

ISBN 9781451658965

1. Leonardo, da Vinci, 1452-1519. 2. Mona Lisa (Painting) 3. Art, Renaissance (Europe) 4. Artists' models. 5. Florence (Italy) -- History -- 1421-1737. 6. Biographies

LC 2013042086

Based on research by Giuseppe Pallanti, author of La Vera Identità della Gioconda. Milan: Skira Editore, 2006.A genius immortalized her. A French king paid a fortune for her. An emperor coveted her. No face has ever captivated so many for so long. Every year more than nine million visitors trek to her portrait in the Louvre. Yet while everyone recognizes her smile, hardly anyone knows her story. This book rests on the premise that the woman in the Mona Lisa is indeed the person identified in its earliest description: Lisa Gherardini (1479-1542), wife of the Florence merchant Francesco del Giocondo. Dianne Haleshas followed facts wherever she could find them -- from the Florence State Archives, to the squalid street where she was born, to the ruins of the convent where she died. Lisa Gherardini was a quintessential woman of her times, caught in a whirl of political upheavals, family dramas, and public scandals. Descended from ancient nobles, she gave birth to six children and died at age sixty-three. Her life spanned the most tumultuous chapters in the history of Florence, decades of war, rebellion, invasion, siege, and conquest--and of the greatest artistic outpouring the world has ever seen. Her story creates an extraordinary tapestry of Renaissance Florence, inhabited by larger-than-legend figures such as Leonardo, Michelangelo, and Machiavelli. Mona Lisa: A Life Discovered takes readers beyond the frame of Leonardo's masterpiece and introduces them to a fully dimensional human being.

"This engaging account of a Renaissance woman will appeal to a general audience." Library Journal.

Delany, Mrs. (Mary), 1700-1788

Peacock, Molly, 1947- The **paper** garden : an artist begins her life's work at 72 / Molly Peacock. Bloomsbury, 2011, c2010. 397 p. : **B**

ISBN 9781608195237

1. Delany, Mrs. (Mary), 1700-1788. 2. Collage. 3. Flower painting and illustration. 4. Creativity in seniors. 5. Women artists -- England. 6. Biographies

Includes index.

Originally published: Toronto : McClelland & Stewart, c2010.

Follows the life of septuagenarian artist Mary Delany, including her invention of mixed media collage late in life and her relationships with such figures as Jonathan Swift, the Duchess of Portland, and King George III.

"The author entwines the story of Delany with private reflections on her own life as an artist and a woman. As Peacock undertook her eccentric quest to discover the life of the woman who created the beautiful paper mosaics that she so admired, she discovered resonant parallels. A lyrical, meditative rumination on art and the blossoming beauty of self that can be the gift of age and love." Kirkus.

Delany, Sarah Louise, 1889-1999

Delany, Sarah Louise, 1889-1999 **Having** our say : the Delany sisters' first 100 years / Sarah and A. Elizabeth Delany ; with Amy Hill

Hearth. Kodansha International, 1993. xiii, 210 p. : B

ISBN 156836010X

1. Delany family 2. Delany, Sarah Louise, 1889-1999. 3. Delany, Annie Elizabeth, 1891-1995. 4. African American women 5. Senior women 6. Aging 7. African American sisters 8. United States -- Race relations. 9. North Carolina -- History. 10. New York (State) -- History 11. Autobiographies and memoirs

LC 93023890

ALA Notable Book, 1994.

Two sisters, both over one hundred years old and the daughters of a man born into slavery, recall the triumphs and tragedies of their lives together, discussing their success as African-American professional women during Harlem's golden age.

"The combination of the two voices, beautifully blended by Ms. Hearth, evokes an epic history, often cruel and brutal, but always deeply humane in their spirited telling of it." New York Times Book Review.

Delisle, Guy

★Delisle, Guy **Pyongyang** : a journey in North Korea / Guy Delisle ; [translated by Helge Dascher]. Drawn & Quarterly, 2005. 176 p. : B

ISBN 1896597890

1. Delisle, Guy Travel North Korea. 2. Canadians in Korea 3. Cartoonists 4. Animators 5. Totalitarianism 6. North Korea -- Social conditions -- 21st century 7. Autobiographies and memoirs 8. Comics and Graphic novels

One of the few Westerners granted access to North Korea documents his observations of the secretive society in this graphic travelogue that depicts the cultural alienation, boredom, and desires of ordinary North Koreans.

"Pyongyang will appeal to multiple audiences: current events buffs, Persepolis fans and those who just love a good yarn." Publishers Weekly.

Deng, Xiaoping, 1904-1997

Pantsov, Alexander V. **Deng** Xiaoping : a revolutionary life / Alexander V. Pantsov, with Steven I. Levine. Oxford University Press, 2015 544 p. B

ISBN 9780199392032

1. Deng, Xiaoping, 1904-1997. 2. Heads of state -- China 3. Communism -- China. 4. China -- History -- 20th century. 5. Biographies

LC 2014042299

Deng Xiaoping joined the Chinese Communist movement as a youth and rose in its ranks to become an important lieutenant of Mao's from the 1930s onward. Two years after Mao's death in 1976, Deng became the de facto leader of the Chinese Communist Party and the prime architect of China's post-Mao reforms. Abandoning the Maoist socio-economic policies he had long fervently supported, he set in motion changes that would dramatically transform China's economy, society, and position in the world.

"Aiming for and largely achieving a balanced perspective, Pantsov and Levine give Deng credit for his accomplishments but do not shy away from his crimes. The result is a nuanced portrait of a genuine reformer who nevertheless kept his foot firmly on the brakes; a man of the people with an authoritarian bent; and, in the end, a man more similar to Mao than he was different." Booklist.

Vogel, Ezra F. **Deng** Xiaoping and the transformation of China / Ezra F. Vogel. Belknap Press of Harvard University Press, 2011. xxiv, 876 p., 22 p. of plates : B

ISBN 9780674055445

1. Deng, Xiaoping, 1904-1997. 2. Heads of state -- China. 3. Communists. 4. Communism. 5. Politicians. 6. China -- Politics and government -- 1976-2002. 7. Biographies

LC 2011006925

Lionel Gelber Prize (Canada), 2012.National Book Critics Circle Award for Biography finalist, 2011.

Denny, Glen

Denny, Glen **Valley** walls : a memoir of climbing and living in Yosemite / Glen Denny. Yosemite Conservancy, 2016 224 p. B

ISBN 9781930238633

1. Photographers 2. Rock climbing. 3. Rock climbers. 4. Yosemite National Park. 5. Autobiographies and memoirs

LC 2015956065

Includes index.

Half a century before the first free ascent of El Capitan's Dawn Wall captivated audiences around the world in 2015, a rag-tag group of innovators were building a foundation for modern American rock climbing from their makeshift home base in Yosemite's historic Camp 4. Photographer Glen Denny was a key figure in that golden age of climbing in the 1950s and 1960s, capturing pioneering feats on camera while tackling challenging ascents himself.

"Climbing newcomers will benefit from the glossary, but the love Denny has for the climbs, climbers, and life during this era make this a must-have for outdoor enthusiasts." Library Journal.

Deraniyagala, Sonali

Deraniyagala, Sonali **Wave** : a memoir of life after the tsunami / Sonali Deraniyagala. Alfred A. Knopf, 2013. 224 p. B

ISBN 9780307962690

1. Deraniyagala, Sonali. 2. Deraniyagala, Sonali Family. 3. Disaster victims -- Sri Lanka 4. Widows 5. Indian Ocean Tsunami, 2004. 6. Bereavement. 7. Sri Lanka. 8. Autobiographies and memoirs

LC 2012040980

"Borzoi Books."

National Book Critics Circle Award for Autobiography/ Memoir finalist

A memoir of the author's experiences as a survivor of the 2004 tsunami that killed her parents, husband, and two young sons recounts her struggles with profound grief and survivor's guilt and her gradual steps toward healing.

Descartes, Rene, 1596-1650

Watson, Richard A., 1931- **Cogito** ergo sum : the life of Rene Descartes / Richard A. Watson. David R. Godine, 2002. viii, 375 p. : B

ISBN 9781567921847

1. Descartes, Rene, 1596-1650. 2. Philosophers -- France 3. Mathematicians 4. Reason 5. Philosophy -- History 6. Biographies

LC 2001040858

"For all of his puckish delight in a juicy anecdote, Watson recognizes and carefully explicates the cultural centrality of Descartes' intellectual legacy. That legacy ensures numerous readers sure to praise a biographer who delivers both the philosopher's cerebral doctrines and his unmistakably human conduct." Booklist.

Di Maio, Vincent J. M., 1941-

Di Maio, Vincent J. M., 1941- **Morgue** : a life in death / Dr. Vincent Di Maio and Ron Franscell ; foreword by Dr. Jan Garavaglia. St. Martin's Press, 2016 304 p. B

ISBN 9781250067142

1. Pathologists 2. Forensic sciences 3. Autopsy 4. Criminal

investigation

LC 2016001125

An award-winning writer and a renowned pathologist describe the most famous and interesting cases of the doctor's career, including the exhuming of Lee Harvey Oswald and the shooting of Trayvon Martin.

"Di Maio and Franscell deliver a well-paced, thoughtful, and absorbing work that will fascinate crime buffs and scholars alike." Publishers Weekly.

DiFelice, Bekah

DiFelice, Bekah **Almost** there : searching for home in a life on the move / Bekah Difelice. NavPress, 2017. 208 p. **B**

ISBN 9781631464713

1. Moving, Household 2. Wanderers and wandering 3. Christian life 4. Life change events 5. Autobiographies and memoirs

LC bl2017026896

Almost There is for those on the move and those who feel restless right where they are. It's for those who struggle with not belonging, with feeling unsettled, with believing that home is out of their reach, at least for the moment. And Almost There is for those who find themselves in a transient lifestyle they didn't expect--say, moving across the country for a new job or the military or an opportunity to begin again.

"This book will appeal broadly to those who have lived a wandering existence, and Christian readers in particular will appreciate DiFelices tangents on the lives of biblical characters ." Publishers Weekly.

DiFranco, Ani

DiFranco, Ani **No** walls and the recurring dream : a memoir / Ani DiFranco. Viking, 2019. 320 p. **B**

ISBN 9780735225176

1. DiFranco, Ani. 2. Women singers -- United States 3. Women social reformers 4. Singers -- United States 5. Social reformers -- United States 6. Autobiographies and memoirs

LC 2019003676

In her new memoir, No Walls and the Recurring Dream, Ani DiFranco recounts her early life from a place of hard-won wisdom, combining personal expression, the power of music, feminism, political activism, storytelling, philanthropy, entrepreneurship, and much more into an inspiring whole.

"DiFranco has defied convention yet remained true to herself. A must for her fans, this riveting, thought-provoking work will also appeal to anyone who enjoys a well-written autobiography." Library Journal.

DiMaggio, Joe, 1914-1999

Cramer, Richard Ben **Joe** DiMaggio : the hero's life / Richard Ben Cramer. Simon & Schuster, 2000. xi, 546 p. : **B**

ISBN 0684853914

1. DiMaggio, Joe, 1914-1999. 2. Monroe, Marilyn, 1926-1962 Relations with men. 3. Engelberg, Morris. 4. New York Yankees (Baseball team) 5. Baseball players 6. Outfielders (Baseball) 7. Batters (Baseball) 8. Men/women relations. 9. Biographies.

LC 00049232

Includes index."

In this biography of the baseball player, Cramer taps every plank in the wall that DiMaggio erected around himself and that protected him from inquiry. In the wall's hollow spots, Cramer locates the girls, finds the Mob guys, and behind the legend of grace and elegance on and off the field discovers a legend who in reality was more often than not graceless and inelegant." The New Yorker.

Positano, Rock G. **Dinner** with Dimaggio : memories of an American hero / Dr. Rock Positano and John Positano ; With a foreword by Francis Ford Coppola. Simon & Schuster, 2017. 288 p. **B**

ISBN 9781501156847

1. DiMaggio, Joe, 1914-1999. 2. Baseball players -- United States 3. Baseball 4. Fame 5. Celebrities 6. Biographies

LC 2016051476

Includes index.

A portrait of the iconic Yankee star by his doctor and friend describes how they supported one another throughout DiMaggio's final years, in an account that discusses such topics as DiMaggio's career-ending injuries and his relationships with first wife Dorothy Arnold and Marilyn Monroe.

"Positano, helped by his brother John, renders a wholly human portrait of an American icon navigating his way through an adoring yet relentlessly demanding public." Booklist.

Dial, Roman

★Dial, Roman The **adventurer's** son : a memoir / Roman Dial. William Morrow & Co, 2020. 368 p. **B**

ISBN 9780062876607

1. Fathers and sons 2. Adventurers 3. Rain forests 4. Wilderness areas 5. Costa Rica 6. Autobiographies and memoirs

LC bl2020000030

An Alaska Pacific University scientist and National Geographic Explorer recounts his two-year effort to uncover the fate of his adventurer son, who in 2014 disappeared into the untracked rainforest of Corcovado National Park.

"In its emotional restraint and careful descriptions of the wild, this is a slow-burning tribute. A poignant, highly moving memoir of tragic circumstances and a lifelong love of exploring." Kirkus

Diamant, Anita

Diamant, Anita **Pitching** my tent : on marriage, motherhood, friendship, and other leaps of faith / Anita Diamant. Scribner, 2005, c2003. xiii, 223 p. ; **B**

ISBN 0743246179

1. Diamant, Anita Anecdotes. 2. Jewish women -- United States 3. Jews -- United States 4. Judaism -- United States. 5. Autobiographies and memoirs.

LC bl2005020665

Reprint. Originally published: 2003.

A collection of essays by the author of The Red Tent and Good Harbor, written during her pre-novelist years as an columnist, considers such themes as the nature of family, the relationship between parents and children, and embracing Judaism in today's culture.

"This collection of short essays, culled primarily from the Boston Globe Sunday Magazine and then reworked [are] organized around such themes as love and marriage, child rearing, friendship and living a religious life. The book's strength lies in its woman-to-woman conversational tone, especially in the opening section about married life and its dark side. These morsels will make a tasty snack for Diamant's admirers." Publishers Weekly.

Diana, Princess of Wales, 1961-1997

Bradford, Sarah, 1938- **Diana** / Sarah Bradford. Penguin Books, 2007, c2006. xviii, 443 p. : **B**

ISBN 0143112465

1. Diana, Princess of Wales, 1961-1997. 2. Charles, Prince of Wales, 1948- 3. Princesses -- Great Britain. 4. Marriage. 5. Divorce. 6. Men/women relations. 7. Biographies

LC bl2007014336

Originally published: New York : Viking, 2006.

Draws on interviews with individuals closest to the late princess to discuss her life behind the scandals, tracing her courtship with Prince Charles, transformation into a high-profile public figure, and the collapse of her marriage.

Brown, Tina **Remembering** Diana : a life in photographs / foreword by Tina Brown. National Geographic, 2017 199 p. : **B**
ISBN 9781426218538
1. Diana, Princess of Wales, 1961-1997 Pictorial works. 2. Princesses -- Great Britain -- Pictorial works.
LC 2017006355
Published to coincide with the 20th anniversary of the tragic death of Diana, Princess of Wales, an elegant book showcases photographs from the National Geographic archive that document the royal's most memorable moments in the spotlight and features reflections from those who knew her best.

Brown, Tina The **Diana** chronicles / Tina Brown. Doubleday, 2007. xvi, 542 p. : **B**
ISBN 9780385517089
1. Diana, Princess of Wales, 1961-1997. 2. Princesses -- Great Britain. 3. Mothers and daughters 4. Female friendship 5. Biographies
LC bl2007007241
Ill. on lining papers.
A portrait of the late Princess Diana examines her relationships with the various women in her life, including her sexually charged mother, scheming grandmother, hated stepmother, competitive sisters, and the "other woman," Camilla Parker Bowles.

★Morton, Andrew, 1953- **Diana** : her true story--in her own words / Andrew Morton. Simon & Schuster Paperbacks, 2017. 448 p., 16 unnumbered p. of plates : **B**
ISBN 9781501169731
1. Diana, Princess of Wales, 1961-1997. 2. Princesses -- Great Britain 3. Celebrities. 4. Fame. 5. Great Britain -- History. 6. Biographies
LC 2017302299
Includes index.
An intimate portrait of the Princess of Wales describes her public and private life, reveals details about her marital problems, and discusses her attitudes toward motherhood and public service

Diaz, Jaquira

Diaz, Jaquira **Ordinary** girls : a memoir / Jaquira Díaz. Algonquin Books of Chapel Hill, 2019. 256 p. **B**
ISBN 9781616209131
1. Diaz, Jaquira Childhood and youth. 2. Multiracial women. 3. Families -- Puerto Rico. 4. Family problems 5. Mental illness 6. Puerto Rico 7. Miami, Florida 8. Autobiographies and memoirs
LC 2019009593
Traces the author's upbringing in the housing projects of Puerto Rico, her mother's battle with schizophrenia, her personal struggles with sexual assault and her efforts to pursue a literary career.

"Her skillful weaving-in of several harrowing deaths that made national headlines, including the Casey Anthony case and the Baby Lollipops Murder, illuminates some eerie similarities and connections to her life. While the story of a typical displaced girl's life could have been tragic, Daz takes charge, changes her trajectory, and tells a tale of an individual who ultimately triumphs." Booklist.

Diaz, Von

Diaz, Von **Coconuts** and collards : recipes and stories from Puerto Rico to the Deep South / Von Diaz. Univ Press of Florida, 2018 192 p. **B**
ISBN 9780813056654
1. Immigration and emigration 2. Immigrants 3. Cooking 4. Recipes 5. Puerto Rico 6. Southern States 7. Autobiographies and memoirs
LC bl2018087290
Includes recipes
When her family moved from Puerto Rico to Atlanta, Von Diaz traded plantains, roast pork, and malta for grits, fried chicken, and sweet tea. Brimming with humor and nostalgia, Coconuts and Collards is a recipe-packed memoir of growing up Latina in the Deep South.

Dickens, Charles, 1812-1870

★Slater, Michael **Charles** Dickens : [a life defined by writing] / Michael Slater. Yale University Press, c2009. xvii, 696 p. : **B**
ISBN 9780300112078
1. Dickens, Charles, 1812-1870. 2. Authors, English -- 19th century 3. Biographies
LC 2009026834
Presents the life of the English author, focusing on his prodigious writings of all types, his public readings, his compassion for the poor and downtrodden of Victorian society, and his charitable works, along with a critical analysis of his major novels.

"This biography actually feels somewhat austere: Slater sticks to the known Gradgrindian facts, emphasizes the writing and public performances, seldom goes in for much scene-painting or gratuitous anecdote, and refuses to speculate unduly without evidence. For anybody who wants to know more about this dynamo of Victorian letters, Michael Slater's superb biography is the one to read." Washington Post Book World.

Tomalin, Claire **Charles** Dickens : a life / Claire Tomalin. Penguin Press, 2011. 496 p. **B**
ISBN 9781594203091
1. Authors, English -- 19th century 2. London, England -- History -- 1800-1950 3. England -- Social life and customs -- 19th century. 4. Biographies
LC 2011031466
Chronicles the story of the 19th-century literary master from the challenges he faced as the imprisoned son of a profligate father, his rise to one of England's foremost novelists and the personal demons that challenged his relationships.

Wilson, A. N., 1950- The **mystery** of Charles Dickens / A. N. Wilson. HarperCollins, 2020. 384 p. **B**
ISBN 9780062954947
1. Authors, English -- 19th century 2. Creation (Literary, artistic, etc.) 3. Fame 4. Suffering 5. Biographies
LC bl2020046150
A lively and insightful biographical celebration of the imaginative genius of Charles Dickens, published in commemoration of the 150th anniversary of his death. Charles Dickens was a superb public performer, a great orator and one of the most famous of the Eminent Victorians. Slight of build, with a frenzied, hyper-energetic personality, Dickens looked much older than his fifty-eight years when he died--an occasion marked by a crowded funeral at Westminster Abbey, despite his waking wishes for a small affair. Experiencing the worst and best of life during the Victorian Age, Dickens was not merely the conduit through whom some of the most beloved characters in literature came into the world. He was one of them.

"Wilson is the perfect choice to write about this complicated soul, showing how reading Dickens, one emerges with a new appreciation of the people one encounters. Even 150 years after his death, Dickens's life and works continue to fascinate." Library Journal

Dickinson, Amy

Dickinson, Amy The **mighty** queens of Freeville : a mother, a daughter, and the people who raised them / Amy Dickinson. Hyperion Books, 2009. 240 p. **B**

ISBN 9781401322854

1. Dickinson, Amy. 2. Dickinson, Amy Family. 3. Dickinson, Amy Homes and haunts Freeville, New York. 4. Extended families. 5. Women. 6. Single mothers 7. Divorced mothers 8. Freeville, New York. 9. Autobiographies and memoirs

LC 2008026525

"In the summertime of 2002, after spending months living off of her credit cards between freelance writing jobs, Dickinson sent in an audition column to the Chicago Tribune and became the paper's replacement for the late Ann Landers. Here, Dickinson traces her own personal history, as well as the history of her mother's family whose members make up the Mighty Queens of Freeville, N.Y., the small town where Dickinson was raised, and where she raised her own daughter between stints in London; New York City; Washington, D.C.; and Chicago. Dickinson writes with an honesty that is at once folksy and intelligent, and brings to life all of the struggles of raising a child (Dickinson was a single mother) and the challenges and rewards of having a supportive extended family." Publishers Weekly.

Dickinson, Amy **Strangers** tend to tell me things : a memoir of love, loss, and living on / Amy Dickinson. Hachette Books, 2016 240 p. **B**

ISBN 9780316352642

1. Advice columnists 2. Family relationships. 3. Men/women relations

LC 2016027999

The voice behind America's most popular advice column "Ask Amy" and the New York Times best-selling author of The Mighty Queens of Freeville returns with her follow-up memoir of family, second chances and finding love.

"In this extension of her debut memoir, Dickinson remains an engagingly chatty, witty, and relatable writer with sage insights." Kirkus.

Dickinson, Bruce, 1958-

Dickinson, Bruce, 1958- **What** does this button do? : an autobiography / Bruce Dickinson. Dey Street Books, 2017. x, 371 pages, 16 unnumbered pages of plates : **B**

ISBN 9780062468130

1. Iron Maiden (Musical group) 2. Singers 3. Rock groups 4. Rock musicians 5. Heavy metal music 6. Great Britain -- Social life and customs -- 20th century 7. Autobiographies and memoirs

LC 2017568208

A memoir by the multifaceted lead vocalist of Iron Maiden traces his myriad experiences outside of the entertainment industry while sharing insight into his solo work, his turbulent childhood, his battle with cancer and his views on the band's enduring cultural influence.

Dickinson, Emily, 1830-1886

★Ackmann, Martha **These** fevered days : ten pivotal moments in the making of Emily Dickinson / Martha Ackmann. W. W. Norton & Company, 2020 288 p. **B**

ISBN 9780393609301

1. Dickinson, Emily, 1830-1886. 2. Poets, American -- 19th century 3. Women poets 4. Creativity in women 5. Writing 6. Amherst, Massachusetts -- History -- 19th century 7. Biographies

LC 2019044493

Shares remarkable insights into the mythologized world of Emily Dickinson through 10 decisive episodes that marked her evolution as a poet, from her religious crisis as a student at Mount Holyoke through her relationship with sister-in-law first reader, Susan.

"Radiant prose, palpable descriptions, and deep empathy for the poet's sensibility make this biography extraordinary." Kirkus

★Gordon, Lyndall **Lives** like loaded guns : Emily Dickinson and her family's feuds / Lyndall Gordon. Viking, 2010. xvii, 491 p., [16] p. of plates : **B**

ISBN 9780670021932

1. Dickinson, Emily, 1830-1886 Family. 2. Family feuds. 3. Poets, American -- 19th century -- Family relationships. 4. Women poets -- United States -- 19th century 5. Biographies

LC 2009046311

Lyndall Gordon, an award-winning biographer, tells the riveting story of the Dickinsons, and reveals Emily as a very different woman from the pale, lovelorn recluse that exists in the popular imagination.

"The author argues that it wasn't heartbreak that kept the poet sequestered, . it was epilepsy, a then-uncontrollable and shameful malady. With one stroke, Gordon recasts Dickinson's entire oeuvre. She then reveals the outrageous treachery of the poet's esteemed brother, Austin, who held his unmarried sisters, wife Susan, and their children hostage to his passion for his ambitious mistress, Mabel Loomis Todd, whose scheming husband encouraged the affair. A jolting and utterly intriguing watershed achievement." Booklist.

Diderot, Denis, 1713-1784

Curran, Andrew S. **Diderot** and the art of thinking freely / Andrew S. Curran. Other Press, 2019. 320 p. **B**

ISBN 9781590516706

1. Diderot, Denis, 1713-1784. 2. Philosophers -- France 3. Enlightenment (European intellectual movement) 4. Intellectual freedom 5. Intellectual life 6. France -- Social life and customs -- 18th century 7. Europe -- Social life and customs -- 18th century 8. Biographies

LC 2018019273

A biography of the prescient philosopher who was jailed in 1749 for atheism describes how he thought about natural selection before Darwin did, mused about the Oedipus complex before Freud and wondered about genetic manipulation centuries before Dolly the Sheep.

Didion, Joan

Daugherty, Tracy The **last** love song : a biography of Joan Didion / Tracy Daugherty. St. Martin's Press, 2015. 560 p. **B**

ISBN 9781250010025

1. Didion, Joan. 2. Authors, American 3. Women authors 4. Biographies

LC 2015017162

Joan Didion lived a life in the public and private eye with her late husband, writer John Gregory Dunne, whom she met while the two were working in New York City when Didion was at Vogue and Dunne was writing for Time. They became wildly successful writing partners when they moved to Los Angeles and co-wrote screenplays and adaptations together. Didion is well-known for her literary journalistic style in both fiction and non-fiction. Some of her most-notable work includes Slouching Towards Bethlehem, Run River, and The Year of Magical Thinking, a National Book Award winner and shortlisted for the Pulitzer Prize, it dealt with the grief surrounding Didion after the loss of her husband and daughter. Daugherty takes readers on a journey back through time, following a young Didion in Sacramento, through to her adult life as a writer interviewing those who know and knew her personally, while maintaining a respectful distance from the reclusive literary great.

Didion, Joan **Where** I was from / Joan Didion. Knopf, 2003. 226 p. **B**

ISBN 0679433325

1. National characteristics, American. 2. California in literature 3. Independence (Personal quality) 4. Self-reliance 5. California -- History. 6. California -- Social conditions. 7. Autobiographies and memoirs

LC 2002043325

The essayist explores American ideals of independence and self-reliance by probing her own life and those of her relatives, discussing how the character of California's settlers created the state as it exists today.

"This is a complex and challenging memoir, difficult to enter into but just as difficult to put down. Those who have long admired the clarity and precision of her prose will not be disappointed with this partly autobiographical, partly historical, but fully engrossing account." Library Journal.

★Didion, Joan The **year** of magical thinking / Joan Didion. A.A. Knopf, c2005. 227 p. **B**

ISBN 140004314X

1. Dunne, John Gregory, 1932- Death and burial. 2. Loss (Psychology) 3. Grief. 4. Girls in comas. 5. Authors, American -- 20th century -- Family relationships. 6. Autobiographies and memoirs

LC 2005045132

National Book Award for Nonfiction, 2005.

Pulitzer Prize for Biography or Autobiography finalist

National Book Critics Circle Award for Autobiography/Memoir finalist

An autobiographical portrait of marriage and motherhood by the acclaimed author details her struggle to come to terms with life and death, illness, sanity, personal upheaval, and grief.

"The author chronicles the year following the death of her husband, fellow writer John Gregory Dunne, from a massive heart attack on December 30, 2003, while the couple's only daughter, Quintana, lay unconscious in a nearby hospital suffering from pneumonia and septic shock. This is an indispensable addition to Didion's body of work and a lyrical, disciplined entry in the annals of mourning literature." Publishers Weekly.

Dillard, Annie

Dillard, Annie An **American** childhood / Annie Dillard. Harper & Row, c1987. 255 p. : **B**

ISBN 0060158050

1. Dillard, Annie Childhood and youth 2. Growing up. 3. Childhood. 4. Authors, American -- 20th century 5. Pittsburgh, Pennsylvania -- Social life and customs. 6. Autobiographies and memoirs

LC BL 99986231

Map on lining papers.

National Book Critics Circle Award for Biography finalist, 1987.

A moving and vivid recollection of the Pulitzer Prize-winning authors childhood in Pittsburgh in the 1950s conveys the keen mind and sense of adventure with which she experienced relatives, neighbors, nature, friends, and changes

"Dillard's luminous prose painlessly captures the pain of growing up in this wonderful evocation of childhood. The events of childhood often loom larger than life; the magic of Dillard's writing is that she sets down typical childhood happenings with their original immediacy and force." Publishers Weekly.

Dillard, Annie The **writing** life / Annie Dillard. Harper & Row, c1989. 111 p. ; **B**

ISBN 9780060161569

1. Dillard, Annie. 2. Authors, American -- 20th century 3. United States -- Social life and customs.

LC 89045034

A best-selling, Pulitzer Prize-winning author looks at her craft and, in a series of illuminating metaphors and anecdotes, paints a picture of a demanding, unpredictable, and sometimes absurd existence

"The author probes the sorcery that levitates her own writing, discussing with clear eye and wry wit how, where and why she writes." Publishers Weekly.

Dinesen, Isak, 1885-1962

★Dinesen, Isak, 1885-1962 **Out** of Africa ; and, Shadows on the grass / Isak Dinesen. Vintage Books, 1989. ix, 462 p. ; **B**

ISBN 9780679724759

1. Dinesen, Isak, 1885-1962 Homes and haunts Kenya. 2. British in Africa. 3. Intellectual life -- Kenya -- 20th century. 4. Rural life -- Kenya. 5. Authors, Danish -- 20th century 6. Kenya -- Description and travel. 7. Autobiographies and memoirs

LC 89040144

In describing her experiences managing a coffee plantation in Kenya, the author provides insights into the nature of African life

Disney, Walt, 1901-1966

Gabler, Neal **Walt** Disney : the triumph of the American imagination / Neal Gabler. Knopf, 2006. xx, 851 p., 32 p. of plates : **B**

ISBN 067943822X

1. Disney, Walt, 1901-1966. 2. Walt Disney Company 3. Animators -- United States 4. Biographies

LC 2006045257

"Although Gabler focuses on corporate matters at the expense of critical treatment of the films, he presents a balanced treatment of the man and his achievements, realistically assessing Disney's considerable impact and offering insight into the hidden, restless soul who constantly challenged himself, risking the financial stability of his empire more than once in his unceasing pursuit of his dreams." Booklist.

Dolan, Timothy Michael

Boyle, Christina An **American** Cardinal : the biography of Cardinal Timothy Dolan / Christina Boyle. St. Martins Press, 2014. 288 p. **B**

ISBN 9781250032874

1. Dolan, Timothy Michael. 2. Catholic Church Clergy. 3. Cardinals -- United States 4. Biographies

LC 2014028470

Chronicles the life of Cardinal Timothy Dolan, the archbishop of New York and the man who might one day become the first American pope.

"All readers, not just Roman Catholics, will be inspired by this story of a Midwestern boy-turned-prominent figure and leaders can learn a lot from his handling of opposition, conflict, and the press." Library Journal.

Dolby, Thomas

Dolby, Thomas The **speed** of sound : breaking the barrier between music and technology / Thomas Dolby. Flatiron Books, 2016. 288 p. **B**

ISBN 9781250071842

1. Dolby, Thomas. 2. Composers. 3. Music and technology. 4. Digital music 5. MP3 (Audio coding standard) -- History. 6. Autobiographies and memoirs

LC 2016021708

The 1980s New Wave star-turned-Silicon Valley entrepreneur traces his disadvantaged early years in a London bedsit, creation of the breakout hit "She Blinded Me With Science" and role in pioneering the use of MP3s in cellphones.

"This stellar book will appeal to students, scholars, and general readers interested in modern technologys startling effects on music and popular culture." Kirkus.

Domino, Fats, 1928-2017

Coleman, Rick **Blue** Monday : Fats Domino and the lost dawn of rock 'n' roll / Rick Coleman. Da Capo Press, 2006. xix, 364 p. : **B**

ISBN 0306814919

1. Rhythm and blues musicians -- United States 2. Rock musicians -- United States

LC bl2006015325

Includes bibliographical references (p. [307]-344) and index.

A noted R&B scholar celebrates the contributions of Fats Domino to the evolution of modern-day rock music, drawing on interviews with many early musical legends--including Lloyd Price, the Clovers, Charles Brown, and others--to examine the career of the legendary musician, the influence of New Orleans, and the impact of rock 'n' roll on the civil rights movement.

"Coleman has crafted a biography of Fats Domino, drawing on new interviews with the pianist himself. From his childhood in New Orleans through the early days of rock'n'roll, when he endured travel difficulties in the segregated South and frequent riots at his concerts, Fats remained a shy but demanding performer and personality. A homesick father who seemed to cherish his family, Fats was also a hard-drinking womanizer, and Coleman tells his story with compassion and honesty up to Fats's survival of Hurricane Katrina in his Ninth Ward home. His argument that rock'n'roll sprung from Fats and the New Orleans sound is hard to dispute, as Fats was playing long before others now credited with starting the revolution. Despite the occasional slips into fandom, this is an essential purchase for any library collecting the history of rock'n'roll." Library Journal.

Dorey-Stein, Beck

Dorey-Stein, Beck **From** the corner of the oval : a memoir / Rebecca Dorey-Stein. Random House Inc., 2018. 304 p. **B**

ISBN 9780525509127

1. Obama, Barack Friends and associates 2. White House, Washington, D.C. Staff 3. Stenographers 4. Presidents -- United States -- Staff 5. Office romance 6. Political culture 7. Washington, D.C. -- Social life and customs -- 21st century 8. United States -- Politics and government -- 2009-2017 9. Autobiographies and memoirs

LC 2017053262

A behind-the-scenes memoir takes readers inside the Obama White House through the eyes of a young staffer learning the ropes, falling in love and finding her place in the world.

"Dorey-Stein relates the highs and lows of the Obama presidency intermixed with those from her personal life in a compulsively readable style--think history lesson meets soap opera. In this poignant, brutally honest, and often-funny work of self-reflection, Dorey-Stein pulls no punches and tells all she learned from and about the president who taught me to look up. " Booklist.

Dorgan, Byron L.

Dorgan, Byron L. The **girl** in the photograph : the true story of a lost Native American child / Byron L. Dorgan. Thomas Dunne Books, 2019. 192 p. **B**

ISBN 9781250173645

1. Native American children 2. Foster children. 3. Child abuse 4. Native American foster children. 5. United States 6. North Dakota 7. Biographies

LC 2019019858

The former North Dakota Senator and author traces the story of a Native American child in a foster-care system that has been tied to widespread abuse, depression and suicide.

Dostoyevsky, Fyodor, 1821-1881

★Frank, Joseph, 1918-2013 **Dostoevsky** : a writer in his time / Joseph Frank. Princeton University Press, 2009. 984 p. **B**

ISBN 9780691128191

1. Dostoyevsky, Fyodor, 1821-1881. 2. Authors, Russian -- 19th century. 3. Writing. 4. Existentialism in literature. 5. Intellectual life -- Russia. 6. Russia -- History -- 19th century. 7. Biographies

LC 2009001418

"Frank displays a brilliant command of Dostoyevsky's heroic endeavors, and his biography reads readily, especially for such a scholarly work." Library Journal.

Doty, James

Doty, James **Into** the magic shop : a neurosurgeon's quest to discover the mysteries of the brain and the secrets of the heart. / James R. Doty. Avery, 2016 304 p. **B**

ISBN 9781594632983

1. Doty, James. 2. Mindfulness (Psychology) 3. Success (Concept) 4. Compassion 5. Poor children 6. Autobiographies and memoirs

LC bl2015058029

Part memoir, part science, part inspiration and part practical instruction, a fascinating volume, drawing on the author's own childhood experiences during which he was taught exercises to ease his own suffering and manifest his greatest desires, shows readers how they can change their lives by first changing their brains and their hearts.

"An optimistic and engagingly well-told life story that incorporates scientific investigation into its altruistic message." Kirkus.

Doty, Mark

Doty, Mark **Dog** years : a memoir / Mark Doty. Harper Collins Publishers, c2007. viii, 215 p. ; **B**

ISBN 006117100X

1. Poets, American -- 20th century 2. Golden retrievers 3. Dog owners 4. Dogs as pets. 5. Autobiographies and memoirs

LC 2006046491

Stonewall Book Award for the Israel Fishman Non-fiction Award, 2008.

Why do dogs speak so profoundly to our inner lives? When poet Doty decides to adopt a dog as a companion for his dying partner, he finds himself bringing home Beau, a large golden retriever, malnourished and in need of loving care. Beau joins Arden, the black retriever, to complete their family. As Beau bounds back into life, the two dogs become Doty's intimate companions, his solace, and eventually the very life force that keeps him from abandoning all hope during the darkest days. Their tenacity, loyalty, and love inspire him when all else fails.

Doughty, Caitlin

Doughty, Caitlin **Smoke** gets in your eyes : and other lessons from the crematory / Caitlin Doughty. W. W. Norton & Company, [2014] 256 p. **B**

ISBN 9780393240238

1. Doughty, Caitlin. 2. Undertakers 3. Death education 4.

Burial. 5. Bloggers 6. United States -- Social life and customs. 7. Autobiographies and memoirs

LC 2014017294

"Not shying away from candid descriptions of corpses, cremation, and putrefaction, Doughty . details postmortem proceedings not to repulse but to reveal our modern society's 'death denial.' " Booklist.

Douglas, Illeana, 1965-

Douglas, Illeana, 1965- **I** blame Dennis Hopper : and other stories from a life lived in and out of the movies / Illeana Douglas. Flatiron Books, 2015. 304 p. **B**

ISBN 9781250052919

1. Actors and actresses -- United States 2. Film industry and trade 3. Family relationships 4. Film actors and actresses -- United States 5. Hollywood, California 6. Autobiographies and memoirs

LC 2015022208

"In 1969, Illeana Douglas' parents saw the film Easy Rider. Like many folks of that generation, the groundbreaking film transformed them. Taking Dennis Hopper's words, "That's what it's all about man", to heart, they abandoned what Illeana had hoped would be her comfortable upper middle class life for a childhood filled with hippies, goats, free spirits, and free love. Illeana writes, "Since it was all out of my control, I began to think of my life as a movie, with a Dennis Hopper like father at the center of it. Years later I would work with Dennis Hopper on the film Search and Destroy".-- Provided by publisher.

"The author's warm portraits and disarming honesty infuse the memoir with an endearing sweetness and charm." Kirkus.

Douglas, John E.

Douglas, John E. The **killer** across the table : unlocking the secrets of serial killers and predators with the FBI's original mindhunter / John E. Douglas and Mark Olshaker. Dey Street Books, 2019. 340 pages ; **B**

ISBN 9780062910639

1. FBI Behavioral Science Unit. 2. FBI agents. 3. Criminal profiling. 4. Serial murder investigation -- United States. 5. Serial murderers -- United States -- Psychology.

LC bl2019008878

The FBI criminal profiler and inspiration for the Mindhunter series shares the stories of four of the most complex predatory killers of his career, offering previously undisclosed insights into his strategies and profiling process.

"Famous as a groundbreaking FBI criminal profiler, a prolific true-crime writer, and the catalyst for Mindhunter on Netflix, Douglas, along with coauthor Olshaker, reveals what hes discerned in the minds of notorious killers." Booklist.

Douglas, Marjory Stoneman, 1890-1998

Davis, Jack E., 1956- An **Everglades** providence : Marjory Stoneman Douglas and the American environmental century / Jack E. Davis. University of Georgia Press, c2009. 616 p. **B**

ISBN 9780820330716

1. Douglas, Marjory Stoneman, 1890-1998. 2. Women environmentalists -- Florida 3. Feminists -- United States 4. Authors, American -- 20th century 5. Nature conservation -- Everglades, Florida 6. Florida.

LC 2008049073

Tells the tale of this suffragist, feminist, and environmentalist who fought for the preservation and protection of the Everglades and, through her due diligence and skillful writing, won the battle that resulted in it becoming a national wilderness area.

"This is both a portrait of one of the 20th century's most important environmental figures and a history of Florida's Everglades. The long-lived Douglas (1890-1998) is best known for the classic The Everglades: River of Grass and her tireless efforts to preserve that region. But she was also a lifelong feminist and social activist who worked to advance human rights. In addition to the rich detail and documentation of Douglas's life, Davis offers an impressive look at America during Douglas's lifetime and the growth of America's environmental movement." Library Journal.

Douglass, Frederick, 1818-1895

★Blight, David W. **Frederick** Douglass : prophet of freedom / David W. Blight. Simon & Schuster, 2018. 864 p. **B**

ISBN 9781416590316

1. Douglass, Frederick, 1818-1895. 2. Abolitionists -- United States 3. African American abolitionists -- United States 4. Slaves 5. Antislavery movements -- United States -- History -- 19th century. 6. United States -- History -- 19th century 7. Biographies.

LC 2018007511

ALA Notable Book, 2019.

Pulitzer Prize for History, 2019.

Chronicles the life of the escaped slave who became one of the greatest orators of his day and a leading abolitionist and writer.

"This magnum opus surpasses previous singular biographies in heft and depth, establishing an essential text for students and educators seeking to understand Douglass's complex and expansive narrative. It will appeal to general audiences and specialists alike." Library Journal.

Dilbeck, D. H. **Frederick** Douglass : America's prophet / D. H. Dilbeck. The University of North Carolina Press, 2018 191 p. : **B**

ISBN 9781469636184

1. Douglass, Frederick, 1818-1895. 2. African American abolitionists. 3. Abolitionists. 4. Faith (Christianity). 5. Christian life 6. United States -- History -- 19th century. 7. Biographies

From his enslavement to freedom, Frederick Douglass was one of America's most extraordinary champions of liberty and equality. Throughout his long life, Douglass was also a man of profound religious conviction.

"Dilbeck investigates Douglass legacy as Americas moral voice and conscience, from his teenage conversion to Christianity to his search for a church that strongly opposed slavery as stridently as he did. The result is a biography that offers an insightful new understanding of an extraordinary man." Booklist.

Douglass, Frederick, 1818-1895 **My** bondage and my freedom / Frederick Douglass ; edited, with a foreword and notes, by John Stauffer. Modern Library, 2003, c1855. lv, 321 p. : **B**

ISBN 0812970314

1. African American abolitionists 2. Abolitionists 3. Anti-slavery movements -- History -- 19th century 4. Fugitive slaves. 5. Maryland -- History -- 19th century 6. United States -- History -- 19th century 7. Autobiographies and memoirs

LC 2003053976

Originally published: New York : Miller, Orton & Mulligan, 1855.In an autobiographical account, the great American reformer of the nineteenth century offers eyewitness insights into slavery, the anti-slavery movement, and their impact on race relations.

Douglass, Frederick, 1818-1895 The **portable** Frederick Douglass / Frederick Douglass ; edited with an introduction and notes by John Stauffer and Henry Louis Gates, Jr. ; general editor: Henry

Louis Gates, Jr.. Penguin Books, 2016 xxxvi, 579 p. ; **B**

ISBN 9780143106814

1. Douglass, Frederick, 1818-1895. 2. African American abolitionists 3. African American orators 4. African Americans -- History 5. Antislavery movements -- United States -- History -- 19th century 6. United States -- History -- 19th century 7. Biographies

LC 2016006199

Presents a newly edited collection of the seminal writings and speeches of a legendary writer, orator and civil rights leader.

Douglass, Frederick, 1818-1895 **Narrative** of the life of Frederick Douglass, an American slave / written by himself ; edited with an introduction by Houston A. Baker, Jr. Penguin Books, 1982. 159 p. : The Penguin American library **B**

ISBN 9780140390124

1. Douglass, Frederick, 1818-1895. 2. Abolitionists -- United States 3. African American abolitionists

LC 82005371

Portrait on lining paper.

The autobiography of the famous abolitionist and statesman who escaped to the North after twenty-one years of enslavement

Stauffer, John, 1965- **Picturing** Fredrick Douglass : an illustrated biography of the nineteenth century's most photographed American / John Stauffer, Zoe Trodd, and Celeste-Marie Bernier Liveright Publishing Corporation, 2015 320 p. **B**

ISBN 9780871404688

1. Douglass, Frederick, 1818-1895. 2. Abolitionists -- United States 3. African American abolitionists 4. Anti-slavery movements. 5. United States -- History -- 19th century. 6. Biographies

LC 2015020546

Picturing Frederick Douglass is a work that promises to revolutionize our knowledge of race and photography in nineteenth-century America. Teeming with historical detail, it is filled with surprises, chief among them the fact that neither George Custer nor Walt Whitman, and not even Abraham Lincoln, was the most photographed American of that century. In fact, it was Frederick Douglass (1818?1895), the ex-slave turned leading abolitionist, eloquent orator, and seminal writer whose fiery speeches transformed him into one of the most renowned and popular agitators of his age.

"The authors have pieced together an illuminating life portrait without extraneous biographical material, focusing intensely on their subject's belief in the strength of photographs." Kirkus.

Downie, David

Downie, David A **passion** for Paris : romanticism and romance in the City of Light / David Downie. St. Martin's Press, 2015. xiv, 304 p. : **B**

ISBN 1250043158

1. Downie, David Travel France Paris. 2. Artists -- France -- Paris. 3. Historic sites -- France -- Paris. 4. Romanticism in art -- France -- Paris. 5. Romanticism -- France -- Paris. 6. Paris (France) -- Buildings, structures, etc. 7. Paris (France) -- Description and travel. 8. Paris (France) -- Intellectual life. 9. Paris (France) -- Social life and customs. 10. Autobiographies and memoirs.

LC 2015007261

A unique combination of memoir, history, and travelogue, this is author David Downie's irreverent quest to uncover why Paris is the world's most romantic city--and has been for over 150 years. Abounding in secluded, atmospheric parks, artists' studios, cafes, restaurants and streets little changed since the 1800s, Paris exudes romance. The art and architecture, the cityscape, riverbanks, and the unparalleled quality of daily life are part of the equation. But the city's allure derives equally from hidden sources: querulous inhabitants, a bizarre culture of heroic negativity, and a rich historical past supplying enigmas, pleasures and challenges. Rarely do visitors suspect the glamor and chic and the carefree atmosphere of the City of Light grew from and still feed off the dark fountainheads of riot, rebellion, mayhem and melancholy--and the subversive literature, art and music of the Romantic Age. Weaving together his own with the lives and loves of Victor Hugo, Georges Sand, Charles Baudelaire, Balzac, Nadar and other great Romantics, Downie delights in the city's secular romantic pilgrimage sites asking, Why Paris, not Venice or Rome--the tap root of 'romance'--or Berlin, Vienna and London--where the earliest Romantics built castles-in-the-air and sang odes to nightingales? Read A Passion for Paris : Romanticism and Romance in the City of Light and find out".-- Provided by publisher.

Downs, Paul

Downs, Paul **Boss** life : surviving my own small business / Paul Downs. Blue Rider Press, 2015 368 p. **B**

ISBN 9780399172335

1. Downs, Paul. 2. Small business 3. New businesses 4. Cabinetmakers 5. Entrepreneurs 6. Autobiographies and memoirs

LC 2015016068

The author of the "You're the Boss" blog at NYTimes.com details the development of his small furniture business and the challenges he has faced along the way.

"This is an invaluable look into operational details for anyone considering starting a business or caught up in the struggle of owning and running one." Booklist.

Doyle, Arthur Conan, Sir, 1859-1930

Doyle, Arthur Conan, Sir, 1859-1930 **Arthur** Conan Doyle: his life in letters / edited by Jon Lellenberg, Daniel Stashower & Charles Foley. Penguin Press, 2008. 720 p. **B**

ISBN 1594201358

1. Doyle, Arthur Conan, Sir, 1859-1930 Correspondence. 2. Authors, Scottish -- 19th century 3. Authors, Scottish -- 20th century 4. Physicians -- Scotland 5. Holmes, Sherlock (Fictitious character) 6. Letters. 7. Autobiographies and memoirs

LC 2007014692

Includes index.

Agatha Award for Best Nonfiction, 2007.

Anthony Award for Best Critical/Nonfiction, 2008.

Edgar Allan Poe Award for Best Critical/Biographical, 2008.

An annotated collection of the esteemed author's private correspondence includes letters shared with his mother that offers insight into his endless search for fulfillment and success outside of the Sherlock Holmes tales, his decision to leave his medical profession to write full time, and his forays into spiritualism.

Sims, Michael, 1958- **Arthur** and Sherlock : Conan Doyle and the creation of Holmes / Michael Sims. Bloomsbury USA, 2017. 320 p. **B**

ISBN 9781632860392

1. Doyle, Arthur Conan, Sir, 1859-1930. 2. Mystery story writers 3. Authors, Scottish -- 19th century 4. Holmes, Sherlock (Fictitious character) 5. Detectives in literature. 6. Biographies

LC 2016033351

The author of The Story of Charlotte's Web explores the rich events behind the creation of young Arthur Conan Doyle's iconic detective, revealing the impact of his early poverty and medical experience on the development of his characters and stories.

"Simss skill and deftness with narrative biography will lead Sherlockians to hope that he continues the story of Conan Doyles life in a future volume." Publishers Weekly.

Doyle, Glennon, 1976-

Doyle, Glennon, 1976- **Love** warrior : a memoir / Glennon Doyle Melton. Flatiron Books, 2016. 288 p. **B**

ISBN 9781250075727

1. Divorced women 2. Self-discovery in women 3. Personal conduct 4. Autobiographies and memoirs

LC 2016016415

A new memoir by the New York Times bestselling author, speaker, philanthropist, and activist, LOVE WARRIOR tells the story of Glennon Doyle Melton's journey of self-discovery after a crisis in her marriage.

"Though the memoir sometimes reads like a self-help book rather than a narrative, it nevertheless tells a compelling story about self-discovery and the nature of mature love. Candid, brave, and generous." Kirkus.

★Doyle, Glennon, 1976- **Untamed** Dial Press, 2020 320 p. **B**

ISBN 9781984801258

1. Self-fulfillment 2. Self-discovery in women 3. Women/women relations 4. Personal conduct 5. Autobiographies and memoirs

LC 2019047945

An activist, speaker and philanthropist offers a memoir wrapped in a wake-up call that reveals how women can reclaim their true, untamed selves by breaking free of the restrictive expectations and cultural conditioning that leaves them feeling dissatisfied and lost.

"This testament to female empowerment and self-love, with an endearing coming-out story at the center, will delight readers." Publishers Weekly

Dresner, Amy

Dresner, Amy **My** fair junkie : a memoir of getting dirty and staying clean / Amy Dresner. Hachette Books, [2017] 240 p. **B**

ISBN 9780316430951

1. Dresner, Amy. 2. Drug addicts 3. Women drug abusers 4. Addiction 5. Alcoholic women 6. California 7. Autobiographies and memoirs

LC 2017016499

A former stand-up comic and prolific online writer chronicles her 20-year battle with sex, drug and alcohol addiction, and what happened when she finally emerged on the other side.

"Dresner brings humility, wit, and sensitivity to a topic many readers are unfamiliar with, and those that are will recognize her truths." Booklist.

Druckerman, Pamela

Druckerman, Pamela **There** are no grown-ups : a midlife coming-of-age story / Pamela Druckerman. Penguin Press, 2018 274 p. **B**

ISBN 9781594206375

1. Forties (Age) 2. Adulthood 3. Aging 4. Middle-aged women 5. Essays 6. Autobiographies and memoirs

LC 2018006194

The best-selling author charts the largely unexplored realities of being a 40-something in today's world, in a latest collection of laugh-out-loud essays that examines the decade as a milestone less associated with midlife than by the disconnects of social media, the French perspectives about libido and the challenges of raising kids while caring for aging parents.

"Half memoir and half ironic how-to guide, Druckerman's book is not only a humorous meditation on the gains and pains of a time in life 'when you become who you are'; it is also a thought-provoking meditation on 'what it means to be a grown-up." Kirkus.

Du Bois, W. E. B. (William Edward Burghardt), 1868-1963

★Lewis, David L., 1936- **W.E.B.** Du Bois : a biography / David Levering Lewis. Henry Holt and Co., 2009. xiv, 893 p. ; **B**

ISBN 9780805088052

1. African American intellectuals 2. African American civil rights workers 3. Civil Rights Movement 4. African Americans -- Civil rights -- History. 5. United States -- History -- 20th century. 6. Biographies

LC 2008000696

"A John Macrae/Holt paperback."

Condensed and updated ed. of: 2 vol. set, originally published 1993-2000.

The two-time Pulitzer Prize-winning biography of the civil-rights pioneer--now in one condensed, updated volume--chronicles Du Bois's long and storied career, detailing the momentous contributions to our national character that still echo today and offering over thirty archival photos.

Du Maurier, Daphne, 1907-1989

Rosnay, Tatiana de, 1961- **Manderley** forever : a biography of Daphne Du Maurier / Tatiana de Rosnay. St Martins Pr., 2017, c2015. 448 p. **B**

ISBN 9781250099136

1. Authors, British 2. Women authors, British -- 20th century 3. Women authors 4. Writing 5. Biographies

LC 2016049032

Originally published as Manderley for ever in 2015 by Albin Michel.

A nonfiction debut by the best-selling author of Sarah's Key traces the life and achievements of classic novelist Daphne du Maurier, sharing creative insights into the master writer's life at different ages and her enduring influence in literature.

"Through De Rosnays novel-like narrative, exhaustive research, and unbridled admiration, du Mauriers spirit comes alive on the page, endearing her to a new generation of fans." Publishers Weekly.

Dubus, Andre, 1959-

Dubus, Andre, 1959- **Townie** : a memoir / Andre Dubus III. W. W. Norton & Co., 2011. 352 p. **B**

ISBN 9780393064667

1. Authors, American -- 20th century 2. Violence. 3. Growing up. 4. Boxers (Sports) 5. Autobiographies and memoirs

LC 2010038029

Acclaimed author Andre Dubus III looks back on the dangerous path he began to take following his parents' split. Once known for his ability to speak with his fists, he shares how he turned his life around.

Duchamp, Marcel, 1887-1968

Tomkins, Calvin, 1925- **Duchamp** : a biography / Calvin Tomkins. H. Holt, 1996. 550 p. : **B**

ISBN 0805008233

1. Duchamp, Marcel, 1887-1968. 2. Artists -- France 3. Modernism (Art) -- Europe. 4. Avant-garde (Aesthetics) -- France. 5. Dadaism -- France. 6. Biographies

LC 96003080

"A John Macrae book."

A portrait of one of the fathers of post-modernism reveals Marcel Duchamp's humor, originality, and charm, as well as the artist's romantic affairs and his influence on contemporary personalities.

"Tomkins organizes the facts of Duchamp's life and work into a sober, coherent whole, and for this alone his book makes valuable reading for anyone seeking to understand how art's cutting edge was honed." New Republic.

Dufu, Tiffany

Dufu, Tiffany **Drop** the ball : achieving more by doing less / Tiffany Dufu, foreword by Gloria Steinem. Flatiron Books, 2017. 288 p. **B**

ISBN 9781250071736

1. Leadership. 2. Women executives. 3. Leadership in women. 4. Businesspeople 5. Autobiographies and memoirs

LC 2016037631

Includes index.

An inspiring memoir by a leading figure in the women's leadership movement counsels women on how to cultivate the essential skills of reevaluating expectations, setting realistic goals and meaningfully engaging with others in order to thrive in personal and professional arenas.

Duleep Singh, Sophia Alexandra, 1876-1948

Anand, Anita **Sophia** : princess, suffragette, revolutionary / Anita Anand. Bloomsbury, 2015. 320 p. **B**

ISBN 9781632860811

1. Women radicals 2. Culture conflict 3. Nobility 4. Socialists 5. Great Britain -- History -- 20th century 6. India -- History -- 20th century 7. Biographies

LC bl2015001991

"Anand writes with a journalist's sense for a solid story and a historian's eye for fascinating anecdotes. Filled with rich detail and walks through little-known avenues of the past, this work is bound to enchant history lovers, those interested in women's studies, Anglophiles, and anyone who enjoys biographies." Library Journal.

Dulles, Allen Welsh, 1893-1969

Grose, Peter, 1934- **Gentleman** spy : the life of Allen Dulles / Peter Grose. University of Mass. Press, 1996. xi, 641 p. : **B**

ISBN 1558490442

1. Dulles, Allen, 1893-1969. 2. United States. Central Intelligence Agency Officials and employees 3. Intelligence service -- United States -- History -- 20th century. 4. Spies -- United States 5. Biographies

LC 96019010

Originally published: Boston : Houghton Mifflin, 1994."This biography of the CIA director under Eisenhower and Kennedy renders the interplay of person and public event and allows readers to enter the dark world of US-sponsored terror and covert paramilitary operations. Grose sets forth in fascinating and often unfamiliar detail the spectacular CIA covert operations: in Iran, Guatemala, Indonesia; the U2 incident; the Bay of Pigs." Choice.

Miller, Scott, 1960- **Agent** 110 : Allen Dulles, American spymaster, and the German underground in World War II / Scott Miller. Simon & Schuster, 2017. 384 p. **B**

ISBN 9781451693386

1. Dulles, Allen Welsh, 1893-1969. 2. United States. Office of Strategic Services 3. Spies 4. Intelligence service. 5. World War II. 6. Secret service 7. Biographies

LC 2016025790

"Simon & Schuster nonfiction original hardcover"--Title page verso.

Presents an account of how OSS spymaster Allen Dulles led a network of disenchanted Germans in a plot to assassinate Hitler and end World War II before the invasion of opportunistic Russian forces.

"Entertaining for both its historical insights into WWII and its dramatic narrative." Kirkus.

Dumas, Thomas Alexandre, 1762-1806

★Reiss, Tom The **black** count : glory, revolution, betrayal, and the real Count of Monte Cristo / Tom Reiss. Crown Trade, 2012. ix, 414 p. : **B**

ISBN 9780307382467

1. Dumas, Thomas Alexandre, 1762-1806. 2. Dumas, Alexandre, 1802-1870. Count of Monte Cristo. 3. Characters and characteristics in literature 4. Soldiers -- France 5. Multiracial men 6. Fathers and sons -- France 7. France -- History -- 18th century 8. Biographies

LC 2012017633

Pulitzer Prize for Biography or Autobiography, 2013.

National Book Critics Circle Award for Biography finalist, 2012.

Traces the story of the mixed-race swordsman and father of novelist Alexandre Dumas, discussing his rise to the French aristocracy, his military triumphs ,and the adventures that inspired such classics as "The Three Musketeers" and "The Count of Monte Cristo."

Duncan, Isadora, 1877-1927

Duncan, Isadora, 1877-1927 **My** life / Isadora Duncan. Liveright, 1972, c1927. 359 p., 10 leaves of plates : **B**

ISBN 0871409429

1. Duncan, Isadora, 1877-1927. 2. Dancers 3. Modern dance. 4. Choreographers 5. Choreography. 6. Autobiographies and memoirs

LC 78102483

The famous dancer and choreographer tells the story of her life, from her enchantment with music and poetry to her love affairs and personal tragedies.

Dunham, Cyrus Grace

Dunham, Cyrus Grace A **year** without a name : a memoir / Cyrus Grace Dunham. Little, Brown & Company, 2019. 171 p. **B**

ISBN 9780316444965

1. Transgender persons 2. Gender identity 3. Identity (Psychology) 4. Gender-nonconforming people 5. Autobiographies and memoirs

LC bl2019023336

Describes the author's experiences as a gender-fluid individual who endured unbearable alienation and how the process of transitioning to their true gender shaped their views on queer identity, family and desire.

Dutta, Sunil

Dutta, Sunil **Stealing** green mangoes : two brothers, two fates, one Indian childhood / Sunil Dutta. Ecco, 2019. 238 p. ; **B**

ISBN 9780062795854

1. Los Angeles, California. Police Department Officials and employees. 2. Brothers 3. East Indian Americans 4. Refugees 5. Police 6. India -- History -- Partition, 1947 7. Autobiographies and memoirs

An Indian refugee-turned-LAPD terrorism expert describes his complicated relationship with his brother, a fugitive and terrorist who the author sought to understand in the wake of a terminal cancer diagnosis.

"An insightful read about the strength of individuals to overcome adversity, reminding us that while our past and family do contribute to our identity, they do not define who we become." Library Journal.

Dworkin, Andrea

Duberman, Martin B. **Andrea** Dworkin : the feminist as revolution-

ary / Martin Duberman. The New Press, 2020. 384 p. **B**
ISBN 9781620975855
1. Dworkin, Andrea. 2. Feminists 3. Women authors 4. Women radicals 5. Feminism 6. United States
LC 2020010657

Fifteen years after her death, Andrea Dworkin remains one of the most important and challenging figures in second-wave feminism. Although frequently relegated to its more radical fringes, Dworkin was without doubt a formidable and influential writer, a philosopher, and an activist-a brilliant figure who inspired and infuriated in equal measure.

"A sympathetic, cleareyed portrait that gives Dworkin her due without smoothing over her rough edges." Kirkus

Dykeman, Wilma

Dykeman, Wilma **Family** of earth : a Southern mountain childhood / Wilma Dykeman. The University of North Carolina Press, 2016. 208 p. **B**
ISBN 9781469630540
1. Dykeman, Wilma. 2. Authors, American -- Southern States 3. Beauty in nature 4. Growing up 5. Fathers and daughters 6. North Carolina 7. Appalachian Region, Southern 8. Autobiographies and memoirs
LC 2015049261

Discovered as a typewritten manuscript only after her death in 2006, Family of Earth allows us to see into the mind of the young author and Appalachian native Wilma Dykeman (1920?2006), who would become one of the American South's most prolific and storied writers.

"A captivating, poetic, difficult-to-categorize book that abundantly showcases the author's talent for making words dance." Kirkus.

Dykstra, Lenny, 1963-

Dykstra, Lenny, 1963- **House** of nails : a memoir of life on the edge / Lenny Dykstra ; with Peter Golenbock. William Morrow, 2016. 352 p. **B**
ISBN 9780062407368
1. New York Mets (Baseball team) 2. Philadelphia Phillies (Baseball team) 3. Professional baseball players 4. Professional baseball. 5. Drug addiction 6. Redemption 7. California 8. Autobiographies and memoirs
LC 2017304573

"Dykstra makes no apologies, offering 'the real truth,' but readers' opinions of him will be harsh." Kirkus.

Dylan, Bob, 1941-

Bell, Ian **Once** upon a time : the lives of Bob Dylan / Ian Bell. Pegasus, 2013 592 p. The lives of Bob Dylan ; **B**
ISBN 9781605984810
1. Singers -- United States 2. Rock musicians -- United States 3. Biographies
LC bl2013042187

In Once Upon a Time, award-winning author Ian Bell draws together the tangled strands of the many lives of Bob Dylan in all their contradictory brilliance. For the first time, the laureate of modern America is set in his entire context: musical, historical, literary, political, and personal.

"This is best described as a fully formed emotional biography, a fascinating read about an artist who, to this day, defends his right of artistic autonomy, refusing to be anyone but himself, whoever that may be." Booklist.

Brown, Donald, 1959- **Bob** Dylan : American troubadour / Donald Brown. Rowman & Littlefield, 2014. 254 p. **B**
ISBN 9780810884205
1. Singers -- United States 2. Rock musicians -- United States 3. Biographies
LC 2013044394

Traces the evolution of the singer's recording career, analyzing the biographical and historical context for each record while providing an analysis of each song.

Dylan, Bob, 1941- **Chronicles.** Bob Dylan. Simon & Schuster, 2004. 304 p. : **B**
ISBN 9780743228152
1. Singers -- United States 2. Folk musicians. 3. Folk music. 4. Autobiographies and memoirs
LC 2004056454

National Book Critics Circle Award for Biography finalist, 2004.

Building on the success of Bob Dylan in His Own Words, an autobiographical portrait of the acclaimed musical performer recounts personal and professional experiences and features black-and-white photography.

"This book will stand as a record of a young man's self-education, as contagious in its frank excitement as the letters of John Keats and as sincere in its ramble as Jack Kerouacs On the Road, to which Dylan frequently refers. A person of Dylans stature could have gotten away with far less; that he has been so thoughtful in the creation of this book is a measure of his talents, and a gift to his fans." Publishers Weekly.

Margotin, Philippe **Bob** Dylan all the songs : the story behind every track / Philippe Margotin, Jean-Michel Guesdon. Black Dog & Leventhal Publishers, 2015 703 p. **B**
ISBN 9781579129859
1. Singers -- United States 2. Rock musicians -- United States 3. United States -- Social life and customs -- 20th century 4. Biographies
LC bl2015041243

A comprehensive account of Bob Dylan's work delivers the full story of every recording session, every album and every single released during his 53-year career .

Dyson, Freeman J.

Dyson, Freeman J. **Maker** of patterns : an autobiography through letters / Freeman Dyson. Liveright Publishing, 2018. 320 p. **B**
ISBN 9780871403865
1. Dyson, Freeman J. Letters 2. Physicists 3. Scientific discoveries 4. Quantum theory 5. Scientists 6. Letters 7. Autobiographies and memoirs
LC 2017055725

The nonagenarian theoretical physicist and author of Disturbing the Universe presents a collection of letters written over a 40-year period that trace his life and the work of leading intellectuals, including J. Robert Oppenheimer, Richard Feynman and Steven Hawking, against a backdrop of the 20th century's major scientific advances.

"Who but Dyson formulates revolutionary physics while riding on a Greyhound bus through Iowa cornfields? In other episodes in this remarkable epistolary autobiography, readers join Dyson as he assesses with Godel equations for a rotating version of Einsteins universe, as he defends Feynmans quantum theorems against Oppenheimers doubts, and as he explores with Bohr the prospects for a nuclear spaceship." Booklist.

Schewe, Phillip F. **Maverick** genius : the pioneering odyssey of Freeman Dyson / Phillip F. Schewe. Thomas Dunne Books,

2013. 352 p. **B**

ISBN 9780312642358

1. Scientists -- United States 2. Physicists -- United States 3. Physics 4. Quantum theory 5. Biographies.

LC 2012041967

A definitive portrait of the scientific visionary who has influenced fields ranging from quantum physics and national defense to space and religion describes his relationships with leading world thinkers and documents his contributions to nuclear rocket technology, the Nuclear Test Ban Treaty and other world-changing endeavors.

Earhardt, Ainsley, 1976-

Earhardt, Ainsley, 1976- The **light** within me / Ainsley Earhardt. HarperCollins, 2018. 304 p. **B**

ISBN 9780062697479

1. Women television journalists 2. Faith (Christianity) 3. Family relationships 4. Christian life 5. Autobiographies and memoirs

LC 2018276398

The Fox News star and #1 New York Times best-selling author offers a powerful, uplifting look at her life and her spiritual journey, reflecting on her family, her faith and her successful career.

Earhart, Amelia, 1897-1937

Butler, Susan, 1932- **East** to the dawn : the life of Amelia Earhart / Susan Butler. Da Capo Press, 1999, c1997. xiv, 489 p. : **B**

ISBN 9780306818370

1. Women pilots 2. Pilots 3. Biographies

LC 98047717

Originally published: Reading, MA : Addison-Wesley, 1997.

A comprehensive biography recounts Earhart's varied life as a social worker, fashion plate, wife, and pilot, and dispels the myths surrounding her disappearance in 1938.

"In this biography of the pilot and women's rights advocate Butler shows a mastery of aviation history, and considerable sophistication about the technology of flight and navigation . The mountain of new material it marshals guarantees East to the Dawn a permanent place on the shelf of Amelia Earhart references." New York Times Book Review.

Winters, Kathleen C. **Amelia** Earhart : the turbulent life of an American icon / Kathleen C. Winters. Palgrave Macmillan, 2010. 256 p. **B**

ISBN 9780230616691

1. Earhart, Amelia, 1897-1937. 2. Women pilots -- United States 3. Pilots -- United States 4. Flight. 5. Biographies

LC 2010020026

"When Amelia Earhart disappeared over the Pacific in 1937, she was at the height of her fame. Fascination with Earhart remains just as strong today, as her mysterious disappearance continues to inspire speculation. In this nuanced and often surprising biography, acclaimed aviation historian Kathleen C. Winters moves beyond the caricature of the spunky, precocious pilot to offer a more complex portrait. Drawing on a wealth of contemporary accounts, airline records, and other original research, this book reveals a flawed heroine who was frequently reckless and lacked basic navigation skills, but who was also a canny manipulator of mass media. Winters details how Earhart and her husband, publisher George Putnam, worked to establish her as an international icon, even as other spectacular pilots went unnoticed. Sympathetic yet unsentimental, this biography helps us to see Amelia Earhart with fresh eyes".-- Provided by publisher.

Earnhardt family

Busbee, Jay **Earnhardt** nation : the full-throttle saga of NASCAR's first family / Jay Busbee. HarperCollins, 2016. 240 p. **B**

ISBN 9780062367716

1. Earnhardt, Dale, 1951-2001 2. NASCAR (Association) 3. Stock car racing. 4. Automobile racing drivers

LC 2016427179

Published to commemorate the 15th anniversary of Earnhardt Sr.'s death, a profile of the influential NASCAR family is set against a backdrop of the history of the world's fastest stock-car-racing organization and traces the achievements of three generations of Earnhardt drivers.

Earp, Wyatt, 1848-1929

Barra, Allen **Inventing** Wyatt Earp : his life and many legends / Allen Barra. Carroll & Graf Publishers, 1998. v, 426 p. : **B**

ISBN 0786705620

1. Earp, Wyatt, 1848-1929. 2. Frontier and pioneer life -- Southwest (United States) 3. Peace officers -- Southwest (United States) 4. United States marshals -- Southwest (United States) 5. Southwest (United States) -- History -- 1848- 6. Biographies

LC 00268780

Tells the entire story of Earp's amazing life, explaining why he became a legend among his contemporaries and how Hollywood reinvented him first as a hero and then as a scoundrel

"Barra is at his best in describing the efforts of assorted Hollywood icons, including John Ford, John Sturges, and Kevin Costner, to depict the real Earp." Booklist.

Boessenecker, John, 1953- **Ride** the devil's herd : Wyatt Earp's epic battle against the West's biggest outlaw gang / John Boessenecker. Hanover Square Press, 2020. 352 p. **B**

ISBN 9781335015853

1. Earp, Wyatt, 1848-1929. 2. Law enforcement 3. Outlaws 4. Gangs 5. Feuds 6. The West (United States) -- History -- 19th century 7. Arizona (Territory) -- History -- 19th century 8. Tombstone, Arizona -- History -- 19th century. 9. O. K. Corral, Arizona -- History 10. Biographies

LC bl2020004581

Documents how a young Wyatt Earp and his brothers waged a successful two-year feud against a loosely organized band of Texas outlaws years before his infamous "Gunfight at the OK Corral.

"A pleasure for thoughtful fans of Old West history, revisionist without being iconoclastic." Kirkus

Tefertiller, Casey, 1952- **Wyatt** Earp : the life behind the legend / Casey Tefertiller ; foreword by Angus Cameron. J. Wiley, 1997. xii, 403 p. : **B**

ISBN 0471189677

1. Earp, Wyatt, 1848-1929. 2. Peace officers -- The West (United States) 3. United States marshals Southwest (United States) 4. Southwest (United States) 5. Tombstone, Arizona -- History -- 19th century. 6. Biographies

LC 97002932

"An engrossing, satisfying inspection of a quintessential figure in American popular culture." Booklist.

Easter, Zac, 1991-2015

Forgrave, Reid, 1979- **Love,** Zac : small-town football and the life and death of an American boy / Reid Forgrave. Algonquin Books of Chapel Hill, 2020 275 p. **B**

ISBN 9781616209087

1. Easter, Zac, 1991-2015. 2. Football players. 3. High school athletes. 4. Football injuries. 5. People with traumatic brain injuries.

6. Iowa. 7. Biographies

LC 2020016842

The story of a young man from small-town Iowa who decided to take his own life rather than continue his losing battle against the traumatic brain injuries he had sustained as a no-holds-barred high school football player, and at the same time a larger story about the hot-button issues that football raises about masculinity and violence, and about what values we want to instill in our kids.

"Awareness about CTE continues to grow, but, as the author suggests, the American 'obsession' with football is still far too complex to do away with the sport or negate the violence that is part of its enduring allure. An intelligent, provocative tale that will give pause to many parents of football players at any level." Kirkus

Eberly, Merl

Tackett, Michael The **baseball** whisperer : a small-town coach who shaped Big League dreams / Michael Tackett. Houghton Mifflin Harcourt, 2016. 288 p. **B**

ISBN 9780544387645

1. Eberly, Merl. 2. Baseball coaches. 3. Baseball. 4. Iowa 5. Biographies

LC 2015037778

A real life Field of Dreams, The Baseball Whisperer is the story of a small Iowa farmtown that over the course of several summers became a powerhouse of collegiate baseball steered by the vision and perseverance of an old ballplayer turned coach who brought kids in from all over the country and taught them how to become ballplayers ? and men.

"One of baseballs most humanizing backstories." Booklist.

Echols, Damien

Echols, Damien **Life** after death / Damien Echols. Penguin, 2012. 384 p. **B**

ISBN 9780399160202

1. Echols, Damien. 2. Misskelley, Jessie. 3. Baldwin, Charles Jason, 1977- 4. Death row. 5. Judicial error. 6. Capital punishment. 7. Prisons. 8. Autobiographies and memoirs

LC 2012026115

A "West Memphis Three" member's account of his 18-year death-row incarceration, made famous by the HBO documentary series Paradise Lost, discusses the justice system flaws that led to his conviction, the abuses he suffered in prison and the trio's vindication in 2011.

Eckhart, Meister, -1327

Harrington, Joel F. (Joel Francis) **Dangerous** mystic : Meister Eckhart's path to the god within / Joel F. Harrington. Penguin Press, 2018. 368 p. **B**

ISBN 9781101981566

1. Eckhart, Meister, -1327. 2. Theologians 3. Mystics 4. Spirituality 5. Heresy 6. Biographies

LC bl2018000973

Looks at the life, times, and thought of Meister Eckhart, the fourteenth-century Christian spiritual leader, and how his thought has become relevant to the modern world.

Eco, Umberto

Eco, Umberto **Confessions** of a young novelist / Umberto Eco. Harvard University Press, 2011. 200 p. **B**

ISBN 9780674058699

1. Writing 2. Fiction writing 3. Authors

LC 2010033172

The author discusses his theories on fiction, lending insight into how his own novels were created.

Eddy, Mary Baker, 1821-1910

★Eddy, Mary Baker, 1821-1910 **Mary** Baker Eddy : speaking for herself / Mary Baker Eddy. Writings of Mary Baker Eddy, c2002. xlv, 183 p. : **B**

ISBN 0879522755

1. Eddy, Mary Baker, 1821-1910. 2. Christian Science -- History 3. Christian Scientists 4. Faith healing -- History 5. Autobiographies and memoirs

LC 2002111766

"Provide[s] a fresh glimpse of the founder of Christian Science." Publishers Weekly.

Edelman, Marian Wright, 1939-

Edelman, Marian Wright, 1939- **Lanterns** : a memoir of mentors / Marian Wright Edelman. Beacon Press, 1999. xxi, 180 p. : **B**

ISBN 9780807072141

1. Edelman, Marian Wright, 1939- Friends and associates. 2. Edelman, Marian Wright, 1939- Philosophy. 3. Mentoring. 4. African American women social reformers 5. Personal conduct. 6. Children -- Personal conduct. 7. Autobiographies and memoirs

LC 99044228

The African American lawyer and president of the Children's Defense Fund describes the positive influences of family, church members, teachers, colleagues, and other social reformers in her life.

"Throughout this absorbing memoir, Edelman's voice resounds with spirituality, a reliance on her faith, and a belief in equality." Booklist.

Edge, Rosalie, 1877-1962

Zaslowsky, Dyan **Rosalie** Edge, hawk of mercy : the activist who saved nature from the conservationists / Dyana Z. Furmansky with a foreword by Bill McKibben & an afterword by Roland C. Clement. University of Georgia Press, c2009. xvii, 312 p., 16 p. of plates : **B**

ISBN 9780820333410

1. Edge, Rosalie, 1877-1962. 2. Environmentalists -- United States 3. Suffragists -- United States 4. Environmentalism 5. Biographies

LC 2009008551

"A biography of the conservationist and suffragette who founded the Hawk Mountain Sanctuary and fought hard for the Olympic National Park. Clearly relishing every moment of Edge's remarkable life, Furmansky vividly enriches environmental history with her inspiring portrait of this indomitable champion of the wild." Booklist.

Edison, Thomas A. (Thomas Alva), 1847-1931

DeGraaf, Leonard **Edison** and the rise of innovation / Leonard DeGraaf ; foreword by Bill Gates. Sterling Signature, 2013. xxvii, 244 p. : **B**

ISBN 9781402767364

1. Edison, Thomas A. (Thomas Alva), 1847-1931. 2. Inventors -- United States 3. Electrical engineers -- United States 4. Inventions. 5. Inventors 6. Biographies

LC bl2013040995

Chronicles the life and work of the inventor through primary and previously unseen sources, including personal and business correspondence, photographs, drawings, advertising materials, and lab notebooks.

"A worthy and visually pleasing mid-length biography recommended for those who prefer Edison the businessman and social phenomenon to the scientist. With a foreword by Bill Gates." Library Journal.

★Morris, Edmund **Edison** / Edmund Morris. Random

House, 2019 783 p. : **B**

ISBN 9780812993110

1. Inventors 2. Determination (Personal quality) 3. Electrical engineers 4. Workaholics 5. Biographies

LC 2019005173

A Pulitzer Prize-winning author presents a new biography of the prolific American inventor-genius, exploring his many roles, including botanist, naval strategist, iron miner, chemist, telegrapher and audio producer, created by virtue of his remarkable inventions.

"Writing in amusing, literate prose that's briskly paced despite a mountain of fascinating detail, Morris sets Edison's achievements against a colorful portrait of his splendid eccentricity -- mostly deaf, he was given to biting phonographs and pianos to divine their acoustics -- whose visionary obsessions drove his businesses near to bankruptcy. The result is an engrossing study of a larger-than-life figure who embodied a heroic age of technology." Publishers Weekly.

Edmonds, Bill

Edmonds, Bill **God** is not here : a soldier's struggle with torture, trauma, and the moral injuries of war / Bill Edmonds. Pegasus Books, 2015 312 p. **B**

ISBN 9781605987743

1. Edmonds, Bill. 2. Coping 3. Post-traumatic stress disorder 4. Military interrogation 5. Right and wrong 6. Iraq 7. Autobiographies and memoirs

LC 2015509270

A former Special Forces captain describes living in Mosul as an advisor to an Iraqi intelligence officer in the days following the abuse scandal at Abu Ghraib and discusses the psychological, spiritual and moral impact it had.

"Edmonds doesn't reach the depth attained in recent books by Ben Fountain, Phil Klay, or Michael Pitre, but he does provide a useful adjunct to the work on PTSD done by Jonathan Shay and other writers and analysts. War is hell, and hell is other people. In this serviceable account, Edmonds assures us that both adage s are true." Kirkus.

Edmundson, Mark, 1952-

Edmundson, Mark, 1952- **Why** football matters : my education in the game / Mark Edmundson. The Penguin Press, [2014] 240 p. **B**

ISBN 9781594205750

1. Football players -- United States 2. Football 3. Character 4. Masculinity 5. Autobiographies and memoirs

LC 2014009726

An acclaimed essayist and author of Why Read? uses his own rite of passage as a high school football player to showcase larger truths about the ways America's game shapes its men.

"Beautifully written and impressively thought out, this smart memoir should appeal to a wide audience." Library Journal.

Edstrom, Erik

Edstrom, Erik **Un-American** : a soldier's reckoning of our longest war / Erik Edstrom. Bloomsbury Publishing, 2020. 304 p. **B**

ISBN 9781635573749

1. United States. Army Officers 2. United States. Army. Infantry Division, 4th 3. Soldiers -- United States 4. Afghan War veterans 5. Conscientious objectors 6. Afghan War, 2001-, American 7. United States -- Military policy 8. Afghanistan -- History -- 2001- 9. Autobiographies and memoirs

LC 2019055362

Before engaging in war, Erik Edstrom asks us to imagine three rarely imagined scenarios: First, imagine your own death. Second, imagine war from "the other side." Third: Imagine what might have been if the war had never been fought. Pursuing these realities through his own combat experience, Erik reaches the unavoidable conclusion about America at war. Un-American is a hybrid of social commentary and memoir that exposes how blind support for war exacerbates the problems it's intended to resolve, devastates the people allegedly being helped, and diverts assets from far larger threats like climate change. Un-American is a revolutionary act, offering a blueprint for redressing America's relationship with patriotism, the military, and military spending.

"An insider's you-are-there look at modern war. Veterans will love it or hate it, but there will be few in between." Kirkus

Edward I, King of England, 1239-1307

Morris, Marc, 1973- A **great** and terrible king : Edward I and the forging of Britain / Marc Morris. Pegasus Books, 2015. 480 p. **B**

ISBN 9781605986845

1. Edward I, King of England, 1239-1307. 2. Rulers 3. Political leadership. 4. Military strategy. 5. Antisemitism. 6. Great Britain -- History -- Edward I, 1272-1307. 7. Biographies

LC 2016303223

Describes the later part of the life of England's King Edward I, who travelled to the Holy Land, conquered Wales, raised one of the greatest armies of the Middle Ages, fathered 15 children and expelled the Jews from his kingdom. By the national best-selling author of The Norman Conquest.

"Highly recommended for scholars and generalists alike interested in the Middle Ages." Library Journal.

Edward III, King of England, 1312-1377

Ormrod, W. M., 1957- **Edward** III / W. Mark Ormrod. Yale University Press, 2012. xx, 721 p., [16] p. of plates : **B**

ISBN 9780300119107

1. Rulers 2. Great Britain -- Rulers 3. Great Britain -- History -- Edward III, 1327-1377 4. Biographies

LC 2011013536

"The long reign of King Edward III of England (1327-77) was filled with dramatic events: the opening of the Hundred Years War, the Black Death, the maturing of Parliament, law, and legal administration. As the author of The Reign of Edward III (CH, Jun'92, 28-5810) and a raft of scholarly papers on Edward and his reign, Ormrod (Univ. of York, UK) has proven himself to be the ideal historian to produce a superlative biography of King Edward. ... Ormrod gets as close to understanding Edward and his reign as anyone is likely to get." Choice.

Edward VII, King of Great Britain, 1841-1910

Hibbert, Christopher, 1924-2008. **Edward** VII : the last Victorian king / Christopher Hibbert. Palgrave Macmillan,, 2007, c1976. 348 p. **B**

ISBN 9781403983770

1. Edward VII, King of Great Britain, 1841-1910. 2. Rulers 3. Monarchy -- Great Britain -- History 4. Great Britain -- History -- Edward VII, 1901-1910 5. Biographies

"First published by J.B. Lippincott Company, 1976"--T.p verso

To his mother, Queen Victoria, he was 'poor Bertie,' to his wife he was 'my dear little man,' while the President of France called him 'a great English king,' and the German Kaiser condemned him as 'an old peacock.' King Edward VII was all these things and more, as Hibbert reveals in this captivating biography. Shedding new light on the scandals that peppered his life, Hibbert reveals Edward's dismal early years under

Victoria's iron rule, his terror of boredom that led to a lively social life at home and abroad, and his eventual ascent to the throne at age 59. Edward is best remembered as the last Victorian king, the monarch who installed the office of Prime Minister.

★Ridley, Jane The **heir** apparent : a life of Edward VII, the playboy prince / Jane Ridley. Random House, 2013 752 p. **B**

ISBN 9781400062553

1. Edward VII, King of Great Britain, 1841-1910. 2. Victoria, Queen of Great Britain, 1819-1901. 3. Rulers 4. Monarchy -- Great Britain -- History 5. Womanizers 6. Gamblers. 7. Great Britain -- History -- Edward VII, 1901-1910 8. Biographies

LC 2013002597

A profile of the early-20th-century British king discusses how he disappointed his mother, Queen Victoria, with his notorious gambling, gluttony and womanizing before his nine-year reign, during which he became an effective leader and diplomat who founded England's modern monarchy.

"Readers who enjoy British history and biographies, royal and otherwise, will enjoy this brilliant biography, as informative as it is absorbing." Library Journal.

Edward, Prince of Wales, 1330-1376

Jones, Michael K. The **Black** Prince : England's greatest medieval warrior / Michael K. Jones. Pegasus Books, 2018. 488 p. **B**

ISBN 9781681777412

1. Princes 2. Warriors 3. Knights and knighthood 4. Command of troops 5. Great Britain -- History -- 14th century 6. Biographies

LC bl2018056219

The remarkable and inspiring story of one of the greatest warrior-princes of the Middle Ages--and an unforgettably vivid portrait of warfare and chivalry in the fourteenth century.

Edwards, Jonathan, 1703-1758

Marsden, George M., 1939- **Jonathan** Edwards : a life / George M. Marsden. Yale University Press, c2003. xx, 615 p. : **B**

ISBN 9780300096934

1. Edwards, Jonathan, 1703-1758. 2. Congregational churches. 3. Theologians 4. Clergy 5. Congregational churches in the United States -- Clergy 6. United States -- History -- Colonial period, 1600-1775 7. Biographies

LC 2002013611

National Book Critics Circle Award for Biography finalist, 2003.

Presents a biography of the controversial eighteenth century theologian.

"In the first full critical biography of Edwards in 60 years, the author humanizes America's greatest colonial clergyman." Booklist.,Clearly sympathetic to his subject without ever becoming an outright apologist for either his character or his theology, Marsden . writes with such verve that he has given us not only the definitive biography but also a narrative that reads like a novelthat most appropriate art form for examining the interior drama of the soul. Commonweal

Eichenwald, Kurt, 1961-

Eichenwald, Kurt, 1961- A **mind** unraveled : a memoir / Kurt Eichenwald. Ballantine Books, [2018] 416 p. **B**

ISBN 9780399593628

1. Eichenwald, Kurt, 1961- Health 2. People with epilepsy 3. Journalists 4. Epilepsy 5. Sick persons 6. Autobiographies and memoirs

LC 2018018965

The author of The Informant traces the decades he spent fighting and hiding the symptoms of epilepsy, a battle involving severe depression and medical mistakes before a dedicated neurologist helped him to survive and thrive.

"Eichenwald has created a universal tale of resilience wrapped in a primal scream against the far-too-savage world. Book clubs will clamor for this tale of survival and call for compassion." Booklist.

Eichmann, Adolf, 1906-1962

Stangneth, Bettina **Eichmann** before Jerusalem : the unexamined life of a mass murderer / Bettina Stangneth ; translated from the German by Ruth Martin. Knopf, 2014, c2011. 608 p. **B**

ISBN 9780307959676

1. Eichmann, Adolf, 1906-1962. 2. Holocaust (1933-1945) 3. Nazis 4. War crime trials -- Jerusalem, Israel. 5. World War II 6. Jerusalem, Israel. 7. Biographies

LC 2014001031

Originally published in German as Eichmann vor Jerusalem by Arche, 2011Cundill Prize in Historical Literature finalist

A total re-assessment of the life of Adolf Eichmann that reveals his activities and notoriety amongst a global network of National Socialists following the collapse of the Third Reich, and permanently undermines Hannah Arendt's often-cited notion of the"banality of evil."

"Stangneth masterfully sifts through the information from these lively social gatherings conducted at journalist Sassens home three years before Eichmanns kidnapping by Israeli agents. A rigorously documented, essential work not only about Eichmann's masterly masquerade, but also about how we come to accept appearances as truth." Kirkus.

Einstein, Albert, 1879-1955

Calaprice, Alice An **Einstein** encyclopedia / Alice Calaprice, Daniel Kennefick, Robert J. Schulmann. Princeton University Press, 2015 xxiii, 347 p. **B**

ISBN 9780691141749

1. Einstein, Albert, 1879-1955. 2. Physicists 3. Relativity (Physics) 4. Unified field theories. 5. Physics. 6. Biographies

LC 2015008233

An Einstein Encyclopedia contains entries on Einstein's birth and death, family and romantic relationships, honors and awards, educational institutions where he studied and worked, citizenships and immigration to America, hobbies and travels, plus the people he befriended and the history of his archives and the Einstein Papers Project.

"This is an extremely well-organized and user-friendly reference title, thoroughly researched and accessible to the general public, students, and scholars alike. Highly recommended for public and academic libraries." Booklist.

Gribbin, John, 1946- **Einstein's** masterwork : 1915 and the general theory of relativity / John Gribbin. Pegasus Books, 2016. 240 p. **B**

ISBN 9781681772127

1. Einstein, Albert, 1879-1955. 2. Physicists -- Germany. 3. Scientists -- Influence 4. General relativity (Physics) 5. Cosmology. 6. Biographies

LC bl2016034583

One of the world's most celebrated science writers reveals the origins of Einstein's General Theory--and provides a greater understanding of who Einstein was at the time of this pivotal achievement.

"Walter Isaacson goes deeper into his life and Dennis Overbye into his work, but readers will find this shorter biography entirely satisfactory." Kirkus.

Isaacson, Walter **Einstein** : his life and universe / Walter Isaacson. Simon & Schuster, 2007. xxii, 675 p., 16 p. of plates : **B**

ISBN 0743264738

1. Einstein, Albert, 1879-1955. 2. Einstein, Albert, 1879-1955 Friends and associates. 3. Physicists 4. Relativity (Physics) 5. Unified field theories. 6. Physics. 7. Biographies

LC 2006051264

ALA Notable Book, 2008.

National Academies Communication Award, 2008.

A narrative portrait based on the complete body of Einstein's papers offers insight into how the iconic thinker's mind worked as well as his contributions to science, in an account that describes his two marriages, his receipt of the Nobel Prize, and the influence of his discoveries on his personal views about morality, politics, and tolerance.

"This is a warm, insightful, affectionate portrait with a human and immensely charming Einstein at its core." New York Times.

Eire, Carlos M. N.

Eire, Carlos M. N. **Learning** to die in Miami : further confessions of a Cuban boy / Carlos Eire. Free Press, 2010. 256 p. **B**

ISBN 9781439181904

1. Eire, Carlos M. N. Childhood and youth. 2. Cuban Americans 3. Child refugees. 4. Immigrants. 5. Assimiliation (Sociology) 6. Miami, Florida. 7. Autobiographies and memoirs

LC 2009052286

Sequel to: Waiting for snow in Havana.

Presents the story of the author's exile in America, where his brother and he relocated as youths from their revolution-torn home in Cuba, struggled with the loss of their cultural identity, and acclimated to American culture.

Eire, Carlos M. N. **Waiting** for snow in Havana : confessions of a Cuban boy / Carlos Eire. Free Press, 2003. 383 p. : **B**

ISBN 0743219651

1. Eire, Carlos M. N. Childhood and youth. 2. Operation Peter Pan. 3. Cuban Americans 4. Child refugees. 5. Identity (Psychology) 6. Havana, Cuba -- Social conditions -- 20th century. 7. Cuba -- History -- Revolution, 1956-1959. 8. Autobiographies and memoirs

LC 2002073875

Sequel to: Learning to Die in Miami.

National Book Award for Nonfiction, 2003.

Carlos Eire's National Book Award-winning memoir of his childhood in 1950s Havana and the overnight upheaval of his world in January 1959, when the Batista government was toppled.

"The author looks beyond the literal to see the mythological themes inherent in the epic struggle for identity that each of our lives represents. As painful as Eire's journey has been, his ability to see tragedy and suffering as a constant source of redemption is what makes this book so powerful." Publishers Weekly.

Eisen, Max

Eisen, Max **By** chance alone : a remarkable true story of courage and survival at Auschwitz / Max Eisen. HarperCollins, 2016 xii, 276 p. : **B**

ISBN 1443449288

1. Eisen, Max. 2. Auschwitz (Concentration camp) 3. Concentration camp inmates. 4. Holocaust survivors. 5. Jews, Czech. 6. Holocaust (1933-1945) 7. Autobiographies and memoirs

Shortlisted for The Charles Taylor Prize for Literary Non-Fiction, 2017

This autobiography of Canadian Max Eisen details the rural Hungarian deportations to Auschwitz-Birkenau, back-breaking slave labour in Auschwitz I, the infamous 'death march' of January 1945, the painful aftermath of liberation, and a journey of physical and psychological healing.

"In the vein of Holocaust memoirs such as Elie Wiesel's Night and Primo Levi's Survival in Auschwitz, this significant new entry offers further documentation of a dark period in history. It will be a solid addition to all World War II collections." Library Journal.

Eisenhower, Dwight D. (Dwight David), 1890-1969

Ambrose, Stephen E. **Eisenhower** : soldier and president / Stephen E. Ambrose. Simon and Schuster, 1990. 635 p., 16 p. of plates : **B**

ISBN 067170107X

1. Eisenhower, Dwight D. (Dwight David), 1890-1969. 2. United States. Army 3. Presidents -- United States 4. Generals -- United States 5. Politicians -- United States 6. Soldiers -- United States

LC 90009701

Condensed version of a two volume work originally published as: Eisenhower. c1983-c1984."Tracing Eisenhower's family background, education, military and political careers, and influence as elder statesman, the author chronicles Eisenhower's triumphs and failures and at the same time provides a vivid picture of the off-duty Ike. This is the definitive one-volume biography of Eisenhower." Publishers Weekly.

Ambrose, Stephen E. The **victors** : Eisenhower and his boys : the men of World War II / Stephen E. Ambrose. Simon & Schuster, 1998. 396 p. : **B**

ISBN 068485628X

1. United States. Army -- History World War II. 2. Western Front (World War II) 3. Soldiers 4. Generals -- United States 5. Command of troops. 6. United States -- History -- 20th century. 7. Biographies

LC 98037808

To re-create the last year of WWII, the author tells the soldiers' stories, drawn from interviews and oral histories from government and private archives.

"The author is a master of letting his subjects tell the story, of standing back and allowing the large lessons to unfold. The result is history with lasting impact." School Library Journal.

Baier, Bret **Three** days in January : Dwight Eisenhower's final mission / Bret Baier with Catherine Whitney. William Morrow, 2017. 320 p. **B**

ISBN 9780062569035

1. Kennedy, John F. (John Fitzgerald), 1917-1963 2. Presidents -- United States -- Transition periods. 3. Politicians -- United States 4. Generals -- United States 5. United States -- Politics and government -- 1953-1961.

LC bl2016051650

Fox News Channel's chief political anchor explores the Presidency of Dwight D. Eisenhower through the lens of his last three days in office in January 1961, revealing Ike to be a model of strong yet principled leadership that is desperately missing in America today.

"A focused and timely study of Eisenhower's significant speech and the sticky transition to JFK's inherited new world." Kirkus.

Eisenhower, Susan, 1951- **How** Ike led : the principles behind Eisenhower's biggest decisions / Susan Eisenhower. Thomas Dunne Books, 2020. 384 p. **B**

ISBN 9781250238771

1. Eisenhower, Dwight D. (Dwight David), 1890-1969 Military

leadership 2. Political leadership 3. National security -- United States 4. Command of troops 5. Ethics 6. United States -- Foreign relations -- 1953-1961 7. United States -- Politics and government -- 1953-1961 8. Biographies

LC 2020006777

How Dwight D. Eisenhower led America through a transformational time - by a DC policy strategist, security expert and his granddaughter. Few people have made decisions as momentous as Eisenhower, nor has one person had to make such a varied range of them. From D-Day to Little Rock, from the Korean War to Cold War crises, from the Red Scare to the Missile Gap controversies, Ike was able to give our country eight years of peace and prosperity by relying on a core set of principles. These were informed by his heritage and upbringing, as well as his strong character and his personal discipline, but he also avoided making himself the center of things. He was a man of judgment, and steadying force. He sought national unity, by pursuing a course he called the "Middle Way" that tried to make winners on both sides of any issue.

"A direct witness to Ike's later years, the author draws on memories of her grandfather, and these highly personal anecdotes supplement her research. Armchair historians will treasure this book." Booklist

Hitchcock, William I. The **age** of Eisenhower : America and the world in the 1950s / William I. Hitchcock. Simon & Schuster, 2018. 512 p. **B**

ISBN 9781439175668

1. Eisenhower, Dwight D. (Dwight David), 1890-1969. 2. Presidents. 3. Cold War 4. United States -- Politics and government -- 1953-1961. 5. United States -- Foreign relations -- 1953-1961. 6. Biographies

LC 2017026867

Citing the enduring popularity of America's 34th President, an original and penetrating assessment of Eisenhower analyzes his considerable influence on the Cold War, today's America and the nature of the presidency itself. By the Pulitzer Prize-finalist author of The Bitter Road to Freedom.

Johnson, Paul, 1928- **Eisenhower** : a life / Paul Johnson. Viking, 2014. 144 p. **B**

ISBN 9780670016822

1. Eisenhower, Dwight D. (Dwight David), 1890-1969. 2. Presidents -- United States 3. Generals -- United States 4. United States -- Politics and government -- 1953-1961. 5. Biographies

LC 2014005313

A portrait of the 34th president places particular emphasis on his years as a five-star general and his two presidential terms, sharing additional coverage of such subjects as his Kansas childhood, West Point education and volatile relationship with Richard Nixon. By the best-selling author of Churchill.

Eisner, Will

Andelman, Bob **Will** Eisner, a spirited life / Bob Andelman. M Press, 2005. 375 p. : **B**

ISBN 1595820116

1. Eisner, Will. 2. Cartoonists -- United States 3. Biographies

LC 2005026326

Includes index.

An account of the life and accomplishments of the innovator of the modern-day comic book and graphic novel celebrates the creator of "The Spirit"--the first super-antihero in comics.

"Besides verifying Eisner's impact on nearly every artist who drew comics in his wake, Andelman shows that Eisner's influence extends to such film directors as Spielberg and Tarantino." Booklist.

Schumacher, Michael, 1950- **Will** Eisner : a dreamer's life in comics / Michael Schumacher. Bloomsbury, 2010. 368 p. **B**

ISBN 9781608190133

1. Eisner, Will. 2. Cartoonists -- United States 3. Cartoons -- United States -- History and criticism 4. Illustrators -- United States 5. United States -- Social life and customs -- 20th century 6. United States -- Social life and customs -- 21st century 7. Biographies

LC 2010011283

Depicts the artist's career over eight decades, from the dawn of comics' Golden Age in the late 1930s to the early 21st century when Pulitzers began being awarded to graphic novels, and features interviews with his family, friends and colleagues

"Propelled by Eisner's geyserlike energy and output, Schumacher keenly chronicles Eisner's brilliant career within a lively history of American comics and creates an inspiring portrait of a perpetually diligent and innovative artist whose belief in comics as fine art fueled a new and fertile creative universe." Booklist.

Eleanor, of Aquitaine, Queen, consort of Henry II, King of England, 1122?-1204

Weir, Alison, 1951- **Eleanor** of Aquitaine : a life / Alison Weir. Ballantine Books, 2001, c1999. xxi, 441 p. : **B**

ISBN 0345434870

1. Eleanor, of Aquitaine, Queen, consort of Henry II, King of England, 1122?-1204. 2. Women rulers -- Great Britain 3. Women rulers -- France 4. Great Britain -- History -- Henry II, 1154-1189. 5. France -- History -- Louis VII, 1137-1180. 6. Biographies

LC BL2001003353

Originally published: London : Jonathan Cape, 1999.

A biography of one of the most influential women of the Middle Ages discusses her marriages to Louis VII of France and Henry II of England, and her later efforts to secure the throne of England for her sons.

"In approaching as complex a subject as feudalism, Weir wears her learning lightly and has a pleasant habit of anticipating all the questions of a curious reader." Publishers Weekly.

Elijah Muhammad, 1897-1975

Evanzz, Karl The **messenger** : the rise and fall of Elijah Muhammad / Karl Evanzz. Pantheon Books, 1999. xv, 667 p. : **B**

ISBN 067944260X

1. Elijah Muhammad, 1897-1975. 2. Black Muslims 3. African Americans 4. Biographies

LC 99011826

A definitive biography of the controversial founder and "prophet" of the Nation of Islam describes Elijah Muhammad's rise to power, his charismatic teachings, his role in the struggle for African-American equality, and the turbulent, contradictory personal life that led to his fall.

"A critical biography of one of America's leading black nationalists of the 20th century. One of the founders of the Nation of Islam (NOI), Muhammad helped convert thousands of African Americans to the religion popularly known as the Black Muslims. Evanzz concludes that Muhammad was essentially a con man who used his considerable powers of persuasion to get rich and seduce women. Especially fascinating is Evanzz's extensive use of FBI files to make his case." Library Journal.

Eliot, George, 1819-1880

Hughes, Kathryn, 1959- **George** Eliot : the last Victorian / Kathryn Hughes. Farrar Straus Giroux, 1999, c1998. xiii, 383

p. : **B**

ISBN 9780374161385

1. Eliot, George, 1819-1880. 2. Authors, English -- 19th century 3. Women authors 4. Creativity in women 5. Biographies

LC 98042926

"First published in 1998 by Fourth Estate, Great Britain"--T.p. verso. James Tait Black Memorial Prize for Biography, 1999.

An illustrated study of the great Victorian novelist details the personal dramas that shaped her work, including her adulterous affair with writer George Henry Lewes, and relates her life to the issues of her day.

"In this biography Hughes shows how George Eliot (nee Mary Anne Evans, 1819-80), in spite of her outwardly anti-Victorian lifestyle, was in fact a true Victorian. A solitary, ascetic child and young woman, she was raised in an upwardly mobile country family. In 1852 she met the married writer and editor George Henry Lewes, with whom she lived until his death in 1878." Library Journal.

Eliot, T. S., (Thomas Stearns), 1888-1965

Crawford, Robert, 1959- **Young** Eliot : from St. Louis to the waste land / Robert Crawford. Farrar Straus & Giroux, 2015 480 p. **B**

ISBN 9780374279448

1. Eliot, T. S., (Thomas Stearns), 1888-1965. 2. Poets, American -- 20th century 3. Biographies

LC 2014047118

Includes index

On the fiftieth anniversary of the death of T. S. Eliot, Robert Crawford presents us with the first volume of a definitive biography of this poetic genius.Young Eliot traces the life of the twentieth century's most important poet from his childhood in St. Louis to the publication of his revolutionary poem The Waste Land.

"Its hard to imagine a literary biography of greater merit being published this year." Booklist.

★Gordon, Lyndall **T.S.** Eliot : an imperfect life / Lyndall Gordon. Norton, 1999, c1998. xv, 721 p., 16 p. of plates : **B**

ISBN 0393047288

1. Eliot, T. S., (Thomas Stearns), 1888-1965. 2. Poets, American -- 20th century 3. Critics -- Great Britain 4. Biographies

LC 98046864

Originally published: London : Vintage, 1998."

Gordon's book is the most authoritative life of Eliot thus far, and is certain to spark new controversies." Publishers Weekly.

Murphy, Russell E. (Russell Elliott) **Critical** companion to T.S. Eliot : a literary reference to his life and work / Russell Elliott Murphy. Facts On File, c2007. x, 614 p. : **B**

ISBN 9780816061839

1. Eliot, T. S. (Thomas Stearns), 1888-1965 Encyclopedias. 2. Poets, American -- 20th century 3. Biographies

LC 2006034076

A guide to the author's life and work presents a brief biography; offers synopses of his writings; and discusses important topics and people and places in his life.

Elizabeth I, Queen of England, 1533-1603

Guy, John **Elizabeth** : the forgotten years / John Guy. Viking, 2016 448 p. **B**

ISBN 9780670786022

1. Elizabeth I, Queen of England, 1533-1603. 2. Women rulers -- Great Britain 3. Great Britain -- History -- Elizabeth I, 1558-1603. 4. Biographies

LC 2016429579

Based on new archival material, a biography of the ambitious Tudor queen focuses on her life at the height of her power, including revolts in Ireland, riots in the London streets of London and a conspiracy to overthrow her.

Hilton, Lisa, 1974- **Elizabeth** : Renaissance prince / Lisa Hilton. Houghton Mifflin Harcourt, 2015. 384 p. **B**

ISBN 9780544577848

1. Machiavelli, Niccolò, 1469-1527 Influence. 2. Elizabeth I, Queen of England, 1533-1603. 3. Women rulers -- Great Britain 4. Great Britain -- History -- Elizabeth I, 1558-1603. 5. Biographies

LC 2015004340

Queen Elizabeth I was all too happy to play on courtly conventions of gender when it suited her "weak and feeble woman's body" to do so for political gain. But in Elizabeth, historian Lisa Hilton offers ample evidence why those famous words should not be taken at face value. With new research out of France, Italy, Russia, and Turkey, Hilton's fresh interpretation is of a queen who saw herself primarily as a Renaissance prince and used Machiavellian statecraft to secure that position.

"Those who enjoyed Hilton's previous books will most likely want to read this one, as will die-hard fans of Elizabeth. Readers seeking a more nuanced look at the queen and Tudor politics should turn instead to works by Antonia Fraser or Alison Weir." Library Journal.

Norton, Elizabeth The **temptation** of Elizabeth Tudor : Elizabeth I, Thomas Seymour, and the making of a virgin queen / Elizabeth Norton. Pegasus Books, 2016. 416 p. **B**

ISBN 9781605989488

1. Elizabeth I, Queen of England, 1533-1603. 2. Seymour, Thomas Seymour, Baron, 1508?-1549 3. Women rulers -- Great Britain 4. Great Britain -- History -- Elizabeth I, 1558-1603. 5. Biographies

LC 2016498384

An analysis of the volatile court life and factors that challenged the youth and early reign of Elizabeth I discusses her attempted seduction by Thomas Seymour, the overwhelming support that favored her sister and the scandals that prompted the creation of her "Virgin Queen" persona.

"Highly recommended for readers interested in British history and the Tudor dynasty. Fans of historical fiction such as Philippa Gregory's Tudor Court series will also find themselves invested in the real-life scandal that befell one of England's most famous queens." Library Journal.

Ronald, Susan **Heretic** queen : Queen Elizabeth I and the wars of religion / Susan Ronald. St. Martin's Press, 2012. 352 p. **B**

ISBN 9780312645380

1. Elizabeth I, Queen of England, 1533-1603 Religion. 2. Catholic Church Relations Protestant churches. 3. Protestant churches Relations Catholic Church. 4. Reformation -- England. 5. War -- Religious aspects. 6. Women rulers -- Great Britain. 7. Diplomacy. 8. England -- Church history -- 16th century. 9. Great Britain -- History -- Elizabeth I, 1558-1603. 10. Biographies.

LC 2012010248

Acclaimed biographer Susan Ronald delivers a stunning account of Elizabeth I that focuses on her role in the Wars of Religion--the battle between Protestantism and Catholicism that tore Europe apart in the sixteenth century.

Weir, Alison, 1951- The **life** of Elizabeth I / Alison Weir. Ballantine, 1998. 532 p. : **B**

ISBN 0345405331

1. Elizabeth I, Queen of England, 1533-1603. 2. Women rulers --

Great Britain 3. Great Britain -- History -- Elizabeth I, 1558-1603. 4. Biographies

LC 98034917

Originally published: London : J. Cape, 1998.

Presents an exhaustively researched biography that reveals the personality, private life, and romantic intrigues of Elizabeth I.

"Weir brings a fine sense of selection and considerable zest to her portrait of the self-styled Virgin Queen." Publishers Weekly.

Elizabeth II, Queen of Great Britain, 1926-

Hardman, Robert **Queen** of the world : Elizabeth II, sovereign and stateswoman / Robert Hardman. Pegasus Books, 2019, c2018. 368 p. **B**

ISBN 9781643130026

1. Windsor, House of 2. Women rulers -- Great Britain 3. Royal houses. 4. Nobility -- Great Britain -- History 5. Monarchy -- Great Britain -- History 6. Great Britain -- Rulers 7. Great Britain -- History -- Elizabeth II, 1952- 8. Biographies

LC bl2018191949

Originally published by Century, 2018.

Written by the renowned royal biographer, Robert Hardman, and with privileged access to the Royal Family and the Royal Household, a brilliant new portrait of the most famous woman in the world and her place in it.

"Throughout, Hardman's analysis is discerning, knowledgeable, and fascinating." Booklist.

Smith, Sally Bedell, 1948- **Elizabeth** the Queen : the life of a modern monarch / Sally Bedell Smith. Random House, 2011. 384 p. **B**

ISBN 9781400067893

1. Women rulers -- England. 2. Monarchy -- Great Britain 3. Royal houses. 4. Leadership in women. 5. Great Britain -- History -- Elizabeth II, 1952- 6. Biographies

LC 2011023661

A tribute to the life and enduring reign of Elizabeth II draws on numerous interviews and previously undisclosed documents to juxtapose the queen's public and private lives.

"A microscopically detailed portrait of the reigning Queen of England." Kirkus.

Williams, Kate, 1974- **Young** Elizabeth : the making of the queen / Kate Williams. Pegasus Books, 2015 336 p. **B**

ISBN 9781605988917

1. Windsor, House of History -- 20th century 2. Royal houses. 3. Nobility -- Great Britain -- History -- 20th century 4. Women rulers 5. Rulers 6. Great Britain -- History -- Elizabeth II, 1952- 7. Biographies

LC 2015452055

A biography of the young princess who, at the impressionable age of eleven, found that she was now heiress to the throne, by the New York Times bestselling author of Becoming Queen Victoria.

"Offering a gracious yet honest viewpoint of the strengths and weaknesses of the longest-reigning monarch, Williams tours Elizabeth's beginning years and illuminates the often overlooked humanity of her personal life." Library Journal.

Ellington, Duke, 1899-1974

Teachout, Terry **Duke** : a life of Duke Ellington / Terry Teachout. Gotham Books, 2013. 496 p. **B**

ISBN 9781592407491

1. Ellington, Duke, 1899-1974. 2. African American jazz musicians 3. Composers. 4. Jazz music. 5. Extramarital affairs 6. Biographies

LC 2013011138

An account of the public and private lives of the eminent jazz artist includes coverage of his slave heritage, the musical talent that inspired some 1,500 compositions and his relationships with numerous lovers. By the author of Pops: A Life of Louis Armstrong.

Ellis, Helen

Ellis, Helen **Southern** lady code : essays / Helen Ellis. Doubleday, 2019. 224 p. **B**

ISBN 9780385543897

1. Manners and customs 2. Popular culture 3. Growing up 4. Women -- Southern States 5. Southern States -- Social life and customs 6. Essays 7. Autobiographies and memoirs

LC 2018019774

The best-selling author presents a riotous collection of essays on the art of living as a "Southern Lady" that explores subjects ranging from marriage and manners to women's health and entertaining.

"In nearly two-dozen essays filled with belly laughs and bits of hard-won wisdom, Ellis self-deprecating wit and tongue-in-cheek charm provide the perfect antidote to bad-hair, or bad-news, days." Booklist.

Ellis, Samantha

Ellis, Samantha **How** to be a heroine : or, what I've learned from reading too much / Samantha Ellis. Vintage Books, 2014. 272 p. **B**

ISBN 9781101872093

1. Ellis, Samantha Books and reading. 2. Women in literature. 3. Feminism 4. Characters and characteristics in literature 5. Self-discovery. 6. Autobiographies and memoirs

LC 2014021162

Taking a retrospective look at the literary ladies, both the characters and writers, whom she has loved since childhood, a playwright and journalist evaluates how her heroines stack up today and shares her experiences growing up in London in a very tightly knit Iraqi-Jewish community.

"The book could equally be titled How to Be a Reader; Ellis is passionate and engaged, railing against writers who shortchange their creations and celebrating those whose characters represent their best selves. She is frank about times she has misread works, and she employs a rigorous feminist lens. Primarily, though, this is a rousing call for women to be the heroines in their own lives, and its good fun, to boot." Booklist.

Ellis, William Henry, 1864-1923

Jacoby, Karl, 1965- The **strange** career of William Ellis : the Texas slave who became a Mexican millionaire / Karl Jacoby. W.W. Norton & Company, 2016. 352 p. **B**

ISBN 9780393239256

1. Ellis, William Henry, 1864-1923. 2. Passing (Identity). 3. Reconstruction (United States history) 4. African Americans 5. Slaves. 6. Mexican-American Border Region 7. United States -- Race relations -- History. 8. Biographies

LC 2016007019

To his contemporaries in Gilded Age Manhattan, Guillermo Eliseo was a fantastically wealthy Mexican, the proud owner of a luxury apartment overlooking Central Park, a busy Wall Street office, and scores of mines and haciendas in Mexico. But for all his obvious riches and his elegant appearance, Eliseo was also the possessor of a devastating secret: he was not, in fact, from Mexico at all. Rather, he had begun life as a slave named William Ellis, born on a cotton plantation in southern Texas during the waning years of King Cotton. After emancipation, Ellis, capitalizing on the Spanish he learned during his childhood along the Mexican border and his ambivalent appearance, engaged in a virtuoso act of reinvention. He crafted an alter ego, the Mexican Guillermo Eliseo, who was able to access many of the privileges denied to African Americans at the time: traveling in first-class train berths, staying in upscale hotels, and eating in the finest restaurants.

"Jacoby's masterly writing places race and its meaning at the center of this essential work. Readers will gain fresh insight into life during Reconstruction as well as the riddle of racial identities." Library Journal.

Ellison, Ralph

★Rampersad, Arnold **Ralph** Ellison : a biography / Arnold Rampersad. Alfred A. Knopf, 2007. 657 p., 24 p. of plates : **B**

ISBN 9780375408274

1. Ellison, Ralph. 2. Authors, American -- 20th century 3. African American authors -- 20th century 4. United States -- Social life and customs -- 20th century 5. Biographies

LC 2006026464

BCALA Literary Award for Nonfiction, 2008.

National Book Award for Nonfiction finalist, 2007.

National Book Critics Circle Award for Biography finalist, 2007.

A critical biography of the author of Invisible Man draws on access to Ellison's personal papers to offer a definitive study of the life, work, and influence of Ralph Ellison, detailing his poverty-stricken Oklahoma youth, his education and involvement in New York's liberal intellectual circles, his personal relationships, and the influence of racism on his life.

Ellsberg, Daniel

Ellsberg, Daniel The **doomsday** machine : confessions of a nuclear war planner / Daniel Ellsberg. Bloomsbury USA, 2017. 416 p. **B**

ISBN 9781608196708

1. Nuclear weapons policy -- History 2. Nuclear strategy -- United States -- History 3. Military secrets 4. Nuclear warfare -- Environmental aspects. 5. Autobiographies and memoirs

LC 2017057657

Andrew Carnegie Medal for Excellence in Non-Fiction finalist, 2018.

From the legendary whistle-blower who revealed the Pentagon Papers, an eyewitness exposé of the dangers of America's Top Secret, seventy-year-long nuclear policy that--chillingly--continues to this day.

"Ellsberg's book is essential for facilitating a national discussion about a vital topic." Library Journal.

Ellsberg, Daniel **Secrets** : a memoir of Vietnam and the Pentagon Papers / Daniel Ellsberg. Penguin Books, 2003, c2002. xiv, 500 p. : **B**

ISBN 0142003425

1. Ellsberg, Daniel. 2. Pentagon Papers Case. 3. Vietnam War, 1961-1975. 4. Autobiographies and memoirs

LC BL2003015126

Originally published: New York : Viking, 2002.

Daniel Ellsberg relates the story of his conversion from a Pentagon official and staunch supporter of America's war against communism to an impassioned anti-war activist. In October 1969, he smuggled classified documents out of his office and made public a top secret study of decision-making in Vietnam. He explains why he published what became known as the Pentagon Papers.

"Ellsberg recalls how he leaked the Pentagon Papers, which documented U.S. foreign-policy failures and deceit in Vietnam from 1945 to 1968. Ellsberg's autobiographical account provides insight into the disturbing abuses of presidential power that plagued the Vietnam/Watergate era." Library Journal.

Elser, Johann Georg, 1903-1945

Ortner, Helmut, 1950- The **lone** assassin : the epic true story of the man who almost killed Hitler / Helmut Ortner ; translated by Ross Benjamin. Skyhorse Pub., c2012. 320 p. **B**

ISBN 9781616083830

1. Elser, Johann Georg, 1903-1945. 2. Hitler, Adolf, 1889-1945 Assassination attempt, 1939 (November 8) 3. Anti-Nazi movement -- Germany 4. Attempted assassination. 5. Attempted murder. 6. Germany -- History -- 1933-1945.

LC 2011049214

Translation of: Der Einzelgänger.

Chronicles the life of the carpenter and watch factory employee who attempted to assassinate Adolf Hitler in 1939 with a homemade bomb.

Elway, John, 1960-

Cole, Jason (Sports writer) **Elway** : a relentless life / Jason Cole. Hachette Books, 2020 368 p. **B**

ISBN 9780316455770

1. Denver Broncos (Football team) 2. Football players 3. Quarterbacks (Football) 4. Executives 5. Competition 6. Biographies

LC 2020013577

Includes index.

This biography of the Hall of Fame quarterback examines his struggles to reach the NFL, the crushing disappointment of losing three Super Bowls, and the eventual triumph of leading the Denver Broncos to two consecutive championships.

"With exclusive recollections of Elway's college football years, Cole delves into the forces that shaped the quarterback and gave him the resiliency to overcome challenges both on and off the field. Recommended for all public library collections, and especially for readers interested in the evolution of sports in the late 20th century." Library Journal

Elwes, Cary, 1962-

Elwes, Cary, 1962- **As** you wish : inconceivable tales from the making of the Princess Bride / Cary Elwes with Joe Layden. Touchstone, 2014. 272 p. **B**

ISBN 9781476764023

1. Princess bride (Motion picture) 2. Films -- Production and direction 3. Actors and actresses 4. Filmmaking 5. Autobiographies and memoirs

LC 2014014652

Includes index.

In a 25th anniversary, behind-the-scenes account of the making of the cult classic film, the lead actor shares never-before-told stories and exclusive photographs as well as interviews with Robin Wright, Billy Crystal and more.

Emerson, Ralph Waldo, 1803-1882

Richardson, Robert D., 1934- **Emerson** : the mind on fire: a biography / Robert D. Richardson, Jr. ; with a frontispiece by Barry Moser. University of California Press, c1995. xiii, 671 p., [16] p. of plates : **B**

ISBN 0520088085

1. Emerson, Ralph Waldo, 1803-1882. 2. Emerson, Ralph Waldo, 1803-1882 Knowledge and learning. 3. Authors, American -- 19th century 4. United States -- Social life and customs -- 19th century. 5. Biographies

LC 94036008

"A centennial book"--Half t.p.

National Book Critics Circle Award for Biography finalist, 1995."

Richardson focuses principally on his subject's inner life, the life of his mind and spirit. But in this subtle portrayal of Emerson the thinker, the reader also sees the clearly limned portrait of Emerson the social activist. A masterful work, this biography will attract the attention of scholars and serious general readers for decades." Booklist.

Wayne, Tiffany K., 1968- **Critical** companion to Ralph Waldo Emerson : a literary reference to his life and work / Tiffany K. Wayne. Facts on File, c2010. xii, 444 p. : **B**

ISBN 9780816073580

1. Emerson, Ralph Waldo, 1803-1882 Handbooks, manuals, etc. 2. Authors, American -- 19th century 3. Biographies

LC 2009024809

"This reference book examines the life and works of a central thinker in American history. . . . It begins with Emerson's biography for context. Part 2 focuses on 140 significant (in the view of scholars) individual works, including 60 poems (most with one to three pages of synopses, critical commentary, and further reading). Part 3 covers related people, places, and topics. . . . The final appendixes offer a chronology of Emerson's life and times, bibliographies of both his works and relevant secondary sources." Choice.

Engel, Richard, 1973-

Engel, Richard, 1973- **And** then all hell broke loose : two decades in the Middle East / Richard Engel. Simon & Schuster, 2016. 400 p. **B**

ISBN 9781451635119

1. Foreign correspondents. 2. War correspondents 3. Middle East -- Politics and government -- 21st century. 4. Autobiographies and memoirs

LC 2015030898

Includes index.

Over two decades Engel has been under fire, blown out of hotel beds, taken hostage. He has watched Mubarak and Morsi in Egypt arrested and condemned, reported from Jerusalem, been through the Lebanese war, covered the whole shooting match in Iraq, interviewed Libyan rebels who toppled Gaddafi, reported from Syria as Al-Qaeda stepped in, was kidnapped in the Syrian crosscurrents of fighting. He goes into Afghanistan with the Taliban and to Iraq with ISIS.

"Clear, candid, and concise, Engels overview of the ongoing battleground should be required reading for anyone desiring a thorough and informed portrait of what the past has created and what the future holds for the Middle East and the world at large." Booklist.

Engels, Friedrich, 1820-1895

Hunt, Tristram, 1974- **Marx's** general : the revolutionary life of Friedrich Engels / Tristram Hunt. Metropolitan Books, 2009. xii, 430 p., 16 p. of plates : **B**

ISBN 9780805080254

1. Engels, Friedrich, 1820-1895. 2. Communism -- History. 3. Communists. 4. Ideology. 5. Political science -- Philosophy. 6. Biographies

LC 2009003845

Elizabeth Longford Prize for Historical Biography, 2010.

A remarkable new biography from one of Britain's leading young historians that recovers the co-founder of communism from the shadows of history, portraying how one of the great "bon viveurs" of Victorian Britain reconciled his exuberant personal life with his radical political philosophy.

Engle, Charlie

Engle, Charlie **Running** man : a memoir / Charlie Engle. Scribner, 2016 288 p. **B**

ISBN 9781476785783

1. Ultramarathon runners. 2. Long-distance runners. 3. Ultramarathon running. 4. Long-distance running. 5. Autobiographies and memoirs

LC bl2016030356

A personal account by a world-class ultra-marathon runner chronicles his globe-spanning races, record-breaking run across the Sahara and struggles with drug addiction and wrongful imprisonment.

"Similar to the journey of self-discovery chronicled in Rich Rolls Finding Ultra (2012), this is a fast-paced, well-written account of a man who accepts pain, pushes beyond imagined limits, and ultimately finds redemption and peace." Booklist.

English, Paul M., 1963-

Kidder, Tracy A **truck** full of money / Tracy Kidder. Random House, 2016 256 p. **B**

ISBN 9780812995244

1. Internet industry and trade. 2. Entrepreneurs 3. Businesspeople 4. Men with bipolar disorder. 5. Biographies

LC 2015050454

The Pulitzer Prize- and National Book Award-winning author of Mountains Beyond Mountains presents the inspiring story of Kayak.com founder Paul English, discussing his struggles with bipolar disorder and rebellious nature while tracing his achievements as an unconventional inventor and entrepreneur.

"While eminently readable as a biography, Kidders book is also a trenchant study of the new American economy and the technological world that built it. More engrossing work from a gifted practitioner of narrative nonfiction." Kirkus.

Ensler, Eve, 1953-

Ensler, Eve, 1953- The **apology** / Eve Ensler. Bloomsbury Publishing, 2019. 208 p. **B**

ISBN 9781635574388

1. Adult child sexual abuse victims 2. Fathers and daughters 3. Abusive men 4. Sexually abused girls 5. Autobiographies and memoirs

LC 2019002247

Examines the themes of abuse and atonement via the author's own experience being both physically and sexually abused.

"This is a powerful and disturbing story that Ensler writes with grace an aplomb." Publishers Weekly.

Ephron, Nora

Ephron, Nora The **most** of Nora Ephron / Nora Ephron. Alfred A. Knopf, 2013. 576 p. **B**

ISBN 9780385350839

1. Ephron, Nora. 2. Women screenwriters. 3. Women authors. 4. Women journalists. 5. Everyday life. 6. Essays. 7. Anthologies. 8. Autobiographies and memoirs

LC 2013016426

A celebration of the work of the late Academy Award-nominated author and screenwriter collects her writings on topics ranging from journalism and feminism to food and aging, in a volume complemented by her notorious Wellesley commencement address and her recent blogs about death.

"Whether Ephron is writing about politics or purses, sexism or souffl, her appeal is her intelligent, incisive sense of humor." Library Journal.

Epstein, Franci

Epstein, Franci **Franci's** war : a woman's story of survival / Franci Rabinek Epstein ; afterword by Helen Epstein. Penguin

Books, 2020. 256 p. **B**

ISBN 9780143135579

1. Epstein, Franci. 2. Theresienstadt (Concentration camp). 3. Bergen-Belsen (Concentration camp) 4. Auschwitz (Concentration camp) 5. Holocaust (1933-1945) -- Prague, Czech Republic 6. Fashion designers 7. Holocaust survivors 8. Czechoslovakia -- History -- 1938-1945.

LC 2019039140

One incredibly strong young woman - a glamorous Jewish fashion designer, who endured the horrors of the Holocaust along with the women prisoners in her tight-knit circle of friends offers powerful testimony in an intense, candid and sometimes funny account of those dark years.

"This devastating account documents a personal slice of Holocaust history." Booklist

Equiano, Olaudah, 1745-1797

★Carretta, Vincent **Equiano,** the African : biography of a self-made man / Vincent Carretta. University of Georgia Press, c2005. xxiv, 436 p. : **B**

ISBN 9780820325712

1. Slaves -- Great Britain 2. Slaves 3. Freed slaves 4. Slave trade 5. United States -- History -- 19th century 6. Biographies

LC 2005011898

Tells the story of the former slave who was the English-speaking world's most renowned person of African descent in the 1700s and is considered the founding father of both the African and the African American literary traditions.

"This is a thoroughly rich, engrossing, and well-researched portrait of an exceptional man and the cause he championed." Booklist.

Erdman, Sarah

Erdman, Sarah **Nine** hills to Nambonkaha : two years in the heart of an African village / Sarah Erdman. Henry Holt, 2003. xi, 322 p. ; **B**

ISBN 0805073817

1. Erdman, Sarah. 2. Peace Corps Cote d'Ivoire 3. Villages -- Africa. 4. Cote d'Ivoire -- Social life and customs. 5. Autobiographies and memoirs

LC 2003044955

"This is an engrossing, well-told tale certain to appeal to armchair travelers and to anyoneespecially womenconsidering international volunteer work." Publishers Weekly.

Eruzione, Mike

Eruzione, Mike The **making** of a miracle : the untold story of the captain of the 1980 Gold Medal-winning U.S. Olympic Hockey team / Mike Eruzione, with Neal Boudette. HarperCollins, 2020. 288 p. **B**

ISBN 9780062960955

1. Olympic Winter Games (13th : 1980 : Lake Placid, N.Y.) 2. Hockey players 3. Hockey teams 4. Olympic medal winners 5. Hockey 6. Autobiographies and memoirs

LC bl2020005267

The captain of the 1980 U.S. Men's Olympic Hockey team traces his blue-collar upbringing in Massachusetts, minor-league achievements and encounters with such individuals as Al Michaels, Herb Brooks and an elite array of Russian Hall of Famers.

"Eruzione recalls what seemed to be a simpler time[rwhen major news came through television, newspapers, or word of mouth, and when the U.S. Olympic team was comprised of scrappy amateurs. This heartwarming memoir will delight more than just hockey fans." Publishers Weekly.

Erway, Cathy

Erway, Cathy The **art** of eating in : how I learned to stop spending and love the stove / Cathy Erway. Gotham Books, 2010. 336 p. **B**

ISBN 9781592405251

1. Erway, Cathy. 2. Cooking, American. 3. Food habits -- United States. 4. Cooking. 5. Autobiographies and memoirs

LC 2009040836

"A fabulous addition to any collection." Library Journal.

Evans, Rachel Held, 1981-2019

Evans, Rachel Held, 1981-2019 **Searching** for Sunday : loving, leaving, and finding the Church / Rachel Held Evans. Thomas Nelson 2015. 240 p. **B**

ISBN 9780718022129

1. Faith (Christianity) 2. Church 3. Spiritual journeys 4. Women -- Religious life 5. Autobiographies and memoirs

LC bl2015015802

Centered around seven sacraments, the author spends a liturgical year trying to discover what being a member of the Christian church really means and why it is so important.

"Elegantly structured and thoughtfully written, Evans's approach to church through the metaphors of the sacraments should please many reading groups and individual seekers." Library Journal.

Evers, Medgar Wiley, 1925-1963

Evers, Medgar Wiley, 1925-1963 The **autobiography** of Medgar Evers : a hero's life and legacy revealed through his writings, letters, and speeches / Medgar Ebers l edited and with commentaries by Myrlie Evers-Willams and Manning Marable. Basic Civitas Books 2005. 352 p. **B**

ISBN 9780465021789

1. African American civil rights workers 2. Civil rights workers 3. Civil Rights Movement 4. African Americans -- Civil rights 5. Mississippi -- Race relations 6. Mississippi -- Politics and government -- 1951- 7. Autobiographies and memoirs

LC oc2007057480

"This is a collection of Evers's unpublished papers and personal collections as well as [his widow] Evers-Williams's recollections. The resulting text resurrects the life, intellectual output, and creative legacy of the slain civil rights hero." Library Journal.

Exmouth, Edward Pellew, Viscount, 1757-1833

Taylor, Stephen, 1948- **Commander** : the life and exploits of Britain's greatest frigate captain / Stephen Taylor. W.W. Norton, 2012. 320 p. **B**

ISBN 9780393071641

1. Great Britain. Royal Navy. Officers 2. Frigates -- Great Britain -- History 3. Ship captains 4. Seafaring life 5. Naval battles 6. Great Britain -- History, Naval -- 18th century 7. Great Britain -- History, Naval -- 19th century 8. Biographies

LC 2012027783

Depicts the adventurous and heroic life story of the British naval officer who started from the bottom and worked his way up to ultimately commanding the HMS Indefatigable during the Revolutionary War and also fought during the French Revolution and Napoleonic Wars.

Fair, Eric

★Fair, Eric **Consequence** : a memoir / Eric Fair. Henry Holt and Company, [2016] 272 p. **B**

ISBN 9781627795135

1. Fair, Eric. 2. Iraq War, 2003-2011, American. 3. Military interrogation 4. Torture -- Iraq. 5. Iraq War, 2003-2011 -- Atrocities. 6. Autobiographies and memoirs

LC 2015031396

In this harrowing and unprecedented memoir, a man questions everything--his faith, his morality, his country--as he recounts his experience with torture as an interrogator in Iraq.

"A startling debut from a haunted individual who wishes he had left Iraq earlier 'with my soul intact.'" Kirkus.

Fairbanks, Douglas, 1883-1939

Goessel, Tracey The **first** king of Hollywood : the life of Douglas Fairbanks / Tracey Goessel. Chicago Review Press, 2015. 560 p. **B**

ISBN 9781613734049

1. Fairbanks, Douglas, 1883-1939. 2. Silent films. 3. Film actors and actresses 4. Biographies

LC 2015018526

The first truly definitive biography of Douglas Fairbanks, the greatest leading man of the silent film era.

"The author draws on the actor's voluminous speeches and public statements, as well as a cache of love letters between Doug and Mary. Sadly, many Fairbanks films have been lost, but this highly recommended book illuminates a vanished era of American film." Library Journal.

Fairchild, David, 1869-1954

Stone, Daniel (Daniel Evan), 1985- The **food** explorer : the true adventures of the globe-trotting botanist who transformed the American dinner table / Daniel Stone. Dutton, 2018. xvi, 397 p., [8] unnumbered p. of plates : **B**

ISBN 9781101990582

1. Fairchild, David, 1869-1954. 2. Botanists 3. Plant introduction 4. Agriculture -- United States 5. Food habits 6. Biographies

LC 2017009136

Documents the adventures and legacy of 19th-century botanist and food explorer David Fairchild to reveal the stories of how diverse crops ranging from avocadoes and mangoes to seedless grapes and pomegranates were introduced to America from faraway cultures.

"An erudite and entertaining historical biography of a food pioneer with particular interest for gastronomes and agriculture enthusiasts." Kirkus.

Falcone, Ben, 1973-

Falcone, Ben, 1973- **Being** a dad is weird : lessons in fatherhood from my family to yours / Ben Falcone. Dey Street Books, 2017 240 p. **B**

ISBN 9780062473622

1. Film producers and directors 2. Fatherhood 3. Fathers 4. Growing up

LC bl2017011670

A lighthearted and intimate look at fatherhood from the director, writer and actor combines stories about his own larger-than-life dad and how his experiences raising two daughters with wife Melissa McCarthy have been shaped by his childhood.

Faliveno, Melissa

Faliveno, Melissa **Tomboyland** / Melissa Faliveno. Little A/ TOPPLE Books, 2020 254 p. **B**

ISBN 9781542014199

1. Faliveno, Melissa. 2. Gender role 3. Social classes and family 4. Desire 5. Identity (Psychology) 6. Essays 7. Autobiographies and memoirs

LC bl2020046072

A fiercely personal and startlingly universal essay collection about the mysteries of gender and desire, of identity and class, of the stories we tell and the places we call home.

"Faliveno, a Sarah Lawrence creative writing instructor, explores identity in her winning debut collection. . . . Readers who prefer to answer their questions about gender and sexuality with more questions will appreciate this perceptive meditation." Publishers Weekly

Faludi, Susan

★Faludi, Susan **In** the darkroom / Susan Faludi. Metropolitan Books, 2016. 432 p. **B**

ISBN 9780805089080

1. Identity (Psychology) 2. Fathers and daughters. 3. Transgender persons 4. Transgender parents 5. Autobiographies and memoirs

LC 2016013605

ALA Notable Book, 2017.

Kirkus Prize for Nonfiction, 2016.

Pulitzer Prize for Biography or Autobiography finalist, 2017.

Pulitzer Prize-winning journalist Susan Faludi had barely heard from her father Steven for over 20 years when she received an email in which Steven came out as transgender. Now called Stefánie Faludi, she wanted to make her daughter's acquaintance all over again. In the Darkroom explores Stef?nie's life, beginning in Budapest after World War I. Susan based this biography on recollections from her childhood, conversations and correspondence with Stefánie, as well as interviews with other family members and friends, Stefánie's surgeon, and other transgender women. In this fascinating account, Susan disentangles fact from fiction in Stefánie's recollections, painting a moving and insightful portrait.-- Description by Katherine Bradley Johnson.

"A moving and penetrating inquiry into manifold struggles for identity, community, a nd authenticity." Kirkus.

Faraday, Michael, 1791-1867

Hirshfeld, Alan The **electric** life of Michael Faraday / Alan Hirshfeld. Walker : 2006. xiv, 258 p. : **B**

ISBN 0802714706

1. Faraday, Michael, 1791-1867. 2. Physicists -- Great Britain 3. Chemists -- Great Britain 4. Electricity -- History 5. Magnetism -- Research -- History 6. Great Britain -- Social life and customs -- 19th century 7. Biographies

LC 2005025533

Tells the story of Michael Faraday, who was a poor, uneducated bookbinder's apprentice who overcame adversity and class prejudice in nineteenth-century England to emerge as the greatest experimental scientist of his day.

"In this biography of the English scientist, the author explains Faraday's status as one of the most inspirational and significant figures of science. A vibrant portrayal that emphasizes Faraday's qualities of wonder, acuity, and diligence, which propelled him to greatness." Booklist.

Farmer, Paul, 1959-

Kidder, Tracy **Mountains** beyond mountains / Tracy Kidder. Random House, 2003. 317 p. **B**

ISBN 9780375506161

1. Physicians. 2. Human rights. 3. Right to medical care. 4. Medical missionaries.

LC 2003041253

ALA Notable Book, 2004.

A portrait of infectious disease expert Dr. Paul Farmer follows the efforts of this unconventional Harvard genius to understand the world's great health, economic, and social problems and to bring healing to humankind.

Farrakhan, Louis

Levinsohn, Florence Hamlish, 1926-1998 **Looking** for Farrakhan / Florence Hamlish Levinsohn. Ivan R. Dee, 1997. xiii, 305 p. ; **B**

ISBN 1566631572

1. Farrakhan, Louis. 2. Black Muslims 3. African Americans 4. Biographies

LC 97011335

Includes index."

Levinsohn's biography, which reflects on the black experience and how it changed young Eugene Walcott into Louis Farrakhan, leader of the Nation of Islam, attempts to make sense of this prominent figure in American politics." Library Journal.

Faulkner, William, 1897-1962

Bloom, Harold **William** Faulkner / edited and with an introduction by Harold Bloom. Bloom's Literary Criticism, c2008. viii, 269 p. ; **B**

ISBN 9780791097861

1. Faulkner, William, 1897-1962 Criticism and interpretation.

LC 2007033754

Presents a collection of critical essays on several works by the American author, including "As I Lay Dying," "The Sound and the Fury," and "Light in August."

Gorra, Michael Edward The **saddest** words : William Faulkner's Civil War / Michael Gorra. Liveright Publishing Corporation, 2020. 400 p. **B**

ISBN 9781631491702

1. Faulkner, William, 1897-1962 Criticism and interpretation 2. Faulkner, William, 1897-1962 Characters African Americans. 3. Literature -- History and criticism 4. African Americans in literature. 5. Southern States in literature 6. Race relations in literature. 7. United States -- History -- Civil War, 1861-1865 -- Literature and the war. 8. United States -- Race relations. 9. Biographies

LC 2020014188

How do we read William Faulkner in the twenty-first century? asks Michael Gorra, in this reconsideration of Faulkner's life and legacy.

"A magisterial, multidisciplinary study of Faulkner that shakes the dust off his canonization." Kirkus

★Parini, Jay **One** matchless time : a life of William Faulkner / Jay Parini. Harper Collins Publishers, 2004. xi, 492 p. **B**

ISBN 0066210720

1. Faulkner, William, 1897-1962. 2. Authors, American -- 20th century 3. Nobel Prize winners 4. Biographies

LC 2004042891

"The author offers a portrait of a man always trying to invent a new mask for himself as well as the portrait of an artist consumed by a desire to tell about the South and its class struggles, its depravity, and its captivity to the double bonds of land and history. Parini examines each of Faulkner's novels, from Soldier's Pay to The Reivers, and connects the Snopses, Sutpens, and Compsons of Faulkner's mythic Yoknapatawpha County foibles, his insecurities, and his inestimable literary achievement." Library Journal.

Rollyson, Carl E. (Carl Edmund) The **life** of William Faulkner. Carl E. Rollyson. University of Virginia Press, 2020. 622 p. **B**

ISBN 9780813944401

1. Authors, American -- 20th century 2. Fiction writing 3. Screenplay writing 4. Films -- Production and direction 5. Biographies

LC 2019032254

Volume 2 of 2-volume series.By the end of volume 1 of The Life of William Faulkner, the young writer had gone from an unpromising, self-mythologizing bohemian to the author of some of the most innovative and enduring literature of the century. The second and concluding volume of Carl Rollyson's ambitious biography finds Faulkner lamenting the many threats to his creative existence: he has inherited only debts?a symptom of the South's faded fortunes?and numerous mouths to feed and funerals to fund. And so he turns to the classic temptation for financially struggling writers?Hollywood. Volume 2 of this monumental work rests on an unprecedented trove of research, giving us the most penetrating and comprehensive life of Faulkner and providing a fascinating look at the author's trajectory from under-appreciated "writer's writer" to world-renowned Nobel laureate and literary icon.

"Rollyson's painstakingly researched and beautifully written biography should be a touchstone for Faulkner scholarship for years to come." Publishers Weekly

Favre, Brett

Pearlman, Jeff **Gunslinger** : the remarkable, improbable, iconic life of Brett Favre / Jeff Pearlman. Houghton Mifflin Harcourt, 2016. 352 p. **B**

ISBN 9780544454378

1. Green Bay Packers (Football team) 2. National Football League 3. Football players. 4. Professional football players. 5. Quarterbacks (Football) 6. Biographies

LC 2016287244

Tells the complete story of NFL quarterback Brett Favre's life, drawing on more than 500 interviews, including many from the people closest to Favre.

Favro, Terri

Favro, Terri **Generation** robot : a century of science fiction, fact, and speculation / Terri Favro. Skyhorse Publishing, 2018. 300 p. **B**

ISBN 9781510723108

1. Technology and civilization 2. Popular culture 3. Science fiction -- History and criticism 4. Technological innovations 5. Autobiographies and memoirs

LC bl2018002037

Covering a century of science fiction, fact and speculation, from the 1950 publication of Isaac Asimov's I, Robot, to the 2050 Singularity when artificial intelligence are predicted to merge, a nostalgic and fascinating book shows how our relationship with robotics and futuristic technologies has shifted over time.

"In every chapter, Favro shows how different actual robots are from many of their counterparts in science fiction. Her books greatest achievement may be to get readers looking at their cell phones, computers, prosthetics, and other gadgets as robots in the real world." Publishers Weekly.

Federer, Roger, 1981-

Hodgkinson, Mark **Fedegraphica** : a graphic biography of the genius of Roger Federer / Mark Hodgkinson. Aurum Press Ltd, 2016. 272 p. : **B**

ISBN 9781781315293

1. Tennis players -- Switzerland 2. Tennis players -- Switzerland --

Pictorial works

LC bl2016022795

Provides a description of the Swiss tennis player's life and career through both text and infographics highlighting statistics of his professional accomplishments.

Feiffer, Jules

Feiffer, Jules **Backing** into forward / Jules Feiffer. Nan A. Talese/Doubleday, 2010. 464 p. **B**

ISBN 9780385531580

1. Authors, American -- 20th century 2. Cartoonists -- United States 3. Cartooning. 4. Drawing. 5. Autobiographies and memoirs

LC 2009021933

"Feiffer is masterful at self-analyzing the skinny Jewish kid from the Bronx who grew up during the Depression, whose sister was a Communist, and whose distant cousin Roy Cohn was a Red-baiter, while he himself was full of insecurities but fortunate enough to luck into the zeitgeist. . . . He offers social commentary and memorable moments from career and family life as he moved from cartooning to screen and playwriting, to authoring children's books, all the while maintaining a wry perspective that shows in the cartoons interspersed throughout this wonderful memoir." Booklist.

Feige, David

Feige, David **Indefensible** : one lawyer's journey into the inferno of American justice / David Feige. Little, Brown and Co., c2006. 276 p. ; **B**

ISBN 031615623X

1. Feige, David. 2. Public defenders -- Bronx, New York City 3. Criminal justice system -- Bronx, New York City. 4. Bronx, New York City -- Social conditions. 5. Autobiographies and memoirs

LC 2006001283

A former Trial Chief of the Bronx Defenders recounts an ordinary day in the life of a South Bronx public defender, citing encounters with a range of factors, from dramatic courtroom battles and threatening defendants to unscrupulous lawyers and vindictive judges.

"The author takes us through a typically harrowing day as a public defender, dealing with arbitrary judges and clients who are often victims of the judicial system. Feige skillfully shares his wisdom and his humanity and sheds light on a justice system that too often works irrationally." Publishers Weekly.

Feinstein, Michael

Feinstein, Michael The **Gershwins** and me : a personal history in twelve songs / Michael Feinstein, with Ian Jackman. Simon & Schuster, 2012. 320 p. **B**

ISBN 9781451645309

1. Gershwin, George, 1898-1937. 2. Gershwin, Ira, 1896-1983. 3. Feinstein, Michael. 4. Popular culture -- History -- 20th century. 5. Songs -- History and criticism. 6. Songwriters 7. Songwriting. 8. United States -- Popular culture -- History -- 20th century. 9. Autobiographies and memoirs

LC 2012006833

A five-time Grammy nominee presents an illustrated tribute to the lives and legacies of the Gershwins that is presented through the stories of 12 of their most enduring songs including "Strike Up the Band" and "Love Is Here to Stay," in a volume that is complemented by a CD of original recordings.

Feldman, Deborah, 1986-

Feldman, Deborah, 1986- **Exodus** / Deborah Feldman. Blue Rider Press, 2014. 288 p. **B**

ISBN 9780399162770

1. Jewish women 2. Women authors 3. Independence in women 4. Single mothers 5. Autobiographies and memoirs

LC 2013046263

The author of the best-selling Unorthodox traces her new life as an independent young woman and single mother searching for an authentic and personal Jewish identity, describing how after leaving her Hasidic community she pursued healing in a circle of like-minded outcasts and misfits.

"The overall effect is captivating, entertaining and informative, providing readers with an honest assessment of the strength of one's convictions and the effect a strict religious background can have on a person. An enthralling account of how one Orthodox Jewish woman turned her back on her religion and found genuineness and validity in her new life." Kirkus.

Feldman, Deborah, 1986- **Unorthodox** : the scandalous rejection of my Hasidic roots / Deborah Feldman. Simon & Schuster, c2012. 272 p. **B**

ISBN 9781439187005

1. Hasidim -- Brooklyn, New York City 2. Self-discovery in women 3. Jewish women. 4. Fundamentalists 5. Brooklyn, New York City 6. New York City 7. Autobiographies and memoirs 8. Books to TV

LC 2011001386

Traces the author's upbringing in a Hasidic community in Brooklyn, describing the strict rules that governed her life, arranged marriage at the age of seventeen, and the birth of her son, which led to her plan to leave and forge her own path in life.

"Born into the insular and exclusionary Hasidic community of Satmar in Brooklyn to a mentally disabled father and a mother who fled the sect, Feldman, as she recounts in this nicely written memoir, seemed doomed to be an outsider from the start. Raised by devout grandparents who forbade her to read in English, the ever-curious child craved books outside the synagogue teaching. Feldman's spark of rebellion started with sneaking off to the library and hiding paperback novels under her bed. She starts to experience panic attacks and the stirrings of her final break with being Hasidic. It's when she finally does get pregnant and wants something more for her child that the full force of her uprising takes hold and she plots her escape. Feldman, who now attends Sarah Lawrence College, offers this engaging and at times gripping insight into Brooklyn's Hasidic community." Publishers Weekly.

Fenn, Lisa

Fenn, Lisa **Carry** on : a story of resilience, redemption, and an unlikely family / Lisa Fenn. Harper Wave, 2016 320 p. **B**

ISBN 9780062427830

1. Crockett, Dartanyon 2. Sutton, Leroy 3. African Americans with disabilities 4. Teenagers who are blind 5. Friendship 6. Wrestlers 7. Cleveland, Ohio. 8. Autobiographies and memoirs

LC 2016012130

An Emmy-winning ESPN producer describes how she developed a surprising, profound and lasting bond with two disabled African-American, inner-city high school wrestlers after filming a segment about them for television.

Fennelly, Beth Ann, 1971-

Fennelly, Beth Ann, 1971- **Heating** & cooling : 52 micro-memoirs / Beth Ann Fennelly. W W Norton & Co Inc 2017. 128 p. **B**

ISBN 9780393609479

1. Women poets 2. Everyday life 3. Mother and child 4. Men/women

relations 5. Autobiographies and memoirs
LC 2017026664

The 52 micro-memoirs in genre-defying Heating & Cooling offer bright glimpses into a richly lived life, combining the compression of poetry with the truth-telling of nonfiction into one heartfelt, celebratory book. Ranging from childhood recollections to quirky cultural observations, these micro-memoirs build on one another to arrive at a portrait of Beth Ann Fennelly as a wife, mother, writer, and deeply original observer of life's challenges and joys.

"A sleek, delightful collection." Kirkus.

Ferlinghetti, Lawrence, 1919-

Ferlinghetti, Lawrence, 1919- **Writing** across the landscape : travel journals 1960/2010 / Lawrence Ferlinghetti ; edited by Giada Diano and Matthew Gleeson. Liveright Publishing Corporation, 2015 552 p. **B**

ISBN 9781631490019

1. Ferlinghetti, Lawrence, 1919-. 2. Ferlinghetti, Lawrence, 1919- Travel. 3. Voyages and travels
LC 2015026292

Presents the travel journals of the legendary poet and best-selling author of Coney Island of the Mind, illustrated with facsimile manuscripts and personal sketches, and offering a peek into the lives of Jack Kerouac, William S. Burroughs and Ezra Pound.

"Avid readers of Ferlinghetti's work will welcome this collection as the 100th anniversary of his birth in 2019 draws ever nearer. It may also provide grist for future biographers." Library Journal.

Fermi, Enrico, 1901-1954

★Schwartz, David N., 1956- The **last** man who knew everything : the life and times of Enrico Fermi, father of the nuclear age / David N. Schwartz. Basic Books, 2017. 448 p. **B**

ISBN 9780465072927

1. Fermi, Enrico, 1901-1954. 2. Manhattan Project (U.S.) 3. Physicists. 4. Quantum theory. 5. Nobel Prize winners. 6. Nuclear physicists. 7. Biographies.
LC 2017020558

A portrait of physicist and innovator Enrico Fermi assesses his pivotal role in achieving a nuclear chain reaction and shares insights into his complex personality, family ties, and relationships with the Italian Fascist Party and the Manhattan Project.

"Though comparable to Segr and Hoerlins The Pope of Physics (2016) as an account of Fermis groundbreaking science, Schwartzs biography delivers a much fuller personal portrait, illuminating how this generous friend to scientific colleagues, this inspiring mentor to students, often proved a difficult husband and negligent father. A sophisticated portrayal of a complex man." Booklist.

Segre, Gino The **pope** of physics : Enrico Fermi and the birth of the atomic age / Gino Segre and Bettina Hoerlin. Henry Holt and Company, 2016. 304 p. **B**

ISBN 9781627790055

1. Fermi, Enrico, 1901-1954. 2. Physicists 3. Scientists 4. Nobel Prize winners 5. Physics 6. Biographies
LC 2016013398

A biography of one of the leading architects of the atomic age touches upon the human dramas that shaped his life as well as his productive and creative pursuit of science that ultimately earned him a Nobel Prize.

"A vivid retelling of events that still shape our lives today." Kirkus.

Feynman, Richard P. (Richard Phillips), 1918-1988

Ottaviani, Jim **Feynman** / written by Jim Ottaviani ; art by Leland Myrick ; coloring by Hilary Sycamore. First Second, 2011. 272 p. **B**

ISBN 9781596432598

1. Feynman, Richard P. (Richard Phillips), 1918-1988. 2. Physicists -- United States 3. Scientists -- United States 4. Nobel Prize winners 5. Biographies 6. Biographical comics 7. Comics and Graphic novels
LC 2010036260

Field, Sally

Field, Sally **In** pieces / Sally Field. Grand Central Publishing, 2018. viii, 404 p. **B**

ISBN 9781538763025

1. Actors and actresses 2. Celebrities 3. Fame 4. Mothers and daughters 5. Autobiographies and memoirs
LC bl2018134673

The Academy Award-winning actress shares insights into her difficult childhood, the artistic pursuits that helped her find her voice and the powerful emotional legacy that shaped her journey as a daughter and mother.

Fillmore, Millard, 1800-1874

Finkelman, Paul, 1949- **Millard** Fillmore : the 13th president, 1850-1853 / Paul Finkelman. Times Books, c2011. 192 p. American presidents series (Times Books) **B**

ISBN 9780805087154

1. Fillmore, Millard, 1800-1874. 2. Presidents -- United States 3. Vice-presidents -- United States 4. Politicians. 5. Civil war 6. United States -- Politics and government -- 1849-1853. 7. United States -- History -- Civil War, 1861-1865 -- Causes. 8. Biographies
LC 2010047174

A portrait of the 13th President traces his rise from virtual obscurity after the sudden death of Zachary Taylor, evaluating his roles in promoting Southern agendas, dividing the Whig party and setting the groundwork for the American Civil War.

"The author describes Millard Fillmore's nearly forgotten presidency by rigidly contrasting him with Abraham Lincoln, another self-made man who wrestled with racial and regional tensions as president. . . . This book is an enlightening view into the often overlooked beginnings of the Civil War, which history buffs and students alike will find enjoyable." Publishers Weekly.

Fincham-Gray, Suzanne

Fincham-Gray, Suzanne **My** patients and other animals : a veterinarian's stories of love, loss, and hope / Suzanne Fincham-Gray. Spiegel & Grau, 2018 288 p. **B**

ISBN 9780812998184

1. Fincham-Gray, Suzanne. 2. Veterinarians. 3. Human/animal relationships 4. Animals 5. Autobiographies and memoirs
LC 2017025329

A memoir of the author's life spent in the company of animals illuminates the universal experiences of loving, healing and losing beloved pets, describing some of the remarkable cases that shaped her career while sharing a veterinarian's perspectives into the many ways that animals change our lives.

Fischer, Bobby, 1943-2008

Brady, Frank, 1934- **Endgame** : the spectacular rise and fall of Bobby Fischer / Frank Brady. Crown, c2010. 304 p. **B**

ISBN 9780307463906

1. Chess players -- United States 2. Chess -- Collection of games.

3. Biographies

LC 2010033840

From an author who wrote one of the bestselling Bobby Fischer books ever and who was himself a friend of Fischer's comes an impressively researched biography that for the first time captures the complete, remarkable arc of the life of the chess master.

"Brady's insightful biography of the legendary chess player focuses more on Fischer's life as a chess champion than on his much-publicized legal troubles and alleged psychological breakdowns. Brady first became friends with Fischer at a chess tournament when they were both children, and he combines a traditional biography with a personal memoir. Brady is uniquely qualified to write this book. Not only is he a seasoned biographer and someone who knew Fischer on a personal level; he's also an accomplished chess player himself, able to convey the game's intricacies to the reader in a clear, uncomplicated manner." Booklist.

Fisher, Carrie

Fisher, Carrie The **princess** diarist / Carrie Fisher. Blue Rider Press, [2016] 257 pages : **B**

ISBN 9780399173592

1. Fisher, Carrie. 2. Film actors and actresses -- United States 3. Film industry and trade 4. Memories. 5. Women with bipolar disorder 6. United States -- Social life and customs -- 20th century 7. United States -- Social life and customs -- 21st century 8. Autobiographies and memoirs

LC 2016054189

The best-selling author and Hollywood icon best known for her Star Wars role shares interconnected essays exploring her life as the child of Tinseltown royalty, adventures on the sets of Star Wars and struggles with bipolar disorder.

"Outspoken, honest commentary of what it's like to be Princess Leia on and off the screen." Kirkus.

Fisher, Carrie **Wishful** drinking / Carrie Fisher. Simon & Schuster, 2008. 176 p. **B**

ISBN 9781439102251

1. Fisher, Carrie. 2. Film actors and actresses -- United States 3. Men/women relations 4. Drug addiction 5. Women with bipolar disorder 6. United States -- Social life and customs -- 20th century 7. United States -- Social life and customs -- 21st century 8. Autobiographies and memoirs

LC bl2008022972

A memoir based on the author's one-woman show describes growing up with celebrity parents, her early success in "Star Wars," battle with addiction and mental illness, turbulent romances, role as a single mother, and struggle for recovery and healing.

★Weller, Sheila **Carrie** Fisher : a life on the edge / Sheila Weller. Sarah Crichton Books/Farrar, Straus and Giroux, 2019. 416 p. **B**

ISBN 9780374282233

1. Fisher, Carrie. 2. Actors and actresses 3. Women authors 4. Families 5. Bipolar disorder 6. Biographies

LC 2019021323

A candid portrait of the beloved Hollywood actress and writer discusses her complicated relationships with her famous parents, her Star Wars fame and her struggles with bipolar disorder and drug addiction.

Fisher, Todd, 1958-

Fisher, Todd, 1958- **My** girls : a lifetime with Carrie and Debbie / Todd Fisher. William Morrow, 2018. x, 388 p., 32 unnumbered p. of plates : **B**

ISBN 9780062792310

1. Fisher, Todd, 1958- Family 2. Reynolds, Debbie 3. Fisher, Carrie 4. Film actors and actresses 5. Film producers and directors 6. Family relationships 7. Brothers and sisters 8. Hollywood, California 9. Autobiographies and memoirs

a personal tribute to the lives of Carrie Fisher and Debbie Reynolds shares poignant stories of the author's experiences growing up with his sister and their mother among Hollywood royalty.

Fishman, Boris, 1979-

Fishman, Boris, 1979- **Savage** feast : three generations, two continents, and a dinner table, a memoir with recipes / Boris Fishman. HarperCollins, 2019 320 p. **B**

ISBN 9780062867896

1. Fishman, Boris, 1979- Family 2. Immigrant families 3. Jews, Eastern European 4. Cooking, Eastern European 5. Food -- Psychological aspects 6. Autobiographies and memoirs

LC 2018277185

The acclaimed author of A Replacement Life shifts between heartbreak and humor in a recipe-filled memoir that is all-at-once a family story, an immigrant story, a love story and an epic meal.

Fisk, Carlton, 1947-

Wilson, Doug, 1961- **Pudge** : the biography of Carlton Fisk / Doug Wilson. St. Martin's Press, 2015. 352 p. **B**

ISBN 9781250065438

1. Baseball players -- United States 2. Baseball. 3. Catchers (Baseball) 4. Catching (Baseball) 5. Biographies

LC 2015027529

The first biography of the Hall of Fame catcher, whose famous home run in the 1975 World Series has been called one of the greatest moment in the history of televised sports

"A well-researched account of a legendary ball player." Library Journal.

FitzGerald, Holly Conklin

FitzGerald, Holly Conklin **Ruthless** river : love and survival by raft on the Amazon's relentless Madre De Dios / Holly FitzGerald. Vintage Books, 2017. 336 p. Vintage Departures **B**

ISBN 9780525432777

1. FitzGerald, Holly Conklin Travel Amazon River Region 2. Married people 3. Survival (after airplane accidents, shipwrecks, etc.) 4. Life change events 5. River travel 6. Peru 7. Bolivia 8. Amazon River 9. Autobiographies and memoirs

LC 2016037102

Holly FitzGerald and her husband, Fitz--married less than two years--set out on a yearlong honeymoon adventure of a lifetime, backpacking around the world. Five months into the trip their plane crash lands in Peru at a penal colony walled in by jungle, and their blissfully romantic journey turns into a terrifying nonstop labyrinth of escape and survival.

"Recommended for fans of survival narratives, coming-of-maturity stories, and travelogues from off the beaten path." Booklist.

Fitzgerald, F. Scott (Francis Scott), 1896-1940

Brown, David S. (David Scott), 1966- **Paradise** lost : a life of F. Scott Fitzgerald / David S. Brown. The Belknap Press of Harvard University Press, 2017. 330 p. **B**

ISBN 9780674504820

1. Fitzgerald, F. Scott (Francis Scott), 1896-1940. 2. Fitzgerald, Zelda, 1900-1948. 3. Authors, American 4. Social classes 5.

Nostalgia 6. Married men 7. Biographies
LC 2016048811

Pigeonholed as a Jazz Age epicurean and an emblem of the Lost Generation, Fitzgerald was at heart a moralist struck by the nation's shifting mood and manners after WWI. Placing him among Progressives such as Charles Beard, Randolph Bourne, and Thorstein Veblen, David Brown reveals Fitzgerald as a writer with an encompassing historical imagination.

Fitzgerald, F. Scott (Francis Scott), 1896-1940 A **life** in letters / F. Scott Fitzgerald ; edited by Matthew J. Bruccoli ; with the assistance of Judith S. Baughman. Simon & Schuster, 1995. xxii, 503 p. : **B**

ISBN 0684801531

1. Fitzgerald, F. Scott (Francis Scott), 1896-1940 Correspondence. 2. Authors, American -- 20th century -- Correspondence. 3. United States -- Social life and customs -- 20th century.
LC 94043901

"A Touchstone book.""

A new collection"--Cover.

A collection of the author's letters displays in his own words his artistic and emotional maturation.

"Essential reading for a full understanding of Fitzgerald as an artist and a man." Library Journal.

Tate, Mary Jo **Critical** companion to F. Scott Fitzgerald : a literary reference to his life and work / Mary Jo Tate ; foreword by Matthew J. Bruccoli. Facts On File, c2007. xvi, 464 p. : **B**

ISBN 9780816064335

1. Fitzgerald, F. Scott (Francis Scott), 1896-1940 Encyclopedias. 2. Authors, American -- 20th century 3. Biographies
LC 2006011393

Rev. ed. of: F. Scott Fitzgerald A to Z. c1998.

Contains extensive updates, including new critical commentary on all Fitzgerald's major novels and short stories. This volume is also illustrated with first-edition dust jackets, portraits of Fitzgerald throughout his life, and pictures of friends, relatives, and contemporaries.

Fitzmaurice, Simon

Fitzmaurice, Simon **It's** not yet dark : a memoir / Simon Fitzmaurice. Houghton Mifflin Harcourt, 2017 176 p. **B**

ISBN 9781328916716

1. People with amyotrophic lateral sclerosis 2. Amyotrophic lateral sclerosis 3. Determination in men 4. Personal conduct 5. Autobiographies and memoirs
LC 2017016109

In 2008, Simon Fitzmaurice was diagnosed with ALS, or Lou Gehrig's disease. He was given four years to live. In 2010, in a state of lung-function collapse, Simon knew with crystal clarity that now was not his time to die. Against all prevailing medical opinion, he chose to ventilate in order to stay alive. In It's Not Yet Dark, the young filmmaker, a husband and father of five small children, draws us deeply into his inner world.

"Fitzmaurice communicates well, making his own case and advocating for the right of the afflicted to make their own choices in how they will live and die. A fine and heartfelt memoir from an author hopeful in his determination to endure against the odds." Kirkus.

Flaherty, Meghan

Flaherty, Meghan **Tango** lessons : a memoir / Meghan Flaherty. Houghton Mifflin Harcourt 2018 320 p. **B**

ISBN 9780544980709

1. Tango (Dance) 2. Intimacy (Psychology) 3. Dancing -- Psychological aspects 4. Self-discovery 5. New York City 6. Autobiographies and memoirs
LC 2017046214

Traces the author's decision to overcome trauma-related intimacy issues by taking dance lessons in New York's vibrant tango underground, where she learned unexpected lessons in strength, balance and love. A first book.

Flaubert, Gustave, 1821-1880

Brown, Frederick, 1934- **Flaubert** : a biography / Frederick Brown. Little, Brown and Co., 2006. 628 p. : **B**

ISBN 9780316118781

1. Flaubert, Gustave, 1821-1880. 2. Authors, French -- 19th century 3. Paris, France 4. Biographies
LC 2005017036

National Book Critics Circle Award for Biography finalist, 2006.

A portrait of the nineteenth-century literary master depicts him as a contradictory artist, in a profile that covers such topics as his celebrated correspondence with George Sand, his character trial after the writing of Madame Bovary, and his volatile relationship with the conservative bourgeoisie.

"The author has put together a judicious work that sticks to the record and relies on expertly chosen passages from Flaubert's brilliant letters and the works of his contemporaries to develop a convincing portrait, brushstroke by brushstroke." New York Times.

Flynn, Nick, 1960-

Flynn, Nick, 1960- **Another** bullshit night in Suck City : a memoir / Nick Flynn. W.W. Norton & Co., 2005. 357 p. : **B**

ISBN 0393329402

1. Flynn, Nick, 1960- Family. 2. Poets, American -- 20th century 3. Homeless persons -- Boston, Massachusetts. 4. Fathers and sons -- Boston, Massachusetts. 5. Children of alcoholics 6. Boston, Massachusetts -- Social life and customs. 7. Massachusetts -- Social life and customs. 8. Autobiographies and memoirs
LC oc2007031151

The movie "Being Flynn" is based on this book.The son of a convicted bank robber and con artist describes their complicated relationship, relating how his father, while in jail, sent the author letters throughout his childhood and turned up in a Boston homeless shelter where the author was a caseworker.

"This memoir describes the years poet Flynn . spent, in his late 20s, working at one of the city's homeless shelters, where his path crisscrossed with his down-and-out father's. Although it's depressing, the book never seems hopeless, because readers know the author has succeeded at doing what his father only pretended to do: write, and write well." Publishers Weekly.

Flynt, Wayne, 1940-

Flynt, Wayne, 1940- **Mockingbird** songs : Harper Lee : a friendship / Wayne Flynt. HarperCollins Publishers, 2017 240 p. **B**

ISBN 9780062660084

1. Lee, Harper 2. Women authors 3. Authors 4. Friendship 5. Letters
LC 2016044095

A portrait of one of America's most beloved authors is presented through reminiscences and letters exchanged with one of her closest friends, describing how their respective experiences with the violent racism of the mid-20th-century American South shaped their families, careers and values.

"Southern historian Flynt (Keeping the Faith) shares his relationship with Harper Lee in a series of affectionate, playful, and mutually admiring letters." Publishers Weekly.

Foer, Esther Safran

Foer, Esther Safran **I** want you to know we're still here : a post-Holocaust memoir / Esther Safran Foer. Tim Duggan Books, 2020. 288 p. **B**

ISBN 9780525575986

1. Foer, Esther Safran Family. 2. Children of Holocaust survivors -- United States 3. Family history 4. Jewish families 5. Loss (Psychology) 6. United States 7. Poland 8. Ukraine 9. Autobiographies and memoirs

LC 2019025860

A Jewish-American community leader and founding CEO of Sixth & I describes her parents' silence on their Holocaust experiences and her visit to the Ukraine in search of her family's stories.

"Foer explores her family with context and detail. Her story will interest readers of historical and personal narratives, especially memoirs and genealogy." Library Journal

Fogerty, John, 1945-

Fogerty, John, 1945- **Fortunate** son : my life, my music / John Fogerty. Little Brown & Co, 2015 320 p. **B**

ISBN 9780316244572

1. Creedence Clearwater Revival 2. Rock musicians -- United States 3. Autobiographies and memoirs

LC bl2015033619

The legendary singer-songwriter and creative force behind Creedence Clearwater Revival, as well as a Grammy-winning solo artist in his own right, presents his long-awaited memoir.

"This isn't just an account of one musician's ups and downs with art and life; Fogerty has created a solid study of popular music over the past 50 years." Publishers Weekly.

Foles, Nick

Foles, Nick **Believe** it : my journey of success, failure, and overcoming the odds / Nick Foles, with Joshua Cooley. The nonfiction imprint of Tyndale House Publishers, Inc., [2018] 288 p. **B**

ISBN 9781496436498

1. Philadelphia Eagles (Football team) 2. Quarterbacks (Football) 3. Football players 4. Determination (Personal quality) 5. Faith (Christianity) 6. Autobiographies and memoirs

LC 2018021881

The author describes how he separates himself from his football career and how his past mistakes have shaped him into the man he is today.

Folger, Henry Clay, 1857-1930

Mays, Andrea E. The **millionaire** and the bard : Henry Folger's obsessive hunt for Shakespeare's first folio / Andrea E. Mays. Simon & Schuster, 2015. 320 p. **B**

ISBN 9781439118238

1. Folger, Henry Clay, 1857-1930. 2. Shakespeare, William, 1564-1616. 3. Book collectors. 4. Millionaires. 5. Businesspeople. 6. Obsession. 7. New York (State) 8. Biographies

LC 2015001458

The Millionaire and the Bard tells the miraculous and romantic story of the making of the First Folio, and of the American industrialist whose thrilling pursuit of the book became a lifelong obsession. When Shakespeare died in 1616 half of his plays died with him. By the time of his death his plays were rarely performed, eighteen of them had never been published, and the rest existed only in bastardized forms that did not stay true to his original language. Seven years later, in 1623, Shakespeare's business partners, companions, and fellow actors, John Heminges and Henry Condell, gathered copies of the plays and manuscripts, edited and published thirty-six of them. This massive book, the First Folio, was intended as a memorial to their deceased friend. They could not have known that it would become one of the most important books ever published in the English language, nor that it would become a fetish object for collectors.

Foner, Moe, 1915-

Foner, Moe, 1915- **Not** for bread alone : a memoir / Moe Foner ; with Dan North ; foreword by Ossie Davis. Cornell University Press, c2002. xv, 142 p. : **B**

ISBN 9780801440618

1. Hospitals -- Employees -- Labor unions -- New York (State) -- History 2. Labor leaders -- New York (State) 3. Biographies

LC 2002005100

Presents an autobiography by a leading player in 1199/SEIU, New York's Health and Human Service Union, and a key strategist in the union's fight for recognition and higher wages for thousands of low-paid hospital workers.

"This memoir focuses on Foner's work on behalf of the union of New York City hospital and healthcare workers, best known by its number1199. Nation,Foner's memoir is a unique window into the evolution of 1199 SEIU from its origins as a tiny conglomeration of drugstore employees into the country's largest healthcare union." Library Journal.

Fontaine, Tessa

Fontaine, Tessa The **electric** woman : a memoir in death-defying acts / Tessa Fontaine. Farrar, Straus and Giroux, 2018. 368 p. **B**

ISBN 9780374158378

1. World of Wonders (Sideshow) 2. Sideshows 3. Circus performers 4. Women circus performers 5. Independence in women 6. Autobiographies and memoirs

LC 2017038360

Tessa Fontaine's astonishing memoir of pushing past fear, The Electric Woman, follows the author on a life-affirming journey of loss and self-discovery-- through her time on the road with the last traveling American sideshow and her relationship with an adventurous, spirited mother.

"This remarkable, beautifully written memoir explores the depth of mother-daughter love and the courageous acts of overcoming fear and accepting change." Publishers Weekly.

Forbes, Sarah, 1982-

Forbes, Sarah, 1982- **Sex** in the museum : my unlikely career at New York's most provocative museum / Sarah Forbes. St. Martin's Press, 2016 224 p. **B**

ISBN 9781250041678

1. Museum of Sex, New York 2. Museum curators 3. Sexuality 4. Sex customs. 5. Sexology. 6. Autobiographies and memoirs

LC 2015038926

Sarah Forbes was a graduate student when she stumbled upon the museum dedicated to "the history, evolution, and cultural significance of human sexuality." She was reluctant when her boyfriend suggested she apply for a job. Little did she know that a part-time position would lead her to her current gig as the Museum's curator. That was twelve years ago. Now Sarah - a mother of two - spends her days examining human sexuality and sexual artifacts.

"A provocative chronicle steeped in eyebrow-raising details and personal honesty." Kirkus.

Ford, Betty, 1918-2011

★McCubbin, Lisa **Betty** Ford : First Lady, women's advocate, survivor, trailblazer / Lisa McCubbin ; foreword by Susan Ford Bales. Gallery Books, 2018. 336 p. **B**

ISBN 9781501164682

1. Betty Ford Center 2. Presidents' spouses -- United States 3. Cancer survivors 4. Women social advocates 5. Women's rights 6. United States -- Social conditions -- 20th century 7. Biographies

LC 2018009239

Drawing on interviews with family, friends, and colleagues, a biography of the groundbreaking, candid, and resilient First Lady discusses her marriage, her determination to speak out on controversial issues, and her founding of the Betty Ford Center.

"This timely biography of Betty Ford will introduce her to millennials and remind others of her importance in championing equal rights for women and speaking out on breast cancer, abortion, depression, and addiction at a time when women, especially a first lady, did not discuss these issues in public." Booklist.

Ford, Henry, 1863-1947

★Baldwin, Neil, 1947- **Henry** Ford and the Jews : the mass production of hate / Neil Baldwin. Public Affairs, c2001. xii, 416 p. : **B**

ISBN 1891620525

1. Ford, Henry, 1863-1947. 2. Antisemitism -- United States. 3. Automobile industry and trade -- United States -- History. 4. Industrialists -- United States 5. Jews -- United States. 6. Biographies

LC 2001041679

Describes how Henry Ford promoted his anti-Semitic views in "The Dearborn Independent" and other publications and examines the response of the Jewish community in America as well as Ford's impact on the spread of anti-Semitism in Europe before World War II.

★Brinkley, Douglas **Wheels** for the world : Henry Ford, his company, and a century of progress, 1903-2003 / Douglas Brinkley. Viking, 2003. xxii, 858 p. : **B**

ISBN 067003181X

1. Ford, Henry, 1863-1947. 2. Ford Motor Company -- History. 3. Model T automobile -- History. 4. Automobile designers -- United States 5. Automobile industry and trade -- History. 6. Mass production -- United States -- History. 7. Biographies

LC 2002033066

An evaluation of the impact of Henry Ford and Ford Motor Company on human civilization discusses the successes of early car models while noting specific ways in which automobile technology has affected industrial labor relations and America's middle class.

"Car lovers will appreciate this amazing account of the birth of the automobile industry, including funny anecdotes about the trusty Model T, the evolution of the V-8 engine, the artistic design of the Thunderbird, sophistication of the Lincoln Continental, and popularity of the Mustang." Booklist.

Watts, Steven, 1952- The **people's** tycoon : Henry Ford and the American century / Steven Watts. A.A. Knopf, 2005. xv, 614 p. : **B**

ISBN 0375407359

1. Ford, Henry, 1863-1947. 2. Industrialists -- United States 3. Businesspeople 4. Automobile industry and trade -- United States -- History. 5. Automobile designers -- United States 6. Biographies

LC 2004048594

"Steven Watts is intelligent, thorough and engaging . in telling the story of an American who not only was influential but remains unavoidable to this day." New York Times Book Review.

Ford, Richard, 1944-

★Ford, Richard, 1944- **Between** them : remembering my parents / Richard Ford. Ecco Press, 2017. 192 p. **B**

ISBN 9780062661883

1. Parent and child 2. Traveling sales personnel 3. Growing up 4. Arkansas 5. Autobiographies and memoirs

LC 2017478573

The Pulitzer Prize-winning author of the Bascombe novels presents a memoir in two parts on the lives of his parents in the Depression-era South that explores their motivations and dreams, his traveling salesman father's early death and the family's transient lives in a series of hotels.

"Illustrated with family photographs, Fords remembrance of his parents is a masterful distillation of sensuous description, psychological intricacy, social insights, and a keen sense of place." Booklist.

Ford, Tanisha C.

Ford, Tanisha C. **Dressed** in dreams : a black girl's love letter to the power of fashion / Tanisha C. Ford. St. Martin's Press, 2019 304 p. **B**

ISBN 9781250173539

1. Ford, Tanisha C. Clothing. 2. Clothing 3. Fashion. 4. African American women -- Clothing. 5. Growing up 6. United States -- Race relations. 7. Autobiographies and memoirs

LC 2019001794

The history of Black American fashion is discussed, including the author's own story of growing up in the Midwest while trying to find her own personal style, and how black fashion has been appropriated by the mainstream America.

"A winning look at black girl fashion and a solid addition for all collections." Library Journal.

Foreman, Tom

Foreman, Tom **My** year of running dangerously : a dad, a daughter, and a ridiculous plan / Tom Foreman. Blue Rider Press, an imprint of Penguin Random House, 2015. 224 p. **B**

ISBN 9780399175473

1. Foreman, Tom. 2. Marathon running. 3. Fathers and daughters. 4. Aging -- Psychological aspects. 5. Long distance runners. 6. Autobiographies and memoirs

LC 2015017237

As a journalist whose career spans three decades, CNN correspondent Tom Foreman has reported from the heart of war zones, riots, and natural disasters. He has interviewed serial killers and been in the line of fire. But the most terrifying moment of his life didn't occur on the job--it occurred at home, when his 18-year old daughter asked, 'How would you feel about running a marathon with me?' At the time, Foreman was approaching 51 years old, and his last marathon was almost 30 years behind him. The race was just sixteen weeks away, but Foreman reluctantly agreed. Training with his daughter, who had just started college, would be a great bonding experience, albeit a long and painful one. My Year of Running Dangerously is Foreman's journey through four half-marathons, three marathons, and one 55-mile race.

"Even the author's long-suffering family had to admit at the end of the season that he was happier, and readers will enjoy running alongside him." Kirkus.

Forhan, Chris, 1959-

Forhan, Chris, 1959- **My** father before me

: a memoir / Chris Forhan. Scribner, 2016. 320 p. **B**

ISBN 9781501131264

1. Forhan, Chris, 1959- Childhood and youth. 2. Forhan, Chris, 1959- Family. 3. Poets, American 4. Fathers and sons -- United States. 5. Suicide -- United States. 6. Fathers -- United States -- Death. 7. Autobiographies and memoirs

LC 2015034743

A multigenerational portrait of the author's Irish-Catholic American family describes how his numerous siblings and he were raised to hide their feelings, recounts his coming-of-age in the 60s and 70s in the wake of his father's suicide and reflects on his adult efforts to reconcile inherited traits.

"Forhan describes his family's healing and acceptance with warmth, humor, and an admirable lack of bitterness." Kirkus.

Forster, E. M. (Edward Morgan), 1879-1970

Kermode, Frank, 1919-2010 **Concerning** E.M. Forster / Frank Kermode. Farrar, Straus and Giroux, 2009. 192 p. **B**

ISBN 9780374298999

1. Forster, E. M. (Edward Morgan), 1879-1970 Criticism and interpretation. 2. Authors, British 3. Writing. 4. Modern literature -- History and criticism 5. Authors, English 6. Biographies

LC 2009039143

Illuminates lesser-known aspects of the forefront novelist's reclusive life and work, drawing on the author's Clark Lectures as delivered at Cambridge University in 2007 on the subject of Forster's own lectures 80 years earlier.

"Overall, Kermode's occasional exasperation with his subject enlivens rather than distorts his eminently fair assessment. Like all good criticism, Concerning EM Forster makes one want to read the books under discussion once more, and it ends on an appropriately affectionate note." Times (London)

Moffat, Wendy, 1955- A **great** unrecorded history : a new life of E.M. Forster / Wendy Moffat. Farrar, Straus and Giroux, 2010. 480 p. **B**

ISBN 9780374166786

1. Forster, E. M. (Edward Morgan), 1879-1970. 2. Forster, E. M. (Edward Morgan), 1879-1970 Relations with men. 3. Forster, E. M. (Edward Morgan), 1879-1970 Friends and associates. 4. Authors, English -- 20th century 5. Gay men 6. English literature -- History and criticism 7. Homosexuality and literature 8. Biographies

LC 2009029504

Shortlisted for the James Tait Black Memorial Prize for Biography, 2010

In a book that draws on first-time interviews with E. M. Forster's friends, the author integrates Forster's public and private lives, shining a light on his life through the lens of his homosexuality, in a biography that invites readers to see Forster, and modern gay history, from a completely new angle.

"In this well-written, intelligent and perceptive biography of Forster . [the author attemps] to draw a picture of a figure who was sensitive, sensuous and kind, an artist who possessed a keen, plain sort of wisdom and lightness of touch that make him, to this day, an immensely influential novelist, almost a prophet. She uses the sources for our knowledge of Forster's sexuality, including letters and diaries, without reducing the mystery and sheer individuality of Forster, without making his sexuality explain everything." New York Times Book Review.

Fosdick, Sarah Graves, 1825-1871

Brown, Daniel, 1951- The **indifferent** stars above : the harrowing saga of a Donner Party bride / Daniel James Brown. William Morrow, 2009. 320 p. **B**

ISBN 9780061348105

1. Fosdick, Sarah Graves, 1825-1871. 2. Brown, Daniel, 1951- Travel The West (United States) 3. Donner Party. 4. Pioneer women -- California 5. Brides -- California 6. Overland journeys to the Pacific 7. Sierra Nevada Mountains 8. The West (United States) -- Description and travel.

LC 2008040646

"In April 1846, as young newlywed Sarah Graves departed her Illinois home on a journey to California, she could not foresee the misery and horror that awaited her. After numerous delays on their difficult westward path, she and her family found themselves dangerously behind schedule as winter loomed, and they decided to join an ill-fated wagon train under the leadership of George Donner. Ending up snowbound and starving in the Sierra Nevada range, the Donner party descended into cannibalism. Never melodramatic or maudlin, Brown's work gracefully balances graphic depictions of extreme privation with humanizing glimpses of the emigrants' everyday hopes and fears." Library Journal.

Foster, Stephen, 1826-1864

Emerson, Ken, 1948- **Doo-dah!** : Stephen Foster and the rise of American popular culture / Ken Emerson. Simon & Schuster, 1997. 400 p. : **B**

ISBN 9780684810102

1. Foster, Stephen, 1826-1864. 2. Composers -- United States 3. Music and society -- United States. 4. Popular culture -- History -- 19th century.

LC 96029816

Offers a study of the classic songwriter whose works included "Oh, Susanna," a man whose music helped to create American popular culture.

"The author explores the roots of early popular music while tracing the tragic life of composer Stephen Collins Foster. He also aims his spotlight at other musical personalities of the period, and provides further illumination of how Foster's songs have been incorporated into popular contemporary melodies. Emerson's exhaustive research . has been meticulously worked into a vivid portrait of 19th-century America." Publishers Weekly.

Fourcade, Marie-Madeleine, 1909-1989

★Olson, Lynne **Madame** Fourcade's secret war : the daring young woman who led France's largest spy network against Hitler / Lynne Olson. Random House, [2019] 384 p. **B**

ISBN 9780812994766

1. Fourcade, Marie-Madeleine, 1909-1989. 2. World War II -- Secret service -- France 3. Women spies -- France 4. Secret service -- France 5. Espionage 6. France -- History -- German occupation, 1940-1945 7. Biographies.

LC 2018049180

The New York Times best-selling author of Citizens of London and Last Hope Island tells the true story of the woman who headed the largest spy network in occupied France during World War II.

"This masterfully told true story reads like fiction and will appeal to readers who devour WWII thrillers la Kristen Hannah's The Nightingale (2015)." Booklist.

Fowlds, Grant

Fowlds, Grant **Saving** the last rhinos : the life of a frontline conservationist / Grant Fowlds and Graham Spence. Pegasus Books, 2020, c2019. 336 p. **B**

ISBN 9781643135069

1. Wildlife conservationists 2. Wildlife conservation 3. Rhinoceros -- Conservation 4. Wildlife refuges 5. South Africa 6. Vietnam 7.

Autobiographies and memoirs
Includes index.
Originally published: Johannesburg, South Africa : Jonathan Ball Publishers, 2019.

What would drive a man to "smuggle" rhino horns back into Africa at great risk to himself? This is just one of the situations Grant Fowlds has put himself in as part of his ongoing fight against poaching, in order to prove a link between southern Africa and the illicit, lucrative trade in rhino horn in Vietnam. Growing up on a farm in the eastern Cape of South Africa, Fowlds developed a deep love of nature, turning his back on hunting to focus on saving wildlife of all kinds and the environment that sustains both them and us. He is a passionate conservationist who puts himself on the front line of protecting rhinos in the wild.

Fox, Amaryllis

★Fox, Amaryllis **Life** undercover : coming of age in the CIA / Amaryllis Fox. Alfred A. Knopf, 2019. 336 p. **B**

ISBN 9780525654971

1. Fox, Amaryllis. 2. United States. Central Intelligence Agency Officials and employees 3. CIA Officials and employees 4. Women intelligence officers 5. Women spies 6. Terrorism -- Prevention 7. Antiterrorists 8. Autobiographies and memoirs

LC 2019009838

A chronicle of an extraordinary life, and of one woman's courage and passion, follows the author as she spends 10 years in the most elite clandestine ops unit of the CIA, hunting down the world's most dangerous terrorist while marrying and becoming a mother.

"Fans of Showtime's Homeland and espionage novels will devour this highly recommended memoir, as will readers interested in counterterrorism, nonprofileration, and peacemaking." Library Journal.

Fox, Michael J., 1961-

Fox, Michael J., 1961- **Always** looking up : the adventures of an incurable optimist / Michael J. Fox. Hyperion, 2009. 288 p. **B**

ISBN 9781401303389

1. Actors and actresses -- Canada 2. Optimism. 3. Parkinson's disease. 4. Self-fulfillment. 5. Autobiographies and memoirs

LC 2008055129

The popular film and television actor evaluates the personal philosophy that has enabled his positive outlook in spite of his battle with degenerative Parkinson's disease, and discusses how he has become a happier person by recognizing the gifts of everyday life.

Fox, Michael J., 1961- **Lucky** man : a memoir / Michael J. Fox. Hyperion, c2002. 260 p. : **B**

ISBN 0786888741

1. Actors and actresses 2. Canadian American actors and actresses 3. Television actors and actresses -- United States 4. People with Parkinson's disease -- Family relationships 5. United States -- Social life and customs -- 21st century 6. Autobiographies and memoirs

LC BL2001012636

The popular actor recounts his childhood in western Canada, his rise in film and television, his diagnosis of Parkinson's disease, and how he has worked to raise awareness of the disease and find a cure.

Fox, Michael J., 1961- **No** time like the future : an optimist considers mortality / Michael J. Fox. Flatiron Books, 2020 viii, 238 p. **B**

ISBN 9781250265616

1. Actors and actresses 2. People with Parkinson's disease 3. Spinal cord -- Wounds and injuries 4. Hope 5. Autobiographies and memoirs

Actor Michael J. Fox shares personal stories and observations about illness and health, aging, the strength of family and friends, and how our perceptions about time affect the way we approach mortality. Thoughtful and moving, but with Fox's trademark sense of humor, his book provides a vehicle for reflection about our lives, our loves, and our losses.

"Back to the Future Fox focuses on issues of hope, fear, toughness, and being realistic as he explains his struggles with Parkinson's and spinal-cord surgery that led to his learning to walk again." Library Journal.

Francis I, King of France, 1494-1547

Frieda, Leonie **Francis** I : the maker of modern France / Leonie Frieda. HarperCollins, 2018 448 p. **B**

ISBN 9780061563096

1. Rulers 2. Princes 3. Monarchy 4. Heads of state 5. France -- History 6. Biographies

LC 2017416947

This biography of Catherine de Medici's father-in-law describes how the aesthete, grand diplomat and contemporary of Machiavelli became the prototype for all Frenchmen and introduced the Renaissance to the country, making it the first European superpower.

Francis, Pope, 1936-

Cool, Michel **Francis,** a new world pope / Michel Cool ; translated by Regan Kramer. William B. Eerdmans Publishing Company, 2013. viii, 120 p. : **B**

ISBN 0802871003

LC 2013020717

"First published in French as François, Pape du Nouveau Monde © 2013 Editions Salvator, Paris."

Describes Pope Francis's journey to the papacy, identifies the most pressing challenges he faces as leader of the Catholic Church, and presents some of his most significant speeches and writings.

Shriver, Mark K. (Mark Kennedy), 1964- **Pilgrimage** : my search for the real Pope Francis / Mark Shriver. Random House, 2016. 256 p. **B**

ISBN 9780812998023

1. Catholic Church Clergy 2. Popes 3. Church and the world 4. Faith (Christianity) 5. Biographies

LC 2016022799

A portrait of Pope Francis and his faith draws on interviews with the men and women who knew him as a child, before he became a priest, or during his years as a bishop, sharing additional insights into the individuals who helped shape his beliefs.

"In this excellent book, Shriver takes readers on a pilgrimage to numerous significant people and places in the life of Pope Francis." Publishers Weekly.

Vallely, Paul **Pope** Francis : the struggle for the soul of Catholicism / Paul Vallely. Bloomsbury USA, 2015, c2013 xxv, 470 p. **B**

ISBN 9781632861153

1. Catholic Church. 2. Jesuits 3. Popes 4. Church and the world 5. Church and social problems 6. Christian church work with poor people 7. Biographies

LC bl2015026821

Previously published in 2013 under the title, Pope Francis: untying the knots

From his first appearance on a Vatican balcony Pope Francis proved himself a Pope of Surprises. With a series of potent gestures, history's first Jesuit pope declared a mission to restore authenticity and integrity to a Catholic Church bedevilled by sex abuse and secrecy, intrigue and in-fighting, ambition and arrogance. He declared it should be 'a poor Church, for the poor'. But there is a hidden past to this modest man with the winning smile. Jorge Mario Bergoglio was previously a bitterly divisive figure. His decade as leader of Argentina's Jesuits left the religious order deeply split. And his behaviour during Argentina's Dirty War, when military death squads snatched innocent people from the streets, raised serious questions -- on which this book casts new light.

"A well-written, balanced portrait of a man leading the church in a new direction. This title will appeal to anyone who seeks a well-rounded study of the current Pope." Library Journal.

Francis, of Assisi, Saint, 1182-1226

Martin, Valerie, 1948- **Salvation** : scenes from the life of St. Francis / Valerie Martin. Knopf, 2001. xii, 268 p. ; **B**

ISBN 0375409831

1. Francis, of Assisi, Saint, 1182-1226. 2. Christian saints -- Assisi, Italy 3. Assisi, Italy. 4. Biographies

LC 00044361

A moving biography of the great saint inspired by a fresco in Italy offers readers a window into the late-medieval world that influenced the teachings and mission of St. Francis of Assisi. By the author of Mary Reilly.

"This portrait will be most interesting to readers who are already familiar with the basic facts of Francis's life and remain open to exploring a new, gritty interpretation of them." Publishers Weekly.

Ugolino, di Monte Santa Maria The **little** flowers of St. Francis of Assisi / written by Ugolino di Monte Santa Maria ; edited by and adapted from a translation by W. Heywood ; with a new preface by Madeleine L'Engle. Vintage Books, 1998. xxxviii, 120 p. ; **B**

ISBN 9780375700200

1. Francis, of Assisi, Saint, 1182-1226 Legends.

LC 97048815

A new introduction by Madeleine L'Engle highlights this inspirational volume, which combines the story of St. Francis of Assisi and his adoption of a life of poverty and humility, with accounts of miracles attributed to the saint.

Frank, Anne, 1929-1945

★Frank, Anne, 1929-1945 The **diary** of a young girl : the definitive edition / Anne Frank; edited by Otto H. Frank and Mirjam Pressler; translated by Susan Massotty Doubleday, c1995. 340 p. **B**

ISBN 9780385473781

1. Holocaust (1933-1945) -- Amsterdam, Netherlands 2. Jewish teenage girls 3. Hidden children (Holocaust) 4. Jews -- Persecutions -- Amsterdam, Netherlands 5. Amsterdam, Netherlands -- Interethnic relations 6. Books to TV 7. Autobiographies and memoirs

LC 9441379

An uncut edition of Anne Frank's diary includes entries originally omitted by her father and provides insight into Anne's relationship with her mother

"This new translation of Frank's famous diary includes material about her emerging sexuality and her relationship with her mother that was originally excised by Frank's father, the only family member to survive the Holocaust." Library Journal.

Frank, Anne, 1929-1945 The **diary** of Anne Frank : the critical edition / prepared by the Netherlands State Institute for War Documentation ; introduced by Harry Paape, Gerrold van der Stroom, and David Barnouw ; with a summary of the report by the Netherlands Forensic Institute ; compiled by H.J.J. Hardy ; edited by David Barnouw and Gerrold van der Stroom ; translated by Arnold J. Pomerans, B.M. Mooyaart-Doubleday and Susan Massotty. Doubleday, 2003. ix, 851 p. : **B**

ISBN 0385508476

1. Frank, Anne, 1929-1945. 2. Holocaust, Jewish (1939-1945) -- Netherlands -- Amsterdam 3. Jews -- Persecutions -- Netherlands -- Amsterdam. 4. Jews -- Netherlands -- Amsterdam 5. Amsterdam (Netherlands) -- Ethnic relations. 6. Diaries. 7. Personal narratives.

LC 2003269527

Translation of: Achterhuis.

A complete collection of Anne Frank writings includes five recently discovered diary pages; her short stories, fables, and personal reminiscences; and her unfinished novel, Cady's Life.

"This volume brings together the three known versions of Frank's diary: the original, a self-edited version... [and] another edited by her father. It also contains ... handwriting and paper analyses, new documentation regarding the Frank family's arrest, and ... information about the diary's troubled publication history." Library Journal. {review of 1989 edition}

Jacobson, Sidney **Anne** Frank : the Anne Frank House authorized graphic biography / Sid Jacobson and Ernie Colon. Hill and Wang, c2010. 152 p. : **B**

ISBN 9780809026852

1. Jewish children -- Amsterdam, Netherlands 2. Jews -- Amsterdam, Netherlands 3. Holocaust (1933-1945) -- Amsterdam, Netherlands 4. Jewish girls -- Amsterdam, Netherlands 5. Amsterdam, Netherlands 6. Biographies 7. Comics and Graphic novels

Drawing on the archives and expertise of the Anne Frank House, the best-selling authors of 9/11 Report: A Graphic Adaptation cover the short-but-inspiring life of the famed Jewish teen memoirist, from the lives of her parents to Anne's years keeping her private diary while hidden from the Nazis to her untimely death in a concentration camp.

Muller, Melissa, 1967- **Anne** Frank : the biography / Melissa Muller ; translated from the German by Rita and Robert Kimber. Metropolitan Books/Henry Holt and Company, 2013. 458 p. **B**

ISBN 9780805087314

1. Jewish children -- Amsterdam, Netherlands 2. Jews -- Amsterdam, Netherlands 3. Holocaust (1933-1945) -- Amsterdam, Netherlands 4. Jewish girls -- Amsterdam, Netherlands 5. Biographies

LC 00266940

"Updated and expanded with new material."

Includes index."

Originally published in Germany in 1998 under the title Das Madchen Anne Frank by Paul List Verlag, Munich; first published in the United States in 1998 by Metropolitan Books; second edition published in Germany in 2012 by S. Fischer Verlag, Frankfurt"--Title page verso.

Moves beyond the girl's internationally beloved biography of life in hiding during the Holocaust to fill in the gaps--where did Anne come from, what was her relationship with her mother, and who betrayed the family to the Nazis.

Frank, Barney, 1940-

★Frank, Barney, 1940- **Frank** : a life in politics from the Great Society to same-sex marriage / Barney Frank. Farrar, Straus and Giroux, 2015. 320 p. **B**

ISBN 9780374280307

1. United States. Congress. House 2. Legislators -- United States 3. Gay legislators 4. Politicians -- United States 5. Gay politicians 6. United States -- Politics and government -- 20th century. 7.

Massachusetts -- Politics and government. 8. Autobiographies and memoirs.

LC 2014040383

Includes index."The candid political memoir of Barney Frank, former House Representative from Massachusetts (Democrat) and a pioneering, openly gay politician".--Provided by publisher.

"Anyone interested in contemporary history or politics will definitely want to read this highly accessible memoir." Library Journal.

Frank, Robert, 1924-

Smith, R. J., 1959- **American** witness : the art and life of Robert Frank / R. J. Smith. Da Capo Press, 2017. 320 p. **B**

ISBN 9780306823367

1. Photographers 2. Biographies

LC bl2017045742

Describes the cross-country family trip by photographer and friend to bohemians and beats, including Jack Kerouac and Allen Ginsberg, that led him to take 27,000 photos, of which 83 ended up in his best-known work, The Americans.

Frankl, Viktor E. (Viktor Emil), 1905-1997

★Frankl, Viktor E. (Viktor Emil), 1905-1997 **Man's** search for meaning / Viktor E. Frankl ; part one translated by Ilse Lasch ; foreword by Harold S. Kushner ; afterword by William J. Winslade. Beacon Press, 2006, c1962. xvi, 165 p. ; **B**

ISBN 9780807014271

1. Frankl, Viktor E. (Viktor Emil), 1905-1997. 2. Holocaust (1933-1945) -- Psychological aspects. 3. Psychologists -- Austria 4. Concentration camp survivors 5. Logotherapy.

LC 2006287144

Originally published as Psycholog erlebt das Konzentrationslager, 1962.

Internationally renowned psychiatrist, Viktor E. Frankl, endured years of unspeakable horror in Nazi death camps. During, and partly because of his suffering, Dr. Frankl developed a revolutionary approach to psychotherapy known as logotherapy. At the core of his theory is the belief that man's primary motivational force is his search for meaning.

Franklin, Aretha, 1942-2018

★Ritz, David **Respect** : the life of Aretha Franklin / David Ritz. Little, Brown and Company, 2014. 560 p. **B**

ISBN 9780316196833

1. Soul musicians 2. Women singers 3. Soul music 4. African American women musicians 5. Biographies

LC 2014018985

An acclaimed music writer offers a complete look at the Queen of Soul, chronicling both her troubles and her triumphs over them.

"[C]ommendable for its depth, much of which comes from interviews with key figures and family members, as well as Ritz's highly readable, captivating style. It's a compelling record of the life of a musical titan and a fascinating picture of the process of recording some of the seminal popular music of our time." Library Journal.

Franklin, Benjamin, 1706-1790

Bunker, Nick **Young** Benjamin Franklin : the birth of ingenuity / Nick Bunker. Alfred A Knopf, 2018. 464 p. **B**

ISBN 9781101874417

1. Franklin, Benjamin, 1706-1790.. 2. Ambition in men 3. Founding Fathers of the United States. 4. Scientists -- United States 5. Printers -- United States 6. United States -- History -- 18th century 7. United States -- History -- Colonial period, 1600-1775 8. Biographies

LC 2017057711

The Pulitzer Prize-finalist author of "Making Haste from Babylon" presents an account of Ben Franklin's early life to share insights into the challenges he overcame in a harsh colonial world and the passion for knowledge that inspired his scientific achievements.

"This thoroughly researched examination of the development of America's earliest preeminent scientist and statesman will appeal to academics and popular history readers." Library Journal.

★Franklin, Benjamin, 1706-1790 **Autobiography,** Poor Richard, and later writings : letters from London, 1757-1775, Paris, 1776-1785, Philadelphia, 1785-1790, Poor Richard's almanack, 1733-1758, The autobiography / Benjamin Franklin. Library of America, 1997. 816 p. ; **B**

ISBN 1883011531

1. Franklin, Benjamin, 1706-1790. 2. Statesmen -- United States 3. United States -- Politics and government -- 1775-1783. 4. United States -- Politics and government -- To 1775. 5. Biographies

LC 97021611

"J.A. Leo Lemay wrote the notes and selected the texts for this volume"--Prelim. paging.Collects Benjamin Franklin's best-known writings, both personal and public, arranged by period and place, and includes scholarly notes.

★Franklin, Benjamin, 1706-1790 The **autobiography** of Benjamin Franklin / introduction by Lewis Leary. Simon & Schuster, 2004. xiv, 143 p. ; **B**

ISBN 0743255062

1. Franklin, Benjamin, 1706-1790. 2. Politicians -- United States 3. Scientists -- United States 4. Inventors -- United States 5. Printers -- United States 6. Autobiographies and memoirs

LC 2003054477

"A Touchstone book."

Considered to be one of the best autobiographies written in colonial America, Franklin portrays a fascinating picture of life in pre-revolutionary Philadelphia. In his own words he describes his life as a printer, inventor, scientist, and politician.

Isaacson, Walter **Benjamin** Franklin : an American life / Walter Isaacson. Simon & Schuster, 2003. x, 590 p., 16 p. of plates : **B**

ISBN 0684807610

1. Franklin, Benjamin, 1706-1790. 2. Politicians -- United States 3. Scientists -- United States 4. Inventors -- United States 5. Printers -- United States 6. United States -- Politics and government -- 1775-1783. 7. United States -- Politics and government -- 1783-1789. 8. Biographies

LC 2003050463

Traces the life of Benjamin Franklin, from his days as a runaway printer to his triumphs as a statesman, inventor, and founding father. Chronicles his tumultuous relationship with his illegitimate son and grandson, his practical marriage, and his flirtations with the ladies of Paris.

"This is a thoroughly researched, crisply written, convincingly argued chronicle that is also studded with little nuggets of fresh information." New York Times Book Review.

Franklin, Missy, 1995-

Franklin, Missy, 1995- **Relentless** spirit : the unconventional raising of a champion / Missy Franklin with

D. A. and Dick Franklin. E. P. Dutton, 2016 320 p. **B**

ISBN 9781101984925

1. Olympic athletes. 2. Families 3. Christian life 4. Parent and child 5. Autobiographies and memoirs

LC 2016046031

The four-time Olympic Gold medalist and her parents trace the inspirational story of how she became both a legendary athlete and a happy and confident woman, achievements that were accomplished by doing things their own way and making the right choices for their family.

"A consistently sunny, family-oriented story of persistence and achievement." Kirkus.

Franklin, Rosalind, 1920-1958

Maddox, Brenda **Rosalind** Franklin : the dark lady of DNA / Brenda Maddox. Harper Collins, 2002. xix, 380 p., 16 p. of plates : **B**

ISBN 0060184078

1. Franklin, Rosalind, 1920-1958. 2. Molecular biologists -- England 3. Women biologists 4. Jewish women scientists -- Great Britain 5. DNA research -- History 6. London, England. 7. Biographies

LC 2002068898

Presents the frequently overlooked story of the woman who helped discover the double helix structure of DNA, detailing the contributions of scientist Rosalind Franklin to the work of Watson, Crick, and Wilkins.

"The author does an excellent job of revisiting Franklin's scientific contributions ... while revealing Franklin's complicated personality." Library Journal.

Franklin, William, 1731-1813

Epstein, Daniel Mark The **loyal** son : the war in Ben Franklin's house / Daniel Mark Epstein. Ballantine Books, 2017. 448 p. **B**

ISBN 9780345544216

1. Franklin, Benjamin, 1706-1790. 2. Franklin, William, 1731-1813. 3. Politicians -- United States 4. Loyalists (United States history) 5. Adult children of politicians 6. Fathers and sons 7. United States -- History -- Revolution, 1775-1783 8. Biographies

LC 2017013553

Discusses the relationship between the Founding Father and his illegitimate son, a relationship that grew strained during the American Revolution.

"A perceptive, gritty portrayal of the frenzy of war and a father and son caught at its tumultuous center." Kirkus.

Frantz, Chris, 1951-

Frantz, Chris, 1951- **Remain** in love : Talking Heads, Tom Tom Club, Tina / Chris Frantz. St. Martin's Press, 2020. 320 p. **B**

ISBN 9781250209221

1. Weymouth, Tina, 1950- 2. Talking Heads (Musical group) 3. Tom Tom Club (Musical group) 4. Drummers. 5. Rock musicians 6. Rock music 7. Popular culture 8. Autobiographies and memoirs

LC 2020002700

Includes index."

Two iconic bands. An unforgettable life. One of the most dynamic groups of the '70s and '80s, Talking Heads, founded by drummer Chris Frantz, his girlfriend Tina Weymouth, and lead singer David Byrne, burst onto the music scene, playing at CBGBs, touring Europe with the Ramones, and creating hits like "Psycho Killer" and "Burning Down the House" that captured the post-baby boom generation's intense, affectless style. In Remain in Love, Frantz writes about the beginnings of Talking Heads-their days as art students in Providence, moving to the sparse Chrystie Street loft Frantz, Weymouth, and Byrne shared where the music that defined an era was written. With never-before-seen photos and immersive vivid detail, Frantz describes life on tour, down to the meals eaten and the clothes worn-and reveals the mechanics of a long and complicated working relationship with a mercurial frontman. At the heart of Remain in Love is Frantz's love for Weymouth: their once-in-a-lifetime connection as lovers, musicians, and bandmates, and how their creativity surged with the creation of their own band Tom Tom Club, bringing a fresh Afro-Caribbean beat to hits like "Genius of Love." Studded with memorable place and names from the era-Grace Jones, Andy Warhol, Stephen Sprouse,Lou Reed, Brian Eno, and Debbie Harry among them-Remain in Love is a frank and open memoir of an emblematic life in music and in love. Edit"-- Provided by publisher.

"Frantz's absorbing, vivid book will reward Talking Heads fans and those interested in the postpunk and 1980s music scene." Library Journal

Franzen, Jonathan

Franzen, Jonathan The **discomfort** zone : a personal history / Jonathan Franzen. Farrar, Straus and Giroux, 2006. 195 p. **B**

ISBN 0374299196

1. Franzen, Jonathan Childhood and youth. 2. Authors, American -- 20th century 3. Teenagers -- Personal conduct 4. Growing up. 5. Misfits (Persons) 6. Autobiographies and memoirs

LC 2006002700

The author describes growing up in a family of all boys in Webster Groves, Missouri, reflecting on such topics as the dynamics of a Christian youth fellowship, his role as the school prankster, his marriage, and the life lessons he has learned from birds.

"For those who admire the razor-sharp jabs Franzen makes at himself and anyone else standing too close, The Discomfort Zone is both a delicious read and a clever showcase for Franzen's talents." Christian Science Monitor.

Frederick II, King of Prussia, 1712-1786

Blanning, T. C. W. **Frederick** the Great : king of Prussia / Tim Blanning. Random House, 2016. 720 p. **B**

ISBN 9781400068128

1. Frederick II, King of Prussia, 1712-1786. 2. Enlightenment (European intellectual movement) 3. Social change. 4. Rulers 5. United States -- History -- French and Indian War, 1754-1763 6. Prussia. 7. Biographies

LC 2015030616

"Originally published by Allen Lane in the UK"--Title page verso. King Frederick II of Prussia, known as "the Great," brilliantly sustained the well-run state he inherited from his father, Frederick I. Yet--in all other respects--the younger Frederick was the opposite of his predecessor, who had physically abused him and rejected the music, art, and philosophy he loved. In this superbly written biography, historian Tim Blanning explores Frederick II's psychology while detailing his life and vividly chronicling his accomplishments. General biography lovers and fans of 18th-century European history will find this an engaging study.

"Readers both casual and scholarly will enjoy this profile for the in-depth examination of its subject, his placement in the historical events of the time, and his future in German history." Library Journal.

MacDonogh, Giles, 1955- **Frederick** the Great : a life in deed and letters / Giles MacDonogh. St. Martin's Press, 2000, c1999. xii, 436 p. : **B**

ISBN 0312253184

1. Prussia -- Rulers 2. Prussia -- History -- Frederick II, the Great, 1740-1786 3. Biographies

LC 00024799

A look at the life of Frederick the Great reveals the often misunderstood king as not only a feared conqueror, but also a patron of the arts and a progressive lawmaker who helped make Berlin one of Europe's great capital cities.

Fredston, Jill A.

Fredston, Jill A. **Rowing** to latitude : journeys along the Arctic's edge / Jill Fredston. North Point Press, 2001. xiii, 289 p. : **B**

ISBN 0374281807

1. Fredston, Jill A. Travel. 2. Rowing -- Arctic regions. 3. Women rowers. 4. Rowers -- United States 5. Men/women relations. 6. Arctic regions -- Description and travel.

LC 2001030049

National Outdoor Book Award for Outdoor Literature, 2002."

The author and her husband, Doug Fesler canoe the Arctic and sub-Arctic coastlines of Alaska, Canada, Greenland, Norway and Sweden for three months out of each year. Fredston ably describes both the big picture--the coastline, encounters with polar bears, the high-stakes game of second-guessing storms and tides--and the details of their travels. A must-read for armchair travelers, as well as a close and loving look at an intimate relationship." Publishers Weekly.

Freitas, Donna

Freitas, Donna **Consent** : a memoir of unwanted attention / Donna Freitas. Little, Brown & Company, 2019. 352 p. **B**

ISBN 9780316450522

1. Women graduate students 2. College teachers 3. Stalkers 4. Mentors 5. Autobiographies and memoirs

LC 2018956641

Donna Freitas delivers a forensic examination of the years she spent stalked by her professor, and uses her nightmarish experience to examine the ways in which we stigmatize, debate, and attempt to understand consent today.

"Any reader interested in current discussions on consent and its importance should pick up this heartfelt and harrowing book." Library Journal.

Fremont, Jessie Benton, 1824-1902

Inskeep, Steve **Imperfect** union : how Jessie and John Frémont mapped the West, invented celebrity, and helped cause the Civil War / Steve Inskeep. Penguin Press, [2020] 480 p. **B**

ISBN 9780735224353

1. Fremont, Jessie Benton, 1824-1902. 2. Fremont, John Charles, 1813-1890. 3. Explorers 4. Pioneer women 5. Pioneers 6. Politicians 7. United States -- History -- 19th century 8. Biographies

LC 2019030462

Steve Inskeep tells the riveting story of John and Jessie Fremont, the husband and wife team who in the 1800s were instrumental in the westward expansion of the United States, and thus became America's first great political couple

"An insightful and welcome biography of consequential Americans." Booklist.

French, Daniel Chester, 1850-1931

Holzer, Harold **Monument** man : the life and art of Daniel Chester French / Harold Holzer. Princeton Architectural Press, 2019. 268 p. **B**

ISBN 9781616897536

1. Artists -- United States 2. Sculptors -- United States -- 19th century. 3. Memorials 4. Lincoln Memorial, Washington, D.C. 5. Washington, D.C. -- Buildings. 6. Biographies

LC 2018007925

The first comprehensive biography of Daniel Chester French, the preeminent artist who created the statue for the Lincoln Memorial among other renowned works, is filled with rich detail and archival photos and coincides with the 50th anniversary of the opening of his country home/studio to the public and a major renovation of the Lincoln Memorial.

"This beautifully written, impeccably researched biography does much to resuscitate French's substantial contributions to American art." Kirkus.

French, Juniper

French, Kelley **Juniper** : the girl who was born too soon / Kelley French and Thomas French. Little Brown & Company, 2016 288 p. **B**

ISBN 9780316324427

1. French, Kelley 2. French, Thomas, 1958- 3. Premature infants. 4. Neonatal intensive care. 5. Children with critical illnesses -- Family relationships. 6. Parenthood. 7. Autobiographies and memoirs

LC bl2016038791

Juniper French was born four months early and weighed 1 pound, 4 ounces. She was the length of a Barbie doll. Her head was smaller than a tennis ball, her skin was nearly translucent, and through her chest you could see her flickering heart. Babies like Juniper, born at the edge of viability, trigger the question: Which is the greater act of love--to save her, or to let her go?

"A fierce and fact-filled love story with few holds barred." Kirkus.

Frenkel, Franoise, 1889-1975

★Frenkel, Franoise, 1889-1975 A **bookshop** in Berlin : the rediscovered memoir of one woman's harrowing escape from the Nazis / Franòise Frenkel ; foreword by Patrick Modiano. Atria Books, 2019, c1945. 304 p. **B**

ISBN 9781501199844

1. Holocaust (1933-1945) 2. Jewish women 3. Women booksellers 4. Refugees, Jewish 5. Berlin, Germany 6. France 7. Autobiographies and memoirs

LC bl2019037959

"First published in France as Rien où poser sa tête by L'Arbalète Gallimard in 2015"

Originally published: Geneva : Jeheber, 1945.

Published quietly in 1945, then rediscovered nearly sixty years later in an attic, A Bookshop in Berlin is a remarkable story of survival and resilience, of human cruelty and human spirit. In the tradition of Suite Française, this book is the tale of a fearless woman whose lust for life and literature refuses to leave her, even in her darkest hours.

"A compelling account of crushing oppression, those who sought to flee it, and those who, at great risk, offered help." Kirkus.

Freud, Sigmund, 1856-1939

Gay, Peter, 1923-2015 **Freud** : a life for our time / Peter Gay. Norton, 2006, 1988. xx, 810 p., 32 p. of plates : **B**

ISBN 9780393328615

1. Freud, Sigmund, 1856-1939. 2. Psychoanalysts -- Austria 3. Jewish men -- Vienna, Austria. 4. Psychoanalysis -- History. 5. Biographies

Originally published: New York : Norton, 1988.

With a new foreword.

National Book Award for Nonfiction finalist, 1988

Pulitzer Prize for Biography or Autobiography finalist

A thorough biographical portrait of the pivotal thinker and practitioner probes many aspects of Freud's life, including his family, his city, his professional challenges, and his innovative and controversial theories.

"This biography provides an updating of our knowledge of the life of the founder of psychoanalysis . and it also delineates the continuing impact of Freud's thought on modern endeavors in a number of fields." Science Books & Films.

★Roudinesco, Elisabeth, 1944- **Freud** : in his time and ours / Elisabeth Roudinesco ; translated by Catherine Porter. Harvard University Press, 2016, c2014. 530 p. **B**

ISBN 9780674659568

1. Freud, Sigmund, 1856-1939. 2. Psychoanalysts 3. Jewish men 4. Biographies

LC 2016013065

"First published as Sigmund Freud en son temps et dans le notre"--Title page verso.

Originally published: Paris : Ed. du Seuil, 2014

Elisabeth Roudinesco's bold reinterpretation of Sigmund Freud is a biography for the twenty-first century--a sympathetic yet impartial appraisal of a genius admired but misunderstood in his time and ours. Alert to tensions in his character and thought, she views Freud less as a scientific thinker than as an interpreter of civilization and culture.

Friedan, Betty, 1921-

Friedan, Betty, 1921- **Life** so far / Betty Friedan. Simon & Schuster, 2000. 399 p. : **B**

ISBN 0684807890

1. Feminists -- United States 2. Feminism -- United States -- History. 3. Gender role 4. Family relationships 5. Autobiographies and memoirs

LC 00023920

"In this memoir, Friedan reminisces over a life of social activism that has included helping to found the National Organization for Women, the National Abortion and Reproductive Rights Action League, and the National Women's Political Caucus, as well as writing the pivotal The Feminine Mystique." Library Journal.

Friedman, Elizebeth, 1892-1980

Fagone, Jason The **woman** who smashed codes : a true story of love, spies, and the unlikely heroine who outwitted America's enemies / Jason Fagone. Dey Street Books, 2017. 288 p. **B**

ISBN 9780062430489

1. Cryptographers 2. Cryptography -- History 3. Military intelligence 4. Codes (Communication) 5. Biographies

LC 2017470719

ALA Notable Book, 2018.

Describes the true story of Elizebeth Smith, a Shakespeare expert, who met and married a groundbreaking cryptologist and worked with him to discover and expose Nazi spy rings in South America by cracking multiple versions of the Enigma machine.

"Riveting, inspiring, and rich in colorful characters, Fagones extensively researched and utterly dazzling title is popular history at its very best and a book club natural." Booklist.

Friedman, Matti

★Friedman, Matti **Pumpkinflowers** : a soldier's story of a forgotten war / Matti Friedman. Algonquin Books of Chapel Hill, 2016. 288 p. **B**

ISBN 9781616204587

1. Friedman, Matti. 2. Soldiers -- Israel. 3. Arab-Israeli conflict. 4. War. 5. Lebanon. 6. Autobiographies and memoirs

LC 2015031466

Canadian Jewish Book Award, 2017.

Shortlisted for The Charles Taylor Prize for Literary Non-Fiction, 2017

Hilary Weston Writers' Trust Prize for Nonfiction finalist, 2016.

Describes the author's harrowing experiences manning a remote Israeli outpost with a regiment of other young soldiers, during a small, unnamed war in the late 1990s that foreshadowed other unwinnable conflicts in the Middle East.

"A haunting yet wry tale of young people at war, cursed by political forces beyond their control, that can stand alongside the best narrative nonfiction coming out of Afghanistan and Iraq." Kirkus.

Friedman, Rachel, 1981-

★Friedman, Rachel, 1981- **And** then we grew up : on creativity, potential, and the imperfect art of adulthood / Rachel Friedman. Penguin Books, 2019. 240 p. **B**

ISBN 9780143132127

1. Adulthood 2. Self-fulfillment 3. Ability 4. Hobbies 5. Autobiographies and memoirs

LC 2019019646

The author describes how her career in the arts was upended by unexpected challenges that compelled her to learn how the creative lives of her contemporaries shaped their relationships and identities.

Friedmann, Jessica

Friedmann, Jessica **Things** that helped : on postpartum depression / Jessica Friedmann. Farrar, Straus and Giroux, 2018, c2017. 272 p. **B**

ISBN 9780374274801

1. Friedmann, Jessica. 2. Postpartum depression 3. Women with depression 4. Coping 5. Mental illness 6. Australian 7. Essays. 8. Autobiographies and memoirs

Originally published: Things that helped : essays. Melbourne, Australia : Scribe Publications. 2017.

In a broad range of essays, an Australian writer--drawing on critical theory, popular culture and her own experiences, navigates her recovery from postpartum depression, while touching on topics of class, race, gender, sexuality, motherhood, creativity and mental illness.

Fromartz, Samuel

★Fromartz, Samuel **In** search of the perfect loaf : a home baker's odyssey / Samuel Fromartz. Viking, 2014. 320 p. **B**

ISBN 9780670025619

1. Fromartz, Samuel. 2. Bread. 3. Baking 4. Cooks 5. Bloggers 6. Autobiographies and memoirs

LC 2014004522

IACP Cookbook Awards, Literary Food Writing, 2015.

The creator of the popular Chewswise blog documents his 2009 assignment to work in a French boulangerie and subsequent travels through America and Europe to learn bread history and science while perfecting his award-winning recipes.

"Richly detailed history and lively anecdotes make this book a consummate celebration of the deceptively simple loaf of bread." Kirkus.

Frost, Robert, 1874-1963

Parini, Jay **Robert** Frost : a life / Jay Parini. Henry Holt, 2000, c1999. xii, 514 p. ; **B**

ISBN 0805063412

1. Poets, American -- 20th century 2. United States -- Social life and customs -- 20th century 3. Biographies

LC BL2003013912

Reprint. Originally published: 1999."

An Owl book."

Based on interviews with Frost's friends and drawing from his personal archives, an account of the poet's life examines his varied literary career, tracing his rise to world fame and offering close readings of his works.

"Rarely has Frost's story been told this dexterously, or with a better understanding of the relation of Frost's personal crises to his accomplishment as a poet." Publishers Weekly.

Fuller, Alexandra, 1969-

Fuller, Alexandra, 1969- **Don't** let's go to the dogs tonight : an African childhood / Alexandra Fuller. Random House, 2001. 301 p. : **B**

ISBN 0375507507

1. Fuller, Alexandra, 1969- Childhood and youth. 2. Girls -- Zimbabwe 3. British in Africa 4. Family relationships. 5. Segregation. 6. Zimbabwe -- History -- Chimurenga War, 1966-1980 7. Zimbabwe -- History -- War for national liberation, 1972-1979. 8. Zimbabwe -- Social life and customs. 9. Autobiographies and memoirs

LC 2001041752

Sequel: Cocktail hour under the tree of forgetfulness.Alexandra Fuller tells the idiosyncratic story of her life growing up white in rural Rhodesia as it was becoming Zimbabwe. The daughter of hardworking, yet strikingly unconventional English-bred immigrants, Alexandra arrives in Africa at the tender age of two. She moves through life with a hardy resilience, even as a bloody war approaches.

"Fuller grew up in Rhodesia (now Zimbabwe) during the civil war, and she watched her parents fight against the local Africans to keep their farm. In a memoir powerful in its frank straightforwardness, she neither apologizes for nor champions her family's views and actions. Instead she gives us an honest, moving portrait of one family struggling to survive tumultuous times." Booklist.

Fuller, Alexandra, 1969- **Leaving** before the rains come / Alexandra Fuller. Penguin Group USA, 2015 256 p. **B**

ISBN 9781594205866

1. Marriage 2. Self-discovery. 3. Self-fulfillment. 4. Divorce. 5. Zimbabwe. 6. Autobiographies and memoirs

LC bl2014055302

A child of the Rhodesian wars and daughter of two deeply complicated parents, Alexandra Fuller is no stranger to pain. But the disintegration of Fuller's own marriage leaves her shattered. Looking to pick up the pieces of her life, she finally confronts the tough questions about her past, about the American man she married, and about the family she left behind in Africa.

"Although her batty and unhinged relatives emerge more vividly than her taciturn husband, Fuller's talent as a storyteller makes this memoir sing." Kirkus.

Fuller, Margaret, 1810-1850

Matteson, John The **lives** of Margaret Fuller : a biography / John Matteson. W W Norton & Co Inc, 2012. 384 p. **B**

ISBN 9780393068054

1. Fuller, Margaret, 1810-1850. 2. Women authors. 3. Social critics. 4. Transcendentalism (New England) 5. Feminists. 6. Biographies

LC 2011040432

A Pulitzer Prize-winning biographer describes the life of the great 19th-century feminist who was a leading figure in the transcendentalist movement, a columnist for Horace Greeley's newspaper and served as the first foreign correspondent for an American newspaper.

Fuller, Tim (Timothy Donald), 1940-2015

Fuller, Alexandra, 1969- **Travel** light, move fast / Alexandra Fuller. Penguin Press, 2019. 272 p. **B**

ISBN 9781594206740

1. Fuller, Alexandra, 1969- Family. 2. Fuller, Tim (Timothy Donald), 1940-2015. 3. British in Africa 4. Coping in women 5. Grief in women 6. Fathers -- Death.

LC 2019000116

The best-selling author of Don't Let's Go to the Dogs Tonight explores how her late father's service during the Rhodesian War, work as a banana farmer in Zambia and preference of unpredictability over security inspired her life.

Gaffigan, Jim

Gaffigan, Jim **Dad** is fat / Jim Gaffigan. Crown Publications, 2013 208 p. **B**

ISBN 9780385349055

1. Parenthood -- Humor. 2. Fatherhood -- Humor. 3. Families -- Humor. 4. Fathers -- Anecdotes 5. Autobiographies and memoirs

LC 2013012076

The popular comedian shares his misadventures as an unlikely father of five, from his formative years in a large Irish-Catholic family, to his middle-of-the-night diaper-changing foibles, to his struggles to lull tyrannical tots to sleep.

Gaffney, Ginger

Gaffney, Ginger **Half** broke : a memoir / Ginger Gaffney. W W Norton & Company, 2020. 256 p. **B**

ISBN 9781324003076

1. Horse trainers 2. Equestrian therapy 3. Prisoners -- Rehabilitation 4. Women horse trainers 5. New Mexico 6. Autobiographies and memoirs

LC 2019030052

A top-ranked horse trainer at an alternative prison ranch in New Mexico describes how her work rehabilitating abandoned horses and traumatized inmates helped her form profound bonds and overcome difficult personal challenges.

"Gaffney's story will delight horse lovers, and her anxieties as an introvert will broaden the appeal of this passionate memoir." Publishers Weekly

Gaiman, Neil

Campbell, Hayley The **art** of Neil Gaiman / Hayley Campbell ; foreword by Audrey Niffenegger. Harper Design, 2014. 320 p. : **B**

ISBN 9780062248565

1. Gaiman, Neil. 2. Novelists, English -- 20th century

LC bl2014015284

With unprecedented access to Neil Gaiman's personal archives, the author gives an insider's glimpse into the artistic inspirations and musings of one of the world's most visionary writers.

Gaines, Chip, 1974-

Gaines, Chip, 1974- **Capital** Gaines : smart things I learned doing stupid stuff / Chip Gaines. W Publishing Group, an imprint of Thomas Nelson, [2017] xiii, 191 p. : **B**

ISBN 9780785216308

1. Fixer upper (Television program). 2. Television personalities 3. Businesspeople 4. Success in business 5. Autobiographies and memoirs

LC bl2017041244

The star of the popular "Fixer Upper" television program shares his personal journey in both business and in life on his way to success as an entrepreneur and television personality.

Galchen, Rivka

Galchen, Rivka **Little** labors / Rivka Galchen. New Directions, 2016. 96 p. **B**

ISBN 9780811225588

1. Women authors 2. Motherhood 3. Infants 4. Literature 5. Autobiographies and memoirs 6. Essays

LC 2015044623

A collection of essays about the ordinary-extraordinary nature of babies and literature.

"The book is an endearing compilation of social criticism, variously contentious, commonplace, funny, and incisive." Publishers Weekly.

Galeano, Eduardo, 1940-2015

Galeano, Eduardo, 1940-2015 **Hunter** of stories / Eduardo Galeano ; translated by Mark Fried. Nation Books, 2017, c2016. xviii, 251 p. **B**

ISBN 9781568589909

1. Authors, Uruguayan 2. Death 3. Personal conduct 4. Essays 5. Autobiographies and memoirs

LC 2017014189

Translation of: El cazador de historiasOriginally published: Mexico City : Siglo Veitiuno Editores,2016

Collects essays, fables, stories, and dialogue written in the final months of the author's life, touching on the themes of death and memory in what is considered to be his final book.

"A worthy addition to the celebrated oeuvre of a writer who remains a towering figure both as an artist and a voice of conscience across Latin America and the world." Publishers Weekly.

Galilei, Galileo, 1564-1642

Heilbron, J. L. **Galileo** / J. L. Heilbron. Oxford University Press, 2010. xiv, 508 p. 16 p. of plates : **B**

ISBN 9780199583522

1. Galilei, Galileo, 1564-1642. 2. Astronomers -- Italy 3. Scientists -- Italy 4. Physicists -- Italy 5. Biographies

LC 2010933141

"This will no doubt become the standard, comprehensive biography. In one of his most inventive sections, [Heilbron] creates a Galilean dialogue on issues of algebra and geometry. Though not easy to read, it brilliantly expresses the ambiguities and blind alleys as Galileo wrestled with the conceptual difficulty of introducing a nongeometrical quantity-time itself into the proportions." New York Times Book Review.

Gammage, Jeff

Gammage, Jeff **China** ghosts : my daughter's journey to America, my passage to fatherhood / Jeff Gammage. William Morrow, c2007. 255 p. : **B**

ISBN 006124029X

1. Gammage, Jeff. 2. Adoptive fathers 3. Adoptive parents 4. International adoption -- China. 5. Population control -- China 6. China -- Social life and customs -- 21st century 7. United States -- Social life and customs -- 21st century

LC 2007061204

Aching to expand from a couple to a family, Jeff and Christine Gammage embarked upon a journey that would carry them through shifting emotions--excitement, exhilaration, fear, apprehension--and miles of red tape and bureaucratic protocol, to a land on the other side of the world where a little girl waited. When they met Jin Yu, a silent, stoic two-year-old, in the smog-choked city of Changsha in Hunan Province, they realized that every frustrating moment of their two-year struggle was worth it. But they also realized that another journey had only begun. Now there was much to experience and learn. This book is a journalist's depiction of the foreign adoption process and a glimpse into a different culture, but more important, it is a heartfelt chronicle ofthe making of a family.--From publisher description.

Gandhi, Mahatma, 1869-1948

Chadha, Yogesh **Gandhi** : a life / Yogesh Chadha. John Wiley, c1997. 546 p. : **B**

ISBN 0471243787

1. Gandhi, Mahatma, 1869-1948 Political and social views. 2. Politicians -- India 3. India -- Politics and government -- 1919-1947- 4. Biographies

LC 97037406

Simultaneously published in the United Kingdom as Rediscovering Gandhi in 1997."

Chadha reexamines Gandhi's life with an eye to restoring its complications and contradictions, noting that to suppress his weaknesses would be to undermine his strengths. And he succeeds in his mission, presenting the great leader not as a holy man but as a humanist and politician." Booklist.

Erikson, Erik H. (Erik Homburger), 1902-1994 **Gandhi's** truth : on the origins of militant nonviolence / Erik H. Erikson. Norton & Co., 1993, c1970. 474 p. **B**

ISBN 0393310345

1. Gandhi, Mahatma, 1869-1948. 2. Nonviolence -- India. 3. Peace movements -- India. 4. India -- History -- 20th century. 5. India -- Politics and government -- 20th century.

LC 92040416

Originally published: New York : Norton, 1970.

Pulitzer Prize for General Nonfiction, 1970.

A Western psychoanalyst and historian presents a detailed examination of the philosophies accepted by Gandhi and his attempts to convert the British through nonviolence.

Gandhi, Mahatma, 1869-1948 An **autobiography** : the story of my experiments with truth / Mohandas K. Gandhi ; translated from the original in Gujarati by Mahadev Desai ; with a foreword by Sissela Bok. Beacon Press, c1993. xxix, 528 p. ; **B**

ISBN 9780807059098

1. Gandhi, Mahatma, 1869-1948. 2. Nationalists -- India 3. Politicians -- India 4. Nationalists -- India 5. Peace activists -- India 6. India -- Politics and government -- 1919-1947. 7. Autobiographies and memoirs

LC 93019758

Includes index.

Originally published: Washington : Public Affairs Press, 1948.

Portrays the life of Gandhi, describes the development of his nonviolent political protest movement, and discusses his religious beliefs.

Gandhi, Rajmohan **Gandhi** : the man, his people, and the empire / Rajmohan Gandhi. University of California Press, 2008, c2006. 754 p. **B**

ISBN 9780520255708

1. Gandhi, Mahatma, 1869-1948. 2. Nationalists -- India 3. Nonviolence -- India. 4. Politicians -- India 5. India -- Politics and government -- 1919-1947. 6. Biographies

LC 2007040986

Originally published: Mohandas : a true story of a man, his people, and an empire. New Delhi : Penguin, 2006."

The author exhibits a deep understanding of the social and political landscape of India, of the cleavages of caste and religion, and of the dynamics of the dominant Congress Party (to which Gandhi had a lifelong allegiance). Rajmohan takes us at a leisurely pace through the broad sweep of Gandhi's personal and public life." Times Literary Supplement.

Guha, Ramachandra **Gandhi** : the years that changed the world: 1914-1948 / Ramachandra Guha. Alfred A. Knopf, 2018. 688 p. **B**

ISBN 9780385532310

1. Gandhi, Mahatma, 1869-1948. 2. Social reformers 3. Social advocates 4. Lawyers 5. Social change 6. India -- Social conditions 7. India -- History -- 20th century 8. Biographies

LC 2018953456

A conclusion to the wide-reaching profile that began with Gandhi Before India covers in scholarly detail Gandhi's arrival in 1915 Bombay and his role in addressing such issues as colonialism, the caste system, religious conflict and the emancipation of women.

★Guha, Ramachandra **Gandhi** before India / Ramachandra Guha. Alfred A Knopf, 2014. 656 p. **B**

ISBN 9780385532297

1. Gandhi, Mahatma, 1869-1948. 2. Social advocates 3. East Indians in South Africa. 4. Lawyers 5. Social reformers 6. South Africa -- History -- 20th century. 7. London, England 8. India 9. Biographies

LC 2013025014

A first volume of a series detailing the life and work of the influential political advocate draws on private papers and other untapped sources to cover his birth in 1869 through his upbringing in Gujarat, discussing his London education and decades as a lawyer in South Africa.

"This first volume in a two-part biography of Gandhi from Guha . proves itself an essential work for its bold purpose, extensive research, and engaging prose." Publishers Weekly.

★Wolpert, Stanley A., 1927- **Gandhi's** passion : the life and legacy of Mahatma Gandhi / Stanley Wolpert. Oxford University Press, 2002, c2001. xii, 308 p. : **B**

ISBN 019515634X

1. Gandhi, Mahatma, 1869-1948. 2. Politicians -- India 3. Nationalists -- India 4. Nonviolence -- India. 5. Nuclear weapons -- India. 6. Biographies

LC bl2005007939

Originally published: Oxford, England : Oxford University Press, 2001.

Celebrates the life and work of India's "Great Soul," focusing on his non-violent struggle to end British imperial domination of India, and offering insight into why modern India has rejected Gandhi's nonviolent idealogies and joined the nuclear arms race.

Gans, Joe

Gildea, William The **longest** fight : in the ring with Joe Gans, boxing's first African American champion / William Gildea. Farrar, Straus and Giroux, c2012. 224 p. **B**

ISBN 9780374280970

1. Gans, Joe. 2. Boxing matches. 3. Boxers (Sports) -- United States 4. African American boxers 5. Boxing.

LC 2011040170

An account of the lesser-known story of early sports hero Jon Gans centers on his epic 1906 boxing match against Oscar "Battling" Nelson, discussing how the competition reflected period racial tensions and the realities endured by African-American athletes.

Garcia Lorca, Federico, 1898-1936

Gibson, Ian, 1939- **Federico** Garcia Lorca : a life / Ian Gibson. Faber and Faber, 1989. xxiv, 551 p. : **B**

ISBN 0571148158

1. Garcia Lorca, Federico, 1898-1936. 2. Authors -- Spain -- 20th century 3. Biographies

LC 91194136

Loosely based on the two-vol. Spanish work: Federico Garcia Lorca. James Tait Black Memorial Prize for Biography, 1989."

Gibson's sense of place is equalled by his sense of person. His recreation of the teeming artistic talent and the caf life of Spain in the 1930s is superb. So effective is Gibson's account of Lorca's vitality and fecundity that along with admiration for the poet's opulent talent, he provokes a fierce outrage at his ultimate fate." Times Literary Supplement.

Garcia Marquez, Gabriel, 1928-2014

Garcia Marquez, Gabriel, 1928-2014 **Living** to tell the tale / Gabriel Garcia Marquez ; translated by Edith Grossman. A.A. Knopf, 2003, c2002. 483 p. : **B**

ISBN 1400041341

1. Garcia Marquez, Gabriel, 1928-2014 Childhood and youth. 2. Authors, Colombian -- 20th century 3. Memories. 4. Small towns. 5. Colombia -- History -- 20th century. 6. Autobiographies and memoirs

LC 2003058924

Originally published in Spanish as Vivir para contarla: Barcelona, Spain : Mondadori, 2002.

The author traces his life from his birth in 1927 to his 1950 proposal to his wife, discussing such topics as his love for Colombia, the impact of literature and music on his life, and how his written works reflect his life.

"Garcia Mrquez tells the entrancing story of his remarkable family, chronicles the turbulence of his troubled country, Colombia, and offers a piquant portrait of himself as a struggling young writer. A resplendent memoir written with compassion and artistry." Booklist.

★Martin, Gerald, 1944- **Gabriel** Garcia Marquez : a life / Gerald Martin. Alfred A. Knopf, 2009. xxiii, 642 p., [16] p. of plates : **B**

ISBN 9780307271778

1. Authors, Colombian -- 20th century 2. Latin Americans 3. Nobel prize winners 4. Authors 5. Biographies

Originally published: London : Bloomsbury, 2008.

Shortlisted for the James Tait Black Memorial Prize for Biography, 2008"

This superbly researched biography is nothing short of a tour de force. . . . This work not only details the life of a great writer but also provides considerable insight into life in Latin America." Library Journal.

Garcia, Amanda Yates

Garcia, Amanda Yates **Initiated** : memoir of a witch / Amanda Yates Garcia. Grand Central Publishing, 2019. 304 p. **B**

ISBN 9781538763056

1. Witches 2. Wiccans 3. Self-discovery in women 4. Witchcraft

LC 2019011190

Based on a podcast.

A writer, artist, professional witch and Oracle of Los Angeles presents this haunting, lyrical memoir in which she describes her journey to return to her body, harness her power and create the magical world she longed for through witchcraft.

Gardener, Helen H. (Helen Hamilton), 1853-1925

Hamlin, Kimberly A **Free** thinker : Helen Hamilton Gardener's audacious pursuit of equality and the vote / Kimberly A. Hamlin. W.W. Norton & Company, 2020 352 p. **B**

ISBN 9781324004974

1. Gardener, Helen H. (Helen Hamilton), 1853-1925. 2. Suffragists -- United States 3. Women intellectuals 4. Women's rights -- History -- 19th century 5. Women authors, American 6. United States -- Social conditions -- 19th century 7. United States -- Social conditions -- 20th century

LC 2019044543

Describes the life of the author, suffragist and civil servant who pretended to be married to her lover, openly opposed sexist piety, debunked "science" that claimed women's brains were inferior and worked tirelessly for the Nineteenth Amendment.

"Based on archival sources and Gardener's own voluminous writings, this highly readable book should provide plenty of new insight into the period and Gardener's fascinating life for general readers, scholars, and aspiring political activists alike." Library Journal

Gardner, Chris (Chris P.)

Gardner, Chris (Chris P.) The **pursuit** of happyness / Chris Gardner with Quincy Troupe and Mim Eichler Rivas. Amistad, c2006. xii, 302 p., 8 p. of plates : **B**

ISBN 0060744863

1. Gardner Rich & Co. 2. Brokers -- United States 3. African American businesspeople 4. Fathers and sons. 5. Homelessness 6. United States -- Social life and customs. 7. Autobiographies and memoirs

LC 2005057203

In a candid memoir, a successful entrepreneur traces his journey from growing up with an abusive stepfather, to life on the streets as a homeless man with a small toddler in tow, to his triumphant battle to the top as a self-made millionaire.

"The author recounts his long walk to Wall Street, a journey that took him from a childhood in the ghettos of Milwaukee to an enormously successful career as a stockbroker in New York city." Library Journal.

Garfunkel, Art, 1941-

Garfunkel, Art, 1941- **What** is it all but luminous : notes from an underground man / Art Garfunkel. Alfred A. Knopf, 2017. 256 p. **B**

ISBN 9780385352475

1. Simon and Garfunkel. 2. Folk musicians 3. Folk music 4. Men/women relations 5. Poetry writing 6. Autobiographies and memoirs

LC 2016037296

Art Garfunkel writes about his life before, during, and after Simon & Garfunkel . . . about their folk-rock music in the roiling age that embraced and was defined by their pathbreaking sound. He writes about growing up in the 1940s and '50s (son of a traveling salesman), a middle class Jewish boy, living in a red brick semi-attached house in Kew Gardens, Queens, a kid who was different--from the age of five feeling his vocal cords "vibrating with the love of sound" . . . meeting Paul Simon in school, the funny guy who made Art laugh; their going on to junior high school together, of being twelve at the birth of rock'n'roll, both of them "captured" by it.

"Sensitive, soulful, sharp-tongued, and serious, Garfunkel vies for a place in the pantheon of singers." Booklist.

Garnett, Edward, 1868-1937

Smith, Helen, 1965- The **uncommon** reader: a life of Edward Garnett / Helen Smith. Farrar, Straus and Giroux, 2017. 496 p. **B**

ISBN 9780374281120

1. Editors 2. Critics 3. Authors 4. Books and reading 5. Biographies

LC 2017025507

A portrait of the influential 20th-century publisher, critic, editor and literary mentor examines his indelible role in the careers of such leading writers as Joseph Conrad, D. H. Lawrence and Edward Thomas, as well as his efforts to establish Russian, American and Australian literature in British readership.

"With Smith's fine sense of pacing and a fascinating subject, her book both delights and informs." Publishers Weekly.

Gates, Henry Louis, 1950-

Gates, Henry Louis, 1950- **Colored** people : a memoir / Henry Louis Gates, Jr. Knopf, 1994. xvi, 216 p. **B**

ISBN 0679421793

1. Gates, Henry Louis, 1950- Childhood and youth. 2. African Americans -- West Virginia -- Social life and customs 3. African American scholars 4. Critics -- United States 5. Growing up. 6. West Virginia. 7. Autobiographies and memoirs

LC 93012256

ALA Notable Book, 1995.

Presents a portrait of Henry Louis Gates, growing up in a West Virginia hill town, presenting a study of his family, his childhood icons, and the social institutions and mores of the time.

"As Gates traces his evolution from Negro to Afro-wearing 'black,' he also traces the evolution of Piedmont (and, by extension, of much of America) at a time when the relationship between the races was being redefined." Newsweek.

Gates, Robert Michael, 1943-

Gates, Robert Michael, 1943- A **passion** for leadership : lessons on change and reform from fifty years of public service / Robert M. Gates. Alfred A. Knopf, 2016. 256 p. **B**

ISBN 9780307959492

1. United States. Secretary of Defense. 2. Leadership. 3. Autobiographies and memoirs

LC 2015010209

The former secretary of defense and author of the best-selling Duty explores why bureaucratic institutions are failing and how they can be transformed through effective leadership, citing the examples of large-scale change in the CIA, Texas A&M University and the Department of Defense.

"Solid advice that should be passed on to leaders at any season of life and particularly helpful to those new to such responsibility." Library Journal.

Gaulle, Charles de, 1890-1970

Jackson, Julian, 1954- **De** Gaulle / Julian Jackson. The Belknap Press of Harvard University Press, 2018. 928 p. **B**

ISBN 9780674987210

1. Presidents -- France 2. Generals -- France 3. World War II 4. French Resistance (World War II) 5. France -- Politics and government -- 20th century 6. Europe -- Politics and government -- 1945- 7. Biographies

LC 2018015618

Simultaneously published in the United Kingdom as A Certain Idea of France: The Life of Charles de Gaulle.Elizabeth Longford Prize for Historical Biography, 2019.

In a definitive biography of the mythic general who refused to accept Nazi domination of France, Julian Jackson captures this titanic figure as never before. Drawing on unpublished letters, memoirs, and resources of the recently opened de Gaulle archive, he shows how this volatile visionary put a broken France back at the center of world affairs.

"A long but excellent, highly useful addition to the library of modern European history as well as the political history of World War II and the Cold War." Kirkus.

Williams, Charles, 1933- The **last** great Frenchman : a life of General de Gaulle / Charles Williams. J. Wiley & Sons, c1993. xvi, 544 p. : **B**

ISBN 0471180718

1. Gaulle, Charles de, 1890-1970. 2. France. Army 3. Presidents -- France 4. Generals -- France 5. Authors, French -- 20th century 6. France -- Politics and government -- 20th century. 7. France -- Foreign relations -- 20th century. 8. France -- History -- 20th century. 9. Biographies

LC 94042881

Traces the life and career of the French general and president from his childhood in Lille, France to his death in 1970.

"The author offers appraisals of de Gaulle's career as soldier, politician and head of state. Williams contrasts the infuriatingly obstinate public figure with the private man, emotional and affectionate in the bosom of his family. Especially interesting is the account of de Gaulle's tender relationship with his retarded daughter. The author also sheds light on de Gaulle's determined anti-Americanism during his final years." Publishers Weekly.

Gautama Buddha

Armstrong, Karen, 1944- **Buddha** / Karen Armstrong. Penguin Books, 2004, c2001. 240 p. **B**

ISBN 0143034367

1. Gautama Buddha. 2. Enlightenment (Buddhism) 3. Buddhism. 4. Spiritual leaders. 5. Biographies

LC bl2004114688

Originally published: New York : Viking, 2001.

A portrait of the Buddha explores his identities both as an archetypal religious icon and as a man, chronicling his journey from his decision to leave a life of ease and power to his attainment of spiritual enlightenment.

"Armstrong interprets the mythologized story of the Buddha's abandonment of his life of comfort and privilege; commitment to practicing advanced forms of yoga and nearly fatal asceticism; enlightenment beneath a bodhi tree; and 45 years of wandering and teaching until his death in 483. And as she does so, she lucidly explains his revelations and influence." Booklist.

Gawande, Atul

Gawande, Atul **Complications** : a surgeon's notes on an imperfect science / Atul Gawande. Metropolitan Books, 2002. x, 269 p. **B**

ISBN 0805063196

1. Gawande, Atul. 2. Hospital patients -- Death. 3. Medical errors. 4. Decision-making. 5. Medicine 6. Essays.

LC 2001055884

"Several of these pieces have appeared, in slightly different form, in the New Yorker and Slate"--T.p. verso.

Also published with the title Complications: notes from the life of a young surgeon.ALA Notable Book, 2003.

National Book Award for Nonfiction finalist, 2002"

The author describes the work of a trainee surgeon. The pieces range from edgy accounts of medical traumas to sobering analyses of doctors' anxieties and burnout. These exquisitely crafted essays, in which medical subjects segue into explorations of much larger themes, place Gawande among the best in the field." Publishers Weekly.

Gawronski, Billy, 1910-1981

Shapiro, Laurie Gwen The **stowaway** : a young man's extraordinary adventure to Antarctica / Laurie Gwen Shapiro. Simon & Schuster, 2018. 256 p. **B**

ISBN 9781476753867

1. Gawronski, Billy, 1910-1981 Travel Antarctica 2. Stowaways 3. Ocean travel 4. Polar expeditions 5. Adventurers 6. Antarctica -- Description and travel 7. New York City 8. Biographies

LC 2017007428

Documents the true story of a New York City teenager who stowed away on an expedition to Antarctica in 1928, tracing how high schooler Billy Gawronski snuck aboard the expedition's flagship and eventually became an international celebrity.

"This coming-of-age story about a strong-willed boy with an insatiable appetite for adventure is evocative of the Hardy Boys and will appeal to both adult and young adult readers." Publishers Weekly.

Gay, Peter, 1923-2015

Gay, Peter, 1923-2015 **My** German question : growing up in Nazi Berlin / Peter Gay. Yale University Press, 1998. xii, 208 p. : **B**

ISBN 0300076703

1. Gay, Peter, 1923-2015. Childhood and youth. 2. Nazism -- Germany. 3. Jews, German -- History -- 1933-1945. 4. Jews -- Persecutions -- Germany. 5. Growing up. 6. Berlin, Germany -- History -- 1933-1945. 7. Autobiographies and memoirs

LC 98026686

The author traces his youth as an assimilated, atheistic Jew during the early years of the Nazi regime, his family's emigration in 1939, and his lingering ambivalent feelings toward Germany and the Germans.

"A searching, sensitive portrait of Gay's youth, as crystalline as memory can be made." Booklist.

Gay, Roxane

★Gay, Roxane **Hunger** : a memoir of (my) body / Roxane Gay. HarperCollins, 2017. 320 p. **B**

ISBN 9780062362599

1. Gay, Roxane. 2. Body image. 3. Self-esteem in women. 4. Self-perception in women. 5. Food habits -- Psychological aspects. 6. Autobiographies and memoirs.

LC bl2016022915

ALA Notable Book, 2018.

Lambda Literary Award for Bisexual Nonfiction, 2018.

Longlisted for the Andrew Carnegie Medal for Excellence in Non-Fiction, 2018.

National Book Critics Circle Award for Autobiography/Memoir finalist, 2017

The best-selling author of Bad Feminist presents a searingly frank memoir of food, weight, self-image and learning how to feed one's hunger in healthy ways, drawing on the popular essays of her long-running Tumblr blog to illuminate the challenges of navigating the boundaries between self-comfort and self-care.

Gaye, Jan

Gaye, Jan **After** the dance : my life with Marvin Gaye / Jan Gaye with David Ritz. HarperCollins 2015 224 p. **B**

ISBN 9780062135513

1. Gaye, Marvin. 2. Gaye, Jan. 3. Singers 4. Musicians' spouses 5. Soul musicians 6. African American singers 7. Autobiographies and

memoirs

LC 2016560527

The second wife of the late, legendary R&B star, describes how she met the Motown superstar when she was 17 and began a torrid love affair and marriage that was eventually shattered by drugs, family dysfunction and the burdens of fame.

"Gaye's explicitly confessional account of her doomed uphill struggle to stay with Marvin is a prime example of how obsessive celebrity worship can so easily (and dangerously) masquerade as enduring love. A fascinating, unsentimental account of a be-careful-what-you-wish-for romance." Kirkus.

Gazzaniga, Michael S.

Gazzaniga, Michael S. **Tales** from both sides of the brain : a life in neuroscience / Michael S. Gazzaniga. Ecco, 2015 272 p. **B**

ISBN 9780062228802

1. Neuroscientists 2. Split brain 3. Intelligence 4. Neuroscience 5. Autobiographies and memoirs

LC bl2015003351

The renowned cognitive neuroscientist who developed the split-brain theory discusses his life and career in science and his quest to understand how the different spheres of the brain can act distinctly and independently of each other. By the author of Who's in Charge.

"For those familiar with the groundbreaking studies that make up the fields backbone, however, the book is a rare opportunity to relive the history of cognitive neuroscience through Gazzanigas knowledgeable and relatable perspective." Choice.

Geddes, Norman Bel, 1893-1958

Szerlip, Barbara The **man** who designed the future : Norman Bel Geddes and the invention of twentieth-century America / B. Alexandra Szerlip. Melville House, 2017. xvii, 396 p. **B**

ISBN 9781612195629

1. Geddes, Norman Bel, 1893-1958. 2. Designers. 3. Design. 4. Biographies

LC 2016050576

A history of American innovation follows a polymath with humble origins who found himself at the center of the worlds of industry, advertising, theater and even gaming, designing everything from the first all-weather stadium to Manhattan's most exclusive nightclub to Futurama, the prescient 1939 exhibit that envisioned how America would look in the not-too-distant future.

"In this fascinating and minutely researched biography, Szerlip brings the brilliant, indefatigable industrial designers imagination to life so we can marvel once more." Booklist.

Gehrig, Lou, 1903-1941

Gehrig, Lou, 1903-1941 The **lost** memoir / Lou Gehrig, Alan D. Gaff. Simon & Schuster, 2020. 224 p. **B**

ISBN 9781982132392

1. Gehrig, Lou, 1903-1941. 2. New York Yankees (Baseball team) 3. Baseball players 4. Professional sports 5. Baseball 6. New York City 7. Autobiographies and memoirs

LC 2019033015

"Portions of this text were previously published in 1927 by The Oakland Tribune as Following the Babe.""

The lost memoir from baseball icon Lou Gehrig-a major historical discovery, published for the first time as a book, with "color commentary" from historian Alan Gaff. In 1927, the legendary Lou Gehrig sat down to write the remarkable story of his life and career. He was at his peak, fresh off a record-breaking season with the fabled '27 World Series champion Yankees. It was an era unlike any other. Gehrig's personal remembrances were published that year as popular weekly columns in The Oakland Tribune. Until now, those pages were lost to history. Lou comes alive in his captivating memoir. It is a heartfelt rags-to-riches tale about a poor kid from New York who grew up to become one of the greatest. He takes us to his childhood home, to Columbia University where he flashed as a prospect, all the way to the dugout at Yankee Stadium where he recounts his first major league hit and bonding with Babe Ruth. There is a real poignancy to this tale. Built like a heavyweight boxer, "Iron Horse" Lou was one of the most powerful men to play the game. Off the field he was a shy, gentle soul. He would die prematurely from ALS, a degenerative neuromuscular disorder now known as Lou Gehrig's Disease. Here is Lou back at bat-Hall of Famer, All Star, and MVP. Lou Gehrig is a monument and tribute to a singular life and career".-- Provided by publisher.

"A baseball icon's rediscovered memoir, enhanced with biographical material by the independent scholar who found it. . . . A simple gem for baseball fans." Kirkus

Robinson, Ray, 1920 December 4- **Iron** horse : Lou Gehrig in his time / Ray Robinson. W.W. Norton, c1990. 300 p. : **B**

ISBN 9780393028577

1. Gehrig, Lou, 1903-1941 Childhood and youth 2. New York Yankees (Baseball team) 3. Baseball players -- United States 4. First base players (Baseball) 5. People with amyotrophic lateral sclerosis 6. Baseball Hall of Fame members. 7. United States -- Social life and customs -- 20th century 8. Biographies

LC 89029272

Chronicles Gehrig's rise from poverty to fame in professional baseball, his remarkable record-breaking career, his happy marriage, and his courage in facing an untimely death from ALS

"Playing in the considerable shadow of Babe Ruth, Lou Gehrig's accomplishments as baseball's Iron Horse include a legendary record of 2, Library Journal.

Gehry, Frank O., 1929-

Goldberger, Paul **Building** art : the life and work of Frank Gehry / Paul Goldberger. Alfred A. Knopf, 2015. 528 p. **B**

ISBN 9780307701534

1. Architecture, American -- 20th century. 2. United States -- Buildings 3. Biographies

LC 2015026562

A biography of the Canadian-born architect Frank Gehry.

"With avid precision and invaluable insight, Goldberger charts the complicated, punishing battles Gehry waged to construct his ambitious, dreamworld buildings, from private homes to Guggenheim Bilbao, the Walt Disney Concert Hall, Facebook headquarters, and beyond. The result is an involving work of significant architectural history and a discerning and affecting portrait of a daring and original master builder." Booklist.

Geist, William

Geist, William **Lake** of the Ozarks : my surreal summers in a vanishing America / Bill Geist. Grand Central Publishing, 2019. 195 p. **B**

ISBN 9781538729809

1. Summer resorts 2. Teenage boys 3. Summer employment 4. Growing up 5. Ozark Mountain region 6. Missouri -- Social life and customs -- 20th century 7. Autobiographies and memoirs

LC 2018048035

A "CBS Sunday Morning" correspondent reflects on his coming of age in the American heartland at a Lake of the Ozarks resort owned by his uncle, and traces his evolution as a man and a writer.

" The book is a quick, pleasant read that effectively reflects how his time at the lodge showed him that life is more difficult and rewarding and fun when you manage to do things your way. Old-fashioned, wistful stories that will appeal to fans of Geist's previous books." Kirkus.

Geithner, Timothy F.

Geithner, Timothy F. **Stress** test : reflections on financial crises / Timothy F. Geithner. Crown Publishing, 2014. 580 p., 16 unnumbered p. of plates : **B**

ISBN 9780804138598

1. United States. Secretary of the Treasury. 2. Financial crises -- United States -- History -- 21st century. 3. Economics. 4. Global Financial Crisis, 2008-2009. 5. United States 6. Autobiographies and memoirs

From the former Treasury Secretary, the definitive account of the unprecedented effort to save the U.S. economy from collapse in the wake of the worst global financial crisis since the Great Depression.

Gelb, Arthur, 1924-2014

Gelb, Arthur, 1924-2014 **City** room / Arthur Gelb. G. P. Putnam's Sons, 2003. 664 p. **B**

ISBN 0399150757

1. New York Times Company. 2. Newspaper editors -- New York City 3. Journalists -- United States 4. Autobiographies and memoirs

LC 2003043154

"A Marian Wood book."

Includes index."

This is a memoir of life at The New York Times by one who spent nearly 50 years there, rising from copy boy to managing editor; {the author} has the power to evoke whole generations of change in the news business, reaching back to the glorious postwar years of manual typewriters, chain smokers, and all-nighters." New York Times Book Review.

Genghis Khan, 1162-1227

Weatherford, J. McIver **Genghis** Khan and the making of the modern world / Jack Weatherford. Crown, c2004. xxxv, 312 p. : **B**

ISBN 9780609610626

1. Genghis Khan, 1162-1227. 2. Mongols -- Rulers 3. Mongols -- History. 4. Biographies

LC 2003020659

Originally published: New York : Crown, 2004.

A re-evaluation of Genghis Khan's rise to power examines the reforms the conqueror instituted throughout his empire and his uniting of East and West, which set the foundation for the nation-states and economic systems of the modern era.

George III, King of Great Britain, 1738-1820

Hadlow, Janice A **royal** experiment : the private life of King George III / Janice Hadlow. Henry Holt and Company, 2014. 512 p. **B**

ISBN 9780805096569

1. George III, King of Great Britain, 1738-1820. 2. Royal houses 3. Home (Social sciences) 4. Fatherhood 5. Families 6. Biographies

LC 2014024707

Documents the American Revolution-era king's radical pursuit of happiness in his private life with Queen Charlotte and their 15 children, describing his resolve to avoid the cruelties of his progenitors, his determined faithfulness and his approaches to parenting.

"Extended forays into the king's periods of madness, which began in 1788 and finally incapacitated him for good in 1811, also diffuse the narrative focus. Unconvincing as revisionist history but enjoyable for its vivid depiction of several varieties of royal lifestyles - and plenty of royal gossip." Kirkus.

Tillyard, S. K. (Stella K.) A **royal** affair : George III and his scandalous siblings / Stella Tillyard. Random House, c2006. xxiv, 352 p., 16 p. of plates : **B**

ISBN 140006371X

1. George III, King of Great Britain, 1738-1820. 2. George III, King of Great Britain, 1738-1820 Family. 3. Nobility -- Great Britain 4. Great Britain -- Rulers 5. Great Britain -- History -- 18th century. 6. Great Britain -- Politics and government -- 1760-1820. 7. Biographies

LC 2006045130

The story of a regal family plagued by scandal and notoriety and trapped by duty, desire, and the protocols of royalty. History remembers King George III of England as the mad monarch who lost America. But as a young man, this poignant figure set aside his own passions in favor of a temperate life as guardian to both his siblings and his country. He would soon learn that his prudently cultivated harmony would be challenged by the impetuous natures of his sisters and brothers. Historians have always been puzzled by George's refusal to give up on America, which forced his government to drag out the Revolutionary War long after it was effectively lost. Biographer Tillyard suggests that the king, seeing the colonists as part of his family, sought to control them in the same way he had attempted to rule his younger siblings.--From publisher description.

"This riveting account reminds us that in the past, the misdemeanors of royals had serious, not simply gossip-rag, implications." Booklist.

Georges, Nicole J.

Georges, Nicole J. **Calling** Dr. Laura : a graphic memoir / Nicole J. Georges. Houghton Mifflin Harcourt, 2013. 288 p. : **B**

ISBN 9780547615592

1. Schlessinger, Laura. 2. Family secrets. 3. Identity (Psychology) 4. Father-separated girls. 5. Truth. 6. Portland, Oregon. 7. Autobiographical comics 8. Alternative comics 9. Autobiographies and memoirs 10. Comics and Graphic novels

LC 2012022389

Lambda Literary Award for LGBT Graphic Novel, 2014"

Georges' quirky, big-faced, and evocative drawings, tempered by a variety of panel sizes, show the bespectacled author as she comes to terms with her mother's lies to her as a child about her father being dead. . . . An excellent graphic memoir offering engaging insights for those who share--or don't share--any of George's worries and traits." Booklist.

Gerald, Casey

Gerald, Casey **There** will be no miracles here : a memoir / Casey Gerald. Riverhead Books, 2018. 352 p. **B**

ISBN 9780735214200

1. African American gay men 2. American dream 3. Success (Concept) 4. Identity (Psychology) 5. Autobiographies and memoirs

LC 2018377393

The co-founder of MBAs Across America describes his upbringing in a black evangelical family, his football recruitment into Yale and the brutal wealth gap that is forcing increasingly large numbers of marginalized groups to redefine the American Dream.

"Hardly a by-the-numbers memoir, this is a powerful book marked by the author's refreshingly complicated and insightful storytelling." Kirkus. Reviews

Gerard, Sarah

Gerard, Sarah **Sunshine** state : Essays / Sarah Gerard. Harper

Perennial, 2017. 208 p. B
ISBN 9780062434876
1. Intimacy (Psychology) 2. Addiction 3. Obsession 4. Religion 5. Florida 6. Essays 7. Autobiographies and memoirs
LC 2017296465

Rising literary star and Los Angeles Times First Fiction Award finalist Sarah Gerard uses her experiences growing up on Florida's gulf coast to illuminate the struggles of modern human survival--physical, emotional, environmental--through a collection of essays exploring intimacy, addiction, obsession, religion, homelessness, and incarceration.

"An intimate journey reveals a Florida few visitors would ever discover." Kirkus.

German, Bill

German, Bill **Under** their thumb : how a nice boy from Brooklyn got mixed up with the Rolling Stones (and lived to tell about it) / Bill German. Villard Books, c2009. 368 p. B
ISBN 9781400066223
1. German, Bill Anecdotes. 2. Rolling Stones Anecdotes. 3. Zines. 4. Journalists. 5. Periodical publishers and publishing 6. Autobiographies and memoirs
LC 2008045533

A coming-of-age memoir offers a bittersweet, insider's view of one of the world's greatest rock bands, describing how the group took him under their wing as a teenager, his participation in the band's private jam sessions and world travels, and his witness to their personal crises and over indulgences.

Geronimo, Apache chief, 1829-1909

★Utley, Robert M., 1929- **Geronimo** / Robert M. Utley. Yale University Press, c2012. 384 p. B
ISBN 9780300126389
1. Geronimo, Apache chief, 1829-1909. 2. Apache Indians 3. Indians of North America. 4. Race relations. 5. Battles. 6. Biographies
LC 2012019521

Spur Award for Biography, 2013.
Western Heritage Award for Outstanding Nonfiction Book, 2013.

This biography of the famous Apache uncovers the truth behind the myths and rumors that enshroud his life, describing how the warrior escaped capture, what his training was like and explains why he was feared by both whites and other Apaches.

"Highly recommended for academic libraries in particular, it will be essential to many public libraries and private readers as well." Library Journal.

Gerrard, Nicci

Gerrard, Nicci The **last** ocean : a journey through memory and forgetting / Nicci Gerrard. Penguin, 2019. 272 p. B
ISBN 9780525521969
1. Alzheimer's disease 2. Dementia 3. Terminal care 4. People with dementia -- Care. 5. Autobiographies and memoirs
LC 2019022660

The award-winning journalist and coauthor of the Nicci French best-sellers presents a lyrical, humane investigation into dementia that explores the journeys of both patients and their loved ones, exposing misguided protocols that contribute to unnecessary end-of-life pain.

"This is a beautifully written, heartfelt look at aging, disease, and death that will both comfort and inspire readers who are living through or fearing such passages." Booklist.

Gershwin, George, 1898-1937

Hyland, William G., 1929- **George** Gershwin : a new biography / William G. Hyland. Praeger, 2003. xv, 279 p. : B
ISBN 9780275981112
1. Gershwin, George, 1898-1937. 2. Composers -- United States 3. Biographies
LC 2003046303

"This fresh and well-researched biography of one of America's great composers is highly recommended for all libraries." Library Journal.

★Pollack, Howard **George** Gershwin : his life and work / Howard Pollack. University of California Press, c2006. xvii, 884 p. : B
ISBN 0520248643
1. Gershwin, George, 1898-1937. 2. Composers -- United States 3. Composition (Music) 4. Music. 5. Pianists. 6. Biographies
LC 2006017926

"This engaging biography is also a tour de force of scholarship." Booklist.

Gerson, Stephane

Gerson, Stephane **Disaster** falls : a family story / Stephane Gerson. Crown, 2017. 256 p. B
ISBN 9781101906699
1. Accidental death 2. Grief 3. Coping 4. Fathers and sons 5. Autobiographies and memoirs
LC 2016016306

Chronicles the aftermath of the author's 8-year-old son's drowning death during a family rafting trip, describing how the tragedy threatened to isolate their surviving family members as they processed wrenching grief in respective ways.

"While asserting that one can never recover from the death of a child, Gerson evocatively describes the process of a struggle that allows him to continue living." Publishers Weekly.

Gessner, David, 1961-

Gessner, David, 1961- **Ultimate** glory : frisbee, obsession, and my wild youth / David Gessner. Riverhead Books, 2017. 304 p. B
ISBN 9780735210561
1. Gessner, David, 1961- Childhood and youth. 2. Ultimate (Game). 3. Competition 4. Athletes -- Training. 5. Outdoor games 6. Autobiographies and memoirs
LC 2016048991

An acclaimed essayist and nature writer describes how he spent his youth playing Ultimate Frisbee and the fierce competition, camaraderie and epic parties he survived while trying to win the national competition in a largely misunderstood sport.

"An anecdotal tour of a sport that has only been around for a few decades but that claims legions of adherents." Kirkus.

Gettleman, Jeffrey, 1971-

Gettleman, Jeffrey, 1971- **Love,** Africa : a memoir of romance, war, and survival / Jeffrey Gettleman. HarperCollins., 2017. 368 p. B
ISBN 9780062284099
1. Journalists 2. War and society 3. Interethnic conflict 4. Political violence 5. East Africa 6. Africa 7. Autobiographies and memoirs
LC 2017299603

The Pulitzer Prize-winning New York Times East Africa bureau chief presents a memoir about finding love and purpose in one of the world's most violent and beautiful regions, tracing his life-long dream of living in Africa and his winding journey toward the personal and professional ambitions of his heart.

"A stark, eye-opening, and sometimes-horrifying portrait by a reporter enthralled by the 'power and magic' of Africa." Kirkus.

Gevisser, Mark

Gevisser, Mark **Lost** and Found in Johannesburg : a memoir / Mark Gevisser. Farrar, Straus and Giroux, 2014. 352 p. **B**

ISBN 9780374176761

1. Gevisser, Mark. 2. Authors, South African -- 20th century 3. Growing up 4. Maps. 5. Gay men 6. Johannesburg, South Africa. 7. Autobiographies and memoirs

LC 2013033018

As a child growing up in apartheid South Africa, Mark Gevisser was obsessed with maps--and with Holmden's Register, Johannesburg's street guide, in particular. He played a game called Dispatcher with this eccentric guide, transporting himself across the city into places that would otherwise be forbidden to him. It was through Dispatcher that he discovered apartheid by realizing that he could not find an access route to the neighboring township of Alexandra and, later, by realizing that Soweto was not mapped at all. This was the beginning of his lifelong obsession with maps and photographs, and what they tell us about borders and boundaries--how we define ourselves by staying within them or by transgressing them. This memoir is an account of getting lost in one's hometown, and then finding oneself as a gay Jewish South African who was raised under apartheid and who eventually married a man of a different race as the country moved toward freedom. Using maps, shards of memory, photographs, and stories, Gevisser constructs a stunning portrait of race and sexuality, heritage and otherness.

"With lots of photos that show the people and places, including the mountains of yellow mine dumps from Joburgs gold, this is a must for those who want to experience the personal reality of apartheid and its aftermath." Booklist.

Gibbs, William Francis

Ujifusa, Steven A **man** and his ship : America's greatest naval architect and his quest to build the S.S. United States / Steven Ujifusa. Simon & Schuster, 2012. 448 p. **B**

ISBN 9781451645071

1. Gibbs, William Francis. 2. Gibbs & Cox -- History 20th century. 3. United States (Steamship) 4. Naval architects. 5. Ocean liners. 6. Steamships. 7. Ship-building. 8. Biographies

LC 2011049883

Documents the story of innovative ship designer William Francis Gibbs, describing the breakthroughs that enabled him to craft high-performance ships of unprecedented versatility.

Gidla, Sujatha, 1963-

Gidla, Sujatha, 1963- **Ants** among elephants : an untouchable family and the making of modern India / Sujatha Gidla. Farrar, Straus and Giroux, 2017. 400 p. **B**

ISBN 9780865478114

1. Gidla, Sujatha, 1963- Childhood and youth. 2. Gidla, Sujatha, 1963- Family. 3. Caste. 4. Inequality 5. Pariahs. 6. Dalits (East Indian Scheduled Castes) 7. India -- Social conditions -- 1947- 8. Kakinada, India 9. Autobiographies and memoirs

LC 2016052857

A woman, born as an "untouchable" into the Indian caste system, describes how she was educated by Canadian missionaries in the 1930s and what it was like growing up in a world full of poverty and injustice but also full of incredible possibility.

"Gidla writes about the heavy topics of poverty, caste and gender inequality, and political corruption with grace and wit . an essential contribution to contemporary Indian literature." Publishers Weekly.

Gies, Miep, 1909-2010

Gies, Miep, 1909-2010 **Anne** Frank remembered : the story of the woman who helped to hide the Frank family / Miep Gies and Alison Leslie Gold. Simon and Schuster Paperbacks, 2009. 264 p., 24 p. of plates : **B**

ISBN 9781416598855

1. Frank, Anne, 1929-1945. 2. Righteous Gentiles in the Holocaust -- Amsterdam, Netherlands 3. Holocaust (1933-1945) -- Amsterdam, Netherlands. 4. World War II -- Jews. 5. Courage in women 6. Amsterdam, Netherlands -- Interethnic relations. 7. Autobiographies and memoirs

LC 2009294295

Includes index.

The reminiscences of Miep Gies, the woman who hid the Frank family in Amsterdam during the Second World War, presents a vivid story of life under Nazi occupation.

"These vignettes and the description of what was happening in Amsterdam provide insight into how the Nazi occupation affected the lives of innocent people, and into the heroism of a remarkable woman, Miep Gies." School Library Journal.

Gilbert, Elizabeth, 1969-

Gilbert, Elizabeth, 1969- **Eat,** pray, love : one woman's search for everything across Italy, India and Indonesia / Elizabeth Gilbert. Viking, 2006. 334 p. **B**

ISBN 9780670034710

1. Gilbert, Elizabeth, 1969- Travel 2. Self-discovery in women. 3. Divorced women. 4. Happiness. 5. Travel writers -- United States 6. Italy -- Description and travel. 7. India -- Description and travel. 8. Indonesia -- Description and travel. 9. Bali (Island) -- Description and travel. 10. Autobiographies and memoirs

LC 2005042435

Traces the author's decision to quit her job and travel the world for a year after suffering a midlife crisis and divorce, a journey that took her to three places in her quest to explore her own nature and learn the art of spiritual balance.

"A probing, thoughtful title with a free and easy style, this work seamlessly blends history and travel for a very enjoyable read." Library Journal.

Gilder, Ginny

Gilder, Ginny **Course** correction : a story of rowing and resilience in the wake of Title IX / Ginny Gilder. Beacon Press, 2015 272 p. **B**

ISBN 9780807074770

1. Rowers -- United States 2. Rowing. 3. Women Olympic athletes 4. Women athletes. 5. Autobiographies and memoirs

LC 2014037358

Course Correction recounts the physical and psychological barriers Gilder overcame as she transformed into an elite athlete who reached the highest echelon of her sport. Set against the backdrop of unprecedented cultural change, Gilder's story personalizes the impact of Title IX, illustrating the life-changing lessons learned in sports but felt far beyond the athletic arena.

Gildiner, Catherine, 1948-

Gildiner, Catherine, 1948- **Good** morning, monster : five heroic journeys to recovery / Catherine Gildiner. St. Martin's Press, 2020. 359 p. **B**

ISBN 9781250271488

1. Women psychologists 2. Psychotherapy patients. 3. Psychic trauma 4. Psychotherapy 5. Autobiographies and memoirs

Previously published: Toronto :A therapist creates moving portraits of five of her most memorable patients, men and women she considers psychological heroes.

"Clinical psychologist Gildiner (Too Close to the Falls) shares heart-wrenching stories of child abuse in this pull-no-punches narrative about five of her patients. . . . These painful accounts will break anyone's heart, and also inspire awe for the ways people who suffered horrific abuse were able to find a measure of recovery." Publishers Weekly

Gilliam, Dorothy Butler, 1936-

Gilliam, Dorothy Butler, 1936- **Trailblazer** : a pioneering journalist's fight to make the media look more like America / Dorothy Butler Gilliam. Center Street, 2019. 360 p. **B**

ISBN 9781546083443

1. Journalists -- United States 2. African American women journalists 3. Women civil rights workers 4. African American women 5. Washington D.C. 6. United States -- Race relations 7. Autobiographies and memoirs

LC 2018034533

The barrier-breaking civil-rights journalist presents a comprehensive view of racial relations and the media in the U.S. that draws on her personal and professional experiences to celebrate the behind-the-scenes victories that have shaped decades of struggle.

"In her compelling memoir, she recounts her trailblazing career during the turbulence of the Vietnam War, the civil rights and womens movements, and Watergate and looks beyond her personal journey to examine efforts to diversify the staffs of news organizations and other challenges currently facing the press." Booklist.

Ginsberg, Allen, 1926-1997

Morgan, Bill, 1949- **I** celebrate myself : the somewhat private life of Allen Ginsberg / Bill Morgan. Viking, 2006. xv, 702 p. : **B**

ISBN 0670037966

1. Ginsberg, Allen, 1926-1997. 2. Poets, American -- 20th century 3. Beat culture 4. United States -- Social life and customs -- 20th century 5. Biographies

LC 2006050045

A portrait of the influential Beat generation poet draws on interviews with friends as well as his journals and correspondence to discuss such topics as his political views, practice of Tibetan Buddhism, and capacity for self-expression.

"Relying heavily on Ginsberg's journals and letters, as well as interviews with close friends, [Morgan] creates here a detailed, revealing portrait of Ginsberg as a gifted poet and flawed human being driven by a fierce hunger for love and an insatiable thirst for fame. This most exhaustive biography to date chronicles Ginsberg's life from cradle to grave, but a major theme is Ginsberg's love life especially his relationship with Peter Orlovsky. Although he became an icon for gay liberation, Ginsberg tended to fall in love with straight men like Jack Kerouac, Neal Cassady, and Orlovsky, which, of course, led to a good deal of rejection and frustration. Morgan's is the first life of Ginsberg to explore this curious paradox in any depth. Cleverly designed, his book includes marginal references to the poems Ginsberg was working on at the time. A monumental work." Library Journal.

Ginsburg, Ruth Bader 1933-2020

Carmon, Irin **Notorious** RBG : the life and times of Ruth Bader Ginsburg / Irin Carmon and Shana Knizhnik. Dey Street Books, 2015. 208 p. **B**

ISBN 9780062415837

1. United States. Supreme Court Justices 2. Judges -- United States 3. Feminists 4. Civil rights -- United States. 5. Women's rights 6. Biographies

LC 2015027547

In an illustrated biography of the feminist icon and legal pioneer, readers can get to know the Supreme Court Justice and fierce Jewish grandmother, who has changed the world despite our struggle with the unfinished business of gender equality and civil rights, standing as a testament to what a little chutzpah can do.

"The brief, cogent excerpts from her court opinions are annotated in plain language by prominent legal academics. Moreover, the authors successfully situate RBG's work within a larger historical context, thereby illustrating her central role in advancing equal rights for all." Library Journal.

★De Hart, Jane Sherron **Ruth** Bader Ginsburg : a life / Jane Sherron de Hart. Alfred A. Knopf, 2018. 752 p. **B**

ISBN 9781400040483

1. United States. Supreme Court Justices 2. Judges -- United States 3. Women judges 4. Jurisprudence 5. Women's rights

LC 2018004415

"The first full life--private; public; legal; philosophical--of the 107th Supreme Court Justice, one of the most profound and profoundly transformative legal minds of our time; a book fifteen years in work, written with the cooperation of Ruth Bader Ginsburg herself and based on many interviews with the Justice, her husband, her children, her friends, and associates."-- Provided by publisher.

"This extensively documented account, incorporating more than 100 pages of chapter notes and a bibliography that cites hundreds of resources, is also quite engaging and very easy to read." Booklist.

★Ginsburg, Ruth Bader. 1933-2020 **My** own words / Ruth Bader Ginsburg with Mary Hartnett and Wendy W. Williams. Simon & Schuster, 2016. 288 p. **B**

ISBN 9781501145247

1. United States. Supreme Court Justices 2. Judges. 3. Civil rights. 4. Women's rights 5. Feminists 6. Autobiographies and memoirs 7. Essays

LC 2016031635

Offers a collection of engaging, serious, and playful writings and speeches from the Supreme Court justice on topics ranging from gender equality and the workings of the Court to Judaism and the value of looking beyond U.S. shores when interpreting the Constitution.

"The variety of subjects is impressive, and Ginsburgs gift for concision enables her to discuss them in enough detail to engage interest while leaving the reader wanting more." Publishers Weekly.

★Rosen, Jeffrey, 1964- **Conversations** with RBG : Ruth Bader Ginsburg on life, love, liberty, and law / Jeffrey Rosen. Henry Holt & Company, 2019. 259 p. **B**

ISBN 9781250235169

1. United States. Supreme Court Justices 2. Judges -- United States 3. Women judges 4. Women Supreme Court justices 5. Biographies

LC 2019020971

The president and chief executive officer of the National Constitution Center offers an intimate look at the life and career of Justice Ruth Bader Ginsburg, in her own words, through an extraordinary series of conversations.

"Libraries with patrons keenly interested in the Supreme Court, especially those serving law, political science, and American history students, will find this a compelling addition. For those eager to add a new resource on the Justice, this book provides a solid introduction to her life and thoughts on the American legal system." Library Journal.

Giraldi, William

Giraldi, William The **hero's** body : a memoir / William Giraldi. Liveright Publishing Corporation, 2016. 288 p. **B**

ISBN 9780871406668

1. Growing up. 2. Masculinity 3. Grief 4. Motorcycle accidents. 5. New Jersey 6. Autobiographies and memoirs

LC 2016019127

Part memoir and part contemplation on what it means to be masculine in the modern world, the author examines his life growing up in a blue collar New Jersey town, where he lost his father in a terrible motorcycle accident and sought solace in bodybuilding.

"A hearty, bittersweet familial chronicle of masculinity drawing on the underappreciated bond between fathers and sons." Kirkus.

Girma, Haben, 1988-

Girma, Haben, 1988- **Haben** : the deafblind woman who conquered Harvard Law / Haben Girma. Twelve, 2019. 256 p. **B**

ISBN 9781538728727

1. Women with disabilities 2. Women who are blind and deaf 3. Determination (Personal quality) 4. Refugees 5. Autobiographies and memoirs

LC 2018050294

Documents the story of the first deaf and blind graduate of Harvard Law School, tracing her refugee parents' harrowing experiences in the Eritrea-Ethiopian war and her development of innovations that enabled her remarkable achievements.

"Articulated in elegant prose, lawyer and activist Girma's struggles navigating an ableist world as a person with disabilities are motivating, heartbreaking, and real." Booklist.

Gisleson, Anne

Gisleson, Anne The **futilitarians** : our year of thinking, drinking, grieving, and reading / Anne Gisleson. Little Brown & Co, 2017 272 p. **B**

ISBN 9780316393904

1. Grief 2. Books and reading 3. Loss (Psychology) 4. Spiritual journeys 5. Autobiographies and memoirs

LC 2017932689

Brought together by author Anne Gisleson and her husband after Hurricane Katrina devastated their hometown, New Orleans, the Existential Crisis Reading Group (the "Futilitarians") discussed literature, traditional religious teachings, and existentialism in response to their shared grief and loss. Their monthly meetings over a year's time considered works by authors as varied as James Baldwin and Shel Silverstein. In Giselson's narrative, the Futilitarians' discussions and her reminiscences portray an inspiring and accessible depiction of human suffering and happiness.

"A graceful narrative that seamlessly interweaves philosophical reflections and intimate revelations." Kirkus.

Glass, Philip, 1937-

Glass, Philip, 1937- **Words** without music : a memoir / Philip Glass. Liveright Publishing Co., 2015 288 p. **B**

ISBN 9780871404381

1. Composers 2. Music 3. Composition (Music) 4. Autobiographies and memoirs

LC 2015000421

While striving to achieve recognition for his musical works, award-winning composer Philip Glass installed drywall, moved furniture, drove a New York City cab, and even taught himself plumbing. Glass eventually became known for his innovative approach to composition, which incorporates multicultural musical, literary, and philosophical influences. He reveals himself in Words Without Music as an engaging storyteller, creating a colloquial, vivid, and unpretentious self-portrait that will appeal to any reader -- not just classical music fans.

"Aspiring musicians and artists will learn much from Glass, as will general readers, musical or not, who will discover an artistic life exceptionally well lived." Booklist.

Gleiberman, Owen

Gleiberman, Owen **Movie** freak : my life watching movies / Owen Gleiberman. Hachette Books, 2016. 304 p. **B**

ISBN 9780316382960

1. Gleiberman, Owen. 2. Films. 3. Film critics 4. Autobiographies and memoirs

LC 2015039430

Includes index.

From a personal obsession with film, to an unorthodox mentorship with the legendary Pauline Kael, to establishing himself with the upstart Entertainment Weekly, Movie Freak is the memoir by veteran film critic Owen Gleiberman that will speak to anyone whose life has been changed by a great film.

"A story of societal change, rich in cultural as well as personal history." Kirkus.

Glenconner, Anne

Glenconner, Anne **Lady** in waiting : my extraordinary life in the shadow of the Crown / Anne Glenconner. Hachette Books, 2020, c2019. 256 p. **B**

ISBN 9780306846366

1. Glenconner, Anne. 2. Margaret, Princess, Countess of Snowdon, 1930-2002. 3. Elizabeth II, Queen of Great Britain, 1926- 4. Ladies-in-waiting 5. Courts and courtiers 6. Royal Family 7. Motherhood 8. Great Britain -- Social conditions -- 20th century. 9. Autobiographies and memoirs

LC bl2020007748

Originally published: London : Hodder & Stoughton, 2019.

The daughter of the 5th Earl of Leicester, unable to inherit her father's estate, describes growing up with royalty, having served as Maid of Honor at Queen Elizabeth's coronation and as lady in waiting to Princess Margaret.

"An insider's look at the world of palaces, princesses, and the pressure of public life . . . A must-have for loyal royal fans." Kirkus

Goddard, Robert Hutchings, 1882-1945

★Clary, David A. **Rocket** man : Robert H. Goddard and the birth of the Space Age / David A. Clary. Hyperion, 2004, c2003. 352 p., 16 p. of plates : **B**

ISBN 0786887052

1. Rocketry -- Research -- United States -- History 2. Space sciences -- Research -- History 3. Aviation -- United States -- History 4. Physicists. 5. United States -- Social life and customs -- 20th century 6. Biographies

LC oc2007100396

Traces the life and times of American rocket pioneer Robert H. Goddard, describing his essential contributions to the science and technology of the twentieth century, the sometimes turbulent life of the visionary genius, and his pivotal role in launching the Space Age.

"Clary presents a clear and relatively straightforward narrative of his subject's life. Readers who come to this generally well-written biography with some knowledge of Goddard's significance will find much of interest to fill out their knowledge of this complex and fascinating scientist for whom NASA's Goddard Space Center is named." Publishers Weekly.

Godel, Kurt, 1906-1978

Goldstein, Rebecca, 1950- **Incompleteness** : the proof and paradox of Kurt Godel / Rebecca Goldstein. W.W. Norton, c2005. 296 p. ; Great discoveries **B**

ISBN 9780393051698

1. Godel, Kurt, 1906-1978. 2. Logicians 3. Proof theory. 4. Biographies

LC 2004023052

Reprint. Originally published: 2005.

A portrait of the eminent twentieth-century mathematician discusses his theorem of incompleteness, relationships with such contemporaries as Albert Einstein, and untimely death as a result of mental instability and self-starvation.

"This is a stimulating exploration of both the power and the limitations of the human intellect." Publishers Weekly.

Goebbels, Joseph, 1897-1945

Longerich, Peter **Goebbels** : a biography / Peter Longerich ; translated by Alan Bance, Jeremy Noakes, Lesley Sharpe. Random House Inc, 2014, c2010. 512 p. **B**

ISBN 9781400067510

1. Nazi Party (Germany) 2. Nazis 3. Antisemitism 4. Nazism 5. Nazi propaganda 6. Germany -- Politics and government -- 1933-1945 7. Biographies

LC 2014004828

Translation from the German.

Originally published: Munich : Siedler Verlag, 2010.

Joseph Goebbels served as Adolf Hitler's Minister of Propaganda, not only crafting the public façade of the Third Reich but micromanaging government approval (or banning) of writers and other artists. In this detailed biography of the second most powerful man in Nazi Germany, historian Peter Longerich examines Goebbels' psychological profile, mines his diaries for descriptions of those around him, and explores his generally unsuccessful efforts to influence Hitler. This thoroughly researched study provides an important contribution to the history of the Third Reich and a fascinating account for biography fans.

"As Longerich acknowledges, his reliance on Goebbel's diaries as a primary source is problematic, since Goebbel's accounts of events and personalities seem designed to impress himself. Still Longerich's efforts to glean the truth from exaggerations and distortions are credible, and this is an outstanding contribution to our understanding of the Nazi regime." Booklist.

Goethe, Johann Wolfgang von, 1749-1832

Armstrong, John, 1966- **Love,** life, Goethe : lessons of the imagination from the great German poet / John Armstrong. Farrar, Straus and Giroux, 2007, c2006. xv, 482 p. : **B**

ISBN 0374299684

1. Goethe, Johann Wolfgang von, 1749-1832 Criticism and interpretation 2. Happiness. 3. Self-fulfillment 4. Germany -- Social life and customs -- 18th century 5. Germany -- Social life and customs -- 19th century 6. Biographies

LC 2006034072

Originally published in 2006 by Allen Lane, Penguin Group, UK , under the title: Love, life, Goethe: how to be happy in an imperfect world.

Examines the major themes of the work of Johann Wolfgang von Goethe in terms of his own life story and explains how his poetry resonates in the present with its depictions of the human yearning for happiness, friendship, and family.

"Armstrong's thoughtful analysis of Goethe's life and works enables readers to fully appreciate the great German poet as an eminently human genius striving for growth and wholeness." Booklist.

Safranski, Rudiger **Goethe** : life as a work of art / Rudiger Safranski ; translated by David Dollenmayer. Liveright Publishing Corporation, 2017. 704 p. **B**

ISBN 9780871404909

1. Goethe, Johann Wolfgang von, 1749-1832. 2. Authors, German 3. German literature -- 18th century -- History and criticism 4. German literature -- 19th century -- History and criticism 5. Germany -- History. 6. Biographies

LC 2017008798

A philosopher and popular biographer highlights the life of the man considered to be the Shakespeare of German literature, relying on his published works, primary sources, and the author|s correspondence with contemporaries to create an illuminating portrait.

"Scholars will welcome this intellectual biography, richly embellished by primary sources and aided by the strong Dollenmayer translation." Publishers Weekly.

Gogh, Vincent van, 1853-1890

Bell, Julian, 1952- **Van** Gogh : a power seething / Julian Bell. New Harvest, 2015. 208 p. **B**

ISBN 9780544343733

1. Gogh, Vincent van, 1853-1890. 2. Painters -- Netherlands 3. Netherlands -- Social life and customs -- 19th century. 4. Biographies

LC bl2015000972

A passionate account of the tortured life and tragic death of the greatest artist of the nineteenth century, by renowned critic and painter Julian Bell.

"Bell describes with glorious acuity the rapid artistic evolution of this self-taught genius propelled by a 'peculiar inner seething,' celebrating with unique fluency Van Goghs 'rapturous vision' and the 'visual electricity' of his masterpieces. A vividly illuminating portrait both for readers versed in Van Gogh and those who are newly curious." Booklist.

Naifeh, Steven W., 1952- **Van** Gogh : the life / Steven Naifeh and Gregory White Smith. Random House, 2011. 800 p. **B**

ISBN 9780375507489

1. Painters -- Netherlands 2. Impressionism (Art) 3. Modern art -- 19th century 4. Artists -- Psychology 5. Biographies

LC 2010053005

The Pulitzer Prize-winning team presents an in-depth, accessible profile that has already been praised by Amsterdam's Van Gogh Museum as a "definitive biography," drawing on newly available primary sources to provide revisionist assessments of the influential artist's turbulent life and genius works.

Goillot, Virginia, 1906-1982

Purnell, Sonia A **woman** of no importance : the untold story of the American spy who helped win WWII / Sonia Purnell. Viking, 2019. 352 p. : **B**

ISBN 9780735225299

1. Women spies -- United States 2. Intelligence officers -- United States 3. French Resistance (World War II) 4. Women's role 5. France -- History -- German occupation, 1940-1945 6. Biographies

LC 2018060359

National Book Critics Circle Award for Biography finalist, 2019

Traces the story of mid-twentieth-century spy Virginia Hall, detailing her pivotal role in coordinating Resistance activities in Europe that helped change the course of World War II.

"Meticulous research results in a significant biography of a trailblazer who now has a CIA building named after her." Kirkus.

Gold, Glen David, 1964-

Gold, Glen David, 1964- **I** will be complete : a memoir / Glen David Gold. Alfred A. Knopf, 2018. 488 p. **B**

ISBN 9781101946398

1. Abandonment (Psychology) 2. Parent and child 3. Growing up 4. Mothers and sons 5. California 6. Autobiographies and memoirs

LC 2017049131

Traces the author's upbringing in the wake of his unconventional mother's destructive choices, detailing the loss of family resources, his mother's get-rich-quick schemes, and his efforts to survive her abandonment at age twelve.

Goldberg, Rita

Goldberg, Rita **Motherland** : growing up with the Holocaust / Rita Goldberg. New Press, 2015. 352 p. **B**

ISBN 9781620970737

1. Jacobsthal, Hilde 2. Holocaust (1933-1945) 3. Holocaust survivors -- United States 4. Family relationships 5. Mothers and daughters 6. Autobiographies and memoirs

LC 2014042769

In a deeply moving second-generation Holocaust memoir, Goldberg introduces the extraordinary story of Hilde Jacobsthal, a close friend of Anne Frank's family who was fifteen when the Nazis invaded Holland. After the arrest of her parents in 1943, Hilde fled to Belgium, living out the war years in an extraordinary set of circumstances--among the Resistance and at Bergen-Belsen after its liberation--that the Guardian newspaper judged worthy of a film script."

"Of course, the family story, and especially the Frank connection, will draw readers (she knew Otto very well, right up to his postwar visits to the U.S.), who will be open to discussion of the big issues of perpetrators, victims, and, especially, bystanders, then and now." Booklist.

Goldblatt, Duchess

Goldblatt, Duchess **Becoming** Duchess Goldblatt : a memoir / Anonymous. Houghton Mifflin Harcourt, 2020. 240 p. **B**

ISBN 9780358216773

1. Twitter (Electronic resource) 2. Anonymous persons 3. Social media 4. Humorous writing 5. Anonyms and pseudonyms 6. Autobiographies and memoirs

LC 2019027260

Becoming Duchess Goldblatt is two stories: that of the reclusive real-life writer who created a fictional character out of loneliness and thin air, and that of the magical Duchess Goldblatt herself, a bright light in the darkness of social media. Fans around the world are drawn to Her Grace's voice, her wit, her life-affirming love for all humanity, and the fun and friendship of the community that's sprung up around her.

"How does a fictional character write a real memoir? Very, very well. . . . She's created a long-term fever dream of humor, compassion, wordplay, and dog photos. A fascinating memoir by a 21st-century original." Kirkus

Goldsmith, George, 1913-

Goldsmith, Martin, 1952- The **inextinguishable** symphony : a true story of music and love in Nazi Germany / Martin Goldsmith. Wiley, c2000. vi, 346 p. : **B**

ISBN 0471350974

1. Goldsmith, Rosemary, 1917-1984. 2. Musicians -- Germany 3. Jews 4. Holocaust (1933-1945) 5. Germany -- History -- 20th century. 6. Biographies

LC 00025955

An account of two Jewish musicians who fell in love while playing for Frankfort's Kulturbund orchestra, which served as a haven for persecuted Jews and as a Nazi propoganda tool, describes how love maintained through the horrors of the Third Reich.

"Goldsmith's weaving together of cultural and personal history constitutes a gripping tale of persecution, intrigue, and love and an insider'sor two insiders' view of a dark time." Booklist.

Goldstein, Meredith

Goldstein, Meredith **Can't** help myself : lessons & confessions from a modern advice columnist / Meredith Goldstein. Grand Central Publishing, 2018. 256 p. **B**

ISBN 9781455543779

1. Love 2. Interpersonal relations 3. Advice columnists 4. Self-fulfillment in women 5. Autobiographies and memoirs

LC 2017041731

Every day, Boston Globe advice columnist Meredith Goldstein takes on the relationship problems of thousands of dedicated readers. They look to her for wisdom on all matters of the heart- how to cope with dating fatigue and infidelity, work romances, tired marriages, true love, and true loss. In her column, she has it all figured out, but in her real life she is a lot less certain. Whether it's her own reservations about the traditional path of marriage and family, her difficulty finding someone she truly connects with, or the evolution of her friendships as her friends start to have their own families, Meredith finds herself looking for insight, just like her readers.

"The book will appeal to loyal readers of advice columnsparticularly Goldsteinsbut be forewarned, this book is a tearjerker." Publishers Weekly.

Golembesky, Michael

Golembesky, Michael **Level** zero heroes : the story of U.S. Marine Special Operations in Bala Murghab, Afghanistan / Michael Golembesky with John R. Bruning. St. Martin's Press, 2014 320 p. **B**

ISBN 9781250030405

1. Golembesky, Michael. 2. United States. Marine Special Operations Command. 3. United States. Marine Corps. 4. Taliban 5. Marines -- United States. 6. Afghan War, 2001-, American. 7. Close air support -- History -- 21st century. 8. Afghanistan 9. Autobiographies and memoirs

LC 2014016597

Follows the members of U.S. Marine Special Operations Team 8222 on their assignment to the remote and isolated Taliban stronghold known as Bala Murghab as they tried to break the Taliban's grip on the valley.

"Readers who enjoy first-person accounts of battles laced with non-stop action will have a tough time putting this one down." Library Journal.

Gooch, Brad, 1952-

Gooch, Brad, 1952- **Smash** cut / Brad Gooch. HarperCollins, 2015. 256 p. **B**

ISBN 9780062354952

1. Brookner, Howard 2. Gay men 3. Gay culture 4. Filmmakers 5. Authors 6. New York City 7. Autobiographies and memoirs

LC 2015460361

Set against the backdrop of 1980s New York City, this colorful and atmospheric tale of wild bohemians, glamorous celebrities and complicated passions follows the author's affair with film director Howard Brookner, which was haunted by addiction, promiscuous sex and infidelity during the AIDS epidemic.

"This candid memoir lovingly evokes a life, and a world, lost." Kirkus

Goodall, Jane, 1934-

★Goodall, Jane, 1934- **Beyond** innocence : an autobiography in letters : the later years / Jane Goodall ; edited by Dale Peterson. Houghton Mifflin, 2001. xiii, 418 p. : **B**

ISBN 0618125205

1. Goodall, Jane, 1934- Correspondence. 2. Primatologists -- Correspondence. 3. Zoologists -- Great Britain 4. Women primatologists. 5. Chimpanzees. 6. Autobiographies and memoirs

LC 00054124

"In this volume of Goodall's letters, a lively portrait is formed through her missives as the young woman rose to the height of her scientific contributions and fame. She became a mother, divorced her first husband, married her second, and lost him to cancer. She was also the first to observe cannibalism in chimps, lost many of her study troop during a polio epidemic, and weathered the kidnapping of a group of her students. This illuminating glimpse into the mind, emotions, and philosophy of an important scientist who also happens to be a celebrated figure will be requested in all libraries." Booklist.

Goodman, Simon

Goodman, Simon The **Orpheus** clock : the search for my family's art treasures stolen by the Nazis / Simon Goodman. Scribner, 2015. 352 p. **B**

ISBN 9781451697636

1. World War II -- Confiscations and contributions -- Germany. 2. Art thefts 3. Nazis 4. Trials 5. Germany -- History -- 20th century. 6. Autobiographies and memoirs

LC 2015017171

The author presents a passionate, gripping, true story of his single-minded quest to reclaim what the Nazis stole from his family, their beloved art collection, and to restore their legacy.

Goodwin, Doris Kearns

Goodwin, Doris Kearns **Wait** till next year : a memoir / Doris Kearns Goodwin. Simon & Schuster, 1997. 261 p. : **B**

ISBN 0684824892

1. Goodwin, Doris Kearns -- Childhood and youth. 2. Brooklyn Dodgers (Baseball team) -- History. 3. Baseball fans 4. Historians -- United States 5. Fathers and daughters. 6. Growing up. 7. Long Island, New York 8. Autobiographies and memoirs

LC 97039766

An eccentric cast of characters populates the autobiography of a young girl who roots for the Brooklyn Dodgers with her father, while her mother suffers from a debilitating illness

"For self-esteem-building female role models, for baseball lore and inning-by-inning action and for a lively trip into the recent American past, you could hardly do better." New York Times Book Review.

Gopnik, Adam

Gopnik, Adam **At** the strangers' gate : arrivals in New York / Adam Gopnik. Alfred A. Knopf, 2017. 272 p. **B**

ISBN 9781400041800

1. Gopnik, Adam Family. 2. City life 3. Authors 4. Husband and wife 5. Books and reading 6. New York City -- Social life and customs -- 20th century. 7. Autobiographies and memoirs

LC 2017016651

"This is a Borzoi book."

The award-winning writer and best-selling author presents a portrait of 1980s New York City to chronicle how its role as a pilgrimage site for young, artistic and ambitious residents was shaped by cultural luminaries, increasing elitism and uneven economic dynamics.

Gorbachev, Mikhail, 1931-

★Taubman, William **Gorbachev** : his life and times / William Taubman. W.W. Norton & Company, 2017. xxv, 852 p. **B**

ISBN 9780393647013

1. Heads of state -- Soviet Union 2. Presidents 3. Cold War 4. Social change 5. Soviet Union -- Politics and government -- 1985-1991 6. Biographies

LC 2017015009

Longlisted for the Andrew Carnegie Medal for Excellence in Non-Fiction, 2018.

National Book Critics Circle Award for Biography finalist, 2017

An extensive portrait of the transformational world leader examines his liberal policies of perestroika and glasnost, his role in ending the Cold War and his unintentional oversight over the collapse of the Soviet Union.

"Taubman (political science, Amherst College) has written a monumental, groundbreaking study of Soviet President Mikhail Sergeyevich Gorbachev." Choice.

Gordievsky, Oleg

★Macintyre, Ben, 1963- The **spy** and the traitor : the greatest espionage story of the Cold War / Ben Macintyre. Crown Publishing, 2018. viii, 358 p. : **B**

ISBN 9781101904190

1. Ames, Aldrich Hazen, 1941- 2. KGB 3. M I 6 4. CIA 5. Cold War 6. Double agents 7. Spies -- Soviet Union 8. Intelligence service -- Soviet Union 9. Biographies

LC 2018024662

Gold Dagger Award for Best Nonfiction of the Year, 2019.

Traces the story of Russian intelligence operative Oleg Gordievsky, revealing how his secret work as an undercover MI6 informant helped hasten the end of the Cold War.

"In a feat of real authorial dexterity, Macintyre accurately portrays the long-game banality of spycraft--the lead time and persistence in planning--with such clarity and propulsive verve that the book often feels like a thriller." Publishers Weekly.

Gorey, Edward, 1925-2000

Dery, Mark **Born** to be posthumous : the eccentric life and mysterious genius of Edward Gorey / Mark Dery. Little Brown & Co, 2018. 496 p. **B**

ISBN 9780316188548

1. Recluses 2. Eccentrics and eccentricities 3. Avant-garde (Aesthetics) 4. Artists 5. United States -- Social life and customs -- 20th century 6. Biographies

LC bl2018192296

The definitive biography of Edward Gorey, the eccentric master of macabre nonsense.

Gornick, Vivian

Gornick, Vivian **Unfinished** business : notes of a chronic re-reader / Vivian Gornick. Farrar, Straus and Giroux, 2020. 160 p. **B**

ISBN 9780374282158

1. Women journalists 2. Books and reading 3. Literature -- History and criticism 4. Change (Psychology) 5. Essays

LC 2019020323

A celebration of passionate reading, of returning again and again to the books that have shaped her at crucial points in her life. In nine essays that traverse literary criticism, memoir, and biography, one of our most celebrated critics writes about the importance of reading--and re-reading--as life progresses.

"Among our most distinguished critics, Gornick uses nine essays blending literary analysis, depth-plumbing memoir, and biography to reconsider the books that have shaped her life." Library Journal

Gotch, Jen, 1971-

Gotch, Jen, 1971- The **upside** of being down : how mental health struggles led to my greatest successes in work and life / Jen Gotch. Gallery Books, 2020. 288 p. **B**

ISBN 9781982108816

1. Businesspeople -- United States 2. People with bipolar disorder 3. Creativity 4. Bipolar disorder 5. Autobiographies and memoirs

LC 2019045250

The founder of the multimillion-dollar lifestyle brand ban.do discusses her history of mental illness and how once it was properly diagnosed, helped to lead her towards a new life of self-awareness, success and joy.

"Anyone who's ever dealt with mental illness will appreciate this forthcoming and empathetic volume." Publishers Weekly

Gottlieb, Lori

Gottlieb, Lori **Maybe** you should talk to someone : a therapist, HER therapist, and our lives revealed / Lori Gottlieb. Houghton Mifflin Harcourt, 2019. 320 p. **B**

ISBN 9781328662057

1. Gottlieb, Lori Health. 2. Psychotherapists. 3. Self-discovery in women. 4. Purpose in life. 5. Psychotherapist and patient. 6. Autobiographies and memoirs.

LC 2018042562

The national advice columnist presents a behind-the-scenes tour of a therapist's world from the perspective of both a patient and a psychotherapist who found answers in her client's journeys.

"Saturated with self-awareness and compassion, this is an irresistibly addictive tour of the human condition." Kirkus.

Gottlieb, Robert, 1931-

Gottlieb, Robert, 1931- **Avid** reader : a life / Robert Gottlieb. Farrar, Straus and Giroux, 2016. 384 p. **B**

ISBN 9780374279929

1. Editors 2. Periodical editors. 3. Publishers and publishing. 4. Books and reading. 5. Autobiographies and memoirs

LC 2015048673

Includes index.

The editor-in-chief of Simon & Schuster writes with wit and candor about becoming the editor of The New Yorker, and the challenges and satisfactions of running America's preeminent magazine.

Gottlieb, Sidney, 1918-1999

Kinzer, Stephen **Poisoner** in chief : Sidney Gottlieb and the CIA search for mind control / Stephen Kinzer. Henry Holt & Company, 2019. 352 p. **B**

ISBN 9781250140432

1. Project MKULTRA 2. CIA -- History 3. Brainwashing 4. Hallucinogenic drugs 5. Human experimentation in medicine 6. Scientists 7. Biographies

LC 2019007076

The award-winning foreign correspondent and author of *All the Shah's Men* documents the remarkable story of the brilliant but controversial chemist who oversaw the CIA's secret drug and mind-control experiments of the mid-20th century.

Gould, Florence, 1895-1983

Ronald, Susan A **dangerous** woman : American beauty, noted philanthropist, Nazi collaborator-- the life of Florence Gould / Susan Ronald. St. Martin's Press, 2018. 416 p. **B**

ISBN 9781250092212

1. Gould, Florence, 1895-1983. 2. Nazi collaborators 3. Socialites. 4. Philanthropists. 5. Americans in Paris, France 6. Biographies

LC bl2017049997

A portrait of the wealthy socialite and patron of the arts details her marriage to railroad heir Frank Jay Gould and her role in creating a luxury hotel and casino empire before becoming a Nazi collaborator in World War II Paris.

"Although Florence's letters and photographs were inaccessible to the author, Ronald compensates with layers of research into the period and surrounding players. While the dense historical detail may deter lay readers, history lovers will welcome this impressive book about a captivating, flawed woman." Publisher's Weekly.

Goya, Francisco, 1746-1828

Hughes, Robert, 1938-2012 **Goya** / Robert Hughes. Alfred A. Knopf, 2003. x, 429 p. : **B**

ISBN 0394580281

1. Goya, Francisco, 1746-1828. 2. Goya, Francisco, 1746-1828 Criticism and interpretation. 3. Men who are deaf 4. Artists -- Spain 5. Spain -- History -- 18th century. 6. Spain -- History -- 19th century. 7. Biographies

LC 2002043281

ALA Notable Book, 2005."

This is a remarkably vital, delectably discursive, and deeply affecting study." Booklist.

★Tomlinson, Janis A. **Goya** : a portrait of the artist / Janis A. Tomlinson. Princeton University Press, 2020 388 p. **B**

ISBN 9780691192048

1. Painters -- Spain 2. Painting, Spanish 3. Painting, Modern 4. Modern art 5. Biographies

LC 2019041721

The life of Francisco Goya (1746-1828) coincided with an age of transformation in Spanish history that brought upheavals in the country's politics and at the court which Goya served, changes in society, the devastation of the Iberian Peninsula in the war against Napoleon, and an ensuing period of political instability. Janis Tomlinson draws on a wide range of documents--including letters, court papers, and a sketchbook used by Goya in the early years of his career--to provide a nuanced portrait of a complex and multifaceted painter and printmaker, whose art is synonymous with compelling images of the people, events, and social revolution that defined his life and era.

"Tomlinson's meticulous distillation of a voluminous number of parish records, drawings, notes, and letters is impressive, and her knowledge of and passion for Goya continually shine through in her writing, making for a fascinating and insightful reading experience. A top-notch biography." Kirkus

Grace, Princess of Monaco, 1929-1982

Jorgensen, Jay, 1964- **Grace** Kelly : Hollywood dream girl / Jay Jorgensen and Manoah Bowman ; designed by Stephen Schmidt. Dey St., 2017 287 p. : **B**

ISBN 9780062643339

1. Grace, Princess of Monaco, 1929-1982 Pictorial works 2. Motion picture actors and actresses -- United States -- Pictorial works 3. Princesses -- Monaco -- Pictorial works

LC 2017278738

"A stunning gallery of more than 400 prized and rare photographs and illustrations, precious childhood snapshots, previously unpublished Edith Head and Helen Rose wardrobe sketches, original portraits, scene stills, on-set candids, wardrobe test shots, vintage magazine covers, and rare reproductions of exhibitor's showmanship manuals showing how film studios marketed Grace Kelly as a star, Grace Kelly captures this beloved luminary's eternal beauty as never before, and is a fresh, celebratory look at herremarkable career and her enduring cultural influence".-- provided by publisher.

Graham, Ashley,

Graham, Ashley, A **new** model : what confidence, beauty, and power really look like / Ashley Graham with Rebecca Paley. Dey Street Books, [2017] xxiii, 198 pages, 8 unnumbered pages of plates : **B**

ISBN 9780062667946

1. Graham, Ashley, 1987- 2. Body image 3. Fashion models 4. Self-acceptance 5. Overweight women 6. Autobiographies and memoirs

LC bl2017011778

The outspoken plus-sized model and body image activist presents a collection of provocative essays that chronicle her life in fashion and offer insight into how ideas around body image are and are not evolving in today's culture.

"Positive, understanding, and uplifting." Booklist.

Graham, Billy, 1918-2018

Martin, William C. (William Curtis), 1937- **Prophet** with honor : the Billy Graham story / William Martin. Zonderkidz, c2013. 144 p. : **B**

ISBN 9780310719359

1. Evangelists -- United States 2. Clergy 3. Evangelicalism. 4. Evangelists. 5. United States -- Religious life and customs -- 20th century 6. Biographies

LC 2009054208

Chronicles Graham's ascent from revivalist preacher to world-reknowned evangelist and discusses Graham's changing views, his relationship with world leaders, his professional accomplishments, and his personal life.

Wacker, Grant, 1945- **America's** pastor : Billy Graham and the shaping of a nation / Grant Wacker. The Belknap Press of Harvard University Press, 2014. 413 p. ; **B**

ISBN 9780674052185

1. Christianity and culture -- United States -- History -- 20th century. 2. Evangelistic work (Christianity) 3. Evangelists 4. Clergy 5. United States 6. Biographies

LC 2014014155

Examines the life of Billy Graham and how he impacted American culture by successfully tapping into broader cultural trends.

"Wacker doesnt shrink, however, from showing how Graham's fascination with presidential politics led him astray repeatedly while allowing that he was a genuine spiritual counselor to the presidents--Lyndon Johnson, in particular. If a great subject deserves a great book, Billy Graham has one." Booklist.

Graham, Mark (Mark A.)

Dreazen, Yochi The **invisible** front : love and loss in an era of endless war / Yochi Dreazen. Crown, 2014. 384 p. **B**

ISBN 9780385347839

1. Graham, Mark (Mark A.) Family. 2. United States. Army 3. Generals -- United States 4. Military psychology. 5. Sons -- Death. 6. Attitudes toward people with mental illnesses 7. United States -- Social conditions. 8. Biographies.

LC 2014007360

An award-winning journalist traces the story of how a military family has channeled grief into advocacy on behalf of victims of mental illness in the aftermath of losing one of their sons in a roadside bombing and the other to suicide.

"Mental health care workers, sociologists, and military historians will find this book a useful first step in a much larger conversation. Readers dealing with mental health issues can take comfort in knowing they are not alone, and others may find motivation in the stories Dreazen relates to help generate change." Library Journal.

Grahame, Kenneth, 1859-1932

Dennison, Matthew The **man** in the willows : the life of Kenneth Grahame / Matthew Dennison. Pegasus Books, 2019. 352 p. **B**

ISBN 9781643130071

1. Grahame, Kenneth, 1859-1932. Wind in the willows. 2. Authors, British 3. Children's literature authors 4. Nature in literature 5. Rural life 6. England 7. Biographies

LC 2018276650

A biography of the author of the children's classic The Wind in the Willows celebrates how the secretary of the Bank of England was inspired by his pastoral wanderings in his country house with his fanciful wife and fragile son.

"Dennisons account of all this is sympathetic but honest, psychologically acute and insightful. It is, withal, a sad story but one that Dennison tells extremely well to his and Grahames credit." Booklist.

Grande, Lance

Grande, Lance **Curators** : behind the scenes of natural history museums / Lance Grande. The University of Chicago Press, 2017. 432 p. **B**

ISBN 9780226192758

1. Grande, Lance. 2. Field Museum of Natural -- History, Chicago. 3. Natural history museum curators. 4. Natural history museums. 5. Excavations (Paleontology) 6. Biologists. 7. Autobiographies and memoirs.

LC 2016032596

Natural history curators oversee the worlds libraries of life, and themselves are full of life and colorful characters. In these pages, readers will get to experience time in the field collecting and identifying, and the magic that happens back at home, as collections are curated, exhibits are mounted, and museum curators engage the public.

"Grande's illumination of the evolving role of the natural history museum and of collection curators completes this passionate memoir and celebration of an essential public resource." Booklist.

Grandmaster Flash

Grandmaster Flash The **adventures** of Grandmaster Flash : my life, my beats / Grandmaster Flash with David Ritz. Harlem Moon, c2008. 272 p. **B**

ISBN 0767924754

1. Grandmaster Flash. 2. Grandmaster Flash and the Furious Five 3. Rap musicians -- United States 4. African American rap musicians 5. African-American disc jockeys 6. African American men -- Family relationships 7. South Bronx, New York City -- Social life and customs -- 20th century 8. South Bronx, New York City -- Social life and customs -- 21st century 9. Autobiographies and memoirs

LC 2007048224

A luminary in the world of hip hop music and a revered musical icon offers a firsthand look at the early days of the hip hop revolution and documents his own musical journey from the mean streets of the

South Bronx, detailing his rise to musical stardom, financial disaster and cocaine addiction, and ultimate redemption with the love of family and friends.

"Grandmaster Flash is best known in conjunction with the Furious Five, the first hip-hop artists inducted into the Rock and Roll Hall of Fame. But before the fame, Joseph Robert Saddler was born into an abusive family in the Bronx. His evolution from a kid spinning records in the streets to hip-hop stardom is an inspiring story filled with heartbreak, determination, and perseverance." Library Journal.

Grant, Cary, 1904-1986

Eyman, Scott, 1951- **Cary** Grant : a brilliant disguise / Scott Eyman. Simon & Schuster, 2020. xi, 556 p. **B**

ISBN 9781501192111

1. Grant, Cary, 1904-1986. 2. Film actors and actresses 3. Men -- England. 4. Acting 5. Interpersonal relations 6. United States 7. Biographies

LC 2020001234

A heavily researched portrait of the Hollywood legend that includes coverage of Grant's early start as a teen acrobat, his complicated relationships and his Golden Era performances.

"Combining existing research with voluminous new interviews and access to Grant's personal papers, this is an informative and entertaining biography of a legendary actor." Library Journal

Grant, Gail Milissa, 1949-

Grant, Gail Milissa, 1949- **At** the elbows of my elders : one family's journey toward civil rights / Gail Milissa Grant. Missouri History Museum : c2008. xix, 251 p. : **B**

ISBN 9781883982669

1. Grant, Gail Milissa, 1949- Family. 2. African American families -- Saint Louis, Missouri 3. Segregation -- United States -- History -- 20th century 4. Civil Rights Movement 5. African Americans -- Civil rights -- History -- 20th century 6. St. Louis, Missouri -- History -- 20th century 7. St. Louis, Missouri -- Race relations 8. United States -- Race relations -- History -- 20th century. 9. Autobiographies and memoirs

LC 2008024219

"This is a fascinating look at the struggles of one black family that mirrored the national struggle for civil rights." Booklist.

Grant, Ulysses S., 1822-1885

★Brands, H. W. The **man** who saved the union : Ulysses Grant in war and peace / H. W. Brands. Doubleday, c2012. 718 p., 16 p. of plates : **B**

ISBN 9780385532419

1. Presidents -- United States 2. Generals -- United States 3. United States -- History -- 19th century 4. Biographies

LC 2011043795

Includes index.

Map on endpapers.An analysis of Ulysses Grant's contributions during the Civil War and his presidency covers his defense of black civil rights, his controversial willingness to sacrifice troops to win, and the heated criticism of his Reconstruction policies.

Bunting, Josiah, 1939- **Ulysses** S. Grant / Josiah Bunting III. Times Books, 2004. xx, 180 p. : American presidents series (Times Books) **B**

ISBN 9780805069495

1. Grant, Ulysses S., 1822-1885. 2. Presidents -- United States 3. United States -- Politics and government -- 1869-1877. 4. Biographies

LC 2004047889

Traces the life and presidency of Ulyssses S. Grant and discusses why he was undervalued as a president.

"This superb book should support those who are gradually moving Grant from the lower to the upper half of rankings of chief executives." Publishers Weekly.

★Chernow, Ron **Grant** / Ron Chernow. Penguin Press, 2017. 928 p. **B**

ISBN 9781594204876

1. Grant, Ulysses S., 1822-1885. 2. Presidents. 3. Generals. 4. United States Civil War, 1861-1865 5. Command of troops 6. United States -- History -- Civil War, 1861-1865 7. United States -- Politics and government -- 1869-1877. 8. Biographies

LC 2017025263

ALA Notable Book, 2018.

Longlisted for the Andrew Carnegie Medal for Excellence in Non-Fiction, 2018.

Presents a meticulously researched portrait of the complicated Civil War general and 18th President, challenging the views of his critics while sharing insights into his prowess as a military leader, the honor with which he conducted his administration and the rise and fall of his fortunes.

"In this sympathetic biography, the author continues the revival of Grant's reputation. At nearly 1,000 pages, Chernow delivers a deeply researched, everything-you-ever-wanted-to-know biography, but few readers will regret the experience." Kirkus.

★Grant, Ulysses S., 1822-1885 The **annotated** memoirs of Ulysses S. Grant / edited with an Introduction by Elizabeth D. Samet. Liveright Publishing Corporation, a division of W. W. Norton & Company, [2019] 1024 p. **B**

ISBN 9781631492440

1. United States. Army 2. Generals -- United States 3. Presidents -- United States 4. United States -- History -- Civil War, 1861-1865 -- Campaigns. 5. United States -- History -- Civil War, 1861-1865 6. United States -- History -- 19th century 7. Autobiographies and memoirs

LC 2018029962

Originally published in 1885 by Mark Twain, this newly annotated edition of General Grant's biography provides detailed historical and cultural contexts to create a more vivid picture of the Civil War era.

"The end result is a very rich reading experience that highlights unexpected connections between events in the text, its historical moment, and its connections to larger cultural themes." Publishers Weekly.

Grant, Ulysses S., 1822-1885 **Memoirs** and selected letters : personal memoirs of U.S. Grant, selected letters 1839-1865 / Ulysses S. Grant. Library of America, 1990. 2 volumes in 1 (1199 pages) : **B**

ISBN 9780940450585

1. Grant, Ulysses S., 1822-1885. 2. United States. Army 3. Generals -- United States 4. Presidents -- United States 5. Biographies

LC 90060013

Letters from Grant to his wife, fellow officers, and government officials accompany his account of his life as a soldier, from West Point to the end of the Civil War

★White, Ronald C. (Ronald Cedric), 1939- **American** Ulysses : a life of Ulysses S. Grant / Ronald C. White, Jr. Random

House, 2016. 816 p. **B**
ISBN 9781400069026
1. Grant, Ulysses S., 1822-1885. 2. Presidents. 3. Generals. 4. United States Civil War, 1861-1865 5. Command of troops 6. United States -- History -- Civil War, 1861-1865 7. United States -- Politics and government -- 1869-1877. 8. Biographies
LC 2015044513

A profile of the Civil War general and eighteenth U.S. president challenges his historical unpopularity, drawing on years of research with primary documents to explore Grant's character as one of generosity, curiosity, and introspection.

"The author portrays a humble, gentle, independent soula writer, in the end, who found his voice writing his extraordinary memoirs just before his death in 1885. An engaging resurrection of Grant featuring excellent maps and character sketches." Kirkus.

Graves, Anthony, 1965-

Graves,Anthony, 1965- **Infinite** hope : how wrongful conviction, solitary confinement and 12 years on death row failed to kill my soul / Anthony Graves. Beacon Press, 2018. 224 p. **B**
ISBN 9780807062524
1. Judicial error. 2. Death row prisoners 3. Criminal justice system. 4. Criminal law. 5. Autobiographies and memoirs
LC 2017035843

Infinite Hope is an argument against the death penalty through one man's personal story. It is about a man enduring a life on death row year after year, when he knows that he is one hundred percent innocent and that his exoneration is unlikely.

"A well-written, matter-of-fact, inspirational account of how a man prevailed against a criminal justice system that is deeply flawed." Kirkus.

Gray, Hanna Holborn

Gray, Hanna Holborn An **academic** life : a memoir / Hanna Holborn Gray. Princeton University Press, 2018. 352 p. **B**
ISBN 9780691179186
1. University of Chicago Presidents 2. Women historians 3. Women college teachers 4. Higher education 5. Universities and colleges 6. Biographies
LC 2017036151

A compelling memoir by the first woman president of a major American university.

Graziano, Rocky, 1922-1990

Sussman, Jeffrey **Rocky** Graziano : fists, fame, and fortune / Jeffrey Sussman. Rowman & Littlefield, [2018] 208 p. **B**
ISBN 9781538102619
1. Boxers (Sports) 2. Boxing 3. Former convicts 4. Athletes 5. Biographies
LC 2017035354

Rocky Graziano, juvenile delinquent, middleweight boxing champion, and comedic actor, was the last great fighter from the golden age of boxing, the era of Joe Louis, Jake LaMotta, and Sugar Ray Robinson. The first biography of Graziano in over 60 years, this book will bring his inspiring story to a new generation of boxing fans.

Green, CeeLo

Green, CeeLo **Everybody's** brother : my story / CeeLo Green with Big Gipp and David Wild Grand Central Pub., 2013 304 p. **B**
ISBN 9781455516674
1. Green, CeeLo. 2. Singers 3. Hip hop culture 4. Musicians 5. Autobiographies and memoirs
LC 2013942951

Describes the life of the vibrant, genre-breaking musician, reality show star, record producer and actor from his difficult childhood in Georgia to his early career with the critically-acclaimed Goodie Mob and through his success with Gnarles Barkley and solo efforts.

Green, Kristen

Green, Kristen **Something** must be done about Prince Edward county : a family, a Virginia town, a civil rights battle / Kristen Green. Harpercollins, 2015 349 p. **B**
ISBN 9780062268679
1. Green, Kristen. 2. School integration 3. Family secrets 4. Race relations 5. Civil rights movement 6. Prince Edward County, Virginia 7. Racism 8. Autobiographies and memoirs
LC 2015295454

Combining hard-hitting investigative journalism and a sweeping family narrative, this provocative true story reveals a little-known chapter of American history: the period after the Brown v. Board of Education decision when one Virginia school system refused to integrate.

"Green's work brims with real-life detail from the journalist's eye and ear and joins the likes of Diane McWhorter's Carry Me Home in further developing the dimensions of the South's desegregation struggleparticularly from the perspective of white communitiesfor general readers and scholars of the late 20th-century civil rights movement." Library Journal.

Green, Robin

Green, Robin The **only** girl : my life and times on the masthead of Rolling Stone / Robin Green. Little Brown & Co 2018 304 p. **B**
ISBN 9780316440028
1. Rolling Stone Magazine 2. Women journalists 3. Periodicals 4. Popular culture -- History -- 1970-1979 5. Sexism in employment 6. Autobiographies and memoirs
LC 2018935533

The only woman writer on the masthead of <I>Rolling Stone</I> magazine in the early 70s provides a raucous and vividly dishy memoir.

"Reading like a real-life road novel, Green's memoir is a must for aspiring writers." Library Journal.

Green, Ryan Speedo

★Bergner, Daniel **Sing** for your life : a story of race, music, and family / Daniel Bergner. Little Brown & Co, 2016 320 p. **B**
ISBN 9780316300674
1. Opera singers 2. Life change events. 3. Child abuse 4. Teenage abuse victims. 5. Virginia 6. Biographies
LC bl2016035233

A chronicle of a young black man's journey from violence to the world's elite opera circles describes Ryan Speedo Green's abuse-marked upbringing and struggles with racism and imprisonment before winning a New York Metropolitan Opera competition.

Greene, Jayson

★Greene, Jayson **Once** more we saw stars : a memoir / Jayson Greene. Alfred A. Knopf, 2019. 256 p. **B**
ISBN 9781524733537
1. Greene, Jayson Family. 2. Children -- Death -- Psychological aspects 3. Bereavement -- Psychological aspects 4. Fathers 5. Grief 6. Manhattan, New York City 7. New York City 8. Autobiographies and memoirs
LC 2018013866

"This is a Borzoi book."

Devastated by his 2-year-old daughter's accidental death, a father in Upper West Side Manhattan navigates unendurable pain and taps the healing power of love to rebuild his shattered family.

"After suffering an unimaginable loss, the author's ability to pursue fatherhood again while still honoring the daughter he lost is a testament to the resilience of the human spirit and its capacity to love. Heartbreaking and inspiring." Library Journal.

Greene, Kate, 1979-

Greene, Kate, 1979- **Once** upon a time I lived on Mars : space, exploration, and life on Earth / Kate Greene. St Martin's Press, 2020 228 p. ; **B**

ISBN 9781250159472

1. United States. National Aeronautics and Space Administration 2. Journalists 3. Social isolation 4. Space sciences -- Research 5. Human behavior 6. Essays 7. Autobiographies and memoirs

An essay collection inspired by the author's four-month stay inside NASA's simulated Martian habitat explores such subjects as humanity's drive to explore, a sibling's disability, the lag time of interplanetary correspondence and the challenges of long-distance marriage.

"Poet and science journalist Greene writes of isolation, deprivation, and boredom in this enlightening account of her sojourn in a habitat mimicking the conditions of a future Mars mission." Publishers Weekly

Greenlaw, Linda, 1960-

Greenlaw, Linda, 1960- The **hungry** ocean : a swordboat captain's journey / Linda Greenlaw. Hyperion, 1999. xiii, 265 p. : **B**

ISBN 0786864516

1. Fishing boat captains 2. Women fishing boat captains 3. Women fishers 4. Ship captains. 5. Newfoundland and Labrador. 6. Canada. 7. Autobiographies and memoirs

LC 98051985

"The author details a 30-day swordfishing trip from Gloucester to the Grand Banks. Greenlaw describes her boat, equipment, and various electronic gear, including the 'temperature bird' that is lowered to measure the temperature at the fishing depth, as well as her technique for finding just the right area to fish. An exciting and detailed look inside the commercial fishing industry." Library Journal.

Greenspan, Alan, 1926-

Greenspan, Alan, 1926- The **age** of turbulence : adventures in a new world / Alan Greenspan. Penguin Press, 2007. 531 p. : **B**

ISBN 1594201315

1. Government economists -- United States. 2. Economists. 3. Economics. 4. United States -- Economic conditions -- 1945- 5. Autobiographies and memoirs

LC 2007013169

The former Federal Reserve Board chairman reveals the financial close call that nearly resulted in an economic disaster after September 11, his efforts to safeguard American interests, and the personal and educational history that informed his choices.

"The former U. S. Federal Reserve Board chair relates his life story, focusing on lessons learned in government service, particularly post-9/11. He also includes political anecdotes, asserts his faith in market capitalism, and shares his predictions for the world of 2030." Library Journal.

Mallaby, Sebastian The **man** who knew : the life and times of Alan Greenspan / Sebastian Mallaby. Penguin Press, 2016. 704 p. **B**

ISBN 9781594204845

1. Board of Governors of the Federal Reserve System (U.S.) 2. Government economists 3. Economists. 4. Monetary policy. 5. Biographies

LC 2016017300

"A Council on Foreign Relations Book."

Traces the life and career of one of the most important economic statesmen of the modern era, describing the array of business and government positions that led to his chairmanship of the Federal Reserve and how the financial crisis of 2008 damaged his reputation.

"He has written a masterful, detailed portrait of one of the leading economic figures of our time." Publishers Weekly.

Woodward, Bob, 1943- **Maestro** : Greenspan's Fed and the American boom / Bob Woodward. Simon & Schuster, 2000. 270 p., 16 p. of plates : **B**

ISBN 0743204123

1. Board of Governors of the Federal Reserve System (U.S.) 2. Economists -- United States 3. Government economists -- United States 4. Monetary policy -- History -- 20th century. 5. Economics. 6. United States -- Economic conditions. 7. Biographies

LC 00052627

Chronicles economic policy through the Clinton presidency, focusing on the role of Alan Greenspan, and discussing Wall Street, technology, and other factors to explain how the current economic arena came into being.

"In a surprisingly short book, Woodward lucidly explains the axes of intellectual and political disagreement over monetary policy, productivity growth, irrational exuberance and more, shedding new light on major conflicts of the Greenspan era and demystifying this most political of ostensibly technical institutions." New York Times Book Review.

Gregory, Rebekah

Gregory, Rebekah **Taking** my life back : my story of faith, determination, and surviving the Boston Marathon bombing / Rebekah Gregory, with Anthony Flacco. Revell, 2017. 320 p. **B**

ISBN 9780800728212

1. Gregory, Rebekah. 2. Boston Marathon Bombing, Boston, Mass., 2013. 3. Boston Marathon 4. People who have had amputations 5. Convalescence. 6. Autobiographies and memoirs

LC 2016048311

A spectator at the 2013 Boston Marathon bombing who suffered the loss of her leg and incurred other debilitating injuries while protecting her son explores how her lengthy journey to recovery has compelled her to explore her faith in unique ways and advanced her resolve to live a meaningful life.

"This is a truly feel-good book that doesnt stint on the challenges that life throws at us." Publishers Weekly.

Grenier, Robert (Robert L.)

Grenier, Robert (Robert L.) **88** days to Kandahar : a CIA diary / Robert L. Grenier. Simon & Schuster, [2014] 288 p. **B**

ISBN 9781476712079

1. CIA 2. Taliban 3. Afghan War, 2001-, American. 4. Intelligence officers -- United States 5. CIA agents 6. United States -- Foreign relations Pakistan 7. Afghanistan -- Politics and government -- 21st century. 8. Pakistan -- Foreign relations United States 9. Autobiographies and memoirs.

LC 2014036555

Includes index.

The director of the American-Afghan war describes how he orchestrated the defeat of the Taliban in the region by forging separate alliances with warlords, Taliban dissidents, and the Pakistani intelligence service.

"This eye-opening account of how things really work in the Middle East and in modern war will appeal to general readers and those interested in political science, war memoirs, contemporary battle accounts, American history, Middle Eastern politics, and books about spies/covert operations." Library Journal.

Gretzky, Wayne, 1961-

Gretzky, Wayne, 1961- **99** : stories of the game / Wayne Gretzky. G. P. Putnam's Sons, 2016 320 p. **B**

ISBN 9780399575471

1. Hockey players. 2. Hockey. 3. Professional hockey 4. Professional hockey players 5. Autobiographies and memoirs

LC 2016036048

One of the greatest sports figures of all time offers candid reflections on the mentors, teammates, and rivals who inspired him and discusses famous moments in hockey history from the viewpoint of one who created many of those moments.

Grey, Jane, Lady, 1537-1554

Tallis, Nicola **Crown** of blood : the deadly inheritance of Lady Jane Grey / Nicola Tallis. Pegasus Books, 2016. 384 p. **B**

ISBN 9781681772448

1. Grey, Jane, Lady, 1537-1554. 2. Tudor, House of 3. Women rulers -- Great Britain 4. Great Britain -- Rulers -- Succession. 5. Great Britain -- History -- Edward VI, 1547-1553. 6. Great Britain -- History -- Mary I, 1553-1558. 7. England -- History -- 16th century 8. Great Britain -- History -- Tudors, 1485-1603 9. Biographies

LC bl2016047401

A history of Lady Jane Grey's often-misunderstood trial and execution places events against a backdrop of the dangerous plots and political intrigues of her time, examining her qualities as a charismatic advocate and martyr of the Protestant faith.

"Readers will share Talli's sympathy with the devout, passive Jane but also approve of her emphasis on the more powerful, ambitious, and unpleasant men and women that surrounded her." Kirkus.

Grey, Joel, 1932-

Grey, Joel, 1932- **Master** of ceremonies : a memoir / Joel Grey. Flatiron Books, 2016. 320 p. **B**

ISBN 9781250057235

1. Actors and actresses 2. Theater -- New York City 3. Jewish-Americans 4. Photographers -- United States 5. Autobiographies and memoirs

LC 2015040157

The Broadway star and Academy Award-winning performer best known for his iconic role as the irascible emcee in Cabaret traces his remarkable life story, documenting his Jewish-American upbringing in 1930s Cleveland, childhood roles, rise to fame and challenging losse

"The diminutive, unforgettable creator of the emcee in Cabaret both on stage and on screen writes frankly of his diverse career, exacting mother, and public embrace of his homosexuality." Kirkus.

Grey, Zane, 1872-1939

Pauly, Thomas H. **Zane** Grey : his life, his adventures, his women / Thomas H. Pauly. University of Illinois Press, 2005. xi, 385 p. : **B**

ISBN 9780252030444

1. Grey, Zane, 1872-1939. 2. Grey, Zane, 1872-1939 Relations with women. 3. Authors, American -- 20th century 4. Adventurers -- United States 5. Extramarital affairs 6. Biographies

LC 2005009413

The first accurate and thorough biography of the man behind the myths of the Old West.

"Pauly explores all facets of the novelist while avoiding devoting too much time to mining the man's novels for nuggets of his life. Grey's personal passions informed his novels, but his books were not mere fictionalized bits and pieces of his life. He was a man who stood apart from his work, and Pauly brings that man robustly to life." Booklist.

Griesinger, Robert Arnold

Lee, Daniel, 1983- The **S.S.** officer's armchair : uncovering the hidden life of a Nazi / Daniel Lee. Hachette Books, 2020. xiv, 303 pages : **B**

ISBN 9780316509091

1. Griesinger, Robert Arnold. 2. Nationalsozialistische Deutsche Arbeiter-Partei. -- Schutzstaffel -- Officers. 3. Nazis 4. Nazism. 5. World War II -- Germany. 6. Germany -- History -- 1933-1945. 7. Biographies

LC 2020935814

Investigates the life of a Stuttgart lawyer-turned-World War II S.S. officer who played a role in the murder of the author's family in the Holocaust.

"Lee's granular focus reveals the mechanisms by which ordinary Germans were drawn into horrific crimes. Even those well-versed in the history of the Holocaust will learn something new." Publishers Weekly

Groberg, Florent, 1983-

Groberg, Florent, 1983- **8** seconds of courage : a soldier's story from immigrant to the Medal of Honor / Flo Groberg and Tom Sileo. Simon & Schuster, 2017. 304 p. **B**

ISBN 9781501165887

1. United States. Army. 2. Afghan War, 2001-, American. 3. Soldiers. 4. Medal of Honor. 5. Immigrants. 6. Autobiographies and memoirs

LC bl2017036478

A personal account by the first immigrant in four decades to receive the Congressional Medal of Honor describes his childhood relocation from France to the U.S., where as a naturalized citizen he joined the military and served multiple tours before he was wounded while protecting his patrol from a suicide bomber.

"In this short, candid book, Groberg . offers insight into the profound sense of duty that drives members of the military while celebrating one man's extraordinary courage." Kirkus.

Grogan, John, 1957-

★Grogan, John, 1957- **Marley** & me : life and love with the world's worst dog / John Grogan. Morrow, 2005. xi, 291 p. : **B**

ISBN 9780060817084

1. Labrador retrievers 2. Dogs as pets. 3. Men and dogs. 4. Dogs. 5. Florida.

LC 2005040010

"Dog lovers will love this account of Grogan's much loved canine." Publishers Weekly.

Grossi, Craig

Grossi, Craig **Craig** & Fred : a Marine, a stray dog, and how they rescued each other / Craig Grossi. William Morrow & Company, 2017. 224 p. **B**

ISBN 9780062693389

1. Dogs 2. Marines 3. Humans and dogs 4. Human/animal relationships 5. Afghanistan 6. Autobiographies and memoirs

LC bl2017033341

A Marine Corps veteran and Purple Heart recipient shares the story of his friendship with a stray dog he met on an Afghan battlefield and how, against military regulations, he worked to bring the dog home, where the pair battled PTSD and began touring America to work with veteran programs.

"Death, violence, and fear are a constant in the battlefield, but Grossi manages to find humor in the midst of horror and life after loss...Positive, encouraging, and inspirational." Kirkus.

Groves, Leslie Richard, 1896-1970

Norris, Robert S. (Robert Stan) **Racing** for the bomb : General Leslie R. Groves, the Manhattan Project's indispensable man / Robert S. Norris. Steerforth Press, c2002. xxi, 722 p. : **B**

ISBN 1586420399

1. Groves, Leslie Richard, 1896-1970. 2. Manhattan Project (U.S.) 3. Generals -- United States 4. Military engineers -- United States 5. Nuclear weapons -- United States -- History. 6. United States -- History, Military -- 20th century. 7. Biographies

LC 2001057629

Follows the World War II race to build the atomic bomb while profiling its top commander, documenting how Colonel Groves drove countless individuals to collecting the necessary funds and materials as well as orchestrated solutions to thousands of technical problems.

"This work will not only serve scholars and general readers equally well but also take its place among the handful of best books about the birth of the atomic age." Booklist.

Gruen, Bob

Gruen, Bob **Right** place, right time : the life of a rock & roll photographer / Bob Gruen. Abrams Press, 2020. xiv, 380 p. : **B**

ISBN 9781419742132

1. Gruen, Bob. 2. Photographers 3. Rock music industry and trade 4. Photographs 5. Rock musicians 6. United States 7. Autobiographies and memoirs

For more than fifty years Gruen has documented the music scene in pictures that have captured the world's attention. Here he tells of his winding, adventure-filled journey in a series of wildly entertaining stories. Gruen offers a unique window into the evolution of American music culture over the last five decades. -- adapted from jacket

"Rock fans will devour this narrative and find its 'you are there' style eminently palpable." Library Journal

Grynszpan, Herschel Feibel, 1921-approximately 1943

Koch, Stephen, 1941 **Hitler's** pawn : the boy assassin and the Holocaust / Stephen Koch. Counterpoint, 2019. 256 p. **B**

ISBN 9781640091443

1. Vom Rath, Ernst, 1909-1938 Assassination 2. Political prisoners 3. Assassins -- France 4. Refugees, Jewish -- France 5. Propaganda 6. Biographies

LC 2018018729

Tells the story of a forgotten 17-year-old Jew who was blamed by the Nazis for the anti-Semitic violence and terror known as the Kristallnacht, the pogrom still seen as an initiating event of the Holocaust.

Gubar, Susan, 1944-

Gubar, Susan, 1944- **Late-life** love : a memoir / Susan Gubar. W.W. Norton & Company, 2018. 272 p. **B**

ISBN 9780393609578

1. Senior women 2. Senior couples 3. Senior romance 4. Seniors -- Psychology 5. Autobiographies and memoirs

LC bl2018183431

An acclaimed writer contemplates and celebrates her relationship with her husband, describing how she learned to confront and deal with the many obstacles faced by senior couples including retirement, adult children, sexuality, and memory issues.

Gubar, Susan, 1944- **Memoir** of a debulked woman : enduring ovarian cancer / Susan Gubar. W.W. Norton, c2012. xiii, 296 p. : **B**

ISBN 9780393073256

1. Gubar, Susan, 1944- Health. 2. Women with ovarian cancer 3. Ovarian cancer. 4. Women with cancer 5. People with cancer 6. Autobiographies and memoirs

LC 2011053073

A woman living with ovarian cancer describes going through debulking surgery, during which parts or whole organs in the lower abdomen are removed, and searches for understanding and offers hope and support to other people in need.

Gucci Mane, 1980-

Gucci Mane, 1980- The **autobiography** of Gucci Mane / with Neil Martinez-Belkin. Simon & Schuster, 2017. 288 p. **B**

ISBN 9781501165320

1. Rap musicians 2. Hip-hop culture 3. Former convicts 4. Addiction 5. Alabama 6. Atlanta, Georgia 7. Autobiographies and memoirs

LC 2017019427

Includes index.

A highly anticipated memoir by the prolific hip-hop artist traces his unlikely path to stardom and personal rebirth, discussing his early years in Alabama and Georgia, his activities as a drug dealer, the experiences that inspired his influential street anthems and his recent prison term.

"Atlanta has always played a significant role in shaping the sound and culture of rap and hip-hop, and the influence of Gucci Mane (n Radric Davis) can't be overstated. .This autobiography, written while he was serving time in a federal prison for possession of a firearm, paints a rich portrait." School Library Journal.

Guevara, Che, 1928-1967

Anderson, Jon Lee **Che** Guevara : a revolutionary life / Jon Lee Anderson. Grove Press, 1997. xv, 814 p. : **B**

ISBN 9780802116000

1. Guevara, Che, 1928-1967. 2. Guerrillas -- Latin America 3. Revolutionaries -- Latin America 4. Revolutions -- Latin America. 5. Latin America -- History -- 20th century. 6. Biographies

LC 97003993

Shortlisted for the James Tait Black Memorial Prize for Biography, 1997

A thorough biography, based on unique access to government documents and extensive interviews with those close to the infamous Latin American rebel, traces Che Guevara's life from its privileged roots to struggles in Cuba and Bolivia.

Guevara, Che, 1928-1967 **Diary** of a combatant : from the Sierra Maestra to Santa Clara, Cuba, 1956-58 / Ernesto Che Guevara ; edited by Maria del Carmen Ariet. Ocean Press, 2013. 358 p., 40 p. of plates : **B**

ISBN 0987077945

1. Guevara, Che, 1928-1967. 2. Cuba -- History -- 1933-1959. 3. Cuba -- Politics and government -- 1933-1959. 4. Autobiographies and memoirs.

LC 2011943989

Translation of: Diario de un combatiente : de la Sierra Maestra a Santa Clara, 1956-1958.

Guggenheim, Peggy, 1898-1979

★Gill, Anton **Art** lover : a biography of Peggy Guggenheim / Anton Gill. Harper Collins, 2003. xvi, 480 p. ; **B**

ISBN 0060196971

1. Guggenheim, Peggy, 1898-1979. 2. Art -- Collectors and collecting 3. Art patrons 4. Self-perception in women. 5. Rich women 6. United States -- Social life and customs -- 20th century. 7. Europe -- Social life and customs -- 20th century. 8. Biographies

LC 2001051731

"Guggenheim was known as much for her sexual exploits as for her championing of modern art, a fact Gill . examines with candor, sensitivity, and mellifluous grace." Booklist.

Guidry, Ron, 1950-

Guidry, Ron, 1950- **Gator** : my life in pinstripes / Ron Guidry. Crown Archetype, [2017] 288 p. **B**

ISBN 9780451499301

1. New York Yankees (Baseball team) 2. Pitchers (Baseball) -- United States 3. Professional baseball players 4. Professional baseball 5. Baseball players 6. Autobiographies and memoirs

LC 2017040975

Includes index.

A legendary Yankees pitcher reflects on his years playing for one of the most storied teams in sports history, tracing his relationships with such contemporaries as Billy Martin, George Steinbrenner and Reggie Jackson.

Guillermoprieto, Alma, 1949-

Guillermoprieto, Alma, 1949- **Dancing** with Cuba : a memoir of the revolution / Alma Guillermoprieto ; translated from the Spanish by Esther Allen. Pantheon Books, 2004. 290 p. **B**

ISBN 0375420932

1. Guillermoprieto, Alma, 1949- Travel Cuba. 2. Modern dance -- Cuba. 3. Dance teachers 4. Revolutions -- Cuba. 5. Cuba -- Description and travel. 6. Cuba -- History -- 1959-1990 7. Autobiographies and memoirs

LC 2003044200

"Guillermoprieto vividly and purposefully recounts her acute discomfort with the strained and ludicrous rhetoric of the revolution, her sorrow over Castro's catastrophic failures, her astonishment at the great valor of Cuba's people, and her gradual recognition of her true calling as a journalist." Booklist.

Gunn, Paul Irvin, 1899-1957

Bruning, John R. **Indestructible** : one man's rescue mission that changed the course of WWII / John R. Bruning. Hachette Books, 2016. 288 p. **B**

ISBN 9780316339407

1. Gunn, Paul Irvin, 1899-1957. 2. Philippine Airlines Officials and employees 3. World War II -- Aerial operations, American. 4. Pilots -- United States 5. Military aviation 6. Americans in the Philippines 7. Philippines -- History -- Japanese occupation, 1942-1945 8. Biographies

LC 2016021715

Chronicles the story of a renegade American pilot consumed by his personal mission to rescue his family from the Japanese in World War II--a man who happened to change the war's very course along the way.

Gunness, Belle, 1859-1908

Schechter, Harold **Hell's** princess : the mystery of Belle Gunness, butcher of men / Harold Schechter. Little A, 2018. 334 p. **B**

ISBN 9781477808955

1. Women serial murderers 2. Violence in women 3. Serial murders 4. Indiana 5. Biographies

LC 2018276362

Hell's Princess is a riveting account of one of the most sensational killing sprees in the annals of American crime: the shocking series of murders committed by the woman who came to be known as Lady Bluebeard.

"This biography of a prolific and brutal serial killer will be of interest to Midwestern regional history buffs as well as true crime fans." Library Journal.

Guo, Xiaolu, 1973-

Guo, Xiaolu, 1973- **Nine** continents : a memoir in and out of China / Xiaolu Guo. Grove Press, 2017. 366 p. **B**

ISBN 9780802127136

1. Authors, Chinese 2. Growing up 3. Moving to a new city 4. Self discovery in women 5. China 6. Autobiographies and memoirs

LC 2017032639

National Book Critics Circle Award for Autobiography, 2017.

An acclaimed, Chinese-born, modern writer describes how she became a citizen of the world after being raised in a fishing village shack by her grandparents, moving into a thriving underground art scene in Beijing and finally winding up in Europe.

"A rich and insightful coming-of-age story of not only a woman, but an artist and the country in which she was born." Kirkus.

Gurwitch, Annabelle

Gurwitch, Annabelle **Wherever** you go, there they are : stories about my family you might relate to / Annabelle Gurwitch. Blue Rider Press, 2017. 304 p. **B**

ISBN 9780399574887

1. Families 2. Family relationships 3. Swindlers and swindling 4. Essays 5. Autobiographies and memoirs

LC 2016052134

The best-selling author of I See You Made an Effort presents a new collection of humorous essays about her family of scam artists, sharing additional insights into the sisterhoods, temporary tribes, communities and cults that have shaped her life.

Gutierrez, Eduardo, 1978-1999

Breslin, Jimmy The **short** sweet dream of Eduardo Gutierrez / Jimmy Breslin. Crown Publishers, 2002. 213 p. **B**

ISBN 0609608274

1. Gutierrez, Eduardo, 1978-1999. 2. Immigrant workers -- New York City 3. Immigrants, Mexican 4. Mexicans in the United States 5. Undocumented workers -- New York City 6. New York City 7. Biographies

LC 2001047283

Includes index.

A portrait of Eduardo Gutierrez, an illegal immigrant worker in the U.S., describes his accidental death in November 1999 at a Brooklyn construction site, in a study of corruption, bad politics, and official indifference.

"A true-life account of an illegal Mexican immigrant who died on a New York construction site, and of the dreary lives and modest ambitions common to Mexicans in this country." New York Times Book Review.

Habsburg, House of

★Rady, Martyn C. The **Habsburgs** : to rule the world / Martyn Rady. Basic Books, 2020. 432 p. B

ISBN 9781541644502

1. Habsburg, House of. 2. Royal houses. 3. Religion and state. 4. Power (Social sciences) 5. Political science. 6. Austria -- History. 7. Holy Roman Empire -- History. 8. Holy Roman Empire -- Civilization. 9. Austria -- Rulers. 10. Spain -- Rulers. 11. Europe -- History. 12. Biographies.

LC 2019042154

Describes the dominance throughout Europe of the Habsburgs, a dynasty that gained control of the Holy Roman Empire in the 1400s and stretched to Hungary and Spain and centuries later to the New World.

"This admirably compact, exceptionally well-written survey will probably be the standard one-volume history of the Habsburg dynasty for years to come." Library Journal

Haddish, Tiffany, 1979-

Haddish, Tiffany, 1979- The **last** black unicorn / Tiffany Haddish. Gallery Books, 2017. 278 p. B

ISBN 9781501181825

1. Women comedians. 2. African Americans. 3. Entertainment industry and trade. 4. African American women comedians 5. Autobiographies and memoirs.

LC 2017038059

The stand-up comedienne presents an uproarious and poignant collection of autobiographical essays that reflect her disadvantaged youth as a foster child in South Central Los Angeles; her discovery of her talent for comedy; and her struggles with gender, race and class boundaries in the entertainment industry.

Hadfield, Chris, 1959-

Hadfield, Chris, 1959- An **astronaut's** guide to life on earth : what going to space taught me about ingenuity, determination, and being prepared for anything / Chris Hadfield. Little, Brown & Co., 2013. 304 p. B

ISBN 9780316253017

1. United States National Aeronautics and Space Administration 2. International Space Station 3. Astronauts. 4. Space flight. 5. Space sciences 6. Former astronauts. 7. Autobiographies and memoirs

LC 2013943519

Astronaut Chris Hadfield, the first Canadian Commander of the International Space Station, presents his own inspiring story and shows how the rest of us can "think like an astronaut" to achieve success and happiness right here on Earth.

"The author emphasizes that becoming an astronaut involved developing physical capabilities and technical skills through tireless practice and a fanatic attention to detail. A page-turning memoir of life as a decorated astronaut." Kirkus.

Hadrian, Emperor of Rome, 76-138

Everitt, Anthony **Hadrian** and the triumph of Rome / Anthony Everitt. Random House, 2009. 432 p. B

ISBN 9781400066629

1. Hadrian, Emperor of Rome, 76-138. 2. Roman emperors 3. Rome -- History -- Hadrian, 117-138. 4. Biographies

LC 2009005683

A meticulously researched profile of the enigmatic Roman emperor places his formative years against a backdrop of first-century events and chronicles his successful efforts to end a century of disorder and warfare. By the best-selling author of Cicero.

"Emperor from 117 to 138 A.D., Hadrian styled himself princeps, or first among equals, and his reversal of his predecessors' expansionist policies contributed to an era of prosperity and relative calm. He was unapologetically Hellenic, a poet and a dabbler in magic, and he kept in his retinue a young male lover whom he later deified. If Hadrian is indeed an enigma, it's because so few accounts of his life have survived, and this is where Everitt--whose books rely heavily on primary sources--runs into difficulty. One gets a clear and compelling sense of Hadrian's times, but the Emperor himself remains tantalizingly unknowable." The New Yorker.

Haffner, Sebastian, 1907-

Haffner, Sebastian, 1907- **Defying** Hitler : a memoir / Sebastian Haffner ; translated from the German by Oliver Pretzel. Farrar, Straus and Giroux, 2002. 309 p. : B

ISBN 0374161577

1. Historians -- Germany 2. Nazism. 3. Germany -- History -- 1918-1933. 4. Autobiographies and memoirs

LC 2002017058

Translation of : Geschichte eines Deutschen.

A memoir on the rise of Nazism in Germany and the lives of ordinary German citizens between the two world wars find the author witnessing such developments as the rise of the First Free Corps, the Hitler Youth movement, the Stresemann years, and Hitler'scoming to power.

"This is a small masterpiece." Booklist.

Hagberg, Eva

Hagberg, Eva **How** to be loved : a memoir of lifesaving friendship / Eva Hagberg Fisher. Houghton Mifflin Harcourt, 2019. 240 p. B

ISBN 9780544991156

1. Hagberg, Eva. 2. People with chronic illnesses 3. People with cancer. 4. Friendship. 5. People with immunologic disease. 6. Autobiographies and memoirs.

LC 2018006363

"A luminous memoir about how friendship saved one woman's life, for anyone who has loved a friend who was sick, grieving, or lost--and for anyone who has struggled to seek help or accept it." Provided by publisher.

" It is the revelation that love can be unconditional and profound that makes this memoir stand out from many similar ones." Kirkus.

Hagel, Chuck, 1946-

Bolger, Daniel P., 1957- **Our** year of war : two brothers, Vietnam, and a nation divided / Daniel P. Bolger. Da Capo Press, 2017. 320 p. B

ISBN 9780306903267

1. Hagel, Tom 2. United States. Department of Defense 3. Vietnam War, 1961-1975. 4. Soldiers 5. Brothers 6. Cabinet officers 7. United States -- History -- 1969- 8. Vietnam -- History -- 1945-1975. 9. Biographies

LC 2017953360

Presents the story of Chuck Hagel--who would one day become U.S. secretary of defense--and his brother, Tom, who went to war in Vietnam, fought in the same unit, and saved each other's life, despite one supporting the war and the other detesting it.

"A crisp account of a messy war, focusing on two Nebraska brothers, one of whom would later become a senator and Secretary of Defense." Kirkus.

Hager, Jenna Bush, 1981-

Hager, Jenna Bush, 1981- **Sisters** first : stories from our wild and wonderful life / Jenna Bush Hager and Barbara Pierce Bush, with a foreword by Laura Bush. Grand Central, 2017 256 p. **B**

ISBN 9781538711415

1. Bush, Barbara Pierce 2. Bush family. 3. Twin sisters. 4. Families -- Political aspects 5. Presidents 6. Growing up

LC 2017471187

The fraternal twin daughters of the 43rd U.S. president share lighthearted and poignant personal stories and reflections from their lives within a powerhouse political dynasty, from their witness to their grandfather's presidency through their subsequent upbringing and work under the eyes of the Secret Service, public and paparazzi.

"The two first daughters emerge as surprisingly well-adjusted, intelligent young women with strong family bonds in this insightful look at life inside the White House." Booklist.

Halbreich, Betty, 1927-

Halbreich, Betty, 1927- **I'll** drink to that : a life in fashion, straight, no chaser / Betty Halbreich, with Rebecca Paley. The Penguin Press, 2014. 320 p. **B**

ISBN 9781594205705

1. Image consultants 2. Clothing 3. Fashion. 4. Beauty 5. Autobiographies and memoirs

LC 2014009695

A personal account by the legendary Bergdorf Goodman personal shopper traces her rise from a cosseted young girl to an influential fashion authority, covering such topics as her difficult marriage, her struggles with depression and her work with Hollywood clients.

"Names are dropped and stories are told in Halbreich's distinctive voice. Fashion mavens will enjoy the industry gossip while mere mortals may benefit from the closet organization tips." Library Journal.

Hale, Robert (Robert Allen), 1941-2008

Kizzia, Tom **Pilgrim's** wilderness : a true story of faith and madness on the Alaska Frontier / Tom Kizzia ; edited by Kevin Doughten. Crown, c2013. 336 p. **B**

ISBN 9780307587824

1. Hale, Robert (Robert Allen), 1941-2008. 2. Criminals 3. Abusive men 4. Dysfunctional families 5. Incest 6. Alaska 7. McCarthy, Alaska

LC 2012016502

Documents the story of Robert "Papa Pilgrim" Hale and the anti-establishment family settlement in remote Alaska that was exposed as a cult-like prison where Hale brutalized and isolated his wife and fifteen children.

"The horror at the heart of this story about religious extremism on the fringes of the last American frontier is slow to reveal itself, but when that horror fully emerges, it will swallow most readers. Provocative and disturbing." Kirkus.

Haley, Alex

Norrell, Robert J. (Robert Jefferson) **Alex** Haley : and the books that changed a nation / Robert J. Norrell. Palgrave Macmillan, 2015 272 p. **B**

ISBN 9781137279606

1. Haley, Alex. 2. African American journalists 3. African American authors 4. Biographies

LC 2015016043

This first biography of Haley follows him from his childhood in relative privilege in deeply segregated small town Tennessee to fame and fortune in high powered New York City. It was in the Navy, that Haley discovered himself as a writer, which eventually led his rise as a star journalist in the heyday of magazine personality profiles. At Playboy Magazine, Haley profiled everyone from Martin Luther King and Miles Davis to Johnny Carson and Malcolm X, leading to their collaboration on The Autobiography of Malcolm X.

"With such a strong focus on the writing of Haley's two major works, this book will appeal primarily to readers who enjoyed or were inspired by The Autobiography of Malcolm X and Roots and wish to learn their backstories." Library Journal.

Hall, Donald, 1928-2018

Hall, Donald, 1928-2018 A **carnival** of losses : notes nearing ninety / Donald Hall. Houghton Mifflin Harcourt, 2018. 144 p. **B**

ISBN 9781328826343

1. Poets 2. Nonagenarians 3. Writing 4. Aging 5. Essays 6. Autobiographies and memoirs

LC 2017049735

Includes index.The noted poet and New York Times best-selling author of Essays After Eighty returns with new reflections on the most recent decade of his life.

Hall, Donald, 1928-2018 **Essays** after eighty / Donald Hall. Houghton Mifflin Harcourt, 2014. 192 p. **B**

ISBN 9780544287044

1. Poets 2. Writing 3. Aging 4. Octogenarians 5. New Hampshire 6. Essays 7. Autobiographies and memoirs

LC 2014016310

A former poet laureate presents a new collection of essays delivering a gloriously unexpected view from the vantage point of very old age.

"America's 14th poet laureate and recipient of the National Medal of the Arts, among countless other honors, Hall offers essays that report meditatively from the 'unknown, unanticipated galaxy' of advanced age. He still lives to write, enjoying life at his ancestral Eagle Pond Farm." Library Journal.

Hall, Sands

★Hall, Sands **Flunk,** start : reclaiming my decade lost in Scientology / Sands Hall. Counterpoint Press, 2018. 368 p. **B**

ISBN 9781619021785

1. Hall, Sands. 2. Scientology 3. Former Scientologists 4. Scientologists 5. Autobiographies and memoirs

LC 2017038728

The compelling story of what drew the author, actress, and musician to Scientology, why she stayed as long as she did, and how she has come to embrace a decade that for years she thought of as lost.

" An early candidate for memoir of the year, this is a thrilling story of one woman's search for truth and her place in the world." Library Journal.

Hallberg, David

Hallberg, David A **body** of work : dancing to the edge and back / David Hallberg. Touchstone, 2017. 400 p. **B**

ISBN 9781476771151

1. Hallberg, David. 2. Bolshoi Ballet Company. 3. Ballet dancers. 4. Ballet. 5. Dancing. 6. Men ballet dancers 7. Autobiographies and memoirs

LC bl2017036576

The first American to join the Bolshoi Ballet as a principal dancer traces his struggles with bullying in childhood, the roles of self-doubt and perfectionism on his performances, and his return from a career-threatening injury.

"Balletomanes and anyone interested in the creative process will appreciate this thoughtful account of the life of an accomplished artist." Booklist.

Halmshaw, Iris Grace

Carter-Johnson, Arabella **Iris** Grace : how Thula the cat saved a little girl and her family / Arabella Carter-Johnson. Skyhorse Publishing, 2017 367 p. **B**

ISBN 9781510719781

1. Carter-Johnson, Arabella 2. Children with autism 3. Human/animal relationships 4. Humans and pets. 5. Cats 6. Autobiographies and memoirs

LC bl2017010839

Describes how a Maine Coon kitten helped a little girl with autism develop the confidence needed to interact with the world.

"Iris story, as told and photographed by her mother, beautifully deciphers the way a child with autism sees and approaches the world, with a deft touch that makes for compelling reading." Booklist.

Hamer, Fannie Lou, 1917-1977

Brooks, Maegan Parker **Fannie** Lou Hamer : America's freedom fighting woman / Maegan Parker Brooks. Rowman & Littlefield, 2020 213 p. **B**

ISBN 9781538115947

1. Hamer, Fannie Lou, 1917-1977. 2. African American women civil rights workers 3. African Americans 4. Civil Rights Movement 5. Civil rights workers 6. Biographies

LC bl2020045808

"Fannie Lou Hamer leapt to America's attention in 1964 when she delivered a stinging indictment of the American promise to the Democratic National Convention. This accessible biography underscores that Hamer's testimony was but one moment within a remarkable life that spanned fifty-nine tumultuous years in the history of American race relations".-- Provided by publisher.

Hamer, Frank, 1884-1955

Boessenecker, John, 1953- **Texas** Ranger : the epic life of Frank Hamer, the man who killed Bonnie and Clyde / John Boessenecker. Thomas Dunne Books, 2016 496 p. **B**

ISBN 9781250069986

1. Hamer, Frank, 1884-1955. 2. Barrow, Clyde, 1909-1934. 3. Parker, Bonnie, 1910-1934. 4. Texas Rangers. 5. Police -- Texas. 6. Law enforcement -- Texas -- History. 7. Biographies

LC 2015048659

Chronicles the life of Frank Hamer, whose extraordinary career as a Texas Ranger made him one of the West's most legendary lawmen.

"Through the extraordinary experiences of this straight-shooting, honor-bound lawman, Boessenecker sets forth a critically needed look at the history of Texas lynchings and race riots while presenting evidence for the murderous nature of Bonnie and Clyde that foreordained their violent deaths." Library Journal.

Hamill, Kirkland

Hamill, Kirkland **Filthy** beasts : a memoir / Kirkland Hamill. Avid Reader Press, 2020. 311 p. **B**

ISBN 9781982122768

1. Hamill, Kirkland Family 2. Rich families 3. Poverty 4. Mothers and sons 5. Family fortunes 6. Bermuda Islands 7. New York City 8. Autobiographies and memoirs

LC bl2020014792

Following a rancorous split from New York's upper-class society, newly divorced Wendy Hamill and her three sons are exiled from the East Coast elite circle. Wendy's middle son, Kirk, is eight when she moves the family to her native Bermuda, leaving the three young boys to fend for themselves as she chases after the highs of her old life: alcohol, a wealthy new suitor, and other indulgences. A fascinating window into the life of extreme privilege and a powerful story of self-acceptance, Filthy Beasts recounts Kirk's unforgettable journey as he confronts his family's many imperfections, accepts his unconventional childhood, and finally comes to terms with his own hidden secrets.

"A stunning, deeply satisfying story about how we outlive our upbringings." Kirkus

Hamilton, Alexander, 1757-1804

★Chernow, Ron **Alexander** Hamilton / Ron Chernow. Penguin Press, 2004. 818 p. **B**

ISBN 9781594200090

1. United States. Secretary of the Treasury. 2. United States. Constitutional Convention (1787) 3. Politicians -- United States 4. United States -- Politics and government -- 1783-1809. 5. Biographies

LC 2003065641

ALA Notable Book, 2005.

National Book Critics Circle Award for Biography finalist, 2004.

The personal life of Alexander Hamilton, an illegitimate, largely self-taught orphan from the Caribbean who rose to become George Washington's aide-de-camp and the first Treasury Secretary of the United States, is captured in a definitive biography.

"Chernow makes fresh contributions to Hamiltoniana: no one has discovered so much about Hamilton's illegitimate origins and harrowed youth; few have been so taken by Hamilton's long-suffering, loving wife, Eliza. This is a fine work that captures Hamilton's life with judiciousness and verve." Publishers Weekly.

Hamilton, Elizabeth Schuyler, 1757-1854

★Mazzeo, Tilar J. **Eliza** Hamilton : the extraordinary life and times of the wife of Alexander Hamilton / Tilar J. Mazzeo. Gallery Books, 2018. 320 p. **B**

ISBN 9781501166303

1. Hamilton, Alexander, 1757-1804 Family 2. Politicians' spouses -- United States 3. Women philanthropists 4. Women and politics 5. Sex scandals 6. Biographies

LC 2018008245

A comprehensive biography of Eliza Hamilton, wife of founding father Alexander Hamilton, chronicles her early years in New York, her married life with Alexander and his tragic death, and her later years as a generous philanthropist.

"Mazzeo (Irena's Children) centers love and devotion in this satisfying cradle-to-grave biography, the first written about the wife of the first U.S. secretary of the treasury." Publishers Weekly.

Hamilton, Gabrielle

Hamilton, Gabrielle **Blood,** bones, and butter : the inadvertent education of a reluctant chef / Gabrielle Hamilton. Random House, c2011. 304 p. ; **B**

ISBN 9781400068722

1. Hamilton, Gabrielle. 2. Cooks -- New York City 3. Restaurateurs -- New York City 4. Cooking. 5. Food habits. 6. New York City. 7. Autobiographies and memoirs

LC 2010017518

James Beard Foundation Book Awards, Writing and Literature, 2012."

Though this book is rhapsodic about foodin every variety, from the humble egg-on-a-roll sandwich served by Greek delis in New York to more esoteric things like fried zucchini agrodolce with fresh mint and hot chili flakesthe book is hardly just for foodies. Ms. Hamilton . is as evocative writing about people and places as she is at writing about cooking." New York Times.

Hamilton, Jeremiah G., -1875

White, Shane **Prince** of darkness : the untold story of Jeremiah G. Hamilton, Wall Street's first black millionaire / Shane White. Palgrave Macmillan, 2015 320 p. **B**

ISBN 9781250070562

1. Hamilton, Jeremiah G., -1875. 2. African American capitalists and financiers 3. African American millionaires 4. African American businesspeople 5. African Americans -- Social conditions -- 19th century. 6. United States -- Race relations -- History -- 19th century. 7. Wall Street, New York City 8. Biographies

LC 2015011416

A prominent historian brings to life the story of a man who defied every convention of his time by becoming Wall Street's first black millionaire in pre-Civil War New York, marrying a white woman, owning railroad stock on trains he was not legally allowed to ride and outsmarting his contemporaries.

"Superb scholarship and a sprightly style recover an unaccountably overlooked life in our history." Kirkus.

Hamilton, Tyler, 1971-

Hamilton, Tyler, 1971- The **secret** race : inside the hidden world of the Tour de France: doping, cover-ups, and winning at all costs / Tyler Hamilton and Daniel Coyle. Bantam Dell, 2012. 304 p. **B**

ISBN 9780345530417

1. Armstrong, Lance 2. Tour de France (Bicycle race) 3. Bicycle racing -- Corrupt practices 4. Doping in sports 5. Athletes -- Drug use. 6. Men with depression 7. Autobiographies and memoirs

LC 2012288990

Hamilton pulls back the curtain on the Tour de France and takes us into the secret world of professional cycling like never before: the doping, the lying, and his years as Lance Armstrong's teammate on U.S. Postal.

Hammarskjold, Dag, 1905-1961

Hammarskjold, Dag, 1905-1961 **Markings** / Dag Hammarskjold ; translated from the Swedish by Leif Sjoberg and W.H. Auden ; foreword by W.H. Auden ; with a new preface by Jimmy Carter. Vintage Books, 2006, c1964. xxiii, 222 p. ; **B**

ISBN 0307277429

1. Hammarskjold, Dag, 1905-1961. 2. United Nations Officials and employees 3. Politicians -- Sweden 4. Biographies

LC 2006041371

Translation of : Vagmarken.Originally published in English: New York : Knopf, 1964.

An inspirational, intimate account of spiritual struggle is based on the personal journal of the U.N. Secretary-General, recording his spiritual growth, self-questioning, and resolutions from 1925 to his untimely death in a plane crash in 1961.

Hampl, Patricia, 1946-

Hampl, Patricia, 1946- The **art** of the wasted day / Patricia Hampl. Penguin Group, 2018 288 p. **B**

ISBN 9780525429647

1. Daydreams 2. Women authors 3. Women's dreams 4. Leisure 5. Autobiographies and memoirs

LC 2017032689

A detailed, thoughtful journey into the necessity of daydreaming and leisure in our continually overbooked lives by making pilgrimages to places of repose and seclusion, including a Benedictine monastery and a trip floating down the Mississippi River in an old cabin cruiser.

"For all the vital, sensuous, enrapturing descriptions that engender a powerful sense of presence, this is also a contemplation of absence and solitude as Hampl tenderly contends with the sudden death of her husband. An exquisite anatomy of mind and an incandescent reflection on nature, being, and rapture." Booklist.

Hampton, Henry, 1940-1998

Else, Jon **True** south : Henry Hampton and "Eyes on the Prize," the landmark television series that reframed the Civil Rights Movement / Jon Else. Viking Press, 2017 352 p. **B**

ISBN 9781101980934

1. Else, Jon 2. Eyes on the prize (Television program) 3. Television programs. 4. civil rights movement 5. Social justice 6. Race (Social sciences) 7. Autobiographies and memoirs 8. Essays.

LC 2016044049

Longlisted for the Andrew Carnegie Medal for Excellence in Non-Fiction, 2018.

Presents the inside story of the making of one of the most important and influential TV shows in history and of its legacy as the film that reframed of the entire history of the Civil Rights movement permanently.

"An illuminating look at racial strife and TV history." Kirkus.

Hampton, Ryan

Hampton, Ryan **American** fix : inside the opioid addiction crisis--and how to end it / Ryan Hampton. St Martins Pr 2018 288 p. **B**

ISBN 9781250196262

1. Addiction 2. Public health 3. Opioid abuse 4. Recovering addicts 5. United States -- Social conditions 6. Autobiographies and memoirs

LC 2018025770

A recovery advocate for the Facing Addiction not-for-profit and former White House staffer traces his own recovery journey while comprehensively explaining the national opioid crisis and his recommendations for addressing it.

"This sobering story by a recovering heroin addict makes a strong case for why tackling the opioid crisis must be a top priority for the country." Booklist.

Hanagarne, Joshua, 1977-

Hanagarne, Joshua, 1977- The **world's** strongest librarian : a memoir of Tourette's, faith, strength, and the power of family / Joshua Hanagarne. Gotham Books, 2013. x, 291 p. ; **B**

ISBN 9781592407873

1. Tourette syndrome 2. Mormons 3. Librarians 4. Tic disorders 5. Autobiographies and memoirs

LC 2012037713

Traces the public librarian author's inspiring story as a Mormon youth with Tourette's Syndrome who after a sequence of radical and ineffective treatments overcame nightmarish tics through education, military service and strength training.

Hanchett, Janelle

Hanchett, Janelle **I'm** just happy to be here : a memoir of renegade mothering / Janelle Hanchett. Hachette Books, 2018. viii, 310 pages ; **B**

ISBN 9780316503778

1. Mothers 2. Motherhood 3. Child rearing 4. Addiction 5. Autobiographies and memoirs

LC 2017952977

From the creator of the blog "Renegade Mothering" a memoir chronicling her tumultuous journey from young motherhood to abysmal addiction and a recovery she never imagined possible.

"Hanchett illuminates how addiction can take over a person's life. She thoughtfully writes about returning to motherhood after periods of absence when her children were young. At times witty, heartbreaking, and enlightening, Hanchett's memoir will resonate with parents and nonparents alike." Booklist.

Handel, Georg Friedrich, 1685-1759

Harris, Ellen T. **George** Frideric Handel : a life with friends / Ellen T. Harris. W. W. Norton & Company, 2014. 496 p. **B**

ISBN 9780393088953

1. Classical music 2. Composers. 3. England -- 18th century 4. Biographies

LC 2014008148

During his lifetime, the sounds of Handel's music reached from court to theater, echoed in cathedrals, and filled crowded taverns, but the man himself - known to most as the composer of Messiah - is a bit of a mystery. Though he took meticulous care of his musical manuscripts and even provided for their preservation on his death, very little of an intimate nature survives.One document - Handel's will - offers us a narrow window into his personal life. In it, he remembers not only family and close colleagues but also neighborhood friends. In search of the private man behind the public figure, Ellen T. Harris has spent years tracking down the letters, diaries, personal accounts, legal cases, and other documents connected to these bequests.

"A readable tale of one of the world's most enigmatic musicians and composers." Publishers Weekly.

Handwerker, Nathan, 1892-1974

Handwerker, Lloyd **Famous** Nathan : a family saga of Coney Island, the American dream, and the search for the perfect hot dog / Lloyd Handwerker, with Gil Reavill. Flatiron Books, 2016 320 p. **B**

ISBN 9781250074546

1. Handwerker, Nathan, 1892-1974. 2. Nathan's Famous. 3. Hot dog stands. 4. Fast food restaurants, chains, etc. 5. Frankfurters. 6. Coney Island, New York City. 7. Biographies

LC 2016001605

Beginning with just five feet of counter space on Coney Island in 1916, Nathan's Famous -- based on the basic principles of quality ingredients, hard work and a price everyone could afford -- soon stretched across the globe, launching the hotdog as an American food staple and Nathan Handwerker to national fame. But the story behind the dog is even tastier... Fleeing Eastern Europe as the shadow of WWI looms large with nothing but twenty dollars in his socks, Nathan arrives in New York with the insatiable desire to make a better life, and within two years he sets up a shop of his own, hawking frankfurters for five cents at the sleepy little beach retreat of Coney Island. As New York booms, pushing trains and patrons to the shore, so too do Nathan's humble hotdogs. Within ten years he has the whole corner, and a brand as recognizable as Coca-Cola and Cracker Jack. Nathan's is famous. But with success comes difficulties, and as Nathan's two sons vie to inherit the family dynasty a story of Biblical proportions plays out, mirroring the corporatization of the American food industry.

Haney, Eric L.

★Haney, Eric L. **Inside** Delta Force : the story of America's elite counterterrorist unit / Eric L. Haney. Delacorte Press, 2002. vii, 324 p., [16] p.of plates : **B**

ISBN 9780385336031

1. United States. Army Commando troops. 2. Green Berets. Delta Force 3. Terrorism -- Prevention. 4. Commando troops 5. Special forces 6. Antiterrorists 7. Biographies 8. Books to TV

LC 2001058408

Adapted into an American television series on CBS (2006-2009): The Unit.

A founding member and veteran of Delta Force goes behind the scenes of the elite counterterrorist unit to describe its grueling selection process, difficult training regimen, and some of its secret missions in various trouble spots around the world.

"The author relates his experiences during the formation and early operations of 1st Special Forces Operational Detachment-Delta. He served three times in Beirut guarding the American ambassador, participated in the invasion of Grenada, served in several Central American countries and narrowly escaped death during the abortive rescue attempt of the American hostages in Iran. Readers of other special forces memoirs will find this one distinctive for Haney's attention to interservice rivalries that he believes compromised several missions, as well as for Haney's nuanced, often disgusted descriptions of the human cost of war." Publishers Weekly.

Hannibal, 247 B.C.-182 B.C.

Hunt, Patrick **Hannibal** / Patrick N. Hunt. Simon & Schuster, 2017. 384 p. **B**

ISBN 9781439102176

1. Generals 2. Command of troops 3. Punic War, 2nd, 218-201 B.C. 4. Military campaigns 5. Carthage (Extinct city) 6. Rome -- History -- Republic, 265-30 B.C. 7. Biographies

LC 2016051474

A portrait of the ancient-world commander includes discussions of his childhood under a master strategist father, his leadership during the Second Punic War and his famed crossing of the Alps with his army and war elephants in an epic battle against Rome.

"This easily digestible and engrossing biography is ideal for general readers with an interest in ancient history." Booklist.

Hansberry, Lorraine, 1930-1965

Nemiroff, Robert **To** be young, gifted, and black : Lorraine Hansberry in her own words / adapted by Robert Nemiroff ; with original drawings and art by Miss Hansberry ; and an introduction by James Baldwin. Signet Classics, 2011, c1969. 271 p. : **B**

ISBN 9780451531780

1. Hansberry, Lorraine, 1930-1965. 2. Women dramatists, American -- 20th century 3. African American dramatists -- 20th century 4. African Americans -- Drama

LC bl2012007490

Originally published: Englewood Cliffs, N.J. : Prentice-Hall, 1969.

Detailing the black experience in mid-twentieth-century America, this candid biography features selections from the works of the late African-American playwright, including play excerpts, autobiographical sketches, poetry, and drawings.

Perry, Imani, 1972- **Looking** for Lorraine : the radiant and radical life of Lorraine Hansberry / Imani Perry. Beacon Press, 2018. 256 p. **B**

ISBN 9780807064498

1. Dramatists, American 2. African American dramatists 3. African American women civil rights workers 4. African American women 5. Biographies

LC 2017055552

Lambda Literary Award for LGBTQ Nonfiction, 2019.

The Hughes-Rogers Professor of African American Studies at Princeton University provides powerful insight into the extraordinary life of the author of A Raisin in the Sun.

"Perrys ardent, expert, and redefining work of biographical discovery brings light, warmth, scope, and enlightening complexity to the spine-straightening story of a brilliant, courageous, seminal, and essential American writer." Booklist.

Hansen, Suzy, 1977-

Hansen, Suzy, 1977- **Notes** on a foreign country : an American abroad in a post-American world / Suzy Hansen. Farrar, Straus and Giroux, 2017. 256 p. **B**

ISBN 9780374280048

1. Hansen, Suzy, 1977- Travel. 2. Foreign correspondents. 3. Americans in Turkey. 4. United States -- Foreign relations Turkey. 5. Turkey -- Foreign relations United States. 6. Autobiographies and memoirs

LC 2016059415

Includes index.

Pulitzer Prize for General Nonfiction finalist, 2018.

In 2007 journalist Suzy Hansen moved to Istanbul, Turkey on a fellowship. Assuming that the rest of the world views the US as generous and benevolent, she was shocked to learn otherwise. In Notes on a Foreign Country, Hansen describes how an ignorance of history and international affairs inform many American self-perceptions. Recalling what she learned about US foreign policy during years spent in the eastern Mediterranean region, Hansen starkly illuminates the problems caused by Americans' unawareness of the rest of the world.

"A mostly illuminating literary debut that shows how Americans' ignorance about the world has made turmoil and terrorism possible." Kirkus.

Harding, Ian, 1986-

Harding, Ian, 1986- **Odd** birds / Ian Harding. St. Martin's Press, 2017. 320 p. **B**

ISBN 9781250117076

1. Bird watching -- Anecdotes. 2. Actors and actresses 3. Bird watchers 4. Determination in men 5. Hollywood, California 6. Autobiographies and memoirs

LC 2017001939

This memoir from an avid birdwatcher and star of Pretty Little Liars discusses his passion as a nature lover and his life's path to celebrity through a series of heartfelt stories, each one featuring a particular bird.

"Harding recounts with charm and enthusiasm his road to success as an actor (including the semester he had to spend portraying a jellyfish) and his rediscovery of the joys of birding." Booklist.

Harding, Thomas, 1968-

Harding, Thomas, 1968- **Kadian** journal : a father's memoir / Thomas Harding. Picador USA, 2017. 288 p. **B**

ISBN 9781250065094

1. Accidental death. 2. Fathers and sons 3. Grief 4. Accidents. 5. Autobiographies and memoirs

LC 2016039171

In July 2012, Thomas Harding's fourteen-year-old son Kadian was killed in a bicycle accident. Shortly afterwards Thomas began to write. This book is the result. Beginning on the day of Kadian's death, and continuing to the one-year anniversary, and beyond, Kadian Journal is a record of grief in its rawest form, and of a mind in shock and questioning a strange new reality.

"Both eloquent and heart-rending, Harding's book is not only a grieving father's testament of love to his dead son. It is also a reminder of the fragility of life and human relationships. An emotionally raw and uncompromising memoir." Kirkus.

Hardwick, Elizabeth, 1916-

Hardwick, Elizabeth, 1916- The **collected** essays of Elizabeth Hardwick / Elizabeth Hardwick ; edited and with an introduction by Darryl Pinckney. New York Review Books, 2017 400 p. **B**

ISBN 9781681371542

1. Civil rights movement 2. Intellectual life 3. Literature -- History and criticism 4. Essays 5. Autobiographies and memoirs

LC 2017014041

Elizabeth Hardwick was one of America's great postwar women of letters, celebrated as a novelist and as an essayist. Until now, however, her slim but remarkable achievement as a writer of short stories has remained largely hidden, with her work tucked away in the pages of the periodicals--such as Partisan Review, The New Yorker, and The New York Review of Books--in which it originally appeared. This first collection of Hardwick's short fiction reveals her brilliance as a stylist and as an observer of contemporary life.

"This wonderful volume of essays about place and time is recommended for libraries with large literature and women's studies collections." Library Journal.

Hardy, Jason Matthew

★Hardy, Jason Matthew The **second** chance club : hardship and hope after prison / Jason Hardy. Simon & Schuster, 2020. 288 p. **B**

ISBN 9781982128593

1. Parolees 2. Parole officers 3. Former convicts -- Rehabilitation 4. Criminals -- Rehabilitation. 5. Louisiana 6. Autobiographies and memoirs

LC 2019035155

A former parole officer shines a bright light on a huge yet hidden part of our justice system through the intertwining stories of seven parolees striving to survive the chaos that awaits them after prison in this illuminating and dramatic book.

"A powerful, necessary book with revelatory passages on nearly every page." Kirkus

Hardy, Thomas, 1840-1928

Hardy, Thomas, 1840-1928 The **collected** letters of Thomas Hardy : further letters 1861-1927 / edited by Michael Millgate and Keith Wilson. Clarendon Press, 2012. 317 p. ; **B**

ISBN 9780199607754

1. Hardy, Thomas, 1840-1928 Correspondence. 2. Authors, English -- 19th century 3. Authors, English -- 20th century 4. Letters

LC 77030355

Includes indexes.

Tomalin, Claire **Thomas** Hardy / Claire Tomalin. Penguin Press, 2007. xxv, 486 p., 16 p. of plates : **B**

ISBN 9781594201189

1. Authors, English -- 19th century 2. Authors, English -- 20th century 3. London, England -- Social life and customs -- 19th century 4. Biographies

LC 2007295886

National Book Critics Circle Award for Biography finalist, 2007.

A portrait of the enigmatic nineteenth-century novelist and poet discusses his humble origins, rise through the London literary scene, and efforts to challenge the sexual and religious conventions of his time.

Hari, Daoud

Hari, Daoud The **translator** : a tribesman's memoir of

Darfur / Daoud Hari. Random House, 2008. 224 p. **B**

ISBN 1400067448

1. Hari, Daoud. 2. Torture 3. Genocide 4. Translators -- Darfur, Sudan 5. Life change events 6. Sudan -- History -- Darfur Conflict, 2003-, Sudanese. 7. Autobiographies and memoirs

LC 2007042308

A young Zaghawa tribesman from the Darfur region of the Sudan describes his escape from the attack that destroyed his village, his struggle for survival, his role as a translator and the dangers he confronted, his ultimate capture, and his new life.

Harjo, Joy, 1951-

Harjo, Joy, 1951- **Crazy** brave : a memoir / Joy Harjo. W. W. Norton, c2012. 208 p. **B**

ISBN 9780393073461

1. Native American women poets. 2. Imagination in women. 3. Self-discovery in women. 4. Identity (Psychology) 5. Autobiographies and memoirs

LC 2012011198

This memoir from the Native American poet and author of She Had Some Horses describes her youth with an abusive stepfather, becoming a single teen mom and how she struggled to finally find inner peace and her creative voice.

Harkness, Ruth

★Croke, Vicki The **lady** and the panda : the true adventures of the first American explorer to bring back China's most exotic animal / Vicki Constantine Croke. Random House, 2005. xix, 372 p. : **B**

ISBN 0375507833

1. Harkness, Ruth. 2. Women explorers 3. Women zoologists 4. Giant panda. 5. Giant panda -- China. 6. China. 7. Biographies

LC 2004051356

"This well-written, exhaustively researched and documented book should be on every library's shelves." Library Journal.

Harper, Michele

Harper, Michele The **beauty** in breaking : a memoir / Michele Harper. Riverhead Books, 2020. xiv, 284 p. ; **B**

ISBN 9780525537380

1. Harper, Michele. 2. Emergency physicians 3. Self-care 4. Psychic healing 5. Medical care 6. Autobiographies and memoirs

LC 2019022440

A female, African American ER physician describes how her own life and encounters with her patients led her to realize that every human is broken and recognizing that and moving towards a place of healing can bring peace and happiness.

"Poignant, helpful, and encouraging, Harper's lessons from life in and outside of the emergency room ultimately teach readers how to trust the healing process." Library Journal

Harpham, Heather Elise, 1967-

Harpham, Heather Elise, 1967- **Happiness** : the crooked little road to semi-ever after: a memoir / Heather Harpham. Henry Holt & Company, 2017. 320 p. **B**

ISBN 9781250131560

1. Harpham, Heather Elise, 1967- Health 2. Newborn Infants 3. Blood -- Diseases 4. Parent and child 5. People with blood disease 6. Autobiographies and memoirs

LC 2016040488

Published in the UK by Oneworld Publications, 2018.

A California girl with wanderlust whose opposites-attract relationship with a homebody writer was significantly compromised by an unplanned pregnancy describes how their baby's serious health disorder prompted the couple to reevaluate their views of family and what they were willing to risk for their child's health.

"Harpham has written a heartfelt exploration of familial bonds and the sometimes incredibly bumpy journey one must take to get to contentment." Publishers Weekly.

Harris, Kate, 1982-

Harris, Kate, 1982- **Lands** of lost borders : a journey on the Silk Road / Kate Harris. Dey Street Books, 2018 320 p. : **B**

ISBN 9780062839343

1. Women travelers 2. Bicycling 3. Voyages and travels. 4. Bicycle touring. 5. Silk Road -- Description and travel. 6. Autobiographies and memoirs

Charles Taylor Prize for Literary Non-Fiction (Canada), 2019.

An Oxford-trained scientist and award-winning writer presents an evocative travelogue and memoir of her journey by bicycle along the Silk Road and how it became synonymous with humanity's exploration of boundaries.

Harris, Neil Patrick, 1973-

Harris, Neil Patrick, 1973- **Neil** Patrick Harris : choose your own autobiography / Neil Patrick Harris. Crown Archetype, 2014. 256 p. **B**

ISBN 9780385346993

1. Actors and actresses -- United States 2. Television actors and actresses -- United States 3. Drama. 4. Singers -- United States 5. Plot-your-own stories. 6. Autobiographies and memoirs. 7. Second person narratives

LC 2014016637

The Emmy Award-winning star of How I Met Your Mother shares his experiences as a child star, Broadway performer and father in an over-the-top, humorous account creatively designed in the style of the popular interactive adventure series.

Harrison, George, 1943-2001

Thomson, Graeme (Writer on music) **George** Harrison : behind the locked door / Graeme Thomson. Overlook Omnibus, 2015 464 p. **B**

ISBN 9781468310658

1. Harrison, George, 1943-2001. 2. Beatles (Musical group) 3. Rock musicians -- England 4. Guitarists 5. Rock groups. 6. Filmmakers. 7. Biographies.

Draws on interviews to track the Beatle through his many changes and conflicts, from schoolboy guitarist to global superstar, and examines his struggle to walk a spiritual path while avoiding the temptations of fame.

"Thomson is especially compelling in his illumination of Harrison's inner life, his robust spirituality, and his deep love of Indian culture." Booklist.

Harrison, Joan, 1907-1994

Lane, Christina **Phantom** lady : Hollywood producer Joan Harrison, the forgotten woman behind Hitchcock / Christina Lane. Chicago Review Press, 2020. 384 pages, 18 unnumbered pages of plates : **B**

ISBN 9781613733844

1. Harrison, Joan, 1907-1994. 2. Hitchcock, Alfred, 1899-1980 Friends and associates. 3. Women film producers and directors 4. Women screenwriters. 5. Women television producers and directors

6. Film actors and actresses. 7. England 8. Hollywood, California 9. Biographies

LC 2019041981

Phantom Lady chronicles the untold story of Joan Harrison, Hollywood's most powerful female writer-producer of the 1940?s. Alfred Hitchcock's confidante and the Oscar-nominated screenwriter of his first American film, Rebecca, she was one of his closest collaborators, critically shaping his brand as the "master of suspense." Forging an image as "the female Hitchcock," Harrison went on to produce numerous Hollywood features before becoming a television pioneer as the producer of Alfred Hitchcock Presents.

"Harrison's story is a compelling one. This superbly written, absorbing biography of a woman succeeding on her own terms will resonate with fans of Hollywood stories, as well as those who appreciate celebrations of previously unsung women." Library Journal

Harrison, Kathryn

Harrison, Kathryn The **kiss** / Kathryn Harrison. Random House, c1997. 207 p. ; **B**

ISBN 9780679449997

1. Women authors -- 20th century 2. Authors, American 3. Incest 4. Adult children -- Family relationships. 5. Autobiographies and memoirs

LC 97153826

The author recounts her sexual affair with her long-absent father, who reappeared when she was in her twenties, and the suffering and eventual readjustment that followed.

Harrison, Kathryn **On** Sunset : a memoir / Kathryn Harrison. Doubleday, [2018] 304 p. **B**

ISBN 9780385542678

1. Harrison, Kathryn Childhood and youth. 2. Authors, American 3. Grandparent and child 4. Growing up 5. California 6. Autobiographies and memoirs

LC 2018019959

The author recounts her childhood in a fading mansion near above Sunset Boulevard and being raised by her eccentric grandfather, a former Alaskan fur-trader, and her grandmother, a Jewish merchant in Shanghai, where she was courted exiled Russian princes.

"Evocative and tender, this delightful memoir pairs the distant past with a safe and sacred time in the authors young life." Publishers Weekly.

Harrison, William Henry, 1773-1841

Collins, Gail **William** Henry Harrison : the 9th president, 1841 / Gail Collins. Times Books/Henry Holt and Co., 2012. 176 p. American presidents series (Times Books) **B**

ISBN 9780805091182

1. Harrison, William Henry, 1773-1841. 2. Whig Party. 3. Presidential election, 1840 4. Political campaigns 5. Politicians. 6. Governors -- Indiana 7. United States -- Politics and government -- 1841-1845. 8. United States -- History -- 1783-1865. 9. Biographies

LC 2011018976

Assesses the president's political career and month-long term in office, including his considerable contributions to the War of 1812 and his role in making permanent changes to the campaign process.

"Although more a journalist than a historian, Collins has done her homework and written a lively, opinionated portrait of early-19th-century America and the modestly talented general who briefly became president." Kirkus.

Harry, Debbie

★Harry, Debbie **Face** it / Debbie Harry. Dey Street Books, 2019. 304 p. **B**

ISBN 9780060749583

1. Harry, Debbie. 2. Blondie (Musical group) 3. Sexual violence victims 4. New wave musicians. 5. Women rock musicians 6. New wave music 7. New York City 8. Autobiographies and memoirs

LC bl2019022982

Complemented by rare photos, a memoir by the iconic performance artist traces seven decades in the entertainment industry while discussing her professional collaborations, struggles with addiction, near-escape from Ted Bundy and Blondie alter-ego.

Harryhausen, Ray

Harryhausen, Ray The **art** of Ray Harryhausen / Ray Harryhausen & Tony Dalton ; with a foreword by Peter Jackson. Billboard Books, 2006, c2005. xi, 230 p. : **B**

ISBN 0823084000

1. Harryhausen, Ray. 2. Animators -- United States 3. Film producers and directors -- United States 4. Autobiographies and memoirs

LC 2005930364

Companion vol. to Ray Harryhausen, an animated life, 2004.

Includes index."First published in Great Britain 2005 by Aurum Press Ltd., London"--T.p. verso."The text is fun and informative, but the main feast here is the art, and the reproductions of the concept drawings and photos of the models are superb." Library Journal.

Hart, Carl

Hart, Carl **High** price : a neuroscientist's journey of self-discovery that challenges everything you know about drugs and society / Carl Hart. HarperCollins 2013 320 p. **B**

ISBN 9780062015884

1. Self-discovery in men 2. Change (Psychology) 3. Neuroscientists 4. College teachers 5. Miami, Florida 6. Autobiographies and memoirs

LC bl2013021952

"An eye-opening, absorbing, complex story of scientific achievement in the face of overwhelming odds." Kirkus.

Hart, Hannah, 1986-

Hart, Hannah, 1986- **Buffering** : unshared tales of a life fully loaded / Hannah Hart. HarperCollins 2016 240 p. **B**

ISBN 9780062457516

1. YouTubers 2. Personal conduct 3. Essays 4. Autobiographies and memoirs

LC bl2016034866

The popular YouTube personality and author of the best-selling My Drunk Kitchen presents a collection of personal narrative essays on faith, family, love, sexuality, self-worth and friendship.

Hart, Kevin, 1979-

Hart, Kevin, 1979- **I** can't make this up : life lessons / Kevin Hart, with Neil Strauss. Simon & Schuster 2017 256 p. **B**

ISBN 9781501155567

1. Comedians 2. African American men 3. Men and success 4. Determination in men 5. Autobiographies and memoirs

LC 2016478508

The award-winning actor and comedian presents an inspirational memoir on the importance of believing in oneself, sharing stories about the addiction and abuse that marked his childhood and how his unique way of looking at the world enabled his survival and successful career.

"A truthful, self-deprecating, and funny look at the hard work behind Harts success." Booklist.

Hartke, Austen

Hartke, Austen **Transforming** : the Bible and the lives of transgender Christians / Austen Hartke. Westminster John Knox Press, 2018. 198 p. **B**

ISBN 9780664263102

1. Trans men 2. Christian men 3. Transgender persons 4. Gender nonconformity 5. Autobiographies and memoirs

LC 2017050167

"Its an informative and illuminating quest, supplemented by an extensive appended list of further reading and resources. This is an important book that fills an urgent need. " Booklist.

Harvey, Samantha, 1975-

Harvey, Samantha, 1975- The **shapeless** unease : a year of not sleeping / Samantha Harvey. Grove Press, 2020. 192 p. **B**

ISBN 9780802148827

1. Insomnia 2. Insomniacs 3. Sleep 4. Health 5. Autobiographies and memoirs

LC 2020010114

First published in 2020 in the United Kingdom by Jonathan Cape, an imprint of Vintage.

The author of The Wilderness describes her year-long bout with insomnia, which was not helped with medication, therapy nor changes in diet or sleeping arrangements in an immersive exploration of memory, writing, influence, the will to survive and death.

"Sleeplessness gets the Susan Sontag illness-as-metaphor treatment in this pensive, compact, lyrical inquiry into the author's nighttime demons. . . . An exquisitely rendered voyage." Kirkus

Hassouri, Paria, 1973-

Hassouri, Paria, 1973- **Found** in transition : a mother's evolution during her child's gender change / Paria Hassouri, MD. New World Library, 2020 215 p. **B**

ISBN 9781608687084

1. Transgender children 2. Parents of transgender children 3. Gender identity 4. Transitioning (Gender identity) 5. Autobiographies and memoirs

LC 2020022089

In this autobiographical narrative, an Iranian-American pediatrician and mother of three is blindsided when one of her children comes out as transgender. As the author grapples with her child's transition from male to female, she is forced to re-examineher ideas of parenting, gender, and personal identity.

"A unique parenting story that has plenty to say about families in general." Kirkus

Hatcher, John Bell

Dingus, Lowell **King** of the dinosaur hunters : the life of John Bell Hatcher and the discoveries that shaped paleontology / Lowell Dingus. Pegasus Books, 2018. 336 p. **B**

ISBN 9781681778655

1. Paleontologists 2. Paleontology -- History 3. Dinosaurs 4. Skeleton 5. Biographies

LC bl2018195446

The acclaimed paleontologist and co-author of Walking on Eggs traces the story of "King of Collectors" John Bell Hatcher, detailing his extraordinary expeditions and pivotal contributions to the world's most significant discoveries and collections.

Hatshepsut, Queen of Egypt 1503-1482 B.C.

Cooney, Kara The **woman** who would be king : Hatshepsut's rise to power in Ancient Egypt / Kara Cooney. Crown, 2014. 320 p. **B**

ISBN 9780307956767

1. Women rulers -- Egypt. 2. Pharaohs 3. Ancient Egypt -- History -- Eighteenth dynasty, ca. 1570-1320 B.C. 4. Biographies

LC 2014000243

A portrait of the longest-reigning woman pharaoh in Ancient Egypt draws on surviving artifacts to consider her unprecedented rise, her achievements and why most of her monuments were destroyed after her death.

"By examining her subject within the context of the stringent gender restrictions of her time and place, [Cooney] attempts to explain the motivations and the thought processes of one of the most successful female leaders of the ancient world." Booklist.

Havel, Vaclav

Havel, Vaclav **To** the Castle and back / Vaclav Havel ; translated from the Czech by Paul Wilson. Alfred A. Knopf, 2007. 383 p. ; **B**

ISBN 0307266419

1. Presidents -- Czechoslovakia 2. Communism. 3. Nationalism -- Czechoslovakia 4. Czechoslovakia -- Politics and government -- 1989-1992. 5. Czech Republic -- Politics and government -- 1993- 6. Autobiographies and memoirs

LC 2007004413

Includes interview with Karel Hvížďala.

The former president of the Czech Republic details his odyssey from dissident playwright to politician, and offers his thoughts on communism, the future of the European Union, the role of national identity in today's world, the war in Iraq, and the United States.

Zantovsky, Michael **Havel** : a life / Michael Zantovsky. Grove, 2014 512 p. **B**

ISBN 9780802123152

1. Presidents -- Czechoslovakia 2. Communism. 3. Dramatists 4. Politicians 5. Czechoslovakia -- Politics and government -- 1989-1992. 6. Czech Republic -- Politics and government -- 1993- 7. Biographies

LC 2015430681

Zantovsky lends a more impartial eye to Havel's subsequent 10-year term as president of the newly formed Czech Republic, when he was no longer at Havel's side, and to the travails of his last years. This moving, perceptive chronicle succeeds in showing the many dimensions of a towering 20th-century figure." Publishers Weekly.

Hawa Abdi, 1947-

Hawa Abdi, 1947- **Keeping** hope alive : one woman, 90,000 lives changed / Hawa Abdi with Sarah J. Robbins. Grand Central Pub., 2013. 240 p. **B**

ISBN 9781455503766

1. Women human rights activists -- Somalia 2. Human rights activists -- Somalia 3. Women gynecologists -- Somalia 4. Gynecologists -- Somalia 5. Somalia 6. Autobiographies and memoirs

LC 2012041781

A memoir by a Nobel Prize nominee about her efforts to advocate on behalf of tens of thousands of fellow citizens in Somalia describes how her physician daughters and she founded a large-scale camp for displaced people from war-torn Mogadishu.

Hawking, Stephen, 1942-2018

Hawking, Stephen, 1942-2018 **My** brief history / Stephen

Hawking. Bantam Books, [2013] 127 p. : **B**

ISBN 9780345535283

1. Physicists -- Great Britain 2. Cosmology. 3. People with disabilities. 4. Physics. 5. Autobiographies and memoirs

LC 2013027938

The famous physicist details the events of his life and career, including attending Oxford and Cambridge, his ALS diagnosis, his study of black holes, and his penning of the bestselling "A Brief History of Time."

"Hawking says it all with charm, intermingling his personal life with abstruse theoretical physics in nontechnical language. Revealing the power of mind over body, this is an enjoyable, entertaining, and inspiring work." Choice.

Mlodinow, Leonard, 1954- **Stephen** Hawking : a memoir of friendship and physics / Leonard Mlodinow. Pantheon Books, 2020 240 p. **B**

ISBN 9781524748685

1. Hawking, Stephen, 1942-2018. 2. Mlodinow, Leonard, 1954- 3. Scientists -- Great Britain 4. Physicists -- Great Britain 5. People with disabilities 6. Friendship 7. Biographies 8. Autobiographies and memoirs

LC 2019049362

The award-winning theoretical physicist and best-selling co-author presents an intimate account of his personal and professional relationship with the late Stephen Hawking throughout nearly two decades of collaborative work.

"This stirring portrait shines a well-deserved spotlight on a little-known victory in the fight for civil rights." Publishers Weekly

Hawthorne, Nathaniel, 1804-1864

Wright, Sarah Bird **Critical** companion to Nathaniel Hawthorne : a literary reference to his life and work / Sarah Bird Wright. Facts On File, c2007. viii, 392 p. : **B**

ISBN 0816055831

1. Hawthorne, Nathaniel, 1804-1864 Handbooks, manuals, etc. 2. Authors, American -- 19th century 3. Biographies

LC 2005034648

An encyclopedic guide to the American poet includes critical entries on his works and characters, biographical information, and influential people and places in his life.

Hayden, Jennifer

Hayden, Jennifer The **story** of my tits / Jennifer Hayden. Top Shelf Productions, 2015 352 p. **B**

ISBN 9781603090544

1. Women cartoonists 2. Breast -- Psychological aspects 3. Women -- Body -- Psychological aspects 4. People with breast cancer 5. Autobiographies and memoirs 6. Autobiographical comics 7. Comics and Graphic novels

LC bl2015041330

Tells the semi-autobiographical tale of one woman's relationship with her breasts, from her innocent childhood conception of them, to her struggle with breast cancer, in which she lost both of them, and beyond.

Hayes, Bill, 1961-

Hayes, Bill, 1961- **Insomniac** city : New York, Oliver, and me / Bill Hayes. Bloomsbury USA, 2017. 288 p. **B**

ISBN 9781620404935

1. Sacks, Oliver, 1933-2015 2. Men/men relations 3. City life 4. Spouses of people with cancer 5. Loss (Psychology) 6. Autobiographies and memoirs

LC 2017017262

The author of Sleep Demons presents a celebration of New York City life and intimate glimpses into his relationship with the late Oliver Sacks, describing how in the aftermath of a partner's death the author moved to the city and unexpectedly fell in love on the eve of Sacks' battle with cancer.

Hazan, Marcella

Hazan, Marcella **Amarcord,** Marcella remembers : the story of a woman who started out to teach science in a small town in Italy, but ended up teaching America how to cook Italian / Marcella and Victor Hazan. Gotham Books, 2008. 320 p. **B**

ISBN 9781592403882

1. Hazan, Marcella. 2. Hazan, Victor. 3. Cooks 4. Cooking, Italian -- History -- 20th century. 5. Italian American women 6. Women immigrants -- United States 7. New York City -- Social life and customs. 8. Italy -- Social life and customs. 9. Autobiographies and memoirs

LC 2007046197

Traces the life story of the best-selling cookbook author from her childhood in a quiet Adriatic Sea fishing town and her family's struggles through World War II to her marriage and her work as a cooking instructor.

"Hazan has selected the best stories from her own life to present Amarcord with all the warmth and humor of a long meal in famiglia made from the choicest ingredients. If you've never been [to] Italy, the time spent with Hazan will have you planning your next vacation faster than you can say manicotti." Christian Science Monitor.

Heaney, Seamus, 1939-

O'Driscoll, Dennis **Stepping** stones : interviews with Seamus Heaney / Dennis O'Driscoll. Farrar, Straus and Giroux, 2008. xxx, 522 p., 16 p. of plates : **B**

ISBN 9780374269838

1. Heaney, Seamus, 1939- Interviews 2. Poets, Irish -- 20th century -- Interviews 3. Nobel Prize winners

LC 2008041252

Includes index.

An account of the life and work of the renowned contemporary poet charts his experiences before and after winning the 1995 Nobel Prize in Literature while discussing the artistic and ethical challenges he faced during the years of the Ulster Troubles.

"The book is a collection of questions and answers, compiled, largely by correspondence, over a period of some seven years. The compiler, Dennis O'Driscoll--a poet, senior tax inspector and strict questioner--persuades you that there will be no tolerance of arrears for Heaney here. The replies are tantamount to, while not pre-empting, an autobiography, by someone who says he inclines to discretion but is not a self-concealing person. This is a forthright though not a confessional book, inclined both to elevated stuff and to jokes." Times Literary Supplement.

Hearst, Patricia, 1954-

★Toobin, Jeffrey **American** heiress : the wild saga of the kidnapping, crimes and trial of Patty Hearst / Jeffrey Toobin. Doubleday, 2016. 368 p. **B**

ISBN 9780385536714

1. Hearst, Patricia, 1954- Trials, litigation, etc. 2. Symbionese Liberation Army. 3. Kidnapping victims 4. Heirs and heiresses 5. Stockholm syndrome. 6. Kidnapping

LC 2016016625

An account of the sensational 1974 kidnapping and trial of Patty Hearst describes the efforts of her family to secure her release, Hearst's baffling participation in a bank robbery and the psychological insights that prompted modern understandings about Stockholm syndrome.

"His thorough research, careful parsing of all the evidence, and superior prose make the book read like a summertime thriller." Publishers Weekly.

Hearst, Phoebe Apperson, 1842-1919

Nickliss, Alexandra M. **Phoebe** Apperson Hearst : a life of power and politics / Alexandra M. Nickliss. Bison Books, an imprint of University of Nebraska Press, 2018. xxx, 630 p. **B**

ISBN 9781496202277

1. Women philanthropists 2. Politicians' spouses 3. Social reformers 4. Family fortunes 5. San Francisco, California 6. San Francisco Bay Area 7. Biographies

LC 2017026677

In Phoebe Apperson Hearst: A Life in Power and Politics Alexandra M. Nickliss offers the first biography of one of the Gilded Age's most prominent and powerful women. A financial manager, businesswoman, and reformer, Phoebe Apperson Hearst was one of the wealthiest and most influential women of the era and a philanthropist, almost without rival, in the San Francisco Bay Area.

Hearst, William Randolph, 1863-1951

Nasaw, David The **chief** : the life of William Randolph Hearst / David Nasaw. Houghton Mifflin, 2000. xv, 687 p. : **B**

ISBN 9780395827598

1. Hearst, William Randolph, 1863-1951. 2. Davies, Marion, 1897-1961. 3. Hearst, Millicent Willson. 4. Publishers and publishing -- United States 5. Newspaper publishers and publishing -- History -- 19th century. 6. Newspaper publishers and publishing -- History -- 20th century. 7. Men/women relations. 8. Biographies

LC 99462122

J. Anthony Lukas Book Prize, 2001.National Book Critics Circle Award for Biography finalist, 2000."

Few publishers have loomed as large in their lifetimes, or cast as long a shadow after death, as William Randolph Hearst. Nasaw's judicious and comprehensive biography sensibly seeks to understand its subject, not to judge him." The New Yorker.

Whyte, Kenneth The **uncrowned** king : the sensational rise of William Randolph Hearst / Kenneth Whyte. Counterpoint, 2009. 546 p., 16 p. of plates : **B**

ISBN 9781582434674

1. Hearst, William Randolph, 1863-1951. 2. Publishers and publishing -- United States 3. Newspaper publishers and publishing -- History -- 19th century. 4. Newspapers -- United States -- History -- 19th century. 5. Newspaper publishers and publishing -- History -- 20th century. 6. New York City -- History -- 1898-1951. 7. Biographies

LC 2008047442

Originally published: Toronto : Random House Canada, 2008.

Traces the unique life of William Randolph Hearst as a successful and controversial figure and the impact his publications had on the world, and offers a detailed examination of his long-fought battle with his rival, Joseph Pulitzer.

"A very worthwhile reexamination of the rise of a flawed but accomplished man." Booklist.

Heath, Robert G. (Robert Galbraith), 1915-1999

Frank, Lone, 1966- The **pleasure** shock : the rise of deep brain stimulation and its forgotten inventor / Lone Frank. E.P. Dutton, [2018] 336 p. ; **B**

ISBN 9781101986530

1. Deep Brain Stimulation 2. Mental illness -- Treatment 3. Physicians 4. Brain -- Research 5. Biographies

LC 2017029957

An assessment of mid-20th-century Tulane psychiatrist Robert G. Heath's brain-pacemaker experiments shares insights into his controversial work with convicts, members of the gay community and the CIA's notorious "mind control" project and how much of his work has been suppressed or adapted as mainstream therapies for mental illness and addiction. By the award-winning author of My Beautiful Genome.

"Frank has written an excellent, balanced portrait of an inventive psychiatrist with a complicated legacy." Publishers Weekly.

Heawood, Sophie

Heawood, Sophie The **hungover** games : a true story / Sophie Heawood. Little, Brown and Company, 2020 304 p. **B**

ISBN 9780316499064

1. Heawood, Sophie. 2. Motherhood 3. Women journalists 4. Single mothers 5. Interpersonal relations 6. Autobiographies and memoirs

LC bl2020045835

An award-winning Yorkshire journalist describes her unconventional experiences with single motherhood, describing how the abandonment of her unplanned child's father compelled her adjustment to a stable and laughably real two-person family.

"Raw and funny, Heawood's memoir celebrates the messiness of life and motherhood with boldness, panache, and unexpected moments of real poignancy. An uncensored and eccentric delight." Kirkus

Hegar, Mary Jennings

Hegar, Mary Jennings **Shoot** like a girl : one woman's dramatic fight in Afghanistan and on the home front / Mary Jennings Hegar. New American Library, 2016 368 p. **B**

ISBN 9781101988435

1. Hegar, Mary Jennings. 2. United States. Air Force Women 3. United States. Air Force Search and rescue operations Afghanistan. 4. Women soldiers 5. Helicopter pilots. 6. Afghan War, 2001-, American. 7. Women's rights 8. United States -- Air National Guard 9. Autobiographies and memoirs

LC 2015047084

An Air National Guard Major describes her experiences after being shot down on a Medevac mission in Afghanistan, recounting the courageous acts that saved lives and earned prestigious decorations before she began efforts to convince the U.S. government to allow women to serve openly on the front lines.

"Hegars inspirational memoir reflects the strength and grace with which she approached her service to her country, whether she was venturing behind enemy lines to rescue wounded soldiers or standing up for womens right to be on the front line." Booklist.

Heinrich, Edward Oscar, 1881-1953

★Dawson, Kate Winkler **American** Sherlock : murder, forensics, and the birth of American CSI / Kate Winkler Dawson. G.P. Putnam's Sons, 2020. 325 p., 8 unnumbered p. of plates : **B**

ISBN 9780525539551

1. Chemists 2. Crime laboratories 3. Criminal evidence 4. Forensic sciences 5. Biographies

LC 2019050904

Describes the life of America's greatest, and first, forensic scientist, who invented tools that are still being used today, including blood spatter analysis, ballistics, lie-detector tests and fingerprints and solved at least two thousand cases during his forty-year career.

"A fascinating book worthy of being associated with the title's literary sleuth. Readers will want a follow-up so they can discover more of Heinrich's cases as told through Dawson's great storytelling." Library Journal

Heisenberg, Werner, 1901-1976

Cassidy, David C., 1945- **Beyond** uncertainty : Heisenberg, quantum physics, and the bomb / David C. Cassidy. Bellevue Literary Press, 2009. 480 p. : **B**

ISBN 1934137138

1. Heisenberg, Werner, 1901-1976. 2. Atomic bomb -- Germany -- History -- 20th century. 3. Physicists -- Germany 4. Biographies

LC 2008039885

Examines the physicist's role in the Nazi atomic bomb project and explores the ethical issue of a scientist's personal responsibility and guilt when serving a military regime.

"This is a biography of the German wunderkind Werner Heisenberg (19011976), who won the 1932 Nobel Prize in physics for revolutionizing the nascent field of quantum physics, first with his matrix interpretation of quantum mechanics, then with his famous uncertainty principle. Exhaustively detailed yet eminently readable, this is an important book." Publishers Weekly.

Hellman, Lillian, 1906-1984

Hellman, Lillian, 1906-1984 **Pentimento** / Lillian Hellman. Back Bay Books, 2000, c1973. 320 p. **B**

ISBN 0316352888

1. Hellman, Lillian, 1906-1984. 2. Women and literature -- United States -- History -- 20th century. 3. Dramatists, American -- 20th century 4. Women dramatists 5. Autobiographies and memoirs

LC BL 00009943

Sequel to: An unfinished woman.Originally published in 1973.

The distinguished American dramatist recalls the people who have colored and shaped her life.

Martinson, Deborah, 1946- **Lillian** Hellman : a life with foxes and scoundrels / Deborah Martinson. Counterpoint, 2005. 480 p. **B**

ISBN 1582433151

1. Hellman, Lillian, 1906-1984. 2. United States. Congress. House. Committee on Un-American Activities 3. Dramatists, American -- 20th century 4. Women dramatists, American -- 20th century 5. Biographies

LC 2005016616

Presents the first biography of the playwright written with the full cooperation of her family, friends, and inner circle, and discusses the life and career of the controversial writer.

"This is a richly thorough, sometimes somber, and fairly objective portrait of an enigmatic individual." Library Journal.

Helman-Minchilli, Elizabeth

Helman-Minchilli, Elizabeth **Eating** Rome : living the good life in the Eternal City / Elizabeth Minchilli. St. Martin's Griffin, 2015 176 p. **B**

ISBN 9781250047687

1. Helman-Minchilli, Elizabeth. 2. Cooking, Italian. 3. Grocery shopping. 4. Restaurants. 5. Dinners and dining. 6. Rome, Italy. 7. Autobiographies and memoirs

LC 2014044288

Elizabeth Minchilli has been eating her way through Rome since she was 12 years old. Join her as she takes you on a stroll through her favorite open air markets; stop by the best gelato shops; order plates full of carbonara and finish the day with a brilliant red Negroni.

"Minchilli is biased toward family-run specialty shops in certain neighborhoods, and she reflects on the changing culinary scene with the rise of the Roman brunch and the closing of many traditional spots." Publishers Weekly.

Hemingway, Ernest, 1899-1961

Blume, Lesley M. M. **Everybody** behaves badly : the true story behind Hemingway's masterpiece The sun also rises / Lesley Blume. Eamon Dolan/Houghton Mifflin Harcourt, 2016. 304 p. **B**

ISBN 9780544276000

1. Hemingway, Ernest, 1899-1961. Sun also rises. 2. Authors, American 3. Biographies

LC 2015037016

In the summer of 1925, Ernest Hemingway and a clique of raucous companions traveled to Pamplona, Spain, for the town's infamous running of the bulls. Then, over the next six weeks, he channeled that trip's maelstrom of drunken brawls, sexual rivalry, midnight betrayals, and midday hangovers into his groundbreaking novel The Sun Also Rises. This revolutionary work redefined modern literature as much as it did his peers, who would forever after be called the Lost Generation. But the full story of Hemingway's legendary rise has remained untold until now. Lesley Blume resurrects the explosive, restless landscape of 1920s Paris and Spain and reveals how Hemingway helped create his own legend.

"Blume's reimagining of 1920s Paris and its scandalous denizens is vivid, spirited, and absorbing." Kirkus.

★Dearborn, Mary V. **Ernest** Hemingway : a biography / Mary V. Dearborn. Knopf, 2017. 752 p. **B**

ISBN 9780307594679

1. Hemingway, Ernest, 1899-1961. 2. Authors, American -- 20th century 3. Journalists -- United States -- 20th century 4. Men -- Psychology 5. Masculinity 6. Biographies

LC 2016015837

A full biography of Ernest Hemingway draws on a wide range of previously untapped material and offers particular insight into the private demons that both inspired and tormented his literary achievements.

"Dearborn's account shines from beginning to end, helped by Hemingway's dramatic life and charismatic personality." Publishers Weekly.

Lynn, Kenneth Schuyler **Hemingway** : life and work / Kenneth S. Lynn. Harvard University Press, 1995, c1987. 702 p. ; **B**

ISBN 9780674387324

1. Hemingway, Ernest, 1899-1961. 2. Authors, American -- 20th century 3. Journalists -- United States -- 20th century 4. Men/women relations. 5. Identity (Psychology) 6. Biographies

LC 95129513

Originally published: New York : Simon and Schuster, 1987.

Pulitzer Prize for Biography or Autobiography finalist"

Taking as his premise Hemingway's glib assertion that the only analyst he relied upon was his portable Corona Number 3, Lynn tracks the exploration of a disordered inner world as Hemingway sought to find some sort of resolution to the agony of his personal conflicts through his cunningly wrought fiction. The man who emerges from Lynn's biography is a vastly more complex and compelling figure than the white-bearded, pontificating Papa of myth." Publishers Weekly.

Mort, T. A. (Terry A.) **Hemingway** at war : Ernest Hemingway's adventures as a World War II correspondent / Terry Mort. Pegasus Books, 2016. 336 p. **B**

ISBN 9781681772479

1. Hemingway, Ernest, 1899-1961. 2. Authors, American 3. Military journalism 4. Journalists 5. War correspondents 6. Biographies

LC 2017299500

An account of Ernest Hemingway's adventures in journalism during World War II explores his early resistance to war journalism, his daring missions with the RAF and French Resistance forces, his role in shaping key understandings about the war and its characters and the impact of the war on his subsequent writings.

Oliver, Charles M. **Critical** companion to Ernest Hemingway : a literary reference to his life and work / Charles M. Oliver. Facts On File, c2007. viii, 630 p. : **B**

ISBN 0816064180

1. Hemingway, Ernest, 1899-1961 Encyclopedias. 2. Novelists, American -- 20th century 3. Biographies

LC 2006007970

Rev. ed. of: Ernest Hemingway A to Z. 1999.

A guide to the author's life and work presents a brief biography, offers synopses of his writings, explores his major and minor characters, and discusses important people, places, and topics in his life.

Reynolds, Nicholas **Writer,** sailor, soldier, spy : Ernest Hemingway's secret adventures, 1935-1961 / Nicholas Reynolds. William Morrow, 2017 336 p. **B**

ISBN 9780062440136

1. United States. Office of Strategic Services 2. Soviet Union. Narodnyi komissariat vnutrennikh del 3. Secret service -- United States. 4. World War II 5. Cold War 6. Authors, American -- 20th century

LC bl2017002589

A former CIA officer and curator of the CIA Museum unveils the astonishing untold story of Nobel Prize-winning author Ernest Hemingway's secret life as a spy for both the American and Soviets before and during World War II.

"Although Reynolds is forced to guess about much of Hemi n gway's secret life as a spy, his conclusions seem consistent with the well-known portrait of the novelist striving to prove his manliness and power." Kirkus.

Heminsley, Alexandra, 1976-

Heminsley, Alexandra, 1976- **Running** like a girl : notes on learning to run / Alexandra Heminsley. Scribner, 2013. 224 p. **B**

ISBN 9781451697124

1. Running. 2. Transformations (Personal) 3. Women runners. 4. Runners. 5. Autobiographies and memoirs

LC 2013018909

A journalist and broadcaster shares her hilarious and inspirational personal journey from a self-proclaimed non-athlete to someone who, after many stumbling, painful efforts, has become a runner, which has transformed her relationships, her body and her life.

Hemon, Aleksandar, 1964-

Hemon, Aleksandar, 1964- The **book** of my lives / Aleksandar Hemon. Farrar, Straus and Giroux, 2013. 240 p. **B**

ISBN 9780374115739

1. Authors 2. Journalists 3. Immigrants. 4. Bosnians in the United States 5. Sarajevo (Bosnia and Hercegovina) 6. Chicago, Illinois. 7. Autobiographies and memoirs

LC 2012034564

National Book Critics Circle Award for Autobiography/Memoir finalist

Essays pay tribute to the two different cities of the author's youth--Sarajevo, until the city came under siege, and then Chicago, where he and his family started a new life, leaving behind everything they had ever known.

Hemon, Aleksandar, 1964- **My** parents : an introduction / Aleksandar Hemon. MCD, Farrar, Straus and Giroux, 2019. 168, 182 p. **B**

ISBN 9780374217433

1. Hemon, Aleksandar, 1964- Family. 2. Immigrants -- Bosnia and Hercegovina. 3. Refugees, Bosnian 4. Memories. 5. Loss (Psychology) 6. Sarajevo (Bosnia and Hercegovina) -- History -- Siege, 1992-1996. 7. Bosnia and Hercegovina -- History. 8. Autobiographies and memoirs.

LC 2018056429

The author shares a two-in-one volume documenting his parents' immigration from Bosnia to Canada and offering a selection of short memories about his family life and childhood friendships in Sarajevo.

"An incisive combination of literature that addresses the function of literature and memories that explore the meaning of memory." Kirkus.

Hendrix, Jimi, 1942-1970

★Cross, Charles R. **Room** full of mirrors : a biography of Jimi Hendrix / Charles R. Cross. Hyperion, 2005. xvi, 384 p. : **B**

ISBN 1401300286

1. Hendrix, Jimi, 1942-1970. 2. Rock musicians -- United States 3. Biographies

LC 2005046362

The image and lifestyle of Jimi Hendrix was larger-than-life, but beyond this was a complex man who struggled to accept his role as an idol. This sensitive, meticulously-researched biography recounts the entire arc of Hendrix's life: from his troubled childhood in Seattle's projects and the early loss of his mother, to his struggles against racial prejudice as a young musician and his rapid ascent to the top of the swinging London scene, and finally to the apex of his career headlining Woodstock in 1969, with his death a year later.

"Admirably comprehensive and well referenced, this is the Hendrix biography to acquire if you can acquire only one." Booklist.

Murray, Charles Shaar **Crosstown** traffic : Jimi Hendrix and the post-war rock'n'roll revolution / Charles Shaar Murray. St. Martin's Press, c1989. viii, 247 p. : **B**

ISBN 9780312042882

1. Rock musicians -- United States 2. African-American rock musicians 3. African American musicians 4. Biographies

LC 89077681

Traces the history and music of Jimi Hendrix and discusses the influence and impact of one of rock music's most innovative guitarists on a generation

"This informed, textured account will be irresistible to devotees of Hendrix and psychedelic rock as well as fans of blues, funk, jazz and rock 'n' roll." Booklist.

★Norman, Philip, 1943- **Wild** thing : the short, spellbinding life of Jimi Hendrix / Philip Norman. Liveright Publishing, 2020. 400 p. **B**

ISBN 9781631495892

1. Rock musicians -- United States 2. Guitarists 3. Rock music 4.

Psychedelic rock music 5. Biographies

LC 2020023464

Published to mark the 50th anniversary of Hendrix's death, a commemorative portrait by the best-selling author of Shout! draws on interviews with friends, lovers, bandmates and family members to include coverage of Hendrix's segregated early performances and historic appearances.

"Essential for music collections and anyone interested in Hendrix or music of the 1960s." Library Journal

Henion, Leigh Ann

Henion, Leigh Ann **Phenomenal** : a hesitant adventurer's search for wonder in the natural world / Leigh Ann Henion. Penguin, 2015 256 p. **B**

ISBN 9781594204715

1. Mothers 2. Motherhood 3. Women journalists. 4. Self-discovery 5. Autobiographies and memoirs

LC 2014036661

In an inspiring memoir, an author, journalist and conflicted young mother, travels the world in search of the most natural phenomena during which she discovers unforgettable truths about motherhood, spirituality and the beauty of nature.

Henry VIII, King of England, 1491-1547

Borman, Tracy **Henry** VIII and the men who made him / Tracy Borman. Grove Press, 2019. 320 p. **B**

ISBN 9780802128430

1. Courts and courtiers 2. Rulers 3. Power (Social sciences) 4. Royal houses 5. Great Britain -- History -- Henry VIII, 1509-1547 6. Great Britain -- Court and courtiers 7. Great Britain -- Politics and government -- 1509-1547. 8. Biographies

LC 2018049543

From acclaimed historian Tracy Borman, a penetrating new portrait of Henry VIII and the men who greatly impacted his life and historic reign.

"A thorough read for all interested in the Tudor era, the Reformation, and the British monarchy" Library Journal.

Weir, Alison, 1951- **Henry** VIII : the king and his court / Alison Weir. Ballantine Books, 2002, c2001. viii, 632 p. : **B**

ISBN 9780345437082

1. Henry VIII, King of England, 1491-1547. 2. Great Britain -- Court and courtiers -- History -- 16th century. 3. Great Britain -- History -- Henry VIII, 1509-1547. 4. Great Britain -- Rulers 5. Biographies

LC BL2002013730

Examines the king's remarkable influence on the laws, customs, culture, and politics of his kingdom and profiles the diverse courtiers, artists, and scholars who surrounded Henry VIII.

"In this biography of the Tudor king, the author examines the minutiae of his daily life and gives prominence to the background players of his court. At times, the weighty detail and numerous characters will make the work inaccessible; however, as a scholarly study it is a significant achievement." Library Journal.

Weir, Alison, 1951- The **six** wives of Henry VIII / Alison Weir. Grove Weidenfeld, 1991. xii, 643 p. : **B**

ISBN 9780802114976

1. Henry VIII, King of England, 1491-1547 Wives. 2. Marriages of royalty and nobility -- Great Britain -- History -- 16th century. 3. Women rulers -- Great Britain 4. Married women -- Great Britain 5. Great Britain -- History -- Henry VIII, 1509-1547.

LC 91029522

Originally published: London : Bodley Head, 1991.

Profiles each of Henry VIII's six wives, describing their backgrounds, personalities, relationship to the king, and ultimate demise, and shows how each reflected the perceptions of women and marriage at the time.

"Wonderfully detailed, extensively researched. The narrative is free flowing, humorous, informative, and readable." School Library Journal.

Henry Frederick Prince of Wales 1594-1612

Fraser, Sarah, 1960- The **prince** who would be king : the life and death of Henry Stuart / Sarah Fraser. William Collins, 2017. xxii, 330 p., 16 unnumbered p. of plates : **B**

ISBN 9780007548088

1. Henry Frederick Prince of Wales 1594-1612. 2. Rulers 3. Great Britain -- History -- James I, 1603-1625. 4. Biographies

LC 2017430284

Henry Stuart's life is the last great forgotten Jacobean tale. Shadowed by the gravity of the Thirty Years' War and the huge changes taking place across Europe in seventeenth-century society, economy, politics and empire, his life was visually and verbally gorgeous.

"Fraser fills a gap in the Stuart story while making the family legacy of regicides, religious wars, and licentiousness even more tragic in context of the story of the king who never was." Publishers Weekly.

Hensley, William L. Iggiagruk

Hensley, William L. Iggiagruk **Fifty** miles from tomorrow : a memoir of Alaska and the real people / William L. Iggiagruk Hensley. Farrar, Straus and Giroux, c2008. 272 p. **B**

ISBN 9780374154844

1. Hensley, William L. Iggiagruk. 2. Inupiat -- Kotzebue, Alaska 3. Childhood -- Kotzebue, Alaska 4. Indians of North America -- Civil rights 5. Inupiat families -- Kotzebue, Alaska 6. Alaska -- Social life and customs -- 20th century 7. Alaska -- Social life and customs -- 21st century 8. Kotzebue, Alaska -- Social life and customs. 9. Autobiographies and memoirs

LC 2008031409

Includes index.

Documents the author's traditional childhood north of the Arctic Circle, his education in the continental U.S., and his lobbying efforts that convinced the government to allocate resources to Alaska's natives in compensation for incursions on their way of life.

Henson, Jim

Jones, Brian Jay **Jim** Henson : the biography / Brian Jay Jones. Ballantine Books, 2013. 672 p. **B**

ISBN 9780345526113

1. Henson, Jim. 2. Muppet show (Television program) 3. Sesame Street (Television program) 4. Puppeteers -- United States 5. Television producers and directors -- United States 6. Television. 7. Biographies

LC 2013024039

Fans of the Muppets -- or TV history at large -- won't want to miss this compelling and informative behind-the-scenes story of "Muppets" inventor, Jim Henson. Henson began work in television in 1955. Joining forces with artist Jane Nebel, whom he later married, Henson enthusiastically developed the signature puppeteering style that landed him on Sesame Street -- and brought the now-famous Muppet Kermit the Frog and many others to the world. Biographer Brian Jay Jones offers the first complete biography of Henson, detailing his personal life, the nature of his creative genius, his collaborations with Frank Oz and other industry stars.

Henson, Taraji P.

Henson, Taraji P. **Around** the way girl : a memoir / Taraji P. Henson. 37 Ink, 2016. 320 p. **B**

ISBN 9781501125997

1. Actors and actresses 2. Academy Award film nominees. 3. Single mothers 4. African American women 5. Autobiographies and memoirs

LC 2016028253

The Academy Award nominee, Golden Globe winner and star of the hit show Empire recalls her beloved screen characters while tracing the story of her life and career, sharing coverage of such topics as her father's Vietnam service, her rise from the violence of the streets of Washington D.C. and her experiences as a single mother.

"Recommended for fans and aspiring actors alike." Library Journal.

Hepburn, Audrey, 1929-1993

Matzen, Robert, 1957- **Dutch** girl : Audrey Hepburn and World War II / Robert Matzen ; foreword by Luca Dotti. Goodknight Books, 2019. 373 p. **B**

ISBN 9781732273535

1. World War II -- Netherlands 2. Teenage girls 3. Anti-Nazi movement 4. Ballet dancers 5. Netherlands -- History -- German occupation, 1940-1945 6. Biographies

LC 2018966886

Twenty-five years after her passing, Audrey Hepburn remains the most beloved of all Hollywood stars, known as much for her role as UNICEF ambassador as for films like Roman Holiday and Breakfast at Tiffany?s. Several biographies have chronicled her stardom, but none has covered her intense experiences through five years of Nazi occupation in the Netherlands. According to her son, Luca Dotti, "The war made my mother who she was."

"A meticulously detailed and researched look at the formative years of an iconic performer; for fans of Hepburn as well as anyone seeking a social history of the Dutch experience of World War II." Library Journal.

Hepburn, Katharine, 1909-2003

Berg, A. Scott (Andrew Scott) **Kate** remembered / A. Scott Berg. Berkley Books, 2004, c2003. xii, 370 p. : **B**

ISBN 0425199096

1. Hepburn, Katharine, 1907-2003. 2. Berg, A. Scott (Andrew Scott) 3. Family relationships 4. Bisexual actresses 5. Film actors and actresses -- United States 6. Film industry and trade 7. United States -- Social life and customs -- 20th century 8. Biographies

LC bl2004110214

Originally published: New York : G.P. Putnam's Sons, c2003.

Recounts the remarkable life of leading lady Katharine Hepburn, presenting a portrait of the four-time Academy Award winner through her intimate conversations and private reflections on love, family, friendship, and show business.

"In this posthumous biography, the author reveals details about such pivotal events as the death of her brother by hanging, her relationships with powerful men like Howard Hughes and John Ford, and her slow, sad decline. Berg's writing is so intimate that readers may feel they are hiding behind a curtain as they listen to the stories he elicits from his subject. Kate herself comes across pretty much the way she did on screen: bossy, courageous, and self-involved." Booklist.

Hepburn, Katharine, 1907-2003

Mann, William J. **Kate** : the woman who was Hepburn / William J. Mann. H. Holt, 2006. xxviii, 621 p., 16 p. of plates : **B**

ISBN 9780805076257

1. Film actors and actresses -- United States 2. Men/women relations. 3. Sexuality. 4. Alcoholic women. 5. Biographies

LC 2006043367

"This will surely be the definitive version of Hepburn's life for decades to come, as it is an outstanding example of painstaking research matched with splendid writing." Publishers Weekly.

Herbert, Frank

★Herbert, Brian **Dreamer** of Dune : the biography of Frank Herbert / Brian Herbert. Tor, 2003. 576 p. : **B**

ISBN 0765306468

1. Herbert, Frank. 2. Authors, American -- 20th century 3. Science fiction writing. 4. Fathers and sons. 5. Eccentric men 6. Biographies

LC 2002042951

"A Tom Doherty Associates book."

A chronicle of the life of the award-winning science-fiction writer, presented by his son, describes Herbert's childhood in Tacoma, Washington, his early years as a reporter and editor, his military service, his struggles to become published, and his creation of numerous works including Dune, The Green Brain, and The Santaroga Barrier.

"This moving, sometimes painfully obsessive biography is an impressive testament of family loyalty and love. A must-read for Herbert fans (both senior and junior), it includes family photos and a bibliography." Publishers Weekly.

Hernandez, Aida

Bobrow-Strain, Aaron, 1969- The **death** and life of Aida Hernandez : a border story / Aaron Bobrow-Strain. Farrar, Straus and Giroux, [2019] 352 p. **B**

ISBN 9780374191979

1. Immigrants 2. Undocumented immigrants 3. Mexicans in the United States 4. Immigrants, Mexican 5. Mexican-American Border Region 6. United States -- Immigration and emigration -- Social aspects 7. Biographies

LC 2018044062

"Bobrow-Strain crafts a gripping narrative that is highly recommended for anyone looking for a better understanding of the policies and emotions surrounding the current debate over immigration and border security." Library Journal.

Hernandez, Daisy

Hernandez, Daisy A **cup** of water under my bed : a memoir / Daisy Hernández. Beacon Press, 2014. 200 p. **B**

ISBN 9780807014486

1. Hernandez, Daisy. 2. Hispanic American women 3. Bisexual women 4. Identity (Psychology) 5. Young women -- Family relationships -- United States. 6. New York City 7. United States -- Social conditions -- 1980- 8. Autobiographies and memoirs

LC 2014000820

It's 1980. Ronald Reagan has been elected president, John Lennon has been shot, and a little girl in New Jersey has been hauled off to English classes. Her teachers and parents and tias are expecting her to become white--like the Italians. This is the opening to A Cup of Water Under My Bed, the memoir of one Colombian-Cuban daughter's rebellions and negotiations with the women who raised her and the world that wanted to fit her into a cubbyhole. From language acquisition to coming out as bisexual to arriving as a reporting intern at the New York Times as the paper is rocked by its biggest plagiarism scandal, Daisy Hernandez chronicles what the women in her community taught her about race, sex, money, and love. This is a memoir about the private nexus of sexuality, immigration, race and class issues, but it is ultimately a daughter's cuento of how to take the lessons from home and shape them into a new, queer life.

Hernandez, Keith

Hernandez, Keith **I'm** Keith Hernandez : a memoir / Keith Hernandez. Little, Brown and Company, 2018. vii, 341 pages : **B**

ISBN 9780316395731

1. New York Mets. 2. Baseball players 3. Professional athletes 4. Baseball 5. Professional baseball players 6. Autobiographies and memoirs

LC 2017963935

The legendary first baseman best known for his World Series win with the New York Mets tells all.

"Often candid and even self-deprecating memories by an athlete who once stood at the summit o f his profession." Kirkus.

Hernandez Castillo, Marcelo, 1988-

Hernandez Castillo, Marcelo, 1988- **Children** of the land : a memoir / Marcelo Hernandez Castillo. HarperCollins, 2020. 288 p. **B**

ISBN 9780062825599

1. United States. Bureau of Immigration and Customs Enforcement 2. Immigrant families 3. Child immigrants 4. Father-separated children 5. Mexican Americans 6. United States -- Immigration and emigration 7. Mexico 8. Autobiographies and memoirs

LC bl2020002598

An award-winning poet chronicles his experiences of growing up undocumented in the United States, describing how his family and his attempt to establish an adult life were heartbreakingly complicated by racist policies.

"Castillo lays bare the inherent unfairness and high psychological toll of the current immigration system on people in both the U.S. and Mexico." Booklist.

Herriman, George, 1880-1944

Tisserand, Michael, 1963- **Krazy** : George Herriman, a life in black and white / Michael Tisserand. HarperCollins, 2016. 560 p. **B**

ISBN 9780061732997

1. Krazy Kat (Comic strip) 2. Comic strip writers. 3. Passing (Identity) 4. Race (Social sciences) 5. New Orleans, Louisiana 6. Biographies

LC bl2016052808

National Book Critics Circle Award for Biography finalist, 2016

A biography of the creator of the wildly popular Krazy Kat comic describes how the 19th-century New Orleans native hid his African-American racial identity in order to advance his art and career.

"Essential reading for comics fans and history buffs, Krazy is a roaring success, providing an indispensable new perspective on turn-of-the-century America." Kirkus.

Herriot, James

Herriot, James **All** creatures great and small / James Herriot. St. Martin's Press, 1992, c1972. 442 p. ; All creatures great and small **B**

ISBN 0312084986

1. Veterinarians -- Yorkshire, England 2. Human/animal relationships 3. Animals. 4. Yorkshire, England -- Social life and customs. 5. Autobiographies and memoirs

LC 92018975

A country veterinary surgeon in Yorkshire describes the joys and trials of his profession and recalls his early career and experiences with his unique clientele.

Herriot, James **Every** living thing / James Herriot. St. Martin's Press, 1992. 342 p. ; **B**

ISBN 031208188X

1. Veterinarians -- Yorkshire, England 2. Animals. 3. Human/animal relationships 4. Yorkshire, England. 5. Autobiographies and memoirs

LC 92018526

"Herriot regales us with additional tales of his veterinary practice in Yorkshire. He picks up his story after World War II, when medicines and treatment have improved, his children are growing up and the family moves to a new house. There are no surprises here, just the expected mix of gentle humor and compassion for animals and people alike. Herriot's many fans will not be disappointed." Publishers Weekly.

Herriot, James **James** Herriot's animal stories / with an introduction by Jim Wright ; and illustrations by Lesley Holmes. St. Martin's Press, 1997. xii, 142 p. : **B**

ISBN 0312168748

1. Veterinarians. 2. Animals. 3. Human/animal relationships 4. Domestic animals. 5. Yorkshire, England. 6. Autobiographies and memoirs

LC 97013863

Ten classic tales of cats, dogs, lambs, horses, cows, and their human counterparts are presented in a collection of the late Yorkshire veterinarian's true-life stories

Herriot, James **James** Herriot's cat stories / James Herriot ; with illustrations by Lesley Holmes. St. Martin's Press, 1994. xiii, 161 p. : **B**

ISBN 0312113420

1. Veterinarians. 2. Cats. 3. Human/animal relationships 4. Humans and cats. 5. Yorkshire, England. 6. Autobiographies and memoirs

LC 94020131

A renowned writer on animals offers a collection of stories about the cats he has known.

Herriot, James **James** Herriot's dog stories / James Herriot. St. Martin's Griffin, 2006, c1986. xxxiii, 426 p. : **B**

ISBN 9780312364526

1. Dogs. 2. Veterinarians. 3. Human/animal relationships 4. Dog owners. 5. Yorkshire, England -- Social life and customs. 6. Autobiographies and memoirs

LC 2007274677

Originally published: New York : St. Martin's Press, 1986.

Here are the complete dog stories from his much-beloved memoirs: a handsome collection of tales, available for the first time in trade paperback, that will warm the hearts of dog lovers around the world. Featuring a special introduction by the author and his own accompanying notes to each specially illustrated story, this tribute from man to dog is a volume no Herriot fan will want to be without. --From publisher description.

"A good choice for dog lovers." School Library Journal.

Herriot, James **James** Herriot's favorite dog stories / James Herriot ; illustrations by Lesley Holmes. St. Martin's Press, 1996. 169 p. : **B**

ISBN 0312146310

1. Dogs. 2. Veterinarians. 3. Human/animal relationships 4. Dogs as pets. 5. Autobiographies and memoirs

LC 96018796

Watercolor illustrations accompany a collection of ten stories about dogs--from border collies and sheepdogs to the exploits of Tricki Woo, the unforgettable Pekinese

"This is a collection of 10 previously published dog stories written in Herriot's heartwarming style. Each tale is accompanied by new attractive watercolor illustrations. A dog-lover's delight." School Library Journal.

Hersch, Fred

Hersch, Fred **Good** things happen slowly : a life in and out of jazz / Fred Hersch. Crown Archetype, 2017 320 p. **B**

ISBN 9781101904343

1. Hersch, Fred. 2. Jazz musicians. 3. Gay musicians. 4. Pianists. 5. Composers. 6. Autobiographies and memoirs

LC 2017028036

The eight-time Grammy-nominated music artist describes his experiences of being one of the first openly gay, HIV-positive musicians in the cloistered, largely African-American jazz world, sharing additional insights into his two-month medically induced coma in 2007, from which he would emerge to create some of the most emotionally compelling music of his career.

"Like much of his music, his memoir is deceptively simple, thoroughly humble, and extraordinarily honest." Booklist.

Hersh, Seymour M., 1937-

★Hersh, Seymour M., 1937- **Reporter** : a memoir / Seymour M. Hersh. Alfred A. Knopf, 2018. 355 p. **B**

ISBN 9780307263957

1. Journalists 2. Investigative journalism 3. Investigative journalists 4. Journalism 5. Autobiographies and memoirs

LC 2017051856

The Pulitzer Prize-winning journalist and National Book Critics Circle Award-winning author presents an account of his decades-long career scooping some of the most high-impact stories of the last half century.

"Rarely has a journalist's memoir come together so well, with admirable measures of self-deprecation, transparent pride, readable prose style, and honesty." Kirkus.

Miraldi, Robert **Seymour** Hersh : scoop artist / Robert Miraldi. Potomac Books, An Imprint of the University of Nebraska Press, [2013] xvii, 415 p. ; **B**

ISBN 9781612344751

1. Journalists 2. Journalism 3. Investigative journalists 4. United States -- Politics and government 5. United States -- Foreign relations 6. Biographies.

LC 2013023619

"A deep biographical treatment of the Pulitzer Prize-winning journalist who is the scourge of those in power. Hersh comes across as a good guy of limited patience when approached by fellow journalists and as a bulldog with sharp teeth when in his reporter mode." Kirkus.

Herzl, Theodor, 1860-1904

Avineri, Shlomo **Herzl's** vision : Theodor Herzl and the foundation of the Jewish state / Shlomo Avineri, translated by Haim Watzman. Bluebridge, 2014 288 p. **B**

ISBN 9781933346984

1. Zionism -- History 2. Zionists 3. Israel -- History. 4. Biographies

LC 2014948524

Originally published in Hebrew, 2013

In this concise, illuminating biography, the renowned Israeli political scientist and public intellectual Shlomo Avineri portraits Herzl's intellectual and spiritual odyssey from a private and marginal individual into a Jewish political leader and shows how it was the political crisis of the Austro-Hungarian Habsburg Empire, torn apart by contending national movements, which convinced Herzl of the need for a Jewish polity. Drawing extensively on Herzl's diaries as well as his published works, Avineri tells the story of how Herzl became, with the Zionist movement that he founded, a player in international politics, and how he harnessed the power of the word to his goals as no other statesman before him had done.

Hetherington, Tim

Huffman, Alan **Here** I am : the story of Tim Hetherington, war photographer / Alan Huffman. Grove Press, 2013. 256 p. **B**

ISBN 9780802120908

1. Photographers 2. Photojournalists 3. War correspondents 4. Libya -- History -- Civil War, 2011- 5. Liberia -- History -- Civil War, 1989-1996 6. Biographies.

LC bl2012046677

Traces the life and career of the award-winning photojournalist whose life was ended in 2011 by a mortar blast while he was covering the Libyan Civil War, honoring his advocacy on behalf of countless war victims while tracing how his achievements reflected the realities of 21st-century war reporting.

Heumann, Judith E.

Heumann, Judith E. **Being** Heumann : an unrepentant memoir of a disability rights activist / Judith Heumann, with Kristen Joiner. Beacon Press, 2019 232 p. **B**

ISBN 9780807019290

1. Heumann, Judith E.. 2. People with disabilities 3. Ableism 4. People with poliomyelitis 5. Physical disabilities. 6. Autobiographies and memoirs

LC 2019026271

An influential disability-rights activist recounts her lifelong battles for education, employment and societal inclusion, in a personal account that includes coverage of her role in advising the Carter administration to help create the Americans with Disabilities Act.

"A driving force in the passage of the Americans With Disabilities Act looks back on a long career of activism. . . . A welcome account of politics in action, and for the best of causes." Kirkus

Hickam, Homer H., 1943-

★Hickam, Homer H., 1943- **Rocket** boys : a memoir / Homer H. Hickam, Jr. Delacorte Press, 1998. xii, 368 p. **B**

ISBN 038533320X

1. United States. National Aeronautics and Space Administration 2. Coal mining towns. 3. Small town life. 4. High school boys. 5. Aerospace engineers 6. United States -- Social life and customs -- 20th century 7. Autobiographies and memoirs

LC 98019304

National Book Critics Circle Award for Biography finalist, 1998.

The author traces the boyhood enthusiasm for rockets that eventually led to a career at NASA, describing how he built model rockets in the family garage in West Virginia, inspired by the launch of the Soviet satellite "Sputnik."

"Even if Hickam stretched the strict truth to metamorphose his memories into Stand By Me-like material for Hollywood . . . the embellishing only converts what is a good story into an absorbing, rapidly readable one that is unsentimental but artful about adolescence, high school, and family life." Booklist.

Hickok, Lorena Alice, 1893-1968

★Golay, Michael, 1951- **America** 1933 : the Great Depression, Lorena Hickok, Eleanor Roosevelt, and the shaping of the New Deal / Michael Golay. Free Press, c2013. 320 p. **B**

ISBN 9781439196014

1. Investigative journalism -- United States -- History 2. Depressions

-- 1929-1941 3. Poverty 4. Journalists 5. United States -- History -- 1933-1945. 6. United States -- Economic conditions -- 1918-1945. 7. United States -- Social conditions -- 1918-1945.

LC 2012041139

Documents the 18-month journey of woman journalist Lorena Hickok during the height of the Great Depression, recounting her experiences and influence in some of the nation's worst-hit regions as documented in almost daily letters written to close friend Eleanor Roosevelt.

Hickok, Wild Bill, 1837-1876

Clavin, Thomas **Wild** Bill : the true story of the American frontier's first gunfighter / Tom Clavin. St. Martin's Press, 2019. 448 p. **B**

ISBN 9781250173799

1. Calamity Jane, 1852-1903 2. Peace officers 3. Frontier and pioneer life 4. Gunfighters 5. Gunfights 6. The West (United States) -- History -- 19th century 7. Biographies

LC 2018041162

The best-selling traces the life of the true James Butler "Wild Bill" Hickok, from his service as a Union spy and lawman to his famous romances and the confrontations that shaped his gunfighter legend.

" Well written, full of vivid characters, and detailed, but built largely from existing literature, this is an accessible celebration of Hickock's life rather than a rigorous deconstruction of his romantic mythos." Booklist.

Hicks, Albert W., approximately 1820-1860

Cohen, Rich The **last** pirate of New York: a ghost ship, a killer, and the birth of a gangster nation / Rich Cohen. Spiegel & Grau, 2019. 224 p. **B**

ISBN 9780399589928

1. Hicks, Albert W., approximately 1820-1860. 2. Criminals -- New York (State) 3. Pirates 4. Murderers 5. Pirates -- New York (State) 6. New York (State) 7. Biographies

LC 2018049488

Documents the story of underworld legend Albert Hick's, chronicling his mid-nineteenth-century crime spree and the plot gone wrong that culminated in an onboard massacre and manhunt in 1860 Coney Island.

"Cohen skillfully narrates Hicks background, criminal career, and the rough-and-tumble world of New York City on the eve of the Civil War. True-crime stories rarely get much better than this one." Booklist.

Higashida, Naoki, 1992-

Higashida, Naoki, 1992- **Fall** down 7 times get up 8 : a young man's voice from the silence of autism / Naoki Higashida ; introduction by David Mitchell ; translated by KA Yoshida and David Mitchell. Random House, 2017. 240 p. **B**

ISBN 9780812997392

1. People with autism 2. Autism 3. Twenties (Age) 4. Adulthood 5. Autobiographies and memoirs

LC 2017004105

A follow-up to The reason I jump, which described the author's experiences as a 13-year-old autistic boy. The author now shares his thoughts and experiences as a 24-year-old living with severe autism.

"In a mix of short essays . Higashida explores aspects of his atypicality, most of it pointing to the fact that he is indeed atypical, indeed unlike most other people, in the depth of his emotional and intellectual strength." Kirkus.

Higashida, Naoki, 1992- The **reason** I jump : the inner voice of a thirteen-year-old boy with autism / Naoki Higashida ; translated by KA Yoshida and David Mitchell. Random House, 2013. 128 p. **B**

ISBN 9780812994865

1. People with autism 2. Autism. 3. Autobiographies and memoirs

LC 2012045703

"Originally published in Japanese by Escor Publishers Ltd. in 2007"--Title page verso.

Written by a thirteen-year-old boy with autism, this book demonstrates how an autistic mind thinks, feels, perceives and responds.

"A a mixture of invaluable anecdotal information, practical advice and whimsical self-expression." Publishers Weekly.

Hilfiger, Tommy

Hilfiger, Tommy **American** dreamer : my life in fashion & business / Tommy Hilfiger with Peter Knobler. Ballantine Books, [2016] 352 p. **B**

ISBN 9781101886212

1. Hilfiger, Tommy. 2. Fashion designers -- United States 3. Fashion 4. Fashion design 5. Businesspeople 6. United States -- Social life and customs -- 20th century. 7. Autobiographies and memoirs

LC 2016023113

Includes index."

An honest, straightforward, mostly entertaining autobiography of the man who created a classic yet hip line of clothing." Kirkus.

Hill, Clint

Hill, Clint **Five** days in November / Clint Hill and Lisa McCubbin. Gallery Books, 2013. 256 p. **B**

ISBN 9781476731490

1. Kennedy, John F. (John Fitzgerald), 1917-1963 Assassination. 2. Kennedy, John F. (John Fitzgerald), 1917-1963 Death and burial. 3. Onassis, Jacqueline Kennedy, 1929-1994. 4. United States. Secret Service Officials and employees 5. Assassination. 6. Secret service -- United States 7. Presidents. 8. United States -- History -- 20th century. 9. Autobiographies and memoirs

LC 2013019272

The retired United States Secret Service agent who is remembered for his courageous actions in the presidential motorcade after JFK was shot shares his memories of the five days leading up to, and after, that tragic day in November 1963. --Publisher.

Hill, Clint **Five** presidents : my extraordinary journey with Eisenhower, Kennedy, Johnson, Nixon, and Ford / Clint Hill with Lisa McCubbin. Gallery Books, 2016. 400 p. **B**

ISBN 9781476794136

1. Hill, Clint. 2. United States. Secret Service Officials and employees 3. Presidents -- Protection 4. Secret service. 5. National security. 6. Safety. 7. United States -- Politics and government. 8. Autobiographies and memoirs

LC 2015050618

A former Secret Service agent reveals his experiences throughout five presidential administrations, sharing anecdotes from some of the twentieth century's most significant historical events.

"An eloquently written travelog through midcentury America from the periphery of political power." Library Journal.

Hill, Clint **Mrs.** Kennedy and me : an intimate memoir / Clint Hill ; with Lisa McCubbin. Gallery Books, 2012. 320 p. **B**

ISBN 9781451648447

1. Hill, Clint. 2. Onassis, Jacqueline Kennedy, 1929-1994 Friends and associates. 3. United States. Secret Service Officials and employees 4. Presidents' spouses -- United States. 5. Secret service. 6. Charisma. 7. United States -- History -- 1960-1969. 8.

Autobiographies and memoirs

LC 2011051017

From 1960 to 1964, Clint Hill was the Secret Service agent assigned to First Lady Jacqueline Kennedy. Telling his story for the first time, Hill recounts Mrs. Kennedy's unfailing grace, intelligence, and spirit during times both joyful and tragic--from the birth of her children to her husband's assassination.

Hill, Joe, 1879-1915

Adler, William M. The **man** who never died : the life, times, and legacy of Joe Hill, American labor icon / William M. Adler. Bloomsbury, c2011. 448 p. **B**

ISBN 9781596916968

1. Hill, Joe, 1879-1915. 2. Industrial Workers of the World. 3. Working class -- Songs and music. 4. Labor movement. 5. Labor organizers. 6. Radical organizations. 7. Biographies

LC 2011009821

Draws on four years of intensive research to present a full-scale portrait of the legendary American songwriter and union hero that offers new evidence supporting his innocence of the crime for which he was executed. By the author of Land of Opportunity.

Hill, Katie, (former Congressional representative)

Hill, Katie, (former Congressional representative) **She** will rise : becoming a warrior in the battle for true equality / Katie Hill. Grand Central Publishing, 2020 x, 305 p. : **B**

ISBN 9781538737002

1. United States. Congress Officials and employees. 2. Misogyny 3. Women politicians 4. Bisexual women 5. Women and politics. 6. United States -- Politics and government. 7. Autobiographies and memoirs

LC 2020938825

Former Congresswoman Katie Hill shares her experience with misogyny and double standards in politics to help women topple the long-standing power structures that prevent them from achieving equality.

"Both thoughtful and thought-provoking, Hill unflinchingly takes responsibility for choices and actions that led to her political demise, while also offering sage advice for those fighting for women's rights in this straightforward and candid memoir-cum-manifesto." Booklist

Hillerman, Tony

Hillerman, Tony **Seldom** disappointed : a memoir / Tony Hillerman. Harper Collins, 2001. viii, 341 p., 8 p. of plates : **B**

ISBN 9780060194451

1. Authors, American -- 20th century 2. Family relationships. 3. Biographies

LC 2001024160

Agatha Award for Best Nonfiction, 2001.

Anthony Award for Best Critical/Nonfiction, 2002.

Starting with his childhood in Oklahoma during the Great Depression, Hillerman's memoir covers a remarkable 76 years. It follows his military service in World War II to his success as an author.

"The entire book will appeal to his fans, but the first half is intensely gripping." Library Journal.

Him, Chanrithy, 1965-

Him, Chanrithy, 1965- **When** broken glass floats : growing up under the Khmer Rouge, a memoir / Chanrithy Him. W.W. Norton, c2000. 330 p. : **B**

ISBN 0393048632

1. Atrocities -- Cambodia. 2. Political refugees -- Cambodia 3. Genocide 4. Political atrocities 5. Cambodia -- Politics and government -- 1975-1979. 6. Autobiographies and memoirs

LC 99058417

A survivor of the Cambodian genocide recounts a childhood in Cambodia, where rudimentary labor camps filled with death and illness were the norm and modern technology, such as cars and electricity, no longer existed.

"Him was 10 in 1975 when the Khmer Rouge overtook her country in what she calls the time of broken glass. Feeling a survivor's responsibility to do so, Him vividly recalls the brutality of the camps, the strict social control, and alienation from family that the Khmer Rouge enforced." Booklist.

Himes, Chester B., 1909-1984

Jackson, Lawrence Patrick **Chester** B. Himes : a biography / Lawrence P. Jackson. Norton & Co., 2017. 448 p. **B**

ISBN 9780393063899

1. African American authors 2. Authors 3. Former convicts 4. Social advocates 5. United States -- Social conditions -- 20th century 6. Biographies

BCALA Literary Award for Nonfiction, 2018.

Edgar Allan Poe Award for Best Critical/Biographical, 2018.

An account of the improbable life of the controversial writer explores Himes' middle-class origins, imprisonment, creative experiences during World War II and eventual escape to Europe, where he became famous for his Harlem detective series and its themes of sexuality, racism and social injustice.

"While two other Himes biographies exist...Jackson succeeds in his bid to offer a definitive life treatment." Booklist.

Himmler, Heinrich, 1900-1945

Breitman, Richard, 1947- The **architect** of genocide : Himmler and the final solution / Richard Breitman. University Press of New England, 1992, c1991 xii, 335 p. ; **B**

ISBN 0874515963

1. Himmler, Heinrich, 1900-1945. 2. Nazis 3. Holocaust (1933-1945) 4. War criminals. 5. Genocide. 6. Germany -- Politics and government -- 1933-1945. 7. Biographies

LC 92053857

Originally published: New York : Knopf, 1991."

Brandeis University Press."Explores the life and character of Heinrich Himmler, and uses revelations about his racial ideology to refute arguments that the Holocaust was unpremeditated.

"This engrossing, detailed study constitutes a powerful refutation of revisionist scholars who claim that Hitler did not plan the Final Solution in advance but instead improvised it out of either military or political frustration." Publishers Weekly.

Hindman, Jessica Chiccehitto

Hindman, Jessica Chiccehitto **Sounds** like Titanic : a memoir / Jessica Chiccehitto Hindman. W. W. Norton & Company, [2019] 256 p. **B**

ISBN 9780393651645

1. Hindman, Jessica Chiccehitto. 2. Violinists -- United States 3. Classical musicians. 4. Musical ability. 5. Classical music -- Performance. 6. Autobiographies and memoirs.

LC 2018044657

National Book Critics Circle Award for Autobiography/Memoir finalist, 2019

Relates how the author, an aspiring violinist, left her Appalachian home to pursue a career in classical music in New York, only to discover that the ensemble she has joined pretends to play over CD recordings, and describes her subsequent identity crisis and disillusionment.

"A tricky, unnerving, consistently fascinating memoir." Kirkus.

Hines, Richard

Hines, Richard **No** way but gentlenesse : a memoir of how Kes, my kestrel, changed my life / Richard Hines. Bloomsbury, 2016 320 p. **B**

ISBN 9781632865021

1. Hines, Richard Childhood and youth 2. Falconry 3. Kestrels 4. Growing up 5. Self-discovery 6. England -- Social life and customs 7. Autobiographies and memoirs

LC 2017301456

In a memoir of one boy's love for a culture lost to time, and his attempt to find salvation in the natural world, the author, who didn't merit a real education and was persecuted by the cruel antics of his English schoolteachers, discovered a love of falconry after stumbling on a nest of kestrels in the ruins of a medieval castle.

Hinton, Anthony Ray

Hinton, Anthony Ray The **sun** does shine : how I found life and freedom on death row / Anthony Ray Hinton, with Lara Love Hardin ; and a foreword by Bryan Stevenson. St. Martin's Press, 2018 255 p. ; **B**

ISBN 9781250124715

1. Hinton, Anthony Ray. 2. Judicial error. 3. Death row. 4. Death row prisoners 5. Trials (Murder). 6. Alabama 7. Autobiographies and memoirs

LC 2017044467

A man who spent thirty years on death row for a crime he did not commit describes how he became a victim of a flawed legal system, recounting the years he shared with fellow inmates who were eventually executed before his exoneration.

Hirohito, Emperor of Japan, 1901-1989

★Bix, Herbert P. **Hirohito** and the making of modern Japan / Herbert P. Bix. Harper Collins, 2000. xi, 800 p., 16 p. of plates : **B**

ISBN 006019314X

1. World War II -- Japan. 2. Monarchy, Japanese. 3. Imperialism, Japanese -- History -- 20th century. 4. Japan -- Rulers. 5. Japan -- Politics and government -- 1926- 6. Japan -- History -- Showa period, 1926-1989. 7. Biographies

LC 99089427

National Book Critics Circle Award for Biography, 2000.

Pulitzer Prize for General Nonfiction, 2001.

In this groundbreaking biography of the Japanese emperor Hirohito, Herbert P. Bix offers the first complete, unvarnished look at the enigmatic leader whose sixty-three-year reign ushered Japan into the modern world. Never before has the full life of this controversial figure been revealed with such clarity and vividness.

"In 1945, fearing that the Japanese would resist American occupation unless the Emperor ordered them to obey, General MacArthur colluded with Hirohito in maintaining that the sovereign had been powerless to control Japan's military leaders. {Bix}, uses newly available sources to argue that Hirohito was a war criminal. An imperialist whose policies reflected his belief in the racial superiority of the Japanese, Hirohito governed by manipulation for almost two decades, and used the threat of Soviet Communism to justify domestic repression and soaring military budgets. The author's virtuoso scholarship and accessible narrative invite us into Hirohito's world." The New Yorker.

Hirsi Ali, Ayaan, 1969-

Hirsi Ali, Ayaan, 1969- **Infidel** / Ayaan Hirsi Ali. Free Press, 2007. xii, 353 p., 8 p. of plates : **B**

ISBN 9780743289689

1. Muslim women's rights. 2. Women refugees. 3. Muslim women. 4. Politicians. 5. Somalia. 6. Netherlands. 7. Autobiographies and memoirs

LC 2006049762

Ultimately a celebration of triumph over adversity, Hirsi Ali's story tells how a bright little girl evolved out of dutiful obedience to become an outspoken, pioneering freedom fighter. As Western governments struggle to balance democratic ideals with religious pressures, no story could be timelier or more significant.

"The circuitous, violence-filled path that led Ms. Hirsi Ali from Somalia to the Netherlands is the subject of Infidel, her brave, inspiring and beautifully written memoir." New York Times.

Hirsi Ali, Ayaan, 1969- **Nomad** : from Islam to America--a personal journey through the clash of civilizations/ Ayaan Hirsi Ali. Free Press, 2010. 304 p. **B**

ISBN 9781439157312

1. Netherlands. Staten-Generaal 2. Muslim women's rights. 3. Women refugees. 4. Somali Americans 5. Muslim women -- United States 6. Netherlands. 7. United States -- Immigration and emigration. 8. Autobiographies and memoirs

LC 2010001481

Includes index.

Picking up where Infidel, her last memoir, left off, Ayaan Hirsi Ali chronicles her struggle with culture shock as she adapts to life in America.

"A thought-provoking book sure to stir as much debate and controversy as Infidel." Booklist.

Hisham, Marwan

Hisham, Marwan **Brothers** of the gun : a memoir of the Syrian war / Marwan Hisham, and Molly Crabapple. One World, 2018. 224 p. **B**

ISBN 9780399590627

1. Assad, Bashar, 1965- 2. Civil war 3. Revolutions 4. Insurgency 5. Military government 6. Syria -- History -- Civil War, 2011- 7. Middle East 8. Autobiographies and memoirs

LC 2017058673

In 2011, Marwan Hisham and his two friends--fellow working-class college students Nael and Tareq--joined the first protests of the Arab Spring in Syria, in response to a recent massacre. Arm-in-arm they marched, poured Coca-Cola into one another's eyes to blunt the effects of tear gas, ran from the security forces, and cursed the country's president, Bashar al-Assad. It was ecstasy. A long-bottled revolution was finally erupting, and freedom from a brutal dictator seemed, at last, imminent. Five years later, the three young friends were scattered: one now an Islamist revolutionary, another dead at the hands of government soldiers, and the last, Marwan, now a journalist in Turkish exile, trying to find a way back to a homeland reduced to rubble.

Hitchcock, Alfred, 1899-1980

Chandler, Charlotte **It's** only a movie : Alfred Hitchcock, a personal biography / Charlotte Chandler. Simon & Schuster, c2005. xvi, 349 p. : **B**

ISBN 0743245083

1. Hitchcock, Alfred, 1899-1980. 2. Film producers and directors -- England 3. Suspense films -- History and criticism 4. Cinematography -- History 5. British in the United States 6. United States -- Social life and customs -- 20th century 7. London, England -- Social life

and customs -- 20th century 8. Biographies

LC 2004052559

Includes index.

A portrait based on interviews with the movie icon, his family members, and his contemporaries profiles him as a devoted family man, notorious practical joker, and an Englishman whose Victorian tastes shaped his films.

"The author reveals several insights into Hitchcock's technical genius, creative worldview and personality. Chandler allows her sources to reminisce at great length, and they tend to tell fascinating stories." Publishers Weekly.

Spoto, Donald, 1941- The **dark** side of genius : the life of Alfred Hitchcock / Donald Spoto ; with a new introduction by the author. Da Capo Press, 1999, c1983. xiv, 594 p. : **B**

ISBN 9780306809323

1. Film producers and directors -- England 2. Film noir -- History and criticism 3. Biographies

LC 99037941

Originally published: Boston, MA : Little, Brown, 1983.

Edgar Allan Poe Award for Best Critical/Biographical, 1984."

This is a vivid and perceptive portrait of a man whose character was as strange and shadowed as his films. Hitchcock's final obsession was secretiveness, but he has been well served by a knowledgeable and revealing biography." Time.

Hitchens, Christopher 1949-2011

Hitchens, Christopher. 1949-2011 **Hitch-22** : a political memoir / Christopher Hitchens. Twelve, 2010. 256 p. **B**

ISBN 9780446540339

1. Intellectuals -- United States 2. Journalists -- United States 3. Authors, American 4. Political journalists 5. United States -- Social life and customs -- 21st century 6. Autobiographies and memoirs

LC 2009051959

National Book Critics Circle Award for Autobiography/ Memoir finalist

The controversial intellectual and author shares his own life story, explaining his contradictory stances on a variety of issues.

"Few authors can rile as easily as Hitchens does, but even his detractors might find it difficult to put down a book so witty, so piercing, so spoiling for a fight. He makes you want to be as good a reader as he is a writer." Booklist.

Hitchens, Christopher. 1949-2011 **Mortality** / Christopher Hitchens. Twelve, 2012. 160 p. **B**

ISBN 9781455502752

1. Hitchens, Christopher. 1949-2011 Health. 2. People with cancer 3. Men with terminal illnesses 4. Mortality. 5. Death. 6. Autobiographies and memoirs

LC 2012014024

Traces the author's battle with esophageal cancer while he continued to write columns on politics and culture for "Vanity Fair," and describes his personal and philosophical view of life and death.

Hitler, Adolf, 1889-1945

★Hitler, Adolf, 1889-1945 **Mein** Kampf / Adolf Hitler ; translated from the German by Ralph Manheim. Houghton Mifflin, c2001. xxii, 694 p. ; **B**

ISBN 0395951054

1. Hitler, Adolf, 1889-1945. 2. Nazi Party (Germany) 3. Nazis. 4. Right-wing extremists. 5. Nazism 6. Germany -- Politics and government -- 20th century. 7. Autobiographies and memoirs

LC 2001051609

"A Mariner book."

Originally published: Boston : Houghton Mifflin, 1943.

With new introd.

A compilation of Hitler's most famous prison writings of 1923--the bible of National Socialism and the blueprint for the Third Reich.

Kershaw, Ian **Hitler** : 1936-1945, nemesis / Ian Kershaw. W.W. Norton, 2000. xxx, 1115 p., 48 p. of plates : **B**

ISBN 9780393049947

1. Hitler, Adolf, 1889-1945. 2. Nazi Party (Germany) 3. Heads of state -- Germany 4. Antisemitism 5. Nazism -- History. 6. Nazis -- Germany 7. Germany -- History -- 1918-1945. 8. Germany -- Politics and government -- 1933-1945. 9. Biographies

Shortlisted for the James Tait Black Memorial Prize for Biography, 2001Draws on previously unused sources, including Joseph Goebbel's diaries, to encompass the the period beginning with the Nazi dictator's attaining absolute power within Germany, through the second World War, to Hitler's suicide.

"Kershaw's two volumes will probably be the standard source for many years." Library Journal.

Kershaw, Ian **Hitler** : a biography / Ian Kershaw. W.W. Norton & Co., 2008. xli, 1029 p., 80 p. of plates : **B**

ISBN 9780393067576

1. Hitler, Adolf, 1889-1945. 2. Nazi Party (Germany) 3. Nazis -- Germany 4. Heads of state -- Germany 5. Dictators -- Germany 6. Politicians -- Germany 7. Germany -- History -- 1918-1945. 8. Germany -- Politics and government -- 1918-1933. 9. Germany -- Politics and government -- 1933-1945. 10. Biographies

LC 2008037294

An abridgement of "Hitler", originally published in two volumes in 1998 (American ed. 1999) and 2000.

A single-volume edition of a classic biographical work traces Hitler's life and addresses key questions about the nature of Nazi radicalism, the Holocaust, and the factors that enabled European society to permit his atrocities.

"This abridgment of the author's two-volume biography on Hitler retains two themes of Kershaw's full-scale original: analyzing the political support the demagogue mustered from the populace and key institutional centers of Germany on his ascent to and exercise of power; and the decisive personal role of Hitler in instigating World War II and genocide. The narrative Kershaw constructs on this foundation is a superb organization and expression of Hitlers chronological arc that plummeted the world into catastrophe and moral trauma, a trajectory informed by Kershaws attention to rationalizations by which people in and outside Germany, whether leaders or led, buried doubts about Hitler until his power was unrestrained, impossible to stop but by war or assassination. Manifestly, Kershaw constitutes core-collection material." Booklist.

Longerich, Peter **Hitler** : a life / Peter Longerich ; translated by Jeremy Noakes and Lesley Sharpe. Oxford University Press, 2019. 912 p. **B**

ISBN 9780190056735

1. Hitler, Adolf, 1889-1945. 2. Nazi Party (Germany) 3. Heads of state -- Germany 4. Nazism 5. Holocaust (1933-1945) 6. Antisemitism 7. Germany -- Politics and government -- 1933-1945. 8. Biographies

LC 2019015905

Acclaimed historian Peter Longerich, author of Goebbels and Heinrich Himmler now turns his attention to Adolf Hitler in this new biography. While many previous portraits have speculated about Hitler's formative years, Longerich focuses on his central role as the driving force of Nazism itself. You cannot separate the man from the monstrous movement he came to embody.

Range, Peter Ross The **unfathomable** ascent : how Hitler came to power / Peter Ross Range. Little, Brown & Company, 2020. 450 p. **B**

ISBN 0316435120

1. Nazi Party (Germany) -- History 2. World leaders 3. Dictators 4. Power (Social sciences) 5. Nationalism 6. Germany -- History -- 1918-1933 7. Germany -- Politics and government -- 1918-1933 8. Biographies

LC bl2020045783

On the night of January 30, 1933, Adolf Hitler leaned out of a spotlit window of the Reich chancellery in Berlin, bursting with joy. The moment seemed unbelievable, even to Hitler. After an improbable political journey that came close to faltering on many occasions, his march to power had finally succeeded. While the path of Hitler's rise has been told in books covering larger portions of his life, no previous work has focused solely on his eight-year climb to rule: 1925-1933.

"This exhaustive account will enlighten even dedicated readers of WWII history." Publishers Weekly

Rosenbaum, Ron **Explaining** Hitler : the search for the origins of his evil / Ron Rosenbaum. Random House, 1998. xlvi, 444 p. **B**

ISBN 9780679431510

1. Hitler, Adolf, 1889-1945 Psychology. 2. Hitler, Adolf, 1889-1945 Family. 3. Motivation (Psychology) 4. Nazism. 5. Nazis. 6. World War II -- Causes. 7. Austria -- Social conditions. 8. Germany -- Politics and government -- 1933-1945. 9. Biographies

LC 97034468

Investigates the heated debate among historians, psychologists, philosophers, and theologians attempting to understand the life and nature of Adolph Hitler

"In this brilliantly skeptical inventory of the world's Hitler-thinking, Rosenbaum analyzes not only the multiple Hitler theories but also the agendas and fantasies that the theorizers bring to their subject." Time.

Ullrich, Volker, 1943- **Hitler** : ascent, 1889-1939 / Volker Ullrich ; translated from the German by Jefferson Chase. Alfred A. Knopf, 2016, c2013. 880 p. **B**

ISBN 9780385354387

1. Hitler, Adolf, 1889-1945. 2. Nazi Party (Germany) 3. Nazism 4. Dictators. 5. Personality. 6. Heads of state. 7. Germany -- History -- 1933-1945. 8. Biographies

LC 2015047202

"A Borzoi book"--Title page verso."

Originally published in Germany ... copyright 2013, S. Fischer Verlag GmbH, Frankfurt am Main"--Title page verso.

Translation of : Adolf Hitler

Draws on previously unseen papers and recent scholarly research to shed new light on the man behind the public persona?from Hitler's childhood and his failures as a young man in Vienna to his First World War experience and his rise as a far-right party leader.

"Above all, in this long but skillfully narrated study, Ullrich reveals Hitler to have been an eminently practical politicianand frighteningly so... one of the best works on Hitler and the origins of the Third Reich to appear in recent years." Kirkus.

Ullrich, Volker, 1943- **Hitler** : downfall, 1939-1945 / Volker Ullrich ; translated from the German by Jefferson Chase. Alfred A. Knopf, 2020, c2018. ix, 838 p. **B**

ISBN 9781101874004

1. Nazism 2. Heads of state -- Germany 3. Dictators 4. Power (Social sciences) 5. Germany -- Politics and government -- 1933-1945 6. Biographies

LC 2019053386

Originally published: Frankfurt : S. Fischer, 2018.

In the summer of 1939 Hitler was at the zenith of his power. The Nazis had consolidated political control in Germany and a series of foreign-policy coups had restored Germany to the status of a major world power. He now embarked on realizing his lifelong ambition: to provide the German people with the resources they needed to flourish and to exterminate those who stood in the way. Yet despite a series of stunning initial triumphs, Hitler's decision to invade the Soviet Union in 1941 turned the tide for good. This is a masterful account of a spectacular downfall, and an essential addition to our understanding of Hitler and the Second World War.

"German historian Ullrich completes his comprehensive biography of the man who is perhaps history's most hated figure. . . . An endlessly revealing look at the Nazi regime that touches on large issues and small details alike." Kirkus

Weber, Thomas, 1974- **Becoming** Hitler : the making of a Nazi / Thomas Weber. Basic Books, 2017. 480 p. **B**

ISBN 9780465032686

1. Hitler, Adolf, 1889-1945. 2. Nazis. 3. Right-wing extremists. 4. Heads of state. 5. Nazism 6. Germany -- Politics and government -- 1918-1933. 7. Biographies

LC 2017022799

Examines Hitler's years in Munich after World War I and his radical transformation from a directionless loner into the leader of Munich's right-wing movement.

"Compelling research and original insights bring a fuller understanding to the mind and motives of the demagogue." Kirkus.

Weber, Thomas, 1974- **Hitler's** first war : Adolf Hitler, the men of the list regiment, and the First World War / Thomas Weber. Oxford University Press, 2010. 416 p. **B**

ISBN 9780199233205

1. Hitler, Adolf, 1889-1945. 2. World War I. 3. Soldiers. 4. Politicians. 5. Draft. 6. Germany -- History. 7. Biographies

LC 2010927224

Offers a profound challenge to the idea that World War I served as the perfect crucible for Hitler's consequent rise.

Ho, Chi Minh, 1890-1969

Duiker, William J., 1932- **Ho** Chi Minh / William J. Duiker. Hyperion, 2000. xix, 695 p., 32 p. of plates : **B**

ISBN 0786863870

1. Communist Party of Vietnam. 2. Viet Cong 3. Vietnam War, 1961-1975. 4. Communism 5. Presidents -- Vietnam 6. Political leadership. 7. Vietnam -- Politics and government -- 1945-1975. 8. Biographies

LC 00026757

Map of Southeast Asia and Pacific Ocean on endpapers.

Describes Ho Chi Minh's poverty-stricken youth, his expatriate years in the U.S., France, and the Soviet Union, and his commitment to the Vietnamese revolution and reunification of Vietnam under Communist rule.

"In this biography the author examines Ho's life primarily in the context of his political activity in Paris, Moscow, southern China, and Vietnam, occasionally spiced with anecdotes of Ho's highly secretive personal life. . . . Duiker handles the complicated political and diplomatic issues with ease, and his narrative, though it sometimes strays from Ho's life to fill in the bigger picture, never bogs down." Booklist.

Hockney, David

Sykes, Christopher Simon, 1948- **David** Hockney : the biography. Christopher Simon Sykes. Nan A. Talese/Doubleday, 2012. 384 p. **B**

ISBN 9780385531443

1. Hockney, David. 2. Artists -- Great Britain 3. Pop art. 4. Gay men. 5. Modern art. 6. Biographies

LC 2011041629

Originally published: Hockney: the biography.

London : Century, the Random House Group, 2011.

A first half of an authorized account of the life and work of the influential British artist and leading proponent of the Pop art genre includes coverage of his education at the Royal College of Art, the role of the 1960s in shaping his vision and his relationship with Peter Schlesinger during the turbulent emergence of gay rights.

Sykes, Christopher Simon, 1948- **David** Hockney : the biography. Christopher Simon Sykes. Nan A. Talese/Doubleday, 2014. 430 p. **B**

ISBN 9780385535908

1. Hockney, David. 2. Artists -- Great Britain 3. Pop art. 4. Gay men. 5. Modern art. 6. Biographies

"Recommended for anyone interested in the remarkable life of this highly regarded painter. Rich with archival detail and the insight of family, friends, and the artist himself, the book is an engaging read." Library Journal.

Hodgman, George

Hodgman, George **Bettyville** : a memoir / George Hodgman. Viking Adult, 2015. 288 p. **B**

ISBN 9780525427209

1. Hodgman, George. 2. Children of aging parents 3. Homecomings 4. Aging parents -- Care 5. Mothers and sons 6. Middle West 7. Missouri. 8. Autobiographies and memoirs

LC 2014038536

National Book Critics Circle Award for Autobiography/ Memoir finalist

A veteran magazine and book editor returns to his hometown of Paris, Missouri, to take care of his aging mother, Betty, a strong-willed woman who speaks her mind and has never really accepted the fact that her son is gay.

"A tender, resolute look at a place, literal and figurative, baby boomers might find themselves." Booklist.

Hodgman, John

Hodgman, John **Medallion** status : true stories from secret rooms / John Hodgman. Viking, 2019. 304 p. **B**

ISBN 9780525561101

1. Hodgman, John. 2. Fame -- Humor. 3. Authors, American 4. Podcasters 5. Fathers and sons. 6. Essays 7. Autobiographies and memoirs

LC 2019024340

The "Judge John Hodgman" podcaster and best-selling author of Vacationland reflects on his unlikely career, the surreal dynamics of moderate fame, the cancellation of his television job and his relationship with his young son.

Hodgman, John **Vacationland** : true stories from painful beaches / John Hodgman. Viking Press, 2017 288 p. **B**

ISBN 9780735224803

1. Voyages and travels 2. Personal conduct 3. Essays 4. Autobiographies and memoirs

LC 2017031760

A memoir of the author's cursed travels through the woods of Massachusetts and coastal Maine, describing his midlife transformation from an idealistic youth to an eccentric family man and his observations on such subjects as the horror of freshwater clams and the evolutionary purpose of the mustache.

"Hodgman is a disarmingly witty storyteller, at once waggish and incisive, droll and tender. Indeed, deep feelings flow beneath the mirth." Booklist.

Hoffa, Jimmy, 1913-1975?

Russell, Thaddeus **Out** of the jungle : Jimmy Hoffa and the remaking of the American working class / Thaddeus Russell. Temple University Press, 2003, c2001. xii, 272 p., 8 p. of plates : **B**

ISBN 1592130275

1. International Brotherhood of Teamsters, Chauffeurs, Warehousemen, and Helpers of America. 2. Labor union officials and employees 3. Labor leaders. 4. Labor movement. 5. Working class. 6. Biographies

LC 2002043556

Originally published: New York : A.A. Knopf, 2001."

Russell makes good use of a range of primary-source materials plus period newspaper accounts and other materials to highlight this story." Library Journal.

Hoffman, Claire

Hoffman, Claire **Greetings** from Utopia Park : surviving a transcendent childhood / Claire Hoffman. HarperCollins, 2016 320 p. **B**

ISBN 9780062338846

1. Growing up 2. Adult children of hippies. 3. Transcendental meditation 4. Autobiographies and memoirs

LC bl2016019226

A journalist describes her experiences as a jaded, skeptical teenager growing up in a secluded utopia in Iowa, Maharishi's National Headquarters for Heaven on Earth, which promoted Transcendental Meditation as a path to peace and enlightenment.

"With honesty and sincerity, this account of coming of age within the ostensible confines of an alternative lifestyle delivers valuable knowledge of another phenomenon of cultural divergence." Library Journal.

Hogan, Linda

Hogan, Linda The **woman** who watches over the world : a native memoir / Linda Hogan. W.W. Norton, 2001. 207 p. **B**

ISBN 0393050181

1. Hogan, Linda. 2. Hogan, Linda Family. 3. Authors, American -- 20th century -- Family relationships. 4. Authors, American -- 20th century 5. Chickasaw Indians 6. Native American authors 7. Biographies

LC 00049005

A Chickasaw woman blends her personal history of struggle with the stories of native women who participated in key events during the Indian Wars more than a century ago.

"In this memoir the author ... expresses a lacerating yet crucial vision of the tragic legacies of the U.S. government's brutal war on Native Americans." Booklist.

Holbrooke, Richard C., 1941-2010

★Packer, George, 1960- **Our** man : Richard Holbrooke and the end of the American century / George Packer. Alfred A. Knopf, 2019. 480 p. **B**

ISBN 9780307958020

1. Holbrooke, Richard C., 1941-2010. 2. Diplomats 3. Ambassadors 4. Politicians 5. Ambition in men 6. United States -- Politics and government -- 20th century 7. Biographies

LC 2018030382

"A Borzoi book."

Pulitzer Prize for Biography or Autobiography finalist, 2020.

National Book Critics Circle Award for Biography finalist, 2019

The National Book Award-winning author of *The Unwinding* draws on firsthand writings in a narrative portrait of the influential American diplomat that explores how his achievements over half a century of history were complicated by his political ambitions.

"An insightful and indispensable rendering of an intriguing and accomplished figure who persisted in the pursuit of peace." Library Journal.

Holiday, Billie, 1915-1959

★Holiday, Billie, 1915-1959 **Lady** sings the blues / Billie Holiday with William Dufty ; [foreword by David Ritz]. Harlem Moon, 2006, c1956. xv, 231 p. : **B**

ISBN 0767923863

1. Holiday, Billie, 1915-1959 Discography. 2. Singers -- United States 3. African American singers 4. Jazz musicians 5. Autobiographies and memoirs

LC bl2006018106

Originally published: New York : Doubleday, 1956.

With a new introduction and rev. discography."

Inside! 10-track tribute CD"--Cover.

Billie Holiday describes her early childhood in an East Baltimore ghetto, her career as an internationally-acclaimed jazz vocalist, and her years spent battling a drug habit.

Holman, James, 1786-1857

Roberts, Jason A **sense** of the world : how a blind man became history's greatest traveler / Jason Roberts. HarperCollins, c2006. xiv, 382 p. : **B**

ISBN 9780007161065

1. Holman, James, 1786-1857. 2. Travelers -- England 3. Voyages and travels. 4. Blindness. 5. Ocean travel. 6. Biographies

LC 2005058166

National Book Critics Circle Award for Biography finalist, 2006.

Offers a portrait of James Holman, a nineteenth-century adventurer renowned for his solo journey around the world, despite a blindness brought on by a mysterious shipboard illness during the Napoleonic Wars.

"Roberts does Holman justice, evoking with grace and wit the tale of this man once lionized as The Blind Traveler." Publishers Weekly.

Holmes, Dave, 1971-

Holmes, Dave, 1971- **Party** of one : a memoir in 21 songs / Dave Holmes. Crown Archetype, an imprint of the Crown Publishing Group, a division of Penguin Random House LLC, 2016. 304 p. **B**

ISBN 9780804187985

1. Holmes, Dave, 1971- Childhood and youth. 2. M T V (Cable television network) 3. Self-acceptance. 4. Gay men -- United States 5. Popular music -- United States -- Miscellanea. 6. Comedians -- United States 7. Coming-of-age stories 8. Autobiographies and memoirs

LC 2015047486

The comic, writer and former MTV VJ presents an uproarious memoir of his experiences as a music geek and social misfit who fumbled his way toward self-acceptance through three decades of music. Illustrations.

"A hilarious and touching coming-of-age story that will strike a particular nerve among Generation Y." Kirkus.

Holmes, Oliver Wendell, Jr., 1841-1935

Budiansky, Stephen **Oliver** Wendell Holmes : a life in war, law, and ideas / Stephen Budiansky. W. W. Norton & Company, 2019. 560 p. **B**

ISBN 9780393634723

1. Holmes, Oliver Wendell, Jr., 1841-1935. 2. United States. Supreme Court Justices 3. Judges -- United States 4. Judicial opinions 5. Judicial review 6. Biographies

LC 2018054671

A portrait of the influential U.S. Supreme Court justice includes coverage of his achievements as a legal scholar, his Civil War service and his often-dissenting but prophetic views on free speech, criminal justice and economic reform.

"This wide-ranging examination of Holmes as an individual and of the law he helped make will appeal to those with an interest in constitutional law as well as to general readers." Publishers Weekly.

Holmes, Richard, 1945-

Holmes, Richard, 1945- **This** long pursuit : reflections of a romantic biographer / Richard Holmes. Pantheon Books, 2017 400 p. **B**

ISBN 9780307379689

1. Biographers. 2. Research 3. Romanticism. 4. Writing 5. Autobiographies and memoirs

LC 2016040528

In this chronicle of his lifelong obsession with discovering, assembling, and re-creating the lives of writers and scientists, Richard Holmes here casts a new eye not only on the Romantic poets and lost women of Romantic science he has long studied, including Margaret Cavendish and Mary Somerville, but on their biographers, as well. He examines the evolution of the myths that have overshadowed certain lives (Percy Shelley's death at sea, Mary Wollstonecraft's paramours, Samuel Taylor Coleridge's opium-fueled lectures), and reveals how the manner in which each generation tells the stories of the lives that came before it shapes and is shaped by a contemporary understanding of human nature.

Hong, Cathy Park

Hong, Cathy Park **Minor** feelings : an Asian American reckoning / Cathy Park Hong. One World, 2020. 206 p. **B**

ISBN 9781984820365

1. Hong, Cathy Park. 2. Asian Americans 3. Asian American women 4. Poets, American 5. Identity (Psychology) 6. Autobiographies and memoirs 7. Essays

LC 2019033869

An award-winning poet and essayist offers a ruthlessly honest, emotionally charged exploration of the psychological condition of being Asian American.

"An extraordinary blend of memoir, cultural criticism, and history that will invite readers from all backgrounds, though especially those who identify as Asian American, to consider the complex relationships between race, family, heritage, and society that shape American lives." Library Journal

Honnold, Alex

★Honnold, Alex **Alone** on the wall / Alex Honnold, with David Roberts. W. W. Norton & Company, 2015. viii, 248 p., 16 unnumbered p. of plates : **B**

ISBN 9780393247626

1. Rock climbing. 2. Rock climbers. 3. Autobiographies and memoirs

The extreme climber famed for his solo ascents without ropes, partners or gear describes his seven most significant achievements, including a free-solo climb up Mexico's Sendero Luminoso and the Fitz Traverse ascent in Patagonia.

Hood, Ann, 1956-

Hood, Ann, 1956- **Kitchen** yarns : notes on life, love, and food / Ann Hood. W.W. Norton & Company, independent publishers since 1923, [2018] 256 p. **B**

ISBN 9780393249507

1. Authors, American 2. Italian American families 3. Cooking -- Psychological aspects 4. Cooking, Italian 5. Providence, Rhode Island 6. Essays 7. Autobiographies and memoirs

LC 2018027425

A collection of personal essays and recipes by the best-selling author of The Knitting Circle reflects on the culinary experiences that shaped her Italian-American childhood and adult family life and includes the award-winning piece, "The Golden Silver Palate."

Hood, Ann, 1956- **Morningstar** : growing up with books / Ann Hood. W. W. Norton & Company, 2017. 192 p. **B**

ISBN 9780393254815

1. Women authors 2. Growing up 3. Books and reading 4. Identity (Psychology) 5. Rhode Island 6. Autobiographies and memoirs

LC 2017015737

The award-winning author reveals the personal stories behind her written works, describing her early years in a Rhode Island mill town and the books that shaped her love of literature, her political views and her travel ambitions.

"Hood has beautifully crafted a very convincing case for discovering literature and getting lost in the pages." Publishers Weekly.

hooks, bell, 1952-

hooks, bell, 1952- **Wounds** of passion : a writing life / bell hooks. H. Holt, 1997. xxiii, 260 p. ; **B**

ISBN 080504146X

1. Women authors, American 2. Feminism. 3. Self-acceptance in women. 4. Writing. 5. Autobiographies and memoirs

LC 97023506

Sequel to: Bone Black.

A powerful memoir tells how one woman writer found her own voice while creating a personal love relationship based on feminist thinking and reflects on the impact of birth control and the women's movement on society.

"In this continuation of the author's autobiography, Hooks chronicles her rigorous education, both in a long, complicated relationship with a fellow writer and as a college and graduate student, experiences that led her away from poetry (her first literary love) to groundbreaking prose that expressed her feminist convictions and views on the status of black women in America." Booklist.

Hoover, Herbert, 1874-1964

Rappleye, Charles **Herbert** Hoover in the White House : the ordeal of the presidency / Charles Rappleye. Simon & Schuster, 2016. 560 p. **B**

ISBN 9781451648676

1. Hoover, Herbert, 1874-1964. 2. Presidents -- United States 3. Political leadership 4. Depressions -- 1929-1941 5. United States -- Politics and government -- 1929-1933.

LC 2015027333

Describes the uphill battle faced by the 31st president, who served his single term during the Great Depression, portraying the man as bright, well-meaning and energetic but ultimately lacking in the tools of leadership.

"A fair, fresh, and fantastic reappraisal of a forgotten figure." Library Journal.

Whyte, Kenneth **Hoover** : an extraordinary life in extraordinary times / Kenneth Whyte. Alfred A. Knopf, 2017. 752 p. **B**

ISBN 9780307597960

1. Hoover, Herbert, 1874-1964. 2. Presidents -- United States 3. Businesspeople 4. Politicians 5. Depressions -- 1929-1941 6. United States -- Politics and government -- 1919-1933 7. Biographies

LC 2017015685

"A Borzoi Book."

National Book Critics Circle Award for Biography finalist, 2017

A portrait of the 31st president traces his difficult childhood and meteoric business career through his significant contributions during World War I and the Great Depression, sharing insights into his less-recognized economic and political achievements.

"With adept explanations of the Depression's complexities and a refreshing sense of objectivity regarding Hoover's approach to combatting it, Whyte portrays a figure to be neither pitied nor reviled, but better understood." Publishers Weekly.

Hoover, J. Edgar, 1895-1972

Gentry, Curt, 1931- **J.** Edgar Hoover : the man and the secrets / Curt Gentry. W.W. Norton, 2001, c1991. 846 p. : **B**

ISBN 0393321282

1. Hoover, J. Edgar, 1895-1972. 2. FBI. 3. FBI agents 4. Police 5. Government executives 6. Biographies

LC BL2001001027

Reprint.

Originally published: 1991.

A biography of the FBI chief reveals connections between Hoover and organized crime, his manipulation of six presidencies, and his assault on civil rights.

"The author has based his account of Hoover on more than 300 interviews and on access to previously classified FBI documents. Gentry paints a portrait of Hoover as the 'indispensable man,' with many provocative revelations about his political dealings." Library Journal.

Hope, Bob, 1903-2003

Quirk, Lawrence J. **Bob** Hope : the road well-traveled / Lawrence J. Quirk. Applause, c1998. viii, 327 p. : **B**

ISBN 1557833532

1. Comedians -- United States 2. Actors and actresses -- United States 3. Adopted children -- United States 4. United States -- Social life and customs -- 20th century 5. Biographies

LC 98087957

Recounts Hope's rise from poverty in England to success as a comedian and actor, and discusses his relationships with his wife, Dolores, and other women, his adopted children, allegations of homophobia, and other details of his private life

"Quirk recaps Hope's life and surveys his relationships with myriad entertainment personalities. This is a good, solid Hollywood bio by a veteran Tinseltown observer." Booklist.

Zoglin, Richard **Hope** : entertainer of the century

/ Richard Zoglin. Simon & Schuster, 2014. 384 p. **B**
ISBN 9781439140277
1. Hope, Bob, 1903-2003. 2. Comedians -- United States 3. Biographies
LC 2014014371

Draws on exclusive reporting to honor Bob Hope's top-rated successes while discussing such topics as his secret first marriage, stint in reform school and ambivalent relationships with fellow stars.

"Not just for Hope fans, Zoglin's work will also appeal to readers interested in the colorful history of American entertainment, in which Hope played a prominent role." Booklist.

Hopkins, Lightnin', 1912-1982

Govenar,AlanB.,1952- **Lightnin'** Hopkins:hislifeandblues/Alan Govenar. Chicago Review Press, c2010. xiv, 334 p. : **B**
ISBN 9781556529627
1. Hopkins, Lightnin', 1912-1982. 2. Blues musicians 3. African American musicians 4. African American blues musicians 5. Blues guitarists. 6. Biographies
LC 2009048798

"An A Cappella book."

Looks at the life, career, and influence of the blues musician, along with a critical analysis of his works and quotations from his lyrics.

Hopper, Edward, 1882-1967

Hopper, Edward, 1882-1967 **Edward** Hopper : the art and the artist / Gail Levin. Norton : 1980. xv, 299 p. : **B**
ISBN 0393315770
1. Hopper, Edward, 1882-1967 Exhibitions 2. Artists -- United States -- Biography. 3. Realism in art. 4. Realism. 5. Autobiographies and memoirs
LC 79027958

Accompanies the exhibition organized by the Whitney Museum and sponsored by Philip Morris Incorporated and the National Endowment for the Arts; to be held at Hayward Gallery, London, Feb. 11-Mar. 29, 1981, and four other museums, Apr. 22, 1981-Feb. 10, 1982.

Covers all phases of the prominent realist's work and reveals aspects of Hopper's personality and life that help explain his artistic development

Hopper, Grace Murray, 1906-1992

★Beyer, Kurt **Grace** Hopper and the invention of the information age / Kurt Beyer. MIT Press, c2009. xii, 389 p. : **B**
ISBN 9780262013109
1. Women computer engineers -- United States 2. Computer science -- United States -- History. 3. Technological innovations. 4. Computer engineers 5. Biographies
LC 2008044229

"In Beyer's fascinating mix of biography and technological history, Grace Hopper comes vividly to life as a navy admiral who launched the art of computer programming." Booklist.

Hopps, Walter

Hopps, Walter The **dream** colony : a life in art / Walter Hopps ; edited by Deborah Treisman, from interviews with Anne Doran ; introduction by Ed Ruscha. Bloomsbury USA, 2017. 288 p. **B**
ISBN 9781632865298
1. Hopps, Walter. 2. Art museum curators. 3. Collectors and collecting. 4. Modern art. 5. Autobiographies and memoirs 6. Interviews
LC 2016055073

A colorful, personal and eye-opening account of the life of Walter Hopps, the innovative, iconoclastic curator of contemporary art, doubles as a panoramic look at art in America in the second half of the 20th century through the eyes of one of the greatest artistic minds of the time.

"Readers interested in 20th-century art will enjoy this memoir by influential gallery owner and curator Walter Hopps (1932-2005)." Library Journal.

Hornbacher, Marya, 1974-

Hornbacher, Marya, 1974- **Wasted** : a memoir of anorexia and bulimia / Marya Hornbacher. Harper Perennial, 2014, c1998. 298 p. ; **B**
ISBN 9780062327031
1. Hornbacher, Marya, 1974- Health. 2. People with anorexia 3. People with bulimia 4. Anorexia nervosa 5. Eating disorders 6. United States -- Social life and customs -- 20th century 7. Autobiographies and memoirs
LC BL 99000897

Originally published: New York : HarperCollins, 1998.

The author shares her lifelong battle with bulimia and anorexia, chronicling her secret life of bingeing and purging and her obsession with food and body image, substance abuse, and sex.

"This is a gritty, unflinching look at eating disorders. Hornbacher is at her best when she zeroes in on the specifics of eating disorders and their origins." New York Times Book Review.

Horne, Lena,

Gavin, James, 1964- **Stormy** weather : the life of Lena Horne / James Gavin. Atria, 2009. 608 p. **B**
ISBN 9780743271431
1. Singers -- United States 2. African American women singers 3. Actors and actresses 4. African American women 5. United States -- Social life and customs -- 20th century. 6. Biographies
LC 2009008170

Profiles the Hollywood actress and singer, evaluating her painful childhood, the challenges she faced as a barrier-breaking African-American performer, and the ways in which she inspired other performers.

"Horne has had a life so rich in ups and downs as to make page after page eventful and suspenseful. This all the more so since the book is also two books in one: a thorough and fluent biography and a history of the slow social rise of black people despite crippling discrimination and stinging humiliationsa history in which Horne's story is embedded." New York Times Book Review.

Hosack, David, 1769-1835

★Johnson, Victoria, 1969- **American** Eden : David Hosack, botany, and medicine in the garden of the early republic / Victoria Johnson. Liveright Publishing Corporation, 2018. 461 p. **B**
ISBN 9781631494192
1. Botany 2. Botanical gardens 3. Physicians 4. Horticulture 5. United States -- History -- 19th century 6. Biographies
National Book Award for Nonfiction finalist, 2018
Pulitzer Prize for History finalist, 2019.

The untold story of Hamilton's--and Burr's--personal physician, whose dream to build America's first botanical garden inspired the young Republic.

"A brilliant evocation of a man and his time. Plant lovers, history buffs, New Yorkaphiles, those interested in early medicine, even Hamiltonians--all will find this engrossing." Library Journal.

Houdini, Harry, 1874-1926

Posnanski, Joe The **life** and afterlife of Harry Houdini /

Joe Posnanski. Avid Reader Press, 2019. xv, 316 p. : **B**

ISBN 9781501137235

1. Houdini, Harry, 1874-1926. 2. Magicians 3. Escape artists 4. Legacies 5. Entertainers 6. United States -- Social life and customs -- 20th century. 7. Biographies

Award-winning journalist Joe Posnanski enters the world of Harry Houdini and his legions of devoted fans in an immersive, entertaining, and magical work on the illusionist's impact on American culture - and why his legacy endures to this day.

House, Callie, 1861-1928

Berry, Mary Frances **My** face is black is true : Callie House and the struggle for ex-slave reparations / Mary Frances Berry. Alfred A. Knopf, 2005. xiv, 314 p. : **B**

ISBN 1400040035

1. House, Callie, 1861-1928. 2. African American women political activists 3. Women political activists -- United States 4. African Americans -- Reparations. 5. Biographies

LC 2004051330

"This is a Borzoi Book"--T.p. verso."

The author unearths the intriguing story of Callie House (1861-1928), a Tennessee washerwoman and seamstress become activist, and the organization she led, the National Ex-Slave Mutual Relief, Bounty and Pension Association... Students and scholars of African-American history, as well as those engaged in the current reparations debates, will be deeply informed by the rise and fall of the Ex-Slave Association." Publishers Weekly.

House, Edward Mandell, 1858-1938

Neu, Charles E. **Colonel** House : a biography of Woodrow Wilson's silent partner / Charles E. Neu. Oxford University Press, 2015. 624 p. **B**

ISBN 9780195045505

1. House, Edward Mandell, 1858-1938. 2. Wilson, Woodrow, 1856-1924 Friends and associates. 3. Versailles, Treaty of, June 28, 1919 (Germany) 4. Politicians 5. World War I 6. Male friendship 7. United States -- Foreign relations -- 1913-1921. 8. United States -- Politics and government -- 1913-1921. 9. Biographies

LC 2014015227

"Neu deems House a 'patient, crafty, and sometimes cynical' in-fighter and 'a shrewd observer of human foibles,' widely admired but faulted by some at the height of his fame for developing an exaggerate d sense of his own importance. A significant, brightly written American story." Kirkus.

Howard, Luke, 1772-1864

Hamblyn, Richard, 1965- The **invention** of clouds : how an amateur meteorologist forged the language of the skies / Richard Hamblyn. Farrar, Straus and Giroux, 2001. x, 403 p. : **B**

ISBN 9780374177157

1. Howard, Luke, 1772-1864. 2. Clouds. 3. Clouds -- Identification. 4. Chemists -- England 5. Meteorology -- England -- History -- 19th century. 6. London, England -- History -- 19th century. 7. Biographies

LC 00068189

Details the true story of a timid young Quaker and amateur meteorologist named Luke Howard who was hurled into the spotlight when he assigned poetic names to the clouds in December 1802, which became a landmark in natural history and meteorology and caused him to become immortalized in the works of the Romantics.

"A remarkable, remarkably pleasing story." Booklist.

Howe, Ben Ryder

Howe, Ben Ryder **My** Korean deli : risking it all for a convenience store / Ben Ryder Howe. Henry Holt and Co., c2010. 320 p. **B**

ISBN 9780805093438

1. Howe, Ben Ryder. 2. Editors -- United States 3. Supplementary employment. 4. Delicatessens 5. Culture conflict 6. New York City -- Social life and customs 7. Brooklyn, New York City -- Social life and customs 8. Autobiographies and memoirs

LC 2010024962

A former senior editor of "The Paris Review" recounts his participation in a family effort to buy and run a Korean convenience store for his in-laws, a pursuit that raised issues about work and family while he shuttled between two divergent cultural arenas.

"The author's wife Gab bought (with the money the couple had saved for a down payment on their first house) her hardworking Korean parents a deli in Brooklyn as a gesture of thanks for all their self-sacrifice. What follows is a series of both comic and tragic vignettes that will leave the reader as surprised as the author about how emotionally invested you can get in a deli. [Howe] delivers a smartly written narrative about love, literature, and the lengths one goes to for family, which turns out to be epically far." Maclean's.

Howe, Gordie, 1928-

Howe, Gordie, 1928- **Mr.** Hockey : my story / Gordie Howe. Penguin Group USA, 2014. 320 p. **B**

ISBN 9780399172915

1. Hockey Hall of Fame. 2. Hockey. 3. Hockey players 4. Sports -- History -- 20th century. 5. Athletes 6. Autobiographies and memoirs.

LC 2015410204

A personal account by the hockey Hall of Famer traces his Depression-era childhood, record-setting career and enduring relationships with his wife and children.

"The author intersperses portions of personal letters he sent to and received from family members. Lots of action, a bit of rumination and few regrets in this unremarkable work by a most remarkable athlete." Kirkus.

Howe, Julia Ward, 1819-1910

Showalter, Elaine The **civil** wars of Julia Ward Howe : a biography / Elaine Showalter. Simon & Schuster, 2016. 352 p. **B**

ISBN 9781451645903

1. Howe, Julia Ward, 1819-1910. 2. Authors, American -- 19th century 3. Women authors, American -- 19th century 4. Feminists -- United States 5. Biographies

LC 2015027331

Describes the life of the woman who wrote The Battle Hymn of the Republic, who worked tirelessly as an outspoken abolitionist and women's rights activist while she wrote and published poems and raised six children.

"A robust and enlightening feminist portrait of a national icon." Booklist.

Howerton, Kristen

Howerton, Kristen **Rage** against the minivan : learning to parent without perfection / Kristen Howerton. Convergent, 2020 xi, 202 p. **B**

ISBN 9781984825162

1. Howerton, Kristen. 2. Motherhood. 3. Child care 4. Motherhood -- Humor. 5. Parenting. 6. Autobiographies and memoirs

LC 2020003348

Having four kids in four years, a licensed marriage and family therapist, in this heartfelt, subversively funny memoir, shares valuable lessons from her journey through motherhood and challenges the idea that there's a "right" way to raise kids.

"A candid and witty alternative to more formulaic parenting books." Kirkus

Huang, Eddie, 1982-

Huang, Eddie, 1982- **Fresh** off the boat : a memoir / Eddie Huang. Spiegel & Grau, c2013. 240 p. **B**

ISBN 9780679644880

1. Restaurateurs -- New York City 2. Taiwanese Americans 3. Ethnic identity 4. Race relations 5. Autobiographies and memoirs 6. Books to TV

LC 2012025704

A Taiwanese-American rebel restaurateur chronicles his rise to success from his difficult childhood in the American South to his turn as a drug dealer who embraced rap culture and more.

Hudson, Clifford

Hudson, Clifford **Master** of none : how a jack-of-all-trades can still reach the top / Clifford Hudson. Harper Business, 2020. 240 p. **B**

ISBN 9780062889034

1. Hudson, Clifford. 2. Career development. 3. Leadership. 4. Success (Concept) 5. Success in business 6. Autobiographies and memoirs

LC 2020014400

A thought-provoking memoir from the former CEO of Sonic discusses whether or not mastery is necessary to succeed, theorizing that expertise is risky and can lead to over-confidence and instead promotes embracing variety and versatility.

"Hudson's book is so enjoyable that readers may not at first realize the trove of valuable advice it contains." Publishers Weekly

Hudson, Rock, 1925-1985

Griffin, Mark, 1968- **All** that Heaven allows : a biography of Rock Hudson / Mark Griffin. HarperCollins 2018 272 p. **B**

ISBN 9780062408853

1. Actors and actresses 2. Closeted gay men 3. People with AIDS 4. Gay men with AIDS 5. Biographies

LC 2018188285

Offers a biography of a deeply complex and widely misunderstood matinee idol of Hollywood's Golden Age.

Hughes, Langston, 1902-1967

★Hughes, Langston, 1902-1967 **I** wonder as I wander : an autobiographical journey / Langston Hughes ; introd. by Arnold Rampersad. Hill and Wang, 1993, c1956. xxii, 405 p. ; **B**

ISBN 0809015501

1. Hughes, Langston, 1902-1967. 2. African American authors -- 20th century 3. Poets, American -- 20th century 4. African American poets 5. Authors, American 6. United States -- History -- 1929-1939. 7. Autobiographies and memoirs

LC 92039307

Originally published: New York : Rinehart, 1956."

A book concerned with the individual, with social issues and with art as it is a part of these things will bring its rewards as a documentary and an important diary." Kirkus.

Rampersad, Arnold The **life** of Langston Hughes: volume I, 1902-1941: I, too, sing America / Arnold Rampersad. Oxford University Press, 2002, c1986. 478 p. : **B**

ISBN 9780195151602

1. Hughes, Langston, 1902-1967. 2. Poets, American -- 20th century 3. African American poets 4. Biographies

LC 2001058766

National Book Critics Circle Award for Biography, 1986.

A biography of the Harlem poet whose works gave voice to the joy and pain of the black experience in America.

★Rampersad, Arnold The **life** of Langston Hughes: volume II, 1941-1967: I dream a world / Arnold Rampersad. Oxford University Press, 2002, c1987. 522 p. : **B**

ISBN 9780195151619

1. Hughes, Langston, 1902-1967. 2. Poets, American -- 20th century 3. African American poets 4. Biographies

LC 2001058766

Pulitzer Prize for Biography or Autobiography finalist

A biography of the Harlem poet whose works gave voice to the joy and pain of the Black experience in America.

Hughes, Ted, 1930-1998

Feinstein, Elaine **Ted** Hughes : the life of a poet / Elaine Feinstein. Norton, 2001. xiv, 273 p. : **B**

ISBN 0393049671

1. Hughes, Ted, 1930-1998. 2. Plath, Sylvia Marriage 3. Poets, English -- 20th century 4. Husband and wife. 5. Men/women relations. 6. Extramarital affairs. 7. Biographies

LC 2001044925

"This biography of the English poet examines Hughes's relationship with his first wife, Sylvia Plath, who committed suicide in 1963 during the acrimonious breakup of their marriage, . {and with} Assia Wevill, the woman for whom Hughes left Plath, and who later killed herself and their child." The Economist.

Humbert, Agnes

Humbert, Agnes **Resistance** : a woman's journal of struggle and defiance in occupied France / Agnes Humbert ; translated by Barbara Mellor. Bloomsbury, 2008. 208 p. **B**

ISBN 9781596915596

1. Humbert, Agnes. 2. Prisoners of war, French -- Germany -- Diaries. 3. World War II -- Prisoners and prisons, German. 4. Forced labor. 5. French Resistance (World War II) 6. France -- History -- German occupation, 1940-1945.

LC 2008016603

Translation of : Notre guerre.

A diary by a key member of the French Resistance during the German occupation of 1940 recounts her group's betrayal to the Gestapo, her imprisonment and deportation to Germany, and the brutal treatment she and her friends endured in labor camps.

Humboldt, Alexander von, 1769-1859

★Wulf, Andrea The **invention** of nature : Alexander von Humboldt's new world / Andrea Wulf. Alfred A. Knopf, 2015 480 p. **B**

ISBN 9780385350662

1. Humboldt, Alexander von, 1769-1859. 2. Scientists -- Germany 3. Naturalists -- Germany 4. Exploration 5. Nature 6. Biographies

LC 2015017505

"THIS IS A BORZOI BOOK"--T.p. verso.Costa Biography Award, 2015.

Royal Society General Prizes for Science Books, 2016

Andrew Carnegie Medal for Excellence in Non-Fiction Finalist, 2016.

Cundill Prize in Historical Literature finalist, 2016

Kirkus Prize for Nonfiction finalist, 2015.

A portrait of the lesser-known German naturalist reveals his ongoing influence on humanity's relationship with the natural world today, discussing such topics as his views on climate change, conservation and nature as a resource for all life. By the author of Founding Gardeners.

"Wulf presents with zest and eloquence the full story of Humboldt's adventurous life and extraordinary achievements, from making science 'accessible and popular' to his early warnings about how deforestation, monoculture agriculture, and industrialization would engender disastrous climate change." Booklist.

Humiston, Grace (Mary Grace), 1869-1948

Ricca, Brad **Mrs.** Sherlock Holmes : the true story of New York's City's greatest female detective and the 1917 missing girl case that captivated a nation / Brad Ricca. St. Martin's Press, 2016. 432 p. **B**

ISBN 9781250072245

1. Humiston, Grace (Mary Grace), 1869-1948. 2. Women private investigators. 3. Missing teenage girls. 4. Cold cases (Criminal investigation) 5. Women lawyers. 6. New York City. 7. Biographies.

Presents the shocking true story of the first female U.S. District Attorney and traveling detective who found missing 18-year-old Ruth Cruger when the entire NYPD had given up.

"Rapid, compelling storytelling informed by rigorous research and enlivened by fecund imagination." Kirkus.

Humphreys, Richard, 1967-

Humphreys, Richard, 1967- **Under** pressure : living life and avoiding death on a nuclear submarine / Richard Humphreys. Hanover Square Press, 2020 267 p. **B**

ISBN 9781335996244

1. United States. Navy 2. Sailors 3. Submarines 4. Nuclear submarines 5. Seafaring life

LC bl2020013351

A former Royal Navy nuclear submariner describes the daily experiences of his military life during the Cold War, a service marked by claustrophobia, disorientation, body odors, cramped conditions and constant fear.

"An amusing addition to the rare genre of submariner memoirs." Kirkus

Hunt, Edward Proctor, 1861-1948

Nabokov, Peter **How** the world moves : the odyssey of an American Indian family / Peter Nabokov. Viking Press, 2015 448 p. **B**

ISBN 9780670024889

1. Pueblo Indians 2. Indians of North America 3. Shamans 4. Rites and ceremonies 5. Southwest (United States) 6. Biographies

LC 2016288005

Narrated through both a multicultural and historical context, a fascinating chronicle of Pueblo Indian life and Anglo/Indian relations over the last century and a half follows Edward Proctor Hunt, who broke with his people's ancient codes to become a shopkeeper and controversial broker between the Indian and white worlds. By the editor of Native American Testimony.

"The pull of the Pueblo was always powerful, and the familial ties and love of ceremony and song were sufficient to bring them back often. The lure of the Land of Enchantment is irresistible, as Nabokov draws us into the simple, cooperative life of the Pueblo Indians and their magnificent territory. A great choice for lovers of the Southwest." Kirkus.

Hurston, Zora Neale

Boyd, Valerie **Wrapped** in rainbows : the life of Zora Neale Hurston / Valerie Boyd. Scribner, 2003. 527 p., 16 p. of plates : **B**

ISBN 0684842300

1. Hurston, Zora Neale. 2. Authors, American -- 20th century 3. African American women -- Southern States 4. Folklorists, American 5. African-American dramatists 6. Southern States 7. Florida. 8. Biographies

LC 2002017011

"A Lisa Drew book."

ALA Notable Book, 2004."

As the author adeptly and passionately analyzes Hurston's revolutionary books, intense spirituality, and myriad adventures, Hurston emerges in all her splendornot only smarter, tougher, and more dazzlingly alive than most people but also freer." Booklist.

★Hurston, Zora Neale **Dust** tracks on a road : the restored text established by the Library of America / Zora Neale Hurston ; with a foreword by Maya Angelou. Harper Perennial Modern Classics, 2006, c1996. xii, 308, 16 p. : **B**

ISBN 0060854081

1. African American women -- Southern States 2. Harlem Renaissance. 3. Folklorists -- United States 4. African American authors -- 20th century 5. Southern States -- Social life and customs. 6. Autobiographies and memoirs

LC 2005052616

"Originally published in 1942 by J.B. Lippincott, Inc. The restored text was published in 1995 by the Library of America as part of Folklore, memoirs & other writings"--T.p. verso."

First Harper Perennial edition published 1996"--T.p. verso.

Presents the story of an African American woman who rose from poverty to become an author who held a prominent place among the artists and intellectuals of the Harlem Renaissance.

Hurston, Zora Neale **Zora** Neale Hurston : a life in letters / Zora Neale Hurston ; collected and edited by Carla Kaplan. Doubleday, 2002. ix, 880 p., 8 p. of plates : **B**

ISBN 0385490356

1. Hurston, Zora Neale Correspondence. 2. Authors, American -- 20th century -- Correspondence. 3. Folklorists, American -- Correspondence. 4. African American authors -- Correspondence. 5. African American women authors -- Correspondence. 6. Letters.

LC 00065671

A collection of more than five hundred letters, written to such people as Langston Hughes, Dorothy West, and many others, paints a portrait of the enigmatic woman who became one of the greatest literary figures in American history.

"These letters reveal a gifted yet complex personality at once humorous, cynical, and analytical." Library Journal.

Jones, Sharon L. (Sharon Lynette) **Critical** companion to Zora Neale Hurston : a literary reference to her life and work / Sharon L. Jones. Facts On File, c2009. xvi, 288 p. : **B**

ISBN 9780816068852

1. Hurston, Zora Neale Handbooks, manuals, etc. 2. African American authors 3. African Americans in literature 4. Biographies

LC 2008010052

An encyclopedic guide to the American author's life and works presents a brief biography, synopses of her writings, critical analysis of her characters and themes, and discusses important people, places, and topics in her life.

Hussein, King of Jordan, 1935-1999

Ashton, Nigel John **King** Hussein of Jordan : a political life / Nigel Ashton. Yale University Press, 2008. 464 p. **B**

ISBN 9780300091670

1. Rulers 2. Political leadership. 3. World politics. 4. Politicians 5. Jordan -- Rulers 6. Jordan -- Politics and government -- 1952-1999. 7. Biographies

LC 2008010803

Drawing on unprecedented access to family archives, an incisive biography illuminates the private King Hussein, his key relationships, and his achievements and disappointments as a central player in Middle Eastern politics, and brings new depth to readers' understanding of the popular and canny king.

Huston, Anjelica

Huston, Anjelica **Watch** me : a memoir / Anjelica Huston. Scribner, 2014. 400 p. **B**

ISBN 9781476760346

1. Nicholson, Jack, 1937- 2. Film actors and actresses. 3. Academy Award film nominees. 4. Women theatrical producers and directors. 5. Autobiographies and memoirs

LC 2014029235

The Academy Award-winning actress and author of the best-selling A Story Lately Told discusses her long-time relationship with Jack Nicholson, her most memorable film appearances and her collaborations with a range of forefront directors.

"This memoir with both substance and flair is a must-read for Huston fans, those who enjoy film, and anyone who wishes to be inspired by a richly textured life well presented. For all entertainment collections." Library Journal.

Huston, John, 1906-1987

Meyers, Jeffrey **John** Huston : courage and art / Jeffrey Meyers. Random House Inc, 2011. 432 p. **B**

ISBN 9780307590671

1. Film industry and trade 2. Film actors and actresses. 3. Film producers and directors 4. Film producers and directors 5. Hollywood, California. 6. Biographies

LC 2010047642

An in-depth profile of the influential director, writer and actor who was responsible for such films as The Maltese Falcon and The African Queen offers insight into his professional achievements as well as his extensive hobbies, five marriages and homes in Mexico and Ireland.

"By balancing the flamboyant life with the landmark works of legendary movie director John Huston, . Meyers reveals how a flawed man produced nearly flawless and indelible films." Booklist.

Huxley, Elspeth, 1907-1997

Huxley, Elspeth Joscelin Grant, 1907-1997 The **flame** trees of Thika : memories of an African childhood / Elspeth Huxley. Penguin Books, 2000, c1959. 280 p.; **B**

ISBN 0141183780

1. Huxley, Elspeth, 1907-1997 Childhood and youth. 2. Authors, English -- 20th century 3. Rural life -- Kenya -- History -- 20th century. 4. British in Kenya -- History -- 20th century. 5. Kenya -- Social life and customs -- 1895-1963. 6. Autobiographies and memoirs 7. Books to TV

LC 99047965

Book adapted into a British television mini-series in seven parts in 1981.

Originally published in 1959, Huxley's autobiography recalls her extraordinary adventures as a child in Africa.

Hynde, Chrissie

Hynde, Chrissie **Reckless** : my life as a Pretender / Chrissie Hynde. Doubleday, 2015 352 p. **B**

ISBN 9780385540612

1. Pretenders (Musical group) 2. Rock musicians 3. Women rock musicians 4. Autobiographies and memoirs

LC 2015027449

A no-holds-barred memoir by the front woman for The Pretenders traces her 1950s childhood in Ohio, her immersion in the music scenes of subsequent decades and her band's instant rise to fame in the heyday of 1980s culture.

Hytner, Nicholas

Hytner, Nicholas **Balancing** acts : behind the scenes at London's National Theatre / Nicholas Hytner. Alfred A. Knopf, 2017. 320 p. **B**

ISBN 9780451493408

1. Hytner, Nicholas. 2. National Theatre (Great Britain). 3. Theatrical producers and directors. 4. Theater. 5. Theater companies 6. Autobiographies and memoirs

LC 2017016630

The former director of London's National Theatre presents a candid, behind-the-scenes memoir about his career directing theater, producing films and opera, and working closely with some of the world's most celebrated actors.

"Arts leaders in general will have something to gain from Hytners endless energy for developing new work and navigating the challenges facing todays cultural sector." Booklist.

Ibadi, Shirin

Ibadi, Shirin **Until** we are free : my fight for human rights in Iran / Shirin Ebadi. Random House, 2016. 224 p. **B**

ISBN 9780812998870

1. Ibadi, Shirin. 2. Lawyers -- Iran 3. Human rights activists 4. Women judges -- Iran 5. Women Nobel Prize winners -- Iran 6. Iran 7. Autobiographies and memoirs

LC 2015027147

The first Muslim woman to win the Nobel Peace Prize recounts how she endured death threats, false accusations targeting her family, arrests, invasions of privacy, home attacks, office seizures and other harassment from the Iranian government for her work as a human rights lawyer.

"The captivating and candid story of a woman who took on the Iranian government and survived, despite every attempt to make her fail." Kirkus.

Ice-T (Musician)

Ice-T (Musician) **Ice** : a memoir of gangster life and redemption--from South Central to Hollywood / Ice-T and Douglas Century. Random House, 2011. 288 p. **B**

ISBN 9780345523280

1. African Americans 2. Gang members 3. African American actors and actresses 4. Teenage fathers. 5. Autobiographies and memoirs

LC 2010041069

The hip-hop artist and television star shares the story of his early life, marked by the deaths of his parents, his involvement in gangs, and the single-minded work ethic that enabled his rise to international fame.

"A fascinating and inspiring story about an African American orphan who beat the odds to become successful, this memoir will appeal to fans of hip-hop and popular culture." Booklist.

Iceberg Slim, 1918-1992

Gifford, Justin, 1975- **Street** poison : the biography of Iceberg Slim / Justin Gifford. Doubleday, 2015. 288 p. **B**

ISBN 9780385538343

1. Iceberg Slim, 1918-1992. 2. African American authors 3. Pimps 4. Drug dealers 5. Prostitution 6. Chicago, Illinois 7. Biographies

LC 2014037252

Pimp-turned-insecticide-salesman-turned-bestselling-author Iceberg Slim (or Robert Peck) died in 1992, apparently penniless despite his influence on generations of black writers, hip hop artists, and popular culture as a whole. This biography of the notorious, complicated writer explores (often in Slim's own words) the violence of his early career and the influence he continues to wield, even though many in the mainstream are unaware of him.

"Recommended for readers of popular fiction and African American literature." Library Journal.

Iftin, Abdi Nor

Iftin, Abdi Nor **Call** me American : a memoir / Abdi Nor Iftin with Max Alexander. Alfred A. Knopf, 2018. 304 p. **B**

ISBN 9781524732196

1. Iftin, Abdi Nor. 2. Somali Americans 3. Immigrants 4. Muslims 5. Radio broadcasters 6. Maine 7. United States -- Immigration and emigration 8. Autobiographies and memoirs

LC 2017043213

"This is a Borzoi Book."

ALA Notable Book, 2019.

A young Somalian, who learned English through American pop culture uses his skills to post secret dispatches to the Internet and NPR after a radical Islamist group comes to power and until he finally wins a visa lottery to emigrate.

Iguodala, Andre, 1984-

Iguodala, Andre, 1984- The **sixth** man : a memoir / Andre Iguodala with Carvell Wallace. Blue Rider Press, 2019. 256 p. **B**

ISBN 9780525533986

1. Golden State Warriors (Basketball team). 2. African American basketball players 3. Professional basketball players 4. Olympic athletes 5. Basketball 6. Autobiographies and memoirs

LC 2018047034

The NBA swingman and All-Star shares insights into his remarkable career, discussing such topics as his 2012 Men's Basketball Olympics gold-medal win, his 2015 NBA championship with the Warriors, and his off-court successes as a Silicon Valley insider.

"There's plenty here about basketball, but the authors move well beyond the scores, hoops, and on-court drama that fill nearly all the pages of similar books. Iguodala is always focused on the relationships and motivations of his teammates and opponents. That insight, he shows, helps him bond with his teammates and defeat his opponents." Booklist.

Ikpi, Bassey

Ikpi, Bassey **I'm** telling the truth, but I'm lying : essays / Bassey Ikpi. Perennial, 2019. 304 p. **B**

ISBN 9780062698346

1. Immigrants 2. African American women authors 3. African American women poets 4. People with Bipolar disorder 5. New York City 6. Oklahoma 7. Nigeria 8. Essays 9. Autobiographies and memoirs

LC 2019457394

A deeply personal collection of essays by the Nigerian-American writer and creator of #NoShameDay explores how her childhood move from Nigeria to Oklahoma was complicated by Bipolar II and anxiety disorders.

"People struggling with mental-health issues will appreciate Ikpi as a talented kindred spirit as she raises such universal questions as: What does it mean to be crazy anyway? Haunting and affirming." Booklist.

Ilgunas, Ken

Ilgunas, Ken **Trespassing** across America : one man's epic, never-done-before (and sort of illegal) hike across the heartland / Ken Ilgunas. Blue Rider Press, 2016. 304 p. **B**

ISBN 9780399175480

1. Ilgunas, Ken Travel 2. Hiking 3. Men and nature 4. Voyages and travels 5. Climate change 6. Autobiographies and memoirs

LC 2016006546

The author recounts his hiking adventure along the proposed route of the Keystone XL pipeline from the Alberta tar sands to the pipeline's end point on the Gulf Coast of Texas.

Irby, Samantha

Irby, Samantha **We** are never meeting in real life : essays / Samantha Irby. Vintage Books, 2017. 256 p. **B**

ISBN 9781101912195

1. Everyday life 2. Misadventures 3. African American women 4. Bloggers 5. Essays 6. Autobiographies and memoirs

LC 2017002278

Sometimes you just have to laugh, even when life is a dumpster fire. With We Are Never Meeting in Real Life, blogger and comedian Samantha Irby turns the serio-comic essay into an art form.

"In her new book of essays, Irby . is once again the inimitably candid, ber-confessional friend readers will happily spend a few hundred pages with." Booklist.

Irving, Apricot Anderson

Irving, Apricot Anderson The **gospel** of trees : a memoir / Apricot Irving. Simon & Schuster, 2018. 384 p. **B**

ISBN 9781451690453

1. Missionaries 2. Expatriates 3. Growing up 4. Expatriate women 5. Haiti 6. Caribbean Area 7. Autobiographies and memoirs

LC 2017049492

A first book by an award-winning writer recounts her childhood as a missionary's daughter in Haiti during a time of complicated and tumultuous foreign intervention, describing how her perspectives on the region transformed as she came of age and how her family struggled with disparate views about her father's absolute approaches to his work.

"With insight and admirable even-handedness, Irving shows the complex forces at play in both the story of Haitis cycle of poverty and the more personal dynamics at play in her family as they struggle mightily to do Gods work." Booklist.

Isabella I, Queen of Spain, 1451-1504

Downey, Kirstin **Isabella** : the warrior queen / Kirstin Downey. Nan A. Talese/Doubleday, 2014. 480 p. **B**

ISBN 9780385534116

1. Isabella I, Queen of Spain, 1451-1504. 2. Catholic Church -- History 15th century. 3. Women rulers -- Spain 4. Inquisition -- Spain. 5. Women politicians 6. Christian women 7. Spain -- History -- Ferdinand and Isabella, 1479-1516. 8. Biographies.

LC 2014003895

Drawing on new scholarship, the Pulitzer Prize-winning author of The Woman Behind the New Deal presents a biography of Isabella of Castile, the controversial Queen of Spain who sponsored Christopher Columbus' journey to the New World, established the Spanish Inquisition and became one of the most influential female rulers in history.

"As one of the most influential political players of the transitional era bridging the Middle Ages and the Renaissance, Isabella has earned her place in the spotlight." Booklist.

Isherwood, Christopher, 1904-1986

Isherwood, Christopher, 1904-1986 **Liberation** : diaries:1970-1983 / Christopher Isherwood ; edited and introduced by Katherine Bucknell. HarperCollins, 2012. 768 p. **B**

ISBN 9780062084743

1. Authors, English -- 20th century -- Diaries 2. Authors, English -- 20th century -- Diaries. 3. Immigrants -- California. 4. British in the United States 5. Hollywood, California. 6. Diaries 7. Autobiographies and memoirs

LC bl2012043187

In this final volume of his diaries, the English-American novelist, whose collaborations with his long-term companion Don Bachardy extended ties in Hollywood and the theatre world, greets advancing age with humor and an unquenchable appetite for the new.

Ishi, -1916

★Kroeber, Theodora **Ishi** in two worlds : a biography of the last wild Indian in North America / Theodora Kroeber ; with a new foreword by Karl Kroeber. University of California Press, 2002 xxiii, 254 p., 14 p. of plates : **B**

ISBN 9780520229402

1. Ishi, -1916. 2. Yana Indians 3. Biographies

LC 2005532000

Ishikawa, Masaji

Ishikawa, Masaji A **river** in darkness : one man's escape from North Korea / Masaji Ishikawa ; translated by Risa Kobayashi and Martin Brown. AmazonCrossing, 2018. 172 p. **B**

ISBN 9781503936904

1. Men -- Japan 2. Defectors 3. Political persecution 4. Classism 5. North Korea -- Social conditions 6. North Korea -- Politics and government 7. Autobiographies and memoirs

LC bl2018000903

In this memoir translated from the original Japanese, Ishikawa candidly recounts his tumultuous upbringing and the brutal thirty-six years he spent living under a crushing totalitarian regime, as well as the challenges he faced repatriating to Japan after barely escaping North Korea with his life.

"Ishikawa relates his painful story with sardonic humor and unwavering familial love even in the depths of despair, making human the often impersonal news coverage of mysterious and threatening North Korea." Booklist.

Ivan IV, the Terrible, Czar of Russia, 1530-1584

Madariaga, Isabel de, 1919- **Ivan** the Terrible : first tsar of Russia / Isabel de Madariaga. Yale University Press, c2005. xxi, 484 p. : **B**

ISBN 0300097573

1. Russia -- Rulers 2. Russia -- History -- Ivan IV, 1533-1584. 3. Biographies

LC 2004029807

"This is a persuasively argued, widely researched and impressively authoritative work that casts new light on the Tsar, his reign, and Russia in the sixteenth century." Times Literary Supplement.

Iversen, Kristen

Iversen, Kristen **Full** body burden : growing up in the nuclear shadow of Rocky Flats / Kristen Iversen. Crown Publishers, c2012. 416 p. **B**

ISBN 9780307955630

1. Iversen, Kristen. 2. Rocky Flats Plant, Colorado Environmental aspects. 3. Rocky Flats Plant, Colorado -- History 4. Rocky Flats Plant, Colorado Health aspects. 5. Nuclear warfare facilities -- Health hazards 6. Secrecy in government 7. Growing up 8. Plutonium -- Health hazards. 9. Jefferson County, Colorado 10. Colorado 11. Autobiographies and memoirs

LC 2011045902

ALA Notable Book, 2013.

A narrative report by a woman who grew up near the Rocky Flats nuclear weapons facility describes the secrets that dominated her childhood, the strange cancers that afflicted her neighbors, her brief employment at Rocky Flats, and the efforts of residents to achieve legal justice.

Ives, Charles, 1874-1954

Swafford, Jan **Charles** Ives : a life with music / Jan Swafford. W.W. Norton, 1996. xv, 525 p. : **B**

ISBN 0393038939

1. Ives, Charles, 1874-1954. 2. Composers -- United States 3. Insurance -- Agents 4. Atonality. 5. Modern music. 6. Biographies

LC 95022549

National Book Critics Circle Award for Biography finalist, 1996."

Ives was a professional organist, a successful insurance executive, a political idealist, and an immensely prolific composer. The author believes that Ives's transcendentalism was central to his identity, ceaselessly inspiring him while also spurring him on to an inevitable physical collapse. Swafford--a composer himself--intersperses his biography with valuable 'entr'actes' of approachable musical analysis, and ends with a ringing endorsement of Ives as an ideal composer for a democratic society." The New Yorker.

Ivester, Jeremy

Ivester, Jo **Once** a girl, always a boy : a family memoir of a transgender journey / Jo Ivestor. She Writes Press, 2020. ii, 328 p. : **B**

ISBN 9781631528866

1. Ivester, Jeremy. 2. Transgender men 3. Gender identity. 4. Transgender people -- Identity. 5. Sex discrimination. 6. Autobiographies and memoirs

LC bl2020046266

"In his mid-twenties, Jeremy Ivester began taking testosterone and had surgery to remove his breasts. This memoir is both Jeremy's and his family's coming out story, told from multiple perspectives-a story of acceptance in a world not quite ready to accept."-- Provided by publisher.

Iyer, Pico

Iyer, Pico **Autumn** light : season of fire and farewells / Pico Iyer. Alfred A. Knopf, 2019. 240 p. **B**

ISBN 9780451493934

1. Iyer, Pico Family 2. Autumn 3. Death 4. Family relationships 5. Married people 6. Japan -- Description and travel 7. Nara-shi, Japan -- Description and travel 8. Autobiographies and memoirs

LC 2018020713

"This is a Borzoi book."

For years, Pico Iyer has split his time between California and Nara, Japan, where he and his Japanese wife, Hiroko, have a small home. But when his father-in-law dies suddenly, calling him back to Japan earlier than expected, Iyer begins to grapple with the question we all have to live with: how to hold on to the things we love, even though we know that we and they are dying. In a country whose calendar is marked with occasions honoring the dead, this question is more urgent than anywhere else.

"Aging, death, and family fracturing are seen through the lens of Japanese culture in this luminous memoir." Publishers Weekly.

Izzard, Eddie

Izzard, Eddie **Believe** me : a memoir of love, death, and jazz chickens / Eddie Izzard, with Laura Zigman. Blue Rider Press, 2017. 400 p. **B**

ISBN 9780399175831

1. Izzard, Eddie. 2. Entertainers. 3. Comedians. 4. Autobiographies and memoirs

LC 2017008493

A wide-ranging memoir by the critically acclaimed British comedian details his childhood in multiple countries, his first performances on the streets of London and the achievements that have marked his international success.

"In this witty and honest memoir, performer Izzard (Dress To Kill) chronicles his life and career thus far." Library Journal.

Jackson family

Jackson family The **Jacksons** : legacy / Jackie, Tito, Jermaine, Marlon, Michael, and Randy Jackson ; with Fred Bronson. Black Dog & Leventhal, 2017. 320 p. **B**

ISBN 9780316473736

1. Jacksons (Musical group) 2. Bands (Music) 3. African American families 4. African American brothers 5. Soul musicians 6. Collective autobiographies and memoirs

LC 2017943146

Written by Jackie, Tito, Jermaine, Marlon and Michael, a first-person visual history of the Jacksons combines exclusive interviews, anecdotes, quotes and previously unseen family archive photos tracing their meteoric rise and history-making tours.

Jackson, Andrew, 1767-1845

★Brands, H. W. **Andrew** Jackson, his life and times / H.W. Brands. Doubleday, 2005. xi, 620 p. : **B**

ISBN 0385507380

1. Jackson, Andrew, 1767-1845. 2. Presidents -- United States 3. Political culture -- United States -- History -- 19th century. 4. Political leadership -- United States -- History -- 19th century. 5. Character. 6. United States -- Politics and government -- 1829-1837. 7. Biographies

LC 2005042178

Explores the life of the first "common man" to become president of the United States, discussing Jackson's early days in South Carolina, his military exploits, and his contributions to the cause of democracy and Manifest Destiny.

Meacham, Jon **American** lion : Andrew Jackson in the White House / Jon Meacham. Random House, 2008. 512 p. **B**

ISBN 9781400063253

1. Jackson, Andrew, 1767-1845 Family. 2. Jackson, Andrew, 1767-1845 Friends and associates. 3. Democratic Party. 4. Presidents -- United States 5. Generals -- United States 6. Political culture -- United States -- History -- 19th century. 7. Political leadership -- United States -- History -- 19th century 8. United States -- Politics and government -- 1829-1837. 9. Biographies

LC 2008023466

Pulitzer Prize for Biography or Autobiography, 2009.Chronicles the life and career of Andrew Jackson, a self-made man who went on to become a military hero and seventh president of the United States, analyzing Jackson's seminal role during a turbulent era in history.

Remini, Robert Vincent, 1921-2013 **Andrew** Jackson / Robert V. Remini ; foreword by General Wesley K. Clark. Palgrave Macmillan, 2008, c1966. 224 p. **B**

ISBN 9780230600157

1. Jackson, Andrew, 1767-1845 Military leadership. 2. United States. Army 3. Tennessee. Militia 4. Presidents -- United States 5. Political leadership -- United States -- History -- 19th century 6. Generals -- United States 7. Command of troops -- Case studies. 8. United States -- History, Military. 9. Biographies

LC 2008000394

Originally published: New York : Twayne Publishers, 1966.

It was Andrew Jackson's military heroism that helped to usher him into the presidency. From the Battle of New Orleans in the War of 1812 to the Indian Wars and his unorthodox presence in the White House, Jackson is one of the most fascinating figures in American history. Here is his life as told by the foremost Jackson historian of our time.

Jackson, Curtis, 1975-

Jackson, Curtis, 1975- **Hustle** harder, hustle smarter / Curtis "50 Cent" Jackson. Amistad, 2020 xviii, 271 p.; **B**

ISBN 9780062953803

1. 50 Cent (Musician) 2. Rap musicians -- United States 3. Television producers and directors -- United States 4. African American businesspeople 5. Success in business. 6. Autobiographies and memoirs

LC bl2020010066

Curtis "50 Cent" Jackson opens up about his amazing comeback--from tragic personal loss to thriving businessman and cable's highest-paid executive--in a unique self-help guide. By the New York Times best-selling author of The 50th Law.

"Savor the celebrity gossip and push through to the lessons of one of hip-hop's most successful businessmen ever." Kirkus

Jackson, Luke, 1988-

Jackson, Luke, 1988- **Freaks,** geeks and Asperger syndrome : a user guide to adolescence / Luke Jackson ; foreword by Tony Attwood. Jessica Kingsley Publishers, 2003. 215 p. : **B**

ISBN 9781843100980

1. Jackson, Luke, 1988- Mental health. 2. Asperger's syndrome -- Patients 3. Asperger's syndrome -- Patients -- Family relationships 4. Asperger's syndrome 5. Autistic children 6. Biographies

LC 2002070930

Offers insights by a teenager with Asperger's syndrome into the difficulties of the disorder, including information on fascinations and obsessions, sensory perception, sleep, bullies, moral dilemmas, eating, and socializing.

"In this terrific book that is sure to inspire other adolescents with the same condition, Library Journal.

Jackson, Luke, 1988- **Sex,** drugs and Asperger's syndrome (ASD) : a user guide to adulthood / Luke Jackson ; foreword by Tony Attwood. Jessica Kingsley Publishers, 2016. 204 p. **B**

ISBN 9781849056458

1. Jackson, Luke, 1988- Mental health. 2. People with Asperger's syndrome -- Family relationships. 3. Autism. 4. Growing up 5.

Asperger's syndrome. 6. Autobiographies and memoirs
LC 2015027315

Includes index."

Jackson's personal and brutally honest take on being an adult with ASD is eye-opening and refreshing. A valuable read for teens and adults with ASD as well as parents, siblings, employers, teachers, caregivers, friends, and partners of those on the spectrum." Library Journal.

Jackson, Michael, 1958-2009

★Greenburg, Zack O'Malley **Michael** Jackson, Inc : the rise, fall and rebirth of a billion-dollar empire / Zack O'Malley Greenburg. Atria Books, 2014. 304 p. **B**

ISBN 9781476705965

1. Jackson, Michael, 1958-2009. 2. Popular music. 3. Music industry and trade 4. Success in business 5. Wealth 6. Biographies
LC 2013045449

Michael Jackson, Inc. reveals the incredible rise, fall, and rise again of Michael Jackson's fortune - driven by the unmatched perfectionism of the King of Pop. Forbes senior editor Zack O'Malley Greenburg uncovers never-before-told stories from interviews with more than 100 people, including music industry veterans Berry Gordy, John Branca, and Walter Yetnikoff; artists 50 Cent, Sheryl Crow, and Jon Bon Jovi; and members of the Jackson family. Other insights come from court documents and Jackson's private notes, some of them previously unpublished.

"A quick-moving yet comprehensive narrative of the singer's career, downfall and unlikely post-mortem second act." Kirkus.

Jackson, Mitchell S.

Jackson, Mitchell S. **Survival** math : notes on an all-American family / Mitchell S. Jackson. Scribner, 2019. 304 p. **B**

ISBN 9781501131707

1. Jackson, Mitchell S. Family 2. African Americans 3. African American neighborhoods 4. Growing up 5. Authors 6. Portland, Oregon 7. Pacific Northwest 8. United States -- Race relations 9. Autobiographies and memoirs
LC bl2019000943

With a poet's gifted ear, a novelist's sense of narrative, and a journalist's unsentimental eye, Mitchell S. Jackson candidly explores his tumultuous youth in the other America. Survival Math takes its name from the calculations Mitchell and his family made to keep safe--to stay alive--in their community, a small black neighborhood in Portland, Oregon blighted by drugs, violence, poverty, and governmental neglect.

"Thanks to Jackson's fresh voice, this powerful autobiography shines an important light on the generational problems of America's oft-forgotten urban communities." Publishers Weekly

Jackson, Richie, 1965-

Jackson, Richie, 1965- **Gay** like me : a father writes to his son / Richie Jackson. Harper, [2020] 176 p. **B**

ISBN 9780062939777

1. Gay men 2. Fathers and sons 3. Gay men -- Identity 4. LGBTQIA parents 5. Autobiographies and memoirs 6. Essays
LC 2019034198

When Jackson's 18-year-old son born through surrogacy came out to him, the successful producer, now in his 50s, was compelled to reflect on his experiences and share his wisdom on life for LGBTQ Americans over the past half-century. Gay Like Me is a celebration of gay identity and parenting, and a powerful warning for his son, other gay men and the world. Jackson looks back at his own journey as a gay man coming of age through decades of political and cultural turmoil. As Ta-Nehisi Coates awakened us to the continued pervasiveness of racism in America in Between the World and Me, Jackson's rallying cry in Gay Like Me is an eye-opening indictment to straight-lash in America.

An invaluable book for all young LGBTQ people [tr heartfelt, wise, and compassionate." Booklist.

Jackson, Shirley, 1916-1965

★Franklin, Ruth **Shirley** Jackson : a rather haunted life / Ruth Franklin. Liveright Publishing Corporation, 2016. 656 p. **B**

ISBN 9780871403131

1. Jackson, Shirley, 1916-1965. 2. Authors, American -- 20th century 3. Women authors, American 4. Women's role 5. Motherhood 6. Vermont 7. Biographies
LC 2016014711

ALA Notable Book, 2017.
Anthony Award for Best Critical/Nonfiction, 2017.
Bram Stoker Award for Best Nonfiction, 2016.
Edgar Allan Poe Award for Best Critical/Biographical, 2017.
National Book Critics Circle Award for Biography, 2016.

Reveals the tumultuous life and inner darkness of the American author, demonstrating how her unique contribution to the Gothic genre came from a focus on domestic horror drawn from an era hostile to women.

"A consistently interesting biography that deftly captures the many selves and multiple struggles of a true American original." Kirkus.

Jackson, Stonewall, 1824-1863

Gwynne, S. C. (Samuel C.), 1953- **Rebel** yell : the violence, passion, and redemption of Stonewall Jackson / S.C. Gwynne. Scribner, 2014. 688 p. **B**

ISBN 9781451673289

1. Jackson, Stonewall, 1824-1863. 2. Confederate States of America. Army 3. Generals -- Confederate States of America 4. Civil war 5. Confederate soldiers 6. United States Civil War, 1861-1865 7. United States -- History -- Civil War, 1861-1865. 8. Biographies
LC 2014010046

National Book Critics Circle Award for Biography finalist, 2014.

In this insightful character study of Confederate General Thomas "Stonewall" Jackson, author S.C. Gwynne weaves incidents from Jackson's life into the chronologically presented account of his Civil War actions. A reserved and deeply religious man, Jackson seemed to be stern, stubborn, and even arbitrary in his military leadership. Yet he was so bold and effective in battle that he was considered the greatest of the Confederacy's leaders. Gwynne's compelling biography is essential reading matter for Civil War and general military history buffs, as well as for anyone who enjoys life stories.

"Gwynne presents Jackson's eccentric personality in biographical episodes that he injects into the arc of Jackson's Civil War campaigns and battles. [The] technique succeeds, thanks to his spry prose and cogent insight, in revealing Jackson's character." Booklist.

Robertson, James I. **Stonewall** Jackson : the man, the soldier, the legend / James I. Robertson, Jr. Macmillan Pub. USA ; c1997. xxiii, 950 p. : **B**

ISBN 0028646851

1. Jackson, Stonewall, 1824-1863. 2. Confederate States of America. Army 3. Generals -- Confederate States of America 4. United States Civil War, 1861-1865 5. Confederate soldiers 6. Command of troops 7. Biographies
LC 96017042

"Robertson's bibliography, which runs to 25 pages of fine print, reveals the solid bedrock on which this work is built; his documentation is a model of thoroughness. The book is illustrated with rare photographs. A highly readable, remarkably interesting study of Jackson as both man and military leader." Choice.

Jackson, Sumner Waldron

Kershaw, Alex **Avenue** of spies : a true story of terror, espionage, and one American family's heroic resistance in Nazi-occupied Paris / Alex Kershaw. Crown, 2015. 304 p. **B**

ISBN 9780804140034

1. French Resistance (World War II) 2. World War II 3. Resistance to military occupation 4. Spies 5. Paris, France -- History, Military -- 20th century. 6. France -- History -- German occupation, 1940-1945. 7. Biographies

LC 2015016861

"Kershaw tells their story in an intense, moving account that also serves to vividly describe the life of ordinary Parisians under the occupation." Booklist.

Jacob, Max, 1876-1944

Warren, Rosanna **Max** Jacob : a life in art and letters / Rosanna Warren. W. W. Norton & Company, 2020 736 p. **B**

ISBN 9780393078855

1. Jacob, Max, 1876-1944. 2. Cubism 3. Poets, French -- 20th century 4. Poetry writing 5. Modernism (Art) -- Europe. 6. Paris, France 7. Biographies

LC 2020017722

A comprehensive portrait of the early 20th-century poet explores how Max Jacob's complex relationships with art, faith and sexuality impacted his life in bohemian Paris and shaped the symbolic themes in his poetry.

"An exemplary work of biography and intellectual history; essential reading for students of literary and artistic modernism." Kirkus

Jacob, Mira, 1973-

Jacob, Mira, 1973- **Good** talk : a memoir in conversations / Mira Jacob. Random House, 2018. 400 p. **B**

ISBN 9780399589041

1. Women authors 2. Interracial families 3. East Indian American women 4. Asian American authors 5. United States -- Social conditions 6. Autobiographies and memoirs 7. Autobiographical comics 8. Comics and Graphic novels

LC 2017021147

National Book Critics Circle Award for Autobiography/Memoir finalist, 2019

An intimate graphic memoir about American identity as it has shaped the author's interracial family in the aftermath of the 2016 elections.

"The narrative spans generations, drawing parallels between Jacob and her son but also highlighting the lack of social progress. Aided by the skillful story structure, Jacob's no-holds-barred vulnerability compels reflection and empathy. The unique art style combines photographic backgrounds with illustrations of characters framed in white, like paper cutouts." School Library Journal.

Jacobs, Harriet, 1818-1896

Yellin, Jean Fagan **Harriet** Jacobs : a life / Jean Fagan Yellin. Basic Civitas Books, c2004. xxi, 394 p. : **B**

ISBN 0465092888

1. Jacobs, Harriet, 1818-1896. 2. Slaves 3. Women slaves 4. African American women authors 5. African American women social reformers 6. United States 7. Biographies

LC 2003017256

"This scholarly account, woven in a reader friendly fashion, restores an heroic woman who lived in an heroic time to history and to us." Publishers Weekly.

Jacobs, Hollye

Jacobs, Hollye The **silver** lining : a supportive and insightful guide to breast cancer / Hollye Jacobs, RN, MS, MSW ; photographs by Elizabeth Messina. Atria Paperback, 2014 xiii, 271 p. : **B**

ISBN 9781476743721

1. Jacobs, Hollye Health. 2. Breast -- Cancer -- Patients -- Psychology 3. Breast -- Cancer 4. Cancer -- Patients -- Attitudes 5. Autobiographies and memoirs.

LC 2013019103

Includes index.

The author draws on her experiences as both a nurse and a patient with breast cancer to share positive insights about the disease's diagnosis, treatments, side effects, and recovery.

"With her humorous and approachable style, Jacobs has written an essential title for patients facing a cancer diagnosis." Library Journal.

Jacobs, Jane, 1916-2006

Kanigel, Robert **Eyes** on the street : the life of Jane Jacobs / Robert Kanigel. Alfred A. Knopf, 2016. 416 p. **B**

ISBN 9780307961907

1. Jacobs, Jane, 1916-2006. 2. City life. 3. Urban planning 4. Urban sociology -- History -- 20th century 5. Urban renewal 6. New York City.

LC 2015050758

Chronicles the life of a noted activist who wrote seven groundbreaking books, including her most famous, The Death and Life of Great American Cities; saved neighborhoods; stopped expressways; was arrested twice; and engaged at home and on the streets in thousands of debatesall of which she won.

Jacques, Juliet

Jacques, Juliet **Trans** : a memoir / Juliet Jacques. Verso, 2016, c2015. viii, 311 p. ; **B**

ISBN 9781784781675

1. Jacques, Juliet. 2. Transgender persons 3. Trans women 4. Transitioning (Gender identity) 5. Transphobia 6. Autobiographies and memoirs

LC 2016033158

Originally published in hardback version in 2015.

Growing up in a time when the transgender experience was hardly acknowledged, the author traces her journey to find herself and documents her transition from male to female, while discussing key issues facing transgender people today.

Jadhav, Narendra, 1953-

★Jadhav, Narendra, 1953- **Untouchables** : my family's triumphant journey out of the caste system in modern India / Narendra Jadhav. Scribner, 2005, c2003. 307 p. ; **B**

ISBN 9780743270793

1. Economists -- Maharashtra, India 2. Monetary reformers -- Maharashtra, India 3. Dalits (East Indian Scheduled Castes) -- Maharashtra, India 4. Dalits (East Indian Scheduled Castes) -- India -- Social conditions -- 20th century. 5. India -- Social life and customs. 6. Autobiographies and memoirs

LC 2005044166

First published in English in 2003 by Penguin Books as Outcaste."

This moving story of perseverance from a sector of India rarely represented to American readers will be a standard text on Indian and Dalit themes for years to come." Library Journal.

Jaeger family

Mendelsohn, Daniel Adam, 1960- The **lost** : a search for six of six million / Daniel Mendelsohn. Harper Collins, 2006. 528 p. **B**

ISBN 0060542977

1. Mendelsohn, Daniel Adam, 1960- 2. Mendelsohn, Daniel, 1960- Family. 3. Jaeger family. 4. Jewish Americans -- Anecdotes. 5. Jews, Ukrainian. 6. Holocaust (1933-1945) -- Ukraine. 7. Shtetl -- Ukraine. 8. Ukraine -- History -- German occupation, 1941-1944 9. Ukraine -- History.

LC 2006041096

National Book Critics Circle Award for Autobiography, 2006.

National Jewish Book Award, 2006.

Sophie Brody Medal, 2007."

Mr. Mendelsohn, an evocative, ruminative writer, brings to life the vanished world not just of prewar Poland but also of his childhood and his extended family." New York Times.

Jaffrey, Madhur

Jaffrey, Madhur **Climbing** the mango trees : a memoir of a childhood in India / Madhur Jaffrey. Alfred A. Knopf, 2006. x, 297 p. : **B**

ISBN 140004295X

1. Jaffrey, Madhur Childhood and youth. 2. Cooks -- India 3. Cooks -- United States 4. Women cooks -- India 5. Cooking, Indic. 6. India -- History -- British occupation, 1765-1947. 7. Autobiographies and memoirs

LC 2006045255

The best-selling author of An Invitation to Indian Cooking offers a charming memoir of growing up in Delhi, India, detailing life in a large family marked by dinners in which forty or more members of her extended family would enjoy the savory dishes of the region, recalling her childhood through the window of the food she experienced.

Jahren, Hope

★Jahren, Hope **Lab** girl / Hope Jahren. Alfred A. Knopf, 2016. 320 p. **B**

ISBN 9781101874936

1. Jahren, Hope. 2. Plants 3. Women scientists 4. Biologists -- United States 5. Geobiology -- Research -- Anecdotes. 6. Autobiographies and memoirs

LC 2015024305

"A Borzoi Book."

National Book Critics Circle Award for Autobiography, 2016.

Hope Jahren, the geobiologist, presents her autobiography.

"Jahren's forthright, beautifully expressed, and galvanizing chronicle deserves the widest possible readership." Booklist.

James, Clive, 1939-2019

James, Clive, 1939-2019 **Latest** readings / Clive James. Yale University Press, 2015 192 p. **B**

ISBN 9780300213195

1. Books and reading. 2. Authors 3. Critics 4. People with cancer 5. Essays 6. Autobiographies and memoirs

LC 2014958943

An esteemed literary critic shares his final musings on books, his children, and his own impending death

"James relishes the limited reading time he has and makes no bones about it, providing sparkling commentary on his old favorites and new discoveries." Publishers Weekly.

James, Eloisa

James, Eloisa **Paris** in love : a memoir / Eloisa James. Random House, c2012. 224 p. **B**

ISBN 9781400069569

1. James, Eloisa. 2. Americans in France. 3. Quality of life. 4. Self-fulfillment 5. Authors, American. 6. Paris, France.

LC 2011040662

Chronicles the year that the author and her family lived in Paris, describing her walking tours of the city, her school-age children's attempts to navigate foreign language schools, and her thoughts on the pleasures and eccentricities of French living.

James, Henry, 1843-1916

Haralson, Eric L. **Critical** companion to Henry James : a literary reference to his life and work / Eric Haralson and Kendall Johnson. Facts On File, c2009. xii, 516 p. : **B**

ISBN 9780816068869

1. Authors, American -- 19th century 2. Literature and society 3. Politics and literature 4. Characters and characteristics in literature 5. United States -- History -- 1865-1921. 6. Biographies

LC 2008036451

A guide to the American novelist includes a chronology of his life, descriptions of the important personalities and issues of his day, and entries which analyze the characters, plots, language, and major themes of his works.

James, Henry, 1843-1916 **Travels** with Henry James / Henry James, foreword by Hendrik Hertzberg, introduction by Michael Anesko. PublicAffairs, 2016. 304 p. **B**

ISBN 9781568585772

1. Voyages and travels 2. Essays

LC 2016030750

Includes index.

Chock full of charm, wit, and biting criticism, this new collection of travel essays by Henry James will reintroduce the novelist as a formidable travel companion--whether for a trip from Lake George to Burlington, an evening at the theater in London, or an afternoon visit to an art exhibit in Paris.

"James devotees will find that his essays are delightful, vivid, and generally uplifting." Publishers Weekly.

James, Jesse, 1847-1882

Stiles, T. J. **Jesse** James : last rebel of the Civil War / T.J. Stiles. A.A. Knopf, 2002. xiii, 510 p., 8 p. of plates : **B**

ISBN 0375405836

1. James, Jesse, 1847-1882. 2. Outlaws -- The West (United States) 3. Guerrillas -- Confederate States of America. 4. Civil war 5. United States Civil War, 1861-1865 6. The West (United States) 7. Missouri -- History -- Civil War, 1861-1865 -- Underground movements. 8. United States -- History -- Civil War, 1861-1865 -- Underground movements. 9. Biographies

LC 2002025493

ALA Notable Book, 2003."

This is a well-written and often surprising reinterpretation of the life of a legendary and enigmatic figure." Booklist.

James, LeBron

Windhorst, Brian **Lebron,** Inc. : the making of a billion-dollar athlete / Brian Windhorst. Grand Central Publishing, 2019 288 p. **B**

ISBN 9781538730874

1. James, LeBron. 2. Cleveland Cavaliers (Basketball team)

3. Professional basketball players. 4. Name-brand products. 5. Marketing. 6. Ambition in men.

LC 2019286139

The best-selling author of Return of the King traces the story of LeBron James' professional journey to becoming a billion-dollar global brand and businessman who has influenced how professional athletes understand their value.

"In his fourth publication on the NBA superstar, sportswriter Windhorst (Return of the King) focuses on the aspirations LeBron James continues to craft off the court. Highly recommended for NBA fans and readers curious about the happenings behind the scenes." Library Journal.

Windhorst, Brian **Return** of the king : Lebron James, the Cleveland Cavaliers, and the greatest comeback in NBA History / Brian Windhorst, and Dave McMenamin. Grand Central Publishing, 2017 288 p. **B**

ISBN 9781478971689

1. James, LeBron. 2. Cleveland Cavaliers (Basketball team) 3. Professional basketball players. 4. Ambition in men. 5. Basketball players. 6. Basketball. 7. Autobiographies and memoirs

LC 2017289063

The inside story of LeBron James's return and ultimate triumph in Cleveland

"This account of how a championship was built is the best NBA book in many years." Booklist.

James, P. D.

James, P. D. **Time** to be in earnest : a fragment of autobiography / P.D. James. Knopf, 2000, c1999. xii, 269 p. **B**

ISBN 037541066X

1. James, P. D.. 2. B B C Worldwide. 3. Great Britain. Parliament. 4. Authors, English -- 20th century -- Diaries. 5. Mystery story writing. 6. Autobiographies and memoirs

LC 99057603

Includes index.

Originally published: London : Faber and Faber, 1999.

Based on the diary she kept for years, a candid autobiography of mystery writer P.D. James retraces her life from her school days in 1930s Cambridge to her membership in the House of Lords and her success as a writer.

"In 1997, on the eve of her 77th birthday noted mystery novelist James decided to keep a diary for the first time ever, recording one year in her life. The result is this fragment of autobiography, a mix of memoir, ruminations on everything from her writing career to Princess Diana's death, and literary criticism." Library Journal.

James, Victoria

James, Victoria **Wine** girl : the obstacles, humiliations, and triumphs of America's youngest sommelier / Victoria James. Ecco Press, 2020. 256 p. **B**

ISBN 9780062961679

1. Women restaurateurs 2. Sommeliers 3. Resilience (Personal quality) 4. Ambition in women 5. Autobiographies and memoirs

LC bl2020007411

The country's youngest sommelier describes her experiences recommending and selling thousands of dollars of wine at a Michelin-starred restaurant where she still contended with groping patrons and abusive bosses in the fast-paced, but toxic restaurant world.

James, William, 1842-1910

Richardson, Robert D., 1934- **William** James : in the maelstrom of American modernism : a biography / Robert D. Richardson. Houghton Mifflin, 2006. xvi, 622 p., 16 p. of plates : **B**

ISBN 0618433252

1. James, William, 1842-1910. 2. Philosophers -- United States 3. United States -- Social life and customs -- 19th century. 4. Biographies

LC 2005037776

Maps on lining papers.

Biographer Richardson has written a moving portrait of James--pivotal member of the Metaphysical Club and author of The Varieties of Religious Experience. The biography, ten years in the making, draws on unpublished letters, journals, and family records.Richardson paints extraordinary scenes from what James himself called the "buzzing blooming confusion" of his life, beginning with childhood, as he struggled to achieve amid the domestic chaos and intellectual brilliance of Father, brother Henry, and sister Alice. James was a beloved teacher who taught courage and risk-taking, and served as mentor to W.E.B. Du Bois, Gertrude Stein, and many other Harvard outsiders. Richardson also illuminates James's hugely influential works. One of the great figures in mysticism here brought richly to life, James is a man "whose leading ideas are still so fresh and challenging that they are not yet fully assimilated by the modern world they helped to bring about."--From publisher description.

"The author's enthusiasm for what he calls the matchless incandescent spirit of William James is contagious." Publishers Weekly.

Jamison, Leslie

★Jamison, Leslie The **empathy** exams : essays / Leslie Jamison. Graywolf Press, 2014. 256 p. **B**

ISBN 9781555976712

1. Pain 2. Empathy 3. Caring 4. Medical care 5. Essays 6. Autobiographies and memoirs

LC 2013946927

"Jamison exhibits at once a journalist's courage to bear witness to acts and conditions that test human limits--incarceration, laboring in a silver mine, ultramarathoning, the loss of a child, devastating heartbreak, suffering from an unacknowledged illness--and a poet's skepticism at her own motives for doing so." Kirkus.

★Jamison, Leslie, 1983- The **recovering** : intoxication and Its aftermath / Leslie Jamison. Little Brown & Co 2018 544 p. **B**

ISBN 9780316259613

1. Sobriety 2. Recovering alcoholics 3. Addiction and creativity 4. Addiction 5. Autobiographies and memoirs

LC 2017946582

The best-selling author of The Empathy Exams presents an exploration of addiction that blends memoir, cultural history, literary criticism and journalistic reportage to analyze the role of stories in conveying the addiction experience, sharing insights based on the lives of genius artists whose achievements were shaped by addiction.

"The bracing, unflinching, and beautifully resonant history of a writer's addiction and hard-won reclamation." Kirkus.

Jang, Lucia

Jang, Lucia **Stars** between the sun and moon : one woman's life in North Korea and escape to freedom / Lucia Jang and Susan McClelland ; with an afterword by Stephan Haggard. Douglas & McIntyre, 2014 287 p. **B**

ISBN 1771620358

1. Jang, Lucia. 2. Totalitarianism 3. Famines 4. Human trafficking 5. Political refugees -- North Korea 6. North Korea -- Social conditions. 7. Autobiographies and memoirs

The memoir of a determined young North Korean woman who endured famine, an unlawful marriage and harsh imprisonment, and who finally managed to escape to Canada.

"An emotional and engrossing work that sheds light on daily life in this opaque country. Highly recommended for readers interested in North Korea as well as those who enjoy inspirational stories. Fans of Barbara Demick's Nothing To Envy will especially appreciate this work." Library Journal.

Jarrett, Valerie

Jarrett, Valerie **Finding** my voice : my journey to the West Wing and the path forward / Valerie Jarrett Viking Press, 2019. 320 p. **B**

ISBN 9780525558132

1. Jarrett, Valerie. 2. Obama, Barack 3. Presidents -- United States -- History -- 21st century 4. African American women 5. Social advocacy 6. Political consultants 7. Autobiographies and memoirs

LC 2019002213

When Valerie Jarrett interviewed a promising young lawyer named Michelle Robinson in July 1991 for a job in Chicago city government, neither knew that it was the first step on a path that would end in the White House. Jarrett soon became Michelle and Barack Obama's trusted personal adviser and family confidante; in the White House, she was known as the one who "got" him and helped him engage his public life. Jarrett joined the White House team on January 20, 2009 and departed with the First Family on January 20, 2017, and she was in the room--in the Oval Office, on Air Force One, and everywhere else--when it all happened. No one has as intimate a view of the Obama Years, nor one that reaches back as many decades, as Jarrett shares in Finding My Voice.

"A modest and insightful addition to a growing shelf of books by insiders from the Obama administration." Kirkus.

Jauhar, Sandeep, 1968-

Jauhar, Sandeep, 1968- **Heart** : a history / Sandeep Jauhar. Farrar Straus & Giroux 2018 272 p. **B**

ISBN 9780374168650

1. Heart -- Surgery 2. Cardiology 3. Medicine -- History 4. Autobiographies and memoirs

LC 2017055262

The leading cardiologist and author of *Doctored* and *Intern* examines the recent dismantling of historical taboos and the development of transformative heart procedures that have changed how we live and what we understand about illness.

Jay-Z, 1969-

Dyson, Michael Eric **Jay-Z** : made in America / Michael Eric Dyson ; with a foreword by Pharrell. St. Martin's Press, 2019. 226 p. : **B**

ISBN 9781250230966

1. Rap musicians 2. Rap music -- History and criticism 3. African American men 4. Fame 5. Biographies

LC 2018561531

Examines the biggest themes of JAY-Z's career, including hustling, and it recognizes the way that he|s always weaved politics into his music, making statements about race, criminal justice and black wealth.

Jayapal, Pramila, 1965-

Jayapal, Pramila, 1965- **Use** the power you have : a brown woman's guide to politics and political change / Pramila Jayapal. The New Press, 2020. 240 p. **B**

ISBN 9781620971437

1. United States. Congress. House 2. Women legislators 3. Legislators 4. East Indian American women 5. Women immigrants 6. United States -- Politics and government -- 1989- 7. Autobiographies and memoirs

LC 2020010661

The first Indian American woman to serve in the House of Representatives and co-chair of the Congressional Progressive Caucus discusses how to achieve a progressive and more inclusive legislative agenda that serves all Americans.

"Passionate and unapologetically leftist, this hopeful book not only chronicles an immigrant's political successes, but, more significantly, the enduring faith in American democracy that inspired them. A passionately articulate memoir and political manifesto." Kirkus

Jefferson, Margo, 1947-

Jefferson, Margo, 1947- **Negroland** : a memoir / Margo Jefferson. Pantheon Books, 2015 288 p. **B**

ISBN 9780307378453

1. Jefferson, Margo, 1947-. 2. African American women. 3. African Americans -- Identity 4. Elite (Social sciences) 5. Racism. 6. Chicago, Illinois 7. Autobiographies and memoirs

LC 2015006843

National Book Critics Circle Award for Autobiography, 2015.

A highly personal meditation on race, sex and American culture by the Pulitzer Prize-winning critic traces her upbringing and education in upper-class African-American circles against a backdrop of the Civil Rights era and its contradictory aftermath.

"Jefferson swings the narrative back and forth through her life, exploring the tides of racism, opportunity, and dignity while also provocatively exploring the inherent contradictions for Jefferson and her family members in working so tirelessly to differentiate themselves." Kirkus.

Jefferson, Thomas, 1743-1826

Bernstein, Richard B., 1956- **Thomas** Jefferson / R.B. Bernstein. Oxford University Press, 2005, c2003. xviii, 253 p. : **B**

ISBN 0195181301

1. Jefferson, Thomas, 1743-1826. 2. Presidents -- United States 3. Biographies

LC bl2006008974

Originally published: New York : Oxford University Press, 2003.

A biography of Thomas Jefferson covers such topics as his life as a Virginia gentleman, his passionate belief in democracy, his defense of slavery, his relationship with Sally Hemings, and his contributions to America as a writer, inventor, and party leader.

"The author provides a . . . view not of Jefferson the politician, but of the man whose ideas changed the world and provided the US with a sense of purpose. This short biography provides a judicious synthesis of the prevailing scholarship on the third president and explores more deeply his views on government and union, slavery, and debt. . . . Its concise form, limited notes, and evenhanded style will appeal to general readers seeking insight into an incredibly complex historical figure." Choice.

Boles, John B. **Jefferson** : architect of American liberty / John B. Boles. Basic Books, 2017. 626 p. **B**

ISBN 9780465094684

1. Jefferson, Thomas, 1743-1826. 2. Founding Fathers of the United States 3. Presidents -- United States 4. Politicians -- United States 5. Revolutions -- United States 6. United States -- Politics and government -- Revolution, 1775-1783. 7. United States -- Politics and government -- Constitutional period, 1789-1809. 8. Biographies

LC bl2017015381

A comprehensive biography of a Founding Father depicts him as an architect, scientist, bibliophile, paleontologist, musician and gourmet and offers new insight into his actions and thoughts about race, abolition, democracy and patriarchal responsibility.

"A fully fleshed biography of Thomas Jefferson (1743-1826) that emphasizes his creative paradoxes and accomplishments." Kirkus.

Burstein, Andrew **Madison** and Jefferson / Andrew Burstein and Nancy Isenberg. Random House, c2010. xxvii, 809 p., 8 p. of plates : **B**

ISBN 9781400067282

1. Jefferson, Thomas, 1743-1826 Friends and associates. 2. Madison, James, 1751-1836 Friends and associates. 3. Founding Fathers of the United States 4. Presidents -- United States 5. Politicians -- United States -- History 6. Politics and culture -- United States -- History 7. United States -- Politics and government -- 18th century 8. United States -- Politics and government -- 19th century 9. Biographies

LC 2010005884

A provocative analysis of the historically pivotal friendship between the third and fourth presidents offers insight into their complex characters while presenting a sobering assessment of how politics were conducted in the country's early years.

"This dual biography promotes Madison from junior partner to full-fledged colleague of the more magnetic Jefferson. According to the authors, Madison's popular image peaked in 1789 as father of the Constitution. But Burstein--and Isenberg--see him as a canny, effective politician for four decades, from the Continental Congress through his two terms as America's fourth president. An important, thoughtful, and gracefully written political history from the viewpoint of the young nation's two most intellectual founding fathers." Publishers Weekly.

Ellis, Joseph J. **American** sphinx: the character of Thomas Jefferson / Joseph J. Ellis. Alfred A. Knopf, 1997. xiv, 365 p. **B**

ISBN 9780679444909

1. Jefferson, Thomas, 1743-1826 Psychology. 2. Politicians -- United States 3. Presidents -- United States 4. Idealism in men. 5. Intellectual life -- United States. 6. United States -- Politics and government -- 1801-1809. 7. United States -- History -- 1783-1825. 8. Biographies

LC 96026171

National Book Award for Nonfiction, 1997.

National Book Critics Circle Award for Biography finalist, 1997.

A character study of Thomas Jefferson.

"Penetrating Jefferson's placid, elegant facade, this extraordinary biography brings the sage of Monticello down to earth without either condemning or idolizing him." Publishers Weekly.

★Gordon-Reed, Annette **Most** blessed of the patriarchs : Thomas Jefferson and the empire of the imagination / Annette Gordon-Reed and Peter S. Onuf. Liveright Publishing Corporation, [2016] xxv, 370 pages : **B**

ISBN 9780871404428

1. Political participation. 2. Political values. 3. Presidents -- United States. 4. United States -- Politics and government -- 1783-1789. 5. United States -- History -- 1783-1815 6. Biographies

LC 2016000927

A noted historian and a leading Jefferson scholar clarify philosophical questions about the Founding Father to trace his youth and development through the inconsistencies attributed to his character and his old age.

"An elegant, astute study that is both readable and thematically rich." Kirkus.

Gordon-Reed, Annette **Thomas** Jefferson and Sally Hemings : an American controversy / Annette Gordon-Reed. University Press of Virginia, 1997. xx, 288 p. ; **B**

ISBN 0813916984

1. Jefferson, Thomas, 1743-1826 Relations with women. 2. Jefferson, Thomas, 1743-1826 Relations with slaves. 3. Hemings, Sally, 1773-1835? 4. Hemings family. 5. Jefferson, Thomas, 1743-1826 Family 6. Monticello (Va.) 7. Slaves. 8. African American families -- Virginia. 9. Multiracial persons 10. African American families. 11. United States -- History -- 1783-1815 12. Virginia -- History. 13. Biographies

LC 96034550

Presents first-hand accounts, memoirs, letters, and recent DNA evidence that points to Thomas Jefferson's thirty-eight-year affair with his slave Sally Hemings, and refutes claims to the contrary.

"Hemings, a slave who was one-quarter African, was also a half sister of Jefferson's deceased wife, and she lived at Monticello for many years. In this understated, brilliant study an African-American law professor examines the allegation that Jefferson was the father of Hemings' children." The New Yorker.

Hitchens, Christopher, 1949-2011 **Thomas** Jefferson : author of America / Christopher Hitchens. Atlas Books, 2005. xiv, 188 p. ; Eminent lives **B**

ISBN 0060598964

1. Jefferson, Thomas, 1743-1826. 2. Presidents -- United States 3. Politicians. 4. Political leadership. 5. United States -- Politics and government -- 1789-1809. 6. Biographies

LC 2005296593

An analysis of the third president's politics and contributions in light of the events that were shaping the development of the United States during his time discusses the impact of the Enlightenment era, the French Revolution, and Jefferson's versatility as a public speaker and writer.

"This opinionated, lively narrative sheds light not only on Jefferson's complex personality but on the politics of his time, making it both a fascinating character study and an excellent review of early American history." Publishers Weekly.

★Meacham, Jon **Thomas** Jefferson : the art of power / Jon Meacham. Random House, 2012. 448 p. **B**

ISBN 9781400067664

1. Presidents -- United States 2. Politicians -- United States 3. Diplomats -- United States 4. Ambition in men 5. United States -- Politics and government -- 1783-1809 6. Biographies

LC 2012013700

Presents a portrait of the third president that considers his early life, role as a Founding Father, and considerable achievements as a master politician.

Jenner, Caitlyn, 1949-

Jenner, Caitlyn, 1949- The **secrets** of my life : a history / Caitlyn Jenner. Grand Central Publishing, 2017 356 p. **B**

ISBN 9781455596751

1. Transgender persons 2. Self-discovery in women 3. Identity (Psychology) 4. Growing up 5. Autobiographies and memoirs

LC 2017000493

The author chronicles her childhood as Bruce Jenner and rise to fame as a gold-medal-winning Olympic decathlete; her marriages and her relationships with her children; her transition; and her experience as the world's most famous transgender woman.

"Painting a life both shallow and deep, painstakingly choreographed and unscripted, Jenner's candid portrait of a self in the remaking is a marvel to behold." Kirkus.

Jeppesen, Travis, 1979-

Jeppesen, Travis, 1979- **See** you again in Pyongyang : a journey into Kim Jong Un's North Korea / Travis Jeppesen. Hachette Books, 2018. 304 p. **B**

ISBN 9780316509152

1. Jeppesen, Travis, 1979- Travel North Korea 2. Kim, Chong-un, 1984- 3. Fascism 4. Dictatorship 5. Isolationism. 6. International relations. 7. North Korea -- History 8. North Korea -- Politics and government 9. Pyongyang, Korea 10. Autobiographies and memoirs 11. Essays

LC bl2018079962

The author, the first American to study at a North Korean university, recounts his experiences living, traveling, and studying in the country to create a multifaceted portrait of Pyongyang in the Kim Jong Un era.

Jerkins, Morgan

Jerkins, Morgan **This** will be my undoing : living at the intersection of black, female, and feminist in (white) America / Morgan Jerkins. HarperPerennial, 2018 272 p. **B**

ISBN 9780062666154

1. Feminism 2. African American women 3. Social advocacy 4. Personal conduct 5. Essays 6. Autobiographies and memoirs

LC 2018303771

An influential literary critic presents a highly anticipated collection of linked essays interweaving incisive commentaries on subjects ranging from pop culture and feminism to black history, misogyny and racism to confront the challenges of being a black woman in today's world.

"Jerkins has penned a complex look at what it means to be an African American woman who subscribes to the tenets of feminism but finds herself marginalized by and chained to a narrative crafted for her, not by her." School Library Journal.

★Jerkins, Morgan **Wandering** in strange lands : a daughter of the Great Migration reclaims her roots / Morgan Jerkins. Harper, 2020. 304 p. **B**

ISBN 9780062873040

1. Jerkins, Morgan Family 2. African American women authors 3. African Americans -- Migrations -- History -- 20th century 4. Family history 5. Ancestors 6. United States -- History 7. United States -- Description and travel 8. Autobiographies and memoirs

LC bl2020016364

Between 1916 and 1970, six million black Americans left their rural homes in the South for jobs in cities in the North, West, and Midwest in a movement known as The Great Migration. But while this event transformed the complexion of America and provided black people with new economic opportunities, it also disconnected them from their roots, their land, and their sense of identity, argues Morgan Jerkins. In this fascinating and deeply personal exploration, she recreates her ancestors' journeys across America, following the migratory routes they took from Georgia and South Carolina to Louisiana, Oklahoma, and California.

"A thrilling, emotional, and engaging ride that almost commands the reader to turn the page. . . . [This] is required reading, accurately widening the lens of American history." Booklist

Jesus Christ

Benedict **Jesus** of Nazareth: Holy Week : from his transfiguration through his death and resurrection / Joseph Ratzinger, Pope Benedict XVI. Ignatius Press, 2011. 384 p. **B**

ISBN 9781586175009

1. Jesus Christ Historicity. 2. Bible. Gospels. 3. Resurrection 4. Faith (Christianity)

LC 2010937202

Sequel to: Jesus of Nazareth: from the baptism in the Jordan to the transfigurationOffers a detailed analysis of Jesus Christ's final week in Jerusalem, examining the political, religious, and scholarly aspects of Jesus' life, teaching, death, and resurrection.

"This is the second volume in [the author's] Jesus of Nazareth series. [This book] is a worthy contribution to the field not only because it was written by a pope, but also because it combines solid scholarship with deep spirituality. As such it joins the Jesus of history to the Christ of faith in an accessible narrative. This volume explores the drama of Holy Week. The focus is on the meaning of the events, with a strong reiteration of recent church teaching against imputing guilt for Jesus' death to the Jews of that time or now." Publishers Weekly.

Chittister, Joan **Following** the path : the search for a life of passion, purpose, and joy / Joan, Sister Chittister. Image, 2012. 188 p. ; **B**

ISBN 9780307953988

1. Jesus Christ. 2. God (Christianity) 3. Ability. 4. Christian life. 5. Purpose in life. 6. United States -- Religion -- 21st century. 7. Autobiographies and memoirs

LC bl2012013838

The author of The Gift of Years aims to help readers find purpose, happiness and fulfillment in their lives.

Fredriksen, Paula **Jesus** of Nazareth, King of the Jews : a Jewish life and the emergence of Christianity / Paula Fredriksen. Knopf, 1999. xxi, 327 p. : **B**

ISBN 0679446753

1. Bible. Gospels Criticism and interpretation 2. Bible. John Criticism and interpretation 3. Christianity. 4. Biographies

LC 99031054

The author of From Jesus to Christ presents a richly textured portrait of the historical Jesus that draws on biblical narratives, the Dead Sea Scrolls, early rabbinic writings, and other sources to create a study of of a man living in the world of late Second Temple Judaism.

Jeter, Derek, 1974-

Jeter, Derek, 1974- **Jeter** unfiltered / Derek Jeter with Anthony Bozza ; photographs by Christopher Anderson. Gallery Books, 2014. 252 p. : **B**

ISBN 1476783667

1. New York Yankees (Baseball team) 2. Baseball players -- United States 3. Baseball -- United States. 4. Autobiographies and memoirs

LC 2014033440

"Jeter Publishing".

A biography of baseball player Derek Jeter.

Jewel, 1974-

Jewel, 1974- **Never** broken : songs are only half the story / Jewel. Blue Rider Press, 2015 336 p. **B**

ISBN 9780399174339

1. Singers -- United States 2. Child abuse victims 3. Alaska 4. Autobiographies and memoirs

LC 2015024911

The best-selling poet and multi-platinum singer and songwriter explores her struggles with abuse at the hands of unconventional and highly creative family members in Alaska before rising to unexpected fame and becoming a parent.

Joan of Arc, Saint, 1412-1431

Castor, Helen **Joan** of Arc : a history / Helen Castor. Harper-

Collins 2015 352 p. **B**

ISBN 9780062384393

1. Women saints -- France 2. Hundred Years' War, 1339-1453. 3. Leadership in women. 4. Women soldiers -- France 5. Europe -- History -- 476-1492. 6. France -- History -- Charles VII, 1422-1461. 7. Biographies

LC 2014029053

Tells the story of the extraordinary peasant girl from Domremy as never told before, revealing a living, breathing woman confronting the challenges of faith and doubt and placing her actions in the context of the larger political and religious conflicts of this period in France.

"Castor carefully combs the record of her interrogation then and rehabilitation 25 years later. An unorthodox yet erudite and elegant biography of this 'massive star.'" Kirkus.

★Gordon, Mary, 1949- **Joan** of Arc / Mary Gordon. Lipper/Viking, 2000. xxv, 180 p. **B**

ISBN 0670885371

1. Joan of Arc, Saint, 1412-1431. 2. Charles VII, King of France, 1403-1461. 3. Women saints -- France 4. Hundred Years' War, 1339-1453. 5. Witchcraft -- France. 6. France -- History -- Charles VII, 1422-1461. 7. Biographies

LC 99055678

"A Lipper/Viking book.""

The strength of this biographical meditation lies in the penultimate chapter, in which Gordon investigates the numerous re-creations of Joan on stage and screen." Publishers Weekly.

Pernoud, Regine, 1909-1998 **Joan** of Arc : her story / Regine Pernoud, Marie-Veronique Clin ; translated and revised by Jeremy duQuesnay Adams ; edited by Bonnie Wheeler. St. Martin's Griffin, 1999, c1998. xxii, 304 p. : **B**

ISBN 9780312227302

1. Joan of Arc, Saint, 1412-1431. 2. Women saints -- France 3. France -- History -- Charles VII, 1422-1461. 4. Biographies

LC BL 00009725

Originally published: New York : St. Martin's Press, 1998.

A truthful look at the French saint follows her life from her childhood to her death when she was burned at the stake for witchcraft.

Jobrani, Maziyar, 1972-

Jobrani, Maziyar, 1972- **I'm** not a terrorist, but I've played one on TV : memoirs of a Middle Eastern funny man / Maz Jobrani. Simon & Schuster, 2014. 208 p. **B**

ISBN 9781476749983

1. Stereotypes (Social psychology) 2. Actors and actresses -- United States 3. Iranian-Americans 4. Comedians -- United States 5. Autobiographies and memoirs

LC 2014015012

A founding member of The Axis of Evil Comedy Tour and regular on Better Off Ted recounts his experiences as an Iranian growing up in America, his efforts to assimilate both cultures and his regular castings as a villain on TV and in movies.

Jobs, Steve, 1955-2011

★Isaacson, Walter **Steve** Jobs : a biography / Walter Isaacson. Simon & Schuster, 2011. 656 p. **B**

ISBN 9781451648539

1. Apple Computer, Inc. -- History. 2. Chief executive officers -- United States 3. Businesspeople -- United States 4. Millionaires -- United States 5. Computer industry and trade -- United States -- History. 6. United States -- Social life and customs -- 20th century 7. Biographies

LC 2011045006

Draws on more than forty interviews with Steve Jobs, as well as interviews with family members, friends, competitors, and colleagues, to offer a look at the co-founder and leading creative force behind the Apple computer company.

"This is an encyclopedic survey of all that Mr. Jobs accomplished, replete with the passion and excitement that it deserves." New York Times Book Review.

Schlender, Brent **Becoming** Steve Jobs : the evolution of a reckless upstart into a visionary leader / Brent Schlender and Rick Tetzeli. Crown Business, 2015 448 p. **B**

ISBN 9780385347402

1. Jobs, Steve, 1955-2011. 2. Apple Computer, Inc. Management. 3. Computer engineers -- United States 4. Businesspeople -- United States 5. Leadership. 6. Computer industry and trade. 7. Biographies

LC 2014031660

An account of how Apple cofounder Steve Jobs became the most famous and visionary CEO in the United States.

"Schlender and Tetzeli's account is unusually intimate thanks to voluminous interviews and Schlender's many personal encounters with Jobs over decades of covering him, and a reverential tone sometimes surfacesas when Jobs's lieutenant Tim Cook offered Jobs his own liver for a transplantin this corrective to Walter Isaacson's more jaundiced biography. But the authors are clear-eyed about Jobs's flaws and give lucid, detailed analyses of his maneuverings and product initiatives; theirs is one of the most nuanced and revealing assessments of Jobs's controversial career." Publishers Weekly.

John Paul II, Pope, 1920-2005

Buttiglione, Rocco, 1948- **Karol** Wojtyla : the thought of the man who became Pope John Paul II / Rocco Buttiglione ; translated by Paolo Guietti and Francesca Murphy. Eerdmans, c1997. xvi, 384 p. ; **B**

ISBN 0802838480

1. John Paul II, Pope, 1920-2005. 2. Catholic theology. 3. Catholic Church and philosophy. 4. Christian sociology (Catholic) 5. Christianity.

LC 97023188

"The author traces the Pope's intellectual development, offering a critique of his literary works and a detailed analysis of how he was influenced by Thomism and phenomenology, which he sought to reconcile while emphasizing individual freedom of conscience. Recommended for general collections for its broad sweep complementary to other biographies on the pope." Library Journal.

Flynn, Raymond L. **John** Paul II : a personal portrait of the pope and the man / Ray Flynn with Robin Moore & Jim Vrabel. St. Martin's Press, 2001. xv, 204 p. : **B**

ISBN 9780312266813

1. Popes -- History -- 20th century 2. Popes 3. Vatican City -- Religious life and customs -- 20th century

LC 00045965

A former U.S. ambassador to the Vatican shares his insights into the pope, revealing how the pontiff reshaped his ofice, and the Church, over the two decades.

"Flynn, the former mayor of Boston and ex-ambassador to the Vatican, tells us . what his book is not: It is not a biography, or an analysis. Flynn views it, rather, as a profile based on his own experiences with Pope John Paul II, dating back to a 1969 visit to Boston of then-Cardinal Karol Wojtyla." National Review.

O'Connor, Garry **Universal** father : a life of Pope John Paul II / Garry O'Connor. Bloomsbury : c2005. xii, 436 p. : **B**

ISBN 1596910968

1. Catholic Church -- History 20th century 2. Catholic Church -- History 21st century 3. Popes 4. Communism and religion. 5. Biographies

LC bl2005008332

Chronicles the life of Pope John Paul II from his childhood and early years as a priest through his twenty-six year papacy, highlighting his opposition to communism, his travels, and changes within the Catholic Church during his reign.

"The text is divided into four distinct phases of Pope John Paul II's life: 1920-1946, 1946-1978, 1978-1990, and 1990-2005. Each phase balances fact with anecdotal evidence, which lends the biography both credibility and charm. This timely and remarkable biography will be sought after by serious readers." Library Journal.

John, Elton

Bego, Mark **Rocket** Man : the life of Elton John / Mark Bego. Pegasus Books, 2020. xiv, 400 pages, 16 unnumbered pages of plates : **B**

ISBN 9781643133133

1. Pop musicians 2. Gay men 3. Pop musicians 4. Addiction 5. Biographies

LC bl2020000150

The colorful and kaleidoscopic life of one of theworld's most original and talented musical artists.

A comprehensive biography, infused with a satisfying dose of dishy gossip." Library Journal.

★John, Elton **Me** : Elton John official autobiography / Elton John. Henry Holt & Company, 2019 320 p. **B**

ISBN 9781250147608

1. Furnish, David 2. Fame 3. Pop musicians 4. Gay men 5. Recovering addicts 6. Autobiographies and memoirs

LC 2019947895

An official autobiography by the influential music artist, published to coincide with the release of Rocketman, includes coverage of John's complicated upbringing in a London suburb, his celebrity collaborations, his struggles with addiction and the establishment of his AIDS Foundation.

"Intimate, with brushes of gossip and hard-won wisdom, this compelling work joins the ranks of other masterly rock memoirs. A must-read for John's many devotees, it will also make fans out of those new to his music." Library Journal

John, King of England, 1167-1216

Morris, Marc, 1973- **King** John : treachery and tyranny in Medieval England: the road to Magna Carta / Marc Morris. Pegasus, 2015 400 p. **B**

ISBN 9781605988856

1. Magna Carta 2. Rulers 3. Civilization, Medieval 4. Political leadership. 5. Command of troops 6. Great Britain -- History -- John, 1199-1216 7. Biographies

LC 2015452049

An authoritative and dramatic new biography paints a vivid picture of the real King John through two interwoven stories, which reveal a dynamic, inventive, relentless and terribly flawed man whose rejection of the Magna Carta led to civil war, foreign invasion and his own demise. By the national best-selling author of The Norman Conquest.

"Describing the kings exactions, Morris shows how they provoked opposition from Englands magnates. Despite Magna Cartas subsequent renown as the foundation of constitutional law, at the time it was a truce surrounded by civil war. That the war ended quickly after John died in 1216 points, suggests Morris, to his personal shortcomings as significant causes of the disasters of his reign. Balanced and dramatic, Morris riveting account will effortlessly attract history readers." Booklist.

Johnson, Andrew, 1808-1875

Gordon-Reed, Annette **Andrew** Johnson : the 17th president, 1865-1869 / Annette Gordon-Reed. Times Books, 2008. 192 p. American presidents series (Times Books) **B**

ISBN 0805069488

1. Johnson, Andrew, 1808-1875. 2. Presidents -- United States 3. African Americans -- Social conditions -- 19th century 4. Politicians -- United States 5. United States -- Politics and government -- 1865-1877. 6. United States -- Race relations 7. Biographies

LC bl2007025255

A portrait of America's seventeenth president describes Andrew Johnson's failed efforts to bring about reconciliation following the Civil War, the antagonism of congressional leaders who sought his impeachment, and his legacy for the present.

Johnson, Charles

Johnson, Charles Richard, 1948- **Grand** : a grandparent's wisdom for a happy life / Charles Johnson. Hanover Square Press, 2020. 256 p. **B**

ISBN 1335015868

1. Grandparent and child 2. Wisdom 3. Personal conduct 4. Happiness 5. Autobiographies and memoirs

LC bl2020010776

A National Book Award winner and MacArthur Genius Fellow Charles Johnson reflects on the joys of being a grandparent in a collection of wisdom and life lessons.

"The National Book Award winner fleshes out 10 ideas on the art of life for his grandson. . . . Johnson digs deep, but he is never obscure, presenting these ideas in context in order to properly explain why he thinks they are important. Demanding, bighearted, and generous--we should all be so lucky to have such a grandfather." Kirkus

Johnson, Jack, 1878-1946

Ward, Geoffrey C. **Unforgivable** blackness : the rise and fall of Jack Johnson / Geoffrey C. Ward. A. A. Knopf, 2004. xi, 492 p. : **B**

ISBN 9780375415326

1. Boxers (Sports) -- United States 2. African American boxers 3. Interracial romance. 4. Boxing -- United States. 5. Biographies

LC 2004048524

Presents the life of the first black heavyweight boxing champion, whose flamboyant personality and defiance of racial stereotypes in the early twentieth century often made him the object of public outrage and a target of law enforcement officials.

"The author brings us back into Johnson's life and times with exquisitely rendered details, and the fight scenes themselves are gripping: fights so bloody that referees have to change shirts midbout, for instance, and a manager who pulls a gun on his fighter to keep him from quitting. The authoritative biography of Johnson for sure, but also one of the best boxing books in recent memory." Booklist.

Johnson, Lady Bird, 1912-2007

Gillette, Michael L. **Lady** Bird Johnson : an oral history / Michael

L. Gillette. Oxford University Press, 2012. 400 p. **B**

ISBN 9780199908080

1. Johnson, Lady Bird, 1912-2007. 2. Johnson, Lyndon B., 1908-1973. 3. United States. Congress. Senate. 4. Women and politics. 5. Women -- Political activity. 6. Presidents' spouses -- United States 7. Campaigning. 8. United States -- Politics and government -- 1945-1989. 9. Biographies 10. Interviews.

LC 2012011580

A fascinating look at the life of Lady Bird Johnson draws largely on 47 recorded oral history interviews, conducted by the author and his colleagues over a span of 18 years.

Johnson, Lyndon B., 1908-1973

★Caro, Robert A. The **passage** of power: the years of Lyndon Johnson / Robert A. Caro. Random House, 2012. xix, 712 p. ; **B**

ISBN 9780679405078

1. Johnson, Lyndon B., 1908-1973. 2. Kennedy, John F. (John Fitzgerald), 1917-1963 Assassination. 3. Vice-presidents 4. Presidents. 5. Politicians. 6. Democrats. 7. United States -- Politics and government. 8. Biographies

American History Book Prize, 2012.

Mark Lynton History Prize, 2013.National Book Critics Circle Award for Biography, 2012.

National Book Award for Nonfiction finalist, 2012

Examines Lyndon Johnson's volatile relationships with John and Robert Kennedy, describes JFK's assassination from Johnson's viewpoint, and recounts his accomplishments as president before they were overshadowed by the Vietnam War.

Peters, Charles, 1926- **Lyndon** B. Johnson : the 36th President, 1963-1969 / Charles Peters ; Arthur M. Schlesinger, Jr., and Sean Wilentz, general editors. Times Books, c2010. 192 p. **B**

ISBN 9780805082395

1. Presidents -- United States 2. Politicians. 3. Liberals. 4. Liberalism. 5. United States -- Politics and government -- 1945-1989. 6. Biographies.

LC 2009045612

Documents the 36th president's time in office and the legacy of his achievements, revealing the insights he gained while serving in the Senate and throughout the Kennedy-Johnson administration and discussing how factors including the Vietnam war drove him from office.

Woods, Randall Bennett, 1944- **Prisoners** of hope : Lyndon B. Johnson, the Great Society, and the limits of liberalism / Randall B. Woods. Basic Books, 2016. 432 p. **B**

ISBN 9780465050963

1. Antipoverty programs -- United States -- History -- 20th century. 2. Social legislation -- United States -- History -- 20th century. 3. Liberalism -- United States -- History -- 20th century. 4. Social change. 5. United States -- Politics and government -- 20th century 6. United States -- Politics and government -- 1963-1969. 7. United States -- Economic policy -- 1961-1971. 8. United States -- Social policy -- 20th century. 9. Biographies

LC 2015040042

Offers a nuanced look at America's most ambitious--and controversial--domestic policy agenda since the New Deal, as well as an intriguing portrait of the president behind it.

"A sympathetic but also gimlet-eyed scholar's look at a towering physical and political presence who learned, to his sorrow, that good intentions were insufficient." Kirkus.

Zeitz, Joshua **Building** the Great Society : inside Lyndon Johnson's White House / Joshua Zeitz. Viking, 2018. xviii, 378 p. ; **B**

ISBN 9780525428787

1. Presidents 2. Liberalism 3. Social change 4. Cabinet officers 5. United States -- Politics and government -- 1963-1969 6. Biographies

LC bl2017046094

An analysis of the Johnson administration reveals how the Great Society programs were put into practice, profiling major figures in the liberal reforms of the 1960s and how they made Johnson's ambitious vision a reality.

"Zeitzs lucid account yields engrossing insights into one of Americas most hopeful, productive, and tragic political eras." Publishers Weekly. Annex

Johnson, Plum

Johnson, Plum **They** left us everything : a memoir / Plum Johnson. Penguin, 2016, c2014. 274 p. **B**

ISBN 9780399184093

1. Johnson, Plum. 2. Caregivers. 3. Children of aging parents. 4. Aging parents -- Care. 5. Parent and adult child. 6. Autobiographies and memoirs

Originally published in Canada (Toronto : Penguin Canada Books, 2014)

Charles Taylor Prize for Literary Non-Fiction (Canada), 2015.

After the death of the author's senile father, and cantankerous ninety-three-year-old mother, she and her three younger brothers must empty and sell the beloved family home. Twenty-three rooms full of history, antiques, and oxygen tanks. The author remembers her loving but difficult parents who could not have been more different: the British father, a handsome, disciplined patriarch who nonetheless could not control his opinionated, extroverted Southern-belle wife who loved tennis and gin gimlets. The task consumes her, becoming more rewarding than she ever imagined.

"It is an uplifting affirmation of human relationships and the cycle of life itself. A warmly candid memoir of navigating family, aging, and death." Kirkus.

Johnson, Robert, 1911-1938

Conforth, Bruce M., 1950- **Up** jumped the devil : the real life of Robert Johnson / Bruce Conforth and Gayle Dean Wardlow. Chicago Review Press, [2019] 320 p. **B**

ISBN 9781641600941

1. Blues musicians 2. Blues (Music) 3. Biographies

LC 2019005127

Robert Johnson is the subject of the most famous myth about the blues: he allegedly sold his soul at the crossroads in exchange for his incredible talent, and this deal led to his death at age 27. But the actual story of his life remains unknown save for a few inaccurate anecdotes. In this definitive biography, the two authors relied on every interview, resource and document, most of it material no one has seen before. As a result, this book not only destroys every myth that ever surrounded Johnson, but also tells a human story of a real person.

★Wald, Elijah **Escaping** the delta : Robert Johnson and the invention of the blues / Elijah Wald. Amistad, 2004. xxvi, 342 p. **B**

ISBN 0060524235

1. Guitarists 2. Blues musicians -- Mississippi 3. Blues (Music) -- Delta region, Mississippi -- History and criticism 4. Biographies

LC 2003052287

A look at the life and music of Robert Johnson and his contributions to the blues describes his obscurity during his own life, his innovative influence on American popular music, and how the history of blues music was shaped by white fans.

"The author writes better than anyone else ever has about the blues. If you read only one book about blues--maybe ever--read this one." Booklist.

Johnson, Samuel, 1709-1784

Boswell, James, 1740-1795 The **life** of Samuel Johnson / James Boswell ; with an introduction by Claude Rawson. Knopf , 1992 liii, 1278 p. : **B**

ISBN 9780679417170

1. Johnson, Samuel, 1709-1784. 2. Authors, English -- 18th century 3. Lexicographers -- Great Britain 4. Biographies

LC 92052915

Boswell's classic biography of the eighteenth-century English lexicographer, critic, and conversationalist.

Martin, Peter, 1940- **Samuel** Johnson : a biography / Peter Martin. Harvard University Press, 2008. 610 p. **B**

ISBN 9780674031609

1. Johnson, Samuel, 1709-1784. 2. Authors, English -- 18th century 3. Intellectual life. 4. England -- History -- 18th century. 5. Biographies

LC 2008011327

"This biography of the English essayist, lexicographer, and literary personality . emphasizes aspects of Johnson not covered by any previously published biographies . notably Johnson's deep depressions; his liberal views on women writers, slavery, and poverty (he was not the complete Tory that others have painted him); and Johnson as a writer whose works deserve to be better known by the general public. Martin covers all the well-known facts and accomplishments of Johnson's life, and he emphasizes the turbulent times in which Johnson lived and the intriguing people he knew. Scholarly but written in an engaging manner and featuring many quotations from Johnson and his friends and acquaintances, this [is a] new portrait of a complex, multifaceted writer and thinker." Library Journal.

Meyers, Jeffrey **Samuel** Johnson : the struggle / Jeffrey Meyers. Basic Books, c2008. 400 p. **B**

ISBN 9780465045716

1. Johnson, Samuel, 1709-1784. 2. Authors, English -- 18th century 3. Lexicographers -- Great Britain 4. Intellectuals -- Great Britain 5. Intellectual life -- Great Britain -- 18th century. 6. Great Britain -- History -- 18th century. 7. Biographies

LC 2008012302

A definitive new biography of Samuel Johnson pays tribute to one of the giants of the English literary tradition in honor of the tricentennial of his birth, shedding new light on his role as a poet, essayist, critic, dictionary-maker, and raconteur, while examining the personal challenges he was forced to overcome to achieve success.

"This biography departs from a strict chronology to narrate significant events and their meaning for Johnson. A central concern involves one of Johnson's darkest secrets, which Meyers says other biographers have evaded: his masochistic sexuality at the hands of his confidante Mrs. Hester Thrale. The biography also speculates on other aspects of Johnson's sex life, both during his marriage to a much older woman and after her death. But Meyers's book is balanced and accomplishes much else." Publishers Weekly.

Johnson, Sophie Lucido

Johnson, Sophie Lucido **Many** love : a memoir of polyamory and finding love(s) / Sophie Lucido Johnson. Touchstone, 2018. 288 p. **B**

ISBN 9781501189784

1. Johnson, Sophie Lucido. 2. Love 3. Polyamory 4. Sex customs 5. Dating (Social customs) 6. Autobiographies and memoirs

LC 2017059117

An illustrated memoir of a woman who gives up her search for "The One" and instead begins an unconventional life of polyamory, shows how she learns to overcome the jealousy and misunderstanding that sometimes comes with such a lifestyle choice.

Johnson-Sirleaf, Ellen, 1938-

Cooper, Helene **Madame** President : the incredible journey of Ellen Johnson Sirleaf / Helene Cooper. Simon & Schuster, 2017. 352 p. **B**

ISBN 9781451697353

1. Women presidents 2. Politicians 3. Leadership in women 4. Sex discrimination against women 5. Liberia -- Politics and government 6. Liberia -- History -- Civil War, 1989-1996 7. Central Africa 8. Biographies

LC 2016042087

The harrowing, but triumphant story of Ellen Johnson Sirleaf, leader of the Liberian women's movement, winner of the Nobel Peace Prize, and the first democratically elected female president in African history.

"A brisk chronicle of a strong-willed, tireless, and determined leader." Kirkus.

Johnston, Ann Dowsett

Johnston, Ann Dowsett **Drink** : the intimate relationship between women and alcohol / Ann Dowsett Johnston. HarperWave, 2013. 256 p. **B**

ISBN 9780062241795

1. Johnston, Ann Dowsett. 2. Women -- Alcohol use 3. Alcoholic women 4. Drinking 5. Addiction 6. Autobiographies and memoirs

LC 2013026103

An exploration of the rise in alcohol consumption and abuse among women in recent years. Drink covers health risks, marketing, current trends and sociological underpinnings of this new epidemic. The author beautifully weaves reportage with her personal recovery story into a compelling and informative narrative addressing one of the most pressing issues for women today

Jokinen, Tom

Jokinen, Tom **Curtains** : adventures of an undertaker-in-training / Tom Jokinen. Da Capo Press, c2010. 279 p. **B**

ISBN 9780306818912

1. Jokinen, Tom. 2. Undertakers 3. Funerals 4. Funeral homes 5. Autobiographies and memoirs

LC bl2010016369

In 2006, CBC journalist Tom Jokinen takes a job as an apprentice undertaker at a Winnipeg funeral home and reveals the changing face of the funeral industry.

Jollett, Mikel

Jollett, Mikel **Hollywood** Park : a memoir / Mikel Jollett. Celadon Books, 2020. 384 p. **B**

ISBN 9781250621566

1. Jollett, Mikel Childhood and youth. 2. Synanon (Foundation) 3. Rock musicians -- United States 4. Cults 5. Growing up 6. Self-discovery 7. United States 8. Autobiographies and memoirs

LC 2020002685

The frontman of indie band The Airborne Toxic Event reveals his upbringing in the infamous Church of Synanon cult, where he endured poverty, addiction and emotional abuse before slowly working his way toward college and a music career.

"In this arresting debut memoir, Jollett, frontman of the indie band Airborne Toxic Event, writes of escaping a California cult named Synanon--where he lived in the 1970s until age five--with his mentally unstable mother and older brother. . . . All this results in a shocking but contemplative memoir about the aftermath of an unhealthy upbringing." Publishers Weekly

Jones, Cleve, 1954-

Jones, Cleve, 1954- **When** we rise : my life in the movement / Cleve Jones. Hachette Books 2016 256 p. **B**

ISBN 9780316315432

1. Gay and Lesbian Movement 2. Gay activists 3. Gay men 4. LGBTQIA rights 5. San Francisco, California 6. Autobiographies and memoirs

LC bl2016046444

Lambda Literary Award for Gay Memoir/Biography, 2017.

The partial inspiration for a forthcoming ABC television miniseries from Oscar-winning screenwriter Dustin Lance Black, longtime LGBTQ and AIDS activist Cleve Jones' memoir is a sweeping, profoundly moving account of his life from sexually liberated 1970s San Francisco, through the AIDS crisis and up to his present-day involvement with the marriage equality battle.

"For those interested in understanding the history of the LGBTQ quest for social justice in America, this work will resonate." Library Journal

Jones, Genevieve (Genevieve Estelle), 1847-1879

Kiser, Joy M., 1947- **America's** other Audubon / Joy M. Kiser. Princeton Architectural Press, 2012. 192 p. **B**

ISBN 9781616890599

1. Jones, Genevieve (Genevieve Estelle), 1847-1879. 2. Ornithologists -- United States 3. Birds -- North America -- Pictorial works. 4. Ornithological illustration -- North America. 5. Birds in art. 6. Biographies

LC 2011039605

Jones, George, 1931-2013

Kienzle, Rich The **grand** tour : the life and music of George Jones / Rich Kienzle. Dey Street Books, 2016 320 p. **B**

ISBN 9780062309914

1. Country musicians -- United States 2. Biographies

LC 2016561296

The veteran country music journalist and author of Southwest Shuffle presents an analysis of the life and career of the influential artist, drawing on archival material, government records and interviews with close associates to discuss his troubled upbringing, struggles with drug abuse and influence on fellow musicians.

"This moving biography keeps Jones's voice alive and underscores his central role in American music history." Publishers Weekly.

Jones, Jim, 1931-1978

Guinn, Jeff The **Road** to Jonestown : Jim Jones and Peoples Temple / Jeff Guinn. Simon & Schuster, 2017 416 p. **B**

ISBN 9781476763828

1. Jones, Jim, 1931-1978. 2. Peoples Temple. 3. Jonestown Mass Suicide, Jonestown, Guyana, 1978. 4. Cults. 5. Suicide. 6. Murder. 7. Biographies

LC 2016051471

A portrait of the influential cult leader behind the Jonestown Massacre examines his personal life, from his extramarital affairs and drug use to his fraudulent faith healing practices and his decision to move his followers to Guyana, sharing astonishing new details about the events leading to the 1978 tragedy.

"A vivid, fascinating revisitation of a time and series of episodes fast receding into history even as their forgotten survivors still walk among us." Kirkus.

Jones, John Paul, 1747-1792

Morison, Samuel Eliot, 1887-1976 **John** Paul Jones : a sailor's biography / Samuel Eliot Morison ; with an introduction by James C. Bradford ; charts and diagrams by Erwin Raisz. Naval Institute Press, 1999, c1959. xxvi, 534 p. : **B**

ISBN 9781557504104

1. United States. Navy 2. Russia. Navy 3. Admirals -- United States 4. Revolutions -- United States 5. American Revolution, 1775-1783 6. Command of troops 7. United States -- History -- Revolution, 1775-1783 -- Naval operations. 8. Biographies

LC 00503558

Originally published: Boston, MA : Little, Brown, 1959. Pulitzer Prize for Biography or Autobiography, 1960.

★Thomas, Evan, 1951- **John** Paul Jones : sailor, hero, father of the American Navy / Evan Thomas. Simon & Schuster, 2003. 383 p., 16 p. of plates : **B**

ISBN 0743205839

1. United States. Navy 2. Admirals -- United States 3. Revolutions -- United States 4. Sailing. 5. Command of troops. 6. United States -- History -- Revolution, 1775-1783 -- Naval operations. 7. Biographies

LC 2003042411

John Paul Jones, at sea and in the heat of battle, was the great American hero of the Age of Sail. He was to history what Patrick O'Brian's Jack Aubrey and C. S. Forester's Horatio Hornblower are to fiction. Ruthless, indomitable, clever; he vowed to sail, as he put it, 'in harm's way.'

"The complex portrait is rendered with nautical precision--the author knows his topsail from his topgallant--and a lively eye for such details as the Enlightenment virtues espoused by Freemasonry or the proper way to kiss a French lady in the eighteenth century." Publishers Weekly.

Jones, Mother, 1837-1930

Gorn, Elliott J., 1951- **Mother** Jones : the most dangerous woman in America / Elliott J. Gorn. Hill and Wang, 2001. xiii, 408 p. : **B**

ISBN 9780809070930

1. Women labor unionists 2. Working class women -- United States 3. Women labor leaders -- United States 4. Labor movement -- United States. 5. Biographies

LC 00044997

Traces Mother Jones's obscure early life as an Irish immigrant, schoolteacher, and dressmaker; details the early deaths of her husband and children; and her role as an agitator who changed the course of the American labor movement.

"Gorn has successfully separated fact from myth . situating Jones's story within a wider cultural frame." Publishers Weekly.

Jones, Nathaniel R., 1926-

Jones, Nathaniel R., 1926- **Answering** the call : an autobiography of the modern struggle to end racial discrimination in America / Judge Nathaniel R. Jones ; foreword by Evelyn

Brooks Higginbotham. The New Press, 2016. 352 p. **B**

ISBN 9781620970751

1. Judges. 2. Civil rights -- United States. 3. Autobiographies and memoirs

LC 2015043150

Judge Nathaniel R. Jones's pathbreaking career was forged in the 1960s: as the first African American assistant U.S. attorney in Ohio; as assistant general counsel of the Kerner Commission; and, beginning in 1969, as general counsel of the NAACP. In that latter role, Jones coordinated attacks against Northern school segregation-a vital, divisive, and poorly understood chapter in the movement for equality-twice arguing in the pivotal U.S. Supreme Court case Bradley v. Milliken, which addressed school desegregation in Detroit. He also led the national response to the attacks against affirmative action, spearheading and arguing many of the signal legal cases of that effort.

"A forthright testimony by a witness to history." Kirkus.

Jones, Saeed

Jones, Saeed **How** we fight for our lives : a memoir / Saeed Jones. Simon & Schuster, 2019. 208 p. **B**

ISBN 9781501132735

1. African American authors 2. Gay authors 3. Growing up 4. Identity (Psychology) 5. Southern states 6. Autobiographies and memoirs

LC 2019002515

Kirkus Prize for Nonfiction, 2019.

Lambda Literary Award for Gay Memoir/Biography, 2020.

Stonewall Book Awards: Israel Fishman Non-fiction Award, 2020.

The co-host of BuzzFeed's AM to DM, award-winning poet and author of Prelude to Bruise documents his coming-of-age as a young, gay, black man in an American South at a crossroads of sex, race and power.

"A memoir of coming to terms that's written with masterful control of both style and material." Kirkus.

Joplin, Janis, 1943-1970

Cooke, John Byrne **On** the road with Janis Joplin / John Byrne Cooke. Berkley Books, 2014 432 p. **B**

ISBN 9780425274118

1. Joplin, Janis, 1943-1970. 2. Cooke, John Byrne 3. Women singers. 4. Women rock musicians. 5. Road managers 6. Autobiographies and memoirs

LC 2014034647

The influential music artist's road manager retraces his eyewitness to Joplin's breakout performance at the Monterey Pop Festival in 1967, pivotal career decisions, appearance at Woodstock, attendance at her high-school reunion and tragic final days.

"Rock music fans will love reading this up-close view of Joplin. The end of the book feels like losing her all over again." Library Journal.

★George-Warren, Holly **Janis** : her life and music / Holly George-Warren. Simon & Schuster, 2019. xv, 377 p., 32 unnumbered p. : **B**

ISBN 9781476793108

1. Joplin, Janis, 1943-1970. 2. Big Brother & the Holding Co. (Musical group) 3. Women singers 4. Rock musicians 5. Social acceptance 6. Blues (Music) 7. Biographies

The Grammy nominee and award-winning co-author of The Road to Woodstock presents an intimate portrait of the counterculture music artist that includes coverage of her conservative upbringing, her extraordinary voice and her boundary-breaking legacy.

"This poignant and ultimately tragic account of an iconic performer is a must for Joplin fans, but anyone who enjoys a good biography will appreciate this exceptional work." Library Journal.

Joplin, Scott, 1868-1917

Berlin, Edward A. **King** of ragtime : Scott Joplin and his era / Edward A. Berlin. Oxford University Press, 1995, c1994. xii, 334 p. : **B**

ISBN 0195101081

1. Joplin, Scott, 1868-1917. 2. Composers -- United States

LC 96107624

"First published in 1994 by Oxford University Press ... First issued as an Oxford University Press paperback, 1995"--T.p. verso.

The story of the popular, critically acclaimed music of Scott Joplin shares a definitive portrait of a man who was part of the first post-Civil War generation of African-American pioneers who escaped poverty and low social status through entertainment.

Jordan, David Starrr, 1851-1931

Miller, Lulu **Why** fish don't exist : a story of loss, love, and the hidden order of life / Lulu Miller. Simon & Schuster, 2020. 192 p. **B**

ISBN 9781501160271

1. Miller, Lulu 2. Naturalists 3. Ichthyologists 4. San Francisco Earthquake and Fire, Calif., 1906 5. Biological specimens -- Collection and preservation 6. United States 7. Biographies 8. Autobiographies and memoirs

LC bl2020012647

The cofounder of NPR's Invisibilia tells the story of a scientist who started over after losing his life's work in the 1906 San Francisco earthquake and discusses whether he is a role model or a cautionary tale.

"Part biography, part science report, and part meditation on how the chaos that caused Miller's existential misery could also bring self-acceptance and a loving wife, this unique book is an ingenious celebration of diversity and the mysterious order that underlies all existence. A quirky wonder of a book." Kirkus

Josephine, Empress of the French, 1763-1814

Williams, Kate, 1974- **Ambition** and desire : the dangerous life of Josephine Bonaparte / Kate Williams. Ballantine Books, 2014. 384 p. **B**

ISBN 9780345522832

1. Josephine, Empress of the French, 1763-1814. 2. Napoleon I, Emperor of the French, 1769-1821 Relations with women. 3. Women rulers -- France 4. Biographies

LC 2014030438

Originally published under the title Josephine: desire, ambition, Napoleon in the United Kingdom by Hutchinson, a member of The Random House Group Limited, London, in 2013.

Biographer Kate Williams, in Ambition and Desire, brings Josephine Bonaparte out from the aura surrounding her husband, Emperor Napoleon Bonaparte, to claim her place on the stage of history. Born to an ordinary but aspiring family on the tiny West Indian island of Martinique, Josephine made her way to Paris, survived the Revolution, became a star of the salons, and married the man who was her match in both brilliance and ambition. This compelling account offers up-close insight into Josephine's passion and achievements as well as her tumultuous relationship with Napoleon.

"Meeting her match in Napolon Bonaparte, Josephine and he embarked on a doomed marital odyssey characterized by personal jealousies and political obsessions. An in-depth portrait of the substantive woman behind the throne." Booklist.

Joyce, James, 1882-1941

★Bowker, Gordon **James** Joyce : a biography / Gordon Bowker. Farrar, Straus and Giroux, 2012. 624 p. **B**

ISBN 9780374178727

1. Authors, Irish -- 20th century 2. Modernism (Literature) 3. Irish in Europe 4. Expatriates 5. Biographies

LC 2011045954

"The extent to which Bowker ties life events, even minor ones, to details in Joyce's works sets this book apart. This is where scholars will benefit as much as Joyce novices who are interested in learning more about this trailblazing author who changed the way fiction is written and read." Library Journal.

Ellmann, Richard, 1918-1987 **James** Joyce / Richard Ellmann. Oxford University Press, 1982, c1959. xviii, 887 p., 54 leaves of plates : **B**

ISBN 0195031032

1. Authors, Irish -- 20th century 2. Biographies

LC 81022455

Originally published: New York : Oxford University Press, 1959.

James Tait Black Memorial Prize for Biography, 1982.

National Book Award for Nonfiction, 1960.

Describes the life of the Irish writer and discusses his works in light of the literary climate in which he lived.

"This is a vast undertaking and continuing achievementmassive, masterly, and definitive, rich in anecdote and detail. It is also extremely readable; the easy, often sympathetic style communicates gracefully not only facts but analysis." Choice.

Fargnoli, A. Nicholas **Critical** companion to James Joyce : a literary reference to his life and work / A. Nicholas Fargnoli, Michael Patrick Gillespie. Facts On File, c2006. xiv, 450 p. : **B**

ISBN 9780816062324

1. Joyce, James, 1882-1941 Handbooks, manuals, etc 2. Novelists, Irish -- 20th century -- Handbooks, manuals, etc 3. Ireland -- In literature Handbooks, manuals, etc.

LC 2005015721

Rev. ed. of: James Joyce A to Z : The essential reference to the life and work. 1995.

Presents a guide to the life and literary accomplishments of the Irish author, including analyses of the contents and characters of each of his works and discussions of places and events in his life which influenced his writing.

O'Brien, Edna **James** Joyce / Edna O'Brien. Viking Penguin, 1999. x, 179 p. **B**

ISBN 0670882305

1. Authors, Irish -- 20th century 2. Modernism (Literature) 3. Biographies

LC 99023214

"A Lipper/Viking book.""

O'Brien tells the story of the aspiring young writer and his downwardly mobile family, his escape to Europe, the constant struggle to scrape together enough money to live on, and finally his relative comfort, thanks to patrons, once Ulysses was published. She also provides thoughtful appreciations of Joyce's major works." Booklist.

Judas Iscariot

★Gubar, Susan, 1944- **Judas** : a biography / Susan Gubar. W.W. Norton, c2009. xxvi, 453 p. : **B**

ISBN 9780393064834

1. Judas Iscariot. 2. Bible 3. Antisemitism. 4. Apostles. 5. Betrayal. 6. Religion. 7. Biographies

LC 2008042967

A cultural and interdisciplinary portrait of the betrayer of Jesus explores the incongruities of his appearances in the Bible as well as historical attitudes that have resulted in his representation of Jewish culture and Judeo-Christian values on money, suicide, and homosexuality.

"An exhaustive, beautifully written cultural history of our favorite wrongdoer, Gubar's work is an immensely rewarding and crucially important book." Library Journal.

Julien, Maude, 1957-

Julien, Maude, 1957- The **only** girl in the world : a memoir / Maude Julien with Ursula Gauthier ; translated from the French by Adriana Hunter. Little, Brown and Company, 2017. 273 p. : **B**

ISBN 9780316466622

1. Child abuse victims 2. Emotionally abused children. 3. Adult child abuse victims 4. Child abusers 5. Autobiographies and memoirs

LC 2017934593

Originally published: Stock, 2014.

Also published in Australia: Melbourne, Vic: Text, 2017.

Describes the author's harrowing upbringing by fanatic parents, who raised her in isolation through traumatic disciplinary exercises designed to "eliminate weakness," and recounts how she eventually escaped with the help of an outsider.

Kaag, John J., 1979-

Kaag, John J., 1979- **American** philosophy : a love story / John Kaag. FSG, 2016. 240 p. **B**

ISBN 9780374154486

1. Philosophy 2. Scholars and academics 3. Intellectual life. 4. Book collectors 5. Autobiographies and memoirs

LC 2016001908

When he stumbles upon a treasure trove of rare books that once belonged to the Harvard philosopher William Ernst Hocking, the author, a disillusioned philosopher at sea in his marriage and career, begins to catalog and preserve this collection and rediscovers the very tenets of American philosophy, seeing them within a 21st-century context.

" Kaag's lively prose, acute self-examination, unfolding romance, and instructive history of philosophy as a discipline make for a surprisingly absorbing book." Kirkus.

Kafka, Franz, 1883-1924

Murray, Nicholas **Kafka** / Nicholas Murray. Yale University Press, 2004. 440 p. : **B**

ISBN 0300106319

1. Authors, Austrian -- 20th century 2. Fathers and sons. 3. Anxiety in men. 4. Biographies

LC 2004107048

"This biography relates Kafka's brief life, trying valiantly to depict a more normal Kafka, a man who lived in society with good friends, enjoyed sex, had wide-ranging intellectual interests and became enamored of Judaism. In Murray's account, Kafka's employer valued him highly, and under the imprint of no less a figure than Kurt Wolff, he experienced some literary success. Despite Murray's best efforts to contain Kafka's idiosyncrasies, though, the writer remains the tormented soul who created out of his personal anxieties and agonies some of the most acclaimed works of the 20th century." Publishers Weekly.

Stach, Reiner **Kafka,** the decisive years / Reiner Stach ; translated from the German by Shelley Frisch. Harcourt, c2005. vi, 581 p. : **B**

ISBN 9780151007523

1. Authors, Austrian -- 20th century 2. Austria -- Social life and

customs -- 20th century 3. Biographies

LC 2005014554

Examines the influential writer's life and work between 1910 and 1915, during which Kafka became fascinated with early Zionism, shared an engagement with Felice Bauer, and wrote such works as "The Metamorphosis" and "The Trial."

"Essential reading for all Kafka devotees." Booklist.

Stach, Reiner **Kafka** : the early years / Reiner Stach ; translated by Shelley Frisch. Princeton University Press, 2016, c2014. 616 p. **B**

ISBN 9780691151984

1. Kafka, Franz, 1883-1924 Childhood and youth. 2. Authors, Austrian -- 20th century 3. Austria -- Social life and customs -- 20th century 4. Biographies

LC 2016021490

Translation of: Kafka, die fruhen Jahre.

Originally published: Frankfurt am Main : S. Fischer, 2014

Addresses how Kafka became Kafka, describing the complex personal, political and cultural circumstances that shaped the young man, as well as a colorful panorama of his wider world, especially the convoluted politics and culture of Prague.

"Brod's detailed reflections, which dominate much of this final volume, will chiefly interest Kafka scholars, but all Kafka devotees will find this biographys insights deeply fulfilling." Publishers Weekly.

Stach, Reiner **Kafka,** the years of insight / Reiner Stach ; translated by Shelley Frisch. Princeton University Press, 2013, c2002. 816 p. **B**

ISBN 9780691147512

1. Kafka, Franz, 1883-1924. 2. Authors, Austrian -- 20th century 3. Writing 4. Terminal illness 5. Family relationships 6. Austria -- Social life and customs -- 20th century 7. Biographies

LC 2012042048

Translation from the German of: Kafka, die Jahre der Erkenntnis.

Originally published: Frankfurt am Main : S. Fischer, 2002."

This well-researched new biography details the last nine years of Franz Kafka's life and explores the personal, social, and political events that shaped his writing." Publishers Weekly.

Kahlo, Frida

Herrera, Hayden **Frida** : a biography of Frida Kahlo / Hayden Herrera. Perennial, 2002, c1983. xiii, 507 p. : **B**

ISBN 9780060085896

1. Kahlo, Frida. 2. Painters -- Mexico 3. Mexico -- Social life and customs. 4. Biographies

LC 80008688

Originally published: New York : Harper & Row, c1983.

An in-depth biography of Mexican artist Frida Kahlo details her haunting and original painting style, her turbulent marriage to muralist Diego Rivera, her association with communism, and her love of Mexican culture and folklore.

Kahlo, Frida The **diary** of Frida Kahlo : an intimate self-portrait / introduction by Carlos Fuentes ; essay and commentaries by Sarah M. Lowe. H.N. Abrams ; 2005, c1995. 295 p. : **B**

ISBN 9780810959545

1. Kahlo, Frida. 2. Painters -- Mexico 3. Surrealism -- Mexico 4. Diaries.

LC bl2005021601

Reprint. Originally published: 1995.

A facsimile of the diary of the twentieth-century Mexican artist, which is accompanied by an English transcription and commentary and more than three hundred illustrations.

"Sprinkled with irony, black humor, even gaiety . this volume is a testament to Kahlo's resilience and courage." Publishers Weekly.

Lozano, Luis-Martin **Frida** Kahlo / [Luis-Martin Lozano ; translated from the Spanish by Mark Eaton and Luisa Panichi]. Bulfinch Press, c2000. 245 p. : **B**

ISBN 0821227661

1. Kahlo, Frida Criticism and interpretation. 2. Artists -- Mexico 3. Women artists -- Mexico 4. Picture books for adults. 5. Biographies

LC 2001089093

"In this illustrated survey of Frida Kahlo's work Lozano . explores her life and paintings in a series of essays that range from a poetic study by noted Mexican cultural critic Carlos Monsivis to a short, prosaic piece written in 1943 by her husband, Diego Rivera, to an academic essay by Lozano himself. Lozano uses Kahlo's own stunning images, offering high-quality reproductions of some of Kahlo's most famous works as well as some of her lesser-known pieces. Previously unseen photos of Kahlo at work in her studio are also included. The detail and clarity of the images is incredible." Library Journal.

Stahr, Celia **Frida** in America : the creative awakening of a great artist / Celia Stahr. St. Martin's Press, 2020. 384 p. **B**

ISBN 9781250113382

1. Kahlo, Frida. 2. Rivera, Diego, 1886-1957 3. Women artists 4. Artists -- Mexico 5. Voyages and travels 6. Expatriate artists. 7. United States 8. San Francisco, California 9. New York City 10. Detroit, Michigan 11. Biographies

LC 2019041724

Describes the years the Mexican artist spent in America beginning in 1930 with her new, older, and already world-famous husband, Diego Rivera, and the impact living in diverse cities of San Francisco, Detroit and New York had on her painting.

"Featuring meticulous research and elegant turns of phrase, Stahr's engrossing account provides scholarly though accessible analysis for both feminists and art lovers." Publishers Weekly

Kakutani, Michiko

Kakutani, Michiko **Ex** libris : 100+ books to read and reread / Michiko Kakutani ; illustrations by Dana Tanamachi. Clarkson Potter, 2020. 301 p. **B**

ISBN 9780525574972

1. Kakutani, Michiko Books and reading. 2. Reading 3. Literature -- Appreciation 4. Critics -- United States 5. Best books. 6. Autobiographies and memoirs 7. Essays

LC 2020007615

The Pulitzer Prize-winning literary critic shares 100 personal, thought-provoking essays on the life-changing works of fiction, nonfiction and poetry she most recommends for the establishment of well-read world citizenship, from The Federalist Papers to the Harry Potter novels.

"Kakutani's recommendations and her 'sense of the shared joys and losses of human experience' are revelations." Publishers Weekly

Kalanithi, Paul

★Kalanithi, Paul **When** breath becomes air / Paul Kalanithi. Random House, 2016 240 p. **B**

ISBN 9780812988406

1. People with cancer 2. Personal conduct 3. Purpose in life 4. Thirties (Age) 5. Autobiographies and memoirs

LC 2015023815

Pulitzer Prize for Biography or Autobiography finalist, 2017.

A young neurosurgeon faced with a terminal diagnosis describes his examination into what truly makes a meaningful life.

"This eloquent, heartfelt meditation on the choices that make life worth living, even as death looms, will prompt readers to contemplate their own values and mortality." Booklist.

Kalb, Bess, 1987-

★Kalb, Bess, 1987- **Nobody** will tell you this but me : a true (as told to me) story / Bess Kalb. Alfred A Knopf, 2020. 224 p. : **B**

ISBN 9780525654711

1. Bell, Bobby 2. Grandmothers -- Anecdotes. 3. Grandmother and granddaughter 4. Women -- Family relationships 5. Independence in women 6. Autobiographies and memoirs

LC 2019026101

The award-winning television writer reflects on her relationship with her loving grandmother, the daughter of immigrants from 19th-century Belarus whose hardships, sacrifices and headstrong nature shaped the author's perspectives on family and career.

"An endearing, bittersweet, and entertainingly fresh take on the family memoir." Kirkus

Kalibbala, Gladys

Yu, Jessica **Garden** of the lost and abandoned : the extraordinary story of one ordinary woman and the children she saves / Jessica Yu. Houghton Mifflin Harcourt, 2017. 372 p. **B**

ISBN 9780544617063

1. Journalists 2. Investigations 3. Abandoned children 4. Altruism 5. Uganda 6. Biographies

LC 2017044919

A portrait of journalist, humanitarian and self-taught detective Gladys Kalibbala describes her high-risk efforts to connect missing and castaway children in Uganda to their families, tracing the influence of her "Lost and Abandoned" newspaper column and her dream of providing safe homes and livelihoods for thousands of street kids.

"This is a powerful and inspiring tale of how one woman can make a tremendous difference in her community." Booklist.

Kaling, Mindy

Kaling, Mindy **Is** everyone hanging out without me? (and other concerns) / Mindy Kaling. Random House Inc., 2011. 224 p. **B**

ISBN 9780307886262

1. Kaling, Mindy. 2. Office (Television program : United States) 3. Actors and actresses 4. Television writers 5. Women comedians 6. Women television personalities 7. Autobiographies and memoirs

LC 2011033922

The writer and actress best known as Kelly Kapoor on "The Office" shares observations on topics ranging from favorite male archetypes and her hatred of dieting to her relationship with her mother and the haphazard creative process in the "Office" writers' room.

Kaling, Mindy **Why** not me? / Mindy Kaling. Crown, 2015. 240 p. **B**

ISBN 9780804138147

1. Kaling, Mindy. 2. Celebrities -- Humor 3. Actors and actresses 4. Television writers 5. Women comedians 6. Autobiographies and memoirs

LC 2015020444

The star of The Mindy Project and author of the best-selling Is Everyone Hanging Out Without Me? presents a second collection of uproarious essays, observations, fears and advice on everything from prisoner fan mail to celebrity interactions.

Kameny, Frank, 1925-2011

★Cervini, Eric, 1992- The **deviant's** war : the homosexual vs. the United States of America / Eric Cervini. Farrar, Straus and Giroux, 2020. 494 p. **B**

ISBN 9780374139797

1. United States. Department of Defense Officials and employees 2. Mattachine Society of Washington -- History 3. Gay men 4. Civil service workers 5. Discrimination in employment 6. Astronomers 7. Biographies

LC 2020003415

In 1957, Frank Kameny, a rising astronomer working for the U.S. Defense Department in Hawaii, received a summons to report immediately to Washington, D.C. The Pentagon had reason to believe he was a homosexual, and after a series of humiliating interviews, Kameny, like countless gay men and women before him, was promptly dismissed from his government job. Unlike many others, though, Kameny fought back. Based on firsthand accounts, recently declassified FBI records, and forty thousand personal documents, Eric Cervini's The Deviant's War unfolds over the course of the 1960s, as the Mattachine Society of Washington, the group Kameny founded, became the first organization to protest the systematic persecution of gay federal employees.

"An absolutely indispensable, highly readable work of history that belongs in every library." Booklist

Kamkwamba, William, 1987-

Kamkwamba, William, 1987- The **boy** who harnessed the wind : creating currents of electricity and hope / William Kamkwamba and Bryan Mealer. William Morrow, 2009. 347 p. **B**

ISBN 9780061730320

1. Inventors -- Malawi 2. Windmills. 3. Wind power. 4. Electric power production. 5. Malawi. 6. Africa. 7. Autobiographies and memoirs

LC bl2009020076

One of the coauthors tells his engaging and inspiring true story of hope, tenacity, and imagination, in which as an African teenager he built a windmill from scraps, creating electricity for his village?and a better life for himself and his family.

"This exquisite tale strips life down to its barest essentials, and once there finds reason for hopes and dreams, and is especially resonant for Americans given the economy and increasingly heated debates over health care and energy policy." Publishers Weekly.

Kan, Karoline, 1989-

Kan, Karoline, 1989- **Under** red skies : three generations of life, loss, and hope in China / Karoline Kan. Hachette Books, 2019. 320 p. **B**

ISBN 9780316412049

1. Kan, Karoline, 1989- Family. 2. Women -- China 3. Intergenerational relations. 4. Social change. 5. Family relationships. 6. China -- Social life and customs. 7. China -- Social conditions -- 1949- 8. Autobiographies and memoirs.

LC 2018036323

Includes index.

Using stories of her own family's history, a former New York Times author offers a personal look at how China is trying to reconcile its impoverished and troubled past with its new role as a world superpower.

"Kan presents an engaging debut memoir that would make an excellent book club choice and has strong YA crossover appeal." Library Journal.

Kandel, Eric R.

Kandel, Eric R. **In** search of memory : the emergence of a new science of mind / Eric R. Kandel. W. W. Norton & Company, c2006. xv, 510 p. : **B**

ISBN 0393058638

1. Neurologists -- United States 2. Medical scientists -- United States 3. Nobel Prizes. 4. Memory. 5. United States -- History -- 20th century. 6. Autobiographies and memoirs

National Academies Communication Award, 2007.

Traces a five-decade convergence of four distinct disciplines including behaviorist psychology, cognitive psychology, neuroscience, and molecular biology; describing how it enabled the development of a new science in the field of memory that has a promising potential for more effective healing.

Kane, Elisha Kent, 1820-1857

McGoogan, Kenneth, 1947- **Race** to the Polar Sea : the heroic adventures of Elisha Kent Kane / Ken McGoogan. Counterpoint, 2008. 320 p. **B**

ISBN 9781582434407

1. Kane, Elisha Kent, 1820-1857. 2. North Pole expeditions. 3. Explorers -- United States 4. Polar expeditions. 5. Survival (after airplane accidents, shipwrecks, etc.) -- Arctic regions. 6. Arctic regions -- Exploration. 7. North Pole. 8. Biographies

LC 2008012045

"With his access to previously unknown Kane logbooks, McGoogan makes an impressive case for the bravery and importance of the explorer who first identified the Greenland ice sheet." Publishers Weekly.

Kang, Mia

Kang, Mia **Knockout** : a memoir / Mia Kang. Abrams Press, 2020 281 p. : **B**

ISBN 9781419743320

1. Fashion models 2. Women martial artists 3. Television personalities 4. Multiracial women 5. Autobiographies and memoirs

LC 2020932370

Mia Kang is many things: a sought-after model, an immigrant, an eating disorder survivor, and a Muay Thai fighter. Knockout is the story of how she eschewed normative body standards and learned to use martial arts to redefine her sense of self-worth. After dealing with bullying, addiction, body dysmorphia, anxiety, depression, and even suicidal thoughts, Mia acknowledges that she is lucky to still be alive to tell readers what she's learned: to not let anyone else dictate who you are supposed to be.

"Knockout is a must-read memoir for the #MeToo era about a resilient young woman who kayos the myth of perfectionism." Booklist

Karadzic, Radovan V., 1945-

Stern, Jessica, 1958- **My** war criminal : personal encounters with an architect of genocide / Jessica Stern. Ecco, 2020. 352 p. **B**

ISBN 9780060889555

1. Stern, Jessica, 1958- 2. War criminals 3. Genocide -- Bosnia and Hercegovina 4. White supremacists 5. War 6. Bosnia and Hercegovina -- History -- 1991- 7. Biographies

LC bl2019037365

An investigation into the nature of violence, terror, and trauma through conversations with a notorious war criminal and hero to white nationalists.

Karajan, Herbert von

Osborne, Richard, 1943- **Herbert** von Karajan : a life in music / Richard Osborne. Northeastern University Press, 2000. x, 851 p. : **B**

ISBN 1555534252

1. Karajan, Herbert von. 2. Conductors (Music) 3. Biographies

LC 99059108

Originally published: London : Chatto & Windus, 1998.".Because Karajan's career developed in Nazi Germany, Osborne dwells at length . on Karajan's involvement with the regime and his postwar exoneration. Drawing on a vast variety of source materials and quoting some in full, Osborne takes us on the enthralling musical journey that was the life of one of the greatest of conductors." Booklist.

Karem, Abraham, 1937-

Whittle, Richard **Predator** : the secret origins of the drone revolution / Richard Whittle. Henry Holt and Co., 2014. 368 p. **B**

ISBN 9780805099645

1. Drone aircraft. 2. Remotely piloted vehicles. 3. Uninhabited combat aerial vehicles. 4. Military aircraft. 5. Biographies

LC 2014014070

The creation of the first weapon in history that can stalk and kill an enemy on the other side of the globe was far more than clever engineering. As Richard Whittle shows in Predator, it was the most profound development in military and aerospace technology since the intercontinental ballistic missile. Once considered fragile toys, drones were long thought to be of limited utility. The Predator itself was resisted at nearly every turn by the military establishment, but a few iconoclasts refused to see this new technology smothered at birth. The remarkable cast of characters responsible for developing the Predator includes a former Israeli inventor who turned his Los Angeles garage into a drone laboratory, two billionaire brothers marketing a futuristic weapon that would combat Communism, a pair of fighter pilots willing to buck their white-scarf fraternity, a cunning Pentagon operator nicknamed "Snake," and a secretive Air Force organization known as Big Safari. When an Air Force team unleashed the first lethal drone strikes in 2001 for the CIA, the military's view of drones changed nearly overnight. Based on five years of research and hundreds of interviews, Predator is a groundbreaking, dramatic account of the creation of a revolutionary weapon that forever changed the way we wage war.

"Military and aviation aficionados will learn from and enjoy this in-depth work that employs a readable, journalistic style." Library Journal.

Karr, Mary

Karr, Mary **Lit** : a memoir / Mary Karr. Harper, 2009. 400 p. **B**

ISBN 9780060596989

1. Karr, Mary Mental health. 2. Karr, Mary Childhood and youth. 3. Karr, Mary Family. 4. Recovering alcoholics -- United States 5. Mental illness -- United States -- Case studies. 6. Alcoholism -- United States -- Case studies. 7. Poets, American -- 20th century 8. Autobiographies and memoirs

LC 2009024810

National Book Critics Circle Award for Autobiography/ Memoir finalist

The author reveals how, shortly after giving birth to a child she adored, she drank herself into the same numbness that nearly devoured her charismatic but troubled mother, reaching the brink of suicide before a spiritual awakening led her to sobriety.

Karski, Jan, 1914-2000

★Karski, Jan, 1914-2000 **Story** of a secret state : my report to the world / Jan Karski ; foreword by Madeleine Albright.

Georgetown University Press, c2013. xxxi, 414 p. **B**

ISBN 9781589019836

1. World War II, Polish. 2. Prisoners of war, Polish 3. Concentration camps 4. Poland -- History -- Occupation, 1939-1945. 5. Autobiographies and memoirs

LC 2012037549

Originally published: 1944."

Briskly paced, this is a gripping and immediate account of Nazi brutality from a brave leader of the resistance. Karski, who died in 2000, was awarded a posthumous Presidential Medal of Freedom in 2012." Publishers Weekly.

Kasinof, Laura

Kasinof, Laura **Don't** be afraid of the bullets : an accidental war correspondent in Yemen / Laura Kasinof. Arcade Publishing, 2014. 304 p. **B**

ISBN 9781628724455

1. Kasinof, Laura. 2. Protest movements -- Yemen (Republic) -- History -- 21st century. 3. Americans in Yemen (Republic) 4. Foreign correspondents -- Yemen (Republic) 5. War correspondents -- Yemen (Republic) 6. Yemen (Republic) -- Politics and government -- 21st century. 7. Yemen (Republic) -- History -- 1990- 8. Sanaa (Yemen) -- Description and travel. 9. Sanaa (Yemen) -- Social conditions -- 21st century. 10. Autobiographies and memoirs

LC 2014019103

"Laura Kasinof studied Arabic in college and moved to Yemen a few years later--after a friend at a late-night party in Washington, DC, recommended the country as a good place to work as a freelance journalist. When she first moved to Sanaa in 2009, she was the only American reporter based in the country. She quickly fell in love with Yemen's people and culture, in addition to finding herself the star of a local TV soap opera. When antigovernment protests broke out in Yemen, part of the revolts sweeping the Arab world at the time, she contacted the New York Times to see if she could cover the rapidly unfolding events for the newspaper. Laura never planned to be a war correspondent, but found herself in the middle of brutal government attacks on peaceful protesters. As foreign reporters were rounded up and shipped out of the country, Laura managed to elude the authorities but found herself increasingly isolated--and even more determined to report on what she saw. Don't be Afraid of the Bullets is a fascinating and important debut by a talented young journalist".-- Provided by publisher.

Katkin, Elizabeth L.,

Katkin, Elizabeth L. **Conceivability** : what I learned exploring the frontiers of fertility / Elizabeth L. Katkin. Simon & Schuster, 2018. 320 p. **B**

ISBN 9781501142369

1. Katkin, Elizabeth L., Health. 2. Conception 3. Infertility -- Treatment 4. Polycystic ovary syndrome (PCOS) 5. In vitro fertilization 6. Autobiographies and memoirs

LC 2017053978

A deeply informative account traces the author's gripping journey through the global fertility industry in search of an answer to her own unexplained infertility, a quest that was shaped by key medical, financial, legal, scientific, emotional and ethical challenges.

Katz, Jon

Katz, Jon **Dog** days : dispatches from Bedlam Farm / Jon Katz. Villard, c2007. 273 p. Bedlam Farm **B**

ISBN 9781400064045

1. Dogs -- New York States -- Anecdotes. 2. Domestic animals -- New York States -- Anecdotes. 3. Human/animal relationships -- New York States -- Anecdotes. 4. Farm life -- New York States -- Anecdotes. 5. Bedlam Farm (West Hebron, N.Y.) Anecdotes. 6. New York (State)

LC 2006052804

Katz learns that living with four dogs on a rural New York farm is one thing. But what happens when you add a couple cows, four donkeys, a growing flock of sheep, a few hens, a temperamental rooster, and even Mother (a barn cat) to the mix?

"This is a collection of stories from upstate New York's Bedlam Farm. Bedlam Farm, a cross between a working and a hobby farm, is the home of the animals that are . [the author's] inspiration. A must-read for all animal lovers." Booklist.

Kaukonen, Jorma

Kaukonen, Jorma **Been** so long : my life and music / Jorma Kaukonen. St. Martin's Press, 2018. 320 p. **B**

ISBN 9781250125484

1. Kaukonen, Jorma. 2. Jefferson Airplane (Musical group) 3. Guitarists 4. Folk musicians 5. Rock musicians 6. Blues musicians 7. Autobiographies and memoirs

LC 2018010693

A memoir by a founding member and lead guitarist of Jefferson Airplane recounts his life and work, from his youth spent living abroad to finding his place in the music world and winning worldwide recognition.

"Entertaining and emotional, alternately exhilarating and depressing, this is a special musician's memoir, and it will strike a resounding chord with fans of classic rock." Booklist.

Keaton, Diane

★Keaton, Diane **Brother** & sister / Diane Keaton. Alfred A. Knopf, 2020. 192 p. **B**

ISBN 9780451494504

1. Keaton, Diane. 2. Film actors and actresses -- United States 3. Brothers and sisters 4. Alcoholics 5. Recluses 6. Autobiographies and memoirs

LC 2019024947

From the beloved film star --a heartfelt memoir about Diane Keaton's relationship with her younger brother, and a poignant exploration of the divergent paths siblings' lives can take.

"Immersive and haunting, this is a must for Keaton's fans and for those seeking to comprehend the nuances of sibling and family relationships." Library Journal

Keats, John, 1795-1821

Gigante, Denise, 1965- The **Keats** brothers : the life of John and George / Denise Gigante. Belknap Press of Harvard University Press, 2011. 550 p. **B**

ISBN 9780674048560

1. Keats, John, 1795-1821. 2. Keats, John, 1795-1821 Family. 3. Keats, George, 1797-1841. 4. Keats, George, 1797-1841 Homes and haunts United States. 5. Poets, English -- 19th century 6. Brothers -- England 7. British in the United States 8. Biographies

LC 2011014487

Motion, Andrew, 1952- **Keats** / Andrew Motion. University of Chicago Press, 1999, c1998. xix, 636 p. : **B**

ISBN 0226542408

1. Keats, John, 1795-1821. 2. Poets, English -- 19th century 3. Biographies

LC 98041014

Originally published: New York : Farrar, Straus and Giroux, 1998."

Motion emphasizes that Keats was no otherworldly creature of exquisite sensibilities but a man whose liberal politics and commitment to medicine animated his aesthetics and enlightened his poetry." Booklist.

Keeling, Ida, 1915-

Keeling, Ida, 1915- **Can't** nothing bring me down : chasing myself in the race against time / Ida Keeling with Anita Diggs. Zondervan, 2018 199 p. : **B**

ISBN 9780310349891

1. Runners. 2. Personal conduct. 3. Faith (Christianity). 4. Life change events. 5. Autobiographies and memoirs

LC 2017041065

The 101-year-old runner describes the obstacles she has faced in her life, from growing up the child of immigrants during the Depression to the murder of her sons, which inspired her to start running at sixty-seven.

Keenan, Jillian

Keenan, Jillian **Sex** with Shakespeare : here's much to do with pain, but more with love / Jillian Keenan. HarperCollins, 2016 352 p. **B**

ISBN 9780062378712

1. Keenan, Jillian. 2. Spanking 3. Fetishism (Sexuality) 4. Sexuality 5. Characters and characteristics in literature 6. Autobiographies and memoirs

LC 2016479925

Published to coincide with the 400th anniversary of Shakespeare's death, a thought-provoking, emotional and hilarious memoir follows the author as she charts her life--and her romances--through the plays of Shakespeare as she wanders the world in search of herself.

"A raunchy memoir revealing a visceral connection to the Bard." Kirkus.

Keflezighi, Meb

Keflezighi, Meb **26** marathons : what I learned about faith, identity, running, and life from my marathon career / Meb Keflezighi, Scott Douglas. Rodale Books, 2019. 256 p. **B**

ISBN 9781635652888

1. Keflezighi, Meb. 2. Determination (Personal quality) 3. Runners 4. Marathon runners 5. Olympic medal winners 6. Autobiographies and memoirs

LC 2018055140

A four-time Olympian marathoner, through a focused narrative, reflects on each of the 26 marathons he's run during his career and shares the lessons on life, family, faith and running he learned along the way.

"26 Marathons is a swift read, guaranteed to be popular with student athletes plus hard-core and recreational runners, who will undoubtedly agree that Meb is an American treasure and running ambassador who never fails to inspire." Booklist.

Keizer, Garret

Keizer, Garret **Getting** schooled : the reeducation of an American teacher / Garret Keizer. Metropolitan Books, 2014. 320 p. **B**

ISBN 9780805096439

1. Keizer, Garret. 2. High schools. 3. High school teachers. 4. Public schools.. 5. Education 6. Vermont 7. Autobiographies and memoirs

LC 2013042594

Perhaps no profession is so constantly discussed, regulated, and maligned by non-practitioners as teaching. The voices of the teachers themselves are conspicuously missing. Defying this trend, teacher and writer Garret Keizer takes us to school -- literally -- in this arresting account of his return to the same rural Vermont high school where he taught fourteen years ago. Much has changed since then -- a former student is his principal, standardized testing is the reigning god, and smoking in the boys' room has been supplanted by texting in the boys' room. More familiar are the effects of poverty, the exuberance of youth, and the staggering workload that technology has done as much to increase as to lighten. Telling the story of Keizer's year in the classroom, Getting Schooled takes us everywhere a teacher might go: from field trips to school plays to town meetings, from a kid's eureka moment to a parent's dark night of the soul. At once fiercely critical and deeply contemplative, Keizer exposes the obstacles that teachers face daily -- and along the way takes aim at some cherished cant: that public education is doomed, that the heroic teacher is the cure for all that ails education, that educational reform can serve as a cheap substitute for societal reformation. Angry, humorous, and always hopeful, Getting Schooled is as good an argument as we are likely to hear for a substantive reassessment of our schools and those who struggle in them.

"[A]t once a sympathetic portrait of a school, a searing indictment of a culture that uses working-class children as cannon fodder, and, unexpectedly, a page-turner." Publishers Weekly.

Keller, Helen, 1880-1968

Herrmann, Dorothy **Helen** Keller : a life / Dorothy Herrmann. A. A. Knopf, 1998. xvi, 394 p. : **B**

ISBN 9780679443544

1. Keller, Helen, 1880-1968. 2. Women who are blind and deaf 3. Biographies

LC 98014556

A full-scale biography draws on the massive archives of Helen Keller's estate and the unpublished memoirs of Keller's teacher, Annie Sullivan, to trace Keller's transformation from a furious girl to a world-renowned figure.

"The author takes us beyond the image of Helen Keller portrayed in The Miracle Worker to unearth a passionate, politically radical woman whose inspiration and teacher, Annie Sullivan, is equally fiery and brilliant. Herrmann brings us into the every day lives of the famous pair, but the story is hardly mundane. . . . Herrmann gives us fascinating details via archives and unpublished memoirs to show how society's view of disabled people was greatly shaped by Keller and Sullivan." Library Journal.

Keller, Helen, 1880-1968 **Helen** Keller : selected writings / edited by Kim E. Nielsen ; consulting editor, Harvey J. Kaye. New York : University Press, c2005. xv, 317 p. : **B**

ISBN 0814758290

1. Keller, Helen, 1880-1968. 2. Deafblind women -- United States. 3. Autobiographies and memoirs.

LC 2004028974

"Published in conjunction with the American Foundation for the Blind."

An intimate portrait of Helen Keller through her life's writing, some published here for the first time.

"Arranged chronologically, the writings are grouped around Keller's primary interests and concerns at various periods of her life. Nielsen pays the most attention to the third (1924-45) and fourth (1945-60) periods, when Keller focused on advocacy for the disabled around the world." Library Journal.

★Keller, Helen, 1880-1968 The **story** of my life / Helen Keller. Modern Library, 2003. xlvi, 343 p. : **B**

ISBN 0679642870

1. Keller, Helen, 1880-1968. 2. Sullivan, Annie, 1866-1936. 3. Women who are blind and deaf 4. Women who are blind 5. Women

who are deaf 6. Women with disabilities 7. Autobiographies and memoirs

LC 2002040971

"With her letters (1887-1901) and a supplementary account of her education, including passages from the reports and letters of her teacher, Anne Mansfield Sullivan, by John Albert Macy."A serious illness destroyed Helen Keller's sight and hearing at the age of two. At seven, she was helped by Anne Sullivan, her beloved teacher and friend. Through sheer determination and resolve, she learned to speak and prepared herself for entry into prep school by age sixteen. Later she enrolled at Radcliffe and graduated with honors. Her motto: "There are no handicaps, only challenges."

Kelly, Megyn

Kelly, Megyn **Settle** for more / Megyn Kelly. HarperCollins 2016. 304 p. **B**

ISBN 9780062494603

1. Trump, Donald, 1946- Views on women 2. Political journalism 3. Sexism 4. Television journalists 5. Political journalists 6. Autobiographies and memoirs

LC 2017295287

The top-rated cable news anchor presents a revelatory memoir that also imparts the values and lessons that have shaped her career, describing her tough-love family, her father's early death, the news events that led to her anchor position and her ongoing feud with Donald Trump.

Kelly, Scott, 1964-

Kelly, Scott, 1964- **Endurance** : a year in space, a lifetime of discovery / Scott Kelly with Margaret Lazarus Dean. Alfred A. Knopf, 2017. 400 p.. **B**

ISBN 9781524731595

1. International Space Station. 2. Astronauts. 3. Space flight 4. Autobiographies and memoirs

LC 2017024799

A memoir by the astronaut who spent a record-breaking year aboard the International Space Station shares candid reminiscences of his voyage, his colorful formative years, and the off-planet journeys that shaped his early career.

"It's fascinating stuff, a tale of aches and pains, of boredom punctuated by terror and worries about what's happening in the dark and back down on Earth." Kirkus.

Kemper, Ellie

Kemper, Ellie **My** squirrel days / Ellie Kemper. Scribner, 2018. 288 p. **B**

ISBN 9781501163340

1. Actors and actresses 2. Celebrities 3. Fame 4. Growing up 5. Autobiographies and memoirs

LC 2018038665

The comedian and star of The Office and Unbreakable Kimmy Schmidt delivers a hilarious and uplifting collection of essays about one pale woman's journey from Midwestern na?f to Hollywood semi-celebrity to outrageously reasonable New Yorker.

Kendi, Ibram X.

★Kendi, Ibram X. **How** to be an antiracist / Ibram X. Kendi. One World, 2019. viii, 305 p. ; **B**

ISBN 9780525509288

1. Identity (Psychology) 2. Ethnic identity 3. Antiracism 4. Racism -- United States -- History. 5. United States -- Race relations. 6. Autobiographies and memoirs

From the National Book Award-winning author comes a bracingly original approach to understanding and uprooting racism and inequality in our society--and in ourselves. Ibram X. Kendi's concept of antiracism reenergizes and reshapes the conversation about racial justice in America--but even more fundamentally, points us toward liberating new ways of thinking about ourselves and each other.

"His prose is thoughtful, sincere, and polished. This powerful book will spark many conversations." Publishers Weekly.

Kennan, George F. (George Frost), 1904-2005

Gaddis, John Lewis **George** F. Kennan : an American life / John Lewis Gaddis. Penguin Press, 2011. 800 p. **B**

ISBN 9781594203121

1. Kennan, George F. (George Frost), 1904-2005. 2. Cold War. 3. Diplomats -- United States 4. Ambassadors -- United States 5. World politics -- 1945-1989. 6. United States -- Foreign relations -- 1945-1989. 7. United States -- Foreign relations Soviet Union. 8. Soviet Union -- Foreign relations United States. 9. Biographies

LC 2011021786

American History Book Prize, 2011.

National Book Critics Circle Award for Biography, 2011.

Pulitzer Prize for Biography or Autobiography, 2012.

Drawing on extensive interviews with George Kennan and exclusive access to his archives, an eminent scholar of the Cold War delivers a revelatory biography of its troubled mastermind.

Kennedy family

Taraborrelli, J. Randy **After** Camelot : an intimate history of the Kennedy family, 1968 to the present / J. Randy Taraborrelli. Grand Central Pub., c2012. 624 p. **B**

ISBN 9780446553902

1. Kennedy family. 2. Rich people. 3. Family relationships. 4. Biographies

LC 2011029518

In this groundbreaking biography of the Kennedys, Taraborrelli brings this complex and dynamic family to life as he recounts the years following the murders of Jack and Bobby. He describes the challenges Bobby's children faced as they grew into adulthood; Eunice and Sargent Shriver's remarkable philanthropic work; the emotional turmoil Jackie faced after JFK's assassination and the complexities of her eventual marriage to Aristotle Onassis; the sudden death of JFK Jr. and the stoicism and grace of his sister, Caroline. He also brings into clear focus the complex and intriguing story of Ted Kennedy and shows how he influenced the sensibilities of the next generation and challenged them to uphold the Kennedy name.

Kennedy, Edward M. (Edward Moore), 1932-2009

Canellos, Peter S., **Last** lion : the fall and rise of Ted Kennedy / the team of the Boston Globe, Bella English ... [et al.] ; edited by Peter S. Canellos. Simon & Schuster, 2009. 480 p. **B**

ISBN 9781439138175

1. United States. Congress. Senate 2. Democratic Party. 3. Legislators -- United States 4. Politicians -- United States 5. Democrats. 6. Liberalism. 7. United States -- Politics and government. 8. Biographies

LC 2008050491

Dismissed as a spent force in politics by the time he reached middle age, Ted Kennedy became the most powerful senator of the last half century and the nation's keeper of traditional liberalism. Perceptive and carefully reported, drawing heavily from candid interviews with the Kennedy family and inner circle, "Last Lion" captures magnificently his life and historic achievements, as well as the personal redemption that he found.

"A respectful but not stuffy . [biography] of Edward Kennedy, the playboy of legendary appetites turned senior statesman. A balanced, nuanced, warts-and-all portrait." Kirkus.

★Gabler, Neal **Catching** the wind : Edward Kennedy and the liberal hour, 1932-1975 / Neal Gabler. Crown, 2020. 928 p. **B**

ISBN 9780307405449

1. Kennedy, Edward M. (Edward Moore), 1932-2009. 2. Kennedy family. 3. United States. Congress. Senate 4. Legislators -- United States 5. Liberals 6. Politicians 7. Liberalism 8. United States -- Politics and government -- 1945-1989. 9. United States -- Politics and government -- 1989- 10. Biographies

LC 2020019328

The epic, definitive biography of Ted Kennedy--an immersive journey through the life of a complicated man and a sweeping history of the fall of liberalism and the collapse of political morality. Edward M. Kennedy was never expected to succeed. The youngest of nine, he lacked his brothers' natural gifts and easy grace. Yet after winning election to the Senate at the tender age of thirty, he became the most consequential legislator of his lifetime, perhaps even American history. A landmark study of legislative genius and a powerful exploration of the man who spent his career upholding his mandate in service of a better America.

"The result of staggering research and expert analysis, Gabler's discerning evaluation of the totality of influences upon one of the twentieth century's most persuasive and popular statesmen is a triumphant achievement and essential reading for everyone fascinated by the Kennedys, politics, and governance." Booklist

Kennedy, Edward M., (Edward Moore), 1932-2009 **True** compass : a memoir / Edward M. Kennedy. Twelve, 2009. x, 532 p., [40] p. of plates : **B**

ISBN 9780446539258

1. Kennedy family 2. United States. Congress. Senate 3. Politicians -- United States 4. Determination (Personal quality) 5. Political leadership 6. Politicians' families. 7. United States -- Politics and government -- 20th century 8. United States -- Politics and government -- 21st century 9. Autobiographies and memoirs

LC 2009931859

In this landmark autobiography, five years in the making, Senator Edward M. Kennedy tells his extraordinary personal story--of his legendary family, politics, and fifty years at the center of national events.

"Mr. Kennedy's conversational gifts as a storyteller and his sense of humor . shine through here, as does his old-school sense of public service and his hard-won knowledge, in his son Teddy Jr.'s words, that even our most profound losses are survivable." New York Times.

Kennedy, John F. (John Fitzgerald), 1917-1963

Brinkley, Alan, 1949-2019 **John** F. Kennedy : the 35th President, 1961-1963 / Alan Brinkley. Times Books : 2012. 224 p. American Presidents series (Times Books) **B**

ISBN 9780805083491

1. Kennedy, John F. (John Fitzgerald), 1917-1963. 2. Presidents -- United States 3. Politicians. 4. Democrats. 5. United States -- Politics and government -- 1961-1963. 6. Biographies

LC 2011043747

Analyzes the contrast between Kennedy's achievements and his legend, tracing the successes and failures of such events as the Bay of Pigs and the Cuban Missile Crisis while exploring the ways in which he reshaped views of the presidency.

Clarke, Thurston **JFK's** last hundred days : the transformation of a man and the emergence of a great president / Thurston Clarke. The Penguin Press, 2013. 384 p. **B**

ISBN 9781594204258

1. Kennedy, John F. (John Fitzgerald), 1917-1963. 2. Presidents -- United States 3. Political leadership -- United States -- Case studies. 4. Change (Psychology) -- Case studies. 5. United States -- Politics and government -- 1961-1963.

LC 2012047456

Clarke reexamines the last months of the President's life to show a man in the midst of great change, finally on the cusp of making good on his extraordinary promise.

Cohen, Andrew, 1955- **Two** Days in June : John F. Kennedy and the 48 Hours that made history / Andrew Cohen. McClelland & Stewart, 2014 404 p. **B**

ISBN 9780771023873

1. Kennedy, John F. (John Fitzgerald), 1917-1963 Oratory 2. Presidents -- United States 3. Political oratory 4. United States -- Politics and government -- 1961-1963. 5. Biographies

LC bl2014049755

"This book is a page-turner. Undoubtedly, Kennedy supporters will love it. More important, it serves as a first-rate introduction to why the president made such a significant impression on the nation and the world despite his brief tenure." Library Journal.

Dallek, Robert **Let** every nation know : John F. Kennedy in his own words / Robert Dallek and Terry Golway. Sourcebooks MediaFusion, 2006. xii, 289 p. : **B**

ISBN 140220647X

1. Kennedy, John F. (John Fitzgerald), 1917-1963. 2. Presidents -- United States 3. Presidents -- United States -- Messages. 4. United States -- Politics and government -- 1961-1963. 5. Speeches, addresses, etc. 6. Biographies

LC 2005037973

A collection of thirty-four of John F. Kennedy's speeches, debates, and interviews offers insight into the ideals, politics, and life of the charismatic president.

"The voice of John F. Kennedy is burned into the brains of people of a certain age. But younger citizens may not be familiar with his ideas and the distinctive way in which he expressed himself. There have been past recordings of JFK's presidential speeches, but this unique package pairs a CD of the speeches with a collection of essays on them by historians Golway and Dallek (the latter wrote his own JFK book, An Unfinished Life, 2003). The result is nothing short of terrific..." Booklist.

Dallek, Robert An **unfinished** life : John F. Kennedy, 1917-1963 / Robert Dallek. Little, Brown, and Co., 2003. x, 838 p., 32 p. of plates : **B**

ISBN 0316172383

1. Presidents -- United States 2. Politicians -- United States 3. Campaigning. 4. United States -- Politics and government -- 1961-1963 5. Biographies

LC 2002116388

Drawing upon previously unavailable material and never-before-opened archives to tell Kennedy's story, we learn for the first time just how sick Kennedy was, what medications he took and concealed from all but a few, and how his medical condition affected his actions as President. We learn for the first time the real story of how Bobby was selected as Attorney General. Dallek reveals what Jack's father did to help his son's election to the presidency, and he follows previously unknown evidence to show what path JFK would have taken in the Vietnam entanglement had he survived.

"The author has written the most accessible, balanced, and scholarly biography yet of JFK. It is the Kennedy biography against which others will be measured." Library Journal.

★Logevall, Fredrik, 1963- **JFK** : coming of age in the American century, 1917-1956 / Fredrik Logevall. Random House, 2020. 816 p. **B**

ISBN 9780812997132

1. Kennedy, John F. (John Fitzgerald), 1917-1963. 2. Kennedy, John F. (John Fitzgerald), 1917-1963 Family. 3. Kennedy family. 4. United States. Congress. Senate 5. Legislators -- Massachusetts 6. Presidents -- United States 7. United States -- Politics and government -- 1945-1989. 8. Massachusetts 9. Biographies

LC 2020003488

Beginning with the three generations of Kennedy men and women who transformed the clan from working-class Irish immigrants to members of Boston's political elite, Volume One spans the first thirty-nine years of JFK's life, from sickly second son to restless Harvard undergraduate and World War II hero, through his ascendance on Capitol Hill and, finally, his decision to run for president.

"This richly detailed portrait sometimes feels romanticized in its evocations of Kennedy's charisma, but Logevall helpfully reminds readers of the considerable substance beneath the glamour. Political history buffs will be enthralled." Publishers Weekly

Morrow, Lance The **best** year of their lives : Kennedy, Johnson, and Nixon in 1948, learning the secrets of power / Lance Morrow. Basic Books, c2005. xl, 312 p. ; **B**

ISBN 0465047238

1. Kennedy, John F. (John Fitzgerald), 1917-1963. 2. Johnson, Lyndon B., 1908-1973 3. Nixon, Richard M. (Richard Milhous), 1913-1994. 4. Legislators -- United States 5. Presidents -- United States 6. United States -- Politics and government -- 1945-1953. 7. United States -- Foreign relations -- 1945-1953.

LC 2005001836

Provides a fresh look at the most pivotal points in the lives of John Kennedy, Lyndon Johnson, and Richard Nixon when they were all ambitious young congressmen in 1948, uncovering a streak of amorality, ruthlessness, and deceit that marked each politician's early career.

"The book succeeds in drawing together three fascinating characters into an illuminating historical intersection. You don't have to agree with all of Morrow's interpretations to be entertained by his lively treatment of three crucial figures during an important time in American history." New York Times Book Review.

Kennedy, John F. Jr., 1960-1999

Andersen, Christopher P. The **good** son : JFK Jr. and the mother he loved / Christopher Andersen. Simon & Schuster, 2014 320 p. **B**

ISBN 9781476775562

1. Kennedy, John F. Jr., 1960-1999. 2. Kennedy family 3. Onassis, Jacqueline Kennedy, 1929-1994. 4. Children of presidents -- United States 5. Mothers and sons 6. Interpersonal relations 7. Biographies

LC 2014024249

At the heart of The Good Son is the most important relationship in JFK Jr.'s life: that with his mother, the beautiful and mysterious Jackie Kennedy Onassis. Andersen explores his reactions to his mother's post-Dallas suicidal depression and growing dependence on prescription drugs (as well as men); how Jackie felt about the women in her son's life, from Madonna and Sarah Jessica Parker, to Daryl Hannah and Carolyn Bessette, to his turbulent marriage; the senseless plane crash the took his life; the aftermath of shock, loss, grief, and confusion; and much more. Offering new insights into the intense, tender, often stormy relationship between this iconic mother and son, The Good Son is a riveting, bittersweet biography for lovers of all things Kennedy.

"Sensitive and astute, Andersen's book offers an intriguing look at a fraught mother-son dynamic that, years after the deaths of both Jackie and John Jr., still has the power to mesmerize. An intimate and compelling look at 'the most brilliant star in the Kennedy firmament.' " Kirkus.

Gillon, Steven M **America's** reluctant prince : the life of John F. Kennedy Jr. / Steven M. Gillon. Dutton, an imprint of Penguin Random House LLC, [2019] 464 p. **B**

ISBN 9781524742386

1. Kennedy, John F., Jr., 1960-1999. 2. Children of presidents -- United States 3. Periodical publishers and publishing 4. Celebrities -- United States 5. Biographies

LC 2019014938

"Through the lens of their decades-long friendship and including exclusive interviews and details from previously classified documents, noted historian and New York Times bestselling author Steven M. Gillon examines John F. Kennedy Jr.'s life and legacy from before his birth to the day he died. Gillon covers the highs, the lows, and the surprising incidents, viewpoints, and relationships that John never discussed publicly, revealing the full story behind JFK Jr.'s complicated and rich life. In the end, Gillon proves that John's life was far more than another tragedy--rather, it's the true key to understanding both the Kennedy legacy and how America's First Family continues to shape the world we live in today." --Provided by publisher.

Kennedy, Joseph P. (Joseph Patrick), 1888-1969

★Nasaw, David The **patriarch** : the remarkable life and turbulent times of Joseph P. Kennedy / David Nasaw. Penguin Press, 2012. 832 p. **B**

ISBN 9781594203763

1. Kennedy, Joseph P. (Joseph Patrick), 1888-1969. 2. Kennedy family. 3. Ambassadors -- United States 4. Politicians -- United States 5. Businesspeople -- United States 6. Biographies

LC 2012027315

Pulitzer Prize for Biography or Autobiography finalist, 2013.

Draws on exclusive access to the subject's records to offer insight into his shrewd financial talents and considerable ambition for his family, discussing the controversies surrounding his character and his role in several mainstream political events.

Kennedy, Kathleen, 1920-1948

Byrne, Paula **Kick** : the true story of Kick Kennedy, JFK's forgotten sister and the heir to Chatsworth / Paula Byrne. Harper, 2016. 352 p. **B**

ISBN 9780062296276

1. Kennedy, Kathleen, 1920-1948. 2. Kennedy family. 3. Socialites 4. Americans in England 5. Aristocracy -- Great Britain 6. Young women 7. Great Britain -- Social life and customs -- 20th century. 8. United States -- Social life and customs -- 20th century. 9. Biographies

LC 2016008270

"Filled with a wealth of revealing new material and insight, the biography of the vivacious, unconventional--and nearly forgotten--young Kennedy sister who charmed American society and the English aristocracy and would break with her family for love."--Provided by publisher.

"At first, the book is less a biography and more a society report of England's upper class, but it evolves into an exciting, heartbreakingly tense love story." Kirkus.

Leaming, Barbara **Kick** Kennedy : the charmed life and tragic death of the favorite Kennedy daughter / Barbara Leaming. Thomas Dunne Books, 2016 368 p. **B**

ISBN 9781250071316

1. Kennedy, Kathleen, 1920-1948. 2. Kennedy family. 3. Socialites -- United States 4. Aristocracy -- Great Britain 5. Americans in London, England 6. Young women 7. Great Britain -- Social life and customs -- 20th century. 8. Biographies

LC 2016007364

Kathleen "Kick" Kennedy was the incandescent life-force of the fabled Kennedy family, her father's acknowledged "favorite of all the children" and her brother Jack's "psychological twin." She was the Kennedy of Kennedys, sure of her privilege, magnetically charming and somehow not quite like anyone else on whatever stage she happened to grace.

"Leaming candidly demystifies the life of one of the least-known Kennedys and vividly illuminates the complex world of British aristocracy." Booklist.

Kennedy, Robert Francis, 1925-1968

Clarke, Thurston The **last** campaign : Robert F. Kennedy and 82 days that inspired America / Thurston Clarke. Henry Holt, 2008. 272 p. **B**

ISBN 0805077928

1. Presidential election, 1968 2. United States -- Politics and government -- 1963-1969.

LC 2007045880

Includes index.

Documents Robert Kennedy's dramatic and ill-fated 1968 presidential campaign, outlining his positions on such issues as the Vietnam War, race, and poverty as well as his private struggles with the assassination of JFK.

"In this account of Robert F. Kennedy's run for president, Clarke follows on Bobby's heels as he plunged headlong into his campaign, from Kansas and Indiana to Oregon and California, throwing off his brother's mantle and becoming at last his own man. He spoke passionately, almost recklessly, inciting crowds to frenzy with his idealistic speeches about the moral shame of Vietnam, the needs of the poor and minorities and the responsibility of each American. Incorporating accounts by a gamut of reporters, politicians, family and Honorary Kennedys, as well as extracts from Bobby's own stunning stump speeches, Clarke compellingly recreates this huge, joyous adenture." Kirkus.

Matthews, Christopher, 1945- **Bobby** Kennedy : a raging spirit / Chris Matthews. Simon & Schuster, 2017. 352 p. **B**

ISBN 9781501111860

1. United States. Congress. Senate. 2. Legislators. 3. Cabinet officers. 4. Politicians 5. United States -- Politics and government -- 1945-1989. 6. Biographies

LC bl2017036574

A portrait of Robert F. Kennedy depicts him as a perpetual family underdog, sharing insights into his decision to join the Navy as a common sailor, his ability to connect with voters from all walks of life, and his assassination during his 1968 campaign.

"A child of that era himself, best-selling Matthews, host of MSNBCs Hardball, regards RFKs legacy through personal recollections and cogently illustrates leadership qualities Kennedy possessed that are sorely lacking in todays divisive culture." Booklist.

Schlesinger, Arthur M. (Arthur Meier), 1917-2007 **Robert** Kennedy and his times / Arthur M. Schlesinger, Jr. Houghton Mifflin, 2002, c1978. xx, 1066 p. ; **B**

ISBN 0618219285

1. Kennedy, Robert Francis, 1925-1968. 2. United States. Congress. Senate 3. Legislators -- United States 4. Politicians -- United States 5. United States -- Politics and government -- 1945-1989. 6. Biographies

LC 2003275770

"A Mariner book."

Originally published: Boston : Houghton Mifflin, 1978. Without ill."

A highly sympathetic and readable political biography covering in depth Robert Kennedy's tenure in public life. At times extremely partisan, at times dispassionate, Schlesinger's study effectively captures Kennedy's impact on national politics and the main currents of American politics during the 1950s and 1960s." Choice.

★Thomas, Evan, 1951- **Robert** Kennedy : his life / Evan Thomas. Simon & Schuster, 2000. 509 p., 16 p. of plates : **B**

ISBN 0684834804

1. Kennedy, Robert Francis, 1925-1968. 2. United States. Congress. Senate 3. Politicians -- United States 4. Legislators -- United States 5. Family relationships. 6. Biographies

LC 00041995

Provides a detailed portrait of a man who was at once kind and cruel, devious and honest, fearful and brave, and one who was centrally engaged in most of the important issues of the postwar era, illuminates his failings as well as his strengths, and places Robert in the complex knot of relationships characteristic of the Kennedy family.

"A solid, judicious life of a politician whose tragic death inspired a generation of what-if history." Booklist.

★Tye, Larry **Bobby** Kennedy : the making of a liberal icon / Larry Tye. Random House, 2016. 608 p. **B**

ISBN 9780812993349

1. Kennedy, Robert Francis, 1925-1968. 2. United States. Congress. Senate 3. Politicians -- United States 4. Legislators -- United States 5. Family relationships. 6. Biographies

LC 2016004991

Draws on unpublished memoirs, unreleased government files, private papers, and interviews with Kennedy's close family and colleagues to chronicle his transformation from 1950s cold warrior to a liberal champion of the working class, the poor, and minorities.

"The author chides RFK for such things as slanting his account of the Bay of Pigs, his perhaps excessive pursuit of Jimmy Hoffa, and his early hawkishness on Vietnam. But the contrary image is clear: a good, if not great man; an unspeakable loss." Kirkus.

Kennedy, Rosemary, 1918-2005

Larson, Kate Clifford **Rosemary** : the hidden Kennedy daughter / Kate Clifford Larson. Houghton Mifflin Harcourt, 2015. 288 p. ; **B**

ISBN 9780547250250

1. Kennedy family. 2. People with developmental disabilities 3. Institutionalized persons 4. Psychosurgery. 5. Frontal lobotomy. 6. Biographies

LC 2015028793

Based on information contained in Rose Kennedy's diaries and correspondence, as well as exclusive family interviews, the author describes the plight of a woman forgotten to history, who was intellectually disabled and kept hidden by the family after she received a lobotomy at age 23.

Kennicott, Philip

Kennicott, Philip **Counterpoint** : a memoir of Bach and mourning / Philip Kennicott. W. W. Norton & Company, 2020. 224 p. **B**

ISBN 9780393635362

1. Bach, Johann Sebastian, 1685-1750 2. Kennicott, Philip. 3. Classical music 4. Bereavement 5. Pianists 6. Music theory 7. Autobiographies and memoirs

LC 2019027075

The Pulitzer Prize-winning Washington Post critic and pianist describes how he navigated loss and a complicated childhood through the masterpieces of Bach, sharing insights into how Bach's genius compositions combine unique counterpoints to evoke transcendent emotion.

Kerkeling, Hape

Kerkeling, Hape **I'm** off then : my journey along the Camino de Santiago / Hape Kerkeling ; translated from the German by Shelley Frisch. Free Press, 2009, c2006. 352 p. **B**

ISBN 9781416553878

1. Kerkeling, Hape Travel Spain. 2. Germans in Spain 3. Spiritual journals 4. Spiritual journeys. 5. Voyages and travels. 6. Northern Spain -- Description and travel 7. Northern Spain -- History, Local. 8. Santiago de Compostela, Spain -- Description and travel. 9. Autobiographies and memoirs

LC 2008051464

Originally published: Munchen : Malik, c2006, with German title Ich bin dann mal weg : meine Reise auf dem Jakobsweg.

An account by a popular German comedian and writer describes his unlikely candidacy for the physically arduous spiritual pilgrimage across the French Alps to the Spanish Shrine of St. James, the loneliness that prompted his quest for meaning, and the deep sense of peace and positive transformation he experienced during his journey.

"Hape Kerkeling, a popular TV talk-show host and cabaret star in his native Germany, cuts loose from the comforts of Düsseldorf and sets off on a hike across the Pyrenees to the grave of St. James at the Cathedral of Santiago de Compostela. Searching for spiritual meaning, this self-described couch potato follows a 1,000-year-old pilgrimage route that lures 100,000 trekkers each year, experiencing almost insufferable heat and physical agony in the process. He skips some of the hardest stretches to hitch rides with local farmers or hop aboard trains, and he avoids fetid pilgrims' hostels whenever possible in favor of the best hotel in town (often not much better). Despite such tactics, this gregarious traveler soon gets into the spirit of things, and his encounters with fellow pilgrims, including a Peruvian shaman with a creepy fondness for Mein Kampf, can be both funny and moving." New York Times Book Review.

Kerouac, Jack, 1922-1969

★Johnson, Joyce, 1935- The **voice** is all : the lonely victory of Jack Kerouac / Joyce Johnson. Viking, c2012. 512 p. **B**

ISBN 9780670025107

1. Kerouac, Jack, 1922-1969. 2. Authors, American -- 20th century 3. Beat culture 4. Beat authors. 5. Beat poets. 6. United States -- Social life and customs -- 20th century. 7. Biographies

LC 2012000603

The National Book Critics Circle Award-winning author of Minor Characters presents a profile of the iconic artist's early years that offers insight into his efforts to bridge his dual cultural heritage while exploring how his French Canadian background enriched his prose, discussing the breakthroughs that inspired such works as On the Road and Visions of Cody.

"Her book is essential reading for anyone interested in a deeper understanding of Kerouac's life and work." Library Journal

Kerry, John, 1943-

Kerry, John, 1943- **Every** day is extra / John Kerry. Simon & Schuster, [2018] 608 p. **B**

ISBN 9781501178955

1. Politicians -- United States 2. Cabinet officers -- United States 3. Presidential candidates 4. Legislators -- United States 5. United States -- Politics and government 6. Autobiographies and memoirs

LC 2018021806

Includes index.

John Kerry tells the story of his life: from son of a diplomat to decorated Vietnam veteran, five-term United States senator, 2004 Democratic presidential nominee and secretary of state for four years.

Kerstetter, Jon

Kerstetter, Jon **Crossings** : a doctor-soldier's story / Jon Kerstetter. Crown Publishing, 2017. 352 p. **B**

ISBN 9781101904374

1. Former physicians 2. Iraq War veterans 3. People who have had strokes 4. Iraq War, 2003-2011 5. Autobiographies and memoirs

LC 2017024442

A Native American doctor shares a poignant memoir on his experiences as a medic and officer in Kosovo, Bosnia and the Iraq War before suffering an injury and stroke on his third tour, which forced him to return home and make a difficult transition to becoming a doctor-patient at home.

"The author's medical perspective on his own condition and critical therapeutic moments adds depth to an already solid story. An inspiring memoir that will be highly useful to readers struggling with PTSD and other wartime injuries." Kirkus.

Kessler, Lauren

Kessler, Lauren **Raising** the barre : big dreams, false starts, and my midlife quest to dance the Nutcracker / Lauren Kessler. Da Capo Press A Member of the Perseus Books Group, 2015 256 p. **B**

ISBN 9780738218311

1. Kessler, Lauren. 2. Nutcracker (Ballet) -- Performance 3. Authors, American 4. Ballet dancers 5. Autobiographies and memoirs

LC 2015026258

An award-winning author's journey to turn off the comfortable cruise-control of midlife and reclaim the daring of her girlhood by dancing in the world's most popular ballet,The Nutcracker, with a professional company.

"An amusingly shrewd memoir of following a lifelong dream." Kirkus.

Keuning-Tichelaar, An, 1922-

Keuning-Tichelaar, An, 1922- **Passing** on the comfort : the war, the quilts, and the women who made a difference / An Keuning-Tichelaar and Lynn Kaplanian-Buller. Good Books, c2005. 186 p. : **B**

ISBN 1561484822

1. Kaplanian-Buller, Lynn. 2. World War II -- Netherlands. 3. World War II, Dutch. 4. Quilting -- United States -- History -- 20th century. 5. World War II -- War work -- United States. 6. Netherlands -- History -- German occupation, 1940-1945. 7. United States -- History -- 20th century

LC 2005001932

Two women--one American, one Dutch--are brought together by a set of worn quilts, made by groups of women half-a-world away, that reveal the diverse stories of women during World War II, including that of An, a young Dutch woman who risked her life repeatedly to care for war-time refugees.

"This is the narrative of a Dutch resistance operation during WWII conducted by Keuning-Tichelaar and her husband, Herman, a Mennonite minister. With the support of their townspeople, the two young newlyweds sheltered and saved the lives of Jewish adults and children, and others in danger from the Nazis. As part of a relief effort, quilts were created by women in North American Mennonite circles and sent to the Netherlands. Beautifully illustrated with 19 color photographs of the quilts, this book describes in an understated voice the harrowing events and the daily acts of courage that Keuning-Tichelaar undertook. When, decades later, coauthor Kaplanian-Buller, a U.S. citizen living in Amsterdam, found the old quilts, she persuaded An to share her story." Publishers Weekly.

Keynes, John Maynard, 1883-1946

Davenport-Hines, R. P. T. (Richard Peter Treadwell), 1953- **Universal** man : the lives of John Maynard Keynes / Richard Davenport-Hines. Basic Books, 2015 352 p. **B**

ISBN 9780465060672

1. Keynes, John Maynard, 1883-1946. 2. Economists -- Great Britain 3. Macroeconomics. 4. Keynesian economics. 5. Economics. 6. Great Britain -- History -- 20th century. 7. Biographies

LC 2015934354

Davenport-Hines revives our understanding of John Maynard Keynes, the twentieth century's most charismatic and revolutionary economist.

"Although this approach necessitates recovering some chronological groundobviously he was a pundit and lover most of his lifethe author is quite successful in avoiding redundancy. The result is that the intellectual, social, professional, and personal aspects of Keynes are described and analyzed both independently and as they interrelated to create a complex and brilliant thinker. This is a splendid biography that will fascinate the general reader and give new insight to the scholar. Summing Up: Highly recommended. Undergraduates through faculty; two-year technical students; general readers." Choice.

Khakpour, Porochista,

★Khakpour, Porochista **Sick** : a memoir / Porochista Khakpour. Harper Perennial, 2018 256 p. **B**

ISBN 9780062428738

1. Khakpour, Porochista, Health. 2. Lyme disease. 3. People with Lyme disease. 4. People with chronic illnesses. 5. Autobiographies and memoirs

LC 2017059572

The author shares her journey as a sufferer of undiagnosed health problems as she, finally diagnosed with late-stage Lyme disease, learns to accept the diagnosis she had searched for over the course of her adult life. .

"Lyme disease is difficult to diagnose, and Khakpours frank memoir will give hope to others who are struggling with this devastating illness." Booklist.

Khalaf, Farida

Khalaf, Farida The **girl** who escaped ISIS : this is my story / Farida Khalaf, Andrea C. Hoffmann. Atria Books, 2016. 224 p. **B**

ISBN 9781501131714

1. ISIS (Islamic State of Iraq and Syria) 2. Former captives 3. Captivity 4. Torture. 5. Autobiographies and memoirs

LC 2016022449

Presents a rare and riveting first-hand account of the terror and torture inflicted by ISIS on young Iraqi Yazidi women, and an inspiring personal story of bravery and resilience in the face of unspeakable horrors

Khan family

Seierstad, Asne, 1970- The **bookseller** of Kabul / Asne Seierstad ; translated from the Norwegian by Ingrid Christophersen. Back Bay Books/Little, Brown, 2004. xvi, 288 p. ; **B**

ISBN 9780316159418

1. Khan family. 2. Seierstad, Asne, 1970- Travel Kabul, Afghanistan. 3. Booksellers -- Kabul, Afghanistan 4. Kabul, Afghanistan -- Social life and customs. 5. Biographies

LC 2006274444

Capturing the harsh realities of life in modern-day Afghanistan and plight of Afghan women, the Norwegian journalist provides a portrait of a committed Muslim man, a bookseller, and his family living in post-Taliban Kabul, Afghanistan.

"The author entered Kabul with Northern Alliance soldiers after they ousted the Taliban. She took the rare opportunity to live with and write a book about the extended family of Sultan Khan, bookseller and entrepreneur. The result, organized around events in the lives of individual members of Khan's large clan . . . provides appropriate information about recent Afghani history, a glimpse from the inside at an Islamic family, and an understanding of the harshness and difficulty of the daily grind in Afghanistan--both under the Taliban and after the U.S. antiterrorist campaign." Booklist.

Khan, Khizr

Khan, Khizr An **American** family : a memoir of hope and sacrifice / Khizr Khan. Random House, 2017 288 p. **B**

ISBN 9780399592492

1. Pakistani Americans 2. Immigrants 3. American dream. 4. Personal conduct 5. Autobiographies and memoirs

LC 2017031372

The Pakistani immigrant-turned-U.S. citizen and Gold Star parent documents the story of his family's pursuit of the American dream, discussing the need to respond to challenges in modern society and advocate for what is most important.

"Khan's aspirational memoir reminds us all why Americans should welcome newcomers from all lands." Kirkus.

Khan, Noor Inayat, 1914-1944

Magida, Arthur J. **Code** name Madeleine : a Sufi spy in Nazi-occupied Paris / Arthur J. Magida. W.W. Norton & Company, [2020] 324 p. **B**

ISBN 9780393635188

1. Khan, Noor Inayat, 1914-1944. 2. French Resistance (World War II) 3. Women spies 4. Espionage 5. Radio operators 6. France -- History -- German occupation, 1940-1945 7. Biographies

LC 2019053511

The dramatic story of Noor Inayat Khan, secret agent for the British in occupied France. During the critical summer months of 1943, Noor Inayat Khan was the only wireless operator transmitting secret messages from Nazi-occupied France to the Special Operations Executive in England. She was a most unlikely spy. As the daughter of an Indian mystic, raised in a household devoted to peaceful reflection on the outskirts of Paris, Khan did not seem destined for wartime heroism. Yet, faced with the evils of Nazism, she could not look away. She volunteered to help the British; was trained in espionage, sabotage, and reconnaissance; and returned to France under cover of night with a new identity and a code name: Madeleine. Khan transmitted countless details crucial to the Allies' success on D-Day, until she was captured and imprisoned by the Gestapo. She attempted two daring escapes before being sent to prison in Germany. Three months after the Allied invasion of France, she was executed at Dachau. Her last word was "liberte."

"Magida delivers a gripping account of a tenacious young woman who demonstrated bravery in the face of extreme evil." Booklist

Khan-Cullors, Patrisse, 1984-

★Khan-Cullors, Patrisse, 1984- **When** they call you a terrorist : a Black Lives Matter memoir / Patrisse Khan-Cullors and Asha Bandele ; with a foreword by Angela Davis. St. Martin's Press, 2018. 280 p. **B**

ISBN 9781250171085

1. African American political activists 2. Civil rights 3. Social movements 4. African American women political activists 5. Autobiographies and memoirs

LC bl2017045690

A memoir by the co-founder of the Black Lives Matter movement explains the movement's position of love, humanity, and justice, challenging perspectives that have negatively labeled the movement's activists while calling for essential political changes.

"With great candor about her complex personal life, Khan-Cullors has created a memoir as compelling as a page-turning novel." Booklist.

Khar, Erin

Khar, Erin **Strung** out : one last hit and other lies that nearly killed me: a memoir / Erin Khar. Park Row Books, 2020. 304 p. **B**

ISBN 9780778309734

1. Drug addicts 2. Heroin addiction 3. Sobriety 4. Denial (Psychology) 5. United States 6. Autobiographies and memoirs

LC bl2020000168

The author shares her story of battling her addiction to heroin and how motherhood helped in her road to recovery. She also discusses the psychology of addiction and why people start taking opioids in the first place.

"This heartbreaking yet heartwarming memoir puts a human face on the drug crisis and the factors that lead to addiction." Publishers Weekly

Khrushchev, Nikita, 1894-1971

Taubman, William **Khrushchev** : the man and his era / William Taubman. Norton, 2003. xx, 876 p. : **B**

ISBN 0393051447

1. Khrushchev, Nikita, 1894-1971. 2. Stalin, Joseph, 1879-1953. 3. Cold War -- History. 4. Heads of state -- Soviet Union 5. Soviet Union -- Politics and government -- 1953-1985. 6. Soviet Union -- Foreign relations -- 1945-1991. 7. Biographies

LC 2002026404

Maps on lining papers.

ALA Notable Book, 2004.

National Book Critics Circle Award for Biography, 2003.

Pulitzer Prize for Biography or Autobiography, 2004.

A portrait of the head of the Soviet Union whose rule followed Stalin's identifies his impact on the country and the rest of the world, citing how his career reflected of the Soviet experience and tracing his efforts to reform communism and ease the cold war.

Kierkegaard, Soren, 1813-1855

Carlisle, Clare **Philosopher** of the heart : the restless life of Soren Kierkegaard / Clare Carlisle. Farrar, Straus and Giroux, 2020, c2019. 368 p. **B**

ISBN 9780374231187

1. Kierkegaard, Soren, 1813-1855. 2. Philosophers 3. Philosophy, Modern. 4. Existentialism. 5. Christianity 6. Biographies

LC 2019055663

A biography of the passionate and challenging philosopher known as the founder of existentialism describes how he explored the questions of existence, being human, the nature of love and Christianity In Copenhagen of the mid 1800s.

"Carlisle (On Habit), reader in philosophy and theology at King's College London, makes an intimidatingly chilly and mercurial figure relatable to readers in this admirable biography." Publishers Weekly

Kiki, 1901-1953

Catel **Kiki** de Montparnasse / Catel & Bocquet ; translated from the Belgian edition by Nora Mahony. SelfMadeHero, 2011. 416 p. : **B**

ISBN 9781906838256

1. Artists' models -- France -- Comic books, strips, etc. 2. Bohemianism 3. Poor families. 4. France. 5. Comics and Graphic novels 6. Biographies

LC 2011431146

In bohemian Montparnasse of the 1920s, Kiki escaped poverty to become one of the most charismatic figures of the avant-garde years between the wars. Partner to Man Ray, and one of the first emancipated women of the 20th century, Kiki made her mark with her freedom of style, word, and thought that could be learned from only one school: the school of life.

Kim, Chong-il, 1942-2011

★Fischer, Paul (Documentary film producer) A **Kim** Jong-Il production : the extraordinary true story of a kidnapped filmmaker, his star actress, and a young dictator's rise to power / Paul Fischer. Flatiron Books, 2015 368 p. **B**

ISBN 9781250054265

1. Kim, Chong-il, 1942-2011. 2. Sin, Sang-ok, 1926-2006 3. Ch'oe, Un-hui, 1930- 4. Propaganda 5. Captives 6. Actors and actresses 7. Film producers and directors 8. North Korea 9. Biographies

LC 2014040366

Before becoming the world's most notorious dictator, Kim Jong-Il ran North Korea's Ministry for Propaganda and its film studios. Conceiving every movie made, he acted as producer and screenwriter. Despite this control, he was underwhelmed by the available talent and took drastic steps, ordering the kidnapping of Choi Eun-Hee (Madam Choi) - South Korea's most famous actress - and her ex-husband Shin Sang-Ok, the country's most famous filmmaker.

"The most compelling facets of this book of astonishments are Fischer's insights into the relationships between Choi, Shin, and their diabolical captor and Fischer's canny perception of how Kim Jong-Il turned his oppressed, corrupt, and starving country into one vast theatrical production of fantasy, deceit, and terror, scripting lives of fear, ignorance, obedience, and deprivation." Booklist.

Kim, Chong-un, 1984-

Fifield, Anna The **great** successor : the divinely perfect destiny of brilliant Comrade Kim Jong Un / Anna Fifield. PublicAffairs, 2019. 288 p. **B**

ISBN 9781541742482

1. Dictators 2. Fascism 3. Isolationism. 4. Communist countries 5. North Korea -- Politics and government

LC 2019004479

A Washington Post journalist with exclusive access to the dictator's inner circle, including an aunt and uncle and a Japanese sushi chef he befriended, paints a fascinating portrait of the most isolated regime in the world.

"A compelling mix of biography, cultural history, and political intrigue." Kirkus.

Pak, Jung H. **Becoming** Kim Jong Un : a former CIA officer's insights into North Korea's enigmatic young dictator / Jung H. Pak. Ballantine Books, 2020. 288 p. : **B**

ISBN 9781984819727

1. Dictatorship 2. Power (Social sciences) 3. Nuclear weapons 4. Ambition 5. North Korea -- Foreign relations 6. North Korea -- History. 7. North Korea -- Politics and government 8. Biographies

LC 2019048665

A CIA analyst's account of the rise of North Korean dictator Kim Jong Un looks at everything from his nuclear ambitions to his summits with President Donald J. Trump.

"An insightful analysis of perhaps the world's most dangerous dystopia." Kirkus

Kim, Il-song, 1912-1994

Harden, Blaine The **great** leader and the fighter pilot : the true story of the tyrant who created North Korea and the young lieutenant who stole his way to freedom / Blaine Harden. Penguin Group USA, 2015. 288 p. **B**

ISBN 9780670016570

1. Kim, Il-song, 1912-1994. 2. No, Kum-Sok. 3. Totalitarianism. 4. Defectors. 5. Communism -- North Korea. 6. Fighter pilots. 7. North Korea -- Foreign relations United States. 8. United States -- Foreign relations North Korea. 9. Biographies

LC 2014038542

Documents the rise of Kim Il Sung, the origins of North Korea's anti-American stance and the daring theft of a Soviet MiG-15 warplane to benefit the United States by fighter pilot No Kum Sok.

Kim, Suki, 1970-

★Kim, Suki, 1970- **Without** you, there is no us : my time with the sons of North Korea's elite / Suki Kim. Crown Publishing, 2014. 272 p. **B**

ISBN 9780307720658

1. Women college teachers 2. Students 3. Totalitarianism 4. Paranoia 5. North Korea 6. Autobiographies and memoirs

LC 2014012730

"The result is a touching portrayal of the student experience in North Korea, which provides readers with a rare glimpse of life in the enigmatic country." Library Journal.

Kimball, Kristin

Kimball, Kristin **Good** husbandry : growing food, love, and family on Essex farm / Kristin Kimball. Scribner, 2019. 288 p. **B**

ISBN 9781501111532

1. Organic farming. 2. Urban-rural migration. 3. Sustainable agriculture 4. Sustainable living. 5. New York (State) 6. Autobiographies and memoirs

LC 2019014660

The author evocatively describes her family's highs and lows throughout five years on Essex Farm that were marked by injury, difficult weather, financial setbacks and renewed commitments.

King, B. B.

★King, B. B. **Blues** all around me : the autobiography of B.B. King / B.B. King with David Ritz. Spike, 1999, c1996. xii, 336 p. : **B**

ISBN 0380807602

1. Blues musicians 2. Autobiographies and memoirs

LC bl2007011853

Originally published: New York : Avon Books, 1996.

The fabled blues guitarist chronicles his youth on a Mississippi cotton farm, years as a disk jockey, experiences with racism and the civil rights movement, romantic relationships, and forty-five years on the road.

"This is one of the best recent pop-music bios. King speaks straight from the soul, it seems, just like he plays the guitar." Booklist.

King, Coretta Scott, 1927-2006

★King, Coretta Scott, 1927-2006, **My** life, my love, my legacy / Coretta Scott King ; as told to the Rev. Dr. Barbara Reynolds. Henry Holt and Company, [2017] 368 p. **B**

ISBN 9781627795982

1. King, Coretta Scott, 1927-2006. 2. King, Martin Luther, Jr., 1929-1968. 3. Civil rights workers -- United States 4. African American women 5. Social reformers -- United States 6. Spouses of clergy 7. United States -- History -- 20th century 8. Autobiographies and memoirs

LC 2016039557

Over the course of many years, Coretta Scott King's close friend, the Rev. Dr. Barbara Reynolds, recorded interviews with King about her experiences. In My Life, My Love, My Legacy, Reynolds assembles these accounts into an authorized biography. From her childhood in segregated Heiberger, Alabama through her college days in Ohio and her classical music studies in Boston, Coretta aspired to be a professional musician. That changed after Martin Luther King Jr persuaded her to marry him, build a family together, and return South to combat Jim Crow. This up-close, graceful narrative offers a vivid depiction of the Kings' lives, especially Coretta's, and the Civil Rights movement.--Description by Katherine Bradley Johnson

"King was undoubtedly a singular woman, and readers will be struck by just how strongly her exceedingly compelling story resonates today. She was much more than just the woman behind the man, and now, in the most eloquent of language, she proves that truth once and for all to generations of readers who will embrace her all over again." Booklist.

King, Martin Luther, Jr., 1929-1968

★Branch, Taylor **At** Canaan's edge : America in the King years, 1965-68 / Taylor Branch. Simon & Schuster, 2006. xiii, 1039 p. : America in the King years ; **B**

ISBN 9780684857121

1. King, Martin Luther, Jr., 1929-1968 Assassination 2. Southern Christian Leadership Conference 3. Voting Rights Act of 1965. 4. Nonviolence -- United States -- History -- 20th century. 5. African Americans -- Civil rights -- History -- 20th century. 6. Civil Rights Movement 7. United States -- History -- 1961-1969. 8. Biographies

LC 2005040177

Sequel to: Pillar of fire.

National Book Award for Nonfiction finalist, 2006.

National Book Critics Circle Award for Biography finalist, 2006.

A comprehensive biography of the last three years of Martin Luther King's life describing the challenges to his leadership and his nonviolent philosophy.

"In this history that follows the life of Martin Luther King from the protest at Selma and the 1966 Meredith March through King's expanding political concern for the poor to his 1968 assassination in Memphis, Tenn., Branch gives us not only the civil rights leader's life but also the rapidly changing pulse of American culture and politics. This magisterial book is a fitting tribute to a magisterial man." Publishers Weekly.

★Branch, Taylor **Parting** the waters : America in the King years, 1954-63 / Taylor Branch. Simon and Schuster, 1988. xii, 1064 p., 32 p. of plates : America in the King years ; **B**

ISBN 0671460978

1. African Americans -- Civil rights 2. Racism. 3. Prejudice. 4. Civil Rights Movement 5. United States -- History -- 1953-1961. 6.

United States -- Social life and customs -- 1950-1960. 7. Biographies
LC 88024033

Sequel: Pillar of Fire.ALA Notable Book, 1990.

National Book Critics Circle Award for Non-Fiction, 1988.

National Book Award for Nonfiction finalist, 1989

Focuses on Martin Luther King, Jr., and the key moments that defined his rise to the forefront of the civil rights movement in America, from Rosa Parks' arrest in Montgomery to King's imprisonment in Birmingham and his triumphant march on Washington.

"The author has searched out the hidden reality and often tragic human drama of the King years. On his best pages, the past, miraculously, seems to spring back to life. King himself appears human, all too human. Yet when the reader is done, his remarkable virtues and ordinary vices seem of a piece, the component parts of a coherent, towering personality." Newsweek.

★Branch, Taylor **Pillar** of fire : America in the King years, 1963-65 / Taylor Branch. Simon & Schuster, 1998. xiv, 746 p. : America in the King years ; **B**

ISBN 0684808196

1. Civil Rights Act of 1964. 2. African Americans -- Civil rights 3. Civil Rights Movement 4. Freedom Riders (Civil rights movement) 5. March on Washington for Jobs and Freedom, 1963. 6. United States -- History -- 1961-1969. 7. United States -- Race relations -- History -- 20th century. 8. Biographies

LC 97046076

Sequel to: Parting the waters.

ALA Notable Book, 1999.

Examines the jailing of Martin Luther King, jr., the end of segregation, and the growing rifts in the civil rights movement that led to calls for a more violent reaction to racism.

"Branch's research is impeccable and his knowledge of his material solid. The book is significant for marshaling so much information, particularly the profiles of all the many individuals involved in the race issues of that time." Booklist.

Flowers, A. R. **I** see the promised land : [a life of Martin Luther King, Jr.] / [text by] Arthur Flowers, [illustrations by] Manu Chitrakar, [design by] Guglielmo Rossi. Tara Books, c2010. 138 p. : **B**

ISBN 9789380340043

1. King, Martin Luther, Jr., 1929-1968. 2. African American men 3. Civil rights workers 4. Baptists -- United States -- Clergy 5. African American civil rights workers 6. Biographies 7. Comics and Graphic novels

LC bl2011000413

Presents in graphic novel format the life of the Baptist minister and Nobel Peace Prize winner who became the leader and orator of the African American civil rights movement before his assassination in 1968.

"A myth-making take on King's life that has both emotional and intellectual impact, the Flowers/Chitrakar collaboration supplies fresh color and richness to the oft-told history of this game-changer." Library Journal.

Honey, Michael K **To** the promised land : Martin Luther King and the fight for economic justice / Michael K. Honey. W.W. Norton & Company, 2018. 224 p. **B**

ISBN 9780393651263

1. Inequality 2. Income distribution 3. Civil Rights Movement 4. Equality 5. Biographies

LC 2017060268

Goes beyond popularized views of Martin Luther King, Jr., to explore his committed advocacy of the poor, the working class ,and unions, as well as his views about nonviolent resistance to all forms of oppression, particularly economic inequality.

"Honey encourages the many who revere his memory to continue his work toward this goal. His book contains both insight and inspiration to activists of many stripes." Publishers Weekly.

Jackson, Troy, 1968- **Becoming** King : Martin Luther King, Jr. and the making of a national leader / Troy Jackson ; introduction by Clayborne Carson. University Press of Kentucky, c2008. xx, 248 p. ; **B**

ISBN 9780813125206

1. King, Martin Luther, Jr., 1929-1968. 2. African American civil rights workers 3. Baptists -- United States -- Clergy 4. African Americans -- Civil rights -- Montgomery, Alabama -- History -- 20th century. 5. Segregation in transportation -- Montgomery, Alabama -- History -- 20th century. 6. Montgomery, Alabama -- Race relations. 7. Montgomery, Alabama -- History -- 20th century 8. Biographies

LC 2008025041

"The author's comprehensive analysis of King's sermons before, during and after the boycott artfully depicts a man in transition, from naive do-gooder to world-changer. Jackson's treatment of Montgomery in the post-boycott era offers new insight into the void in leadership and the fractious infighting among the movement's luminaries after King departed the scene. An informed investigation of the struggles that defined a time and place-and the man who gave them a voice." Kirkus.

Joseph, Peniel E The **sword** and the shield : the revolutionary lives of Malcolm X and Martin Luther King Jr. / Peniel E. Joseph. Basic Books, 2020. 368 p. **B**

ISBN 9781541617865

1. King, Martin Luther, Jr., 1929-1968. 2. Malcolm X, 1925-1965 3. Civil Rights Movement 4. Social advocates 5. Identity (Psychology) -- Political aspects 6. African Americans -- Identity 7. United States -- History -- 20th century 8. United States -- Race relations

LC 2019051608

"The Sword and the Shield is a dual biography of Malcolm X and Martin Luther King that transforms our understanding of the twentieth century's most iconic African American leaders. Peniel E. Joseph reveals a nuanced portrait of two men who, despite markedly different backgrounds, inspired and pushed each other throughout their adult lives. This is a strikingly revisionist biography, not only of Malcolm and Martin, but also of the movement and era they came to define".--Provided by publisher.

"An authoritative dual biography from a leading scholar of African American history." Kirkus

King, Martin Luther, Jr., 1929-1968 The **autobiography** of Martin Luther King, Jr. / edited by Clayborne Carson. Intellectual Properties Management in association with Warner Books, 1998. xi, 400 p. : **B**

ISBN 0446524123

1. King, Martin Luther, Jr., 1929-1968. 2. African Americans 3. African American civil rights workers 4. Civil rights workers 5. Baptists -- Clergy 6. Autobiographies and memoirs

LC 98035704

Drawing on King's unpublished writings and other materials, a civil rights scholar assembles a first-person narrative of King's life

"Carson, director of Martin Luther King Jr. Papers Project, brings together selections from King's writings, speeches, and recordings to create this fascinating 'autobiography' of the famed civil rights leader and Nobel Peace Prize winner. The writings trace King's struggles with religion, philosophy, and the racial politics of the U.S." Booklist.

Rosenbloom, Joseph, 1944- **Redemption** : Martin Luther King Jr.'s last 31 hours / Joseph Rosenbloom. Beacon Press, 2018 289 p. **B**

ISBN 9780807083383

1. King, Martin Luther, Jr., 1929-1968 Assassination. 2. African American civil rights workers. 3. Civil Rights Movement. 4. Civil rights. 5. Biographies

LC 2017024226

A deeply intimate chronicle of the last 31 hours of Martin Luther King Jr.'s life draws on dozens of interviews with Memphis insiders and recently released archival materials to share insights into his personal and political activities as well as his marital difficulties at the same time James Earl Ray orchestrated his assassination.

Sokol, Jason The **heavens** might crack : the death and legacy of Martin Luther King, Jr. / Jason Sokol. Basic Books, 2018. 320 p. **B**

ISBN 9780465055913

1. King, Martin Luther, Jr., 1929-1968 Assassination. 2. African American civil rights workers. 3. Civil Rights Movement. 4. Civil rights. 5. Biographies

LC 2017042658

"On April 4, 1968, Martin Luther King Jr. was fatally shot as he stood on the balcony of the Lorraine Motel in Memphis. At the time of his murder, King was a polarizing figure--scorned by many white Americans, worshipped by some African Americans and liberal whites, and deemed irrelevant by many black youth. In The Heavens Might Crack, historian Jason Sokol traces the diverse responses, both in America and throughout the world, to King's death. Whether celebrating or mourning, most agreed that the final flicker of hope for a multiracial America had been extinguished. A deeply moving account of a country coming to terms with an act of shocking violence, The Heavens Might Crack is essential reading for anyone seeking to understand America's fraught racial past and present".-- Provided by publisher.

Wexler, Stuart **Killing** King : racial terrorists, James Earl Ray, and the plot to assassinate Martin Luther King Jr. / Stuart Wexler and Larry Hancock. Counterpoint Press, 2018. 304 p. **B**

ISBN 9781619029194

1. King, Martin Luther, Jr., 1929-1968 Assassination. 2. Ray, James Earl, 1928-1998. 3. Conspiracies -- United States -- History -- 20th century. 4. African American civil rights workers. 5. Civil Rights Movement. 6. Civil rights. 7. Biographies

LC 2017054596

Uncovering previously unknown FBI files and sources, as well as new forensics, the authors of America's Secret Jihad convincingly make the case that Martin Luther King was assassinated by a clear and long simmering conspiracy orchestrated by the racial terrorists who were responsible for the Mississippi Burning murders

King, Stephen, 1947-

King, Stephen, 1947- **On** writing : a memoir of the craft / Stephen King. Scribner, 2000. 288 p. **B**

ISBN 9780684853529

1. Authors, American -- 20th century 2. Horror story writing. 3. Writing. 4. Autobiographies and memoirs

LC 00030105

Bram Stoker Award for Best Nonfiction, 2000.

Locus Award for Best Nonfiction/Related/Reference Book, 2001.

The author shares his insights into the craft of writing and offers a humorous perspective on his own experience as a writer.

"The author recounts his life from early childhood through the aftermath of the 1999 accident that nearly killed him. Along the way, King touts the writing philosophies of William Strunk and Ernest Hemingway, advocates a healthy appetite for reading, expounds upon the subject of grammar, critiques a number of popular writers, and offers the reader a chance to try out his theories. . . . Recommended for anyone who wants to write and everyone who loves to read." Library Journal.

Kingsolver, Barbara

★Kingsolver, Barbara **Animal,** vegetable, miracle : a year of food life / Barbara Kingsolver, with Steven L. Hopp and Camille Kingsolver ; original drawings by Richard A. Houser. Harper Collins, 2007. 370 p. : **B**

ISBN 9780060852559

1. Hopp, Steven L., 1954- 2. Natural foods. 3. Farm life -- Appalachian Region, Southern -- Anecdotes. 4. Rural life -- Appalachian Region, Southern -- Anecdotes. 5. Agriculture -- Appalachian Region, Southern -- Anecdotes. 6. Appalachian Region, Southern -- Social life and customs 7. Autobiographies and memoirs

LC 2006053516

ALA Notable Book, 2008.

Green Prize for Sustainable Literature, 2008.

James Beard Foundation Book Awards, Writing and Literature, 2008.

Follows the author's family's efforts to live on locally- and home-grown foods, an endeavor through which they learned lighthearted truths about food production and the connection between health and diet.

"This is a serious book about important problems. Its concerns are real and urgent. It is clear, thoughtful, often amusing, passionate and appealing. It may give you a serious case of supermarket guilt, thinking of the energy footprint left by each out-of-season tomato, but you'll also find unexpected knowledge and gain the ability to make informed choices about whatand howyou're willing to eat. " Washington Post Book World.

Kingston, Maxine Hong

Kingston, Maxine Hong The **woman** warrior ; China men / Maxine Hong Kingston ; with an introduction by Mary Gordon. Everyman's Library, 2005. xxix, 541 p. ; **B**

ISBN 9781400043842

1. Kingston, Maxine Hong Childhood and youth. 2. Kingston, Maxine Hong Family. 3. Authors, American -- 20th century 4. Chinese Americans -- History. 5. Chinese Americans -- California 6. Chinese Americans -- California -- Social life and customs. 7. California 8. Autobiographies and memoirs

LC 2004061143

Originally published: The woman warrior.

New York : Knopf, 1976.

China men. New York : Knopf, 1980.

Collects two works by the author that focus on the lives of Chinese Americans, the first of which reccounts her childhood in a tradition-bound Chinese family.

Kinsman, Kat, 1972-

Kinsman, Kat, 1972- **Hi,** anxiety : life with a bad case of nerves / Kat Kinsman. Dey Street, 2016. viii, 221 pages ; **B**

ISBN 9780062369680

1. Anxiety in women. 2. Determination (Personal quality) 3. Women with depression 4. Anxiety. 5. Autobiographies and memoirs

LC 2016030635

An analysis of the role of anxiety in the life of the award-winning editor-in-chief of the Tasting Table website expands on her high-profile CNN article to explore her adolescent diagnosis with depression and her daily struggles with making choices and pursuing treatment.

Kipling, Rudyard, 1865-1936

Gilmour, David, 1952- The **long** recessional : the imperial life of Rudyard Kipling / David Gilmour. Farrar, Straus and Giroux, 2002. xii, 351 p., 16 p. of plates : **B**

ISBN 0374187029

1. Kipling, Rudyard, 1865-1936. 2. Authors, English -- 19th century 3. Imperialism in literature. 4. Imperialism. 5. Postcolonialism. 6. Biographies

LC 2002100585

Elizabeth Longford Prize for Historical Biography, 2003."

The author offers a brief, sympathetic, well-informed, and highly readable account of Kipling." Library Journal.

Ricketts, Harry **Rudyard** Kipling : a life / Harry Ricketts. Carroll & Graf, 2001. xii, 434 p., 16 p. of plates : **B**

ISBN 0786708301

1. Kipling, Rudyard, 1865-1936. 2. Authors, English -- 19th century 3. Authors, English -- 20th century 4. England -- Social life and customs -- 19th century 5. England -- Social life and customs -- 20th century 6. Biographies

LC 2002277531

The first full-scale study of Rudyard Kipling in decades provides an incisive reassessment of the life and literary work of an author who had a profound influence on twentieth-century English literature.

Kirkby, Bruce, 1968-

Kirkby, Bruce, 1968- **Blue** sky kingdom : an epic family journey to the heart of the Himalaya / Bruce Kirkby. Pegasus Books, 2020 295 p. **B**

ISBN 9781643135687

1. Kirkby, Bruce, 1968- Family 2. Television personalities 3. Families 4. Voyages and travels 5. Family travel 6. Himalaya Mountains 7. Tibet 8. Autobiographies and memoirs

Bruce Kirkby had fallen into a pattern of looking mindlessly at his phone for hours, flipping between emails and social media, ignoring his children and wife, when a thought struck him. This wasn't living; this wasn't him. This moment of clarity started a chain reaction which ended with a grand plan: he was going to take his wife and two young sons, jump on a freighter and head for the Himalayas. Bruce and his family had a remarkable three months journey, where they would end up living amongst the Lamas of Zanskar Valley, one of the last places on earth where Himalayan Buddhism is still practiced freely in its original setting.

"A breathtaking journey, both geographical and internal, Kirkby's blending of travelog of an already fascinatingly remote locale and personal family experience is unique and luminous. Will appeal to a wide range of readers." Library Journal

Kissinger, Henry, 1923-

Ferguson, Niall **Kissinger** : the idealist, 1923-1968 / Niall Ferguson. Penguin Group USA, 2015 560 p. **B**

ISBN 9781594206535

1. United States. Secretary of State. 2. Politicians -- United States 3. National security advisors 4. Negotiation. 5. Jewish men. 6. United States -- History -- 20th century. 7. United States -- Foreign relations. 8. Biographies

LC 2015373204

A definitive portrait of the American statesman, based on unprecedented access to his private papers, challenges common misconceptions to trace Kissinger's beliefs to philosophical idealism.

"It will surprise many readers how quickly Kissinger finds his principles incompatible with the Kennedy-Johnson policy in Vietnam, and how reluctant he is to serve under the devious Nixon. A sophisticated portrait, certain to stir debate--and to heighten expectations for the sequel." Booklist.

★Gewen, Barry The **inevitability** of tragedy : Henry Kissinger and his world / Barry Gewen. W.W. Norton & Company, 2020. 448 p. **B**

ISBN 9781324004059

1. Cabinet officers 2. Politicians 3. International relations 4. Diplomacy 5. United States -- Foreign relations 6. Biographies

LC 2019050503

A revisionist portrait of the diplomatic advisor under the Nixon and Ford administrations illuminates the controversies and fundamental ideas behind his policies, discussing how Kissinger's views were partly shaped by his experiences as a Jewish-German refugee.

"Masterly work on the making of Henry Kissinger?and what American foreign policy can learn from his dark experience and pessimistic outlook." Kirkus

Klarsfeld, Beate, 1939-

Klarsfeld, Beate, 1939- **Hunting** the truth : memoirs of Beate and Serge Klarsfeld / Beate and Serge Klarsfeld ; translated from the French by Sam Taylor. Farrar, Straus and Giroux, 2018. 454 p. **B**

ISBN 9780374279820

1. Klarsfeld, Serge, 1935- 2. Nazi hunters 3. Husband and wife 4. War criminals 5. Political activists 6. Autobiographies and memoirs

LC 2017035981

Includes index."

Originally published in 2015 by Fayard/Flammarion, France, as Memoires."

A pair of European activists present the dramatic story of their work as Nazi hunters, describing their respective upbringings as survivors of persecution and their 50-year effort to expose, apprehend and prosecute Nazi war criminals, from torturer Klaus Barbie to Gestapo chief Kurt Kischka

"A masterful work of historical importance." Booklist.

Klebold, Sue

Klebold, Sue A **mother's** reckoning : living in the aftermath of tragedy / Sue Klebold. Crown, 2016. 272 p. **B**

ISBN 9781101902752

1. Klebold, Dylan, 1981-1999. 2. Columbine High School (Littleton, Colo.). 3. Child murderers 4. School shootings -- Colorado 5. Parent and child 6. Teenagers with emotional illnesses 7. Autobiographies and memoirs

LC 2015018513

The mother of one of the two shooters at Columbine High School draws on personal recollections, journal entries and video recordings to piece together what led to her son's unpredicted breakdown and share insights into how other families might recognize warning signs.

"Klebold's painful memoir unfolds with more sorrow than drama; readers will be left with the sense that even the 'best' mother cannot know what her child may be feeling or thinking." Booklist.

Klein, Jessi, 1975-

Klein, Jessi, 1975- **You'll** grow out of it / Jessi Klein. Grand

Central Publishing, 2016. 256 p. **B**

ISBN 9781455531189

1. Women comedians 2. Tomboys 3. Bungling and bunglers. 4. Femininity 5. Autobiographies and memoirs

LC 2016009270

Humorous and poignant stories from the "Inside Amy Schumer" head writer's awkward youth include entries on her tomboy pursuits of femininity, her emulation of Oprah, and the dangers of wedding websites.

"This uplifting and uproarious collection of personal essays will be repeatedly shared among friends." Publishers Weekly.

Kleiss, N. Jack

Kleiss, N. Jack **Never** call me a hero : a legendary American dive-bomber pilot remembers the battle of Midway / N. Jack Kleiss, Timothy Orr, Laura Orr. HarperCollins, 2017. 368 p. **B**

ISBN 9780062692054

1. Midway, Battle of, 1942 2. Bomber pilots 3. Battles 4. Air battles 5. Autobiographies and memoirs

LC bl2017015836

In an eyewitness account of the Battle of Midway by one of its key participants, an American dive-bomber pilot discusses how he sank two Japanese carriers and struck a third, playing a decisive individual role in determining the outcome of the battle.

Klemperer, Victor, 1881-1960

★Klemperer, Victor, 1881-1960 **I** will bear witness: a diary of the Nazi years, 1942-1945 / Victor Klemperer ; translated from the German by Martin Chalmers. Random House, 2000, c1995. 556 p. The Diaries of Victor Klemperer ; **B**

ISBN 9780375502408

1. Klemperer, Victor, 1881-1960. 2. Holocaust (1933-1945) -- Germany 3. Jews, German -- History -- 1933-1945. 4. College teachers -- Germany. 5. Philologists -- Germany -- Diaries. 6. Germany -- History -- 1933-1945 Sources. 7. Dresden, Germany.

LC 98015429

Originally published as Ich will Zeugnis ablegen bis zum letzten: Berlin : Aufbau-Verlag, 1995.

ALA Notable Book, 2000.

National Book Critics Circle Award for Biography finalist, 2000.

A second volume of the author's firsthand account of life in Nazi Germany chronicles the worst years of the war, including the bombing of Dresden and his escape from deportation to a Jewish concentration camp by advancing American troops.

"Never has the isolation of living in a world that wishes one's people dead been rendered with greater pathos. Every act of cruelty as well as every gesture of kindness is scrupulously recorded." The Nation.

Klinsmann, Jurgen

Kirschbaum, Erik **Soccer** without borders : Jurgen Klinsmann, coaching the U.S. men's national soccer team and the quest for the World Cup / Erik Kirschbaum, Jurgen Klinsmann. Picador USA, 2016. 224 p. **B**

ISBN 9781250098313

1. World Cup (Soccer) 2. Soccer coaches. 3. Soccer 4. Autobiographies and memoirs

LC 2016002387

Includes index.

A controversial U.S men's soccer coach reveals his thoughts on building a winning soccer team.

"Kirschbaum provides a welcome sketch of Klinsmann, a thoughtful man of the world who has for years lived in California and who cannot be pigeonholed as merely a European trying to remake American soccer in the Old World image." Kirkus.

Knausgaard, Karl Ove, 1968-

Knausgaard, Karl Ove, 1968- **Autumn** / Karl Ove Knausgaard, translated by Ingvild Burkey. Penguin Group USA, 2017, c2015 224 p. Four seasons encyclopedia ; **B**

ISBN 9780399563300

1. Authors 2. Autumn 3. Fathers and daughters 4. Fetus. 5. Autobiographies and memoirs 6. Letters

LC 2017031387

Translation of: Om høsten.Originally published, 2015

A first entry in a planned four-part autobiographical series by the award-winning author of Out of the World is comprised of sensory letters written to his unborn daughter that describe his childhood and daily life with his wife and older children in rural Sweden.

"An engagingly wide-ranging set of meditations." Kirkus.

Knausgaard, Karl Ove, 1968- **Winter** / Karl Ove Knausgaard ; with illustrations by Lars Lerin. Penguin Press, 2018. 240 p. Four seasons encyclopedia ; **B**

ISBN 9780399563331

1. Authors 2. Fathers and daughters 3. Fatherhood 4. Fetus. 5. Autobiographies and memoirs 6. Letters

LC bl2017045697

Continues the author's autobiographical quartet based on the seasons and collects daily meditations and letters addressed directly to his unborn daughter and how her prenatal development reshaped his perspectives on everyday objects.

"A winningly interior journey into the most interior of seasons." Kirkus.

Knight, Christopher Thomas, 1965-

Finkel, Michael The **stranger** in the woods : the extraordinary story of the North Pond hermit / Michael Finkel. Alfred A. Knopf, 2017. 240 p. **B**

ISBN 9781101875681

1. Solitude. 2. Eccentrics and eccentricities. 3. Wilderness survival 4. Hermits 5. Maine 6. Biographies

LC 2016029910

"This is a Borzoi book"--Title page verso.

Documents the true story of a man who endured a hardscrabble, isolated existence in a tent in the Maine woods, never speaking with others and surviving by stealing supplies from nearby cabins, for 27 years, in a portrait that illuminates the survival means he developed and the reasons behind his solitary life.

"With inevitable comparisons to Jon Krakauer's Into the Wild, this book will appeal to recreational readers interested in outdoor adventure, survival stories, or escaping the mainstream." Library Journal.

Knight, Philip H., 1938-

Knight, Philip H., 1938- **Shoe** dog : a memoir by the creator of Nike / Phil Knight. Simon & Schuster, 2016 384 p. **B**

ISBN 9781501135910

1. Nike 2. Entrepreneurship. 3. Entrepreneurs 4. Businesspeople 5. Shoes 6. Autobiographies and memoirs

LC 2016010080

The influential founder and CEO of Nike shares the inside story of the company's early days as an intrepid startup and its evolution to one of the world's most iconic and profitable brands, offering insights into his own experiences as a young man who envisioned a company that would be run in atypical ways.

"Has anyone else ever written as evocatively about selling shoes? Well, George Pelecanos wrote a crime novel called Shoedog, and there's a character in it who sells shoes with a definite flair, but that's really something very different. And, yet, maybe not. Pelecanos brings his street characters to vivid life and makes us care about them. Remarkably, Knight does the same thing for a giant corporation--certainly an even more formidable task." Booklist.

Koh, EJ, 1988-

Koh, EJ, 1988- The **magical** language of others : a memoir / E.J. Koh. Tin House Books, [2020] 203 p. **B**

ISBN 9781947793385

1. Mothers and daughters 2. Generation gap 3. Teenage girls 4. Asian Americans 5. United States 6. South Korea 7. Japan 8. Autobiographies and memoirs 9. Letters

LC 2019031239

Left behind when work requires her parents to return to Korea, a teen poet reconnects with family history to manage the impact of absent caregivers on her sense of self. By the award-winning author of A Lesser Love.

"Both creative tribute and personal reckoning, this is a finely wrought, linguistically rich, provocative memoir." Booklist.

Kois, Dan

Kois, Dan **How** to be a family : the year I dragged my kids around the world to find a new way to be together / Dan Kois. Little, Brown & Company, 2019. 320 p. **B**

ISBN 9780316552622

1. Kois, Dan Family 2. Journalists 3. Families 4. Voyages and travels 5. Family travel 6. Autobiographies and memoirs

LC bl2019028227

A father humorously recounts the year his family spent trying to get out of the rut of their busy, overscheduled East Coast lives by living in New Zealand, the Netherlands, Costa Rica and small-town Kansas.

Koker, David, 1921-

Koker, David, 1921- **At** the edge of the abyss : a concentration camp diary, 1943-1944 / David Koker ; edited by Robert Jan van Pelt ; translated from the Dutch by Michiel Horn and John Irons. Northwestern University Press, c2012. xii, 396 p. : **B**

ISBN 0810126362

1. Koker, David, 1921-. 2. Vught (Concentration camp). 3. Prisoners of war -- Netherlands 4. World War II 5. Autobiographies and memoirs.

LC 2011026584

"Originally published in Dutch by G. A. van Oorschot as Dagboek geschreven in Vught, 1977."

Konnikova, Maria

Konnikova, Maria The **biggest** bluff : how I learned to pay attention, master the odds, and win / Maria Konnikova. Penguin Press, 2020. 400 p. **B**

ISBN 9780525522621

1. Konnikova, Maria. 2. Seidel, Erik, 1959- 3. Poker players 4. Human behavior. 5. Gambling -- United States 6. Mentors 7. Autobiographies and memoirs

LC 2020002627

Includes index."

How a New York Times bestselling author and New Yorker contributor parlayed a strong grasp of the science of human decision-making and a woeful ignorance of cards into a life-changing run as a professional poker player, under the wing of a legend of the game.

"A smart and subtle delight--highly recommended for fans of cards and brain-hacking alike." Kirkus

Koufax, Sandy, 1935-

Leavy, Jane **Sandy** Koufax : a lefty's legacy / Jane Leavy. Harper Collins, c2002. xxii, 282 p. : **B**

ISBN 0060195339

1. Baseball players -- United States 2. Jewish Americans 3. Jewish American men 4. Baseball players -- United States -- Interviews 5. United States -- Social life and customs -- 20th century 6. Biographies

LC 2002068722

Includes index.

Draws on more than four hundred interviews with friends, teammates, and opponents to present a portrait of the distinguished baseball pitcher.

"The author delivers an honest and exquisitely detailed examination of a complex man." Publishers Weekly.

Kozol, Jonathan

Kozol, Jonathan The **theft** of memory : losing my father one day at a time / Jonathan Kozol. Crown Publishers 2015. 352 p. **B**

ISBN 9780804140973

1. Kozol, Harry L., 1906- 2. People with Alzheimer's disease 3. Alzheimer's disease 4. Neurologists 5. Adult children of people with Alzheimer's disease 6. Autobiographies and memoirs

LC 2014041699

A deeply personal account of the life of the author's father--a nationally renowned neurologist who, after a life of helping to establish emerging fields in mental health, succumbed to Alzheimer's disease.

"The author's approach is shrewd yet warmly empathetic; he is curious about how the mind's gradual breakdown exposes its machinery, and raptly attuned to the emotional effects of these changes on his parents and himself. The result is a clear-eyed and deeply felt meditation on the aspects of family that age does not ravage." Publishers Weekly.

Kramer, Clara

Kramer, Clara **Clara's** war : one girl's story of survival / Clara Kramer with Stephen Glantz. Ecco, c2009. xii, 339 p., [8] p. of plates : **B**

ISBN 9780061728600

1. Kramer, Clara. 2. Holocaust (1933-1945) -- Poland. 3. Jews, Polish -- History. 4. World War II -- Poland. 5. Antisemitism -- Poland. 6. Poland -- History -- 1918-1945. 7. Autobiographies and memoirs

"Originally published in Great Britain in 2008 by Ebury Press, an imprint of Ebury Publishing, a Random House Company"--T.p. verso.

An account based on the subject's personal record of the months during which she hid from Nazis in an underground bunker with seventeen others includes coverage of such topics as the characteristics of their unlikely protector Mr. Beck, the house fire that threatened everyone's survival, and Beck's affair with Clara's cousin.

"Based on her wartime diary, which she kept while hiding in a basement in Poland, Kramer's book vividly recalls the tensions within her hidden community after the Nazis overtook the town of Zolkiew in 1942. Of particular interest are revelations about the family who hid the Kramers, particularly how an anti-Semitic Polish householder demonstrated great courage in shielding Jews in his basement." Library Journal.

Kramer, Jane

Kramer, Jane The **reporter's** kitchen / Jane Kramer. St Martins Press, 2017 320 p. **B**

ISBN 9781250074379

1. Food 2. Food habits 3. Cooking 4. Essays 5. Autobiographies and

memoirs

LC 2017024876

A volume of culinary essays by The New Yorker journalist and accomplished home cook also draws on her extensive international travels and includes chef profiles, a reflection on how her husband and she hosted a July Thanksgiving in Umbria, and a piece on how she helped an acclaimed Danish chef foraged for edible sea grass on the Nordic coast.

"Eloquent and charmingly loquacious, Kramer's essays are sharp and insightful. A joyous feast of food, travel, and human relationships." Kirkus. Reviews

Kranz, Gene

Kranz, Gene **Failure** is not an option : mission control from Mercury to Apollo 13 and beyond / Gene Kranz. Simon & Schuster, c2000. 415 p. : **B**

ISBN 0743200799

1. Kranz, Gene Career in aerospace engineering. 2. United States National Aeronautics and Space Administration. 3. Space flight -- United States -- History 4. Astronautics -- United States -- History. 5. United States -- History -- 20th century 6. United States -- Social life and customs -- 20th century 7. Autobiographies and memoirs

LC 00027720

Includes index.

The man who headed the "tiger team" that saved the Apollo 13 astronauts gives an insider's view of NASA Mission Control, from the early years of trying to catch up with the Russians to the end of the manned spaced program.

"A welcome contribution to the history of space flight. More than any previous book, it gives the view of that history as lived by the brotherhood of Mission Control. The writing, like Kranz himself, is brisk, unadorned and informative, but warmed from time to time by characteristic expressions of irony and humor." New York Times Book Review.

Kreider, Tim

Kreider, Tim **I** wrote this book because I love you : essays / Tim Kreider. Simon & Schuster, 2018 256 p. **B**

ISBN 9781476738994

1. Men/women relations 2. Interpersonal relations 3. Friendship 4. Love 5. Essays 6. Autobiographies and memoirs

LC 2017049097

A writer for The New York Times and creator of a popular comic strip explores his relationships with women in a collection of essays that ruminate on his troubles finding lasting love, his commitment issues and his valued female friendships.

"Kreider's clever hand and philosophic--rather than solipsistic--viewpoint place him in a different realm than writers like David Sedaris and David Foster Wallace who share his affection for details, uncommon settings, and nuance." Publishers Weekly.

Kreuger, Ivar, 1880-1932

Partnoy, Frank The **match** king : Ivar Kreuger, the financial genius behind a century of Wall Street scandals / Frank Partnoy. Public Affairs, 2009. 356 p. **B**

ISBN 9781586487430

1. Civil engineers -- Sweden 2. Investment banking -- Corrupt practices 3. Fraud -- History 4. Suicide -- History 5. Sweden -- Social life and customs -- 20th century 6. United States -- Social life and customs -- 20th century 7. Biographies

LC 2009926224

Frank Partnoy delivers a thrilling history lesson about an era and a nearly century-old Wall Street scandal rooted in unscrupulous investment banking and derivative hedge funds techniques developed by one man--Ivar Kreuger. Kreuger made his fortune in the 1920s by raising money from American investors to lend to European governments in exchange for match monopolies. Then he suddenly committed suicide in 1932. As his fraudulent schemes unravelled in the wake of his death, the so-called "Kreuger crash" began, bankrupting millions and leading to the enactment of the securities laws of 1933 and 1934.

"The author delivers a thrilling account of the grandfather of all Ponzi and Madoff schemesIvar Kreuger (1880-1932), who made his fortune in the 1920s by raising money from American investors to lend to European governments in exchange for match monopolies. A fascinating depiction of a man and his era." Publishers Weekly.

Krug, Nora

★Krug, Nora **Belonging** : a German reckons with history and home / Nora Krug. Scribner, 2018. 288 p. **B**

ISBN 9781476796628

1. Krug, Nora Family 2. Families -- History 3. German Americans 4. World War II -- Germany 5. Guilt 6. Germany -- History -- 20th century 7. Autobiographies and memoirs 8. Autobiographical comics 9. Comics and Graphic novels

LC bl2018187724

National Book Critics Circle Award for Autobiography, 2018.

A graphic memoir by an award-winning artist tells the story of her attempt to confront the hidden truths of her family's wartime past in Nazi Germany and to comprehend the forces that have shaped her life, her generation and history.

"The narrative is a deeply personal--and deeply moving--dive into national legacy and family history, with more text than most graphic novels and a graphic presentation that mixes documentary photographs, illustrations, and memories that predate the author's birth." Kirkus.

Kruk, Herman, 1897-1944

Kruk, Herman, 1897-1944 The **last** days of the Jerusalem of Lithuania : chronicles from the Vilna ghetto and the camps, 1939-1944 / Herman Kruk ; edited and introduced by Benjamin Harshav ; translated by Barbara Harshav. YIVO Institute for Jewish Research, 2002, c1961. lii, 732 p. : **B**

ISBN 0300044941

1. Kruk, Herman, 1897-1944. 2. Klooga (Concentration camp) 3. Jews -- Persecutions -- Vilnius, Lithuania. 4. Holocaust (1933-1945) -- Vilnius, Lithuania. 5. Jewish resistance and revolts 6. World War II 7. Vilnius, Lithuania -- Interethnic relations.

LC 2002016736

Originally published in Yiddish as Togbukh fun Vilner geto: New York : Yivo, 1961."

This is a major addition to Holocaust literature and Jewish history. In 1961 a Yiddish edition of the Vilna diaries was published. This larger new edition has been painstakingly assembled from those diaries and other documents and writings by Kruk that were widely scattered and only found since the 1961 edition; Harshav has also added a wealth of new footnotes." Publishers Weekly.

Kugler, Rob

Kugler, Rob A **dog** named Beautiful : a Marine, a dog, and a long road trip home / Rob Kugler. Flatiron Books, [2019] 288 p. **B**

ISBN 9781250164254

1. Kugler, Rob Travel United States 2. United States. Marine Corps 3. Marines 4. Iraq War veterans 5. Dogs 6. Dogs with disabilities 7. Autobiographies and memoirs

LC 2019002979

A medically retired Marine describes the role of his beloved chocolate lab in his recovery from war injuries and the loss of his brother, recounting the poignant road journey they shared in the final months of his dog's life.

Kuo, Michelle

Kuo, Michelle **Reading** with Patrick : a teacher, a student, and a life-changing friendship / Michelle Kuo. Random House, 2017. 304 p. **B**

ISBN 9780812997316

1. Kuo, Michelle. 2. Prisoners -- Education. 3. Alternative schools. 4. Books and reading. 5. Literacy. 6. United States -- Race relations. 7. Autobiographies and memoirs

LC 2016036759

A former alternative school teacher and Harvard Law School fellow shares the story of her work with a gifted student who was imprisoned for murder in the Mississippi Delta and whose education she continued through classic works of literature.

"Honest, thoughtful, and humane, Kuo's book is not only a testament to a remarkable friendship, but a must-read for anyone interested in social justice and race in America. Thoughtfully provocative reading." Kirkus.

Kupperman, Joel

Kupperman, Michael **All** the answers / Michael Kupperman. Simon & Schuster 2018 224 p. **B**

ISBN 9781501166433

1. Quiz kids (Radio program) 2. Child prodigies 3. Child celebrities 4. Fathers and sons 5. Fame 6. Biographical comics 7. Biographies 8. Comics and Graphic novels

LC bl2018080304

"Kupperman's solid, line-heavy drawings, which impart credibility to the preposterous concepts of his humorous strips, are equally effective at conveying this real-life drama. His clear-eyed yet touching portrait of his father serves as a a powerful indictment of celebrity culture." Booklist.

Kurosawa, Akira, 1910-1998

Kurosawa, Akira, 1910-1998 **Something** like an autobiography / Akira Kurosawa ; translated by Audie E. Bock. Vintage Books, 1983, c1982. xiii, 205 p., 8 p. of plates : **B**

ISBN 0394714393

1. Kurosawa, Akira, 1910-1998. 2. Film directors and producers -- Japan 3. Autobiographies and memoirs

LC 82048900

Translation of: Gama no abura.

Includes index.

The distinguished filmmaker chronicles his life from his birth in 1910 to the worldwide success in 1951 of his film "Rashomon" and provides a provocative account of the Japanese film industry.

"This is a fascinating, moving record of one man's pursuit of excellence in a single art." New York Times Book Review.

Kurtz, Glenn

Kurtz, Glenn **Three** minutes in Poland : discovering a lost world in a 1938 family film / Glenn Kurtz. Farrar, Straus and Giroux, 2014. 288 p. **B**

ISBN 9780374276775

1. Kurtz, Glenn Family 2. Jews, Polish 3. Holocaust (1933-1945) 4. Small towns -- Poland 5. Amateur films 6. Poland -- History -- 20th century 7. Autobiographies and memoirs

LC 2014008516

The author's search for the annihilated Polish community captured in his grandfather's 1938 home movie. From this brief film, Glenn Kurtz creates a riveting exploration of memory, loss, and improbable survival--a monument to a lost world.

"Engrossing detective work and chance encounters--one casual online viewer recognized a 13-year-old boy in the film as her still-living grandfather--allowed Kurtz to assemble a vibrant portrait of Jewish Nasielsk, its homely shops, proud synagogue, quarreling Hasidim and Zionists, impish kids, and, not least, of its harrowing war-time dissolution. He also explores the resurrection of the communitys history, as survivors find images of loved ones lost for generations and forge new bonds." Publishers Weekly.

Kushner, David, 1968-

Kushner, David, 1968- **Alligator** candy : a memoir / David Kushner. Simon & Schuster, 2016 256 p. **B**

ISBN 9781451682533

1. Grief 2. Brothers of murder victims 3. Families of murder victims 4. Murder 5. Florida 6. Autobiographies and memoirs

LC 2015022792

An NPR culture commentator and Rolling Stone contributing editor documents the story of his brother's murder at the hands of two drifters and his family's efforts to survive and seek justice against a backdrop of 1970s parenting dynamics and media hype.

"This emotional account invites readers to journey down a path that at first is in the shade but eventually wanders through strands of sunlight. You will hold those close to you tight after reading. For fans of true crime, books about getting past tragedy, and memoirs." Library Journal.

Kuzmic, Kristina

Kuzmic, Kristina **Hold** on, but don't hold still : hope and humor from my seriously flawed life / Kristina Kuzmic. Viking, 2020. 272 p. **B**

ISBN 9780525561842

1. Busy parents 2. Single mothers 3. Parenting 4. Motherhood 5. Autobiographies and memoirs

LC 2019031040

The popular family lifestyle guru traces her journey from an immigrant high-school student and single mother to a social-media influencer and grateful recipient of support by Oprah Winfrey, sharing heartfelt advice for today's overworked moms on how to achieve self-acceptance.

"Her candor is refreshing, a necessary voice amid the noise many parents face. Kuzmic writes with heart, and her authenticity will resonate with readers as they tag along on her journey." Booklist

Kyle, Taya, 1974-

Kyle, Taya, 1974- **American** wife : love, war, faith, and renewal / Taya Kyle, ; with Jim DeFelice. William Morrow, 2015 240 p. **B**

ISBN 9780062398086

1. Kyle, Chris, 1974-2013 2. Widows 3. Military spouses 4. Husband and wife 5. Bereavement 6. Autobiographies and memoirs

LC 2016304090

The widow of late SEAL sniper Chris Kyle describes their shared military service, her husband's murder at the height of his fame and the author's struggles to persevere and raise their children as a single parent.

Kym, Min

Kym, Min **Gone** : a girl, a violin, a life unstrung / Min Kym. Crown, 2017. 240 p. **B**

ISBN 9780451496072

1. Violinists 2. Loss (Psychology) 3. Stealing 4. Music 5. Autobiographies and memoirs

LC 2016054104

The child prodigy-turned-violin virtuoso describes how her career was upended by the 2010 theft of her beloved 1696 Stradivarius, revealing how the instrument represented her senses of self and music and how its displacement triggered revelations about art, passion and what it means to do what one loves.

"A pellucid memoir of letting go and coming to terms." Kirkus.

La Tour du Pin Gouvernet, Henriette Lucie Dillon, marquise de, 1770-1853

Moorehead, Caroline **Dancing** to the precipice : the life of Lucie de la Tour du Pin, eyewitness to an era / Caroline Moorehead. HarperCollins, 2009. 544 p. **B**

ISBN 9780061684418

1. La Tour du Pin Gouvernet, Henriette Lucie Dillon, marquise de, 1770-1853. 2. Nobility -- France 3. Aristocracy -- France 4. Monarchy, French -- History -- 18th century 5. France -- Social life and customs -- 1789-1815. 6. France -- History -- Reign of Terror, 1793-1794 7. United States -- Social life and customs -- 1783-1865. 8. Biographies

LC bl2009012224

Originally published: London : Chatto & Windus, 2009.

Shares the story of a turn-of-the-nineteenth-century social chronicler, from her early years among the French and British nobility to her first-hand witness to such events as the demise of the French monarchy and the Reign of Terror.

"In 1820, at the age of forty-nine, Lucie Dillon, the Marquise de la Tour du Pin, started writing her memoirs, an endeavor that went on for thirty years and produced one of the great monuments of French history. Lucie began life as an aristocrat, dbuting at Versailles at the age of eleven; at the beginning of the Terror, as friends and relatives fell to the guillotine, she fled France with her husband and children. Resilient and resourceful, the family thrived on a farm in upstate New York, where Lucie churned butter, traded with Indians, and played hostess to Talleyrand. A return to France brought Lucie and her husband into Napoleon's inner circle; in later years, following an exile in London, they found favor with the restored Bourbon monarchy. Moorehead's biography, drawing on a trove of previously unpublished correspondence, captures the rhythm of the radical contrasts in her subject's life." The New Yorker.

LaMarche, Una

LaMarche, Una **Unabrow** : misadventures of a late bloomer / Una LaMarche. Plume, 2015. 272 p. **B**

ISBN 9780142181447

1. LaMarche, Una. 2. Young women. 3. Personal conduct. 4. Growing up 5. Self-discovery. 6. Autobiographies and memoirs 7. Coming-of-age stories 8. Essays

LC 2014021212

The book June Cleaver would have written if she spent more time drinking and less time vacuuming. As a girl, Una LaMarche was as smart as she was awkward. She was blessed with a precocious intellect, a love of all things pop culture, and eyebrows bushier than Frida Kahlo's. Adversity made her stronger...and funnier. In UNABROW, Una shares the cringe-inducing lessons she's learned from a life as a late bloomer, including the seven deadly sins of DIY bangs, how not to make your own jorts, and how to handle pregnancy, plucking, and the rites of passage during which your own body is your worst frenemy.

"LaMarche is entertaining and fresh; readers will want to savor this sassy, offbeat commentary." Publishers Weekly.

Lacks, Henrietta, 1920-1951

★Skloot, Rebecca, 1972- The **immortal** life of Henrietta Lacks / Rebecca Skloot. Crown Publishers, 2009. x, 369 p., 8 p. of plates : **B**

ISBN 9781400052172

1. Lacks, Henrietta, 1920-1951 Health. 2. People with cancer 3. Cell culture. 4. Medical ethics. 5. Scientific discoveries. 6. Biographies

LC 2009031785

ALA Notable Book, 2011.

National Academies Communication Award, 2011.

Documents the story of how scientists took cells from an unsuspecting descendant of freed slaves and created a human cell line that has been kept alive indefinitely, enabling discoveries in such areas as cancer research, in vitro fertilization and gene mapping.

Lafayette, Marie Joseph Paul Yves Roch Gilbert Du Motier, marquis de, 1757-1834

Auricchio, Laura The **Marquis** : Lafayette reconsidered / Laura Auricchio. Alfred A. Knopf, Inc., 2014. 400 p. **B**

ISBN 9780307267559

1. Generals -- United States 2. Politicians -- France 3. Strategic alliances (Military) 4. Generals -- France 5. United States -- History -- Revolution, 1775-1783 -- French participation 6. France -- History -- 1789-1815 7. Biographies

LC 2013046386

Describes the rise and fall of the Marquis de Lafayette, the French hero who aided the colonists during the American Revolution, but who lost everything during the French Revolution due to his views that the monarchy needed to be reformed, not abolished.

"A first-rate work that should appeal to history readers of all kinds." Library Journal.

Vowell, Sarah, 1969- **Lafayette** in the somewhat United States / Sarah Vowell. Riverhead Books, 2015. 288 p. **B**

ISBN 9781594631740

1. Diplomats 2. Generals -- France 3. Revolutions -- United States 4. French in America 5. United States -- History -- Revolution, 1775-1783 -- French participation 6. Biographies

LC 2015024639

A portrait of the French hero of the American Revolution, the Marquis de Lafayette, discusses his nonpartisan influence on a fledgling United States, his relationships with the Founding Fathers, and his contributions during the contentious 1824 presidential election.

"In this crash course on the fledgling nation's teenaged French general, undoubtedly the only American Revolution narrative to offhandedly drop a Ferris Bueller reference, Vowell . retains her familiar casual tone and displays her crow-like ability to find the shiny, nearly forgotten historical details." Publishers Weekly.

Lahidji, Changiz, 1950-

Lahidji, Changiz, 1950- **Full** battle rattle : my story as the longest-serving special forces A-Team soldier in American history / Changiz Lahidji and Ralph Pezzullo. St. Martin's Press, 2018. 352 p. **B**

ISBN 9781250121158

1. Special forces 2. Iranian Americans 3. Special operations (Military science) 4. Persian Gulf War, 1991 5. Autobiographies and memoirs

LC 2017037543

The Special Forces veteran and first Muslim Green Beret shares the stories of his contributions to history-shaping operations, including the Iran hostage rescue of 1980, the 1993 conflict that inspired "Black Hawk Down," and the locating of Osama Bin Laden.

Lahiri, Jhumpa

Lahiri, Jhumpa **In** other words / Jhumpa Lahiri ; translated from the Italian by Ann Goldstein. Alfred A. Knopf, 2016, c2015. 240 p. **B**

ISBN 9781101875551

1. Lahiri, Jhumpa Travel. 2. Italian language. 3. Language and culture. 4. Language and languages. 5. Voyages and travels 6. Italy -- Description and travel. 7. Autobiographies and memoirs 8. Bilingual materials English/Italian

LC 2015020998

Translated from the Italian of: In altre parole.

Originally published: Parma : Guanda, 2015.

The author traces her enduring love affair with the Italian language that prompted her family's move to Rome, where her efforts to master the language as a writer shaped her feelings of belonging and exile.

"Lahiri's unexpected metamorphosis provides a captivating and insightful lesson in the power of language to transform." Publishers Weekly.

Lahti, Christine

Lahti, Christine **True** stories from an unreliable eyewitness : a feminist coming of age / Christine Lahti. HarperCollins, 2018 224 p. **B**

ISBN 9780062663672

1. Actors and actresses 2. Growing up 3. Aging 4. Acting 5. Hollywood, California 6. Autobiographies and memoirs

LC bl2018003905

A collection of interrelated personal stories by the actress best known for her work on such productions as "Chicago Hope" and "The Blacklist" focuses on the milestones of her childhood, early career, and midlife while reflecting on the realities of being a woman in Hollywood.

"Her style is irreverent, bawdy, and laugh-out-loud funny, but she doesnt shirk from painful subjects, including family mental illness. Lahti is one of those rare celebrities who not only has a fascinating life but who can also tell a relatable story with humility and humor." Booklist.

Laing, Olivia

★Laing, Olivia The **lonely** city : adventures in the art of being alone / Olivia Laing. Picador, 2016. 352 p. **B**

ISBN 9781250039576

1. Laing, Olivia. 2. Loneliness. 3. Artists -- Psychology. 4. City life -- Psychological aspects. 5. Loners. 6. Autobiographies and memoirs.

LC 2015037147

What does it mean to be lonely? How do we live, if we're not intimately involved with another human being? How do we connect with other people, particularly if our sexuality or physical body is considered deviant or damaged? Does technology draw us closer together or trap us behind screens? Olivia Laing explores these questions by travelling deep into the work and lives of some of the century's most original artists, among them Andy Warhol, David Wojnarowicz, Edward Hopper, Henry Darger and Klaus Nomi. Part memoir, part biography, part dazzling work of cultural criticism, The Lonely City is not just a map, but a celebration of the state of loneliness.

"Laing's writing becomes expansive, exploring their biographies, sharing art analysis, and weaving in observations from periods of desolation that was at times 'cold as ice and clear as glass.' " Publishers Weekly.

Lake, Dianne

Lake, Dianne **Member** of the family : my story of Charles Manson, life inside his cult, and the darkness that ended the Sixties / Dianne Lake, and Deborah Herman. William Morrow, 2017. 336 p. **B**

ISBN 9780062695574

1. Manson, Charles, 1934-2017 2. Cults 3. Child abuse victims 4. Growing up 5. Brainwashing 6. Autobiographies and memoirs

LC 2017277072

An inside account by the youngest member of Charles Manson's cult describes her involuntary indoctrination by her parents at age 14 and the manipulation, psychological control and physical abuse that she endured before she was rescued and adopted by the police officer who arrested her.

Lakshmi, Padma

Lakshmi, Padma **Love,** loss, and what we ate / Padma Lakshmi. Ecco Press, 2016 325 p. ; **B**

ISBN 9780062202611

1. Cooks 2. Immigrants 3. Television personalities 4. Immigrant families 5. Autobiographies and memoirs

The host of the Emmy Award-winning Top Chef presents a memoir about her immigrant childhood and complicated life in front of the camera, tracing her formative experiences in her grandmother's South India kitchen and her relationships with people who influenced her culinary skills and career.

Lalami, Laila, 1968-

Lalami, Laila, 1968- **Conditional** citizens : on belonging in America / Laila Lalami. Pantheon Books, 2020. 208 p. **B**

ISBN 9781524747169

1. Citizenship 2. Discrimination 3. Naturalization 4. Immigrants, Arab 5. United States -- Immigration and emigration 6. United States -- History -- 21st century 7. Autobiographies and memoirs

LC 2019037549

A Pulitzer Prize finalist recounts her unlikely journey from Moroccan immigrant to U.S. citizen, using it as a starting point for her exploration of the rights, liberties and protections that are traditionally associated with American citizenship.

"In this eloquent and troubling account, novelist and National Book Award-finalist Lalami (The Other Americans) draws on her personal history as 'an immigrant, a woman, an Arab, and a Muslim' to argue that becoming a U.S. citizen does not necessarily mean becoming 'an equal member of the American family' . . . . This profound inquiry into the American immigrant experience deserves to be widely read." Publishers Weekly

Lamar, Kendrick, 1987-

Moore, Marcus J. The **butterfly** effect : how Kendrick Lamar ignited the soul of Black America / Marcus J. Moore. Atria Books, 2020 278 p. **B**

ISBN 9781982107581

1. Rap musicians 2. African American men 3. Fame 4. Influence (Literary, artistic, etc.) 5. United States 6. Biographies

A cultural portrait of the 13-time Grammy Award- and Pulitzer Prize-winning rap superstar documents his coming-of-age as an artist, his genius as a lyricist and his profound impact on today's racially fraught America.

"Fans will likely devour this title despite its problems, and the work has crossover appeal to young adult readers, who will be stirred by Lamar's professional and personal journey." Library Journal

Lamarr, Hedy, 1913-2000

Rhodes, Richard, 1937- **Hedy's** folly : the life and breakthrough inventions of Hedy Lamarr, the most beautiful woman in the world / Richard Rhodes. Doubleday, c2011. 336 p. **B**

ISBN 9780385534383

1. Lamarr, Hedy, 1913-2000. 2. Actors and actresses. 3. Film actors

and actresses. 4. Spread spectrum communications. 5. Inventors.

LC 2011021746

Describes the lesser-known technological talents of actress Hedy Lamarr and the collaborative work with avant-garde composer George Antheil that eventually led to the development of spread-spectrum radio, cell phones, and GPS systems.

"Here's a recipe that might surprise you: take a silver-screen sex goddess (Hedy Lamarr), an avant-garde composer (George Antheil), a Hollywood friendship, and mutual technological curiosity, and mix well. What results is a patent for spread-spectrum radio, which has impacted the development of everything from torpedoes to cell phones and GPS technologies. This surprising and long-forgotten story is brought to life . [by Rhodes,] who deftly moves between Nazi secrets, scandalous films, engineering breakthroughs, and musical flops to weave a taut story that straddles two very different worlds the entertainment industry and wartime weaponry and yet somehow manages to remain a delectable read." Library Journal.

Shearer, Stephen Michael, 1951- **Beautiful** : the life of Hedy Lamarr / Stephen Michael Shearer. Thomas Dunne Books, 2010. 432 p. **B**

ISBN 9780312550981

1. Spread spectrum communications 2. Film actors and actresses 3. Women inventors 4. Biographies

LC 2010013058

"This biography chronicles the life of Hollywood legend Hedy Lamarr, from her cosseted childhood in an assimilated Jewish family in Austria to her early breaks in Max Reinhardt's internationally famous theater company; her scandalous, career-launching nude scene in the Czech film Ecstasy; her tortured first marriage to Jewish Nazi arms manufacturer Friedrich Mandl (dubbed an honorary Aryan by the Third Reich); and her daring escape from the sadistic Mandl and Nazi Germany to Los Angeles and MGM. One finishes the book feeling that one has read a complete portrait of Hedy Lamarr, actor and inventor, a biography that reveals, with drama and wit, how much more there was to this complex, brilliant woman than her ethereal natural beauty." Booklist.

Lamott, Anne

Lamott, Anne **Almost** everything : notes on hope / Anne Lamott. Riverhead Books, 2018. 192 p. **B**

ISBN 9780525537441

1. Spirituality. 2. Hope -- Religious aspects. 3. Life -- Religious aspects. 4. Anxiety 5. Autobiographies and memoirs

LC 2018013899

Presents an inspirational guide to the role of hope in everyday life and explores essential truths about how to overcome burnout and suffering by deliberately choosing joy.

Lamott, Anne **Small** victories : spotting improbable moments of grace / Anne Lamott. Riverhead Books, a member of Penguin Group (USA), 2014. 256 p. **B**

ISBN 9781594486296

1. Lamott, Anne. 2. Christian life 3. Hope. 4. Joy -- Religious aspects -- Christianity. 5. Grace (Christian theology) 6. Essays 7. Autobiographies and memoirs

LC 2014026967

Anne Lamott writes about community, family and faith in essays that are wise, irreverent, funny and poignant - a style that has become her trademark. Now in Small Victories, Lamott has once again written a brilliant and insightful book that offers a message of hope that celebrates the triumph of light over the darkness in our lives. Our victories over hardships and pain may be small, they may be infrequent, but they keep us going and they often come from the most unexpected places: within ourselves. Lamott shows how we can forgive thoughtless family members; spotlights the value of turning toward love even in the most hopeless situations (the death of a loved one, a cancer diagnosis), and shows how to find the joy in getting lost in traffic while racing to the aid of a sick friend.

"Lamott confronts each situation with humor and rectitude and shows readers how she found something redeeming in each one. Sage advice on finding beauty and happiness in life despite bad circumstances." Kirkus.

Lancaster, Burt, 1913-1994

Buford, Kate **Burt** Lancaster : an American life / Kate Buford. Knopf, 2000. ix, 447 p. : **B**

ISBN 9780679446033

1. Lancaster, Burt, 1913-1994. 2. United States. Congress. House. Committee on Un-American Activities 3. Film actors and actresses -- United States 4. Men/women relations. 5. Biographies

LC 99037351

"Lancaster's decades-long political involvement with liberal causes (and his constant run-ins with the House Un-American Activities Committee in the 1950s) are a central theme in this well-researched and engaging biography, which also details the artist's acting career, his turns as a producer and his personal life." Publishers Weekly.

Lance, Rachel

Lance, Rachel **In** the waves : my quest to solve the mystery of a Civil War submarine / Rachel Lance. Dutton, 2020. 400 p. **B**

ISBN 9781524744151

1. H.L. Hunley (Submarine). 2. Submarines, American -- History 3. Submarines -- United States -- History -- 19th century. 4. Underwater archaeology -- Charleston, South Carolina. 5. Shipwrecks -- United States -- History -- 19th century. 6. United States -- History -- Civil War, 1861-1865 -- Naval operations 7. Charleston, South Carolina -- Antiquities. 8. Autobiographies and memoirs

LC 2019021230

An inventive woman scientist recounts the 1864 sinking of the Confederate submarine, H.L. Hunley, recounting her efforts to uncover what actually happened when the sub was discovered 131 years later with its hull and victims still intact.

"Lance delivers a lively, if often technical, description of the many experiments, models, calculations, and explosions that persuaded her and her doctoral committee that this is what happened to the Hunley. An entertaining account of research that solved a historical mystery." Kirkus

Lancon, Philippe

Lancon, Philippe **Disturbance** : surviving Charlie Hebdo / Philippe Lancon ; translated from the French by Steven Rendall. Europa Editions, 2019, c2018. 448 p. **B**

ISBN 9781609455569

1. Victims of terrorism 2. Journalists -- France 3. Wounds and injuries 4. Life change events 5. France 6. Paris, France

Translation of: Le lambeauOriginally published: Paris : Gallimard, 2018

A survivor of the Charlie Hebdo terrorist attack in January 2015 describes key events while discussing how the attack, his long-term recovery and the writings of classic authors reshaped his relationship with journalism and the world.

Land, Stephanie

★Land, Stephanie **Maid** : hard work, low pay, and a

mother's will to survive / Stephanie Land ; foreword by Barbara Ehrenreich. Hachette Books, 2019. 288 p. **B**

ISBN 9780316505116

1. Household employees 2. Working poor people 3. Poverty 4. Working class 5. United States -- Social conditions 6. Autobiographies and memoirs

LC 2018954908

An economic hardship journalist describes the years she worked in low-pay domestic work under wealthy employers, contrasting the privileges of the upper-middle class to the realities of the overworked laborers supporting them.

"Writer Land's vivid and visceral yet nearly unrelenting memoir covers three dark years in the life of a single mother raising her young daughter, Mia, on the unlivable wages that come with the physically and emotionally grueling work of contract housekeeping." Library Journal.

Landrieu, Mitch

Landrieu, Mitch **In** the shadow of statues : a white Southerner confronts history / Mitch Landrieu. Viking Press, 2018. 224 p. **B**

ISBN 9780525559443

1. Racism 2. Race relations 3. Social change 4. Inequality 5. New Orleans, Louisiana 6. Southern States 7. Autobiographies and memoirs

LC 2018006748

The New Orleans mayor who removed Confederate statues from the city confronts the racism that shapes many Americans and argues for white America to reckon with its past.

Landry, Tom

Ribowsky, Mark The **last** cowboy : a life of Tom Landry / Mark Ribowsky. Liveright Pub. Corp., c2013. 720 p. **B**

ISBN 9780871403339

1. Dallas Cowboys (Football team) 2. National Football League. 3. Professional football. 4. Professional football coaches. 5. Christian men. 6. Biographies

LC 2013034731

A biography of the legendary professional football coach and strategist. After playing with the AAFC Yankees and NFL Giants, then as defensive coach of the Giants, Landry spent thirty years as head coach of the Dallas Cowboys, including twenty consecutive winning seasons. Discusses his relations to players, including those not sharing his temperament and background.

Lang, Maya

Lang, Maya **What** we carry : a memoir / Maya Shanbhag Lang. The Dial Press, 2020 288 p. **B**

ISBN 9780525512394

1. East Indian American women 2. Mothers and daughters 3. People with Alzheimer's disease 4. Postpartum depression 5. Autobiographies and memoirs

LC 2019018845

The author of The Sixteenth of June offers a memoir about immigrants and their native-born children, the complicated love between mothers and daughters, and the surprising discovery of strength.

"Readers interested in examining their own family stories, or those who experienced the struggles of new parenthood or reversed parenting roles, will connect deeply with Lang's beautiful memoir." Library Journal

Lang, Michael

Lang, Michael The **road** to Woodstock / Michael Lang. Ecco, 2009. 304 p. **B**

ISBN 9780061576553

1. Sound recording executives and producers 2. Woodstock Festival, 1969 3. Peace movements -- United States -- History 4. Counterculture. 5. United States -- History -- 20th century 6. Autobiographies and memoirs

LC 2011477461

A fortieth anniversary tribute to the first Woodstock event, written by its co-creator, describes the events of the historical three-day performance, in an account that features rare photographs and recollections by such artists as the Grateful Dead, Crosby Stills & Nash, and The Who.

Lange, Dorothea, 1895-1965

Gordon, Linda **Dorothea** Lange : a life beyond limits / Linda Gordon. W.W. Norton, 2009. 560 p. **B**

ISBN 9780393057300

1. Lange, Dorothea, 1895-1965. 2. Photographers -- United States 3. Documentary photography -- United States -- History -- 20th century. 4. Photography. 5. Photographs. 6. United States -- Social life and customs -- 20th century Pictorial works. 7. Biographies

LC 2009019639

WILLA Literary Awards: Scholarly Nonfiction, 2010.

Charts the iconic photographer's life from her struggles with polio and family experiences to her early career in San Francisco and rise to a chronicler of the Great Depression and World War II, exploring her growing radicalization while showcasing rare and previously suppressed images.

"Gordon's elegant biography is testament to Lange's gift for challenging her country to open its eyes." New York Times Book Review.

Lanier, Heather Kirn

Lanier, Heather Kirn **Raising** a rare girl : a memoir / Heather Lanier. Penguin Press, 2020. 336 p. **B**

ISBN 9780525559634

1. Lanier, Fiona, 2011- 2. Mothers of children with disabilities 3. Wolf-Hirschhorn syndrome -- Patients 4. Genetic disorders in children 5. Human chromosome abnormalities. 6. United States 7. Autobiographies and memoirs

LC 2019042870

The award-winning author describes her unique journey raising a daughter with ultra-rare Wolf-Hirschhorn syndrome, her observations about society's callous attitudes toward disability and her efforts to help her child walk, talk and survive.

"A poet and creative nonfiction professor grapples with motherhood and the meaning of life in this memoir of raising her developmentally challenged daughter. . . . A book of pluck, spirit, and great emotion with an appealing perspective on the value of each human life." Kirkus

Lansdale, Edward Geary, 1908-1987

★Boot, Max, 1968- The **road** not taken : Edward Lansdale and the American tragedy in Vietnam / Max Boot. Liveright Publishing Corporation, 2018 784 p. **B**

ISBN 9780871409416

1. Vietnam War, 1961-1975 2. Intelligence officers 3. Generals 4. Military intelligence 5. Biographies

LC bl2017046061

Pulitzer Prize for Biography or Autobiography finalist, 2019.

In chronicling the adventurous life of legendary CIA operative Edward Lansdale, the author aims to reframe readers' understanding of the Vietnam War.

"A probing, timely study of wrong turns in the American conduct of the Vietnam War." Kirkus.

Lanzmann, Claude

Lanzmann, Claude The **Patagonian** hare : a memoir / Claude Lanzmann ; translated from the French by Frank Wynne. Farrar, Straus and Giroux, 2012. 496 p. **B**

ISBN 9780374230043

1. Lanzmann, Claude. 2. Film producers and directors 3. Journalists -- France 4. Memories. 5. Autobiographies and memoirs

LC 2011048058

The author traces his life in film and journalism, describing his early experiences as an underground soldier in occupied Paris, his affair with Simone de Beauvoir, and the making of his seminal documentary Shoah.

Laplante, Edgar, 1888-

Willetts, Paul **King** con : the bizarre adventures of the Jazz Age's greatest impostor / Paul Willetts. Random House Inc 2018 304 p. **B**

ISBN 9780451495815

1. Fraud 2. Vaudeville performers 3. Swindlers and swindling 4. False personation 5. Biographies

LC 2018014380

A portrait of charismatic vaudeville performer and 1920s con artist Edgar LaPlante describes how he amassed millions through a fraudulent charity, his seduction of a wealthy Austrian countess and his friendships with celebrities and powerful world leaders.

"With the rise of identity theft, celebrity worship, and manipulative s o cial media, this sprightly story of a legendary con artist's outrageous successes becomes a cautionary tale for the digital age." Kirkus.

Larsen, Bob

Futterman, Matthew **Running** to the edge : a band of misfits and the guru who unlocked the secrets of speed / Matthew Futterman. Doubleday, 2019. 288 p. **B**

ISBN 9780385543743

1. Track and field coaches 2. Running -- Training 3. Speed 4. Physical fitness 5. Biographies

LC 2018049020

In the dusty hills above San Diego, Bob Larsen became America's greatest running coach. Starting with a ragtag group of high school cross country and track runners, Larsen set out on a decades-long quest to find the secret of running impossibly fast, for longer distances than anyone thought possible. Running to the Edge is a riveting account of Larsen's journey, and his quest to discover the unorthodox training secrets that would lead American runners (elite and recreational) to breakthroughs never imagined.

"A fascinating look at the history of U.S. distance running with plenty of grit, innovative approaches, near disasters, and fun." Library Journal.

Larsen, Nella

Hutchinson, George, 1953- **In** search of Nella Larsen : a biography of the color line / George Hutchinson. Belknap Press of Harvard University Press, 2006. x, 611 p. : **B**

ISBN 9780674021808

1. Larsen, Nella. 2. Authors, American -- 20th century 3. Women authors -- 20th century 4. Danish American women 5. West Indian Americans 6. Harlem, New York City -- History -- 20th century. 7. Biographies

LC 2005058129

Born to a Danish seamstress and a West Indian cook, Larsen lived her life in the shadows of America's racial divide. Hutchinson exposes the truths and half-truths surrounding her, and the complex reality they mask and mirror. His book is a cultural biography of the color line as lived by a person who embodied all its ambiguities and complexities.

Laughlin, James, 1914-1997

Laughlin, James, 1914-1997 The **luck** of friendship : the letters of Tennessee Williams and James Laughlin / James Laughlin and Tennessee Williams, edited by Peggy Fox and Thomas Keith. W. W. Norton & Company, 2018. 352 p. **B**

ISBN 9780393246209

1. Williams, Tennessee, 1911-1983 2. Male friendship 3. Authors 4. Publishers and publishing 5. Interpersonal relations 6. Letters 7. Autobiographies and memoirs

The chronicle of Tennessee Williams and James Laughlin's unlikely yet enduring literary and personal relationship.

"The rivers of mutual affection, admiration, and artistry form a powerful confluence in these deeply affecting exchanges." Kirkus.

Lawrence, D. H. (David Herbert), 1885-1930

Worthen, John **D.H.** Lawrence : the early years, 1885-1912 / John Worthen. Cambridge University Press, c1991. xxx, 626 p. : The Cambridge biography--D.H. Lawrence, 1885-1930 **B**

ISBN 0521437725

1. Lawrence, D. H., 1885-1930 Childhood and youth. 2. Authors, English -- 20th century 3. Biographies

LC 90023423

Recounts the novelist's early years as a teacher in London, and reveals how his sexual experiences, which included an intense relationship with an older married woman, affected his literary career

"This first volume of Cambridge's three-volume life of Lawrence, . takes the young writer through his elopement with Frieda. This persuasive biography is compulsive good reading from cover to cover. A major event in modern literary studies." Library Journal.

Worthen, John **D.** H. Lawrence : the life of an outsider / John Worthen. Counterpoint, c2005. xxvi, 518 p. : **B**

ISBN 9781582433417

1. Lawrence, D. H. (David Herbert), 1885-1930. 2. Authors, English -- 20th century 3. Mothers and sons 4. Men/women relations. 5. Marriage. 6. Biographies

Originally published: London : Allen Lane, 2005.

A portrait of one of the twentieth century's most radical and misunderstood writers follows Lawrence from his awkward youth in Nottinghamshire, through his turbulent relationship with Frieda and the years of exile abroad, to his premature death at the age of 44.

"Using as a unifying theme Lawrence's perpetual status as an outsider, both in working-class Nottinghamshire and in the English literary world, Worthen gives us the full sweep of this groundbreaking writer's utterly unconventional, often torturous, and occasionally rhapsodic life." Booklist.

Lawrence, Ernest Orlando, 1901-1958

Hiltzik, Michael A. **Big** science : Ernest Lawrence, the cyclotron, and the birth of the military-industrial complex / Michael Hiltzik. Simon & Schuster, 2015 448 p. **B**

ISBN 9781451675757

1. Lawrence, Ernest Orlando, 1901-1958. 2. Cyclotrons. 3. Physicists -- United States 4. Military-industrial complex. 5. Biographies

LC 2014017463

The birth of Big Science can be traced to Berkeley, California, nearly nine decades ago, when a resourceful young scientist with a talent for physics and an even greater talent for promotion pondered his new invention and declared, "I'm going to be famous!" Ernest Orlando Lawrence's cyclotron would revolutionize nuclear physics, but that was only the beginning of its impact. It would change our understanding of the basic building blocks of nature. It would help win World War II. Its influence would be felt in academia and international politics. It was the beginning of Big Science.

Lawrence, T. E. (Thomas Edward), 1888-1935

Anderson, Scott, 1959- **Lawrence** in Arabia : war, deceit, imperial folly and the making of the modern Middle East / Scott Anderson. Doubleday, 2013. 577 p. **B**

ISBN 9780385532921

1. Lawrence, T. E. (Thomas Edward), 1888-1935. 2. Great Britain. Army 3. World War I 4. Soldiers -- Great Britain 5. Military campaigns 6. Middle East -- History -- 1914-1923. 7. Turkey

LC 2012049719

ALA Notable Book, 2014.

National Book Critics Circle Award for Biography finalist, 2013.

A narrative chronicle of World War I's Arab Revolt explores the pivotal roles of a small group of adventurers and low-level officers who orchestrated a secret effort to control the Middle East, demonstrating how they instigated jihad against British forces, built an elaborate intelligence ring and forged ties to gain valuable oil concessions.

★Brown, Malcolm, 1930- **T.E.** Lawrence / Malcolm Brown. New York University Press, 2003. 160 p. : **B**

ISBN 0814799205

1. Lawrence, T. E. (Thomas Edward), 1888-1935. 2. Orientalists -- Great Britain 3. Soldiers -- Great Britain 4. Command of troops 5. Great Britain -- History. 6. Middle East -- History. 7. Middle East -- History -- 20th century. 8. Biographies

LC 2003051387

A historical portrait of the soldier and leader most widely known as Lawrence of Arabia discusses his illegitimacy, relationships with contemporaries, adventurous nature, wartime experiences, deeply held faith, sexual ambiguity, and efforts for peace.

"The book is a major literary work." Publishers Weekly.

Lawrence, T. E. (Thomas Edward), 1888-1935 **Seven** pillars of wisdom : a triumph / T.E. Lawrence. Anchor Books, 1991. 784 p. **B**

ISBN 9780385418959

1. World War I 2. Military campaigns 3. Soldiers -- Great Britain 4. British in the Middle East 5. Arabian Peninsula -- Social life and customs 6. Autobiographies and memoirs

"Originally published in a private edition by the George Doran Publishing Company in 1926"--T.p. verso.

The classic account of the Arab tribes' guerrilla warfare against Turkish forces during World War I and of Lawrence's part in and reflections on that warfare.

Sattin, Anthony The **young** T. E. Lawrence / Anthony Sattin. W. W. Norton & Company, 2015, c2014. 352 p. **B**

ISBN 9780393242669

1. Soldiers -- Great Britain 2. Archaeologists -- Great Britain 3. World War I 4. Military campaigns 5. Arabian Peninsula. 6. Middle East. 7. Arab countries. 8. Biographies.

LC 2014032063

"First published in Great Britain in 2014 under the title "Young Lawrence : a portrait of the legend as a young man."

A biography focusing on T. E. Lawrence--better known as Lawrence of Arabia--in his 20s presents the untold story of the awkward archaeologist from Oxford who, upon first visiting "The East," fell in love with Arab culture and found his life's mission, and draws upon surviving letters, diaries and accounts from close confidantes to bring his extraordinary journeys to life.

"Recommended as an insightful, gracefully written, and sensitive account that explains how a shy, private young man developed into a widely known and revered 'hero' who was never comfortable with his fame." Library Journal.

Lawson, Jenny, 1979-

Lawson, Jenny, 1979- **Furiously** happy : a funny book about horrible things / Jenny Lawson. Flatiron Books, 2015. 352 p. **B**

ISBN 9781250077004

1. Women with depression 2. Self-acceptance 3. Anxiety. 4. Depression 5. Autobiographies and memoirs

LC 2015022196

"Lawson's goal is not to offend, although that might happen to some readers, but to lay bare the truth about her struggles in life so that others can benefit. She does a solid job exposing the hidden nature of mental illness by putting a direct spotlight on her own issues, thereby illuminating an often taboo subject. Her amusing essays open up a not-so-funny topic: mental illness in its many guises. Kudos to Lawson for being a flagrant and witty spokesperson for this dark subject matter." Kirkus.

Le Carre, John, 1931-

★Le Carre, John, 1931- The **pigeon** tunnel : stories from my life / John Le Carre. Viking, 2016. 400 p. **B**

ISBN 9780735220775

1. Spies in literature. 2. Authors, English. 3. Autobiographies and memoirs

LC 2016299972

The author of such best-selling suspense novels as A Delicate Truth shares personal anecdotes from his life, discussing subjects ranging from his Cold War-era service in British intelligence to his work as a writer in Russia before and after the collapse of the Berlin Wall.

"The author's self-deprecating humor and wit are never far away, and he proves a most elegant and genial host on this tour of his life and work." Publishers Weekly.

Le Guin, Ursula K., 1929-2018

Le Guin, Ursula K., 1929-2018 **Ursula** K. Le Guin : conversations on writing / Ursula K. Le Guin with David Naimon. Tin House Books, 2018. 150 p. **B**

ISBN 9781941040997

1. Le Guin, Ursula K., 1929-2018 Interviews 2. Le Guin, Ursula K., 1929-2018 Authorship 3. Women authors, American 4. Authors, American 5. Writing 6. Literature -- History and criticism. 7. United States -- Civilization 8. Interviews

LC 2018003429

Locus Award for Best Nonfiction/Related/Reference Book, 2019.

In a series of interviews with David Naimon, Le Guin discusses craft, aesthetics, and philosophy in her fiction, poetry, and nonfiction respectively. The discussions provide ample advice and guidance for writers of every level, but also give Le Guin a chance to sound off on some of her favorite subjects: the genre wars, the patriarchy, the natural world, and what, in her opinion, makes for great writing.

"Readers and writers who have enjoyed Le Guin in her many forms throughout the years will likely relish the intimate insights the novelist shares. That said, the interviews are freely available online for those interested in listening to Le Guin's words in her own voice." Library Journal.

Le Roux, Paul Calder

Ratliff, Evan The **mastermind** : drugs, empire, murder, betrayal / Evan Ratliff. Random House, [2019] xxxi, 446 p. **B**

ISBN 9780399590412

1. Criminals 2. Drug traffic 3. Computer crimes 4. Crime bosses 5. Biographies

LC 2018035751

It all started as an online prescription drug network, supplying hundreds of millions of dollars' worth of painkillers to American customers. It would not stop there. Before long, the business had turned into a sprawling multinational conglomerate engaged in almost every conceivable aspect of criminal mayhem. The man behind it all, pulling the strings from a laptop in Manila, was Paul Calder Le Roux?a reclusive programmer turned criminal genius who could only exist in the networked world of the twenty-first century, and the kind of self-made crime boss that American law enforcement had never imagined.

"Sifting through detail after nefarious detail, Ratliff serves up a taut narrative that limns a portrait of a sociopath whose powers were most definitely used to evil ends. A wholly engrossing story that joins the worlds of El Chapo and Edward Snowden; both disturbing and memorable." Kirkus.

Shannon, Elaine **Hunting** Leroux : the inside story of the DEA takedown of a criminal genius and his empire / Elaine Shannon. William Morrow, 2019 xiv, 354 p., [16] p. of plates : **B**

ISBN 9780062859136

1. Computer crimes 2. Organized crime -- Technological innovations. 3. Undercover operations 4. Criminals 5. Biographies

The story of Paul LeRoux, the twisted-genius entrepreneur and cold-blooded killer who brought revolutionary innovation to international crime, and the exclusive inside story of how the DEA's elite, secretive 960 Group brought him down

LeDuff, Charlie

LeDuff, Charlie **Detroit** : an American autopsy / Charlie LeDuff. Penguin Press, 2013. 272 p. **B**

ISBN 9781594205347

1. LeDuff, Charlie. 2. Journalists 3. Investigative journalism. 4. Local government. 5. Inner city. 6. Detroit, Michigan -- Social conditions. 7. Autobiographies and memoirs

LC 2012030924

The Pulitzer Prize-winning author presents an expose of bureaucratic corruption and systemic arson in his home city of Detroit, tracing his work with a local fire brigade and his investigations into the daily lives of politicians, police officials, businesspeople and homeowners who are working to save the troubled city.

LeFavour, Cree

LeFavour, Cree **Lights** on, rats out : a memoir / Cree LeFavour. Grove Press, 2017. 244 p. **B**

ISBN 9780802125965

1. Young women 2. Self-harm 3. Psychiatrists 4. Self-injurious behavior 5. Autobiographies and memoirs

LC 2016048377

A young college graduate one year into her increasingly obsessive treatment with a psychiatrist begins to organize her days around a compulsion to harm herself with lit cigarettes. By the James Beard Award-nominated author of Fish.

"A searing, brilliant memoir revealing the therapeutic process and its ability 'to turn our ghosts into ancestors.' " Booklist.

LeMond, Greg

De Vise, Daniel The **comeback** : Greg Lemond, the true king of American cycling, and a legendary Tour de France / Daniel de Visé. Atlantic Monthly Press, 2018. 432 p. **B**

ISBN 9780802127945

1. LeMond, Greg. 2. Tour de France (Bicycle race). 3. Bicycle racing 4. Bicyclists 5. Bicycling 6. Biographies

LC 2017061342

Traces the dramatic life story of the first American Tour de France winner, covering such topics as his complicated family life, the hunting accident that nearly ended his cycling career and his confrontation with Lance Armstrong over performance-drug allegations.

Leadbelly, 1885-1949

Wolfe, Charles K. The **life** and legend of Leadbelly / Charles Wolfe and Kip Lornell. Harper Collins Publishers, c1992. xv, 333 p. : **B**

ISBN 9780060168629

1. Blues musicians -- United States 2. Biographies

LC 92052606

A biography of the legendary folk and blues singer discusses his influences, his close relationships with folk greats Woody Guthrie and Pete Seeger, and his involvement in left-wing politics and the labor movement

"Drawing on a variety of primary and secondary sources, including numerous interviews, Wolfe and Lornell attempt to separate fact from fiction. Photographs, informative notes, and a full discography are valuable additions." Choice.

Leahy, William D.

O'Brien, Phillips Payson, 1963- The **second** most powerful man in the world : the life of Admiral William D. Leahy, Roosevelt's Chief of Staff / Phillips Payson O'Brien. E.P. Dutton, [2019] viii, 531 p. **B**

ISBN 9780399584800

1. United States. Office of Strategic Services 2. United States. Joint Chiefs of Staff 3. Presidents -- United States -- Staff 4. Admirals -- United States 5. White House chiefs of staff 6. Biographies

LC 2018016899

A portrait of the influential presidential advisor explores his less-recognized but pivotal role in shaping administrative and military decisions during World War II, revealing his evolving leadership throughout the critical transition to the Truman White House.

" A lucid, opinionated life of a man who exerted far greater influence than historians give him credit forand a book sure to invite spirited argument from historians who disagree." Kirkus.

Lear, Edward, 1812-1888

Peck, Robert McCracken, 1952- The **natural** history of Edward Lear (1812-1888) / Robert McCracken Peck ; with a foreword by David Attenborough. David R. Godine, Publisher, 2016. 223 p. : **B**

ISBN 1567925839

1. Lear, Edward, 1812-1888. 2. Artists -- Great Britain 3. Natural history illustration. 4. Natural history illustrators -- Great Britain 5. Poets, English -- 19th century 6. Biographies

LC 2016016171

Edward Lear, known as an author of nonsense verse, was also an artist and natural history illustrator.

Lear, Norman

Lear, Norman **Even** this I get to experience / Norman Lear. Penguin Books, 2014. 464 p. **B**

ISBN 9781594205729

1. Television programs 2. Television producers and directors. 3.

Television 4. Autobiographies and memoirs
LC 2014032903

The legendary creator of iconic television programs All in the Family, Sanford and Son, Maude, Good Times, The Jeffersons, and Mary Hartman, Mary Hartman, Norman Lear remade our television culture, while leading a life of unparalleled political, civic, and social involvement. Sharing the wealth of Lear's ninety years, Even This I Get to Experience is a memoir as touching and remarkable as the life he has led.

"A big-hearted, richly detailed chronicle of comedy, commitment and a long life lived fully." Kirkus.

Leary, Timothy, 1920-1996

Minutaglio, Bill The **most** dangerous man in America : Timothy Leary, Richard Nixon & the hunt for the fugitive king of LSD / Bill Minutaglio and Steven L. Davis. Twelve, 2018 400 p. **B**

ISBN 9781455563586

1. Leary, Timothy, 1920-1996. 2. Weather Underground Organization. 3. Fugitives. 4. Escapes. 5. Psychologists. 6. Radicalism. 7. United States -- Politics and government -- 1969-1974. 8. Biographies
LC 2017032575

Presents an account of Timothy Leary's 1970 prison escape and run from the law, detailing the events that led to his incarceration, his support by the terrorist group Weather Underground and his targeting by Richard Nixon.

"Minutaglio and Davis are superb storytellers, and throughout the narrative, they nimbly move between their two converging subjects. Their account is expertly detailed and blessedly fat-free." Kirkus.

Leavitt, Henrietta Swan, 1868-1921

Johnson, George, 1952 January 20- **Miss** Leavitt's stars : the untold story of the woman who discovered how to measure the universe / George Johnson. W.W. Norton, c2005. xiv, 162 p. : Great discoveries **B**

ISBN 9780393051285

1. Leavitt, Henrietta Swan, 1868-1921. 2. Astrometry -- History. 3. Women astronomers -- United States 4. Astronomical photometry. 5. Astronomy -- United States -- History -- 20th century. 6. United States -- Social life and customs -- 20th century 7. Biographies
LC 2005002823

Recounts the story of Radcliffe-educated Henrietta Swan Leavitt, who in the face of ill health and progressing hearing loss discovered a new law that enabled astronomers to use variable stars in order to measure the universe.

"This book is a fine tribute to a remarkable woman of science." Publishers Weekly.

Lecorgne, Constant, 1832-1886

Ball, Edward, 1958- **Life** of a Klansman : a family history in white supremacy / Edward Ball. Farrar Straus & Giroux, 2020 400 p. **B**

ISBN 9780374186326

1. Lecorgne, Constant, 1832-1886. 2. Lecorgne family. 3. White League (La.) 4. Ku-Klux Klan 5. Reconstruction (United States history) -- Louisiana -- New Orleans. 6. Racism -- Louisiana -- New Orleans -- History -- 19th century. 7. White supremacy movements -- Louisiana -- New Orleans -- History -- 19th century. 8. Creoles (Louisiana) -- History -- 19th century. 9. New Orleans, Louisiana -- Race relations 10. Autobiographies and memoirs
LC 2020003403

Presents a trenchant exploration of a family's legacy of white supremacy, detailing how Louisiana carpenter Constant Lecorgne joined the KKK to promote fanatical racism in post-Civil War America.

"The result is a clear-eyed work of historical reclamation and an intimate, self-lacerating take on memory and collective responsibility." Publishers Weekly

Ledyard, John, 1751-1789

Gifford, Bill **Ledyard** : in search of the first American explorer / Bill Gifford. Harcourt, c2007. 331 p. **B**

ISBN 0151012180

1. Ledyard, John, 1751-1789. 2. Explorers -- United States 3. United States -- Social life and customs -- 18th century. 4. Biographies 5. Biographies

"This book makes an important contribution to the existing literature through its personal approach to Ledyard's life. Few of Ledyard's letters and journals remain . . . but, by using most of what's available and tracking down details through his own travels, the author paints a fascinating portrait of the man he calls the archetype of the restless American wanderer." New York Times Book Review.

Lee, Bruce, 1940-1973

★Polly, Matthew **Bruce** Lee : a life / Matthew Polly. Simon & Schuster, 2018 672 p. **B**

ISBN 9781501187629

1. Lee, Bruce, 1940-1973. 2. Martial artists. 3. Actors and actresses. 4. Martial arts. 5. Films. 6. Biographies
LC 2018013592

Featuring rarely seen photos, a first authoritative biography of the martial arts film legend traces his early years in Hong Kong cinema, his work as a celebrity trainer and his stereotype-breaking achievements.

"A fascinating story of a remarkable figure in popular culture, this is the biography Bruce Lees legion of fans have been waiting for." Booklist.

Lee, Frances Glessner, 1878-1962

★Goldfarb, Bruce **18** tiny deaths : the untold story of Frances Glessner Lee and the invention of modern forensics / Bruce Goldfarb. Sourcebooks, 2020 336 p. **B**

ISBN 9781492680475

1. Lee, Frances Glessner, 1878-1962. 2. Women forensic scientists 3. Forensic scientists -- United States 4. Forensic sciences -- History 5. Crime scenes 6. United States 7. Biographies
LC 2019031080

An account of the life of the woman best known for creating the Nutshell Studies of Unexplained Death dioramas describes her transition from a wealthy socialite to a leader in modern forensics whose methods are still used today.

"A stand-out addition to any library's true-crime collection." Booklist

Lee, Gypsy Rose, 1914-1970

Abbott, Karen, 1973- **American** rose : a nation laid bare : the life and times of Gypsy Rose Lee / Karen Abbott. Random House, 2010. 320 p. **B**

ISBN 9781400066919

1. Lee, Gypsy Rose, 1914-1970. 2. Stripteasers -- United States 3. Authors, American -- 20th century 4. Burlesque. 5. Biographies
LC 2010015081

"Imaginative and engaging, Abbott's biography of the celebrated stripper, who died in 1970 at age 59, also proves a well-informed look at the evolution of musical theater in the early 20th century." Publishers Weekly.

Lee, Harper

Crespino, Joseph **Atticus** Finch: the biography : Harper Lee, her father, and the making of an American icon / Joseph Crespino. Basic Books, 2018. 288 p. **B**

ISBN 9781541644946

1. Lee, Harper. To kill a mockingbird. 2. Lee, Harper. Go set a watchman. 3. Finch, Atticus (Fictitious character). 4. Authors, American -- 20th century. 5. Women authors. 6. Biographies

LC 2017056457

"Who was the real Atticus Finch? The publication of Go Set a Watchman in 2015 forever changed how we think about Atticus Finch. Once seen as a paragon of decency, he was reduced to a small-town racist. How are we to understand this transformation? In Atticus Finch, historian Joseph Crespino draws on exclusive sources to reveal how Harper Lee's father provided the central inspiration for each of her books.

Lee, Helie, 1964-

Lee, Helie, 1964- **In** the absence of sun : a Korean American woman's promise to reunite three lost generations of her family / Helie Lee. Harmony Books, c2002. 342 p., [8] p. of plates : **B**

ISBN 0609609343

1. Lee family 2. Yi family. 3. Baek, Hongyong, 1912- Family. 4. Korean Americans 5. Families 6. California Genealogy. 7. North Korea Genealogy.

LC 2002001680

"Lee's Still Life with Rice (1996) was a novelized account of her grandmother's life and escape from what would become North Korea. As she now recounts her and her father's struggles to get other people out of the North, she continues to wrestle with her own Korean heritage-in particular, the paternalistic and patronizing attitudes toward women." Booklist.

Lee, Hyeonseo

Lee, Hyeonseo The **girl** with seven names : a North Korean defector's story / Hyeonseo Lee, with David John. HarperCollins, 2015 320 p. **B**

ISBN 9780007554836

1. Political refugees -- North Korea 2. Defectors. 3. North Korea 4. Autobiographies and memoirs

LC bl2015035054

An extraordinary insight into life under one of the world's most ruthless and secretive dictatorships ? and the story of one woman's terrifying struggle to avoid capture/repatriation and guide her family to freedom.

"Remarkable bravery fluently recounted." Kirkus.

Lee, Li-Young, 1957-

Lee, Li-Young, 1957- The **winged** seed : a remembrance / Lee Li-Young. Simon & Schuster, 1995. 205 p. **B**

ISBN 0671707086

1. Poets, American -- 20th century 2. Chinese Americans 3. Refugees, Chinese 4. Growing up. 5. Autobiographies and memoirs

LC 94037072

"In this fourth collection by [the author], timely immigration issues drive such poems as Self-Help for Fellow Refugees, but Lee swiftly folds them into broader inquiries about inheritance, memory and loss. Lee's ringing clarity and his compelling life story have brought him uncommonly loyal readers: this volume should swell their ranks. A CD of Lee reading many of the poems is included." Publishers Weekly.

Lee, Richard Henry, 1732-1794

Unger, Harlow G., 1931- **First** founding father : Richard Henry Lee and the call to independence / Harlow Giles Unger. Da Capo Press, 2017. 320 p. **B**

ISBN 9780306825613

1. Lee, Richard Henry, 1732-1794. 2. United States. Declaration of Independence Signers 3. Politicians 4. Founding fathers of the United States. 5. Revolutions -- United States 6. American Revolution, 1775-1783 7. United States -- History -- Revolution, 1775-1783 8. Biographies

LC 2017040744

Before Washington, before Jefferson, before Franklin or John Adams, there was Lee--Richard Henry Lee, the First Founding Father. Richard Henry Lee was the first to call for independence, and the first to call for union. He was "father of our country" as much as George Washington, securing the necessary political and diplomatic victories in the Revolutionary War. Lee played a critical role in holding the colonial government together, declaring the nation's independence, and ensuring victory for the Continental Army by securing the first shipments of French arms to American troops. Next to Washington, Lee was arguably the most important American leader in the war against the British.

"Unger's thorough research, smooth narrative, and placement of Lee in the context of 18th-century America will inform both general readers and historians." Choice.

Lee, Robert E. (Robert Edward), 1807-1870

★Blount, Roy **Robert** E. Lee / Roy Blount, Jr. Lipper/Viking, 2003. 210 p. **B**

ISBN 0670032204

1. Confederate States of America. Army 2. Generals -- Confederate States of America 3. Command of troops. 4. Confederate soldiers 5. Leadership in men. 6. United States -- History -- Civil War, 1861-1865 -- Campaigns 7. Biographies

LC 2002032423

A portrait of the Civil War leader delves into his family history and personality to reveal the human behind the general, documenting how the lessons he learned from his elders were applied on the battlefield.

"Blount's concise writing keeps his biography trim and succinct, and his admiration for the subject allows for enjoyable reading." Booklist.

Fellman, Michael The **making** of Robert E. Lee / Michael Fellman. Johns Hopkins University Press, 2003, c2000. xx, 360 p. : **B**

ISBN 9780801874116

1. Lee, Robert E. (Robert Edward), 1807-1870. 2. Lee, Robert E. (Robert Edward), 1807-1870 Political and social views. 3. Confederate States of America. Army 4. Generals -- Confederate States of America 5. Gentry -- Southern States 6. Biographies

LC 2002043290

"Originally published in hardcover by Random House, Inc., New York, 2000"--T.p. verso.

"With rigorous research and unprecedented insight into Robert E. Lee's personal and public lives, Michael Fellman here uncovers the intelligent, ambitious, and often troubled man behind the legend, exploring his life within the social, cultural, and political context of the nineteenth-century American South." Provided by publisher

Freeman, Douglas Southall, 1886-1953 **Lee** : an abridgement in one volume of the four-volume R.E. Lee / Douglas Southall Freeman ; Richard Harwell ; with a new foreword by James M. McPherson. Collier Books ; 1993, c1961. xxiii, 601 p. : **B**

ISBN 0684829533

1. Lee, Robert E. (Robert Edward), 1807-1870. 2. Generals -- Confederate States of America 3. Generals -- United States 4.

Command of troops 5. Biographies

LC 93006528

Originally published: New York : Scribner, 1961.

Includes index."

Students of history will continue to want and to use the original four-volume work but most general readers will find this abridgment more convenient and adequate to their interest. All footnotes and all of the appendix have been omitted as well as details of Civil War action that are not necessary to show the main course of Lee's life and action." Booklist.

Horn, Jonathan, 1982- The **man** who would not be Washington : Robert E. Lee's Civil War and his decision that changed American history / Jonathan Horn. Scribner, 2015. 384 p. **B**

ISBN 9781476748566

1. Confederate States of America. Army 2. Generals -- United States 3. Command of troops. 4. Leadership in men. 5. Generals -- Confederate States of America 6. Confederate States of America. 7. Biographies

LC 2014029702

In The Man Who Would Not Be Washington, former White House speechwriter Jonathan Horn reveals how the officer most associated with Washington went to war against the union that Washington had forged. This extensively researched and gracefully written biography follows Lee through married life, military glory, and misfortune.

"In tracing Lee's biography, Horn establishes the powerful connection that both Lee and Washington had to slavery and the complex meaning of both states' rights and the Founding Fathers to white Southerners of Lee's generation. Historians will find little that is new, but undergraduates will consider it informative. Summing Up: Recommended. Public and undergraduate libraries." Choice.

Korda, Michael, 1933- **Clouds** of glory : the life and legend of Robert E. Lee / Michael Korda. HarperCollins, 2014. 640 p. **B**

ISBN 9780062116291

1. Lee, Robert E. (Robert Edward), 1807-1870. 2. Confederate States of America. Army 3. Generals -- United States 4. Military history 5. Civil war 6. Command of troops 7. United States -- History -- Civil War, 1861-1865 8. United States -- Politics and government -- 1783-1865. 9. Biographies

LC 2014415636

Accompanied by stunning illustrations and in-text battle maps, this unrivaled biography of the brilliant general analyzes Lee's command during the Civil War, exploring his responsibility for the fatal stalemate at Antietam, his defeat at Gettysburg and his failed strategy for winning the war.

"Korda examines the life of Robert E. Lee from start to finish, illuminating not just the man, but his extended family and the society which produced him." Publishers Weekly.

Thomas, Emory M., 1939- **Robert** E. Lee : a biography / Emory M. Thomas. W.W. Norton, 1997, c1995. 472 p. : **B**

ISBN 0393316319

1. Confederate States of America. Army 2. Generals -- United States 3. Command of troops. 4. Leadership in men. 5. Generals -- Confederate States of America 6. Confederate States of America. 7. Biographies

LC bl 99787828

Originally published: New York : W.W. Norton, 1995.

Providing a thorough examination of the life of Robert E. Lee, a biography finds meaning in Lee's successes and failures and portrays him as a man struggling with personal inner torments who found release in the responsibilities of war.

"Civil War historian Thomas presents Lee as neither an icon nor a flawed figure, but rather as a man who made the best of his lot, whose comic vision of life ultimately shaped him into an individual who was both more and less than his legend." Publishers Weekly.

Lee, Stan, 1922-2018

Fingeroth, Danny, A **marvelous** life : the amazing story of Stan Lee / Danny Fingeroth. St. Martin's Press, 2019. 320 p. **B**

ISBN 9781250133908

1. Marvel comics (New York, N.Y.) 2. Comic book writers. 3. Superhero comics -- History and criticism. 4. Comic book illustrators. 5. Comic books, strips, etc. -- Publishing. 6. Biographies

LC 2019031647

The definitive biography of the beloved--often controversial--co-creator of many legendary superheroes, A Marvelous Life: The Amazing Story of Stan Lee presents the origin of "Stan the Man," who spun a storytelling web of comic book heroic adventures into a pop culture phenomenon: the Marvel Universe.

"Lee remains a pivotal figure in the superhero genre that's come to dominate popular culture, and Fingeroth, a comics veteran who worked closely with Lee, gives evenhanded treatment to his accomplishments and foibles." Booklist

Leibovitz, Liel **Stan** Lee : a life in comics / Liel Leibovitz. Yale University Press, 2020 viii, 179 p. : **B**

ISBN 9780300230345

1. Marvel comics (New York, N.Y.) 2. Comic book writers. 3. Jewish American men 4. Superhero comics -- History and criticism. 5. Comic book illustrators. 6. Biographies

LC 2019950942

A meditation on the deeply Jewish and surprisingly spiritual roots of Stan Lee and Marvel Comics.

"Fans of the legendary comic book writer and publisher will devour this expert mix of biography and literary analysis." Publishers Weekly

Riesman, Abraham **True** believer : the rise and fall of Stan Lee / Abraham Riesman. Crown, 2020 416 p. **B**

ISBN 9780593135716

1. Lee, Stan, 1922-2018. 2. Cartoonists 3. Comic book writers. 4. Popular culture -- Influence 5. Superhero comics -- History and criticism. 6. Biographies

LC 2020016622

Includes index."

The definitive, revelatory biography of Marvel Comics creator Stan Lee, an artist and entrepreneur who reshaped global pop culture at a steep personal cost. Stan Lee-born Stanley Martin Lieber in 1922--is one of the most beloved and influential entertainers to emerge from the twentieth century. True Believer chronicles every triumph and every misstep of an extraordinary life, and leaves it to readers to decide whether Lee lived up to the responsibilities of his own talent.

"This detailed, clear-eyed examination pulls back the curtain on one of America's great storytellers and is sure to reignite debates over Lee's legacy." Publishers Weekly

Lefevre, Didier, 1957-2007

Guibert, Emmanuel The **photographer** : into war-torn Afghanistan with Doctors Without Borders / illustrated by Emmanuel Guibert ; written by Didier Lefevre and Frederic Lemercier ; translated from the French by Alexis Siegel. First

Second, 2009. xi, 267 p. : **B**

ISBN 9781596433755

1. Lefevre, Didier, 1957-2007. 2. Médecins sans frontières (Association) 3. Photojournalists -- France. 4. Medical care -- Afghanistan. 5. Humanitarian assistance -- Afghanistan. 6. Afghanistan -- History -- Soviet occupation, 1979-1989 -- Medical care. 7. Autobiographical comics 8. Comics and Graphic novels 9. Autobiographies and memoirs

LC 2012288469

ALA Notable Book, 2010.

In 1986, Afghanistan was torn apart by a war with the Soviet Union. This graphic novel/photo-journal is a record of one reporter's arduous and dangerous journey through Afghanistan, accompanying the Doctors Without Borders.

"The graphic novel combines traditional comic art with some of the four thousand photographs Lefevre shot while in Afghanistan. . . . Many images will stay with readers as both horrifying and glorious. The Afghan children being treated for burns, bullet wounds, and shrapnel are page by page next to the beauty of the Afghan mountainous landscapes. . . . [This book] has a powerful message and images of a part of the world that should be discussed more often." Voice of Youth Advocates.

Lefevre, John

Lefevre, John **Straight** to hell : true tales of deviance, debauchery, and billion-dollar deals / John Lefevre. Atlantic Monthly Press, 2015. 288 p. **B**

ISBN 9780802123305

1. Investment banking 2. Bankers 3. Corporate culture 4. Investment bankers 5. Autobiographies and memoirs

LC 2015460485

The investment banker behind the popular Twitter account @GSElevator offers a behind-the-scenes account of his wild life of excess.

"This will appeal readily to heterosexual males with an inflated sense of entitlement and a mental age below 30, particularly those working in large corporations." Library Journal.

Legendre, Gertrude Sanford, 1902-2000

Finn, Peter, 1962- A **guest** of the Reich : the story of American heiress Gertrude Legendre and her dramatic captivity and daring escape from Nazi Germany / Peter Finn. Pantheon Books, [2019] 256 p. **B**

ISBN 9781524747336

1. Legendre, Gertrude Sanford, 1902-2000. 2. United States. Office of Strategic Services -- History 3. Women spies -- United States 4. World War II -- Women 5. Women prisoners of war 6. Heirs and heiresses 7. Germany -- History -- 1933-1945 8. Biographies

LC 2019002112

The co-author of The Zhivago Affair traces the experiences of the American heiress who joined the OSS and was captured behind enemy lines in 1944 before orchestrating her daring escape from the Nazis into Switzerland.

"This riveting account of a little-known historical personality will appeal to World War II and general history fans alike." Library Journal.

Legler, Casey

★Legler, Casey **Godspeed** : a memoir / Casey Legler. Atria Books, 2018. 192 p. **B**

ISBN 9781501135750

1. Women with Autism 2. Olympic athletes 3. Teenagers with depression 4. Teenagers -- Drug use 5. Autobiographies and memoirs

LC 2018022193

A coming-of-age memoir by a former Olympic swimmer describes the crippling loneliness that marked her athletic childhood and her struggles with addiction and self-destructiveness prior to her diagnosis with autism.

"A coming-of-age drama captured through poetic prose and convincing honesty." Kirkus.

Lehrer, Riva, 1958-

Lehrer, Riva, 1958- **Golem** girl : a memoir / Riva Lehrer. One World, 2020 448 p. **B**

ISBN 9781984820303

1. Artists with disabilities 2. Intersectionality 3. Empowerment (Social sciences) 4. Sexuality

LC 2020012800

Memoir of an artist born with disabilities who searches for freedom and connection in a society afraid of strange bodies.

"Painter Lehrer applies the same unflinching gaze for which her portraits are known to a lifetime with spina bifida in this trenchant debut memoir of disability and queer culture." Publishers Weekly

Leibniz, Gottfried Wilhelm, Freiherr von, 1646-1716

Nadler, Steven M., 1958- The **best** of all possible worlds : a story of philosophers, God, and evil / Steven Nadler. Farrar, Straus and Giroux, 2008. 320 p. **B**

ISBN 9780374229986

1. Leibniz, Gottfried Wilhelm, Freiherr von, 1646-1716. 2. Malebranche, Nicolas, 1638-1715. 3. Arnauld, Antoine, 1612-1694. 4. God 5. Philosophers -- Germany 6. Philosophy, Modern -- 17th century. 7. Good and evil. 8. Germany -- History -- 17th century 9. France -- History -- 17th century 10. Biographies

LC 2008029143

Traces the development of modern philosophical and religious thought as influenced by the friendship shared by German philosopher and mathematician Gottfried Wilhelm Leibniz and philosopher-theologians Antoine Arnauld and Nicolas de Malebranche, who in spite of disparate views shared a passionate concern about the resolution of evil.

"This book is written simply and clearly, without condescension, flashiness or oversimplification. But it's a demanding book nonetheless, and you need to pay attention. You'll be amply rewarded if you do." Washington Post Book World.

Leite, David

Leite, David **Notes** on a banana : a memoir of food, love, and manic depression / David Leite. HarperCollins, 2017. 272 p. **B**

ISBN 9780062414373

1. Men with bipolar disorder 2. Cooks 3. Cooking 4. Self-discovery 5. Massachusetts 6. Autobiographies and memoirs

LC bl2017007293

The founder of the James Beard Award-winning website Leite's Culinaria presents a candid, humorous story of family, food, mental illness and sexual identity.

"In this coming-of-age story and chronicle of self-acceptance, Leite impressively finds honesty and humor in the darkest of circumstances, making this a strong debut memoir. A brave and moving tale of food, family, and psychology." Kirkus.

Leitzel, Lillian

Jensen, Dean **Queen** of the air : a true story of love and tragedy at the Circus / Dean N. Jensen. Crown, 2013. 320 p. **B**

ISBN 9780307986566

1. Codona, Alfredo 2. Ringling Brothers and Barnum and Bailey Circus. 3. Circus 4. Circus performers 5. Acrobatics. 6. Women circus performers 7. United States -- Social life and customs -- 20th

century 8. Biographies

LC 2012018066

Traces the story of world-famous trapeze artist Leitzel and her star-crossed love affair with Alfredo Codona of the famous Flying Codona Brothers, chronicling her disadvantaged youth, three marriages, and achievements with the Ringling Bros and Barnum & Bailey Circus.

Lemay, Mimi

★Lemay, Mimi **What** we will become : a mother, a son, and a journey of transformation / Mimi Lemay. Houghton Mifflin Harcourt, 2019 320 p. **B**

ISBN 9780544965836

1. Parents of transgender children 2. Transgender children 3. Motherhood 4. Gender identity 5. Autobiographies and memoirs

LC 2019013136

A mother's memoir of her transgender child's odyssey, and her journey outside the boundaries of the faith and culture that shaped her.

"This is a vital and engrossing book about how to live an authentic life. Well suited for readers interested in gender and generational family dynamics." Library Journal

Lenin, Vladimir Il'ich, 1870-1924

Pomper, Philip **Lenin's** brother : the origins of the October Revolution / Philip Pomper. W.W. Norton & Co., 2010. 304 p. **B**

ISBN 9780393070798

1. Lenin, Vladimir Il'ich, 1870-1924 Family. 2. Lenin, Vladimir Il'ich, 1870-1924 Political and social views. 3. Revolutionaries -- Russia 4. Brothers -- Russia 5. Revolutions. 6. Terrorists -- Russia 7. Soviet Union -- History -- Revolution, 1917-1921 -- Causes. 8. Biographies

LC 2009027390

Drawing on the family archives of Vladimir Lenin, originally Vladimir Ulyanov, the author traces the transformation of the Communist leader's brother, Alexander, from a humble student to a terrorist plotting the assassination of the tsar and delves into how the failed plot and Alexander's subsequent execution shaped the ideals and motivations of Lenin.

"In 1887, the future leader of the Russian revolution, Vladimir Ulyanov (later Lenin), was 17 when his 21-year-old brother was hanged for his role in a bungled attempt to assassinate Czar Alexander III. Historians consider this the seminal event that launched Lenin's career as a revolutionary. [The author] delivers an absorbing and surprisingly detailed account of Alexander Ulyanov's short life and even shorter career (four months) as a terrorist." Publishers Weekly.

Sebestyen, Victor, 1956- **Lenin** : the man, the dictator, and the master of terror / Victor Sebestyen. Pantheon, 2017. 592 p. **B**

ISBN 9781101871638

1. Lenin, Vladimir Il'ich, 1870-1924 2. Revolutionaries -- Soviet Union 3. Dictators -- Soviet Union 4. State-sponsored terrorism -- Soviet Union -- History. 5. Communism. 6. Russia -- Politics and government -- 1894-1917. 7. Soviet Union -- Politics and government -- 1917-1936. 8. Biographies

LC 2017008076

Draws on diaries, memoirs, and private letters written by both the controversial dictator and his friends to explore how Vladimir Lenin's personal life, including key relationships with women, shaped his politics and role in launching the Russian Revolution.

"Sebestyen is to be commended for bringing the true Lenin to life for historians to consider. His study will rank with those of Richard Pipes and Robert Service in modern historiography." Choice.

Service, Robert, 1947- **Lenin--a** biography / Robert Service. Harvard University Press, 2000. xxv, 561 p. : **B**

ISBN 0674003306

1. Lenin, Vladimir Il'ich, 1870-1924. 2. Heads of state -- Soviet Union 3. Revolutionaries -- Russia 4. Communism. 5. Communists. 6. Russia -- Politics and government -- 1894-1917. 7. Soviet Union -- Politics and government -- 1917-1936. 8. Biographies

LC 00021394

A biography of the first Soviet leader delves into his heavily mythologized life to show why he was so feared, respected, and loved in Russia.

Lennon, John, 1940-1980

Connolly, Ray, 1940- **Being** John Lennon : a restless life / Ray Connolly. W W Norton & Co Inc., 2018 448 p. **B**

ISBN 9781643130538

1. Beatles (Musical group) 2. Musicians 3. Rock musicians 4. Celebrities 5. Popular culture -- History -- 1960-1969 6. Great Britain 7. England 8. Biographies

LC bl2018188289

Provides an intimate yet unsparing biography of one of the greatest and most mythologized musicians of the 20th century.

"A welcome new perspective on an endlessly influential and compelling artist " Booklist.

Greenberg, Keith Elliot, 1959- **December** 8, 1980 : the day John Lennon died / Keith Elliot Greenberg. Backbeat Books, 2010. 240 p. **B**

ISBN 9780879309633

1. Lennon, John, 1940-1980 Assassination. 2. Rock musicians. 3. Rock music. 4. Assassination. 5. Fans (Persons) 6. New York City. 7. New York City -- Social life and customs -- 20th century.

LC 2010031425

"Greenberg's definitive and unforgettable inquiry into John Lennon's death illuminates the cruel mysteries of madness, and, more resonantly, all the qualities that made Lennon such an exceptional and compelling artist." Booklist.

Norman, Philip, 1943- **John** Lennon : the life / Philip Norman. Ecco, c2008. 864 p. **B**

ISBN 9780060754013

1. Lennon, John, 1940-1980. 2. Beatles (Musical group) 3. Rock musicians 4. Rock music. 5. Celebrities 6. England -- Social life and customs -- 20th century. 7. Biographies

LC 2008004684

A comprehensive portrait of the rock icon covers topics ranging from Lennon's traumatic childhood in the care of his aunt and the Beatles' unprecedented rise to the in-fighting during the Yoko years and his early death in 1980.

"This work's ambitious range proves to be its strength, enveloping you in ways that a quicker read could not. [This] is a gift of a book, heartfelt and heart-rending." Christian Science Monitor.

Riley, Tim, 1960- **Lennon** : the man, the myth, the music - the definitive life / Tim Riley. Hyperion, 2011. 800 p. **B**

ISBN 9781401324520

1. Lennon, John, 1940-1980. 2. Beatles (Musical group) 3. Rock musicians -- England 4. Rock music. 5. Musicians 6. Biographies

LC 2011015657

Granted access to previously untapped files from the city of Liverpool and the Liverpool College of Art, the author, a renowned music historian and journalist, challenges many popular assumptions about the Beatle's life by presenting an authoritative examination of John Lennon's life and creative legacy.

"Here is Lennon in the fullness of his diffracted personality, across the spectrum of his phases and faces. Leather John, mugging sailors in Hamburg A Lennon punch felled him to his knees is superseded by Beatle John, mugging for the world's press. Beatle John contains both Ed Sullivan John, yodeling harmonies and bending his knees in awkward demi-plis, and Revolver John, acidhead, sleepyhead, drug dormouse, singing in that cold little cocoon voice (Riley calls it timefrozen) about floating downstream and not wanting to be woken up. Then there's Imagine John, the drooping sage. And finally, of course, John the martyr." New York Times Book Review.

Lennox, Margaret Douglas, Countess of, 1515-1578

Weir, Alison, 1951- The **lost** Tudor princess : the life of Margaret Douglas of Scotland / Alison Weir. Ballantine Books, 2016. 432 p. **B**

ISBN 9780345521392

1. Lennox, Margaret Douglas, Countess of, 1515-1578. 2. Henry VIII, King of England, 1491-1547 Family. 3. Mary, Queen of Scots, 1542-1587 Family. 4. Nobility -- Great Britain -- History -- 16th century. 5. Great Britain -- History -- Tudors, 1485-1603. 6. Biographies

LC 2015037958

A profile of the niece of Henry VIII reveals her lesser-known contributions to period politics, covering her two affairs, arrangement of her son's marriage to Mary Queen of Scots and role in securing the throne for James VI.

"An abundantly detailed history from an author steeped in England's past." Kirkus.

Lenz, Frank G.

Herlihy, David V. The **lost** cyclist : the epic tale of an American adventurer and his mysterious disappearance / David V. Herlihy. Houghton Mifflin Harcourt, c2010. 320 p. **B**

ISBN 9780547195575

1. Bicyclists -- United States 2. Bicycling. 3. Missing persons.

LC 2009028857

Includes index.

A cycling historian traces the epic journey of 1880s high-wheel racer Frank Lenz to cycle around the world as a correspondent for Outing magazine, an effort during which his murder sparked an international outcry and an ensuing investigation by fellow cyclist William Sachtleben.

Leon, Donna

Leon, Donna **My** Venice and other essays / Donna Leon. Atlantic Monthly Press, 2013. 240 p. **B**

ISBN 9780802120366

1. Americans in Venice, Italy. 2. Everyday life. 3. Venice, Italy 4. Essays 5. Autobiographies and memoirs

LC 2015295832

The author of the international best-selling Commissario Guido Brunetti series, which is set in Italy, presents more than 50 humorous, passionate and insightful essays about her life in Venice that also explore her family history, her former life in New Jersey and the idea of the Italian man.

Leonard, Sugar Ray, 1956-

Kimball, George, 1943-2011 **Four** kings : Leonard, Hagler, Hearns, Duran, and the last great era of boxing / George Kimball. McBooks Press, c2008. 275 p. **B**

ISBN 9781590131626

1. Hearns, Thomas. 2. Hagler, Marvelous Marvin, 1954- 3. Duran, Roberto, 1951- 4. Boxers (Sports) -- United States 5. Boxing -- United States -- History. 6. Boxing matches -- United States -- History. 7. United States -- Social life and customs.

LC 2008013825

"The author resurrects Sugar Ray Leonard, Marvin Hagler, Thomas Hearns, and Roberto Duran from the mists of memory, re-creating the nine bouts the middleweights fought against one another in the 1980s. A great boxing book." Booklist.

Leonardo, da Vinci, 1452-1519

★Isaacson, Walter **Leonardo** da Vinci / Walter Isaacson. Simon & Schuster, 2017. 576 p. **B**

ISBN 9781501139154

1. Leonardo, da Vinci, 1452-1519. 2. Artists 3. Scientists 4. Gifted persons 5. Biographies

LC 2017020817

Longlisted for the Andrew Carnegie Medal for Excellence in Non-Fiction, 2018.

The best-selling author of Benjamin Franklin draws on da Vinci's remarkable notebooks as well as new discoveries about his life and work in a narrative portrait that connects the master's art to his science, demonstrating how da Vinci's genius was based on the skills and qualities of everyday people, from curiosity and observation to imagination and fantasy.

"Encompassing in its coverage, robust in its artistic explanations, yet written in a smart, conversational tone, this is both a solid introduction to the man and a sweeping saga of his genius." Booklist.

Nuland, Sherwin B. **Leonardo** da Vinci / Sherwin B. Nuland. Viking, 2000. 170 p. : **B**

ISBN 0670893919

1. Leonardo, da Vinci, 1452-1519. 2. Artists -- Italy 3. Scientists -- Italy 4. Intellectual life. 5. Science. 6. Italy -- History -- 1492-1559. 7. Biographies

LC 00032061

"A Lipper/Viking book."

Attempts to unlock the secret of the great Renaissance man's love of art and science.

Leonowens, Anna Harriette Crawford, 1834-1914

Landon, Margaret Mortenson, 1903-1993 **Anna** and the King of Siam / Margaret Landon ; illustrated by Margaret Ayer. Harper Perennial, 2000, c1944. xiii, 395 p. : **B**

ISBN 0060954884

1. Leonowens, Anna Harriette Crawford, 1834-1914. 2. Mongkut, King of Siam, 1804-1868 3. Governesses -- Thailand 4. Women authors 5. Women journalists 6. British in Thailand 7. Thailand -- Court and courtiers. 8. Thailand -- Social life and customs. 9. Biographies

LC BL 00002177

Originally published: New York : The John Dow Co., 1944.

Examines the life of Anna Leonowens, an English woman who served as a tutor for the court of King Mongkut of Siam

Lerner, Betsy

Lerner, Betsy The **bridge** ladies : a memoir / Betsy Lerner. Harper Wave, [2016] 272 p. **B**

ISBN 9780062354464

1. Lerner, Betsy. 2. Mothers and daughters 3. Female friendship 4.

Bridge (Game) 5. Literary agents -- United States 6. United States -- Social life and customs. 7. Autobiographies and memoirs
LC 2015043022

A fifty-year-old bridge game, and the secrets it held, provides an unexpected way to cross the generational divide between the author and her mother.

Lessing, Doris May, 1919-2013

★Lessing, Doris May, 1919-2013 **Under** my skin : my autobiography to 1949 / Doris Lessing. Harper Collins, 1994. 419 p. : **B**

ISBN 9780060171506

1. Lessing, Doris May, 1919-2013 Childhood and youth. 2. Authors, English -- 20th century 3. Women communists -- Great Britain 4. British in Zimbabwe 5. Growing up. 6. Zimbabwe -- Social conditions. 7. England. 8. Autobiographies and memoirs
LC 94020051

Sequel: Walking in the shade.

James Tait Black Memorial Prize for Biography, 1994.

The author recounts her childhood in Persia and Southern Rhodesia, difficult adolescence, two marriages, political activity, and growth as a writer.

"In this immediate, vivid, beautifully paced memoir, Doris Lessing sets the individual against history, the personal against the general, and shows, by the example of her own life set down honestly, how biography and fiction mesh, how fiction transmutes the personal to the general, how the particular experience illuminates the universe." London Review of Books.

Lester, C. N.

Lester, C. N. **Trans** like me : conversations for all of us / C.N. Lester. Seal Press, 2018, c2017. 240 p. **B**

ISBN 9781580057851

1. Transgender persons 2. Gender identity 3. LGBTQIA rights 4. Genderqueer 5. Autobiographies and memoirs
LC 2017051262

Originally published: London : Virago, 2017.

Discusses the most important and high-profile narratives around the trans community and examines what these narratives mean in terms of cultural progress.

Levesque, Emily

Levesque, Emily The **last** stargazers : the enduring story of astronomy's vanishing explorers / Emily Levesque. Sourcebooks, 2020. xvi, 313 p. **B**

ISBN 9781492681076

1. Levesque, Emily. 2. Astronomy 3. Women astronomers 4. Astronomical observatories 5. Astronomy -- History 6. Autobiographies and memoirs
LC 2020005285

Amidst the lonely quiet of stargazing to wild bears loose in the observatory, these love stories of astronomy show how scientists are going beyond the machines to infuse important creativity and intimate passion into the stars, inspiring future generations to peer skyward in pursuit of the universe's secrets.

Levi, Primo,

Angier, Carole, 1943- The **double** bond : Primo Levi, a biography / Carole Angier. Farrar, Straus and Giroux, 2002. xxvi, 898 p. : **B**

ISBN 0374113157

1. Authors, Italian -- 20th century 2. Chemists -- Italy 3. Jews, Italian 4. Holocaust survivors -- Italy 5. Biographies
LC 2002104433

"Angier's long, gripping narrative of Levi's time in Auschwitz synthesizes the best of his memoirs, poetry, fiction, essays, and scientific writing. A compelling biography and a must for all Holocaust collections." Booklist.

Levi, Primo The **periodic** table / Primo Levi ; translated from the Italian by Raymond Rosenthal ; with an introduction by Neal Ascherson. Alfred A. Knopf, 1996, c1984 xxv, 241 p. : **B**

ISBN 9780805210415

1. Auschwitz (Concentration camp) 2. Chemists. 3. Chemical elements. 4. Periodic table of the elements 5. Jewish men. 6. Italy 7. Germany 8. Autobiographies and memoirs.
LC 96008920

Originally published in the U.S., in translation : New York : Schocken Books, 1984.

One of Italy's leading men of letters, a chemist by profession, writes about incidents in his life in which one or another of the elements figured in such a way as to become a personal preoccupation,

"This curious memoir, organized in 21 chapters from Argon to Zinc, ransacks the periodic table of the elements for strained metaphors as it traces one adolescent's search for identity. Levi ironically portrays himself as a young aspiring chemist eager to fathom nature's secrets." Publishers Weekly.

★Levi, Primo, **Survival** in Auschwitz : the Nazi assault on humanity / Primo Levi ; translated from the Italian by Stuart Woolf ; including "A conversation with Primo Levi by Philip Roth." Simon & Schuster, 1996, c1993. 187 p. ; **B**

ISBN 0684826801

1. Auschwitz (Concentration camp) 2. World War II, Italian. 3. Holocaust (1933-1945) -- Italy 4. Italy 5. Germany
LC bl2005012360

"A Touchstone book."

Translation of : Se questo e un uomo.

Originally published: New York : Collier Books, 1993.

Also published with the title If This is a man.The author describes his twenty month ordeal in the Nazi death camp.

Levy, Ariel, 1974-

Levy, Ariel, 1974- The **rules** do not apply / Ariel Levy. Random House, 2017. 224 p. **B**

ISBN 9780812996937

1. Women journalists 2. Ambition in women 3. Marriage 4. Gender role 5. Autobiographies and memoirs
LC 2016043502

A New Yorker staff writer and author of Female Chauvinist Pigs shares a profound, hopeful memoir of her own experiences with devastating loss to council fellow survivors about the healing aspects of accepting difficult life challenges that are beyond our control.

"Levys generous portrait of modern feminismat turns bleak, heartrending, inspired, and hopefulspeaks strongly and directly to readers." Booklist.

Levy, Deborah

Levy, Deborah The **cost** of living : a working autobiography / Deborah Levy. Bloomsbury, 2018 128 p. **B**

ISBN 9781635571912

1. Middle-aged women 2. Gender role 3. Lifestyles 4. Divorce 5. Autobiographies and memoirs
LC 2018276218

Drawing on her own experience of attempting to live with pleasure, value and meaning, the two-time Booker Prize finalist, in a "living autobiography," critiques the roles that society assigns to us and reflects on the politics of breaking with the usual gendered rituals.

"This timely look at how women are viewed (and often dismissed) by society will resonate with many readers, but particularly with those who have felt marginalized or undervalued." Publishers Weekly.

Levy, Reynold

Levy, Reynold **They** told me not to take that job : tumult, betrayal, heroics, and the transformation of Lincoln Center / Reynold Levy. PublicAffairs, 2015 xvii, 349 p. : **B**

ISBN 9781610393614

1. Levy, Reynold. 2. Lincoln Center for the Performing Arts, New York City 3. Performing arts -- New York City -- Management. 4. Businesspeople 5. Leadership. 6. Success (Concept) 7. Autobiographies and memoirs

LC 2014049065

The president of the Lincoln Center for the Performing Arts reveals the real story behind the $1.2 billion reinvention of Lincoln Center, and the trials and triumphs along with way, providing unique lessons for leaders in all kinds of organizations.

Lewin, Walter H. G.

★Lewin, Walter H. G. **For** the love of physics : from the end of the rainbow to the edge of time - a journey through the wonders of physics / Walter Lewin, Warren Goldstein, contributor. Simon & Schuster, 2011. 288 p. **B**

ISBN 9781439108277

1. Massachusetts Institute of Technology 2. Physicists -- Massachusetts 3. Physics -- Study and teaching 4. College teachers -- Massachusetts 5. Universities and colleges -- Faculty 6. Massachusetts -- Social life and customs

LC 2010047737

A memoir of the MIT physics professor best known for his YouTube-aired lectures also offers a tour of some of the most engaging discoveries in physics, covering such topics as why lightning strikes and how musical harmony happens.

Lewis, Bernard, 1916-

Lewis, Bernard, 1916- **Notes** on a century : reflections of a Middle East historian / Bernard Lewis with Buntzie Ellis Churchill. Viking, 2012. 384 p. **B**

ISBN 9780670023530

1. Middle East specialists -- Great Britain 2. Area specialists 3. Historiography -- Middle East 4. Middle East -- History -- 20th century. 5. Middle East -- History -- 21st century. 6. Autobiographies and memoirs

LC 2011049267

Includes index.

Presents the life and career of the Middle East specialist, from his professional relationships with world leaders to his accomplishments in world politics, and offers the author's analysis of the political transformation of the region.

Lewis, C. S. (Clive Staples), 1898-1963

McGrath, Alister E., 1953- **C.** S. Lewis : a life : eccentric genius, reluctant prophet / Alister McGrath. Tyndale House Publishers, c2013. 350 p. **B**

ISBN 9781414339351

1. Lewis, C. S. (Clive Staples), 1898-1963. 2. Authors, English -- 20th century 3. Biographies

LC 2012033140

ECPA Christian Book Awards, Non-Fiction, 2014.

Chronicles the life and career of the eccentric British author.

Wilson, A. N., 1950- **C.S.** Lewis : a biography / A.N. Wilson. Norton, 1990. xviii, 334 p., [8] p. of plates : **B**

ISBN 0393028135

1. Authors, English -- 20th century 2. Anglicans -- England 3. Biographies

LC 89027361

"First published in Great Britain 1990"--T.p. verso."

The mixture presented in Wilson's biography of the life of learning, the college life at Magdalen where he taught, of domestic drama and bad temper, religion, and sex, is irresistible." New York Review of Books.

Lewis, Damien

Lewis, Damien The **dog** who could fly : the incredible true story of a WWII airman and the four-legged hero who flew at his side / Damien Lewis. Atria Books, 2014. 304 p. **B**

ISBN 9781476739144

1. Great Britain. Royal Air Force 2. Dogs -- War use. 3. Military pilots 4. World War II 5. German shepherd dog 6. Great Britain -- History -- 20th century 7. Autobiographies and memoirs

LC 2014015567

A U.S. release of a popular UK account by the best-selling co-author of Sergeant Rex documents the true story of a World War II Royal Air Force service dog who aided missions and survived close calls before saving the life of his closest human companion.

"A heartwarming and well-paced man-and-his-dog story. Lewis has captured the spirit of the era and told the story using Bozdech's manuscript as source material without making it maudlin or sentimental." Publishers Weekly.

Lewis, John, 1940-2020

★Lewis, John, 1940-2020 **March.** John Lewis, Andrew Aydin, and Nate Powell. Top Shelf Productions, 2013. 121 p. : March ; **B**

ISBN 9781603093002

1. King, Martin Luther, Jr., 1929-1968. 2. Civil Rights Movement -- Alabama. 3. Politicians 4. Racism -- Alabama. 5. Protests, demonstrations, vigils, etc. 6. Alabama -- Race relations. 7. United States -- Social conditions -- 20th century. 8. Autobiographical comics 9. Comics and Graphic novels 10. Autobiographies and memoirs

Coretta Scott King Honor Book for Authors, 2014.

A first-hand account of the author's lifelong struggle for civil and human rights spans his youth in rural Alabama, his life-changing meeting with Martin Luther King, Jr., and the birth of the Nashville Student Movement.

"This is superb visual storytelling that establishes a convincing, definitive record of a key eyewitness to significant social change." School Library Journal.

★Lewis, John, 1940-2020 **March.** John Lewis, Andrew Aydin, and Nate Powell. Top Shelf Productions, 2015. 160 p. : March ; **B**

ISBN 9781603094009

1. Student Nonviolent Coordinating Committee (U.S.) 2. Civil Rights Movement 3. Protests, demonstrations, vigils, etc. 4. Politicians 5. Racism 6. United States -- Social conditions -- 20th century. 7. Autobiographical comics 8. Comics and Graphic novels

9. Autobiographies and memoirs
Eisner Awards, Best Reality-Based Work, 2016.
Street Lit Book Award Medal: Graphic Novel, 2016
Harvey Awards, Best Graphic Album - Original, 2016.

The award-winning, best-selling series returns, as John Lewis' story continues through Freedom Rides and the legendary 1963 March on Washington.

"Heroism and steadiness of purpose continue to light up Lewis' frank, harrowing account of the civil rights movement's climactic days. . . . The contrast between the dignified marchers and the vicious, hate-filled actions and expressions of their tormentors will leave a deep impression on readers." Kirkus.

★Lewis, John, 1940-2020 **March.** John Lewis with Andrew Aydin ; art by Nate Powell. Top Shelf Productions, 2016. 246 p. : March ; **B**

ISBN 9781603094023

1. Student Nonviolent Coordinating Committee (U.S.) 2. Civil Rights Movement 3. Protests, demonstrations, vigils, etc. 4. Politicians 5. Racism 6. United States -- Social conditions -- 20th century. 7. Autobiographical comics 8. Comics and Graphic novels 9. Autobiographies and memoirs

Series complete in 3 volumes.
Eisner Awards, Best Reality-Based Work, 2017.
Flora Stieglitz Straus Award, 2017.
National Book Award for Young People's Literature, 2016.
SEE-IT Award finalist, 2017.

Congressman John Lewis, one of the key figures of the civil rights movement, joins co-writer Andrew Aydin and artist Nate Powell to bring the lessons of history to vivid life for a new generation, urgently relevant for today's world.

"Though Lewis and Aydin throw a lot at readers in this volume, their message, helped along seamlessly and splendidly by Powell's fantastic, cinematic artwork, is abundantly clear: the victories of the civil rights movement, symbolized in particular by Barack Obama's inauguration, are hard-won and only succeeded through the dogged dedication of a wide variety of people." Booklist.

★Lewis, John, 1940-2020 **Walking** with the wind : a memoir of the movement / John Lewis with Michael D'Orso. Simon & Schuster, 1998. 496 p. : **B**

ISBN 0684810654

1. United States. Congress. House 2. Student Nonviolent Coordinating Committee (U.S.) 3. Civil Rights Movement 4. Civil rights workers -- United States 5. African American civil rights workers 6. Legislators -- United States 7. Biographies

LC 98003040

Includes index.
Robert F. Kennedy Book Award, 1999.

The highest black elected official in America, the congressman looks back on his life from his childhood on a Alabama cotton farm to his fight for civil rights, to his enduring commitment to the ideals of Martin Luther King, Jr.

"A classic, invaluable blockbuster history of the civil-rights movement." Kirkus

Meacham, Jon **His** truth is marching on : John Lewis and the power of hope / Jon Meacham ; afterword by John Lewis. Random House, 2020. xii, 354 p. : **B**

ISBN 9781984855022

1. United States. Congress. House 2. African American politicians 3. African American civil rights workers 4. Civil Rights Movement 5. African Americans -- Civil rights 6. Biographies

LC 2020024320

John Lewis, who at age twenty-five marched in Selma, Alabama, and was beaten on the Edmund Pettus Bridge, was a visionary and a man of faith. Drawing on decades of wide-ranging interviews with Lewis, Jon Meacham writes of how this great-grandson of a slave and son of an Alabama tenant farmer was inspired by the Bible and his teachers in nonviolence, Reverend James Lawson and Martin Luther King, Jr., to put his life on the line in the service of what Abraham Lincoln called "the better angels of our nature." Integral to Lewis's commitment to bettering the nation was his faith in humanity and in God - and an unshakable belief in the power of hope.

"A well-crafted testament to a tumultuous time in American history and to one of the brave men who helped shape the world we know today." Library Journal

Lewis, Matt, 1974-

Lewis, Matt, 1974- **Last** man off : a true story of disaster and survival on the Antarctic seas / Matt Lewis. Plume, 2015. 256 p. **B**

ISBN 9780147515346

1. Sudur Havid (Fishing boat). 2. Shipwrecks -- Antarctic Ocean. 3. Survival at sea -- Antarctic Ocean. 4. Severe storms -- Antarctic Ocean. 5. Marine biologists 6. Antarctic Ocean. 7. Autobiographies and memoirs

LC 2015004920

"Originally published in Great Britain by Viking, 2014"--Title page verso.

There's nothing that armchair adventure lovers relish more than a gripping true story of disaster and heroism, and Last Man Off delivers all that against a breathtaking backdrop of icebergs and killer whales. On June 6, 1998, twenty-three-year-old Matt Lewis had just started his dream job as a scientific observer aboard a deep-sea fishing boat in the waters off Antarctica. As the crew haul in the line for the day, a storm begins to brew. When the captain vanishes and they are forced to abandon ship, Lewis leads the escape onto three life rafts, where the battle for survival begins.

"A darkly exhilarating memoir of tragedy at sea." Kirkus.

Leyva, Selenis, 1972

Leyva, Selenis, 1972- **My** sister : how one sibling's transition changed us both / Selenis Leyva and Marizol Leyva. Bold Type Books, 2020. 256 p. **B**

ISBN 9781541762954

1. Leyva, Marizol 2. Trans women 3. Sisters 4. Transitioning (Gender identity) 5. Transgender persons 6. United states 7. Autobiographies and memoirs

LC bl2020007657

This memoir, written by two sisters who alternate chapters, describes how the younger sibling struggled with her identity and transitioned to a trans woman and activist with the help of her sister's unwavering support.

"The love between the Leyva sisters is clear throughout this warmly recommended memoir. Its beautiful, conversational style should resonate with a broad range of readers." Library Journal

Li, Charles N., 1940-

Li, Charles N., 1940- The **bitter** sea : coming of age in a China before Mao / Charles N. Li. Harper Collins, 2008. x, 283 p., 8 p. of plates : **B**

ISBN 0061346640

1. Linguists -- United States 2. Chinese Americans -- California

3. Nationalists -- China -- History 4. Childhood -- China 5. China -- History -- 1949-1976. 6. Asia -- History -- 1945- 7. California -- Social life and customs -- 20th century 8. Autobiographies and memoirs

LC 2007025697

The author documents his childhood in post-World War II China as the son of a wealthy government official, the crippling dissolution of his family's wealth when the Nationalists came to power, and his efforts to become an independent Chinese American.

Li, Yiyun, 1972-

Li, Yiyun, 1972- **Dear** friend, from my life I write to you in your life / Yiyun Li. Random House, 2017. 224 p. **B**

ISBN 9780399589096

1. Li, Yiyun, 1972- Mental health. 2. Authors, American -- 21st century 3. People with depression 4. Books and reading 5. Writing 6. Essays. 7. Autobiographies and memoirs.

LC 2016017675

A memoir of the author's struggle with depression and suicidal thoughts includes reflections on the life-affirming solace she found in the journals, diaries, and fiction of other writers, including William Tervor, Katherine Mansfield, and Philip Larkin.

Liddell, Eric, 1902-1945

Hamilton, Duncan, 1958- **For** the glory : Eric Liddell's journey from Olympic champion to modern martyr / Duncan Hamilton. Penguin Group USA, 2016 320 p. **B**

ISBN 9781594206207

1. Liddell, Eric, 1902-1945. 2. Runners 3. Missionaries. 4. Prisoners of war 5. Christian missionaries 6. Biographies

LC 2016449372

In the 1924 Olympics, devout Scottish sprinter Eric Liddell refused to run in his race -- the 100 meter -- because it fell on a Sunday. Instead, he spent the months leading up to the Olympics training for the 400, which no one expected him to win. But win he did, and his victory was later immortalized in the 1981 film Chariots of Fire. But this was only the beginning of his sacrifices and his principled stance -- at the peak of his career, Liddell went on to dedicate his life to missionary work in China, where he ultimately died in a Japanese work camp.

Liebling, A. J. (Abbott Joseph), 1904-1963

Liebling, A. J. (Abbott Joseph), 1904-1963 **World** War II writings / A.J. Liebling. Library of America, c2008. xiii, 1089 p. : **B**

ISBN 9781598530186

1. New Yorker (New York, N.Y. : 1925) 2. Journalists -- United States 3. War correspondents -- United States 4. Western Front (World War II) 5. World War II 6. Europe -- History -- 20th century. 7. Essays. 8. Autobiographies and memoirs

LC 2007938791

"This volume brings together three books along with 26 uncollected New Yorker pieces and two excerpts from The Republic of Silence (1947)"--Jacket.

A collection of World War II accounts by the influential journalist and author includes "The Road Back to Paris," "Mollie and Other War Pieces," and "Normandy Revisited," in a volume that also features twenty-nine previously uncollected New Yorker articles.

"The war brought out the best in [Liebling]. Here he . relied on straightforward observation, delivered in a style less mannered than Hemingway's, less sentimental than Ernie Pyle's, less excitable than Michael Herr's. It's the kind of writing that looks easy, except that very few war correspondents have ever done it so well." New York Times Book Review.

Lil' Wayne

Lil' Wayne **Gone** 'til November : a journal of Rikers Island / Lil Wayne. Penguin Group USA, 2016 160 p. **B**

ISBN 9780735212114

1. Imprisonment 2. Prisoners. 3. Rap musicians. 4. Autobiographies and memoirs

LC 2016561294

The Grammy Award-winning rap superstar details the circumstances that led to his year-long incarceration at Rikers Island and his experiences during his imprisonment, sharing intimate insights into his daily rituals, interactions with other inmates and efforts to stay positive.

Limonov, Eduard

Carrere, Emmanuel, 1957- **Limonov** : the outrageous adventures of the radical Soviet poet who became a bum in New York, a sensation in France, and a political antihero in Russia / Emmanuel Carrere ; translated by John Lambert. Farrar, Straus and Giroux, 2014, c2011. 336 p. **B**

ISBN 9780374192013

1. Adventurers 2. Politics and culture 3. Authors, Russian 4. Poets, Russian 5. Biographies

LC 2014004040

Translation from the French of: Limonov.

Originally published: 2011."

A thrilling page-turner that also happens to be the biography of one of Russia's most controversial figures."-- Provided by publisher.

Lincoln, Abraham, 1809-1865

★Blumenthal, Sidney, 1948- **All** the powers of Earth : the political life of Abraham Lincoln, 1856-1860 / Sidney Blumenthal. Simon & Schuster, 2019. 512 p. **B**

ISBN 9781476777283

1. Politicians 2. Legislators 3. Ambition in men 4. Debates and debating 5. United States -- History -- 19th century 6. Biographies

Third volume of author's work on the life of Abraham Lincoln, following A self-made man and Wrestling with his angel.After a period of depression that he would ever find his way to greatness, Lincoln takes on the most powerful demagogue in the country, Stephen Douglas, in the debates for a senate seat. He sidelines the frontrunner William Seward, a former governor and senator for New York, to cinch the new Republican Party's nomination. All the Powers of Earth is the political story of all time. Lincoln achieves the presidency by force of strategy, of political savvy and determination. This is Abraham Lincoln, who indisputably becomes the greatest president and moral leader in the nation's history. But he must first build a new political party, brilliantly state the anti-slavery case and overcome shattering defeat to win the presidency.

Blumenthal, Sidney, 1948- A **self-made** man : the political life of Abraham Lincoln, 1809-1849 / Sidney Blumenthal. Simon & Schuster 2016 608 p. **B**

ISBN 9781476777252

1. Presidents -- United States 2. Ambition in men 3. Political leadership 4. Childhood 5. United States -- History -- 1815-1865. 6. Biographies

LC bl2017022882

"In this engrossing life-and-times study of the formative years of Abraham Lincoln (1809-65), before he became a national figure, political journalist and historian Blumenthal (The Strange Death of Republican America) takes the reader deep into Illinois and national politics to locate the character and content of Lincoln's ideas, interests, and identity, and to understand his driving ambition to succeed in law and politics. In doing so, the author makes the important point that Lincoln gained empathy and understanding of the people from his own self-awareness and need to escape his own origins of relative poverty and hard struggle. If Blumenthal sometimes loses Lincoln in his detailed accounting of patronage, politicking, and personalities, great and small, he effectively shows that the president's Illinois was a proving ground for the politics of expansion, economic development, nativism, anti-Mormonism, and slavery that both reflected and affected national concerns. Lincoln, the self-made man, is revealed as tried-and-true, ready for the troubled times that came in the years leading up to the Civil War." Library Journal.

Blumenthal, Sidney, 1948- **Wrestling** with his angel : the political life of Abraham Lincoln, 1849-1856 / Sidney Blumenthal. Simon & Schuster, 2017. 576 p. **B**

ISBN 9781501153785

1. Presidents -- United States 2. Ambition in men 3. Debates and debating 4. Political oratory 5. United States -- History -- 1815-1865. 6. Biographies

LC bl2017019319

This book follows Blumenthal's "A Self-Made Man: the Political Life of Abraham Lincoln, 1809-1849", 2016.

The second volume of this acclaimed biography of the 16th president explores how he rebounded from the disintegration of the Whig Party and took on the anti-Immigration party in Illinois to clear a path for a new Republican Party.

"A painstakingly researched portrait of the political landscape as the country inched toward civil war." Kirkus.

Brookhiser, Richard **Founders'** son : a life of Abraham Lincoln / Richard Brookhiser. Basic Books, 2014. 288 p. **B**

ISBN 9780465032945

1. Lincoln, Abraham, 1809-1865. 2. Founding Fathers of the United States -- Influence 3. Presidents -- United States 4. United States -- Politics and government -- 1861-1865. 5. Autobiographies and memoirs

LC 2014021173

"This highly accessible read will appeal most to readers who desire to learn more about Lincoln and especially the ideas, dogmas, and dreams that moved him to his public career and life in the White House." Library Journal.

Burlingame, Michael, 1941- **Abraham** Lincoln: a life / Michael Burlingame. Johns Hopkins University Press, 2008. 2 v. **B**

ISBN 9780801889936

1. Lincoln, Abraham, 1809-1865. 2. Presidents -- United States 3. Politicians -- United States 4. Political leadership -- United States -- History. 5. Civil war 6. United States -- History -- Civil War, 1861-1865. 7. United States -- Politics and government -- 1861-1865. 8. United States -- History -- 1815-1865. 9. Biographies

LC 2007052919

"The author has produced the finest Lincoln biography in more than 60 years. Future Lincoln books cannot be written without it, and from no other book can a general reader learn so much about Abraham Lincoln." Publishers Weekly.

Carwardine, Richard **Lincoln** : a life of purpose and power / Richard Carwardine. Alfred A. Knopf, 2006, c2003. xv, 394 p. : **B**

ISBN 1400044561

1. Lincoln, Abraham, 1809-1865. 2. Presidents -- United States 3. Civil war 4. United States Civil War, 1861-1865 5. United States -- History -- Civil War, 1861-1865. 6. United States -- Politics and government -- 1861-1865. 7. United States -- Politics and government -- 1815-1861. 8. Biographies

LC 2005047230

Originally published: London : Pearson Education, 2003.

A portrait of America's sixteenth president follows Lincoln's life and career during his rise to political power and his years in the White House, arguing that he looked beyond the political system to find support in his struggle to end slavery.

"This book is not only analytical and smart, it's also delightfully readableand it will surely emerge as one of the most important Lincoln books to be published this decade." Publishers Weekly.

Donald, David Herbert, 1920- **Lincoln** / David Herbert Donald. Simon & Schuster, 1995. 714 p., 32 p. of plates : **B**

ISBN 0684808463

1. Lincoln, Abraham, 1809-1865. 2. Presidents -- United States 3. Politicians -- United States -- History -- 19th century 4. Civil war 5. United States Civil War, 1861-1865 6. United States -- History -- 19th century. 7. United States -- History -- Civil War, 1861-1865. 8. Biographies

LC 95004782

ALA Notable Book, 1996."

This biography examines: Lincoln's relationship with his father; his romance with Ann Rutledge; his bouts of hypo, which amounted at times almost to clinical depression; his marriage; his political ambition; his attitudes toward slavery and black people; his relations with radical Republicans during the Civil War; the mistakes and successes of his wartime leadership." The Atlantic.

★Foner, Eric, 1943- **Our** Lincoln : new perspectives on Lincoln and his world / edited by Eric Foner. W.W. Norton & Co., 2008. 256 p. **B**

ISBN 9780393067569

1. Lincoln, Abraham, 1809-1865. 2. Lincoln, Abraham, 1809-1865 Political and social views. 3. Lincoln, Abraham, 1809-1865 Military leadership. 4. Presidents -- United States 5. Political leadership. 6. Command of troops. 7. Family relationships. 8. United States -- History -- 19th century. 9. United States -- History -- Civil War, 1861-1865. 10. United States -- Politics and government -- 1861-1865. 11. Essays.

LC 2008017096

"Historians collectively situate Lincoln's ideas, interests, and policies and the meanings various people from abolitionists to neo-Confederates have found in Lincoln, from the microscopic to a wider historical context of politics, culture, and memory. Essays explore such topics as presidential leadership, civil liberties, citizenship and rights, democratic politics, mass-produced imagery, African colonization, antislavery, race, religion, family life, writing sensibilities and style, and the need to claim Lincoln for one's own cause. The eloquent and compelling results show how and why Lincoln was both a man of his time and a man for all time." Library Journal.

Freehling, William W., 1935- **Becoming** Lincoln : plunges and recoveries during an epic pre-Civil War climb / William W. Freehling. University of Virginia Press, [2018] 376 p. **B**

ISBN 9780813941561

1. Lincoln, Abraham, 1809-1865. 2. Lincoln, Abraham, 1809-1865 Political career before 1861. 3. Lincoln, Abraham, 1809-1865 Political and social views. 4. Lincoln, Abraham, 1809-1865 Oratory. 5. Presidents -- United States 6. Lawyers. 7. Fathers and sons. 8. Books and reading. 9. United States -- History -- Civil War, 1861-1865 -- Causes. 10. Biographies.

LC 2017061669

Traces Lincoln from his tough childhood through incarnations as a bankrupt with few prospects, a superb lawyer, a canny two-party politician, a great orator, a failed state legislator, and a losing senatorial candidate, to becoming the president who ended slavery.

"Built on Freehling's vast knowledge of the time period, this commendable biography shows the geographical division of opinions leading up to war and the life events that made the man who saved the union." Kirkus.

Gienapp, William E. **Abraham** Lincoln and Civil War America : a biography / William E. Gienapp. Oxford University Press, 2002. xiii, 239 p. : **B**

ISBN 0195150996

1. Lincoln, Abraham, 1809-1865. 2. Lincoln, Abraham, 1809-1865 Military leadership. 3. Presidents -- United States 4. United States -- Politics and government -- 1861-1865. 5. Biographies

LC 2001050056

"In spite of the book's size, its discriminating history of Lincoln's life is surprisingly rich, and the narrative of his presidency and the unfolding of the war is crisp and coherent." Bookmarks.

Holzer, Harold A **just** and generous nation : Abraham Lincoln and the fight for American opportunity / Harold Holzer and Norton Garfinkle. Basic Books, 2015. 288 p. **B**

ISBN 9780465028306

1. Lincoln, Abraham, 1809-1865 Political and social views. 2. Equality -- Economic aspects. 3. Economic development. 4. Social mobility. 5. United States Civil War, 1861-1865 6. United States -- History -- Civil War, 1861-1865 -- Causes. 7. United States -- Politics and government -- 1861-1865. 8. Biographies

LC 2015022842

The eminent historian Harold Holzer and the noted economist Norton Garfinkle present a groundbreaking new account of the beliefs that inspired our sixteenth president to go to war when the Southern states seceded from the Union. Rather than a commitment to eradicating slavery or a defense of the Union, they argue, Lincoln's guiding principle was the defense of equal economic opportunity. Lincoln firmly believed that the government's primary role was to ensure that all Americans had the opportunity to better their station in life. As president, he worked tirelessly to enshrine this ideal within the federal government. He funded railroads and canals, supported education, and, most importantly, issued the Emancipation Proclamation, which opened the door for former slaves to join white Americans in striving for self-improvement.

"This review of Lincoln's thoughts and actions and examination of subsequent administrations' willingness to promote and secure the American Dream will generate much-needed debate on the history, efficacy, and morality of government's role and responsibility in shaping an economy of fairness and growth. The future of America depends on that question." Library Journal.

Holzer, Harold, The **Lincoln** anthology : great writers on his life and legacy from 1860 to now / edited by Harold Holzer. Library of America, 2009. 800 p. **B**

ISBN 9781598530339

1. Lincoln, Abraham, 1809-1865. 2. Presidents. 3. Political leadership. 4. United States -- Politics and government. 5. Anthologies.

LC bl2009006162

A volume of writings on the sixteenth president includes works of fiction, history, and poetry by figures ranging from Churchill and Grant to Tolstoy and Twain, in a collection that offers insight into the ways in which American history and culture have contributed to the sixteenth president's legendary persona.

Holzer, Harold **Lincoln** and the power of the press : the war for public opinion / Harold Holzer. Simon & Schuster, 2014. 832 p. **B**

ISBN 9781439192719

1. Lincoln, Abraham, 1809-1865 Relations with journalists. 2. Press and politics. 3. Public relations. 4. United States Civil War, 1861-1865 5. United States -- History -- Civil War, 1861-1865. 6. United States -- Politics and government -- 1861-1865. 7. Biographies

LC 2014021392

Includes index.

Mark Lynton History Prize, 2015.

Lincoln believed that "with public sentiment nothing can fail; without it, nothing can succeed." Harold Holzer makes a significant contribution to our understanding of Lincoln's leadership by showing us how deftly he managed his relations with the press of his day to move public opinion forward to preserve the Union and abolish slavery.

McGinty, Brian **Lincoln's** greatest case : the river, the bridge, and the making of America / Brian McGinty. Liveright Publishing Corporation, A Division of W.W. Norton & Company, 2015. 320 p. **B**

ISBN 9780871407849

1. Lincoln, Abraham, 1809-1865. 2. Presidents -- United States. 3. Trials. 4. Lawyers. 5. Steamboats 6. Biographies

LC 2014036938

It may seem unlikely that a single liability suit, the?Effie Afton?case, could help launch Abraham Lincoln's political career while determining the future of rail transportation in the U.S. However, in?Lincoln's Greatest Case, legal historian Brian McGinty demonstrates how Lincoln's courtroom performance assured that trains would win over steamboats in the competition to dominate inland transportation. His intelligence, wit, and skill during the trial also helped convince political supporters that he could be a successful campaigner. This detailed and intriguing account illuminates a critical moment in transportation history and a pivotal event in Lincoln's ascent to the presidency.

"McGinty's book gives us the best accounting of Lincoln, the lawyer, to date. Highly recommended." Library Journal.

★McPherson, James M. **Abraham** Lincoln : a presidential life / James M. McPherson. Oxford University Press, c2009. xi, 79 p. ; **B**

ISBN 9780195374520

1. Lincoln, Abraham, 1809-1865. 2. Presidents -- United States 3. Politicians -- United States 4. Political leadership -- United States -- History. 5. Biographies

LC 2008035623

McPherson follows Abraham Lincoln from his early frontier days to his turbulent years in the White House.

"McPherson, America's leading authority on Lincoln and his times, demonstrates his complete command of his subject in this concise but remarkably rich and perceptive biography. . . . This little book is bigger than its pages and should be in every library, schoolhouse, and home." Library Journal.

Pryor, Elizabeth Brown **Six** encounters with Lincoln : a president confronts democracy and Its demons / Elizabeth Brown Pryor. Viking Press, 2017. 400 p. **B**

ISBN 9780670025909

1. Character 2. Ideology 3. Conversation 4. Social behavior 5. Biographies

LC 2016042837

Explores the psychology, character and leadership of the 16th President as evidenced by six lesser-known encounters with his constituents, from an awkward meeting with Army officers on the eve of the Civil War to a White House conversation with a fierce abolitionist.

"Deeply researched, telling moments in the life of arguably the most written-about man in American history." Kirkus.

★Reynolds, David S., 1948- **Abe** : Abraham Lincoln in his times / David S. Reynolds. Penguin Press, 2020. xx, 1066 p. : **B**

ISBN 9781594206047

1. Lincoln, Abraham, 1809-1865. 2. Ideology 3. Growing up 4. Influence (Literary, artistic, etc.) 5. Presidents -- United States 6. United States -- Politics and government -- 1861-1865. 7. United States -- Social life and customs -- 19th century. 8. Biographies

LC 2019047287

The award-winning author of Walt Whitman's America presents an immersive portrait of the 16th President, from his younger life in the decades before the Civil War through his emergence as a progressive political leader and advocate for human justice.

"Reynolds' biography moves Lincoln's life ever forward, inserting digressions without slowing the narrative pace. Even readers who think they know Lincoln's life deeply will find new insights here. This is sure to win a wide audience." Booklist

Sandburg, Carl, 1878-1967 **Abraham** Lincoln : the prairie years and the war years / Carl Sandburg. Harcourt, 2002 xiv, 762 p. : **B**

ISBN 9780156027526

1. Lincoln, Abraham, 1809-1865. 2. Presidents -- United States 3. Biographies

LC bl2006010116

"A Harvest book."

Symonds, Craig L. **Lincoln** and his admirals / Craig L. Symonds. Oxford University Press, 2008. 448 p. **B**

ISBN 9780195310221

1. Lincoln, Abraham, 1809-1865 Military leadership. 2. Welles, Gideon, 1802-1878. 3. Fox, Gustavus Vasa, 1821-1883. 4. United States. Navy -- History 19th century. 5. Presidents -- United States 6. Naval history -- 19th century 7. Naval battles 8. Command of troops -- United States 9. United States -- History -- Civil War, 1861-1865 -- Naval operations. 10. United States -- History, Naval -- 19th century.

LC 2008004251

A prize-winning historian reveals how Abraham Lincoln managed the men who ran the naval side of the Civil War and transformed himself into one of the greatest naval strategists of his age, in a unique and riveting account of the commander-in-chief during the Civil War.

White, Ronald C. (Ronald Cedric), 1939- **A.** Lincoln : a biography / Ronald C. White, Jr. Random House Pub. Group, 2009. 816 p. **B**

ISBN 9781400064991

1. Lincoln, Abraham, 1809-1865. 2. Presidents -- United States 3. Political leadership. 4. Politicians -- United States 5. United States -- Politics and government -- 1861-1865. 6. Biographies

LC 2008028840

A biography of America's sixteenth president portrays Lincoln as a man of integrity whose moral compass holds the key to understanding his life, examining his speeches, his ideas on slavery, his religious odyssey, and his role as Commander-in-Chief.

"In this biography, the author follows the familiar trajectory of the 16th President's life; what's unique is his insight into the moral and intellectual framework of Lincoln's thinking. An exceptional work that belongs in every public and academic library." Library Journal.

Lincoln, Mary Todd, 1818-1882

Clinton, Catherine, 1952- **Mrs.** Lincoln : a life / Catherine Clinton. Harpercollins, 2009 viii, 415 p. : **B**

ISBN 9780060760403

1. Lincoln, Mary Todd, 1818-1882. 2. Presidents' spouses -- United States 3. Women 4. Biographies.

LC 2009294632

A major profile of the sixteenth president's first lady evaluates how her life reflected nineteenth-century America, covering such topics as her well-connected aristocratic family, her experiences as a southerner married to a northern politician, and her struggles with the tragic losses of her child and husband.

Lindbergh, Anne Morrow, 1906-2001

Hertog, Susan **Anne** Morrow Lindbergh : her life / Susan Hertog. Anchor Books, 2000, c1999. 608 p. **B**

ISBN 9780385720076

1. Lindbergh, Charles A. (Charles Augustus), 1902-1974 Marriage. 2. Authors, American -- 20th century 3. Women pilots -- United States 4. Pilots' spouses -- United States 5. United States -- Social life and customs -- 20th century. 6. Biographies

LC BL 00014496

Originally published: New York : Nan A. Talese, c1999.

Drawing on more than five years of interviews and access to personal family papers and correspondence, this fascinating biography offers a stunning portrait of a world-famous couple and their marriage, the tragic kidnapping and murder of their infant son, and Lindbergh's links to the German Reich.

"This sympathetic portrayal of Anne as a wife, mother, poet and feminist may well find a readership more interested in a talented woman's creative struggle than in the oft-told Lindbergh story." Publishers Weekly.

Winters, Kathleen C. **Anne** Morrow Lindbergh : first lady of the air / Kathleen C. Winters. Palgrave Macmillan, 2006. 256 p. **B**

ISBN 9781403969323

1. Lindbergh, Anne Morrow, 1906-2001. 2. Lindbergh, Charles A. (Charles Augustus), 1902-1974 Family. 3. Women pilots -- United States 4. Authors, American -- 20th century 5. Biographies

LC 2006043290

Presents a compelling portrait of Anne Morrow, the wife of Charles Lindbergh and an aviation pioneer in her own right, reconstructing her adventure-filled life within the context of the dangerous early days of aviation's golden age.

"Winters shows in great detail that Lindbergh accomplished this under the glare of an unremitting spotlight, and in the company of an often-demanding spouse. That the author is able to bring something new to the Lindbergh story is impressive, and she does it through both technical explanations of Lindbergh's accomplishments and Anne's own words about her flying exploits, marriage, and writing." Booklist.

Lindbergh, Charles A. (Charles Augustus), 1902-1974

Lindbergh, Charles A. (Charles Augustus), 1902-1974 The **spirit** of St. Louis / Charles A. Lindbergh. Scribner, 2003, c1953. xii, 562 p. **B**

ISBN 9780743237055

1. Lindbergh, Charles A. (Charles Augustus), 1902-1974 Childhood and youth 2. Spirit of St. Louis (Airplane) 3. Transatlantic flights. 4. Pilots -- United States 5. Aviation -- United States -- History 6. United States -- Social life and customs -- 20th century. 7. United States -- History -- 20th century. 8. Autobiographies and memoirs

LC bl2010026935

Originally published: New York : Scribner, 1953.

Pulitzer Prize for Biography or Autobiography, 1954.

Presents Lindbergh's own account of his historic transatlantic solo flight in 1927.

Lindgren, Astrid, 1907-2002

Andersen, Jens, 1955- **Astrid** Lindgren : the woman behind Pippi Longstocking / Jens Andersen, translated by Caroline Waight. Yale University Press, 2018, c2014 360 p. **B**

ISBN 9780300226102

1. Children's literature authors 2. Authors, Swedish 3. Longstocking, Pippi (Fictitious character) 4. Biographies

LC 2017940326

Translation of: Denna dagen, ett liv: En biografi över Astrid Lindgren Originally published: Sweden : Nordstedts, 2014

The first English?language biography of Astrid Lindgren provides a moving and revealing portrait of the beloved Scandinavian literary icon whose adventures of Pippi Longstocking have influenced generations of young readers all over the world.

"Andersen incisively and resonantly chronicles the evolution of Lindgrens progressive work and its impact, along with her influence as a childrens-book editor and environmental activist, bringing to new light a writer as empowered and exhilarating as her most cherished creation." Booklist.

Lindhout, Amanda

★Lindhout, Amanda A **house** in the sky : a memoir / Amanda Lindhout, Sara Corbett. Scribner, 2013. 288 p. **B**

ISBN 9781451645606

1. Lindhout, Amanda. 2. Journalists -- Canada 3. Hostages -- Somalia 4. Voyages and travels. 5. Captivity. 6. Somalia -- History -- 1991- 7. Autobiographies and memoirs

LC 2013016015

Documents the author's backpacking tours through some of the world's most dangerous and war-ridden regions, describing her work as a fledgling television reporter, her brutal 15-month incarceration in Somalia and her founding of a non-profit organization to promote aid, development and education.

Linne, Carl von, 1707-1778

Blunt, Wilfrid, 1901-1987 **Linnaeus** : the compleat naturalist / Wilfrid Blunt ; with an introduction by William T. Stearn. Princeton University Press, c2001. 264 p. : **B**

ISBN 0691096368

1. Linne, Carl von, 1707-1778. 2. Naturalists -- Sweden 3. Biographies

LC 2001097706

Originally published: The compleat naturalist. New York : Viking Press, 1971. With new introd.

Lipska, Barbara K.

Lipska, Barbara K. The **neuroscientist** who lost her mind : my tale of madness and recovery / Barbara K. Lipska with Elaine McArdle. Houghton Mifflin Harcourt, 2018. 224 p. **B**

ISBN 9781328787309

1. People with melanoma 2. Brain metastasis. 3. Cancer 4. Neuroscientists. 5. Autobiographies and memoirs

LC 2017046211

Describes how the author, a leading expert on the neuroscience of mental illness, endured months of terrifying symptoms related to a brain melanoma before immunotherapy enabled a cure, recounting in vivid detail her recollection of the experience and what it revealed about the role of mental illness, brain injury and age on behavior, personality and memory.

Lispector, Clarice

Moser, Benjamin **Why** this world : a biography of Clarice Lispector / Benjamin Moser. Oxford University Press, 2009. viii, 479 p., 16 p of plates : **B**

ISBN 9780195385564

1. Lispector, Clarice. 2. Authors, Brazilian -- 20th century 3. Women authors -- 20th century 4. Brazil -- History -- 20th century 5. Biographies

LC 2008055639

National Book Critics Circle Award for Biography finalist, 2009.

Uses previously unknown manuscripts and numerous interviews to explore the life and work of the Brazilian author.

Lister, Joseph, Baron, 1827-1912

Fitzharris, Lindsey, 1982- The **butchering** art : Joseph Lister's quest to transform the grisly world of Victorian medicine / Lindsey Fitzharris. Scientific American / Farrar, Straus and Giroux, 2017. 288 p. **B**

ISBN 9780374117290

1. Lister, Joseph, Baron, 1827-1912. 2. Surgeons. 3. Surgery. 4. Medicine -- History. 5. Physicians -- History. 6. Biographies

LC 2016059275

ALA Notable Book, 2018.

A dramatic account of how 19th-century Quaker surgeon Joseph Lister developed an antiseptic method that indelibly changed medicine, describes the practices and risks of early operating theaters as well as the belief systems of Lister's contemporaries.

Liston, Sonny, 1932-1970

Assael, Shaun The **murder** of Sonny Liston : Las Vegas, heroin, and heavyweights / Shaun Assael. Blue Rider Press, 2016. 352 p. **B**

ISBN 9780399169755

1. Liston, Sonny, 1932-1970. 2. Heroin. 3. Boxers (Sports). 4. Police cover-ups. 5. Organized crime 6. Las Vegas, Nevada.

LC 2016016232

Includes index.

An investigation into the unsolved death of Heavyweight Champion Sonny Liston is set against a backdrop of the Vegas mob battles, drug wars and boxing glory days of the early 1970s and shares the insights of close associates who doubted official rulings that his death was due to a drug overdose.

Litt, David, 1986-

Litt, David, 1986- **Thanks,** Obama : my hopey changey White House years / David Litt. Ecco, 2017. 256 p. **B**

ISBN 9780062568458

1. Obama, Barack Friends and associates 2. Presidents -- United States -- Staff 3. Speechwriters 4. Humorists 5. United States -- Politics and government -- 2009-2017 6. Washington, D.C. -- Social

life and customs -- 21st century 7. Autobiographies and memoirs
LC 2017019330

The senior comic speechwriter and presidential advisor presents an account of his college education through his years working with Barack Obama, sharing behind-the-scenes anecdotes and his reflections on Obama's legacy in the age of Trump.

Little Richard, 1932-

White, Charles, 1942- The **life** and times of Little Richard : the quasar of rock / Charles White. Da Capo, 1994. xvi, 282 p. : **B**

ISBN 0306805529

1. Rock musicians -- United States 2. Biographies
LC 93048054

Includes index.Previous ed.: New York : Harmony Books, 1984.

Lively, Penelope, 1933-

Lively, Penelope, 1933- **Life** in the garden / Penelope Lively. Viking, 2018. 208 p. **B**

ISBN 9780525558378

1. Authors, English -- 20th century 2. Gardening 3. Thought and thinking 4. Women authors 5. Autobiographies and memoirs
LC 2018013220

Penelope Lively takes up her key themes of time and memory, and her lifelong passions for art, literature, and gardening in this philosophical and poetic memoir.

Lloyd Webber, Andrew, 1948-

Lloyd Webber, Andrew, 1948- **Unmasked** : a memoir / Andrew Lloyd Webber. HarperCollins, 2018 272 p. **B**

ISBN 9780062424204

1. Composers 2. Musicals 3. Theater 4. Autobiographies and memoirs
LC 2017568260

Published to coincide with his 70th birthday, a memoir by the award-winning composer, producer and impresario of some of the most recognized musicals in theater history traces his half-century career, sharing insights into his eccentric, diverse family; his Oxford education; his creative process; and the events that shaped his characters and productions.

Lloyd, Carli, 1982-

Lloyd, Carli, 1982- **When** nobody was watching : my hard-fought journey to the top of the soccer world / Carli Lloyd, with Wayne Coffey. Houghton Mifflin Harcourt, 2016. 256 p. **B**

ISBN 9780544814622

1. Women soccer players 2. Soccer players 3. Soccer 4. Professional athletes 5. Autobiographies and memoirs
LC 2016036411

The celebrated star of the U.S. women's national soccer team chronicles her amazing journey to the top.

"This book is a remarkable portrait of the relentless drive and sacrifice required to truly be the best." Booklist.

Lobo, Julio, 1898-

Rathbone, John Paul The **sugar** king of Havana : the rise and fall of Julio Lobo, Cuba's last tycoon / John Paul Rathbone. Penguin Press, 2010. 336 p. **B**

ISBN 9781594202582

1. Sugar industry and trade -- History 2. Businesspeople -- Cuba 3. Rich men. 4. Exiles. 5. Cuba -- History -- 1895- 6. Biographies
LC 2010013790

Documents the career of an influential Cuban sugar magnate whose life mirrored the turbulent course of post-independence Cuba's republic, discussing his celebrity affairs, brushes with death, and strained relationship with Che Guevara.

Locke, Alain LeRoy, 1886-1954

★Stewart, Jeffrey C., 1950- The **new** Negro : the life of Alain Locke / Jeffrey C. Stewart. Oxford University Press, 2018 962 p. **B**

ISBN 9780195089578

1. Locke, Alain LeRoy, 1886-1954. 2. African-American philosophers. 3. Harlem Renaissance. 4. Intellectual life 5. African American intellectuals. 6. New York City 7. Harlem, New York City 8. Biographies
LC 2017026626

BCALA Literary Award for Nonfiction, 2019.
National Book Award for Nonfiction, 2018.
Pulitzer Prize for Biography or Autobiography, 2019.

In The New Negro: The Life of Alain Locke, Jeffrey C. Stewart offers the definitive biography of the father of the Harlem Renaissance, based on the extant primary sources of his life and on interviews with those who knew him personally. He narrates the education of Locke, including his becoming the first African American Rhodes Scholar and earning a PhD in philosophy at Harvard University, and his long career as a professor at Howard University.

"Those who love biographies or reading about important yet undercelebrated Americans will enjoy Stewart's comprehensive, richly contextualized portrait of a key writer, educator, philosopher, and supporter of the arts." Booklist.

Locke, Tembi, 1970-

Locke, Tembi, 1970- **From** scratch : a memoir of love, Sicily, and finding home / Tembi Locke. Simon & Schuster, 2019. x, 339 p. ; **B**

ISBN 9781501187650

1. Grief in women 2. Interracial marriage 3. Family traditions 4. Widows 5. Sicily, Italy 6. Autobiographies and memoirs
LC 2019002516

A poignant and transporting cross-cultural love story set against the lush backdrop of the Sicilian countryside, where one woman discovers the healing powers of food, family, and unexpected grace in her darkest hour.

Lockwood, Belva Ann Bennett, 1830-1917

Norgren, Jill **Belva** Lockwood : the woman who would be president / Jill Norgren. New York University Press, 2007. xviii, 311 p. : **B**

ISBN 9780814758342

1. Lockwood, Belva Ann Bennett, 1830-1917. 2. Lawyers 3. Women lawyers 4. Ambition in women. 5. Biographies
LC 2006034486

"Those with interests in women's, political, social, and cultural history will enjoy Lockwood." Choice.

Lockwood, Patricia

Lockwood, Patricia **Priestdaddy** : a memoir / Patricia Lockwood. Riverhead Books, 2017. 352 p. **B**

ISBN 9781594633737

1. Catholic Church. 2. Homecomings 3. Nonconformists 4. Catholics 5. Father and adult daughter 6. Autobiographies and memoirs
LC 2016029241

Thurber Prize for American Humor, 2018.
Kirkus Prize for Nonfiction finalist, 2017.

The author of Motherland Fatherland Homelandsexuals presents a darkly comic memoir about her relationship with her unconventional married Catholic priest father, describing emblematic moments from her youth and the crisis that led the author and her non-religious husband to briefly live in her parents' rectory.

"Lockwood magically combines laugh-aloud moments with frank discussions of social issues and shows off her poets skills with lovely, metaphor-filled descriptions that make this memoir shine." Booklist.

Loh, Sandra Tsing

Loh, Sandra Tsing The **madwoman** and the Roomba : my year of domestic mayhem / Sandra Tsing Loh. W.W. Norton & Company, [2020] xv, 276 p. **B**

ISBN 9780393249200

1. Women authors, American 2. Middle-aged women 3. Aging 4. Femininity 5. Autobiographies and memoirs

LC 2019052108

Middle age, for Sandra Tsing Loh, feels more like living a disorganized 25-year-old's life in an 85-year-old's malfunctioning body. With raucous wit and carefree candor, Loh recounts the struggles of leaning in, staying lean, and keeping her family well-fed and financially afloat?all those burdens of running a household that still, all-too-often, fall to women.

"Loh's voice is laugh-out-loud hilarious, and her fun house perspective on the foibles of middle age are intelligent and effervescent. Fans of her previous memoir and her NPR program The Loh Down on Science will delight in this outing." Publishers Weekly

Lombardi, Vince, 1913-1970

Eisenberg, John, 1956- **That** first season : how Vince Lombardi took the worst team in the NFL and set it on the path to glory / John Eisenberg. Houghton Mifflin Harcourt, 2009. 304 p. **B**

ISBN 9780618904990

1. Lombardi, Vince, 1913-1970. 2. Green Bay Packers (Football team) -- History. 3. National Football League. 4. Football coaches -- United States 5. Professional football coaches 6. Professional football. 7. Professional football coaching.

LC 2009028269

Celebrating the fiftieth anniversary of Vince Lombardi's first season in Green Bay, the author chronicles the coach's first year as head coach with the franchise he would reinvent and etch forever in football history, in a book based on interviews and thorough research.

London, Jack, 1876-1916

Labor, Earle, 1928- **Jack** London : an American life / Earle Labor. Farrar, Straus and Giroux, 2013. 496 p. **B**

ISBN 9780374178482

1. London, Jack, 1876-1916. 2. Authors, American -- 19th century 3. Writing. 4. Authors, American -- 20th century 5. Biographies

LC 2012050948

Spur Award for Biography, 2014."

The first authorized biography of a great American novelist".-- Provided by publisher.

Reesman, Jeanne Campbell **Jack** London, photographer / Jeanne Campbell Reesman, Sara S. Hodson, & Philip Adam. University of Georgia Press, c2010. xiv, 271 p. : **B**

ISBN 9780820329673

1. London, Jack, 1876-1916 Archives 2. Henry E. Huntington Library and Art Gallery Photograph collections. 3. Photographers -- United States 4. Authors, American -- 20th century

LC 2010005973

Examines the photography of the famed American author, from his photojournalist exploits in London, Veracruz, and the South Seas to his documentation of the 1906 San Francisco Earthquake.

Longfellow, Henry Wadsworth, 1807-1882

★Basbanes, Nicholas A., 1943- **Cross** of snow : a life of Henry Wadsworth Longfellow / Nicholas A. Basbanes. Alfred A. Knopf, 2020. x, 461 p. **B**

ISBN 9781101875148

1. Poets, American -- 19th century 2. Translators 3. Creation (Literary, artistic, etc.) 4. Influence (Literary, artistic, etc.) 5. Biographies

LC 2019028002

"This is a Borzoi Book" -- t.p. verso.

In Cross of Snow, the result of more than twelve years of research, including access to never-before-examined letters, diaries, journals, notes, Nicholas Basbanes reveals the life, the times, the work--the soul--of the man who shaped the literature of a new nation with his countless poems, sonnets, stories, essays, translations, and whose renown was so wide-reaching that his deep friendships included Charles Dickens, Nathaniel Hawthorne, Ralph Waldo Emerson, Julia Ward Howe, and Oscar Wilde.

"A revelatory exploration of Longfellow's life and art. . . . A welcome new biography of the iconic 19th-century poet." Kirkus

Longworth, Alice Roosevelt, 1884-1980

Cordery, Stacy A. **Alice** : Alice Roosevelt Longworth, American princess and Washington power broker / Stacy A. Cordery. Viking, 2007. 608 p. **B**

ISBN 9780670018338

1. Longworth, Alice Roosevelt, 1884-1980. 2. Roosevelt, Theodore, 1858-1919 Family. 3. Children of presidents -- United States 4. Women and politics. 5. Intellectual life. 6. United States -- History. 7. Biographies

LC 2006103087

A portrait of Teddy Roosevelt's daughter relates such facts as her tempestuous teen years and flouting of social conventions in order to promote women's rights, her infidelity-tested marriage to Nicholas Longworth, and her criticism of FDR's New Deal programs.

"An authoritative, intriguing portrait of a first daughter who broke the mold." Publishers Weekly.

Lopez, Barry Holstun, 1945-

Lopez, Barry Holstun, 1945- **Horizon** / Barry Lopez. Alfred A. Knopf, 2019. xiv, 572 p. **B**

ISBN 9780394585826

1. Lopez, Barry Holstun, 1945- Travel 2. Authors, American 3. Travel writers 4. Travelers 5. Voyages and travels

LC 2018033323

The National Book Award-winning author of Arctic Dreams presents a lyrical, intellectual account of his world travels and the extraordinary encounters with people, animals and natural elements that shaped his life.

Lopez, Nadia

Lopez, Nadia The **bridge** to brilliance : how one principal in a tough community is inspiring the world / Nadia Lopez with Rebecca Paley. Viking Press, 2016 288 p. **B**

ISBN 9781101980255

1. School principals. 2. Inner city schools 3. Life change events 4. Motivation in education. 5. Autobiographies and memoirs

LC 2016287199

When thirteen-year-old Vidal Chastanet told photographer Brandon Stanton that his principal ,"Ms. Lopez," was the person who most influenced his life, it was the pebble that started a whirlwind for Nadia Lopez and her small, new public school in one of Brooklyn's most wretched communities. The posting on Stanton's wildly popular site Humans of New York (HONY) went mega-viral. Lopez--not long before on the verge of quitting--found herself in the national spotlight and headed for a meeting with Obama, as well as the beneficiary of a million-dollar IndieGoGo campaign for the school. Here is her first-person account of what it took to get to that moment.

"Filled with narratives about overcoming adversity and of seeing the good where others see only trouble, and success where others see failure, this feel-good story will resonate with just about any reader." Library Journal.

Louis XIV, King of France, 1638-1715

Fraser, Antonia, 1932- **Love** and Louis XIV : the women in the life of the Sun King / Antonia Fraser. Nan A. Talese, Doubleday, 2006. xxviii, 388 p. : **B**

ISBN 0385509847

1. Louis XIV, King of France, 1638-1715. 2. Monarchy, French. 3. Paramours. 4. Mothers and sons 5. Favorites, Royal -- France. 6. France -- Rulers. 7. France -- History -- Louis XIV, 1643-1715. 8. France -- Moral conditions -- History -- 17th century. 9. Biographies

LC 2006044674

A study of the life and reign of the Sun King looks at the world of King Louis XIV from the perspective of his intimate relationships with the women in his life, from his mother, Anne of Austria, and his official queen, Marie-Therese, to his many mistresses--including Louise de la Valliere, Athenais, marquise de Montespan, and Francoise de Maintenon.

"One of the most enveloping popular histories of the current publishing season." Booklist.

Mansel, Philip, 1951- **King** of the world : the life of Louis XIV / Philip Mansel. University of Chicago Press, 2020, c2019. 608 p. **B**

ISBN 9780226690896

1. Louis XIV, King of France, 1638-1715. 2. Chateau de Versailles (Versailles, France) 3. Rulers 4. Courts and courtiers 5. Monarchy, French 6. Aristocracy -- France. 7. France -- History -- Louis XIV, 1643-1715. 8. France 9. Biographies

Originally published: London : Allen Lane, 2019."

An impressive, comprehensive biography of the Sun King--a must-add to any Francophile's library." Kirkus

Louis, Joe, 1914-1981

Roberts, Randy **Joe** Louis : hard times man / Randy Roberts. Yale University Press, c2010. 352 p. **B**

ISBN 9780300122220

1. Louis, Joe, 1914-1981. 2. Boxers (Sports) -- United States 3. African American boxers 4. Boxing -- United States. 5. Biographies

LC 2010015422

Through meticulous research and first-hand interviews, the author presents Joe Louis's impact on boxing and the U.S., revealing an athlete who carefully managed his public image and who actually had complex relationships with both the black and white communities, including mobsters.

"In this biography of the American boxer, Roberts handles the boxing action with professional aplomb, and he knows when to cut away to tell us something of consequence and when to return to the ring. The author ably chronicles Louis's rise from Alabama cotton fields to the cavernous Yankee Stadium, where celebrities glittered in the ringside seats for his big fights; the development of the mass media (boxing was enormously popular on radio); Louis's career in the U.S. Army; and his sad decline, amid unpayable debts and mental illness. All legendary athletes should hope for treatment by such capable, compassionate hands." Kirkus.

Louvin, Charlie, 1927-2011

Louvin, Charlie, 1927-2011 **Satan** is real : the ballad of the Louvin Brothers / Charlie Louvin and Benjamin Whitmer. HarperCollins, 2012. 297 p. **B**

ISBN 9780062069030

1. Louvin, Charlie, 1927-2011. 2. Louvin, Ira, 1924-1965. 3. Louvin Brothers 4. Country music. 5. Family relationships. 6. Country music industry and trade. 7. United States -- Popular culture -- History -- 20th century. 8. Autobiographies and memoirs

LC 2012563500

The story of musical brothers Charlie and Ira Louvin--the first a church-going gospel singer, the second a hard drinking, mandolin-smashing hellraiser who was banned from performing at the Grand Ole Opry after his wife shot him for trying to choke her.

Lovato, Roberto

Lovato, Roberto **Unforgetting** : a memoir of family, migration, gangs, and revolution in the Americas / Roberto Lovato. HarperCollins 2020 304 p. **B**

ISBN 9780062938473

1. Journalists 2. Families -- El Salvador 3. Immigration and emigration 4. Violence in gangs 5. San Francisco, California 6. El Salvador 7. Autobiographies and memoirs

LC bl2020018268

A journalistic memoir detailing the author's firsthand experiences with immigration, gang life and guerilla warfare explores the violence that shaped generations of his impoverished Salvadoran family to connect today's immigration crisis to the realities of everyday families.

"In a memoir that is at once profoundly personal and historically significant, accomplished journalist and scholar Lovato digs deep into his own troubled past to embark on the superhuman task of unforgetting the tortured history entwining his family, El Salvador, and the United States of América. . . . This mix of memoir and history is an essential chronicle, solidly researched and carefully sourced, and enriched with some poetry and plenty of hard-won wisdom." Booklist

Lovelace, Ada King, Countess of, 1815-1852

Essinger, James, 1957- **Ada's** algorithm : how Lord Byron's daughter Ada Lovelace launched the digital age / James Essinger. Melville House, [2014] 288 p. **B**

ISBN 9781612194080

1. Lovelace, Ada King, Countess of, 1815-1852. 2. Babbage, Charles, 1791-1871. 3. Women mathematicians 4. Computers -- History 5. Algorithms 6. Mathematicians 7. Great Britain -- History -- 19th century 8. Biographies

LC 2014021837

"Based on ten years of research and filled with fascinating characters and observations of the period, not to mention numerous illustrations, Essinger tells Ada's fascinating story in unprecedented detail to absorbing and inspiring effect".-- Provided by publisher.

"Essinger (Spellbound: The Surprising Origins and Astonishing Secrets of English Spelling, 2007, etc.) presents Ada's story with great enthusiasm and rich detail, painting her life as one that was rich with opportunity and access but stifled by sexism. Ada continues to inspire, and by using her own voice via letters and research, the author brings her to life for a new generation of intrepid female innovators. A robust, engaging and exciting biography." Kirkus.

Lowe, George, 1924-2013

Lowe, George, 1924-2013 **Letters** from Everest : a New Zealander's account of the epic first ascent / George Lowe. HarperCollins, 2013. 176 p. **B**

ISBN 9781775540335

1. Lowe, George, 1924-2013. 2. Mount Everest Expedition, 1953. 3. Mountaineers -- Correspondence. 4. Mountaineering -- History. 5. Male friendship 6. Mount Everest. 7. New Zealand. 8. Letters. 9. Autobiographies and memoirs

"In this touching book, unpublished letters from the George Lowe collection are brought together for the first time to describe the day-to-day moments of the historic 1953 Everest expedition. Lowe met Hillary while working in New Zealand's Southern Alps just after the war and struck up a friendship. Little did he know it would be the beginning of a journey to the highest altitudes and latitudes of the planet." --From publisher description

Lowell, Robert, 1917-1977

Jamison, Kay Redfield **Robert** Lowell, setting the river on fire : a study of genius, mania, and character / Kay Redfield Jamison. Alfred A. Knopf, 2017. 560 p. **B**

ISBN 9780307700278

1. Poets, American -- 20th century 2. Bipolar disorder 3. Creativity 4. Men with bipolar disorder 5. Biographies

LC 2016028281

ALA Notable Book, 2018.

Pulitzer Prize for Biography or Autobiography finalist, 2018.

Presents an account of the life of the major American poet while sharing psychological insights into the relationship between bipolar illness and creative genius.

"A deeply informed investigation of a poet's suffering and creative triumph." Kirkus.

Mariani, Paul **Lost** puritan : a life of Robert Lowell / Paul Mariani. W.W. Norton, 1996, c1994. 527 p. : **B**

ISBN 0393313743

1. Poets, American -- 20th century 2. Biographies

LC BL 99775162

Reprint. Originally published: 1994.

Traces the life and career of the Pulitzer Prize-winning poet, discusses his influence on modern poetry, and looks at the manic depression and alcoholism that marred his personal life

Lowman, Margaret

Lowman, Margaret **Life** in the treetops : adventures of a woman in field biology / Margaret D. Lowman. Yale University Press, 1999. xvi, 219 p. : **B**

ISBN 0300078188

1. Ecologists 2. Women ecologists 3. Women biologists 4. Biologists 5. Autobiographies and memoirs

LC 98048691

Map of canopy sites on end papers.

Includes index."

Lowman gives a funny, unassuming and deeply idiosyncratic chronicle of her trials and triumphs as a field biologist of tree canopies and other ecosystems in Australia, New England, Belize, Panama and elsewhere." New York Times Book Review.

Lucas, George, 1944-

Jones, Brian Jay **George** Lucas : a life / Brian Jay Jones. Little Brown & Co., 2016 viii, 550 p., 16 unnumbered p. of plates : **B**

ISBN 9780316257442

1. Star Wars (Motion picture) 2. Film producers and directors -- United States 3. Film industry and trade 4. Filmmaking 5. Indiana Jones films 6. Biographies

Traces the story of the man behind such blockbuster franchises as Star Wars and Indiana Jones, offering insight into the challenges he overcame and his influential legacy.

Luce, Henry Robinson, 1898-1967

★Brinkley, Alan, 1949-2019 The **publisher** : Henry Luce and his American century / Alan Brinkley. Alfred A. Knopf, 2010. 528 p. **B**

ISBN 9780679414445

1. Journalists -- United States 2. Publishers and publishing 3. Periodicals -- United States -- History and criticism. 4. Publishers and publishing 5. Biographies

LC 2009038834

Pulitzer Prize for Biography or Autobiography finalist

A profile of the media giant founder of such magazines as "Time," "Life," and "Fortune" documents his childhood as the son of missionaries, university years, and prescient beliefs that transformed the magazine industry.

Lumet, Sidney, 1924-2011

Spiegel, Maura **Sidney** Lumet : a life / Maura Spiegel. St Martins Pr 2019 384 p. **B**

ISBN 9781250030153

1. Lumet, Sidney, 1924-2011. 2. Film producers and directors -- United States 3. Television producers and directors 4. Filmmaking 5. Films 6. United States 7. Biographies

LC 2019031704

A portrait of the influential, five-time Oscar-nominated director shares insights into his use of gritty realism in his stage and television productions as well as his acclaimed work on such Hollywood films as 12 Angry Men and Serpico.

"A likely definitive exploration of the director's distinguished career?of great interest to budding filmmakers and film enthusiasts." Kirkus

Lunden, Joan

Lunden, Joan **Had** I known : a memoir of survival / Joan Lunden. Harper, 2015. 304 p. **B**

ISBN 9780062404084

1. Lunden, Joan. 2. Women cancer survivors 3. Breast cancer 4. People with breast cancer 5. Women television journalists 6. Autobiographies and memoirs

LC bl2015029745

"And Lunden's fans will enjoy learning more about her life. With longtime coauthor and friend Morton, Lunden offers a chatty book with an empowering message for women with breast cancer." Booklist.

Lundquist, Verne

Lundquist, Verne **Play** by play : calling the wildest games in sports -- from SEC football to college basketball, the Masters and more / Verne Lundquist. HarperCollins 2018 320 p. **B**

ISBN 9780062684448

1. Sportscasters 2. Sports 3. Sportscasting 4. Professional sports 5. Autobiographies and memoirs

LC bl2018134709

An award-winning sportscaster chronicles his life and career, touching on such iconic sports moments as Jack Nicklaus' 1986 Masters victory, the attack on Nancy Kerrigan and the Dallas Cowboy victories of the 1970s.

Lussu, Emilio, 1890-1975

Lussu, Emilio, 1890-1975 A **soldier** on the southern front : the classic Italian memoir of World War I / Emilio Lussu ; translated from the Italian by Gregory Conti. Rizzoli Ex Libris, 2014. x, 278 p. ; **B**

ISBN 0847842789

1. Lussu, Emilio, 1890-1975. 2. Soldiers -- Italy -- Sette Comuni 3. World War I 4. World War I -- Campaigns -- Italy -- Sette Comuni. 5. Autobiographies and memoirs.

LC bl2014009001

A rediscovered Italian classic documenting the author's experiences as an infantryman on a series of near-absurd missions concocted with tragic results by tactically unskilled commanders offers a rare perspective of the Italian front.

"A compelling read that enters the mind of a man at the front, exposed daily to terrible scenes and decisions that change who he is." Library Journal.

Luther, Martin, 1483-1546

Bainton, Roland H. (Roland Herbert), 1894-1984 **Here** I stand : a life of Martin Luther / Roland H. Bainton. Abingdon Press, 1990 336 p. : **B**

ISBN 9780687168958

1. Luther, Martin, 1483-1546. 2. Reformation -- Germany 3. Lutheran Church -- Germany -- Clergy

LC 90045795

A biography of the German monk, whose protest against some of the doctrines of the Catholic Church led to the Protestant Reformation

Hendrix, Scott H. **Martin** Luther : visionary reformer / Scott H. Hendrix. Yale University Press, 2015 xxi, 341 p., 16 unnumbered p. of plates : **B**

ISBN 9780300166699

1. Luther, Martin, 1483-1546. 2. Reformation -- Germany 3. Biographies

LC 2015017636

Chronicles the life of the sixteenth century German friar whose public conflict with the Catholic Church triggered the Protestant Reformation.

"This carefully documented, fast-paced telling will delight readers of biography, history, and fiction; historians, theologians, and psychologists may gain deeper insights into how flaws in personality and the zeitgeist itself often prejudice the pursuit of truth." Library Journal.

Metaxas, Eric **Martin** Luther : the man who rediscovered God and changed the world / Eric Metaxas. Viking, 2017. 416 p. **B**

ISBN 9781101980019

1. Luther, Martin, 1483-1546. 2. Reformation 3. Religious reformers 4. Lutheran Church -- Clergy 5. Protestantism 6. Germany -- Church history -- 16th century 7. Biographies

LC 2017025388

Published to coincide with the 500th anniversary of the Reformation, a portrait of the influential religious figure shares insight into the purpose and influence of Martin Luther's famous 95 Theses while exploring his specific role in inspiring modern ideas about faith, virtue and freedom.

"A masterful portrait of a seminal figure." Booklist.

Oberman, Heiko Augustinus **Luther** : man between God and the Devil / Heiko A. Oberman ; translated by Eileen Walliser-Schwarzbart. Yale University Press, 2006, c1989. xx, 380 p. : **B**

ISBN 0300103131

1. Luther, Martin, 1483-1546. 2. Reformation -- Germany 3. Reformation -- Germany. 4. Germany -- Church history -- 16th century. 5. Biographies

LC oc2007039341

Translation of: Luther : Mensch zwischen Gott und Teufel."

The author posits that to understand Luther the reformer is to first realize he was a medieval man for whom Satan was as real as God and human. By placing Luther back into the context of his own age, Oberman strips away any simplistic, post-Enlightenment notions of Luther as the savior of humanity from the darkest obscurantism of the Catholic Church. A triumph of scholarship that brings Luther to life in all of his furious, outspoken, and violent passion." Booklist.

Roper, Lyndal **Martin** Luther : renegade and prophet / Lyndal Roper. Random House, 2017. 400 p. **B**

ISBN 9780812996197

1. Reformation 2. Lutheran Church -- Clergy 3. Protestantism 4. Germany -- History

LC 2016027660

In Martin Luther, Oxford University historian Lyndal Roper provides a detailed biography of the great Reformation. Presenting well-known history in a fresh and engaging manner, Roper relates Luther's family background, depicts key friendships, and discusses important influences on his theological evolution. Candidly and with restraint, she examines his uncompromising stances on such significant matters as his rejection of humanism and his anti-Semitic proclamations. Both scholars and general readers will appreciate the this balanced and insightful portrait.

"This volume will be of great appeal to scholars, but it is also extremely readable and will find a welcome audience among history enthusiasts." Publishers Weekly.

Schilling, Heinz, 1942- **Martin** Luther : rebel in an age of upheaval / Heinz Schilling. Oxford University Press, 2017, c2013. 576 p. **B**

ISBN 9780198722816

1. Luther, Martin, 1483-1546. 2. Reformation 3. Christianity -- History. 4. Lutheran Church -- Clergy 5. Protestantism 6. Germany -- Church history -- 16th century. 7. Biographies

LC bl2017027857

Translated from the German Martin Luther: rebell in einer zeit des umbruchs by Rona Johnston Gordon.

Originally published by Verlag in 2013.In this comprehensive and balanced biography we see Luther as a rebel, but not as a lone hero; as a soldier in a mighty struggle for the universal reform of Christianity and its role in the world. The foundation of Protestantism changed the religious landscape of Europe, and subsequently the world, but the author chooses to show Luther not simply as a reformer, but as an individual.

Wilson, Derek, 1935- **Out** of the storm : the life and legacy of Martin Luther / Derek Wilson. St. Martin's Press, 2008. 416 p. **B**

ISBN 9780312375881

1. Luther, Martin, 1483-1546. 2. Church history -- 16th century. 3. Religion. 4. Religious leaders 5. Biographies

LC 2007039331

A definitive portrait of the renegade monk whose activities helped ignite the Protestant Reformation and transformed the face of Europe provides a revealing study of the complex life, motivations, convictions, and religious, social, and cultural legacy of Martin Luther for both his own time and later eras.

"A nuanced portrait of a perplexing titan." Booklist.

Luttrell, Marcus

Luttrell, Marcus **Lone** survivor : the eyewitness account of Operation Redwing and the lost heroes of SEAL Team 10 / Marcus Luttrell with Patrick Robinson. Little, Brown, 2007. 390 p., 8 p. of plates : **B**

ISBN 0316067598

1. Luttrell, Marcus. 2. United States. Navy. SEALs 3. United States. Navy. Officers. 4. Afghan War, 2001-, American. 5. Soldiers 6. Military campaigns 7. Survival 8. Afghanistan 9. Autobiographies and memoirs

LC 2007921207

The leader, and only survivor, of a team of U.S. Navy SEALs sent to northern Afghanistan to capture a well-known al Qaeda leader chronicles the events of the battle that killed his teammates and offers insight into the training of this elite group of warriors.

Lutz, Robert A.

Lutz, Robert A. **Car** guys vs. bean counters : the battle for the soul of American business / Bob Lutz. Portfolio/Penguin, c2011. xii, 241 p., 16 p. of plates : **B**

ISBN 9781591844006

1. General Motors Corporation. 2. Automobile industry and trade executives 3. Automobile industry and trade -- United States. 4. New products -- United States. 5. Corporate culture -- United States 6. Autobiographies and memoirs

LC 2011010720

Includes index.

A forefront car industry leader describes how he was pulled out of retirement to turn around a bankrupt General Motors in 2008, recounting how he transitioned the company away from office politics and penny pinching.

Lynch, David, 1946-

Lynch, David, 1946- **Room** to dream : a life in art / David Lynch and Kristina McKenna. Random House, 2018. xii, 577 p. : **B**

ISBN 9780399589195

1. Film producers and directors 2. Filmmaking 3. Creation (Literary, artistic, etc.) 4. Creativity 5. Autobiographies and memoirs

LC 2017058580

The extraordinary and highly anticipated memoir from visionary filmmaker David Lynch. In this memoir, David Lynch opens up about a lifetime of extraordinary creativity, the friendships he has made along the way and the struggles he has faced, sometimes successful, sometimes not, to bring his projects to fruition. Part memoir, part biography, Room to Dream interweaves Lynch's own reflections on his life with the story of those times, as told by Kristine McKenna, drawing from extensive & explosive interviews with ninety of Lynch's friends, family members, actors, agents, musicians and collaborators. Lynch responds to each recollection and reveals the inner story of the life behind the art.

"An incandescently detailed and complexly enlightening chronicle of a fervent, uncompromising life devoted to 'pure creativity.'" Booklist.

Lynn, Loretta

Lynn, Loretta **Still** woman enough : a memoir / Loretta Lynn with Patsy Bale Cox. Hyperion, c2002. xix, 244 p. : **B**

ISBN 0786866500

1. Country musicians -- United States 2. United States -- Social life and customs -- 20th century. 3. Autobiographies and memoirs

LC BL2002000807

At head of title: Loretta Lynn.

The celebrated country singer discusses her turbulent relationship with Doo, the man she married at the age of thirteen, revealing a woman whose loyalty, spirit, and determination allowed her to triumph in the face of adversity.

"In this sequel to Coal miner's daughter, Lynn mostly focuses on her marriage and the trials and pleasures of Nashville stardom, including fond recollections of friends like Conway Twitty and Tammy Wynette. Though her grammar may make purists flinch . Lynn's literary voice is as natural and endearing as her songs." Publishers Weekly.

★Lynn, Loretta **Me** & Patsy kickin' up dust : my friendship with Patsy Cline / Loretta Lynn, with Patsy Lynn Russell ; foreword by Dolly Parton. Grand Central Publishing, 2020. xiii, 222 p. **B**

ISBN 9781538701669

1. Cline, Patsy, 1932-1963 2. Women country musicians 3. Country music 4. Female friendship 5. Friends' death 6. Autobiographies and memoirs

LC bl2020007341

Includes index.

Loretta Lynn and the late Patsy Cline are legends--country icons and sisters of the heart. For the first time ever Loretta tells their story: a celebration of their music and their relationship up until Patsy's tragic and untimely death. Full of laughter and tears, this eye-opening, heartwarming memoir paints a picture of two stubborn, spirited country gals who'd be damned if they'd let men or convention tell them how to be. Tender and fierce, Me & Patsy Kickin' Up Dust is an up-close-and-personal portrait of a friendship that defined a generation and changed country music indelibly--and a meditation on love, loss and legacy.

"Fans will pounce on beloved country superstar Lynn's memoir about her bond with sister icon Patsy Cline." Booklist

Lythcott-Haims, Julie

Lythcott-Haims, Julie **Real** American : a memoir / Julie Lythcott-Haims. Henry Holt & Co., 2017. 192 p. **B**

ISBN 9781250137746

1. Multiracial persons 2. Race awareness 3. Identity (Psychology) 4. Racism -- United States 5. Autobiographies and memoirs

LC 2017009272

Shares the story of the author's biracial upbringing in an America where ubiquitous and socially accepted racist norms constantly challenged her self-esteem, prompting her award-winning career in education and her perspectives on wisdom and the healing power of community.

"A compelling and important addition to any collection of personal narratives by women of color." Library Journal.

Maathai, Wangari

Maathai, Wangari **Unbowed** : a memoir / Wangari Muta Maathai. Alfred A. Knopf, 2006. xvii, 314 p. : **B**

ISBN 0307263487

1. Maathai, Wangari. 2. Green Belt Movement (Society : Kenya) 3. Kikuyu (African people) 4. Women environmentalists -- Kenya 5. Women politicians -- Kenya 6. Nobel Prize winners 7. Kenya 8. Autobiographies and memoirs

Includes index.

Hurston/Wright Legacy Award: Nonfiction, 2007.

The recipient of the 2004 Nobel Peace Prize describes her life as a feminist, political activist, and environmentalist in Kenya, detailing her determination to receive an education despite the odds, her confrontations with the brutal Moi government, the 1977 establishment of the Green Belt Movement, her role in the transformation of Kenya's government, and her hope for the future.

Mabanckou, Alain, 1966-

Mabanckou, Alain, 1966- The **lights** of Pointe-Noire : a memoir / Alain Mabanckou ; translated by Helen Stevenson. The New Press, 2016, c2013. 202 p. **B**

ISBN 9781620971901

1. Mabanckou, Alain, 1966-. 2. Authors, Congolese. 3. Homecomings 4. Congo (Brazzaville) 5. Pointe-Noire (Kouilou, Congo) 6. Autobiographies and memoirs

LC 2015032791

Translation of Lumieres de Pointe-Noire, 2013

Finalist for the Man Booker International Prize 2015

Alain Mabanckou left Congo in 1989, at the age of twenty-two, not to return until a quarter of a century later. When at last he returns home to Pointe-Noire, a bustling port town on Congo's south-eastern coast, he finds a country that in some ways has changed beyond recognition: the cinema where, as a child, Mabanckou gorged on glamorous American culture has become a Pentecostal temple, and his secondary school has been re-named in honour of a previously despised colonial ruler. But many things remain unchanged, not least the swirling mythology of Congolese culture which still informs everyday life in Pointe-Noire. Mabanckou though, now a decorated French-Congolese writer and esteemed professor at UCLA, finds he can only look on as an outsider at the place where he grew up.

"Mabanckou blurs past and present further with a subtle writing style that involves a variety of techniques. It's no wonder he has won multiple awards. He is an artisteven of the memoir form." Library Journal.

MacArthur, Douglas, 1880-1964

Borneman, Walter R., 1952- **MacArthur** at war : World War II in the Pacific / Walter R. Borneman. Little, Brown and Co., 2016. viii, 594 p., 16 unnumbered p. of plates : **B**

ISBN 9780316405324

1. World War II 2. Command of troops 3. Military strategy 4. Military history 5. Biographies

LC 2016931808

The author of the national best-seller The Admirals chronicles General Douglas MacArthur's amazing rise during World War II.

"An able researcher and fluent writer, Borneman holds solid appeal for the military history audience." Booklist.

Frank, Richard B., 1947- **MacArthur** : a biography / Richard B. Frank ; foreward by General Wesley K. Clark. Palgrave MacMillan, 2007. 224 p. **B**

ISBN 1403976589

1. MacArthur, Douglas, 1880-1964 Military leadership. 2. MacArthur, Douglas, 1880-1964. 3. Generals -- United States 4. Command of troops 5. United States -- History -- 20th century. 6. United States -- Social life and customs -- 20th century. 7. Biographies

Profiles five-star general Douglas MacArthur, focusing on his contributions to military strategy and leadership, his role as an early proponent of the Air Force as an integral part of modern warfare, and his management of peace during the U.S. occupation of Japan.

"A good starting point for generalists." Library Journal.

★Herman, Arthur, 1956- **Douglas** MacArthur : American warrior / Arthur Herman. Random House, 2016. 880 p. **B**

ISBN 9780812994889

1. United States. Army 2. Generals. 3. United States -- History, Military -- 20th century 4. Biographies

LC 2015039817

The Pulitzer Prize finalist and author of Gandhi & Churchill goes beyond the mythologies of the World War II general to illuminate his strengths and weaknesses, placing his career against a backdrop of history while discussing how he shaped his character to meet national needs.

"Herman presents a superb reexamination of MacArthur and his role in American history." Booklist.

Perry, Mark, 1950- The **most** dangerous man in America : the making of Douglas MacArthur / Mark Perry. Basic Books, 2014. 384 p. **B**

ISBN 9780465013289

1. Generals -- United States 2. Leadership 3. World War II 4. Military campaigns 5. Japan 6. United States -- History -- 20th century. 7. Biographies

LC 2014004629

This biography of the brilliant, but egotistical and rebellious military commander describes the secrets to his success on the Pacific stage of World War II as well as the personal and professional challenges he faced to get there.

"While much has been written on the general topic, Perry is strong on discussing MacArthur's relationship with FDR as well as his fellow officers in the Pacific." Library Journal.

MacDonald, Jeffrey R., 1943-

McGinniss, Joe, 1942-2014 **Fatal** vision / Joe McGinniss. G. P. Putnam's Sons, 1983. 663 p. **B**

ISBN 0399128166

1. Murderers 2. Murder -- North Carolina. 3. Wife-killing. 4. Child murders. 5. North Carolina.

LC 82024127

A study of a brutal multiple murder and its bizarre aftermath focuses on Jeffrey MacDonald, who was convicted, in 1979, of the murders of his pregnant wife and two small daughters nine years earlier.

MacNicol, Glynnis, 1974-

MacNicol, Glynnis, 1974- **No** one tells you this : a memoir / Glynnis MacNicol. Simon & Schuster, [2018] 256 p. **B**

ISBN 9781501163135

1. Self-fulfillment in women 2. Forties (Age) 3. Single women 4. Women journalists 5. New York City 6. New York (State) 7. Autobiographies and memoirs

LC 2018000331

The co-founder of TheList describes the discrimination she endured as a successful careerwoman without a spouse or child, tracing her midlife journey of self-discovery and how it challenged her beliefs about love, death, sex, friendship and loneliness.

"No typical fortysomething (how many of us would move to Wyoming at the drop of a hat?), MacNicol is relatable, and the joy she finds in her life, lived on her own terms, is striking." Booklist.

Machado, Carmen Maria

★Machado, Carmen Maria **In** the dream house : a memoir / Carmen Maria Machado. Graywolf Press 2019. 247 p. ; **B**

ISBN 9781644450031

1. Family violence. 2. Dysfunctional families. 3. Psychic trauma. 4. Lesbians. 5. Autobiographies and memoirs.

Lambda Literary Award for LGBTQ Nonfiction, 2020.Shares the story of the author's relationship with an abusive partner and how it was shaped by her religious upbringing, her sexual orientation and inaccurate cultural beliefs about psychological trauma.

Machiavelli, Niccolo, 1469-1527

Benner, Erica **Be** like the fox : Machiavelli in his world / Erica Benner. W. W. Norton & Company, 2017 384 p. **B**

ISBN 9780393609721

1. Machiavelli, Niccolo, 1469-1527. 2. Intellectuals. 3. Intellectual life. 4. Ideology. 5. Political scientists. 6. Italy -- History -- 1492-1559. 7. Florence, Italy -- History -- 1421-1737. 8. Biographies

LC 2017000694

The dramatic, myth-shattering story of how Machiavelli, the most misunderstood thinker of all time, fought to change his corrupt world.

Boucheron, Patrick **Machiavelli** : the art of teaching people what to fear / Patrick Boucheron ; translated from the French by Willard Wood. Other Press, 2020, c2017. 176 p. **B**

ISBN 9781590519523

1. Political scientists 2. Diplomats 3. Political ethics 4. Political science -- Philosophy 5. Biographies

LC 2019025723

Originally published in French as Un ete avec Machiavel in 2017 by Editions des Equateurs, Paris.In a series of poignant vignettes, a preeminent historian makes a compelling case for Machiavelli as an unjustly maligned figure with valuable political insights that resonate as strongly today as they did in his time. Whenever a tempestuous period in history begins, Machiavelli is summoned, because he is known as one for philosophizing in dark times. In fact, since his death in 1527, we have never ceased to read him to pull ourselves out of torpors. But what do we really know about this man apart from the term invented by his detractors to refer to that political evil, Machiavellianism? With verve and a delightful erudition, Patrick Boucheron sheds light on the life and works of this unclassifiable visionary, illustrating how we can continue to use him as a guide in times of crisis.

"Readers looking to learn more about the thinker, as well as those seeking an introduction, will find this creative work appealing." Library Journal

Unger, Miles **Machiavelli** : a biography / Miles J. Unger. Simon & Schuster, 2011. 384 p. **B**

ISBN 9781416556282

1. Machiavelli, Niccolo, 1469-1527. 2. Intellectuals. 3. Political scientists. 4. Power (Social sciences) 5. Politicians -- Italy. 6. Italy -- History -- 1492-1559. 7. Florence, Italy -- History -- 1421-1737. 8. Biographies

LC 2010054130

An authoritative exploration of the Florentine intellectual includes coverage of his relationships with contemporaries ranging from Leonardo da Vinci and Michelangelo to Cesare Borgia and Pope Alexander VI, his personal philosophies about power and violence and the legacy of such written works as The Prince. By the author of Magnifico.

Viroli, Maurizio **Niccolo's** smile : a biography of Machiavelli / Maurizio Viroli ; translated from the Italian by Antony Shugaar. Hill and Wang, 2002, c2000. xv, 271 p. : **B**

ISBN 0374528004

1. Machiavelli, Niccolo, 1469-1527. 2. Authors, Italian -- 16th century 3. Intellectuals -- Italy -- Florence 4. Statesmen -- Italy -- Florence 5. Florence (Italy) -- Politics and government -- 1421-1737. 6. Biographies

LC bl2011018280

Originally published: New York : Farrar, Straus and Giroux, 2000.

A biography of the Italian known as the founder of modern political thought explores Niccolo Machiavelli's childhood, relationships, and travels, and his ideas on the role of a citizen as a member of a family and part of a republic.

"This biography of the Italian political philosopher traces his life from respected secretary of the Florentine republic, dispatched on crucial diplomatic missions to Europe's most illustrious courts, to forgotten commoner. Viroli provides a detailed, historical background for Machiavelli's personal triumphs and woes. But the strength of this work lies in his ceaseless concentration on Machiavelli the man, who comes alive on each page." Publishers Weekly.

Mackay, John William, 1831-1902

Crouch, Gregory, 1966- The **bonanza** king : John Mackay and the battle over the greatest riches in the American West / Gregory Crouch. Scribner, 2018. 384 p. **B**

ISBN 9781501108198

1. Gold mines and mining -- California -- History -- 19th century 2. Gold rush. 3. Prospecting. 4. Prospectors. 5. The West (United States) 6. Biographies

LC bl2018055915

Traces the rags-to-riches frontier story of Irish immigrant John Mackay, describing how in mid-19th-century Nevada he outmaneuvered the pernicious "Bank Ring" monopoly and thousands of rivals to take control of the nation-changing Comstock Lode.

Maclean, Donald Duart, 1913-1983

Philipps, Roland A **spy** named orphan : the enigma of Donald Maclean / Roland Philipps. W W Norton & Company, 2018 416 p. **B**

ISBN 9780393608571

1. Maclean, Donald Duart, 1913-1983. 2. Spies 3. Secret service. 4. Great Britain. 5. Biographies

LC 2017060974

Drawing on a wealth of previously classified files and unseen family papers, the author meticulously documents the extraordinary story of one of the most treacherous spies of the Cold War era and a key member of the infamous "Cambridge Five" spy ring.

Macleod, Janice

MacLeod, Janice A **Paris** year : my day-to-day adventures in the most romantic city in the world / Janice MacLeod. St. Martin's Griffin, 2017. 272 p. **B**

ISBN 9781250130129

1. Voyages and travels 2. Paris, France 3. France 4. Diaries 5. Autobiographies and memoirs

LC 2017004257

Part memoir and part visual journey through the streets of modern-day Paris, France, A Paris Year chronicles, day by day, one woman's French sojourn in the world's most beautiful city. Beginning on her first day in Paris, Janice MacLeod, the author of the best-selling book, Paris Letters, began a journal recording in illustrations and words, nearly every sight, smell, taste, and thought she experienced in the City of Light. The end result is more than a diary: it's a detailed and colorful love letter toone of the most romantic and historically rich cities on earth. Combining personal observations and anecdotes with stories and facts about famous figures in Parisian history, this visual tale of discovery, through the eyes of an artist, is sure to delight, inspire, and charm.

"MacLeod's (Paris Letters) outsider view of Paris is a lovely portrayal of the romantic city, as she shares her experiences living there as an expat." Library Journal.

Madden, T Kira,

Madden, T Kira **Long** live the tribe of fatherless girls : a memoir / T Kira Madden. Bloomsbury, 2019. 309 p. **B**

ISBN 9781635571851

1. Madden, T Kira, Childhood and youth. 2. Growing up 3. Dysfunctional families 4. Upper class 5. Women authors, American 6. Boca Raton, Florida 7. Autobiographies and memoirs

LC 2018016519

An acclaimed literary essayist presents this raw and redemptive debut memoir about coming of age and reckoning with desire as a queer, biracial teenager in Boca Raton, Florida, where she, the only child of parents continually battling drug and alcohol addictions, found loving friendships with fatherless girls.

"A searing, lyrical debut memoir about addiction, abuse, race, and the sexualization and objectification of young women. This coming-of-age work of forgiveness, family, and love will leave an indelible mark on all who read it." Library Journal.

Madison, Deborah

Madison, Deborah An **onion** in my pocket : my life with vegetables / Deborah Madison. Alfred A. Knopf, 2020. 320 p. **B**

ISBN 9780525656012

1. Madison, Deborah. 2. Cooks -- United States 3. Food writers -- United States 4. Vegetarianism 5. Vegetarian cooking 6. California 7. San Francisco, California 8. Autobiographies and memoirs

LC 2019039918

Thanks to her beloved cookbooks and groundbreaking work as the chef at Greens Restaurant in San Francisco, Deborah Madison, though not a vegetarian herself, has long been revered as this country's leading authority on vegetables. But before she became a household name, Madison spent almost twenty years as an ordained Buddhist priest, coming of age in the midst of counterculture San Francisco. In this charmingly intimate and refreshingly frank memoir, she tells her story--and with it the story of the vegetarian movement--for the very first time.

"A renowned vegetarian chef and cookbook author returns with a menu of memories about her life, profession, and passions. . . . A savory journey through kitchens, ingredients, meals, cookbooks, family, and colleagues--all composing the author's heart." Kirkus

Madison, Dolley, 1768-1849

Allgor, Catherine, 1958- A **perfect** union : Dolley Madison and the creation of the American nation / Catherine Allgor. Henry Holt & Co., 2006. x, 493 p. : **B**

ISBN 9780805073270

1. Madison, Dolley, 1768-1849. 2. Presidents' spouses -- United States 3. Women and politics -- United States -- History. 4. Men/women relations. 5. United States -- Politics and government -- 1783-1865. 6. Biographies

LC 2005055127

An in-depth study of the early days of the American republic offers an intriguing portrait of the life of a remarkable American woman, profiling the seminal role played by Dolley Madison amid the turbulent and complex political, social, and cultural world of the early nineteenth century.

Madison, James, 1751-1836

Broadwater, Jeff **James** Madison : a son of Virginia and a founder of the nation / Jeff Broadwater. University of North Carolina Press, 2012. 320 p. **B**

ISBN 9780807835302

1. Madison, James, 1751-1836. 2. Presidents -- United States 3. Politicians -- United States 4. Ideology. 5. United States -- Politics and government -- 1809-1817. 6. United States -- Politics and government -- 1789-1815.

LC 2011035946

Focuses on Madison's role in the battle for religious freedom in Virginia, his contributions to the adoption of the Constitution and the Bill of Rights, his place in the evolution of the party system, his relationship with Dolley Madison, his performance as commander in chief during the War of 1812 and his views on slavery.

Cheney, Lynne V. **James** Madison : a life reconsidered / Lynne Cheney. Viking Adult, 2014. 576 p. **B**

ISBN 9780670025190

1. Madison, James, 1751-1836. 2. United States. Constitution. 3. Founding Fathers of the United States. 4. Presidents -- United States 5. Politicians -- United States 6. War of 1812 7. United States -- Politics and government -- 1809-1817. 8. United States -- Politics and government -- 1789-1815. 9. Biographies

LC 2013047837

A portrait of the fourth U.S. president offers insight into his pivotal contributions as a Founding Father, covering such topics as his political philosophy and his role as the intellectual force behind the Constitution.

"Cheney conclusively demonstrates through the historical record that Madison, in word and deed, was a primary figure in shaping early American development." Publishers Weekly.

Feldman, Noah, 1970- The **three** lives of James Madison : genius, partisan, president / Noah Feldman. Random House, 2017. 944 p. **B**

ISBN 9780812992755

1. Madison, James, 1751-1836. 2. Democratic Party -- History. 3. United States. Constitution Signers. 4. Founding fathers of the United States. 5. Presidents. 6. Politicians. 7. Political leadership. 8. United States -- Politics and government. 9. Biographies

LC 2017000125

A controversial assessment of what the author identifies as the three distinct arcs of the fourth American President's career explores how he redefined the United States in each of his political roles through his design of the Constitution, co-founding of the Democratic-Republican Party and invention of wartime economic sanctions.

"With its lively prose and political acumen, this biography will be of interest to general-history readers and scholars alike." Publishers Weekly.

Stewart, David O. **Madison's** gift : five partnerships that built America / David O. Stewart. Simon & Schuster, 2015. 432 p. **B**

ISBN 9781451688580

1. Madison, James, 1751-1836. 2. Founding Fathers of the United States. 3. Presidents -- United States. 4. Politicians. 5. United States -- History -- 1783-1865. 6. Biographies

LC 2014021393

James Madison, one of the Founders of the U.S. and its fourth president, seems to fade into the background in comparison with his revolutionary comrades, who were physically taller and more extroverted. However, Madison was a brilliant writer and skilled collaborator, making him indispensable to the success of the new republic the Founders were designing. In?Madison's Gift, acclaimed author David Stewart highlights Madison's abilities and details his work with five collaborators -- four other Founders and his wife Dolley.

Wills, Garry, 1934- **James** Madison / Garry Wills. Times Books, 2002. xx, 184 p. American presidents series (Times Books) **B**

ISBN 0805069054

1. Madison, James, 1751-1836. 2. Democratic Party -- History. 3. Presidents -- United States 4. Politicians -- United States 5.

Political leadership. 6. War of 1812 7. United States -- Politics and government -- 1809-1817. 8. United States -- History -- 1809-1817. 9. United States -- History -- War of 1812. 10. Biographies

LC 2002019692

"The author maintains that Madison possessed qualities that served him well early in his career but proved to be a handicap during his Presidency. . . . Written with flair, this clear and balanced account is based on a sure handling of the material." Library Journal.

Madonna, 1958-

Simone, Alina, 1974- **Madonnaland** : and other detours into fame and fandom / Alina Simone. University of Texas Press, 2016. 138 p. **B**

ISBN 9780292759466

1. Music, American 2. Singers 3. Women musicians 4. Popular music 5. Biographies

LC 2015028441

Filled with fresh insights about the music business, fandom, and what it takes to become a superstar, Madonnaland is as much a book for people who, like Simone, prefer "dark rooms, coffee, and state-subsidized European films filled with existential despair" as it is for people who can't get enough of Madonna. --From publisher description.

Magdalena, Carlos

Magdalena, Carlos The **plant** messiah : adventures in search of the world's rarest species / Carlos Magdalena. Doubleday, 2018. 272 p. **B**

ISBN 9780385543613

1. Horticulturists 2. Botanists 3. Rare and endangered plants. 4. Plant conservation. 5. Autobiographies and memoirs

LC 2017027303

In The Plant Messiah, Magdalena takes readers from the Amazon to the jungles of Mauritius to deep within the Australian Outback in search of the rare and the vulnerable. Back in the lab, we watch as he develops groundbreaking, left-field techniques for rescuing species from extinction, encouraging them to propagate and thrive once again. Along the way, he offers moving, heartfelt stories about the secrets contained within these incredible organisms.

"Magdalenas paean to flora is bound to enthrall readers and get them thinking more fully about plants." Publishers Weekly.

Magellan, Ferdinand, 1480?-1521

Bergreen, Laurence **Over** the edge of the world : Magellan's terrifying circumnavigation of the globe / Laurence Bergreen. Morrow, 2003. xvi, 458 p. : **B**

ISBN 0066211735

1. Magellan, Ferdinand, 1480?-1521. 2. Trips around the world. 3. Explorers -- Portugal 4. Exploration. 5. Expeditions.

LC 2003050143

Colored map on endpapers.

A chronicle of Ferdinand Magellan's sixteenth-century voyage around the world draws on first-person accounts and describes his crew's experiences with mutiny, navigation, death, and Magellan's ruthless leadership.

"The author tells a well-rounded story of Magellan, not just that of the romanticized hero but also that of the explorer's darker side. . . . Fascinating reading for history buffs, and a great story that rivals any seagoing adventure." Booklist.

Mah, Adeline Yen, 1937-

Mah, Adeline Yen, 1937- **Falling** leaves : the true story of an unwanted Chinese daughter / Adeline Yen Mah. Wiley, 1998, c1997. ix, 278 p. : **B**

ISBN 0471247421

1. Chinese Americans -- California 2. Women physicians -- California 3. Immigrants, Chinese 4. California 5. China -- Social life and customs. 6. China -- History -- 1949-1976. 7. Autobiographies and memoirs

LC 97040144

Originally published: Falling leaves return to their roots. London : M. Joseph, 1997.

Includes index."

Although the focus of this memoir is the author's struggle to be loved by a family that treated her cruelly, it is more notable for its portrait of the domestic affairs of an immensely wealthy, Westernized Chinese family in Shanghai as the city evolved under the harsh strictures of Mao and Deng. In recounting this painful tale, Yen Mah's unadorned prose is powerful, her insights keen and her portrait of her family devastating." Publishers Weekly.

Mahjoub, Jamal, 1960-

Mahjoub,Jamal,1960-A**line**intheriver:Khartoum,cityofmemory/ Jamal Mahjoub. Bloomsbury Publishing, 2018 401 p. : **B**

ISBN 9781408885468

1. Mahjoub, Jamal, 1960- Travel Sudan 2. Manners and customs 3. Identity (Psychology) 4. Homecomings 5. Authors 6. Sudan -- Politics and government 7. Khartoum, Sudan -- History 8. Autobiographies and memoirs

LC 2019300509

Includes index.

Traces the author's early memories of Khartoum and his studies into Sudan's past as well as the factors that triggered and perpetuated the civil war after it gained independence in 1956.

Maier, Vivian, 1926-2009

Bannos, Pamela, 1959- **Vivian** Maier : a photographer's life and afterlife / Pamela Bannos. The University of Chicago Press, 2017. 352 p. ; **B**

ISBN 9780226470757

1. Maier, Vivian, 1926-2009. 2. Women photographers. 3. Street photography. 4. Photography 5. Biographies

LC 2017022051

Who was Vivian Maier? Many people know her as the reclusive Chicago nanny who wandered the city for decades, constantly snapping photographs, which were unseen until they were discovered in a seemingly abandoned storage locker. They revealed her to be an inadvertent master of twentieth-century American street photography. Not long after, the news broke that Maier had recently died and had no surviving relatives. Soon the whole world knew about her preternatural work, shooting her to stardom almost overnight.

"Bannos's biography is a vital contribution to understanding the historical relevance of Maiers work and an important challenge to the way in which Maiers work and legacy have been represented thus far." Publishers Weekly.

Mailer, Norman

Dearborn, Mary V. **Mailer** : a biography / Mary V. Dearborn. Houghton Mifflin, 1999. viii, 478 p. : **B**

ISBN 0395736552

1. Authors, American -- 20th century 2. Journalists -- United States 3. United States -- Social life and customs -- 1945- 4. Biographies

LC 99032214

"Dearborn supplies a close reading of one of the most controversial American writers of the postwar era. Mailer's body of work, beginning with his career-defining first novel, The Naked and the Dead (1948), is analyzed with remarkable insight. Mailer's notorious personal life is also examined, as Dearborn sorts through the various preoccupations that have obsessed the writer over five decades in the literary spotlight." Booklist.

Lennon, Michael **Norman** Mailer : a double life / J. Michael Lennon. Simon & Schuster, 2013. 960 p. **B**

ISBN 9781439150191

1. Mailer, Norman. 2. Authors, American -- 20th century 3. Journalists -- United States 4. United States -- Social life and customs -- 1945- 5. Biographies

LC 2013005097

Drawing on extensive interviews and unpublished letters, as well as his own encounters with Mailer, this authoritative biography of the eminent novelist, journalist and controversial public figure chronicles his entire career and his self-conscious effort to create a distinctive identity for himself.

"Detailed and anecdotal without being gossipy . and a must-read for students and admirers of Mailer's work." Kirkus.

Mailer, Norris Church

Mailer, Norris Church A **ticket** to the circus : a memoir / Norris Church Mailer. Random House, 2010. 336 p. **B**

ISBN 9781400067947

1. Mailer, Norris Church Marriage. 2. Mailer, Norman Marriage. 3. Authors' spouses -- United States 4. Husband and wife. 5. Marriage. 6. Authors, American -- 20th century 7. Autobiographies and memoirs

LC 2009033941

The wife of Norman Mailer shares the story of her life and more than three-decade marriage, marked by her early years in Arkansas, her relationship with a young Bill Clinton and her experiences as a parent. By the author of Cheap Diamonds.

"The author adds a fat new sheaf to the public dossier on her late husband, Norman Mailer, and tells an involving coming-of-age story to boot. The book will be of interest to anyone who works in a university marriage lab. It also shows that Norman wasn't the only talented raconteur in the family." New York Times Book Review.

Mailhot, Terese Marie

Mailhot, Terese Marie **Heart** berries : a memoir / Terese Marie Mailhot. Counterpoint Press, 2018 160 p. **B**

ISBN 9781619023345

1. Mailhot, Terese Marie Health. 2. Native American women. 3. First Nations (Canada) 4. Indian reservations 5. Mothers and daughters 6. Autobiographies and memoirs

LC 2017051069

Terese Mailhot's debut memoir chronicles her struggle to balance the beauty of her Native heritage with the often desperate and chaotic reality of life on the reservation.

Majorana, Ettore

Magueijo, Joao A **brilliant** darkness : the extraordinary life and disappearance of Ettore Majorana, the troubled genius of the nuclear age / Joao Magueijo. Basic Books, 2009. xxi, 280 p. : **B**

ISBN 9780465009039

1. Majorana, Ettore. 2. Majorana, Ettore Legends. 3. Nuclear physicists. 4. Physics -- History -- 20th century. 5. Nuclear fission. 6. Missing persons. 7. Biographies

LC 2009037678

A theoretical physicist documents the story of the 1930s nuclear physicist and his mysterious disappearance, tracing his research group's discovery of atomic fission in 1934 while investigating theories about Majorana's alleged suicide, murder or kidnapping.

"The author paints the life of a twenty something math prodigy who joined Enrico Fermi, Emilio Segre, and the other Via Panisperna Boys who in 1934 discovered nuclear fusion. The author could have easily fallen into the jargon of his profession to describe the work of a fellow scientist, but he does not. His clear explanation of Majorana's insight into nuclear physics, often accompanied with drawings and illustrations, will appeal to a wide audience." Library Journal.

Malcolm X, 1925-1965

★Malcolm X, 1925-1965 The **autobiography** of Malcolm X / with the assistance of Alex Haley ; introduction by M.S. Handler ; epilogue by Alex Haley. Ballantine Books, 1992, c1965. xv, 527 p. **B**

ISBN 0345376714

1. Black Muslims 2. African Americans 3. Autobiographies and memoirs

LC 91093124

Book made into a movie called Malcolm X.

Originally published: New York : Grove Press, 1965."

Alex Haley did his job with sensitivity and with devotion. {The book} will have a permanent place in the literature of the Afro-American struggle." New York Review of Books.

★Marable, Manning, 1950-2011 **Malcolm** X : a life of reinvention / Manning Marable. Viking, 2011. 594 p., 16 p. of plates : **B**

ISBN 9780670022205

1. Black Muslims 2. Black nationalism -- United States 3. African American civil rights workers 4. Muslims -- United States 5. United States -- History -- 20th century 6. Biographies

LC 2010025768

ALA Notable Book, 2012.

Pulitzer Prize for History, 2012.

Andrew Carnegie Medal for Excellence in Non-Fiction finalist, 2012.

National Book Critics Circle Award for Biography finalist, 2011.

Pulitzer Prize for Biography or Autobiography finalist, 2012.

Shortlisted for the James Tait Black Memorial Prize for Biography, 2011

National Book Award for Nonfiction finalist, 2011

An authoritative biography of Malcolm X draws on new research to trace his life from his troubled youth through his involvement in the Nation of Islam, his activism in the world of Black Nationalism, and his assassination.

"This is an account of the lives of Malcolm X (1925-1965), including his years as a street hustler in Boston and Harlem, his time in prison where voracious reading led to his transformation into a the devout follower of Elijah Muhammad's Nation of Islam (NOI), his rise as the NOI's chief minister, and, finally, his split from Elijah Muhammad and his acceptance of all people who would work for African American human and economic rights." Library Journal.

★Payne, Les, 1941- The **dead** are arising : the life of Malcolm X / Les Payne and Tamara Payne. Liveright Publishing Corporation, 2020 640 p. **B**

ISBN 9781631491665

1. Nation of Islam 2. Black Muslims 3. Black nationalism -- United States. 4. African American Muslims 5. African American civil rights workers 6. United States -- History -- 20th century 7. United

States -- Race relations 8. Biographies

LC 2020029637

National Book Award for Nonfiction, 2020.

A revisionary portrait of the iconic civil rights leader draws on hundreds of hours of interviews with surviving family members, intelligence officers and political leaders to offer new insights into Malcolm X's Depression-era youth, religious conversion and 1965 assassination.

"This gripping read delivers penetrating explanations and fresh insights into previously unexamined dimensions of Malcolm X and his becoming and being El-hajj Malik El Shabazz within the context of Black life." Library Journal

Perry, Bruce **Malcolm** : the life of a man who changed Black America / Bruce Perry. Station Hill, c1991. xv, 542 p. : **B**

ISBN 9780882681030

1. Black Muslims 2. African Americans 3. United States -- Race relations. 4. Biographies

LC 90023350

Traces the life of the influential Black leader, describes the people who helped shape his philosophy, and looks at the circumstances that led to his murder.

"Perry traces Malcolm X's footsteps from birth in 1925 to death in 1965, using several hundred interviews to fill in detail and correct the autobiography Alex Haley edited. Probing what he labels as the deep-seated and hidden causes that made Malcolm who and what he was, Perry produces a portrait of an emotionally abused and abandoned boy who grew to manipulate his fearful helplessness into emotional and political power." Library Journal.

Malek, Alia, 1974-

Malek, Alia, 1974- The **home** that was our country : a memoir of Syria / Alia Malek. Nation Books, 2017. 304 p. **B**

ISBN 9781568585321

1. Malek, Alia, 1974- Family. 2. City life 3. Arab Spring, 2010- 4. Exile. 5. Home (Concept) 6. Damascus, Syria 7. Syria -- History -- Civil War, 2011- 8. Autobiographies and memoirs

LC 2016037114

In The Home that Was My Country, Syrian-American journalist Alia Malek chronicles her return to her family home in Damascus and the history of the Jabban apartment building. Here, generations of Christians, Jews, Muslims, and Armenians lived, worked, loved, and suffered in close quarters. In telling the story of her family over the course of the last century, Alia brings to light the triumphs and failures that have led Syria to where it is today.

"Moving and insightful, Malek's memoir combines sharp-eyed observations of Syrian politics, only occasionally overdone, with elegiac commentary on home, exile, and a bygone era. Provocative, richly detailed reading." Kirkus.

Mallory, George, 1886-1924

Davis, Wade **Into** the silence : the Great War, Mallory, and the conquest of Everest / Wade Davis. A. A. Knopf, c2011. 672 p. **B**

ISBN 9780375408892

1. Mallory, George, 1886-1924. 2. Mount Everest Expedition, 1924 3. Mountaineers -- Great Britain 4. World War I -- Great Britain -- Influence. 5. Mountaineering. 6. Mount Everest.

LC 2011013888

"A Borzoi book."

Samuel Johnson Prize for Non-Fiction, 2012.

Shortlisted for The Charles Taylor Prize for Literary Non-Fiction

Governor General's Literary Awards, English-language Nonfiction finalist

Recounts George Mallory's attempt to scale Mount Everest in the early 1920s, and how, in the aftermath of World War I, the expedition became a symbol of national pride and hope.

Maloney, Rosie

Calcaterra, Regina **Girl** unbroken : a sister's harrowing story of survival from the streets of Long Island to the farms of Idaho / Regina Calcaterra and Rosie Maloney. William Morrow & Co., 2016. 288 p. **B**

ISBN 9780062412584

1. Maloney, Rosie. 2. Calcaterra, Regina 3. Child abuse. 4. Sisters. 5. Child abuse victims 6. Farm life 7. Long Island, New York 8. Idaho 9. Biographies

LC bl2016044777

"As engrossing as Etched in Sand, this book is a testament to Maloneys remarkable resilience and a moving tribute to the unbreakable bond of love she shared with her siblings. Courageous and emotionally intense." Kirkus.

Manchester, William, 1922-2004

Manchester, William, 1922-2004 **Goodbye,** darkness : a memoir of the Pacific war / William Manchester. Back Bay Books/ Little, Brown and Company, 2002, c1980. 401 p. : **B**

ISBN 9780316501118

1. United States. Marine Corps. 2. World War II 3. Soldiers -- United States 4. Authors, American -- 20th century 5. Marines. 6. Pacific Ocean. 7. Autobiographies and memoirs

LC bl 99780144

Originally published: Boston : Little, Brown, 1980.

Pulitzer Prize for General Nonfiction finalist

The author relates his experiences as a Marine Corps sergeant in World War II, recalling the horrors of Guadalcanal and Okinawa.

"This memoir arises from a 1978 trip the author made to Pacific battlefields, seeking to exorcise three decades of nightmares dating to wartime days as a Marine Corps sergeant. First tracing his family background, youth, enlistment, training, and embarkation from San Diego, Manchester unravels a memoir featuring historical reconstruction, disjointed flash-forwards, shocking vignettes, {and} redoubtable vocabulary." Choice.

Mandela, Nelson, 1918-2013

Brand, Christo **Mandela** : my prisoner, my friend / Christo Brand. Thomas Dunne Books, 2014. xv, 272 p., [16] p. of plates : **B**

ISBN 9781250055262

1. African National Congress of South Africa 2. Anti-apartheid Movement -- South Africa. 3. Prison guards -- South Africa 4. Political prisoners -- South Africa 5. Civil rights workers -- South Africa 6. Presidents -- South Africa 7. South Africa. 8. South Africa -- Politics and government. 9. Biographies

LC 2014026586

"The author quickly recounts Mandela's general biography, including the Rivonia trial for sabotage that landed him in prison, but this is really a tale of two men and their shared humanity in an inhumane place. A worthy addition to the canon of Mandela literature that details a relationship that many knew about but few truly understood." Kirkus.

Mandela, Nelson, 1918-2013 **Conversations** with myself / Nelson Mandela. Farrar Straus & Giroux, 2010. 288 p. **B**

ISBN 9780374128951

1. Politicians. 2. Leadership in men. 3. Social advocates. 4. Anti-

apartheid activists.

LC 2010933174

Draws on the author's personal archive of never-before-seen papers to offer unique access to the private world of the incomparable world leader, who worked from prison to end apartheid in South Africa.

"This volume of personal papers . adds much that has never been said before about Nelson Mandela, including diary entries from his time in the underground, debates about passive resistance and guerrilla warfare, letters from prison, and recorded reminiscences with former fellow prisoners." Booklist.

★Mandela, Nelson, 1918-2013 **Dare** not linger : the Presidential years / Nelson Mandela with Mandla Langa; prologue by Graca Machel. Farrar Straus & Giroux 2017. 320 p. **B**

ISBN 9780374134716

1. Anti-apartheid Movement South Africa 2. Presidents -- South Africa 3. Anti-apartheid activists 4. Politicians. 5. Social advocates. 6. South Africa -- Politics and government -- 1948-1994. 7. Autobiographies and memoirs

LC 2017036979

A sequel to the best-selling Long Walk to Freedom completes the Nobel Prize Laureate's unfinished memoirs and is complemented by notes and speeches written by Mandela during his historic presidency.

"Essential to students of Mandela's political career as well as of modern African history." Kirkus.

Mandela, Nelson, 1918-2013 **In** his own words / Nelson Mandela ; edited by Kader Asmal, David Chidester, Wilmot James. Little, Brown and Co., 2003. xlii, 558 p. : **B**

ISBN 0316110191

1. African National Congress of South Africa 2. Presidents -- South Africa 3. Nobel Prize winners 4. Political prisoners -- South Africa 5. Politicians. 6. South Africa -- Race relations. 7. South Africa -- Politics and government -- 20th century. 8. Autobiographies and memoirs 9. Speeches, addresses, etc. 10. Essays.

LC 2004107807

Includes index.

A collection of speeches by the South African leader includes pieces that marked such moments in his life as his imprisonment and release, his acceptance of the Nobel Peace Prize, and his election as South Africa's first black president.

"This collection of Mandela's speeches shows why he remains a universal hero. This volume will be in great demand for the personal drama, the history, and, yes, for the inspiring moral values." Booklist.

★Mandela, Nelson, 1918-2013 **Long** walk to freedom : the autobiography of Nelson Mandela / Nelson Mandela. Little, Brown, 1994. 558 p., 24 p. of plates : **B**

ISBN 9780316545853

1. Anti-apartheid Movement South Africa 2. Presidents -- South Africa 3. Anti-apartheid activists 4. Politicians. 5. Social advocates. 6. South Africa -- Politics and government -- 1948-1994. 7. Autobiographies and memoirs

LC 94079980

Includes index.

Film adaptation entitled Mandela: Long walk to freedom (2013)

The leader of South Africa's antiapartheid movement chronicles his life, including his tribal years, his time spent in prison, and his return to lead his people.

"This book provides important new evidence to the forty-year story of apartheid, as seen by its most formidable opponent. And there is enough candour to provide insights into the nature of leadership." Times Literary Supplement.

Mandela, Nelson, 1918-2013 **Mandela** : an illustrated autobiography / Nelson Mandela. Little, Brown, 1996. 208 p. : **B**

ISBN 0316550388

1. Presidents -- South Africa 2. Politicians -- South Africa 3. Social advocates. 4. Anti-apartheid activists. 5. South Africa -- Politics and government -- 1948-1994. 6. South Africa -- Politics and government -- 1994- 7. Autobiographies and memoirs

"This is an illustrated and abridged edition of Long walk to freedom: the autobiography of Nelson Mandela ..."--T.p. verso.

Includes index.

Photographs from Mandela's childhood, career, imprisonment, and presidency are accompanied by text from his memoir "Long walk to freedom".

"The photos, from a variety of archives and journalistic sources, ably illustrate Mandela and, even more so, the South Africa around him." Library Journal.

Smith, David James, 1956- **Young** Mandela : the revolutionary years / David James Smith. Little, Brown, c2010. 416 p. **B**

ISBN 9780316035484

1. African National Congress of South Africa 2. Anti-apartheid Movement South Africa -- History. 3. Apartheid -- South Africa -- History. 4. Anti-apartheid movements 5. Political prisoners -- South Africa 6. Civil rights workers -- South Africa 7. South Africa -- Politics and government -- 1961-1978. 8. Biographies

LC 2010031883

In the twilight of his life, Nelson Mandela is a national hero, a world leader, and a household name. While many people know the story of Mandela's imprisonment, release, and role in reuniting South Africa, few have studied his childhood and upbringing. Here, journalist David James Smith chronicles the childhood that shaped Nelson (born Rolihlahla) into a man and reveals several little-known facts about the great leader.

"Smith's focus is on Mandela's legal training and practice, his relationship with the multiracial ANC, and his early revolutionary years leading up to his arrest, trial, and conviction for sabotage and treason, followed by his sentencing to life in prison on Robben Island in 1964. Smith leaves Mandela there at age 46." Library Journal.

Mandel'shtam, Nadezhda, 1899-1980

Mandel'shtam, Nadezhda, 1899-1980 **Hope** against hope : a memoir / Nadezhda Mandelstam ; translated from the Russian by Max Hayward ; with an introduction by Clarence Brown and "Nadezhda Mandelstam (1899-1980): an obituary" by Joseph Brodsky. Modern Library, 1999. xxv, 442 p. ; **B**

ISBN 0375753168

1. Mandel'shtam, Nadezhda, 1899-1980. 2. Mandel'shtam, Osip, 1891-1938. 3. Poets, Russian -- 20th century 4. Soviet Union -- Intellectual life -- 1917-1970. 5. Soviet Union -- Politics and government -- 1917-1936. 6. Soviet Union -- Politics and government -- 1936-1953. 7. Biographies

LC 98047833

Includes index."

Mandelstam tells the story of her family's experiences of hardship in Soviet Russia under Stalin. What is remarkable about the book is not just its content but also its authorial voice, which, in Max Hayward's deft translation, is so unique and consistent that the reader can get a sense of it by opening the book at random and reading almost any paragraph. Although Hope Against Hope is a painful book to read, one of the things that makes it bearable, apart from its sheer beauty, is a kind of unquenchable spirit and optimism that keeps rising to the surface, compounding the more mysterious consolations of art." Harper's

Mankell, Henning, 1948-2015

Mankell, Henning, 1948-2015 **Quicksand** : what it means to be a human being / Henning Mankell. Vintage Books, 2017 320 p. **B**

ISBN 9780525432159

1. Authors, Swedish 2. Death 3. People with cancer 4. Coping 5. Autobiographies and memoirs 6. Essays

LC bl2016057757

The late activist and best-selling author of the Kurt Wallander mysteries explores in a sequence of intimate vignettes the myriad experiences of a life richly lived through his relationships and writings as evaluated after his 2014 lung cancer diagnosis.

"This book is a compelling attempt to leave behind something for future civilizations to stumble upon, to piece together what it meant to be a human in the 21st century." Library Journal.

Mankiller, Wilma Pearl, 1945-

Mankiller, Wilma Pearl, 1945- **Mankiller** : a chief and her people / Wilma Mankiller and Michael Wallis. St. Martin's Griffin, 2000, c1993. xxvi, 310 p. : **B**

ISBN 9780312206628

1. Cherokee women 2. Cherokee Indians

LC bl2004112427

Originally published: New York : St. Martin's Press, 1993. With a new afterword by the author.

An updated edition of this best selling memoir reviews not only the experiences of a former Chief of the Cherokee nation, but also the shifting events of the last five years, which have included a kidney transplant and political struggles within the nation. Reissue.

Mankoff, Robert

Mankoff, Robert **How** about never--is never good for you? : my life in cartoons / Bob Mankoff. Henry Holt & Company, 2014 304 p. **B**

ISBN 9780805095906

1. Mankoff, Robert. 2. New Yorker (New York, N.Y. : 1925) 3. Cartoonists -- United States 4. Cartoons. 5. Periodical editors -- United States 6. Growing up 7. Comics and Graphic novels 8. Autobiographies and memoirs

LC 2013021129

Memoir in cartoons by the longtime cartoon editor of The New Yorker.

People tell Bob Mankoff that as the cartoon editor of The New Yorker he has the best job in the world. Never one to beat around the bush, he explains to us, in the opening of this singular, delightfully eccentric book, that because he is also a cartoonist at the magazine he actually has two of the best jobs in the world. With the help of myriad images and his funniest, most beloved cartoons, he traces his love of the craft all the way back to his childhood, when he started doing funny drawings at the age of eight. Throughout, we see his commitment to the motto "Anything worth saying is worth saying funny."

Mann, Sally, 1951-

★Mann, Sally, 1951- **Hold** still : a memoir with photographs / Sally Mann. Little, Brown and Company, 2015. xiv, 482 p. : **B**

ISBN 9780316247764

1. Photographers 2. Photography. 3. Families 4. Family secrets. 5. Virginia. 6. Autobiographies and memoirs.

LC bl2015017753

Andrew Carnegie Medal for Excellence in Non-Fiction, 2016.

National Book Award for Nonfiction finalist, 2015"

Here photographer Mann chronicles her rich and eccentric family history, told through the exploration of old documents and images stored away in her attic. Raw and darkly humorous, Mann's writing is consistently honest and poignant as she depicts her beloved Virginia farm, her childhood, her parents, and her children." Library Journal.

Manson, Charles, 1934-2017

★Guinn, Jeff **Manson** : the life and times of Charles Manson / Jeff Guinn. Simon & Schuster, [2013] 352 p. **B**

ISBN 9781451645163

1. Mass murderers -- California 2. Criminals -- United States 3. Prisoners -- United States 4. Murder -- California 5. United States -- Social life and customs -- 20th century. 6. Biographies

LC 2012050176

Guinn's biography answers lingering questions about the Manson Family murders, while delivering stunning revelations about the life of America's most notorious psychopath.

Mansoor, Peter R., 1960-

Mansoor, Peter R., 1960- **Baghdad** at sunrise : a Brigade Commander's war in Iraq / Peter R. Mansoor ; foreword by Donald Kagan and Frederick Kagan. Yale University Press, CT, 2008. 416 p. **B**

ISBN 9780300140699

1. Iraq War, 2003-2011, American 2. World politics. 3. Military history. 4. War. 5. United States -- Armed Forces 6. United States -- History, Military 7. Autobiographies and memoirs

LC 2008007366

An on-the-ground commander describes his brigade's first year in Iraq after the U.S. forces seized Baghdad in the spring of 2003, and explains what went right and wrong as the U.S. military confronted an insurgency, in a firsthand analysis of success and failure in Iraq.

"This is a unique contribution to the burgeoning literature on the Iraq war. The critique is balanced, perceptive and merciless." Publishers Weekly.

Mantle, Mickey, 1931-1995

Castro, Tony **Mantle** : the best there ever was / Tony Castro. Rowman & Littlefield, [2019] 272 p. **B**

ISBN 9781538122211

1. Mantle, Mickey, 1931-1995. 2. New York Yankees (Baseball team) -- History. 3. Baseball players -- United States 4. Baseball 5. Dysfunctional families 6. Alcoholics 7. Biographies

LC 2018056819

"Distributed by NATIONAL BOOK NETWORK"--T.p. verso.

This book brings to life the story of Mickey Mantle, presenting a fully-rounded portrait of a complex, misunderstood national hero. It includes never-before-published details from Mantle's widow and offers illuminating insight into his career using modern analytics, arguing that he should be considered the greatest ballplayer of all time.

"Castro was Mantle's friend, and he uses that relationship to bring an intimacy to the book. Mantles life story has been told many times, but its never received as loving a treatment as this one." Booklist.

Leavy, Jane The **last** boy : Mickey Mantle and the end of America's childhood / Jane Leavy. Harper, c2010. xxiv, 456 p., [16] p. of plates : **B**

ISBN 9780060883522

1. New York Yankees (Baseball team) -- History 2. Baseball Hall of Fame members 3. Baseball players -- United States 4. Outfielders

(Baseball) 5. Baseball -- History -- 20th century 6. United States -- Social life and customs -- 20th century 7. Biographies

LC 2010525670

Drawing on more than five hundred interviews with loved ones and fellow baseball players, the author crafts a deeply personal biography of the Yankee great, weaving her own memories of the major league slugger with an authoritative account of his life onand off the field.

"This is unlike any biography on the sports shelf. Leavy, in exploring her own ambivalent feelings toward Mantle, permits readers to experience the same confusing emotions that many of those around him felt: proud to bask in his reflected glory but too intimidated to confront him. A masterpiece of sports biography." Booklist.

Roberts, Randy, 1951- A **season** in the sun : the rise of Mickey Mantle / Randy Roberts and Johnny Smith. Basic Books, 2018 304 p. **B**

ISBN 9780465094424

1. Mantle, Mickey, 1931-1995. 2. New York Yankees (Baseball team) -- History. 3. Baseball players. 4. Baseball 5. Biographies

LC 2017038834

An account of Mickey Mantle's historic 1956 season describes how he navigated injuries, alcoholism and his detractors to become a heroic idol in postwar America, sharing insights into his complex personality on and off the field. By the authors of Blood Brothers.

"Highly recommended for fans of sports, Americana, and those seeking an informative historical read." Library Journal.

Mao, Zedong, 1893-1976

Chang, Jung, 1952- **Mao** : the unknown story / Jung Chang, Jon Halliday. Knopf, 2005. xiii, 814 p. : **B**

ISBN 0679422714

1. Heads of state -- China 2. Totalitarianism -- China. 3. Communism -- China. 4. China -- History -- 1949-1976. 5. Biographies

LC 2004063826

"Originally published in Great Britain by Jonathan Cape, London"--T.p. verso."

This is a magisterial work. This biography supplies substantial . information and presents it all in a stylish way that will put it on bedside tables around the world." New York Times Book Review.

★Pantsov, Alexander, 1955- **Mao** : the real story / Alexander V. Pantsov with Steven I. Levine. Simon & Schuster, 2012, c2007. 736 p. **B**

ISBN 9781451654479

1. Mao, Zedong, 1893-1976. 2. Heads of state. 3. Communists. 4. Revolutions -- China. 5. Politicians. 6. China -- Politics and government -- 1949-1976. 7. Biographies

LC 2011053113

Originally published in Russian: Moskva : Molodaia Gvardiia, 2007, under title Mao Tzedun.

Draws on extensive, previously unavailable Russian documents to reveal surprising details about Mao Zedong's rise to power and leadership in China, providing coverage of such topics as his health, alleged affairs and controversial political decisions. Co-written by the author of The Bolsheviks and the Chinese Revolution 1919-1927.

"The Great Helmsman fully fleshed, still complicated and ever provocative." Kirkus.

Short, Philip **Mao** : a life / Philip Short. Henry Holt, 2000. xiii, 782 p. : **B**

ISBN 9780805031157

1. Heads of state -- China 2. Genocide -- China. 3. Communism -- China -- History. 4. Revolutions -- China. 5. China -- Politics and government -- 1949-1976. 6. China -- History -- 1949-1976. 7. China -- History -- Cultural Revolution, 1966-1976 8. Biographies

LC 99041839

"A John Macrae book."

Originally published in 1999 in Great Britain by Hodder & Stoughton.

A portrait of Mao explores the life of the peasant who rose to the position of "chairman" of China's communist party and absolute ruler of the country, overseeing both brilliant reform and terrible butchery during his long reign.

"This biography takes Mao from his 1893 birth in the village of Shaoshan to school in Changsha, where he trained to be a teacher, and then into revolutionary activity, the long fight with Chiang Kai-shek, and leadership of the most populous nation on Earth." Booklist.

Maravich, Pete, 1947-1988

Kriegel, Mark **Pistol** : the life of Pete Maravich / Mark Kriegel. Free Press, c2007. viii, 381 p., 16 p. of plates : **B**

ISBN 0743284976

1. Maravich, Pete, 1947-1988. 2. Professional basketball players. 3. Professional basketball. 4. Basketball players 5. Basketball. 6. United States -- Social life and customs -- 20th century. 7. Biographies

LC 2006051526

Recounts the life and achievements of the troubled 1970s basketball star, from his relationship with his obsessive father and unbroken college scoring record to the personal demons that challenged his life and his evangelical Christian faith.

March de la Torre, Aleida

March de la Torre, Aleida **Remembering** Che : my life with Che Guevara / Aleida March. Ocean Press, 2012. viii, 168 p. : **B**

ISBN 9780987077936

1. Guevara, Che, 1928-1967 2. Revolutionaries' spouses 3. Revolutionaries. 4. Husband and wife. 5. Widows. 6. Latin America -- History. 7. Cuba -- History -- 1959-1990. 8. Cuba -- History -- 1990- 9. Autobiographies and memoirs

LC bl2012014280

Reveals the life of Che Guevara through the eyes of his widow, including the start of their romance and her reaction to his assassination in Bolivia.

Marchione, Anthony James, 1925-1945

Harding, Stephen, 1952- **Last** to die : a defeated empire, a forgotten mission, and the last American killed in World War II / Stephen Harding. Da Capo Press, 2015. 288 p. **B**

ISBN 9780306823381

1. Marchione, Anthony James, 1925-1945. 2. United States. Army Air Forces. Photo Reconnaissance Squadron, 20th 3. United States. Army Air Forces Aerial gunners 4. Soldiers 5. World War II. 6. Military campaigns 7. Japan 8. Biographies

LC 2015003486

In a book based on interviews with people who were there, combined with official histories of America and Japan, the author describes the final days of World War II and the tragic death of Sergeant Anthony J. Marchione, the last U.S. soldier killed during the war.

"Harding treats the youth with admiration and affection that elicit compassion without becoming cloying or melodramatic. This is a superb look at the life and death of one young man among millions of others who loved, were loved by others, and died too soon." Booklist.

Marciano, Rocky, 1923-1969

Stanton, Mike, 1957- **Unbeaten** : Rocky Marciano's fight for perfection in a crooked world / Mike Stanton. Henry Holt and Company, 2018. 384 p. ; **B**

ISBN 9781627799195

1. Marciano, Rocky, 1923-1969. 2. Boxers (Sports) 3. Boxing 4. Immigrants 5. Corruption 6. Biographies

LC 2017057871

Presents a revelatory portrait of the legendary heavyweight champion that covers his rise from an Italian immigrant family, his signature "Suzie Q" punch, and his struggles with the sport's corrupt elements.

"This meticulously documented and well-written work should stand for both fans and scholars as Marciano's definitive biography." Library Journal.

Marconi, Guglielmo, marchese, 1874-1937

Raboy, Marc, 1948- **Marconi** : the man who networked the world / Marc Raboy. Oxford University Press, 2016 592 p. **B**

ISBN 9780199313587

1. Marconi, Guglielmo, marchese, 1874-1937. 2. Inventors 3. Electrical engineers. 4. Radio. 5. Wireless telegraph -- Marconi system -- History. 6. Biographies

LC 2015042075

Governor General's Literary Awards, English-language Non-fiction finalist, 2016

Shortlisted for The Charles Taylor Prize for Literary Non-Fiction, 2017

Guglielmo Marconi is one of the most enigmatic figures in the history of technology. Inventor, entrepreneur, statesman and diplomat, Marconi shaped the age of electronic media more than any other. Before the dawn of the 20th century, he envisaged a world of seamless, wireless communication, and set out to create it using all the tools at his disposal--guile, charm, and visionary genius. Between 1896 and 1937, Marconi was at the heart of every major innovation in electronic communication.

"A comprehensive portrait of a complicated man, Raboys meticulous, judicious work merits anchorage on science-history shelves." Booklist.

Mardini, Yusra

Mardini, Yusra **Butterfly** : from refugee to Olympian, my story of rescue, hope, and triumph / Yusra Mardini. St. Martin's Press, 2018 256 p. **B**

ISBN 9781250184405

1. Mardini, Yusra. 2. Olympic Games (31st : 2016 : Rio de Janeiro, Brazil). 3. Women swimmers. 4. Olympic athletes 5. Refugees 6. Resilience in women. 7. Autobiographies and memoirs

LC 2017061098

"First published in the United Kingdom by Bluebird, an imprint of Pan Macmillan"--T.p. verso.

Traces the author's life-changing rescue of a boatload of fellow refugees and how it inspired her to compete on the 2016 Refugee Olympic Team in Rio de Janeiro, tracing her subsequent work with the UN as a Goodwill Ambassador and her advocacy on behalf of people who have been forced from their homes by war.

Margaret, Princess, Countess of Snowdon, 1930-2002

Brown, Craig, 1957- **Ninety-nine** glimpses of Princess Margaret / Craig Brown. Farrar, Straus and Giroux, 2018, c2017. 432 p. **B**

ISBN 9780374906047

1. Margaret, Princess, Countess of Snowdon, 1930-2002. 2. Princesses -- Great Britain 3. Reputation 4. Fame 5. Biographies

LC 2018008784

"Originally published in 2017 by 4th Estate, an imprint of HarperCollinsPublishers, Great Britain, as Ma'am Darling: 99 Glimpses of Princess Margaret."

James Tait Black Memorial Prize for Biography, 2017

National Book Critics Circle Award for Biography finalist, 2018

Combining interviews, parodies, dreams, parallel lives, diaries, announcements, lists, catalogues and essays on Princess Margaret, the author offers a kaleidoscopic experiment in biography and a witty meditation on fame and art, snobbery and deference, bohemia and high society.

"Readers wanting a straightforward biography should look elsewhere, but those interested in a sometimes hilarious, sometimes gloomy view of Princess Margaret through a variety of lenses, or a look at how popular representation shapes our view of a public figure should snap up this book." Library Journal.

Margery, 1888-1941

Jaher, David The **witch** of Lime Street : seance, seduction, and Houdini in the spirit world / David Jaher. Crown Publishers, 2015. 432 p. **B**

ISBN 9780307451064

1. Margery, 1888-1941. 2. Houdini, Harry, 1874-1926. 3. Doyle, Arthur Conan, Sir, 1859-1930 4. Spiritualists -- United States 5. Spiritualism -- United States -- History -- 20th century. 6. Women mediums -- United States 7. Competition

LC 2015009392

"Through a combination of feminine seduction and illusionist skill that even Houdini admired, Crandon became the one psychic to almost win the respect of the scientific community and outshine Houdini as an entertainer. Jaher's narrative style is as engaging as his character portraits are colorful. Together, they bring a bygone age and its defining spiritual obsessions roaring to life. Fascinating, sometimes thrilling, reading." Kirkus.

Marie Antoinette, Queen, consort of Louis XVI, King of France, 1755-1793

Fraser, Antonia, 1932- **Marie** Antoinette : the journey / Antonia Fraser. Nan A. Talese, Doubleday, 2001. xxii, 512 p. : **B**

ISBN 038548948X

1. Women rulers -- France. 2. Monarchy, French. 3. Rulers. 4. France -- History -- Louis XVI, 1774-1793. 5. France -- Rulers. 6. Biographies

LC 2001023493

Illustrated with unpaged color plates."

A well-researched biography that may cause one to rethink the role in which history has cast Marie Antoinette." Library Journal.

Marie-Benoit, de Bourg d'Ire, 1895-1990

Zuccotti, Susan, 1940- **Pere** Marie-Benoit and Jewish rescue : how a French priest together with Jewish friends saved thousands during the Holocaust / Susan Zuccotti. Indiana University Press, 2013. 264 p. **B**

ISBN 9780253008534

1. Marie-Benoit, de Bourg d'Ire, 1895-1990. 2. Franciscans France 3. World War II -- Jews -- Rescue -- France 4. Righteous Gentiles in the Holocaust 5. Priests 6. Holocaust (1933-1945) -- France. 7. Marseille -- History. 8. France -- History -- German occupation, 1940-1945. 9. Biographies

LC 2012047187

Unlike many Catholics of the time, Franciscan priest Père Marie-Benoît vehemently opposed anti-Semitism and championed protection for the Jews. He rescued thousands of Jews during World War II by sheltering refugees in France, and assisted Italian Jews after his transfer to Rome. This compelling biography illuminates both his individual efforts and the work of many who opposed the Holocaust.

Maris, Roger, 1934-1985

Clavin, Thomas **Roger** Maris : baseball's reluctant hero / Tom Clavin and Danny Peary. Simon & Schuster, 2010. 422 p. **B**

ISBN 9781416589280

1. Maris, Roger, 1934-1985. 2. New York Yankees (Baseball team) 3. Professional baseball players. 4. Professional baseball. 5. Baseball players 6. Baseball. 7. Biographies

LC 2009039722

A portrait of the baseball legend who broke Babe Ruth's single-season home-run record describes his childhood in North Dakota, his glory years with the Yankees and the ways in which he was unfairly targeted by the media and adversarial fans.

"As is evident from the occasionally worshipful prose, the authors . all but genuflect at the mention of the name Maris. But to their credit, they do make a compelling and relentless argument, and by book's end what emerges is a sympathetic portrait of a man who was shamefully wronged, a man who endured patently unfair treatment, and who defiantly persevered." Philadelphia Inquirer.

Markham, Beryl, 1902-1986

Markham, Beryl, 1902-1986 **West** with the night / Beryl Markham. North Point Press, 2013. xv, 293 p. ; **B**

ISBN 9780865477636

1. Markham, Beryl, 1902-1986. 2. Women pilots 3. Horse breeders. 4. British in Africa. 5. Horse breeding. 6. East Africa -- Description and travel 7. Autobiographies and memoirs

LC 2013498448

Originally published: Boston : Houghton, Mifflin, 1942.

The author describes growing up in an Africa that no longer exists, training and breeding race horses, flying mail to Sudan, and being the first woman to fly the Atlantic from east to west.

Markle, Meghan, 1981-

Morton, Andrew, 1953- **Meghan** : a Hollywood princess / Andrew Morton. Grand Central Publishing, 2018. 288 p. **B**

ISBN 9781538747353

1. Henry, Prince, grandson of Elizabeth II, Queen of Great Britain, 1984- 2. Princes. 3. Princesses. 4. Royal houses. 5. Social classes. 6. Great Britain -- Social life and customs -- 21st century 7. Biographies

LC 2018289013

From the New York Times best-selling author of Diana: Her True Story comes a biography of Meghan Markle, the American actress who won Prince Harry's heart.

Marlowe, Christopher, 1564-1593

★Honan, Park **Christopher** Marlowe : poet & spy / Park Honan. Oxford University Press, 2005. xv, 421 p. : **B**

ISBN 9780198186953

1. Marlowe, Christopher, 1564-1593. 2. Dramatists, English -- Early modern, 1500-1700 3. England -- Social life and customs -- 16th century. 4. Biographies

LC 2005019761

The life of Christopher Marlowe, one of the great playwrights of his age, as well as a secret agent and the central figure in a murder mystery, is explored in this richly detailed biography, which includes new facts about his youth, sojourn at Cambridge, continental adventures, turbulent personal life, and mysterious death.

"The author sheds light on the much-speculated (and previously erroneously reported) aspects of Marlowe's life without neglecting its more ordinary features (his stable two-parent upbringing, his diligent scholarship at Cambridge) or destroying the poet's aura of intrigue." Publishers Weekly.

Nicholl, Charles The **reckoning** : the murder of Christopher Marlowe / Charles Nicholl. University of Chicago Press, 1995, c1992. 413 p. : **B**

ISBN 0226580245

1. Marlowe, Christopher, 1564-1593 Death and burial. 2. Dramatists, English -- 16th century. 3. Murder -- London, England -- History -- 16th century. 4. Murder victims -- Great Britain. 5. Spies -- Great Britain -- History -- 16th century 6. London, England -- History -- 16th century.

LC 95003004

Originally published: London : J. Cape, 1992.

Gold Dagger Award for Best Nonfiction of the Year, 1992.

James Tait Black Memorial Prize for Biography, 1992.

An investigation into the death of Christopher Marlowe, the sixteenth-century author tragically stabbed to death in a lodging house, reveals the secrets behind the enigmatic literary legend.

"A remarkable piece of scholarship, this work carefully reconstructs the events leading up to the murder with all the excitement and suspense of a modern mystery novel; at the same time it vividly conveys the energy and color of Elizabethan England." Library Journal.

Marsh, Henry

Marsh, Henry **Admissions** : life as a brain surgeon / Henry Marsh. Thomas Dunne Books, 2017 288 p. **B**

ISBN 9781250127266

1. Neurosurgeons 2. Medical care -- Accessibility. 3. Community health services 4. Brain -- Surgery 5. Autobiographies and memoirs

LC 2017023778

National Book Critics Circle Award for Autobiography/Memoir finalist, 2017"

Another thoughtful, painful, utterly fascinating mixture of nut-and-bolts brain surgery with a compassionate, workaholic surgeon's view of medicine around the world and his own limitations." Kirkus.

Marsh, Henry **Do** no harm : stories of life, death and brain surgery / Henry Marsh. Thomas Dunne Books, 2015, c2014. 304 p. **B**

ISBN 9781250065810

1. Neurosurgeons 2. Brain -- Surgery 3. Physician and patient 4. Surgery 5. Autobiographies and memoirs

LC 2015002573

Originally published: London : Weidenfeld & Nicolson, 2014."

One of the best books ever about a life in medicine, Do No Harm boldly and gracefully exposes the vulnerability and painful privilege of being a physician." Booklist.

Marshall, George C. (George Catlett), 1880-1959

Roll, David L., 1940- **George** Marshall : Defender of the Republic / David L. Roll. Dutton Caliber, 2019. 704 p. **B**

ISBN 9781101990971

1. Marshall, George C. (George Catlett), 1880-1959. 2. United States. Army 3. World War II 4. Generals -- United States 5. Political leadership -- United States 6. Marshall Plan, 1948-1952 7. United States -- History, Military -- 20th century. 8. United States -- Politics and government -- 1901-1953. 9. United States -- Foreign relations

-- 20th century. 10. Biographies

LC 2018055675

Traces the story of the distinguished U.S. soldier and statesman, examining his role in influencing two world wars and America's emergence as a global superpower.

"This well-written and captivating book will stand as the definitive biography of Marshall." Publishers Weekly.

Unger, Debi **George** Marshall : an interpretive biography / Debi Unger, Irwin Unger, Stanley Hirshson. HarperCollins, 2014 560 p. **B**

ISBN 9780060577193

1. Marshall, George C., (George Catlett), 1880-1959. 2. United States. Army 3. United States. Secretary of State. 4. Generals -- United States 5. Politicians -- United States 6. Marshall Plan, 1948-1952. 7. Command of troops 8. Biographies

LC 2015413285

This interpretive biography of George C. Marshall follows his life from his childhood in Western Pennsylvania and his military training at the Virginia Military Institute to his role during and after World War II and his death in 1959 at the age of seventy-eight. It brings to light the virtuous historical role models who inspired him, including George Washington and Robert E. Lee, and his relationships with the Washington political establishment, military brass, and foreign leaders, from Harry Truman to Chiang Kai-shek. It explores Marshall's successes and failures during World War II, and his contributions through two critical years of the emerging Cold War - including the transformative Marshall Plan, which saved Western Europe from Soviet domination, and the failed attempt to unite China's nationalists and communists.

"The authors praise him [Marshall] for his management of the vast military expansion and his ability to cope with the difficulties inherent in controlling a giant military coalition. His decisions regarding the implementation of D-Day and the planned invasion of Japan are justifiably questioned, as are his choices as the Cold War commenced. This is an excellent reexamination of Marshall's career that is ideal for general readers." Booklist.

Marshall, John, 1755-1835

★Paul, Joel R **Without** precedent : Chief Justice John Marshall and his times / Joel Richard Paul. Riverhead Books, 2018 448 p. **B**

ISBN 9781594488238

1. Marshall, John, 1755-1835. 2. United States. Supreme Court 3. Judges. 4. Biographies

LC 2017016049

A portrait of the influential chief justice, statesman, and diplomat illuminates his pivotal role in the establishment of the Constitution and Supreme Court and recounts his work as an advisor to multiple presidents.

"This masterly work elucidates the indelible imprint that Marshall made on the U.S. Constitution and its subsequent interpretation." Library Journal.

Smith, Jean Edward **John** Marshall : definer of a nation / Jean Edward Smith. H. Holt & Co., 1996. xi, 736 p. : **B**

ISBN 9780805013894

1. Marshall, John, 1755-1835. 2. United States. Supreme Court Justices 3. United States. Supreme Court Chief Justices 4. Judges -- United States 5. United States -- History. 6. Biographies 7. Biographies

LC 96015072

"A Marian Wood book."

Chronicles the life, career, and contributions of the man who sat on the United States Supreme Court for thirty-five years and who was instrumental in molding the court into the powerful body it is today.

"Mr. Smith's splendid biography deserves a large readership mostly because it has recovered Marshall the man." New York Times Book Review.

Unger, Harlow G., 1931- **John** Marshall : the chief justice who saved the nation / Harlow Giles Unger. Da Capo Press, 2014. 384 p. **B**

ISBN 9780306822209

1. Marshall, John, 1755-1835. 2. United States. Supreme Court Justices 3. Judges -- United States 4. Judges. 5. Biographies

LC 2014008405

A soul-stirring biography of John Marshall, the young Republic's great chief justice who led the Supreme Court to power and brought law and order to the nationIn the political turmoil that convulsed America after George Washington's death, the surviving Founding Fathers went mad--literally pummeling each other in Congress and challenging one another to deadly duels in their quest for power...

Marshall, Paule, 1929-

Marshall, Paule, 1929- **Triangular** Road : a memoir / Paule Marshall. BasicCivitas Books, c2008. 192 p. **B**

ISBN 9780465013593

1. Hughes, Langston, 1902-1967. 2. African American authors 3. Women and literature -- United States -- History -- 20th century. 4. Intellectual life -- African Americans 5. African Americans 6. United States -- Social life and customs -- 20th century. 7. Autobiographies and memoirs

LC 2008036671

"Though fiction may have pride of place in . [the author's] heart, Triangular Road reveals a strong gift for self-scrutiny made all the more revealing by quiet humor and what appears to be complete honesty." Washington Post.

Marshall, Thurgood, 1908-1993

Gibson, Larry S., 1942- **Young** Thurgood : the making of a Supreme Court Justice / Larry S. Gibson. Prometheus Books, 2012. 390 p. **B**

ISBN 9781616145712

1. United States. Supreme Court Officials and employees 2. United States. Supreme Court -- History 3. Judges -- United States 4. African Americans -- Civil rights. 5. Civil rights 6. African American judges 7. United States -- Social life and customs -- 20th century 8. United States -- History -- 20th century 9. Biographies

LC 2012027517

The only biography of Thurgood Marshall endorsed by his immediate family covers his whole life, from his upbringing to his landmark work with the NAACP and his appointment as the first African-American justice of the Supreme Court.

★Haygood, Wil **Showdown** : Thurgood Marshall and the Supreme Court nomination that changed America / Wil Haygood. Alfred A. Knopf, 2015. 480 p. **B**

ISBN 9780307957191

1. Marshall, Thurgood, 1908-1993. 2. United States. Supreme Court. 3. United States. Supreme Court Chief Justices. 4. Judges -- Selection and appointment -- United States -- History -- 20th century. 5. African American judges 6. Civil rights -- United States. 7. Judges -- United States 8. United States -- Politics and government -- 1945-

1989 9. Biographies

LC 2014044440

The author of The Butler presents a revelatory biography of the first African-American Supreme Court justice?one of the giants of the civil rights movement, and one of the most transforming Supreme Court justices of the 20th century.

"The behind-the-scenes look at the hard-fought battle that Lyndon Johnson and his supporters waged on Marshalls behalf creates suspense, even though readers will already know of their ultimate success." Publishers Weekly.

Marshall, Thurgood, 1908-1993 **Thurgood** Marshall : his speeches, writings, arguments, opinions, and reminiscences / edited by Mark V. Tushnet ; foreword by Randall Kennedy. Lawrence Hill Books, c2001. xxvi, 548 p. The library of Black America **B**

ISBN 9781556523861

1. Marshall, Thurgood, 1908-1993. 2. United States. Supreme Court Justices 3. Judges -- United States 4. Racism -- Law and legislation

LC 2001016793

A collection of the first African American Supreme Court justice includes his arguments for school desegregation cases, reports on racism and race riots in the Army, notes on the history of civil rights, and opinions on several issues.

"In a career ranging from his trial and appellate work for the NAACP to his tenure as an associate justice of the Court, Marshall wrought revolutionary changes in U.S. law and politics, and this collection of his legal briefs, writings, speeches, and judicial opinions, plus a never-before-published oral interview, gives us a superior analysis of the advocate, the democrat, the dissenter, and the unflagging fighter for equality." Library Journal.

Starks, Glenn L., 1966- **Thurgood** Marshall : a biography / Glenn L. Starks, F. Erik Brooks. Greenwood, 2012. 168 p. Greenwood biographies **B**

ISBN 9780313349164

1. Marshall, Thurgood, 1908-1993. 2. United States. Supreme Court. Justices 3. African American judges 4. Judges -- United States 5. African Americans 6. Biographies

LC 2011051894

Includes index."

This book provides a detailed examination of the life and legal legacy of Supreme Court Justice Thurgood Marshall, including a discussion of the many legal cases in which he was involved"-- Provided by publisher.

Williams, Juan **Thurgood** Marshall : American revolutionary / Juan Williams. Times Books, 1998. xviii, 459 p. : **B**

ISBN 9780812920284

1. Marshall, Thurgood, 1908-1993. 2. United States. Supreme Court Justices. 3. Judges -- United States 4. Civil rights workers -- United States 5. African American judges 6. School desegregation decision, 1954. 7. Biographies

LC 98009735

Presents a biography of the first African American appointed to the Supreme Court, from his crusade against segregation to his friendships with other famous Black figures.

"Williams presents Marshall as a revolutionary of grand vision, but this well-rounded portrait of the man also addresses his vanities and warts, from his ascension to his deflation and subsequent redemption. This is a must read for all Americans concerned with the struggle for civil and individual rights." Booklist.

Martin, Billy, 1928-1989

Pennington, Bill, 1956- **Billy** Martin : baseball's flawed genius / Bill Pennington. Houghton Mifflin Harcourt, 2015. 496 p. **B**

ISBN 9780544022096

1. Martin, Billy, 1928-1989. 2. New York Yankees (Baseball team) -- History. 3. Professional baseball managers -- United States 4. Baseball players 5. Professional baseball teams. 6. Baseball -- History 7. Biographies

LC 2014039677

A portrait of the 1950s New York Yankees second baseman explores the athletic and leadership genius behind his mercurial personality and controversial antics, tracing his shantytown upbringing and conflict-marked relationships.

"Pennington analyzes the ongoing conflict that was Billy Martin--including his relationships with equally complex individuals such as George Steinbrenner and Reggie Jackson--from all sides (Billys varied career is covered chronologically, but it's the Yankee years, however sporadic, that matter) and with balance and impressive depth." Booklist.

Martin, Mary, 1913-1990

Kaufman, David, 1951- **Some** enchanted evenings : the glittering life and times of Mary Martin / David Kaufman. St. Martin's Press, 2016. 304 p. **B**

ISBN 9781250031754

1. Martin, Mary, 1913-1990. 2. Hagman, Ben 3. Halliday, Richard, 1905-1973 4. Film actors and actresses -- United States 5. Women singers -- United States 6. Musicals -- New York City 7. Singers 8. Biographies

LC 2015047863

A biography of the American actress, singer and Broadway star describes her childhood in Texas, her early marriage and subsequently quick divorce and her arrival in New York City, where she became a huge star of the Great White Way

"A warm and well-researched... appreciation of one of the stage's most beloved performers and, on the evidence here, least interesting legends." Kirkus.

Martin, Steve, 1945-

Martin, Steve, 1945- **Born** standing up : a comic's life / Steve Martin. Scribner, 2007. 224 p. **B**

ISBN 1416553649

1. Entertainers -- United States 2. Comedians -- United States 3. Stand-up comedians 4. Stand-up comedy. 5. Autobiographies and memoirs

LC 2007027143

The author shares the stories of his years in stand-up comedy in a humorous memoir that recalls a first job selling guidebooks at Disneyland, his early magic and comedy act, his years of honing his craft, and the sacrifice, discipline, and originality ittook to take him to the top.

"This book does a sharp-witted job of breaking down the step-by-step process that brought [the author] from Disneyland, where he spent his version of a Dickensian childhood as a schoolboy employee, to both the pinnacle of stardom and the brink of disaster. . . . Even for readers already familiar with Mr. Martin's solemn side, [this] is a surprising book: smart, serious, heartfelt and confessional without being maudlin." New York Times.

Martin, Trayvon, 1995-2012

Fulton, Sybrina **Rest** in power : the enduring life of Trayvon Martin - a parents' story of love, injustice, and the birth of a movement / Sybrina Fulton and Tracy Martin. Spiegel & Grau,

2017. 288 p. **B**
ISBN 9780812997231
1. Racism. 2. Injustice. 3. Civil rights 4. Violence against minorities. 5. Biographies
LC 2017002840
Sybrina Fulton and Tracy Martin, Trayvon Martin's parents, chronicle their reactions to their son's death as they recount the details of his final days, the trial of the man who killed him, and subsequent events. They build a loving portrait of their son as they relate the memories of family and friends. Telling Trayvon's story in alternating chapters, they provide information that's missing from news reports and offer food for thought in the national controversy that followed this death and the subsequent deaths in Ferguson, MO, Charleston, SC, and other places.

"Given the unconscionable shooting deaths of young black men, many by police, that followed Trayvon's, this galvanizing testimony from parents who channeled their sorrow into action offers a deeply humanizing perspective on the crisis propelling a national movement." Booklist.

Martin, Wednesday

Martin, Wednesday **Primates** of Park Avenue: a memoir / Wednesday Martin, Ph.D. Simon & Schuster, 2015. 256 p. **B**
ISBN 9781476762623
1. Martin, Wednesday. 2. Mothers -- New York City 3. Primates -- Behavior -- Miscellanea. 4. Interpersonal relations -- New York City 5. City life -- New York City 6. Upper East Side, New York City 7. New York City -- Social life and customs. 8. Autobiographies and memoirs
LC 2014041481
"This anthropological journey into the wilds of New York City's most exclusive zip code could have easily devolved into condescension, but instead it proves that mothers everywhere want the same thing: health and happiness for their progeny." Library Journal.

Martinez, Jose Manuel, 1962-

★Garrison, Jessica The **devil's** harvest : a ruthless killer, a terrorized community, and the search for justice in California's Central Valley / Jessica Garrison. Hachette Books, [2020] 336 p. **B**
ISBN 9780316455688
1. Drug dealers 2. Murderers -- California -- Case studies. 3. Serial murders -- California -- Case studies. 4. Crimes against immigrants 5. Central Valley, California
LC 2019055804
Jose Martinez, a ruthless drug cartel hitman, ravaged California's Central Valley with murder after murder while their police forces did nothing. Widely known as a loving father and devoted son, he was also a merciless murderer and responsible for numerous kidnappings and illegal shipments of drugs and weapons. The Devil's Harvest presses upon moral questions haunting our politically divided country: why do some deaths-and some lives-matter more than others?

"Garrison, former Los Angeles Times reporter and Buzzfeed News West Coast investigations editor, delivers in her debut an expertly researched account of the life and alleged crimes of Jose Manuel Martinez, one of America's most prolific hit men. . . . This is essential reading for true crime buffs." Publishers Weekly

Martini, Adrienne, 1971-

Martini, Adrienne, 1971- **Somebody's** gotta do it : why cursing at the news won't save the nation, but your name on a local ballot can / Adrienne Martini. Henry Holt and Company, 2020 240 p. **B**
ISBN 9781250247636
1. Women politicians 2. Politicians -- New York State 3. Local elections 4. Campaign management 5. United States -- Politics and government -- 2017- 6. New York (State) -- Politics and government 7. Autobiographies and memoirs
LC 2019039991
Both funny and instructive, this memoir is about a progressive woman - a knitter, runner, mom and resident of rural Otsego County in upstate New York - who ran for office and won, and then realized the critical importance of the job.

"Using humor and anecdotes, Martini shows the importance of running for local office and helps provide a broader understanding of local government. Readers interested in learning about government organization and policy, and those who might want to run for office one day will enjoy the insights and lessons offered throughout." Library Journal

Marton, Kati

Marton, Kati **Enemies** of the people : my family's journey to America / Kati Marton. Simon & Schuster, 2009. x, 272 p. **B**
ISBN 9781416586128
1. Marton, Kati Childhood and youth. 2. Marton, Endre, 1910-2005. 3. Marton, Ilona, d. 2004. 4. Hungary. Allamvedelmi Hatosag. 5. Journalists -- Budapest, Hungary 6. Political prisoners -- Hungary 7. World War II -- Budapest, Hungary. 8. Hungarian Americans 9. Budapest, Hungary -- History 10. Hungary -- History -- 1945-1989. 11. Biographies
LC 2009014480
National Book Critics Circle Award for Autobiography/Memoir finalist

Relates the author's eyewitness account of her parents' arrests in Cold War Budapest, Hungary, and the terrible separation that followed, drawing on secret police files to reveal how her family was betrayed by friends and colleagues.

Marx, Karl, 1818-1883

Liedman, Sven-Eric, 1939- A **world** to win : the life and works of Karl Marx / Sven-Eric Liedman. Verso, 2018, c2015 832 p. **B**
ISBN 9781786635044
1. Marxism 2. Communists 3. Communism -- History -- 19th century 4. Philosophers 5. Biographies
LC 2018003399
Originally published as Karl Marx: En Biografi by Albert Bonniers F'rlag, 2015.

Sperber, Jonathan, 1952- **Karl** Marx : a nineteenth-century life / Jonathan Sperber. Liveright Pub. Corp., c2013. 512 p. **B**
ISBN 9780871404671
1. Marx, Karl, 1818-1883. 2. Communists -- Germany 3. Philosophers -- Germany 4. Exiles, German 5. Intellectuals -- Germany 6. Biographies
LC 2012044951
Pulitzer Prize for Biography or Autobiography finalist

This biography of the philosopher and political revolutionary describes his childhood and family life along with his public life as an agitator and dissident and compares him to his contemporaries including Napoleon III, Bismarck, Adam Smith and Charles Darwin.

Wheen, Francis **Karl** Marx : a life / Francis Wheen. Norton,

2000, c1999. 431 p. : B
ISBN 039304923X
1. Marx, Karl, 1818-1883. 2. Communists -- Germany 3. Exiles, German 4. Intellectuals -- Germany 5. Communism. 6. Biographies
LC 99087466
Originally published: London : Fourth Estate, 1999."
Following Marx from his childhood in Trier, Germany, through his exile in London, Wheen takes readers from hovel to grand house, from the International Working Man's Association to Capital, from obscurity to notoriety and back again." Publishers Weekly.

Mary, Blessed Virgin, Saint

Hazleton, Lesley 1945- **Mary** : a flesh-and-blood biography of the Virgin Mother / Lesley Hazleton. Bloomsbury, 2004. vii, 246 p. ; B
ISBN 1582342369
1. Motherhood. 2. Biographies
LC 2003017403
A portrait of the human side of Mary, the mother of Jesus, draws on Judaic and Christian history, theology, and anthropology, to reconstruct the life of a young peasant girl, through her diverse roles as mother, teacher, wise woman and healer, activist, and more, exploring her grief over the deah of her son and how she transformed that pain into renewal and wisdom.
"Hazleton takes readers through an impressive array of historical, cultural, literary, and spiritual topics. This book is an easy read, and Hazleton's stream-of-consciousness style is intriguing." Library Journal.

Mary, Queen of Scots, 1542-1587

Fraser, Antonia, 1932- **Mary,** Queen of Scots / Antonia Fraser. Delta Trade Paperbacks, 2001, c1993. xv, 613 p. : B
ISBN 038531129X
1. Mary, Queen of Scots, 1542-1587. 2. Women rulers -- Scotland 3. Monarchy -- Great Britain 4. Catholic women. 5. Monarchy. 6. Scotland -- History -- Mary Stuart, 1542-1567. 7. Great Britain -- History -- Elizabeth I, 1558-1603. 8. Biographies
LC 2001278458
Originally published: New York : Delta, 1993.
James Tait Black Memorial Prize for Biography, 1969.
A biography of Mary Queen of Scots captures the essence of the impulsive and beautiful Scottish queen who lost a throne for love and whose power struggle with Elizabeth I of England ended with her beheading.

Mary, Queen, consort of George V, King of Great Britain, 1867-1953

Edwards, Anne, 1927- **Matriarch** : Queen Mary and the House of Windsor / Anne Edwards. W. Morrow, 1984. 527 p., 32 p. of plates : B
ISBN 0688035116
1. Mary, Queen, consort of George V, King of Great Britain, 1867-1953. 2. Windsor, House of 3. Women rulers -- Great Britain 4. Royal houses. 5. Great Britain -- History -- 20th century. 6. Biographies
LC 84060447

Marzano-Lesnevich, Alexandria

Marzano-Lesnevich, Alexandria The **fact** of a body : a murder and a memoir / Alexandria Marzano-lesnevich. Flatiron Books, [2017] viii, 326 pages ; B
ISBN 9781250080547
1. Law students 2. Family secrets 3. Psychic trauma 4. Capital punishment 5. Autobiographies and memoirs
LC 2017003049
Lambda Literary Award for Lesbian Memoir/Biography, 2018.
A National Endowment for the Arts fellow documents the story of how a summer job at a Louisiana law firm and the case of a convicted murderer and child molester changed her views about the death penalty and forced her to confront traumatic secrets in her own family.
"She poses a greater philosophical and legal question of one's past and how that determines cause in an exquisite and thought-provoking comparison study." Library Journal.

Mason, C. Nicole, 1976-

Mason, C. Nicole, 1976- **Born** bright : a young girl's journey from nothing to something in America / C. Nicole Mason. St. Martin's Press, [2016] 242 p. B
ISBN 9781250069924
1. Poverty 2. Children of teenage parents 3. Inequality 4. African American women 5. Autobiographies and memoirs
LC 2016003704
The author describes the path she took to escape poverty, after being raised by a 16-year-old single mother in 1970s Los Angeles, and examines the conditions that make it nearly impossible for others to replicate her journey.
"This firsthand account of a passage out of poverty will inspire readers interested in the strength of the human spirit in overcoming formidable obstacles." Library Journal.

Mason, George, 1725-1792

★Broadwater, Jeff **George** Mason : forgotten founder / Jeff Broadwater. University of North Carolina Press, c2006. xii, 329 p. : B
ISBN 0807830534
1. Mason, George, 1725-1792. 2. United States. Constitution. 1st-10th Amendments. 3. Politicans -- United States 4. Constitutional history 5. Revolutions -- United States 6. American Revolution, 1775-1783 7. United States -- History -- Colonial period, 1600-1775 8. United States -- History -- Revolution, 1775-1783. 9. United States -- History -- Confederation, 1783-1789. 10. Virginia -- History -- Colonial period, 1600-1775 11. Virginia -- History -- 1775-1865. 12. Biographies
LC 2006010729
"Because Mason left little evidence of his private life, there are blurred edges in the portrait that Broadwater paints, but overall this is an exemplary biography: sympathetic but dispassionate, thorough but not cluttered, convincing in its interpretations and arguments. It leaves no doubt that Mason deserves to be returned to the esteem and reputation he enjoyed during his lifetime, but in no way is it hagiography." Washington Post Book World.

Massimino, Mike, 1962-

Massimino, Mike, 1962- **Spaceman** : an astronaut's unlikely journey to unlock the secrets of the universe / Mike Massimino. Crown, 2016 320 p. B
ISBN 9781101903544
1. United States. National Aeronautics and Space Administration 2. Astronauts -- United States 3. Space programs -- United States. 4. Space flight 5. Astronautics 6. Autobiographies and memoirs
LC 2016011667
A memoir by an unlikely astronaut who helped save the Hubble telescope describes his early attempts to gain admission into NASA, his first spacewalks, the loss of his fellow astronauts in the Columbia disaster,

his decision not to return to space and his ongoing support of future space-travel ventures.

"This is an engaging and uplifting memoir thats sure to give readers a deeper appreciation for the U.S. space program and inspire some future astronauts." Publishers Weekly.

Masters, Alexander

Masters, Alexander A **life** discarded : 148 diaries found in the trash / Alexander Masters. Farrar Straus & Giroux, 2016 192 p. **B**

ISBN 9780374178185

1. Notebooks. 2. Searching 3. Investigations 4. Diary writing 5. Autobiographies and memoirs

LC 2016027560

Shortlisted for the James Tait Black Memorial Prize for Biography, 2016

In a true, shocking, heartbreaking and often humorous story of an ordinary life, an award-winning biographer, after discovering 148 discarded notebooks overflowing with urgent handwriting starting in 1952 and ending half a century later, presents an unforgettable biographical detective story.

Masters, Jarvis Jay, 1962-

Sheff, David The **Buddhist** on death row : how one man found light in the darkest place / David Sheff. Simon & Schuster, 2020. 320 p. **B**

ISBN 9781982128456

1. California State Prison at San Quentin 2. Buddhists -- United States 3. Death row prisoners 4. Meditation 5. Buddhist meditation 6. United States 7. Biographies

LC 2019040344

The #1 New York Times bestselling author of Beautiful Boy explores the transformation of Jarvis Jay Masters who became one of America's most respected Buddhist practitioners during his two decades in solitary confinement in San Quentin.

"An indelible portrait of an incarcerated man finding new life and purpose behind bars." Kirkus

Mastromonaco, Alyssa

Mastromonaco, Alyssa **Who** thought this was a good idea? : and other questions you should have answers to when you work in the White House / Alyssa Mastromonaco with Lauren Oyler. Twelve, 2017. 256 p. **B**

ISBN 9781455588220

1. Mastromonaco, Alyssa. 2. Obama, Barack 3. White House chiefs of staff. 4. Presidents -- United States. 5. Bureaucracy -- United States. 6. Politicians -- United States. 7. United States -- Politics and government -- 1989-1993. 8. Autobiographies and memoirs

LC 2016050683

The former deputy chief of staff to President Barack Obama presents an intimate, whimsical and admiring portrait of the 44th commander-in-chief while sharing candid advice for today's young women professionals

"The memoir abounds with intimate glimpses of Washington, D.C., celebrities . and cheerfully dispensed survival strategies." Kirkus.

Matar, Hisham, 1970-

★Matar, Hisham, 1970- The **return** : fathers, sons, and the land in between / Hisham Matar. Random House, 2016. 256 p. **B**

ISBN 9780812994827

1. Authors, American 2. Missing persons 3. Kidnapping victims 4. Loss (Psychology) 5. Cairo, Egypt 6. Libya 7. Autobiographies and memoirs

LC 2015047925

Pulitzer Prize for Biography or Autobiography, 2017.

National Book Critics Circle Award for Autobiography/Memoir finalist, 2016

The award-winning author of Anatomy of a Disappearance describes his journey home to Libya after a 30-year absence due to his family's political exile and his father's kidnapping in Cairo, and his inextinguishable hopes that his father will be found alive.

"A beautifully written, harrowing story of a son's search for his father and how the impact of inexplicable loss can be unrelenting while the strength of family and cultural ties can ultimately sustain." Kirkus.

Matisse, Henri, 1869-1954

Spurling, Hilary **Matisse** the master : a life of Henri Matisse, the conquest of colour, 1909-1954 / Hilary Spurling. A.A. Knopf, 2005. xxi, 512 p. : **B**

ISBN 0679434291

1. Matisse, Henri, 1869-1954. 2. Artists -- France -- 20th century 3. Sculptors, French 4. Painters -- France 5. Painting, French -- 20th century. 6. Biographies

LC 2004051074

Sequel to: The unknown Matisse.

Whitbread Book Award for Biography, 2005.

Whitbread Book of the Year Award, 2005.

Chronicles the later years of the influential artist, interweaving analyses of his work with a study of Matisse's relationships with family and friends, trips around the world, the women in his life, and the continuing influences on the evolution of his art.

"Spurling's rich, flexible style is well attuned to the rigors and flights of Matisse's creative life." Publishers Weekly.

Spurling, Hilary The **unknown** Matisse : a life of Henri Matisse, the early years, 1869-1908 / Hilary Spurling. Alfred A. Knopf, 1998. xxv, 480 p., 24 p. of plates : **B**

ISBN 0679434283

1. Matisse, Henri, 1869-1954. 2. Artists -- France 3. Avant-garde (Aesthetics) -- France -- History -- 19th century. 4. Painters -- France 5. Family relationships. 6. France -- History -- 19th century. 7. Biographies

LC 97046816

Sequel: Matisse the master."

This volume makes for a gripping read and reveals much about the artist's early development." Publishers Weekly.

Matsuhisa, Nobuyuki

Matsuhisa, Nobuyuki **Nobu** : a memoir / Nobuyuki Matsuhisa. Atria, 2017, c2014. xvii, 206 p. : **B**

ISBN 9781501122798

1. Restaurateurs 2. Cooks 3. Cooking 4. Dinners and dining 5. Autobiographies and memoirs

LC 2017024524

"Originally published in Japanese in 2014 by Diamond Publishing as The Smiling Faces of My Guests Mean Everything."

The celebrity chef and international restaurateur shares the story of his life, from his devotion to his family to his struggles with depression, while reflecting on the philosophies that have made him one of the world's most respected culinary artists.

"A passionate chef with an open mind and a big heart, Matsuhisa shares lessons in humility, gratitude, and empathy that will stick with readers long after theyve finished the final chapter." Publishers Weekly.

Maugham, W. Somerset (William Somerset), 1874-1965

Hastings, Selina, 1945- The **secret** lives of Somerset Maugham : a biography / Selina Hastings. Random House, c2010. 672 p. **B**

ISBN 9781400061419

1. Maugham, W. Somerset (William Somerset), 1874-1965. 2. Authors, English -- 20th century 3. Gay men -- England 4. Gay husbands 5. Homosexuality and literature 6. England -- Social life and customs -- 20th century 7. Biographies

LC 2009035797

National Book Critics Circle Award for Biography finalist, 2010.

Draws on exclusive access to the literary master's private papers and interviews with his daughter to share insights into such topics as his work as a British spy and private homosexuality, in a profile that is complemented by previously unpublished photographs.

"This steady-eyed biography of an extraordinary, extravagant, generous and bitter artist will not only fascinate its readers but encourage some to go to his work for the first time." Times Literary Supplement.

Mauldin, William Henry, 1921-

DePastino, Todd **Bill** Mauldin : a life up front / Todd DePastino. W.W. Norton, 2008. 320 p. **B**

ISBN 0393061833

1. Cartoonists -- United States 2. Biographies

LC 2007040494

Traces the World War II military service of the two-time Pulitzer Prize-winning creator of the popular "Up Front" cartoon, offering insight into his work's reflection of soldier life, in an account that features more than ninety classic cartoons and rare photographs.

"Thoroughly researched and sprightly written, DePastino's balanced biography is a solid introduction to an American original. Classic Mauldin cartoons are an entertaining bonus." Publishers Weekly.

Maupin, Armistead

★Maupin, Armistead **Logical** family : a memoir / Armistead Maupin. HarperCollins 2017. 400 p. **B**

ISBN 9780062391223

1. Gay men 2. Transformations, Personal 3. Interpersonal conflict 4. Belonging 5. Autobiographies and memoirs

LC 2017276332

The best-selling author of the Tales of the City series chronicles his odyssey from the old South to freewheeling San Francisco, a personal journey that shaped his evolution from a curious youth to a groundbreaking writer and gay rights pioneer.

"Engaging reminiscences from an ebullient storyteller." Kirkus.

May, Meredith

May, Meredith The **honey** bus : a memoir of loss, courage and a girl saved by bees / Meredith May. Park Row, 2019. 352 p. **B**

ISBN 9780778307785

1. Growing up 2. Beekeeping 3. Grandfather and granddaughter 4. Family relationships 5. Autobiographies and memoirs

LC bl2019009438

Meredith May recalls the first time a honeybee crawled on her arm. She was five years old, her parents had recently split and suddenly she found herself in the care of her grandfather, an eccentric beekeeper who made honey in a rusty old military bus in the yard. That first close encounter was at once terrifying and exhilarating for May, and in that moment she discovered that everything she needed to know about life and family was right before her eyes, in the secret world of bees.

"Journalist May mines her deeply upsetting personal history in this sharply visceral memoir." Booklist.

Mayakovsky, Vladimir, 1893-1930

Almereyda, Michael, **Night** wraps the sky : writings by and about Mayakovsky / edited by Michael Almereyda. Farrar, Straus and Giroux, 2008. xxvii, 272 p. : **B**

ISBN 9780374281359

1. Mayakovsky, Vladimir, 1893-1930. 2. Poets, Russian -- 20th century 3. Men/women relations 4. Suicide victims 5. Russia -- History -- 20th century 6. Biographies

LC 2007046662

"A compendium of all things Mayakovsky: new translations of his poems and essays, eyewitness accounts, photographs, and artwork from his circle. A reconsideration of the poet for the post-Soviet world."''The book further explores Mayakovsky's relationships with Lili Brik and Tatiana Yakovleva, explains his propaganda work, and addresses his mixture of the surreal, the lyric, and the sarcastic; the text is generously illustrated with photographs of Mayakovsky's friends and contemporaries and artworks of the times." Library Journal.

Mayer, Frederick, 1921-2016

Lichtblau, Eric **Return** to the Reich : a Holocaust refugee's secret mission to defeat the Nazis / Eric Lichtblau. Houghton Mifflin Harcourt, 2019. 304 p. **B**

ISBN 9781328528537

1. Mayer, Frederick, 1921-2016. 2. United States. Office of Strategic Services Officials and employees 3. Spies 4. World War II 5. Jews, German 6. Immigrants -- United States 7. Germany 8. Austria 9. Biographies

LC 2019009834

The remarkable story of Fred Mayer, a German-born Jew who escaped Nazi Germany only to return as an American commando on a secret mission behind enemy lines. Growing up in Germany, Freddy Mayer witnessed the Nazis' rise to power. When he was sixteen, his family made the decision to flee to the United States--they were among the last German Jews to escape, in 1938. In America, Freddy tried enlisting the day after Pearl Harbor, only to be rejected as an "enemy alien" because he was German. He was soon recruited to the OSS, the country's first spy outfit before the CIA. Freddy, joined by Dutch Jewish refugee Hans Wynberg and Nazi defector Franz Weber, parachuted into Austria as the leader of Operation Greenup, meant to deter Hitler's last stand.

Mayer, Louis B., 1885-1957

★Eyman, Scott, 1951- **Lion** of Hollywood : the life and legend of Louis B. Mayer / Scott Eyman. Simon & Schuster, 2005. 596 p. : **B**

ISBN 0743204816

1. Mayer, Louis B., 1885-1957. 2. Metro-Goldwyn-Mayer. 3. Film producers and directors -- United States 4. Film industry and trade 5. Filmmakers. 6. Hollywood, California. 7. Biographies

LC 2005042472

Draws on interviews and previously unavailable archival resources to chronicle Louis B. Mayer's life from his early years in the Russian shtetls, to his rise to the head of MGM, to his embittered exile.

"Eyman's extensive knowledge of old Hollywood, his scrupulous research and his refusal to indict the often-pilloried Mayer make this biography an often revelatory delight." Publishers Weekly.

Mayes, Frances

Mayes, Frances A **year** in the world : journeys of a passionate traveller / Frances Mayes. Broadway Books, 2006.

xx, 420 p. : **B**
ISBN 0767910052
1. Mayes, Frances Travel 2. Travel writers -- United States 3. Voyages and travels. 4. Travelers. 5. Women travelers.
LC 2005050831
Map on endpapers.
Celebrating the wonders, benefits, and experiences of travel, the best-selling author of Under the Tuscan Sun shares a collection of narrative essays in which she details her travels to Spain, Portugal, France, Britain, Turkey, Greece, southern Italy, and North Africa, interweaving personal insights with commentary on art, history, landscape, culture, and tradition.
"Befitting her gifts as a poet, Mayes' prose shines with evocative imagery, bringing life to every subject she encounters across her peripatetic year." Booklist.

Mayes, Frances **Under** magnolia : a Southern memoir / Frances Mayes. Crown, 2014. 320 p. **B**
ISBN 9780307885913
1. Mayes, Frances. 2. Families 3. Growing up 4. Interpersonal relations 5. Voyages and travels 6. Georgia 7. Southern states 8. Autobiographies and memoirs
LC 2013042448
The best-selling author shares the story of her youth in the American South and her decision to return to the places that shaped her early ideals, a journey marked by her regional travels and growing appreciation for Southern writers.
"With her trademark skill for capturing the essence of place and time, Mayes candidly reveals a youth riddled with psychological abuse and parental neglect that, nevertheless, ignited a fiery passion for adventure and self-discovery." Booklist.

Mayes, Frances **Under** the Tuscan sun : at home in Italy / Frances Mayes. Chronicle Books, 1996. 280 p. ; **B**
ISBN 9780811808422
1. Mayes, Frances. 2. Americans in Italy. 3. Women travelers. 4. Divorced women. 5. Cooking, Italian. 6. Tuscany, Italy -- Description and travel. 7. Tuscany, Italy -- Social life and customs. 8. Autobiographies and memoirs
LC 96015137
Excerpts from this book appeared in the New York Times, Ploughshares, and House Beautiful.
Sequel: Bella Tuscany.
The poet and travel writer describes her experiences in Tuscany during the restoration of her countryside villa.
"Casual and conversational, [Ms. Mayes's] chapters are filled with craftsmen and cooks, with exploratory jaunts into the countryside--but what they all boil down to is an intense celebration of what she calls 'the voluptuousness of Italian life.' Occasionally, this leads to the sort of gushy observations you might expect from a besotted lover. But more often it produces an appealing and very vivid snapshot imagery." New York Times Book Review.

Mayfield, Katherine, 1958-
Mayfield, Katherine, 1958- The **undertaker's** daughter / Katherine Mayfield Gallery Books, 2015. 368 p. **B**
ISBN 9781476757285
1. Undertakers 2. Growing up 3. Fathers and daughters. 4. Intergenerational friendship 5. Kentucky 6. Autobiographies and memoirs
LC 2014006727
After Kate Mayfield was born, she was taken directly to a funeral home. Her father was an undertaker, and for thirteen years the family resided in a place nearly synonymous with death. A place where the living and the dead entered their house like a vapor. The place where Kate would spend the entirety of her childhood. In a memoir that reads like a Harper Lee novel, Mayfield draws the reader into a world of Southern mystique and ghosts.
"Mayfield's secret life forced her to lie and sneak around, and her teenage angst was only compounded by the brutal revelation from her sister Evelyn, a thoroughly unpleasant bully, that her father was a serial philanderer and a drunk. Mayfield fashions a poignant send-off to Jubilee in this thoughtfully rendered work." Publishers Weekly.

Maynard, Joyce, 1953-
Maynard, Joyce, 1953- The **best** of us : a memoir / Joyce Maynard. Bloomsbury USA, 2017. 448 p. **B**
ISBN 9781635570342
1. Women authors 2. Marriage 3. Married men -- Death 4. Romantic love 5. Autobiographies and memoirs
LC 2016058363
In a memoir of learning to understand true love through the experience of loss, the author describes finding the love of her life in her late fifties, only to lose him to pancreatic cancer less than three years into their marriage.
"This haunting story, penned by a master wordsmith, is a reminder to savor every loved one and every day." Booklist.

Mays, Willie, 1931-
Hirsch, James S. **Willie** Mays : the life, the legend / James S. Hirsch, authorized by Willie Mays. Scribner, 2010. 416 p. **B**
ISBN 9781416547907
1. New York Giants (Baseball team) 2. Baseball players -- United States 3. Professional baseball. 4. African American baseball players 5. Professional baseball players. 6. Biographies
LC 2009049214
A biography authorized by the baseball great offers a gripping account of Willie Mays's life, drawn from interviews with the icon, as well as friends, family members and teammates.
"This is a superb baseball book, but it's also a riveting narrative of Mays' life and times, ranging from his penchant for fancy suits to urban development in New York City to the giddy cult of celebrity. In the mid-1950s, Willie Mays was as famous as anyone in the country, gracing the cover of Time and other magazines and appearing on numerous television shows. More impressive and what distinguishes this book from the run-of-the-mill sports biography is Hirsch's extensive and cogent take on race relations and the civil-rights movement both within and outside of baseball." Seattle Times.

Mays, Willie, 1931- **24** : life stories and lessons from the Say Hey Kid / Willie Mays and John Shea. St. Martin's Press, 2020. 272 p. **B**
ISBN 9781250230423
1. Baseball players -- United States 2. Professional baseball players 3. Personal conduct 4. Racism 5. Autobiographies and memoirs
LC 2019058386
Includes index.
A man widely regarded as one the greatest all-around players in baseball history reflects on his lifetime of experience meeting challenges with positivity, integrity and triumph.
"This definitive work about a living legend is a must-buy for baseball fans." Publishers Weekly

Mbeki, Thabo
Gevisser, Mark A **legacy** of liberation : Thabo Mbeki and the

future of the South African dream / Mark Gevisser. Palgrave Macmillan, 2009. 400 p. **B**

ISBN 9780230611009

1. Mbeki, Thabo. 2. Mbeki, Thabo Influence. 3. Presidents -- South Africa 4. Political leadership -- South Africa -- Case studies. 5. South Africans -- Social conditions. 6. South Africa -- Politics and government -- 1994- 7. South Africa -- Race relations.

LC 2008050763

"This is a biography of South Africa's second president. Gevisser traces Mbeki's family back several generations, from colonial disposession through the struggle for liberation. Mbeki's life story has the makings of a gripping tale. Gevisser writes well, particularly when he is witness to an event, when his narrative leaps off the page." New York Times Book Review.

McBee, Thomas Page

McBee, Thomas Page **Man** alive : a true story of violence, forgiveness and becoming a man / Thomas Page McBee. City Lights Books, [2014] 172 p. ; **B**

ISBN 9780872866249

1. McBee, Thomas Page. 2. Trans men 3. Transgender persons 4. Transitioning (Gender identity) 5. Adult child abuse victims 6. Autobiographies and memoirs

LC 2014022173

Lambda Literary Award for Transgender Nonfiction

On the cusp of a life-changing decision to transition from female to male, the author focuses on two of the men who impacted his life, seeking to understand what it truly means to be a man.

"Full of bravery and clear, far-sighted compassion and devoid of sentiment, victimization, and clich, McBees meditations bring him a hard-won sense of selfone that is bound to inspire any reader who has struggled with internal dissonance." Publishers Weekly.

McBride, Regina, 1956-

McBride, Regina, 1956- **Ghost** songs : a memoir / Regina McBride. Tin House Books, 2016. 350 p. **B**

ISBN 9781941040430

1. Authors, American -- 20th century 2. Ghosts 3. Grief in women 4. Coping in women 5. Autobiographies and memoirs

LC 2016006743

"A wrenchingly lyrical memoir of family and tragedy." Kirkus.

McBride, Sarah, 1990-

★McBride, Sarah, 1990- **Tomorrow** will be different : love, loss, and the fight for trans equality / Sarah McBride. Crown Archetype, 2018 288 p. **B**

ISBN 9781524761479

1. Transgender persons. 2. Civil rights. 3. Identity (Psychology). 4. Personal conduct 5. Autobiographies and memoirs

LC 2017040046

The national press secretary for the Human Rights Campaign presents a memoir about her struggles with gender identity and relationships against a backdrop of the transgender equality movement.

"All readers will find this book enlightening. Those struggling with gender identity, and their families and friends, will find hope in McBride's words." Library Journal.

McBride-Jordan, Ruth, 1921-

McBride, James, 1957- The **color** of water : a Black man's tribute to his white mother / James McBride. Riverhead Books, 1996. xiii, 228 p. : **B**

ISBN 1573220221

1. McBride, James, 1957- 2. Multiracial persons 3. Interracial marriage. 4. Jewish women. 5. Mothers. 6. New York City 7. Biographies

LC 95037243

ALA Notable Book, 1997.

A young African American man describes growing up as one of twelve children of a white mother and Black father, and discusses his mother's contributions to his life and his confusion over his own identity.

"Told with humor and clear-eyed grace, McBride's memoir is not only a terrific story, it's a subtle contribution to the current debates on race and identity. The sheer strength of spirit, pain and humor of McBride and his mother as they wrestled with different aspects of race and identity is vividly told." The Nation.

McCabe, Andrew (Andrew George), 1968-

McCabe, Andrew (Andrew George), 1968- The **threat** : how the FBI protects America in the age of terror and Trump / Andrew G. McCabe. St Martins Pr 2019 288 p. **B**

ISBN 9781250207579

1. Mueller, Robert S., III, 1944- 2. Trump, Donald, 1946- 3. FBI 4. Political corruption 5. FBI agents 6. Law enforcement 7. Terrorism -- Prevention 8. United States -- Politics and government 9. Autobiographies and memoirs

LC 2018419333

The former deputy director of the FBI details how law enforcement battles terror threats, Russian crime and attacks by the White House itself on the U.S. Constitution.

"This polished combination career retrospective, manifesto about the FBI's value, and rebuttal to Donald Trump's smears tells former FBI director McCabe's side of the story." Publishers Weekly.

McCall, Nathan

McCall, Nathan **Makes** me wanna holler : a young black man in America / Nathan McCall. Random House, 1994. viii, 404 p. ; **B**

ISBN 0679412689

1. McCall, Nathan. 2. Former convicts 3. African Americans 4. Journalists -- United States 5. African American teenagers 6. Virginia 7. Autobiographies and memoirs

LC 93030654

An African-American journalist recalls his troubled childhood, his rehabilitation while in prison, and his successful career.

McCandless, Christopher Johnson, 1968-1992

Krakauer, Jon **Into** the wild / Jon Krakauer. Villard Books, c1996. 207 p. : **B**

ISBN 9780679428503

1. McCandless, Christopher Johnson, 1968-1992. 2. Wilderness survival. 3. Idealism in men. 4. Adventurers -- United States 5. Young men -- United States 6. Alaska. 7. The West (United States) 8. Biographies 9. Pacific Northwest literature

LC 95020008

"Christopher McCandless was a disaffected, idealistic young man who trekked into the Alaskan wilderness in search of transcendence and perished there. This narrative, which ponders his journey and inner life with sympathy and imagination, has YA appeal on many levels." Booklist.

McCarthy, Joseph, 1908-1957

★Tye, Larry **Demagogue** : the life and long shadow of Senator

Joe McCarthy / Larry Tye. Houghton Mifflin Harcourt, 2020 608 p. **B**

ISBN 9781328959720

1. McCarthy, Joseph, 1908-1957 Influence. 2. McCarthy, Joseph, 1908-1957. 3. United States. Congress. Senate 4. Anti-communist movements -- United States -- History. 5. Legislators -- United States 6. Subversive activities 7. Politicians 8. United States -- Politics and government -- 20th century 9. Biographies

LC 2019024932

The definitive biography of the most dangerous demagogue in American history, based on first-ever access to his personal and professional papers, medical and military records, and recently-unsealed transcripts of his closed-door Congressional hearings.

"A definitive biography that will stand the test of time." Library Journal

Wicker, Tom **Shooting** star : the brief arc of Joe McCarthy / Tom Wicker. Harcourt, 2006. 212 p. **B**

ISBN 015101082X

1. McCarthy, Joseph, 1908-1957. 2. United States. Congress. Senate 3. Legislators -- United States 4. Anti-communist movements -- United States -- History -- 20th century. 5. Internal security -- United States -- History -- 20th century. 6. United States -- Politics and government -- 1945-1953. 7. United States -- Politics and government -- 1953-1961. 8. Biographies

LC 2005020990

Joe McCarthy first became visible to the nation on February 9, 1950, when he delivered a Lincoln Day address to local Republicans in Wheeling, West Virginia. That night he declared, "I have here in my hand a list of 205 [members of the Communist Party] still working and shaping policy in the State Department." Anticommunism was already a cause embraced by the Republican Party as a whole; McCarthy tapped into this current and turned it into a flood. Little more than five years later, after countless hearings and stormy speeches and after incalculable damage to ordinary Americans and the nation itself, McCarthy's Senate colleagues voted 67-22 to censure him for his reckless accusations and fabrications. We know today that not one prosecution resulted from McCarthy's investigations into communists in the U.S. government.--Publisher description.

"This perceptive, well-written book should have wide appeal." Choice.

McClelland, Mac

McClelland, Mac **Irritable** hearts : a PTSD love story / Mac McClelland. Flatiron Books, 2015 320 p. **B**

ISBN 9781250052896

1. McClelland, Mac. 2. Post-traumatic stress disorder. 3. Journalists -- United States -- Biography. 4. Earthquakes -- Psychological aspects. 5. Haiti Earthquake, Haiti, 2010. 6. Autobiographies and memoirs

LC 2014034163

In 2010, human rights reporter Mac McClelland left Haiti after covering the devastation of the earthquake. Back home, she finds herself imagining vivid scenes of violence and can't sleep or stop crying. It becomes clear that she is suffering from Post Traumatic Stress Disorder, triggered by her trip and seemingly exacerbated by her experiences in the other charged places she'd reported from. The bewilderment about this sudden loss of self-control is magnified by her feelings for Nico, a French soldier she met in Haiti who despite their brief connection seems to have found a place in her confused heart. While we most often connect it to veterans, PTSD is more often caused by other manner of trauma, and can even be contagious--close proximity to those afflicted can trigger it in those around them.

McCloskey, Jim (Minister)

★McCloskey, Jim (Minister) **When** truth is all you have : a memoir of faith, justice, and freedom for the wrongly convicted / Jim McCloskey with Philip Lerman ; foreword by John Grisham. Doubleday, 2020. 304 p. **B**

ISBN 9780385545037

1. Centurion Ministries. 2. Social advocates 3. Judicial error 4. Faith (Christianity) 5. Christian church work with prisoners. 6. Autobiographies and memoirs

LC 2019054453

The founder of the Centurion Ministries, the first American organization dedicated to freeing the wrongly imprisoned, describes his life-changing advocacy of an innocent convict and his establishment of a movement that has freed dozens of victims.

"This will be essential for collections focused on social justice, the wrongly convicted, and spiritual transformation." Library Journal

McColl, Sarah

McColl, Sarah **Joy** enough / Sarah McColl. Liveright Pub. Corp., 2019. 160 p. **B**

ISBN 9781631494703

1. Mothers and daughters 2. Grief 3. Loss (Psychology) 4. Enjoyment 5. Autobiographies and memoirs

LC 2018026979

An editor-in-chief of Yahoo Food presents a life-affirming memoir of her experiences with dual loss, recounting how she endured the end of her marriage and her mother's cancer diagnosis by reconnecting with her childhood home and preparing elaborate, nourishing meals.

"McColl's resonant first book is resplendent with love, and the hope she finds in discovering that her unfathomable grief also carved a space for more profound joy " Booklist.

McCourt, Alphie

McCourt, Alphie A **long** stone's throw / Alphie McCourt. Sterling & Ross Publishers, 2008. 384 p. **B**

ISBN 9780981453552

1. McCourt, Alphie. 2. Irish Americans -- New York City 3. Immigrants -- New York City 4. Drinking -- Social aspects. 5. Alcoholic men -- New York City, 6. New York City. 7. Limerick, Ireland. 8. Autobiographies and memoirs

LC 2008032672

The youngest brother of authors Frank and Malachy McCourt describes his flight from his native Ireland in pursuit of his literary siblings, struggles with alcoholism, and efforts to raise a daughter with health challenges.

"Alphie is the youngest of the four McCourt brothers and the third--after Frank and Malachy--to pen a memoir about his life in Ireland and the U.S. McCourt always finds irony in life and his tales of the bar and restaurant business and its clientele are laugh-out-loud funny. Sensitive, lyrical, funny, stubborn, impetuous, McCourt writes with a steady hand, a joyful heart, and an Irishman's sense of life's absurdities." Publishers Weekly.

McCourt, Frank

McCourt, Frank **'Tis** : a memoir / Frank McCourt. Scribner, 1999. 367 p. **B**

ISBN 9780684848785

1. McCourt, Frank Family. 2. McCourt family. 3. High school teachers. 4. Immigrants, Irish 5. Self-acceptance. 6. Irish Americans 7. New York City 8. Autobiographies and memoirs

LC 99031280

Sequel to: Angela's ashes.

A sequel to Angela's Ashes picks up the sometimes harrowing tale of McCourt's youth as he immigrates from Ireland to America, joins the Army, goes to college, and begins building a life.

"This volume takes McCourt from his arrival in America and subsequent service in the Korean War through the mid-1980s. This memoir features a mesmerizing narrative fraught with sufferings. It triumphs by effecting a genuinely comic meditation upon human frailty, grace and possibility." Publishers Weekly.

★McCourt, Frank **Angela's** ashes : a memoir / Frank McCourt. Scribner, 1996. 364 p. : **B**

ISBN 9780684874357

1. Growing up -- Limerick, Ireland 2. Poor families -- Limerick, Ireland 3. Children of alcoholics -- Limerick, Ireland 4. Irish Americans 5. Limerick, Ireland 6. Autobiographies and memoirs

LC 96005335

Sequel: 'Tis.

ALA Notable Book, 1997.

The author recounts his childhood in Depression-era Brooklyn as the child of Irish immigrants who decide to return to worse poverty in Ireland when his infant sister dies.

"An extraordinary work in every way. McCourt magically retrieves love, dignity, and humor from a childhood of hunger, loss, and pain." Kirkus.

McCourt, Frank **Teacher** man : a memoir / Frank McCourt. Scribner, 2005. 258 p. ; **B**

ISBN 9780743243773

1. High school teachers -- New York City 2. Teaching. 3. Self-acceptance. 4. Education. 5. New York City -- Social life and customs 6. Autobiographies and memoirs

LC 2005054113

The author describes his coming of age as a teacher, storyteller, and writer, a personal journey during which he spent fifteen years finding his voice in the classroom, and came to terms with the undervalued importance of teaching.

"Full of gritty specifics, never preachy, often hilarious, McCourt's book thrusts you right into the hormones-and-catcalls chaos of the classroom--where learning is not just a mystery but a flat-out miracle." Newsweek.

McCourt, Malachy, 1931-

McCourt, Malachy, 1931- A **monk** swimming : a memoir / Malachy McCourt. Hyperion, c1998. 290 p. ; **B**

ISBN 9780786863983

1. Irish Americans 2. Actors and actresses 3. Alcoholism 4. Immigrants, Irish 5. New York City. 6. Autobiographies and memoirs

LC 97046720

The actor-brother of Frank McCourt offers an entertaining, witty memoir of life in New York City during the freewheeling 1960s, detailing his quest for fame and fortune, family life, battle with alcoholism, and reunion with his long-estranged father.

"The memoir, which covers ground through 1963, will have readers smiling and laughing constantly." Publishers Weekly.

McCourt, Malachy, 1931- **Death** need not be fatal / Malachy McCourt, with Brian McDonald. Center Street, 2017 259 p. **B**

ISBN 9781478917069

1. Senior men. 2. Death -- Psychological aspects. 3. Aging -- Psychological aspects. 4. Autobiographies and memoirs

LC 2017001094

The Irish American actor, writer, politician, bon vivant, and younger brother of author Frank McCourt discusses the role death has played in his life and describes his perception of his own impending demise.

"Veering at times into philosophical inquiry, addiction narrative, celebrity tell-all, and a tender appraisal of brotherly rivalry, McCourt continually returns to themes of acceptance, gratitude, and love." Booklist.

McCourt, Malachy, 1931- **Singing** my him song / Malachy McCourt. Harper Collins Publishers, c2000. 242 p. ; **B**

ISBN 9780060195939

1. Green Party U S A. 2. Irish Americans 3. Actors and actresses 4. Alcoholism 5. Immigrants, Irish 6. New York (State) -- Social life and customs -- 20th century 7. Los Angeles, California -- Social life and customs -- 20th century 8. Limerick, Ireland -- Social life and customs -- 20th century 9. Autobiographies and memoirs

LC 00059774

The author continues his life story beginning in 1963, discussing his careers in show business and politics, his battle with alcoholism, finding true love, and a cancer diagnosis.

McCracken, Elizabeth

McCracken, Elizabeth An **exact** replica of a figment of my imagination : a memoir / Elizabeth McCracken. Little, Brown, c2008. 184 p. **B**

ISBN 9780316027670

1. McCracken, Elizabeth. 2. Authors, American -- 20th century 3. Americans in France. 4. Parents of stillborn infants. 5. Grief. 6. France -- Social life and customs. 7. Autobiographies and memoirs

LC 2008005032

The author traces her marriage and relocation to France at the height of her writing career, her devastation over her stillborn son in her ninth month of pregnancy, and her heart-wrenching grieving process.

McCullers, Carson, 1917-1967

Shapland, Jenn, 1987- **My** autobiography of Carson McCullers : a memoir / Jenn Shapland. Tin House Books, 2020. xv, 266 p. **B**

ISBN 9781947793286

1. Shapland, Jenn, 1987- 2. McCullers, Carson, 1917-1967. 3. Women authors 4. Authors, American -- 20th century 5. Bisexual women 6. Bisexual women authors 7. Autobiographies and memoirs

LC 2019031475

A writer draws on an intimate correspondence between McCullers and a woman named Annemarie to share previously unknown insights into the 20th-century novelist's private life, her approaches to queer fiction and the influence of her time at Yaddo.

"Celebrating McCullers, love, and the idea that every story told includes something of its teller, Shapland writes an involving literary journey of the self." Booklist

McCurley, T. Mark

McCurley, T. Mark **Hunter** killer : inside America's unmanned air war / T. Mark Mccurley, Kevin Maurer. Penguin Group USA, 2014. 352 p. **B**

ISBN 9780525954439

1. McCurley, T. Mark. 2. Drone aircraft. 3. Technology and war. 4. Remotely piloted vehicles. 5. Weapons. 6. Middle East -- Military relations United States. 7. United States -- Military relations Middle East. 8. Autobiographies and memoirs.

LC 2015016824

An insider's tour of the U.S. military's secret Remotely Piloted Aircraft program discusses how drones work and their potential for neutralizing security threats.

"The author ably chronicles the tedious, routine work involving 'days drenched in blood,' and he gives a good sense of the evolution of the RPA since the 1990s and the intensive human element necessary to command it. An illuminating tale of a pilot on the cutting edge." Kirkus.

McDaniel, Hattie, 1895-1952

Jackson, Carlton **Hattie** : the life of Hattie McDaniel / Carlton Jackson. Madison Books, c1990. xii, 220 p., 16 p. of plates : **B**

ISBN 1568330049

1. McDaniel, Hattie, 1895-1952. 2. Film actors and actresses -- United States 3. African American film actors and actresses 4. Biographies

LC 89030903

Includes index.

Traces the life and career of the first Black actress to win an Academy Award, looks at her work in radio, and describes her relationships with her fellow actors

"For those of us who knew her only as Mammy in Gone with the Wind, Hattie McDaniel's life story holds lots of surprises. She was also a singer, songwriter, and radio, stage, and TV performer. With an anecdotal style, the author clears up a lot of errors concerning her career." Booklist.

Watts, Jill, 1958- **Hattie** McDaniel : black ambition, white Hollywood / Jill Watts. Amistad, c2005. xi, 352 : **B**

ISBN 0060514906

1. McDaniel, Hattie, 1895-1952. 2. Film actors and actresses -- United States 3. African American women 4. African American actors and actresses 5. Race relations 6. Biographies

LC 2005042126

An exploration of Hollywood racism as reflected in the life and career of the actress best known for her portrayal of "Mammy" in "Gone with the Wind" describes her denigration in spite of her Oscar-winning performance, her controversial decision to stickto stereotypical roles, and her successful efforts to integrate a Los Angeles neighborhood.

"Watts is both sympathetic and honest: we pity McDaniel and her unenviable position, but at the same time, see how her intense careerism drove her often to accommodate rather than challenge film industry racism. Watts' research is extensive, her writing clear and accessible, and her book a thorough, engaging, intelligent piece of historical scholarship." Women's Review of Books.

McDougall, Christopher, 1962-

McDougall, Christopher, 1962- **Running** with Sherman : the donkey with the heart of a hero / Christopher McDougall. Alfred A. Knopf, 2019. 352 p. **B**

ISBN 9781524732363

1. Donkeys 2. Human-animal relationships 3. Animal rescue 4. Pack burro racing 5. Pennsylvania 6. Autobiographies and memoirs

LC 2019009852

"This is a Borzoi book."

When Chris McDougall agreed to take in a donkey from an animal hoarder, he thought it would be no harder than the rest of the adjustments he and his family had made after moving from Philadelphia to the heart of Pennsylvania Amish country. But when he arrived, Sherman was in such bad shape he could barely move, and his hair was coming out in clumps. Chris decided to undertake a radical rehabilitation program designed not only to heal Sherman's body but to heal his mind as well. It turns out the best way to soothe a donkey is to give it a job, and so Chris decided to teach Sherman how to run. He'd heard about burro racing--a unique type of race where humans and donkeys run together in a call-back to mining days--and decided he and Sherman would enter the World Championship in Colorado.

McGlynn, David, 1976-

McGlynn, David, 1976- **One** day you'll thank me : lessons from an unexpected fatherhood / David McGlynn. Counterpoint Press, [2018] 208 p. **B**

ISBN 9781640090392

1. McGlynn, David, 1976- Family 2. Authors, American 3. Fatherhood 4. Father and child 5. Fathers and sons 6. Autobiographies and memoirs

LC 2017052590

Fatherhood caught David McGlynn by surprise. His sons arrived in quick succession:the first when the author was a dirt-poor student and the second not long after he'd moved his family across the country to start a new job in bucolic Wisconsin. As a result, McGlynn found himself colliding with fatherhood, at once scared to death and utterly thrilled. Just like many new fathers, he hopes he's doing the right thing--but he's never quite sure.

McGowan, Rose, 1973-

McGowan, Rose, 1973- **Brave** / Rose McGowan. HarperOnes, 2018. 288 p. **B**

ISBN 9780062655981

1. Actors and actresses 2. Feminism 3. Sexual harassment 4. Social advocacy 5. Autobiographies and memoirs

LC bl2017049932

The actress and award-winning director traces her childhood escape from an Italian cult and her rise in Hollywood, describing how she endured nightmarish exposure and sexualization before committing herself to feminist causes.

"Frank and bold, this memoir is a resounding wakeup call to the entertainment industry and to society as a whole." Publishers Weekly.

McInerny, Nora

McInerny, Nora The **hot** young widows club : lessons on survival from the front lines of grief / Nora McInerny. TED Books/Simon & Schuster, 2019. 128 p. **B**

ISBN 9781982109981

1. McInerny, Nora. 2. Death. 3. Grief. 4. Bereavement. 5. Loss (Psychology) 6. Autobiographies and memoirs.

LC bl2019011698

The author, whose husband died young of brain cancer, provides wise, heartfelt, and humorous advice for those grieving the loss of a loved one, and offers suggestions for how to help people who are grieving.

McKean, Thomas, 1734-1817

McKean, David (Director of policy planning) **Suspected** of independence : the life of Thomas Mckean, America's first power broker / David McKean. PublicAffairs, 2016. 320 p. **B**

ISBN 9781610392211

1. McKean, Thomas, 1734-1817. 2. United States. Declaration of Independence Signers 3. United States. Continental Congress. 4. Founding Fathers of the United States. 5. Politicians. 6. Governors. 7. American Revolution, 1775-1783 8. United States -- History -- Revolution, 1775-1783 9. Biographies

LC 2016005686

Thomas McKean was America's first political operator - a man who installed himself at the center of every major political event of his time. In an extraordinary career that spanned almost half a century, McKean represented Pennsylvania and Delaware to the Stamp Act Congress and both Continental Congresses, and was instrumental in the creation of both the Articles of Confederation and the Constitution. He was one of the first to lobby for independence from British rule, the last to sign the Declaration of Independence, and was briefly the second President of Congress while George Washington was away.

"His story has been long in coming and worth the wait. For students of the Revolutionary era, the author delivers a useful biography of a significant player in the birth pangs of the new nation." Kirkus.

McKellen, Ian

O'Connor, Garry **Ian** McKellen : a biography / Garry O'Connor. St. Martin's Press, 2019. 352 p. **B**

ISBN 9781250223883

1. McKellen, Ian. 2. Actors and actresses -- Great Britain 3. Film actors and actresses -- United States 4. Gay men 5. LGBTQIA rights 6. Biographies

LC 2019032544

A biography of the esteemed actor follows his career, which includes roles in over 400 plays and films, from his debut in London's West End in 1964 to playing Gandalf in the Lord of the Rings film adaptations.

McKeon, Kathy

McKeon, Kathy **Jackie's** girl : my life with the Kennedy family / Kathy McKeon. Simon & Schuster, 2017. 320 p. **B**

ISBN 9781501158940

1. Kennedy family 2. Onassis, Jacqueline Kennedy, 1929-1994 3. Personal assistants 4. Immigrants, Irish 5. Nannies 6. Mentors 7. Autobiographies and memoirs

LC 2017003981

A coming-of-age memoir by a young woman who was Jackie Kennedy's personal assistant and sometime nanny for 13 years describes her witness to several historical events and the lessons about life and love she learned from the beloved First Lady.

"Celebrity watchers who covet an insiders role will find McKeons frank yet benevolent memoir to be both a sobering reality check and an engaging foray into the ever-fascinating world of the Kennedy dynasty." Booklist.

McKinley, William, 1843-1901

Merry, Robert W., 1946- **President** McKinley : Architect of the American Century / Robert W. Merry. Simon & Schuster, 2017. 448 p. **B**

ISBN 9781451625448

1. McKinley, William, 1843-1901. 2. Presidents -- United States 3. United States -- Politics and government -- 1897-1901. 4. Biographies

LC 2016050943

"In this great American story, acclaimed historian Robert Merry resurrects the presidential reputation of William McKinley, which loses out to the brilliant and flamboyant Theodore Roosevelt who succeeded him after his assassination. He portrays McKinleya's a chief executive of consequence whose low place in the presidential rankings does not reflect his enduring accomplishments and the stamp he put on the country's future role in the world".-- Provided by publisher.

"Critics or admirers of McKinleys presidency will agree it was a momentous one and that Merry's is a fair-minded profile of its central actor." Booklist.

McLane, Maureen N.

McLane, Maureen N. **My** poets / Maureen N. McLane. Farrar, Straus and Giroux, 2012. 273 p. ; **B**

ISBN 9780374217495

1. Poetry -- Influence. 2. Poetry -- History and criticism. 3. Books and reading 4. Essays 5. Autobiographies and memoirs

LC 2011041208

National Book Critics Circle Award for Autobiography/Memoir finalist

Combines criticism and memoir to examine the poets that had the greatest effect on the author's life, including Chaucer and Shelley.

McLaughlin, Rhett

McLaughlin, Rhett **Rhett** & Link's book of mythicality : a field guide to curiosity, creativity, & tomfoolery / Rhett McLaughlin and Link Neal ; with Jake Greene. Crown Archetype, 2017. 269 p. : **B**

ISBN 9780451496294

1. McLaughlin, Rhett. 2. Neal, Link. 3. Internet personalities -- United States 4. YouTube (Electronic resource)

LC 2017046617

"From the YouTube superstars and creators of Good Mythical Morning comes the ultimate guide to living a "Mythical" life, featuring stories and photos from their lifelong friendship, as well as awesomely illustrated tips for laughing more, learning more, and never taking yourself too seriously".-- Provided by publisher.

McLuhan, Marshall, 1911-1980

Coupland, Douglas **Marshall** McLuhan : you know nothing of my work! / Douglas Coupland. Atlas & Co., c2010. v, 216 p. ; **B**

ISBN 9781935633167

1. McLuhan, Marshall, 1911-1980. 2. Mass media specialists -- Canada 3. Mass media -- Social aspects. 4. Popular culture. 5. Canada -- Social life and customs -- 20th century 6. Biographies

Surveys the life and career of the social theorist best known for the quotation, "The medium is the message," who helped shape the culture of the 1960s and predicted the future of television and the rise of the Internet.

"The book rewards by refusing to slip into the numbing vortex of academic discourse, taking a fizzy, pop-culture approach to explaining a deep thinker, one who ended up popularized almost in spite of himself." New York Times Book Review.

McMurtry, Larry

McMurtry, Larry **Books** : a memoir / Larry McMurtry. Simon & Schuster, 2008. 272 p. **B**

ISBN 9781416583349

1. McMurtry, Larry Childhood and youth. 2. Antiquarian booksellers -- United States 3. Books and reading 4. Authors, American -- 20th century 5. Book collecting. 6. United States -- Social life and customs -- 20th century 7. Autobiographies and memoirs

LC 2008010565

The author recounts his lifelong love affair with books, from his largely "bookless" boyhood and discovery of literature as a young man, to the evolution of his writing career and his passion as a book collector who opens bookstores of rare and collectible volumes.

McMurtry, Larry **Walter** Benjamin at the Dairy Queen : reflections at sixty and beyond / Larry McMurtry. Simon & Schuster, 1999. 204 p. : **B**

ISBN 0684854961

1. McMurtry, Larry Books and reading 2. McMurtry, Larry Homes and haunts Texas. 3. Authors, American -- 20th century 4. Reminiscing in old age 5. Books and reading -- United States. 6. Antiquarian booksellers -- United States 7. Texas -- History -- 20th

century 8. Autobiographies and memoirs 9. Essays.

LC 99019346

The Pulitzer Prize-winning author presents a memoir of his odyssey from rancher's son to critically acclaimed novelist, in a reminiscence set against the backdrop of the Lone Star State.

"When McMurtry recalls reading 'Don Quixote' as a thirteen-year-old on a Texas ranch and imagining himself as a character in the novel, other obsessional readers will immediately feel a kinship with this author. His appealing ruminations about his life and work as a reader, writer, and bookseller explore the differences between 'dense and empty, open and closed, new country and old cities, no society and old society'the bare land in which he was reared and the crowded universe of literature." The New Yorker.

McRaven, William H. (William Harry), 1955-

McRaven, William H. (William Harry), 1955- **Sea** stories : my life in Special Operations / Admiral William H. McRaven, U.S. Navy Retired. Grand Central Publishing, 2019. 352 p. **B**

ISBN 9781538729748

1. United States. Navy 2. United States. Navy. SEALs 3. Admirals 4. Special operations (Military science) 5. Raids (Military science) 6. Commando troops 7. Autobiographies and memoirs

LC 2019931174

A memoir from an accomplished military leader recounts stories of bravery and heroism from his career as a Navy SEAL and commander of America's Special Operations Forces.

"McRaven, a retired U.S. Navy admiral, follows his self-help guide, Make Your Bed, in which he shared principles for success learned during his more than 30 years as a Navy SEAL, with this collection of fascinating stories from his time as commander of the Special Operations Forces. McRavens war stories deliver remarkable insight into the life of a wartime leader." Publishers Weekly.

McTell, Blind Willie, 1901-

Gray, Michael, 1946- **Hand** me my travelin' shoes : in search of Blind Willie McTell / Michael Gray. Bloomsbury, 2009. 448 p. **B**

ISBN 9781556529757

1. Blues musicians 2. People who are blind 3. African American musicians 4. Blues (Music) 5. Georgia -- Social life and customs. 6. Biographies

LC 2009022329

Shortlisted for the James Tait Black Memorial Prize for Biography, 2007"

Less a conventional biography than a mixture of history, travelogue and detective story, Gray paints an evocative portrait of an artist who defied blues stereotypes." Kirkus.

McWilliam, Candia, 1955-

McWilliam, Candia, 1955- **What** to look for in winter : a memoir in blindness / Candia McWilliam. Harper, 2012, c2011. xvi, 440 p. ; **B**

ISBN 9780062094506

1. Women authors, Scottish 2. Vision disorders. 3. Blindness -- Psychological aspects 4. Life change events 5. Autobiographies and memoirs

Originally published: London : Jonathan Cape, 2011.

Hawthornden Prize, 2011.

Candia McWilliam had just joined the judging panel of the Man Booker Prize for Fiction in 2006 when she started to lose her sight. In 'What To Look For In Winter', we see her rifling through her many selves for that elusive thing, a sense of self, as all the time she searches the wilder shores of medicine for a cure for her blindness.

Mda, Zakes

Mda, Zakes **Sometimes** there is a void : memoirs of an outsider / Zakes Mda. Farrar, Straus and Giroux, 2012. 561 p. ; **B**

ISBN 9780374280949

1. Mda, Zakes Childhood and youth. 2. Authors, South African -- 20th century 3. Exiles. 4. Immigrants. 5. Social advocates. 6. South Africa. 7. Autobiographies and memoirs

LC 2011020817

Includes index.

Originally published: South Africa : Penguin Books, 2011.

Chronicles the author's life as an artist, family man, and teacher against a backdrop of political turbulence in South Africa, providing coverage of such topics as his childhood exile, his three marriages, and the literature that inspired his achievements.

Mead, Margaret, 1901-1978

Mead, Margaret, 1901-1978 **Blackberry** winter : my earlier years / Margaret Mead. Simon & Schuster, 1984, c1972. 305 p. : **B**

ISBN 0671216422

1. Mead, Margaret, 1901-1978. 2. Women anthropologists -- United States 3. Autobiographies and memoirs

LC 83020373

Includes index.

Reprint. Originally published: New York : Morrow, 1972."

About one-third of Mead's autobiography covers the years before she became an anthropologist and another third her field work in Samoa, in New Guinea, among the Omaha Indians, and in Bali. The concluding chapters . describe in subjective detail her role as mother and grandmother." Choice.

Mead, Rebecca

★Mead, Rebecca **My** life in Middlemarch / Rebecca Mead. Crown, 2014. 304 p. **B**

ISBN 9780307984760

1. Eliot, George, 1819-1880. Middlemarch. 2. Mead, Rebecca Books and reading. 3. Books and reading. 4. Reading. 5. Readers 6. Women journalists 7. Autobiographies and memoirs

LC 2013011477

Published by The Text Publishing Company; Melbourne, Victoria in 2014 under the title: The road to Middlemarch: my life with George Eliot.

In this memoir, journalist and New Yorker staff writer Rebecca Mead, draws out the intricate ways in which the themes of George Eliot's Middlemarch -- "one of the few English novels written for grown-up people," according to Virginia Woolf -- have run through her own life. Mead also draws an uncanny portrait of the ways in which Eliots's life resonates with her own through a fascinating reading of Eliot's biography. For those who wonder about the power of literature to shape our lives, this book is a must-read.

"A rare and remarkable fusion of techniques that draws two women together across time and space." Kirkus.

Meagher, Thomas Francis, 1823-1867

★Egan, Timothy The **immortal** Irishman : the Irish revolutionary who became an American hero / Timothy Egan. Houghton Mifflin Harcourt, 2016. 384 p. **B**

ISBN 9780544272880

1. Meagher, Thomas Francis, 1823-1867. 2. United States. Army Officers 3. United States. Army of the Potomac. Irish Brigade 4. Generals -- United States 5. Revolutionaries -- Ireland 6. Irish Americans 7. Governors 8. United States -- History -- Civil

War, 1861-1865 9. Ireland -- History -- Famine, 1845-1852. 10. Biographies.

LC 2015037256

Places the improbable life of revolutionary hero Thomas Francis Meagher against a backdrop of Irish-American history, detailing his leadership during Irish uprisings, service with the Irish Brigade in the Civil War, and achievements as the territorial governor of Montana.

Mealer, Bryan

Mealer, Bryan The **kings** of Big Spring : God, oil, and one family's search for the American dream / Bryan Mealer. Flatiron Books, 2018. 384 p. **B**

ISBN 9781250058911

1. Mealer, Bryan Family. 2. Oil industry and trade. 3. Rich people. 4. Family fortunes. 5. Drug addiction. 6. Big Spring, Texas. 7. Texas. 8. Biographies

LC bl2017050135

Traces the story of the author's family, whose fortunes and prospects became subject to the Texas oil boom of the 1980s and its related glamour, corruption, drug affiliations, and risks.

"As tribute to the grit of the rural poor, as social history of dirt-and-oil Texas, and as rambunctious family saga, this work triumphs." Library Journal.

Mecom, Jane, 1712-1794

Lepore, Jill, 1966- **Book** of ages : the life and opinions of Jane Franklin / Jill Lepore. Alfred A. Knopf, 2013. 480 p. **B**

ISBN 9780307958341

1. Franklin, Benjamin, 1706-1790. 2. Women -- United States -- Social conditions -- 18th century. 3. Brothers and sisters. 4. Letter writing 5. Boston, Massachusetts -- History -- 18th century 6. Biographies

LC 2013001012

Mark Lynton History Prize, 2014.

National Book Award for Nonfiction finalist, 2013

A revelatory portrait of the founding father's youngest sister, Jane, draws on correspondences, artifacts and recently discovered portraits to reveal how in spite of obscurity and poverty she was, like her brother, a passionate reader, gifted writer and shrewd political commentator who made insightful observations about an early America.

Medici, House of

Parks, Tim **Medici** money : banking, metaphysics, and art in fifteenth-century Florence / Tim Parks. W.W. Norton & Company, 2005. xii, 273 p. : **B**

ISBN 0393058271

1. Medici, House of. 2. Medici, House of Art patronage. 3. Banks and banking -- Florence, Italy -- History. 4. European Renaissance -- Italy. 5. Art, Italian -- Florence, Italy. 6. Art, Renaissance (Europe) -- Florence, Italy. 7. Florence, Italy -- History -- 1421-1737. 8. Biographies

LC 2004030516

"Atlas Books."

An account of the Renaissance era's preeminent financiers describes how the Medicis built their fortune, documenting the political, diplomatic, and metaphysical tools that enabled them to retain their wealth and become art patrons and nobles.

"The general reader will learn from this book a great deal about the era, and those who bestrode it, without getting bogged down in excessive scholarly detail." National Review.

Meeink, Frank

Meeink, Frank **Autobiography** of a recovering skinhead : the Frank Meeink story / as told to Jody M. Roy. Hawthorne Books & Literary Arts, 2009. xv, 350 p. ; **B**

ISBN 9780979018824

1. Meeink, Frank. 2. Skinheads. 3. Neo-Nazis. 4. Hate groups. 5. Neo-Nazism. 6. Autobiographies and memoirs

LC 2009027527

Recounts the author's youth as a violent skinhead, leading a notorious white supremacist gang in Philadelphia before he reconciled his racism in prison and, once released, fought to spread tolerance with the Anti-Defamation League.

"Stories of personal redemption don't get much more interesting than this one, and the gritty first-person narrative . . . draws the reader into Meeink's story, giving it an immediacy and a visceral intensity that makes us feel as though we've lived a bit of his life. Readers should be warned that the book is unflinchingly straightforward: some of the language is quite raw, and some of the imagery quite graphic." Booklist.

Mehra, Nishta

Mehra, Nishta **Brown,** white, black : an American family at the intersection of race, gender, sexuality, and religion / Nishta Mehra. Picador, [2019] 224 p. **B**

ISBN 9781250133557

1. Mehra, Nishta. 2. Identity (Psychology) 3. Intersectionality. 4. Interracial families. 5. Interfaith families. 6. United States -- Race relations. 7. Autobiographies and memoirs.

LC 2018024338

Describes how the author's experiences as an Indian-American, the wife of a white Christian woman and the mother of an adopted black son have been challenged by rigid cultural family norms.

"Mehra (The Pomegranate King) blends memoir and cultural analysis to dive into the complex realities of race, gender, ethnicity, sexuality, and the constructs that surround these topics." Library Journal.

Meiji, Emperor of Japan, 1852-1912

Keene, Donald **Emperor** of Japan : Meiji and His world, 1852-1912 / Donald Keene. Columbia University Press, c2002. xiii, 922 p. : **B**

ISBN 023112340X

1. Meiji, Emperor of Japan, 1852-1912. 2. Rulers 3. Japan -- History -- Meiji period, 1868-1912. 4. Japan -- Rulers 5. Biographies

LC 2001028826

"This is a biography-cum-history of Emperor Meiji and his times. Meiji's reign saw Japan become fully industrialized under a brand new constitution, and with new economic and educational systems adopted. Despite the book's massive scale, Keene's graceful writing holds the reader's interest throughout." Booklist.

Meir, Golda Mabovitz, 1898-1978

Klagsbrun, Francine **Lioness** : Golda Meir and the nation of Israel / Francine Klagsbrun. Schocken Books, 2017 864 p. **B**

ISBN 9780805242379

1. Meir, Golda Mabovitz, 1898-1978. 2. Women prime ministers. 3. Zionists. 4. Women politicians. 5. Zionism. 6. Israel -- Politics and government. 7. Autobiographies and memoirs

LC 2017004908

A biography of the fourth prime minister of Israel, an iron-willed, chain-smoking grandmother, follows her childhood in Milwaukee to joining a kibbutz in Palestine and ending up in a series of public-service positions before her political career took off.

"With hundreds of books on Meir available, this one stands out with its depth of resources and research, building a convincing case that Meir's achievements are still relevant." Library Journal.

Mekhennet, Souad

Mekhennet, Souad **I** was told to come alone : my journey behind the lines of jihad / Souad Mekhennet. Henry Holt and Co., 2017. 304 p. **B**

ISBN 9781627798976

1. Emwazi, Mohammed, -2015. 2. Mekhennet, Souad. 3. ISIS (Islamic State of Iraq and Syria) 4. Islam 5. Women journalists 6. Foreign correspondents 7. Jihad 8. Autobiographies and memoirs

LC 2016054740

Washington Post national security correspondent Souad Mekhennet is a Muslim who grew up in Germany. Viewed by Muslims as an interviewer they can trust, she often has access to significant newsmakers who won't meet with other Western journalists. In I Was Told to Come Alone, Mekhennet traces her life and career, offering insight into the experiences of Arabs and Muslims living in Europe. She also vividly portrays the people she's interviewed (including several jihadis) and the places of conflict she's visited as a reporter.

"A riveting memoir and a literary bombshell that effectively eviscerates every preconception, misconception, and prejudice readers have about the Arab world, I Was Told to Come Alone reinforces the singular significance of journalism, especially foreign journalism, at a time when it is facing its greatest challenges." Booklist.

Melinek, Judy

Melinek, Judy **Working** stiff : two years, 262 bodies, and the making of a medical examiner / Judy Melinek, MD and T.J. Mitchell. Scribner, 2014 288 p. **B**

ISBN 9781476727257

1. Melinek, Judy. 2. Forensic pathologists -- New York City 3. Coroners -- New York City 4. Death 5. Autobiographies and memoirs

LC 2014017610

A New York City forensic pathologist and her Harvard-educated husband describe her experiences as a student and doctor throughout the events of September 11, the subsequent anthrax bio-terrorism attack and the disastrous crash of Flight 587.

"Though some sections call for a strong stomach, armchair detectives and would-be forensic pathologists will find Melinek's well-written account to be inspiring and engaging." Publishers Weekly.

Mellon, Andrew W. (Andrew William), 1855-1937

★Cannadine, David, 1950- **Mellon** : an American life / David Cannadine. A.A. Knopf, 2006. xvi, 779 p., 48 p. of plates : **B**

ISBN 0679450327

1. Mellon, Andrew W. (Andrew William), 1855-1937. 2. United States. Department of the Treasury Officials and employees 3. Politicians -- United States 4. Cabinet officers -- United States 5. Diplomats -- United States 6. Bankers -- United States 7. United States -- Politics and government -- 1901-1953. 8. Biographies

LC 2006045116

Shortlisted for the James Tait Black Memorial Prize for Biography, 2006

A portrait of Andrew Mellon describes his rise to the heights of political and financial power, his controversial role as treasury secretary under three presidents, and his remarkable philanthropy and gift to America of the National Gallery of Art.

Mellon, Paul, Mrs

Gordon, Meryl **Bunny** Mellon : the life of an American style legend / Meryl Gordon. Grand Central Publishing, 2017. 400 p. **B**

ISBN 9781455588749

1. Mellon, Paul, Mrs. 2. Gardeners 3. Philanthropists 4. Upper class 5. Upper class women 6. United States -- History -- 20th century 7. Biographies

LC 2017016493

Drawing on Bunny Mellon's letters, diaries, and appointment books, as well as extensive interviews, the author chronicles the life of the style icon and aristocrat who designed the White House Rose Garden and was a living witness to twentieth-century U.S. history.

"Readers interested in gardening, art, and interior design will drool over Bunnys fine tastes, and her ease at fulfilling every one of them, but all lovers of biographies will marvel at Gordons portrayal of Bunnys long life, and the significant figures who buzzed in and out of it." Booklist.

Melville, Herman, 1819-1891

Delbanco, Andrew, 1952- **Melville** : his world and work / Andrew Delbanco. Knopf, 2005. xxiii, 415 p. : **B**

ISBN 0375403140

1. Melville, Herman, 1819-1891. 2. Literature and society -- United States -- History -- 19th century. 3. Social problems in literature. 4. Authors, American -- 19th century 5. Writing. 6. Biographies

LC 2005040919

Chronicles the life and career of American author Herman Melville, uncovering autobiographical elements in his diverse works, discussing the historical and cultural implications of his writing, and assessing his accomplishments as a writer.

"This is sure to elicit new appreciation for Melville's work and could well be the best one-volume biography for some time to come." Library Journal.

Hardwick, Elizabeth **Herman** Melville / Elizabeth Hardwick. Viking, 2000. ix, 161 p. ; **B**

ISBN 0670891584

1. Melville, Herman, 1819-1891. 2. Authors, American -- 19th century 3. United States -- Social life and customs -- 19th century 4. Biographies

LC 00036510

"A Lipper/Viking book."

The life story of the nineteenth-century author furnishes an analysis of all of Melville's writings and depicts his days as a whaleship deckhand and his bitterness over the public's failure to embrace his master work, Moby-Dick.

"Interweaving critical readings of his fiction and poetry with events in Melville's life, Hardwick offers glimpses into his tortured writing career, his sometimes difficult family life, and his ambivalent relationship with his friend Nathaniel Hawthorne." Library Journal.

Parker, Hershel **Herman** Melville : a biography. Hershel Parker. Johns Hopkins University Press, 1996. xx, 941 p., 32 p. of plates : **B**

ISBN 9780801854286

1. Melville, Herman, 1819-1891. 2. Authors, American -- 19th century 3. Biographies

Pulitzer Prize for Biography or Autobiography finalist"

This, the first volume of a two-volume biography of Melville, ends in 1851, when the author presented to his . friend Nathaniel Hawthorne an inscribed pre-publication copy of Moby-Dick." The Atlantic.

Parker, Hershel **Herman** Melville : a biography. Hershel Parker.

Johns Hopkins University Press, 2002. xvii, 997 p. : B
ISBN 9780801868924
1. Melville, Herman, 1819-1891. 2. Authors, American -- 19th century 3. Biographies

A second volume in the biography chronicles Melville's life from the conclusion of Moby Dick to his death forty years later, documenting the negative reviews that overshadowed his work, his decision to turn to magazine fiction, and his achievements as a poet, as culled from family letters, diary entries, and newspaper articles.

Shelden, Michael **Melville** in love : the secret life of Herman Melville and the muse of Moby-dick / Michael Shelden. Ecco, 2016. 271 p., 8 unnumbered p. of plates : B
ISBN 9780062418982
1. Authors, American -- 19th century 2. Extramarital affairs 3. Books and reading 4. United States -- History -- 19th century 5. Biographies
LC bl2016023427

A Pulitzer finalist in Biography, drawing on new archival research, tells the story of Melville's passionate, obsessive and clandestine affair with a married woman with whom he formed an illicit and enduring romantic and intellectual bond that gave him the courage and wherewithal to write Moby Dick.

"Written for a general audience, this well-paced, enjoyable read is a must for Melville fans." Library Journal.

Melville, Wilma

Melville, Wilma **Hero** dogs : how a pack of rescues, rejects, and strays became America's greatest disaster-search partners / Wilma Melville with Paul Lobo. St. Martin's Press, 2019. 336 p. B
ISBN 9781250179913
1. Melville, Wilma. 2. National Disaster Search Dog Foundation (United States) 3. Dogs -- Training. 4. Search and rescue operations. 5. Dog rescue. 6. Search dogs. 7. Autobiographies and memoirs.
LC 2018039819

Recounts how the author turned a band of shelter dogs into one of America's foremost disaster-response teams during such catastrophes as the Oklahoma City bombing, the Septemner 11 terrorist attacks, and Hurricane Katrina.

"Melville, a canine search-and-rescue handler who was inspired to launch the National Disaster Search Dog Foundation (SDF) after volunteering to help look for Oklahoma City bombing survivors in 1995, shares the struggles of establishing and maintaining the organization." Publishers Weekly.

Melvin, Leland

Melvin, Leland **Chasing** space : an astronaut's story of grit, grace, and second chances / Leland Melvin. HarperCollins, 2017. 256 p. B
ISBN 9780062496720
1. Astronauts 2. Football players 3. African American astronauts 4. African American football players 5. Autobiographies and memoirs
LC bl2017011674

An uplifting memoir by the former NASA astronaut and NFL wide receiver traces his personal journey from the gridiron to the stars, examining the intersecting roles of community, perseverance and grace that create opportunities for success.

"The author makes his seemingly larger-than-life experiences relatable to readers, emphasizing how his hard work and confidence were crucial to his success." School Library Journal.

Mencken, H. L. (Henry Louis), 1880-1956

Rodgers, Marion Elizabeth **Mencken** : the American iconoclast / Marion Elizabeth Rodgers. Oxford University Press, 2005. ix, 662 p. : B
ISBN 0195072383
1. Mencken, H. L. (Henry Louis), 1880-1956. 2. American Mercury. 3. Authors, American -- 20th century 4. Journalists -- United States 5. Editors -- United States 6. Political journalism. 7. Baltimore, Maryland 8. Biographies
LC 2005047786

H. L. Mencken, the 20th century's greatest newspaper journalist, a famous wit, and a fearless iconoclast, fought for civil liberties and free speech yet held paradoxical views of minorities and was conflicted as a German-American during World War II. Marion Rodgers frames the public man and the private man within the context of his era, and covers the many love affairs that made him known as "The German Valentino," as well as his happy marriage at age 50 to Sarah Haardt, and his pivotal role in introducing James Joyce, F. Scott Fitzgerald, and Langston Hughes to the American literary scene.

Mendel, Gregor, 1822-1884

★Henig, Robin Marantz The **monk** in the garden : the lost and found genius of Gregor Mendel, the father of genetics / Robin Marantz Henig. Houghton Mifflin, 2000. viii, 292 p. : B
ISBN 0395977657
1. Mendel, Gregor, 1822-1884. 2. Geneticists -- Austria 3. Scientists -- Austria 4. Genetics -- History. 5. Research. 6. Biographies
LC 00024341

National Book Critics Circle Award for Biography finalist, 2000."

The author explores Mendel's personality and experiments. The latter lasted but a few years in the 1850s and 1860s, ending when Mendel became the abbot of his monastery in what is now Brno in the Czech Republic. Henig crisply conveys how the laws of inheritance that Mendel derived from his statistical analysis remained unnoticed until several botanists who discovered them independently in 1900 also learned that Mendel found them first. This biography itself rediscovers a scientist often mentioned but insuffcently known." Booklist.

Mendeleyev, Dmitry Ivanovich, 1834-1907

Gordin, Michael D. A **well-ordered** thing : Dmitrii Mendeleev and the shadow of the periodic table / Michael D. Gordin. Basic Books, c2004. xx, 364 p. : B
ISBN 9780465027750
1. Mendeleyev, Dmitry Ivanovich, 1834-1907. 2. Chemists -- Russia 3. Periodic law. 4. Chemistry. 5. Russia -- History -- 19th century. 6. Biographies
LC 2003025533

The story of Dmitrii Mendeleev is told in full for the first time, illuminating the role of this remarkable man of science in bringing the Russian Empire out of the dark ages during the nineteenth century, thus paving the way for the rationalism of the Soviet Union.

Mendelsohn, Daniel Adam, 1960-

Mendelsohn, Daniel Adam, 1960- An **odyssey** : a father, a son, and an epic / Daniel Mendelsohn. Alfred A. Knopf, 2017. 256 p. B
ISBN 9780385350594
1. Homer. Odyssey 2. Mendelsohn, Jay, 1929-2012 3. Father and adult son 4. Books and reading 5. Voyages and travels 6. Loss (Psychology) 7. Autobiographies and memoirs
LC 2017011844

Presents the story of a father and son's transformative shared journey in reading in the wake of the father's late-in-life enrollment in his son's undergraduate seminar, where the two engaged in debates over how to interpret Homer's classic masterpiece.

"Mendelsohn weaves family history and trenchant literary analysis into a luminous whole." Publishers Weekly.

Mengele, Josef, 1911-1979

Marwell, David George **Mengele** : unmasking the "Angel of Death" / David G. Marwell. W. W. Norton & Company, [2020] 496 p. **B**

ISBN 9780393609530

1. Mengele, Josef, 1911-1979. 2. Waffen-SS. 3. Auschwitz (Concentration camp). 4. War criminals -- Germany 5. World War II -- Atrocities -- Poland. 6. Physicians -- Germany. 7. Nazi hunters 8. Biographies

LC 2019033220

A gripping portrait of the infamous Nazi doctor, written by the former Justice Department official who proved his death, draws on victim interviews and visits to crime scenes to detail Mengele's university studies and brutal wartime experiments.

"With a distinctive blend of history and political intrigue, Marwell creates a thorough account of one of the most well-known war criminals in history and the efforts to bring him to justice. A worthy addition to Holocaust scholarship." Library Journal.

Merkin, Daphne

Merkin, Daphne **This** close to happy : a reckoning with depression / Daphne Merkin. Farrar, Straus and Giroux, 2017. 304 p. **B**

ISBN 9780374140366

1. Merkin, Daphne Mental health 2. Women with depression 3. Depression -- Treatment 4. Coping in women 5. People with depression 6. Autobiographies and memoirs

LC 2016025616

A former New Yorker staff writer and award-winning author draws on her journalistic essays on depression to trace her lifelong battle with the disease, marked by her wealthy but inconsistent family and her numerous pursuits in therapy and hospitalization.

Merrill, James Ingram

Hammer, Langdon, 1958- **James** Merrill : life and art / Langdon Hammer. Knopf, 2015. 512 p. **B**

ISBN 9780375413339

1. Merrill, James Ingram. 2. Poets, American -- 20th century 3. Gay poets 4. Gay men 5. Biographies

LC 2014029325

"A Borzoi book."

Lambda Literary Award for Gay Memoir/Biography, 2016

The first biography of one of the most important poets in the second half of the twentieth century, whose life story is unparalleled in its narrative interest. The story of James Merrill (1926-1995) is that of a young man escaping, but inevitably reproducing, the energies and obsessions of glamorous, powerful parents (his father founded Merrill Lynch); of a gay man inventing his identity against a shifting social and sexual backdrop; and of a brilliantly gifted poet testing the redemptive potential of his art.

"While certainly organized for readers who adore biographies and life dramas, this will strongly appeal to those who love to discover where art springs from life." Library Journal.

Merton, Thomas, 1915-1968

Elie, Paul, 1965- The **life** you save may be your own : an American pilgrimage / Paul Elie. Farrar, Straus and Giroux, 2003. xiii, 554 p. : **B**

ISBN 0374256802

1. Merton, Thomas, 1915-1968. 2. Day, Dorothy, 1897-1980 3. Percy, Walker, 1916-1990. 4. O'Connor, Flannery 5. Christianity and literature -- United States -- History -- 20th century. 6. Catholics in literature. 7. Catholic authors -- 20th century -- Criticism and interpretation 8. Authors, American -- 20th century 9. United States -- Social life and customs -- 20th century. 10. Biographies

LC 2002192522

National Book Critics Circle Award for Biography finalist, 2003.

The author explores the lives of Thomas Merton, Dorothy Day, Walker Percy, and Flannery O'Connor to search for evidence that their "Christ haunted" Catholic backgrounds inspired them to write, in a study of the spiritual and literary pilgrimage of these four great American Catholic writers.

"This thoroughly researched and well-sourced work deserves attention from students of history, literature and religion, but it will be of special significance to Catholic readers interested in the expression of faith in the modern world." Publishers Weekly.

Merton, Thomas, 1915-1968 The **intimate** Merton : his life from his journals / edited by Patrick Hart and Jonathan Montaldo. HarperSanFrancisco, c1999. xvii, 374 p. : **B**

ISBN 0062516299

1. Merton, Thomas, 1915-1968. 2. Trappists United States 3. Trappists United States.

LC 99033239

Includes index.

Culling the beloved Trappist monk's journals for evidence of spiritual transformation, the author finds evidence aplenty, revealing Merton's passionate explorations of spirituality and the contemplative life, his relationship with Buddhism, his role in the 1960s anti-war movement, and much more.

★Merton, Thomas, 1915-1968 The **seven** storey mountain / Thomas Merton. Harcourt Brace, 1998, c1948. xxiii, 467 p. ; **B**

ISBN 0151004137

1. Merton, Thomas, 1915-1968. 2. Catholic Church. 3. Trappists United States 4. Faith in men. 5. Faith (Christianity) 6. Authors, American 7. Christian writing. 8. Autobiographies and memoirs

LC 98198169

Includes index.

Originally published: New York : Harcourt, Brace, 1948."

The Seven Storey Mountain is the extraordinary spiritual testament of Thomas Merton (1915-1968), a man who experienced life to its fullest in the world before entering a Trappist monastery. By the end of his life, he had become one of the twentieth century's best known and loved Christian voices. This autobiography deals not with what happens to a man, but what happens inside his soul"--Clifton Fadiman, from the publisher's web site.

"The autobiography of a poet who became a convert to Catholicism and at the age of 26 after a full and traveled world career as student and teacher, entered a Trappist monastery." Publishers Weekly.

Messineo, Janet

Messineo, Janet **Casting** into the light : tales of a fishing life / Janet Messineo. Pantheon Books, 2019. 320 p. **B**

ISBN 9781524747640

1. Messineo, Janet. 2. Fishing 3. Women fishers 4. Salt-water fishing 5. Striped bass fishing. 6. Autobiographies and memoirs

LC 2018052725

The champion surfcaster and Martha's Vineyard Times columnist traces her efforts to break barriers in a strictly male sport, describing its unspoken ethics while sharing insider strategies on surf-fishing techniques, lures, baits and locations.

"An inspirational memoir of one womans self-discovery while pursuing the elusive catch." Booklist.

Messud, Claire, 1966-

Messud, Claire, 1966- **Kant's** little Prussian head and other reasons why I write : an autobiography in essays / Claire Messud. W. W. Norton & Company, 2020 xxi, 306 p. **B**

ISBN 9781324006756

1. Authors, American -- 20th century 2. Authors, American -- 21st century 3. Family relationships 4. Influence (Literary, Artistic, etc.) 5. Essays 6. Autobiographies and memoirs

LC 2020018802

The award-winning author celebrates family, art and literature in essays that explore such subjects as her childhood relocation to Australia, her father's death in Beirut and her favorite paintings at Boston's Museum of Fine Arts.

"Powerful and inspirational: Messud is as fine a critic as she is a novelist." Kirkus

Mezrich, Joshua D.

Mezrich, Joshua D. **When** death becomes life : notes from a transplant surgeon / Joshua D. Mezrich. HarperCollins, 2019 368 p. **B**

ISBN 9780062656209

1. Transplantation of organs, tissues, etc. 2. Surgeons 3. Medicine 4. Organ donors 5. Autobiographies and memoirs

LC bl2018192007

A portrait of the extraordinary field of organ transplantation draws on a century of advancement to discuss its pioneers, science and ethical challenges as well as the ways that organ transplants have revolutionized medical care.

"The author presents a history of a procedure, the invention of breakthrough treatments such as dialysis, and the development of medications to prevent rejection. Woven into this history are personal accounts of success, failure, perfect procedures, and frightening complications. Mezrich relieves the tension with humor, balancing clinical perspective with heart-rending stories, and through it all maintains enthusiasm and wonder at the process." Library Journal.

Micheaux, Oscar, 1884-1951

McGilligan, Patrick **Oscar** Micheaux : the great and only : the life of America's first black filmmaker / Patrick McGilligan. HarperCollins, c2007. vii, 402 p., [16] p. of plates : **B**

ISBN 9780060731397

1. African American film producers and directors 2. Race relations -- Filmography 3. African Americans in the performing arts -- History 4. Independent films -- United States -- History and criticism 5. United States -- Social life and customs -- 20th century 6. Biographies

LC 2007060735

Traces the life and career of a pioneering director from the genre of African-American cinema, discussing his childhood in the homesteading communities of South Dakota, his direction of numerous silent and sound films at a time before black-produced movies could be shown in white theaters, and his lesser-known influence on American black culture.

"McGilligan's prose style may be pedestrian, but he organizes his biographical materials into a lively, readable tale." New York Times Book Review.

Michelangelo Buonarroti, 1475-1564

Hirst, Michael **Michelangelo.** The Achievement of Fame, 1475-1534 Michael Hirst. Yale University Press, 2012. x, 438 p. : **B**

ISBN 9780300118612

1. Michelangelo Buonarroti, 1475-1564. 2. Artists -- Italy 3. Art, Italian. 4. Biographies

LC 2011042294

This first book in a two-volume history of the great artist covers his rise to prominence, an era during which her created the statue Pietà, the giant marble David, the Sistine Ceiling frescoes, the new sacristy and library for the Medici family at San Lorenzo, and the monumental tomb for Pope Julius II in Rome.

★Unger, Miles **Michelangelo** : a life in six masterpieces / Miles J. Unger. Simon & Schuster, 2014. 448 p. **B**

ISBN 9781451678741

1. Michelangelo Buonarroti, 1475-1564. 2. Vatican. Sistine Chapel. 3. Vatican City. San Pietro in Vaticano (Basilica). 4. Artists -- Italy 5. European Renaissance. 6. Biographies

LC 2013045778

The life of perhaps the most famous, most revolutionary artist in history, told through the stories of six of his magnificent masterpieces.

Miletich, Patrick Jay, 1968-

Wertheim, L. Jon **Blood** in the cage : mixed martial arts, Pat Miletich, and the furious rise of the UFC / L. Jon Wertheim. Houghton Mifflin Harcourt, 2009. 288 p. **B**

ISBN 9780618982615

1. UFC (Mixed martial arts event) 2. Martial artists -- United States 3. Mixed martial arts. 4. Self-defense 5. Martial arts 6. United States -- Social life and customs -- 21st century 7. Autobiographies and memoirs

LC 2008036764

An inside look at the growing sport of mixed martial arts chronicles the life and career of Pat Miletich, a pioneer of mixed martial arts and six-time UFC champion, against the backdrop of the rise of the Ultimate Fighting Championship.

Mill, John Stuart, 1806-1873

Mill, John Stuart, 1806-1873 **Autobiography** / John Stuart Mill ; edited with an introduction by John M. Robson. Penguin Books, 1989. 234 p. ; **B**

ISBN 9780140433166

1. Mill, John Stuart, 1806-1873. 2. Philosophers -- England 3. Autobiographies and memoirs

LC 91103446

"First published 1873."

Millan, Cesar

Millan, Cesar **Cesar** Millan's lessons from the pack : stories of the dogs who changed my life / Cesar Millan, with Melissa Jo Peltier. National Geographic Society, 2017. 234 p. : **B**

ISBN 9781426216138

1. Dogs 2. Humans and dogs 3. Human/animal relationships 4. Dogs -- Behavior 5. Autobiographies and memoirs

LC 2016044868

Millan looks at the positive effects that having and training dogs has on their owners, and shares personal stories of how the dogs in his life have given him important lessons in respect, confidence, resilience, and authenticity.

"Famed dog behavior expert Millan goes from teacher to student in this touching and informative tribute to the dogs hes loved and learned from." Booklist.

Millay, Edna St. Vincent, 1892-1950

Milford, Nancy **Savage** beauty : the life of Edna St. Vincent Millay / Nancy Milford. Random House, 2001. xviii, 550 p., 32 p. of plates : **B**

ISBN 039457589X

1. Millay, Edna St. Vincent, 1892-1950. 2. Poets, American -- 20th century 3. Women poets, American -- 20th century 4. Women and literature -- United States -- History -- 20th century. 5. Bohemianism -- Greenwich Village, New York City. 6. Greenwich Village, New York City -- Social life and customs -- 20th century. 7. Biographies

LC 2001018598

"In 1923, Edna St. Vincent Millay became the first woman to win the Pulitzer Prize for poetry. To write her biography, Milford . persuaded Millay's younger sister and sole heir, Norma, to give her access to hundreds of Millay's personal papers, letters, and notebooks. Selecting from this extraordinary collection, Milford meticulously integrates Millay's major poems, letters received and sent, reactions of friends, and comments from extensive interviews with Norma into an orderly and affecting narrative." Library Journal.

Miller, Adrienne

Miller, Adrienne **In** the land of men : a memoir / Adrienne Miller. Ecco, 2020. 336 p. **B**

ISBN 9780062682413

1. Miller, Adrienne. 2. Wallace, David Foster. 3. Esquire. 4. Periodical editors 5. Women periodical editors -- United States 6. Periodicals 7. Women editors 8. New York City 9. Autobiographies and memoirs

LC 2019028856

The author traces her coming of age in the male-dominated 1990s literary world, discussing her relationship with David Foster Wallace and her achievements as the first female literary editor of Esquire.

"This intriguing memoir about the literary life of a female editor working in the 'last-hurrah days' of print magazine publishing will appeal to book nerds and fans of David Foster Wallace." Publishers Weekly

Miller, Arthur, 1915-2005

Bigsby, Christopher William Edgar, 1941- **Arthur** Miller : 1915-1962 / Christopher Bigsby. Harvard University Press, 2009. 776 p. **B**

ISBN 9780674035058

1. Miller, Arthur, 1915-2005. 2. Dramatists, American -- 20th century 3. United States -- Social life and customs -- 20th century 4. Biographies

LC 2009002489

Shortlisted for the James Tait Black Memorial Prize for Biography, 2008"

A richly detailed, revealing look at the making of a playwright and a man." Kirkus.

Gottfried, Martin **Arthur** Miller : his life and work / Martin Gottfried. Da Capo Press, 2004, c2003. x, 484 p. : **B**

ISBN 0306813777

1. Dramatists, American -- 20th century 2. United States -- Social life and customs -- 20th century. 3. Biographies

LC bl2006031045

Originally published: 2003.

A portrait of the American playwright draws on interviews with colleagues, friends, and family to create a study of Arthur Miller, from his childhood in Depression-era New York City, through his rise to critical acclaim, to the present day.

"This is an uncomfortable, challenging work, forbidding us any bien-pensant ease, and we should be grateful for it." Times Literary Supplement.

Miller, Chanel

★Miller, Chanel **Know** my name : a memoir / Chanel Miller. Viking, 2019. viii, 357 p. ; **B**

ISBN 9780735223707

1. Miller, Chanel. 2. Injustice 3. Rape victims 4. Courage in women 5. Rape in universities and colleges. 6. Autobiographies and memoirs

LC bl2019028329

National Book Critics Circle Award for Autobiography, 2019

Miller (previously known as Emily Doe) reclaims her identity to tell her story of trauma, transcendence, and the power of words. She tells of her struggles with isolation and shame during the aftermath and the trial, reveals the oppression victims face in even the best-case scenarios, and illuminates a culture biased to protect perpetrators.

"A much-needed memoir giving voice to those who must be heard. Miller's writing stands apart." Library Journal

Miller, Donald, 1971-

Miller, Donald, 1971- **Blue** like jazz : nonreligious thoughts on Christian spirituality / Donald Miller. T. Nelson, c2003. ix, 243 p. : **B**

ISBN 0785263705

1. Christianity. 2. Spirituality. 3. Faith (Christianity) 4. Christian life

LC 2003002223

A minister who has been a frequent radio, TV, and college guest speaker recounts his zealous early life pursuit of the Christian life and his experiences of emptiness and spiritual detachment, tracing his quest to connect with a God he perceived as distant.

Miller, Jonah

Stabiner, Karen **Generation** chef : risking it all for a new American dream / Karen Stabiner. Avery Pub., 2016. 288 p. **B**

ISBN 9781583335802

1. Restaurateurs. 2. Restaurants 3. Cooks. 4. Gastronomy. 5. Biographies

LC 2016026428

A Columbia University food journalism instructor illuminates the challenges faced by today's elite chefs through the experiences of a young chef's make-or-break first year at a new restaurant, detailing how he put his future on the line to pursue an ambitious culinary dream.

"Stabiner takes the reader beyond the shiny surface of food celebrity and Instagrammed plates to expose the beating hearts of those who get up every day to create something inspiring for strangers to consume." Publishers Weekly.

Miller, Lee, 1907-1977

★Burke, Carolyn **Lee** Miller : a life / Carolyn Burke. Knopf, 2005. xv, 426 p. : **B**

ISBN 9780375401473

1. Miller, Lee, 1907-1977. 2. Photographers -- United States 3. Photojournalists -- United States 4. Women photographers -- United States 5. Fashion models -- United States 6. Biographies

LC 2004043844

National Book Critics Circle Award for Biography finalist, 2005.

A detailed profile of Lee Miller offers a multifaceted study of the iconic model, photographer, muse, journalist, mother, sexual adventuress, and gourmet cook, documenting her love affair with artist Man Ray, her unconventional marriages, and her troubled personal life.

"This sympathetic tribute sheds further light on the lives of this highly original, often misunderstood woman." The Economist.

Miller, Stephen (Political advisor)

Guerrero, Jean **Hatemonger** : Stephen Miller, Donald Trump, and the white nationalist agenda / Jean Guerrero. William Morrow & Company, 2020. 336 p. **B**

ISBN 9780062986719

1. Presidents -- United States -- Staff 2. Political consultants 3. Speechwriters 4. Immigration policy 5. United States -- Politics and government 6. United States -- Immigration and emigration 7. Biographies

LC bl2020015865

Stephen Miller is one of the most influential advisors in the White House. He has crafted Donald Trump's speeches, designed immigration policies that ban Muslims and separate families, and outlasted such Trump stalwarts as Steve Bannon and Jeff Sessions. But he's remained an enigma. Until now. Investigative journalist and author Jean Guerrero charts the thirty-four-year-old's astonishing rise to power, drawing from more than one hundred interviews with his family, friends, adversaries and government officials. Hatemonger unveils the man driving some of the most divisive confrontations over what it means to be American - and what America will become.

"An unsparing portrait of the young architect of Trumpian nationalism. . . . A readable study in the banality of evil, even if it comes clothed in bespoke suits." Kirkus

Mills, Dan, 1968-

Mills, Dan, 1968- **Sniper** one : on scope and under siege with a sniper team in Iraq / Dan Mills. St. Martin's Press, 2008. 352 p. **B**

ISBN 9780312531263

1. Great Britain. Army. 2. Iraq War, 2003-2011, British. 3. Snipers. 4. British in Iraq. 5. Soldiers -- Great Britain 6. Iraq -- Military relations. 7. Great Britain -- Armed Forces. 8. Autobiographies and memoirs

LC 2008020438

A decorated member of the Princess of Wales' Royal Regiment recounts his 2004 tour of duty in Iraq, a six-month service of peaceful intentions that were violently altered by hostile attacks by the people of Al Amarah.

"When a battalion of the Prince of Wales' Royal Regiment landed in Iraq in 2004, Mills commanded the 18 men of the sniper platoon. His gripping combat narrative covers how the platoon did more than its share of the fighting during the months when the Iraqis virtually besieged the battalion." Booklist.

Mills, Judy A.

Mills, Judy A. **Blood** of the tiger : a story of conspiracy, greed, and the battle to save a magnificent species / J.A. Mills. Beacon Press, 2015. 296 p. **B**

ISBN 9780807074961

1. Tigers 2. Rare and endangered animals 3. Environmental protection groups and agencies 4. Environmentalists 5. China 6. Autobiographies and memoirs

LC 2014015760

"Set against the backdrop of China's reawakening and ascendance to world dominance, Blood of the Tiger tells of a global fight to rein in the forces of greed on behalf of one of the world's most endangered species".-- Provided by publisher.

"The author provides a list of resources for readers inspired to take action, in addition to a substantial set of notes. A telling inside view of 20 years in international tiger conservation work, including the successes, failures and the work that is still required." Kirkus.

Mills, Marja

Mills, Marja The **mockingbird** next door : life with Harper Lee / Marja Mills. The Penguin Press, 2014. 288 p. **B**

ISBN 9781594205194

1. Lee, Harper 2. Authors, American -- 20th century 3. Sisters 4. Small towns 5. Alabama. 6. Autobiographies and memoirs

LC 2013039938

A journalist who befriended the notoriously quiet and private author of "To Kill a Mockingbird" describes her personal friendship with Harper Lee and her sister and how she eventually moved in next door to the two women and become part of their life in Alabama.

Milne, A. A. (Alan Alexander), 1882-1956

Thwaite, Ann **Goodbye** Christopher Robin : A. A. Milne and the making of Winnie-the-Pooh / Ann Thwaite ; with a preface by Frank Cottrell-Boyce. St. Martin's Griffin, 2017. xxxi, 254 p., 8 unnumbered p. of plates : **B**

ISBN 1250190908

1. Milne, A. A. (Alan Alexander), 1882-1956. 2. Milne, A. A. (Alan Alexander), 1882-1956. Winnie-the-Pooh. 3. Milne, Christopher, 1920-1996. 4. Authors, English -- 20th century 5. Biographies. 6. Children's stories -- Authorship. 7. Fathers and sons -- Great Britain -- History -- 20th century. 8. Biographies

LC 2017041098

"First published in Great Britain under the title A.A. Milne : his life by Faber & Faber. Previously published in Great Britain as this abridged edition by Pan Books, an imprint of Pan Macmillan.""

Goodbye Christopher Robin: A.A. Milne and the Making of Winnie-the-Pooh is drawn from Ann Thwaite's Whitbread Award-winning biography of A. A. Milne , one of England's most successful writers. After serving in the First World War, Milne wrote a number of well-received plays, but his greatest triumph came when he created Winnie-the-Pooh, Piglet, Tigger, Eeyore and, of course, Christopher Robin, the adventurous little boy based on his own son. Goodbye Christopher Robin inspired the film directed by Simon Curtis and starring Domhnall Gleeson, Margot Robbie and Kelly Macdonald. It offers the reader a glimpse into the relationship between Milne and the real-life Christopher Robin, whose toys inspired the magical world of the Hundred Acre Wood. Goodbye Christopher Robin is a story of celebrity, a story of both the joys and pains of success and, ultimately, the story of how one man created a series of enchanting tales that brought hope and comfort to an England ravaged by the First World War".-- Provided by publisher.

Milton, John, 1608-1674

Hawkes, David, 1964- **John** Milton : a hero of our time / David Hawkes. Counterpoint, 2010. 356 p. **B**

ISBN 9781582434377

1. Milton, John, 1608-1674. 2. Milton, John, 1608-1674 Political and social views. 3. Milton, John, 1608-1674 Influence. 4. Poets, English -- Early modern, 1500-1700 5. Authors, English -- 17th century. 6. England -- History -- 17th century. 7. Great Britain -- History -- Stuarts, 1603-1714. 8. Biographies

This biography of the author of Paradise Lost examines his unorthodox and iconoclastic views on politics, economics and sex during a time of great religious and political upheaval in England, and discusses the modern-day relevance of his ideas.

Min, Anchee, 1957-

★Min, Anchee, 1957- The **cooked** seed : a memoir / Anchee Min. Bloomsbery, 2013 320 p. **B**

ISBN 9781596916982

1. Revolutions -- China. 2. Second chances 3. Communism -- China. 4. Growing up. 5. China -- History -- Cultural Revolution, 1966-1976. 6. Autobiographies and memoirs

LC 2013015953

Traces the author's journey from the painful deprivations of her homeland to the sudden bounty of the United States, where she endured five jobs, crime, and a painful marriage before the birth of a daughter inspired her writing career.

Min, Anchee, 1957- **Red** Azalea / Anchee Min. Anchor Books, 2006, c1994. xiv, 306 p. ; **B**

ISBN 1400096987

1. Revolutions -- China. 2. Communism -- China. 3. Growing up. 4. Actors and actresses. 5. China -- History -- Cultural Revolution, 1966-1976. 6. Autobiographies and memoirs

LC 2006271433

"With a new preface".--Cover."Originally published in hardcover in a slightly different form in the United States by Pantheon Books ... New York, in 1994"--T.p. verso.

A woman who grew up in China during its Cultural Revolution describes the grueling physical labor she endured on Red Fire Farm, her forced segregation from men, her sexual relationship with her platoon leader, and her introduction to acting.

"In this memoir of growing up in China during the Cultural Revolution, sexual freedom becomes a powerful political as well as literary statement." New York Times Book Review.

Mingus, Charles, 1922-1979

Gabbard, Krin **Better** git it in your soul : an interpretive biography of Charles Mingus / Krin Gabbard. University of California Press, 2016 323 p. **B**

ISBN 9780520260375

1. Mingus, Charles, 1922-1979. 2. Composers 3. Jazz musicians. 4. Bass players. 5. Biographies 6. Essays

LC 2015031907

This biography traces the output of jazz master Charles Mingus--his recordings, his compositions, and his writings--highlighting key moments in his life and musicians who influenced him and were influenced by him.

"A solid addition to the literature of jazz." Booklist.

Mirvis, Tova

Mirvis, Tova The **book** of separation : a memoir / Tova Mirvis. Houghton Mifflin Harcourt, 2017. 288 p. **B**

ISBN 9780544520523

1. Authors, American -- 20th century 2. Self-discovery in women 3. Jewish women. 4. Jews 5. Autobiographies and memoirs

LC 2017015328

The memoir of a woman who leaves her faith and her marriage and sets out to navigate the terrifying, liberating terrain of a newly mapless world.

Miskjian, Stepan, 1886-1974

Mackeen, Dawn Anahid The **hundred-year** walk : an Armenian odyssey / Dawn Anahid Mackeen. Houghton Mifflin Harcourt, 2012. 288 p. **B**

ISBN 9780618982660

1. Miskjian, Stepan, 1886-1974. 2. Mackeen, Dawn Anahid Family. 3. Armenian genocide, 1915-1923. 4. Crimes against humanity. 5. Refugees, Armenian. 6. Armenians in Turkey -- History. 7. Turkey -- History -- 20th century. 8. Armenia -- History -- 20th century. 9. Biographies.

LC 2015016713

During and after World War I, the Ottoman government killed over a million Armenians in one of the first modern genocides. One survivor was Stepan Miskjian; he escaped from a caravan leading him to slaughter, walked 1,000 miles across Turkey and Syria, and later wrote journals about his experiences. Using those journals as a starting point, his granddaughter, journalist Dawn Anahid MacKeen retraced his footsteps, learning about her grandfather, her roots, herself, and the Middle East in the process. Deftly combining history and travelogue, MacKeen provides a harrowing and inspirational tale.

"Powerful, terrible stories about what people are willing to do to other peoplebut leavened with hope and, ultimately, forgiveness." Kirkus.

Mitchell, Jerry

★Mitchell, Jerry **Race** against time : a reporter reopens the unsolved murder cases of the civil rights era / Jerry Mitchell. Simon & Schuster, 2020. 320 p. **B**

ISBN 9781451645132

1. Mitchell, Jerry. 2. Ku Klux Klan 3. Investigative journalists. 4. Cold cases (Criminal investigation) 5. Trials (Murder) 6. Civil rights workers 7. Southern states 8. Mississippi 9. Alabama 10. Autobiographies and memoirs

LC 2019030562

An award-winning investigative journalist recounts the 1964 "Mississippi Burning" murders of three civil rights workers by the KKK, describing his role in reopening the case and bringing its mastermind and participating Klansmen to justice.

"A fine work of investigative journalism and an essential addition to the history of the civil rights movement." Kirkus

Mitchell, Joan, 1926-1992

Albers, Patricia **Joan** Mitchell : lady painter / Patricia Albers. Alfred A. Knopf, 2011. 544 p. **B**

ISBN 9780375414374

1. Mitchell, Joan, 1926-1992. 2. Abstract expressionism. 3. Abstract expressionists. 4. Women painters. 5. Painters -- United States 6. Biographies

LC 2011000457

"A Borzoi book.""

This is a biography of Joan Mitchell (192592), a major 20th-century American artist. This significant biography covers all aspects of Mitchell's life, including her synesthesia, eidetic memory, alcoholism, troubled relationships, and art. Filled with intimate details of her complex personality and unconventional lifestyle, this is a conscientiously objective yet sympathetic portrait of the lady painter and the social and cultural contexts in which she became a successful artist in the male-dominated Parisian and New York art worlds." Library Journal.

Mitchell, Joni, 1943-

Hoskyns, Barney, **Joni** : the anthology / edited by Barney Hoskyns. Picador, 2017. 320 p. **B**

ISBN 9781250148629

1. Folk music 2. Women musicians 3. Popular music 4. Folk musicians 5. Anthologies 6. Biographies

LC 2017027146

A tribute to the legendary singer songwriter is comprised of 60 detailed magazine articles that capture her journey as an artist and span her entire career, from her first performance at the Troubadour in 1968 to a 1998 interview with MOJO.

"This intriguing anthology captures the essence of award-winning songwriter/performer Joni Mitchell as both individual and artist. The book's concept is singular, and the selection and structuring of the material well done." Library Journal.

Yaffe, David, 1973- **Reckless** daughter : a portrait of Joni Mitchell / David Yaffe. Sarah Crichton Books, Farrar, Straus and Giroux, 2017. 544 p. **B**

ISBN 9780374248130

1. Folk music 2. Women musicians 3. Folk musicians 4. Biographies

LC 2017024370

A portrait of the music-culture icon shares insight into her use of experimental lyrics while revealing the inspirations behind her most famous songs, from her youth on the Canadian prairie to her early marriage and the child she gave up for adoption.

"A shimmering portrait of one artists life, illusions and all." Booklist.

Mitford, Nancy, 1904-1973

Thompson, Laura, 1964- **Life** in a cold climate : Nancy Mitford: the biography / Laura Thompson. Review, 2003. xvi, 432 p., 16 unnumbered p. of plates : **B**

ISBN 9780747245742

1. Mitford, Nancy, 1904-1973 Correspondence 2. Women authors -- 20th century 3. Women biographers 4. London, England -- Social life and customs -- 20th century. 5. France -- Social life and customs -- 20th century. 6. Biographies

LC oc2007097745

"Highly recommended for fans of literary biographies, as well as those interested in British history and dramas. The combination of poetic prose and dedicated research makes this an accessible an delightful read." Library Journal.

Mithridates VI Eupator, King of Pontus, ca. 132-63 B.C.

Mayor, Adrienne, 1946- The **Poison** King : the life and legend of Mithridates, Rome's deadliest enemy / Adrienne Mayor. Princeton University Press, 2009. 472 p. **B**

ISBN 9780691126838

1. Poisoning.. 2. Rulers. 3. Conquerors. 4. Rome -- History -- Mithridatic Wars, 88-63 B.C. 5. Pontus -- Rulers 6. Pontus -- History. 7. Mediterranean Region -- History, Military. 8. Black Sea Region -- History, Military. 9. Biographies

LC 2009015050

National Book Award for Nonfiction finalist, 2009

Mayor delivers an account of Mithradates, the ruthless visionary who began to challenge Rome's power in 120 B.C. Machiavelli praised his military genius. Kings coveted his secret elixir against poison. Poets celebrated his victories, intrigues, and panache. But until now, no one has told the full story of his incredible life.

"This is a reappraisal of Mithradates's character and a detailed account of his scientific pursuits, notably his in-depth studies of poison. [The author places] him in his proper context as a Greco-Persian ruler following in the footsteps of his purported ancestor Alexander the Great. The most compelling aspect of this book is Mayor's engaging style. A true storyteller, she makes Mithradates's world come alive." Library Journal.

Mitnick, Kevin D. (Kevin David), 1963-

Mitnick, Kevin D. (Kevin David), 1963- **Ghost** in the wires : my adventures as the world's most wanted hacker / Kevin Mitnick with William L. Simon. Little, Brown and Company, 2011. 368 p. **B**

ISBN 9780316037709

1. Hackers. 2. Computer crimes. 3. Computer security 4. Information superhighway.

LC 2010043461

Kevin Mitnick is one of the world's foremost computer hackers. He infiltrated some of the most complicated and advanced computer systems before the law finally caught up with him. Here, Mitnick chronicles his three years on the run from the FBI, during which he worked odd jobs, kept tabs on his pursuers, and continued to hack into systems throughout the world.

Mizrahi, Isaac

Mizrahi, Isaac **I.M.** : a memoir / Isaac Mizrahi. Flatiron Books, [2019] 384 p. **B**

ISBN 9781250074089

1. Mizrahi, Isaac. 2. Fashion designers. 3. Popular culture. 4. Gay men. 5. Syrian Americans. 6. Autobiographies and memoirs.

LC 2018029257

A memoir by the multifaceted pop culture icon discusses his experiences as a gay youth in a Syrian Jewish Orthodox family, his education at LaGuardia High School for Performing Arts, and the making of his documentary, "Unzipped."

"There isn't a phony note in this memoir from fashion designer Mizrahi, who comes to us as he is, no holds barred, with a forthrightness that should appeal to readers of all stripes." Library Journal.

Moaveni, Azadeh, 1976-

Moaveni, Azadeh, 1976- **Honeymoon** in Tehran : two years of love and danger in Iran / Azadeh Moaveni. Random House, 2009. 340 p. ; **B**

ISBN 9781400066452

1. Women journalists -- 21st century 2. Politics and culture -- Iran 3. Men/women relations 4. Culture conflict 5. Iran -- Social life and customs -- 21st century 6. Autobiographies and memoirs

LC 2009278110

The Iranian-American author describes her return to Iran as a reporter for "Time" magazine, her marriage to an Iranian man, the repressive Iranian society and its impact, and her family's decision to leave Iran.

"This perfect blend of political commentary and social observation is an excellent choice for readers interested in going beyond the headlines to gain an in-depth understanding of twenty-first-century Iran." Booklist.

Moaveni, Azadeh, 1976- **Lipstick** jihad : a memoir of growing up Iranian in America and American in Iran / Azadeh Moaveni. PublicAffairs, 2005. xi, 249 p. ; **B**

ISBN 1586481932

1. Iranian American women 2. Iranian-Americans 3. Iranian-Americans -- Identity 4. Iran -- Social conditions -- 1979-1997. 5. Iran -- Social conditions -- 1997- 6. United States -- Social life and customs -- 20th century 7. Autobiographies and memoirs

LC 2004043184

The story of the Iranian-American author's search for identity between two cultures torn apart by a violent history paints a portrait of Iran's next generation.

"Moaveni, an Iranian-American who grew up in California, decided to embark on a journey in spring 2000 to rediscover her Iranian heritage. In this account, she . . . conveys the tensions she observed between the fundamentalist mullahs and younger Iranians, who are pushing for a more Westernized, modern Iran. . . . A charming and informative memoir." Library Journal.

Mochi, approximately 1841-1881

Enss, Chris, 1961- **Mochi's** war : the tragedy of Sand Creek / Chris Enss and Howard Kazanjian. TwoDot, [2015] 192 p. **B**

ISBN 9780762760770

1. Mochi, approximately 1841-1881. 2. Sand Creek Massacre, November 29, 1864 3. Cheyenne Indians -- Wars, 1864. 4. Indians of North America -- Relations with European Americans 5. Massacres 6. Sand Creek Massacre National Historic Site (Colorado). 7. Biographies

LC 2015005372

As with many incidents in American history, the victors wrote the first version of history--turning the tragedy of the Sand Creek Massacre into a heroic feat by the Colorado militia tasked with moving the Cheyenne onto reservations. The truth of those events has made Colonel John Chivington's name infamous in Colorado and American history, and this dramatic and poignant reflection on the events leading to the tragic events of the massacre and the ensuing years of violence offers new perspectives with the hindsight of more than a century and a half of repercussions by telling the story of one of the women, a Cheyenne named Mochi, who became swept up in the cycle of war and vengeance that ensued.

"Highly recommended for adult readers of Western and Native American history, this biographical account provides a counterpoint to the many works that have mythologized such women as Pocahontas and Sacajawea." Library Journal.

Mock, Janet, 1983-

Mock, Janet, 1983- **Redefining** realness : my path to womanhood, identity, love & so much more / Janet Mock. Pocket Books, 2014. 320 p. **B**

ISBN 9781476709123

1. Transgender persons 2. Identity (Psychology) 3. Multiracial women 4. Femininity 5. Autobiographies and memoirs

LC 2013047625

A journalist and activist who was profiled in a 2011 Marie Claire feature outlines bold perspectives on the realities of being young, multiracial, economically challenged and transgender in today's America, recounting her disadvantaged youth and decision to undergo gender reassignment surgery at the age of 18 before pursuing a career and falling in love.

Mockett, Marie Mutsuki

Mockett, Marie Mutsuki **Where** the dead pause, and the Japanese say goodbye : a journey / Marie Mutsuki Mockett. W W Norton, 2015. 352 p. **B**

ISBN 9780393063011

1. Funerals 2. Pilgrims and pilgrimages 3. Death 4. Grief in women 5. Japan -- Description and travel 6. Autobiographies and memoirs

LC 2014032438

A woman describes her journey visiting Zen priests and performing rituals after the death of both her Japanese grandfather and her American father and her inability to bury them at her family's Buddhist temple in the wake of the Fukushima nuclear disaster.

"Mocketts involving and revelatory chronicle of Japanese spirituality in a time of crisis greatly enriches our perceptions of both a unique culture and the human longing for connection with the dead." Booklist.

Modigliani, Amedeo, 1884-1920

Secrest, Meryle **Modigliani** : a life / Meryle Secrest. Alfred A. Knopf, 2011. 384 p. **B**

ISBN 9780307263681

1. Modigliani, Amedeo, 1884-1920. 2. Painters -- Italy 3. Modernism (Art) 4. Tuberculosis. 5. People with tuberculosis 6. Paris, France. 7. Biographies

LC 2010045357

"A Borzoi book."

A full-scale profile of the celebrated modernist artist includes coverage of his upbringing as a Sephardic Jewish youth by a impoverished Italian family, his considerable training and the ways in which his private battles with tuberculosis shaped his achievements.

Moe, John

Moe, John The **hilarious** world of depression / John Moe. St. Martin's Press, 2020 256 p. **B**

ISBN 9781250209283

1. People with depression 2. Mental health 3. Family and suicide 4. Self-destructive behavior 5. Autobiographies and memoirs

LC 2019058396

Based on a podcast.

The host of the podcast The Hilarious World of Depression offers a moving portrait of what it means to be depressed.

"Moe's edifying, enjoyable take on the realities of living with depression will uplift any reader." Publishers Weekly

Moghul, Haroon

Moghul, Haroon **How** to be a Muslim : an American story / Haroon Moghul. Beacon Press, 2017. 256 p. **B**

ISBN 9780807020746

1. Moghul, Haroon. 2. Muslim American men 3. Islam -- Social aspects 4. Identity (Psychology) 5. Faith (Islam) 6. Autobiographies and memoirs

LC 2016041078

A young Muslim leader shares his quest to forge a unique American Muslim identity that reflected his beliefs and personality in a post-9/11 world where he, in a society that fears Muslims, struggled with his faith and searching for intellectual forebears, as well as suffered with the onset of bipolar disorder.

"Highly recommended for its candor and relatability, this book will invite readers to fathom what it means to grasp Islamand religion and spirituality in general." Publishers Weekly.

Mohammed Bin Salman, Crown Prince of Saudi Arabia, 1985-

Hubbard, Ben (Journalist) **MBS** : the rise to power of Mohammed Bin Salman / Ben Hubbard. Tim Duggan Books, [2020]. 359 p. ; **B**

ISBN 9781984823823

1. Princes -- Saudi Arabia 2. Assassination 3. Ambition in men 4. Inheritance and succession 5. Saudi Arabia -- Politics and government -- 21st century. 6. Biographies

LC bl2020006712

"This account is, by far, the best characterization of this mercurial leader, along with his varied alliances and how he came to develop them ... An important and keen assessment of the Saudi Crown Prince that should be on every bookshelf." Library Journal

Molina, Benjamin

Molina, Bengie, 1974- **Molina** : the story of the father who raised an unlikely baseball dynasty / Bengie Molina with Joan Ryan. Simon & Schuster, 2015. 256 p. **B**

ISBN 9781451641042

1. Molina, Benjamin. 2. Molina, Bengie, 1974- 3. Fathers -- Puerto Rico. 4. Fathers and sons. 5. Baseball -- Puerto Rico. 6. Baseball

players 7. Puerto Rico 8. Biographies

LC 2014043223

A Major League Baseball player tells the inspiring true story of his father, a poor Puerto Rican factory worker who, against all odds, raised on of the greatest baseball dynasties of all time: three sons who have each earned two World Series rings.

"This memoir will appeal to any baseball fan as well as patrons from Puerto Rican communities." Library Journal.

Momus, 1960-

Momus, 1960- **Niche** : a memoir in pastiche / Momus. Farrar, Straus and Giroux, 2020. 320 p. **B**

ISBN 9780374144081

1. Musicians 2. Songwriters 3. Bloggers 4. Popular culture 5. Autobiographies and memoirs

LC 2020012290

Rather than one avuncular tell-all relayed in his own voice, Momus has structured the narrative of his life as a typically atypical mockery of the rock-bio oral history. Instead of using living witnesses, Momus assumes the voices of 217 dead authors and artists and forces them to speak for and about him. From these dramatic monologues?sometimes unreliable, often comical?there gradually emerges a picture of one eccentric star's life across three continents and in his own, remarkable, niche.

"This is that rare show-biz memoir that's both entertaining and a literary triumph." Publishers Weekly

Monet, Claude, 1840-1926

★King, Ross, 1962- **Mad** enchantment : Claude Monet and the painting of the water lilies / Ross King. Bloomsbury USA, 2016. 384 p. **B**

ISBN 9781632860125

1. Monet, Claude, 1840-1926 Criticism and interpretation. 2. Monet, Claude, 1840-1926 Last years. 3. Water lilies in art. 4. Painters -- France 5. Impressionism (Art) 6. Artists. 7. Biographies

LC 2015049404

Charles Taylor Prize for Literary Non-Fiction (Canada), 2017.

Hilary Weston Writers' Trust Prize for Nonfiction finalist, 2016.

Examines the life of the artist Claude Monet with a focus on the paintings of the water lilies in his garden at Giverny.

"Never before has the full drama and significance of Monets magnificent Water Lilies been conveyed with such knowledge and perception, empathy and wonder." Booklist.

Monk, Thelonious, 1917-1982

Kelley, Robin D. G. **Thelonious** Monk : the life and times of an American original / Robin D. G. Kelley. Free Press, 2009. 608 p. **B**

ISBN 9780684831909

1. Jazz musicians 2. Jazz music 3. African American musicians 4. Musicians 5. Biographies

LC 2009008526

Hurston/Wright Legacy Award: Nonfiction, 2010.

A comprehensive profile of the enigmatic jazz pianist and composer offers insight into his antebellum origins, his participation in the Great Migration north, and the mid-twentieth-century cultural upheavals that shaped his personal and creative life.

"The author knows music, especially Monk's music, and his descriptions of assorted studio and live dates, along with what Monk is up to musically throughout, are handled expertly. Likewise, the characters in Monk's life and career are well served. The genius of modern music has gotten the passionate, and compassionate, advocate he deserves." New York Times Book Review.

Monroe, James, 1758-1831

Unger, Harlow G., 1931- The **last** founding father : James Monroe and a nation's call to greatness / Harlow Giles Unger. Da Capo Press, 2009. xii, 388 p. : **B**

ISBN 9780306818080

1. Monroe, James, 1758-1831. 2. Presidents -- United States 3. Politicians -- United States 4. Founding Fathers of the United States. 5. Diplomats. 6. United States -- Politics and government -- 1817-1825. 7. United States -- Politics and government -- 1783-1865. 8. Biographies

LC 2009026195

Recounts the life of the fifth president from his fierce participation in critical Revolutionary War battles through his political contributions, documenting his efforts toward securing the nation's durability and his mentorship under the first four presidents.

Monroe, Marilyn, 1926-1962

Casillo, Charles **Marilyn** Monroe : the private life of a public icon / Charles Casillo. St. Martin's Press, August 2018. 336 p. **B**

ISBN 9781250096869

1. People with bipolar disorder 2. Film actors and actresses 3. Foster children 4. Fame 5. Biographies

LC 2018004352

Includes index.

The author of *The Marilyn Diaries* draws on new research and interviews to reveal how Monroe's traumatic childhood contributed to her struggle with bipolar disorder and impacted her career and personal life.

"Beginning with Monroe's illegitimate birth and impoverished childhood in and out of foster homes and orphanages, Casillo traces the deep roots of Monroe's essential feelings of inadequacy and longing for acceptance." Booklist.

★Taraborrelli, J. Randy The **secret** life of Marilyn Monroe / J. Randy Taraborrelli. Grand Central Pub., 2009. 576 p. **B**

ISBN 9780446580823

1. Monroe, Marilyn, 1926-1962. 2. Film actors and actresses -- United States 3. Mental illness -- Hollywood, California 4. Men/women relations 5. Mothers and daughters -- United States 6. United States -- History -- 20th century 7. Hollywood, California -- History -- 20th century 8. Biographies.

LC 2008044704

Includes index.

A profile of the iconic actress explores the roles of the influential women in her life, including her mentally ill mother, in an account that also discusses Monroe's own struggles with mental illness, her estranged father, and the Kennedys.

"For this biography, the author delves beneath the legend of Marilyn Monroe to uncover the stark facts of the life and times of a singularly vulnerable woman woefully unequipped to deal with the quotidian business of normal life, much less the pressures of a Hollywood career and international celebrity. A painful and engrossing account of the profoundly damaged personality at the heart of the world's greatest sex symbol." Kirkus.

Montaigne, Michel de, 1533-1592

Bakewell, Sarah **How** to live--or--a life of Montaigne : in one question and twenty attempts at an answer / Sarah Bakewell.

Other Press, c2010. ix, 389 p. : B
ISBN 9781590514252
1. Montaigne, Michel de, 1533-1592. 2. Montaigne, Michel de, 1533-1592 Philosophy. 3. Authors, French -- 16th century 4. Life -- Philosophy 5. Intellectuals -- France 6. France -- History -- 16th century 7. Biographies
LC 2010026896
Originally published: London : Chatto & Windus, 2010.
National Book Critics Circle Award for Biography, 2010.
Examines the essays of Michel de Montaigne that explored the search for the meaning of life, and profiles the philosopher using the questions he posed and the answers he explored.
"In a wide-ranging intellectual career, Michel de Montaigne found no knowledge so hard to acquire as the knowledge of how to live this life well. By casting her biography of the writer as 20 chapters, each focused on a different answer to the question How to live? Bakewell limns Montaigne's ceaseless pursuit of this most elusive knowledge. Embedded in the 20 life-knowledge responses, readers will find essential factswhen and where Montaigne was born, how and whom he married, how he became mayor of Bordeaux, how he managed a public life in a time of lethal religious and political passions. Because Montaigne's capacious mirror still captivates many, this insightful life study will win high praise from both scholars and general readers." Booklist.

Montalvan, Luis Carlos
Montalvan, Luis Carlos **Until** Tuesday : a wounded warrior and the golden retriever who saved him / Luis Carlos Montalvan, with Bret Witter. Hyperion, 2011. 272 p. B
ISBN 9781401324292
1. Montalvan, Luis Carlos. 2. Veterans 3. Service dogs -- United States. 4. Post-traumatic stress disorder 5. Human/animal relationships 6. Autobiographies and memoirs
LC 2010051147
"Tuesday has a personality that shines. I am not kidding when I say it is common for people to pull out their cell phones and take pictures of and with him. Tuesday is that kind of dog. And then, in passing, they notice me, the big man with the tight haircut. There is nothing about me--even the straight, stiff way I carry myself--that signals disabled. Until people notice the cane in my left hand, that is, and the way I lean on it every few steps. Then they realize my stiff walk and straight posture aren't just pride, and that Tuesday isn't just an ordinary dog. He walks directly beside me, for instance, so that my right leg always bisects his body. He nuzzles me when my breathing changes, and he moves immediately between me and the object--a cat, an overeager child, a suspiciously closed door--any time I feel apprehensive. Because beautiful, happy-go-lucky, favorite-of-the-neighborhood Tuesday isn't my pet; he's my service dog." Captain Luis Montalvan returned home from his second tour of duty in Iraq, having survived stab wounds, a traumatic brain injury, and three broken vertebrae. But the pressures of civilian life and his injuries proved too much to bear. Physical disabilities, agoraphobia, and crippling PTSD drove him to the edge of suicide. That'swhen he met Tuesday - his best friend forever. Tuesday came with his own history of challenges: from the Puppies Behind Bars program, to a home for troubled boys, to the streets of Manhattan, Tuesday blessed many lives on his way to Luis. Until Tuesday unforgettably twines the story of man and dog".-- Provided by publisher.
"Montalvan's mixture of memoir, military history, and pet story results in an urgently important tale." Booklist.

Montana, Joe, 1956-
Dunnavant, Keith **Montana** : the biography of football's Joe Cool / Keith Dunnavant. Thomas Dunne Books, 2015 352 p. B
ISBN 9781250017840
1. Football players -- United States 2. Quarterbacks (Football) 3. Football
LC 2015019171
A portrait of the three-time Superbowl MVP and Pro Football Hall of Famer traces his career against a backdrop of late-20th-century America, from his working class childhood in Pennsylvania and years at Notre Dame through his remarkable achievements in San Francisco and beyond.
"Well written and researched, this title will be of interest to a wide range of sports fans." Library Journal.

Montgomery, Sy
Montgomery, Sy The **good** good pig : the extraordinary life of Christopher Hogwood / Sy Montgomery. Ballantine Books, c2006. 228 p., 8 p. of plates : B
ISBN 0345481372
1. Montgomery, Sy. 2. Pigs. 3. Human/animal relationships -- New Hampshire -- Anecdotes. 4. Pet owners -- New Hampshire 5. Pigs as pets -- New Hampshire -- Anecdotes. 6. New Hampshire -- Social life and customs. 7. Autobiographies and memoirs
LC 2005057094
An ardent nature lover and author of Journey of the Pink Dolphins describes her unique friendship with a pig named Christopher Hogwood, a once sickly piglet who helped her develop a new relationship with neighbors in her small-town community that gave her an anchor to family and home.
"Anyone who has ever loved a pet can enjoy reading about the relationship between Montgomery and her Christopher." Science Books & Films.

Montross, Christine
Montross, Christine **Falling** into the fire : a psychiatrist's encounters with the mind in crisis / Christine Montross. Penguin Press, 2013. 224 p. B
ISBN 9781594203930
1. Montross, Christine. 2. Mental illness 3. Psychotherapy 4. Physician and patient 5. Medical personnel 6. Autobiographies and memoirs
LC 2013007699
"Diagnoses rest upon a physicians knowledge and judgment but also clinical intuition. We are all fragile and vulnerable creatures. Compassion counts." Booklist.

Moody, Rick
Moody, Rick The **long** accomplishment : a memoir of hope and struggle in matrimony / Rick Moody. Henry Holt & Company, 2019. 352 p. B
ISBN 9781627798440
1. Moody, Rick Marriage 2. Authors, American 3. Marriage 4. Husband and wife 5. Remarriage 6. Autobiographies and memoirs
LC 2018044743
The author shares a month-by-month account of a harrowing year of his life, marked by his second marriage, depression, addiction, miscarriages, robberies and the deaths of friends.
"Despite the digressions, this is a revealing, intimate memoir?and a moving love letter from Moody to his wife." Publishers Weekly.

Mooney, Jonathan
Mooney, Jonathan **Normal** sucks : how to live, learn, and thrive outside the lines / Jonathan Mooney. Henry Holt & Com-

pany, [2019] 245 p. **B**

ISBN 9781250190161

1. Children with learning disabilities 2. Normality (Psychology) 3. Teaching 4. Education

LC 2018053025

A writer diagnosed with dyslexia and ADHD as a child explores the toll the system takes on kids who are not "normal" and advocates for a revolution in the way we think about diversity, abilities and disabilities.

"In this engaging, eye-opening read, popular speaker and author Mooney (The Short Bus, 2007) shares his memories of navigating life with ADD and dyslexia, combined with his unique upbringing, and provides an invaluable history of and perspective on neurodiversity." Booklist.

Mooney, Paul, 1941-

Mooney, Paul, 1941- **Black** is the new white / Paul Mooney. Simon Spotlight Entertainment, 2009. 272 p. **B**

ISBN 9781416587958

1. Television comedy writers -- United States 2. African American comedians 3. African-American celebrities. 4. United States -- Social life and customs -- 21st century 5. Autobiographies and memoirs

LC 2009019572

A contributor to Chappelle's Show, The Richard Pryor Show, Saturday Night Live, and may other programs recounts his many experiences with Pryor and describes his life as a TV writer, in a memoir that combines personal narrative with sharp, witty social insights.

Moore, Colten

Moore, Colten **Catching** the sky / Colten Moore , Keith O'Brien. 37 Ink, 2016. 256 p. **B**

ISBN 9781501117244

1. ESPN X-Games 2. Extreme sports 3. Snowmobiles 4. Brothers -- Death 5. Athletes 6. Autobiographies and memoirs

LC bl2016000903

Family bonds and brotherly love shine in a poignant and exciting memoir as richly layered and emotionally complex as Into Thin Air and Friday Night Lights when, in the wake of the devastating freestyle snowmobile accident that killed his older brother Caleb at Aspen's Winter X Games, Colten Moore returns to win gold.

"Moore's well-written memoir will enthrall fans of extreme sports, the X Games, and those trying to find their way after losing a loved one." Library Journal.

Moore, Darnell L., 1976-

Moore, Darnell L., 1976- **No** ashes in the fire : coming of age black and free in America / Darnell L. Moore. Nation Books, 2018 224 p. **B**

ISBN 9781568589480

1. African American men 2. Black Lives Matter movement 3. Prejudice 4. Race relations 5. Autobiographies and memoirs

LC 2017046505

Lambda Literary Award for Gay Memoir/Biography, 2019.

The editor-at-large of CASSIUS and original Black Lives Matter organizer describes his own direct experiences with prejudice, violence and repression; his search for intimacy in the gay neighborhoods of his youth and his participation in key civil movements where he found his calling as an advocate on behalf of society's marginalized people.

Moore, Marianne, 1887-1972

★Moore, Marianne, 1887-1972 The **selected** letters of Marianne Moore / Marianne Moore ; Bonnie Costello, general editor ; Celeste Goodridge and Cristanne Miller, associate editors. Knopf, 1997. xv, 597 p. : **B**

ISBN 0679439099

1. Moore, Marianne, 1887-1972 Correspondence. 2. Poets, American -- 20th century -- Correspondence. 3. Women poets -- United States -- 20th century -- Correspondence. 4. Single women. 5. Letters.

LC 96052200

Includes index.

Letters to Moore's family, friends, and fellow writers depict her views on life and poetry.

Moore, Mary Tyler, 1937-2017

Moore, Mary Tyler, 1937-2017 **Growing** up again : confronting my diabetes / Mary Tyler Moore. St. Martin's Press, c2009. 240 p. **B**

ISBN 9780312376314

1. Moore, Mary Tyler, 1937-2017 Health. 2. Women with diabetes 3. Actors and actresses -- United States 4. Health. 5. Autobiographies and memoirs

LC 2008037579

The actress describes her forty-year battle with Type-1 diabetes, an effort that was influenced by alcoholism, her career, and her personal and professional relationships.

"While working on The Dick Van Dyke Show, . [the author] was diagnosed with juvenile (Type 1) diabetes and quickly discovered that managing the disease is a full-time job. Moore details the daily challenges she faces to maintain healthy blood sugar levels. Moore's humor, authoritative information, and honest evaluation of her own experiences with diabetes make this work essential for diabetes and consumer health collections." Library Journal.

Moore, Michael Scott

Moore, Michael Scott The **desert** and the sea : 977 days captive on the Somali pirate coast / Michael Scott Moore. HarperWave, 2018. 451 pages ; **B**

ISBN 9780062449177

1. Hostages 2. Pirates -- Somalia -- 21st century. 3. Terrorism -- Somalia 4. Hostage taking 5. Somalia 6. Autobiographies and memoirs

LC bl2018072609

A journalist and the author chroncles his three years of captivity by Somali pirates, offering an exploration of foreign policy, religious extremism and the costs of survival in the process.

Moore, Susanna

Moore, Susanna **Miss** aluminum : a memoir / Susanna Moore. Farrar, Straus and Giroux, 2020. 240 p. **B**

ISBN 9780374279714

1. Moore, Susanna. 2. Authors, American 3. Celebrities 4. Mothers -- Death. 5. Fashion models 6. California 7. Los Angeles, California 8. Hollywood, California 9. Autobiographies and memoirs

LC 2019046741

The author of The Life of Objects describes how she used a friend's trunk of expensive clothing to establish a career in 1963 Hollywood before embarking on a determined effort to uncover the truth about her mother's death.

"Moore was perched at the periphery of Hollywood's fast lane, which makes for a tantalizing tale, told in a seductive and provocative voice." Booklist

Moore, Wayetu

Moore, Wayetu The **dragons,** the giant, the women : a mem-

oir / Wayetu Moore. Graywolf Press, 2020. 272 p. **B**
ISBN 9781644450314
1. Civil war 2. Refugees 3. Families 4. Race (Social sciences) 5. Liberia 6. United States 7. Autobiographies and memoirs
LC bl2020013303

The author shares her experiences of escaping the First Liberian Civil War and building a life in the United States, shining the light on the great political and personal forces that continue to affect many migrants around the world.

"Readers will be both enraptured and heartbroken by Moore's intimate yet epic story of love for family and home." Publishers Weekly

Moore, Wes, 1978-

Moore, Wes, 1978- The **other** Wes Moore : the story of one name and two fates / Wes Moore ; afterword by Tavis Smiley. Spiegel & Grau, 2010. 256 p. **B**
ISBN 9780385528191
1. Moore, Wes, 1978- Childhood and youth. 2. Moore, Wes, 1975- Childhood and youth. 3. Teenagers -- Personal conduct. 4. African American teenage boys 5. Violence. 6. Father-separated boys. 7. Baltimore, Maryland -- Social conditions -- 20th century. 8. Autobiographies and memoirs
LC 2009041663

BCALA Literary Award for Nonfiction, 2011.

Traces the parallel lives of two youths with the same name in the same community, describing how the author grew up to be a Rhodes Scholar and promising business leader while his counterpart suffered a life of violence and imprisonment.

Moore, Wes, 1978- The **work** : my search for a life that matters / Wes Moore. Spiegel & Grau, 2014. 208 p. **B**
ISBN 9780812993578
1. Baltimore 2. Community activists 3. African American men 4. Purpose in life 5. Determination in men 6. Autobiographies and memoirs
LC 2013038679

The delinquent-turned-Oxford scholar picks up after the events of his best-selling The Other Wes Moore to trace his search for purpose in Afghanistan, on Wall Street and in the White House, sharing inspirational stories by others who found meaning in a life in service

"This is a beautifully philosophical look at the expectation that work should bring meaning to our lives through service to others." Booklist.

Moorer, Allison

Moorer, Allison **Blood** : a memoir / Allison Moorer. Da Capo Press, 2019. 320 p. **B**
ISBN 9780306922688
1. Moorer, Allison. 2. Women country musicians 3. Family violence 4. Children of murder victims 5. Children of murderers 6. Autobiographies and memoirs 7. Alabama
LC 2018057263

An award-winning musician shares the story of how her parents' murder-suicide forever changed both her life and that of her sister and explores the meaning of inheritance, destiny, shame, and trauma and how the tragedy shaped her art.

Morales, Angela

Morales, Angela The **girls** in my town : essays / Angela Morales. University of New Mexico Press, 2016. 176 p. **B**
ISBN 9780826356628
1. Growing up 2. Mexican American families 3. Dysfunctional families 4. Autobiographies and memoirs 5. Essays
LC 2015020149

Girls in My Town creates an unforgettable portrait of a family in Los Angeles. Reaching back to her grandmother's childhood and navigating through her own girlhood and on to the present, Angela Morales contemplates moments of loss and longing, truth and beauty, motherhood and daughterhood.

"Essays that are as thematically ambitious as they are deeply personal." Kirkus.

Moran, Caitlin, 1975-

★Moran, Caitlin, 1975- **How** to be a woman / Caitlin Moran. Harper Perennial, 2012, c2011. 305 p. **B**
ISBN 9780062124296
1. Women -- Social conditions -- 21st century. 2. Femininity 3. Femininity (Philosophy) 4. Feminine beauty (Aesthetics) 5. Autobiographies and memoirs
LC 2012372347

Originally published: London : Ebury Press, 2011."

In her brilliant, original voice, Moran successfully entertains and enlightens her audience with hard-won wisdom and wit." Publishers Weekly.

Moran, Caitlin, 1975- **More** than a woman / Caitlin Moran. Harper, 2020. 255 p. **B**
ISBN 9780062893710
1. Women -- Social conditions -- 21st century. 2. Femininity 3. Feminism 4. Aging 5. Autobiographies and memoirs 6. Essays
LC 2020018256

As timely as it is hysterically funny, this memoir/manifesto will have readers laughing out loud, blinking back tears, and redefining their views on feminism and the patriarchy. More Than a Woman is a brutally honest, scathingly funny, and absolutely necessary take on the life of the modern woman, and one that only Caitlin Moran can provide.

"Moran handles weighty topics with lightness and a welcoming spirit, delivering straight talk with empathy, humor, and hope." Booklist

Moran, Rachel

Moran, Rachel **Paid** for : my journey through prostitution / Rachel Moran. W.W. Norton & Company, Inc., 2015. 304 p. **B**
ISBN 9780393351972
1. Moran, Rachel. 2. Prostitutes -- Dublin, Ireland 3. Prostitution -- Ireland. 4. Gender role 5. Ireland 6. Autobiographies and memoirs
LC 2015009736

A former teen prostitute describes the fears she and others had working on the streets and in brothels and speaks to the psychological damage that accompanies prostitution and the estrangement from one's body.

"Moran's thoughtful, highly readable, and provocative treatise shines a necessary light on a dark and underdiscussed topic." Kirkus.

Morgan, Daniel, 1736-1802

Zambone, Albert Louis, 1969- **Daniel** Morgan : a revolutionary life / Albert Louis Zambone. Westholme Publishing, 2018. 376 p. **B**
ISBN 9781594163159
1. Generals -- United States -- History -- 18th century 2. Command of troops 3. American Revolution, 1775-1783 4. Military history 5. United States -- History -- Revolution, 1775-1783. 6. Biographies
LC 2020275151

Based on a podcast.

A Major New Biography of a Man of Humble Origins Who Became One of the Great Military Leaders of the American Revolution.

In Daniel Morgan: A Revolutionary Life, the first biogra?phy of this iconic figure in forty years, historian Albert Louis Zambone presents Morgan as the quintessential American everyman, who rose through his own dogged determination from poverty and obscurity to become one of the great battlefield commanders in American history.

"Zambone is careful to avoid speculating on gaps in the record and diligently reviews primary documents, such as store ledgers listing quotidian purchases. The resulta look at a consequential but now-obscure figure who came from, as Zambone puts it, the often-silent ranks of the colonial poorwill fascinate readers." Publishers Weekly.

Morgan, Leslie, 1965-

Morgan, Leslie, 1965- The **naked** truth : a memoir / Leslie Morgan. Simon & Schuster, [2019] 272 p. **B**

ISBN 9781501174100

1. Divorced women 2. Middle-aged women -- Sexuality 3. Men/women relations 4. Sexuality 5. Autobiographies and memoirs

LC 2019000817

When Leslie Morgan divorced after a twenty-year marriage, both her self-esteem and romantic optimism were shattered. She was determined to avoid the cliché of the "lonely, middle-aged divorcee" lamenting her stretch marks and begging her kids to craft her online dating profile. Instead, Leslie celebrated her independence with an audacious plan: she would devote a year to seeking out five lovers in hopes of unearthing the erotic adventures and authentic connections long missing from her life.

"A formidable, addictive storyteller, Morgan provides a highly stimulating story of a midlife education in the messiness of modern sex and love." Kirkus.

Morgan, William, 1928-1961

Sallah, Michael The **Yankee** comandante : the untold story of courage, passion, and one American's fight to liberate Cuba / Michael Sallah, Mitch Weiss. Lyons Press, an imprint of Rowman & Littlefield, [2015] 304 p. **B**

ISBN 9780762792870

1. Morgan, William, 1928-1961. 2. Revolutionaries 3. Communism -- Cuba. 4. Double agents 5. Political prisoners 6. Cuba -- History -- Revolution, 1956-1959 7. Biographies

LC 2014033720

"Olga lives today in the U.S., and Sallah and Weiss interviewed her extensively. They also make clear Morgan's flaws: he had at least three wives and several children by them; was court martialed by the U.S. Army, serving time in prison; and was employed by and associated with known mobsters. Though the tale does not end happily, it's a romantic and entertaining read." Publishers Weekly.

Morris, David J., 1971-

Morris, David J., 1971- The **evil** hours : a biography of post-traumatic stress disorder / David J. Morris. Houghton Mifflin Harcourt, 2015. 336 p. **B**

ISBN 9780544086616

1. Morris, David J., 1971- Mental health 2. Post-traumatic stress disorder 3. War -- Psychological aspects 4. Soldiers -- Psychology 5. Combat -- Psychological aspects 6. Autobiographies and memoirs

LC 2014034487

"An Eamon Dolan Book."

An examination of the role of PTSD in American life by an ex-Marine, war correspondent and PTSD patient shares discussions of its widespread impact on families and the taboos that challenge its treatments.

"Though its incidence among combat veterans has brought post-traumatic stress disorder to the fore, the National Institute of Mental Health estimates that one in every 30 American adults suffers from the condition. Seasoned war correspondent Morris, also a former marine infantry officer with PTSD, here draws on personal experience, interviews, and scientific studies to present the big picture." Library Journal.

Morris, Jan, 1926-2020

Morris, Jan, 1926-2020 A **writer's** house in Wales / Jan Morris. National Geographic, 2002. 143 p. : **B**

ISBN 0792265238

1. Morris, Jan, 1926-2020 Homes and haunts Wales. 2. Home (Concept) 3. Villages -- Wales. 4. Wales -- Social life and customs. 5. Autobiographies and memoirs

LC 2001044731

The author describes Trefan Morys, her country house in Wales, and looks at Welsh culture, history, and symbols.

"The author reflects on her home in Wales, its beautiful setting and the nature of being Welsh. This slim and charming volume offers a crisp account of the turbulent history of the Welsh and their battle to maintain their language and culture in the shadow of their more powerful neighbor." Publishers Weekly.

Morris, Mark, 1956-

Morris, Mark, 1956- **Out** loud : a memoir / Mark Morris and Wesley Stace. Penguin Books, 2019. 384 p. **B**

ISBN 9780735223073

1. Dancers 2. Choreographers 3. Dance companies 4. Gay men 5. New York City 6. Autobiographies and memoirs

LC 2019947748

The acclaimed choreographer traces his rise from humble origins to the pinnacle of the performing-arts world, discussing his formation of the Mark Morris Dance Group and his celebrated collaborations with such artists as Mikhail Baryshnikov and Yo-Yo Ma.

Morrison, Jim, 1943-1971

Riordan, James **Break** on through : the life and death of Jim Morrison / James Riordan and Jerry Prochnicky. Morrow, c1991. 544 p., 32 p. of plates : **B**

ISBN 0688088295

1. Morrison, Jim, 1943-1971. 2. Doors (Musical group) 3. Rock musicians -- United States 4. Biographies

LC 90026580

An in-depth portrait of Jim Morrison examines the complex early family life of the controversial musician, the intellectual roots of his music, his wild life with The Doors, his romances, and his mysterious death

"This look at the life and work of Jim Morrison is well documented and avoids unfounded speculation and unnecessary tales of debauchery common to many other rock 'n' roll biographies. An excellent biography of a true rock icon." Choice.

Moses (Biblical leader)

Zornberg, Avivah Gottlieb **Moses** : a human life / Avivah Gottlieb Zornberg. Yale University Press, 2016. 224 p. **B**

ISBN 9780300209624

1. Bible. Old Testament 2. Religious leaders 3. Spiritual leaders 4. Judaism -- History. 5. Prophets 6. Biographies

LC bl2016048642

An unprecedented portrait of Moses's inner world and perplexing character, by a distinguished biblical scholar.

"A meaty, worthwhile biography by a great interpreter of Jewish texts." Kirkus.

Moses, Robert, 1888-1981

Caro, Robert A. The **power** broker : Robert Moses and the fall of New

York / Robert A. Caro. Knopf, 1974. ix, 1246 p. : B
ISBN 0394480767
1. Moses, Robert, 1888-1981. 2. Public works. 3. Political corruption. 4. Roads -- Design and construction. 5. Civil service workers 6. New York City -- History -- 20th century. 7. Biographies
LC 73020751
Pulitzer Prize for Biography or Autobiography, 1975."
This is a biographical critique of the man who in four decades as a public official built most of the parks, bridges and highways in and around New York City." Newsweek

Motley, Eric L. (Eric Lamar), 1972-

Motley, Eric L. (Eric Lamar), 1972- **Madison** Park : a place of hope / Eric L. Lamar Motley. Harpercollins Christian Pub, 2017. 320 p. B
ISBN 9780310349631
1. African Americans. 2. American dream. 3. Faith (Christianity) 4. Presidents -- Staff. 5. Alabama. 6. Madison Park, Alabama. 7. Autobiographies and memoirs.
LC 2018304566
A special assistant to George W. Bush and executive vice president of The Aspen Institute think tank chronicles his vibrant coming of age in a small Alabama community founded by freed slaves, where he learned valuable lessons about helping others, embracing faith and fighting racial injustice.

Mowat, Farley

Mowat, Farley **Born** naked / Farley Mowat. Houghton Mifflin, 1994, c1993. 256 p. : B
ISBN 9780395689271
1. Mowat, Farley Childhood and youth 2. Childhood. 3. Authors, Canadian -- 20th century 4. Families 5. Canada. 6. Autobiographies and memoirs
Originally published: Toronto : Key Porter Books, 1993.
The author highlights a period of his idyllic youth, revealing the mischievous, inquisitive boy whose fascination with wildlife brought him great joy and his family plenty of tolerant embarrassment.
"There are no dull pages here; every man, woman, child, and animal mentioned even casually makes an impression. Highly recommended to all those who like good writing." Library Journal.

Mowat, Farley **High** latitudes : a northern journey / Farley Mowat. Key Porter, c2002. xii, 300 p. ; B
ISBN 9781616086022
1. Mowat, Farley Travel Canada, Northern. 2. Natural history -- Canada, Northern. 3. Winter sports 4. Inuit -- Canada, Northern -- Social life and customs 5. Canada, Northern -- Description and travel. 6. Canada, Northern -- Environmental conditions. 7. Autobiographies and memoirs
LC 2002489957
Includes index.
A chronicle of Farley Mowat's 1966 journey across northern Canada.
"In 1966, Mowat's publisher, Jack McClelland, sent Mowat into northern Canada to research an illustrated volume on the region. This book is the tale of that journey. Hopscotching by creaky plane from one isolated settlement to another, Mowat witnesses the devastation being wrought on the native peoples by encroaching white men, lured by a mirage of the north's supposedly limitless minerals and the raw beauty of the land and its people. A cavalcade of vivid, fiction-worthy characters fills these pages. Voiced with a passionate sense of justice, this work is stirring reading from the bard of the Canadian north." Publishers Weekly.

Mozart, Wolfgang Amadeus, 1756-1791

Einstein, Alfred, 1880-1952 **Mozart** : his character, his work / Alfred Einstein ; translated by Arthur Mendel and Nathan Broder. Oxford University Press, 1962. viii, 492 p. : B
ISBN 9780195007329
1. Mozart, Wolfgang Amadeus, 1756-1791. 2. Composers, Austrian
LC BL 99727331
Translation of: Mozart, sein Charakter, sein Werk.
Originally published: 1945."
The author's examination of the events of Mozart's life in relation to his character, and even more, his analysis of the sources, models, and methods of the musician's creative processes are penetrating and illuminating." Christian Science Monitor.

Gutman, Robert W. **Mozart** : a cultural biography / Robert W. Gutman. Harcourt Brace, 1999. xxii, 839 p. : B
ISBN 015100482X
1. Mozart, Wolfgang Amadeus, 1756-1791. 2. Composers -- Austria 3. Biographies
LC 99031953
An exhaustively researched account of a great composer's life offers new perspectives and interpretations, placing him within the context of his times, discussing the musical genres he worked in, and giving a clear picture of the man behind the legends.

Haupt, Lyanda Lynn **Mozart's** starling / Lyanda Lynn Haupt. Little Brown & Co., 2017. 256 p. B
ISBN 9780316370899
1. Haupt, Lyanda Lynn 2. Starlings 3. Birds as pets 4. Naturalists 5. Composers 6. Autobiographies and memoirs
LC bl2017011192
A naturalist describes how Wolfgang Amadeus Mozart was enchanted by the intelligence and playful spirit of a starling in a Viennese shop and took it home for a family pet and discusses a natural history of the frequently reviled bird.
"This hard-to-put-down, charming blend of science, biography, and memoir illuminating the little-known story of the composer and his beloved bird is enlivened by the immediacy of Haupts tales of Carmen, and brimming with starling information, travelogues, and historical details about Mozarts Vienna." Booklist.

Suchet, John, 1944- **Mozart** : the man revealed / John Suchet. Pegasus Books, 2017. 288 p. : B
ISBN 9781681775098
1. Mozart, Wolfgang Amadeus, 1756-1791. 2. Composers -- Austria 3. Genius 4. Classical music. 5. Musicians 6. Biographies
LC bl2017030785
The illustrated life-story of the world's most beloved composer, bringing vividly to life the man himself, his influences, achievements, and the glittering milieu of the Habsburg empire in eighteenth-century Europe.
"Rich with wit and warmth, this compact biography is thoroughly enchanting." Kirkus.

Mufleh, Luma

St. John, Warren **Outcasts** united : a refugee team, an American town / Warren St. John. Spiegel & Grau, c2009. 320 p. B
ISBN 9780385522038
1. Mufleh, Luma. 2. Soccer coaches 3. Child refugees 4. Social change. 5. Refugees, African. 6. Georgia -- Social life and customs 7. Clarkston, Georgia -- Social life and customs
LC 2008040697

Documents the lives of a wildly diverse group of young kids who unite as a team under the leadership of their American-educated Jordanian coach, against the backdrop of a fading American town struggling to make a haven for its new arrivals--refugees.

Muhammad, Ibtihaj, 1985-

Muhammad, Ibtihaj, 1985- **Proud** : my fight for an unlikely American dream / Ibtihaj Muhammad, with Lori L. Tharps. Hachette Books, 2018. xiii, 270 p. : **B**

ISBN 9780316518963

1. Fencers 2. Women fencers 3. African American women 4. Muslim women 5. Autobiographies and memoirs

LC bl2018135206

Shares the life story of the Olympic fencer, including how she overcame feeling out of place in her sport and how she became the first American woman to compete in the Olympics wearing a hijab. As the only woman of color and the only religious minority on Team USA's saber fencing squad, Ibtihaj had to chart her own path to success and Olympic glory.

Muhammad, Prophet, d. 632

Armstrong, Karen, 1944- **Muhammad:** a prophet for our time / Karen Armstrong. Atlas Books, 2006. 249 p. : Eminent lives **B**

ISBN 0060598972

1. Muhammad, Prophet, d. 632. 2. Islam -- 21st century. 3. Religious leaders 4. Muslims. 5. Biographies

LC 2006045864

A meticulously researched account of the works and lasting influence of the prophet Muhammad discusses his life at the end of the sixth and beginning of the seventh centuries, offering insight into his establishment of a faith that was to have a profound impact on world history.

"Readers of these pages cannot escape the genius of Muhammad and his aim for peace and compassion among nations and among Muslims themselves. . . . Recommended for all libraries." Library Journal.

Hazleton, Lesley, 1945- The **first** Muslim : the story of Muhammad / Lesley Hazleton. Riverhead Books, 2013. 320 p. **B**

ISBN 9781594487286

1. Prophets 2. Religious leaders 3. Islam -- History 4. Islam -- Origin 5. Biographies

LC 2012038501

Biographer Lesley Hazleton offers an engaging, well-researched historical portrait of the Prophet Muhammad. The First Muslim offers a welcome introduction to the character and personality of this famous spiritual leader, while vividly portraying his life's major events -- including his abandonment as an infant, his marriage to a much older widow, the mystical revelation he experienced (later transcribed as the Quran), and the political challenges he faced during the early development of Islam.

Muir, John, 1838-1914

★Heacox, Kim **John** Muir and the ice that started a fire : how a visionary and the glaciers of Alaska changed America / Kim Heacox. Lyons Press, 2014. 264 p. **B**

ISBN 9780762792429

1. Muir, John, 1838-1914. 2. Nature conservation. 3. Glaciers -- Alaska. 4. Geology. 5. Climate change -- Alaska. 6. Alaska 7. Biographies

LC 2013050235

John Muir and the Ice That Started a Fire takes two of the most compelling elements in the narrative of wild America, John Muir and Alaska, and combines them into a brisk and engaging biography.John Muir was a fascinating man who was many things: inventor, scientist, revolutionary, druid (a modern day Celtic priest), husband, son, father and friend, and a shining son of the Scottish Enlightenment -- both in temperament and intellect. Kim Heacox, author of The Only Kayak, bring us a story that evolves as Muir's life did, from one of outdoor adventure into one of ecological guardianship. Muir went from impassioned author to leading activist. He would popularize glaciers unlike anybody else, and be to glaciers what Jacques Cousteau would be to the oceans and Carl Sagan to the stars The book also offers an environmental caveat on global climate change and the glaciers' retreat alongside a beacon of hope: Muir shows us how one person changed America, helped it embrace its wilderness, and in turn, gave us a better world. Heacox takes us into how Muir changed our world, advanced the science of glaciology and popularized geology.

"The book is an engaging and informative look at Muir and his life's work, as well as a timely call to action that poses difficult questions to the reader and the philosophies that underpin modern life." Publishers Weekly.

Muir, John, 1838-1914 **Nature** writings : the story of my boyhood and youth, my first summer in the Sierra, the mountains of California, Stickeen, selected essays / John Muir. Library of America : 1997. 888 p. : **B**

ISBN 1883011248

1. Muir, John, 1838-1914. 2. Natural history -- United States. 3. Naturalists -- United States 4. Environmentalists -- United States 5. Autobiographies and memoirs 6. Essays.

LC 96009664

Includes index."

This compilation of Muir's writings combines The Story of My Boyhood and Youth, My First Summer in the Sierra, The Mountains of California, Stickeen, and a number of his essays along with illustrations, a chronology of his life, and scholarly notes." Library Journal.,Muir is at his best . when he is looking intently at something, walking around it, sniffing the air, looking again. As a writer he is a kind of visionary sensualist, a seer who reveals what lies in plain sight. Commentary

Muir, John, 1838-1914 The **story** of my boyhood and youth / John Muir. Sierra Club Books, 1988, c1965. xii, 162 p. ; **B**

ISBN 0871567490

1. Muir, John, 1838-1914 Childhood and youth. 2. Sierra Club 3. Naturalists -- United States 4. Wildlife conservationists. 5. Environmentalists. 6. Wildlife conservation. 7. Biographies

LC 88023988

Includes index.

Originally published: Madison, University of Wisconsin Press, 1965

The American naturalist relates incidents from his boyhood in Scotland and the central Wisconsin wilderness

Worster, Donald, 1941- A **passion** for nature ; the life of John Muir / Donald Worster. Oxford University Press, 2008. 528 p. **B**

ISBN 9780195166828

1. Muir, John, 1838-1914. 2. Naturalists -- United States 3. Environmentalists -- United States 4. Nature. 5. Environmentalism. 6. Biographies

LC 2008001441

"The author draws on John Muir's (1838-1914) correspondence and writings to offer an enlightening biography of the influential naturalist. Competently documented, this all-inclusive biography explains the life and times of a figure known to all who love nature and will appeal to general readers and anyone interested in the early roots of today's green movement and its founding fathers." Library Journal.

Mulgrew, Kate, 1955-

Mulgrew, Kate, 1955- **Born** with teeth : a memoir / Kate Mulgrew. Little Brown & Co 2015 320 p. **B**

ISBN 9780316334310

1. Growing up 2. Actors and actresses 3. Adoption 4. unplanned pregnancy 5. Autobiographies and memoirs

LC 2015930445

A star known for her strong female roles in Star Trek: Voyager and Orange Is the New Black offers a deeply moving account of the price and rewards of a passionate life.

"Mulgrew's enjoyable narrative is compelling as she portrays her decades of acting work, personal triumphs and heartbreaks, and her mesmerizing life." Library Journal.

Mulgrew, Kate, 1955- **How** to forget : a daughter's memoir / Kate Mulgrew. William Morrow & Co., 2019 288 p. **B**

ISBN 9780062846815

1. Mulgrew, Kate, 1955- Family 2. Parents -- Death 3. Actors and actresses 4. Parent and adult child 5. Loss (Psychology) 6. Iowa 7. Autobiographies and memoirs

LC 2019014753

The award-winning actress known for her roles in such productions as <I>Orange Is the New Black</I> describes how, after attending her parents' deaths, she uncovered painful secrets that challenged her understanding of her unconventional Irish-Catholic family.

"In her first memoir, Born with Teeth, stage and screen actress Mulgrew (Star Trek: Voyager; Orange Is the New Black) discussed her longing for the daughter she gave up for adoption. With this follow-up, she examines a different form of longingthat of her parents' approval." Library Journal.

Mullally, Megan

Offerman, Nick, 1970- The **greatest** love story ever told : an oral history / Nick Offerman and Megan Mullally. Penguin Group USA 2018 320 p. **B**

ISBN 9781101986677

1. Offerman, Nick, 1970- 2. Couples 3. Actors and actresses 4. Men/women relations 5. Dating (Social customs) 6. Los Angeles, California 7. Autobiographies and memoirs

LC 2018410359

The popular comedic couple trace the story of their relationship, sharing anecdotes, family photos and secrets that reveal how they overcame considerable social differences through their shared values and mutual love of music and laughter.

Mumler, William H.

Manseau, Peter The **apparitionists** : a tale of phantoms, fraud, photography, and the man who captured Lincoln's ghost / Peter Manseau. Houghton Mifflin Harcourt, 2017. 352 p. **B**

ISBN 9780544745971

1. Photographers 2. Psychics 3. Paranormal phenomena 4. Spiritualism 5. Biographies

LC 2017018074

The story of "spirit photographer" William Mumler documents how his images of the ghosts of loved ones were highly sought and infamously denounced, tracing the story of his successful defense against charges of fraud, the yet-unsolved mystery behind his photography and what his successes reveal about period culture.

Munch, Edvard, 1863-1944

Prideaux, Sue **Edvard** Munch : behind the Scream / Sue Prideaux. Yale University Press, 2005. xiii, 391 p., [112] p. of plates : **B**

ISBN 0300110243

1. Munch, Edvard, 1863-1944. 2. Artists -- Norway 3. Painters -- Norway 4. Art, Norwegian. 5. Painting. 6. Biographies

LC 2005012040

James Tait Black Memorial Prize for Biography, 2005."

Prideaux's treatment is very effective and her writing, cohesive, clear, and often compelling." Library Journal.

Ustvedt, Oystein **Edvard** Munch : an inner life / Oystein Ustvedt ; translated from the Norwegian by Alison McCullough. Thames & Hudson, 2020 223 p. : **B**

ISBN 9780500295762

1. Modernism (Art) 2. Artists -- Norway. 3. Painters -- Norway 4. Art, Norwegian. 5. Biographies

LC 2019949015

A renowned expert on Edvard Munch delivers this wonderfully illustrated volume on the life and work of the great artist.

"A beautifully produced introduction to a celebrated artist." Kirkus

Munster, Pamela N.

Munster, Pamela N. **Twisting** fate : my journey with BRCA--from breast cancer doctor to patient and back / Pamela N. Munster, MD ; foreword by Siddhartha Mukherjee. The Experiment, [2018] 272 p. **B**

ISBN 9781615194780

1. Munster, Pamela N. Health. 2. BRCA genes. 3. People with breast cancer 4. Oncologists 5. Women physicians 6. Autobiographies and memoirs

LC 2018020072

A forefront oncologist shares the story of her own battle with breast cancer and how it transformed her perspectives as a doctor, describing her research team's groundbreaking work on the BRCA gene and how to live with its mutations.

"Told from the unique perspective of a compassionate physician being treated for the very disease she has spent her life treating, this medical narrative is utterly engrossing." Publishers Weekly.

Murad, Nadia

Murad, Nadia. The **last** girl : my story of captivity, and my fight against the Islamic State / Nadia Murad ; foreword by Amal Clooney. Tim Duggan Books/Crown Publishing, 2017. 320 p. **B**

ISBN 9781524760434

1. ISIS (Islamic State of Iraq and Syria) 2. Women refugees 3. Human trafficking 4. Survival 5. Social advocacy 6. Iraq 7. Autobiographies and memoirs

LC 2017028775

A human rights activist and Nobel Peace Prize nominee traces the harrowing and ultimately inspiring story of her captivity by the Islamic State, describing how militants massacred the people of her Iraqi farming village, killing most of her family members and forcing her into prostitution before she escaped and became an advocate for human rights.

" Murad provides a rare glimpse into the rich culture of the Yazidi. Her memoir is powerful and heart-breaking and will inspire the world to action." Library Journal.

Murakami, Haruki, 1949-

Murakami, Haruki, 1949- **What** I talk about when I talk about running : a memoir / Haruki Murakami ; translated from the Japanese by Philip Gabriel. Alfred A. Knopf, 2008. 192 p. **B**

ISBN 9780307269195

1. New York City Marathon 2. Authors, Japanese -- 21st century

3. Marathon runners 4. Marathon running. 5. Distance running -- Training 6. Japan -- Social life and customs -- 21st century 7. Autobiographies and memoirs

LC 2008017774

"Originally published in Japan ... by Bungeishunju, Ltd., Tokyo, in 2007"--T.p. verso.

Title is a translation of Hashiru koto ni tsuite kataru toki ni boku no kataru koto.

The Japanese writer recalls his four-month preparation for the 2005 New York City marathon, interweaving his reflections on the meaning of running in his life, his thoughts on the writing process and his career, and his experiences as an author and as anathlete.

Murdoch, Iris

Bayley, John, 1925-2015 **Elegy** for Iris / John Bayley. St. Martin's Press, 1999. 275 p. : **B**

ISBN 0312198647

1. Murdoch, Iris Marriage. 2. Bayley, John, 1925-2015 Marriage. 3. University of Oxford. 4. People with Alzheimer's disease 5. Husband and wife. 6. Critics -- Great Britain 7. Authors, English -- 20th century 8. Autobiographies and memoirs

LC 98040895

This book was made into a movie entitled Iris.

The author describes life with his wife, Iris Murdoch, and her struggle with Alzheimer's disease.

"This splendid book enlarges our imagination of the range and possibilities of love." New York Times Book Review.

Conradi, Peter J., 1945- **Iris** : the life of Iris Murdoch / Peter J. Conradi. Norton, 2002, c2001. xxix, 706 p. : **B**

ISBN 039332401X

1. Murdoch, Iris. 2. Authors, English -- 20th century 3. Philosophers -- Great Britain 4. Great Britain -- Social life and customs -- 20th century 5. Biographies

LC BL2002013388

Originally published under title: Iris Murdoch.

London : HarperCollins Publishers, 2001.

Traces the life and career of the philosopher and novelist, from her student days at Oxford, through her marriage to John Bayley, to Murdoch's influence on literary England, from 1940 to the present day.

"Rich footnoting leads the reader to expansions on the narrative as well as to the authority behind the biographer's statements. Scholars need this text, but it will also intrigue lay readers." Library Journal.

Murphy, John Cullen

Murphy, Cullen **Cartoon** county : my father and his friends in the golden age of make-believe / Cullen Murphy. Farrar, Straus and Giroux, 2017. 256 p. **B**

ISBN 9780374298555

1. Murphy, John Cullen. 2. Cartoonists. 3. Cartoons 4. Biographies

LC 2017001316

A history of the cartoonists and illustrators from the Connecticut School, written by the son of the artist behind the popular strips "Prince Valiant" and "Big Ben Bolt," explores the achievements and pop-culture influence of these artists in the aftermath of World War II.

"Part memoir, part cultural history, part treasure trove of drawings and photographs, many previously unpublishedand all thoroughly delightful as a celebration of the golden age of newspaper comics." Kirkus.

Murray, Daniel Alexander Payne, 1852-1925

Taylor, Elizabeth Dowling The **original** Black elite : Daniel Murray and the story of a forgotten era / Elizabeth Dowling Taylor. Amistad Press, 2017. 240 p. **B**

ISBN 9780062346094

1. Library of Congress. 2. Elite (Social sciences) 3. African-American social advocates. 4. African Americans -- Political activity. 5. Washington, D.C. 6. Biographies

LC bl2017003834

In this outstanding cultural biography, the author of the New York Times bestseller A Slave in the White House chronicles a critical yet overlooked chapter in American history: the inspiring rise and calculated fall of the black elite, from Emancipation through Reconstruction to the Jim Crow Era?embodied in the experiences of an influential figure of the time, academic, entrepreneur, and political activist and black history pioneer Daniel Murray.

"The level of detail and research sheds light on a period that is mostly forgotten, revealing much-needed insight into African Americans' role and response in the shaping of American culture and politics." Library Journal.

Murray, James A. H., 1837-1915

Winchester, Simon The **professor** and the madman : a tale of murder, insanity, and the making of the Oxford English dictionary / Simon Winchester. HarperCollins, 1998. xi, 242 p. : **B**

ISBN 0060175966

1. Murray, James A. H., 1837-1915. 2. Minor, William Chester, 1834-1920. 3. Oxford English dictionary. 4. Oxford English dictionary History. 5. Lexicography -- History. 6. Lexicographers -- England 7. Psychiatric hospital patients -- England 8. Dictionaries -- History and criticism. 9. Biographies

LC 98010204

National Book Critics Circle Award for Nonfiction finalist, 1998.

Describes how more than ten thousand definitions were submitted for the first Oxford English Dictionary from Dr. W.C. Minor, an American Civil War criminal who was considered both a genius and a lunatic.

"The author relates the story of the Oxford English Dictionary's first editor and the expatriate American murderer who contributed more than 10,000 quotations as examples. Best of all, among the entertaining tangents one learns a great deal about the making of that grandest of all reference works." Library Journal.

Murray, Liz, 1980-

Murray, Liz, 1980- **Breaking** night : my journey from homeless to Harvard / Liz Murray. Hyperion, 2010. 352 p. **B**

ISBN 9780786868919

1. Harvard University. 2. Children of drug abusers. 3. Life change events. 4. Determination in women. 5. Homeless persons 6. New York City. 7. Autobiographies and memoirs

LC 2010013679

The author offers an emotional account of her-amazing journey from a 15-year-old living on the streets and eating garbage to her acceptance into Harvard, a feat that prompted a Lifetime movie and a successful motivational-speaking career.

Murray, Pauli, 1910-1985

★Rosenberg, Rosalind, 1946- **Jane** Crow : the life of Pauli Murray / Rosalind Rosenberg. Oxford University Press, 2017. 512 p. **B**

ISBN 9780190656454

1. Murray, Pauli, 1910-1985. 2. Social reformers -- United States 3. Civil Rights Movement. 4. Women's movement. 5. Social justice. 6. United States -- History -- 20th century. 7. Biographies.

LC 2017000717

This comprehensive and accessible biography of 20th-century lawyer and African American activist Pauli Murray is a detailed chronicle of her life and achievements, along with a history of the civil rights and feminist movements and early views of intersectionality.

"Rosenberg shows how Murray pursued an intersectional activism, repeatedly identifying the ways in which race, class, and gender worked together to constrain opportunity. The biography also deftly explores Murray's relationships and private struggles with identity. From childhood, Murray understood herself to be male, repeatedly seeking (unsuccessfully) medical treatment for gender dysphoria; she was also attracted to, and formed lasting relationships with, women during an era when both same-sex attraction and transgender identity were suspect categories. Placing Murray in historical context with practiced ease, Rosenberg weaves these many threads together into an authoritative narrative that will introduce Murray to many future generations." Publishers Weekly.

Murrow, Edward R., 1908-1965

Edwards, Bob, 1947- **Edward** R. Murrow and the birth of broadcast journalism / Bob Edwards. Wiley, c2004. xiii, 174 p. ; **B**

ISBN 0471477532

1. Journalists -- United States 2. Journalism -- United States -- 20th century 3. War correspondents -- United States -- History -- World War II. 4. Broadcasting -- United States -- History. 5. United States -- Social life and customs -- 20th century 6. Biographies

LC 2003021223

An account of one of the most important names in twentieth-century journalism examines Murrow's role in pioneering broadcast media, the famous stories that he covered, and his influential career, as well as evaluating the decline of broadcast news since the 1980s.

"Edwards brings to life the early days of radio and television and the innovations that Murrow sparked. . . . Readers interested in journalism will enjoy this slim book." Booklist.

Mussolini, Benito, 1883-1945

Bosworth, R. J. B. **Mussolini** / R.J.B. Bosworth. Arnold, 2002. xv, 584 p., 16 p. of plates : **B**

ISBN 0340731443

1. Heads of state -- Italy 2. Dictators -- Italy 3. Fascism -- Italy -- History. 4. Fascists. 5. Italy -- Politics and government -- 1922-1945. 6. Biographies

"This is the definitive study of the Italian dictator and belongs in every public and academic library with a strong European history collection." Library Journal.

Mutter, Thomas D. (Thomas Dent), 1811-1859

★Aptowicz, Cristin O'Keefe **Dr.** Mutter's marvels : a true tale of intrigue and innovation at the dawn of modern medicine / Cristin O'Keefe Aptowicz. Gotham Books, 2014 371 p. : **B**

ISBN 9781592408702

1. Mutter, Thomas D. (Thomas Dent), 1811-1859. 2. Mutter Museum. 3. Humanists. 4. Surgeons 5. Physicians 6. Surgery. 7. Biographies.

LC 2014014747

A portrait of the brilliant and eccentric medical innovator who revolutionized American surgery and founded America's most famous medical oddities museum describes his advocacy for clean and compassionate patient care in spite of his numerous detractors.

"In her deftly crafted narrative, the author provides an absorbing account of the charismatic surgeon's life and career as well as a vivid look at the medical practices and prejudices of his time." Kirkus.

Myers, Kyl

Myers, Kyl **Raising** them : our adventure in gender creative parenting / Kyl Myers. Topple Books/Little A, 2020 229 p. ; **B**

ISBN 9781542003674

1. Myers, Kyl Family 2. Gender identity 3. Child rearing 4. Options, alternatives, choices 5. Parents 6. Autobiographies and memoirs

LC bl2020046614

A sociologist, exploring the science of gender and sex and the adulthood gender inequities that start in childhood, shares the joy of watching her own child develop their own agency to grow happily and healthy toward their own gender and expression.

"An enlightening, much-needed resource for parents hoping to raise their children without limitations." Kirkus

Myles, Eileen

Myles, Eileen **Afterglow** : a dog memoir / Eileen Myles. Grove Press, 2017 224 p. **B**

ISBN 9780802127099

1. Human/animal relationships 2. Pit bull terriers 3. Pet owners 4. Humans and pets 5. Autobiographies and memoirs

LC 2017008720

In 1990, Myles chose Rosie from a litter on the street, and their connection instantly became central to the writer's life and work. During the course of their sixteen years together, Myles was madly devoted to the dog's wellbeing, especially in her final days. Starting from the emptiness following Rosie's death, Afterglow (a dog memoir) launches a heartfelt and fabulist investigation into the true nature of the bond between pet and pet-owner.

"Poetic, heartrending, soothing, and funny, this is a mind-expanding contemplation of creation, the act and the noun, and the creatures whose deaths we presume will precede ours but whose lives make our own better beyond reason." Booklist.

Nabokov, Vladimir Vladimirovich, 1899-1977

Boyd, Brian, 1952- **Vladimir** Nabokov : the American years / Brian Boyd. Princeton University Press, [1993?], c1991. xiv, 783 p. : **B**

ISBN 0691024715

1. Nabokov, Vladimir Vladimirovich, 1899-1977 Criticism and interpretation. 2. Authors, American -- 20th century 3. Authors, Russian -- 20th century 4. Authors 5. Fame. 6. United States -- Social life and customs -- 20th century 7. Biographies.

LC BL 00005842

Reprint. Originally published: 1991.

Boyd, Brian, 1952- **Vladimir** Nabokov : the Russian years / Brian Boyd. Princeton University Press, c1990. xii, 607 p., 24 p. of plates : **B**

ISBN 9780691067940

1. Nabokov, Vladimir Vladimirovich, 1899-1977. 2. Authors, American -- 20th century 3. Authors, Russian -- 20th century 4. Biographies

LC 90008040

Retraces Nabokov's early years and offers an introduction to his work and the world he lived in.

Nabokov, Vladimir Vladimirovich, 1899-1977 **Speak,** memory : an autobiography revisited / Vladimir Nabokov ; with an introduction by Brian Boyd. Alfred A. Knopf, 1999. xxxv, 268 p. : **B**

ISBN 9780375405532

1. Refugees, Russian 2. Russian Americans 3. Authors, Russian --

20th century 4. Jews, Russian 5. Autobiographies and memoirs
LC 98049237

The author recounts his Russian childhood, his family's flight to England in 1919, and emigre life in Paris and Berlin.

★Pitzer, Andrea The **secret** history of Vladimir Nabokov / Andrea Pitzer. Pegasus Books : 2013 xv, 432 p., 16 p. of plates : B

ISBN 1605984116

1. Nabokov, Vladimir Vladimirovich, 1899-1977 Criticism and interpretation. 2. Authors, American -- 20th century 3. Authors, Russian -- 20th century 4. Art and politics 5. Biographies
LC 2014427844

Argues that the famous Russian-American novelist, accused of turning a blind eye to the horrors of history, hid this disturbing information within his fiction.

"Drawing on new biographical material and her sharp critical senses, Pitzer reveals the tightly woven subtext of the novels, always keen to shine a light where the deception is not obvious. Though no substitute for Brian Boyd's definitive two-volume biography, this is a brilliant examination that adds to the understanding of an inspiring and enigmatic life." Kirkus.

Nadar, Felix, 1820-1910

Begley, Adam The **great** Nadar : the man behind the camera / Adam Begley. Tim Duggan Books, 2017. 256 p. B

ISBN 9781101902608

1. Photographers 2. Celebrities 3. Balloons (Aeronautics) 4. Ballooning 5. Paris, France 6. Biographies
LC 2016045382

Includes index.

A portrait of the fabled Parisian photographer, adventurer and pioneer discusses his bohemian youth, larger-than-life studio, pioneering exploits as a balloonist and photography sessions with such famed subjects as Victor Hugo, Gustave Courbet and Alexandre Dumas.

"Told in a pleasant, conversational style, this title is not only filled with curious, whimsical details about a lively figure, it is also is a very readable narrative." Library Journal.

Nafisi, Azar

★Nafisi, Azar **Reading** Lolita in Tehran : a memoir in books / Azar Nafisi. Random House, 2003. 347 p. B

ISBN 0375504907

1. Nafisi, Azar. 2. Khomeini, Ruhollah, 1902-1989. 3. State-sponsored terrorism -- Iran. 4. Self-discovery in women. 5. Books and reading -- Iran. 6. English language teachers -- Iran. 7. Iran -- History -- Islamic revolution, 1979-1997. 8. Iran -- Social life and customs. 9. Tehran, Iran 10. Iran.
LC 2002036724

From 1995-97 in Iran, Azar Nafisi gathered with seven of her former students, all young women, to read and discuss forbidden works of Western literature. Reserved at first, the women soon learned to speak their minds and share their repressed dreams.

"A spirited tribute both to the classics of world literature and to resistance against oppression." Kirkus.

★Nafisi, Azar **Things** I've been silent about : a memoir in moments / Azar Nafisi. Random House, 2008. 368 p. B

ISBN 9781400063611

1. Nafisi, Azar. 2. Nafisi, Azar Family. 3. Family relationships. 4. Muslim women. 5. Immigrants. 6. Women -- Iran 7. Iran. 8. Autobiographies and memoirs
LC bl2008026872

A memoir offers a portrait of the author's family and childhood in Iran, centered around her powerful mother and her manipulative fictions about herself, as she reflects on women's choices and her own struggle to free herself from her mother's influence.

Naipaul, V. S. (Vidiadhar Surajprasad), 1932-2018

French, Patrick, 1966- The **world** is what it is : the authorized biography of V.S. Naipaul / Patrick French. Knopf, 2008. 480 p. B

ISBN 9781400044054

1. Authors, Trinidadian -- 20th century 2. Nobel Prize winners 3. Brahmins 4. Writing. 5. Trinidad and Tobago. 6. Biographies
LC 2008006988

Hawthornden Prize, 2009.

National Book Critics Circle Award for Biography, 2008."

This book is a prodigious achievement, a wonderful biography, a justification for the art of biography itself." Times Literary Supplement.

Naipaul, V. S. (Vidiadhar Surajprasad), 1932-2018 **Between** father and son : family letters / V. S. Naipaul ; edited by Gillon Aitken. Alfred A. Knopf, 2000. xi, 297 p. B

ISBN 0375407308

1. Naipaul, V. S. (Vidiadhar Surajprasad), 1932-2018 Correspondence. 2. Naipaul, V. S. (Vidiadhar Surajprasad), 1932-2018 Family. 3. University of Oxford Students. 4. College students -- Great Britain 5. Authors, Trinidadian -- 20th century 6. Authors, Trinidadian -- 20th century -- Correspondence. 7. Brothers and sisters. 8. Letters. 9. Biographies
LC 99031089

"In 1950, at the age of 17, famous-writer-in-the-making V. S. Naipaul ventured to Oxford University in England on a scholarship supplied by the government of his native Trinidad. He and his father maintained a rich, full correspondence during his time away, and these letters fortunately have been gathered into book form." Booklist.

Naipaul, V. S. (Vidiadhar Surajprasad), 1932-2018 **Reading** & writing : a personal account / V.S. Naipaul. New York Review of Books, 2000. 64 p. ; B

ISBN 0940322382

1. Naipaul, V. S. (Vidiadhar Surajprasad), 1932- Books and reading. 2. Naipaul, V. S. (Vidiadhar Surajprasad), 1932- Authorship. 3. East Indians in Trinidad and Tobago -- Social life and customs. 4. Authors, Trinidadian -- 20th century 5. Trinidadians in England 6. Books and reading. 7. Autobiographies and memoirs
LC 99049615

"The author elegantly expresses hard-earned wisdom about literature and culture, the political stakes of history and the relationship between the writer and the world." New York Times Book Review.

Namath, Joe Willie, 1943-

★Namath, Joe Willie, 1943- **All** the way : football, fame, and redemption / Joe Namath with Don Yaeger. Little, Brown and Company, 2018. 320 p. B

ISBN 9780316421102

1. National Football League 2. Football players -- United States 3. Quarterbacks (Football) 4. Men -- Religious life 5. Recovering alcoholics 6. Autobiographies and memoirs
LC bl2018167851

The NFL icon who first brought show business to sports relates the story of his spectacular rise and reign as "Broadway Joe" and discusses his struggles with alcoholism and the redemption he found in God later in life.

"In time for the 50th anniversary of Namath's leading the New York Jets to a huge upset victory in the Super Bowl, here's a memoir recounting the football player's rise to stardom, glamorous social life, and post-retirement struggles with injuries and alcoholism." Library Journal.

Napoleon I, Emperor of the French, 1769-1821

Broers, Michael **Napoleon** : soldier of destiny / Michael Broers. Pegasus Books, 2015, c2014. 608 p. Napoleon (Michael Broers) ; **B**

ISBN 9781605988726

1. Generals -- France 2. Politicians -- France 3. Command of troops 4. France -- Rulers. 5. France -- History -- 1789-1815. 6. France -- Politics and government -- 1789-1815. 7. Biographies

LC 2016303202

Originally published: London : Faber and Faber, 2014.All previous lives of Napoleon have relied more on the memoirs of others than on his own uncensored words. This is the first life of Napoleon, in any language, that makes full use of his newly released personal correspondence compiled by the Napoleon Foundation in Paris.

"Highly recommended for general readers and scholars alike." Library Journal.

Broers, Michael **Napoleon** : the spirit of the age 1805-1810 / Michael Broers. Pegasus Books, 2018. 544 p. Napoleon (Michael Broers) ; **B**

ISBN 9781681776699

1. Generals -- France 2. Politicians -- France 3. Command of troops 4. France -- Rulers. 5. France -- History -- 1789-1815. 6. France -- Politics and government -- 1789-1815. 7. Biographies

LC 2017278630

The second volume in this dynamic three-part life of Napoleon, covering the tumultuous years of 1805 to 1810?marking the zenith of Napoleon's power and military might across Europe.

Gueniffey, Patrice **Bonaparte** : 1769-1802 / Patrice Gueniffey ; translated by Steven Rendall. The Belknap Press ofHarvard University Press, 2015, c2013. 992 p. **B**

ISBN 9780674368354

1. Generals -- France 2. Politicians -- France 3. Command of troops 4. France -- Rulers. 5. France -- History -- 1789-1815. 6. France -- Politics and government -- 1789-1815. 7. Biographies

LC 2014034162

Originally published in French under the same title, 2013

In the first volume of thorough biography of Napoleon Bonaparte, the author looks at the life of Napoleon from his boyhood in Corsica to his meteoric rise during the Italian and Egyptian campaigns to his proclamation as Consul for Life in 1802.

★Johnson, Paul, 1928- **Napoleon** / Paul Johnson. Viking, 2002. xii, 190 p. ; **B**

ISBN 9780670030781

1. Napoleon I, Emperor of the French, 1769-1821. 2. Generals -- France 3. Politicians -- France 4. Rulers. 5. Emperors -- France 6. France -- Rulers. 7. France -- History -- 1789-1815. 8. France -- Politics and government -- 1789-1815. 9. Biographies

LC 2001045605

"A Penguin life.""

A Lipper/Viking book.""

Johnson presents a concise appraisal of Napoleon's career and a precise understanding of his enigmatic character. The author views Napoleon, not as an idea man whose ideology was the ladder by which he propelled himself to heights of power, but as an opportunist who took advantage of a series of events and situations he could manipulate into achieving supreme control." Booklist.

★Roberts, Andrew, 1963- **Napoleon** : a life / Andrew Roberts. Viking Press, 2014, c2014. 976 p. **B**

ISBN 0670025321

1. Rulers. 2. Generals. 3. Courts and courtiers. 4. Political leadership. 5. France -- History -- 1789-1815. 6. France -- Politics and government -- 1789-1815. 7. Biographies.

LC 2013497791

Originally published under the title Napoleon the Great: London : Allen Lane 2014.

In this voluminous biography of Napoleon Bonaparte, historian Andrew Roberts relates the Corsican general's early life and traces the details of his military campaigns. Arguing that Napoleon was an effective statesman and an intellectual as well as a brilliant commander, Roberts strives to refute the conclusions of less admiring biographers. He also highlights Napoleon's influence on later military strategists. Though this is a long work, Napoleon will appeal to a wide range of readers.

"Other opinionated observers . consider Napoleon a self-absorbed opportunist plagued by his incompetent economics, pugnacious foreign policy, totalitarian government and massive propaganda, but Roberts offers a solid reconsideration." Kirkus.

Schom, Alan **Napoleon** Bonaparte / Alan Schom. Harper Collins, 1997. xxii, 888 p. : **B**

ISBN 9780060172145

1. Corsica -- History -- 1789-1794. 2. Napoleonic Wars, 1800-1815. 3. Command of troops 4. France -- Rulers 5. France -- History -- Revolution, 1789-1799. 6. Biographies

LC 97005805

Map of Europe in 1789, before Napoleon, and in 1814 before his defeat at Waterloo on endpapers.The product of more than ten years of exhaustive research, a unique, single-volume biography by a historian and scholar traces Napoleon's spectacular rise and fall, his campaigns of conquest, his reorganization of France's government, and his personal life.

"Schom's judgments have all the more impact for being brief and infrequent. What really interests him is telling the story of the man who made universal rules for others but recognized none for himself. He tells it straightforwardly and well; and not, thankfully, at the multivolume length he believes the subject still really requires." Times Literary Supplement.

Zamoyski, Adam **Napoleon** : a life / Adam Zamoyski. Basic Books, 2018. 800 p. **B**

ISBN 9780465055937

1. France. Army -- History Napoleonic Wars, 1800-1815 2. Napoleonic Wars, 1800-1815. 3. Generals -- France 4. Politicians -- France. 5. Command of troops 6. France -- Rulers. 7. France -- History -- 1789-1815. 8. France -- Politics and government -- 1789-1815. 9. Biographies

LC 2018015891

Describes the life of Napoleon, who was born poor, became an army general at 26 and let his love of an older woman transform him into a military commander who was crowned Emperor of France by age 35.

Napoleon III, Emperor of the French, 1808-1873

Strauss-Schom, Alan The **shadow** emperor : a biography of Napoleon III / Alan Strauss-schom. St Martin's Press, 2018

592 p. **B**
ISBN 9781250057785
1. Napoleon III, Emperor of the French, 1808-1873. 2. Rulers 3. France -- Rulers 4. Biographies
LC 2017060757

In the first full biography of Napoleon III by an American historian, Strauss-Schom uses his years of primary source research to explore the major cultural, sociological, economical, financial, international, and militaristic long-lasting effects of France's most polarizing emperor. Louis-Napoleon's achievements have been mixed and confusing, even to historians. He completely revolutionized the infrastructure of the state and the economy, but at the price of financial scandals of imperial proportions.

"Highly recommended for readers of European history and historical biography." Library Journal.

Napoli, Lisa, 1963-

Napoli, Lisa, 1963- **Radio** shangri-la : what I learned in Bhutan, the happiest kingdom on Earth / Lisa Napoli. Crown Publishers, 2010. 304 p. **B**
ISBN 9780307453020
1. Napoli, Lisa, 1963- -- Travel -- Bhutan. 2. Women travelers. 3. Bhutan -- Description and travel. 4. Autobiographies and memoirs
LC 2009049176

Describes how a midlife crisis and chance encounter prompted the author's relocation to Bhutan, where she volunteered at the country's first youth radio station and witnessed the self-proclaimed "world's happiest country's" first steps into the modern world.

"The author provides a readable account of her life-changing decision to leave the comforts of her cosmopolitan Los Angeles life and serve as a volunteer at Kuzoo FM 90, a radio station for young people in the remote Himalayan kingdom of Bhutan. Disillusioned with her love life and fed up with her job as a public-radio commentator, Napoli took a chance on a mysterious stranger's offer of unpaid work in a country where [b]eing, not having and [h]appiness above wealth were the prevailing national philosophies. The author's authentic voice and light, pleasant cultural insights make for a refreshingly uplifting book." Kirkus.

Narayan, Shoba

Narayan, Shoba The **milk** lady of Bangalore : an unexpected adventure / Shoba Narayan. Algonquin Books of Chapel Hill, 2018. 224 p. **B**
ISBN 9781616206154
1. Narayan, Shoba. 2. Community life. 3. Cows -- Social aspects. 4. Milk -- Social aspects. 5. Women cookbook authors. 6. India -- Social life and customs. 7. Autobiographies and memoirs
LC 2017023398

A writer and cookbook author describes her return to Bangalore and how she bonded with the local milk lady, offered to buy her a new cow and gained a new perspective on the spiritual and historical role the animal plays in India.

"An absolute joy to read. Through her close encounters with the bovine kind, Narayan shows how Indian traditions are incorporated into contemporary ways of life." Library Journal.

Nash, Ogden, 1902-1971

Parker, Douglas M., 1935- **Ogden** Nash : the life and work of America's laureate of light verse / Douglas M. Parker ; with a foreword by Dana Gioia. Ivan R. Dee, 2005. xiv, 316 p. ; **B**
ISBN 156663637X
1. Nash, Ogden, 1902-1971. 2. Poets, American -- 20th century 3. Humorous poetry, American -- History and criticism 4. Poetry writing. 5. United States -- Social life and customs -- 20th century. 6. Biographies
LC 2004059912

Looks at the life, career, and writings of the American poet.

"Parker's is a useful, highly readable biography of one of America's best-loved poets." Publishers Weekly.

Nasr, Amir Ahmad

Nasr, Amir Ahmad **My** Isl@m : how fundamentalism stole my mind--and doubt freed my soul / Amir Ahmad Nasr. St. Martin's Press, 2013. 304 p. **B**
ISBN 9781250016799
1. Nasr, Amir Ahmad. 2. Fundamentalism 3. Muslims 4. Blogs 5. Internet 6. Sudan 7. Qatar 8. Malaysia 9. Autobiographies and memoirs
LC 2013004044

Sudanese-born Malaysian author Amir Ahmad Nasr shares a conversational account of his expatriate upbringing and the evolution of his Muslim faith. Through internet bloggers in Egypt, Nasr discovered that not all Muslims shared the fundamentalist religious and political beliefs he'd learned in his youth. Through the metaphor of a love affair, My Isl@m (based on Nasr's own popular blog) relates how his faith has changed through the years. Readers needn't know much about Islam to enjoy his smart yet accessible views.

Nawaz, Zarqa

Nawaz, Zarqa **Laughing** all the way to the mosque / Zarqa Nawaz. Little Brown & Co 2016, c2014 241 p. **B**
ISBN 1443416932
1. Little mosque on the prairie (Television program) 2. Women television producers and directors 3. Muslim women 4. Muslims -- Canada -- Social life and customs 5. Muslims -- Ethnic identity 6. Autobiographies and memoirs

Originally published in Canada (Toronto : HarperCollins Canada, [2014])

A humorous account of growing up in a traditionally Muslim household in Canada.

"Nawaz's self-deprecating wit is endearing, and her simple, factual tone provides education without ever being boring. This memoir provides an important glimpse into the everyday life of a Western Muslim family, but, even better, it is a laugh-out-loud story that everyone can enjoy." Publishers Weekly.

Nayeri, Dina

★Nayeri, Dina The **ungrateful** refugee : what immigrants never tell you / Dina Nayeri. Catapult, 2019. 336 p. **B**
ISBN 9781948226424
1. Child refugees 2. Girls -- Iran 3. Immigrant families -- United States 4. Assimilation (Sociology) 5. Autobiographies and memoirs
LC bl2019020952

Kirkus Prize for Nonfiction finalist, 2019.

The author of Refuge draws on first-person testimonies in an urgent portrait of the refugee crisis that reveals how it happened and the harmful ways that Western governments respond to the inhumane conditions refugees endure.

"Nayeri is unflinching when it comes to the realities of refugee life. The larger notion of the refugee story is considered, and Nayeri deftly explores the balance between truth and storytelling when it comes to the expectations of both the telling and the hearing of these accounts." Library Journal.

Neel, Alice, 1900-1984

Hoban, Phoebe **Alice** Neel : the art of not sitting pretty / Phoebe Hoban. St. Martin's Press, 2010. 416 p. **B**

ISBN 9780312607487

1. Neel, Alice, 1900-1984. 2. Women artists -- United States 3. Gender role 4. Portrait painting. 5. Artists 6. Biographies

LC 2010035781

Documents the life of the leading 20th-century artist from her turn-of-the-century upbringing and education at the Philadelphia School of Design for Women to the development of her controversial political views and the role of the feminist movement in enabling her recognition.

Nehru, Jawaharlal, 1889-1964

Brown, Judith M. (Judith Margaret), 1944- **Nehru** : a political life / Judith M. Brown. Yale University Press, c2003. xvi, 407 p. : **B**

ISBN 0300092792

1. Nehru, Jawaharlal, 1889-1964. 2. Prime ministers -- India 3. India -- Politics and government -- 20th century. 4. Biographies

LC 2003005807

Tharoor, Shashi, 1956- **Nehru** : the invention of India / Shashi Tharoor. Arcade Pub., c2003. xix, 282 p. ; **B**

ISBN 9781559706971

1. Nehru, Jawaharlal, 1889-1964. 2. Prime ministers -- India 3. India -- Politics and government -- 20th century. 4. Biographies

LC 2003058274

The author of India: From Midnight to the Millennium provides a close-up portrait of Jawaharlal Nehru, India's first prime minister, the influential politician who led his newly independent nation from colonialism into the modern world, and his lasting legacy in terms of India's history and world role.

"The author touches on key points in Nehru's life: his English education, the importance of guidance he received from his father and Gandhi, his prison years during the drive for independence, and his administration of the new Indian republic. He neatly pulls together the essence of Nehru's beliefs in democratic institution building, pan-Indian secularism, Socialist democratic economy, and the foreign policy of non-alignment. If readers could choose only one narrative about Nehru, this would suffice." Library Journal.

Nelson, John, 1892-1993

Nelson, James Carl The **remains** of Company D : a story of the Great War / James Carl Nelson. St. Martin's Press, 2009. 384 p. **B**

ISBN 9780312551001

1. Nelson, John, 1892-1993. 2. United States. Army. Infantry Regiment, 28th (1901-1957) 3. United States. Army Military life -- History 20th century. 4. Soldiers -- United States 5. World War I, American. 6. Cantigny, Battle of, 1918. 7. Argonne, Battle of the, France, 1918 8. France.

LC 2009016931

A compelling tale of battle rooted in one man's search for his grandfather's legacy, this work follows the members of Company D, 28th Infantry Regiment, United States First Division, from enlistment to combat to the effort to recover their remains, focusing on three major battles during World War I.

"This outstanding book paints the portrait of a small military unit, in this case, Company D of the Twenty-eighth Infantry Regiment in World War I. Nelson orients the narrative around his grandfather, who lived to 101 despite serious wounds and awakened Nelson's interest in WWI by what he did not say about his experiences. Nelson set out to tell the Company D story from official records and the documents and reminiscences left behind by dozens of other veterans. [The author] writes so clearly about the background, especially trench warfare, that even readers with minimal WWI knowledge will feel educated as well as fascinated." Booklist.

Nelson, Maggie, 1973-

★Nelson, Maggie, 1973- The **Argonauts** / Maggie Nelson. Graywolf Press, 2015. 160 p. **B**

ISBN 9781555977078

1. Interpersonal relations 2. Gender identity 3. Pregnancy 4. Love. 5. Autobiographies and memoirs

LC bl2015017696

The Argonauts is a genre-bending memoir, a work of "autotheory" offering fresh, fierce, and timely thinking about desire, identity, and the limitations and possibilities of love and language. At its center is a romance: the story of the author's relationship with the artist Harry Dodge. This story, which includes Nelson's account of falling in love with Dodge, who is fluidly gendered, as well as her journey to and through a pregnancy, offers a firsthand account of the complexities and joys of (queer) family-making.

Nelson, Willie, 1933-

★Patoski, Joe Nick, 1951- **Willie** Nelson : an epic life / Joe Nick Patoski. Little, Brown, c2008. 800 p. **B**

ISBN 9780316017787

1. Country musicians -- United States 2. Musicians 3. Biographies

LC 2007044984

Draws on more than one hundred interviews with the iconic country-music artist and his intimates to trace his rise from humble Depression-era roots to one of the genre's most famous figures, in a profile that covers such topics as his first performance at age four, his education in a series of Texas bars, and his brushes with the law.

"This impressive, entertaining chronicle of Willie Nelson's life is replete with exactly what you'd expecthonky-tonk, long nights on the open road, whiskey, womanizing and weed--but [the author] looks beyond country music trappings to find the funny, talented, determined man who became an unlikely icon." Publishers Weekly.

Nemat, Marina

Nemat, Marina **Prisoner** of Tehran : a memoir / Marina Nemat. Free Press, c2007. ix, 306 p. ; **B**

ISBN 1416537422

1. Nemat, Marina. 2. Women political prisoners -- Iran 3. Political prisoners -- Iran 4. Iran -- Politics and government -- 1979-1997. 5. Autobiographies and memoirs

LC 2006050191

An autobiography of Marina Nemat, who was arrested at the age of 16 on false charges by Iranian Revolutionary Guards, tortured in Tehran's notorious Evin prison, and sentenced to death for "political crimes."

"The author's story is not so much a political history lesson than it is a memoir of faith and love, a protest against violence that cannot be silenced. . . . Her persistence in standing for goodness is a lesson for us all." Christian Science Monitor.

Neruda, Pablo, 1904-1973

★Feinstein, Adam **Pablo** Neruda : a passion for life / Adam Feinstein. Bloomsbury, 2004. xii, 497 p. : **B**

ISBN 1582344108

1. Neruda, Pablo, 1904-1973. 2. Authors, Chilean -- 20th century 3. Chile -- Social life and customs -- 20th century 4. Biographies

LC 2004000715

A biography of the Chilean author and poet traces his odyssey from a poverty-stricken youth, through his participation in the Spanish Civil War and exile from his own country, to his remarkable literary endeavors.

"Feinstein undoubtedly researched every existent source and found new ones, and the result is a detailed and accurate biography. This is a necessary book, with many beautiful photos." Publishers Weekly.

Nesmith, Michael

Nesmith, Michael **Infinite** Tuesday : an autobiographical riff / Michael Nesmith. Random House Inc., 2017. 352 p. **B**

ISBN 9781101907504

1. Monkees (Musical group) 2. Musicians 3. Songwriters 4. Christian scientists 5. Spiritual life 6. Autobiographies and memoirs

LC 2016058926

An idiosyncratic memoir by the Monkees icon, songwriter and music-video innovator traces his experiences as a wild youth and celebrity before finding peace and creative wholeness through the teachings of Christian Science and his collaborations with like-minded fellow artists.

"This selectively revealing, insightful memoir casts the cerebral Monkee as a spiritual seeker and self-deprecating visionary." Kirkus.

Ness, Eliot

Collins, Max Allan **Eliot** Ness and the mad butcher : hunting America's deadliest unidentified serial killer at the dawn of modern criminology / Max Allan Collins, A. Brad Schwartz. William Morrow & Company, [2020] 576 p. **B**

ISBN 9780062881977

1. Detectives 2. Public officials 3. Serial murderers 4. Serial murder investigation 5. Cleveland, Ohio 6. Biographies

LC 2020005488

In 1934, the nation's most legendary crime-fighter - fresh from taking on the greatest gangster in American history - arrived in Cleveland, a corrupt and dangerous town about to host a world's fair. It was to be his coronation, as well as the city's. Instead, terror descended, as headless bodies started turning up. The young detective, already battling the mob and crooked cops, found his drive to transform American policing subverted by a menace largely unknown to law enforcement: a serial murderer. As Ness zeroed in on a suspect powerful forces thwarted his quest for justice. In this battle between a flawed hero and a twisted monster - by turns horror story, political drama, and detective thriller - Collins and Schwartz find an American tragedy, classic in structure, epic in scope.

"A successful blend of history and suspense, this volume will appeal to readers interested in true crime and law enforcement. Readers intrigued by the Mad Butcher may also enjoy James Jessen Badal's In the Wake of the Butcher." Library Journal

Netanyahu, Binyamin

Kaspit, Ben The **Netanyahu** years / Ben Caspit ; translated by Ora Cummings. Dunne Books, 2017, c1997 480 p. **B**

ISBN 9781250087058

1. Politicians 2. Prime ministers -- Israel 3. Arab-Israeli conflict 4. Political leadership 5. Israel -- Politics and government -- 1993- 6. Middle East -- Politics and government 7. Biographies

LC 2017010999

Translation of: Netanyahu

Originally published: Tel Aviv : Alfa Tiqsoret, 1997

Benjamin Netanyahu is currently serving his fourth term in office as Prime Minister of Israel, the longest serving Prime Minister in the country's history. Now Israeli journalist Ben Caspit puts Netanyahu's life under a magnifying glass, focusing on his last two terms in office. Caspit covers a wide swath of topics, including Netanyahu's policies, his political struggles, and his fight against the Iranian nuclear program, and zeroes in on Netanyahu's love/hate relationship with the American administration, America's Jews, and his alliances with American business magnates. A timely and important book, The Netanyahu Years is a primer for anyone looking to understand this world leader.

"As captured in Cummings's remarkably fluid translation, Caspit's detailed, clear account covers Israel's domestic-policy disputes and Netanyahu's impact as a world leader." Publishers Weekly.

Neumann, Adam

Wiedeman, Reeves **Billion** dollar loser : the epic rise and spectacular fall of Adam Neumann and WeWork / Reeves Wiedeman. Little Brown & Company, 2020 304 p. **B**

ISBN 9780316461368

1. Neumann, Adam. 2. Businesspeople 3. Real estate business 4. Immigrants 5. Business failures 6. United States 7. Biographies

LC 2020940737

Includes index.

Moving between New York real estate, Silicon Valley venture capital, and the very specific force field of spirituality and ambition erected by Adam Neumann himself, Billion Dollar Loser lays bare the internal drama inside WeWork. Based on more than two hundred interviews, this book chronicles the breakneck speed at which WeWork's CEO built and grew his company along with Neumann's relationship to a world of investors, including Masayoshi Son of Softbank, who fueled its chaotic expansion into everything from apartment buildings to elementary schools.

"Readers will feel like they are in the room with Neumann and his beleaguered colleagues during every twist and turn of this fascinating corporate train wreck." Publishers Weekly

Neumann, Hanus Stanislav, 1921-2001

Neumann, Ariana **When** time stopped : a memoir of my father's war and what remains / Ariana Neumann. Scribner, 2020. 352 p. **B**

ISBN 9781982106379

1. Neumann, Hanus Stanislav, 1921-2001. 2. Newman family. 3. Neumann, Ariana 4. Jews, Czech. 5. Holocaust (1933-1945) -- Czechoslovakia 6. Holocaust survivors 7. Families 8. Berlin, Germany 9. Czechoslovakia 10. Venezuela 11. Biographies

LC 2019045041

A Venezuelan foreign correspondent describes the harrowing early experiences of her father, an only survivor of their Jewish-Czechoslovakian family, who hid from the Gestapo in plain sight before starting over in South America.

"Neumann's eloquent, skillfully researched book will appeal to many, especially those interested in family histories and the lives of Holocaust survivors." Library Journal

Nevins, Sheila

Nevins, Sheila **You** don't look your age : and other fairy tales / Sheila Nevins. Flatiron Books, 2017. 272 p. **B**

ISBN 9781250111302

1. Career development 2. Personal conduct 3. Aging 4. Women 5. Essays 6. Autobiographies and memoirs

LC 2017003050

A famed television producer and president of HBO Documentary Films shares frank but lighthearted advice for today's women on how to navigate the challenges of pursuing a career in a man's world, balancing the responsibilities of a working parent, aging in a youth-obsessed culture and thriving as a feminist in a dynamic marriage.

Newman, Kurt

Newman, Kurt **Healing** children : a surgeon's stories from the frontiers of pediatric medicine / Kurt, M.d. Newman. Viking Press, 2017 384 p. **B**

ISBN 9780525428831

1. Pediatric surgeons. 2. Children -- Surgery 3. Physicians 4. Sick children 5. Autobiographies and memoirs

LC 2017025373

A medical memoir by a forefront pediatric surgeon presents a case for treating children very differently from adults, tracing decades of advancement in pediatrics to counsel parents and caregivers on how to recognize the unique health needs and healing potential of young patients.

"Written primarily as a guide for parents navigating the unpredictable health of their children, the book also addresses the future of pediatric care, as Newman delves into the most innovative therapies and initiatives in development." Kirkus.

Newman, Nathaniel

Newman, Magdalena M. **Normal** : a mother and her beautiful son / Magdalena Newman ; with Hilary Liftin. Houghton Mifflin Harcourt, 2020. 256 p. **B**

ISBN 9781328593122

1. Newman, Nathaniel. 2. Newman, Magdalena M. 3. Mothers and sons. 4. Medical genetics 5. Genetic disorders in children. 6. Treacher Collins syndrome 7. Washington (State) 8. Seattle, Washington 9. Autobiographies and memoirs

LC 2019023276

A moving memoir from the mother of a child with Treacher Collins Syndrome.

"Readers looking for an inspiring story about the power of the human spirit will find one here." Publishers Weekly.

Newton, Isaac, 1642-1727

Gleick, James **Isaac** Newton / James Gleick. Pantheon Books, 2003. xii, 272 p. : **B**

ISBN 0375422331

1. Newton, Isaac, 1642-1727. 2. Physicists -- Great Britain 3. Scientists -- Great Britain 4. Mathematicians -- Great Britain 5. Biographies

LC 2002192696

Pulitzer Prize for Biography or Autobiography finalist"

This is now the biography of choice for the interested layman. Gleick copes with the complex tapestry of Newton's interests by teasing them apart into individual chapters, assembled into a smooth chronological flow. Newton the man emerges from the shadows." New York Times Book Review.

Westfall, Richard S. The **life** of Isaac Newton / Richard S. Westfall. Cambridge University Press, 1994, c1993. xv, 328 p. : **B**

ISBN 0521477379

1. Newton, Isaac, Sir, 1642-1727. 2. Physicists -- Great Britain 3. Physics -- History. 4. Science -- History. 5. Biographies

LC BL 99757695

Reprint. Originally published: 1993.

Ngugi wa Thiong'o, 1938-

Ngugi wa Thiong'o, 1938- **In** the house of the interpreter : a memoir / Ngugi wa'Thiong'o. Pantheon Books, 2012. 272 p. **B**

ISBN 9780307907691

1. Ngugi wa Thiong'o, 1938- Childhood and youth. 2. Ngugi wa Thiong'o, 1938- Family. 3. Authors, Kenyan -- 20th century 4. Imperialism, British -- Kenya 5. Resistance to government 6. Kikuyu (African people) 7. Kenya -- History -- 1895-1963 8. Kenya -- History -- Mau Mau Emergency, 1952-1960, Kenyan. 9. Kenya -- Colonial influence. 10. Kenya -- Social conditions -- 20th century. 11. Autobiographies and memoirs

LC 2012013986

Follows: Dreams in a time of war (2010).

National Book Critics Circle Award for Autobiography/ Memoir finalist

The second volume of memoirs from the renowned Kenyan novelist, poet and playwright covers his high school years at the end of British colonial rule in Africa, during the Mau Mau Uprising.

Ngugi wa Thiong'o, 1938- **Wrestling** with the devil : a prison memoir / Ngugi Wa Thiong'o. The New Press, 2018. 248 p. : **B**

ISBN 9781620973332

1. Ngugi wa Thiong'o, 1938- Caitaani mutharaba-ini. 2. Imprisonment 3. Prisoners 4. Political prisoners 5. Prisons 6. Kenya 7. Autobiographies and memoirs

Never before published in America, a novelist and memoirist who was thrown in a Kenyan jail without charge recounts the drama and challenges of writing a novel while under 24-four-hour surveillance, capturing the pain of being cut off from his family as well as the spirit of defiance that defines hope.

"At once exhilarating and defiant, wa Thiongos memoir is a thought provoking document of a grim time in Kenyan history." Publishers Weekly.

Nicholas II, Emperor of Russia, 1868-1918

Service, Robert, 1947- The **last** of the tsars : Nicholas II and the Russia Revolution / Robert Service. Pegasus Books, 2017. 496 p. **B**

ISBN 9781681775012

1. Nicholas II, Emperor of Russia, 1868-1918. 2. Rulers 3. Revolutions -- Russia 4. Russia -- Rulers 5. Russia -- History -- Nicholas II, 1894-1917. 6. Soviet Union -- History -- Revolution, 1917-1921 7. Biographies

LC bl2017033722

A riveting account of the last eighteen months of Tsar Nicholas II's life and reign from one of the finest Russian historians writing today.

"A compelling work; organized, concise, and chilling." Kirkus.

Nichols, Donald

Harden, Blaine **King** of spies : the dark reign of America's spymaster in Korea / Blaine Harden. Viking Press, 2017. 288 p. **B**

ISBN 9780525429937

1. Korean War, 1950-1953 2. Spies 3. Intelligence service 4. War -- Psychological aspects 5. Korea -- Foreign relations United States 6. United States -- Foreign relations Korea 7. Biographies

LC 2017025386

Describes the story of army mechanic Donald Nichols, who was recruited by the Army's Counter-Intelligence Corps to get close with South Korea's first president, Syngman Rhee, and become a key player in the war effort during the North Korean invasion.

"The author ably connects his ominous central figure to the larger mysterious, unresolved narrative of the Korean conflict. An engrossing hidden history of wartime espionage, with elements of derring-do and moral barbarity." Kirkus.

Nichols, Mike

Carter, Ash (Editor) **Life** isn't everything : Mike Nichols, as remembered by 103 of his closest friends / Ash Carter and Sam Kashner. Henry Holt and Company, 2019. 368 p. **B**

ISBN 9781250112873

1. Film producers and directors 2. Filmmakers 3. Biographies

LC 2019031319

Includes index.

An up-close and personal portrait of legendary filmmaker, theater director, and comedian Mike Nichols, drawing on candid conversations with his closest friends in show business and the arts-from Dustin Hoffman and Meryl Streep to Natalie Portman and Lorne Michaels.

Nidetch, Jean

Meltzer, Marisa, 1977- **This** is big : how the founder of Weight Watchers changed the world -- and me / Marisa Meltzer. Little, Brown and Company, 2020. xi, 290 p. ; **B**

ISBN 9780316414005

1. Meltzer, Marisa, 1977- 2. Weight Watchers International. 3. Weight control 4. Diet 5. Dieting 6. Diet industry and trade 7. Biographies 8. Autobiographies and memoirs

LC 2019945559

Marisa Meltzer began her first diet at the age of five. Fast forward nearly four decades, Marisa comes across an obituary for Jean Nidetch, the Queens, New York housewife who founded Weight Watchers in 1963. Weaving Jean's incredible story as weight loss maven and pathbreaking entrepreneur with Marisa's own journey through Weight Watchers, she chronicles the deep parallels, and enduring frustrations, in each woman's decades-long efforts to lose weight and keep it off.

"A straightforward memoir of struggling with obesity and finding inspiration from the founder of Weight Watchers ? Her story will resonate with readers who have struggled with weight and body image issues." Kirkus

Nietzsche, Friedrich Wilhelm, 1844-1900

Kaag, John J., 1979- **Hiking** with Nietzsche : on becoming who you are / John Kaag. Farrar, Straus, and Giroux, 2018. 256 p. **B**

ISBN 9780374170011

1. Hiking 2. Philosophy 3. Mountaineering 4. Self 5. Swiss Alps -- Description and travel 6. Autobiographies and memoirs

LC 2017057604

In an illuminating Alpine trek though the Swiss peaks, the author, drawing on two separate journeys--one when he was 19 and one 17 years later--channels the spirit of Freidrich Nietzche as he searches for meaning.

"A wonderful introduction to Nietzsche set against the unique backdrop of the landscape and cities he experienced. The tone and writing style make it accessible to general readers, while the content will reward those familiar with Nietzsche as well." Library Journal.

Prideaux, Sue **I** am dynamite! : a life of Nietzsche / Sue Prideaux. Tim Duggan Books, 2018. 480 p. **B**

ISBN 9781524760823

1. Nietzsche, Friedrich Wilhelm, 1844-1900. 2. Philosophers -- Germany 3. Intellectuals 4. Ethics 5. Philosophy 6. Biographies

LC bl2018167887

Hawthornden Prize, 2019.

Illuminates the life of the famous philosopher and the events and people--including his family members, composer Richard Wagner and former lover Lou Salomé--that helped shape his brilliant, eccentric, but also deeply troubled mind.

Nightingale, Florence, 1820-1910

Bostridge, Mark **Florence** Nightingale : the making of an icon / Mark Bostridge. Farrar, Straus and Giroux, 2008. 672 p. **B**

ISBN 9780374156657

1. Nightingale, Florence, 1820-1910. 2. Nurses -- England 3. Crimean War, 1853-1856. 4. Great Britain -- History -- 19th century. 5. Biographies

LC 2008031424

Elizabeth Longford Prize for Historical Biography, 2009.

A profile of the iconic Victorian social reformer evaluates her scandalous decision to break with the conventions of her privileged class to work as a nurse, the myths surrounding her, and the controversial nature of her achievements.

"Bostridge presents a well-researched, and comprehensive biography of Nightingale, drawing heavily on letters, diaries, and other primary sources in a successful effort to create a balanced and authentic portrait of the woman, not the myth. Beginning with moving depictions of Nightingale's struggles to be allowed to pursue her calling despite her family's objections, Bostridge skillfully illuminates the spiritual and philosophical motivations that drove Nightingale's impassioned and lifelong dedication to the causes of nursing and public health reform." Library Journal.

Nimitz, Chester W. (Chester William), 1885-1966

Borneman, Walter R., 1952- The **admirals** : Nimitz, Halsey, Leahy, and King--the five-star admirals who won the war at sea / Walter R. Borneman. Little, Brown and Co., 2012. 512 p. **B**

ISBN 9780316097840

1. Nimitz, Chester W. (Chester William), 1885-1966. 2. Halsey, William Frederick, 1882-1959. 3. Leahy, William D. 4. King, Ernest Joseph, 1878-1956. 5. United States. Navy 6. United States. Navy -- History 20th century. 7. Admirals -- United States 8. Naval art and science -- History -- 20th century. 9. Command of troops. 10. World War II -- Naval operations, American.

LC 2011032394

"Borneman deftly manipulates multiple narrative strands and a wealth of detail. He vividly fleshes out the numerous vain, ambitious men vying for power at the top and examines their important decisions and lasting ramifications." Kirkus.

Nir, Sarah Maslin, 1983-

Nir, Sarah Maslin, 1983- **Horse** crazy : the story of a woman and a world in love with an animal / Sarah Maslin Nir. Simon and Schuster, 2020. 384 p. **B**

ISBN 9781501196232

1. Equestrians 2. Horses 3. Horse owners 4. Women journalists 5. United States 6. Autobiographies and memoirs

LC 2019058615

Includes index.

Horse Crazy is a fascinating, funny, and moving love letter to these graceful animals and the people who-like her-are obsessed with them. It is also a coming-of-age story of Nir growing up an outsider within the world's most elite inner circles, and finding her true north in horses. Nir takes us into the lesser-known corners of the riding world and profiles some of its most captivating figures.

"This thoughtful, well-researched book offers a charming portrait of horses in America as well as of a woman who found self-acceptance in their graceful company. A bighearted debut book sure to please horse lovers." Kirkus

Nixon, Richard M. (Richard Milhous), 1913-1994

Dallek, Robert **Nixon** and Kissinger : partners in power / Robert Dallek. Harper Collins Publishers, c2007. xii, 740 p. : **B**

ISBN 0060722304

1. Nixon, Richard M. (Richard Milhous), 1913-1994. 2. Kissinger, Henry, 1923- 3. Presidents -- United States. 4. Politicians -- United States. 5. United States -- Foreign relations -- 1945-1989.

LC 2006052100

Pulitzer Prize for History finalist, 2008.

A dual portrait of the late former president and the former Secretary of State describes the ambitious drives that motivated them, offering insight into the tumultuous relationship that shaped their respective foreign policy agendas.

"A look behind the scenes at this quintessential pair of power brokers and their lasting influence, for good and ill, on the political stage." Bookmarks.

★Farrell, John A. (John Aloysius) **Richard** Nixon : the life / John A. Farrell. Doubleday, 2017. 752 p. **B**

ISBN 9780385537353

1. Presidents -- United States 2. Politicians 3. Power (Social sciences) 4. Watergate Scandal 5. United States -- Politics and government -- 1945-1989 6. Biographies

LC 2016049856

American History Book Prize, 2017.

Longlisted for the Andrew Carnegie Medal for Excellence in Non-Fiction, 2018.

Pulitzer Prize for Biography or Autobiography finalist, 2018.

An extensively researched portrait of the 37th president by the biographer of Clarence Darrow traces Nixon's early political ambitions in his post-military years, his early achievements as a senator and vice president and his forward-thinking ideas in health care, poverty, civil rights, the environment and foreign affairs.

Thomas, Evan, 1951- **Being** Nixon : a man divided / Evan Thomas. Random House, 2015. 656 p. **B**

ISBN 9780812995367

1. Nixon, Richard M. (Richard Milhous), 1913-1994. 2. Presidents -- United States 3. Political leadership. 4. Politicians 5. United States -- Politics and government -- 1969-1974. 6. Biographies

LC 2015009669

"Thomas doesn't shy away from showing Nixon at his worst, acknowledging Nixon's penchant for the maudlin, his self-pity, his fear of confrontation, and his often poisonous rivalry with Henry Kissinger. Thomas is generous to his subject, contextualizing Nixon and often teasing out his well-concealed desire to do the right thing." Publishers Weekly.

Weiner, Tim **One** man against the world : the tragedy of Richard Nixon / Tim Weiner. Henry Holt and Company, 2015. 352 p. **B**

ISBN 9781627790833

1. Presidents -- United States 2. Politicians -- United States 3. United States -- Politics and government -- 1969-1974. 4. Biographies

LC 2015012381

A crucial new look at the greatest political suicide in history, One Man Against the World leaves us not only with new insight into this tumultuous period, but also into the motivations and demons of an American president who saw enemies everywhere, and, thinking the world was against him, undermined the foundations of the country he had hoped to lead.

"Those seeking to understand America in the second half of the twentieth century and, distressingly, beyond would do well to begin here. The tragedy was not Nixon's alone, but his role in it has never been portrayed more vividly." Booklist.

Woodward, Bob, 1943- The **final** days / Bob Woodward, Carl Bernstein. Simon and Schuster Paperbacks, 2005, c1976. 470 p. : **B**

ISBN 0743274067

1. Nixon, Richard M. (Richard Milhous), 1913-1994 Impeachment 2. Nixon, Richard M. (Richard Milhous), 1913-1994 Resignation 3. Political corruption. 4. Watergate Scandal. 5. Government cover-ups. 6. Presidents -- United States. 7. United States -- Politics and government -- 20th century. 8. United States -- History -- 20th century.

LC 2005282821

Includes index.

The Washington Post reporters draw on interviews, leaks, and investigations to reconstruct the events and circumstances, in and outside the White House, during the unsettled and unsettling final weeks of the Nixon administration.

Noah, Trevor, 1984-

★Noah, Trevor, 1984- **Born** a crime : stories from a South African childhood / Trevor Noah. Spiegel & Grau, 2016. 224 p. **B**

ISBN 9780399588174

1. Comedians 2. Television personalities 3. Race relations 4. Growing up 5. South Africa 6. Essays 7. Autobiographies and memoirs

LC 2016031399

Thurber Prize for American Humor, 2017.

Trevor Noah, host of The Daily Show, shares his remarkable story of growing up in South Africa, with a black South African mother and a white European father at a time when it was against the law for a mixed-race child like him to exist. In a country where racism barred blacks from social, educational, and economic opportunity, Trevor surmounted staggering obstacles and created a promising future for himself, thanks to his mother's unwavering love and indomitable will.

Noguchi, Isamu, 1904-1988

Herrera, Hayden **Listening** to stone : the art and life of Isamu Noguchi / Hayden Herrera. Farrar, Straus and Giroux, 2015. 512 p. **B**

ISBN 9780374281168

1. Noguchi, Isamu, 1904-1988. 2. Artists 3. Modern art -- 20th century. 4. Sculptors 5. Sculpture, American -- 20th Century. 6. Biographies

LC 2014031274

From the author of Arshile Gorky, a major biography of the great American sculptor that redefines his legacy.

"Herrera adroitly shows that Noguchi was more than just a sculptor--he was a skilled craftsman, a heartbreaker, and a philosopher of design." Publishers Weekly.

Nolte, Nick

Nolte, Nick **Rebel** : my life outside the lines / Nick Nolte. HarperCollins, 2015 320 p. **B**

ISBN 9780062219572

1. Nolte, Nick. 2. Film actors and actresses 3. Film industry and trade 4. Actors and actresses 5. Autobiographies and memoirs

LC 2017278529

The three-time Academy Award nominee traces his half century in Hollywood, describing his extreme character-creation efforts as a method actor, the substance abuse issues that have overshadowed his life and his experiences as a father.

"Long since on the wagon and an obviously thoughtful man, Nolte seems to share the reader's surprise that he lived long enough to take that role. Better than the usual run of actor memoirs and plenty of fun to boot." Kirkus.

Norris, Gloria

Norris, Gloria **Kookooland** / Gloria Norris. Regan Arts, 2016 304 p. **B**

ISBN 9781941393604

1. Norris, Gloria. 2. Fathers and daughters 3. Growing up 4. Manipulation (Social sciences) 5. Violence 6. Autobiographies and memoirs

LC 2015930624

After her father--a wiseguy who relies on charm, snappy wit and an unyielding belief that he is above the law--commits an unspeakable act of violence, young Gloria Norris, in an unconventional coming-of-age-memoir, sets herself on a path away from the cycle of violence whirling around her to carve out a good life on her terms.

"A tumble through a tumultuous time, in which the heroine inexplicably, beautifully lands on her feet." Booklist.

Norris, Mary (Editor)

Norris, Mary (Editor) **Between** you and me : confessions of a comma queen / Mary Norris. W W Norton & Co 2015. 240 p. **B**

ISBN 9780393240184

1. New Yorker (New York, N.Y. : 1925) 2. Editors 3. Writing 4. Language and languages -- Grammars. 5. Autobiographies and memoirs

LC 2014043252

A New Yorker copy veteran presents laugh-out-loud descriptions of some of the most common and vexing errors in language and usage, drawing on examples from classic literature and pop culture while sharing anecdotes from her work with celebrated writers.

"In countless laugh-out-loud passages, Norris displays her admirable flexibility in bending rules when necessary. She even makes her serious quest to uncover the reason for the hyphen in the title of the classic novel Moby-Dick downright hilarious. A funny book for any serious reader." Kirkus.

Norris, Michele

Norris, Michele The **grace** of silence : a memoir / Michele Norris. Pantheon Books, 2010. 288 p. **B**

ISBN 9780307378767

1. Norris, Michele. 2. Norris, Michele Family. 3. African American journalists 4. African American women 5. Race relations 6. Racism. 7. Autobiographies and memoirs

LC 2010019285

A host of NPR's "All Things Considered" traces her ancestry in America's South and how it reflects the nation's turbulent efforts toward racial equality, a heritage that has influenced her awareness about character, silence, and integration.

"In examining her personal roots for this memoir, African American Norris . found some skeletons in her family's closet. For example, she discovered that in the early 20th century her grandmother had dressed as Aunt Jemina to pitch pancake flour to the wives of white farmers in the Midwest. Using her skills as an investigative reporter, Norris also pieces together details of an incident in 1946 when her father was shot by a white policeman in Birmingham, AL. Norris's family history offers Americans of all races a moving and revealing account of the obstacles facing several generations of middle-class African Americans in the pre-Civil Rights era." Library Journal.

Northup, Solomon, 1808-1863?

★Northup, Solomon, 1808-1863? **Twelve** years a slave / Solomon Northup ; introduction by Ira Berlin ; general editor Henry Louis Gates, Jr. Penguin Books, 2012, c1853. xxxvi, 240 p. : **B**

ISBN 9780143106708

1. Slaves 2. Slavery -- Louisiana -- History -- 19th century. 3. African Americans 4. Plantation life -- Louisiana -- History -- 19th century. 5. United States -- History -- 19th century 6. Autobiographies and memoirs

LC 2012012550

Originally published: 1853.

Describes the life of Solomon Northup, a free Black man from Saratoga, N.Y., who was kidnapped in 1841 and forced into slavery in Louisiana for twelve years.

Novacek, Michael J.

Novacek, Michael J. **Time** traveler : in search of dinosaurs and ancient mammals from Montana to Mongolia / Michael Novacek. Farrar, Straus and Giroux, 2002. x, 368 p. : **B**

ISBN 0374278806

1. Paleontology -- Field work. 2. Fossils -- Collectors and collecting. 3. Dinosaurs. 4. Paleontologists -- United States 5. Autobiographies and memoirs

LC 2001040438

"The author first describes the youthful experiences that inspired him to become a paleontologist. Then Novacek launches into his various expeditions. Interweaving his adventures with explanations of where his finds fit into the geologic past, Novacek has combined the comedic with the informative in this entertaining survey of his career." Booklist.

Nuland, Sherwin B.

Nuland, Sherwin B. **Lost** in America : a journey with my father / Sherwin B. Nuland. Knopf, 2003. 209 p. **B**

ISBN 0375412948

1. Nuland, Sherwin B. Family. 2. Nudelman, Meyer. 3. Fathers and sons. 4. Jewish Americans -- New York City 5. Immigrants, Jewish 6. Father and child. 7. Bronx, New York City 8. Biographies

LC 2002040795

The author offers an account of his father's life, from the turn-of-the-century arrival of a young immigrant from Russia to his struggle against poverty, tragedy, and illness, and explores how his father's life influenced his own.

"Written with enormous empathy, yet without a hint of sentimentality, Nuland's memoir is both heartbreaking and breathtaking." Publishers Weekly.

Nur Jahan, Empress, consort of Jahangir, Emperor of Hindustan, d. 1645

★Lal, Ruby **Empress** : the astonishing reign of Nur Jahan / Ruby Lal. W.W. Norton & Company, 2018. 320 p. **B**

ISBN 9780393239348

1. Women rulers -- Mogul Empire 2. Civilization, Islamic 3. Muslim women 4. Mogul Empire 5. India -- History 6. Biographies

LC 2018003419

Presents a deeply researched portrait of the seventeenth-century Mughal Empire ruler that illuminates her genius as a designer, architect, politician, hunter, and partner.

"A page-turning, eye-opening biography that shatters our impressions of India as established by the British Raj." Kirkus.

Nureyev, Rudolf, 1938-1993

Kavanagh, Julie, 1952- **Nureyev** : the life / Julie Kavanagh. Pantheon Books, 2007. 782 p. **B**

ISBN 0375405135

1. Nureyev, Rudolf, 1938-1993. 2. Ballet dancers -- Russia 3.

Celebrities 4. Ballet. 5. Defectors. 6. Russia 7. United States 8. Biographies

LC 2006038137

A definitive portrait of the iconic ballet dancer describes Nureyev's Soviet youth, his dramatic 1961 defection to the West, the extraordinary performances that transformed him into an international celebrity, his flamboyant lifestyle, his major influence on the modern history of dance, his notorious sexual escapades, and the AIDS that claimed his life in 1993.

"In this biography of the Russian ballet dancer, the author chronicles Nureyev's many tempestuous relationships, including his legendary work with Margot Fonteyn and his formative affair with the outstanding Danish dancer Erik Bruhn. Kavanagh's consummate biography will stand as a pillar in dance history." Booklist.

Nusseibeh, Sari

Nusseibeh, Sari **Once** upon a country : a Palestinian life / Sari Nusseibeh ; with Anthony David. Farrar, Straus and Giroux, 2007. viii, 542 p., 8 p. of plates : **B**

ISBN 9780374299507

1. Nusseibeh, Sari. 2. Palestinians. 3. Arab-Israeli conflict. 4. Nationalism. 5. Palestine -- Politics and government -- 1945-

LC 2006013272

A Palestinian scholar and leader offers a look at the troubling recent history of his country and the Middle East from a Palestinian perspective, sharing his rationale for promoting a two-state solution to the problems affecting the region.

Nutter, Tommy, 1943-1992

Richardson, Lance, 1984- **House** of Nutter : the rebel tailor of Savile Row / Lance Richardson. Crown Archetype, 2018. 336 p. **B**

ISBN 9780451496461

1. Nutter, Tommy, 1943-1992. 2. Fashion designers -- Great Britian 3. Fashion 4. Popular culture 5. Photographers 6. Biographies

LC 2017045881

Describes the life and career of the Savile Row tailor and his photographer brother who influenced the fashion of the swinging cultural revolution that took place in the late 60s and early 70s, influencing everyone from Bianca Jagger to the Beatles.

Nyad, Diana

Nyad, Diana **Find** a way / Diana Nyad. Knopf, 2015. 304 p. **B**

ISBN 9780385353618

1. Nyad, Diana. 2. Women swimmers 3. Swimmers 4. Marathon swimming. 5. Swimming. 6. Autobiographies and memoirs

LC 2015009932

"A Borzoi book."

On September 2, 2013, at the age of 64, Diana Nyad emerged onto the shores of Key West after completing a 110 mile, 53 hour, record-breaking swim through shark-infested waters from Cuba to Florida. Her memoir shows why, at 64 she was able to achieve what she couldn't at 30 and how her repeated failures contributed to her success.

"Particularly effective in its ability to portray the complex psychology of an extreme endurance athlete, Nyad's moving account is well suited for readers interested in open-water swimming, endurance sports, athletes' memoirs, or age-defying adventures." Library Journal.

Nye, Bill

Nye, Bill **Everything** all at once : how to unleash your inner nerd, tap into radical curiosity and solve any problem / Bill Nye ; edited by Corey S. Powell. Rodale Books, 2017. 384 p. **B**

ISBN 9781623367916

1. Nye, Bill. 2. Critical thinking. 3. Science. 4. Misfits (Persons) 5. Social change. 6. Essays 7. Autobiographies and memoirs

LC 2017022105

Everyone has an inner nerd just waiting to be awakened by the right passion. In Everything All at Once, Bill Nye will help you find yours. With his call to arms, he wants you to examine every detail of the most difficult problems that look unsolvable?that is, until you find the solution. Bill shows you how to develop critical thinking skills and create change, using his "everything all at once" approach that leaves no stone unturned.

"Bow-tied nerd superhero Nye (Unstoppable: Harnessing Science to Change the World, 2015, etc.) serves up a tasty combination of memoir and manifesto." Kirkus.

O'Brady, Colin

★O'Brady, Colin The **impossible** first : from fire to ice - crossing Antarctica alone / Colin O'Brady. Scribner, 2020. 288 p. **B**

ISBN 9781982133115

1. Expeditions -- Arctic regions. 2. Wilderness survival -- Arctic regions. 3. Exploration 4. Quests 5. Antarctica -- Exploration 6. Autobiographies and memoirs

LC bl2020000113

A multiple world-record holder and premier endurance athlete recounts his triumphant recovery from a disabling burn accident in early adulthood and his inspiring 932-mile solo crossing of Antarctica.

"An unforgettable memoir of perseverance, survival, daring to dream big, and showing the world how to make the impossible possible." Booklist

O'Brian, Patrick, 1914-2000

King, Dean **Patrick** O'Brian : a life revealed / Dean King. H. Holt, 2000. xviii, 397 p., [16] p. of plates : **B**

ISBN 0805059768

1. O'Brian, Patrick, 1914-2000. 2. Authors, English -- 20th century 3. Historical fiction writing. 4. Sea story writing. 5. Biographies

LC 99048495

A biography of author Patrick O'Brian, the creator of the popular Aubrey-Maturin historical novels, describes the personal life of the reclusive eccentric who radically altered his own identity.

O'Brien, Edna

O'Brien, Edna **Country** girl / Edna O'Brien. Little Brown, 2013, c2012. x, 339 p. : **B**

ISBN 9780316122702

1. O'Brien, Edna. 2. Women authors -- 20th century 3. Authors, Irish -- 20th century 4. Ambition in women. 5. Interpersonal relations. 6. Ireland -- Social life and customs -- 20th century. 7. Autobiographies and memoirs

LC 2012047510

Originally published in 2012 (London: Faber and Faber, 2012.)"

While O'Brien overly devotes her time to cataloguing the notable actors, writers, and politicians of her acquaintance, the accounts of her childhood and her descriptions of Ireland soar with a lyricism reminiscent of Joyce." Library Journal.

O'Brien, Jack, 1939-

O'Brien, Jack, 1939- **Jack** be nimble : the accidental education of an unintentional director / Jack O'Brien. Farrar, Straus and

Giroux, 2013. 368 p. **B**
ISBN 9780865478985
1. Theatrical producers and directors -- United States 2. Television producers and directors -- United States 3. Theater 4. Theatrical producers and directors 5. Autobiographies and memoirs
LC 2012048077
Includes index."

A memoir from Jack O'Brien, one of America's best-loved theater directors and winner of three Tonys".-- Provided by publisher.

"Highly recommended for lovers of the theater and those interested in acting and directing." Library Journal.

O'Brien, Tim, 1946-

O'Brien, Tim, 1946- **Dad's** maybe book / Tim O'Brien. Houghton Mifflin Harcourt, 2019. 400 p. **B**
ISBN 9780618039708
1. O'Brien, Tim, 1946- Family 2. Authors, American 3. Fatherhood 4. Fathers and sons 5. Advice 6. Autobiographies and memoirs
LC 2019002551

In 2003, already an older father, National Book Award-winning novelist Tim O'Brien resolved to give his young sons what he wished his own father had given to him--a few scraps of paper signed "Love, Dad." Maybe a word of advice. Maybe a sentence or two about some long-ago Christmas Eve. Maybe some scattered glimpses of their rapidly aging father, a man they might never really know. For the next fifteen years, the author talked to his sons on paper, as if they were adults, imagining what they might want to hear from a father who was no longer among the living. The result is Dad's Maybe Book, a funny, tender, wise, and enduring literary achievement that will squeeze the reader's heart with joy and recognition.

O'Connor, Flannery

★Gooch, Brad, 1952- **Flannery** : a life of Flannery O'Connor / Brad Gooch. Little, Brown and Co., 2008. 464 p. **B**
ISBN 9780316000666
1. Medical genetics. 2. Women authors, American -- 20th century 3. Friendship letter writing 4. Short story writing 5. United States -- Social life and customs -- 20th century 6. Milledgeville, Georgia -- Social life and customs -- 20th century 7. Biographies
LC 2008028504
National Book Critics Circle Award for Biography finalist, 2009.

Evaluates the ways in which the mid-twentieth-century novelist reflected American culture and influenced literature, in a portrait that includes coverage of her relationships with such contemporaries as Robert Lowell, Elizabeth Hardwick, and James Dickey.

O'Connor, Sandra Day, 1930-

Biskupic, Joan **Sandra** Day O'Connor : how the first woman on the Supreme Court became its most influential justice / Joan Biskupic. ECCO, c2005. x, 419 p. : **B**
ISBN 0060590181
1. United States. Supreme Court -- History 2. United States. Supreme Court Justices 3. Women judges -- United States 4. Women Supreme Court Justices 5. Women and politics -- United States -- History -- 20th century 6. United States -- Social life and customs -- 20th century 7. United States -- History -- 20th century 8. Biographies
LC 2005052103

Uses interviews with hundreds of legal and political insiders and information from formerly-private papers of the justices, chronicles the life and career of the first female justice on the United States Supreme Court.

"The author offers an insightful biography of perhaps the most influential associate justice in recent history." Library Journal.

Hirshman, Linda R. **Sisters** in law : how Sandra Day O'Connor and Ruth Bader Ginsburg went to the Supreme Court and changed the world / Linda Hirshman. HarperCollins, [2015] 320 p. **B**
ISBN 9780062238467
1. Ginsburg, Ruth Bader. 1933-2020 2. United States. Supreme Court Justices. 3. United States. Supreme Court. 4. Judges -- United States 5. Civil rights -- United States. 6. Women's rights 7. Women judges -- United States 8. United States -- Politics and government -- 1945-1989 9. Biographies
LC 2015002577

An account of the intertwined lives of the first and second woman Supreme Court justices examines their respective religious and political beliefs while sharing insights into how they have influenced interpretations of the Constitution to promote equal rights for women.

★Thomas, Evan, 1951- **First** : Sandra Day O'Connor, an American life / Evan Thomas. Random House, 2019. 416 p. **B**
ISBN 9780399589287
1. United States. Supreme Court Justices 2. Sexism 3. Women judges. 4. Women and politics -- United States -- History -- 20th century 5. Determination in women 6. Biographies
LC 2018040502

Based on exclusive interviews and access to the Supreme Court archives, an authoritative portrait of America's first female Supreme Court justice covers her convention-breaking achievements and role in shaping decades of American law.

"This highly readable biography shows the underlying factors motivating O'Connor both on and off the Court. It will have considerable popular appeal to both political scientists and historians, as well as general readers interested in how America's government interacts with the public in resolving political issues related to the law." Library Journal.

O'Faolain, Nuala

O'Faolain, Nuala **Are** you somebody : the accidental memoir of a Dublin woman / Nuala O'Faolain. H. Holt, 1998, c1996. 215 p. **B**
ISBN 0805056637
1. Women journalists -- Ireland 2. Journalists -- Ireland 3. Authors, Irish -- 20th century 4. Autobiographies and memoirs
LC 97029725
Includes columns originally published in the Irish times.
Originally published: Dublin : New Island Books, 1996."
This is a moving and painfully honest memoir." Library Journal.

O'Farrell, Maggie, 1972-

O'Farrell, Maggie, 1972- **I** am, I am, I am : seventeen brushes with death / Maggie O'Farrell. Alfred A. Knopf, 2018. 224 p. **B**
ISBN 9780525520221
1. Near-death experience 2. Accidents 3. Sick persons 4. Vulnerability. 5. Essays 6. Autobiographies and memoirs
LC 2017028597

Presents a memoir told entirely in seventeen near-death experiences stemming from a dangerous childhood illness, accidents, an encounter with a disturbed person, and the author's daily efforts to protect her daughter from the vulnerabilities of a high-risk condition.

"OFarrells intrepidness and determination are awe-inspiring, her experiences overwhelming, and her writing impeccable. This is a memoiristic tour de force." Booklist.

O'Grey, Eric

O'Grey, Eric **Walking** with Peety : the dog who saved my life / Eric O'Grey, with contributor Mark Dagostino. Grand Central Publishing, 2017. xv, 299 p., 8 unnumbered p. of plates : **B**

ISBN 9781478971160

1. Weight loss 2. Adopted dogs 3. Overweight men 4. Dogs 5. Autobiographies and memoirs

An inspirational speaker discusses how he overcame high-risk challenges with obesity and Type-2 diabetes by rescuing an equally at-risk shelter dog who shared his journey of recovery during a transformative year's worth of rehabilitating walks.

"This feel-good, easy-to-read book, coauthored with Dagostino and lightly sprinkled with scripture, is sure to inspire many readers." Booklist.

O'Keeffe, Georgia, 1887-1986

Drohojowska-Philp, Hunter, 1952- **Full** bloom : the art and life of Georgia O'Keeffe / Hunter Drohojowska-Philp. W.W. Norton, c2004. 630, 48 p. of plates : **B**

ISBN 0393058530

1. O'Keeffe, Georgia, 1887-1986. 2. Painters -- United States 3. Women painters -- United States 4. United States -- Social life and customs -- 20th century. 5. Biographies

LC 2003026071

Offers a portrait of the twentieth-century woman artist through discussions of her marriage to art photography pioneer Alfred Stieglitz, the impact of his infidelity on her psyche, and her relocation to New Mexico, where she created her signature works.

"O'Keeffe lived a long, adventurous, and profoundly productive life, and Drohojowska-Philp charts her triumphs over adversity in an involving, revelatory biography that attains the grand scope and depth her subject deserves." Booklist.

Robinson, Roxana **Georgia** O'Keeffe : a life / Roxana Robinson. Harper & Row, c1989. x, 639 p. : **B**

ISBN 9780060159658

1. O'Keeffe, Georgia, 1887-1986. 2. Artists -- United States 3. Women artists -- United States 4. Biographies

LC 89045061

"An Edward Burlingame book."

Includes index.

The first biography written with the full cooperation of the O'Keeffe family examines the artist's long and distinguished career, her personal relationships, and her significance in terms of American art and the women's movement.

"This biography, the first to draw on sources unavailable during O'Keeffe's lifetime and the first to be granted her family's cooperation offers a persuasive feminist analysis of the life and work of an iconic figure in American art. [The author's] detailed, sensitive critique of O'Keeffe's work . alternates with an absorbing, intimate narrative of O'Keeffe's personal life." Publishers Weekly.

O'Neil, Buck, 1911-2006

Posnanski, Joe The **soul** of baseball : a road trip through Buck O'Neil's America / Joe Posnanski. W. Morrow, c2007. 276 p. ; **B**

ISBN 0060854030

1. O'Neil, Buck, 1911-2006 Travel 2. Posnanski, Joe Travel 3. Negro leagues -- History. 4. African American baseball players 5. African American baseball coaches 6. First base players (Baseball) 7. United States -- Social life and customs -- 20th century 8. United States -- Description and travel. 9. Biographies

LC 2007296667

Documents the author's cross-country travels at the side of Negro Leagues champion Buck O'Neil, a journey during which the pair sought to recapture their love of the game, remembered O'Neil's history-making career, and explored the numerous challenges that the sport has overcome.

O'Neill, Eric, 1973-

O'Neill, Eric, 1973- **Gray** day : my undercover mission to expose America's first cyber spy / Eric O'Neill. Crown Publishers, 2019. viii, 291 p. **B**

ISBN 9780525573524

1. Hanssen, Robert. 2. FBI 3. Cyber intelligence (Computer security). 4. FBI agents 5. Moles (Spies) 6. Spies -- Russia

LC 2018038605

A cybersecurity expert and former FBI operative traces his undercover mission to capture a notorious Russian mole, describing how under the guise of a computer tech he gathered evidence against his own boss, exposing America's vulnerability to Russian cyberespionage.

O'Neill, Eugene, 1888-1953

Dowling, Robert M., 1970- **Critical** companion to Eugene O'Neill : a literary reference to his life and work / Robert M. Dowling. Facts On File, c2009. 2 v. (xiv, 818 p.) : **B**

ISBN 9780816066759

1. O'Neill, Eugene, 1888-1953 Criticism and interpretation 2. Dramatists. 3. Characters and characteristics in literature 4. Literature and society 5. Writing. 6. Biographies

LC 2008024135

A guide to the American playwright includes a chronology of his life, descriptions of the important personalities and issues of his day, and entries which analyze the characters, plots, language, and major themes of his works.

"These volumes are wonderfully organized and very easy to use. . . . Entries are of a length to provide a good background of O'Neill's works and life." Booklist.

Dowling, Robert M., 1970- **Eugene** O'Neill : a life in four acts / Robert M. Dowling. Yale University Press, 2014 448 p. **B**

ISBN 9780300170337

1. O'Neill, Eugene, 1888-1953. 2. Dramatists, American -- 20th century 3. Theater 4. Biographies

LC 2014014634

"A major new biography of the Nobel Prize-winning playwright whose brilliantly original plays revolutionized American theater".-- Provided by publisher.

"A well-rounded portrait of the playwright that can serve as a comprehensive introduction while also considering previously unknown facets of O'Neill's life and work." Library Journal.

Gelb, Arthur, 1924-2014 **By** women possessed : a life of Eugene O'Neill / Arthur Gelb and Barbara Gelb. G.P. Putnam's Sons, an imprint of Penguin Random House, 2016. 880 p. **B**

ISBN 9780399159114

1. O'Neill, Eugene, 1888-1953 Relations with women. 2. Dramatists, American -- 20th century 3. Men/women relations 4. Theater 5. Biographies

LC 2016008421

"A Marian Wood book."

In a final volume on the troubled life and brilliant works of a Nobel Prize-winning American playwright, readers are taken on a tour through both a magical moment in American theater and into the stormy world of a genius, following him though his great successes, his failures and the long 12-year period during which nothing he wrote was produced.

"This is a compelling examination of one of the 20th centurys most passionate and troubled minds, and a prime example of expert, diligent, and wryly editorial biographical research." Publishers Weekly.

O'Neill, Robert, 1976-

O'Neill, Robert, 1976- The **operator** : firing the shots that killed Osama Bin Laden and my years as a SEAL Team Warrior / Robert O'Neill. Scribner, 2017. 320 p. **B**

ISBN 9781501145032

1. Bin Laden, Osama, 1957-2011. 2. United States. Navy. SEALs 3. Qaida (Organization) 4. Special forces. 5. Afghan War, 2001- 6. Commando operations 7. War on Terrorism, 2001-2009 8. Afghanistan 9. Autobiographies and memoirs

LC 2017007867

One of America's most elite soldiers discusses his 400-mission career.

Oates, Joyce Carol, 1938-

Oates, Joyce Carol, 1938- The **lost** landscape : a writer's coming of age / Joyce Carol Oates. Ecco Press, 2015. 352 p. **B**

ISBN 9780062408679

1. Women authors, American 2. Growing up 3. Autobiographies and memoirs

LC 2016304587

The Lost Landscape is Joyce Carol Oates? vivid chronicle of her hardscrabble childhood in rural western New York State. From memories of her relatives, to those of a charming bond with a special red hen on her family farm; from her first friendships to her earliest experiences with death. Oates explores the world through the eyes of her younger self, an imaginative girl eager to tell stories about the world and the people she meets. While reading Alice in Wonderland changed a young Joyce forever and inspired her to view life as a series of endless adventures, growing up on a farm taught her harsh lessons about sacrifice, hard work, and loss.

"Given the popularity of Oates previous memoir, this spellbinding coming-of-age narrative, backed by an author tour and an extensive media campaign, will be a veritable readers magnet." Booklist.

Oates, Joyce Carol, 1938- A **widow's** story : a memoir / Joyce Carol Oates. Ecco, 2011. 432 p. **B**

ISBN 9780062015532

1. Women authors, American 2. Grief -- Psychological aspects 3. Widows 4. Marriage 5. United States 6. Autobiographies and memoirs

LC 2011381200

"In a narrative as searing as the best of her fiction, Oates describes the aftermath of her husband Ray's unexpected death from pneumonia. Scattershot moments stand out the day she cancels their 30-year subscription to The New York Times, unable to bear the sight of his favorite paper; her fury at the tulips, harbingers of spring, pushing through the snow (Too soon! This is too soon!); the night she weans herself from Lorazepam. A Widow's Story is the painful, scorchingly angry journey of a woman struggling to live in a house from which meaning has departed, like air leaking from a balloon. " Entertainment Weekly.

Obama, Barack

Alter, Jonathan The **promise** : President Obama, year one / Jonathan Alter. Simon & Schuster, 2010. 384 p. **B**

ISBN 9781439101193

1. Obama, Barack. 2. Democratic Party. 3. Presidents -- United States 4. Politicians -- United States 5. Democrats. 6. Self-confidence. 7. United States -- Politics and government -- 2001-2009 8. Biographies

LC 2010020438

The author of the best-selling book The Defining Moment: FDR's Hundred Days and the Triumph of Hope offers an up-close look at the Obama presidency, as that chief executive grappled with such problems as the hard-hit economy, the war in Afghanistan, health-care reform and more.

D'Antonio, Michael A **consequential** president : the legacy of Barack Obama / Michael D'Antonio. Thomas Dunne Books, 2017. 304 p. **B**

ISBN 9781250081391

1. Obama, Barack Influence. 2. Presidents 3. United States -- Politics and government -- 2009-2017 4. Biographies

LC 2016045029

In response to criticism and disappointment from the Left, the author offers a bold assessment of the lasting successes and major achievements of President Obama. Includes 47 charts and graphs. By a Pulitzer Prize-winning author.

"Obama's historic presidency during a time of great divisiveness in Washington and the country is an important time in American history, and DAntonio offers a terrific summary." Booklist.

Garrow, David J., 1953- **Rising** star : the making of Barack Obama / David Garrow. William Morrow, 2017 960 p. **B**

ISBN 9780062641830

1. United States. Congress. Senate 2. Presidents -- United States 3. African Americans 4. Politicians' families. 5. United States -- Politics and government 6. Hawaii 7. Chicago, Illinois 8. Biographies

LC 2017033946

The Pulitzer Prize-winning author of Bearing the Cross presents a definitive account of Barack Obama's life before his presidency, sharing insights into his formative years in Honolulu and Jakarta, his influential associates and his community work in Chicago.

"An exhaustive epic of Barack Obama's trajectory to the presidency." Kirkus.

Kantor, Jodi, 1975- The **Obamas** / Jodi Kantor. Little Brown & Co, 2011. 352 p. **B**

ISBN 9780316098755

1. Obama, Barack. 2. Obama, Michelle, 1964- 3. White House, Washington, D.C. 4. Presidents -- United States. 5. Presidents' spouses -- United States. 6. Husband and wife. 7. Politicians. 8. Washington, D.C. 9. Biographies

LC 2011940240

Explores the Obama family's transition into the White House, capturing the emotions and personalities beneath the public facade as the president and the First Lady deal with their new roles.

★Maraniss, David **Barack** Obama : the story / David Maraniss. Simon & Schuster, 2012. 448 p. **B**

ISBN 9781439160404

1. Obama, Barack Childhood and youth. 2. Obama, Barack Family. 3. Obama, Barack Travel Africa 4. Presidents -- United States 5. African Americans 6. Politicians' families. 7. United States -- Politics and government 8. Hawaii 9. Biographies

LC 2011052983

Based on interviews with the President himself and a wealth of letters, journals, and other documents, Maraniss' account spans Obama's childhood and political beginnings. Offering startling new insights, Maraniss reveals a man who struggled with his race and identity at a young age, but later embraced his strong character and ambition to rise to America's highest seat of power.

★Obama, Barack **Dreams** from my father : a story of race and inheritance / Barack Obama. Crown Publishers, 2007, c1995. xvii, 442 p. ; **B**

ISBN 9780307383419

1. Obama, Barack. 2. African American legislators 3. African Americans 4. Multiracial persons 5. Racism -- United States. 6. Chicago, Illinois -- Race relations. 7. United States -- Race relations. 8. Kenya -- Social conditions. 9. Autobiographies and memoirs

LC 2007271892

Originally published: New York : Times Books, c1995.

With new introd.

The son of an African father and white American mother discusses his childhood in Hawaii, his struggle to find his identity as an African American, and his life accomplishments.

"The author offers an account of his life's journey that reflects brilliantly on the power of race consciousness in America. . . . Obama writes well; his account is sensitive, probing, and compelling." Choice. [review of 1995 edition]

★Obama, Barack A **promised** land / Barack Obama. Crown Publishers, 2020. 784 p. **B**

ISBN 9781524763169

1. Obama, Barack. 2. Presidents -- United States 3. Determination in men 4. Hope 5. African American politicians 6. United States -- Politics and government -- 2009-2017. 7. United States -- Politics and government -- 2001-2009 8. Autobiographies and memoirs 9. Autobiographies and memoirs

LC bl2020046605

A deeply personal account of history in the making--from the president who inspired us to believe in the power of democracy.

Obama, Barack The **audacity** of hope : thoughts on reclaiming the American dream / Barack Obama. Crown Publishers, 2006. 375 p. **B**

ISBN 9780307237699

1. Obama, Barack. 2. United States. Congress. Senate 3. Democratic Party. 4. National characteristics, American. 5. Political science -- Philosophy. 6. Legislators -- United States. 7. African American legislators. 8. United States -- Politics and government -- Philosophy. 9. United States -- Politics and government -- 2001-2009

LC 2006028967

Includes index.

BCALA Literary Award for Nonfiction, 2007.

The junior senator from Illinois discusses how to transform U.S. politics, calling for a return to America's original ideals and revealing how they can address such issues as globalization and the function of religion in public life.

★Remnick, David The **bridge** : the life and rise of Barack Obama / David Remnick. Alfred A. Knopf, 2010. x, 656 p., [16] p. of plates : **B**

ISBN 9781400043606

1. Obama, Barack. 2. Democratic Party. 3. Democrats. 4. Presidents -- United States 5. African American politicians 6. Community organizers. 7. United States -- Politics and government -- 2001-2009 8. Biographies

LC 2010922697

Examines the experiences of Barack Obama's life and explores the ambition behind his rise to the presidency, from his relationship with his parents to how social and racial tensions influenced his philosophy.

"Writing with emotional precision and a sure knowledge of politics, Mr. Remnick situates Mr. Obama's career firmily within a historical context. He puts Mr. Obama's life and political philosophy in perspective with the civil rights movement that shaped his imagination, as well as the power politics of Chicago, and the politics of race as it has been played out, often nastily, on the state and national stages." New York Times.

Obama, Michelle, 1964-

★Obama, Michelle, 1964- **Becoming** / Michelle Obama. Crown, 2018. 400 p. **B**

ISBN 9781524763138

1. Presidents' spouses -- United States 2. African American women lawyers 3. African American lawyers 4. African American women 5. United States -- Politics and government -- 2009-2017. 6. Autobiographies and memoirs.

LC bl2018183323

An intimate memoir by the former First Lady chronicles the experiences that have shaped her remarkable life, from her childhood on the South Side of Chicago through her setbacks and achievements in the White House.

"There are no dramatic revelations and not much overt politics here, but fans of the Obamas will find an interesting, inspiring saga of quiet social revolutions." Publishers Weekly.

Slevin, Peter **Michelle** Obama : a life / Peter Slevin. Alfred A. Knopf, 2015 384 p. **B**

ISBN 9780307958822

1. Presidents' spouses -- United States 2. African American women 3. Politicians' spouses -- United States 4. Presidential candidates' spouses 5. Biographies

LC 2014041100

Here is the first comprehensive account of the life and times of Michelle Obama, a woman of achievement and purpose?and the most unlikely first lady in modern American history.

"She is one of his greatest assets in public office and an important foil to criticism that he is not black enough. Slevin delivers a somewhat fawning portrait, but when necessary, he is willing to criticize and reveal his subject's missteps." Kirkus.

★Swarns, Rachel L. **American** tapestry : the story of the black, white, and multiracial ancestors of Michelle Obama / Rachel L. Swarns. HarperCollins, 2012. 400 p. **B**

ISBN 9780061999864

1. Presidents' spouses -- United States 2. Ancestors 3. Families -- History 4. Generations -- United States -- History 5. Biographies

LC 2012454035

Illuminating the lives of the ordinary people who fought for freedom in the Revolutionary and Civil Wars, this intimate family history traces the compelling story of Michelle Obama's ancestors, taking readers on a journey from slavery to the White House in five generations that bears witness to our changing nation.

"The result is an engrossing book that demonstrates a lot of research, dedication, and care. Recommended to all readers interested in biographies that employ genealogical research, as well as readers in African American heritage and history." Library Journal.

Obrist, Hans-Ulrich

Obrist, Hans-Ulrich **Ways** of curating / Hans Ulrich Obrist with Asad Reza. Faber & Faber, 2014. 176 p. **B**

ISBN 9780865478190

1. Art museums 2. Art curators 3. Museum curators 4. Museums 5. Autobiographies and memoirs

LC 2014016970

The world's most influential contemporary-art curator explores the history and practice of his craft.

"An essential title for museum professionals, curators, and students aspiring to these professions." Library Journal.

Ocasio-Cortez, Alexandria, 1989-

Gupta, Prachi **AOC** : Fighter, phenom, changemaker / Prachi Gupta. Workman Publishing, [2019] 132 pages : **B**

ISBN 9781523510375

1. United States. Congress. House 2. Women politicians 3. Women legislators 4. Democrats. 5. Women and politics. 6. United States -- Politics and government -- 1989- 7. Biographies

LC bl2019037416

A celebratory biography of Alexandria Ocasio-Cortez (aka "AOC"), the youngest congresswoman in United States history, detailing not only her life but the movement she has energized.

"Gupta's reporting is as sharp and galvanizing as her subject. A beautiful tribute to a contemporary firebrand." Booklist.

Jones, Brenda (Communications director) **Alexandria** Ocasio-Cortez : the life, times, and rise of "AOC" / Brenda Jones and Krishan Trotman. Plume, 2020. xviii, 186 p. **B**

ISBN 9780593189856

1. United States. Congress. House 2. Hispanic American women 3. Women legislators 4. Women politicians 5. Feminists 6. New York City 7. United States -- Politics and government -- 21st century 8. Biographies

LC 2020012468

Not long ago, no one could even imagine a twenty-eight-year-old Latina upstart running for Congress representing Queens and the Bronx: It required facing the city's nearly all-white, all-male political machine. But since Alexandria Ocasio-Cortez graced the scene in all her bartending, tweet-talking, mold-breaking glory, the face of politics in the twenty-first century has changed. Today, Ocasio-Cortez is a foremost advocate for progress, whipping up support among her colleagues and gaining the secret admiration of her foes. She's jousting with an outrageous president and a conservative media sphere that place her under relentless attack. Why? Because they fear her gift for speaking truth to power.

Lopez, Lynda, 1971- **AOC** : the fearless rise and powerful resonance of Alexandria Ocasio-Cortez / edited by Lynda Lopez. St. Martin's Press, 2020. 240 p. **B**

ISBN 9781250257413

1. Ocasio-Cortez, Alexandria, 1989- -- Influence. 2. United States. Congress. House 3. Hispanic Americans -- Political activity. 4. Political participation. 5. Social justice. 6. Political change. 7. United States -- Politics and government -- 2017- 8. New York City 9. Essays. 10. Biographies.

LC 2020005577

Tracing the remarkable political career of the New York congresswoman and her role in a growing Puerto Rican activist movement, a diverse collection features essays by such contributors as Carmen Rita Wong and Maria Cristina Gonzlez Noguera.

"While there are several articles about Ocasio-Cortez, this book dives deep into her background, image, and ideas, and comes up with important insights. For readers interested in aspiring to politics." Library Journal

Ocker, J. W.

Ocker, J. W. A **season** with the witch : the magic and mayhem of Halloween in Salem, Massachusetts / J.W. Ocker. Countryman Press, 2016. 240 p. **B**

ISBN 9781581573398

1. Witches 2. Wiccans 3. Halloween 4. Tourism 5. Salem, Massachusetts -- History 6. Autobiographies and memoirs

LC 2016023647

Edgar Award-winning travel writer spends an autumn living in one of America's spookiest tourist destinations: Salem, Massachusetts

"The result is a fresh, fun glimpse of a town that has come to grips with its sordid history and prospered. Armchair travelers will enjoy the trip." Booklist.

Odetta, 1930-2008

Zack, Ian **Odetta** : a life in music and protest / Ian Zack. Beacon Press, 2020. 276 p. **B**

ISBN 9780807035320

1. Odetta, 1930-2008. 2. African American women singers 3. Civil Rights Movement 4. Folk singers -- United States. 5. Women singers -- United States 6. United States 7. Biographies

LC 2019056298

The untold story of the woman whose music and afro inspired a generation, whose voice provided a soundtrack for the unfolding civil rights movement of the 1950s and '60s.

"A much-needed biography of a crucial American artist and activist." Booklist

Odette, 1912-1995

Loftis, Larry **Code** name : Lise : the true story of World War II's most highly decorated woman / Larry Loftis. Gallery Books, an imprint of Simon & Schuster, Inc., 2019 320 p. **B**

ISBN 9781501198656

1. Odette, 1912-1995. 2. Women spies -- Great Britain 3. World War II 4. Secret service 5. Spies 6. Biographies.

LC 2018028438

"The extraordinary true story of Odette Sansom, the British spy who operated in occupied France and fell in love with her commanding officer during World War II--perfect for fans of Unbroken, The Boys in the Boat, and Code Girls."--Provided by publisher.

"Reading like a thrilling spy novel and the most exciting sort of nonfictionwell researched, well written, and fast paced enough to keep the pages turningthis will interest fans of the history of espionage, World War II history, military history, women's history, and biography." Library Journal.

Odum, Eugene P. (Eugene Pleasants), 1913-2002

Craige, Betty Jean **Eugene** Odum : ecosystem ecologist & environmentalist / Betty Jean Craige. University of Georgia Press, c2001. xxii, 226 p. : **B**

ISBN 0820322814

1. Odum, Eugene P. (Eugene Pleasants), 1913-2002. 2. Ecologists -- United States 3. Environmentalists -- United States 4. Environmentalism -- United States. 5. United States -- Environmental conditions 6. Biographies

"A captivating biography of one of the most influential ecologists of the twentieth century. An enjoyable book for both the professional interested in the history of modern ecology and the layperson interested in the impact Odum's vision of ecology has had on environmentalism." Choice.

Oelhafen, Ingrid von

Oelhafen, Ingrid von **Hitler's** stolen children : the shocking true story of the Nazi kidnapping conspiracy / Ingrid von Oelhafen & Tim Tate with Dr. Dorothee Schmitz-Koster. Collins, 2020. ix, 275 p. : **B**

ISBN 9781443460637

1. Oelhafen, Ingrid von. 2. Lebensborn e.V. (Germany) 3. World War II -- Children 4. World War II -- Germany. 5. Eugenics -- Germany -- History -- 20th century. 6. Kidnapping. 7. Germany -- History -- 1933-1945. 8. Autobiographies and memoirs.

Originally published under the title: Hitler's forgotten children. London : Elliott and Thompson, 2015.

Also published: New York : Berkley Caliber, 2016.

The author shares her story of being taken from her family in St. Sauerbrunn in what was then Yugoslavia and brought to Germany to be "Germanized" in the Lebensborn program.

"This riveting, raw, and heart-wrenching story of misplaced identity and one woman's quest to find peace and hope in the darkest of times will intrigue a variety of readers interested in a mix of history nestled among personal memoir." Library Journal.

Offutt, Chris, 1958-

★Offutt, Chris, 1958- **My** father, the pornographer : a memoir / Chris Offutt. Atria Books, [2016] 304 p. **B**

ISBN 9781501112461

1. Offutt, Chris, 1958- Family. 2. Novelists, American -- 20th century -- Family relationships. 3. Fathers and sons -- United States. 4. Pornography -- United States. 5. Secrets 6. Autobiographies and memoirs

LC 2015027503

After inheriting 400 novels of pornography written by his father in the 1970s and ?80s, critically acclaimed author Chris Offutt sets out to make sense of a complicated father-son relationship in this carefully observed, beautifully written memoir.

"Highly readable and moving, this title will enthrall readers from page one." Library Journal.

Oher, Michael

Lewis, Michael (Michael M.) The **blind** side : evolution of a game / Michael Lewis. W. W. Norton, 2006. 299 p. **B**

ISBN 9780393061239

1. Oher, Michael. 2. University of Mississippi Football. 3. Football -- Offense. 4. Football players. 5. Football -- Defense. 6. College sports -- United States. 7. Biographies

Follows one young man from his impoverished childhood with a crack-addicted mother, through his discovery of the sport of football, to his rise to become one of the most successful, highly-paid players in the NFL.

"The author describes the NFL's ever-growing obsession with left tackles as a means to counter defenders who seem to grow bigger, stronger, and more vicious each season. He juxtaposes that narrative with the unlikely story of [football player] Michael Oher. . . . The book works on three levels. First as a shrewd analysis of the NFL; second, as an expose of the insanity of big-time college football recruiting; and, third, as a moving portrait of the positive effect that love, family, and education can have in reversing the path of a life that was destined to be lived unhappily and, most likely, end badly." Booklist.

Okun, Alanna

Okun, Alanna The **curse** of the boyfriend sweater : essays on crafting / Alanna Okun. Flatiron Books, 2018. 224 p. **B**

ISBN 9781250095619

1. Knitting 2. Knitters 3. Handicraft 4. Hobbies 5. Essays 6. Autobiographies and memoirs

LC 2017045150

In a collection of essays about art, craft and mental health, the author shares the many lessons she has learned through crafting and how the art and physicality of making things has helped her cope with life's internal trauma.

Ollestad, Norman

Ollestad, Norman **Crazy** for the storm : a memoir of survival / Norman Ollestad. Ecco, c2009. 288 p. **B**

ISBN 9780061766725

1. Ollestad, Norman Childhood and youth. 2. Ollestad, Norman Family. 3. Ollestad, Norman, 1935-1979. 4. Airplane accident victims 5. Airplane accidents -- California. 6. Surfers -- California 7. Skiing

LC 2008053675

On February 19th, 1979, blinded by a blizzard, a small chartered plane crashed into the side of a massive mountain. Eleven-year-old Norman Ollestad, his father, his father's girlfriend, and the pilot were in the crash. After a nine-hour nightmare, only little Norman remained alive. Here, Norman Ollestad chronicles his harrowing experience and epic fight for survival.

"In the winter of 1979, the 11-year-old Ollestad survived a plane crash in which his father and his father's girlfriend were killed. Alternating with young Norman's nine-hour trek to safety are scenes from the year preceding the crash, when the boy took a surfing trip with his father through the jungle along Mexico's Pacific coast. The flashbacks sections are the most fascinating parts of the book, and Ollestad ably captures the contrast between his charismatically cool father, Norman Sr., and his bullying stepfather-to-be, Nick. [He] presents a captivating account of high-altitude disaster that nicely dovetails with his coming-of-age story in '70s California. Deep and resonant." Kirkus.

Olmsted, Frederick Law, 1822-1903

Rybczynski, Witold A **clearing** in the distance : Frederick Law Olmsted and America in the nineteenth century / Witold Rybczynski. Scribner, 1999. 480 p., 16 p. of plates : **B**

ISBN 0684824639

1. Olmsted, Frederick Law, 1822-1903. 2. Landscape architects, American 3. Landscape architecture -- United States -- History -- 19th century. 4. Parks -- United States -- History. 5. Parks -- Design and construction. 6. United States -- Civilization. 7. Central Park, New York City. 8. Prospect Park, Brooklyn, New York City. 9. Biographies

LC 99018094

ALA Notable Book, 2000.

J. Anthony Lukas Book Prize, 2000."

Rybczynski, celebrated for his sparkling prose as well as for his deep knowledge of architectural history, adeptly chronicles the life of the man who 'was a landscape architect before that profession was founded.'" Booklist.

Olson, Loren A.

Olson, Loren A. **Finally** out : letting go of living straight / Loren A. Olson, MD. Oak Lane Press, 2017 xiii, 286 p. : **B**

ISBN 0997961430

1. Olson, Loren A.. 2. Coming out (Sexual orientation). 3. Middle-aged gay men -- United States 4. Autobiographies and memoirs.

LC bl2017036116

The author relates his story of coming out at the age of forty, discussing how his sexuality evolved over the course of his life and offering advice to other men who are coming out in midlife.

"Olson's in-depth yet accessible, candid and useful guidance should prove popular with LGBTQ readers as well as those interested in psychiatry." Booklist.

Omar, Qais Akbar

Omar, Qais Akbar A **fort** of nine towers : an Afghan childhood / Qais Akbar Omar. Farrar, Straus and Giroux, 2013. 384 p. **B**

ISBN 9780374157647

1. Taliban 2. Rug industry and trade 3. Rug merchants 4. Child carpet weavers 5. Afghanistan -- Social conditions -- 20th century 6. Autobiographies and memoirs

LC 2012034566

Middle East Book Award, Honorable Mention, 2013

This memoir from a carpet designer in Kabul describes his childhood before the Mujahedin took over, being kidnapped, camping in caves and his employing neighborhood girls while teaching them literature and science in his secret shop under Taliban rule.

Onassis, Jacqueline Kennedy, 1929-1994

Kaplan, Alice Yaeger **Dreaming** in French : the Paris years of Jacqueline Bouvier Kennedy, Susan Sontag, and Angela Davis / Alice Kaplan. University of Chicago Press, c2012. 272 p. **B**

ISBN 9780226424385

1. Sontag, Susan, 1933-2004 2. Davis, Angela Y., 1944- 3. Americans in France 4. Intellectual life -- Women 5. College students 6. American women in France 7. France -- Social life and customs -- 20th century 8. Paris, France -- Social life and customs -- 20th century 9. United States -- Civilization -- French influences 10. Biographies

LC 2011026598

Looks at how the magical city of Paris, France, changed the lives and outlooks of three notable American women. By the author of The Collaborator: The Trial & Execution of Robert Brasillach.

Leaming, Barbara **Jacqueline** Bouvier Kennedy Onassis : the life of Jacqueline Kennedy Onassis / Barbara Leaming. Thomas Dunne Books, [2014] 352 p. : **B**

ISBN 9781250017642

1. Onassis, Jacqueline Kennedy, 1929-1994. 2. Celebrities -- United States 3. Presidents' spouses -- United States 4. People with post-traumatic stress disorder 5. Families of murder victims. 6. Biographies.

LC 2014026768

Traces the pattern of Jacqueline Onassis' life from her youth to her transformation into a deft political wife and unique First Lady, and examines her thirty-year struggle with PTSD after the assassination of her husband, John F. Kennedy.

"Leaming tells a heart-wrenching story of a woman who not only endured a horrific event but also struggled to recover and was often misunderstood as she eventually carved out a life of her own making." Booklist.

Leaming, Barbara **Mrs.** Kennedy : the missing history of the Kennedy years / Barbara Leaming. Simon & Schuster, 2002, c2001. x, 406 p. : **B**

ISBN 9780743227490

1. Onassis, Jacqueline Kennedy, 1929-1994. 2. Presidents' spouses -- United States 3. Men/women relations. 4. United States -- Politics and government -- 1961-1963. 5. Biographies

LC BL2002012436

"A Touchstone book."

Originally published: New York : Free Press, 2001.

A portrait of Jacqueline Kennedy during the thousand days of JFK's administration sheds new light on her life as both a woman and as First Lady, revealing struggles for herself, her marriage, and her husband's presidency.

"Asserting that Jacqueline Kennedy's role in shaping her husband's presidency has been under-examined, Leaming . offers a corrective in this intimate look at a very private woman. Initially inclined to keep herself as much in the background as possible, says Leaming, Jacqueline Kennedy became an increasingly visible and vocal first lady as she realized how effective she could be as an image maker. It's in this capacity that Leaming convincingly depicts her as being instrumental in shaping the course of her husband's administration." Publishers Weekly.

Onassis, Jacqueline Kennedy, 1929-1994 **Historic** conversations on life with John F. Kennedy / Jacqueline Kennedy ; interviews with Arthur M. Schlesinger, Jr., 1964 ; foreword by Caroline Kennedy ; introduction and annotations by Michael Beschloss. Hyperion, c2011. xxxii, 368 p. : **B**

ISBN 9781401324254

1. Onassis, Jacqueline Kennedy, 1929-1994 Interviews. 2. Kennedy, John F. (John Fitzgerald), 1917-1963. 3. Presidents' spouses -- United States -- Interviews 4. Presidents -- United States 5. United States -- History -- 20th century 6. Autobiographies and memoirs

LC bl2011025216

Issued in slipcase.

Presents the annotated transcription and original audio for the 1964 interviews with Jacqueline Kennedy on her experiences and impressions as the wife of John F. Kennedy, offering an intimate and detailed account of the man and his times.

Onwuachi, Kwame

★Onwuachi, Kwame **Notes** from a young Black chef : a memoir / Kwame Onwuachi with Joshua David Stein. Alfred A. Knopf, 2019. 288 p. **B**

ISBN 9781524732622

1. Top chef (Television program) 2. African American cooks 3. Restaurateurs. 4. Determination in men 5. Cooking, African American 6. Bronx, New York City 7. Nigeria 8. Autobiographies and memoirs

LC 2018036747

The Top Chef star traces his culinary coming-of-age in both the Bronx and Nigeria, discussing his eclectic training in acclaimed restaurants while sharing insights into the racial barriers that have challenged his career.

"A solid choice for fans of celebrity chef and pop culture memoirs." Library Journal.

Oppenheimer, Frank, 1912-1985

Cole, K. C. **Something** incredibly wonderful happens : an intimate biography of Frank Oppenheimer / K.C. Cole. Houghton Mifflin Harcourt, 2009. xiv, 396 p., 8 p. of plates : **B**

ISBN 9780151008223

1. Oppenheimer, Frank, 1912-1985. 2. Exploratorium 3. Physicists -- United States 4. Atomic bomb -- United States -- History 5. Nuclear physics -- Research -- United States -- History 6. McCarthyism 7. United States -- History -- 20th century 8. United States -- Social life and customs -- 20th century 9. Biographies

LC 2008052954

A portrait of the brother of famed physicist Robert Oppenheimer describes his own scientific contributions to the atomic bomb, his reemergence after the Red Scare, and his triumphant creation of the influential Exploratorium museum.

Oppenheimer, J. Robert, 1904-1967

Bernstein, Jeremy, 1929- **Oppenheimer** : portrait of an enigma / Jeremy Bernstein. Ivan R. Dee, c2004. xi, 223 p. : **B**

ISBN 1566635691

1. Oppenheimer, J. Robert, 1904-1967. 2. Nuclear physicists -- United States 3. Nuclear physics -- History. 4. Physicists -- United States 5. Jewish American men 6. Biographies

LC 2003066652

Traces the life and works of nuclear physicist J. Robert Oppenheimer, discussing his role in the creation of the atomic bomb.

"The author recounts Oppenheimer's eclectic life as it evolved in the US through his education and service at several prestigious institutions. The book is not a review of Oppenheimer's contributions to physics or the development of the atomic bomb; rather, it provides insight into the human side of a brilliant individual, all things considered. Of course, his leadership of the Manhattan Project, and his persecution by Congress for alleged communist sympathies, defined Oppenheimer's career. Bernstein provides personalized insights into both." Choice.

Bird, Kai **American** Prometheus : the triumph and tragedy of J. Robert Oppenheimer / Kai Bird and Martin J. Sherwin. A.A. Knopf, 2005. xiii, 721 p. : **B**

ISBN 0375412026

1. Oppenheimer, J. Robert, 1904-1967. 2. Oppenheimer, J. Robert, 1904-1967 -- Childhood and youth. 3. Manhattan Project (U.S.) -- History 4. Physicists -- United States 5. Atomic bomb -- United States -- History. 6. Science -- Political aspects. 7. Physics -- History -- 20th century. 8. United States -- History -- 20th century. 9. Biographies

LC 2004061535

National Book Critics Circle Award for Biography, 2005.

Pulitzer Prize for Biography or Autobiography, 2006."

The authors explore Oppenheimer's life from his youth as a child prodigy through his radical political activities in the 1930s, and on to the Manhattan Project and its political fallout. The humanity of the troubled man behind the porkpie hat emerges on every page of this unquestionably definitive account." Booklist.

★Monk, Ray **Robert** Oppenheimer : a life inside the center / Ray Monk. Doubleday, 2013. 848 p. **B**

ISBN 9780385504072

1. Oppenheimer, J. Robert, 1904-1967. 2. Physicists -- United States 3. Atomic bomb -- United States -- History -- 20th century. 4. Intellectual life -- 20th century. 5. Biographies

LC 2012046045

Explores the complex intellectual life of the innovator of the atomic bomb, providing coverage of such topics as his sympathy toward Communism, his lead over the Manhattan Project, and his Jewish faith.

Ormes, Jackie, 1911-1985

Goldstein, Nancy, 1942- **Jackie** Ormes : the first African American woman cartoonist / Nancy Goldstein. University of Michigan Press, c2008. ix, 225 p. : **B**

ISBN 9780472116249

1. Ormes, Jackie, 1911-1985. 2. Cartoonists -- United States 3. African American women cartoonists 4. African Americans 5. African American cartoonists 6. Biographies

LC 2007035395

Looks at the life and career of the first African American woman cartoonist.

"In the first book devoted to Ormes, Goldstein not only recounts with enthusiasm the trailblazing cartoonist's remarkable story from her birth in Pittsburgh to her celebrity-filled life in Chicago but also keenly analyzes Ormes' influential cartoons and the role black newspapers played in the struggle for racial equality. With a generous selection of Ormes' 'forward-looking' cartoons resurrected for the first time, this is one exciting and significant book." Booklist.

Orner, Peter

Orner, Peter **Am** I alone here? : notes on living to read and reading to live / Peter Orner. Catapult, 2016. 276 p. **B**

ISBN 9781936787258

1. Books and reading 2. Authors, American 3. Personal conduct 4. Autobiographies and memoirs

LC bl2016045831

A collection of 41 short essays about reading and life reflects the acclaimed writer's beliefs about the role of stories in shaping his identity and includes entries on the censoring of the works of Isaac Babel and Zora Neale Hurston, the paradoxical loneliness of Franz Kafka and the dubious insanity of Robert Walser.

"Book lovers will devour these genuine, personal tales about literature and reading." Kirkus.

Orr, Bobby, 1948-

Orr, Bobby, 1948- **Orr** : my story / Bobby Orr. Putnam Adult, [2013] 320 p. **B**

ISBN 9780399161759

1. Boston Bruins (Hockey team) -- History. 2. Hockey players -- Canada 3. Hockey. 4. Canada. 5. Autobiographies and memoirs

LC 2013024246

A personal account by the record-breaking NHL defenseman traces his rise from a small-town youth to one of the most acclaimed names in hockey and discusses the events that inspired his career, the financially ruinous betrayal by his agent, and his views on the game today.

Orwell, George, 1903-1950

Meyers, Jeffrey **Orwell** : wintry conscience of a generation / Jeffrey Meyers. W.W. Norton & Co., c2000. xvi, 380 p. : **B**

ISBN 039304792X

1. Orwell, George, 1903-1950. 2. Authors, English -- 20th century 3. Literature and society -- England -- History -- 20th century. 4. Politics and literature -- Great Britain -- History -- 20th century. 5. Journalists -- Great Britain 6. England -- Social life and customs -- 20th century. 7. Biographies

LC 00038020

Drawing on the collected works of the visionary writer, as well as interviews with family and friends and unpublished materials in the Orwell Archive, the author paints a vivid portrait of the writer who penned, 1984 and other modern classics.

"With wit and acumen, Meyers portrays a complex, eccentric, intelligent, and unbending man hard on family and friends, a writer of singular gifts, and a 'prophetic moralist' whose vision continues to illuminate society's dark side." Booklist.

Quinn, Edward, 1932- **Critical** companion to George Orwell : a literary reference to his life and work

/ Edward Quinn. Facts On File, c2009. xi, 450 p. : **B**

ISBN 9780816070916

1. Authors, English -- 20th century 2. Journalists -- Great Britain 3. Literature and society -- England -- History -- 20th century. 4. Politics and literature -- Great Britain -- History -- 20th century. 5. Great Britain -- Social life and customs -- 20th century 6. Biographies

LC 2008026727

A guide to the English novelist includes a chronology of his life, descriptions of the important personalities and issues of his day, and entries which analyze the characters, plots, language, and major themes of his works.

"This volume provides a review of Orwell's life and covers all his novels, nonfiction, and other writings. . . . It is a superb resource for those desiring an introduction to George Orwell, the man and the writer." Booklist.

Osborne, John, 1929-1994

Heilpern, John **John** Osborne : the many lives of the angry young man / John Heilpern. Alfred A. Knopf, 2007, c2006. xv, 527 p., 16 p. of plates : **B**

ISBN 0375403159

1. Dramatists, English -- 20th century 2. Mothers and sons -- Great Britain 3. Great Britain -- Social life and customs -- 20th century 4. Autobiographies and memoirs

LC 2006046575

Originally published: London : Chatto & Windus, 2006.

Based on intimate journals and letters, a biography of the late dramatist explores his youth, brief journalism career, work in the theater, and his turbulent personal life, and offers a critical analysis of his contributions to twentieth-century theater.

"Heilpern draws on Osborne's bleak private notebooks to generate acute readings of his often autobiographical plays. Sympathy for the man and admiration for the work don't blind Heilpern to his subject's outsized flaws. Osborne had a talent for invective and could be cruelly intolerant in matters large and small. He threatened theatre critics with physical violence by way of anonymous seaside postcards. Stung by his teenage daughter's indifference to high culture, he damned her as criminally commonplace and never spoke to her again. Without excusing such breathtaking abuse, Heilpern makes a compelling case for Osborne as a necessary truthteller and unyielding advocate of individualism in conformist times." The New Yorker.

Osbourne, Ozzy, 1948-

Osbourne, Ozzy, 1948- **I** am Ozzy / Ozzy Osbourne; Chris Ayres, contributor. Grand Central Pub., 2010 320 p. **B**

ISBN 9780446569897

1. Rock musicians -- England 2. Heavy metal music. 3. Men -- Personal conduct 4. Rock music 5. Autobiographies and memoirs

LC 2009937230

The Black Sabbath front man and reality TV star discusses his working class upbringing, his decision to quit a factory job for a life in music, his alcohol and substance excesses, his brushes with death and STDs, and the surreal experience of becoming a grandfather.

Otlet, Paul, 1868-1944

Wright, Alex **Cataloging** the world : Paul Otlet and the birth of the Information Age / Alex Wright. Oxford University Press, 2014. 384 p. **B**

ISBN 9780199931415

1. Otlet, Paul, 1868-1944. 2. Librarians 3. Information organization 4. Knowledge 5. Information management 6. Belgium 7. Biographies

LC 2013035233

"Wright ends his illuminating story in the present, where Otlet's thoughts about the connection of information to knowledge, and knowledge to insight, are still urgent." Kirkus.

Owen, Mark

Owen, Mark **No** easy day : the firsthand account of the mission that killed Osama Bin Laden : the autobiography of a Navy SEAL / Mark Owen with Kevin Maurer. Dutton, c2012. xiii, 316 p. : **B**

ISBN 9780525953722

1. Bin Laden, Osama, 1957-2011. 2. United States. Navy. SEALs 3. Qaida (Organization) 4. Afghan War, 2001- 5. Commando operations 6. War on Terrorism, 2001-2009 7. Special operations (Military science) 8. Afghanistan 9. Autobiographies and memoirs

LC bl2012031043

Examines the mission that killed Osama Bin Laden, details the selection and training process for one of the most elite units in the military, and describes previously unreported missions that illustrate the life and work of a SEAL and the evolution of the team after the events of September 11.

Owen, Mark **No** hero : the evolution of a Navy SEAL / Mark Owen, Kevin Maurer. Dutton, 2014. 336 p. **B**

ISBN 9780525954521

1. United States. Navy. SEALs 2. Former Navy SEALs. 3. Combat 4. Military missions 5. War 6. Autobiographies and memoirs

LC 2015300011

Recounts definitive moments from the author's career as a Navy SEAL, discussing the missions that had the greatest personal meaning for him and explaining the lessons and values he hopes to pass on to the next generation.

Owens, Delia

Owens, Delia The **eye** of the elephant : an epic adventure in the African wilderness / Delia and Mark Owens. Houghton Mifflin, 1992. viii, 305 p. : **B**

ISBN 0395423813

1. Owens, Delia. 2. Owens, Mark. 3. Wildlife conservation -- Africa. 4. Elephants -- Africa. 5. Wildlife conservationists -- United States 6. Autobiographies and memoirs

LC 92017691

Two naturalists describe how a battle to save the elephants of Africa turned into a fight for their lives when commercial poachers heard of their work.

Oz, Amos

Oz, Amos A **tale** of love and darkness / Amos Oz ; translated from the Hebrew by Nicholas de Lange. Harcourt, 2004, c2002. 538 p. **B**

ISBN 0151008787

1. Oz, Amos Childhood and youth. 2. Authors, Israeli 3. Antisemitism. 4. Zionism. 5. Family relationships. 6. Jerusalem, Israel 7. Autobiographies and memoirs

LC 2004007302

Originally published in Hebrew as Sipur al ahavah ve-hoshekh: Jerusalem : Keter, 2002.

The award-winning author recounts his boyhood in war-torn Jerusalem of the 1940s and 1950s, his mother's tragic suicide when he was twelve, his decision to join a kibbutz and change his name, and his participation in Israel's political upheavals.

Ozawa, Seiji, 1935-

Murakami, Haruki, 1949- **Absolutely** on music : conversations / Haruki Murakami with Seiji Ozawa ; translated from the Japanese by Jay Rubin. Alfred A. Knopf, 2016, c2011. 288 p. **B**

ISBN 9780385354349

1. Conductors (Music) -- Interviews. 2. Music -- History and criticism. 3. Writing 4. Male friendship 5. Autobiographies and memoirs

LC 2016008866

Originally published as Ozawa Seiji-san to, ongaku ni tsuite hanashi o suru: Tokyo : Shinchosha, 2011.

A deeply personal, intimate conversation about music and writing illuminates the perspectives and shared interests of the internationally acclaimed, best-selling author of Colorless Tsukuru Tazaki and His Years of Pilgrimage and his close friend, the former conductor of the Boston Symphony Orchestra.

"A work that general readers will enjoy and the musical cognoscenti will devour." Kirkus.

Pablo Cruz, Rosayra

Pablo Cruz, Rosayra The **book** of Rosy : a mother's story of separation at the border / Rosayra Pablo Cruz and Julie Schwietert Collazo. HarperOne, 2020. 240 p. **B**

ISBN 9780062941923

1. Pablo Cruz, Rosayra. 2. Schwietert Collazo, Julie. 3. Undocumented immigrants 4. Refugees 5. Separated friends, relatives, etc. 6. Mother and child. 7. United States -- Immigration and emigration 8. Collective autobiographies and memoirs 9. Multiple perspectives

LC 2019050658

A searing critique of the Trump administration-induced immigration crisis, written by a mother who was separated from her children and the American who helped reunite the family, shares timely insights into the injustices of today's migrant experience.

"This wrenching story brings to vivid life the plight of the many families separated at the U.S.-Mexico border. . . . Disturbing and unforgettable." Publishers Weekly

Pace, Kristin Knight

Pace, Kristin Knight **This** much country / Kristin Knight Pace. Grand Central Pub., 2019 320 p. **B**

ISBN 9781538762400

1. Yukon Quest International Sled Dog Race 2. Dogsledding 3. Women athletes 4. Transformations, Personal 5. Sled dogs 6. Alaska 7. Yukon Territory 8. Autobiographies and memoirs

LC bl2019005337

A memoir from one of the few women to have completed both the Yukon Quest and the Iditarod chronicles how she learned how to run sled dogs in one of the most remote places on earth.

"An honest, heartfelt, and exciting memoir and a must-read for all nature lovers seeking a glimpse into a truly Alaskan adventure." Booklist.

Padgett, Jason

Padgett, Jason **Struck** by genius : how a brain injury made me a mathematical marvel / Jason Padgett and Maureen Ann Seaberg. Houghton Mifflin Harcourt 2014 256 p. **B**

ISBN 9780544045606

1. Padgett, Jason. 2. Psychic trauma. 3. Synesthesia 4. Savant syndrome. 5. Social acceptance 6. Autobiographies and memoirs

LC 2013041065

After a violent mugging forever altered the way his brain works, the author, the first documented case of acquired savant syndrome with mathematical synesthesia, recounts how he overcame huge setbacks and embraced his unique gifts.

"A beautiful, inspiring and intimate account of Padgett's struggles and breakthroughs. An exquisite insider's look into the mysteries of consciousness." Kirkus.

Padilla Peralta, Dan-el

Padilla Peralta, Dan-el **Undocumented** : a Dominican boy's odyssey from a homeless shelter to the Ivy League / Dan-el Padilla Peralta. Penguin Press, 2015 320 p. **B**

ISBN 9781594206528

1. Undocumented immigrants. 2. Homeless boys. 3. Immigrants 4. Dominicans (Dominican Republic) 5. Autobiographies and memoirs

LC 2015460103

A Princeton University salutatorian describes his experiences as an undocumented immigrant youth in New York City, relating his efforts as a scholarship student in a private school that sharply contrasted with his street life in East Harlem.

Pagels, Elaine H., 1943-

★Pagels, Elaine H., 1943- **Why** religion? : a personal story / Elaine Pagels. Ecco, an imprint of HarperCollinsPublishers, 2018. 256 p. **B**

ISBN 9780062368539

1. Coping in women 2. Faith (Christianity) 3. Loss (Psychology) 4. Grief 5. Autobiographies and memoirs

LC bl2018183665

The author of "The Gnostic Gospels" draws on personal experiences and the perspectives of neurologists, anthropologists, and historians to illuminate the enduring capacity of faith in explaining and meeting the challenges of the twenty-first century.

"Pagels treats readers to the examined life behind her intellectual feats with extreme grace and depth. This luminous memoir strips religion to its elementary particles: love, suffering, and mystery." Publishers Weekly.

Painter, Nell Irvin

Painter, Nell Irvin **Old** in art school : a memoir of starting over / Nell Painter. Counterpoint Press, 2018. 320 p. **B**

ISBN 9781640090613

1. Artists 2. Senior artists 3. Adults -- School re-entry 4. African American women artists 5. Autobiographies and memoirs

LC 2017055407

National Book Critics Circle Award for Autobiography/Memoir finalist, 2018

A Princeton University historian describes her post-retirement decision to study art, a venture that compelled her to find relevance in the undervalued masters she loves, the obstacles faced by women artists and the challenges of balancing art and life.

Palahniuk, Chuck

Palahniuk, Chuck **Consider** this : moments in my writing life after which everything was different / Chuck Palahniuk. Grand Central Publishing, 2020. 288 p. **B**

ISBN 9781538717950

1. Palahniuk, Chuck. 2. Authors, American -- 20th century 3. Authors 4. Writing 5. Creative writing. 6. Autobiographies and memoirs

LC 2019036414

With advice grounded in years of careful study and a keenly observed life, Palahniuk combines practical advice and concrete examples from beloved classics, his own books, and a"kitchen-table MFA" culled from an evolving circle of beloved authors and artists, with anecdotes, postcards from the road, and much more.

"Fans will appreciate the insight into his own work, ... his tributes to friends and forebears, and how he delivers gracious and encouraging wisdom in his characteristically conversational style." Booklist.

Palak'ean, Grigoris, 1876-1934

Palakean, Grigoris, 1876-1934 **Armenian** Golgotha / Grigoris Balakian ; translated by Peter Balakian with Aris Sevag. Alfred A. Knopf, 2009. xli, 509 p. : **B**

ISBN 9780307262882

1. Palak'ean, Grigoris, 1876-1934. 2. Armenian genocide, 1915-1923 3. Armenians in Turkey -- History -- 20th century 4. Armenian genocide survivors. 5. Genocide -- Turkey -- History -- 20th century 6. Turkey -- History -- 20th century 7. Autobiographies and memoirs

LC 2008039957

On April 24, 1915, the author, along with some 250 other intellectuals and leaders of Constantinople's Armenian community, were arrested in the launch of a systematic attempt to eliminate the Armenian minority from Anatolia while countless deportation caravans of Armenians were tortured, raped, slaughtered and mutilated on their way to the Syrian deserts.

"Both a memoir and an attempt at a history of the genocide, it assumes considerable familiarity with Ottoman politics, but remains fascinating firsthand testimony to a monumental crime." The New Yorker.

Palladio, Andrea, 1508-1580

Rybczynski, Witold The **perfect** house : a journey with the Renaissance architect Andrea Palladio / Witold Rybczynski. Scribner, c2002. xvii, 266 p. : **B**

ISBN 0743205863

1. Palladio, Andrea, 1508-1580. 2. Architecture, Renaissance -- Italy. 3. Architects -- Italy 4. Biographies

LC 2002066838

"With its intriguing biographical detail, precise descriptions of design elements, and engaging insights into daily life in the 16th century, Rybczynski's book is a small but lasting gift to the reader." Library Journal.

Palm, Angela

★Palm, Angela **Riverine** : a memoir from anywhere but here / Angela Palm. Graywolf, 2016. 224 p. **B**

ISBN 9781555977467

1. Belonging 2. Discontent 3. Rural life 4. Friendship. 5. Indiana 6. Essays 7. Autobiographies and memoirs

LC 2015953721

An award-winning collection of essays on place, young love and crime reflects on the author's upbringing on the banks of the Kankakee River in rural Indiana, where annual floods shaped community dreams and her love for a boy who was sentenced to prison for life for murder.

"All in all, this is a memoir to linger over, savor and study." Publishers Weekly.

Palmer, Arnold, 1929-2016

Callahan, Tom **Arnie** : The life of Arnold Palmer / Tom Callahan. HarperCollins, 2017. 304 p. **B**

ISBN 9780062439727

1. Golfers 2. Golf -- Anecdotes. 3. Professional golfers -- United States 4. Biographies

LC 2017002983

A veteran sportswriter a author of His Father's Son: Earl and Tiger Woods shines a spotlight on one of the greatest golfers ever to play the game, Arnold Palmer.

"Sportswriter Callahan . breezily floats from story to story across the life of legendary golfer Arnold Palmer, describing dashing Palmers enduring appeal from the moment he burst onto the new television screens of the 1950s." Publishers Weekly.

Palmer, Arnold, 1929-2016 A **golfer's** life / Arnold Palmer, with James Dodson. Ballantine Books, 1999. xi, 420 p. : **B**

ISBN 9780345414816

1. Masters Golf Tournament 2. British Open (Golf tournament) 3. U.S. Open (Golf tournament) 4. Golfers 5. Golf. 6. Husband and wife. 7. Men/women relations. 8. Autobiographies and memoirs

LC 98051681

Includes index.

The respected golfer recounts his life on and off the course, from his upbringing as the son of a country club groundskeeper to his battle with cancer at the age of sixty-eight.

"Palmer's immense popularity is widely credited with rescuing professional golf in the late 1950s and 1960s. Written with humor and candor, the book recounts Palmer's friendships and rivalries with the greats of the game, his enduring marriage to Winnie Palmer, his legendary triumphs and disasters, and his battle against cancer." Library Journal.

Palmer, Arnold, 1929-2016 A **life** well played : my stories / Arnold Palmer. St. Martin's Press, 2016 224 p. **B**

ISBN 9781250085948

1. Golfers. 2. Personal conduct. 3. Golf.

LC 2016013252

The golfing master reevaluates his many life experiences, sharing details about familiar stories while offering new anecdotes and his time-tested insights into relationships, business success, and living a life of integrity.

"A heartfelt, sincere, miniself-portrait by a man who epitomizes class." Kirkus.

Palmer, Hannah, 1978-

Palmer, Hannah, 1978- **Flight** path : a search for roots beneath the world's busiest airport / Hannah Palmer. Hub City Press, 2017. 224 p. **B**

ISBN 9781938235283

1. Hartsfield-Jackson Atlanta International Airport. 2. Cities and towns -- Growth. 3. Airports. 4. Urban planning. 5. Land use. 6. Atlanta, Georgia -- History. 7. Clayton County, Georgia -- Local history. 8. Fulton County, Georgia -- Local history. 9. Autobiographies and memoirs.

LC 2016037303

"This thoroughly engaging memoir takes a deeply personal look at the neighborhoods around Atlantas Hartsfield-Jackson International Airport." Booklist.

Pamuk, Orhan, 1952-

Pamuk, Orhan, 1952- **Istanbul** : memories and the city / Orhan Pamuk ; translated from the Turkish by Maureen Freely. Knopf, 2005. xii, 384 p. : **B**

ISBN 9781400040957

1. Art and society. 2. Architecture and society. 3. Civilization, Islamic -- Byzantine influences. 4. Istanbul, Turkey -- Description and travel. 5. Turkey -- History. 6. Istanbul, Turkey -- Social life and customs. 7. Autobiographies and memoirs

LC 2004061537

National Book Critics Circle Award for Autobiography/ Memoir finalist

A portrait of one of the world's most complex and diverse cities interweaves the history of Istanbul with observations and reflections on the city's landmarks, art, people, institutions, and great spaces.

"The author mingles personal memoir with cultural history, and a fascinating read it is too for anyone who has even the slightest acquaintance with this fabled bridge between east and west." The Economist.

Panagore, Peter Baldwin

Panagore, Peter Baldwin **Heaven** is beautiful : how dying taught me that death is just the beginning / Peter Baldwin Panagore. Hampton Roads Pub. Co. : Distributed by Red Wheel-Weiser, 2015. 256 p. **B**

ISBN 9781571747341

1. Near-death experience 2. Spiritual journeys 3. Snow and ice climbing 4. Hypothermia 5. Autobiographies and memoirs

LC bl2015042483

In 1980, Peter Panagore had a near-death experience when he became trapped on a mountain while ice climbing in Alberta. In Heaven is beautiful, he describes that experience, the minutes he spent on the other side, and how it changed his life.

"Readers who have a fascination with near-death experiences and mysticism will be drawn into Panagore's remembrances of dying on the side of that mountain and the unexplainable feelings he encountered, and may find comfort in his assurance that death is not to be feared." Publishers Weekly.

Pao, Ellen K.

Pao, Ellen K. **Reset** : my fight for inclusion and lasting change / Ellen Pao. Spiegel & Grau, 2017. 288 p. **B**

ISBN 9780399591013

1. Whistle blowers 2. Women executives 3. Sex discrimination 4. Internet industry and trade 5. Autobiographies and memoirs

LC 2017301132

The co-founder of the award-winning diversity nonprofit Project Include shares the full story behind her landmark 2015 whistleblower lawsuit against powerhouse venture capitalist firm Kleiner Perkins, exploring what her case and refusal to settle revealed about Silicon Valley discrimination and complicity in revenge porn and online harassment.

Paperny, Anna Mehler

Paperny, Anna Mehler **Hello** I want to die please fix me : depression in the first person / Anna Mehler Paperny. The Experiment, 2020, c2019. 352 p. **B**

ISBN 9781615194926

1. Mental health 2. Depression 3. Mental illness 4. Women with depression 5. Autobiographies and memoirs

LC bl2020009832

Originally published: Toronto : Random House Canada, 2019.

Hilary Weston Writers' Trust Prize for Nonfiction finalist, 2019.

An investigative report on how depression is treated today shares stories from the author's personal journey with suicidal depression and draws on interviews with patients and experts to explore how current systems need to change.

"An eye-opening and humane book treatment of a difficult subject." Kirkus

Papp, Joseph, 1921-1991

★Turan, Kenneth **Free** for all : Joe Papp, the public, and the greatest theater story ever told / Kenneth Turan and Joseph Papp. Broadway, 2009. 648 p. **B**

ISBN 9780767931687

1. Joseph Papp Public Theater (New York, N.Y.) 2. Theatrical producers and directors -- United States 3. Jewish Americans 4. Actors and actresses -- United States -- Interviews. 5. Biographies.

LC 2008050887

An oral history of the New York Shakespeare Festival and the Public Theater draws on interviews with 160 celebrity contributors including Meryl Streep, James Earl Jones and Kevin Kline to trace the pivotal artistic contributions of producer and director Joe Papp.

"A wonderful book that clearly and powerfully shows that Papp's own story was the most enduring drama he ever produced." Kirkus.

Parazynski, Scott

Parazynski, Scott The **sky** below / Scott Parazynski, with Susy Flory. Little A, 2017. 284 p. **B**

ISBN 9781503936706

1. Former astronauts. 2. Adventurers. 3. Voyages and travels 4. Exploration 5. Autobiographies and memoirs

LC bl2017031594

A man who was a NASA astronaut for 17 years discusses his amazing life, including a global ozone-mapping mission, serving as John Glenn's crewmate, a death-defying spacewalk, becoming the only astronaut to summit Mt. Everest and much more.

"A genial, readable account of mountain climbing, spaceship travel, and other adventures." Kirkus.

Parcells, Bill, 1941-

Parcells, Bill, 1941- **Parcells** : a football life / Bill Parcells, Nunyo Demasio. Crown Publishing, 2014. 400 p. **B**

ISBN 9780385346351

1. National Football League. 2. New York Giants (Football team) 3. New England Patriots (Football team) 4. New York Jets (Football team) 5. Dallas Cowboys (Football team) 6. Professional football coaches 7. Professional football teams 8. Football 9. Autobiographies and memoirs

LC 2014027830

Bill Parcells may be the most iconic football coach of our time. During his decades-long tenure as an NFL coach, he turned failing franchises into contenders. He led the ailing New York Giants to two Super Bowl victories, turned the New England Patriots into an NFL powerhouse, reinvigorated the New York Jets, brought the Dallas Cowboys back to life, and was most recently enshrined in the Pro Football Hall of Fame. Taking readers behind the scenes with one of the most influential and fascinating coaches the NFL has ever known, PARCELLS will take a look back at this coach's long, storied and influential career, offer a nuanced portrayal of the complex man behind the coach, and examine the inner workings of the NFL.

Pardlo, Gregory

Pardlo, Gregory **Air** traffic : a memoir of ambition and manhood in America / Gregory Pardlo. Alfred A. Knopf, 2018. 256 p. **B**

ISBN 9781524731762

1. Pardlo, Gregory Family. 2. Fathers and sons. 3. African American families 4. Growing up 5. Personal conduct 6. Autobiographies and memoirs

LC 2017047413

"Endlessly introspective, wide-ranging, and lucid, Pardlos fearless inventory stuns with beautifully written, fully saturated snapshots of rich and complicated familial love." Booklist.

Parini, Jay

Parini, Jay The **art** of teaching / Jay Parini. Oxford University Press, 2005. xi, 160 p. ; **B**

ISBN 9780195169690

1. Parini, Jay. 2. College teachers -- United States 3. College teaching -- Vocational guidance 4. Autobiographies and memoirs.

LC 2004005443

In a deeply personal memoir filled with humor, encouragement, and hard-won wisdom about the teacher's craft, the distinguished critic and author furnishes valuable insights into the many challenges educators face, as well as a discussion of such topics as politics in the classroom, the importance of a disciplined approach to life, fostering relationships with students, and balancing one's teaching load with research and writing.

"The author offers musings about teaching's demands and what it takes to not lose one's other, creative self while meeting those demands in this memoir-cum-advice book for novice instructors. This warm guide should inform, entertain, and inspire young teachers as they seek to waken a student to his or her potential." Publishers Weekly.

Parini, Jay **Borges** and me : an encounter / Jay Parini. Doubleday, 2020 320 p. **B**

ISBN 9780385545822

1. Parini, Jay. 2. Borges, Jorge Luis, 1899-1986. 3. Authors -- 20th century. 4. Authors, Argentine 5. Americans in Scotland. 6. Vocation 7. Scotland 8. Autobiographies and memoirs

LC 2019038775

In 1971 Jay Parini was an aspiring poet and graduate student of literature at University of St Andrews in Scotland. One day his friend and mentor, Alastair Reid, asked Jay if he could play host for a "visiting Latin American writer" while he attended to business in London. That "writer" turned out to be the blind and aged and eccentric master of literary compression and metaphysics, Jorge Luis Borges.

"Essential for Borges's legions of fans, as well as those who enjoy literary memoirs by experimental writers whose works play a bit more loosely with the facts." Library Journal

Park, Sooyong

Park, Sooyong **Great** soul of Siberia : passion, obsession, and one man's quest for the world's most elusive tiger / Sooyong Park, foreword by John Vaillant. Greystone Books, 2015 340 p. **B**

ISBN 9781771641135

1. Siberian tigers. 2. Rare and endangered animals. 3. Animal behavior. 4. Zoologists. 5. Autobiographies and memoirs

LC bl2015049847

In The Great Soul of Siberia, renowned tiger researcher Sooyong Park tracks three generations of Siberian tigers living in remote southeastern Russia. Reminiscent of the way Timothy Treadwell (the so-called Grizzly Man) immersed himself in the lives of bears, Park sets up underground bunkers to observe the tigers, living thrillingly close to these beautiful but dangerous apex predators. At the same time, he draws from twenty years of experience and research to focus on the Siberian tigers? losing battle against poaching and diminishing habitat.

"Living in solitary confinement during the brutal winter months, waiting patiently for Bloody Mary to appear, Park felt he had gained access to 'the intimate depths of nature,' and he shares this intimacy with readers. A heartfelt memoir that reflects the author's respect and love for a wild and pitiless world." Kirkus.

Park, Yeonmi

Park, Yeonmi **In** order to live : a North Korean's journey to freedom / Yeonmi Park. Penguin Group USA, 2015 288 p. **B**

ISBN 9781594206795

1. Political refugees -- North Korea 2. Defectors. 3. Slaves. 4. Teenage girls 5. North Korea 6. Autobiographies and memoirs

LC 2015509352

A young North Korean defector and activist describes her father's imprisonment by the regime of Kim Jong-Il, her enslavement in China and her walk through the freezing Gobi Desert to freedom in South Korea, where she dedicated her life to human rights activism.

Parker, Bonnie, 1910-1934

Guinn, Jeff **Go** down together : the true, untold story of Bonnie and Clyde / Jeff Guinn. Simon & Schuster, 2009. 480 p. **B**

ISBN 9781416557067

1. Parker, Bonnie, 1910-1934. 2. Barrow, Clyde, 1909-1934. 3. Crime in the news media 4. Criminals -- United States 5. Thieves 6. Thieves 7. Biographies

LC 2008053342

"As Guinn relates, Bonnie and Clyde didn't commit many of the acts--particularly the murders--they were accused of. Their crime spree only lasted from spring 1932 to May 1934. But in the worst of the Depression, Americans ate up accounts of the Barrow exploits as a form of entertainment. The gang fed the newspapers terrific stuff, including the staged photo of Bonnie holding a gun and smoking a cigar. For folks living hardscrabble lives, the fact that the gang robbed the same bankers who were foreclosing on their farms made the exploits of Bonnie and Clyde even sweeter. Guinn succeeds marvelously in recreating the spirit of the times, the desperation of unemployment and financial ruin." PopMatters.

Parker, Charlie, 1920-1955

Crouch, Stanley **Kansas** City lightning : the rise and times of Charlie Parker / Stanley Crouch. It Books, 2013. 448 p. **B**

ISBN 9780062005595

1. Parker, Charlie, 1920-1955. 2. Smith, Buster, 1904-1991 3. Jazz musicians 4. Jazz music 5. Saxophonists. 6. Musicians 7. Kansas City, Missouri 8. New York City 9. Biographies

LC 2013015773

The first of two volumes based on the life of one of the most talented and influential musicians of the 20th century reaches back past the legend to reveal Charlie Parker the wunderkind who was raised in the midst of the Depression in the wide-open town of Boss Tom Pendergast's Kansas City.

Parker, Dorothy, 1893-1967

Meade, Marion, 1934- **Dorothy** Parker : what fresh hell is this? / Marion Meade. Villard Books, 1988, c1987. xix, 459 p., 16 p. of plates : **B**

ISBN 0394544404

1. Parker, Dorothy, 1893-1967. 2. Authors, American -- 20th century 3. Women and literature -- United States -- History -- 20th century. 4. Biographies

LC 87040189

She was known for her outrageous one-liners, her ruthless theatre criticism, her clever verses and bittersweet stories. But there was another side to Dorothy Parker: a private life set on a course of destruction through two divorces, a string of painful affairs, a lifelong problem with alcohol, and several suicide attempts.

Parker, Lara (Writer and editor)

Parker, Lara (Writer and editor) **Vagina** problems : endometriosis, painful sex, and other taboo topics / Lara Parker. St. Martin's Griffin, 2020 240 p. **B**

ISBN 9781250240682

1. Parker, Lara (Writer and editor) Health. 2. Endometriosis. 3. Women -- Health 4. Women -- Empowerment 5. Chronic pain. 6. Autobiographies and memoirs

LC 2020024208

With unflinching honesty, Lara Parker, the Deputy Director for BuzzFeed, shares her day-to-day challenges of living, working, and loving with chronic pain caused by endometriosis in this raw, darkly humorous, and hopeful memoir.

"A solid purchase for public and consumer health libraries." Library Journal

Parker, Quanah, Comanche chief, 1847-1911

Gwynne, S. C. (Samuel C.), 1953- **Empire** of the summer moon : Quanah Parker and the rise and fall of the Comanches, the most powerful Indian tribe in American history / S.C. Gwynne. Scribner, c2010. 336 p. **B**

ISBN 9781416591054

1. Comanche Indians. 2. Indians of North America -- Wars. 3. Battles. 4. Frontier and pioneer life -- The West (United States) 5. The West (United States) -- History -- 19th century. 6. The West (United States) -- History -- 1890-1945.

LC 2009049747

National Book Critics Circle Award for Nonfiction finalist, 2010.

Pulitzer Prize for General Nonfiction finalist, 2011."

A welcome contribution to the history of Texas, Westward expansion and Native America." Kirkus.

Parks, Rosa, 1913-2005

Brinkley, Douglas **Rosa** Parks / Douglas Brinkley. Viking, 2000. 246 p. ; **B**

ISBN 0670891606

1. Parks, Rosa, 1913-2005. 2. African-American women civil rights workers -- Montgomery, Alabama 3. Civil Rights Movement. 4. Social advocates. 5. Civil rights workers -- Montgomery, Alabama 6. Montgomery, Alabama -- Race relations. 7. Montgomery, Alabama 8. Biographies

LC 00035916

"A Lipper/Viking book."

A portrait of the African-American woman who is immortalized for refusing to surrender her bus seat to a white passenger examines who Rosa Parks was before, during, and after her historic act and how her action contributed to the end of the Jim Crow laws.

Theoharis, Jeanne The **rebellious** life of Mrs. Rosa Parks / Jeanne Theoharis. Beacon Press, c2012. 360 p. **B**

ISBN 9780807050477

1. Parks, Rosa, 1913-2005. 2. Civil Rights Movement. 3. African American women civil rights workers 4. African-American social advocates. 5. Civil rights workers. 6. Montgomery, Alabama. 7. Biographies

LC 2012031992

Examines the historical icon's six decades of activism, challenging perceptions of her as an accidental actor in the civil rights movement.

Parks, Tim

Parks, Tim **Teach** us to sit still : a skeptic's search for health and healing / Tim Parks. Rodale, 2011. xiii, 322 p. : **B**

ISBN 9781609611583

1. Parks, Tim Health. 2. Authors, English. 3. Chronic pain -- Treatment 4. Mind and body therapies. 5. Alternative medicine. 6. Autobiographies and memoirs

LC 2011008512

Originally published: London : Harvill Secker, 2010.

Recounts how the author took up breathing exercises and meditation when traditional methods failed to meet the needs of a debilitating health condition, a journey during which he began to question everything he once believed and gained an understanding of the relationship between the mind and body.

"In a hallmark of conversion narratives, the original mania reproduces itself as a mirror image: in the old days, hyperbolically anxious; in the new, hyperbolically anxious to enumerate the old anxiety. To his credit, Parks doesn't pretend otherwise. Moreover, his personal account, never preachy, engages some serious matters about contemporary life, notably what it's like to be a patient, as nearly all of us, sooner or later, are or will be." New York Times Book Review.

Parravani, Christa

Parravani, Christa **Her** : a memoir / Christa Parravani. Henry Holt and Co., c2013. 288 p. **B**

ISBN 9780805096538

1. Parravani, Christa. 2. Parravani, Cara. 3. Identity (Psychology) 4. Identical twins. 5. Women with depression 6. Grief in women. 7. Autobiographies and memoirs

LC 2012029499

Relates the author's life with her identical twin sister, Cara, the downward spiral due to depression and drugs that resulted Cara's early death, and the author's determination to defy the odds that she herself would die within two years of her twin.

"A finely wrought achievement of grace, emotional honesty, and self-possession." Publishers Weekly.

Parravani, Christa **Loved** and wanted : a memoir of choice, children, and womanhood / Christa Parravani. Henry Holt and Company, 2020. 224 p. **B**

ISBN 9781250756848

1. Parravani, Christa. 2. Mothers 3. Reproductive rights 4. Women college teachers 5. Parenthood 6. United States 7. Autobiographies and memoirs

LC 2020018815

The university professor and best-selling author of Her recounts how an unplanned pregnancy at age 40 was further complicated by state policies that limit women's access to reproductive choices and adequate child health care.

"This is a powerful account of what many women face in the U.S. today." Publishers Weekly

Parsons, Jack, 1914-1952

Pendle, George, 1976- **Strange** angel : the otherworldly life of rocket scientist John Whiteside Parsons / George Pendle. Harcourt, c2005. 350 p. : **B**

ISBN 015100997X

1. Parsons, Jack, 1914-1952. 2. Rocketry -- Research -- United States -- History 3. Occultists -- United States 4. Aeronautical engineers -- United States 5. United States -- Social life and customs -- 20th century 6. Biographies

LC 2004010666

Traces the life story of the rocket scientist whose work was dismissed after his accidental death revealed his occult beliefs, discussing his contributions to rocketry and his participation in the occult community of 1930s Los Angeles.

"Marshaling a cast of characters ranging from Robert Millikan to L. Ron Hubbard, Pendle offers a fascinating glimpse into a world long past, a story that would make a compelling work of fiction if it weren't so astonishingly true." Publishers Weekly.

Passarlay, Gulwali

Passarlay, Gulwali The **lightless** sky : a twelve-year-old refugee's harrowing escape from Afghanistan and his extraordinary journey across half the world / Gulwali Passarlay. HarperCollins 2016 256 p. **B**

ISBN 9780062443878

1. Passarlay, Gulwali. 2. Taliban 3. Refugees 4. Violence 5. Survival 6. Refugees, Afghan. 7. Afghanistan -- Social conditions -- 2001- 8. Autobiographies and memoirs

LC 2015042841

Documents the author's traumatic flight from Afghanistan to the West at the age of 12, describing how he escaped from Taliban recruiters that killed his father, his journey over mountains through eight countries and his endurance against hunger, brutality and imprisonment.

"A vivid, timely story of survival. If spies live in boredom punctuated by flashes of terrifying action, then refugees on the run live in constant high anxiety punctuated by flashes of horror and panic." Kirkus.

Pataki, Allison

Pataki, Allison **Beauty** in the broken places : a memoir of love, faith, and resilience / Allison Pataki. Random House, 2018 272 p. **B**

ISBN 9780399591655

1. Pataki, Allison. 2. People who have had strokes 3. Husband and wife 4. Convalescence 5. Caregivers 6. Autobiographies and memoirs

LC 2017058576

The best-selling author of The Accidental Empress describes how, while on a vacation during her pregnancy, her healthy 35-year-old surgical resident husband suffered a rare and life-threatening stroke that placed everything they had worked for in jeopardy, a struggle she navigated by writing daily letters to her husband that helped her make sense of challenges and fall in love with him all over again. Illustrations.

"In this powerful and immersive memoir, Pataki relives the harrowing year that followed her husbands stroke in June 2015." Publishers Weekly.

Patchett, Ann

Patchett, Ann **This** is the story of a happy marriage / Ann Patchett. HarperCollins, 2013 320 p. **B**

ISBN 9780062236678

1. Authors, American. 2. Women authors 3. Childhood. 4. Growing up. 5. Essays 6. Autobiographies and memoirs

LC bl2013040463

Inviting readers into her personal life, the New York Times best-selling author of State of Wonder and Bel Canto shares the stories of the people, places, ideals and art to which she has remained indelibly committed.

Patchett, Ann **Truth** & beauty : a friendship / Ann Patchett. Harper Collins, 2004. 257 p. **B**

ISBN 9780060572143

1. Patchett, Ann, 1963- Friends and associates. 2. Grealy, Lucy Friends and associates. 3. Friendship. 4. People with Ewing's sarcoma 5. Women with cancer 6. People with disfigurements 7. Autobiographies and memoirs

LC 2003067586

The author describes her intimate twenty-year friendship with the late Lucy Grealy, tracing their introduction at a writer's workshop, the integral part their friendship played in their writing careers, and her witness to Grealy's medical deterioration.

"As young writers. Patchett and Lucy Grealy began an intense friendship that lasted until Grealy's tragic death. With intimacy, grace, and humor, Patchett's memoir captures Lucy's exuberance and her roller-coaster struggles with disfigurement and depression." Booklist.

Patel, Eboo, 1975-

Patel, Eboo, 1975- **Acts** of faith : the story of an American Muslim, the struggle for the soul of a generation / Eboo Patel. Beacon Press, c2007. xix, 189 p. ; **B**

ISBN 0807077267

1. Interfaith Youth Core. 2. Muslims -- United States 3. Religious pluralism. 4. Interfaith relations. 5. East Indian Americans 6. United States -- Interethnic relations. 7. United States -- Religious life and customs. 8. Autobiographies and memoirs

LC 2007009064

The author, a young American Muslim of Indian background, juxtaposes his college years as an angry young radical with a description of how he came to see the possibilities of religious pluralism and founded the Interfaith Youth Core.

"The author, a founder of the Interfaith Youth Core, traces the personal journey that led to the group's formation and introduces readers to its philosophy." Kirkus

Paterniti, Michael

Paterniti, Michael **Love** and other ways of dying : essays / Michael Paterniti. Dial Press, 2015 xvii, 437 p. ; **B**

ISBN 9780385337021

1. Paterniti, Michael. 2. Self-discovery 3. Life change events 4. Essays 5. Autobiographies and memoirs

LC 2014033162

Presents a collection of essays that celebrate the many ways in which stories can profoundly change how people experience and see the world.

"A wide variety of places and people are given Paterniti's trademark scrutiny here, and the resulting essays are illuminating and pleasantly verbose." Library Journal.

Paterson, Katherine

Paterson, Katherine **Stories** of my life / Katherine Paterson. Dial Books for Young Readers, 2014. 288 p. **B**

ISBN 9780803740433

1. Paterson, Katherine. 2. Authors, American -- 20th century 3. Children's literature writing 4. Autobiographies and memoirs

LC 2013042628

An uplifting personal account by the Newbery Medal- and National Book Award-winning author shares intimate stories about the experiences that inspired her novels, from her early childhood in China to her marriage to a minister and relationships with four children.

"Written in a conversational style, these 'kitchen sink stories' will perhaps be received best by professional adults and readers who grew up with her books; much of what she recounts is about the distant past, courtship, and motherhood. What absolutely shines through is Paterson's warm, self-effacing humor, and the extraordinary humility of a writer who has won two National Book Awards, two Newbery Medals, and the Hans Christian Andersen Medal." Publishers Weekly.

Patterson, Floyd

★Stratton, W. K. 1955- **Floyd** Patterson : the fighting life of boxing's invisible champion / W. K. Stratton. Houghton Mifflin Harcourt, 2012. 286 p. **B**

ISBN 9780151014309

1. Patterson, Floyd. 2. Boxers (Sports) -- United States 3. African American boxers 4. Boxing. 5. Biographies

LC 2012017319

Documents the inspiring story of the civil rights activist, Olympic gold medalist, and history's youngest World Heavyweight Champion, placing his career against a backdrop of boxing's golden age while analyzing misunderstood aspects of his character.

"Stratton's attention to detail is impressive, and he seems to have uncovered every little tidbit about Patterson's life both in and out of the ring, making this warm biography a must for boxing fanatics. An engaging, breezy portrait of an underappreciated boxing giant." Kirkus.

Patterson, Jodie, 1970-

Patterson, Jodie, 1970- The **bold** world : a memoir of family and transformation / Jodie Patterson. Ballantine Books, 2019 352 p. **B**

ISBN 9780399179013

1. Transgender persons 2. Intersectionality 3. Mother and child 4. Social acceptance 5. Autobiographies and memoirs

LC 2018039475

A respected activist, entrepreneur, and writer draws on inspiration from her ten-year-old transgender child in an exploration of identity, gender, authenticity, and race as they have shaped generations of her African American family.

Patterson, Pat

Patterson, Pat **Accepted** : how the first gay superstar changed WWE / Pat Patterson with Bertrand Hebert, foreword by Vince McMahon. ECW Press, 2016 320 p. **B**

ISBN 9781770412934

1. World Wrestling Entertainment, Inc. 2. Professional wrestlers. 3. Professional wrestling. 4. Entertainers. 5. Entertainment industry and trade 6. Autobiographies and memoirs

LC bl2016032588

The WWE Hall of Famer describes how he was rejected by his family for his sexual orientation and moved to the United States in the 1960s, where, in spite of language and discriminatory challenges, he applied his creative and athletic talents to climb to the upper ranks of sports entertainment.

"Patterson is a very good storyteller, and his tales from the road about well-known personalities such as the fun-seeking Andre the Giant and the forever-young-at-heart Ray Stevens are wonderfully told, and many of the wrestlers time-killing pranks are laugh-out-loud funny." Publishers Weekly.

Patton, George S., 1885-1945

Brighton, Terry **Patton,** Montgomery, Rommel : masters of war / Terry Brighton. Crown Publishers, [2009], c2008. xix, 426 p. : **B**

ISBN 9780307461544

1. Montgomery of Alamein, Bernard Law Montgomery, Viscount, 1887-1976. 2. Rommel, Erwin, 1891-1944. 3. Generals -- United States 4. World War II. 5. Military campaigns. 6. Military history. 7. North Africa. 8. Europe.

LC bl2009031129

Originally published: Masters of battle.

London : Viking, 2008.

An account of World War II as it was experienced by three influential commanders draws on primary source materials to evaluate their explosive relationships with one another, their command talents, and their enthusiasm for publicity.

"Brighton shows how during the period between the wars, each refined his skills, which included reading one another's published treatises on the subject of mobile warfare. The author pulls no punches in revealing their flaws as well. Very highly recommended." Library Journal.

Patton, George S., 1885-1945 **War** as I knew it / George S. Patton, Jr. ; annotated by Paul D. Harkins ; with a new introduction by Rick Atkinson. Houghton Mifflin Co., 1995, c1947. xxii, 425 p. : **B**

ISBN 0395735297

1. Patton, George S., 1885-1945. 2. United States. Army 3. Western Front (World War II) 4. Generals -- United States 5. Battles 6. World War II 7. North Africa -- History -- 20th century 8. Europe -- History -- 20th century 9. Autobiographies and memoirs

LC 95196167

Originally published: Boston, MA : Houghton Mifflin, 1947.

Transcripts from General Patten's war diary covering his campaigns in Sicily, France, and Germany.

Paul, Pamela

Paul, Pamela **My** life with Bob : flawed heroine keeps book of books, plot ensues. / Pamela Paul. Henry Holt and Company, 2017. 272 p. **B**

ISBN 9781627796316

1. Books. 2. Books and reading 3. Reading. 4. Introspection. 5. Autobiographies and memoirs

LC 2016046990

The New York Times Book Review editor reveals how for 28 years she has maintained a personal journal recording every book she has ever read, sharing literature-influenced experiences that shaped her personal and professional life.

"Paul is inspired to question why we read, how we read, what we read, and how reading helps us create our own narratives. Readers will be drawn to this witty and authentic tribute to the extraordinary power of books." Publishers Weekly.

Paul, the Apostle, Saint

Borg, Marcus J. The **first** Paul : reclaiming the radical visionary behind the church's conservative icon / Marcus J. Borg and John Dominic Crossan. HarperOne, 2009. 240 p. **B**

ISBN 9780061430725

1. Bible. Epistles of Paul Criticism and interpretation 2. Apostles 3. Religious leaders. 4. Christianity. 5. Religion. 6. Biographies

LC bl2009001936

Challenges mainstream beliefs about the apostle Paul that credit him with supporting early church agendas on such issues as slavery, the subordination of women, and homosexuality.

"The great epistolary apostle is revealed as neither anti-Semitic, anti-sex, nor misogynist, but a preacher of social and political equality." Booklist.

Murphy-O'Connor, J. (Jerome), 1935- **Paul** : a critical life / Jerome Murphy-O'Connor. Oxford University Press, 1996. xvi, 416 p. : **B**

ISBN 9780198267492

1. Christian saints -- Tarsus, Turkey 2. Apostles 3. Evangelists 4. Converts to Christianity from Judaism. 5. Biographies

LC 95049173

"This is likely to become the standard work on Paul's life for the next generation and is warmly recommended as such." Choice.

Wright, N. T. (Nicholas Thomas) **Paul** : a biography / N.T. Wright. HarperOne, 2018. 464 p. **B**

ISBN 9780061730580

1. Paul, the Apostle, Saint. 2. Bible. New Testament 3. Christian saints. 4. Christian church history -- Primitive and early church, 30-600 5. Apostles. 6. Biographies

LC 2017027846

In this definitive biography, renowned Bible scholar, Anglican bishop, and bestselling author N. T. Wright offers a radical look at the apostle Paul, illuminating the humanity and remarkable achievements of this intellectual who invented Christian theology?transforming a faith and changing the world.

"A very human Paul, brought to life by an experienced teacher and pastoran excellent introduction for general readers." Kirkus.

Pauling, Linus, 1901-1994

Pauling, Linus, 1901-1994 **Linus** Pauling : in his own words : selected writings, speeches, and interviews / edited by Barbara Marinacci ; introduction by Linus Pauling. Simon & Schuster, c1995. 320 p. ; **B**

ISBN 0684813874

1. Pauling, Linus, 1901-1994. 2. Science -- History. 3. Scientists -- United States 4. Biographies

LC 95031123

"A Touchstone book."

Selected writings share the late scientist's views on chemistry, education, the structure of matter, proteins, nuclear politics, fallout, and nutritional medicine.

"This book attempts to follow the life and career of Dr. Pauling through his own writings, interspersed with narrative by the editor. The book succeeds wonderfully. Linus Pauling is unique among modern scientists, both for winning two Nobel Prizes and for his political and social views. Through his writings, the breadth and depth of his work become clear to the reader." Science Books & Films.

Paulsen, Gary

★Paulsen, Gary **Winterdance** : the fine madness of running the Iditarod / Gary Paulsen. Harcourt Brace, c1994. 256 p. ; **B**

ISBN 9780151262274

1. Paulsen, Gary. 2. Iditarod Trail Sled Dog Race, Alaska. 3. Mushers -- Alaska 4. Endurance sports 5. Autobiographies and memoirs

LC 93042096

Paulsen and his team of dogs endured snowstorms, frostbite, dogfights, moose attacks, sleeplessness, and hallucinations in the relentless push to go on.

"This book is primarily an account of Paulsen's first Iditarod and its frequent life-threatening disasters. However, the book is more than a tabulation of tribulations; it is a meditation on the extraordinary attraction this race holds for some men and women." Library Journal.

Pavlychenko, Liudmyla Mykhailivna, 1916-1974

Pavlychenko, Liudmyla Mykhailivna, 1916-1974 **Lady** Death : the memoirs of Stalin's sniper / Lyudmila Pavlichenko ; foreword by Martin Pegler; translated by David Foreman; edited by Alla Igorevna Begunova. Greenhill Books, 2018, c2015. 252 p. **B**

ISBN 9781784382704

1. Soviet Union. Army. 2. Snipers 3. World War II -- Soviet Union. 4. Women soldiers 5. Ukraine 6. Autobiographies and memoirs

LC bl2018184916

"First published by Veche Publishers (Moscow) in 2015 as 'I - sniper : in battles for Sevastopol and Odessa'"--Title page verso.

The wartime memoir of Lyudmila Pavlichenko is a remarkable document: the publication of an English language edition is a significant coup. Pavlichenko was World War II's best scoring sniper and had a varied wartime career that included trips to England and America.In June 1941, when Hitler launched Operation Barbarossa, she left her university studies, ignored the offer of a position as a nurse, to become one of Soviet Russia's 2000 female snipers.Less than a year later she had 309 recorded kills, including 29 enemy sniper kills. She was withdrawn from active duty after being injured. She was also regarded as a key heroic figure for the war effort.

"Lady Death reads like a novel, and it is a rare war story by a patriot whose determination to fight for her country is inspiring and should firmly put to rest any doubts about women in combat. There is no question that this is a significant historical document, but it is also a gripping narrative (which includes her memories of travel in the U.S.) that devotees of history, especially WWII, should absolutely not miss." Booklist.

Paxson, Margaret

Paxson, Margaret The **plateau** / Maggie Paxson. Riverhead Books, [2019] 368 p. **B**

ISBN 9781594634758

1. Paxson, Margaret. 2. Villages -- France 3. Refugees 4. Altruism 5. Asylum, Right of 6. Le Chambon-sur-Lignon, France 7. France -- History -- 20th century 8. Autobiographies and memoirs

LC 2018050747

In a remote pocket of Nazi-held France, ordinary people risked their lives to rescue many hundreds of strangers, mostly Jewish children. Was this a fluke of history, or something more? Anthropologist Maggie Paxson, certainties shaken by years of studying strife, arrives on the Plateau to explore this phenomenon: What are the traits that make a group choose selflessness?

"Throughout, Paxson keeps asking questions and probing, never settling for assumptions. An elegant, intensive study that grapples with an enormous idea: how to be good." Kirkus.

Payne, Ethel L.

Morris, James McGrath **Eye** on the struggle : Ethel Payne, the first lady of the black press / James McGrath Morris. Amistad, 2015 x, 466 p., 16 unnumbered p. of plates : **B**

ISBN 9780062198853

1. Women journalists 2. African American women 3. Civil rights workers 4. Biographies

LC 2015296496

Describes the life and career of the journalist and network news commentator who publicly asked President Eisenhower to support desegregation and covered such important civil rights events as the Montgomery Bus Boycott and the desegregation crisis in Little Rock.

"Morris straight-ahead chronicle of Paynes extraordinary front-line life reveals how invincible and incisive she was as she forthrightly combined journalism with advocacy and made the most of the box seat on history she fought so ardently and courageously to occupy." Booklist.

Peace, Robert, 1980-2010

★Hobbs, Jeff, 1980- The **short** and tragic life of Robert Peace : a brilliant young man who left Newark for the Ivy League but did not survive / Jeff Hobbs. Scribner, 2014. 384 p. **B**

ISBN 9781476731902

1. Peace, Robert, 1980-2010. 2. Hobbs, Jeff, 1980- 3. Yale University 4. Street life 5. Working class African Americans 6. African American college students 7. College students 8. Newark, New Jersey 9. New Haven, Connecticut 10. Biographies

LC 2014001213

"Writing with novelistic detail and deep insight, Hobbs, who was Peace's roommate at Yale, registers the disadvantages his friend faced while avoiding hackneyed fatalism and sociology. Hobbs reveals a man whose singular experience and charisma made him simultaneously an outsider and a leader in both New Haven and Newark." Publishers Weekly.

Peale, Charles Willson, 1741-1827

Staiti, Paul J. **Of** arms and artists : the American Revolution through painters' eyes / Paul Staiti. Bloomsbury Press, 2016. 320 p. **B**

ISBN 9781632864659

1. Peale, Charles Willson, 1741-1827. 2. Copley, John Singleton, 1738-1815. 3. Trumbull, John, 1756-1843. 4. West, Benjamin, 1738-1820. 5. Stuart, Gilbert, 1755-1828. 6. American Revolution, 1775-1783 7. Painting -- Political aspects -- United States -- History -- 18th century. 8. Art history 9. Art and history 10. United States -- History -- Revolution, 1775-1783

LC 2016007703

A vibrant and original perspective of the American Revolution through the stories of five great artists of the Revolutionary period who contributed greatly to America's founding spirit paints a new picture of this era, deepening our understanding of the whirlwind out of which the United States emerged.

Peck, Annie S. (Annie Smith), 1850-1935

Kimberley, Hannah A **woman's** place is at the top : a biography of Annie Smith Peck, queen of the climbers / Hannah Kimberley. St. Martin's Press, [2017] 320 p. **B**

ISBN 9781250084002

1. Peck, Annie S. (Annie Smith), 1850-1935. 2. Women mountaineers. 3. Women explorers. 4. Gender role. 5. Mountaineering -- History. 6. Biographies.

LC 2017010843

Presents the life of the little-known early feminist, independent thinker and accomplished adventurer who became a political speaker and writer for women's suffrage and was the first person to conquer Mount Huascaran and raced Hiram Bingham to climb Mount Coropuna in 1911.

"Peck was a dynamic and compelling woman, and her story will be hard to resist for armchair travelers and fans of hidden history." Booklist.

Pelosi, Nancy, 1940-

★Ball, Molly **Pelosi** / Molly Ball. Henry Holt & Comapny, 2020. 345 p. **B**

ISBN 9781250252869

1. United States. Congress. House Speakers 2. United States. Congress. House Leadership -- History 3. Women legislators 4. Women politicians 5. Leadership in women 6. Influence (Psychology) 7. United States -- Politics and government 8. Biographies

LC 2020930617

She's the iconic leader who puts Donald Trump in his place, the woman with the toughness to take on a lawless president and defend American democracy. Ever since the Democrats took back the House in the 2018 midterm elections, Nancy Pelosi has led the opposition with strategic mastery and inimitable elan. It's a remarkable comeback for the veteran politician who for years was demonized by the right and taken for granted by many in her own party. Ball's portrait takes readers inside the life and times of this historic and underappreciated figure. Based on exclusive interviews with the Speaker and deep background reporting, Ball shows Pelosi through a thoroughly modern lens to explain how this extraordinary woman has met her moment.

"A cradle-to-today portrait of a master politician. . . . A top-notch political biography." Kirkus.

Pelosi, Nancy, 1940- **Know** your power : a message to America's daughters / Nancy Pelosi with Amy Hill Hearth. Doubleday, 2008. 192 p. **B**

ISBN 9780385525862

1. United States. Congress. House Speakers 2. United States. Congress. House 3. Women legislators -- United States 4. Legislators -- United States 5. Women -- Personal conduct 6. Inspiration in women 7. United States -- Politics and government -- 21st century 8. Autobiographies and memoirs

LC bl2008011863

One of America's most powerful political leaders describes her personal odyssey to the heights of American political power as the first female Speaker of the House and offers encouragement and inspiration to women to follow their dreams.

"In this graceful personal and political history, Pelosi describes growing up as the daughter of a congressman in an Italian-American Catholic world . and her burgeoning political interest. Pelosi's book is a simply crafted acknowledgment of the support of her family, mentors and helpful colleagues without rhetorical flourishes, insider scandal or intimate revelationsa gentle account from a tough politician." Publishers Weekly.

Pembroke, William Marshal, Earl of, 1144?-1219

Asbridge, Thomas S. The **greatest** knight : the remarkable life of William Marshal, the power behind five English thrones / Thomas Asbridge. Ecco Press, 2014. 256 p. **B**

ISBN 9780062262059

1. Knights and knighthood. 2. England -- History -- Medieval period, 1066-1485. 3. Great Britain -- History -- 12th century. 4. Biographies

LC 2015431306

A renowned scholar brings to life medieval England's most celebrated knight, William Marshal - who served under such rulers as Queen Eleanor of Aquitaine, Richard the Lionheart and his infamous brother, John - providing an unprecedented and intimate view of this age and the legendary warrior class that shaped it.

"Matters did not improve after Henry's death, so Marshal's career comes across as a relentless series of intrigues, battles, atrocities, truces quickly broken, internal revolts and treason that often included Marshal for reasons the author must guess because historical evidence is lacking. A valuable biography of an important figure in a distant, violent, barely comprehensible era." Kirkus.

Penn, William, 1644-1718

Murphy, Andrew R., 1967- **William** Penn : a life / Andrew R. Murphy. Oxford University Press, 2019. 460 p. **B**

ISBN 9780190234249

1. Pioneers 2. Quakers 3. Colonies 4. Colonialism 5. Pennsylvania -- History -- Colonial period, 1600-1775 6. Great Britain -- Politics and government -- 1660-1688 7. Biographies

LC 2018016591

The first major biography of William Penn in more than 40 years, and the first to make full use of Penn's private papers, presents a complex portrait of a man who, despite his importance, has remained an elusive figure.

"Well crafted and thoroughly researched, the writing style here is more academic than narrative. Yet, for anyone desiring comprehensive knowledge of Penn's life, this is the book to read." Library Journal.

Pepin, Jacques, 1935-

Pepin, Jacques, 1935- The **apprentice** : my life in the kitchen / Jacques Pépin. Houghton Mifflin, 2003. viii, 318 p. : **B**

ISBN 0618197370

1. French Culinary Institute. 2. Cooking. 3. Cooks -- France 4. Food habits -- France. 5. Family relationships. 6. Autobiographies and memoirs

LC 2002192158

Includes index."

Pepin relates how his interest in food and culinary techniques developed into passions for cooking and teaching. He does this deftly, neatly capturing personalities and events with clear, concise writing." Library Journal.

Pepys, Samuel, 1633-1703

★Pepys, Samuel, 1633-1703 The **diary** of Samuel Pepys / edited and with a preface by Richard Le Gallienne; introduction by Robert Louis Stevenson. Modern Library, 2001. xxxv, 310 p. ; **B**

ISBN 0679642218

1. Pepys, Samuel, 1633-1703. 2. Cabinet officers -- Great Britain 3. Great Britain -- History -- Charles II, 1660-1685 -- Sources. 4. Great Britain -- Social life and customs -- 17th century Sources. 5. Diaries.

LC 00054817

Diary entries by the tailor's son who rose up through the royal ranks describe his experiences in London from 1660 to 1669, and explore the political and cultural scene during the Restoration, the Plague, and the Great Fire of London.

Tomalin, Claire **Samuel** Pepys : the unequalled self / Claire Tomalin. A.A. Knopf, 2002. xxxiii, 470 p., 24 p. of plates : **B**

ISBN 0375411437

1. Pepys, Samuel, 1633-1703. 2. Great Britain. Royal Navy Officers. 3. Cabinet officers -- Great Britain 4. Authors, British -- 17th century 5. English diaries -- History and criticism 6. Great Britain -- History -- Stuarts, 1603-1714. 7. Great Britain -- Social life and customs -- 17th century. 8. Great Britain -- History -- Restoration, 1660-1688. 9. Diaries. 10. Biographies

LC 2002075701

Whitbread Book Award for Biography, 2002.
Whitbread Book of the Year Award, 2002."

Tomalin mines the diary, and she also expands upon the characters and events, great and small, that affected Pepys' life and livelihood to bring the man and his milieu to lifepungently as well as vibrantly." Booklist.

Perelman, Grigori, 1966-

Gessen, Masha **Perfect** rigor : a genius and the mathematical breakthrough of the century / Masha Gessen. Houghton Mifflin Harcourt, 2009. xi, 242 p. ; **B**

ISBN 9780151014064

1. Mathematicians -- Russia. 2. Mathematics. 3. Poincare conjecture. 4. Recluses. 5. Russia. 6. Biographies

LC 2009014742

Relates the story of the mathematical genius who solved one of the world's greatest intellectual puzzles--the Poincare conjecture--but could not cope with the reality of human affairs, causing him to withdraw first from the field he loved, and then fromthe world in general.

"The story of Russian mathematical prodigy Grigory Perelman, who solved a problem that had stumped everyone for a centurythen walked away from his chosen field. [The author] paints a fascinating picture of the Soviet math establishment and of the mind of one of its most singular products. An engrossing examination of an enigmatic genius." Kirkus.

Perkins, Frances, 1882-1965

Downey, Kirstin The **woman** behind the New Deal : the life of Frances Perkins, FDR's Secretary of Labor and his moral conscience / Kirstin Downey. Nan A. Talese, c2009. 480 p. **B**

ISBN 9780385513654

1. United States. Department of Labor 2. Women cabinet officers -- United States 3. Women social reformers -- United States 4. United States -- History -- 20th century.

LC 2008023208

Presents a portrait of the first female cabinet member and one of the most influential women of the twentieth century, whose efforts to improve the lives of America's working people resulted in such initiatives as unemployment insurance and Social Security.

"Like many biographers, Downey . . . is enamored of her subject. But her fascination serves her well, allowing her to construct an intriguing catalog of Perkins's achievements and explore the influences that held sway in her life, a psychological approach lacking in previous Perkins biographies. Here Perkins's triumphs and tragedies are compiled into a compelling narrative that never loses its scholarly touch." Library Journal.

Perkins, John, 1945-

Perkins, John, 1945- The **new** confessions of an economic hit man / John Perkins. Berrett-Koehler Publishers, Inc., 2016. 336 p. **B**

ISBN 9781626566743

1. United States. National Security Agency. 2. Chas. T. Main, Inc. 3. World Bank Developing countries. 4. Economists -- United States 5. Energy consultants -- United States 6. Intelligence officers -- United States 7. Business -- Corrupt practices. 8. Autobiographies and memoirs

LC 2015036436

In a new edition that includes 15 new chapters, a former chief economist at an international consulting firm describes how he and others were paid large sums of money to cheat countries out of trillions of dollars using false economics, bribes, surveillance and even assassination.

"An intriguing, vivid account of Perkins's 'living on the edge' experiences, this fascinating read is of the truth-is-stranger-than-fiction variety." Library Journal.

Perry, Imani, 1972-

Perry, Imani, 1972- **Breathe** : a letter to my sons / Imani Perry. Beacon Press, 2019. 184 p. **B**

ISBN 9780807076552

1. African American mothers 2. African American educators 3. African American families. 4. African American boys 5. United States -- Race relations. 6. Autobiographies and memoirs

LC 2019003863

A Princeton University professor of African-American studies explores the terror, grace and beauty of coming of age as a Black person in contemporary America, sharing insights into what it means to parent children in a persistently unjust world.

"Deeply intergenerational, the book blurs intended audiences to call all of us to face up to legacies of injustice while insisting on the grace and conviviality necessary to imagine just futures. A masterfully poetic and intimate work that anchors mothering within the long-standing tradition of black resistance and resourcefulness. " Kirkus.

Perry, Michael, 1964-

Perry, Michael, 1964- **Montaigne** in barn boots : an amateur ambles through philosophy / Michael Perry. HarperCollins,

2017 288 p. B

ISBN 9780062230560

1. Montaigne, Michel de, 1533-1592. 2. Farmers 3. Farm life 4. Philosophy 5. Personal conduct 6. Wisconsin 7. Autobiographies and memoirs

LC 2017277954

The author reflects on the lessons he has gleaned from French Renaissance philosopher Michel de Montaigne, contrasting his own life to that of the intellectual and explaining how de Montaigne's views shaped his perspectives on everything from faith to race to sex.

Perry, Tyler

Perry, Tyler **Higher** is waiting : passages of inspiration / Tyler Perry. Spiegel & Grau, 2017 208 p. B

ISBN 9780812989342

1. Faith (Christianity) 2. Hope 3. Integrity -- Religious aspects -- Christianity. 4. Determination (Personal quality) 5. New Orleans, Louisiana 6. Autobiographies and memoirs

LC 2017034266

The cinematic innovator behind Tyler Perry Studios traces his youth in New Orleans through his successful career, in an uplifting account of his spiritual awakening that explains how his faith has enriched his life and sustained him in hard times.

Peters, Robert Parkins

Sisman, Adam The **professor** and the parson : a story of desire, deceit, and defrocking / Adam Sisman. Counterpoint, 2020, c2019. 288 p. B

ISBN 9781640093287

1. Swindlers and swindling 2. Fraud 3. Impostors 4. Priest impersonators 5. Biographies

LC 2019026530

Originally published: London : Profile Books, 2019.

The author describes his investigation into the true life of fraudulent priest Robert Parkin Peters and how he cheated his way through bigamous marriages, religious posts and academic positions.

"A captivating true tale that makes even the most intricate con-artist movies look cartoonish." Kirkus

Petersen, Andrea

Petersen, Andrea **On** edge : a journey through anxiety / Andrea Petersen. Crown, [2017] 336 p. B

ISBN 9780553418576

1. Petersen, Andrea Mental health. 2. Anxiety disorders 3. Anxiety in women 4. Mental health 5. Neuroscience 6. Autobiographies and memoirs

LC 2016050111

A compassionate account of living with anxiety, complemented by deep reportage on the science of anxiety disorders, traces the author's personal journey of trying to understand and manage her own case from neuroscientific, spiritual and genetic perspectives.

"Sensitive and frank personal views on anxiety backed by substantial research and analysis of the evolution of treatment methods and drugs to alleviate symptoms." Kirkus.

Petroski, Henry

Petroski, Henry The **house** with sixteen handmade doors : a tale of architectural choice and craftsmanship / Henry Petroski, with photographs by Catherine Petroski. W. W. Norton & Company, 2014 384 p. B

ISBN 9780393242041

1. Phinney, Robert Edgar, 1915-1989 2. Architecture 3. House construction. 4. Architecture, Domestic -- Designs and plans 5. Building. 6. Autobiographies and memoirs

LC 2014006423

"Though this fascinating history of a house includes painstaking attention to woodcrafting techniques that may excite professional and amateur architects and carpenters a bit more than general readers, the book is replete with Petroski's usual fascinating details and elegant prose." Booklist.

Petrushevskaia, Liudmila

Petrushevskaia, Liudmila The **girl** from the Metropol Hotel : growing up in communist Russia / Ludmilla Petrushevskaya ; translated from the Russian with an introduction by Anna Summers. Penguin Books, 2017, c2006 176 p. B

ISBN 9780143129974

1. Petrushevskaia, Liudmila. 2. Hotel Metropol (Moscow, Russia) -- History 20th century. 3. Authors, Russian -- 20th century. 4. Communism. 5. Growing up. 6. Moscow, Russia -- Social conditions 7. Soviet Union -- History -- 1925-1953. 8. Autobiographies and memoirs

LC 2016031256

Original Russian edition: 2006.

National Book Critics Circle Award for Autobiography/Memoir finalist, 2017

A memoir from the Russian author, describes waiting in bread lines with her Bolshevik family who once lived across the street from the Kremlin and being raised by her aunt and grandmother after her mother left.

Pham, Thong Van

★Pham, Andrew X., 1967- The **eaves** of heaven : a life in three wars / Andrew X. Pham on the behalf of my father Thong Van Pham. Harmony Books, 2008. 320 p. B

ISBN 9780307381200

1. Pham, Thong Van. 2. Vietnamese Americans 3. Refugees -- United States 4. Vietnam War, 1961-1975 -- Refugees. 5. Immigration and emigration 6. Vietnam -- History -- 20th century. 7. Biographies

LC 2007033894

National Book Critics Circle Award for Autobiography/Memoir finalist.

A memoir by the award-winning author offers a portrait of his father's experiences over the course of three wars--the French occupation of Indochina, the World War II Japanese invasion, and the Vietnam War--as he captures the trials of everyday life in Vietnam amid the tragedy, violence, and turbulence of war.

Phelps-Roper, Megan, 1986-

Phelps-Roper, Megan, 1986- **Unfollow** : a memoir of loving and leaving the Westboro Baptist Church / Megan Phelps-Roper. Farrar, Straus, and Giroux, 2019. 304 p. B

ISBN 9780374275839

1. Westboro Baptist Church (Topeka, Kan.). 2. Christianity and politics 3. Christian women 4. Extremism 5. Homophobia 6. Autobiographies and memoirs

LC 2019018856

The activist granddaughter of the founder of Topeka's Westboro Baptist Church describes her work as their Twitter spokeswoman and how her dialogues with critics challenged her to question and eventually denounce the church's extreme views on homosexuality.

Philby, Kim, 1912-1988

Macintyre, Ben, 1963- A **spy** among friends : Kim Philby's great betrayal / Ben Macintyre. Crown, 2014. 384 p. **B**

ISBN 9780804136631

1. Philby, Kim, 1912-1988. 2. Elliott, Nicholas, 1916-1994 3. Angleton, James, 1917-1987 4. KGB British operations. 5. Spies -- Great Britain 6. Double agents 7. Betrayal 8. Spies -- Soviet Union 9. Soviet Union -- History -- 1953-1991. 10. Great Britain -- History -- 20th century. 11. Biographies

LC 2014003296

Elizabeth Longford Prize for Historical Biography, 2015.

The revelation in 1963 that British MI6 agent Kim Philby had betrayed Britain to the Soviets for decades rocked the Western intelligence community. In A Spy Among Friends, acclaimed journalist Ben Macintyre portrays Philby's extensive career and analyzes both his motives for selling out his country and why his treason went undetected for so long. This fascinating account delves into the gentlemen's club that was MI6 at the time Philby worked there -- upper-crust acceptance of a man who was "one of us" protected Philby from exposure. Anyone interested in Cold War history or the annals of spycraft will find Macintyre's account both riveting and chilling.

"A tale of espionage, alcoholism, bad manners and the chivalrous code of spies--the real world of James Bond, that is, as played out by clerks and not superheroes." Kirkus.

Philip II, King of Spain, 1527-1598

Kamen, Henry **Philip** of Spain / Henry Kamen. Yale University Press, 1997. xiii, 384 p. : **B**

ISBN 0300070810

1. Philip II, King of Spain, 1527-1598. 2. Spain -- History -- Philip II, 1556-1598. 3. Spain -- Politics and government -- 16th century. 4. Spain -- Rulers 5. Biographies

LC 96052421

Reassesses King Philip II's reputation as narrow-minded tyrant, describes the major events of his reign, and presents a more rounded depiction of his personality.

"Kamen's prose is lucid, succinct, and thorough. In humanizing a man too often viewed as a cardboard tyrant, Kamen has made a valuable contribution to European historiography." Booklist.

Philipps, Busy, 1979-

Philipps, Busy, 1979- **This** will only hurt a little / Busy Philipps. Touchstone, 2018. 288 p. **B**

ISBN 9781501184710

1. Instagram (Electronic resource) 2. Freaks and geeks (Television program) 3. Dawson's Creek (Television program) 4. Cougar town (Television program) 5. Television actors and actresses -- United States 6. Acting 7. Fame 8. Celebrities 9. Autobiographies and memoirs

LC bl2018167913

Presents a memoir by the comedic actress known for her roles on "Freaks and Geeks," "Dawsons Creek," and "Cougar Town," who has become a breakout star on Instagram.

"... actress Philipps presents a candid look at her life in and out of the spotlight, all told through her unflinchingly authentic, no-filter voice." Library Journal.

Phillip, Arthur, 1738-1814

Keneally, Thomas A **commonwealth** of thieves : the improbable birth of Australia / Thomas Keneally. Nan A. Talese, Doubleday, 2006, c2005. 385 p. : **B**

ISBN 9780385514590

1. Phillip, Arthur, 1738-1814. 2. Prisoners -- Australia -- History. 3. Convict ships -- Australia -- History. 4. Penal colonies -- Australia -- History. 5. Frontier and pioneer life -- Australia. 6. Australia -- History -- 18th century. 7. Australia -- History -- 19th century. 8. Biographies

LC 2006044470

Originally published: Milson Point, N.S.W. : Random House Australia, 2005.

A history of the European settlement of Australia tells the story of Captain Arthur Phillip, who was empowered to govern a colony comprised primarily of unskilled criminals and petty thieves, disgruntled military men, and a sometimes hostile native population.

"This book offers an engaging treatment of a subject which over the years has provoked a long and sometimes heated debate." Times Literary Supplement.

Phillips, Sam, 1923-2003

★Guralnick, Peter **Sam** Phillips : the man who invented rock 'n' roll / Peter Guralnick. Little, Brown and Company, 2015. 752 p. **B**

ISBN 9780316042741

1. Phillips, Sam, 1923-2003. 2. Sound recording executives and producers -- United States 3. Sound recording industry and trade 4. Music industry and trade 5. Music 6. Biographies.

LC 2015024690

Draws on interviews and firsthand personal observations extending throughout a twenty-five-year period with both Phillips and legendary Sun Records artists to explain the label's unique and influential integration of new music styles.

"The author emphasizes Phillips's contributions to rock and roll's 1950s emergence in the racially charged South and his personal and professional relationships with not only the many famous singers and musicians who benefited commercially and artistically from his vision, encouragement, and technical skills but also the obscure rockabilly, blues, country, and pop artists who were given an opportunity to express themselves on vinyl. This long but consistently engaging book offers a more detailed and intimate account than Kevin and Tanja Crouch's Sun King and is recommended to fans of early American popular music." Library Journal.

Philpott, Mary Laura

Philpott, Mary Laura **I** miss you when I blink : essays / Mary Laura Philpott. Atria, [2019] 288 p. **B**

ISBN 9781982102807

1. Philpott, Mary Laura. 2. Adulthood. 3. Middle age 4. Contentment 5. Middle-aged women 6. Essays 7. Autobiographies and memoirs

LC 2018030497

The Emmy Award-winning co-host of A Word on Words presents a memoir-in-essays that lightheartedly addresses the conflicting pressures of modern adulthood, revealing how periodic self-reinventions can offer necessary renewal and healthy perspective.

"Readers with their own sets of anxieties should be charmed by the authors friendly tone, warm sense of humor, and relatable experiences." Booklist.

Piaf, Edith, 1915-1963

Burke, Carolyn **No** regrets : the life of Edith Piaf / Carolyn Burke. Alfred A. Knopf, 2011. 304 p. **B**

ISBN 9780307268013

1. Piaf, Edith, 1915-1963. 2. Fame. 3. Singers -- France 4. Women singers 5. Biographies

LC 2010035229

"The author focuses on the internationally renowned French vocalist and lyricist best known for the song La Vie en Rose. Piaf is commonly associated with la chanson raliste, realistic songs that speak to the underprivileged. Burke's contextual detail and attention to research will appeal to scholars, and her masterful storytelling will engage readers." Library Journal.

Piazza, Jo

Piazza, Jo **How** to be married : what I learned from real women on six continents about surviving my first (really hard) year of marriage / Jo Piazza. Harmony Books, [2017] 320 p. **B**

ISBN 9780451495556

1. Authors, American -- 21st century 2. Newlyweds 3. Married women 4. Marriage -- Cross-cultural studies. 5. Autobiographies and memoirs

LC 2016036609

A lighthearted narrative on what it takes to make a great marriage traces the author's haphazard first year as a newlywed and how it contrasted with traditional notions that rarely move past weddings, a journey marked by insights from married women of other cultures.

Picasso, Pablo, 1881-1973

Leal, Brigitte The **ultimate** Picasso / Brigitte Leal, Christine Piot, Marie-Laure Bernadac ; preface by Jean Leymarie. Harry N. Abrams, 2003. 551 p. : **B**

ISBN 9780810991149

1. Picasso, Pablo, 1881-1973. 2. Artists -- France

LC 2003007773

Presents a concise version of a retrospective of Picasso's work, presenting more than 1,200 reproductions that include paintings, drawings, lithographs, ceramics, and sculpture, covering every major period in the artist's life.

Penrose, Roland, Sir **Picasso,** his life and work : His Life and Work / Roland Penrose. University of California Press, 1981. xviii, 517 p., 32 p. of plates : **B**

ISBN 9780520042070

1. Picasso, Pablo, 1881-1973. 2. Artists -- France

LC 80054015

Includes index.

Smee, Sebastian The **art** of rivalry : four friendships, betrayals, and breakthroughs in modern art / Sebastian Smee. Random House, 2016. 256 p. **B**

ISBN 9780812994803

1. Picasso, Pablo, 1881-1973 Friends and associates. 2. Matisse, Henri, 1869-1954 Friends and associates. 3. Manet, Edouard, 1832-1883 Friends and associates. 4. Degas, Edgar, 1834-1917 Friends and associates. 5. Pollock, Jackson, 1912-1956 Friends and associates. 6. De Kooning, Willem, 1904-1997 Friends and associates. 7. Freud, Lucian Friends and associates. 8. Bacon, Francis, 1909-1992 Friends and associates. 9. Artists -- Psychology. 10. Modern art 11. Friendship 12. Creation (Literary, artistic, etc.). 13. Biographies

LC 2015050361

Includes index.

Traces the stories of four pairs of artists whose relationships shaped and spurred their achievements and the cultural world, profiling the psychologically tense relationships of Picasso and Matisse, Manet and Degas, Pollack and de Kooning, and Lucian Freud and Francis Bacon.

"This ambitious and impressive work is an utterly absorbing read about four important relationships in modern art." Publishers Weekly.

Unger, Miles **Picasso** and the painting that shocked the world / Miles J. Unger. Simon & Schuster, 2018. 336 p. **B**

ISBN 9781476794211

1. Picasso, Pablo, 1881-1973 Criticism and interpretation 2. Picasso, Pablo, 1881-1973. Demoiselles d'Avignon 3. Artists 4. Painters 5. Modern art 6. Creation (Literary, artistic, etc.) 7. Biographies

LC 2017022812

Traces the story of Picasso's rise from an obscure young painter in Barcelona to one of the most influential artists of the 20th century, documenting the events of his first visit to Paris, his emergence as a leader of a group of bohemian artists, his gradual recognition by collectors and the 1906 creation of the disturbing masterpiece, Les Demoiselles d'Avignon.

"This engrossing book chronicles with precision and enthusiasm a painting with lasting impact in todays art world." Publishers Weekly.

Pilate, Pontius, 1st cent

Schiavone, Aldo **Pontius** Pilate : deciphering a memory / Aldo Schiavone ; translated by Jeremy Carden. Liveright Publishing, 2017, c2016. 224 p. **B**

ISBN 9781631492358

1. Pilate, Pontius, 1st cent. 2. Jesus Christ Crucifixion 3. Public officials 4. Prophets 5. Executions and executioners 6. Crucifixion 7. Judaea (Region) 8. Rome -- History -- Empire, 30 B.C.-476 A.D. 9. Biographies

LC 2016056360

Originally published: Turin : Einaudi, 2016.

The classicist and author of Spartacus: Revealing Antiquity presents a revisionist portrait of the controversial biblical figure that reconstructs the social, religious and political climates behind his fateful encounters with Jesus.

"A levelheaded, engaging reading of the Gospels and historical account that forms a solid sense of this pivotal personage and his role on the epic stage." Kirkus.

Pilecki, Witold, 1901-1948

Fairweather, Jack The **volunteer** : one man, an underground army, and the secret mission to destroy Auschwitz / Jack Fairweather. Custom House, 2019 xvi, 505 p. : **B**

ISBN 9780062561411

1. Auschwitz (Concentration camp) 2. Prisoners 3. Espionage 4. Holocaust victims 5. Insurgency 6. Biographies

Costa Book of the Year Award, 2019.

Costa Biography Award, 2019.

Documents the remarkable true story of an ill-fated Polish resistance fighter's infiltration of Auschwitz to sabotage the camp from within, chronicling his daring escape to smuggle evidence of murderous Nazi activities to Allied forces.

Pinchot, Gifford, 1865-1946

Miller, Char, 1951- **Gifford** Pinchot and the making of modern environmentalism / Char Miller. Shearwater Books, 2001. 458 p. : **B**

ISBN 1559638222

1. Pinchot, Gifford, 1865-1946. 2. United States. Forest Service. 3. Environmentalists -- United States 4. Politicians -- United States 5. Conservation of natural resources -- United States -- History. 6. Forestry -- History. 7. Biographies

LC 2001005665

National Outdoor Book Award for History/Biography, 2002."

Charismatic, progressive, and controversial, Gifford Pinchot (1865-1946) established and directed the Forest Service under Theodore Roosevelt, lobbied hard for responsible logging practices, expressed prescient warnings about pollution, and called for sustainable energy. Miller's animated biography portrays Pinchot in all his fervor, and environmentalism in all its complexity." Booklist.

Pine, Emilie

Pine, Emilie **Notes** to self : essays / Emilie Pine. The Dial Press, [2018] 192 p. **B**

ISBN 9781984855459

1. Pine, Emilie. 2. Children of alcoholics -- Ireland 3. Rape victims -- Ireland 4. Sexism. 5. Feminism. 6. Essays. 7. Autobiographies and memoirs.

LC 2019004557

"Originally published in Ireland by Tramp Press in 2018"--T.p. verso.

In this vivid and powerful collection of essays, Emilie Pine boldly confronts the past to better understand herself, her relationships and her role in society.

Pinfield, Matt

Pinfield, Matt **All** these things that I've done : my insane, improbable rock life / Matt Pinfield, with Mitchell Cohen. Scribner, 2016 288 p. **B**

ISBN 9781476793894

1. M T V (Cable television network) 2. Popular music 3. Television personalities 4. Autobiographies and memoirs

LC 2016024686

A memoir from a music personality, TV host and MTV and VH1 veejay chronicles the songs and artists that informed and molded his childhood and teenage years to ultimately inspire his career, relationships and life and shares his stories from the front lines of rock and roll.

"His own recurring struggles with addiction flesh out the narrative, grounding his enthusiasm for music in an awareness of the somber side of the rock lifestyle. His encyclopedic knowledge of contemporary sounds makes the memoir as informative as it is personal." Publishers Weekly.

Piniella, Lou, 1943-

Piniella, Lou, 1943- **Lou** : fifty years of kicking dirt, playing hard, and winning big in the sweet spot of baseball / Lou Piniella and Bill Madden. Harper, 2017 342 pages, 16 unnumbered leaves of plates : **B**

ISBN 9780062660794

1. New York Yankees (Baseball team) 2. Major League Baseball (Organization) 3. Baseball players 4. Baseball 5. Baseball managers 6. Professional athletes 7. Autobiographies and memoirs

LC 2017302410

A candid memoir by the beloved New York Yankee reflects on his nearly half-century career as a player and manager while sharing insights and stories from some of his most memorable moments with many of the biggest names in Major League Baseball.

Pinter, Harold, 1930-

Fraser, Antonia, 1932- **Must** you go? : my life with Harold Pinter / Antonia Fraser. Nan A. Talese/Doubleday, 2010. 336 p. **B**

ISBN 9780385532501

1. Fraser, Antonia, 1932- 2. Dramatists, English -- 20th century 3. Authors, English -- 20th century 4. Husband and wife. 5. Interpersonal relations. 6. Biographies

LC 2010007374

"Must you go?" is the story of a thirty-year marriage, beginning with a scandalous affair while both Antonia and Harold were married to other people, and ending with Harold's death from cancer on Christmas Eve in 2008.

"The author simultaneously creates a tender portrait of an exciting marriage, and a deliciously detailed account of living in the thick of creativity and fame." Entertainment Weekly.

Pirsig, Robert M.

Pirsig, Robert M. **Zen** and the art of motorcycle maintenance : an inquiry into values / Robert Pirsig. Quill, 1999, c1974. xiv, 436 p. ; **B**

ISBN 0688171664

1. Fathers and sons 2. Self 3. Philosophy, Western 4. Voyages and travels 5. United States 6. Autobiographical fiction

LC 2002278394

Originally published: New York : Morrow, 1974.

With new introd. and reader's guide.

While cycling through the Western States, a disillusioned American questions the meaning of existence after confronting the ghost of his former, uninstitutionalized self.

Pivnik, Sam, 1926-

Pivnik, Sam, 1926- **Survivor** : Auschwitz, the Death March, and my fight for freedom / Sam Pivnik. St. Martin's Press, 2013, c2012 320 p. **B**

ISBN 9781250029522

1. Holocaust (1933-1945) 2. Holocaust survivors 3. Jews, Polish 4. Concentration camps. 5. Autobiographies and memoirs

LC 2012474461

Documents the extraordinary story of the author's survival of the Holocaust, relating his harrowing endurance of ghetto establishments in his home town of Bedzin after the Nazi invasion of Poland, his torturous six-month imprisonment at Auschwitz and his near escapes from subsequent wartime brutalities.

Pla, Josep, 1897-1981

Pla, Josep, 1897-1981 The **gray** notebook / Josep Pla. New York Review Books, [2013] 704 p. **B**

ISBN 9781590176719

1. Pla, Josep, 1897-1981. 2. Authors, Catalan -- 20th century 3. Authors -- 20th century 4. Young men 5. Families -- Spain. 6. Barcelona, Spain -- Social life and customs. 7. Spain -- Social life and customs -- 20th century. 8. Diaries. 9. Autobiographies and memoirs

LC 2013028497

Translation of Quadern Gris.

Translated from the Catalan by Peter Bush."

Pla . is considered one of the greatest writers of Catalan language, and this beautiful translation lets English readers glory in the quiet strength of his words." Kirkus.

Plath, Sylvia

★Clark, Heather **Red** comet: the short life and blazing art of Sylvia Plath / Heather Clark. Alfred A. Knopf, 2020. 1120 p. **B**

ISBN 9780307961167

1. Plath, Sylvia. 2. Women Poets 3. Poets, American 4. Women and literature 5. Women with depression 6. Biographies

LC 2019041635

The highly anticipated new biography of Sylvia Plath that focuses on her remarkable literary and intellectual achievements, while restoring the woman behind the long-held myths about her life and art.

"Clark's in-depth scholarship and fine writing result in a superb work that will deliver fresh revelations to Plath's many devoted fans." Publishers Weekly

Plath, Sylvia The **letters** of Sylvia Plath : Volume 1: 1940-1956 / Sylvia Plath ; edited by Peter K. Steinberg and Karen V. Kukil. Harper, 2017. 800 p. **B**

ISBN 9780062740434

1. Plath, Sylvia Correspondence 2. Women poets 3. Women authors

4. Women college students 5. Marriage 6. Letters

While her renown as one of the twentieth century's most influential poets is beyond dispute, Plath was also one of its most captivating correspondents. The Letters of Sylvia Plath is the breathtaking compendium of this prolific writer's correspondence with more than 120 people, including family, friends, contemporaries, and colleagues.

Plath, Sylvia The **unabridged** journals of Sylvia Plath, 1950-1962 : Transcripts from the Original Manuscripts at Smith College / edited by Karen V. Kukil. Anchor Books, 2000. x, 732 p., 24 p. of plates : **B**

ISBN 0385720254

1. Plath, Sylvia. 2. Poets, American -- 20th century 3. Diaries.

LC 00042024

"Transcribed from the original manuscripts at Smith College."An uncensored collection of the late poet's complete journals as recorded during the last twelve years of her life includes previously unpublished material and chronicles her personal and literary struggles.

Winder, Elizabeth **Pain,** parties, work : Sylvia Plath in New York, summer 1953 / Elizabeth Winder. HarperCollins, 2013. 272 p. **B**

ISBN 9780062085498

1. Poets, American -- 20th century 2. Women poets, American -- 20th century 3. Periodicals 4. Internship programs 5. New York City 6. Biographies

LC bl2013008794

Marking the 50th anniversary of Sylvia Plath's death, this brilliant biography captures a moment in time - the month she spent in New York City in June of 1953 as a Guest Editor for Mademoiselle's prestigious annual College issue.

Plummer, Christopher

Plummer, Christopher **In** spite of myself : a memoir / Christopher Plummer. Knopf, 2008. 608 p. **B**

ISBN 9780679421627

1. Plummer, Christopher. 2. Actors and actresses -- Canada 3. Social classes. 4. Rich families. 5. Canada -- Social life and customs. 6. Autobiographies and memoirs

LC 2008031229

"An entertaining self-portrait by one of today's most acclaimed actors details his privileged Canadian upbringing, his early acting days, his roles with the Royal Shakespeare Company, his film career, the legendary performers with whom he has worked, and

"The author is an enchanting observer of the showbiz cavalcade, drawing vivid thumbnails of everyone from Laurence Olivier to Lenny Bruce and tossing off witty anecdotes . like the most effortless ad libs. The result is a sparkling star turn from a born raconteur for whom all the world is indeed a stage." Publishers Weekly.

Poe, Edgar Allan, 1809-1849

Ackroyd, Peter, 1949- **Poe** : a life cut short / Peter Ackroyd. Nan A. Talese/Doubleday, 2008. 224 p. **B**

ISBN 9780385508001

1. Poe, Edgar Allan, 1809-1849. 2. Authors, American -- 19th century 3. Authors -- 19th century 4. United States -- Social life and customs -- 19th century. 5. Biographies

LC 2008018244

Includes index.

A portrait of enigmatic American writer Edgar Allan Poe examines his literary accomplishments--lyrical poetry, macabre tales, invention of the first fictional detective, and pioneer of the science fiction and fantasy genres--and legacy in terms of his turbulent, sometimes sordid life.

Collins, Paul, 1969- **Edgar** Allan Poe : the fever called living / Paul Collins. New Harvest, 2014. 144 p. **B**

ISBN 9780544261877

1. Poe, Edgar Allan, 1809-1849. 2. Authors, American -- 19th century 3. Crime writing. 4. Adopted boys 5. Biographies

LC 2013024777

Describes the personal and professional life of the master of the horror genre behind "The Raven," including a discussion of his rocky relationship with his wealthy adoptive father and his time spent working as an editor and reviewer.

"Although Collins doesn't provide much new information, the clean, crisp narrative presents the puzzling Poe as a deeply troubled and toweringly talented artist." Kirkus.

Silverman, Kenneth **Edgar** A. Poe : mournful and never-ending remembrance / Kenneth Silverman. HarperCollins, 1991. ix, 564 p. **B**

ISBN 0060167157

1. Poe, Edgar Allan, 1809-1849. 2. Authors, American -- 19th century 3. Mystery story writers. 4. Biographies

LC 90056397

Edgar Allan Poe Award for Best Critical/Biographical, 1992.

A look at the life and work of Edgar Allan Poe traces his life from his childhood as an adopted son, to his experiences in the U.S. Army, to his career as a journalist, editor, and writer, and discusses his influence on literature.

"The author explains how Poe's early life influenced his work. He details Poe's turbulent career as poet, short story writer, and editor . and traces his literary development through bouts of alcoholism and hallucinations and disputes with literary rivals. An excellent addition to the literature that furthers understanding of America's gothic tale-teller." Library Journal.

Sova, Dawn B. **Critical** companion to Edgar Allan Poe : a literary reference to his life and work / Dawn B. Sova. Facts on File, c2007. viii, 458 p. : **B**

ISBN 9780816064083

1. Poe, Edgar Allan, 1809-1849 Encyclopedias. 2. Authors, American -- 19th century 3. Biographies

LC 2006029466

Rev. ed. of: Edgar Allan Poe, A to Z. c2001.

An encyclopedic guide to the American author's life and works presents a brief biography, offers synopses of his writings, and critical analysis of his characters and major themes; and discusses important people, places, and topics in his life.

"Biographical, historical, and critical material on Poe's life and work is presented in alphabetical order in three sections. The entries on Poe's works each provide a synopsis, a publication history, and character descriptions, while major works such as The Cask of Amontillado and The Purloined Letter have . . . [a] commentary and . . . further-reading suggestions." School Library Journal.

Walsh, John Evangelist, 1927-2015 **Midnight** dreary : the mysterious death of Edgar Allan Poe / John Evangelist Walsh. Rutgers University Press, 1998. xvi, 199 p. : **B**

ISBN 9780813526058

1. Poe, Edgar Allan, 1809-1849 Death and burial. 2. Missing persons. 3. Death. 4. Authors, American -- 19th century. 5. Authors, American

-- 19th century -- Death.

LC 98024043

A reconstruction of the unsolved, real-life mystery surrounding the death of Edgar Allan Poe examines the last days of the author's life and his mysterious death in Baltimore.

"Walsh has undertaken a superbly informed speculation on the week proceeding the mysterious death of Edgar Allan Poe 150 years ago." Library Journal.

Poehler, Amy, 1971-

Poehler, Amy, 1971- **Yes** please / Amy Poehler. It Books, 2014. 288 p. **B**

ISBN 9780062268341

1. Women comedians -- United States 2. Television actors and actresses -- United States 3. Comedians 4. Actors and actresses -- Anecdotes. 5. Autobiographies and memoirs

LC 2014469870

The actress best known for her work on "Parks and Recreation" and "Saturday Night Live" reveals personal stories and offers her humorous take on such topics as love, friendship, parenthood, and her relationship with Tina Fey.

Pogrebin, Abigail

Pogrebin, Abigail **My** Jewish year : 18 holidays, one wondering Jew / Abigail Pogrebin ; foreword by A. J. Jacobs. Fig Tree Books, 2017. 225 p. **B**

ISBN 9781941493205

1. Judaism 2. Faith (Judaism) 3. Jewish holidays 4. Jewish families. 5. Autobiographies and memoirs

LC bl2017009327

Although she grew up following some holiday rituals, Pogrebin realized how little she knew about their foundational purpose and contemporary relevance; she wanted to understand what had kept these holidays alive and vibrant, some for thousands of years. Her curiosity led her to embark on an entire year of intensive research, observation, and writing about the milestones on the religious calendar.

"A sentimental journey through Judaic practice and thought." Kirkus.

Poitier, Sidney

Goudsouzian, Aram **Sidney** Poitier : man, actor, icon / Aram Goudsouzian. University of North Carolina Press, c2004. xii, 480 p. : **B**

ISBN 0807828432

1. Actors and actresses -- United States 2. African American actors and actresses 3. Biographies

LC 2003019372

"The author traces Poitier's journey from life as the son of a poor Bahamian farmer to celebrity status in the States as a trailblazing actor who has received as much criticism as praise for his portrayal of dignified and stoical black men." Booklist.

★Poitier, Sidney The **measure** of a man : a spiritual autobiography / Sidney Poitier. Harper San Francisco, 2000. xiii, 255 p., 8 p. of plates : **B**

ISBN 0062516078

1. African American actors and actresses 2. Faith in men. 3. Spirituality. 4. Actors and actresses. 5. Autobiographies and memoirs

LC 99088322

Includes index.

The acclaimed actor reveals the depth, passion, and intellectual fervor that have driven his life and career, citing the elements of his childhood that gave him his sense of worth, family, and ethics and how these qualities are essential to spiritual development.

"Poitier attempts to unravel for himself his own remarkable life story, looking at early life experiences, his family, and various themes that he believes have contributed to his success. Measure is not a chronological autobiography; the book emphasizes themes that have shaped his life. Poitier's tale is an affirmation of the value of morality and personal integrity in leading a successful, fulfilling life." Booklist.

Polk, James K. (James Knox), 1795-1849

Borneman, Walter R., 1952- **Polk** : the man who transformed the presidency and America / Walter R. Borneman. Random House, 2008. 448 p. **B**

ISBN 1400065607

1. Polk, James K. (James Knox), 1795-1849. 2. Presidents -- United States 3. Politicians. 4. Leadership in men. 5. United States -- Politics and government -- 1845-1849. 6. Biographies

LC 2007014040

A biography of a misunderstood and under-appreciated American president follows the political career of James K. Polk and the events of his administration, including the acceptance of Texas into the union and the expansion of presidential powers.

"The author presents a birth-death biography of Polk. Borneman has a pleasing style and makes fine use of primary sources that all demonstrate why Polk is habitually ranked as one of the ten best presidents by historians." Library Journal.

Merry, Robert W., 1946- A **country** of vast designs : James K. Polk and the conquest of the American continent / Robert Merry. Simon & Schuster, 2009. 592 p. **B**

ISBN 9780743297431

1. Polk, James K. (James Knox), 1795-1849. 2. Presidents -- United States 3. Politicians -- United States 4. United States -- Politics and government -- 1845-1849. 5. United States -- Territorial expansion. 6. Biographies

LC 2009024131

"Merry's chronicle is filled with excellent insights into the critical events and fine portrayals of a cast of statesmen, warriors, and scheming rogues. [This is] an outstanding addition to American history collections." Booklist.

Polk, Sarah Childress, 1803-1891

Greenberg, Amy S., 1968- **Lady** first : the world of first lady Sarah Polk / Amy S. Greenberg. Alfred A. Knopf, [2019] 400 p. **B**

ISBN 9780385354134

1. Polk, Sarah Childress, 1803-1891. 2. Polk, James K. (James Knox), 1795-1849 3. Presidents' spouses -- United States 4. Political intrigue. 5. Women's rights. 6. Power (Social sciences) 7. United States -- Politics and government -- 1845-1849. 8. Biographies.

LC 2018010748

An exploration of Sarah Polk's political savvy and contributions to American feminism details the contradictions attributed to her character, her wartime achievements, and her influence in Washington politics during her husband's presidency.

"This is an in-depth, telling account of a largely overlooked woman who was able to effect profound influence while working within the constraints of her time and place." Booklist.

Pollard, Robert, 1957-

Cutter, Matthew **Closer** you are : the story of Robert Pollard and Guided by Voices / Matthew Cutter. Da Capo Press, 2018.

352 p. **B**

ISBN 9780306825767

1. Guided by Voices (Musical group). 2. Rock musicians -- United States 3. Biographies.

LC 2017060942

In an authorized biography of the founder of Guided by Voices, his story is told in its entirety and draws upon interviews with his friends, family and bandmates, as well as with the consummate artist himself.

"Though Cutters attention to detail (especially with regard to gigs and recordings) drags the narrative in spots, he has captured the raucous and squalling voice of a powerful American songwriter." Publishers Weekly.

Pollen, Bella

Pollen, Bella **Meet** me in the in-between / Bella Pollen. Grove Press, 2017. 320 p. **B**

ISBN 9780802126580

1. Identity (Psychology) 2. Self-awareness 3. Life change events 4. Belonging 5. Autobiographies and memoirs

LC 2016056295

A woman describes her experience growing up between her transatlantic parents and discusses how it made her adventurous spirit bloom, ultimately resulting in her early marriage to a charismatic mafioso and her falling in with a crowd of Mexican smugglers who loved Pink Floyd.

"Hers is a memoir of an indelible life full of incredible adventures." Booklist.

Pollock, Jackson, 1912-1956

Solomon, Deborah **Jackson** Pollock : a biography / Deborah Solomon. Cooper Square Press, 2001, c1987. 287 p. : **B**

ISBN 9780815411826

1. Pollock, Jackson, 1912-1956. 2. Painters -- United States 3. Artists -- United States 4. Abstract expressionism -- United States. 5. Abstract expressionists -- United States. 6. United States -- Social life and customs -- 20th century. 7. Biographies

LC 2001028915

Originally published: New York : Simon and Schuster, 1987."

A concisely written biography; the footnotes indicate solid research." Library Journal.

Polo, Marco, 1254-1323?

Belliveau, Denis, 1964- **In** the footsteps of Marco Polo : a companion to the public television film / Denis Belliveau and Francis O'Donnell. Rowman & Littlefield Publishers : 2008. 256 p. **B**

ISBN 9780742556836

1. Polo, Marco, 1254-1323? Travel Asia. 2. Belliveau, Denis, 1964- Journeysl Asia. 3. O'Donnell, Francis Travel Asia. 4. Voyages and travels. 5. Explorers. 6. Adventurers. 7. Asia -- Description and travel.

LC 2008023411

An illustrated companion volume to a PBS documentary traces the authors' two-year expedition to answer the question about Marco Polo's alleged visit to China, a venture that was fraught with the perils and turmoil of the Middle East and natural threats. TV tie-in.

Bergreen, Laurence **Marco** Polo : from Venice to Xanadu / Laurence Bergreen. A.A. Knopf, 2007. 415 p. : **B**

ISBN 140004345X

1. Polo, Marco, 1254-1323? Travel 2. Explorers -- Italy 3. Voyages and travels. 4. Voyages and travels 5. Europe -- History -- 13th century 6. Asia -- Description and travel. 7. Biographies

LC 2007021860

A portrait of the thirteenth-century explorer, adventurer, and global traveler follows Marco Polo from his youth in Venice to his journey to Asia and role in the court of Kublai Khan, to his return to Europe, and discusses his influence on the history of his era.

"The author gives a full-blooded rendition of Polo's astonishing journey. It is richly researched and vividly conveyed. " Washington Post Book World.

Pomerantsev, Peter

Pomerantsev, Peter **Nothing** is true and everything is possible : the surreal heart of the new Russia / Peter Pomerantsev. PublicAffairs, 2014. 256 p. **B**

ISBN 9781610394550

1. Pomerantsev, Peter. 2. Homecomings 3. Television producers 4. Social change -- Russia 5. Social problems -- Russia 6. Russia -- Social conditions -- 1991- 7. Russia -- History -- 1991- 8. Russia -- Economic conditions -- 1991- 9. Autobiographies and memoirs

LC 2014018638

RSL Ondaatje Prize, 2016.

Nothing Is True and Everything is Possible is a journey into the glittering, surreal heart of 21st century Russia: into the lives of oligarchs convinced they are messiahs, professional killers with the souls of artists, Bohemian theater directors turned Kremlin puppet-masters, supermodel sects, post-modern dictators, and playboy revolutionaries. This is a world erupting with new money and new power, changing so fast it breaks all sense of reality, where life is seen as a whirling, glamorous masquerade where identities can be switched and all values are changeable. It is a completely new type of society where nothing is true and everything is possible--yet it is also home to a new form of authoritarianism, built not on oppression but avarice and temptation.

Pompadour, Jeanne Antoinette Poisson, marquise de, 1721-1764

Lever, Evelyne **Madame** de Pompadour : a life / Evelyne Lever ; translated from the French by Catherine Temerson. Farrar, Straus and Giroux, 2002. viii, 310 p. : **B**

ISBN 9780374113087

1. Pompadour, Jeanne Antoinette Poisson, marquise de, 1721-1764. 2. Louis XV, King of France, 1710-1774 Relations with women. 3. Favorites, Royal -- France. 4. Mistresses -- France 5. Courts and courtiers. 6. Paramours 7. France -- History -- Louis XV, 1715-1774. 8. Biographies

LC 2002022811

A portrait of the famous mistress of Louis XV traces the political and personal intricacies of her relationship with the king, her impact on period culture, and friendships with top artists, writers, and philosophers.

"Lever has crafted a detailed and fascinating portrait of the woman who pretty well ran France from 1745 to 1764." Publishers Weekly.

Ponzi, Charles

Zuckoff, Mitchell **Ponzi's** scheme : the true story of a financial legend / Mitchell Zuckhoff. Random House, c2005. xiii, 390 p. : **B**

ISBN 1400060397

1. Ponzi, Charles. 2. Swindlers and swindling -- United States. 3. Ponzi schemes -- United States -- History. 4. White collar crime.

LC 2004046770

A look at the career of the man who developed the most famous scheme in American finance explains how, in 1920, Charles Ponzi raked in millions of dollars from investors by promising them he could double their investments in three months.

"The author chronicles Ponzi's mercurial rise and fall as he conjured up one get-rich-quick scheme after another. Zuckoff provides not only a definitive portrait of Ponzi's life but also insights into immigrant life and the social world of early 20th-century Boston." Publishers Weekly.

Pop, Iggy, 1947-

Trynka, Paul **Iggy** Pop : open up and bleed / Paul Trynka. Broadway Books, c2007. 371 p. : B

ISBN 0767923197

1. Bowie, David, 1947-2016 2. Punk rock musicians -- United States 3. Punk rock music. 4. Biographies

LC 2006030216

Born James Newell Osterberg Jr., Iggy Pop transcended life in Ypsilanti, Michigan, to become a member of the punk band the Stooges, earning the nickname "the Godfather of Punk." He is one of the most riveting and reckless performers in music history, with a commitment to his art that is perilously total. But his personal life was often a shambles, as he struggled with drug addiction, mental illness, and the ever-problematic question of commercial success in the music world. That he is even alive today, let alone performing with undiminished energy, is a wonder. Biographer Trynka spent time with Iggy's childhood friends, lovers, and fellow musicians, and has spoken to dozens of musicians who count Iggy as an influence, and portrays in detail Iggy's relationship with his enigmatic friend and mentor David Bowie. He also interviewed Iggy himself. What emerges is a psychological study of a Jekyll/Hyde personality.--From publisher description.

"Drawing from original interviews with Iggy (n James Newell Osterberg Jr.) and his countless accomplices over the years, Trynka . has constructed a comprehensive portrait of the seemingly indestructible rock provocateur, one that touches all the familiar bases in recounting Iggy's riotous ascent from suburban Michigan schoolboy to frontman of the Stooges to solo artist with an intermittently transcendent career to composer of a drug-inspired hit song that became the jingle for a luxury cruise line." New York Times Book Review.

Porter, Carolyn

Porter, Carolyn **Marcel's** letters : a font and the search for one man's fate / Carolyn Porter. Skyhorse Publishing, 2017. 352 p. B

ISBN 9781510719330

1. Heuzé, Marcel, 1912-1992 2. Father-separated families 3. Historical research 4. Letter writing 5. Graphic designers 6. France -- History -- German occupation, 1940-1945 7. Germany -- History -- 1933-1945 8. Minnesota 9. Biographies

LC 2017001221

A graphic designer's search for inspiration leads to a cache of letters and the mystery of one man's fate during World War II.

"Porters captivating memoir describes her journey to find answers, noting how her fascination with Marcel proved infectious as she faces obstacle after obstacle and enlists the help of experts to discover the fate that awaited him." Booklist.

Porter, Cole, 1891-1964

McBrien, William **Cole** Porter : a biography / William McBrien. Alfred A. Knopf, 1998. xiii, 459 p. : B

ISBN 0394582357

1. Porter, Cole, 1891-1964. 2. Composers -- United States 3. Gay men -- United States 4. Songwriters -- Musical films 5. Marriage. 6. Biographies

LC 97046116

"In this biography of the American songwriter, the author weaves a complex and groundbreaking portrait of Porter, interspersed with lyrics and 72 illustrations, recounting his affluent upbringing in Peru, Ind., and his emergence in the 1930s as the musical theater's reigning sophisticate. This astute biography will help to create a standard-setting portrait of Porter as a homosexual artist in a heterosexual world." Publishers Weekly.

Posey, Parker, 1968-

Posey, Parker, 1968- **You're** on an airplane : a self-mythologizing memoir / Parker Posey. Blue Rider Press, 2018. 256 p. B

ISBN 9780735218192

1. Actors and actresses 2. Fame 3. Advice 4. Acting 5. Autobiographies and memoirs

LC 2018288327

The "Queen of the Indies" star of such productions as Waiting for Guffman shares insider perspectives on a life in entertainment, exploring the therapeutic activities that enrich her life and her relationships with forefront directors.

"Resilient and fiercely observant, Posey is an unflinchingly honest and entertaining interpreter of her many stories." Kirkus.

Potter, Beatrix, 1866-1943

Lear, Linda J., 1940- **Beatrix** Potter : a life in nature / Linda Lear. St. Martin's Press, 2007. xix, 583 p. 32 p. of plates : B

ISBN 0312369344

1. Potter, Beatrix, 1866-1943. 2. Authors 3. Illustrators -- Great Britain 4. Children's stories -- History and criticism 5. Children's literature authors -- 20th century 6. Lake District (England) -- Social life and customs -- 20th century 7. Biographies

LC 2006051245

Details the life of the children's author and illustrator who created such memorable characters as Peter Rabbit, Jemima Puddle-Duck, and Tom Kitten.

"This is a meticulously researched and brilliantly recreated life that . is endlessly fascinating and often illuminating. It is altogether a remarkable achievement." Booklist.

Poulenc, Francis, 1899-1963

Johnson, Graham, 1950- **Poulenc** : the life in the songs / Graham Johnson ; translations of the song texts by Jeremy Sams. Liveright Publishing, 2020. 672 p. B

ISBN 9781631495236

1. Composers -- France 2. Orchestral music -- History and criticism 3. Classical music -- 20th century -- History and criticism 4. Gay men 5. Biographies

LC 2020010683

Francis Poulenc (1899-1963) is widely acknowledged as one of the twentieth century's most significant masters of vocal music ?solo, choral, and operatic-- quite apart from his achievements in instrumental spheres. But what it cost him, and the determined bravery it took for his unusual talent to thrive, has always been underestimated. In this seminal biography, which will serve as the definitive guide to the songs, acclaimed collaborative pianist Graham Johnson shows that it is in Poulenc's extraordinary songs, and seeing how they fit into his life ?which included crippling guilt on account of his sexuality? that we discover Poulenc heart and soul. With the insight that comes from a lifetime of performing this music, Johnson provides an essential volume for singers, pianists, listeners, and readers interested in the artistic milieu of modernism in the first half of the twentieth century.

"This astute biography will be a boon to Poulenc fans and classical music buffs alike." Publishers Weekly

Pound, Ezra, 1885-1972

Moody, Anthony David **Ezra** Pound : poet : a portrait of the man and his work, 1885-1920 / A. David Moody. Oxford University Press, 2007 xv, 507 p. ; **B**

ISBN 9780199215577

1. Pound, Ezra, 1885-1972. 2. Poets, American -- 20th century 3. Biographies

LC 2007021413

Includes index.

Discusses the life of the poet, including his youthful ambition, his education in America, and his years in the London literary scene.

Powell, Anthony, 1905-2000

Spurling, Hilary **Anthony** Powell : dancing to the music of time / Hilary Spurling. Alfred A. Knopf, 2018, c2017. 480 p. **B**

ISBN 9780525521341

1. Authors 2. Authors, English -- 20th century 3. Biographies

LC 2017051875

Originally published: London : Penguin Books, 2017.

Examines the life of the English literary figure best known for his 12-volume comedic work that examines political, cultural and military life in the mid-20th century and who was friends with Evelyn Waugh, Henry Green and George Orwell.

Powell, Colin, 1937-

√ DeYoung, Karen, 1949- **Soldier** : the life of Colin Powell / Karen DeYoung. Knopf, 2006. 610 p., 8 leaves of plates : **B**

ISBN 1400041708

1. Powell, Colin, 1937- Childhood and youth. 2. Powell, Colin, 1937- Family. 3. Powell family. 4. United States. Department of State 5. United States. Army 6. Politicians -- United States 7. Generals -- United States 8. African American generals. 9. Command of troops 10. United States -- History. 11. Biographies

LC 2006045288

A biography of the soldier-statesman follows Colin Powell's life from his Jamaican roots and youth in the Bronx, through his decorated career in the Army and as Chairman of the Joint Chiefs of Staff, to his role as Secretary of State and departure from the post.

"This is a diligent, sympathetic, but not uncritical full-scale biography." New York Review of Books.

★Powell, Colin, 1937- **It** worked for me : in life and leadership / Colin L. Powell, Tony Koltz. HarperCollins, 2012. 320 p. **B**

ISBN 9780062135124

1. Leadership in men. 2. Command of troops. 3. Success (Concept) 4. Generals. 5. Autobiographies and memoirs

LC 2012002970

"An inspiring and useful memoir from a significant figure in 21st-century American politics." Kirkus.

Powell, Colin, 1937- **My** American journey / Colin L. Powell, with Joseph E. Persico. Ballantine Books, 2003. x, 675 p., 42 p. of plates : **B**

ISBN 0345466411

1. United States. Army 2. United States. Joint Chiefs of Staff 3. Generals -- United States 4. African American generals. 5. Leadership in men. 6. African American soldiers 7. Autobiographies and memoirs

LC 2003269724

"Updated to include his remarks to the United Nations on the crisis in Iraq"--Cover.

Includes index.

The former Secretary of State recalls his youth, his military service, and his rise to the heights of America's political and military elite.

"This is an endearing and well-written book. It will make you like Colin Powell." New York Times Book Review.

Powell, John Wesley, 1834-1902

Ross, John F., 1958- The **promise** of the Grand Canyon : John Wesley Powell's perilous journey and his vision for the American West / John F. Ross. Viking Press, 2018. 400 p. **B**

ISBN 9780525429876

1. Naturalists 2. Explorers 3. National parks and reserves 4. Geologists 5. Grand Canyon 6. Colorado River 7. Biographies

LC bl2018125383

When John Wesley Powell became the first person to navigate the entire Colorado River, through the Grand Canyon, he completed what Lewis and Clark had begun nearly 70 years earlier--the final exploration of continental America. The son of an abolitionist preacher, a Civil War hero (who lost an arm at Shiloh), and a passionate naturalist and geologist, in 1869 Powell tackled the vast and dangerous gorge carved by the Colorado River and known today (thanks to Powell) as the Grand Canyon.

"If you've ever used a topographic map, thank Powell. His legacy deserves more attention, and Ross's biography stands to correct this. For all readers, especially lovers of science, history, and adventure." Library Journal.

Powell, Julie

Powell, Julie **Julie** and Julia : 365 days, 524 recipes, 1 tiny apartment kitchen / Julie Powell. Little, Brown and Co., 2005. 309 p. **B**

ISBN 031610969X

1. Powell, Julie. 2. Child, Julia. Mastering the art of French cooking. 3. Women cooks -- Anecdotes. 4. Cooking, French. 5. Food habits -- United States. 6. Marriage. 7. Autobiographies and memoirs

LC 2005007974

The author recounts how she escaped the doldrums of an unpromising career by mastering every recipe in Julia Child's 1961 classic, "Mastering the Art of French Cooking," a year-long endeavor that transformed her life.

"Both home cooks and devotees of Bridget Jones-style dishing will be caught up in Powell's funny, sharp-tongued but generous writing." Publishers Weekly.

Power, Carla

Power, Carla **If** the oceans were ink : an unlikely friendship and a journey to the heart of the Qur'an / Carla Power. Henry Holt and Company, 2015. 320 p. **B**

ISBN 9780805098198

1. Power, Carla. 2. Muslim women. 3. Converts to Islam. 4. Islam. 5. Religion. 6. Autobiographies and memoirs

LC 2014017543

Pulitzer Prize for General Nonfiction finalist, 2016.

National Book Award for Nonfiction finalist, 2015

If the Oceans Were Ink is Carla Power's eye-opening story of how she and her longtime friend Sheikh Mohammad Akram Nadwi found a way to confront ugly stereotypes and persistent misperceptions that were cleaving their communities. Their friendship between a secular American and a madrasa-trained sheikh had always seemed unlikely, but now they were frustrated and bewildered by the battles being fought in their names. Both knew that a close look at the Quran would reveal a faith that preached peace and not mass murder; respect for women and not oppression. And so they embarked on a year long journey through the controversial text.

"Powers narrative offers an accessible and enlightening route into a topic fraught with misunderstanding." Publishers Weekly.

Power, Marianne

Power, Marianne **Help** me! : one woman's quest to find out if self-help really can change your life / Marianne Power. Grove Press, 2019, c2018. 384 p. **B**

ISBN 9780802129062

1. Women -- Psychology 2. Self-help psychology 3. Self-improvement 4. Self-fulfillment 5. Autobiographies and memoirs

LC 2018045957

Originally published in the UK by Pan Macmillan, 2018."

Some of her plights are hilarious; others are almost unbearably poignant. Self-help seekers will be moved and entertained by Powers over-the-top exploits " Booklist.

Power, Samantha

Power, Samantha The **education** of an idealist : a memoir / Samantha Power. Dey Street Books, 2019. xii, 580 p. : **B**

ISBN 9780062820693

1. United Nations Officials and employees 2. Human rights policy 3. Ambassadors -- United States 4. Irish American women 5. Immigrants, Irish 6. United States -- Politics and government. 7. United States -- Foreign relations. 8. Autobiographies and memoirs

The Pulitzer Prize winner and former U.N. Ambassador traces her journey from an Irish immigrant to a human rights activist, sharing insights into her career as a war correspondent and her influential views on foreign policy.

Powers, J. F. (James Farl), 1917-1999

Powers, J. F. (James Farl), 1917-1999 **Suitable** accommodations : an autobiographical story of family life : the letters of J. F. Powers, 1942-1963 / edited by Katherine A. Powers. Farrar, Straus and Giroux, 2013. 480 p. **B**

ISBN 9780374268060

1. Authors, American -- 20th century. 2. Families 3. Catholics. 4. Independence (Personal quality) 5. Letters. 6. Autobiographies and memoirs

LC 2013010997

Includes index.

This collection of letters from the late "comic writer of genius" starts with prison, where he spent more than a year as a conscientious objector, and moves through his courtship, his marriage, his struggle with faith and his increasingly bizarre search for suitable accommodations.

Powers, Ron

Powers, Ron **No** one cares about crazy people : the chaos and heartbreak of mental health in America / Ron Powers. Hachette Books, 2017. 384 p. ; **B**

ISBN 9780316341172

1. Powers, Ron Family 2. Schizophrenia 3. Health policy -- United States 4. People with mental illnesses 5. People with schizophrenia 6. Autobiographies and memoirs

LC 2016046019

The journalist and co-author of True Compass offers a fast-paced, carefully researched narrative of the social history of mental illness, focusing specifically on schizophrenia, the taboos that compromise mental health care and the way the disease has devastated his own family.

"Readers will surely be moved by this double portrait of one familys days of happiness and sorrow, and the worlds halting and flawed attempts to care for troubled people." Publishers Weekly.

Pratchett, Terry

Pratchett, Terry A **slip** of the keyboard : collected nonfiction / Terry Pratchett ; introduction by Neil Gaiman. Doubleday, 2014. 336 p. **B**

ISBN 9780385538305

1. Pratchett, Terry. 2. Life. 3. Popular culture. 4. Fantasy writing. 5. Animal welfare. 6. Autobiographies and memoirs. 7. Essays.

LC 2014011949

A collection of essays and other non fiction from Terry Pratchett, spanning the whole of his writing career from his early years to the present day. Terry Pratchett has earned a place in the hearts of readers the world over with his bestselling Discworld series -- but in recent years he has become equally well-known and respected as an outspoken campaigner for causes including Alzheimer's research and animal rights. A Slip of the Keyboard brings together for the first time the finest examples of Pratchett's non fiction writing, both serious and surreal: from musings on mushrooms to what it means to be a writer (and why banana daiquiris are so important); from memories of Granny Pratchett to speculation about Gandalf's love life, and passionate defences of the causes dear to him. With all the humour and humanity that have made his novels so enduringly popular, this collection brings Pratchett out from behind the scenes of the Discworld to speak for himself -- man and boy, bibliophile and computer geek,champion of hats, orangutans and Dignity in Dying.

"The essays, letters, speeches, and articles feature all the wit and charm of his beloved novels and allow readers a more personal look at Pratchett's life and beliefs. In a mere 336 pages, Pratchett ruminates on the underappreciated role of fantasy fiction and its importance in the literary world; the trick to becoming a successful author (hint: there isn't one); the care and feeding of authors while on book tours; and his work with fellow writer and friend Neil Gaiman." Booklist.

Prejean, Helen

Prejean, Helen **River** of fire : my spiritual journey / Sister Helen Prejean, C.S.J.. Random House, 2019. 320 p. **B**

ISBN 9781400067305

1. Sisters of Saint Joseph 2. Catholic Church 3. Nuns 4. Faith (Christianity) 5. Social advocacy 6. Social justice 7. Autobiographies and memoirs

LC 2018051678

In this revelatory, intimate memoir from the author of Dead Man Walking, the nation's foremost leader in efforts to abolish the death penalty shares the story of her growth as a spiritual leader, speaks out about the challenges of the Catholic Church, and shows that joy and religion are not mutually exclusive.

"Informing and entertaining, Prejeans exceptional memoir will be of special interest to Catholics and social justice advocates." Publishers Weekly.

Presley, Elvis, 1935-1977

Alden, Ginger **Elvis** and Ginger : Elvis Presley's fiancee and last love finally tells her story / Ginger Alden. Berkley Publishing Group, 2014. 400 p. **B**

ISBN 9780425266335

1. Alden, Ginger. 2. Rock musicians -- United States 3. Young women -- Relations with older men 4. Engaged persons 5. Rock music 6. Biographies

LC 2014009089

Breaking her thirty-year silence, the former fiancée to Elvis Presley tells the story of her whirlwind romance with the King and what it was like being in Graceland when fifty thousand mourners arrived to pay their respects.

"It's an outpouring of affection for a man who has stayed in the author's mind all these years, a way for her to show the world the Elvis she knew. The book has a pretty much guaranteed readership, as many Elvis fans will read anything and everything that appears in print about their idol." Booklist.

Connolly, Ray, 1940- **Being** Elvis : a lonely life / Ray Connolly. Liveright Publishing Corporation, 2016. 368 p. **B**

ISBN 9781631492808

1. Presley, Elvis, 1935-1977. 2. Singers -- United States 3. Rock musicians -- United States 4. Rock music 5. Biographies

LC 2016054735

Taking a fresh look at the 20th-century icon who fundamentally transformed American culture, a veteran rock journalist, with a narrative formed by interviews over many years, explores the extravagance and irrationality inherent in the Elvis mythology, offering a thoughtful celebration of an immortal life.

"Connolly carefully and sympathetically paints the many faces of Presley, faces eventually shrouded in despair." Kirkus.

★Guralnick, Peter **Careless** love : the unmaking of Elvis Presley / Peter Guralnick. Little, Brown, 1999. xv, 767 p. : **B**

ISBN 9780316332224

1. Presley, Elvis, 1935-1977. 2. United States. Army. 3. Rock musicians -- United States 4. Marriage. 5. Faith in men. 6. Prescription drug abuse. 7. Biographies

LC 98025778

Sequel to: Last train to Memphis.

Recounts the second half of Elvis Presley's life, from his army service in 1958 Germany through his death in 1977, and focuses on his relationship with manager Colonel Tom Parker.

"This second and concluding volume of Guralnick's biography of the rock star covers Elvis's hitch in the army through his death in 1977. . . . The breadth of Guralnick's research is nothing short of amazing, and his lyrical narrative presents an empathetic portrait of a man struggling with drugs, sex, family, personal eccentricities, money, and the delicate web of relationships surrounding any famous figure." Library Journal.

Mason, Bobbie Ann **Elvis** Presley / Bobbie Ann Mason. Viking, 2003. x, 178 p. : **B**

ISBN 0670031747

1. Presley, Elvis, 1935-1977. 2. Rock musicians -- United States 3. Biographies

LC 2002028873

"A Lipper/Viking book."

Charts the life of the rock-and-roll music star from his childhood experiences as a devoted son from a small town to the achievements that changed the nation's musical culture.

Victor, Adam, 1964- The **Elvis** encyclopedia / Adam Victor. Overlook Duckworth, 2008. 598 p. : **B**

ISBN 1585675989

1. Presley, Elvis, 1935-1977 Encyclopedias.

LC bl2009003376

A comprehensive and in-depth tribute to the iconic rock-and-roll legend provides complete coverage of every aspect of his life, from his disadvantaged youth and meteoric rise to fame to his marriage to Priscilla and untimely death, in a detailed resource complemented by hundreds of photographs.

Zoglin, Richard **Elvis** in Vegas : the heyday and reinvention of the Las Vegas show / Richard Zoglin. Simon & Schuster, 2019. 320 p. **B**

ISBN 9781501151194

1. Popular music -- History and criticism. 2. Entertainment industry and trade 3. Rock musicians 4. Rock music 5. Las Vegas, Nevada -- History. 6. United States -- Popular culture -- History -- 20th century 7. Biographies

LC 2018057437

Tells the story of how Las Vegas saved Elvis and Elvis saved Las Vegas in the greatest musical comeback of all time.

"Elvis fans will enjoy this richly sourced look at one of the most consequential performances of his career and his lasting legacy in the city that hosted him." Publishers Weekly.

Preston, Douglas J.

Preston, Douglas J. The **lost** city of the monkey god : a true story / Douglas Preston. Grand Central Publishing, 2017. 336 p. **B**

ISBN 9781455540006

1. Preston, Douglas J. Travel Mosquitia (Nicaragua and Honduras) 2. Extinct cities 3. Jungles 4. Excavations (Archaeology) 5. Wildlife 6. Mosquitia (Nicaragua and Honduras) -- Description and travel 7. Honduras 8. Autobiographies and memoirs

LC 2016037247

Though he's probably better known as the co-author of the suspenseful Pendergast novels, Douglas Preston also writes thrilling nonfiction. In his latest real-life adventure tale, he gives us a compelling, high-octane account of his travels in Honduras' Mosquitia area, where he's part of a team looking for evidence of the fabled Ciudad Blanca (The White City) aka "The Lost City of the Monkey God" -- but the group has to deal with unfriendly soldiers, parasites, jaguars, snakes, insects, and more.

Preston, Katherine, 1984-

Preston, Katherine, 1984- **Out** with it : how stuttering helped me find my voice / Katherine Preston. Atria Books, 2013. 272 p. **B**

ISBN 9781451676587

1. Preston, Katherine, 1984- Health. 2. Young women 3. Self-perception. 4. Stuttering. 5. Stutterers. 6. Autobiographies and memoirs

LC 2012048984

"A fresh, engaging account of a young woman's journey, first to find a cure for a lifelong struggle with stuttering, and ultimately to embrace the voice that has defined her character".-- Provided by publisher.

Prince

Greenman, Ben **Dig** if you will the picture : funk, sex, god and genius in the music of Prince / Ben Greenman. Henry Holt and Company, 2017. 304 p. **B**

ISBN 9781250128379

1. Rock musicians -- United States 2. Popular music composers 3. Popular music -- Social aspects 4. Musicians 5. Biographies

LC 2016054759

Presents a unique and kaleidoscopic look into the life, legacy and electricity of the pop legend Prince and his wide-ranging impact on our culture.

"As much a fan boy as an authority, rock journalist Greenman . investigates Princes development as an artist, his career trajectory, his massive creative output, and his numerous side projects." Booklist.

Shahidi, Afshin **Prince** : a private view / Afshin Shahidi ; foreword by Beyonce Knowles-Carter. St. Martin's Press,

2017. xvi, 235 p. : **B**

ISBN 9781250134431

1. Prince Portraits. 2. Rock musicians -- United States -- Portraits. 3. Rock musicians -- United States -- Portraits. 4. Photographers -- United States -- Catalogs. 5. Illustrated books

LC 2017032068

The photographer who was a trusted friend to and long-time collaborator with Prince presents 250 photos of the late artist, taken between 2001 and 2010, that provide never-before-seen glimpses into his personal and professional life.

Prior-Palmer, Lara

Prior-Palmer, Lara **Rough** magic : riding the world's loneliest horse race / Lara Prior-Palmer. Catapult, 2019. 224 p. **B**

ISBN 9781948226196

1. Horse racing 2. Women and horses 3. Competition 4. Young women 5. Mongolia 6. Autobiographies and memoirs

LC 2018950159

For fans of Helen Macdonald's H Is for Hawk, this is the extraordinary debut memoir of a young woman who traveled to Mongolia to compete in the world's longest, toughest horse race, and emerged as its youngest and first-ever female winner.

"First-time author Prior-Palmer transforms from hopeless 19-year-old underdog into surprising champion of the grueling 2013 Mongol Derby in this exhilarating, visceral account of her attempt to win a 1,000-kilometer horse race across the Mongolian countryside." Publishers Weekly.

Proulx, Annie

Proulx, Annie **Bird** cloud : a memoir / Annie Proulx. Simon & Schuster 2011 320 p. **B**

ISBN 9780743288804

1. Proulx, Annie. 2. Women authors 3. Natural areas 4. House construction 5. Wyoming. 6. Autobiographies and memoirs

LC 2011389064

The author describes her purchase of six hundred wilderness acres in Wyoming and construction of a library-centric home where she contemplated her rich family history, including a river boat captain ancestor who met historical figures.

"Proulx bought a 640-acre nature preserve by the North Platte River in Wyoming and started building her dream house, a project that took years and went hundreds of thousands of dollars over budget. In her bustling account, Proulx salivates over the prospect of a Japanese soak tub, polished concrete floor, solar panels, and luxe furnishings that often turn into pricey engineering fiascoes. [This] is a fine evocation of place that becomes a meditation on the importance of a home, however harsh and evanescent." Publishers Weekly.

Proust, Marcel, 1871-1922

Carter, William C., 1941- **Marcel** Proust : a life / William C. Carter. Yale University Press, 2000. xiv, 946 p. : **B**

ISBN 0300081456

1. Proust, Marcel, 1871-1922. 2. Authors, French -- 20th century 3. Biographies

LC 99053701

"Excavating biographic details out of such material as untranslated memoirs and recently collected letters, Carter . accounts for the daily affairs of this social butterfly-turned-hypochondriac and shut-in. Proust's romances and infatuations, his political action during the Dreyfus affair, and his literary runs-ins with Anatole France and André Gide, as well as larger issues such as his homosexuality, all receive lengthy treatment." Publishers Weekly.

Pryor, Richard

Henry, David, 1958- **Furious** cool : Richard Pryor and the world that made him / David Henry and Joe Henry. Algonquin Books of Chapel Hill, 2013 400 p. **B**

ISBN 9781616200787

1. Comedians -- United States 2. African American comedians 3. African American actors and actresses 4. Film actors and actresses -- United States 5. Biographies

LC 2013019665

Provides a rare glimpse into the life of an outrageously human, fearlessly black, openly angry and profanely outspoken comedic genius whose humble beginnings as the child of a prostitute helped shaped him into one of the most influential and outstanding performers of our time.

"A beautifully written account of the troubled life of a manic genius." Booklist.

Przybylo, Henry Jay

Przybylo, Henry Jay **Counting** backwards : a doctor's notes on anesthesia / Henry Jay Przybylo. W.W. Norton & Company, 2017 256 p. ; **B**

ISBN 9780393254433

1. Przybylo, Henry Jay. 2. Anesthesiologists. 3. Anesthesia. 4. Physicians. 5. Medicine 6. Autobiographies and memoirs

LC 2017018049

An anesthesiologist with more than thirty years of experience explores the most common but most mysterious procedure in medicine, telling intimate stories that explore the nature of consciousness, the politics of pain relief, and the wonder of modern medicine.

"Przybylo offers a rare and thoughtful look behind the scenes of this crucial yet arcane specialization." Publishers Weekly.

Ptacin, Mira

Ptacin, Mira **Poor** your soul : a memoir / Mira Ptacin. Soho Press, 2016. 320 p. **B**

ISBN 9781616956349

1. Ptacin, Mira. 2. Ptacin, Mira Family. 3. Women authors, American 4. First pregnancy. 5. Loss (Psychology). 6. Bereavement 7. Autobiographies and memoirs

LC 2015028123

A woman describes her road to hope and recovery as she intertwines her own story of the loss of a baby due to a birth defect, with that of her mother, who lost the son she adopted after emigrating from Poland.

"Ptacin's memoir is a raw and absorbing story of family fortitude and a young woman's struggle to confront and accept the unexpected." Publishers Weekly.

Puccini, Giacomo, 1858-1924

Berger, William, 1961- **Puccini** without excuses : a refreshing reassessment of the world's most popular composer / William Berger. Vintage Books, 2005. 471 p. ; **B**

ISBN 1400077788

1. Puccini, Giacomo, 1858-1924. Operas. 2. Classical music 3. Composers -- Italy -- 19th century 4. Operas -- Stories, plots, etc. 5. Italy -- Social life and customs -- 19th century 6. Biographies

LC 2005046157

A critical analysis of the life and work of the popular operatic composer reassesses Puccini's role in the history of music and his enduring legacy, in a study that encompasses a biographical profile, detailed discussions of each of his operatic works, recommended recordings and videos, trivia and anecdotes, and a helpful glossary.

"The author sets Puccini within his times before discussing the circumstances of each opera's premiere and famous interpreters of the roles, providing character lists and synopses and fleshing all this out with musical commentary. Chapters on opera production and the genre's relation to film are useful. Berger's lucid yet hardly dispassionate views are designed to elicit strong reactions, so this is not the first place one should go for an unbiased introduction to the composer's oeuvre. But the author's grounding information is helpful for the novice, and he refers to some of the current authoritative sources." Library Journal.

Pujol, Juan,

Talty, Stephan **Agent** Garbo : how a brilliant, eccentric spy tricked Hitler and saved D-Day / Stephan Talty. Houghton Mifflin Harcourt, 2012. 320 p. **B**

ISBN 9780547614816

1. World War II. 2. Spies -- Great Britain 3. Espionage -- History -- 20th century 4. Secret service -- Great Britain -- History -- 20th century 5. London, England -- History -- 20th century 6. Germany -- Politics and government -- 1933-1945 7. Biographies

LC 2012005470

Describes the life of Juan Pujol, a poultry farmer who opposed the Nazis and concocted a series of staggering lies that lead to his becoming one of Germany's most valued spies, while actually acting as a double-agent for the Allies.

Pulitzer, Joseph, 1847-1911

Morris, James McGrath **Pulitzer** : a life in politics, print, and power / James McGrath Morris. Harper, 2010. 576 p. **B**

ISBN 9780060798697

1. Journalists -- United States 2. Journalists 3. Mass media -- Ownership. 4. Newspaper publishers and publishing 5. Biographies

LC 2009027501

"Comprehensive biography of media mogul Joseph Pulitzer".--Provided by publisher.

Purkayastha, Ian, 1992-

Purkayastha, Ian, 1992- **Truffle** Boy : my unexpected journey through the exotic food underground / Ian Purkayastha with Kevin West. Hachette Books, 2016. 304 p. **B**

ISBN 9780316383950

1. Truffles. 2. Gourmet food industry and trade 3. Businesspeople. 4. Restaurant management 5. Autobiographies and memoirs

LC 2016008650

In a recipe-augmented biography, a purveyor of truffles and other highly-desired specialty foods explains how he built a devoted clientele of New York's chicest chefs and restaurateurs.

Pushkin, Aleksandr Sergeevich, 1799-1837

★Binyon, T. J. **Pushkin** : a biography / T.J. Binyon. Knopf, 2003. xxix, 727 p., 16 p. of plates : **B**

ISBN 9781400041107

1. Pushkin, Aleksandr Sergeevich, 1799-1837. 2. Poets, Russian -- 19th century 3. Men/women relations. 4. Marriage. 5. Biographies

LC 2003112113

Samuel Johnson Prize for Nonfiction, 2003."

The author argues that Pushkin's political views and rebellious temper were a continual source of trouble, inviting criticism and condemnation his entire life and eventually ending it in 1837 when he was fatally wounded in a duel with George D'Anthes. A stunning achievement, this thorough biography is sure to become the definitive account of Pushkin's life for years to come and will appeal to the scholar and general reader alike." Library Journal.

Putin, Vladimir Vladimirovich, 1952-

Myers, Steven Lee The **new** tsar : the rise and reign of Vladimir Putin / Steven Lee Myers. Alfred A. Knopf, 2015. 416 p. **B**

ISBN 9780307961617

1. Political leadership. 2. Presidents -- Russia. 3. Power (Social sciences). 4. Russia -- Politics and government -- 1991- 5. Russia -- Social conditions -- 1991- 6. Biographies

LC 2015010720

"A Borzoi book"--Title page verso.

Tells the epic tale of the rise to power of Russia's current president of his emergence from shrouded obscurity and deprivation to become one of the most consequential and complicated leaders in modern history.

Putin, Vladimir Vladimirovich, 1952- **First** person : an astonishingly frank self-portrait by Russia's president Vladimir Putin / with Nataliya Gevorkyan, Natalya Timakova, and Andrei Kolesnikov ; translated by Catherine A. Fitzpatrick. PublicAffairs, c2000. xiii, 206, 1 p., 16 p. of plates ; **B**

ISBN 9781586480189

1. Putin, Vladimir Vladimirovich, 1952- Interviews. 2. Soviet Union. Komitet gosudarstvenno bezopasnosti -- History. 3. Presidents -- Russia (Federation) 4. Presidents -- Russia (Federation) -- Interviews. 5. Intelligence service -- Soviet Union -- History. 6. Russia (Federation) -- Politics and government -- 1991- 7. Soviet Union -- History. 8. Soviet Union -- Politics and government.

LC 00132549

Reveals the childhood, education, and personal life of Russia's newest president through interviews with Vladimir Putin, his wife, staff, and friends.

Pyle, Ernie, 1900-1945

Tobin, James, 1956- **Ernie** Pyle's war : America's eyewitness to World War II / James Tobin. Free Press, 1997. 312 p. : **B**

ISBN 0684836424

1. Pyle, Ernie, 1900-1945. 2. War correspondents -- United States 3. Journalists. 4. World War II 5. Journalism -- Objectivity. 6. Pacific Ocean. 7. Biographies

LC 97006165

National Book Critics Circle Award for Biography, 1997."

Living and working among the troops he so vividly chronicled, Pyle offered a unique insider's perspective of the harsh reality experienced by the common soldier during World War II. A respectful and insightful biography of a giant among journalists." Booklist.

Qashu, Sayed, 1975-

Qashu, Sayed, 1975- **Native** : dispatches from an Israeli-Palestinian life / Sayed Kashua ; translated from the Hebrew by Ralph Mandel. Grove Press, 2016. 304 p. **B**

ISBN 9780802124555

1. Arab-Israeli conflict. 2. Palestinians -- Israel 3. Prejudice 4. Israel 5. Essays 6. Autobiographies and memoirs

LC bl2016000992

Translation from the Hebrew of: Ben haaretz."

A wickedly ironic but humane collection." Kirkus.

Quin, Tegan, 1980-

Quin, Tegan, 1980- **High** school / Tegan and Sara. Farrar, Straus and Giroux, 2019. 384 p. **B**

ISBN 9780374169947

1. Quin, Sara, 1980- 2. Tegan and Sara. 3. Twin sisters. 4. Singers -- Canada 5. Musicians -- Canada 6. Autobiographies and memoirs

LC 2019014934

Award-winning identical twin music artists Tegan and Sara share the coming-of-age story of their high school years, detailing how their early relationships, family tragedies and high expectations shaped their rise to celebrated musicians and global LGBTQ icons.

Quindlen, Anna

★Quindlen, Anna **Nanaville** : Adventures in Grandparenting / Anna Quindlen. Random House, [2019] 160 p. **B**

ISBN 9780812996104

1. Quindlen, Anna Family. 2. Grandmothers 3. Grandparent and child 4. Grandmother and child 5. Happiness 6. Autobiographies and memoirs

LC 2018052184

Before mommy blogs were even invented, Anna Quindlen became a go-to writer on the joys and challenges of motherhood in her nationally syndicated column. Now she's taking the next step and going full Nana in the pages of this lively and moving book about: her grandchildren, her children, and her new and remarkable role.

"The author imparts sensible advice with self-deprecating humor and sincere gratitude for the bounty of her life. A warmhearted memoir sure to appeal to other new grandmothersand Quindlen's many fans." Kirkus.

Quinones-Hinojosa, Alfredo

Quinones-Hinojosa, Alfredo **Becoming** Dr. Q : my journey from migrant farm worker to brain surgeon / Alfredo Quinones-Hinojosa ; with Mim Eichler Rivas. University of California Press, c2011. 317 p., 24 p. of plates : **B**

ISBN 9780520271180

1. Quinones-Hinojosa, Alfredo. 2. Neurosurgeons 3. Mexican Americans -- Mexico 4. Nervous system -- Surgery 5. Immigrants -- Mexico 6. Autobiographies and memoirs

LC 2011011531

"When the callow Quiones-Hinojosa, or Dr. Q, made up his mind to pursue a better life and, especially, an education in the U.S., no border or barrier could have kept him from his destiny: a fate that led eventually to his becoming a Johns Hopkins University neurosurgeon, professor, and brain-cancer research scientist. Indeed, the brash teenager left all that was familiar in his native Mexico and, with less than $70 in his pocket, climbed the fence. In fact, he scaled it twice because he was caught the first time and sent back. Quiones-Hinojosa's story is gripping, inspiring, and just plain awesome." Booklist.

Radtke, Kristen

Radtke, Kristen **Imagine** wanting only this / Kristen Radtke. Pantheon Books, 2017. 277 p. : **B**

ISBN 9781101870839

1. Radtke, Kristen Travels 2. Women travelers 3. Extinct cities 4. Life change events 5. Young women 6. Comics and Graphic novels 7. Autobiographical comics 8. Autobiographies and memoirs

LC 2016034575

When Kristen Radtke was in college, the sudden death of a beloved uncle and, not long after his funeral, the sight of an abandoned mining town marked the beginning moments of a lifelong fascination with ruins and with people and places left behind. Over time, this fascination deepened until it triggered a journey around the world in search of ruined places.

"A fantastic example of the graphic novels possibilities as a literary medium, this work is visually imperfect, lyrically beautiful, and unquestionably brave." Library Journal.

Rahr, Guido

Malarkey, Tucker **Stronghold** : one man's quest to save the world's wild salmon / Tucker Malarkey. Spiegel & Grau, 2019. 352 p. **B**

ISBN 9781984801692

1. Salmon 2. Wildlife conservation 3. Fishery conservation 4. Pacific salmon 5. Oregon 6. Alaska 7. Russia 8. Biographies

LC 2018047731

A nonfiction debut by the author of the best-selling An Obvious Enchantment documents the story of fly fisherman and environmentalist Guido Rahr and his dangerous mission to protect the world's last major salmon habitat.

"This fascinating account of Rahr's crusade to get a multinational salmon conservation effort off the ground will be an enjoyable read for those interested in wilderness conservation and salmon ecology." Library Journal.

Rakoff, Joanna Smith, 1972-

Rakoff, Joanna Smith, 1972- **My** Salinger year / Joanna Rakoff. Alfred A. Knopf, 2014. 272 p. **B**

ISBN 9780307958006

1. Salinger, J. D. (Jerome David), 1919-2010 2. Literature -- Publishing. 3. Authors, American -- 21st century 4. Literary agents 5. Fan mail 6. New York City 7. Coming-of-age stories 8. Autobiographies and memoirs

LC 2013026931

Traces the author's experiences in 1990s New York as the assistant to the agent of J. D. Salinger, a job that contrasted with her threadbare personal life and was enriched by the famous writer's fan letters. By the award-winning author of A Fortunate Age.

"As Rakoff recounts her funny and wrenching personal predicaments, she also charts the quiet battle of attrition between the values of the old publishing world, personal and impassioned, and the aggressively invasive corporate imperative. An intriguing look at the ever-fascinating Salinger and a gracefully incisive tale of love and literature, creativity and survival." Booklist.

Raleigh, Walter, 1552?-1618

Gallay, Alan, 1957- **Walter** Ralegh : architect of empire / Alan Gallay. Basic Books, 2019. 576 p. **B**

ISBN 9781541645790

1. Elizabeth I, Queen of England, 1533-1603 2. Explorers -- Great Britain 3. Courts and courtiers 4. Colonists 5. Poets 6. Great Britain -- Colonies. 7. Great Britain -- History -- Elizabeth I, 1558-1603. 8. Great Britain -- History -- James I, 1603-1625 9. United States -- History -- Colonial period, 1600-1775 10. Biographies

LC 2019010985

The award-winning author of The Indian Slave Trade examines the life of the court poet, colonizer and favorite of Elizabeth I against a backdrop of his hermetic philosophical beliefs and his vision of a universal English empire.

Ramanujan Aiyangar, Srinivasa, 1887-1920

Kanigel, Robert The **man** who knew infinity : a life of the genius, Ramanujan / Robert Kanigel. C. Scribner's, c1991. ix, 438 p. : **B**

ISBN 0684192594

1. Ramanujan Aiyangar, Srinivasa, 1887-1920. 2. Hardy, G. H. (Godfrey Harold), 1877-1947. 3. Mathematicians -- India 4. Mathematicians -- Great Britain 5. Genius -- History -- 20th century 6. India -- Social life and customs -- 20th century 7. Great Britain

-- Social life and customs -- 20th century 8. Biographies

LC 90049788

National Book Critics Circle Award for Biography finalist, 1991."

Kanigel deserves high praise for a work of arduous research and rare insight." Booklist.

Ramey, Sarah

Ramey, Sarah The **lady's** handbook for her mysterious illness : a memoir / Sarah Ramey. Doubleday 2020 304 p. **B**

ISBN 9780385534079

1. Ramey, Sarah Health. 2. Reflex sympathetic dystrophy 3. Chronic diseases. 4. Sexism in medicine. 5. Women -- Health. 6. Autobiographies and memoirs

LC 2019018299

The funny, defiant memoir of Sarah Ramey's years-long battle with a mysterious illness that doctors thought was all in her head--but wasn't. A revelation and an inspiration for millions of women whose legitimate health complaints are ignored.

"A visceral, scathing, erudite read that digs deep into how modern medicine continues to fail women and what can be done about it." Booklist

Ramos, Isaias

Connolly, Daniel The **book** of Isaias : a child of Hispanic immigrants seeks his own America / Daniel Connolly. St. Martin's Press, 2016. 272 p. **B**

ISBN 9781250083067

1. Ramos, Isaias. 2. Mexican American students 3. Children of immigrants 4. Minority college students 5. Universities and colleges -- Admission 6. Memphis, Tennessee 7. Biographies

LC 2016018423

"Connolly unearths the human element behind one of todays most debated issues, asking expert and everyday readers alike to consider how the immigrant experience is affecting one of the fastest-growing youth populations in the nation." Publishers Weekly.

Ramos, Jason A.

Ramos, Jason A. **Smokejumper** : a memoir by one of America's most select airborne firefighters / Jason A. Ramos and Julian Smith. HarperCollins 2015 336 p. **B**

ISBN 9780062319623

1. Smokejumpers 2. Smokejumping 3. Wildfires 4. Fire fighting 5. Autobiographies and memoirs

LC 2015007015

An insider account of the high-risk world of elite wilderness firefighters who parachute into deep-wilderness fire zones reveals the unique skills that smokejumpers must employ to fight dangerous fires and stay alive.

"Most of us avoid jumping from the frying pan into the fire, but as an elite smokejumper with the Department of the Interior Ramos does it regularly, often alone or with just one partner." Library Journal.

Ramos, Jorge, 1958-

Ramos, Jorge, 1958- **Stranger** : the challenge of a Latino immigrant in the Trump era / Jorge Ramos. Vintage Books, 2018. 192 p. **B**

ISBN 9780525563792

1. Immigrants -- Public opinion 2. Immigration and emigration 3. Citizenship 4. Racism 5. United States -- Immigration and emigration 6. Autobiographies and memoirs

LC bl2018012491

Simultaneously published in Spanish by Vintage Español.

In this personal manifesto, Ramos sets out to examine what it means to be a Latino immigrant, or just an immigrant, in present-day America. Using current research and statistics, with a journalist's nose for a story, and interweaving his own personal experience, Ramos shows us the changing face of America while also trying to find an explanation for why he, and millions of others, still feel like strangers in this country.

" An insightful read about prejudice against Latinx individuals in America. Readers of politics and culture will find Ramos's book enlightening." Library Journal.

Ramsay, Gordon

Ramsay, Gordon **Roasting** in Hell's Kitchen : temper tantrums, F words, and the pursuit of perfection / Gordon Ramsay. Harper Collins, 2007, c2006. 287 p. **B**

ISBN 9780061191985

1. Ramsay, Gordon. 2. Cooks -- England 3. Childhood -- Great Britain 4. Anger in men 5. Cooking 6. Great Britain -- Social life and customs -- 21st century 7. Autobiographies and memoirs

LC bl2007006460

Includes index.

Originally published: New York : Harper Entertainment, 2006.

An outspoken celebrity chef from the "Hell's Kitchen" reality television show describes his relationships with his violent father and mercurial mentor, his experiences with a host of celebrity patrons, and his work in several famous restaurants.

Ramsey, Franchesca, 1983-

Ramsey, Franchesca, 1983- **Well,** that escalated quickly : memoirs and mistakes of an accidental activist / Franchesca Ramsey. Grand Central Publishing, 2018. 288 p. **B**

ISBN 9781538761038

1. YouTube (Electronic resource) 2. Twitter (Electronic resource) 3. Bloggers 4. Social media 5. Television personalities 6. Communication and technology 7. Autobiographies and memoirs

LC 2017055221

"In this sharp, funny, and incredibly timely collection of personal essays, veteran video blogger and star of MTV's Decoded, Franchesca Ramsey explores race, identity, online activism, and the downfall of real communication in the age of Twitter rants and call-out wars".--Provided by publisher.

Rand, Ayn

Heller, Anne Conover **Ayn** Rand and the world she made / Anne C. Heller. Nan A. Talese/Doubleday, 2008. 592 p. **B**

ISBN 9780385513999

1. Rand, Ayn. 2. Authors, American -- 20th century 3. Philosophers -- United States 4. Objectivism (Philosophy) 5. Authors, American 6. Biographies

LC 2008027638

A portrait of the influential writer and philosopher examines her contributions to American culture and politics, offering insight into her childhood in Russia, successful literary career, and passionate advocacy of laissez-faire capitalism.

"The author has delivered a thoughtful, flesh-and-blood portrait of an extremely complicated and self-contradictory woman, coupling this character study with literary analysis and plumbing the quirkier depths of Rand's prodigious imagination." New York Times.

Rand, Ayn **Journals** of Ayn Rand / edited by David Harriman ; foreword by Leonard Peikoff. Plume Books, 1999, c1997.

xviii, 727 p. : **B**

ISBN 9780452278875

1. Rand, Ayn Diaries. 2. Objectivism (Philosophy) 3. Women novelists, American -- 20th century -- Diaries 4. Women philosophers -- United States -- Diaries

LC BL 99012111

Includes index.

Originally published: New York : Dutton, 1997.

The private journals of one of the most influential writers of the twentieth century reveal the progression of Rand's literary and philosophical ideals.

"This work offers almost everything the author ever wrote to herself. As intriguing yet sometimes numbing as her fiction, the book, which covers the years from 1927 to the mid-1970s, contains her first philosophical stabs, notes on her novels, HUAC testimony against alleged Hollywood communists, and her unfinished projects." Publishers Weekly.

Rand, Ayn **Letters** of Ayn Rand / edited by Michael S. Berliner ; introduction by Leonard Peikoff. Dutton, c1995. xxi, 681 p. : **B**

ISBN 0525939466

1. Rand, Ayn Correspondence. 2. Authors, American -- 20th century -- Correspondence. 3. Philosophers -- United States -- Correspondence. 4. Objectivism (Philosophy) 5. United States -- Social life and customs -- 20th century.

LC 94023646

Includes index."

Imbued with her fiercely held beliefs, the letters most devoted to politics and philosophy fairly blaze off the page. Regardless of one's opinion of her thinking, her letters add greatly to our understanding of a most exceptional woman of letters." Booklist.

Rankin, Lissa, 1969-

Rankin, Lissa, 1969- The **anatomy** of a calling : a doctor's journey from the head to the heart and a prescription for finding your life's purpose / Lissa, Rankin. Rodale, 2015 288 p. **B**

ISBN 9781623365745

1. Self-discovery 2. Spiritual journeys. 3. Women physicians. 4. Autobiographies and memoirs

LC 2015040863

The best-selling author of Mind Over Medicine presents a spiritual narrative written to inspire readers to discover their personal heroic calling, sharing the story of her own transformative experience of self-awareness that led to her career as a healer.

"Readers who seek more information and methodology regarding mind/body healing and health through diverse spiritual practices will find Rankins story fascinating." Publishers Weekly.

Rannells, Andrew

Rannells, Andrew **Too** much is not enough : a memoir of fumbling toward adulthood / Andrew Rannells. Crown Publishing, 2019. xii, 251 p. ; **B**

ISBN 9780525574859

1. Actors and actresses 2. Young men 3. Ambition 4. Acting 5. Broadway, New York City 6. New York City 7. Autobiographies and memoirs

The star of Broadway's The Book of Mormon and HBO's Girls presents a heartfelt coming-of-age memoir that recounts how, as a fiercely ambitious but sexually confused Midwestern teen, he haphazardly pursued his theatrical dreams in 1997 New York City.

"In a spirited debut saturated with personality and frank humor, Rannells tells the stories of his youth growing up as the fourth of five siblings in Omaha, Nebraska." Kirkus.

Rao, Cheeni

Rao, Cheeni **In** Hanuman's hands : a memoir of recovery and redemption / Cheeni Rao. HarperOne, c2008. 416 p. **B**

ISBN 9780060736620

1. Rao, Cheeni. 2. Drug addicts -- Rehabilitation. 3. Young men 4. East Indian Americans 5. Hindus -- United States 6. Autobiographies and memoirs

LC 2008055421

A descendant of Brahmin priests combines his own story of encountering western culture with the mythic tales of his Hindu ancestors to describe how he fell subject to the temptations of sex, crime, and drugs while attending an elite New England college before hitting bottom and finding the inspiration to recover through visions of the mischievous monkey god Hanuman.

Rapp Black, Emily

Rapp Black, Emily The **still** point of the turning world / Emily Rapp. The Penguin Press, 2013. 224 p. **B**

ISBN 9781594205125

1. Tay-Sachs Disease. 2. Children with terminal illnesses -- Family relationships. 3. Parents 4. Mothers 5. Autobiographies and memoirs

LC 2012039516

Relates how the author's hopes for her infant son were shattered when he was diagnosed with a fatal degenerative disorder at nine months, and describes how she coped with her grief by studying great works of art, literature, philosophy, and theology.

Rapping, Jonathan

Rapping, Jonathan **Gideon's** promise : a public defender movement to transform criminal justice / Jonathan Rapping. Beacon Press, 2020. 256 p. **B**

ISBN 9780807064627

1. Rapping, Jonathan. 2. Gideon's Promise (Organization) 3. Legal assistance to poor people. 4. Public defenders -- United States. 5. Criminal justice system. 6. Judicial system. 7. United States -- Social conditions. 8. Autobiographies and memoirs.

LC 2019059060

Drawing from his own experiences as well as cutting-edge research in the fields or organizational and cultural psychology, a public defender, revealing the pervasive issues inherent in our current system of public defense, lays the foundation for how model public defense programs should work to end mass incarceration.

"Rapping, a MacArthur 'genius grant' recipient and former public defender, describes in this impressive debut the history and philosophy of Gideon's Promise, his criminal justice reform organization. . . . This optimistic, well-articulated account is a must-read for policy makers and criminal-justice advocates." Publishers Weekly

Rasputin, Grigori Efimovich, 1869-1916

★Smith, Douglas, 1962- **Rasputin** : faith, power, and the twilight of the Romanovs / Douglas Smith. Farrar, Straus and Giroux, 2016. 544 p. **B**

ISBN 9780374240844

1. Romanov, House of. 2. Mystics -- Russia 3. Courts and courtiers 4. Aristocracy 5. Scandals 6. Russia -- History -- Nicholas II, 1894-1917 7. Russia -- Politics and government -- 1894-1917. 8. Biographies

LC 2016027558

Shortlisted for the James Tait Black Memorial Prize for Biography, 2016.

On the 100th anniversary of his murder, a biography of the mystical faith healer and close friend of the last Tsar of Russia describes his strange rise to power, his penchant for debauchery and his involvement in the end of the Romanov dynasty.

Rather, Dan

Rather, Dan **Rather** outspoken : my life in the news / Dan Rather. Grand Central Pub., 2012. 320 p. **B**

ISBN 9781455502417

1. Rather, Dan. 2. C B S News. 3. C B S evening news (Television program) 4. Broadcast journalists. 5. Television journalism. 6. Television journalists 7. Journalists. 8. Autobiographies and memoirs

LC 2011052227

The noted broadcast journalist traces his career while reflecting on the historical events of his time, sharing new insights into such topics as the Abu Ghraib scandal, the George W. Bush Air National Guard controversy, and JFK's assassination.

Ravin, Idan

Ravin, Idan The **hoops** whisperer : on the court and inside the heads of basketball's best players / Idan Ravin. Gotham Books, 2014 viii, 246 p. ; **B**

ISBN 9781592408917

1. National Basketball Association 2. Athletes -- Training. 3. Basketball 4. Autobiographies and memoirs

Sharing his unorthodox drills and improvisational techniques in action, professional basketball's hottest trainer, recounting his own inspirational journey, reveals how faith, effort, dedication and passion can transform any player into a superstar--and anyone into a success.

Reagan, Ronald

Brands, H. W. **Reagan** : the life / H. W. Brands. Doubleday, 2015. 816 p. **B**

ISBN 9780385536394

1. Presidents -- United States 2. United States -- Politics and government -- 1981-1989. 3. Biographies

LC 2014038054

The two-time Pulitzer Prize nominee and author of Traitor to His Class explores the 40th president's indelible role in preserving democracy and shaping present-day America, detailing his early life, improbable rise and presidential achievements.

"This is a detailed look at a president who sparked much controversy and affection and it belongs in most collections of presidential biography." Booklist.

Reagan, Ronald **Reagan** : a life in letters / edited, with an introduction and commentary by Kiron K. Skinner, Annelise Anderson, Martin Anderson ; with a foreword by George P. Shultz. Free Press, 2004, c2003. xx, 935 p. ; **B**

ISBN 0743219678

1. Reagan, Ronald Correspondence. 2. Presidents -- United States 3. United States -- Politics and government -- 1945-1989 Sources. 4. Correspondence.

LC bl2004115990

Reprint. Originally published: 2003.

A collection of letters from the former president offers insight into his public and private life of more than seventy years, from his early struggles and Hollywood achievements to his political career.

"This volume consists of a sampling of the former president's copious outpouring of personal letters, from his childhood to the onset of Alzheimer's after the presidency. The editors . arrange the letters thematically, introduce each chapter with a brief commentary, and introduce each letter with a sentence or two of explanation. The editors have done an admirable job in compiling these documents. Their commentary is exactly as it might have been had Ronald Reagan been able to produce this volume himself." Choice.

Reagan, Ronald The **Reagan** diaries / Ronald Reagan ; edited by Douglas Brinkley. Harper Collins, 2007. xiv, 767 p. : **B**

ISBN 006087600X

1. Reagan, Ronald. 2. Republican Party. 3. Presidents -- United States -- Diaries. 4. Politicians. 5. Republicans. 6. Cold War. 7. United States -- Politics and government -- 1981-1989. 8. Diaries.

LC bl2007006078

Includes index.

Culled from his handwritten daily diaries, an account of the fortieth president's eight years in the oval office offers insight into his character as well as the behind-the-scenes factors that contributed to such events as his first inauguration and the end of the Cold War.

"There is a kind of touching banality to many of the entries, as though Reagan were just another CEO writing about corporate life at the top, albeit corporate life that revolved around nuclear and hostage negotiations. Edited by Douglas Brinkley . , the book shows a Reagan almost sweetly amazed by small trappings of office. Reading these diaries, Americans will find it easier to understand how Reagan did what he did for so long: by steady work, and a steadfast commitment to the job at hand." Newsweek.

★Spitz, Bob **Reagan** : an American journey / Bob Spitz. Penguin Press, [2018] 608 p. **B**

ISBN 9781594205316

1. Reagan, Ronald. 2. Presidents -- United States 3. Conservatism -- United States. 4. Film actors and actresses 5. United States -- Politics and government -- 1981-1989. 6. Biographies

LC 2018019603

Draws on hundreds of interviews and previously unavailable documents to present a post-partisan biography of the fortieth president that offers insight into Reagan's universal appeal and transformative leadership.

"In visiting his final years, readers share the pathos of Reagans descent into dementia and feel the intense sorrow of the millions who mourn his passing. Candid, complete, compelling." Booklist.

Rebanks, James

Rebanks, James The **shepherd's** life : modern dispatches from an ancient landscape / James Rebanks. Flatiron Books, 2015. xviii, 292 p. : **B**

ISBN 9781250060242

1. Rebanks, James. 2. Shepherds. 3. Rural life 4. Lake District (England) 5. Autobiographies and memoirs

Originally published in Canada (Toronto : Doubleday Canada, 2015)

A shepherd in the Lake District of northern England shares his way of life in this memoir about living and farming in a storied landscape.

Red Cloud, 1822-1909

Drury, Bob The **heart** of everything that is : the untold story of Red Cloud, an American legend / Bob Drury and Tom Clavin. Simon & Schuster, 2013 400 p. **B**

ISBN 9781451654660

1. Oglala Indians 2. Red Cloud's War, 1866-1867. 3. Indians of North America 4. Government relations with indigenous peoples 5.

Biographies

LC 2013003200

Draws on Red Cloud's autobiography, which was lost for nearly a hundred years, to present the story of the great Oglala Sioux chief who was the only Plains Indian to defeat the United States Army in a war.

"The authors offer a battle-and-skirmish account of Sioux leader Red Cloud's war on the whites who invaded the Great Plains, though their narrative is strong on ethnohistorical matters as well. A well-researched and -written account of an often overlooked figure in the history of the Indian Wars." Kirkus.

Redding, Otis, 1941-1967

Gould, Jonathan, 1951- **Otis** Redding : an unfinished life / Jonathan Gould. Crown Publishing, 2017. 464 p. **B**

ISBN 9780307453945

1. Redding, Otis, 1941-1967. 2. Soul musicians 3. Creativity in men 4. African American musicians 5. Soul music 6. Southern States -- Social life and customs -- 20th century 7. Biographies

LC 2016043388

Coinciding with the 50th anniversary of the artist's performance at the 1967 Monterey Pop Festival, this definitive biography traces his short life and career from his childhood in Georgia, his recording contract with Stax and the plane crash that took his life.

"Better late than never, the soul master receives his considerable due in this superbly researched and written biography." Kirkus.

Ribowsky, Mark **Dreams** to remember : Otis Redding, Stax Records, and the transformation of Southern soul / Mark Ribowsky. Liveright Publishing Corporation, 2015 336 p. **B**

ISBN 9780871408730

1. Redding, Otis, 1941-1967. 2. Soul musicians. 3. Soul music. 4. Musicians 5. Biographies

LC 2015009097

The author of The Supremes: A Saga of Motown Dreams discusses soul icon Otis Redding and the southern music he helped popularize.

"Unlike other performers who died far too young, Redding's death did not come out of abuse, and though he suffered, it was a universal human suffering--a pain in the heart that, partnered with unerring musical instinct, personal strength, and a little tenderness, he transformed into art. Ribowsky goes into the seamy side of the record business but also the sheer beauty and magic of the sixties soul music that Redding epitomized." Booklist.

Reed, Lou. 1942-2013

DeCurtis, Anthony **Lou** Reed : a life / Anthony DeCurtis. Little, Brown and Company, 2017. 448 p. **B**

ISBN 9780316376556

1. Velvet Underground (Musical group). 2. Songwriters 3. Singers. 4. Rock musicians. 5. Biographies

LC 2017008817

A portrait of the lead singer and songwriter for the Velvet Underground cites his foundational role in the alternative rock genre while examining the contradictions, reinventions and extremes that marked his personal and professional endeavors.

Rehm, Diane

Rehm, Diane **On** my own / Diane Rehm. Alfred A. Knopf, 2016. 128 p. **B**

ISBN 9781101875285

1. Rehm, Diane. 2. Rehm, John B. Health. 3. Radio broadcasters 4. Widows 5. Bereavement. 6. Loss (Psychology). 7. Autobiographies and memoirs

LC 2015023006

The NPR radio host recounts her late husband's long battle with Parkinson's and her efforts to reconstruct a life without him, describing how she found inspiration in the examples of widowed colleagues and her advocacy of the Right to Die movement.

"Rehm's forthright memoir, which probes the process of loss, grief, and renewal, will find a wide audience with fans of her show as well as many others facing this profound passage." Publishers Weekly.

Rehman, Sabeeha

Rehman, Sabeeha **Threading** my prayer rug : one woman's journey from Pakistani Muslim to American Muslim / Sabeeha Rehman. Arcade Publishing, 2016. 304 p. **B**

ISBN 9781628726633

1. Rehman, Sabeeha. 2. Pakistani Americans 3. Muslim women -- United States 4. Muslims -- United States 5. Interfaith relations 6. Autobiographies and Memoirs

LC 2016007676

"This enthralling story of the making of an American is also a timely meditation on religion and culture. Threading My Prayer Rug is a richly textured reflection on what it is to be a Muslim in America today."-- Provided by publisher.

Reichl, Ruth

Reichl, Ruth **Comfort** me with apples : more adventures at the table / Ruth Reichl. Random House, 2001. 302 p. **B**

ISBN 0375501959

1. Reichl, Ruth. 2. Women food writers. 3. Cooking. 4. Food and courtship. 5. Food habits -- United States. 6. Autobiographies and memoirs

LC 00053355

Sequel to: Tender at the bone."

In this second installment of her memoirs, {Reichl} retraces her route from married life on a commune in late-seventies Berkeley to her first job as a food critic, dining at expensive restaurants in Los Angeles with her glamorous editor. Reichl writes with gusto, and her story has all the ingredients of a modern fairy tale: hard work, weird food, and endless curiosity." The New Yorker.

Reichl, Ruth **Garlic** and sapphires : the secret life of a critic in disguise / Ruth Reichl. Penguin Press, 2005. 333 p. ; **B**

ISBN 1594200319

1. Reichl, Ruth. 2. Restaurant critics -- United States 3. Food writers -- United States 4. Cooking. 5. Food. 6. Autobiographies and memoirs

LC 2004051362

Includes index.

The editor-in-chief of "Gourmet" recounts her visits to some of the world's most acclaimed restaurants, both as herself and as an anonymous diner in disguise, to offer insight into the differences in her dining experiences.

"Reichl's ability to experience meals in such a dramatic way brings an infectious passion to her memoir. Reading this work . ensures that the next time readers sit down in a restaurant, they'll notice things they've never noticed before." Publishers Weekly.

Reichl, Ruth **My** kitchen year : 136 recipes that saved my life / Ruth Reichl. Random House, 2015. 320 p. **B**

ISBN 9781400069989

1. Reichl, Ruth. 2. Women food writers. 3. Cooking 4. Coping in women 5. Women editors 6. United States -- Social life and customs

-- 21st century 7. Essays. 8. Autobiographies and memoirs
LC 2014029197

"Reichl has written some classics in food literature, including Tender at the Bone (1998); therefore, much attention will be accorded her latest book." Booklist.

★Reichl, Ruth **Save** me the plums : my gourmet memoir / Ruth Reichl Random House, 2019. 266 p. **B**

ISBN 9781400069996

1. Reichl, Ruth. 2. Restaurant critics -- United States 3. Food writers -- United States 4. Cooking. 5. Food. 6. Autobiographies and memoirs

LC 2018025584

The six-time James Beard Award-winning journalist and best-selling author of My Kitchen Year chronicles her groundbreaking tenure as editor-in-chief of Gourmet magazine and her work with legendary fellow epicureans to transform how America thinks about food.

"This look back in time will appeal to Reichl's many fans, foodies, as well as general readers. It's part elegy, part picaresque for a recent history that already feels like another era after the Great Recession and the evolution of digital publishing." Library Journal.

Reid, Constance

Reid, Constance **Slacks** and calluses : our summer in a bomber factory / Constance Bowman ; illustrated by Clara Marie Allen ; introduced by Sandra M. Gilbert. Smithsonian Institution Press, c1999. xiv, 181 p. : **B**

ISBN 156098368X

1. Reid, Constance. 2. Allen, Clara Marie Anecdotes. 3. B-24 bomber -- Design and construction -- Anecdotes. 4. Aircraft industry and trade workers 5. World War II -- United States -- Anecdotes. 6. United States -- Social life and customs Anecdotes. 7. Collective autobiographies and memoirs

LC 99031365

Originally published: Slacks and callouses.

1st ed. New York : Toronto : Longmans, Green & Co., 1944.

Provides an account of how two women assumed wartime roles working on a production line at a B-24 bomber plant during World War II

Reinhardt, Django, 1910-1953

Dregni, Michael, 1961- **Django** : the life and music of a Gypsy legend / Michael Dregni. Oxford University Press, 2004. 326 p. : **B**

ISBN 019516752X

1. Reinhardt, Django, 1910-1953. 2. Guitarists -- France 3. Jazz musicians -- France 4. Romanies -- Music -- History and criticism 5. Jazz -- France -- History and criticism. 6. Biographies

LC 2004006214

The first major critical biography of the great jazz musician chronicles the colorful life of guitarist Django Reinhardt, including his long musical relationship with violinist Stephane Grapelli and his wanderings around Europe and the United States.

"This biography does its complex subject justice. And even when Dregni dallies overlong on some byways, his immersion in the period's history enriches his storytelling and our understanding. The panoramic results present Django Reinhardt as he has never been seen." New York Times Book Review.

Reles, Abe, 1906-1941

Cannell, Michael T. A **brotherhood** betrayed : the man behind the rise and fall of Murder, Inc. / Michael Cannell. Minotaur Books, 2020 336 p. **B**

ISBN 9781250204387

1. Reles, Abe, 1906-1941. 2. Assassins -- New York City 3. Mafia -- New York City -- Case Studies 4. Mafiosi 5. Murder -- New York City -- History 6. New York City 7. Biographies

LC 2020017246

The riveting true story of the rise and fall of Murder, Inc. and the executioner-turned-informant whose mysterious death became a turning point in Mob history.

"Readers interested in a non-sensationalized treatment of a major chapter in American crime will be riveted." Publishers Weekly

Rembrandt Harmenszoon van Rijn, 1606-1669

Blom, Onno **Young** Rembrandt : a biography / Onno Blom ; translated from the Dutch by Beverley Jackson. W. W. Norton & Company, 2020, c2019. 288 p. : **B**

ISBN 9780393531794

1. Rembrandt Harmenszoon van Rijn, 1606-1669. 2. Painters 3. Painters -- Netherlands 4. Painting, Dutch. 5. Childhood 6. Netherlands -- Civilization -- 17th century. 7. Netherlands -- Social life and customs. 8. Biographies

LC 2020024524

Originally published: London : Pushkin Press, 2019."

A captivating exploration of the little-known story of Rembrandt's formative years by a prize-winning biographer. Rembrandt van Rijn's early years are as famously shrouded in mystery as Shakespeare's, and his life has always been an enigma. How did a miller's son from a provincial Dutch town become the greatest artist of his age? How in short, did Rembrandt become Rembrandt?

"This portrait will delight both casual art fans and connoisseurs alike." Publishers Weekly

Renkl, Margaret

Renkl, Margaret **Late** migrations : a natural history of love and loss / Margaret Renkl ; with art by Billy Renkl. Milkweed Editions, 2019. 248 p. **B**

ISBN 9781571313782

1. Renkl, Margaret. 2. Families 3. Children of aging parents 4. Nature 5. Caregivers 6. Southern States 7. Essays 8. Autobiographies and memoirs

LC 2018044003

ALA Notable Book, 2020.

The widely followed New York Times opinion writer presents a collection of brief essays on the natural world, her Alabama childhood, her complicated parents and her transition to the role of a caregiver.

"It is a fine feat, this book. Renkl intimately knows that this life thrives on death and chooses to sing the glory of being alive all the same." Booklist.

Renoir, Auguste, 1841-1919

White, Barbara Ehrlich **Renoir** : an intimate biography / Barbara Ehrlich White. Thames & Hudson, 2017. 246 p. **B**

ISBN 9780500239575

1. Artists -- France 2. Painters -- France 3. Impressionism (Art) 4. Painting. 5. France -- History -- 19th century 6. Biographies

LC 2017931859

"Studded with stirring quotations from unpublished letters and embellished with reproductions of many of Renoirs most-beloved works, this is a jewel of a biography, and it will be treasured by anyone interested in art." Booklist.

Retta

Retta **So** close to being the sh*t, y'all don't even know / Retta. St. Martin's Press, 2018. 224 p. **B**

ISBN 9781250109347

1. Retta. 2. Actors and actresses. 3. Comedians. 4. Personal conduct. 5. Growing up. 6. Essays 7. Autobiographies and memoirs

LC 2017056742

The Hollywood star of hit series as Parks and Recreation and Girlfriends' Guide to Divorce presents an uproarious collection of essays that trace her upbringing by hardworking Liberian parents, the events that shifted her career focus from medicine to comedy and the ways that her successes have been shaped by fear and circumstance.

Revuelta Clews, Natalia, 1925-

Gimbel, Wendy **Havana** dreams : a story of Cuba / Wendy Gimbel. A.A. Knopf, 1998. 234 p. : **B**

ISBN 9780679430537

1. Castro, Fidel, 1926-2016 Relations with women 2. Fernandez Revuelta, Alina, 1956- 3. Mistresses -- Cuba 4. Women -- Cuba. 5. Cuba -- History -- 1933-1959. 6. Cuba -- History -- 1959-1990 7. Cuba -- Social life and customs -- 1959-

LC 98014571

A portrait of four generations of Cuban women, members of the Revuelta family.

"Gimbel succeeds in showing the complexity of family relationships resulting from the Cuban revolution, which extends into two countries." Library Journal.

Reynolds, Debbie

Reynolds, Debbie **Make** 'em laugh : short-term memories of longtime friends / Debbie Reynolds, with Dorian Hannaway. William & Morrow & Co., 2015. 272 p. **B**

ISBN 9780062416636

1. Celebrities -- Anecdotes. 2. Women celebrities. 3. Motherhood. 4. Friendship. 5. Autobiographies and memoirs.

LC bl2015040779

"Reynolds, who refers to herself as a comic (hence the books title), has done some outstanding film work with Singin in the Rain at the forefront but what's most impressive here is her (almost always) upbeat outlook and her fond regard for the deep friendships she has forged throughout her life. This isn't exactly a showbiz memoir; it's more of a memory book by a woman who has lived a rich life that happened to involve Hollywood." Booklist.

Rezaian, Jason

Rezaian, Jason **Prisoner** : my 544 days in an Iranian prison--solitary confinement, a sham trial, high-stakes diplomacy, and the extraordinary efforts it took to get me out / Jason Rezaian. HarperCollins, 2019. 320 p. **B**

ISBN 9780062691576

1. Hostages 2. Journalists 3. Political prisoners 4. Diplomatic negotiations in international disputes 5. Iran -- Politics and government 6. Autobiographies and memoirs

LC bl2018191914

The former Tehran bureau chief describes how he was kept hostage for 18 months on trumped-up charges of espionage and rendered a pawn in high-stakes diplomatic talks that became a part of the Iran nuclear deal.

"At a time when journalists find themselves increasingly under fire, both abroad and at home, Rezaian's dedication to his craft is an inspiring homage to the fearlessness of these intrepid purveyors of truth " Booklist.

Rhodes, Benjamin J., 1977-

Rhodes, Benjamin J., 1977- The **world** as it is : a memoir of the Obama White House / Ben Rhodes. Random House, 2018 xx, 450 p., 8 unnumbered p. of plates : **B**

ISBN 9780525509356

1. Obama, Barack Friends and associates 2. White House, Washington, D.C. Staff 3. Presidents -- United States -- Staff 4. Political science 5. Political culture 6. Washington, D.C. -- Social life and customs -- 21st century 7. United States -- Politics and government -- 2009-2017 8. Autobiographies and memoirs

From one of Barack Obama's closest aides comes a behind-the-scenes account of his presidency--and how idealism can confront harsh reality and still survive.

Rhodes, William R.

Rhodes, William R. **Banker** to the world : leadership lessons from the front lines of global finance / William R. Rhodes. McGraw-Hill, c2011. xxiii, 249 p. ; **B**

ISBN 9780071704250

1. Bankers -- United States 2. International banking 3. International finance. 4. Leadership.

LC 2010032040

A former executive of Citigroup explains what he learned during his long tenure at the company, including the lessons he learned in crisis management, effective and responsible leadership and the importance of diplomacy in negotiation.

Rice, Anne, 1941-

Rice, Anne, 1941- **Called** out of darkness : a spiritual confession / Anne Rice. Alfred A. Knopf, 2008. 256 p. **B**

ISBN 9780307268273

1. Rice, Anne, 1941- Homes and haunts New Orleans, Louisiana. 2. Women authors, American -- 20th century 3. Faith in women. 4. Religious conversion 5. Moral development. 6. Autobiographies and memoirs

LC 2008020192

The author presents a personal journey of faith that records her New Orleans Catholic childhood; loss of faith and involvement with secular humanism; and her eventual return, after thirty-eight years as an atheist, to New Orleans and a belief in Christ.

Rice, Condoleezza, 1954-

Rice, Condoleezza, 1954- **Extraordinary,** ordinary people : a memoir of family / Condoleezza Rice. Crown, 2010. 352 p. **B**

ISBN 9780307587879

1. African American families 2. African American women 3. Race relations 4. African American women politicians 5. Birmingham, Alabama -- Race relations 6. Autobiographies and memoirs

LC 2010021645

The personal story of the former Secretary of State traces her childhood in segregated Alabama, describes the influence of people who shaped her life, and pays tribute to her parents' characters and sacrifices.

Rice, Condoleezza, 1954- **No** higher honor : a memoir of my years in Washington / Condoleeza Rice. Crown Pub., 2011. 384 p. **B**

ISBN 9780307587862

1. United States. Secretary of State 2. United States. National Security Council. 3. African American women 4. African American women politicians 5. African American women cabinet officers 6. Presidents -- United States -- Staff 7. United States -- Politics and

government -- 2001-2009 8. Autobiographies and memoirs
LC 2011534059

A former national security advisor and Secretary of State offers the story of her eight years serving at the highest levels of government, including the difficult job she faced in the wake of 9/11.

Richard III, King of England, 1452-1485

Skidmore, Chris, 1981- **Richard** III : England's most controversial king / Chris Skidmore. St. Martin's Press, 2017. 400 p. **B**

ISBN 9781250045485

1. Rulers 2. Monarchy 3. Power (Social sciences) 4. Great Britain -- History -- Richard III, 1483-1485 5. Biographies
LC 2017061096

"First published in Great Britain by Weidenfeld & Nicolson, an imprint of The Orion Publishing Group Ltd, an Hachette UK company; First U.S. Edition: April 2018."

Drawing on new manuscript evidence, an acclaimed historian presents this first full biography of Richard III for 50 years, which reassesses his life and times and examines in intense detail his inner nature and complex relations to unravel the mystery of the last English monarch to die on the battlefield.

Richards, Cecile

Richards, Cecile **Make** trouble : standing up, speaking out, and finding the courage to lead-- my life story / Cecile Richards with Lauren Peterson. Touchstone, 2018. 288 p. **B**

ISBN 9781501187599

1. Richards, Cecile. 2. Planned Parenthood Federation of America. 3. Women political activists. 4. Leadership in women. 5. Women's rights. 6. Social justice. 7. Autobiographies and memoirs
LC 2017061243

The president of Planned Parenthood and daughter of the late Texas Governor Ann Richards shares the story of her lifetime spent fighting for women's rights and social justice, offering insight into her work as a labor organizer, the challenges of balancing her career with her family responsibilities and her views about the importance of taking risks, making mistakes and standing up for what is right.

Richards, Keith, 1943-

★Richards, Keith, 1943- **Life** / Keith Richards ; contributions by James Fox. Little Brown & Co, 2010. 564 p., 32 p. of plates : **B**

ISBN 9780316034388

1. Rolling Stones (Musical group) 2. Rock musicians. 3. Rock music. 4. Rock groups. 5. Bands (Music) 6. Autobiographies and memoirs
LC 2010934918

Includes index.

The lead guitarist for The Rolling Stones recounts his life, from a youth obsessed with Chuck Berry to the formation of the Stones and their subsequent stardom, and discusses his problems with drugs, the death of Brian Jones, and his relationship with Mick Jagger.

"This autobiography of the Rolling Stones guitarist is way more than a revealing showbiz memoir. It is also a high-def, high-velocity portrait of the era when rock 'n' roll came of age, a raw report from deep inside the counterculture maelstrom of how that music swept like a tsunami over Britain and the United States. It's an eye-opening all-nighter in the studio with a master craftsman disclosing the alchemical secrets of his art. And it's the intimate and moving story of one man's long strange trip over the decades, told in dead-on, visceral prose without any of the pretense, caution or self-consciousness that usually attend great artists sitting for their self-portraits." New York Times Book Review.

Richards, Susan, 1949-

Richards, Susan, 1949- **Chosen** by a horse : a memoir / Susan Richards. Soho Press, c2006. 248 p. ; **B**

ISBN 9781569474198

1. Horses -- New York (State) -- Anecdotes. 2. Women horse owners -- New York (State) 3. Women and horses. 4. Human/animal relationships -- New York (State) -- Anecdotes. 5. New York (State) 6. Autobiographies and memoirs
LC 2005052337

Tells the story of a woman whose hurts from a difficult past are healed with the help of the companionship and affection of a formerly abused horse for which she has agreed to care.

"Richards adopts an emaciated mare and her foal, overriding the small voice telling her that she already has three horses to care for and a herniated disk. Her experience with her new charges proves profoundly instructive in terms of how love can foster growth of the human spirit and help in overcoming pain and loss. The abused mare, Lay Me Down, proves to be one of those rare creatures that remain gentle despite years of mistreatment, responding profoundly to the kind treatment that is part of everyday life for Richards' animals. Fascinated by the affection this animal accords a stranger, Richards notes the mare's courage and slowly begins to emulate it in her own life, opening up to a love affair and its aftermath." Booklist.

Richards, Susan, 1950-

Richards, Susan, 1950- **Lost** and found in Russia : lives in the post-Soviet landscape / Susan Richards. Other Press, 2010. 320 p. **B**

ISBN 9781590513484

1. Richards, Susan, 1950- Travel Soviet Union 2. Social change. 3. Post-communism 4. Russia -- Description and travel 5. Siberia -- Description and travel. 6. Russia -- History -- 1991-
LC 2010011464

First published in the United Kingdom by I.B. Tauris & Co. Ltd."

A patiently crafted glimpse through a crack in the wardrobe of the devastation wrought on Russian society during the turbulent post-Communist '90s." Kirkus.

Richardson, John, 1924-2019

Richardson, John, 1924-2019 The **sorcerer's** apprentice : Picasso, Provence, and Douglas Cooper / John Richardson. Alfred A. Knopf, 1999. viii, 318 p. : **B**

ISBN 9780375400339

1. Cooper, Douglas, 1911-1984 2. Picasso, Pablo, 1881-1973. 3. Art historians -- Great Britain 4. Gay men -- Great Britain 5. Art, French -- 20th century -- Provence, France. 6. Art -- Collectors and collecting -- France. 7. Autobiographies and memoirs
LC 99027200

The story of Douglas Cooper--the brilliant, controversial art expert and collector who assembled the world's most important private collection of cubist paintings--is told for the first time, with details on Cooper's relationship with Picasso and other great artists of the period.

"Picasso biographer John Richardson has written a concise account of the first half of his own life and notably of his long relationship as a young man with the Cubist art historian and collector Douglas Cooper. The account concentrates on the dozen years, from early 1949 to the end of 1960, when Richardson lived with Cooper, visiting museums and monuments all over Europe, meeting the great artists and other personalities of the day, and restoring the colonnaded Chateau de Castille in the south of France." New York Times Book Review.

Richardson, Micheal Ray

Rosen, Charles **Sugar** : Micheal Ray Richardson, eighties excess, and the NBA / Charley Rosen. University of Nebraska Press, 2018. 183 p. **B**

ISBN 9781496202161

1. Richardson, Micheal Ray. 2. National Basketball Association -- History 3. Basketball players 4. Professional athletes 5. Fame 6. Money 7. Biographies

LC 2017038778

By constructing his various lines of narration around the polarizing figure of Richardson--equal parts basketball savant, drug addict, and pariah--Rosen illuminates some of the more unseemly aspects of the NBA during the 1980s, going behind the scenes to provide an account of what the league's darker side was like during its celebrated golden age.

Richmond Mouillot, Miranda

Richmond Mouillot, Miranda A **fifty-year** silence : love, war, and a ruined house in France / Miranda Richmond Mouillot. Crown Publishers, 2015. 288 p. **B**

ISBN 9780804140645

1. Richmond Mouillot, Miranda. 2. Richmond Mouillot, Miranda Family. 3. Jews 4. Grandparents 5. Holocaust survivors 6. Divorced persons 7. France 8. United States 9. Autobiographies and memoirs

LC 2014015315

"A memoir by a young woman who travels to France to uncover the truth about her grandparents' mysterious and irrevocable estrangement and pieces together the extraordinary story of their wartime experiences".--Provided by publisher.

"The corrosive effects of the Holocaust--upon those directly involved and generations thereafter--are illustrated vividly in this candid saga of familial love and misunderstanding." Library Journal.

Rickey, Branch, 1881-1965

Breslin, Jimmy **Branch** Rickey / Jimmy Breslin. Viking, 2011. 160 p. **B**

ISBN 9780670022496

1. Rickey, Branch, 1881-1965. 2. Brooklyn Dodgers (Baseball team) 3. Baseball 4. Baseball team owners -- United States 5. Professional baseball. 6. Biographies

LC 2010035008

Traces the efforts of the 1940s Brooklyn Dodgers president and general manager to promote baseball integration, describing his role in bringing Jackie Robinson to the team while sharing background information on Rickey's youth, times, and career.

"Breslin reveals much about the development of baseball, the Dodgers' last years in Brooklyn, and the struggle to overcome the national pastime's racism while tracing the life, deeds, and some (but not all) of Branch Rickey's warts. A breezy read, this Penguin Life is nonetheless insightful, humorous, and biting at times as it traces how the man dubbed the Mahatma by sportswriters emerged from obscurity as an Idaho lawyer to develop the baseball farm system, multiple MLB winners, Vero Beach spring training, the scientific teaching of skills, and the MLB expansion that brought New York the Mets." Library Journal.

Ride, Sally

Sherr, Lynn **Sally** Ride : America's first woman in space / Lynn Sherr. Simon & Schuster, 2014. 320 p. **B**

ISBN 9781476725765

1. Ride, Sally. 2. Space programs -- International competition 3. Sexism 4. Women physicists 5. Lesbians 6. Biographies.

LC 2013039647

Sally Ride, the first American woman to go into space, competed successfully in the male-dominated profession of physics and became an inspiration to girls who dreamed of science careers. Journalist Lynn Sherr, drawing on materials provided by Ride's family and friends as well as official records and Sherr's own friendship with Ride, offers a moving and sensitive portrait of this pioneer who guarded her private life -- her long-term lesbian relationship only became known through her obituary.

Rideau, Wilbert

Rideau, Wilbert **In** the place of justice : a story of punishment and deliverance / Wilbert Rideau. Alfred A. Knopf, 2010. 384 p. **B**

ISBN 9780307264817

1. Rideau, Wilbert. 2. Angola Prison, Louisiana 3. African American prisoners -- Louisiana 4. Prisoners -- Louisiana -- Social conditions -- 20th century. 5. Criminal justice system -- Louisiana -- History -- 20th century. 6. Corruption investigation -- Louisiana -- History -- 20th century. 7. Louisiana -- History -- 20th century. 8. Autobiographies and memoirs

LC 2009038526

Includes index.

A journalist who spent forty-four years in Louisiana prisons relates the crime that put him behind bars and how he worked to redeem himself, exposed a profoundly corrupt penal system, and fought to reform it.

Rieder, Travis

Rieder, Travis **In** pain : a bioethicist's personal struggle with opioids / Travis Rieder. Harper, 2019. xiii, 297 pages ; **B**

ISBN 9780062854643

1. Opioids 2. Pain 3. Pain -- Treatment 4. Drug withdrawal symptoms. 5. Autobiographies and memoirs

LC bl2019015139

A bioethicist's eloquent and riveting memoir of opioid dependence and withdrawal is a harrowing personal reckoning and clarion call for change not only for government but medicine itself, revealing the lack of crucial resources and structures to handle this insidious nationwide epidemic.

"With this smart, r iveting, real-life account, the author proves himself a convincing and effective advocate for opioid use reform. A harrowing cautionary narrative that speaks to patients and physicians alike on the ugly reality of the enduring opioid epidemic." Kirkus.

Riefenstahl, Leni

Bach, Steven **Leni** : the life and work of Leni Riefenstahl / Steven Bach. A.A. Knopf, 2007. x, 386 p., 32 p. of plates : **B**

ISBN 0375404007

1. Riefenstahl, Leni. 2. Propaganda. 3. Nazism and film. 4. Nazism and art. 5. Film producers and directors 6. Germany -- History -- 1933-1945 7. Biographies

LC 2006049323

Leni Riefenstahl, the woman best known as "Hitler's filmmaker," is one of the most controversial personalities of the twentieth century. Her story is one of huge talent and huger ambition, one that probes the sometimes blurred borders dividing art and beauty from truth and humanity. Two of her films, Olympia and Triumph of the Will, are universally regarded as among the greatest and most innovative documentaries ever made, but they are also insidious glorifications of Hitler and the Third Reich. Relying on new sources--including interviews with her colleagues and intimate friends, as well as on previously unknown recordings of Riefenstahl herself--biographer Bach untangles the truths and lies behind this gifted woman's lifelong self-vindication as an apolitical artist who claimed she knew nothing of the Holocaust and denied her complicity with the criminal regime she both used and sanctified.--From publisher description.

"This is a lively, incisive look at a compelling and somewhat appalling figure who demonstrated that beauty isn't always truth." Publishers Weekly.

Trimborn, Jurgen, 1971- **Leni** Riefenstahl : a life / Jurgen Trimborn ; translated from the German by Edna McCown. Faber and Faber, 2007. xii, 375 p. of plates : **B**

ISBN 0374184933

1. Riefenstahl, Leni. 2. Propaganda. 3. Nazism and film. 4. Nazism and art. 5. Film producers and directors 6. Germany -- History -- 1933-1945. 7. Germany -- Social life and customs -- 20th century. 8. Biographies

LC 2006013263

A revealing portrait of the controversial filmmaker examines Riefenstahl's remarkable contributions to the cinematic art, her relationship with Adolf Hitler, the two monumental films she created for him--Triumph of the Will and Olympia--and her refusal to be held accountable for her role in the Holocaust and the atrocities of the Nazi regime.

"Trimborn interviewed Riefenstahl in 1997, when he was twenty-five, having already spent six years of 'intensive labor' on the project, and he briefly entertained the quixotic hope of writing a definitive book with her blessing and collaboration. Unwilling to misrepresent himself as a hagiographer, he was doomed to fail, though his disappointment does not seem to have warped his fair-mindedness. [The author's] aim was to correct the murky published record and the 'attitudes' of his compatriots. One has to admire the sniperlike precision with which he takes out fugitive falsehoods that have lived under cover for a century." The New Yorker.

Riess, Jana

Riess, Jana **Flunking** sainthood : a year of breaking the Sabbath, forgetting to pray, and still loving my neighbor / Jana Riess. Paraclete Press, c2011. x, 179 p. ; **B**

ISBN 9781557256607

1. Riess, Jana. 2. Women authors 3. Spiritual life -- Christianity. 4. Perfection -- Religious aspects -- Christianity. 5. Failure (Psychology) 6. Autobiographies and memoirs

LC 2011022595

"The author intended to devote an entire year (a year-long experiment) to mastering 12 different spiritual challenges, including praying at fixed times during the day, exhibiting gratitude, observing the Sabbath, practicing hospitality according to the rules set by St. Benedict, abstaining from eating meat, and amply demonstrating her generosity. But nothing turned out as planned. Although her spiritual quest falls far short, she can still proffer spiritual lessons. Anyone who has failed to live up to expectations, which means most everyone, will love this book." Booklist.

Riggs, Nina

★Riggs, Nina The **bright** hour : a memoir of living and dying / Nina Riggs. Simon & Schuster, 2017. 310 p. ; **B**

ISBN 9781501169359

1. Riggs, Nina. 2. People with breast cancer 3. People with terminal illnesses 4. Death -- Psychological aspects. 5. Family and death 6. Autobiographies and memoirs

LC 2017007161

Discussing motherhood, marriage, friendship, and the legacy of her great-great-great grandfather, Ralph Waldo Emerson, the author, who has been diagnosed with terminal breast cancer, explores what makes a meaningful life when one has limited time.

"In this tender memoir Riggs displays a keen awareness of and reverence for all the moments of lifeboth the light, and the dark, 'the cruel, and the beautiful.' " Publishers Weekly.

Rin-Tin-Tin (Dog)

★Orlean, Susan **Rin** Tin Tin : the life and the legend / Susan Orlean. Simon & Schuster, 2011. 320 p. **B**

ISBN 9781439190135

1. German shepherd dog 2. Working dogs. 3. Dogs in films. 4. Dogs in the performing arts. 5. Animal biographies

LC 2011024476

Chronicles the rise of the iconic German shepherd character while sharing the stories of the real WWI dog and the canine performer in the 1950s television show, and explores Rin Tin Tin's relevance in the military and popular culture.

Rinella, Steven

Rinella, Steven **Meat** eater : adventures from the life of an American hunter / Steven Rinella. Spiegel & Grau, c2012. 272 p. **B**

ISBN 9780385529815

1. Rinella, Steven. 2. Hunters 3. Hunting -- United States -- History. 4. Nature

LC 2012018129

The author of American Buffalo and host of the Sportsman Channel's MeatEater presents a treasury of engaging facts about the natural world and history of hunting that also chronicles his evolution as a sportsman, exploring such topics as Manifest Destiny, the ethics of killing and humanity's responsibility toward prey.

Ripert, Eric

Ripert, Eric **32** yolks : from my mother's table to working the line / Eric Ripert, with Veronica Chambers. Random House, 2016. 304 p. **B**

ISBN 9780812992984

1. Ripert, Eric. 2. Ripert, Eric Childhood and youth. 3. Cooks -- Paris, France 4. Restaurateurs -- Paris, France 5. Cooking, French. 6. Cooking -- Paris, France 7. Paris, France 8. Autobiographies and memoirs

LC 2015050280

The chef and co-owner of the New York restaurant Le Bernardin and a regular guest judge on Bravo's Top Chef shares how the events from his childhood prompted him to learn to cook and find happiness as he was finally able to share his lifelong love of food with other people.

"Readers may know Ripert as the meditative host of the PBS series Avec Eric; a fan-favorite judge on Bravo's Top Chef; and the owner of Le Bernardin, a French seafood restaurant in New York. His roots, however, are far from that calm and thoughtful adult. This memoir tells of Ripert's tumultuous childhood in France where a love of excellent food was instilled in him early on. Although the loving descriptions of flavors and cooking techniques will make some long for recipes, this narrative sheds light on the carefully controlled chaos behind the scenes at several top restaurants in the 1970s and 1980s." Library Journal.

Rippon, Adam, 1989-

Rippon, Adam, 1989- **Beautiful** on the outside : a memoir / Adam Rippon. Grand Central Publishing, 2019. 245 p., 16 unnumbered p. of plates : **B**

ISBN 9781538732403

1. Figure skaters 2. Olympic medal winners 3. Figure skating 4. Gay men 5. Autobiographies and memoirs

LC bl2019022961

The medal-winning Olympics figure skater reveals the early poverty and discrimination that challenged his career as an openly gay athlete, describing his homeschooled childhood in Pennsylvania and the setbacks and successes that shaped his achievements.

Rivera, Diego, 1886-1957

Marnham, Patrick **Dreaming** with his eyes open : a life of Diego Rivera / Patrick Marnham. Knopf, 1998. 350 p. : **B**

ISBN 9780679430421

1. Rivera, Diego, 1886-1957. 2. Painters -- Mexico 3. Murals -- Mexico -- History -- 20th century. 4. Men/women relations. 5. Mexico (City) -- History 6. Biographies

LC 98006145

Explores the the life and work of the controversial Diego Rivera, his education, the influence of his native Mexico, his relationship with Frida Kahlo, and his creative artistry.

"For the browsing public as well as specialists in European, Latin American, and American modern art, this book is not to be overlooked." Library Journal.

Rivera, Mariano, 1969-

Rivera, Mariano, 1969- The **closer** : my story / Mariano Rivera with Wayne Coffey. Little Brown & Co, 2014. 288 p. **B**

ISBN 9780316400732

1. Baseball players 2. Christian life 3. Baseball 4. Pitchers (Baseball) 5. Autobiographies and memoirs

LC 2014934754

"[I]n this entertaining, admirably subdued autobiography, the glory is God's: Rivera's story brims with examples of his faith." Publishers Weekly.

Rivers, Joan

Bennetts, Leslie, 1949- **Last** girl before freeway : the life, loves, losses, and liberation of Joan Rivers / Leslie Bennetts. Little, Brown and Company, 2016. 304 p. **B**

ISBN 9780316261302

1. Comedians -- United States 2. Women comedians 3. Entertainers -- United States 4. Television producers and directors -- United States 5. Autobiographies and memoirs

LC 2016938566

A portrait of the influential comedienne explores her enduring cultural legacy, discussing subjects ranging from her husband's suicide and her feud with Johnny Carson to her numerous cosmetic surgeries and her controversial death in 2014.

Roa, John

Roa, John A **practical** way to get rich... and die trying : a memoir about risking it all / John Roa. Viking, 2020 xvi, 302 p. **B**

ISBN 9781984881229

1. Entrepreneurs 2. Young men 3. New businesses 4. Ambition in men 5. Autobiographies and memoirs

LC 2020020015

A young tech entrepreneur presents a cautionary tale about his rise the top of the industry and the toll it took on him, from excessive drug and alcohol use to his eventual psychotic breakdown.

"For young entrepreneurs seeking to win the glittering--but personally destructive--startup game, it is essential reading. A candid and disturbing memoir of the ups and downs of entrepreneurship." Kirkus

Roach, Margaret

Roach, Margaret A **way** to garden : a hands-on primer for every season / Margaret Roach. Timber Press, 2019. 336 p. **B**

ISBN 9781604698770

1. Roach, Margaret Philosophy. 2. Gardens 3. Growth (Plants) 4. Gardening. 5. Women gardeners. 6. Autobiographies and memoirs

LC 2018043086

"Readers will appreciate Roach's focus on gardening as a way anyone can help make the world a better place and her approach, combining horticultural how-to and woo-hoo (her term), which balances precise learned information with ones own intuition." Booklist.

Robbins, Tom, 1932-

Robbins, Tom, 1932- **Tibetan** peach pie : a true account of an imaginative life / Tom Robbins. Ecco, 2014. 224 p. **B**

ISBN 9780062267405

1. Books and reading 2. Men/women relations 3. Drug use 4. Voyages and travels 5. Autobiographies and memoirs

LC 2014434624

Internationally bestselling novelist and American icon Tom Robbins delivers the long awaited tale of his wild life and times, both at home and around the globe.

"Each piece stands on its own, but when read side by side they develop into a powerful argument about magic and the necessity of imaginative, interior worlds." Library Journal.

Robert I, King of Scots, 1274-1329

Penman, Michael A. **Robert** the Bruce : King of Scots / Michael Penman. Yale University Press, 2014. vii, 443 p., 16 unnumbered p. of plates ; **B**

ISBN 0300148720

1. Robert I, King of Scots, 1274-1329. 2. Scotland -- History -- Robert I, 1306-1329. 3. Scotland -- Kings and rulers

LC 2014007172

"Robert the Bruce (1274–1329) famously defeated the English at Bannockburn and became the hero king responsible for Scottish independence. In this fascinating new biography of the renowned warrior, Michael Penman focuses on Robert's kingship in the fifteen years that followed his triumphant victory and establishes Robert as not only a great military leader but a great monarch." --From publisher description.

Roberts, David, 1943-

Roberts, David, 1943- **Limits** of the known / David Roberts. W W Norton & Company, 2018 336 p. **B**

ISBN 9780393609868

1. Mountaineering. 2. Adventurers. 3. Purpose in life. 4. People with cancer 5. Autobiographies and memoirs

LC 2017048507

The mountaineer and award-winning author of Alone on the Ice and The Lost World of the Old Ones recounts his search for meaning in the quests of history's famed explorers, drawing partially on his own relationship with extreme-risk adventure and serious illness to share insights into what may have motivated landmark expeditions and ascents.

"Roberts conveys the exhilaration and vitality of adventuring as well as the agony and anger of a cancer diagnosis with equal aplomb, making for a moving narrative that speaks to the glories of the human spirit and the limitations of the human body." Publishers Weekly.

Roberts, Eric A., 1907-1972

Hutton, Robert (Journalist) **Agent** Jack : the true story of MI5's secret Nazi hunter / Robert Hutton. St. Martin's Press, 2019. 336 p. **B**

ISBN 9781250221766

1. Roberts, Eric A., 1907-1972. 2. M I 5 3. Spies -- Great Britain 4. Intelligence officers -- Great Britain 5. World War II -- Military intelligence. 6. Nazi collaborators 7. Biographies

LC 2019032549

Documents the lesser-known story of World War II bank clerk-turned-MI5 spy Eric Roberts, tracing his gripping undercover effort to infiltrate England's communist party while constructing an information network of hundreds of British Nazi sympathizers.

Roberts, John G., 1955-

Biskupic, Joan The **Chief** : the life and turbulent times of Chief Justice John Roberts / Joan Biskupic. Basic Books, [2019] 336 p. **B**

ISBN 9780465093274

1. United States. Supreme Court Chief Justices. 2. United States. Supreme Court 3. Constitutional law. 4. Conservatives. 5. Judicial system. 6. Judges -- United States 7. Biographies

LC 2018039502

An incisive biography of the Supreme Court's enigmatic chief justice takes readers inside the momentous legal decisions of his tenure so far

"Digging into the life career of the elusive chief justice, CNN legal analyst Biskupic, who was the Supreme Court correspondent at the Washington Post and has written biographies on Sonia Sotomayor, Antonin Scalia, and Sandra Day O'Connor, is perfectly positioned to dissect the first decade-plus tenure of Chief Justice John Roberts." Kirkus.

Roberts, Keena

Roberts, Keena **Wild** life : dispatches from a childhood of baboons and button-downs / Keena Roberts. Grand Central Publishing, 2019. 352 p. **B**

ISBN 9781538745151

1. Growing up 2. Adolescence 3. Belonging 4. Girls 5. Africa 6. Botswana 7. United States 8. Philadelphia, Pennsylvania 9. Autobiographies and memoirs

LC 2019021573

Keena Roberts split her adolescence between the wilds of an island camp in Botswana and the even more treacherous halls of an elite Philadelphia private school.

Robertson, Robbie

Robertson, Robbie **Testimony** / Robbie Robertson. Crown Archetype, [2016] 336 p. **B**

ISBN 9780307889782

1. Robertson, Robbie. 2. Rock musicians -- Canada 3. Rock groups 4. Rock music 5. Multiracial men 6. United States -- Social life and customs -- 20th century 7. Canada -- Social life and customs -- 20th century 8. Autobiographies and memoirs

LC 2016031782

A memoir by the influential rock artist traces his half-Jewish, half-Mohawk upbringing in Toronto, his early years with rockabilly legend Ronnie Hawkins, the rise of The Band, the stories behind his iconic songs and The Band's famous farewell concert, The Last Waltz.

"This book will enrich and delight any rock fan." Library Journal.

Robeson, Eslanda Goode, 1896-1965

Ransby, Barbara **Eslanda** : the large and unconventional life of Mrs. Paul Robeson / Barbara Ransby. Yale University Press, c2013. 448 p. **B**

ISBN 9780300124347

1. Robeson, Eslanda Goode, 1896-1965. 2. Robeson, Paul, 1898-1976. 3. Women social advocates. 4. Women anthropologists. 5. Independence in women. 6. African-American anthropologists. 7. Biographies

LC 2012022359

Chronicles the eventful life of the anthropologist, journalist, and women's rights advocate, exploring her world travels, friendships with notables and world leaders, and defiant McCarthy committee testimony.

Robeson, Paul, 1898-1976

Robeson, Paul, 1898-1976 **Here** I stand / Paul Robeson ; with a preface by Lloyd L. Brown and a new introduction by Sterling Stuckey. Beacon Press, 1988, c1958. xxxvi, 121 p. : **B**

ISBN 9780807064450

1. Robeson, Paul, 1898-1976. 2. African Americans

LC 87047882

The much beleaguered black singer's 1958 statement on the Negro culture in America is introduced by a short background history

Robeson, Paul, Jr., 1927-2014 The **undiscovered** Paul Robeson : an artist's journey, 1898-1939 / Paul Robeson, Jr. Wiley, c2001. 400 p. ; **B**

ISBN 9780471242659

1. Robeson, Paul, 1898-1976. 2. Robeson, Paul, 1898-1976 Childhood and youth. 3. African Americans 4. Singers -- United States 5. Actors and actresses -- United States 6. Political activists -- United States 7. Biographies

LC 2001017656

A biography of Paul Robeson, who overcame racial discrimination to become a world-famous African-American athlete, actor, singer, and civil rights activist.

"Extensively illustrated with personal photographs, this is a unique account of a brilliant but troubled man." Library Journal.

Robespierre, Maximilien, 1758-1794

McPhee, Peter, 1948- **Robespierre** : a revolutionary life / Peter McPhee. Yale University Press, c2012. 299 p. **B**

ISBN 9780300118117

1. Robespierre, Maximilien, 1758-1794. 2. Revolutionaries. 3. Politicians. 4. Ruthlessness in men. 5. Lawyers. 6. France -- History -- Revolution, 1789-1799. 7. France -- History -- Reign of Terror, 1793-1794. 8. France -- Politics and government -- 1789-1799. 9. Biographies

LC 2011027640

Chronicles the life and times of the French Revolutionary figure, looking at little known aspects, including his nervousness, lust for power, and role in "the Terror."

Robinson, Betty, 1911-1999

Montillo, Roseanne **Fire** on the track : Betty Robinson and the triumph of the early Olympic women / Roseanne Montillo. Crown, 2017. 304 p. **B**

ISBN 9781101906156

1. Robinson, Betty, 1911-1999. 2. Women Olympic athletes. 3. Women runners. 4. Running 5. Sexism in sports. 6. Biographies

LC 2017008783

Describes the life of the pioneering women's track star, who won gold at the 1928 Olympic Games in Amsterdam, only to nearly die in a plane crash and then miraculously rehab her way back onto the 1936 Olympic team.

"Robinson's life story and important role in breaking down barriers for women has already been optioned for film; this well-balanced biography and history of a groundbreaking female track star recalls a time and an athlete worth celebrating." Library Journal.

Robinson, Jackie, 1919-1972

Kashatus, William C., 1959- **Jackie** and Campy : the untold story of their rocky relationship and the breaking of baseball's color line / William C. Kashatus. University of Nebraska Press,

[2014] 296 p. **B**

ISBN 9780803246331

1. Robinson, Jackie, 1919-1972. 2. Campanella, Roy, 1921-1993. 3. African American baseball players 4. Baseball players -- United States 5. Male friendship -- United States -- History. 6. African Americans -- Civil rights. 7. United States -- Race relations -- History -- 20th century. 8. Biographies.

LC 2013033133

"Kashatus has written a superb narrative of sports, race, and politics in the 1950s and '60s, and also tells of the bittersweet consequences in Jackie and Campy's lives." Publishers Weekly.

Robinson, Jackie, 1919-1972 **I** never had it made / Jackie Robinson as told to Alfred Duckett. G. P. Putnam's Sons, 1972. 287 p. **B**

ISBN 0399110216

1. Robinson, Jackie, 1919-1972. 2. Major League Baseball (Organization) 3. Racism in sports -- History. 4. Racism in baseball -- History. 5. Baseball players. 6. African Americans 7. Autobiographies and memoirs

LC 75175272

In relating his life, Robinson reveals the struggles of a black athlete in the white-dominated world of American sports

"The hard nut of this moving book, however, is the young Jackie Robinson digging in against the profanity of prejudice in that public arena we had the temerity to call the national game before he arrived." Kirkus.

Robinson, Sugar Ray, 1920-1989

★Haygood, Wil **Sweet** thunder : the life and times of Sugar Ray Robinson / Wil Haygood. Alfred A. Knopf, c2009. 416 p. **B**

ISBN 9781400044979

1. Boxers (Sports) -- United States 2. Boxing. 3. African American athletes 4. Biographies

LC 2009005534

"A Borzoi book."

Documents the rise of the iconic boxer against a backdrop of the mid-twentieth century, describing his Harlem youth and emergence as a symbol of black America while offering insight into his athletic talents and his relationships with such figures as Langston Hughes, Lena Horne, and Miles Davis.

Robison, John Elder

Robison, John Elder **Look** me in the eye : my life with Asperger's / John Elder Robison. Crown Publishers, c2007. 304 p. **B**

ISBN 0307395987

1. Robison, John Elder Mental health. 2. People with Asperger's syndrome 3. People with autism 4. Asperger's syndrome. 5. Autism. 6. United States -- Social life and customs. 7. Autobiographies and memoirs

LC 2007013139

The author describes life growing up different in an odd family, his unusual talents, his struggle to live a "normal" life, his diagnosis at the age of forty with Asperger's syndrome, and the dramatic changes that have occurred since that diagnosis.

"Robison's memoir is must reading for its unblinking (as only an Aspergian can) glimpse into the life of a person who had to wait decades for the medical community to catch up with him." Booklist.

Robison, John Elder **Switched** on : a memoir of brain change and emotional awakening / John Elder Robison. Spiegel & Grau, 2015. 304 p. **B**

ISBN 9780812996890

1. Robison, John Elder Mental health. 2. People with Asperger's syndrome 3. Asperger's syndrome 4. Brain 5. Emotions 6. Autobiographies and memoirs

LC 2015014112

A follow-up to the best-selling Look Me in the Eye continues the story of the author's struggles with autism, recounting how, after undergoing an experimental brain therapy, he began to experience empathy in ways that challenged his perceptions about his relationships, memories and sense of identity.

"Fascinating for its insights into Aspergers and research, this engrossing record will make readers reexamine their preconceptions about this syndrome and the future of brain manipulation." Booklist.

Rockefeller, John D. (John Davison), 1839-1937

Chernow, Ron **Titan** : the life of John D. Rockefeller, Sr. / Ron Chernow. Random House, 1998. xxii, 774 p. : **B**

ISBN 9780679438083

1. Rockefeller family. 2. Standard Oil Company. 3. Capitalists and financiers -- United States 4. Industrialists -- United States 5. Philanthropists -- United States 6. United States -- History -- 1865-1921. 7. Biographies

LC 97033117

ALA Notable Book, 1999.

National Book Critics Circle Award for Biography finalist, 1998.

John D. Rockefeller, Sr., history's first billionaire and the patriarch of America's most famous dynasty, is an icon whose true nature has eluded three generations of historians.

"This book is a triumph of the art of biography. Unflaggingly interesting, it brings John D. Rockefeller Sr. to life through sustained narrative portraiture of the large-scale, 19th-century kind." New York Times Book Review.

Rockefeller, Nelson Aldrich, 1908-1979

Smith, Richard Norton, 1953- **On** his own terms : a life of Nelson Rockefeller / Richard Norton Smith. Random House Inc., 2014. 640 p. : **B**

ISBN 9780375505805

1. Rockefeller, Nelson Aldrich, 1908-1979. 2. Republicans 3. Vice presidents -- United States 4. Philanthropists 5. Politicians -- United States 6. United States -- Politics and government -- 20th century 7. Biographies.

LC 2013497351

A Pulitzer Prize finalist offers a sweeping portrait of one of the 20th century's most significant politicians, businessmen and philanthropists. Illustrations. Tour. Family tree provided online.

Rockwell, Norman, 1894-1978

Solomon, Deborah **American** mirror : the life and art of Norman Rockwell / Deborah Solomon. Farrar, Straus and Giroux, 2013. 512 p. **B**

ISBN 9780374113094

1. Rockwell, Norman, 1894-1978. 2. Painters -- United States 3. Illustrators -- United States 4. Depression. 5. Mental illness. 6. Biographies

LC 2013021682

Includes index.

The celebrated critic and author of Utopia Parkway presents a portrait of the classic 20th-century American artist that explores his achievements and influence as a long-time illustrator for The Saturday

Evening Post, sharing additional insights into his unexpectedly complex private life.

"Praised for her biographies of Jackson Pollock and Joseph Cornell, noted art critic Solomon makes a surprise leap to rock-solid Americana artist Norman Rockwell. But as she says, Rockwell painted a history of the American people that had never happened, and she goes on to detail his not-so-apple-pie personality." Library Journal.

Rodgers, Richard, 1902-1979

Purdum, Todd S. **Something** wonderful : Rodgers and Hammerstein's Broadway revolution / Todd S. Purdum. Henry Holt & Company, 2018. x, 386 pages, 16 unnumbered pages of plates : **B**

ISBN 9781627798341

1. Hammerstein, Oscar, 1895-1960 2. Theater -- Broadway, New York City 3. Composers 4. Dramatists 5. Musical writing 6. Biographies

LC 2017044836

A revelatory portrait of the creative partnership that transformed musical theater and provided the soundtrack to the American Century.

"Purdum's anecdote-filled account is a sterling primer on the influential duo, both for newcomers to their work and to those looking to rekindle an old flame." Publishers Weekly.

Rodriguez, Daniel, 1988-

Rodriguez, Daniel, 1988- **Rise** : a soldier, a dream, and a promise kept / Daniel Rodriguez ; contributions by Joe Layden. Houghton Mifflin Harcourt, 2014 256 p. **B**

ISBN 9780544365605

1. United States. Army 2. Clemson Tigers (Football team) 3. Afghan War, 2001-, American. 4. Iraq War, 2003-2011, American. 5. College football 6. Soldiers -- United States 7. Autobiographies and memoirs

LC 2014016742

A soldier who fought in one of the bloodiest battles in Afghanistan, and against all odds, lived to pursue his dream of playing Division 1 college football tells his story for the first time.

"This is an uncommonly solid memoir. Recommended for all readers, particularly those interested in sports and military books." Library Journal.

Rodriguez, Deborah

Rodriguez, Deborah **Kabul** Beauty School : an American woman goes behind the veil / Deborah Rodriguez ; with Kristin Ohlson. Random House, c2007. 275 p. ; **B**

ISBN 1400065593

1. Rodriguez, Deborah. 2. Kabul Beauty School. 3. Women -- Kabul, Afghanistan -- Social life and customs -- 21st century. 4. Muslim women -- Kabul, Afghanistan -- Social conditions -- 21st century. 5. Beauty shops -- Social aspects -- Kabul, Afghanistan. 6. Hairdressers 7. Kabul, Afghanistan -- Social life and customs -- 21st century. 8. Autobiographies and memoirs

LC 2006050384

Soon after the fall of the Taliban, in 2001, Deborah Rodriguez went to Afghanistan as part of a humanitarian aid group. Surrounded by people whose skills--as doctors, nurses, and therapists--seemed eminently more practical than her own, Rodriguez, a hairdresser and mother from Michigan, despaired of being of any real use. Yet she found she had a gift for befriending Afghans, and once her profession became known she was eagerly sought out by Westerners desperate for a good haircut and by Afghan women, who have a long and proud tradition of running their own beauty salons. Thus the idea for the Kabul Beauty School was born. Within that small haven, the line between teacher and student quickly blurred as these vibrant women shared with Rodriguez their stories and their hearts, ultimately giving her the strength to leave her own unhealthy marriage and allow herself to love again, Afghan style.

"Rodriguez's experiences will delight readers as she recounts such tales as two friends acting as parents and negotiating a dowry for her marriage to an Afghan man or her students puzzling over a donation of a carton of thongs. Most of all, they will share her admiration for Afghan women's survival and triumph in chaotic times." School Library Journal.

Rodriguez, Richard

Rodriguez, Richard **Darling** : a spiritual autobiography / Richard Rodriguez. Viking, 2013. 256 p. **B**

ISBN 9780670025305

1. Catholic Church United States 2. Pilgrims and pilgrimages, Christian -- Israel 3. Religion. 4. Gay men 5. Catholic men 6. United States -- Religion. 7. Essays.

LC 2013017046

"With compassion and profundity of vision, Rodriguez offers a compelling view of modern spirituality that is as multifaceted as it is provocative." Kirkus.

Rodriguez, Richard **Hunger** of memory : the education of Richard Rodriguez : an autobiography. Bantam Books, 2004, c1982. 212 p. ; **B**

ISBN 0553382519

1. Rodriguez, Richard. 2. Bilingual education. 3. Second-language acquisition. 4. Mexican Americans -- California 5. Growing up. 6. California -- Social life and customs -- 20th century. 7. Autobiographies and memoirs

LC 2004269979

Previously published: Boston : D.R. Godine, 1982.

A personal account of what it has cost the author, nonmonetarily, to be educated beyond his origins as the son of Mexican immigrants rejects affirmative action and bilingualism as benign errors.

Rogers, Fred

King, Maxwell The **good** neighbor : the life and work of Fred Rogers / Maxwell King. Abrams Press, 2018. 320 p. **B**

ISBN 9781419727726

1. Mister Rogers' neighborhood (Television program) 2. Television personalities 3. Children's television personalities 4. Television programs for children 5. Values 6. Biographies

LC bl2018134511

Drawing on original interviews, oral histories and archival documents, the author traces the iconic children's program host's personal, professional, and artistic life through decades of work.

"Grown-up fans, pop culture enthusiasts, and anyone interested in the history of educational television and child development will be inspired. An excellent and timely addition to most collections." Library Journal.

Rogers, Jimmy

Goins, Wayne E. **Blues** all day long : the Jimmy Rogers story / Wayne Everett Goins ; foreword by Kim Wilson. University of Illinois Press, 2014 416 p. **B**

ISBN 9780252080173

1. Rogers, Jimmy. 2. Guitarists -- United States 3. Jazz musicians 4. African American musicians -- 20th century 5. Biographies

LC 2014007477

A member of Muddy Waters' legendary late 1940s-1950s band, Jimmy Rogers pioneered a blues guitar style that made him one of the most revered sidemen of all time. Rogers also had a significant if star-crossed career as a singer and solo artist for Chess Records, releasing the classic singles "That's All Right" and "Walking By Myself." In Blues All Day Long, Wayne Everett Goins mines seventy-five hours of interviews with Rogers' family, collaborators, and peers to follow a life spent in the blues.

"Goins enthusiastically tracks Rogers' early years playing in the juke-joint South and his arrival in Chicago in 1945, where he began his dynamic, downright telepathic collaboration with Muddy Waters. Fluent in the blues vernacular, Goins gleans fresh facts and vivid memories from dozens of lively interviews to capture the energy and struggles of the Chicago blues scene, from Maxwell Street to the Chess Records studios, as he tracks the ups and downs of devoted family man Rogers career with Waters, Little Walter, Howlin Wolf, and many others. Rogers story, including his retreat from music during the 1960s, triumphant return, and international stardom, is engrossing, and Goins zeal and nimble expressiveness are thrilling as he praises Rogers' special brand of lyrics, his irresistible, buttery-smooth vocal quality, and his highly sophisticated melodic, harmonic, and rhythmic style while celebrating Rogers' timeless passion and conviction." Booklist.

Rogers, Robbie

Rogers, Robbie **Coming** out to play / Robbie Rogers with Eric Marcus. Penguin Books, 2014. 256 p. **B**

ISBN 9780143126614

1. Rogers, Robbie. 2. Gay athletes 3. Coming out (Sexual or gender identity) 4. Soccer players 5. Gay men 6. Autobiographies and memoirs

LC 2014011229

Robbie Rogers knows better than most that keeping secrets can crush you. But for much of his life Robbie lived in paralyzing fear that sharing his big secret would cost him the love of his family and his career as a professional soccer player. So he never told anyone what was destroying his soul, both on and off the field. In Coming Out to Play, Robbie takes readers on his incredible journey from terrified teenager to a trailblazing out and proud professional soccer player for the L.A. Galaxy, who has embraced his new identity as a role model and champion for those still struggling with the secrets that keep them from living their dreams.

"Rogers's debut is great inspiration for people of all ages struggling with shame and grappling with identity issues with regard to sexuality or otherwise. Those who enjoy memoir and stories of people who overcome difficulty will embrace this account." Library Journal.

Roiphe, Anne, 1935-

Roiphe, Anne, 1935- **Art** and madness : a memoir of love without reason / Anne Roiphe. Nan A. Talese/Doubleday, c2011. 208 p. **B**

ISBN 9780385531641

1. Women authors, American -- 20th century 2. Intellectual life. 3. Husband and wife. 4. Marriage. 5. Autobiographies and memoirs

LC 2010028051

"Roiphe's narrative moves in punchy, spare episodes, nonchronologically and erratically, veering from past to present tense, and requiring effort on the part of the reader. Yet she is a masterly writer: her work presents vivid, priceless snapshots of the roiling era of Communist hysteria, faddish homosexuality, male privilege, and the heartbreaking fragility of talented men and their dreams of fame." Publishers Weekly.

Roiphe, Anne, 1935- **Epilogue** / Anne Richardson Roiphe. Harpercollins, 2008. 256 p. **B**

ISBN 9780061254628

1. Grief. 2. Married men -- Death 3. Widows 4. Loneliness in women. 5. Autobiographies and memoirs

LC 2008034530

As the death of her husband truly sinks in, Anne Roiphe begins her vignette-constructed memoir. An acclaimed writer, Roiphe now commences a new chapter of her life, one of firsts and singularity. This is her story of renewal, self-awareness, and acceptance.

Roker, Al, 1954-

Roker, Al, 1954- **Been** there, done that : family wisdom for modern times / Al Roker, Deborah Roberts with Laura Morton. New American Library, 2016 256 p. **B**

ISBN 9780451466365

1. Roker, Al, 1954- Anecdotes. 2. Roberts, Deborah, 1960- Anecdotes. 3. Parenting -- Anecdotes. 4. Family life -- Anecdotes. 5. African American television newscasters and commentators

LC 2015031342

The best-selling Today show personality and his news-journalist wife share life lessons, wisdom and family anecdotes on subjects ranging from growing up in the segregated South and weight loss to what they have learned from the elderly and child members of their family.

"Despite Roker's tendency toward hackneyed 'dad jokes' and sometimes trite observations (e.g., technology can get in the way of genuine interactions), this is an entertaining, encouraging read and a sweet testament to the couple's devotion to their marriage and family." Publishers Weekly.

Rooney, Andrew A., 1920-2011

Rooney, Andrew A., 1920-2011 **My** war / Andy Rooney. PublicAffairs, 2000, c1995. xiii, 333 p. : **B**

ISBN 1586480103

1. United States. Army 2. World War II, American. 3. War correspondents -- United States 4. Bomber pilots -- United States -- History -- World War II 5. War -- Psychological aspects. 6. United States 7. Autobiographies and memoirs

LC 00059228

Originally published: New York : Random House, 1995.

The author recounts his experiences as a young reporter to "Stars and Stripes," the American forces' daily newspaper in Europe, including his personal account of the liberation and entry into Buchenwald.

"The author relates how he became a notable combat journalist in WW II, a war he calls 'the ultimate experience for anyone in it.' For the Army newspaper Stars and Stripes, he covered the air war over Germany, the D-Day invasion of Normandy and the Allied drive into Germany. Rooney's simple, ruminative style . grips the reader as he describes famous events of the war." Publishers Weekly.

Roosevelt family

Peyser, Marc **Hissing** cousins : the untold story of Eleanor Roosevelt and Alice Roosevelt Longworth / Marc Peyser and Timothy Dwyer. Nan A. Talese / Doubleday 2015. 336 p. **B**

ISBN 9780385536011

1. Roosevelt, Eleanor, 1884-1962. 2. Longworth, Alice Roosevelt, 1884-1980. 3. Power (Social sciences) 4. Jealousy 5. Cousins 6. Presidents' spouses -- United States 7. Biographies

LC 2014026766

A provocative dual portrait of first cousins Eleanor Roosevelt and Alice Roosevelt Longworth discusses how their tangled lives were shaped by 20th-century history and politics, sharing insights into their childhoods, respective beliefs and adversarial relationship.

"Peyser and Dwyer's detailed and witty double biography is hard to put down, a fascinating look at an era and two exceptionally strong, intelligent women." Booklist.

Roosevelt, Eleanor, 1884-1962

Burns, Eric **Someone** to watch over me : a portrait of Eleanor Roosevelt and the tortured father who shaped her life / Eric Burns. Pegasus Books, 2017. 304 p. **B**

ISBN 9781681773285

1. Roosevelt, Eleanor, 1884-1962 Family. 2. Roosevelt, Elliot Bulloch, 1860-1894 3. Fathers and daughters 4. Presidents' spouses -- United States 5. Independence in women. 6. Biographies

LC 2017276796

A fresh and sensitive examination of Eleanor Roosevelt--one of the most remarkable Americans in history--and the tortured father who would inspire and shape her future leadership and advocacy.

"Using personal letters and the little information that is known of his relationship with Eleanor . the author underscores the crucial connection between her success and idolization of her father." Library Journal.

Cook, Blanche Wiesen **Eleanor** Roosevelt. Blanche Wiesen Cook. Viking, 1999. 686 p. **B**

ISBN 9780670844982

1. Roosevelt, Eleanor, 1884-1962. 2. Roosevelt, Franklin D. (Franklin Delano), 1882-1945 3. Presidents' spouses -- United States 4. Women social advocates 5. Feminism. 6. Husband and wife. 7. Washington, D.C. -- History -- 1933-1945. 8. New England -- History -- 20th century. 9. Biographies

The second volume in the best-selling biography of America's visionary First Lady examines Eleanor Roosevelt's growing influence on the history and policy of America during the White House years and the Depression, as she championed racial justice, women's rights, and more.

"Cook is unafraid to take on difficult issues . thus rendering the biography not simply a riveting read but also a profoundly moving and wise account of how history has been shaped by the intricacies of the human heart, mind and spirit." Publishers Weekly.

★Cook, Blanche Wiesen **Eleanor** Roosevelt Blanche Weisen Cook Viking, 2016 720 p. **B**

ISBN 9780670023950

1. Roosevelt, Eleanor, 1884-1962. 2. Roosevelt, Franklin D. (Franklin Delano), 1882-1945 3. Presidents' spouses -- United States 4. Women social advocates 5. Feminism. 6. Husband and wife. 7. Washington, D.C. -- History 8. New England -- History -- 20th century. 9. Biographies

LC 87040632

A concluding volume to the definitive portrait of Eleanor Roosevelt traces her post-World War II years, covering subjects ranging from FDR's death and the founding of the UN through her efforts to promote key initiatives in spite of limited support and her death in 1962.

"All this makes for fascinating reading, and it highlights for students of history how the world has changed since ERs time. And how it has not." Booklist.

★Michaelis, David, 1957- **Eleanor** : a life / David Michaelis. Simon & Schuster, 2020. xx, 698 p., 32 unnumbered p. of numbered plates ; **B**

ISBN 9781439192016

1. Roosevelt, Eleanor, 1884-1962. 2. Roosevelt, Franklin D. (Franklin Delano), 1882-1945 3. Presidents' spouses -- United States 4. Women social advocates 5. Feminism. 6. Independence in women. 7. United States -- History -- 1933-1945. 8. Biographies

Presents a breakthrough portrait of Eleanor Roosevelt, America's longest-serving First Lady, an avatar of democracy whose ever-expanding agency as diplomat, activist, and humanitarian made her one of the world's most widely admired and influential women.

"Biographer Michaelis (Schulz and Peanuts) presents a compulsively readable and exhaustively researched portrait of one of the most admired women of the 20th century. . . . This jam-packed biography is a must-read for 20th-century history buffs." Publishers Weekly

★Quinn, Susan, 1940- **Eleanor** and Hick : the love affair that shaped a First Lady / Susan Quinn. Penguin Press, 2016. 448 p. **B**

ISBN 9781594205408

1. Hickok, Lorena Alice, 1893-1968 2. Presidents' spouses 3. Female friendship 4. Women/women relations 5. Women journalists 6. Collective autobiographies and memoirs

LC 2016303873

An intimate account of the close relationship between First Lady Eleanor Roosevelt and reporter Lorena Hickok shares compassionate insights into how their more than three-decade friendship transformed their lives and empowered them to play significant roles in one of the most tumultuous periods in American history.

"A relentlessly captivating study of two remarkable individuals who helped extend the roles of American women in the public policy realm." Kirkus.

Roosevelt, Franklin D. (Franklin Delano), 1882-1945

Brands, H. W. **Traitor** to his class : the privileged life and radical presidency of Franklin Delano Roosevelt / H.W. Brands. Doubleday, 2008. 888 p., 16 p. of plates : **B**

ISBN 9780385519588

1. Roosevelt, Franklin D. (Franklin Delano), 1882-1945. 2. Presidents -- United States 3. Depressions -- 1929-1941 4. New Deal (1933-1939) 5. Political culture -- United States -- History -- 20th century. 6. United States -- Politics and government -- 1933-1945. 7. Biographies

LC 2008015164

Pulitzer Prize for Biography or Autobiography finalist

A biography of Franklin Delano Roosevelt examines his political leadership in a dark time of Depression and war, his championship of the poor, his revolutionary New Deal legislation, and his legacy for the future.

"A thoroughly readable, scrupulously fair assessment of the one president who could inspire a Mt. Rushmore makeover." Kirkus.

Brinkley, Douglas **Rightful** heritage : Franklin D. Roosevelt and the land of America / Douglas Brinkley. HarperCollins, 2016 752 p. **B**

ISBN 9780062089236

1. Presidents -- United States 2. New Deal (1933-1939) 3. Nature conservation -- United States -- History 4. Wildlife conservationists.

LC bl2016003042

The New York Times best-selling author of The Wilderness Warrior examines the environmental legacy of FDR and the New Deal, evaluating the creation of the Civilian Conservation Corps and the dozens of State Park systems that were protected by his decisions.

"Brinkley vividly tracks Roosevelt's 'political know-how, legislative muscle, and fearlessness' from a unique and important perspective in this engrossing and richly illuminating portrait of one of the American environments most ardent and effective champions." Booklist.

★Dallek, Robert **Franklin** D. Roosevelt : a political life / Robert Dallek. Viking, [2017] 704 p. **B**

ISBN 9780525427902

1. Roosevelt, Franklin D. (Franklin Delano), 1882-1945. 2. Presidents -- United States 3. Political science -- United States

-- History 4. Political leadership 5. Politicians 6. United States -- Politics and government -- 1933-1945. 7. United States -- Politics and government -- 1919-1933.

LC 2017032686

A wide-ranging portrait of the 32nd President focuses on his career as an incomparable politician and dealmaker whose unusual skills served to unite divided factions, initiate essential reforms and transform America into an international superpower.

"The result is a comprehensive retelling of a major American life that will rank among the standard biographies of its subject." Publishers Weekly.

Smith, Jean Edward **FDR** / Jean Edward Smith. Random House, c2007. xx, 858 p. : **B**

ISBN 1400061210

1. Roosevelt, Franklin D. (Franklin Delano), 1882-1945. 2. Presidents -- United States 3. United States -- History 4. Biographies

LC 2006043087

Presents a multi-faceted study of the complex American president, detailing his diverse roles as commander-in-chief, leader of a social revolution, and statesman, and exploring his personal life and the physical disabilities that he hid from the general public.

"Smith's FDR is at once a careful, intelligent synopsis of the existing Roosevelt scholarship (the sheer bulk of which is huge) and a meticulous reinterpretation of the man and his record. Smith pays more attention to Roosevelt's personal life than have most previous biographers. He is openly sympathetic yet ready to criticize when that is warranted, and to do so in sharp terms; he conveys the full flavor and import of Roosevelt's career without ever bogging down in detail. " Washington Post Book World.

Roosevelt, Quentin, 1897-1918

Burns, Eric The **golden** lad : the haunting story of Quentin and Theodore Roosevelt / Eric Burns. Pegasus Books, 2016. 300 p. **B**

ISBN 9781605989518

1. Roosevelt, Theodore, 1858-1919 2. Fathers and sons 3. World War I 4. Biographies

LC 2017304306

Theodore Roosevelt is one of the most fascinating and written-about presidents in American history--yet the most poignant tale about this larger-than-life man has never been told.

"Burns's unique, stirring account of America's most colorful president allows Teddy Roosevelt, the man and father, to step off the page." Publishers Weekly.

Roosevelt, Theodore, 1858-1919

Brinkley, Douglas The **wilderness** warrior : Theodore Roosevelt and the crusade for America / Douglas Brinkley. Harpercollins, 2009. xv, 940 p. : **B**

ISBN 9780060565282

1. Roosevelt, Theodore, 1858-1919 Views on nature 2. Presidents -- United States 3. Nature conservation -- United States -- History 4. Wildlife conservationists. 5. Environmentalists. 6. Biographies.

LC 2009291902

Green Prize for Sustainable Literature: Adult Nonfiction, 2010.

National Outdoor Book Award for History/Biography, 2009.

Evaluates Theodore Roosevelt's role in launching modern conservationsim, identifying the contributions of such influences as James Audubon and John Muir while describing how Roosevelt's exposure to natural wonders in his early life shaped his environmental values.

"The author has absorbed a huge amount of research, but encyclopedic inclusiveness and repetition occasionally mar narrative movement. But this book has Rooseveltian energy. It is largehearted, full of the vitality of its subject and a palpable love for the landscape it describes." New York Times Book Review.

DiSilvestro, Roger L. **Theodore** Roosevelt in the Badlands : a young politician's quest for recovery in the American West / Roger L. Di Silvestro. Walker & Co., 2011. 320 p. **B**

ISBN 9780802717214

1. Roosevelt, Theodore, 1858-1919. 2. Presidents -- United States 3. Frontier and pioneer life -- North Dakota. 4. Ranch life -- North Dakota -- History -- 19th century. 5. Biographies

LC 2010044297

A history of the 26th President's turbulent years spent as a rancher in the Dakota Territory Badlands reveals how his experiences shaped his subsequent values as a conservationist and his role in influencing national perspectives on wildlife and the cattle industry.

McCullough, David **Mornings** on horseback / David McCullough. Simon & Schuster, 1982, c1981. 445 p., 32 p. of plates : **B**

ISBN 9780671447540

1. Roosevelt, Theodore, 1858-1919 Childhood and youth. 2. Presidents -- United States

LC BL 99925995

Reprint. Originally published: 1981.

Includes index.

Examines the life of Theodore Roosevelt from age ten to twenty-seven, focusing on the influence of his family relationships and experiences on his growth to manhood.

"Based on diligent and thorough research, with emphasis on family, physical ailments, and friends, and written with verve and color, this is a stimulating book that will appeal to the general reader." Library Journal.

★Morris, Edmund **Colonel** Roosevelt / Edmund Morris. Random House, 2010. 976 p. **B**

ISBN 9780375504877

1. Roosevelt, Theodore, 1858-1919. 2. Presidents -- United States 3. Politicians -- United States 4. Progressivism (United States politics) 5. United States -- Politics and government -- 1909-1913. 6. United States -- Politics and government -- 1913-1921. 7. Biographies

LC 2010005890

Sequel to: Theodore Rex.

Presents a chronicle of the last ten years of Theodore Roosevelt's life to cover his African safaris, return to public life, involvement with the Progressive movement, campaign for president in 1912, and various brushes with death.

★Morris, Edmund The **rise** of Theodore Roosevelt / Edmund Morris. Modern Library, 2001, c1979. xxxiv, 920 p. : **B**

ISBN 0375756787

1. Roosevelt, Theodore, 1858-1919. 2. Presidents -- United States 3. Politicians -- United States. 4. Nobel Prize winners 5. Wildlife conservationists 6. United States -- Politics and government -- 1901-1909. 7. New York (State) -- Politics and government -- 1865-1950 8. New York (State) -- Governors 9. Biographies

LC 2001030520

Sequel: Theodore Rex."

Revised and updated".--Cover.Originally published: New York : Coward, McCann & Geoghegan, 1979.

Pulitzer Prize for Biography or Autobiography, 1980.

Focuses on Roosevelt's pre-presidential career, covering the period between 1858 to 1901, during which time Roosevelt built himself up from a frail asthmatic youth to a robust man with varied interests.

"This first volume of a three volume study of the life and times of Theodore Roosevelt covers Roosevelt's life up to the age of 42, when an assassin's bullet elected him the youngest president in the nation's history." Booklist.

★Morris, Edmund **Theodore** Rex / Edmund Morris. Random House, 2001. x, 772 p. : **B**

ISBN 0394555090

1. Roosevelt, Theodore, 1858-1919. 2. Presidents -- United States 3. Politicians -- United States 4. Conservation of natural resources -- United States -- History. 5. Nobel Prize winners 6. United States -- Politics and government -- 1901-1909. 7. Panama Canal -- History. 8. Philippines -- History -- Colonial period (American), 1898-1946. 9. Biographies

LC 2001019366

Sequel to: The Rise of Theodore Roosevelt.

Sequel: Colonel Roosevelt.

ALA Notable Book, 2003.

Describes Theodore Roosevelt's presidency as he faced the challenges of a new century in which the United States would become a world power, and discusses his accomplishments and failures, the enemies he made, and his family life.

"Morris excels at placing TR in the context of his time, showing how he out maneuvered powerful but ossified opponents from the Gilded Age and trumped isolationists by averting war, in the process winning the first Nobel Peace Prize." Library Journal.

★Ward, Geoffrey C. The **Roosevelts** : an intimate history / Geoffrey C. Ward ; based on a documentary film by Ken Burns ; with a preface by Ken Burns ; picture research by Susanna Steisel ; design by Maggie Hinders. Alfred A. Knopf, 2014. 528 p. **B**

ISBN 9780307700230

1. Roosevelt, Theodore, 1858-1919 Influence. 2. Roosevelt, Franklin D. (Franklin Delano), 1882-1945 Influence. 3. Roosevelt, Eleanor, 1884-1962 Influence. 4. Presidents -- United States 5. Presidents' spouses -- United States 6. United States -- Politics and government -- 20th century. 7. United States -- Social conditions -- 20th century. 8. Biographies

LC 2014019251

An extraordinarily vivid and personal portrait of a great American political family and its impact on the United States serves as the tie-in volume to the PBS documentary to air in the fall of 2014.

"Starting with Teddy's asthma-plagued youth and ending with Eleanor's death in 1962, every aspect of their lives and legacies is touched upon. Hundreds of photos, newspaper clippings, and accompanying captions flesh out the story, which expands to cover their friends and family, enemies, and (alleged) lovers." Publishers Weekly.

Rorschach, Hermann, 1884-1922

Searls, Damion The **inkblots** : Hermann Rorschach, his iconic test, and the power of seeing / Damion Searls. Crown Publishing, [2017] 416 p. **B**

ISBN 9780804136549

1. Rorschach, Hermann, 1884-1922. 2. Psychiatrists -- Switzerland. 3. Psychological tests 4. Psychology 5. Rorschach Test. 6. Biographies

LC 2016028995

Documents the lesser-known story of the creator of the psychological test developed to reveal key aspects of human personality, sharing insights into how his inkblots were carefully designed and rose to prominence after his early death.

"Searls shows persuasively how the creation and reinvention of inkblots has reflected psychologists' scientific and cultural perspectives." Kirkus.

Rose, Pete, 1941-

Rose, Pete, 1941- **Play** hungry : the making of a baseball player / Pete Rose. Penguin Press, 2019. xi, 290 p. **B**

ISBN 9780525558675

1. Baseball players 2. Baseball 3. Success (Concept) 4. Determination (Personal quality)

LC 2018056333

Includes index.

A personal account by the iconic but controversial baseball athlete shares firsthand insights into the role of his father in his successes, the most memorable moments from his career and the scandal that resulted in his lifetime ban.

"Pete's vivid recollections of his early years, growing up in the forties and fifties, point out the profound difference between then and now for most kids. The title says it all. This is how a hungry kid became one of the greatest ball players of all time. Essential reading for baseball fans, controversy and all." Publishers Weekly.

Rosenberg, David, 1961-2014

Glaser, Gabrielle **American** baby : a mother, a child, and the shadow history of adoption / Gabrielle Glaser. Viking, 2020. 352 p. **B**

ISBN 9780735224681

1. Katz, Margaret Erle 2. Adopted children 3. Adoption 4. Adoption agencies 5. Corruption 6. New York City

LC 2020005338

A history of adoption in postwar America explores the impact of "Baby Boom" values and limited birth control on the life of a pregnant teen who was forced by the institutions of the 1960s to give up her rights.

"A searing narrative that combines the detailed saga of one unwed teenage mother with deep research on all aspects of a scandalous adoption industry." Kirkus

Rosenberg, Justus, 1921-

Rosenberg, Justus, 1921- The **art** of resistance : my four years in the French underground: a memoir / Justus Rosenberg. William Morrow, 2020. 320 p. **B**

ISBN 9780062742193

1. Fry, Varian, 1908-1967 2. French Resistance (World War II) 3. Anti-Nazi movement 4. World War II -- Underground movements 5. World War II -- Jews -- Rescue 6. France -- History -- German occupation, 1940-1945. 7. Autobiographies and memoirs

LC bl2019037347

Includes index.

In this World War II memoir set in Nazi-occupied France a story of bravery, daring, adventure, survival and romance a former Eastern European Jew remembers his flight from the Holocaust and his extraordinary four years in the French underground.

Rosenbloom, Stephanie

Rosenbloom, Stephanie **Alone** time : four seasons, four cities, and the pleasures of solitude / Stephanie Rosenbloom. Viking, [2018] 288 p. **B**

ISBN 9780399562303

1. Rosenbloom, Stephanie Travel 2. Solitude 3. Travelers 4. Women travelers 5. Voyages and travels 6. New York City 7. Autobiographies

and memoirs

LC 2018011925

A wise, passionate account of the pleasures of travelling solo. In our increasingly frantic daily lives, many people are genuinely fearful of the prospect of solitude, but time alone can be both rich and restorative, especially when travelling. Through on-the-ground reporting and recounting the experiences of artists, writers, and innovators who cherished solitude, Stephanie Rosenbloom considers how being alone as a traveller--and even in in one's own city--is conducive to becoming acutely aware of the sensual details of the world--patterns, textures, colors, tastes, sounds--in ways that are difficult to do in the company of others. --From publisher description

Rosenfelt, David

Rosenfelt, David **Dogtripping** : 25 rescues, 11 volunteers, and 3 RVs on our canine cross-country adventure / David Rosenfelt. St Martins Press, 2013. 288 p. **B**

ISBN 9781250014696

1. Authors, American 2. Dogs 3. Human/animal relationships 4. Cross-country automobile trips 5. Autobiographies and memoirs

LC 2013009168

Traveling goes to the dogs in this funny, heartwarming book. As if driving from California to Maine isn't ambitious enough, crime novelist David Rosenfelt and his wife -- who run a dog rescue foundation -- add 25 dogs to the mix, setting of with rescue volunteers in three RVs. The author's trademark self-deprecating humor shines in this charming (although occasionally sad) portrait of their "dogged" cross-country journey, as he reflects on wonderful canines he has known and loved, and explores how he became involved in dog rescue.

"Spirited and absolutely absorbing reading for fans of canine capers." Booklist.

Rosenthal, Jason

Rosenthal, Jason **My** wife said you may want to marry me : a memoir / Jason B. Rosenthal. HarperCollins, 2020. 228 p. **B**

ISBN 9780062940599

1. Rosenthal, Amy Krouse 2. Widowers 3. Loss (Psychology) 4. Family and death 5. Women authors 6. Autobiographies and memoirs

LC bl2020007400

The "Journey Through Loss and Grief" TED Talk presenter and co-author of Dear Boy, traces the death of his wife, "Modern Love" columnist Amy Krouse Rosenthal, and his subsequent efforts to cope and honor Amy's final wish. Surveying his life before, with, and after Amy, Jason ruminates on love, the pain of watching a loved one suffer, and what it means to heal--how he and their three children, despite their profound sorrow, went on. Jason's emotional journey offers insights on dying and death and the excruciating pain of losing a soulmate, and illuminates the lessons he learned.

"Rosenthal's gut-wrenching, honest, and uplifting memoir offers reassurance and connection to readers experiencing their own losses." Booklist

Rosenthal, Joe, 1911-2006

Bradley, James, 1954- **Flags** of our fathers / James Bradley with Ron Powers. Bantam Books, 2000. 376 p. : **B**

ISBN 0553111337

1. United States. Marine Corps 2. United States. Navy 3. Iwo Jima, Battle of, 1945. 4. World War II 5. Military campaigns 6. Photographs. 7. Iwo Jima, Japan -- History, Military -- World War II. 8. Pacific Area. 9. Biographies

LC 00025803

"This is the story of the most famous photograph to come out of World War II, the flag-raising on Mount Suribachi during the Battle of Iwo Jima in February 1945. Bradley is the son of one of the six men immortalized in that remarkable photo, and his gripping narrative, vivid descriptions, and heartfelt style make this a powerful story of courage, humility, and tragedy." Library Journal.

Ross, Barney, 1909-

Century, Douglas **Barney** Ross / Douglas Century. Nextbook : c2006. xvii, 215 p. : **B**

ISBN 0805242236

1. Boxers (Sports) -- United States 2. Boxing -- United States -- History 3. Drug addiction 4. Weapons industry and trade -- Israel 5. United States -- Social life and customs -- 20th century 6. Biographies

LC 2005049939

A profile of one of the most colorful sports figures of the twentieth century follows the life and career of boxer Barney Ross, from his youth as the child of Eastern European immigrants in a tough Chicago neighborhood and his hardscrabble early life, to his successful boxing career, exploits as a combat Marine during World War II, campaign against drug abuse, and fervent support of a Jewish state.

Ross, Elizabeth Griscom, 1752-1836

Miller, Marla **Betsy** Ross and the making of America / Marla R. Miller. Henry Holt, 2010. 480 p. **B**

ISBN 9780805082975

1. Ross, Elizabeth Griscom, 1752-1836. 2. Revolutionaries -- United States 3. Patriotism. 4. Women revolutionaries 5. Flags -- United States -- History. 6. Philadelphia, Pennsylvania -- History -- Revolution, 1775-1783. 7. United States -- History -- Revolution, 1775-1783. 8. Biographies

LC 2009035385

Cundill Prize in Historical Literature finalist

A comprehensively researched portrait of the iconic Revolutionary War figure draws on new sources to describe the fabled creation of the first flag while reconstructing her true life behind her seamstress legend and offering insight into the roles of period artisan families.

Ross, Marion, 1928-

Ross, Marion, 1928- **My** days : happy and otherwise / Marion Ross, with David Laurell ; foreword by Ron Howard. Kensington Publishing, 2018. 320 p. **B**

ISBN 9781496715159

1. Happy days (Television program) 2. Television actors and actresses 3. Celebrities 4. Motherhood 5. Characters and characteristics in television 6. Autobiographies and memoirs

LC 2017955111

The real-life woman behind the Happy Days mom tells the amazing story of her life and career.

"Happy Days fans will enjoy the anecdotes about the show, but Ross's perseverance also serves as a primer for aspiring actors." Library Journal.

Ross, Steve, (Graphic novelist)

Ross, Steve, (Holocaust survivor) **From** broken glass : my story of finding hope in Hitler's death camps to inspire a new generation / Steve Ross, with Brian Wallace and Glenn Frank. Hachette Books, 2018. xix, 266 pages, 8 unnumbered pages of plates : **B**

ISBN 9780316513043

1. Holocaust (1933-1945) 2. Holocaust survivors 3. Social advocates

4. World War II

LC 2017963705

A survivor of the Holocaust describes how--by observing and enduring inconceivable cruelty as well as by receiving compassion from caring fellow prisoners--he learned of the human capacity to rise above even the bleakest circumstances, and later used that knowledge to help underprivileged youth in Boston for more than 40 years.

Rossini, Gioacchino, 1792-1868

Servadio, Gaia **Rossini** / Gaia Servadio. Carroll & Graf Publishers, 2003. xii, 244 p. : **B**

ISBN 9780786711956

1. Rossini, Gioacchino, 1792-1868. 2. Composers -- Italy 3. Operas -- Italy -- History and criticism 4. Classical music -- 19th century -- History and criticism 5. Sacred music -- History and criticism 6. Italy -- History -- 19th century 7. Biographies

LC 2003043563

Recounts the life of the nineteenth century Italian composer of such works as "The Barber of Seville" and "William Tell."

"This is a deeply rewarding book, written with real personality and much scholarship." Publishers Weekly.

Roth, Henry

Kellman, Steven G., 1947- **Redemption** : the life of Henry Roth / Steven G. Kellman. W.W. Norton, c2005. 371 p., 16 p. of plates : **B**

ISBN 0393057798

1. Roth, Henry. 2. Authors, American -- 20th century 3. Biographies

LC 2005011979

A portrait of the twentieth-century American literary icon describes his incest-marked childhood on the Jewish Lower East Side through his later years in New Mexico, in a volume based on uncovered FBI files and interviews with personal friends and family members.

"The author traces Roth's fascinating career from his birth in Galicia, Austria-Hungary, to his final years in New Mexico. He focuses on his experience of New York's Lower East Side and Jewish and Irish Harlem. This biography should be included in all public library and academic collections." Library Journal.

Roth, Joseph, 1894-1939

Roth, Joseph, 1894-1939 **Joseph** Roth : a life in letters / translated and edited by Michael Hofmann. W. W. Norton, c2012. 512 p. **B**

ISBN 9780393060645

1. Roth, Joseph, 1894-1939 Correspondence. 2. Authors, Austrian -- 20th century 3. Letters 4. Autobiographies and memoirs

LC 2011032677

The tumultuous and calamitous life of the Austrian writer best known for The Radetzky March is described through translations of the author's own letters that recall his father's and wife's mental illnesses, numerous mistresses and travel to Paris.

Roth, Philip, 1933-2018

Roth, Philip, 1933-2018 The **facts** : a novelist's autobiography / Philip Roth. Farrar, Straus & Giroux, 1988. 195 p. ; **B**

ISBN 0374152128

1. Authors, American -- 20th century -- Biography. 2. Authors, American 3. Jewish Americans 4. Autobiographies and memoirs

LC 88014187

The author looks back on five important periods of his life and differentiates his life from his biographically based fiction.

Rothko, Mark, 1903-1970

Cohen-Solal, Annie, 1948- **Mark** Rothko : toward the light in the chapel / Annie Cohen-Solal. Yale University Press, 2015. 224 p. **B**

ISBN 9780300182040

1. Rothko, Mark, 1903-1970. 2. Painters -- United States 3. Jewish men 4. Immigrants 5. Art 6. Biographies

LC 2014037767

First published in French as Mark Rothko by Actes Sud (Arles, France, 2013)."

Mark Rothko was not only one of the most influential American painters of the twentieth century; he was a scholar, an educator, and a deeply spiritual human being. Born Marcus Yakovlevich Rotkovitch, he emigrated from the Russian Empire to the United States at age ten, already well educated in the Talmud and carrying with him bitter memories of the pogroms and persecutions visited upon the Jews of Latvia. Few artists have achieved success as quickly, and by the mid-twentieth century, Rothko's artwork was being displayed in major museums throughout the world. In May 2012 his painting Orange, Red, Yellow was auctioned for nearly $87 million, setting a new Christie's record. Author Annie Cohen-Solal gained access to archival materials no previous biographer had seen. As a result, her book is an extraordinarily detailed portrait of Rothko the man and the artist, an uncommonly successful painter who was never comfortable with the idea of his art as a commodity".-- Provided by publisher.

"A defining and affecting tribute to a modern master." Booklist.

Roulston, Marjorie Hillis

Scutts, Joanna The **extra** woman : how Marjorie Hillis led a generation of women to live alone and like it / Joanna Scutts. Liveright Publishing Corporation, [2018] 288 p. **B**

ISBN 9781631492730

1. Roulston, Marjorie Hillis. Live alone and like it. 2. Single women 3. Living alone 4. Authors 5. Feminists 6. Biographies

LC 2017027416

From the flapper to The Feminine Mystique, the author presents a cultural history of single women in the city through the reclaimed life of glamorous guru Marjorie Hillis.

"A sparklingly intelligent and well-researched cultural history." Kirkus.

Roundtree, Dovey Johnson, 1914-2018

★Roundtree, Dovey Johnson, 1914-2018 **Mighty** justice : my life in civil rights / Dovey Johnson Roundtree and Katie McCabe ; foreword by Tayari Jones. Algonquin Books of Chapel Hill, 2019. xii, 273 p., 8 unnumbered p. of plates : **B**

ISBN 9781604731323

1. Social advocates 2. Civil rights 3. Women lawyers 4. Civil Rights Movement 5. United States -- Social conditions 6. Autobiographies and memoirs

Originally published in 2009 by The University Press of Mississippi under title: Justice older than the law : the life of Dovey Johnson Roundtree.

Includes discussion questions (pages [267]-269).

Legendary African American civil rights attorney Dovey Johnson Roundtree recounts her trailblazing life in this inspiring, beautifully told story that shows how one remarkable woman changed history, and how urgent it is to continue her work today.

"This eye-opening, accessible book documents the life of a trailblazing human rights advocate." Publishers Weekly.

Rousey, Ronda

Rousey, Ronda **My** fight / your fight / Ronda Rousey. Regan Arts, 2015 288 p. **B**

ISBN 9781941393260

1. UFC (Mixed martial arts event) 2. Women martial artists. 3. Martial artists -- United States 4. Mixed martial arts. 5. Self-defense 6. Autobiographies and memoirs

LC 2015930623

The undefeated UFC champion and Hollywood star charts her difficult journey to fame, revealing her tragic childhood, her secrets behind her achievements and her experiences as a pioneering woman athlete.

"The book is just too long; it could have been more than 50 pages shorter, and Rousey would still have inspired her readers. But her warrior mentality is always evident, and one of her more helpful pieces of advice is to feel angry, not sad, after a loss. She urges would-be elite athletes--and really, anyone--to set goals, then become obsessed with elevating them. Plainspoken, often repetitive, and always fiery. Rousey is a fierce yet endearing role modeland a woman possessed." Kirkus.

Rousseau, Jean-Jacques, 1712-1778

★Damrosch, Leopold **Jean-Jacques** Rousseau : restless genius / Leo Damrosch. Houghton Mifflin Co., 2005. x, 566 p. : **B**

ISBN 0618446966

1. Rousseau, Jean-Jacques, 1712-1778. 2. Rousseau, Jean-Jacques, 1712-1778 Childhood and youth. 3. Burke, Edmund, 1729-1797 4. Authors, French -- 18th century 5. Personal conduct. 6. Human nature. 7. Reason -- History. 8. Biographies

LC 2005013579

National Book Award for Nonfiction finalist, 2005"

A delight to read, Damrosch comes as close to Rousseau's authentic self as we are likely to get." New York Times Book Review.

Rousseau, Jean-Jacques, 1712-1778 **Confessions** / Jean-Jacques Rousseau ; edited and introduced by P.N. Furbank. Knopf, c1992. xli, 320, 306 p. ; **B**

ISBN 067940998X

1. Rousseau, Jean-Jacques, 1712-1778. 2. Authors, French -- 18th century 3. Biographies

LC 91053194

Rowbottom, Allie

Rowbottom, Allie **Jell-O** girls : a family history / Allie Rowbottom. Little Brown & Co 2018 288 p. **B**

ISBN 9780316510615

1. Rowbottom, Allie Family 2. Jell-O Company 3. Rich families 4. Families -- History 5. Food industry and trade -- History 6. Wealth -- Psychological aspects 7. Autobiographies and memoirs

LC bl2018100750

A descendant of the Jell-O dynasty traces the privilege, addiction and illness that has impacted generations of her family, tracing her late mother's obsessive research into a link between their family's lifestyle and poor health.

" In this compassionate, feminist-flavored memoir, Rowbottom both distances and broadens the family story by setting it in the context of the changes in the lives of American women over the past century, as reflected in the marketing and sales of Jell-O. First viewed as a sweet treat and later as a dietary aid, the dessert serves as an oddly apt reflection of women's concurrent, ambivalent relationships to their appetites and bodies." Booklist.

Rudd, Mark

Rudd, Mark **Underground** : my life with SDS and the Weathermen / Mark Rudd. William Morrow, 2009. 352 p. **B**

ISBN 9780061472756

1. Rudd, Mark. 2. Protest movements 3. Social advocates 4. Radicals -- United States 5. Revolutions. 6. United States -- History -- 20th century. 7. Autobiographies and memoirs

LC 2010292486

A leader of the Columbia University student uprising of 1968 and fugitive member of the notorious Weather Underground describes how he and his friends helped to organize the Days of Rage protests in 1969 and plotted to overthrow the government in a failed bombing attempt.

Rufus, Rob

Rufus, Rob **Die** young with me : a memoir / Rob Rufus. Touchstone Books, 2016. 320 p. **B**

ISBN 9781501142611

1. Rufus, Rob. 2. Punk rock musicians -- United States 3. Teenagers with cancer 4. Resilience (Personal quality) 5. Punk rock music 6. West Virginia 7. Appalachian region 8. Autobiographies and memoirs

LC 2016005363

The author describes growing up in rural West Virginia and starting a punk band with his twin brother, only to be diagnosed with stage four cancer, which forced him to discover his inner strength.

"By refusing to abandon hope, easy though it would have been to do so, Rufus' memoir makes a valuable contribution to the literature of healing and recovery." Kirkus.

Ruiz, Miguel, 1952-

Ruiz, Miguel, 1952- The **Toltec** art of life and death : living your life as a work of art / Don Miguel Ruiz and Barbara Emrys. Harper Elixir, 2017. xv, 391p. ; **B**

ISBN 9780062390936

1. Near-death experiences 2. Spiritual biography

LC bl2017014788

Includes reader's guide.

The author describes the mystical Toltec journey he took throughout a heart attack-induced nine-week coma, relating his encounters with the people, ideas, and events that transformed his life.

"Readers might find it difficult to follow Ruiz's winding road to the truth, but will come away from this book with a deeper understanding of life's complexities." Publishers Weekly.

Rush, Benjamin, 1746-1813

Fried, Stephen, 1958- **Rush** : revolution, madness, and Benjamin Rush, the visionary doctor who became a founding father / Stephen Fried. Crown Publishing, 2018. 416 p. **B**

ISBN 9780804140065

1. Founding fathers of the United States 2. Physicians 3. Revolutionaries 4. Social advocacy 5. Biographies

ALA Notable Book, 2019.

The remarkable story of Benjamin Rush, medical pioneer and one of our nation's most provocative and unsung Founding Fathers. In the summer of 1776, fifty-six men put their quills to a dangerous document they called the Declaration of Independence. Among them was a thirty-year-old doctor named Benjamin Rush. One of the youngest signatories, he was also, among stiff competition, one of the most visionary.

Rush, Chris, 1956-

Rush, Chris, 1956- The **light** years : a memoir / Chris Rush.

Farrar, Straus and Giroux, 2019. 352 p. **B**
ISBN 9780374294410
1. Drug use 2. Growing up 3. Artists -- United States 4. Counterculture 5. Autobiographies and memoirs
LC 2018020669

A coming-of-age memoir documents the author's descent into the counterculture of the 1970s, relating his preadolescent exposure to LSD, his teenage pursuit of kinship in the communes of the American West, and the factors that nearly ended his life.

Rushdie, Salman

★Rushdie, Salman **Joseph** Anton : a memoir / Salman Rushdie. Random House, 2012. 656 p. **B**
ISBN 9780812992786
1. Rushdie, Salman. Satanic verses. 2. Hiding. 3. Ayatollahs. 4. Death threats. 5. Islam. 6. Autobiographies and memoirs
LC 2012372283

Shortlisted for the James Tait Black Memorial Prize for Biography, 2012.

For the first time, author Salman Rushdie tells the story of his nine years spent underground, moving from house to house, an armed police protection team living with him at all times, and of how he regained his freedom.

Rushin, Steve

Rushin, Steve **Sting-ray** afternoons : a memoir / Steve Rushin. Little, Brown & Co., 2017. 352 p. **B**
ISBN 9780316392235
1. Growing up 2. Sportswriters. 3. Childhood 4. Family relationships 5. Minnesota 6. United States -- Social life and customs -- 20th century 7. Autobiographies and memoirs
LC 2016958350

A bittersweet memoir of the author's 1970s childhood nostalgically tours the era's products, history and cultural rebirth, sharing laugh-out-loud observations of his family life as it was shaped by influences ranging from the Steve Miller Band and Saturday morning cartoons to Bic pens and Schwinn Sting-Ray bikes.

"Rushin's everykid upbringing and the touchstones of childhood he recounts make Sting-Ray Afternoons a fun-filled and charming trip." Booklist.

Russo, Gianni, 1943-

Russo, Gianni, 1943- **Hollywood** godfather : my life in the movies and the mob / Gianni Russo, with Patrick Picciarelli. St. Martin's Press, 2019. 304 p. **B**
ISBN 9781250181398
1. Actors and actresses 2. Former gang members 3. Organized crime 4. Acting 5. Autobiographies and memoirs
LC 2018030147

Includes index.

The mobster-turned-actor best known for his performance in The Godfather describes the real-life Mafia experiences that informed his character, from his childhood in Little Italy to his role in the death of a Colombian drug cartel member.

"In this robust, fast-paced memoir, Russo describes his life going from being a real-life mobster to landing a role playing one in The Godfather." Publishers Weekly.

Russo, Richard, 1949-

Russo, Richard, 1949- **Elsewhere** / Richard Russo. Alfred A. Knopf, Inc., 2012. 288 p. **B**
ISBN 9780307959539
1. Authors, American 2. Mothers and sons 3. Poverty 4. Poor families 5. New York (State) 6. Autobiographies and memoirs
LC 2012016354

The Pulitzer Prize-winning author of Empire Falls presents an upbeat personal account of his youth, his parents and the 1950s upstate New York town they struggled to escape, recounting the encroaching poverty and illness that challenged everyday life and the dreams his mother instilled that inspired his career.

Russo, Vito

Schiavi, Michael R. **Celluloid** activist : the life and times of Vito Russo / Michael Schiavi. The University of Wisconsin Press, c2011. xiii, 361 p. : **B**
ISBN 9780299282301
1. Gay & Lesbian Alliance Against Defamation (New York, N.Y.) -- History 20th century. 2. ACT UP New York (Organization) -- History 20th century. 3. Gay men. 4. Gay activists 5. Homosexuality in films. 6. Film historians -- United States 7. Biographies.
LC 2010044627

"Conventionally academic but complex portrait of an undeservedly obscure gay author and activist." Kirkus.

Ruth, Babe, 1895-1948

Creamer, Robert W. **Babe** : the legend comes to life / Robert W. Creamer. Simon & Schuster, 1992. 443 p. : **B**
ISBN 9780671760700
1. Ruth, Babe, 1895-1948. 2. Baseball players 3. Biographies
LC 91039086

"A Fireside book."I
ncludes index.

The truth behind the famous Ruth stories analyzes the astounding statistics with detailed information on specific games, and describes Ruth's varied, often volatile, relations with those around him, from fellow players to fans, friends, and reporters. From Babe Ruth's early days in a Baltimore orphanage, to the glory days with the Yankees, to his final years, Robert W. Creamer has drawn an indelible protrait of a true folk hero.

★Leavy, Jane The **big** fella : Babe Ruth and the world he created / Jane Leavy. Harper, 2018. 320 p. **B**
ISBN 9780062380227
1. Ruth, Babe, 1895-1948. 2. Baseball players -- United States 3. Professional baseball 4. Celebrities 5. Fame
LC bl2018167865

National Book Critics Circle Award for Biography finalist, 2018

A portrait of Babe Ruth and his partnership with business manager Christy Walsh traces how their strategies, achievements and notoriety established a blueprint for modern athletic stardom.

"A skilled strategist and nearly peerless player, Ruth proves himself worthy of, yes, yet another biography, this one warts-and-all but still admiring. Sparkling, exemplary sports biography, shedding new light on a storied figure in baseball history." Kirkus.

Rutherford, Ernest, 1871-1937

Reeves, Richard, 1936- A **force** of nature : the frontier genius of Ernest Rutherford / Richard Reeves. W. W. Norton & Co., c2008. 207 p., 16 p. of plates : **B**
ISBN 039305750X
1. Rutherford, Ernest, 1871-1937. 2. Physicists -- England 3. Radioactivity. 4. Nuclear fission. 5. Physics -- History 6. England

-- History -- 20th century 7. New Zealand -- History -- 20th century 8. Biographies

LC 2007033184

"Atlas books."

A scholarly profile of a leading twentieth-century experimental physicist covers such topics as his discovery of the atom's orbital structure and contributions to splitting the atom to his receipt of the Nobel Prize and other honors.

"The author re-introduces Ernest Rutherford, one of the founding geniuses of nuclear physics. This biography does an outstanding job of capturing the excitement and almost breathless pace of physics research in the 20th century's first four decades." Publishers Weekly.

Ryan, Bob, 1946-

Ryan, Bob, 1946- **Scribe** : my life in sports / Bob Ryan. Bloomsbury, 2014. 288 p. **B**

ISBN 9781620405062

1. Boston globe 2. Sportswriters -- United States 3. Sports 4. Sports journalism 5. Autobiographies and memoirs

LC 2014012348

Includes index.

The colorful, captivating, endlessly entertaining memoir by one of America's greatest sportswriters--a gift for sports fans everywhere.

"This thoroughly engaging book is recommended to all sports enthusiasts, especially readers interested in Boston-area teams." Library Journal.

Ryan, Donald P.

Ryan, Donald P. **Beneath** the sands of Egypt : adventures of an unconventional archaeologist / Donald P. Ryan. Harpercollins, 2010. 352 p. **B**

ISBN 9780061732829

1. Archaeologists. 2. Archaeology. 3. Egyptology. 4. Excavations (Archaeology) 5. Ancient Egypt -- History -- 30 B.C.-640 A.D. 6. Valley of the Kings, Egypt -- Antiquities. 7. Ancient Egypt -- History -- 332-30 B.C. 8. Autobiographies and memoirs

LC 2010020355

"Ryan, the archaeologist who rediscovered tomb KV 60 in the Valley of the Kings (later identified as the final resting place of the pharoah Hatshepsut), takes us through his life, career, and numerous expeditions. It's a thrilling book, not because it's full of Indiana Jones heroics but because Ryan's enthusiasm for what he does (more dirt-sifting than bull-whip-wielding) is manifested on every page; and . . . he catches us up in his excitement, makes us wish we weren't just reading about this stuff but were actually doing it. . . . This wonderful adventure story should be must reading for anyone aspiring to become an archaeologist, but even those of us who harbor no such dreams will be aching to get a little dirt under our fingernails." Booklist.

Ryan, Evelyn

Ryan, Terry, 1946-2007 The **prize** winner of Defiance, Ohio : how my mother raised 10 kids on 25 words or less / Terry Ryan ; foreword by Suze Orman. Simon & Schuster, 2001. 351 p. **B**

ISBN 0743211227

1. Ryan, Evelyn Family. 2. Ryan family. 3. Contests 4. Family relationships. 5. Motherhood. 6. Family violence 7. Ohio 8. Defiance, Ohio. 9. Autobiographies and memoirs

LC 2001018379

The Prize Winner of Defiance, Ohio introduces Evelyn Ryan, an enterprising woman who kept poverty at bay with wit, poetry, and perfect prose during the "contest era" of the 1950s and 1960s. Standing up to the church, her alcoholic husband, and antiquated ideas about women, Evelyn turned every financial challenge into an opportunity for innovation, all the while raising her six sons and four daughters with the belief that miracles are an everyday occurrence.

"The author recounts the life of her mother, a small-town Ohio housewife in the nineteen-fifties who lived on the brink of dire poverty, thanks to a brood of ten kids and an ineffectual drunk of a husband. Since Evelyn couldn't work outside her home, she worked inside it, penning hundreds of product jingles and entering them in the national contests that drove the advertising industry of the day." The New Yorker.

Rynecki, Moshe, 1881-1943

Rynecki, Elizabeth **Chasing** portraits : a great-granddaughter's quest for her lost art legacy / Elizabeth Rynecki. NAL, New American Library, 2016 304 p. **B**

ISBN 9781101987667

1. Rynecki, Moshe, 1881-1943. 2. Jewish artists. 3. Art, Polish -- 20th century. 4. Arts, Jewish 5. Jews in art. 6. Biographies

LC 2016012588

The memoir of one woman's emotional quest to find the art of her Polish-Jewish great-grandfather, lost during World War II. Moshe Rynecki's body of work reached close to eight hundred paintings and sculptures before his life came to a tragic end. It was his great-granddaughter Elizabeth who sought to rediscover his legacy, setting upon a journey to seek out what had been lost but never forgotten.

"A wonderful story beautifully told. Rynecki's yearslong search, successes, frustrations, and failures are a study in perseverance." Kirkus.

Saban, Nick

Burke, Monte **Saban** : the making of a coach / Monte Burke. Simon & Schuster, [2015] 320 p. **B**

ISBN 9781476789934

1. Saban, Nick. 2. University of Alabama Football -- History. 3. Football coaches -- United States 4. Leadership in men. 5. Football coaches 6. College football 7. Biographies

LC 2015018182

A portrait of the influential and controversial University of Alabama football coach shares insights into his winning "Process," his early coaching years at the college and professional levels, and the defining events that shaped his career.

"With Sabans wins and losses over the years having been covered extensively in the media, Burke wisely focuses on the man rather than the play-by-play, and the result is a genuinely insightful look at a fierce competitor who nevertheless seems to care for his players both on and off the field." Booklist.

Sabar, Yona

Sabar, Ariel **My** father's paradise : a son's search for his Jewish past in Kurdish Iraq / Ariel Sabar. Algonquin Books of Chapel Hill, 2008. 348 p. **B**

ISBN 9781565124905

1. Sabar, Yona. 2. Sabar, Ariel. 3. Jews, Kurdish -- Zakhu, Iraq. 4. Father and adult son. 5. Family relationships. 6. Judaism -- Relations -- Islam. 7. Iraq -- Description and travel.

LC 2008024811

National Book Critics Circle Award for Autobiography, 2008."

This is an engaging account of a wonderful, enlightening journey, a voyage with the power to move readers deeply even as it stretches across differences of culture, family, and memory." Christian Science Monitor.

Sacagawea

★Clark, Ella Elizabeth, 1896- **Sacagawea** of the Lewis and Clark expedition / Ella E. Clark and Margot Edmonds. University of California Press, c1979. viii, 171 p., 1 leaf of plates : **B**

ISBN 9780520050600

1. Sacagawea. 2. Lewis and Clark Expedition (1804-1806) 3. Shoshoni women

LC 78065466

Includes index.

Uses previously unknown information about Sacagawea's later years to separate fact from myth about the courageous Indian woman who accompanied the Lewis and Clark Expedition

Sacks, Oliver, 1933-2015

★Sacks, Oliver, 1933-2015 **Everything** in its place : first loves and last tales / Oliver Sacks. Alfred A. Knopf, 2019. 320 p. **B**

ISBN 9780451492890

1. Sacks, Oliver, 1933-2015. 2. Neurologists 3. Science 4. Human behavior 5. Essays.

LC 2018022660

"This is a Borzoi book.""

From the best-selling author of Gratitude and On the Move, a final volume of essays that showcases Sacks's broad range of interests--from his passions for ferns, swimming, and horsetails, to his final case histories exploring schizophrenia, dementia, and Alzheimer's. Oliver Sacks, scientist and storyteller, is beloved by readers for his neurological case histories, his fascination and familiarity with human behavior at its most unexpected and unfamiliar. Everything In Its Place is a celebration of Sacks's myriad interests, all told with his characteristic compassion, erudition, and luminous prose".-- Provided by publisher.

"The essays in this final volume from late, great neurologist Sacks move from his love of ferns, swimming, and horsetails to his final case histories investigating schizophrenia, dementia, and Alzheimer's." Library Journal.

Sacks, Oliver, 1933-2015 **On** the move : a memoir / Oliver Sacks. Alfred A. Knopf, 2015. 416 p. **B**

ISBN 9780385352543

1. Neurologists. 2. Physicians 3. Drug addiction 4. Autobiographies and memoirs

LC 2015001870

"This is a Borzoi book."

An autobiography of the British neurologist Oliver Sacks.

"An engaging and candid introduction to a man who transcended the life of a clinical practitioner to become a medical storyteller and humanitarian." Choice.

Sacks, Oliver, 1933-2015 **Uncle** Tungsten : memories of a chemical boyhood / Oliver Sacks. Alfred A. Knopf, 2001. viii, 337 p. : **B**

ISBN 9780375404481

1. Neurologists -- England 2. Family relationships. 3. Psychoses. 4. Growing up. 5. Biographies

LC 2001033738

Includes index.

The scientific wonder of youth is skillfully evoked in this memoir by the distinguished neurologist and author of Awakenings in which he describes his fascination with metals, gases, and chemicals, especially "Uncle Tungsten," and with unravelling the complex mysteries of the world around.

"Sacks' first scientific love was chemistry, and he presents an avid history of the field within a memoir that pays tribute to his uncle, who welcomed Sacks into his lab, thus encouraging his passion for chemistry and learning." Booklist.

Weschler, Lawrence **And** how are you, Dr. Sacks? : a biographical memoir of Oliver Sacks / Lawrence Weschler. Farrar, Straus and Giroux, 2019. 352 p. **B**

ISBN 9780374236410

1. Weschler, Lawrence 2. Neurologists -- England 3. Neurologists -- United States 4. Scientists 5. Gay men 6. Biographies 7. Autobiographies and memoirs

LC 2018060824

The New Yorker veteran and author of Mr. Wilson's Cabinet of Wonder draws on decades of friendship to trace the lesser-known early story of the brilliant neurologist and author of The Man Who Mistook His Wife for a Hat.

Sackville-West, V. (Victoria), 1892-1962

Dennison, Matthew **Behind** the mask : the life of Vita Sackville-West / Matthew Dennison. St. Martin's Press, 2015. 416 p. **B**

ISBN 9781250033949

1. Sackville-West, V. (Victoria), 1892-1962. 2. Authors, English -- 20th century 3. Aristocracy. 4. Eccentrics and eccentricities 5. Gardeners. 6. Sissinghurst Garden, England -- History. 7. Biographies

LC 2015002466

In this new biography of Vita Sackville-West, Matthew Dennison traces the triumph and contradictions of Vita's extraordinary life. His narrative charts a fascinating course from Vita's lonely childhood at Knole, through her affectionate but 'open' marriage to Harold Nicolson (during which both husband and wife energetically pursued homosexual affairs, Vita most famously with Virginia Woolf), and through Vita's literary successes and disappointments, to the famous gardens the couple created at Sissinghurst. The book tells how, from her privileged world of the aristocracy, Sackville-West brought her penchant for costume, play-acting and rebellion to the artistic vanguard of modern Britain.

"Dennison downplays Vita's relationship with Woolf as a smoldering and significant writerly friendship. His narrative is utterly absorbing in its attention to the minutiae of property, inheritance, houses, clothing, and letters. All the while, the author extracts from Vita's writing rich autobiographical detail. A lively, vigorously written biography of a singular character that beckons readers urgently back to Sackville-West's writing." Kirkus.

Sagan, Carl, 1934-1996

Poundstone, William **Carl** Sagan : a life in the cosmos / William Poundstone. Henry Holt, 1999. xvii, 473 p. : **B**

ISBN 0805057668

1. Sagan, Carl, 1934-1996. 2. Astronomers -- United States 3. Biographies

LC 99014615

Chronicles the astronomer's rise to scientific celebrity, describing his gift of enthusiastic communication and his conflicts with the academic establishment.

"This is an exhaustive and detailed account, especially when discussing Sagan's original scientific work and influences." Library Journal.

Said, Kurban

Reiss, Tom The **Orientalist** : solving the mystery of a strange and a dangerous life / Tom Reiss. Random House, 2005. xxvii, 433 p. : **B**

ISBN 1400062659

1. Said, Kurban. 2. Bey, Essad, 1905- 3. Ehrenfels, Elfriede 1894- 4.

Authors, German -- 20th century 5. Germany. 6. Biographies

LC 2004050928

ALA Notable Book, 2006."

The author takes the reader through his own search for the truth; through the twists of 20th-century history in Russia and Germany, and hence though the life-story itself. This would be hard work if the interweaving of biography, investigation and geopolitics were not so elegant." The Economist.

Saks, Elyn R., 1955-

Saks, Elyn R., 1955- The **center** cannot hold : my journey through madness / Elyn R. Saks. Hyperion, c2007. 340 p. ; **B**

ISBN 9781401301385

1. University of Southern California. School of Law 2. People with schizophrenia -- Family relationships. 3. Women with schizophrenia 4. College teachers -- California 5. Schizophrenia -- Treatment 6. California -- Social life and customs -- 20th century 7. Autobiographies and memoirs

LC bl2007018825

A memoir of paranoid schizophrenia by an accomplished professor recounts her first symptoms at the age of eight, her efforts to hide the severity of her condition, and the obstacles she has overcome in the course of her treatment and marriage.

Salinger, J. D. (Jerome David), 1919-2010

Beller, Thomas **J.D.** Salinger : the escape artist / Thomas Beller. New Harvest, 2014. 192 p. **B**

ISBN 9780544261990

1. Salinger, J. D. (Jerome David), 1919-2010. 2. Authors, American -- 20th century 3. Biographies

LC 2013045583

Three years after his death at ninety-one, J.D. Salinger remains our most mythic writer. The Catcher in the Rye (1951) became an American classic, and he was for a long time the writer for The New Yorker. Franny and Zooey and Raise High the Roof Beam, Carpenters introduced, by way of the Glass family, a new type in contemporary literature: the introspective, voluble cast of characters whose stage is the Upper East Side of New York. But fame proved a burden, and in 1963 Salinger fled to New Hampshire, spending the next half century in isolation. Beller has followed his subject's trail, from his Park Avenue childhood to his final refuge, barnstorming across New England to visit various Salinger shrines, interviewing just about everyone alive who ever knew Salinger. The result is a quest biography in the tradition of Geoff Dyer's Out of Sheer Rage, a book as much about the biographer as about the subject--two vivid, entertaining stories in one.

"Beller's prose is conversational and intimate, and his admiration for his subject is evident." Library Journal.

★Slawenski, Kenneth **Salinger** : a life / Kenneth Slawenski. Random House, 2010. 464 p. **B**

ISBN 9781400069514

1. Salinger, J. D. (Jerome David), 1919-2010. 2. Authors, American -- 20th century 3. Writing. 4. Creativity. 5. Biographies

LC 2010008926

Examines the life of the reclusive author of "Catcher in the Rye," including his encounters with celebrities, his love life, his devotion to Eastern religion, and his conflicted relationship with his success.

Salk, Jonas, 1914-1995

Jacobs, Charlotte **Jonas** Salk : a life / Charlotte DeCroes Jacobs. Oxford University Press, 2015 512 p. **B**

ISBN 9780199334414

1. Salk, Jonas, 1914-1995. 2. Virologists. 3. Poliomyelitis vaccine. 4. Influenza vaccines. 5. AIDS (Disease) 6. Biographies

LC 2014040267

The first full biography of Jonas Salk offers a complete picture of the enigmatic figure, from his early years working on an influenza vaccine--for which he never fully got credit--to his seminal creation of the Polio vaccine, up through his later work to find a cure for AIDS.

"Throughout, the author demonstrates a deep understanding of the character and the nature of science in the latter half of the 20th century. Jacobs makes a convincing case that Salk was a shy man who never succeeded in making the scientific or personal connections that could bring happiness, but his idealism proved a boon to mankind." Kirkus.

Salzman, Mark, 1959-

Salzman, Mark, 1959- **Iron** & silk / Mark Salzman. Vintage Books, 1987, c1986. 211 p. ; **B**

ISBN 0394755111

1. Salzman, Mark, 1959- Travel China. 2. Martial arts -- China. 3. Martial artists -- China. 4. English language teachers -- China. 5. China -- Description and travel. 6. China -- Social life and customs. 7. Autobiographies and memoirs

LC 87040085

Reprint. Originally published: New York : Random House, 1986.

The author recounts his experiences in China, as the sole private pupil to Pan Quingfu, China's foremost martial artist, discusses his relationships with the diverse Chinese people he came to know

"This book is not so much a treatise on modern Chinese mores as a series of telling vignettes. [The author] describes his encounter with Pan Qingfu, the country's foremost master of wushu, the traditional Chinese martial art." Time.

Samaras, Tim

Hargrove, Brantley The **man** who caught the storm : the life of legendary tornado chaser Tim Samaras / Brantley Hargrove. Simon & Schuster, 2018 320 p. **B**

ISBN 9781476796093

1. Tornadoes 2. Storm chasers 3. Weather forecasting. 4. Disasters. 5. Biographies

LC 2018014605

Documents the life and achievements of late engineer and storm chaser Tim Samaras, describing his development of innovative new tools and his life-risking efforts in pursuit of scientific information that has transformed the field of meteorology.

"An exemplar of narrative nonfiction; readers from all across the spectrum will enjoy this title." Library Journal.

Samer, 1992 or 1993-

Samer, 1992 or 1993- The **Raqqa** diaries : escape from "Islamic State" / Samer; edited by Mike Thomson and John Neal, translated by Ibrahim Nader, illustrated by Scott Coelho. Interlink Books, 2017 106 p. **B**

ISBN 9781566560054

1. ISIS (Islamic State of Iraq and Syria) 2. Atrocities. 3. Refugees, Syrian 4. Raqqah, Syria 5. Syria -- History -- Civil War, 2011-. 6. Autobiographies and memoirs 7. Diaries

LC bl2017032381

"Samer (a pseudonym) is twenty-four years old. Having escaped Raqqa, he is living in a refugee camp in northern Syria." -- from book jacket

This diary was smuggled out of Syria and translated from the Arabic.A young activist chronicles his experience in Raqqa following its capture by Daesh and describes how he eventually fled to a refugee camp in northern Syria.

Samuelsson, Marcus

Samuelsson, Marcus **Yes,** chef / Marcus Samuelsson. Random House, 2012. 336 p. **B**

ISBN 9780385342605

1. Samuelsson, Marcus. 2. Cooks -- United States 3. Swedish Americans 4. Interracial adoption 5. Cooks -- Ethiopia 6. Autobiographies and memoirs

LC 2011042220

IACP Cookbook Awards, Literary Food Writing, 2013.

James Beard Foundation Book Awards, Writing and Literature, 2013.

The "Top Chef: Masters" winner and James Beard Award-winning proprietor of Harlem's Red Rooster traces his Ethiopian birth, upbringing by an adoptive family in Sweden and rise to a famous New York chef, sharing personal insights into his challenges as a black man in a deeply prejudiced industry.

"This distinctive and compelling memoir has all the elements of a good story: humor, travel, and a young individual overcoming obstacles via a passionate calling." Library Journal.

Sanchez, Aaron

Sanchez, Aaron **Where** I come from : life lessons from a Latino chef / Aaron Sanchez. Abrams Press, [2019] xxi, 261 pages ; **B**

ISBN 9781419738029

1. Mexican Americans 2. Celebrity chefs 3. Cooking 4. Cooks 5. El Paso, Texas 6. New York City 7. New Orleans, Louisiana 8. Autobiographies and memoirs

LC 2018958855

The award-winning co-star of MasterChef shares stories from his family life and culinary journey, detailing his upbringing by a fiercely talented restaurateur mother and his work beside some of New York's most distinguished chefs.

Sand, George, 1804-1876

Eisler, Benita **Naked** in the marketplace : the lives of George Sand / Benita Eisler. Counterpoint, a member of the Perseus Books Group, c2006. viii, 308 p. ; **B**

ISBN 1582433496

1. Sand, George, 1804-1876. 2. Authors, French -- 19th century 3. France -- History -- 19th century 4. Biographies

LC 2006021684

"Eisler's portrait of this woman of many firsts brings Sand and her boldly improvised life forward more vividly than ever before." Booklist.

Harlan, Elizabeth **George** Sand / Elizabeth Harlan. Yale University Press, c2004. xx, 376 p. ; **B**

ISBN 9780300104172

1. Sand, George, 1804-1876. 2. Authors, French -- 19th century 3. France -- Social life and customs -- 19th century. 4. Biographies

LC 2004010315

"Sand, nee, Aurore Dupin, left her husband and two children in provincial France and successfully launched herself as a self-supporting writer in Paris, donning men's clothing to ease passage into the professional world and taking a pseudonym to protect her aristocratic family's name. Sand took on many lovers, among them poet Alfred de Musset and composer Frederic Chopin. Yet despite Sand's outward daring, as Harlan shows, she obsessed over her identity, as both a woman and an aristocrat. Harlan sensitively analyzes the gaps and idiosyncrasies in her subject's heavily self-edited correspondence, autobiography and novels to uncover a fresh portrait of this volatile, imaginative woman of letters." Publishers Weekly.

Jack, Belinda **George** Sand : a woman's life writ large / Belinda Jack. Vintage Books, 2001, c1999. xiv, 395 p. : **B**

ISBN 0679779183

1. Sand, George, 1804-1876. 2. Women authors -- France -- 19th century 3. Authors, French -- 19th century 4. France -- Social life and customs -- 19th century 5. Biographies

LC BL2002002064

Originally published: Great Britain : Chatto & Windus, 1999.

Follows Sand's life from her birth in 1804 through her work as a minister of propaganda during the Revolution of 1848, her relationship with Chopin, and her work in the radical politics of her day.

"Prodigious author, cross-dresser, lover of Chopin and Alfred de Musset, intimate of (among others) Liszt, Balzac, Dumas (pre and fils), Turgenev, and Flaubert (who cried twice at her funeral), Sand was both before her time and quintessentially of it. Jack's nuanced, moving assessment of the writer's early years . is the strongest section of this packed life. When Sand moves onto a larger stage, Jack's style becomes breathless, as if she could barely keep up with her flamboyant subject." The New Yorker.

Sanders, Bernard

Rall, Ted **Bernie** / Ted Rall. Seven Stories Press, 2016. 208 p. **B**

ISBN 9781609806989

1. Sanders, Bernard. 2. United States. Congress 3. Legislators -- United States 4. Presidential candidates 5. Socialists -- United States 6. Politicians. 7. United States -- Politics and government -- 1989- 8. Biographical comics. 9. Comics and Graphic novels 10. Biographies.

LC 2015046626

Discusses the life of the presidential candidate and the decline of leftist politics in the Democratic Party.

Sanger, Margaret, 1879-1966

Baker, Jean H. **Margaret** Sanger : a life of passion / Jean H. Baker. Hill and Wang, 2011. 368 p. **B**

ISBN 9780809094981

1. Women social reformers. 2. Birth control. 3. Women's rights. 4. Feminists. 5. Biographies

LC 2011008439

A portrait of a forefront leader in the birth control movement seeks to restore her position in feminist history in an account that includes coverage of such topics as the nursing experiences that inspired her beliefs, her pioneering of a first family-planning clinic and her relationships with such figures as John Reed, Mabel Dodge and H. G. Wells.

Santana, Carlos

Santana, Carlos The **universal** tone : my life / Carlos Santana. Little, Brown and Company, 2014. viii, 535 pages : **B**

ISBN 9780316244923

1. Santana, Carlos. 2. Santana (Musical group) 3. Music, Latin American 4. Guitarists -- United States 5. Mexican Americans 6. Rock musicians -- United States 7. United States -- Popular culture -- History -- 20th century 8. Autobiographies and memoirs

LC bl2014043161

An intimate account by the rock music artist traces his hardscrabble youth in Mexico and early days as a promising guitarist through his influential collaborations with fellow Latin stars.

"An appreciative and unpretentious chronicle, this is required reading for Santana fans and devotees of classic rock legends." Kirkus.

Sarao, Navinder Singh

Vaughan, Liam, 1979- **Flash** crash : a trading savant, a global manhunt, and the most mysterious market crash in history / Liam Vaughan. Doubleday, 2020. 336 p. **B**

ISBN 9780385543651

1. Stock market 2. Financial crises 3. White collar crime 4. Brokers

LC 2020005099

Describes the story of a trading prodigy who amassed millions playing the markets like a video game from his working-class West London childhood home until he unwittingly started The Flash Crash and the FBI showed up at his door.

"A cleareyed, smart account that merits high rank in the library of computer crime." Kirkus

Sardy, Marin

Sardy, Marin The **edge** of every day : sketches of schizophrenia / Marin Sardy. Pantheon Books, 2019. 304 p. **B**

ISBN 9781524746933

1. Schizophrenia. 2. People with schizophrenia 3. Family and mental illness. 4. People with schizophrenia -- Family relationships. 5. Alaska 6. Anchorage, Alaska 7. Autobiographies and memoirs

LC 2018042987

Shares highly informed meditations into how the author's childhood in Anchorage, her literary career, and the lives of beloved family members have been impacted by hereditary schizophrenia.

Sargent, John Singer, 1856-1925

★Herdrich, Stephanie L **Sargent** : the masterworks / Stephanie L. Herdrich. Rizzoli Electa, 2018. 221 p. : **B**

ISBN 9780847862399

1. Sargent, John Singer, 1856-1925. 2. Painters -- United States 3. Painting -- United States 4. Biographies

LC bl2018053091

"This visual feast of Sargent's most acclaimed creations is time well spent for art students and curious general readers." Library Journal

Sarsour, Linda, 1980-

Sarsour, Linda, 1980- **We** are not here to be bystanders : a memoir of love and resistance / Linda Sarsour ; foreword by Harry Belafonte. 37 INK, Simon & Schuster, 2020. xii, 253 p. **B**

ISBN 9781982105167

1. Muslim women -- United States 2. Civil rights workers 3. Women political activists 4. Palestinian Americans 5. Autobiographies and memoirs

LC 2019030321

On a chilly spring morning in Brooklyn, nineteen-year-old Linda Sarsour stared at her reflection, dressed in a hijab for the first time. She saw in the mirror the woman she was growing to be--a young Muslim American woman unapologetic in her faith and her activism, who would discover her innate sense of justice in the aftermath of 9/11. Now heralded for her award-winning leadership of the Women's March on Washington, in We Are Not Here to Be Bystanders Linda Sarsour offers a poignant story of community and family. From the Brooklyn bodega her father owned, where Linda learned the real meaning of intersectionality, to protests in the streets of Washington DC, Linda's experience as a daughter of Palestinian immigrants is a moving portrayal of what it means to find one's voice and use it for the good of others.

"An incredible, galvanizing story of the power of participation." Booklist

Sartre, Jean-Paul, 1905-1980

Sartre, Jean-Paul, 1905-1980 **We** have only this life to live : selected essays, 1939/1975 / Jean-Paul Sartre ; edited by Ronald Aronson and Adrian van den Hoven. New York Review Books, 2013. 600 p. **B**

ISBN 9781590174937

1. Sartre, Jean-Paul, 1905-1980. 2. Essays. 3. Autobiographies and memoirs

LC 2013001043

This is the first gathering of Sartre's essays in English to draw on all ten volumes of Situations, the title under which Sartre collected his essays during his life, while also featuring previously uncollected work, including the reports Sartre filed during his 1945 trip to America. Here Sartre writes about Faulkner, Bataille, Giacometti, Fanon, the liberation of France, torture in Algeria, existentialism and Marxism, friends lost and found, and much else. We Have Only This Life to Live provides an indispensable, panoramic view of the world of Jean-Paul Sartre.

Satrapi, Marjane, 1969-

★Satrapi, Marjane, 1969- The **complete** Persepolis / Marjane Satrapi. Pantheon Books, c2007. 341 p. : **B**

ISBN 9780375714832

1. Children and war -- Iran 2. Teenage girls 3. Women's rights -- Iran 4. Women's role -- Iran 5. Iran -- History -- Islamic revolution, 1979-1997. 6. Tehran, Iran. 7. Iran -- Social life and customs -- 20th century 8. Autobiographies and memoirs 9. Autobiographical comics 10. Comics and Graphic novels

LC 2007060106

Contains the author's Persepolis (2003) and Persepolis 2 (2004)The great-granddaughter of Iran's last emperor and the daughter of ardent Marxists describes growing up in Tehran in a country plagued by political upheaval and vast contraditions between public and private life.

Sattouf, Riad

Sattouf, Riad, The **Arab** of the future : growing up in the Middle East (1978-1984) : a graphic memoir / Riad Sattouf. Metropolitan Books, 2015. 160 p. : **B**

ISBN 9781627793445

1. Sattouf, Riad Childhood and youth 2. Qaddafi, Muammar 3. Assad, Hafez, 1930-2000 4. Growing up. 5. Dictatorship. 6. Cartoonists -- France 7. Boys. 8. Libya. 9. Middle East. 10. Autobiographical comics. 11. Comics and Graphic novels

LC 2014041152

Sequel: The Arab of the future 2 Translated from the French Arabe du futur by Sam Taylor.

The author recounts his nomadic childhood growing up in rural France, Gaddafi's Libya, and Assad's Syria, under the roof of his father, a Syrian Pan-Arabist, who drags his family along in his pursuit of grandiose dreams for the Arab nation.

"Caught between his parents, Sattouf makes the best of his situation by becoming a master observer and interpreter, his clean, cartoonish art making a social and personal document of wit and understanding." Publishers Weekly.

Sattouf, Riad The **Arab** of the future 2 : a graphic memoir : a childhood in the Middle East (1984-1985) / Riad Sattouf. Metropolitan Books, 2016. 154 p. : **B**

ISBN 9781627793513

1. Assad, Hafez, 1930-2000 2. Antisemitism 3. Growing up. 4. Dictatorship. 5. Boys. 6. Syria 7. Middle East. 8. Comics and Graphic novels 9. Autobiographical comics.

LC bl2016039900

Sequel to: The Arab of the future In a graphic account of his childhood, the author, now settled in his father's hometown of Homs, gets to go to school, where he dedicates himself to becoming a true Syrian in the country of the dictator Hafez Al-Assad, and the rest of his family also strains to fit in, until a single brutal act forces the family to make a dramatic change.

"Rather than being incongruous with the oppressive society and grim events he depicts, Sattouf's broadly cartoonish drawing style imparts a level of attachment that makes his story bearable." Booklist.

Saunders, Gerda

Saunders, Gerda **Memory's** last breath : field notes on my dementia / Gerda Saunders. Hachette Books, 2017. 256 p. **B**

ISBN 9780316502627

1. Saunders, Gerda. 2. People with dementia 3. Alzheimer's disease. 4. Aging 5. Autobiographies and memoirs

LC 2017003005

A former literature professor offers an unsparing account of her life with dementia and what it is like to be an intellectual person who is aware of her irreversible cognitive decline.

Saunders, John, 1955-2016

Saunders, John, 1955-2016 **Playing** hurt : my journey from despair to hope / John Saunders, with John U. Bacon. Da Capo Press, 2017. 320 p. **B**

ISBN 9780306824739

1. Sportscasters. 2. People with depression. 3. Depression 4. Coping 5. Autobiographies and memoirs

LC 2017285301

An autobiography of sportscaster John Saunders who suffered from depression.

"A story that merits both sympathy and attention." Kirkus.

Scales, Helen

Scales, Helen **Eye** of the shoal : a fish-watcher's guide to life, the ocean and everything / Helen Scales. Bloomsbury Sigma, 2018. 320 p. **B**

ISBN 9781472936844

1. Marine biologists 2. Fishes 3. Marine ecology 4. Oceans 5. Autobiographies and memoirs

LC bl2018108386

"Popular science books don't get much better than this accessible and eye-opening look at fish by marine biologist Scales (Spirals in Time)." Publishers Weekly.

Scalia, Antonin, 1936-2016

Murphy, Bruce Allen **Scalia** : a court of one / Bruce Allen Murphy. Simon & Schuster, 2014. 592 p. **B**

ISBN 9780743296496

1. United States. Supreme Court Justices 2. Judges -- United States 3. Constitutional law 4. Law 5. United States -- Politics and government 6. Biographies

LC 2013042971

A deeply researched portrait of the controversial Supreme Court justice includes coverage of his impressive career achievements, his appointment in 1986 and his party-dividing resolve to support agendas from an ethical, rather than political, perspective.

"Murphy details Scalia's behind-the-scenes angling to push himself as the leading advocate for originalism and to get on the Supreme Court. But his scathing critiques set him at odds with conservatives, most notably Sandra Day O'Connor, pushing many to the center. Murphy offers a highly engaged, well-researched analysis of a brash justice whose single-mindedness may ultimately reduce his legacy." Booklist.

Schefter, Adam

Schefter, Adam The **man** I never met / Adam Schefter, with Michael Rosenberg. St Martins Pr 2018 208 p. **B**

ISBN 9781250161895

1. Blended families 2. Loss (Psychology) 3. September 11 Terrorist Attacks, 2001 4. Widows 5. Autobiographies and memoirs

LC 2018013698

The influential ESPN personality describes how his wife lost her first husband during the World Trade Center attacks, how he bonded with his young stepson and how their family has made September 11 an anniversary of hope and healing.

"Schefter's book is affecting not only for the story it tells of how the author learned to honor his wife's husband as 'the fifth member of [his] family,' but also for how it shows a man growing into a mature understanding of the true meaning of love and sacrifice." Kirkus.

Scheinman, Ted, 1985-

Scheinman, Ted, 1985- **Camp** Austen : my life as an accidental Jane Austen superfan / Ted Scheinman. Farrar, Straus and Giroux, 2018. 176 p. **B**

ISBN 9780865478213

1. Austen, Jane, 1775-1817 2. Women authors, English 3. Graduate students 4. Role playing 5. Literature -- History and criticism 6. Autobiographies and memoirs

LC 2017038310

The senior editor of Pacific Standard magazine traces his upbringing as the son of a devoted Jane Austen scholar whose education was marked by literary tributes and his own contributions as the organizer of UNC-Chapel Hill's Jane Austen Summer Camp, where devotees engage in study and roleplaying.

"While Scheinman is clearly an astute reader of Austen he includes numerous analyses of Austens life and work that are insightful and often quite funny this is also a fascinating window into a man's experience in a largely female realm. Scheinman is a wonderful guide to the world of Austen, and this honest and thoughtful discussion of the role Austen's works have played in his family will delight any Janeite." Booklist.

Schemel, Patty, 1967-

Schemel, Patty, 1967- **Hit** so hard : a memoir / Patty Schemel. Da Capo Press, 2017. 288 p. **B**

ISBN 9780306825071

1. Hole (Musical group) 2. Women rock musicians 3. Drummers 4. Drug addiction 5. Fame 6. Autobiographies and memoirs

LC bl2017045182

The former drummer for Hole provides a front-seat view into the life of Courtney Love and Kurt Cobain, her one-time housemates, and describes her own addictions to heroin that resulted in being fired, homelessness, multiple stints in rehab and petty theft and prostitution.

Schenone, Laura

Schenone, Laura The **dogs** of Avalon : the race to save animals in peril / Laura Schenone. W W Norton & Co Inc, 2017. 320 p. **B**

ISBN 9780393073584

1. SPCA International 2. Greyhounds 3. Animal rescue 4. Animal welfare 5. Dog rescue 6. Ireland 7. Autobiographies and memoirs

LC 2017013983

After adopting a greyhound, an Irish woman embarks on a quest to stop the abuse being done to the breed after they no longer can run fast enough during dog races, becoming the head of the Irish SPCA and creating a healing sanctuary.

"An engrossing account of greyhounds, their owners, and their champions." Kirkus.

Scheyer, Moriz, 1886-1949

Scheyer, Moriz, 1886-1949 **Asylum:** a survivor's flight from Nazi-occupied Vienna through wartime France / Moriz Scheyer ; translated from the German, with an epilogue and essay and notes, by the author's grandson, P.N. Singer. Little Brown and Company, 2016. 305 pages : **B**

ISBN 9780316272889

1. Holocaust survivors 2. Jews, Austrian 3. World War II. 4. Holocaust (1933-1945) 5. France -- History -- German occupation, 1940-1945 6. Autobiographies and memoirs

LC bl2016032052

A recently discovered account reveals an Austrian Jewish writer's flight, persecution and clandestine life in wartime France.

"A well-written book full of desperate hope, intense fear, and a demand for vigilance against the mentality of hate." Kirkus.

Schiaparelli, Elsa, 1890-1973

Secrest, Meryle **Elsa** Schiaparelli : a biography / Meryle Secrest. Alfred A. Knopf, 2014. 352 p. **B**

ISBN 9780307701596

1. Schiaparelli, Elsa, 1890-1973. 2. Clothing industry and trade 3. Fashion designers 4. Women fashion designers 5. Fashion design 6. Biographies

LC 2014025820

"The first biography of the grand couturier, surrealist, and embattled figure (her medium was apparel), whose extraordinary work has stood the test of time".-- Provided by publisher.

"Richly illustrated and endlessly intriguing, Secrest's biography illuminates the 'daredevil swagger' of Schiaparelli's clothes and the oft-besieged couturier's inexhaustible tenacity and dazzling creativity." Booklist.

Schiff, Dorothy, 1903-1989

Nissenson, Marilyn, 1939- The **lady** upstairs : Dorothy Schiff and the New York Post / Marilyn Nissenson. St. Martin's Press, 2007. xii, 500 p., 16 p. of plates : **B**

ISBN 0312313101

1. Schiff, Dorothy, 1903-1989. 2. New York Post. 3. Journalists -- United States 4. Publishers and publishing -- United States -- History -- 20th century 5. New York City -- Social life and customs -- 20th century 6. Biographies

LC 2006053087

Traces the life and career of the socialite newspaper publisher who owned the New York Post throughout the mid-twentieth century, from her origins in a German-Jewish banking family and the influence of the Depression on her political views to her choices in editorial writers and her role in the reportage of crucial historical events.

Schindler, Oskar, 1908-1974

Crowe, David **Oskar** Schindler : the untold account of his life, wartime activities, and the true story behind the list / David M. Crowe. Westview Press, 2004. xi, 766 p. : **B**

ISBN 081333375X

1. Schindler, Oskar, 1908-1974. 2. Righteous Gentiles in the Holocaust. 3. Holocaust (1933-1945) 4. Biographies

LC 2004013879

A portrait of the controversial Oskar Schindler looks at the myths and realities of every aspect of his life, from Nazi Party member, opportunist, and spy to bon vivant and rescuer of twelve hundred Jews.

"This book is essential in understanding one of the most extraordinary figures from the Holocaust." Booklist.

Schlegle, Ernie

Manzione, Gianmarc **Pin** action : small-time gangsters, high-stakes gambling, and the teenage hustler who became a bowling champion / Gianmarc Manzione. Pegasus Books, 2014 336 p. **B**

ISBN 9781605986456

1. Bowling 2. Gambling 3. Organized crime 4. Swindlers and swindling 5. New York City 6. Biographies

LC 2015410656

Traces the rise of con artist-turned-bowling champion Ernie Schlegel against a backdrop of gritty 1960s and 1970s New York, profiling the sport of action bowling and the contributors who shaped his achievements.

"This well-researched account is for those who remember the glory days of bowling. Others will be fascinated by the gritty side of the sport, which few knew existed." Library Journal.

Schlesinger, Arthur M., Jr. (Arthur Meier), 1917-2007

★Aldous, Richard **Schlesinger** : the imperial historian / Richard Aldous. W.W. Norton & Co., 2017. 448 p. **B**

ISBN 9780393244700

1. Schlesinger, Arthur M., Jr. (Arthur Meier), 1917-2007. 2. Historians. 3. Biographies

LC 2017019909

The first major biography of preeminent historian and intellectual Arthur Schlesinger Jr., a defining figure in Kennedy's White House.

"Aldous correctly links 'The Vital Center' to Schlesinger's growing discomfort with the treacherous conventional political cant of 'left' and 'right.' Amid the global struggle against totalitarianism, Schlesinger charged, liberals everywhere had to disown communism just as sharply as conservatives had to disown fascism. In defense of democracy, the book also presented a critique of political perfectionism." New York Review of Books.

Schlesinger, Arthur M. (Arthur Meier), 1917-2007 A **life** in the twentieth century : innocent beginnings, 1917-1950 / Arthur M. Schlesinger, Jr. Houghton Mifflin, 2000. 576 p. : **B**

ISBN 0395707528

1. Historians -- United States 2. Growing up. 3. Intellectual life -- 20th century. 4. Autobiographies and memoirs

LC 00061322

Includes index."

Schlesinger's autobiography, skillfully interweaving the personal and the historical, is elegantly simple and marvellously clear. Complex thoughts are set forth with a lucidity that conceals the depth of the intellectual analysis. Wit, humour and the resources of a natural storyteller sweep the reader along." The Economist.

Schmidle, Nicholas

Schmidle, Nicholas **To** live or to perish forever : two tumultuous years in Pakistan / Nicholas Schmidle. Henry Holt and Co., 2009. 272 p. **B**

ISBN 9780805089387

1. Schmidle, Nicholas Travel Pakistan. 2. Taliban 3. Journalists -- United States 4. Terrorism -- Pakistan 5. Radicalism 6. War -- Pakistan 7. Pakistan -- Politics and government -- 1971- 8. Pakistan

-- Description and travel.

LC 2008048373

"Schmidle offers a gripping, grim account of his two years as a journalism fellow in Pakistan, where his travels took him into the most isolated and unfriendly provinces, and into the thick of interests and beliefs that impede that nation's peace and progress. Schmidle has, with this effort, established himself as a fresh, eloquent and informed contributor to the ongoing dialogue regarding Pakistan, terrorism and the strategic importance of engaging Central Asia in efforts toward peace and stability." Publishers Weekly.

Schmidt, Franz, d. 1634

Harrington, Joel F. (Joel Francis) The **faithful** executioner : life and death, honor and shame in the turbulent sixteenth century / Joel F. Harrington. Farrar, Straus and Giroux, 2013. 368 p. **B**

ISBN 9780809049929

1. Schmidt, Franz, d. 1634. 2. Executions and executioners 3. Criminal justice system -- History. 4. Criminal procedure -- History. 5. Capital punishment -- History. 6. Nuremberg, Germany -- Social life and customs -- 16th century. 7. Diaries. 8. Biographies.

LC 2012029017

Includes index."

A work of nonfiction that explores the thoughts and experiences of one early modern executioner, Nuremberg's Frantz Schmidt (1555-1634), through his own words - a rare personal journal, in which he recorded and described all the executions and corporal punishments he administered between 1573 and his retirement in 1617"-- Provided by publisher.

Schneerson, Menachem Mendel, 1902-1994

Telushkin, Joseph, 1948- **Rebbe** : the life and teachings of Menachem M. Schneerson, the most influential rabbi in modern history / Joseph Telushkin. HarperWave, 2014. 544 p. **B**

ISBN 9780062318985

1. Rabbis -- New York City 2. Religious leaders -- United States 3. Jewish leadership 4. Hasidism -- History. 5. Brooklyn, New York City 6. United States -- Religious life and customs -- 20th century 7. Biographies

LC 2015370576

"The book is rich with accounts of encounters with the Rebbe, including, besides his own followers, Jews of many denominations, secular Israeli leaders, American politicians, students of philosophy, and non-Jews. What stands out is Schneerson's engagement with the principles by which he managed to wield a considerable and controversial influence upon the American cultural scene and the Jewish world." Publishers Weekly.

Schon, Jan Hendrik, 1970-

Reich, Eugenie Samuel **Plastic** fantastic : how the biggest fraud in physics shook the scientific world / Eugenie Samuel Reich. Palgrave Macmillan, 2009. 266 p. ; **B**

ISBN 9780230224674

1. Physicists -- Germany. 2. Science fraud. 3. Superconductors -- Research. 4. Scandals.

LC 2008051801

Traces the infamous fraudulent discovery of physicist Jan Henrik Schon, a star researcher from Bell Laboratories who claimed to have developed technology that would enable the creation of virtually limitless computer chips, in an account that evaluates the motivations for his scam and how it successfully duped some of the scientific community's most informed minds.

Schorr, Daniel, 1916-2010

Schorr, Daniel, 1916-2010 **Staying** tuned : a life in journalism / Daniel Schorr. Pocket Books, c2001. xiv, 354 p. : **B**

ISBN 0671020870

1. Schorr, Daniel, 1916-2010. 2. Journalists -- United States 3. Journalists -- United States 4. Broadcast journalism. 5. Autobiographies and memoirs

LC 2001021014

The legendary journalist recalls his distinguished career, from the golden age of broadcast news to the high-tech world of the twenty-first century, as he recounts his involvement in a variety of seminal historical events, including the rise of the Berlin Wall, the Cold War, the Civil Rights movement, Watergate, and the rise of CNN.

"Schorr's memoir is as much an inside look at the famous world figures of the latter half of the twentieth century as it is the story of one man's life and career." Booklist.

Schreiber, Flora Rheta, 1918-1988

Schreiber, Flora Rheta, 1918-1988 **Sybil** / Flora Rheta Schreiber. Warner Books, 1974, c1973. 460 p. : **B**

ISBN 0808505173

1. Schreiber, Flora Rheta, 1918-1988. 2. Dissociative identity disorder 3. People with mental illnesses 4. Autobiographies and memoirs

LC BL 99747888

Includes index.

Originally published: Chicago : Regnery, 1973.

Records the life of a young woman who assumed sixteen personalities, possibly due to abuse by her neurotic mother, and describes the events and outcome of her eleven years in psychoanalysis.

"This is the true story of Sybil I. Dorsett, a battered child possessed by 16 different personalities. The author skillfully evokes Sybil's patient work during 11 years of psychoanalysis and her eventual success in integrating these selves into a unified personality." Library Journal.

Schriever, Bernard A.

Sheehan, Neil A **fiery** peace in a cold war : Bernard Schriever and the ultimate weapon / Neil Sheehan. Random House, c2009. 560 p. **B**

ISBN 9780679422846

1. United States. Air Force Officers 2. Cold War. 3. Military engineers -- United States 4. Intercontinental ballistic missiles -- Design and construction -- History. 5. Intercontinental ballistic missiles -- United States -- History.

LC 2009002247

The Pulitzer- and National Book Award-winning author of A Bright Shining Lie chronicles the mid-twentieth-century effort to prevent the Soviet Union from acquiring nuclear superiority, in an account that describes the pivotal contributions of Bernard Schriever, Eisenhower, and Stalin.

Schultz, Philip

Schultz, Philip **My** dyslexia / Philip Schultz. W. W. Norton & Co., 2011. 128 p. **B**

ISBN 9780393079647

1. Schultz, Philip. 2. Poets, American 3. People with dyslexia 4. Dyslexia. 5. Creativity. 6. Autobiographies and memoirs

LC 2011015859

Schultz traces his difficult childhood and his new understanding of his early years. In doing so, he shows how a boy who did not learn to read until he was eleven went on to become a prizewinning poet by sheer force of determination. His balancing act, life as a member of a family with not one but two dyslexics, countered by his intellectual and creative successes as a writer, reveals an inspiring story of the strengths of the human mind.

"Schultz paints a precise and compelling picture of how his brain works, how he sees himself, and how he thinks others have seen him throughout his life. . . . His affecting prose will inspire compassion and leave readers with an understanding not only of dyslexia, but of the lifelong challenges that someone with disabilities may face." Publishers Weekly.

Schulz, Charles M. (Charles Monroe), 1922-2000

★Michaelis, David, 1957- **Schulz** and Peanuts / David Michaelis. Harper Collins, 2007. 672 p. **B**

ISBN 0066213932

1. Cartoonists -- United States 2. Peanuts (Comic strip) 3. United States -- Social life and customs. 4. Biographies

LC bl2007016508

A portrait of the late creator of the "Peanuts" comic strip evaluates how his career was shaped by his midwestern working-class origins, family losses, and wartime experiences, offering insight into how familiar storylines closely reflected Schulz's private life.

"It is Mr. Michaelis's achievement in these pages that he leaves us with both a shrewd appreciation of Schulz's minimalist art and a sympathetic understanding of Schulz the man." New York Times.

Schuman, Rebecca

Schuman, Rebecca **Schadenfreude,** a love story : me, the Germans, and 20 years of attempted transformations, unfortunate miscommunications, and humiliating situations that only they have words for / Rebecca Schuman. Flatiron Books, 2017. 288 p. **B**

ISBN 9781250077578

1. Schuman, Rebecca. 2. Journalists. 3. Voyages and travels 4. National characteristics, German. 5. Germany -- Description and travel.

LC 2016038531

A debut book by the education columnist for Slate traces her experiences as a Jewish teen intellectual whose fateful relationship with a boy who introduced her to Kafka inspired her love for German language and culture.

"Schuman's engrossing book is a feast of honesty, humility and humor, all the hallmarks of great confessional literature." Publishers Weekly.

Schumann, Robert, 1810-1856

Chernaik, Judith **Schumann** : the faces and the masks / Judith Chernaik. Alfred A. Knopf, 2018. 336 p. **B**

ISBN 9780451494467

1. Schumann, Robert, 1810-1856. 2. Composers -- Germany 3. Classical music 4. Mental illness 5. Musicians 6. Biographies

LC 2017060796

"This is a Borzoi Book published by Alfred A. Knopf."

Drawing on unpublished archive material, as well as more established materials, the author traces the life and music of a major composer and key figure of Romanticism, who has been the subject of major controversy since his early death in a mental asylum.

Geck, Martin **Robert** Schumann : the life and work of a romantic composer / Martin Geck ; translated by Stewart Spencer. The University of Chicago Press, 2012. 304 p. **B**

ISBN 9780226284699

1. Schumann, Robert, 1810-1856. 2. Composers -- Germany 3. Musicians 4. Music 5. Biographies

LC 2012007981

Originally published as Robert Schumann: Mensch und Musiker der Romantik, 2010 by Siedler Verlag.

Schumer, Amy

Schumer, Amy The **girl** with the lower back tattoo / Amy Schumer. Gllery Books, 2016. 352 p. **B**

ISBN 9781501139888

1. Celebrities 2. Gender role 3. Women comedians 4. Women -- Humor. 5. Essays.

LC 2016299978

An uproarious collection of no-holds-barred personal essays by the Emmy Award-winning comedian reflects on her raucous childhood antics, her hard-won rise in the entertainment industry and her struggles to maintain the courage to approach the world in unstintingly honest ways.

"A hilarious and effective memoir from a woman with zero inhibitions." Kirkus.

Schwartz, Morris S.

Albom, Mitch, 1958- **Tuesdays** with Morrie : an old man, a young man, and life's greatest lesson / Mitch Albom. Doubleday, 1997. 192 p. ; **B**

ISBN 0385484518

1. Brandeis University Faculty. 2. Death -- Psychological aspects -- Case studies. 3. Friendship. 4. Purpose in life. 5. Men with terminal illnesses 6. United States -- Social life and customs. 7. Autobiographies and memoirs

LC 96052535

A sportswriter conveys the wisdom of his late mentor, professor Morrie Schwartz, recounting their weekly conversations as Schwartz lay dying.

"As a student at Brandeis University in the late 1970s, Albom was especially drawn to his sociology professor, Morris Schwartz. On graduation he vowed to keep in touch with him, which he failed to do until 1994, when he saw a segment about Schwartz on the TV program Nightline, and learned that he had just been diagnosed with Lou Gehrig's disease. By then a sports columnist for the Detroit Free Press . Albom was idled by the newspaper strike in the Motor City and so had the opportunity to visit Schwartz in Boston every week until the older man died. Their dialogue is the subject of this moving book." Publishers Weekly.

Schwarz, Geraldine

Schwarz, Geraldine **Those** who forget : my family's story in Nazi Europe--a memoir, a history, a warning / Geraldine Schwarz ; translated from the French by Laura Marris. Scribner, 2020, c2017. 320 p. **B**

ISBN 9781501199080

1. Schwarz, Geraldine Family 2. Schwarz family 3. Holocaust (1933-1945) 4. Journalists -- France 5. Families -- History 6. World War II -- Europe 7. France -- History -- 1945- 8. France -- History -- German occupation, 1940-1945 9. Germany -- History -- 1933-1945. 10. Germany -- History -- 1945- 11. Autobiographies and memoirs

LC 2020004934

Originally published: Paris : Flammarion, 2017.

During World War II, Geraldine Schwarz's German grandparents were neither heroes nor villains; they were merely Mitlaufer--those who followed the current. Once the war ended, they wanted to bury the past under the wreckage of the Third Reich. Decades later, while delving through filing cabinets in the basement of their apartment building in Mannheim, Schwarz discovers that in 1938, her paternal grandfather Karl took advantage of Nazi policies to buy a business from a Jewish family for a low price. She finds letters from the only survivor of this family (all the others perished in Auschwitz), demanding reparations. But Karl Schwarz refused to acknowledge his responsibility. Geraldine starts to question the past: How guilty were her grandparents? What makes us complicit?

"In searing yet engaging prose, Schwarz makes her case for the need for memory work in this highly recommended read for fans of memoirs and World War II history." Library Journal

Schweitzer, Albert, 1875-1965

Schweitzer, Albert, 1875-1965 **Out** of my life and thought : an autobiography / Albert Schweitzer ; foreword by Jimmy Carter ; new foreword by Lachlan Forrow ; translated by Antje Bultmann Lemke. Johns Hopkins University Press, 2009. xx, 272 p. : **B**

ISBN 0801894123

1. Schweitzer, Albert, 1875-1965. 2. Missionaries, medical -- Gabon -- Lambarene (Moyen-Ogooue) 3. Musicians -- Europe 4. Theologians -- Europe 5. Strasbourg (France) 6. Autobiographies and memoirs.

LC 2009925674

Sciolino, Elaine

Sciolino, Elaine The **Seine** : the river that made Paris / Elaine Sciolino. W.W. Norton & Company, 2019. 304 p. **B**

ISBN 9780393609356

1. Rivers 2. River life 3. History 4. Harbors 5. Seine Valley -- Description and travel. 6. Seine Valley -- Social life and customs. 7. Seine River. 8. Paris, France -- Description and travel. 9. Paris, France -- History. 10. France -- Description and travel. 11. Autobiographies and memoirs

LC 2019025988

The former New York Times Paris bureau chief and author of the best-selling The Only Street in Paris presents a vibrant tour of the Seine that traces its rich history and the stories of contributors from all walks of life.

Scott, Harriet, approximately 1820-1876

VanderVelde, Lea **Mrs.** Dred Scott : a life on slavery's frontier / Lea VanderVelde. Oxford University Press, 2009. viii, 480 p., 6 p. of plates : **B**

ISBN 9780195366563

1. Scott, Harriet, approximately 1820-1876. 2. Scott, Dred, 1809-1858 Family. 3. Scott, Dred, 1809-1858 Trials, litigation, etc. 4. Women slaves 5. Slaves 6. Race relations. 7. United States -- History -- 19th century. 8. Biographies

LC 2008027920

A life of Harriet Scott, Dred's wife and co-litigant in the case, uses sources only recently brought to light to explore the reasons and ways that slaves used the courts to establish their freedom.

"Through Harriet Scott's life, the author is able to create a valuable portrait of the development of slavery on the U.S. frontier during an era in which that scourge was leading the country toward civil war. Despite the wealth of historical knowledge presented, the heart of this well-researched work is the tragic tale of how a loving family's effort to gain their freedom was brutally rejected by Supreme Court justices bent on maintaining the institution of slavery at all costs." Library Journal.

Scott-Heron, Gil, 1949-2011

Scott-Heron, Gil, 1949-2011 The **last** holiday : a memoir / Gil Scott Heron. Grove Press, 2012. 384 p. **B**

ISBN 9780802129017

1. African American singers 2. Social justice. 3. Music and society. 4. African American poets 5. Autobiographies and memoirs

LC 2012289233

A personal account by the late musician and poet traces the story of his life, career, and history-making 1981 tour at the side of Stevie Wonder to raise support for the establishment of Martin Luther King, Jr. Day.

Scovell, Nell

Scovell, Nell **Just** the funny parts : and a few hard truths about sneaking into the Hollywood boys' club / Nell Scovell. Dey Street Books, 2018. 288 p. **B**

ISBN 9780062473486

1. Television writers 2. Sex discrimination against women 3. Entertainment industry and trade 4. Popular culture 5. Hollywood, California 6. Autobiographies and memoirs

LC bl2018000687

The veteran television writer and creator of Sabrina the Teenage Witch shares insights into Hollywood's sexual politics throughout the past 30 years through anecdotes involving some of the industry's biggest names, including Mark Harmon, Bette Midler, David Letterman, Candice Bergen and Conan O'Brien.

"Scovell comes across as a smart, energetic, determined woman, someone who is always shooting for greater success and who really hates it when she fails at something. A revealing and timely portrait of a professional writer and the industry in which she works." Booklist.

Seager, Sara

★Seager, Sara The **smallest** lights in the universe : a memoir / Sara Seager. Crown, 2020 304 p. **B**

ISBN 9780525576259

1. Seager, Sara. 2. Women astrophysicists 3. Widows 4. Extrasolar planets. 5. Astrophysicists. 6. Autobiographies and memoirs

LC 2020007803

In this luminous memoir, an MIT astrophysicist must reinvent herself in the wake of tragedy and discovers the power of connection on this planet, even as she searches our galaxy for another Earth.

"This thoughtful and affecting memoir of navigating life after loss reads like a comforting novel, inspiring others to follow their dreams and never give up on the possibilities of discovery and self-reflection. Readers seeking women's biographies and studies in planetary science will relish this heartfelt story." Library Journal

Searcey, Dionne

Searcey, Dionne **In** pursuit of disobedient women : a memoir of love, rebellion, and family, far away / Dionne Searcey. Ballantine Books, 2020 288 p. : **B**

ISBN 9780399179853

1. Searcey, Dionne. 2. New York Times. 3. Journalists. 4. Family and work 5. Journalists 6. Women -- Political activity. 7. Senegal -- Politics and government. 8. West Africa -- Politics and government. 9. Autobiographies and memoirs.

LC 2019038588

An award-winning West Africa bureau chief for The New York Times describes her family's four-year relocation to Senegal, where she witnessed the extraordinary lives and struggles of women shaped by war, globalization and an outdated patriarchy.

"Well-written and illuminating, Searcey's memoir introduces readers to life in contemporary West Africa and the work of overseas reporting." Booklist

Searcy, David, 1946-

Searcy, David, 1946- **Shame** and wonder : essays / David Searcy. Random House, [2016] viii, 228 pages : **B**

ISBN 9780812993943

1. West Texas 2. Essays 3. Autobiographies and memoirs

LC 2014046233

A debut essay collection features expansive, deeply personal musings on such topics as the relationship between nature and beauty, the hidden depths of Scrooge McDuck and the author's childhood dreams of space travel.

"While the narrative style may not be for everyone, readers who appreciate it will enjoy this collection." Library Journal.

Sedaris, David

★Sedaris, David The **best** of me / David Sedaris. Little Brown & Company, 2020 ix, 388 p. **B**

ISBN 9780316628242

1. Sedaris, David. 2. Family relationships 3. Brothers and sisters 4. Families 5. Childhood 6. Essays. 7. Autobiographies and memoirs

LC 2020942220

The American humorist, author and radio contributor presents shares his most memorable work in a collection of stories and essays that feature him shopping for rare taxidermy, hitchhiking with a quadriplegic and hand-feeding a carnivorous bird.

"This is the perfect introduction for the uninitiated, while Sedaris's fans will enjoy rediscovering old favorites." Publishers Weekly

★Sedaris, David **Calypso** / David Sedaris. Little Brown & Company, 2018 288 p. **B**

ISBN 9780316392389

1. Families 2. Autobiographies and memoirs 3. Essays.

LC 2017950359

A latest collection of personal essays by the best-selling author of Let's Explore Diabetes with Owls and Me Talk Pretty One Day shares even more revealing and intimate memories from his upbringing and family life.

"The author's fans and newcomers alike will be richly rewarded by this sidesplitting collection." Publishers Weekly.

Sedaris, David **Dress** your family in corduroy and denim / David Sedaris. Little, Brown, 2004. 257 p. ; **B**

ISBN 9780316143462

1. Sedaris, David. 2. Families -- Humor. 3. Essays. 4. Autobiographies and memoirs

LC 2003065673

Lambda Literary Award for Humor, 2004.

In a collection of essays, the Rooster gets married at an uproarious wedding, an estrangement occurs over a rubber vs. plastic debate, and the author gets the upper hand during a slumber party game of strip poker.

"The author has a unique ability to supply exactly the right details to bring every funny, awkward, ludicrous, painful, horrible real-life moment into harrowingly crisp focus." Booklist.

★Sedaris, David **Theft** by finding : diaries 1977-2002 / David Sedaris. Little, Brown & Co., 2017. 528 p. **B**

ISBN 9780316154727

1. Personal conduct 2. Family relationships 3. Diaries 4. Anthologies

LC 2016959026

Longlisted for the Andrew Carnegie Medal for Excellence in Non-Fiction, 2018.

An anthology of personal favorite diary entries by the best-selling author of Let's Explore Diabetes with Owls features excerpts that have inspired his famed autobiographical essays and shares insights into the intimate arenas of his life.

"A candid, socially incisive, and sharply amusing chronicle of the evolution of an arresting comedic artist." Booklist.

Seeger, Pete, 1919-2014

★Dunaway, David King **How** can I keep from singing? : the ballad of Pete Seeger / David King Dunaway. Villard, 2008. 560p. **B**

ISBN 0345506081

1. Folk singers -- United States 2. Folk music, American. 3. Biographies

LC 2007041814

Seeger's private papers and numerous interviews with his friends, family, and fellow musicians provide material for a newly revised, detailed portrait of the famous folk singer, tracing his career and influence as a singer, surveying his political development, and including never-before-published photographs from the singer's archives.

"The focus of Seeger's life has been on using music as a force for social change. But he is perhaps best known as the major banjo-playing folksinger who pioneered the folk music revival that flowered in the 1960s. This excellent book provides a well-written and extensively researched account, not only of Seeger's life, but also of the social and political movements of the times in which he lived. An extensive bibliography and discography add to the book's usefulness." Library Journal.

Wilkinson, Alec, 1952- The **protest** singer : an intimate portrait of Pete Seeger / Alec Wilkinson. Alfred A. Knopf, 2009. 176 p. **B**

ISBN 9780307269959

1. Folk singers -- United States 2. Music -- Political aspects. 3. Folk music, American 4. Peace movements -- United States -- History 5. United States -- Social life and customs -- 20th century 6. United States -- Social life and customs -- 21st century 7. Biographies

LC 2008054387

Presents a portrait of the folk singer, tracing his career and influence as a singer and surveying his political development.

Seek, Amy, 1977-

Seek, Amy, 1977- **God** and Jetfire : confessions of a birth mother / Amy Seek. Farrar, Straus and Giroux, 2015. 256 p. **B**

ISBN 9780374164454

1. Open adoption. 2. Motherhood. 3. Families 4. Birthmothers 5. Autobiographies and memoirs

LC 2014044643

"Seek's prose is lyrical, at times heart-wrenching, as she deeply explores her pain, regret, and longing. The author provides an informative view of open adoption (its advantages as well as its drawbacks). There is nothing prescriptive or commonplace about this true story of a mother who has to learn as all parents must both how to embrace, and how to let go." Publishers Weekly.

Seinfeld, Jerry

★Seinfeld, Jerry **Is** this anything? / Jerry Seinfeld. Simon & Schuster, 2020 480 p. **B**

ISBN 9781982112691

1. Stand-up comedians 2. Stand-up comedy 3. Comic routine writing 4. Humorous writing 5. Autobiographies and memoirs

LC bl2020022074

Since his first performance at the legendary New York nightclub "Catch a Rising Star" as a twenty-one-year-old college student in fall of 1975, Jerry Seinfeld has written his own material and saved everything. For this book, Seinfeld has selected his favorite material, organized decade by decade. In page after hilarious page, one brilliantly crafted observation after another, readers will witness the evolution of one of the great comedians of our time and gain new insights into the thrilling but unforgiving art of writing stand-up comedy.

"This sharply observed, life-in-gags treasure trove offers essential reading for comedy fans, from a master of the form." Publishers Weekly

Selgin, Peter

Selgin, Peter The **inventors** : a memoir / Peter Selgin. Hawthorne Books, 2016 232 p. **B**

ISBN 9780989360470

1. Selgin, Peter. 2. Teacher-student relationships 3. Fathers and sons. 4. Autobiographies and memoirs

LC 2015030856

Both Selgin's father and the man he calls "the teacher" led remarkable lives. Among other things, Paul Selgin invented the first dollar bill-changing-machine and helped design the so-called proximity fuse, which hastened the end of World War II. As for the teacher, he became a forceful advocate for human rights and diversity, championing the cause of indigenous peoples and refuges from Southeast Asia, while insisting that they not forget their history - ironically, since the teacher did everything he could to obliterate his own. As Selgin discovers only after their deaths, for very different reasons both men felt compelled to reinvent themselves. The Inventors is the story of how these two charismatic men shaped the author's life. It's also the story of a relationship between a boy and his teacher, a relationship that was equal parts inspiring and destructive.

"A reflective investigation of the self, memory, and invention." Kirkus.

Selim I, Sultan of the Turks, 1470-1520

★Mikhail, Alan, 1979- **God's** shadow : Sultan Selim, his Ottoman empire, and the making of the modern world / Alan Mikhail. Liveright Publishing Corporation, 2020 496 p. **B**

ISBN 9781631492396

1. Selim I, Sultan of the Turks, 1470-1520. 2. Ayse Gulbahar Hatun, consort of Bayezid II, Sultan of the Turks, -1505. 3. Turkey -- History -- Selim I, 1512-1520. 4. Turkey -- History -- 1453-1683 5. Turkey -- History -- Ottoman Empire, 1288-1918.

LC 2020010516

The Ottoman Empire was a hub of flourishing intellectual fervor, geopolitical power, and enlightened pluralistic rule. At the helm of its ascent was the omnipotent Sultan Selim I (1470-1520), who, with the aid of his extraordinarily gifted mother, Gülbahar, hugely expanded the empire, propelling it onto the world stage. Alan Mikhail centers Selim's Ottoman Empire and Islam as the very pivots of global history, redefining world-changing events.

"A wonderful, exciting, engaging, scholarly yet accessible work for all readers of world history, a book that addresses a critical but often overlooked axis of global history." Library Journal

Sellers, Bakari, 1984-

Sellers, Bakari, 1984- **My** vanishing country : a memoir / Bakari Sellers. Amistad, 2020 224 p. **B**

ISBN 9780062917454

1. South Carolina. General Assembly. House of Representatives. 2. African American legislators 3. Racism 4. Legislators -- South Carolina 5. Rural African Americans. 6. Denmark, South Carolina 7. Autobiographies and memoirs

LC 2019040021

The CNN analyst and record-setting South Carolina State Representative chronicles the past, present and likely future of the American South, discussing his father's civil rights heroism and the ignored harsh realities of the black working class.

"A strong voice for social justice emerges in an engaging memoir." Kirkus

Selvaratnam, Tanya

Selvaratnam, Tanya **Assume** nothing : a story of intimate violence / Tanya Selvaratnam. Henry Holt and Company, 2020. 288 p. **B**

ISBN 9781250214249

1. Schneiderman, Eric T., 1954- 2. Abused women. 3. Abusive men. 4. Partner abuse. 5. Family violence. 6. United States -- Social conditions. 7. Autobiographies and memoirs.

The author shares her harrowing experiences with abuse at the hands of a top law enforcer to expose the realities of partner violence while counseling readers on how to recognize, expose and end domestic abuse.

"Selvaratnam (The Big Lie) deftly combines memoir and research to deliver a timely, must-read analysis of domestic violence. . . . A critical and timely piece in the era of the #metoo movement, this work will appear to a wide audience." Library Journal

Semmelweis, Ignac Fulop, 1818-1865

Nuland, Sherwin B. The **doctors'** plague : germs, childbed fever, and the strange story of Ignac Semmelweis / Sherwin B. Nuland. W. W. Norton, 2004, c2003. 205 p. : **B**

ISBN 039332625X

1. Semmelweis, Ignac Fulop, 1818-1865. 2. Germ theory of disease. 3. Communicable diseases. 4. Epidemics. 5. Medicine.

LC bl2005020475

"Atlas books."

Reprint. Originally published: 2003.

Analyzes how doctor Ignac Semmelweis's reforms of the medical field led to his discovery of the correlation between hand washing and reduced infection, recounting how his work contributed to the establishment of germ theory.

Sendak, Maurice

Cott, Jonathan **There's** a mystery there : the primal vision of Maurice Sendak / Jonathan Cott. Doubleday, [2017] 256 p. : **B**

ISBN 9780385540438

1. Children's literature authors 2. Children's book illustrators 3. Creativity 4. Imagination 5. Biographies 6. Interviews

LC 2016050812

A penetrating examination of the creative inspirations and legacy of children's book genius Maurice Sendak draws on the author's masterful 1976 Rolling Stone interview to reveal the torments and formative life experiences that shaped Sendak's complicated body of work.

Sendlerowa, Irena, 1910-2008

★Mazzeo, Tilar J. **Irena's** children : the extraordinary story of the woman who saved 2,500 children from the Warsaw ghetto / Tilar J. Mazzeo. Gallery Books, 2016. 320 p. **B**

ISBN 9781476778501

1. Sendlerowa, Irena, 1910-2008. 2. Righteous Gentiles in the Holocaust -- Poland. 3. Ghettoes, Jewish -- Poland. 4. Holocaust (1933-1945) -- Children. 5. Jews, Polish. 6. Warsaw, Poland -- History -- Occupation, 1939-1945. 7. Poland -- History -- 20th

century. 8. Biographies.

LC 2015051244

The best-selling author of The Widow Cliquot presents the story of a Holocaust rescuer to reveal the formidable risks she took to her own safety to save some 2,500 children from death and deportation in Nazi-occupied Poland during World War II.

"Mazzeo chronicles a ray of hope in desperate times in this compelling biography of a brave woman who refused to give up." Kirkus.

Seton, Elizabeth Ann, Saint, 1774-1821

Barthel, Joan **American** saint : the life of Elizabeth Seton / Joan Barthel ; foreword by Maya Angelou. Thomas Dunne Books, 2014. 304 p. **B**

ISBN 9780312571627

1. Seton, Elizabeth Ann, Saint, 1774-1821. 2. Catholic women 3. Christian saints 4. Women's rights 5. Rich families 6. Biographies

LC 2013030995

Mother Elizabeth Seton was canonized by the Catholic Church in 1975, 200 years after her birth to a prominent Episcopalian family in New York City. In American Saint, Joan Barthel, a professor of American Studies at Wake Forest University, engagingly highlights the significance of Elizabeth's contributions to American education, the Catholic Church, and women's roles in the Church. Barthel relates Elizabeth's rejection by New York society after her conversion to Catholicism, her relocation to Maryland, her struggles within the Church, and her eventual triumph in founding the first American women's religious order and establishing the first parochial school.

"A biography of the first American saint. offering a rounded portrait of an ambitious woman who struggled mightily to fulfill the tenets of her faith: to be obedient, merciful and good." Kirkus.

Seuss, Dr

★Jones, Brian Jay **Becoming** Dr. Seuss : Theodor Geisel and the making of an American imagination / Brian Jay Jones. Dutton, [2019] 448 p. **B**

ISBN 9781524742782

1. Seuss, Dr. 2. Authors, American -- 20th century 3. Illustrators -- United States 4. Children's literature authors, American -- 20th century 5. Children's book illustrators -- United States -- 20th century 6. Biographies

LC 2018059288

A full-scale portrait of Theodor Geisel, best known as American icon Dr. Seuss, shares insights into his successful early career as a radical political cartoonist and the complicated genius that informed his beliefs on such subjects as empathy and environmentalism.

"This attractive biography should be on the bedside reading table of thousands of Dr. Seuss lovers, and deservedly so." Library Journal.

Morgan, Judith **Dr.** Seuss & Mr. Geisel : a biography / Judith & Neil Morgan. Da Capo Press, 1996, 1995. xix, 345 p. : **B**

ISBN 030680736X

1. Seuss, Dr. 2. Authors, American -- 20th century 3. Illustrators -- United States 4. Illustration of books -- United States -- 20th century. 5. Children's literature writing 6. United States -- Social life and customs -- 20th century 7. Biographies

LC 96019313

Reprint. Orginally published: 1995.

Includes index.

Traces the life and career of the creator of the Grinch and the Cat in the Hat and examines his lasting contributions to the world of children's literature.

"Fans of The Cat in the Hat, The Grinch Who Stole Christmas and other classics may be surprised to learn that Dr. Seuss was terrified of children and had none of his own, and that writing verse was a supreme effort for him. While children's literature is Ted Geisel's principal claim to fame, his creative life was multifarious, including an apprenticeship with film director and army major Frank Capra during WWII and stints in advertising. The authors deftly evoke the settings where Geisel lived and worked." Publishers Weekly.

Seward, William Henry, 1801-1872

Stahr, Walter **Seward** : Lincoln's indispensable man / Walter Stahr. Simon & Schuster, 2012. 608 p. **B**

ISBN 9781439121160

1. Seward, William Henry, 1801-1872. 2. United States. Department of State 3. United States. Congress. Senate. 4. Republican Party. 5. Cabinet officers -- United States 6. Politicians -- United States 7. Republicans. 8. Governors. 9. United States -- Foreign relations -- 1861-1865. 10. United States -- Politics and government -- 1861-1865. 11. New York (State) -- Governors 12. Biographies

LC 2011052984

A in-depth profile of the leader of the 16th President's "Team of Rivals" examines his considerable political roles including those of a progressive Governor of New York, Secretary of State and Lincoln's advisor during the Civil War, offering insight into his status as a polarizing figure and his pivotal contributions to keeping Britain and France from formally recognizing the Confederacy.

Sexton, Anne, 1928-1974

Middlebrook, Diane Wood **Anne** Sexton : a biography / Diane Wood Middlebrook. Vintage Books, 1992, c1991. xxiii, 498 p. : **B**

ISBN 0679741828

1. Sexton, Anne, 1928-1974. 2. Poets, American -- 20th century 3. Mental illness 4. Parent abuse 5. Incest 6. United States -- Social life and customs -- 20th century 7. Biographies

LC 92050093

Originally published: Boston : Houghton Mifflin Co., 1991.

National Book Award for Nonfiction finalist, 1991

National Book Critics Circle Award for Biography finalist, 1991.

Explores the work and tormented life of the American poet, a woman who struggled with mental illness throughout her career, finally taking her own life in 1974.

"Ms. Middlebrook has written a wonderful book: just, balanced, insightful, complex in its sympathies and in its judgment of Sexton both as a person and as a writer." New York Times Book Review.

Shackleton, Ernest Henry, Sir, 1874-1922

Smith, Michael, 1946- **Shackleton** : by Endurance we conquer / Michael Smith. Oneworld, 2014. 400 p. **B**

ISBN 9781780745725

1. Shackleton, Ernest Henry, Sir, 1874-1922. 2. Endurance (Ship) 3. Exploration. 4. South Pole expeditions. 5. Polar expeditions. 6. Explorers. 7. Antarctica -- Exploration. 8. South Pole -- Exploration. 9. Biographies.

LC bl2014048451

Ernest Shackleton is one of history's great explorers, who became a leading figure in Antarctic discovery. Brings a fresh perspective to the heroic age of Polar exploration dominated by Shackleton's complex, compelling and enduringly fascinating story.

"Shackleton is admired for his leadership skills while his repeated off-ice failures are overlooked or unknown. Smith offers a fascinating assessment of his subject, one that will be enjoyed by readers of biographies, polar literature, and adventure stories." Library Journal.

Shah, Saira

Shah, Saira The **storyteller's** daughter / Saira Shah. Alfred A. Knopf, 2003. 253 p. ; **B**

ISBN 9780375415319

1. Shah, Saira. 2. Women -- Afghanistan -- Social conditions -- 20th century. 3. Afghanistan -- Description and travel. 4. Afghanistan -- Social life and customs. 5. Afghanistan -- History -- 20th century.

LC 2004295126

The British-born woman who filmed "Beneath the Veil," a groundbreaking documentary about Afghanistan, shares her journey of self discovery as a woman caught between the Western world and the land of her father's family.

"The author weaves oral traditions with history to describe life as an Afghani raised in the West but with solid roots in the East. . . . We learn about Shah's documentary work in Afghanistan, the power of myth through which Afghanistan's tradition is born, the brave work of peoples and organizations such as the Revolutionary Association of the Women of Afghanistan (RAWA), and the West's (and even East's) misconceptions regarding Muslim teachings. . . . This rare personal and historic account of the region is a great addition to public and academic libraries." Library Journal.

Shahani, Aarti Namdev

Shahani, Aarti Namdev **Here** we are : American dreams, American nightmares / Aarti Namdev Shahani. Celadon Books, 2019. 320 p. **B**

ISBN 9781250204752

1. Racism 2. Immigrants 3. American dream 4. Drug cartels 5. New York City 6. Autobiographies and memoirs

LC bl2019023083

An award-winning NPR correspondent presents a heartfelt memoir about the immigrant experience in modern America, detailing her education as a scholarship student at an elite Manhattan prep school and her father's victimization by a notorious drug cartel.

Shakespeare, William, 1564-1616

Bate, Jonathan **Soul** of the age : a biography of the mind of William Shakespeare / Jonathan Bate. Random House, 2009. xix, 471 p. **B**

ISBN 9781400062065

1. Shakespeare, William, 1564-1616. 2. Dramatists, English -- Early modern, 1500-1700 3. Intellectual life -- England -- 16th century. 4. Intellectual life -- England -- 17th century. 5. England -- Civilization -- 16th century 6. England -- Civilization -- 17th century. 7. Biographies

LC 2008016561

Tells the story of the great dramatist while deducing the crucial events of Shakespeare's life, connecting those events to his world and work, and revealing how this unsurpassed artist came to be.

"In this biography of Shakespeare, the author uses the Bard's own Seven Ages of Man speech from As You Like It to envision him as an infant, a school boy, a lover, a soldier, a justice, a pantaloon, and an old man entering oblivion. The result is a fresh new way to look at Shakespeare and a welcome reminder of what literary biography can still do." Library Journal.

Bryson, Bill **Shakespeare** : the world as stage / Bill Bryson. Atlas Books, 2007. 208 p. **B**

ISBN 0060740221

1. Shakespeare, William, 1564-1616. 2. Dramatists, English -- Early modern, 1500-1700 3. Theater. 4. Authors, English 5. England -- Social life and customs -- 16th century. 6. England -- Social life and customs -- 17th century. 7. Biographies

LC 2007021647

"In this addition to the Eminent Lives series, bestselling author Bryson...does what he does best: marshaling the usual little facts that others might overlook--for example, that in Shakespeare's day perhaps 40% of women were pregnant when they got married--to paint a portrait of the world in which the Bard lived and prospered... Bryson is a pleasant and funny guide to a subject at once overexposed and elusive--as Bryson puts it, 'he is a kind of literary equivalent of an electron--forever there and not there.'" Publishers Weekly.

Greenblatt, Stephen, 1943- **Will** in the world : how Shakespeare became Shakespeare / Stephen Greenblatt. W. W. Norton, 2004. 430 p. : **B**

ISBN 9780393050578

1. Shakespeare, William, 1564-1616. 2. Dramatists, English -- Early modern, 1500-1700 3. Poets, English -- Early modern, 1500-1700 4. Theater -- England -- History -- 16th century. 5. Intellectual life -- England -- 16th century. 6. England -- History -- 16th century. 7. Biographies

LC 2004011512

National Book Award for Nonfiction finalist, 2004

National Book Critics Circle Award for Biography finalist, 2004.

Pulitzer Prize for Biography or Autobiography finalist, 2005.

A portrait of Elizabethan England and how it contributed to the making of William Shakespeare discusses how he moved to London lacking money, connections, and a formal education and rose to became his age's foremost playwright.

"Greenblatt is at his best when he merges his gifts as a literary critic and scholar with his instincts as a biographer. He writes with real subtlety and skill about the sonnets. He also writes very well about the climate of fear and the use of public punishment and torture in Elizabethan and early Jacobean England, and how this enters into the very spirit of Shakespeare's work." New York Times Book Review.

Shapiro, James, 1955- The **year** of Lear : Shakespeare in 1606 / James Shapiro. Simon & Schuster, 2015 384 p. **B**

ISBN 9781416541646

1. Shakespeare, William, 1564-1616 Tragedies 2. Shakespeare, William, 1564-1616 Criticism and interpretation 3. Gunpowder Plot, 1605 4. Religious persecution 5. Literature and society 6. Drama 7. England -- History -- 17th century 8. Biographies

LC 2015031731

Published in Great Britain under the title: 1606: William Shakespeare and the Year of Lear.

James Tait Black Memorial Prize for Biography, 2015

Looks at the year 1606, in which Shakespeare created three of his great tragedies, examining how the tumultuous events and cultural conflicts of that year helped shape these works, and affected Shakespeare on a personal level.

"His well-written, scholarly exploration will stand as a n influential work that is a joy to read." Kirkus.

★Wells, Stanley, 1930- **Shakespeare** : for all time / Stanley Wells. Oxford University Press, c2003. xxi, 442 p. : **B**

ISBN 9780195160932

1. Shakespeare, William, 1564-1616 Criticism and interpretation History. 2. Shakespeare, William, 1564-1616. 3. Dramatists, English -- Early modern, 1500-1700 4. Stratford-upon-Avon (England) 5. Biographies

LC 2002027412

Looks at the life, career, works, and influence of William Shakespeare.

Shakur, Tupac, 1971-1996

Dyson, Michael Eric **Holler** if you hear me : searching for Tupac Shakur / Michael Eric Dyson. Basic Civitas Books, 2006, c2001. 292 p. : **B**

ISBN 0465017282

1. Rap musicians -- United States

LC bl2006028334

Originally published: c2001.

With a new pref. by the author.

Explores the legacy of rap artist Tupac Shakur, arguing that his icon status as the "black James Dean" is an enduring one.

"Dyson's discussion goes beyond slogans and poses to the actualities of thug life and the consequences of Shakur's passions and allegiances. Piquant and analytical." Booklist.

Shannon, Claude Elwood, 1916-2001

Soni, Jimmy A **mind** at play : how Claude Shannon invented the information age / Jimmy Soni and Rob Goodman. Simon & Schuster, 2017. 384 p. **B**

ISBN 9781476766683

1. Shannon, Claude Elwood, 1916-2001. 2. Mathematicians -- United States 3. Electrical engineers -- United States 4. Information theory 5. Technological innovations 6. Biographies

LC 2016050944

Chronicles the life and times of the lesser-known Information Age intellect, revealing how his discoveries and innovations set the stage for the digital era, influencing the work of such collaborators and rivals as Alan Turing, John von Neumann and Vannevar Bush.

"A welcome and inspiring account of a largely unsung herounsung because, the authors suggest, he accomplished something so fundamental that it's difficult to imagine a world without it." Kirkus.

Shannon, Lisa, 1975-

Shannon, Lisa, 1975- **Thousand** sisters : my journey of hope into the worst place on Earth to be a woman / Lisa Shannon ; foreword by Zainab Salbi. Seal Press, 2010. 300 p. **B**

ISBN 9781580052962

1. Human rights. 2. Women and war. 3. Women refugees. 4. War victims. 5. Congo (Democratic Republic) 6. Autobiographies and memoirs

LC 2009025391

The founder of the organization Run for Congo Women describes her visit to Congo and recounts the extreme hardships and tragic events in the lives of the women she meets there.

"Shannon presents images of the uncensored horror stories that, to many Congolese, have become regrettably routine: Congo's vile colonial history and the Rwandan genocide spillover that has caused the murders of more than five million Congolese people; children forced to kill and rape in their own communities; daily child deaths from easily curable illnesses; grisly murders of men and children in front of their wives and mothers; families burned alive inside their homes; women who must choose between rape and watching their children starve. Juxtaposing brutality with beauty, Shannon's direct prose is a stirring reminder that these horrors are real and ongoing. An alarming and inspiring message that will hopefully spur much-needed action." Kirkus.

Shapiro, Dani

Shapiro, Dani **Hourglass** : time, memory, marriage / Dani Shapiro. Alfred A. Knopf, 2017. 144 p. **B**

ISBN 9780451494481

1. Marriage 2. Women authors, American 3. Authors, American -- 20th century 4. Memory 5. Autobiographies and memoirs

LC 2016029345

An intimate and life-affirming memoir by the best-selling author of Still Writing explores themes of marriage, memory, the frailty of bonds and the time accretion of sorrow and love.

"A sharply observed and frequently moving memoir of a marriage." Kirkus.

★Shapiro, Dani **Inheritance** : a memoir of genealogy, paternity, and love / Dani Shapiro. Alfred A. Knopf, 2019. 256 p. **B**

ISBN 9781524732714

1. Shapiro, Dani. 2. Fathers and daughters 3. Paternity 4. Jewish women -- Identity 5. Genealogy 6. Autobiographies and memoirs

LC 2018024082

National Jewish Book Award, 2019."

The acclaimed and beloved author of Hourglass now gives us a new memoir about identity, paternity, and family secrets--a real-time exploration of the staggering discovery she made last year about her father, and her struggle to piece together the hidden story of her own life".--Provided by publisher.

"This beautifully written, thought-provoking genealogical mystery will captivate readers from the very first pages." Publishers Weekly.

Sharapova, Maria, 1987-

Sharapova, Maria, 1987- **Unstoppable** : my life so far / Maria Sharapova. Sarah Crichton Books, Farrar, Straus and Giroux, 2017 304 p. **B**

ISBN 9780374279790

1. Tennis players. 2. Women tennis players. 3. Tennis. 4. Autobiographies and memoirs

LC 2017017149

The five-time Grand Slam winner presents the remarkable story of how her father relocated her at the age of 7 from their native Russia to America to develop her tennis talents before she embarked on a record-setting career shaped by astonishing competitions, her provocative beliefs and her recent fight to return to the court.

"Unstoppable is an inspiring memoir about coming-of-age within the elite tennis community and a tribute to the unconditional support from families and coaches who make success possible." Booklist.

Sharp, Waitstill, 1902-1984

Joukowsky, Artemis **Defying** the Nazis : the Sharps war / Artemis Joukowsky. Beacon Press, [2016] 272 p. **B**

ISBN 9780807071823

1. Sharp, Waitstill, 1902-1984. 2. Sharp Cogan, Martha, 1905-1999. 3. Righteous Gentiles in the Holocaust 4. World War II -- Jews -- Rescue 5. Holocaust (1933-1945) 6. Unitarians 7. Prague, Czech Republic

LC 2016007704

The official companion to the 2016 Ken Burns PBS film tells the little-known story of the Sharps, an otherwise ordinary couple whose faith and commitment to social justice inspired them to undertake dangerous rescue and relief missions across war-torn Europe, saving the lives of countless refugees, political dissidents, and Jews on the eve of World War II.

"A harrowing and ultimately inspirational tribute to a brave couple." Booklist.

Shatner, William

Shatner, William **Live** long and-- : what I learned along the way / William Shatner ; with David Fisher. Thomas Dunne

Books, 2018. 224 p. **B**
ISBN 9781250166692
1. Star Trek (Television program) 2. Actors and actresses -- Canada 3. Quality of life 4. Personal conduct 5. Men and success 6. Autobiographies and memoirs
LC 2018012331

The "Star Trek" legend reflects on his career and the health scare that informed and reinforced his beliefs about living a good life, sharing engaging stories about his childhood, personal setbacks, and iconic successes.

" Anyone who has read a Shatner book or seen him speak in person is familiar with his anecdotal, conversational style, and although there aren't a lot of Star Trek memories referenced here, fans will enjoy Shatner's musings on his passions and adventures." Booklist.

Shatner, William **Spirit** of the horse : a celebration in fact and fable / William Shatner. Thomas Dunne Books, 2017. 304 p. **B**
ISBN 9781250130020
1. Horses 2. Human/animal relationships 3. Equestrianism 4. Equestrian therapy 5. Autobiographies and memoirs
LC 2017001073

William Shatner describes the effect horses have had on his life and on the lives of others, and pairs this with some of his favourite stories about horses, which include nonfiction and fiction, myth and folktale, and prose and verse.

"Shatner puts forth a lovely look at the influence and importance of horses." Booklist.

Shaw, Artie, 1910-2004

Nolan, Tom **Three** chords for beauty's sake : the life of Artie Shaw / Tom Nolan. W.W. Norton, c2010. xv, 430 p., 8 p. of plates : **B**
ISBN 9780393062014
1. Shaw, Artie, 1910-2004. 2. Jazz musicians 3. Jazz band leaders 4. Biographies
LC 2010006301

Depicts the Swing Era jazz clarinetist and big band leader who broke racial barriers by hiring African American musicians, wrote three books, had frequent "retirements" and had seven wives, including Lana Turner and Ava Gardner.

"In this biography of the swing clarinetist-bandleader Nolan, who interviewed Shaw and many of his band mates and intimates, appraises his difficult subject with a cool eye. His briskly written work lauds the musician's instrumental virtuosity and ambitious conceptions, but the author cuts Shaw no slack about his many personal failingshis arrogance, anger, selfishness, egocentricity and his horrific relationships with parents, wives and children. It's a multidimensional portrait of a brilliant yet self-absorbed autodidact who could never find happiness or satisfaction, even when his greatest fantasies of fame and success were realized. An exemplary work of jazz biography." Kirkus.

Shaw, Bernard, 1856-1950

Peters, Sally **Bernard** Shaw : the ascent of the superman / Sally Peters. Yale University Press, c1996. xvi, 328 p. : **B**
ISBN 0300075006
1. Shaw, Bernard, 1856-1950. 2. Homosexuality and literature -- Great Britain -- History -- 19th century. 3. Homosexuality and literature -- Great Britain -- History -- 20th century. 4. Dramatists, Irish -- 20th century 5. Men/women relations in literature. 6. Biographies
LC 95037248

A biography of the playwright speculates that he was secretly homosexual and examines his literary ambitions and austere lifestyle.

"An exploration of the ambiguities and passions that formed this great playwright and thinker. Shaw's sexuality, always a good topic of speculation, is studied here, but one wishes for more insights and in-depth analysis. Peters does devote a chapter to Shaw's close relationship with the actor and playwright Harley Granville Barker, mainly from Shaw's point of view. One may not agree with Peter's conclusions, but they will prove to be of interest to anyone studying Shaw." Library Journal.

Shaya, Alon

Shaya, Alon **Shaya** : An odyssey of food, my journey back to Israel / Alon Shaya. Alfred A. Knopf, 2018. xxiii, 412 p. **B**
ISBN 9780451494160
1. Shaya, Alon. 2. Cooks. 3. Cooking, Israeli. 4. Identity (Philosophical concept) 5. Growing up 6. Autobiographies and memoirs
LC 2017010159

"This is a Borzoi book."

Includes index.

Mixing together stories of place, of people and of the food that connects them with a memoir of one man's culinary sensibility, the founder of Domenica, Pizza Domenica and Shaya Restaurants describes how food saved his life and how, through a path of twists and turns, his celebrated cuisine the food of his native Israel with a New Orleans kick came to be.

"This is a must-read book for up-and-coming chefs, and a worthy addition to the chef-memoir genre." Publishers Weekly.

Shears, Jake

Shears, Jake **Boys** keep swinging : a memoir / Jake Shears. Atria Books, 2018. 288 p. **B**
ISBN 9781501140129
1. Shears, Jake. 2. Scissor Sisters 3. Singers 4. Growing up 5. Rock musicians 6. Rock music 7. Autobiographies and memoirs
LC 2017038858

The lead singer of the multi-platinum band Scissor Sisters explores his development as a young artist, his coming-of-age in the American West, his entry into New York City's dynamic music scene, and the band's rise to international fame in the early 2000s.

Sheehan, Jason

Sheehan, Jason **Cooking** dirty : a story of life, sex, love and death in the kitchen / Jason Sheehan. Farrar, Straus and Giroux, 2009. 368 p. **B**
ISBN 9780374289218
1. Sheehan, Jason. 2. Cooks -- United States 3. Food writers -- United States 4. Cooking. 5. Kitchens. 6. Autobiographies and memoirs
LC 2008047158

Describes the James Beard Award-winning author's experiences in a series of kitchens from a pizzeria and a French colonial to an all-night diner and a crab shack, jobs during which he fraternized with cooking staffs throughout numerous professional and personal challenges.

"Sheehan's memoir is emphatically not about the glam end of cooking or celebrity chefs, but about a straight blue-collar gig, where the kitchens are staffed by the kind of guys who get off on the fact that the work is insanely grueling. The war stories are as profane and outrageous as you'd expect, and Sheehan finds just the right balance between bravado and humility." Publishers Weekly.

Sheehy, Gail, 1937-2020

Sheehy, Gail, 1937-2020 **Daring** : my passages / Gail Sheehy.

William Morrow & Co., 2014. 416 p. **B**

ISBN 9780062291691

1. Women journalists 2. Ambition in women 3. Women authors 4. Autobiographies and memoirs

LC 2014034090

In an inspiring story of the unconventional life of a writer who dared, the best-selling author of the self-help classic Passages candidly recounts her challenges and victories as a groundbreaking female journalist in the 1960s, reflects on ambition and shares her own major life passages.

"Sheehy gives readers a distinct glimpse into some of the most important events of the last 40 years. Her perspective on the women's movement and the decline of print journalism is especially compelling." Library Journal.

Shelley, Mary Wollstonecraft, 1797-1851

★Montillo, Roseanne The **lady** and her monsters : a tale of dissections, attempts to reanimate dead tissue, and the writing of Mary Shelley's Frankenstein / Roseanne Montillo. Willam Morrow, c2013. 320 p. **B**

ISBN 9780062025814

1. Shelley, Mary Wollstonecraft, 1797-1851. Frankenstein. 2. Women and literature -- England -- History -- 19th century 3. Women authors, English -- History -- 19th century 4. Horror stories -- History and criticism 5. Frankenstein's monster (Fictitious character) 6. Biographies

LC 2012021509

Blending grotesque 19th-century science with literary creation, this fascinating volume, tracing the origins of the greatest horror story of all time, explores how Shelley and her contemporaries were intrigued by the occultists and scientists who risked everything to advance our understanding of human anatomy and medicine.

"Fraught with suicides, superstitions, natural disasters, and love affairs, the life of Mary Shelley shares much emotionally with the harrowing tale of her great protagonist, Victor Frankenstein. A delicious and enticing journey into the origins of a masterpiece." Publishers Weekly.

Sampson, Fiona **In** search of Mary Shelley : the girl who wrote Frankenstein / Fiona Sampson. Pegasus Books, 2018. 368 p. **B**

ISBN 9781681777528

1. Women authors 2. Literature -- History and criticism 3. Young women 4. Poets 5. Biographies

LC bl2018087125

Published to coincide with the 200th anniversary of Frankenstein, a major new biography of Mary Shelley, written by an award-winning poet, shares literary insight into Shelley's firsthand experiences throughout her infamously turbulent life.

Shen, Aisling Juanjuan, 1974-

Shen, Aisling Juanjuan, 1974- A **tiger's** heart : the story of a modern Chinese woman / Aisling Juanjuan Shen. Soho Press, 2009. 320 p. **B**

ISBN 9781569475867

1. Gender role 2. Chinese American women 3. Immigrants -- United States 4. Chinese Americans 5. China. 6. Yangtze River 7. Autobiographies and memoirs

LC 2009005426

"Like a suspense novel, this book is impossible to put down. All readers interested in China, as well as memoir fans (especially of success stories), must read this astonishing title." Library Journal.

Shepard, Sadia

Shepard, Sadia The **girl** from foreign : a search for shipwrecked ancestors, lost loves and forgotten histories / Sadia Shepard. Penguin Press, 2008. 384 p. **B**

ISBN 9781594201516

1. Shepard, Sadia Family. 2. Women authors -- 21st century 3. Jews -- Identity 4. Converts to Islam 5. Jewish women. 6. India -- Description and travel 7. United States -- Social life and customs -- 21st century 8. Autobiographies and memoirs

LC 2008003912

The daughter of a white Christian father and a Pakistani Muslim mother relates her journey to an insular Jewish community in India in search of her grandmother's secret history.

Sheridan, Philip Henry, 1831-1888

★Wheelan, Joseph **Terrible** swift sword : the life of General Philip H. Sheridan / Joseph Wheelan. Da Capo Press, 2012. 352 p. **B**

ISBN 9780306820274

1. Cavalry. 2. Civil war. 3. Leadership. 4. Total war. 5. United States -- History -- Civil War, 1861-1865 6. Biographies

LC 2012018587

"A sympathetic portrait of ""Grant's most dependable troubleshooter."" Kirkus.

Sherman, Anna (Anne Katherine), 1970-

Sherman, Anna (Anne Katherine), 1970- The **bells** of old Tokyo : meditations on time and a city / Anna Sherman. Picador, 2019. 337 p. ; **B**

ISBN 9781250206404

1. Time 2. Bells 3. Change 4. Tokyo, Japan 5. Japan -- History. 6. Japan -- Social life and customs 7. Autobiographies and memoirs

LC 2019016492

Explores the history and culture of Tokyo as the author searches for eight lost bells that used to mark neighborhoods and time before Western-style clocks were common and introduces readers to residents both past and present and their contributions.

"Highly recommended for anyone who has visited or is planning to visit Tokyo. Readers will gain insight into the history, culture, and language of Japan as well as ideas on city hot spots." Library Journal.

Sherman, William Tecumseh, 1820-1891

Fellman, Michael **Citizen** Sherman : a life of William Tecumseh Sherman / Michael Fellman. University Press of Kansas, 1997, c1995. xiv, 486 p. : **B**

ISBN 9780700608409

1. United States. Army 2. Generals -- United States 3. Biographies

LC 94041087

Originally published: Random House, 1995.

Biography of Civil War General William T. Sherman, focusing on his early life, military career, and family relationships.

McDonough, James L., 1934- **William** Tecumseh Sherman : in the service of my country : a life / James Lee McDonough. W. W. Norton & Co., 2016. 832 p. : **B**

ISBN 9780393241570

1. Sherman, William Tecumseh, 1820-1891. 2. United States. Army 3. Generals -- United States 4. Personal conduct 5. Command of troops 6. United States -- History -- Civil War, 1861-1865 7. United States -- History -- Civil War, 1861-1865 -- Campaigns. 8.

Biographies

LC 2016007023

A biography of the lauded general explores his involvement in the Civil War's most decisive battles, his good friendship with Ulysses S. Grant, his strained marriage, the loss of his young son and his plague of personal debts.

Woodworth, Steven E. **Sherman** / Steven E. Woodworth ; foreword by Wesley K. Clark. Palgrave Macmillan, 2009. xiv, 198 p., 8 p. of plates : **B**

ISBN 9780230610248

1. United States. Army 2. Generals -- United States 3. Military history -- 19th century 4. War -- History -- 19th century 5. Unionists (United States Civil War) 6. United States -- History -- Civil War, 1861-1865 -- Campaigns 7. Biographies

LC 2008022060

A portrait of controversial Civil War general William Tecumseh Sherman examines his military career, his outstanding command of military strategy, the criticism he sustained for his implacable "scorched earth" conduct against the South, and his legacy interms of modern military conduct.

"An excellent brief life of a major and controversial figure." Booklist.

Sherrod, Shirley, 1948-

Sherrod, Shirley, 1948- The **courage** to hope : how I stood up to the right wing media, the Obama administration, and the forces of fear / Shirley Sherrod ; with Catherine Whitney. Atria Books, 2012. 320 p. **B**

ISBN 9781451650945

1. United States. Department of Agriculture 2. Mass media -- Objectivity. 3. Courage in women. 4. African American farmers. 5. Farmers. 6. Georgia -- Rural conditions. 7. Autobiographies and memoirs

LC 2011050718

Traces how the author was forced to resign from the USDA in the wake of unsubstantiated accusations, tracing the media and legal efforts that enabled her ultimate vindication and drew apologies from the NAACP and the White House.

Shin, Dong-hyuk

Harden, Blaine **Escape** from Camp 14 : one man's remarkable odyssey from North Korea to freedom in the west / Blaine Harden. Viking, 2012. 256 p. **B**

ISBN 9780670023325

1. Shin, Dong-hyuk. 2. Political prisoners. 3. Concentration camps. 4. Escapes. 5. Forced labor. 6. North Korea -- Politics and government. 7. Biographies

LC 2011037555

Presents a dramatic account by one of the few survivors born in North Korea's infamous political prison camps, describing the brutal conditions he was forced to endure as a child, his witnessing of his family's executions, and his harrowing escape.

Shopsin, Tamara

Shopsin, Tamara **Arbitrary** stupid goal / Tamara Shopsin. MCD/Farrar Straus & Giroux, 2017. 336 p. **B**

ISBN 9780374105860

1. City life 2. Restaurateurs 3. Family businesses 4. Families 5. Greenwich Village, New York City -- Social life and customs -- 20th century 6. New York City -- Social life and customs -- 20th century 7. Autobiographies and memoirs

LC 2016059399

An offbeat memoir by the New Yorker illustrator and cook from New York City's Shopsin's eatery profiles the tight-knit, pre-fashion Greenwich Village of her bohemian 1970s childhood and her relationship with her big-hearted, tall-tale-telling father.

"Deeply nostalgic but not at all mawkish, Shopsin's supremely charming and affecting memoir of growing up in a pre-gentrified Greenwich Village will enchant fans of restaurant lore and postwar New York history alike." Booklist.

Short, Martin, 1950-

Short, Martin, 1950- **I** must say : my life as a humble comedy legend / Martin Short. HarperCollins, 2014 320 p. **B**

ISBN 9780062309525

1. Saturday night live (Television program) 2. Comedians -- Canada 3. Actors and actresses 4. Autobiographies and memoirs

LC 2014028617

A memoir by Canadian comedian, Martin Short, known for his work on SCTV and Saturday night live, his roles in a number of great comedy films, and his memorable theatrical appearances.

"A true vaudevillian, Short is always on as he delivers funny anecdotes from a diffuse and storied career." Kirkus.

Shorter, Frank, 1947-

Shorter, Frank, 1947- **My** marathon : reflections on a gold medal life / Frank Shorter with John Brant. Rodale, c2016. xviii, 254 p. : **B**

ISBN 9781623367244

1. United States Anti-Doping Agency 2. Runners -- United States 3. Marathon running. 4. Child abuse. 5. Doping in sports 6. Autobiographies and memoirs

LC bl2016027627

Includes index.

The Olympian and founder of the United States Anti-Doping Agency discusses his life, including his athletic triumphs and the abuse he and his siblings suffered at the hands of his father.

Shraya, Vivek, 1981-

Shraya, Vivek, 1981- **I'm** afraid of men / Vivek Shraya. Penguin Canada, 2018. 96 p. **B**

ISBN 9780735235939

1. Transgender persons 2. Gender identity 3. Gender role 4. Masculinity 5. Autobiographies and memoirs

LC 2019410566

A trans artist explores how masculinity was imposed on her as a boy and continues to haunt her as a girl--and how we might reimagine gender for the twenty-first century.

Shrewsbury, Elizabeth Hardwick Talbot, Countess of, 1527?-1608

Hubbard, Kate, 1963- **Devices** and desires : Bess of Hardwick and the building of Elizabethan England / Kate Hubbard. HarperCollins Publishers, [2019] 320 p. **B**

ISBN 9780062302991

1. Shrewsbury, Elizabeth Hardwick Talbot, Countess of, 1527?-1608. 2. Countesses -- England 3. Nobility -- Great Britain 4. Political intrigue. 5. Women landowners -- Great Britain 6. Great Britain -- History -- Elizabeth, 1558-1603 7. Biographies.

LC 2018043843

The critically acclaimed author of Serving Victoria illuminates the life of the little-known Bess of Hardwick--next to Queen Elizabeth I, the richest and most powerful woman in 16th-century England.

"In this engaging, well-researched biography, Hubbard (Serving Victoria) showcases the independent nature and innate business sense of Elizabeth, Countess of Shrewsbury (better known as Bess of Hardwick; 15271608), through the lens of her passion for large-scale architecture." Publishers Weekly.

Shriver, Eunice Kennedy

★McNamara, Eileen **Eunice** : the Kennedy who changed the world / Eileen McNamara. Simon & Schuster, 2018. 320 p. **B**

ISBN 9781451642261

1. Shriver, Eunice Kennedy. 2. Kennedy family. 3. Eunice Kennedy Shriver National Institute of Child Health and Human Development (U.S.). 4. Special Olympics, Inc. 5. Women philanthropists. 6. Philanthropists. 7. Biographies

LC 2017046517

Examines the life of Eunice Kennedy Shriver, covering her Stanford education, her inspirational relationship with her sister Rosemary, her advocacy on behalf of disabled citizens, and her role as founder of the Special Olympics.

"Along with providing insights into Eunices roles as wife, mother, sister, and daughter, McNamara uses her journalistic prowess to produce a complete and detailed portrait of this spirited and magnetic activist." Booklist.

Shriver, Timothy P.

Shriver, Timothy P. **Fully** alive : discovering what matters most / Timothy P. Shriver. Sarah Crichton Books, 2014 304 p. **B**

ISBN 9780374280918

1. Shriver family 2. Special Olympics. 3. Sports for people with disabilities 4. Athletes with disabilities 5. People with disabilities 6. Autobiographies and memoirs

LC 2014020245

The chairman of Special Olympics shares inspiring stories about athletes with intellectual disabilities who have become champions in the face of seeming powerlessness and vulnerability, sharing additional insight into the Shriver family and their dedication to advocacy.

"Sincere, profound and deeply satisfying." Kirkus.

Shteyngart, Gary, 1972-

★Shteyngart, Gary, 1972- **Little** failure : a memoir / Gary Shteyngart. Random House, 2014. 369 p. **B**

ISBN 9780679643753

1. Growing up 2. Jews, Russian 3. Russians in the United States 4. Immigrants, Russian 5. Queens, New York City 6. Autobiographies and memoirs

LC 2013013217

National Book Critics Circle Award for Autobiography/ Memoir finalist

Traces the author's uproarious experiences as a young bullied Jewish-Russian immigrant in Queens, his haphazard college pursuits and his initial forays into a literary career.

"An immigrant's memoir like few others, with as sharp an edge and as much stylistic audacity as the author's well-received novels." Kirkus.

Shula, Don, 1930-

Ribowsky, Mark **Shula** : the coach of the NFL's greatest generation / Mark Ribowsky. Liveright Publishing Corporation, a division of W.W. Norton & Company, [2019] 400 p. **B**

ISBN 9781631494604

1. Miami Dolphins (Football team). 2. Baltimore Colts (Football team) 3. National Football League 4. Football coaches -- United States 5. Professional football coaches 6. Children of immigrants 7. Professional football players 8. Biographies

LC 2019014727

Spanning seven decades, the notorious loss of Super Bowl III, and an historic undefeated season with the Dolphins, Shula is the definitive biography of a coaching legend.

"Ribowsky's excellent biography will thrill football fans of all allegiances." Publishers Weekly.

Shultz, Melissa

Shultz, Melissa **From** mom to me again : how I survived my first empty-nest year and reinvented the rest of my life / Melissa T. Shultz. Sourcebooks, Inc., 2016 xx, 197 p. : **B**

ISBN 1492618438

1. Shultz, Melissa. 2. Empty nesters -- United States. 3. Motherhood -- United States. 4. Parents -- United States. 5. Self-realization in women -- United States. 6. Autobiographies and memoirs.

LC 2016001340

The author describes her struggle with an empty nest after her children went away to college, but also how she ultimately reinvented her friendships, career, and herself.

Sickles, Daniel Edgar, 1819-1914

Keneally, Thomas **American** scoundrel : the life of the notorious Civil War General Dan Sickles / Thomas Keneally. Nan A. Talese, Doubleday, 2002. xii, 397 p. **B**

ISBN 9780385501392

1. Sickles, Daniel Edgar, 1819-1914. 2. United States. Congress. House 3. United States. Army 4. Legislators -- United States 5. Politicians -- United States 6. Murder -- Washington, D.C. 7. Generals -- United States 8. Biographies

LC 2001043078

"A frequently spellbinding recitation of the career of a totally awful politician, crook, adulterer and murderer who was no good as a general either." New York Times Book Review.

Silver, Elizabeth L., 1978-

Silver, Elizabeth L., 1978- The **tincture** of time : a memoir of (medical) uncertainty / Elizabeth L. Silver. Penguin Press, 2017. 256 p. **B**

ISBN 9781101981443

1. Children with critical illnesses -- Family relationships. 2. Parenthood. 3. Coping 4. Medical care. 5. Autobiographies and memoirs

LC 2016043492

An account of the author's family experiences in the wake of her newborn daughter's baffling stroke traces the ensuing year of testing, treatments, and stress that challenged her faith in medicine and compelled her investigation into historical and alternate practices.

"The attempt to balance personal trauma with wider cultural reference is a tricky challenge, but this will resonate with anyone who has experienced diagnostic difficulties." Kirkus.

Simon, Carly

Simon, Carly **Boys** in the trees : a memoir / Carly Simon. Flatiron Books, 2015 304 p. **B**

ISBN 9781250095893

1. Simon, Carly. 2. Women singers. 3. Singers. 4. Popular music. 5.

Autobiographies and memoirs

LC 2015038193

The successful singer-songwriter describes her life growing up amidst the glamour of literary New York with her father who co-founded Simon & Schuster, her path to art and music, her marriage to James Taylor and her famously cryptic song lyrics.

"Memoirs by rock icons of the 1960s and '70s are flying fast and furious these days. This is one of the best, lively and memorable. Check the new album that accompanies the book, too." Kirkus.

Simon, Marie, 1922-1998

Simon, Marie, 1922-1998 **Underground** in Berlin : a young woman's extraordinary tale of survival in the heart of Nazi Germany / Marie Simon, translated by Anthea Bell Little Brown & Co., 2015, c2014 368 p. **B**

ISBN 9780316382090

1. Jews, German 2. Hiding. 3. Deception 4. Holocaust (1933-1945) -- Psychological aspects. 5. Berlin, Germany 6. Autobiographies and memoirs

LC 2015935821

Also published: Toronto : Knopf Canada, 2015.

In this absorbing memoir, author Marie Jalowicz Simon relates her experiences as a hidden Jew in Berlin during World War II. In 1941, when she realized that the SS was likely to round her up for deportation to a concentration camp, she disappeared into the city, relying on family and friends to help her survive to the end of the war. Simon's son Hermann transcribed his mother's unusual odyssey from her tape recordings. This emotionally touching but unsentimental account expresses hope for the future.

Simon, Neil, 1927-2018

Simon, Neil, 1927-2018 The **play** goes on : a memoir / Neil Simon. Simon & Schuster, 1999. 348 p. : **B**

ISBN 0684846918

1. Dramatists, American -- 20th century 2. Spouses -- Death. 3. Autobiographies and memoirs

LC 99036449

Continues the author's Rewrites.

Includes index.

The renowned American playwright reveals how, following the death of his wife, he found creative inspiration in his career and a new relationship.

Simon, Neil, 1927-2018 **Rewrites** : a memoir / Neil Simon. Simon & Schuster, 1998, c1996. 397 p. : **B**

ISBN 0684835622

1. Dramatists, American -- 20th century 2. Autobiographies and memoirs

LC BL 98004301

"A Touchstone book."

Reprint. Originally published: c1996.

Includes index.

The playwright recounts his painful childhood, his many influences, anecdotes from his career, and the devastating death of his wife.

"This is a gentleman's autobiography, and Simon never stoops to dishing the dirt on his show biz cronies." Library Journal.

Simon, Paul, 1941-

Hilburn, Robert **Paul** Simon : the life / Robert Hilburn. Simon & Schuster, 2018 439 p., 16 unnumbered p. of plates : **B**

ISBN 9781501112126

1. Simon and Garfunkel. 2. Rock musicians 3. Biographies

LC 2018015535

An intimate, candid portrait of the two-time Rock and Roll Hall of Fame member and first songwriter recipient of the Gershwin Prize, written with rare input by Simon himself, discusses his creative process, his marriages, his decision to leave Simon and Garfunkel and the challenges and sacrifices of living life at an ultimate level of music artistry.

Simon, Scott

Simon, Scott **Unforgettable** : a mother's final days and the lessons that last a lifetime / Scott Simon. Flatiron Books, 2015 256 p. **B**

ISBN 9781250061133

1. Mothers and sons 2. Radio personalities. 3. Self-discovery. 4. Death 5. Autobiographies and memoirs

LC 2015002582

When NPR's Scott Simon began tweeting from his mother's hospital room in July 2013, he didn't know that his missives would soon spread well beyond his 1.2 million Twitter followers. Squeezing the magnitude of his final days with her into 140-character updates, Simon's evocative and moving meditations spread virally. Over the course of a few days, Simon chronicled his mother's death and reminisced about her life, revealing her humor and strength, and celebrating familial love. UNFORGETTABLE, expands on those famous tweets.

"Simon appreciates how generously Patti is treated by the staff at the hospital, which brings up memories of the 'lovely' men who courted her. He takes his quirky, devoted, gracious mother on her own terms, and his work shimmers as a touching tribute." Publishers Weekly.

Simone, Nina, 1933-2003

Cohodas, Nadine **Princess** Noire : the tumultuous reign of Nina Simone / Nadine Cohodas. Pantheon Books, 2010. 464 p. **B**

ISBN 9780375424014

1. Simone, Nina, 1933-2003. 2. Singers 3. African American singers 4. Civil rights. 5. Cabarets. 6. Biographies

LC 2009022252

A portrait of the mid-20th-century singer traces the challenges she faced acquiring her education, her 1959 debut at New York City's Town Hall and her relationships with such contemporaries as Lorraine Hansberry and James Baldwin.

"Looking at every aspect of Simone's work, from stage decorum to audience interaction, the author offers many rich insights into her subject's conflicted emotional world. Throughout, she nurtures the reader's empathy for the artist but takes care to avoid unfounded speculation on racism or gender bias. In fact, this is a 360-degree profile of Simone, offering solid critical insights at every turn." Choice.

Simpson, J. A., 1953-

Simpson, J. A., 1953- The **word** detective : searching for the meaning of it all at the Oxford English Dictionary / John Simpson. Basic Books, 2016 336 p. **B**

ISBN 9780465060696

1. Simpson, J. A., 1953-. 2. Oxford English dictionary. 3. Lexicographers -- Great Britain 4. Dictionaries -- History and criticism. 5. Lexicography. 6. Autobiographies and memoirs

LC 2016025594

Includes index.

The Word Detective is John Simpson's memoir as the former Chief Editor of the Oxford English Dictionary (OED). Simpson takes us from his first encounter with the dictionary in the old-fashioned world of Oxford in 1976 through to his retirement as Chief Editor thirty-seven years later. Simpson introduces us to the dusty basement archives and the traditional OED afternoon tea ceremony, and recounts the personal adventures of a life well lived, from marriage, to the birth of his two daughters. Simpson presents lexicography as an examination of the links between our language and our history.

Sinatra, Frank, 1915-1998

★Friedwald, Will, 1961- **Sinatra!** the song is you : a singer's art / Will Friedwald. Da Capo Press, 1997. 559 p. : **B**

ISBN 0306807424

1. Sinatra, Frank, 1915-1998. 2. Vocal music, American 3. Singers -- United States 4. United States -- Social life and customs -- 20th century 5. Biographies

LC 96043855

Originally published: New York : Scribner, 1995."

Friedwald's commentary is alert and perceptive, and even more valuable is the wealth of pointed reminiscence drawn from interviews he has done with musicians who worked closely with Mr. Sinatra." New York Times Book Review.

★Kaplan, James, 1951- **Sinatra** : the chairman / James Kaplan. Doubleday, 2015. 928 p. Frank Sinatra (James Kaplan) ; **B**

ISBN 9780385535397

1. Sinatra, Frank, 1915-1998. 2. Singers -- United States 3. Jazz music. 4. Jazz singers. 5. Biographies.

LC 2015008973

Presents a behind-the-scenes examination of the life and career of the legendary performer that offers insight into his prolific accomplishments, multidimensional character, and complex relationships.

"An appropriately big book for an oversized artistic presence." Kirkus.

Singer, Isaac Bashevis, 1904-1991

Singer, Isaac Bashevis, 1904-1991 **More** stories from my father's court / Isaac Bashevis Singer ; translated from the Yiddish by Curt Leviant. Farrar, Straus and Giroux, c2000. 215 p. ; **B**

ISBN 0374213437

1. Singer, Isaac Bashevis, 1904-1991 Childhood and youth. 2. Jews, Eastern European 3. Jewish way of life. 4. Family relationships 5. Rabbis -- Poland. 6. Poland -- History -- 20th century. 7. Essays. 8. Autobiographies and memoirs

LC 00037583

Originally published in Yiddish in the Daily Forward, (1950s).

The author offers a collection of twenty-eight stories depicting events in his father's rabbinical court in pre-war Warsaw.

Sinise, Gary

Sinise, Gary **Grateful** American : a journey from self to service / Gary Sinise with Marcus Brotherton. Nelson Books, [2019] 272 p. **B**

ISBN 9781400208128

1. Sinise, Gary. 2. Actors and actresses -- United States 3. Veterans 4. Disabled veterans 5. Helpfulness in men 6. United States 7. Autobiographies and memoirs

LC 2018032657

Gary Sinise shares the never-before-told story of his journey from trouble-making Chicago kid to cofounder of the legendary Steppenwolf Theater Company, world-famous actor, and tireless advocate for America's active duty defenders, veterans, and first responders.

Sitting Bull, 1831-1890

Utley, Robert M., 1929- **Sitting** Bull : the life and times of an American patriot / Robert M. Utley. Henry Holt & Co, 2008 464 p. **B**

ISBN 080508830X

1. Indians of North America -- Great Plains (United States) -- History 2. Dakota Indians 3. Dakota Indians -- History. 4. Chiefs (Political anthropology) -- North America 5. The West (United States) -- History -- 19th century. 6. Biographies

LC bl2008012894

"This book is well written, strongly documented, and fairly reasoned to satisfy even specialists within the field. It surpasses all previous biographies of Sitting Bull." Choice.

Yenne, Bill, 1949- **Sitting** Bull / Bill Yenne. Westholme, 2008. 448 p. **B**

ISBN 9781594160608

1. Dakota warriors 2. Chiefs (Political anthropology) -- North America 3. Dakota Indians 4. Dakota Indians -- History -- 19th century 5. The West (United States) -- History -- 19th century. 6. Biographies

LC 2012450110

Documents the life of Sitting Bull, from his youth as a warrior and rise as a tribal elder to his failed efforts to save Lakota land and culture through nonviolence and negotiations.

"In this biography, the author captures the extraordinary life of Plains Indian leader Sitting Bull while providing new insight into the nomadic culture of the Lakota." Publishers Weekly.

Skelton, Marc, 1974-

Skelton, Marc, 1974- **Pounding** the rock : basketball dreams and real life in a Bronx high school / Marc Skelton. Doubleday, a division of Penguin Random House LLC, [2019] 256 p. **B**

ISBN 9780385542654

1. Fannie Lou Hamer Freedom High School (New York, N.Y) Basketball 2. Fannie Lou Hamer Panthers (Basketball team) 3. High school basketball 4. Basketball coaches 5. Inner city schools 6. Basketball 7. Bronx, New York City -- Social conditions 8. New York City -- Social conditions 9. Autobiographies and memoirs

LC 2018027159

An account of the Bronx Fannie Lou Hamer Panthers' 2016-2017 season shares insights into how a small, working-class high school has become a symbol of regeneration and how its coach inspires the team to balance their championships with academics.

"Skelton's game accounts are exciting and reveal details about his players, their lives, and off-court challenges." Kirkus.

Skiles, Wes

Hauserman, Julie **Drawn** to the deep : the remarkable underwater explorations of Wes Skiles / Julie Hauserman. University Press of Florida, 2018. 240 p. **B**

ISBN 9780813056982

1. Underwater photography 2. Divers 3. Cave diving 4. Photographers 5. Biographies

LC 2018933358

National Outdoor Book Award for History/Biography, 2019.

This book is the inspiring story of an explorer and activist who uncovered environmental abuses, advanced the field of underwater photography, and astonished the world with unprecedented views of the secret depths of the planet.

Skinner, B. F., 1904-1990

Bjork, Daniel W. **B.F.** Skinner : a life / Daniel W. Bjork. Basic Books, c1993. xiv, 298 p., 8 p. of plates : **B**

ISBN 0465006116

1. Psychologists -- United States 2. Behaviorism (Psychology) -- History 3. Verbal behavior 4. Psychology -- History -- 20th century 5. United States -- History -- 20th century 6. Biographies

LC 92054522

The first major biography of the preeminent psychologist traces Skinner's life and work and places his contributions within the American tradition of utopian and social-political debate.

"Bjork places Skinner squarely in the context of the US social, technological, and political history. Although heavily documented, Bjork's book is very readable because documentation is in endnotes. A handsome, well-indexed work, with an excellent bibliography." Choice.

Slahi, Mohamedou Ould

Slahi, Mohamedou Ould **Guantanamo** diary / Mohamedou Ould Slahi, edited by Larry Siems Little, Brown and Company, 2015. 400 p. **B**

ISBN 9780316328685

1. Guantanamo Bay Detention Camp 2. Prisoners of war -- Guantanamo Bay Naval Base, Cuba. 3. Detention of persons -- United States. 4. Torture victims 5. War on Terrorism, 2001-2009 6. Guantanamo Bay Naval Base, Cuba. 7. United States -- Politics and government. 8. Autobiographies and memoirs

LC 2014023763

Since 2002, Mohamedou Slahi has been imprisoned at the detention camp at Guantanamo Bay, Cuba. In all these years, the United States has never charged him with a crime. A federal judge ordered his release in March 2010, but the U.S. government fought that decision, and there is no sign that the United States plans to let him go. Three years into his captivity Slahi began a diary, recounting his life before he disappeared into U.S. custody, "his endless world tour" of imprisonment and interrogation, and his daily life as a Guantanamo prisoner.

Slate, Jenny

★Slate, Jenny **Little** weirds / Jenny Slate. Little, Brown and Company, 2019. ix, 224 pages ; **B**

ISBN 9780316485340

1. Loss (Psychology) 2. Growing up 3. Female friendship 4. Self-care 5. Autobiographies and memoirs 6. Essays

LC 2019933749

The actress, stand-up comedian and best-selling children's book author explores her internal self, dreams and insecurities through bursts of writing on a wide range of subjects from heartbreak and divorce, to the smell of honeysuckle and a French-kissing rabbit.

"This volume mixes the oddball self-examination of Jenny Lawson with moments of poetic insight. Recommended for lovers of fizzy memoirs." Library Journal.

Slouka, Mark

★Slouka, Mark **Nobody's** son : a memoir / Mark Slouka. W. W. Norton & Company, 2016. 304 p. **B**

ISBN 9780393292305

1. Slouka, Mark Family. 2. Mothers and sons. 3. Family secrets. 4. Refugees 5. Czech Americans. 6. Autobiographies and memoirs

LC 2016018257

The son of Czechoslovakian parents who were smuggled out of their country to escape the Nazis, only to endure postwar Communist purges traces the experiences of the war's refugees and the author's own efforts to reconnect with his mother through a labyrinth of trauma, displacement and denial.

Slowinski, Joseph

James, Jamie. 1951- The **snake** charmer : a life and death in pursuit of knowledge / Jamie James. Hyperion, 2008. 272 p. **B**

ISBN 1401302130

1. Slowinski, Joseph. 2. Herpetologists -- United States 3. Snakes -- Study and teaching 4. Rattlesnakes -- Study and teaching 5. Boa constrictors -- Study and teaching 6. Everglades, Florida -- Description and travel 7. Peru -- Description and travel 8. Burma -- Description and travel 9. United States -- Social life and customs -- 20th century 10. United States -- Social life and customs -- 21st century 11. Biographies

LC 2007048987

Traces the life and death of Joe Slowinski, a renowned herpetologist who had been a leading expert on Asia's venomous snakes, in a profile that documents his groundbreaking work and the dramatic final hours of his life after he had been bitten by a krait.

"James recounts the gritty and sad story of Joe Slowinski, a flamboyant and well-known herpetologist who died in Burma in 2001, aged 38, from the poisonous bite of a krait snake. This book is both a tribute to Slowinski's spirit and scientific accomplishments, and a cautionary tale about the dangers of an overly passionate ambition." Publishers Weekly.

Smalls, Robert, 1839-1915

Lineberry, Cate **Be** free or die : the amazing story of Robert Smalls' escape from slavery to Union hero / Cate Lineberry. St. Martin's Press, 2017. 288 p. **B**

ISBN 9781250101860

1. Smalls, Robert, 1839-1915. 2. Planter (Steamship) 3. United States. Congress. House 4. African Americans 5. Ship captains 6. Fugitive slaves 7. Slavery 8. South Carolina -- History -- 19th century 9. United States -- History -- Civil War, 1861-1865 10. United States -- History -- 19th century 11. Biographies

LC 2017004245

Describes the amazing hijacking of a Confederate steamer in 1862 by a 23-year-old slave who avoided the heavily armed troops stationed in Charleston Harbor and delivered the vessel to Union forces, earning his freedom.

"This is unquestionably a remarkable story, and journalist Lineberry . ably tells it as a microcosm of the war." Kirkus.

Smarsh, Sarah

★Smarsh, Sarah **Heartland** : a memoir of working hard and being broke in the richest country on Earth / Sarah Smarsh. Simon & Schuster 2018 304 p. **B**

ISBN 9781501133091

1. Poverty 2. Working class 3. Income distribution 4. Classism 5. Kansas 6. Autobiographies and memoirs

LC 2017301189

National Book Award for Nonfiction finalist, 2018

Kirkus Prize for Nonfiction finalist, 2018.

Reveals one woman's experience of working-class poverty with a startlingly observed, eye-opening and topical personal story.

"Will appeal to readers who enjoy memoirs and to sociologists. While Smarsh ends on a hopeful note, she offers a searing indictment of how the poor are viewed and treated in this country." Library Journal.

Smiley, Jane

Smiley, Jane **Thirteen** ways of looking at the novel / Jane Smiley. Knopf, 2005. x, 591 p. ; **B**

ISBN 1400040590

1. Smiley, Jane. 2. Authors, American -- 20th century. 3. Books and reading -- United States. 4. Fiction writing. 5. Fiction -- History and

criticism

LC 2005045181

"The book is roughly divided into three sections: the first classifies the novel, beginning with the most simple of definitions (e.g., it's long, in prose, has a protagonist), and adds moral and aesthetic complexity as it moves along. The second section consists of a primer for fledgling novelists. The result is a thorough reflection on the art and craft of the novel from one of its best-known contemporary practitioners." Publishers Weekly.

Smith, Adam, 1723-1790

Norman, Jesse **Adam** Smith : father of economics / Jesse Norman. Basic Books, 2018. 432 p. **B**

ISBN 9780465061976

1. Economists -- Great Britain 2. Economics -- Philosophy 3. Capitalism -- Moral and ethical aspects 4. Capitalism and democracy 5. Biographies

LC 2018015933

Previously published in the UK as Adam Smith: what he thought, and why it matters by Penguin Random House.

Adam Smith (1723-1790) is now widely regarded as the greatest economist of all time. But what he really thought, and the implications of his ideas, remain fiercely contested. Was he an eloquent advocate of capitalism and individual freedom? A prime mover of "market fundamentalism"? An apologist for human selfishness? Or something else entirely? Political philosopher Jesse Norman dispels the myths and caricatures, and provides a far more complex portrait of the man.

"It's hard to imagine an American politician writing with the same depth and grasp of an inordinately complex subject, but Norman pulls it off quite capably. A worthy addition to the literature surrounding Smith and that of modern conservative thought." Kirkus.

Smith, Alfred Emanuel, 1873-1944

Finan, Christopher M., 1953- **Alfred** E. Smith : the happy warrior / Christopher M. Finan. Hill and Wang, 2002. x, 396 p., 16 p. of plates : **B**

ISBN 0809030330

1. Smith, Alfred Emanuel, 1873-1944. 2. Presidential candidates 3. Presidential election, 1928 4. Irish Americans 5. Catholics -- United States 6. New York (State) -- Governors 7. New York (State) -- Politics and government -- 1865-1950 8. United States -- Politics and government -- 1901-1953. 9. Biographies

LC 2002019476

"Finan writes well, but for an occasional lapse into anachronism." New York Times Book Review.

Smith, Bren

Smith, Bren **Eat** like a fish : my adventures as a fisherman turned restorative ocean farmer / Bren Smith. Alfred A. Knopf, 2019. 336 p. **B**

ISBN 9780451494542

1. Aquaculture 2. Sustainable agriculture 3. Seaweed 4. Fishers 5. Autobiographies and memoirs

LC 2018050112

James Beard Foundation Book Awards, Writing and Literature, 2020.

Green Prize for Sustainable Literature: Adult Nonfiction, 2020.

Through tales that span from his childhood in Newfoundland to his early years on the high seas aboard commercial fishing trawlers, from pioneering new forms of ocean farming to surfing the frontiers of the food movement, Smith introduces the world of sea-based agriculture, and advocates getting ocean vegetables onto American plates. Here he shows how we can transform our food system while enjoying delicious, nutritious, locally grown food, and how restorative ocean farming has the potential to create millions of new jobs and protect our planet in the face of climate change, rising populations, and finite food resources.

"Part memoir, part treatise on the life of a professional fisherman, part manual for the future of eating worldwide, this unique book cannot help but make readers think long and hard about the fate of the earth as it faces the challenges of global warming and the outlook for feeding the planet." Booklist.

Smith, Claire Bidwell

Smith, Claire Bidwell The **rules** of inheritance : a memoir / Claire Bidwell Smith. Hudson Street Press, c2012. 304 p. **B**

ISBN 9781594630880

1. Smith, Claire Bidwell. 2. Grief. 3. Loss (Psychology) 4. Children of people with cancer 5. Social isolation. 6. Autobiographies and memoirs

LC 2011025136

At age fourteen, Claire Bidwell Smith--an only child--learned that both of her parents had cancer. The fear of becoming a family of one before she came of age compels Claire to make a series of fraught choices, set against the glittering backdrop of New York and Los Angeles--and the pall of regret. When the inevitable happens, and Claire is alone in the world, she is inconsolable at the revelation that suddenly she is no one's special person. It is only when Claire eventually falls in love, marries, and becomes a mother that she emerges from the fog of grief.

Smith, Daniel B., 1977-

Smith, Daniel B., 1977- **Monkey** mind : a memoir of anxiety / Daniel B. Smith. Simon & Schuster, c2012. 288 p. **B**

ISBN 9781439177303

1. Smith, Daniel B., 1977- Mental health. 2. Anxiety disorders. 3. Anxiety in men. 4. Anxiety. 5. People with mental illnesses 6. Autobiographies and memoirs

LC 2011025971

The author of Muses, Madmen, and Prophets shares affirming, personal insights into the experiences of anxiety in today's world, evocatively describing its painful coherence and absurdities while sharing the stories of sufferers to illustrate anxiety's intellectual history and influence.

Smith, Joseph 1805-1844

Beam, Alex **American** crucifixion : the murder of Joseph Smith and the fate of the Mormon church / Alex Beam. Public Affairs, 2014. 352 p. **B**

ISBN 9781610393133

1. Mormon Church -- History 19th century 2. Mormons 3. Polygamy. 4. Assassination. 5. Mormon polygamy 6. Illinois 7. Nauvoo, Illinois

LC 2014004063

Journalist Alex Beam, a Boston Globe columnist and contributor to The Atlantic, examines the life of Latter Day Saints' founder Prophet Joseph Smith as well as the events that led to his group's move to Utah in the mid-1840s. While still in Illinois, Smith's ambitions grew, and he prepared to run for the U.S. presidency -- but having led the Mormons to settle there after fleeing Missouri, he provoked violent backlash against his doctrines and was arrested and ultimately killed by gunfire while awaiting trial for perjury and polygamy. Beam's thoroughly researched and balanced narration of Smith's rise and fall will captivate anyone interested in American history, especially the history of religion.

"Beam offers a captivating saga of Smith's rise and fall and of a colorful cast of characters who contributed to the internal politics and rivalries that led to Smith's death and drove the Mormons forward to their destiny." Booklist.

Bushman, Richard L. **Joseph** Smith : rough stone rolling / Richard Lyman Bushman, with the assistance of Jed Woodworth. Alfred A. Knopf, 2005. xxiv, 740 p. : **B**

ISBN 1400042704

1. Smith, Joseph, 1805-1844. 2. Mormons 3. Biographies

LC 2004061613

Presents the life of the founder of the Church of Latter Day Saints, from his hardscrabble early life in rural New York, to the visions that inspired The Book of Mormon, and his untimely death at the hands of a mob in 1844.

"In this biography of the founder of the Mormon church, the author stresses the boy seer's thoroughly ordinary origins born to a hard-pressed New England farm family and denied all but the rudiments of a formal education to emphasize the marvel of the religious revolution he brought about. A deft portrait of a deeply controversial figure." Booklist.

Remini, Robert Vincent, 1921-2013 **Joseph** Smith / Robert V. Remini. Viking, 2002. xv, 190 p. ; **B**

ISBN 067003083X

1. Smith, Joseph, 1805-1844. 2. Mormon Church -- History 19th century 3. Visions (Christianity) 4. Mormons -- United States 5. Assassination -- Religious aspects -- Christianity 6. United States -- Religious life and customs -- 19th century 7. Biographies

LC 2001056762

Chronicles the life of the founder of the Mormon Church from his birth in 1805, through the visions he started receiving at age fourteen, to his assassination in 1844.

"A masterful evenhanded precis that will engross history and religion readers alike." Booklist.

Smith, Lee, 1944-

★Smith, Lee, 1944- **Dimestore** : a writer's life / Lee Smith. Algonquin Books of Chapel Hill, 2016 224 p. **B**

ISBN 9781616205027

1. Smith, Lee, 1944-. 2. Growing up 3. Authors, American 4. Women authors 5. Grundy, Virginia. 6. Autobiographies and memoirs

LC 2015023739

In her first work of nonfiction, the author recounts her early days in the small coal town of Grundy, Virginia--and beyond.

"In this candid, wistful, appreciative, and beguiling memoir, Smith offers a distinctive and intimate look at one writers beginnings." Booklist.

Smith, Mary-Ann Tirone, 1944-

Smith, Mary-Ann Tirone, 1944- **Girls** of tender age : a memoir / Mary-Ann Tirone Smith. Free Press, c2006. 285 p. : **B**

ISBN 0743279778

1. Smith, Mary-Ann Tirone, 1944- Childhood and youth. 2. Smith, Mary-Ann Tirone, 1944- Homes and haunts Hartford, Connecticut 3. Authors, American -- 20th century 4. Growing up. 5. Child sexual abusers -- Hartford, Connecticut 6. Authors, American -- Homes and haunts -- Hartford, Connecticut 7. Hartford, Connecticut -- Social life and customs. 8. Autobiographies and memoirs

LC 2005051376

Traces the author's experiences of growing up in a small-town community under the shadows of a severely autistic brother and a violent serial pedophile who eventually murdered one of the writer's young classmates.

"This memoir, an unsentimental view of life in a post-World War II working-class family, is interspersed with the story of Bob Malm, a serial pedophile who brutally murdered a fifth-grade classmate of hers in December 1953. This poignant memoir belongs in all collections." Library Journal.

Smith, Mychal Denzel, 1986-

Smith, Mychal Denzel, 1986- **Invisible** man, got the whole world watching : a young black man's education / Mychal Denzel Smith. Nation Books, 2016 320 p. **B**

ISBN 9781568585284

1. African American men 2. Racism 3. Identity (Psychology) 4. African Americans 5. Autobiographies and memoirs

LC 2016655096

A prominent journalist and contributing writer to The Nation magazine describes his education and the experiences of black masculinity against a backdrop of the Obama administration, the death of Trayvon Martin, the career of LeBron James and other pivotal influences that have shaped race relations in today's America.

"This is a commanding read that deserves a place in all libraries. It will make a great book group discussion, especially when paired with Coates's memoir." School Library Journal.

Smith, Patti

★Smith, Patti **Just** kids / Patti Smith. Ecco, 2010. 304 p. **B**

ISBN 9780066211312

1. Smith, Patti. 2. Mapplethorpe, Robert, 1946-1989. 3. Chelsea Hotel 4. Women rock musicians. 5. Women poets. 6. Musicians. 7. Songwriters 8. Brooklyn, New York City 9. New York City 10. Autobiographies and memoirs

LC 2010279646

ALA Notable Book, 2011.

National Book Award for Nonfiction, 2010.

National Book Critics Circle Award for Autobiography/Memoir finalist

An artist and musician recounts her romance, lifetime friendship, and shared love of art with Robert Mapplethorpe, in a memoir that includes such influential artists as Bob Dylan, Allen Ginsberg, Andy Warhol, and William Burroughs.

"This is one of the best books ever written on becoming an artistnot the race for online celebrity and corporate sponsorship that often passes for artistic success these days, but the far more powerful, often difficult journey toward the ecstatic experience of capturing radiance of imagination on a page or stage or photographic paper." Washington Post.

★Smith, Patti **Year** of the monkey / Patti Smith. Alfred A. Knopf, 2019. 176 p. **B**

ISBN 9780525657682

1. Smith, Patti. 2. Poets, American -- 20th century 3. Women rock musicians 4. Wanderers and wandering 5. Chinese zodiac 6. Autobiographies and memoirs

LC 2019009856

From the *National Book Award*-winning author of *Just Kids* and *M Train* comes a memoir in which dreams and reality are vividly woven into a tapestry of one transformative year.

"Fans of Smith's extensive body of work and those who enjoy well-crafted personal narratives will find much to love in this brief and vibrant book." Library Journal

Smith, Patti **M** train / Patti Smith. Alfred A. Knopf, 2015. 272 p. **B**

ISBN 9781101875100

1. Smith, Patti. 2. Women rock musicians. 3. Creativity in women. 4. Loss (Psychology) 5. Authors. 6. Biographies.

LC 2015012904

ALA Notable Book, 2016.

The Rock and Roll Hall of Fame inductee presents reflections on her inner life from the unique perspectives of the cafes and cultural haunts she has visited and worked in around the world.

Smith, Tracy K.

Smith, Tracy K. **Ordinary** light : a memoir / Tracy K. Smith. Alfred A. Knopf, 2015 352 p. **B**

ISBN 9780307962669

1. Children of people with cancer 2. Growing up 3. Grief 4. African American women 5. Autobiographies and memoirs

LC 2014026185

National Book Award for Nonfiction finalist, 2015

The youngest of five children, Tracy K. Smith was raised with limitless affection and a firm belief in God by a stay-at-home mother and an engineer father. But just as Tracy is about to leave home for college, her mother is diagnosed with cancer, a condition she accepts as part of God's plan. Ordinary Light is the story of a young woman struggling to fashion her own understanding of belief, loss, history, and what it means to be black in America.

"Smith holds our intellectual and emotional attention ever so tightly as she charts her evolving thoughts on the divides between races, generations, economic classes, and religion and science and celebrates her lifesaving discovery of poetry as 'soul language.' " Booklist.

Smith, William, 1769-1839

Winchester, Simon The **map** that changed the world : William Smith and the birth of modern geology / Simon Winchester ; illustrations by Soun Vannithone. Harper Collins, 2001. xix, 329 p., 2 p. of plates : **B**

ISBN 0060193611

1. Smith, William, 1769-1839. 2. Geologists -- Great Britain 3. Cartographers. 4. Cartography. 5. Geology, Stratigraphic -- History. 6. Great Britain -- History. 7. Biographies

LC 2001016603

The world's coal and oil industry, its gold mining, its highway systems, and its railroad routes were all derived entirely from the creation of William Smith's first map. Simon Winchester unfolds the poignant sacrifice behind this world-changing discovery.

"In the early years of the nineteenth century, William Smith created the first geological map of Great Britain, a time-consuming, solitary project that helped establish geology as one of the fundamental fields of study. Winchester tells Smith's story, including the dramatic ups and downs of his personal life. This is just the kind of creative nonfiction that elevates a seemingly arcane topic into popular fare." Booklist.

Smithson, James, 1765-1829

Ewing, Heather P. The **lost** world of James Smithson : science, revolution, and the birth of the Smithsonian / Heather Ewing. Bloomsbury : 2007. 432 p. : **B**

ISBN 1596910291

1. Smithson, James, 1765-1829. 2. Smithsonian Institution -- History. 3. Scientists -- Great Britain 4. Philanthropists 5. Museums. 6. Great Britain -- Social life and customs -- 18th century 7. United States -- Social life and customs -- 19th century 8. United States -- History -- 19th century 9. Biographies

LC bl2007011507

Chronicles the life of James Smithson as a scientist, suspected spy, gambler, radical revolutionary, and philanthropist, telling the story of his remarkable bequest and the controversy it spawned.

"The author provides a readable and informative perspective on late Enlightenment chemistry, backing it up with extensive archival research and forays into secondary literature on science." Times Literary Supplement.

Smoyer, Clarence, 1923-

Makos, Adam **Spearhead** : an American Tank Gunner, his enemy, and a collision of lives in World War II / Adam Makos. Ballantine Books, 2019 xiii, 393 p., 32 unnumbered p. of plates : **B**

ISBN 0804176728

1. United States. Army Officers 2. United States. Army. Armored Regiment, 32nd 3. M26 (Tank) -- History. 4. Panther (Tank) -- History. 5. Tank crews -- United States 6. World War II -- Campaigns -- Western Front. 7. Biographies

LC 2018039460

"Clarence Smoyer began the war as a gentle giant, a factory worker from Pennsylvania coal country reluctant to unleash the power of the Sherman tank he crewed. But as his tank platoon fought its way from Normandy to the Rhine and beyond, and he watched his friends cut down one by one, he learned to kill with deadly accuracy and efficiency. His fight would climax in Cologne, in the shadow of the great cathedral, where he took a shot immortalized by a chance photograph--and where he would later forge a friendship with the German tanker he tragically dueled soon after."--Provided by publisher.

Smyth, Katharine, 1981-

Smyth, Katharine, 1981- **All** the lives we ever lived : seeking solace in Virginia Woolf / Katharine Smyth. Crown, 2019 308 p. : **B**

ISBN 1524760625

1. Woolf, Virginia, 1882-1941. To the lighthouse. 2. Fathers and daughters -- United States 3. Fathers -- Death. 4. Grief. 5. Autobiographies and memoirs.

LC 2018289715

An intimate work of memoir and literary criticism describes how the author found literary solace and insights in Virginia Woolf's <I>To the Lighthouse</I> while mourning a beloved parent's death.

"A work of incisive observation and analysis, exquisite writing, and an attempt to determine if there is any revelation that could lessen loss, that could help to make the fact of death okay." Kirkus.

Snare, John

★Cumming, Laura The **vanishing** Velazquez : a 19th century bookseller's obsession with a lost masterpiece / Laura Cumming. Scribner, 2016. 320 p. **B**

ISBN 9781476762159

1. Snare, John. 2. Velazquez, Diego, 1599-1660. 3. Booksellers. 4. Portrait painting. 5. Biographies

LC 2015040220

Originally published: London : Chatto & Windus, 2016 as "The Vanishing Man: In Pursuit of Velazques".

James Tait Black Memorial Prize for Biography, 2016

Describes the true story of a provincial bookseller who discovered an incredible portrait of King Charles I at a liquidation auction and his lifelong quest to prove it was painted by Diego Velazquez.

"Snares story is noteworthy, but it is Cummings spirited and clever narration that makes this enigma utterly engrossing." Publishers Weekly.

Socrates, 469-399 B.C.

★Hughes, Bettany The **hemlock** cup : Socrates, Athens, and the search for the good life / Bettany Hughes. A.A. Knopf, 2011. 384 p. **B**

ISBN 9781400041794

1. Philosophers -- Greece. 2. Ancient philosophers. 3. Intellectual

life. 4. Athens, Greece. 5. Ancient Greece. 6. Biographies
LC 2010045486

A dual portrait of the classical philosopher and fifth-century B.C. Athens draws on the latest sources to offer insight into the period's daily realities and elements ranging from the gymnasia and the red-light district to the battlefields and the teeming Agora where Socrates frequently spoke and was condemned to death. By the author of Helen of Troy.

"For decades, while his city underwent war and hardship and defeat and civil war and political restructuring, Socrates settled himself in the agora and talked of inner things, the essence of things. Some of his words were taken down by acolytes such as Plato and Xenophon; some of his mannerisms were mocked by playwrights such as Aristophanes; the master himself, a man Hughes claims we can all benefit from getting to know a little better, wrote nothing, but his recorded dialogues, his Socratic method of relentless questioning, have become indispensable pieces of our Western mental furniture. Hughes revisits all of this with the panache of a born explainer, enthusiastically filling out the world of ancient Athens. She takes readers through the torturous birth and early crises of Athenian democracy, and she's refreshingly evenhanded about the resentment such a democracy might feel toward somebody like Socrates." Washington Post.

Johnson, Paul, 1928- **Socrates** : a man for our times / Paul Johnson. Viking, 2011. 240 p. **B**

ISBN 9780670023035

1. Philosophy, Ancient. 2. Ancient philosophers. 3. Philosophers. 4. Philosophy. 5. Ancient Greece -- History -- To 146 B.C. 6. Biographies
LC 2011019767

Illuminates key tenets in the influential philosopher's beliefs through the story of his life, tracing his middle-class existence against a vibrant backdrop of fifth century B.C. Athens while sharing intimate analyses of specific aspects of his personality.

Waterfield, Robin, 1952- **Why** Socrates died : dispelling the myths / Robin Waterfield. W. W. Norton & Co., 2009. 288 p. **B**

ISBN 9780393065275

1. Socrates, 469-399 B.C. Trials, litigation, etc. 2. Socrates, 469-399 B.C. Death and burial. 3. Ethics. 4. Death. 5. Trials. 6. Executions and executioners. 7. Ancient Greece -- History -- To 146 B.C. 8. Ancient Greece -- History -- Macedonian Expansion, 359-323 B.C.
LC 2009004317

A revisionist account of the trial and execution of the philosopher draws on Greek sources to separate truth from myth, offering insight into Socrates' character as a deeply moral thinker whose convictions strongly contrasted those of his former student, Alcibaides.

"The author sets out to explain why Socrates died: he discusses his trial, but also offers an informed and well-written account of classical Athenian history." Times Higher Education.

Solnit, Rebecca

★Solnit, Rebecca **Recollections** of my nonexistence : a memoir / Rebecca Solnit. Viking, 2020. 256 p. **B**

ISBN 9780593083338

1. Solnit, Rebecca. 2. Women authors, American 3. Women intellectuals 4. Feminism 5. Writing 6. San Francisco, California 7. Autobiographies and memoirs
LC 2019022497

In Recollections of My Nonexistence, Rebecca Solnit describes her formation as a writer and as a feminist in 1980s San Francisco, in an atmosphere of gender violence on the street and throughout society and the exclusion of women from cultural arenas. She tells of being poor, hopeful, and adrift in the city that became her great teacher, and of the small apartment that, when she was nineteen, became the home in which she transformed herself. Beyond being a memoir, Solnit's book is also a passionate argument: that women are not just impacted by personal experience, but by membership in a society where violence against women pervades.

"This is a thinking person's book about writing, female identity, and freedom by a powerful and motivating voice for change." Publishers Weekly

Solomon, Andrew, 1963-

★Solomon, Andrew, 1963- **Far** and away : reporting from the brink of change, seven continents, twenty-five years / Andrew Solomon. Scribner, 2016 464 p. **B**

ISBN 9781476795041

1. Life change events 2. Social change. 3. Autobiographies and memoirs
LC 2016304584

A volume of essays by the National Book Award and National Books Critics' Circle Award-winning author of Far From the Tree chronicles his activist stint on the Moscow barricades in 1991, his 2002 account of cultural rebirth in post-Taliban Afghanistan and other stories of profound change.

"Agile, informative, even revelatory pieces that, together, show us both the great variety of humanity and the interior of a gifted writer's heart." Kirkus.

Solomon, Andrew, 1963- The **noonday** demon : an atlas of depression / Andrew Solomon. Scribner, 2001. 569 p. **B**

ISBN 068485466X

1. Depression. 2. Melancholy. 3. People with depression. 4. People with mental illnesses 5. Autobiographies and memoirs
LC 2001018884

Lambda Literary Award for Biography/Autobiography, 2001.

National Book Award for Nonfiction, 2001.

ALA Notable Book, 2002.

Pulitzer Prize for General Nonfiction finalist

A journey of incomparable range and resonance into the most pervasive of family secrets, The Noonday Demon examines depression in personal, cultural, and scientific terms.

"The author draws on his own life story and other sources for a deeply moving and provocative exploration of depression." Booklist.

Solomonov, Michael

★Solomonov, Michael **Zahav** : a world of Israeli cooking / Michael Solomonov and Steven Cook ; produced by Dorothy Kalins ; photography by Mike Persico ; design by Don Morris Design. Houghton Mifflin Harcourt, [2015] 368 p. : **B**

ISBN 9780544373280

1. Solomonov, Michael. 2. Recipes. 3. Cooking, Israeli. 4. Cooks 5. Cooking, Middle Eastern. 6. Israel -- Social life and customs 7. Philadelphia, Pennsylvania -- Social life and customs 8. Autobiographies and memoirs.
LC 2015004346

"A Rux Martin book."

Includes index."

Readers with an adventurous palate and an open mind will be richly rewarded by this terrific debut." Publishers Weekly.

Soloway, Jill

Soloway, Jill **She** wants it : desire, power, and toppling the patri-

archy / Jill Soloway. Crown Archetype, [2018] 288 p. **B**
ISBN 9781101904749
1. Soloway, Jill. 2. Gender identity 3. Coming out (Sexual or gender identity) 4. Women television producers and directors. 5. Gender-nonconforming people 6. Autobiographies and memoirs
LC 2018022379

The creator of "Transparent" shares the poignant story of how her parent came out as transgender, compelling the author to challenge the male-dominated landscape of Hollywood to create her Emmy- and Golden Globe-winning series.

"This is an honest look at Soloways mind-opening journey, which allowed for deeper understanding of Hollywood's patriarchy as well as of the author's own gender, art, and self." Booklist.

Sone, Monica Itoi, 1919-2011

Sone, Monica Itoi, 1919-2011 **Nisei** daughter / Monica Sone University of Washington Press, 2014, c1953. xvii, 238 p. ; **B**
ISBN 9780295993553
1. Japanese Americans -- Seattle, Washington 2. Japanese Americans -- Forced removal and incarceration, 1942-1945 3. Seattle, Washington 4. Autobiographies and memoirs
LC 79004921

Tells the story of a Japanese-American woman growing up in Seattle in the 1930s who was subjected to relocation during World War II

Sontag, Susan, 1933-2004

★Moser, Benjamin **Sontag** : her life and work / Benjamin Moser. Ecco Press, 2019. 832 p. **B**
ISBN 9780062896391
1. Women authors 2. Women intellectuals 3. Feminists 4. Radicalism 5. Biographies
LC 2018044760

Pulitzer Prize for Biography or Autobiography, 2020.

The author of Why This World chronicles the life story of the 20th-century activist and intellectual, sharing insights into Sontag's private life and indelible influence on modern politics, feminism and gender diversity.

"A nuanced, authoritative portrait of a legendary artist." Kirkus.

Rollyson, Carl E. (Carl Edmund) **Susan** Sontag : the making of an icon / Carl Rollyson and Lisa Paddock. W.W. Norton, c2000. xiv, 370 p. : **B**
ISBN 0393049280
1. Sontag, Susan, 1933-2004. 2. Authors, American -- 20th century 3. Women and literature -- United States -- History -- 20th century. 4. Biographies
LC 00020402

Delves beneath the surface to examine the forces that made Sontag an international icon, exploring her public persona and private passions, including the strategies behind her meteoric rise to fame and her political moves and missteps.

"The authors have unearthed a deluge of information on Sontag's personal lifeon her early years and family life, her lesbianism. her relationship with son David Rieff and her battles with breast cancer. While the authors provide an intelligent, though not strikingly original, analysis of her work, they are best at detailing how Sontag and her publishers have marketed her image as much as her thought." Publishers Weekly.

Sorensen, Theodore C.

Sorensen, Theodore C. **Counselor** : a life at the edge of history / Ted Sorensen. Harper, c2008. 576 p. **B**
ISBN 0060798718
1. Kennedy, John F. (John Fitzgerald), 1917-1963 Friends and associates. 2. Political consultants -- United States 3. Speechwriters -- United States 4. Lawyers -- United States 5. Politicians -- United States 6. United States -- Politics and government -- 1961-1963. 7. Autobiographies and memoirs
LC 2007047328

A prominent international lawyer and former advisor to JFK recounts their conversations during some of the most decisive moments of the thirty-fifth president's career, including the Bay of Pigs, the Cuban Missile Crisis, and the writing of "Profiles in Courage."

"This book is instantly essential for any student of the period. It fills gaps in the historical record; it vividly conveys life inside the administration; and it generously dishes anecdotes." Washington Post Book World.

Soros, George

Tamkin, Emily The **influence** of Soros : politics, power, and the struggle for an open society / Emily Tamkin. HarperCollins, 2020. 320 p. **B**
ISBN 9780062972637
1. Soros, George Influence. 2. Soros Foundation. 3. Open Society Foundations. 4. International relations 5. Business and politics 6. Philanthropy 7. Conspiracy theories. 8. Biographies
LC 2020002225

A journalistic investigation into the career and activities of Hungarian-American hedge fund tycoon George Soros examines the origins of his influence and the truth about the conspiracies attributed to his philanthropic pursuits.

"Readers who enjoy political history and international relations will find this book informative and useful." Library Journal

Sotomayor, Sonia, 1954-

★Sotomayor, Sonia, 1954- **My** beloved world : a memoir / Sonia Sotomayor. Knopf, 2013. 320 p. **B**
ISBN 9780307594884
1. United States. Supreme Court Justices. 2. Hispanic-American judges 3. Judges -- United States 4. Women judges 5. Hispanic American women 6. Autobiographies and memoirs
LC 2012031797

Appointed to the Supreme Court in 2009, Sonia Sotomayor became the first Latina to achieve this high judicial office. My Beloved World offers a moving portrait of her gritty South Bronx neighborhood and her extended Puerto Rican family, as well as details of the many challenges she has faced during her formative years and early career. This open, eloquent memoir describes how she overcame poverty, her father's early death, and even the onset of her own early health issues to excel in school, attend Princeton and Yale Law School -- while still remaining true to her heritage.

"Graceful, authoritative memoir from the country's first Hispanic Supreme Court justice. . . . The author's text forms a cultural patchwork of memories and reflections as she mines the nuances of her parents' tumultuous relationship, fondly recalls family visits in Puerto Rico and offers insight on a judicial career that's just beginning when the memoir ends. . . . Mature, life-affirmative musings from a venerable life shaped by tenacity and pride." Kirkus.

Soyinka, Wole

Soyinka, Wole The **open** sore of a continent : a personal narrative of the Nigerian crisis / Wole Soyinka. Oxford University Press, 1996. vi, 170 p. ; **B**

ISBN 0195105575

1. Soyinka, Wole Homes and haunts Nigeria. 2. Authors, Nigerian -- 20th century 3. State-sponsored terrorism 4. Authoritarianism 5. Political activists. 6. Nigeria -- Politics and government -- 1960- 7. Autobiographies and memoirs

LC 96008757

Includes index."

Soyinka begins with the 1995 murder of dissident writer Ken Saro-Wiwa and works his way back through the grim, almost unbelievable history of Nigeria's brutal despots. As he describes various forms of systematic humiliation, torture, murder, 'ethnic cleansing,' greed, ecological destruction, and all the other 'spoils of power,' Soyinka interprets his personal experiences of protest, harassment, incarceration, and exile within a broad framework of historical and literary references." Booklist.

Soyinka, Wole **You** must set forth at dawn : a memoir / Wole Soyinka. Random House, 2006. xx, 499 p. : **B**

ISBN 037550365X

1. Authors, Nigerian -- 20th century 2. Political prisoners -- Nigeria 3. Political activists 4. Nigeria -- Politics and government. 5. Autobiographies and memoirs

LC 2005051923

A memoir by Africa's first Nobel laureate for literature continues the story that began in his childhood autobiography "Ake" as Soyinka describes the adventures and mishaps of his adulthood, including his frequent exile from his homeland, his celebrated literary work, and his advocacy for political and human rights.

Spaak, Suzanne

Nelson, Anne, 1954- **Suzanne's** children : a daring rescue in Nazi Paris / Anne Nelson. Simon & Schuster, 2017 xvi, 318 p. **B**

ISBN 9781501105326

1. Spaak, Suzanne. 2. Holocaust (1933-1945). 3. Righteous Gentiles in the Holocaust. 4. World War II 5. French Resistance (World War II)

LC 2017008567

Documents the courageous story of Belgian Catholic and political family insider Suzanne Spaak, who joined the Resistance during the Nazi occupation of Paris and who used her fortune and status to enlist wealthy and powerful allies, ultimately sacrificing her life to save hundreds of Jewish children from deportation to Auschwitz.

"This heartfelt story is almost a model for how popular history should be written; it will satisfy lovers of history, Jewish history in particular." Library Journal.

Spark, Muriel

Stannard, Martin, 1947- **Muriel** Spark : the biography / Martin Stannard. W.W. Norton & Co., 2010. 627 p. **B**

ISBN 9780393051742

1. Spark, Muriel. 2. Authors, Scottish -- 20th century 3. Women authors, Scottish 4. Converts to Catholicism. 5. Women and religion. 6. Scotland -- Social life and customs -- 20th century. 7. Biographies

LC 2009047982

Originally published: London : Weidenfeld & Nicolson, c2009.

Shortlisted for the James Tait Black Memorial Prize for Biography, 2009"

This is among the richest and most satisfying literary biographies of our time: not only a portrait of the artist herself but also a rendering of her literary and social context and a judicious examination of her works." Wall Street Journal.

Speaker, Tris

Gay, Timothy M. **Tris** Speaker : the rough-and-tumble life of a baseball legend / Timothy M. Gay. University of Nebraska Press, c2005. xii, 314 p. : **B**

ISBN 9780803222069

1. Speaker, Tris. 2. Center fielders (Baseball) 3. Baseball managers. 4. Scandals. 5. Baseball players -- United States 6. United States -- Social life and customs -- 20th century. 7. Biographies

LC 2005016975

"This is a look at the Hall of Fame center fielder, whose colorful personality and remarkable talent were overshadowed by contemporaries like Ty Cobb and Cy Young. Gay has insured the righting of history with this biography. A worthwhile read for any sports fan." Publishers Weekly.

Spector, Phil, 1940-

★Brown, Mick, 1950- **Tearing** down the wall of sound : the rise and fall of Phil Spector / Mick Brown. Alfred A. Knopf, 2007. viii, 452 p. : **B**

ISBN 1400042194

1. Sound recording executives and producers -- United States 2. Men -- Personal conduct 3. Trials (Murder) -- Los Angeles, California 4. Men 5. United States -- Social life and customs -- 21st century 6. Los Angeles, California -- Social life and customs -- 21st century 7. Biographies

LC 2007004819

Originally published: London : Bloomsbury, 2007.

Phil Spector, born in the Bronx in 1940, grew up an outsider despised by his peers. Yet after his family moved to California, he learned everything he could about music, formed a band, and had a number-one hit with "To know him is to love him." He quickly became the top producer of early rock and roll, originator of such girl groups as the Ronettes, a millionaire by twenty-one, owner of his own label by twenty-two. Hit followed hit, and for all of them he used a new technique called the "wall of sound." But the reign of the boy-man who owned pop culture seemed doomed by the "British Invasion," and he spiraled into paranoid isolation and peculiar behavior. Though he seemed to improve for a time, even returning to the recording studio to work, it didn't last, and in 2003, the actress Lana Clarkson was found at his home, dead by gunshot.

"Stacked with incredible anecdotes, Brown's entertaining and nuanced portrait lifts the fog of myth and outright falsehood (including Spector's own) that have obscured the celebrity producer (like an enormous, gravity-defying wig) through the years." Publishers Weekly.

Speer, Albert, 1905-1981

Fest, Joachim C., 1926-2006 **Speer** : the final verdict / Joachim Fest ; translated from the German by Ewald Osers and Alexandra Dring. Harcourt, c2001. x, 419 p. : **B**

ISBN 0297646168

1. Speer, Albert, 1905-1981. 2. Architects -- Germany 3. Nazis -- Germany 4. Biographies

LC 2001430585

Originally published in German with the same title: Berlin : Alexander Fest, 1999.

A portrait of Germany's World War II Armaments Minister considers his rise from unemployed architect to designer of the Third Reich's most important buildings, personal relationship with Hitler, and considerable ambition.

"This is a valuable, important biography, but perhaps it is an effort to explain the unexplainable." Booklist.

Speer, Albert, 1905-1981 **Inside** the Third Reich : memoirs / Albert Speer ; translated from the German by Richard and Clara

Winston ; introduction by Eugene Davidson. Simon & Schuster, 1997, c1970. xx, 596 p. : **B**

ISBN 0684829495

1. Speer, Albert, 1905-1981. 2. Hitler, Adolf, 1889-1945. 3. Nazis. 4. Architects -- Germany 5. War criminals -- Germany 6. Germany -- Politics and government -- 1933-1945. 7. Autobiographies and memoirs

LC BL 99791720

"A Touchstone book."

Originally published: New York : Macmillan, 1970.

The author presents a detailed account of his fifteen-year association with the German Fuhrer.

Spiegel, Renia, 1924-1942

Spiegel, Renia, 1924-1942, **Renia's** diary : a Holocaust journal / Renia Spiegel, Elizabeth Bellak, Sarah Durand, Deborah Lipstadt ; translated by Anna Blasiak, Marta Dziurosz. St. Martin's Press, September 2019. 176 p. **B**

ISBN 9781250244024

1. Spiegel, Renia, 1924-1942. 2. Holocaust (1933-1945) -- Poland 3. Holocaust victims 4. Antisemitism 5. Jewish ghettos -- Poland 6. Poland -- History -- Occupation, 1939-1945.

LC 2019024270

A first English-language translation of teen holocaust victim Renia Spiegel's secret journal chronicles her witness to the Nazi invasion of Poland, her Jewish family's forced relocation to the Przemsyl ghetto and her attempt to go into hiding.

"This family's epic, layered story of survival serves as an important Holocaust document." Publishers Weekly.

★Spiegelman, Art **Co-mix** : a retrospective of comics, graphics, and scraps / Art Spiegelman Drawn & Quarterly, 2013. 192 p. : **B**

ISBN 9781770461147

1. Spiegelman, Art. 2. Comic books, strips, etc. -- History and criticism. 3. Comic book illustrators 4. Comic book writers 5. Comic book illustration. 6. Biographical comics 7. Comics and Graphic novels 8. Anthologies. 9. Biographies.

LC bl2013040412

"Maus did much to 'legitimize' comics to the wider world, but this thoughtfully curated, elegantly presented volume is an even more convincing testament to the potential of the medium." Booklist.

Spiegelman, Art

★Spiegelman, Art **Maus** : a survivor's tale / Art Spiegelman. Pantheon Books, 1997. 295 p. : **B**

ISBN 0679406417

1. Spiegelman, Vladek, 1906-1982 2. Auschwitz (Concentration camp) 3. Children of Holocaust survivors 4. Fathers and sons 5. Holocaust (1933-1945) -- Poland 6. Holocaust survivors 7. Autobiographies and memoirs 8. Comics and Graphic novels

LC 96032796

A son struggles to come to terms with the horrific story of his parents and their experiences during the Holocaust and in postwar America, in an omnibus edition of Spiegelman's two-part, Pulitzer Prize-winning best-seller.

"An undisputed classic and award-winning title (including a Pulitzer Prize in 1992) in which renowned cartoonist Spiegelman depicts his father's experiences as a World War II Nazi concentration camp survivor." Library Journal.

Spiegelman, Art **MetaMaus** : a look inside a modern classic / Art Spiegelman. Pantheon Books, c2011. 320 p. **B**

ISBN 9780375423949

1. Spiegelman, Art. 2. Spiegelman, Art. Maus. 3. Cartoonists -- United States 4. Modern literature -- 20th century -- History and criticism 5. Comic book writing 6. Jewish Americans 7. Autobiographies and memoirs

LC 2010052045

National Jewish Book Award, 2011.

A New Yorker contributor and co-founder of RAW traces the creative process that went into his Pulitzer Prize-winning classic, revealing the inspirations for his work while providing on an accompanying DVD a reference copy of The Complete Maus and audio interviews with his father.

"Informative about everything you may or may not have thought to ask about Maus and the Spiegelmans, this exhaustive purgative has been well organized and packaged and succeeds in being grimly entertaining, indeed almost addictive." Library Journal.

Spiegelman, Nadja

★Spiegelman, Nadja **I'm** supposed to protect you from all this : a memoir / Nadja Spiegelman. Riverhead Books, 2016. 288 p. **B**

ISBN 9781594631924

1. Spiegelman, Nadja. 2. Mouly, Francoise 3. Mothers and daughters. 4. Autobiographies and memoirs

LC 2016010834

The daughter of Maus creator Art Spiegelman and New Yorker art director Francoise Mouly describes her coming-of-age discovery of her mother's complicated childhood, her investigation into four generations of family women and her own efforts to reinvent herself in New York.

Spiegelman, Willard

Spiegelman, Willard **Senior** moments : looking back, looking ahead / Willard Spiegelman. Farrar, Straus and Giroux, 2016. 208 p. **B**

ISBN 9780374261221

1. Spiegelman, Willard. 2. Authors, American 3. College teachers 4. Aging -- Psychological aspects. 5. Reminiscing in old age 6. Essays. 7. Autobiographies and memoirs

LC 2015048666

An English professor and the former editor-in-chief of Southwest Review presents a collection of essays that describe the normal, and inevitable, aging process with candidness, humor, wisdom and elegance.

"Readers of a similar age will savor his delight in language and life as he ponders the past and peers into the future." Booklist.

Spielberg, Steven, 1947-

Haskell, Molly **Steven** Spielberg : a life in films / Molly Haskell. Yale University Press, 2017. 224 p. **B**

ISBN 9780300186932

1. Film producers and directors 2. Filmmaking 3. Jewish way of life 4. Films 5. Biographies

LC bl2016052714

A biography of the popular and talented film director describes how his unique and evocative gift for storytelling evolved from experiences in his own life, including his parents? traumatic divorce and his return to Judaism after his son was born.

"Compact, incisive, and wittya great starting point for those interested in Spielberg's life and art." Kirkus.

Spillman, Rob

Spillman, Rob **All** tomorrow's parties / Rob Spillman. Grove

Press, 2016. 400 p. **B**

ISBN 9780802124838

1. Authors 2. Creativity in men 3. Voyages and travels 4. Nonconformists 5. New York City 6. Berlin, Germany 7. West Berlin, Germany 8. East Berlin, Germany 9. Autobiographies and memoirs

LC 2016591800

In All Tomorrow's Parties, Spillman traces his past to craft a deeply affecting coming-of-age portrait of an artist's life that serves as an exhilarating cultural tour of the last quarter century through the lens of two transforming cities, drawing on musical inspiration from the Sex Pistols to Sonic Youth and the words of literary heroes such as Paul Bowles and Ken Kesey.

"Musically and culturally astute, this well-structured book is a delightful coming-of-age story couched within a travel narrative that deftly evokes one of the major historical moments of the 20th century. A richly detailed and always engaging memoir on artistic discovery." Kirkus.

Sprague, Kate Chase, 1840-1899

Oller, John **American** queen : the rise and fall of Kate Chase Sprague, Civil War "Belle of the North" and gilded age woman of scandal / John Oller. Da Capo Press, [2014] 288 p. **B**

ISBN 9780306822803

1. Sprague, Kate Chase, 1840-1899. 2. Chase, Salmon P. (Salmon Portland), 1808-1873. 3. Sprague, William, 1830-1915. 4. Socialites. 5. Ambition in women 6. Scandals 7. Extramarital affairs 8. Washington (D.C.) -- Social life and customs -- 19th century 9. United States -- Politics and government -- 19th century. 10. Biographies

LC 2014012054

Kate Chase, the charismatic daughter of Abraham Lincoln's treasury secretary, enjoyed unprecedented political power for a woman. As her widowed father's hostess, she set up a rival "court" against Mary Lincoln in hopes of making her father president and herself his First Lady. To facilitate that goal, she married one of the richest men in the country, the handsome "boy governor" of Rhode Island, in the social event of the Civil War. But when William Sprague turned out to be less of a prince as a husband, she found comfort in the arms of a powerful married senator. The ensuing scandal ended her virtual royalty, leaving her a social outcast who died in poverty. Yet in her final years she would find both greater authenticity and the inner peace that had always eluded her.

"Oller's work is less the story of a woman's political rise and fall and more one that reveals how the social limitations of the past created tragic outcomes for talented females. A well-researched, thoughtful biography of a woman who 'became entirely her own person, a rare feat for women of her day.'" Kirkus.

Springsteen, Bruce

Carlin, Peter Ames **Bruce** : the innocence, the darkness, the rising / Peter Ames Carlin. Simon & Schuster, 2012. 416 p. **B**

ISBN 9781439191828

1. Springsteen, Bruce. 2. E Street Band. 3. Singers -- United States 4. Rock musicians -- United States. 5. Rock music -- United States. 6. Popular music. 7. United States -- Popular culture -- History -- 20th century 8. Biographies

LC 2012020890

Carlin has produced the definitive biography of the Boss himself--rock legend Bruce Springsteen. Drawing upon unfettered access to the singer as well as his closest friends and colleagues, Carlin examines the depths of this iconic figure and his considerable music catalog.

"The author presents his subject as a supremely gifted musician and truly heroic figure, albeit one with a lot on his troubled mind." Kirkus.

★Springsteen, Bruce **Born** to run / Bruce Springsteen. Simon & Schuster, 2016. 512 p. **B**

ISBN 9781501141515

1. Springsteen, Bruce. 2. Rock musicians -- United States 3. Rock music 4. Men and success. 5. Celebrities 6. United States -- Popular culture -- History -- 20th century. 7. Autobiographies and memoirs

LC 2016016742

In a personal account inspired by the remarkable 2009 Super Bowl halftime show, a Rock and Roll Hall of Famer traces his life from his childhood in a Catholic New Jersey family and the musical experiences that prompted his career to the rise of the E Street Band and the stories behind some of his most famous songs.

"A superb memoir by any standard, but one of the best to have been written by a rock star." Kirkus.

Spurrier, Steve, 1945-

Spurrier, Steve, 1945- **Head** ball coach : my life in football, doing it differently--and winning / Steve Spurrier with Buddy Martin. Blue Rider Press, 2016 416 p. **B**

ISBN 9780399574665

1. Football coaches 2. Football 3. Former professional football players. 4. Autobiographies and memoirs

LC 2016029233

College football's most colorful, endearing, and successful pioneer, Steve Spurrier, shares his story of a life in football -- from growing up in Tennessee to winning the Heisman Trophy to playing and coaching in the pros to leading the Florida Gators to six SEC Championships and a National Championship to elevating the South Carolina program to new heights -- and coaching like nobody else.

Stack, Megan K.

Stack, Megan K. **Every** man in this village is a liar : an education in war / Megan K. Stack. Doubleday, c2010. 240 p. **B**

ISBN 9780385527163

1. Stack, Megan K. Travel Middle East. 2. War on Terrorism, 2001-2009 3. Terrorism -- Middle East -- History -- 21st century. 4. War and society -- Middle East. 5. Women war correspondents -- United States 6. Middle East -- History, Military -- 21st century. 7. Middle East -- Social conditions -- 21st century. 8. Middle East -- Description and travel. 9. Autobiographies and memoirs

LC 2009034473

National Book Award for Nonfiction finalist, 2010".

As a 25-year-old correspondent for the Los Angeles Times, Stack covered Afghanistan in the days immediately following 9/11, then traveled to other outposts in the war on terror, from Iraq to Iran, Libya, and Lebanon. In a disquieting series of essays, Stack now takes readers deep into the carnage where she was exposed to the insanity, innocence, and inhumanity of wars with no beginning, middle, or end. Her soaring imagery sears itself into the brain, in acute and accurate tales that should never be forgotten by the wider world, and yet always are." Booklist.

Stalin, Joseph, 1879-1953

Conquest, Robert **Stalin** : breaker of nations / Robert Conquest. Penguin Books, 1992, c1991. xvii, 346 p. : **B**

ISBN 0140169539

1. Stalin, Joseph, 1879-1953. 2. Politicians -- Soviet Union 3. Communists. 4. Soviet Union -- Politics and government. 5. Soviet Union -- History -- 1917-1953. 6. Biographies

LC 91028782

Reprint. Originally published: New York : Viking, 1991.

A portrait of the Soviet leader describes Stalin's childhood, his roles as student, revolutionary, and communist theoretician, his clash with Lenin, the great Terror, and the Nazi-Soviet pact.

"Intended for the general reader, [this work] provides a superb portrait of the man who terrorized his country for 30 years. Briskly written, authoritative yet not pedantic, filled with interesting incidents and anecdotes, [it] makes for fascinating reading." New York Times Book Review.

Khlevniuk, Oleg V. **Stalin** : new biography of a dictator / Oleg V. Khlevniuk ; translated by Nora S. Favorov. Yale University Press, 2015. 384 p. **B**

ISBN 9780300163889

1. Stalin, Joseph, 1879-1953. 2. Heads of state -- Soviet Union 3. Dictators -- Soviet Union 4. Political leadership. 5. Soviet Union -- Politics and government -- 1936-1953. 6. Biographies

LC 2014039237

"Readers with an interest in Soviet history, and those who can't wait for the next two volumes of Kotkin's Stalin, will appreciate this well-documented portrayal of a man whose despotic rule reverberates in Russia to this day." Library Journal.

★Kotkin, Stephen **Stalin** : paradoxes of power, 1878-1928 / Stephen Kotkin. Penguin Press, 2014 512 p. **B**

ISBN 9781594203794

1. Communist Party of the Soviet Union -- History 2. Heads of state -- Russia 3. Communism 4. Socialism 5. Russia -- History -- 20th century 6. Europe -- History -- 20th century 7. Soviet Union -- History -- Revolution, 1917-1921 8. Biographies

Pulitzer Prize for Biography or Autobiography finalist, 2015.

A first volume in an extensively researched portrait of the Soviet dictator provides intimate coverage of such topics as his rise from humble origins, the inner geography of the Bolshevik regime and the early formation of Stalin's fabricated trial process.

★Kotkin, Stephen **Stalin** : waiting for Hitler 1929-1941 / Stephen Kotkin. Penguin Press, 2017. 1154 p. **B**

ISBN 9781594203800

1. Communist Party of the Soviet Union -- History 2. Heads of state -- Russia 3. Communism 4. Socialism 5. Famines 6. Russia -- History -- 20th century 7. Europe -- History -- 20th century 8. Soviet Union -- History -- 1925-1953 9. Biographies

LC bl2017044852

Mark Lynton History Prize, 2018.History of the world during the build-up to World War II from the vantage point of Joseph Stalin's sea of power, exploring how in the aftermath of achieving dictatorial power over the Soviet Empire, Stalin formally ordered the systematic collectivization of the world's largest peasant economy.

"The John P. Birkelund Professor in History and International Affairs at Princeton University, Kotkin offers his second in a magisterial three-volume biography of Soviet leader Joseph Stalin, following Pulitzer Prize finalist Stalin. Vol. 1: Paradoxes of Power, 1878-1928." Library Journal.

Radzinskii, Edvard **Stalin** : the first in-depth biography based on explosive new documents from Russia's secret archives / Edvard Radzinsky ; translated by H.T. Willetts. Doubleday, [1997], c1996. xii, 607 p. : **B**

ISBN 0385479549

1. Stalin, Joseph, 1879-1953. 2. Heads of state -- Soviet Union 3. Soviet Union -- History -- 1925-1953. 4. Biographies

LC BL 99794376

Anchor Books imprint on spine.

Reprint. Originally published: c1996.

Presents a new version of the life of the Soviet dictator based on recently recovered documents.

"For this biography of the Soviet ruler the author has examined mountains of rare archival sources and interviewed many who lived through decades of Stalinist (mis)rule. The result is the best general biography of Stalin to date. Radzinsky strips away layer after layer of myth, falsehood, and enigma to produce a riveting portrait of a man whose primary role model was Ivan the Terrible." Library Journal.

★SebagMontefiore, Simon, 1965- **Stalin** : the court of the red tsar / Simon Sebag Montefiore. Knopf, 2004. xxvii, 785 p. : **B**

ISBN 9781400042302

1. Stalin, Joseph, 1879-1953. 2. Kremlin, Moscow. 3. Heads of state -- Soviet Union 4. Stalinism. 5. Communism -- History. 6. Doctors' Plot, 1953. 7. Soviet Union -- History -- 1925-1953. 8. Biographies

LC 2003027390

Originally published: London : Weidenfeld & Nicolson, 2003.

A biography of the Soviet dictator and the men and women who surrounded him focuses on the foundation of human, psychological, and physical supports that encouraged him through the early days of Communism, World War II, and the Great Terror.

"In the relentless detail, the mood-setting descriptions of the leader's surroundings, the sketches of the people around him and in Stalin's own words, pranks and tempers, Montefiore gives us not only the most intimate view of the general secretary that we have to date but a rounded and complex portrait of a man who could go from charming to lethal in the space of a few seconds." The Nation.

★Sebag-Montefiore, Simon, 1965- **Young** Stalin / Simon Sebag Montefiore. Alfred A. Knopf, 2007. xxxii, 460 p., 32 p. of plates : **B**

ISBN 1400044650

1. Stalin, Joseph, 1879-1953. 2. Heads of state -- Soviet Union 3. Dictators -- Soviet Union 4. Russia -- History -- 20th century 5. Biographies

LC 2007029220

Costa Biography Award, 2007.

Shortlisted for the James Tait Black Memorial Prize for Biography, 2007

Examines the turbulent early years of a man who would become the personification of twentieth-century evil, detailing his poverty-stricken youth, religious training, role as a fanatical revolutionary, many love affairs, and evolution into a murderous tyrant.

Service, Robert, 1947- **Stalin** : a biography / Robert Service. Belknap Press of Harvard University Press, 2005. xviii, 715 p., 24 p. of plates : **B**

ISBN 0674016971

1. Stalin, Joseph, 1879-1953. 2. Heads of state -- Soviet Union 3. Soviet Union -- History -- 1925-1953. 4. Biographies

LC 2004061115

"This book covers Stalin's life from his early, troubled years in a small town in Georgia to the pinnacle of power in the Kremlin. By providing such a rich and complex portrait of the dictator and the Soviet system, Service humanizes Stalin without ever diminishing the extent of the atrocities he unleashed upon the Soviet population." Publishers Weekly.

Suny, Ronald Grigor **Stalin** : passage to revolution / Ron-

ald Grigor Suny. Princeton Univ Press, 2020. 856 p. **B**
ISBN 9780691182032
1. Stalin, Joseph, 1879-1953. 2. Communists 3. Heads of state 4. Dictators 5. Soviet Union -- History -- 1917-1953 6. Biographies
LC 2019034217

This is the definitive biography of Joseph Stalin from his birth to the October Revolution of 1917, a panoramic and often chilling account of how an impoverished, idealistic youth from the provinces of tsarist Russia was transformed into a cunning and fearsome outlaw who would one day become one of the twentieth century's most ruthless dictators.

"A comprehensive, deeply researched study of one of the world's most brutal dictators as he took the paths that would lead him to power." Kirkus

Stallworth, Ron

Stallworth, Ron **Black** Klansman : race, hate, and the undercover investigation of a lifetime / Ron Stallworth. Flatiron Books, 2018, c2014. 191 p., 8 unnumbered p. of plates : **B**
ISBN 9781250299048
1. Ku-Klux Klan -- History 2. African American police 3. Undercover operations 4. White supremacy movements 5. Hate groups 6. Colorado -- History -- 20th century 7. Autobiographies and memoirs
LC 2018003659

"Originally published in 2014 under the same title by Police and Fire Publishing"--Title page verso.

Relates how African American detective Ron Stallworth went undercover to investigate the Ku Klux Klan in Colorado Springs in 1978, describing how he disrupted Klan activities and exposed white supremacists in the military during the months-long investigation.

Staniforth, Nate

Staniforth, Nate **Here** is real magic : a magician's search for wonder in the modern world / Nate Staniforth. Bloomsbury, 2018. 288 p. **B**
ISBN 9781632864246
1. Staniforth, Nate. 2. Magicians. 3. Sense of wonder. 4. Magic 5. Autobiographies and memoirs
LC 2017016409

Chronicling his evolution from an obsessed young magician to a broken wanderer and back again, the former host of the Discovery Channel's international hit TV show Breaking Magic tells the story of his rediscovery of astonishment and the importance of wonder in everyday life.

"The result is a personal story that conjures up the wonder and magic of life without any trickery or deceit." Publishers Weekly.

Stanley, Paul

Stanley, Paul **Backstage** pass : the Starchild's all-access guide to the good life / Paul Stanley. Harperone, 2019 256 p. **B**
ISBN 9780062820280
1. Kiss (Musical group) 2. Rock musicians -- United States 3. Self improvement 4. Rock groups -- United States 5. Rock music 6. United States -- Social life and customs -- 20th century 7. Autobiographies and memoirs
LC 2019004755

The legendary front man and rhythm guitarist of KISS offers an anecdotal tour of his personal life and celebrity relationships, offering insights into the creative perspectives that have shaped his career and family dynamics.

Stanton, Edwin M. (Edwin McMasters), 1814-1869

Marvel, William **Lincoln's** autocrat : the life of Edwin Stanton / William Marvel. The University of North Carolina Press, 2015. 624 p. **B**
ISBN 9781469622491
1. Stanton, Edwin M. (Edwin McMasters), 1814-1869. 2. Lincoln, Abraham, 1809-1865 Friends and associates. 3. United States. War Department 4. Cabinet officers -- United States 5. Politicians -- United States 6. Reconstruction (United States history) 7. United States Civil War, 1861-1865 8. United States -- History -- Civil War, 1861-1865 9. Biographies
LC 2014032690

Edwin M. Stanton (1814-1869), one of the nineteenth century's most impressive legal and political minds, wielded enormous influence and power as Lincoln's Secretary of War during most of the Civil War and under Johnson during the early years of Reconstruction. In the first full biography of Stanton in more than fifty years, William Marvel offers a detailed reexamination of Stanton's life, career, and legacy.

"A complex work that will appeal to Civil War scholars and general readers who want a deeper treatment of Stanton than found in Doris Kearns Goodwin's Team of Rivals." Library Journal.

★Stahr, Walter **Stanton** : Lincoln's war secretary / Walter Stahr. Simon & Schuster, 2017 480 p. **B**
ISBN 9781476739304
1. Stanton, Edwin M. (Edwin McMasters), 1814-1869. 2. Lincoln, Abraham, 1809-1865 Friends and associates. 3. United States. War Department 4. Cabinet officers 5. Politicians 6. Reconstruction (United States history) 7. United States Civil War, 1861-1865 8. United States -- History -- Civil War, 1861-1865 9. Biographies
LC 2017022628

Walter Stahr, award-winning author of the New York Times bestseller Seward, tells the story of Abraham Lincoln's indispensable Secretary of War, Edwin Stanton, the man the president entrusted with raising the army that preserved the Union.

"A lively, lucid, and opinionated history, and his research supports his skepticism on some historical claims. The book should be Stanton's definitive biography for some time to come." Kirkus.

Stanton, Elizabeth Cady, 1815-1902

Ginzberg, Lori D. **Elizabeth** Cady Stanton : an American life / Lori D. Ginzberg. Hill and Wang, 2009. 272 p. **B**
ISBN 9780809094936
1. Stanton, Elizabeth Cady, 1815-1902. 2. Feminists -- United States 3. Women's rights -- History -- 19th century. 4. Suffrage. 5. Suffragist Movement -- United States -- History. 6. United States -- History -- 19th century. 7. Biographies
LC 2008054395

Historian Lori D. Ginzberg narrates the life of a woman of great charm, enormous appetite, and extraordinary intellectual gifts who turned the limitations placed on women like herself into a universal philosophy of equal rights.

"Ginzberg has produced a readable and realistic account of the life of one of the most important feminists and intellectuals of the 19th century, a woman who was at once an abolitionist who could sound like a racist and an advocate of civil rights for women whose language often reeked of elitism." Library Journal.

Staples, Mavis

Kot, Greg **I'll** take you there : Mavis Staples, the Staple Singers, and the march up freedom's highway / Greg Kot. Scribner,

2014. 320 p. **B**

ISBN 9781451647853

1. Staples, Mavis. 2. Staple Singers (Musical group) 3. Gospel musicians -- United States 4. Women gospel singers. 5. Civil Rights Movement 6. Biographies

LC 2013032633

Though Mavis Staples has recently enjoyed a career resurgence as a solo artist, she's probably best known for singing with her family on the church circuit in Chicago before they made their way up the charts with songs like "I'll Take You There." In addition to describing their movements though gospel, R&B, and even disco, author Greg Kot also details friendships with other artists, like Bob Dylan and Aretha Franklin, and their involvement with the civil rights movement. Check out I'll Take You There for full immersion in the Mavis Staples sound.

"Kot's effort remains clear and respectful and takes us deep into the golden age of Mavis and her marvelously talented group." Publishers Weekly.

Stark, Lizzie

Stark, Lizzie **Pandora's** DNA : tracing the breast cancer genes through history, science, and one family tree / Lizzie Stark. Chicago Review Press, [2014] 336 p. **B**

ISBN 9781613748602

1. Stark, Lizzie Health. 2. Mastectomy 3. Coping in women 4. Breast cancer -- Genetic aspects 5. BRCA genes. 6. Autobiographies and memoirs

LC 2014018310

ALA Notable Book, 2015.

Would you cut out your healthy breasts and ovaries if you thought it might save your life? That's not a theoretical question for journalist Lizzie Stark's relatives, who grapple with the horrific legacy of cancer built into the family DNA. It is a BRCA mutation that has robbed most of her female relatives of breasts, ovaries, peace of mind, or life itself. In Pandora's DNA, Stark uses her family's experience to frame a larger story about the so-called breast cancer genes, exploring the morass of legal quandaries, scientific developments, medical breakthroughs, and ethical concerns that surround the BRCA mutations.

"The book is a must-read for women questioning whether to be tested for the BRCA mutations and for women considering their options after testing positive. A gutsy, deeply revealing account that more than fulfills the promise of the subtitle." Kirkus.

Starr, Ringo, 1940-

Starr, Ringo, 1940- **Photograph** / Ringo Starr. Genesis Publications, 2015 304 p. **B**

ISBN 9781905662333

1. Beatles (Musical group) 2. Rock musicians -- England 3. Drummers 4. Rock music 5. Autobiographies and memoirs

LC bl2015040020

The world-famous drummer opens his photographic archives to share memories of his childhood, his time with The Beatles and beyond.

Stavis, R. H.

Stavis, R. H. **Sister** of darkness : the chronicles of a modern exorcist / Rachel H. Stavis, with Sarah Durand. Dey Street Books, 2017. 320 p. **B**

ISBN 9780062656148

1. Exorcism. 2. Exorcists. 3. Psychic trauma. 4. Good and evil. 5. Autobiographies and memoirs

LC 2017278044

A rare non-denominational exorcist, the subject of a forthcoming major motion picture, shares the story of her work wrestling hostile entities from infected souls, in an account that also offers her insights into how pain and trauma can make people vulnerable to energy-draining negative forces.

Stefanovic, Sofija

Stefanovic, Sofija **Miss** ex-Yugoslavia : a memoir / Sofija Stefanovic. Atria Books 2018 256 p. **B**

ISBN 9781501165740

1. Authors 2. Immigrants 3. Subcultures 4. Women authors 5. Australia 6. Yugoslavia 7. Autobiographies and memoirs

LC 2017045539

A memoir from the Manhattan-based Serbian-Australian writer and host of a best-selling literary salon describes growing up amidst ethnic tensions and violent totalitarian leaders as well as rock music, terrible crushes and protest rallies.

Stein, Gertrude, 1874-1946

Malcolm, Janet **Two** lives : Gertrude and Alice / Janet Malcolm. Yale University Press, 2007. 240 p. **B**

ISBN 9780300125511

1. Stein, Gertrude, 1874-1946. 2. Toklas, Alice B., 1877-1967. 3. Authors, American -- 20th century 4. Americans in France. 5. Intellectual life -- Paris, France -- 20th century. 6. Biographies

LC 2007012085

Presents an investigation of the lives and works of Gertrude Stein and Alice B. Toklas.

"This is a vital addition to Stein criticism as well as an important work that critiques the political responsibility of the artist (even a genius) to the larger world." Publishers Weekly.

Steinbeck, John, 1902-1968

Souder, William, 1949- **Mad** at the world : a life of John Steinbeck / William Souder. W. W. Norton & Company, 2020 xiv, 446 p. **B**

ISBN 9780393292268

1. Steinbeck, John, 1902-1968. 2. Authors, American. 3. Empathy in men 4. Misanthropy 5. Injustice. 6. Biographies

LC 2020017019

Explores how John Steinbeck's complicated persona and firsthand struggles through the depths of the Great Depression gave him deeply empathic perspectives that shaped his politics and his evocative characters and themes.

"Steinbeck fans could not ask for a more nuanced account of this troubled giant of American literature." Publishers Weekly

Steinbeck, John, 1902-1968 **Travels** with Charley : in search of America / John Steinbeck. Penguin Books, 2002, c1962. 214 p. : **B**

ISBN 0142000701

1. Steinbeck, John, 1902-1968 Travel United States. 2. Authors, American -- 20th century. 3. Automobile travel. 4. Men and dogs. 5. Poodles. 6. United States -- Description and travel.

LC 2001055444

"John Steinbeck centennial edition (1902-2002)."

Originally published: New York : Viking Press, 1962.

Author John Steinbeck was 58 when he set out to rediscover the country he had been writing about for so many years. With his elderly French poodle, Charley, he embarked on a quest across America, from the northermost tip of Maine to California's Monterey Peninsula. Traveling the interstates and the country roads, they stopped to smell America: truckers and strangers, old friends and new acquaintances. Steinbeck's poignant, perceptive reflections reveal the American character: a blend of unexpected kindnesses and racial hostilities, loneliness and humor.

Steinberg, Avi

Steinberg, Avi The **happily** ever after : a memoir of an unlikely romance novelist / Avi Steinberg. Nan A. Talese/Doubleday, 2020. 272 p. **B**

ISBN 9780385540254

1. Journalists 2. Romance writing 3. Romance writers 4. Divorced men 5. Autobiographies and memoirs

LC 2019049254

Is romance dead? Is that why there are so many vampires in today's romance novels? When Avi Steinberg's love life took a grim turn, he did what he always does: He consulted his old books, the usual cast of Great (Very Serious, Usually Male) Authors. And he immediately realized that these books were part of the problem. Instead, he began to read romances, the books he--like so many of us--have been conditioned to dismiss as "trashy." What he discovered was a genre that was tremendously diverse and daring, along with a vast network of innovative writers who were keeping the novel as alive as ever. His own relationship problems, he realized, came down to a failure of his imagination. And so he set out on a quest to write and publish a romance novel and to find real-life love.

"A journalist offers insight into the romance genre while recounting his own unexpected transformation into a romance novelist. . . . A quirky and informative memoir." Kirkus

Steinberg, Saul, 1914-1999

Bair, Deirdre **Saul** Steinberg : a biography / Deirdre Bair. Nan A. Talese/Doubleday, 2012. 752 p. **B**

ISBN 9780385524483

1. United States. Navy Officers 2. New Yorker (New York, N.Y. : 1925) 3. Artists 4. Cartoonists 5. Immigrants 6. World War II 7. Biographies

LC 2011050601

A definitive portrait of one of The New Yorker's most iconic artists includes coverage of his education in Milan, extensive service during World War II, marriage to artist Hedda Sterne and relationships with such contemporaries as Saul Bellow, Vladimir Nabokov and Le Corbusier. By the National Book Award-winning author of Samuel Beckett.

Steinem, Gloria, 1934-

Steinem, Gloria, 1934- **My** life on the road / Gloria Steinem Random House, 2015 304 p. **B**

ISBN 9780679456209

1. Feminists. 2. Women 3. Feminism -- United States. 4. Intersectionality 5. Biographies

LC 2015010718

A feminist activist and co-founder of Ms. magazine presents a memoir comprised of reflections on definitive events in her career, from her time on the campaign trail and interactions with forefront political leaders to her visits to India and her encounters with "civilian" feminists.

"Illuminating and inspiring, this book presents a distinguished woman's exhilarating vision of what it means to live with openness, honesty, and a willingness to grow beyond the apparent confinement of seemingly irreconcilable polarities. An invigoratingly candid memoir from a giant of women's rights." Kirkus.

Stengel, Casey, 1890-1975

Appel, Marty **Casey** Stengel : the greatest character in baseball / Marty Appel. Doubleday, [2017] 336 p. **B**

ISBN 9780385540476

1. Baseball managers 2. Baseball players 3. Baseball 4. Biographies

LC 2016027618

Never-before-published family documents and new interviews enhance this detailed biography of quirky, legendary baseball player-turned-manager Casey Stengel, who led the New York Yankees to eight pennants and was known for keeping a live sparrow under his hat during ball games. Other ballplayers, like Yogi Berra and Mickey Mantle, appear throughout, and while the focus is on baseball, author Marty Appel chronicles Stengel's full life off the field as well (including a brief, pre-baseball stint in dentistry).

Creamer, Robert W. **Stengel** : his life and times / Robert W. Creamer. University of Nebraska Press, [1996], c1984. 349 p. : **B**

ISBN 0803263678

1. Stengel, Casey, 1890-1975 Anecdotes 2. Professional baseball managers 3. Baseball players -- United States 4. Baseball -- History -- 20th century 5. United States -- Social life and customs -- 20th century 6. Biographies

LC 95040143

Originally published: New York : Simon and Schuster, c1984. With new introd."Bison books"--P. preceding t.p.

Includes index."

Casey Stengel is remembered as either the shrewd, innovative New York Yankee manager who won 10 pennants and seven World Series from 1949 to 1960 or as the seemingly senile, aged master of malaprop who (mis)-managed the legendarily inept New York Mets in the early 1960s. Creamer . dissolves the apparently disparate images and melds them into an inclusive vision of an unexpectedly complex man." Booklist.

Stern, Amanda

Stern, Amanda **Little** panic : dispatches from an anxious life / Amanda Stern. Grand Central Publishing, 2018. viii, 389 pages : **B**

ISBN 9781538711927

1. Anxiety 2. Growing up 3. Anxiety in women 4. Fear 5. Autobiographies and memoirs

LC 2017963706

Presents a relatable, darkly comic memoir about her lifelong struggles with anxiety, tracing her upbringing by a bohemian mother and sanitized, affluent father in a transforming New York City.

Stern, Fritz, 1926-

Stern, Fritz, 1926- **Five** Germanys I have known / Fritz Stern. Farrar, Straus and Giroux, 2006. 546 p. : **B**

ISBN 0374155402

1. Historians -- Germany -- History -- 20th century. 2. Historians -- Germany 3. Germany -- History -- 20th century. 4. Autobiographies and memoirs

LC 2006000060

Includes index.

A dual memoir and history by a celebrated scholar explores the dilemma posed by Germany's status as both a civilized nation and a country responsible for some of the western world's greatest horrors, in an account that profiles his homeland as the Weimar, the Third Reich, the postwar West and East Germanys, and a unified country after 1990.

"In this memoir, Stern looks back over the five Germanys his generation has seenthe Weimar Republic, Nazi tyranny, the post-1945 Federal Republic, the Soviet-controlled German Democratic Republic and, lastly, the reunited Germany of the presentand explains how he came to reconcile himself with his birth country (which his Jewish family fled in 1938) as it has come to terms with its new place in today's more cohesive and peaceful Europe. The book's intriguing structure makes it a wonderful combination of history, memoir, analysis and even poetry." Publishers Weekly.

Stevens, John Paul, 1920-2019

Stevens, John Paul, 1920-2019 The **making** of a justice : reflections on my first 94 years / John Paul Stevens. Little Brown & Co 2019 560 p. **B**

ISBN 9780316489645

1. United States. Supreme Court. 2. Judges. 3. Federal judges. 4. Criminal justice system. 5. Federal courts. 6. Autobiographies and memoirs

LC 2018962439

The former Supreme Court justice provides a personal account of his youth, his early days in private practice, and some of the most important Supreme Court decisions from his thirty-four-year tenure.

Stevenson, Bryan

★Stevenson, Bryan **Just** mercy : a story of justice and redemption / Bryan Stevenson. Spiegel & Grau, 2014. x, 336 p. ; **B**

ISBN 9780812994520

1. Justice 2. Redemption 3. Lawyers 4. Social advocates 5. Alabama 6. Autobiographies and memoirs

ALA Notable Book, 2015.

Andrew Carnegie Medal for Excellence in Non-Fiction, 2015.

Kirkus Prize for Nonfiction finalist, 2014.

The founder of the Equal Justice Initiative in Montgomery, Alabama recounts his experiences as a lawyer working to assist those desperately in need, reflecting on his pursuit of the ideal of compassion in American justice.

"Stevenson details changes in victims rights, incarceration of juveniles, death penalty reforms, inflexible sentencing laws, and the continued practices of injustice that see too many juveniles, minorities, and mentally ill people imprisoned in a frenzy of mass incarceration in the U.S. A passionate account of the ways our nation thwarts justice and inhumanely punishes the poor and disadvantaged." Booklist.

Stewart, Rory

Stewart, Rory The **prince** of the marshes : and other occupational hazards of a year in Iraq / Rory Stewart. Harvest Books, 2007, c2006. 432 p. **B**

ISBN 0156032791

1. Stewart, Rory. 2. British in Iraq. 3. Iraq War, 2003-2011 4. Governors. 5. Strategic alliances (Military) 6. Iraq -- Description and travel. 7. Iraq -- Social life and customs -- 21st century. 8. Autobiographies and memoirs

LC bl2007009349

Originally published: Orlando, FL : Harcourt, 2006.

Recounts how the author, a British diplomat, was named deputy governor of Amarah and Nasiriya in southern Iraq at the end of 2003, an appointment during which he negotiated hostage releases, held elections, and worked to organize a social infrastructure for millions of beleaguered Iraqi citizens.

"In 2003, Stewart, a former British diplomat, joined the Coalition Provisional Authority in Iraq and was posted to the southern province of Maysan, where he found himself the de-facto governor of a restive populace whose allegiances were split among fifty-four political parties, twenty major tribes, and numerous militias. Stewart's account of his attempts to placate the various local figures who continually threaten to kill each other, or him, is both shrewd and self-deprecating." The New Yorker.

Stilwell, Joseph Warren, 1883-1946

Tuchman, Barbara W. (Barbara Wertheim), 1912-1989 **Stilwell** and the American experience in China, 1911-45 / Barbara W. Tuchman. Grove Press, 2001, c1970. xv, 621 p. : **B**

ISBN 0802138527

1. Stilwell, Joseph Warren, 1883-1946. 2. Military attaches -- United States. 3. World War II -- China. 4. International relations. 5. Revolutions -- China. 6. United States -- Foreign relations China. 7. China -- Foreign relations United States. 8. China -- History -- 1912-1949. 9. China -- Politics and government -- 1912-1949.

LC 2001040154

Originally published: New York : Macmillan, 1970.

Pulitzer Prize for General Nonfiction, 1972.

Joseph Stilwell was the military attaché to China in 1935 to 1939, commander of United States forces, and allied chief of staff to Chiang Kai-shek in 1942-44. His story unfolds against the background of China's history, from the revolution of 1911 to the turmoil of World War II, when China's Nationalist government faced attack from Japanese invaders and Communist insurgents.

Stoker, Bram, 1847-1912

★Skal, David J. **Something** in the blood : the untold story of Bram Stoker, the man who wrote Dracula / David J. Skal. Liveright, 2015 448 p. **B**

ISBN 9781631490101

1. Stoker, Bram, 1847-1912. 2. Authors, English -- 19th century 3. Theatrical managers -- Great Britain 4. Horror story writing. 5. Dracula, Count (Fictitious character) 6. Biographies

LC 2016028093

A groundbreaking biography reveals the haunted origins of the man who created Dracula and traces the psychosexual contours of late Victorian society.

"An engagingly written, well-documented biography of a famous writer we all think we know, even if we really dont." Booklist.

Stokes, Rose Pastor, 1879-1933

Hochschild, Adam **Rebel** Cinderella : from rags to riches to radical, the epic journey of Rose Pastor Stokes / Adam Hochschild. Houghton Mifflin Harcourt, 2020. 304 p. **B**

ISBN 9781328866745

1. Feminists 2. Women socialists 3. Women political activists 4. Protests, demonstrations, vigils, etc. 5. New York City 6. United States -- History -- 1900-1945 7. United States -- Politics and government 8. Biographies

LC 2019027932

From the bestselling author of King Leopold's Ghost and Spain in Our Hearts comes the astonishing but forgotten story of an immigrant sweatshop worker who married an heir to a great American fortune and became one of the most charismatic radical leadersof her time.

"Hochschild's captivating and fast-paced biography is a true delight and an excellent addition to women's history shelves." Booklist

Stone, Alex

Stone, Alex **Fooling** Houdini : magicians, mentalists, math geeks, and the hidden powers of the mind / Alex Stone. Harper, 2012. 320 p. **B**

ISBN 9780061766213

1. Stone, Alex. 2. Magicians -- United States 3. Magic -- Psychological aspects. 4. Magic tricks 5. Magic -- Social aspects. 6. Autobiographies and memoirs

LC 2011041927

A biography of magician Alex Stone, his quest to join the ranks of master magicians and the interesting characters he meets along the way.

Stone, I. F. (Isidor Feinstein), 1907-1989

Guttenplan, D. D. **American** radical : the life and times of I. F. Stone / D. D. Guttenplan. Farrar, Straus and Giroux, 2009. 592 p. **B**

ISBN 9780374183936

1. Stone, I. F. (Isidor Feinstein), 1907-1989. 2. Journalists -- United States -- 20th century 3. Investigative journalists -- United States 4. Jewish Americans 5. Jewish American men 6. Biographies

LC 2009009667

"Guttenplan's lively biography brings back to life a man whose work has often been forgotten but whose writing and life provide a model for the kind of freethinking journalism missing in society today." Publishers Weekly.

★MacPherson, Myra **All** governments lie : the life and times of rebel journalist I.F. Stone / Myra MacPherson. Scribner, 2006. xxvi, 564 p., 8 p. of plates : **B**

ISBN 0684807130

1. Stone, I. F., 1907-1989. 2. Journalists -- United States 3. Biographies

LC 2006042389

A portrait of the twentieth-century independent journalist offers insight into his outspoken, five-decade pursuit of truthful, anti-establishment journalism, in an account that includes coverage of his denouncements of Cold War policies, McCarthyism, and the Vietnam Gulf of Tonkin incident.

"This biography interweaves his life and journalism within the context of the social and political era, providing an engaging overview of a complex man who challenged his contemporaries. Many of the political issues Stone confronted will resonate with today's readers." Library Journal.

Stone, Oliver

Stone, Oliver **Chasing** the light : writing, directing, and surviving Platoon, Midnight Express, Scarface, Salvador, and the movie game / Oliver Stone. Houghton Mifflin Harcourt, 2020. 304 p. **B**

ISBN 9780358346234

1. Stone, Oliver. 2. Film producers and directors -- United States 3. Screenwriters 4. Vietnam veterans 5. Screenplay writing 6. New York City 7. Autobiographies and memoirs

LC 2020003631

Includes index.

A memoir by the controversial and outspoken Oscar-winning director and screenwriter includes coverage of his complicated New York childhood, service in Vietnam, cocaine addiction and creative struggles and triumphs in 1970s and 1980s Hollywood.

"In the often tacky world of movie memoirs, Stone's will stand out for its hard-earned insights, integrity, and grace." Kirkus

Stone, Robert, 1937-

Bell, Madison Smartt **Child** of light : a biography of Robert Stone / Madison Smartt Bell. Doubleday, 2020. 608 p. **B**

ISBN 9780385541602

1. Authors, American -- 20th century 2. Writing 3. Drug addiction 4. Interpersonal relations 5. Biographies

LC 2019022780

A portrait of American novelist Robert Stone traces his relationship with a mentally unstable mother, his military service, his Stanford education, his membership in the Merry Pranksters and the publication of such novels as the award-winning <I>Dog Soldiers</I>.

"Perhaps not the last word on Stone but essential for students and fans of the writer's works." Kirkus

Stossel, Scott

Stossel, Scott **My** age of anxiety : fear, hope, dread, and the search for peace of mind / Scott Stossel. Alfred A. Knopf, 2013. 416 p. **B**

ISBN 9780307269874

1. Stossel, Scott. 2. Anxiety. 3. Panic attacks 4. Anxiety disorders. 5. Anxiety -- Treatment. 6. Autobiographies and memoirs

LC 2013006336

The author recounts his lifelong battle with anxiety, showing the many manifestations of the disorder as well as the countless treatments that have been developed to counteract it, and provides a history of the efforts to understand this common form of mental illness.

"[T]he author's beautiful prose and careful research combine to make this book informative, thoughtful and fun to read. Powerful, eye-opening and funny." Kirkus.

Stowe, Harriet Beecher, 1811-1896

Hedrick, Joan D., 1944- **Harriet** Beecher Stowe : a life / Joan D. Hedrick. Oxford University Press, 1994. xviii, 507 p. : **B**

ISBN 0195066391

1. Women and literature -- United States -- History -- 19th century. 2. Authors, American -- 19th century 3. Abolitionists -- United States -- History 4. Women abolitionists 5. Biographies

LC 93016610

Pulitzer Prize for Biography or Autobiography, 1995."

This biography brings to life not just the complex and fascinating woman and writer but also the 19th-century America that shaped her and was in turn shaped by her. Hedrick manages to weave into his immensely readable biography a history teeming with the domestic detail of the famous Beecher clan, the settling of the West, and the impact of the Civil War and the abolition movement." Library Journal.

Strauss, Richard, 1864-1949

Kennedy, Michael, 1926- **Richard** Strauss / Michael Kennedy. Clarendon Press, 1995. 250 p. **B**

ISBN 0198165811

1. Strauss, Richard, 1864-1949. 2. Composers -- Germany -- 19th century 3. Germany -- Social life and customs -- 19th century 4. Biographies

LC 95021613

Strayed, Cheryl, 1968-

★Strayed, Cheryl, 1968- **Wild** : from lost to found on the Pacific Crest Trail / Cheryl Strayed. Alfred A. Knopf, 2012. 315 p. : **B**

ISBN 9780307592736

1. Strayed, Cheryl, 1968- Travel Pacific Crest Trail. 2. Authors, American -- 21st century 3. Hiking -- Pacific Crest Trail 4. Loss (Psychology) 5. Grief in women 6. Pacific Crest Trail -- Description and travel. 7. Autobiographies and memoirs

LC 2011033752

Ttraces the personal crisis the author endured after the death of her mother and a painful divorce, which prompted her ambition to undertake a dangerous 1,100-mile solo hike that both drove her to rock bottom and helped her to heal.

Strayhorn, Billy

Claerbaut, A. Alyce, **Strayhorn** : an illustrated life / edited by

A. Alyce Claerbaut and David Schlesinger. Bolden, 2015. xii, 196 p. : B

ISBN 9781932841985

1. Strayhorn, Billy. 2. Composers -- United States 3. Jazz musicians -- United States 4. Composers -- United States -- Pictorial works 5. Jazz musicians -- United States -- Pictorial works

LC 2015021651

Featuring commentary from Lena Horne, Clark Terry, Nancy Wilson, Terell Stafford and more, an array of essays, photos and ephemera celebrates one of the most significant yet under-appreciated contributors to 20th century American music, describing his triumph over adversity, early success and open homosexuality. Includes timeline and list of recommended resources.

Streisand, Barbra

Mann, William J. **Hello,** gorgeous : becoming Barbra Streisand / William J. Mann. Houghton Mifflin Harcourt, 2012. 496 p. B

ISBN 9780547368924

1. Streisand, Barbra. 2. Women singers -- United States 3. Jewish American women 4. Film actors and actresses -- United States 5. Women entertainers 6. United States -- Social life and customs -- 20th century. 7. Biographies

LC 2012016364

Traces the formative years of the Academy Award-winning actress and platinum album music artist, providing coverage of such topics as her relationship with her mother, her marriage to Elliott Gould and the making of Funny Girl against a backdrop of the birth of off-off-Broadway.

Strindberg, August, 1849-1912

Prideaux, Sue **Strindberg** : a life / Sue Prideaux. Yale University Press, c2012. 371 p. B

ISBN 9780300136937

1. Strindberg, August, 1849-1912. 2. Authors, Swedish -- 19th century 3. Dramatists. 4. Poets. 5. Authors. 6. Biographies

LC 2011038050

The author looks at the life of the playwright best known for the work Miss Julie, paying special attention to how real life inspired the ideas, premises and characters of his plays and other literary works.

Stritch, Elaine

Jacobs, Alexandra (Editor) **Still** here : the madcap, nervy, singular life of Elaine Stritch / Alexandra Jacobs. Farrar, Straus and Giroux, 2019. 352 p. B

ISBN 9780374268091

1. Actors and actresses 2. Alcoholic women 3. Theater -- Broadway, New York City 4. Women entertainers -- United States 5. New York City 6. United States -- Social life and customs -- 20th century 7. Biographies

LC 2019020220

A full chronicle of the Tony Award-winning star's life and career includes coverage of her upbringing in Depression-era Detroit, her psychologically fraught creative collaborations, her struggles with addiction and her Tony Award-winning performances.

Stuart, Granville, 1834-1918

Milner, Clyde A., 1948- **As** big as the West : the pioneer life of Granville Stuart / Clyde A. Milner II and Carol A. O'Connor. Oxford University Press, 2008. xvi, 430 p., 32 p. of plates : B

ISBN 9780195127096

1. Stuart, Granville, 1834-1918. 2. Pioneers -- Montana 3. Frontier and pioneer life -- Montana. 4. Ranchers -- Montana 5. Ranch life -- Montana -- History. 6. Biographies

LC 2008011980

A narrative biography traces Granville Stuart's trajectory from his youth in an Iowa agricultural settlement, to his rough-and-tumble life in Montana and his rise to prominence as a public figure in the American West, in a study that illuminates the conflicting realities of the frontier.

Stuart, Jeb, 1833-1864

Wert, Jeffry D. **Cavalryman** of the lost cause : a biography of J.E.B. Stuart / Jeffry D. Wert. Simon & Schuster, 2008. 512 p. B

ISBN 9780743278195

1. Stuart, Jeb, 1833-1864. 2. Confederate States of America. Army 3. Confederate States of America. Army. Cavalry 4. Generals -- Confederate States of America 5. Military history -- 19th century 6. Military strategy -- History -- 19th century. 7. Interpersonal relations. 8. United States -- History -- Civil War, 1861-1865 -- Campaigns 9. United States -- History -- Civil War, 1861-1865 -- Cavalry operations. 10. Biographies

LC 2007051552

A balanced portrait of the controversial Confederate cavalryman describes his military contributions, contentious relationships with his staff and subordinates, and battlefield death at the age of thirty-one.

Styron, William, 1925-2006

Styron, William, 1925-2006 **Darkness** visible : a memoir of madness / William Styron. Vintage Books, 1992, c1990. 84 p. ; B

ISBN 0679736395

1. Styron, William, 1925-2006 Mental health 2. People with depression. 3. Authors, American 4. Men with depression 5. Mental illness 6. United States -- Social life and customs 7. Autobiographies and memoirs

LC 91050032

Originally published: New York : Random House, c1990.

The author chronicles his descent into depression, discussing not only his own experience and recovery but also how others can find help

"The book's virtues considerable are twofold. First, it is a pitiless and chastened record of a nearly fatal human trial far commoner than assumed, and then a literary discourse on the ways and means of our cultural discontents." Publishers Weekly.

Styron, William, 1925-2006 **My** generation : collected nonfiction / William Styron ; edited by James L. W. West III. Random House, [2015] 624 p. B

ISBN 9780812997057

1. Authors, American. 2. United States -- Social life and customs 3. Essays. 4. Autobiographies and memoirs

LC 2014038029

Includes index."

Including significant previously uncollected material, My Generation is the definitive gathering of the fruits of this beloved writer's five decades of public life. Here is the William Styron unafraid to peer into the darkest corners of the 20th century or to take on the complex racial legacy of the United States. But here too is Styron writing about his daily walk with his dog, musing on the Modern Library's "100 Greatest Books," and offering personal insight into the extraordinary array of noted contemporary figures he interacted with over the course of an illustrious career. These are the people and events, tragic and joyful, historical and intimate, that aroused Styron's unrivalled curiosity"-- Provided by publisher.

"Elegant and entertaining, the writings in My Generation compose a definitive volume that will appeal to a broad audience. Summing Up: Highly recommended. Lower-division undergraduates through faculty; general readers." Choice.

Sullivan, Ed, 1901-1974

Maguire, James, 1959- **Impresario** : the life and times of Ed Sullivan / James Maguire. Billboard Books, 2006. vii, 344 p. : **B**

ISBN 9780823079629

1. Sullivan, Ed, 1901-1974. 2. Ed Sullivan show (Television program) 3. Television personalities -- United States 4. Biographies.

LC 2005933953

Sultan, Tim

Sultan, Tim **Sunny's** nights : lost and found at a bar on the edge of the world / Tim Sultan. Random House, [2016] 224 p. **B**

ISBN 9781400067275

1. Sultan, Tim. 2. Bartenders -- New York City 3. Bars (Drinking establishments) 4. Friendship 5. Bartending 6. Brooklyn, New York City -- Social life and customs. 7. Red Hook, New York -- Social life and customs. 8. Autobiographies and memoirs

LC 2015019985

An ode to the dive bars of New York and the author's friendships with some of the world's most charismatic bar owners describes their remarkable celebrity encounters against a backdrop of a rapidly transforming urban community.

Summitt, Pat Head, 1952-2016

Cornelius, Maria M. The **final** season : the perseverance of Pat Summitt / Maria M. Cornelius foreword by Candace Parker. The University of Tennessee Press, 2016 xvii, 311 p. ; **B**

ISBN 9781621902720

1. Summitt, Pat Head, 1952-2016. 2. Lady Volunteers (Basketball team). 3. Basketball coaches -- United States 4. Alzheimer's disease -- Patients

LC 2016009421

Includes index.

Summitt, Pat Head, 1952- **Sum** it up : 1,098 victories, a couple of irrelevant losses, and a life in perspective / Pat Summitt with Sally Jenkins. Crown, 2013. 256 p. **B**

ISBN 9780385346870

1. Women basketball coaches -- United States 2. College basketball 3. Basketball for women 4. People with Alzheimer's disease -- United States 5. Autobiographies and memoirs

LC 2012050333

Describes how Summitt's upbringing helped her to develop a balanced coaching style that contributed to the Tennessee Vols record-breaking wins, recounting her recent personal battle against early onset Alzheimer's disease.

Sundaram, Anjan

Sundaram, Anjan **Bad** news : last journalists in a dictatorship / Anjan Sundaram. Doubleday, [2015] 208 p. **B**

ISBN 9780385539562

1. Sundaram, Anjan Travel Rwanda. 2. Journalism -- Study and teaching 3. Journalists 4. Censorship 5. Despotism 6. Rwanda 7. Africa 8. Autobiographies and memoirs

LC 2015005625

The author recounts his time spent in Kigali, Rwanda running a journalists' training program. He also provides an account of a country still trapped in political and social turmoil.

Sundberg, Kelly, 1977-

Sundberg, Kelly, 1977- **Goodbye,** sweet girl : a story of domestic violence and survival / Kelly Sundberg. HarperCollins, 2018 272 p. **B**

ISBN 9780062497673

1. Family violence. 2. Abusive men 3. Abused women 4. Violence against women 5. Autobiographies and memoirs

LC bl2018094994

The author describes her abusive marriage to a man who was funny, warm and supportive but also vengeful and violent and how she finally rejected the abuse, accepted responsibility for herself and decided that she deserved better.

Suskind, Owen

Suskind, Ron **Life,** animated : a story of sidekicks, heroes, and autism / Ron Suskind. Kingswell, 2014. 320 p. **B**

ISBN 9781423180364

1. Suskind, Owen. 2. Suskind, Ron. 3. Disney, Walt, 1901-1966 Characters 4. Children with autism 5. Parents of children with autism 6. Communication 7. Interpersonal relations 8. Autobiographies and memoirs

LC 2014006760

Tells the real-life story of Owen Suskind, the son of the Pulitzer Prize-winning journalist who, unable to speak for years, memorized dozens of Disney movies and turned them into a language to express love and loss, kinship and brotherhood.

"The Disney effect may be distinctive to this experience, but the family dynamic should resonate with a much wider readership." Kirkus.

Sutherland, Amy

Sutherland, Amy **Rescuing** Penny Jane : one shelter volunteer, countless dogs, and the quest to find them all homes / Amy Sutherland. HarperCollins, 2017 304 p. **B**

ISBN 9780062377234

1. Animal rescue 2. Animal shelter workers. 3. Animal shelters. 4. Animal welfare 5. Autobiographies and memoirs

LC bl2017006986

A best-selling author and columnist for the Boston Globe describes what it was like working at an animal shelter helping to train scared, aggressive and previously-neglected dogs eventually find love and permanent homes.

"An inside look at the experiences of shelter dogs that is sure to appeal to dog and animal lovers." Kirkus.

Swift, Graham, 1949-

Swift, Graham, 1949- **Making** an elephant : writing from within / Graham Swift. Random House Inc., 2009. 240 p. **B**

ISBN 9780307270993

1. Authors, English 2. Writing. 3. Male friendship 4. Authors 5. Autobiographies and memoirs 6. Essays

LC 2009014052

In his first nonfiction work, the Booker Prize-winning author presents a varied selection of essays, poetry, and interviews that chronicle his struggles to become a published author, his relations with other writers, and his insights on the writing profession.

"Out from behind the scrim of fiction, Swift is highly entertaining, at once welcoming and teasing, clever and probing." Booklist.

Swift, Jonathan, 1667-1745

★Damrosch, Leopold **Jonathan** Swift : his life and his world / Leo Damrosch. Yale University Press, 2013. 592 p. **B**

ISBN 9780300164992

1. Swift, Jonathan, 1667-1745. 2. Authors, Irish -- 18th century 3. Satirists. 4. Ireland 5. England -- Politics and government -- 18th century. 6. Biographies

LC 2013013063

National Book Critics Circle Award for Biography, 2013.
Pulitzer Prize for Biography or Autobiography finalist
Kirkus Prize for Nonfiction finalist, 2014."
A rich and rewarding portrait of an irreplaceable genius." Kirkus.

Stubbs, John, 1977- **Jonathan** Swift : the reluctant rebel / John Stubbs. W. W. Norton & Company, 2017. 752 p. **B**

ISBN 9780393239423

1. Swift, Jonathan, 1667-1745. 2. Satirists 3. Authors, Irish -- 18th century 4. Social critics 5. Social classes 6. Ireland -- Politics and government -- 18th century. 7. England -- Politics and government -- 18th century. 8. Biographies

LC 2016038238

A detailed portrait of the man behind "Gulliver's Travels" traces his early loss of a parent, the contradictions that marked his character, and his achievements as a political writer and dean of St. Patrick's Cathedral in Dublin.

"Though his last years were sad, his trajectory as a literary artist had been steadily upward, as Stubbs ever more engrossing, superlatively literate exposition demonstrates." Booklist.

Swofford, Anthony

Swofford, Anthony **Jarhead** : a Marine's chronicle of the Gulf War and other battles / Anthony Swofford. Scribner, 2003. 260 p. **B**

ISBN 0743235355

1. Swofford, Anthony. 2. United States. Marine Corps. Marines, 7th. Battalion, 2nd. Surveillance and Target Acquisition Platoon. 3. Snipers 4. Soldiers -- United States 5. Persian Gulf War, 1991, American 6. Marines 7. Autobiographies and memoirs

LC 2002030866

Swofford weaves his experience of the Gulf War in the early 1990s with vivid accounts of boot camp, reflections on the mythos of the marines, and remembrances of battles with lovers and family.

"This book offers an unflinching portrayal of the loneliness and brutality of modern warfare and sophisticated analyses of--and visceral reactions to--its politics." Publishers Weekly.

Sybil, 1923-1998

Nathan, Debbie **Sybil** exposed : the extraordinary story behind the famous multiple personality case / Debbie Nathan. Free Press, 2011. xxi, 297 p. : **B**

ISBN 9781439168271

1. Sybil, 1923-1998 Mental health. 2. Mason, Shirley, 1923-1998. 3. People with dissociative identity disorder 4. Dissociative disorders 5. Women with mental illnesses 6. Personality disorders 7. Biographies

LC 2011009164

Documents the stories of the three women behind the famous multiple-personality-disorder case, contending that a large portion of the story was fabricated by a willing patient, her psychiatrist and an ambitious journalist who took advantage of a public that was psychologically primed to believe their claims.

Sylvester II, Pope, 945?-1003

Brown, Nancy Marie The **abacus** and the cross : the story of the Pope who brought the light of science to the Dark Ages / Nancy Marie Brown. Basic Books, c2010. 368 p. **B**

ISBN 9780465009503

1. Religion and science -- History -- To 1500. 2. Popes. 3. Religious leaders. 4. Civilization, Medieval 5. Biographies

LC 2010036361

Traces the achievements of medieval Pope Sylvester II, revealing his lesser-known role in promoting scientific awareness throughout turn-of-the-first-millennium Catholicism, in a report that includes coverage of his humble origins and introduction of Arabic numerals to Europe.

"As readably knowledgeable about Gerbert's political fortunes as about his intellectual influence, Brown is a lively narrator and interesting interpreter of Gerbert's life and world. This portrait gives both the science and the history audiences something to talk about." Booklist.

Szegedy-Maszak, Marianne, 1955-

Szegedy-Maszak, Marianne, 1955- **I** kiss your hands many times : hearts, souls, and wars in Hungary / Marianne Szegedy-Maszak. Spiegel & Grau, [2013] 400 p. **B**

ISBN 9780385524858

1. Szegedy-Maszak, Marianne, 1955- Family 2. Refugees, Hungarian. 3. World War II -- Hungary. 4. Holocaust (1933-1945) -- Hungary. 5. Jews, Hungarian. 6. Hungary 7. Biographies 8. Love letters

LC 2012043179

Traces how the author's parents' World War II romance was challenged by her father's arrest for anti-Fascist views before they left communist Budapest for America, in an account based on love letters exchanged between 1940 and 1947.

Taft, Helen Herron, 1861-1943

Anthony, Carl Sferrazza **Nellie** Taft : the unconventional first lady of the ragtime era / Carl Sferrazza Anthony. William Morrow, c2005. x, 534 p. : **B**

ISBN 0060513829

1. Taft, Helen Herron, 1861-1943. 2. Taft, William H. (William Howard), 1857-1930 3. Presidents' spouses -- United States 4. Biographies

LC 2004052553

A portrait of the early twentieth-century First Lady describes her bold determination to fulfill a then-untraditional political and public role at the side of her husband, noting her part in the emergence of the Progressive era.

"This lively biography provides an illuminating glimpse into the life of an until-now underappreciated First Lady." Booklist.

Talley, Andre Leon

★Talley, Andre Leon The **chiffon** trenches : a memoir / Andre Leon Talley. Ballantine Books, 2020 xv, 284 p. : **B**

ISBN 9780593129258

1. Talley, Andre Leon. 2. Vogue (New York, N.Y.) 3. Clothing industry and trade 4. African Americans 5. Fashion editors -- United States 6. Fashion 7. Autobiographies and memoirs

LC 2019055525

A revealing memoir by a noted style icon captures the fashion world from the inside out, in its most glamorous and most cutthroat moments.

"Though the text brims with gossipy anecdotes, Talley mixes the serious and the saucy with equal heft. Though his legacy speaks for itself, this balanced, entertaining memoir is dramatic proof in print. A heartfelt and often eyebrow-raising memoir perfect for armchair fashionistas or high-fashion insiders." Kirkus

Talusan, Meredith

Talusan, Meredith **Fairest** : a memoir / Meredith Talusan. Viking, [2020] 320 p. **B**

ISBN 9780525561309

1. Harvard University Students 2. Gender identity 3. Passing (Identity) 4. Transgender persons 5. Filipino Americans 6. Autobiographies and memoirs

LC 2019031336

"A heartrending immigrant memoir and a uniquely intersectional coming-of-age story of a life lived in duality and the in-between, and how one navigates through race, gender, and the search for love".-- Provided by publisher.

"This elegant memoir examining whiteness, womanhood, and the shaping of identity will resonate with readers of any community, LGBTQ or not." Publishers Weekly

Tamblyn, Amber

★Tamblyn, Amber **Era** of ignition : coming of age in a time of rage and revolution / Amber Tamblyn. Crown Archetype, 2019. 272 p. **B**

ISBN 9781984822987

1. Tamblyn, Amber. 2. Actors and actresses 3. Feminists 4. Transformations, personal 5. Women's rights 6. Essays 7. Autobiographies and memoirs

LC 2018047443

The activist poet and Emmy-nominated actress presents a passionate, deeply personal exploration of feminism in today's divisive world that recalls a turning point in her life that helped her take control of her own destiny.

"A personal and passionate story about making a world ""that is nourished, healed, and flourishing."""" Kirkus.

Tammet, Daniel, 1979-

Tammet, Daniel, 1979- **Born** on a blue day : inside the extraordinary mind of an autistic savant : a memoir / Daniel Tammet. Free Press, 2007, c2006. ix, 226 p. : **B**

ISBN 9781416535072

1. Tammet, Daniel, 1979- Mental health. 2. People with autism 3. Savant syndrome. 4. Asperger's syndrome 5. Synesthesia 6. England -- Social life and customs. 7. Autobiographies and memoirs

LC 2006041331

Originally published: London : Hodder & Stoughton, 2006.

An autistic savant with genius-level mathematical talents describes how he was shunned by his classmates in spite of his super-human capacity for math and language and offers insight into how he experiences the world.

"This autobiography is as fascinating as Benjamin Franklin's and John Stuart Mill's, both of which are, like his, about the growth of a mind." Booklist.

Tan, Amy

Tan, Amy The **opposite** of fate : a book of musings / Amy Tan. G. P. Putnam's Sons, 2003. 398 p. : **B**

ISBN 0399150749

1. Tan, Amy. 2. Tan, Amy Family. 3. Fate and fatalism. 4. Authors, American -- 20th century -- Family relationships. 5. Chinese Americans 6. Authors, American -- 20th century 7. Essays.

LC 2003047190

The author reflects on her family's Chinese American legacy, her experiences as a writer, her survival of natural disasters, and her struggle to manage three family members afflicted with brain disease.

"No matter how much readers already revere Tan, their appreciation for her will grow tenfold after experiencing these provocative and unforgettable revelations." Booklist.

★Tan, Amy **Where** the past begins : a writer's memoir / Amy Tan. Ecco Press, 2017. 224 p. **B**

ISBN 9780062319296

1. Authors, American 2. Writing 3. Creativity 4. Women authors 5. Autobiographies and memoirs

LC 2017036982

Longlisted for the Andrew Carnegie Medal for Excellence in Non-Fiction, 2018.

The best-selling author of such novels as The Joy Luck Club presents an intimate memoir on her life as a writer that explores formative experiences from her childhood and her evolving perspectives on the symbiotic relationship between fiction and emotional memory.

"In her ambushing and revealing memoir, beloved novelist Tan . chronicles with striking candor, sharp wit, and storytelling magic stranger-than-fiction traumas." Booklist.

Taseer, Aatish

★Taseer, Aatish, 1980- **Stranger** to history : a son's journey through Islamic lands / Aatish Taseer. Graywolf Press, 2012, c2009. xxiii, 323 p. : **B**

ISBN 9781555976286

1. Taseer, Aatish Travel Islamic countries. 2. Muslims -- Attitudes. 3. Islam -- 21st century. 4. Fundamentalism 5. Islam 6. Islamic countries -- Religious life and customs.

LC 2012936228

Originally published: Melbourne : Text Publishing Co., 2009."

This well-constructed travel memoir offers subtle political insight, well-drawn characters, lush detail, and poignant personal narrative. A welcome blend of journalism, travel writing, and memoir; strongly recommended." Library Journal.

Tate, Christie

★Tate, Christie **Group** : how one therapist and a circle of strangers saved my life Simon & Schuster 2020 288 p. **B**

ISBN 9781982154615

1. People with bulimia 2. Group psychotherapy. 3. Psychotherapists 4. Eating disorders 5. Chicago, Illinois 6. Texas 7. Autobiographies and memoirs

LC bl2020022051

A top law school graduate struggling with suicidal thoughts and an eating disorder describes her reluctant participation in a therapeutic support group that taught her the meaning of human connection and intimacy. A first book.

"Tate delivers a no-holds-barred account of her five-plus years in group therapy in this dazzling debut memoir." Publishers Weekly

Taussig, Rebekah

Taussig, Rebekah **Sitting** pretty : the view from my ordinary resilient disabled body / Rebekah Taussig. HarperOne, 2020 224 p. **B**

ISBN 9780062936790

1. Taussig, Rebekah. 2. Disability rights advocates 3. Identity (Psychology) 4. Ableism 5. Barrier-free design 6. Autobiographies and memoirs 7. Essays

LC 2019056133

From disability advocate with a PhD in disability studies and creative nonfiction, and creator of the Instagram account @ sitting pretty, an essay collection based on a lifetime of experiences in a paralyzed body, tackling themes of identity, accessibility, bodies, and representation.

"An invaluable, eye-opening look at disability from a firsthand perspective." Booklist

Taylor, Barbara Brown

Taylor, Barbara Brown **Holy** envy : finding God in the faith of others / Barbara Brown Taylor. HarperOne, 2019. 240 p. **B**

ISBN 9780062406569

1. Taylor, Barbara Brown. 2. Religions. 3. Interfaith relations 4. Spirituality. 5. Spiritual life 6. United States -- Religious life and customs -- 21st century 7. Autobiographies and memoirs

LC 2018033141

The award-winning author recounts her inspirational discoveries of finding the sacred in unexpected places while teaching the world's religions to undergraduate students in Baptist rural Georgia.

"Taylor effectively reminds us that religion is more than beliefs, that it involves our deepest selves and is the fabric of our shared lives." Library Journal.

Taylor, Benjamin, 1952-

Taylor, Benjamin, 1952- The **hue** and cry at our house : a year remembered / Benjamin Taylor. Penguin Books, [2017. 208 p. **B**

ISBN 9780143131649

1. Kennedy, John F. (John Fitzgerald), 1917-1963 Assassination 2. Authors, American -- 20th century 3. Growing up 4. Coping 5. Children with Asperger's syndrome 6. Fort Worth, Texas 7. Texas 8. Autobiographies and memoirs

LC 2016049441

Includes index.

The author describes growing up in Fort Worth, Texas during the 1950s and 1960s and discusses in detail what it was like learning about President Kennedy's assassination and the impact it had on his friends, family and the entire community.

"In this skillful blend of dialogue between youth and maturity, Taylor sums up the value and quality of the years of his treasured past and unforgettable present, while stressing the sanctity of life." Publishers Weekly.

Taylor, Chucky, 1977-

Dwyer, Johnny **American** warlord : the true story / Johnny Dwyer. Alfred A. Knopf, 2015. 336 p. **B**

ISBN 9780307273482

1. Taylor, Charles Ghankay. 2. Political violence -- Liberia. 3. Warlords 4. War crimes 5. Soldiers -- Liberia. 6. Liberia -- History -- Civil War, 1989-1996 -- Atrocities. 7. Liberia -- History -- Civil War, 1999-2003 -- Atrocities. 8. Liberia -- Politics and government -- 1980- 9. Biographies

LC 2014025451

Tells the story of "Chucky" Taylor, a young American who lost his soul in Liberia, the country where his African father was a ruthless warlord and dictator.

"Dwyer deftly captures both the larger implications of Taylor's reign and the human-scaled horror of his son's descent: Chucky's story had been improbable and at times surreal, but its brutality was real. A dark triumph—a meticulous geopolitical narrative and gripping tale of an American son lost to evil." Kirkus.

Taylor, Cory, 1955-2016

Taylor, Cory, 1955-2016 **Dying** : a memoir / Cory Taylor. Tin House Books, 2017, c2016. 141 p. ; **B**

ISBN 9781941040706

1. People with terminal illnesses 2. Death -- Psychological aspects. 3. Australian 4. Autobiographies and memoirs

Originally published: Melbourne, Vic. : Text Publishing Company, 2016.

Shortlisted for the Stella Prize

At the age of sixty, Cory Taylor is dying of melanoma-related brain cancer. Her illness is no longer treatable. As she tells us in her remarkable last book, she now weighs less than her neighbour's retriever. Written in the space of a few weeks, in a tremendous creative surge, this powerful and beautifully written book is a clear-eyed account of what dying has taught Cory: she describes the tangle of her feelings, she reflects on her life, and she remembers the lives and deaths of her parents. She tells us why she would like to be able to choose the circumstances of her own death.

"This slender volume brings a fresh point of view to end-of-life care, the concept of having a sense of control over the unknown, and the role of chance in life." Publishers Weekly.

Taylor, Elizabeth, 1932-2011

Kashner, Sam **Furious** love : Elizabeth Taylor, Richard Burton, and the marriage of the century / Sam Kashner & Nancy Schoenberger. Harpercollins, 2010. 512 p. **B**

ISBN 9780061562846

1. Burton, Richard, 1925-1984 2. Film actors and actresses -- United States 3. Actors and actresses -- Wales. 4. Marriages of celebrities 5. Entertainers -- United States 6. United States -- Social life and customs -- 20th century 7. Biographies

LC 2010006732

"In this dual biography of the two legendary film stars, the authors draw upon new information, including interviews with Elizabeth Taylor and with the Burton family, to capture the famously passionate and tumultuous relationship between the legendary couple. It's a mesmerizing tale, but it's also sad, and sometimes ugly, as the two stars engaged in vicious fights, nursed their jealousies and insecurities, and descended into alcoholism while outwardly living a life of glamour and sophistication." Booklist.

Taylor, Jill Bolte, 1959-

Taylor, Jill Bolte, 1959- **My** stroke of insight : a brain scientist's personal journey / Jill Bolte Taylor. Viking, 2008, c2006. 183 p : **B**

ISBN 9780670020744

1. Neuroscientists 2. People who have had strokes 3. Strokes. 4. Brain. 5. Autobiographies and memoirs

Self-published in 2006.

Traces the Harvard brain scientist author's massive left-hemisphere stroke at the age of thirty-seven, during which she observed the disparate functioning of her right and left brain and came into a realization that she could tap feelings of calm and well-being from her kinesthetic right hemisphere to promote her recovery and a positive outlook.

Taylor, Justin, 1982-

Taylor, Justin, 1982- **Riding** with the ghost : a memoir / Justin Taylor. Random House, 2020 240 p. **B**

ISBN 9780593129296

1. Authors, American -- 21st century 2. Authors, American -- 21st century -- Family relationships. 3. Fathers and sons -- United States. 4. Faith 5. Autobiographies and memoirs

LC 2019041738

The acclaimed author describes how his father's unsuccessful suicide attempt amidst struggles to keep his marriage together while fighting long-term illness and depression forced him to confront and reckon with troubles in his own life.

"A greater literary achievement than Taylor's impressive fiction." Kirkus

Taylor, Marshall Walter, 1878-1932

Balf, Todd **Major** : a black athlete, a white era, and the fight to be the world's fastest human being / Todd Balf. Crown Publishers, 2008. 320 p. **B**

ISBN 0307236587

1. Bicyclists -- United States 2. African-American bicyclists 3. Bicycle racing -- History. 4. United States -- History -- 20th century 5. Biographies

LC 2007020747

Includes index.A portrait of turn-of-the-twentieth-century cyclist Major Taylor, the first great African-American sports celebrity, describes his remarkable sports career, his virtuous and devout lifestyle, and his competition with such white rivals as Floyd McFarland.

"The author chronicles the life of the unlikeliest of stars in the early years of cycling: Marshall Major Taylor. Taylor was an incomparable athlete, poet and celebrity, but he was also a black man living during a time when the scars of the Civil War and slavery were still fresh in the minds of Americans. Balf . . . does great work presenting the complex nature of Taylor's life, including his upbringing in poverty in Indianapolis, the years he was treated as a son by a rich white family, the fans who both worshipped and vilified him and his close relationships with his white trainer and promoter." Publishers Weekly.

Kranish, Michael The **world's** fastest man : the extraordinary life of cyclist Major Taylor, America's first Black sports hero / Michael Kranish. Scribner, 2019. 388 p. **B**

ISBN 9781501192593

1. Bicyclists -- United States 2. African Americans 3. Racism in sports 4. Bicycle racing 5. Biographies

LC 2019006827

The award-winning author traces the lesser-known story of Major Taylor, who broke racial barriers at the height of the Jim Crow era by becoming the world's fastest and most famous bicyclist.

"Both inspiring and heartbreaking, this is an essential contribution to sports history and an excellent companion to Todd Balf's equally strong Major (2008)." Booklist.

Tea, Michelle

★Tea, Michelle **Against** memoir : complaints, confessions & criticism / Michelle Tea. Amethyst Editions/The Feminist Press at the City University of New York, 2018. 300 p. **B**

ISBN 9781936932184

1. Tea, Michelle. 2. Authors, American 3. Lesbian authors 4. Gender identity 5. Gender role 6. Essays

LC 2017049287

A queer countercultural icon divulges on all things artistic, romantic, and neurotic in this collection of essays.

"Author and poet Tea (Without a Net) covers the gamut of her experience in this unputdownable antimemoir, which consists of previously published articles, talks, essays, and reviews but mostly recollections of her experience as a queer activist." Library Journal.

Tecumseh, Shawnee chief, 1768-1813

Eckert, Allan W. A **sorrow** in our heart : the life of Tecumseh / Allan W. Eckert. Bantam Books, 1993, c1992. xv, 1068 p. : **B**

ISBN 055356174X

1. Tecumseh, Shawnee chief, 1768-1813. 2. Indians of North America -- Wars -- 1750-1815. 3. Indians of North America -- Northwest, Old -- History. 4. Shawnee Indians 5. Biographies

LC BL 99752181

Reprint. Originally published: 1992.

A biography of the Shawnee leader describes his vision to unite North American tribes into one Indian nation capable of forcing back the encroaching white settlers.

Teege, Jennifer, 1970-

Teege, Jennifer, 1970- **My** grandfather would have shot me : a Black woman discovers her family's Nazi past / Jennifer Teege and Nikola Sellmair, translated by Carolin Sommer. The Experiment, 2015, c2013 288 p. **B**

ISBN 9781615192533

1. Goth, Amon, 1908-1946 2. Plaszow (Concentration camp) 3. Grandfather and granddaughter. 4. Multiracial women 5. Nazis 6. Life change events 7. Autobiographies and memoirs

LC 2014046242

Originally published under the title Amon : mein Grossvater hätte mich erschossen, 2013

A German-Nigerian woman discovers, while examining a library book, that her grandfather, Amon Goeth, was portrayed in Schindler's List as the central villain of the Plaszów concentration camp, responsible for brutally murdering thousands of people.

"Originally published in German as Amon: mein Grossvater htte mich erschossen, Teege's account is an important addition to narratives written by descendants of war criminals. A gripping read, highly recommended for anyone interested in history, memoirs, and biography." Library Journal.

Teffi, N. A. (Nadezhda Aleksandrovna), 1872-1952

Teffi, N. A. (Nadezhda Aleksandrovna), 1872-1952 **Memories** : from Moscow to the Black Sea / Teffi ; translated by Robert and Elizabeth Chandler, Anne-Marie Jackson and Irina Steinberg ; introduction by Edythe Haber. New York Review Books, 2016. 240 p. ; **B**

ISBN 9781590179512

1. Women authors, Russian. 2. Soviet Union -- History -- Revolution, 1917-1921 3. Autobiographies and memoirs

LC 2015043142

Originally published in Russian as Vospominaniia, 1980

Considered Teffi's single greatest work, Memories: From Moscow to the Black Sea is a deeply personal account of the author's last months in Russia and Ukraine, suffused with her acute awareness of the political currents churning around her, many of which have now resurfaced.

Tegmark, Max

Tegmark, Max **Our** mathematical universe : my quest for the ultimate nature of reality / Max Tegmark. Alfred A. Knopf, 2013. 432 p. **B**

ISBN 9780307599803

1. Tegmark, Max. 2. Cosmology. 3. Mathematical physics 4. Astronomy. 5. Parallel universes 6. Autobiographies and memoirs

LC 2013016020

Max Tegmark leads us on an astonishing journey through past, present, and future, and through the physics, astronomy and mathematics that are the foundation of his work, most particularly his hypothesis that our physical reality is a mathematical structure and his theory of the ultimate multiverse. In a dazzling combination of both popular and groundbreaking science, he not only helps us grasp his often mind-boggling theories (his website gives a flavor of how they might boggle the mind), but he also shares with us some of the often surprising triumphs and disappointments that have shaped his life as a scientist.

"Lively and lucid, the narrative invites general readers into debates over computer models for brain function, over scientific explanations of consciousness, and over prospects for finding advanced life in other galaxies." Booklist.

Teigen, Chrissy

Teigen, Chrissy **Cravings:** Hungry for more / Chrissy Teigen. Clarkson Potter, 2018. 240 p. **B**

ISBN 9781524759728

1. Cooking. 2. Cooks. 3. Recipes. 4. Quick and easy cooking 5. Autobiographies and memoirs

LC 2017061197

A follow-up to Cravings is presented in the form of a culinary diary about the Sports Illustrated model's family life and features healthier, flavor-forward adaptations of recipes for such fare as pancakes, onion dip and banana bread.

Teller, Edward, 1908-2003

★Goodchild, Peter **Edward** Teller : the real Dr. Strangelove / Peter Goodchild. Harvard University Press, 2004. xxv, 469 p. : **B**

ISBN 0674016696

1. Physicists -- United States 2. Atomic bomb -- United States -- History. 3. Biographies

LC 2004054257

"This is a biography of the father of the hydrogen bomb, a witness against J. Robert Oppenheimer in the latter's security hearing, and, finally, an ardent promoter of the Cold War arms race. {The author} studied a wide range of primary and secondary sources and interviewed many people on both sides of the controversies that swirled around Teller. The result is a remarkably well-balanced study of a notoriously prickly and opinionated person." Library Journal.

Temple, O. (Olive), 1880-1936

Ricca, Brad **Olive** the lionheart : lost love, imperial spies, and one woman's journey to the heart of Africa / Brad Ricca. St. Martin's Press, 2020. 320 p. **B**

ISBN 9781250207012

1. Temple, O. (Olive), 1880-1936 Travel Africa 2. Temple, O. (Olive), 1880-1936 Correspondence 3. Alexander, Boyd, 1873-1910 Correspondence 4. Talbot, Percy Amaury, 1877-1945 Travel Africa 5. Women explorers 6. Married women 7. Voyages and travels 8. Husband and wife 9. Africa -- Description and travel 10. Africa -- Social life and customs -- 20th century 11. London, England 12. Biographies

LC 2020010731

In 1910, Olive MacLeod, a thirty-year-old, redheaded Scottish aristocrat, received word that her fiancé, the famous naturalist Boyd Alexander, was missing in Africa. So she went to find him. Olive the Lionheart is the thrilling true story of her astonishing journey. Drawing on Olive's own letters and secret diaries, Olive the Lionheart is a love story that defies all boundaries, set against the backdrop of a beautiful, unconquerable Africa.

"Biographer Ricca (Mrs. Sherlock Holmes) delivers an illuminating portrait of Scottish aristocrat Olive MacLeod, who set out in 1910, at age 30, to find her fiancé, the naturalist Boyd Alexander, after he went missing in Africa. . . . Fans of women's history and adventure stories will cheer this engrossing account." Publishers Weekly

Tenzin Priyadarshi

Tenzin Priyadarshi **Running** toward mystery : the adventure of an unconventional life / the Venerable Tenzin Priyadarshi and Zara Houshmand. Spiegel & Grau, 2019. 272 p. **B**

ISBN 9781984819857

1. Tenzin Priyadarshi. 2. Buddhist monks 3. Mentoring 4. Mentors 5. Scholars and academics 6. India 7. United States 8. Autobiographies and memoirs

LC 2019021238

A revered monk and teacher as well as president and CEO of The Dalai Lama Center for Ethics and Transformative Values shares the spiritual journey that led him to where he is today.

"The purpose of this memoir, which is highly recommended for all spirituality collections, is not to impress but to inspire readers to find a thread connecting them to humanity and the courage to explore the many facets of oneself. A cross between Paramahansa Yogananda's Autobiography of a Yogi and Pema Chödrön's When Things Fall Apart, this more than succeeds." Library Journal

Teresa, Mother, 1910-1997

Spink, Kathryn **Mother** Teresa : a complete authorized biography / Kathryn Spink. Harper San Francisco, c1997. xiv, 306 p. ; **B**

ISBN 9780062508256

1. Missionaries of Charity -- History. 2. Nuns -- Calcutta, India 3. Women and religion -- India. 4. Calcutta, India -- Religious life and customs -- 20th century 5. Biographies

LC 97041349

Includes index.

Traces the life of the Catholic nun who devoted her life to the poor, sick, and social outcasts of Calcutta.

Tesla, Nikola, 1856-1943

Carlson, W. Bernard **Tesla** : inventor of the electrical age / W. Bernard Carlson. Princeton University Press, [2013] 500 p. **B**

ISBN 9780691057767

1. Tesla, Nikola, 1856-1943. 2. Electrical engineers -- United States 3. Inventors -- United States 4. Electric power -- History. 5. Electrical engineering -- History 6. Biographies

LC 2012049608

Draws on original documents from Tesla's private and public life to place the engineer within the cultural and technological context of his time, focusing on his inventions as well as the creation and maintenance of his celebrity.

Munson, Richard **Tesla** : inventor of the modern / Richard Munson. W.W. Norton & Company, [2018] 320 p. **B**

ISBN 9780393635447

1. Inventors 2. Electrical engineers 3. Electrical engineering 4. Serbian Americans 5. Biographies

LC 2017055596

Describes how the formerly unappreciated scientist and inventor with the bizarre personal life and enigmatic behavior contributed so much to our modern world, including plans for cell phones, the internet, death-ray weapons and interstellar communications in the early 1900s.

"A lucid, expertly researched biography of the brilliant Nikola Tesla (1856-1943), a contemporary and competitor of Thomas Edison who was equally celebrated during his life." Kirkus.

Tester, Jon, 1956-

Tester, Jon, 1956- **Grounded** : a senator's lessons on winning back rural America / Jon Tester, US senator for Montana, with Aaron Murphy. Ecco Press, 2020 406 p. **B**

ISBN 9780062977489

1. United States. Congress. Senate 2. Legislators 3. Farmers 4. Rural life 5. Responsibility 6. United States -- Politics and government 7. Autobiographies and memoirs

LC 2020033859

Senator Jon Tester is a rare voice in Congress. He is the only United States senator who manages a full-time job outside of the Senate - as a farmer. But what has really come to distinguish Tester in the Senate is his commitment to accountability, his ability to stand up to Donald Trump, and his success in, time and again, winning red state voters back to the Democratic Party. The media and Democrats too often discount rural people as Trump supporters; Tester knows better. His voice is vital to the public discourse as we seek to understand the issues that are important to rural and working-class America in not just the 2020 election but also for years to come.

"Montana senator Tester's candid and appealing debut interweaves autobiography and insights into the issues and values that resonate with rural voters. . . . This political memoir stands apart from the pack." Publishers Weekly

Tey, Josephine, 1896 or 1897-1952

Thomson, Jennifer, 1980- **Josephine** Tey : a life / Jennifer Morag Henderson. Dufour Editions 2016, c2015. 420 p. **B**

ISBN 9781910124703

1. Tey, Josephine, 1896 or 1897-1952. 2. Women authors, Scottish -- 20th century 3. Authors, Scottish -- 20th century 4. Biographies

Originally published: Dingwall, Scotland : Sandstone Press, 2015.

Josephine Tey was the pen-name of Elizabeth MacKintosh (1896-1952). Born in Inverness, MacKintosh lived several 'lives': best known as Golden Age Crime Fiction writer 'Josephine Tey', she was also successful novelist and playwright 'Gordon Daviot'.

Tharp, Marie

Felt, Hali **Soundings** : the remarkable woman who mapped the ocean floor / Hali Felt. Henry Holt and Co., 2012. 304 p. **B**

ISBN 9780805092158

1. Tharp, Marie. 2. Cartographers -- United States 3. Women cartographers -- United States 4. Submarine topography. 5. Geomorphologists -- United States 6. Biographies

LC 2011044178

Includes index."

A compelling portrait of one of the most interesting "forgotten" women of the twentieth century, the scientist who mapped, for the first time, the ocean floor. Until Marie Tharp's groundbreaking work in the 1950s, the floor of the ocean was a mystery--then, as now, we knew less about the ocean than we did about outer space. In a time when women in the scientific community were routinely dismissed, Tharp's work changed our understanding of the earth's geologic evolution. While her partner, Bruce Heezen, went on expeditions to collect soundings (records of sonar pings measuring the ocean's depth across its entire expanse), Tharp turned this data into beautiful and controversial maps that laid the groundwork for proving the theory of continental drift. Tharp's maps showed for the first time that the continents were moving and had always been moving and that what had happened over eons under the sea was as "visible" now as looking at the same phenomenon on land. Her maps have been called some of "the most remarkable achievements in modern cartography" and yet no one knows her name. The brilliant young writer Hali Felt captures the romance of scientific discovery and brings to vivid life this pioneering scientist who changed the way we view the earth".-- Provided by publisher.

Thatcher, Margaret

Moore, Charles, 1956- **Margaret** Thatcher : at her zenith : in London, Washington and Moscow / Charles Moore. Alfred A. Knopf, 2016. 821 p. Margaret Thatcher: the authorized biographies ; **B**

ISBN 9780307958969

1. Conservative Party (Great Britain) 2. Women prime ministers -- Great Britain 3. Women politicians -- Great Britain. 4. Political leadership -- Great Britain 5. Prime ministers -- Great Britain 6. Great Britain -- Politics and government -- 20th century 7. Biographies

LC 2013020670

Presents the life of Britain's former Prime Minister, covering her humble beginnings as the daughter of a grocer, education at Oxford, rise in the Coservative party, election as Prime Minister in 1979, and major events in her term up to the Falklands War of 1982.

"A chronology of world events, copious notes, and an extensive bibliography enhance an exhaustive narrative that will fascinate students of contemporary British history and politics." Booklist.

★Moore, Charles, 1956- **Margaret** Thatcher : the authorized biography, from Grantham to the Falklands / Charles Moore. Alfred A. Knopf, 2013. 859 p. Margaret Thatcher: the authorized biographies ; **B**

ISBN 9780307958945

1. Conservative Party (Great Britain) 2. Women prime ministers -- Great Britain 3. Women politicians -- Great Britain. 4. Political leadership -- Great Britain 5. Prime ministers -- Great Britain 6. Great Britain -- Politics and government -- 20th century 7. Biographies

LC 2013020670

Elizabeth Longford Prize for Historical Biography, 2014.

With unequaled authority and dramatic detail, the first volume of Charles Moore's authorized biography of Margaret Thatcher reveals as never before the early life, rise to power, and first years as prime minister of the woman who transformed Britain and the world in the late twentieth century.

Theroux, Paul

Theroux, Paul **Figures** in a landscape : people and places : essays: 2001-2016 / Paul Theroux. Houghton Mifflin Harcourt, 2018. 400 p. **B**

ISBN 9780544870307

1. Theroux, Paul Travel. 2. Authors, American. 3. Voyages and travels 4. Essays

LC 2017045486

"An Eamon Dolan book."

In the spirit of his much-loved Sunrise with Seamonsters and Fresh Air Fiend, Paul Theroux's latest collection of essays leads the reader through a dazzling array of sights, characters, and experiences, as Theroux applies his signature searching curiosity to a life lived as much in reading as on the road.

Thomas, Abigail

Thomas, Abigail **What** comes next and how to like it : a memoir / Abigail Thomas. Simon & Schuster 2015 240 p. **B**

ISBN 9781476785059

1. Thomas, Abigail. 2. Authors, American -- 20th century 3. Loss (Psychology) 4. Married men -- Death 5. Best friends 6. Autobiographies and memoirs

LC 2015295750

The New York Times best-selling author of A Three Dog Life presents an uplifting memoir about her life after the devastating loss of her husband, changes in a once-platonic friendship, her daughter's illness and the death of a beloved dog.

"This episodic memoir is full of love and life. Readers will identify with the feelings and the people even as they realize how different they are, how wondrous." Booklist.

Thomas, Clarence, 1948-

Robin, Corey, 1967- The **enigma** of Clarence Thomas / Corey Robin. Metropolitan Books, Henry Holt and Company, 2019. 208 p. **B**

ISBN 9781627793834

1. United States. Supreme Court Justices 2. Racism 3. Conservatism 4. Judges -- United States 5. Political questions and judicial power -- United States. 6. United States -- Politics and government. 7. Biographies

LC 2019012026

An analysis of the controversial Supreme Court justice examines Thomas' opinions against a backdrop of his autobiographical and political writings, revealing his pessimistic beliefs about the absolute racism of white people and the impossibility of progress.

Thomas, Dylan, 1914-1953

Thomas, Dylan, 1914-1953 A **child's** Christmas in Wales / Dylan Thomas ; with woodcuts by Ellen Raskin. New Directions Pub., 2007. 51 p. : **B**

ISBN 0811217310

1. Thomas, Dylan, 1914-1953 Childhood and youth. 2. Thomas, Dylan, 1914-1953 Homes and haunts Wales. 3. Christmas -- Wales. 4. Poets, Welsh -- 20th century 5. Wales -- Social life and customs. 6. Autobiographies and memoirs.

LC 2007024727

Captures a child's-eye view, and an adult's fond memories, of a magical time of presents, aunts and uncles, the frozen sea, and in the best of circumstances, newly fallen snow.

"For any season of the year the language is enchanting and the poetry shines with an unearthly radiance." New York Times Book Review.

Thomas, Edward, 1878-1917

Hollis, Matthew **Now** all roads lead to France : a life of Edward Thomas / Matthew Hollis. W. W. Norton & Company, 2012. 416 p. **B**

ISBN 9780393089073

1. Frost, Robert, 1874-1963 Friends and associates 2. Poets, English -- 20th century 3. World War I 4. Modernism (Literature) -- Great Britain 5. British in France 6. Biographies

LC 2012015784

Describes the last five years of the First World War poet's life, discussing his close friendship with Robert Frost, his work and his marriage and his decision to fight in the war which ultimately took his life in France 1917.

Thomas, Elizabeth Marshall, 1931-

Thomas, Elizabeth Marshall, 1931- **Growing** old : notes on aging with something like grace / Elizabeth Marshall Thomas. HarperOne, 2020 224 p. **B**

ISBN 9780062956439

1. Aging -- United States. 2. Seniors -- United States -- Social conditions 3. Seniors -- United States 4. Memory 5. United States -- Social life and customs -- 21st century 6. Autobiographies and memoirs

LC 2019016989

Part memoir and part life-affirming map all of us may follow to embrace our later years with grace and dignity, this look at the social and historical traditions related to aging explores a wide range of issues connected with growing older.

"With wit and humor, Thomas thoughtfully conveys the realities of aging. This fully absorbing memoir will especially resonate with readers over 65 and those who work with geriatric populations, yet all readers should find much wisdom to be gained from this warm offering." Library Journal

Thomas, R. Eric

Thomas, R. Eric **Here** for it : or, how to save your soul in America; essays / R. Eric Thomas. Ballantine Books, 2020. 272 p. **B**

ISBN 9780525621034

1. Thomas, R. Eric. 2. Authors, American 3. Journalists -- United States 4. African American gay men 5. Christian gay men and lesbians 6. United States -- Social conditions -- 21st century. 7. Essays 8. Autobiographies and memoirs

LC 2019037442

A humorist and playwright provides a heartfelt and humorous memoir-in-essays about growing up seeing the world differently, finding unexpected hope and every awkward, extraordinary stumble along the way.

"A laugh-out-loud memoir that is strongly recommended for everyone." Library Journal

Thomas, a Becket, Saint, 1118?-1170

Guy, John, 1952 November 17- **Thomas** Becket : warrior, priest, rebel : a 900 year old story retold / John Guy. Random House, c2011. 512 p. **B**

ISBN 9781400069071

1. Christian saints. 2. Christian martyrs. 3. Political leadership. 4. Rebels. 5. Great Britain -- History -- Henry II, 1154-1189 6. Biographies

LC 2011042794

Places the life of Thomas Becket against the violent 12th-century clashes between church and state, tracing his early achievements as Henry II's chancellor and eventual elevation to Archbishop of Canterbury before being exiled, murdered and ultimately canonized for his stance against the king's dictates.

Thompson, Hunter S.

Denevi, Timothy **Freak** kingdom : Hunter S. Thompson's manic ten-year crusade against American fascism / Timothy Denevi. PublicAffairs, [2018] 416 p. **B**

ISBN 9781541767942

1. Nixon, Richard M. (Richard Milhous), 1913-1994 2. Presidential elections -- History 3. Journalists 4. Political campaigns 5. Politicians 6. United States -- Politics and government -- 1945-1989 7. Biographies

LC 2018015549

This brilliantly told and dramatic story chronicles Hunter S. Thompson's crusade against Richard Nixon and how his fevered effort to expose institutional injustice hastened his own decline but led to some of the best political writing in our history.

McKeen, William, 1954- **Outlaw** journalist : the life and times of Hunter S. Thompson / William McKeen. Norton, c2008. 448 p. **B**

ISBN 9780393061925

1. Thompson, Hunter S., 1937- Friends and associates 2. Journalists -- United States 3. Alcoholic men -- United States 4. Journalism

-- United States -- 20th century 5. Hallucinogenic drugs 6. United States -- Social life and customs -- 20th century 7. Biographies
LC 2008013214

McKeen chronicles the mesmerizing life of legendary Gonzo journalist and Fear and loathing in Las Vegas author Hunter S. Thompson. Thompson's childhood is detailed, along with his explosive relationship with his editors at Playboy and Rolling Stone, his drug use, his controversial persona, and life at his secluded Colorado home.

★Thompson, Hunter S. **Fear** and loathing in America : the brutal odyssey of an outlaw journalist, 1968-1976 / Hunter S. Thompson ; foreword by David Halberstam ; edited by Douglas Brinkley. Simon & Schuster, 2000. xxv, 756 p. : **B**

ISBN 068487315X

1. Thompson, Hunter S. Correspondence 2. Rolling Stone Magazine. 3. Journalists -- United States -- Correspondence. 4. Political journalism. 5. Journalism 6. United States -- History -- 20th century. 7. Letters.
LC 00047012

Sequel to: The proud highway."

During the period covered in this collection, Thompson was a vital, deliriously erratic force in journalism, covering the turbulent 1968 Democratic National Convention in Chicago, the 1968 election of Richard M. Nixon, the 1972 campaign, Watergate, the falls of Nixon and Saigon." New York Times Book Review.

Wenner, Jann **Gonzo** : the life of Hunter S. Thompson / Jann Wenner and Corey Seymour ; introduction by Johnny Depp. Little, Brown, 2007. 496 p. **B**

ISBN 0316005274

1. Thompson, Hunter S. Friends and associates. 2. Journalists -- United States 3. Biographies
LC 2007011693

Includes index.

Draws on interviews with the revolutionary writer's friends, families, and other intimates to offer insight into his Kentucky childhood, literary achievements, and fast-paced lifestyle that led to his tragic suicide.

"This oral biography is a look at the turbulent life of Gonzo journalism pioneer Hunter S. Thompson (1937-2005). This fine, fond biography amuses, inspires, outrages and haunts at all the right momentsand sometimes all at once." Publishers Weekly.

Thompson, Juan F.

Thompson, Juan F. **Stories** I tell myself : growing up with Hunter S. Thompson / Juan F. Thompson. Alfred A. Knopf, 2015. 320 p. **B**

ISBN 9780307265357

1. Thompson, Hunter S. 2. Thompson, Hunter S. Family. 3. Authors, American -- 20th century 4. Fathers and sons 5. Drug abuse 6. Gonzo journalism. 7. Biographies
LC 2015006934

A detailed and intimate description of the life of the manic, drug-fueled, charismatic and sensitive wildman of American journalism, known for his fearless style covering everything from biker gangs to presidential elections, as told by his only son.

"The son of the legendary gonzo journalist recalls his turbulent but exciting years swimming in the wake of a most mercurial creature." Kirkus.

Thoreau, Henry David, 1817-1862

Dann, Kevin T., 1956- **Expect** great things : the life and search of Henry David Thoreau / Kevin Dann. TarcherPerigee, 2017 400 p. **B**

ISBN 9780399184666

1. Thoreau, Henry David, 1817-1862. 2. Authors, American -- 19th century 3. Naturalists -- United States 4. Philosophers -- United States 5. Spirituality in literature. 6. Biographies
LC 2016023294

"To coincide with the bicentennial of Thoreau's birth in 2017, this biography by naturalist and historian Kevin Dann fills a gap in our understanding of one modern history's most important spiritual visionaries by capturing the fullarc of Thoreau's life as a mystic, spiritual seeker, and explorer in transcendental realms.

"For all Thoreau devotees, who will welcome the sympathetic overview of the author's full life and enthusiasms." Library Journal.

Sullivan, Robert, 1963- The **Thoreau** you don't know : what the prophet of environmentalism really meant / Robert Sullivan. HarperCollins Publishers, 2009. 368 p. **B**

ISBN 9780061710315

1. Thoreau, Henry David, 1817-1862. 2. Authors, American -- 19th century 3. Naturalists -- United States 4. Environmentalism. 5. Biographies
LC 2008034495

Includes index.

An alternate profile of the iconic American and environmental writer explores Thoreau's contributions as an activist, organizer, and adventurer who was more social than his reclusive persona suggested.

"The author endeavors to free Henry David Thoreau from his calcified reputation as a cantankerous hermit and nature worshipper. Sounding like your favorite teacher who manages to make history fun and relevant, Sullivan vibrantly portrays the sage of Walden as a geeky, curious, compassionate fellow of high intelligence and deep feelings who loved company, music, and long walks." Booklist.

★Thoreau, Henry David, 1817-1862 **Walden,** or, Life in the woods / Henry David Thoreau ; with an introduction by Verlyn Klinkenborg. Knopf : Distributed by Random House, c1992. xxxi, 295 p. ; **B**

ISBN 0679418962

1. Thoreau, Henry David, 1817-1862 Homes and haunts Massachusetts Walden Woods. 2. Authors, American -- 19th century 3. Natural history -- Massachusetts -- Walden Woods. 4. Solitude. 5. Wilderness areas -- Massachusetts -- Walden Woods. 6. Walden Woods (Mass.) -- Social life and customs. 7. Biographies
LC 92054444

Originally published: Boston, Ticknor and Fields, 1854.

Presents Thoreau's reflections on his experience living alone in the woods surrounding Walden Pond as well as his philosophy concerning man's need to reevaluate life and commune with nature.

★Walls, Laura Dassow **Henry** David Thoreau : a life / Laura Dassow Walls. The University of Chicago Press, 2017. 640 p. ; **B**

ISBN 9780226344690

1. Authors, American. 2. Intellectuals. 3. Naturalists. 4. United States -- Social life and customs -- 19th century 5. Biographies
LC 2016053416

Kirkus Prize for Nonfiction finalist, 2017.

Traces the life of the extraordinary poet, best known for his meditations on nature at Walden Pond, who also spent time with good friend and neighbor Ralph Waldo Emerson and worked as a manual laborer, an inventor and a radical political activist.

"A superbly researched and written literary portrait that broadens our understanding of the great American writer and pre-eminent naturalist who has too long been regarded as a self-righteous scold." Kirkus.

Thorp, Edward O.

Thorp, Edward O. A **man** for all markets : from Las Vegas to Wall Street, how I beat the dealer and the market / Edward O. Thorp. Random House, [2017] 256 p. **B**

ISBN 9781400067961

1. Investment advisers 2. Gambling 3. Statistics 4. Mathematicians -- United States 5. Autobiographies and memoirs

LC 2016026545

Includes index.

The incredible real-life story of the card-counting mathematics professor who taught the world how to beat the dealer and helped start a revolution on Wall Street.

"Readers who like to read the life stories of ambitious, creative, and successful people with fascinating stories to tell should be steered in this books direction." Booklist.

Thorpe, Jeremy

Preston, John, 1953- A **very** English scandal : sex, lies and a murder plot at the heart of the establishment / John Preston. Other Press, 2016. 352 p. **B**

ISBN 9781590518144

1. Thorpe, Jeremy. 2. Thorpe, Jeremy Sexual behavior. 3. Thorpe, Jeremy Trials, litigation, etc. 4. Great Britain. Parliament. 5. Politicians -- Great Britain 6. Scandals 7. Trials (Conspiracy) 8. Government cover-ups 9. Great Britain -- Politics and government -- 1964-1979. 10. Biographies

LC 2016005086

Includes index."

A behind-the-scenes look at the desperate, scandalous private life of a British member of Parliament and champion manipulator, and the history-making trial that exposed his dirty secrets to the world." Provided by publisher.

"Though knee-deep in politics, scandal, and betrayal, the book also conveys the sobering, grim reality of lives destroyed by dirty politics and homophobic culture." Publishers Weekly.

Thorpe, Jim, 1887-1953

Buford, Kate **Native** American son : the life and sporting legend of Jim Thorpe / Kate Buford. Alfred A. Knopf, 2010. 448 p. **B**

ISBN 9780375413247

1. Thorpe, Jim, 1887-1953. 2. Athletes -- United States 3. Native American athletes -- United States 4. Indians of North America. 5. Biographies

LC 2010012815

"Borzoi Book."

Chronicles defining moments in the career of the preeminent American athlete, from his contributions to college football and gold-medal wins at the 1912 Olympics to his role in shaping professional football and baseball, in a portrait that also discusses his private struggles and political views.

★Crawford, Bill, 1955- **All** American : the rise and fall of Jim Thorpe / Bill Crawford. John Wiley & Sons, c2004. iv, 284 p. : **B**

ISBN 0471557323

1. Thorpe, Jim, 1887-1953. 2. Athletes -- United States 3. Native-American athletes 4. Native-American Olympic medal winners 5. Baseball players -- United States 6. United States -- Social life and customs -- 20th century 7. Biographies

LC 2004014376

A biography of Jim Thorpe, one of the greatest all-around athletes in history.

"This terse, punchy biography of sports legend Thorpe (1888-1953) illuminates the current debate over the exploitation of unpaid college athletes by moneymaking, headline-grabbing educational institutions." Publishers Weekly.

Thubron, Colin, 1939-

Thubron, Colin, 1939- **To** a mountain in Tibet / Colin Thubron. Harper, 2011. 288 p. **B**

ISBN 9780061768262

1. Thubron, Colin, 1939- Travel Tibet. 2. Mountains. 3. Bereavement. 4. Pilgrims and pilgrimages. 5. Travelers 6. Tibet -- Description and travel. 7. Mount Kailas -- Description and travel. 8. Autobiographies and memoirs

LC 2010043013

Offers an intimate travelogue of the author's trek to Kailas, the holiest mountain in Tibet, in the wake of the death of his mother and the loss of his family.

"Emotional subtlety and vivid evocations of the people and places are only part of what makes the book so enjoyable. The present-tense narration allows readers to make discoveries alongside Thubron, which adds immeasurably to the intimacy and immediacy of the reading experience. A powerful and hauntingly elegiac hybrid of travelogue and memoir." Kirkus.

Thucydides, 460?-395? B.C.E.

Kagan, Donald **Thucydides** : the reinvention of history / Donald Kagan. Viking, 2009. 272 p. **B**

ISBN 9780670021291

1. Thucydides, 460?-395? B.C.E. History of the Peloponnesian War. 2. Historians. 3. Civilization, Ancient. 4. Intellectual life -- Greece -- To 146 B.C. 5. Ancient history. 6. Greece -- History -- Peloponnesian War, 431-404 B.C. -- Historiography. 7. Greece -- Historiography. 8. Biographies

LC 2009008368

A Yale professor's reassessment of the life and contributions of the ancient revisionist historian places him in a context of his time, citing the pivotal influence of his refusal to credit the gods or individuals with the societal events documented in The Peloponnesian War.

Thunberg, Greta, 2003-

Ernman, Malena **Our** house is on fire : scenes of a family and a planet in crisis / Malena and Beata Ernman, Svante and Greta Thunberg. Penguin Books, 2020, c2018. 279 p. ; **B**

ISBN 9780143133575

1. Nature -- Effect of humans on 2. Teenage girl social advocates 3. Environmentalism 4. Climate change 5. Collective autobiographies and memoirs

LC 2020003131

Originally published in Swedish as Scener ur hjartat by Bokforlaget Polaris, Stockholm, 2018."

Written by a remarkable family and told through the voice of an iconoclastic mother, Our House Is on Fire is the story of how they fought their problems at home by taking global action. And it is the story of how Greta decided to go on strike from school, igniting a worldwide rebellion".-- Provided by publisher.

"A collective portrait of activist Greta Thunberg's family, encompassing not only climate change, but also issues of mental health. In this moving text, Swedish opera singer Malena Ernman, her husband, Svante

Thunberg, and their daughters, Greta and Beata, stitch together vignettes about 'burned-out people on a burned out planet.' . . . An impassioned call to action and a vulnerable family portrait of neurodiversity." Kirkus

Tiptree, James Jr., 1915-1987

Phillips, Julie **James** Tiptree, Jr. : the double life of Alice B. Sheldon / Julie Phillips. St. Martin's Press, 2006. vi, 469 p., 16 p. of plates : **B**

ISBN 0312203853

1. Authors, American -- 20th century 2. Women science fiction authors 3. Biographies

LC 2006040095

Hugo Award for Best Related Non-Fiction Book, 2007.

Locus Award for Best Nonfiction/Related/Reference Book, 2007.

National Book Critics Circle Award for Biography, 2006.

ALA Notable Book, 2007.

A profile of the successful woman author who hid behind the male pen name of James Tiptree, Jr., to publish popular short works of science fiction in the 1970s describes her childhood explorations of Africa with her mother, work as an intelligence officer during World War II, and shocking suicide.

Titian, 1477-1576

Hale, Sheila **Titian** : his life / Sheila Hale. HarperCollins, 2012. 704 p. **B**

ISBN 9780060598761

1. Titian, 1477-1576. 2. Painters -- Italy 3. Painting, Renaissance (Europe) 4. Painting, Italian -- 16th century. 5. Art, Renaissance (Europe) 6. Venice, Italy -- History -- 16th century. 7. Biographies

LC bl2012044871

A full-length biography of a leading painter of the Italian High Renaissance takes into account recent historical art research and scholarship and examines all contemporary accounts of Titian's life and work, attempting to explain the evolution of his complex methods.

Hudson, Mark **Titian** : the last days / Mark Hudson. St Martins Press, 2009. xiv, 304 p. **B**

ISBN 9780802710765

1. Titian, 1477-1576. 2. Artists 3. Painters 4. Art. 5. Italy -- History -- 16th century. 6. Biographies

LC bl2009034120

The author of Coming Back Brockens and The Music in My Head offers a compelling portrait of the life, work and meaning of Titian, a respected 16th-century painter, in a book with an eight-page color insert.

"At the time of his deathfrom plague, in Venice in 1576Titian had been one of the most celebrated artists in Europe for most of the century, the revered portrait painter of popes, emperors, and kings. But in his final works, as plague swept Venice, Titian, then in his mid-eighties, began confronting darker themes, including his own mortality. Hudson focusses his book on this group of paintings, now largely lost, and discusses Titian's career with humor, enlivening a potentially staid subject." The New Yorker.

Tito, 2000-

Mainardi, Diogo, 1962- The **fall** : a father's memoir in 424 steps / Diogo Mainardi ; translated from the Portuguese by Margaret Jull Costa. Other Press, [2014], c2012. 160 p. **B**

ISBN 9781590517000

1. Tito, 2000- Health. 2. Mainardi, Diogo, 1962- 3. Cerebral palsy 4. Fathers and sons 5. Life change events 6. People with disabilities 7. Venice, Italy 8. Autobiographies and memoirs

LC 2014005571

"Originally published in Portuguese as: A Queda: As memorias de um pai em 424 passos in 2012 by Editora Record, Rio de Janeiro, Brazil."

Originally published: Rio de Janiero : Editora Record, 2012."

Tito emerges as collaborator in the booknot as a cause or a type or a symbol but as a happy, well-adjusted, well-loved individual with a life well worth living. A singularly compelling memoir." Kirkus.

Tizon, Alex

Tizon, Alex **Big** little man : in search of my Asian self / Alex Tizon. Houghton Mifflin Harcourt, 2014. 272 p. **B**

ISBN 9780547450483

1. Tizon, Alex. 2. Filipino Americans. 3. Asian Americans -- Ethnic identity. 4. Gender role -- United States. 5. Masculinity -- United States. 6. United States -- Interethnic relations. 7. Autobiographies and memoirs

LC 2013045020

Alex Tizon's family emigrated from the Philippines when he was four. He quickly learned to be ashamed of his face, his color, his physical size. In movies and on television he saw Asian men as 'servants, villains, or geeks, one-dimensional, powerless, sneaky little men.' His fierce and funny observations of sex and the Asian American male include the story of his own college life in the 1980s, a tortured tutorial on just how little sex appeal accrued to the Asian man.

Tjipombo, Tupa

Tjipombo, Tupa **I** am not your slave : a memoir / Tupa Tjipombo, Chris Lockhart. Lawrence Hill Books, 2020. 256 p. **B**

ISBN 9781641602372

1. Tjipombo, Tupa. 2. Human trafficking victims 3. Sexual slavery 4. Human trafficking 5. Rape 6. Africa 7. Dubai 8. Autobiographies and memoirs

LC 2019029549

I Am Not Your Slave is the true story of a young African girl who was abducted from southwestern Africa and funneled through an extensive yet almost completely unknown human-trafficking network spanning the entire African continent. As she is transported from the point of her abduction on a remote farm and channeled to her ultimate destination in Dubai, her three-year odyssey exposes the brutal horrors of a modern day middle passage.

"In this harrowing, unsparing memoir, the author documents unimaginable brutality against women with dignity and grace and provides readers with an urgent education about the devastating scope of human trafficking in the modern world. Difficult but necessary reading." Kirkus.

Tobia, Jacob, 1991-

Tobia, Jacob, 1991- **Sissy** : a coming-of-gender story / Jacob Tobia. G. P. Putnam's Sons, [2019] 320 p. **B**

ISBN 9780735218826

1. Gender identity 2. Gender-nonconforming people 3. Coming out (Sexual or gender identity) 4. Growing up 5. Autobiographies and memoirs

LC 2018041589

A gender-diverse cultural influencer on both the Forbes "30 Under 30" and "OUT 100" lists examines how their religious, political and educational experiences revealed the need for greater cultural inclusion and anti-discrimination legislation that acknowledges the gender spectrum.

"TV producer and performer Tobia, who uses the pronouns they/them, recounts their journey from shy, closeted gender-nonconforming kid to out-and-proud young genderqueer LGBTQ activist in this hilarious and candid memoir. Tobia thoughtfully and accessibly captures the anguish of being placed inside boxes that dont fithow gender hurts us all by creating prisons of identity, with both kids and adults policing and bullying those who fail to conform." Publishers Weekly.

Tocqueville, Alexis de, 1805-1859

Epstein, Joseph, 1937- **Alexis** de Tocqueville : democracy's guide / Joseph Epstein. Harper Collins Atlas Books, c2006. 208 p. ; Eminent lives **B**

ISBN 0060598980

1. Tocqueville, Alexis de, 1805-1859 Political and social views. 2. Historians -- France 3. Politicians -- France -- 19th century 4. Politicians -- Europe 5. Democracy. 6. France -- History -- 19th century 7. Biographies

LC 2006047175

"The author provides an examination of the man, his works, his influence, his times and what we can learn from Democracy in America. . . . As an introduction to the man and a primer for his works, Epstein's book is admirable." Publishers Weekly.

Todd, Mabel Loomis, 1856-1932

Dobrow, Julie, **After** Emily : two remarkable women and the legacy of America's greatest poet / Julie Dobrow. W.W. Norton & Company, [2018] 384 p. **B**

ISBN 9780393249262

1. Dickinson, Emily, 1830-1886 2. Todd, Mabel Loomis, 1856-1932. 3. Bingham, Millicent Todd, 1880-1968. 4. Women poets 5. Women editors 6. Mother and adult daughter 7. Poetry -- History and criticism 8. United States -- History -- 19th century 9. Biographies

LC 2018016671

Describes the lives of Mabel Loomis Todd and her daughter, Millicent Todd Bingham, who transcribed, edited, and promoted the work of Emily Dickinson despite growing legal issues and Mabel's complicated relationships with the Dickinsons.

"Dobrow's intimate portrait of these artistically talented and intelligent women, based largely on their extensive, detailed diaries and correspondence, reveals fallible women who painstakingly attempted to share an extraordinary poets vision." Booklist.

Tolokonnikova, Nadezhda, 1989-

Tolokonnikova, Nadezhda, 1989- **Rules** for rulebreakers : a Pussy Riot guide to revolution / Nadya Tolokonnikova. HarperOne, 2018. 256 p. **B**

ISBN 9780062741585

1. Pussy Riot (Musical group) 2. Art and politics 3. Punk rock music 4. Punk rock musicians 5. Feminism 6. Autobiographies and memoirs

LC 2017059217

From a life of inspired action and creative rebellion, a feminist artist, activist and Pussy Riot founder shares her core principles and formative experiences, offering inspiration for opposing authoritarian leaders and governments that threaten to suppress individual rights and freedoms.

Tolstoy, Leo, graf, 1828-1910

★Bartlett, Rosamund **Tolstoy** : a Russian life / Rosamund Bartlett. Houghton Mifflin Harcourt, c2011. 500 p. **B**

ISBN 9780151014385

1. Tolstoy, Leo, graf, 1828-1910. 2. Authors, Russian -- 19th century 3. Authors 4. Intellectual life. 5. Rebels. 6. Russia -- History -- 19th century. 7. Biographies

LC 2010050015

Draws on key Russian sources and extensive new materials to trace the influential 19th-century literary master's life and legacy, providing coverage of such topics as his early life, his troubled relationship with his wife and his evocative portrayals of beloved Russian landscapes.

Blaisdell, Robert **Creating** Anna Karenina : Tolstoy and the birth of literature's most enigmatic heroine / Bob Blaisdell. Pegasus Books, 2020. xxiii, 389 p., 8 unnumbered p. of plates : **B**

ISBN 9781643134628

1. Tolstoy, Leo, graf, 1828-1910. Anna Karenina 2. Characters and characteristics in literature 3. Authors, Russian 4. Creation (Literary, artistic, etc.) 5. Fiction writing 6. Biographies

"The story behind the origins of Anna Karenina and the turbulent life and times of Leo Tolstoy".-- Provided by publisher.

"Tolstoy comes to life as a complex individual defying easy classification. Tolstoy's fans will relish learning from, and, occasionally, arguing with Blaisdell's opinions. This passionate book is almost impossible to put down." Publishers Weekly

Tomine, Adrian, 1974-

Tomine, Adrian, 1974- The **loneliness** of the long-distance cartoonist / Adrian Tomine. Drawn and Quarterly, 2020. 168 p. **B**

ISBN 9781770463950

1. Cartoonists 2. Self-consciousness 3. Embarrassment in men 4. Fame 5. Autobiographical comics 6. Comics and Graphic novels 7. Autobiographies and memoirs

LC bl2020017911

Illustrated by the author.

A comedic memoir about fandom, fame, and other embarrassments from the life of a New York Times bestseller.

"Subtle, provocative, and sharply drawn--a portrait of the perpetually dissatisfied artist." Kirkus

Toorpakai, Maria, 1990-

Toorpakai, Maria, 1990- A **different** kind of daughter : the girl who hid from the Taliban in plain sight / Maria Toorpakai with Katharine Holstein. Twelve, 2016. 256 p. **B**

ISBN 9781455591411

1. Taliban. 2. Passing (Identity) 3. Escapes -- Pakistan. 4. Women's rights -- Pakistan. 5. Squash players -- Pakistan 6. Pakistan -- Social conditions. 7. Autobiographies and memoirs

LC 2015050405

A woman from an oppressive Pakistani tribal region, where women playing sports is forbidden, discusses how she passed as a boy in order to play the sports she loved, thus becoming a lightning rod of freedom in her country's fierce battle over women's rights, as well as the subject of a forthcoming 2016 documentary.

"This astonishing and inspirational memoir chronicles more than Maria's life; it also relates the story of her parents, an incredible couple, who, despite the odds, fought for the betterment and education of themselves, their children, and the Pakistani people." Library Journal.

Torres, Alissa

Torres, Alissa **American** widow / Alissa Torres ; illustrated by Choi. Villard, 2008. 224 p. **B**

ISBN 9780345500694

1. Torres, Alissa. 2. Widows -- New York City 3. September 11 Terrorist Attacks, 2001 4. Pregnancy. 5. Family relationships. 6. New York City -- Social life and customs. 7. Autobiographical comics 8. Comics and Graphic novels 9. Autobiographies and memoirs

LC 2008008396

Created in the format of a graphic novel, a deeply personal memoir recalls the author's whirlwind romance, courtship, and marriage to

Eddie Torres, a one-time illegal alien who had worked his way up the ladder of success to take a dream job at Cantor Fitzgerald, only to die in the World Trade Center attacks, leaving his wife pregnant with their first child.

"The author's tragedy of errors inspires anger on her behalf, although the story is calmly and beautifully told. Choi's simple and attractive line art is set off by turquoise wash, yielding to a full-color photo at the end when Alissa embraces her life anew" Library Journal.

Toulouse-Lautrec, Henri de, 1864-1901

Frey, Julia Bloch, 1943- **Toulouse-Lautrec** : a life / Julia Frey. Phoenix Giants, 1995, c1994. xxii, 597 p. : **B**

ISBN 1857993632

1. Artists -- France 2. France -- Social life and customs -- 19th century. 3. Biographies

LC BL 00006387

Originally published: London : Weidenfeld and Nicolson, 1994.

National Book Critics Circle Award for Biography finalist, 1994."

The author chronicles Toulouse-Lautrec's transformation from a pampered invalid into one of the most radical of the fin de siecle artists. Her sensitive, eloquent, and richly illustrated biography has brought the real Toulouse-Lautrec out from behind the scrim of myth." Booklist.

Toussaint Louverture, 1743-1803

★Bell, Madison Smartt **Toussaint** Louverture : a biography / Madison Smartt Bell. Pantheon Books, c2007. 333 p. : **B**

ISBN 0375423370

1. Revolutionaries -- Haiti 2. Generals -- Haiti 3. Haiti -- History -- Revolution, 1791-1804 4. Biographies

LC 2006045848

Map on lining papers.

Presents a biography of Toussaint Louverture that captures the frequently contradictory and complex life of the leader of the late-eighteenth-century Haitian Revolution that became the only successful slave revolt in history.

"This is the best biography of Toussaint yet, in large part because Bell does not shy away from the man's contradictions." New York Times Book Review.

★Girard, Philippe R **Toussaint** Louverture : a revolutionary life / Philippe Girard. Basic Books, [2016] 352 p. **B**

ISBN 9780465094134

1. Toussaint Louverture, 1743-1803. 2. Revolutionaries -- Haiti 3. Generals -- Haiti 4. Slavery -- History -- 18th century. 5. Slave resistance and revolts -- Haiti. 6. Haiti -- History -- Revolution, 1791-1804 7. Caribbean Area. 8. Biographies

LC 2016018088

A definitive biography of one of the most influential men in history, based on meticulous research from archives across the world and in multiple languages, chronicles how the lowly freedman transformed himself into a revolutionary hero and the mastermind of the bloody slave revolt of 1791.

Hazareesingh, Sudhir **Black** spartacus : the epic life of Toussaint Louverture / Sudhir Hazareesingh. Farrar, Straus and Giroux, 2020. xxvi, 427 p. : **B**

ISBN 9780374112660

1. Toussaint Louverture, 1743-1803. 2. Revolutionaries 3. Slave resistance and revolts -- Haiti. 4. Leadership in men. 5. Generals 6. Haiti -- History -- Revolution, 1791-1804. 7. Biographies

LC 2020012455

Drawing on groundbreaking archival research and a keen interpretive lens, this brilliant work of both biography and intellectual history is a new interpretation of the life of the Haitian revolutionary Toussaint Louverture.

"Mauritian British historian Hazareesingh presents a deeply researched, energetic, and comprehensively reenvisioned study of the extraordinary life and still-growing influence of Haiti's liberator and founding father." Booklist

Tracy, Spencer, 1900-1967

Curtis, James, 1953- **Spencer** Tracy : a biography / James Curtis. Alfred A. Knopf, 2011. 1024 p. **B**

ISBN 9780307262899

1. Tracy, Spencer, 1900-1967. 2. Actors and actresses -- United States 3. Faith in men 4. Men/women relations 5. Alcoholism 6. Biographies

LC 2011014719

"The author presents an exhaustive and exhausting biography of the legendary Hollywood star, famed for his uncanny naturalism and authority on camera and best remembered for the series of films he made with longtime companion Katharine Hepburn. A monumental, definitive biography of one the finest film actors in the history of the medium." Kirkus.

Tran, G. B. (Gia-Bao), 1976-

Tran, G. B. (Gia-Bao), 1976- **Vietnamerica** : a family's journey / G. B. Tran. Villard Books, 2011. 279 p. : **B**

ISBN 9780345508720

1. Tran, G. B. (Gia-Bao), 1976- Family 2. Vietnam War, 1961-1975 -- Refugees. 3. Families -- History 4. Immigrants, Vietnamese 5. Vietnamese Americans. 6. Vietnam 7. United States 8. Comics and Graphic novels 9. Autobiographical comics 10. Autobiographies and memoirs

A memoir in graphic novel format about the author's experiences as the son of Vietnamese immigrants who fled to America during the fall of Saigon describes how he learned his tragic ancestral history and the impact of the Vietnam War on his family while visiting their homeland years later.

"The comic utilizes a dizzying barrage of effects to depict the characters' confusing experience: different lettering styles, realistic action set against full-page government posters, sound effects swirling from panel to panel, action-packed panoramas breaking apart as South Vietnam collapses." Publishers Weekly.

Tran, Phuc, 1974-

Tran, Phuc, 1974- **Sigh,** gone : a misfit's memoir of great books, punk rock, and the fight to fit in / Phuc Tran. Flatiron Books, 2020. 306 p. **B**

ISBN 9781250194718

1. Vietnamese Americans 2. Teenage immigrants 3. Misfits (Persons) 4. Books and reading 5. Pennsylvania 6. Autobiographies and memoirs

LC 2019047906

In 1975, during the fall of Saigon, Phuc Tran immigrates to America along with his family. By sheer chance they land in Carlisle, Pennsylvania, a small town where the Trans struggle to assimilate into their new life. In this coming-of-age memoir told through the themes of great books such as The Metamorphosis, The Scarlet Letter, The Iliad, and more, Tran navigates the push and pull of finding and accepting himself despite the challenges of immigration, feelings of isolation, and teenage rebellion, all while attempting to meet the rigid expectations set by his immigrant parents.

"This high-impact, emotional memoir about growing up in a Vietnamese immigrant family refracts the author?s angry adolescence through a prism of classic literature." Publishers Weekly

Travis, Randy

Travis, Randy **Forever** and ever, amen : a memoir of music, faith, and braving the storms of life / Randy Travis with Ken Abraham. Nelson Books, [2019] 304 p. **B**

ISBN 9781400207985

1. Travis, Randy. 2. Country musicians 3. Fame 4. Faith (Christianity) 5. People who have had strokes 6. Autobiographies and memoirs

LC 2018046406

The long-awaited, deeply personal story of one of American music's greatest icons, a remarkable tale of the utmost heights of fame and success, the deepest lows of life's sorrows, and a miraculous return from the brink of death---told as only Randy Travis can.

"Travis writes honestly about his ups and downs as well as his serious health problems and closes on a hopeful note. For Travis many fans and all who love country music." Booklist.

Trebek, Alex, 1940-2020

Trebek, Alex, 1940-2020 The **answer** is ... : reflections on my life / Alex Trebek. Simon & Schuster, 2020. 290 p. : **B**

ISBN 9781982157999

1. Jeopardy! (Television program) 2. Television personalities 3. Television game shows 4. Television game show hosts 5. Quiz shows 6. Autobiographies and memoirs

LC 2020938903

Longtime <I>Jeopardy!</I> host and television icon Alex Trebek reflects on his life and career.

"Readers will likely come away from the memoir feeling even more comfortable with the author than they already did. An amiable, enjoyable series of glimpses into the life of an avuncular figure." Kirkus

Trebincevic, Kenan, 1980-

Trebincevic, Kenan, 1980- The **Bosnia** list : a memoir of war, exile, and return / Kenan Trebincevic and Susan Shapiro. Penguin Books, 2014. 320 p. **B**

ISBN 9780143124573

1. Yugoslav War, 1991-1995 2. Muslims 3. Interethnic conflict 4. Refugees 5. Bosnia and Hercegovina 6. Autobiographies and memoirs

LC 2013035345

"This poignant, searing memoir chronicles Kenan's miraculous escape from the brutal ethnic cleansing campaign that swept the former Yugoslavia. After two decades in the United States, Kenan honors his father's wish to visit their homeland, making a list ofwhat he wants to do there. Kenan decides to confront the former next door neighbor who stole from his mother, see the concentration camp where his Dad and brother were imprisoned and stand on the grave of his first betrayer to make sure he's really dead.Back in the land of his birth, Kenan finds something more powerful-and shocking-than revenge".-- Provided by publisher.

"An engaging memoir of war trauma and the redemption to be found in confronting it." Kirkus.

Trillin, Alice Stewart

★Trillin, Calvin **About** Alice / Calvin Trillin. Random House, c2006. 78 p. ; **B**

ISBN 9781400066155

1. Trillin, Calvin, Marriage 2. Trillin, Alice Stewart. 3. Authors' spouses -- United States 4. People with cancer 5. Husband and wife. 6. Authors, American -- 20th century 7. Biographies

LC 2006045573

The best-selling author celebrates the life of a remarkable woman who played a vital role in the author's life.

Trotsky, Leon, 1879-1940

Service, Robert, 1947- **Trotsky** : a biography / Robert Service. Belknap Press of Harvard University Press, 2009. xxii, 600 p., 24 p. of plates : **B**

ISBN 9780674036154

1. Trotsky, Leon, 1879-1940. 2. Revolutionaries -- Soviet Union 3. Communism -- Soviet Union -- History. 4. Exiles -- Russia 5. Politicians -- Soviet Union 6. Russia -- Politics and government -- 1894-1917. 7. Soviet Union -- Politics and government -- 1917-1936. 8. Biographies

LC 2009025417

Trotsky is perhaps the most intriguing and, given his prominence, the most understudied of the Soviet revolutionaries. Using new archival sources, Robert Service offers new insights. He discusses Trotsky's fractious relations with the leaders he was trying to unify; his attempt to disguise his political closeness to Stalin; and his role in the early 1920s as the progenitor of political and cultural Stalinism. Trotsky evinced a surprisingly glacial and schematic approach to making revolution. Service recounts Trotsky's role in the botched German revolution of 1923; his willingness to subject Europe to a Red Army invasion in the 1920s; and his assumption that peasants could easily be pushed onto collective farms. Although Trotsky's followers clung to the stubborn view of him as a pure revolutionary and a powerful intellect unjustly hounded into exile by Stalin, the reality is very different.--From publisher description.

Trotter, William Monroe, 1872-1934

★Greenidge, Kerri **Black** radical : the life and times of William Monroe Trotter / Kerri K. Greenidge. Liveright Publishing Corporation, a division of W.W. Norton & Co., [2020] xxii, 408 p. **B**

ISBN 9781631495342

1. Trotter, William Monroe, 1872-1934. 2. Boston Guardian 3. African American radicals 4. African American civil rights workers 5. African American journalists 6. Journalists 7. United States -- Race relations -- History 8. Biographies

LC 2019037416

A portrait of the lesser-known, turn-of-the-20th-century civil rights activist explores how he used his influence as an emancipator and the editor of the Guardian to promote gradualist politics and rally black working-class Americans throughout the post-Reconstruction era. This long-overdue biography reestablishes William Monroe Trotter's essential place next to Douglass, Du Bois, and King in the pantheon of American civil rights heroes.

"A must-read for both scholars and general readers interested in the civil rights movement." Library Journal

Truman, Harry S., 1884-1972

Baime, A. J. (Albert J.) The **accidental** president : Harry S. Truman and the four months that changed the world / A. J. Baime. Houghton Mifflin Harcourt, 2017 352 p. **B**

ISBN 9780544617346

1. Truman, Harry S., 1884-1972. 2. Political leadership. 3. Cold War 4. Presidents 5. United States -- Politics and government -- 1945-1953. 6. United States -- Foreign relations -- 1945-1953. 7. Biographies

LC 2017044086

A suspenseful chronicle of the 33rd president's first four months in office traces his unlikely rise to the Oval Office and his pivotal contributions to major decisions, from the founding of the United Nations and the Nazi surrender to the liberation of concentration camps and the decision to drop the bomb.

Dallek, Robert **Harry** S. Truman : the 33rd President, 1945-1953 / Robert Dallek ; edited by Arthur M. Schlesinger and Sean Wilentz. Times Books, 2008. 208 p. American presidents series (Times Books) **B**

ISBN 9780805069389

1. Truman, Harry S., 1884-1972. 2. Presidents -- United States 3. Politicians 4. United States -- Politics and government -- 1945-1953.

LC 2008010193

Traces the thirty-third president's unlikely rise to power and his role in bringing America into the nuclear age, covering his perspectives on civil rights, his clashes with Douglas MacArthur over the conduct of the Korean War, and his reelection in 1948.

"This book is the best starting point for knowledge of Truman's life and for an astute assessment of his career." Publishers Weekly.

Donald, Aida DiPace **Citizen** soldier : a life of Harry S. Truman / Aida D. Donald. Basic Books, c2012. 224 p. **B**

ISBN 9780465031207

1. Truman, Harry S., 1884-1972. 2. Presidents -- United States 3. Soldiers -- United States 4. United States -- Politics and government -- 1945-1953. 5. Biographies

LC 2012025583

Depicts the life of America's 33rd president, from his impoverished start with his farming family, through enlisting in the army in 1917 and numerous failed business ventures to beginning a political career in Missouri that ultimately led to the presidency.

"With her research and historical expertise, Donald, former editor-in-chief of Harvard University Press, has succeeded in making Truman much more than a silent commander of a failed watch, into a fully formed man of sizable defects and masterful achievements." Publishers Weekly.

McCullough, David G. **Truman** / David McCullough. Simon & Schuster, 1992. 1117 p. : **B**

ISBN 0671456547

1. Truman, Harry S., 1884-1972. 2. CIA -- History. 3. United States. Department of Defense 4. Presidents -- United States 5. Politicians -- United States -- History -- 20th century 6. Marshall Plan, 1948-1952. 7. Anti-Communism. 8. United States -- Politics and government -- 1945-1953. 9. United States -- History -- 1945-1953. 10. Biographies

LC 92005245

ALA Notable Book, 1993.

Lionel Gelber Prize (Canada), 1992.

Pulitzer Prize for Biography or Autobiography, 1993.

National Book Award for Nonfiction finalist, 1992

National Book Critics Circle Award for Autobiography/Memoir finalist, 1992.

A biography of the thirty-third U.S. president explores Truman's brutal frontier childhood, his education, his dogged optimism, and his rise through the ranks of the Pendergast machine that controlled Missouri politics.

"This biography of the 33rd president not only conveys in rich detail Truman's accomplishments as a politician and statesman, but also reveals the character and personality of this constantly-surprising manas schoolboy, farmer, soldier, merchant, county judge, senator, vice president and chief executive. The book relates how Truman overcame the stigma of business failure and debt . . . and acquired a reputation for honesty, reliability and common sense." Publishers Weekly.

Trump, Donald, 1946-

D'Antonio, Michael **Never** enough : Donald Trump and the pursuit of success / Michael D'Antonio Thomas Dunne Books, 2015. 400 p. **B**

ISBN 9781250042385

1. Businesspeople -- United States 2. Presidential candidates. 3. Public relations -- United States -- Case studies. 4. Success in business -- United States -- Case studies. 5. United States -- Social life and customs. 6. Biographies

LC 2015916088

Reprinted in 2016 under the title The truth about Trump

An unauthorized biography of the controversial businessman recounts his early days in development while reviewing the unorthodox approach that brought him success and that fuels his insatiable quest for power.

Kranish, Michael **Trump** revealed : an American journey of ambition, ego, money, and power / Michael Kranish and Marc Fisher. Scribner, 2016 384 p. **B**

ISBN 9781501155772

1. Trump, Donald, 1946- Political and social views. 2. Presidential candidates. 3. Businesspeople 4. Presidential election, 2016 5. United States -- Politics and government -- 2009-2017 6. Biographies

LC 2016032645

A biography of Donald Trump is reported by a team of award-winning Washington Post journalists and co-authored by investigative political reporter Michael Kranish and senior editor Marc Fisher.

"The most definitive book about Trump to date." Booklist.

★Trump, Mary L. **Too** much and never enough : how my family created the world's most dangerous man / Mary Trump. Simon & Schuster, 2020. 225 p. ; **B**

ISBN 9781982141462

1. Trump family. 2. Presidents. 3. Businesspeople. 4. Dysfunctional families. 5. Fathers and sons. 6. United States -- History -- 21st century. 7. United States -- Politics and government -- 2017- 8. Biographies.

LC bl2020015126

Includes index.

In this revelatory, authoritative portrait of Donald J. Trump and the toxic family that made him, Mary L. Trump, a trained clinical psychologist and Donald's only niece, shines a bright light on the dark history of their family in order to explain how her uncle became the man who now threatens the world's health, economic security, and social fabric.

"Trump, a trained clinical psychologist and the niece of President Donald Trump, delivers a concise and damning account of her family's dysfunctions and their role in shaping her uncle's toxic blend of cruelty, incompetence, and vainglory." Publishers Weekly

Trump, Melania, 1970-

Jordan, Mary, 1960- The **art** of her deal : the untold story of Melania Trump / Mary Jordan. Simon & Schuster, 2020. vii, 341 p. : **B**

ISBN 9781982113407

1. Trump, Donald, 1946- 2. Presidents' spouses. 3. Ambition in women. 4. Independence in women. 5. Decision-making. 6. Biographies.

"Traces Melania's journey from Slovenia, where her family stood out for their nonconformity, to her days as a fledgling model known for steering clear of the industry's hard-partying scene, to a tiny living space in Manhattan she shared platonically with a male photographer, to the long, complicated dating dance that finally resulted in her marriage to Trump."--Provided by publisher.

"Interesting and fair . . . meticulously researched . . . as complete a portrait as we can expect of the current first lady." Kirkus

Trussoni, Danielle

Trussoni, Danielle The **fortress** : a love story / Danielle Trussoni. Dey Street Books, 2016. 320 p. **B**

ISBN 9780062459008

1. Grozni, Nikolai 2. Romantic love 3. Moving to a new country 4. Marital conflict 5. Second chances 6. Bulgaria 7. France 8. Autobiographies and memoirs

LC 2017285211

The author discusses her marriage, focusing on the time her and her husband moved to the south of France in a effort to save their relationship.

"Told over a 10-year period in Iowa, Bulgaria, Providence, and southern France, The Fortress is an immersive and honest portrayal of human nature bound by commitment." Booklist.

Truth, Sojourner, d. 1883

★Painter, Nell Irvin **Sojourner** Truth : a life, a symbol / Nell Irvin Painter. W.W. Norton, 1996. xii, 370 p. : **B**

ISBN 0393027392

1. African American abolitionists 2. Fugitive slaves 3. Interracial friendship. 4. Feminists 5. United States -- History -- 1783-1865. 6. United States -- History -- 1865-1898. 7. Biographies

LC 95047595

ALA Notable Book, 1997.

BCALA Literary Award for Nonfiction, 1997."

Painter persuasively offers us the real woman behind the myth." Publishers Weekly.

Tubman, Harriet, 1820?-1913

Clinton, Catherine, 1952- **Harriet** Tubman : the road to freedom / Catherine Clinton. Little, Brown, 2004. xiii, 272 p. **B**

ISBN 9780316144926

1. Slaves 2. African American women 3. Underground Railroad. 4. Anti-slavery movements -- History -- 19th century. 5. United States -- History -- 19th century. 6. Biographies

LC 2003056185

"Clinton turns sobriquets into meaningful descriptors of a unique person. In her hands, a familiar legend acquires human dimension with no diminution of its majesty and power." Publishers Weekly.

★Dunbar, Erica Armstrong **She** came to slay : the life and times of Harriet Tubman / Erica Armstrong Dunbar. Simon & Schuster, 2019. xiv, 157 p. **B**

ISBN 9781982139599

1. African American women abolitionists. 2. African American women 3. Underground Railroad. 4. Women spies. 5. United States -- History -- 19th century. 6. Biographies.

A lively, informative and illustrated tribute to one of the most exceptional women in American history--Harriet Tubman--looks at a heroine whose fearlessness and activism still resonates today.

"With illustrations and catchy asides enhancing the conversational style, this smoothly readable narrative tells a story kept alive through oral tradition for decades. Perfect for Tubman novices but also enjoyable historical reading for those who already know most of the stories." Kirkus.

Humez, Jean McMahon, 1944- **Harriet** Tubman : the life and the life stories / Jean M. Humez. University of Wisconsin Press, c2003. xii, 471 p. : **B**

ISBN 9780299191207

1. Slaves 2. African American women 3. Underground Railroad. 4. Intellectual life -- African American women 5. United States -- History -- 19th century 6. Biographies

LC 2003005676

Larson, Kate Clifford **Bound** for the promised land : Harriet Tubman, portrait of an American hero / Kate Clifford Larson. Ballantine, c2004. 402 p. **B**

ISBN 0345456270

1. Underground Railroad. 2. Fugitive slaves 3. Slaves 4. Anti-slavery movements -- History -- 19th century. 5. United States -- History -- 19th century. 6. Biographies

"Using a clear writing style, Larson does an excellent job of placing Tubman in the context of her times." School Library Journal.

Turing, Alan Mathison, 1912-1954

Copeland, B. Jack, 1950- **Turing** : pioneer of the information age / Jack Copeland. Oxford University Press, 2012. 300 p. : **B**

ISBN 9780199639793

1. Turing, Alan Mathison, 1912-1954. 2. Artificial intelligence. 3. World War II -- Cryptography. 4. Mathematicians -- England 5. Military intelligence. 6. Great Britain -- History -- 20th century. 7. Biographies

LC bl2013024746

In the centenary of Alan Turing's birth, we celebrate the life and work of one of the greatest scientists of the 20th century. Best known for the role he played in cracking German secret code Enigma during World War Two, and the personal tragedy of his death aged only 41, this is an insight into to the man, his work, and his legacy.

Leavitt, David, 1961- The **man** who knew too much : Alan Turing and the invention of the computer / David Leavitt. W. W. Norton, c2006. 319 p. : **B**

ISBN 0393052362

1. Turing, Alan Mathison, 1912-1954. 2. Mathematicians -- Great Britain 3. Gay men -- Legal status, laws, etc. -- Great Britain. 4. Artificial intelligence -- History. 5. Computers -- History 6. Great Britain -- History -- 20th century

LC 2005018034

"Atlas books."

Outlines the English mathematician's efforts in devising a programmable calculating machine, his work in cracking the Nazi Enigma code, and how the revelation of his homosexuality led to his tragic imprisonment and suicide.

"The author succeeds in drawing a wonderfully vivid picture of his shy, dry, brilliant hero." National Review.

Turner, J. M. W., 1775-1851

★Moyle, Franny **Turner** : The extraordinary life and momentous times of J.M.W. Turner / Franny Moyle. Penguin Group USA, 2016. 400 p. **B**

ISBN 9780735220928

1. Landscape painters 2. Painters 3. Artists -- Great Britain 4. Landscape painting 5. Biographies

LC 2016043479

Chronicles the life of one of Western art's most admired, misunderstood and celebrated painters.

"This excellent biography shows the benefits, and the pitfalls, of such single-minded obsession." Kirkus.

Turner, Ted

Auletta, Ken **Media** man : Ted Turner's improbable empire / Ken Auletta. Norton, c2004. 205 p. : **B**

ISBN 9780393051681

1. Turner, Ted. 2. Businesspeople -- United States 3. Sports team owners 4. Telecommunication -- United States 5. United States -- Social life and customs -- 21st century 6. Biographies

LC 2004012215

Traces the rise and fall of the cable network mogul, relating his transformation of a small Atlanta network into a national cable superstation, invention of the first twenty-four-hour CNN news channel, and eventual ousting after selling his company to Time Warner.

Turner, Tina, 1939-

★Turner, Tina, 1939- **My** love story : a memoir / Tina Turner. Atria Books, 2018. 320 p. **B**

ISBN 9781501198243

1. Rock musicians -- United States 2. Women singers 3. African American women musicians 4. Autobiographies and memoirs

LC bl2018167903

The rock & roll legend examines her illustrious career and complicated personal life, from her darkest hours to her happiest moments.

"She married German music producer Erwin Bach in 2013, and her gratitude for his loving support, especially when she faced serious health and family issues, shines throughout, as do her optimism, perseverance, and faith. Full-color and black-and-white photos beautifully enhance the text. Fans of Turner will especially enjoy this memorable, engaging life story." Library Journal.

Tutankhamen, King of Egypt

Brier, Bob The **murder** of Tutankhamen : a true story / Bob Brier. G. P. Putnam's Sons, c1998. xx, 264 p. : **B**

ISBN 9780399143830

1. Tutankhamen, King of Egypt. 2. Tutankhamen, King of Egypt Death and burial. 3. Egypt -- Rulers 4. Ancient Egypt -- History -- Eighteenth dynasty, ca. 1570-1320 B.C. 5. Biographies

LC 97049193

A look at the last days of the ancient Egyptian pharaoh draws on new medical and archaeological evidence that suggests that Tutankhamen suffered a brutal, untimely death that led to subsequent palace and political intrigue.

"By combining known historical events with evidence gathered by advanced technologies, Brier has recreated the suspenseful story of religious upheaval and political intrigue that likely resulted in the murder of the teenage King Tutankhamen." Booklist

Twain, Mark, 1835-1910

Powers, Ron **Mark** Twain : a life / Ron Powers. Free Press, 2005. xi, 722 p. : **B**

ISBN 0743248996

1. Twain, Mark, 1835-1910. 2. Authors, American -- 19th century 3. Humorists -- United States -- 19th century 4. Journalists -- United States 5. Insecurity in men. 6. Biographies

LC 2005048816

National Book Critics Circle Award for Biography finalist, 2005.

Presents a biography of Mark Twain that embodies the totality of the man in his many moods and phases of life as youth, son and brother, writer, friend, husband, and celebrity.

"A masterful biography of interest to both general readers and academics." Booklist.

Scharnhorst, Gary The **life** of Mark Twain : the early years, 1835-1871 / Gary Scharnhorst. University of Missouri Press, 2018 xxxi, 686 p. **B**

ISBN 9780826221445

1. Twain, Mark, 1835-1910. 2. Authors. 3. Storytelling. 4. Literature and society. 5. Humorists. 6. Biographies

This book begins the first multi-volume biography of Samuel Clemens to appear in over a century. In the succeeding years, Clemens biographers have either tailored their narratives to fit the parameters of a single volume or focused on a particular period or aspect of Clemens's life, because the whole of that epic life cannot be compressed into a single volume. In The Life of Mark Twain, Gary Scharnhorst has chosen to write a complete biography plotted from beginning to end, from a single point of view, on an expansive canvas.

"Besides ferreting out truths Clemens himself concealed, Scharnhorst announces his intention to challenge the misleading perspectives of previous biographersincluding those academic specialists whose single-volume tomes deliver skeletal portraits of a robust figure. The signal achievement manifested in this volume will leave readers eagerly awaiting its sequels." Booklist.

Scharnhorst, Gary The **life** of Mark Twain : the middle years, 1871-1891 / Gary Scharnhorst. University of Missouri Press, 2019. 802 p. **B**

ISBN 9780826221896

1. Twain, Mark, 1835-1910. 2. Authors. 3. Storytelling. 4. Literature and society. 5. Humorists. 6. Biographies

LC 2018049235

The second volume of Gary Scharnhorst's three-volume biography chronicles the life of Samuel Langhorne Clemens between his move with his family from Buffalo to Elmira (and then Hartford) in spring 1871 and their departure from Hartford for Europe in mid-1891. During this time he wrote and published some of his best-known works, including Roughing It, The Gilded Age, The Adventures of Tom Sawyer, A Tramp Abroad, The Prince and the Pauper, Life on the Mississippi, Adventures of Huckleberry Finn, and A Connecticut Yankee in King Arthur's Court.

"This painstakingly researched narrative explores the shifting circumstances and evolving motivations of a great author at the peak of his creative powers.." Booklist.

Shelden, Michael **Mark** Twain : man in white : the grand adventure of his final years / Michael Shelden. Random House, 2010. 528 p. **B**

ISBN 9780679448006

1. Twain, Mark, 1835-1910. 2. Authors, American -- 19th century 3. Humorists -- United States -- 19th century 4. Writing. 5. United States -- History -- 19th century. 6. Biographies

LC 2009019719

Drawing heavily on Twain's own letters and journals, Shelden illuminates Mark Twain's twilight years in this account of the legendary author's life, recounting both Twain's private family experiences and his larger-than-life public image.

★Twain, Mark, 1835-1910 **Autobiography** ofMark Twain : volume 1 / Harriet Elinor Smith, editor ; associate editors: Benjamin Griffin, Victor Fischer, Michael B. Frank, Sharon K. Goetz, Leslie Myrick. University of California Press, c2010- 760 p. **B**

ISBN 9780520267190

1. Twain, Mark, 1835-1910. 2. Authors. 3. Humorists -- United States -- 19th century 4. Intellectual life -- 19th century 5. Storytelling. 6. Autobiographies and memoirs

LC 2009047700

"A publication of the Mark Twain Project of the Bancroft Library."

In the first complete and uncensored edition of his autobiography, one of America's foremost authors and humorists relates experiences lived, people encountered, places visited, and judgments rendered throughout his lifetime.

"Laced with Twain's unique blend of humor and vitriol, the haphazard narrative is engrossing, hugely funny, and deeply revealing of its author's mind." Publishers Weekly.

★Twain, Mark, 1835-1910 **Autobiography** of Mark Twain : volume 2 / Harriet Elinor Smith, editor ; associate editors: Benjamin Griffin, Victor Fischer, Michael B. Frank, Sharon K. Goetz, Leslie Myrick. University of California Press, 2013 xix, 733 p. **B**

ISBN 9780520272781

1. Twain, Mark, 1835-1910. 2. Authors. 3. Humorists -- United States -- 19th century 4. Intellectual life -- 19th century 5. Storytelling. 6. Autobiographies and memoirs

LC bl2013041739

The second volume of Mark Twain's uncensored autobiography continues to describe the events of the author's life in his own humorous and opinionated voice, including his preoccupation with money and his dislike of the politicians of his day.

"Twain traveled extensively and befriended many luminaries, and his colorful experiences give the book the same Dickensian scope as the first volume, and presents a vivid picture of America in the 19th century and Twain's indelible mark on it." Publishers Weekly.

★Twain, Mark, 1835-1910 **Autobiography** of Mark Twain : volume 3 / Mark Twain ; Harriet Elinor Smith, editor ; associate editors: Benjamin Griffin, Victor Fischer, Michael B. Frank. University of California Press, 2015. 792 p. **B**

ISBN 9780520279940

1. Twain, Mark, 1835-1910. 2. Authors. 3. Humorists -- United States -- 19th century 4. Intellectual life -- 19th century 5. Storytelling. 6. Autobiographies and memoirs

LC bl2015038084

A concluding volume of the literary master's uncensored collection of writings on his inner and outer life features his daily dictations from March 1907 to December 1909 and cover his honorary degrees from Oxford, critical assessments of Theodore Roosevelt and controversial "Ashcroft-Lyon Manuscript."

Zacks, Richard **Chasing** the last laugh : Mark Twain's raucous and redemptive round-the-world comedy tour / Richard Zacks. Doubleday, 2016. 352 p. **B**

ISBN 9780385536448

1. Twain, Mark, 1835-1910. 2. Authors, American -- 19th century 3. Humorists -- United States -- 19th century 4. Biographies

LC 2015036843

In 1895, at age sixty, Mark Twain was dead broke and miserable--his recent novels had been critical and commercial failures, and he was bankrupted by his inexplicable decision to run a publishing company. His wife made him promise to pay every debt back in full, so Twain embarked on an around-the-world comedy lecture tour that would take him from the dusty small towns of the American West to the faraway lands of India, South Africa, Australia, and beyond. Twain remained abroad for five years, a time of struggle and wild experiences -- and ultimately redemption, as he rediscovered his voice as a writer and humorist, and returned, wiser and celebrated. As he said in his famous reply to an article about his demise, "the report of my death is an exaggeration."

"Zacks's narrative is well-researched with rich detail...and it will strike ardent Twain fans and history lovers as fresh and inspiring." Publishers Weekly.

Tweedy, Jeff, 1967-

Tweedy, Jeff, 1967- **Let's** go (so we can get back) : a memoir of recording and discording with Wilco, etc. / Jeff Tweedy. Dutton, [2018] 336 p. **B**

ISBN 9781101985267

1. Wilco (Musical group) 2. Alternative rock musicians 3. Guitarists. 4. Anxiety in men. 5. Prescription drug abuse 6. Autobiographies and memoirs.

The singer, guitarist, and songwriter, best known for this work with the bands Uncle Tupelo and Wilco, opens up about his past, his songs, the music and the people that have inspired him.

Twombly, Cy, 1928-2011

Rivkin, Joshua **Chalk** : the art and erasure of Cy Twombly / Joshua Rivkin. Melville House, 2018. 464 p. **B**

ISBN 9781612197180

1. Twombly, Cy, 1928-2011. 2. Artists -- United States 3. Modernism (Art) 4. Painting. 5. Sculpture. 6. Biographies.

LC 2018034338

"The first book to explore the life of Cy Twombly, one of the most-important and influential artists of the Twentieth Century Cy Twombly was a man obsessed with myth and history--including his own. Shuttling between his stunning homes in Italy and the United States, where he perfected his room-size canvases, he managed his public image carefully and rarely gave interviews. Upon first seeing Twombly's remarkable paintings, author Joshua Rivkin became obsessed himself with the mysterious artist, and beganchasing every lead, big or small--anything that might illuminate who Twombly really was. Now, after unprecedented archival research and years of interviews, Rivkin has reconstructed Twombly's life, from his time at the legendary Black Mountain College, to his canonization in a 1979 Whitney retrospective; from his heady explorations of Rome in the 1950s with Robert Rauschenberg, to the ongoing efforts to shape his legacy after his death. Including previously unpublished photographs, Chalk presents a more personal and searching type of biography than we've ever encountered, and brings to life a more complex Twombly than we've ever known".-- Provided by publisher.

Tyler, Carol

Tyler, Carol **You'll** never know. C. Tyler. Fantagraphics, 2009. 104 p. You'll never know ; **B**

ISBN 9781606991442

1. World War II veterans. 2. Fathers and daughters. 3. Family relationships. 4. Families 5. War comics. 6. Comics and Graphic novels 7. Autobiographical comics 8. Autobiographies and memoirs

LC 2014378054

The complete three-volume series You'll Never Know was collected under the title Soldier's Heart: The Campaign to Understand My WWII Veeran Father: a Daughter's Memoir in 2015.

A good and decent man is the first of a 3-part graphic memoir chronicling the author's relationship with her World War II veteran father, and how his war experience shaped her childhood and affected her relationships in adulthood.

Tyler, John, 1790-1862

★Crapol, Edward P. **John** Tyler : the accidental president / Edward P. Crapol. University of North Carolina Press, c2006.

332 p. : **B**
ISBN 0807830410
1. Tyler, John, 1790-1862. 2. Presidents -- United States 3. United States -- Politics and government -- 1841-1845. 4. Biographies
LC 2005037963

"In this biography of the former U.S. president, the author argues that Tyler was in fact a terrifically strong president who helped strengthen the executive branch. This balanced, fascinating volume will introduce a new generation of readers to an oft-ignored president." Publishers Weekly.

May, Gary, 1944- **John** Tyler / Gary May. Times Books/ Henry Holt and Co., 2008. xviii, 183 p. ; **B**
ISBN 0805082387
1. Tyler, John, 1790-1862. 2. Governors -- Virginia 3. Legislators -- United States 4. Presidents -- United States 5. Vice-Presidents -- United States 6. United States -- Politics and government -- 1815-1861. 7. Virginia -- Politics and government -- 1775-1865. 8. Biographies
LC 2008018131

Traces the events of the tenth executive leader's presidency from his unexpected ascent after the premature death of William Henry Harrison and unpopular veto of a proposed Bank of the United States to his indirect role in promoting secession.

Tynan, Tracy

Tynan, Tracy **Wear** and tear : the threads of my life / Tracy Tynan. Scribner, 2016. 320 p. **B**
ISBN 9781501123689
1. Tynan, Tracy. 2. Fashion designers. 3. Autobiographies and memoirs
LC 2015031108

The memoirs of a celebrity costume designer describe her upbringing in the fashionable celebrity circles of her literary parents, her family's artistic but traumatizing approaches to shopping and how the fashion-savvy perspectives of her early years shaped her relationships and career.

"Each of the three-dozen gemlike chapters cover an episode built around a specific piece of clothing, from a designer crepe de chine gown to a maroon plaid dress to a tiny pink knitted cap, a gift of love for Tynan's premature baby. The sum total is an absorbing memoir well-told from a singular perspective." Library Journal.

Tyson, Mike, 1966-

Tyson, Mike, 1966- **Iron** ambition : my life with Cus D'Amato / Mike Tyson. Blue Rider Press, 2017 320 p. **B**
ISBN 9780399177033
1. D'Amato, Cus. 2. Boxers (Sports) -- United States 3. Boxing trainers 4. Mentors 5. Coach and athlete 6. Autobiographies and memoirs
LC 2017007907

The former heavyweight champion and best-selling memoirist presents an intimate look at the life and leadership lessons of the legendary boxing trainer, exploring D'Amato's pivotal role in the careers of multiple World Champions and his legal adoption of Tyson in the aftermath of the latter's mother's death.

"A belated but welcome homage to a boxing legend who died shortly before Tyson's career took off." Kirkus.

Tyson, Neil deGrasse

Tyson, Neil deGrasse **Letters** from an astrophysicist / Neil deGrasse Tyson. W W Norton & Company, 2019. 247 p. **B**
ISBN 9781324003311
1. Tyson, Neil deGrasse Correspondence 2. Cosmology. 3. Astronomy -- Miscellanea. 4. Astrophysics -- Miscellanea. 5. Science 6. Letters
LC 2019030198

Astrophysicist Neil deGrasse Tyson has attracted one of the world's largest online followings with his fascinating, widely accessible insights into science and our universe. Now, Tyson invites us to go behind the scenes of his public fame by revealing his correspondence with people across the globe who have sought him out in search of answers. In this hand-picked collection of 101 letters, Tyson draws upon cosmic perspectives to address a vast array of questions about science, faith, philosophy, life, and of course, Pluto. His succinct, opinionated, passionate, and often funny responses reflect his popularity and standing as a leading educator.

Tyson, Timothy B.

Tyson, Timothy B. **Blood** done sign my name : a true story / Timothy B. Tyson. Crown Publishers, 2004. vii, 355 p. **B**
ISBN 9780609610589
1. Tyson, Timothy B. Childhood and youth. 2. Crimes against African Americans -- Oxford, North Carolina -- History -- 20th century. 3. Murder -- Oxford, North Carolina -- History -- 20th century. 4. Trials (Murder) -- Oxford, North Carolina. 5. Riots -- Oxford, North Carolina -- History -- 20th century. 6. Oxford, North Carolina -- Race relations. 7. Autobiographies and memoirs
LC 2003019804

National Book Critics Circle Award for Nonfiction finalist, 2004.

Thirty years after the murder of a black man by a Klansman and his acquittal by an all-white jury, the author returns to his hometown of Oxford, North Carolina, to make sense of what happened, interweaving his own childhood memories and the real world of modern-day Oxford with interviews with participants on both sides, shedding new light on the struggle for racial justice.

"A significant work of memoir and social history; for public and academic libraries." Library Journal.

U-God, 1970-

U-God, 1970- **Raw** : my journey into the Wu-Tang / Lamont "U-God" Hawkins. Picador, 2018. 304 p. **B**
ISBN 9781250191168
1. Wu-Tang Clan (Musical group). 2. Rap musicians. 3. Rap music. 4. Music industry and trade. 5. Autobiographies and memoirs
LC 2017047146

A dramatic account of the lesser-known story behind the meteoric rise of the Wu-Tang Clan, written by one of its founding members, traces his early years in 1970s Brownsville, New York, and how he and his fellow group members escaped the projects to make hip-hop history.

"Hawkins is a wonderful storyteller who spares no detail (he writes of using plastic wrap as a prophylactic), and his willingness to share his wisdom in nonsaccharine terms yields an inspirational coming-of-age story." Publishers Weekly.

Ulander, Perry A., 1948-

Ulander, Perry A., 1948- **Walking** point : from the ashes of the Vietnam War / Perry A. Ulander. North Atlantic Books, 2016 252 p. **B**
ISBN 9781623170127
1. United States. Army. Airborne Brigade, 173rd 2. United States. Army Military life -- History 3. Soldiers -- United States 4. Vietnam War, 1961-1975 5. Marijuana 6. Drug use 7. Autobiographies and

memoirs

LC 2015022372

"This intimate memoir by an American GI who served in Vietnam offers a powerful narrative for readers with an interest in the effects of war and violence, American involvement in Vietnam and how trauma can be a catalyst for transformation".--Provided by publisher.

"Ulander's fine memoir should take a place among the best works in the Vietnam War autobiographical canon." Publishers Weekly.

Ullman, Ellen

Ullman, Ellen **Life** in code : a personal history of technology / Ellen Ullman. MCD, Farrar, Straus and Giroux, 2017. 320 p. **B**

ISBN 9780374534516

1. Computer programmers -- United States 2. Computer programming -- History 3. Internet -- History 4. Technology and civilization 5. Autobiographies and memoirs

LC 2017012764

The award-winning author of Close to the Machine shares insights into the past half century of online development to explore how digital technology has lost its innocence, changing life in unexpected and sometimes sinister ways.

"Neither technophilic nor technophobic, this collection creates a time-lapse view of the rapid development of technology in recent years and provides general readers with much-needed grounding for the sweeping changes of the revolution underway." Publishers Weekly.

Ullmann, Otto, 1925-2005

Asbrink, Elisabeth **And** in the Vienna woods the trees remain : the heartbreaking true story of a family torn apart by war / Elisabeth Asbrink ; translated from the Swedish by Saskia Vogel. Other Press, 2020. 320 p. **B**

ISBN 9781590519172

1. Ullmann, Otto, 1925-2005. 2. Refugees, Jewish 3. World War II 4. Holocaust (1933-1945) 5. Antisemitism 6. Sweden -- History -- 20th century 7. Biographies

LC 2019019275

Winner of the August Prize, an intricate weave of documents, substantive narrative, and emotional commentary that centers on a young Jewish refugee's friendship with the future founder of IKEA.

"Top-notch microcosmic World War II history and an excellent illustration of the immense power of the written word." Kirkus.

Unferth, Deb Olin

Unferth, Deb Olin **Revolution** : the year I fell in love and went to join the war / Deb Olin Unferth. Henry Holt, 2011. 224 p. **B**

ISBN 9780805093230

1. Unferth, Deb Olin Travel Central America. 2. Revolutionaries. 3. Engaged persons 4. Voyages and travels. 5. Authors, American -- 21st century 6. Central America -- Description and travel.

LC 2010023471

National Book Critics Circle Award for Autobiography/ Memoir finalist.

The award-winning author examines the summer she ran away from college to join the Sandinista revolutionaries in Nicaragua, describing the romantic affair with a Christian idealist that prompted the journey, their inability to find people who welcomed them and their struggles with disillusionment.

Ung, Loung

Ung, Loung **First** they killed my father : a daughter of Cambodia remembers / Loung Ung. Harper Perennial, 2006, c2000. 238 p. : **B**

ISBN 9780060856267

1. Ung, Loung. 2. Khmer Rouge. 3. Atrocities -- Cambodia. 4. Refugees, Cambodian. 5. Women refugees. 6. Refugees. 7. Cambodia -- Politics and government -- 1975-1979. 8. Autobiographies and memoirs

LC bl2006011138

Sequel: Lucky child.Originally published: New York : HarperCollinsPublishers, 2000.

Chronicles the brutality of the Khmer Rouge in Cambodia, from the author's forced "evacuation" of Phnom Penh in 1975 to her family's subsequent movements from town to town and eventual separation.

Ung, Loung **Lucky** child : a daughter of Cambodia reunites with the sister she left behind / Loung Ung. Harper Perennial, 2006, c2005. xv, 268 p. : **B**

ISBN 0060733950

1. Ung, Loung. 2. Ung, Chou. 3. Cambodian Americans 4. Cambodian American women. 5. Refugees -- United States 6. Sisters. 7. Cambodia 8. Autobiographies and memoirs

LC bl2006030732

Sequel to: First they killed my father.Sequel: Lulu in the sky.

Originally published: New York : HarperCollins, 2005.

Describes the Ung family's experiences of relocation from war-torn Cambodia and assimilation in Vermont, a transition marked by leaving a sibling behind and the family's struggles to forge a new life in a very different society.

"This book is alternately heart-wrenching and heartwarming, as it follows the parallel lives of Loung Ung and her closest sister, Chou, during the 15 years it took for them to reunite." Publishers Weekly.

Ungern-Sternberg, Roman, 1885-1921

Palmer, James, 1978- The **bloody** white baron : the extraordinary story of the Russian nobleman who became the last Khan of Mongolia / James Palmer. Basic Books, 2009. 288 p. **B**

ISBN 9780465014484

1. Ungern-Sternberg, Roman, 1885-1921. 2. Eccentrics and eccentricities. 3. Military art and science. 4. Psychopathology. 5. Antisemites. 6. Soviet Union -- History -- 20th century. 7. Mongolia -- History. 8. Biographies

LC 2008937254

Chronicles the life and campaigns of the brutal nobleman who led a group of White Russians, Siberians, Japanese, and native Mongolians in conquering Mongolia in 1920, spreading antisemitism, violence, and genocide in his wake, and dreamed of driving the communists out of Moscow and restablishing the Mongolian Empire.

Union, Gabrielle

Union, Gabrielle **We're** going to need more wine : stories that are funny, complicated, and true / Gabrielle Union. Dey Street Books, 2017 304 p. **B**

ISBN 9780062693983

1. Actors and actresses 2. African American women 3. Women social advocates 4. Rape victims 5. Essays 6. Autobiographies and memoirs

LC 2017277365

"This sparkling book collects amusing and heartbreaking stories from the life of actress Union (Being Mary Jane)." Publishers Weekly.

Updike, John

★Begley, Adam **Updike** / Adam Begley. Harper, 2014. 576

p. **B**

ISBN 9780061896453

1. Updike, John. 2. Authors, American -- 20th century. 3. American literature -- 20th century. 4. Biographies.

LC 2013039246

Updike is Adam Begley's masterful, much-anticipated biography of one of the most celebrated figures in American literature: Pulitzer Prize-winning author John Updike--a candid, intimate, and richly detailed look at his life and work.In this magisterial biography, Adam Begley offers an illuminating portrait of John Updike, the acclaimed novelist, poet, short-story writer, and critic who saw himself as a literary spy in small-town and suburban America, who dedicated himself to the task of transcribing "middleness with all its grits, bumps and anonymities.".

"Begley draws on deep research and interviews with the author and his circle to chart his early influences--in particular his ambitious mother, Linda--and rigorously explore the heavily autobiographical dimensions of his fiction and poetry." Publishers Weekly.

Valadon, Suzanne, 1865-1938

Hewitt, Catherine **Renoir's** dancer : the secret life of Suzanne Valadon / Catherine Hewitt. St. Martin's Press, 2018. 368 p. **B**

ISBN 9781250157652

1. Valadon, Suzanne, 1865-1938. 2. Women painters. 3. Artists' models 4. Illegitimacy 5. Painters. 6. Biographies

LC 2017041095

Describes how the illegitimate daughter of an impoverished linen maid in rural France became a famous model for Renoir and other impressionists of the era and was also a talented artist herself who refused to be confined by gender or tradition.

"A well-researched tribute to and resurrection of a master of fin de sicle art." Kirkus.

Valenti, Jessica

★Valenti, Jessica **Sex** object : a memoir / Jessica Valenti. Dey Street Books, 2016 224 p.. **B**

ISBN 9780062435088

1. Feminism. 2. Women. 3. Autobiographies and memoirs

LC 2016017749

The founder of Feministing.com and a columnist for The Guardian US exploring drugs, sex, harassment, assault, bad boyfriends, abortions, work, family and other topics shares funny, embarrassing, painful and sometimes illegal moments from her own life that illuminate what it's like to be a woman today.

"An entertaining and shocking memoir from a leading feminist writer." Booklist.

Vampira, 1921-2008

Poole, W. Scott, 1971- **Vampira** : dark goddess of horror / W. Scott Poole. Soft Skull Press, 2014 320 p. **B**

ISBN 9781593765439

1. Vampira, 1921-2008. 2. Entertainers -- United States 3. Women's role 4. Horror films 5. Camp (Aesthetics) 6. Biographies

LC 2014014147

The new book from award-winning historian W. Scott Poole is a whip-smart piece of pop culture detailing the story of cult horror figure Vampira that actually tells the much wider story of 1950s America and its treatment of women and sex, as well as capturing a fascinating swath of Los Angeles history. In Vampira Poole gives us the eclectic life of the dancer, stripper, actress, and artist Maila Nurmi, who would reinvent herself as Vampira during the backdrop of 1950s America. A veteran of the New York stage and late nights at Hollywood's hipster hangouts, Nurmi would eventually be linked to Elvis, Orson Welles, and James Dean, as well as stylist and photographer Rudi Gernreich, founder of the Mattachine Society and designer of the thong. Thanks to rumors of a romance between Vampira and James Dean, his tragic death inspired the circulation of stories that she had cursed him and, better yet, had access to his dead body for use in her dark arts. Vampira is a wildly compelling tour through a forgotten piece of pop cultural history, one with both cultish and literary merit, sure to capture the imagination of Vampira fans new and old.

"Before there was Dr. Morgus, Svengoolie, and Elvira, there was the titular Vampira. This stone-cold winner belongs in every American studies collection." Library Journal.

Van Buren, Martin, 1782-1862

Widmer, Edward L. **Martin** Van Buren / Ted Widmer. Times Books, 2005. 189 p. American presidents series (Times Books) **B**

ISBN 0805069224

1. Van Buren, Martin, 1782-1862. 2. Presidents -- United States 3. United States -- Politics and government -- 1837-1841. 4. Biographies

LC 2004053652

Examines the life and presidency of Martin Van Buren, describing his failed efforts to control such issues as slavery and the great banking panic of 1837.

"The author keenly evokes the environment that enabled Van Buren to thrive." New York Times Book Review.

Van Buren, Peter

Van Buren, Peter **We** meant well : how I helped lose the war for the hearts and minds of the Iraqi people / Peter Van Buren. Metropolitan Books, c2011. 288 p. **B**

ISBN 9780805094367

1. Van Buren, Peter. 2. Postwar reconstruction -- Iraq. 3. Iraq War, 2003-2011 -- Public opinion. 4. Public opinion -- Iraq. 5. Iraq -- Foreign relations United States 6. United States -- Foreign relations Iraq 7. Autobiographies and memoirs

LC 2011008821

A State Department insider reveals what he believes to be costly and misguided efforts by American forces to reconstruct Iraq, arguing that taxpayer money was used for numerous initiatives designed to provide employment and morale to Iraqi citizens, but ultimately failed to acknowledge cultural and wartime truths.

Van Es, Bart

Van Es, Bart The **cut** out girl : a story of war and family, lost and found / Bart Van Es. Penguin Press, 2018. 304 p. **B**

ISBN 9780735222243

1. De Jong, Hesseline 2. Van Es, Bart Family 3. Jews, Dutch 4. World War II -- Netherlands 5. Holocaust (1933-1945) -- Children 6. Child Holocaust survivors 7. Netherlands -- History -- German occupation, 1940-1945 8. Autobiographies and memoirs

LC 2018006209

Costa Biography Award, 2018.

Costa Book of the Year Award, 2018.

The author describes his friendship with an 80-year-old woman in Amsterdam who was smuggled as a child into his grandfather's family during the Nazi occupation and together they confront the dark truth of the Dutch cooperation in rounding up the Jews.

Van Ness, Jonathan

Van Ness, Jonathan **Over** the top : a raw journey to self-love / Jonathan Van Ness. HarperOne, 2019. 304 p. **B**

ISBN 9780062906373

1. Queer eye (Television program : 2018-) 2. Gay men 3. Growing up 4. Television personalities 5. Identity (Psychology) 6. Autobiographies and memoirs

LC bl2019020845

The style-expert star of *Queer Eye* shares deeply personal stories from his Midwestern childhood, revealing how he channeled his passions and setbacks into the positive energy that shaped his signature brand.

Van Vechten, Carl, 1880-1964

★White, Edward, 1981- The **tastemaker** : Carl Van Vechten and the birth of modern America / Edward White. Farrar, Straus and Giroux, 2014. 384 p. **B**

ISBN 9780374201579

1. Van Vechten, Carl, 1880-1964. 2. Authors, American 3. Photographers 4. Journalists 5. Homosexuality 6. New York City 7. Biographies

LC 2013034003

"A revealing biography of the influential and controversial cultural titan who embodied an era".-- Provided by publisher.

"In orderly chapters, White tackles this complicated, multifaceted, tremendously fascinating and contradictory subject. A vigorous, fully fleshed biography of an important contributor to American culture." Kirkus.

Vanasco, Jeannie

Vanasco, Jeannie **Things** we didn't talk about when I was a girl : a memoir / Jeannie Vanasco. Tin House Books, 2019 357 p. **B**

ISBN 9781947793453

1. Rape victims 2. Sexual violence 3. Sexual harassment of women 4. Sex crimes 5. Autobiographies and memoirs

LC 2019013796

A part-memoir, part-true-crime account and testament to female friendship describes how the author navigated sexual trauma by contacting her former friend and rapist, who agreed to come forward and explore how biases shape sexual violence and its perceptions.

Vance, J. D.

★Vance, J. D. **Hillbilly** elegy : a memoir of a family and culture in crisis / J. D. Vance. HarperCollins 2016 352 p. **B**

ISBN 9780062300546

1. Poor families 2. Working class 3. Communities 4. Upward mobility 5. Autobiographies and memoirs

LC 2016304613

Kirkus Prize for Nonfiction finalist, 2016.

Shares the poignant story of the author's family and upbringing, describing how they moved from poverty to an upwardly mobile clan that included the author, a Yale Law School graduate, while navigating the demands of middle-class life and the collective demons of the past.

"Both heartbreaking and heartwarming, this memoir is akin to investigative journalism." Library Journal.

Vanderbilt, Cornelius, 1794-1877

Renehan, Edward, 1956- **Commodore** : the life of Cornelius Vanderbilt / Edward J. Renehan, Jr. Basic Books, c2007. xx, 364 p., 16 p. of plates : **B**

ISBN 0465002552

1. Vanderbilt, Cornelius, 1794-1877. 2. Businesspeople 3. Railroads -- United States -- History. 4. Biographies

LC 2007022392

Presents the life and accomplishments of the steamship and railroad entrepreneur, focusing on his success in building the first integrated railroad system in the Northeast and in establishing New York City as a financial capital.

"A warts and more warts portrait of a brilliantly successful, genuinely despicable man." Kirkus.

★Stiles, T. J. The **first** tycoon : the epic life of Cornelius Vanderbilt / T.J. Stiles. Alfred A. Knopf, 2009. 752 p. **B**

ISBN 9780375415425

1. Vanderbilt, Cornelius, 1794-1877. 2. Businesspeople -- United States 3. Millionaires -- United States 4. Railroads -- United States -- History -- 19th century. 5. Steamboats -- United States -- History -- 19th century. 6. United States -- History -- 19th century. 7. Biographies

LC 2008047879

National Book Award for Nonfiction, 2009.

Pulitzer Prize for Biography or Autobiography, 2010."

This is a mighty and mighty confident work, one that moves with force and conviction and imperious wit through Vanderbilt's noisy life and times. This is state-of-the-art biography, crisper and more piquant than a 600-page book has any right to be." New York Times.

Vanhoenacker, Mark

Vanhoenacker, Mark **Skyfaring** : a journey with a pilot / Mark Vanhoenacker. Knopf, 2015. 288 p. **B**

ISBN 9780385351812

1. Airplanes -- Piloting 2. Aviation 3. Pilots 4. Autobiographies and memoirs

LC 2014041159

Drawing from the fields of history, politics, geography, meteorology, ecology and physics, a pilot and writer reminds us of the strange combinations of forces that make modern air travel possible.

"The author loves travel and encountering new cities and situations, and his job makes this possible for him. This is a delightful and entertaining work, a genuine pleasure to read, and likely to be enjoyed by all. Highly recommended. Summing Up: Highly recommended. All levels." Choice.

Vann, John Paul, 1924-1972

Sheehan, Neil A **bright** shining lie : John Paul Vann and America in Vietnam / Neil Sheehan. Random House, 1989, c1988. 861 p. **B**

ISBN 9780679724148

1. Vann, John Paul, 1924-1972. 2. United States. Army Officers 3. Vietnam War, 1961-1975 -- United States. 4. Soldiers -- United States 5. Biographies

National Book Award for Nonfiction, 1988.

Pulitzer Prize for General Nonfiction, 1989.

Robert F. Kennedy Book Award, 1989.

National Book Critics Circle Award for Nonfiction finalist, 1988.

Pulitzer Prize for Biography or Autobiography finalist, 1989.

Pulitzer Prize for History finalist, 1989.

When he came to Vietnam in 1962, Lieutenant Colonel John Paul Vann was the one clear-sighted participant in an enterprise riddled with arrogance and self-deception, a charismatic soldier who put his life and career on the line in an attempt to convince his superiors that the war should be fought another way. By the time he died in 1972, Vann had embraced the follies he once decried. He died believing that the war had been won. In this book, a monument of history and biography ... a journalist tells the story of John Vann ... and of the tragedy which destroyed the country and squandered so much of America's young manhood and resources.

"The author tells the story of the war through the focus of John Paul Vann, an army officer who faced down South Vietnamese politicians and American generals to expose the corruption that undermined our efforts and later was President Nixon's civilian adviser in Vietnam until he was killed in a helicopter crash in 1972. It is a dramatic device that lets Mr. Sheehan bring the very palpable feel of the war to us with passionate power." New York Times Book Review.

Vargas, Jose Antonio

Vargas, Jose Antonio **Dear** America : notes of an undocumented citizen / Jose Antonio Vargas. Dey Street Books, 2018. 320 p. **B**

ISBN 9780062851352

1. Vargas, Jose Antonio. 2. Journalists -- United States 3. Immigrants. 4. Political activists. 5. Human rights activists. 6. Autobiographies and memoirs

LC bl2018134469

The journalist and immigration-rights activist presents a memoir relating how he was sent from the Philippines to the U.S. as a child, his discovery of his undocumented status as a teenager, and his decision to reveal his immigration status publicly in 2011.

Varty, Boyd

Varty, Boyd **Cathedral** of the wild : an African journey home / Boyd Varty. Random House, 2014. 336 p. **B**

ISBN 9781400069859

1. Varty, Boyd. 2. Wildlife conservation 3. Wildlife conservationists 4. Wildlife refuges 5. Families 6. Londolozi Game Reserve (South Africa) 7. South Africa 8. Autobiographies and memoirs

LC 2013022706

Lions, tigers, and baboons, oh my! Growing up at the Londolozi private game reserve in South Africa, Boyd Varty's childhood included plenty of excitement (hosting Nelson Mandela after his 1990 release from prison) and danger (such as a black mambo slithering over his 11-year-old legs). And there was also a lot of love from his fascinating family, made up of a visionary, conservation-minded father, a renowned filmmaking uncle, a caring but not-easily-shaken mother, and a sister who was his beloved companion and playmate. In this dramatic memoir, Varty reflects on his time with Mandela, shares campfire stories of his family and their adventures, and documents his own tale of personal evolution, which saw him travel around the world only to come back home again.

"An intense, insightful memoir that brings together several wise observations about the relationship between nature and humanity." Publishers Weekly.

Vasari, Giorgio, 1511-1574

Rowland, Ingrid D. (Ingrid Drake) The **collector** of lives : Giorgio Vasari and the invention of art / Ingrid Rowland and Noah Charney. W.W. Norton & Company, 2017. 400 p. **B**

ISBN 9780393241310

1. Vasari, Giorgio, 1511-1574. 2. Artists -- Italy 3. Biographers -- Italy 4. Renaissance -- Italy. 5. Art history 6. Biographies

LC 2017026667

Giorgio Vasari (1511-1574) was a man of many talents-a sculptor, painter, architect, writer, and scholar-but he is best known for Lives of the Artists, which singlehandedly established the canon of Italian Renaissance art. Before Vasari's extraordinary book, art was considered a technical skill, and artists were mere decorators and craftsmen. It was through Vasari's visionary writings that Raphael, Leonardo, and Michelangelo came to be regarded as great masters of life as well as art, their creative genius celebrated as a divine gift.

Lauded by Sarah Bakewell as "insightful, gripping, and thoroughly enjoyable," The Collector of Lives reveals how one Renaissance scholar completely redefined how we look at art.

"Rowland and Charney do more than deliver a richly detailed life of this singular Renaissance figure. They raise intriguing questions about how tastes and standards develop." Kirkus.

Vaughan, Sarah, 1924-1990

Hayes, Elaine M. **Queen** of Bebop : the musical lives of Sarah Vaughan / Elaine M. Hayes. Ecco Press, 2017. 320 p. **B**

ISBN 9780062364685

1. Vaughan, Sarah, 1924-1990. 2. Women jazz musicians. 3. Bebop music. 4. Popular music. 5. Jazz musicians 6. Biographies

LC bl2017020231

Sarah Vaughan dropped out of school to become a jazz singer; her win at Amateur Night at the Apollo Theater landed her a gig singing with Earl Hines' band, where she performed with Dizzy Gillespie, Charlie Parker, and Billy Eckstine at the dawn of bebop. A champion of civil rights, with a voice like honey and a mouth that earned her the nickname "Sailor," Vaughan was a rare woman in a male-oriented business, a strong and successful performer despite mismanagement by the men in her life. Queen of Bebop?provides an insightful look at her life and career -- and the legacy she left behind.

"A deeply illuminating and unforgettable biography of a true American master." Booklist.

Vaughan, Stevie Ray, 1954-1990

★Paul, Alan, 1966- **Texas** flood : the inside story of Stevie Ray Vaughan / Alan Paul and Andy Aledort. St. Martin's Press, 2019. 368 p. **B**

ISBN 9781250142832

1. Vaughan, Stevie Ray, 1954-1990. 2. Guitarists 3. Blues musicians 4. Fame 5. Drug addiction 6. Biographies 7. Oral histories

LC 2018055443

Includes index.

An unstinting account of the guitar legend's life and career draws on firsthand insights from family members and loved ones to discuss topics ranging from Vaughan's creative endeavors and battles with addiction to his tumultuous marriage and fatal helicopter crash.

"In this definitive oral history, Paul (One Way Out: The Inside Story of the Allman Brothers Band) and musician and teacher Aledort trace the life and music of guitarist Stevie Ray Vaughan (1954-1990)...Fans will be thrilled with this intelligent, informative, and enlightening biography of the guitar great." Publishers Weekly.

Vavilov, N. I., 1887-1943

Pringle, Peter The **murder** of Nikolai Vavilov : the story of Stalin's persecution of one of the great scientists of the twentieth century / Peter Pringle. Simon & Schuster, 2008. 416 p. **B**

ISBN 0743264983

1. Stalin, Joseph, 1879-1953. 2. Plant breeders -- Soviet Union 3. Plant geneticists -- Soviet Union 4. Political purges -- Soviet Union -- History -- 20th century. 5. Political atrocities -- Soviet Union -- History -- 20th century.

LC 2008003510

Documents the early years of the genetic revolution as a period marked by one of the most relevant scientific scandals of the twentieth century and the tragic murder of leading Soviet geneticist Nikolai Vavilov by the Stalin regime.

"This is a must-read to grasp the ultimate, disasterous effect of politics trumping science." Science Books & Films.

Verant, Samantha

Verant, Samantha **How** to make a French family : a memoir of love, food, and faux pas / Samantha Verant. Sourcebooks, 2017. 320 p. **B**

ISBN 9781492638490

1. Verant, Samantha. 2. Americans in France. 3. Blended families. 4. Stepmothers. 5. Recipes. 6. France. 7. Autobiographies and memoirs.

LC 2016032663

The author of Seven Letters from Paris describes how she relocated to southwestern France in midlife, where her efforts to be a loving stepmother were shaped by culture clashes and the region's sophisticated culinary traditions.

"Verant combines one part second chance at romance, on part travelogue, and nearly three dozen recipes in this heartfelt account of how she... started life over in France with an instant family. " Publishers Weekly.

Verdi, Giuseppe, 1813-1901

Berger, William, 1961- **Verdi** with a vengeance : an energetic guide to the life and complete works of the king of opera / William Berger. Vintage Books, 2000. viii, 497 p. : **B**

ISBN 037570518X

1. Verdi, Giuseppe, 1813-1901. Operas. 2. Classical music 3. Composers -- Italy -- 19th century 4. Italy -- Social life and customs -- 19th century 5. Biographies

LC 00042261

Provides background on the artist's childhood and struggle with success, scene-by-scene analyses of such operas as Aida, La traviata, and Don Carlos, and a discussion on his musical recordings.

"The author provides a brief overview of the composer's life and times and examines the connections between contemporary politics and Verdi's creative output. A glossary and recommended recordings, films, and soundtracks are included. Informative and eminently readable for the novice and scholar alike." Library Journal.

Suchet, John, 1944- **Verdi** : the man revealed / John Suchet. Pegasus Books, 2018 288 p. **B**

ISBN 9781681777689

1. Verdi, Giuseppe, 1813-1901. 2. Composers -- Italy 3. Classical music 4. Italy 5. Biographies

LC 2019565070

Describes the life and career of Italy's greatest operatic composer, whose obsession with perfection drove his collaborators to incredible frustration and was also a landowner, farmer, politician and was outspoken in promoting Italian independence and criticizing the church.

"Obviously, music lovers will want this volume, but the subject is so lively and the presentation so attractive that it will appeal to all who value a solid biography." Library Journal.

Verney family

Tinniswood, Adrian The **Verneys** : a true story of love, war, and madness in seventeenth-century England / Adrian Tinniswood. Jonathan Cape, 2007. xxii, 570 p., 16 p. of plates : **B**

ISBN 1594489483

1. Verney family. 2. Gentry -- Great Britain -- History -- 17th century -- Correspondence. 3. Families -- Great Britain -- History -- 17th century -- Sources. 4. Archives. 5. Great Britain -- History -- Stuarts, 1603-1714 6. Buckinghamshire, England -- History -- 17th century. 7. Buckinghamshire, England -- Social life and customs -- 17th century. 8. Biographies

LC 2007000911

Traces the story of the seventeenth-century English family as drawn from their personal letters and other documents, discussing how their experiences reflected the realities of period gentry life, in an account that includes coverage of their relationships with Parliament and the royal family.

Vespucci, Amerigo, 1451-1512

★Fernandez-Armesto, Felipe **Amerigo** : the man who gave his name to America / Felipe Fernandez-Armesto. Random House, c2007. xxi, 231 p. : **B**

ISBN 9781400062812

1. Vespucci, Amerigo, 1451-1512. 2. Explorers -- Spain 3. Explorers -- Portugal 4. Explorers -- Italy 5. America -- Name. 6. Western Hemisphere -- Exploration -- Spanish. 7. Western Hemisphere -- Exploration -- Portuguese. 8. Western Hemisphere -- Exploration -- Italian. 9. Florence, Italy 10. Biographies

LC 2006051739

In this groundbreaking work, leading historian Felipe Fernandez-Armesto tells the story of our hemisphere as a whole, showing why it is impossible to understand North, Central, and South America in isolation without turning to the intertwining forces that shape the region.

"Faced by unreliable sources, Fernandez-Armesto sticks to what can be said of Vespucci with confidence, and wisely opts to paint a rich portrait of the times rather than speculate about details that may never be known." Times Literary Supplement.

Victoria, Queen of Great Britain, 1819-1901

★Baird, Julia (Julia Woodlands) **Victoria** the queen : an intimate biography of the woman who ruled an empire / Julia Baird. Random House, 2016. 704 p. **B**

ISBN 9781400069880

1. Victoria, Queen of Great Britain, 1819-1901. 2. Women rulers -- Great Britain 3. Husband and wife 4. Women's role 5. Loss (Psychology) 6. Great Britain -- History -- Victoria, 1837-1901. 7. Biographies

LC 2015025297

"Baird does not turn a blind eye on Victoria's darker sides, including her willfulness, selfishness, and self-pity. But that simply adds dimensions to a significant character." Booklist.

Cadbury, Deborah **Queen** Victoria's matchmaking : the royal marriages that shaped Europe / Deborah Cadbury. PublicAffairs, 2017. 320 p. **B**

ISBN 9781610398466

1. Victoria, Queen of Great Britain, 1819-1901 Family 2. Women rulers 3. Matchmaking 4. Marriage 5. Arranged marriage 6. Biographies

LC 2017952726

An exploration of the role in which Queen Victoria exerted the most international power and influence: as a matchmaking grandmother.

"British historian and documentarian Cadbury (Princes at War) energetically reveals the extent of Queen Victorias meddling in the marriage arrangements of her grandchildren in order to create the familys ideal British-German alliance." Publishers Weekly.

Erickson, Carolly, 1943- **Her** little majesty : the life of Queen Victoria / Carolly Erickson. Simon & Schuster, c1997. 304 p. : **B**

ISBN 0684807653

1. Victoria, Queen of Great Britain, 1819-1901. 2. Women rulers -- Great Britain 3. Great Britain -- History -- Victoria, 1837-1901. 4. Biographies

LC 96035041

A multilayered portrait of Queen Victoria describes the life and reign of a monarch who ruled for sixty-four years

"Erickson has a knack for plucking pithy quotes, and the essentials of the queen's life are often deftly set out." Publishers Weekly.

Hibbert, Christopher, 1924-2008 **Queen** Victoria : a personal history / Christopher Hibbert. Basic Books, c2000. xviii, 557 p., 32 p. of plates : **B**

ISBN 0465067611

1. Victoria, Queen of Great Britain, 1819-1901. 2. Women rulers -- Great Britain 3. Great Britain -- History -- Victoria, 1837-1901. 4. Biographies

LC 2001269136

Commemorating the centennial of Queen Victoria's death, a thought-provoking profile of the famed British monarch examines the complex life, reign, and personality of a woman who sat on the throne for sixty-four years. By the author of George III.

"Hibbert explores the life and reign of the British monarch based on primary sources, particularly the 60 million words of Victoria's letters and journals. As a result, he renders Victoria and her familial and political relationships with deliciously gossipy and often touching intimacy." New York Times Book Review.

★Wilson, A. N., 1950- **Victoria** : a life / A. N. Wilson. Penguin Press, 2014. 624 p. **B**

ISBN 9781594205996

1. Victoria, Queen of Great Britain, 1819-1901. 2. Women rulers -- Great Britain. 3. Great Britain -- History -- Victoria, 1837-1901. 4. Biographies

LC 2014013973

Queen Victoria reigned over Britain and its Empire for 64 years, becoming the namesake for a whole era and overseeing significant political developments in her government. Her children married important royalty throughout Europe, extending her influence well past her death in 1901. Victoria's life was darkened by the great sadness of Prince Consort Albert's premature demise, but also notable for her collaboration with a series of effective prime ministers. Biographer A.N. Wilson's fluid and balanced account brings Victoria's complex personality to life, portraying her as an interesting woman and successful monarch.

"[F]ew if any previous biographers have viewed her as incisively and absorbingly as Wilson does in his lengthy but smoothly flowing treatment of the queens long life. [He] sees Victoria as a woman who battled demons and emerged from her various darknesses victorious as a functioning woman and monarch." Booklist.

Worsley, Lucy **Queen** Victoria : twenty-four days that changed her life / Lucy Worsley. St. Martin's Press, 2019. 288 p. **B**

ISBN 9781250201423

1. Women rulers -- Great Britain 2. Gender role 3. Monarchy 4. Rulers 5. Great Britain -- History -- Victoria, 1837-1901 6. Biographies

LC 2018039820

The BBC historian presenter and best-selling author of Courtiers explores the life and myriad roles of Queen Victoria as they reflected her defiance of gender conventions and defining position in a time of extraordinary change and political resistance.

"Fans of biography and history, especially related to British history should find this fascinating reading. Those interested in Queen Victoria will find this to be a wonderful addition to the literature." Library Journal.

Vidal, Gore, 1925-2012

Parini, Jay **Empire** of self : a life of Gore Vidal / Jay Parini. Doubleday, 2015. 512 p. **B**

ISBN 9780385537568

1. Vidal, Gore, 1925-2012. 2. Authors, American -- 20th century 3. Gay men 4. Popular culture -- History -- 20th century 5. Celebrities 6. Biographies

LC 2015004719

An authorized profile of the influential 20th-century American novelist and cultural figure explores the private psychological and sexual aspects of his character behind his celebrity while examining his relationships and the secrets that shaped his beliefs.

"It's difficult to paint an appealing picture of a narcissist, but Parini has produced a balanced account of a man of immense talent who sometimes used it wisely and other times didn't. Lively and insightful, this book should find favor among lovers of literature and biography. It's got heart." Library Journal.

Vidal, Gore, 1925-2012 **Point** to point navigation : a memoir, 1964 to 2006 / Gore Vidal. Doubleday, c2006. 277 p. : **B**

ISBN 0385517211

1. Authors, American -- 20th century 2. United States -- Social life and customs 3. Autobiographies and memoirs

LC 2006011644

In a follow-up to his best-selling Palimpsest, the iconoclastic novelist and critic continues the story of his eventful life, chronicling his odyssey through the worlds of literature, TV, film, theater, politics, and international society; his encounters with celebrities from every arena; and the illness and death of his long-time partner, Howard Austen.

Villa, Pancho, 1878-1923

Katz, Friedrich The **life** and times of Pancho Villa / Friedrich Katz. Stanford University Press, 1998. xv, 985 p. : **B**

ISBN 0804730458

1. Villa, Pancho, 1878-1923. 2. Revolutionaries -- Mexico 3. Social movements -- Mexico -- History. 4. Mexico -- History -- Revolution, 1910-1920. 5. Chihuahua, Mexico (State) -- History. 6. Biographies

LC 97047271

"The author traces Pancho Villa's rise from relatively obscure outlaw to national leader of the Mexican Revolution (1910-20) and his subsequent decline to guerrilla leader. .{This} is likely to be the definitive account of Villa for years to come." Library Journal.

Villani, Cedric, 1973-

Villani, Cedric, 1973- **Birth** of a theorem : a mathematical adventure / Cedric Villani, translated by Malcolm DeBevoise ; illustrations by Claude Gondard. Faber and Faber, Inc. an affiliate of Farrar, Straus and Giroux, 2015, c2012. 288 p. **B**

ISBN 9780865477674

1. Mathematicians -- France 2. Mathematics -- History 3. Theories 4. Scientific discoveries. 5. Autobiographies and memoirs

LC 2014031268

Originally published as Theoreme vivant, 2012.

An intimate look inside a mathematician's mind as he wrestles with the theorem that will make his reputation Cedric Villani is a rock-star mathematician. An intellect of unusual depth and breadth, he is the director of France's greatest mathematics research institute. In 2010 he received the Fields Medal, the most coveted prize in mathematics, for his proofs resolving one of the most controversial theories of classical physics. Birth of a Theorem is his own account of the year leading up to the award. It invites readers inside the mind of a genius as he wrestles with the most important work of his career. But you don't have to understand nonlinear Landau damping to love Birth of a Theorem.

"And though readers will marvel at his remarkable genius, they will also recognize how much Villani depends on loving family ties, congenial friendships, and supportive institutions to nurture that genius. A rare portal into stratospheric mathematics." Booklist.

Viloria, Hida

Viloria, Hida **Born** both : an intersex life / Hida Viloria. Hachette Books, 2017. 352 p. **B**

ISBN 9780316347846

1. People who are intersex 2. LGBTQIA rights 3. Intersexuality 4. LGBTQIA persons 5. Autobiographies and memoirs

LC 2016030284

In Born Both, author Hida Viloria provides an up-close account of he/r life as an intersex person and a chronicle of he/r activism. Although s/he was raised as a girl, s/he learned at age 20 that he/r genitalia were not typically female, eventually discovering the intersex community. This courageous memoir offers affirmation for intersex people and their friends and family, as well as information for intersex advocates.

"This brave and empowering book deserves a wide audience." Library Journal.

Vincent, Leah

Vincent, Leah **Cut** me loose : sin and salvation after my ultra-Orthodox girlhood / Leah Vincent. Nan A. Talese, 2014. 240 p. **B**

ISBN 9780385538091

1. Vincent, Leah. 2. Jewish women. 3. Fundamentalists 4. Judaism 5. Self fulfillment 6. Coming-of-age stories. 7. Autobiographies and memoirs

LC 2013016764

Recounts the author's experiences after her fundamentalist Jewish family cut her off at the age of sixteen for exchanging letters with a male friend traces her downward spiral into promiscuity and self-destruction in New York City.

Vogt, William, 1902-1968

Mann, Charles C The **wizard** and the prophet : two remarkable scientists and their dueling visions of tomorrow's world / Charles C. Mann. Alfred A. Knopf, 2018. 384 p. **B**

ISBN 9780307961693

1. Vogt, William, 1902-1968. 2. Borlaug, Norman E. (Norman Ernest), 1914-2009. 3. Environmental sciences -- History -- 20th century. 4. Food security. 5. Water-supply 6. Energy. 7. Biographies

LC 2017024776

Two influential scientists, William Vogt (1902-1968), and Norman Borlaug (1914-2009), and their approaches to environmental problems.

"This unique, encompassing, clarifying, engrossing, inquisitive, and caring work of multifaceted research, synthesis, and analysis humanizes the challenges and contradictions of modern environmentalism and our struggle toward a viable future." Booklist.

Volpe, Joseph

Volpe, Joseph The **toughest** show on Earth : my rise and reign at the Metropolitan Opera / Joseph Volpe with Charles Michener. Knopf, 2006. x, 304 p. : **B**

ISBN 0307262855

1. Volpe, Joseph. 2. Metropolitan Opera, New York City 3. Opera producers and directors -- United States 4. New York City -- Social life and customs -- 21st century 5. Autobiographies and memoirs

LC 2005057932

On the eve of his retirement as general manager of The Metropolitan Opera, the outspoken culture czar offers a behind-the-scenes glimpse of life at one of the world's great operatic houses, recalling the political and artistic intrigues in which he has played a part, the business of running a cultural institution, and his collaboration with noted musicians, singers, directors, and conductors.

Voltaire, 1694-1778

★Pearson, Roger **Voltaire** almighty : a life in pursuit of freedom / Roger Pearson. Bloomsbury, 2005. xxxii, 447 p. : **B**

ISBN 1582346305

1. Voltaire, 1694-1778. 2. Authors, French -- 18th century 3. France -- Social life and customs -- 18th century. 4. Biographies

LC 2005053027

Shortlisted for the James Tait Black Memorial Prize for Biography, 2005.

Presents the life of the French philosopher, discussing his literary and philosophical writings, his tumultuous relationships with some of the rulers and thinkers of his day, and his lasting influence on French culture.

"The author has composed a lively and thorough account of the illustrious philosophe's chaotic life." Choice.

Von Bremzen, Anya

Von Bremzen, Anya **Mastering** the art of Soviet cooking : a memoir of love and longing / Anya von Bremzen. Crown Publishers, 2013 320 p. **B**

ISBN 9780307886811

1. Von Bremzen, Anya. 2. Food writers -- United States 3. Women cooks -- Soviet Union 4. Food habits -- Soviet Union. 5. Cooking, Russian -- History -- 20th century. 6. Soviet Union -- Social life and customs. 7. Russia -- Social conditions -- 1991- 8. Moscow, Russia 9. Autobiographies and memoirs

LC 2013007787

A multi-generational memoir by a celebrated food writer captures the flavors of the mid-20th-century Soviet experience, tracing her upbringing by an anti-Soviet mother, her witness to the political events that led to the empire's collapse and the parallel food universes of her life that evinced both simple and sumptuous fare.

"With anecdotes, history and recipes, the author delivers a lively, precisely detailed cultural chronicle." Kirkus.

Von Furstenberg, Diane

Von Furstenberg, Diane The **woman** I wanted to be / Diane von Furstenberg. Simon & Schuster, 2014. 416 p. **B**

ISBN 9781451651546

1. Von Furstenberg, Diane Family. 2. Women -- Identity. 3. Women fashion designers -- United States 4. Fashion designers -- United States 5. Businesspeople -- United States 6. Autobiographies and memoirs

LC 2014033232

The influential fashion designer and author of Diane: A Signature Life describes her pursuit of a creativity and independence, providing coverage of such topics as her childhood in Brussels, her struggles with cancer and her creation of a genre-defining dress design.

"This is a fascinating glimpse into the life of one of the fashion worlds most enduring stars that will fascinate fashionistas and fans of strong, creative women." Publishers Weekly.

Vonnegut, Kurt

Shields, Charles J., 1951- **And** so it goes : Kurt Vonnegut, a life / Charles Shields. Henry Holt and Co., 2011. 528 p. **B**

ISBN 9780805086935

1. Vonnegut, Kurt. 2. Authors, American -- 20th century 3. Authors, American -- 20th century -- Correspondence 4. United States -- Social life and customs -- 20th century 5. United States -- Social life and customs -- 21st century 6. Biographies

LC 2010045173

The first authorized biography of the influential American writer, examines Vonnegut's life from his childhood to his death in 2007 and explores how the author changed the conversation of American literature.

"Kurt Vonnegut had a chip on his shoulder when it came to the critics. Despite being one of the most popular writers of his generation, he routinely complained that his work was overlooked, or miscast as high-concept, middle-brow fiction. The publication of Charles J. Shields's fascinating new biography . probably won't put this beef to rest, at least among his loyalists. But it does provide a definitive and disturbing account of the late author, whose ambition and talent transformed him from an obscure science fiction writer to a countercultural icon." Boston Globe.

★Vonnegut, Kurt A **man** without a country / Kurt Vonnegut; edited by Daniel Simon. Seven Stories Press, 2005. ix, 146 p.: **B**

ISBN 158322713X

1. Vonnegut, Kurt. 2. Authors, American -- 20th century 3. United States -- Politics and government -- 2001-2009 4. Autobiographies and memoirs 5. Essays.

LC 2005014967

In a collection of brief autobiographical essays, the renowned novelist offers his views on art, politics, and everyday life in America.

"The author discusses politics, human nature, and other topics in this collection of articles written over the last five years, many from the alternative magazine In These Times." Publishers Weekly.

Vowell, Sarah, 1969-

Vowell, Sarah, 1969- **Assassination** vacation / Sarah Vowell. Simon & Schuster, 2005. 258 p. : **B**

ISBN 0743260031

1. Vowell, Sarah, 1969- Travel United States. 2. Presidents -- United States -- Assassination. 3. Assassins 4. Historic sites -- United States. 5. Presidents -- United States 6. United States -- History, Local. 7. United States -- Description and travel.

LC 2004059134

In this engaging and highly unusual travelogue, journalist Sarah Vowell explores the history of American presidential assassinations. From the Florida Keys all the way to Alaska, Vowell visits assassination sites, museums, prisons, monuments, and even a religious commune. Along the way she shares strange-but-true historical facts -- for instance, did you know that Robert Todd Lincoln, "a.k.a. Jinxy McDeath," was present at several presidential assassinations? -- and offers keen observations about history, politics, and the connection of the past to the present.

Vreeland, Diana, 1903-1989

Stuart, Amanda Mackenzie **Empress** of fashion : a life of Diana Vreeland / Amanda Mackenzie Stuart. HarperCollins, 2012. 400 p. **B**

ISBN 9780061691744

1. Fashion periodical editors -- United States 2. Fashion -- United States -- History -- 20th century. 3. Women periodical editors -- United States 4. Fashion periodicals 5. United States -- Social life and customs -- 20th century. 6. Autobiographies and memoirs

LC bl2012038528

This rare glimpse into the life of the innovative fashion editor of Harper's Bazaar and the legendary editor-in-chief of Vogue who, redefining women's sense of beauty and style, launched the careers of such timeless beauties Lauren Bacall and Lauren Hutton, explores her originality, her tenacity and her inimitable sensibility.

Wade, Becky

Wade, Becky **Run** the world : my 3,500-mile journey through running cultures around the globe / Becky Wade. William Morrow, 2016. 288 p. **B**

ISBN 9780062416438

1. Runners 2. Marathon running. 3. Cross-country runners. 4. Marathon runners. 5. Autobiographies and memoirs

LC 2017304785

An elite marathoner describes the year she spent running over 3,500 miles in nine different countries, living with host families and exploring diverse running communities and cultures all over the globe.

"Every so often a book comes along that becomes a cult classic for competitive runners but also has appeal to a broader audience... and this terrific debut is sure to join their ranks." Booklist.

Wagner family

Carr, Jonathan, 1942- The **Wagner** clan : the saga of Germany's most illustrious and infamous family / Jonathan Carr. Atlantic Monthly Press, 2007 400 p. **B**

ISBN 0871139758

1. Wagner family. 2. Wagner, Richard, 1813-1883 Family 3. Composers -- Germany -- 19th century. 4. Antisemitism. 5. Ambition 6. Germany -- Social life and customs -- 19th century. 7. Germany -- Social life and customs -- 20th century. 8. Biographies

LC 2011560972

"Carr's sprightly, fluent narrative places the family in its historical and intellectual context without reducing it to the symbolic effigy it has often become." Publishers Weekly.

Wagner, Alex

Wagner, Alex **Futureface** : a family mystery, an epic quest, and the secret to belonging / Alex Wagner. One World, 2018. xii, 338 p. : **B**

ISBN 9780812997941

1. Women journalists 2. Interethnic families 3. Women -- Identity 4. Ethnic identity 5. Autobiographies and memoirs

An Atlantic senior editor and former host of NOW with Alex Wagner documents her international travels in search of answers to the mystery of her ancestry and broader questions about the American experience of race and immigration, evaluating the cost of today's obsession with race and identity and whether or not it is possible for society to forge an all-inclusive future.

Wagner, Richard, 1813-1883

Ross, Alex, 1968- **Wagnerism** : art and politics in the shadow of music / Alex Ross. Farrar, Straus and Giroux, 2020. 784 p. **B**

ISBN 9780374285937

1. Wagner, Richard, 1813-1883 Influence. 2. Influence (Literary, artistic, etc.) 3. Composers -- Germany 4. Operas -- History and criticism 5. Music and literature

LC 2020012449

A large-canvas narrative history, charting the impact of the cultural titan Wagner on art and politics. Ross will show how various artists-composers, novelists, poets, filmmakers-wrestled with the legacy of Wagner in the twentieth century.

"With this multifaceted jewel of a book, Ross has produced a monumental study of Wagner's legacy." Library Journal

Wainwright, Loudon, III, 1946-

Wainwright, Loudon, III, 1946- **Liner** notes : on parents & children, exes & excess, death & decay & a few of my other favorite things / Loudon Wainwright III. Blue Rider Press, [2017] 288 p. **B**

ISBN 9780399177026

1. Singers 2. Creativity 3. Alcoholism 4. Actors and actresses

LC 2017020391

The influential Grammy Award-winning singer, songwriter and actor shares meditative personal reflections on relationships and creativity, tracing the struggles with alcoholism, infidelity and competitiveness that have challenged his celebrity family.

"A very funny and candid memoir, in an occasionally cringeworthy sort of way." Kirkus.

Walder, Tracy

Walder, Tracy The **unexpected** spy : from the CIA to the FBI, my secret life taking down some of the world's most notorious terrorists / Tracy Walder ; with Jessica Anya Blau. St. Martin's Press, 2020. xii, 249 pages ; **B**

ISBN 9781250230980

1. Walder, Tracy. 2. CIA -- Officials and employees 3. FBI -- Officials and employees. 4. Intelligence service -- United States. 5. Women spies -- United States 6. Terrorism -- Prevention 7. War on Terrorism, 2001-2009. 8. Autobiographies and memoirs

LC 2019036365

Offers a riveting account of a young woman who went straight from her college sorority to the CIA, where she hunted terrorists and weapons of mass destruction.

"Walder's fast-paced and intense narrative opens a window into life in two of America's major intelligence agencies." Publishers Weekly

Waldman, Ayelet

Waldman, Ayelet A **really** good day / Ayelet Waldman. Alfred A. Knopf, 2017. 256 p. **B**

ISBN 9780451494092

1. Waldman, Ayelet Health. 2. People with bipolar disorder 3. Bipolar disorder -- Treatment 4. People with depression 5. Hallucinogenic drugs -- Therapeutic use. 6. Autobiographies and memoirs

LC 2016023416

A lighthearted account of the author's experiment with microdoses of LSD in an effort to treat a debilitating mood disorder details what she has learned about the misunderstood drug and how she believes psychedelics can be appropriately used as therapeutic medicines.

"This great read will attract open-minded psychology buffs, contemporary biography readers, and those keen to hear a new voice discuss issues associated with so-called illicit drugs in America." Library Journal.

Walker, Alice, 1944-

Walker, Alice, 1944- The **same** river twice : honoring the difficult / Alice Walker. Scribner, c1996. 302 p. ; **B**

ISBN 9780684814193

1. Walker, Alice, 1944- Color purple Film adaptations 2. Authors, American -- 20th century 3. Screenwriters -- United States -- 20th century 4. Film adaptations -- History and criticism. 5. African American authors 6. Autobiographies and memoirs

LC 95030056

Chronicles the experiences of Alice Walker in the aftermath of the publication of The Color Purple and its winning of the Pulitzer Prize, as illustrated by essays, journal entries, and the author's never-used screenplay.

"This book finds the Pulitzer Prize-winning author still grappling with criticism of the film version of her novel The Color Purple. Walker's memoir pieces together assorted journal entries, magazine clippings, occasional photographs and even her original screenplay to form an intimate scrapbook of the period." Publishers Weekly.

Walker, C. J., 1867-1919

Bundles, A'Lelia **On** her own ground : the life and times of Madam C.J. Walker / A'Lelia Bundles. Scribner, 2001. 415 p. : **B**

ISBN 0684825821

1. Walker, C. J., 1867-1919. 2. African American women executives 3. African American businesspeople 4. Cosmetics industry and trade -- History 5. Hair care for African-American women. 6. Biographies 7. Books to TV.

LC 00057372

"A Lisa Drew book."

This book is being made into a TV show called Self Made."

Bundles presents a biography of her great-great-grandmother, who was born Sarah Breedlove on a Louisiana plantation in 1867 and whose name subsequently became synonymous with hair straightening and black wealth." Library Journal.

Walker, Mary, d. 1872

Nathans, Sydney **To** free a family : the journey of Mary Walker / Sydney Nathans. Harvard University Press, 2011. 360 p. **B**

ISBN 9780674062122

1. Walker, Mary, d. 1872. 2. Fugitive slaves. 3. Women slaves. 4. Family reunions. 5. African American women 6. Cambridge, Massachusetts. 7. Orange County, North Carolina.

LC 2011023122

Recounts the story of Mary Walker, who fled slavery in 1848 then spent the next 17 years trying to recover her family from the North.

Wall, Duncan

Wall, Duncan The **ordinary** acrobat : a journey into the wondrous world of the circus, past and present / Duncan Wall. Alfred A. Knopf, 2013. 320 p. **B**

ISBN 9780307271723

1. Wall, Duncan. 2. Circus. 3. Acrobats. 4. Acrobatics. 5. Circus performers. 6. Autobiographies and memoirs

LC 2012038250

Duncan Wall recounts his experience as a student at the Ecole Nationale des Arts du Cirque and looks at the evolution of the circus, including the innovative Cirque du Soleil.

Wallace, David Foster

Max, D. T. (Daniel T.) **Every** love story is a ghost story : a life of David Foster Wallace / D.T. Max. Viking, 2012. 336 p. **B**

ISBN 9780670025923

1. Wallace, David Foster. 2. Authors, American -- 20th century 3. Men with depression 4. Suicide victims 5. Biographies

LC 2012008488

Includes index.

Profiles the life of the influential and tormented literary figure, drawing on conversations with family and friends as well as hundreds of unpublished letters, manuscripts, and audio recordings to offer insight into his authentic writing style and his 2008 suicide.

Wallace, Jackie

★Jackson, Ted **You** ought to do a story about me : addiction, an unlikely friendship, and the endless quest for redemption / Ted Jackson. Dey Street Books, 2020 332 p. **B**

ISBN 9780062935670

1. Wallace, Jackie. 2. Jackson, Ted. 3. Former professional football players 4. Homeless men 5. African American men 6. Racism 7. New Orleans, Louisiana 8. Louisiana 9. Biographies

LC bl2020015853

Documents the photojournalist author's 30-year friendship with former NFL star Jackie Wallace, describing the losses and addiction that led the three-time Super Bowl star to homelessness on the streets of New Orleans.

"This story of a unique bond between two friends deserves wide readership in public libraries and is an ideal choice for book groups and discussions." Library Journal

Wallace, Perry (Law professor)

Maraniss, Andrew **Strong** inside : Perry Wallace and the collision of race and sports in the South / Andrew Maraniss. Vanderbilt University Press, 2014. x, 467 p. **B**

ISBN 9780826520234

1. Vanderbilt University Basketball -- History. 2. Vanderbilt Commodores (Basketball team) -- History. 3. African American basketball players 4. Racism in sports. 5. College basketball. 6. Basketball 7. United States -- Social life and customs -- 20th century. 8. Southern States -- Race relations. 9. Biographies

LC 2014015257

Strong Inside is the dramatic, untold story of Perry Wallace, a brilliant student and talented athlete who became the first African-American basketball player in the SEC at Vanderbilt University during the tumultuous late 1960s. The fast-paced, richly detailed biography places Wallace's struggles and ultimate success into the larger contexts of civil rights and race relations in the South.

"Nuanced and complex, Strong Inside is an invaluable resource for studying the state of race relations in the US, both past and present." Choice.

Walls, Jeannette

★Walls, Jeannette The **glass** castle : a memoir / Jeannette Walls. Scribner, 2005. 288 p. **B**

ISBN 0743247531

1. Walls, Jeannette Childhood and youth. 2. Dysfunctional families -- United States -- Case studies. 3. Eccentrics and eccentricities. 4. Growing up. 5. Children of alcoholics 6. Welch, West Virginia 7. Autobiographies and memoirs

ALA Notable Book, 2006.

The child of an alcoholic father and an eccentric artist mother discusses her family's nomadic upbringing, during which she and her siblings fended for themselves while their parents outmaneuvered bill collectors and the authorities.

"Shocking, sad, and occasionally bitter, this gracefully written account speaks candidly, yet with surprising affection, about parents and about the strength of family ties--for both good and ill." Booklist.

Walsh, Bill, 1931-2007

Harris, David, 1946- The **genius** : how Bill Walsh reinvented football and created an NFL dynasty / David Harris. Random House, c2008. 400 p. **B**

ISBN 9781400066650

1. Walsh, Bill, 1931-2007. 2. San Francisco 49ers (Football team) 3. National Football League 4. Football coaches -- United States 5. Professional football. 6. Football teams. 7. Biographies

LC 2008016566

Offers a portrait of football coach Bill Walsh, who transformed the San Francisco 49ers, the NFL's worst team in 1979, into a football powerhouse through a combination of organization innovation, player management, and determination.

"Walsh was one of the NFL's greatest coaches, and Harris' book does him justice." Booklist.

Walsh, Mikey

Walsh, Mikey **Gypsy** boy : my life in the secret world of the Romany Gypsies / Mikey Walsh. Thomas Dunne Books, 2012. 288 p. **B**

ISBN 9780312622084

1. Walsh, Mikey. 2. Young gay men -- England 3. Romanies -- England -- Social life and customs. 4. Child abuse 5. Homosexuality 6. England -- Social life and customs. 7. Autobiographies and memoirs

LC 2011038168

"First published in Great Britain by Hodder & Stoughton"--T.p. verso.

The son of a Romany Gypsy champion bareknuckle boxer shares the story of his upbringing in England, his realization of his sexual orientation, and how his circumstances were shaped by his culture's absolute beliefs.

Walters, Barbara, 1931-

Walters, Barbara, 1931- **Audition** : a memoir / Barbara Walters. Alfred A. Knopf, 2008. 448 p. **B**

ISBN 030726646X

1. Journalists -- United States 2. Women journalists 3. Insecurity in women. 4. Self-acceptance in women. 5. Autobiographies and memoirs

LC 2008005843

Includes index.

The television journalist chronicles the people, events, and forces that have shaped her life, discussing her relationships with family, friends, and others; her struggle to succeed in a man's world; and the interviews she has conducted during her forty-year career.

"Alternating between tales of her personal struggles, professional achievements and insider anecdotes about the celebrities and world leaders she's interviewed, this mammoth memoir's energy never flags." Publishers Weekly.

Walton, Bill, 1952-

Walton, Bill, 1952- **Back** from the dead / Bill Walton. Simon & Schuster, 2016. 288 p. **B**

ISBN 9781476716862

1. Men with spinal cord injuries 2. Basketball players. 3. Sportscasters. 4. Autobiographies and memoirs

LC 2015031712

Includes index.

An NBA sports star and cultural icon discusses his catastrophic spinal collapse in 2007, the excruciating pain he suffered and his slow recovery, as well as his childhood, sports career and the political and cultural upheaval of the 1960s.

"This memoir is defined by trials as much as successes and will appeal to readers who appreciated Walton as player and commentator." Library Journal.

Walton, Sam, 1918-

Walton, Sam, 1918- **Sam** Walton, made in America : my story / Sam Walton with John Huey. Bantam Books, 1993, c1992. xiii, 346 p. : **B**

ISBN 9780553562835

1. Wal-Mart (Firm) -- History. 2. Businessmen -- United States -- Biography. 3. Discount stores (Retail trade) -- United States -- History. 4. Millionaires -- United States -- Biography.

LC BL 99738358

Includes index.

Originally published: New York : Doubleday, 1992.

In an account of his rise to the top of the American retail business, the reminiscences of the billionaire retailer are combined with interviews with Walton's family and friends

Wambach, Abby, 1980-

Wambach, Abby, 1980- **Forward** : a memoir / Abby Wambach. Dey Street Books, 2016 240 p. **B**

ISBN 9780062466983

1. Women soccer players 2. Soccer 3. Soccer players 4. Autobiographies and memoirs

LC 2016037369

The U.S. Women's national team captain - winner of the 2015 World Cup and the highest international goal scorer of all time - shares her story, her struggles and her worldview in a memoir that is also a rousing call to arms to dream big and fight for a better world.

"A cut above the standard sports memoir." Booklist.

Warburg family

Chernow, Ron The **Warburgs** : the twentieth-century odyssey of a remarkable Jewish family / Ron Chernow. Random House, 1993. xvii, 820 p. : **B**

ISBN 9780679418238

1. Warburg family. 2. Jews, German. 3. Jewish Americans 4. Bankers. 5. Jewish American families 6. Biographies

LC 93016599

ALA Notable Book, 1994.

Presents a monumental portrait of the powerful Warburg banking dynasty, tracing this remarkable Jewish family's odyssey from post-World War I Germany through the rise of Hitler and beyond.

Warburg, Siegmund, Sir, 1902-1982

Ferguson, Niall **High** financier : the lives and times of Siegmund Warburg / Niall Ferguson. Penguin Group USA, 2010. 560 p. **B**

ISBN 9781594202469

1. Warburg, Siegmund, Sir, 1902-1982. 2. Capitalists and financiers. 3. Economists. 4. Economic policy. 5. Economics. 6. Europe -- Economic conditions -- 1945- 7. Biographies

LC 2010018353

"Ferguson draws a richly vivid portrait of this unusual banker, an intellectual who read the Latin and Greek classics in the original and preferred Nietzsche to newspapers." New York Times Book Review.

Ward, Clarissa, 1980-

Ward, Clarissa, 1980- **On** all fronts : the education of a journalist / Clarissa Ward. Penguin Press, 2020. 384 p. **B**

ISBN 9780525561477

1. Television journalists -- United States 2. War correspondents -- United States 3. Women journalists 4. Iraq War, 2003-2011, American. 5. Syria -- History -- Civil War, 2011- 6. Autobiographies and memoirs

LC 2019049839

Includes index.

The five-time Emmy Award-winning CNN chief international correspondent draws on the wrenching stories of soldiers, civilians and rebels in war-torn Syria to illuminate the human cost of Bashar al Assad's reign of terror and its personal impact on her family.

"Ward's journalism skills shine, putting readers on the front lines. Readers interested in the life stories of intrepid women journalists and the nature of investigative, international journalism will be captivated by this engrossing account." Library Journal

Ward, Ferdinand De Wilton, 1851-1925

Ward, Geoffrey C. A **disposition** to be rich : how a small-town pastor's son ruined an American president, brought on a Wall Street crash, and made himself the best-hated man in the United States / Geoffrey C. Ward. Alfred A. Knopf, 2012. 432 p. **B**

ISBN 9780679445302

1. Ward, Ferdinand De Wilton, 1851-1925. 2. Grant, Ulysses S., 1822-1885 3. Capitalists and financiers -- United States 4. Swindlers and swindling -- United States -- History -- 19th century 5. Financial crises -- United States -- History 6. Ponzi schemes 7. New York (State) -- History -- 19th century 8. Rochester, New York -- History -- 19th century 9. United States -- History -- 1865-1898

LC 2011035140

"This is a Borzoi book"--T.p. verso.

Documents the story of Gilded Age con artist Ferdinand Ward, recounting how his large-scale pyramid operation and other sensational schemes triggered one of the greatest financial scandals in American history.

Ward, Jesmyn

★Ward, Jesmyn **Men** we reaped : a memoir / Jesmyn Ward. Bloomsbury, 2013. 272 p. **B**

ISBN 9781608195213

1. Ward, Jesmyn. 2. African American women authors 3. Rural poor people. 4. Children of single parents 5. Death. 6. Mississippi. 7. Autobiographies and memoirs

LC 2013013600

National Book Critics Circle Award for Autobiography/ Memoir finalist

A National Book Award winner recounts the loss of five young men in her life to drugs, accidents, suicide and the bad luck that can follow people who live in poverty, particularly black men, sharing her experiences of living through the dying as she searches through answers in her community.

"Ward's candid account is full of sadness and hope that takes readers out of their comfort zone and proves that education and hard work are the way up for the young and downtrodden." Library Journal.

Warhol, Andy, 1928-1987

★Gopnik, Blake **Warhol** Ecco Press, 2020. 864 p. **B**

ISBN 9780062298393

1. Warhol, Andy, 1928-1987. 2. Artists -- United States 3. Pop art -- United States 4. Pop artists -- United States 5. Nonconformists 6. United States -- Social life and customs -- 20th century. 7. Biographies

LC bl2020012640

From his impoverished childhood as the son of Slovak immigrants in 1930s Pittsburgh, to finding commercial success as an advertising illustrator, to his painstaking pivot into fine art to becoming one of the first people to bring a queer aesthetic out into the open; Warhol shows us how deliberately Andy Warhol reflected the changing winds of commercialism, capitalism and celebrity in the 1960s that still underpin our world today.

"Warhol fans and pop art enthusiasts alike will find this an endlessly engrossing portrait." Publishers Weekly

Wariner, Ruth

Wariner, Ruth The **sound** of gravel : a memoir / Ruth Wariner. Flatiron Books, 2016. 352 p. **B**

ISBN 9781250077691

1. Wariner, Ruth. 2. Church of the Firstborn of the Fulness of Times 3. Mormon women 4. Polygamy -- Religious aspects 5. Resilience

in women 6. Mormons 7. Mexico 8. California 9. Autobiographies and memoirs

LC 2015037663

An account of the author's coming-of-age in a polygamist Mormon Doomsday cult describes her childhood on a Mexico hills farm as one of her father's more than 40 welfare-dependent children, the extreme religious beliefs that haunted her daily life and her escape in the aftermath of a devastating tragedy.

"With power and insight, Wariners tale shows a road to escape from the most confining circumstances." Booklist.

Warren, Cat

Warren, Cat **What** the dog knows : the science and wonder of working dogs / Cat Warren. Simon & Schuster, 2013. 320 p. **B**

ISBN 9781451667318

1. Warren, Cat. 2. Working dogs 3. Search dogs 4. Human/animal relationships 5. Volunteers 6. Autobiographies and memoirs

LC 2013012006

"A Touchstone book."

Explores the world of working dogs, as well as canine intelligence and training, as the author and her German shepherd, Solo, work with forensic anthropologists, detectives, and dog handlers to find the bodies of the missing.

"Warren writes with verve and provides rare insight into our working partnership with canines." Kirkus.

Warren, Elizabeth

Felix, Antonia **Elizabeth** Warren : Her fight. Her work. Her life. / Antonia Felix. Sourcebooks Inc., 2018 464 p. **B**

ISBN 9781492665281

1. United States. Congress. Senate 2. Women politicians 3. Politicians -- United States 4. Political culture 5. United States -- Politics and government 6. Biographies

LC 2018010616

Traces the iconic senator's rise from her hardscrabble origins in the American Midwest to a leader in progressive politics, sharing stories from her career, as well as her insights into the economic realities of today.

"A complementary portrayal of a compelling political personality. Recommended for readers interested in Senator Warren, politics, and the lives of inspirational women." Library Journal.

Warren, Elizabeth A **fighting** chance / Elizabeth Warren. Henry Holt & Company, 2014 384 p. **B**

ISBN 9781627790529

1. Women senators 2. Women politicians. 3. Global Financial Crisis, 2008-2009. 4. United States -- Politics and government 5. Autobiographies and memoirs

LC 2014000776

A chronicle of the Massachusetts senator's two-decade career in Washington describes her childhood pursuit of an education, early exposure to the dysfunctional political process, high-risk advocacy of better bankruptcy laws and competitive run for public office.

"Warren emerges as a committed advocate with real world sensibility, who tasted tough economic times at an early age and did not forget its bitterness." Publishers Weekly.

Washington, Booker T., 1856-1915

Harlan, Louis R. **Booker** T. Washington : the making of a Black leader, 1856-1901 / Louis R. Harlan. Oxford University Press, 1972. xi, 379 p. : **B**

ISBN 9780195019155

1. Washington, Booker T., 1856-1915. 2. African American men 3. African American educators 4. Intellectual life -- African Americans 5. African Americans -- Social conditions -- 19th century

LC 72077499

Examines the black educator's life, paying special attention to his role in party politics, presidential legislation, and the freedman's struggle for equality.

Harlan, Louis R. **Booker** T. Washington : the wizard of Tuskegee, 1901-1915 / Louis R. Harlan. Oxford University Press, 1983. xiv, 548 p. : **B**

ISBN 0195032020

1. Tuskegee Institute. 2. African Americans 3. Educators -- United States 4. Middle class African Americans 5. Leadership in men. 6. United States -- History -- 20th century. 7. Biographies

LC 82014547

Pulitzer Prize for Biography or Autobiography, 1984.

A chronicle of Washington's last fifteen years reviews his accomplishments and explains how he gained strong political influence.

"Having avoided the pitfalls of white guilt and black rage and the temptation to judge the past by standards of the present, Mr. Harlan deserves honors for his remarkable achievement." New York Times Book Review.

Norrell, Robert J. (Robert Jefferson) **Up** from history : the life of Booker T. Washington / Robert J. Norrell. Belknap Press of Harvard University Press, 2009. xi, 508 p. : **B**

ISBN 9780674032118

1. Washington, Booker T., 1856-1915. 2. Tuskegee Institute -- History 3. African American men 4. African American educators 5. Intellectual life -- African Americans 6. African Americans -- Education 7. United States -- History -- 19th century 8. United States -- History -- 20th century 9. Biographies

LC 2008032599

A definitive biography of Booker T. Washington focuses on his efforts to support the cause of black people in the segregated South by promoting an economic independence and development of moral character in order to integrate blacks into American life and to overcome exploitation and discrimination.

★ Washington, Booker T., 1856-1915 **Up** from slavery / Booker T. Washington. Penguin Books, 1986, c1901. liii, 332 p. ; **B**

ISBN 9780140390513

1. Tuskegee Institute. 2. African Americans 3. Educators -- United States 4. Social advocates 5. Race relations 6. Autobiographies and memoirs

LC 8516712

Originally published: New York : Doubleday, Page, & Co., 1901.

The African-American educator documents his struggle for freedom and self-respect and his fight to establish industrial training and educational programs for black Americans.

Washington, George, 1732-1799

Breen, T. H. **George** Washington's journey : the president forges a new nation / T. H. Breen. Simon & Schuster, 2016 320 p. **B**

ISBN 9781451675429

1. Presidents -- United States 2. American Revolution, 1775-1783 3. United States -- History -- Revolution, 1775-1783. 4. Biographies

LC 2015007283

An assessment of the first President's lesser-known achievements as a political strategist describes his 13-state plan for establishing a people-centric federal government that would prevent national fragmentation and promote independence.

"Breen's superb chronicle offers glimpses into Washington's love of his country and its people, and his willingness to meet them on their own terms to secure the unity of the new republic." Publishers Weekly.

Brookhiser, Richard **Founding** father : rediscovering George Washington / Richard Brookhiser. Free Press, c1996. 230 p. ; **B**

ISBN 0684822911

1. Washington, George, 1732-1799. 2. United States. Continental Army 3. Presidents -- United States 4. Generals -- United States 5. United States -- History -- 18th century. 6. Biographies

LC 95050650

A revisionist biography of George Washington chronicles his quarter-century career in public life, from his heroic deeds as a leader through the legacy that has been passed down to his political descendants

Calloway, Colin G. (Colin Gordon), 1953- The **Indian** world of George Washington : the first President, the first Americans, and the birth of the nation / Colin G. Calloway. Oxford University Press, [2018] 712 p. **B**

ISBN 9780190652166

1. Washington, George, 1732-1799 Relations with Indians. 2. Government relations with indigenous peoples 3. Presidents -- United States 4. Indians of North America 5. American Revolution, 1775-1783 6. United States -- History -- French and Indian War, 1754-1763. 7. United States -- History -- Revolution, 1775-1783. 8. Biographies

LC 2017028686

National Book Award for Nonfiction finalist, 2018"

An authoritative, sweeping, and fresh new biography of the nation's first president, Colin G. Calloway's book reveals fully the dimensions and depths of George Washington's relations with the First Americans."--Provided by publisher.

Chernow, Ron **Washington** : a life / Ron Chernow. Penguin Press, 2010. 800 p. **B**

ISBN 9781594202667

1. Washington, George, 1732-1799. 2. United States. Continental Army 3. Presidents -- United States 4. Generals -- United States 5. Political leadership. 6. United States -- History -- 18th century. 7. Biographies

LC 2010019154

ALA Notable Book, 2011.

American History Book Prize, 2010.

Pulitzer Prize for Biography or Autobiography, 2011.

A comprehensive account of the life of George Washington negates the stereotype of a stolid, unemotional man and instead reveals a dashing, passionate man of fiery opinions and many moods who fiercely guarded his private life.

Coe, Alexis **You** never forget your first : a biography of George Washington / Alexis Coe. Viking Books, 2020. 320 p. **B**

ISBN 9780735224100

1. Presidents -- United States 2. Generals 3. Political leadership 4. Command of troops 5. Biographies

LC 2019045005

A whimsically irreverent portrait of America's first President includes coverage of Washington's entitled upbringing by a single mother, his dog "Sweetlips," his numerous military defeats and the partisan nightmares that spun from his back-stabbing cabinet.

"Evenhanded and engaging, this biography brings fresh insight to one of America's most written-about leaders." Kirkus

★Ellis, Joseph J. **His** Excellency : George Washington / Joseph J. Ellis. Alfred A. Knopf, 2004. xiv, 320 p. : **B**

ISBN 1400040310

1. Washington, George, 1732-1799. 2. United States. Continental Army 3. Presidents -- United States 4. Generals -- United States 5. Politicians -- United States 6. Soldiers -- United States 7. United States -- History -- Colonial period, 1600-1775. 8. United States -- History -- French and Indian War, 1754-1763 9. United States -- History -- Revolution, 1775-1783. 10. United States -- History -- Confederation, 1783-1789. 11. Biographies

LC 2004046576

From the French and Indian War to Mount Vernon, from the American Revolution to the presidency, Ellis delivers what will stand the test of time as the definitive biography of an American icon.

"The author offers a magisterial account of the life and times of George Washington, celebrating the heroic image of the president whom peers like Jefferson and Madison recognized as their unquestioned superior while acknowledging his all-too-human qualities." Publishers Weekly.

Flexner, James Thomas, 1908-2003 **George** Washington and the new nation, 1783-1793 / James Thomas Flexner. Little, Brown, 1970. xi, 466 p. : **B**

ISBN 9780316286008

1. Washington, George, 1732-1799. 2. Presidents -- United States. 3. United States -- History -- 1783-1815. 4. United States -- Politics and government -- 1783-1809. 5. Biographies

LC 78117042

Detailed narrative of Washington's career from his return to Mount Vernon following the Revolutionary War through his first term as president.

Flexner, James Thomas, 1908-2003 **George** Washington: anguish and farewell 1793-1799 / James Thomas Flexner. Little, Brown, 1972. xii, 554 p. : **B**

ISBN 0316286028

1. Washington, George, 1732-1799. 2. Presidents -- United States 3. Generals -- United States 4. United States -- History -- 1783-1815 5. United States -- Politics and government -- 1783-1809. 6. Biographies

LC 72006875

Profiles Washington from his second term as president to his death, focusing on his struggles to unite the new republic.

Flexner, James Thomas, 1908-2003 **George** Washington: the forge of experience, 1732-1775 / James Thomas Flexner. Little, Brown, 1965. x, 390 p. : **B**

ISBN 9780316285971

1. Washington, George, 1732-1799. 2. Generals -- United States 3. Command of troops 4. United States -- History -- Colonial period, 1600-1775. 5. Biographies

LC 65021361

A biography of America's first President from birth to the beginning of the Revolutionary War, portraying the personal qualities which contributed to his greatness.

Horn, Jonathan, 1982- **Washington's** end : the final years and forgotten struggle / Jonathan Horn. Scribner, 2020. 384 p. **B**

ISBN 9781501154232

1. Presidents -- United States 2. Retirement 3. Command of troops 4. Diplomacy 5. United States -- Politics and government -- 1783-1809. 6. Biographies

LC bl2020000195

Historian and former White House speechwriter Jonathan Horn tells the astonishing true story of George Washington's forgotten last years--the personalities, plotting, and private torment that unraveled America's first post-presidency. Horn reveals that the quest to surrender power proved more difficult than Washington imagined and brought his life to an end he never expected. The statesman who had staked his legacy on withdrawing from public life would feud with his successors and find himself drawn back into military command. The patriarch who had dedicated his life to uniting his country would leave his name to a new capital city destined to become synonymous with political divisions.

"An outstanding biographical work on one of America's most prominent leaders. Highly recommended for those who want to better understand the early republic." Library Journal

Larson, Edward J. (Edward John) The **return** of George Washington : 1783-1789 / Edward Larson. William Morrow & Company, 2014. 400 p. **B**

ISBN 9780062248671

1. United States. Constitutional Convention (1787) 2. Founding Fathers of the United States 3. Presidents -- United States. 4. United States -- Politics and government -- 1783-1789. 5. Biographies

LC 2013497765

Documents Washington's lesser-known decision to come out of retirement to lead the Constitutional Convention and become America's first president, discussing his vital role in addressing key financial and policy challenges.

"Larson identifies Washington's three goals'respect abroad, prosperity at home, and development westward'and includes an account of an inaugural dish that makes turducken seem unambitious. Profound, even affectionate, scholarship infuses every graceful sentence." Kirkus.

Randall, Willard Sterne **George** Washington : a life / Willard Sterne Randall. Henry Holt & Co., 1997. ix, 548 p. : **B**

ISBN 9780805027792

1. Washington, George, 1732-1799. 2. United States. Continental Army 3. Founding Fathers of the United States. 4. Presidents -- United States 5. Generals -- United States 6. Leadership in men. 7. Biographies

LC 97019125

"A John Macrae book."

Explores Washington's life from a personal rather than political perspective, sharing the story of his life as a man rather than a leader.

"Chronicling less the adaptive leader of the struggling rebellion or the persuasive conciliator of the infant republic, Randall . portrays instead the vain, restless, ambitious provincial who got tremendously lucky. Altogether human, Randall's demythologized Washington comes vividly to life." Publishers Weekly.

Stark, Peter, 1954- **Young** Washington : how wilderness and war forged America's founding father / Peter Stark. Ecco, 2018. 384 p. **B**

ISBN 9780062416063

1. Washington, George, 1732-1799 Childhood and youth. 2. Generals. 3. Presidents. 4. Politicians 5. Military history 6. United States -- History -- French and Indian War, 1754-1763 7. Biographies

LC 2017052000

A portrait of the first U.S. president's early years shares insights into how his service in the British military and his stationing in the brutal wilderness of the Ohio Valley shaped his nascent leadership and indirectly fed the conflict that led to the French and Indian War.

Washington, George, 1732-1799 **Writings** / George Washington ; [selected by John H. Rhodehamel]. Library of America : c1997. xxiii, 1149 p. ; The Library of America ; **B**

ISBN 188301123X

1. Washington, George, 1732-1799 Archives. 2. United States -- History -- Revolution, 1775-1783 -- Sources. 3. United States -- Politics and government -- 1775-1783 -- Sources. 4. United States -- Politics and government -- 1783-1809 -- Sources. 5. Virginia -- History -- Colonial period, ca. 1600-1775 -- Sources.

LC 96009665

Bringing together 450 letters, orders, addresses, and other significant historical documents penned by America's first president during the course of his life, a substantial anthology is arranged chronologically beginning with a journal written at age sixteen.

Washington, Martha, 1731-1802

Brady, Patricia, 1943- **Martha** Washington : an American life / Patricia Brady. Viking, 2005. 276 p., [16] p. of plates : **B**

ISBN 0670034304

1. Washington, Martha, 1731-1802. 2. Presidents' spouses -- United States 3. Biographies

LC 2004061242

Challenges popular misconceptions to profile the nation's original first lady as the widowed mother of two children who became Washington's beloved partner and a mainstay in his powerful and stressful life, drawing on numerous sources to reveal her contributions to American character as well as her passionate commitment to her family.

Washington, Mary Ball, 1708-1789

Saxton, Martha The **widow** Washington : the life of Mary Washington / Martha Saxton. Farrar, Straus and Giroux, 2019. 379 p. **B**

ISBN 9780809097012

1. Washington, Mary Ball, 1708-1789. 2. Washington, George, 1732-1799 Family. 3. Presidents -- United States -- Mothers. 4. Mothering 5. Mothers and sons 6. Orphans 7. Virginia -- History -- Colonial period, ca. 1600-1775. 8. United States -- History -- Colonial period, ca. 1600-1775. 9. United States -- History -- Revolution, 1775-1783. 10. Biographies

LC 2018056295

"Biography of Mary Ball Washington, George Washington's mother. Places her life as an orphan, a young wife in rural Virginia, a slaveholder, a widow, and mother to the first president in the context of the changing economic circumstances and cultural values of colonial Virginia and a young nation".-- Provided by publisher.

"All readers will value this vivid account that corrects Mary's record and reveals the dilemmas and distorted sensibility of Virginian slaveholding white women, along with the devastation caused by the Revolutionary War. " Library Journal.

Shirley, Craig **Mary** Ball Washington : the untold story of George Washington's mother / Craig Shirley. Broadside, 2019. 400 p. **B**

ISBN 9780062456519

1. Washington, Mary Ball, 1708-1789. 2. Presidents -- United States -- Mothers. 3. Mothering 4. Mothers and sons 5. Widows -- United States 6. Virginia -- History -- Colonial period, ca. 1600-1775. 7.

United States -- History -- Colonial period, 1600-1775 8. United States -- History -- Revolution, 1775-1783. 9. Biographies

LC 2019021060

In Mary Ball Washington, New York Times bestselling author Craig Shirley uncovers startling details about the inner workings of the Washington family. He vividly brings to life a resilient widow who single-handedly raised six children and ran a large farm at a time when most women's duties were relegated to household matters. Throughout, Shirley compares and contrasts mother and son, illuminating the qualities they shared and the differences that divided them.

Wasserman, Lew

Bruck, Connie **When** Hollywood had a king : the reign of Lew Wasserman, who leveraged talent into power and influence / Connie Bruck. Random House, 2003. xiv, 512 p. : **B**

ISBN 0375501681

1. Wasserman, Lew. 2. M C A Inc. 3. Chief executive officers -- United States 4. Businesspeople 5. Labor unions -- Musicians. 6. Chicago, Illinois 7. Hollywood, California 8. Biographies

LC 2003041418

"Those who are interested in comprehensive details about the inner workings of the entertainment industry its history, business, customs, people, and gossip will find this a fascinating read and a solid resource." Library Journal.

Waters, Alice

Waters, Alice **Coming** to my senses : the making of a counterculture cook / Alice Waters. Clarkson Potter, 2017. 304 p. **B**

ISBN 9780307718280

1. Chez Panisse 2. Women cooks 3. Restaurants 4. Restaurateurs 5. Food 6. Berkeley, California 7. California 8. Autobiographies and memoirs

LC bl2017029928

The executive chef of Chez Panisse in California presents the story of her tumultuous culinary journey, describing her efforts to promote distinctive flavors in a time of uniform convenience foods, her achievements within the bohemian 1960s cultural circuit and her ongoing reflections as the head of one of the world's most influential restaurants.

"Chef, restaurateur, activist, and author Waters writes about her childhood and formative years leading up to the opening of her iconic Berkeley, CA, restaurant Chez Panisse." Library Journal.

Waters, Ethel, 1900-1977

Bogle, Donald **Heat** wave : the life and career of Ethel Waters / Donald Bogle. HarperCollins, 2011. 352 p. **B**

ISBN 9780061241734

1. Singers -- United States 2. African American singers 3. African American women 4. Biographies

LC 2010029230

The best-selling author of Dorothy Dandridge examines the life and legacy of theatrical star Ethel Waters.

Waters, John, 1946-

Waters, John, 1946- **Carsick** : John Waters hitchhikes across America / John Waters. Farrar, Straus and Giroux, 2014. 288 p. **B**

ISBN 9780374298630

1. Waters, John, 1946- Travel 2. Film producers and directors -- United States 3. Hitchhiking -- United States. 4. United States -- Description and travel. 5. United States -- Social life and customs -- 21st century

LC 2013034093

Want to take a bawdy ride across the United States? Then pick up Carsick! Mixing in a bit of fiction before hitting the road for real (it begins with vividly imagined best-case and worst-case scenarios), 66-year-old filmmaker and cult legend John Waters -- who made Pink Flamingos, Hairspray, etc. -- traces his 2012 cross-country hitchhiking trip. With a motley group of unsuspecting drivers, including a gentle farmer (who thinks Waters is a hobo), an indie band (who tweet about the encounter), and the author's unexpected hero (who's a 20-year-old Republican politician!), he has a great time and makes it from his house in Baltimore to his apartment in San Francisco in one piece.

"For more than half of this account of his 2012 cross-country journey . [Waters] imagines what lies in store, with dueling full-length novellas that spin best and worst case scenarios. [A] sweet and funny ride." Kirkus.

Waters, John, 1946- **Mr.** know-it-all : the tarnished wisdom of a filth elder / John Waters. Farrar, Straus and Giroux, 2019. 288 p. **B**

ISBN 9780374214968

1. Film producers and directors -- United States 2. Aging 3. Nonconformists 4. Fame 5. Autobiographies and memoirs 6. Essays

LC 2018057165

The newest essay collection from the New York Times-bestselling John Waters, reflecting on how to overcome newfound responsibility and rebel in the autumn of your years.

"In this delightful hybrid memoir/advice book, film director Waters shares highlights from his 40-year career and musings on a random assortment of subjects, including music, architecture, and the best vacation spots." Publishers Weekly.

Waters, John, 1946- **Role** models / John Waters. Farrar, Straus and Giroux, 2010. 256 p. **B**

ISBN 9780374251475

1. Waters, John, 1946- Sources. 2. Influence (Literary, artistic, etc.) 3. Film producers and directors -- United States 4. Screenwriters -- United States 5. Artists -- United States 6. Essays.

LC 2009042211

"The cult film director of such productions as Hairspray and Pink Flamingos presents irreverent literary profiles of the figures who influenced his life and work, from martyr Saint Catherine of Siena to English novelist Denton Welch."

"The famed cult-film director recalls the famous and not-so-famous people he has idolized over the years. In this consistently charming and witty collection of essays, he fondly remembers the many artists he has admired throughout his life, from stars, such as Little Richard, to such near-unknown figures as the 1960s Baltimore stripper Lady Zorro. An impressive, heartfelt collection by a true American iconoclast." Kirkus.

Waters, Maxine

Andrews-Dyer, Helena **Reclaiming** her time : the power of Maxine Waters / Helena Andrews-Dyer and R. Eric Thomas ; with illustrations by Sabrina Dorsainvil. Dey Street Books, 2020 256 p. **B**

ISBN 9780062992031

1. United States. Congress. House 2. African American women legislators 3. Social justice 4. African American women politicians 5. Women legislators -- United States 6. Biographies

LC 2020008250

To millions nationwide, Congresswoman Maxine Waters is a hero of the resistance and an icon, serving eye rolls, withering looks, and sharp retorts to any who dare waste her time on nonsense. But behind the Auntie Maxine meme is a seasoned public servant and she's not here to play.

Throughout her forty years in public service and eighty years on earth, U.S. Representative for California's 43rd district has been a role model, a crusader for justice, a game-changer, a trailblazer, and an advocate for the marginalized who has long defied her critics, including her most vocal detractor, Donald J. Trump. And she's just getting started. Featuring inspiring highlights from her personal life and political career, beloved memes, and testimonies from her many friends and fans, Reclaiming Her Time is a funny, warm, and admiring portrait of a champion who refuses to stay silent in the face of corruption and injustice.

"Their buoyant and zesty portrait of the woman known as 'Auntie Maxine' is perfect for the vivacious, unconventional, tireless, and essential Waters." Booklist

Jones, Brenda (Communications director) **Maxine** Waters : the life, times and rise of "Auntie Maxine" / Brenda Jones and Krishan Trotman. Plume, 2020 208 p. **B**

ISBN 9780593189870

1. Waters, Maxine. 2. United States. Congress. House 3. African American women legislators 4. Women legislators 5. African American women politicians 6. Women politicians. 7. Los Angeles, California 8. United States -- Politics and government -- 21st century 9. Biographies

LC 2020012467

Part of a four-book series celebrating women in congress, this biography of the representative for California's 43rd congressional district describes growing up with a single mother in Missouri to forging a new political path for young people of color.

"A spirited tribute to an impressive woman." Kirkus

Watt, Lauren Fern

Watt, Lauren Fern **Gizelle's** bucket list : my life with a very large dog / Lauren Fern Watt. Simon & Schuster, 2017. 224 p. **B**

ISBN 9781501123658

1. Watt, Lauren Fern. 2. Dogs 3. Mastiff 4. Women and dogs 5. Dog owners 6. Autobiographies and memoirs

LC 2016033521

A lightbeat, epic account of how the 20-something author brought her giant English Mastiff to her first tiny New York apartment after college, while navigating boyfriends, first jobs, her mother's illness and a bucket list that involves her dog's participation.

"As much a story about growing up as about letting go of things that cannot be changed, Watt's book is also a reminder of the profound healing connection that can exist between humans and the pets they love. A tender, heartfelt story." Kirkus.

Watts, Shannon

Watts, Shannon **Fight** like a mother : how a grassroots movement became the gun lobby's worst nightmare--and how women everywhere can organize to bring about change / Shannon Watts. HarperOne, [2019] 272 p. **B**

ISBN 9780062892560

1. Gun control 2. School shootings 3. Mothers -- Political activity 4. Mass shootings 5. Autobiographies and memoirs

LC 2019006368

The founder of Moms Demand Action for Gun Sense in America traces the story of how her rallying call to action grew into a powerful women's movement for protecting children from gun violence.

"The founder of Moms Demand Action for Gun Sense in America offers advice for women looking to take up that causeor any other." Kirkus.

Watts, Tom

Hoskyns, Barney **Lowside** of the road : a life of Tom Waits / Barney Hoskyns. Bantam Dell Pub Group, 2009. 288 p. **B**

ISBN 9780767927086

1. Watts, Tom. 2. Songwriters 3. Rock musicians 4. Rock music. 5. Biographies

LC 2009455678

A superb rock journalist and biographer delves into the life of one of the most revered and critically acclaimed singer-songwriters alive today, making sense of the life and career of the beloved icon, from the beginning of his career on the margins of the 1970s Los Angeles rock scene to his place among such greats as Bob Dylan and Neil Young.

"This book lights up and whirls like one of the greasy carnival rides in Mr. Waits's own sprawling oeuvre . Mr. Hoskyns rummaged through Mr. Waits's interviews, pored through the historical record and talked to those who were willing to speak. Thus his unauthorized biography mirrors, in some ways, Mr. Waits's own junkyard aesthetic. Mr. Hoskyns picks up what shards of Mr. Waits's life he can find and holds them to the light, turning them eagerly in his hands." New York Times Book Review.

Waugh family

Waugh, Alexander **Fathers** and sons : the autobiography of a family / Alexander Waugh. Nan A. Talese, [2007], c2004. 472 p. : **B**

ISBN 0385521502

1. Waugh, Evelyn, 1903-1966 Family. 2. Waugh family. 3. Authors, English -- 20th century 4. Fathers and sons -- Great Britain 5. Great Britain -- Social life and customs -- 20th century 6. Collective autobiographies and memoirs

LC 2007005239

Originally published: London : Headline, 2004.

The grandson of Evelyn Waugh explores the complex dynamics of father-son relationships in his family that have produced four generations of successful authors, tracing the influences that have linked fathers and sons across the generations.

"The scion of an illustrious--and fabulously eccentric--English literary dynasty referees four generations of father-son antagonisms in this scintillating family memoir. Waugh ... focuses on the fraught relationship between his great-grandfather, prominent critic and publisher Arthur Waugh, and Arthur's son, the famous novelist Evelyn. If this tome were merely an excuse to reprint some of Evelyn's hilarious jottings, it would be well worth the price, but it's also an absorbing study of how writers process their most painfully formative experiences." Publishers Weekly.

Waugh, Evelyn, 1903-1966

Eade, Philip **Evelyn** Waugh : a life revisited / Philip Eade. Henry Holt and Co., 2016. 432 p. **B**

ISBN 9780805097603

1. Waugh, Evelyn, 1903-1966. 2. Authors, English -- 20th century 3. Homosexuality. 4. Family relationships. 5. Nervous breakdown. 6. Biographies

LC 2016019839

Marking a half-century since the English author's death, this biography sheds new light on his difficult relationship with his overly-sentimental father; his exploration of homosexuality at Oxford; and his disastrous first marriage, checkered military career and extreme nervous breakdown.

"Eade offers up a softer portrait of Waugh that might help bring him some new readers, which he deserves." Kirkus.

Wayne, John, 1907-1979

Eliot, Marc **American** titan : searching for John Wayne / Marc

Eliot. Dey Street Books, 2014. 352 p. **B**

ISBN 9780062269003

1. Wayne, John, 1907-1979. 2. Film actors and actresses -- United States 3. Western films. 4. Biographies

LC 2014014183

From the New York Times best-selling biographer of Jimmy Stewart and Clint Eastwood comes a major, in-depth look at one of the most enduring American film icons of all time.

"But given that it tells the same story without any unique insights, the book can't help coming across as a bit been there, done that. Still, it's a solidly written account of Wayne's life and does a credible job with the question of how the legend affected Wayne, the person. Libraries with room on the shelves for two new Wayne biographies should slide this one in beside Eyman's work." Booklist.

Eyman, Scott, 1951- **John** Wayne : the life and legend / Scott Eyman. Simon & Schuster, 2014. 512 p. **B**

ISBN 9781439199589

1. Wayne, John, 1907-1979. 2. Film actors and actresses -- United States 3. Western film actors and actresses. 4. Western films. 5. Popular culture -- History -- 20th century. 6. United States 7. Biographies

LC 2013032604

"A revelatory biography of the enduringly popular John Wayne that draws on more than 100 interviews as well as exclusive access to the files of Wayne's film production company to answer the question why he became and remains an iconic American figure".-- Provided by publisher.

"Insightful, exhaustive and engrossinga definitive portrait of the man and the legend." Kirkus.

Webb, Jimmy

Webb, Jimmy The **cake** and the rain : an autobiography / Jimmy Webb. St. Martin's Press, 2017. 346 pages : **B**

ISBN 9781250058416

1. Songwriters 2. Musicians 3. Songwriting 4. Popular music 5. Autobiographies and memoirs

LC 2017000908

The Grammy Award-winning songwriter, author, and youngest inductee into the National Songwriters' Hall of Fame traces his religious upbringing in Oklahoma, struggles with addiction and meteoric successes with artists ranging from The Supremes and The Fifth Dimension to Johnny Cash and Art Garfunkel.

"Webb writes in a comfortable, conversational way, as though hes telling a few close friends some stories from his fascinating life, and the book makes a great way for a music fan to pass a few hours." Booklist.

Weegee, 1899-1968

★Bonanos, Christopher, 1969- **Flash** : the making of Weegee the Famous / Christopher Bonanos. Henry Holt and Company, 2018. 336 p. **B**

ISBN 9781627793063

1. Weegee, 1899-1968. 2. Photojournalists 3. Crime scenes 4. Photographers 5. Biographies

LC 2017041202

Includes index.

National Book Critics Circle Award for Biography, 2018.

Arthur Fellig's ability to arrive at a crime scene just as the cops did was so uncanny that he renamed himself "Weegee," claiming that he functioned as a human Ouija board. Weegee documented better than any other photographer the crime, grit, and complex humanity of midcentury New York City. In Flash, we get a portrait not only of the man (both flawed and deeply talented, with generous appetites for publicity, women, and hot pastrami) but also of the fascinating time and place that he occupied.

"Bonanos has meticulously researched every aspect of Weegee's life, filling this fascinating and lively account with amusing and touching anecdotes and photographs carefully selected to illustrate Weegee's work and life." Library Journal.

Weiner, Jennifer

Weiner, Jennifer **Hungry** heart : adventures in life, love, and writing / Jennifer Weiner. Atria Books, 2016. 320 p. **B**

ISBN 9781476723402

1. Weiner, Jennifer. 2. Authors, American. 3. Femininity 4. Growing up 5. Father-deserted families 6. Essays 7. Autobiographies and memoirs

LC 2016022112

"You fall down. You get hurt. You get up again. You know Jennifer Weiner as many things: a bestselling author, a Twitter phenomenon, and "an unlikely feminist enforcer" (The New Yorker). She's also a mom, a daughter, and a sister; a former rower and current runner; a best friend and a reality TV junkie. Here, in her first foray into nonfiction, she takes the raw stuff of her personal life and spins it into a collection of essays on womanhood.

"Like her enormously popular commercial fiction, from its very first page this memoir will enthusiastically reach out to female readers and swiftly draw them close." Publishers Weekly.

Weisman, Eliot

Weisman, Eliot The **way** it was : my life with Frank Sinatra / Eliot Weisman. Hachette Books, 2017 320 p. **B**

ISBN 9780316470087

1. Sinatra, Frank, 1915-1998. 2. Managers, booking agents, etc. 3. Autobiographies and memoirs

LC bl2017044202

Frank Sinatra's long-time manager and friend, who was one of the singer's most trust confidantes and advisors, tells the story of the final years of the iconic entertainer from the perspective from within his inner circle.

Weiss, Piper, 1978-

Weiss, Piper, 1978- **You** all grow up and leave me : a memoir of teenage obsession / Piper Weiss. William Morrow, 2018. 304 p. **B**

ISBN 9780062456571

1. Teenage girls 2. Child sexual abusers 3. Violence against women 4. Coaching (Athletics) 5. Autobiographies and memoirs

LC 2017025491

Combining research, interviews, and personal records, You All Grow Up and Leave Me explores the psychological manipulation by child predators their ability to charm their way into seemingly protected worlds and the far-reaching effects their actions have on those who trust them most.

"Weiss has crafted a dark and brooding yet brisk and eloquently written memoir, and her vivid coming-of-age narration shines a spotlight on the precarious relationship between teenagers and adults and everything that can go awry in between. A bristling, harrowing journey into the life of a stalker and his unsuspecting victims." Kirkus.

Weller, George, 1907-2002

Weller, George, 1907-2002 **Weller's** war : a legendary correspondent's saga, on five continents, of World War II / George Weller, ed-

ited by Anthony Weller. Random House, 2009. 608 p. **B**
ISBN 9780307406552
1. War correspondents -- United States -- History -- World War II. 2. World War II, American 3. Pulitzer Prizes 4. Journalists -- United States -- 20th century 5. Europe 6. Asia 7. Autobiographies and memoirs
LC 2008039988
"Weller's war reporting won him the Pulitzer Prize in 1943. Here, his son assembles many of his dispatches, which add tremendously to our understanding of the war at ground level, the people's war." Library Journal.

Welles, Orson, 1915-1985

Callow, Simon, 1949- **Orson** Welles : Hello Americans / Simon Callow. Viking, 2006. 528 p. : Orson Welles (Simon Callow) **B**
ISBN 9780670872565
1. Welles, Orson, 1915-1985. 2. Film producers and directors -- United States 3. Actors and actresses -- United States 4. Newspapers -- Political aspects -- United States 5. Film industry and trade -- Hollywood, California -- History 6. United States -- Social life and customs -- 20th century 7. Biographies
LC 95037138
A second volume in the biographical series about the legendary director traces the years after Citizen Kane to offer insight into Welles's increasing inability to function within the movie industry's structure, tracing his contributions to such films as The Magnificent Ambersons and The Lady from Shanghai, as well as his efforts in radio comedy, spectacular theater, and newspaper politics.
"Destined to be the definitive word. Highly recommended." Library Journal.

★Callow, Simon, 1949- **Orson** Welles : One-man band / Simon Callow. Viking, 2016, c2015. 466 p. : Orson Welles (Simon Callow) **B**
ISBN 9780670024919
1. Welles, Orson, 1915-1985. 2. Film producers and directors -- United States 3. Actors and actresses -- United States 4. Filmmakers 5. Film industry and trade -- Hollywood, California -- History 6. Biographies
LC bl2016013489
Originally published: London : Jonathan Cape, 2015.
In the third installment in his four-volume survey of Orson Welles' life and work, a celebrated British actor traces Welles' self-exile from America and his realization that he could only function to his own satisfaction as an independent film-maker, a one-man band, which committed him to a perpetual cycle of money-raising.
"Welles rightly imagined that people would never stop writing about him after he died. Callow continues to set the standard in this increasingly crowded field." Kirkus.

Jaglom, Henry, 1939- **My** lunches with Orson : conversations between Henry Jaglom and Orson Welles / edited by Peter Biskind. Henry Holt & Co 2013. 240 p. **B**
ISBN 9780805097252
1. Jaglom, Henry, 1939- 2. Welles, Orson, 1915-1985. 3. Film producers and directors 4. Films, American -- Production and direction 5. Filmmaking 6. Conversation 7. Autobiographies and memoirs
LC 2013000291
Based on long-lost recordings, a set of revealing conversations between the film historian author and the iconic cultural provocateur unstintingly reflects on topics ranging from politics and literature to the shortcomings of his friends and the many films Welles wanted to make.

Lebo, Harlan **Citizen** Kane : a filmmaker's journey / Harlan Lebo. Thomas Dunne Books, 2016. 368 p. **B**
ISBN 9781250077530
1. Welles, Orson, 1915-1985. 2. Citizen Kane (Motion picture) Production and direction. 3. Film producers and directors 4. Biographies.
LC 2015045237
In commemoration of the film's 75th anniversary, describes how newcomer Orson Welles won an unprecedented contract that gave him total creative control over his masterpiece, the dispute over who wrote the script and the plot by William Randolph Hearst to destroy the project.
"Lebo's book is highly readable; it's dense, lucid, and page-turning. Fans of Welles and classic Hollywood will be delighted by this comprehensive, intelligent work." Publishers Weekly.

McGilligan, Patrick **Young** Orson : the years of luck and genius on the path to Citizen Kane / Patrick McGilligan. HarperCollins ; 2015. 352 p. **B**
ISBN 9780062112484
1. Welles, Orson, 1915-1985. 2. Citizen Kane (Motion picture) Production and direction. 3. Film producers and directors 4. Men and success. 5. Ambition in men. 6. Radio producers and directors 7. Biographies.
LC 2016297780
"Exhaustively researched but well-paced and stuffed with beguiling detail, this is a vivid, sympathetic portrait of Welless youthful promise and achievement, before the misfires and compromises of his later years." Publishers Weekly.

Wellington, Arthur Wellesley, Duke of, 1769-1852

Hibbert, Christopher, 1924-2008 **Wellington** : a personal history / Christopher Hibbert. Addison Wesley, 1997. xiii, 460 p., 24 p. of plates : **B**
ISBN 9780201632323
1. Wellington, Arthur Wellesley, Duke of, 1769-1852. 2. Politicians -- Great Britain 3. Generals -- Great Britain 4. Prime Ministers -- Great Britain -- 19th century 5. Military strategy -- Great Britain. 6. Great Britain -- Politics and government -- 19th century. 7. Great Britain -- History, Military -- 19th century. 8. Biographies
LC 97017285
Looks at the private life of the great British general who defeated Napoleon at the Battle of Waterloo.
"Altogether, Wellington does not quite pass the niceness test. He was a difficult man, a major military figure, a minor Prime Minister and in sum a historically important legend. Hibbert skillfully brings out all these characteristics." New York Times Book Review.

Wells, Ida B., 1862-1931

★Giddings, Paula **Ida** : a sword among lions : Ida B. Wells and the campaign against lynching / Paula J. Giddings. Amistad, 2008. xii, 800 p., 16 p. of plates : **B**
ISBN 9780060519216
1. Wells, Ida B., 1862-1931. 2. African American women 3. African American women civil rights workers 4. African American women social reformers 5. Lynching -- United States -- History 6. United States -- Race relations 7. United States -- History -- 20th century 8. Biographies
LC bl2008005797
BCALA Literary Award for Nonfiction, 2009.

National Book Critics Circle Award for Biography finalist, 2008.

Traces the life and legacy of the nineteenth-century activist and pioneer, documenting her birth into slavery and upbringing in the Victorian-era South, where she became a journalist and pioneer for civil rights and suffrage, in an account that also describes her determination to counter lynching activities.

"An iconic figure in American history, Wells was not always celebrated by her contemporaries for her groundbreaking activism because of her assertive politics and difficult personality. . . . Giddings offers a look at how Wells' own self-assertion affected her relationships with family, friends, colleagues, and the broader American public as she evolved as a woman and an activist. . . . With meticulous research, including Wells' own diary, Giddings brings to life one of the most fascinating women in American history, giving readers a real feel for the texture and context of Wells' life." Booklist.

Welteroth, Elaine, 1986-

Welteroth, Elaine, 1986- **More** than enough : claiming space for who you are (no matter what they say) / Elaine Welteroth. Viking, 2019. 272 p. **B**

ISBN 9780525561583

1. Teen Vogue (New York, N.Y.) 2. African American women journalists 3. Personal conduct 4. Determination in women 5. Multiracial women 6. Autobiographies and memoirs

LC 2019002372

In this part-manifesto, part-memoir, the revolutionary editor who infused social consciousness into the pages of Teen Vogue explores what it means to come into your own -- on your own terms.

"Welteroth's inspiring debut follows her personal and professional trajectories as she unpacks her ascent to becoming editor-and-chief of Teen Vogue in 2017 and details her experience as a black woman in media. From humble beginnings as a brown girl boss running a makeshift hair salon out of her Newark, Calif., cul-de-sac home, Welteroth built an illustrious editorial career as she worked her way up through increasingly substantial roles at Ebony and Glamour magazines." Publishers Weekly.

Welty, Eudora, 1909-2001

Marrs, Suzanne **Eudora** Welty : a biography / Suzanne Marrs. Harcourt, 2005. xix, 652, 16 p. of plates : **B**

ISBN 0151009147

1. Welty, Eudora, 1909-2001. 2. Authors, American -- 20th century 3. Women authors, American -- 20th century 4. Men/women relations. 5. Female friendship 6. Biographies

LC 2004030490

"This book belongs on the shelf beside its subject's own work. Neither hagiography nor pathography, it is, you feel, the thoroughly respectful and straightforward biography its honest, modest, intensely private subject would have wanted." New York Times Book Review.

Waldron, Ann **Eudora** : a writer's life / Ann Waldron. Anchor Books, 1999, c1998. xiv, 398 p. : **B**

ISBN 9780385476485

1. Women authors, American -- 20th century -- Biography.

LC BL 99012407

Originally published: New York : Doubleday, 1998.

The first biography of the great southern writer cuts through the myth surrounding her life and reveals her as a serious literary talent whose friends included Katherine Ann Porter and Elizabeth Bowen, and whose chief rival was Carson McCullers.

Welty, Eudora, 1909-2001 **One** writer's beginnings / Eudora Welty. Simon & Schuster, 2020, c1984. 128 p. **B**

ISBN 9781982151775

1. Welty, Eudora, 1909-2001 Childhood and youth. 2. Women authors. 3. Writing. 4. Authors, American -- 20th century 5. Creativity. 6. Mississippi -- Social life and customs. 7. Autobiographies and memoirs

LC 91019527

Originally published: Cambridge, Mass. : Harvard University Press, 1984.

National Book Award for Nonfiction finalist, 1984.

National Book Critics Circle Award for Biography finalist, 1984.

With a new introduction, this updated edition of the award-winning and best-selling author's classic book of guidance for aspiring writers is part memoir, offering a vivid glimpse into life in early 1900s Mississippi, and part an exploration of cultivating creativity.

"Less shapely or focused than Welty's stories, and a little too wispy in its self-portrait--but a welcome, often-eloquent arrival nonetheless, for Welty readers and writing students in about equal measure." Kirkus.

Wenner, Jann

Hagan, Joe, 1971- **Sticky** fingers : the life and times of Jann Wenner and Rolling stone magazine / Joe Hagan. Alfred A. Knopf, 2017. 560 p. **B**

ISBN 9781101874370

1. Wenner, Jann. 2. Rolling Stone Magazine 3. Editors -- United States 4. Publishers and publishing 5. Rock music 6. Celebrities 7. Biographies

LC 2017018102

The biography of founder, editor, and publisher of Rolling stone magazine Jann Wenner.

"This biographical chronicle of the cultural evolution from the 1960s to the present is a must-read for counterculture enthusiasts and historians." Library Journal.

Werner, Ruth, 1907-2000

★Macintyre, Ben, 1963- **Agent** Sonya : Moscow's most daring wartime spy / Ben Macintyre. Crown, 2020. 400 p. **B**

ISBN 9780593136300

1. Werner, Ruth, 1907-2000. 2. Soviet Union. Glavnoe razvedyvatel'noe upravlenie. 3. Spies -- Soviet Union 4. Spies -- Great Britain 5. Women spies -- Soviet Union 6. Nuclear weapons -- History -- 20th century. 7. Biographies

LC 2020019326

Reveals the story of the female spy hidden in plain sight who set the stage for the Cold War--one of the last great intelligence secrets of the 20th century.

"[MacIntyre's] fast-paced historical account reads like a novel, with surprising twists and turns, and will thrill readers until the very last page. Readers who enjoy the writings of Neal Bascomb or Candice Millard, and fans of historical fiction will relish this book." Library Journal

Wesley, John, 1703-1791

★Tomkins, Stephen, 1968- **John** Wesley : a biography / Stephen Tomkins. Wm. B. Eerdmans Pub. Co., 2003. 208 p. ; **B**

ISBN 0802824994

1. Wesley, John, 1703-1791. 2. Christian theologians 3. Methodist Church -- England -- Clergy 4. England -- Religious life and customs -- 18th century 5. Biographies

LC 2003054328

"In this biography of the founder of the Methodist religion Tomkins presents a keenly engaging portrait of a great man full of contradictoriness. Wesley insisted he was loyal to the Church of England yet consented to his followers setting up establishments and engaging in practices that flouted Anglican authority. He altered the face of Christianity in the West by inspiring modern evangelicalism and Pentecostalism. A fascinating figure, fascinatingly limned." Booklist.

West, Jerry, 1938-

West, Jerry, 1938- **West** by West : my charmed, tormented life / Jerry West and Jonathan Coleman. Little, Brown and Co., 2011. 336 p. **B**

ISBN 9780316053495

1. Los Angeles Lakers (Basketball team) 2. Professional basketball. 3. Basketball players. 4. Basketball coaches. 5. Basketball. 6. Autobiographies and memoirs

LC 2011019736

Includes index.

The coach responsible for the championship-winning success of the Lakers for the past 40 years describes his difficult childhood, being a star player at West Virginia University, his career and his relationships with sports legends from Wilt Chamberlain to Shaquille O'Neal.

Westaby, Stephen

Westaby, Stephen **Open** heart : a cardiac surgeon's stories of life and death on the operating table / Stephen Westaby. Basic Books, [2017] 320 p. ; **B**

ISBN 9780465094837

1. Cardiologists 2. Artificial heart 3. Heart -- Surgery 4. Surgeons 5. Autobiographies and memoirs

LC 2016058151

Includes index.

A veteran Oxford heart surgeon imparts the hard-won lessons of a life lived on the brink, sharing the stories of remarkable cases from his career while revealing why heart procedures have never become routine.

"Intense and sometimes-stunning stories of the heart, delivered from the heart." Booklist.

Westheimer, Ruth, 1928-

Westheimer, Ruth, 1928- The **doctor** is in : Dr. Ruth on love, life, and joie de vivre / Ruth Westheimer, Pierre A. Lehu. Amazon Publishing, 2015 191 p. **B**

ISBN 9781477828366

1. Sex counselors and therapists 2. Personal conduct. 3. Optimism. 4. Life skills 5. Autobiographies and memoirs

LC bl2015020100

Everyone knows Dr. Ruth as America's most famous and trusted sex therapist, but few people know she was raised in an orphanage in Switzerland, narrowly escaping death during the Holocaust?or that she was an ace sniper in the Israeli amy. After years spent as a professor in Paris, Dr. Ruth came to America with big dreams and even bigger chutzpah. And, at the age of eighty-seven, she is as feisty as ever. Through intimate and funny stories, Dr. Ruth sheds light on how she's learned to live a life filled with joie de vivre.

"While Westheimer has covered some of this ground previously, her wit and brassy style breathe new life into familiar self-help material." Publishers Weekly.

Westover, Tara

★Westover, Tara **Educated** : a memoir / Tara Westover. Random House, 2018 384 p. **B**

ISBN 9780399590504

1. Westover, Tara. 2. Survivalism. 3. Home schooling. 4. Family violence victims 5. Women college students. 6. Idaho -- Rural conditions. 7. Autobiographies and memoirs

LC 2017037645

ALA Notable Book, 2019.

National Book Critics Circle Award for Autobiography/Memoir finalist, 2018

Traces the author's experiences as a child born to survivalists in the mountains of Idaho, describing her participation in her family's paranoid stockpiling activities and her resolve to educate herself well enough to earn an acceptance into a prestigious university and the unfamiliar world beyond.

"In its keen exploration of family, history, and the narratives we create for ourselves, Educated becomes more than just a success story." Booklist.

Wetherall, Tyler, 1983-

Wetherall, Tyler, 1983- **No** way home : a memoir of life on the run / Tyler Wetherall. St. Martin's Press, 2018. 320 p. **B**

ISBN 9781250112194

1. Children of criminals 2. Fathers and daughters 3. Fugitives 4. Hiding 5. Autobiographies and memoirs

LC 2017049579

A New York writer presents a memoir of her childhood spent on the run in a series of homes in five different countries under an assumed name, describing her discovery of her father's fugitive status and his half-billion-dollar marijuana smuggling operation, her self-destructive youth and her efforts to reconcile her family's past with her own realities.

White, Bill, 1934-

White, Bill, 1934- **Uppity** : my untold story about the games people play / Bill White with Gordon Dillow. Grand Central Pub., c2011. 304 p. **B**

ISBN 9780446555258

1. New York Yankees (Baseball team) 2. St. Louis Cardinals (Baseball team) 3. Sportscasters. 4. African-American sportscasters. 5. Baseball players -- United States 6. African American baseball players 7. Autobiographies and memoirs

LC 2010038025

Includes index.

A baseball great shares stories about his rise from the minor leagues of the Deep South to the major leagues, despite the racism he had to deal with along the way, and discusses his career as a broadcaster and president of the National League.

White, E. B. (Elwyn Brooks), 1899-1985

Elledge, Scott **E.B.** White : a biography / Scott Elledge. Norton, 1986. xvii, 400 p. : **B**

ISBN 0393303055

1. Authors, American -- 20th century 2. Children's literature writing -- 20th century. 3. United States -- Social life and customs -- 20th century 4. Biographies

LC 85029807

A biography of the popular American children's author recounts his childhood, his education at Cornell, and his long association with the New Yorker magazine.

"The author is fair, respectful, thorough, entertaining, skillful and unpedantic. He has performed a splendid exercise in scholarship and literary analysis, and the result is fun." New York Times Book Review.

White, E. B. (Elwyn Brooks), 1899-1985 **Letters** of E. B. White / E.B. White ; rev. and updated by Martha White ; foreword by John Updike ; originally collected and edited by Dorothy Lobrano Guth. Harper Collins, 2006, c1976. xv, 713 p., [24] p. of plates : **B**

ISBN 9780060757083

1. White, E. B. (Elwyn Brooks), 1899- Correspondence. 2. Authors,

American -- 20th century -- Correspondence. 3. Letters.
LC 200643490

Includes bibliographical references and index.

Updated to include newly released letters written between 1976 and 1985, a thirtieth anniversary edition shares the New Yorker writer's and classic author's thoughts about such topics as the uncertainty of the future, his marriage, and his relationships with such colleagues as James Thurber, Groucho Marx, and John Updike.

White, Edmund, 1940-

White, Edmund, 1940- **City** boy : my life in New York during the 1960s and 70s / Edmund White. Bloomsbury USA, 2009. 304 p. **B**

ISBN 9781596914025

1. White, Edmund, 1940- Homes and haunts New York City. 2. Authors, American -- 20th century 3. Gay men -- United States 4. Gay culture. 5. Intellectual life -- New York City -- 20th century. 6. New York City -- History -- 20th century. 7. Autobiographies and memoirs

LC 2009012493

National Book Critics Circle Award for Autobiography/ Memoir finalist

A memoir based on the author's experiences as a cultural and intellectual insider in 1970s New York describes the philosophical and political debates in which he participated, the sophisticated performances he attended, and his encounters with such figures as Susan Sontag and Harold Brodkey.

White, Edmund, 1940- The **unpunished** vice : a life of reading / Edmund White. Bloomsbury USA, 2018. 320 p. **B**

ISBN 9781635571172

1. White, Edmund, 1940- Books and reading. 2. Authors, American -- 20th century 3. Books and reading 4. Biographers 5. Literature -- Appreciation 6. Autobiographies and memoirs

LC 2017036149

The acclaimed author describes the key role that reading played throughout his life and helped shape his tastes, memories and gave him enjoyment, providing light and laughter in his darkest times.

White, Michael, 1956-

White, Michael, 1956- **Travels** in Vermeer : a memoir / Michael White. Persea Books, 2015. 192 p. **B**

ISBN 9780892554379

1. Vermeer, Johannes, 1632-1675 2. Influence (Literary, artistic, etc.) 3. Poets 4. Painters 5. Art 6. Autobiographies and memoirs

LC 2014016180

"A Karen and Michael Braziller Book.""

An enchanting book about the transformative power of art." Kirkus.

Whitley, Hiram C., 1834-1875

Lane, Charles, 1961- **Freedom's** detective : the Secret Service, the Ku Klux Klan and the man who masterminded America's first War on Terror / Charles Lane. Hanover Square Press, 2019. 352 p. **B**

ISBN 9781335006851

1. Whitley, Hiram C., 1834-1875. 2. United States. Secret Service -- History 19th century. 3. Ku-Klux Klan -- History 19th century. 4. Intelligence service. 5. Undercover operations. 6. Terrorism investigation. 7. African Americans -- Suffrage. 8. United States -- History -- 19th century. 9. Biographies.

LC bl2019003970

Chronicles the story of the Reconstruction-era Secret Service and its battle against the KKK's effort to suppress the emancipated African-American vote, sharing particular insights into the career of controversial Secret Service chief, Hiram C. Whitley.

"A detail laden, arduously researched chronicle that delineates an important early era of the Secret Service." Kirkus.

Whitman, Walt, 1819-1892

Callow, Philip **From** noon to starry night : a life of Walt Whitman / Philip Callow. I.R. Dee, 1992. xvi, 394 p. : **B**

ISBN 0929587952

1. Whitman, Walt, 1819-1892. 2. Poets, American -- 19th century 3. Biographies

LC 92005311

A biography of the great American poet draws upon a broad range of sources and quotes liberally from Whitman's poetry to discuss his many jobs, his sexual fluidity, his solitariness, and his work

"Infused with tenderness and respect, this fine biography deciphers the complexity of Whitman's sexuality and passionate creativity while celebrating his abiding compassion and grandeur of spirit." Booklist.

Oliver, Charles M. **Critical** companion to Walt Whitman : a literary reference to his life and work / Charles M. Oliver. Facts on File, c2006. viii, 408 p. : **B**

ISBN 9780816057689

1. Whitman, Walt, 1819-1892. 2. Poets, American -- 19th century

LC 2005004172

An encyclopedic guide to the American poet includes entries on his works and characters, biographical information, influential people in his life, important places, and literary terms relevant to his writings.

Wickersham, Joan

Wickersham, Joan The **suicide** index : putting my father's death in order / Joan Wickersham. Harcourt, c2008. 336 p. **B**

ISBN 9780151014903

1. Wickersham, Joan. 2. Women authors, American 3. Suicide. 4. Survivors of suicide victims -- Psychology 5. Adult children -- Psychology. 6. United States -- Social life and customs -- 20th century 7. Autobiographies and memoirs

LC 2007029299

ALA Notable Book, 2009.

National Book Award for Nonfiction finalist, 2008"

Wickersham's memoir unravels the twisted branches of family ties in the aftermath of her father's suicide as she attempts to answer the question, Why did he do it? Wickersham's effort is worth the read. This book is beautifully written and haunts the reader long after it's closed. Recommended." Library Journal.

Wideman, John Edgar

Wideman, John Edgar **Hoop** roots / John Edgar Wideman. Houghton Mifflin, 2001. 242 p. **B**

ISBN 0395857317

1. Wideman, John Edgar Childhood and youth. 2. Authors, American -- 20th century 3. African American authors 4. African-Americans and basketball. 5. Basketball. 6. Autobiographies and memoirs

LC 2001026455

"Wideman examines his lifelong relationship with basketball. He argues that basketball first allowed him to set his own standard in a white world that often imposes definitions of success on black people. A poignant, thought-provoking memoir." Booklist.

Wiener, Anna, 1987-

★Wiener, Anna, 1987- **Uncanny** valley : a memoir / Anna Wiener. 2020. 320 p. **B**

ISBN 9780374278014

1. High technology industry and trade 2. New businesses 3. Overdoing things 4. Computer industry and trade 5. Silicon Valley, California 6. Santa Clara County, California -- Social conditions. 7. Autobiographies and memoirs

LC 2019021999

The author chronicles her experience at a big-data startup in the heart of the Silicon Valley bubble: a world of surreal extravagance, dubious success and fresh-faced entrepreneurs hell-bent on domination, glory and, of course, progress.

"A funny, highly informative, and terrifying read." Kirkus.

Wiesel, Elie, 1928-2016

Burger, Ariel, **Witness** : lessons from Elie Wiesel's classroom / Ariel Burger. Houghton Mifflin Harcourt, 2018. 256 p. **B**

ISBN 9781328802699

1. Wiesel, Elie, 1928-2016. 2. Teacher-student relationships 3. Teachers 4. Holocaust survivors 5. Holocaust (1933-1945) 6. Autobiographies and memoirs

LC 2018006868

National Jewish Book Award, 2018.

Ariel Burger first met Elie Wiesel at age fifteen. They studied together and taught together. Witness chronicles the intimate conversations between these two men over decades, as Burger sought counsel on matters of intellect, spirituality, and faith, while navigating his own personal journey from boyhood to manhood, from student and assistant to rabbi and, in time, teacher. In this profoundly hopeful, thought-provoking, and inspiring book, Burger takes us into Elie Wiesel's classroom, where the art of listening and storytelling conspire to keep memory alive. As Wiesel's teaching assistant, Burger gives us a front-row seat witnessing these remarkable exchanges in and out of the classroom.The act of listening, of sharing these stories, makes of us, the readers, witnesses"-- Provided by publisher.

Wiesel, Elie, 1928-2016 **All** rivers run to the sea : memoirs / Elie Wiesel. Knopf, 1995. 432 p., [8] p. of plates : **B**

ISBN 0679439161

1. Authors, Jewish 2. Holocaust (1933-1945) 3. Holocaust survivors 4. Authors, French -- 20th century 5. Autobiographies and memoirs

LC 95017607

Includes index.

Translation of : Tous les fleuves vont a la mer."

Wiesel's immensely moving, unforgettable memoir has the searing intensity of his novels and autobiographical tales." Publishers Weekly.

★Wiesel, Elie, 1928-2016 **And** the sea is never full : memoirs, 1969- / Elie Wiesel ; translated from the French by Marion Wiesel. Schocken Books, c2000. x, 429 p., [8] p. of plates : **B**

ISBN 0805210296

1. Authors, Jewish 2. Holocaust survivors 3. Holocaust (1933-1945) -- Public opinion. 4. Jews -- Politics and government -- 1948- 5. Autobiographies and memoirs

LC 00030129

Includes index."

This concluding volume begins when the author is age 40. He continues his travels . and he continues to write, his books including Souls on fire, Four Hasidic Masters, Twilight, and more. Wiesel is the most significant writer to have made the Holocaust the major theme of his work, just as it has been of major importance to his life. The horror of the Holocaust can be felt in this memoir with an intensity beyond words." Booklist.

★Wiesel, Elie, 1928-2016 **Night** / Elie Wiesel ; foreword by Francois Mauriac ; translated from the French by Stella Rodway. Hill and Wang, [1960]. 116 p. ; **B**

ISBN 0809073501

1. Birkenau Extermination Camp. 2. Auschwitz (Concentration camp) 3. God (Judaism) 4. Jewish teenage boys. 5. Guilt in teenage boys. 6. Concentration camp survivors 7. Transylvania, Romania. 8. Germany -- History -- 1933-1945. 9. Autobiographies and memoirs

LC 60014910

Sequel: Dawn.

Reprinted in 2017 with updated front and back matter to include speeches and essays commemorating his recent death.Originally published in Yiddish in a more expanded version, under title (transliterated: Un di velt hot geshvign)

A terrifying account of the Nazi death camp horror that turns a young Jewish boy into an agonized witness to the death of his family.

Wiesenthal, Simon

Pick, Hella **Simon** Wiesenthal : a life in search of justice / Hella Pick. Northeastern University Press, 1996. xvii, 349 p. : **B**

ISBN 155553273X

1. Holocaust survivors 2. Jews 3. War criminals. 4. Austria -- Politics and government -- 1945- 5. Vienna, Austria 6. Biographies

LC 96011808

A thorough biography of the controversial, internationally renowned Nazi-hunter chronicles his survival in thirteen Nazi-concentration camps, his quests for Adolf Eichmann, Josef Mengele, and others, and his support for former Austrian president Kurt Waldheim. UP.

"This biography has interesting things to say about forgiveness, including an extraordinary hallucinogenic encounter with a dying SS officer, and conveys a broadly sympathetic picture of a man capable of distinguishing between individuals and their political rhetoric." Times Literary Supplement.

★Wiesenthal, Simon The **sunflower** : on the possibilities and limits of forgiveness / Simon Wiesenthal ; with a symposium edited by Harry James Cargas and Bonny V. Fetterman. Schocken Books, 1998. xii, 289 p. ; **B**

ISBN 0805210601

1. Wiesenthal, Simon. Sonnenblume. 2. World War II, Jewish. 3. Forgiveness (Judaism) 4. Concentration camps. 5. Genocide. 6. Autobiographies and memoirs

LC 99198049

Author Simon Wiesenthal inquires into the possibilities and limits of compassion, forgiveness, justice, and human responsibility among a diverse group of fifty-three men and women, including Holocaust survivors, victims of attempted genocide, psychiatrists, political leaders, and more.

"The responses to the author's question are as varied as their authors. The mystery of evil and atonement remain, and the reader is left challenged on these most basic issues of meaning in human life." Publishers Weekly.

Wilberforce, William, 1759-1833

Hague, William, 1961- **William** Wilberforce : the life of the great anti-slave trade campaigner / William Hague. Harcourt,

2008. 608 p. **B**
ISBN 9780151012671
1. Wilberforce, William, 1759-1833. 2. Legislators -- Great Britain 3. Slave trade 4. Abolitionists -- Great Britain 5. Philanthropists -- Great Britain 6. Great Britain -- Politics and government -- 1760-1820. 7. Great Britain -- Politics and government -- 1820-1830. 8. Biographies
LC 2007045981
"First published in Great Britain by HarperCollinsPublishers"--T.p. verso."
Hague describes how Wilberforce, dedicating his political life to moral causes ... decided on two: the reformation of manners, as he confided to his diary, and the abolition of African slavery. Wilberforce's campaign against vice had scant historical effect, but that against slavery in British realms arguably prodded the Western world toward abolition. Why Wilberforce's effort (trade in slaves was banned in 1807; abolition occurred in 1834) followed a tortuous path becomes understandable as Hague explains the parliamentary practicalities that Wilberforce faced. Incorporating Wilberforce's domestic life, Hague's effort is a well-rounded portrait of the pioneering British abolitionist." Booklist.

Wilde, Oscar, 1854-1900

Ellmann, Richard, 1918-1987 **Oscar** Wilde / Richard Ellmann. Knopf, 1988, c1987. xvii, 680 p. [32] p. of plates : **B**
ISBN 9780394554846
1. Authors, Irish -- 19th century 2. Poets, Irish -- 19th century 3. Dramatists, Irish -- 19th century. 4. Sexuality. 5. Ireland. 6. Biographies
LC 88207185
Originally published: London : H. Hamilton, 1987.
National Book Critics Circle Award for Biography, 1988.
Pulitzer Prize for Biography or Autobiography, 1989.
Presents an in-depth study of the complex and tragic life of Oscar Wilde and a tribute to his inimitable wit and brilliant writings
"Wilde's life epitomizes the classic formula for a tragic history, the man who, by hubris, falls from greatness. In Mr. Ellmann's hands, the story becomes as compelling as fiction while never deviating from the facts. Humour and elegance illuminate the accounts of Wilde's family, his friends and the enemies he earned." The Economist.

O'Sullivan, Emer The **fall** of the house of Wilde : Oscar Wilde and his family / Emer O'Sullivan. Bloomsbury, 2016 416 p. **B**
ISBN 9781608199877
1. Wilde, Oscar, 1854-1900 Family 2. Authors, Irish -- 19th century 3. Family relationships 4. Eccentrics and eccentricities. 5. Homosexuality -- Law and legislation 6. Great Britain -- History -- Victoria, 1837-1901 7. Biographies
LC bl2016044570
A first-ever biography of Oscar Wilde that places him within the context of his family and social and historical milieu finally tells the whole story of one of the most prominent characters of the late 19th century whose trial for indecency heralded decadence's demise - and his own.
"OSullivan's impressively comprehensive biography is equal parts political history, literary criticism, and Shakespearean tragedy." Publishers Weekly.

Wilder, Billy, 1906-2002

Brackett, Charles, 1892-1969 **It's** the pictures that got small : Charles Brackett on Billy Wilder and Hollywood's golden age / edited by Anthony Slide. Columbia University Press, 2014. 368 p. **B**
ISBN 9780231167086
1. Brackett, Charles, 1892-1969. 2. Wilder, Billy, 1906-2002. 3. Film producers and directors 4. Screenwriters -- United States 5. Diaries 6. Autobiographies and memoirs
LC 2014015801
In this annotated collection of writings taken from dozens of Brackett's unpublished diaries, leading film historian Anthony Slide clarifies Brackett's critical contribution to Wilder's films and Hollywood history while enriching our knowledge of Wilder's achievements in writing, direction, and style.
"Though the diary format is not for all readers, anyone interested in the golden age of film should enjoy this very entertaining and illustrative look at the film industry of the 1930s and 1940s." Library Journal.

Wilder, Laura Ingalls, 1867-1957

★Fraser, Caroline **Prairie** fires : the American dreams of Laura Ingalls Wilder / Caroline Fraser. Metropolitan Books, 2017. 480 p. **B**
ISBN 9781627792769
1. Wilder, Laura Ingalls, 1867-1957. 2. Authors, American -- 20th century 3. Women pioneers -- United States 4. Frontier and pioneer life -- United States. 5. Biographies
LC 2017028870
Includes index.
National Book Critics Circle Award for Biography, 2017.
Pulitzer Prize for Biography or Autobiography, 2018.
A comprehensive historical portrait of Laura Ingalls Wilder draws on unpublished manuscripts, letters, diaries and official records to fill in the gaps in Wilder's official story, sharing lesser-known details about her pioneer experiences while challenging popular misconceptions about how her books were ghostwritten.
"A vivid portrait of frontier life and one of its most ardent celebrants." Kirkus.

McDowell, Marta The **world** of Laura Ingalls Wilder : the frontier landscapes that inspired the Little House books / Marta McDowell. Timber Press, 2017. 390 p. **B**
ISBN 9781604697278
1. Wilder, Laura Ingalls, 1867-1957 Homes and haunts 2. Wilder, Laura Ingalls, 1867-1957. Little house books. 3. Women authors, American 4. Pioneer women 5. Frontier and pioneer life 6. Family farms 7. Middle West 8. United States 9. Biographies
LC 2016057864
Complemented by historical and contemporary photos, a celebration of Wilder's unique relationship with the American frontier reflects on the pioneer spirit of her time and the natural world that was integral to her stories.
"McDowell's warm descriptions of the author, her times, and the plants she loved provide a wonderful companion to Wilder's books, while instructions on growing a Little House inspired garden add an interactive component." Publishers Weekly.

Wilder, Laura Ingalls, 1867-1957 **Pioneer** girl : the annotated autobiography / Laura Ingalls Wilder ; Pamela Smith Hill, editor. South Dakota Historical Society Press, [2014] 400 p. **B**
ISBN 9780984504176
1. Wilder, Laura Ingalls, 1867-1957. 2. Frontier and pioneer life 3. Women authors 4. Pioneer women 5. Authors, American. 6. United States 7. Autobiographies and memoirs
LC 2014027174
"A publication of the Pioneer Girl Project".

Laura Ingalls Wilder's unedited, and unpublished, draft of her autobiography that was written for an adult audience and eventually served as the foundation for her popular Little House on the Prairie series includes not-safe-for-children tales that feature stark scenes of domestic abuse, love triangles gone awry and a man who lit himself on fire while drunk off whiskey.

"Lengthy footnotes make the manuscript somewhat tricky to navigate, but Hill's comments are cogent and her arguments strong, and this will be welcomed wherever there are Wilder fans. Illustrated with maps, photos, and artwork, and appended with additional manuscripts and an extensive bibliography." Booklist.

Wilder, Laura Ingalls, 1867-1957 The **selected** letters of Laura Ingalls Wilder / William Anderson HarperCollins 2016 320 p. **B**

ISBN 9780062419682

1. Wilder, Laura Ingalls, 1867-1957. 2. Authors 3. Writing 4. Letters

LC 2016591797

A single-volume collection of personal writings by the beloved American author spans 60 years of her life and shares deeply personal insights into her experiences, beliefs, family dynamics and career.

Wilder, Thornton, 1897-1975

★Niven, Penelope **Thornton** Wilder : a life / Penelope Niven. HarperCollins, 2012. 800 p. **B**

ISBN 9780060831363

1. Wilder, Thornton, 1897-1975. 2. Authors, American -- 20th century. 3. Dramatists, American -- 20th century 4. Family relationships 5. Creativity in men 6. Biographies

LC 2012532027

Drawn from thousands of pages of letters, journals, manuscripts and other documents, this brilliant biography of the three-time Pulitzer Prize-winning playwright and novelist explores his public persona, his private relationships and his complicated family.

Wilderson, Frank B., III, 1956-

Wilderson, Frank B., III, 1956- **Afropessimism** / Frank B. Wilderson III. Liveright Publishing Corporation, a division of W.W. Norton and Company, 2020. 352 p. **B**

ISBN 9781631496141

1. African American intellectuals 2. African Americans -- Identity 3. Racism. 4. Minorities -- United States -- Social conditions 5. Autobiographies and memoirs

LC 2019051446

The award-winning author of Incognegro offers an account of the non-analogous experience of being black by theorizing the black experiences through a lens of perpetual and incomparable slavery that flourishes in today's world.

"An essential contribution to any discussion of race and likely to be a standard text in cultural studies for years to come." Kirkus

Willan, Anne

Willan, Anne **One** souffle at a time : a memoir of food and France / Anne Willan ; with Amy Friedman. St. Martin's Press, 2013 viii, 305 p. : **B**

ISBN 9780312642174

1. Willan, Anne. 2. Ecole de cuisine La Varenne 3. Women cooks 4. Cooking, French. 5. Cooking schools. 6. British in France. 7. France -- Social life and customs -- 20th century. 8. Autobiographies and memoirs

LC 2013004043

Includes index.

Includes recipes.

IACP Cookbook Awards, Literary Food Writing, 2014.

A collection of life stories and 50 recipes from the founder of La Varenne Cooking School shares upbeat, no-nonsense guidelines on the secrets of French cooking interspersed with reminiscences about the author's fish-out-of-water culinary training. By the author of The Art of French Provincial Cooking.

"A charming, if not revelatory, portrait of a woman determined to bring French cuisine to a wider audience, with emphasis on traditional, accessible recipes that respect the intellectual side of cookery." Kirkus.

Williams, Caroline, 1975-

Williams, Caroline, 1975- **My** plastic brain : one woman's year-long journey to discover if science can improve her mind / Caroline Williams. Prometheus Books, 2018, c2017. 320 p. **B**

ISBN 9781633883918

1. Neuroplasticity. 2. Brain -- Regeneration. 3. Neuroscience 4. Stress 5. Autobiographies and memoirs

LC 2017047080

Originally published under title: Override : my quest to go beyond brain training and take control of my mind. London, United Kingdom : Scribe Publications, 2017.

Exploring "neuroplasticity" by volunteering herself as a test subject, a science journalist with access to cutting-edge experts and facilities around the world challenges researchers to make real changes to the function and performance of her brain and shares her intimate journey with readers to discover what neuroscience can really do for us.

Williams, Hank, Sr., 1923-1953

★Hemphill, Paul, 1936- **Lovesick** blues : the life of Hank Williams / Paul Hemphill. Viking, 2005. 207 p. ; **B**

ISBN 0670034142

1. Country musicians -- United States 2. Biographies

LC 2004065113

Traces the life and career of the mid-twentieth-century country music star, from his sickly and fatherless childhood and musical education by an African-American street singer, to his early gigs in Depression-era rural honky-tonks and rise to Grand Ole Opry star, in an account that also discusses his struggles with alcoholism and early death.

"This is the finest work of literature about Williams yet written." Booklist.

Ribowsky, Mark **Hank** : the short life and long country road of Hank Williams / Mark Ribowsky. Liveright Publishing Corporation, 2016. 384 p. **B**

ISBN 9781631491573

1. Country musicians. 2. Addicts 3. Addiction 4. Country music 5. Biographies

LC 2016026928

Presents a portrait of one of country musics founding fathers, from his difficult childhood in 1920s Alabama, to his early success and rise to stardom, his fiery relationship with his wife, and the drug and alcohol abuse that led to his death at the age of twenty-nine.

Williams, Jay

Williams, Jay **Life** is not an accident : a memoir of reinvention / Jay Williams. HarperCollins, 2015. 304 p. **B**

ISBN 9780062327987

1. Williams, Jay. 2. Basketball players 3. Accident victims 4. Motorcycle accidents. 5. Determination in men. 6. Autobiographies and memoirs.

LC 2015050965

In a candid, no-holds-barred memoir, the former Chicago Bulls' top draft pick talks about the accident that ended his career and sent him down a new path, shares behind-the-scenes details of life as an All-American and speaks out about corruption in the NBA.

"Recommended for anyone interested in a behind-the-scenes look at the lives of college basketball and NBA players." Library Journal.

Williams, Mary 1967-

Williams, Mary, 1967- The **lost** daughter / Mary Williams. Blue Rider Press, 2013. 320 p. **B**

ISBN 9780399160868

1. Fonda, Jane, 1937- 2. Black Panther Party. 3. Interracial adoption. 4. Adopted teenage girls. 5. Dysfunctional families. 6. African American teenage girls. 7. Oakland, California -- Race relations -- History. 8. Autobiographies and memoirs

LC 2013001245

The adopted daughter of Jane Fonda describes her youth in politically charged 1970s Oakland, California, her daunting prospects in the face of her dysfunctional family and the ways in which a positive, structured home life enabled her world travels and eventual reconnection with her biological family.

Williams, Mary Mildred, 1847-1921

Morgan-Owens, Jessie **Girl** in black and white : the story of Mary Mildred Williams and the abolition movement / Jessie Morgan-Owens. W.W. Norton & Company, [2019] 272 p. **B**

ISBN 9780393609240

1. Williams, Mary Mildred, 1847-1921. 2. Williams, Mary Mildred, 1847-1921. Family. 3. Child slaves 4. Freed slaves 5. Photographs 6. Color of African Americans 7. United States -- Race relations -- History -- 19th century 8. Biographies

LC 2018053655

Presents the lesser-known story of slave Mary Mildred Williams, whose fair-skinned appearance rendered her the poster child of the American abolitionist movement and influenced the line where white sympathy was drawn and recognized. Illustrations.

Williams, Patricia (Comedian)

Williams, Patricia (Comedian) **Rabbit** : the autobiography of Ms. Pat / Patricia Williams with Jeannine Amber Dey Street Books, 2017. 256 p. **B**

ISBN 9780062407306

1. Children of alcoholic mothers 2. Growing up 3. Teenage mothers 4. Comedians 5. Atlanta, Georgia 6. Autobiographies and memoirs

LC 2017486713

The popular comedian traces her youth in Atlanta's most troubled neighborhood at the height of the crack epidemic, discussing the experiences with an alcoholic mother, four siblings, petty crime and prostitution that led to her becoming a mother at age 13 before resolving to secure a better life for her children.

"Both savagely honest and often genuinely funny, this is the story of how a resilient woman survived a harrowing early life and found unexpected salvation through humor. Sassy, inspiring, and uplifting." Kirkus.

Williams, Richard, 1942-

Williams, Richard, 1942- **Black** and white : the way I see it / Richard Williams with Bart Davis. Atria Books, 2014. 320 p. **B**

ISBN 9781476704203

1. Williams, Serena, 1981- Family. 2. Williams, Venus, 1980- Family. 3. Tennis coaches 4. Tennis 5. Daughters 6. Families 7. Autobiographies and memoirs

LC 2013033646

"The gripping story of Richard Williams, the father who raised and trained two of the greatest women in sports, Venus and Serena. He achieved greatness in spite of hardship and disadvantages to become a successful businessman, family man and tennis coach".-- Provided by publisher.

Williams, Robin, 1951-2014

★Itzkoff, Dave **Robin** / Dave Itzkoff. Henry Holt and Company, 2018. 400 p. **B**

ISBN 9781627794244

1. Comedians 2. Actors and actresses 3. Men with depression 4. Suicide 5. Biographies

LC 2017050678

The New York Times culture reporter and author of Mad as Hell presents a compelling portrait of Robin Williams that illuminates his comic brilliance, conflicting emotions and often misunderstood character, sharing insights into the gift for improvisation that shaped his wide range of characters, his struggles with addiction and depression and his relationships with friends and family members.

"The book has some nifty trivia (first choices to play Mork from Ork were John Byner and Dom DeLuise), but this isnt one of those skimming-the-surface Hollywood bios. Its a meaty, well-researched, moving story of a man who could never quite come to terms with his own brilliance." Booklist.

Williams, Roger, 1604?-1683

Barry, John M., 1947- **Roger** Williams and the creation of the American soul : church, state, and the birth of liberty / John M. Barry. Viking, c2012. 464 p. : **B**

ISBN 9780670023059

1. Williams, Roger, 1604?-1683. 2. Christian theologians 3. Baptists -- Rhode Island 4. Freedom of religion 5. Christianity -- History 6. Rhode Island -- History -- Colonial period, 1600-1775 7. United States -- History -- Colonial period, 1600-1775 8. Biographies

LC 2011032995

Barry explores the development of the fundamental ideas of church and state through the story of Roger Williams. The first to link religious freedom to individual liberty, Williams helped shape the balance of religion and politics seen in America today.

Gaustad, Edwin S. (Edwin Scott) **Roger** Williams / Edwin S. Gaustad. Oxford University Press, 2005. x, 150 p. : **B**

ISBN 019518369X

1. Williams, Roger, 1604?-1683. 2. Baptists -- Rhode Island 3. Freedom of religion -- Rhode Island -- History -- 17th century. 4. Pioneers -- Rhode Island 5. Puritans -- Rhode Island 6. Rhode Island 7. Rhode Island -- Church history -- 17th century. 8. Rhode Island -- History -- Colonial period, ca. 1600-1775. 9. Biographies

LC 2004025246

A biography of Roger Williams paints a portrait of a man who became an original and passionate advocate for religous freedom and a rare New England colonist who took seriously the culture and legal rights of Native Americans.

Williams, Ted, 1918-2002

Bradlee, Ben, Jr The **kid** : the immortal life of Ted Williams / Ben Bradlee, Jr. Little, Brown, and Company, 2013. 864 p. **B**

ISBN 9780316614351

1. Williams, Ted, 1918-2002. 2. Baseball players -- United States 3.

Batting (Baseball) 4. Baseball -- Records. 5. Biographies
LC 2013028253

A biography of the baseball legend discusses his status as the best hitter in the history of the sport, his five years away from baseball to serve as a Marine pilot in WWII and Korea, and how he spent most of his life hiding his Mexican heritage.

"Sprawling, entertaining life of the baseball great, renowned as a sports hero while leading a life as checkered as Babe Ruth's or Ty Cobb's." Kirkus.

Williams, Tennessee, 1911-1983

Lahr, John, 1941- **Tennessee** Williams : mad pilgrimage of the flesh / John Lahr. W. W. Norton & Company, 2014. 784 p. **B**

ISBN 9780393021240

1. Williams, Tennessee, 1911-1983. 2. Dramatists, American -- 20th century 3. Gay men 4. Authors 5. Celebrities 6. Biographies
LC 2014022281

Lambda Literary Award for Gay Memoir/Biography
National Book Critics Circle Award for Biography, 2014.
National Book Award for Nonfiction finalist, 2014

A biography of one of America's most treasured playwrights describes the writer's public persona as well as his more personal life, including conflicts with his family, his sexuality and multiple affairs and even his misreported death.

"Drawing on vast archival sources and unpublished manuscripts, as well as interviews, memoirs and theater history, he fashions a sweeping, riveting narrative.There is only one word for this biography: superb." Kirkus.

Williams, Thomas Chatterton, 1981-

Williams, Thomas Chatterton, 1981- **Self-portrait** in black and white : unlearning race / Thomas Chatterton Williams. W.W. Norton & Company, [2019] 192 p. **B**

ISBN 9780393608861

1. Multiracial persons 2. Race (Social sciences) 3. Identity (Psychology) 4. Race awareness. 5. United States -- Race relations. 6. Autobiographies and memoirs
LC 2019020819

The award-winning cultural critic and author of Losing My Cool draws on his controversial op-ed about the "one drop" rule that shaped his experiences and identity beliefs as a mixed-race youth who looked white but was treated as black.

Willner, Nina, 1961-

Willner, Nina, 1961- **Forty** autumns : a family's story of courage and survival on both sides of the Berlin Wall / Nina Willner. William Morrow, 2016. 384 p. **B**

ISBN 9780062410313

1. Military intelligence officers -- United States 2. Separated friends, relatives, etc. 3. Cold War 4. Women intelligence officers 5. Berlin, Germany -- History -- 1945-1990. 6. East Germany 7. Autobiographies and memoirs
LC 2016038924

Author Nina Willner, the first female U.S. Army intelligence officer to work in East Germany, had a whole family living behind the Iron Curtain. While her mother Hanna had escaped from East Berlin in 1948, marrying an American and raising her children there, all Hanna's relatives remained behind. In Forty Autumns, Willner relates their story: both her grandfather's brutal "re-education" in a mental institution and the family's loving solidarity in the face of Communist oppression. The Berlin Wall's destruction in 1989 allowed Hanna's first reunion with her relatives in 40 years. Gripping, heartrending, and inspiring, this combined history and family memoir relates the history of the Cold War in personal terms.

"A poignant and engrossing, occasionally harrowing, family memoir." Kirkus.

Willughby, Francis, 1635-1672

Birkhead, Tim The **wonderful** Mr. Willughby : the first true ornithologist / Tim Birkhead. Bloomsbury, 2018. 288 p. **B**

ISBN 9781408878484

1. Willughby, Francis, 1635-1672. 2. Ornithologists -- England 3. Naturalists -- England 4. Biographies
LC 2018018017

Describes the too-short life and career of the man who helped found the Royal Society and accelerated science in the 1600s through his study of birds and his identification system that categorized them by distinguishing features.

"In spite of Willughby's short life, Birkhead ably constructs a full time line of his influence on modern science. For readers, especially ornithologists, with deep interests in natural history and the history of science." Library Journal.

Wilson, Brian, 1942-

Wilson, Brian, 1942- **I** am Brian Wilson : a memoir / Brian Wilson with Ben Greenman. Da Capo Press, 2016 320 p. **B**

ISBN 9780306823060

1. Beach Boys (Musical group) 2. Rock musicians -- United States 3. Men with mental illnesses 4. Creativity in men 5. Music 6. Autobiographies and memoirs
LC 2016030071

The memoirs of the legendary co-founder of the Beach Boys offer insights into his difficult relationship with his father, the women in his life, his parenting experiences, and the events that inspired his music.

Wilson, Chris, 1978-

Wilson, Chris, 1978- The **Master** Plan : my journey from life in prison to a life of purpose / Chris Wilson ; with Bret Witter. G.P. Putnam's Sons, 2019. 416 p. **B**

ISBN 9780735215580

1. Former convicts 2. Self-fulfillment 3. Personal conduct 4. Purpose in life 5. Maryland 6. Autobiographies and memoirs
LC 2018041588

The inspiring, instructive, and ultimately triumphant memoir of a man who used hard work and a Master Plan to turn a life sentence into a second chance.

"Wilson engagingly tells his riveting story while also exposing corrupt justice practices and the ways that society consistently works against former convicts, especially black men." Booklist.

Wilson, Katherine, 1974-

Wilson, Katherine, 1974- **Only** in Naples : lessons in food and famiglia from my Italian mother-in-law / Katherine Wilson. Random House, 2016. 304 p. **B**

ISBN 9780812998160

1. Wilson, Katherine, 1974- Marriage. 2. Wilson, Katherine, 1974- Family. 3. Americans in Italy 4. Cultural differences 5. Cooking -- Naples, Italy 6. Daughters-in-law -- Family relationships -- Naples, Italy 7. Naples, Italy -- Social life and customs. 8. Autobiographies and memoirs
LC 2015016098

After graduating from college, well-to-do Katherine Wilson left Washington, D.C. and headed to Naples, Italy for an unpaid internship at the American Consul. Though Naples was considered "dirty and dangerous" by her friends and family, she discovered that people either loved or hated the city, and she loved it. Not only did she learn to eat better (she'd been a binge eater), but she was embraced by an Italian family and their chic, well-connected matriarch, Raffaella, who taught Wilson about Neapolitan culture and how to cook delicious local foods -- and eventually lessons about marriage and motherhood when Wilson married her son. This lighthearted, charming look at Italian life includes recipes.

"Each experience, each delicious meal is insightfully described as the reader follows Wilsons path toward carnale, becoming confident and comfortable in ones own skin." Booklist.

Wilson, Woodrow, 1856-1924

★Berg, A. Scott (Andrew Scott) **Wilson** / A. Scott Berg. G.P. Putnam's Sons, 2013. 800 p. **B**

ISBN 9780399159213

1. Wilson, Woodrow, 1856-1924. 2. Presidents -- United States 3. World War I. 4. Democrats. 5. World politics. 6. United States -- Politics and government -- 1913-1921. 7. Biographies

LC 2013009339

This biography of the 28th President of the United States from the Pulitzer Prize-winning author of Lindbergh includes details from recently-discovered papers that highlight the character of the scholar-leader who shepherded his country through the first World War.

"Berg portrays Wilson as an utterly new kind of chief executive, in a mold that has yet to be refilled. Readable, authoritative and, most usefully, inspiring." Kirkus.

★Brands, H. W. **Woodrow** Wilson / H.W. Brands. Times Books, 2003. xvi, 169 p. : **B**

ISBN 0805069550

1. Wilson, Woodrow, 1856-1924. 2. Presidents -- United States 3. International relations. 4. Idealism in men. 5. War -- Causes. 6. United States -- Politics and government -- 1913-1921. 7. Biographies

LC 2002041393

Offers an account of the administration of Woodrow Wilson, detailing Wilson's unusual route to the White House, his campaign against corporate interests, his influential shaping of American foreign policy, and his political successes and failures.

"The author presents Wilson as a moralistic, idealistic intellectual who came to the presidency well versed in domestic policy but sadly lacking in knowledge and experience of international affairs, a leader who ultimately sacrificed his health and his presidential legacy in a doomed battle with Sen. Henry Cabot Lodge to have the League of Nations ratified. Brands's brief, skillful life of the President is recommended for all public libraries." Library Journal.

Cooper, John Milton **Woodrow** Wilson : a biography / John Milton Cooper, Jr. Alfred A. Knopf, 2009. viii, 702 p., 16 p. of plates : **B**

ISBN 9780307265418

1. Wilson, Woodrow, 1856-1924. 2. League of Nations -- History. 3. Presidents -- United States 4. World War I. 5. Democrats. 6. World politics. 7. United States -- Politics and government -- 1913-1921. 8. Biographies

LC 2009019097

Pulitzer Prize for Biography or Autobiography finalist.

This thoroughly researched one-volume profile of America's 28th president is universally hailed for its scholarship and insight into the life and career of one of the nation's most polarizing leaders.

"Cooper exhibits complete command of his materials, a sure knowledge of the man and a nuanced understanding of a presidency almost Shakespearean in its dimensions." Kirkus.

O'Toole, Patricia The **moralist** : Woodrow Wilson and the world he made / Patricia O'Toole. Simon & Schuster, 2018 512 p. **B**

ISBN 9780743298094

1. Wilson, Woodrow, 1856-1924. 2. Political leadership. 3. Presidents. 4. United States -- Foreign relations -- 1913-1921. 5. Biographies

LC 2018006628

An in-depth portrait of the 28th President argues that controversial decisions by the Wilson administration established unprecedented levels of American overreach in foreign affairs, examining the challenges, leadership, failures and health setbacks that shaped the Paris Peace Conference of 1919 and founded the League of Nations.

Windsor, Edie

Windsor, Edie A **wild** and precious life : a memoir / Edie Windsor, with Joshua Lyon. St. Martin's Press, 2019. xiii, 274 p. : **B**

ISBN 9781250195135

1. Lesbians 2. Social advocates 3. LGBTQIA rights 4. Gay activists 5. Autobiographies and memoirs

Edie Windsor became internationally famous when she sued the US government, seeking federal recognition for her marriage to Thea Spyer, her partner of more than four decades. The Supreme Court ruled in Edie's favor, a landmark victory that set the stage for full marriage equality in the US. Beloved by the LGBTQ community, Edie embraced her new role as an icon; she had already been living an extraordinary and groundbreaking life for decades.

Windsor, Edward, Duke of, 1894-1972

★Ziegler, Philip **King** Edward VIII : a biography / Philip Ziegler. Ballantine Books, 1992, c1990. xvi, 552 p. : **B**

ISBN 0345375637

1. Windsor, Edward, Duke of, 1894-1972. 2. Great Britain -- History -- Edward VIII, 1936. 3. Great Britain -- Kings and rulers

LC BL 99724218

Originally published: New York : Knopf, 1991.Drawing on Edward VIII's diaries and love letters and on the private papers of Chamberlain, Churchill, and Baldwin, this biography reveals the man who gave up a throne for love

Windsor, House of

Novis, Constance, **Queen** Elizabeth II and the Royal Family / editors, Constance Novis, Helen Fewster. DK Publishing, 2015. 311 p. : **B**

ISBN 9781465438003

1. Elizabeth II, Queen of Great Britain, 1926- 2. Windsor, House of. 3. Monarchy -- Great Britain -- History. 4. Great Britain -- Kings and rulers -- History. 5. Great Britain -- History.

LC 2015487921

Includes index.Traces the line of the Windsor House, profiling such events and people as Princess Margaret and Prince Charles, the wedding of Prince William and Kate, and the Queen's jubilees, providing details on the private and personal lives of the queen and her family.

Windsor, Wallis Warfield, Duchess of, 1896-1986

Morton, Andrew, 1953- **Wallis** in love : the untold life of the Duchess of Windsor, the woman who changed the monarchy / Andrew Morton. Grand Central Publishing, 2018. 368 p. **B**

ISBN 9781455566976

1. Windsor, Wallis Warfield, Duchess of, 1896-1986. 2. Windsor,

Edward, Duke of, 1894-1972 Marriage. 3. Nobility. 4. Marriages of royalty and nobility. 5. Great Britain -- History -- 20th century 6. Biographies

LC 2017034572

A portrait of the woman for whom Edward VIII infamously abdicated the British throne draws on journal entries, letters, and other previously unseen records to analyze her complex personality against the backdrop of Jazz Age London.

Winfrey, Oprah, 1954-

Winfrey, Oprah, 1954- The **wisdom** of Sundays : life-changing insights from Super Soul conversations / Oprah Winfrey. Flatiron Books, 2017. 224 p. **B**

ISBN 9781250138064

1. Spirituality. 2. Growth (Psychology) 3. Purpose in life 4. Love 5. Essays 6. Autobiographies and memoirs

LC 2017022445

A lavishly designed, photographic chronicle of the Emmy Award-winning global media leader's spiritual journey describes the inspirational wisdom and insights she has received from spiritual leaders who have been featured on Super Soul Sunday broadcasts.

Winkfield, Jimmy, 1882-1974

Drape, Joe **Black** maestro : the epic life of an American legend / Joe Drape. Morrow, c2006. 280 p. **B**

ISBN 0060537299

1. Winkfield, Jimmy, 1882-1974. 2. African American jockeys. 3. Jockeys 4. Horse racing -- United States -- History. 5. Horse racing -- Europe -- History. 6. United States -- Social life and customs -- 20th century. 7. Europe -- Social life and customs -- 20th century. 8. Biographies

Presents the life of African-American jockey Jimmy Winkfield, who after winning the Kentuck Derby, emigrated to Europe and became a wealthy horse racer and trainer in Russia and France, until forced by circumstance to return to America and racial discrimination.

Winslow family

Fraser, Rebecca The **Mayflower** : the families, the voyage, and the founding of America / Rebecca Fraser. St. Martin's Press, 2017. 384 p. **B**

ISBN 9781250108562

1. Winslow, Edward, 1595-1655 2. Winslow, Josiah, 1629?-1680 3. Mayflower (Ship) 4. Pilgrims (New England settlers) 5. Colonists 6. Survival 7. Trading companies 8. Massachusetts -- History -- Colonial period, 1626-1775 9. Collective biographies

LC 2017026873

With the aid of contemporary documents, the author brings to life an ordinary family, the Winslows, made less ordinary by their responses to the challenges of the New World after their passage on the Mayflower, in a book that looks at the First Thanksgiving and the Winslows conflicted relationship with the Wampanoag Indians.

Winslow, Emily (Emily Carroll)

Winslow, Emily (Emily Carroll) **Jane** Doe January : my twenty-year search for truth and justice / Emily Winslow. William Morrow, [2016] 320 p. **B**

ISBN 9780062434807

1. Rape victims 2. Authors, American -- 21st century 3. Rape investigation 4. Trials (Rape) 5. Autobiographies and memoirs.

LC 2015046675

One of the victims of a serial rapist offers a gripping chronicle of the criminal's prosecution.

Winters, Richard D.

Alexander, Larry, 1951- **Biggest** brother : the life of Major D. Winters, the man who led the band of brothers / Larry Alexander. NAL Caliber, c2005. xxii, 287 p. : **B**

ISBN 0451215109

1. United States. Army 2. United States. Army. Parachute Infantry Regiment, 506th. Company E -- History. 3. Soldiers -- United States 4. World War II -- Campaigns -- Western Front. 5. World War II -- Regimental histories -- United States. 6. Biographies

LC 2004027330

A tribute complemented by the insights of family, friends, and fellow veterans chronicles the war-time accomplishments of Major Richard D. Winters, the skillful leader of the Band of Brothers, the legendary fighting unit of World War II.

"This is the story of what distinguished Easy Company from other first-class field units: its leadership, in the person of Major Richard Winters, its commander. Alexander is especially good at showing how Winters' sense of responsibility developed as a student, an enlistee, in OCS, and as an officer. He also gives a detailed picture of the army of 60-plus years ago, and the process that turned thousands of young civilians into the men who beat the Germans." Booklist.

Winterson, Jeanette, 1959-

Winterson, Jeanette, 1959- **Why** be happy when you could be normal? / Jeanette Winterson. Grove Press, 2012, c2011. 230 p. **B**

ISBN 9780802120106

1. Winterson, Jeanette, 1959- Childhood and youth. 2. Winterson, Jeanette, 1959- Family. 3. Adopted children -- England 4. Birthparents -- Identification. 5. Adoptees -- Identity 6. Conflict in families. 7. Manchester, England 8. Autobiographies and memoirs

Originally published: London : Jonathan Cape, 2011.

Lambda Literary Award for Lesbian Memoir/BiographyALA Notable Book, 2013.

The author of the best-selling Oranges Are Not the Only Fruit traces her life-long search for happiness as the adopted daughter of Pentecostal parents who raised her in a north England industrial town through practices of fierce control and paranoia, an experience that prompted her to search for her biological mother and turn for solace to the literary world.

Winthrop, John, 1588-1649

Bremer, Francis J. **John** Winthrop : America's forgotten founding father / Francis J. Bremer. Oxford University Press, c2003. xviii, 478 p. : **B**

ISBN 0195149130

1. Winthrop, John, 1588-1649. 2. Puritans -- Massachusetts 3. Colonists. 4. Governors. 5. Puritans -- Massachusetts -- History -- 17th century. 6. Massachusetts -- Governors 7. Massachusetts -- History -- Colonial period, 1600-1775. 8. Great Britain -- History -- Tudors, 1485-1603. 9. Great Britain -- History -- Early Stuarts, 1603-1649. 10. England -- Church history -- 16th century. 11. England -- Church history -- 17th century. 12. Biographies

LC 2002038143

The first full-length biography of the first governor of the Massechusetts Bay Colony delves deeply into the life of this seminal figure in the formation of American society and culture.

"Bremer's definitive biography gracefully portrays Winthrop as a man of his time, whose influence in the new colony grew out of his own struggles to establish his identity before he left England." Publishers Weekly.

Winton, Tim, 1960-

Winton, Tim, 1960- **Island** home : a landscape memoir / Tim Winton. Milkweed Editions, 2017, c2015. 241 p. ; **B**

ISBN 9781571311245

1. Authors, Australian -- 20th century 2. Authors 3. Humans -- Effect of environment on 4. Nature 5. Australia -- Description and travel. 6. Australian 7. Autobiographies and memoirs

LC 2017002185

Originally published: Melbourne, Vic. : Hamish Hamilton, 2015.

Australian Book Industry Awards, General Non Fiction Book of the Year, 2016."

For over thirty years, the author has written novels in which the natural world is as much a living presence as any character. In this beautiful, evocative, and sometimes provocative memoir, he explores Australia's unique landscape, and how that singular place has shaped him and his writing".-- Provided by publisher.

"The worlds largest island deserves nothing less than Winton's beautifully curated, intimate, environmentally sensitive history." Booklist.

Withers, Ernest C., 1922-2007

Lauterbach, Preston **Bluff** City : the secret life of photographer Ernest Withers / Preston Lauterbach. W. W. Norton & Company, 2019. 288 p. **B**

ISBN 9780393247923

1. African American photographers 2. African American civil rights workers 3. FBI informants 4. Civil Rights Movement 5. Biographies

LC 2018032872

Tells the little-known story of iconic photographer Ernest Withers, whose work both captured and influenced the 1950s and 1960s civil rights movement, while he also acted as an informant for the FBI.

Witherspoon, Reese, 1976-

Witherspoon, Reese, 1976- **Whiskey** in a teacup : what growing up in the South taught me about life, love, and baking biscuits / Reese Witherspoon. Touchstone, 2018. 288 p. **B**

ISBN 9781501166273

1. Cooking, American -- Southern style. 2. Growing up -- Southern states 3. Etiquette 4. Film actors and actresses -- United States 5. Tennessee 6. Southern States 7. Autobiographies and memoirs

LC 2018022538

Includes recipes from the author and her family.

The award-winning actress reflects on her Southern heritage and how it is infused into every part of her life, and shares some of her grandmother Dorothea's favorite recipes and traditions.

"Sincere descriptions of making family and friends comfortable in her home whether for book club night or a holiday are punctuated with almost 50 uncomplicated, sentimental recipes (like her grandmother's tea punch) and playlists of favorite music." Library Journal.

Wittgenstein family

Waugh, Alexander The **House** of Wittgenstein : a family at war / Alexander Waugh. Doubleday, c2009. 352 p. **B**

ISBN 9780385520607

1. Wittgenstein family. 2. Families -- History 3. Dysfunctional families 4. Eccentrics and eccentricities -- Vienna, Austria 5. Family problems -- Austria 6. Vienna, Austria -- History 7. Biographies

LC 2008033312

"Waugh tells the story of the downfall of the wealthy Wittgenstein family. He follows the intellectually and musically gifted Wittgenstein children as history conspires to rob them of one of Europe's largest fortunes. Waugh weaves the family's story around that of the fourth son, Paul: losing his arm in the Great War, Paul gained international acclaim as a left-handed concert pianist; at that time, his brother Ludwig's notoriety was limited to a small circle at Cambridge. With the rise of the Nazis, the Wittgenstein siblings were declared racially Jewish and held hostage for their wealth--a peril that ratchets up the book's tension and contributes to the already tragic atmosphere haunting the family. Waugh sifted through letters and journals held in archives and private collections for this masterfully researched work that brings the characters of this previously untold story to life. He moves seamlessly among historical circumstance, personal relations, and the world of classical composition and performance." Library Journal.

Wizenberg, Molly

Wizenberg, Molly **Delancey** : a man, a woman, a restaurant, a marriage / Molly Wizenberg. Simon & Schuster, 2014. 336 p. **B**

ISBN 9781451655094

1. Wizenberg, Molly. 2. Pettit, Brandon. 3. Delancey (Pizzeria : Seattle, Wash.) 4. Husband and wife 5. Restaurants 6. Pizzerias 7. Restaurateurs 8. Autobiographies and memoirs

LC 2013034429

Includes index.

Includes recipes.

The Orangette blogger and author describes how her husband's decision to open and run a pizza restaurant sparked the first crisis in their young marriage.

"Wizenberg candidly describes her fears and doubts, as well as her struggles with trying to be a supportive wife." Library Journal.

★Wizenberg, Molly **Fixed** stars / Molly Wizenberg. Abrams Books, 2020. 256 p. **B**

ISBN 9781419742996

1. Wizenberg, Molly. 2. Questioning (Sexual or gender identity) 3. Coming out (Sexual or gender identity) 4. Married women -- Sexuality 5. Women -- Sexuality 6. Autobiographies and memoirs

LC bl2020018888

A best-selling memoirist describes how, as a married woman with a toddler, she found herself drawn to a female attorney during jury duty and began to question her identity and desires and let go of ideals that no longer fit.

"An essential addition that will resonate with fans of Wizenberg's earlier memoirs and anyone probing the complicated ways that sexuality and traditional family life overlap or diverge." Library Journal

Wodehouse, P. G. (Pelham Grenville), 1881-1975

McCrum, Robert **Wodehouse** : a life / Robert McCrum. W.W. Norton & Co., 2004. xiii, 530 p., 16 p. of plates : **B**

ISBN 0393051595

1. Wodehouse, P. G. (Pelham Grenville), 1881-1975. 2. Jeeves and Wooster. 3. Authors, English -- 20th century 4. Songwriters 5. Humorous writing. 6. Biographies

LC 2004018562

"The author takes the reader from Wodehouse's school days at Dulwich to his successful work as a Broadway lyricist and a master storyteller of Edwardian times who gave us Bertie Wooster and Jeeves to his darkest hour during World War II and final years of semi-exile in America. He offers his most spirited and convincing analysis in countering accusations that Wodehouse knowingly collaborated with the Nazis. This work is thoroughly researched and well written; it will please Wodehouse aficionados and general readers alike." Library Journal.

Wolff, Tobias, 1945-

Wolff, Tobias, 1945- **This** boy's life : a memoir / Tobias Wolff.

Atlantic Monthly Press, 1989. 288 p. **B**

ISBN 0871132486

1. Wolff, Tobias, 1945- Childhood and youth. 2. Authors, American -- 20th century 3. Growing up 4. Family violence. 5. Stepfathers. 6. Washington (State) 7. Autobiographies and memoirs 8. Pacific Northwest literature.

LC 88017600

National Book Critics Circle Award for Biography finalist, 1989.

The author chronicles the tumultuous events of his early life, discussing his parents' divorce, the nomadic wanderings with his mother that followed, and the strange and eventful process of growing up.

"The novelist and short story writer offers an engrossing and candid look into his childhood and adolescence in his first book of nonfiction. In unaffected prose he recreates scenes from his life that sparkle with the immediacy of narrative fiction. The result is an intriguingly guileless book, distinct from the usual reflective commentary of autobiography." Library Journal.

Wollstonecraft, Mary, 1759-1797

Gordon, Lyndall **Vindication** : a life of Mary Wollstonecraft / Lyndall Gordon. Harper Collins, 2005. x, 562 p. **B**

ISBN 0060198028

1. Wollstonecraft, Mary, 1759-1797. 2. Authors, English -- 18th century 3. Women authors, English -- 18th century 4. Feminists -- Great Britain 5. Men/women relations. 6. Biographies

LC 2005040237

Published simultaneously in Great Britain as Mary Wollstonecraft."

The author tackles this formidable woman with grace, clarity and much new research. Gordon relates Wollstonecraft's story with the same potent mixture of passion and reason her subject personified." New York Times Book Review.

Wong, Ali

★Wong, Ali **Dear** girls : intimate tales, untold secrets, and advice for living your best life / Ali Wong. Random House, 2019. 224 p. **B**

ISBN 9780525508830

1. Wong, Ali. 2. Comedians -- United States 3. Women comedians 4. Television writers -- United States 5. Mothers and daughters 6. Letters 7. Autobiographies and memoirs

LC 2019022835

"In her hit Netflix comedy special Baby Cobra, an eight-month pregnant Ali Wong resonated so heavily that she became a popular Halloween costume. Wong told the world her remarkably unfiltered thoughts on marriage, sex, Asian culture, working women, and why you never see new mom comics on stage but you sure see plenty of new dads. The sharp insights and humor are even more personal in this completely original collection. She shares the wisdom she's learned from a life in comedy and reveals stories from her life off stage, including the brutal singles life in New York (i.e. the inevitable confrontation with erectile dysfunction), reconnecting with her roots (and drinking snake blood) in Vietnam, tales of being a wild child growing up in San Francisco, and parenting war stories. Though addressed to her daughters, Ali Wong's letters are absurdly funny, surprisingly moving, and enlightening (and disgusting) for all".-- Provided by publisher.

"Wong brings the same dedication here, where mistakes inspire wisecracking wisdom. A down-to-earth collection that is raw but not irreverent." Kirkus.

Wood, Damon, 1969-

Wood, Damon, 1969- **Working** for the man, playing in the band : my years with James Brown / Damon Wood, with Phil Carson. ECW Press, [2018] 279 p. **B**

ISBN 9781770413856

1. Brown, James, 1933-2006 2. Soul music 3. Guitarists 4. Musicians 5. Soul musicians 6. Autobiographies and memoirs

LC 2019393707

Guitarist Damon Wood spent six-and-a-half years playing for James Brown and the Soul Generals. Damon's narrative of this dramatic period in James Brown's illustrious career will fascinate his millions of fans.

"An insider's account that will delight both Brown fans and those interested in what it's like working for such a dedicated showman. Kudos to Wood for delivering the inside scoop on a demanding performer with exacting standards who brought it, every night." Library Journal.

Wood, Grant, 1891-1942

Evans, R. Tripp, 1968- **Grant** Wood : a life / R. Tripp Evans. Alfred A. Knopf, 2010. xii, 402 p., 8 p. of plates : **B**

ISBN 9780307266293

1. Wood, Grant, 1891-1942. 2. Painters -- United States 3. Regionalism in art. 4. Homosexuality 5. Midwest Regionalism (Art) 6. Iowa -- History -- 20th century 7. United States -- History -- 20th century 8. Biographies

LC 2010018019

"Evans transforms our view of painter Grant Wood and his all-American paintings, including American Gothic, in a revelatory and heartrending biography of an artist forced to conceal his homosexuality." Booklist.

Wood, Henrietta, approximately 1818-1912

McDaniel, W. Caleb (William Caleb), 1979- **Sweet** taste of liberty : a true story of slavery and restitution in America / W. Caleb McDaniel. Oxford University Press, 2019. 288 p. **B**

ISBN 9780190846992

1. Slavery 2. Women freed slaves 3. Restitution 4. Sheriffs 5. Cincinnati, Ohio 6. United States -- History -- 19th century 7. Biographies

LC 2018047090

Pulitzer Prize for History, 2020."

In this gripping study, Rice University historian McDaniel recounts the painful but triumphant story of one enslaved woman's long fight for justice. . . . McDaniel tells this story engrossingly and accessibly. This is a valuable contribution to Reconstruction history with clear relevance to current debates about reparations for slavery." Publishers Weekly

Wooden, John, 1910-2010

Davis, Seth **Wooden** : a coach's life / Seth Davis. Times Books, 2014. 576 p. **B**

ISBN 9780805092806

1. Wooden, John, 1910-2010. 2. U C L A Bruins (Basketball team) -- History. 3. University of California, Los Angeles Basketball -- History. 4. Athletic coaches -- United States 5. Basketball coaching. 6. College basketball. 7. Basketball. 8. Biographies

LC 2013020209

Includes index.

A provocative assessment of legendary UCLA coach John Wooden by the best-selling author of When March Went Mad draws on hundreds of interviews from all periods of his career to offer insight into his driving ambition, divided relationships and hard-won lessons.

"Davis has avoided stultifying, game-by-game detail (but does offer genuinely exciting accounts of several key games) and has provided a multidimensional, nearly cradle-to-grave portrait of a highly successful and revered coach and teacher, in the process delivering a history of the evolution of college basketball and profiles of many of its stars." Booklist.

Woodfox, Albert

Woodfox, Albert **Solitary** : unbroken by four decades in solitary confinement. My story of transformation and hope. / Albert Woodfox. Grove Press, 2019. 320 p. **B**

ISBN 9780802129086

1. Angola Prison, Louisiana 2. Black Panther Party. 3. Solitary confinement 4. False imprisonment 5. Judicial error 6. Racism 7. Louisiana 8. Autobiographies and memoirs

LC 2018045958

Hurston/Wright Legacy Award: Nonfiction, 2020.
Pulitzer Prize for General Nonfiction finalist, 2020.
National Book Award for Nonfiction finalist, 2019.

Chronicles the author's extraordinary achievements as an activist during and after spending 40 years in solitary confinement for a crime he did not commit, describing how he has committed his post-exoneration life to prison reform.

"Woodfox's shocking memoir of his years in prison, mostly under solitary confinement, is a testament to the human spirit and a scathing indictment of the justice system." Booklist.

Woodhull, Victoria C. (Victoria Claflin), 1838-1927

Goldsmith, Barbara **Other** powers : the age of suffrage, spiritualism, and the scandalous Victoria Woodhull / Barbara Goldsmith. A.A. Knopf, 1998. xv, 531 p. : **B**

ISBN 9780394555362

1. Woodhull, Victoria C. (Victoria Claflin), 1838-1927. 2. Feminists -- United States 3. Women -- Suffrage -- United States -- History. 4. Suffragists -- United States -- History. 5. Women's rights and spiritualism. 6. Biographies

LC 97049464

Interweaves the stories of important figures of America's Victorian era with the life of Victoria Woodhull, a pioneering female politician and onetime prostitute.

"Victoria Woodhull was a charismatic and notorious figure in the struggle for women's rights in the years following the Civil War. She was the first woman to address Congress and the first woman to run for president. Goldsmith . has successfully woven together a history of Woodhull's life with the lives of the powerful she touched." Library Journal.

Woods, Tiger

Bamberger, Michael, 1960- The **second** life of Tiger Woods / Michael Bamberger. Avid Reader Press, 2020. 288 p. **B**

ISBN 9781982122829

1. Golfers 2. Athletes 3. Personal conduct 4. Scandals 5. Biographies

LC bl2020004900

Presents an intimate account of Tiger Woods's comeback that discusses the golf champion's high-risk back surgery, 2017 DUI arrest, rehabilitation and triumphant 2019 Masters victory.

"In all, this may be the most insightful and evenhanded book written yet about one of the signature athletes of the last 25 years." Booklist

★Benedict, Jeff **Tiger** Woods / Jeff Benedict and Armen Keteyian. Simon & Schuster, 2018. xix, 490 p. ; **B**

ISBN 9781501126420

1. Golfers 2. Athletes 3. Celebrities 4. African American men 5. Biographies

LC bl2018038015

A behind-the-scenes portrait of the golf star's meteoric rise and fall from grace draws on interviews from every aspect of Wood's life to reveal the true Tiger Woods.

"Journalists and coauthors Benedict and Keteyian (both, The System) have deconstructed the carefully crafted movie script that has been Tiger Woods's life." Library Journal.

Callahan, Tom **In** search of Tiger : a journey through golf with Tiger Woods / Tom Callahan. Three Rivers Press, 2004, c2003. viii, 245 p. : **B**

ISBN 1400051401

1. Professional Golfers' Association of America 2. Golfers -- United States 3. Golf -- Anecdotes. 4. Professional golfers -- United States 5. Fathers and sons -- United States 6. United States -- Social life and customs -- 21st century 7. Biographies

LC bl2006006234

Includes index.

Originally published: New York : Crown, c2003.

A look at Tiger Woods from age twenty to twenty-seven follows him through golf tournaments and captures the relationship between Tiger and his father while revealing the key influences in his life and career.

"The author examines Tiger's early years, how he got to the top of his game and his vision for the future. Anecdotes and insider insights highlight portraits of major Tiger victories. This is a comprehensive examination of the man, his talent, his competition and the world of professional golf, a must-read for fans and players alike." Publishers Weekly.

Woods, Tiger The **1997** Masters : my story / Tiger Woods, with Lorne Rubenstein. Grand Central Pub., 2017. 256 p. **B**

ISBN 9781455543588

1. Masters Golf Tournament History. 2. Professional golfers. 3. Golf -- Tournaments. 4. Autobiographies and memoirs

LC bl2017002359

Published to coincide with the 20th anniversary of Tiger Woods' historic win at the 1997 Masters, an account of the pro golfer's historic career shares previously unknown stories and the ways his record-setting win changed both the sport and his life on and off the course.

"An in-depth, inside look at the legendary golfer's historic 1997 Masters win." Kirkus.

Woolf, Leonard, 1880-1969

★Glendinning, Victoria **Leonard** Woolf : a biography / Victoria Glendinning. Free Press, c2006. 498 p. : **B**

ISBN 0743246535

1. Woolf, Leonard, 1880-1969. 2. Political scientists -- Great Britain 3. Publishers and publishing -- Great Britain 4. Authors, English -- 20th century 5. Socialists -- Great Britain 6. Great Britain -- History -- 20th century. 7. Biographies

LC 2006049784

An account of the life and career of the Bloomsbury political intellectual and husband of Virginia Woolf covers his comfortable Jewish childhood, role in inspiring the League of Nations, and relationships with such figures as E.M. Forster and T.S. Eliot.

"Glendinning's generous biography does not ignore that Woolf could be grumpy and was too often cheeseparing, but her account does justice to his range of passions, his literary and political contributions and, above all, his human goodness he was a man who knew how to live." New Statesman.

Woolf, Virginia, 1882-1941

Briggs, Julia **Virginia** Woolf : an inner life / Julia Briggs. Harcourt, Inc., c2005. xiv, 527 p. : **B**

ISBN 0151011435

1. Woolf, Virginia, 1882-1941 Criticism and interpretation 2. Women and literature -- England -- History -- 20th century. 3. Autobiography

in literature. 4. Self in literature. 5. England -- Social life and customs -- 20th century 6. Essays 7. Biographies

LC 2005016048

Originally published: London : Allen Lane, 2005.

A portrait of the twentieth-century writer reveals how her life was centered on her writing; drawing on letters, diaries, and essays to explain how her written works reflect her formative experiences and creative philosophies.

"That this book is a must for Woolf fans goes without saying, but it is also a must for anyone interested in the nature of female consciousness at its most self-aware and the workings of artistic sensibility at their most illuminating." Publishers Weekly.

★Lee, Hermione **Virginia** Woolf / Hermione Lee. A.A. Knopf, 1997, c1996. xiii, 893 p. : **B**

ISBN 0679447075

1. Woolf, Virginia, 1882-1941. 2. Authors, English -- 20th century 3. Biographies

LC 96217613

Originally published: London: Chatto & Windus, 1996.

National Book Critics Circle Award for Biography finalist, 1997."

Lee re-creates the world Woolf was born into in 1882, a maze of formalities and reticences, and then leads us through changes that, slow in coming but shocking in effect, made all that seem light-years away by the time Woolf was 50. She convinces us that Woolf, contrary to previous assumptions, reveled in a deep intimacy with her husband, Leonard. Finally, she makes a persuasive case for the underlying sanity of this woman as she battled her own madness and shows the brilliant literary uses she made of her instability." New York Times Book Review.

Woolf, Virginia, 1882-1941 A **moment's** liberty : the shorter diary / Virginia Woolf ; abridged and edited by Anne Olivier Bell ; introduction by Quentin Bell. Harcourt Brace Jovanovich, 1992, c1990. xii, 516 p. ; **B**

ISBN 0156619121

1. Woolf, Virginia, 1882-1941 Diaries. 2. Novelists, English -- 20th century -- Diaries.

LC BL 99724925

Includes index.

Reprint. Originally published: c1990.

Selections from the diaries of Virginia Woolf share her observations on English social life, literature, politics, and her own work.

"The diaries here may appeal to a larger audience, not least because each year represented is prefaced by a wonderfully succinct overview. Here are Woolf's superbly drawn portraits of Max Beerbohm, T.S. Eliot, John Maynard Keynes, Katherine Mansfield--and her occasionally acerbic remarks on what they said and did. But the diaries are also a repository for luminous thoughts on birds and weather, the pleasures of walking or listening to music." Publishers Weekly.

Woolf, Virginia, 1882-1941 **Moments** of being / Virginia Woolf ; edited, with an introduction and notes, by Jeanne Schulkind. Grafton Books, 1989, c1976. 249 p. ; **B**

ISBN 0586073264

1. Woolf, Virginia, 1882-1941. 2. Authors, English -- 20th century 3. Women authors, British 4. Autobiographies and memoirs

LC 91111059

Originally published: London : Chatto and Windus, 1976.Six autobiographical pieces that span her entire career reveal the underlying unity of Woolf's art, thought, and sensibility and the unusual degree to which she integrated personal experiences within her fiction.

Wordsworth, William, 1770-1850

Bate, Jonathan **Radical** Wordsworth : the poet who changed the world / Jonathan Bate. Yale University Press, 2020. xxii, 586 p., 16 unnumbered p. of plates : **B**

ISBN 9780300169645

1. Poets, English -- 19th century 2. Influence (Literary, artistic, etc.) 3. Romanticism in art 4. Nature (Aesthetics) 5. Biographies

LC 2020931386

"First published in 2020 in Great Britain by William Collins"--Title page verso.

Published in time for the 250th anniversary of William Wordsworth's birth, this is the biography of a great poetic genius, a revolutionary who changed the world. He and his fellow Romantics changed forever the way we think about childhood, the sense of the self, our connection to the natural environment, and the purpose of poetry. But his was also a revolutionary life in the old sense of the word, insofar as his art was of memory, the return of the past, the circling back to childhood and youth. This beautifully written biography is purposefully fragmentary, momentary, and selective, opening up what Wordsworth called "the hiding-places of my power."

"In this energetic literary biography, Bate (Shakespeare and the English Romantic Imagination), a senior research fellow at Oxford University, places William Wordsworth's work in the context of his life. . . . Appealingly conveying his own love of and frustrations with Wordsworth, Bate demonstrates in his delightful volume how, flaws and all, the poet 'made a difference' in the way future generations would think and feel." Publishers Weekly

Johnston, Kenneth R. The **hidden** Wordsworth : poet, lover, rebel, spy / Kenneth R. Johnston. W.W. Norton, 1998. xxii, 965 p. : **B**

ISBN 0393046230

1. Wordsworth, William, 1770-1850 Childhood and youth. 2. Wordsworth, William, 1770-1850 Relations with women. 3. Poets, English -- 19th century 4. Revolutionaries -- Great Britain 5. Spies -- Great Britain 6. Romanticism in poetry -- Great Britain. 7. Biographies

LC 97040317

Maps depicting 'Wordsworth's London, 1791-1795' and 'Wordsworth's Paris, 1791-1793' on endpapers.

Shortlisted for the James Tait Black Memorial Prize for Biography, 1998"

This volume focuses on the poet's first thirty-six years, the tumultuous decades immortalized in 'The Prelude.' Johnston's spacious, absorbing argument that Wordsworth's moments of emotion recollected in tranquillity were themselves rather less than tranquil is amply supported by a thorough documentation of the multifarious life and times of the young poet, at Hawkshead, at Cambridge, in Grasmere, and abroad." The New Yorker.

Worley, Jennifer

Worley, Jennifer **Neon** girls : a stripper's education in protest and power / Jennifer Worley. HarperPerennial, 2020 261 p. : **B**

ISBN 9780062971326

1. Worley, Jennifer. 2. Stripteasers 3. Women labor unionists 4. Labor activists 5. Feminism 6. San Francisco, California -- Social life and customs 7. Autobiographies and memoirs

A former San Francisco stripper gives an account of how she led her fellow dancers to create the first strippers' union in the world and take control of the operation of their club.

"A fast-paced, engaging book that readers with an interest in feminist thought, memoirs, and labor activism will enjoy." Library Journal

Wouk, Herman, 1915-2019

Wouk, Herman, 1915-2019 **Sailor** and fiddler : reflections of a 100-year-old author / Herman Wouk. Simon & Schuster, 2016 256 p. **B**

ISBN 9781501128547

1. Authors, American 2. Writing 3. Aging 4. Autobiographies and memoirs

LC 2015037994

The Pulitzer Prize-winning cultural literary master reflects on his life and times from the unique vantage point of 100 years of age, covering such topics as his work on Fred Allen's radio shows, his World War II military service, his long-time marriage and the surprising inspirations behind his written works.

"Wouk is jaunty and wise in this sparkling memoir of a well-lived life of literature, fame, and love." Booklist.

Wray, Fay, 1907-2004

Riskin, Victoria **Fay** Wray and Robert Riskin : a Hollywood memoir / Victoria Riskin. Pantheon Books, [2019] 400 p. **B**

ISBN 9781524747282

1. Wray, Fay, 1907-2004. 2. Riskin, Robert, 1897-1955. 3. Film actors and actresses. 4. Screenwriters. 5. Film producers and directors. 6. Comedy films. 7. Biographies.

LC 2018027978

The daughter of the actress best known for "King Kong" and the screenwriter for "It Happened One Night" presents a memoir that describes her parents' lives and work, her father's collaborations with Frank Capra, and his early death.

Wright, Frank Lloyd, 1867-1959

★Huxtable, Ada Louise **Frank** Lloyd Wright / Ada Louise Huxtable. Lipper/Viking, 2004. xvii, 251 p. : **B**

ISBN 0670033421

1. Wright, Frank Lloyd, 1867-1959. 2. Architects -- United States 3. Biographies

LC 2004046477

Provides a portrait of the American architect, describing his personal life, his career as a builder and craftsman, his architectural achievements, and his influence on the world of art and architecture.

"The eventfulness of the extraordinary life and the refreshing intelligence and craft of the author make this book a pleasure to read. That I found myself on occasion arguing with the text only proves the provocative quality of Huxtable's exploration." New York Times Book Review.

Secrest, Meryle **Frank** Lloyd Wright / Meryle Secrest. Harper Perennial, 1993, c1992. xviii, 634 p. : **B**

ISBN 0060975679

1. Wright, Frank Lloyd, 1867-1959. 2. Architects -- United States 3. Architecture, American. 4. Biographies

LC 92056269

Originally published: 1st ed. New York : Knopf, 1992.

A biography of the acclaimed architect describes Wright's Midwest boyhood, his apprenticeship with Louis Sullivan, his travels to Europe and subsequent success there, his three marriages, his work, and more.

"A portrait of a complex, often contradictory architect. Secrest writes with authority and compassion about Wright's long and turbulent career. Her exhaustive scholarship provides fresh insights into Wright's personality." Library Journal.

Wright, James Arlington, 1927-1980

Blunk, Jonathan **James** Wright : a life in poetry / Jonathan Blunk. Farrar, Straus and Giroux, 2017. 528 p. **B**

ISBN 9780374178598

1. Wright, James Arlington, 1927-1980. 2. Poets, American. 3. Biographies

LC 2017003852

The sweeping authorized biography of one of America's most complex, influential, and enduring poets.

"A much-needed, engaging, and discerning biography that should help Wright find a new generation of readers." Kirkus.

Wright, Lawrence, 1947-

Wright, Lawrence, 1947- **God** save Texas : a journey into the soul of the Lone Star State / Lawrence Wright. Alfred A. Knopf, 2018. 304 p. **B**

ISBN 9780525520108

1. Wright, Lawrence, 1947- Travel Texas 2. States 3. Culture 4. Texas -- Description and travel 5. Texas -- Social life and customs 6. Texas -- Politics and government 7. Texas -- Economic conditions 8. Autobiographies and memoirs

LC 2017031324

National Book Critics Circle Award for Nonfiction finalist, 2018

The Pulitzer Prize-winning author of The Looming Tower explores the history, culture and politics of Texas while challenging popular stereotypes, offering insight into how the state boasts some of the highest rates of diversity, technology exports and growth as well as the lowest tax models and government regulations.

"Wrights large-scale portrait, which reveals how Texas is only growing in influence, is comprehensive, insightful, and compulsively entertaining." Publishers Weekly.

Wright, Orville, 1871-1948

★McCullough, David G. The **Wright** brothers / David McCullough. Simon & Schuster 2015. 650 p. **B**

ISBN 9781476728742

1. Wright, Orville, 1871-1948. 2. Wright, Wilbur, 1867-1912. 3. Aeronautics -- United States -- History -- 20th century. 4. Flight -- History -- 20th century. 5. Wright Flyer (Airplane) 6. Airplanes -- History -- 20th century. 7. Biographies

LC 2014046049

ALA Notable Book, 2016.

Chronicles the dramatic story-behind-the-story about the Wright brothers, sharing insights into the disadvantages that challenged their lives and their mechanical ingenuity.

"McCullough's usual warm, evocative prose makes for an absorbing narrative; he conveys both the drama of the birth of flight and the homespun genius of America's golden age of innovation." Publishers Weekly.

Wright, Richard, 1908-1960

Rowley, Hazel **Richard** Wright : the life and times / Hazel Rowley. Henry Holt and Co., 2001. x, 626 p. : **B**

ISBN 9780805047769

1. Wright, Richard, 1908-1960. 2. Authors, American -- 20th century 3. African American authors 4. Race relations. 5. Racism. 6. Biographies

LC 00054249

"A John Macrae book."

Traces Wright's rise from a Mississippi sharecropper's shack to international fame, describing his writings, his role as an outspoken critic of racism, his expatriate life, and his relationship with other notables of his time.

"he strength of {this book} is {the} painstaking research. Rowley . has a daunting dedication to primary sources and her documentation is meticulous." New York Times Book Review.

★Wright, Richard, 1908-1960 **Black** boy : (American hunger) : a record of childhood and youth / Richard Wright ; foreword by Edward P. Jones. Harper Collins Publishers, 2005, c1945. x, 419 p. ; **B**

ISBN 0060834005

1. Wright, Richard, 1908-1960 Childhood and youth. 2. Wright, Richard, 1908-1960 Homes and haunts Mississippi. 3. African Americans -- Mississippi -- Social life and customs. 4. Racism -- Mississippi 5. Authors, American -- Homes and haunts -- Mississippi. 6. Authors, American -- 20th century 7. Mississippi -- Social conditions. 8. Autobiographies and memoirs

LC 2005052698

"The restored text established by the Library of America."

Originally published: New York : Harper & Brothers, 1945.

Traces the author's coming of age in the Jim Crow-era South, a period during which he struggled to survive while journeying from innocence to adulthood.

Wright, iO Tillett

Wright, iO Tillett **Darling** days : a memoir / iO Tillett Wright. Ecco Press, 2016. 224 p. **B**

ISBN 9780062368201

1. Gender role 2. Gender identity 3. Growing up 4. Adult children of divorced parents 5. Lower East Side, New York City. 6. Autobiographies and memoirs

LC bl2016038051

The author describes her search for an authentic sense of self and gender identity in a coming of age biography set in the 1980s and 1990s urban bohemia of New York's Lower East Side, where punk rock, poverty and heroin met art and glamour.

"It's unclear how this engagingly reckless soul found the poise to launch a publishing, acting, and writing career; she just seemed to be doing it by her late teens. If Wright can pull it off, there's hope for just about everybody. An earnest and heartfelt memoir cloaked under a battle-toughened exterior." Kirkus.

Wyeth, Andrew, 1917-2009

Wyeth, Andrew, 1917-2009 **Andrew** Wyeth : autobiography / introduction by Thomas Hoving ; with commentaries by Andrew Wyeth as told to Thomas Hoving. Bulfinch Press ; c1995. 168 p. : **B**

ISBN 9780821225691

1. Wyeth, Andrew, 1917-2009. 2. Painters -- United States 3. Exhibition catalogs 4. Autobiographies and memoirs

LC 94048305

Published on the occasion of the retrospective exhibition "Andrew Wyeth: autobiography" at the Nelson-Atkins Museum of Art, Kansas City, Sept. 29-Nov. 26, 1995.

A comprehensive edition of the artist's work reproduces 138 paintings, including Wyeth's most recognized works, along with his comments about each one and reflections on his life

"Each painting is accompanied by commentary from the artist that lends insight into his life and character. Several nude studies are included." Booklist. [review of 1995 edition]

Wyeth, N. C. (Newell Convers), 1882-1945

Michaelis, David, 1957- **N.C.** Wyeth : a biography / David Michaelis. Knopf, 1998. x, 555 p. : **B**

ISBN 9780679426264

1. Wyeth, N. C. (Newell Convers), 1882-1945. 2. Painters -- United States 3. Illustrators -- United States 4. Family relationships. 5. Biographies

LC 98006143

A lavishly illustrated, full-scale portrait of the distinguished American illustrator describes N. C. Wyeth's attitude toward his own art, his close family ties, his complex personality, and his influence on the artistic careers of his famed son, Andrew, and grandson, Jamie.

"Michaelis's work is an outstanding example of the biographer's art. Integrating Wyeth's complex personal and psychological life with his artistic oeuvre, Michaelis creates a portrait of both the artist and the man." Library Journal.

Wynette, Tammy, 1942-1998

McDonough, Jimmy **Tammy** Wynette : tragic country queen / Jimmy McDonough. Viking, 2010. 448 p. **B**

ISBN 9780670021536

1. Wynette, Tammy, 1942-1998. 2. Country musicians -- United States 3. Country music. 4. Women musicians. 5. Women country musicians. 6. Biographies

LC 2009042565

"A full-scale profile of the iconic country-music performer documents her small-town upbringing, struggles with addiction and high-profile divorce in a rapidly evolving Nashville."

"Mr. McDonough is crazy about Wynette but also detached enough to see her clearly, writing with obvious respect for both her life and art. You bookish types, as Mr. McDonough describes his readers, will surely want to listen to her sing on the basis of this book's recommendations. With an emphatic sense of her place in country musicat the top of the heap, casting a shadow big enough to obscure today's woefully synthetic assembly-line singershe combines a love of her overlooked and minor classics with a compelling big-picture life story. His opinions are often corroborated by the colorfully authentic voices of those who knew her well and marveled at her moxie." New York Times.

Yang, Kao Kalia, 1980-

Yang, Kao Kalia, 1980- The **song** poet : a memoir of my father / Kao Kalia Yang. Metropolitan Books, 2016. 304 p. **B**

ISBN 9781627794947

1. Yang, Bee, 1958- 2. Yang, Kao Kalia, 1980- Family. 3. Hmong Americans 4. Singers 5. Fathers and daughters 6. Songs, Hmong 7. Autobiographies and memoirs

LC 2015032156

National Book Critics Circle Award for Autobiography/Memoir finalist, 2016.

The author delivers a powerful memoir of her father, a Hmong song poet who sacrificed his gift for his children's future in America.

"Yang powerfully demonstrates that much of what society doesn't hold valuable gifts and talents that don't translate into monetary or educational success still carry immense value, if only we choose to see it." Library Journal.

Yasuke (Black Samuraï)

Lockley, Thomas **African** samurai : the true story of Yasuke, a legendary black warrior in feudal Japan / Thomas Lockley and Geoffrey Girard. Hanover Square Press, 2019 368 p. **B**

ISBN 9781335141026

1. Oda, Nobunaga, 1534-1582 2. Samurai 3. Warriors 4. Africans in Japan 5. War 6. Japan -- History -- Period of civil wars, 1480-1603 7. Biographies

LC bl2019004187

Published in the UK under the title Yasuke: the true story of the legendary African samurai.

Traces the remarkable life story of history's first foreign-born samurai, detailing his near-mythical journey from a boy soldier in late-16th-century Northern Africa to the heights of Japanese society, where his presence triggered cultural riots.

"The title may seem rather implausible, but Lockley and Girard dispel any doubts as they tell the remarkable story of this legendary, world-traveling African warrior in the war-torn islands of sixteenth-century Japan." Booklist.

Yeats, W. B. (William Butler), 1865-1939

Brown, Terence, 1944- The **life** of W.B. Yeats : a critical biography / Terence Brown. Blackwell, 1999. xiii, 410 p., [8] p. of plates : B

ISBN 9780631182986

1. Poets, Irish -- 19th century 2. Poets, Irish -- 20th century 3. Ireland -- Intellectual life -- 19th century. 4. Ireland -- Intellectual life -- 20th century. 5. Biographies

LC 99028388

"In this biography Brown places Yeats's work as poet and dramatist in its political and socialas well as personal-- and erotic-- context." New York Times Book Review.

Foster, R. F., 1949- **W.B.** Yeats : a life / R.F. Foster. Oxford University Press, 1997-2003. 2 v. : B

ISBN 0192117351

1. Poets, Irish -- 19th century 2. Poets, Irish -- 20th century 3. Intellectual life -- Ireland. 4. Biographies

LC 96031671

James Tait Black Memorial Prize for Biography, 1997.

The first volume in an exhaustive biography covers the poet's first fifty years, revising previous assumptions about Yeats's background, his relationships with Maude Gonne and other women, and his role in shaping modern Irish identity.

Yellow Bird, Lissa

★Murdoch, Sierra Crane **Yellow** Bird : oil, murder, and a woman's search for justice in Indian country / Sierra Crane Murdoch. Random House, 2020. 400 p. B

ISBN 9780399589157

1. Clarke, Kristopher 2. Native American women 3. Oil workers 4. Missing persons investigation 5. Women former convicts 6. Fort Berthold Indian Reservation, North Dakota 7. North Dakota 8. Biographies

LC 2019022833

Tells the true crime story of a murder on an Indian reservation, and the unforgettable Arikara woman who becomes obsessed with solving it.

"Required reading for all fans of true crime, particularly those interested in the intersections of poverty and environmental justice, along with Native studies." Library Journal

Yelverton, Therese, Viscountess Avonmore, 1832?-1881

Schama, Chloe **Wild** romance : a Victorian story of a marriage, a trial, and a self-made woman / Chloe Schama. Walker & Co., 2009. 320 p. B

ISBN 9780802717368

1. Yelverton, Therese, Viscountess Avonmore, 1832?-1881. 2. Avonmore, William Charles Yelverton, Viscount, 1824-1883 Trials, litigation, etc. 3. Yelverton, Therese, Viscountess Avonmore, 1832?-1881 Travel. 4. Trials (Bigamy) 5. Aristocracy -- England 6. Bigamy -- England -- History -- 19th century. 7. Upper class women -- England 8. England -- Social life and customs -- 19th century.

LC 2009044758

Tells the story of Theresa Longworth, a Victorian Englishwoman whose husband abandoned her, forcing her to prove in court that they were ever married, in a book that conveys riveting courtroom drama, full of steamy accusations and intrigue, as well as Longworth's life afterward as a successful unmarried author and speaker.

"Schama details the bigamy trial of William Charles Yelverton, which dominated the front pages of Irish, Scottish, and British newspapers in 1861. Although the story of Yelverton and his first wife, Theresa Longworth, practically tells itself through court documents, letters, and public opinion, Schama adds a journalist's touch in her story development. The latter part of the book deals with Theresa's later life in America as a self-made woman still haunted by her past." Library Journal.

Yip-Williams, Julie, 1976-2018

★Yip-Williams, Julie, 1976-2018 The **unwinding** of the miracle : a memoir of life, death, and everything that comes after / Julie Yip-Williams. Random House, [2019] 256 p. B

ISBN 9780525511359

1. Vietnamese Americans 2. Women with cancer 3. Colon cancer 4. Boat people (Southeast Asian refugees) 5. Autobiographies and memoirs

LC 2018031944

An unconventional memoir by a young mother with Stage IV metastatic cancer describes her experiences as a blind Vietnamese political refugee-turned-Harvard-educated lawyer before terminal illness inspired her blog to share the real-world guidance she wished she had.

"Her writing is honest and, by turns, angry, humorous, and heartbreaking, especially when she talks about her two little girls, who are just starting elementary school. Even though readers know the ending--the prologue indicates that if theyre reading this, she's already gone--every bit of new bad news hits like a blow to the gut." Booklist.

Young, Brigham, 1801-1877

Arrington, Leonard J. **Brigham** Young : American Moses / Leonard J. Arrington. Knopf, 1986. xvii, 522, 16 p. of plates : B

ISBN 9780394510224

1. Young, Brigham, 1801-1877. 2. Mormon Church Presidents 3. Religious leaders -- United States 4. Mormons 5. Biographies

LC 84048650

National Book Critics Circle Award for Biography finalist, 1985.

An historian of the Mormon Church draws on diaries and letters not available to previous biographers to profile the controversial church leader.

Turner, John G. **Brigham** Young, pioneer prophet / John G. Turner. The Belknap Press of Harvard University Press, 2012. 490 p. B

ISBN 9780674049673

1. Young, Brigham, 1801-1877. 2. Mormon Church. 3. Mormons. 4. Faith in men. 5. Biographies

LC 2012015555

"There aren't enough superlatives for this book. It will remain the standard biography for a long time. Because of its thorough documentation, academics will take it seriously, while general readers will appreciate its clarity of prose and argument." Library Journal.

Young, Damon (Editor-in-chief of Very Smart Brothas)

★Young, Damon (Editor-in-chief of Very Smart Brothas) **What** doesn't kill you makes you blacker : a memoir in essays / Damon Young. Ecco Press. 2019. 320 p. B

ISBN 9780062684301

1. African Americans -- Identity 2. Identity (Psychology) 3. Race relations 4. Growing up 5. Pittsburgh, Pennsylvania 6. United States

-- Race relations. 7. Autobiographies and memoirs 8. Essays.

LC bl2019000961

The co-founder of VerySmartBrothas.com presents a provocative and humorous memoir-in-essays that explores the direct impact of racism on his life, the shifting definition of Black male identity and the ongoing realities of white supremacy.

"Young uses pop culture references and personal stories to look at a life molded by structural racism, the joy of having a family that holds together in a crisis, and the thrill of succeeding against difficult odds. Youngs charm and wit make these essays a pleasure to read; his candid approach makes them memorable." Publishers Weekly.

Young, Matt, 1986-

★Young, Matt, 1986- **Eat** the apple : a memoir / Matt Young. Bloomsbury USA, 2018 224 p. **B**

ISBN 9781632869500

1. United States. Marine Corps 2. Military life. 3. Iraq War, 2003-2011, American. 4. Marines. 5. Personal conduct 6. Autobiographies and memoirs

LC 2017011843

A combat veteran and writing instructor traces the darkly comic story of his youth and masculinity as they were shaped in an age of continuous war, describing how he joined the Marines as a way to temper his reckless nature before enduring three Iraq deployments.

"Youngs visceral prose, honed in college and writing programs after his tours of duty, confronts shame, guilt, and pain without flinching yet is beyond sympathetic to its subject; it is another act of service." Booklist.

Young, R. J. (Writer)

Young, R. J. (Writer) **Let** it bang : a young black man's reluctant odyssey into guns / R. J. Young. Houghton Mifflin Harcourt 2018 224 p. **B**

ISBN 9781328826336

1. Gun ownership 2. Racism 3. Race relations 4. Guns 5. Autobiographies and memoirs

LC 2018012248

A story of race, guns, and self-protection in America today is delivered through the quest of a young black man learning to shoot a handgun better than a white person.

Young, Steve, 1961-

Young, Steve, 1961- QB : my life behind the spiral / Steve Young with Jeff Benedict. Houghton Mifflin Harcourt, 2016 416 p. **B**

ISBN 9780544845763

1. Football players. 2. Quarterbacks (Football). 3. Football 4. Mormons 5. Autobiographies and memoirs

LC 2016024863

Includes index.

A memoir by the NFL Hall of Famer shares insights into what it takes to become an elite professional quarterback, describing his unlikely rise in sports as a devout Mormon and high-achieving student with an eidetic memory, the media pressure, his infamous confrontation with Joe Montana and the other factors that challenged his career.

Yousafzai, Malala, 1997-

★Yousafzai, Malala, 1997- **I** am Malala : the story of the girl who stood up for education and was shot by the Taliban / Malala Yousafzai with Christina Lamb. Little, Brown, & Co., 2013. viii, 327 p., 16 unnumbered p. of plates **B**

ISBN 9780316322409

1. Taliban 2. Girls -- Education 3. Children's rights 4. Victims of crimes 5. Women's rights 6. Pakistan 7. Autobiographies and memoirs

Describes the life of a young Pakistani student who advocated for women's rights and education in the Taliban-controlled Swat Valley who survived an assassination attempt and became the youngest nominee for the Nobel Peace Prize.

Yousafzai, Ziauddin

Yousafzai, Ziauddin **Let** her fly : a father's journey / Ziauddin Yousafzai with Louise Carpenter ; foreword by Malala Yousafzai. Little, Brown and Company, 2018. 144 p. **B**

ISBN 9780316450508

1. Yousafzai, Ziauddin. 2. Yousafzai, Malala, 1997- Family. 3. Taliban. 4. Political activists -- Pakistan 5. Educators -- Pakistan 6. Girls -- Education -- Pakistan. 7. Fathers and daughters. 8. Autobiographies and memoirs.

LC bl2018183646

The father of Malala Yousafzai traces his journey from an unconfident, stammering little boy living in a mud hut in Pakistan to a man who has broken with tradition and proven there are many faces of feminism.

"Yousafzai isn't just a Pakistani diplomat, educator, educational activist, and human rights campaigner; he's also the father of Nobel laureate Malala Yousafzai. Here he explains what he has learned from his daughter." Library Journal.

Zamperini, Louis, 1917-

Hillenbrand, Laura **Unbroken** : a World War II story of survival, resilience, and redemption / Laura Hillenbrand. Random House, 2010. xviii, 473 p. : **B**

ISBN 9781400064168

1. United States. Army Air Forces. 307th Heavy Bombardment Group. 2. World War II -- Prisoners and prisons, Japanese. 3. Prisoners of war, American 4. Post-traumatic stress disorder 5. Distance runners -- United States 6. Pacific Area. 7. California 8. Japan -- History, Military -- 20th century 9. Biographies

LC 2010017517

ALA Notable Book, 2012.

Relates the story of a U.S. airman who survived when his bomber crashed into the sea during World War II, spent forty-seven days adrift in the ocean before being rescued by the Japanese Navy, and was held as a prisoner until the end of the war.

"Hillenbrand's triumph is that in telling Louie's story . she tells the stories of thousands whose suffering has been mostly forgotten. She restores to our collective memory this tale of heroism, cruelty, life, death, joy, suffering, remorselessness, and redemption." Publishers Weekly.

Zapata, Emiliano, 1879-1919

Womack, John, Jr., 1937- **Zapata** and the Mexican Revolution / John Womack, Jr. Knopf, 1969, c1968 xi, 435, xxi p. **B**

ISBN 9780394708539

1. Zapata, Emiliano, 1879-1919. 2. Revolutionaries -- Mexico 3. Mexico -- History -- 1910-1946.

LC 68023947

A biography of the Mexican patriot who organized and led his rural community in resistance to the central government.

Zapruder, Abraham

Zapruder, Alexandra **Twenty-six** seconds : a personal history of the Zapruder film / Alexandra Zapruder. Twelve, [2016] 272 p. **B**

ISBN 9781455574810

1. Kennedy, John F. (John Fitzgerald), 1917-1963 Assassination. 2.

Kennedy, John F. (John Fitzgerald), 1917-1963 In films 3. Zapruder, Abraham. 4. Ethical problems 5. Public interest 6. Memory -- Political aspects 7. Films and history 8. Biographies

LC 2016025786

The lesser-known family story behind Abraham Zapruder's film footage of the Kennedy assassination and its lasting impact, told by Zapruder's granddaughter, draws on personal records and previously sealed archives to trace the film's role in the media, courts, government and arts community.

"This well-written exploration of conspiracy, propriety, copyright, and public good versus private gain is seen through the prism of the worlds most famous home movie." Publishers Weekly.

Zaske, Sara

Zaske, Sara **Achtung** baby : an American mom on the German art of raising self-reliant children / Sara Zaske. Picador, 2018 ix, 239 p. ; **B**

ISBN 9781250160171

1. Zaske, Sara. 2. Parenting. 3. Self-reliance in children. 4. Parent and child. 5. Moving to a new country 6. Germany 7. Autobiographies and memoirs

LC 2017032099

When Sara Zaske moved from Oregon to Berlin with her husband and toddler, she knew the transition would be challenging, especially when she became pregnant with her second child. She was surprised to discover that German parents give their children a great deal of freedom?much more than Americans. In Berlin, kids walk to school by themselves, ride the subway alone, cut food with sharp knives, and even play with fire. German parents did not share her fears, and their children were thriving. Was she doing the opposite of what she intended, which was toraise capable children? Why was parenting culture so different in the States?

"An entertaining, informative, and enlightening narrative on the German methods of parenting that will have many in the U.S. reconsidering how they're raising their children." Kirkus.

Zeamer, Jay, Jr., 1918-2007

Drury, Bob **Lucky** 666 : the impossible mission / Bob Drury and Tom Clavin. Simon & Schuster, 2016 352 p. **B**

ISBN 9781476774855

1. Zeamer, Jay, Jr., 1918-2007. 2. United States. Army Air Forces. Bombardment Group, 22nd. 3. Bomber pilots. 4. B-17 bomber. 5. World War II -- Aerial operations, American. 6. Biographies

LC 2016017924

The authors of the #1 New York Times best-selling The Heart of Everything That Is traces the lesser-known story of a daredevil bomber pilot and his misfit crew who in 1943 engaged the Japanese in what became history's longest dogfight, changing the course of the war through their heroic acts of sacrifice.

"Drury and Clavin offer a vivid slice of war history that WWII buffs and anyone who admires true acts of heroism will find riveting." Booklist.

Zemurray, Samuel, 1877-1961

Cohen, Rich The **fish** that ate the whale : the life and times of America's banana king / Rich Cohen. Farrar, Straus and Giroux, 2012. 320 p. **B**

ISBN 9780374299279

1. Zemurray, Samuel, 1877-1961. 2. United Fruit Company 3. Businesspeople 4. Jewish Americans 5. Banana industry and trade 6. Corporations, American -- Corrupt practices 7. New Orleans, Louisiana 8. Biographies

LC 2011041207

Traces the rise of Samuel Zemurray from a penniless youth to one of the world's wealthiest and most powerful men, offering insight into his capitalist talents and the ways in which his life reflected the best and worst of American business dealings.

Zenger, John Peter, 1697-1746

★Kluger, Richard **Indelible** ink : the trials of John Peter Zenger and the birth of America's free press / Richard Kluger. W.W. Norton & Company, c2016. xxi, 346 p. **B**

ISBN 9780393245462

1. Journalism -- United States -- 18th century 2. Freedom of the press -- United States 3. Trials (Libel) 4. Freedom of speech 5. New York City -- History -- Colonial period, 1600-1775 6. Great Britain -- Colonies North America -- History -- 18th century 7. Biographies

LC 2016011040

The story of the battle to legalize free expression in America describes the strict censorship throughout colonization and the efforts of New York printer John Peter Zenger to avoid imprisonment for criticizing a corrupt politician.

"Event by compelling event, readers follow Zenger through the drama that eventually landed him in jail on libel chargesbefore a liberty-loving jury freed him with a 1735 verdict signaling a clear American commitment to the unfettered reporting that can check abuse of power." Booklist.

Zhukov, Georgii Konstantinovich, 1896-1974

Roberts, Geoffrey, 1952- **Stalin's** general : the life of Georgy Zhukov / Geoffrey Roberts. Random House, c2012. 448 p. **B**

ISBN 9781400066926

1. Zhukov, Georgii Konstantinovich, 1896-1974. 2. Command of troops. 3. Military strategy. 4. Exiles. 5. World War II -- Soviet Union. 6. Soviet Union -- History -- 1925-1953. 7. Biographies

LC 2011040663

A profile of the Soviet general credited with a decisive role in key World War II victories compares his legend with his achievements while surveying his eventful post-war experiences as Krushchev's disgraced defense minister.

Ziegfeld, Florenz, 1869-1932

Mordden, Ethan, 1947- **Ziegfeld** : the man who invented show business / Ethan Mordden. St. Martin's Press, 2008. 352 p. **B**

ISBN 9780312375430

1. Ziegfeld, Florenz, 1869-1932. 2. Ziegfeld Follies (Musical show) 3. Theatrical producers and directors -- United States 4. Performing arts -- History 5. Men/women relations 6. Impresarios -- United States 7. United States -- Social life and customs -- 19th century 8. United States -- Social life and customs -- 20th century 9. Biographies

LC 2008028746

An account of the life and legacy of the creator of the Follies covers such topics as his vision of the Ziegfeld Girl, development of landmark productions including Showboat, and role in the careers of numerous stars, from Marilyn Miller and Will Rogers to Eddie Cantor and Fanny Brice.

"In his witty, well-researched biography of the great producer Florenz Ziegfeld, Mordden discusses Ziegfeld's extraordinary eye for talent and transforming approach to staging musicals." Booklist.

Zimmerman, Eilene

Zimmerman, Eilene **Smacked** : a story of white-collar ambition, addiction, and tragedy / Eilene Zimmerman. Random House, [2020] 288 p. **B**

ISBN 9780525511007

1. Zimmerman, Eilene. 2. Zimmerman, Peter, -2015. 3. Lawyers 4. Drug addicts 5. Drug addiction 6. White collar workers 7. United States 8. Autobiographies and memoirs

LC 2019029770

Drawing on extensive research and interviews to paint a picture of drug dependence today in a moneyed, upwardly mobile world, a journalist pieces together the mysteries surrounding her ex-husband's unexpected death from drug abuse.

"Zimmerman's wrenching story and her extensive research into the hidden crisis of white-collar drug addiction will resonate with many readers." Publishers Weekly

Zimmerman, Paul

Zimmerman, Paul **Dr.** Z : the lost memoirs of an irreverent football writer / Paul Zimmerman ; edited by Peter King. Triumph Books, 2017. 280 p. **B**

ISBN 9781629374642

1. Zimmerman, Paul. 2. Sportswriters -- United States 3. Football -- United States. 4. Athletes 5. Sports 6. United States -- Social life and customs -- 20th century 7. Autobiographies and memoirs

LC 2017009840

Dr. Z's memoir is a rich package of personalities, stories never shared about such characters as Vince Lombardi, Walter Payton, Lawrence Taylor, and Johnny Unitas. Even Joe Namath, with whom Zimmerman had a legendary and well-documented 23-year feud, saw fit to eventually unburden himself to the remarkable scribe.

Zinn, Howard, 1922-2010

Duberman, Martin B. **Howard** Zinn : a life on the left / Martin Duberman. New Press : 2012. 352 p. **B**

ISBN 9781595586780

1. Zinn, Howard, 1922-2010. 2. Zinn, Howard, 1922-2010 Political and social views. 3. Historians -- United States 4. Political activists 5. Authors 6. Radicals 7. Biographies

LC 2012017592

A portrait of the life and achievements of the progressive activist, author, and teacher examines his roles as an anti-war veteran, an iconic contributor to the civil rights movement, and dedicated white professor at a historically black college.

Zweibel, Alan

Zweibel, Alan **Laugh** lines : my life helping funny people be funnier : a cultural memoir / Alan Zweibel ; foreword by Billy Crystal. Abrams Press, 2020. 336 p. **B**

ISBN 9781419735288

1. Comedians 2. Television writers 3. Humorous writing 4. Television comedies 5. Autobiographies and memoirs

LC bl2020046065

Alan Zweibel started his comedy career selling jokes for seven dollars apiece to the last of the Borscht Belt standups. Then one night, despite bombing on stage, he caught the attention of Lorne Michaels and became one of the first writers at Saturday Night Live, where he penned classic material for Gilda Radner, John Belushi, and all of the original Not Ready For Prime Time Players. From SNL, he went on to have a hand in a series of landmark shows--from It's Garry Shandling's Show to Curb Your Enthusiasm. Throughout the pages of Laugh Lines Zweibel weaves together his own stories and interviews with his friends and contemporaries, including Richard Lewis, Eric Idle, Bob Saget, Mike Birbiglia, Sarah Silverman, Judd Apatow, Dave Barry, Carl Reiner, and more.

"Comics and comedy fans alike will delight in this hilarious and self-deprecating memoir." Publishers Weekly

Zweig, Stefan, 1881-1942

Prochnik, George The **impossible** exile : Stefan Zweig at the end of the world / George Prochnik. Other Press, 2014 408 p. **B**

ISBN 9781590516126

1. Zweig, Stefan, 1881-1942. 2. Authors, Austrian -- 20th century 3. Authors, Jewish -- 20th century 4. Suicide. 5. Exiles. 6. Germany -- Politics and government -- 1933-1945. 7. Biographies

LC 2013025383

National Jewish Book Award, 2014."

Intelligent, reflective and deeply sad portrait of a man tragically cut adrift by history." Kirkus.

AUTHOR, TITLE, AND SUBJECT INDEX

This index to the books in the Classified Collection includes title and subject entries and added entries for illustrators, joint authors, and editors of works entered under title, all arranged in one alphabet.

The number or symbol in bold face type at the end of each entry refers to the Dewey Decimal Classification where the main entry for the book will be found. Works classed in B (Biography) will be found under the headings for the biographies' subject.

Hughes, L. Selected poems of Langston Hughes **811**
Jazz poems **808.81**
Johnson, J. Complete poems **811**
Jones, S. Prelude to bruise **811**
Komunyakaa, Y. Talking dirty to the gods **811**
Komunyakaa, Y. Warhorses **811**
Lewis, R. Voyage of the Sable Venus and other poems **811**
Mackey, N. Splay anthem **811**
Matthews, A. Simulacra **811**
May, J. Hum **811**
Pardlo, G. Digest **811**
Parker, M. There are more beautiful things than Beyonce **811**
Phillips, R. Heaven **811**
Reed, J. Indecency **811**
Shockley, E. Semiautomatic **811**
Smith, P. Incendiary art **811.54**
Smith, P. Shoulda been Jimi Savannah **811**
Smith, T. The body's question **811**
Smith, T. Duende **811**
Smith, T. Life on Mars **811**
Walker, A. Hard times require furious dancing **811**
Wheatley, P. The poems of Phillis Wheatley **811**
Wicker, M. Silencer **811**
Wilson, R. Farther traveler **818**

African American poetry **811.008**

AFRICAN AMERICAN POETS
African American poetry **811.008**
Hughes, L. I wonder as I wander **B**
Jackson, A. A surprised queenhood in the new black sun **B**
Rampersad, A. The life of Langston Hughes volume I, 1902-1941 I, too, sing America **B**
Rampersad, A. The life of Langston Hughes volume II, 1941-1967 I dream a world **B**
Scott-Heron, G. The last holiday **B**

AFRICAN AMERICAN POETS -- 20TH CENTURY
Clifton, L. Mercy **811**

AFRICAN AMERICAN POLICE
Forman, J. Locking up our own **364.973**
Stallworth, R. Black Klansman **B**

AFRICAN AMERICAN POLITICAL ACTIVISTS
Cleaver, E. Target zero **B**
Khan-Cullors, P. When they call you a terrorist **B**
Sharpton, A. Rise up **973.933**

AFRICAN AMERICAN POLITICIANS
Cummings, E. We're better than this **B**
Dray, P. Capitol men **973.8**
Meacham, J. His truth is marching on **B**
Obama, B. A promised land **B**
Remnick, D. The bridge **B**
Sharpton, A. Rise up **973.933**

AFRICAN AMERICAN PRESS
Michaeli, E. The Defender **071**

AFRICAN AMERICAN PRISONERS
Alexander, M. The new Jim Crow **364.973**
Bailey, I. My brother Moochie **B**

AFRICAN AMERICAN PRISONERS -- LOUISIANA
Rideau, W. In the place of justice **B**

AFRICAN AMERICAN QUILTMAKERS -- ALABAMA -- WILCOX COUNTY -- EXHIBITIONS
Gee's Bend **704**

AFRICAN AMERICAN QUILTS -- ALABAMA -- WILCOX COUNTY -- EXHIBITIONS
Gee's Bend **704**

AFRICAN AMERICAN QUILTS -- SOCIAL ASPECTS -- HISTORY -- 19TH CENTURY
Tobin, J. Hidden in plain view **973.7**

AFRICAN AMERICAN RADICALS
Greenidge, K. Black radical **B**

AFRICAN AMERICAN RAP MUSICIANS
Grandmaster Flash The adventures of Grandmaster Flash **B**

AFRICAN AMERICAN SCHOLARS
Gates, H. Colored people **B**

AFRICAN AMERICAN SINGERS
Bogle, D. Heat wave **B**
Cohodas, N. Princess Noire **B**
Gaye, J. After the dance **B**
Holiday, B. Lady sings the blues **B**
Keiler, A. Marian Anderson **B**
Scott-Heron, G. The last holiday **B**

AFRICAN AMERICAN SINGERS -- UNITED STATES
Belafonte, H. My song **B**

AFRICAN AMERICAN SINGLE MOTHERS
Austin, N. Motherhood so white **B**

AFRICAN AMERICAN SISTERS
Delany, S. Having our say **B**

AFRICAN AMERICAN SOCIAL ADVOCATES
Mckesson, D. On the other side of freedom **323.092**

AFRICAN AMERICAN SOLDIERS
Buckley, G. American patriots **355**
Egerton, D. Thunder at the gates **973.7**
Hervieux, L. Forgotten **940.54**
Kaplan, A. The interpreter **940.54**
Powell, C. My American journey **B**
Taylor, A. The internal enemy **975.5**

AFRICAN AMERICAN SOLDIERS -- HISTORY -- 19TH CENTURY
Ash, S. Firebrand of liberty **973.7**
Tuccille, J. The roughest riders **973.8**

AFRICAN AMERICAN SOLDIERS -- HISTORY -- 20TH CENTURY
Slotkin, R. Lost battalions **940.4**

AFRICAN AMERICAN SOLDIERS -- HISTORY -- PICTORIAL WORKS
Fighting for freedom **355.0089**

AFRICAN AMERICAN SOLDIERS -- HISTORY
Buckley, G. American patriots **355**
Tuccille, J. The roughest riders **973.8**

AFRICAN AMERICAN SOLDIERS -- PORTRAITS
Fighting for freedom **355.0089**

AFRICAN AMERICAN SOUND RECORDING EXECUTIVES AND PRODUCERS

AUTHOR, TITLE, AND SUBJECT INDEX
EIGHTEENTH EDITION

Andrews, J. Home **B**
Andrews, J. Home work **B**
Angel, K. Unmastered **B**
Angelou, M. I know why the caged bird sings **B**
Angelou, M. Mom & me & mom **B**
Angelou, M. A song flung up to heaven **B**
Ankiel, R. The phenomenon **B**
Annan, K. Interventions **B**
Ansary, M. West of Kabul, east of New York **B**
Anselmo, L. My (part-time) Paris life **B**
Antunes, A. The fat man and infinity **B**
Apatow, J. Sick in the head **B**
Arana, M. American chica **B**
Araton, H. Our last season **B**
Arena, B. What's wrong with US? **B**
Arkin, A. An improvised life **B**
Armstrong, K. The spiral staircase **B**
Aron, N. Good morning, destroyer of men's souls **B**
Arsenault, K. Mill town **B**
Atlas, J. The shadow in the garden **B**
Atleework, K. Miracle country **B**
Attenborough, D. Adventures of a young naturalist **B**
Augustine, S. Confessions **B**
Aung San Suu Kyi Freedom from fear **B**
Auster, P. Report from the interior **B**
Austin, N. Motherhood so white **B**
Austin, P. Beautiful eyes **B**
Auvinen, K. Rough beauty **B**
Avery, S. Ice capades **B**
Axelrod, D. Believer **B**
Axelrod, H. The point of vanishing **B**
B., D. Epileptic **B**
Bacall, L. By myself and then some **B**
Badkhen, A. Walking with Abel **B**
Bailey, B. The splendid things we planned **B**
Bailey, E. The sound of a wild snail eating **B**
Bailey, I. My brother Moochie **B**
Bailey, L. Because we are bad **B**
Bair, D. Parisian lives **B**
Baker, N. Substitute **B**
Baldwin, A. Nevertheless **B**
Ball, E. Life of a Klansman **B**
Ball, L. Love, Lucy **B**
Ballard, J. Miracles of life **B**
Banville, J. Time pieces **B**
Barbarisi, D. Dueling with kings **B**
Bard, E. Lunch in Paris **B**
Barkan, A. Eyes to the wind **B**
Barlow, J. Mother American night **B**
Barnes, J. Levels of life **B**
Barnes, J. Nothing to be frightened of **B**
Barnett, E. Quitter **B**
Barnett, K. The spark **B**
Barr, N. Seeking enlightenment-- hat by hat **B**
Bartolo, P. Tears of salt **B**
Basie, C. Good morning blues **B**
Bass, R. The traveling feast **B**
Bass, R. Why I came West **B**
Bastianich, L. My American dream **B**
Baszile, J. The Black girl next door **B**
Bauermeister, E. House lessons **B**
Bauman, J. Stronger **B**
Bayley, J. Elegy for Iris **B**
Baylor, E. Hang time **B**
Beah, I. A long way gone **B**
Beard, A. In the water they can't see you cry **B**
Beasley, S. Don't kill the birthday girl **B**
Beavan, C. No impact man **B**
Bechdel, A. Fun home **B**
Belafonte, H. My song **B**
Belcourt, B. A history of my brief body **B**
Bell, L. Claiming ground **B**
Benincasa, S. Real artists have day jobs **B**
Benjamin, A. Let me not be mad **B**
Benmosche, B. Good for the money **B**
Bennett, A. Keeping on keeping on **B**
Bennetts, L. Last girl before freeway **B**
Berg, E. I'll be seeing you **B**
Berg, R. No house to call my home **B**
Bergen, C. A fine romance **B**
Berlin, L. Welcome home **B**
Bernard, E. Black is the body **B**
Bernstein, J. Famous father girl **B**
Betz-Hamilton, A. The less people know about us **B**
Bialosky, J. Poetry will save your life **B**
Bianchi, A. Becoming an ally to the gender expansive child **B**
Biden, J. Promise me, Dad **B**
Biden, J. Where the light enters **B**
Bilal, W. Shoot an Iraqi **B**
Bizot, F. The gate **B**
Black Elk, Black Elk speaks **B**
Black, D. Mama's boy **B**
Black, M. A better man **B**
Blair, T. A journey **B**
Blanco, R. The prince of Los Cocuyos **B**
Boeheim, J. Bleeding orange **B**
Boggs, B. The art of waiting **B**
Bolz-Weber, N. Accidental saints **B**
Bonner, B. The book of Atlantis Black **B**
Bontinck, D. Rescued from ISIS **B**
Bosker, B. Cork dork **B**
Boston, S. Lucky dog **B**
Bourdain, A. Kitchen confidential **B**
Bourdain, A. Medium raw **B**
Bouton, K. Shouting won't help **B**
Bowdler, M. Is rape a crime? **B**
Bowie on Bowie **B**
Bown, M. The world's most travelled man **B**
Boyd, G. My Times in black and white **B**
Boylan, J. Good boy **B**
Boylan, J. I'm looking through you **B**
Brackett, C. It's the pictures that got small **B**
Brady, J. The coldest war **B**

AUTHOR, TITLE, AND SUBJECT INDEX
EIGHTEENTH EDITION

Villani, C. Birth of a theorem B
Viloria, H. Born both B
Vincent, L. Cut me loose B
Volpe, J. The toughest show on Earth B
Von Bremzen, A. Mastering the art of Soviet cooking B
Von Furstenberg, D. The woman I wanted to be B
Vonnegut, K. A man without a country B
Wade, B. Run the world B
Wagner, A. Futureface B
Walder, T. The unexpected spy B
Waldman, A. A really good day B
Walker, A. The same river twice B
Wall, D. The ordinary acrobat a journey into the wondrous world of the circus, past and present B
Walls, J. The glass castle B
Walsh, M. Gypsy boy B
Walters, B. Audition B
Walton, B. Back from the dead B
Wambach, A. Forward B
Ward, C. On all fronts B
Ward, J. Men we reaped B
Wariner, R. The sound of gravel B
Warren, C. What the dog knows B
Warren, E. A fighting chance B
Washington, B. Up from slavery B
Waters, A. Coming to my senses B
Waters, J. Mr. know-it-all B
Watt, L. Gizelle's bucket list B
Watts, S. Fight like a mother B
Webb, J. The cake and the rain B
Weiner, J. Hungry heart B
Weisman, E. The way it was B
Weiss, P. You all grow up and leave me B
Weller, G. Weller's war B
Welteroth, E. More than enough B
Welty, E. One writer's beginnings B
Wertheim, L. Blood in the cage B
Weschler, L. And how are you, Dr. Sacks? B
West, J. West by West B
Westaby, S. Open heart B
Westheimer, R. The doctor is in B
Westover, T. Educated B
Wetherall, T. No way home B
White, B. Uppity B
White, E. City boy B
White, E. The unpunished vice B
White, M. Travels in Vermeer B
Whittington, H. Raising Ryland 362.7
Wickersham, J. The suicide index B
Wideman, J. Hoop roots B
Wiener, A. Uncanny valley B
Wiesel, E. All rivers run to the sea B
Wiesel, E. And the sea is never full B
Wiesel, E. Night B
Wiesenthal, S. The sunflower B
Wilder, L. Pioneer girl B
Wilderson, F. Afropessimism B
Willan, A. One souffle at a time B
Williams, C. My plastic brain B
Williams, M. The lost daughter B
Williams, P. Rabbit B
Williams, R. Black and white B
Williams, T. Self-portrait in black and white B
Willner, N. Forty autumns B
Wilson, B. I am Brian Wilson B
Wilson, C. The Master Plan B
Wilson, K. Only in Naples B
Windhorst, B. Return of the king B
Windsor, E. A wild and precious life B
Winfrey, O. The wisdom of Sundays B
Winterson, J. Why be happy when you could be normal? B
Winton, T. Island home B
Witherspoon, R. Whiskey in a teacup B
Wizenberg, M. Delancey B
Wizenberg, M. Fixed stars B
Wolff, T. This boy's life B
Wong, A. Dear girls B
Wood, D. Working for the man, playing in the band B
Woodfox, A. Solitary B
Woods, T. The 1997 Masters B
Woolf, V. Moments of being B
Worley, J. Neon girls B
Wouk, H. Sailor and fiddler B
Wright, L. God save Texas B
Wright, R. Black boy B
Wright, i. Darling days B
Wyeth, A. Andrew Wyeth B
X, Malcolm The autobiography of Malcolm X B
Yang, K. The song poet B
Yip-Williams, J. The unwinding of the miracle B
Young, D. What doesn't kill you makes you blacker B
Young, M. Eat the apple B
Young, R. Let it bang B
Young, S. QB B
Yousafzai, M. I am Malala B
Zaske, S. Achtung baby B
Zimmerman, E. Smacked B
Zimmerman, P. Dr. Z B
Zweibel, A. Laugh lines B

AUTOBIOGRAPHIES AND MEMOIRS

Addario, L. Of love & war B
Barnett, B. A knock at midnight B
Billings, J. Rejoicing in lament B
Block, F. The thorn necklace B
Bolick, K. Spinster B
Brennan-Jobs, L. Small fry B
Brodak, M. Bandit B
Brown, R. You can't go wrong doing right B
Bryant, K. The Mamba mentality B
Burton, S. Empty B
Connors, P. A song for the river B
Diamant, A. Pitching my tent B
Downie, D. A passion for Paris B
Frank, B. Frank B

B

Gardiner, J. Bach **B**
Gardiner, J. Bach **B**
Geck, M. Johann Sebastian Bach **B**
Kennicott, P. Counterpoint **B**
Wolff, C. Johann Sebastian Bach **B**
Wolff, C. Johann Sebastian Bach **B**
BACH, JOHANN SEBASTIAN, 1685-1750 CRITICISM AND INTERPRETATION
Geck, M. Johann Sebastian Bach **B**
BACH, JOHANN SEBASTIAN, 1685-1750. SUITES
Siblin, E. The cello suites **787.4**
BACH, MARIA, 1896-1978
Porter, C. Five lives in music **920**
BACHELOR (TELEVISION PROGRAM)
Kaufman, A. Bachelor nation **791.45**
Bachelor nation Kaufman, A. **791.45**
BACK -- DISEASES -- TREATMENT
Deyo, R. Watch your back! **617.5**
The **back** chamber Hall, D. **811**
The **back** channel Burns, W. **B**
Back from the dead Walton, B. **B**
BACK IN THE DAY BAKERY (SAVANNAH, GA.)
Day, C. Back in the Day Bakery, made with love **641.81**
Back in the Day Bakery, made with love Day, C. **641.81**
The **back** in the swing cookbook Unell, B. **641.5**
Back pocket pasta Henry, C. **641.82**
The **back** roads to March Feinstein, J. **796.323**
Back to normal Gnaulati, E. **618.92**
Back to school Rose, M. **374**
BACK TO THE FUTURE FILMS HISTORY AND CRITICISM
Gaines, C. We don't need roads **791.43**
BACKACHE -- TREATMENT
Deyo, R. Watch your back! **617.5**
Backing into forward Feiffer, J. **B**
BACKMAN, FREDRIK, 1981-
Backman, F. Things my son needs to know about the world **B**
Backman, F. Things my son needs to know about the world **B**
The **backpacker's** handbook Townsend, C. **796.51**
BACKPACKING
Baggett, J. The lost girls **910.4**
Fletcher, C. The man who walked through time **917.91**
Harvey, M. The National Outdoor Leadership School's wilderness guide **796.51**
Townsend, C. The backpacker's handbook **796.51**
BACKPACKS
Sandqvist, A. Heavy-duty sewing **646.2**
Backstage pass Stanley, P. **B**
The **backyard** astronomer's guide Dickinson, T. **522**
The **backyard** beekeeper Flottum, K. **638**
Backyard building Stiles, J. **690**
Backyard guide to the night sky Schneider, H. **523.8**
The **backyard** homestead **641**
BACKYARDS
Tougias, R. Birder on Berry Lane **598**
BACON, FRANCIS, 1909-1992 FRIENDS AND ASSOCIATES
Smee, S. The art of rivalry **B**
BACTERIA
Ben-Barak, I. The invisible kingdom **579**
Collen, A. 10% human **612.3**
Rosen, W. Miracle cure **615.7**
Tetro, J. The germ files **571.2**
BACTERIA -- HEALTH ASPECTS
Finlay, B. Let them eat dirt **616.9**
BACTERIA
Bad advice Offit, P. **362.1**
Bad blood Carreyrou, J. **338.7**
The **bad** food bible Carroll, A. **613.2**
Bad Indians Miranda, D. **305.8009794**
Bad land Raban, J. **978**
Bad news Sundaram, A. **B**
Bad paper Halpern, J. **332.70973**
Bad pharma Goldacre, B. **615.1**
Bad science Goldacre, B. **500**
The **bad-ass** librarians of Timbuktu Hammer, J. **025.8**
BADKHEN, ANNA, 1976-
Badkhen, A. Walking with Abel **B**
BAEK, HONGYONG, 1912- FAMILY
Lee, H. In the absence of sun **B**
BAER, MAX, 1909-1959
Schaap, J. Cinderella Man **B**
Bagehot Grant, J. **B**
BAGEHOT, WALTER, 1826-1877
Grant, J. Bagehot **B**
BAGGETT, JENNIFER TRAVEL
Baggett, J. The lost girls **910.4**
Baghdad at sunrise Mansoor, P. **B**
BAGHDAD, IRAQ -- HISTORY
Kennedy, H. When Baghdad ruled the Muslim world **953**
BAGHDAD, IRAQ -- POLITICS AND GOVERNMENT
Newton, M. Enemy of the state **345.567**
BAGHDAD, IRAQ -- SOCIAL LIFE AND CUSTOMS
Ciezadlo, A. Day of honey **B**
BAGS
Sandqvist, A. Heavy-duty sewing **646.2**
Bags Alicia, A. **646.4**
Bags and totes Johnson, L. **646.4**
BAILEY FAMILY
Bailey, B. The splendid things we planned **B**
BAILEY, BLAKE, 1963-
Bailey, B. The splendid things we planned **B**
BAILEY, BLAKE, 1963- CHILDHOOD AND YOUTH
Bailey, B. The splendid things we planned **B**
BAILEY, BLAKE, 1963- FAMILY
Bailey, B. The splendid things we planned **B**
BAILEY, ELISABETH
Bailey, E. The sound of a wild snail eating **B**
BAILEY, ISSAC J
Bailey, I. My brother Moochie **B**
BAILEY, ISSAC J. FAMILY

Billion-dollar ball Gaul, G. 796.332
Billionaire at the barricades Ingraham, L. 324.973
The **billionaire's** vinegar Wallace, B. 641.2
Billions and billions Sagan, C. 500
Billy Martin Pennington, B. B
Billy the Kid Wallis, M. B
BILLY, THE KID
Gardner, M. To hell on a fast horse B
Wallis, M. Billy the Kid B
BILLY, THE KID PICTORIAL WORKS
Wallis, M. Billy the Kid B
BILOTT, ROBERT, 1965-
Bilott, R. Exposure 344.04
BILTMORE ESTATE (ASHEVILLE, N.C.)
Kiernan, D. The last castle 975.6
BIN LADEN FAMILY
Coll, S. The Bin Ladens 920
BIN LADEN, OSAMA, 1957-2011
Bergen, P. Manhunt 363.325
Coll, S. Ghost wars 958.104
Coll, S. The Bin Ladens 920
Levy, A. The exile B
O'Neill, R. The operator B
Owen, M. No easy day B
Scheuer, M. Osama bin Laden B
Soufan, A. Anatomy of terror 363.325
The **Bin** Ladens Coll, S. 920
Bing Crosby (Gary Giddins) ; [series] Giddins, G.
BINGHAM, HIRAM, 1875-1956
Adams, M. Turn right at Machu Picchu 985
Heaney, C. Cradle of gold B
BINGHAM, HIRAM, 1875-1956 TRAVEL PERU
Bingham, H. Lost city of the Incas 985
BINGHAM, MILLICENT TODD, 1880-1968
Dobrow, J. After Emily B
BINION, TED, DIED 1998
McManus, J. Positively Fifth Street 795.41
BIODEGRADATION
Doughty, C. Will my cat eat my eyeballs? 306.9
BIODIVERSITY
Bondar, C. Wild sex 591.56
Fraser, C. Rewilding the world 333.95
Sustaining life 333.95
Thomas, C. Inheritors of the Earth 575
Wagner, A. Arrival of the fittest 572.8
Wilson, E. A window on eternity 333.95
Wilson, E. The diversity of life 333.95
Wohlleben, P. The secret wisdom of nature 508
BIODIVERSITY CONSERVATION
Dinerstein, E. The kingdom of rarities 596
Wilson, E. Half-earth 333.95
Biodynamic gardening Waldin, M. 635
BIOETHICS
Anthes, E. Frankenstein's cat 616.02
BIOFEEDBACK
Carroll, S. The Serengeti rules 570
BIOGEOGRAPHY
De Queiroz, A. The monkey's voyage 570
BIOGRAPHERS
Atlas, J. The shadow in the garden B
Caro, R. Working B
Holmes, R. This long pursuit B
White, E. The unpunished vice B
BIOGRAPHERS -- GREAT BRITAIN
Martin, P. A life of James Boswell B
BIOGRAPHERS -- ITALY
Rowland, I. The collector of lives B
BIOGRAPHERS -- UNITED STATES
Bailey, B. The splendid things we planned B
BIOGRAPHICAL COMICS
Delisle, G. Hostage B
Derf My friend Dahmer 741.5
Dorian, P. Lon Chaney speaks B
Guibert, E. Alan's war B
Kleist, R. Johnny Cash B
Kupperman, M. All the answers B
Ottaviani, J. Feynman B
Rall, T. Bernie B
Santiago, W. "21" B
Spiegelman, A. Co-mix B
Spiegelman, A. In the shadow of no towers 741.5
Voloj, J. Ghetto brother 741.5
BIOGRAPHIES
AOC B
Abbott, K. American rose B
Ackmann, M. These fevered days B
Ackroyd, P. Charlie Chaplin B
Ackroyd, P. Chaucer B
Ackroyd, P. Poe B
Adler, W. The man who never died B
Ahamed, L. Lords of finance 920
Albers, P. Joan Mitchell B
Alden, G. Elvis and Ginger B
Aldous, R. Schlesinger B
Alexander, L. Biggest brother B
Alford, T. Fortune's fool B
Alinder, M. Ansel Adams B
Allgor, C. A perfect union B
Alter, J. His very best B
Alter, J. The promise B
Ambrose, S. The victors B
Anand, A. Sophia B
Andelman, B. Will Eisner, a spirited life B
Andersen, C. The good son B
Andersen, J. Astrid Lindgren B
Andersen, J. Hans Christian Andersen B
Anderson, J. Che Guevara B
Andrews-Dyer, H. Reclaiming her time B
Angier, C. The double bond B
Anolik, L. Hollywood's Eve B
Anthony, C. Nellie Taft B
Appel, M. Casey Stengel B
Applegate, D. The most famous man in America B
Aptowicz, C. Dr. Mutter's marvels B

Guinn, J. Go down together B
Guinn, J. Manson B
Guinn, J. The Road to Jonestown B
Guinn, J. The vagabonds 920
Gupta, P. AOC B
Gura, P. The life of William Apess, Pequot B
Guralnick, P. Careless love B
Guralnick, P. Dream boogie B
Guralnick, P. Sam Phillips B
Gussow, M. Edward Albee B
Gutman, R. Mozart B
Guttenplan, D. American radical B
Guy, J. Elizabeth B
Guy, J. Thomas Becket B
Gwynne, S. Rebel yell B
Hadlow, J. A royal experiment B
Hagan, J. Sticky fingers B
Hagstrom, R. The Warren Buffett way B
Hague, W. William Wilberforce B
Hale, S. Titian B
Hales, D. Mona Lisa B
Hamblyn, R. The invention of clouds B
Hamilton, D. For the glory B
Hammarskjold, D. Markings B
Hammer, L. James Merrill B
Handwerker, L. Famous Nathan B
Haney, E. Inside Delta Force B
Haralson, E. Critical companion to Henry James B
Harden, B. Escape from Camp 14 B
Harden, B. King of spies B
Harden, B. The great leader and the fighter pilot B
Harding, S. Last to die B
Hardman, R. Queen of the world B
Hardwick, E. Herman Melville B
Hargrove, B. The man who caught the storm B
Harlan, E. George Sand B
Harlan, L. Booker T. Washington B
Harman, C. Charlotte Bronte B
Harman, C. Jane's fame B
Harrington, J. Dangerous mystic B
Harrington, J. The faithful executioner B
Harris, D. The genius B
Harris, E. George Frideric Handel B
Haskell, M. Steven Spielberg B
Hastings, S. The secret lives of Somerset Maugham B
Hauserman, J. Drawn to the deep B
Hawkes, D. John Milton B
Hayes, E. Queen of Bebop B
Haygood, W. Showdown B
Haygood, W. Sweet thunder B
Hazareesingh, S. Black spartacus B
Hazleton, L. Mary B
Hazleton, L. The first Muslim B
Heacox, K. John Muir and the ice that started a fire B
Heaney, C. Cradle of gold B
Hedrick, J. Harriet Beecher Stowe B
Heidler, D. Henry Clay B
Heilbron, J. Galileo B
Heller, A. Ayn Rand and the world she made B
Helm, S. A life in secrets B
Hemphill, P. Lovesick blues B
Hendershot, H. Open to debate B
Hendrix, S. Martin Luther B
Henig, R. The monk in the garden B
Hennessy, K. Dorothy Day B
Henry, D. Furious cool B
Herbert, B. Dreamer of Dune B
Herdrich, S. Sargent B
Herman, A. Douglas MacArthur B
Herrera, H. Frida B
Herrera, H. Listening to stone B
Herrmann, D. Helen Keller B
Hertog, S. Anne Morrow Lindbergh B
Hewitt, C. Renoir's dancer B
Hibbert, C. Edward VII B
Hibbert, C. Queen Victoria B
Hibbert, C. Wellington B
Hilburn, R. Johnny Cash B
Hilburn, R. Paul Simon B
Hillenbrand, L. Unbroken B
Hillerman, T. Seldom disappointed B
Hilsum, L. In extremis B
Hilton, L. Elizabeth B
Hiltzik, M. Big science B
Hiney, T. Raymond Chandler B
Hirsch, J. Willie Mays B
Hirshey, G. Not pretty enough B
Hirshfeld, A. Eureka man B
Hirshfeld, A. The electric life of Michael Faraday B
Hirshman, L. Sisters in law B
Hirst, M. Michelangelo. B
Historians on Hamilton 782.1
Hitchcock, W. The age of Eisenhower B
Hitchens, C. Thomas Jefferson B
Hoban, P. Alice Neel B
Hobbs, J. The short and tragic life of Robert Peace B
Hochschild, A. Rebel Cinderella B
Hoffman, A. My happiness bears no relation to happiness B
Hogan, L. The woman who watches over the world B
Hollis, M. Now all roads lead to France B
Holmes, R. African queen B
Holton, W. Abigail Adams B
Holzer, H. A just and generous nation B
Holzer, H. Lincoln and the power of the press B
Holzer, H. Monument man B
Honan, P. Christopher Marlowe B
Honey, M. To the promised land B
Hope, B. Blood and oil B
Horn, J. The man who would not be Washington B
Horn, J. Washington's end B
Horwitz, T. Midnight rising B
Hoskyns, B. Lowside of the road B
Hough, R. Captain James Cook B

C

CHILD SEXUAL ABUSE -- DRAMA
Shanley, J. Doubt **812**
CHILD SEXUAL ABUSE -- UNITED STATES
Bass, E. The courage to heal **616.85**
CHILD SEXUAL ABUSE BY CLERGY
Betrayal **261.8**
CHILD SEXUAL ABUSE INVESTIGATION
Rabinowitz, D. No crueler tyrannies **345.73**
CHILD SEXUAL ABUSERS
Barr, J. Start by believing **364.15**
Weiss, P. You all grow up and leave me **B**
CHILD SEXUAL ABUSERS -- HARTFORD, CONNECTICUT
Smith, M. Girls of tender age **B**
CHILD SLAVES
Morgan-Owens, J. Girl in black and white **B**
CHILD SOLDIERS
Aleksievich, S. Last witnesses **940.53**
CHILD SOLDIERS -- SIERRA LEONE
Beah, I. A long way gone **B**
CHILD WAR VICTIMS
Aleksievich, S. Last witnesses **940.53**
CHILD WELFARE
Beam, C. To the end of June **362.73**
CHILD WELFARE -- NEW YORK CITY
Bernstein, N. The lost children of Wilder **362.73**
CHILD WELFARE -- UNITED STATES
Clinton, H. It takes a village **305.23**
Madrick, J. Invisible Americans **362.7086**
CHILD WITNESSES
Rabinowitz, D. No crueler tyrannies **345.73**
Stargardt, N. Witnesses of war **940.53**
A **child's** Christmas in Wales Thomas, D. **B**
CHILD, JULIA
Barr, L. Provence, 1970 **641**
Child, J. Julia and Jacques cooking at home **641.594**
Child, J. My life in France **B**
Conant, J. The lotus eaters **940.54**
Prud'homme, A. France is a feast **778**
Prud'homme, A. The French chef in America **B**
Spitz, B. Dearie **B**
CHILD, JULIA CORRESPONDENCE
As always, Julia **641.5092**
CHILD, JULIA. MASTERING THE ART OF FRENCH COOKING
Powell, J. Julie and Julia **B**
CHILD, PAUL, 1902-1994
Conant, J. The lotus eaters **940.54**
Prud'homme, A. France is a feast **778**
CHILD-FREE LIFESTYLE
Blackstone, A. Childfree by choice **306.874**
CHILD-SEPARATED FATHERS
Holroyd, M. A book of secrets **306.874**
CHILDBIRTH
Bhattacharya, S. The baby book **649.1**
Harshe, J. Birth without fear **618.2**
McConville, B. On becoming a mother **306.874**
Murkoff, H. What to expect when you're expecting **618.2**
Nilsson, L. A child is born **612.6**
The pregnancy encyclopedia **618.2**
Rowland, K. Whoa, baby! **618.2**
Simkin, P. The birth partner **618.2**
Vincent, P. Baby catcher **618.2**
CHILDBIRTH AT HOME
Silbernagel, S. The many faces of home birth **618.4**
Childfree by choice Blackstone, A. **306.874**
CHILDHOOD
Auster, P. Report from the interior **B**
Blom, O. Young Rembrandt **B**
Blumenthal, S. A self-made man **B**
Calcaterra, R. Etched in sand **B**
Dillard, A. An American childhood **B**
Griffiths, J. A country called childhood **305.23**
Mowat, F. Born naked **B**
Patchett, A. This is the story of a happy marriage **B**
Rushin, S. Sting-ray afternoons **B**
Sedaris, D. The best of me **B**
CHILDHOOD -- CHICAGO, ILLINOIS
Common (Musician) One day it'll all make sense **B**
CHILDHOOD -- CHINA
Li, C. The bitter sea **B**
CHILDHOOD -- CZECHOSLOVAKIA
Albright, M. Prague winter **B**
CHILDHOOD -- GREAT BRITAIN
Ramsay, G. Roasting in Hell's Kitchen **B**
CHILDHOOD -- IRELAND
Heaney, S. District and circle **821**
CHILDHOOD -- KOTZEBUE, ALASKA
Hensley, W. Fifty miles from tomorrow **B**
CHILDHOOD -- UNITED STATES -- HISTORY
Mintz, S. Huck's raft **305.23**
CHILDHOOD LEUKEMIA
Keene, N. Childhood leukemia **618.92**
Childhood leukemia Keene, N. **618.92**
CHILDLESSNESS
Blackstone, A. Childfree by choice **306.874**
CHILDREN
Levy, A. Huck Finn's America **813**
The **children** Halberstam, D. **323.1**
CHILDREN -- BEHAVIOR MODIFICATION
Glickman, E. Your kid's a brat and it's all your fault **649**
CHILDREN -- BOOKS AND READING
Newman, N. Raising passionate readers **649**
Paul, P. How to raise a reader **649**
CHILDREN -- BOOKS AND READING
Manglik, G. Muslims in story **809**
CHILDREN -- BOOKS AND READING -- UNITED STATES
Dorr, C. LGBTQAI+ books for children and teens **028.7**
CHILDREN -- CROSS-CULTURAL STUDIES
Griffiths, J. A country called childhood **305.23**
CHILDREN -- DEATH
Hirsch, E. Gabriel **811**

Seaver, B. The joy of seafood 641.6
Seaver, B. For cod & country 641.6
Seaver, B. Two if by sea 641.6
Selengut, B. Good fish 641.6
Stein, R. Rick Stein's complete seafood 641.6

COOKING (SMOKED FOODS)
Disbrowe, P. Food52 any night grilling 641.7
Franklin, A. Franklin barbecue 641.7

COOKING (SMOKED FOODS)
Byres, T. Smoke 641.5
Raichlen, S. Project smoke 641.6

COOKING (SOURDOUGH)
Ford, B. New world sourdough 641.81

COOKING (SPICES)
Arokiasamy, C. The spice merchant's daughter 641.6
Bevill, A. World spice at home 641.6
Duguid, N. Burma 641.595
Hemphill, I. The spice & herb bible 641.3
Lakshmi, P. The encyclopedia of spices and herbs 641.3
Selengut, B. How to taste 641.5973
Seneviratne, S. The new sugar and spice 641.86
Sharma, N. Season 641.6
Sodha, M. Made in India 641.595

COOKING (SUGAR)
Yosses, B. The sweet spot 641.86

COOKING (TEA)
Gascoyne, K. Tea 641.3

COOKING (TRUFFLES)
Jacobs, R. The truffle underground 381

COOKING (VARIETY MEATS)
McLagan, J. Odd bits 641.3

COOKING (VEGETABLES)
Andres, J. Vegetables unleashed 641.5
Anthony, M. V is for vegetables 641.6
Bittman, M. How to cook everything vegetarian 641.5
Bloomfield, A. A girl and her greens 641.6
Chernila, A. Eating from the ground up 641.6
Chernila, A. Eating from the ground up 641.6
Complete book of home preserving 641.4
Dinki, N. Meat on the side 641.3
EatingWell vegetables 641.6
Firth, H. Bosh! 641.5
Hamshaw, G. Food **52** vegan 641.5
Kafka, B. Vegetable love 641.6
Knauer, I. The farm cooking school 641.5
La Place, V. Verdura 641.6
Landau, R. Vedge 641.6
Lang, R. The Southern vegetable book 641.6
Liddon, A. Oh she glows every day cookbook 641.5
Madison, D. Vegetable literacy 641.6
Mangini, C. The vegetable butcher 641.6
McFadden, J. Six seasons 641.5
Ottolenghi, Y. Plenty 641.6
Ottolenghi, Y. Plenty more 641.6
Prescott, M. Food is the solution 613.2
Sarno, C. The wicked healthy cookbook 651.56
Thug Kitchen 641.5
Turner, K. But I could never go 641.5
Vegetables from an Italian garden 641.6
Vegetables illustrated 641.6
Vinton, S. Put 'em up! 641.6
Wells, P. Salad as a meal 641.8
Wells, P. Vegetable harvest 641.6

COOKING (WILD FOODS)
Gibbons, E. Stalking the wild asparagus 581.6
Viljoen, M. Forage, harvest, feast 641.6

COOKING (WILD FOODS) -- TECHNIQUE
Canterbury, D. The Bushcraft field guide to trapping, gathering, & cooking in the wild 641.6

COOKING (YOGURT)
Caldwell, G. Homemade yogurt & kefir 641.6
Rule, C. Yogurt culture 641.6

COOKING -- ALASKA
Dixon, K. The Tutka Bay Lodge cookbook 641.5979

COOKING -- ANECDOTES
Foose, M. Screen doors and sweet tea 641.5975
Ha, R. Cook Korean! 641.595
Lebovitz, D. My Paris kitchen 641.594
Weir, J. Kitchen gypsy 641.5

COOKING -- BLOGS
Galarza, D. Beyond the plate 641.5092

COOKING -- CALIFORNIA
Moore, R. This is Camino 641.5979

COOKING -- EAST AFRICA
Hassan, H. In Bibi's kitchen 641.596

COOKING -- ENCYCLOPEDIAS
Larousse gastronomique 641.3

COOKING -- ENGLAND -- LONDON
Crapanzano, A. The London cookbook 641.594

COOKING -- EQUIPMENT AND SUPPLIES
The best of America's test kitchen 2018 641.5

COOKING -- EUROPE, EASTERN
Hercules, O. Mamushka 641.594

COOKING -- FRANCE
Thorisson, M. A kitchen in France 641.594

COOKING -- FRANCE -- MEDOC
Thorisson, M. French country cooking 641.594

COOKING / GENERAL
Clark, M. Cook this now 641.5973

COOKING -- GERMANY
Rosin, F. Modern German cookbook 641.594

COOKING -- GREECE
Kochilas, D. Ikaria 641.594

COOKING -- GULF STATES
Buffett, L. Gumbo love 641.5975

COOKING -- HISTORY
Fernandez-Armesto, F. Near a thousand tables 641.3
Sitwell, W. A history of food in 100 recipes 641.509
Willan, A. The cookbook library 641.509
Wilson, B. Consider the fork 643
Wrangham, R. Catching fire 394.1

COOKING -- HISTORY -- 20TH CENTURY
101 classic cookbooks ; 641.5

COOKING -- HOUSTON, TEXAS

Anthony, M. The Gramercy Tavern cookbook **641.5973**
The best chicken recipes **641.665**
The best of America's test kitchen **2018** **641.5**
The best recipe **641.5**
Barber, D. The third plate **641.3**
Bastianich, L. Lidia's Italian-American kitchen **641.594**
Batali, M. America farm to table **641.5973**
Batali, M. Mario Batali big American cookbook **641.5973**
Beard, J. James Beard's American cookery **641.5**
Beard, J. The essential James Beard cookbook **641.5973**
Besh, J. Cooking from the heart **641.5973**
Birdsall, J. The man who ate too much **B**
Brennan, K. Keepers **641.5973**
Bruni, F. A meatloaf in every oven **641.82**
Clark, M. Cook this now **641.5973**
Cook's Country eats local **641.5973**
Cook's illustrated revolutionary recipes **641.5973**
Cunningham, M. The Fannie Farmer cookbook **641.5973**
Deetz, K. Bound to the fire **641.59**
DiSpirito, R. Now eat this! **641.5**
Dufresne, W. wd~**50** **641.5973**
Erway, C. The art of eating in **B**
Estrine, D. Harvest to heat **641.5973**
Falk, D. The hungry fan's game day cookbook **641.5973**
Flay, B. Brunch @ Bobby's **641.5**
The food of a younger land **394.1**
Freedman, P. American cuisine **641.5973**
Friedman, A. Chefs, drugs and rock & roll **647.95**
Goin, S. The A.O.C. cookbook **641.5973**
The Good Housekeeping cookbook **641**
Goodall, T. The ultimate student cookbook **641.5**
Guarnaschelli, A. The home cook **641.5973**
Hamilton, G. Prune **641.3**
Hesser, A. Food52 **641.5975**
Holland, T. Brown sugar kitchen **641.5973**
Humm, D. I [heart] New York **641.59747**
The new American plate cookbook **641.5**
The immigrant cookbook **641.59**
Kamp, D. The United States of Arugula **641**
Kasper, L. The Splendid table's, how to eat supper **641.5**
Keller, T. Ad Hoc at home **641.5973**
Kim, H. My Korea **641.595**
Knauer, I. The farm cooking school **641.5**
Krishna, P. Indian-ish **641.595**
Langholtz, G. America **641.5973**
Lohman, S. Eight flavors **641.5973**
Lopez-Alt, J. The food lab **664**
Lundy, R. Victuals **641.5974**
McBride, M. Martina's kitchen mix **641.5973**
Mitchell, A. Eating in the middle **641.3**
Moore, C. Little Flower baking **641.81**
Moulton, S. Sara Moulton's home cooking **101** **641.5973**
The new family cookbook **641.5973**
Parks, S. Bravetart **641.86**
Perelman, D. Smitten kitchen every day **641.5**
Peternell, C. A recipe for cooking **641.5**
Phillips, M. Chelsea Market cookbook **641.59747**
Rich, S. Rich table **641.5973**
Ridge, B. The Beekman 1802 heirloom dessert cookbook **641.59747**
Rombauer, I. Joy of cooking **641.5973**
Rombauer, I. Joy of cooking **641.5973**
Rosen, A. Bring it! **641.5973**
Sappington, A. Heartlandia **641.5973**
Selengut, B. How to taste **641.5973**
Sifton, S. Thanksgiving **641.5**
Thielen, A. The New Midwestern table **641.5977**
Tosi, C. Milk bar life **641.86**
Voltaggio, B. Home **641.5973**
Walker, D. Danielle Walker's Eat what you love **641.3**
Workman, K. Dinner solved! **641.5**
Yeh, M. Molly on the range **641.5973**

COOKING, AMERICAN -- ALASKA
Wilson, M. The Alaska from scratch cookbook **641.5**

COOKING, AMERICAN -- CALIFORNIA
Guzman, G. Nopalito **641.5972**

COOKING, AMERICAN -- CALIFORNIA STYLE
Avila, W. Guerrilla Tacos **641.84**
Balla, N. Bar Tartine **641.5979**
Brioza, S. State Bird Provisions **641.5979**
Hirigoyen, G. Pintxos **641.8**
Kinch, D. Manresa **641.5979**
Kostow, C. A new Napa cuisine **651.57**
Moore, R. This is Camino **641.5979**
Prueitt, E. Tartine all day **641.5979**
Rosenthal, M. Cooking my way back home **641.5979**
Valladolid, M. Casa Marcela **641.5979**
Wangler, J. Season **641.5979**

COOKING, AMERICAN -- HISTORY
The food of a younger land **394.1**

COOKING, AMERICAN -- HISTORY -- 20TH CENTURY
Barr, L. Provence, 1970 **641**
Ziegelman, J. A square meal **641.5973**

COOKING, AMERICAN -- LOUISIANA
Besh, J. My New Orleans **641.5976**

COOKING, AMERICAN -- LOUISIANA STYLE
Chase, L. The Dooky Chase cookbook **641.5976**
Link, D. Real Cajun **641.5976**
Toups, I. Chasing the gator **641.5976**

COOKING, AMERICAN -- MIDDLE WEST
Thielen, A. The New Midwestern table **641.5977**
Yeh, M. Molly on the range **641.5973**

COOKING, AMERICAN -- MIDWESTERN STYLE
Brownson, J. Dinner at home **641.5977**
Sever, S. Midwest made **641.5977**

COOKING, AMERICAN -- NEW ENGLAND STYLE
Dojny, B. The New England cookbook **641.5974**
Jennings, M. Homegrown **641.5974**
Sewall, J. The New England kitchen **641.5974**

COOKING, AMERICAN -- NEW ORLEANS, LOUISIANA
Besh, J. My New Orleans **641.5976**

COOKING, AMERICAN -- NORTH CAROLINA
Howard, V. Deep Run roots **641.5975**

COOKING, ITALIAN -- HISTORY -- 20TH CENTURY
Hazan, M. Amarcord, Marcella remembers **B**
COOKING, ITALIAN -- NORTHERN STYLE
Necchio, V. Veneto **641.594**
COOKING, ITALIAN -- TUSCAN STYLE
Buford, B. Heat **B**
Rogers, R. River Cafe London **641.594**
COOKING, ITALIAN -- VENETIAN STYLE
Necchio, V. Veneto **641.594**
COOKING, ITALIAN AMERICAN
Carmellini, A. Urban Italian **641.594**
De Laurentiis, G. Giada's kitchen **641.594**
COOKING, JAPANESE
Cole, T. Uchi **641.595**
Goulding, M. Rice, noodle, fish **394.1**
Orkin, I. The gaijin cookbook **641.595**
Orkin, I. Ivan Ramen **641.595**
Sakai, S. Japanese home cooking **641.595**
Shimbo, H. Hiroko's American kitchen **641.595**
COOKING, JEWISH
Sussman, A. Sababa **641.5**
COOKING, KOREAN
Ha, R. Cook Korean! **641.595**
Hong, D. Koreatown **641.595**
Joo, J. Korean food made simple **641.595**
Kim, B. Korean BBQ **641.595**
Kim, H. My Korea **641.595**
Lee, C. Quick & easy Korean cooking **641.5**
Maangchi,. Maangchi's big book of Korean cooking **641.595**
Maangchi Maangchi's real Korean cooking **641.595**
West, D. K food **641.595**
COOKING, KOSHER
Marks, G. The world of Jewish cooking **641.5**
COOKING, LATIN AMERICAN
Kijac, M. The South American table **641.598**
Presilla, M. Gran cocina latina **641.5972**
Van Aken, N. New World kitchen **641.598**
COOKING, LEBANESE
Abood, M. Rose water & orange blossoms **641.595**
Massaad, B. Man'oushe **641.595**
Roden, C. Arabesque **641.59**
Sageer, J. Julie Taboulie's Lebanese kitchen **641.595**
COOKING, LOW-SALT
Goldman, J. Sodium girls limitless low-salt cookbook **641.5**
Terry, B. Vegan Soul kitchen **641.5**
COOKING, MALAYSIAN
Arokiasamy, C. The Malaysian kitchen **641.595**
COOKING, MEDITERRANEAN
Acquista, A. The Mediterranean family table **641.59**
David, E. A book of Mediterranean food **641.59**
Goldstein, J. The new Mediterranean Jewish table **641.5**
Helou, A. Mediterranean street food **641.59**
Jenkins, N. The new Mediterranean diet cookbook **641.59**
Lawson, N. At my table **641.59**
Ottolenghi, Y. Nopi **641.595**
Ottolenghi, Y. Ottolenghi **641.59**
Psilakis, M. How to roast a lamb **641.59**
Psilakis, M. Live to eat **641.59**
Ronnen, T. Crossroads **641.59**
Sageer, J. Julie Taboulie's Lebanese kitchen **641.595**
Shulman, M. Mediterranean harvest **641.5**
Speck, M. Ancient grains for modern meals **641.598**
Wadi, S. The new Mediterranean table **641.59**
Weir, J. Kitchen gypsy **641.5**
Wolfert, P. The slow Mediterranean kitchen **641.59**
Wolfert, P. Mediterranean clay pot cooking **641.59**
COOKING, MEXICAN
Bayless, R. Rick Bayless's Mexican kitchen **641.5972**
Bayless, R. Rick Bayless Mexico one plate at a time **641.5972**
Bayless, R. Authentic Mexican **641.5972**
Bayless, R. Fiesta at Rick's **641.5972**
Bayless, R. Mexican everyday **641.5972**
Bayless, R. More Mexican everyday **641.5972**
Camara, G. My Mexico City kitchen **641.5972**
Carrillo Arronte, M. Mexico **641.5972**
Gerson, F. Mexican ice cream **641.86**
Gerson, F. My sweet Mexico **641.5972**
Gerson, F. Mexican ice cream **641.86**
Guzman, G. Nopalito **641.5972**
Hernandez, E. Turnip greens & tortillas **641.5972**
Holtz, D. Tacopedia **641.8**
Jamison, C. The border cookbook **641.5979**
Jinich, P. Mexican today **641.5972**
Kennedy, D. The essential cuisines of Mexico **641.5972**
Kennedy, D. From my Mexican kitchen **641.5972**
Presilla, M. Gran cocina latina **641.5972**
Santibanez, R. Truly Mexican **641.5972**
Stupak, A. Tacos **641.84**
Tellez, L. Eat Mexico **641.5972**
Valladolid, M. Casa Marcela **641.5979**
Werner, E. Hartwood **641.5972**
COOKING, MEXICAN AMERICAN
Casares, S. The enchilada queen cookbook **641.5926872073**
Centeno, J. Ama **641.5979**
Cramby, J. Tex-mex from scratch **641.5972**
Trejo, D. Trejo's tacos **641.5979**
COOKING, MIDDLE EASTERN
Bishara, R. Levant **641.59**
Bishara, R. Olives, lemons & za'atar **641.59**
Ghayour, S. Bazaar **641.5**
Ghayour, S. Persiana **641.595**
Helou, A. Feast **641.595**
Khan, Y. Zaitoun **641.595**
Maffei, Y. My halal kitchen **641.595**
Ottolenghi, Y. Jerusalem **641.5**
Ottolenghi, Y. Nopi **641.595**
Ottolenghi, Y. Ottolenghi **641.59**
Ottolenghi, Y. Ottolenghi Simple **641.5**
Packer, S. Honey & Co. **641.595**
Roden, C. The new book of Middle Eastern food **641.595**
Solomonov, M. Israeli soul **641.595**

E

AUTHOR, TITLE, AND SUBJECT INDEX
EIGHTEENTH EDITION

ETHOLOGISTS -- GREAT BRITAIN
Dawkins, R. Brief candle in the dark **B**
ETIQUETTE
Forni, P. The civility solution **395**
Goodman, R. How to behave badly in Elizabethan England **942.05**
Martin, J. Miss Manners' guide to excruciatingly correct behavior **395**
Post, L. Emily Post's etiquette **395**
Witherspoon, R. Whiskey in a teacup **B**
ETIQUETTE -- UNITED STATES
Alkon, A. Good manners for nice people **395**
Dresser, N. Multicultural manners **395**
ETIQUETTE
The **etymologicon** Forsyth, M. **422**
ETYMOLOGY
Bragg, M. The adventure of English **420**
Crystal, D. The story of English in 100 words **422**
Hitchings, H. The secret life of words **422**
Mugglestone, L. Lost for words **423**
EUCLIDES
Berlinski, D. The king of infinite space **516.2**
Rudman, P. The Babylonian theorem **510.9**
Eudora Waldron, A. **B**
Eudora Welty Marrs, S. **B**
Eugene O'Neill Dowling, R. **B**
Eugene Odum Craige, B. **B**
Eugene Onegin Pushkin, A. **891.71**
EUGENICS
Collins, M. Admit one **811**
Okrent, D. The guarded gate **344.73**
EUGENICS -- GERMANY -- HISTORY -- 20TH CENTURY
Oelhafen, I. Hitler's stolen children **B**
EUGENICS -- LAW AND LEGISLATION -- UNITED STATES
Cohen, A. Imbeciles **344.7304**
EUGENICS -- UNITED STATES -- HISTORY -- 20TH CENTURY
Nourse, V. In reckless hands **344.7304**
Eunice McNamara, E. **B**
EUNICE KENNEDY SHRIVER NATIONAL INSTITUTE OF CHILD HEALTH AND HUMAN DEVELOPMENT (U.S.)
McNamara, E. Eunice **B**
EURASIA -- COMMERCE -- HISTORY
Frankopan, P. The Silk Roads **909**
Eureka Orzel, C. **500**
The **Eureka** factor Kounios, J. **612.8**
Eureka man Hirshfeld, A. **B**
Europa MacLennan, J. **940**
EUROPA (GEOGRAFIE). GTT
Brosens, K. European tapestries in the Art Institute of Chicago **746.3**
EUROPE
Brighton, T. Patton, Montgomery, Rommel **B**
Dorren, G. Lingo **409**
Freely, J. The flame of Miletus **509.38**
Grayling, A. The age of genius **940.2**
Guibert, E. Alan's war **B**
Lower, W. Hitler's furies **940.53**
MacLennan, J. Europa **940**
Nicolson, A. Why Homer matters **883**
Pettegree, A. The book in the Renaissance **070.5**
Pye, M. The edge of the world **940.1**
Stone, N. World War One **940.3**
Svensson, P. The book of eels **597**
Weller, G. Weller's war **B**
Europe Flannery, T. **508.4**
EUROPE -- ANTIQUITIES
Von Petzinger, G. The first signs **302.2**
EUROPE -- CHURCH HISTORY -- 600-1500
Asbridge, T. The crusades **909.07**
Phillips, J. Holy warriors **909.07**
EUROPE -- CIVILIZATION
Barzun, J. From dawn to decadence **940.2**
Blanning, T. The pursuit of glory **940.2**
Ortega y Gasset, J. The revolt of the masses **901**
EUROPE -- CIVILIZATION -- 21ST CENTURY
Caldwell, C. Reflections on the revolution in Europe **304.8**
EUROPE -- CIVILIZATION -- ISLAMIC INFLUENCES
Caldwell, C. Reflections on the revolution in Europe **304.8**
EUROPE -- COLONIES AFRICA -- HISTORY -- 19TH CENTURY
Pakenham, T. The scramble for Africa, 1876-1912 **960.3**
EUROPE -- COLONIES AFRICA -- HISTORY -- 20TH CENTURY
Pakenham, T. The scramble for Africa, 1876-1912 **960.3**
EUROPE -- COMMERCE
Bown, S. Merchant kings **338.8**
EUROPE -- DESCRIPTION AND TRAVEL
Egan, T. A pilgrimage to eternity **263**
Mak, G. In Europe **940.5**
O'Brien, M. Mrs. Adams in winter **B**
EUROPE -- ECONOMIC CONDITIONS -- 1945-
Ferguson, N. High financier **B**
Judt, T. Postwar **940.55**
Steil, B. The Marshall Plan **338.91**
EUROPE -- EMIGRATION AND IMMIGRATION -- HISTORY -- 21ST CENTURY
McDonald-Gibson, C. Cast away **305.9**
EUROPE -- ETHNIC RELATIONS -- HISTORY -- 20TH CENTURY
Gerwarth, R. The vanquished **940.5**
EUROPE -- FOREIGN ECONOMIC RELATIONS UNITED STATES
Steil, B. The Marshall Plan **338.91**
EUROPE -- FOREIGN RELATIONS
Judt, T. Postwar **940.55**
EUROPE -- FOREIGN RELATIONS ISLAMIC EMPIRE
Asbridge, T. The crusades **909.07**
EUROPE -- FOREIGN RELATIONS UNITED STATES

Grunwald, M. The swamp 975.9
EVERLEIGH CLUB
Abbott, K. Sin in the Second City 306.7409773
EVERLEIGH, ADA
Abbott, K. Sin in the Second City 306.7409773
EVERLEIGH, MINNA
Abbott, K. Sin in the Second City 306.7409773
EVERS, JOHNNY
Rapp, D. Tinker to Evers to Chance 796.357
EVERS, MEDGAR WILEY, 1925-1963
Evers, M. The autobiography of Medgar Evers B
EVERT, CHRIS, 1955-
Howard, J. The rivals 796.342
Every body yoga Stanley, J. 613.7
Every book its reader Basbanes, N. 028
Every day is extra Kerry, J. B
Every drop for sale Rothfeder, J. 333.91
Every grain of rice Dunlop, F. 641.595
Every landlord's legal guide Stewart, M. 346.7304
Every living thing Herriot, J. B
Every love story is a ghost story Max, D. B
Every man in this village is a liar Stack, M. B
Every patient tells a story Sanders, L. 616.07
Every shut eye ain't asleep 811
Every word is a bird we teach to sing Tammet, D. 402
Everybody behaves badly Blume, L. B
Everybody had an ocean McKeen, W. 781.6609
Everybody lies Stephens-Davidowitz, S. 302.23
Everybody loves our town Yarm, M. 781.66
Everybody matters Chapman, B. 658.4
Everybody's brother Green, C. B
The **everyday** baker Dodge, A. 641.81
Everyday chic Sims, M. 642
The **everyday** DASH diet cookbook Heller, M. 613.2
Everyday Dorie Greenspan, D. 641.5
Everyday greatness Covey, S. 170
EVERYDAY LIFE
Carlsen, S. A walk around the block 31
Crosley, S. Look alive out there B
DePalma, A. The Cubans 920
Didion, J. South and West 818
Ellenberg, J. How not to be wrong 510
Ephron, N. The most of Nora Ephron B
Fennelly, B. Heating & cooling B
Havrilesky, H. What if this were enough? 152.4
Irby, S. We are never meeting in real life B
Kakalios, J. The physics of everyday things 530
Leon, D. My Venice and other essays B
Nhat Hanh, T. The art of living 294.3
Picard, L. Chaucer's people 942.03
Sanders, E. Eating the sun 520
Shankle, M. Church of the small things 248.8
The **everyday** meat guide Venezia, R. 641.3
The **everyday** parenting toolkit Kazdin, A. 649
Everyone is Italian on Sunday Ray, R. 641.594
Everything all at once Nye, B. B
Everything below the waist Block, J. 613
Everything I know about love Alderton, D. B
Everything in its place Sacks, O. B
Everything is broken Larkin, E. 959.105
Everything is f*cked Manson, M. 152.4
Everything is obvious Watts, D. 153.4
Everything to gain Carter, J. B
Everything we have Mueller, G. 940.54
Everything you need to know about social media Van Susteren, G. 302.30285
Everything you wanted to know about Indians but were afraid to ask Treuer, A. 909
Everything's trash, but it's okay Robinson, P. 814
Everywhere I look Garner, H. 820
Evicted Desmond, M. 339.4
EVICTION
Desmond, M. Evicted 339.4
The **evil** hours Morris, D. B
EVOLUTION
Arbesman, S. The half-life of facts 501
Ayala, F. Darwin's gift to science and religion 576.8
Browne, E. Darwin's Origin of species 576.8
Brusatte, S. The rise and fall of the dinosaurs 567.9
Costa, J. Darwin's backyard 576.8
Dawkins, R. A devil's chaplain 500
Dawkins, R. An appetite for wonder B
Dawkins, R. Science in the soul 500
Dawkins, R. The greatest show on Earth 576.8
De Queiroz, A. The monkey's voyage 570
Denworth, L. Friendship 158.2
DeSalle, R. The brain 612.8
Dunbar, R. Human evolution 155.7
Gould, S. The flamingo's smile 508
Gould, S. The structure of evolutionary theory 576.8
Gribbin, J. Almost everyone's guide to science 500
Harari, Y. Homo deus 909.83
Harari, Y. Sapiens 909
Harman, O. Evolutions 201
Hawking, S. The grand design 530.14
Hazen, R. The story of Earth 550
Hoffman, D. The case aganist reality 121
Johnson, P. Darwin B
Keller, M. Charles Darwin's on the origin of species 576.8
Kenneally, C. The first word 400
Leakey, R. The origin of humankind 573.2
Lister, A. Darwin's fossils 576.8
Losos, J. Improbable destinies 576.8
Margulis, L. Symbiotic planet 576.8
Meredith, M. Born in Africa 960
Mitteldorf, J. Cracking the aging code 612.6
O'Connor, M. Resurrection science 591.68
Pagel, M. Wired for culture 303.4
Pinker, S. The blank slate 155.2
Prothero, D. The story of life in 25 fossils 560
Pyenson, N. Spying on whales 599.5
Ridley, M. The evolution of everything 303.48
Rutherford, A. A brief history of everyone who ever

LaFarge, A. Chasing Chopin **B**
Spurling, H. The unknown Matisse **B**
Weber, C. Proust's duchess **920**
White, B. Renoir **B**

FRANCE -- HISTORY -- 20TH CENTURY
Aczel, A. The artist and the mathematician **B**
Brian, D. The Curies **920**
Helm, S. A life in secrets **B**
Kaplan, A. The interpreter **940.54**
Paxson, M. The plateau **B**
Vinen, R. 1968 **909.82**
Williams, C. The last great Frenchman **B**

FRANCE -- HISTORY -- CHARLES VII, 1422-1461 DRAMA
Shaw, B. Saint Joan **822**

FRANCE -- HISTORY -- CHARLES VII, 1422-1461
Castor, H. Joan of Arc **B**
Gordon, M. Joan of Arc **B**
Pernoud, R. Joan of Arc **B**

FRANCE -- HISTORY -- CONSULATE AND FIRST EMPIRE, 1799-1815
Coote, S. Napoleon and the Hundred Days **940.2**
Fraser, F. Pauline Bonaparte **B**

FRANCE -- HISTORY -- GERMAN OCCUPATION, 1914-1918
Sebba, A. Les Parisiennes **305.40944**

FRANCE -- HISTORY -- GERMAN OCCUPATION, 1940-1945
Kaiser, C. The cost of courage **920**
Humbert, A. Resistance **B**
Kershaw, A. Avenue of spies **B**
King, D. Death in the city of light **364.152**
Magida, A. Code name Madeleine **B**
Mazzeo, T. The hotel on Place Vendome **647.94**
Moorehead, C. A train in winter **940.53**
Moorehead, C. Village of secrets **944**
Olson, L. Madame Fourcade's secret war **B**
Porter, C. Marcel's letters **B**
Purnell, S. A woman of no importance **B**
Rosenberg, J. The art of resistance **B**
Scheyer, M. Asylum **B**
Schwarz, G. Those who forget **B**
Smith, J. The liberation of Paris **940.54**
Zuccotti, S. Pere Marie-Benoit and Jewish rescue **B**

FRANCE -- HISTORY -- LOUIS VII, 1137-1180
Weir, A. Eleanor of Aquitaine **B**

FRANCE -- HISTORY -- LOUIS XIV, 1643-1715
Fraser, A. Love and Louis XIV **B**
Mansel, P. King of the world **B**

FRANCE -- HISTORY -- LOUIS XV, 1715-1774
Lever, E. Madame de Pompadour **B**

FRANCE -- HISTORY -- LOUIS XVI, 1774-1793
Fraser, A. Marie Antoinette **B**

FRANCE -- HISTORY -- REIGN OF TERROR, 1793-1794
McPhee, P. Robespierre **B**
Moorehead, C. Dancing to the precipice **B**

FRANCE -- HISTORY -- RESTORATION, 1814-1830
Coote, S. Napoleon and the Hundred Days **940.2**

FRANCE -- HISTORY -- REVOLUTION, 1789-1799
Chaffin, T. Revolutionary brothers **920**
Gaines, J. For liberty and glory **973.4**
McPhee, P. Liberty or death **944.04**
McPhee, P. Robespierre **B**
Mostert, N. Line upon a wind **940.2**
Popkin, J. A new world begins **944.04**
Schama, S. Citizens **944.04**
Schom, A. Napoleon Bonaparte **B**
Winik, J. The great upheaval **973.3**

FRANCE -- HISTORY -- REVOLUTION, 1789-1799 -- CAUSES
Burke, E. Reflections on the revolution in France **944.04**

FRANCE -- HISTORY -- REVOLUTION, 1789-1799 -- INFLUENCE
Murray, W. A savage war **973.7**

FRANCE -- HISTORY -- THIRD REPUBLIC, 1870-1940
Brown, F. For the soul of France **944.081**
Read, P. The Dreyfus affair **944.081**

FRANCE -- HISTORY -- TO 987
Wilson, D. Charlemagne **B**

FRANCE -- HISTORY, LOCAL
Caro, I. Paris to the past **944**

FRANCE -- HISTORY, MILITARY
Mosier, J. The myth of the Great War **940.4**
Philbrick, N. In the hurricane's eye **973.3**
Walker, W. Betrayal at Little Gibraltar **940.4**

FRANCE -- HISTORY, MILITARY -- 1328-1589
Fiennes, R. Agincourt **944.02542**
Green, D. The Hundred Years War **944**

FRANCE -- HISTORY, MILITARY -- 1789-1815
Cornwell, B. Waterloo **940.2**

FRANCE -- HISTORY, MILITARY -- 19TH CENTURY
Esdaile, C. Napoleon's wars **940.2**

FRANCE -- HISTORY, MILITARY -- 20TH CENTURY
Arnold, J. Jungle of snakes **355.02**
Herwig, H. The Marne, 1914 **940.4**
Ousby, I. The road to Verdun **940.4**
Sacco, J. The Great War **940.4**

FRANCE -- HISTORY, NAVAL -- 19TH CENTURY
Adkin, M. The Trafalgar companion **940.27**

FRANCE -- MORAL CONDITIONS -- HISTORY -- 17TH CENTURY
Fraser, A. Love and Louis XIV **B**

FRANCE. NAVY
Philbrick, N. In the hurricane's eye **973.3**

FRANCE -- NOBILITY
Tuchman, B. A distant mirror **944**

FRANCE -- POLITICS AND GOVERNMENT -- 1789-1799
Burke, E. Reflections on the revolution in France **944.04**
McPhee, P. Robespierre **B**

FRANCE -- POLITICS AND GOVERNMENT -- 1789-1815
Broers, M. Napoleon **B**
Broers, M. Napoleon **B**
Gueniffey, P. Bonaparte **B**
Johnson, P. Napoleon **B**

G

Glenconner, A. Lady in waiting **B**
Glengarry Glen Ross Mamet, D. **812**
GLENN, ELIZABETH ELLIOTT LUMPKIN, 1880 OR 1881-1963
Hall, J. Sisters and rebels **920**
Glitter and glue Corrigan, K. **B**
Glitterville's handmade Christmas Brown, S. **745.594**
Glitterville's handmade Halloween Brown, S. **745.594**
The **global** age Kershaw, I. **940.55**
Global crisis Parker, G. **909**
GLOBAL ENVIRONMENTAL CHANGE
Barnosky, A. Tipping point for planet earth **304.2**
Dumanoski, D. The end of the long summer **551.6**
Hertsgaard, M. Hot **304.2**
Holthaus, E. The future earth **363.738**
Klare, M. All hell breaking loose **355.20973**
Kolbert, E. Field notes from a catastrophe **363.738**
Macdougall, J. Frozen Earth **551.7**
Nesbit, J. This is the way the world ends **363.7**
Pfeiffer, M. Lyme **616.9**
Robinson, M. Climate justice **363.7**
Wallace-Wells, D. The uninhabitable Earth **304.2**
GLOBAL ENVIRONMENTAL CHANGE -- HISTORY
Rich, N. Losing Earth **363.738**
GLOBAL ENVIRONMENTAL CHANGE -- PSYCHOLOGICAL ASPECTS
Lifton, R. The climate swerve **155.9**
GLOBAL FINANCIAL CRISIS, 2008-2009
Benmosche, B. Good for the money **B**
Blinder, A. After the music stopped **330.973**
Dayen, D. Chain of title **330.973**
Ferguson, C. Predator nation **330.973**
Geithner, T. Stress test **B**
Howard, T. The mortgage wars **332.7**
Kaiser, R. Act of Congress **346.73**
King, M. The end of alchemy **330.12**
Lanchester, J. I.O.U. **330.9**
McLean, B. All the devils are here **330.973**
Morgenson, G. Reckless endangerment **332.7**
Warren, E. A fighting chance **B**
A **global** history of architecture Ching, F. **720.9**
GLOBAL TEMPERATURE CHANGES
Kolbert, E. Field notes from a catastrophe **363.738**
GLOBAL WARMING
Alley, R. Earth **621**
Fagan, B. The long summer **551.6**
Flannery, T. The weather makers **363.738**
Foer, J. We are the weather **636**
Ghosh, A. The great derangement **809**
Goodell, J. How to cool the planet **551.6**
Gore, A. An inconvenient truth **363.738**
Hertsgaard, M. Hot **304.2**
Kolbert, E. Field notes from a catastrophe **363.738**
Lappe, A. Diet for a hot planet **363.738**
Manson, M. Everything is f*cked **152.4**
McKibben, B. Eaarth **304.2**
McKibben, B. The end of nature **304.2**
Nesbit, J. This is the way the world ends **363.7**
Nuccitelli, D. Climatology versus pseudoscience **577.27**
Pollack, H. A world without ice **551.31**
Raygorodetsky, G. The archipelago of hope **304.2**
Scigliano, E. The big thaw **550**
Wallace-Wells, D. The uninhabitable Earth **304.2**
GLOBAL WARMING -- ENVIRONMENTAL ASPECTS
Lynas, M. Six degrees **551.6**
GLOBAL WARMING -- HISTORY
Rich, N. Losing Earth **363.738**
GLOBAL WARMING -- PREVENTION
Berners-Lee, M. How bad are bananas? **363.738**
GLOBALIZATION
The atlas of global conservation **333.95**
Emmerson, C. 1913 **909.82**
Friedman, T. Thank you for being late **303.48**
Greene, J. Moral tribes **170**
Gore, A. The future **303.4**
Hickel, J. The divide **330.9**
Immerwahr, D. How to hide an empire **973**
Mishra, P. Age of anger **909.8**
Newman, K. The accordion family **306.874084**
GLOBALIZATION (ECONOMICS)
Foer, F. How soccer explains the world **327.1**
GLOBALIZATION (ECONOMICS) -- DEVELOPING COUNTRIES
Stiglitz, J. Globalization and its discontents **337**
GLOBALIZATION (ECONOMICS) -- EMPLOYMENT EFFECTS
Macy, B. Factory man **338.7**
GLOBALIZATION -- SOCIAL ASPECTS
Naim, M. The end of power **303.3**
Globalization and its discontents Stiglitz, J. **337**
GLOBE THEATRE (LONDON, ENGLAND : 1599-1644)
Shapiro, J. A year in the life of William Shakespeare, 1599 **822**
GLOMAR EXPLORER (SHIP)
Dean, J. The taking of K-129 **910.91**
The **glorious** cause Middlekauff, R. **973.3**
A **glorious** enterprise Peck, R. **508**
The **glorious** foods of Greece Kochilas, D. **641.594**
Glorious French food Peterson, J. **641.594**
The **glorious** pasta of Italy Marchetti, D. **641.82**
Glorious shade Carey, J. **635.9**
Glory Bethencourt, K. **779.2**
GLOUCESTER, MASSACHUSETTS -- HISTORY ANECDOTES
Kurlansky, M. The last fish tale **639.2**
Gluten-free & vegan pie Katzinger, J. **641.3**
Gluten-free baking at home Larsen, J. **641.5**
GLUTEN-FREE DIET
Ahern, S. Gluten-free girl every day **641.5**
Cavallari, K. True roots **641.5**
Conners, R. Bakerita **641.81**
Cristofano, J. Eat well, be well **641.5**
Esposito, J. Jennifer's Way kitchen **641.5**
Goyoaga, A. Cannelle et Vanille **641.5**

Hochschild, A. Bury the chains **326**
Holway, T. The flower of empire **727**
McCalman, I. Darwin's armada **576.8**

GREAT BRITAIN -- HISTORY -- 20TH CENTURY
Anand, A. Sophia **B**
Copeland, B. Turing **B**
Corera, G. Operation Columba **940.54**
Davenport-Hines, R. Universal man **B**
Edwards, A. Matriarch **B**
Glendinning, V. Leonard Woolf **B**
Korda, M. With wings like eagles **940.54**
Leavitt, D. The man who knew too much **B**
Lewis, D. The dog who could fly **B**
Macintyre, B. A spy among friends **B**
Macintyre, B. Agent Zigzag **B**
Mayer, C. Born to be king **B**
Moore, W. No man's land **940.4**
Morton, A. Wallis in love **B**
Purnell, S. Clementine **B**
Ruane, K. Churchill and the bomb in war and Cold War **355.02**
Smith, S. Prince Charles **B**
Vinen, R. 1968 **909.82**
Wallach, J. Desert queen **B**
Wilson, K. Blood and fears **940.54**

GREAT BRITAIN -- HISTORY -- ANGLO-SAXON PERIOD, 449-1066
Ackroyd, P. The death of King Arthur **823**
Morris, M. The Norman Conquest **942.02**

GREAT BRITAIN -- HISTORY -- ANNE, 1702-1714
Somerset, A. Queen Anne **B**

GREAT BRITAIN -- HISTORY -- BOMBING, 1940-1945
Larson, E. The splendid and the vile **940.54**

GREAT BRITAIN -- HISTORY -- CHARLES II, 1660-1685 -- SOURCES
Pepys, S. The diary of Samuel Pepys **B**

GREAT BRITAIN -- HISTORY -- CHARLES II, 1660-1685
Jordan, D. The king's revenge **941.06**
Mortimer, I. The time traveler's guide to Restoration Britain **941.06**
Uglow, J. A gambling man **B**

GREAT BRITAIN -- HISTORY -- EARLY STUARTS, 1603-1649
Bremer, F. John Winthrop **B**

GREAT BRITAIN -- HISTORY -- EDWARD I, 1272-1307
Morris, M. A great and terrible king **B**

GREAT BRITAIN -- HISTORY -- EDWARD III, 1327-1377
Ormrod, W. Edward III **B**

GREAT BRITAIN -- HISTORY -- EDWARD VI, 1547-1553
Rounding, V. The burning time **272**
Tallis, N. Crown of blood **B**

GREAT BRITAIN -- HISTORY -- EDWARD VII, 1901-1910
Carter, M. George, Nicholas and Wilhelm **940.3**
Hibbert, C. Edward VII **B**
Ridley, J. The heir apparent **B**

GREAT BRITAIN -- HISTORY -- EDWARD VIII, 1936
Cadbury, D. Princes at war **920**
Ziegler, P. King Edward VIII **B**

GREAT BRITAIN -- HISTORY -- ELIZABETH I, 1558-1603
Fraser, A. Mary, Queen of Scots **B**
Gallay, A. Walter Ralegh **B**
Guy, J. Elizabeth **B**
Hilton, L. Elizabeth **B**
Mortimer, I. The time traveler's guide to Elizabethan England **942.05**
Norton, E. The temptation of Elizabeth Tudor **B**
Ronald, S. Heretic queen **B**
Weir, A. The life of Elizabeth I **B**

GREAT BRITAIN -- HISTORY -- ELIZABETH II, 1952-
Bates, S. Royalty Inc **920**
Hardman, R. Queen of the world **B**
Smith, S. Elizabeth the Queen **B**
Williams, K. Young Elizabeth **B**

GREAT BRITAIN -- HISTORY -- ELIZABETH, 1558-1603
Hubbard, K. Devices and desires **B**

GREAT BRITAIN -- HISTORY -- GEORGE III, 1760-1820
Foreman, A. Georgiana, Duchess of Devonshire **B**
Morrison, R. The Regency years **941.07**

GREAT BRITAIN -- HISTORY -- GEORGE IV, 1820-1830
Koch, B. Mad and bad **920**

GREAT BRITAIN -- HISTORY -- GEORGE V, 1910-1936
Clay, C. King, Kaiser, Tsar **920**
Nicolson, J. The perfect summer **942.083**

GREAT BRITAIN -- HISTORY -- GEORGE VI, 1936-1952
Alexander, E. Love in the Blitz **942.1**
Cadbury, D. Princes at war **920**
Purnell, S. Clementine **B**

GREAT BRITAIN -- HISTORY -- HENRY II, 1154-1189
Guy, J. Thomas Becket **B**
Weir, A. Eleanor of Aquitaine **B**

GREAT BRITAIN -- HISTORY -- HENRY VII, 1485-1509
Gristwood, S. Blood sisters **942.04092**

GREAT BRITAIN -- HISTORY -- HENRY VIII, 1509-1547
Bolt, R. A man for all seasons **822**
Borman, T. Henry VIII and the men who made him **B**
Borman, T. Thomas Cromwell **B**
Fraser, A. The wives of Henry VIII **920**
Lipscomb, S. The king is dead **942.05**
MacCulloch, D. Thomas Cromwell **B**
Porter, L. Katherine the queen **B**
Rounding, V. The burning time **272**
Starkey, D. Six wives **920**
Weir, A. Henry VIII **B**
Weir, A. The six wives of Henry VIII **B**

GREAT BRITAIN -- HISTORY -- INVASIONS
Pocock, T. The terror before Trafalgar **940.2**

GREAT BRITAIN -- HISTORY -- JAMES I, 1603-1625
Fraser, A. Faith and treason **942.06**
Fraser, S. The prince who would be king **B**
Gallay, A. Walter Ralegh **B**
Woolley, B. The king's assassin **941.06**

GREAT BRITAIN -- HISTORY -- JOHN, 1199-1216
Morris, M. King John **B**

Hardwick, E. The dolphin letters, 1970-1979 **811**

HARDWICK, ELIZABETH, 1916-

Hardwick, E. The collected essays of Elizabeth Hardwick **B**

HARDWICK, VERMONT -- ECONOMIC CONDITIONS -- 21ST CENTURY

Hewitt, B. The town that food saved **338.1**

HARDY, G. H. (GODFREY HAROLD), 1877-1947

Kanigel, R. The man who knew infinity **B**

HARDY, JASON MATTHEW

Hardy, J. The second chance club **B**

HARDY, THOMAS, 1840-1928

Hardy, T. The collected letters of Thomas Hardy **B**

Tomalin, C. Thomas Hardy **B**

HARDY, THOMAS, 1840-1928 CORRESPONDENCE

Hardy, T. The collected letters of Thomas Hardy **B**

HARE KRISHNA MOVEMENT

Das, G. The way of the monk **294.5**

HARI, DAOUD

Hari, D. The translator **B**

HARJO, JOY, 1951-

Harjo, J. Crazy brave **B**

HARKNESS, RUTH

Croke, V. The lady and the panda **B**

HARLAN, JOHN MARSHALL, 1833-1911

Luxenberg, S. Separate **342.7308**

Harlem Gill, J. **974.7**

HARLEM (NEW YORK, N.Y.)

Samuelsson, M. The Red Rooster Cookbook **641.59747**

HARLEM (NEW YORK, N.Y.) -- INTELLECTUAL LIFE

Wall, C. Women of the Harlem renaissance **810**

HARLEM RENAISSANCE -- INFLUENCE

Abdul-Jabbar, K. On the shoulders of giants **B**

HARLEM RENAISSANCE

Bernard, E. Carl Van Vechten and the Harlem Renaissance **813**

Hurston, Z. Dust tracks on a road **B**

Stewart, J. The new Negro **B**

HARLEM, NEW YORK CITY

Day, D. Dapper Dan **B**

Gill, J. Harlem **974.7**

Stewart, J. The new Negro **B**

HARLEM, NEW YORK CITY -- 20TH CENTURY

Bernard, E. Carl Van Vechten and the Harlem Renaissance **813**

HARLEM, NEW YORK CITY -- ECONOMIC CONDITIONS

Tough, P. Whatever it takes **362.74**

HARLEM, NEW YORK CITY -- HISTORY -- 20TH CENTURY

Hutchinson, G. In search of Nella Larsen **B**

HARLEM, NEW YORK CITY -- SOCIAL CONDITIONS

Brown, C. Manchild in the promised land **B**

HARLESTON FAMILY

Ball, E. The sweet hell inside **920**

Harley-Davidson **629.227**

HARLEY-DAVIDSON MOTORCYCLE

Harley-Davidson **629.227**

HARLEY-DAVIDSON MOTORCYCLE -- HISTORY

Harley-Davidson **629.227**

HARNACK-FISH, MILDRED, 1902-1943

Thomas, G. Defying Hitler **920**

Harper's anthology of 20th century Native American poetry **811**

HARPER'S FERRY, WEST VIRGINIA -- HISTORY -- JOHN BROWN'S RAID, 1859

Brands, H. The zealot and the emancipator **920**

Horwitz, T. Midnight rising **B**

Reynolds, D. John Brown, abolitionist **B**

Meyer, E. Five for freedom **973.7**

HARPER, MICHELE

Harper, M. The beauty in breaking **B**

The **HarperCollins** Bible dictionary **220.3**

HARPHAM, HEATHER ELISE, 1967-

Harpham, H. Happiness **B**

HARPHAM, HEATHER ELISE, 1967- HEALTH

Harpham, H. Happiness **B**

Harriet Beecher Stowe Hedrick, J. **B**

Harriet Jacobs Yellin, J. **B**

Harriet Tubman Clinton, C. **B**

Harriet Tubman Humez, J. **B**

HARRIMAN ALASKA EXPEDITION (1899)

Adams, M. Tip of the iceberg **B**

HARRIMAN, W. AVERELL (WILLIAM AVERELL), 1891-1986

Fullilove, M. Rendezvous with destiny **973.917092**

HARRIMAN, WILLIAM AVERELL, 1891-1986

Olson, L. Citizens of London **940.54012**

HARRINGTON, SHAWN

Bradburd, R. All the dreams we've dreamed **796.323**

HARRIOT, THOMAS, 1560-1621

Arianrhod, R. Thomas Harriot **509.2**

HARRIS, DOLL, 1913-2001

Reeder, L. Dust Bowl girls **920**

HARRIS, JESSICA B

Harris, J. My soul looks back **641.59**

HARRIS, KATE, 1982-

Harris, K. Lands of lost borders **B**

Harris, K. Lands of lost borders **B**

HARRIS, NEIL PATRICK, 1973-

Harris, N. Neil Patrick Harris **B**

HARRISON, AUSTEN ST . BARBE, 1891-1976

Hoffman, A. Till we have built Jerusalem **920**

HARRISON, GEORGE, 1943-2001

Brown, C. 150 glimpses of the Beatles **920**

Harrison, G. George Harrison on George Harrison **782.42166092**

Thomson, G. George Harrison **B**

HARRISON, JIM, 1937-2016

Harrison, J. A really big lunch **641.01**

HARRISON, JOAN, 1907-1994

Lane, C. Phantom lady **B**

HARRISON, JOHN, 1693-1776

Sobel, D. Longitude **526**

I

JEWS, ETHIOPIAN -- ISRAEL -- HISTORY -- 20TH CENTURY
Berg, R. Red Sea spies **327.125694**
JEWS, ETHIOPIAN -- SUDAN -- HISTORY -- 20TH CENTURY
Berg, R. Red Sea spies **327.125694**
JEWS, EUROPEAN
Wasserstein, B. On the eve **305.892**
JEWS, FRENCH -- SOCIAL LIFE AND CUSTOMS
Nathan, J. Quiches, kugels, and couscous **641.5**
JEWS, GERMAN
Chernow, R. The Warburgs **B**
Lichtblau, E. Return to the Reich **B**
Simon, M. Underground in Berlin **B**
JEWS, GERMAN -- HISTORY -- 1933-1945
Friedlander, S. Nazi Germany and the Jews **940.53**
Gay, P. My German question **B**
Gilbert, M. Kristallnacht **940.53**
Klemperer, V. I will bear witness a diary of the Nazi years, 1942-1945 **B**
JEWS, HUNGARIAN
Szegedy-Maszak, M. I kiss your hands many times **B**
JEWS, ISRAELI
Shavit, A. My promised land **956.05**
JEWS, ISRAELI -- IDENTITY
La Guardia, A. War without end **956.9405**
JEWS, ITALIAN
Angier, C. The double bond **B**
JEWS, KURDISH -- ZAKHU, IRAQ
Sabar, A. My father's paradise **B**
JEWS, POLISH
Gross, J. Neighbors **940.53**
Kurtz, G. Three minutes in Poland **B**
Mazzeo, T. Irena's children **B**
Pivnik, S. Survivor **B**
Rosenfeld, O. In the beginning was the ghetto **940.53**
JEWS, POLISH -- HISTORY
Kramer, C. Clara's war **B**
JEWS, RUSSIAN
Gessen, M. Where the Jews aren't **957**
Nabokov, V. Speak, memory **B**
Shteyngart, G. Little failure **B**
JEWS, SOVIET
Brent, J. Stalin's last crime **947.084**
JEWS, SPANISH -- HISTORY
Lowney, C. A vanished world **946**
JEWS, UKRAINIAN
Mendelsohn, D. The lost **B**
JFK Logevall, F. **B**
JFK's last hundred days Clarke, T. **B**
Jheronimus Bosch Fischer, S. **759.9492**
JIHAD
Abouzeid, R. No turning back **B**
Bergen, P. United States of Jihad **363.3250973**
Lambert, M. God's armies **956**
Lewis, B. The crisis of Islam **297.7**
McMeekin, S. The Berlin-Baghdad express **940.3**
Mekhennet, S. I was told to come alone **B**
Jill Wiseman's beautiful beaded ropes Wiseman, J. **745.594**
Jim Brown Zirin, D. **B**
Jim Cramer's get rich carefully Cramer, J. **332.024**
Jim Henson Jones, B. **B**
Jim Trelease's read-aloud handbook Trelease, J. **372.4**
Jimmy Buffett White, R. **B**
JINNAH, MAHOMED ALI, 1876-1948
Hajari, N. Midnight's furies **954.04**
Jitney Wilson, A. **812**
JOAL-FADIOUT, SENEGAL -- SOCIAL CONDITIONS
Badkhen, A. Fisherman's blues **307.76**
Joan Mitchell Albers, P. **B**
Joan of Arc Castor, H. **B**
Joan of Arc Gordon, M. **B**
Joan of Arc Pernoud, R. **B**
JOAN OF ARC, SAINT, 1412-1431
Castor, H. Joan of Arc **B**
Gordon, M. Joan of Arc **B**
Pernoud, R. Joan of Arc **B**
JOAN, OF ARC, SAINT, 1412-1431 DRAMA
Shaw, B. Saint Joan **822**
Job Greenstein, E. **223**
JOB APPLICATIONS
Sandberg, S. Lean in **658.4**
JOB CREATION -- UNITED STATES -- HISTORY -- 20TH CENTURY
Taylor, N. American made **331.13**
JOB HUNTING
Aujla, D. 50 ways to get a job **650.14**
Bolles, R. What color is your parachute? **331.12**
Kay, A. This is how to get your next job **650.14**
Mackay, H. Use your head to get your foot in the door **650.14**
Raskin, D. The dirty little secrets of getting your dream job **650.14**
Sandberg, S. Lean in **658.4**
Yate, M. Knock 'em dead cover letters **650.14**
Yate, M. Knock 'em dead resumes **650.14**
JOB HUNTING -- UNITED STATES
Anders, G. You can do anything **650.1**
JOB HUNTING -- UNITED STATES -- HISTORY -- 21ST CENTURY
Chideya, F. The episodic career **650.1**
JOB SATISFACTION
Crawford, M. Shop class as soulcraft **331**
Hallowell, E. Shine **658.3**
Johnson, J. WorkParty **650.1**
Lyons, D. Lab rats **302.3**
Shell, G. Springboard **650.1**
JOB SATISFACTION -- PSYCHOLOGICAL ASPECTS
Webb, C. How to have a good day **650.1**
JOB VACANCIES -- UNITED STATES -- INFORMATION SERVICES
Jerrard, J. Crisis in employment **025.5**
JOBRANI, MAZIYAR, 1972-
Jobrani, M. I'm not a terrorist, but I've played one on

McPherson, J. Battle cry of freedom **973.7**
McPherson, J. This mighty scourge **973.7**
Mostert, N. Line upon a wind **940.2**
Murray, W. A savage war **973.7**
Neiberg, M. Potsdam **940.53**
O'Donnell, P. Washington's immortals **973.3**
The Oxford illustrated history of the Third Reich **943.086**
Philbrick, N. Bunker Hill **973.3**
Philbrick, N. Valiant ambition **973.3**
Roberts, A. Masters and commanders **940.5322**
Scott, J. Target Tokyo **940.54**
Stark, P. Young Washington **B**
Stone, N. World War One **940.3**
Vogel, S. Through the perilous fight **973.5**
Ward, G. The Civil War **973.7**
The West Point history of World War II. **940.53**
Wilson, K. Blood and fears **940.54**
Zambone, A. Daniel Morgan **B**

MILITARY HISTORY -- 19TH CENTURY

Ash, S. Firebrand of liberty **973.7**
Goodheart, A. 1861 **973.7**
Sides, H. Blood and thunder **978**
Snow, R. Iron dawn **973.7**
Talty, S. The illustrious dead **940.2**
Wert, J. Cavalryman of the lost cause **B**
Woodworth, S. Sherman **B**

MILITARY HISTORY -- 20TH CENTURY

Arnold, J. Jungle of snakes **355.02**
Englund, P. The beauty and the sorrow **940.309**
Faber, D. Munich, 1938 **940.53**
Hastings, M. Retribution **940.54**
Hedges, C. War is a force that gives us meaning **355.02**
Haynes, F. The lions of Iwo Jima **940.54**
Kilcullen, D. The accidental guerrilla **355.4**
Nelson, J. The Polar Bear expedition **947.084**
Thompson, M. The white war **940.3**

MILITARY HISTORY -- 21ST CENTURY

Kilcullen, D. The accidental guerrilla **355.4**

MILITARY HISTORY -- PICTORIAL WORKS

War **355.0209**

MILITARY HISTORY, MODERN

Kennedy, P. The rise and fall of the great powers **909.82**

MILITARY HISTORY

The book of war **355**
Voices of war **355**
The West Point history of the Civil War **973.7**
The West Point history of World War II. **940.53**
Atkinson, R. An army at dawn **940.54**
Atkinson, R. Crusade **956.7044**
Atkinson, R. In the company of soldiers **956.7044**
Atkinson, R. The day of battle **940.54**
Bacevich, A. America's war for the greater Middle East **956.05**
Beevor, A. D-day **940.54**
Boot, M. War made new **355.0209**
Brighton, T. Patton, Montgomery, Rommel **B**
Burke, E. Reflections on the revolution in France **944.04**
Cohen, E. Conquered into liberty **355.009747**
Cotton, T. Sacred duty **355.6**
Crowley, R. City of fortune **945**
Evans, R. The Third Reich at war **940.53**
Feifer, G. The great gamble **958.104**
France, J. Perilous glory **355**
Gardner, M. Rough riders **973.91**
Giangreco, D. Hell to pay **940.54**
Goldsworthy, A. Pax Romana **930**
Hanson, V. The soul of battle **355**
Hanson, V. The father of us all **355.0209**
Hastings, M. Catastrophe 1914 **940.3**
Holland, J. Battle of Britain **940.54**
Hopkins, W. The Pacific War **940.54**
Kagan, D. The Peloponnesian War **930**
Keegan, J. Fields of battle **970**
Keegan, J. The American Civil War **973.7**
Klein, M. A call to arms **940.53**
Korda, M. With wings like eagles **940.54**
Lieven, D. Russia against Napoleon **940.2**
Mansoor, P. Baghdad at sunrise **B**
McElya, M. The politics of mourning **975.5**
McNamara, R. In retrospect **959.704**
McPherson, J. For cause and comrades **973.7**
McPherson, J. Drawn with the sword **973.7**
Morgan, T. Valley of death **959.704**
Morris, I. War! what is it good for? **303.6**
Nolan, C. The allure of battle **355.409**
Norman, M. Tears in the darkness **940.54**
Olson, L. Citizens of London **940.54012**
Parker, G. Global crisis **909**
Plokhy, S. Yalta **940.53**
Preston, D. Eight days at Yalta **940.53**
Reeves, R. Daring young men **943**
Snow, P. When Britain burned the White House **975.3**
Stephenson, M. The last full measure **305.9**
Ward, G. The Vietnam War **959.704**
Weinberg, G. A world at arms **940.53**

MILITARY INTELLIGENCE

Andrew, C. The secret world **327.1209**
Boot, M. The road not taken **B**
Copeland, B. Turing **B**
Draper, R. To start a war **956.7044**
Fagone, J. The woman who smashed codes **B**
Hastings, M. The secret war **940.54**
Macintyre, B. Operation Mincemeat **940.54**
Meltzer, B. The first conspiracy **973.4**
Soufan, A. The black banners declassified **363.325**

MILITARY INTELLIGENCE -- GREAT BRITAIN

Neitzel, S. Soldaten **940.54**

MILITARY INTELLIGENCE -- SOVIET UNION

Ohler, N. The Bohemians **940.53**

MILITARY INTELLIGENCE OFFICERS -- UNITED STATES

Willner, N. Forty autumns **B**

MILITARY INTERROGATION

Edmonds, B. God is not here **B**

Winchester, S. The professor and the madman **B**

MURRAY, LIZ, 1980-

Murray, L. Breaking night **B**

MURRAY, PAULI, 1910-1985

Rosenberg, R. Jane Crow **B**

MURRAY, PAULI, 1910-1985 FRIENDS AND ASSOCIATES

Bell-Scott, P. The firebrand and the First Lady **920**

MURROW, EDWARD R., 1908-1965

Edwards, B. Edward R. Murrow and the birth of broadcast journalism **B**

Edwards, B. Edward R. Murrow and the birth of broadcast journalism **B**

Olson, L. Citizens of London **940.54012**

MUSCLES -- ANATOMY -- ENCYCLOPEDIAS

Liebman, H. Encyclopedia of exercise anatomy **613.7**

MUSE, TOBY

Muse, T. Kilo **363.4509861**

MUSEE DU LOUVRE -- HISTORY

Gardner, J. The Louvre **700.9**

The **muses** go to school **700.71**

MUSEUM CURATORS

Forbes, S. Sex in the museum **B**

Obrist, H. Ways of curating **B**

Stourton, J. Kenneth Clark **B**

MUSEUM OF MODERN ART (NEW YORK, N.Y.) PHOTOGRAPH COLLECTIONS

Photography at MoMA. **770**

MUSEUM OF SEX, NEW YORK

Forbes, S. Sex in the museum **B**

A **museum** of their own Holladay, W. **704**

MUSEUM THEFTS -- NORWAY

Dolnick, E. The rescue artist **364.16**

MUSEUMS

Conniff, R. House of lost worlds **069**

Ewing, H. The lost world of James Smithson **B**

Holladay, W. A museum of their own **704**

The J. Paul Getty Museum and its collections **708.19**

Obrist, H. Ways of curating **B**

Wilkins, R. Long road to hard truth **069**

MUSHERS -- ALASKA

Paulsen, G. Winterdance **B**

MUSHROOM GROWING

Russell, S. The essential guide to cultivating mushrooms **635**

MUSHROOMS

Jacobs, R. The truffle underground **381**

Russell, S. The essential guide to cultivating mushrooms **635**

MUSHROOMS -- NORTH AMERICA -- IDENTIFICATION

McKnight, K. A field guide to mushrooms, North America **579.6**

MUSHROOMS -- NORTH AMERICA -- PICTORIAL WORKS

McKnight, K. A field guide to mushrooms, North America **579.6**

MUSIC

A basic music library **16.78**

Adams, J. Hallelujah junction **B**

Burton-Hill, C. Year of wonder **780.9**

Dyer, G. Otherwise known as the human condition **824.914**

Geck, M. Robert Schumann **B**

Gioia, T. Delta blues **781.6430976**

Glass, P. Words without music **B**

Guralnick, P. Looking to get lost **920**

Guralnick, P. Sam Phillips **B**

Kym, M. Gone **B**

McNally, D. On Highway **61** **781.64**

Morris, E. This living hand **973**

Pollack, H. George Gershwin **B**

Ratliff, B. The jazz ear **781.65092**

Wilson, B. I am Brian Wilson **B**

Music **780.9**

Music Gioia, T. **780.9**

MUSIC -- 18TH CENTURY -- HISTORY AND CRITICISM

Rosen, C. The classical style **780.9**

MUSIC -- 19TH CENTURY -- HISTORY AND CRITICISM

Sachs, H. The Ninth **784.2**

MUSIC -- 20TH CENTURY -- BIO-BIBLIOGRAPHY -- DICTIONARIES

Musicians & composers of the 20th century **780.92**

MUSIC -- 20TH CENTURY -- HISTORY AND CRITICISM

Day, T. A century of recorded music **780**

Young, R. Electric Eden **781.62**

MUSIC -- DICTIONARIES

All music guide to classical music **016.78026**

Hoffman, M. The NPR classical music companion **780.3**

MUSIC -- DISCOGRAPHY

All music guide to classical music **016.78026**

MUSIC -- HISTORY

Wald, E. American epic **781.64**

MUSIC -- HISTORY AND CRITICISM

Bullock, D. David Bowie made me gay **780.86**

Chinen, N. Playing changes **781.6509**

Duncan, D. Country music **781.642**

Grout, D. A history of western music **780.9**

Kundera, M. Encounter **809**

Mannes, E. The power of music **781**

Mauceri, J. For the love of music **781.1**

Moody, R. On celestial music **780.9**

Murakami, H. Absolutely on music **B**

Music **780.9**

Ross, A. Listen to this **780**

The Oxford American book of great music writing **781.64**

Ward, G. Jazz **781.65**

MUSIC -- INFLUENCE

Cross, C. Here we are now **782.42166092**

Doggett, P. Electric shock **781.64**

Wald, E. Dylan goes electric! **782.42164**

Wald, E. How the Beatles destroyed rock 'n' roll **781.64**

N

-- HISTORY
Light, M. 100 suns **779**
NUCLEAR WEAPONS -- UNITED STATES
Schlosser, E. Command and control **363.17**
NUCLEAR WEAPONS -- UNITED STATES -- HISTORY
Norris, R. Racing for the bomb **B**
NUCLEAR WEAPONS DEVELOPMENT
Nelson, C. The age of radiance **539.7**
NUCLEAR WEAPONS DEVELOPMENT -- MORAL AND ETHICAL ASPECTS
Preston, D. Before the fallout **303.48**
NUCLEAR WEAPONS POLICY -- HISTORY
Ellsberg, D. The doomsday machine **B**
NUDELMAN, MEYER
Nuland, S. Lost in America **B**
Nudge Thaler, R. **330.01**
NULAND, SHERWIN B
Nuland, S. Lost in America **B**
NULAND, SHERWIN B. FAMILY
Nuland, S. Lost in America **B**
NUMBER CONCEPT
Bellos, A. Here's looking at Euclid **513**
Clegg, B. Are numbers real? **510**
Posamentier, A. Numbers **513.5**
NUMBER THEORY
Ash, A. Elliptic tales **515**
Clegg, B. Are numbers real? **510**
Parker, M. Things to make and do in the fourth dimension **510**
Singh, S. The Simpsons and their mathematical secrets **510**
NUMBER THEORY -- HISTORY
Livio, M. The equation that couldn't be solved **512**
NUMBER THEORY -- POPULAR WORKS
Conway, J. The book of numbers **512**
NUMBERS
Aczel, A. Finding zero **513.5**
Havil, J. The irrationals **512.7**
Livio, M. The golden ratio **516.2**
Parker, M. Things to make and do in the fourth dimension **510**
Posamentier, A. Numbers **513.5**
Tammet, D. Thinking in numbers **510**
Numbers Posamentier, A. **513.5**
NUMBERS -- SOCIAL ASPECTS
Bellos, A. Here's looking at Euclid **513**
The **numbers** game Anderson, C. **796.334**
Numbers rule Szpiro, G. **510**
NUMERALS
Aczel, A. Finding zero **513.5**
NUMERATION -- HISTORY
Tammet, D. Thinking in numbers **510**
NUMEROLOGY -- HISTORY
Gardner, M. Did Adam and Eve have navels? **500**
NUNS
Prejean, H. River of fire **B**
NUNS -- CALCUTTA, INDIA
Spink, K. Mother Teresa **B**
NUNS -- DRAMA
Shanley, J. Doubt **812**
NUR JAHAN, EMPRESS, CONSORT OF JAHANGIR, EMPEROR OF HINDUSTAN, D. 1645
Lal, R. Empress **B**
NUREMBERG WAR CRIME TRIALS, 1946-1949
Sands, P. East West Street **345**
NUREMBERG, GERMANY -- SOCIAL LIFE AND CUSTOMS -- 16TH CENTURY
Harrington, J. The faithful executioner **B**
Nureyev Kavanagh, J. **B**
NUREYEV, RUDOLF, 1938-1993
Kavanagh, J. Nureyev **B**
NURSE AND PATIENT
Brown, T. The shift **B**
NURSERY RHYMES
Brown, M. Marc Brown's playtime rhymes **398.8**
The Oxford dictionary of nursery rhymes **398.8**
NURSES
Brown, T. The shift **B**
Case, M. How to treat people **B**
Lineberry, C. The secret rescue **940.54**
NURSES -- ENGLAND
Bostridge, M. Florence Nightingale **B**
NURSING
Case, M. How to treat people **B**
The **nursing** mother's companion Huggins, K. **649**
NURTURING BEHAVIOR
Taylor, S. The tending instinct **304.5**
NUSSBAUM, EMILY, 1966-
Nussbaum, E. I like to watch **791.45**
NUSSEIBEH, SARI
Nusseibeh, S. Once upon a country **B**
NUTCRACKER (BALLET) -- PERFORMANCE
Kessler, L. Raising the barre **B**
NUTRITION
Barrett, P. Trim healthy mama trim healthy table **613.2**
Bittman, M. The food matters cookbook **641.3**
Britton, S. Naturally nourished **641.5**
Campbell, T. The China study **613.2**
Carroll, A. The bad food bible **613.2**
Curry, K. Fit men cook **641.5**
Davis, B. Becoming vegan **613.2**
DiSpirito, R. Rocco's healthy+delicious **641.3**
Fuhrman, J. Eat to live quick & easy cookbook **641.5**
Hartwig, M. Food freedom forever **613.2**
Hartwig, M. The whole30 fast & easy **641.5**
Hartwig, M. The Whole30 slow cooker **641.5**
Hay, D. Life in balance **641.5**
Hunt, L. Help yourself **641.5**
Kass, S. Eat a little better **641.3**
Krieger, E. The food you crave **641.5**
Le, S. One hundred million years of food **641.3**
Masley, S. The better brain solution **612.8**
Moody, L. Healthier together **641.5**
The new American plate cookbook **641.5**

PAROLE OFFICERS
Hardy, J. The second chance club **B**
PAROLEES
Hardy, J. The second chance club **B**
PARQUE NACIONAL DA GORONGOSA (MOZAMBIQUE)
Hanes, S. White man's game **333.95**
Wilson, E. A window on eternity **333.95**
PARRADO, NANDO, 1949-
Parrado, N. Miracle in the Andes **982**
PARRAVANI, CARA
Parravani, C. Her **B**
PARRAVANI, CHRISTA
Parravani, C. Her **B**
Parravani, C. Loved and wanted **B**
PARSONS, JACK, 1914-1952
Pendle, G. Strange angel **B**
PART-TIME EMPLOYMENT
Mulcahy, D. The gig economy **650.1**
The **particle** at the end of the universe Carroll, S. **539.7**
Particle physics brick by brick Still, B. **539.7**
PARTICLES (NUCLEAR PHYSICS)
Bowen, M. The telescope in the ice **522**
Butterworth, J. Atom land **539.7**
Carroll, S. The particle at the end of the universe **539.7**
Close, F. The infinity puzzle **530.14**
Gilder, L. The age of entanglement **530.12**
Kumar, M. Quantum **530.12**
Lederman, L. Beyond the god particle **539.7**
Randall, L. Warped passages **530**
Randall, L. Knocking on heaven's door **500**
Still, B. Particle physics brick by brick **539.7**
PARTIES
Hudson, K. Pretty fun **642**
PARTIES
Hudson, K. Pretty fun **642**
The **parties** versus the people Edwards, M. **320.973**
Parting the waters Branch, T. **B**
PARTISANSHIP
Safer, J. I love you, but I hate your politics **158.2**
PARTISANSHIP -- POLITICAL ASPECTS -- UNITED STATES
Zelizer, J. Burning down the house **328.73**
PARTITO NAZIONALE FASCISTA (ITALY)
Corner, P. The Fascist Party and popular opinion in Mussolini's Italy **945.091**
PARTNER ABUSE
Ali, N. I am Nujood, age 10 and divorced **B**
Selvaratnam, T. Assume nothing **B**
PARTON, DOLLY, 1946- INFLUENCE
Smarsh, S. She come by it natural **782.421642092**
PARTY AFFILIATION -- SOCIAL ASPECTS
Safer, J. I love you, but I hate your politics **158.2**
PARTY DECORATIONS
Calderone, A. Cook beautiful **641.5**
Party of one Holmes, D. **B**
PASCAL, BLAISE, 1623-1662 CORRESPONDENCE
Devlin, K. The unfinished game **519.2**
The **passage** of power Caro, R. **B**
Passage to Juneau Raban, J. **917.98**
PASSARLAY, GULWALI
Passarlay, G. The lightless sky **B**
PASSENGER SHIPS
Larson, E. Dead wake **940.4**
PASSENGER SHIPS -- HISTORY -- 20TH CENTURY
Henry, J. Great White Fleet **387.24309710904**
PASSING (FOOTBALL)
Gwynne, S. The perfect pass **920**
PASSING (IDENTITY)
Jacoby, K. The strange career of William Ellis **B**
Talusan, M. Fairest **B**
Tisserand, M. Krazy **B**
Toorpakai, M. A different kind of daughter **B**
Passing on the comfort Keuning-Tichelaar, A. **B**
The **passion** economy Davidson, A. **330.9**
A **passion** for leadership Gates, R. **B**
A **passion** for nature ; the life of John Muir Worster, D. **B**
A **passion** for Paris Downie, D. **B**
Passionate minds Pierpont, C. **810.9**
PASSOVER COOKING
Amster, L. The New York Times passover cookbook **641.5**
PASTA
Louis, J. Pasta by hand **641.82**
Pasta Carluccio, A. **641.82**
Pasta by hand Louis, J. **641.82**
Pasta Grannies Bennison, V. **641.594**
Pasta modern Segan, F. **641.82**
PASTA PRODUCTS -- ITALY
Zanini De Vita, O. Encyclopedia of pasta **664**
PASTA PRODUCTS -- ITALY -- HISTORY
Zanini De Vita, O. Encyclopedia of pasta **664**
PASTEL DRAWING -- TECHNIQUE
Eagle, E. Pastel painting atelier **741.2**
McKinley, R. Pastel pointers **741.2**
Price, M. Painting with pastels **741.2**
Pastel painting atelier Eagle, E. **741.2**
Pastel pointers McKinley, R. **741.2**
PASTERNAK, BORIS LEONIDOVICH, 1890-1960 CENSORSHIP
Finn, P. The Zhivago affair **891.73**
PASTERNAK, BORIS LEONIDOVICH, 1890-1960 -- DOKTOR ZHIVAGO
Finn, P. The Zhivago affair **891.73**
PASTORAL COUNSELING (JUDAISM)
Kushner, H. When bad things happen to good people **296.3**
PASTORAL POETRY
Virgil, 7. The eclogues of Virgil **871**
PASTRY
Ansel, D. Dominique Ansel **641.86**
Barrow, C. When pies fly **641.86**
Barrow, C. Pie squared **641.86**
Beranbaum, R. Rose's baking basics **641.81**

Reynaud, S. Pies and tarts for dinner and dessert **641.86**
Ricciardi, H. Magpie **641.86**
Weinstein, B. A la mode **641.86**
Pies and tarts for dinner and dessert Reynaud, S. **641.86**
PIG FARMING
Estabrook, B. Pig tales **636.4**
Pig tales Estabrook, B. **636.4**
The **pigeon** tunnel Le Carre, J. **B**
PIGS AS PETS
Jenkins, S. Happily ever Esther **920**
PIGS AS PETS -- NEW HAMPSHIRE -- ANECDOTES
Montgomery, S. The good good pig **B**
PIGS
Montgomery, S. The good good pig **B**
PILATE, PONTIUS, 1ST CENT
Schiavone, A. Pontius Pilate **B**
PILATES
Isacowitz, R. Pilates **613.7**
Pilates Isacowitz, R. **613.7**
Pilates for breast cancer survivors Aaronson, N. **616.99**
PILECKI, WITOLD, 1901-1948
Fairweather, J. The volunteer **B**
PILGRIM (BRIG)
Dana, R. Two years before the mast **B**
Pilgrim at Tinker Creek Dillard, A. **508**
Pilgrim's wilderness Kizzia, T. **B**
Pilgrimage Shriver, M. **B**
A **pilgrimage** to eternity Egan, T. **263**
PILGRIMS (NEW ENGLAND SETTLERS)
Bradford, W. Of Plymouth Plantation, 1620-1647 **974.4**
Bunker, N. Making haste from Babylon **974.4**
Fraser, R. The Mayflower **B**
Philbrick, N. Mayflower **973.2**
Silverman, D. This land is their land **974.4**
Whittock, M. Mayflower lives **974.4**
PILGRIMS AND PILGRIMAGES
Egan, T. A pilgrimage to eternity **263**
Feiler, B. Walking the Bible **915**
Mockett, M. Where the dead pause, and the Japanese say goodbye **B**
Mullins, E. The four roads to Heaven **263**
Thubron, C. To a mountain in Tibet **B**
PILGRIMS AND PILGRIMAGES, CHRISTIAN
Langland, W. Piers Plowman **821**
PILGRIMS AND PILGRIMAGES, CHRISTIAN -- ISRAEL
Rodriguez, R. Darling **B**
Pilgrims in their own land Marty, M. **200**
Pilgrims of the vertical Taylor, J. **796.52**
PILLAGE
Childs, C. Finders keepers **930**
Felch, J. Chasing Aphrodite **930**
Rydell, A. The book thieves **027**
Pillar of fire Branch, T. **B**
PILLARS OF ISLAM
Ramadan, T. Introduction to Islam **297**
Pillows, curtains, & shades step by step **747**
PILOTS
Butler, S. East to the dawn **B**
Chivers, C. The fighters **920**
Hampton, D. The flight **629.13**
Jackson, J. Atlantic fever **629.13**
Vanhoenacker, M. Skyfaring **B**
PILOTS -- UNITED STATES
Barbree, J. Neil Armstrong **B**
Bruning, J. Indestructible **B**
Groom, W. The aviators **920**
Hardesty, V. Black wings **920**
Lindbergh, C. The spirit of St. Louis **B**
Wilson, K. Blood and fears **940.54**
Winters, K. Amelia Earhart **B**
PILOTS AND PILOTAGE
Chapman piloting & seamanship **623.88**
PILOTS' SPOUSES -- UNITED STATES
Hertog, S. Anne Morrow Lindbergh **B**
Pilsner Acitelli, T. **338.7**
PIMPS
Gifford, J. Street poison **B**
Pin action Manzione, G. **B**
PINCHOT, GIFFORD, 1865-1946
Egan, T. The big burn **973.911**
Miller, C. Gifford Pinchot and the making of modern environmentalism **B**
PINCUS, GREGORY, 1903-1967
Eig, J. The birth of the pill **920**
PINDAR TRANSLATIONS INTO ENGLISH
Pindar The complete odes **885**
PINE RIDGE INDIAN RESERVATION, SOUTH DAKOTA
Bunnell, D. Good Friday on the rez **B**
PINE, EMILIE
Pine, E. Notes to self **B**
PINFIELD, MATT
Pinfield, M. All these things that I've done **B**
PINIELLA, LOU, 1943-
Piniella, L. Lou **B**
Pink brain, blue brain Eliot, L. **612.6**
The **pink** line Gevisser, M. **306.76**
PINKERTON'S NATIONAL DETECTIVE AGENCY
Meltzer, B. The Lincoln conspiracy **973.7092**
PINKERTON, ALLAN, 1819-1884
Meltzer, B. The Lincoln conspiracy **973.7092**
Waller, D. Lincoln's spies **973.7**
PINN, RONALD
O'Hagan, A. The secret life **920**
PINTER, HAROLD, 1930-
Fraser, A. Must you go? **B**
Pintxos Hirigoyen, G. **641.8**
PIONEER FAMILIES
McCullough, D. The pioneers **920**
Pioneer girl Wilder, L. **B**
The **pioneer** woman cooks Drummond, R. **641.5**
PIONEER WOMEN
Inskeep, S. Imperfect union **B**
McDowell, M. The world of Laura Ingalls Wilder **B**

Hennessey, S. Unmaking the presidency **973.933092**
Hitchens, C. Thomas Jefferson **B**
Kaspit, B. The Netanyahu years **B**
Kennedy, E. True compass **B**
Khlevniuk, O. Stalin **B**
Kurtz-Phelan, D. The China mission **951.04**
The Lincoln anthology **B**
Mazower, M. Hitler's empire **940.53**
McPherson, J. Tried by war **973.7092**
Morris, M. A great and terrible king **B**
Morris, M. King John **B**
Myers, S. The new tsar **B**
Newton, M. Enemy of the state **345.567**
O'Toole, P. The moralist **B**
Ostrovsky, A. The invention of Russia **947.086**
Our Lincoln **B**
Pakula, H. The last empress **B**
Posner, E. The demagogue's playbook **306.20973**
Raphael, R. Mr. president **352.230973**
Rappleye, C. Herbert Hoover in the White House **B**
Reynolds, D. Waking giant **973.5**
Roberts, A. Napoleon **B**
Ryback, T. Hitler's private library **27**
Sherratt, Y. Hitler's philosophers **193**
Shesol, J. Supreme power **347.73**
Sweeney, J. North Korea undercover **951.9305**
Thomas, E. Being Nixon **B**
Traub, J. John Quincy Adams **B**
White, R. A. Lincoln **B**
Wills, G. James Madison **B**
Wills, G. Lincoln at Gettysburg **973.7**
Wolff, M. Fire and fury **973.933092**
Woodward, B. Fear **973.933092**

POLITICAL LEADERSHIP -- GREAT BRITAIN
Moore, C. Margaret Thatcher **B**
Moore, C. Margaret Thatcher **B**

POLITICAL LEADERSHIP -- PHILOSOPHY
Bueno de Mesquita, B. The dictator's handbook **303.3**
Viroli, M. How to choose a leader **303.3**

POLITICAL LEADERSHIP -- SOUTH AFRICA -- CASE STUDIES
Gevisser, M. A legacy of liberation **B**

POLITICAL LEADERSHIP -- UNITED STATES
Emanuel, R. The nation city **352.23**
Goodwin, D. Leadership in turbulent times **973.09**
Roll, D. George Marshall **B**
Souza, P. Shade **973.932092**

POLITICAL LEADERSHIP -- UNITED STATES -- CASE STUDIES
Clarke, T. JFK's last hundred days **B**
Goodwin, D. Team of rivals **973.7**
Mann, J. The rebellion of Ronald Reagan **973.927092**

POLITICAL LEADERSHIP -- UNITED STATES -- HISTORY
Avlon, J. Washington's farewell **973.4**
Beschloss, M. Presidents of war **355.00973**
Burlingame, M. Abraham Lincoln **B**
McPherson, J. Abraham Lincoln **B**

POLITICAL LEADERSHIP -- UNITED STATES -- HISTORY -- 19TH CENTURY
Brands, H. Andrew Jackson, his life and times **B**
Meacham, J. American lion **B**
Remini, R. Andrew Jackson **B**

POLITICAL LEADERSHIP -- UNITED STATES -- HISTORY -- 20TH CENTURY
Winik, J. 1944 **940.53**

POLITICAL OBLIGATION
Sunstein, C. Impeachment **342.73**

POLITICAL ORATORY
Blumenthal, S. Wrestling with his angel **B**
Cohen, A. Two Days in June **B**

Political order and political decay Fukuyama, F. **320.1**

POLITICAL PARTICIPATION
AOC **B**
Abrams, S. Our time is now **324.60973**
Can it happen here? **320.473**
Achen, C. Democracy for realists **320.973**
Barkan, A. Eyes to the wind **B**
Cadava, G. The Hispanic Republican **324.2734089**
Gordon-Reed, A. Most blessed of the patriarchs **B**
Ingraham, L. Billionaire at the barricades **324.973**
Lupick, T. Fighting for space **362.29150971133**
Palmieri, J. She proclaims **305.42**
Sanders, S. No, you shut up **323.173**
Waldman, M. The fight to vote **324.6**

POLITICAL PARTICIPATION -- PHILOSOPHY
Viroli, M. How to choose a leader **303.3**

POLITICAL PARTICIPATION -- UNITED STATES
Litt, D. Democracy in one book or less **321.8**
Moscatello, C. See Jane win **320.082**
Tomasky, M. If we can keep it **320.973**

POLITICAL PARTIES
Dionne, E. Why the right went wrong **320.520973**
Fountain, B. Beautiful country burn again **324.973**
Kaplan, D. The most dangerous branch **347.73**
Kornacki, S. The red and the blue **306.20973**
Nussbaum, M. The monarchy of fear **306.20973**
Pfeiffer, D. Yes we (still) can **320.973**
Taibbi, M. Hate Inc. **302.230973**
Tocqueville, A. Democracy in America **320.973**
Wood, G. Friends divided **920**

POLITICAL PARTIES -- GERMANY -- HISTORY -- 20TH CENTURY
Turner, H. Hitler's thirty days to power **943.086**

POLITICAL PARTIES -- UNITED STATES
Avlon, J. Washington's farewell **973.4**
Edwards, M. The parties versus the people **320.973**
Stevens, S. It was all a lie **324.2734**

POLITICAL PARTIES -- UNITED STATES -- HISTORY
Morone, J. Republic of wrath **320.973**

POLITICAL PERSECUTION
Amis, M. Koba the dread **947.084**
Applebaum, A. Iron curtain **947**
Gessen, M. The future is history **947.086**

Q

R

S

SOCIAL BEHAVIOR IN ANIMALS
Bekoff, M. Wild justice **591.5**
Goodall, J. In the shadow of man **599.8**
Wood, L. The last giants **599.67**
SOCIAL BEHAVIOR IN CHIMPANZEES
Goodall, J. In the shadow of man **599.8**
SOCIAL BEHAVIOR IN INSECTS
Holldobler, B. The superorganism **595.7**
SOCIAL CHANGE
Aczel, A. The artist and the mathematician **B**
Adichie, C. We should all be feminists **305.42**
Bidwell, D. When one religion isn't enough **261.2**
Blanning, T. Frederick the Great **B**
Bordewich, F. Congress at war **324.2734**
Brill, S. Tailspin **306.0973**
Brinkley, J. Cambodia's curse **959.604**
Buckley, G. The Black Calhouns **920**
Burak, A. Power play **794.8**
Chemaly, S. Rage becomes her **155.3**
Cooke, J. The other side of paradise **972.91**
Cowen, T. The complacent class **305.5**
Demick, B. Eat the Buddha **951**
Dower, J. Ways of forgetting, ways of remembering **940.53**
Dyson, M. What truth sounds like **305.800973**
Englund, W. March 1917 **940.5309**
Ferguson, N. The square and the tower **302.309**
Figes, O. A people's tragedy **947.08**
Fountain, B. Beautiful country burn again **324.973**
Fraser, A. The King and the Catholics **941.07**
Guha, R. Gandhi **B**
Hartman, S. Wayward lives, beautiful experiments **305.48**
Herman, A. 1917 **940.3**
Hessler, P. The buried **962.05**
Ingrassia, P. Engines of change **629.222**
Kan, K. Under red skies **B**
Kelly, H. Jane Austen, the secret radical **823**
Kennedy, R. RFK **973.92**
Klineberg, S. Prophetic city **303.40973**
Landrieu, M. In the shadow of statues **B**
McPherson, J. The war that forged a nation **973.7**
Moore, S. Paradise of the Pacific **996.9**
Mortimer, I. Millennium **909**
Moss, D. Democracy **320.473**
Naim, M. The end of power **303.3**
Nye, B. Everything all at once **B**
O'Rourke, P. None of my business **332**
Owens, L. Love and rage **152.4**
Perry, I. May we forever stand **782.25**
Popkin, J. A new world begins **944.04**
Reid-Henry, S. Empire of democracy **320**
Reiss, B. Wild nights **616.8**
Richards, S. Lost and found in Russia **B**
Russell, G. The ship of dreams **910.91**
Sharma, R. The rise and fall of nations **330.9**
Simon, J. Eisenhower vs. Warren **347.73**
Solomon, A. Far and away **B**
St. John, W. Outcasts united **B**
Szablowski, W. Dancing bears **947.086**
Taubman, W. Gorbachev **B**
Toffler, A. Future shock **303.4**
Traister, R. Good and mad **305.420973**
Woods, R. Prisoners of hope **B**
Zeitz, J. Building the Great Society **B**
Zoepf, K. Excellent daughters **305.42**
SOCIAL CHANGE -- CASE STUDIES
Diamond, J. Collapse **304.2**
SOCIAL CHANGE -- CHINA
Osnos, E. Age of ambition **951.06**
SOCIAL CHANGE -- EASTERN EUROPE -- HISTORY -- 20TH CENTURY
Kotkin, S. Uncivil society **947**
SOCIAL CHANGE -- EUROPE
Jarausch, K. Out of ashes **940.5**
SOCIAL CHANGE -- INDIA -- HISTORY -- 20TH CENTURY
Karnad, R. Farthest field **940.54**
Raghavan, S. India's war **940.54**
SOCIAL CHANGE -- MIDDLE EAST
MacFarquhar, N. The media relations department of Hizbollah wishes you a happy birthday **965.04**
SOCIAL CHANGE -- PSYCHOLOGICAL ASPECTS
Pipher, M. The green boat **303.4**
SOCIAL CHANGE -- RUSSIA
Pomerantsev, P. Nothing is true and everything is possible **B**
SOCIAL CHANGE -- SOUTHERN STATES -- HISTORY -- 19TH CENTURY
Johnson, W. River of dark dreams **305.800977**
SOCIAL CHANGE -- SOVIET UNION -- HISTORY
Kotkin, S. Uncivil society **947**
SOCIAL CHANGE -- UNITED STATES
Chang, J. We gon' be alright **305.800973**
Gray, E. A girl's guide to joining the resistance **303.48**
Zoellner, T. The national road **973**
SOCIAL CHANGE -- UNITED STATES -- HISTORY -- 19TH CENTURY
Howe, D. What hath God wrought **973.5**
SOCIAL CHANGE -- UNITED STATES -- HISTORY -- 20TH CENTURY
Tirella, J. Tomorrow-land **607**
Ziegelman, J. A square meal **641.5973**
SOCIAL CLASSES
Biss, E. Having and being had **306.3**
Brown, D. Paradise lost **B**
Cadillac Man Land of the lost souls **B**
Clancy, T. The Clancys of Queens **B**
Cowen, T. The complacent class **305.5**
Eddo-Lodge, R. Why I'm no longer talking to white people about race **305.8**
Frank, T. Rendezvous with oblivion **306.20973**
Freeland, C. Plutocrats **305.5**
Fritzsche, P. Hitler's first hundred days **943.086**
Galeano, E. Mirrors **909**

Huang, Y. Charlie Chan **B**
Jobrani, M. I'm not a terrorist, but I've played one on TV **B**
Orth, S. Couchsurfing in Iran **955.06**
Sandler, L. One and only **306.874**
Tanenbaum, L. I am not a slut **305.235**
Young, K. Bunk **177**

STEREOTYPES (SOCIAL PSYCHOLOGY) -- SOCIAL ASPECTS
Nugent, B. American nerd **305.9**

STERN, AMANDA
Stern, A. Little panic **B**
Stern, A. Little panic **B**

STERN, FRITZ, 1926-
Stern, F. Five Germanys I have known **B**
Stern, F. Five Germanys I have known **B**

STERN, JESSICA, 1958-
Stern, J. My war criminal **B**

STESICHORUS. GRYONIS ADAPTATIONS
Carson, A. Red doc> **811**

Steve Jobs Isaacson, W. **B**

STEVEDORES
Fisher, J. On the Irish waterfront **331.7**

Steven Raichlen's BBQ USA Raichlen, S. **641.5**
Steven Raichlen's Planet Barbecue! Raichlen, S. **641.7**
Steven Spielberg Haskell, M. **B**

STEVENS, GEORGE, 1904-1975
Harris, M. Five came back **791.4302**

STEVENS, JOHN CHRISTOPHER, 1960-2012
Richter, P. The ambassadors **327.73017**

STEVENS, JOHN PAUL, 1920-2019
Stevens, J. The making of a justice **B**
Stevens, J. The making of a justice **B**

STEVENSON, BRYAN
Stevenson, B. Just mercy **B**
Stevenson, B. Just mercy **B**

STEWART, CHRIS, 1950- HOMES AND HAUNTS ALPUJARRA REGION, SPAIN
Stewart, C. Driving over lemons **946**

STEWART, JAMES, 1908-1997
Eyman, S. Hank and Jim **920**

STEWART, RORY
Stewart, R. The prince of the marshes **B**

STEWS
One pot **641.82**
Volger, L. Bowl **641.81**

Stickmaking handbook Jones, A. **736**
Sticks and stones Bazelon, E. **302.34**
Sticky fingers Hagan, J. **B**

STIEGLITZ, ALFRED, 1864-1946
Burke, C. Foursome **920**

STIEGLITZ, ALFRED, 1864-1946 CATALOGS
Alfred Stieglitz **770**

Stiff Roach, M. **611**

STIGMA (SOCIAL PSYCHOLOGY)
Fessler, P. Carville's cure **362.19699**

Stiletto network Ryckman, P. **331.4**
Still foolin' 'em Crystal, B. **B**
Still here Jacobs, A. **B**
Still life Milgrom, M. **590.75**
Still life with two dead peacocks and a girl Seuss, D. **811.6**
The **still** point of the turning world Rapp Black, E. **B**
Still woman enough Lynn, L. **B**

STILL-LIFE IN ART
Seuss, D. Still life with two dead peacocks and a girl **811.6**

STILLS (MOTION PICTURES) -- UNITED STATES
Longworth, K. Hollywood frame by frame **791.430973**

Stilwell and the American experience in China, 1911-45 Tuchman, B. **B**

STILWELL, JOSEPH WARREN, 1883-1946
Tuchman, B. Stilwell and the American experience in China, 1911-45 **B**

STIMSON, HENRY L. (HENRY LEWIS), 1867-1950
Jordan, J. American warlords **920**

Sting like a bee Montville, L. **B**
The **sting** of the wild Schmidt, J. **595.7**
Sting-ray afternoons Rushin, S. **B**
Stirring up fun with food Gellar, S. **641.5**
Stitch 'n bitch Stoller, D. **746.43**
Stitch 'n bitch superstar knitting Stoller, D. **746.43**
Stitches Small, D. **B**

STITCHES (SEWING)
Chanin, N. The geometry of hand-sewing **746.44**
Knight, E. 500 crochet stitches **746.43**
Knight, E. 750 knitting stitches **746.43**

STOCK CAR RACING
Busbee, J. Earnhardt nation **B**

STOCK MARKET
Henriques, D. A first-class catastrophe **332.64**
Nations, S. A history of the United States in five crashes **338.5**
Perino, M. The hellhound of Wall Street **330.973**
Schroeder, A. The snowball **B**
Shiller, R. Irrational exuberance **332.63**
Vaughan, L. Flash crash **B**

STOCK MARKET -- UNITED STATES -- HISTORY -- 20TH CENTURY
Mahar, M. Bull! **332.64**

STOCK MARKET CRASH, OCTOBER 1929
Galbraith, J. The great crash, 1929 **338.5**
Kennedy, D. Freedom from fear **973.91**
Perino, M. The hellhound of Wall Street **330.973**

STOCK MARKET CRASH, OCTOBER 1987
Henriques, D. A first-class catastrophe **332.64**

STOCKHOLDERS
Gramm, J. Dear chairman **659.2**

STOCKHOLM SYNDROME
King, D. Six days in August **364.15**
Toobin, J. American heiress **B**

STOCKHOLM, SWEDEN
King, D. Six days in August **364.15**

STOCKS
Bernstein, W. The investor's manifesto **332.6**

Shachtman, T. Absolute zero and the conquest of cold 536
THEROUX, ALEXANDER TRAVEL ESTONIA
Theroux, A. Estonia 947.98086
THEROUX, JESSICA TRAVEL ITALY
Theroux, J. Cooking with Italian grandmothers 641.594
THEROUX, PAUL
Theroux, P. On the plain of snakes 917
Theroux, P. Figures in a landscape **B**
THEROUX, PAUL TRAVEL
Theroux, P. Figures in a landscape **B**
THEROUX, PAUL TRAVEL AFRICA
Theroux, P. Dark star safari 916
THEROUX, PAUL TRAVEL ASIA
Theroux, P. The great railway bazaar 915
THEROUX, PAUL TRAVEL CHINA
Theroux, P. Riding the iron rooster 915
THEROUX, PAUL TRAVEL OCEANIA
Theroux, P. The happy isles of Oceania 919
THEROUX, PAUL TRAVEL SOUTH AMERICA
Theroux, P. The old Patagonian express 917
THEROUX, PAUL TRAVEL SOUTHERN STATES
Theroux, P. Deep South 975
These are my rivers Ferlinghetti, L. 811
These fevered days Ackmann, M. **B**
These truths Lepore, J. 973
THESSALONIKE, GREECE -- HISTORY
Mazower, M. Salonica, city of ghosts 949.5
They are already here Scoles, S. 001.942
They bled blue Turbow, J. 796.357
They can live in the desert but nowhere else Suny, R. 956.6
They fought like demons Blanton, D. 973.7
They left us everything Johnson, P. **B**
They made America Evans, H. 609.2
They marched into sunlight Maraniss, D. 959.704
They poured fire on us from the sky Deng, A. 962.404
They said it couldn't be done Coffey, W. 796.357
They told me not to take that job Levy, R. **B**
Thick Cottom, T. 301.092
THIEVES
Bilefsky, D. The last job 364.16
Guinn, J. Go down together **B**
Guinn, J. Go down together **B**
Johnson, K. The feather thief 364.16
Leerhsen, C. Butch Cassidy **B**
Thieves' road Mort, T. 978.3
The **thin** light of freedom Ayers, E. 975.5
Thing explainer Munroe, R. 500
The **thing** with feathers Strycker, N. 598
Things I should have told my daughter Cleage, P. **B**
Things I've been silent about Nafisi, A. **B**
Things my son needs to know about the world Backman, F. **B**
Things that are Leach, A. 508
Things that helped Friedmann, J. **B**
Things that make white people uncomfortable Bennett, M. 305.896
The **things** they cannot say Sites, K. 355.0092
Things to make and do in the fourth dimension Parker, M. 510
Things we didn't talk about when I was a girl Vanasco, J. **B**
Think Blackburn, S. 100
Think and grow rich Hill, N. 650.1
Think before you like Harrison, G. 302.30285
Think better, live better Osteen, J. 248.4
Think like a feminist Hay, C. 305.42
Think like a freak Levitt, S. 153.43
Think like a rocket scientist Varol, O. 650.1
Thinking differently Flink, D. 371.9
Thinking in bets Duke, A. 658.4
Thinking in numbers Tammet, D. 510
Thinking machines Dormehl, L. 006.309
A **thinking** person's guide to America's national parks 333.78
Thinking with type Lupton, E. 686.2
Thinking, fast and slow Kahneman, D. 153.4
The **third** chapter Lawrence-Lightfoot, S. 305.260973
The **third** coast Dyja, T. 977.3
The **third** plate Barber, D. 641.3
The **third** rainbow girl Eisenberg, E. 364.152
The **Third** Reich Burleigh, M. 943.086
The **third** reich Childers, T. 943.086
The **Third** Reich at war Evans, R. 940.53
The **Third** Reich in power, 1933-1939 Evans, R. 943.086
Thirteen days Kennedy, R. 327.73
Thirteen days in September Wright, L. 956.04
Thirteen ways of looking at a Black man Gates, H. 920.71
Thirteen ways of looking at the novel Smiley, J. **B**
THIRTIES (AGE)
Kalanithi, P. When breath becomes air **B**
Thirty million words Suskind, D. 612.8
The **Thirty** Years War Wilson, P. 940.2
THIRTY YEARS' WAR, 1618-1648
Wilson, P. The Thirty Years War 940.2
This ain't the summer of love Waksman, S. 781.66
This America Lepore, J. 320.973
This blessed earth Genoways, T. 630.9
This blue McLane, M. 811
This book is overdue! Johnson, M. 021.2
This boy's life Wolff, T. **B**
This chair rocks Applewhite, A. 155.67
This changes everything Klein, N. 363.738
This close to happy Merkin, D. **B**
This cold heaven Ehrlich, G. 998.2
This explains everything 500
This far by faith Williams, J. 200
This fight is our fight Warren, E. 305.5
This house has fallen Maier, K. 966.905
This I believe 170
This I believe II 170
This idea is brilliant Brockman, J. 500
This is big Meltzer, M. **B**
This is Camino Moore, R. 641.5979
This is Chance! Mooallem, J. 363.34

McDougall, C. Born to run **796.42**

Ulysses and us Kiberd, D. **823**

Ulysses S. Grant Bunting, J. **B**

Un-American Cahan, R. **940.53**

Un-American Edstrom, E. **B**

The **unabridged** journals of Sylvia Plath, 1950-1962 Plath, S. **B**

Unabrow LaMarche, U. **B**

The **unbanking** of America Servon, L. **332.10973**

Unbeaten Stanton, M. **B**

Unbound Stein, A. **306.76**

Unbowed Maathai, W. **B**

Unbroken Hillenbrand, L. **B**

Uncanny valley Wiener, A. **B**

Uncentering the Earth Vollmann, W. **B**

Uncertain justice Tribe, L. **342.73**

UNCERTAINTY

Chodron, P. Fail, fail again, fail better **158.1**

Uncivil society Kotkin, S. **947**

Uncle Tom or new Negro? **370**

Uncle Tungsten Sacks, O. **B**

UNCLES -- HAITI

Danticat, E. Brother, I'm dying **B**

Uncommon carriers McPhee, J. **388**

The **uncommon** reader Smith, H. **B**

Unconditional love Isay, J. **306.874**

The **unconquered** Wallace, S. **981**

UNCONVENTIONAL WARFARE

Arnold, J. Jungle of snakes **355.02**

Boot, M. Invisible armies **355.02**

Kilcullen, D. The accidental guerrilla **355.4**

Romesha, C. Red Platoon **958.104**

UNCONVENTIONAL WARFARE -- PALESTINE -- HISTORY -- 20TH CENTURY

Hoffman, B. Anonymous soldiers **956.94**

The **uncrowned** king Whyte, K. **B**

Undaunted courage Ambrose, S. **917**

Undecided Morgan, G. **331.702**

Undeniable Nye, B. **576.8**

Under a flaming sky Brown, D. **977.6**

Under another sky Higgins, C. **930**

Under his very windows Zuccotti, S. **940.53**

Under magnolia Mayes, F. **B**

Under milk wood Thomas, D. **822**

Under my skin Lessing, D. **B**

Under pressure Damour, L. **155.5**

Under pressure Humphreys, R. **B**

Under red skies Kan, K. **B**

Under the black flag Cordingly, D. **910.4**

Under the knife Laar, A. **617**

Under the lights and in the dark Oxenham, G. **796.334**

Under the sea wind Carson, R. **578.77**

Under the stars White, D. **796.54**

Under the surface Wilber, T. **333.8**

Under the Tuscan sun Mayes, F. **B**

Under their thumb German, B. **B**

UNDERCOVER OPERATIONS

Friedman, M. Spies of no country **327.12095694**

Lane, C. Freedom's detective **B**

Jacobsen, A. Surprise, kill, vanish **327.1273**

Mendez, A. Argo **955.05**

Shannon, E. Hunting Leroux **B**

Stallworth, R. Black Klansman **B**

Underground Hunt, W. **624.1**

Underground Murakami, H. **364.15**

Underground Rudd, M. **B**

UNDERGROUND AREAS

Hunt, W. Underground **624.1**

Tabor, J. Blind descent **796.52**

UNDERGROUND CONSTRUCTION

Hunt, W. Underground **624.1**

UNDERGROUND ECOLOGY

Wolfe, D. Tales from the underground **577.5**

The **underground** girls of Kabul Nordberg, J. **305.309581**

Underground in Berlin Simon, M. **B**

The **underground** is massive Matos, M. **781.648**

UNDERGROUND PRESS PUBLICATIONS

Ostertag, B. People's movements, people's press **071**

UNDERGROUND RAILROAD

Bordewich, F. Bound for Canaan **973.7**

Clinton, C. Harriet Tubman **B**

Dunbar, E. She came to slay **B**

Foner, E. Gateway to freedom **973.7**

Humez, J. Harriet Tubman **B**

Larson, K. Bound for the promised land **B**

Tobin, J. From midnight to dawn **973.7**

Tobin, J. Hidden in plain view **973.7**

Walters, K. The underground railroad **973.7**

The **underground** railroad Walters, K. **973.7**

The **Underground** Railroad Snodgrass, M. **973.7**

UNDERSTANDING (PERSONAL QUALITY)

Angelou, M. Wouldn't take nothing for my journey now **814**

Understanding celiac disease Ali, N. **616.3**

Understanding comics McCloud, S. **741.5**

Understanding exposure Peterson, B. **771**

Understanding hepatitis Ali, N. **616.3**

Understanding Iran Polk, W. **955**

Understanding media McLuhan, M. **302.23**

Understanding the Book of Mormon Hardy, G. **289.3**

Understanding the NICU **618.92**

Understanding the world Rendgen, S. **741.6**

Understanding wood Hoadley, R. **684**

Understanding world religions Hexham, I. **200**

The **undertaker's** daughter Mayfield, K. **B**

UNDERTAKERS

Doughty, C. Smoke gets in your eyes **B**

Doughty, C. Will my cat eat my eyeballs? **306.9**

Jokinen, T. Curtains **B**

Mayfield, K. The undertaker's daughter **B**

Mitford, J. The American way of death revisited **338.4**

UNDERWATER ARCHEOLOGY

Beneath the seven seas **930**

Easter, G. The tsarina's lost treasure **910.91**

Ulander, P. Walking point **B**
UNITED STATES -- ARMY -- AIRBORNE DIVISION, 101ST
Atkinson, R. In the company of soldiers **956.7044**
Frederick, J. Black hearts **956.7044**
UNITED STATES -- ARMY -- AMERICAN EXPEDITIONARY FORCES -- HISTORY
Eisenhower, J. Yanks **940.4**
UNITED STATES -- ARMY -- HISTORY
Hogeland, W. Autumn of the Black Snake **970.004**
UNITED STATES -- ARMY -- HISTORY 19TH CENTURY
Donovan, J. A terrible glory **973.8**
Sides, H. Blood and thunder **978**
UNITED STATES -- ARMY -- HISTORY CIVIL WAR, 1861-1865
McPherson, J. For cause and comrades **973.7**
UNITED STATES -- ARMY -- HISTORY WORLD WAR I
Eisenhower, J. Yanks **940.4**
UNITED STATES -- ARMY -- HISTORY WORLD WAR II
Ambrose, S. Citizen soldiers **940.54**
Ambrose, S. The victors **B**
Cross, R. Operation Dragoon **940.54**
UNITED STATES -- ARMY AFRICAN AMERICAN TROOPS
Slotkin, R. Lost battalions **940.4**
UNITED STATES -- ARMY AFRICAN AMERICAN TROOPS -- HISTORY 19TH CENTURY
Egerton, D. Thunder at the gates **973.7**
UNITED STATES -- ARMY AFRICAN AMERICAN TROOPS -- HISTORY PICTORIAL WORKS
Fighting for freedom **355.0089**
UNITED STATES -- ARMY AIR FORCES
Ambrose, S. The wild blue **940.54**
Nelson, C. The first heroes **940.54**
Zuckoff, M. Lost in Shangri-la **940.54**
UNITED STATES -- ARMY AIR FORCES -- HISTORY WORLD WAR II
Nelson, C. The first heroes **940.54**
UNITED STATES -- ARMY AIR FORCES. 307TH HEAVY BOMBARDMENT GROUP
Hillenbrand, L. Unbroken **B**
UNITED STATES -- ARMY AIR FORCES. BOMBARDMENT GROUP, 22ND
Drury, B. Lucky 666 **B**
UNITED STATES -- ARMY AIR FORCES. PHOTO RECONNAISSANCE SQUADRON, 20TH
Harding, S. Last to die **B**
UNITED STATES -- ARMY AIR FORCES. SQUADRON, 741ST
Ambrose, S. The wild blue **940.54**
UNITED STATES -- ARMY AIR FORCES AERIAL GUNNERS
Harding, S. Last to die **B**
UNITED STATES -- ARMY COMMANDO TROOPS
Couch, D. Sua sponte **356**
Haney, E. Inside Delta Force **B**
UNITED STATES -- ARMY MEDICAL SERVICE
Lineberry, C. The secret rescue **940.54**
UNITED STATES -- ARMY MILITARY LIFE
Atkinson, R. In the company of soldiers **956.7044**
Finkel, D. The good soldiers **956.7044**
UNITED STATES -- ARMY MILITARY LIFE -- HISTORY
Ulander, P. Walking point **B**
UNITED STATES -- ARMY MILITARY LIFE -- HISTORY 20TH CENTURY
Nelson, J. The remains of Company D **B**
UNITED STATES -- ARMY OF THE POTOMAC -- IRISH BRIGADE
Egan, T. The immortal Irishman **B**
UNITED STATES -- ARMY OFFICERS
Edstrom, E. Un-American **B**
Egan, T. The immortal Irishman **B**
Kaplan, A. The interpreter **940.54**
Makos, A. Spearhead **B**
Sheehan, N. A bright shining lie **B**
Showalter, D. Patton and Rommel **920**
UNITED STATES -- ARMY RECRUITING, ENLISTMENT, ETC.
Slotkin, R. Lost battalions **940.4**
UNITED STATES -- ARMY SCOUTS
Burns, M. The only one living to tell **B**
UNITED STATES -- ARMY SPECIAL OPERATIONS FORCES
Blehm, E. Legend **B**
UNITED STATES -- ARMY WOMEN
Thorpe, H. Soldier girls **956.7044**
UNITED STATES -- ARMY -- AMERICAN EXPEDITIONARY FORCES
Carroll, A. My fellow soldiers **940.4**
Yockelson, M. Forty-seven days **940.4**
UNITED STATES -- ARMY -- ANTI-ARICRAFT BARRAGE BALLOON BATTALION, 320TH -- HISTORY
Hervieux, L. Forgotten **940.54**
UNITED STATES -- ARMY -- ARMORED REGIMENT, 32ND
Makos, A. Spearhead **B**
UNITED STATES -- ARMY -- ARMY OF THE POTOMAC
Sears, S. Lincoln's lieutenants **920**
UNITED STATES -- ARMY -- CAVALRY, 7TH
Connell, E. Son of the morning star **973.8**
Connell, E. Son of the morning star **973.8**
UNITED STATES -- ARMY -- CHEMICAL WARFARE SERVICE
Emery, T. Hellfire boys **358**
UNITED STATES -- ARMY -- CORPS, 10TH
Weintraub, S. A Christmas far from home **951.904**
UNITED STATES -- ARMY -- DIVISION, 77TH -- HISTORY
Roberts, R. War fever **974.4**
UNITED STATES -- ARMY -- ENGINEER REGIMENT, 30TH (GAS AND FLAME)
Emery, T. Hellfire boys **358**
UNITED STATES -- ARMY -- GAS REGIMENT, 1ST
Emery, T. Hellfire boys **358**

UNITED STATES -- HISTORY -- 21ST CENTURY

UNITED STATES -- HISTORY -- CIVIL WAR, 1861-1865

Hendrickson, P. The living and the dead **959.704**
Kilcullen, D. The accidental guerrilla **355.4**
Klare, M. All hell breaking loose **355.20973**
Mazzetti, M. The way of the knife **356**
McNamara, R. In retrospect **959.704**
Nelson, M. The three-cornered war **978**
Olson, L. Those angry days **940.53**
Woodward, B. State of denial **973.931**

UNITED STATES -- MILITARY POLICY -- 20TH CENTURY
Hopkins, W. The Pacific War **940.54**

UNITED STATES -- MILITARY POLICY -- DECISION MAKING
Woodward, B. The commanders **327.73**

UNITED STATES -- MILITARY POLICY -- HISTORY -- 21ST CENTURY
Scahill, J. Dirty wars **355.00973**

UNITED STATES -- MILITARY POLICY -- RELIGIOUS ASPECTS
Preston, A. Sword of the spirit, shield of faith **322**

UNITED STATES -- MILITARY RELATIONS
Gates, R. Exercise of power **973.929**
Johnson, A. Night in the American village **305.40952**
McDonell, N. The bodies in person **956.7044**

UNITED STATES -- MILITARY RELATIONS CHINA
Allison, G. Destined for war **327.73051**

UNITED STATES -- MILITARY RELATIONS IRAN
Crist, D. The twilight war **327.73055**

UNITED STATES -- MILITARY RELATIONS MIDDLE EAST
McCurley, T. Hunter killer **B**

UNITED STATES -- MILITARY RELATIONS PHILIPPINES
Capozzola, C. Bound by war **355**

UNITED STATES -- MILITARY RELATIONS SOVIET UNION
Ambinder, M. The brink **355.5**
Nelson, J. The Polar Bear expedition **947.084**

UNITED STATES -- MILITIA -- HISTORY -- 18TH CENTURY
Breen, T. American insurgents, American patriots **973.3**

UNITED STATES -- MORAL CONDITIONS
Callahan, D. The cheating culture **174**
Edelman, M. The measure of our success **649**
Talese, G. The voyeur's motel **306.770973**

UNITED STATES -- NATIONAL ADVISORY COMMISSION ON CIVIL DISORDERS
Gillon, S. Separate and unequal **363.32**

UNITED STATES -- NATIONAL ADVISORY COMMITTEE FOR AERONAUTICS
Teitel, A. Breaking the chains of gravity **629.4**

UNITED STATES -- NATIONAL AERONAUTICS AND SPACE ADMINISTRATION
Anderson, C. The ordinary spaceman **B**
Barbree, J. Neil Armstrong **B**
Cassutt, M. The astronaut maker **B**
Dean, M. Leaving orbit **B**
Donovan, J. Shoot for the moon **629.45**
Greene, K. Once upon a time I lived on Mars **B**
Hardesty, V. Black wings **920**
Hickam, H. Rocket boys **B**
Hubbard, S. Exploring Mars **523.4**
Massimino, M. Spaceman **B**
Nelson, C. Rocket men **629.45**
Smith, A. Moondust **920**
Tyson, N. Space chronicles **629.4**
Ward, P. Life as we do not know it **576.839**

UNITED STATES -- NATIONAL AERONAUTICS AND SPACE ADMINISTRATION -- HISTORY
Teitel, A. Fighting for space **920**
Wolfe, T. The right stuff **629.4**

UNITED STATES -- NATIONAL AERONAUTICS AND SPACE ADMINISTRATION -- NASA
Kluger, J. Disaster strikes! **363.12**

UNITED STATES -- NATIONAL AERONAUTICS AND SPACE ADMINISTRATION OFFICIALS AND EMPLOYEES
Lee Shetterly, M. Hidden figures **510.92**
Paul, R. We could not fail **920**

UNITED STATES -- NATIONAL AERONAUTICS AND SPACE ADMINISTRATION OFFICIALS AND EMPLOYEES -- HISTORY
Paul, R. We could not fail **920**

UNITED STATES -- NATIONAL PARK SERVICE -- HISTORY
Duncan, D. The national parks **333.78**
Egan, T. The big burn **973.911**

UNITED STATES -- NATIONAL SECURITY AGENCY
Gellman, B. Dark mirror **327.12730092**
Greenwald, G. No place to hide **327.12**
Harris, S. @WAR **355.3**
Perkins, J. The new confessions of an economic hit man **B**

UNITED STATES. NATIONAL SECURITY AGENCY -- HISTORY
Budiansky, S. Code warriors **327.73047**

UNITED STATES. NATIONAL SECURITY COUNCIL
Gans, J. White House warriors **355**
Rice, C. No higher honor **B**

UNITED STATES -- NATURAL HISTORY
Schweid, R. Consider the eel **597**

UNITED STATES -- NAVAL SPECIAL WARFARE DEVELOPMENT GROUP
Chesney, W. No ordinary dog **B**

UNITED STATES -- NAVAL SPECIAL WARFARE DEVELOPMENT GROUP -- HISTORY
Darack, E. The final mission of Extortion 17 **958.104**

UNITED STATES -- NAVY
Borneman, W. The admirals **B**
Bradley, J. Flags of our fathers **B**
Humphreys, R. Under pressure **B**
McRaven, W. Sea stories **B**
Morison, S. John Paul Jones **B**
Prados, J. Storm over Leyte **940.54**
Thomas, E. John Paul Jones **B**

V

VONNEGUT, KURT HANDBOOKS, MANUALS, ETC
Farrell, S. Critical companion to Kurt Vonnegut **813**
Voodoo histories Aaronovitch, D. **909.08**
Voodoo science Park, R. **509**
VOROBYOV, NIKO TRAVEL
Vorobyov, N. Dopeworld **364.1**
VOTER REGISTRATION
Smith, E. Thank you for voting **324.973**
Wehle, K. What you need to know about voting and why **324.60973**
VOTER SUPPRESSION
Abrams, S. Our time is now **324.60973**
VOTING
DuBois, E. Suffrage **324.6**
Greenberg, L. We are indivisible **321.8**
Hasen, R. Election meltdown **324.973**
Lichtman, A. The embattled vote in America **324.6**
Litt, D. Democracy in one book or less **321.8**
MacLean, N. Democracy in chains **320.530973**
Smith, E. Thank you for voting **324.973**
Waldman, M. The fight to vote **324.6**
Ware, S. Why they marched **920**
Wehle, K. What you need to know about voting and why **324.60973**
VOTING RESEARCH
Salvanto, A. Where did you get this number? **303.3**
VOTING RIGHTS ACT OF 1965
Anderson, C. One person, no vote **324.6**
Berman, A. Give us the ballot **324.6**
Branch, T. At Canaan's edge **B**
Kotz, N. Judgment days **323**
VOWELL, SARAH, 1969-
Vowell, S. Assassination vacation **B**
VOWELL, SARAH, 1969- TRAVEL UNITED STATES
Vowell, S. Assassination vacation **B**
A **voyage** long and strange Horwitz, T. **970.01**
Voyage of mercy Puleo, S. **363.8**
The **voyage** of the Beagle Darwin, C. **508**
Voyage of the Sable Venus and other poems Lewis, R. **811**
VOYAGER PROJECT
Scott, J. The vinyl frontier **629.4**
VOYAGES AND TRAVELS
Adams, M. Tip of the iceberg **B**
Adams, M. Turn right at Machu Picchu **985**
Alford, J. Hot, sour, salty, sweet **641.5**
Ambrose, S. Undaunted courage **917**
An innocent abroad **910.4**
Ash, J. A Byzantine journey **915**
Atkins, W. The immeasurable world **910.915**
Bain, A. Ultimate travel **910.91**
Bass, R. The traveling feast **B**
Baxter, J. The most beautiful walk in the world **914.404**
Belliveau, D. In the footsteps of Marco Polo **B**
Bergreen, L. Marco Polo **B**
Bergreen, L. Marco Polo **B**
Berlin, L. Welcome home **B**
Bewes, D. Slow train to Switzerland **914.94**
Black, G. On the Ganges **954**
Boissoneault, L. The last voyageurs **917**
Bown, M. The world's most travelled man **B**
Bown, S. The last Viking **B**
Bryson, B. A walk in the woods **917**
Bryson, B. In a sunburned country **919**
Bryson, B. Notes from a small island **914**
Bryson, B. The road to Little Dribbling **914**
Buettner, D. Sovietrek **947.086**
Butcher, T. Chasing the devil **916**
Caputo, P. The longest road **973.93**
Castner, B. Disappointment river **B**
Chamberlin, S. On the trail **796.510973**
Chatwin, B. In Patagonia **918**
Chatwin, B. The songlines **919.4**
Cole, T. Blind spot **770**
Cole, T. Known and strange things **824**
Conover, T. The routes of man **388.1**
Coyne, T. A course called Scotland **B**
Denson, A. Cool Tokyo guide **915.204**
Duke, L. Mandela, Mobutu, and me **968.06**
Dyer, G. White sands **824**
Elliot, J. An unexpected light **915**
Elliot, J. Mirrors of the unseen **915**
Fallows, J. Our towns **306.0973**
Fatland, E. Sovietistan **915.804**
Faulkner, S. Bitterroot **978**
Feiler, B. Walking the Bible **915**
Ferlinghetti, L. Writing across the landscape **B**
Foer, J. Atlas Obscura **910.4**
Frazier, I. Great Plains **917**
Frazier, I. Travels in Siberia **957**
Gill, A. To America with love **973.93**
Gorra, M. The bells in their silence **914.304**
Grann, D. The lost city of Z **918.1**
Green, B. Boltzmann's tomb **500**
Griffiths, T. Slicing the silence **919**
Harris, K. Lands of lost borders **B**
Henry, J. Great White Fleet **387.243**
Hessler, P. Country driving **303.48**
Hodgman, J. Vacationland **B**
Hoffman, C. The lunatic express **910.4**
Homer Odyssey **883**
Homer The Odyssey **883**
Homer The Odyssey **883**
Horwitz, T. Spying on the South **917**
Housden, R. Saved by beauty **955**
Ilgunas, K. Trespassing across America **B**
Iyer, P. A beginner's guide to Japan **952.05**
Iyer, P. The man within my head **823**
James, H. Travels with Henry James **B**
Jenkins, P. A walk across America **917**
Jenkins, P. Looking for Alaska **979.8**
Kavenna, J. The ice museum **919.804**
Keahey, J. Sicilian splendors **914**
Kerkeling, H. I'm off then **B**

W

X

Y

Z